Longman
Anagram
Dictionary

Longman
anagram
Dictionary

Longman
Anagram
Dictionary

R J Edwards

Longman

Longman Group Limited,
Longman House, Burnt Mill, Harlow,
Essex CM20 2JE, England
and Associated Companies throughout the world.

First published 1985

British Library Cataloguing in Publication Data
Edwards, R.J. (Rik J.)
  Anagram dictionary.
   1. Anagrams—Glossaries, vocabularies, etc.
   I. Title
   793.73'   GV1507.A5

   ISBN 0-582-89202-3

Set in APS5 Univers

Printed in Great Britain
by Hazell, Watson & Viney Ltd, Aylesbury.

Author's preface

The *Longman Anagram Dictionary* has been de-
signed to solve any anagram within seconds, so it
should prove indispensable to crossword solvers and
word-game enthusiasts alike.

Over 100,000 words have been taken from the Longman Word Bank. To these has been added a unique
list of some 70,000 phrases, in as many variations as
possible, both common and obscure, which may
appear in cryptic crosswords.

It is very easy to use. Take the letters suspected of
forming an anagram, and arrange them in
alphabetical order. Then look up the resulting jumble
in the appropriate length section of the dictionary. The
solution will appear on the right.

For example, suppose the clue reads 'Reached an
arrangement for Ted and Anita' (8). This suggests the
solution is an anagram of the letters T,E,D,A,N,I,T,A.
Arrange these letters alphabetically; this gives
AADEINTT, which we find in the eight-letter section as
ATTAINED.

The method is the same where the answer is a phrase.
Suppose the clue reads 'Rome's roles varied approx-
imately' (4,2,4). So we need an anagram of the letters
R,O,M,E,S,R,O,L,E,S. This gives EELMOORRSS, which we
find in the ten-letter section as MORE OR LESS.

In some cases, more than one solution will be given for
a certain combination of letters. Where this occurs,
choose whichever solution fits in with the rest of the
clue, or with the letters already written in the crossword
frame.

The *Longman Anagram Dictionary* can also help with
word games, puzzles and competitions – it will prove a
trusty friend in every puzzler's home.

Rik Edwards

About the author

Rik Edwards was born in 1956 and was educated
in Watford and at the University of Warwick. In
addition to compiling books for the word-game
enthusiast, his interests include popular music and
misprinted bank notes.

How to spot anagrams

Crossword compilers have many ways of indicating the use of an anagram, and the solver may find the following summary useful.

Usually, the anagram clue is in three parts: the letters making up the anagram; some indication that the letters must be rearranged (ie an 'anagram signal'); and some indication of the meaning of the solution.

Thus in 'Horsemen find unusually rare firs', 'rare firs' provides the letters in the anagram, 'unusually' is the anagram signal, and 'Horsemen' refers loosely to the meaning of the solution – 'Farriers'. In this case 'find' is a link – we can 'find' farriers by rearranging 'rare firs'.

There is virtually no limit to the ingenuity of the compilers in finding anagram signals, and they will usually find one which fits in well with the rest of the clue. No list of anagram signals can claim to be complete, but the following is probably as comprehensive as any published, and the user should get a full idea of the kind of signal he can expect.

about	chaos	derange(d)	get(s) face-lift
accident(al)	chop(ped) up	different(ly)	go to pieces
adapt(ed)	clumsy	disarray	go(ne) off
aimless	cocktail	disaster	
alter(ed)	collapse(d)	disguise(d)	hidden
alternative	combination	dislocate(d)	hotchpotch
amok	come(s) to	disorder(ed)	
anew	comic(al)	disorganise(d)	in
another	compose(d)	disturb(ed)	in a bad way
another way	concoct(ed)	drunk(en)	in a fashion
anyway	confuse(d)		in a heap
around	confusion	eccentric	in a mess
arrange(d)	constitution	enough for	in knots
arrangement	construct(ed)	erratic(ally)	in pieces
assorted	construction	error	incorrect(ly)
	cook(ed)	eruption	ingredients
bad(ly)	correct(ed)	explosion	injure(d)
become(s)	correction		involve(d)
becoming	crack(ed) up	fashion(ed)	
bend(s)	crash(ed)	fickle	jerky
bent	crazy	flaw(ed)	jerkily
bizarre	crumple(d)	fluster(ed)	jumble(d)
break(s)	crush(ed)	foolish(ly)	
break(ing)	cunning(ly)	fracas	kind
break out		fresh	kind of
broken	damage(d)	from	
	dance(d)		liquid
change(d)		get(s)	
			mad(ly)
			make(s)

manage(d)
management
mangle(d)
maybe
melt(ed)
mess(ed)
messy
misapplied
misbehave(d)
miserable
mix(ed)
mixture
mix-up
mobile
muddle(d)

new
new order
new style

odd(ly)
off
order(ed)
organise(d)
out (of)
out of order

perhaps
permutation
pervert(ed)

poor(ly)
possible
potential(ly)

queer(ly)

rearrange(d)
rebuilt
recast
refine(d)
reform(ed)
remodel(led)
reorder(ed)
reorganise(d)
repair(ed)
resettle(d)
reshape(d)
resolve(d)
revise(d)
revolution
rewritten
riot(ous)
rough(ly)
ruin(ed)
run amok

sad
scatter(ed)
scramble(d)
scruffy

shake(n)
shape(d)
shatter(ed)
shift(ed)
shuffle(d)
smash(ed)
sort of
spoil(t)
stew
stir(red)
storm(y)
strange(ly)
stumbling
subtle
subvert(ed)
swap
swirling
switch(es)

throw(n)
toss(ed)
tousle(d)
transform(ed)
transport(ed)
treacherous
trouble(d)
turbulent
turn(ed)
turn(ed) out

twist(ed)
twisting

unorthodox
unruly
unstable
untidy
unusual(ly)
upset
uses

vandalise(d)
vary
varied
variety
various(ly)
version
violent(ly)

wander(ing)
weird
went off
went to pieces
wild(ly)
wobbly
woolly
wreck(ed)
wrong(ly)

AAB	BAA	**ADY**	DAY	**AIR**	AIR	**AOV**	AVO	**BGO**	BOG
AAH	AHA	**AEG**	AGE		RIA		OVA		GOB
ABC	A B C	**AEK**	KEA	**AIS**	AIS	**AOZ**	AZO	**BGU**	BUG
	ABC	**AEL**	ALE	**AIT**	AIT	**APP**	PAP	**BHO**	HOB
	CAB		IFA		TAI	**APR**	PAR	**BHU**	HUB
ABD	BAD	**AEN**	ANE	**AIV**	VIA		RAP	**BIJ**	JIB
	DAB	**AEP**	APE	**A.IM**	IAM	**APS**	ASP	**BIK**	KIR
ABF	FAB		PEA	**AJP**	JAP		PAS	**BIL**	LIB
ABG	BAG	**AER**	ARE	**AJR**	JAR		SAP	**BIN**	BIN
	GAB		EAR		RAJ		SPA		NIB
ABH	BAH		ERA	**AJT**	JAT	**APT**	APT	**BIO**	IBO
ABJ	JAB	**AES**	SAE	**AJW**	JAW		PAT		OBI
ABL	ALB		SEA	**AJY**	JAY		TAP	**BIR**	RIB
	LAB	**AET**	ATE	**AKO**	KOA	**APW**	PAW	**BIS**	SIB
ABN	BAN		EAT		OAK	**APX**	PAX	**BIT**	BIT
	NAB		ETA	**AKR**	ARK	**APY**	PAY	**BIZ**	DIZ
ABO	ABO		TEA	**AKS**	ASK		PYA	**BJO**	JOB
	BOA	**AEV**	AVE		KAS		YAP	**BLO**	LOB
ABP	BAP	**AEW**	AWE		SKA	**APZ**	ZAP	**BMO**	MOB
ABR	BAR	**AEX**	AXE	**AKT**	KAT	**AQU**	QUA	**BMU**	BUM
	BRA	**AEY**	AYE	**AKU**	AUK	**ART**	ART	**BNO**	NOB
ABT	BAT		YEA	**AKW**	KWA		RAT	**BNU**	BUN
	TAB	**AFG**	FAG	**AKY**	YAK		TAR		NUB
ABY	BAY	**AFH**	FAH	**ALL**	ALL	**ARW**	RAW	**BOO**	BOO
ACD	CAD	**AFN**	FAN	**ALM**	LAM		WAR	**BOP**	BOP
ACE	ACE	**AFO**	OAF	**ALO**	LAO	**ARY**	RAY	**BOR**	ORB
ACH	CHA	**AFR**	FAR	**ALP**	ALP	**ASS**	ASS		ROB
ACL	LAC		FRA		LAP	**AST**	SAT	**BOS**	SOB
ACM	CAM	**AFT**	AFT		PAL	**ASW**	SAW	**BOW**	BOW
	MAC		FAT	**ALS**	SAL		WAS	**BOX**	BOX
ACN	CAN	**AFY**	FAY	**ALV**	LAV	**ASX**	SAX	**BOY**	BOY
ACP	CAP	**AGG**	GAG	**ALW**	AWL	**ASY**	SAY		YOB
ACR	ARC	**AGH**	HAG		LAW	**ATT**	TAT	**BPU**	PUB
	CAR	**AGJ**	JAG	**ALX**	LAX	**ATU**	TAU	**BRU**	BUR
ACS	SAC	**AGL**	GAL	**ALY**	LAY	**ATV**	VAT		RUB
ACT	ACT		LAG	**AMM**	MAM	**ATW**	TAW	**BSU**	BUS
	CAT	**AGM**	MAG	**AMN**	MAN		TWA		SUB
ACV	VAC	**AGN**	NAG	**AMO**	MOA	**ATX**	TAX	**BTU**	BUT
ACW	CAW	**AGO**	AGO	**AMP**	AMP	**AWX**	WAX		TUB
ACY	CAY		GOA		MAP	**AWY**	WAY	**BUY**	BUY
ADD	ADD	**AGP**	GAP	**AMR**	ARM		YAW	**CDO**	COD
	DAD	**AGR**	GAR		MAR				DOC
ADF	FAD		RAG		RAM	**BBE**	EBB	**CDU**	CUD
ADG	DAG	**AGS**	GAS	**AMS**	MAS	**BBI**	BIB	**CEI**	ICE
	GAD		SAG	**AMT**	MAT	**BBO**	BOB	**CEP**	CEP
ADH	DAH	**AGT**	GAT	**AMW**	MAW	**BBU**	BUB	**CES**	SEC
	HAD		TAG	**AMY**	MAY	**BCO**	COB		ETC
ADI	AID	**AGW**	WAG		YAM	**BCU**	CUB		TEC
ADL	LAD	**AGY**	GAY	**ANP**	NAP	**BDE**	BED	**CEU**	CUE
ADM	DAM	**AHH**	HAH		PAN		DEB	**CGI**	CIG
	MAD	**AHM**	HAM	**ANR**	RAN	**BDI**	BID	**CGO**	COG
ADN	AND	**AHN**	HAN	**ANS**	SAN	**BDO**	BOD	**CHI**	CHI
	DAN	**AHP**	PAH	**ANT**	ANT	**BDU**	BUD	**CHO**	OCH
	DNA	**AHR**	RAH		TAN		DUB	**CIP**	PIC
	NAD	**AHS**	ASH	**ANV**	VAN	**BEE**	BEE	**CIS**	CIS
ADO	ADO		HAS	**ANW**	AWN	**BEG**	BEG		SIC
ADP	DAP	**AHT**	HAT		WAN	**BEL**	BEL	**CIT**	TIC
	PAD	**AHW**	HAW	**ANY**	ANY	**BEN**	NEB	**CIY**	ICY
ADR	RAD	**AHY**	HAY		NAY	**BET**	BET	**CLO**	COL
ADS	ADS		YAH	**AOR**	OAR	**BEW**	WEB	**CMU**	CUM
	SAD	**AIL**	AIL	**AOT**	OAT	**BEY**	BYE	**CMW**	CWM
ADW	DAW	**AIM**	AIM		TAO	**BFI**	FIB	**CNO**	CON
	WAD	**AIN**	AIN			**BFO**	FOB	**COO**	COO
						BGI	BIG		

Code	Word	Code	Word	Code	Word	Code	Word	Code	Word
COP	COP	DRY	DRY	EKN	KEN	FIX	FIX	HWY	WHY
COR	COR	DST	DT'S	EKR	ERK	FLU	FLU	IKL	ILK
	ROC	EEF	FEE	EKY	KEY	FLY	FLY	IKN	INK
COS	COS	EEG	GEE		KYE	FNU	FUN		KIN
COT	COT	EEK	EKE	ELL	ELL	FOP	FOP	IKP	KIP
COW	COW	EEL	EEL	ELM	ELM	FOR	FOR	IKR	IRK
COX	COX		LEE	ELO	LEO		FRO	IKS	SKI
COY	COY	EEN	E'EN		OLE	FOT	OFT	IKT	KIT
CPU	CUP		EEN	ELT	LET	FOU	FOU	ILL	ILL
CRU	CUR		NEE	ELU	LEU		UFO	ILM	MIL
CRY	CRY	EEP	PEE	ELV	LEV	FOX	FOX	ILN	NIL
CTU	CUT	EER	E'ER	ELY	LEY	FRU	FUR	ILO	OIL
DDI	DID		ERE		LYE	FRY	FRY	ILP	LIP
DDO	ODD	EES	SEE	EMN	MEN	FTU	FUT	ILT	LIT
DDU	DUD	EET	TEE	EMR	REM	GGI	GIG	IMN	NIM
DEF	FED	EEV	EVE	EMS	EMS	GHO	HOG	IMP	IMP
DEH	EDH	EEW	EWE	EMT	MET	GHU	HUG	IMR	MIR
	HE'D		WEE	EMU	EMU		UGH		RIM
DEI	DIE	EEY	EYE	EMW	MEW	GIJ	JIG	IMS	ISM
	IDE	EEZ	ZEE	ENO	EON	GIN	GIN	IMV	VIM
DEK	KED	EFF	EFF		ONE	GIP	PIG	IMX	MIX
DEL	LED	EFI	FIE	ENP	PEN	GIR	RIG	INN	INN
DEN	DEN	EFL	ELF	ENS	ENS	GIS	GI'S	INO	ION
	END	EFN	FEN		SEN		GIS	INP	NIP
DEO	DOE	EFO	FOE	ENT	NET	GIT	GIT		PIN
	ODE	EFR	REF		TEN	GIW	WIG	INS	SIN
DEP	PED	EFT	EFT	ENW	NEW	GJO	JOG	INT	NIT
DER	RED	EFU	FEU		WEN	GJU	JUG		TIN
DET	TED	EFW	FEW	ENY	YEN	GLO	LOG	INV	VIN
DEU	DUE	EFY	FEY	ENZ	ZEN	GLU	LUG	INW	WIN
DEW	DEW	EFZ	FEZ	EOR	ORE	GMU	GUM	INX	NIX
	WED	EGG	EGG		ROE		MUG	INY	YIN
DEY	DYE	EGI	GIE	EOT	TOE	GMY	GYM	IPP	PIP
DEZ	ZED	EGK	KEG	EOV	VOE	GNO	NOG	IPR	RIP
DFI	FID	EGL	GEL	EOW	OWE	GNU	GNU	IPS	PIS
DGI	DIG		LEG		WOE		GUN		PSI
	GID	EGM	GEM	EPP	PEP	GOO	GOO		SIP
DGO	DOG	EGN	GEN	EPR	PER	GOT	GOT	IPT	PIT
	GOD	EGO	EGO		REP		TOG		TIP
DGU	DUG	EGP	PEG	EPS	EPS	GOY	GOY	IPX	PIX
DHI	HID	EGR	ERG		ESP	GPU	PUG	IPY	YIP
DHO	DOH	EGT	GET	EPT	PET	GPY	GYP	IPZ	ZIP
	HOD		TEG	EPW	PEW	GRU	RUG	IRS	SIR
DIK	KID	EGV	VEG	EPY	YEP	GTU	GUT	IST	ITS
DIL	LID	EGY	GEY	ERR	ERR		TUG		SIT
DIM	DIM	EHI	HIE	ERT	RET		VUG		TIS
	MID	EHM	HEM	ERU	RUE	GUV	GUV	ISX	SIX
DIN	DIN	EHN	HEN	ERV	REV	GUY	GUY	ITT	TIT
DIO	IDO	EHO	HOE	ERY	RYE	HHU	HUH	ITW	TWI
DIP	DIP	EHP	HEP		YER	HIM	HIM		WIT
DIR	RID	EHR	HER	EST	SET	HIP	HIP	IVY	IVY
DIS	IDS	EHS	HE'S	ESU	SUE		PHI	IWZ	WIZ
DIT	DIT		SHE		USE	HIS	HIS	JOT	JOT
DIY	YID	EHT	ETH	ESW	SEW	HIT	HIT	JOY	JOY
DJS	DJS		HET	ESX	SEX	HMO	OHM	JTU	JUT
DLO	OLD		THE	ESY	YES	HMU	HUM	KOS	KOS
DMO	DOM	EHU	HUE	ETV	VET	HNO	NOH	KOW	WOK
	MOD	EHW	HEW	ETW	WET	HNU	HUN	KRU	KRU
DMU	MUD	EHX	HEX	ETX	TEX	HOO	OHO	KSY	SKY
DNO	DON	EHY	HEY	ETY	YET		OOH	LMO	MOL
	NOD	EIL	LEI	EVX	VEX	HOP	HOP		OLM
DNU	DUN		LIE	EWY	YEW	HOR	RHO	LMU	LUM
DOP	POD	EIP	PIE	FFO	OFF	HOS	SOH	LOO	LOO
DOR	ROD	EIR	IRE	FGI	FIG	HOT	HOT	LOP	LOP
DOS	DO'S	EIT	TIE	FGO	FOG		THO	LOS	SOL
	DOS	EIV	VIE	FGU	FUG	HOW	HOW	LOT	LOT
	SOD	EJO	JOE	FIL	FIL		WHO	LOW	LOW
DOT	DOT	EJT	JET	FIN	FIN	HOY	HOY		OWL
	TOD	EJW	JEW	FIR	FIR	HSY	SHY	LOX	LOX
DOU	DUO	EKL	ELK	FIS	IFS	HTU	HUT	LPU	PUL
DPU	PUD		LEK	FIT	FIT	HTY	THY	LPY	PLY

LSY	SLY	PSU	PUS
LUX	LUX		SUP
MMO	MOM		UPS
MMU	MUM	PSY	SPY
MNO	MON	PTU	PUT
MNU	MUN		TUP
MOO	MOO	PUY	PUY
MOP	MOP	PXY	PYX
	POM	RTU	RUT
MOR	MOR	RTY	TRY
MOT	MOT	RWY	WRY
	TOM	33U	3U3
MOW	MOW	STY	STY
MRU	RUM	TTU	TUT
MSU	MUS	TUU	UTU
	SUM		
MTU	TUM		
NNU	NUN		
NOR	NOR		
	NOR		
NOS	NOS		
	SON		
NOT	NOT		
	TON		
NOW	NOW		
	OWN		
	WON		
NOY	YON		
NPU	PUN		
NRU	RUN		
	URN		
NSU	NUS		
	SUN		
NTU	NUT		
	TUN		
OOR	ROO		
OOT	TOO		
OOW	WOO		
OOZ	ZOO		
OPP	POP		
OPR	PRO		
OPS	OPS		
	POS		
	SOP		
OPT	OPT		
	POT		
	TOP		
OPX	POX		
ORT	ROT		
	TOR		
ORU	OUR		
ORW	ROW		
OST	SOT		
OSU	SOU		
OSW	SOW		
OSX	SOX		
OSY	SOY		
OTT	TOT		
OTU	OUT		
OTW	OWT		
	TOW		
	TWO		
OTY	TOY		
OUY	YOU		
OVW	VOW		
OWW	WOW		
OWY	YOW		
PPU	PUP		
PRY	PRY		

AABL	BAAL	ABCK	BACK	ABLW	BAWL	ACES	ACES	ACOX	COAX
AABR	ARAB	ABCR	CRAB	ABLY	ABLY		CASE		COXA
AABS	BAAS	ABCS	CABS	ABMO	AMBO	ACET	CATE	ACPR	CARP
AACP	PACA		SCAB	ABMR	BARM	ACEV	CAVE	ACPS	CAPS
AADD	DADA	ABCU	CUBA	ABNR	BARN	ACFF	CAFF	ACPT	PACT
AADM	ADAM	ABDE	ABED		BRAN	ACFL	CALF	ACRS	ARCS
AADT	DATA		BADE	ABNS	BANS	ACFT	FACT		CARS
AAER	AREA		BEAD		NABS	ACGR	CRAG		SCAR
AAFL	ALFA	ABDL	BALD	ABNU	BUNA	ACHI	CHAI	ACRT	CART
AAFR	AFAR	ABDN	BAND	ABOR	BOAR	ACHK	HACK	ACRW	CRAW
AAGG	GAGA	ABDR	BARD		BORA	ACHM	MACH	ACRY	RACY
AAGL	ALGA		BRAD	ABOS	ABOS	ACHP	CHAP	ACRZ	CZAR
	GALA		DRAB		BOAS	ACHR	ARCH		Z CAR
AAGN	NAGA	ABDS	BADS	ABOT	BOAT		CHAR	ACSS	SACS
AAGR	AGAR		DABS	ABPS	BAPS	ACHS	CASH	ACST	ACTS
	RAGA	ABDU	BAUD	ABRS	BARS	ACHT	CHAT		CAST
AAGS	SAGA		DAUB		BRAS	ACHW	CHAW		CATS
AAHH	HA HA	ABDW	BAWD	ABRT	BRAT	ACHY	ACHY		SCAT
	HA-HA	ABEK	BAKE		T BAR	ACIL	LAIC	ACSV	VACS
AAHK	HAKA		BEAK		T-BAR	ACIM	MICA	ACSW	CAWS
AAHM	AMAH	ABEL	ABLE	ABRW	BRAW	ACIN	INCA	ACSY	CAYS
AAHR	HAAR		BALE	ABRY	BRAY	ACIO	CIAO	ACTT	TACT
AAHY	AYAH	ABEM	BEAM	ABSS	BASS	ACIP	PICA	ACVY	CAVY
AAIR	ARIA	ABEN	BANE	ABST	BAST	ACIS	ASCI	ADDE	DEAD
AAJR	AJAR		BEAN		BATS	ACJK	JACK		EDDA
AAJV	JAVA	ABER	BARE		STAB	ACKL	CALK	ADDO	DADO
AAKK	KAKA		BEAR		TABS		LACK	ADDS	ADDS
AAKM	KAMA		BRAE	ABSW	SWAB	ACKM	MACK		DADS
AAKN	AKAN	ABES	BASE	ABSY	BAYS	ACKP	PACK	ADDY	D DAY
AAKR	ARAK	ABET	ABET	ABTU	ABUT	ACKR	CARK		DYAD
AAKT	KATA		BATE		TUBA		RACK	ADEF	DEAF
	TAKA		BEAT	ACCD	AC DC	ACKS	CASK		FADE
AAKV	KAVA		BETA	ACCE	CECA		SACK	ADEG	AGED
AALM	ALMA	ABEU	BEAU	ACCO	COCA	ACKT	TACK		EGAD
	LAMA	ABFL	FLAB	ACDE	ACED	ACKW	WACK	ADEH	HADE
AALN	ANAL	ABGN	BANG		DACE	ACKY	YACK		HEAD
AALR	ALAR	ABGR	BRAG	ACDH	CHAD	ACLL	CALL	ADEI	AIDE
AALS	ALAS		GARB	ACDI	ACID	ACLM	CALM		IDEA
AALT	TAAL		GRAB		CADI		CLAM	ADEJ	JADE
	TALA	ABGS	BAGS	ACDL	CLAD	ACLN	CLAN	ADEL	DALE
AALV	LAVA		GABS	ACDO	CODA	ACLO	COAL		DEAL
AAMM	MA'AM	ABHL	BLAH	ACDR	CARD		COLA		LADE
	MAMA	ABHS	BASH	ACDS	CADS	ACLP	CLAP		LEAD
AAMN	MANA	ABHT	BAHT	ACEF	CAFE	ACLR	CARL	ADEM	DAME
AAMY	MAYA		BATH		FACE	ACLS	LACS		EDAM
AANN	ANNA	ABIL	BAIL	ACEG	CAGE	ACLT	TALC		MADE
AANO	ANOA	ABIM	IAMB	ACEH	ACHE	ACLW	CLAW		MEAD
AANR	ARAN	ABIN	BANI		EACH	ACLX	CALX	ADEN	DANE
AAPP	PAPA	ABIS	BIAS	ACEK	CAKE	ACLY	ACYL		DEAN
AAPR	PARA	ABIT	BAIT	ACEL	ALEC		CLAY	ADEO	ODEA
AAPT	TAPA	ABJM	JAMB		LACE		LACY	ADEP	APED
AART	RATA	ABJS	JABS	ACEM	ACME	ACMO	COMA	ADER	DARE
AARU	AURA	ABKL	BALK		CAME	ACMP	CAMP		DEAR
AASV	VASA	ABKN	BANK		MACE	ACMR	CRAM		READ
AATT	TA TA	ABKR	BARK	ACEN	ACNE		MARC	ADET	DATE
AATX	TAXA	ABKS	BASK		CANE	ACMS	CAMS		EDTA
AAWY	AWAY	ABLL	BALL	ACEP	CAPE		MACS	ADEV	VADE
ABBE	BABE	ABLM	BALM		PACE	ACNS	CANS		VEDA
ABBL	BLAB		LAMB	ACER	ACER		SCAN	ADEW	AWED
ABBR	BARB	ABLO	BOLA		ACRE	ACNT	CANT		WADE
ABBU	BABU	ABLS	ALBS		CARE	ACNY	CYAN	ADEX	AXED
ABBY	BABY		LABS		RACE	ACOP	CAPO	ADEZ	ADZE
ABCH	BACH		SLAB			ACOT	COAT		DAZE

Code	Word	Code	Word	Code	Word	Code	Word	Code	Word
ADFS	FADS	ADRW	DRAW	AELL	LEAL	AEPR	APER	AFLM	FLAM
ADFT	DAFT		WARD	AELM	LAME		PARE	AFLN	FLAN
ADGL	GLAD	ADRY	DRAY		MALE		PEAR	AFLO	FOAL
ADGO	DAGO		YARD		MEAL		RAPE		LOAF
	GOAD	ADSW	DAWS	AELN	ELAN		REAP	AFLP	FLAP
ADGR	DRAG		WADS		LANE	AEPS	APES	AFLR	FARL
ADGS	DAGS	ADSY	DAYS		LEAN		APSE	AFLT	FLAT
	GADS	ADVY	DAVY	AELO	ALOE		PEAS	AFLW	FLAW
ADGU	GAUD		V DAY	AELP	LEAP	AEPT	PATE	AFLX	FLAX
ADGW	GAWD	AEES	EASE		PALE		PEAT	AFLY	FLAY
ADHJ	HADJ	AEFK	FAKE		PEAL		TAPE	AFMO	FOAM
ADHL	DHAL	AEFL	FLEA		PLEA	AEPV	PAVE	AFMR	FARM
ADHN	HAND		LEAF	AELR	EARL	AEPX	APEX	AFNS	FANS
ADIN	HARD	AEFM	FAME		RALE	AERR	RARE	AFNW	FAWN
ADHS	DASH	AEFR	FARE		REAL		REAR	AFOR	AFRO
	SHAD		FEAR	AELS	ALES	AERS	ARES		FARO
ADIK	KADI		FRAE		LASE		EARS		FORA
ADIL	DAIL	AEFS	SAFE		LEAS		ERAS	AFOS	OAFS
	DIAL	AEFT	FATE		SALE		RASE		SOFA
	LAID		FEAT		SEAL		SEAR	AFOY	OFAY
ADIM	AMID		FETA	AELT	LATE		SERA	AFPR	FRAP
	MAID	AEFZ	FAZE		TALE	AERT	RATE	AFRT	RAFT
ADIP	PAID	AEGG	GAGE		TEAL		TARE	AFRU	FRAU
ADIQ	QADI	AEGL	GAEL	AELV	LAVE		TEAR	AFRY	FRAY
ADIR	ARID		GALE		LEVA	AERU	UREA	AFST	FAST
	RAID	AEGM	GAME		VALE	AERV	AVER		FATS
ADIS	AIDS	AEGN	GEAN		VEAL		RAVE	AFSY	FAYS
	DAIS	AEGP	GAPE		VELA	AERW	WARE	AFTU	TUFA
	SAID		PAGE	AELW	WALE		WEAR	AFTW	WAFT
ADIT	ADIT	AEGR	GEAR		WEAL	AERY	YEAR	AGGN	GANG
ADIV	AVID		RAGE	AELX	AXEL	AERZ	EZRA	AGGO	AGOG
	DIVA	AEGS	AGES		AXLE		RAZE	AGGS	GAGS
ADIW	WADI		SAGE	AELY	YALE	AESS	SEAS	AGHN	HANG
ADKN	DANK	AEGT	GATE	AELZ	LAZE	AEST	EAST	AGHS	GASH
ADKR	DARK	AEGU	AGUE		ZEAL		EATS		HAGS
ADKY	DYAK	AEGV	GAVE	AEMN	AMEN		ETAS		SHAG
ADLN	LAND	AEGW	WAGE		MANE		SATE	AGHT	GHAT
ADLO	LOAD	AEGZ	GAZE		MEAN		SEAT	AGIM	MAGI
ADLR	LARD	AEHK	HAKE		NAME		SETA	AGIN	AGIN
ADLS	LADS	AEHL	HALE	AEMR	MARE		TEAS		GAIN
ADLU	AULD		HEAL		REAM	AESV	SAVE	AGIO	AGIO
	DUAL		HELA	AEMS	MESA		VASE	AGIR	RAGI
	LAUD	AEHM	AHEM		SAME	AESX	AXES	AGIT	GAIT
ADLY	LADY		HAEM		SEAM		SEAX	AGIV	VAGI
ADMN	DAMN		HAME	AEMT	MATE	AESY	AYES	AGJS	JAGS
ADMP	DAMP	AEHP	HEAP		MEAT		EASY	AGKW	GAWK
ADMR	DRAM	AEHR	HARE		TAME		EYAS	AGLL	GALL
ADMS	DAMS		HEAR		TEAM		YEAS	AGLN	LANG
ADMU	DUMA		RHEA	AEMX	EXAM	AETT	TEAT	AGLO	GAOL
ADNO	DONA	AEHS	SHEA	AEMZ	MAZE	AETW	WETA		GOAL
ADNR	DARN	AEHT	HATE	AENO	A ONE	AETZ	ZETA	AGLS	GALS
	NARD		HEAT		AEON	AEVW	WAVE		LAGS
	RAND	AEHV	HAVE	AENP	NAPE	AFFF	FAFF		SLAG
ADNS	NADS	AEHY	YEAH		NEAP	AFFG	GAFF	AGLU	GAUL
	SAND	AEHZ	HAZE		PANE	AFFW	WAFF	AGMP	GAMP
ADNW	DAWN	AEIL	ILEA	AENR	EARN	AFGL	FLAG	AGMR	GRAM
	WAND	AEJN	JEAN		NEAR	AFGN	FANG	AGMS	MAGS
ADOP	DOPA	AEJP	JAPE	AENS	SANE	AFGR	FRAG	AGMY	GAMY
ADOR	ROAD	AEKL	KALE	AENT	ANTE		GRAF	AGNP	PANG
ADOS	SODA		LAKE		NEAT	AFGS	FAGS	AGNR	GRAN
ADOT	TOAD		LEAK	AENV	NAVE	AFHL	HALF		RANG
ADOW	WOAD	AEKM	KAME		VANE	AFHS	FASH	AGNS	NAGS
ADPR	PARD		MAKE		VENA	AFHT	HAFT		SANG
ADPS	DAPS	AEKP	PEAK	AENW	ANEW	AFIL	FAIL		SNAG
	PADS	AEKR	RAKE		WANE	AFIN	FAIN	AGNT	GNAT
ADQU	QUAD	AEKS	KEAS		WEAN		NAIF		TANG
ADRS	RADS		SAKE	AEOR	AERO	AFIR	FAIR	AGNW	GNAW
	SARD	AEKT	TAKE	AEOT	TOEA	AFIT	FIAT	AGNY	YANG
ADRT	DART		TEAK			AFIW	WAIF	AGOS	GOAS
	DRAT	AEKW	WAKE			AFKL	FLAK		SAGO
	TRAD		WEAK			AFLL	FALL		

AGOT	GOAT / TOGA
AGOY	YOGA
AGPS	GAPS / GASP
AGPW	GAWP
AGOU	QUAG
AGRS	RAGS
AGRU	GAUR
AGRY	GRAY
AGSS	SAGS
AGST	GATS / STAG / TAGS
AGSW	SWAG / WAGS
AGSY	GAYS
AHHS	HASH / SHAH
AHHT	HATH
AHIL	HAIL / HILA
AHIR	HAIR
AHIS	SHIA
AHIT	THAI
AHJJ	HAJJ
AHKL	LAKH
AHKN	ANKH / HANK / KHAN
AHKR	HARK
AHKT	KHAT
AHKW	HAWK
AHLL	HALL
AHLO	HALO
AHLS	LASH
AHLT	HALT / LATH
AHLU	HAUL / HULA
AHMR	HARM
AHMS	HAMS / MASH / SHAM
AHMT	MATH
AHMW	WHAM
AHNS	HANS
AHNT	THAN
AHOP	OPAH
AHOR	HOAR
AHOT	OATH
AHOW	WHOA
AHOX	HOAX
AHOY	AHOY
AHPR	HARP
AHPS	HASP / PASH
AHPT	PATH
AHRS	RASH
AHRT	HART / RATH / TAHR / THAR
AHSS	SASH
AHST	HAST / HATS / TASH
AHSW	HAWS / SHAW / WASH
AHSY	ASHY / HAYS
AHTT	THAT
AHTW	THAW / WHAT
AHYZ	HAZY
AIIL	ILIA
AIJL	JAIL
AIJN	JAIN
AIJO	JIAO
AIKL	ILKA
AIKN	AKIN / KINA
AIKP	PAKI / PIKA
AIKS	SAKI
AILM	MAIL / MALI
AILN	LAIN / NAIL
AILP	PAIL / PALI
AILR	ARIL / LAIR / LARI / LIAR / LIRA / RAIL / RIAL
AILS	AILS / LIAS / SAIL / SIAL
AILT	ALIT / TAIL / TALI
AILV	VIAL
AILW	WAIL
AILX	AXIL
AIMM	IMAM / MAIM
AIMN	MAIN / MINA
AIMR	AMIR / RIMA
AIMS	AIMS
AIMX	MAXI
AINP	NIPA / PAIN
AINR	IRAN / RAIN / RANI
AINT	AIN'T / ANTI
AINV	VAIN
AINW	WAIN
AINZ	NAZI
AIOT	IOTA
AIPR	PAIR
AIQR	IRAQ
AIRS	AIRS / RIAS / SARI
AIRY	AIRY
AIST	AITS / ASTI
AISV	SIVA / VISA
AISX	AXIS
AISY	I SAY
AITT	AT IT
AITV	VITA
AITW	WAIT
AITX	TAXI
AIVV	VIVA
AJLR	JARL
AJMS	JAMS
AJPS	JAPS
AJRS	JARS
AJST	JATS
AJSW	JAWS
AJSY	JAYS
AJZZ	JAZZ
AKLN	KLAN / LANK
AKLO	KOLA
AKLR	LARK
AKLT	TALK
AKLW	WALK
AKMO	AMOK / MAKO
AKMR	MARK
AKMS	MASK
AKNO	KAON / KOAN
AKNP	KNAP
AKNR	NARK / RANK
AKNS	SANK
AKNT	TANK
AKNY	YANK
AKOR	OKRA
AKOS	KOAS / OAKS / SOAK
AKOY	KAYO
AKPR	PARK
AKRS	ARKS
AKRT	KART
AKSS	ASKS
AKST	KATS / TASK
AKSU	AUKS / SKUA
AKSY	YAKS
AKTY	KYAT
ALLM	MALL
ALLP	PALL
ALLT	TALL
ALLW	WALL
ALLY	ALLY
ALMM	MALM
ALMO	LOAM
ALMP	LAMP / PALM
ALMR	MARL
ALMS	ALMS / LAMS / SLAM
ALMT	MALT
ALMU	ALUM / MAUL
ALMY	AMYL
ALNO	LOAN
ALNP	PLAN
ALNU	ULNA
ALNW	LAWN
ALOP	OPAL
ALOR	ORAL
ALOS	ALSO / LAOS
ALOT	ALTO
ALOV	OVAL
ALOW	ALOW / AWOL
ALPP	LAPP / PALP
ALPS	ALPS / LAPS / PALS / SLAP
ALPT	PLAT
ALPU	PULA
ALPW	PAWL
ALPY	PLAY
ALRY	ARYL
ALSS	LASS
ALST	LAST / SALT / SLAT
ALSV	LAVS / SLAV
ALSW	AWLS / LAWS
ALSY	LAYS / SLAY
ALTX	XTAL
ALWY	YAWL
ALYZ	LAZY
AMMO	AMMO
AMMS	MAMS
AMNO	MOAN
AMNU	MAUN
AMNX	MANX
AMNY	MANY / MYNA
AMOR	ROAM
AMOS	AMOS / MOAS / SOMA
AMOT	ATOM / MOAT
AMPR	PRAM / RAMP
AMPS	AMPS / MAPS / SAMP / SPAM
AMPT	TAMP
AMPU	PUMA
AMPV	VAMP
AMRS	ARMS / MARS / RAMS
AMRT	MART / TRAM
AMRU	ARUM
AMRW	WARM
AMRY	ARMY
AMSS	MASS
AMST	MAST / MATS
AMSW	MAWS / SWAM
AMSX	XMAS
AMSY	MAYS / YAMS
AMTT	MATT
AMYZ	MAZY
ANNO	ANON
ANOR	ROAN
ANOV	NOVA
ANOX	AXON
ANPS	NAPS / PANS / SNAP / SPAN
ANPT	PANT
ANPU	PUNA
ANPW	PAWN
ANRT	RANT / TARN
ANRW	WARN
ANRY	NARY / YARN
ANST	ANTS / TANS
ANSU	ANUS
ANSV	VANS
ANSW	AWNS / SAWN / SWAN
ANTU	AUNT / TUNA
ANTW	WANT
ANUY	YUAN
ANVY	NAVY
ANWY	WANY / YAWN
ANYZ	ZANY
AOPR	PROA
AOPS	SOAP
AOPT	ATOP
AORR	ROAR
AORS	OARS / SOAR
AORT	ROTA / TARO
AORV	ARVO
AOST	OAST / OATS
AOSV	AVOS
AOSY	SOYA
AOTU	AUTO
AOTZ	A TO Z
AOVW	AVOW
APPS	PAPS
APPU	PUPA
APPY	YAPP
APRR	PARR
APRS	RAPS / RASP / SPAR
APRT	PART / PRAT / RAPT / TRAP
APRU	PRAU
APRW	WARP / WRAP
APRY	PRAY
APSS	ASPS / PASS / SAPS / SPAS
APST	PAST / PATS / SPAT / TAPS
APSU	UPAS
APSW	PAWS / SWAP / WASP

APSY	PAYS	BDEN	BEND	BESY	BYES	BLOW	BLOW	CDHI	CHID
	SPAY	BDEO	BODE	BETU	TUBE		BOWL	CDIK	DICK
	YAPS	BDER	BRED	BETY	BYTE	BLRU	BLUR	CDIS	DISC
APSZ	ZAPS	BDES	BEDS	BEUZ	ZEBU		BURL	CDKO	DOCK
APUY	YAUP		DEBS	BEVY	BEVY	BLSU	SLUB	CDKU	DUCK
APWY	YAWP	BDET	DEBT	BFFI	BIFF	BMNU	NUMB	CDLO	CLOD
AQUY	QUAY	BDIN	BIND	BFFU	BUFF	BMOO	BOOM		COLD
ARST	ARTS	BDIR	BIRD	BFIS	FIBS	BMOS	MOBS	CDOR	CORD
	RATS		DRIB	BFMU	BUMF	BMOT	TOMB	CDOS	CODS
	STAR	BDIS	BIDS	BFOS	FOBS	BMOU	UMBO		DOCS
	TARS		DIBS	BGIL	GLIB	BMOW	WOMB	CDRU	CRUD
	TSAR	BDLO	BOLD	BGIO	IGBO	BMPU	BUMP		CURD
ARSU	SURA	BDMU	DUMB	BGIH	BRIG	BMSU	BUMS	CDSU	SCUD
	URSA	BDNO	BOND	BGLO	GLOB	BNOO	BOON	CDTU	DUCT
ARSW	WARS	BDNU	BUND	BGNO	BONG	DNOR	BORN	CEER	CERE
ARSY	RAYS	BDOS	BODS	BGNU	BUNG	BNOS	NOBS		CREE
ARTT	TART	BDOU	DOUB	BGOS	BOGS		SNOB	CEFH	CHEF
ARTW	WART	BDOY	BODY		GOBS	BNUY	BONY	CEFL	CLEF
ARTY	ARTY	BDRU	DRUB	BGOY	BOGY	BNRU	BURN	CEGL	CLEG
	TRAY	BDSU	BUDS		GO BY	BNSU	BUNS	CEHK	HECK
ARTZ	TZAR		DUBS		GO-BY		NUBS	CEHO	ECHO
ARVY	VARY	BEEF	BEEF		GOBY		SNUB		OCHE
ARWY	AWRY	BEEN	BEEN	BGRU	GRUB	BNTU	BUNT	CEHT	ETCH
	WARY	BEEP	BEEP	BGSU	BUGS	BOOR	BOOR		TECH
ARXY	X RAY	BEER	BEER	BHLU	BUHL	BOOS	BOOS	CEHW	CHEW
	X-RAY	BEES	BEES	BHOO	HOBO	BOOT	BOOT	CEHZ	CHEZ
ARZZ	RAZZ	BEET	BEET	BHOS	BOSH	BOOY	BOYO	CEIL	LICE
ASSW	SAWS	BEGI	GIBE		HOBS	BOPS	BOPS	CEIM	MICE
ASSY	SAYS	BEGR	BERG	BHOT	BOTH	BORS	ORBS	CEIN	NICE
ASTT	TATS	BEGS	BEGS	BHRU	BUHR		ROBS	CEIP	EPIC
ASTU	TAUS	BEGY	GYBE	BHSU	BUSH		SORB		PICE
ASTV	VAST	BEHR	HERB		HUBS	BORT	BORT	CEIR	CIRE
	VATS	BEIJ	JIBE			BORW	BROW		RICE
ASTW	SWAT	BEIK	BIKE	BIIS	IBIS	BOSS	BOSS	CEIS	ICES
	TAWS		KIBE	BIJS	JIBS		SOBS	CEIT	CITE
	WAST	BEIL	BILE	BIKL	BILK	BOSW	BOWS	CEIV	VICE
ASTY	STAY	BEIN	BINE	BIKR	BIRK		SWOB	CEKN	NECK
ASWY	SWAY	BEIR	BIER	BILL	BILL	BOSY	BOYS	CEKO	COKE
	WAYS		BRIE	BILM	LIMB		YOBS	CEKP	PECK
	YAWS	BEIS	BISE	BILO	BOIL	BOTU	BOUT	CEKR	RECK
ATTU	TAUT	BEIT	BITE	BILP	BLIP	BOTY	TOBY	CELL	CELL
ATTW	TWAT	BEIX	IBEX	BILS	LIBS	BOUY	BUOY	CELO	COLE
	WATT	BEKR	BERK	BIMR	BRIM	BOXY	BOXY	CELT	CELT
AVWY	WAVY		KERB	BINS	BINS	BPRU	BURP	CELU	CLUE
AWXY	WAXY	BELL	BELL		NIBS	BPSU	PUBS	CELW	CLEW
BBEE	BEEB	BELO	BOLE	BINT	BINT	BRRU	BURR	CEMO	COME
BBEL	BLEB		LOBE	BIOR	BIRO	BRSU	BURS	CEMY	CYME
BBES	EBBS	BELP	PLEB		BRIO		RUBS	CENO	CONE
BBEU	BUBE	BELS	BELS	BIOS	IBOS	BRTU	BRUT		ONCE
BBIS	BIBS	BELT	BELT		OBIS	BRUY	BURY	CENT	CENT
BBLO	BLOB	BELU	BLUE	BIOT	OBIT		RUBY	CEOP	COPE
BBLU	BULB	BELW	BLEW	BIRS	RIBS	BSSU	SUBS	CEOR	CORE
BBMO	BOMB	BEMR	BERM	BIRT	BRIT	BSTU	BUST	CEOT	COTE
BBOO	BOOB	BENO	BONE	BISS	SIBS		BUTS	CEOV	COVE
BBOS	BOBS	BENR	BREN	BIST	BITS		STUB	CEPS	SPEC
BBOU	BUBO	BENS	NEBS	BITT	BITT		TUBS	CEPU	PUCE
BBSU	BUBS	BENT	BENT	BJOS	JOBS	BSUY	BUSY	CERT	CERT
BCEI	BICE	BEOO	OBOE	BKLU	BULK		BUYS	CERU	CURE
BCEK	BECK	BEOR	BOER	BKNO	KNOB	BTTU	BUTT		ECRU
BCEU	CUBE		BORE	BKNU	BUNK	BUZZ	BUZZ	CERW	CREW
BCHU	CHUB		ROBE	BKOO	BOOK	CCHI	CHIC	CEST	SECT
BCIR	CRIB	BEOT	TO BE		KOBO	CCKO	COCK		TECS
BCKU	BUCK		TO-BE	BKRU	BURK	CCOO	COCO	CESU	CUES
BCLO	BLOC	BEOY	OBEY	BKSU	BUSK	CDEE	CEDE	CESY	SYCE
BCLU	CLUB	BERS	SERB	BLLO	BOLL	CDEI	CEDI	CETU	CUTE
BCMO	COMB	BERV	VERB	BLLU	BULL		DICE	CFFU	CUFF
BCOS	COBS	BERW	BREW	BLOO	OBOL		ICED	CFIO	COIF
BCRU	CURB	BERY	BYRE	BLOS	LOBS	CDEK	DECK		FOCI
BCSU	CUBS	BEST	BEST		SLOB	CDEO	CODE	CFIS	FISC
BDEI	BIDE		BETS	BLOT	BLOT		COED	CFLO	FLOC
BDEL	BLED	BESW	WEBS		BOLT	CDEU	DUCE	CGHU	CHUG

CGIS	CIGS	CLRU	CURL
CGLO	CLOG	CLTU	CULT
CGOS	COGS	CMOR	CORM
CHIK	HICK	CMSU	SCUM
CHIN	CHIN	CMSW	CWMS
	INCH	CNNO	CONN
CHIP	CHIP	CNOO	COON
CHIR	RICH	CNOR	CORN
CHIS	CHIS	CNOS	CONS
CHIT	CHIT	CNOU	UNCO
	ITCH	CNOY	CONY
CHKO	HOCK	CNSY	SYNC
CHLO	LOCH	COOP	CO-OP
CHMU	CHUM		COOP
	MUCH		POCO
CHOP	CHOP	COOS	COOS
CHOS	COSH	COOT	COOT
CHOU	OUCH	COPR	CROP
CHOW	CHOW	COPS	COPS
CHSU	SUCH	COPT	COPT
CIKK	KICK	COPU	COUP
CIKL	LICK	COPY	COPY
CIKM	MICK	CORS	ROCS
CIKN	NICK	CORW	CROW
CIKP	PICK	COST	COST
CIKR	RICK		COTS
CIKS	SICK		SCOT
CIKT	TICK	COSW	COWS
CIKW	WICK		SCOW
CIKY	ICKY	COSY	COSY
CILO	COIL	COYZ	COZY
	LOCI	CPSU	CUPS
CILP	CLIP		CUSP
CINO	COIN	CRSU	CURS
	ICON	CRSY	SCRY
CINZ	ZINC	CRTU	CURT
CIOR	COIR	CRUX	CRUX
CIOT	OTIC	CSSU	CUSS
CIPS	PICS	CSTU	CUTS
	SPIC		SCUT
CIPT	PICT	CSTY	CYST
CIRU	URIC	DDEE	DEED
CIST	CIST	DDEM	MEDD
	TICS	DDER	REDD
CITY	CITY	DDEU	DUDE
CJKO	JOCK	DDEY	EDDY
CKLO	LOCK	DDOO	DODO
CKLU	LUCK	DDOS	ODDS
CKMO	MOCK	DDRU	RUDD
CKMU	MUCK	DDSU	DUDS
CKNO	CONK		SUDD
	NOCK	DEEF	FEED
CKOO	COOK	DEEG	EDGE
CKOP	POCK	DEEH	HEED
CKOR	CORK	DEEM	DEEM
	ROCK		DEME
CKOS	SOCK		MEDE
CKPU	PUCK	DEEN	DENE
CKRU	RUCK		EDEN
CKSU	SUCK		NEED
CKTU	TUCK	DEEP	DEEP
CLLU	CULL	DEER	DEER
CLMU	CULM		REED
CLOO	COOL	DEES	SEED
	LOCO	DEET	TEED
CLOP	CLOP	DEEW	WEED
CLOS	COLS	DEEY	EYED
CLOT	CLOT	DEFL	FLED
	COLT	DEFN	FEND
CLOW	COWL	DEFS	FEDS
CLOY	CLOY		

DEFT	DEFT	DENY	DENY
DEFU	FEUD		DYNE
DEFY	DEFY	DEOP	DOPE
DEGI	GIED	DEOR	DOER
DEGL	GELD		REDO
DEGO	DOGE		RODE
DEGR	DREG	DEOS	DOES
DEGY	EDGY		DOSE
DEHI	HIDE		ODES
DEHL	HELD	DEOT	DOTE
DEHO	HOED		TOED
DEHR	HERD	DEOV	DOVE
DEHS	SHED	DEOW	OWED
DEHU	HUED	DEOZ	DOZE
DEHY	HYDE	DEPS	PEDS
DEIK	DIKE		SPED
DEIL	DELI	DEPU	DUPE
	IDLE	DERS	REDS
	LIED	DERU	RUDE
DEIM	DIME		RUED
	IDEM	DERV	DERV
DEIN	DINE	DERW	DREW
DEIP	PIED	DERY	DREY
DEIR	DIRE		DYER
	RIDE	DEST	TEDS
DEIS	DIES	DESU	DUES
	IDES		SUED
	SIDE		USED
DEIT	DIET	DESW	DEWS
	EDIT		WEDS
	TIDE	DESY	DYES
	TIED	DESZ	ZEDS
DEIV	DIVE	DETU	DUET
	VIDE	DEWY	DEWY
	VIED	DFFO	DOFF
DEIW	WIDE	DFFU	DUFF
DEJU	JUDE	DFIN	FIND
DEKS	DESK	DFIS	FIDS
	KEDS	DFLO	FOLD
DEKU	DUKE	DFNU	FUND
DEKY	DYKE	DFOO	FOOD
DELL	DELL	DFOR	FORD
DELM	MELD	DGIL	GILD
DELN	LEND	DGIR	GIRD
DELO	DOLE		GRID
	LODE	DGIS	DIGS
DELP	PLED		GIDS
DELS	LEDS	DGLO	GOLD
	SLED	DGNO	DONG
DELU	DUEL	DGNU	DUNG
DELV	VELD	DGOO	GOOD
DELW	LEWD	DGOS	DOGS
	WELD		GODS
DEMN	MEND	DGRU	DRUG
DEMO	DEMO	DGSU	DUGS
	DOME	DHIN	HIND
	MODE	DHIS	DISH
DEMR	DERM	DHLO	HOLD
DEMY	DEMY	DHOO	HOOD
DENO	DONE	DHOS	HODS
	NODE		SHOD
DENR	REND	DHOT	DOTH
DENS	DENS	DHOW	DHOW
	ENDS	DHTU	THUD
	SEND	DIIM	MIDI
DENT	DENT	DIIN	NIDI
	TEND	DIJN	DJIN
DENU	DUNE	DIKN	KIND
	NUDE	DIKR	DIRK
DENV	VEND		
DENW	WEND		

DIKS	DISK
	KIDS
	SKID
DILL	DILL
DILM	MILD
DILO	IDOL
	LIDO
DILS	LIDS
	SILD
	SLID
DILW	WILD
DILY	IDLY
DIMN	MIND
DIMO	MODI
DIMS	DIMS
DINO	DO IN
	NODI
DINR	RIND
DINS	DINS
DINT	DINT
DINW	WIND
DIOT	DO IT
DIOV	VOID
DIPR	DRIP
DIPS	DIPS
DIQU	QUID
DIRS	RIDS
DIRT	DIRT
DIST	DITS
DISY	YIDS
DITY	TIDY
DJOO	DOJO
DJOU	JUDO
DJUY	JUDY
DKNU	DUNK
DKRU	KURD
DKSU	DUSK
DKUU	KUDU
DLLO	DOLL
DLLU	DULL
DLMO	MOLD
DLOP	PLOD
DLOR	LORD
DLOS	SOLD
DLOT	DOLT
	TOLD
DLOU	LOUD
	LUDO
DLOW	WOLD
DLUY	DULY
DMOO	DOOM
	MOOD
DMOR	DORM
DMOS	DOMS
	MODS
DMPU	DUMP
DMRU	DRUM
DNOP	POND
DNOR	DR. NO
DNOS	DONS
	NODS
DNOT	DON'T
DNOU	UNDO
DNOW	DOWN
DNSU	DUNS
DNWY	WYND
DOOR	DOOR
	ROOD
DOOT	TO DO
	TO-DO
DOOW	WOOD

DOPR	DORP, DROP, PROD
DOPS	PODS
DOPU	DO UP
DORS	RODS
DORT	TROD
DORU	DOUR
DORW	WORD
DORY	DORY
DOSS	DOSS, SODS
DOST	DOST, DOTS, TODS
DOSU	DUOS
DOXY	DOXY
DOYZ	DOZY
DPSU	PUDS, SPUD
DRSU	SURD
DRSY	DRYS
DRUU	URDU
DSSU	SUDS
DSTU	DUST, STUD
DTUY	DUTY
EEEP	EPEE
EEFL	FEEL, FLEE
EEFR	FREE, REEF
EEFS	FEES
EEFT	FEET, FETE
EEGH	GHEE
EEGL	GLEE
EEGN	GENE
EEGO	OGEE
EEHL	HEEL
EEHM	HEME
EEHR	HERE
EEHT	THEE
EEHW	WHEE
EEIR	ERIE
EEJP	JEEP
EEJR	JEER
EEJT	JETE
EEKK	KEEK
EEKL	KEEL, LEEK
EEKM	MEEK
EEKN	KEEN, KNEE
EEKP	KEEP, PEEK, PEKE
EEKR	REEK
EEKS	SEEK
EEKW	WEEK
EELP	PEEL, PELE
EELR	LEER, REEL
EELS	EELS, ELSE, LEES
EELY	EELY
EEMR	MERE
EEMS	SEEM
EEMT	MEET, METE, TEEM
EENN	NENE
EENP	NEEP, PEEN
EENR	NE'ER
EENS	SEEN, SENE
EENT	TEEN
EENV	EVEN, NEVE
EEPP	PEEP
EEPR	PEER
EEPS	PEES, SEEP
EEPW	WEEP
EERS	ERSE, SEER, SERE
EERT	TREE
EERV	EVER, VEER
EERW	EWER, WERE
EERY	EYER, EYRE
EESS	SEES
EEST	TEES
EESV	EVES
EESW	EWES, WEES
EESX	EXES
EESY	EYES
EESZ	ZEES
EETW	TWEE
EFFI	FIEF, FIFE
EFFS	EFFS
EFFT	TEFF
EFHT	HEFT
EFIL	FILE, LIEF, LIFE
EFIN	FINE
EFIR	FIRE, RIFE
EFIV	FIVE
EFIW	WIFE
EFKR	KERF
EFLL	FELL
EFLO	FLOE
EFLP	PELF
EFLS	SELF
EFLT	FELT, LEFT
EFLU	FLUE, FUEL
EFLW	FLEW
EFLX	FLEX
EFMU	FUME
EFNR	FERN
EFNS	FENS
EFOR	FORE
EFOS	FOES
EFRS	REFS, SERF
EFRT	FRET
EFST	EFTS, FEST
EFSU	FEUS, FUSE
EFTW	WEFT
EFUZ	FUZE
EGGS	EGGS
EGGY	YEGG
EGHU	HUGE
EGIR	GIER
EGIS	EGIS, GIES
EGIV	GIVE
EGKS	KEGS
EGLN	GLEN
EGLO	LOGE, OGLE
EGLS	GELS, LEGS
EGLU	GLUE, LUGE
EGLY	GLEY
EGMR	GERM
EGMS	GEMS
EGMU	GEUM
EGNO	GONE
EGNS	GENS
EGNT	GENT
EGOR	ERGO, GOER, GORE, OGRE
EGOS	EGOS, GOES
EGPS	PEGS
EGRS	ERGS
EGRU	URGE
EGRW	GREW
EGRY	GREY
EGST	GEST, GETS, TEGS
EHIK	HIKE
EHIR	HEIR, HIRE
EHIS	HIES
EHIV	HIVE
EHLL	HE'LL, HELL
EHLM	HELM
EHLO	HOLE
EHLP	HELP
EHLR	HERL
EHMO	HOME
EHMP	HEMP
EHMS	HEMS, MESH
EHMT	THEM
EHNO	HONE
EHNS	HENS
EHNT	THEN
EHNW	HEWN, WHEN
EHOP	HOPE
EHOR	HERO
EHOS	HOES, HOSE, SHOE
EHOV	HOVE
EHOW	HOWE
EHPW	PHEW
EHPY	HYPE
EHRR	HERR
EHRS	HERS
EHST	ETHS
EHSU	HUES
EHSW	HEWS, SHEW
EHSY	HEYS
EHTW	THEW, WHET
EHTY	THEY
EHWW	WHEW
EHWY	WHEY
EIJV	JIVE
EIKL	LIKE
EIKM	MIKE
EIKN	KINE
EIKP	KEPI, PIKE
EIKT	KITE, TIKE
EILM	LIME, MILE
EILN	LIEN, LINE
EILP	PILE, PLIE
EILR	LIRE, RILE
EILS	ISLE, LEIS, LIES
EILT	TILE
EILU	LIEU
EILV	EVIL, LIVE, VEIL, VILE, VLEI
EILW	LWEI, WILE
EILX	ILEX
EIMM	MIME
EIMN	MIEN, MINE
EIMR	EMIR, MIRE, RIEM, RIME
EIMS	SEMI
EIMT	EMIT, ITEM, MITE, TIME
EINN	NINE
EINP	PEIN, PINE
EINR	ERIN, REIN
EINS	SINE
EINT	TINE
EINV	NEVI, VEIN, VINE
EINW	WINE
EINZ	ZEIN
EIPP	PIPE
EIPR	PIER, RIPE
EIPS	PIES
EIPW	WIPE
EIRS	IRES, RISE, SIRE
EIRT	RITE, TIER, TIRE
EIRV	RIVE, VIER
EIRW	WEIR, WIRE
EIST	SITE, TIES
EICV	VICE, VISE
EISW	WISE
EISZ	SIZE
EITU	ETUI
EITX	EXIT
EITY	YETI
EIVW	VIEW
EJKO	JOKE
EJKR	JERK
EJLL	JELL
EJLO	JOEL
EJNO	JEON
EJNU	JUNE
EJOS	JOES
EJOV	JOVE
EJOY	JOEY
EJSS	JESS
EJST	JEST, JETS
EJSU	JESU
EJSW	JEWS
EJTU	JUTE
EKLP	KELP
EKLS	ELKS, LEKS
EKLT	KELT
EKLU	LUKE
EKMO	MOKE
EKNR	KERN
EKNS	KENS
EKNU	NUKE
EKNW	KNEW
EKOP	POKE
EKOS	SOKE
EKOW	WOKE
EKOY	YOKE
EKPR	PERK
EKPS	KESP, SKEP
EKPT	KEPT
EKPU	PUKE
EKRS	ERKS
EKRT	TREK
EKSW	SKEW
EKSY	KEYS
EKTY	TYKE
ELLS	ELLS, SELL
ELLT	TELL
ELLW	WELL
ELLY	YELL
ELMO	MOLE
ELMS	ELMS
ELMT	MELT
ELMU	MULE
ELMW	MEWL
ELNO	LONE, NOEL

9

ELNS	LENS
ELNT	LENT
ELNU	LUNE
ELOP	LOPE
	POLE
ELOR	LORE
	ROLE
ELOS	LEOS
	LOSE
	SLOE
	SOLE
ELOV	LOVE
	VOLE
ELPT	PELT
ELPU	PULE
ELPY	YELP
ELRU	LURE
	RULE
ELRY	LYRE
	RELY
ELSS	LESS
ELST	LEST
	LETS
ELSU	LUES
	SLUE
ELSW	SLEW
	WELS
ELSY	LEYS
	LYES
	LYSE
ELTT	LETT
ELTU	LUTE
ELTW	WELT
ELUY	YULE
ELVY	LEVY
EMMO	MEMO
EMMY	EMMY
EMNO	OMEN
EMNU	MENU
EMOP	MOPE
	POEM
	POME
EMOR	MORE
EMOS	SOME
EMOT	MOTE
	TOME
EMOU	MOUE
EMOV	MOVE
EMOW	MEOW
EMPR	PERM
EMPT	TEMP
EMRS	REMS
EMRT	TERM
EMSS	MESS
EMST	STEM
EMSU	EMUS
	MUSE
EMSW	MEWS
	SMEW
EMTU	MUTE
ENNO	NEON
	NONE
ENOP	NOPE
	OPEN
	PEON
	PONE
ENOR	ONER
ENOS	EONS
	NOES
	NOSE
	ONES
ENOT	NOTE
	TONE
ENOV	OVEN
ENOX	OXEN
ENOZ	ZONE
ENPS	PENS
ENPU	NUPE
ENRT	RENT
	TERN
ENRU	RUNE
ENRW	WREN
ENSS	NESS
ENST	NEST
	NETS
	SENT
	STEN
	TENS
ENSW	NEWS
	SEWN
	WENS
ENSY	SYNE
	YENS
ENTT	TENT
ENTU	TUNE
ENTV	VENT
ENTW	NEWT
	WENT
ENTX	NEXT
ENVY	ENVY
EOOZ	OOZE
EOPP	PEPO
	POPE
EOPR	PORE
	ROPE
EOPS	EPOS
	PESO
	POSE
EOPT	POET
	TOPE
EOPX	EXPO
EORS	EROS
	ORES
	ROES
	ROSE
	SORE
EORT	ROTE
	TORE
EORU	EURO
	ROUE
EORV	OVER
	ROVE
EORW	WORE
EORY	YORE
EORZ	ZERO
EOST	TOES
EOSW	OWES
	WOES
EOTT	TOTE
EOTV	VETO
	VOTE
EOTY	EYOT
EOVW	WOVE
EOYZ	OYEZ
EPPR	PREP
	REPP
EPPS	PEPS
EPRS	REPS
EPRT	PERT
EPRU	PERU
	PURE
EPRY	PREY
	PYRE
EPST	PEST
	PETS
	STEP
EPSW	PEWS
	SPEW
EPSY	ESPY
EPTW	WEPT
EPTY	TYPE
ERRS	ERRS
ERST	REST
	RETS
ERSU	RUES
	RUSE
	SUER
	SURE
	USER
ERSV	REVS
ERSY	RYES
ERTU	TRUE
ERTV	VERT
ERTW	WERT
ERTY	TREY
	TYRE
ERVY	VERY
ESST	SETS
ESSU	SUES
	USES
ESSW	SEWS
ESTT	SETT
	STET
	TEST
ESTU	SUET
ESTV	VEST
	VETS
ESTW	STEW
	WEST
	WETS
ESTX	SEXT
ESTZ	ZEST
ESWY	YEWS
ESXY	SEXY
ETTX	TEXT
ETVX	VEXT
FFGU	GUFF
FFHU	HUFF
FFIJ	JIFF
FFIM	MIFF
FFIN	NIFF
FFIR	RIFF
FFIT	TIFF
FFIY	IFFY
FFLU	LUFF
FFMU	MUFF
FFOT	TOFF
FFPU	PUFF
FFRU	RUFF
FFTU	TUFF
FGIS	FIGS
FGIT	GIFT
FGLO	FLOG
	GOLF
FGLU	GULF
FGOO	GOOF
FGOR	FROG
FGOS	FOGS
FGSU	FUGS
FHII	HI FI
	HI-FI
FHIS	FISH
FHNO	FOHN
FHOO	HOOF
FIIJ	FIJI
FIKN	FINK
FILL	FILL
FILM	FILM
FILO	FOIL
FILP	FLIP
FILS	FILS
FILT	FLIT
	LIFT
FIMR	FIRM
FINN	FINN
FINO	FINO
	INFO
FINR	FIRN
FINS	FINS
FIRS	FIRS
FIRT	FRIT
	RIFT
FIST	FIST
	FITS
	SIFT
FISU	SUFI
FIZZ	FIZZ
FKLO	FOLK
FKNU	FUNK
FKOR	FORK
FLLU	FULL
FLOO	FOOL
FLOP	FLOP
FLOT	LOFT
FLOU	FOUL
FLOW	FLOW
	FOWL
	WOLF
FLRU	FURL
FLUX	FLUX
FMOR	FORM
	FROM
FMUY	FUMY
FNOT	FONT
FOOP	POOF
FOOR	ROOF
FOOT	FOOT
FOOW	WOOF
FOPR	PROF
FOPS	FOPS
FOPU	POUF
FORT	FORT
FORU	FOUR
FOST	SOFT
FOSU	UFOS
FOTT	TOFT
FOXY	FOXY
FRSU	FURS
	SURF
FRTU	TURF
FRUY	FURY
FSSU	FUSS
FTTU	TUFT
FUZZ	FUZZ
GGHO	HOGG
GGIS	GIGS
GGNO	GONG
GGOO	GO-GO
GGOR	GROG
GGUV	VUGG
GHHI	HIGH
GHIN	NIGH
GHIS	SIGH
GHIW	WHIG
GHNU	HUNG
GHOS	GOSH
	HOGS
GHOT	GOTH
GHOY	YOGH
GHSU	GUSH
	HUGS
GHTU	THUG
GHUV	VUGH
GIJS	JIGS
GIKN	KING
GILL	GILL
GILN	LING
GILR	GIRL
GILT	GILT
GILU	UGLI
GIMN	MING
GIMR	GRIM
GINO	GO IN
GINP	PING
GINR	GIRN
	GRIN
	RING
GINS	GINS
	SIGN
	SING
	SNIG
GINW	WING
GINZ	ZING
GIOR	GIRO
GIOT	GO IT
GIOY	YOGI
GIPR	GRIP
	PRIG
GIPS	PIGS
GIRS	RIGS
GIRT	GIRT
	GRIT
	TRIG
GIST	GIST
	GITS
GISW	SWIG
	WIGS
GITW	TWIG
GJOS	JOGS
GJSU	JUGS
GKNU	GUNK
GLLU	GULL
GLMU	GLUM
GLNO	LONG
GLNU	LUNG
GLOO	LOGO
GLOS	LOGS
	SLOG
GLOW	GLOW
GLPU	GULP
	PLUG
GLSU	LUGS
	SLUG
GLTU	GLUT
GLUY	UGLY
GMOO	MOOG
GMOS	SMOG
GMSU	GUMS
	MUGS
	SMUG
GMSY	GYMS

GNOO	GO ON	HLLU	HULL	IKKN	KINK	ILWY	WILY	IPSY	I SPY
	GOON	HLMO	HOLM	IKKR	KIRK	IMNS	NIMS		I-SPY
	NO GO	HLOS	HOLS	IKLL	KILL	IMNT	MINT		YIPS
	NO-GO	HLOT	HOLT	IKLM	MILK	IMNX	MINX	IPSZ	ZIPS
GNOP	PONG		LOTH	IKLN	KILN	IMOT	OMIT	IPTU	TUPI
GNOS	NOGS	HLOW	HOWL		LINK	IMPP	PIMP	IPTY	PITY
	SNOG	HLOY	HOLY	IKLO	KILO	IMPR	PRIM	IQTU	QUIT
	SONG	HLRU	HURL	IKLS	SILK	IMPS	IMPS	IQUZ	QUIZ
GNOT	TONG	HLSU	LUSH	IKLT	KILT		SIMP	IRSS	SIRS
GNOW	GOWN		SHUL	IKMN	MINK	IMRS	MIRS	IRST	STIR
GNRU	RUNG	HMNY	HYMN	IKMR	MIRK		RIMS	IRTW	WRIT
GNSU	GNUS	HMOO	HOMO	IKMS	SKIM	IMRT	TRIM	IRWY	WIRY
	GUNS		MOHO	IKNO	IKON	IMRU	RIMU	ISST	SITS
	SNUG	HMOS	OHMS		OINK	IMRV	MIRV	ISTT	TITS
	SUNG	HMOT	MOTH	IKNP	PINK	IMRY	MIRY	ISTU	SUIT
GNTU	TUNG	HMOW	WHOM	IKNR	RINK		RIMY	ISTW	WITS
GOOS	GOOS	HMOY	HOMY	IKNS	INKS	IMSS	ISMS	ISWZ	SWIZ
GOOT	GO TO	HMPU	HUMP		SINK		MISS	ITTW	TWIT
	TOGO	HMSU	HUMS		SKIN	IMST	MIST	IZZZ	ZIZZ
GOPU	GO UP		MUSH	IKNT	KNIT	IMSW	SWIM	JJUU	JU JU
GORT	GROT	HMTY	MYTH	IKNW	WINK	IMTT	MITT		JUJU
GORW	GROW	HNOP	PHON	IKNY	INKY	INNS	INNS	JKNU	JUNK
GORY	GORY	HNOR	HORN	IKPS	KIPS	INOP	PION	JKOY	JOKY
	GYRO	HNOS	NOSH		SKIP	INOR	IRON	JLOT	JOLT
	ORGY	HNSU	HUNS		SPIK	INOS	IONS	JLOW	JOWL
GOST	TOGS		SHUN	IKRS	IRKS		SION	JLUY	JULY
GOSW	WOGS	HNTU	HUNT		KRIS	INOT	INTO	JMPU	JUMP
GOSY	GOYS	HOOP	HOOP		RISK		NOT I	JOSS	JOSS
GOTU	GOUT		POOH	IKSS	KISS	INOV	VINO	JOST	JOTS
GPSU	PUGS	HOOS	SHOO		SKIS	INOW	WINO	JOSY	JOYS
GPSY	GYPS	HOOT	HOOT	IKST	KITS	INOY	YONI	JRUY	JURY
GRSU	RUGS	HOOY	YO HO		SKIT	INOZ	ZION	JSTU	JUST
GRTU	TRUG	HOPS	HOPS	ILLM	MILL	INPS	NIPS		JUTS
GRUU	GURU		POSH	ILLO	LI-LO		PINS	KKOO	KOOK
GSTU	GUST		SHOP	ILLP	PILL		SNIP	KLOO	LOOK
	GUTS	HOPW	WHOP	ILLR	RILL		SPIN	KLOY	YOLK
	TUGS	HOPY	HYPO	ILLS	ILLS	INPT	PINT	KLRU	LURK
GSUV	GUVS	HORT	THRO		SILL	INPY	PINY	KLSU	SULK
GSUY	GUYS	HORU	HOUR	ILLT	LILT	INQU	QUIN	KMNO	MONK
HHOO	HO-HO	HOST	HOST		TILL	INRU	RUIN	KMRU	MURK
HHSU	HUSH		SHOT	ILLW	WILL	INSS	SINS	KMSU	MUSK
HIKS	SIKH		TOSH	ILLY	LILY	INST	ISN'T	KNOO	NOOK
HIKT	KITH	HOSW	HOWS	ILMO	LIMO		NITS	KNOT	KNOT
HILL	HILL		SHOW	ILMP	LIMP		SNIT	KNOW	KNOW
HILT	HILT	HOSY	HOYS	ILMS	MILS		TINS	KNPU	PUNK
HIMS	SHIM	HOTU	THOU		SLIM	INSW	WINS	KNRU	KNUR
HIMW	WHIM	HPSU	PUSH	ILMT	MILT	INTT	TINT	KNSU	SUNK
HINS	SHIN	HPTU	PHUT	ILMY	LIMY	INTU	UNIT	KOOR	ROOK
HINT	HINT	HRSU	RUSH	ILNO	LINO	INTW	TWIN	KOOT	KOTO
	THIN	HRTU	HURT		LION	INTY	TINY		TOOK
HINW	WHIN		RUTH		LOIN	INUZ	ZUNI	KOPR	PORK
HIPS	HIPS		THRU	ILNT	LINT	INVY	VINY	KOPY	POKY
	PISH	HSSU	HUSS	ILNY	INLY	INWY	WINY	KORW	WORK
	SHIP	HSTU	HUTS		LINY	IOPT	TOPI	KORY	YORK
HIPT	PITH		SHUT	ILOR	ROIL	IORS	SORI	KOSU	SOUK
HIPW	WHIP		THUS	ILOS	OILS	IORT	RIOT	KOSW	WOKS
HISS	HISS		TUSH		SILO		TIRO	KPUU	PUKU
HIST	HIST	HSWY	WHYS		SOIL		TORI	KRSU	KRUS
	HITS	IIKW	KIWI	ILOT	LOTI		TRIO		RUSK
	THIS	IILP	PILI		TOIL	IPPS	PIPS	KRTU	TURK
HISW	WISH	IIMN	MINI	ILOV	VIOL	IPQU	QUIP	KRUU	KURU
HITW	WHIT	IIMP	IMPI	ILOY	OILY	IPRS	RIPS	KSTU	TUSK
	WITH	IINS	NISI	ILPS	LIPS	IPRT	TRIP	LLLO	LOLL
HIWZ	WHIZ	IINT	IN IT		LISP	IPSS	SIPS	LLLU	LULL
HJNO	JOHN	IIRS	IRIS		SLIP	IPST	PITS	LLMO	MOLL
HKLO	KOHL	IITT	TITI	ILST	LIST		SPIT	LLMU	MULL
HKLU	HULK	IJKN	JINK		SILT		TIPS	LLNU	NULL
HKNO	HONK	IJNN	JINN		SLIT	IPSV	SPIV	LLOP	POLL
HKNU	HUNK	IJNO	JOIN	ILSY	SYLI	IPSW	WISP	LLOR	ROLL
HKOO	HOOK	IJNX	JINX	ILTT	TILT			LLOT	TOLL
HKSU	HUSK			ILTW	WILT			LLPU	PULL

LLUU	LULU	MOSS	MOSS	OOSW	WOOS	PRSY	SPRY
LMOO	LOOM	MOST	MOST	OOSZ	ZOOS	PSSU	PUSS
LMOS	MOLS		MOTS	OOTT	OTTO		SUPS
	OLMS		TOMS		TOOT	PSTU	PUTS
LMOT	MOLT	MOSU	SUMO	OOTZ	ZOOT		TUPS
LMPU	LUMP	MOSW	MOWS	OOUZ	OUZO	PSUY	PUYS
	PLUM	MOUV	OVUM	OOYY	YO YO	PTTU	PUTT
LMSU	LUMS	MPPU	PUMP		YO-YO	RSTU	RUST
	SLUM	MPRU	RUMP	OOYZ	OOZY		RUTS
LNOO	LOON	MPSU	SUMP	OPPR	PROP	RSUU	URUS
LNOY	ONLY	MRSU	RUMS	OPPS	POPS	RTUY	YURT
LNXY	LYNX	MSSU	MUSS	OPRS	PROS	SSSU	SUSS
LOOP	LOOP		SUMS	OPRT	PORT	STTU	TUTS
	POLO	MSTU	MUST	OPRU	POUR	TTUU	TUTU
	POOL		SMUT		ROUP		
LOOS	LOOS		TUMS	OPRW	PROW		
	SOLO	MSUW	SWUM	OPRY	ROPY		
	SOOL	MTTU	MUTT	OPSS	SOPS		
LOOT	LOOT	NNOO	NOON	OPST	OPTS		
	TOOL	NNOR	NORN		POST		
LOOW	WOOL	NNOU	NON U		POTS		
LOPP	PLOP		NON-U		SPOT		
LOPS	LOPS		NOUN		STOP		
	SLOP	NNSU	NUNS		TOPS		
LOPT	PLOT		SUNN	OPSU	OPUS		
LOPY	PLOY	NNWY	WYNN		SOUP		
	POLY	NOOS	SO ON	OPSW	SWOP		
LORT	ROTL		SOON		WOPS		
LORU	LOUR	NOOT	ONTO	OPSY	POSY		
LOSS	LOSS		TOON	OPTU	POUT		
LOST	LOST	NOPR	PORN	OPTY	TYPO		
	LOTS	NOPS	PONS	OPXY	POXY		
	SLOT	NOPU	UPON	ORRT	TORR		
LOSU	SOUL	NOPY	PONY	ORST	ROTS		
LOSW	LOWS	NORT	TORN		SORT		
	OWLS	NORW	WORN		TORS		
	SLOW	NOSS	SONS	ORSU	OURS		
LOTU	LOUT	NOST	SNOT		SOUR		
LOTV	VOLT		TONS	ORSW	ROWS		
LOWY	YOWL	NOSU	NOUS	ORSY	ROSY		
LPPU	PULP		ONUS	ORTT	TORT		
LPRU	PURL	NOSW	OWNS		TROT		
LPSU	PLUS		SNOW	ORTU	ROUT		
LRSU	SLUR		SOWN		TOUR		
LSTU	LUST	NOSY	NOSY	ORTW	TROW		
	SLUT	NOTU	UNTO		WORT		
LTUZ	LUTZ	NOTW	NOWT	ORTY	TORY		
LUUZ	ZULU		TOWN		TROY		
MMOS	MOMS		WONT		TYRO		
MMSU	MUMS	NOTY	TONY	ORUX	ROUX		
MNOO	MONO	NOXY	ONYX	ORUY	YOUR		
	MOON	NPSU	PUNS	ORXY	ORYX		
MNOR	MORN		SPUN	OSST	SOTS		
	NORM	NPTU	PUNT		TOSS		
MNOU	MUON	NPUY	PUNY	OSSU	SOUS		
MNOW	MOWN	NRSU	RUNS	OSSW	SOWS		
MOOR	MOOR		URNS	OSSY	SOYS		
	MORO	NRTU	RUNT	OSTT	TOTS		
	ROOM		TURN	OSTU	OUST		
MOOS	MOOS	NSSU	SUNS		OUTS		
MOOT	MOOT	NSTU	NUTS	OSTW	STOW		
MOOZ	ZOOM		STUN		SWOT		
MOPP	POMP		TUNS		TOWS		
MOPR	PROM	OOPP	POOP		TWOS		
	ROMP	OOPR	POOR	OSTY	TOYS		
MOPS	MOPS	OOPS	OOPS	OSVW	VOWS		
	POMS	OORS	ROOS	OSWW	WOWS		
MOPY	YOMP	OORT	ROOT	OTTU	TOUT		
MORS	MORS	OOSS	SO SO	PPSU	PUPS		
MORT	MORT		SO-SO	PRRU	PURR		
MORW	WORM	OOST	SOOT	PRSU	SPUR		

AAABK	KAABA	AAEKP	APEAK	AAIPS	PAISA	AANST	SANTA	ABDEO	ABODE	ABEFL	FABLE
AABCL	CABAL	AAEKW	AWAKE	AAIRS	ARIAS		SATAN		ADOBE	ABEGL	BAGEL
AABDE	BAAED	AAELP	PALEA	AAIRT	ATRIA	AANSU	SAUNA	ABDER	BARED		GABLE
AABEM	ABEAM	AAELR	AREAL		TIARA	AAORT	AORTA		BEARD	ABEGN	BEGAN
	AMEBA	AAEMZ	AMAZE	AAITW	AWAIT	AAPPS	PAPAS		BREAD	ABEGR	BARGE
AABHI	BAHAI	AAENP	PAEAN	AAJLP	JALAP	AAPPW	PAPAW		DEBAR	ABEGT	BEGAT
AABIL	LABIA	AAENR	ARENA	AAJNP	JAPAN	AAPRO	PARAO	ABDES	BASED	ABEHO	BOHEA
AABIR	BRAAI	AAERS	AREAS	AAKKS	KAKAS	AAPRT	APART		BEADS		OBEAH
AABIZ	BAIZA	AACRW	AWARE	AAKKY	KAYAK		AT PAR	ABDET	BATED	ABEHT	BATHE
AABLN	BANAL	AAEST	AT SEA	AAKLO	KOALA	AAPST	PASTA	ABDEU	DAUBE	ABEIZ	BAIZE
AABLR	LABRA	AAFFJ	JAFFA	AAKLP	KALPA	AAQRT	QATAR	ABDEY	BAYED	ABEKL	BLEAK
AABLS	BAALS	AAFIM	MAFIA	AAKLR	KRAAL	AARRS	ARRAS		BEADY	ABEKR	BAKER
	BALAS	AAFIN	NAAFI	AAKMR	KARMA	AARRU	AURAR	ABDIL	AD LIB		BRAKE
	BALSA	AAFLT	FATAL		MAKAR	AARRY	ARRAY		AD-LIB		BREAK
	BASAL	AAFNU	FAUNA	AAKNS	AKANS	AARST	RASTA	ABDIR	BRAID	ABEKS	BAKES
AABLT	TABLA	AAGHL	GALAH	AAKNT	TANKA		RATAS		RABID		BEAKS
AABMM	MAMBA	AAGHN	GHANA	AAKNZ	KAZAN	AARSU	AURAS	ABDLN	BLAND	ABELL	BE ALL
AABMS	SAMBA	AAGIN	AGAIN	AAKPP	KAPPA	AARTT	ATTAR	ABDLY	BADLY		BE-ALL
AABNW	BWANA	AAGIS	SAIGA	AAKPR	PARKA		TATAR	ABDNR	BRAND		LABEL
	NAWAB	AAGIT	TAIGA	AAKRT	KARAT	AARTW	AT WAR	ABDNS	BANDS	ABELM	AMBLE
AABRS	ARABS	AAGJN	GANJA	AALLM	LLAMA	AASSY	ASSAY	ABDNY	BANDY		BLAME
	SABRA	AAGLL	ALGAL	AALLU	ALULA	AASTV	AVAST	ABDOR	BOARD	ABELR	ABLER
AACCO	CACAO		GALLA	AALLY	ALLAY	ABBCY	CABBY		BROAD		BLARE
AACDH	DACHA	AAGLN	LAGAN	AALMR	ALARM	ABBEK	KEBAB		DOBRA		BLEAR
AACEP	APACE	AAGLS	AI GAS	AALMS	LAMAS	ABBEL	BABEL	ABDRS	BARDS	ABELS	BALES
AACFI	FACIA		GALAS	AALMT	MALTA	ABBES	BABES		BRADS		BLASE
AACKL	ALACK	AAGLV	VAGAL	AALMY	MALAY	ABBGY	GABBY		DRABS		SABLE
AACLL	CALLA	AAGMM	GAMMA	AALNS	NASAL	ABBIR	RABBI	ABDRY	DARBY	ABELT	BLEAT
AACLN	CANAL		MAGMA	AALNT	NATAL	ABBLS	BLABS	ABDSU	BAUDS		TABLE
AACLV	CAVAL	AAGNP	PAGAN	AALNV	NAVAL	ABBLU	BABUL		DAUBS	ABELY	BELAY
AACMO	MACAO		PANGA	AALNY	NYALA		BUBAL	ABDSW	BAWDS		
AACMW	MACAW	AAGNR	GRANA	AALPP	APPAL	ABBMO	A BOMB	ABDWY	BAWDY		
AACNZ	ANZAC	AAGNS	NAGAS		PAPAL	ABBNO	NABOB	ABDYY	BY DAY		
AACPS	PACAS	AAGOR	AGORA	AALPY	PLAYA	ABBOT	ABBOT				
AACRS	SACRA	AAGRS	AGARS	AALPZ	LA PAZ	ABBRS	BARBS				
AACRT	CARAT	AAGSS	SAGAS		PLAZA	ABBSU	BABUS				
AACUV	VACUA	AAGUV	GUAVA	AALRT	ALTAR	ABBTY	TABBY				
AADEG	ADAGE	AAHHS	HA-HAS		RATAL	ABBYY	YABBY				
AADEH	AHEAD	AAHJR	RAJAH	AALRU	AURAL	ABCCY	BACCY				
AADFR	FARAD	AAHKS	HAKAS	AALRV	LARVA	ABCEH	BEACH				
AADGG	DAGGA	AAHLL	ALLAH	AALRZ	LAZAR	ABCEL	CABLE				
AADGR	GARDA	AAHLP	ALPHA	AALST	ATLAS	ABCER	BRACE				
AADHL	HADAL	AAHMS	AMAHS	AALSV	LAVAS		CABER				
AADIL	DALAI	AAHNS	HANSA	AALWY	ALWAY	ABCHT	BATCH				
AADIN	NAIAD	AAHPS	PASHA	AAMMM	MAMMA	ABCIN	CABIN				
AADKY	DAYAK	AAHRS	HAARS	AAMMS	MAMAS	ABCIR	BARIC				
AADLS	SALAD	AAHSU	HAUSA	AAMNN	MANNA		CARIB				
AADMM	MADAM	AAHSW	AWASH	AAMNT	ATMAN	ABCIS	BASIC				
AADMN	AD MAN	AAHSY	AYAHS		MANTA	ABCKL	BLACK				
	ADMAN	AAILN	LIANA	AAMNY	MAYAN	ABCKS	BACKS				
AADMR	DAMAR	AAILS	ALIAS	AAMOR	AROMA	ABCNO	BACON				
	DRAMA	AAILV	AVAIL	AAMOS	OMASA	ABCNU	CUBAN				
AADNP	PANDA	AAILX	AXIAL		SAMOA	ABCOR	CAROB				
AADPT	ADAPT	AAIMN	AMNIA	AAMPP	PAMPA		COBRA				
AADRR	RADAR		ANIMA	AAMPR	PRAAM	ABCRS	CRABS				
AADRW	AWARD		MANIA	AAMSS	AMASS	ABCRT	BRACT				
AADTY	ADYTA	AAIMR	MARIA	AAMSY	MAYAS	ABCSS	SCABS				
AAEGL	ALGAE	AAIMS	MASAI	AANNN	NANNA	ABCSU	SCUBA				
	GALEA	AAINP	APIAN	AANNS	ANNAS	ABDEG	BADGE				
AAEGN	AN AGE	AAINR	ARIAN	AANRS	SARAN		DEBAG				
AAEGP	AGAPE		NAIRA	AANRT	ANTRA	ABDEI	ABIDE				
AAEGT	AGATE	AAINS	ASIAN		RAN AT	ABDEK	BAKED				
AAEGV	AGAVE	AAINV	AVIAN	AANRY	ARYAN	ABDEL	BLADE				

ABELZ	BLAZE	ABJNO	BANJO	ABSSY	ABYSS	ACEHL	CHELA	ACEST	CASTE
ABEMR	AMBER	ABJOT	JABOT	ABSTU	ABUTS		LEACH		CATES
	BREAM	ABKLN	BLANK		TABUS	ACEHN	ENCHA	ACESU	CAUSE
ABEMS	BEAMS	ABKLS	BALKS		TUBAS	ACEHP	CHAPE		SAUCE
ABEMY	BEAMY	ABKLU	BAULK	ABTTY	BATTY		CHEAP	ACESV	CAVES
	EMBAY	ABKNS	BANKS	ABWYY	BYWAY		PEACH	ACETT	TACET
	MAYBE	ABKRS	BARKS	ACCDE	DECCA	ACEHR	REACH	ACETU	ACUTE
ABENO	BEANO	ABKRY	BRAKY	ACCDY	CYCAD	ACEHS	ACHES	ACETX	EXACT
ABENS	BANES	ABKSS	BASKS	ACCEH	CACHE		CHASE	ACETZ	AZTEC
	BEANS	ABLLS	BALLS	ACCEL	CECAL		THECA	ACFFH	CHAFF
ABEOT	E BOAT	ABLLU	BULLA	ACCEM	MECCA	ACEHT	CHEAT	ACFFS	CAFFS
ABEOV	ABOVE	ABLLY	BALLY	ACCHO	COACH		TEACH	ACFIL	CALIF
ABERR	BARER	ABLMS	BALMS	ACCHT	CATCH	ACEIM	AMICE	ACFLO	FOCAL
	BARRE		LAMBS	ACCIR	CIRCA	ACEIN	NAICE	ACFLS	CALFS
ABERS	BARES	ABLMU	ALBUM	ACCIT	CACTI	ACEIR	ERICA	ACFNR	FRANC
	BASER	ABLMY	BALMY	ACCKL	CLACK	ACEKR	CRAKE	ACFNY	FANCY
	BEARS	ABLOR	LABOR	ACCKR	CRACK		CREAK	ACFPU	F.A. CUP
	BRAES		LOBAR	ACCOO	COCOA	ACEKS	CAKES	ACFRS	SCARF
	SABRE	ABLOS	BOLAS	ACCUY	YUCCA	ACELM	CAMEL	ACFRT	CRAFT
ABERV	BRAVE	ABLRU	LUBRA	ACDDY	CADDY		MACLE	ACFRY	FARCY
ABERY	BY EAR	ABLRW	BRAWL	ACDEF	FACED	ACELN	CLEAN	ACFST	FACTS
ABERZ	BRAZE	ABLSS	SLABS	ACDEG	CADGE		LANCE	ACGIM	MAGIC
	ZEBRA	ABLST	BLAST		CAGED	ACELP	PLACE	ACGIN	ACING
ABESS	BASES	ABLSW	BAWLS	ACDEH	ACHED	ACELR	CARLE	ACGIR	CIGAR
ABEST	ABETS	ABLTU	TUBAL	ACDEK	CAKED		CLEAR	ACGLN	CLANG
	BASTE	ABLWY	BY LAW	ACDEL	DECAL	ACELS	LACES	ACGNO	CONGA
	BATES		BYLAW		LACED		SCALE	ACGOR	CARGO
	BEAST	ABLYY	LAY BY	ACDEN	ACNED	ACELT	CLEAT	ACGRS	CRAGS
	BEATS		LAY-BY		CANED		ECLAT		SCRAG
	BETAS	ABMMO	MAMBO		DANCE	ACELV	CALVE	ACGSS	CS GAS
	TABES	ABMOS	AMBOS	ACDEP	PACED	ACEMO	CAMEO	ACHHT	HATCH
ABESU	ABUSE		SAMBO	ACDER	CADRE		COMAE	ACHIM	MICAH
	BEAUS	ABMRU	BURMA		CARED	ACEMR	CREAM	ACHIN	CHAIN
ABESY	BY SEA		RUMBA		CEDAR	ACEMS	ACMES		CHINA
ABETU	BEAUT		UMBRA		RACED		CAMES	ACHIO	CHIAO
ABEUX	BEAUX	ABMRY	BARMY	ACDES	CASED		MACES	ACHIR	CHAIR
ABGGY	BAGGY	ABNNS	BANNS	ACDET	ACTED	ACENO	CANOE	ACHIS	CHAIS
ABGHN	BHANG	ABNOR	BARON		CADET		OCEAN	ACHIT	AITCH
ABGNO	GABON	ABNOT	BATON	ACDEV	CAVED	ACENP	PECAN	ACHKL	CHALK
ABGNS	BANGS	ABNRS	BARNS	ACDEW	CAWED	ACENR	CRANE	ACHKS	HACKS
ABGRS	BRAGS	ABNRT	BRANT	ACDEY	DECAY		NACRE		SHACK
	GARBS	ABNRU	BURAN	ACDHR	CHARD	ACENS	CANES	ACHKW	WHACK
	GRABS		UNBAR	ACDIR	ACRID	ACENT	ENACT	ACHLO	LOACH
ABHIS	SAHIB		URBAN	ACDIS	ACIDS	ACEOX	COXAE	ACHLR	LARCH
ABHIT	HABIT	ABNRW	BRAWN		ASDIC	ACEPR	CAPER	ACHLS	CLASH
ABHOR	ABHOR	ABNRY	BARNY	ACDIT	DICTA		PACER	ACHLT	LATCH
ABHRS	BRASH	ABNTU	BANTU	ACDLS	CLADS		RECAP	ACHMO	MACHO
ABHST	BAHTS	ABOOT	TABOO		SCALD	ACEPS	CAPES		MOCHA
	BATHS	ABOQT	Q BOAT	ACDLU	DUCAL		PACES	ACHMP	CHAMP
ABIIL	ALIBI	ABORR	ARBOR	ACDNY	CANDY		SCAPE	ACHMR	CHARM
ABIIT	TIBIA	ABORS	BOARS	ACDOS	CODAS		SPACE		MARCH
ABIKT	BATIK	ABORT	ABORT	ACDOT	OCTAD	ACEPT	EPACT	ACHMS	CHASM
ABILN	BLAIN		BOART	ACDRS	CARDS	ACERR	RACER	ACHMT	MATCH
ABILR	BRAIL		TABOR	ACDTU	DUCAT	ACERS	ACRES	ACHNR	RANCH
	LIBRA	ABORV	BRAVO	ACEEK	ACKEE		CARES	ACHNT	CHANT
ABILS	BAILS	ABORX	BORAX	ACEEP	PEACE		CARSE		NATCH
	BASIL	ABOSS	BASSO	ACEES	CEASE		RACES	ACHOP	POACH
ABILT	BALTI	ABOST	BOAST	ACEFH	CHAFE		SCARE	ACHOR	ROACH
ABILY	LIBYA		BOATS	ACEFL	FECAL		SERAC	ACHOS	CHAOS
ABIMS	IAMBS		SABOT	ACEFR	FACER	ACERT	CARET	ACHOV	HAVOC
ABIMT	AMBIT	ABOTU	ABOUT		FARCE		CATER	ACHPR	PARCH
ABINR	BAIRN		U BOAT	ACEFS	CAFES		CRATE	ACHPS	CHAPS
	BRAIN		U-BOAT		FACES		REACT		PASCH
ABINS	BASIN	ABQSU	SQUAB	ACEFT	FACET		RECTA	ACHPT	PATCH
ABIOT	BIOTA	ABRSS	BRASS	ACEGL	GLACE		TRACE	ACHRR	CHARR
ABIRR	BRIAR	ABRST	BRATS	ACEGR	GRACE	ACERV	CARVE	ACHRS	CHARS
ABIRY	BY AIR		T BARS	ACEGS	CAGES		CAVER		CRASH
ABISS	BASIS	ABRSU	BURSA	ACEGY	CAGEY		CRAVE	ACHRT	CHART
	BASSI	ABRSY	BRAYS	ACEHK	CHEKA	ACERZ	CRAZE	ACHRY	CHARY
ABIST	BAITS	ABSST	STABS		HACEK	ACESS	CASES	ACHST	CHATS
ABJMS	JAMBS	ABSSW	SWABS						

ACHSW	CHAWS / SCHWA
ACHTW	WATCH
ACHTY	YACHT
ACIIL	CILIA / ILIAC
ACILL	LILAC
ACILM	CLAIM / MALIC
ACILS	SALIC
ACILT	TICAL
ACILV	CAVIL
ACILX	CALIX
ACIMN	MANIC
ACIMR	MICRA
ACINN	INCAN
ACINP	PANIC
ACINR	CAIRN
ACINS	INCAS
ACINT	ACTIN / ANTIC / CAN IT!
ACIOT	COATI
ACIOZ	AZOIC
ACIPR	CARPI
ACIPS	ASPIC / SPICA
ACIRT	ARTIC
ACIRU	AURIC / CAURI / CURIA
ACIRV	VICAR
ACITT	ATTIC / TACIT
ACJKS	JACKS
ACKKN	KNACK
ACKLN	CLANK
ACKLO	CLOAK
ACKLS	CALKS / LACKS / SLACK
ACKLU	CAULK
ACKMS	MACKS / SMACK
ACKMU	AMUCK
ACKNR	CRANK
ACKNS	SNACK
ACKOR	CROAK
ACKPS	PACKS
ACKQU	QUACK
ACKRS	CARKS / RACKS
ACKRT	TRACK
ACKRW	WRACK
ACKSS	CASKS / SACKS
ACKST	STACK / TACKS
ACKSW	WACKS
ACKSY	YACKS
ACKTY	TACKY
ACKWY	WACKY
ACLLO	LOCAL
ACLLS	CALLS / SCALL
ACLMP	CLAMP
ACLMS	CALMS / CLAMS
ACLNS	CLANS
ACLNU	LUCAN
ACLOP	COPAL
ACLOR	CAROL / CORAL
ACLOS	COALS / COLAS
ACLOT	OCTAL
ACLOV	VOCAL
ACLOX	COXAL
ACLOZ	COLZA
ACLPS	CLAPS / CLASP / SCALP
ACLRW	CRAWL
ACLRY	CLARY / LYCRA
ACL33	CLA33
ACLSU	CAULS / CLAUS
ACLSW	CLAWS
ACLSY	CLAYS / SCALY
ACLXY	CALYX
ACMMO	COMMA
ACMOR	CAROM / MACRO
ACMOS	COMAS
ACMPR	CRAMP
ACMPS	CAMPS / SCAMP
ACMPY	CAMPY
ACMRS	CRAMS / SCRAM
ACMSU	SUMAC
ACNNO	CANON
ACNNY	CANNY / NANCY
ACNOP	CAPON
ACNOR	ACORN
ACNOS	OSCAN
ACNOT	CANTO
ACNSS	SCANS
ACNST	CANST / CANTS / SCANT
ACOOP	A POCO
ACOPR	COPRA
ACOPS	CAPOS
ACORS	OSCAR
ACORT	ACTOR
ACOST	COAST / COATS / COSTA
ACOTT	COTTA
ACPPU	CUPPA
ACPRS	CARPS / CRAPS / SCARP / SCRAP
ACPST	PACTS
ACPSU	SCAUP
ACPTU	ACT UP
ACRRY	CARRY
ACRSS	CRASS / SCARS
ACRST	CARTS
ACRSY	SCARY
ACRSZ	CZARS / Z CARS
ACRTT	TRACT
ACRYZ	CRAZY
ACSST	CASTS / SCATS
ACSSU	ASCUS
ACSTT	TACTS
ACSTU	SCUTA
ACSUY	SAUCY
ACTTY	CATTY
ADDDE	ADDED
ADDDY	DADDY
ADDEF	FADED
ADDEI	AIDED
ADDEJ	JADED
ADDEL	ADDLE / LADED
ADDER	ADDER / DARED / DREAD
ADDET	DATED
ADDEV	VEDDA
ADDEW	WADED
ADDEZ	DAZED
ADDFY	FADDY
ADDNY	DANDY
ADDOT	ADD TO
ADDPU	ADD UP
ADDPY	PADDY
ADDRY	DRYAD
ADDSY	DYADS
ADDWY	WADDY
ADEEM	EDEMA
ADEER	EARED
ADEES	EASED
ADEEV	EVADE
ADEFK	FAKED
ADEFM	FAMED
ADEFR	FARED
ADEFS	FADES
ADEFT	DEFAT / FATED
ADEFZ	FAZED
ADEGG	GAGED
ADEGL	GLADE
ADEGM	GAMED
ADEGP	GAPED / PAGED
ADEGR	GRADE / RAGED
ADEGS	DEGAS
ADEGT	GATED
ADEGW	WADGE / WAGED
ADEGZ	GAZED
ADEHR	HARED / HEARD
ADEHS	HADES / HEADS / SHADE
ADEHT	DEATH / HATED
ADEHW	HAWED
ADEHX	HEXAD
ADEHY	HAYED / HEADY
ADEHZ	HAZED
ADEIL	AILED / IDEAL
ADEIM	AIMED / AMIDE / MEDIA
ADEIR	AIDER / AIRED / REDIA
ADEIS	A SIDE / AIDES / ASIDE / IDEAS
ADEIU	ADIEU
ADEIZ	AZIDE
ADEJP	JAPED
ADEJS	JADES
ADEJW	JAWED
ADEKL	DALEK
ADEKN	KNEAD / NAKED
ADEKR	DRAKE / RAKED
ADEKS	ASKED
ADEKW	WAKED
ADELL	LADLE
ADELM	LAMED / MEDAL
ADELN	ELAND / LADEN
ADELP	PEDAL / PLEAD
ADELR	ALDER
ADELS	DALES / DEALS / LADES / LASED / LEADS
ADELT	DEALT / DELTA
ADELV	LAVED
ADELW	WEALD
ADELY	DELAY
ADELZ	LAZED
ADEMN	AD MEN / ADMEN / NAMED
ADEMR	ARMED / DERMA / DREAM
ADEMS	DAMES / MEADS
ADEMT	MATED / TAMED
ADEMZ	MAZED
ADENO	ANODE
ADENS	DANES / DEANS / SEDAN
ADENV	VANED / VENDA
ADENW	AWNED / WANED
ADEOR	ADORE / OARED
ADEPR	DRAPE / PADRE / PARED / RAPED
ADEPS	SPADE
ADEPT	ADEPT / PATED / TAPED
ADEPV	PAVED
ADEPW	PAWED
ADEPY	PAYED
ADERR	DARER / DREAR
ADERS	DARES / DEARS / RASED / READS
ADERT	DATER / RATED / TARED / TRADE / TREAD
ADERV	RAVED
ADERW	WADER / WARED
ADERY	DEARY / RAYED / READY
ADERZ	RAZED
ADEST	DATES / SATED / STEAD
ADESV	SAVED
ADESW	SAWED / WADES
ADESZ	ADZES / DAZES
ADETW	TAWED
ADETX	TAXED
ADEVW	WAVED
ADEVY	V E DA'
ADEWX	WAXED
ADEWY	YAWED
ADFRT	DRAFT
ADFRU	FRAUD
ADFRW	DWARF
ADGLN	GLAND
ADGMO	DOGMA / GO MA
ADGNO	DONGA / GONAD
ADGNR	DRANG / GRAND
ADGOS	DAGOS / GOADS
ADGOU	GOUDA
ADGRS	DRAGS
ADGRU	GUARD
ADGSU	GAUDS
ADGSW	GAWDS
ADGUY	GAUDY
ADHIJ	HADJI / JIHAD
ADHIM	MAHDI
ADHIP	APHID
ADHIT	HAD IT
ADHNO	HAD ON
ADHNS	HANDS
ADHNT	HADN'T
ADHNY	HANDY
ADHOR	HOARD
ADHPU	HAD UP
ADHRS	HARDS / SHARD
ADHRY	HARDY / HYDRA
ADHST	HADST
ADHSU	SADHU
ADHSY	SHADY
ADIIN	INDIA
ADIIO	OIDIA
ADIIR	RADII
ADIKN	KINDA
ADIKS	KADIS

Key	Word(s)
ADILN	LADIN
ADILP	PLAID
ADILR	DRAIL / LAIRD
ADILS	DIALS
ADILT	TIDAL
ADILV	VALID
ADILY	DAILY
ADIMN	ADMIN
ADIMO	AMIDO
ADIMS	MAIDS
ADIMT	ADMIT
ADIMX	ADMIX
ADINR	DINAR / DRAIN / NADIR
ADINV	DIVAN / VIAND
ADINY	DAY IN
ADIOP	PODIA
ADIOR	RADIO
ADIOU	AUDIO
ADIOV	AVOID
ADIOZ	AZIDO / DIAZO
ADIPR	RAPID
ADIPS	SAPID
ADIPV	VAPID
ADIQS	QADIS
ADIRS	RAIDS
ADIRT	TRIAD
ADIRX	RADIX
ADIRY	DAIRY / DIARY
ADIRZ	IZARD
ADIST	ADITS / STAID
ADISV	DIVAS
ADISY	DAISY
ADITU	AUDIT
ADITV	DAVIT
ADJSU	JUDAS
ADKLS	SKALD
ADKNR	DRANK
ADKOV	VODKA
ADKRS	DARKS
ADKRY	DARKY
ADKSY	DYAKS
ADLLO	DO ALL
ADLLY	DALLY
ADLMO	DOLMA / DOMAL / MODAL
ADLMY	MADLY
ADLNO	NODAL
ADLNS	LANDS
ADLOP	L-DOPA
ADLOS	LOADS
ADLOU	ALOUD
ADLRS	LARDS
ADLRW	DRAWL
ADLRY	LARDY
ADLSU	LAUDS
ADLSY	SADLY
ADLTU	ADULT
ADMNO	MONAD / NOMAD
ADMNS	DAMNS
ADMPS	DAMPS
ADMRS	DRAMS
ADMTU	DATUM
ADNNO	DONNA
ADNOR	ADORN / RADON
ADNOS	DONAS
ADNRS	DARNS / NARDS
ADNRW	DRAWN
ADNRY	RANDY
ADNSS	SANDS
ADNST	STAND
ADNSU	SUDAN
ADNSW	DAWNS / WANDS
ADNSY	SANDY
ADNTU	DAUNT
ADOPT	ADOPT
ADORS	ROADS / SAROD
ADOSS	SODAS
ADOST	TOADS
ADOTY	TOADY / TODAY
ADPPU	PAD UP
ADPRS	PARDS
ADQSU	QUADS / SQUAD
ADRST	DARTS / TRADS
ADRSU	SUDRA
ADRSW	DRAWS / SWARD / WARDS
ADRSY	DRAYS / YARDS
ADRTY	TARDY
AEEGL	EAGLE
AEEGR	AGREE / EAGER / EAGRE
AEEHV	HEAVE
AEEIR	AERIE
AEELS	EASEL / LEASE
AEELT	ELATE
AEELV	LEAVE
AEEMN	ENEMA
AEEMR	AMEER
AEENT	EATEN
AEENV	VENAE
AEEPS	PEASE
AEEPY	PAYEE
AEERS	ERASE / SAREE
AEERT	ARETE / EATER
AEESS	EASES
AEEST	SETAE / TEASE
AEESV	EAVES
AEETX	EXEAT
AEEVW	WEAVE
AEFFG	GAFFE
AEFGO	OF AGE
AEFHS	SHEAF
AEFIR	AFIRE
AEFKL	FLAKE
AEFKN	KENAF
AEFKR	FAKER / FREAK
AEFKS	FAKES
AEFLL	FELLA
AEFLM	FLAME
AEFLR	FERAL / FLARE
AEFLS	FALSE / FLEAS / LEAFS
AEFLT	FETAL
AEFLY	LEAFY
AEFMR	FRAME
AEFNR	FRENA
AEFNT	FANTE
AEFOR	AFORE
AEFOV	FOVEA
AEFRS	FARES / FEARS / SAFER
AEFRT	AFTER
AEFRW	WAFER
AEFRY	FAERY / FAYRE
AEFSS	SAFES
AEFST	FATES / FEAST / FEATS
AEFSZ	FAZES
AEGGR	EGGAR
AEGGS	GAGES
AEGGU	GAUGE
AEGHP	PHAGE
AEGIL	AGILE
AEGIM	IMAGE
AEGIS	AEGIS
AEGLL	LEGAL
AEGLM	GLEAM
AEGLN	ANGEL / ANGLE / GLEAN
AEGLP	PLAGE
AEGLR	GLARE / LAGER / LARGE / REGAL
AEGLS	GAELS / GALES
AEGLT	AGLET
AEGLV	GAVEL
AEGLY	AGLEY
AEGLZ	GLAZE
AEGMM	GEMMA
AEGMN	MANGE
AEGMO	OMEGA
AEGMR	GAMER / MARGE
AEGMS	GAMES
AEGNO	GENOA
AEGNR	ANGER / RANGE
AEGNT	AGENT
AEGNV	VEGAN
AEGPR	GAPER / GRAPE
AEGPS	GAPES / PAGES
AEGRS	GEARS / RAGES / SAGER / SARGE
AEGRT	GRATE / GREAT / TERGA
AEGRU	ARGUE / AUGER
AEGRV	GRAVE
AEGRW	WAGER
AEGRY	GAYER
AEGRZ	GAZER / GRAZE
AEGSS	GASES / SAGES
AEGST	GATES / STAGE
AEGSU	USAGE
AEGSW	SWAGE / WAGES
AEGSZ	GAZES
AEGTT	GET AT
AEGUV	VAGUE
AEGUZ	GAUZE
AEHHT	HEATH
AEHKS	HAKES / SHAKE
AEHLR	HALER
AEHLS	HEALS / LEASH / SHALE
AEHLT	LATHE
AEHLV	HALVE
AEHLW	WHALE / WHEAL
AEHLZ	HAZEL
AEHMN	HE-MAN
AEHMR	HAREM
AEHMS	HAMES / SHAME / SHEMA
AEHNN	HENNA
AEHNS	ASHEN
AEHNT	NEATH / THANE
AEHNV	HAVEN
AEHNY	HYENA
AEHOS	HOSEA
AEHPR	RAPHE
AEHPS	HEAPS / PHASE / SHAPE
AEHRS	HARES / HEARS / RHEAS / SHARE / SHEAR
AEHRT	EARTH / HATER / HEART
AEHRV	HAVER
AEHRW	WHARE
AEHRZ	HAZER
AEHSS	ASHES
AEHST	HASTE / HATES / HEATS
AEHSV	HAVES / SHAVE
AEHSW	HAWSE
AEHSZ	HAZES
AEHTT	THETA
AEHTW	WHEAT
AEHVY	HEAVY
AEIKL	ALIKE
AEILL	ILEAL
AEILN	ALIEN
AEILR	ARIEL
AEILS	AISLE
AEILV	ALIVE
AEIMN	AMINE
AEIMR	RIMAE
AEIMZ	MAIZE
AEINN	INANE
AEINS	ANISE
AEINT	ATE IN / EAT IN / TINEA
AEINV	NAIVE
AEIPS	PAISE / SEPIA
AEIPT	PIETA
AEIRR	AIRER
AEIRS	ARIES / ARISE / RAISE / SERAI
AEIRT	IRATE
AEIRZ	ZAIRE
AEITT	ATE IT / EAT IT
AEIVW	WAIVE
AEJKS	JAKES
AEJMS	JAMES
AEJNS	JEANS
AEJPS	JAPES
AEKLN	ANKLE
AEKLS	LAKES / LEAKS / SLAKE
AEKLY	LEAKY
AEKMR	MAKER
AEKMS	KAMES / MAKES
AEKNO	OAKEN
AEKNS	SNAKE / SNEAK
AEKNT	TAKEN
AEKNV	KNAVE
AEKNW	WAKEN
AEKNY	KENYA
AEKOR	KOREA
AEKOW	AWOKE
AEKPS	PEAKS / SPAKE / SPEAK
AEKPY	PEAKY
AEKQU	QUAKE
AEKRR	RAKER
AEKRS	ASKER / RAKES / SAKER
AEKRT	TAKER
AEKRW	WAKER / WREAK
AEKSS	SAKES
AEKST	SKATE / STAKE / STEAK / TAKES
AEKSU	UKASE
AEKSW	ASKEW / WAKES
AEKTW	TWEAK
AELLP	LAPEL
AELLY	ALLEY
AELMM	LEMMA

AELMP	AMPLE, MAPLE
AELMR	LAMER, REALM
AELMS	LAMES, MALES, MEALS
AELMT	METAL
AELMY	MEALY
AELNO	ALONE
AELNP	NEPAL, PANEL, PENAL, PLANE
AELNR	LEARN, RENAL
AELNS	ELSAN, LANES, LEANS
AELNT	LEANT
AELNV	NAVEL, VENAL
AELOS	ALOES
AELPP	APPLE
AELPR	PALER, PEARL
AELPS	LAPSE, LEAPS, PALES, PEALS, PLEAS, SALEP, SEPAL
AELPT	LEAPT, LEPTA, PETAL, PLATE, PLEAT
AELQU	EQUAL
AELRS	EARLS, LASER, RALES, REALS, SERAL
AELRT	ALERT, ALTER, ARTEL, LATER, RATEL, TALER
AELRV	LAVER, RAVEL, VELAR
AELRW	WALER
AELRX	LAXER, RELAX
AELRY	EARLY, LAYER, RELAY
AELSS	LASES, SALES, SEALS
AELST	LEAST, SETAL, SLATE, STALE, STEAL, TALES, TEALS, TESLA
AELSV	LAVES, SALVE, SLAVE, VALES, VALSE
AELSW	WALES, WEALS
AELSX	AXELS, AXLES
AELSZ	LAZES
AELTU	ALEUT
AELTV	VALET
AELTX	EXALT, LATEX
AELUV	VALUE
AELVV	VALVE
AELVY	VEALY
AEMNR	NAMER
AEMNS	MANES, MANSE, MEANS, NAMES
AEMNT	MEANT
AEMRR	REARM
AEMRS	MARES, MASER, REAMS, SMEAR
AEMRT	MATER, TAMER
AEMRZ	MAZER
AEMSS	MASSE, MESAS, SEAMS
AEMST	MATES, MEATS, STEAM, TAMES, TEAMS
AEMSU	AMUSE
AEMSX	EXAMS
AEMSY	SEAMY
AEMSZ	MAZES, SMAZE
AEMTT	MATTE
AEMTY	ETYMA, MATEY, MEATY
AEMUV	MAUVE
AENNP	PANNE
AENNS	SENNA
AENNT	ANENT
AENNX	ANNEX
AENOP	PAEON
AENOS	AEONS, AS ONE, AT ONE, ATONE, OATEN
AENOV	NOVAE
AENPS	ASPEN, NAPES, PANES
AENPT	PATEN
AENQU	QUEAN
AENRS	EARNS, NARES, NEARS, SANER, SNARE
AENRT	AREN'T
AENRV	RAVEN
AENRY	YEARN
AENST	ANTES, NATES, NEATS
AENSV	AVENS, NAVES, VANES
AENSW	WANES, WEANS
AENSZ	SENZA
AENWX	WAXEN
AENWY	WANEY
AEOPR	OPERA
AEORS	AROSE
AEORT	ORATE
AEOSS	OASES
AEOST	TO SEA
AEOTV	OVATE
AEPPR	PAPER
AEPPU	PUPAE
AEPRR	PARER
AEPRS	PARES, PARSE, PEARS, PRASE, RAPES, REAPS, SPARE, SPEAR
AEPRT	APTER, PATER, PRATE, TAPER
AEPRV	PAVER
AEPRY	PAYER, REPAY
AEPSS	APSES, PASSE
AEPST	PASTE, PATES, SEPTA, SPATE, TAPES
AEPSU	PAUSE
AEPSV	PAVES
AEPTU	ATE UP, EAT UP, TAUPE
AEPTY	PEATY
AERRR	RARER
AERRS	REARS
AERRV	RAVER
AERSS	RASES, SEARS
AERST	ASTER, RATES, STARE, TARES, TEARS
AERSV	AVERS, RAVES, SAVER
AERSW	SAWER, SWEAR, WARES, WEARS
AERSY	SAYER, YEARS
AERSZ	RAZES
AERTT	TREAT
AERTU	URATE
AERTV	AVERT
AERTW	WATER
AERTX	EXTRA, TAXER
AERUZ	AZURE
AERVV	VARVE
AERVW	WAVER
AERWY	WEARY
AESSS	ASSES
AESST	ASSET, EASTS, SATES, SEATS
AESSV	SAVES, VASES
AESSX	SAXES
AESSY	ESSAY
AESTT	STATE, TASTE, TEATS, TESTA
AESTU	SAUTE
AESTV	STAVE
AESTW	SWEAT, TAWSE, WASTE
AESTX	TAXES
AESTY	AS YET, YEAST
AESUV	SUAVE
AESVW	WAVES
AESWX	WAXES
AFFFS	FAFFS
AFFGS	GAFFS
AFFIX	AFFIX
AFFLO	OFFAL
AFFLU	LUFFA
AFFQU	QUAFF
AFFST	STAFF
AFFTY	TAFFY
AFGHU	FAUGH
AFGIN	FAGIN
AFGLS	FLAGS
AFGLU	FUGAL
AFGNS	FANGS
AFGOR	GO FAR
AFGRT	GRAFT
AFHIT	FAITH
AFHLS	FLASH
AFHRW	WHARF
AFHST	HAFTS, SHAFT
AFIKR	FAKIR
AFILL	FLAIL
AFILN	FINAL
AFILP	PILAF
AFILR	FLAIR, FRAIL
AFILS	FAILS
AFINR	INFRA
AFINT	FAINT, FANTI
AFIRR	FRIAR
AFIRS	FAIRS, FARSI
AFIRT	AFRIT
AFIRY	FAIRY
AFIST	FIATS
AFISW	WAIFS
AFKLN	FLANK
AFKLS	FLASK
AFKLY	FLAKY
AFKNR	FRANK
AFLLS	FALLS
AFLLU	FULLA
AFLMS	FLAMS
AFLMY	FLAMY
AFLNS	FLANS
AFLOO	ALOOF
AFLOR	FLORA
AFLOS	FOALS, LOAFS, SOL FA, SOL-FA
AFLOT	ALOFT, FLOAT
AFLPS	FLAPS
AFLRS	FARLS
AFLST	FLATS
AFLSW	FLAWS
AFLSY	FLAYS
AFLTU	FAULT
AFLTY	FATLY
AFLUW	AWFUL
AFMOS	FOAMS
AFMOY	FOAMY
AFMRS	FARMS
AFNNY	FANNY
AFNSU	SNAFU
AFNSW	FAWNS
AFOOT	AFOOT
AFORS	AFROS, FAROS, SO FAR
AFORY	FORAY
AFOSS	FOSSA, SOFAS
AFOST	FATSO
AFPRS	FRAPS
AFRST	RAFTS
AFRSW	SWARF
AFRSY	FRAYS
AFSST	FASTS
AFSTW	WAFTS
AFTTY	FATTY
AGGIN	AGING
AGGJY	JAGGY
AGGNS	GANGS
AGGOR	AGGRO
AGHIZ	GHAZI
AGHLU	LAUGH
AGHMO	OGHAM
AGHNS	GNASH, HANGS
AGHNW	WHANG
AGHPR	GRAPH
AGHSS	SHAGS
AGHST	GHATS
AGHTU	AUGHT
AGIKN	KIANG
AGILL	GLIAL
AGILN	ALGIN, ALIGN, LINGA
AGILR	ARGIL, GLAIR, GRAIL
AGILS	SIGLA
AGILY	GAILY
AGIMO	IMAGO
AGIMS	SIGMA

Code	Word(s)
AGINP	APING
AGINR	GRAIN
AGINS	GAINS
AGINT	GIANT
AGINW	AWING
AGINX	AXING
AGIOS	AGIOS
AGIST	GAITS
AGKSW	GAWKS
AGKWY	GAWKY
AGLLO	ALGOL
AGLLS	GALLS
AGLNO	ALONG
AGLNS	GLANS
	SLANG
AGLOP	GALOP
AGLOR	ARGOL
	GORAL
	LARGO
AGLOS	GAOLS
	GOALS
AGLOT	GLOAT
AGLOW	AGLOW
AGLRU	GLAUR
AGLSS	GLASS
	SLAGS
AGLSU	GAULS
AGMMU	GUMMA
AGMMY	GAMMY
AGMNO	AMONG
	MANGO
AGMNY	MANGY
AGMPS	GAMPS
AGMRS	GRAM'S
	GRAMS
AGMSU	MAGUS
AGMTU	GAMUT
AGNNO	GONNA
AGNOP	GO NAP
AGNOR	ARGON
	GROAN
	ORGAN
AGNOT	TANGO
	TONGA
AGNOU	GUANO
AGNOW	GOWAN
	WAGON
AGNOY	AGONY
AGNPR	PRANG
AGNPS	PANGS
AGNRS	GRANS
AGNRT	GRANT
AGNRY	ANGRY
	RANGY
AGNSS	SNAGS
AGNST	ANGST
	GNATS
	STANG
	TANGS
AGNSU	ANGUS
AGNSW	GNAWS
AGNTU	GAUNT
AGNTW	TWANG
AGNTY	TANGY
AGORT	ARGOT
	GROAT
AGOSS	SAGOS
AGOST	GOATS
	TOGAS
AGOTT	GOT AT
	GOTTA
AGPPY	GAPPY
AGPRS	GRASP
AGPRY	GRAPY
AGPSS	GASPS
AGPSW	GAWPS
AGQSU	QUAGS
AGRSS	GRASS
AGRSU	ARGUS
	GAURS
	SUGAR
AGRSY	GRAYS
AGRUU	AUGUR
AGRVY	GRAVY
AGSST	STAGS
AGSSU	GAUSS
AGSSW	SWAGS
AGSSY	GASSY
AGSTY	STAGY
AGSUV	VAGUS
AGUYZ	GAUZY
AHHOO	HOO-HA
AHHPY	HYPHA
AHHRS	HARSH
AHHSS	SHAHS
AHIIT	HAITI
AHIJJ	HAJJI
AHIKK	KHAKI
AHIKM	HAKIM
AHIKU	HAIKU
AHILP	PHIAL
AHILR	HILAR
AHILS	HAILS
AHIPS	APHIS
	APISH
	SPAHI
AHIRS	HAIRS
AHIRY	HAIRY
AHIST	HAS IT
	SAITH
	THAIS
AHISV	SHIVA
AHJJS	HAJJS
AHJNO	JONAH
AHKLS	LAKHS
AHKNS	ANKHS
	HANKS
	KHANS
	SHANK
AHKNT	THANK
AHKOS	SHAKO
AHKRS	HARKS
	SHARK
AHKST	KHATS
AHKSW	HAWKS
AHKSY	SHAKY
AHLLO	HALLO
	HOLLA
AHLLS	HALLS
	SHALL
AHLMU	HAULM
AHLNU	UHLAN
AHLOS	HALOS
	SHOAL
AHLOT	LOATH
AHLPS	PLASH
AHLPY	PHYLA
AHLSS	SLASH
AHLST	HALTS
	LATHS
	SHALT
AHLSU	HAULS
	HULAS
AHLSW	SHAWL
AHMMY	HAMMY
AHMNU	HUMAN
	NAHUM
AHMRS	HARMS
	MARSH
AHMSS	SHAMS
	SMASH
AHMST	MATHS
AHMSW	SHAWM
	WHAMS
AHNOS	HAS ON
AHNST	HASN'T
AHNTU	HAUNT
AHOOY	YAHOO
AHORS	HOARS
AHORT	TORAH
AHORY	HOARY
AHOST	OATHS
AHOSX	XHOSA
AHPPY	HAPPY
AHPRS	HARPS
	SHARP
AHPRY	HARPY
AHPSS	HASPS
AHPST	PATHS
	STAPH
AHPSU	HAS UP
AHPSW	PSHAW
AHPUW	WHAUP
AHQSU	QUASH
AHRRY	HARRY
AHRST	HARTS
	RATHS
	TRASH
AHRTW	WRATH
AHRXY	HYRAX
AHSST	STASH
AHSSW	SHAWS
	SWASH
AHSTW	SWATH
	THAWS
AHSTY	HASTY
AHSWY	WASHY
AIIQR	IRAQI
AIJLS	JAILS
AIJNS	JAINS
AIJOU	OUIJA
AIKMU	UMIAK
AIKNS	ASK IN
	KINAS
AIKOP	OKAPI
AIKPS	PAKIS
	PIKAS
AIKRT	KRAIT
AIKRU	KAURI
AIKSS	SAKIS
AIKST	SAKTI
AILLN	ALL IN
	ALL-IN
AILLV	VILLA
AILMS	ISLAM
	MAILS
	SALMI
AILMT	TAMIL
AILNP	PLAIN
AILNS	NAILS
	SLAIN
	SNAIL
AILNT	INTAL
	LATIN
AILNV	ANVIL
AILNW	IN LAW
	IN-LAW
AILNY	INLAY
	LAY IN
AILOV	VIOLA
AILPP	PALPI
	PIPAL
AILPR	APRIL
AILPS	PAILS
AILPT	PLAIT
AILPU	PILAU
AILQU	QUAIL
AILRS	ARILS
	LAIRS
	LIARS
	LIRAS
	RAILS
	RIALS
AILRT	TRAIL
	TRIAL
AILRV	RIVAL
	VIRAL
AILRY	LAIRY
	RIYAL
AILSS	SAILS
	SIALS
	SISAL
AILST	TAILS
AILSW	WAILS
AILSX	AXILS
AILTV	VITAL
AILTY	ITALY
	LAITY
AIMMS	IMAMS
	MAIMS
AIMMX	MAXIM
AIMNO	AMINO
AIMNS	MAINS
	MINAS
AIMNY	IN MAY
AIMNZ	NIZAM
AIMOR	MAORI
AIMOW	MIAOW
AIMOX	AXIOM
AIMRS	AMIRS
AIMSS	AMISS
AIMST	TAMIS
AIMSV	MAVIS
AIMSW	SWAMI
AIMSX	MAXIS
AIMTY	AMITY
AINNO	ANION
AINNP	PINNA
AINNR	RAN IN
AINOP	PIANO
AINOT	TAINO
AINPS	PAINS
	SPAIN
AINPT	INAPT
	PAINT
AINRS	NARIS
	RAINS
	RANIS
AINRT	TRAIN
AINRV	INVAR
AINRY	RAINY
AINST	ANTIS
	SAINT
	SAT IN
	SATIN
	STAIN
AINSV	SAVIN
AINSW	SAW IN
	SWAIN
AINSZ	NAZIS
AINTT	TAINT
	TITAN
AINTW	TWAIN
AINUX	AUXIN
AINWY	WAY IN
AIOPT	PATIO
AIORT	RATIO
AIORY	ORIYA
AIOSS	OASIS
AIOST	IOTAS
AIPPP	PAPPI
AIPRS	PAIRS
	PARSI
AIPRT	TAPIR
AIPSS	APSIS
AIPTT	PITTA
AIPZZ	PIZZA
AIQSU	QUASI
AIRRS	ARRIS
AIRRW	WIRRA
AIRSS	ARSIS
	SARIS
AIRST	ASTIR
	SITAR
	STAIR
	STRIA
	TARSI
AIRSY	SYRIA
AIRSZ	SIZAR
AIRTT	TRAIT
AIRVX	VARIX
AISSV	VISAS
AISTV	VISTA
AISTW	WAIST
	WAITS
AISTX	TAXIS
AISVV	VIVAS
AISXX	X-AXIS
AISXY	Y-AXIS
AISXZ	Z-AXIS
AITTV	VITTA
AJLRS	JARLS
AJLRU	JURAL
AJMMY	JAMMY
AJMNO	JAM ON
AJMOR	MAJOR
AJNTU	JAUNT
	JUNTA
AJYZZ	JAZZY
AKKLU	KULAK
AKKOP	KAPOK
AKKPU	PUKKA
AKLLY	ALKYL
AKLNP	PLANK
AKLNS	KLANS
AKLNU	LUKAN
AKLNY	LANKY
AKLOP	POLKA
AKLOS	SKOAL
AKLRS	LARKS
AKLST	STALK
	TALKS

AKLSW	LAWKS, WALKS	ALMPS	LAMPS, PALMS, PLASM, PSALM	ALSSY	SLAYS	ANOWY	NO WAY, NOWAY	APRST	PARTS, PRATS, SPRAT, STRAP, TRAPS
AKMOS	MAKOS	ALMPY	AMPLY, PALMY	ALSTU	TALUS	ANPPY	NAPPY	APRSU	PRAUS, SUPRA
AKMOU	OAKUM	ALMQU	QUALM	ALSTX	XTALS	ANPRU	RAN UP	APRSW	WARPS, WRAPS
AKMRS	MARKS	ALMRU	MURAL	ALSTY	SALTY, SLATY	ANPRW	PRAWN	APRSY	PRAYS, SPRAY
AKMSS	MASKS	ALMRY	MARLY	ALSUU	USUAL	ANPSS	SNAPS, SPANS	APRTY	PARTY
AKMUZ	MUZAK	ALMSS	SLAMS	ALSWY	YAWLS	ANPST	PANTS	APSST	PASTS, SPATS
AKNOR	KORAN, KRONA	ALMST	MALTS, SMALT	ALTUV	VAULT	ANPSW	PAWNS, SPAWN	APSSW	SWAPS, WASPS
AKNOS	KAONS, KOANS	ALMSU	ALUMS, MAULS	ALTWZ	WALTZ	ANPSY	PANSY	APSSY	SPAYS
AKNPR	PRANK	ALMTY	MALTY	ALUUV	UVULA	ANPTU	UNAPT	APSTU	SAT UP, SPUTA, STUPA
AKNPS	KNAPS, SPANK	ALNNU	ANNUL	ALUVV	VULVA	ANQRU	QURAN	APSTY	PASTY, PATSY
AKNRS	NARKS, RANKS	ALNOP	NOPAL	AMMMO	MOMMA	ANRST	RANTS, TARNS, TRANS	APSUY	YAUPS
AKNST	STANK, TANKS	ALNOR	LORAN	AMMMY	MAMMY	ANRSW	WARNS	APSWY	WASPY, YAWPS
AKNSW	SWANK	ALNOS	LOANS, SALON	AMMNY	MY MAN	ANRSY	YARNS	APTTY	PATTY
AKNSY	SNAKY, YANKS	ALNOT	TALON, TONAL	AMMRS	SMARM	ANRTU	RUN AT	AQRTU	QUART
AKOOR	KAROO	ALNOY	LAY ON	AMMTY	TAMMY	ANRUU	NAURU	AQSTU	SQUAT
AKOOZ	KAZOO	ALNOZ	ZONAL	AMNNO	NO MAN	ANSSW	SWANS	AQSUW	SQUAW
AKOPY	YAPOK	ALNPS	PLANS	AMNNU	UNMAN	ANSTU	AUNTS	AQSUY	QUAYS
AKOSS	SOAKS	ALNPT	PLANT	AMNOR	MANOR, ROMAN	ANSTW	WANTS	ARRSU	SURRA
AKOSY	KAYOS	ALNRS	SNARL	AMNOS	MASON, MOANS	ANSTY	NASTY, TANSY	ARRTY	TARRY
AKOTY	TOKAY	ALNRU	LUNAR, ULNAR	AMNOW	WOMAN	ANSWY	YAWNS	ARSST	STARS, TRASS, TSARS
AKPRS	PARKS, SPARK	ALNST	SLANT	AMNSY	MYNAS	ANTTU	TAUNT	ARSTT	START, TARTS
AKPRY	PARKY	ALNSW	LAWNS	AMOPR	PRO-AM	ANTTY	NATTY	ARSTU	SUTRA
AKPTU	KAPUT	ALNUY	UNLAY	AMORS	ROAMS	ANTUV	VAUNT	ARSTW	STRAW, WARTS
AKPWY	PAWKY	ALNWY	LAWNY, WANLY	AMORU	AMOUR	ANTWY	TAWNY	ARSTY	SATYR, STRAY, TRAYS
AKQRU	QUARK	ALOPR	PAROL, POLAR	AMORY	MAYOR	ANVVY	NAVVY	ARSTZ	TZARS
AKRST	KARST, KARTS, STARK	ALOPS	OPALS	AMOST	ATOMS, MOATS, STOMA	AOPPP	POPPA	ARSUV	VARUS
AKRSY	SARKY	ALORS	ORALS, SOLAR	AMOTZ	MATZO	AOPPR	APPRO	ARSUY	SAURY
AKRTU	KRAUT	ALORV	VOLAR	AMPRS	PRAMS, RAMPS	AOPRS	PROAS, SAPOR	ARSXY	X RAYS, X-RAYS
AKRUY	YURAK	ALORY	ROYAL	AMPRT	TRAMP	AOPRT	APORT, OP ART	ARTTY	RATTY, TARTY
AKRYZ	KARZY	ALOSS	LASSO	AMPSS	SPASM	AOPSS	SOAPS	ARTWY	WARTY
AKSST	TASKS	ALOST	ALTOS	AMPST	STAMP, TAMPS	AOPSY	SOAPY	ASSTW	SWATS
AKSSV	KVASS	ALOSV	OVALS, SALVO	AMPSU	PUMAS	AOPTT	AT TOP	ASSTY	STAYS
AKSTY	KYATS	ALOTT	TOTAL	AMPSV	VAMPS	AOPTY	ATOPY	ASSWY	SWAYS
ALLLY	ALLYL	ALOTV	VOLTA	AMPSW	SWAMP	AOPTZ	TOPAZ	ASTTW	TWATS, WATTS
ALLMO	MOLAL	ALOVV	VOLVA	AMRRY	MARRY	AOQTU	QUOTA	ASTTY	TASTY
ALLMS	SMALL	ALPPS	LAPPS, PALPS	AMRST	MARTS, SMART, TRAMS	AORRS	ROARS	ASVVY	SAVVY
ALLNO	LLANO	ALPPU	PUPAL	AMRSU	ARUMS	AORRW	ARROW	ATTTY	TATTY
ALLNU	NULLA	ALPPY	APPLY	AMRSW	SWARM, WARMS	AORRZ	RAZOR	BBBOY	BOBBY
ALLOT	ALLOT, ATOLL	ALPSS	SLAPS	AMSST	MASTS	AORSS	SAROS, SOARS	BBCEU	CUBEB
ALLOW	ALLOW	ALPST	PLATS, SPLAT	AMSSY	MASSY	AORST	ROAST, ROTAS, TAROS	BBCHU	CHUBB
ALLOY	ALLOY, LOYAL	ALPSW	PAWLS	AMSTT	MATTS	AORTT	TAROT	BBCOY	COBBY
ALLPS	PALLS, SPALL	ALPSY	PALSY, PLAYS, SPLAY	AMSTY	MAYST	AORTW	TO WAR	BBCUY	CUBBY
ALLPU	ALL UP, ALL-UP	ALPTY	APTLY, TYPAL	ANNNY	NANNY	AORVY	OVARY	BBDEE	EBBED
ALLPY	PALLY	ALPUY	LAY UP	ANNOR	RAN ON	AOSSY	SAY SO, SAY-SO, SOYAS	BBDEY	DEBBY
ALLRY	RALLY	ALRRU	RURAL	ANNOY	ANNOY	AOSTT	STOAT, TOAST	BBEIL	BIBLE
ALLST	STALL	ALRSY	ARYLS	ANNSU	SUNNA	AOSTU	AUTOS	BBEIR	BRIBE
ALLSW	WALLS	ALRTU	ULTRA	ANOPR	APRON	AOSTW	SAW TO	BBELS	BLEBS
ALLSY	SALLY	ALRTW	TRAWL	ANOPT	ON TAP, PANTO	AOSVW	AVOWS	BBEMO	BOMBE
ALLTY	TALLY	ALRWY	RAWLY	ANORS	ARSON, ROANS, SONAR	AOSVY	SAVOY	BBEOP	BEBOP
ALLWY	WALLY	ALSST	LASTS, SALTS, SLATS	ANORT	RAN TO	APPSU	PUPAS		
ALLXY	LAXLY	ALSSV	SLAVS	ANORW	ROWAN	APPSY	SAPPY		
ALMNY	MANLY			ANORY	RAYON	APPUY	PAY UP		
ALMOR	MOLAR, MORAL			ANOST	SAT ON	APPYZ	ZAPPY		
ALMOS	LOAMS			ANOSV	NOVAS	APRRY	PARRY		
ALMOY	LOAMY			ANOSX	AXONS	APRSS	RASPS, SPARS		
				ANOTX	TAXON				
				ANOTY	ATONY				

Code	Word	Code	Word	Code	Word	Code	Word	Code	Word
BBEWY	WEBBY	BDEIJ	JIBED	BEERW	WEBER	BELUY	BLUEY	BGOSU	BOGUS
BBHMO	H BOMB	BDEIK	BIKED	BEERY	BEERY	BEMOR	OMBRE	BGOTY	GOT BY
	H-BOMB	BDEIM	IMBED	BEEST	BEETS	BEMOS	BESOM	BGRSU	GRUBS
BBHOY	HOBBY	BDEIN	IN BED		BESET	BEMRS	BERMS	BGRUY	RUGBY
BBHUY	HUBBY	BDEIP	BIPED	BEFGO	BEFOG	BEMRU	UMBER	BHIRT	BIRTH
BBILO	BILBO	BDEIR	BIDER	BEFIR	BRIEF	BEMSU	SEBUM	BHLSU	BLUSH
BBLOS	BLOBS		BRIDE		FIBRE	BENOR	BONER	BHMOR	RHOMB
BBLOY	LOBBY	BDEIS	B SIDE	BEFIT	BEFIT		BORNE	BHMPU	BUMPH
BBLRU	BLURB		BIDES	BEGIL	BILGE	BENOS	BONES	BHMRU	RHUMB
BBLSU	BULBS	BDEIT	BIDET	BEGIN	BEGIN	BENOT	T BONE	BHMTU	THUMB
BBMOS	BOMBS		DEBIT		BEING		T-BONE	BHOOS	HOBOS
BBOOS	BOOBS	BDELN	BLEND		BINGE	BENOY	EBONY	BHOOT	BOOTH
BBOOY	BOOBY	BDELO	LOBED	BEGIO	BOGIE	BENOZ	BONZE	BHORT	BROTH
	YOBBO	BDEMO	DEMOB	BEGIR	GIBER	BENRT	BRENT		THROB
BBPUY	PUBBY	BDENO	BONED	BEGIS	GIBES	BENST	BENTS	BHOTY	BOTHY
BBSUY	BUSBY	BDENS	BENDS	BEGIY	BEIGY	BEOOS	OBOES	BHRSU	BRUSH
BBTUY	TUBBY	BDENY	BENDY	BEGLO	BOGLE	BEOOZ	BOOZE		SHRUB
BCCIU	CUBIC	BDENZ	Z BEND		GLOBE	BEOPR	PROBE	BHSUY	BUSHY
BCCIY	BICCY	BDEOO	BOOED	BEGLU	BUGLE	BEORR	BORER	BIIMN	NIMBI
BCDEU	CUBED	BDEOR	BORED		BULGE	BEORS	BOERS	BIINT	BIT IN
BCEEH	BEECH		ROBED	BEGNU	BEGUN		BORES	BIIOR	ORIBI
BCEER	REBEC	BDEOS	BODES	BEGOT	BEGOT		BROSE	BIJOU	BIJOU
BCEEX	XEBEC	BDEOT	TO BED	BEGOY	BOGEY		ROBES	BIKKY	BIKKY
BCEHL	BELCH	BDEOW	BOWED	BEGRS	BERGS		SOBER	BIKLN	BLINK
BCEHN	BENCH	BDEOX	BOXED	BEGSY	GYBES	BEORW	BOWER	BIKLS	BILKS
BCEHO	BOCHE	BDERY	DERBY	BEGTY	GET BY	BEORX	BOXER	BIKNR	BRINK
BCEKS	BECKS	BDEST	DEBTS	BEGUZ	UZBEG	BEOSX	BOXES	BIKRS	BIRKS
BCELO	COBLE	BDESU	DEBUS	BEHRS	HERBS	BEOSY	OBEYS		BRISK
BCEMO	COMBE	BDETU	DEBUT	BEHRT	BERTH	BEPSU	PUBES	BILLR	BRILL
BCENO	BONCE	BDFII	BIFID	BEIJS	JIBES	BERRY	BERRY	BILLS	BILLS
BCERU	CUBER	BDGOY	BY GOD!	BEIKS	BIKES	BERSS	SERBS	BILLY	BILLY
BCESU	CUBES	BDHIO	DHOBI		KIBES	BERSU	REBUS	BILMO	LIMBO
BCHIR	BIRCH	BDILN	BLIND	BEILL	LIBEL	BERSV	VERBS	BILMP	BLIMP
BCHIT	BITCH	BDILU	BUILD	BEIMO	BIOME	BERSW	BREWS	BILMS	LIMBS
BCHNU	BUNCH	BDINO	NO BID	BEIMU	IMBUE	BERSY	BYRES	BILOR	BROIL
BCHOR	BROCH	BDINS	BINDS	BEINN	BENIN	BERTU	BRUTE	BILOS	BOILS
BCHOT	BOTCH	BDINU	IN BUD	BEINR	BRINE		REBUT	BILPS	BLIPS
BCHSU	CHUBS	BDIPU	BID UP	BEINS	BINES		TUBER	BILSS	BLISS
BCHTU	BUTCH	BDIRS	BIRDS	BEIRR	BRIER	BERUX	EXURB	BILSY	SIBYL
BCIKR	BRICK		DRIBS	BEIRS	BIERS	BERUY	BUYER	BILTU	BUILT
BCIKY	BICKY	BDLNO	BLOND	BEIRT	BITER	BESST	BESTS	BILTZ	BLITZ
BCILM	CLIMB	BDLOO	BLOOD		TRIBE	BESSU	BUSES	BIMRS	BRIMS
BCIOR	BORIC	BDNOS	BONDS	BEIST	BITES	BESTU	TUBES	BINOR	ROBIN
BCIPU	PUBIC	BDNOU	BOUND	BEISV	VIBES	BESTY	BYTES	BINOS	BISON
BCIRS	CRIBS	BDNSU	BUNDS	BEITZ	ZIBET	BETTU	BUTTE	BINRU	BRUIN
BCITU	CUBIT	BDNUU	BUNDU	BEKLO	BLOKE	BEVVY	BEVVY		BURIN
BCKLO	BLOCK	BDOOR	BROOD	BEKOR	BROKE	BFFIS	BIFFS		RUB IN
BCKOR	BROCK	BDOTU	DOUBT	BEKRS	BERKS	BFFIU	BUFFI	BINRY	BRINY
BCKOU	BUCKO	BDRSU	DRUBS		KERBS	BFFLU	BLUFF	BINST	BINTS
BCKSU	BUCKS	BEEFS	BEEFS	BEKRU	BURKE	BFFOU	BUFFO	BINUY	BUY IN
BCLOO	COBOL	BEEFY	BEEFY	BEKUZ	UZBEK	BFFSU	BUFFS		BUY-IN
BCLOS	BLOCS	BEEGI	BEIGE	BELLS	BELLS	BFIOR	FIBRO	BIORS	BIROS
BCLSU	CLUBS	BEEGL	GLEBE	BELLY	BELLY	BFLYY	FLY BY	BIORT	ORBIT
BCMOO	COMBO	BEEGR	GREBE	BELMU	UMBEL		FLYBY	BIOST	OBITS
	COOMB	BEEGT	BEGET	BELNO	NOBLE	BGGOY	BOGGY	BIPSU	PUBIS
BCMOS	COMBS	BEEHT	THEBE	BELNT	BLENT	BGGUY	BUGGY	BIQSU	SQUIB
BCMRU	CRUMB	BEEIL	BELIE	BELOS	BOLES	BGHIT	BIGHT	BIRST	BRITS
BCRSU	CURBS	BEELL	BELLE		LOBES	BGHOU	BOUGH	BIRTU	BRUIT
	SCRUB	BEELP	BLEEP	BELOT	BOTEL	BGHRU	BURGH	BISSY	BYSSI
BDDEI	BIDED	BEELR	REBEL	BELOU	BOULE	BGIMR	MR. BIG	BISTT	BITTS
BDDEO	BODED	BEELT	BETEL	BELOW	BELOW	BGINO	BINGO	BITTY	BITTY
BDDIY	BIDDY		LET BE		BOWEL	BGINR	BRING	BJMOU	JUMBO
BDDUY	BUDDY	BEELV	BEVEL		ELBOW	BGIOS	IGBOS	BKLSU	BULKS
BDEEL	BLEED	BEELZ	BEZEL	BELPS	PLEBS	BGIOT	BIGOT	BKLUY	BULKY
BDEEM	EMBED	BEEMR	BERME	BELRU	BLUER	BGIRS	BRIGS	BKNOS	KNOBS
BDEER	BREED		EMBER		RUBLE	BGLOS	GLOBS	BKNSU	BUNKS
BDEGI	GIBED	BEEOS	OBESE	BELRY	BERYL	BGLUY	BULGY	BKOOR	BROOK
BDEGO	BODGE	BEEPS	BEEPS	BELSS	BLESS	BGMOU	GUMBO	BKOOS	BOOKS
BDEGU	BUDGE	BEERS	BEERS	BELST	BELTS	BGNOO	BONGO	BKOSY	BOSKY
	DEBUG	BEERT	BERET		BLEST	BGNOS	BONGS	BKRSU	BURKS
BDEGY	GYBED	BEERV	BREVE	BELSU	BLUES	BGNSU	BUNGS	BKSSU	BUSKS

Code	Word(s)
BLLOS	BOLLS
BLLSU	BULLS
BLLUY	BULLY
BLMOO	BLOOM
BLMPU	PLUMB
BLNOW	BLOWN
BLNOY	NOBLY
BLNTU	BLUNT
BLOSS	SLOBS
BLOST	BLOTS / BOLTS
BLOSU	BOLUS
BLOSW	BLOWS / BOWLS
BLOWY	BLOWY
BLRSU	BLURS / BURLS
BLRTU	BLURT
BLRUY	BURLY
BLSSU	SLUBS
BLTUY	BUTYL
BMOOR	BROOM
BMOOS	BOOMS / BOSOM
BMOST	TOMBS
BMOSU	UMBOS
BMOSW	WOMBS
BMOUX	BUXOM
BMPSU	BUMPS
BMPUY	BUMPY
BNNOY	BONNY
BNNUY	BUNNY
BNOOR	BORON
BNOOS	BOONS / BOSON
BNORU	BOURN / RUB ON
BNORW	BROWN
BNOSS	SNOBS
BNOSU	BONUS / BOSUN
BNRSU	BURNS
BNRTU	BRUNT / BURNT
BNSSU	SNUBS
BNSTU	BUNTS
BOORS	BOORS
BOORT	ROBOT
BOOST	BOOST / BOOTS
BOOSY	BOYOS
BOOTY	BOOTY
BOOWX	OX BOW / OXBOW
BOOYZ	BOOZY
BOPUW	UP BOW
BORRU	BURRO
BORSS	SORBS
BORST	BORTS
BORSW	BROWS
BOSSW	SWOBS
BOSSY	BOSSY
BOSTU	BOUTS
BOSUY	BUOYS
BPRSU	BURPS
BPRUU	RUB UP
BPTUY	PUT BY
BPUUY	BUY UP
BRRSU	BURRS
BRRUY	BURRY
BRSTU	BURST
BSSTU	BUSTS / STUBS
BSTTU	BUTTS
BSTUY	BUSTY
BTTUU	BUTUT
BTTUY	BUTTY
CCCIO	COCCI
CCEER	RECCE
CCEHK	CHECK
CCEHZ	CZECH
CCEIR	CERIC
CCELY	CYCLE
CCEMU	CECUM
CCHIK	CHICK
CCHIN	CINCH
CCHKO	CHOCK
CCHKU	CHUCK
CCHNO	CONCH
CCHOU	COUCH
CCIIV	CIVIC
CCIKL	CLICK
CCIKR	CRICK
CCILO	COLIC
CCIMO	COMIC
CCINO	CONIC
CCINY	CYNIC
CCKLO	CLOCK
CCKLU	CLUCK
CCKOR	CROCK
CCKOS	COCKS
CCKOY	COCKY
CCKRU	CRUCK
CCOOS	COCOS
CCORU	OCCUR
CDDEE	CEDED
CDDEI	DICED / EDDIC
CDDEO	CODED
CDDUY	CUDDY
CDEER	CEDER / CREED
CDEES	CEDES
CDEEU	DEUCE / EDUCE
CDEHI	CHIDE
CDEIM	MEDIC
CDEIR	CIDER / CRIED / DICER
CDEIS	DICES
CDEIT	CITED / EDICT
CDEIV	VEDIC / VICED
CDEIY	DICEY
CDEKS	DECKS
CDENO	CONED
CDENS	SCEND
CDENU	DUNCE
CDEOO	COOED
CDEOP	COPED
CDEOR	CODER / CORED / CREDO / DECOR
CDEOS	CODES
CDEOU	COUDE / DOUCE
CDEOV	COVED
CDEOW	COWED
CDEOX	CODEX
CDEOY	DECOY
CDERU	CRUDE / CURED
CDERY	CYDER / DECRY
CDHIL	CHILD
CDHIT	DITCH
CDHOR	CHORD
CDHTU	DUTCH
CDHUY	DUCHY
CDIIN	INDIC
CDIIO	IODIC
CDIKS	DICKS
CDIKY	DICKY
CDILU	LUCID
CDIOR	DORIC
CDIOS	DISCO
CDIOT	DICOT
CDIPU	CUPID
CDISS	DISCS
CDKOS	DOCKS
CDKSU	DUCKS
CDKUY	DUCKY
CDLOS	CLODS / COLDS / SCOLD
CDLOU	CLOUD / COULD
CDNOO	CODON
CDORS	CORDS / SCROD
CDORW	CROWD
CDRSU	CRUDS / CURDS
CDRUY	CURDY
CDSSU	SCUDS
CDSTU	DUCTS
CEEEM	EMCEE
CEEFN	FENCE
CEEFS	FECES
CEEHK	CHEEK
CEEHL	LEECH
CEEHN	HENCE
CEEHP	CHEEP
CEEHR	CHEER
CEEIN	NIECE
CEEIP	PIECE
CEEJT	EJECT
CEEKR	CREEK
CEELR	CREEL
CEELT	ELECT
CEELX	EXCEL
CEELY	LYCEE
CEEMR	CREME
CEENP	PENCE
CEENS	CENSE / SCENE
CEEOO	COOEE
CEEPR	CREEP / CREPE
CEERS	CERES / CREES / SCREE
CEERT	ERECT / TERCE
CEFGL	G CLEF
CEFHI	CHIEF / FICHE
CEFHS	CHEFS
CEFHT	FETCH
CEFKL	FLECK
CEFLS	CLEFS
CEFLT	CLEFT
CEFOR	FORCE
CEGIN	GENIC
CEGKO	GECKO
CEGLS	CLEGS
CEHIL	CHILE
CEHIM	CHIME
CEHIN	CHINE / NICHE
CEHIT	ETHIC
CEHIV	CHIVE
CEHKO	CHOKE
CEHKS	HECKS
CEHKT	KETCH
CEHLW	WELCH
CEHLY	CHYLE
CEHMY	CHYME
CEHNT	TENCH
CEHNW	WENCH
CEHOP	EPOCH
CEHOR	CHORE / OCHRE
CEHOS	CHOSE
CEHPR	PERCH
CEHRT	CHERT / RETCH
CEHRU	RUCHE
CEHSS	CHESS
CEHST	CHEST
CEHSW	CHEWS
CEHTU	CHUTE
CEHTV	VETCH
CEHTY	TECHY
CEHWY	CHEWY
CEIIN	ICENI
CEIIR	ICIER
CEIJU	JUICE
CEILM	CLIME / MELIC
CEILN	CLINE
CEILO	OLEIC
CEILR	RELIC
CEILS	SLICE
CEIMN	MINCE
CEIMR	CRIME
CEINO	ON ICE
CEINR	NICER
CEINS	SINCE
CEINW	WINCE
CEIOV	VOICE
CEIPR	PRICE
CEIPS	EPICS / SPICE
CEIRR	CRIER
CEIRS	CRIES
CEIRT	RECTI / TRICE
CEIRU	CURIE
CEIST	CITES
CEISV	VICES
CEITU	CUTIE
CEITV	CIVET / EVICT
CEITW	TWICE
CEKLR	CLERK
CEKNS	NECKS / SNECK
CEKNV	V NECK
CEKOR	OCKER
CEKOS	COKES
CEKPS	PECKS / SPECK
CEKRS	RECKS
CEKRW	WRECK
CELLO	CELLO
CELLS	CELLS
CELNO	CLONE
CELNU	UNCLE
CELOS	CLOSE / COLES
CELOV	CLOVE
CELOY	COLEY
CELPU	CUPEL
CELRU	CRUEL / LUCRE / ULCER
CELST	CELTS
CELSU	CLUES
CELSW	CLEWS
CELTY	CETYL
CEMOR	COMER
CEMOS	COMES
CEMOT	COMET
CEMRY	MERCY
CENNO	NONCE
CENOP	PONCE
CENOR	CRONE / ONCER
CENOS	CONES / SCONE
CENOT	CENTO / CONTE
CENOU	ON CUE / OUNCE
CENOV	COVEN
CENOY	CONEY
CENST	CENTS / SCENT
CEOPS	COPES / COPSE / SCOPE
CEOPU	COUPE
CEORR	CORER / CRORE
CEORS	CORES / SCORE
CEORT	RECTO
CEORV	COVER
CEORW	COWER
CEOST	COTES
CEOSV	COVES
CEOSX	COXES
CEOTT	OCTET
CEOTV	COVET
CEOVY	COVEY
CEPRT	CREPT
CEPRY	CREPY
CEPSS	SPECS
CERRU	CURER / RECUR
CERSS	CRESS
CERST	CERTS / CREST
CERSU	CRUSE / CURES / CURSE / SUCRE
CERSW	CREWS / SCREW

CERTU	CRUET	CHITY	ITCHY	CIMOS	OSMIC	CLOOR	COLOR	DDEIS	SIDED
	CURET	CHIVY	VICHY	CIMPR	CRIMP	CLOOS	COOLS	DDEIT	TIDED
	CUTER	CHKNU	CHUNK	CIMSU	MUSIC		LOCOS	DDEIV	DIVED
	TRUCE	CHKOO	CHOKO	CINOS	COINS	CLOOY	COOLY	DDEKY	DYKED
CERUV	CURVE	CHKOS	HOCKS		ICONS	CLOPS	CLOPS	DDEMO	DOMED
CESST	SECTS		SHOCK		SCION	CLOST	CLOTS	DDEOP	DOPED
CESTU	CUTES	CHKSU	SHUCK		SONIC		COLTS	DDEOR	ODDER
	SCUTE	CHLMU	MULCH	CINOT	TONIC	CLOSU	LOCUS	DDEOS	DOSED
CFFHU	CHUFF	CHLNU	LUNCH	CINPU	PUNIC	CLOSW	COWLS	DDEOT	DOTED
CFFIL	CLIFF	CHLNY	LYNCH	CINRU	INCUR		SCOWL	DDEOZ	DOZED
CFFOS	SCOFF	CHLOS	LOCHS		RUNIC	CLOSY	CLOYS	DDEPU	DUPED
CFFSU	CUFFS	CHLOT	CLOTH	CINSU	INCUS	CLOTU	CLOUT	DDERS	REDDS
	SCUFF	CHLRU	CHURL	CINSZ	ZINCS	CLOYY	COYLY	DDERU	UDDER
CFHIL	FILCH		LURCH	CINTU	CUT IN	CLRSU	CURLS	DDESU	DUDES
CFHIN	FINCH	CHMNU	MUNCH		TUNIC	CLRUY	CURLY	DDETY	TEDDY
CFHIU	FICHU	CHMOO	MOOCH	CIOPT	COP IT	CLSTU	CULTS	DDGIY	GIDDY
CFIIN	FICIN	CHMOP	CHOMP		OP CIT	CMORS	CORMS	DDGOY	DODGY
CFIIS	SCI-FI	CHMPU	CHUMP		OPTIC	CMORU	MUCRO	DDIIN	DID IN
CFIKL	FLICK	CHMSU	CHUMS		PICOT	CMPRU	CRUMP	DDIIT	DID IT
CFILO	FOLIC	CHNOT	NOTCH		TOPIC	CMRSU	SCRUM	DDILO	DILDO
CFIOS	COIFS	CHNPU	PUNCH	CIORU	CURIO	CMSSU	SCUMS	DDIMY	MIDDY
CFISU	SUFIC	CHNRU	CHURN	CIOST	STOIC	CMSUU	MUCUS	DDINU	UNDID
CFKLO	FLOCK	CHNSY	SYNCH	CIOTX	TOXIC	CNNOS	CONNS	DDIRU	DRUID
CFKOR	FROCK	CHOOP	POOCH	CIPRS	CRISP	CNOOR	CROON	DDIST	DIDST
CFMOY	COMFY	CHOPR	PORCH		SCRIP	CNOOS	COONS	DDLOY	ODDLY
CFORT	CROFT	CHOPS	CHOPS	CIPRY	PRICY	CNOPY	PONCY	DDMUY	MUDDY
CFOSU	FOCUS	CHOPU	POUCH	CIPSS	SPICS	CNORS	CORNS	DDNOY	NODDY
CFRSU	SCURF	CHORT	TORCH	CIPST	PICTS		SCORN	DDOOS	DODOS
CFSUU	FUCUS	CHOSU	HOCUS	CIPSY	SPICY	CNORW	CROWN	DDOTY	TODDY
CGHIN	CHING	CHOSW	CHOWS	CISST	CISTS	CNORY	CORNY	DDOWY	DOWDY
CGHLU	GULCH	CHOTU	TOUCH	CISSY	CISSY		CRONY	DDRSU	RUDDS
CGHOU	COUGH	CHOUV	VOUCH	CISTU	CUTIS	CNOTU	COUNT	DDRUY	RUDDY
CGHSU	CHUGS	CHOUX	CHOUX		ICTUS	CNTUU	UNCUT	DDSSU	SUDDS
CGIIN	ICING	CHPSY	PSYCH	CITTU	CUT IT	COOPS	CO-OPS	DEEFF	EFFED
CGILN	CLING	CHRRU	CHURR	CIVVY	CIVVY		COOPS	DEEFR	DEFER
CGILO	LOGIC	CHRSU	CRUSH	CJKOS	JOCKS		SCOOP		FREED
CGINU	CUING	CHSUY	CUSHY	CKKNO	KNOCK	COOPT	CO-OPT	DEEFS	FEEDS
CGIOR	CORGI	CIILT	LICIT	CKLNO	CLONK	COOST	COOTS	DEEFT	FETED
CGIOY	YOGIC	CIILV	CIVIL	CKLOS	LOCKS		SCOOT	DEEGG	EGGED
CGIRU	UGRIC	CIILY	ICILY	CKLPU	PLUCK	COPRS	CORPS	DEEGH	HEDGE
CGLNU	CLUNG	CIIMM	MIMIC	CKLUY	LUCKY		CROPS	DEEGK	KEDGE
CGLOS	CLOGS	CIINO	IONIC	CKMOS	MOCKS	COPRU	CROUP	DEEGL	LEDGE
CGNOO	CONGO	CIIRR	CIRRI		SMOCK	COPST	COPTS	DEEGO	GEODE
CHHIT	HITCH	CIJUY	JUICY	CKMUY	MUCKY	COPSU	COUPS	DEEGR	EDGER
CHHIW	WHICH	CIKKS	KICKS	CKNOS	CONKS	COPUY	COYPU		GREED
CHHNU	HUNCH	CIKLN	CLINK		NOCKS	CORSS	CROSS	DEEGS	EDGES
CHHOO	HOOCH	CIKLS	LICKS	CKNSU	SNUCK	CORSU	SCOUR		SEDGE
CHHTU	HUTCH		SLICK	CKOOR	CROOK	CORSW	CROWS	DEEGW	WEDGE
CHIKN	CHINK	CIKMS	MICKS	CKOOS	COOKS	CORTU	COURT	DEEHS	HEEDS
CHIKO	HOICK	CIKNS	NICKS	CKOPS	POCKS	COSST	COSTS	DEEHW	HEWED
CHIKS	HICKS		SNICK	CKOPY	POCKY		SCOTS	DEEHX	HEXED
CHIKT	THICK	CIKPR	PRICK	CKORS	CORKS	COSSW	SCOWS	DEEIL	ELIDE
CHILL	CHILL	CIKPS	PICKS		ROCKS	COSTU	SCOUT	DEEIN	DIENE
CHILM	MILCH	CIKPY	PICKY	CKORY	CORKY	CPRTY	CRYPT	DEEIR	EIDER
CHILO	CHOLI	CIKQU	QUICK		ROCKY	CPSSU	CUSPS	DEEIX	DEXIE
CHILZ	ZILCH	CIKRS	RICKS	CKOSS	SOCKS	CPTUU	CUT UP	DEEJW	JEWED
CHIMO	OHMIC	CIKRT	TRICK	CKOST	STOCK	CRRUY	CURRY	DEEKN	KNEED
CHIMP	CHIMP	CIKRW	WRICK	CKPSU	PUCKS	CRSTU	CRUST	DEEKY	KEYED
CHIMU	HUMIC	CIKST	STICK	CKRSU	RUCKS	CRUVY	CURVY	DEELR	ELDER
CHINP	PINCH		TICKS	CKRTU	TRUCK	CSSTU	SCUTS	DEELU	ELUDE
CHINS	CHINS	CIKSW	WICKS	CKSSU	SUCKS	CSSTY	CYSTS	DEELV	DELVE
CHINW	WINCH	CILNO	NICOL	CKSTU	STUCK	CTTUY	CUTTY	DEEMN	EMEND
CHIOR	CHOIR	CILNT	CLINT		TUCKS	DDEEG	EDGED	DEEMS	DEEMS
	ICHOR	CILOS	COILS	CLLSU	CULLS	DDEEN	ENDED		DEMES
CHIPR	CHIRP	CILOW	WILCO		SCULL	DDEES	DEEDS		MEDES
CHIPS	CHIPS	CILPS	CLIPS	CLMOU	LOCUM	DDEGO	DODGE	DEEMT	METED
CHIPT	PITCH	CILRY	LYRIC	CLMPU	CLUMP	DDEIK	DIKED	DEEMW	MEWED
CHIRR	CHIRR	CILSU	SULCI	CLMSU	CULMS	DDEIN	DINED	DEENR	ENDER
CHIST	CHITS	CILTY	LYTIC	CLMTU	MULCT	DDEIO	DIODE	DEENS	DENES
CHISU	CUISH	CIMNU	CUMIN	CLNOO	COLON	DDEIR	DRIED		DENSE
CHITW	WITCH	CIMOR	MICRO	CLNOW	CLOWN		REDID		NEEDS

Code	Words
DEENU	ENDUE
DEENY	NEEDY
DEEOP	EPODE
DEEOR	ERODE
DEEPS	DEEPS / SPEED
DEERR	ERRED
DEERS	DEERS / REEDS / SEDER
DEERT	DETER / TREED
DEERY	REEDY
DEESS	SEEDS
DEEST	STEED
DEESU	SUEDE
DEESW	SEWED / SWEDE / WEEDS
DEESX	DESEX / SEXED
DEESY	SEEDY
DEETU	ETUDE
DEETW	TWEED
DEEUX	EXUDE
DEEVX	VEXED
DEEWY	WEEDY
DEFGO	DEFOG
DEFGU	FUDGE
DEFIL	FIELD / FILED
DEFIN	FIEND / FINED
DEFIR	FIRED / FRIED
DEFIT	FETID
DEFIX	FIXED
DEFIY	DEIFY / EDIFY
DEFJL	FJELD
DEFLT	DELFT
DEFMU	FUMED
DEFNS	FENDS
DEFOX	FOXED
DEFPU	FED UP
DEFSU	FEUDS / FUSED
DEGIL	GELID / GLIDE
DEGIM	MIDGE
DEGIN	DEIGN
DEGIO	GEOID
DEGIR	DIRGE / RIDGE
DEGIU	GUIDE
DEGJU	JUDGE
DEGLO	LODGE
DEGLS	GELDS
DEGLY	LEDGY
DEGNU	NUDGE
DEGOP	PODGE
DEGOR	GO RED / GORED
DEGOS	DOGES
DEGOT	GODET
DEGOW	WODGE
DEGRS	DREGS
DEGRU	URGED
DEGSY	SEDGY
DEGUY	GUYED
DEHIK	HIKED
DEHIR	HIDER / HIRED
DEHIS	HIDES / SHIED
DEHIV	HIVED
DEHLO	HOLED
DEHMO	HOMED
DEHNO	HONED
DEHOP	EPHOD / HOPED
DEHOR	HORDE
DEHOS	HOSED / SHOED
DEHOT	DOETH
DEHPT	DEPTH
DEHRS	HERDS / SHERD / SHRED
DEHSS	SHEDS
DEIIM	IMIDE
DEIIV	IVIED
DEIIX	DIXIE
DEIJV	JIVED
DEIKL	LIKED
DEIKN	INKED
DEIKR	IRKED
DEIKS	DIKES / SKIED
DEILM	LIMED
DEILN	LED IN / LINED
DEILO	OILED / OLDIE
DEILP	PILED / PLIED
DEILR	IDLER / RILED
DEILS	DELIS / IDLES / SIDLE / SLIDE
DEILT	TILDE / TILED
DEILV	DEVIL / LIVED
DEILW	WIELD / WILED
DEILY	YIELD
DEIMM	MIMED
DEIMN	DENIM / MINED
DEIMR	DIMER / MIRED / RIMED
DEIMS	DEISM / DIMES
DEIMT	DEMIT / TIMED
DEIMX	MIXED
DEINP	PINED
DEINR	DINER / IN RED
DEINS	DINES / SNIDE
DEINT	END IT / TINED
DEINU	INDUE
DEINW	WIDEN / WINED
DEINX	INDEX / NIXED
DEIOV	VIDEO
DEIOX	OXIDE
DEIPP	PIPED
DEIPR	PRIDE / PRIED
DEIPS	SPIED
DEIPT	TEPID
DEIRR	DIRER / DRIER / RIDER
DEIRS	DRIES / RIDES / SIRED
DEIRT	TIRED / TRIED
DEIRV	DIVER / DRIVE / RIVED
DEIRW	WEIRD / WIDER / WIRED
DEISS	SIDES
DEIST	DEIST / DIETS / EDITS / SITED / TIDES
DEISV	DIVES / VISED
DEISW	WIDES
DEIOZ	OIZED
DEITY	DEITY
DEJKO	JOKED
DEKKO	DEKKO
DEKNO	KENDO
DEKNU	NUKED
DEKOP	POKED
DEKOY	YOKED
DEKPU	PUKED
DEKSS	DESKS
DEKSU	DUKES
DEKSY	DYKES / SKYED
DELLS	DELLS
DELLW	DWELL
DELMO	MODEL
DELMS	MELDS
DELNO	LED ON / LODEN / OLDEN
DELNS	LENDS
DELOP	LOPED / POLED
DELOR	OLDER
DELOS	DOLES / LODES / SOLED
DELOV	LOVED
DELOW	DOWEL / LOWED
DELOY	YODEL
DELPU	DUPLE / LED UP / PULED
DELRU	LURED / RULED
DELRY	REDLY
DELSS	SLEDS
DELSU	DUELS / DULSE / SLUED
DELSW	WELDS
DELSY	LYSED
DELTV	VELDT
DELTW	DWELT
DEMMO	MODEM
DEMNO	DEMON
DEMNS	MENDS
DEMOO	MOOED
DEMOP	MOPED
DEMOS	DEMOS / DOMES / MODES
DEMOU	ODEUM
DEMOV	MOVED
DEMOW	MOWED
DEMRS	DERMS
DEMRU	DEMUR
DEMSU	MUSED / SEDUM
DEMTU	MUTED
DENNO	DONNE / END ON / NO END / ON END
DENOR	DRONE
DENOS	NODES / NOSED / SONDE
DENOT	NOTED / TONED
DENOW	ENDOW / OWNED
DENOY	DOYEN
DENOZ	DOZEN / ZONED
DENPS	SPEND
DENPU	END UP / UPEND
DENRS	RENDS
DENRT	TREND
DENRU	UNDER
DENSS	SENDS
DENST	DENTS / TENDS
DENSU	DUNES / NUDES
DENSV	VENDS
DENSW	WENDS
DENSY	DYNES
DENTU	TUNED
DENUU	UNDUE
DENWY	WENDY
DEOOR	RODEO
DEOOW	WOOED
DEOOZ	OOZED
DEOPR	DOPER / PORED / ROPED
DEOPS	DOPES / POSED / SPODE
DEOPT	DEPOT / OPTED / TOPED
DEOPY	DOPEY
DEORR	ORDER
DEORS	DOERS
DEORT	DOTER
DEORV	DROVE / ROVED
DEORW	DOWER / ROWED
DEORX	REDOX
DEORZ	DOZER
DEOSS	DOSES
DEOST	DOEST / DOTES
DEOSU	DOUSE
DEOSV	DOVES
DEOSW	DOWSE / SOWED
DEOSZ	DOZES
DEOTT	TOTED
DEOTU	OUTED
DEOTV	VOTED
DEOTW	TOWED
DEOTY	TOYED
DEOVW	VOWED
DEOWW	WOWED
DEPPU	UPPED
DEPRU	DRUPE / DUPER / PRUDE
DEPSU	DUPES / PSEUD
DEPTY	TYPED
DERRU	RUDER
DERRY	DRYER
DERSS	DRESS
DERSY	DREYS
DERUZ	DRUZE
DESTU	DUETS
DETUV	DUVET
DFFOS	DOFFS
DFFSU	DUFFS
DFILU	FLUID
DFINS	FINDS
DFINU	FUNDI
DFIOR	FIORD
DFIRT	DRIFT
DFJOR	FJORD
DFLOO	FLOOD / OF OLD
DFLOS	FOLDS
DFNOR	FROND
DFNOU	FOUND
DFNSU	FUNDS
DFOOR	DO FOR
DFOOS	FOODS
DFORS	FORDS
DGGOO	DOGGO
DGGOY	DOGGY
DGHOU	DOUGH
DGIIR	RIGID
DGIIT	DIGIT
DGILS	GILDS
DGILU	GUILD
DGINO	DINGO / DOING
DGINR	GRIND
DGINY	DINGY / DYING
DGIRS	GIRDS / GRIDS
DGLOS	GOLDS
DGLOY	GODLY
DGMOY	MY GOD!
DGNOS	DONGS
DGNUY	DUNGY
DGOOS	GOODS
DGOOY	GOODY

Code	Word	Code	Word	Code	Word	Code	Word	Code	Word
DGOPY	PODGY	DIPRS	DRIPS	DOPRU	PROUD	EEHNW	WHEEN	EEMOT	EMOTE
DGORU	GOURD	DIQSU	QUIDS	DORSS	DROSS	EEHPS	SHEEP	EEMRR	MERER
DGPUY	PUDGY		SQUID	DORSW	SWORD	EEHRS	HERES	EEMRS	MERES
DGRSU	DRUGS	DIRST	DIRTS		WORDS		SHEER	EEMRT	METER
DHIIN	HINDI	DIRTY	DIRTY	DORTU	TUDOR	EEHRT	ETHER		METRE
DHIMU	HUMID	DITTY	DITTY	DORWX	X-WORD		THERE	EEMRY	EMERY
DHINS	HINDS	DIVVY	DIVVY	DORWY	DOWRY		THREE	EEMSS	SEEMS
DHINU	HINDU	DIYZZ	DIZZY		ROWDY	EEHRW	HEWER	EEMST	MEETS
DHIOT	DHOTI	DJOOS	DOJOS		WORDY		WHERE		METES
DHIOY	HYOID	DKNRU	DRUNK	DOTTY	DOTTY	EEHRX	HEXER		TEEMS
DHIRT	THIRD	DKNSU	DUNKS	DPPUY	DUPPY	EEHST	SHEET	EEMYY	MY EYE!
DHISY	DISHY	DKOSU	KUDOS	DPRUY	DRY UP		THESE	EENNS	NENES
DHITW	WIDTH	DKRSU	KURDS	DPSSU	SPUDS	EEHSX	HEXES	EENPR	PREEN
DHLOS	HOLDS	DKSUU	KUDUS	DRSSU	SURDS	EEHTT	TEETH	EENPS	NEEPS
DHNOU	HOUND	DKSUY	DUSKY	DRSTU	DURST	EEILT	ELITE		PEENS
DHOOS	HOODS	DLLOR	DROLL	DSSTU	DUSTS	EEILX	EXILE		PENES
DHORW	DR. WHO	DLLOS	DOLLS		STUDS	EEINR	ERNIE	EENQU	QUEEN
DHORY	HYDRO	DLLOY	DOLLY	DSSUY	SUDSY	EEINS	SEE IN	EENRS	SNEER
DHOSW	DHOWS	DLLSU	DULLS	DSTUY	DUSTY		SEINE	EENRT	ENTER
DHOWY	HOWDY	DLLUY	DULLY		STUDY	EEIRS	ERIES		TERNE
DHSTU	THUDS	DLMOS	MOLDS	EEEGS	GEESE	EEIRY	EYRIE	EENRU	ENURE
DIILP	LIPID	DLMOU	MOULD	EEEIR	EERIE	EEISV	SIEVE	EENRV	NERVE
DIILV	LIVID	DLOOR	DROOL	EEELM	MELEE	EEISZ	SEIZE		NEVER
DIIMO	IDIOM	DLOPS	PLODS	EEELV	LEVEE	EEJLW	JEWEL	EENRW	NEWER
DIIMS	MIDIS	DLORS	LORDS	EEEPS	EPEES	EEJPS	JEEPS		RENEW
DIIMT	TIMID	DLORW	WORLD	EEEPT	TEPEE	EEJRS	JEERS	EENSS	SENSE
DIINR	INDRI	DLOST	DOLTS	EEEPV	PEEVE	EEJST	JETES	EENST	TEENS
DIIOT	IDIOT	DLOUW	WOULD	EEERV	REEVE	EEKKS	KEEKS		TENSE
DIIVV	VIVID	DLRYY	DRYLY	EEFLS	FEELS	EEKLN	KNEEL	EENSU	ENSUE
DIJNN	DJINN	DMMUY	DUMMY		FLEES	EEKLS	KEELS	EENSV	EVENS
DIKNR	DRINK	DMNOU	MOUND	EEFLT	FLEET		LEEKS		NEVES
DIKNS	KINDS	DMOOS	DOOMS	EEFMM	FEMME		SLEEK		SEVEN
DIKNY	DINKY		MOODS	EEFRR	FREER	EEKNS	KEENS	EENTT	TENET
DIKRS	DIRKS	DMOOU	DUOMO		REFER		KNEES	EENTV	EVENT
DIKSS	DISKS	DMOOY	MOODY	EEFRS	FREES	EEKOP	PEKOE	EENTW	TWEEN
	SKIDS	DMORS	DORMS		REEFS	EEKOV	EVOKE	EENTY	TEENY
DILLR	DRILL	DMPSU	DUMPS	EEFRV	FEVER	EEKPS	KEEPS	EENUV	VENUE
DILLS	DILLS	DMPUY	DUMPY	EEFRW	FEWER		PEEKS	EENWY	WEENY
DILLY	DILLY	DMRSU	DRUMS	EEFRY	REEFY		PEKES	EEOPT	TOPEE
	IDYLL	DMRUU	DURUM	EEFST	FETES	EEKRS	ESKER	EEOST	SEE TO
DILMS	MILDS	DNNOU	DUNNO	EEFSU	FUSEE		REEKS	EEOXY	OX EYE
DILMY	DIMLY	DNNUY	DUNNY	EEFSZ	FEZES	EEKRY	REEKY		OXEYE
DILOS	IDOLS	DNOOR	DONOR	EEFUZ	FUZEE	EEKSS	SEEKS	EEPPS	PEEPS
	LIDOS		RONDO	EEGHN	HENGE	EEKST	SKEET	EEPRS	PEERS
	SOLID	DNOOS	SNOOD	EEGIL	LIEGE	EEKSW	WEEKS		PERSE
DILOY	DOILY	DNOOT	DO NOT	EEGIN	GENIE	EELLV	LEVEL		SPREE
DILRU	LURID		TONDO	EEGIS	SIEGE	EELNO	LEONE	EEPRT	PETER
DILRY	DRILY	DNOPS	PONDS	EEGKR	GREEK	EELNW	NEWEL	EEPRU	PUREE
DILSS	SILDS	DNOPU	POUND	EEGLS	GLEES	EELOP	ELOPE		RUPEE
DILSW	WILDS	DNORU	ROUND	EEGLY	ELEGY	EELPR	LEPER	EEPSS	SEEPS
DIMNO	MID ON	DNORW	DROWN	EEGMR	MERGE		REPEL	EEPST	STEEP
	MID-ON	DNOST	DON'TS	EEGNR	GENRE	EELPS	PEELS	EEPSW	SWEEP
DIMNS	MINDS	DNOSU	NODUS		GREEN		PELES		WEEPS
DIMOU	ODIUM		SOUND	EEGNS	GENES		SLEEP	EEPWY	WEEPY
DIMST	MIDST	DNOSW	DOWNS	EEGNT	GENET	EELPX	EXPEL	EEQRU	QUEER
DIMTU	TUMID	DNOSY	SYNOD	EEGNW	NGWEE	EELRS	LEERS	EEQUU	QUEUE
DINOT	TONDI	DNOUW	WOUND	EEGOS	GO SEE		REELS	EERSS	SEERS
DINRS	RINDS	DNOWY	DOWNY		OGEES	EELRV	ELVER	EERST	ESTER
DINST	DINTS	DNSWY	WYNDS	EEGPU	GEE-UP		LEVER		RESET
DINSU	NIDUS	DOOPR	DROOP	EEGRS	SERGE		REVEL		STEER
DINSW	WINDS	DOORS	DOORS	EEGRT	EGRET	EELST	SLEET		STERE
DINWY	WINDY		ROODS		GREET		STEEL		TERSE
DIOOV	OVOID	DOORU	ODOUR	EEGRV	VERGE		STELE		TREES
DIOOZ	ZOOID	DOOST	STOOD	EEGST	EGEST	EELSV	ELVES	EERSU	REUSE
DIORT	DROIT		TO-DOS	EEHLS	HEELS	EELTU	ELUTE	EERSV	SERVE
DIOST	SOD IT!	DOOSW	WOODS	EEHLT	LETHE	EELTX	TELEX		SEVER
DIOSV	VOIDS	DOOTU	OUTDO	EEHLV	HELVE	EEMMR	EMMER		VEERS
DIOTT	DITTO	DOOWY	WOODY	EEHLW	WHEEL	EEMMT	EMMET		VERSE
DIOTV	DIVOT	DOPRS	DORPS	EEHMN	HE-MEN	EEMNS	SEMEN	EERSW	EWERS
DIOWW	WIDOW		DROPS	EEHMT	THEME	EEMNY	ENEMY		SEWER
DIPPY	DIPPY		PRODS	EEHNS	SHEEN		YEMEN	EERSY	EYRES

Code	Word	Code	Word	Code	Word	Code	Word	Code	Word
EERTV	EVERT	EFMOR	FORME	EGLPU	LEG UP	EHKOT	THE O.K.	EIKKS	KIKES
	REVET	EFMRU	FEMUR		LEG-UP	EHKOY	HOKEY	EIKLN	LIKEN
EERTX	EXERT	EFMSU	FUMES	EGLRU	GRUEL	EHLLO	HELLO	EIKLS	LIKES
EERUV	REVUE	EFNOR	FREON	EGLSU	GLUES	EHLLS	HELL'S	EIKMS	MIKES
EERVV	VERVE	EFNOT	OFTEN		GULES		SHELL	EIKNO	KOINE
EERVY	EVERY	EFNRS	FERNS		LUGES	EHLMS	HELMS	EIKNS	SKEIN
EESSX	SEXES	EFNRY	FERNY	EGLSY	GLEYS	EHLOS	HOLES	EIKNY	IN KEY
EESTW	SWEET	EFORT	FETOR	EGLUY	GLUEY		SHEOL	EIKPS	KEPIS
EESVX	VEXES		FORTE	EGMMY	GEMMY	EHLOT	HELOT		PIKES
EETTW	TWEET	EFORY	FOYER	EGMNO	GNOME		HOTEL		SPIKE
EFFIS	FIEFS	EFORZ	FROZE	EGMRS	GERMS		THOLE	EIKRS	SKIER
	FIFES	EFOSS	FOSSE	EGMRY	GERMY	EHLOV	HOVEL	EIKRY	KYRIE
EFFOR	OFFER	EFOSX	FOXES	EGMSU	GEUMS	EHLOW	WHOLE	EIKSS	SKIFS
EFGIN	FEIGN	EFRRY	FERRY	EGNOR	GONER	EHLOY	HOLEY	EIKST	KITES
EFGIR	GRIEF		FRYER		NEGRO	FHLPS	HELPS		OKITE
EFGLU	GUELF	EFRSS	SERFS	EGNOS	SEGNO	EHLPW	WHELP		TIKES
EFGOR	FORGE	EFRST	FRETS	EGNOT	GET ON	EHLRS	HERLS	EIKSV	SKIVE
EFGOY	FOGEY	EFRUZ	FURZE	EGNST	GENTS	EHLSW	WELSH	EIKOY	OKIEY
EFGUU	FUGUE	EFSST	FESTS	EGNSU	GENUS	EHLTY	ETHYL	EILLS	LISLE
EFHIT	THIEF	EFSSU	FUSES		NEGUS		LYTHE	EILMN	LIMEN
EFHLS	FLESH	EFSTU	FETUS	EGOOS	GOOSE	EHLXY	HEXYL	EILMP	IMPEL
	SHELF	EFSTW	WEFTS	EGOOY	GOOEY	EHMNY	HYMEN	EILMR	MILER
EFHNO	FOEHN	EFSUZ	FUZES	EGOPR	GROPE	EHMOR	HOMER	EILMS	LIMES
EFHRS	FRESH	EGGIU	GIGUE	EGOPY	POGEY		HOMES		MILES
EFHST	HEFTS	EGGLY	LEGGY	EGORR	ROGER	EHMOY	HOMEY		SLIME
EFHTT	THEFT	EGGNU	GUNGE	EGORS	GOERS	EHMPS	HEMPS		SMILE
EFHTY	HEFTY	EGGOR	GORGE		GORES	EHMRT	THERM	EILMU	ILEUM
EFIKN	KNIFE	EGGOU	GOUGE		GORSE	EHMRU	RHEUM	EILMY	LIMEY
EFILN	ELFIN	EGGSY	YEGGS		OGRES	EHMRY	RHYME	EILNN	LINEN
EFILR	FILER	EGHIN	HINGE	EGORT	ERGOT	EHMST	METHS	EILNR	LINER
	FLIER		NEIGH	EGORU	ROGUE	EHMTY	THYME	EILNS	LIENS
	LIFER	EGHIT	EIGHT		ROUGE	EHNOP	PHONE		LINES
	RIFLE	EGHIW	WEIGH	EGORV	GROVE	EHNOR	HERON	EILNT	INLET
EFILS	FILES	EGHNT	THEGN	EGOSS	GESSO	EHNOS	HONES		LET IN
	FLIES	EGHRU	HUGER	EGOST	GOEST		SHONE	EILNV	LIVEN
EFILT	FILET	EGIIN	GENII	EGOUV	VOGUE	EHNOY	HONEY	EILNY	LINEY
EFIMT	METIF	EGIJR	REJIG	EGPRU	PURGE	EHNRY	HENRY	EILOR	OILER
EFINR	FINER	EGIKR	GRIKE	EGPTU	GET UP	EHNTT	TENTH		ORIEL
	INFER	EGILT	GILET		GETUP	EHOOY	HOOEY	EILOT	LIE TO
EFINS	FINES		LEG IT	EGPTY	EGYPT	EHOPR	HOPER		TOILE
EFINT	FEINT		LEGIT	EGRRU	URGER	EHOPS	HOPES	EILOV	OLIVE
EFIRR	FIRER	EGILU	GUILE	EGRSU	SURGE	EHORS	HORSE		VIOLE
	FRIER	EGIMR	GRIME		URGES		SHORE		VOILE
EFIRS	FIRES	EGINR	NIGER	EGRSY	GREYS	EHORT	OTHER	EILPR	PERIL
	FRIES		REIGN	EGSST	GESTS		THROE	EILPS	PILES
	SERIF	EGINS	SENGI	EGSSU	GUESS	EHORV	HOVER		PLIES
EFIRT	REFIT		SINGE	EGSTU	GUEST	EHORW	WHORE		SPIEL
EFIRV	FIVER	EGINT	GET IN	EHIKR	HIKER	EHOSS	HOSES		SPILE
EFIRX	FIXER		TINGE	EHIKS	HIKES		SHOES	EILPU	LIE UP
EFIRY	FIERY	EGINV	GIVEN	EHILT	LITHE	EHOST	ETHOS	EILRS	RILES
	REIFY	EGINW	WINGE	EHILW	WHILE		THOSE		SLIER
EFISV	FIVES	EGINY	EYING	EHILX	HELIX	EHOSU	HOUSE	EILRT	LITER
EFISX	FIXES	EGIOV	OGIVE	EHIMN	HEM IN	EHOSV	SHOVE		LITRE
EFKLU	FLUKE	EGIPR	GRIPE	EHINR	RHINE	EHOSW	HOWES		TILER
EFKRS	KERFS	EGIRS	GRISE	EHINS	SHINE		WHOSE	EILRV	LIVER
EFLLS	FELLS	EGIRT	TIGER	EHINT	THINE	EHPRY	HYPER		LIVRE
EFLLY	FELLY	EGIRV	GIVER	EHINW	WHINE	EHPSY	HYPES		VILER
EFLMU	FLUME	EGIST	GIEST	EHIRR	HIRER	EHRSU	USHER	EILSS	ISLES
EFLNO	FELON	EGISU	GUISE	EHIRS	HEIRS	EHRSW	SHREW	EILST	ISLET
EFLOS	FELOS	EGISV	GIVES		HIRES	EHRSY	SHYER		ISTLE
	FLOES	EGITT	GET IT		SHIER	EHRTW	THREW		STILE
EFLPS	PELFS	EGKRY	GRYKE		SHIRE	EHRTZ	HERTZ		TILES
EFLRU	FLEUR	EGLMO	GOLEM	EHIRT	THEIR	EHSSW	SHEWS	EILSU	ILEUS
EFLRY	FLYER	EGLMU	GLUME	EHISS	SHIES	EHSTW	WHETS		LIEUS
EFLST	FELTS	EGLNS	GLENS	EHIST	HEIST	EIILN	LIE IN	EILSV	EVILS
EFLSU	FLUES	EGLNU	LUNGE	EHISV	HIVES		LIE-IN		LIVES
	FUELS	EGLOR	OGLER	EHITT	TITHE	EIILP	PILEI	EILSW	LEWIS
	FUSEL	EGLOS	LOGES	EHITW	WHITE	EIINT	TIE IN		WILES
EFLSW	FLEWS		OGLES		WITHE		TIE-IN	EILSX	LEXIS
EFLTU	FLUTE	EGLOT	LET GO	EHKLW	WHELK	EIIPX	PIXIE	EILTT	TITLE
EFLTY	LEFTY	EGLOV	GLOVE	EHKMR	KHMER	EIJSV	JIVES		

Code	Word	Code	Word	Code	Word	Code	Word	Code	Word
EIMMR	MIMER	EINSW	SINEW	EISSZ	SIZES	ELLTY	TELLY	ELRUX	LUREX
EIMMS	MIMES		SWINE	EISTU	ETUIS	ELMMU	LUMME	ELSSU	SLUES
EIMNR	MINER		WINES		SUITE	ELMNO	LEMON	ELSSW	SLEWS
EIMNS	MIENS	EINSX	NIXES	EISTX	EXIST		MELON	ELSSY	LYSES
	MINES	EINTU	UNITE		EXITS	ELMNU	LUMEN	ELSTT	LETTS
EIMOR	MOIRE		UNTIE	EISTY	YETIS	ELMOR	MOREL	ELSTU	LUTES
EIMOV	MOVIE	EINTW	TWINE	EISVW	VIEWS	ELMOS	MOLES	ELSTW	WELTS
EIMOX	MOXIE	EINVX	VIXEN		WIVES	ELMOT	MOTEL	ELSTY	STYLE
EIMPR	PRIME	EINVY	VEINY	EITTW	TWITE	ELMOU	OLEUM	ELSUX	LUXES
EIMPT	TEMPI	EINWY	WINEY	EJKOP	KOPJE	ELMPU	PLUME	ELTUX	EXULT
EIMRS	EMIRS	EINWZ	WIZEN	EJKOR	JOKER	ELMRU	LEMUR	ELTWY	WETLY
	MIRES	EIOPS	POISE	EJKOS	JOKES	ELMST	MELTS	EMMOS	MEMOS
	MISER	EIORS	OSIER	EJKOY	JOKEY		SMELT	EMMSY	EMMYS
	RIEMS	EIORV	VIREO	EJKRS	JERKS	ELMSU	MULES	EMNNO	NOMEN
	RIMES	EIPPR	PIPER	EJKRY	JERKY	ELMSW	MEWLS	EMNNU	NUMEN
EIMRT	MERIT	EIPPS	PIPES	EJLLS	JELLS	ELMUV	VELUM	EMNOS	MESON
	MITRE	EIPQU	EQUIP	EJLLY	JELLY	ELMUY	MULEY		OMENS
	REMIT		PIQUE	EJLOU	JOULE	ELMXY	XYLEM	EMNOV	VENOM
	TIMER	EIPRR	PRIER	EJLPU	JULEP	ELNOR	ENROL	EMNOW	WOMEN
EIMRX	MIXER		RIPER	EJMMY	JEMMY		LONER	EMNOY	MONEY
EIMSS	SEMIS	EIPRS	PIERS	EJNNY	JENNY	ELNOS	NOELS	EMNRU	RUMEN
EIMST	EMITS		PRIES	EJNOS	JONES	ELNOT	LENTO	EMNSU	MENUS
	ITEMS		PRISE	EJNOY	ENJOY		LET ON	EMOOR	ROMEO
	METIS		SPIRE	EJOSY	JOEYS	ELNOV	NOVEL	EMOOS	MOOSE
	MITES	EIPRT	TRIPE	EJRRY	JERRY	ELNSU	LUNES	EMOPR	MOPER
	SMITE	EIPRV	VIPER	EJRWY	JEWRY	ELNWY	NEWLY		PROEM
	TIMES	EIPRW	WIPER	EJSST	JESTS	ELOOS	LOOSE	EMOPS	MOPES
EIMSX	MIXES	EIPRZ	PRIZE	EJSSU	JESUS	ELOPR	LOPER		POEMS
EINNP	PENNI	EIPSS	SPIES	EJSTU	JUTES		PROLE		POMES
EINNR	INNER	EIPST	PISTE	EJTTY	JETTY	ELOPS	LOPES	EMOPT	TEMPO
	RENIN		SPITE	EKLLN	KNELL		POLES	EMOPY	MYOPE
EINNS	NINES		STIPE	EKLNT	KNELT		SLOPE	EMORR	ORMER
EINNU	ENNUI	EIPSW	SWIPE	EKLOY	YOKEL	ELOPU	LOUPE	EMORS	MORES
EINNV	VENIN		WIPES	EKLPS	KELPS	ELORS	LORES		MORSE
EINOP	OPINE	EIPTT	PETIT		SKELP		LOSER	EMORT	METRO
EINOS	EOSIN	EIPTU	TIE UP	EKLST	KELTS		ROLES	EMORV	MOVER
	NOISE		TIE-UP	EKMOS	MOKES	ELORV	LOVER		VOMER
EINOT	TOE-IN	EIPTW	PEWIT		SMOKE	ELORW	LOWER	EMORW	MOWER
EINOV	OVINE	EIPTY	PIETY	EKNOR	KRONE		ROWEL	EMOST	MOTES
EINPR	RIPEN	EIQRU	QUIRE	EKNOT	TOKEN	ELOSS	LOESS		SMOTE
EINPS	PEINS	EIQTU	QUIET	EKNOW	WOKEN		LOSES		TOMES
	PENIS		QUITE	EKNRS	KERNS		SLOES	EMOSU	MOUES
	PINES	EIRRS	RISER	EKNSU	NUKES		SOLES		MOUSE
	SNIPE	EIRRT	TRIER	EKOPR	POKER	ELOST	STOLE	EMOSV	MOVES
	SPINE	EIRRV	RIVER	EKOPS	POKES	ELOSU	LOUSE	EMOSW	MEOWS
EINPT	INEPT	EIRRW	WIRER		SPOKE		OUSEL	EMOSY	MOSEY
EINPY	PINEY	EIRRY	EYRIR	EKOPY	POKEY	ELOSV	LOVES	EMOTT	MOTET
EINRS	REINS	EIRSS	RISES	EKOST	STOKE		SOLVE		MOTTE
	RESIN		SIRES	EKOSY	YOKES		VOLES		TOTEM
	RINSE	EIRST	RITES	EKPRS	PERKS	ELOTT	TO LET	EMOZZ	MEZZO
	RISEN		TIERS	EKPRY	PERKY	ELOTW	OWLET	EMPRS	PERMS
	SERIN		TIRES	EKPSS	KESPS		TOWEL		SPERM
	SIREN		TRIES		SKEPS	ELOTX	EXTOL	EMPST	TEMPS
EINRT	INERT	EIRSV	RIVES	EKPSU	PUKES	ELOUV	OVULE	EMPSU	SPUME
	INTER		VIERS	EKPSY	PESKY	ELOUZ	OUZEL	EMPTT	TEMPT
	NITRE	EIRSW	WEIRS	EKRRY	KERRY	ELOVW	VOWEL	EMPTY	EMPTY
	TRINE		WIRES	EKRST	TREKS	ELOVY	LOVEY	EMRRY	MERRY
EINRU	INURE		WISER	EKSSW	SKEWS	ELPRY	REPLY	EMRST	TERMS
	URINE	EIRSX	SIXER	EKSTY	TYKES	ELPST	PELTS	EMRSU	MUSER
EINRV	RIVEN	EIRTT	TITER	EKSYY	SKYEY		SLEPT		SERUM
EINSS	SINES		TITRE	ELLMS	SMELL		SPELT	EMRUX	MUREX
EINST	INSET		TRITE	ELLNS	SNELL	ELPSU	PULES	EMSST	STEMS
	SET IN	EIRTU	UTERI	ELLNY	NELLY		PULSE	EMSSU	MUSES
	SET-IN	EIRTV	RIVET	ELLPS	SPELL	ELPSY	YELPS	EMSSY	MESSY
	STEIN	EIRTW	WRITE	ELLQU	QUELL	ELPTU	LET UP	EMSTU	MUTES
	TINES	EISST	SITES	ELLSS	SELLS		LETUP	ENNOO	NO ONE
EINSU	IN USE		STIES	ELLST	TELLS	ELRRU	RULER	ENNOS	NONES
EINSV	VEINS	EISSU	ISSUE	ELLSW	SWELL	ELRSU	LURES	ENNOT	TENON
	VINES	EISSV	VISES		WELLS		RULES		TONNE
		EISSW	WISES	ELLSY	YELLS	ELRSY	LYRES	ENNOX	XENON
		EISSX	SIXES	ELLTU	TULLE		SLYER	ENNPY	PENNY

Code	Word(s)
ENOOR	RONEO
ENOOS	NOOSE
ENOOZ	OZONE
ENOPR	PRONE
ENOPS	OPENS, PEONS
ENOPU	ONE UP
ENOPY	PEONY
ENORS	NORSE, SENOR, SNORE
ENORT	NOTER, TENOR, TONER
ENORW	OWNER
ENORZ	ZONER
ENOSS	NOSES
FNOST	NOTES, ONSET, SET ON, STONE, TONES
ENOSV	OVENS
ENOSW	SEW ON
ENOSY	NOSEY
ENOSZ	ZONES
ENOVW	WOVEN
ENOVY	ENVOY
ENPRU	PRUNE
ENPST	SPENT
ENPTY	N-TYPE
ENQRU	QUERN
ENRRU	RERUN
ENRST	RENTS, STERN, TERNS
ENRSU	NURSE, RUNES
ENRSW	WRENS
ENRTU	TUNER
ENRTY	ENTRY
ENRVY	NERVY
ENSST	NESTS, STENS
ENSTT	TENTS
ENSTU	TUNES
ENSTV	VENTS
ENSTW	NEWTS
ENSUV	NEVUS, VENUS
ENSUX	NEXUS, UNSEX
ENSWY	NEWSY
ENTTY	NETTY
EOOPV	POOVE
EOORW	WOOER
EOOSZ	OOZES
EOPPS	PEPOS, POPES
EOPRR	ROPER
EOPRS	PORES, POSER, PROSE, ROPES, SPORE
EOPRT	PORTE, TOPER, TROPE
EOPRV	PROVE
EOPRW	POWER
EOPSS	PESOS, POSES, POSSE
EOPST	ESTOP, POETS, STOEP, STOPE, TOPES
EOPSX	EXPOS
EOPSY	POESY, SEPOY
EOPXY	EPOXY
EOQTU	QUOTE, TOQUE
EORRR	ERROR
EORRS	SORER
EORRV	ROVER
EORRW	ROWER
EORSS	ROSES, SORES
EORST	ROTES, STORE
EORSU	EUROS, ROUES, ROUSE
EORSV	OVERS, ROVES, SERVO, VERSO
EORSW	SOWER, SWORE, WORSE
EORSZ	ZEROS
EORTT	OTTER, TORTE
EORTU	OUTER, OUTRE, ROUTE
EORTV	OVERT, TROVE, VOTER
EORTW	TOWER, WROTE
EORTY	TOYER
EORVW	VOWER
EORXX	XEROX
EOSSU	SOUSE
EOSTT	SET TO, SET-TO, TOTES
EOSTV	STOVE, VETOS, VOTES
EOSTY	EYOTS
EPPPY	PEPPY
EPPRU	UPPER
EPPTY	P-TYPE
EPRRU	PURER
EPRRY	PERRY
EPRSS	PRESS
EPRST	STREP
EPRSU	PURSE, SPRUE, SUPER
EPRSY	PREYS, PYRES
EPRTU	ERUPT
EPRTW	TWERP
EPRUV	REV UP
EPRXY	PYREX
EPSST	PESTS, STEPS
EPSSW	SPEWS
EPSTU	SET UP, SET-UP, STUPE, UPSET
EPSTW	SWEPT
EPSTY	TYPES
EPSUU	USE UP
EPSXY	PYXES
EPTTY	PETTY
EQRUY	QUERY
EQSTU	QUEST
ERRSU	SURER
ERRTU	TRUER
ERRTY	TERRY
ERSST	RESTS, TRESS
ERSSU	RUSES, SUERS, USERS
ERSTW	STREW, TREWS, WREST
ERSTY	TYRES
ERTTU	UTTER
ESSTT	SETTS, STETS, TESTS
ESSTV	VESTS
ESSTW	STEWS
ESSTY	STYES
ESSTZ	ZESTS
ESTTV	T V SET
ESTTX	TEXTS
ESTTY	TESTY
ESTYZ	ZESTY
FFFLU	FLUFF
FFGOO	GO OFF
FFGRU	GRUFF
FFGSU	GUFFS
FFHIT	FIFTH
FFHIW	WHIFF
FFHOW	HOWFF
FFHSU	HUFFS
FFHUY	HUFFY
FFIJS	JIFFS
FFIJY	JIFFY
FFIKS	SKIFF
FFIMS	MIFFS
FFINO	IN OFF, IN-OFF
FFINS	NIFFS, SNIFF
FFINY	NIFFY
FFIQU	QUIFF
FFIRS	RIFFS
FFIST	STIFF, TIFFS
FFITY	FIFTY
FFLSU	LUFFS
FFMSU	MUFFS
FFNOO	ON-OFF
FFNSU	SNUFF
FFOST	TOFFS
FFPSU	PUFFS
FFPUY	PUFFY
FFRSU	RUFFS
FFSTU	STUFF
FGGOY	FOGGY
FGGUY	FUGGY
FGHIT	FIGHT
FGILN	FLING
FGINU	FUNGI
FGIRT	GRIFT
FGIST	GIFTS
FGLNU	FLUNG
FGLOS	FLOGS
FGLSU	GULFS
FGOOR	FORGO, GO FOR
FGOOS	GOOFS
FGOOY	GOOFY
FGORS	FROGS
FHIIS	HI-FIS, HI FIS
FHILT	FILTH
FHIRT	FIRTH
FHIST	SHIFT
FHISY	FISHY
FHLSU	FLUSH
FHOOS	HOOFS
FHORT	FORTH, FROTH
FIINS	FINIS
FIINT	FIT IN
FIINX	INFIX
FIKNS	FINKS
FIKRS	FRISK
FILLR	FRILL
FILLS	FILLS
FILLY	FILLY
FILMS	FILMS
FILMY	FILMY
FILNT	FLINT
FILNY	FLY-IN
FILOO	FOLIO
FILOS	FOILS
FILPS	FLIPS
FILRT	FLIRT
FILST	FLITS, LIFTS
FILSU	FUSIL
FILTY	FITLY
FIMOT	MOTIF
FIMRS	FIRMS
FIMTU	MUFTI
FINNS	FINNS
FINNU	IN FUN
FINNY	FINNY
FINOS	FINOS
FINOT	FIT ON
FINOX	FIX ON
FINRS	FIRNS
FINTU	UNFIT
FINTY	NIFTY
FINUY	UNIFY
FIOST	FOIST
FIPTU	FIT UP, FIT-UP
FIPUX	FIX UP
FIRST	FIRST, FRITS, RIFTS
FIRTU	FRUIT
FIRTZ	FRITZ
FIRZZ	FRIZZ
FISST	FISTS, SIFTS
FISTW	SWIFT
FIYZZ	FIZZY
FKLNU	FLUNK
FKLOS	FOLKS
FKLUY	FLUKY
FKNSU	FUNKS
FKNUY	FUNKY
FKORS	FORKS
FLLOY	FOLLY
FLLSU	FULLS
FLLUY	FULLY
FLMPU	FLUMP
FLNOW	FLOWN
FLOOR	FLOOR
FLOOS	FOOLS
FLOOW	WOLOF
FLOPS	FLOPS
FLORU	FLOUR
FLOSS	FLOSS
FLOST	LOFTS
FLOSU	FOULS
FLOSW	FLOWS, FOWLS
FLOTU	FLOUT
FLOTY	LOFTY
FLRSU	FURLS
FLTUY	FLUTY
FMORS	FORMS
FMORU	FORUM
FMPRU	FRUMP
FNNUY	FUNNY
FNORT	FRONT
FNORW	FROWN
FNOST	FONTS
FNOTU	FOUNT
FOOPR	PROOF
FOOPS	POOFS, SPOOF
FOORS	ROOFS
FOOST	FOOTS
FOOSW	WOOFS
FOOTY	FOOTY
FOPRS	PROFS
FOPSU	POUFS
FORRU	FUROR
FORST	FORTS, FROST
FORSU	FOURS
FORTY	FORTY
FOSTY	SOFTY
FPRUY	FRY UP, FRY-UP
FRRUY	FURRY
FRSSU	SURFS
FRSTU	TURFS
FRTUY	TURFY
FRUYZ	FURZY
FSSUY	FUSSY
FSTTU	TUFTS
FSTUY	FUSTY
FTTUY	TUFTY
FUYZZ	FUZZY
GGHOS	HOGGS
GGILO	GOLGI
GGINO	GOING
GGIOT	GIGOT
GGIPY	PIGGY
GGMUY	MUGGY
GGNOS	GONGS
GGNUY	GUNGY
GGOSY	SOGGY
GGUVY	VUGGY
GHHIS	HIGHS

GHHIT	THIGH	GINVY	VYING	GOPRU	GROUP	HITWY	WHITY	HOPSY	HYPOS
GHILT	LIGHT	GINYZ	ZINGY	GOPRY	PORGY		WITHY	HOPTU	HOT UP
GHIMT	MIGHT	GIORR	RIGOR	GOPTU	GOT UP	HJNOS	JOHNS	HOQTU	QUOTH
GHINT	NIGHT	GIORS	GIROS	GORSS	GROSS	HKLSU	HULKS	HORST	HORST
	THING	GIORV	VIRGO	GORST	GROTS	HKMOU	HOKUM		SHORT
GHINY	HYING	GIOSY	YOGIS	GORSW	GROWS		KHOUM	HORSU	HOURS
GHIRT	GIRTH	GIOTT	GOT IT	GORSY	GORSY	HKNOS	HONKS	HORTT	TROTH
	RIGHT	GIPRS	GRIPS		GYROS	HKNSU	HUNKS	HORTW	THROW
GHISS	SIGHS		PRIGS	GORSZ	GROSZ	HKOOS	HOOKS		WORTH
GHIST	SIGHT		SPRIG	GORTU	GROUT		SHOOK		WROTH
GHISW	WHIGS	GIPRU	RIG UP	GOSTU	GUSTO	HKOOY	HOOKY	HOSST	HOSTS
GHITT	TIGHT	GIPSY	GIPSY	GOSTY	STOGY	HKSSU	HUSKS		SHOTS
GHLLY	GHYLL	GIRST	GIRTS	GOTUY	GOUTY	HKSUY	HUSKY	HOSSW	SHOWS
GHLOU	GHOUL		GRIST	GPPUY	GUPPY	HLLOO	HOLLO	HOSTU	SHOUT
	LOUGH		GRITS	GPSYY	GYPSY	HLLOU	HULLO		SOUTH
GHLPY	GLYPH	GISST	GISTS	GRSTU	TRUGS	HLLOY	HOLLY		THOUS
GHNOT	THONG	GISSW	SWIGS	GRSUU	GURUS	HLLSU	HULLS	HOSWY	SHOWY
GHORU	ROUGH	GISTU	G SUIT	GSSTU	GUSTS	HLMOS	HOLMS	HOTUY	YOUTH
GHOST	GHOST	GISTW	TWIGS	GSTUY	GUSTY	HLMPY	LYMPH	HPSUY	PUSHY
	GOTHS	GKNOO	KONGO		GUTSY	HLOPX	PHLOX	HQRSU	QURSH
GHOSU	SOUGH	GKNSU	GUNKS	HHHUU	UH HUH	HLORW	WHORL	HRRUY	HURRY
GHOTU	OUGHT	GLLOY	GOLLY		UH-HUH	HLOSS	SLOSH	HRSTU	HURTS
	TOUGH	GLLSU	GULLS	HHISW	WHISH	HLOST	HOLTS	HRSUY	RUSHY
GHRSU	SHRUG	GLLUY	GULLY	HHMOU	HO HUM		SLOTH	HRTTU	TRUTH
GHSTU	THUGS	GLMOO	GLOOM	HHMPU	HUMPH	HLOSW	HOWLS	HSSTU	SHUTS
GHSUY	GUSHY	GLMOU	MOGUL	HHORU	H HOUR	HLOTY	HOTLY	HSSUY	HUSSY
GIILV	VIGIL	GLNOS	LONGS	HHSSU	SHUSH	HLPSU	PLUSH	IIJNN	JINNI
GIJNO	JINGO	GLNSU	LUNGS	HIIRS	IRISH	HLPSY	SYLPH	IIKNN	IN INK
GIKNS	KINGS		SLUNG	HIKNT	THINK	HLRSU	HURLS		KININ
GILLO	GO ILL	GLOOS	LOGOS	HIKRS	SHIRK	HLSSU	SLUSH	IIKSW	KIWIS
GILLR	GRILL	GLOOW	GO LOW	HIKSS	SIKHS	HLSYY	SHYLY	IILLV	VILLI
GILLS	GILLS	GLOOY	OLOGY	HIKST	KITHS	HMNOT	MONTH	IILMT	LIMIT
GILNO	LINGO	GLORW	GROWL	HIKSW	WHISK	HMNPY	NYMPH	IILMU	ILIUM
GILNS	SLING	GLORY	GLORY	HILLS	HILLS	HMNSY	HYMNS	IIMMN	MINIM
GILNT	GLINT	GLOSS	GLOSS	HILLY	HILLY	HMOOP	OOMPH	IIMNS	MINIS
GILNU	LUNGI		SLOGS	HILMU	HILUM	HMOPR	MORPH	IIMNX	MIX IN
GILNY	LYING	GLOSW	GLOWS	HILOT	LITHO	HMOST	MOTHS	IIMPS	IMPIS
GILOO	IGLOO	GLPSU	GULPS		THIOL	HMOTU	MOUTH	IINST	SIT IN
GILRS	GIRLS		PLUGS	HILRW	WHIRL	HMPSU	HUMPS		SIT-IN
GILST	GILTS	GLSSU	SLUGS	HILST	HILTS	HMPTU	THUMP	IIORT	TORII
GILSU	UGLIS	GLSTU	GLUTS	HILTT	TILTH	HMPUY	HUMPY	IIPPT	PIPIT
GILTU	GUILT	GMMUY	GUMMY	HIMRT	MIRTH	HMRRY	MYRRH	IISTV	VISIT
GIMNY	MINGY	GMNOO	MONGO	HIMSS	SHIMS	HMRTU	THRUM	IJKNS	JINKS
GIMOS	GISMO	GMNOU	MUNGO	HIMST	SMITH	HMSTU	MUSTH	IJLST	JILTS
GIMOY	GOYIM	GMOOR	GROOM	HIMSW	WHIMS	HMSTY	MYTHS	IJNNS	JINNS
GIMOZ	GIZMO	GMOOS	MOOGS	HINNT	NINTH	HMSUU	HUMUS	IJNNU	INJUN
GIMPY	PIGMY	GMPRU	GRUMP	HINNY	HINNY	HMSUY	MUSHY	IJNOS	JOINS
GIMRY	GRIMY	GMPUU	MUG UP	HINOP	HOP IN	HNOOS	SHOON	IJNOT	JOINT
GINOR	GROIN	GMPYY	PYGMY	HINOR	RHINO	HNOOW	NOHOW	IJOST	JOIST
GINOT	GOT IN	GNNUY	GUNNY	HINSS	SHINS	HNOPS	PHONS	IKKNS	KINKS
	INGOT	GNOOS	GOONS	HINST	HINTS	HNOPY	PHONY		SKINK
	TIGON	GNOOT	GOT ON		THINS	HNORS	HORNS	IKKNY	KINKY
	TO-ING	GNOOW	GO NOW	HINSW	WHINS		SHORN	IKKOS	KIOSK
GINOW	OWING	GNOOY	GOONY	HINSY	SHINY	HNORT	NORTH	IKKRS	KIRKS
GINPS	PINGS	GNOPR	PRONG	HINWY	WHINY		THORN	IKKRU	KUKRI
GINPU	GIN UP	GNOPS	PONGS	HIOPP	HIPPO	HNORY	HORNY	IKLLR	KRILL
GINRS	GIRNS	GNORW	GROWN	HIOPT	HOP IT	HNOSW	SHOWN	IKLLS	KILLS
	GRINS		WRONG		TOPHI	HNSSU	SHUNS		SKILL
	RINGS	GNOSS	SNOGS	HIORU	HOURI	HNSTU	HUNTS	IKLMS	MILKS
GINRU	RUING		SONGS	HIOST	HOIST		SHUNT	IKLMY	MILKY
GINRW	WRING	GNOST	TONGS	HIPQS	Q-SHIP	HOOPS	HOOPS	IKLNS	KILNS
GINSS	SIGNS	GNOSW	GOWNS	HIPSS	SHIPS	HOOPT	PHOTO		LINKS
	SINGS	GNOUY	YOUNG	HIPST	PITHS	HOOPW	WHOOP		SLINK
	SNIGS	GNRSU	RUNGS	HIPSW	WHIPS	HOOSS	SHOOS	IKLOS	KILOS
GINST	STING	GNRTU	GRUNT	HIPTY	PITHY	HOOST	HOOTS	IKLRS	SKIRL
GINSU	SUING	GNRUW	WRUNG	HIRRS	SHIRR		SHOOT	IKLSS	SILKS
GINSV	V SIGN	GNSSU	SNUGS	HIRRW	WHIRR	HOOSW	WHOSO	IKLST	KILTS
GINSW	SWING	GNSTU	STUNG	HIRST	SHIRT		WOOSH	IKLSY	SILKY
	WINGS	GNSUW	SWUNG	HISSW	SWISH	HOOTT	TOOTH	IKMNS	MINKS
GINSZ	ZINGS	GOOTU	GO OUT	HISTW	WHIST	HOPSS	SHOPS	IKMPS	SKIMP
GINTY	TYING		OUTGO	HISTX	SIXTH	HOPSW	WHOPS		

Code	Word	Code	Word	Code	Word	Code	Word	Code	Word
IKMRS	MIRKS	ILOSV	VIOLS	INOTW	IN TOW	ISSTU	SITUS	LLMOS	MOLLS
	SMIRK	ILOSY	SOILY	INOTX	TOXIN		SUITS	LLMSU	MULLS
IKMRY	MIRKY	ILPPU	PUPIL	INPPU	PIN UP	ISTTW	TWIST	LLNSU	NULLS
IKMSS	SKIMS	ILPSS	LISPS		PINUP		TWITS	LLOPS	POLLS
IKNOP	PINKO		SLIPS	INPPY	NIPPY	ISTXY	SIXTY	LLORS	ROLLS
IKNOS	IKONS	ILPST	SPILT	INPRT	PRINT	ITTTU	TUTTI	LLORT	TROLL
	OINKS		SPLIT	INPSS	SNIPS	ITTTY	TITTY	LLOST	TOLLS
IKNPR	PRINK	ILPSU	PILUS		SPINS	ITTWX	TWIXT	LLOSY	LYSOL
IKNPS	PINKS	ILPTU	LIT UP	INPST	PINTS	ITTWY	WITTY	LLOWY	LOWLY
IKNRS	RINKS		TULIP	INPSY	SPINY	ITYZZ	TIZZY	LLPSU	PULLS
IKNSS	SINKS	ILQTU	QUILT	INPTU	INPUT	JKNSU	JUNKS	LLRTU	TRULL
	SKINS	ILRSW	SWIRL		PUT IN	JKNUY	JUNKY	LLSUY	SULLY
IKNST	KNITS	ILRTW	TWIRL	INPUZ	UNZIP	JLLOY	JOLLY	LLSYY	SLYLY
	SKINT	ILSST	LISTS	INQSU	QUINS	JLOST	JOLTS	LMOOS	LOOMS
	STINK		SILTS	INQTU	QUINT	JLOSW	JOWLS	LMOOT	MOLTO
IKNSW	WINKS		SLITS	INRSU	RUINS	JLOTY	JOLTY	LMOST	MOLTS
IKPSS	SKIPS	ILSSY	LYSIS	INSST	SNITS	JMPSU	JUMPS		SMOLT
	SPIKS	ILSTT	STILT	INSSU	SINUS	JMPUY	JUMPY	LMOTU	MOULT
IKPSY	SPIKY		TILTS	INSTT	STINT	JNOTU	JUNTO	LMPPU	PLUMP
IKQRU	QUIRK	ILSTW	WILTS		TINTS	JORRU	JUROR	LMPSU	LUMPS
IKRRS	SKIRR	ILSTY	SILTY	INSTU	UNITS	JOSTU	JOUST		PLUMS
IKRSS	RISKS		STYLI	INSTW	TWINS	KKLSU	SKULK		SLUMP
IKRST	SKIRT	IMNOR	MINOR	INSUZ	ZUNIS	KKNSU	SKUNK	LMPUY	LUMPY
	STIRK	IMNST	MINTS	INTUY	UNITY	KKOOS	KOOKS	LMSSU	SLUMS
IKRSY	RISKY	IMNSU	MINUS	IOOST	ISOTO	KKOOY	KOOKY	LNNOY	NYLON
IKRTU	TURKI	IMOPR	PRIMO		SOOTI	KLLNO	KNOLL	LNOOR	ORLON
IKSST	SKITS	IMOPU	OPIUM	IOPRR	PRIOR	KLLSU	SKULL	LNOOS	LOONS
IKTTY	KITTY	IMOST	MOIST	IOPST	POSIT	KLNOP	PLONK	LNOOY	LOONY
ILLMS	MILLS		OMITS		TOPIS	KLNPU	PLUNK	LNOPY	PYLON
ILLOS	LI-LOS	IMOSU	SUOMI	IOPSU	PIOUS	KLNRU	KNURL	LOOOV	OVOLO
ILLPS	PILLS	IMOTV	VOMIT	IOPTV	PIVOT	KLNSU	SLUNK	LOOPR	ORLOP
	SPILL	IMPPR	PRIMP	IOQTU	QUOIT	KLOOS	LOOKS	LOOPS	LOOPS
ILLQU	QUILL	IMPPS	PIMPS	IORRS	ORRIS	KLOSY	YOLKS		POOLS
ILLRS	RILLS	IMPRS	PRISM	IORST	RIOTS	KLOYY	YOLKY		SLOOP
ILLRT	TRILL	IMPUX	MIX UP		TORSI	KLRSU	LURKS		SPOOL
ILLSS	SILLS		MIX-UP		TRIOS	KLSSU	SULKS	LOOPY	LOOPY
ILLST	LILTS	IMPWY	WIMPY	IORSV	VISOR	KLSUY	SULKY	LOOSS	SOLOS
	STILL	IMRST	TRIMS	IORVY	IVORY	KMNOS	MONKS		SOOLS
	TILLS	IMRSU	RIMUS	IORVZ	VIZOR	KMOOS	SMOKO	LOOST	LOOTS
ILLSW	SWILL	IMRSV	MIRVS	IOSUX	SIOUX	KMOSY	SMOKY		SLOOT
	WILLS	IMSST	MISTS	IOTTW	TO WIT	KMRUY	MURKY		STOOL
ILLSY	SILLY	IMSSW	SWIMS	IPPTU	TIP UP	KMSUY	MUSKY		TOOLS
	SLILY	IMSSY	MISSY	IPPUZ	ZIP-UP	KNNOW	KNOWN	LOOSW	WOOLS
ILLTW	TWILL	IMSTT	MITTS	IPPYZ	ZIPPY	KNOOS	NOOKS	LOOTT	LOTTO
ILMOS	LIMOS	IMSTY	MISTY	IPQSU	QUIPS		SNOOK	LOPPS	PLOPS
ILMPS	LIMPS	INNNY	NINNY	IPRST	SPIRT	KNOST	KNOTS	LOPPY	POLYP
ILMPY	IMPLY	INNOO	ONION		SPRIT	KNOSW	KNOWS	LOPRW	PROWL
ILMSS	SLIMS	INNOP	PINON		STRIP	KNOSY	YONKS	LOPSS	SLOPS
ILMST	MILTS	INNOU	UNION		TRIPS	KNOTU	KNOUT	LOPST	PLOTS
ILMSY	SLIMY	INNPU	UNPIN	IPRSU	SIRUP	KNOTY	TONKY	LOPSY	PLOYS
ILMTY	MILTY	INNPY	PINNY	IPRSY	SPIRY	KNOWY	WONKY		POLYS
ILNOS	LIONS	INNRU	INURN	IPRTW	TWIRP	KNPSU	PUNKS	LOPTU	PLUTO
	LOINS		RUN IN	IPRVY	PRIVY		SPUNK		POULT
ILNPU	LUPIN	INNSU	SUNNI	IPSST	SPITS	KNRSU	KNURS	LORRY	LORRY
ILNST	LINTS	INNTY	TINNY	IPSSV	SPIVS	KNRTU	TRUNK	LORSU	LOURS
ILNSY	LYSIN	INOPP	POP IN	IPSSW	WISPS	KNSTU	STUNK	LORUY	LOURY
ILNTU	UNTIL	INOPS	PIONS	IPSTU	SIT UP	KOOPS	SPOOK	LOSST	SLOTS
ILNTY	LINTY	INOPT	PINTO		TUPIS	KOORS	ROOKS	LOSSU	SOULS
ILNVY	VINYL		PITON	IPSTY	TIPSY	KOOST	KOTOS	LOSSW	SLOWS
ILOOP	POLIO		POINT	IPSWY	WISPY		STOOK	LOSSY	LOSSY
ILOPS	SPOIL	INOQU	QUOIN	IPSXY	PYXIS	KOPRY	PORKY	LOSTU	LOTUS
ILOPT	PILOT	INORS	IRONS	IPTTU	PUTTI	KORST	STORK		LOUTS
ILOPU	POILU		ROSIN	IQRTU	QUIRT		TORSK	LOSTV	VOLTS
ILOPX	OXLIP	INORT	INTRO	IQSTU	QUITS	KORSW	WORKS	LOSUY	LOUSY
ILORS	LORIS		NITRO	IRSST	STIRS	KORSY	YORKS	LOSWY	YOWLS
	ROILS	INORY	IRONY	IRSTW	WRIST	KRSSU	RUSKS	LOTYZ	ZLOTY
ILORZ	ZORIL	INOST	SIT ON		WRITS	KRSTU	TURKS	LPPSU	PULPS
ILOSS	SILOS	INOSV	VINOS	IRSUV	VIRUS	KSSTU	TUSKS	LPPUY	PULPY
	SOILS	INOSW	WINOS	IRTYZ	RITZY	LLLOS	LOLLS	LPRSU	PURLS
ILOST	TOILS	INOSY	NOISY	ISSSW	SWISS	LLLOY	LOLLY		SLURP
ILOSU	LOUIS			ISSSY	SISSY	LLLSU	LULLS	LPSUU	LUPUS

LRSSU	SLURS	NOPTU	PUT ON	OPSTU	POUTS
LRSUY	SURLY		PUT-ON		SPOUT
LRTUY	TRULY		TON UP		STOUP
LRWYY	WRYLY		TON-UP	OPSTY	TYPOS
LSSTU	LUSTS	NOPUW	OWN UP	OPSUY	SOUPY
	SLUTS	NORST	SNORT	OPTTU	PUTTO
LSTUY	LUSTY		SWORN	OPTTY	POTTY
LSUUZ	ZULUS	NORTU	RUN TO	OPTUW	TWO UP
MMMUY	MUMMY	NORTY	TRY ON		TWO-UP
MMOPY	POMMY		TRY-ON	ORRSY	SORRY
MMOTY	TOMMY	NOSSW	SNOWS	ORRWY	WORRY
MMPSU	MUMPS	NOSSY	SONSY	ORSST	SORTS
MMRUY	RUMMY	NOSTU	SNOUT	ORSSU	SORUS
MMTUY	TUMMY	NOSTW	TOWNS		SOURS
MMUYY	YUMMY		WONTS	ORSTT	TORTS
MNOOR	MORON	NOSTY	STONY		TROTS
MNOOS	MOONS	NOSWY	SNOWY	ORSTU	ROUTS
MNOOY	MOONY	NPRSU	SPURN		TORUS
MNORS	MORNS	NPRUU	RUN UP		TOURS
	NORMS		RUN-UP	ORSTW	TROWS
MNORU	MOURN	NPSTU	PUNTS		WORST
MNOTU	MOUNT	NPSUU	SUN UP		WORTS
MOOPR	PROMO		SUNUP	ORSTY	STORY
MOORS	MOORS	NRSTU	RUNTS		TYROS
	MOROS		TURNS	ORSUY	YOURS
	ROOMS	NRTUU	U TURN	ORTTU	TROUT
MOORT	MOTOR		U-TURN		TUTOR
MOORV	VROOM	NRTUY	RUNTY	OSSTU	OUSTS
MOORY	ROOMY	NSSTU	STUNS	OSSTW	STOWS
MOOST	MOOTS	NSTTU	STUNT		SWOTS
MOOSZ	ZOOMS	NTTUY	NUTTY	OSTTU	STOUT
MOOTT	MOTTO	OOPPS	POOPS		TOUTS
MOPPU	MOP UP	OOPRS	SPOOR	PPPUY	PUPPY
	MOP-UP	OOPRT	TROOP	PPTUU	PUT UP
MOPRS	PROMS	OOPRV	PROVO		PUT-UP
	ROMPS	OOPST	STOOP	PRRSU	PURRS
MOPST	STOMP	OOPSW	SWOOP	PRSSU	SPURS
MOPSY	YOMPS	OOPTT	POTTO	PRSTU	SPURT
MORST	MORTS		TO POT		TURPS
	STORM	OORRT	ROTOR	PRSUU	USURP
MORSW	WORMS	OORST	ROOST	PRSUY	PURSY
MORWY	WORMY		ROOTS		SYRUP
MOSSY	MOSSY		TORSO	PSSUY	PUSSY
MOSUY	MOUSY	OORTY	ROOTY	PSTTU	PUTTS
MPPSU	PUMPS	OOSST	SOOTS	PTTUY	PUTTY
MPRTU	TRUMP	OOSTT	OTTOS	RSSTU	RUSTS
MPSSU	SUMPS		TOOTS		TRUSS
MPSTU	STUMP	OOSTY	SOOTY	RSTTU	STRUT
MPSUU	SUM UP	OOSYY	YO YOS		TRUST
MPSUY	SPUMY		YO-YOS	RSTTY	TRYST
MRSTU	STRUM	OOWYZ	WOOZY	RSTUY	RUSTY
MSSTU	MUSTS	OPPPU	POP-UP		YURTS
	SMUTS	OPPPY	POPPY	RSUUY	USURY
MSSUY	MUSSY	OPPRS	PROPS	STTUU	TUTUS
MSTTU	MUTTS	OPPSY	POPSY		
MSTUY	MUSTY		SOPPY		
MUYZZ	MUZZY	OPPTU	TOP UP		
NNORS	NORNS	OPPYY	YOPPY		
NNORU	RUN ON	OPRST	PORTS		
	RUN-ON		SPORT		
NNOSU	NOUNS		STROP		
NNOSY	SONNY	OPRSU	POURS		
NNRUY	RUNNY		ROUPS		
NNTUY	TUNNY	OPRSW	PROWS		
NOOPS	SNOOP	OPRSY	PROSY		
	SPOON	OPRXY	PROXY		
NOOPT	ON TOP	OPSST	POSTS		
NOOSW	SWOON		SPOTS		
NOOTW	ON TOW		STOPS		
		OPSSU	SOUPS		
		OPSSW	SWOPS		

AAABCL	CABALA	AABGRT	RATBAG	AACGIM	AGAMIC
AAABKL	KABALA	AABHIS	BAHA'IS	AACGIR	AGARIC
AAABLT	BALATA	AABHKS	KASBAH	AACGIU	GUAIAC
AAABNN	RANANA	AABHMR	BRAHMA	AACHIM	CHAIMA
AAABRZ	BAZAAR	AABIKN	ABNAKI	AACHKW	KWACHA
AAACCI	ACACIA	AABILL	LABIAL	AACHNS	ASH CAN
AAACDN	CANADA	AABILM	BAALIM	AACHRT	CATHAR
AAACLP	ALPACA	AABILU	ABULIA	AACHTT	ATTACH
AAACMR	MARACA	AABIMZ	ZAMBIA	AACHTY	CATHAY
AAACPT	PATACA	AABINN	BANIAN	AACILP	APICAL
AAADMR	ARMADA	AABINZ	BANZAI	AACILR	RACIAL
AAADNP	PANADA	AABLMS	BALSAM	AACILT	ALTAIC
AAAELZ	AZALEA	AABLOV	LAVABO	AACIMN	CAIMAN
AAAGLM	MALAGA	AABLST	BASALT		MANIAC
AAAGNN	NAGANA	AABLTU	ABLAUT	AACINR	ARNICA
AAAGNP	PA'ANGA		TABULA		CARINA
AAAHLL	HALALA	AABMMS	MAMBAS		CRANIA
AAAHNV	HAVANA	AABMNR	BARMAN	AACIRV	CAVIAR
AAAITX	ATAXIA	AABMNT	BANTAM	AACISS	CASSIA
AAAJMP	PAJAMA		BATMAN	AACITX	ATAXIC
AAAKKN	KANAKA	AABNNY	BANYAN	AACJKL	JACKAL
AAAKRW	ARAWAK	AABNSW	NAWABS	AACKRR	ARRACK
AAALMS	SALAAM	AABRSS	SABRAS	AACKTT	ATTACK
AAAMNN	MANANA	AACCDI	CICADA	AACLLS	CALLAS
AAAMNP	PANAMA	AACCEL	CAECAL	AACLMU	MACULA
AAAMNS	AS A MAN	AACCHH	CHA CHA	AACLNR	CARNAL
AAAMRS	SAMARA		CHA-CHA	AACLNS	CANALS
AAAMRY	AYMARA	AACCIL	CICALA	AACLNU	LACUNA
AAANNS	ANANAS	AACCKK	ACK ACK	AACLOT	CATALO
AAAPPY	PAPAYA		ACK-ACK	AACLPR	CARPAL
AAARTV	AVATAR	AACCLO	CLOACA	AACLPS	PASCAL
AABBBO	BAOBAB	AACCNN	CAN CAN	AACLRS	LASCAR
AABBLO	BALBOA		CANCAN		RASCAL
AABBST	SABBAT	AACCOS	CACAOS		SACRAL
AABCHS	CASBAH	AACDEF	FACADE		SCALAR
AABCIM	CAMBIA	AACDER	ARCADE	AACLSU	CASUAL
AABCIR	ARABIC	AACDHR	CHADAR		CAUSAL
AABCMN	CABMAN	AACDHS	DACHAS	AACLTU	ACTUAL
AABCRS	SCARAB	AACDIR	ACARID	AACMNY	CAYMAN
AABDER	ABRADE	AACDLU	CAUDAL	AACMRT	TARMAC
	BAD EAR	AACDMP	MADCAP	AACMSW	MACAWS
AABDEU	AUBADE	AACDNR	CANARD	AACNPT	CAT NAP
AABDHT	BAD HAT	AACDRY	ARCADY		CATNAP
AABDIN	INDABA	AACEFL	FAECAL	AACNRY	CANARY
AABDLL	BALLAD	AACEFR	CARAFE	AACNST	SANCTA
AABDLM	LAMBDA	AACEHP	APACHE	AACNSV	CANVAS
AABDMN	BAD MAN	AACEHT	CHAETA	AACNSZ	ANZACS
AABDOR	ABOARD	AACEIR	AIR ACE	AACNTV	VACANT
	ABROAD	AACELP	PALACE	AACPPY	PAPACY
AABDRT	TABARD	AACELT	ACETAL	AACRST	CARATS
AABDWY	BAD WAY	AACEMR	CAMERA	AACRTV	CRAVAT
AABEGT	TEA BAG	AACENP	CANAPE	AADDIL	LA-DI-DA
AABELR	ARABLE	AACENR	ARCANE	AADEGM	DAMAGE
AABELT	ABLATE	AACENT	CATENA	AADEGN	AGENDA
AABELZ	ABLAZE	AACERS	CAESAR	AADEGS	ADAGES
AABEMN	AMEBAN	AACETV	CAVEAT	AADEKW	AWAKED
AABEMO	AMOEBA		VACATE	AADEMM	MADAME
AABERZ	ZAREBA	AACFIL	FACIAL	AADEMN	MAENAD
AABFIN	FABIAN	AACFIS	FACIAS	AADEMZ	AMAZED
AABGGR	RAGBAG		FASCIA	AADEPR	PARADE
AABGGS	GASBAG	AACFLU	FACULA	AADFIR	AFRAID
AABGIM	GAMBIA	AACFNT	CAFTAN	AADFRS	FARADS
AABGIN	BAAING	AACFRS	FRACAS	AADGHO	HAD A GO

AADGIO	ADAGIO	AAEGSV	SAVAGE	AAGIPR	AIR GAP
AADGIR	GARDAI	AAEGTU	GATEAU	AAGIRS	AIR GAS
AADGNU	UGANDA	AAEHKP	PAKEHA	AAGIST	TAIGAS
AADGOP	PAGODA	AAEHKT	TAKAHE	AAGJRS	GAS JAR
AADHIL	DAHLIA	AAEHLM	HAEMAL	AAGJRU	JAGUAR
AADHMR	DHARMA	AAEHNY	HYAENA	AAGLLP	PLAGAL
AADHNT	AT HAND	AAEILR	AERIAL	AAGLLS	GALLAS
AADHRZ	HAZARD	AAEILX	ALEXIA	AAGLNO	ANGOLA
AADILR	RADIAL	AAEIMN	ANEMIA	AAGLNR	RAGLAN
AADILS	DALASI	AAEINT	TAENIA	AAGLNS	LAGANS
AADIMN	MAIDAN	AAEIRS	SEA AIR	AAGLST	STALAG
AADINO	ADONAI	AAEKLN	ALKANE	AAGLXY	GALAXY
AADINR	RADIAN	AAEKNW	AWAKEN	AAGMNS	GAS MAN
AADINS	NAIADS	AAEKRT	KARATE	AAGMRY	MAGYAR
AADINV	NAVAID	AAEKSW	AWAKES		MARGAY
AADINY	IN A DAY	AAELLP	PAELLA	AAGNNO	GOANNA
AADIST	STADIA		PALEAL	AAGNOR	ANGORA
AADJLN	JANDAL	AAELLU	ALULAE	AAGNPR	PARANG
AADKMS	DAMASK	AAELMT	MALATE	AAGNPS	PAGANS
AADKOT	DAKOTA	AAELNN	ANNEAL		PANGAS
AADLLN	AND ALL	AAELOR	AREOLA	AAGNRY	ANGARY
AADLLY	ALL DAY	AAELPP	APPEAL	AAGNUY	GUYANA
AADLMY	MALADY	AAELPT	PALATE	AAGORS	AGORAS
AADLNO	ANODAL	AAELRV	LARVAE	AAGOWY	GO AWAY
AADLNS	SANDAL	AAELTV	VALETA	AAGPPR	GRAPPA
AADLNU	LANDAU	AAEMMM	MAMMAE	AAGPST	GAS TAP
AADLNV	VANDAL	AAEMNP	APE-MAN	AAGRVY	VAGARY
AADLOP	APODAL	AAEMNS	SEAMAN	AAGSUV	GUAVAS
AADLRU	RADULA	AAEMNX	AXEMAN	AAHHLV	HALVAH
AADLSS	SALADS	AAEMSZ	AMAZES	AAHHWW	HAW-HAW
AADMMN	MAD MAN	AAENNZ	ZENANA	AAHIIS	ISAIAH
	MADMAN	AAENOP	APNOEA	AAHIPR	PARIAH
AADMMR	DAMMAR	AAENPS	PAEANS		RAPHIA
AADMMS	MADAMS	AAENPV	PAVANE	AAHJRR	JARRAH
AADMRS	DRAMAS	AAENRS	ARENAS	AAHJRS	RAJAHS
	MADRAS	AAENSU	NAUSEA	AAHKKL	KHALKA
AADMRU	MARAUD	AAEORT	AORTAE	AAHKST	SHAKTA
AADMSS	AD MASS	AAEPPR	APPEAR	AAHLLW	WALLAH
	ADMASS	AAERRR	ARREAR	AAHLRS	ASHLAR
AADMYY	MAY DAY	AAERRT	ERRATA	AAHMMM	HAMMAM
	MAYDAY	AAESTV	AVESTA	AAHMNS	SHAMAN
AADNPS	PANDAS		SAVATE	AAHMRS	ASHRAM
AADNRW	RWANDA	AAESWY	SEAWAY	AAHMST	ASTHMA
AADNTW	AT DAWN	AAFFIR	AFFAIR	AAHNOV	NAVAHO
AADNYY	ANY DAY		RAFFIA	AAHNPS	ASHPAN
AADPST	ADAPTS	AAFFJS	JAFFAS	AAHNPT	PATHAN
AADPYY	PAY DAY	AAFFRY	AFFRAY	AAHNSS	HANSAS
	PAYDAY	AAFGHN	AFGHAN	AAHPPR	PARAPH
AADRSW	AWARDS	AAFINR	FARINA	AAHPSS	PASHAS
AADRTU	DATURA	AAFINS	NAAFIS	AAHPTY	APATHY
AAEELP	PALEAE	AAFIRS	SAFARI	AAHRSS	HARASS
AAEERS	SEA-EAR	AAFKNT	KAFTAN	AAHSSU	HAUSAS
AAEERT	AERATE	AAFLNU	FAUNAL	AAHSSY	SASHAY
AAEEST	AT EASE	AAFLOT	AFLOAT	AAHTTT	AT THAT
AAEEYY	AYE AYE	AAFMNT	FAT MAN	AAIINS	IN ASIA
	AYE-AYE	AAFNNT	FAN-TAN	AAIKLL	ALKALI
AAEFLM	AFLAME	AAFNSU	FAUNAS	AAILLP	PALLIA
AAEFNU	FAUNAE	AAGGHI	HAGGAI	AAILLX	AXILLA
AAEGGR	GARAGE	AAGGLO	GALAGO	AAILMN	ANIMAL
AAEGGV	GAVAGE	AAGGQU	QUAGGA		LAMINA
AAEGLN	ANLAGE	AAGGRS	SAGGAR		MANILA
	GALENA	AAGHLS	GALAHS	AAILMP	IMPALA
AAEGLR	LAAGER	AAGHNR	HANGAR	AAILMS	SALAMI
AAEGLS	GALEAS	AAGHOS	HAS A GO	AAILMW	MALAWI
AAEGLV	LAVAGE	AAGHST	AGHAST	AAILNS	LIANAS
AAEGMN	MANAGE	AAGILN	AGNAIL		SALINA
AAEGMR	GEMARA	AAGILR	ARGALI	AAILNY	INYALA
AAEGOR	AGORAE	AAGILV	GAVIAL	AAILPS	PALAIS
AAEGPS	AGAPES	AAGINN	ANGINA	AAILRT	ATRIAL
AAEGRV	RAVAGE	AAGINU	IGUANA		LARIAT
AAEGST	AGATES	AAGINV	VAGINA	AAILSS	ASSAIL

Code	Word	Code	Word	Code	Word
AAILSV	AVAILS	AALNRT	ANTRAL	ABBCRY	CRABBY
	SALIVA	AALNSS	NASALS	ABBCSY	SCABBY
	SALVIA	AALNST	ASLANT	ABBDDE	DABBED
AAIMMS	MIASMA	AALOPY	PAYOLA	ABBDEG	GABBED
AAIMMX	MAXIMA	AALORT	AORTAL	ABBDEI	BABIED
AAIMNR	AIRMAN	AALOVW	AVOWAL	ABBDEJ	JABBED
	MARIAN	AALPPS	APPALS	ABBDEL	DABBLE
	MARINA	AALPRY	PARLAY	ABBDEN	NABBED
AAIMNS	MANIAS	AALPSY	PLAYAS	ABBDER	BARBED
AAIMRR	AIR ARM	AALPSZ	PLAZAS	ABBDET	TABBED
AAIMSS	MASAIS	AALPTY	AT PLAY	ABBDJO	BAD JOB
AAINOX	ANOXIA	AALRST	ALTARS	ABBDOY	BAD BOY
AAINPP	PAPAIN		ASTRAL	ABBDUY	BAD BUY
AAINPT	PATINA		TARSAL	ABBEEW	BAWBEE
	TAIPAN	AALRSY	SALARY	ABBEGL	GABBLE
AAINRS	NAIRAS	AALRSZ	LAZARS	ABBEGR	GABBER
AAINTT	ATTAIN	AALSSV	VASSAL	ABBEIS	BABIES
AAINTW	TAIWAN	AALSTT	AT LAST	ABBEIY	YABBIE
AAINWY	IN A WAY	AALSWY	ALWAYS	ABBEJR	JABBER
AAIPRU	AU PAIR	AALTUV	VALUTA	ABBEKS	KEBABS
AAIPRY	APIARY	AALWYY	WAYLAY	ABBELR	BARBEL
AAIPSS	PAISAS	AAMMRR	MARRAM		RABBLE
AAIPZZ	PIAZZA	AAMMTT	TAM-TAM	ABBELU	BAUBLE
AAIRST	TARSIA	AAMNOS	SAMOAN	ABBERR	BARBER
	TIARAS	AAMNOT	TO A MAN	ABBERT	RABBET
AAIRVY	AVIARY	AAMNOZ	AMAZON	ABBESY	ABBEYS
AAIRWY	AIRWAY	AAMNPS	SAMPAN	ABBFLY	FLABBY
AAISTW	AWAITS	AAMNRT	MANTRA	ABBGOR	GABBRO
AAJJMR	JAM JAR	AAMNTX	TAXMAN	ABBGRY	GRABBY
AAJMPY	PYJAMA	AAMORS	AROMAS	ABBHOO	HABOOB
AAJNNO	JOANNA		MASORA	ABBHSY	SHABBY
AAJNOV	NAVAJO	AAMPPS	PAMPAS	ABBILL	LIB-LAB
AAJNPS	JAPANS	AAMPRS	PRAAMS	ABBIRS	RABBIS
AAJRSW	SWARAJ	AAMQSU	SQUAMA	ABBIRT	RABBIT
AAKKMR	MARKKA	AAMRTU	TRAUMA	ABBLSU	BABULS
AAKKOP	KAKAPO	AANNNS	NANNAS		BUBALS
AAKKSY	KAYAKS	AANNRU	ANURAN	ABBMOO	BAMBOO
AAKLOS	KOALAS	AANOPR	ON A PAR	ABBMOS	A BOMBS
AAKLRS	KRAALS	AANOST	SONATA	ABBMOY	BOMBAY
AAKMNU	MANUKA	AANPRT	TARPAN	ABBNOO	BABOON
AAKMRS	MAKARS	AANPST	SNAP AT	ABBNOS	NABOBS
AAKMTU	MAKUTA	AANQTU	QUANTA	ABBORS	ABSORB
AAKNOR	ANORAK	AANRRT	ARRANT	ABBOST	ABBOTS
AAKNWZ	KWANZA	AANRSY	ARYANS	ABBOTY	BY BOAT
AAKPRS	PARKAS	AANRTT	RATTAN	ABBRSU	BUSBAR
AAKRST	KARATS		TANTRA	ABCCLU	BUCCAL
AALLMS	LLAMAS		TARTAN	ABCDEK	BACKED
AALLNY	ANALLY	AANRTZ	TARZAN	ABCDER	BRACED
AALLPP	PALPAL	AANSST	SANTAS	ABCDIR	BARDIC
AALLRU	ALULAR	AANSSU	SAUNAS	ABCDTU	ABDUCT
AALLRV	LARVAL	AANSTV	SAVANT	ABCEEM	BECAME
AALLSY	ALLAYS	AANSTW	TSWANA	ABCEHL	BLEACH
AALMMM	MAMMAL	AANSTZ	STANZA	ABCEHR	BREACH
AALMMS	LAMMAS	AANWYY	ANYWAY	ABCEHT	THE A B C
AALMNP	NAPALM	AAORRU	AURORA	ABCEIM	AMEBIC
AALMNU	MANUAL	AAORST	AORTAS	ABCEJT	ABJECT
AALMNW	LAWMAN	AAOTTV	OTTAVA	ABCEKR	BACKER
AALMNY	LAYMAN	AAPPSW	PAPAWS	ABCELM	BECALM
AALMOR	AMORAL	AAPPWW	PAWPAW	ABCELS	CABLES
AALMPR	PALMAR	AAPSST	PASTAS	ABCEMN	CABMEN
AALMPS	PLASMA	AAQRSU	QUASAR	ABCEMR	CAMBER
AALMRS	ALARMS	AARRSY	ARRAYS	ABCEMY	CAME BY
AALMRU	ALARUM	AARRTT	TARTAR	ABCENO	BEACON
AALMSU	ULAMAS	AARSST	RASTAS	ABCERR	BRACER
AALMSY	MALAYS	AARSTT	STRATA	ABCERS	BRACES
AALNNS	ANNALS	AARSTY	ASTRAY		CABERS
AALNNU	ANNUAL	AASSSY	ASSAYS	ABCFIR	FABRIC
AALNOT	ATONAL	AASSTV	AVASTS	ABCFNO	CONFAB
AALNOX	AXONAL	ABBBEL	BABBLE	ABCGIM	BIG MAC
AALNPR	PLANAR	ABBCIR	BICARB	ABCGKO	GO BACK
AALNPT	PLATAN	ABBCOT	BOBCAT	ABCHLN	BLANCH

ABCHNR	BRANCH	ABDELM	BEDLAM	ABEEMR	BEAMER
ABCHOR	BROACH		BELDAM	ABEENT	BEATEN
ABCHPU	HUB CAP		BLAMED	ABEEOR	AEROBE
	HUBCAP		LAMBED	ABEERR	BEARER
ABCIIM	IAMBIC	ABDELO	ALBEDO	ABEERT	BEATER
ABCIKN	BACK IN		DOABLE		BERATE
ABCILT	BALTIC	ABDELR	BALDER		REBATE
ABCINS	CABINS		BLARED	ABEERV	BEAVER
ABCIRS	CARIBS	ABDELS	BLADES	ABEERW	BEWARE
ABCISS	BASICS	ABDELW	BAWLED	ABEFFL	BAFFLE
ABCKLS	BLACKS	ABDELZ	BLAZED	ABEFHL	BEHALF
ABCKPU	BACK UP	ABDEMN	BAD MEN	ABEFLL	BEFALL
	BACKUP	ABDENN	BANNED	ABEFLM	FLAMBE
ABCLLY	CALL BY	ABDENP	BED PAN	ABEFLS	FABLES
ABCLMY	CYMBAL		BEDPAN	ABEFPR	PREFAB
ABCLNO	BLANCO	ABDENR	BANDER	ABEGGR	BEGGAR
ABCLOT	COBALT	ABDEOS	ABODES	ABEGLM	GAMBLE
ABCMOP	MOB CAP		ADOBES	ABEGLN	BANGLE
ABCMOR	CRAMBO	ABDEOT	BOATED	ABEGLR	GARBLE
ABCMOT	COMBAT	ABDEPY	PAYBED	ABEGLS	BAGELS
ABCNOR	CARBON	ABDERR	BARRED		GABLES
ABCORS	CAROBS	ABDERS	BEARDS	ABEGLU	BELUGA
	COBRAS		BREADS	ABEGNR	BANGER
ABCORX	BOXCAR		DEBARS		GRABEN
ABCORY	CARBOY		SABRED	ABEGOR	BORAGE
ABCRST	BRACTS	ABDERU	DAUBER	ABEGOZ	GAZEBO
ABDDEE	BEADED	ABDERV	ADVERB	ABEGRS	BARGES
ABDDEI	ABIDED		BRAVED	ABEHLR	HERBAL
	BADDIE	ABDERY	BRAYED	ABEHOS	OBEAHS
ABDDEL	BLADED	ABDERZ	BRAZED	ABEHRS	BASHER
ABDDEN	BAD END	ABDEST	BASTED	ABEHRT	BATHER
	BANDED	ABDESU	ABUSED		BREATH
ABDDEU	DAUBED		DAUBES	ABEHSS	BASHES
ABDDEY	DAY BED	ABDETT	BATTED	ABEHST	BATHES
	DAYBED	ABDFOR	FORBAD	ABEIIL	BAILIE
ABDDGO	BAD DOG	ABDGLO	GO BALD	ABEIIT	TIBIAE
ABDDHU	BUDDHA	ABDHNY	BY HAND	ABEILL	BELIAL
ABDEEH	BEHEAD	ABDHRY	HARD BY		LABILE
ABDEEK	BEAKED	ABDILR	BRIDAL		LIABLE
ABDEEL	BEADLE		RIBALD	ABEILR	BAILER
ABDEEM	BEAMED	ABDILS	AD LIBS	ABEILS	ABSEIL
ABDEES	DEBASE		AD-LIBS	ABEILT	ALBEIT
	SEA BED	ABDINR	RIBAND	ABEILV	VIABLE
ABDEET	DEBATE	ABDINT	BANDIT	ABEILW	BEWAIL
ABDEEY	BAD EYE	ABDIRS	BRAIDS	ABEILY	BAILEY
ABDEFL	FABLED		DISBAR	ABEINS	SABINE
ABDEGG	BAD EGG	ABDJOY	DAY JOB	ABEINT	BEAT IN
	BAGGED	ABDLLY	BALDLY	ABEIRS	BRAISE
ABDEGL	GABLED	ABDLNY	BY LAND		RABIES
ABDEGN	BANGED	ABDLOT	BAD LOT	ABEIRT	BAITER
ABDEGO	BODEGA	ABDLRY	DRABLY	ABEISS	BIASES
ABDEGR	BADGER	ABDNOT	NOT BAD	ABEITT	BEAT IT
	BARGED	ABDNOU	ABOUND	ABEJOR	JERBOA
ABDEGS	BADGES	ABDNRS	BRANDS	ABEJRU	ABJURE
	DEBAGS	ABDNRY	BRANDY	ABEKLR	BALKER
ABDEHS	BASHED	ABDOOT	TOO BAD	ABEKLS	BLEAKS
ABDEHT	BATHED	ABDORS	ADSORB	ABEKMN	EMBANK
ABDEIL	BAILED		BOARDS	ABEKMR	EMBARK
	BALDIE		BROADS	ABEKNR	BANKER
ABDEIR	ABIDER	ABDORY	BY ROAD	ABEKRR	BARKER
	AIR BED	ABDRRU	DURBAR	ABEKRS	BRAKES
ABDEIS	ABIDES	ABDRSU	ABSURD		BREAKS
	BIASED	ABDRWY	BAWDRY	ABEKRY	BAKERY
ABDEIT	BAITED	ABEEGL	BEAGLE	ABEKST	BASKET
ABDEKL	BALKED	ABEEGR	BARGEE	ABELLS	LABELS
ABDEKN	BANKED	ABEEHV	BEHAVE	ABELLT	BALLET
ABDEKR	BARKED	ABEEIL	BAILEE	ABELLU	BULLAE
	BRAKED	ABEEKR	BEAKER	ABELMM	EMBALM
	DEBARK	ABEEKT	BETAKE		
ABDEKS	BASKED	ABEELN	BALEEN		
ABDELL	BALLED		ENABLE		

ABELMR	BLAMER
	LAMBER
	MARBLE
	RAMBLE
ABELMS	AMBLES
	BLAMES
ABELNU	NEBULA
	UNABLE
ABELOR	BOREAL
ABELOT	BOATEL
	LOBATE
	OBLATE
ABELRR	BARREL
ABELRS	BLARES
	BLEARS
ABELRV	VERBAL
ABELRW	BAWLER
	WARBLE
ABELRY	BARELY
	BARLEY
	BLEARY
ABELRZ	BLAZER
ABELSS	SABLES
ABELST	ABLEST
	BLEATS
	STABLE
	TABLES
ABELSU	SUABLE
	USABLE
ABELSY	BASELY
	BELAYS
ABELSZ	BLAZES
ABELTT	BATTLE
	TABLET
ABEMNO	BEMOAN
ABEMNR	BARMEN
ABEMNT	BATMEN
ABEMNY	BY NAME
ABEMRS	AMBERS
	BREAMS
ABEMRU	UMBRAE
ABEMSY	EMBAYS
ABENNR	BANNER
ABENOS	BEANOS
ABENRR	BARREN
ABENRT	BANTER
ABENRU	URBANE
ABENRY	BARNEY
	NEAR BY
	NEARBY
ABENRZ	BRAZEN
ABENST	ABSENT
ABENTT	BATTEN
ABENTU	BUTANE
ABENTZ	BEZANT
ABEORT	BOATER
	BORATE
ABEOST	E BOATS
ABEPRU	BEAR UP
ABEPTU	BEAT UP
	UPBEAT
ABEQRU	BARQUE
ABEQSU	BASQUE
ABERRS	BARRES
ABERRT	BARTER
ABERRV	BRAVER
ABERRZ	BRAZER
ABERSS	SABRES
ABERST	BAREST
	BASTER
	BREAST
ABERSU	ABUSER
	BURSAE
ABERSV	BRAVES
ABERSZ	BRAZES
	ZEBRAS
ABERTT	BATTER
ABERTY	BETRAY
ABERUU	BUREAU
ABESSS	BASSES
ABESST	BASEST
	BASSET
	BASTES
	BEASTS
ABESSU	ABUSES
ABESTT	AT BEST
ABESTU	BEAUTS
ABETTU	BATTUE
	BEAUTY
ABFGLU	BAGFUL
ABFHLY	BY HALF
ABFILU	FIBULA
ABFOTX	FOX BAT
ABGIIL	GALIBI
ABGIKN	BAKING
ABGIKT	KIT BAG
	KITBAG
ABGILM	GIMBAL
ABGIMT	GAMBIT
ABGIMY	BIGAMY
ABGINO	GABION
ABGINR	BARING
ABGINS	BASING
ABGINT	BATING
ABGINY	BAYING
ABGIWY	BIG WAY
ABGLLO	GLOBAL
ABGLMO	GAMBOL
ABGLOR	BROLGA
ABGMUY	MAYBUG
ABGNNO	BANG ON
	BANG-ON
ABHIKT	BHAKTI
ABHINS	BANISH
ABHIOP	PHOBIA
ABHIST	HABITS
ABHMRU	RHUMBA
ABHMSU	AMBUSH
ABHNTU	BHUTAN
ABHORS	ABHORS
ABHOST	BATHOS
ABHOTX	HAT BOX
ABHOXY	HAYBOX
ABHPTY	BYPATH
ABIILS	ALIBIS
ABIILT	TIBIAL
ABIIST	TIBIAS
ABIJOW	OJIBWA
ABIKKU	KABUKI
ABIKMO	AKIMBO
ABILMU	LABIUM
ABILNO	ALBINO
	ALBION
ABILNR	LIBRAN
ABILNS	BLAINS
ABILNY	LIBYAN
ABILOR	BAILOR
ABILRS	BRAILS
	LIBRAS
ABILRT	TRIBAL
ABILRU	BURIAL
ABILRY	BY RAIL
ABILRZ	BRAZIL
ABILSS	BASILS
ABILVY	VIABLY
ABIMNN	BINMAN
ABIMRU	BARIUM
ABIMST	AMBITS
ABIMSU	IAMBUS
ABINOS	BONSAI
ABINOT	OBTAIN
ABINRS	DAIRNS
	BRAINS
ABINRY	BINARY
	BRAINY
ABINSS	BASINS
ABIORR	BARRIO
ABIORS	ISOBAR
ABIRRS	BRIARS
ABIRSU	AIR BUS
	AIRBUS
ABITXY	BY TAXI
ABJJOO	JOJOBA
ABJNOS	BANJOS
ABJOST	JABOTS
ABKLMO	BOKMAL
ABKLNS	BLANKS
ABKLSU	BAULKS
ABKNNO	BANK ON
ABLLNO	NO BALL
	NO-BALL
ABLLOT	BALLOT
ABLLTU	ALL BUT
ABLMOP	APLOMB
ABLMOW	MOB LAW
ABLMRU	LABRUM
	LUMBAR
	UMBRAL
ABLMSU	ALBUMS
ABLMTY	TYMBAL
ABLNOZ	BLAZON
ABLORU	LABOUR
ABLOST	OBLAST
ABLPRU	BURLAP
ABLPYY	BYPLAY
ABLRSU	BURSAL
	LUBRAS
ABLRSW	BRAWLS
ABLRTU	BRUTAL
ABLSST	BLASTS
ABLSTY	STABLY
ABLSUY	USABLY
ABLSWY	BYLAWS
ABLSYY	LAY BYS
	LAY-BYS
ABMMOS	MAMBOS
ABMNOW	BOWMAN
ABMNSU	BUSMAN
ABMOSS	SAMBOS
ABMOTW	WOMBAT
ABMRSU	RUMBAS
	SAMBUR
	UMBRAS
ABMRTY	BY TRAM
ABNORS	BARONS
ABNORY	BARONY
	BARYON
ABNOST	BATONS
ABNOTY	BOTANY
ABNRST	BRANTS
ABNRSU	UNBARS
ABNRTU	TURBAN
ABNRUU	AUBURN

Code	Word	Code	Word	Code	Word
ABNRWY	BRAWNY	ACCSTU	CACTUS	ACDERT	CARTED
ABNSTU	BANTUS	ACCSUU	CAUCUS		CRATED
ABOOST	TABOOS	ACCSUY	YUCCAS		REDACT
ABOQST	Q BOATS	ACDDEE	DECADE		TRACED
ABORRS	ARBORS	ACDDEG	CADGED	ACDERV	CARVED
ABORRU	ARBOUR	ACDDEI	CADDIE		CRAVED
ABORRW	BARROW	ACDDEN	DANCED	ACDERZ	CRAZED
ABORST	ABORTS	ACDDER	CARDED	ACDEST	CADETS
	BOARTS	ACDDEU	ADDUCE	ACDESU	CAUSED
	TABORS	ACDDIN	CANDID		SAUCED
ABORSV	BRAVOS	ACDDIT	ADDICT	ACDESY	DECAYS
ABORTU	RUBATO	ACDDIY	DYADIC	ACDHMR	DRACHM
	TABOUR	ACDDTU	ADDUCT	ACDHOR	CHADOR
ABORUY	YORUBA	ACDEEF	DEFACE	ACDHRS	CHARDS
ABOSSS	BASSOS	ACDEES	CEASED	ACDIIM	AMIDIC
ABOSST	BOASTS	ACDEFH	CHAFED	ACDIJU	JUDAIC
	SABOTS	ACDEGR	CADGER	ACDILP	PLACID
ABOSTU	U BOATS		GRACED	ACDILY	ACIDLY
	U-BOATS	ACDEGS	CADGES	ACDINO	ADONIC
ABPRTU	ABRUPT	ACDEHK	HACKED		ANODIC
ABPSSY	BY PASS	ACDEHR	ARCHED	ACDINR	RANCID
	BYPASS	ACDEHS	CASHED	ACDIOZ	ZODIAC
	PASS BY		CHASED	ACDIPS	CAPSID
ABQSSU	SQUABS	ACDEHT	DETACH	ACDLSS	SCALDS
ABRRSU	BURSAR	ACDEHW	CHAWED	ACDLTY	DACTYL
ABRSSU	BURSAS	ACDEIR	CARDIE	ACDNOR	DACRON
ABRSSY	BRASSY	ACDEIV	ADVICE	ACDORW	COD WAR
ABSUWY	SUBWAY	ACDEJK	JACKED		COWARD
ABSWYY	BYWAYS	ACDEKL	CALKED	ACDOST	OCTADS
ACCCLO	COCCAL		LACKED	ACDSTU	DUCATS
ACCDEE	ACCEDE	ACDEKP	PACKED	ACEEFF	EFFACE
ACCDII	ACIDIC	ACDEKR	CARKED	ACEEFS	FAECES
ACCDOR	ACCORD		RACKED	ACEEFX	CEEFAX
ACCDSY	CYCADS	ACDEKS	SACKED	ACEEGI	ICE AGE
ACCEHN	CHANCE	ACDEKT	TACKED	ACEEHL	CHELAE
ACCEHS	CACHES	ACDELL	CALLED	ACEEHT	THECAE
ACCEHT	CACHET	ACDELM	CALMED	ACEEIP	APIECE
ACCEIL	CELIAC	ACDELN	CANDLE	ACEEJT	EJECTA
ACCEIP	ICE CAP		LANCED	ACEEKS	ACKEES
	IPECAC	ACDELP	PLACED	ACEELN	ENLACE
ACCEIT	ACETIC	ACDELR	CRADLE	ACEELR	CEREAL
ACCEKL	CACKLE		CREDAL	ACEELV	CLEAVE
ACCELN	CANCEL	ACDELS	DECALS	ACEEMN	MENACE
ACCELS	CALCES		SCALED	ACEEMR	AMERCE
ACCEMU	CAECUM	ACDELV	CALVED		RACEME
ACCENR	CANCER	ACDELW	CLAWED	ACEEMZ	ECZEMA
ACCENT	ACCENT	ACDEMP	CAMPED	ACEENR	CAREEN
ACCEPT	ACCEPT		DECAMP	ACEENS	ENCASE
ACCERS	SCARCE	ACDENN	CANNED		SEANCE
ACCERU	ACCRUE	ACDENO	CANOED	ACEENT	CETANE
ACCESS	ACCESS		DEACON	ACEEPS	ESCAPE
ACCESU	ACCUSE	ACDENR	CRANED	ACEERR	CAREER
ACCGNO	COGNAC		DANCER	ACEERS	CREASE
ACCHIK	CHIACK		NACRED	ACEERT	CREATE
ACCHNO	CONCHA	ACDENS	ASCEND	ACEESS	CEASES
ACCHNY	CHANCY		DANCES	ACEFFT	AFFECT
ACCHOU	CACHOU	ACDENT	CADENT	ACEFHR	CHAFER
ACCHTY	CATCHY		CANTED	ACEFHS	CHAFES
ACCIIN	INCAIC		DECANT	ACEFIL	FACILE
ACCILO	CALICO	ACDEOT	COATED	ACEFIN	FIANCE
ACCILT	LACTIC	ACDEOX	COAXED	ACEFIS	FACIES
ACCIMM	MICMAC	ACDEPP	CAPPED	ACEFNR	FRANCE
ACCINY	CYANIC	ACDEPR	CARPED	ACEFPU	FACE UP
ACCIRT	ARCTIC		REDCAP	ACEFRS	FACERS
ACCITT	TACTIC	ACDEPS	SPACED		FARCES
	TIC TAC	ACDERR	CARDER	ACEFSS	FASCES
ACCKLS	CLACKS	ACDERS	CADRES	ACEFST	FACETS
ACCKNU	CANUCK		CEDARS	ACEFSU	FAUCES
ACCKRS	CRACKS		SACRED	ACEFTU	FAUCET
ACCOST	ACCOST		SCARED	ACEGHN	CHANGE
ACCRUY	CURACY			ACEGHR	CHARGE

ACEGHU	GAUCHE	ACEKPR	PACKER	ACENOS	CANOES
ACEGIL	GAELIC	ACEKPT	PACKET		OCEANS
ACEGLN	GLANCE	ACEKRS	CRAKES	ACENOT	AT ONCE
ACEGLS	GLACES		CREAKS		OCTANE
ACEGLY	LEGACY		SACKER		ONE ACT
ACEGNU	UNCAGE	ACEKRT	RACKET	ACENPR	PRANCE
ACEGNY	AGENCY		TACKER	ACENPS	PECANS
ACEGOS	SOCAGE	ACEKRY	CREAKY	ACENRS	CRANES
ACEGOW	COWAGE	ACEKST	CASKET		NACRES
ACEGRS	GRACES	ACELLO	LOCALE	ACENRT	CANTER
ACEHIS	CHAISE	ACELLR	CALLER		CARNET
ACEHKL	HACKLE		CELLAR		CENTRA
ACEHKR	HACKER		RECALL		NECTAR
ACEHLP	CHAPEL	ACELMR	CALMER		RECANT
	PLEACH		MARCEL		TRANCE
ACEHLS	LACHES	ACELMS	CAMELS	ACENRV	CARVEN
ACEHLT	CHALET		MACLES		CAVERN
	THECAL		MESCAL		CRAVEN
ACEHMS	SACHEM	ACELMU	MACULE	ACENST	ASCENT
	SCHEMA	ACELNR	LANCER		ENACTS
ACEHNS	ENCASH	ACELNS	CLEANS		SECANT
ACEHOR	CHOREA		LANCES		STANCE
	ORACHE	ACELNT	CANTLE	ACENSU	USANCE
ACEHPR	PREACH		LANCET	ACEOPW	COWPEA
ACEHPS	CHAPES	ACELNU	UNLACE	ACEORS	COARSE
	CHEAPS	ACELOR	ORACLE	ACEORT	COATER
ACEHRR	ARCHER	ACELOS	SOLACE	ACEOST	COSTAE
ACEHRS	ARCHES	ACELOT	LOCATE	ACEOSW	SEA COW
	CHASER	ACELOV	ALCOVE	ACEOSX	COAXES
	ESCHAR		COEVAL	ACEOTV	AVOCET
	SEARCH	ACELOW	ACE LOW		OCTAVE
ACEHRX	EXARCH	ACELPR	CARPEL	ACEPRS	CAPERS
ACEHSS	CASHES		PARCEL		ESCARP
	CHASES		PLACER		PARSEC
	CHASSE	ACELPS	PLACES		RECAPS
ACEHST	CHASTE	ACELPU	LACE-UP		SCRAPE
	CHEATS	ACELQU	CALQUE		SPACER
	SACHET		CLAQUE	ACEPRT	CARPET
	SCATHE	ACELRR	CARREL	ACEPRU	APERCU
ACEHSW	CASHEW	ACELRS	CLEARS	ACEPSS	SCAPES
ACEILM	MALICE		SCALER		SPACES
ACEILP	EPICAL		SCLERA	ACEPST	ASPECT
	PLAICE	ACELRT	CARTEL		EPACTS
ACEILR	ECLAIR		CLARET	ACEPSY	SPACEY
ACEILX	LEXICA		RECTAL	ACEPTU	TEA CUP
ACEIMN	ANEMIC	ACELRV	CARVEL	ACEQSU	CASQUE
	CAME IN	ACELSS	SCALES	ACERRS	RACERS
	CINEMA	ACELST	CASTLE		SCARER
	ICE MAN		CLEATS	ACERRT	CARTER
	ICEMAN		ECLATS		CRATER
ACEIMS	AMICES	ACELSU	CLAUSE		TRACER
ACEIMT	CAME IT	ACELSV	CALVES	ACERRU	CURARE
ACEINN	CANINE	ACELSX	CALXES	ACERRV	CARVER
ACEINR	IN CARE	ACELTT	CATTLE	ACERSS	CARESS
ACEINS	CASEIN	ACELTY	ACETYL		CARSES
	IN CASE	ACELYY	CLAYEY		SCARES
ACEIPS	APICES	ACEMNO	CAME ON	ACERST	CARETS
	SPICAE	ACEMNP	ENCAMP		CASTER
ACEIRS	CARIES	ACEMNU	ACUMEN		CATERS
	ERICAS	ACEMOP	POMACE		CRATES
ACEIRU	CURIAE	ACEMOS	CAMEOS		REACTS
ACEISV	CAVIES	ACEMOT	CAME TO		RECAST
	VESICA	ACEMPR	CAMPER		TRACES
ACEITV	ACTIVE	ACEMPU	CAME UP	ACERSU	CAUSER
ACEJKT	JACKET	ACEMRS	CREAMS		CESURA
ACEJLO	CAJOLE		SCREAM		SAUCER
ACEKLM	MACKLE	ACEMRY	CREAMY	ACERSV	CARVES
ACEKLR	CALKER	ACENNR	CANNER		CAVERS
ACEKLT	TACKLE	ACENNU	NUANCE		CRAVES
ACEKLY	LACKEY	ACENOR	CORNEA	ACERSY	SCAREY
ACEKNR	CANKER			ACERSZ	CRAZES

ACERTT	T T RACE	ACHINS	CASH IN	ACILRT	RICTAL
ACERTU	CURATE		CHAINS	ACILRU	CURIAL
ACESST	CASTES		IN CASH		URACIL
ACESSU	CAUSES	ACHIPS	PHASIC		URALIC
	SAUCES	ACHIPT	HAPTIC	ACILRY	RACILY
ACESTU	CUESTA		PHATIC	ACILST	TICALS
ACESTX	EXACTS	ACHIQU	QUAICH	ACILSV	CAVILS
ACESTZ	AZTECS	ACHIRS	CHAIRS		SLAVIC
ACESUY	CAYUSE		RACHIS	ACIMNO	ANOMIC
ACFFHS	CHAFFS	ACHKKU	CHUKKA		MANIOC
ACFFHY	CHAFFY	ACHKLS	CHALKS	ACIMNT	MANTIC
ACFGIN	FACING	ACHKLY	CHALKY	ACIMOR	ROMAIC
ACFILS	CALIFS	ACHKOW	WHACKO	ACIMOS	MOSAIC
	FISCAL	ACHKRU	CHUKAR	ACIMOT	ATOMIC
ACFINT	IN FACT	ACHKSS	SHACKS	ACIMPS	SCAMPI
ACFIOS	FIASCO	ACHKSW	WHACKS	ACIMPT	IMPACT
ACFIPY	PACIFY	ACHKTW	THWACK	ACIMRS	RACISM
ACFLNO	FALCON	ACHKWY	WHACKY	ACIMST	MASTIC
ACFLNU	CANFUL	ACHLNU	LAUNCH	ACINNT	TANNIC
ACFLPU	CAPFUL		NUCHAL	ACINOS	CASINO
ACFLRU	CARFUL	ACHLOR	CHORAL	ACINOT	ACTION
	FULCRA	ACHLRY	ARCHLY		ATONIC
ACFNRS	FRANCS	ACHMMY	CHAMMY		CATION
ACFORT	ACT FOR	ACHMNU	MANCHU	ACINOX	ANOXIC
	FACTOR	ACHMOR	CHROMA		AXONIC
ACFRRY	FAR CRY	ACHMPS	CHAMPS	ACINPS	PANICS
ACFRSS	SCARFS	ACHMRS	CHARMS	ACINPT	CATNIP
ACFRST	CRAFTS	ACHMSS	CHASMS	ACINRS	CAIRNS
ACFRTY	CRAFTY	ACHMSU	SUMACH	ACINRU	URANIC
ACGGIN	CAGING	ACHNOR	ANCHOR	ACINST	ACTINS
ACGGRY	CRAGGY		ARCHON		ANTICS
ACGHIN	ACHING	ACHNPU	PAUNCH		NASTIC
ACGHOT	GOTCHA	ACHNST	CHANTS	ACINTT	INTACT
ACGHOU	GAUCHO		SNATCH	ACINUV	VICUNA
ACGHTU	CAUGHT		STANCH	ACIOPT	COPITA
ACGIKN	CAKING	ACHNTU	NAUTCH	ACIORS	SCORIA
ACGILL	GALLIC	ACHOOT	CAHOOT	ACIORT	AORTIC
ACGILN	LACING	ACHOSV	HAVOCS	ACIOST	SCOTIA
ACGILR	GARLIC	ACHOUV	AVOUCH	ACIPRY	PIRACY
ACGILS	GLACIS	ACHPRS	SCARPH	ACIPSS	SPICAS
ACGILY	CAGILY	ACHPTY	PATCHY	ACIQTU	ACQUIT
ACGIMS	MAGICS	ACHRRS	CHARRS	ACIRST	ARTICS
ACGINN	CANING	ACHRST	CHARTS		CRISTA
ACGINO	AGONIC		STARCH		RACIST
ACGINP	PACING	ACHSTU	CUSHAT	ACIRSU	CAURIS
ACGINR	CARING	ACHSTW	SWATCH	ACIRSV	VICARS
	RACING	ACHSTY	YACHTS	ACIRSY	SYRIAC
ACGINS	CASING	ACHTTY	CHATTY	ACIRTU	URATIC
ACGINT	ACTING	ACIILS	SIALIC	ACISSS	CASSIS
ACGINV	CAVING		SILICA	ACISTT	ATTICS
ACGINW	CAWING	ACIILT	ITALIC		STATIC
ACGIRS	CIGARS	ACIIMN	AMINIC	ACITUY	ACUITY
ACGIRT	TRAGIC	ACIINN	NIACIN	ACITVY	CAVITY
ACGLMP	G CLAMP	ACIKMR	KARMIC	ACJKPU	JACK UP
ACGLNO	CALGON	ACIKNP	PACK IN	ACKKNS	KNACKS
ACGLNS	CLANGS	ACIKNT	CATKIN	ACKLNS	CLANKS
ACGLNY	GLYCAN		NATICK	ACKLOP	POLACK
ACGMPR	G-CRAMP	ACILLN	CALL IN	ACKLOS	CLOAKS
ACGNOR	GARCON		CLINAL	ACKLSS	SLACKS
ACGNOS	CONGAS	ACILLS	LILACS	ACKLSU	CAULKS
	GASCON		SCILLA	ACKMSS	SMACKS
ACGORS	CARGOS	ACILMS	CLAIMS	ACKNPU	UNPACK
ACGORU	COUGAR	ACILMX	CLIMAX	ACKNRS	CRANKS
ACGRSS	SCRAGS	ACILNO	ALNICO	ACKNRY	CRANKY
ACGTTU	CATGUT		OILCAN	ACKNSS	SNACKS
ACHHNU	HAUNCH	ACILNR	CARLIN	ACKOPY	YAPOCK
ACHHTT	THATCH	ACILNU	UNCIAL	ACKORS	CROAKS
ACHIIS	ISCHIA	ACILOR	LORICA	ACKORY	CROAKY
ACHIJK	HIJACK	ACILOS	SOCIAL	ACKPPU	PACK UP
ACHILP	CALIPH	ACILOT	COITAL	ACKQSU	QUACKS
ACHILT	CHITAL	ACILOX	OXALIC	ACKRST	TRACKS

Code	Word	Code	Word	Code	Word
ACKRSW	WRACKS	ACNOTU	TOUCAN	ADDEMN	DAMNED
ACKSST	STACKS	ACNOTW	ANT COW		DEMAND
ACLLMY	CALMLY	ACNSST	SCANTS		MADDEN
ACLLNO	CLONAL	ACNSTU	TUSCAN	ADDEMO	MADE DO
	ON CALL	ACNSTY	SCANTY	ADDEMP	DAMPED
ACLLOR	COLLAR	ACOOTV	OCTAVO	ADDEMR	MADDER
ACLLOS	LOCALS	ACOPPT	TOP CAP	ADDENR	DANDER
ACLLOW	CALLOW	ACOPRT	CAPTOR		DARNED
ACLLPU	CALL UP	ACOPTW	COWPAT	ADDENS	SADDEN
	CALL-UP	ACORRT	CARROT		SANDED
ACLLSU	CALLUS		TROCAR	ADDENW	DAWNED
ACLMMY	CLAMMY	ACORSS	ACROSS	ADDEOR	ADORED
ACLMPS	CLAMPS		OSCARS		DEODAR
ACLMTU	TALCUM	ACORST	ACTORS	ADDEOS	DADOES
ACLNUY	LUNACY		CASTOR	ADDEPP	DAPPED
ACLOPU	COPULA		CO-STAR	ADDEPR	DRAPED
	CUPOLA		SCROTA	ADDEPS	SPADED
ACLORR	CORRAL	ACORTV	CAVORT	ADDERS	ADDERS
ACLORS	CAROLS	ACORYZ	CORYZA		DREADS
	CORALS	ACOSST	COASTS		SADDER
ACLORU	OCULAR	ACOSTT	AT COST	ADDERT	DARTED
ACLOST	COSTAL	ACOTTU	ACT OUT		TRADED
ACLOSV	VOCALS	ACPPRY	CRAPPY	ADDERW	WADDER
ACLOUY	LUCAYO	ACPPSU	CUPPAS		WARDED
ACLPSS	CLASPS	ACPRSS	SCARPS	ADDERY	YARDED
	SCALPS		SCRAPS	ADDGIN	ADDING
ACLRRU	CRURAL	ACPRSU	CARPUS	ADDGIO	GADOID
ACLRSW	CRAWLS	ACPSSU	SCAUPS	ADDGIP	GIDDAP
	SCRAWL	ACPSTU	ACTS UP	ADDGMO	MAD DOG
ACLRWY	CRAWLY		CATSUP	ADDGOY	DOG DAY
ACLSSY	CLASSY	ACRRWY	WAR CRY	ADDHOO	DOODAH
ACMMOS	COMMAS	ACRSTT	TRACTS	ADDHSU	SADDHU
ACMNNO	CON MAN	ACSTTY	SCATTY	ADDIKZ	ZADDIK
	CONMAN	ADDDEG	GADDED	ADDILL	DID ALL
ACMNOO	MONACO	ADDDEL	ADDLED	ADDIMY	MIDDAY
ACMNOR	MACRON	ADDDEN	ADDEND	ADDLOY	DAY OLD
ACMNOS	MASCON	ADDDEP	PADDED	ADDORT	DOTARD
ACMNOW	COWMAN	ADDDEW	WADDED	ADDOST	ADDS TO
ACMOOT	OTOMAC	ADDDOO	DOODAD		AT ODDS
ACMORS	CAROMS	ADDEEH	HEADED	ADDPSU	ADDS UP
	MACROS	ADDEEL	LEADED	ADDRSY	DRYADS
ACMOST	COMSAT	ADDEEN	DEADEN	ADEEFL	LEAFED
	MASCOT	ADDEER	DEADER	ADEEFM	DEFAME
ACMOSU	MUCOSA	ADDEEV	EVADED	ADEEFN	DEAFEN
ACMOTT	TOMCAT	ADDEGG	DAGGED	ADEEFR	DEAFER
ACMPRS	CRAMPS	ADDEGO	GOADED		FEARED
ACMPSS	SCAMPS	ADDEGR	GADDER	ADEEFT	DEFEAT
ACMPSU	CAMPUS		GRADED	ADEEGG	DEGAGE
ACMRSS	SCRAMS	ADDEHI	HADDIE	ADEEGR	AGREED
ACMRSU	SACRUM	ADDEHN	HANDED		DRAGEE
ACMSSU	SUMACS	ADDEHS	DASHED		GEARED
ACMSTU	MUSCAT		SHADED	ADEEHL	HEALED
ACMUUV	VACUUM	ADDEIL	LADDIE	ADEEHP	HEAPED
ACNNNO	CANNON	ADDEIM	DIADEM	ADEEHR	ADHERE
ACNNOS	CANONS	ADDEIN	DANDIE		HEADER
ACNNOT	CAN NOT	ADDEIR	RAIDED	ADEEHT	HEATED
	CANNOT	ADDELN	DANDLE	ADEEHV	HEAVED
	CANTON		LANDED	ADEEIL	AEDILE
ACNNOY	CANYON	ADDELO	LOADED	ADEEIM	MEDIAE
ACNNRY	CRANNY	ADDELP	PADDLE	ADEEIR	REDIAE
ACNOOR	CORONA	ADDELR	LADDER	ADEEIT	IDEATE
	RACOON		LARDED	ADEEJY	DEEJAY
ACNOPS	CAPONS		RADDLE	ADEEKL	LEAKED
ACNOPY	CANOPY	ADDELS	ADDLES	ADEEKP	PEAKED
ACNORS	ACORNS		SADDLE	ADEELN	LEADEN
ACNORT	CANTOR	ADDELU	LAUDED		LEANED
	CARTON	ADDELW	DAWDLE	ADEELP	LEAPED
ACNORY	CRAYON		WADDLE		PEALED
ACNOST	CANTOS	ADDELY	DEADLY	ADEELR	DEALER
	SNO-CAT	ADDEMM	DAMMED		LEADER
ACNOTT	OCTANT				

ADEELS	LEASED / SEALED
ADEELT	ELATED
ADEEMN	DEMEAN
ADEEMO	OEDEMA
ADEEMR	DEAR ME! / REAMED / REMADE
ADEEMS	SEAMED
ADEEMT	TEAMED
ADEENN	ENNEAD / NA-DENE
ADEENR	EARNED / ENDEAR / NEARED
ADEENW	WEANED
ADEEPR	REAPED
ADEERR	DEARER / READER / REARED
ADEERS	ERASED / RED SEA / RESEDA / SEARED
ADEERV	EVADER
ADEERW	DRAWEE
ADEEST	SEATED / SEDATE / TEASED
ADEESV	EVADES
ADEETT	TEATED
ADEEVW	WEAVED
ADEFFF	FAFFED
ADEFFG	GAFFED
ADEFGG	FAGGED
ADEFGN	FAG END / FANGED
ADEFGO	GO DEAF
ADEFHS	FASHED
ADEFHT	HAFTED
ADEFIL	AFIELD / FAILED
ADEFIN	FADE-IN
ADEFKL	FLAKED
ADEFLM	FLAMED
ADEFLO	FOALED / LOAFED
ADEFLR	FLARED
ADEFLU	FEUDAL
ADEFLY	DEAFLY / FLAYED
ADEFMO	FOAMED
ADEFMR	FARMED / FRAMED
ADEFNN	FANNED
ADEFNW	FAWNED
ADEFOR	FEDORA
ADEFRT	DAFTER / RAFTED
ADEFRY	DEFRAY / FRAYED
ADEFST	FASTED
ADEFTT	FATTED
ADEFTW	WAFTED
ADEGGG	GAGGED
ADEGGJ	JAGGED
ADEGGL	LAGGED
ADEGGN	GANGED / NAGGED
ADEGGR	DAGGER / RAGGED
ADEGGS	SAGGED
ADEGGT	GADGET / TAGGED
ADEGGU	GAUGED
ADEGGW	WAGGED
ADEGHN	HANGED
ADEGHS	GASHED
ADEGIN	GAINED
ADEGIT	GAITED
ADEGKW	GAWKED
ADEGLL	GALLED
ADEGLN	ANGLED / DANGLE
ADEGLO	AGE-OLD / GAOLED / OLD AGE
ADEGLR	GLARED
ADEGLS	GLADES
ADEGLZ	GLAZED
ADEGMT	GET MAD
ADEGNR	DANGER / GANDER / GARDEN / RANGED
ADEGNT	TANGED
ADEGNW	GNAWED
ADEGOR	DOG-EAR
ADEGOS	DAGOES / DOSAGE / SEA DOG / SEA GOD / SEADOG
ADEGOT	DOTAGE / TOGAED
ADEGPP	GAPPED
ADEGPS	GASPED
ADEGPW	GAWPED
ADEGRR	GRADER / RED RAG / REGARD
ADEGRS	GRADES
ADEGRT	GRATED
ADEGRU	ARGUED
ADEGRV	GRAVED
ADEGRY	GRAYED
ADEGRZ	GRAZED
ADEGSS	GASSED
ADEGST	STAGED
ADEGSW	SWAGED / WADGES
ADEHHS	HASHED
ADEHIL	HAILED / HALIDE
ADEHIR	HAIRED
ADEHKR	HARKED
ADEHKW	HAWKED
ADEHLN	HANDLE
ADEHLO	HALOED
ADEHLR	HERALD
ADEHLS	LASHED
ADEHLT	HALTED / LATHED
ADEHLU	HAULED
ADEHLV	HALVED
ADEHLW	WHALED
ADEHMM	HAMMED
ADEHMR	HARMED
ADEHMS	MASHED / SHAMED
ADEHNO	HEAD ON / HEAD-ON
ADEHNP	DAPHNE
ADEHNR	HANDER / HARDEN
ADEHOR	OH DEAR!
ADEHOX	HOAXED
ADEHPR	HARPED
ADEHPS	PHASED / SHAPED
ADEHPT	HEPTAD
ADEHPU	HEAD-UP / HEAD UP
ADEHRR	HARDER
ADEHRS	SHARED
ADEHRT	DEARTH / HATRED / THREAD
ADEHSS	DASHES / SASHED / SHADES
ADEHST	DEATHS / HASTED
ADEHSV	SHAVED
ADEHSW	WASHED
ADEHSX	HAD SEX / HEXADS
ADEHSY	HYADES
ADEHTW	THAWED
ADEHYY	HEYDAY
ADEIJL	JAILED
ADEILL	ALLIED
ADEILM	MAILED / MEDIAL
ADEILN	DANIEL / DEAL IN / DENIAL / LEAD IN / LEAD-IN / NAILED
ADEILO	EIDOLA
ADEILR	ARILED / DERAIL / RAILED
ADEILS	IDEALS / LADIES / SAILED
ADEILT	DETAIL / DILATE / TAILED
ADEILW	WAILED
ADEIMM	MAIMED
ADEIMN	MAIDEN / MEDIAN
ADEIMR	ADMIRE
ADEIMS	AMIDES
ADEIMT	MADE IT
ADEINO	NO IDEA
ADEINP	PAINED
ADEINR	RAINED
ADEINT	DETAIN
ADEINV	INVADE
ADEIOR	ROADIE
ADEIOT	IODATE
ADEIPR	DIAPER / PAIRED / REPAID
ADEIRR	RAIDER
ADEIRS	RAISED
ADEIRT	TIRADE
ADEIRV	VARIED
ADEISS	ASIDES / DASSIE

ADEISU	ADIEUS	ADELRS	ALDERS	ADENRT	ARDENT
ADEISV	ADVISE	ADELRY	DEARLY		RANTED
	VISAED	ADELST	DELTAS		RED ANT
ADEISZ	AZIDES		DESALT	ADENRU	UNREAD
ADFITV	DATIVE		LASTED	ADENRW	WANDER
ADEITW	WAITED		SALTED		WARDEN
ADEITX	TAXIED		SLATED		WARNED
ADEIUX	ADIEUX		STALED	ADENRY	YARNED
ADEIVW	WAIVED	ADELSV	SALVED	ADENSS	SEDANS
ADEJMM	JAMMED		SLAVED	ADENSU	SUNDAE
ADEJRR	JARRED	ADELSY	DELAYS	ADENTT	ATTEND
ADEJRU	ADJURE	ADELUV	VALUED	ADENTV	ADVENT
ADEJUV	DÉJÀ VU	ADELVV	VALVED	ADENTW	WANTED
ADEKKY	YAKKED	ADELZZ	DAZZLE	ADENWY	NEW DAY
ADEKLR	LARKED	ADEMMN	DAMN ME!		YAWNED
ADEKLS	DALEKS		MAD MEN	ADEOPP	PEA POD
	SLAKED		MADMEN	ADEOPR	COAPED
ADEKLT	TALKED	ADEMMR	DAMMER	ADEORR	ROARED
ADEKLW	WALKED		RAMMED	ADEORS	ADORES
ADEKMO	MAKE DO	ADEMNN	MANNED		SOARED
ADEKMR	MARKED	ADEMNO	DAEMON	ADEORT	ORATED
ADEKMS	MASKED		MOANED	ADEOTT	TO DATE
ADEKNR	DANKER	ADEMNP	DAMPEN	ADEOVW	AVOWED
	DARKEN	ADEMNR	DARN ME!	ADEPPR	DAPPER
	NARKED		REMAND		RAPPED
	RANKED	ADEMNS	AMENDS	ADEPPS	SAPPED
ADEKNS	KNEADS		DESMAN	ADEPPT	TAPPED
	SNAKED	ADEMNT	TANDEM	ADEPPY	YAPPED
ADEKNT	TANKED	ADEMNU	UNMADE	ADEPPZ	ZAPPED
ADEKNY	YANKED	ADEMOP	POMADE	ADEPRR	DRAPER
ADEKOS	SOAKED	ADEMOR	RADOME	ADEPRS	DRAPES
ADEKOY	KAYOED		ROAMED		PADRES
ADEKPR	PARKED	ADEMOT	MOATED		PARSED
ADEKQU	QUAKED	ADEMOW	MEADOW		RASPED
ADEKRR	DARKER	ADEMPP	MAPPED		SPARED
ADEKRS	DRAKES	ADEMPR	DAMPER		SPREAD
ADEKST	SKATED	ADEMPT	TAMPED	ADEPRT	DEPART
	STAKED	ADEMPU	MADE UP		PARTED
ADELLN	END ALL		MADE-UP		PETARD
ADELLP	PALLED	ADEMPV	VAMPED		PRATED
ADELLS	LADLES	ADEMRR	MARRED	ADEPRU	READ UP
ADELLU	ALLUDE	ADEMRS	DREAMS	ADEPRW	WARPED
ADELLW	WALLED	ADEMRT	DREAMT	ADEPRY	PRAYED
ADELMM	LAMMED	ADEMRW	WARMED	ADEPSS	PASSED
ADELMP	PALMED	ADEMRY	DREAMY		SPADES
ADELMR	DERMAL	ADEMSS	MASSED	ADEPST	PASTED
	MARLED	ADEMST	MASTED	ADEPSU	PAUSED
ADELMS	DAMSEL	ADEMSU	AMUSED	ADEPSY	SPAYED
	MEDALS		MEDUSA	ADEPTT	PATTED
ADELMT	MALTED	ADEMTT	MATTED	ADEPTU	UPDATE
ADELMU	MAULED	ADENNP	PANNED	ADEPUY	YAUPED
ADELNO	LEAD ON	ADENNT	TANNED	ADEPWY	YAWPED
	LOANED	ADENNU	DUENNA	ADERRS	DARERS
ADELNP	PLANED	ADENOS	ANODES	ADERRT	DARTER
ADELNR	DARNEL	ADENOT	ATONED		RETARD
ADELNS	ELANDS		DONATE		TARRED
ADELNT	DENTAL	ADENOY	ONE DAY		TRADER
ADELOP	PEDALO	ADENPP	APPEND	ADERRW	DRAWER
ADELOR	LOADER		NAPPED		REWARD
	ORDEAL	ADENPR	PANDER		WARDER
ADELPP	DAPPLE	ADENPT	PANTED		WARRED
	LAPPED		PEDANT	ADERRY	DREARY
ADELPR	PEDLAR		PENTAD	ADERST	DATERS
ADELPS	LAPSED	ADENPW	PAWNED		STARED
	PEDALS	ADENPX	EXPAND		TRADES
	PLEADS	ADENRR	DARNER		TREADS
ADELPT	PLATED		ERRAND	ADERSW	SAW RED
ADELPU	LEAD UP	ADENRS	SANDER		WADERS
ADELPW	DEWLAP		SNARED	ADERTT	RATTED
ADELPY	PLAYED				TETRAD
ADELRR	LARDER			ADERTV	ADVERT

ADERVV	VARVED	ADHNNO	ON HAND	ADINSY	DAYS IN
ADERXY	X-RAYED	ADHNNU	UNHAND		IN DAYS
ADERZZ	RAZZED	ADHNOR	HADRON	ADINTY	DAINTY
ADESST	STEADS	ADHNOT	HAD NOT	ADIORS	RADIOS
ADESTT	STATED		TO HAND	ADIORT	ADROIT
	TASTED	ADHNOW	AND HOW!	ADIOSS	SAID SO
ADESTU	SAUTED	ADHNSY	SHANDY	ADIOSV	AVOIDS
ADESTV	STAVED	ADHORS	HOARDS	ADIPPU	PAID UP
ADESTW	WASTED	ADHOSW	SHADOW		PAID-UP
ADESTY	STAYED	ADHOTU	HAD OUT	ADIPRS	RAPIDS
	STEADY	ADHPRU	HARD UP	ADIPSX	SPADIX
ADETTT	TATTED		PURDAH	ADIRRS	SIRDAR
ADETTV	VATTED	ADHRSS	SHARDS	ADIRRY	DRY AIR
ADFFOR	AFFORD	ADHRSY	HYDRAS	ADIRST	TRIADS
ADFFOY	OFF DAY	ADHSSU	SADHUS	ADIRSU	RADIUS
ADFGIN	FADING	ADIIKO	AIKIDO	ADIRSZ	IZARDS
ADFGLY	GADFLY	ADIILN	INLAID	ADIRVZ	VIZARD
ADFHNU	HAD FUN	ADIIMR	MID AIR	ADIRWZ	WIZARD
ADFIRT	ADRIFT		MIDAIR	ADISST	SADIST
ADFIRY	FRIDAY	ADIINN	INDIAN	ADISTU	AUDITS
ADFLTY	DAFTLY	ADIINV	AVIDIN	ADISTV	DAVITS
ADFRST	DRAFTS	ADIJNO	ADJOIN	ADISYY	SAYYID
ADFRSU	FRAUDS	ADIKKO	KODIAK	ADJNOR	JORDAN
ADFRSW	DWARFS	ADIKMO	MIKADO	ADJSTU	ADJUST
ADGGOT	DOG-TAG	ADIKNP	KIDNAP	ADKLNY	DANKLY
ADGGOY	GAY DOG	ADIKTT	DIKTAT	ADKLRY	DARKLY
ADGGRY	DRAGGY	ADILLP	PALLID	ADKLSS	SKALDS
ADGHOR	GO HARD	ADILMS	DISMAL	ADLLOP	OLD PAL
ADGIIN	AIDING	ADILMY	MILADY	ADLLOR	DOLLAR
ADGILN	LADING	ADILNN	INLAND	ADLLOS	SOD ALL
	LIGAND	ADILNO	LADINO	ADLLUY	DUALLY
ADGILO	ALGOID		LAID ON	ADLMNO	ALMOND
ADGIMY	DIGAMY	ADILNR	ALDRIN		DOLMAN
ADGINR	DARING	ADILNS	ISLAND		OLD MAN
ADGINT	DATING	ADILNU	UNLAID	ADLMOS	DOLMAS
ADGINW	WADING	ADILPS	PLAIDS	ADLMPY	DAMPLY
ADGINZ	DAZING	ADILPU	LAID UP	ADLMTU	TALMUD
ADGIRV	GRAVID	ADILRS	DRAILS	ADLMYY	MY LADY
ADGLLO	OLD LAG		LAIRDS	ADLNNO	ON LAND
ADGLLY	GLADLY	ADILRZ	LIZARD	ADLNOO	DOOLAN
ADGLNS	GLANDS	ADILST	DISTAL	ADLNOP	POLAND
ADGLOP	LAP DOG	ADILVY	AVIDLY	ADLNOR	DRALON
	LAPDOG	ADIMMT	DAMMIT		LARDON
ADGLOY	DAYGLO	ADIMNO	DAIMON	ADLNOU	UNLOAD
ADGMOS	DOGMAS		DOMAIN	ADLNPU	UPLAND
ADGMOT	GOT MAD	ADIMNT	DAMN IT!	ADLOPU	LOAD UP
ADGNOR	DRAGON	ADIMOT	DIATOM	ADLORS	DORSAL
ADGNOS	DONGAS	ADIMRS	DISARM	ADLOSW	DOWLAS
	GONADS	ADIMRU	RADIUM	ADLRSW	DRAWLS
ADGNRS	GRANDS	ADIMRY	MYRIAD	ADLRWY	DRAWLY
ADGORW	WAR GOD	ADIMSS	SADISM		DRY LAW
ADGPRU	DRAG UP	ADIMST	ADMITS	ADLSTU	ADULTS
ADGRSU	GUARDS		AMIDST	ADMNOR	RANDOM
ADHHIT	HADITH	ADIMSY	DISMAY	ADMNOS	DAMSON
ADHHIW	WHIDAH	ADIMWY	MIDWAY		MONADS
ADHHOW	HOWDAH	ADINOP	IN A POD		NOMADS
ADHHWY	WHYDAH	ADINOR	DORIAN	ADMNOY	DYNAMO
ADHIJS	HADJIS		INROAD		MONDAY
ADHIMR	DIRHAM		ORDAIN	ADMNUY	MAUNDY
ADHIMS	MAHDIS	ADINOS	ADONIS	ADMORR	RAMROD
ADHINN	HAND IN	ADINPT	PANDIT	ADMORU	MADURO
	HAND-IN	ADINPU	UNPAID	ADMOSU	DO A SUM
	IN HAND	ADINQR	QINDAR	ADMSTU	DATUMS
ADHINS	DANISH	ADINRS	DINARS	ADMTUY	ADYTUM
	SANDHI		DRAINS	ADNNOS	DONNAS
ADHIOR	HAIRDO	ADINRT	DARN IT!	ADNOPR	PARDON
ADHIPS	APHIDS	ADINRU	DURIAN	ADNOPT	DOPANT
ADHIRS	RADISH	ADINRW	DRAW IN	ADNORS	ADORNS
ADHLOT	OLD HAT		INWARD	ADNORU	AROUND
ADHLRY	HARDLY	ADINSU	UNSAID	ADNORW	DRAW ON
ADHMOR	DO HARM	ADINSV	DIVANS		ONWARD

ADNRST	STRAND
ADNRTU	TUNDRA
ADNSST	STANDS
ADNSTU	DAUNTS
ADNSTY	DYNAST
ADNSUY	SUNDAY
ADOPRY	PARODY
ADOPST	ADOPTS
ADORRU	ARDOUR
ADORTW	TOWARD
ADOTUY	DAY OUT
ADPPSU	PADS UP
ADPRUW	DRAW UP
	UPWARD
ADQSSU	SQUADS
ADRSSW	SWARDS
ADRTWY	TAWDRY
AEEFIR	FAERIE
AEEFLM	FEMALE
AEEFOV	FOVEAE
AEEFRR	FEARER
AEEFRT	AFREET
AEEGGN	ENGAGE
	ENGAGE
AEEGGR	REGGAE
AEEGJR	JAEGER
AEEGJT	JET AGE
AEEGLL	ALLEGE
AEEGLP	PELAGE
AEEGLR	REGALE
AEEGLS	EAGLES
AEEGLT	EAGLET
	GELATE
	LEGATE
AEEGLU	LEAGUE
AEEGMM	GEMMAE
AEEGMN	MANEGE
	MENAGE
AEEGMR	MEAGRE
AEEGMT	GAMETE
AEEGNR	ENRAGE
	GENERA
AEEGNT	NEGATE
AEEGNV	AVENGE
	GENEVA
AEEGOP	APOGEE
AEEGOT	GOATEE
AEEGRS	AGREES
	EAGRES
	GREASE
AEEGRV	GREAVE
AEEGSW	SEWAGE
AEEHHW	HEE-HAW
AEEHLR	HEALER
AEEHLX	EXHALE
AEEHNP	PEAHEN
AEEHNT	ETHANE
AEEHNV	HEAVEN
AEEHNX	HEXANE
AEEHRR	HEARER
	REHEAR
AEEHRS	HEARSE
AEEHRT	AETHER
	HEATER
	REHEAT
AEEHRV	HEAVER
AEEHRY	HEAR YE!
AEEHSV	HEAVES
	SHEAVE
AEEILM	MEALIE
AEEIMN	MEANIE
AEEIPS	SEA PIE
AEEIRS	AERIES
	EASIER
AEEKLN	ALKENE
AEEKMR	REMAKE
AEEKNW	WEAKEN
AEEKNY	YANKEE
AEEKRT	RETAKE
AEEKRU	EUREKA
AEEKRW	WEAKER
AEELLL	ALLELE
AEELLM	MALLEE
AEELMN	ENAMEL
AEELNR	LEANER
AEELNT	LATEEN
AEELNV	LEAVEN
AEELOT	OLEATE
AEELPR	LEAPER
	REPEAL
AEELPS	ASLEEP
	ELAPSE
	PLEASE
	SAPELE
AEELRS	SEALER
AEELRT	ELATER
	RELATE
AEELRV	LEAVER
	REVEAL
AEELSS	EASELS
	LEASES
AEELST	ELATES
	TEASEL
AEELSV	LEAVES
AEELSW	WEASEL
AEELTU	ELUATE
	LUTEAE
AEELTV	VELETA
AEELTZ	TEAZEL
	TEAZLE
AEELWY	LEEWAY
AEEMNR	MEANER
AEEMNS	ENEMAS
AEEMNX	AXEMEN
AEEMPR	AMPERE
AEEMRR	REAMER
AEEMRS	SEAMER
AEEMSS	SESAME
AEEMSV	SAVE ME
AEENNT	NEATEN
AEENRR	EARNER
	NEARER
AEENRT	NEATER
AEENRW	WEANER
AEENST	SATEEN
	SENATE
AEENSU	UNEASE
AEENUV	AVENUE
AEEOTT	TO A TEE
AEEPPR	RAPPEE
AEEPRR	REAPER
AEEPRT	REPEAT
AEEPST	PESETA
AEEPSU	EASE UP
AEEPSW	PESEWA
AEEPSX	APEXES
AEEPVY	PEAVEY
AEEQTU	EQUATE
AEERRR	REARER
AEERRS	ERASER
AEERRT	TEARER
	TERRAE
AEERRW	WEARER
AEERSS	ERASES
	SAREES
AEERST	EASTER
	SEATER
	TEASER
AEERSV	AVERSE
AEERTX	AERTEX
AEERVW	WEAVER
AEESST	TEASES
AEESSW	SEESAW
AEESSY	EYASES
AEESTT	ESTATE
	TEA SET
	TESTAE
AEESTX	EXEATS
AEESVW	WEAVES
AEFFGR	GAFFER
AEFFGS	GAFFES
AEFFIP	PIAFFE
AEFFLR	RAFFLE
AEFFLW	WAFFLE
AEFFRZ	ZAFFRE
AEFGLN	FLANGE
AEFGNR	GRAFEN
AEFGOR	FORAGE
AEFGOS	SEA FOG
AEFHLL	FELLAH
AEFHRS	AFRESH
AEFHRT	FATHER
AEFILL	FAILLE
AEFILN	FINALE
AEFIMN	FAMINE
AEFINN	FENIAN
AEFINR	IN FEAR
AEFIRR	FAIRER
AEFIST	FIESTA
AEFITX	FIXATE
AEFJNT	FAN-JET
AEFKLR	FLAKER
AEFKLS	FLAKES
AEFKRS	FREAKS
AEFKRY	FAKERY
	FREAKY
AEFLLN	FALLEN
AEFLLS	FELLAS
AEFLMR	FLAMER
AEFLMS	FLAMES
AEFLNX	FLAXEN
AEFLOR	LOAFER
AEFLOT	FOETAL
	OF LATE
AEFLOV	FOVEAL
AEFLRS	FALSER
	FLARES
AEFLRT	FALTER
AEFLRU	EARFUL
	FERULA
AEFLST	FESTAL
AEFLSY	SAFELY
AEFLTY	FEALTY
AEFMNT	FAT MEN
AEFMOR	FEMORA
AEFMRR	FARMER
	FRAMER
AEFMRS	FRAMES
AEFNOR	NO FEAR
AEFNRU	FRAUEN
AEFNRW	FAWNER
AEFNST	FANTES
	FASTEN

AEFNSU	UNSAFE
AEFNTT	FATTEN
AEFOSS	FOSSAE
AEFPPR	FRAPPE
AEFRRT	RAFTER
AEFRRY	RAREFY
AEFRST	AFTERS
	FASTER
	STRAFE
AEFRSW	WAFERS
AEFRSY	FAYRES
AEFRTT	FATTER
AEFRTW	WAFTER
AEFSST	FEASTS
	SAFEST
AEFSTY	SAFETY
AEGGGL	GAGGLE
AEGGHL	HAGGLE
AEGGIN	AGEING
AEGGLR	GARGLE
	LAGGER
AEGGLW	WAGGLE
AEGGNR	GANGER
	GRANGE
	NAGGER
AEGGNU	GANGUE
AEGGRT	GARGET
AEGGRU	GAUGER
AEGGRW	WAGGER
AEGGSU	GAUGES
AEGGWW	GEWGAW
AEGHIR	HEGIRA
AEGHIS	GEISHA
AEGHIW	AWEIGH
AEGHMO	HOMAGE
AEGHNR	HANGER
AEGHRT	GATHER
AEGHSS	GASHES
AEGILN	GENIAL
	LINAGE
AEGILO	GOALIE
AEGILS	SILAGE
AEGILT	LIGATE
AEGILV	GLAIVE
AEGIMN	ENIGMA
	GAMINE
AEGIMP	MAGPIE
AEGIMR	GAMIER
	MAIGRE
	MIRAGE
AEGIMS	IMAGES
AEGINR	GAINER
	IN GEAR
	REGAIN
	REGINA
AEGINS	EASING
AEGINU	GUINEA
AEGINV	GAVE IN
AEGIRT	GAITER
	TRIAGE
AEGIRV	ARGIVE
AEGIRW	EARWIG
AEGISV	VISAGE
AEGITY	GAIETY
AEGJLN	JANGLE
AEGJST	GAS JET
AEGKRW	GAWKER
AEGKST	GASKET
AEGLLU	ULLAGE
AEGLLY	GALLEY
AEGLMN	MANGLE

AEGLMS	GLEAMS
AEGLMY	GAMELY
	GLEAMY
AEGLNR	ANGLER
	REGNAL
AEGLNS	ANGELS
	ANGLES
	GLEANS
AEGLNT	TANGLE
AEGLNU	LANGUE
AEGLNW	WANGLE
AEGLOR	GALORE
AEGLOT	LEGATO
AEGLOV	LOVAGE
AEGLPS	PLAGES
AEGLPU	PLAGUE
AEGLRR	LARGER
AEGLRS	GLARES
	LAGERS
	LARGES
AEGLRT	TERGAL
AEGLRV	GRAVEL
AEGLRZ	GLAZER
AEGLSV	GAVELS
AEGLSY	SAGELY
AEGLSZ	GLAZES
AEGMMR	GAMMER
AEGMMS	SMEGMA
AEGMNR	ENGRAM
	GERMAN
	MANGER
AEGMNS	MANGES
AEGMNT	MAGNET
AEGMRS	MARGES
AEGMST	GAMEST
AEGMUY	MAGUEY
AEGMUZ	ZEUGMA
AEGNNO	NONAGE
AEGNNT	GANNET
AEGNOR	ONAGER
	ORANGE
AEGNOS	GENOAS
AEGNRR	GARNER
	RANGER
AEGNRS	ANGERS
	RANGES
	SERANG
AEGNRT	ARGENT
	GARNET
AEGNRV	GRAVEN
AEGNRW	GNAWER
AEGNST	AGENTS
AEGNSV	VEGANS
AEGOPT	POTAGE
AEGORT	ORGEAT
AEGOST	GO EAST
AEGOSY	EASY GO
	GO EASY
AEGOTU	OUTAGE
AEGOTW	TOWAGE
AEGOVY	VOYAGE
AEGPRS	GAPERS
	GASPER
	GRAPES
AEGPRT	PARGET
AEGPUV	GAVE UP
AEGRRT	GARRET
	GARTER
	GRATER
AEGRRU	ARGUER
AEGRRV	GRAVER

AEGRRZ	GRAZER
AEGRSS	GASSER
AEGRST	GRATES
	GREATS
	STAGER
AEGRSU	ARGUES
	AUGERS
AEGRSV	GRAVES
AEGRSW	WAGERS
AEGRSY	GREASY
AEGRSZ	GRAZES
AEGRTT	TARGET
AEGRTU	TUAREG
AEGRTY	GYRATE
AEGRUV	VAGUER
AEGSST	SAGEST
	STAGES
AEGSSU	USAGES
AEGSSW	SWAGES
AEGSTT	GETS AT
AEGSTY	GAYEST
AEGSUZ	GAUZES
AEHHLT	HEALTH
AEHHPR	RHAPHE
AEHHPY	HYPHAE
AEHHRS	REHASH
AEHHRT	HEARTH
AEHHSS	HASHES
AEHHST	HEATHS
	SHEATH
AEHHTY	HEATHY
AEHHVY	YAHVEH
AEHHWY	YAHWEH
AEHIJR	HEJIRA
AEHIKN	HANKIE
AEHILN	INHALE
AEHILR	HAILER
AEHILS	SHEILA
AEHILT	HALITE
AEHIMN	HAEMIN
AEHINR	HERNIA
AEHINT	IN HEAT
AEHINW	WAHINE
AEHIRZ	HAZIER
AEHIST	SAITHE
AEHITV	HAVE IT
AEHJMT	THE JAM
AEHKNR	HANKER
	HARKEN
AEHKNS	SHAKEN
AEHKRS	SHAKER
AEHKRW	HAWKER
AEHKSS	SHAKES
AEHLLT	LETHAL
AEHLMT	HAMLET
AEHLOS	HALOES
AEHLOT	LOATHE
AEHLRS	HALERS
	LASHER
AEHLRT	HALTER
	LATHER
	THALER
AEHLRU	HALERU
AEHLRW	WHALER
AEHLSS	HASSLE
	LASHES
AEHLST	HASLET
	LATHES
	SHELTA
AEHLSV	HALVES

AEHLSW	WHALES	AEIKNT	INTAKE	AEIPRT	PIRATE
	WHEALS		TAKE IN		PRATIE
AEHLSZ	HAZELS	AEIKRS	KAISER	AEIPST	PIETAS
AEHLTW	WEALTH	AEIKTT	TAKE IT	AEIPZZ	PIAZZE
AEHMMR	HAMMER	AEILLM	MALLEI	AEIRRS	AIRERS
AEHMMY	MAYHEM	AEILLN	LINEAL		RAISER
AEHMNT	ANTHEM	AEILLS	ALLIES		SIERRA
AEHMNU	HUMANE	AEILMN	MENIAL	AEIRRV	ARRIVE
AEHMOT	AT HOME	AEILMP	IMPALE	AEIRRW	WARIER
AEHMPR	HAMPER	AEILMS	MESIAL	AEIRSS	ARISES
AEHMRS	HAREMS	AEILNO	EOLIAN		RAISES
	MASHER	AEILNP	ALPINE	AEIRST	SATIRE
AEHMSS	MASHES		NEPALI		STRIAE
	SHAMES		PINEAL	AEIRSV	VARIES
AEHNNS	HENNAS	AEILNR	LINEAR	AEIRTT	ATTIRE
AEHNOV	HAVE ON		NAILER		RATITE
AEHNPP	HAPPEN	AEILNS	ALIENS	AEIRTW	WAITER
AEHNPT	HAPTEN		SALINE	AEIRVW	WAIVER
AEHNRT	ANTHER		SILANE		WAIVER
	THENAR	AEILNT	ENTAIL	AEISST	SIESTA
AEHNST	HASTEN		TINEAL	AEISSU	AUSSIE
	THANES	AEILNV	ALEVIN	AEISSV	AVISES
AEHNSV	HAVENS		VALINE	AEISSZ	ASSIZE
	SHAVEN		VEINAL	AEISTT	EATS IT
AEHNSY	HYENAS		VENIAL	AEISTV	VITAES
AEHNTV	HAVEN'T	AEILPS	ESPIAL	AEISTX	TAXIES
AEHORS	ASHORE		LIPASE	AEISVW	WAIVES
	HOARSE	AEILRR	RAILER	AEITTT	TATTIE
AEHORX	HOAXER	AEILRS	ARIELS	AEITTV	VITTAE
AEHOSX	HOAXES		ISRAEL	AEJMRT	RAM JET
AEHPPU	HEAP UP		SERIAL		RAMJET
AEHPRR	HARPER	AEILRT	RETAIL	AEJMST	JETSAM
AEHPRS	PHRASE	AEILRW	WAILER	AEJPRS	JASPER
	SERAPH	AEILRZ	LAZIER	AEKKNR	KRAKEN
	SHAPER	AEILSS	AISLES	AEKLNR	LANKER
	SHERPA	AEILSY	EASILY		RANKLE
AEHPSS	PASHES		ELYSIA	AEKLNS	ANKLES
	PHASES	AEIMMR	MAIMER	AEKLNT	ANKLET
	SHAPES	AEIMNO	ANOMIE	AEKLNY	ALKYNE
AEHPST	SPATHE	AEIMNR	AIRMEN	AEKLRT	TALKER
AEHPTU	HEAT UP		MARINE	AEKLRW	WALKER
AEHPUV	HAVE UP		REMAIN	AEKLSS	SLAKES
AEHRRS	RASHER	AEIMNS	AMINES	AEKLWY	WEAKLY
	SHARER	AEIMNT	INMATE	AEKMNU	UNMAKE
AEHRRT	RATHER	AEIMRS	ARMIES	AEKMPU	MAKE UP
AEHRSS	RASHES	AEINNP	PENNIA		MAKE-UP
	SHARES		PINNAE	AEKMRR	MARKER
	SHEARS	AEINNS	INSANE		REMARK
AEHRST	EARTHS		SIENNA	AEKMRS	MAKERS
	HEARTS	AEINNT	INNATE	AEKMRT	MARKET
AEHRSV	HAVERS	AEINPR	RAPINE	AEKNOR	KOREAN
	SHAVER	AEINPT	PINETA	AEKNOT	TAKE ON
AEHRSW	WASHER	AEINRS	ARISEN	AEKNOW	AWOKEN
	WHARES	AEINRT	RETAIN	AEKNRR	RANKER
AEHRTT	THREAT		RETINA	AEKNRT	TANKER
AEHRTW	THE WAR	AEINRV	NAIVER	AEKNSS	SNAKES
	WREATH		RAVINE		SNEAKS
AEHRTY	EARTHY		VAINER	AEKNSV	KNAVES
	HEARTY	AEINRW	WEAR IN	AEKNSW	WAKENS
AEHSSS	SASHES	AEINRZ	ZANIER	AEKNSY	SNEAKY
AEHSST	HASTES	AEINST	EATS IN	AEKORS	SOAKER
	TASHES		TISANE	AEKOSY	KAYOES
AEHSSV	SHAVES	AEINSV	NAVIES	AEKOTT	TAKE TO
AEHSSW	WASHES	AEINSZ	ZANIES	AEKPRR	PARKER
AEHSSX	HAS SEX	AEINTU	AUNTIE	AEKPSS	SPEAKS
AEHSTW	SWATHE	AEINTV	NATIVE	AEKPTU	TAKE UP
	WHEATS	AEIOPT	OPIATE		UPTAKE
AEIILS	LIAISE	AEIPRR	RAPIER	AEKPUW	WAKE UP
AEIJLR	JAILER		REPAIR	AEKQRU	QUAKER
AEIJLZ	JEZAIL	AEIPRS	ASPIRE	AEKQSU	QUAKES
AEIKMT	MAKE IT		PRAISE		SQUEAK

AEKRSS	SAKERS
AEKRST	SKATER
	STRAKE
	STREAK
	TAKERS
AEKRSW	WAKERS
	WREAKS
AEKSST	SKATES
	STAKES
	STEAKS
AEKSTW	TWEAKS
AELLLY	LEALLY
AELLMT	MALLET
AELLMY	LAMELY
AELLNO	ALL ONE
AELLNY	LEANLY
AELLOR	LOREAL
AELLPS	LAPELS
AELLPT	L PLATE
	PALLET
AELLPY	PALELY
AELLRT	TALLER
AELLRU	ALLURE
	LAUREL
AELLRW	WALLER
AELLRY	REALLY
AELLST	ALL SET
	SALLET
AELLSY	ALLEYS
	SALLEY
AELLTU	LUTEAL
AELLTW	WALLET
AELLTY	LATELY
AELLVY	VALLEY
AELMMS	LEMMAS
AELMNT	LAMENT
	MANTLE
	MENTAL
AELMNW	LAWMEN
AELMNY	LAYMEN
	MEANLY
	NAMELY
AELMOR	MORALE
AELMPR	PALMER
AELMPS	MAPLES
	SAMPLE
AELMRS	REALMS
AELMRT	ARMLET
AELMRU	MAULER
AELMRV	MARVEL
AELMST	LAMEST
	METALS
	SAMLET
AELMSU	SAMUEL
AELMSY	MEASLY
AELMTU	AMULET
	MULETA
AELMTY	TAMELY
AELNNR	LANNER
AELNOP	ONE LAP
AELNOS	ON SALE
AELNOT	LEAN TO
	LEAN-TO
AELNPP	PEN PAL
AELNPR	PLANER
AELNPS	PANELS
	PLANES
AELNPT	PLANET
	PLATEN
AELNRS	LEARNS

AELNRT	ANTLER
	LEARNT
	RENTAL
AELNRU	NEURAL
	UNREAL
AELNRV	VERNAL
AELNRY	NEARLY
AELNSS	ELSANS
AELNSV	NAVELS
AELNSY	SANELY
AELNTT	LATENT
	TALENT
AELNTU	ELUANT
AELNTY	NEATLY
AELOPR	PAROLE
AELOPS	ASLOPE
AELOPT	PELOTA
AELORS	SOLERA
AELOSV	LOAVES
AELOTZ	ZEALOT
AELPPR	RAPPEL
AELPPS	APPLES
AELPPT	LAPPET
AELPPU	LEAP UP
	PAPULE
AELPQU	PLAQUE
AELPRR	PARREL
AELPRS	PEARLS
AELPRT	PALTER
	PLATER
AELPRU	PLEURA
AELPRY	PARLEY
	PEARLY
	PLAYER
	REPLAY
AELPSS	LAPSES
AELPST	PALEST
	PASTEL
	PETALS
	PLATES
	PLEATS
	SEPTAL
	STAPLE
AELPSU	SEAL UP
AELQSU	EQUALS
	SQUEAL
AELRRY	RARELY
AELRSS	LASERS
AELRST	ALERTS
	ALTERS
	LASTER
	RATELS
	SALTER
	SLATER
	STALER
	STELAR
	TALERS
AELRSV	LAVERS
	RAVELS
	SALVER
	SERVAL
	SLAVER
AELRSW	WALERS
AELRSY	LAYERS
	RELAYS
	SLAYER
AELRTT	LATTER
	RATTLE
AELRTV	TRAVEL
	VARLET

AELRTY	ELYTRA
	LYRATE
	REALTY
AELRUV	VALUER
AELRWY	LAWYER
AELRYY	YEARLY
AELRZZ	RAZZLE
AELSSS	LASSES
AELSST	SLATES
	STALES
	STEALS
	TASSEL
	TESLAS
AELSSV	SALVES
	SLAVES
	VALSES
AELSTT	LATEST
AELSTU	SALUTE
AELSTV	VALETS
	VESTAL
AELSTX	EXALTS
	LAXEST
AELSTY	LYSATE
AELSUV	VALUES
AELSUX	SEXUAL
AELSVV	VALVES
AELSYZ	SLEAZY
AELTTT	TATTLE
AELTTW	WATTLE
AELTUX	LUXATE
AELUUV	UVULAE
AELUVV	VULVAE
AEMMNR	MERMAN
AEMMRR	RAMMER
AEMMRY	YAMMER
AEMMST	STEMMA
AEMNNO	ONE MAN
	ONE-MAN
AEMNNP	PENMAN
AEMNNR	MANNER
AEMNOR	MOANER
AEMNOT	OMENTA
AEMNOY	YEOMAN
AEMNPR	PREMAN
AEMNQU	MANQUE
AEMNRT	MARTEN
AEMNRU	MANURE
AEMNST	STAMEN
AEMNSY	YES MAN
	YES-MAN
AEMNTX	TAXMEN
AEMORR	REMORA
	ROAMER
AEMORS	RAMOSE
AEMOSS	SAMSOE
AEMPPR	MAPPER
	PAMPER
AEMPRT	TAMPER
AEMPRV	REVAMP
	VAMPER
AEMQRU	MARQUE
AEMQSU	MASQUE
AEMRRS	REARMS
AEMRRW	WARMER
AEMRSS	MASERS
	SMEARS
AEMRST	MASTER
	MATERS
	STREAM
AEMRSU	AMUSER
AEMRSY	SMEARY

46

Code	Word(s)
AEMRTT	MATTER
AEMRTU	MATURE
AEMSSS	MASSES
AEMSST	STEAMS
AEMSSU	AMUSES
	ASSUME
AEMSSX	XMASES
AEMSTT	MATTES
	TAMEST
AEMSTU	MEATUS
AEMSTY	MATEYS
	MAYEST
	STEAMY
AEMSUV	MAUVES
AEMSYZ	ZYMASE
AEMTTU	MUTATE
AENNOV	NOVENA
AENNOY	ANYONE
AENNRT	TANNER
AENNSS	SENNAS
AENNTT	TENANT
AENOPS	PAEONS
AENOPW	WEAPON
AENOPY	PAEONY
AENORS	REASON
	SENORA
AENORT	ORNATE
AENORW	WEAR ON
AENOSS	SEASON
AENOST	ATONES
AENOTT	NOTATE
AENOTZ	ZONATE
AENOWY	ONE WAY
	ONE-WAY
AENPPR	RAPPEN
AENPRT	ENTRAP
	PARENT
	TREPAN
AENPRY	NAPERY
AENPRZ	PANZER
AENPST	PATENS
AENPTT	PATENT
	PATTEN
AENPTU	PEANUT
AENQSU	QUEANS
AENRRS	SNARER
AENRRT	ERRANT
	RANTER
AENRRW	WARNER
	WARREN
AENRSS	SARSEN
	SNARES
AENRST	ASTERN
	STERNA
AENRSV	RAVENS
AENRSW	ANSWER
AENRSY	SENARY
	YEARNS
AENRTT	NATTER
AENRTU	NATURE
	TEA URN
AENRTV	TAVERN
AENRWY	YAWNER
AENSST	ASSENT
	SANEST
AENSSU	ANUSES
AENSTU	UNSEAT
AENSUV	NAEVUS
AENSUY	UNEASY
AENSWY	SAWNEY
AENTTU	ATTUNE
	NUTATE
	TAUTEN
AENTTX	EXTANT
AENTTY	TETANY
AEOPQU	OPAQUE
AEOPRS	OPERAS
AEOPRT	PROTEA
AEOPTT	TEA POT
	TEAPOT
AEOPTY	TEAPOY
AFORRS	SOARER
AEORSS	SEROSA
AFORST	ORATES
AEORSU	AROUSE
AEORTT	ROTATE
AEORVW	AVOWER
AEOTTU	ATE OUT
	EAT OUT
AEOUVZ	ZOUAVE
AEPPRS	PAPERS
	SAPPER
AEPPRT	TAPPER
AEPPRU	PAUPER
AEPPRY	PAPERY
	PREPAY
	YAPPER
AEPPTT	TAPPET
AEPPTU	PUPATE
AEPRRS	RASPER
AEPRRT	PARTER
	PRATER
AEPRRU	REAR UP
AEPRRW	PREWAR
	WARPER
AEPRRY	PRAYER
AEPRSS	PARSES
	PASSER
	REPASS
	SPARES
	SPARSE
	SPEARS
AEPRST	PRATES
	REPAST
	TAPERS
AEPRSX	PRAXES
AEPRSY	REPAYS
AEPRTT	PATTER
AEPRTU	TEAR UP
	UPRATE
AEPRTX	PRETAX
AEPRUV	RAVE UP
	RAVE-UP
AEPRUY	YAUPER
AEPRWY	YAWPER
AEPSSS	PASSES
AEPSST	PASTES
	SPATES
	STAPES
AEPSSU	PAUSES
AEPSTT	APTEST
AEPSTU	EATS UP
AEPSUV	SAVE UP
AEQRSU	SQUARE
AEQRUV	QUAVER
AEQSUY	QUEASY
AERRST	ARREST
	RAREST
	RASTER
AERRSV	RAVERS
AERRTT	TARTER
AERRTY	ARTERY
AERSST	ASSERT
	ASTERS
	STARES
AERSSU	ASSURE
AERSSV	SAVERS
AERSSW	SAWERS
	SWEARS
	WRASSE
AERSTT	AT REST
	STATER
	TASTER
	TREATS
AERSTV	AVERTS
	STARVE
	VASTER
AFRSTW	WASTER
	WATERS
AERSTX	EXTRAS
	TAXERS
AERSTY	STAYER
AERSTZ	ERSATZ
AERSUV	SUAVER
AERSUZ	AZURES
AERSVW	WAVERS
AERSWY	SAWYER
	SWAYER
AERSZZ	RAZZES
AERTTT	TATTER
AERTTU	TAUTER
AERTTY	TREATY
	YATTER
AERTWY	WATERY
AESSSS	ASSESS
AESSST	ASSETS
	STASES
AESSSY	ESSAYS
AESSTT	STATES
	TASTES
AESSTV	STAVES
AESSTW	SWEATS
	WASTES
AESSTY	YEASTS
AESTTT	ATTEST
AESTTU	ASTUTE
	STATUE
AESTWY	SWEATY
AESTYY	YEASTY
AFFFOR	FAR OFF
	FAR-OFF
AFFGUW	GUFFAW
AFFIKR	KAFFIR
AFFIMR	AFFIRM
AFFIRT	TARIFF
AFFLOS	OFFALS
AFFLOY	LAY OFF
	LAYOFF
AFFLSU	LUFFAS
AFFLWY	WAFFLY
AFFNOR	RAN OFF
AFFOPY	PAY OFF
	PAYOFF
AFFOSW	SAW OFF
	SAW-OFF
AFFQSU	QUAFFS
AFFSST	STAFFS
AFGGOT	FAGGOT
AFGIKN	FAKING
AFGINO	IN A FOG
AFGINR	FARING
AFGINS	FAGINS

AFGINT	FATING	AFLSTU	FAULTS	AGILMN	LAMING
AFGINZ	FAZING		FLATUS		LINGAM
AFGISY	GASIFY	AFLSWY	SAWFLY		MALIGN
AFGLNO	FLAGON	AFLTUY	FAULTY	AGILMY	GAMILY
AFGLNU	FUNGAL	AFMNOT	FANTOM	AGILNO	IN-GOAL
AFGLRU	FRUGAL	AFMORT	FORMAT	AGILNP	PALING
AFGOST	GO FAST	AFMOSU	FAMOUS	AGILNS	ALGINS
AFGRST	GRAFTS	AFNSSU	SNAFUS		ALIGNS
AFGRUY	ARGUFY	AFOORT	TOO FAR		LASING
AFHILN	IN HALF	AFOPRY	PAY FOR		LINGAS
AFHIMS	FAMISH	AFORRW	FARROW		SIGNAL
AFHIOS	OAFISH	AFORSY	FORAYS	AGILNU	LINGUA
AFHIRS	SHARIF	AFORTU	FAR OUT	AGILNV	LAVING
AFHIST	FAITHS		FAR-OUT	AGILNZ	LAZING
AFHLOO	LOOFAH	AFORUV	FAVOUR	AGILOR	AIR LOG
AFHLSY	FLASHY	AFRSTU	FRUSTA		GLORIA
AFHMOT	FATHOM	AGGGIN	GAGING	AGILOV	OGIVAL
AFHNSU	HAS FUN	AGGHIS	HAGGIS	AGILRS	GLAIRS
AFHORS	SHOFAR	AGGHNO	GO HANG		GRAILS
AFHRSW	WHARFS	AGGHSY	SHAGGY	AGIMNN	NAMING
AFHSST	SHAFTS	AGGILO	LOGGIA	AGIMNR	ARMING
AFIIJN	FIJIAN	AGGIMN	GAMING		MARGIN
AFIILL	FILIAL	AGGINP	GAPING	AGIMNT	MATING
AFIILN	FINIAL		PAGING		TAMING
AFIINX	IN A FIX	AGGINR	RAGING	AGIMNY	MAYING
AFIKRS	FAKIRS	AGGINT	GATING	AGIMNZ	MAZING
AFILLN	FALL IN	AGGINW	WAGING	AGIMST	STIGMA
AFILLS	FLAILS	AGGINZ	GAZING	AGIMWW	WIGWAM
AFILMU	FAMULI	AGGIWW	WIGWAG	AGINNO	GAIN ON
AFILMY	FAMILY	AGGIZZ	ZIGZAG	AGINNR	RANG IN
AFILNS	FINALS	AGGLWY	WAGGLY	AGINNT	ANTING
AFILNV	FLAVIN	AGGMOT	MAGGOT	AGINNW	AWNING
AFILOR	FOLIAR	AGGNPU	GANG UP		WANING
AFILPS	PILAFS	AGGNSY	SNAGGY	AGINOR	OARING
AFILRS	FLAIRS	AGGQUY	QUAGGY	AGINPR	PARING
AFILRY	FAIRLY	AGHILT	ALIGHT		RAPING
AFIMNY	INFAMY	AGHINR	HARING	AGINPT	TAPING
AFIMRY	RAMIFY	AGHINT	HANG IT!	AGINPV	PAVING
AFIMSS	MASSIF		HATING	AGINPW	PAWING
AFINNN	FINNAN	AGHINW	HAWING	AGINRR	RARING
AFINNT	INFANT	AGHINY	HAYING	AGINRS	GRAINS
AFINRU	UNFAIR	AGHINZ	HAZING		RASING
AFINST	FAINTS	AGHIRS	GARISH	AGINRT	RATING
	FANTIS	AGHIRT	ARIGHT		TARING
AFINYZ	NAZIFY	AGHISU	AGUISH	AGINRU	AIR GUN
AFIRRS	FRIARS	AGHISZ	GHAZIS		UGRIAN
AFIRRY	FRIARY	AGHKRU	GURKHA	AGINRV	RAVING
AFIRSS	FARSIS	AGHLLU	GULLAH	AGINRW	WARING
AFIRTY	RATIFY	AGHLOS	GALOSH	AGINRY	GRAINY
AFJLRU	JARFUL	AGHLSU	LAUGHS		RAYING
AFKLNS	FLANKS	AGHNNO	HANG ON	AGINRZ	RAZING
AFKLSS	FLASKS	AGHNPU	HANG UP	AGINSS	ASSIGN
AFKNRS	FRANKS		HANG-UP	AGINST	GIANTS
AFKORS	ASK FOR	AGHNSW	WHANGS		SATING
AFLLOR	FLORAL	AGHNTU	NAUGHT	AGINSV	SAVING
	FOR ALL	AGHPRS	GRAPHS	AGINSY	SAYING
AFLLOW	FALLOW	AGHRRY	GHARRY	AGINTW	TAWING
AFLLPU	LAPFUL	AGHTTU	TAUGHT	AGINTX	TAXING
AFLLTY	FLATLY	AGIILN	AILING	AGINVW	WAVING
AFLLUW	LAWFUL		NILGAI	AGINWX	WAXING
AFLMNU	MANFUL	AGIIMN	AIMING	AGINWY	YAWING
AFLMOR	FORMAL	AGIINR	AIRING	AGIORU	GIAOUR
AFLMRU	ARMFUL	AGIJNP	JAPING	AGIORV	VIRAGO
	FULMAR	AGIJNW	JAWING	AGIOTU	AGOUTI
AFLMYY	MAYFLY	AGIJSW	JIGSAW	AGIRST	GRATIS
AFLNOT	FONTAL	AGIKMN	MAKING	AGIRTU	GUITAR
AFLNTU	FLAUNT	AGIKNR	RAKING	AGJLNY	JANGLY
AFLOSS	SOL-FAS	AGIKNS	ASKING	AGJNOR	JARGON
AFLOST	FLOATS		GASKIN	AGKORT	GO-KART
AFLRTU	ARTFUL		KIANGS	AGLLNO	GALLON
		AGIKNT	TAKING	AGLLOP	GALLOP

AGLNOS	AS LONG	AHILLP	PHALLI	AHNSTU	HAUNTS
	SLOGAN	AHILLT	THALLI		SUN HAT
AGLNOU	LANUGO	AHILNR	RHINAL		SUNHAT
AGLNRU	LANGUR	AHILNU	HAUL IN	AHNSTY	SHANTY
AGLNSS	SLANGS	AHILPS	PALISH	AHNTTU	U THANT
AGLNSY	SLANGY		PHIALS	AHOORY	HOORAY
AGLOOW	GO AWOL	AHILRY	HILARY	AHOOSY	YAHOOS
AGLOPS	GALOPS	AHILSS	SALISH	AHOPRS	PHASOR
AGLORS	GORALS	AHILSV	LAVISH	AHOPST	PASHTO
	LARGOS	AHILTW	WITHAL		PATHOS
AGLOSS	GLOSSA	AHILYZ	HAZILY		POTASH
AGLOST	GLOATS	AHIMNT	HIT MAN	AHOPTT	TOP HAT
AGLRSU	GLAURS	AHIMOR	MOHAIR	AHORRW	HARROW
AGLRUV	VULGAR	AHIMPS	MISHAP	AHORTT	THROAT
AGLSSY	GLASSY	AHINPT	HAT PIN	AHORTU	AUTHOR
AGLSUV	VALGUS	AHINSV	VANISH	AHORTX	THORAX
AGMMNO	GAMMON	AHINTT	TIN HAT	AHOSSX	XHOSAS
AGMMNU	MAGNUM	AHIORT	HOT AIR	AHOSTT	SHOT AT
AGMMSU	GUMMAS		THORIA	AHOSTU	HAS OUT
AGMNNU	GUNMAN	AHIPRS	PARISH	AHOSTW	SO WHAT?
AGMNOS	MANGOS	AHIPRU	RUPIAH	AHOTWZ	HOWZAT
AGMNRU	GRANUM	AHIRRS	HARRIS	AHPRSS	SHARPS
AGMOOY	OOGAMY		SIRRAH	AHPRTU	PRUTAH
AGMORS	ORGASM	AHIRSV	RAVISH	AHPSST	STAPHS
AGMOYZ	ZYGOMA	AHIRTW	WRAITH	AHPSUW	WASH UP
AGMPUZ	GAZUMP	AHISTT	THAT IS		WHAUPS
AGNNOT	TONGAN	AHISTU	HIATUS	AHQSSU	SQUASH
AGNNRY	GRANNY	AHJNOS	JONAHS	AHRRUY	HURRAY
AGNOQU	QUANGO	AHJOSU	JOSHUA	AHRSSU	HUSSAR
AGNORS	GROANS	AHKMOW	MOHAWK	AHRSTT	STRATH
	ORGANS	AHKNPU	PUNKAH	AHRSTW	WRATHS
	SARONG	AHKNRS	SHRANK	AHRSTY	TRASHY
AGNORY	ORANGY	AHKNSS	SHANKS	AHRTTW	THWART
AGNOST	TANGOS	AHKNST	THANKS	AHSSTU	TUSSAH
AGNOSU	GUANOS	AHKOSS	SHAKOS	AHSSTW	SWATHS
AGNOSW	GOWANS	AHKRSS	SHARKS	AIILRY	AIRILY
	WAGONS	AHLLMU	MULLAH	AIIMMN	MINIMA
AGNOTU	NOUGAT	AHLLNU	NULLAH	AIIMNS	SIMIAN
AGNPRS	PRANGS	AHLLOO	HALLOO	AIIMPR	IMPAIR
	SPRANG	AHLLOS	HALLOS	AIINNV	IN VAIN
AGNPRU	RANG UP		HOLLAS	AIINNZ	ZINNIA
AGNRST	GRANTS	AHLLOW	HALLOW	AIINRS	RAISIN
AGNRTY	GANTRY	AHLLRT	THRALL	AIINTT	TITIAN
AGNRUY	RAY GUN	AHLLUX	HALLUX	AIIPTW	WAPITI
AGNSTW	TWANGS	AHLMNY	HYMNAL	AIIQRS	IRAQIS
AGNTTY	GNATTY	AHLMOS	SHALOM	AIIRTV	TRIVIA
AGNTWY	TWANGY	AHLMSU	HAULMS	AIJLOV	JOVIAL
AGOORT	AGOROT	AHLOOP	HOOP-LA	AIJNOV	JOVIAN
AGORST	GROATS	AHLORT	HARLOT	AIJOSU	OUIJAS
AGORSY	ARGOSY	AHLOSS	SHOALS	AIKLNO	KAOLIN
AGORTU	RAGOUT	AHLPSS	SPLASH	AIKLNW	WALK IN
AGOTTU	TAUTOG	AHLPSU	LASH UP		WALK-IN
AGPRSS	GRASPS	AHLPSY	PLASHY	AIKLSU	SALUKI
AGRSSU	SUGARS	AHLRSY	RASHLY	AIKLTU	LIKUTA
AGRSSY	GRASSY	AHLSSW	SHAWLS	AIKNNP	NAPKIN
AGRSUU	AUGURS	AHMMSY	SHAMMY	AIKNNS	SANK IN
AGRSUY	SUGARY	AHMNNU	NUMNAH	AIKNPR	PARKIN
AGRUUY	AUGURY	AHMNOS	HANSOM	AIKNSS	ASKS IN
AGSTUU	AUGUST	AHMNSU	HUMANS	AIKOPS	OKAPIS
AHHKOO	HOOKAH	AHMOOP	OOMPAH	AIKORT	TROIKA
AHHLPY	HYPHAL	AHMOTU	MAHOUT	AIKRST	AT RISK
AHHOOS	HOO-HAS	AHMRSY	MARSHY		KRAITS
AHHRRU	HURRAH	AHMRTW	WARMTH	AIKRSU	KAURIS
AHHRST	THRASH	AHNNSY	SHANNY	AIKTUW	KUWAIT
AHIILT	LITHIA	AHNOOT	ON OATH	AILLMU	ALLIUM
AHIINT	TAHINI	AHNOPR	ORPHAN	AILLNW	WALL IN
AHIJJS	HAJJIS	AHNORS	SHORAN	AILLPR	PILLAR
AHIKMS	HAKIMS	AHNOST	HAS NOT	AILLSV	VILLAS
AHIKOW	KOWHAI	AHNOWY	ANY HOW	AILLTW	AT WILL
AHIKRS	RAKISH		ANYHOW	AILLYZ	LAZILY
AHIKST	SHAKTI	AHNRTW	THRAWN	AILMNR	MARLIN

AILMNU	ALUMNI	AIMNSZ	NAZISM	AIPRTY	PARITY
	LUMINA		NIZAMS	AIPRUY	PYURIA
AILMNY	MAINLY	AIMOPT	OPTIMA	AIPSST	PASTIS
AILMOS	SOMALI	AIMOPY	MYOPIA	AIPSTT	PAST IT
AILMOT	MALOTI	AIMORS	MAORIS	AIPSTW	SAW-PIT
AILMPR	PRIMAL	AIMOST	MAOIST	AIPSZZ	PIZZAS
AILMRT	MITRAL		TAOISM	AIPTUW	WAIT UP
AILMSS	MISSAL	AIMOSW	MIAOWS	AIRRTY	RARITY
AILMST	TAMILS	AIMOSX	AXIOMS	AIRSST	SISTRA
AILMSX	SMILAX	AIMPRT	ARMPIT		SITARS
AILMSY	MISLAY		IMPART		STAIRS
AILMTU	ULTIMA	AIMPSS	PASSIM	AIRSTT	ARTIST
AILMUV	VALIUM	AIMQSU	MAQUIS		STRAIT
AILNNP	PINNAL	AIMRTU	ATRIUM		STRATI
AILNNU	ANNULI	AIMRTX	MATRIX		TRAITS
AILNPS	PLAINS	AIMSTU	AUTISM	AISSST	ASSIST
	SPINAL	AINNNT	TANNIN		STASIS
AILNPT	PLAINT	AINNOS	ANIONS	AISSTV	VISTAS
	PLIANT	AINNOT	ANOINT	AISSTW	WAISTS
AILNPY	IN PLAY		NATION	AJLOPY	JALOPY
AILNRT	TRINAL	AINNPS	PINNAS	AJMNOS	JAMS ON
AILNRU	URINAL	AINNTW	WANT IN	AJMOPT	JAM POT
AILNSS	SNAILS	AINNUZ	ZUNIAN	AJMORS	MAJORS
AILNST	IN LAST	AINOPS	PIANOS	AJMPTU	JUMP AT
	LAST IN	AINORT	RATION	AJNORT	TROJAN
	LATINS	AINORW	IN A ROW	AJNOST	ST. JOAN
AILNSV	ANVILS	AINOST	TAINOS	AJNSTU	JAUNTS
	SILVAN	AINOSU	SIOUAN		JUNTAS
AILNSW	IN LAWS	AINPRS	SPRAIN	AJNTUY	JAUNTY
	IN-LAWS	AINPRT	IN PART	AJPRTU	RAJPUT
AILNSY	INLAYS	AINPST	PAINTS	AKKLSU	KULAKS
AILNTY	LITANY	AINPSV	SPAVIN	AKLLNY	LANKLY
AILNVY	VAINLY	AINPTU	TUPIAN	AKLLSY	ALKYLS
AILNYZ	ZANILY	AINPTY	PAINTY	AKLNOW	WALK ON
AILORS	SAILOR	AINQTU	QUAINT		WALK-ON
AILORT	TAILOR	AINRST	INSTAR	AKLNOX	KLAXON
AILOSV	VALOIS		STRAIN	AKLNPS	PLANKS
	VIOLAS		TRAINS	AKLNRY	RANKLY
AILOTX	OXTAIL	AINRTU	IN A RUT	AKLOOT	LOOK AT
AILPPS	PIPALS		NUTRIA	AKLOPS	POLKAS
AILPRS	APRILS	AINRTY	IN TRAY	AKLOSV	SLOVAK
	SPIRAL	AINSST	SAINTS	AKLPUW	WALK UP
AILPST	PLAITS		SATINS	AKLSST	STALKS
AILPSU	PILAUS		STAINS	AKLSTY	STALKY
AILQSU	QUAILS	AINSSV	SAVINS	AKMNSU	UNMASK
AILRST	TRAILS	AINSSW	SWAINS	AKMPRU	MARKUP
	TRIALS	AINSTT	TAINTS	AKMRST	ST. MARK
AILRSV	RIVALS		TITANS	AKNOOT	NOOTKA
AILRSY	RIYALS	AINSTU	AUSTIN	AKNORU	KORUNA
AILRTU	RITUAL	AINSTY	SANITY	AKNPRS	PRANKS
AILRTY	ARTILY		SATINY	AKNPSS	SPANKS
AILRWY	WARILY	AINSUX	AUXINS	AKNSSW	SWANKS
AILSTV	VITALS	AINTVY	VANITY	AKNSWY	SWANKY
AILSUV	VISUAL	AIOPRV	PAVIOR	AKOORR	KARROO
AILVWY	WAVILY	AIOPST	PATIOS	AKOOSZ	KAZOOS
AIMMOS	MAOISM		PATOIS	AKOPSY	YAPOKS
	MIMOSA	AIOPTU	UTOPIA	AKORTW	AT WORK
AIMMSX	MAXIMS	AIORST	AORIST	AKOSTU	ASK OUT
AIMNNO	AMNION		RATIOS	AKPRSS	SPARKS
	MINOAN		SATORI	AKQRSU	QUARKS
	NOMINA	AIORSY	ORIYAS	AKQSUW	SQUAWK
AIMNNT	TINMAN	AIOSTT	TAOIST	AKRSTU	KRAUTS
AIMNNU	NUMINA	AIPPRR	RIPRAP	AKSWYY	SKYWAY
AIMNPT	PIT MAN	AIPPRY	PAPYRI	ALLMOS	SLALOM
	PITMAN	AIPPST	PAPIST	ALLMOW	MALLOW
AIMNRS	IN ARMS	AIPRSS	PARSIS	ALLMSS	SMALLS
AIMNRT	MARTIN	AIPRST	RAPIST	ALLNOS	LLANOS
AIMNRU	RUMINA		TAPIRS	ALLNSU	NULLAS
AIMNST	MANTIS	AIPRSV	PARVIS	ALLOOP	PALOLO
	MATINS	AIPRSW	RIPSAW	ALLOPR	PALLOR
AIMNSU	ANIMUS	AIPRSX	PRAXIS	ALLOPW	WALLOP

ALLORY	ORALLY	ALPPSU	PALPUS	AMRRTY	MARTYR
ALLOST	ALLOTS		SLAP-UP	AMRSST	SMARTS
	ATOLLS	ALPPUY	PLAY UP	AMRSSW	SWARMS
ALLOSW	ALLOWS	ALPRRU	LARRUP	AMRSTU	STRUMA
	SALLOW	ALPRSU	PULSAR	ANNOPS	SNAP-ON
ALLOSY	ALLOYS	ALPRSW	SPRAWL	ANNORT	NATRON
ALLOTU	ALL OUT	ALPRTY	PALTRY	ANNOST	SONANT
	ALL-OUT		PARTLY	ANNOSY	ANNOYS
ALLOTW	TALLOW	ALPSST	SPLATS	ANNOTW	WANTON
ALLOUY	YOU-ALL	ALPSSY	SPLAYS	ANNOTY	TANNOY
ALLOVY	OVALLY	ALPSTU	ST. PAUL	ANNRTY	TRANNY
ALLOWW	WALLOW	ALPSUY	LAYS UP	ANNSTU	SUNTAN
ALLOWY	LAY LOW	ALRSTU	LUSTRA	ANOORT	RATOON
ALLPRU	PLURAL	ALRSTW	TRAWLS	ANOPRS	APRONS
ALLPSS	SPALLS	ALRSTY	STYLAR		PARSON
ALLPUW	WALL UP	ALRSUW	WALRUS	ANOPRT	PATRON
ALLQSU	SQUALL	ALRTTY	TARTLY	ANOPSS	PASS ON
ALLSST	STALLS	ALRUUV	UVULAR	ANOPST	PANTOS
ALLSTY	LASTLY	ALRUVV	VULVAR	ANORRW	NARROW
ALLUVV	VULVAL	ALSTUV	VAULTS	ANORSS	SONARS
ALMNOR	NORMAL	ALSTVY	VASTLY	ANORSV	SOVRAN
ALMNOS	SALMON	ALSUUV	UVULAS	ANORSW	ROWANS
ALMORS	MOLARS	ALSUVV	VULVAS	ANORTU	OUTRAN
	MORALS	ALTTUY	TAUTLY		RAN OUT
ALMORT	MORTAL	ALTUUV	TUVALU	ANORTY	NOTARY
ALMORU	MORULA	ALTUVY	VAULTY	ANORWY	NORWAY
ALMOST	ALMOST	AMMMNO	MAMMON	ANOSSX	SAXONS
	STOMAL	AMMMOS	MOMMAS	ANOSTX	TAXONS
ALMPSS	PSALMS	AMMORT	MARMOT	ANOSXY	SAXONY
ALMQSU	QUALMS	AMMOSU	OMASUM	ANPPSY	SNAPPY
ALMRSU	MURALS	AMMOXY	MYXOMA	ANPRSW	PRAWNS
ALMRWY	WARMLY	AMMPUW	WAMPUM	ANPRTY	PANTRY
ALMSST	SMALTS	AMMRSS	SMARMS	ANPRUW	UNWRAP
ALMSUY	ASYLUM	AMMRSY	SMARMY	ANPSSW	SPAWNS
ALMTUU	MUTUAL	AMMSTU	SUMMAT	ANRSTU	RUNS AT
	UMLAUT	AMNNOR	NORMAN		SATURN
ALNNSU	ANNULS	AMNNOY	ANONYM	ANRSUU	URANUS
ALNOOS	SALOON	AMNOOR	MAROON	ANRSUY	SUNRAY
ALNOPY	NO PLAY	AMNOPT	TAMPON	ANRTTU	TRUANT
	PLAY ON	AMNORS	MANORS	ANRTTY	TYRANT
ALNOSS	SALONS		RANSOM	ANRUWY	RUNWAY
ALNOST	TALONS		ROMANS		UNWARY
ALNOSY	LAYS ON	AMNORT	MATRON	ANSTTU	TAUNTS
ALNOTV	VOLANT	AMNORY	ROMANY	ANSTUV	VAUNTS
ALNPST	PLANTS	AMNOSS	MASONS	ANSTXY	SYNTAX
ALNRSS	SNARLS	AMNOTU	AMOUNT	ANSYZZ	SNAZZY
ALNRSY	SNARLY	AMNOTY	MAY NOT	AOOPTT	POTATO
ALNRXY	LARYNX	AMNRTU	ANTRUM	AOORRT	ORATOR
ALNSST	SLANTS	AMNTTU	MUTANT	AOOTTT	TATTOO
ALNSTU	SULTAN	AMNTUU	AUTUMN	AOPPPS	POPPAS
ALNSUY	UNLAYS	AMOOTT	TOMATO	AOPPRS	APPROS
ALNSVY	SYLVAN	AMOPRS	PRO-AMS	AOPPRT	POP ART
ALNTUW	WALNUT	AMOPTU	MAP OUT	AOPRRT	PARROT
ALOPPR	POPLAR	AMORRT	MORTAR		RAPTOR
ALOPRT	PATROL	AMORRU	ARMOUR	AOPRRU	UPROAR
	PORTAL	AMORRW	MARROW	AOPRST	PASTOR
ALOPST	POSTAL	AMORSS	MORASS	AOPRUV	VAPOUR
ALOQTU	LOQUAT	AMORST	STROMA	AOPTUY	PAY OUT
ALORSV	SALVOR		TO ARMS		PAY-OUT
ALORSY	ROYALS	AMORSU	AMOURS	AOQRTU	QUARTO
ALORTU	TORULA	AMORSY	MAYORS	AOQSTU	QUOTAS
ALORUV	OVULAR	AMOSST	STOMAS	AORRST	ROSTRA
	VALOUR	AMOSTT	AT MOST	AORRSW	ARROWS
ALOSSS	LASSOS	AMOSTZ	MATZOS	AORRSY	ROSARY
ALOSSV	SALVOS	AMPRST	TRAMPS	AORRSZ	RAZORS
ALOSTT	TOTALS	AMPRUW	WARM UP	AORRTY	ROTARY
ALOTUW	OUTLAW		WARM-UP	AORRWY	YARROW
ALOTUY	LAY OUT	AMPSSS	SPASMS	AORSST	ASSORT
	LAYOUT	AMPSST	STAMPS		ROASTS
	OUTLAY	AMPSSW	SWAMPS	AORSTT	STATOR
		AMPSWY	SWAMPY	AORSTX	STORAX

AORSUU	AUROUS	BBDEOS	SOBBED	BCEEHR	BREECH
AORSUV	SAVOUR	BBDERU	DUBBER	BCEEKT	BECKET
AORSVY	SAVORY		RUBBED	BCEEMO	BECOME
AORTVY	VOTARY	BBDESU	SUBBED	BCEEQU	QUEBEC
AOSSSY	SAYS SO	BBDETU	TUBBED	BCEERS	REBECS
AOSSTT	STOATS	BBDINO	DOBBIN	BCEHLN	BLENCH
	TOASTS	BBDINU	DUBBIN	BCEHOS	BOCHES
AOSTTU	SAT OUT	BBDKUY	DYBBUK	BCEHRU	CHERUB
AOSTUW	SAW OUT	BBEELP	PEBBLE	BCEIKR	BICKER
AOTUWY	WAY OUT	BBEERR	BERBER	BCEIOR	CORBIE
	WAY-OUT	BBEEYY	BYE-BYE	BCEIOX	ICE BOX
AOTWWY	TWO WAY	BBEFIR	FIBBER		ICEBOX
	TWO-WAY	BBEGIN	EBBING	BCEIPS	BICEPS
APPPSU	PAPPUS	BBEGIR	GIBBER	BCEIRS	SCRIBE
APPRUW	WRAP UP	BBEGIT	GIBBET	BCEIST	BISECT
APPSSU	PASS UP	BBEGLO	GOBBLE	BCEJOT	OBJECT
APPSUY	PAYS UP	BBEGOT	GOBBET	BCEKLU	BUCKLE
APRSST	SPRATS	BBEHLO	HOBBLE	BCEKNO	BECKON
	STRAPS	BBEIIM	IMBIBE	BCEKTU	BUCKET
APRSSY	SPRAYS	BBEIJR	JIBBER	BCELOR	CORBEL
APRSTY	PASTRY	BBEIKL	KIBBLE	BCELOS	COBLES
APRTTU	TART UP	BBEILN	NIBBLE	BCELOU	BOUCLE
APSTUY	STAY UP	BBEILS	BIBLES	BCEMOO	COOMBE
AQRRUY	QUARRY	BBEIRR	BRIBER	BCEMOR	COMBER
AQRSTU	QUARTS	BBEIRS	BRIBES	BCEMOS	COMBES
AQRTUZ	QUARTZ	BBELMU	BUMBLE	BCEMOY	COME BY
AQSSTU	SQUATS	BBELNO	NOBBLE	BCEMRU	CUMBER
AQSSUW	SQUAWS	BBELNU	NUBBLE	BCENOS	BONCES
ARRSTY	STARRY	BBELOW	LOW EBB	BCENOU	BOUNCE
ARSSST	STRASS		WOBBLE	BCERSU	CUBERS
ARSSTT	STARTS	BBELPY	PEBBLY	BCGINU	CUBING
ARSSTU	TARSUS		PLEBBY	BCHIOP	PHOBIC
ARSSTW	STRAWS	BBELRU	BURBLE	BCHITY	BITCHY
ARSSTY	SATYRS		LUBBER	BCHLOT	BLOTCH
	STRAYS		RUBBLE	BCHNRU	BRUNCH
ARSTTU	STUART	BBEMNU	BENUMB	BCHNUY	BUNCHY
ARSTUU	TAURUS	BBEMOR	BOMBER	BCHOOR	BROOCH
ARSTUX	SURTAX	BBEMOS	BOMBES	BCHORS	BORSCH
ARSTWY	STRAWY	BBEORR	ROBBER	BCHOTY	BOTCHY
ARSTXY	STYRAX	BBEOSU	BUBOES	BCIILM	LIMBIC
ASSTTU	STATUS	BBERRU	RUBBER	BCIINO	BIONIC
BBBDEO	BOBBED	BBETUY	BY TUBE	BCIINU	INCUBI
BBBEIR	BIBBER	BBGINO	GIBBON	BCIIOT	BIOTIC
BBBELO	BOBBLE	BBGIOY	BIG BOY	BCIKRS	BRICKS
BBBELU	BUBBLE	BBGRUY	GRUBBY	BCILMS	CLIMBS
BBBEOR	BOBBER	BBHIOT	HOBBIT	BCILPU	PUBLIC
BBBHUU	HUBBUB	BBHMOS	H BOMBS	BCIMOR	BROMIC
BBBINO	BOBBIN		H-BOMBS	BCIMSU	CUBISM
BBBLUY	BUBBLY	BBHNOO	HOBNOB	BCIRRU	RUBRIC
BBCELO	COBBLE	BBIKOS	SKIBOB	BCISTU	CUBIST
BBCEOR	COBBER	BBINOR	RIBBON		CUBITS
BBCEOW	COBWEB	BBKNOY	KNOBBY	BCKLOS	BLOCKS
BBCHSU	CHUBBS	BBLLUU	BULBUL	BCKLUY	BY LUCK
BBCHUY	CHUBBY	BBLNUY	NUBBLY	BCKORS	BROCKS
BBDDEU	DUBBED	BBLOWY	BY-BLOW	BCKPUU	BUCK UP
BBDEEW	WEBBED		WOBBLY	BCMOOS	COMBOS
BBDEFI	FIBBED	BBLRSU	BLURBS		COOMBS
BBDEGU	BED BUG	BBMRUY	BRUMBY	BCMORY	CORYMB
	BEDBUG	BBNNOO	BONBON	BCMRSU	CRUMBS
BBDEIJ	JIBBED	BBNOSY	SNOBBY	BCNOOR	BRONCO
BBDEIL	DIBBLE	BBNOTU	NOBBUT	BCNOTU	COBNUT
BBDEIN	NIBBED	BBOOSY	YOBBOS	BCNOUY	BOUNCY
BBDEIR	BRIBED	BBORTU	BURBOT	BCOOWY	COWBOY
	DIBBER	BBRSUU	SUBURB	BCRSSU	SCRUBS
	RIBBED	BBSTUY	STUBBY	BDDDEE	BEDDED
BBDEJO	JOBBED	BCDEEK	BEDECK	BDDDEU	BUDDED
BBDELO	LOBBED	BCDEIO	BODICE	BDDEER	BEDDER
BBDEMO	BOMBED	BCDEKU	BUCKED	BDDEGO	BODGED
	MOBBED	BCDEMO	COMBED	BDDEGU	BUDGED
BBDEOO	BOOBED	BCDERU	CURBED	BDDEIN	BIDDEN
BBDEOR	ROBBED	BCDIOU	CUBOID	BDDEIR	BIDDER

BDDENO	BONDED	BDEKRU	BURKED	BDNOTU	OBTUND
BDDIOR	DO BIRD	BDEKSU	BUSKED	BDOORS	BROODS
BDDISU	DISBUD	BDELLU	BULLED	BDOORY	BROODY
BDDJOO	ODD JOB	BDELNO	BLONDE	BDOPRY	DROP BY
BDEEEF	BEEFED	BDELNS	BLENDS	BDORWY	BYWORD
BDEEEN	NEED BE	BDELNU	BUNDLE	BDOSTU	DOUBTS
BDEEEP	BEEPED	BDELOO	BOODLE	BEEEFL	FEEBLE
BDEEGG	BEGGED	BDELOT	BOLTED	BEEELT	BEETLE
BDEEHL	BEHELD	BDELOU	DOUBLE	BEEEPR	BEEPER
BDEEIL	EDIBLE	BDELOW	BOWLED	BEEERZ	BREEZE
BDEEIS	BESIDE	BDELRU	BURLED	BEEESV	BEEVES
BDEEIT	BETIDE	BDEMMU	BUMMED	BEEFIL	BELIEF
BDEELL	BELLED	BDEMOO	BOOMED	BEEFLL	BEFELL
BDEELN	BLENDE	BDEMOS	DEMOBS	BEEFLT	LEFT BE
BDEELS	BLEEDS	BDEMOW	WOMBED	BEEFLY	BEE FLY
BDEELT	BELTED	BDEMOY	EMBODY		FEEBLY
BDEEMS	EMBEDS	BDEMPU	DUMPED	BEEFOR	BEFORE
BDEENO	BE DONE	BDEMRU	DUMBER	BEEFRT	BEREFT
BDEENR	BENDER	BDENNU	UNBEND	BEEGIS	BEIGES
BDEEOY	OBEYED	BDENOR	BONDER	BEEGLS	GLEBES
BDEERS	BREEDS	BDENOY	BEYOND	BEEGLY	LEG BYE
BDEERW	BREWED	BDENRU	BURDEN	BEEGNO	BEGONE
BDEEST	BESTED		BURNED	BEEGRS	GREBES
BDEETT	BETTED	BDENTU	BUNTED	BEEGRU	BURGEE
BDEFFU	BUFFED	BDEOOT	BOOTED	BEEGST	BEGETS
BDEGGU	BUGGED	BDEOOZ	BOOZED	BEEHLT	BETHEL
BDEGIL	BILGED	BDEOPP	BOPPED	BEEHOV	BEHOVE
BDEGIN	BIG END	BDEOPR	PROBED	BEEHRW	HEBREW
BDEGIR	BRIDGE	BDEORR	BORDER	BEEHRY	HEREBY
BDEGIU	BUDGIE	BDEORS	DESORB	BEEHST	BEHEST
BDEGLU	BUGLED		SORBED	BEEILR	BELIER
	BULGED	BDEORT	DEBTOR	BEEILS	BELIES
BDEGNU	BUNGED	BDEOSS	BOSSED	BEEILZ	BELIZE
BDEGOS	BODGES	BDEOTU	BED OUT	BEEIMR	BIREME
BDEGSU	BUDGES	BDEOUY	BUOYED	BEEIST	BETISE
	DEBUGS	BDEPRU	BURPED	BEEISV	BEVIES
BDEGTU	BUDGET	BDERRU	BURRED	BEEISX	IBEXES
BDEHIN	BEHIND	BDESSU	BUSSED	BEEKRS	BREEKS
BDEHLO	BEHOLD	BDESTU	BUSTED	BEEKRU	REBUKE
BDEHOT	HOTBED		DEBUTS	BEELLS	BELLES
BDEHSU	BUSHED	BDESUU	SUBDUE	BEELMM	EMBLEM
BDEIIM	IBIDEM	BDETTU	BUTTED	BEELPS	BLEEPS
BDEIIR	BIRDIE	BDEUZZ	BUZZED	BEELRS	REBELS
BDEIKL	BILKED	BDFIOR	FORBID	BEELRT	TREBLE
BDEILL	BILLED	BDGINO	BODING	BEELST	BETELS
BDEILM	LIMBED	BDHIOS	DHOBIS		LETS BE
BDEILO	BOILED	BDHIRY	HYBRID	BEELSV	BEVELS
	BOLIDE	BDIILO	LIBIDO	BEELSZ	BEZELS
BDEILR	BRIDLE	BDIIMR	MIDRIB	BEEMMR	MEMBER
BDEIMS	IMBEDS	BDIITT	TIDBIT	BEEMRS	BERMES
BDEIMU	IMBUED	BDIKNO	BODKIN		EMBERS
BDEINR	BINDER	BDILNS	BLINDS	BEEMSU	BEMUSE
	BRINED	BDILOY	BODILY	BEEOOT	BOOTEE
	INBRED	BDILSU	BUILDS	BEEORR	REBORE
BDEINT	IN DEBT	BDIMOR	MORBID	BEERRV	REVERB
BDEINU	BEDUIN	BDINNU	UNBIND	BEERRW	BREWER
BDEIOR	BORIDE	BDINPU	BIND UP	BEERST	BERETS
BDEIOS	BODIES	BDINTY	BY DINT	BEERSV	BREVES
BDEIPS	BIPEDS	BDIOTU	OUTBID	BEERTT	BETTER
BDEIRS	BIDERS	BDIPSU	BIDS UP	BEERTV	BREVET
	BRIDES	BDIRTU	TURBID	BEERYZ	BREEZY
	DEBRIS	BDKLOO	KOBOLD	BEESST	BESETS
BDEIRU	BURIED	BDLLOY	BOLDLY		ST. BEES
BDEIST	BED-SIT	BDLMUY	DUMBLY	BEFFRU	BUFFER
	BIDETS	BDLNOS	BLONDS		REBUFF
	DEBITS	BDLOOS	BLOODS	BEFFTU	BUFFET
BDEISU	BUSIED	BDLOOY	BLOODY	BEFGOS	BEFOGS
BDEKLU	BULKED		OLD BOY	BEFHOO	BEHOOF
BDEKNU	BUNKED	BDLOUY	DOUBLY	BEFILO	FOIBLE
	DEBUNK	BDNOOY	NOBODY	BEFIRS	BRIEFS
BDEKOO	BOOKED	BDNOSU	BOUNDS		FIBRES

BEFIST	BEFITS	BEINTT	BITTEN	BELSUY	BLUESY
BEFLMU	FUMBLE	BEIOOT	BOOTIE		BLUEYS
BEFLRY	BELFRY	BEIORS	RIBOSE	BELTUU	TUBULE
BEFLWY	FLEW BY	BEIOST	TOBIES	BEMMRU	BUMMER
BEGGIR	BIGGER	BEIOTW	BOW TIE	BEMNOT	ENTOMB
BEGGLO	BOGGLE	BEIQSU	BISQUE	BEMNOW	BOWMEN
BEGGOX	EGG BOX	BEIRRS	BRIERS	BEMNRU	NUMBER
BEGILO	OBLIGE	BEIRRY	BRIERY	BEMNSU	BUSMEN
BEGILR	GERBIL	BEIRST	BESTIR	BEMOOR	BOOMER
BEGILS	BILGES		BISTRE	BEMORS	OMBRES
BEGINN	BENIGN		BITERS		SOMBRE
BEGINS	BEGINS		TRIBES	BEMORY	EMBRYO
	BEINGS	BEIRSU	BRUISE	BEMOSS	BESOMS
	BINGES		BURIES		EMBOSS
BEGIOO	BOOGIE		BUSIER	BEMPRU	BUMPER
BEGIOS	BOGIES		RUBIES	BEMRSU	UMBERS
	GOBIES	BEIRTT	BITTER	BENNOT	BONNET
BEGIOU	BOUGIE	BEISSU	BUSIES	BENNSU	BUNSEN
BEGLNO	BELONG	BEISTZ	ZIBETS	BENNTU	UNBENT
BEGLNU	BUNGLE	BEITUY	UBIETY	BENORR	REBORN
BEGLOS	BOGLES	BEJJUU	JUJUBE	BENORS	BONERS
	GLOBES	BEJLMU	JUMBLE	BENORT	BRETON
BEGLOT	GOBLET	BEJOVY	BY JOVE!	BENORU	BOURNE
BEGLOW	BOW LEG	BEKLOS	BLOKES	BENORZ	BRONZE
BEGLRU	BUGLER	BEKNOR	BROKEN	BENOST	T BONES
	BURGLE	BEKNRU	BUNKER		T-BONES
BEGLSU	BUGLES	BEKOOR	BOOKER	BENOTY	BETONY
	BULGES	BEKOOT	BETOOK	BENRRU	BURNER
BEGNOY	BYGONE	BEKORR	BROKER	BENRTU	BUNTER
	GONE BY	BEKRSU	BURKES		BURNET
BEGORU	BROGUE		BUSKER	BENTWY	WENT BY
BEGOSY	BOGEYS	BELLOU	BOULLE	BEOORZ	BOOZER
	GOES BY		LOBULE	BEOOSZ	BOOZES
BEGRRU	BURGER	BELLOW	BELLOW	BEOPPR	BOPPER
BEGSTY	GETS BY	BELLTU	BULLET	BEOPRR	PROBER
BEHILT	BLITHE	BELLUY	BLUELY	BEOPRS	PROBES
BEHKRY	KHYBER	BELMMU	MUMBLE	BEOPRU	BORE UP
BEHLMU	HUMBLE	BELMOW	BLOW ME!	BEORRS	BORERS
BEHLSU	BUSHEL		WOMBLE		RESORB
BEHOOS	HOBOES	BELMRU	LUMBER	BEORSS	SOBERS
BEHORT	BOTHER		RUMBLE	BEORST	SORBET
BEHOTX	THE BOX	BELMSU	UMBELS		STROBE
BEHRST	BERTHS		UMBLES	BEORSU	BOURSE
BEHSSU	BUSHES	BELMTU	TUMBLE	BEORSW	BOWERS
BEIINT	BITE IN	BELNNY	BLENNY		BROWSE
BEIISS	IBISES	BELNOR	NOBLER	BEORSX	BOXERS
BEIKLR	BILKER	BELNOS	NOBLES	BEORTT	BETTOR
BEIKOO	BOOKIE	BELNOZ	BENZOL	BEORVV	BOVVER
BEILLS	LIBELS	BELOOR	BOLERO	BEORWY	BOWERY
BEILLT	BILLET	BELOPU	PUEBLO		BOWYER
BEILMN	NIMBLE	BELORT	BOLTER	BEOSSS	BOSSES
BEILMO	EMBOLI	BELORU	ROUBLE		OBSESS
	MOBILE	BELORW	BLOWER	BEOSTT	OBTEST
BEILMR	LIMBER		BOWLER	BEOSTU	OBTUSE
BEILMY	BLIMEY	BELOST	BOTELS	BEOSTW	BESTOW
BEILNU	IN BLUE	BELOSU	BLOUSE	BEOTUY	YOU BET!
	NUBILE		BOULES	BEPRSU	SUPERB
BEILNY	BY-LINE	BELOSW	BOWELS	BEPRUW	BREW UP
BEILOR	BOILER		ELBOWS	BERSTU	BRUTES
BEILOT	BOLETI	BELOTT	BOTTLE		BUSTER
BEIMNN	BINMEN	BELPTU	BELT UP		REBUTS
BEIMOZ	ZOMBIE	BELPUW	BLEW UP	BERSUX	EXURBS
BEIMRT	TIMBER	BELRRU	BURLER	BERSUY	BUYERS
	TIMBRE	BELRSU	RUBLES	BERTTU	BUTTER
BEIMRU	ERBIUM	BELRTU	BUTLER	BERUZZ	BUZZER
	IMBRUE	BELRTY	TREBLY	BESSTU	SUBSET
BEIMSU	IMBUES	BELSTU	BLUEST	BESTTU	BUTTES
BEINOR	BONIER		BUSTLE	BESUZZ	BUZZES
BEINOV	BOVINE		SUBLET	BFFFOO	FOB OFF
BEINRS	BRINES		SUBTLE	BFFINO	BOFFIN
BEINRU	BRUNEI			BFFIOT	BIT OFF

BFFLSU	BLUFFS	BIKNSU	BUSKIN	BNOSUW	SUNBOW
BFFOSU	BUFFOS	BILLNO	BILLON	BNOTTU	BUTTON
BFFOUY	BUY OFF	BILLOW	BILLOW	BNOTUY	BOUNTY
BFGOOW	FOGBOW	BILLOY	BILLY-O	BNPRUU	BURN-UP
BFIILR	FIBRIL	BILMNY	NIMBLY	BOOOTT	TO BOOT
BFIINR	FIBRIN	BILMPS	BLIMPS	BOOPTY	POTBOY
BFIMOR	BIFORM	BILOPU	BOIL UP	BOORRW	BORROW
BFIORS	FIBROS	BILORS	BROILS	BOORST	ROBOTS
BFLOTY	BOTFLY	BILORV	BOVRIL	BOOSST	BOOSTS
BFLOUX	BOXFUL	BILOTW	BLOW IT	BOOSWX	OX BOWS
BFLTUU	TUBFUL	BILRTY	TRILBY		OXBOWS
BFOOTY	BY FOOT	BILSSY	SIBYLS	BOOWWW	BOW WOW
BGGIIN	GIBING	BILSUY	BUSILY		BOWWOW
BGGIIW	BIGWIG	BIMNSU	NIMBUS	BOPSTY	BY POST
BGGINY	GYBING	BIMSTU	SUBMIT	BOPUUY	BUOY UP
BGHIIT	BLIGHT	BINNOR	INBORN	BORRSU	BURROS
BGHIRT	BRIGHT	BINNOU	BUNION	BORRUW	BURROW
BGHMUU	HUMBUG	BINOOT	BONITO	BORSTU	ROBUST
BGHOSU	BOUGHS	BINORS	ROBINS	BORTTU	TURBOT
BGHOTU	BOUGHT	BINORT	BRITON	BORTUU	RUB OUT
BGHRSU	BURGHS	BINRSU	BURINS	BOTUUY	BUY OUT
BGIIJN	JIBING		RUBS IN	BPRSUU	RUBS UP
BGIIKN	BIKING	BINSUY	BUYS IN	BPSTUU	BUST UP
BGIINT	BITING	BINTTU	BUTT IN		BUST-UP
BGILLY	CLIBLY	BIOORZ	BORZOI	BPSTUY	PUTS BY
BGILNO	GLOBIN	BIOOST	OBOIST	BPSUUY	BUYS UP
	GOBLIN	BIOPRT	PROBIT	BRSSTU	BURSTS
BGILNU	BLUING	BIOPSY	BIOPSY	BSSSUY	BYSSUS
BGINNO	BONING	BIORST	BISTRO	CCCILY	CYCLIC
BGINOO	BOOING		ORBITS	CCCOSU	COCCUS
BGINOR	BORING	BIOTTW	TWO BIT	CCCOXY	COCCYX
	ROBING		TWO-BIT	CCDEER	RECCED
BGINOW	BOWING	BIQSSU	SQUIBS	CCDEKO	COCKED
BGINOX	BOXING	BIRSTU	BRUITS	CCDEOT	DECOCT
BGINRS	BRINGS	BJLOOT	JOB LOT	CCEEHR	CRECHE
BGINTU	TUBING	BJMOSU	JUMBOS	CCEEOR	COERCE
BGIOPT	BIG TOP	BKMNUU	BUNKUM	CCEERS	RECCES
BGIOST	BIGOTS	BKOOPU	BOOK UP	CCEHIL	CHICLE
BGLNOO	OBLONG	BKOORS	BROOKS		CLICHE
BGMOSU	GUMBOS	BLLORY	BROLLY	CCEHIO	CHOICE
BGNOOS	BONGOS	BLMNUY	NUMBLY		ECHOIC
BGNPUU	BUNG UP	BLMOOS	BLOOMS	CCEHIT	HECTIC
BGOORU	BURGOO	BLMOOY	BLOOMY	CCEHKS	CHECKS
BGOSTU	GO BUST	BLMOSY	SYMBOL	CCEHLN	CLENCH
BHIKOS	KIBOSH	BLMPSU	PLUMBS	CCEHLO	CLOCHE
BHILSU	BLUISH	BLNOTU	UNBOLT	CCEHSZ	CZECHS
BHIMOR	RHOMBI	BLNSTU	BLUNTS	CCEIIL	ICICLE
BHIOPS	BISHOP	BLOOTT	BLOTTO	CCEIIN	ICENIC
BHIOSY	BOYISH	BLOOWY	LOWBOY	CCEILR	CIRCLE
BHIPSY	BY SHIP	BLOPUW	BLOW UP		CLERIC
BHIRST	BIRTHS		BLOWUP	CCEILT	CELTIC
BHIRSU	HUBRIS	BLOSWY	BLOWSY	CCEINS	SCENIC
BHKOOY	BY HOOK	BLRRUY	BLURRY	CCEIPT	PECTIC
BHLMUY	HUMBLY	BLSTUY	BUTYLS	CCEIRU	ERUCIC
BHMORS	RHOMBS		SUBTLY	CCEKLO	COCKLE
BHMRSU	RHUMBS	BMMRUY	BRUMMY	CCEKOP	COPECK
BHMSTU	THUMBS	BMNOOT	BON MOT	CCEKOR	COCKER
BHOOST	BOOTHS	BMOORS	BROOMS	CCELRY	CYCLER
BHORST	THROBS	BMOOSS	BOSOMS	CCELSY	CYCLES
BHRSSU	SHRUBS	BMOOSY	BOSOMY	CCENOS	SCONCE
BIIIKN	BIKINI	BMOOTT	BOTTOM	CCEORS	SOCCER
BIIJTU	JIBUTI	BMOOTY	TOMBOY	CCERSU	CRUCES
BIIKTZ	KIBITZ	BNNORU	UNBORN	CCHHII	CHICHI
BIINOT	BIOTIN	BNOOSS	BOSONS	CCHHRU	CHURCH
BIISTV	VIBIST	BNORSU	BOURNS	CCHIKS	CHICKS
BIITTT	TITBIT		RUBS ON	CCHILN	CLINCH
BIJOSU	BIJOUS		SUBORN	CCHILY	CHICLY
BIJOUX	BIJOUX	BNORSW	BROWNS	CCHIOR	CHORIC
BIKLNS	BLINKS	BNORYY	BRYONY	CCHIPU	HICCUP
BIKLNU	IN BULK	BNORYZ	BRONZY	CCHKOS	CHOCKS
BIKNRS	BRINKS	BNOSSU	BOSUNS	CCHKSU	CHUCKS

CCHLTU	CLUTCH
CCHNOS	CONCHS
CCHNOY	CONCHY
CCHNRU	CRUNCH
CCHORS	SCORCH
CCHORT	CROTCH
CCHORU	CROUCH
CCHOST	SCOTCH
CCHRTU	CRUTCH
CCHSTU	SCUTCH
CCIILN	CLINIC
CCIINO	ICONIC
CCIINP	PICNIC
CCIINZ	ZINCIC
CCIIPR	PICRIC
CCIIRT	CITRIC
	CRITIC
CCIISV	CIVICS
CCIKLS	CLICKS
CCIKRS	CRICKS
CCILNO	CLONIC
CCILTU	CULTIC
CCIMOS	COMICS
	COSMIC
CCIMRY	CYMRIC
CCINSY	CYNICS
CCIOPT	COPTIC
CCIPRU	CUPRIC
CCIRSU	CIRCUS
CCISTY	CYSTIC
CCKLOO	O'CLOCK
CCKLOS	CLOCKS
CCKLSU	CLUCKS
CCKOOU	CUCKOO
CCKOPU	COCK UP
	COCK-UP
CCKORS	CROCKS
CCKRSU	CRUCKS
CCLOTU	OCCULT
CCNOOO	COCOON
CCNORU	CONCUR
CCOOOR	ROCOCO
CCOPUY	OCCUPY
CCORSU	CROCUS
	OCCURS
CCOSTU	STUCCO
CCSSUU	CUSCUS
CDDEEI	DECIDE
CDDEEK	DECKED
CDDEEO	DECODE
CDDEEU	DEDUCE
	DEUCED
	EDUCED
CDDEHI	CHIDED
CDDEIU	CUDDIE
CDDEKO	DOCKED
CDDEKU	DUCKED
CDDELO	CODDLE
CDDELU	CUDDLE
CDDEOR	CORDED
CDDETU	DEDUCT
	DUCTED
CDDLOY	CLODDY
CDDLUY	CUDDLY
CDDRUY	CRUDDY
CDEEEM	EMCEED
CDEEER	DECREE
	RECEDE
CDEEES	SECEDE
CDEEEX	EXCEED
CDEEFN	FENCED
CDEEFT	DEFECT
CDEEHO	ECHOED
CDEEHT	ETCHED
CDEEHW	CHEWED
CDEFIN	EDENIC
CDEEIP	PIECED
CDEEIT	DECEIT
CDEEIV	DEVICE
CDEEKL	DECKLE
CDEEKN	NECKED
CDEEKO	DECOKE
CDEEKP	PECKED
CDEEKR	DECKER
	RECKED
CDEELW	CLEWED
CDEENO	ENCODE
CDEENS	CENSED
CDEENT	DECENT
CDEERS	CEDERS
	CREEDS
	SCREED
CDEERU	REDUCE
CDEERW	CREWED
CDEESU	DEUCES
	SEDUCE
CDEETT	DETECT
CDEFFU	CUFFED
CDEFNU	FECUND
CDEFOR	FORCED
CDEGGO	COGGED
CDEGIN	CEDING
CDEGIO	GEODIC
CDEGLU	CUDGEL
CDEGOR	CODGER
CDEHIL	CHILDE
CDEHIM	CHIMED
CDEHIN	CHINED
	INCHED
	NICHED
	DREICH
CDEHIS	CHIDES
CDEHIT	ITCHED
CDEHKO	CHOKED
	HOCKED
CDEHNR	DRENCH
CDEHOS	COSHED
CDEHOU	DOUCHE
CDEHRU	RUCHED
CDEIKK	KICKED
CDEIKL	LICKED
CDEIKM	MEDICK
CDEIKN	NICKED
CDEIKP	PICKED
CDEIKR	DICKER
	RICKED
CDEIKT	TICKED
CDEIKW	WICKED
CDEIKY	DICKEY
CDEILO	COILED
	DOCILE
CDEILS	SLICED
CDEIMN	MINCED
CDEIMO	MEDICO
CDEIMS	MEDICS
CDEINO	COINED
	IN CODE
	NO DICE
CDEINR	CINDER
CDEINU	INDUCE
CDEINW	WINCED
CDEIOP	COPIED
CDEIOV	VOICED
CDEIPR	PRICED
CDEIPS	SPICED
CDEIPT	DEPICT
CDEIRS	DICERS
	SCRIED
CDEIRT	CREDIT
	DIRECT
	TRICED
CDEIRY	DRY ICE
CDEIST	EDICTS
CDEKLO	LOCKED
CDEKMO	MOCKED
CDEKNO	CONKED
	NOCKED
	ON DECK
CDEKOO	COOKED
CDEKOR	CORKED
	DOCKER
	ROCKED
CDEKOS	SOCKED
CDEKOT	DOCKET
CDEKRU	RUCKED
CDEKSU	SUCKED
CDEKTU	TUCKED
CDELLU	CULLED
CDELNO	CLONED
CDELOO	COOLED
CDELOR	COLDER
CDELOS	CLOSED
CDELOW	COWLED
CDELOY	CLOYED
CDELRU	CURDLE
	CURLED
CDELTU	DULCET
CDEMOO	COMEDO
CDEMOY	COMEDY
CDENNO	CONNED
CDENOP	PONCED
CDENOR	CORNED
CDENOS	SECOND
CDENOT	DOCENT
CDENSS	SCENDS
CDENSU	DUNCES
CDEOOP	COOPED
CDEOPP	COPPED
CDEORR	CORDER
	RECORD
CDEORS	CODERS
	CREDOS
	SCORED
CDEORW	CROWED
CDEOST	COSTED
CDEOSU	ESCUDO
CDEOSY	DECOYS
CDEPPU	CUPPED
CDERRU	CRUDER
CDERSU	CURSED
CDERSY	DESCRY
CDERUV	CURVED
CDESSU	CUSSED
CDFINU	FUNDIC
CDFIOU	FUCOID
CDFIOY	CODIFY
CDGIIN	DICING
CDGINO	CODING
CDHIOR	ORCHID
CDHORS	CHORDS
CDIIIM	IMIDIC
CDIIIR	IRIDIC
CDIINT	INDICT

CDIIOX	OXIDIC	CEEIPR	PIECER	CEFORR	FORCER
CDIIOY	IDIOCY		PIERCE	CEFORS	FORCES
CDIISV	VISCID		RECIPE		FRESCO
CDIKNO	IN DOCK	CEEIPS	PIECES	CEFRUW	CURFEW
CDILNO	CODLIN		SPECIE	CEGGPU	EGG CUP
CDIMTU	DICTUM	CEEIRS	CERISE		EGGCUP
CDINOO	CONOID	CEEIRT	RECITE	CEGHIO	CHIGOE
CDINOR	NORDIC		TIERCE	CEGINR	CRINGE
CDINSY	SYNDIC	CEEISX	EXCISE	CEGINU	CUEING
CDINTU	INDUCT	CEEITX	EXCITE	CEGKOS	GECKOS
CDIOSS	DISCOS	CEEJRT	REJECT	CEGLRY	CLERGY
CDIOST	DICOTS	CEEJST	EJECTS	CEGNOR	CONGER
CDISSU	DISCUS	CEEKPR	PECKER	CEGNOT	COGENT
CDJNOU	JOCUND	CEEKRS	CREEKS	CEGNTY	CYGNET
CDKNOU	UNDOCK	CEELNR	CRENEL	CEGORR	GROCER
CDLLOY	COLDLY	CEELOR	CREOLE	CEHIIN	ECHINI
CDLOSS	SCOLDS	CEELOU	COULEE	CEHIKY	HICKEY
CDLOSU	CLOUDS	CEELRS	CREELS	CEHILN	LICHEN
CDLOUY	CLOUDY	CEELRT	TERCEL	CEHILS	CHISEL
CDMNOO	CONDOM	CEELRV	CLEVER	CEHIMR	CHIMER
CDNOOR	CON ROD	CEELRW	CREWEL	CEHIMS	CHIMES
	CONDOR	CEELRY	CELERY	CEHINR	ENRICH
	CORDON	CEELST	ELECTS		RICHEN
CDNOUW	DUN COW		SELECT	CEHINS	CHINES
CDOORT	DOCTOR	CEELSX	EXCELS		INCHES
CDORSW	CROWDS	CEELSY	LYCEES		NICHES
CEEEFL	FLEECE	CEEMNT	CEMENT	CEHINT	ETHNIC
CEEEGR	GREECE	CEEMRR	MERCER	CEHIOR	HEROIC
CEEEHS	CHEESE	CEEMRS	CREMES	CEHIPR	CIPHER
CEEEMS	EMCEES	CEEMRT	CERMET	CEHIQU	QUICHE
CEEENO	EOCENE	CEENOR	ENCORE	CEHIRR	RICHER
CEEFFO	COFFEE	CEENPT	PECTEN	CEHIRS	RICHES
CEEFFT	EFFECT	CEENRS	CENSER	CEHIRT	THRICE
CEEFHL	FLECHE		SCREEN	CEHIST	ETHICS
CEEFIR	FIERCE	CEENRT	CENTER		ITCHES
CEEFLY	FLEECY		CENTRE	CEHISV	CHIVES
CEEFNN	FENNEC		RECENT	CEHKOR	CHOKER
CEEFNR	FENCER		TENREC	CEHKOS	CHOKES
CEEFNS	FENCES	CEENSS	CENSES	CEHKOY	CHOKEY
CEEFSU	FESCUE		SCENES		HOCKEY
CEEHIL	LICHEE	CEEORV	CORVEE	CEHKST	SKETCH
CEEHIS	SEICHE	CEEPRS	CREEPS	CEHLOR	CHOLER
CEEHKL	HECKLE		CREPES	CEHLOT	CLOTHE
CEEHKS	CHEEKS	CEEPRY	CREEPY	CEHLOU	LOUCHE
CEEHKY	CHEEKY		CREPEY	CEHLPS	SCHLEP
CEEHLR	LECHER	CEEPTX	EXCEPT	CEHMMY	CHEMMY
CEEHLY	LYCHEE		EXPECT	CEHMOR	CHROME
CEEHMS	SCHEME	CEERSS	CESSER	CEHNOS	CHOSEN
CEEHNT	THENCE		RECESS	CEHNQU	QUENCH
CEEHNW	WHENCE	CEERST	ERECTS	CEHNRT	TRENCH
CEEHOR	COHERE		SECRET	CEHNRW	WRENCH
	REECHO		TERCES	CEHNST	STENCH
CEEHOS	ECHOES	CEERSU	CERUSE	CEHNUU	EUNUCH
CEEHOY	ECHOEY		RESCUE	CEHOOS	CHOOSE
CEEHPS	CHEEPS		SECURE	CEHORS	CHORES
	SPEECH	CEERTT	TERCET	CEHORT	HECTOR
CEEHQU	CHEQUE	CEESSX	EXCESS		ROCHET
CEEHRS	CHEERS	CEESUX	EXCUSE		TROCHE
CEEHRT	ETCHER	CEFFIO	COIFFE	CEHOSS	COSHES
CEEHRU	EUCHRE		OFFICE	CEHOTU	TOUCHE
CEEHRW	CHEWER	CEFFOR	COFFER	CEHPRY	CYPHER
CEEHRY	CHEERY	CEFHIS	CHIEFS	CEHPSY	PSYCHE
CEEHST	ETCHES		FICHES	CEHRRY	CHERRY
CEEHSW	ESCHEW	CEFHLT	FLETCH	CEHRSU	RUCHES
CEEHSY	CHEESY	CEFHNR	FRENCH	CEHRTW	WRETCH
CEEIMN	ICEMEN	CEFIKL	FICKLE	CEHRTY	CHERTY
CEEIMT	EMETIC	CEFINT	INFECT	CEHSST	CHESTS
CEEINN	NICENE	CEFIRR	FERRIC	CEHSTU	CHUTES
CEEINS	NIECES	CEFKLS	FLECKS	CEHSTY	CHESTY
CEEINT	ENTICE	CEFLOS	FO'C'SLE		SCYTHE
CEEINV	EVINCE	CEFLST	CLEFTS	CEHTTY	TETCHY

CEIIKR	ICKIER	CEINPR	PINCER	CEKRSW	WRECKS
CEIIKS	SICKIE		PRINCE	CEKRTU	TUCKER
CEIILT	ELICIT	CEINPT	INCEPT	CEKTTU	TUCKET
CEIINS	INCISE		PECTIN	CELLOS	CELLOS
CEIINT	INCITE	CEINQU	QUINCE	CELLOT	COLLET
CEIIST	CITIES	CEINRT	CRETIN	CELLRU	CULLER
	ICIEST	CEINST	INCEST	CELMOO	COELOM
CEIISV	CIVIES		INSECT	CELMOP	COMPEL
CEIJNT	INJECT		NICEST	CELMOY	COMELY
CEIJSU	JUICES	CEINSU	INCUSE	CELMSU	MUSCLE
CEIKKR	KICKER	CEINSW	WINCES	CELNOR	CORNEL
CEIKLM	MICKLE	CEINTY	NICETY	CELNOS	CLONES
CEIKLN	NICKEL	CEINWY	WINCEY	CELNOV	CLOVEN
CEIKLP	PICKLE	CEIOOT	COOTIE	CELNSU	UNCLES
CEIKLS	SICKLE	CEIOPR	COPIER	CELNTU	LUCENT
CEIKLT	KELTIC	CEIOPS	COPIES	CELOOR	COOLER
	TICKLE	CEIOPT	POETIC		LOCOER
CEIKMY	MICKEY	CEIORR	CORRIE	CELOOT	OCELOT
CEIKNR	NICKER	CEIORS	COSIER	CELOPU	COUPLE
CEIKNS	SICKEN	CEIORT	EROTIC	CELORS	CLOSER
CEIKOO	COOKIE	CEIORW	COWRIE		CRESOL
CEIKPR	PICKER	CEIORZ	COZIER	CELORT	LECTOR
CEIKPT	PICKET	CEIOSS	COSIES	CELORV	CLOVER
CEIKRS	SICKER	CEIOSV	VOICES		VELCRO
CEIKRT	TICKER	CEIOSZ	COZIES	CELOSS	CLOSES
CEIKRW	WICKER	CEIOTX	EXOTIC	CELOST	CLOSET
CEIKRY	CRIKEY	CEIPPT	PEPTIC	CELOSU	COLEUS
CEIKTT	TICKET	CEIPRR	PRICER	CELOSV	CLOVES
CEIKTW	WICKET	CEIPRS	CRIPES	CELOSX	SCOLEX
CEILLO	COLLIE		PRECIS	CELOSY	COLEYS
	OCELLI		PRICES	CELOTT	TOLTEC
CEILMS	CLIMES	CEIPRY	PRICEY	CELPSU	CUPELS
CEILNP	PENCIL	CEIPSS	PISCES	CELPUU	CUPULE
CEILNS	CLINES		SPICES	CELRRU	CURLER
CEILNT	CLIENT	CEIPST	SEPTIC	CELRSU	ULCERS
CEILNU	NUCLEI	CEIPTU	CUP TIE	CELRTU	CUTLER
CEILNY	NICELY		CUP-TIE	CELRUU	CURULE
CEILOO	COOLIE	CEIQRU	CIRQUE	CELRUW	CURLEW
CEILOP	POLICE	CEIRRS	CRIERS	CELTTU	CUTLET
CEILOR	RECOIL	CEIRSS	CRISES	CELTUY	CUTELY
CEILPS	SPLICE		SCRIES	CEMNNO	CON MEN
CEILPV	PELVIC	CEIRST	STERIC		CONMEN
CEILPY	CLYPEI		TRICES	CEMNOO	COME ON
CEILQU	CLIQUE	CEIRSU	CRUISE		COME-ON
CEILRS	RELICS		CURIES	CEMNOW	COWMEN
	SLICER	CEIRVX	CERVIX	CEMOOT	COME TO
CEILRT	RELICT	CEISSU	CUISSE	CEMOPU	COME UP
	TRICEL	CEISTU	CUTIES	CEMORS	COMERS
CEILSS	SLICES	CEISTV	CIVETS	CEMOST	COMETS
CEILSU	SLUICE		EVICTS	CEMOSY	CYMOSE
CEILSV	CLEVIS	CEJKOY	JOCKEY	CEMRTU	RECTUM
CEILTU	LUETIC	CEJOOS	JOCOSE	CENOPS	ON SPEC
CEIMMO	COMMIE	CEKKOP	KOPECK		PONCES
CEIMNO	COME IN	CEKLOR	LOCKER	CENOPU	POUNCE
	INCOME	CEKLOT	LOCKET	CENORR	CORNER
CEIMNR	MINCER	CEKLRS	CLERKS	CENORS	CENSOR
CEIMNS	MINCES	CEKLSU	SUCKLE		CRONES
CEIMOT	COME IT	CEKMOR	MOCKER		ONCERS
CEIMOX	MEXICO	CEKMRU	MUCKER	CENORT	CORNET
CEIMPU	PUMICE	CEKNOR	CONKER	CENOSS	SCONES
CEIMRS	CRIMES		RECKON	CENOST	CENTOS
CEIMRT	METRIC	CEKOOR	COOKER		CONTES
CEIMRU	CERIUM	CEKOPT	POCKET	CENOSU	OUNCES
CEIMSU	CESIUM	CEKORR	CORKER	CENOSV	COVENS
	MISCUE		ROCKER	CENOVX	CONVEX
CEINOR	COINER	CEKORS	OCKERS	CENOVY	CONVEY
CEINOS	COSINE	CEKORT	ROCKET	CENSST	SCENTS
	OSCINE	CEKOST	SOCKET	CENSSU	CENSUS
CEINOT	NOETIC	CEKPRU	PUCKER	CENSTY	ENCYST
	NOTICE	CEKPSS	SPECKS	CEOOPR	COOPER
CEINOV	NOVICE	CEKRSU	SUCKER		

CEOOTY	COYOTE	CFLPUU	CUPFUL	CHISTT	STITCH
	OOCYTE	CFORRY	CRY FOR	CHISTW	SWITCH
CEOPPR	COPPER	CFORST	CROFTS	CHITTW	TWITCH
CEOPRS	CORPSE	CFRSUY	SCURFY	CHITTY	TITCHY
CEOPRU	RECOUP	CGHHOU	CHOUGH	CHITWY	WITCHY
CEOPSS	COPSES	CGHILT	GLITCH	CHIVVY	CHIVVY
CEOPSU	COUPES	CGHIOT	GOTHIC	CHKMOO	MOHOCK
CEORRS	CRORES	CGHORU	GROUCH	CHKNSU	CHUNKS
	SCORER	CGHOSU	COUGHS	CHKNUY	CHUNKY
CEORRT	RECTOR	CGIINS	ICINGS	CHKOOS	CHOKOS
CEORSS	CROSSE	CGIINT	CITING	CHKOSS	SHOCKS
	SCORES	CGIKNO	COKING	CHKSSU	SHUCKS
CEORST	CORSET	CGIKOS	GO SICK	CHLOOS	SCHOOL
	ESCORT	CGILNS	CLINGS	CHLORS	SCHORL
	RECTOS	CGILNU	CLUING	CHLOST	CLOTHS
	SCOTER	CGILNY	CLINGY	CHLOSU	SLOUCH
	SECTOR	CGIMNO	COMING	CHMMUY	CHUMMY
CEORSU	COURSE		GNOMIC	CHMOOS	SMOOCH
	SOURCE	CGINNO	CONING	CHMOPS	CHOMPS
CEORSV	COVERS	CGINOP	COPING	CHMOSU	SO MUCH
CEORSW	COWERS	CGINOR	CORING	CHMPSU	CHUMPS
	ESCROW	CGINOV	COVING	CHNOOP	PONCHO
CEORTT	COTTER	CGINOW	COWING	CHNPUY	PUNCHY
CEORTV	COVERT	CGINOX	COXING	CHNRSU	CHURNS
	VECTOR	CGINRU	CURING	CHOORT	COHORT
CEORTX	CORTEX	CGINRY	CRYING	CHOOSY	CHOOSY
CEOSST	COSSET	CGIOOT	COGITO	CHOPPY	CHOPPY
CEOSSU	SCOUSE	CGIORS	CORGIS	CHOPSY	PSYCHO
CEOSTT	OCTETS	CGIRTU	TUGRIC	CHORSU	CHORUS
CEOSTV	COVETS	CGLLOY	GLYCOL	CHOTUY	TOUCHY
CEPRSU	SPRUCE	CGNSUY	SCUNGY	CHPSTU	PUTSCH
CERRSU	CURERS	CHHIOR	CHI-RHO	CHRRSU	CHURRS
	RECURS	CHIILL	CHILLI	CHSSSU	SCHUSS
CERSST	CRESTS	CHIILT	LITCHI	CIILMU	CILIUM
CERSSU	CRUSES		LITHIC	CIIMMS	MIMICS
	CURSES	CHIINT	CHITIN	CIIMOT	MIOTIC
	CUSSER	CHIKNS	CHINKS	CIIMTV	VICTIM
CERSSW	SCREWS	CHIKOS	HOICKS	CIINOP	PIONIC
CERSTU	CRUETS	CHIKRS	KIRSCH	CIINOR	IRONIC
	CURETS	CHIKST	KITSCH	CIINOT	COIN IT
	RECTUS		THICKS	CIINRT	NITRIC
	TRUCES	CHILLS	CHILLS	CIIRSS	CRISIS
CERSUV	CURVES	CHILLY	CHILLY	CIKKPU	KICK UP
CERSUX	CRUXES	CHILOR	ORCHIL	CIKLNO	LOCK IN
CERSWY	SCREWY	CHILRY	RICHLY	CIKLNS	CLINKS
CERTTU	CUTTER	CHIMPS	CHIMPS	CIKLNU	IN LUCK
CESSSU	CUSSES	CHIMRS	CHRISM	CIKLSS	SLICKS
CESTTU	CUTEST		SMIRCH	CIKLSY	SICKLY
CFFHSU	CHUFFS	CHIMSS	SCHISM	CIKMNU	MUCK IN
CFFILS	CLIFFS	CHIMTY	THYMIC	CIKNOP	PICK ON
CFFILY	CLIFFY	CHINOP	PHONIC	CIKNOT	ON TICK
CFFINO	COFFIN	CHINOT	CHITON	CIKNPU	UNPICK
CFFORY	CRY OFF	CHINPU	CHIN UP!	CIKNPY	PYKNIC
CFFOSS	SCOFFS	CHINRU	URCHIN	CIKNSS	SNICKS
CFFOTU	CUT OFF	CHINST	SNITCH	CIKNSU	SUCK IN
	CUTOFF	CHINTZ	CHINTZ	CIKNTU	TUCK IN
	OFFCUT	CHIOPR	ORPHIC		TUCK-IN
CFFRSU	SCRUFF	CHIOPT	PHOTIC	CIKOSY	YOICKS
CFFSSU	SCUFFS	CHIORS	CHOIRS	CIKPPU	PICK UP
CFHILN	FLINCH		ORCHIS		PICKUP
CFHILT	FLITCH	CHIOSZ	SCHIZO	CIKPRS	PRICKS
CFHISU	FICHUS	CHIPPY	CHIPPY	CIKQSU	QUICKS
CFIILM	FILMIC	CHIPRS	CHIRPS	CIKRST	TRICKS
CFIINN	FINNIC	CHIPRY	CHIRPY	CIKRSW	WRICKS
CFIKLS	FLICKS	CHIPSY	PHYSIC	CIKRTU	TURKIC
CFILOR	FROLIC	CHIPTY	PHYTIC	CIKRTY	TRICKY
CFIMOR	FORMIC	CHIQTU	QUITCH	CIKSST	STICKS
CFIMOT	COMFIT	CHIRRS	CHIRRS	CIKSTY	STICKY
CFISTU	FUSTIC	CHIRST	CHRIST	CILLOU	LOCULI
CFKLOS	FLOCKS	CHIRUZ	ZURICH	CILMUU	CUMULI
CFKORS	FROCKS	CHISST	SCHIST	CILNOP	CLIP-ON

CILNOU	UNCOIL	CKOSST	STOCKS	CORTUY	CRY OUT
CILNST	CLINTS	CKOSTY	STOCKY		OUTCRY
CILOOT	COOL IT	CKRSTU	STRUCK	COSSTU	SCOUTS
CILOPU	COIL UP		TRUCKS	COTTUU	CUT OUT
CILOPY	POLICY	CKRSUU	RUCKUS		CUTOUT
CILORT	LICTOR	CLLOOP	COLLOP	CPRSTY	CRYPTS
CILOSY	COSILY	CLLOOY	COOLLY	CPRSUY	CYPRUS
CILQUY	CLIQUY	CLLORS	SCROLL	CPSTUU	CUTS UP
CILRSY	LYRICS	CLLSSU	SCULLS	CRRSUY	SCURRY
CIMMOS	COMMIS	CLMNOU	COLUMN	CRSSTU	CRUSTS
CIMMOT	COMMIT	CLMOPY	COMPLY	CRSTUY	CRUSTY
CIMNOR	MICRON	CLMOSU	LOCUMS		CURTSY
CIMNOU	MUONIC	CLMPSU	CLUMPS	CRSUVY	SCURVY
CIMNSU	CUMINS	CLMPUY	CLUMPY	DDDEEE	DEEDED
CIMOPY	MYOPIC	CLMSTU	MULCTS	DDDEEI	EDDIED
CIMOST	SITCOM	CLMSUY	CLUMSY	DDDEER	REDDED
CIMOTY	COMITY	CLNOOS	COLONS	DDDEET	TEDDED
	MYOTIC		CONSOL	DDDEEW	WEDDED
CIMPRS	CRIMPS	CLNOOY	COLONY	DDDEGO	DODGED
	SCRIMP	CLNOSU	CLONUS	DDDEIK	KIDDED
CIMRUU	CURIUM		CONSUL	DDDEIL	DIDDLE
CIMSTY	MYSTIC	CLNOSW	CLOWNS		LIDDED
CINNOU	NUNCIO	CLNRUU	UNCURL	DDDEIR	RIDDED
CINOOP	COIN-OP	CLOORS	COLORS	DDDELO	DODDLE
CINOOZ	OZONIC	CLOORU	COLOUR	DDDENO	NODDED
CINORT	CITRON	CLOSSW	SCOWLS	DDDEOP	PODDED
CINORZ	ZIRCON	CLOSTU	CLOUTS	DDDEOR	DODDER
CINOSS	SCIONS		LOCUST	DDDEOS	SODDED
CINOST	TOCSIN	CLOSTY	COSTLY	DDEEEH	HEEDED
	TONICS	CLOTUW	LOW-CUT	DDEEEM	DEEMED
CINOSU	COUSIN	CLPRUU	CURL UP	DDEEEN	NEEDED
CINPSU	PUNICS	CLPSTU	SCULPT	DDEEES	SEEDED
CINRSU	INCURS	CLRTUY	CURTLY	DDEEEW	WEEDED
CINSTU	CUTS IN	CLSSUU	SULCUS	DDEEFI	DEFIED
	TUNICS	CLSTUU	CULTUS	DDEEFN	DEFEND
CIOOPT	OCTOPI	CMMNOO	COMMON		FENDED
CIOPRT	TROPIC	CMMRUY	CRUMMY	DDEEGH	HEDGED
CIOPST	COPS IT	CMMSUY	SCUMMY	DDEEGK	KEDGED
	OPTICS	CMOOSS	COSMOS	DDEEGL	GELDED
	PICOTS	CMOSTU	CUSTOM	DDEEGR	DREDGE
	TOPICS	CMOSUU	MUCOUS	DDEEGW	WEDGED
CIORSU	CURIOS	CMPRSU	CRUMPS	DDEEHL	HEDDLE
CIORTT	TRICOT		SCRUMP	DDEEHR	HERDED
CIORTV	VICTOR	CMRSSU	SCRUMS	DDEEIL	ELIDED
CIOSST	STOICS	CMSTUU	SCUTUM	DDEEIN	DENIED
CIOSTU	COITUS	CNOOPU	COUPON		INDEED
CIPRSS	CRISPS	CNOORS	CROONS	DDEEIR	DERIDE
	SCRIPS	CNOORT	CROTON	DDEEIS	EDDIES
CIPRST	SCRIPT	CNOOST	NOSTOC	DDEEIT	DIETED
CIPRSY	CRISPY	CNOOTT	COTTON		EDITED
CIRRSU	CIRRUS	CNOOTY	TYCOON	DDEELM	MEDDLE
CIRSTT	STRICT	CNOOVY	CONVOY		MELDED
CIRSTU	CITRUS	CNOPSW	C. P. SNOW	DDEELP	PEDDLE
	RICTUS	CNORSS	SCORNS	DDEELU	DELUDE
	RUSTIC	CNORSW	CROWNS		ELUDED
CISSUV	VISCUS	CNOSTU	COUNTS	DDEELV	DELVED
CISTTU	CUTS IT	CNOTUY	COUNTY	DDEELW	WELDED
CKKNOS	KNOCKS	COOPPU	COOP UP	DDEEMN	MENDED
CKLNOS	CLONKS	COOPSS	SCOOPS	DDEEMO	DEMODE
CKLNOU	UNLOCK	COOPST	CO-OPTS	DDEENP	DEPEND
CKLOPU	LOCK UP	COOPTU	COP-OUT	DDEENR	REDDEN
	LOCK-UP	COOPWX	COW POX	DDEENT	DENTED
	LOCKUP		COWPOX		TENDED
CKLPSU	PLUCKS	COOSST	SCOOTS	DDEENU	DENUDE
CKLPUY	PLUCKY	COPRSU	CORPUS		ENDUED
CKMOPU	MOCK-UP	COPRTY	CRYPTO	DDEENV	VENDED
CKMOSS	SMOCKS	COPRUY	CROUPY	DDEENW	WENDED
CKNORU	UNCORK	COPSUY	COYPUS	DDEEOR	ERODED
CKOOPU	COOK UP	CORRSU	CURSOR	DDEERR	REDDER
CKOORS	CROOKS	CORSSU	SCOURS	DDEERT	TEDDER
CKOPRU	CORK UP	CORSTU	COURTS	DDEEUX	EXUDED

DDEFFO	DOFFED	DDEOOS	DODOES	DEEFIS	DEFIES
DDEFGU	FUDGED	DDEOOW	WOODED	DEEFLL	FELLED
DDEFIL	FIDDLE	DDEORW	WORDED	DEEFLT	FELTED
DDEFLO	FOLDED	DDEOST	ODDEST	DEEFLX	FLEXED
DDEFLU	FUDDLE	DDEOSU	DOUSED	DEEFNR	FENDER
DDEFNU	FUNDED	DDEOSW	DOWSED	DEEFRS	DEFERS
DDEFOR	FODDER	DDEOTT	DOTTED	DEEFRT	DEFTER
	FORDED	DDERRU	RUDDER	DEEFSU	DEFUSE
DDEGGO	DOGGED	DDERSU	UDDERS	DEEGGL	LEGGED
DDEGIL	GILDED	DDESTU	DUSTED	DEEGGP	PEGGED
	GLIDED	DDFILY	FIDDLY	DEEGHR	HEDGER
DDEGIR	GIRDED	DDFIOR	DID FOR	DEEGHS	HEDGES
	RIDGED	DDGLOO	OLD DOG	DEEGIR	EDGIER
DDEGIU	GUIDED	DDGOOO	DO GOOD	DEEGKS	KEDGES
DDEGJU	JUDGED	DDHISU	DUDISH	DEEGLL	GELLED
DDEGLO	LODGED	DDHOSY	SHODDY	DEEGLN	LEGEND
DDEGLU	GUDDLE	DDIIKK	DIK-DIK	DEEGLP	PLEDGE
DDEGMO	DODGEM	DDIKSY	SKIDDY	DEEGLR	LEDGER
DDEGINO	DUG END	DDILNR	DIRNDL	DEEGLS	LEDGES
	DOG-END	DDILOS	DILDOS		SLEDGE
DDEGNU	NUDGED	DDILTY	TIDDLY	DEEGLU	DELUGE
DDEGOR	DODGER	DDINOT	DID NOT	DEEGMM	GEMMED
DDEGOS	DODGES	DDIORS	SORDID	DEEGMR	MERGED
DDEGRU	DRUDGE	DDIORT	DO DIRT	DEEGNO	ON EDGE
DDEHIN	HIDDEN	DDIOTU	OUTDID	DEEGNR	GENDER
DDEHIS	DISHED	DDIOTY	ODDITY	DEEGNU	DENGUE
DDEHLU	HUDDLE	DDIRSU	DRUIDS	DEEGOS	GEODES
DDEHOO	HOODED		SIDDUR	DEEGRV	VERGED
DDEIIK	KIDDIE	DDLOOT	ODD LOT	DEEGRY	GREEDY
DDEIIO	IODIDE	DDMMUU	DUMDUM		GREYED
DDEIIT	TIDIED	DDNOOS	ODDS ON	DEEGSS	SEDGES
DDEIIV	DIVIDE		ODDS-ON	DEEGSW	WEDGES
DDEIKR	KIDDER	DDNOOW	DO DOWN	DEEHLM	HELMED
DDEILM	MIDDLE	DDOTUY	DO DUTY	DEEHLP	HELPED
DDEILP	PIDDLE	DEEEFR	FEEDER	DEEHMM	HEMMED
DDEILR	RIDDLE		REEFED	DEEHMS	MESHED
DDEILS	SIDLED	DEEEGR	DEGREE	DEEHRT	THREE-D
DDEILW	WIDDLE	DEEEHL	HEELED	DEEHSW	SHEWED
DDEIMM	DIMMED	DEEEJR	JEERED	DEEILR	LIEDER
DDEIMN	MIDDEN	DEEEKK	KEEKED		RELIED
	MINDED	DEEEKL	KEELED	DEEILS	DIESEL
DDEINN	DINNED	DEEEKN	KEENED		ELIDES
DDEINR	RIDDEN	DEEEKP	PEEKED	DEEILV	LEVIED
	RINDED	DEEEKR	REEKED		VEILED
DDEINU	INDUED	DEEELN	NEEDLE	DEEILX	EXILED
DDEINW	WINDED	DEEELP	PEELED	DEEILY	EYELID
DDEIOS	DIODES	DEEELR	LEERED	DEEIMP	IMPEDE
DDEIOV	DEVOID		REELED	DEEIMS	DEMISE
	VOIDED	DEEELT	DELETE	DEEINN	IN NEED
DDEIPP	DIPPED	DEEEMR	REDEEM	DEEINP	IN DEEP
DDEIPR	PRIDED	DEEEMS	SEEMED	DEEINR	DENIER
DDEJRU	JUDDER	DEEEMT	TEEMED		NEREID
DDEKNU	DUNKED	DEEENP	DEEPEN		REINED
DDELLU	DULLED		PEENED	DEEINS	DENIES
DDELMO	MOLDED	DEEENV	EVENED		DIENES
DDELMU	MUDDLE		VENDEE		SEINED
DDELNO	NODDLE	DEEEPP	PEEPED	DEEINV	ENDIVE
	OLD NED	DEEEPR	DEEPER		ENVIED
DDELOO	DOODLE		PEERED		VEINED
DDELOR	LORDED	DEEEPS	SEEPED	DEEIPS	ESPIED
DDELOT	TODDLE	DEEEPV	PEEVED	DEEIRS	DESIRE
DDELPU	PUDDLE	DEEERS	SEE RED		EIDERS
DDEMOO	DOOMED		SEEDER		RESIDE
DDEMPU	DUMPED	DEEERV	REEVED	DEEIRT	DIETER
DDENNO	DONNED		VEERED		TIERED
DDENNU	DUNNED	DEEERW	WEEDER	DEEIRV	DERIVE
DDENOR	DRONED	DEEFGL	FLEDGE	DEEIRW	DEWIER
	NODDER	DEEFHT	HEFTED	DEEISV	DEVISE
DDENOS	SODDEN	DEEFIL	DEFILE		SIEVED
DDENOW	DOWNED	DEEFIN	DEFINE	DEEISX	DEXIES
DDENSU	SUDDEN	DEEFIR	DEFIER	DEEISZ	SEIZED

DEEITY	TIE-DYE	DEEOPS	DEPOSE	DEFINS	FIENDS
DEEIVW	VIEWED		EPODES	DEFIOT	FOETID
DEEJKR	JERKED	DEEORS	ERODES	DEFIRR	RED FIR
DEEJLL	JELLED		REDOES	DEFIRT	RIFTED
DEEJST	JESTED	DEEORT	TEREDO	DEFIRV	FERVID
DEEJTT	JETTED	DEEORZ	ZEROED	DEFIST	FISTED
DEEKNN	KENNED	DEEOTV	DEVOTE		SIFTED
DEEKOV	EVOKED		VETOED	DEFITT	FITTED
DEEKPR	PERKED	DEEPPP	PEPPED	DEFIZZ	FIZZED
DEEKSW	SKEWED	DEEPRU	PUREED	DEFJLS	FJELDS
DEELLW	WELLED	DEEPRY	PREYED	DEFKNU	FUNKED
DEELLY	YELLED	DEEPSS	SPEEDS	DEFKOR	FORKED
DEELMT	MELTED	DEEPSW	SPEWED	DEFLLU	FULLED
DEELMW	MEWLED	DEEPSY	SPEEDY	DEFLNO	ENFOLD
DEELMY	MEDLEY	DEEPTT	PETTED		FONDLE
DEELNR	LENDER	DEEPTU	DEPUTE	DEFLOO	FOOLED
DEELNS	LENSED	DEERST	DESERT	DEFLOR	FOLDER
DEELOP	ELOPED		DETERS	DEFLOT	LOFTED
DEELPT	PELTED		RESTED	DEFLOU	FOULED
DEELPY	DEEPLY	DEERSU	REUSED	DEFLOW	FLOWED
	YELPED	DEERSV	SERVED		FOWLED
DEELRS	ELDERS		VERSED		WOLFED
DEELRV	DELVER	DEERTT	RETTED	DEFLRU	FURLED
DEELRW	LEWDER	DEERTX	DEXTER	DEFLTU	FLUTED
	WELDER	DEERVV	REVVED	DEFLTY	DEFTLY
DEELST	ELDEST	DEESST	STEEDS	DEFLUX	FLUXED
DEELSU	ELUDES	DEESSW	SWEDES	DEFMOR	DEFORM
DEELSV	DELVES	DEESTT	DETEST		FORMED
DEELSW	SLEWED		SETTED	DEFNOR	FONDER
DEELTU	ELUTED		TESTED	DEFNOU	FONDUE
	TELEDU	DEESTU	ETUDES	DEFNRU	REFUND
DEELTW	WELTED	DEESTV	VESTED	DEFOOR	ROOFED
DEEMNR	MENDER	DEESTW	STEWED	DEFOOT	FOOTED
DEEMNS	EMENDS		TWEEDS	DEFOOW	WOOFED
DEEMOT	DEMOTE	DEESUX	EXUDES	DEFORX	RED FOX
	EMOTED	DEETTV	VETTED	DEFRRU	FURRED
DEEMOW	MEOWED	DEETWY	TWEEDY	DEFRTU	TURFED
DEEMPR	PERMED	DEFFHU	HUFFED	DEFSSU	FUSSED
DEEMPT	TEMPED	DEFFIM	MIFFED	DEFTTU	TUFTED
DEEMRT	TERMED	DEFFIR	DIFFER	DEGGHO	HOGGED
DEEMRU	DEMURE	DEFFIT	TIFFED	DEGGHU	HUGGED
DEEMRY	REMEDY	DEFFLU	DUFFEL	DEGGIJ	JIGGED
DEEMSS	MESSED		LUFFED	DEGGIN	EDGING
DEENNO	DONNEE	DEFFMU	MUFFED	DEGGIP	PIGGED
DEENNP	PENNED	DEFFNO	OFFEND	DEGGIR	DIGGER
DEENNT	NEEDN'T	DEFFPU	PUFFED		RIGGED
DEENNY	YENNED	DEFFRU	DUFFER	DEGGIW	WIGGED
DEENOP	OPENED		RUFFED	DEGGJO	JOGGED
DEENOR	REDONE	DEFGGO	FOGGED	DEGGJU	JUGGED
DEENOT	DENOTE	DEFGIR	FRIDGE	DEGGLO	DOGLEG
DEENPX	EXPEND	DEFGIT	FIDGET		LOGGED
DEENRR	RENDER		GIFTED	DEGGLU	LUGGED
DEENRS	DENSER	DEFGLU	GULFED	DEGGMU	MUGGED
	SENDER	DEFGOO	GOOFED	DEGGOR	GORGED
DEENRT	RENTED	DEFGOR	FORGED	DEGGOT	TOGGED
	TENDER	DEFGOS	DEFOGS	DEGGOU	GOUGED
DEENRU	ENDURE	DEFGSU	FUDGES	DEGGPU	PUGGED
	ENURED	DEFHIS	FISHED	DEGGRU	GRUDGE
DEENRV	NERVED	DEFHOO	HOOFED		RUGGED
DEENSS	SENSED	DEFIKN	KNIFED	DEGGTU	TUGGED
DEENST	NESTED	DEFILL	FILLED	DEGHIN	HINGED
	TENSED	DEFILM	FILMED	DEGHIS	SIGHED
DEENSU	ENDUES	DEFILO	FOILED	DEGHSU	GUSHED
	ENSUED	DEFILR	RIFLED	DEGILL	GILLED
DEENSW	SWEDEN	DEFILS	FIELDS	DEGILN	DINGLE
DEENTT	DETENT	DEFILT	LIFTED	DEGILR	GILDER
	NETTED	DEFIMR	FIRMED		GIRDLE
	TENTED	DEFINN	FINNED		GLIDER
DEENTV	VENTED	DEFINO	DO FINE	DEGILS	GLIDES
DEENTX	EXTEND	DEFINR	FINDER	DEGILY	EDGILY
			FRIEND	DEGIMS	MIDGES

DEGIMT	MIDGET	DEHISS	DISHES	DEIKNY	KIDNEY
DEGINN	ENDING		HISSED	DEIKPP	KIPPED
	GINNED	DEHISW	WISHED	DEIKPS	SPIKED
DEGINP	PINGED	DEHITT	TITHED	DEIKRS	RISKED
DEGINR	GIRNED	DEHITW	WHITED	DEIKRU	DUIKER
	RINGED	DEHKNO	HONKED	DEIKSS	KISSED
DEGINS	DEIGNS	DEHKOO	HOOKED	DEIKST	SKITED
	DESIGN	DEHKSU	HUSKED	DEIKSV	SKIVED
	SIGNED	DEHLLU	HULLED	DEIKTT	KITTED
	SINGED	DEHLNO	HELD ON	DEILLM	MILLED
DEGINW	WINGED	DEHLOR	HOLDER	DEILLT	LILTED
DEGINY	DYEING	DEHLOW	HOWLED		TILLED
DEGINZ	ZINGED	DEHLPU	HELD UP	DEILLW	WILLED
DEGIOO	GOODIE		UPHELD	DEILMP	DIMPLE
DEGIPR	GRIPED	DEHLRU	HURDLE		LIMPED
DEGIRR	GIRDER		HURLED	DEILMR	MILDER
	RIDGER	DEHMMU	HUMMED	DEILMS	MISLED
DEGIRS	DIRGES	DEHMNY	HYMNED		SLIMED
	RIDGES	DEHMOT	METHOD		SMILED
DEGIRT	GET RID	DEHMPU	HUMPED	DEILMW	MILDEW
	GIRTED	DEHNOP	PHONED	DEILNN	LINDEN
DEGIRU	GUIDER	DEHNOR	HORNED	DEILNO	INDOLE
DEGIST	DIGEST	DEHNOS	NOSHED	DEILOP	DIPOLE
DEGISU	GUIDES	DEHNOY	HOYDEN	DEILON	ROILED
DEGJSU	JUDGES	DEHNTU	HUNTED	DEILOS	OLDIES
DEGLLU	GULLED	DEHOOP	HOOPED		SOILED
DEGLNO	GOLDEN	DEHOOS	SHOOED	DEILOT	LIED TO
	LONGED	DEHOOT	HOOTED		TOILED
DEGLNU	GULDEN	DEHOPP	HOPPED	DEILPP	LIPPED
	LUNGED	DEHOPS	EPHODS	DEILPS	DISPEL
DEGLOR	LODGER	DEHORS	HORDES		LISPED
DEGLOS	LODGES		HORSED		SPILED
DEGLOT	GET OLD		SHORED	DEILRS	SLIDER
DEGLOV	GLOVED	DEHORT	RED HOT	DEILRV	DRIVEL
DEGLOW	GLOWED		RED-HOT	DEILRW	WILDER
DEGLPU	GULPED	DEHORW	WHORED	DEILRY	DIRELY
DEGLSU	SLUDGE	DEHOST	HOSTED	DEILSS	SIDLES
DEGMMU	GUMMED	DEHOSU	HOUSED		SLIDES
DEGMSU	SMUDGE	DEHOSV	SHOVED	DEILST	IDLEST
DEGNNU	GUNNED	DEHOSW	SHOWED		LISTED
DEGNOP	PONGED	DEHPST	DEPTHS		SILTED
DEGNRU	GERUND	DEHPSU	PUSHED		TILDES
DEGNSU	NUDGES	DEHRSS	SHERDS	DEILSV	DEVILS
DEGOOS	GOOSED		SHREDS	DEILSW	WIELDS
DEGOPR	GROPED	DEHRSU	RUSHED	DEILSY	YIELDS
DEGOPS	PODGES	DEHRSW	SHREWD	DEILTT	TILTED
DEGOPY	PYE-DOG	DEIIMS	IMIDES		TITLED
DEGORU	DROGUE	DEIINO	IODINE	DEILTU	DILUTE
	GOURDE	DEIINS	INSIDE	DEILTW	WILTED
	ROUGED	DEIINT	INDITE	DEILWY	DEWILY
DEGOST	GODETS		TIED IN		WIDELY
	STODGE	DEIINV	DIVINE	DEIMMR	DIMMER
DEGOSY	YE GODS	DEIIOS	IODISE		RIMMED
DEGPPY	GYPPED	DEIIOZ	IODIZE	DEIMMU	MEDIUM
DEGPRU	PURGED	DEIIPT	PITIED	DEIMNO	MONIED
DEGRSU	SURGED	DEIIRS	IRIDES	DEIMNP	IMPEND
DEGRTU	TRUDGE	DEIIRT	TIDIER	DEIMNR	MINDER
DEGSTU	GUSTED	DEIIST	TIDIES		REMIND
DEGTTU	GUTTED	DEIISX	DIXIES	DEIMNT	MINTED
DEHHSU	HUSHED	DEIJKN	JINKED	DEIMOR	DO RE MI
DEHILL	HILLED	DEIJLT	JILTED		DORMIE
DEHILS	SHIELD	DEIJNO	JOINED	DEIMOT	DO TIME
DEHINR	HINDER	DEIJSU	JUDIES	DEIMPR	PRIMED
DEHINS	SHINED	DEIKLL	KILLED	DEIMPU	MUD PIE
DEHINT	HINTED	DEIKLM	MILKED	DEIMRS	DERMIS
DEHINW	WHINED	DEIKLN	KINDLE		DIMERS
DEHIOO	HOODIE		LINKED	DEIMRT	MITRED
DEHIPP	HIPPED	DEIKNP	PINKED	DEIMSS	MISSED
DEHIPT	PITHED	DEIKNR	KINDER	DEIMST	DEMIST
DEHIRT	DITHER		RED INK		DEMITS
		DEIKNW	WINKED		MISTED

DEIMTU	TEDIUM	DEIPTU	TIED UP	DELOOS	LOOSED
DEINNO	DONE IN	DEIRRS	DERRIS		OODLES
DEINNP	PINNED		DRIERS		SOOLED
DEINNR	DINNER		RIDERS	DELOOT	LOOTED
DEINNS	SINNED	DEIRRV	DRIVER		TOLEDO
DEINNT	DENTIN	DEIRST	DIREST		TOOLED
	INDENT		DRIEST	DELOOW	WOOLED
	INTEND		STRIDE	DELOPP	LOPPED
	TINNED	DEIRSV	DIVERS	DELOPR	POLDER
DEINOP	OPINED		DRIVES	DELOPS	SLOPED
DEINOR	IRONED	DEIRTV	DIVERT	DELOPY	DEPLOY
DEINOS	DOES IN	DEISST	DEISTS	DELORS	SOLDER
	NO-SIDE		DESIST	DELORU	LOUDER
	NOISED	DEISSU	DISUSE		LOURED
	ON SIDE		ISSUED	DELOST	OLDEST
	ONSIDE	DEISTU	DUTIES	DELOSU	SOULED
	SIDE ON		SUITED	DELOSV	SOLVED
	SIDE-ON	DEISTV	DIVEST	DELOSW	DOWELS
DEINOT	DONE IT	DEISTW	WIDEST		SLOWED
DEINPP	NIPPED	DEIZZZ	ZIZZED	DELOSY	YODELS
DEINPS	SNIPED	DEJKNU	JUNKED	DELOTT	DETTOL
	SPINED	DEJLOT	JOLTED		DOTTLE
DEINRS	DINERS	DEJMPU	JUMPED		LOTTED
	RINSED	DEJOTT	JOTTED	DELOTU	LED OUT
DEINRT	TINDER	DEJTTU	JUTTED	DELOWY	YOWLED
DEINRU	INURED	DEKKOS	DEKKOS	DELOYY	DOYLEY
	RUINED	DEKLOO	LOOKED	DELPPU	PULPED
DEINRV	DRIVEN	DEKLOY	YOLKED	DELPRU	PURLED
DEINRW	DREW IN	DEKLRU	LURKED	DELPSU	PULSED
	REWIND	DEKMOS	SMOKED	DELPUX	DUPLEX
	WINDER	DEKNOY	DONKEY	DELRUY	RUDELY
DEINST	ENDS IT	DEKNOZ	ZONKED	DELSTU	LUSTED
DEINSU	INDUES	DEKOOR	ROOKED	DELSTY	STYLED
	UNDIES	DEKOPS	SPOKED	DEMMOS	MODEMS
DEINTT	TINTED	DEKORW	WORKED	DEMMSU	SUMMED
DEINTU	UNITED	DEKORY	YORKED	DEMNOO	MOONED
	UNTIED	DEKOST	STOKED	DEMNOR	MODERN
DEINTW	TWINED	DEKRSY	RED SKY	DEMNOS	DEMONS
DEIOPR	PERIOD	DEKSTU	TUSKED	DEMOOR	MOORED
DEIOPS	POISED	DELLLO	LOLLED		ROOMED
DEIORS	DORIES	DELLLU	LULLED	DEMOOT	MOOTED
DEIORT	EDITOR	DELLMU	MULLED	DEMOOZ	ZOOMED
	TIE-ROD	DELLOP	POLLED	DEMOPP	MOPPED
	TRIODE	DELLOR	ROLLED	DEMOPR	ROMPED
DEIORV	VOIDER	DELLOT	TOLLED	DEMOPS	MOPEDS
DEIORW	WEIRDO	DELLOW	DO WELL	DEMOPY	YOMPED
DEIORZ	DOZIER	DELLPU	PULLED	DEMORR	DORMER
DEIOST	DOES IT	DELLRU	DULLER	DEMORW	WORMED
DEIOSV	VIDEOS	DELLSW	DWELLS	DEMOST	MODEST
DEIOSX	DOXIES	DELLWY	LEWDLY	DEMOSU	MOUSED
	OXIDES	DELMNO	DOLMEN	DEMPPU	PUMPED
DEIOTU	DIE OUT		OLD MEN	DEMPRU	DUMPER
DEIPPP	PIPPED	DELMOO	LOOMED	DEMPSU	SPUMED
DEIPPR	DIPPER	DELMOS	MODELS	DEMRRU	MURDER
	RIPPED		SELDOM	DEMRSU	DEMURS
DEIPPS	SIPPED	DELMOT	MODEL T	DEMSSU	MUSSED
DEIPPT	TIPPED		MOLTED	DENNOT	TENDON
DEIPPY	YIPPED	DELMOU	MODULE	DENNOU	UNDONE
DEIPPZ	ZIPPED	DELMOY	MELODY	DENNPU	PUNNED
DEIPQU	PIQUED	DELMPU	LUMPED	DENNSU	SUNNED
DEIPRS	PRIDES		PLUMED	DENOOS	NODOSE
	PRISED	DELNOO	NOODLE		NOOSED
	SPIDER	DELNOR	RONDEL	DENOOW	WOODEN
	SPIRED	DELNOS	LODENS	DENOPR	PONDER
DEIPRZ	PRIZED	DELNOU	LOUDEN	DENOPU	DONE UP
DEIPSS	PISSED		NODULE	DENORR	DRONER
DEIPST	SPITED	DELNUY	NUDELY	DENORS	DRONES
	STIPED	DELOOP	LOOPED		SNORED
DEIPSU	UPSIDE		POODLE	DENORT	RODENT
DEIPSW	SWIPED		POOLED	DENORU	UNDOER
DEIPTT	PITTED			DENORV	VENDOR

DENORW	DOWNER	DEORTU	DETOUR	DGHOOT	HOT DOG
	DREW ON		ROUTED	DGHOSU	DOUGHS
	WONDER		TOURED	DGHOUY	DOUGHY
DENORY	YONDER	DEORTW	TROWED	DGIIKN	DIKING
DENOST	DOESN'T	DEORUV	DEVOUR	DGIILN	IDLING
	STONED	DEOSSS	DOSSES	DGIINN	DINING
DENOSU	UNDOES	DEOSST	TOSSED	DGIINO	INDIGO
DENOSW	ENDOWS	DEOSSU	DOUSES	DGIINP	PIDGIN
	SNOWED		SOUSED	DGIINR	RIDING
DENOSY	DOYENS	DEOSSW	DOWSES	DGIINS	SIDING
DENOSZ	DOZENS	DEOSTU	OUSTED	DGIINT	TIDING
DENOTW	WONTED	DEOSTW	STOWED	DGIINV	DIVING
DENPRU	PRUNED	DEOSUX	EXODUS	DGIIST	DIGITS
DENPSS	SPENDS	DEOTTU	TOUTED	DGIKNY	DYKING
DENPSU	ENDS UP	DEOTUV	DEVOUT	DGILOW	GO WILD
	SEND UP	DEOTUX	TUXEDO	DGILSU	GUILDS
	SEND-UP	DEPPPU	PUPPED	DGIMNO	DOMING
	UPENDS	DEPPSU	SPED UP	DGINOP	DOPING
DENPTU	PUNTED		SUPPED	DGINOS	DOINGS
DENRST	TRENDS	DEPPTU	TUPPED		DOSING
DENRSU	NURSED	DEPRRU	PURRED	DGINOT	DOTING
	SUNDER	DEPRSU	PRUDES		TIN GOD
DENRTU	TURNED		PURSED	DGINOU	GUIDON
DENRTY	TRENDY	DEPRUW	DREW UP	DGINOZ	DOZING
DENSUU	UNUSED	DEPRUY	DUPERY	DGINPU	DUPING
DENSUW	SUNDEW	DEPSSU	PSEUDS	DGINRS	GRINDS
DENTTU	NUTTED	DEPSUU	USED UP	DGINRU	DURING
DEOOPP	POOPED	DEPSUY	PSEUDY	DGINRY	DRYING
DEOORS	RODEOS	DEPTTU	PUTTED	DGIORT	GOT RID
DEOORT	ROOTED	DEPTUY	DEPUTY	DGIOTW	GODWIT
DEOORV	DO OVER	DERRSY	DRYERS	DGIRTU	TURGID
	OVERDO	DERRUY	RUDERY	DGLOOT	GOT OLD
DEOOST	SOOTED	DERSSU	DURESS	DGLOOY	GOODLY
DEOOTT	TOOTED	DERSSY	DRESSY	DGLSUY	SLUDGY
DEOPPP	POPPED	DERSTU	DUSTER	DGMSUY	SMUDGY
DEOPPS	SOPPED		RUDEST	DGNOOR	DRONGO
DEOPPT	TOPPED		RUSTED	DGNOOS	GODSON
DEOPRS	SPORED	DERTTU	RUTTED	DGNOOW	GO DOWN
DEOPRT	DEPORT	DESSSU	SUSSED		GODOWN
	PORTED	DESTUV	DUVETS	DGNORU	GROUND
	RED TOP	DETTTU	TUTTED	DGNOSU	SUN GOD
DEOPRU	POURED	DFFIMO	MID OFF	DGOOOS	SO GOOD
DEOPRV	PROVED		MID-OFF	DGOOPT	TOP DOG
DEOPRW	POWDER	DFFNOO	NOD OFF	DGOOTY	TOY DOG
DEOPST	DEPOTS	DFFOOS	SOD OFF!	DGORSU	GOURDS
	DESPOT	DFGIIR	FRIGID	DGOSTY	STODGY
	POSTED	DFIIRT	TRIFID	DGOTUU	DUGOUT
DEOPSU	DOES UP	DFIKNO	KIND OF	DHIIPS	HISPID
	PSEUDO	DFILNO	INFOLD	DHIISW	WIDISH
DEOPTT	POTTED	DFILOR	FLORID	DHILOS	OLDISH
DEOPTU	POUTED	DFILSU	FLUIDS	DHILOT	HOLD IT
DEOQTU	QUOTED	DFIMOY	MODIFY	DHIMOS	MODISH
DEORRS	ORDERS	DFIORS	FIORDS	DHINSU	HINDUS
DEORRU	DOURER	DFIRST	DRIFTS	DHINSY	SHINDY
	ORDURE	DFIRTY	DRIFTY	DHIORR	HORRID
DEORRV	DROVER	DFJORS	FJORDS	DHIOST	DHOTIS
DEORRW	REWORD	DFLNOU	UNFOLD	DHIOSV	DOVISH
DEORSS	DOSSER	DFLNOY	FONDLY	DHIPSU	DISH UP
DEORST	SORTED	DFLOOS	FLOODS	DHIRST	THIRDS
	STORED	DFLOPU	FOLD UP	DHIRSY	DRYISH
	STRODE	DFLRYY	DRY FLY	DHISTW	WIDTHS
DEORSU	DOUSER	DFNORS	FRONDS	DHLNOO	HOLD ON
	ROUSED	DFNOSU	FOUNDS	DHLOPU	HOLD UP
	SOURED	DFNSUU	FUNDUS		HOLDUP
DEORSV	DROVES	DFOORX	OXFORD		UPHOLD
DEORSW	DOWERS	DGGNOU	DUGONG	DHLOSU	SHOULD
	DOWSER		GUN DOG	DHMTUU	MUD HUT
	DOWSE		GUNDOG	DHNOSU	HOUNDS
	DROWSE	DGGOPU	PUG DOG	DHOOOO	HOODOO
DEORTT	ROTTED	DGHIIN	HIDING	DHOORT	HOT ROD
		DGHINY	DINGHY	DHORSU	SHROUD

DHORSY	HYDROS	DLLOOP	DOLLOP	EEEIPW	WEEPIE
DHORTU	DROUTH	DLLOPU	DOLL UP	EEEIRR	EERIER
DIIKNN	IN KIND	DLLORY	DROLLY	EEEITY	EYETIE
DIILMP	LIMPID		LORDLY	EEEJRR	JEERER
DIILOS	SOLIDI	DLLOUY	LOUDLY	EEEKKR	KEEKER
DIILQU	LIQUID	DLMOOT	OLD TOM	EEEKLU	EKUELE
DIILST	DISTIL	DLMOOU	MODULO	EEEKMR	MEEKER
DIILTY	TIDILY	DLMOSU	MOULDS	EEEKNR	KEENER
DIIMNU	INDIUM	DLMOUY	MOULDY	EEEKPR	KEEPER
DIIMOS	IDIOMS	DLNOOT	TOLD ON	EEEKRS	SEEKER
DIIMOU	OIDIUM	DLNOPU	DUNLOP	EEELMS	MELEES
DIIMTW	DIMWIT	DLNOSU	UNSOLD	EEELNV	ELEVEN
DIIMTY	DIMITY	DLNOTU	UNTOLD	EEELPR	PEELER
DIINNW	WIND IN	DLNUUY	UNDULY	EEELSS	LESSEE
DIINRS	INDRIS	DLOOPS	PODSOL	EEELSV	LEVEES
DIIOST	IDIOTS	DLOOPZ	PODZOL		SLEEVE
DIKLNY	KINDLY	DLOORS	DROOLS	EEELTY	EYELET
DIKMNU	DINKUM	DLOORU	DOLOUR	EEEMRT	MEETER
DIKNNU	UNKIND	DLORSW	WORLDS	EEEMST	ESTEEM
DIKNRS	DRINKS	DLORUY	DOURLY	EEEMTU	EMEUTE
DILLMY	MILDLY	DMNOOY	MONODY	EEENRS	SERENE
DILLRS	DRILLS	DMNOSU	MOUNDS	EEENRT	ENTREE
DILLSY	IDYLLS	DMOOSU	DUOMOS	EEENRV	EVENER
DILLWY	WILDLY	DMOOSY	SODOMY		VENEER
DILMOR	MILORD	DMORWY	MY WORD!	EEENSZ	SNEEZE
DILMOU	MODULI	DNNOOW	DOWN ON	EEEPPR	PEEPER
DILMPY	DIMPLY	DNOOPR	DROP ON	EEEPRW	WEEPER
DILNNU	DUNLIN	DNOORS	DONORS	EEEPST	TEPEES
DILOPT	POT LID		RONDOS	EEEPSV	PEEVES
DILOPY	PLOIDY	DNOORT	TROD ON	EEERRV	REVERE
DILORT	LORD IT	DNOPSU	POUNDS	EEERSV	REEVES
DILOSS	SOLIDS	DNORSU	ROUNDS		SEVERE
DILOST	STOLID	DNORSW	DROWNS	EEERTT	TEETER
DILOWX	WILD OX	DNORTU	ROTUND		TERETE
DIMNOO	DOMINO		UNTROD	EEERVW	WEEVER
DIMNSU	NUDISM	DNOSSU	SOUNDS	EEESTT	SETTEE
DIMOPU	PODIUM	DNOSSY	SYNODS	EEFFOS	SEE OFF
DIMOSU	SODIUM	DNOSUW	WOUNDS	EEFFOT	TEE OFF
DIMOSW	WISDOM	DNRRUY	DRY RUN		TOFFEE
DIMSST	MIDSTS	DNRSUY	SUNDRY	EEFFSU	EFFUSE
DINNUW	UNWIND	DOOOOV	VOODOO	EEFGIN	FEEING
DINOOR	INDOOR	DOOPRS	DROOPS	EEFGRU	REFUGE
DINOPR	DROP IN	DOOPRY	DROOPY	EEFHIR	HEIFER
DINOPU	DUPION	DOORSU	ODOURS	EEFHOR	HEREOF
DINOSW	DISOWN	DOOSTU	OUTDOS	EEFILN	FELINE
DINOWW	WINDOW	DOPRSY	DROPSY	EEFILR	RELIEF
DINPTU	PUNDIT	DORRTY	DRY ROT	EEFINR	FERINE
DINPUW	UPWIND	DORSSW	SWORDS		REFINE
	WIND UP	DORSSY	DROSSY	EEFIRZ	FRIEZE
DINSTU	NUDIST	DORSWX	X-WORDS	EEFLLO	FELLOE
DINTUY	NUDITY	DORSWY	DROWSY	EEFLLR	FELLER
	UNTIDY	DORTUY	DRY OUT	EEFLNN	FENNEL
DIOOPS	ISOPOD	DPSTUU	DUST UP	EEFLNS	FLENSE
DIOORT	TOROID		DUST-UP	EEFLRU	FERULE
DIOOSU	IODOUS				REFUEL
	ODIOUS	DRSTUY	STURDY	EEFLRX	REFLEX
DIOOSZ	ZOOIDS	EEEEGG	GEE-GEE	EEFLRY	FREELY
DIOPRT	TORPID	EEEEHT	TEE-HEE	EEFLST	FLEETS
	TRIPOD	EEEEPT	TEEPEE	EEFLSX	FLEXES
DIORRT	TORRID	EEEEWW	WEE-WEE	EEFLTT	FETTLE
DIOSTT	DITTOS	EEEFFT	EFFETE	EEFLUY	EYEFUL
DIOSTU	STUDIO	EEEFLR	FEELER	EEFPRR	PREFER
DIOSTV	DIVOTS	EEEFRR	REEFER	EEFRRS	REFERS
DIOSWW	WIDOWS	EEEFRZ	FREEZE	EEFRRT	FERRET
DIPPRY	DRIPPY	EEEGMR	EMERGE	EEFRST	FESTER
DIPRTU	PUTRID	EEEGNR	RENEGE		FREEST
DIPSTU	STUPID	EEEGRZ	GEEZER	EEFRSU	REFUSE
DIQSSU	SQUIDS	EEEHLR	HEELER	EEFRSV	FEVERS
DJNNOO	DONJON	EEEHNT	ETHENE	EEFRTT	FETTER
DKNRSU	DRUNKS	EEEHST	SEETHE	EEFRTU	REFUTE
DKOOOO	KOODOO	EEEHTT	TEETHE	EEFSSU	FUSEES
		EEEHWZ	WHEEZE		

EEFSTW	FEWEST	EEHPRS	HERPES	EEJSSS	JESSES
EEFSUZ	FUZEES		SPHERE	EEJSTT	JET SET
EEGGLP	PEG LEG	EEHRSS	SHEERS		JET-SET
EEGHLT	THE LEG	EEHRST	ESTHER	EEKKLR	LEKKER
EEGHNS	HENGES		ETHERS	EEKLMY	MEEKLY
EEGILS	LIEGES		THREES	EEKLNN	KENNEL
EEGIMR	EMIGRE	EEHRSY	HERESY	EEKLNR	KERNEL
	REGIME	EEHRTT	TETHER	EEKLNS	KNEELS
EEGINN	ENGINE	EEHRTW	WETHER	EEKLNY	KEENLY
EEGINS	GENIES	EEHSST	SHEETS	EEKLRT	KELTER
	SEEING		THESES	EEKLSS	SLEEKS
EEGINY	EYEING	EEHWYY	WHEYEY	EEKLTT	KETTLE
EEGIRV	GRIEVE	EEHWYZ	WHEEZY	EEKLWY	WEEKLY
EEGISS	EGISES	EEIKLP	KELPIE	EEKMRS	KERMES
	SIEGES	EEIKNP	KEEP IN	EEKNOP	KEEP ON
EEGKRS	GREEKS	EEILNP	PENILE	EEKNOT	KETONE
EEGLMU	LEGUME	EEILNR	LIERNE	EEKORV	REVOKE
EEGLNO	ONE LEG	EEILNS	ENSILE	EEKOSV	EVOKES
EEGLNT	GENTLE		SENILE	EEKPPU	KEEP UP
EEGMNO	GENOME	EEILRS	RELIES		UPKEEP
EEGMRR	MERGER	EEILRV	RELIVE	EEKPRU	PERUKE
EEGMRS	MERGES		REVILE	EEKRSS	ESKERS
EEGNOP	PONGEE	EEILRY	EERILY	EEKRSW	SKEWER
EEGNRS	GENRES	EEILST	ELITES	EEKRSY	KERSEY
	GREENS	EEILSV	LEVIES	EELLOP	POLLEE
EEGNRT	REGENT	EEILSX	EXILES	EELLOV	O LEVEL
EEGNRY	ENERGY		ILEXES	EELLPT	PELLET
	GREENY	EEILTV	LEVITE	EELLRS	SELLER
EEGNST	GENETS	EEILVW	WEEVIL	EELLRT	TELLER
	GENTES	EEIMNR	ERMINE	EELLRY	YELLER
EEGRRT	REGRET	EEIMPR	EMPIRE	EELLSV	LEVELS
EEGRRV	VERGER		EPIMER		S LEVEL
EEGRSS	EGRESS	EEIMRT	METIER	EELMPT	PELMET
	SERGES	EEIMST	SEMITE		TEMPLE
EEGRST	EGRETS	EEINNS	SEEN IN	EELMRY	MERELY
	GREETS	EEINPR	REPINE	EELMSY	SEEMLY
EEGRSV	VERGES	EEINQU	EQUINE	EELMTT	METTLE
EEGRSY	GEYSER	EEINRS	NEREIS	EELMTY	MEETLY
EEGRTT	GETTER		SERINE	EELNNT	LENTEN
EEGSST	EGESTS	EEINRT	ENTIRE	EELNOV	ELEVON
EEGSTT	GET SET	EEINRV	ENVIER	EELNPS	SPLEEN
EEHINR	HEREIN	EEINRW	WIENER	EELNRT	RELENT
	INHERE	EEINSS	SEES IN	EELNRU	UNREEL
EEHINT	THEINE		SEINES	EELNSS	LENSES
EEHIRT	EITHER	EEINSV	ENVIES		LESSEN
EEHITV	THIEVE	EEINTV	VENITE	EELNST	NESTLE
EEHKLS	SHEKEL	EEIORS	SOIREE	EELNSW	NEWELS
EEHLMP	HELP ME	EEIPPY	YIPPEE	EELNTT	NETTLE
EEHLMT	HELMET	EEIPRX	EXPIRE	EELNUV	VENULE
EEHLPR	HELPER	EEIPSS	ESPIES	EELNVY	EVENLY
EEHLSV	HELVES	EEIPTT	PETITE	EELNXY	XYLENE
	SHELVE	EEIPTW	PEEWIT	EELOPP	PEOPLE
EEHLSW	WHEELS	EEIRRS	SIRREE	EELOPR	ELOPER
EEHMMR	HEMMER	EEIRRT	ETRIER	EELOPS	ELOPES
EEHMNP	HEMPEN		RETIRE	EELORS	OR ELSE
EEHMNS	ENMESH	EEIRRW	REWIRE	EELOVV	EVOLVE
EEHMSS	MESHES	EEIRSS	SERIES	EELPRS	LEPERS
EEHMST	THEMES	EEIRSV	REVISE		REPELS
EEHMUX	EXHUME	EEIRSX	SEXIER	EELPRT	PETREL
EEHNOR	HEREON	EEIRSY	EYRIES	EELPRY	YELPER
EEHNPW	NEPHEW	EEIRVV	REVIVE	EELPSS	SLEEPS
EEHNRR	HERREN	EEIRVW	REVIEW	EELPST	PESTLE
EEHNRT	NETHER		VIEWER	EELPSV	PELVES
EEHNSS	SHEENS	EEISSV	SIEVES	EELPSX	EXPELS
EEHNSY	SHEENY	EEISSZ	SEIZES	EELPSY	SLEEPY
EEHORS	HEROES	EEJJNU	JEJUNE	EELQSU	SEQUEL
EEHORT	HERETO	EEJKRR	JERKER	EELRSS	LESSER
	HETERO	EEJLSW	JEWELS	EELRSV	ELVERS
EEHOSX	HEXOSE	EEJNNT	JENNET		LEVERS
EEHPPR	HEPPER	EEJRST	JESTER		REVELS
		EEJRSY	JERSEY	EELRTT	LETTER

EELRTW	WELTER	EENSSU	ENSUES	EERSTT	SETTER
EELSST	SLEETS	EENSSV	SEVENS		STREET
	STEELS	EENSTT	TENETS		TESTER
	STELES	EENSTV	EVENTS	EERSTU	RETUSE
EELSSV	SELVES	EENSTW	NEWEST	EERSTV	EVERTS
	VESSEL	EENSTY	TEENSY		REVETS
EELSTT	SETTLE	EENSUV	VENUES	EERSTW	WESTER
EELSTU	ELUTES	EENSYZ	SNEEZY	EERSTX	EXERTS
EELSTV	SVELTE	EENTTX	EXTENT	EERSUV	REVUES
EELSTY	SLEETY	EENTUX	EXEUNT	EERSVW	SWERVE
	STEELY	EEOPRS	REPOSE	EERTTT	TETTER
EELTVV	VELVET	EEOPSS	EPOSES	EERTTW	WETTER
EELTVW	TWELVE	EEOPST	TOPEES	EERTUY	TUYERE
EEMMNR	MERMEN	EEOPSX	EXPOSE	EERTVX	VERTEX
EEMMRS	EMMERS	EEOPTU	TOUPEE	EESSTT	SESTET
EEMMST	EMMETS	EEOPTY	PEYOTE		TESTES
EEMNNP	PENMEN	EEORST	STEREO		TSETSE
EEMNOT	TONEME	EEORSV	EVER SO	EESSTW	SWEETS
EEMNOY	YEOMEN		SOEVER	EESTTU	SUTTEE
EEMNSS	MENSES	EEORSZ	ZEROES	EESTTW	TWEETS
EEMNSY	YES MEN	EEORTV	VETOER	EESTTX	SEXTET
	YES-MEN	EEORUV	OEUVRE	EFFGIN	EFFING
EEMNYZ	ENZYME	EEOSST	SEES TO	EFFGIY	EFFIGY
EEMOPT	METOPE	EEOSTU	SEE OUT	EFFGOR	GOFFER
EEMORT	METEOR	EEOSTV	VETOES	EFFGOT	GET OFF
	REMOTE	EEOSUY	YOU SEE	EFFHOT	THE OFF
EEMORV	REMOVE	EEOSXY	OX EYES	EFFILP	PIFFLE
EEMOST	EMOTES		OXEYES	EFFILR	RIFFLE
EEMPRS	SEMPRE	EEPPPR	PEPPER	EFFKOY	OFF KEY
EEMPRT	TEMPER	EEPPST	STEPPE		OFF-KEY
EEMPTX	EXEMPT	EEPRRY	PREYER	EFFLMU	MUFFLE
EEMRST	MEREST	EEPRSS	SPREES	EFFLOT	LET OFF
	METERS	EEPRST	PESTER	EFFLRU	RUFFLE
	METRES		PETERS	EFFLUX	EFFLUX
EEMRSU	RESUME		PRESET	EFFNOO	ONE OFF
EEMSSS	MESSES	EEPRSU	PERUSE		ONE-OFF
EENNRT	RENNET		PUREES	EFFOPU	POUFFE
	TENNER		RUPEES	EFFORS	OFFERS
EENNST	SENNET	EEPRSV	VESPER	EFFORT	EFFORT
EENNSU	UNSEEN	EEPRSW	SPEWER	EFFOST	OFFSET
EENNUV	UNEVEN	EEPRTT	PETTER		SET OFF
EENOPR	OPENER	EEPRTU	REPUTE		SET-OFF
	REOPEN	EEPRTW	PEWTER	EFFPRU	PUFFER
EENOPS	PEONES	EEPRTX	EXPERT	EFFRSU	SUFFER
EENOPT	POTEEN	EEPSSS	SEPSES	EFFTTU	TUFFET
EENORW	ERE NOW	EEPSST	STEEPS	EFGINR	FINGER
EENOST	SEEN TO	EEPSSW	SWEEPS		FRINGE
EENOTW	TOWNEE	EEPSTT	SEPTET	EFGINS	FEIGNS
EENOVZ	EVZONE	EEPTTU	PUTTEE	EFGINT	FETING
EENPRS	PREENS	EEQRSU	QUEERS	EFGIRS	GRIEFS
EENPRT	REPENT	EEQRUU	QUEUER	EFGIRU	FIGURE
EENQSU	QUEENS	EEQSUU	QUEUES	EFGLNU	ENGULF
EENRRT	RENTER	EEQUXY	EXEQUY	EFGLOR	GOLFER
EENRSS	SNEERS	EERRST	RESTER	EFGLOT	LEFT GO
EENRST	ENTERS		TERSER	EFGLSU	GUELFS
	NESTER	EERRSU	REUSER	EFGOOR	FOREGO
	RESENT	EERRSV	REVERS	EFGORR	FORGER
	TENSER		SERVER	EFGORS	FORGES
EENRSU	ENSURE	EERRTU	URETER	EFGORT	FORGET
	ENURES	EERRTV	REVERT	EFGOSY	FOGEYS
EENRSV	NERVES	EERSST	ESTERS	EFGSUU	FUGUES
EENRSW	RENEWS		RESETS	EFHILS	ELFISH
EENRTT	NETTER		STEERS	EFHIRS	FISHER
	TENTER		STERES	EFHISS	FISHES
EENRTU	NEUTER	EERSSU	REUSES	EFHIST	FETISH
	TENURE	EERSSV	SERVES	EFHLOP	OF HELP
	TUREEN		SEVERS	EFHLSY	FLESHY
EENRVY	VENERY		SEVRES	EFHOOR	HOOFER
EENSSS	NESSES		VERSES	EFHRRU	FUHRER
	SENSES	EERSSW	SEWERS	EFHSTT	THEFTS
EENSST	TENSES			EFIINT	FINITE

EFIKNS	KNIFES	EFLRUU	RUEFUL	EGHINS	HINGES
EFILLN	FELL IN	EFLRUX	REFLUX		NEIGHS
EFILLR	FILLER	EFLSTU	FLUTES	EGHINW	WHINGE
	REFILL	EFLSUU	USEFUL	EGHINX	HEXING
EFILLT	FILLET	EFLSUX	FLUXES	EGHIRS	SIGHER
EFILNO	OLEFIN	EFMNOT	FOMENT	EGHIST	EIGHTS
EFILNY	FINELY	EFMNRU	FRENUM	EGHISW	WEIGHS
EFILPR	PILFER	EFMORR	FORMER	EGHITW	WEIGHT
EFILRR	RIFLER		REFORM	EGHITY	EIGHTY
EFILRS	FLIERS	EFMORS	FORMES	EGHLMP	PHLEGM
	LIFERS	EFMRSU	FEMURS	EGHLNT	LENGTH
	RIFLES	EFNOOT	OF NOTE	EGHLUY	HUGELY
EFILRT	FILTER	EFNORS	FREONS	EGHMOO	GO HOME
	LIFTER	EFNORZ	FROZEN	EGHNOU	ENOUGH
	TRIFLE	EFNOST	SOFTEN	EGHNRU	HUNGER
EFILRU	IREFUL	EFNRYZ	FRENZY	EGHOPR	GOPHER
EFILST	FILETS	EFOORT	FOOTER	EGHOTT	GHETTO
	ITSELF	EFOORW	WOOFER	EGHRSU	GUSHER
	STIFLE	EFORRU	FURORE	EGHSSU	GUSHES
EFILTT	LEFT IT	EFORST	FOREST	EGHSTU	HUGEST
EFILTU	FUTILE		FOSTER	EGIILL	GILLIE
EFILWY	WIFELY		SOFTER	EGIILR	GIRLIE
EFILZZ	FIZZLE	EFORSY	FOYERS	EGIIMN	GEMINI
EFIMRR	FIRMER	EFOSSS	FOSSES	EGIINP	PIEING
EFIMST	METIFS	EFOSTU	FOETUS	EGIINT	IGNITE
EFINOR	ON FIRE	EFRRSU	SURFER		TIEING
EFINRS	INFERS	EFRRSY	FRYERS	EGIINV	GIVE IN
EFINRY	FINERY	EFRSSU	FUSSER	EGIJLN	JINGLE
EFINST	FEINTS	EFRSUZ	FURZES	EGIJNW	JEWING
	FINEST	EFRTUU	FUTURE	EGIJRS	REJIGS
	INFEST	EFSSSU	FUSSES	EGIKNY	KEYING
EFINSU	INFUSE	EFSUZZ	FUZZES	EGIKRS	GRIKES
EFIORX	FOXIER	EGGGIL	GIGGLE	EGILLR	GRILLE
EFIOST	SOFTIE	EGGGIN	EGGING	EGILLU	LIGULE
EFIPRX	PREFIX	EGGGLO	GOGGLE	EGILMN	MINGLE
EFIPUV	FIVE UP	EGGGNO	EGG NOG	EGILMT	GIMLET
EFIRRS	FERRIS		EGGNOG	EGILNO	LEGION
	FRIERS	EGGHOT	HOGGET	EGILNR	LINGER
EFIRSS	SERIFS	EGGIJL	JIGGLE	EGILNS	SINGLE
EFIRST	REFITS	EGGIJR	JIGGER	EGILNT	TINGLE
	SIFTER	EGGILN	NIGGLE	EGILPT	PIGLET
	STRIFE	EGGILO	LOGGIE	EGILRS	GRILSE
EFIRSU	FURIES	EGGILW	WIGGLE	EGILRU	REGULI
EFIRSV	FIVERS	EGGIMO	MOGGIE		UGLIER
EFIRSX	FIXERS	EGGINR	GINGER	EGILRV	VERLIG
EFIRTT	FITTER		NIGGER	EGILST	GILETS
	TITFER	EGGIRR	RIGGER		LEGS IT
EFIRVY	VERIFY	EGGISU	GIGUES	EGILSU	GUILES
EFISTY	FEISTY	EGGJLO	JOGGLE	EGILTU	GLUTEI
EFISZZ	FIZZES	EGGJLU	JUGGLE	EGIMMR	MEGRIM
EFKLSU	FLUKES	EGGJOR	JOGGER	EGIMNT	METING
EFLLOW	FELLOW	EGGLOR	LOGGER	EGIMNW	MEWING
EFLLRU	FULLER	EGGLOT	TOGGLE	EGIMOS	EGOISM
EFLLTY	LET FLY	EGGLOW	WOGGLE	EGINNO	GONE IN
EFLMSU	FLUMES	EGGLRU	GURGLE	EGINNR	GINNER
EFLMSY	MYSELF		LUGGER	EGINNS	ENSIGN
EFLNNU	FUNNEL	EGGMRU	MUGGER	EGINOP	PIGEON
EFLNOS	FELONS	EGGNTU	NUGGET	EGINOR	IGNORE
EFLNOT	TEFLON	EGGORR	GORGER		REGION
EFLNOY	FELONY	EGGORS	GORGES	EGINOS	GOES IN
EFLNTU	FLUENT	EGGORT	GORGET		SOIGNE
EFLOOT	FOOTLE	EGGORU	GOUGER	EGINOT	TOEING
EFLORT	FLORET	EGGORY	GO GREY	EGINOW	WIGEON
EFLORU	FOULER	EGGOSU	GOUGES	EGINPP	PIGPEN
EFLORW	FLOWER	EGGRRU	RUGGER	EGINRR	ERRING
	FOWLER	EGHHIR	HIGHER		RINGER
EFLORX	FLEXOR	EGHHIT	EIGHTH	EGINRS	REIGNS
EFLOUW	WOEFUL		HEIGHT		RESIGN
EFLPRU	PURFLE				SIGNER
EFLRSY	FLYERS	EGHIIN	HIEING		SINGER
EFLRTU	FLUTER	EGHILS	SLEIGH	EGINRW	WINGER
		EGHINO	HOEING		

EGINRY	IN GREY	EGNOSS	SEGNOS	EHINRS	RHINES
EGINSS	GNEISS	EGNOST	GETS ON		SHINER
	SINGES	EGNOTT	GOTTEN		SHRINE
EGINST	GETS IN	EGNOTU	TONGUE	EHINRW	WHINER
	INGEST	EGNOXY	OXYGEN	EHINSS	SHINES
	SIGNET	EGNRTU	URGENT	EHINSW	NEWISH
	TINGES	EGNRTY	GENTRY		WHINES
EGINSU	GENIUS	EGNSTU	SET GUN	EHINTW	WHITEN
EGINSW	WINGES	EGNSUU	UNGUES	EHINTZ	ZENITH
EGINSX	SEXING	EGOORV	GO OVER	EHINWY	WHINEY
EGINTW	TWINGE		GROOVE	EHIOPT	OPHITE
EGIORR	GORIER	EGOOST	GOES TO	EHIORS	HORSIE
EGIORS	ORGIES		STOOGE	EHIPPR	HIPPER
EGIORT	GOITRE	EGOOSY	GOOSEY	EHIPRS	PERISH
EGIOST	EGOIST	EGOPRR	GROPER	EHIRSS	SHIRES
	GOES IT	EGOPRS	GROPES	EHIRST	THEIRS
	STOGIE	EGOPSU	GOES UP	EHIRSV	SHIVER
EGIOSV	OGIVES	EGOPTU	PEG OUT		SHRIVE
EGIPPR	GRIPPE	EGORRS	ROGERS	EHIRSW	WISHER
EGIPRR	GRIPER	EGORRW	GROWER	EHIRTT	TITHER
EGIPRS	GRIPES	EGORSU	GROUSE	EHIRTV	THRIVE
EGIPUV	GIVE UP		ROGUES	EHIRTW	WHITER
EGIRST	TIGERS		ROUGES		WITHER
EGIRSU	REGIUS		RUGOSE		WRITHE
EGISSU	GUISES	EGORSV	GROVES	EHIRTZ	ZITHER
EGISTT	GETS IT	EGOSTT	GOT SET	EHISSS	HISSES
EGJLNU	JUNGLE	EGOSTW	GO WEST	EHISST	HEISTS
EGKMSU	MUSKEG	EGOSUV	VOGUES		SHIEST
EGLLOW	GO WELL	EGOTTU	GET OUT		THESIS
EGLLTU	GULLET	EGOTUY	GET YOU!	EHISSW	WISHES
EGLMOS	GOLEMS	EGOTYZ	ZYGOTE	EHISTT	THEIST
EGLMSU	GLUMES	EGPRSU	PURGES		TITHES
EGLNNU	GUNNEL		SPURGE	EHISTW	WHITES
EGLNOR	LONGER	EGPRUW	GREW UP		WITHES
EGLNOU	LOUNGE	EGPSTU	GETS UP	EHITWY	WHITEY
EGLNPU	PLUNGE	EGRRSU	URGERS	EHKLPT	KLEPHT
EGLNSU	LUNGES	EGRSSU	SURGES	EHKLSW	WHELKS
EGLNTU	GLUTEN	EGRTTU	GUTTER	EHKMRS	KHMERS
EGLNTY	GENTLY	EGSSTU	GUESTS	EHKNOR	HONKER
EGLOPR	PROLEG		GUSSET	EHKOOR	HOOKER
EGLOPS	GOSPEL			EHKORS	KOSHER
EGLORU	REGULO	EHHIKS	SHEIKH	EHLLOR	HOLLER
EGLORW	GLOWER	EHHIRT	HITHER	EHLLOS	HELLOS
EGLOST	LET'S GO	EHHLLO	OH HELL!	EHLLRU	HULLER
	LETS GO	EHHNPY	HYPHEN	EHLLSS	SHELLS
		EHHOTW	THE WHO	EHLLSY	SHELLY
EGLOSV	GLOVES	EHHRST	THRESH	EHLMOP	PHLOEM
EGLOUY	EULOGY	EHHSSU	HUSHES	EHLMOY	HOMELY
EGLPRU	GULPER	EHIIPP	HIPPIE	EHLMTY	METHYL
EGLPSU	LEG-UPS	EHIIST	SHIITE	EHLNOP	PHENOL
EGLRSU	GRUELS	EHIJSW	JEWISH	EHLNPY	PHENYL
EGLRYY	GREYLY	EHIKNO	HONKIE	EHLORW	HOWLER
EGLTUU	TELUGU	EHIKRS	SHRIEK	EHLOST	HELOTS
EGLUZZ	GUZZLE		SHRIKE		HOSTEL
EGMMRU	GUMMER	EHILMU	HELIUM		HOTELS
EGMNNU	GUNMEN	EHILOR	HOLIER	EHLOSV	HOVELS
EGMNOR	MONGER	EHILOS	HOLIES		SHOVEL
EGMNOS	GNOMES		ISOHEL	EHLPPU	HELP UP
EGMNTU	NUTMEG	EHILOT	EOLITH	EHLPSW	WHELPS
EGMORU	MORGUE	EHILRS	RELISH	EHLRRU	HURLER
EGMRTU	TERGUM	EHILRT	LITHER	EHLRSU	LUSHER
EGNNOO	GONE ON	EHILSV	ELVISH	EHLRTU	HURTLE
EGNNOU	GUENON	EHILSW	WHILES	EHLSSU	LUSHES
EGNNRU	GUNNER	EHIMNR	MENHIR	EHLSTT	SHTETL
EGNOOS	GOES ON	EHIMNS	HEMS IN	EHLSTU	HUSTLE
EGNOOT	GONE TO	EHIMNT	HIT MEN		SLEUTH
EGNOPS	SPONGE	EHIMNU	INHUME	EHLSTY	SHELTY
EGNOPU	GONE UP	EHIMRT	HERMIT	EHMNSY	HYMENS
EGNORS	GONERS	EHIMRU	HUMERI	EHMORS	HOMERS
EGNORV	GOVERN	EHIMST	THEISM	EHMORT	MOTHER
EGNORW	GREW ON	EHINOR	HEROIN	EHMRRY	RHYMER
EGNORY	GROYNE		ON HIRE		

EHMRST	THERMS	EIILZZ	LIZZIE	EILLMO	MOLLIE
EHMRSU	RHEUMS	EIIMNT	IN TIME	EILLMR	MILLER
EHMRSY	RHYMES	EIINOS	IONISE	EILLMT	MILLET
EHMRUY	RHEUMY	EIINOZ	IONIZE	EILLMU	ILLUME
EHMSSU	MUSHES	EIINPT	TIE PIN	EILLNO	NIELLO
EHNOOP	NO HOPE		TIEPIN	EILLNT	LENTIL
EHNOPS	PHONES	EIINRT	TINIER		LINTEL
EHNOPY	PHONEY	EIINST	SENITI		
EHNORS	HERONS		TIE-INS	EILLNW	WELL IN
	NOSHER		TIES IN	EILLOT	TOLLIE
	SENHOR	EIINSZ	IN SIZE	EILLOW	LIE LOW
EHNORT	HORNET	EIINTV	INVITE	EILLPU	PILULE
	THRONE	EIINVW	IN VIEW	EILLRT	TILLER
EHNOSS	NOSHES	EIIPRT	PITIER	EILLRW	WILLER
EHNOST	HONEST	EIIPST	PITIES	EILLSU	ILL-USE
EHNOSY	HONEYS	EIIPSX	PIXIES	EILLTT	LITTLE
EHNRSY	HENRYS	EIIRRW	WIRIER	EILLVY	EVILLY
EHNRTU	HUNTER	EIIRSS	IRISES		LIVELY
EHOOPO	HOOPOE	EIIRVZ	VIZIER		VILELY
EHOOPR	HOOPER	EIJKNO	IN JOKE	EILMNR	MERLIN
EHOOPY	PHOOEY	EIJKNR	JERKIN	EILMNS	SIMNEL
EHOORT	HOOTER	EIJKNU	JUNKIE	EILMNY	MYELIN
EHOORV	HOOVER	EIJMNO	JOIN 'EM	EILMOT	MOTILE
EHOOST	SOOTHE	EIJNNO	EN JOIN	EILMPP	PIMPLE
EHOOSV	HOOVES	EIJNNU	IN JUNE	EILMPR	LIMPER
EHOPPR	HOPPER	EIJNOR	JOINER		PRELIM
EHOPRS	POSHER		REJOIN	EILMPS	IMPELS
EHOPRT	POTHER	EIJNRU	INJURE		SIMPLE
EHORSS	HORSES	EIJNST	IN JEST	EILMPW	WIMPLE
	SHORES	EIJNSX	JINXES	EILMRS	MILERS
EHORST	OTHERS	EIJNTY	JITNEY		SMILER
	THROES	EIJRSU	JURIES	EILMRT	MILTER
EHORSV	HOVERS	EIJRTT	JITTER	EILMSS	SLIMES
	SHOVER	EIJSTU	JESUIT		SMILES
	SHROVE	EIKKOO	KOOKIE	EILMSU	MUESLI
EHORSW	SHOWER	EIKLLR	KILLER	EILMSY	LIMEYS
	WHORES	EIKLLY	LIKELY		SMILEY
EHORSY	HORSEY	EIKLMR	MILKER	EILMTY	TIMELY
EHORTT	HOTTER	EIKLNR	LINKER	EILMZZ	MIZZLE
	TOTHER	EIKLNS	LIKENS	EILNNO	ON LINE
EHORTV	THROVE		SILKEN		ON-LINE
EHORTX	EXHORT	EIKLNT	TINKLE	EILNNS	LINENS
EHORTY	THEORY	EIKLNU	UNLIKE	EILNNT	LINNET
EHOSSU	HOUSES	EIKLNV	KELVIN	EILNOP	PILE ON
EHOSSV	SHOVES	EIKLNW	WELKIN		PINOLE
EHPRSU	PUSHER		WINKLE	EILNOS	INSOLE
EHPRYZ	ZEPHYR	EIKLRT	KILTER		LESION
EHPSSU	PUSHES		KIRTLE	EILNOV	IN LOVE
EHRRSU	RUSHER	EIKLTT	KITTLE	EILNPP	NIPPLE
EHRRSY	SHERRY	EIKMOS	ESKIMO	EILNPS	SPINEL
EHRRWY	WHERRY	EIKMST	KISMET		SPLINE
EHRSSU	RHESUS	EIKNOV	INVOKE	EILNPT	PINTLE
	RUSHES	EIKNPT	KEPT IN	EILNPU	LINE UP
	USHERS	EIKNRS	SINKER		LINE-UP
EHRSSW	SHREWS	EIKNRT	TINKER		LINEUP
EHSSTY	SHYEST	EIKNSS	SKEINS		LUPINE
EIIKNP	PINKIE	EIKNSV	KNIVES	EILNRS	LINERS
EIILLN	NIELLI	EIKNTT	KITTEN	EILNRT	LINTER
EIILLS	LILIES	EIKOOR	ROOKIE	EILNST	ENLIST
EIILLW	WILLIE	EIKOPR	POKIER		INLETS
EIILMS	SIMILE	EIKPPR	KIPPER		LETS IN
EIILMU	MILIEU	EIKPRS	SPIKER		LISTEN
EIILNN	IN LINE	EIKPSS	SPIKES		SILENT
EIILNR	INLIER	EIKRSS	KISSER		TINSEL
EIILNS	LIES IN		SKIERS	EILNSV	LIVENS
EIILNU	IN LIEU	EIKRST	STRIKE		SNIVEL
EIILNV	LIVE IN	EIKRSV	SKIVER	EILNSY	LYSINE
EIILOR	OILIER	EIKRSY	KYRIES	EILNTY	LENITY
EIILRV	VIRILE	EIKSSS	KISSES	EILNUV	UNVEIL
EIILRW	WILIER	EIKSST	SKITES	EILOOR	ORIOLE
EIILRX	ELIXIR	EIKSSV	SKIVES	EILOOT	OOLITE
				EILOPS	PILOSE

EILOPT	PIOLET	EIMNTU	MINUET	EINPPR	NIPPER
	POLITE		MINUTE	EINPPS	PEPSIN
EILORT	LOITER	EIMNTY	ENMITY	EINPRS	SNIPER
	TOILER	EIMNZZ	MIZZEN	EINPRU	PUNIER
EILOST	LIES TO	EIMOPS	IMPOSE		PURINE
	TOILES	EIMORS	ISOMER		UNRIPE
EILOSV	OLIVES	EIMOSS	MIOSES	EINPSS	SNIPES
EILOTT	TOILET	EIMOST	SOMITE		SPINES
EILOTV	VIOLET	EIMOSV	MOVIES	EINPST	IN STEP
EILPPR	RIPPLE	EIMOTT	TO TIME		INSTEP
EILPPT	TIPPLE	EIMOTV	MOTIVE		SPINET
EILPPU	PILE UP	EIMOTY	MOIETY		STEP IN
	PILEUP	EIMPRR	PRIMER		STEP-IN
EILPRS	LISPER	EIMPRS	PRIMES	EINPSU	PUISNE
	PERILS		SIMPER		SUPINE
	PLIERS	EIMPRT	PERMIT	EINPTY	IN TYPE
EILPRT	LET RIP	EIMPRU	IMPURE	EINQSU	SEQUIN
	TRIPLE		UMPIRE	EINQUU	UNIQUE
EILPRY	RIPELY	EIMPTU	IMPUTE	EINRRS	RINSER
EILPSS	PLISSE	EIMRRT	TRIMER	EINRRU	RUINER
	SPIELS	EIMRSS	MISERS	EINRSS	RESINS
	SPILES		REMISS		RINSES
EILPSU	LIES UP	EIMRST	MERITS		SIRENS
	PILEUS		MISTER	EINRST	INSERT
EILPSV	PELVIS		MITRES		INTERS
EILPUV	LIVE UP		REMITS		SINTER
EILRST	LITERS		SMITER		STRINE
	LITRES		TIMERS		TRINES
	TILERS	EIMRSX	MIXERS	EINRSU	INSURE
EILRSV	LIVERS	EIMRSY	MISERY		INURES
	LIVRES	EIMSSS	MISSES		URSINE
	SILVER	EIMSST	SMITES	EINRTT	TINTER
	SLIVER		TMESIS	EINRTU	TRIUNE
EILRTT	LITTER	EIMSSU	MISUSE		UNITER
	TILTER	EIMSSX	SEXISM	EINRTV	INVERT
EILRTU	RUTILE	EIMSTY	STYMIE	EINRTW	TWINER
EILRVY	LIVERY	EINNNR	RENNIN		WINTER
	VERILY	EINNOP	OPEN IN	EINRVY	VINERY
EILSST	ISLETS	EINNOS	NOSE IN	EINRWY	WINERY
	SLIEST	EINNOT	INTONE	EINSST	INSETS
	STILES	EINNPT	TENPIN		SETS IN
EILSTT	TITLES	EINNPW	NEW PIN		STEINS
EILSTV	VILEST	EINNRS	SINNER	EINSSW	SINEWS
EILSVW	SWIVEL	EINNRT	INTERN	EINSTU	UNITES
EILSWY	WISELY		TINNER		UNTIES
EILSXY	SEXILY	EINNRW	WINNER	EINSTV	INVEST
EILSZZ	SIZZLE	EINNSS	NISSEN	EINSTW	TWINES
EILTTT	TITTLE	EINNST	SENNIT		WISENT
EILTVY	LEVITY		TENNIS	EINSUW	UNWISE
EIMMNU	IMMUNE	EINNTT	INTENT	EINSUX	UNISEX
EIMMOP	POMMIE	EINNTU	IN TUNE	EINSVX	VIXENS
EIMMOR	MEMOIR		TUNE IN	EINSWY	SINEWY
EIMMRS	MERISM	EINNTV	INVENT	EINSWZ	WIZENS
	SIMMER	EINNTW	WENT IN	EINTTW	WENT IT
EIMMRU	IMMURE	EINNTY	NINETY	EINTTY	ENTITY
EIMNNT	TINMEN	EINOPR	ORPINE	EIOOST	OTIOSE
EIMNNX	MENINX	EINOPS	OPINES	EIOPPY	YOPPIE
EIMNOO	MOONIE		PONIES	EIOPSS	POISES
EIMNOR	MERINO	EINOPT	POINTE		POSIES
EIMNOS	MONIES	EINORS	NOSIER	EIOPST	POSTIE
EIMNOT	NO TIME		SENIOR	EIOPTT	TIPTOE
	ON TIME	EINORT	ORIENT	EIORRS	ROSIER
EIMNOV	MOVE IN	EINORW	WORE IN	EIORRT	RIOTER
EIMNPT	PIT MEN	EINORZ	ZERO IN	EIORSS	OSIERS
	PITMEN	EINOSS	ENOSIS	EIORST	SORTIE
EIMNRT	MINTER		EOSINS		TORIES
EIMNRU	MURINE		NOISES	EIORSV	VIREOS
EIMNRV	VERMIN		OSSEIN	EIOSTV	SOVIET
EIMNSX	MINXES	EINOSW	NOWISE	EIOTVV	VOTIVE
EIMNTT	MITTEN	EINOTX	NO EXIT	EIPPPU	PIPE UP
		EINOVW	WOVE IN	EIPPRR	RIPPER

EIPPRS	PIPERS	EJLOSU	JOULES	ELMNOS	LEMONS
	SIPPER	EJLPSU	JULEPS		MELONS
EIPPRT	TIPPER	EJMPRU	JUMPER		SOLEMN
EIPPRZ	ZIPPER	EJNOSY	ENJOYS	ELMNOT	LOMENT
EIPPST	SIPPET	EJORTT	JOTTER		MOLTEN
EIPPTT	TIPPET	EKLLNS	KNELLS	ELMNOY	LEMONY
EIPQSU	EQUIPS	EKLNOS	KELSON	ELMNPU	LUMPEN
	PIQUES	EKLOOR	LOOKER	ELMNSU	LUMENS
EIPQTU	PIQUET	EKLOSY	YOKELS	ELMOPY	EMPLOY
EIPRRS	PRIERS	EKLOWY	LOW KEY	ELMORS	MORELS
	SPRIER		LOW-KEY		MORSEL
EIPRSS	PRISES	EKLRRU	LURKER	ELMOST	MOLEST
	SPIRES	EKLSTU	ST. LUKE		MOTELS
EIPRST	ESPRIT	EKMNOY	MONKEY	ELMOTT	MOTTLE
	PRIEST	EKMORS	SMOKER	ELMOTY	MOTLEY
	RIPEST	EKMOSS	SMOKES	ELMOUV	VOLUME
	SPRITE	EKMSTU	MUSKET	ELMPPU	PEPLUM
	STRIPE	EKNNOT	NEKTON	ELMPRU	RUMPLE
FIPRSU	RISE UP	EKNNSU	SUNKEN	ELMPSU	PLUMES
EIPRSV	VIPERS	EKNOPS	SPOKEN	ELMRSU	LEMURS
EIPRSW	WIPERS	EKNOPT	KEPT ON	ELMRTY	MYRTLE
EIPRSZ	PRIZES	EKNORR	KRONER	ELMSST	SMELTS
EIPRTV	PRIVET	EKNORW	KNOWER	ELMSSU	MUSSEL
EIPRTY	PYRITE	EKNOST	TOKENS	ELMTUY	MUTLEY
EIPRXY	EXPIRY	EKNOUY	UNYOKE	ELMUZZ	MUZZLE
EIPSSS	SEPSIS	EKOORT	RETOOK	ELNNOS	NELSON
	SPEISS	EKOPRR	PORKER	ELNNRU	RUNNEL
EIPSST	SPITES	EKOPRS	POKERS	ELNNTU	TUNNEL
	STIPES	EKOPSS	SPOKES	ELNOOS	LOOSEN
EIPSSW	SWIPES	EKOPUW	WOKE UP	ELNOPT	LEPTON
EIPSTU	TIE-UPS	EKORRW	REWORK	ELNOPY	OPENLY
	TIES UP		WORKER	ELNORS	ENROLS
EIPSTW	PEWITS	EKORRY	YORKER		LONERS
EIQRSU	QUIRES	EKORST	STOKER	ELNOSS	LESSON
	RISQUE		STROKE	ELNOST	LETS ON
	SQUIRE	EKOSST	STOKES		STOLEN
EIQRUV	QUIVER	EKPPTU	KEPT UP		TELSON
EIQSTU	QUIETS	EKRRSY	SKERRY	ELNOSV	NOVELS
EIQTUY	EQUITY	EKRSTU	TUSKER		SLOVEN
EIRRSS	RISERS	EKRTUY	TURKEY	ELNOZZ	NOZZLE
EIRRST	TRIERS	ELLMOW	MELLOW	ELNPTU	PENULT
EIRRSV	RIVERS	ELLMRU	MULLER	ELNPTY	PLENTY
EIRRSW	WIRERS	ELLMSS	SMELLS	ELNSSU	UNLESS
EIRRTW	WRITER	ELLMSY	SMELLY	ELNSXY	LYNXES
EIRSST	RESIST	ELLMTU	MULLET	ELNUZZ	NUZZLE
	SISTER	ELLMUV	VELLUM	ELOOPR	LOOPER
EIRSSU	ISSUER	ELLNOP	POLLEN	ELOORS	LOOSER
EIRSSX	SIXERS	ELLNOT	TELL ON	ELOORT	LOOTER
EIRSTT	SITTER	ELLNOY	LONELY		RETOOL
EIRSTV	RIVETS	ELLNSU	SULLEN		ROOTLE
	STRIVE	ELLNUU	LUNULE	ELOOSS	LOOSES
EIRSTW	WRITES	ELLNUW	UNWELL	ELOOTT	TOOTLE
EIRTTT	TITTER	ELLOPR	POLLER	ELOPPR	LOPPER
EIRTTV	TRIVET	ELLOPX	POLLEX		PROPEL
EIRTUV	VIRTUE	ELLORR	ROLLER	ELOPPS	PEPLOS
EIRTVY	VERITY	ELLOSY	SOLELY	ELOPPT	TOPPLE
EISSSU	ISSUES	ELLOVY	LOVELY	ELOPRS	PROLES
EISSTT	TESTIS		VOLLEY	ELOPRT	PETROL
EISSTU	SUITES	ELLOWY	YELLOW	ELOPRV	PLOVER
	TISSUE	ELLPSS	SPELLS	ELOPSS	SLOPES
EISSTV	ST. IVES	ELLPTU	PULLET	ELOPSU	LOUPES
EISSTW	WISEST	ELLPUW	WELL UP	ELOPTU	TUPELO
EISSTX	EXISTS	ELLPUY	PULLEY	ELOPTY	PEYOTL
	SEXIST	ELLQSU	QUELLS	ELORRS	SORREL
EISZZZ	ZIZZES	ELLSSW	SWELLS	ELORSS	LESSOR
EJKNOO	NO JOKE	ELMMOP	POMMEL		LOSERS
EJKNRU	JUNKER	ELMMOS	MOSLEM	ELORST	OSTLER
EJKNTU	JUNKET	ELMMPU	PUMMEL		STEROL
EJKOPS	KOPJES	ELMNOR	MERLON	ELORSV	LOVERS
EJKORS	JOKERS				SOLVER
EJLOST	JOSTLE				

ELORSW	LOWERS	
	ROWELS	
	SLOWER	
ELORSY	SORELY	
ELORTV	REVOLT	
ELORTW	TROWEL	
ELORUV	LOUVRE	
	VELOUR	
ELORVY	OVERLY	
ELORWY	LOWERY	
ELOSSS	LOSSES	
ELOSST	STOLES	
ELOSSU	LOUSES	
	OUSELS	
ELOSSV	SOLVES	
ELOSTU	SOLUTE	
	TOUSLE	
ELOSTW	LOWEST	
	OWLETS	
	TOWELS	
ELOSTX	EXTOLS	
ELOSUV	OVULES	
ELOSUZ	OUZELS	
ELOSVW	VOWELS	
	WOLVES	
ELOTTU	LET OUT	
	LET-OUT	
	OUTLET	
ELOTUV	VOLUTE	
ELPPRU	PURPLE	
ELPPSU	SUPPLE	
ELPRRU	PURLER	
ELPRSU	PULSER	
ELPRTY	PELTRY	
	PERTLY	
ELPRUY	PURELY	
ELPSST	SPELTS	
ELPSSU	PLUSES	
	PULSES	
ELPSTU	LETS UP	
ELPSUX	PLEXUS	
ELPUZZ	PUZZLE	
ELRRSU	RULERS	
ELRSTU	LUSTRE	
	RESULT	
	RUSTLE	
	SUTLER	
	ULSTER	
ELRSTY	STYLER	
ELRSUY	SURELY	
ELRTTU	TURTLE	
ELRUWZ	WURZEL	
ELSSTU	TUSSLE	
ELSSTY	SLYEST	
	STYLES	
ELSTTY	STYLET	
ELSTUX	EXULTS	
ELSTUZ	LUTZES	
EMMMRU	MUMMER	
EMMNOT	MOMENT	
EMMORY	MEMORY	
EMMRRU	RUMMER	
EMMRSU	SUMMER	
EMMSUU	MUSEUM	
EMNOOV	MOVE ON	
EMNOPY	EPONYM	
EMNORS	SERMON	
EMNORT	MENTOR	
EMNOSS	MESONS	
EMNOSY	MONEYS	
EMNOTY	ETYMON	
EMNRSU	RUMENS	
EMOORR	ROOMER	
EMOORS	MOROSE	
	ROMEOS	
EMOORX	EXMOOR	
EMOOSS	OSMOSE	
EMOPPR	MOPPER	
EMOPPT	MOPPET	
EMOPRR	ROMPER	
EMOPRS	PROEMS	
EMOPRT	PRO TEM	
EMOPST	TEMPOS	
EMOPSY	MYOPES	
EMOPUV	MOVE UP	
EMOQSU	MOSQUE	
EMORRS	ORMERS	
EMORRT	TREMOR	
EMORRW	WORMER	
EMORST	METROS	
EMORSU	MEROUS	
	MOUSER	
EMOSSS	MOSSES	
EMOSSU	MOUSES	
	MOUSSE	
EMOSSY	MOSEYS	
EMOSTT	MOTETS	
	MOTTES	
	TOTEMS	
EMOSZZ	MEZZOS	
EMPRSS	SPERMS	
EMPSSU	MESS UP	
	SPUMES	
EMPSTT	TEMPTS	
EMPSTU	SEPTUM	
EMRSSS	MESSRS	
EMRSSU	SERUMS	
EMRSTU	MUSTER	
	STUMER	
EMRTTU	MUTTER	
EMSSSU	MUSSES	
EMSSTY	SYSTEM	
ENNNOP	PENNON	
ENNORU	NEURON	
ENNORW	RENOWN	
ENNOST	SONNET	
	TENONS	
	TONNES	
ENNOSW	NO NEWS	
	SEWN ON	
ENNOTW	NEWTON	
	WENT ON	
ENNPTU	PUNNET	
ENNRRU	RUNNER	
ENOOPR	OPERON	
ENOORS	RONEOS	
	SOONER	
ENOORW	WORE ON	
ENOOSS	NOOSES	
ENOOSZ	SNOOZE	
ENOOTW	ONE-TWO	
ENOPPU	OPEN UP	
ENOPRS	PERSON	
ENOPRV	PROVEN	
ENOPST	PONTES	
ENOPSU	NOSE UP	
ENOPTT	POTENT	
	TOP TEN	
ENORRS	SNORER	
ENORRY	ORNERY	
ENORSS	SENORS	
	SENSOR	
	SNORES	
ENORST	NESTOR	
	TENORS	
	TENSOR	
	TONERS	
ENORSW	WORSEN	
ENORSZ	ZONERS	
ENORTT	ROTTEN	
	TORTEN	
ENOSST	ONSETS	
	SETS ON	
	STONES	
ENOSSU	ONUSES	
ENOSSW	SEWS ON	
ENOSTX	SEXTON	
ENOSUV	VENOUS	
ENOSVY	ENVOYS	
ENOSXY	ONYXES	
ENOTTU	TENUTO	
	TEUTON	
ENOTTW	WENT TO	
ENPPTU	PENT-UP	
ENPRSU	PRUNES	
ENPRTU	PUNTER	
ENPRUY	PENURY	
ENPSTU	SENT UP	
ENPTUU	TUNE UP	
ENPTUW	WENT UP	
ENQRSU	QUERNS	
ENRRSU	RERUNS	
ENRRTU	RETURN	
	TURNER	
ENRSST	STERNS	
ENRSSU	NURSES	
ENRSTU	TUNERS	
	UNREST	
ENRSTW	STREWN	
ENRSTY	SENTRY	
ENRSUU	UNSURE	
ENRTTU	NUTTER	
ENRTUU	UNTRUE	
ENSSTU	SUNSET	
ENTTWY	TWENTY	
EOOPPS	OPPOSE	
EOOPRR	POORER	
EOOPSV	POOVES	
EOORRT	ROOTER	
	TORERO	
EOORSV	ROOVES	
EOORSW	WOOERS	
EOORTT	TOOTER	
EOPPPR	POPPER	
EOPPPT	POPPET	
EOPPRR	PROPER	
EOPPRT	TOPPER	
EOPPRY	POPERY	
	PYROPE	
EOPRRT	PORTER	
	PRETOR	
	REPORT	
EOPRRU	POURER	
EOPRSS	POSERS	
	SPORES	
EOPRST	PORTES	
	POSTER	
	PRESTO	
	TOPERS	
EOPRSU	POSEUR	
	ROSE UP	

74

EOPRSV	PROVES	EPPSTU	STEP UP	FFNSSU	SNUFFS
EOPRSW	POWERS		STEP-UP	FFNSUY	SNUFFY
EOPRSY	OSPREY	EPRRSU	PURSER	FFOOPP	POP OFF
EOPRTT	POTTER	EPRRSY	SPRYER	FFOPTU	PUT OFF
EOPRTU	POUTER	EPRSST	STREPS	FFORUX	FOX FUR
	TORE UP	EPRSSU	PURSES	FFSSTU	STUFFS
	TROUPE		SPRUES	FFSTUY	STUFFY
EOPRTX	EXPORT	EPRSTU	ERUPTS	FGHILT	FLIGHT
EOPRTY	POETRY		PUREST	FGHIRT	FRIGHT
EOPSSS	POSSES		REST UP	FGHIST	FIGHTS
EOPSST	ESTOPS	EPRSTW	TWERPS	FGHOTU	FOUGHT
	POSSET	EPRSUU	PURSUE	FGIILN	FILING
	PTOSES	EPRSUV	REVS UP	FGIINN	FINING
	STOEPS	EPRTTU	PUTTER	FGIINR	FIRING
	STOPES	EPRTTY	PRETTY	FGIINX	FIXING
EOPSSU	OPUSES	EPRUVY	PURVEY	FGILNS	FLINGS
	SPOUSE	EPSSSU	PUSSES	FGILNY	FLYING
EOPSSY	SEPOYS	EPSSTU	SETS UP	FGILUY	UGLIFY
EOPSTX	SEXPOT		STUPES	FGIMNU	FUMING
EOQRTU	ROQUET		UPSETS	FGINOR	FRO-ING
	TORQUE	EPSSUU	USES UP	FGINOX	FOXING
EOQSTU	QUOTES	EQSSTU	QUESTS	FGINRY	FRYING
EORRRS	ERRORS	ERRSUU	USURER	FGINSU	FUSING
EORRRT	TERROR	ERRSUV	SURREY	FGIRST	GRIFTS
EORRRY	ORRERY	ERRTTU	TURRET	FGJLUU	JUGFUL
EORRST	RESORT	ERSSST	STRESS	FGKNUU	KUNG FU
	ROSTER	ERSSTU	RUSSET	FGNSUU	FUNGUS
	SORTER		SUREST	FGNUUY	FU-YUNG
	STORER	ERSSTW	WRESTS	FGOORT	FORGOT
EORRSU	SOURER	ERSSUV	VERSUS	FHIINS	FINISH
EORRSV	ROVERS	ERSTTU	TRUEST	FHILTY	FILTHY
EORRTT	RETORT		UTTERS	FHIMUY	HUMIFY
	ROTTER	ERSTUU	SUTURE	FHIOOT	HOOF IT
EORRTV	TROVER		UTERUS	FHIRST	FIRTHS
EORRZZ	ROZZER	ERSTUV	TURVES		SHRIFT
EORSST	SOREST	ERSTUY	SURETY	FHIRTT	THRIFT
	STORES	ERSTVY	VESTRY	FHISST	SHIFTS
	TOSSER	ERSUVY	SURVEY	FHISTU	SHUFTI
EORSSU	ROUSES	ESSSSU	SUSSES	FHISTY	SHIFTY
	SEROUS	ESSTTV	T V SETS	FHORST	FROTHS
EORSSV	SERVOS	FFFLOY	FLY OFF	FHORTU	FOURTH
	VERSOS	FFFLSU	FLUFFS	FHORTY	FROTHY
EORSSW	SOWERS	FFFLUY	FLUFFY	FHPRUY	FURPHY
EORSTT	OTTERS	FFGINO	OFFING	FIIKNR	FIRKIN
	TORTES	FFGOOT	GOT OFF	FIILLN	FILL IN
EORSTU	OUSTER	FFHIOS	OFFISH		INFILL
	ROUTES	FFHIST	FIFTHS	FIILLP	FILLIP
	SOUTER	FFHISW	WHIFFS	FIILVY	VILIFY
EORSTV	STROVE	FFHOOP	HOP OFF	FIIMNR	INFIRM
	TROVES	FFHOSW	HOWFFS	FIIMST	MISFIT
	VOTERS	FFIINT	TIFFIN	FIINST	FITS IN
EORSTW	TOWERS	FFIKSS	SKIFFS	FIITXY	FIXITY
EORSTY	OYSTER	FFILLU	FULFIL	FIIVVY	VIVIFY
	STOREY	FFILTU	FITFUL	FIKRSS	FRISKS
	TOYERS	FFIMNU	MUFFIN	FIKRSY	FRISKY
EORSVW	VOWERS	FFINOS	IN-OFFS	FILLPU	FILL UP
EORTTT	TOTTER	FFINPU	PUFFIN	FILLRS	FRILLS
EORTTX	EXTORT	FFINSS	SNIFFS	FILLRY	FRILLY
EORTVX	VORTEX	FFINSY	SNIFFY	FILLUW	WILFUL
EORUVY	VOYEUR	FFIOPR	RIP OFF	FILMRY	FIRMLY
EORWWZ	WOWZER		RIP-OFF	FILMSY	FLIMSY
EOSSST	TOSSES	FFIOPT	TIP OFF	FILNOR	FLORIN
EOSSSU	SOUSES		TIP-OFF	FILNOW	INFLOW
EOSSTT	SET-TOS	FFIOST	SOFFIT	FILNOY	IF ONLY
	SETS TO	FFIQSU	QUIFFS	FILNST	FLINTS
EOSSTV	STOVES	FFISST	STIFFS	FILNSU	SINFUL
EOSTTU	OUTSET	FFISUX	SUFFIX	FILNTU	TINFUL
	SET OUT	FFLOTY	FYLFOT	FILNTY	FLINTY
EPPPTU	PUPPET	FFNORU	FOR FUN	FILNUX	INFLUX
EPPRSU	SUPPER		RUN OFF	FILOOS	FOLIOS
	UPPERS		RUNOFF	FILOSS	FOSSIL

FILOXY	FOXILY	FORSWY	FROWSY	GHNSUY	GUN SHY
FILPTU	UPLIFT	FPRSUY	FRY-UPS		GUN-SHY
FILRST	FLIRTS	GGGILY	GIGGLY	GHOPTU	GO PHUT
FILRTY	FLIRTY	GGGORY	GROGGY	GHORSU	ROUGHS
FILSSU	FUSILS	GGHHIO	GO HIGH	GHORTU	TROUGH
FIMNOR	IN FORM	GGIIRR	GRIGRI	GHORTW	GROWTH
	INFORM	GGIKNO	GINKGO	GHOSST	GHOSTS
FIMOST	MOTIFS	GGILNO	OGLING	GHOSSU	SOUGHS
FIMSSU	SUFISM	GGILNU	GLUING	GHOSTU	SOUGHT
FINORT	FORINT	GGILNY	NIGGLY		TOUGHS
FINOST	FITS ON	GGILOO	GIGOLO	GHRSSU	SHRUGS
FINOSU	FUSION	GGILWY	WIGGLY	GIIJNV	JIVING
FINOTY	NOTIFY	GGINNO	NIGNOG	GIIKLN	LIKING
FINRUY	IN FURY		NOGGIN	GIIKNN	INKING
FINSTU	UNFITS	GGINOR	GORING	GIIKNR	IRKING
FIOOTT	FOOT IT		GRINGO	GIIKNS	SKIING
FIOPRT	PROFIT	GGINOS	GOINGS	GIIKNV	VIKING
FIOSST	FOISTS	GGINRU	URGING	GIILMN	LIMING
FIOSSY	OSSIFY	GGINUY	GUYING	GIILNN	LIGNIN
FIOTTU	FIT OUT	GGIOST	GIGOTS		LINING
	OUTFIT	GGITWY	TWIGGY	GIILNO	OILING
FIPRUY	PURIFY	GGLOOO	GOOGOL	GIILNP	PILING
FIPSTU	FITS UP	GGLOOY	GOOGLY	GIILNR	RILING
FIPTYY	TYPIFY	GGMOSY	SMOGGY	GIILNT	TILING
FIRSST	FIRSTS	GGNOOR	GORGON	GIILNV	LIVING
FIRSTU	FRUITS	GGOOOO	GOO-GOO	GIILNW	WILING
FIRTUY	FRUITY	GHHILY	HIGHLY	GIILOR	OIL RIG
FIRYZZ	FRIZZY	GHHIPU	HIGH UP	GIILSV	VIGILS
FISSTW	SWIFTS		HIGH-UP	GIIMMN	MIMING
FJLOUY	JOYFUL	GHHIST	THIGHS	GIIMNN	MINING
FKLNSU	FLUNKS	GHHOTU	THOUGH	GIIMNR	MIRING
FKLNUY	FLUNKY	GHIIKN	HIKING		RIMING
FKLOSY	FOLKSY	GHIINR	HIRING	GIIMNT	TIMING
FLLOOW	FOLLOW	GHIINV	HIVING	GIIMNX	MIXING
FLLOUY	FOULLY	GHIKNT	KNIGHT	GIINNN	INNING
FLMORY	FORMYL	GHILNO	HOLING	GIINNP	PINING
FLMPSU	FLUMPS	GHILPT	PLIGHT	GIINNR	RING IN
FLNRUU	UNFURL	GHILST	LIGHTS	GIINNW	WINING
FLOORS	FLOORS		SLIGHT	GIINNX	NIXING
FLOOYZ	FLOOZY	GHIMNO	HOMING	GIINOR	ORIGIN
FLOPPY	FLOPPY	GHIMTY	MIGHTY	GIINPP	PIPING
	POP FLY	GHINNO	HONING	GIINPW	WIPING
FLOPTU	POTFUL	GHINOP	HOPING	GIINRS	RISING
FLOPUU	FOUL UP	GHINOS	HOSING		SIRING
	FOUL-UP	GHINST	NIGHTS	GIINRT	TIRING
FLORSU	FLOURS		THINGS	GIINRV	VIRGIN
FLORUY	FLOURY	GHINSY	SHYING	GIINRW	WIRING
FLOSSY	FLOSSY	GHINTY	NIGHTY	GIINST	SITING
FLOSTU	FLOUTS	GHIOPZ	PHIZOG	GIINSV	VISING
FLOSTY	SOFTLY	GHIORT	RIGHTO	GIINSZ	SIZING
FLPRUU	FURL UP	GHIOSY	GOYISH	GIJKNO	JOKING
FLRRUY	FLURRY	GHIOTW	GO WITH	GIJLNY	JINGLY
FLRSUU	SULFUR	GHIRST	GIRTHS	GIKNNU	NUKING
FMNOOR	ON FORM		RIGHTS	GIKNOP	POKING
FMOOTY	MY FOOT!	GHIRTW	WRIGHT	GIKNOY	YOKING
FMORSU	FORUMS	GHISST	SIGHTS	GIKNPU	PUKING
FMPRSU	FRUMPS	GHISTT	TIGHTS	GIKRTU	TUGRIK
FMPRUY	FRUMPY	GHLLSY	GHYLLS	GILLRS	GRILLS
FNOOOT	ON FOOT	GHLOOS	GOLOSH	GILLUY	GLUILY
FNORST	FRONTS	GHLOPU	PLOUGH		UGLILY
FNORSW	FROWNS	GHLOSU	GHOULS	GILMNU	LIGNUM
FNOSTU	FOUNTS		LOUGHS	GILMRY	GRIMLY
FOOPRS	PROOFS		SLOUGH	GILMSU	SIGLUM
FOOPSS	SPOOFS	GHLPSY	GLYPHS	GILNOP	LOPING
FOORST	SORT OF	GHNNOU	HUNG ON		POLING
FOPRUU	FOUR UP	GHNORT	THRONG	GILNOS	LOSING
FORRUW	FURROW	GHNOST	THONGS		SOLING
FORSST	FROSTS	GHNOSU	SHOGUN	GILNOU	OIL GUN
FORSTW	FROWST	GHNOTU	NOUGHT	GILNOV	LOVING
FORSTY	FROSTY	GHNPUU	HUNG UP	GILNOW	LOWING
FORSUU	RUFOUS	GHNRUY	HUNGRY		

GILNPU	PLUG IN	GINSUX	SIX-GUN	HHMPSU	HUMPHS
	PULING	GIOOTT	GO TO IT	HHMRTY	RHYTHM
GILNPY	PLYING	GIOPSS	GOSSIP	HHOOSW	WHOOSH
GILNRU	LURING	GIOPST	SPIGOT	HHPSUU	HUSH UP
	RULING	GIORRU	RIGOUR	HHRSTU	THRUSH
GILNSS	SLINGS	GIORSV	VIRGOS	HIIMPS	IMPISH
GILNST	GLINTS	GIORTU	RIG OUT	HIIMSS	SHIISM
GILNSU	LUNGIS		RIGOUT	HIIMST	MISHIT
	SLUING	GIORUV	VIGOUR	HIINTW	WITHIN
GILNSY	LYSING	GIPPRY	GRIPPY	HIITTW	WITH IT
	SINGLY	GIPRSS	SPRIGS		WITH-IT
GILNTY	TINGLY	GIPRSU	RIGS UP	HIJSTU	JUTISH
GILOOS	IGLOOS	GIPSTY	PIG STY	HIKMUZ	MUZHIK
GILRSY	GRISLY		PIGSTY	HIKNRS	SHRINK
GILTUY	GUILTY	GIRTTY	GRITTY	HIKNST	THINKS
GIMNOO	MOOING	GJLNUY	JUNGLY	HIKOOT	HOOK IT
GIMNOP	MOPING	GKLOOO	GO LOOK	HIKRSS	SHIRKS
GIMNOV	MOVING	GLLMUY	GLUMLY	HIKSSW	WHISKS
GIMNPU	IMPUGN	GLLOOP	GOLLUP	HIKSWY	WHISKY
GIMNSU	MUSING	GLMNOO	MONGOL	HILLPU	UPHILL
GIMNTU	MUTING	GLMOOS	GLOOMS	HILLRS	SHRILL
GIMOSS	GISMOS	GLMOOY	GLOOMY	HILLRT	THRILL
GIMOSZ	GIZMOS	GLMOSU	MOGULS	HILMOS	HOLISM
GINNOS	NOSING	GLMSUY	SMUGLY	HILMOY	HOMILY
	SIGN ON	GLNNOO	LONG ON	HILMSU	MULISH
GINNOT	NOTING	GLNOOO	OOLONG	HILNPT	PLINTH
	TONING	GLNOOO	30 LONG	HILNTY	THINLY
GINNOW	OWNING	GLNPUU	UNPLUG	HILOPS	POLISH
GINNOZ	ZONING	GLNSUY	SNUGLY	HILOST	LITHOS
GINNRU	RUNG IN	GLOOOY	OOLOGY	HILOSW	OWLISH
GINNTU	TUNING	GLOOSW	GO SLOW	HILRSW	WHIRLS
GINOOW	WOOING		GO SLOW	HILRWY	WHIRLY
GINOOZ	OOZING	GLOPTU	PUTLOG	HILSTW	WHILST
GINOPR	PORING	GLORSW	GROWLS	HIMMSY	SHIMMY
	ROPING	GLOSSY	GLOSSY	HIMNOY	HOMINY
GINOPS	POSING	GMNNOO	GNOMON	HIMORS	ROMISH
GINOPT	OPTING	GMNOSU	MUNGOS	HIMPRS	SHRIMP
	TOPING	GMOOPR	POGROM	HIMRST	MIRTHS
GINORS	GRISON	GMOORS	GROOMS	HIMSST	SMITHS
	GROINS	GMPRSU	GRUMPS	HIMSTY	SMITHY
	SIGNOR	GMPRUY	GRUMPY	HIMSWY	WHIMSY
GINORV	ROVING	GMPSUU	MUGS UP	HINNST	NINTHS
GINORW	ROWING	GMPSUY	GYPSUM	HINNWY	WHINNY
GINOST	INGOTS	GNNSUU	UNSUNG	HINOOS	SHOO-IN
	STINGO	GNOORT	TROGON	HINOPS	HOPS IN
	TIGONS	GNOORW	GROW ON		SIPHON
	TO-INGS	GNOPPU	POPGUN	HINORS	RHINOS
GINOTT	TOTING	GNOPRS	PRONGS	HINOST	SHINTO
GINOTU	OUTING	GNOPSY	SPONGY	HINOSW	SHOW IN
GINOTV	VOTING	GNORST	STRONG	HINPSU	PUNISH
GINOTW	TOWING	GNORSW	WRONGS		UNSHIP
GINOTY	TOYING	GNORUV	GUVNOR	HINPSX	SPHINX
GINOVW	VOWING	GNOTUY	TOY GUN	HINRSU	INRUSH
GINOWW	WOWING	GNPRSU	SPRUNG		RUSH IN
GINPPU	UPPING	GNPRUU	RUNG UP	HINSTY	SHINTY
GINPRS	SPRING	GNRSTU	GRUNTS	HINSUV	VISHNU
GINPRU	RING UP		STRUNG	HIOOSV	SHIVOO
GINPRY	PRYING	GNSTUU	TUNGUS	HIOPPS	HIPPOS
GINPSU	SIGN UP	GOOPST	STOP-GO		POPISH
GINPSY	SPYING	GOORTT	GROTTO	HIOPST	HOPS IT
GINPTU	PIGNUT	GOORVY	GROOVY	HIOPTT	HOT TIP
GINPTY	TYPING	GOOTTU	GOT OUT	HIORSU	HOURIS
GINPUZ	ZIP GUN	GOPRSU	GROUPS	HIOSST	HOISTS
GINRST	STRING	GOPRUW	GROW UP	HIPPSU	UPPISH
GINRSW	WRINGS	GORRTU	TURGOR	HIPPWY	WHIPPY
GINRTY	TRYING	GORSTU	GROUTS	HIPQSS	Q-SHIPS
GINSST	STINGS	GORSYZ	GROSZY	HIPRST	THRIPS
GINSSV	V SIGNS	GORTTU	ROTGUT	HIQSSU	SQUISH
GINSSW	SWINGS	GORTTY	GROTTY	HIRRSS	SHIRRS
GINSTY	STINGY	GSYYYZ	SYZYGY	HIRRSW	WHIRRS
GINSUU	UNGUIS	HHISTW	WHISHT	HIRSST	SHIRTS

HIRSTT	T SHIRT	HOPRTY	TROPHY
	T-SHIRT	HOPSSY	HYSSOP
	THIRST	HOPSTU	SHOT UP
HIRSTY	SHIRTY		TOPHUS
	THYRSI		UPSHOT
HIRTTY	THIRTY	HOPSUW	SHOW UP
HISSTW	WHISTS	HORSST	HORSTS
HISSTX	SIXTHS		SHORTS
HISSWY	SWISHY	HORSTW	THROWS
HISTTU	SHUT IT!		WORTHS
HISTTY	STITHY	HORSTY	SHORTY
HJNNOY	JOHNNY	HORTWY	WORTHY
HJNOST	ST. JOHN	HOSSTU	SHOUTS
HKNOOU	UNHOOK	HOSTUY	YOUTHS
HKNRSU	SHRUNK	HOSTVW	T V SHOW
HKOOPU	HOOK UP	HPPSUU	PUSH UP
	HOOKUP	HPRSUU	RUSH UP
HLLOOS	HOLLOS		UPRUSH
HLLOOW	HOLLOW	HPSTUU	PUSHTU
HLLOWY	WHOLLY		SHUT UP!
HLLSUY	LUSHLY	HPSTUY	TYPHUS
HLMOTY	THYMOL	HRSTTU	STRUTH
HLMPSY	LYMPHS		THRUST
HLMPUY	PHYLUM		TRUTHS
HLNOUY	UNHOLY	IIJNNO	JOIN IN
HLOPSS	SPLOSH	IIJNNS	JINNIS
HLORSW	WHORLS	IIKNNS	SINK IN
HLORUY	HOURLY	IIKNSS	SISKIN
HLOSST	SLOTHS	IIKPST	SKIP IT!
HLPSSY	SYLPHS	IILLMU	LIMULI
HLPSUY	PLUSHY	IILLOY	OILILY
HLSSUY	SLUSHY	IILLWY	WILILY
HMMSUU	HUMMUS	IILMST	LIMITS
HMNOPY	NYMPHO	IILNOV	VIOLIN
HMNOST	MONTHS	IILNST	INSTIL
HMNPSY	NYMPHS	IILNTY	TINILY
HMOOST	SMOOTH	IILPST	PISTIL
HMOOSW	WHOMSO	IILRWY	WIRILY
HMOPRS	MORPHS	IILTTW	TWILIT
HMORUU	HUMOUR	IIMMNS	MINIMS
HMOSTU	MOUTHS	IIMMNU	MINIUM
HMOTUY	MOUTHY	IIMNNO	MINION
HMPSTU	THUMPS	IIMNOU	IONIUM
HMRSTU	THRUMS	IIMNRT	IN TRIM
HMSTUY	THYMUS	IIMOSS	MIOSIS
HNNOOP	PHONON	IINNOP	PINION
HNOOPT	PHOTON	IINOSV	VISION
HNOORT	THORON	IINPPP	PIPPIN
HNOORU	HONOUR	IINSST	INSIST
HNOOSW	ON SHOW		SIT-INS
HNOOWW	HOW NOW		SITS IN
HNOPSU	NOSH-UP	IINTTU	INTUIT
	PUSH ON	IINTTW	NITWIT
HNOPSY	SYPHON	IIPPPP	PIP-PIP
HNOPTY	PYTHON	IIPPST	PIPITS
HNORST	THORNS	IIPPUU	PIUPIU
HNORSU	ONRUSH	IIPRST	SPIRIT
HNORTW	THROWN	IISSTV	VISITS
HNORTY	THORNY	IJKMOU	MOUJIK
HNOTWY	WHY NOT?	IJLNUY	IN JULY
HNRTUU	UNHURT	IJMNPU	JUMP IN
HNSSTU	SHUNTS	IJNNSU	INJUNS
HOOOOY	YOO-HOO	IJNORU	JUNIOR
HOOOTT	TOO HOT	IJNOST	JOINTS
HOOPST	PHOTOS	IJNRUY	INJURY
HOOPSW	WHOOPS	IJOSST	JOISTS
HOOPTT	HOT POT	IJRSTU	JURIST
HOORRR	HORROR	IKKNSS	SKINKS
HOOSST	SHOOTS	IKKOSS	KIOSKS
HOOSSW	SWOOSH	IKKRSU	KUKRIS
HOOTTY	TOOTHY	IKKUUY	KIKUYU

IKLLSS	SKILLS
IKLNOO	LOOK IN
	LOOK-IN
IKLNPU	LINK UP
	LINKUP
IKLNSS	SLINKS
IKLNSY	SLINKY
IKLNTY	TINKLY
IKLOPY	POKILY
IKLRSS	SKIRLS
IKLSSU	SUSLIK
IKMNOO	KIMONO
IKMPSS	SKIMPS
IKMPSY	SKIMPY
IKMRSS	SMIRKS
IKMSSU	KUMISS
IKNNSU	SUNK IN
IKNNSY	SKINNY
IKNOOT	TOOK IN
IKNOPS	PINKOS
IKNORW	WORK IN
	WORK-IN
IKNPRS	PRINKS
IKNSST	STINKS
IKNSTY	STINKY
IKOOTT	TOOK IT
IKQRUY	QUIRKY
IKRRSS	SKIRRS
IKRSST	SKIRTS
	STIRKS
IKRSSU	RUSSKI
IKSVVY	SKIVVY
ILLMPY	LIMPLY
ILLMSY	SLIMLY
ILLNOR	ROLL IN
ILLNPU	PULL-IN
ILLOPW	PILLOW
ILLOWW	WILLOW
ILLPSS	SPILLS
ILLQSU	QUILLS
	SQUILL
ILLRST	TRILLS
ILLSST	STILLS
ILLSSW	SWILLS
ILLSTW	TWILLS
ILLSTY	STILLY
ILLSUV	VILLUS
ILMMSU	MUSLIM
ILMNOU	MOULIN
ILMNSU	MUSLIN
ILMOSS	LISSOM
ILMOTU	ULTIMO
ILMPPY	PIMPLY
ILMPRY	PRIMLY
ILMPSY	SIMPLY
ILMPTU	LUMP IT
ILMRTY	TRIMLY
ILMSTU	LITMUS
ILMTUU	TUMULI
ILMYZZ	MIZZLY
ILNOOT	LOTION
ILNOPP	POPLIN
ILNOPS	SLIP ON
	SLIP-ON
ILNOSS	IN LOSS
ILNOST	TONSIL
ILNOSY	NOSILY
ILNOTW	WILTON
ILNPRU	PURLIN
ILNPST	SPLINT
ILNPSU	LUPINS

ILNSTU	INSULT	INNRTU	IN TURN	IQRSTU	QUIRTS
	SUNLIT		TURN IN		SQUIRT
ILOPRX	PROLIX	INOOPS	POISON	IRSSTW	WRISTS
ILOPRY	PYLORI	INOOPT	OPTION	IRSTWY	WRISTY
ILOPSS	SPOILS		POTION	ISSTTW	TWISTS
ILOPST	PILOTS	INOORS	ORISON	ISTTWY	TWISTY
	PISTOL	INOPPS	POPS IN	JLSTUY	JUSTLY
	SPOILT	INOPRS	PRISON	JMNOPU	JUMP ON
ILOPSU	POILUS	INOPST	PINTOS	JMPPUU	JUMP UP
ILOPSX	OXLIPS		PISTON	JNOSTU	JUNTOS
ILOPTY	POLITY		PITONS	JNSTUU	UNJUST
ILOQRU	LIQUOR		POINTS	JOOSUY	JOYOUS
ILORSY	ROSILY	INOPTT	TIN-POT	JORRSU	JURORS
ILPPSU	PUPILS	INOQSU	QUOINS	JOSSTU	JOUSTS
	SLIP UP	INORSS	ROSINS		JUST SO
	SLIP-UP	INORST	INTROS	KKLSSU	SKULKS
ILPPSY	SLIPPY	INORSW	IN ROWS	KKNSSU	SKUNKS
ILPPTU	PULPIT	INORTT	TRITON	KLLNOS	KNOLLS
ILPPTY	TRIPLY	INOSST	SITS ON	KLLOSY	SKOLLY
ILPSST	SPLITS	INOSTX	TOXINS	KLLSSU	SKULLS
ILPSTU	TULIPS	INOSUV	VINOUS	KLNOOO	LOOK ON
ILQSTU	QUILTS	INPPSU	PIN UPS	KLNOPS	PLONKS
ILRSSW	SWIRLS		PINS UP	KLNPSU	PLUNKS
ILRSTW	TWIRLS		PINUPS	KLNRSU	KNURLS
ILRSTY	LYRIST	INPRST	PRINTS	KLOOOT	LOOK TO
ILRSWY	SWIRLY		SPRINT	KLOOPU	LOOK UP
ILRTWY	TWIRLY	INPRTU	TURNIP	KLRTUU	KULTUR
ILSSTT	STILTS	INPSTU	INPUTS	KMOSUX	MUSK OX
IMMNOS	MONISM		PUTS IN		MUSK-OX
IMMOOS	SIMOOM	INPSUZ	UNZIPS	KNOOOT	TOOK ON
IMMOSU	OSMIUM	INQSTU	SQUINT	KNOORR	KRONOR
IMMSTU	SUMMIT	INQSUY	QUINSY	KNOORW	WORK ON
IMNNOW	MINNOW	INRSXY	SYRINX	KNOOSS	SNOOKS
IMNNTU	MUNTIN	INRTWY	WINTRY	KNORRU	KRONUR
IMNOOR	MORION	INSSTT	STINTS	KNORUY	KORUNY
IMNOOS	SIMOON	IOPPTT	TIP-TOP	KNOSTU	KNOUTS
IMNOOT	MOTION	IOPRRS	PRIORS	KNOTTY	KNOTTY
IMNORS	MINORS	IOPRRY	PRIORY	KNPSUY	SPUNKY
IMNOST	INMOST	IOPRST	PROSIT	KNRSTU	TRUNKS
	MONIST		TRIPOS	KOOOTT	TOOK TO
IMNOSY	MYOSIN	IOPSST	POSITS	KOOPSS	SPOOKS
	SIMONY		PTOSIS	KOOPSY	SPOOKY
IMNTUY	MUTINY	IOPSTT	STOP IT	KOOPTU	TOOK UP
IMOPRS	PRIMOS	IOPSTV	PIVOTS	KOOSST	STOOKS
IMOPRT	IMPORT	IOPTTU	UP TO IT	KOOTWW	KOWTOW
IMOPST	IMPOST	IOQSTU	QUOITS	KOPRUW	WORK UP
IMORRR	MIRROR	IORSSV	VISORS	KORSST	STORKS
IMORRS	MORRIS	IORSTU	SUITOR	LLLOOP	LOLLOP
IMOSSY	MYOSIS	IORSVZ	VIZORS	LLNOOR	ROLL ON
IMOSTV	VOMITS	IOSTTU	SIT OUT		ROLL-ON
IMOTTT	TOMTIT	IOSTTW	STOW IT!	LLNOPU	PULL ON
IMPPRS	PRIMPS	IOTTUW	OUTWIT		PULL-ON
IMPRSS	PRISMS	IPPRTU	TRIP UP	LLNORU	UNROLL
IMPRSU	PRIMUS	IPPSSU	PISS-UP	LLOOWY	WOOLLY
	PURISM	IPPSTU	TIPS UP	LLOPRU	ROLL UP
IMPSUX	MIX-UPS	IPPTUY	UPPITY		ROLL-UP
IMQRSU	SQUIRM	IPRRTU	IRRUPT	LLORST	STROLL
IMRSTU	TRUISM	IPRSST	SPIRTS		TROLLS
IMSSSU	MISSUS		SPRITS	LLOSWY	SLOWLY
INNOOS	ONIONS		STIRPS	LLPPUU	PULL UP
INNOOT	NOTION		STRIPS		PULL-UP
INNOPS	PINONS	IPRSSY	PRISSY	LLRSTU	TRULLS
INNORW	WORN IN	IPRSTU	PURIST	LMMOUX	LUMMOX
INNOSU	UNIONS		SPRUIT	LMMPUY	PLUMMY
	UNISON		STIR UP	LMMSUY	SLUMMY
INNOWW	WINNOW	IPRSTW	TWIRPS	LMOORU	ORMOLU
INNPSU	UNPINS	IPRSTY	STRIPY	LMOSTU	MOULTS
INNRSU	INURNS	IPRSUY	SIRUPY	LMOSTY	MOSTLY
	RUN-INS	IPRTUY	PURITY	LMPPSU	PLUMPS
	RUNS IN	IPSSTU	SITS UP	LMPSSU	SLUMPS
		IPSTTY	TYPIST	LMTTUU	TUMULT

LNNOSY	NYLONS	NNORTU	TURN ON	ORSTTU	TROUTS
LNOOPY	POLONY		TURN-ON		TUTORS
LNOOST	STOLON	NNORUW	UNWORN	ORTTUY	TRY OUT
LNOPSY	PYLONS	NOOPRT	PRONTO		TRYOUT
LNOPTU	PLUTON		PROTON	PPSTUU	PUTS UP
LNRUUY	UNRULY	NOOPSS	SNOOPS	PRRSUY	SPURRY
LOOOSV	OVOLOS		SPOONS	PRSSTU	SPURTS
LOOPRY	POORLY	NOOPST	SPOT ON	PRSSUU	USURPS
LOOPSS	SLOOPS		SPOT-ON	PRSUYY	SYRUPY
	SPOOLS	NOORTU	ON TOUR	RSSTTU	STRUTS
LOOSST	SLOOTS	NOOSSW	SWOONS		TRUSTS
	STOOLS	NOOSTY	SNOOTY	RSSTTY	TRYSTS
LOOSTT	LOTTOS	NOOTTU	NOT OUT	RSTTUY	TRUSTY
LOOVVX	VOLVOX	NOPRTU	TORN UP		
LOPPRY	PROPYL	NOPSTU	PUTS ON		
LOPPSY	POLYPS		UNSTOP		
	SLOPPY	NOPSUW	OWNS UP		
LOPRSW	PROWLS	NOPTUW	UPTOWN		
LOPRTY	PORTLY	NORSST	SNORTS		
LOPSTU	POULTS	NORSTU	RUNS TO		
LOPSUW	SLOW UP	NORTUU	OUTRUN		
LOPTWY	TWO-PLY		RUN OUT		
LORSUY	SOURLY	NOSSTU	SNOUTS		
LOSTYZ	ZLOTYS	NOSTTY	SNOTTY		
LPPSUY	SUPPLY	NOSTUY	SNOUTY		
LPRSSU	SLURPS	NPRSSU	SPURNS		
LPRSYY	SPRYLY	NPRSUU	RUN-UPS		
LRRSUY	SLURRY		RUNS UP		
LRSTUY	SULTRY	NPRTUU	TURN UP		
LRUUXY	LUXURY		TURN-UP		
LSSTUY	STYLUS		UPTURN		
MMNOOR	MORMON	NRSTUU	U TURNS		
MMNOSU	SUMMON		U-TURNS		
MMOOPP	POM-POM	NSSTTU	STUNTS		
MMOOTT	TOM TOM	OOPPRT	TROPPO		
	TOM-TOM	OOPPTU	POP OUT		
MMOPRS	MRS. MOP	OOPPVX	VOX POP		
MMRRUU	MURMUR	OOPRRT	TORPOR		
MMUUUU	MUU MUU	OOPRSS	SPOORS		
MMUUYY	YUM-YUM	OOPRST	TROOPS		
MNOOPP	POMPON	OOPRSU	POROUS		
MNOORS	MORONS	OOPRSV	PROVOS		
MNORSU	MOURNS	OOPRTU	UPROOT		
MNOSTU	MOUNTS	OOPSST	STOOPS		
MNOTTU	MUTTON	OOPSSW	SWOOPS		
MOORRW	MORROW	OOPSTT	POTTOS		
MOORST	MOTORS	OOPWWW	POW WOW		
MOOSTT	MOTTOS		POWWOW		
MOPPRT	PROMPT	OORRST	ROTORS		
MOPPSU	MOPS UP	OORRSW	SORROW		
MOPSST	STOMPS	OORSST	ROOSTS		
MOPSSU	POSSUM		TORSOS		
MOQRUU	QUORUM	OOSTTY	TOOTSY		
MORRUU	RUMOUR	OPPPRU	PROP UP		
MORSST	STORMS	OPPSTU	STOP UP		
MORSTY	STORMY		TOPS UP		
MORTUU	TUMOUR	OPRSST	SPORTS		
MOSTTU	UTMOST		STROPS		
MPRSTU	TRUMPS	OPRSTU	SPROUT		
MPRSUU	RUMPUS		STUPOR		
MPSSTU	STUMPS	OPRSTY	SPORTY		
MPSSUU	SUMS UP	OPRTTU	PRUTOT		
MPSTUU	SPUTUM	OPSSTU	SPOUTS		
MPSTUY	STUMPY		STOUPS		
MRSSTU	STRUMS		TOSS UP		
MSTTUY	SMUTTY		TOSS-UP		
NNOORW	WORN ON	OPSTTY	SPOTTY		
NNOOWW	NOW, NOW	OPTTUU	OUTPUT		
NNORSU	RUN-ONS		PUT OUT		
	RUNS ON	ORSSTW	WORSTS		

AAABBCL	CABBALA	AAAHNPS	HAS A NAP	AABCOTT	CATBOAT
AAABBIL	ALI BABA	AAAHNSV	HAVANAS	AABDDEL	ADDABLE
AAABBMR	BAMBARA	AAAIKLT	LATAKIA	AABDDER	ABRADED
AAABCLS	CABALAS	AAAILMR	MALARIA	AABDDHN	DAB HAND
AAABERY	BAY AREA	AAAILPS	APLASIA	AABDDIN	BAND AID
AAABHMS	BAHAMAS	AAAIQRU	AQUARIA		BAND-AID
AAABILN	ALBANIA	AAAJMPS	PAJAMAS	AABDDLN	BAD LAND
AAABINR	ARABIAN	AAAKKMR	MARKKAA	AABDDOR	BAD ROAD
AAABLMT	TAMBALA	AAAKKNS	KANAKAS	AABDEGN	BANDAGE
AAABMOS	ABOMASA	AAAKRSW	ARAWAKS	AABDEHT	HAD A BET
AAABMST	MASTABA	AAALLPT	PALATAL	AABDELL	BALLADE
AAABNNS	BANANAS	AAALMNY	MALAYAN	AABDELT	ABLATED
AAABRSZ	BAZAARS	AAALMRS	MARSALA		DATABLE
AAACCIS	ACACIAS	AAALMSS	SALAAMS	AABDELW	WADABLE
AAACCLR	CARACAL	AAALNRY	RAY ALAN	AABDEMN	BAD NAME
AAACCRS	CASCARA	AAAMNPS	PANAMAS	AABDENU	BANDEAU
AAACDIN	ACADIAN	AAAMRSS	SAMSARA	AABDERR	ABRADER
AAACDIR	ARCADIA	AAAMRSY	AYMARAS	AABDERS	ABRADES
AAACDMM	MACADAM	AAANNSV	SAVANNA	AABDESU	AUBADES
AAACENP	PANACEA	AAANRTT	TANTARA	AABDGHN	HANDBAG
AAACHLZ	CHALAZA	AAANRWY	RAN AWAY	AABDGNS	SAND BAG
AAACIJM	JAMAICA	AAAPPRT	APPARAT		SANDBAG
AAACIMR	ARAMAIC	AAAPPSY	PAPAYAS	AABDHIO	OBADIAH
AAACLLS	LA SCALA	AAARSTV	AVATARS	AABDHJO	HAD A JOB
AAACLMN	ALMANAC	AAARTTT	RAT-A-TAT	AABDHNT	HATBAND
AAACLNT	CATALAN	AAARTTU	TUATARA	AABDIIS	BASIDIA
AAACLPS	ALPACAS	AABBCDK	BAD BACK	AABDINS	INDABAS
AAACMRS	MARACAS	AABBCEG	CABBAGE	AABDLLS	BALLADS
	MASCARA	AABBCRY	BABY CAR	AABDLRW	BRADAWL
AAACNRR	RAN A CAR	AABBEGN	BEANBAG	AABDNRS	SAND BAR
AAACNRV	CARAVAN	AABBEWY	EBB AWAY		SANDBAR
AAACNST	CANASTA	AABBGGR	GRAB BAG	AABDORV	BRAVADO
AAACNTT	CANTATA	AABBHST	SABBATH	AABDRRW	DRAWBAR
AAACRWY	CARAWAY		SHABBAT	AABDRST	BASTARD
AAACSSV	CASSAVA	AABBMRU	RUM BABA	AABDSWY	BAD WAYS
AAADFGH	HAD A FAG	AABBRRY	BARBARY	AABEELT	EATABLE
AAADGQU	AQUADAG	AABBRTY	TAR BABY	AABEEMO	AMOEBAE
AAADHNP	HAD A NAP	AABBSST	SABBATS	AABEFFL	AFFABLE
AAADILX	ADAXIAL	AABBSTY	BABY-SAT	AABEFGL	FLEABAG
AAADKNN	KANNADA	AABCDST	BAD CAST	AABEFLY	BAY LEAF
AAADLMN	MANDALA	AABCELN	BALANCE	AABEGGG	BAGGAGE
AAADMNR	RAMADAN	AABCELP	CAPABLE	AABEGGR	GARBAGE
AAADMNT	ADAM ANT	AABCELT	ACTABLE	AABEGLR	ALGEBRA
	ADAMANT	AABCEMR	MACABRE	AABEGRR	BARRAGE
AAADMRS	ARMADAS	AABCERT	ABREACT	AABEGSS	BAGASSE
AAAEGNP	APANAGE		CABARET	AABEGST	TEA BAGS
AAAEIMN	ANAEMIA	AABCFKR	FAR BACK	AABEHST	HAS A BET
AAAELSZ	AZALEAS	AABCILM	CAMBIAL	AABEIKN	IKEBANA
AAAETWY	ATE AWAY	AABCINR	CARIBAN	AABEILM	AMIABLE
	EAT AWAY	AABCIOP	COPAIBA	AABEILT	LABIATE
AAAFFLL	ALFALFA	AABCIRS	ARABICS	AABEIRS	AIR BASE
AAAFGHS	HAS A FAG	AABCITX	TAXI CAB		ARABISE
AAAFIRT	RATAFIA		TAXICAB	AABEIRZ	ARABIZE
AAAFRWY	FAR AWAY	AABCKLY	LAY BACK	AABEJLL	JELLABA
	FARAWAY	AABCKNR	CAB RANK	AABELLS	SALABLE
AAAGHKN	AGA KHAN		RAN BACK	AABELMT	TAMABLE
AAAGIPT	PATAGIA	AABCKPY	PAY BACK	AABELNT	BALANTE
AAAGLMM	AMALGAM	AABCKRR	BARRACK	AABELPR	PARABLE
AAAGMNR	ANAGRAM	AABCKST	SAT BACK	AABELPY	PAYABLE
AAAHHKL	HALAKAH	AABCKWY	WAY BACK	AABELRT	RATABLE
AAAHIPS	APHASIA	AABCLPY	CAPABLY	AABELRY	LAY BARE
AAAHMMT	MAHATMA	AABCORT	ACROBAT	AABELST	ABLATES
AAAHMRT	MARATHA	AABCOST	TABASCO	AABELSV	SAVABLE

AABELTU	TABLEAU	AACCDES	CASCADE	AACEHPS	APACHES
	TABULAE		SACCADE	AACEHRT	TRACHEA
AABELTX	TAXABLE	AACCDIR	CARDIAC	AACEHTT	ATTACHE
AABELTY	LAY A BET	AACCDIS	CICADAS	AACEHTU	CHATEAU
AABEMNO	AMOEBAN	AACCELO	CLOACAE	AACEHWY	EACH WAY
AABEMOS	AMOEBAS	AACCEST	SACCATE	AACEIMN	ANAEMIC
AABERST	ABREAST	AACCHHS	CHA-CHAS	AACEIMR	AMERICA
AABERTY	BETA RAY	AACCHIR	ARCHAIC	AACEINR	CARINAE
AABFFLY	AFFABLY	AACCHLN	CLACHAN	AACEIRR	AIR RACE
AABFILU	FABLIAU	AACCILM	ACCLAIM	AACEIRS	AIR ACES
AABGGRS	RAGBAGS	AACCILS	CICALAS	AACEIRV	AVARICE
AABGGSS	GASBAGS	AACCIOR	CARIOCA		CAVIARE
AABGILM	MAILBAG	AACCKRR	CARRACK	AACEKMM	ACK EMMA
AABGINR	BARGAIN	AACCLLO	CLOACAL	AACEKNP	PANCAKE
AABGRST	RATBAGS	AACCLLT	CAT CALL	AACEKNS	ASKANCE
AABHHIW	WAHHABI		CATCALL	AACELLT	LACTEAL
AABHIIL	BALI HAI	AACCLRU	CARACUL	AACELMN	MANACLE
AABHIMS	BAHAISM	AACCNVY	VACANCY	AACELMR	CARAMEL
AABHINR	BAHRAIN	AACCORU	CURACAO	AACELMS	CALM SEA
AABHIST	BAHAIST	AACCOTT	TOCCATA	AACELMU	MACULAE
AABHITT	HABITAT	AACCRSS	CARCASS	AACELNU	LACUNAE
AABHJOS	HAS A JOB	AACDDER	ARCADED	AACELNV	VALANCE
AABHKSS	KASBAHS	AACDDIN	CANDIDA	AACELPS	PALACES
AABHMNR	BRAHMAN	AACDEEM	ACADEME	AACELPT	PLACATE
AABHMTT	BATH MAT	AACDEFS	FACADES	AACELRV	CARAVEL
AABHOST	SABAOTH	AACDEHR	CHARADE	AACELST	ACETALS
AABHSUU	BAUHAUS	AACDEHT	CATHEAD	AACELSW	CASE LAW
AABIIMN	NAMIBIA	AACDELN	CANDELA	AACELTT	LACTATE
AABIJNP	PANJABI	AACDELR	CALDERA	AACELTV	CLAVATE
AABIKNS	ABNAKIS	AACDEMY	ACADEMY	AACEMMR	MACRAME
AABILLR	BARILLA	AACDENV	ADVANCE	AACEMNV	CAVE MAN
AABILLS	LABIALS	AACDENZ	CADENZA		CAVEMAN
AABILMS	BAALISM	AACDERS	ARCADES	AACEMQU	MACAQUE
AABILMY	AMIABLY	AACDERV	CADAVER	AACEMRS	CAMERAS
AABILNS	BASINAL	AACDERY	DAY CARE	AACEMTT	CAT MEAT
AABILOU	ABOULIA	AACDETU	CAUDATE	AACENPS	CANAPES
AABILRS	BASILAR	AACDETV	VACATED	AACENRS	SARACEN
AABIMMR	MARIMBA	AACDFIR	FARADIC	AACENST	CATENAS
AABINNS	BANIANS	AACDHMR	DRACHMA	AACENTZ	AZTECAN
AABINOU	OUABAIN	AACDHRS	CHADARS	AACERRT	RAT RACE
AABINST	ABSTAIN	AACDILR	RADICAL	AACERSS	CAESARS
AABIRST	ARABIST	AACDINT	ANTACID	AACERST	CATSEAR
AABKNRT	TANBARK	AACDINV	VANADIC	AACERSU	CAESURA
AABKOOZ	BAZOOKA	AACDIRS	ACARIDS	AACERTT	TEA CART
AABLLNY	BANALLY		ASCARID	AACERTU	ARCUATE
AABLLPT	PAT-BALL	AACDJKW	JACKDAW	AACESTV	CAVEATS
AABLLST	BALLAST	AACDKSS	SAD SACK		VACATES
AABLLSY	BASALLY	AACDLNS	SCANDAL	AACETTU	ACTUATE
AABLLWY	WALLABY	AACDLOR	CARLOAD	AACFILS	FACIALS
AABLMSS	BALSAMS	AACDLPR	PLACARD		FASCIAL
AABLMSY	ABYSMAL	AACDNRS	CANARDS	AACFILU	FAUCIAL
AABLNTT	BLATANT	AACDOOV	AVOCADO	AACFINR	AFRICAN
AABLORT	ABLATOR	AACDRSZ	CZARDAS	AACFINT	FANATIC
AABLOSV	LAVABOS	AACEEGR	ACREAGE	AACFISS	FASCIAS
AABLRTU	TABULAR	AACEEHR	EARACHE	AACFLLY	FALLACY
AABLRTY	RATABLY	AACEEHT	CHAETAE	AACFLPT	FLAT CAP
AABLSST	BASALTS	AACEEKT	TEA CAKE	AACFLTU	FACTUAL
AABLSSY	ABYSSAL	AACEENT	CATENAE	AACFNST	CAFTANS
AABLSTU	ABLAUTS	AACEEPT	AT PEACE	AACFRST	FAST CAR
AABMNOT	BOATMAN	AACEETT	ACETATE	AACGILL	GLACIAL
AABMNST	BANTAMS	AACEFIS	FASCIAE	AACGILM	MAGICAL
	BATSMAN	AACEFLT	FALCATE	AACGLOS	COAL GAS
AABMORU	MARABOU	AACEFLU	FACULAE	AACGLOU	COAGULA
AABMRRS	MARS BAR	AACEFRS	CARAFES	AACGNOU	GUANACO
AABMRSS	SAMBARS	AACEGIP	AGAPEIC	AACHIKL	HALAKIC
AABMRTU	TAMBURA	AACEGKP	PACKAGE	AACHILM	MALACHI
AABNNOZ	BONANZA	AACEGNR	CARNAGE	AACHIMR	AMHARIC
AABNNSY	BANYANS	AACEGRT	CARTAGE	AACHIMS	CHIASMA
AABOTTY	ATTABOY	AACEHLT	CHAETAL	AACHINT	ACANTHI
AABOSUU	SUB-AQUA	AACEHNP	PANACHE	AACHIPS	APHASIC
AABRRUV	BRAVURA	AACEHNR	ARCHEAN	AACHIPT	CHAPATI

AACHIRT	CATHARI	AACMRST	TARMACS	AADEMMN	MAN MADE
	CITHARA	AACNPST	CAPSTAN		MAN-MADE
AACHKSW	HACKSAW		CAT NAPS		MANMADE
AACHLPS	PASCHAL		CATNAPS	AADEMMS	MADAMES
AACHNRY	ANARCHY	AACNRRU	RUN A CAR	AADEMNO	ADENOMA
AACHPSY	PAY CASH	AACNRTU	CURTANA	AADEMNS	MAENADS
AACHRRT	CATARRH	AACNSSV	CANVASS	AADEMNT	MANDATE
AACHRST	CATHARS	AACPSTW	CAT'S-PAW	AADEMRW	MADE WAR
AACHRSW	CAR WASH	AACRSTV	CRAVATS	AADEMSS	AMASSED
AACHRTY	HAY CART	AACRTTT	ATTRACT	AADEMWY	MADE WAY
AACHRWY	ARCHWAY	AACRTUY	ACTUARY	AADENNT	ANDANTE
AACIIST	ASIATIC	AACTUWY	CUT AWAY	AADENRV	VERANDA
AACIITV	VIATICA		CUTAWAY	AADENTV	VEDANTA
AACIKLR	CLARKIA	AADDDEN	ADDENDA	AADEPRR	PARADER
AACILNR	ACRILAN	AADDEES	DEAD SEA	AADEPRS	PARADES
	CRANIAL	AADDEFI	DEAF-AID	AADEPRT	ADAPTER
AACILOS	ASOCIAL	AADDEGM	DAMAGED	AADERRW	AWARDER
AACILOX	COAXIAL	AADDEIL	ALIDADE	AADERRY	ARRAYED
AACILPT	CAPITAL	AADDEMN	DEAD MAN	AADERSY	DARE SAY
AACILRR	RAILCAR	AADDENP	DEADPAN		DARESAY
AACIMNS	CAIMANS	AADDEOR	DEODARA		
	MANIACS	AADDEPR	PARADED	AADESSY	ASSAYED
AACINOR	OCARINA	AADDEPT	ADAPTED	AADFGLY	FLAG DAY
AACINPS	CAPSIAN	AADDERW	AWARDED	AADFHIT	HAD A FIT
AACINPT	CAPTAIN	AADDHRY	HARD DAY	AADFHLY	HALF DAY
AACINRS	ARNICAS	AADDIMS	DADAISM	AADFLSU	ALFA SUD
	CARINAS	AADDIST	DADAIST	AADFSTY	FAST DAY
AACINST	SATANIC	AADDKRY	DARK DAY	AADGGHR	HAGGARD
AACINTV	VATICAN	AADDLMO	OLD ADAM	AADGGLR	LAGGARD
AACIOPT	TAPIOCA	AADDLYY	LADY DAY	AADGIMR	DIAGRAM
AACIQTU	AQUATIC	AADDRST	DASTARD	AADGIOS	ADAGIOS
AACIRSS	ASCARIS	AADEEFR	DEAF EAR	AADGLLW	GADWALL
AACISTT	ASTATIC	AADEERT	AERATED	AADGLNO	GONADAL
AACJKLS	JACKALS	AADEFHT	FATHEAD	AADGLNR	GARLAND
AACJKRT	JACK TAR	AADEFHW	HAD A FEW	AADGLRU	GRADUAL
AACJKSS	JACKASS	AADEGGR	GARAGED	AADGMNR	GRANDMA
AACKLTW	CAT WALK	AADEGHO	GO AHEAD	AADGNPR	GRANDPA
	CATWALK		GO AHEAD	AADGOPR	PODAGRA
AACKNRS	RANSACK	AADEGMN	MANAGED	AADGOPS	PAGODAS
AACKPRR	CAR PARK	AADEGMR	DAMAGER	AADHIKP	HAD A KIP
AACKSTT	ATTACKS	AADEGMS	DAMAGES	AADHILS	DAHLIAS
AACLLNU	LACUNAL	AADEGNR	GRENADA	AADHINP	DAPHNIA
AACLLSU	CLAUSAL	AADEGNS	AGENDAS	AADHIWY	HID AWAY
AACLMPR	ARC LAMP	AADEGRT	AT GRADE	AADHLRY	HALYARD
AACLMRU	MACULAR		GRADATE	AADHMNR	HARD MAN
AACLMSU	MACULAS	AADEGRV	RAVAGED	AADHNPR	HARDPAN
AACLNNU	CANNULA	AADEGRY	YARDAGE	AADHNRR	RAN HARD
AACLNRU	LACUNAR	AADEGSV	SAVAGED	AADHNRS	HANSARD
AACLNSU	LACUNAS	AADEHMN	HEADMAN	AADHNSW	HANDSAW
AACLOST	CATALOS	AADEHMS	ASHAMED	AADHRSZ	HAZARDS
	COASTAL	AADEHMY	MADE HAY	AADHRTY	HAD A TRY
AACLOTT	CATTALO	AADEHRW	WARHEAD	AADHRWY	HARD WAY
AACLPRT	CALTRAP	AADEHWY	HEADWAY	AADIIRR	AIR RAID
AACLPSS	PASCALS	AADEILV	AVAILED	AADILMR	ADMIRAL
AACLPSU	SCAPULA	AADEIMR	MADEIRA	AADILNP	PALADIN
AACLPTY	PLAYACT	AADEIMT	ADAMITE	AADILPS	APSIDAL
AACLRSS	LASCARS	AADEINS	NAIADES	AADILRS	RADIALS
	RASCALS	AADEIRT	RADIATE	AADILWY	WAYLAID
	SCALARS	AADEITW	AWAITED	AADIMNS	MAIDANS
AACLRVY	CALVARY	AADEIWY	DIE AWAY	AADIMOR	DIORAMA
	CAVALRY	AADEKLR	KRAALED	AADINRS	RADIANS
AACLSSU	CASUALS	AADELLY	ALLAYED	AADINRT	RADIANT
AACLSTT	LAST ACT	AADELMR	ALARMED	AADINSV	NAVAIDS
AACLSUV	VASCULA	AADELNR	ADRENAL	AADKNRT	TANKARD
AACLTTU	TACTUAL	AADELNW	DANELAW	AADKOST	DAKOTAS
AACMNNT	MANN ACT	AADELRU	RADULAE	AADKRWW	AWKWARD
AACMNSY	CAYMANS	AADELRW	RAW DEAL	AADLLMN	DAMN ALL
AACMNTX	MANX CAT	AADELRY	ALREADY	AADLLMR	MALLARD
AACMORS	SARCOMA	AADELTU	ADULATE	AADLLMS	SMALL AD
AACMRRT	TRAMCAR	AADELTY	TEA LADY	AADLLPU	PALUDAL
AACMRSS	SARCASM			AADLMNU	LADANUM
				AADLNRY	LANYARD

AADLNSS	SANDALS	AAEGILR	ALGERIA	AAEILSS	ALIASES
AADLNSU	LANDAUS		REGALIA	AAEIMMT	IMAMATE
AADLNSV	VANDALS	AAEGINV	VAGINAE	AAEIMNS	AMNESIA
AADLNTX	LAND TAX	AAEGISS	ASSEGAI	AAEIMNT	AMENTIA
AADLOPY	PAYLOAD	AAEGITT	AGITATE		ANIMATE
AADLPPU	APPLAUD	AAEGKLS	GAS LEAK	AAEIMPY	PYAEMIA
AADLRRU	RADULAR	AAEGKNT	TANKAGE	AAEIMRU	URAEMIA
AADLRSU	RADULAS	AAEGKOS	SOAKAGE	AAEIMTV	AMATIVE
AADLSTY	LAST DAY	AAEGLMN	GAMELAN	AAEINPT	PATINAE
AADMNNO	MADONNA	AAEGLNN	ANLAGEN	AAEINST	TAENIAS
AADMNOR	ROADMAN	AAEGLNS	ANLAGES	AAEIPRS	SPIRAEA
AADMNRS	MANSARD		LASAGNE	AAEIPTT	APATITE
AADMNRY	DRAYMAN	AAEGLRR	REALGAR	AAEIRST	ATRESIA
	YARDMAN	AAEGLRS	LAAGERS	AAEIRVW	AIRWAVE
AADMOPR	ROAD MAP	AAEGLRT	AT LARGE	AAEISTT	SATIATE
AADMORT	MATADOR	AAEGLSV	SALVAGE	AAEKLNT	ALKANET
AADMRRY	YARDARM	AAEGMNR	MANAGER	AAEKMNW	WEAK MAN
AADMRSU	MARAUDS	AAEGMNS	MANAGES	AAEKMRR	EARMARK
AADMRWY	WARM DAY	AAEGMNT	GATE MAN	AAEKMRS	SEAMARK
AADMRZZ	MAZZARD		MAGENTA	AAEKMRW	MAKE WAR
AADMSXY	XMAS DAY		MAGNATE	AAEKMWY	MAKE WAY
AADNORR	ANDORRA	AAEGMPR	RAMPAGE	AAEKNSW	AWAKENS
AADNORY	ANYROAD	AAEGMRW	WAR GAME	AAEKPRT	PARTAKE
AADNRTY	TANYARD	AAEGMSS	MASSAGE	AAEKSTT	AT STAKE
AADNRVW	VANWARD	AAEGNOP	APOGEAN	AAELLLM	LAMELLA
AADOPRS	PARADOS	AAEGNPT	PAGEANT	AAELLPT	PATELLA
AADOPRT	ADAPTOR	AAEGNRR	ARRANGE	AAELLRS	ALL EARS
AADOPRX	PARADOX	AAEGNRT	TANAGER	AAELLRT	LATERAL
AADORTX	ROAD TAX	AAEGNTT	GET A TAN	AAELLRY	AREALLY
AADPRWY	DRAW PAY	AAEGNTV	VANTAGE	AAELLSW	SEA WALL
AADPSYY	PAYDAYS	AAEGPRR	PARERGA		SEAWALL
AADQRTU	QUADRAT	AAEGPRW	WARPAGE	AAELMMT	LEMMATA
AADRSTY	DAYSTAR	AAEGPSS	PASSAGE	AAELMNS	AMESLAN
AADRWWY	WAYWARD	AAEGQUY	QUAYAGE	AAELMNU	ALUMNAE
AAEEFGL	LEAFAGE	AAEGRRS	RARE GAS	AAELMOT	OATMEAL
AAEEFLT	TEA LEAF	AAEGRRV	RAVAGER	AAELMPT	PALMATE
AAEEFPY	PAY A FEE	AAEGRST	TEAR GAS	AAELMSY	AMYLASE
AAEEGKL	LEAKAGE	AAEGRSV	RAVAGES	AAELNNS	ANNEALS
AAEEGLT	GALEATE		SAVAGER	AAELNRS	ARSENAL
AAEEGRV	AVERAGE	AAEGRTT	REGATTA	AAELNST	SEALANT
	GAVE EAR	AAEGRWW	WAGE WAR	AAELNSY	ANALYSE
AAEEHRT	HETAERA	AAEGSSU	ASSUAGE	AAELNWY	LANEWAY
AAEEINT	TAENIAE		SAUSAGE	AAELNYZ	ANALYZE
AAEEKLS	SEAKALE	AAEGSSV	SAVAGES	AAELORR	AREOLAR
AAEEKTW	WEAK TEA	AAEGSTU	GATEAUS	AAELOTX	OXALATE
AAEELLP	PALE ALE	AAEGSTW	WASTAGE	AAELPPR	APPAREL
AAEELLR	REAL ALE	AAEGTTW	WATTAGE	AAELPPS	APPEALS
AAEELNS	SEA-LANE	AAEGTUX	GATEAUX	AAELPPT	PALPATE
AAEELOR	AREOLAE	AAEGTWY	GATEWAY	AAELPRV	PALAVER
AAEEMNT	EMANATE		GET AWAY	AAELPST	PALATES
	ENEMATA		GETAWAY	AAELPTU	PLATEAU
	MANATEE	AAEGVWY	GAVE WAY	AAELPTY	APETALY
AAEEPPS	APPEASE	AAEHILP	APHELIA	AAELRST	TARSEAL
AAEERST	AERATES	AAEHKMY	MAKE HAY	AAELRTZ	LAZARET
AAEFFNR	FANFARE	AAEHKNT	KHANATE	AAELSST	ATLASES
AAEFFTT	TAFFETA	AAEHKPS	PAKEHAS		SALT SEA
AAEFHSW	HAS A FEW	AAEHKSW	SEA HAWK	AAELSTT	AT LEAST
AAEFIRR	AIR FARE	AAEHLRT	TREHALA	AAELSUX	ASEXUAL
	AIRFARE	AAEHNSY	HYAENAS	AAEMMMT	MAMMATE
AAEFKLO	OAK LEAF	AAEHRSY	HEARSAY	AAEMNNS	SANE MAN
AAEFMRT	FERMATA	AAEHRTT	AT HEART	AAEMNSY	SAY AMEN
AAEFMTT	FAT MEAT	AAEHSTT	HASTATE	AAEMQSU	SQUAMAE
AAEFNST	SANTA FE	AAEIKMT	TAKE AIM	AAEMRTU	AMATEUR
AAEFRRW	WARFARE	AAEILLX	AXILLAE	AAEMRTW	RAW MEAT
AAEFRST	FAR EAST	AAEILMN	LAMINAE	AAEMSSS	AMASSES
AAEGGNO	ANAGOGE	AAEILMS	MALAISE	AAENNNT	ANTENNA
AAEGGOS	AGES AGO		SEA MAIL	AAENPST	PEASANT
AAEGGRS	GARAGES	AAEILNN	ALANINE	AAENPSV	PAVANES
AAEGHLU	HAULAGE	AAEILNO	AEOLIAN	AAENRRT	NARRATE
AAEGHOV	HAVE A GO	AAEILNR	AIR LANE	AAENRTU	TAUREAN
		AAEILRS	AERIALS	AAENRTY	ANY RATE

AAENRUW	UNAWARE	AAGLMPS	GAS LAMP	AAILLLP	PALLIAL
AAENSTV	AVESTAN	AAGLNOY	ANALOGY	AAILLMN	MANILLA
AAEORRT	AERATOR	AAGLNRS	RAGLANS	AAILLMX	MAXILLA
AAEORRU	AURORAE	AAGLNRU	ANGULAR	AAILLNV	VANILLA
AAEPPRS	APPEARS	AAGLSST	STALAGS	AAILLPP	PAPILLA
AAEPPRT	PARAPET	AAGMMRR	GRAMMAR	AAILLSX	AXILLAS
AAERRRS	ARREARS	AAGMMTU	GUMMATA	AAILLUV	ALLUVIA
AAERRRY	ARRAYER	AAGMNRT	TANGRAM	AAILLXY	AXIALLY
AAERSSY	ASSAYER	AAGMNSW	SWAGMAN	AAILMMN	MAILMAN
AAERTTX	TAX RATE	AAGMOPY	APOGAMY	AAILMMS	LAMAISM
AAERTTY	TEA TRAY	AAGMRSY	MAGYARS		MIASMAL
AAERTXY	TAX YEAR		MARGAYS	AAILMMX	MAXIMAL
AAESSWY	SEAWAYS	AAGNNOS	GOANNAS	AAILMNR	LAMINAR
AAFFILX	AFFIXAL	AAGNOPR	PARAGON	AAILMNS	ANIMALS
AAFFIRS	AFFAIRS	AAGNORS	ANGORAS		LAMINAS
AAFFRSY	AFFRAYS	AAGNORZ	ORGANZA	AAILMNU	ALUMINA
AAFGHIN	AFGHANI	AAGNOTT	GOT A TAN	AAILMNV	MAIL VAN
AAFGHNS	AFGHANS	AAGNPRS	PARANGS	AAILMOS	SOMALIA
AAFGORR	FARRAGO	AAGNRRY	GRANARY	AAILMRT	MARITAL
AAFHIST	HAS A FIT	AAGNRTV	VAGRANT		MARTIAL
AAFHLMO	HALF A MO	AAGORSU	SAGUARO	AAILMSS	SALAMIS
AAFHLPY	HALF PAY	AAGOTWY	GOT AWAY	AAILMST	LAMAIST
AAFHLWY	HALF WAY	AAHHNPT	NAPHTHA	AAILNOP	PIANOLA
	HALFWAY	AAHHOPR	PHARAOH	AAILNOT	LAOTIAN
AAFIILR	FILARIA	AAHIJNR	HARIJAN	AAILNOV	VALONIA
AAFILNT	FANTAIL	AAHIKPS	HAS A KIP	AAILNRU	URALIAN
AAFINNT	INFANTA	AAHILMT	THALAMI	AAILNSS	SALINAS
AAFINUX	FAUX-NAI	AAHILPV	PAHLAVI	AAILNTV	LATVIAN
AAFIPRT	PARFAIT	AAHIMRT	MARATHI		VALIANT
AAFIRSS	SAFARIS	AAHINPR	PIRANHA	AAILNTY	ANALITY
AAFIRWY	FAIR WAY	AAHINST	ASHANTI	AAILORS	SOLARIA
	FAIRWAY	AAHINSV	SHAVIAN	AAILORV	VARIOLA
AAFKNST	KAFTANS	AAHIPRS	PARIAHS	AAILOST	SOLATIA
AAFLLTY	FATALLY	AAHJRRS	JARRAHS	AAILPRT	PARTIAL
	LAY FLAT	AAHKMSY	YASHMAK		PATRIAL
AAFLTTU	AT FAULT	AAHLLOS	HALLOAS	AAILPST	SPATIAL
AAFLWYY	FLY AWAY	AAHLLSW	WALLAHS	AAILPZZ	PALAZZI
	FLYAWAY	AAHLLWY	HALLWAY	AAILRRV	ARRIVAL
AAFMNST	FANTASM	AAHLMRS	MARSHAL	AAILRST	LARIATS
	FAST MAN	AAHLNPX	PHALANX	AAILRTV	TRAVAIL
AAFNSTY	FANTASY	AAHLNRW	NARWHAL	AAILRWY	RAILWAY
AAFPRTT	FAT PART	AAHLNTU	NAHUATL	AAILSSS	ASSAILS
AAFPSUX	FAUX PAS	AAHLPRS	PHRASAL	AAILSSV	SALIVAS
AAGGILN	GANGLIA	AAHLPST	ASPHALT	AAILSSW	WASSAIL
AAGGLOT	TAGALOG	AAHMMMS	HAMMAMS	AAIMMNO	AMMONIA
AAGGNWY	GANGWAY	AAHMNNU	HANUMAN	AAIMMSS	MIASMAS
AAGGQSU	QUAGGAS	AAHMOPR	AMPHORA	AAIMNOR	ROMANIA
AAGHILR	GHARIAL	AAHMRSS	ASHRAMS	AAIMNOS	ANOSMIA
AAGHLTU	LAUGH AT	AAHNNOS	HOSANNA	AAIMNOT	ANIMATO
AAGHMNN	HANGMAN	AAHNOSV	NAVAHOS	AAIMNRS	MARINAS
AAGHNRS	HANGARS	AAHNPSS	ASHPANS	AAIMNRT	MARTIAN
AAGILLN	LINGALA	AAHNPST	PATHANS		TAMARIN
AAGILNN	ANGINAL	AAHNRTX	ANTHRAX	AAIMNRX	MARXIAN
AAGILNS	AGNAILS	AAHORSW	HAS A ROW	AAIMNST	STAMINA
AAGILNV	VAGINAL	AAHPPRS	PARAPHS	AAIMOTW	WAIT A MO
AAGILSV	GAVIALS	AAHPRTW	WARPATH	AAIMRRW	WARM AIR
AAGILTW	WAGTAIL	AAHPSTU	AT A PUSH	AAIMRSU	SAMURAI
AAGIMNS	GAS MAIN	AAHPTWY	PATHWAY	AAIMSTV	ATAVISM
AAGIMNZ	AMAZING	AAHRSTY	ASHTRAY	AAINNRV	NIRVANA
AAGINOS	AGNOSIA		HAS A TRY	AAINORV	OVARIAN
AAGINRR	ARRAIGN	AAHRTTW	ATHWART	AAINPST	AT PAINS
AAGINRS	SANGRIA	AAHSSSY	SASHAYS		PATINAS
AAGINRU	GUARANI	AAIILMR	AIR MAIL	AAINRST	ARTISAN
AAGINST	AGAINST		AIRMAIL		TSARINA
AAGINSU	IGUANAS	AAIILNT	ITALIAN	AAINRSU	SAURIAN
AAGINSV	VAGINAS	AAIINNR	IRANIAN	AAINRSV	SAVARIN
AAGINSY	GAINSAY	AAIIRVV	VIVARIA	AAINRTV	VARIANT
AAGJRSU	JAGUARS	AAIJNNP	IN JAPAN	AAINSTT	ATTAINS
AAGKMSS	GAS MASK	AAIKLLS	ALKALIS	AAINWWY	AWAY WIN
AAGLLNT	GALLANT	AAIKNNT	KANTIAN	AAIORTV	AVIATOR
AAGLLVY	VAGALLY	AAIKPPR	PAPRIKA		

AAIPPTT	PIT A PAT	AAMMNNS	MANS MAN	ABBDGIN	BIG BAND
	PIT-A-PAT	AAMMNNX	MANXMAN		DABBING
AAIPRSU	AU PAIRS	AAMMNTY	TAMMANY	ABBDIKY	BABY KID
AAIPRTT	PARTITA	AAMMSTT	TAM-TAMS	ABBDKOO	BAD BOOK
AAIPSZZ	PIAZZAS	AAMNORS	OARSMAN	ABBDMOR	BOMBARD
AAIQSSU	QUASSIA	AAMNOSS	SAMOANS	ABBDNOX	BANDBOX
AAIQTUV	AQUAVIT	AAMNOSZ	AMAZONS	ABBDOSY	BAD BOYS
AAIRSTU	AUSTRIA	AAMNOTT	ATOM ANT	ABBDSUY	BAD BUYS
AAIRSWY	AIRWAYS	AAMNOTY	ANATOMY	ABBEESW	BAWBEES
AAISTTV	ATAVIST	AAMNPRT	MAN TRAP	ABBEGLR	GABBLER
AAJJMRS	JAM JARS		MANTRAP	ABBEGLS	GABBLES
AAJKLWY	JAYWALK		RAMPANT	ABBEGNO	BOGBEAN
AAJMPSY	PYJAMAS	AAMNPSS	SAMPANS	ABBEGRR	GRABBER
AAJMRTT	JAM TART	AAMNPTY	TYMPANA	ABBEGRU	BUGBEAR
AAJNNSU	SAN JUAN	AAMNRST	MANTRAS	ABBEIST	TABBIES
AAJNOSV	NAVAJOS	AAMNRTY	ARMY ANT	ABBEISY	YABBIES
AAJNRUY	JANUARY	AAMORSV	SAMOVAR	ABBEJRS	JABBERS
AAJOPSU	SAPAJOU	AAMORTY	AMATORY	ABBELLR	BARBELL
AAKKLRU	KARAKUL	AAMOSTT	STOMATA	ABBELMR	BRAMBLE
AAKKMRS	MARKKAS	AAMPPRT	RAMPART	ABBELRS	BARBELS
AAKKOPS	KAKAPOS	AAMRSTU	TRAUMAS		RABBLES
AAKLWWY	WALKWAY	AAMRTWY	TRAMWAY	ABBELRU	BARBULE
AAKMNOR	RAN AMOK	AAMSSTU	SATSUMA	ABBELSU	BAUBLES
AAKMRUZ	MAZURKA	AANNOTT	ANNATTO	ABBERRS	BARBERS
AAKNORS	ANORAKS	AANNRSU	ANURANS	ABBERST	RABBETS
AAKPRWY	PARKWAY	AANOSST	SONATAS		STABBER
AAKRTUY	AUTARKY	AANPRST	RAN PAST	ABBERSW	SWABBER
AALLLNS	LALLANS		SPARTAN	ABBGGIN	BIG BANG
AALLMNT	TALL MAN		TARPANS		GABBING
AALLMPU	AMPULLA	AANPSST	PASSANT	ABBGIJN	JABBING
AALLMWX	MAX WALL		SNAPS AT	ABBGINN	NABBING
AALLNSY	NASALLY	AANQRTU	QUARTAN	ABBGINR	BARBING
AALLPPY	PAPALLY	AANRRTW	WARRANT	ABBGINT	TABBING
AALLPST	LAST LAP	AANRSTT	RATTANS	ABBGINY	BABYING
AALLRST	ALL STAR		TARTANS	ABBGMOO	GO A BOMB
	ALL-STAR	AANRUWY	RUN AWAY	ABBGOOU	BUGABOO
AALLRUY	AURALLY		RUNAWAY	ABBGORS	GABBROS
AALMMMS	MAMMALS	AANSSTV	SAVANTS	ABBHISY	BABYISH
AALMNOY	ANOMALY	AANSSTW	TSWANAS	ABBHNTU	BATH BUN
AALMNPS	NAPALMS	AANSSTZ	STANZAS	ABBHOOS	HABOOBS
AALMNST	LAST MAN	AAOPRRT	PRO RATA	ABBHRRU	RHUBARB
AALMNSU	MANUALS	AAORRSU	AURORAS	ABBIIMN	BAMBINI
AALMORY	MAYORAL	AAPPSWW	PAWPAWS	ABBILOT	BOBTAIL
AALMPRY	PALMYRA	AAPRTWY	PARTWAY	ABBIMNO	BAMBINO
AALMSTY	LAST MAY	AAPTUWY	PUT AWAY	ABBIRST	RABBITS
AALNNRU	ANNULAR	AAQRSSU	QUASARS	ABBIRTY	RABBITY
AALNNSU	ANNUALS	AARRSTT	TARTARS	ABBISTY	BABY-SIT
AALNORS	ALSO RAN	ABBBDEL	BLABBED	ABBLLOY	BALL BOY
	ALSO-RAN	ABBBELR	BABBLER	ABBLMRY	BRAMBLY
AALNORW	WAR LOAN		BLABBER	ABBMOOS	BAMBOOS
AALNPRT	PLANTAR	ABBBELS	BABBLES	ABBMOST	BOMBAST
AALNPST	PLATANS	ABBBITT	BABBITT	ABBMOTU	BUMBOAT
	SALTPAN	ABBBMOY	BOMB BAY	ABBNOOS	BABOONS
AALNRTU	NATURAL	ABBBOYY	BABY BOY	ABBNRTU	BRAN TUB
AALNSTU	SULTANA	ABBCDER	CRABBED	ABBORSS	ABSORBS
AALNSTY	ANALYST	ABBCDES	SCABBED	ABBRSSU	BUSBARS
AALOPRS	PARASOL	ABBCEIS	CABBIES	ABCCEIR	ACERBIC
AALOPSY	PAYOLAS	ABBCIKT	BACKBIT		BRECCIA
AALOPZZ	PALAZZO	ABBCKUY	BUY BACK	ABCCILU	CUBICAL
AALORRU	AURORAL	ABBCMOR	CAR BOMB	ABCCIMR	CAMBRIC
AALORSU	AROUSAL	ABBCOST	BOBCATS	ABCCIOR	BORACIC
AALPPRU	PAPULAR	ABBCRYY	CRY BABY	ABCCKTU	CUT BACK
AALPPUY	PAY PAUL		CRYBABY		CUTBACK
AALPRSY	PARLAYS	ABBDDET	BAD DEBT	ABCCOOT	TOBACCO
AALPSTU	SPATULA	ABBDEGR	GRABBED	ABCDDLO	BAD COLD
AALRSTU	AUSTRAL	ABBDELR	DABBLER	ABCDEEH	BEACHED
AALSSSV	VASSALS		DRABBLE	ABCDEEL	DEBACLE
AALSSTU	ASSAULT	ABBDELS	DABBLES	ABCDEHU	DEBAUCH
AALSSUU	AS USUAL	ABBDERR	DRABBER	ABCDEIR	CARBIDE
AALSWYY	WAYLAYS	ABBDEST	STABBED	ABCDEKL	BLACKED
AAMMMRY	MAMMARY	ABBDESW	SWABBED	ABCDELO	CODABLE

ABCDEMP	CAMP BED	ABCGIKN	BACKING	ABDDGOS	BAD DOGS
ABCDEOR	BROCADE	ABCGILN	CABLING	ABDDHSU	BUDDHAS
ABCDERT	BRACTED	ABCGINR	BRACING	ABDDINS	DISBAND
ABCDERU	CUDBEAR	ABCGKLO	BACKLOG	ABDDLLO	ODDBALL
ABCDIIS	DIBASIC	ABCGKOT	GOT BACK	ABDDLOY	DO BADLY
ABCDILR	BALDRIC	ABCGORY	GO BY CAR	ABDDMOO	BAD MOOD
ABCDIOR	C. B. RADIO	ABCHIKT	HIT BACK	ABDEEFL	FEEL BAD
ABCDKLU	BAD LUCK	ABCHILS	CHABLIS	ABDEEHS	BEHEADS
ABCDNOS	ABSCOND	ABCHIOT	COHABIT	ABDEEHV	BEHAVED
ABCDOOR	CORDOBA	ABCHNRY	BRANCHY	ABDEEIR	BEADIER
ABCDSTU	ABDUCTS	ABCHOSX	CASH BOX	ABDEELM	BELDAME
ABCEEHS	BEACHES	ABCHPSU	HUB CAPS	ABDEELN	ENABLED
ABCEEMR	EMBRACE		HUBCAPS	ABDEELR	BLEARED
ABCEENS	ABSENCE	ABCIILL	BACILLI	ABDEELS	BEADLES
ABCEERR	CEREBRA	ABCIILN	ALBINIC	ABDEELT	BELATED
ADCEEGU	BECAUSE	ABCIIMN	MINI CAB		BLEATED
ABCEGIR	BIG RACE		MINICAB	ABDEELY	BELAYED
	RIB CAGE	ABCIIOR	CIBORIA		DYEABLE
ABCEGKT	GET BACK	ABCIIOT	ABIOTIC	ABDEEMN	BEAM END
ABCEGOS	DOSCAGE	ABCIJNO	JACOBIN	ABDEEMR	BREAMED
ABCEHIR	HEBRAIC	ABCIKLN	IN BLACK	ABDEEMT	BEDMATE
ABCEHMR	CHAMBER	ABCIKNW	WIN BACK	ABDEEMY	EMBAYED
	CHAMBRE	ABCIKST	SIT BACK	ABDEERS	DEBASER
ABCEHST	BATCHES	ABCIKSY	SICK BAY	ABDEERT	BERATED
ABCEIKL	LIE BACK	ABCILRS	SCRIBAL		DEBATER
ABCEILM	ALEMBIC	ABCIMMU	CAMBIUM		REBATED
	CEMBALI	ABCINOT	BOTANIC	ABDEESS	DEBASES
ABCEILR	CALIBRE	ABCIORU	CARIBOU	ABDEEST	DEBATES
ABCEILT	CITABLE	ABCIOUV	BIVOUAC	ABDEETT	ABETTED
ABCEIMO	AMOEBIC	ABCJJKO	JACK JOB	ABDEFLT	FELT BAD
ABCEINR	CARBINE	ABCKLLO	BALLOCK	ABDEFOR	FORBADE
ABCEINT	CABINET	ABCKLLY	BLACKLY	ABDEGGR	BRAGGED
ABCEIOR	AEROBIC	ABCKLPU	BLACK UP	ABDEGGS	BAD EGGS
ABCEIOT	ICE BOAT	ABCKMRU	BUCKRAM	ABDEGHI	BIG HEAD
	ICEBOAT	ABCKNNO	BANNOCK		BIGHEAD
ABCEIRS	ASCRIBE	ABCKNOW	WON BACK	ABDEGII	BIG IDEA
ABCEISS	ABSCISE	ABCKNRU	RUN BACK	ABDEGIL	BIG DEAL
	SCABIES	ABCKORW	BACK ROW	ABDEGIN	BEADING
ABCEITT	TABETIC	ABCKOTU	BACK OUT	ABDEGIR	ABRIDGE
ABCEKLN	BLACKEN		OUTBACK		BRIGADE
ABCEKLR	BLACKER	ABCKPSU	BACKS UP	ABDEGNO	BONDAGE
ABCEKNR	BRACKEN		BACKUPS	ABDEGOS	BODEGAS
ABCEKRS	BACKERS	ABCKPTU	PUT BACK	ABDEGRS	BADGERS
ABCEKRT	BRACKET	ABCKSTU	SACKBUT	ABDEHIT	HABITED
ABCEKST	SET BACK	ABCLLOX	CALL BOX	ABDEHLR	HALBERD
	SETBACK	ABCLLOY	CALL BOY	ABDEHNT	THE BAND
ABCEKTW	WETBACK		CALLBOY	ABDEHOW	BOWHEAD
ABCELLU	BULLACE	ABCLLSY	CALLS BY	ABDEHOY	HEAD BOY
	CUE BALL	ABCLMSY	CYMBALS	ABDEHRT	BREADTH
ABCELMO	CEMBALO	ABCLNOS	BLANCOS	ABDEHSU	SUBHEAD
ABCELMR	CLAMBER	ABCLNOY	BALCONY	ABDEILN	BAD LINE
ABCELMS	BECALMS	ABCLRUY	CURABLY	ABDEILP	BIPEDAL
ABCELOP	PLACEBO	ABCMOST	COMBATS		PIEBALD
ABCELOV	VOCABLE	ABCNORS	CARBONS	ABDEILR	BRAILED
ABCELRU	CURABLE	ABCORRW	CROWBAR	ABDEILS	BALDIES
ABCELSU	BASCULE	ABCORSX	BOXCARS		DISABLE
ABCEMRS	CAMBERS	ABCORSY	CARBOYS	ABDEILU	AUDIBLE
ABCENOS	BEACONS	ABDDEER	BEARDED	ABDEIMO	AMEBOID
ABCENOW	COWBANE	ABDDEES	DEBASED	ABDEIMT	BAD TIME
ABCENRU	UNBRACE	ABDDEET	DEBATED	ABDEINR	BANDIER
ABCEOOS	CABOOSE	ABDDEIL	ADDIBLE		BRAINED
ABCERRS	BRACERS	ABDDEIN	BANDIED	ABDEINS	BANDIES
ABCESSS	ABSCESS	ABDDEIR	BRAIDED		BASINED
ABCFFKO	BACK OFF	ABDDEIS	BADDIES	ABDEINW	BAD WINE
ABCFIKN	FINBACK	ABDDELR	BLADDER	ABDEIRR	BRAIDER
ABCFILO	BIFOCAL	ABDDENR	BRANDED	ABDEIRS	AIR BEDS
ABCFIRS	FABRICS	ABDDEOR	BOARDED		BRAISED
ABCFKLY	FLYBACK		ROAD BED		SEABIRD
ABCFLNU	FAN CLUB		ROADBED	ABDEIRW	BAWDIER
ABCFNOS	CONFABS	ABDDESY	DAY BEDS	ABDEISS	BIASSED
ABCGHKO	HOGBACK		DAYBEDS	ABDEJRU	ABJURED

ABDEKLN	BLANKED	ABDLMOR	LOMBARD	ABEFFMO	OFF BEAM
ABDEKLU	BAULKED	ABDLORY	BROADLY	ABEFFOT	BEAT OFF
ABDEKRS	DEBARKS	ABDLRUY	DURABLY		OFFBEAT
ABDELLR	RED BALL	ABDMNNO	BONDMAN	ABEFILR	FRIABLE
ABDELMR	MARBLED	ABDNOOR	ON BOARD	ABEFILU	FIBULAE
ABDELMS	BELDAMS	ABDNOPR	PROBAND	ABEFILX	FIXABLE
ABDELNO	OLD BEAN	ABDNORW	WAR BOND	ABEFIRT	FAR BE IT
ABDELNR	BLANDER	ABDNOSU	ABOUNDS	ABEFITY	BEATIFY
ABDELOS	ALBEDOS	ABDNOSY	SANDBOY	ABEFLLS	BEFALLS
ABDELOT	BLOATED	ABDNOYY	ANYBODY	ABEFLLU	BALEFUL
	LOBATED	ABDNRTU	BAD TURN	ABEFLLY	FLYABLE
ABDELRU	DURABLE	ABDNSTY	STAND BY	ABEFLNU	BANEFUL
ABDELRW	BRAWLED		STANDBY	ABEFORR	FORBEAR
	WARBLED	ABDOPRU	BOARD UP	ABEFPRS	PREFABS
ABDELRY	DRYABLE	ABDORSS	ADSORBS	ABEFRSU	BUS FARE
ABDELST	BALDEST	ABDORST	BAD SORT	ABEGGIM	BIG GAME
	BLASTED	ABDRRSU	DURBARS	ABEGGIR	BAGGIER
	STABLED	ABDRSTU	BUSTARD	ABEGGMO	GAMBOGE
ABDEMNO	ABDOMEN	ABDRUZZ	BUZZARD	ABEGGRR	BRAGGER
	BAD OMEN	ABDSUYY	BUSY DAY	ABEGGRS	BEGGARS
ABDEMOV	BAD MOVE	ABEEELV	LEAVE BE	ABEGGRU	BURGAGE
ABDEMRU	BERMUDA	ABEEERV	BEREAVE	ABEGGRY	BEGGARY
ABDENOR	BROADEN	ABEEFGO	BE OF AGE	ABEGHNS	SHEBANG
ABDENPS	BED PANS	ABEEFLO	BEEFALO	ABEGILN	BELGIAN
	BEDPANS	ABEEGHR	HERBAGE		BENGALI
ABDENRR	BRANDER	ABEEGLL	GABELLE	ABEGIMN	BEAMING
ABDENRS	BANDERS		GELABLE		BIG NAME
ABDENSS	BADNESS	ABEEGLR	BARE LEG		BIG-NAME
ABDENSW	BAD NEWS		BEAGLER	ABEGIMR	GAMBIER
ABDEOOT	TABOOED	ABEEGLS	BEAGLES	ABEGIMT	MEGABIT
ABDEORR	BOARDER	ABEEGRS	BARGEES	ABEGINO	BEGONIA
	BROADER	ABEEHNN	HENBANE	ABEGINR	BEARING
ABDEORT	ABORTED	ABEEHNS	BANSHEE	ABEGINT	BEATING
ABDEOST	BOASTED		HAS-BEEN	ABEGIPP	BAGPIPE
ABDEPST	BAD STEP	ABEEHNT	BENEATH	ABEGIRS	BIG EARS
ABDEPSY	PAYBEDS	ABEEHRT	BREATHE	ABEGJOT	GET A JOB
ABDERSU	DAUBERS	ABEEHRV	BEHAVER	ABEGKOS	BOSKAGE
ABDERSV	ADVERBS	ABEEHSV	BEHAVES	ABEGLMR	GAMBLER
ABDERUY	BUY DEAR	ABEEHTY	EYEBATH		GAMBREL
ABDERVY	VERY BAD	ABEEILS	BAILEES	ABEGLMS	GAMBLES
ABDETTU	ABUTTED	ABEEIMT	TIE-BEAM	ABEGLNS	BANGLES
ABDFIIR	BID FAIR	ABEEKLR	BLEAKER	ABEGLRR	GARBLER
ABDFMOR	BAD FORM	ABEEKNT	BETAKEN	ABEGLRS	GARBLES
ABDGIIN	ABIDING	ABEEKPS	BESPEAK	ABEGLSU	BELUGAS
ABDGIKN	BAD KING	ABEEKRR	BREAKER	ABEGMOR	EMBARGO
ABDGILN	BALDING	ABEEKRS	BEAKERS	ABEGMPU	PUB GAME
ABDGINN	BANDING	ABEEKST	BETAKES	ABEGMRU	UMBRAGE
ABDGINR	BRIGAND	ABEELLY	EYEBALL	ABEGNRS	BANGERS
ABDGINS	BAD SIGN	ABEELMW	EWE LAMB		GRABENS
ABDGINU	DAUBING	ABEELNS	ENABLES	ABEGOOV	GO ABOVE
ABDGINW	WINDBAG	ABEELNT	TENABLE	ABEGOPT	PEAT BOG
ABDGLOY	GO BADLY	ABEELNU	NEBULAE	ABEGOPY	PAGE BOY
ABDGLUY	LADYBUG	ABEELOR	EAR LOBE	ABEGORR	BEGORRA
ABDHILS	BALDISH		EARLOBE	ABEGORX	GEARBOX
ABDHMTU	MUD BATH	ABEELQU	EQUABLE	ABEGOSZ	GAZEBOS
ABDHNSU	HUSBAND	ABEELRT	BLEATER	ABEHIRS	BEARISH
ABDHOST	BAD SHOT	ABEELSU	SEA BLUE	ABEHITU	HABITUE
ABDIKRS	BAD RISK	ABEEMRS	BEAMERS	ABEHKNT	THE BANK
ABDILRY	RABIDLY	ABEENRV	VERBENA	ABEHKRU	HAUBERK
ABDILUY	AUDIBLY	ABEEORS	AEROBES	ABEHLMS	SHAMBLE
ABDILWY	BAWDILY	ABEERRS	BEARERS	ABEHLRS	HERBALS
ABDINOR	INBOARD	ABEERST	BEATERS	ABEHLRT	BLATHER
ABDINOY	IN A BODY		BERATES		HALBERT
ABDINRS	RIBANDS		REBATES	ABEHRRS	BRASHER
ABDINST	BANDITS	ABEERSV	BEAVERS	ABEHRSS	BASHERS
ABDIORY	BY RADIO	ABEERTT	ABETTER		BRASHES
ABDIPRU	UPBRAID	ABEERTY	BAY TREE	ABEHRST	BATHERS
ABDIRSS	DISBARS	ABEESTT	BEATEST		BREATHS
ABDKOOY	DAY BOOK	ABEESWX	BEESWAX	ABEHRTY	BREATHY
ABDLLNY	BLANDLY	ABEFFLR	BAFFLER		BY HEART
ABDLLOR	BOLLARD	ABEFFLS	BAFFLES	ABEIILR	LIBERIA

ABEIILS	BAILIES	ABEKSST	BASKETS	ABENSTT	BATTENS
ABEIINN	BIENNIA	ABELLNT	NETBALL	ABEOOTV	OBOVATE
ABEIINR	IBERIAN	ABELLNW	NEW BALL	ABEOPRT	PROBATE
ABEIJNS	BASENJI	ABELLOV	LOVABLE	ABEOQRU	BAROQUE
ABEIKLL	LIKABLE	ABELLRU	RUBELLA	ABEORRW	BOER WAR
ABEIKLS	SKIABLE	ABELLST	BALLETS	ABEORST	BOASTER
ABEIKNR	BREAK IN	ABELMMS	EMBALMS		BOATERS
ABEIKNT	BEATNIK	ABELMNT	LAMBENT		BORATES
ABEILLO	LOBELIA	ABELMNU	ALBUMEN	ABEORSV	BRAVOES
ABEILLP	PLIABLE	ABELMOV	MOVABLE	ABEORTT	ABETTOR
ABEILLR	BRAILLE	ABELMRR	RAMBLER	ABEORTU	BEAR OUT
	LIBERAL	ABELMRS	BLAMERS	ABEOTTU	BEAT OUT
ABEILLV	LIVABLE		MARBLES	ABEPRSU	BEARS UP
ABEILMR	BALMIER		RAMBLES	ABEPSTU	BEATS UP
ABEILMT	BIMETAL	ABELMRT	LAMBERT		UPBEATS
	TIMBALE	ABELMRY	BRAMLEY	ABEQRSU	BARQUES
ABEILNP	BIPLANE	ABELMTU	MUTABLE	ABEQSSU	BASQUES
ABEILNS	LESBIAN	ABELNNO	LEBANON	ABERRST	BARTERS
ABEILRS	BAILERS	ABELNOO	BOOLEAN	ABERRSU	SABREUR
ABEILRT	LIBRATE	ABELNOT	NOTABLE	ABERRVY	BRAVERY
	TRIABLE	ABELNOY	BALONEY	ABERSSS	BRASSES
ABEILRW	WIRABLE	ABELNPY	BY PLANE	ABERSST	BASTERS
ABEILSS	ABSEILS	ABELNRU	NEBULAR		BREASTS
ABEILST	BESTIAL	ABELNRY	BLARNEY	ABERSSU	ABUSERS
	STABILE	ABELNSU	BUS LANE	ABERSTT	BATTERS
ABEILSW	BEWAILS		NEBULAS	ABERSTV	BRAVEST
ABEILSY	BAILEYS	ABELNTU	TUNABLE	ABERSTY	BARYTES
ABEILSZ	SIZABLE	ABELNTY	TENABLY		BETRAYS
ABEILVV	BIVALVE	ABELOPT	POTABLE	ABERSUU	BUREAUS
ABFIMNT	AMBIENT	ABELORT	BLOATER	ABERSWY	SWEAR BY
ABEIMRR	BARMIER	ABELORU	RUBEOLA	ABERTTU	ABUTTER
ABEINRS	SERBIAN	ABELOST	BOATELS	ABERTTY	BATTERY
ABEINRW	WINE BAR		OBLATES	ABERUUX	BUREAUX
ABEINSS	SABINES	ABELOSV	ABSOLVE	ABESSST	BASSETS
ABEINST	BEATS IN	ABELOTU	BALE OUT	ABESSSY	ABYSSES
ABEINTT	TIBETAN	ABELQUY	EQUABLY	ADFFIIL	BAILIFF
ABFIOTW	TIE A BOW	ABELRRS	BARRELS	ABFFLOU	BUFFALO
ABEIPST	BAPTISE	ABELRRW	BRAWLER	ABFGGLO	GOLF BAG
ABEIPTZ	BAPTIZE		WARBLER	ABFHLSU	BASHFUL
ABEIRRR	BARRIER	ABELRST	BLASTER	ABFIILR	BIFILAR
ABEIRRT	ARBITER		STABLER	ABFILRU	FIBULAR
	RAREBIT	ABELRSV	VERBALS	ABFILSU	FIBULAS
ABEIRRZ	BIZARRE	ABELRSW	BAWLERS	ABFIMOR	FIBROMA
	BRAZIER		WARBLES	ABGGGIN	BAGGING
ABEIRSS	BRAISES	ABELRSZ	BLAZERS	ABGGILY	BAGGILY
ABEIRST	BAITERS	ABELRTT	BATTLER	ABGGINN	BANGING
ABEIRTT	BATTIER	ABELRVY	BRAVELY	ABGGINR	BARGING
	BIRETTA	ABELSST	STABLES	ABGGKOO	GAG BOOK
ABEIRTU	AIR TUBE	ABELSTT	BATTLES	ABGHINS	BASHING
ABEIRTV	VIBRATE		TABLETS	ABGHINT	BATHING
ABEIRUX	EXURBIA	ABELSTY	BEASTLY	ABGIILN	BAILING
ABEISTT	BATISTE		LAY BETS	ABGIILS	GALIBIS
ABEISUV	ABUSIVE	ABELTWY	BELTWAY	ABGIINS	BIASING
ABEITUX	BAUXITE	ABEMNOS	AMBONES	ABGIINT	BAITING
ABEJLUY	BLUE JAY		BEMOANS	ABGIKLN	BALKING
ABEJNOS	BANJOES	ABEMNOT	BOATMEN	ABGIKLT	BIG TALK
ABEJNOW	JAWBONE	ABEMNST	BATSMEN		TALK BIG
ABEJORS	JERBOAS		BEST MAN	ABGIKNN	BANKING
ABEJRRU	ABJURER	ABEMNSU	SUNBEAM	ABGIKNR	BARKING
ABEJRSU	ABJURES	ABEMORT	BROMATE		BRAKING
ABEKLLY	BLEAKLY	ABEMSSY	EMBASSY	ABGIKNS	BASKING
ABEKLNR	BLANKER	ABENNRS	BANNERS	ABGIKST	KIT BAGS
ABEKLNT	BLANKET	ABENORT	BARONET		KITBAGS
ABEKLNU	BELA KUN	ABENOSY	SOYBEAN	ABGILLN	BALLING
ABEKLRS	BALKERS	ABENOTY	BAYONET	ABGILLS	GAS BILL
ABEKLSY	KABYLES	ABENQTU	BANQUET	ABGILMN	AMBLING
ABEKMRS	EMBARKS	ABENRST	BANTERS		BLAMING
ABEKNRS	BANKERS	ABENRSY	BARNEYS		LAMBING
ABEKPRU	BREAK UP	ABENRSZ	BRAZENS	ABGILMS	GIMBALS
	BREAKUP	ABENRUX	EXURBAN	ABGILNR	BLARING
ABEKRRS	BARKERS	ABENSST	ABSENTS	ABGILNW	BAWLING

ABGILNZ	BLAZING
ABGIMST	GAMBITS
ABGINNN	BANNING
ABGINNT	BANTING
ABGINOS	GABIONS
ABGINOT	BOATING
ABGINRR	BARRING
ABGINRS	SABRING
ABGINRV	BRAVING
ABGINRY	BRAYING
ABGINRZ	BRAZING
ABGINST	BASTING
ABGINSU	ABUSING
ABGINTT	BATTING
ABGIPRT	BIG PART
ABGJOOT	GOT A JOB
ABGKORW	WORKBAG
ABGLMOS	GAMBOLS
ABGLMOU	LUMBAGO
ABGLORS	BROLGAS
ABGLRRU	BURGLAR
ABGMSUY	MAYBUGS
ABGNOPR	PROBANG
ABGNOTU	GUNBOAT
ABGOOTU	GO ABOUT
ABGOPST	POST BAG
	POSTBAG
ABGOTTU	TUG BOAT
ABHHIPT	HIP BATH
ABHHOOP	POOH-BAH
ABHHOTT	HOT BATH
ABHIINT	INHABIT
ABHILNO	HOBNAIL
ABHILOS	ABOLISH
ABHILTU	HALIBUT
ABHIMNR	BRAHMIN
ABHIOPS	PHOBIAS
ABHIORS	BOARISH
ABHIRTT	AT BIRTH
ABHLRSY	BRASHLY
ABHMNSU	BUSHMAN
ABHMRSU	RHUMBAS
ABHORRU	HARBOUR
ABHOTUY	HAUTBOY
ABHPSTY	BYPATHS
ABHSTUW	WASH TUB
	WASHTUB
ABIILMU	BULIMIA
ABIILOV	BOLIVIA
ABIILRY	BILIARY
ABIILTY	ABILITY
ABIJLNR	BRINJAL
ABIJNPU	PUNJABI
ABIJOSW	OJIBWAS
ABIJOWY	OJIBWAY
ABIKLMR	MILK BAR
ABILLMP	LIP BALM
ABILLMY	BALMILY
ABILLNP	PINBALL
ABILLPY	PLIABLY
ABILLSW	SAWBILL
ABILLSY	SYLLABI
ABILLWX	WAXBILL
ABILLWY	WAYBILL
ABILMNU	ALBUMIN
ABILMOX	MAILBOX
ABILNOS	ALBINOS
ABILNSY	LIBYANS
ABILOPR	BIPOLAR
	PARBOIL
ABILORS	BAILORS

ABILORT	ORBITAL
ABILORV	BOLIVAR
ABILOTU	BAIL OUT
ABILRRY	LIBRARY
ABILRSU	BURIALS
ABILSTT	BLAST IT
ABILSYZ	SIZABLY
ABIMNRU	UMBRIAN
ABIMOSS	BIOMASS
ABIMPST	BAPTISM
ABINORR	IRON BAR
ABINORS	SORBIAN
ABINORW	RAINBOW
ABINOST	BASTION
	OBTAINS
ABINOTT	NOT A BIT
ABINRTV	VIBRANT
ABINRTY	BY TRAIN
ABIORRS	BARRIOS
ABIORSS	ISOBARS
ABIORTV	VIBRATO
ABIPRTT	BIT PART
ABIPSTT	BAPTIST
ABISSST	BASSIST
ABJKMOS	SJAMBOK
ABKLLNY	BLANKLY
ABKLOOW	LAW BOOK
ABKLRUW	BULWARK
ABKMNOO	BOOKMAN
ABKNNOS	BANKS ON
ABLLLUY	LULLABY
ABLLNOO	BALLOON
ABLLNOS	NO-BALLS
ABLLOST	BALLOTS
ABLLOTY	TALL BOY
	TALLBOY
ABLLOVY	LOVABLY
ABLLPSU	BALLS-UP
ABLMNOU	UMBONAL
ABLMOOT	TOMBOLA
ABLMPUU	PABULUM
ABLMSTY	TYMBALS
ABLMTUY	MUTABLY
ABLNORW	BARN OWL
ABLNOSZ	BLAZONS
ABLNOTY	NOTABLY
ABLOPYY	PLAYBOY
ABLORST	BORSTAL
ABLORSU	LABOURS
ABLOTUW	BAWL OUT
ABLPSYY	BYPLAYS
ABLRTUU	TUBULAR
ABLSSTU	LAST BUS
ABMOORR	BARROOM
ABMORTU	TAMBOUR
ABMOSTW	WOMBATS
ABMRSSU	SAMBURS
ABNOORZ	BORAZON
ABNOOSS	BASSOON
ABNORSY	BARYONS
ABNOTUY	BUOYANT
ABNRSTU	TURBANS
ABOOPSX	SOAP BOX
	SOAPBOX
ABOORTW	ROWBOAT
ABOOTTW	TOW BOAT
ABORRSU	ARBOURS
ABORRSW	BARROWS
ABORSSU	SUB ROSA
ABORSTU	RUBATOS
	TABOURS

ABORSUY	YORUBAS
ABRRSSU	BURSARS
ABRRSUY	BURSARY
ABRSTUU	ARBUTUS
ABSSUWY	SUBWAYS
ABSUWZZ	BUZZ SAW
ACCDDEE	ACCEDED
ACCDEEN	CADENCE
ACCDEER	ACCEDER
ACCDEES	ACCEDES
ACCDEHN	CHANCED
ACCDEHO	COACHED
ACCDEIU	CADUCEI
ACCDEKL	CLACKED
ACCDEKO	COCKADE
ACCDEKR	CRACKED
ACCDERU	ACCRUED
ACCDESU	ACCUSED
ACCDFIL	FLACCID
ACCDHIL	CHALCID
ACCDORS	ACCORDS
ACCEERT	ACCRETE
ACCEFLU	FELUCCA
ACCEGOS	SOCCAGE
ACCEHIL	CALICHE
	CHALICE
ACCEHIN	CHICANE
ACCEHLN	CHANCEL
ACCEHLO	COCHLEA
ACCEHNO	CONCHAE
ACCEHNR	CHANCRE
ACCEHNS	CHANCES
ACCEHOR	COACHER
ACCEHOS	COACHES
ACCEHRT	CATCHER
ACCEHST	CATCHES
ACCEHTT	CATHECT
ACCEHTU	CATECHU
ACCEILN	CALCINE
ACCEILO	COELIAC
ACCEILS	CALICES
ACCEILT	CALCITE
ACCEIMR	CERAMIC
	RACEMIC
ACCEINO	COCAINE
	OCEANIC
ACCEINV	VACCINE
ACCEIPR	CAPRICE
ACCEIPS	ICE CAPS
ACCEIST	ASCETIC
ACCEKLR	CACKLER
	CLACKER
	CRACKLE
ACCEKLS	CACKLES
ACCEKOP	PEACOCK
ACCEKOS	SEA-COCK
ACCEKRR	CRACKER
ACCELNO	CONCEAL
ACCELNS	CANCELS
ACCELOR	CORACLE
ACCELSU	SACCULE
ACCELSY	CALYCES
ACCEMNO	MECCANO
ACCENOV	CONCAVE
ACCENPT	PECCANT
ACCENRS	CANCERS
ACCENST	ACCENTS
ACCEPRY	PECCARY
ACCEPST	ACCEPTS
ACCERRS	SCARCER

ACCERSU	ACCRUES	ACDDHIS	CADDISH
	ACCUSER	ACDDHKO	HADDOCK
ACCESSU	ACCUSES	ACDDHRU	CHUDDAR
ACCFIIP	PACIFIC	ACDDIRS	DISCARD
ACCFILY	CALCIFY	ACDDIST	ADDICTS
ACCGNOS	COGNACS	ACDDKOP	PADDOCK
ACCHIKS	CHIACKS	ACDDLOY	COLD DAY
ACCHIOT	CHAOTIC	ACDDSTU	ADDUCTS
ACCHITT	CATCH IT	ACDEEES	DECEASE
ACCHKOY	HAYCOCK	ACDEEFF	EFFACED
ACCHLNO	CONCHAL	ACDEEFR	DEFACER
ACCHNOT	CATCH ON		RED FACE
ACCHOSU	CACHOUS	ACDEEFS	DEFACES
ACCHOTW	CHOCTAW	ACDEEFT	FACETED
ACCHPTU	CATCH UP	ACDEEHL	CHALDEE
	CATCHUP		LEACHED
ACCHRRU	CURRACH	ACDEEHP	PEACHED
ACCHRST	SCRATCH	ACDEEHR	REACHED
ACCIILN	ACLINIC	ACDEEHT	CHEATED
ACCIINT	ACTINIC	ACDEEIT	ICED TEA
ACCIIST	ASCITIC	ACDEEKR	CREAKED
	SCIATIC	ACDEELN	CLEANED
ACCIKRS	CARSICK		ENLACED
ACCILLU	CALCULI	ACDEELR	CLEARED
ACCILMO	COMICAL		CREEDAL
ACCILMU	CALCIUM		DECLARE
ACCILNO	CONICAL	ACDEELV	CLEAVED
	LACONIC	ACDEEMN	MENACED
ACCILNY	CYNICAL	ACDEEMR	AMERCED
ACCILOR	CALORIC		CREAMED
ACCILOS	CALICOS	ACDEENS	ENCASED
ACCILOV	VOCALIC	ACDEENT	ENACTED
ACCILRU	CRUCIAL	ACDEENV	VENDACE
ACCILRY	ACRYLIC	ACDEEPR	CAPERED
ACCILSS	CLASSIC	ACDEEPS	ESCAPED
ACCILST	CLASTIC	ACDEERS	CREASED
ACCILSU	SACCULI	ACDEERT	CATERED
ACCIMMS	MICMACS		CREATED
ACCIMOT	COMATIC		REACTED
ACCINRU	CRUCIAN	ACDEERU	DUE CARE
ACCISTT	TACTICS	ACDEERY	DECAYER
ACCISTU	CAUSTIC	ACDEETU	EDUCATE
ACCKLRY	CRACKLY	ACDEETX	EXACTED
ACCKOSS	CASSOCK	ACDEFFH	CHAFFED
	COSSACK	ACDEFIN	FANCIED
ACCKPRU	CRACK UP	ACDEFOP	PO-FACED
	CRACK-UP	ACDEFOT	DE FACTO
ACCMOPT	COMPACT	ACDEFPU	FACED UP
ACCNOOR	RACCOON	ACDEFRS	SCARFED
ACCNOTT	CONTACT	ACDEFRT	CRAFTED
ACCNOTU	ACCOUNT	ACDEGHN	CHANGED
ACCOPTY	COPY CAT	ACDEGHR	CHARGED
	COPYCAT	ACDEGLN	CLANGED
ACCOSST	ACCOSTS		GLANCED
ACDDDEU	ADDUCED	ACDEGNO	DECAGON
ACDDEEF	DEFACED	ACDEGNU	UNCAGED
ACDDEES	DECADES	ACDEGOR	CORDAGE
ACDDEEY	DECAYED		DOG RACE
ACDDEHR	CHEDDAR	ACDEGRS	CADGERS
ACDDEIN	CANDIED	ACDEHHT	HATCHED
ACDDEIS	CADDIES	ACDEHIN	CHAINED
ACDDEIU	DECIDUA		ECHIDNA
ACDDEIY	ACID DYE	ACDEHIP	EDAPHIC
ACDDELN	CANDLED	ACDEHIR	CHAIRED
ACDDELO	CLADODE	ACDEHIX	HEXADIC
ACDDELS	SCALDED	ACDEHKL	CHALKED
ACDDEOP	DECAPOD	ACDEHKW	WHACKED
ACDDERR	RED CARD	ACDEHLS	CLASHED
ACDDERU	ADDUCER	ACDEHLT	LATCHED
ACDDESU	ADDUCES	ACDEHMP	CHAMPED
ACDDETU	CUT DEAD		

ACDEHMR	CHARMED		
	MARCHED		
ACDEHMT	MATCHED		
ACDEHNR	RANCHED		
ACDEHNT	CHANTED		
ACDEHOP	POACHED		
ACDEHOT	CATHODE		
ACDEHPP	CHAPPED		
ACDEHPR	PARCHED		
ACDEHPT	PATCHED		
ACDEHRR	CHARRED		
ACDEHRS	CRASHED		
ACDEHRT	CHARTED		
ACDEHST	SCATHED		
ACDEHTT	CHATTED		
ACDEHTW	WATCHED		
ACDEHTY	YACHTED		
ACDEILL	CEDILLA		
ACDEILM	CLAIMED		
	DECIMAL		
	DECLAIM		
	MEDICAL		
ACDEILN	ICELAND		
ACDEILR	RADICLE		
ACDEILT	CITADEL		
	DELTAIC		
	DIALECT		
	EDICTAL		
ACDEIMY	MEDIACY		
ACDEINR	CAIRNED		
ACDEINS	CANDIES		
ACDEINY	CYANIDE		
ACDEIRR	CARRIED		
ACDEIRS	CARDIES		
	RADICES		
	SIDECAR		
ACDEIST	DIE-CAST		
ACDEISV	ADVICES		
ACDEITT	DICTATE		
ACDEITY	EDACITY		
ACDEJLO	CAJOLED		
ACDEKLM	MACKLED		
ACDEKLN	CLANKED		
ACDEKLO	CLOAKED		
ACDEKLS	SLACKED		
ACDEKLU	CAULKED		
ACDEKMS	SMACKED		
ACDEKNR	CRANKED		
ACDEKNS	SNACKED		
ACDEKOR	CROAKED		
ACDEKQU	QUACKED		
ACDEKRT	TRACKED		
ACDEKRW	WRACKED		
ACDEKST	STACKED		
ACDELMP	CLAMPED		
ACDELNO	CELADON		
ACDELNR	CANDLER		
ACDELNS	CALENDS		
	CANDLES		
ACDELNU	UNLACED		
ACDELOS	SOLACED		
ACDELOT	LOCATED		
ACDELPP	CLAPPED		
ACDELPS	CLASPED		
	SCALPED		
ACDELRS	CRADLES		
ACDELRW	ARC-WELD		
	CRAWLED		
ACDELSS	CLASSED		
ACDELST	CASTLED		
ACDELWW	DEWCLAW		

ACDEMMR	CRAMMED	ACDIMMU	CADMIUM	ACEELRT	ELECTRA
ACDEMOR	COMRADE	ACDIMNO	MONADIC		TREACLE
ACDEMPR	CRAMPED		NOMADIC	ACEELRV	CLEAVER
ACDEMPS	DECAMPS	ACDIMNY	DYNAMIC	ACEELST	CELESTA
	SCAMPED	ACDIOPR	PARODIC	ACEELSV	CLEAVES
ACDENNS	SCANNED		PICADOR	ACEEMNS	MENACES
ACDENNU	NUANCED	ACDIORR	CORRIDA	ACEEMNV	CAVE MEN
ACDENOR	ONE CARD	ACDIORT	CAROTID		CAVEMEN
ACDENOS	DEACONS	ACDIQRU	QUADRIC	ACEEMRR	CREAMER
ACDENPR	PRANCED	ACDIRST	DRASTIC	ACEEMRS	AMERCES
ACDENRS	DANCERS	ACDIRTU	AIR DUCT	ACEEMRT	CREMATE
ACDENRU	DURANCE	ACDISTX	TAX DISC	ACEENNP	PENANCE
ACDENRY	ARDENCY	ACDITUV	VIADUCT	ACEENNT	CANTEEN
ACDENSS	ASCENDS	ACDJNTU	ADJUNCT	ACEENNY	CAYENNE
ACDENST	DECANTS	ACDKLOP	PADLOCK	ACEENOT	ACETONE
	DESCANT	ACDKMPU	MUDPACK	ACEENRS	CAREENS
	SCANTED	ACDKNVY	VAN DYCK	ACEENRT	CRENATE
ACDEORR	CORRADE	ACDLLUY	DUCALLY	ACEENSS	ENCASES
ACDEORT	ART DECO	ACDLNOR	CALDRON		SEANCES
	CORDATE	ACDLOPT	COLD TAP	ACEENSW	NEW CASE
	RED COAT	ACDLORW	COLD WAR	ACEENTU	CUNEATE
	REDCOAT	ACDLSTY	DACTYLS	ACEEPRS	ESCAPER
ACDEORU	ECUADOR	ACDMMNO	COMMAND	ACEEPSS	ESCAPES
ACDEOST	COASTED	ACDNORU	CANDOUR	ACEERRS	CAREERS
ACDEOUV	COUVADE	ACDORSW	COWARDS	ACEERRT	CATERER
ACDEPRS	REDCAPS	ACDRSTU	CUSTARD		RETRACE
	SCARPED	ACEEEPS	ESCAPEE		TERRACE
	SCRAPED	ACEEEUV	EVACUEE	ACEERSS	CREASES
ACDEPTU	ACTED UP	ACEEFFR	EFFACER	ACEERST	CREATES
ACDERRS	CARDERS	ACEEFFS	EFFACES	ACEERTX	EXCRETA
	SCARRED	ACEEFIN	FAIENCE	ACEESTT	CASETTE
ACDERST	REDACTS		FIANCEE	ACEESTY	CAT'S-EYE
ACDERSU	CRUSADE	ACEEFNW	NEW FACE		CATS EYE
	USED CAR	ACEEFPR	PREFACE	ACEFFFO	FACE-OFF
ACDERTT	DETRACT	ACEEGIL	ELEGIAC	ACEFFMO	CAME OFF
ACDERTU	TRADUCE	ACEEHHT	CHEETAH	ACEFFST	AFFECTS
ACDESTT	SCATTED	ACEEHIV	ACHIEVE	ACEFHMR	CHAMFER
ACDFIIT	FATIDIC	ACEEHLR	LEACHER	ACEFHRS	CHAFERS
ACDFIIY	ACIDIFY	ACEEHLS	LEACHES	ACEFILM	MALEFIC
ACDFRTY	DRY FACT	ACEEHLT	CHELATE	ACEFINN	FINANCE
ACDGGIN	CADGING	ACEEHMT	MACHETE	ACEFINR	FANCIER
ACDGINN	DANCING	ACEEHNN	ENHANCE	ACEFINS	FANCIES
ACDGINR	CARDING	ACEEHNO	EACH ONE		FASCINE
ACDGORT	DOG CART	ACEEHNS	ACHENES		FIANCES
ACDHIIL	CHILIAD		ENCHASE	ACEFITY	ACETIFY
ACDHIMR	DHARMIC	ACEEHPR	CHEAPER	ACEFLRU	CAREFUL
ACDHIRY	DIARCHY	ACEEHPS	PEACHES	ACEFNRU	FURNACE
ACDHLMO	COLD HAM	ACEEHRS	REACHES	ACEFOTU	OUTFACE
ACDHLOP	OLD CHAP	ACEEHRT	CHEATER	ACEFPSU	FACES UP
ACDHLOR	CHORDAL		HECTARE	ACEFPUU	EUFA CUP
ACDHMOU	MUCH ADO		TEACHER	ACEFRRT	REFRACT
ACDHMRS	DRACHMS	ACEEHST	ESCHEAT	ACEFRRU	FARCEUR
ACDHNOW	COWHAND		TEACHES	ACEFRSU	SURFACE
ACDHOPR	POCHARD	ACEEHTT	THECATE	ACEFRTU	FACTURE
ACDHORR	ORCHARD	ACEEILP	CALIPEE	ACEFSTU	FAUCETS
ACDHORS	CHADORS	ACEEILT	ELEATIC	ACEGHHI	ACE HIGH
ACDHRYY	DYARCHY	ACEEINP	IN PEACE	ACEGHNR	CHANGER
ACDIIIN	INDICIA	ACEEISV	VESICAE	ACEGHNS	CHANGES
ACDIINO	CONIDIA	ACEEKNP	KNEECAP	ACEGHOU	GOUACHE
ACDIINV	DA VINCI	ACEELLN	NACELLE	ACEGHOW	COWHAGE
ACDIIRT	TRIADIC	ACEELMP	EMPLACE	ACEGHRR	CHARGER
ACDIITY	ACIDITY	ACEELMR	RECLAME	ACEGHRS	CHARGES
ACDIKLS	SKALDIC	ACEELNR	CLEANER	ACEGILN	ANGELIC
ACDILNO	NODICAL	ACEELNS	CLEANSE		ANGLICE
ACDILOP	PLACOID		ENLACES		GALENIC
ACDILOR	COLD AIR		SCALENE	ACEGILP	PELAGIC
	CORDIAL	ACEELNV	ENCLAVE	ACEGILR	GLACIER
ACDILOT	COTIDAL	ACEELPR	PERCALE		GRACILE
ACDILRY	ACRIDLY		REPLACE	ACEGIMR	GEMARIC
ACDILTW	WILD CAT	ACEELRR	CLEARER		GRIMACE
	WILDCAT	ACEELRS	CEREALS	ACEGIMT	GAMETIC

ACEGINO	COINAGE	ACEHMST	MATCHES	ACEILRV	CLAVIER
ACEGINR	GRECIAN	ACEHNNT	ENCHANT	ACEILST	CASTILE
ACEGINS	CEASING	ACEHNRR	RANCHER		ELASTIC
ACEGIPT	PIT CAGE	ACEHNRS	RANCHES		LATICES
ACEGKLO	LOCKAGE	ACEHNRT	CHANTER	ACEILSV	VESICAL
ACEGKLR	GRACKLE		TRANCHE	ACEILTT	LATTICE
ACEGKOR	CORKAGE	ACEHNST	CHASTEN		TACTILE
ACEGLLO	COLLAGE	ACEHOPR	POACHER	ACEIMNO	ENCOMIA
ACEGLNO	CONGEAL	ACEHOPS	POACHES	ACEIMNR	CARMINE
ACEGLNR	CLANGER	ACEHPRS	PARCHES	ACEIMNS	AMNESIC
ACEGLNS	GLANCES	ACEHPRT	CHAPTER		CINEMAS
ACEGLOU	CAGOULE	ACEHPST	PATCHES	ACEIMNX	MEXICAN
ACEGNOT	COGNATE	ACEHQUU	QUECHUA	ACEIMST	SEMATIC
ACEGNSU	UNCAGES	ACEHRRS	ARCHERS	ACEIMSU	CAESIUM
ACEGORS	CARGOES	ACEHRRT	CHARTER	ACEINNP	PINNACE
	CORSAGE	ACEHRRY	ARCHERY	ACEINNR	CANNIER
	SOCAGER	ACEHRSS	CHASERS	ACEINNS	CANINES
ACEGORU	COURAGE		CRASHES		NANCIES
ACEGOTT	COTTAGE	ACEHRSX	EXARCHS	ACEINNT	ANCIENT
ACEGSTU	SCUTAGE	ACEHRSY	HYRACES	ACEINOT	ACONITE
ACEHHRT	HATCHER	ACEHRTT	CHATTER	ACEINPS	INSCAPE
ACEHHRU	HACHURE		RATCHET		PISCEAN
ACEHHST	HATCHES	ACEHRTW	WATCHER	ACEINRS	ARSENIC
ACEHHTT	HATCHET	ACEHRXY	EXARCHY	ACEINRT	CERTAIN
ACEHILL	HELICAL	ACEHSST	SACHETS	ACEINTT	TETANIC
ACEHILR	CHARLIE		SCATHES	ACEINTX	INEXACT
ACEHILT	ETHICAL	ACEHSSW	CASHEWS	ACEINTZ	ZINCATE
ACEHIMN	MACHINE	ACEHSTT	THE ACTS	ACEIORS	SCORIAE
ACEHIMP	IMPEACH	ACEHSTW	WATCHES	ACEIORT	EROTICA
ACEHIMR	CHIMERA	ACEIILS	LAICISE	ACEIOTX	EXOTICA
ACEHINR	IN REACH	ACEIILT	CILIATE	ACEIPRS	SCRAPIE
ACEHINT	TEACH-IN	ACEIILZ	LAICIZE	ACEIPRT	PARETIC
ACEHIPT	HEPATIC	ACEIINN	ICENIAN	ACEIPST	ASEPTIC
ACEHIRR	HIRE CAR	ACEIKLS	SACLIKE		SPICATE
ACEHIRS	CASHIER	ACEIKMR	KERAMIC	ACEIPSU	AUSPICE
ACEHIRV	ARCHIVE	ACEIKMX	CAKE MIX	ACEIPSZ	CAPSIZE
ACEHISS	CHAISES	ACEIKNT	CAKE TIN	ACEIPTV	CAPTIVE
ACEHIST	AITCHES	ACEIKPX	PICK AXE	ACEIQRU	ACQUIRE
ACEHKLS	HACKLES		PICKAXE	ACEIRRR	CARRIER
	SHACKLE	ACEIKRT	TACKIER	ACEIRRS	CARRIES
ACEHKNY	HACKNEY	ACEIKRW	WACKIER		SCARIER
ACEHKOT	HOT CAKE	ACEIKSS	SEASICK	ACEIRRT	ERRATIC
ACEHKRW	WHACKER	ACEILLL	ALLELIC	ACEIRRW	AIR CREW
ACEHKST	HACKEST	ACEILLX	LEXICAL		AIRCREW
ACEHLLS	SHELLAC	ACEILMN	MELANIC	ACEIRRZ	CRAZIER
ACEHLLT	HELLCAT	ACEILMR	CLAIMER	ACEIRST	CRISTAE
ACEHLMY	ALCHEMY		MIRACLE		STEARIC
ACEHLNN	CHANNEL		RECLAIM	ACEIRSU	SAUCIER
ACEHLNO	CHALONE	ACEILMT	CLIMATE	ACEIRSV	VARICES
ACEHLOP	EPOCHAL		METICAL		VISCERA
ACEHLOR	CHOLERA	ACEILMX	EXCLAIM	ACEIRTT	CATTIER
	CHORALE	ACEILMY	MYCELIA		CITRATE
ACEHLOS	LOACHES	ACEILNP	CAPELIN	ACEISST	ASCITES
ACEHLOT	CHOLATE		IN PLACE	ACEISTT	STATICE
ACEHLPS	CHAPELS		PANICLE	ACEISTV	ACTIVES
ACEHLPT	CHAPLET		PELICAN	ACEITTV	CAVETTI
ACEHLPY	CHEAPLY	ACEILNR	CARLINE	ACEITUX	AUXETIC
ACEHLRS	CLASHER	ACEILNS	IN SCALE	ACEJKST	JACKETS
	LARCHES		SANICLE	ACEJLOR	CAJOLER
	RASCHEL	ACEILNU	CAULINE	ACEJLOS	CAJOLES
ACEHLSS	CLASHES	ACEILOR	CALORIE	ACEKKNR	KNACKER
ACEHLST	CHALETS		LORICAE	ACEKLMS	MACKLES
	LATCHES	ACEILPR	CALIPER	ACEKLNS	SLACKEN
	SATCHEL		REPLICA	ACEKLPT	PLACKET
ACEHLTT	CHATTEL	ACEILPS	SPECIAL	ACEKLRS	SLACKER
ACEHMNO	MACH ONE	ACEILPT	PLICATE	ACEKLRT	TACKLER
ACEHMRR	CHARMER	ACEILRS	ECLAIRS	ACEKLRU	CAULKER
	MARCHER		SCALIER	ACEKLST	TACKLES
ACEHMRS	MARCHES	ACEILRT	ARTICLE	ACEKLSY	LACKEYS
ACEHMRT	MATCHER		RECITAL	ACEKMRS	SMACKER
ACEHMSS	SACHEMS	ACEILRU	AURICLE	ACEKNRS	CANKERS

Code	Word(s)
ACEKPST	PACKETS
ACEKRRT	TRACKER
ACEKRST	RACKETS / TACKERS
ACEKSST	CASKETS
ACELLMO	CALOMEL
ACELLNY	CLEANLY
ACELLOR	OCELLAR
ACELLOS	CALLOSE / LOCALES
ACELLOT	COLLATE
ACELLPS	SCALPEL
ACELLRS	CALLERS / CELLARS / RECALLS / SCLERAL
ACELLRU	CURE-ALL
ACELLRY	CLEARLY
ACELMNR	MR. CLEAN
ACELMOU	LEUCOMA
ACELMRS	MARCELS
ACELMSS	MESCALS
ACELMST	CALMEST
ACELMSU	MACULES
ACELMTU	CALUMET
ACELNNU	UNCLEAN
ACELNOR	CORNEAL
ACELNPU	CLEAN UP / CLEANUP
ACELNRS	LANCERS
ACELNRT	CENTRAL
ACELNRU	NUCLEAR / UNCLEAR
ACELNRY	LARCENY
ACELNST	CANTLES / LANCETS
ACELNSU	UNLACES
ACELNTY	LATENCY
ACELNVY	VALENCY
ACELOPT	POLE CAT / POLECAT
ACELORS	ORACLES / SOLACER
ACELORT	LOCATER
ACELOSS	SOLACES
ACELOST	LACTOSE / LOCATES / TALCOSE / TO SCALE
ACELOSV	ALCOVES
ACELOSW	ACES LOW
ACELOTY	ACOLYTE
ACELOUV	VACUOLE
ACELPPR	CLAPPER
ACELPRS	CLASPER / PARCELS / PLACERS / SCALPER
ACELPRT	PLECTRA
ACELPRU	CLEAR UP
ACELPRY	PRELACY
ACELPSU	CAPSULE / LACE-UPS / SCALE UP / SPECULA
ACELQRU	LACQUER
ACELQSU	CLAQUES
ACELRRS	CARRELS
ACELRRW	CRAWLER
ACELRSS	SCALERS
ACELRST	CARTELS / CLARETS / SCARLET
ACELRSU	SECULAR
ACELRTT	CLATTER
ACELSSS	CLASSES
ACELSST	CASTLES
ACELSSU	CLAUSES
ACELSTU	SULCATE
ACELSUX	EXCUSAL
ACELSXY	CALYXES
ACELTTU	LATE CUT
ACELTUY	ACUTELY
ACELTXY	EXACTLY
ACEMMRR	CRAMMER
ACEMNOR	ROMANCE
ACEMNPS	ENCAMPS
ACEMNRW	CREWMAN
ACEMOPR	COMPARE
ACEMOPS	POMACES
ACEMOSU	MUCOSAE
ACEMOTU	CAME OUT
ACEMPRS	CAMPERS / SCAMPER
ACEMRSS	SCREAMS
ACENNOT	CONNATE
ACENNRS	CANNERS / SCANNER
ACENNRY	CANNERY
ACENNST	NASCENT
ACENNSU	NUANCES
ACENNTY	TENANCY
ACENORS	COARSEN / CORNEAS
ACENORT	NO TRACE
ACENOTV	CENTAVO
ACENPRR	PRANCER
ACENPRS	PRANCES
ACENPTY	PATENCY
ACENRSS	ANCRESS
ACENRST	CANTERS / CARNETS / NECTARS / RECANTS / SCANTER / TRANCES
ACENRSV	CAVERNS
ACENRTT	RENT ACT
ACENRTU	CENTAUR
ACENRTY	NECTARY
ACENSST	ASCENTS / SECANTS / STANCES
ACENSTU	NUTCASE
ACEOPSW	COWPEAS
ACEORRS	COARSER
ACEORRT	CREATOR / REACTOR
ACEORST	COASTER / COATERS
ACEORSU	CAROUSE
ACEORTV	OVERACT
ACEORTW	ATE CROW / EAT CROW
ACEORTX	EXACTOR
ACEOSSU	CASEOUS
ACEOSTT	COSTATE
ACEOSTU	ACETOUS
ACEOSTV	AVOCETS / OCTAVES
ACEOSTW	TWO ACES
ACEOSTY	TEA COSY
ACEOTTV	CAVETTO
ACEOTUU	AUTOCUE
ACEPRRS	SCARPER / SCRAPER
ACEPRSS	ESCARPS / PARSECS / SCRAPES / SPACERS
ACEPRST	CARPETS / PRECAST / SPECTRA
ACEPRSU	APERCUS
ACEPRTU	CAPTURE
ACEPRUV	CARVE UP / CARVE-UP
ACEPSST	ASPECTS
ACEPSTU	CUSPATE / TEA CUPS
ACEQSSU	CASQUES
ACERRSS	CRASSER / SCARERS
ACERRST	CARTERS / CRATERS / TRACERS
ACERRSV	CARVERS
ACERRTT	RETRACT
ACERRTY	TRACERY
ACERRUV	VERRUCA
ACERSST	CASTERS / RECASTS
ACERSSU	CAUSERS / CESURAS / SAUCERS
ACERSSV	SCARVES
ACERSTT	SCATTER / T T RACES
ACERSTU	CURATES
ACERTTU	CUT RATE
ACERTTX	EXTRACT
ACERTTY	CATTERY
ACERTUY	CAUTERY
ACESSTU	CUESTAS
ACESSTY	ECSTASY
ACESSUY	CAYUSES
ACESTTY	TESTACY
ACFFILT	AFFLICT
ACFFIRT	TRAFFIC
ACFFLLO	CALL OFF
ACFFOST	CAST OFF / CAST-OFF / CASTOFF
ACFGHIN	CHAFING
ACFGINS	FACINGS
ACFHIST	CATFISH
ACFHISU	FUCHSIA
ACFHLNU	FLAUNCH
ACFIILN	FINICAL
ACFILNY	FANCILY
ACFILRY	CLARIFY
ACFILSS	FISCALS
ACFIMOR	FORMICA
ACFIMRU	FUMARIC
ACFIMSS	FASCISM
ACFINNY	INFANCY
ACFINOT	FACTION
ACFINRT	FRANTIC / INFARCT
ACFIOPR	FAIR COP
ACFIRSY	SCARIFY
ACFISST	FASCIST

ACFKLOR	FOR LACK	ACGMNOP	CAMPONG	ACHNSTU	STAUNCH
ACFKLSU	SACKFUL	ACGNOOT	OCTAGON	ACHNSTY	SNATCHY
ACFLLOR	CALL FOR	ACGNORS	GARCONS	ACHOOST	CAHOOTS
ACFLLOY	FOCALLY	ACGNOSS	GASCONS	ACHOPRY	CHARPOY
ACFLNOS	FALCONS	ACGORSU	COUGARS	ACHORSU	AUROCHS
ACFLPSU	CAPFULS	ACGORYZ	GO CRAZY	ACHOSTW	CAT SHOW
ACFLRSU	CARFULS	ACHIILS	ISCHIAL	ACHPPTU	PATCH UP
ACFLRUU	FURCULA	ACHIIMT	HAMITIC	ACHPRSS	SCARPHS
ACFLTTU	TACTFUL	ACHIINN	IN CHINA	ACHPTUZ	CHUTZPA
ACFLTUY	FACULTY	ACHIINT	CHIANTI	ACHRSTY	STARCHY
ACFORST	ACTS FOR	ACHIIPS	PACHISI	ACHSSTU	CUSHATS
	FACTORS	ACHIJKS	HIJACKS	ACHTTVW	WATCH T.V.
ACFORTU	ACT FOUR	ACHIJNT	JACINTH	ACIIKRS	AIRSICK
	FUR COAT	ACHIKRY	HAY RICK	ACIILMM	MIMICAL
ACFORTY	FACTORY		HAYRICK	ACIILMS	ISLAMIC
ACGGINR	GRACING	ACHILLP	PHALLIC		LAICISM
ACGGRSY	SCRAGGY	ACHILLT	THALLIC	ACIILNS	SALICIN
ACGHIKN	HACKING	ACHILOS	SCHOLIA	ACIILNV	VICINAL
ACGHIMO	OGHAMIC	ACHILPS	CALIPHS	ACIILRY	CILIARY
ACGHINR	ARCHING	ACHILRY	CHARILY	ACIILSS	LIASSIC
	CHAGRIN	ACHILSY	CLAYISH	ACIILST	ITALICS
ACGHINS	CASHING	ACHIMNO	MOHICAN	ACIIMMS	MIASMIC
	CHASING	ACHIMNR	IN MARCH	ACIINNO	ANIONIC
ACGHINW	CHAWING		RICH MAN	ACIINOV	AVIONIC
	CHIN-WAG	ACHIMOS	CHAMOIS	ACIINPS	PISCINA
ACGHIPR	GRAPHIC	ACHIMOX	CHAMOIX	ACIINTT	TITANIC
ACGHOSU	GAUCHOS	ACHIMST	TACHISM	ACIINUX	AUXINIC
ACGHRRU	CURRAGH	ACHINNU	UNCHAIN	ACIIPPR	PRIAPIC
ACGIILN	ALGINIC	ACHINPS	SPINACH	ACIKLLY	ALKYLIC
ACGIJKN	JACKING	ACHINTT	THIN CAT	ACIKLTY	TACKILY
ACGIKLN	CALKING	ACHINTX	XANTHIC	ACIKLWY	WACKILY
	LACKING	ACHINTY	CYNTHIA	ACIKNOR	KORANIC
ACGIKNP	PACKING	ACHIORT	CHARIOT	ACIKNPS	PACKS IN
ACGIKNR	CARKING		HARICOT	ACIKNPY	PANICKY
	RACKING	ACHIPPS	SAPPHIC	ACIKNST	CATKINS
ACGIKNS	SACKING	ACHIPST	SPATHIC	ACIKPSX	SIX-PACK
ACGIKNT	TACKING	ACHIRTU	HAIR CUT	ACIKRST	KARSTIC
ACGILLN	CALLING		HAIRCUT	ACIKSTT	STICK AT
ACGILLO	LOGICAL	ACHIRTY	CHARITY	ACILLLY	ALLYLIC
ACGILMN	CALMING	ACHISSS	CHASSIS	ACILLNS	CALLS IN
ACGILNN	LANCING	ACHISTT	TACHIST	ACILLRY	LYRICAL
ACGILNP	PLACING	ACHITTW	WATCH IT	ACILMNO	NO CLAIM
ACGILNS	LACINGS	ACHKLPU	CHALK UP		NO-CLAIM
	SCALING	ACHKMMO	HAMMOCK	ACILMPY	CAMPILY
ACGILNV	CALVING	ACHKOPS	HOPSACK	ACILMSU	MUSICAL
ACGILNW	CLAWING	ACHKOSS	HASSOCK	ACILNNY	CANNILY
ACGIMNO	COAMING	ACHKPSU	SHACK UP	ACILNOR	CLARION
ACGIMNP	CAMPING	ACHKRSU	CHUKARS	ACILNOS	OILCANS
ACGINNN	CANNING	ACHKSTW	THWACKS	ACILNOU	INOCULA
ACGINNR	CRANING	ACHLLOO	ALCOHOL	ACILNPY	PLIANCY
ACGINNT	CANTING	ACHLLOR	CHLORAL	ACILNRS	CARLINS
ACGINOR	ORGANIC	ACHLNOY	HALCYON	ACILNSS	IN CLASS
ACGINOS	AGONICS	ACHLNTU	AT LUNCH	ACILNTU	LUNATIC
ACGINOT	COATING		UNLATCH	ACILNUV	VINCULA
ACGINOX	COAXING	ACHLORS	SCHOLAR	ACILOOR	AIR-COOL
ACGINPP	CAPPING	ACHLORT	TROCHAL	ACILOPT	CAPITOL
ACGINPR	CARPING	ACHLOSW	SALCHOW		OPTICAL
ACGINPS	SPACING	ACHLOTY	LOCH TAY		TOPICAL
ACGINRS	SCARING	ACHMNOR	MONARCH	ACILOSS	SOCIALS
ACGINRT	CARTING	ACHMNOT	NO MATCH	ACILOTT	COAL TIT
	CRATING	ACHMNSU	MANCHUS	ACILOTV	VOLTAIC
	TRACING	ACHMOPR	CAMPHOR	ACILPST	PLASTIC
ACGINRV	CARVING	ACHMOST	STOMACH	ACILPTY	TYPICAL
	CRAVING	ACHMOTW	MACH TWO	ACILRTU	CURTAIL
ACGINST	ACTINGS	ACHMPTU	MATCH UP	ACILRTY	CLARITY
	CASTING	ACHNNOS	CHANSON	ACILRYZ	CRAZILY
ACGINSU	CAUSING	ACHNORS	ANCHORS	ACILSTU	ST. LUCIA
	SAUCING	ACHNOVY	ANCHOVY	ACILSUY	SAUCILY
ACGIRST	GASTRIC	ACHNPUY	PAUNCHY	ACILTTY	CATTILY
ACGLMPS	G CLAMPS	ACHNRTY	CHANTRY		TACITLY
ACGLNOV	LONG VAC	ACHNRUY	RAUNCHY	ACILTUV	VICTUAL

ACIMNOP	CAMPION	ACKPPSU	PACKS UP	ACNRTUY	TRUANCY
ACIMNOR	ROMANIC	ACKSTTU	STUCK AT	ACNSSTU	SANCTUS
ACIMNOS	ANOSMIC	ACLLLOY	LOCALLY		TUSCANS
	MASONIC	ACLLOOR	COROLLA	ACOOPRR	CORPORA
ACIMNRU	CRANIUM	ACLLOPS	SCALLOP	ACOOPTT	TOP COAT
ACIMNTT	CATMINT	ACLLORS	COLLARS		TOPCOAT
ACIMNTY	CITY MAN	ACLLORU	LOCULAR	ACOORTU	TOURACO
ACIMOPT	APOMICT	ACLLOSU	CALLOUS	ACOPRRT	CAR PORT
ACIMOSS	MOSAICS	ACLLOTU	CALL OUT		CARPORT
ACIMOST	SOMATIC	ACLLOVY	VOCALLY	ACOPRST	CAPTORS
ACIMPRY	PRIMACY	ACLLPSU	CALLS UP	ACOPSTW	COWPATS
ACIMPST	IMPACTS	ACLMNUY	CALUMNY	ACORRST	CARROTS
ACIMSST	MASTICS	ACLMORU	CLAMOUR		TROCARS
	MISCAST	ACLNOOR	CORONAL	ACORRTT	TRACTOR
ACINNOT	CONTAIN	ACLNOOT	COOLANT	ACORRTU	CURATOR
ACINNST	STANNIC	ACLNOOV	VOLCANO	ACORRTY	CARROTY
	TIN CANS	ACLNORW	CORN LAW	ACORSST	CASTORS
ACINOPT	CAPTION	ACLNPSU	UNCLASP		CO-STARS
ACINOQU	COQUINA	ACLNSTY	SCANTLY	ACORSTU	SURCOAT
ACINORR	CARRION	ACLOPRT	CALTROP	ACORSTV	CAVORTS
ACINOSS	CAISSON	ACLOPSU	CUPOLAS	ACORSTW	TWO CARS
	CASINOS	ACLOPSY	CALYPSO	ACORSUU	RAUCOUS
ACINOST	ACTIONS	ACLORRS	CORRALS	ACOSTTU	ACTS OUT
	CATIONS	ACLORST	SCROTAL		CAST OUT
ACINOSY	SYCONIA	ACLORSU	OCULARS		OUTCAST
ACINOTU	AUCTION	ACLORYZ	CORYZAL	ACOSTTW	TWO ACTS
	CAUTION	ACLPRTY	CRYPTAL	ACOSUUV	VACUOUS
ACINRTT	TANTRIC	ACLRSSW	SCRAWLS	ACPPRSY	SCRAPPY
ACINRTU	CURTAIN	ACLRSSY	CRASSLY	ACPSSTU	CATSUPS
ACIOPRS	PROSAIC	ACLRSTU	CRUSTAL	ADDDEEN	DEAD END
ACIOPRT	APRICOT	ACLRSTY	CRYSTAL		DEAD-END
ACIOPST	COPITAS	ACLRSWY	SCRAWLY	ADDDEEO	DO A DEED
ACIOPTY	OPACITY	ACLSSTU	CUTLASS	ADDDEER	DREADED
ACIORRS	CORSAIR	ACMNOPR	CRAMPON	ADDDEIS	DADDIES
ACIORSU	CARIOUS	ACMNOPY	COMPANY	ADDDEIW	WADDIED
	CURIOSA	ACMNORS	MACRONS	ADDDELP	PADDLED
ACIORTT	RICOTTA	ACMNORY	ACRONYM	ADDDELR	RADDLED
	RIOT ACT	ACMNOSS	MASCONS	ADDDENS	ADDENDS
ACIOSST	SCOTIAS	ACMNSTU	SANCTUM	ADDDEOT	ADDED TO
ACIPRSY	PISCARY	ACMOOST	SCOTOMA		ODD DATE
ACIPRVY	PRIVACY	ACMOPSS	COMPASS	ADDDEPU	ADDED UP
ACIPSST	SPASTIC	ACMOPTU	CAMP OUT	ADDDOOS	DOODADS
ACIPTUY	PAUCITY	ACMOSST	COMSATS	ADDEEFM	DEFAMED
ACIQRTU	QUARTIC		MASCOTS	ADDEEGR	DEGRADE
ACIQSTU	ACQUITS	ACMOSSU	MUCOSAS	ADDEEHR	ADHERED
ACIRSST	RACISTS	ACMOSTT	TOMCATS		REDHEAD
ACIRSSU	CUIRASS	ACMQTUU	CUMQUAT	ADDEEIR	READIED
ACIRSTY	SATYRIC	ACMSSTU	MUSCATS	ADDEEIT	IDEATED
ACISSTT	STATICS	ACMSUUV	VACUUMS	ADDEEKN	KNEADED
ACISSTU	CASUIST	ACNNNOS	CANNONS	ADDEELP	PLEADED
ACISSTV	SITS VAC	ACNNNUY	UNCANNY	ADDEELR	RED LEAD
ACISTTU	CAT SUIT	ACNNOST	CANTONS	ADDEELY	DELAYED
	CATSUIT	ACNNOSY	CANYONS	ADDEEMN	AMENDED
ACITUVY	VACUITY	ACNOORS	CORONAS		DEAD MEN
ACJKKSY	SKYJACK		RACOONS	ADDEEMR	DREAMED
ACJKLOW	LOCKJAW	ACNOORT	CARTOON	ADDEENR	RED DEAN
ACJKOPT	JACKPOT	ACNOPSW	SNOWCAP	ADDEENS	DEADENS
ACJKPSU	JACKS UP	ACNORRU	RANCOUR	ADDEERR	DREADER
ACJLORU	JOCULAR	ACNORRY	CARRY ON	ADDEERT	TREADED
ACJMNTU	MUNTJAC		CARRY-ON	ADDEEST	DEAD SET
ACKKLMU	KALMUCK		CARRYON		DEADEST
ACKLLOP	POLLACK	ACNORST	CANTORS		SEDATED
ACKLLSY	SLACKLY		CARTONS	ADDEETU	DUE DATE
ACKLMOR	ARM LOCK	ACNORSY	CRAYONS	ADDEFIN	FADED IN
ACKLOOR	OARLOCK	ACNORTU	COURANT	ADDEFRT	DRAFTED
ACKLOPS	POLACKS	ACNOSST	SNO-CATS	ADDEFRU	DEFRAUD
ACKLORW	WARLOCK	ACNOSTT	OCTANTS	ADDEFRW	DWARFED
ACKMOTT	MATTOCK	ACNOSTU	CONATUS	ADDEGGR	DRAGGED
ACKNPSU	UNPACKS		TOUCANS	ADDEGHO	GODHEAD
ACKOPSY	YAPOCKS	ACNRRTU	CURRANT	ADDEGJU	ADJUDGE
ACKOPTU	PACK OUT	ACNRSWY	SCRAWNY	ADDEGLN	GLADDEN

Code	Word(s)
ADDEGOR	DAGO RED
ADDEGRU	GUARDED
ADDEHIR	DIE HARD
	DIE-HARD
ADDEHLN	HANDLED
ADDEHLO	OLD HEAD
ADDEHNO	HAD DONE
ADDEHOR	HOARDED
ADDEILL	DALLIED
	DIALLED
ADDEILO	OLD IDEA
ADDEILP	PLAIDED
ADDEILS	LADDIES
ADDEILT	DILATED
ADDEIMR	ADMIRED
ADDEIMO	DIADEMS
ADDEINO	ADENOID
ADDEINR	DANDIER
	DRAINED
ADDEINS	DANDIES
ADDEINU	UNAIDED
ADDEINV	INVADED
ADDEIOR	RADIOED
ADDEIOT	TOADIED
ADDEIOV	AVOIDED
ADDEIPS	PADDIES
ADDEISV	ADVISED
ADDEISW	WADDIES
ADDEITU	AUDITED
ADDEJRU	ADJURED
ADDEKRR	DARK RED
ADDELLU	ALLUDED
ADDELNS	DANDLES
ADDELOS	DO DEALS
ADDELPR	PADDLER
ADDELPS	PADDLES
ADDELRS	LADDERS
	RADDLES
	SADDLER
ADDELRW	DAWDLER
	DRAWLED
	WADDLER
ADDELSS	SADDLES
ADDELST	STADDLE
ADDELSW	DAWDLES
	SWADDLE
	WADDLES
ADDELTW	TWADDLE
ADDELTY	DATEDLY
ADDELYZ	DAZEDLY
ADDEMNS	DEMANDS
	MADDENS
ADDEMRS	MADDERS
ADDENOR	ADORNED
ADDENOT	DONATED
ADDENOU	DUODENA
ADDENPU	PUDENDA
ADDENSS	SADDENS
ADDENTU	DAUNTED
	UNDATED
ADDEOPT	ADOPTED
ADDEORS	DEODARS
ADDEPTU	UPDATED
ADDERSS	ADDRESS
ADDERSW	SWARDED
	WADDERS
ADDERTT	DRATTED
ADDESST	SADDEST
ADDFHIS	FADDISH
ADDFIMS	FADDISM
ADDFINY	DANDIFY
ADDFIST	FADDIST
ADDGGIN	GADDING
ADDGILN	ADDLING
ADDGINP	PADDING
ADDGINW	WADDING
ADDGMNO	GODDAMN
ADDGMOS	MAD DOGS
ADDGOOY	GOOD DAY
ADDGOSY	DOG DAYS
ADDHIKS	KADDISH
ADDHIMR	DID HARM
ADDHITY	HYDATID
ADDHLNO	OLD HAND
ADDHSSU	SADDHUS
ADDIINS	DISDAIN
ADDIKTY	KATYDID
ADDIKTZ	TZADDIK
ADDILMN	MIDLAND
ADDILMO	OLD MAID
ADDIMNO	DIAMOND
ADDIMSU	DID A SUM
ADDINOR	ANDROID
ADDLLOY	OLD LADY
ADDLLRU	DULLARD
ADDLNRY	DRY LAND
ADDLOSY	LAY ODDS
ADDOOSS	DOS-A-DOS
ADDORST	DOTARDS
ADDQSUY	SQUADDY
ADEEEFY	FEDAYEE
ADEEEPS	DEEP SEA
ADEEESW	SEAWEED
ADEEFHT	THE DEAF
ADEEFKR	FREAKED
ADEEFLR	FEDERAL
ADEEFLS	FEEL SAD
ADEEFLT	DEFLATE
ADEEFMR	DEFAMER
ADEEFMS	DEFAMES
ADEEFNS	DEAFENS
ADEEFRT	DRAFTEE
ADEEFST	DEAFEST
	DEFEATS
	FEASTED
ADEEFTY	FETE DAY
ADEEGGH	EGGHEAD
ADEEGGN	ENGAGED
ADEEGLL	ALLEGED
ADEEGLM	GLEAMED
ADEEGLN	GLEANED
ADEEGLR	REGALED
ADEEGLT	GELATED
ADEEGLU	LEAGUED
ADEEGLY	GLAD EYE
ADEEGMN	END GAME
ADEEGNR	ANGERED
	DERANGE
	ENRAGED
	GRANDEE
	GRENADE
ADEEGNT	NEGATED
ADEEGNV	AVENGED
ADEEGRS	DRAGEES
	GREASED
ADEEGRW	RAGWEED
	WAGERED
ADEEGSS	DEGASES
ADEEHIR	HEADIER
ADEEHLX	EXHALED
ADEEHMN	HEADMEN
ADEEHNN	HENNAED
ADEEHPR	EPHEDRA
ADEEHRR	REHEARD
ADEEHRS	ADHERES
	HEADERS
	SHEARED
ADEEHRT	EARTHED
	HEARTED
	RED HEAT
ADEEHRV	HAVERED
ADEEHST	HEADEST
	HEADSET
ADEEHSV	SHEAVED
ADEEHTT	THE DATE
ADEEIJT	JADEITE
ADEEILN	DELAINE
ADEEIMT	MEDIATE
ADEEINN	ADENINE
ADEEINS	ANISEED
ADEEINW	NEW IDEA
ADEEIRR	READIER
ADEEIRS	DEARIES
	READIES
ADEEIRW	WEARIED
ADEEISS	DISEASE
	SEASIDE
ADEEIST	IDEATES
ADEEITV	DEVIATE
ADEEJSY	DEEJAYS
ADEEKNR	KNEADER
ADEEKNS	SNEAKED
ADEEKNW	WAKENED
ADEEKRW	WREAKED
ADEEKTW	TWEAKED
ADEEKWY	WEEKDAY
ADEELLS	ALLSEED
ADEELMR	EMERALD
ADEELNR	LEARNED
ADEELNW	NEW DEAL
ADEELPR	PEARLED
	PLEADER
ADEELPS	ELAPSED
	PLEASED
ADEELPT	PLEATED
ADEELRS	DEALERS
	LEADERS
ADEELRT	ALERTED
	ALTERED
	RELATED
	TREADLE
ADEELRW	LEEWARD
ADEELRX	RELAXED
ADEELRY	DELAYER
	LAYERED
	RELAYED
ADEELTX	EXALTED
ADEELUV	DEVALUE
ADEEMNR	MEANDER
ADEEMNS	DEMEANS
ADEEMRR	DREAMER
	REARMED
ADEEMRS	SMEARED
ADEEMRT	RED MEAT
ADEEMST	STEAMED
ADEEMSU	MADE USE
	MEDUSAE
ADEEMWY	MAYWEED
ADEENNS	ENNEADS
ADEENNX	ANNEXED
ADEENPR	RAN DEEP
ADEENRS	ENDEARS
ADEENRV	RAVENED

ADEENRY	DEANERY	ADEFLST	FELT SAD	ADEGORS	DOG-EARS
	YEAR-END	ADEFLTT	FLATTED	ADEGORW	DOWAGER
	YEARNED	ADEFLTU	DEFAULT	ADEGOSS	DOSAGES
ADEENST	EAST END		FAULTED		SEA DOGS
	END SEAT	ADEFMNU	MADE FUN		SEADOGS
ADEENTT	DENTATE	ADEFMOR	MADE FOR	ADEGOVY	VOYAGED
ADEEOPT	ADOPTEE	ADEFNSU	SNAFUED	ADEGPRS	GRASPED
ADEEPPR	PAPERED	ADEFOOS	SEAFOOD	ADEGPRU	UPGRADE
ADEEPRS	SPEARED	ADEFORS	FEDORAS	ADEGRRS	RED RAGS
ADEEPRT	PREDATE	ADEFORY	FORAYED		REGARDS
	RED TAPE	ADEFOTU	FADE OUT	ADEGRRU	GUARDER
	TAPERED		FADE-OUT	ADEGRSS	GRASSED
ADEEPRV	DEPRAVE	ADEFPPR	FRAPPED	ADEGRSU	SUGARED
	PERVADE	ADEFRRT	DRAFTER	ADEGRTY	GYRATED
ADEEPST	AT SPEED	ADEFRST	STRAFED		TRAGEDY
ADEEPSU	EASED UP	ADEFRSY	DEFRAYS	ADEGRUU	AUGURED
ADEEQTU	EQUATED	ADEFSTT	DAFTEST	ADEGSSU	DEGAUSS
ADEERRS	READERS	ADEFSTY	FAST DYE	ADEHHOT	HOTHEAD
ADEERRT	RETREAD	ADEGGHS	SHAGGED	ADEHILN	INHALED
	TREADER	ADEGGLR	DRAGGLE	ADEHILS	HALIDES
ADEERRV	AVERRED	ADEGGNS	SNAGGED	ADEHILY	HEADILY
ADEERRW	WEAR RED	ADEGGRS	DAGGERS	ADEHINP	PINHEAD
ADEERST	DEAREST	ADEGGST	GADGETS	ADEHINR	HANDIER
ADEERSV	ADVERSE	ADEGGSW	SWAGGED	ADEHIPR	RAPHIDE
	EVADERS	ADEGHIN	HEADING	ADEHIPS	APHIDES
ADEERSW	DRAWEES	ADEGHLU	LAUGHED		DIPHASE
ADEERTT	TREATED	ADEGHNS	GNASHED	ADEHIPT	PITHEAD
ADEERTV	AVERTED	ADEGHNW	WHANGED	ADEHIRR	HARDIER
ADEERTW	WATERED	ADEGHPR	GRAPHED		HARRIED
ADEERVW	WAVERED	ADEGILN	ALIGNED		RED HAIR
ADEESST	SEDATES		DEALING	ADEHIRS	SHADIER
ADEESSY	ESSAYED		LEADING	ADEHIRW	RAWHIDE
ADEESTU	DUE EAST	ADEGILO	GEOIDAL	ADEHKNT	THANKED
	SAUTEED	ADEGILT	LIGATED	ADEHLLO	HALLOED
ADEESTW	SWEATED	ADEGINR	GRAINED		HOLLAED
ADEETUX	EXUDATE		READING	ADEHLNR	HANDLER
ADEFFHO	HEAD OFF	ADEGINV	EVADING	ADEHLNS	HANDLES
ADEFFIP	PIAFFED	ADEGINW	WINDAGE	ADEHLOS	SHOALED
ADEFFIX	AFFIXED	ADEGIOT	GODETIA	ADEHLOT	LOATHED
ADEFFLO	LEAD OFF	ADEGIRU	GAUDIER	ADEHLOW	LEW HOAD
	LEAD-OFF	ADEGISU	GAUDIES	ADEHLPS	PLASHED
ADEFFMO	MADE OFF	ADEGISV	VISAGED	ADEHLRS	HERALDS
ADEFFOR	READ OFF	ADEGJLN	JANGLED	ADEHLSS	SLASHED
ADEFFQU	QUAFFED	ADEGKRT	GET DARK	ADEHLTY	DEATHLY
ADEFFST	STAFFED	ADEGLMN	MANGLED		THE LADY
ADEFGGL	FLAGGED	ADEGLMO	LAME DOG	ADEHMMS	SHAMMED
ADEFGGR	FRAGGED	ADEGLNN	ENGLAND	ADEHMMW	WHAMMED
ADEFGLN	FLANGED	ADEGLNO	DONEGAL	ADEHMSS	SMASHED
ADEFGLR	RED FLAG	ADEGLNR	DANGLER	ADEHNNO	ONE HAND
ADEFGNS	FAG ENDS		GNARLED	ADEHNOS	HAS DONE
ADEFGOR	FORAGED	ADEGLNS	DANGLES	ADEHNRS	HANDERS
ADEFGRT	GRAFTED		GLANDES		HARDENS
ADEFHIL	HAD LIFE		SLANGED	ADEHNRU	UNHEARD
ADEFHIS	DEAFISH	ADEGLOT	GLOATED	ADEHNST	HANDSET
ADEFHLS	FLASHED	ADEGLPU	PLAGUED	ADEHNTU	HAUNTED
ADEFHOR	HEAD FOR	ADEGLSS	GLASSED	ADEHOPX	HEXAPOD
ADEFHST	SHAFTED	ADEGMNO	GONE MAD	ADEHOTW	TOWHEAD
ADEFILL	FLAILED	ADEGMOS	GOES MAD	ADEHPRS	PHRASED
ADEFINS	FADE-INS	ADEGMOT	DOG TEAM	ADEHPST	HEPTADS
	FADES IN	ADEGMST	GETS MAD	ADEHQSU	QUASHED
ADEFINT	DEFIANT	ADEGNNU	DUNNAGE	ADEHRST	HARD-SET
	FAINTED	ADEGNOR	GROANED		HARDEST
ADEFINY	FINE DAY	ADEGNPR	PRANGED		THREADS
ADEFIRS	FAR SIDE	ADEGNRR	GRANDER	ADEHRTY	HYDRATE
ADEFITX	FIXATED	ADEGNRS	DANGERS		THE YARD
ADEFKLN	FLANKED		GANDERS		THREADY
ADEFKNR	FRANKED		GARDENS	ADEHSST	STASHED
ADEFLLU	FALL DUE	ADEGNRT	DRAGNET	ADEHSTW	SWATHED
ADEFLLW	DEWFALL		GRANTED	ADEHSYY	HEYDAYS
ADEFLOT	FLOATED	ADEGNTW	TWANGED		
ADEFLPP	FLAPPED	ADEGOOR	GOOD EAR		

ADEIILS	DAILIES	ADEINRT	DETRAIN	ADELLOS	DOES ALL
	LIAISED		TRADE IN	ADELLOW	ALLOWED
	SEDILIA		TRADE-IN	ADELLOY	ALLOYED
ADEIINR	DENARII		TRAINED	ADELLPS	SPALLED
ADEIIRS	DAIRIES	ADEINRV	INVADER	ADELLRU	ALLURED
	DIARIES	ADEINST	DETAINS	ADELLST	STALLED
ADEIISS	DAISIES		INSTEAD	ADELLSU	ALLUDES
ADEIJSU	JUDAISE		STAINED	ADELMMS	SLAMMED
ADEIJUZ	JUDAIZE	ADEINSV	INVADES	ADELMNR	MANDREL
ADEIKLM	LIKE MAD	ADEINTT	TAINTED	ADELMNT	MANTLED
ADEIKNS	ASKED IN	ADEINTV	DEVIANT	ADELMOR	EARLDOM
ADEIKRS	DARKIES	ADEIOPS	ADIPOSE	ADELMOS	DAMOSEL
ADEILLR	DALLIER	ADEIORS	ROADIES	ADELMOZ	DAMOZEL
	RALLIED	ADEIORV	AVOIDER	ADELMRS	MEDLARS
ADEILLS	DALLIES	ADEIORX	EXORDIA	ADELMSS	DAMSELS
	SALLIED	ADEIOST	IODATES	ADELNNP	PLANNED
ADEILLT	TALLIED		TOADIES	ADELNOS	LEADS ON
ADEILLY	IDEALLY	ADEIPPR	PREPAID	ADELNOT	TALONED
ADEILMM	DILEMMA	ADEIPRR	PARRIED	ADELNPT	PLANTED
ADEILMP	IMPALED	ADEIPRS	ASPIRED	ADELNRS	DARNELS
	IMPLEAD		DESPAIR		SLANDER
ADEILMS	MISDEAL		DIAPERS		SNARLED
	MISLEAD		PRAISED		
ADEILNN	ANNELID	ADEIPRT	PIRATED	ADELNRU	LAUNDER
	LINDANE	ADEIPSS	APSIDES	ADELNST	DENTALS
ADEILNS	DEALS IN	ADEIRRS	DEAR SIR		SLANTED
	DENIALS		RAIDERS	ADELNTW	WETLAND
	LEAD INS	ADEIRRT	TARDIER	ADELOPR	LEOPARD
	LEADS IN		TARRIED		PAROLED
ADEILNT	DEALT IN	ADEIRRV	ARRIVED	ADELOPS	PEDALOS
	TAIL END	ADEIRST	ASTRIDE	ADELOPT	TADPOLE
ADEILOP	OEDIPAL		DISRATE	ADELORS	ORDEALS
ADEILOR	DARIOLE		TIRADES		SEA LORD
ADEILPP	APPLIED	ADEIRSU	RESIDUA		SEA-LORD
ADEILPR	LIP-READ	ADEIRSV	ADVISER	ADELORT	LEOTARD
	PREDIAL	ADEIRSX	RADIXES	ADELORU	ROULADE
ADEILPS	PALSIED	ADEIRTT	ATE DIRT	ADELOSS	LASSOED
ADEILPT	PLAITED		ATTIRED	ADELOTU	LEAD OUT
ADEILQU	QUAILED		EAT DIRT	ADELPPS	DAPPLES
ADEILRS	DERAILS	ADEIRTV	DRIVE AT		SLAPPED
ADEILRT	TRAILED	ADEIRTY	DIETARY	ADELPRS	PEDLARS
ADEILRY	READILY	ADEISSS	DASSIES	ADELPRY	PEDLARY
ADEILST	DETAILS	ADEISSV	ADVISES	ADELPST	STAPLED
	DILATES	ADEISTV	DATIVES	ADELPSU	LEADS UP
ADEILSV	DEVISAL	ADEISTW	WAISTED	ADELPSW	DEWLAPS
ADEILSY	DIALYSE	ADEISVV	SAVVIED	ADELPSY	SPLAYED
ADEILUZ	DUALIZE	ADEISWY	WAYSIDE	ADELPTT	PLATTED
ADEIMMR	MERMAID	ADEITUZ	DEUTZIA	ADELPTY	ADEPTLY
ADEIMNR	AMERIND	ADEITWY	TIDEWAY	ADELRRS	LARDERS
ADEIMNS	MAIDENS	ADEJMPS	P. D. JAMES	ADELRRW	DRAWLER
	MEDIANS	ADEJNTU	JAUNTED	ADELRTW	TRAWLED
	SIDEMAN	ADEJRSU	ADJURES	ADELRTX	DEXTRAL
ADEIMNT	MEDIANT	ADEJSSU	JUDASES	ADELRZZ	DAZZLER
ADEIMOW	MIAOWED	ADEKLNP	PLANKED	ADELSST	DESALTS
ADEIMRR	ADMIRER	ADEKLNS	KALENDS	ADELSTT	SLATTED
	MARRIED	ADEKLNY	NAKEDLY	ADELSTU	SALUTED
ADEIMRS	ADMIRES	ADEKLST	STALKED	ADELSZZ	DAZZLES
	MISREAD	ADEKMNR	DENMARK	ADELTTW	WATTLED
ADEIMST	MISDATE	ADEKMOS	MAKES DO	ADELTUV	VAULTED
ADEIMTY	DAY TIME	ADEKNPP	KNAPPED	ADELTUX	LUXATED
ADEINOR	ANEROID	ADEKNPS	SPANKED	ADELTWZ	WALTZED
ADEINOS	ANODISE	ADEKNRS	DARKENS	ADEMMRS	SMARMED
	NO IDEAS	ADEKNST	DANKEST	ADEMNNU	MUNDANE
ADEINOZ	ANODIZE	ADEKNSU	UNASKED		NUDE MAN
ADEINPS	SAND PIE	ADEKNSW	SWANKED		UNNAMED
ADEINPT	PAINTED	ADEKNVY	VAN DYKE	ADEMNOR	ROADMEN
ADEINRR	DRAINER		VANDYKE	ADEMNOS	DAEMONS
	RANDIER	ADEKPRS	SPARKED	ADEMNPS	DAMPENS
ADEINRS	SANDIER	ADEKRST	DARKEST	ADEMNRS	REMANDS
	SARDINE	ADELLMU	MEDULLA		
		ADELLNO	DONE ALL		

ADEMNRU	DURAMEN	ADENSTY	TEN DAYS	ADFIMNY	DAMNIFY
	MANURED	ADENSWY	ENDWAYS	ADFIOPR	PAID FOR
	MAUNDER	ADENTTU	ATTUNED	ADFIORS	FAIR DOS
	UNARMED		TAUNTED	ADFIRSY	FRIDAYS
ADEMNRY	DRAYMEN	ADENTUV	VAUNTED	ADFLMOO	DAMFOOL
	YARDMEN	ADENTXY	NEXT DAY		MAD FOOL
ADEMNSS	DESMANS	ADEOORT	TOO DEAR	ADFLMPU	MUDFLAP
	MADNESS	ADEOPPS	PEA PODS	ADFLMTU	MUD FLAT
ADEMNST	TANDEMS	ADEOPRT	ADOPTER		MUDFLAT
ADEMNSU	MEDUSAN	ADEORRS	ADORERS	ADFLNSY	SAND FLY
ADEMNTW	WENT MAD	ADEORRW	ARROWED	ADFLORU	FOULARD
ADEMOPS	POMADES	ADEORST	ROASTED	ADFNNOT	FONDANT
ADEMORS	RADOMES	ADEORSU	AROUSED	ADFOOPT	FOOTPAD
ADEMOSW	MEADOWS	ADEORTT	ROTATED	ADFORRW	FORWARD
ADEMOSY	SAMOYED	ADEORTU	READOUT		FROWARD
	SOME DAY	ADEORTV	DROVE AT	ADGGGIN	DAGGING
ADEMOTU	MADE OUT	ADEORTY	YEAR DOT	ADGGHNO	HANGDOG
ADEMPRS	DAMPERS	ADEOSTT	TOASTED	ADGGINO	GOADING
ADEMPRT	TRAMPED	ADEPPRT	TRAPPED	ADGGINR	GRADING
ADEMPST	DAMPEST	ADEPPRW	WRAPPED		NIGGARD
	STAMPED	ADEPPSW	SWAPPED	ADGGOST	DOG-TAGS
ADEMPSW	SWAMPED	ADEPPTU	PUPATED	ADGGOSY	GAY DOGS
ADEMRRU	EARDRUM	ADEPRRS	DRAPERS	ADGHHIY	HIGH DAY
ADEMRRY	RED ARMY		SPARRED	ADGHILO	HIDALGO
ADEMRST	SMARTED	ADEPRRY	DRAPERY	ADGHINN	HANDING
ADEMRSW	SWARMED	ADEPRSS	SPREADS	ADGHINS	DASHING
ADEMRTU	MATURED	ADEPRST	DEPARTS		SHADING
ADEMSSU	ASSUMED		PETARDS	ADGHIPR	DIGRAPH
	MEDUSAS	ADEPRSU	READS UP	ADGHNNU	HANDGUN
ADENNOY	ANNOYED	ADEPRSY	SPRAYED	ADGHOOR	ROAD HOG
	ANODYNE	ADEPRTU	UPRATED	ADGHRTU	DRAUGHT
ADENNPS	SPANNED	ADEPRUV	RAVED UP	ADGIILT	DIGITAL
ADENNSU	DUENNAS	ADEPRWY	DREW PAY	ADGIINO	GONIDIA
ADENNSW	SWANNED	ADEPSTU	UPDATES	ADGIINR	RAIDING
ADENOPR	OPERAND	ADEPSUV	SAVED UP	ADGIIPY	PYGIDIA
ADENOPS	DAPSONE	ADEQRSU	SQUARED	ADGILLN	LADLING
ADENOPY	OPEN DAY	ADERRST	DARTERS	ADGILNN	LANDING
ADENORT	DARE NOT		RED STAR	ADGILNO	LOADING
	TRADE ON		RETARDS	ADGILNR	DARLING
	TREAD ON		STARRED		LARDING
ADENORU	RONDEAU		TRADERS	ADGILNS	LADINGS
ADENORY	ONE YARD	ADERRSW	DRAWERS		LIGANDS
ADENOST	DONATES		REWARDS	ADGILNU	LANGUID
ADENOTT	NOTATED		WARDERS		LAUDING
ADENOTZ	ZONATED	ADERSSU	ASSURED	ADGILUY	GAUDILY
ADENPPS	APPENDS	ADERSTT	STARTED	ADGIMMN	DAMMING
	SNAPPED	ADERSTV	ADVERTS	ADGIMNN	DAMNING
ADENPRR	PARDNER		STARVED	ADGIMNP	DAMPING
ADENPRS	PANDERS	ADERSTW	STEWARD	ADGIMNW	WING DAM
ADENPST	PEDANTS		STRAWED	ADGINNR	DARNING
	PENTADS	ADERSTY	REST DAY	ADGINNS	SANDING
ADENPSW	SPAWNED		STRAYED	ADGINNW	DAWNING
ADENPSX	EXPANDS	ADERSVW	DWARVES	ADGINOR	ADORING
ADENRRS	DARNERS	ADESTTW	SWATTED		GORDIAN
	ERRANDS	ADESTUY	TUESDAY		RAIN GOD
ADENRRY	REYNARD	ADFFHNO	HAND OFF	ADGINPP	DAPPING
ADENRSS	SANDERS		HANDOFF	ADGINPR	DRAPING
ADENRST	RED ANTS		OFF HAND	ADGINPS	SPADING
ADENRSU	ASUNDER		OFFHAND	ADGINRS	DARINGS
	DANSEUR	ADFFHOS	DASH OFF	ADGINRT	DARTING
ADENRSW	WANDERS	ADFFILO	LAID OFF		TRADING
	WARDENS	ADFFIOP	PAID OFF	ADGINRW	DRAWING
ADENRTV	VERDANT	ADFFIST	DISTAFF	ADGINRY	YARDING
ADENRTX	DEXTRAN	ADFFLOO	OFF-LOAD	ADGINWY	GWYNIAD
ADENRTY	RENT DAY	ADFFORS	AFFORDS	ADGIRZZ	GIZZARD
ADENRYY	YARN-DYE	ADFFORW	DRAW OFF	ADGKORT	GOT DARK
ADENSSS	SADNESS		WARD OFF	ADGLLOR	RAG DOLL
ADENSSU	SUNDAES	ADFFOSY	OFF DAYS	ADGLLOS	OLD LAGS
ADENSSW	SAD NEWS	ADFHLNU	HANDFUL	ADGLMNO	MANGOLD
ADENSTT	ATTENDS	ADFILLU	FLUIDAL	ADGLNOO	GONDOLA
ADENSTV	ADVENTS	ADFILNN	FINLAND	ADGLNOY	LONG DAY

ADGLNRY	GRANDLY	ADIIPXY	PYXIDIA	ADINRSW	DRAWS IN
ADGLOPS	LAP DOGS	ADIIRST	DIARIST		INWARDS
	LAPDOGS	ADIIRTY	ARIDITY	ADINSTT	DISTANT
ADGMNOO	GOOD MAN	ADIJMSU	JUDAISM	ADINTTY	DITTANY
	MOGADON	ADIJNOS	ADJOINS	ADIOPRR	AIR-DROP
ADGNOOR	DRAGOON	ADIKMNN	MANKIND		AIRDROP
	GADROON	ADIKMOS	MIKADOS	ADIOPRT	PAROTID
ADGNORS	DRAGONS	ADIKNNR	DRANK IN	ADIOPTU	PAID OUT
ADGNORU	AGROUND	ADIKNPS	KIDNAPS	ADIORSV	ADVISOR
	ON GUARD		SKIDPAN	ADIORTU	AUDITOR
ADGNOSS	SAD SONG	ADIKSTT	DIKTATS	ADIOSVW	DISAVOW
ADGNRRU	GURNARD	ADILLMM	MILLDAM	ADIPPTU	PUT PAID
ADGOOWY	GOOD WAY	ADILLOW	LAID LOW	ADIPRTY	DAY TRIP
ADGORST	DOG STAR	ADILLPY	LILY PAD		PAY DIRT
ADGORTU	DRAG OUT	ADILLTY	TIDALLY	ADIRSTY	SATYRID
ADGPRSU	DRAGS UP	ADILLVY	VALIDLY	ADIRSUY	DYSURIA
ADHHIRT	HARD HIT	ADILMNU	MAUDLIN	ADIRSVZ	VIZARDS
	HIT HARD	ADILMOP	DIPLOMA	ADIRSWZ	WIZARDS
ADHHMOS	SHAHDOM	ADILMOY	AMYLOID	ADISSST	SADISTS
ADHHOSW	HOWDAHS	ADILMPS	PLASMID	ADISSXY	SIX DAYS
ADHIIKS	DASHIKI	ADILMSU	DUALISM	ADJNNOU	DON JUAN
ADHIKRS	DARKISH	ADILNOR	ORDINAL	ADJNORU	ADJOURN
ADHILNY	HANDILY	ADILNOS	LADINOS	ADJSSTU	ADJUSTS
ADHILOP	HAPLOID	ADILNRU	DIURNAL	ADKLMRU	MUDLARK
ADHILOY	HOLIDAY	ADILNRW	RAN WILD	ADKNPRU	DRANK UP
	HYALOID	ADILNSS	ISLANDS	ADLLLOT	ALL TOLD
ADHILSY	SHADILY	ADILNSU	SUN DIAL		TOLD ALL
ADHIMMS	MAHDISM		SUNDIAL	ADLLMOY	MODALLY
ADHIMPS	DAMPISH	ADILOOZ	ZOOIDAL	ADLLNOW	LOWLAND
ADHIMRS	DIRHAMS	ADILOPR	DIPOLAR	ADLLNOY	NODALLY
	MIDRASH	ADILOPW	LOW-PAID	ADLLOPR	POLLARD
ADHIMST	MAHDIST	ADILORT	DILATOR	ADLLOPS	OLD PALS
ADHINNS	HAND-INS	ADILOTU	LAID OUT	ADLLORS	DOLLARS
	HANDS IN	ADILPRY	RAPIDLY	ADLLORW	LAW LORD
ADHINPS	SHIN PAD	ADILPST	PLASTID	ADLLOST	OLD SALT
ADHINPU	DAUPHIN	ADILPSY	DISPLAY	ADLMNOS	ALMONDS
ADHINPW	HIND PAW	ADILPTU	PLAUDIT	ADLMORU	MODULAR
ADHIORS	HAIRDOS	ADILPVY	VAPIDLY	ADLNOOR	LARDOON
ADHIPTY	HAD PITY	ADILQSU	SQUALID	ADLNOPU	POUNDAL
ADHISTY	THIS DAY	ADILRSZ	LIZARDS	ADLNORU	NODULAR
ADHLLLO	HOLDALL	ADILRTY	TARDILY	ADLNOSU	UNLOADS
ADHLLNO	HOLLAND	ADILSTU	DUALIST	ADLNOSY	SYNODAL
ADHLOYY	HOLY DAY	ADILSTY	STAIDLY	ADLNOWY	LAY DOWN
ADHMNOO	MANHOOD	ADILTUY	DUALITY	ADLNPSU	UPLANDS
ADHMRSU	MAD RUSH	ADIMNOS	DAIMONS	ADLNRUY	LAUNDRY
ADHNNSU	UNHANDS		DOMAINS	ADLNTWY	TYNWALD
ADHNORS	HADRONS	ADIMOST	DIATOMS	ADLOPSU	LOADS UP
ADHNOTU	HAND OUT		MASTOID	ADLORRW	WAR LORD
	HAND-OUT	ADIMPRY	PYRAMID		WARLORD
	HANDOUT	ADIMRSS	DISARMS	ADLORUY	OUR LADY
ADHNPSU	HANDS UP	ADIMRSY	MYRIADS	ADLOSSW	SODS LAW
ADHNRRU	RUN HARD	ADIMSST	DISMAST	ADMNOOR	DOORMAN
ADHNRTU	HARD NUT	ADIMSSY	DISMAYS	ADMNOOW	WOODMAN
ADHNRTY	HYDRANT	ADIMSTU	STADIUM	ADMNOQU	QUONDAM
ADHOORT	TOO HARD	ADINNOR	ANDIRON	ADMNORT	DORMANT
ADHOPRT	HARD TOP	ADINNRS	INNARDS		MORDANT
	HARDTOP	ADINNRW	DRAWN IN	ADMNOSS	DAMSONS
ADHOPST	DASHPOT		INDRAWN	ADMNOSU	OSMUNDA
ADHOSSW	SHADOWS	ADINNST	STAND IN	ADMNOSY	DYNAMOS
ADHOSTU	DASH OUT		STAND-IN		MONDAYS
ADHOSWY	SHADOWY	ADINOPR	PONIARD	ADMNSTU	DUSTMAN
ADHPPSU	HAD PUPS	ADINORS	DORIANS	ADMOORT	DOOR MAT
ADHPRSU	PURDAHS		INROADS		DOORMAT
ADHPRTU	HARD PUT		ORDAINS	ADMOPSS	DOMPASS
ADHRRTY	TRY HARD		SADIRON	ADMORRS	RAMRODS
ADIIMN	IDI AMIN	ADINOTX	OXIDANT	ADMORST	STARDOM
ADIILMS	MISLAID	ADINOUY	YOU AND I	ADMRSSY	DRY MASS
ADIILNO	LIANOID	ADINPST	PANDITS	ADMRSTU	DURMAST
ADIILNV	INVALID		SANDPIT		MUSTARD
ADIINNS	INDIANS	ADINRSU	DURIANS	ADNNOOS	AND SO ON
ADIINSU	INDUSIA				

ADNNORW	DRAWN ON	AEEGGNS	ENGAGES	AEEHIRV	HEAVIER
	RAN DOWN	AEEGHNN	GEHENNA	AEEHISV	HEAVIES
ADNOORT	DONATOR	AEEGHNW	WHANGEE	AEEHKNR	HEARKEN
	TORNADO	AEEGHRT	THE RAGE	AEEHLNT	LETHEAN
ADNOOSS	SO-AND-SO	AEEGHST	THE AGES	AEEHLOR	EAR HOLE
ADNOPRS	PARDONS	AEEGILL	GALILEE	AEEHLRT	HALTERE
ADNOPST	DOPANTS	AEEGILM	MILEAGE		LEATHER
ADNORSW	DRAWS ON	AEEGILN	LINEAGE	AEEHLRV	LE HAVRE
	ONWARDS	AEEGILP	EPIGEAL	AEEHLSS	LEASHES
ADNORTU	ROTUNDA	AEEGIMP	GAME PIE	AEEHLSX	EXHALES
ADNOSTT	STAND TO	AEEGIPR	RIPE AGE	AEEHLSY	EYELASH
ADNOSTU	ASTOUND	AEEGIRV	GIVE EAR	AEEHLTT	ATHLETE
ADNOSTW	SAT DOWN	AEEGJRS	JAEGERS	AEEHMNT	METHANE
ADNOWWY	WAY DOWN	AEEGKRW	RAG WEEK	AEEHMST	THE SAME
ADNPPUU	UP-AND-UP	AEEGLLS	ALLEGES	AEEHNPS	PEAHENS
ADNPRUW	DRAWN UP	AEEGLLZ	GAZELLE	AEEHNPT	HEPTANE
ADNPSTU	DUST PAN	AEEGLMN	MELANGE	AEEHNRT	EARTHEN
	DUSTPAN	AEEGLNR	ENLARGE		HEARTEN
	STAND UP		GENERAL	AEEHNSV	HEAVENS
	STAND-UP		GLEANER	AEEHNSW	SHAWNEE
ADNRSST	STRANDS	AEEGLNS	SENEGAL	AEEHNTW	WHEATEN
ADNRSTU	TUNDRAS	AEEGLNT	ELEGANT	AEEHNTZ	THE NAZE
ADNSSTY	DYNASTS	AEEGLNU	EUGLENA	AEEHOTV	HEAVE TO
ADNSSUY	SUNDAYS	AEEGLNV	EVANGEL	AEEHPRS	RESHAPE
ADNSTYY	DYNASTY	AEEGLOV	LEAVE GO	AEEHPTT	PET HATE
ADOOPPS	SODA POP	AEEGLRS	REGALES	AEEHPUV	UPHEAVE
ADOOPSW	SAPWOOD	AEEGLRU	LEAGUER	AEEHRRS	REHEARS
ADOORWY	DOORWAY	AEEGLRY	EAGERLY		SHEARER
ADORRSU	ARDOURS	AEEGLSS	AGELESS	AEEHRSS	HEARSES
ADORSTW	TOWARDS		SEA LEGS	AEEHRST	ASH TREE
ADORSUU	ARDUOUS	AEEGLST	EAGLETS		HEATERS
ADORTTU	DART OUT		GELATES		REHEATS
ADORTUW	DRAW OUT		LEGATES	AEEHRSW	WHEREAS
	OUTWARD	AEEGLSU	LEAGUES	AEEHRTT	THEATER
ADOSTWY	TWO DAYS	AEEGLSV	SELVAGE		THEATRE
ADPRSUW	DRAWS UP	AEEGLTV	VEGETAL		THEREAT
	UPWARDS	AEEGMMT	GEMMATE	AEEHRTW	WEATHER
ADSSTUW	SAWDUST	AEEGMNR	GERMANE		WHEREAT
AEEEGLT	LEGATEE	AEEGMNS	MANEGES		WREATHE
AEEEGNT	TEEN AGE		MENAGES	AEEHSSV	SHEAVES
	TEENAGE	AEEGMNT	GATE MEN	AEEHSTT	THE EAST
AEEEGPR	PEERAGE	AEEGMSS	MESSAGE	AEEHSVX	HAVE SEX
AEEEGPS	SEEPAGE	AEEGMST	GAMETES	AEEHSWY	EYEWASH
AEEELRS	RELEASE	AEEGNNV	GENEVAN	AEEIKLP	APELIKE
AEEELTV	ELEVATE	AEEGNOP	ONE PAGE	AEEIKLR	LEAKIER
AEEFFOS	EASE OFF		PAGE ONE	AEEIKPR	PEAKIER
AEEFGRS	SERFAGE		PEONAGE	AEEILMS	MEALIES
AEEFHRT	FEATHER	AEEGNPT	PAGE TEN	AEEILNS	SEA LINE
AEEFILR	LEAFIER	AEEGNRS	ENRAGES	AEEILPT	PILEATE
AEEFIRS	FAERIES	AEEGNRT	NEGATER	AEEILRR	EARLIER
	FREESIA		REAGENT	AEEILRS	REALISE
AEEFLLT	LEAFLET	AEEGNRV	AVENGER	AEEILRT	ATELIER
AEEFLMS	FEMALES		ENGRAVE	AEEILRZ	REALIZE
AEEFLNW	NEW LEAF	AEEGNST	NEGATES	AEEILTV	LEAVE IT
AEEFLRT	LEFT EAR	AEEGNSV	AVENGES	AEEIMNS	MEANIES
	REFLATE	AEEGNTV	VENTAGE		NEMESIA
AEEFLRW	WELFARE	AEEGORV	OVER AGE	AEEIMNT	MATINEE
AEEFLSU	EASEFUL	AEEGPRS	PRESAGE	AEEIMNX	EXAMINE
AEEFMNR	FREE MAN	AEEGRRS	GREASER	AEEIMPT	MEAT PIE
	FREEMAN	AEEGRRT	GREATER	AEEIMRS	SEAMIER
AEEFNRR	RAN FREE	AEEGRRW	WAGERER	AEEIMRT	EMIRATE
AEEFORS	FAROESE	AEEGRSS	GREASES		MEATIER
AEEFOTV	FOVEATE	AEEGRSV	GREAVES	AEEIMSS	SIAMESE
AEEFRRT	FERRATE	AEEGSTT	GESTATE	AEEIMTT	TEA TIME
AEEFRST	FEASTER		TAGETES		TEATIME
AEEFRTU	FEATURE	AEEGTTZ	GAZETTE	AEEINNT	EATEN IN
AEEFRTX	TAX FREE	AEEHHNT	HEATHEN	AEEINRT	RETINAE
	TAX-FREE	AEEHHRT	HEATHER		TRAINEE
AEEFRWY	FREEWAY	AEEHHST	SHEATHE	AEEINST	ETESIAN
AEEFSTW	SWEET F. A.	AEEHHSW	HEE-HAWS	AEEINTT	EATEN IT
AEEGGLT	GATELEG	AEEHINR	HERNIAE	AEEINTV	NAIVETE

AEEINVW	WEAVE IN
AEEIPTX	EXPIATE
AEEIRRW	WEARIER
AEEIRST	SERIATE
AEEIRSW	WEARIES
AEEIRTT	ITERATE
AEEISST	EASIEST
AEEISVV	EVASIVE
AEEIUVX	EXUVIAE
AEEKLNS	ALKENES
AEEKMNW	WEAK MEN
AEEKMRS	REMAKES
AEEKMRT	MEERKAT
AEEKMSU	MAKE USE
AEEKNNN	NANKEEN
AEEKNRS	SNEAKER
AEEKNRT	RETAKEN
AEEKNRW	WAKENER
AEEKNSY	YANKEES
AEEKORT	OAK TREE
AEEKPRS	SPEAKER
AEEKRST	RETAKES
AEEKSTW	WEAKEST
AEELLMS	MALLEES
AEELLSY	ALL EYES
AEELLWY	WALLEYE
AEELMNP	EMPANEL
	EMPLANE
AEELMNS	ENAMELS
AEELMPX	EXAMPLE
	EXEMPLA
AEELMSS	MEASLES
AEELMST	MALTESE
AEELMSX	MALE SEX
AEELMTU	EMULATE
AEELNNO	LANE ONE
AEELNNP	ENPLANE
AEELNOS	ON LEASE
AEELNOV	ON LEAVE
AEELNRR	LEARNER
AEELNRT	ETERNAL
AEELNRW	RENEWAL
AEELNST	LEANEST
AEELNSV	ENSLAVE
	LEAVENS
AEELOPR	PAROLEE
AEELOPX	POLEAXE
AEELORU	AUREOLE
AEELPRR	PEARLER
AEELPRS	RELAPSE
	REPEALS
AEELPRT	PLEATER
	PRELATE
AEELPRU	PLEURAE
AEELPSS	ELAPSES
	PLEASES
AEELPTT	PALETTE
	PELTATE
AEELQSU	SEQUELA
AEELRRT	ALTERER
	RELATER
AEELRRX	RELAXER
AEELRSS	SEALERS
AEELRST	ELATERS
	RELATES
	STEALER
AEELRSV	REVEALS
	SEVERAL
AEELRSX	RELAXES
AEELRTX	EXALTER
AEELRUV	REVALUE

AEELSST	TEASELS
AEELSTU	ELUATES
AEELSTX	LATEXES
AEELTTY	LAYETTE
AEELTVW	WAVELET
AEEMMPY	EMPYEMA
AEEMMRT	AMMETER
AEEMNNO	ANEMONE
AEEMNNP	PEN NAME
AEEMNNS	SANE MEN
AEEMNPT	PET NAME
AEEMNST	MEANEST
AEEMOSW	AWESOME
AEEMPRS	AMPERES
AEEMPRT	TEMPERA
AEEMPTU	AMPUTEE
AEEMQRU	MARQUEE
AEEMRRS	REAMERS
	SMEARER
AEEMRSS	SEAMERS
AEEMRST	STEAMER
AEEMRSU	MEASURE
AEEMRTY	MAY TREE
AEEMSTW	MAE WEST
AEENNOT	NEONATE
AEENNPT	PENTANE
AEENNRS	ENSNARE
AEENNST	NEATENS
AEENNSX	ANNEXES
AEENOPS	OPEN SEA
AEENORY	ONE YEAR
	YEAR ONE
AEENPST	PENATES
	PESANTE
AEENPSX	EXPANSE
AEENPTU	EATEN UP
AEENRRS	EARNERS
AEENRRY	YEARNER
AEENRST	EARNEST
	EASTERN
	NEAREST
AEENRSW	WEANERS
AEENRTT	ENTREAT
	TERNATE
AEENRTV	VETERAN
AEENRWY	NEW YEAR
AEENSST	ENTASES
	SENATES
	SENSATE
AEENSTT	NEAT SET
	NEATEST
AEENSUV	AVENUES
AEENVWW	NEW WAVE
AEEOPRT	OPERATE
AEEORST	ROSEATE
	TEA ROSE
AEEORTV	OVERATE
	OVEREAT
AEEORVW	OVERAWE
AEEOSTU	EASE OUT
AEEPPRR	PAPERER
	PREPARE
AEEPRRY	PER YEAR
AEEPRSS	ASPERSE
	PARESES
AEEPRST	REPEATS
AEEPRTX	EX PARTE
AEEPRTZ	TRAPEZE
AEEPSST	PESETAS
AEEPSSU	EASES UP
AEEPSSW	PESEWAS

AEEPSTT	SEPTATE
AEEPSVY	PEAVEYS
AEEQSTU	EQUATES
AEERRSS	ERASERS
AEERRST	RARE SET
	SERRATE
	TEARERS
AEERRSU	ERASURE
AEERRSW	SWEARER
	WEARERS
AEERRTT	RETREAT
	TREATER
AEERRTW	WATERER
AEERRVW	WAVERER
AEERSST	EASTERS
	SEATERS
	TEASERS
	TESSERA
AEERSSY	ESSAYER
AEERSTT	RESTATE
AEERSTU	AUSTERE
AEERSTW	SWEATER
AEERSVW	WEAVERS
AEECCGW	SEESAWS
AEESSTT	ESTATES
	TEA SETS
AEESTTT	TESTATE
AEFFGIL	FIG LEAF
AEFFGIR	GIRAFFE
AEFFGRS	GAFFERS
AEFFIPR	PIAFFER
AEFFIPS	PIAFFES
AEFFIST	TAFFIES
AEFFISX	AFFIXES
AEFFKMO	MAKE OFF
AEFFKOP	OFF PEAK
	OFF-PEAK
AEFFKOR	RAKE OFF
	RAKE-OFF
AEFFKOT	TAKE OFF
	TAKE-OFF
	TAKEOFF
AEFFLLY	FLY LEAF
	FLYLEAF
AEFFLNS	SNAFFLE
AEFFLOS	SEAL OFF
AEFFLRS	RAFFLES
AEFFLRU	FEARFUL
AEFFLRW	WAFFLER
AEFFLSW	WAFFLES
AEFFLTU	FATEFUL
AEFFORT	TEAR OFF
AEFFORW	WEAR OFF
AEFFQRU	QUAFFER
AEFFRST	STAFFER
AEFGGMR	FARM EGG
AEFGHLT	THE FLAG
AEFGILN	FINAGLE
	LEAFING
AEFGILO	FOLIAGE
AEFGILR	FRAGILE
AEFGINR	FEARING
AEFGIRS	GAS FIRE
AEFGIRT	FRIGATE
AEFGITU	FATIGUE
AEFGINR	FLANGER
AEFGLNS	FLANGES
AEFGLOT	FLOTAGE
AEFGNOR	FAR GONE
	FAR-GONE
	GONE FAR

AEFGOOT	FOOTAGE	AEFLMRT	LEFT ARM	AEGGRSW	SWAGGER
AEFGORR	FORAGER	AEFLNRU	FLANEUR		WAGGERS
AEFGORS	FOR AGES		FRENULA	AEGGRTY	GARGETY
	FORAGES		FUNERAL	AEGGRWY	WAGGERY
	GOES FAR	AEFLNTT	FLATTEN	AEGGSWW	GEWGAWS
AEFGORT	GO AFTER	AEFLOPW	PEAFOWL	AEGHHIS	HIGH SEA
AEFGORV	FORGAVE	AEFLORS	FOR SALE	AEGHHIT	HIGH TEA
AEFGRRT	GRAFTER		LOAFERS	AEGHILN	HEALING
AEFHILS	HAS LIFE	AEFLORT	FLOATER	AEGHINP	HEAPING
AEFHISS	SEA FISH	AEFLOUV	OF VALUE	AEGHINR	HEARING
AEFHIST	FISH TEA	AEFLPPR	FLAPPER	AEGHINT	HEATING
AEFHLLT	THE FALL	AEFLPRS	FELSPAR	AEGHISS	GEISHAS
AEFHLNO	ONE HALF	AEFLPRU	FLARE UP	AEGHLNO	HALOGEN
AEFHLRS	FLASHER		FLARE-UP	AEGHLRU	LAUGHER
AEFHLSS	FLASHES	AEFLPRY	PALFREY	AEGHMNN	HANGMEN
AEFHLTT	FELT HAT	AEFLRSS	FAR LESS	AEGHNOX	HEXAGON
	THE FLAT	AEFLRST	FALTERS	AEGHNRS	HANGERS
AEFHLTU	HATEFUL	AEFLRSU	EARFULS	AEGHNSS	GNASHES
AEFHNUV	HAVE FUN		FERULAS	AEGHOST	HOSTAGE
AEFHRRT	FARTHER		REFUSAL	AEGHRST	GATHERS
AEFHRST	FATHERS	AEFLRTT	FLATTER	AEGIIMN	IMAGINE
AEFHRTY	THE FRAY	AEFLRTU	TEARFUL	AEGIINR	NIGERIA
AEFIIRS	FAIRIES	AEFLRZZ	FRAZZLE	AEGIKLN	LEAKING
AEFIKLN	FANLIKE	AEFLSST	FALSEST		LINKAGE
AEFIKLR	FLAKIER	AEFLSTY	FLY EAST	AEGIKNP	PEAKING
AEFILLM	ILL FAME	AEFMNOR	FORAMEN	AEGIKNS	SINKAGE
AEFILLT	LIE FLAT		FOREMAN	AEGIKPR	GARPIKE
AEFILMN	INFLAME	AEFMNOW	WON FAME	AEGIKRW	GAWKIER
AEFILNS	FINALES	AEFMNRU	FRAENUM	AEGILLL	ILLEGAL
AEFILNT	INFLATE	AEFMNST	FAST MEN	AEGILLP	PILLAGE
AEFILNV	FLAVINE	AEFMORR	FAR MORE	AEGILLT	TILLAGE
AEFILOT	FOLIATE		FOREARM	AEGILLV	VILLAGE
AEFILPT	FLEA PIT	AEFMPRU	FRAME UP	AEGILLY	AGILELY
	FLEAPIT		FRAME-UP	AEGILMT	TIME LAG
AEFILRR	FRAILER	AEFMRRS	FARMERS	AEGILNN	GIN LANE
AEFILRU	AIR FLUE	AEFNOPR	PROFANE		LEANING
	FAILURE	AEFNOST	FAST ONE	AEGILNP	PEALING
AEFILSS	FALSIES	AEFNRSU	UNSAFER	AEGILNR	ENGRAIL
AEFILSW	SAW LIFE	AEFNRSW	FAWNERS		REALIGN
AEFILTT	FLATTIE	AEFNRTW	WENT FAR	AEGILNS	LEASING
AEFIMNN	FINE MAN	AEFNSST	FASTENS		SEALING
AEFIMNR	FIREMAN		FATNESS	AEGILNT	ELATING
AEFIMNS	FAMINES	AEFNSTT	FATTENS		GELATIN
AEFIMNW	WIN FAME	AEFORRY	FORAYER		GENITAL
AEFIMRR	FIREARM	AEFORSW	FORESAW	AEGILOS	GOALIES
AEFINNS	FENIANS	AEFOSST	FATSOES	AEGILRZ	GLAZIER
AEFINNT	INFANTE		FOSSATE	AEGILST	LIGATES
AEFINNZ	FANZINE	AEFRRST	RAFTERS	AEGILSV	GLAIVES
AEFINRR	REFRAIN		STRAFER	AEGIMNN	MEANING
AEFINRT	FAINTER	AEFRRVY	VERY FAR	AEGIMNR	MANGIER
	FINE ART	AEFRSST	STRAFES		REAMING
AEFIQRU	AQUIFER	AEFRSTW	FAR WEST	AEGIMNS	ENIGMAS
AEFIRRR	FARRIER		FRETSAW		GAMINES
AEFIRST	FAIREST		WAFTERS		SEAMING
	SET FAIR	AEFSSTT	FASTEST	AEGIMNT	MINTAGE
AEFIRSX	FAIR SEX		SET FAST		TEAMING
AEFIRTT	FATTIER	AEFSTTT	FATTEST	AEGIMOS	IMAGOES
AEFISST	FIESTAS	AEGGGLS	GAGGLES	AEGIMPR	EPIGRAM
AEFISTT	FATTIES	AEGGGLU	LUGGAGE	AEGIMPS	MAGPIES
AEFISTX	FIXATES	AEGGHLR	HAGGLER	AEGIMRR	ARMIGER
AEFJNST	FAN-JETS	AEGGHLS	HAGGLES	AEGIMRS	MIRAGES
AEFKLNR	FLANKER	AEGGINR	GEARING	AEGIMRT	MIGRATE
AEFKLUW	WAKEFUL	AEGGISW	SWAGGIE		RAGTIME
AEFKMNU	MAKE FUN	AEGGLRS	GARGLES	AEGIMRY	IMAGERY
AEFKMOR	MAKE FOR	AEGGLRY	GREYLAG	AEGIMST	GAMIEST
AEFKNRR	FRANKER	AEGGLSW	WAGGLES	AEGIMSV	MISGAVE
AEFKORS	FORSAKE	AEGGLSY	LAY EGGS	AEGINNR	EARNING
AEFLLLT	LET FALL	AEGGNRS	GANGERS		ENGRAIN
AEFLLNN	FLANNEL		GRANGES		IN ANGER
AEFLLTT	FLATLET	AEGGRST	STAGGER		IN RANGE
AEFLMOR	FEMORAL	AEGGRSU	GAUGERS		NEARING

AEGINNT	ANTEING	AEGLOTV	VOLTAGE	AEGORST	STORAGE
	ANTIGEN	AEGLPPR	GRAPPLE	AEGORTU	OUTRAGE
	GENTIAN	AEGLPRT	LEG TRAP		TOUAREG
	NEAT GIN	AEGLPRU	EAR PLUG	AEGORVY	VOYAGER
	NET GAIN		EARPLUG	AEGOSSU	GASEOUS
AEGINNU	GUANINE		PLAGUER	AEGOSTW	STOWAGE
AEGINNV	ANGEVIN	AEGLPSU	PLAGUES	AEGOSVY	VOYAGES
AEGINNW	WEANING	AEGLPUY	PLAGUEY	AEGOTTV	GAVOTTE
AEGINOR	IRON AGE	AEGLRRU	REGULAR	AEGOTUV	GAVE OUT
AEGINOS	AGONIES	AEGLRSS	LARGESS	AEGPRRS	GRASPER
	AGONISE	AEGLRST	LARGEST	AEGPRSS	GASPERS
AEGINOZ	AGONIZE	AEGLRSV	GRAVELS	AEGPRST	PARGETS
AEGINPR	REAPING	AEGLRTY	GREATLY	AEGPSTU	UPSTAGE
AEGINRR	ANGRIER	AEGLRVY	GRAVELY	AEGRRST	GARRETS
	EARRING	AEGLSSS	GLASSES		GARTERS
	GRAINER	AEGLSTT	GESTALT	AEGRRSU	ARGUERS
	REARING	AEGLTUV	VULGATE	AEGRRUV	GRAVURE
AEGINRS	ERASING	AEGLUVY	VAGUELY	AEGRSSS	GASSERS
	REGAINS	AEGMMRS	GAMMERS		GRASSES
	SEARING	AEGMMRU	RUMMAGE	AEGRSST	STAGERS
AEGINRT	TEARING	AEGMNOS	MANGOES	AEGRSTT	TARGETS
AEGINRV	VINEGAR	AEGMNOT	MAGNETO	AEGRSTU	TUAREGS
AEGINRW	WEARING		MEGATON	AEGRSTY	GYRATES
AEGINST	EASTING		MONTAGE	AEGSSSU	GAUSSES
	SEATING	AEGMNRS	ENGRAMS	AEGSTUV	VAGUEST
	TEASING		GERMANS	AEGTTTU	GUTTATE
AEGINSU	GUINEAS		MANGERS	AEHHHST	THE SHAH
AEGINTV	VINTAGE	AEGMNRT	GARMENT	AEHHILS	SHEILAH
AEGINTZ	TZIGANE	AEGMNRY	GERMANY	AEHHJOV	JEHOVAH
AEGIPRS	PIG'S EAR	AEGMNST	MAGNETS	AEHHLTY	HEALTHY
AEGIPSX	PAGE SIX	AEGMNSW	SWAGMEN	AEHHNRS	HARSHEN
AEGIRRZ	GRAZIER	AEGMNTU	AUGMENT	AEHHPRS	RHAPHES
AEGIRSS	GASSIER		MUTAGEN	AEHHRRS	HARSHER
AEGIRST	GAITERS	AEGMOOR	MOORAGE	AEHHRST	HEARTHS
	SEAGIRT	AEGMOXY	EXOGAMY	AEHHSST	SHEATHS
AEGIRSW	EARWIGS	AEGMPSU	GAME'S UP	AEHHSTW	THE WASH
AEGISSV	VISAGES	AEGMRTW	GET WARM	AEHIIRR	HAIRIER
AEGIVWY	GIVE WAY	AEGMSUZ	ZEUGMAS	AEHIKNS	HANKIES
AEGJLNS	JANGLES	AEGNNOP	GONE NAP	AEHIKRS	SHAKIER
AEGJSST	GAS JETS	AEGNNOT	TONNAGE	AEHIKSW	WEAKISH
AEGKSST	GASKETS	AEGNNRT	REGNANT	AEHILMO	HEMIOLA
AEGLLLY	LEGALLY	AEGNNST	GANNETS	AEHILNO	IN A HOLE
AEGLLNO	GALLEON	AEGNNTT	TANGENT	AEHILNR	HERNIAL
AEGLLOR	ALLEGRO	AEGNOOR	OREGANO		INHALER
AEGLLRY	ALLERGY	AEGNOPS	GOES NAP	AEHILNS	INHALES
	GALLERY	AEGNORR	GROANER	AEHILNY	HYALINE
	LARGELY	AEGNORS	ONAGERS	AEHILPR	HARELIP
	REGALLY		ORANGES	AEHILRU	HAULIER
AEGLLSU	SULLAGE	AEGNORT	NEGATOR	AEHILSS	SHEILAS
AEGLLSY	GALLEYS	AEGNORW	WAGONER	AEHILTY	HYALITE
AEGLLTU	GLUTEAL	AEGNOST	ON STAGE	AEHILVY	HEAVILY
AEGLMNS	MANGLES	AEGNOSV	GAS OVEN	AEHIMNY	HYMENIA
AEGLMPU	PLUMAGE	AEGNOSY	NOSEGAY	AEHIMRS	MISHEAR
AEGLNOT	TANGELO	AEGNOTW	TEA GOWN	AEHIMSS	MESSIAH
AEGLNPR	GRAPNEL	AEGNPRT	TREPANG	AEHIMST	ATHEISM
AEGLNPS	SPANGLE	AEGNRRS	GARNERS	AEHINPR	HEPARIN
AEGLNRS	ANGLERS		RANGERS	AEHINPS	IN SHAPE
AEGLNRU	GRANULE	AEGNRRT	GRANTER	AEHINRS	HERNIAS
AEGLNRW	WANGLER	AEGNRST	ARGENTS	AEHINRT	HAIR NET
	WRANGLE		GARNETS	AEHINSS	HESSIAN
AEGLNST	TANGLES		STRANGE		IN ASHES
AEGLNSU	ANGELUS	AEGNSSY	GAYNESS	AEHINST	IN HASTE
AEGLNSW	WANGLES	AEGOORT	ROOTAGE	AEHIORR	HOARIER
AEGLNTT	GANTLET	AEGOPRS	GO SPARE	AEHIORS	AIR HOSE
AEGLNUW	GUNWALE	AEGOPRT	PORTAGE	AEHIPPR	HAPPIER
AEGLOPR	PERGOLA		TOP GEAR	AEHIPPT	EPITAPH
AEGLORT	GLOATER	AEGOPST	GESTAPO	AEHIPRS	HARPIES
AEGLORW	LOW GEAR		POSTAGE	AEHIRRR	HARRIER
AEGLOSS	GLOSSAE		POTAGES	AEHIRRS	HARRIES
AEGLOST	LEGATOS	AEGOPTT	POTTAGE	AEHIRST	HASTIER
AEGLOSV	LOVAGES	AEGOPTW	PAGE TWO	AEHIRWY	HAYWIRE

Code	Word(s)
AEHISTT	ATHEIST
	STAITHE
AEHISTZ	HAZIEST
AEHISVY	YESHIVA
AEHKNRS	HANKERS
AEHKNRT	THANKER
AEHKOSS	SHAKOES
AEHKOST	THE OAKS
AEHKOTY	THE OKAY
AEHKPSU	SHAKE UP
	SHAKE-UP
AEHKRSS	SHAKERS
AEHKRSW	HAWKERS
AEHLLLL	ALL HELL
AEHLLNW	NEW HALL
AEHLLOP	ALL HOPE
AEHLLUV	HELLUVA
AEHLMNO	MANHOLE
AEHLMNY	HYMENAL
AEHLMOR	ARMHOLE
AEHLMOT	HOT MEAL
AEHLMRT	THERMAL
AEHLMRU	HUMERAL
AEHLMST	HAMLETS
AEHLNOT	ETHANOL
AEHLNRT	ENTHRAL
AEHLNSU	UNLEASH
AEHLORT	LOATHER
	RAT HOLE
AEHLOST	LOATHES
AEHLOTV	THE OVAL
AEHLPRS	SPHERAL
AEHLPSS	HAPLESS
	PLASHES
AEHLPSY	SHAPELY
AEHLRSS	SLASHER
AEHLRST	HALTERS
	LATHERS
	SLATHER
	THALERS
AEHLRSW	WHALERS
AEHLRTY	EARTHLY
	LATHERY
AEHLSSS	ASHLESS
	HASSLES
	SLASHES
AEHLSST	HATLESS
AEHLSTT	STEALTH
AEHLTWY	WEALTHY
AEHMMOR	RAM HOME
AEHMMRS	HAMMERS
AEHMNOR	MENORAH
AEHMNST	ANTHEMS
AEHMPRS	HAMPERS
AEHMPTY	EMPATHY
AEHMRSS	MARSHES
	SMASHER
AEHMRST	HAMSTER
AEHMRTY	THE ARMY
AEHMSSS	SMASHES
AEHMSTW	WEST HAM
AEHMTTW	MATTHEW
AEHMUZZ	MEZUZAH
AEHNNPY	HA'PENNY
AEHNOPT	PHAETON
	PHONATE
AEHNORS	HOARSEN
	SENHORA
AEHNORT	ANOTHER
	ON EARTH

Code	Word(s)
AEHNOTV	HAVE NOT
	HAVE-NOT
AEHNPPS	HAPPENS
AEHNPRS	SHARPEN
AEHNPRT	PANTHER
AEHNRSS	HARNESS
AEHNRST	ANTHERS
AEHNRTU	HAUNTER
	UNEARTH
AEHNRTX	NARTHEX
AEHNSST	HASTENS
AEHNSWY	SAY WHEN
AEHNTVY	THE NAVY
AEHOPST	TEA SHOP
AEHORRS	HOARSER
AEHORRW	WAR HERO
AEHORST	EARSHOT
AEHORTT	TO HEART
AEHOSTT	HOT SEAT
AEHOTTZ	THE A TO Z
AEHOTUV	HAVE OUT
AEHPPRS	PERHAPS
AEHPPSU	HEAPS UP
	SHAPE UP
AEHPRRS	HARPERS
	SHARPER
AEHPRSS	PHRASES
	SERAPHS
	SHAPERS
	SHERPAS
AEHPRTY	THERAPY
AEHPSST	SPATHES
AEHPSTU	HEATS UP
AEHQSSU	QUASHES
AEHRRSS	RASHERS
AEHRRTU	URETHRA
AEHRSST	RASHEST
	TRASHES
AEHRSSV	SHAVERS
AEHRSSW	HAWSERS
	WASHERS
AEHRSTT	SHATTER
	THE ARTS
	THREATS
AEHRSTV	HARVEST
AEHRSTW	SWATHER
	WREATHS
AEHRSVW	WHARVES
AEHRSXY	HYRAXES
AEHRTUU	HAUTEUR
AEHSSST	STASHES
AEHSSTW	SWATHES
AEHSTUX	EXHAUST
AEIIKNT	KAINITE
AEIILNN	ANILINE
AEIILNR	AIR LINE
	AIRLINE
AEIILRS	ISRAELI
AEIILSS	LIAISES
AEIILST	LAITIES
AEIIMTT	IMITATE
AEIINNS	ASININE
AEIINRT	INERTIA
AEIIPPR	AIR PIPE
AEIIPRR	PRAIRIE
AEIIRRV	RIVIERA
AEIITTV	VITIATE
AEIJLNV	JAVELIN
AEIJLRS	JAILERS
AEIJLSZ	JEZAILS
AEIJMMR	JAMMIER

Code	Word(s)
AEIJMNS	JASMINE
AEIJRZZ	JAZZIER
AEIKLLT	TAKE ILL
AEIKLMN	MANLIKE
AEIKLMR	ARMLIKE
AEIKLNR	LANKIER
AEIKLRT	RATLIKE
AEIKLRW	WARLIKE
AEIKLST	TALKIES
AEIKLSW	SAWLIKE
	WALKIES
AEIKLWX	WAXLIKE
AEIKMNR	RAMEKIN
AEIKMST	MAKES IT
	MISTAKE
AEIKNNS	SNEAK IN
AEIKNNT	TAKEN IN
AEIKNPS	SEA-PINK
AEIKNRT	KERATIN
AEIKNST	INTAKES
	TAKES IN
AEIKNTT	TAKEN IT
AEIKNTY	KYANITE
AEIKPRR	PARKIER
AEIKRSS	KAISERS
AEIKRSZ	KARZIES
AEILLMN	MANILLE
AEILLMT	ALL-TIME
AEILLOV	ALVEOLI
AEILLPR	PALLIER
AEILLRS	RALLIES
AEILLRT	LITERAL
AEILLSS	SALLIES
AEILLST	TALLIES
AEILLSW	WALLIES
AEILLUV	ELUVIAL
AEILLVX	VEXILLA
AEILMMN	MAILMEN
AEILMMS	MELISMA
AEILMNN	MELANIN
AEILMNP	IMPANEL
	MANIPLE
AEILMNR	MANLIER
	MARLINE
	MINERAL
AEILMNS	MENIALS
	SEMINAL
AEILMNT	AILMENT
	ALIMENT
AEILMNV	EVIL MAN
AEILMPR	LEMPIRA
	PALMIER
AEILMPS	IMPALES
AEILMRS	REALISM
AEILMRT	MARLITE
AEILMSS	AIMLESS
AEILNNY	INANELY
AEILNOP	OPALINE
AEILNOR	AILERON
AEILNOS	SEA LION
AEILNOT	ELATION
AEILNPR	PLAINER
	PRALINE
AEILNPS	ALPINES
	NEPALIS
	SPANIEL
AEILNPT	PANTILE
AEILNPU	PAULINE
AEILNPX	AXLE PIN
	EXPLAIN

AEILNRT	LATRINE	
	RATLINE	
	RELIANT	
	RETINAL	
	TRENAIL	
AEILNRV	ELINVAR	
	RAVELIN	
AEILNRX	RELAXIN	
AEILNSS	SALINES	
AEILNST	ELASTIN	
	ENTAILS	
	SALIENT	
AEILNSW	IN WALES	
AEILNSX	LANE SIX	
AEILNSY	ELYSIAN	
AEILNTV	VENTAIL	
AEILNVY	NAIVELY	
AEILOST	ISOLATE	
AEILOTV	VIOLATE	
AEILPPR	APPLIER	
AEILPPS	APPLIES	
AEILPRT	AT PERIL	
	PLAITER	
AEILPRV	PREVAIL	
AEILPSS	ESPIALS	
AEILPST	TALIPES	
AEILPSY	PAISLEY	
AEILQTU	LIQUATE	
	TEQUILA	
AEILRRT	TRAILER	
AEILRSS	AIRLESS	
	SERIALS	
AEILRST	REALIST	
	RETAILS	
	SALTIER	
	SALTIRE	
AEILRSW	WAILERS	
AEILRTY	IRATELY	
	REALITY	
AEILRVV	REVIVAL	
AEILRWY	WEARILY	
AEILSST	SET SAIL	
AEILSTZ	LAZIEST	
AEILTVV	TEL AVIV	
AEILUVX	EXUVIAL	
AEIMMMS	MAMMIES	
AEIMMNS	MISNAME	
AEIMMPP	PIP EMMA	
AEIMMRT	MARMITE	
AEIMMST	TAMMIES	
AEIMNOR	MORAINE	
AEIMNOT	AMNIOTE	
AEIMNPR	PERMIAN	
AEIMNRR	MARINER	
AEIMNRS	MARINES	
	REMAINS	
	SEMINAR	
AEIMNRT	MINARET	
	RAIMENT	
AEIMNRV	VERMIAN	
AEIMNRW	WIREMAN	
AEIMNSS	SAMISEN	
AEIMNST	INMATES	
	STEAM IN	
AEIMNSW	WISE MAN	
AEIMNTV	VIETNAM	
AEIMNTY	AMENITY	
	ANY TIME	
AEIMOPR	EMPORIA	
AEIMOST	ATOMISE	
AEIMOTZ	ATOMIZE	
AEIMPRT	PRIMATE	
AEIMPRV	VAMPIRE	
AEIMPSS	IMPASSE	
AEIMPST	PASTIME	
AEIMRRS	MARRIES	
AEIMRST	MAESTRI	
AEIMRTU	MURIATE	
AEIMRTW	WARTIME	
AEIMSSS	MESSIAS	
AEIMSSV	MASSIVE	
	MAVISES	
AEIMSTT	AT TIMES	
	ETATISM	
AEIMSTW	TIME WAS	
AEIMSTZ	MESTIZA	
AEINNNS	NANNIES	
AEINNOT	ETONIAN	
AEINNPR	PANNIER	
AEINNPT	PINNATE	
AEINNRS	INSANER	
AEINNRT	ENTRAIN	
AEINOPR	OPEN AIR	
	OPEN-AIR	
AEINOSV	EVASION	
AEINOTT	ATE INTO	
	FAT INTO	
AEINPPP	PANPIPE	
AEINPPS	NAPPIES	
AEINPRS	PERSIAN	
AEINPRT	PAINTER	
	PERTAIN	
AEINPSS	PANSIES	
AEINPST	PANTIES	
	SAPIENT	
AEINPTT	PATIENT	
AEINPTU	PETUNIA	
AEINQTU	ANTIQUE	
AEINRRT	TERRAIN	
	TRAINER	
AEINRST	IN TEARS	
	NASTIER	
	RETAINS	
	RETINAS	
	RETSINA	
	STAINER	
	STEARIN	
AEINRSV	RAVINES	
AEINRSW	SWEAR IN	
	WEARS IN	
AEINRSY	IN YEARS	
AEINRTT	NATTIER	
	NITRATE	
	TERTIAN	
AEINRTU	TAURINE	
	URINATE	
AEINRVV	VERVAIN	
AEINSST	ENTASIS	
	SESTINA	
	TANSIES	
AEINSTT	IN STATE	
	INSTATE	
	SATINET	
AEINSTU	AUNTIES	
	SINUATE	
AEINSTV	NAIVEST	
	NATIVES	
	VAINEST	
AEINSTZ	ZANIEST	
AEINSVV	NAVVIES	
AEINSWY	EASY WIN	
AEINTVY	NAIVETY	
AEINTXY	ANXIETY	
AEIOPST	OPIATES	
AEIOQSU	SEQUOIA	
AEIORSV	OVARIES	
AEIPPRS	APPRISE	
	SAPPIER	
AEIPPRZ	ZAPPIER	
AEIPRRS	ASPIRER	
	PARRIES	
	PRAISER	
	RAPIERS	
	REPAIRS	
AEIPRSS	ASPIRES	
	PARESIS	
	PRAISES	
AEIPRST	PARTIES	
	PIASTRE	
	PIRATES	
	PRATIES	
	SEA TRIP	
	TRAIPSE	
AEIPRSY	PAY RISE	
AEIPRTT	PARTITE	
AEIPRTV	PRIVATE	
AEIPRTW	WIRETAP	
AEIPRXY	PYREXIA	
AEIPSSS	ASEPSIS	
AEIPSST	PASTIES	
	PATSIES	
AEIPSSV	PASSIVE	
AEIPSTT	PATTIES	
AEIPTXY	EPITAXY	
AEIQRUV	AQUIVER	
AEIRRRV	ARRIVER	
AEIRRSS	ARRISES	
	SIERRAS	
AEIRRST	TARRIES	
	TARSIER	
AEIRRSV	ARRIVES	
AEIRRTT	RATTIER	
AEIRSST	SATIRES	
AEIRSTT	ARTIEST	
	ARTISTE	
	ATTIRES	
	STRIATE	
	TASTIER	
AEIRSTW	WAITERS	
	WARIEST	
AEIRSVW	WAIVERS	
AEIRTTT	TATTIER	
	TITRATE	
AEIRTUZ	AZURITE	
AEIRTVY	VARIETY	
AEISSST	SIESTAS	
AEISSSU	AUSSIES	
AEISSSZ	ASSIZES	
AEISSTU	AT ISSUE	
AEISSUX	AUXESIS	
AEISSVV	SAVVIES	
AEISTTT	ETATIST	
	TATTIES	
AEISTTU	SITUATE	
AEISTTY	SATIETY	
AEISTVW	WAVIEST	
AEJJLNU	JEJUNAL	
AEJLOSU	JEALOUS	
AEJMRST	RAMJETS	
AEJMSST	ST.JAMES	
AEJMSTY	MAJESTY	
AEJNOSS	SAN JOSE	
AEJOOPS	JOE SOAP	

AEJPRSS	JASPERS	AELLRTY	ALERTLY	AELNRTU	NEUTRAL
AEJPRSY	JASPERY	AELLSST	SALLETS	AELNRTV	VENTRAL
AEKLNRS	RANKLES	AELLSSW	LAWLESS	AELNRUV	UNRAVEL
AEKLNST	ANKLETS	AELLSSY	SALLEYS	AELNSSU	SENSUAL
	LANKEST	AELLSTT	TALLEST	AELNSSW	AWNLESS
AEKLNSY	ALKYNES	AELLSTW	WALLETS	AELNSSX	LAXNESS
AEKLOTU	LEAK OUT	AELLSTY	STALELY	AELNSTT	TALENTS
AEKLPPT	PEP TALK	AELLSVY	VALLEYS	AELNSTU	ELUANTS
AEKLPRS	SPARKLE	AELLTUU	ULULATE	AELOORS	AEROSOL
AEKLRST	STALKER	AELMMOY	MYELOMA		ROSEOLA
	TALKERS	AELMMRT	TRAMMEL	AELOOTT	TOO LATE
AEKLRSW	WALKERS	AELMMSY	MALMSEY	AELOPRS	PAROLES
AEKMNSU	UNMAKES	AELMMTU	MUMETAL	AELOPRT	PROLATE
AEKMOTU	MAKE OUT	AELMNOR	ALMONER	AELOPRV	OVERLAP
AEKMPSU	MAKES UP	AELMNOT	OMENTAL	AELOPST	APOSTLE
AEKMRRS	REMARKS	AELMNRU	NUMERAL	AELORRT	REALTOR
AEKMRST	MARKETS	AELMNSS	MANLESS		RELATOR
AEKNNOT	TAKEN ON	AELMNST	LAMENTS	AELORSS	LASSOER
AEKNORS	KOREANS		MANTLES		SEROSAL
AEKNOST	TAKES ON	AELMNTT	MANTLET	AELORST	OESTRAL
AEKNOTT	TAKEN TO	AELMOPU	AMPOULE	AELORTU	TORULAE
AEKNPPR	KNAPPER	AELMOPY	MAYPOLE	AELORTV	LEVATOR
AEKNPRS	SPANKER	AELMORS	MORALES	AELORTW	LOW RATE
AEKNPSU	SNEAK UP	AELMORU	MORULAE	AELORUU	ROULEAU
AEKNPTU	TAKEN UP	AELMORV	REMOVAL	AELORVY	OVERLAY
AEKNPUW	WAKEN UP	AELMOST	MALTOSE	AELOSSS	LASSOES
AEKNRRS	RANKERS	AELMOSY	AMYLOSE	AELOSSV	SALVOES
AEKNRST	TANKERS	AELMOTT	MATELOT	AELOSTV	SOLVATE
AEKNRVY	KNAVERY	AELMPRS	PALMERS	AELOSTZ	ZEALOTS
AEKORSS	SOAKERS		SAMPLER	AELOSUZ	ZEALOUS
AEKOSTT	TAKES TO	AELMPRT	TEMPLAR	AELOSVY	SAVELOY
AEKOTTU	TAKE OUT		TRAMPLE	AELOTUV	OVULATE
AEKPPSU	SPEAK UP	AELMPRY	LAMPREY	AELPPRS	RAPPELS
AEKPRRS	SPARKER	AELMPSS	SAMPLES	AELPPST	LAPPETS
AEKPSSY	PASS KEY	AELMRSS	ARMLESS	AELPPSU	PAPULES
	PASSKEY	AELMRST	ARMLETS	AELPPTU	LEAPT UP
AEKPSTU	TAKES UP	AELMRSV	MARVELS	AELPQSU	PLAQUES
AEKPSUW	WAKES UP	AELMRTT	MARTLET	AELPRRS	PARRELS
AEKQRSU	QUAKERS	AELMSST	SAMLETS	AELPRST	PALTERS
AEKQSSU	SQUEAKS	AELMSTU	AMULETS		PLASTER
AEKQSUY	SQUEAKY	AELNNPR	PLANNER		PSALTER
AEKRRST	STARKER	AELNNRS	LANNERS		STAPLER
AEKRSST	SKATERS	AELNNRT	LANTERN	AELPRSU	PERUSAL
	STRAKES	AELNNRU	UNLEARN		PLEURAS
	STREAKS	AELNNTU	ANNULET	AELPRSY	PARLEYS
AEKRSTY	STREAKY	AELNOPT	POLENTA		PARSLEY
AELLLLT	TELL ALL	AELNOPU	APOLUNE		REPLAYS
AELLLOV	LOVE ALL	AELNORT	LATER ON		SPARELY
AELLMNT	TALL MEN	AELNORV	VERONAL	AELPRTT	PLATTER
AELLMNU	LUMENAL	AELNOST	LEAN TOS		PRATTLE
AELLMRS	SMALLER		LEAN-TOS	AELPSSS	SAPLESS
AELLMST	MALLETS	AELNOTW	LANE TWO	AELPSST	PASTELS
AELLMSU	MALLEUS	AELNPPS	PEN PALS		STAPLES
AELLMWX	MAXWELL	AELNPPY	PLAY PEN	AELPSSU	SEALS UP
AELLNOV	NOVELLA		PLAYPEN	AELPSSY	PAY LESS
AELLNPY	PENALLY	AELNPRT	PLANTER	AELPSTT	LET PAST
AELLNRW	RAN WELL		REPLANT	AELPSTU	PULSATE
AELLNVY	VENALLY	AELNPRY	PLENARY		STEAL UP
AELLORS	ROSELLA	AELNPSS	NAPLESS	AELQRRU	QUARREL
AELLORV	ALL OVER	AELNPST	PLANETS	AELQSSU	SQUEALS
	ALLOVER		PLATENS	AELQTUZ	QUETZAL
	OVERALL		TEN LAPS	AELRRSU	SURREAL
AELLPRU	PLEURAL	AELNPTX	EXPLANT	AELRRTT	RATTLER
AELLPST	L PLATES	AELNPTY	APLENTY	AELRRTW	TRAWLER
	PALLETS		PENALTY	AELRSST	ARTLESS
AELLPSU	LES PAUL	AELNQUU	UNEQUAL		SALTERS
AELLQUY	EQUALLY	AELNRRS	SNARLER		SLATERS
AELLRST	STELLAR	AELNRST	ANTLERS	AELRSSV	SALVERS
AELLRSU	ALLURES		RENTALS		SLAVERS
	LAURELS		SALTERN	AELRSSY	RAYLESS
AELLRSW	WALLERS		STERNAL		SLAYERS

AELRSTT	RATTLES	AEMQRSU	MARQUES	AENRRSW	WARNERS
	STARLET	AEMQSSU	MASQUES		WARRENS
	STARTLE	AEMRRST	ARMREST	AENRRTY	TERNARY
AELRSTU	SALUTER		SMARTER	AENRSSW	ANSWERS
AELRSTV	TRAVELS	AEMRRSW	SWARMER		RAWNESS
	VARLETS	AEMRRTU	ERRATUM	AENRSTT	NATTERS
AELRSTW	WASTREL	AEMRSST	MASTERS	AENRSTU	NATURES
AELRSUV	VALUERS		STREAMS		SAUNTER
AELRSVY	SLAVERY	AEMRSSU	MASSEUR		TEA URNS
AELRSWY	LAWYERS	AEMRSTT	MATTERS	AENRSTV	SERVANT
AELRSZZ	RAZZLES	AEMRSTU	MATURES		TAVERNS
AELRTTT	TARTLET		STRUMAE		VERSANT
	TATTLER	AEMRSTW	WARMEST	AENRSWY	YAWNERS
AELRTUV	VAULTER	AEMRSTY	MASTERY	AENRTTU	TAUNTER
AELRTWZ	WALTZER	AEMRTTY	MATTERY	AENRTUV	VAUNTER
AELSSST	TASSELS	AEMSSSU	ASSUMES	AENSSST	ASSENTS
AELSSTT	STALEST	AEMSTTT	MATTEST	AENSSTU	UNSEATS
AELSSTU	SALUTES	AENNNPT	PENNANT	AENSTTU	ATTUNES
AELSTTT	TATTLES	AENNORY	ANNOYER		TAUTENS
AELSTTW	WATTLES	AENNOSV	NOVENAS		TETANUS
AELSTTY	STATELY	AENNOTU	TONNEAU	AENSTTX	SEXTANT
AELSTUX	LUXATES	AENNPRS	SPANNER	AEOOPPS	PAPOOSE
AELSTWZ	WALTZES	AENNPTW	WENT NAP	AEOPPPS	PAPPOSE
AELSUVY	SUAVELY	AENNRST	TANNERS	AEOPPRV	APPROVE
AELTTUX	TEXTUAL	AENNRTT	ENTRANT	AEOPPSU	PEA SOUP
AELTVXY	LEVY TAX	AENNRTY	TANNERY	AEOPQRU	OPAQUER
ACMMNNX	MANXMEN	AENNSST	ST. ANNE'S	AEOPRRT	PRAETOR
AEMMNOT	MOMENTA	AENNSSW	WANNESS		PRORATE
AEMMRST	STAMMER	AENNSTT	TENANTS	AEOPRRV	OVER PAR
AEMMRSY	YAMMERS	AENOPPR	ON PAPER	AEOPRST	ESPARTO
AEMMSTU	SUMMATE		PROPANE		PROTEAS
AEMNNOS	NO MEANS	AENOPRS	PERSONA		SEAPORT
	NO NAMES	AENOPRT	ONE PART	AEOPRTT	TOP RATE
AEMNNOT	MONTANE		OPERANT	AEOPRTW	WAR POET
AEMNNOU	NOUMENA		PRONATE	AEOPRVY	OVERPAY
AEMNNRS	MANNERS		PROTEAN	AEOPRWY	ROPEWAY
AEMNNRT	REMNANT		TRAP ONE	AEOPSTT	TEA POTS
AEMNNTX	NEXT MAN	AENOPRW	OPEN WAR		TEAPOTS
AEMNORS	OARSMEN	AENOPSW	WEAPONS	AEOQRTU	EQUATOR
	SAN REMO	AENORRV	OVERRAN		QUORATE
AEMNORU	ENAMOUR		RAN OVER	AEOQSUU	AQUEOUS
AEMNOTV	OVERMAN	AENORSS	REASONS	AEORRSS	SOARERS
AEMNORY	ANYMORE		SENORAS	AEORRST	ROASTER
AEMNOTT	TOMENTA	AENORST	ONE STAR	AEORSSU	AROUSES
AEMNPTY	PAYMENT		SENATOR	AEORSSW	SOW'S EAR
AEMNRRU	MANURER		TREASON	AEORSTT	ROTATES
AEMNRST	MARTENS	AENORSW	WEARS ON		TOASTER
	SMARTEN	AENOSSS	SEASONS	AEORSVW	AVOWERS
AEMNRSU	MANURES	AENOSTT	NO TASTE		OVERSAW
	SURNAME		NOTATES		SAW OVER
AEMNSST	STAMENS	AENOSTU	SOUTANE	AEORTUW	OUTWEAR
AEMNSTY	AMNESTY	AENOSTW	NO SWEAT		WEAR OUT
AEMNTXY	NEXT MAY	AENOUUV	NOUVEAU	AEORTVX	OVERTAX
AEMOORT	TEAROOM	AENPPRS	SNAPPER	AEOSTTU	EATS OUT
AEMOORW	WOOMERA	AENPRRT	PARTNER	AEPPRRT	TRAPPER
AEMOOSV	VAMOOSE	AENPRST	ENTRAPS	AEPPRRW	WRAPPER
AEMOPPR	PAMPERO		PARENTS	AEPPRSS	SAPPERS
AEMOPRW	WAR POEM		PASTERN	AEPPRST	TAPPERS
AEMOPRY	MORE PAY		TREPANS	AEPPRSU	PAUPERS
	PAY MORE	AENPRSW	SPAWNER	AEPPRSW	SWAPPER
AEMORRS	REMORAS	AENPRSZ	PANZERS	AEPPRSY	PREPAYS
AEMORRV	OVERARM	AENPRTT	PATTERN		YAPPERS
AEMORST	MAESTRO	AENPRTY	PAY RENT	AEPPSTT	TAPPETS
AEMPPRS	PAMPERS	AENPRUV	PARVENU	AEPPSTU	PASTE-UP
AEMPRRT	TRAMPER	AENPSST	APTNESS		PUPATES
AEMPRST	STAMPER	AENPSSY	SYNAPSE	AEPQRTU	PARQUET
	TAMPERS	AENPSTT	PATENTS	AEPRRSS	SPARSER
AEMPRSV	REVAMPS		PATTENS	AEPRRSU	REARS UP
	VAMPERS		TEN PAST	AEPRRSW	WARPERS
AEMPRTU	TEMPURA	AENPSTU	PEANUTS	AEPRRSY	PRAYERS
AEMPTTT	ATTEMPT	AENRRSS	SNARERS		SPRAYER

AEPRRTU	RAPTURE	AFFLOPY	PLAY OFF	AFILLNS	FALLS IN
AEPRSST	REPASTS		PLAY-OFF	AFILLNY	FINALLY
AEPRSSY	PESSARY	AFFLOSY	LAYOFFS	AFILLPT	PITFALL
AEPRSTT	PATTERS		LAYS OFF	AFILLPU	PAILFUL
	SPATTER	AFFNORS	SAFFRON	AFILLRY	FRAILLY
	TAPSTER	AFFNORT	AFFRONT	AFILLUV	FLUVIAL
AEPRSTU	PASTURE	AFFNORW	WARN OFF	AFILLUW	WAILFUL
	TEARS UP	AFFNOSW	SAWN-OFF	AFILMOY	FOAMILY
	UPRATES	AFFOPSS	PASS OFF	AFILMPY	AMPLIFY
AEPRSUV	RAVE-UPS	AFFOPSY	PAYOFFS	AFILNPU	PAINFUL
	RAVES UP		PAYS OFF	AFILNTY	FAINTLY
AEPRSUY	YAUPERS	AFFOSSW	SAW-OFFS	AFILORW	AIRFLOW
AEPRSWY	YAWPERS	AFGGGIN	FAGGING	AFILOTX	FOXTAIL
AEPSSUV	SAVES UP	AFGGOST	FAGGOTS	AFILQUY	QUALIFY
AEPSTTU	UPSTATE	AFGHHIS	HAGFISH	AFILRTY	FRAILTY
AEQRRSU	SQUARER	AFGHINT	HAFTING	AFILSSY	SALSIFY
AEQRRTU	QUARTER	AFGHIRS	GARFISH	AFILSTU	FISTULA
AEQRSSU	SQUARES	AFGHRTU	FRAUGHT	AFILSTY	FALSITY
AEQRSUV	QUAVERS	AFGIILN	FAILING	AFIMOOS	MAFIOSO
AEQRTTU	QUARTET	AFGIINR	FAIRING	AFIMSSS	MASSIFS
AEQRUVY	QUAVERY	AFGIKLN	FLAKING	AFIMSUV	FAUVISM
AERRSST	ARRESTS	AFGILLN	FALLING	AFINNST	INFANTS
	RASTERS	AFGILMN	FLAMING	AFINORS	INSOFAR
AERRSSU	ASSURER	AFGILNO	FOALING	AFINORT	NOT FAIR
AERRSTT	STARTER		LOAFING	AFINSTU	FUSTIAN
AERSSST	ASSERTS	AFGILNR	FLARING	AFIORTW	WAIT FOR
AERSSSU	ASSURES	AFGILNT	FATLING	AFISSTY	SATISFY
AERSSTT	STATERS	AFGILNU	GAINFUL	AFISTUV	FAUVIST
	TASTERS	AFGILNY	FLAYING	AFITTUY	FATUITY
AERSSTV	STARVES	AFGILRU	FIGURAL	AFKLNRY	FRANKLY
AERSSTW	WASTERS	AFGIMNO	FOAMING	AFKLNTU	TANKFUL
AERSSTY	STAYERS	AFGIMNR	FARMING	AFKLOWY	FOLKWAY
AERSSWY	SAWYERS		FRAMING	AFKORSS	ASKS FOR
	SWAYERS	AFGIMNY	MAGNIFY	AFLLOOY	ALOOFLY
AERSTTT	TARTEST	AFGINNN	FANNING	AFLLOSW	FALLOWS
	TATTERS	AFGINNW	FAWNING	AFLLOTU	FALL OUT
AERSTTU	STATURE	AFGINRT	RAFTING		FALLOUT
AERSTTW	SWATTER	AFGINRY	FRAYING		OUTFALL
AERSTTY	YATTERS	AFGINST	FASTING	AFLLPUY	PLAYFUL
AERSTUY	ESTUARY	AFGINTT	FATTING	AFLLUWY	AWFULLY
AESSTTT	ATTESTS	AFGINTW	WAFTING	AFLMORU	FORMULA
AESSTTU	STATUES	AFGIRTY	GRATIFY	AFLMORW	WOLFRAM
AESSTTV	VASTEST	AFGLLUY	FALL GUY	AFLMOST	FLOTSAM
AESSTUV	SUAVEST		FUGALLY	AFLMRSU	ARMFULS
AESTTTU	STATUTE	AFGLNOS	FLAGONS		FULMARS
	TAUTEST	AFGLRUW	GULF WAR	AFLMSUU	FAMULUS
AFFFGIN	FAFFING	AFGMNOR	FROGMAN	AFLMTUY	MY FAULT
AFFFLLO	FALL OFF	AFHIIRS	FAIRISH	AFLNORT	FRONTAL
	FALLOFF	AFHILTW	HALF WIT	AFLNSTU	FLAUNTS
AFFGGIN	GAFFING		HALF-WIT	AFLNTUY	FLAUNTY
AFFGNOR	RANG OFF	AFHIMNU	HAFNIUM	AFLOPTT	FLATTOP
AFFGSUW	GUFFAWS	AFHINOS	FASHION	AFLORUV	FLAVOUR
AFFHIRS	RAFFISH	AFHIORS	OARFISH	AFLOTTU	FLAT OUT
AFFHLLY	FLY HALF	AFHISSW	SAWFISH		FLAT-OUT
	FLY-HALF	AFHISTT	FATTISH	AFLPSTY	FLYPAST
AFFHOST	HATS OFF	AFHISWY	FISHWAY	AFLRTUY	TRAYFUL
AFFIKRS	KAFFIRS	AFHLMRU	HARMFUL	AFMNOOT	FOOTMAN
AFFILMN	FILM FAN	AFHLNOT	NOT HALF	AFMNORT	FORMANT
AFFILOT	TAIL OFF	AFHLOOS	LOOFAHS	AFMNOST	FANTOMS
AFFILSY	FALSIFY	AFHLOTY	HAY LOFT	AFMNRTU	TURFMAN
AFFIMRS	AFFIRMS	AFHMOST	FATHOMS	AFMORRT	ART FORM
AFFIMST	MASTIFF	AFHORTW	WHAT FOR	AFMORST	FORMATS
AFFINRU	FUN FAIR	AFIIJNS	FIJIANS	AFMORTU	FARM OUT
	RUFFIAN	AFIILNS	FINIALS	AFMORTX	TAX FORM
AFFINTY	TIFFANY	AFIILNT	TAIL FIN	AFNORRT	FORTRAN
AFFIOPR	PAIR OFF	AFIILOR	AIRFOIL	AFOOSTT	TOO FAST
AFFIRST	TARIFFS	AFIILRT	AIRLIFT	AFOPRSS	PASS FOR
AFFJMPU	JAM PUFF	AFIIMOS	MAFIOSI	AFOPRSY	PAYS FOR
AFFKLOW	WALK OFF	AFIINRS	FRISIAN	AFOPRTX	FOX TRAP
AFFKMOR	MARK OFF	AFILLLL	FALL ILL	AFORRSW	FARROWS
AFFLLOR	FALL FOR	AFILLNP	PINFALL	AFORSUV	FAVOURS

AFORUWY	FOUR-WAY	AGHILNV	HALVING	AGIKLNS	SLAKING
AFOSTUU	FATUOUS	AGHILNW	WHALING	AGIKLNT	TALKING
AFPRRUW	FUR WRAP	AGHILOT	GOLIATH	AGIKLNW	WALKING
AGGGGIN	GAGGING	AGHILRS	LARGISH	AGIKLWY	GAWKILY
AGGGIJN	JAGGING	AGHILRT	ALRIGHT	AGIKMNR	MARKING
AGGGILN	LAGGING	AGHILST	ALIGHTS	AGIKMNS	MAKINGS
AGGGINN	GANGING	AGHILSU	GAULISH		MASKING
	NAGGING	AGHIMMN	HAMMING	AGIKNNR	NARKING
AGGGINR	RAGGING	AGHIMNR	HARMING		RANKING
AGGGINS	SAGGING	AGHIMNS	MASHING	AGIKNNS	SNAKING
AGGGINT	TAGGING		SHAMING	AGIKNNT	TANKING
AGGGINU	GAUGING	AGHINOX	HOAXING	AGIKNNY	YANKING
AGGGINW	WAGGING	AGHINPR	HARPING	AGIKNOS	SOAKING
AGGHHIS	HAGGISH	AGHINPS	PHASING	AGIKNOY	KAYOING
AGGHIMN	GINGHAM		SHAPING	AGIKNPR	PARKING
AGGHINN	HANGING	AGHINRS	GARNISH	AGIKNQU	QUAKING
AGGHINS	GASHING		SHARING	AGIKNRS	SARKING
AGGHISW	WAGGISH	AGHINST	HASTING	AGIKNRT	KARTING
AGGHNOV	VAN GOGH	AGIINSU	ANGUISH		KING RAT
AGGIINN	GAINING	AGHINSV	SHAVING	AGIKNSS	GASKINS
AGGIINV	GINGIVA	AGHINSW	WASHING	AGIKNST	SKATING
AGGIKNW	GAWKING	AGHINTT	AT NIGHT		STAKING
AGGILLN	GALLING	AGHINTW	THAWING		TAKINGS
AGGILNN	ANGLING	AGHIOST	GOATISH	AGILLMU	GALLIUM
AGGILNO	GAOLING	AGHJMNO	MAH-JONG	AGILLNP	PALLING
AGGILNR	GLARING	AGHJNOY	JOHN GAY	AGILLNU	LINGUAL
AGGILNZ	GLAZING	AGHKOSW	GOSHAWK	AGILLNW	WALLING
AGGILOS	LOGGIAS	AGHKRSU	GURKHAS	AGILLNY	ALLYING
AGGINNR	RANGING	AGHLLSU	GULLAHS	AGILLOR	GORILLA
AGGINNU	UNAGING	AGHLMPU	GALUMPH	AGILLSU	LUGSAIL
AGGINNW	GNAWING	AGHLOSU	GOULASH	AGILMMN	LAMMING
AGGINPS	GASPING	AGHLSTY	GHASTLY	AGILMNP	PALMING
AGGINPW	GAWPING	AGHNNOS	HANGS ON	AGILMNR	MARLING
AGGINRS	GAS RING	AGHNOTU	HANG OUT	AGILMNS	LINGAMS
AGGINRT	G RATING		HANGOUT		MALIGNS
	GRATING	AGHNPSU	HANG-UPS	AGILMNT	MALTING
AGGINRU	ARGUING		HANGS UP	AGILMNU	MAULING
AGGINRV	GRAVING	AGHNRUY	HUNGARY	AGILNNO	LOANING
AGGINRY	GRAYING	AGHNSTU	NAUGHTS	AGILNNP	PLANING
AGGINRZ	GRAZING	AGHNTUY	NAUGHTY	AGILNNS	LINSANG
AGGINSS	GASSING	AGHORTW	WARTHOG	AGILNOT	ANTILOG
AGGINST	STAGING	AGIIJLN	JAILING	AGILNPP	LAPPING
AGGINSW	SWAGING	AGIIKLT	GLAIKIT	AGILNPS	LAPSING
AGGISWW	WIGWAGS	AGIILMN	MAILING		PALINGS
AGGISZZ	ZIGZAGS	AGIILNN	NAILING		SAPLING
AGGLNOO	GO ALONG	AGIILNR	RAILING	AGILNPT	PLATING
	LONG AGO	AGIILNS	SAILING	AGILNPW	LAPWING
	LONG-AGO	AGIILNT	TAILING	AGILNPY	PLAYING
AGGMORR	GROGRAM	AGIILNW	WAILING	AGILNRY	ANGRILY
AGGMOST	MAGGOTS	AGIILPT	PIGTAIL	AGILNSS	SIGNALS
AGGMOTY	MAGGOTY	AGIILTY	AGILITY	AGILNST	LASTING
AGGNPSU	GANGS UP	AGIIMMN	MAIMING		SALTING
AGHHHIT	HIGH HAT	AGIIMMS	IMAGISM		SLATING
AGHHIIM	AIM HIGH	AGIIMOR	ORIGAMI		STALING
AGHHIMN	HANG HIM	AGIIMST	IMAGIST	AGILNSV	SALVING
AGHHINR	RAN HIGH	AGIINNP	PAINING		SLAVING
AGHHINS	HASHING	AGIINNR	INGRAIN	AGILNSY	SLAYING
AGHHIPY	HIGH PAY		RAINING	AGILNUV	VALUING
AGHHIRT	HIGH ART	AGIINPR	PAIRING	AGILOPT	GALIPOT
AGHHIWY	HIGHWAY	AGIINPT	TAIPING	AGILORS	GIRASOL
AGHHOSW	HOGWASH	AGIINRS	RAISING		GLORIAS
AGHHTUY	HAUGHTY	AGIINSV	VISAING	AGILSTY	STAGILY
AGHIILN	HAILING	AGIINTW	WAITING	AGILUYZ	GAUZILY
AGHIKNR	HARKING	AGIINTX	TAXIING	AGIMMNR	RAMMING
AGHIKNW	HAWKING	AGIINVW	WAIVING	AGIMNNN	MANNING
AGHIKSW	GAWKISH	ACIJMMN	JAMMING	AGIMNNO	MOANING
AGHILNO	HALOING	AGIJNNU	JUNGIAN	AGIMNOR	ROAMING
AGHILNS	LASHING	AGIJNRR	JARRING	AGIMNOT	MOATING
AGHILNT	HALTING	AGIJSSW	JIGSAWS	AGIMNPP	MAPPING
	LATHING	AGIKKNY	YAKKING	AGIMNPT	TAMPING
AGHILNU	HAULING	AGIKLNR	LARKING	AGIMNPV	VAMPING

AGIMNRR	MARRING	AGINSSY	SAYINGS	AHHIMNS	MISHNAH
AGIMNRS	MARGINS	AGINSTT	STATING	AHHKOOS	HOOKAHS
AGIMNRT	M RATING		TASTING	AHHLRSY	HARSHLY
	MIGRANT	AGINSTW	WASTING	AHHOPRT	HAP'ORTH
AGIMNRW	WARMING	AGINSTY	STAYING	AHIILOR	HAIR OIL
AGIMNSS	MASSING		STYGIAN	AHIILSW	SWAHILI
AGIMNST	MASTING	AGINSWY	SWAYING	AHIINPR	HAIRPIN
AGIMNSU	AMUSING	AGINTTT	TATTING	AHIINRT	THIN AIR
AGIMNTT	MATTING	AGINTTV	VATTING	AHIIPRS	AIRSHIP
AGIMSST	STIGMAS	AGINTXY	TAXYING	AHIISTX	.. HIT A SIX
AGIMSWW	WIGWAMS	AGINWWX	WAXWING	AHIKLSY	SHAKILY
AGINNNP	PANNING	AGIORSU	GIAOURS	AHIKMNS	KHAMSIN
AGINNNT	TANNING	AGIORSV	VIRAGOS	AHIKMSW	MAWKISH
AGINNOS	GAINS ON	AGIOSTU	AGOUTIS	AHIKNOS	KHOISAN
AGINNOT	ATONING	AGIOUUY	OUGUIYA	AHIKNRS	KRISHNA
AGINNOY	IN AGONY	AGIPRST	AT GRIPS	AHIKNSV	KNAVISH
AGINNPP	NAPPING	AGIRSTU	GUITARS	AHILLNT	ANT HILL
AGINNPT	PANTING	AGIRTVY	GRAVITY		ANTHILL
AGINNPW	PAWNING	AGJLMOS	LOGJAMS	AHILLST	ALL THIS
AGINNRS	SNARING	AGJLRUU	JUGULAR		TALLISH
AGINNRT	RANTING	AGJNOOR	JARGOON	AHILLTT	TALLITH
AGINNRW	WARNING	AGKMNOP	KAMPONG	AHILMMY	HAMMILY
AGINNRY	YARNING	AGLLNOO	GALLOON	AHILNPS	PLANISH
AGINNSW	AWNINGS	AGLLNOS	GALLONS	AHILNSU	HAULS IN
AGINNTW	WANTING	AGLLOPS	GALLOPS	AHILPPS	LAPPISH
AGINNWY	YAWNING	AGLLOSW	GALLOWS	AHILPPY	HAPPILY
AGINOPS	SOAPING	AGLLOTT	GLOTTAL	AHILPSY	APISHLY
AGINORR	ROARING	AGLMNOR	LONG ARM	AHILSSV	SLAVISH
AGINORS	SIGNORA	AGLMORU	GLAMOUR	AHILSTY	HASTILY
	SOARING	AGLNOOS	LAGOONS	AHIMNNS	MANNISH
AGINORT	ORATING	AGLNOOW	OWN GOAL	AHIMNNT	THIN MAN
AGINORV	VIRGOAN	AGLNORU	LANGUOR	AHIMNNU	INHUMAN
AGINOST	AGONIST	AGLNOSS	SLOGANS	AHIMNOT	MANIHOT
AGINOVW	AVOWING	AGLNOSU	LANUGOS	AHIMOPR	MORPHIA
AGINPPR	RAPPING	AGLNOSW	SANG LOW	AHIMPSS	MISHAPS
AGINPPS	SAPPING	AGLNOWY	LONG WAY	AHIMPTU	HAM IT UP
AGINPPT	TAPPING	AGLNRSU	LANGURS	AHIMRST	MITHRAS
AGINPPY	YAPPING	AGLNTUY	GAUNTLY	AHIMRSW	WARMISH
AGINPPZ	ZAPPING	AGLOOPY	APOLOGY	AHIMSWY	YAHWISM
AGINPRS	PARINGS	AGLOSSS	GLOSSAS	AHIMTUZ	AZIMUTH
	PARSING	AGMMNOS	GAMMONS	AHIMTVZ	MITZVAH
	RASPING	AGMMNSU	MAGNUMS	AHINNST	TANNISH
	SPARING	AGMNORU	ORGANUM	AHINPSS	SPANISH
AGINPRT	PARTING	AGMNOST	AMONGST	AHINPST	HAT PINS
	PRATING	AGMNSTU	MUSTANG	AHINPTY	PYTHIAN
AGINPRW	WARPING	AGMNSTY	GYMNAST	AHINRST	TARNISH
AGINPRY	PRAYING	AGMNSYY	SYNGAMY	AHINRSU	IAN RUSH
AGINPSS	PASSING	AGMOPRR	PROGRAM	AHINRSV	VARNISH
AGINPST	PASTING	AGMORRW	RAGWORM	AHINRTW	IN WRATH
AGINPSU	PAUSING	AGMORSS	ORGASMS	AHINSTT	TIN HATS
AGINPSY	SPAYING	AGMORTW	GOT WARM	AHIOPXY	HYPOXIA
AGINPTT	PATTING	AGMOSYZ	ZYGOMAS	AHIORSW	AIR SHOW
AGINPUY	YAUPING	AGMPRSU	GRAMPUS	AHIPRST	HARPIST
AGINPWY	YAWPING	AGMPSUZ	GAZUMPS	AHIPRSU	RUPIAHS
AGINRRT	R RATING	AGNNNOO	NONAGON	AHIPRSW	WARSHIP
	TARRING	AGNNOOR	ORGANON	AHIPSSW	WASPISH
AGINRRW	WARRING	AGNOQSU	QUANGOS	AHIPSTY	HAS PITY
AGINRST	GASTRIN	AGNORRT	GRANTOR	AHIPSWW	WHIPSAW
	RATINGS	AGNORSS	SARONGS	AHIPSWY	SHIPWAY
	STARING	AGNORSW	WAR SONG	AHIRSTT	TARTISH
AGINRSU	AIR GUNS	AGNORTU	RANG OUT	AHIRSTW	TRISHAW
	UGRIANS	AGNOSTU	SANG OUT		WRAITHS
AGINRSV	RAVINGS	AGNRSUY	RAY GUNS	AHISTTT	THAT'S IT!
AGINRTT	RATTING	AGOPPST	STOPGAP	AHISTTW	WHATSIT
AGINRTV	V RATING	AGORRTW	RAGWORT	AHISTWY	THIS WAY
AGINRTX	X RATING	AGORRTY	GYRATOR	AHJOTZZ	HOT JAZZ
AGINRVY	VARYING	AGORSTU	RAGOUTS	AHKLMOO	HOLM OAK
AGINRXY	X-RAYING	AGOSUYZ	AZYGOUS	AHKMOSW	MOHAWKS
AGINRZZ	RAZZING	AGRUUUY	URUGUAY	AHKNPSU	PUNKAHS
AGINSSS	ASSIGNS	AHHHISS	HASHISH	AHLLMOR	HAM ROLL
AGINSSV	SAVINGS	AHHIKSW	HAWKISH	AHLLMSU	MULLAHS

AHLLNSU	NULLAHS	AIILLNV	VILLAIN	AILMNOY	ALIMONY
AHLLOOS	HALLOOS	AIILMMN	MINIMAL	AILMNPS	PLASMIN
AHLLOST	SHALLOT	AIILMRS	SIMILAR	AILMNPT	IMPLANT
AHLLOSW	HALLOWS	AIILMRY	MILIARY	AILMNPU	IN A LUMP
	SHALLOW	AIILNNT	IN LATIN	AILMNRS	MARLINS
AHLLOTY	TALLY HO	AIILNOP	LIN PIAO	AILMOPT	OPTIMAL
	TALLY-HO	AIILNOS	LIAISON	AILMOSS	SOMALIS
AHLLPSU	PHALLUS	AIILNPR	IN APRIL	AILMPRU	PRIMULA
AHLLRST	THRALLS	AIILNPT	PINTAIL	AILMPST	PALMIST
AHLLSTU	THALLUS	AIILNPU	NAUPLII	AILMRST	MISTRAL
AHLMNPY	NYMPHAL	AIILNTU	NAUTILI	AILMSSS	MISSALS
AHLMNSY	HYMNALS	AIILNTY	LAY IN IT	AILMSSY	MISLAYS
AHLMNUY	HUMANLY	AIILORV	RAVIOLI	AILNORT	ON TRIAL
AHLMORU	HUMORAL	AIILQSU	SILIQUA	AILNOTT	IN TOTAL
AHLMOSW	OHMS I AW	AIILRTV	TRIVIAL	AILNOTY	LAY IT ON
AHLOOPS	HOOP-LAS	AIIMMNS	ANIMISM	AILNPST	PLAINTS
AHLORST	HARLOTS	AIIMNPT	TIMPANI	AILNPSX	SALPINX
AHLORWY	HOLY WAR	AIIMNRT	MARTINI	AILNPTU	NUPTIAL
AHLOSTU	LASH OUT	AIIMNST	ANIMIST	AILNPTY	INAPTLY
AHLPRSY	SHARPLY	AIIMNTU	MINUTIA		PTYALIN
AHLPSSY	SPLASHY	AIIMNTV	VITAMIN	AILNQTU	QUINTAL
AHMMMOT	MAMMOTH	AIIMPRS	IMPAIRS	AILNRSU	INSULAR
AHMNNTU	MANHUNT	AIINNRT	IN TRAIN		URINALS
AHMNOPT	PHANTOM	AIINNTW	IN TWAIN	AILNSTY	NASTILY
AHMNORS	ROMANSH	AIINNTY	INANITY		SAINTLY
AHMNORU	MAN-HOUR	AIINPRS	ASPIRIN	AILNTTY	NATTILY
AHMNORY	HARMONY		IN PAIRS	AILOPRS	POLARIS
AHMNOSS	HANSOMS		IN PARIS	AILOPST	TOPSAIL
AHMNOSW	SHOWMAN	AIINPST	PIANIST	AILOPSY	SOAPILY
AHMNRYY	HYMNARY	AIINRSS	RAISINS	AILOPTT	TALIPOT
AHMOOPS	OOMPAHS	AIINSTU	TUNISIA	AILOPTV	PIVOTAL
	SHAMPOO	AIIPSTW	WAPITIS	AILOQTU	ALIQUOT
AHMOSTU	MAHOUTS	AIISSVV	VIS-A-VIS	AILORSS	SAILORS
AHMOTTZ	MATZOTH	AIJJMMS	JIMJAMS	AILORST	TAILORS
AHMPSSU	SMASH UP	AIJLYZZ	JAZZILY	AILORTY	ORALITY
	SMASH-UP	AIJNORT	JANITOR	AILOTTU	TAIL OUT
AHMRSTU	RUSH MAT	AIKLLNY	LANKILY	AILPPRU	PUPILAR
AHNOOPR	HARPOON	AIKLMMN	MILKMAN	AILPPSY	PAY SLIP
AHNOPRS	ORPHANS	AIKLMNN	LINKMAN		PAYSLIP
AHNORSX	SAXHORN	AIKLMNS	KLANISM	AILPRSS	SPIRALS
AHNOSTW	WHAT'S ON	AIKLNSW	WALKS IN	AILPSWY	SLIPWAY
AHNOTTW	WHAT NOT	AIKLNSY	SNAKILY	AILQTUY	QUALITY
	WHATNOT	AIKLSSU	SALUKIS	AILRRVY	RIVALRY
AHNPPUY	UNHAPPY	AIKLSSY	SKYSAIL	AILRSTU	RITUALS
AHNPRXY	PHARYNX	AIKMNNS	KINSMAN	AILRSTY	TRYSAIL
AHNSSTU	SUN HATS	AIKMOOT	TOOK AIM	AILRTTU	TITULAR
	SUNHATS	AIKMSST	SAKTISM	AILRTUV	VIRTUAL
AHOORSY	HOORAYS	AIKNNPS	NAPKINS	AILSSTV	SLAVIST
AHOOSTT	SHOOT AT	AIKNPRS	PARKINS	AILSTTY	TASTILY
AHOPRTY	ATROPHY	AIKOSUY	I ASK YOU	AILSTUW	LAW SUIT
AHOPSTT	TOP HATS	AIKPRRT	PRAKRIT		LAWSUIT
AHORRSW	HARROWS	AILLMNU	LUMINAL	AIMMMUX	MAXIMUM
AHORSTT	THROATS	AILLMOP	OIL LAMP	AIMMNTU	MANUMIT
AHORSTU	AUTHORS	AILLMPU	PALLIUM	AIMMOSS	MIMOSAS
AHORTTY	THROATY	AILLMSW	SAW MILL	AIMMOST	ATOMISM
AHOSTUW	WASH OUT		SAWMILL	AIMMRSX	MARXISM
	WASHOUT	AILLMYY	MAY LILY	AIMNNOR	IRON MAN
AHPPSSU	HAS PUPS	AILLNNO	LANOLIN	AIMNNOS	AMNIONS
AHPRRTY	PHRATRY	AILLNPY	PLAINLY		MANSION
AHPSTUW	WHATS UP?	AILLNST	INSTALL		MINOANS
AHQSSUY	SQUASHY	AILLNSW	WALLS IN		ONANISM
AHRSSSU	HUSSARS	AILLORZ	ZORILLA	AIMNOPR	RAMPION
AHRSSTT	STRATHS	AILLPRS	PILLARS	AIMNOPT	MAINTOP
AHRSTTW	THWARTS	AILLPRU	PILULAR		TAMPION
AHRSTWY	SWARTHY	AILLPUV	PLUVIAL	AIMNRST	MARTINS
AIIILMT	MILITIA	AILLOSU	SQUILLA	AIMNRTV	VARMINT
AIIILNT	INITIAL	AILLSTY	SALTILY	AIMNRUU	URANIUM
AIIJMNS	JAINISM	AILLTVY	VITALLY	AIMNSTU	TSUNAMI
AIIKMNN	MANIKIN	AILMMOR	IMMORAL	AIMOPST	IMPASTO
AIILLLP	LAPILLI	AILMNNO	NOMINAL	AIMORST	AMORIST
AIILLMN	LIMINAL	AILMNOS	OSMANLI	AIMOSST	MAOISTS

AIMOSTT	ATOMIST	AJLLMOR	JAM ROLL	ALMNNUY	UNMANLY
AIMPPRU	AIR PUMP	AJLLRUY	JURALLY	ALMNOOP	LAMPOON
AIMPRRY	PRIMARY	AJLMMPU	PLUM JAM	ALMNORS	NORMALS
AIMPRST	ARMPITS	AJLNORU	JOURNAL	ALMNOSS	SALMONS
	IMPARTS	AJMNRUY	JURYMAN	ALMNOWY	WOMANLY
AIMQRSU	MARQUIS	AJMNSTU	JUST MAN	ALMNPSU	SUN LAMP
AIMRSST	TSARISM	AJMOPST	JAM POTS		SUNLAMP
AIMRSTU	ATRIUMS	AJMOSTU	JUST A MO	ALMNSUU	ALUMNUS
AIMRSTX	MARXIST	AJMPSTU	JUMPS AT	ALMORST	MORTALS
AIMSSTT	STATISM	AJNOOTT	NOT A JOT		STROMAL
AINNOOX	OXONIAN	AJNORST	TROJANS	ALMOSSW	LOW MASS
AINNOPS	SAPONIN	AJPRSTU	RAJPUTS	ALMOTTU	MULATTO
AINNORT	RAN INTO	AKKLRSY	SKYLARK	ALMRSTY	SMARTLY
AINNOST	ANOINTS	AKLLNOW	KNOW ALL	ALMSSUY	ALYSSUM
	NATIONS		KNOW-ALL		ASYLUMS
AINNSTT	INSTANT	AKLLORW	ALL WORK	ALMSTUU	UMLAUTS
AINNSTW	WANTS IN	AKLMORW	LOW MARK	ALNNSUU	ANNULUS
AINNTUY	ANNUITY	AKLNOSW	WALK-ONS	ALNOOPT	PLATOON
AINOORT	ORATION		WALKS ON	ALNOORT	ORTOLAN
AINOOTV	OVATION	AKLNOSX	KLAXONS	ALNOOSS	SALOONS
AINOPPT	APPOINT	AKLOOST	LOOKS AT	ALNOOTT	NOT A LOT
AINOPSS	PASSION	AKLOSSV	SLOVAKS	ALNOPPY	PANOPLY
AINOPTU	OPUNTIA	AKLOTTU	TALK OUT	ALNOPSY	PLAYS ON
	UTOPIAN	AKLOTUW	WALK OUT	ALNPRSU	SNARL-UP
AINORRT	RAN RIOT		WALKOUT	ALNPTUY	UNAPTLY
AINORST	IN A SORT	AKLPSUW	WALKS UP	ALNSSTU	SULTANS
	RATIONS	AKLRSTY	STARKLY	ALNSTUW	WALNUTS
AINOSTT	STATION	AKMNORU	RUN AMOK	ALNSUUU	UNUSUAL
AINOSUX	ANXIOUS	AKMNORW	WORKMAN	ALOOPRW	POOR LAW
AINOSVY	SYNOVIA	AKMNSSU	UNMASKS	ALOPPRS	POPLARS
AINPPRS	PARSNIP	AKMORST	OSTMARK	ALOPPRU	POPULAR
AINPQTU	PIQUANT	AKMORTU	MARK OUT	ALOPRRU	PARLOUR
AINPRSS	SPRAINS	AKMORUY	MARK YOU	ALOPRST	PATROLS
AINPRST	IN PARTS	AKMPRSU	MARKUPS		PORTALS
	SPIRANT	AKMQTUU	KUMQUAT	ALOPRSU	PARLOUS
AINPRTU	PURITAN	AKMRSTU	MUSK RAT	ALOPSTW	TWO LAPS
AINRRTY	TRINARY		MUSKRAT	ALOPTUY	OUTPLAY
AINRRUY	URINARY	AKNOPTT	TANK TOP		PLAY OUT
AINRSST	INSTARS	AKNORSU	KORUNAS	ALOQRRU	RORQUAL
	STRAINS	AKNORTU	OUTRANK	ALOQRSU	SQUALOR
AINRSSU	RUSSIAN	AKOOPRT	PARTOOK	ALOQSTU	LOQUATS
AINRSTT	TRANSIT	AKORRTW	ARTWORK	ALORRST	ROSTRAL
AINRSTU	NUTRIAS	AKORWWX	WAXWORK	ALORSSV	SALVORS
AINRTUY	UNITARY	AKOSSTU	ASKS OUT	ALORSTU	TORULAS
AINSSTU	SUSTAIN	AKQSSUW	SQUAWKS	ALORSTW	LAST ROW
AIOPRRT	AIRPORT	AKSSWYY	SKYWAYS	ALORTYY	ROYALTY
AIOPRSV	PAVIORS	ALLLOYY	LOYALLY	ALOSTTU	LAST OUT
AIOPRTT	PATRIOT	ALLMNPU	PULLMAN		OUTLAST
AIOPRTY	TOPIARY	ALLMORY	MORALLY	ALOSTUW	OUTLAWS
AIORRRW	WARRIOR	ALLMOSS	SLALOMS	ALOSTUY	LAYOUTS
AIORRTT	TRAITOR	ALLMOSW	MALLOWS		LAYS OUT
AIORSTV	TRAVOIS	ALLNOOW	WALLOON		OUTLAYS
AIORSUV	SAVIOUR	ALLNOTY	TONALLY	ALPPSUY	PLAYS UP
	VARIOUS	ALLNTUU	ULULANT	ALPRRSU	LARRUPS
AIOSSTT	TAOISTS	ALLOOPS	PALOLOS	ALPRSSU	PULSARS
AIOSTTW	SAW TO IT	ALLOOTX	AXOLOTL	ALPRSSW	SPRAWLS
AIPPRRS	RIPRAPS	ALLOPRY	PAYROLL	ALPSSTU	ST. PAUL'S
AIPPSST	PAPISTS	ALLOPSW	WALLOPS	ALQSTUY	SQUATLY
AIPRSST	RAPISTS	ALLORYY	ROYALLY	ALRSTUU	SUTURAL
AIPRSSW	RIPSAWS	ALLOSSW	SALLOWS	AMMORST	MARMOTS
AIPRSTX	TRAP SIX	ALLOSWW	SWALLOW	AMMRSUY	SUMMARY
AIPSSTW	SAW-PITS		WALLOWS	AMNNORS	NORMANS
AIPSTUW	WAITS UP	ALLOTTY	TOTALLY	AMNNOSW	SNOWMAN
AIRSSTT	ARTISTS	ALLOTWY	TALLOWY	AMNNOSY	ANONYMS
	STRAITS	ALLOTYY	LOYALTY	AMNNOTY	ANTONYM
	TSARIST	ALLPSUW	WALLS UP	AMNOOPR	POOR MAN
AIRSTVY	VARSITY	ALLQSSU	SQUALLS	AMNOORS	MAROONS
AISSSST	ASSISTS	ALLQSUY	SQUALLY	AMNOORT	MOONRAT
AISSTTT	STATIST	ALLRRUY	RURALLY	AMNOOTT	OTTOMAN
AISTUVY	SUAVITY	ALLRSTU	LUSTRAL	AMNOOTY	TOO MANY
AJKMNNU	JUNK MAN	ALLSUUY	USUALLY	AMNOPRY	PARONYM

114

AMNOPST	POSTMAN	AORSSTT	STATORS	BBEGINW	WEBBING
	TAMPONS	AORSSUV	SAVOURS	BBEGIRS	GIBBERS
AMNORSS	RAMSONS	AORSSUY	OSSUARY	BBEGIST	GIBBETS
	RANSOMS	AORSTTW	AT WORST	BBEGLOR	GOBBLER
AMNORST	MATRONS		TWO STAR	BBEGLOS	GOBBLES
	TRANSOM	AORSUVY	SAVOURY	BBEGOST	GOBBETS
AMNORSY	MASONRY	AOSSUYY	SAYS YOU!	BBEGRRU	GRUBBER
AMNOSTU	AMOUNTS	AOSTTUY	OUTSTAY	BBEHIOS	HOBBIES
AMNQTUU	QUANTUM	APPRRUU	PURPURA	BBEHISU	HUBBIES
AMNRTTU	TANTRUM	APPRSUW	WRAPS UP	BBEHLOS	HOBBLES
AMNSTTU	MUTANTS	APPRSUY	PAPYRUS	BBEHMOT	THE BOMB
AMNSTUU	AUTUMNS	APRSSSU	SURPASS	BBEHOOP	BOB HOPE
AMOOPRT	TAPROOM	APRSTTU	START UP	BBEIIMR	IMBIBER
AMOORSU	AMOROUS		TARTS UP	BBEIIMS	IMBIBES
AMOORXY	OXYMORA		UPSTART	BBEIKLS	KIBBLES
AMOPSTT	TOPMAST	APSSTUY	STAYS UP	BBEILNR	NIBBLER
AMOPSTU	MAPS OUT	APSTTUY	STAY PUT	BBEILNS	NIBBLES
AMORRST	MORTARS	ARSSTTU	STRATUS	BBEILOS	BILBOES
AMORRSU	ARMOURS	BBBDELO	BOBBLED		LOBBIES
AMORRSW	MARROWS	BBBEIOS	BOBBIES	BBEILOT	BIBELOT
AMORRUY	ARMOURY	BBBEIRS	BIBBERS	BBEILQU	QUIBBLE
AMORRWY	MARROWY	BBBELOS	BOBBLES	BBEIOOS	BOOBIES
AMORSSY	MORASSY	BBBELRU	BLUBBER	BBEIRRS	BRIBERS
AMPRSUW	WARM UPS	BBBELCU	BUBBLES	BBEIRRY	BRIBERY
	WARMS UP	BBBGINO	BOBBING	BBEIRTU	TUBBIER
AMRRSTY	MARTYRS	BBBINOS	BOBBINS	BBEISSU	BUSBIES
AMRSSTU	STRUMAS	BBOOIKO	BIBCOCK	BBEJORS	JOBBERS
AMRSTTU	STRATUM	BBCDEIR	CRIBBED	BBEJORY	JOBBERY
ANNOSTY	TANNOYS	BBCDELO	COBBLED	BBEKLNO	KNOBBLE
ANNOTTW	WANT NOT	BBCDELU	CLUBBED	BBEKLOS	BLESBOK
ANNRTYY	TYRANNY	BBCEIRR	CRIBBER	BBELLOY	BELL BOY
ANOOPPR	ON APPRO	BBCELOR	CLOBBER		BELLBOY
ANOOPRS	SOPRANO		COBBLER	BBELMRU	BUMBLER
ANOORST	RATOONS	BBCELOS	COBBLES	BBELMSU	BUMBLES
ANOPRRS	SPORRAN	BBCEORS	COBBERS	BBELNOR	NOBBLER
ANOPRSS	PARSONS	BBCEOSW	COBWEBS	BBELNOS	NOBBLES
ANOPRST	PATRONS	BBCGINU	CUBBING	BBELNSU	NUBBLES
ANORRSW	NARROWS	BBCINOU	BUBONIC	BBELORS	SLOBBER
ANORSSV	SOVRANS	BBCRSUY	SCRUBBY	BBELORW	WOBBLER
ANORSUU	URANOUS	BBDDEIL	DIBBLED	BBELOSW	WOBBLES
ANOTTUW	WANT OUT	BBDDERU	DRUBBED	BBELRSU	BURBLES
ANPRSTU	RUN PAST	BBDEEIT	EBB TIDE		LUBBERS
	SUN TRAP	BBDEELP	PEBBLED	BBELSTU	STUBBLE
	SUNTRAP	BBDEGLO	GOBBLED	BBEMNSU	BENUMBS
ANPRSUW	UNWRAPS	BBDEGRU	GRUBBED	BBEMORS	BOMBERS
ANRSTTU	TRUANTS	BBDEGSU	BED BUGS	BBEORRY	ROBBERY
ANRSTTY	TYRANTS		BEDBUGS	BBERRSU	RUBBERS
ANRSUWY	RUNWAYS	BBDEHLO	HOBBLED	BBERRUY	RUBBERY
AOOPPRS	APROPOS	BBDEIIM	IMBIBED	BBFGIIN	FIBBING
AOOPRTT	TAP ROOT	BBDEIKL	KIBBLED	BBGIIJN	JIBBING
	TAPROOT	BBDEILO	BILOBED	BBGIINN	NIBBING
AOORRST	ORATORS		LOBBIED	BBGIINR	BRIBING
AOORRTY	ORATORY	BBDEILR	DRIBBLE		RIBBING
AOOSTTT	TATTOOS	BBDEILS	DIBBLES	BBGIJNO	JOBBING
AOPPRRT	RAPPORT	BBDEIRS	DIBBERS	BBGILNO	LOBBING
AOPPRST	POP STAR	BBDEKNO	KNOBBED	BBGIMNO	BOMBING
AOPRRST	PARROTS	BBDEKNU	BUNK BED		MOBBING
	RAPTORS	BBDELRU	BURBLED	BBGINOO	BOOBING
AOPRRSW	SPARROW	BBDENSU	SNUBBED	BBGINOR	ROBBING
AOPRRTY	PORTRAY	BBDEOSW	SWOBBED	BBGINOS	GIBBONS
AOPRSST	PASTORS	BBDESTU	STUBBED		SOBBING
AOPRSTW	POSTWAR	BBDGINU	DUBBING	BBGINRU	RUBBING
AOPRSUV	VAPOURS	BBDINOS	DOBBINS	BBGINSU	GUBBINS
AOPRTTW	TRAP TWO	BBDINSU	DUBBINS		SUBBING
AOPSSTU	PASS OUT	BBDKSUY	DYBBUKS	BBGINTU	TUBBING
AOPSTTU	SPAT OUT	BBEELPS	PEBBLES	BBGIOSU	GIBBOUS
AOPSTUY	AUTOPSY	BBEERRS	BERBERS	BBGIOSY	BIG BOYS
	PAY-OUTS	BBEESUY	BUSY BEE	BBHIMOS	MOBBISH
	PAYS OUT	BBEESYY	BYE-BYES	BBHIOST	HOBBITS
AOQRSTU	QUARTOS	BBEFIOV	FIVE BOB	BBHIRSU	RUBBISH
AORSSST	ASSORTS	BBEGILR	GLIBBER	BBHIRTY	BY BIRTH

BBHNOOS	HOBNOBS	BCEHRTU	BUTCHER	BCISSTU	CUBISTS
BBHRSUY	SHRUBBY	BCEHSTU	BUTCHES	BCJKMUU	JUMBUCK
BBIKOSS	SKIBOBS		THE CUBS	BCKLLOU	BULLOCK
BBIKTUZ	KIBBUTZ	BCEIIKR	BRICKIE	BCKOORY	BY CROOK
BBINORS	RIBBONS	BCEIIKS	BICKIES	BCKOTTU	BUTTOCK
BBKLNOY	KNOBBLY	BCEIKRS	BICKERS	BCKOTUX	TUCK BOX
BBLLSUU	BULBULS	BCEILMO	EMBOLIC	BCKPSUU	BUCKS UP
BBLOSUU	BULBOUS	BCEILMR	CLIMBER	BCLMOOU	COULOMB
BBLOSWY	BY-BLOWS	BCEIMNO	COMBINE	BCLMRUY	CRUMBLY
BBLSTUY	STUBBLY	BCEIMOR	MICROBE	BCMOSTU	COMBUST
BBMOOTU	BOMB OUT	BCEINOZ	BENZOIC	BCNOORS	BRONCOS
BBNNOOS	BONBONS	BCEIORS	CORBIES	BCNOSTU	COBNUTS
BBNOORU	BOURBON	BCEIRRS	SCRIBER	BCOOSWY	COWBOYS
BBOOOTY	BOOT BOY	BCEIRSS	SCRIBES	BCOOTTY	BOYCOTT
BBORSTU	BURBOTS	BCEISST	BISECTS	BDDDIIR	DID BIRD
BBRSSUU	SUBURBS	BCEJOST	OBJECTS	BDDEEES	SEEDBED
BCCEEIU	ICE CUBE	BCEJSTU	SUBJECT	BDDEEIS	BEDSIDE
BCCEIIS	BICCIES	BCEKLOR	BLOCKER	BDDEEIT	BETIDED
BCCEILU	CUBICLE	BCEKLRU	BUCKLER		DEBITED
BCCEILY	BICYCLE	BCEKLSU	BUCKLES	BDDEELN	BLENDED
BCCILOU	BUCOLIC	BCEKNOS	BECKONS	BDDEEOX	DEED BOX
BCCILUY	CUBICLY	BCEKORT	BROCKET	BDDEERS	BEDDERS
BCCISUU	SUCCUBI	BCEKORU	ROEBUCK	BDDEGIN	BEDDING
BCCMOOX	COXCOMB	BCEKOSU	BUCKOES	BDDEGIR	BRIDGED
BCCMSUU	SUCCUMB	BCEKSTU	BUCKETS	BDDEIIS	BIDDIES
BCCNOOR	CORN COB	BCELLOW	COWBELL	BDDEILN	BLINDED
	CORNCOB	BCELMRU	CRUMBLE	BDDEILR	BRIDLED
BCDEEHL	BELCHED	BCELMSU	SCUMBLE	BDDEIRS	BIDDERS
BCDEEHN	BENCHED	BCELNOU	ONE CLUB	BDDEISU	BUDDIES
BCDEEIL	DECIBEL	BCELORS	CORBELS	BDDELOO	BLOODED
BCDEEKS	BEDECKS	BCEMOOS	COOMBES	BDDELOU	DOUBLED
BCDEHIR	BIRCHED	BCEMORS	COMBERS	BDDENOU	BOUNDED
BCDEHIT	BITCHED	BCEMOSY	COMES BY	BDDENOW	BED DOWN
BCDEHNU	BUNCHED	BCEMRSU	CUMBERS	BDDEOOR	BROODED
BCDEHOT	BOTCHED	BCENORU	BOUNCER	BDDEOTU	DOUBTED
BCDEHOU	DEBOUCH	BCENOSU	BOUNCES	BDDESUU	SUBDUED
BCDEIKR	BRICKED	BCEOORT	OCTOBER	BDDGIIN	BIDDING
BCDEIKS	SICKBED	BCEORSU	OBSCURE	BDDGINU	BUDDING
BCDEILM	CLIMBED	BCESTTU	BEST CUT	BDDGIOR	BIRD DOG
BCDEIOS	BODICES	BCFKORU	BUCK FOR	BDDILOR	OLD BIRD
BCDEIRS	SCRIBED	BCFLOUW	WOLF CUB	BDDISSU	DISBUDS
BCDEKLO	BLOCKED	BCFSSUU	SUBFUSC	BDDJOOS	ODD JOBS
BCDEKOR	BEDROCK	BCGIITY	BIG CITY	BDEEELP	BLEEPED
BCDEMRU	CRUMBED	BCGIKNU	BUCKING	BDEEELR	BLEEDER
BCDENOU	BOUNCED	BCGIMNO	COMBING	BDEEERR	BREEDER
BCDKORU	BURDOCK	BCGINRU	CURBING	BDEEERZ	BREEZED
BCEEEHN	BEECHEN	BCHIKOU	CHIBOUK	BDEEFIR	BRIEFED
BCEEEHS	BEECHES	BCHIMOR	RHOMBIC		DEBRIEF
	BESEECH	BCHIMTU	BIT MUCH	BDEEHOV	BEHOVED
BCEEFLU	CLUB FEE	BCHINOR	BRONCHI	BDEEHRT	BERTHED
BCEEGIR	ICEBERG	BCHIOPR	PIBROCH	BDEEILL	BELLIED
BCEEHLS	BELCHES	BCHIPTU	BITCH UP	BDEEILV	BEDEVIL
BCEEHNR	BENCHER	BCHLOTY	BLOTCHY	BDEEIMT	BED TIME
BCEEHNS	BENCHES	BCHOOSY	COSH BOY	BDEEINR	INBREED
BCEEKST	BECKETS	BCHORST	BORSCHT	BDEEIRR	BERRIED
BCEELRT	TREBLE C		BORTSCH	BDEEIRS	DERBIES
BCEEMOS	BECOMES	BCIILSY	SIBYLIC	BDEEISS	BESIDES
BCEENOS	OBSCENE	BCIINOS	BIONICS	BDEEIST	BETIDES
BCEFORY	BY FORCE	BCIISTU	BISCUIT		SIDE BET
BCEHINR	BIRCHEN	BCILMPU	PLUMBIC	BDEEKOR	BO DEREK
BCEHINT	BENTHIC	BCILNOU	LION CUB	BDEEKRU	REBUKED
BCEHIOR	BRIOCHE	BCINOOR	BORONIC	BDEELNR	BLENDER
BCEHIRS	BIRCHES		CON BRIO	BDEELNS	BLENDES
BCEHIST	BITCHES	BCINOOS	BOSONIC	BDEELOV	BELOVED
BCEHITW	BEWITCH	BCINOOX	COIN BOX	BDEELOW	ELBOWED
BCEHKTU	THE BUCK		COIN-BOX	BDEELRT	RED BELT
BCEHNSU	BUNCHES	BCINORU	RUBICON		TREBLED
BCEHORS	BROCHES	BCINORY	BYRONIC	BDEELSS	BLESSED
BCEHORT	BOTCHER	BCINSUU	INCUBUS	BDEEMRU	UMBERED
BCEHOST	BOTCHES	BCIRRSU	RUBRICS	BDEEMSU	BEMUSED
BCEHRSU	CHERUBS	BCIRTUY	BUTYRIC	BDEENPR	PREBEND

BDEENRS	BENDERS	BDELOUW	WOULD-BE	BDLOOOT	OLD BOOT		
BDEEORR	REBORED	BDELRRU	BLURRED	BDLOOSY	OLD BOYS		
BDEEORS	BEDSORE	BDELSTU	BUSTLED	BDLORWY	BLOW DRY		
	SOBERED	BDEMNNO	BONDMEN		BLOW-DRY		
BDEESTT	TEST-BED	BDEMOOR	BEDROOM	BDMNUUU	UMBUNDU		
BDEFFLU	BLUFFED		BOREDOM	BDNNOUU	UNBOUND		
BDEGHOU	BOUGHED	BDEMSTU	DUMBEST	BDNOORW	DO BROWN		
BDEGILO	OBLIGED	BDENNOU	BOUNDEN	BDNOOTU	NO DOUBT		
BDEGIOT	BIGOTED	BDENNSU	UNBENDS	BDNOOWW	BOW DOWN		
BDEGIRS	BRIDGES	BDENORU	BOUNDER		DOWN BOW		
BDEGISU	BUDGIES		REBOUND		DOWN-BOW		
BDEGLRU	BURGLED	BDENORW	BROWNED	BDNOPUU	BOUND UP		
BDEGOOT	GOOD BET	BDENORZ	BRONZED	BDNORUW	RUB DOWN		
BDEGOOY	GOODBYE	BDENOSY	BEYONDS		RUBDOWN		
BDEGSTU	BUDGETS	BDENOUW	UNBOWED	BDNOSTU	OBTUNDS		
BDEHINS	BEHINDS	BDENRSU	BURDENS	BDOOOWX	BOXWOOD		
BDEHLMU	HUMBLED	BDENSTU	SUBTEND	BDOOSTY	STOOD BY		
BDEHLOS	BEHOLDS	BDEOORR	BROODER	BDOPRSY	DROPS BY		
RDEHLSU	BLUSHED	BDEOOST	BOOSTED	BDORSWY	BYWORDS		
BDEHMTU	THUMBED	BDEOPST	BED POST	BEEEEGS	BEE GEES		
BDEHOST	HOTBEDS		BEDPOST	BEEEFIR	BEEFIER		
BDEHRSU	BRUSHED	BDEORRS	BORDERS		FREEBIE		
BDEIIRS	BIRDIES	BDEORRY	BY ORDER	BEEEFLR	FEEBLER		
BDEIKLN	DLINKED	BDEORSS	DESORBS	BEEEFTW	WEBFEET		
BDEILLO	BODE ILL	BDEORST	DEBTORS	BEEEGIS	BESIEGE		
BDEILLR	ILL-BRED	BDEORSU	ROSEBUD	BEEEHIV	BEE HIVE		
BDEILLU	BULLIED	BDEORSW	BROWSED		BEEHIVE		
BDEILNR	BLINDER	BDEORTU	DOUBTER	BEEEHNS	SHEBEEN		
	BRINDLE		OBTRUDE	BEEEIKL	BEELIKE		
BDEILOR	BROILED		REDOUBT	BEEEILN	BEELINE		
BDEILOS	BOLIDES	BDEORUY	RUDE BOY	BEEEILV	BELIEVE		
BDEILRS	BRIDLES	BDEOSTU	BEDS OUT	BEEEJLZ	JEZEBEL		
BDEILRU	BUILDER	BDERSUU	SUBDUER	BEEELPR	BLEEPER		
BDEIMMR	BRIMMED	BDESSUU	SUBDUES	BEEELST	BEETLES		
BDEIMOR	BROMIDE	BDFIILY	BIFIDLY	BEEENNZ	BENZENE		
BDEIMRU	IMBRUED	BDFIIOR	FIBROID	BEEENTW	BETWEEN		
BDEINOU	BEDOUIN	BDFIORS	FORBIDS	BEEEPRS	BEEPERS		
BDEINRS	BINDERS	BDGGINO	BODGING	BEEERSZ	BREEZES		
BDEINSU	BEDUINS	BDGGINU	BUDGING	BEEFGIN	BEEFING		
BDEIORS	BORIDES	BDGIINN	BINDING	BEEFGIT	BIG FEET		
	DISROBE	BDGINNO	BONDING	BEEFILR	FEBRILE		
BDEIORT	ORBITED	BDGIORW	BIG WORD	BEEFILS	BELIEFS		
BDEIORV	OVERBID	BDGJOOO	GOOD JOB	BEEFINT	BENEFIT		
BDEIORZ	ZEBROID	BDGLLOU	BULLDOG	BEEFIRR	BRIEFER		
BDEIOSY	DISOBEY	BDGNOOW	BOG DOWN	BEEFIRS	FRISBEE		
BDEIOWY	WIDE BOY	BDGOOOY	GOOD BOY	BEEGILL	LEGIBLE		
BDEIRSU	BRUISED	BDGOOUY	GOOD BUY	BEEGILO	OBLIGEE		
BDEISST	BED-SITS	BDHIRSY	HYBRIDS	BEEGILU	BEGUILE		
BDEISSU	SUBSIDE	BDHOOOY	BOYHOOD	BEEGINP	BEEPING		
BDEISTU	SUBEDIT	BDIILOR	OILBIRD	BEEGINU	BEGUINE		
BDEITUY	DUBIETY	BDIILOS	LIBIDOS	BEEGLSY	LEG BYES		
BDEKNOO	BOOK END	BDIIMRS	MIDRIBS	BEEGMRU	BEER MUG		
	BOOKEND	BDIISTT	TIDBITS	BEEGRSU	BURGEES		
BDEKNSU	DEBUNKS	BDIKNOS	BODKINS	BEEGRTU	BEER GUT		
BDEKOOR	BROOKED	BDILLNY	BLINDLY	BEEHLRT	BLETHER		
BDELMOO	BLOOMED	BDILPUU	BUILD UP	BEEHLST	BETHELS		
BDELMPU	PLUMBED		BUILDUP	BEEHLTU	THE BLUE		
BDELNOR	BLONDER	BDINNSU	UNBINDS	BEEHOOV	BEHOOVE		
BDELNOS	BLONDES	BDINOOR	BRIDOON	BEEHORT	THE ROBE		
BDELNOW	BEND LOW	BDINOTU	IN DOUBT	BEEHOSV	BEHOVES		
BDELNRU	BLUNDER	BDINPSU	BINDS UP	BEEHRST	SHERBET		
BDELNSU	BUNDLES	BDINRSU	SUNBIRD	BEEHRSW	HEBREWS		
BDELNTU	BLUNTED	BDINRUU	BURUNDI	BEEHRTY	THEREBY		
BDELORU	BOULDER	BDINSTU	DUSTBIN	BEEHRWY	WHEREBY		
	DOUBLER	BDIOORU	BOUDOIR	BEEHSTT	THE BEST		
BDELORW	LOWBRED	BDIOSTU	OUTBIDS	BEEHTTU	THE TUBE		
BDELOST	BOLDEST	BDIOSUU	DUBIOUS	BEEIJLU	JUBILEE		
BDELOSU	DOUBLES	BDIRSTU	DISTURB	BEEIKLW	WEBLIKE		
BDELOTT	BLOTTED	BDISSUY	SUBSIDY	BEEILLS	BELLIES		
BDELOTU	BLUE DOT	BDKLOOS	KOBOLDS	BEEILNY	BYE-LINE		
	DOUBLET	BDLLOUY	DULL BOY	BEEILTT	LET IT BE		

BEEILTU	BLUE TIE	BEGIIMT	BIG TIME	BEIIKKS	BIKKIES
BEEIMRS	BIREMES		BIG-TIME	BEIILLS	BILLIES
BEEINNZ	BENZINE	BEGILLN	BELLING	BEIILRS	RISIBLE
BEEINOT	EBONITE	BEGILLY	LEGIBLY	BEIILSV	VISIBLE
BEEINRZ	ZEBRINE	BEGILMU	BELGIUM	BEIINST	BITES IN
BEEIQTU	BE QUIET	BEGILNO	IGNOBLE	BEIIRTT	BITTIER
BEEIQUZ	BEZIQUE	BEGILNT	BELTING	BEIKLNR	BLINKER
BEEIRRS	BERRIES	BEGILNU	BLUEING	BEIKLNU	BLUE INK
BEEISST	BETISES	BEGILNY	BELYING	BEIKLOS	OBELISK
BEEISVV	BEVVIES	BEGILOS	OBLIGES	BEIKLRS	BILKERS
BEEKNOT	BETOKEN	BEGILRS	GERBILS	BEIKLRU	BULKIER
BEEKOPS	BESPOKE	BEGILST	GIBLETS	BEIKNOR	BROKE IN
BEEKRRS	BERSERK	BEGINOY	OBEYING	BEIKOOS	BOOKIES
BEEKRSU	REBUKES	BEGINRR	BRINGER	BEIKOTX	BOX KITE
BEELMMS	EMBLEMS	BEGINRW	BREWING	BEIKRRS	BRISKER
BEELMRT	TREMBLE	BEGINSS	BIGNESS	BEIKRST	BRISKET
BEELMSS	BLESS ME!	BEGINST	BESTING	BEILLST	BILLETS
BEELNNO	ENNOBLE	BEGINTT	BETTING	BEILLSU	BULLIES
BEELNUX	BENELUX	BEGIOOS	BOOGIES	BEILMNR	NIMBLER
BEELOTY	EYEBOLT	BEGIOSU	BOUGIES	BEILMOR	EMBROIL
BEELRST	TREBLES	BEGJNUU	JUNE BUG	BEILMOS	MOBILES
BEELSSS	BLESSES	BEGKOOR	GO BROKE	BEILMRS	LIMBERS
BEEMMRS	MEMBERS	BEGLLOU	GLOBULE	BEILMRT	TIMBREL
BEEMRSU	BURMESE	BEGLMRU	GRUMBLE	BEILMSU	SUBLIME
BEEMSSU	BEMUSES	BEGLNOS	BELONGS	BEILMSY	BY MILES
BEEOOST	BOOTEES	BEGLNRU	BUNGLER	BEILNOW	BOWLINE
BEEORRS	REBORES	BEGLNSU	BUNGLES	BEILNSY	BY-LINES
BEEORRU	BOURREE	BEGLOOT	BOOTLEG	BEILNTZ	BLINTZE
BEEORSV	OBSERVE	BEGLOOW	GO BELOW	BEILOQU	OBLIQUE
	OBVERSE	BEGLORY	GLORY BE!	BEILORR	BROILER
	VERBOSE	BEGLOST	GOBLETS	BEILORS	BOILERS
BEEORWY	EYEBROW	BEGLOSW	BOW LEGS	BEILRRU	BURLIER
BEEQSTU	BEQUEST		BOWLEGS	BEILRST	BLISTER
BEERRSV	REVERBS	BEGLRSU	BUGLERS		BRISTLE
BEERRSW	BREWERS		BURGLES	BEILRTT	BRITTLE
BEERRWY	BREWERY	BEGNNRU	BREN GUN	BEILRTY	LIBERTY
BEERSSU	REBUSES	BEGNOOS	BONGOES	BEILSTW	BLEWITS
BEERSTT	BETTERS	BEGNORU	BURGEON	BEILSTZ	BLITZES
BEERSTV	BREVETS	BEGNOSY	BYGONES	BEILTTU	BLUE TIT
BEERSTW	BESTREW	BEGORSU	BROGUES	BEIMNOR	BROMINE
BEERTTU	BURETTE	BEGRRSU	BURGERS	BEIMNTU	BITUMEN
BEFFIOT	BITE OFF	BEGRSSU	BURGESS	BEIMOSZ	ZOMBIES
BEFFLOW	BLEW OFF	BEHIITX	EXHIBIT	BEIMPRU	BUMPIER
BEFFLRU	BLUFFER	BEHIKNT	BETHINK	BEIMRST	TIMBERS
BEFFRSU	BUFFERS	BEHILMS	BLEMISH	BEIMRSU	IMBRUES
	REBUFFS	BEHILMT	THIMBLE	BEIMRTU	TERBIUM
BEFFSTU	BUFFETS	BEHILOS	BOLSHIE	BEINNOR	BONNIER
BEFGIIL	FILIBEG	BEHINOP	HIP BONE	BEINNOZ	BENZOIN
BEFGIRU	FIREBUG		HIPBONE	BEINNSU	BUNNIES
BEFHOOS	BEHOOFS	BEHIOST	BOTHIES	BEINORW	BROWNIE
BEFILNO	LOBE-FIN	BEHIRRT	REBIRTH	BEINOST	BONIEST
BEFILOS	FOIBLES	BEHIRSU	BUSHIER	BEINRSU	SUBERIN
BEFILRT	FILBERT	BEHLLOP	BELL HOP	BEINRTT	BITTERN
BEFILRY	BRIEFLY		BELLHOP	BEINRTU	TRIBUNE
BEFILSU	FUSIBLE	BEHLMRU	HUMBLER		TURBINE
BEFILSY	FLIES BY	BEHLMSU	HUMBLES	BEIOOST	BOOTIES
BEFINOR	BONFIRE	BEHLORT	BROTHEL	BEIORRT	ORBITER
BEFIORX	FIREBOX	BEHLOTW	BLEW HOT	BEIORSS	BOSSIER
BEFITUX	TUBIFEX	BEHLRSU	BLUSHER	BEIOSTW	BOW TIES
BEFLMRU	FUMBLER	BEHLSSU	BLUSHES	BEIOSTY	OBESITY
BEFLMSU	FUMBLES		BUSHELS	BEIQRTU	BRIQUET
BEFOORR	FORBORE	BEHMNSU	BUSHMEN	BEIRRSU	BRUISER
BEFOOTW	WEBFOOT	BEHNOPY	BY PHONE	BEIRSST	BESTIRS
BEFORRX	BRER FOX	BEHNOST	BENTHOS	BEIRSSU	BRUISES
BEFOSUX	FUSE BOX	BEHOORT	THEORBO	BEIRSTT	BITTERS
BEGGGIN	BEGGING	BEHOPRT	POT HERB	BEIRSTU	BUSTIER
BEGGIST	BIGGEST		POTHERB	BEIRTTU	TRIBUTE
BEGGISU	BUGGIES	BEHORRT	BROTHER	BEIRTVY	BREVITY
BEGGLOS	BOGGLES	BEHORST	BOTHERS	BEISSTU	BUSIEST
BEGHRRU	BURGHER	BEHORTT	BETROTH	BEISTTU	BUTTIES
		BEHRSSU	BRUSHES	BEITTWX	BETWIXT

BEJJSUU	JUJUBES	BEMNRSU	NUMBERS	BFLLOWY	BLOWFLY
BEJKOUX	JUKE BOX	BEMOORS	BOOMERS		FLYBLOW
	JUKEBOX	BEMORST	MOBSTER	BFLNOWY	FLOWN BY
BEJLMSU	JUMBLES	BEMORSY	EMBRYOS	BFLOSUX	BOXFULS
BEJLOSS	JOBLESS	BEMPRSU	BUMPERS	BGGGINU	BUGGING
BEKLOOT	BOOKLET	BEMSSUU	SUBSUME	BGGHIIS	BIGGISH
BEKLSUY	BLUE SKY	BENNOOS	NO BONES	BGGIILN	BILGING
	SKY BLUE	BENNORW	NEWBORN	BGGIILR	BIG GIRL
BEKMNOO	BOOKMEN	BENNOST	BONNETS	BGGIISW	BIGWIGS
BEKNORS	BONKERS	BENNSSU	BUNSENS	BGGILNU	BUGLING
BEKNRSU	BUNKERS	BENORRW	BROWNER		BULGING
BEKOORS	BOOKERS	BENORST	BRETONS	BGGINNU	BUNGING
BEKOOST	SET BOOK		SORBENT	BGGINOY	GOING BY
BEKOPRU	BROKE UP	BENORSU	BOURNES	BGGINSU	BIG GUNS
BEKORRS	BROKERS	BENORSZ	BRONZES	BGHHIOY	HIGHBOY
BEKRSSU	BUSKERS	BENOSSU	BONUSES	BGHILST	BLIGHTS
BELLMOT	TOM BELL	BENOSWY	NEWSBOY	BGHILTY	BLIGHTY
BELLOSU	LOBULES	BENRRSU	BURNERS	BGHINSU	BUSHING
	SOLUBLE	BENRSTU	BUNTERS	BGHINTY	BY NIGHT
BELLOSW	BELLOWS		BURNETS	BGHIOST	BIG SHOT
BELLOUV	VOLUBLE	BEOOPUZ	BOOZE-UP	BGHIRTU	BIG HURT
BELLSTU	BULLETS	BEOORST	BOOSTER	BGHISTY	BY SIGHT
BELMMRU	MUMBLER	BEOORSZ	BOOZERS	BGHMORU	HOMBURG
BELMMSU	MUMBLES	BEOORTU	BORE OUT	BGHMSUU	HUMBUGS
BELMNSU	NUMBLES	BEOPPRS	BOPPERS	BGHOORU	BOROUGH
BELMOOR	BLOOMER	BEOPRRV	PROVERB	BGHORTU	BROUGHT
BELMOPR	PROBLEM	BEOPRSU	SOBER UP	BGIIKLN	BILKING
BELMORU	MOB RULE	BEOQSUY	OBSEQUY	BGIILLN	BILLING
BELMOSU	EMBOLUS	BEOQTUU	BOUQUET	BGIILMN	LIMBING
BELMOSW	WOMBLES	BEORRSS	RESORBS	BGIILNO	BOILING
BELMPRU	PLUMBER	BEORRSW	BROWSER	BGIILNS	SIBLING
BELMRRU	RUMBLER	BEORSST	SORBETS	BGIIMNU	IMBUING
BELMRSU	LUMBERS		STROBES	BGIINNR	BRING IN
	RUMBLES	BEORSSW	BROWSES		BRINING
	SLUMBER	BEORSTT	BETTORS	BGIJNOY	BY JINGO!
BELMRTU	TUMBLER	BEORSWY	BOWYERS	BGIKLNU	BULKING
	TUMBREL		SWORE BY	BGIKLOO	LOOK BIG
BELMRTY	TREMBLY	BEOSSTT	OBTESTS	BGIKNNU	BUNKING
BELMSTU	STUMBLE	BEOSSTW	BESTOWS	BGIKNOO	BOOKING
	TUMBLES	BEPRRTU	PERTURB	BGIKNOR	BROKING
BELNOOY	BOLONEY	BEPRSUW	BREWS UP	BGIKNRU	BURKING
BELNOST	NOBLEST	BEPRTUY	PUBERTY	BGIKNSU	BUSKING
BELNOTW	BENT LOW	BEORSUU	BRUSQUE	BGILLNU	BULLING
BELNRTU	BLUNTER	BERSSTU	BUSTERS	BGILMOU	GUMBOIL
BELOOPR	BLOOPER	BERSTTU	BUTTERS	BGILNOS	GOBLINS
BELOORS	BOLEROS	BERSTUV	SUBVERT	BGILNOT	BILTONG
BELOPSU	PUEBLOS	BERSUZZ	BUZZERS		BOLTING
BELORST	BOLSTER	BERTTUY	BUTTERY	BGILNOW	BLOWING
	BOLTERS	BESSSTU	SUBSETS		BOWLING
	LOBSTER	BFFFOOS	FOBS OFF	BGILNOY	IGNOBLY
BELORSU	ROUBLES	BFFGINU	BUFFING	BGILNRU	BURLING
BELORSW	BLOWERS	BFFINOS	BOFFINS	BGILOOR	OBLIGOR
	BOWLERS	BFFKNOU	BUNK OFF	BGILOOY	BIOLOGY
BELORSY	SOBERLY	BFFLOOW	BLOW OFF	BGIMMNU	BUMMING
BELORTT	BLOTTER	BFFMOPU	BUMP OFF	BGIMNOO	BOOMING
	BOTTLER	BFFNOOU	BUFFOON	BGIMNPU	BUMPING
BELORTU	TROUBLE	BFFOSUY	BUYS OFF	BGINNOR	BRING ON
BELOSSU	BLOUSES	BFFOUZZ	BUZZ OFF	BGINNRU	BURNING
BELOSTT	BOTTLES	BFGHIIS	BIG FISH	BGINNTU	BUNTING
BELOSTU	BOLETUS	BFGIILM	BIG FILM	BGINOOT	BOOTING
BELOTUW	BLEW OUT	BFGIORU	BIG FOUR	BGINOOZ	BOOZING
BELPSTU	BELTS UP	BFGIOTX	GIFT BOX	BGINOPP	BOPPING
BELRRSU	BURLERS	BFGOOSW	FOGBOWS	BGINOPR	PROBING
BELRSTU	BLUSTER	BFHIRSU	FURBISH	BGINORS	SORBING
	BUTLERS	BFIILRS	FIBRILS	BGINORT	BRING TO
	SUBTLER	BFIINOR	FIRROIN	BGINOSS	BOSSING
BELSSTU	BUSTLES	BFIIOTT	BIT OF IT	BGINOUY	BUOYING
	SUBLETS	BFILMRU	BRIMFUL	BGINPRU	BRING UP
BEMMRSU	BUMMERS	BFIORSU	FIBROUS		BURPING
BEMNOST	ENTOMBS	BFKLOOU	BOOKFUL	BGINRRU	BURRING
BEMNOSU	UMBONES	BFLLOUW	BOWLFUL	BGINRUY	BURYING

BGINSSU	BUSSING	BILOPSU	BOILS UP	BOOPSTY	POSTBOY		
BGINSUY	BUSYING	BILORST	BRISTOL		POTBOYS		
BGINTTU	BUTTING	BILOSSU	SUBSOIL	BOORRSW	BORROWS		
BGINUZZ	BUZZING	BILOSTW	BLOWS IT	BOPSSTU	BUS STOP		
BGIORTY	BIGOTRY	BILPTUU	BUILT UP		BUS-STOP		
BGJOTUY	TOBY JUG		BUILT-UP	BOPSUUY	BUOYS UP		
BGKLOOO	LOG BOOK	BILRSTY	BRISTLY	BORRSUW	BURROWS		
	LOGBOOK	BIMNOSU	OMNIBUS	BORSTTU	TURBOTS		
BGLMRUY	GRUMBLY	BIMRSUX	BRUXISM	BORSTUU	RUBS OUT		
BGLNOOW	LONGBOW	BIMSSTU	SUBMITS	BOSTUUY	BUYS OUT		
BGLNOUW	BLOWGUN	BINNOSU	BUNIONS	BPSSTUU	BUST-UPS		
BGLOSSU	BUGLOSS	BINOOST	BONITOS		BUSTS UP		
BGMOOTU	GUMBOOT	BINORST	BRITONS	CCCDIOO	COCCOID		
BGNPSUU	BUNGS UP	BINRSTU	BURST IN	CCCEHIO	CHOC-ICE		
BGPRSUU	GRUBS UP	BINSTTU	BUTTS IN	CCCNOOT	CONCOCT		
BHIIINT	INHIBIT	BINSTUU	SUBUNIT	CCDEEHK	CHECKED		
BHIINSS	HIS NIBS	BIOORSZ	BORZOIS	CCDEENO	CONCEDE		
BHIIRST	BRITISH	BIOOSST	OBOISTS	CCDEENY	DECENCY		
BHIKOOS	BOOKISH	BIOOSUV	OBVIOUS	CCDEEOR	COERCED		
BHILLSU	BULLISH	BIOPRST	PROBITS	CCDEESU	SUCCEED		
BHILPSU	PUBLISH	BIOPRTY	PROBITY	CCDEHIL	CLICHED		
BHILSUY	BUSHILY	BIORRTW	RIBWORT	CCDEHIN	CINCHED		
BHIMORT	THROMBI	BIORSST	BISTROS	CCDEHKO	CHOCKED		
BHIMSTU	BISMUTH	BIORSTT	BISTORT	CCDEHKU	CHUCKED		
BHINRSU	BURNISH	BIOSTTW	TWO BITS	CCDEHOU	COUCHED		
BHIOORS	BOORISH	BISSSTU	SUBSIST	CCDEIIT	DEICTIC		
BHIOPSS	BISHOPS	BJLOOST	JOB LOTS	CCDEIKL	CLICKED		
BHIRSTU	BRUTISH	BJNOOSW	SNOW JOB	CCDEIKR	CRICKED		
BHLOOTW	BLOW HOT	BJORUXY	JURY BOX	CCDEIMO	COMEDIC		
BHLRSUU	BULRUSH	BKOOPSU	BOOKS UP	CCDEIOS	CODICES		
BHMORSU	RHOMBUS	BKOORWX	WORKBOX	CCDEIOT	DOCETIC		
BHNORTY	BRYTHON	BLLNTUY	BLUNTLY	CCDEKLO	CLOCKED		
BHPRSUU	BRUSH UP	BLLOSUU	BULLOUS	CCDEKLU	CLUCKED		
	BRUSHUP	BLLOSUY	SOLUBLY	CCDEKOR	CROCKED		
BIIKNS	BIKINIS	BLLOUVY	VOLUBLY	CCDELOU	OCCLUDE		
BIIKLOT	KILOBIT	BLMOOSS	BLOSSOM	CCDENOS	SCONCED		
BIILLNO	BILLION	BLMOSSY	SYMBOLS	CCDENOU	CONDUCE		
BIILMRU	LIBRIUM	BLNOORW	LOW BORN	CCDEOST	DECOCTS		
BIILNTU	BUILT-IN		LOWBORN	CCDHIIL	CICHLID		
	INBUILT	BLNOOSU	BLOUSON	CCDIILO	CODICIL		
BIILOSU	BILIOUS	BLNOPUW	BLOWN UP	CCDIIOR	CRICOID		
BIILSVY	VISIBLY	BLNOSTU	UNBOLTS	CCDILOY	CYCLOID		
BIILTTY	BITTILY	BLOOOTX	TOOL BOX	CCDKLOU	CUCKOLD		
BIIMNOU	NIOBIUM		TOOLBOX	CCDNOOR	CONCORD		
BIIMNSU	MINIBUS	BLOOQUY	OBLOQUY	CCDNOTU	CONDUCT		
BIINORT	IN ORBIT	BLOORWW	LOWBROW	CCEEHKR	CHECKER		
BIINOTT	BIT INTO	BLOOSWY	LOWBOYS	CCEEHRS	CRECHES		
BIINRTU	RUB IT IN	BLOOTUW	BLOW OUT		SCREECH		
BIINTTY	TINY BIT		BLOWOUT	CCEEILN	LICENCE		
BIISSTV	VIBISTS		BOWL OUT	CCEEINS	SCIENCE		
BIISTTT	TITBITS	BLOPSTU	SUBPLOT	CCEEIRV	CREVICE		
BIJNOSU	SUBJOIN	BLOPSUW	BLOWS UP	CCEELRY	RECYCLE		
BIKLLUY	BULKILY		BLOWUPS	CCEENRY	RECENCY		
BIKLNOT	INKBLOT	BMNOOST	BON MOTS	CCEEORS	COERCES		
BIKLRSY	BRISKLY	BMNOOSU	UNBOSOM	CCEERSY	SECRECY		
BIKMNPU	BUMPKIN	BMOOORX	BOXROOM	CCEGNOY	COGENCY		
BIKNSSU	BUSKINS	BMOOSTT	BOTTOMS	CCEHIKN	CHECK IN		
BILLMSU	BULLISM	BMOOSTY	TOMBOYS		CHICKEN		
BILLNOU	BULLION	BMORSTY	BY STORM		IN CHECK		
BILLOPX	PILL BOX	BNNRSUU	SUNBURN	CCEHILS	CLICHES		
	PILLBOX	BNORSSU	SUBORNS	CCEHINO	CONCHIE		
BILLOSW	BILLOWS	BNORSUU	BURNOUS	CCEHINS	CINCHES		
BILLOWY	BILLOWY	BNORSWY	SWORN BY	CCEHIOR	CHOICER		
BILMNOO	IN BLOOM	BNORTUU	BURN OUT		CHOREIC		
BILMPUY	BUMPILY	BNOSSUW	SUNBOWS	CCEHIOS	CHOICES		
BILMRTU	TUMBRIL	BNOSTTU	BUTTONS	CCEHKLU	CHUCKLE		
BILNNOY	BONNILY	BNPRSUU	BURN-UPS	CCEHKPU	CHECK UP		
BILNORU	BURN OIL	BNRSTUY	BY TURNS		CHECKUP		
BILNOTU	BOTULIN	BOOOPRY	POOR BOY	CCEHLOS	CLOCHES		
BILNOTW	BLOWN IT	BOOPSTX	POSTBOX	CCEHNOS	CONCHES		
BILOOYZ	BOOZILY			CCEHORT	CROCHET		

CCEHOSU	COUCHES	CCILNOO	COLONIC	CDEEEIV	DECEIVE
CCEIIKP	ICE PICK	CCILNOU	COUNCIL	CDEEEJT	EJECTED
CCEIILS	ICICLES	CCILOOP	PICCOLO	CDEEELT	ELECTED
CCEIIRT	ICTERIC	CCILSTY	CYCLIST	CDEEEPR	PRECEDE
CCEIKOR	COCKIER	CCIMOTY	MYCOTIC	CDEEERR	DECREER
CCEIKOS	COCKIES	CCINOTV	CONVICT	CDEEERS	DECREES
CCEIKRT	CRICKET	CCIOORS	SIROCCO		RECEDES
CCEILNU	NUCLEIC	CCIOPTU	OCCIPUT		SECEDER
CCEILPT	P-CELTIC	CCIPRTY	CRYPTIC	CDEEERT	ERECTED
CCEILRR	CIRCLER	CCIRSUY	CIRCUSY	CDEEESS	SECEDES
CCEILRS	CIRCLES	CCKLNOO	CLOCK ON	CDEEESX	EXCEEDS
	CLERICS	CCKOOSU	CUCKOOS	CDEEFHT	FETCHED
CCEILRT	CIRCLET	CCKOPSU	COCKS UP	CDEEFII	EDIFICE
CCEILST	CELTICS	CCLOSTU	OCCULTS	CDEEFKL	FLECKED
CCEILSY	CYCLISE	CCMOOOR	MOROCCO	CDEEFLT	DEFLECT
CCEILTU	CUTICLE	CCNOOOS	COCOONS	CDEEFST	DEFECTS
CCEILYZ	CYCLIZE	CCNOOTU	COCONUT	CDEEHIP	CEPHEID
CCEINOR	CORNICE	CCNORSU	CONCURS	CDEEHIS	DEHISCE
CCEINOS	CONCISE	CCNOSSU	CONCUSS	CDEEHLW	WELCHED
CCEINOT	CONCEIT	CCOOORS	ROCOCOS	CDEEHMS	SCHEMED
CCEINRT	CENTRIC	CCORSUU	SUCCOUR	CDEEHNW	WENCHED
CCEIOPP	COPPICE	CCORSUY	SUCCORY	CDEEHOR	COHERED
CCEIOPT	ECTOPIC	CCOSSTU	STUCCOS	CDEEHPR	PERCHED
CCEIPST	SCEPTIC	CDDDEEI	DECIDED	CDEEHRT	RETCHED
CCEKLOR	CLOCKER	CDDDEEO	DECODED	CDEEHRU	EUCHRED
CCEKLOS	COCKLES	CDDDEEU	DEDUCED	CDEEIIT	EIDETIC
CCEKNOY	COCKNEY	CDDDESU	SCUDDED	CDEEILN	DECLINE
CCEKOPS	COCKPS	CDDEEEI	DECREED	CDEEILP	PEDICEL
CCEKORT	CROCKET		RECEDED		PEDICLE
CCELLOT	COLLECT	CDDEEES	SECEDED	CDEEIMN	ENDEMIC
CCELNOY	CYCLONE	CDDEEIR	DECIDER	CDEEINO	CODEINE
CCELNUY	LUCENCY		DECRIED	CDEEINT	ENTICED
CCELRSY	CYCLERS	CDDEEIS	DECIDES	CDEEINV	EVINCED
CCEMNOO	COMECON	CDDEEKO	DECOKED	CDEEIOS	DIOCESE
CCENNOR	CONCERN	CDDEENO	ENCODED	CDEEIOV	DEVOICE
CCENNOT	CONNECT	CDDEENS	DESCEND	CDEEIPR	PIERCED
CCENOPT	CONCEPT		SCENDED	CDEEIRR	DECRIER
CCENORT	CONCERT	CDDEEOR	DECODER	CDEEIRS	DECRIES
CCENOSS	SCONCES	CDDEEOS	DECODES	CDEEIRT	RECITED
CCENOTV	CONVECT	CDDEEOY	DECOYED	CDEEIST	DECEITS
CCEOOTT	COCOTTE	CDDEERU	REDUCED	CDEEISV	DEVICES
CCEORRT	CORRECT	CDDEESU	DEDUCES	CDEEISX	EXCISED
CCERTUW	CREW CUT		SEDUCED	CDEEITV	EVICTED
CCESSSU	SUCCESS	CDDEEUW	CUDWEED	CDEEITX	EXCITED
CCFIRUY	CRUCIFY	CDDEHIN	CHIDDEN	CDEEKLR	CLERKED
CCGHINO	GNOCCHI	CDDEHIT	DITCHED	CDEEKLS	DECKLES
CCGIKNO	COCKING	CDDEHRU	CHUDDER	CDEEKOS	DECOKES
CCGILNY	CYCLING	CDDEILM	MIDDLE C	CDEEKPS	SPECKED
CCHHRUY	CHURCHY	CDDEINU	INDUCED	CDEEKRW	WRECKED
CCHIKNU	CHUCK IN	CDDEISU	CUDDIES	CDEELPU	DECUPLE
CCHIKTU	CHUCK IT	CDDELOR	CODDLER	CDEELSU	SECLUDE
CCHIMOR	CHROMIC	CDDELOS	CODDLES	CDEELUX	EXCLUDE
CCHINOR	CHRONIC		SCOLDED	CDEENOR	ENCODER
CCHIORY	CHICORY	CDDELOU	CLOUDED		ENCODED
CCHIPSU	HICCUPS	CDDELSU	CUDDLES	CDEENOS	ENCODES
CCHIPSY	PSYCHIC	CDDEORW	CROWDED	CDEENRT	CENTRED
CCHKLOS	SCHLOCK	CDDESTU	DEDUCTS		RED CENT
CCHKPUU	CHUCK UP	CDDIIIO	DIDICOI	CDEENST	DESCENT
CCHNRSU	SCRUNCH	CDDIIOS	DISCOID		SCENTED
CCHNRUY	CRUNCHY	CDDIIRU	DRUIDIC	CDEEOPR	PROCEED
CCIIILS	SILICIC	CDDIKOP	PIDDOCK	CDEEORV	COVERED
CCIILNS	CLINICS	CDDIORS	DISCORD	CDEEORW	COWERED
CCIILPR	CIRCLIP	CDDKORU	RUDDOCK	CDEEOST	CESTODE
CCIINPS	PICNICS	CDDKORY	DRY DOCK	CDEEOTV	COVETED
CCIIRST	CRITICS	CDEEEFL	FLEECED	CDEERRU	REDUCER
CCIIRTU	CIRCUIT	CDEEEFN	DEFENCE	CDEERST	CRESTED
CCIKLNO	CLOCK IN	CDEEEHK	CHEEKED	CDEERSU	REDUCES
CCIKLOW	COWLICK	CDEEEHL	LEECHED		RESCUED
CCIKLOY	COCKILY	CDEEEHP	CHEEPED		SECURED
	COLICKY	CDEEEHR	CHEERED		SEDUCER
CCIKOPT	COCKPIT	CDEEEHS	CHEESED	CDEERSW	SCREWED

CDEESSU	SEDUCES
CDEESSY	ECDYSES
CDEESTT	DETECTS
CDEESUX	EXCUSED
CDEFFHU	CHUFFED
CDEFFIO	COIFFED
CDEFFOS	SCOFFED
CDEFFSU	SCUFFED
CDEFHIL	FILCHED
CDEFIIT	DEFICIT
CDEFIKL	FLICKED
CDEFINO	CONFIDE
CDEFKLO	FLOCKED
CDEFKOR	DEFROCK
CDEFNTU	DEFUNCT
CDEFOSU	DEFOCUS
CDEGGHU	CHUGGED
CDEGGLO	CLOGGED
CDEGHOU	COUGHED
CDEGIKN	DECKING
CDEGINR	CRINGED
CDEGINU	EDUCING
CDEGLOT	GET COLD
CDEGLSU	CUDGELS
CDEGORS	CODGERS
CDEHHIT	HITCHED
CDEHHNU	HUNCHED
CDEHIIL	CEILIDH
CDEHIIN	ICH DIEN
CDEHIKO	HOICKED
CDEHILL	CHILLED
CDEHILP	DELPHIC
CDEHINO	HEDONIC
CDEHINP	PINCHED
CDEHINW	WINCHED
CDEHIOW	COWHIDE
CDEHIPP	CHIPPED
CDEHIPR	CHIRPED
CDEHIPT	PITCHED
CDEHIRR	CHIRRED
CDEHIST	DITCHES
CDEHISU	DUCHIES
CDEHKOS	SHOCKED
CDEHKSU	SHUCKED
CDEHLNU	LUNCHED
CDEHLNY	LYNCHED
CDEHLOT	CLOTHED
	THE COLD
CDEHLRU	LURCHED
CDEHMMU	CHUMMED
CDEHMNU	MUNCHED
CDEHMOO	MOOCHED
CDEHMOP	CHOMPED
CDEHNOT	NOTCHED
CDEHNPU	PUNCHED
CDEHNRU	CHUNDER
	CHURNED
CDEHOPP	CHOPPED
CDEHOPU	POUCHED
CDEHORW	CHOWDER
	COWHERD
CDEHOSU	DOUCHES
CDEHOTU	TOUCHED
CDEHOUV	VOUCHED
CDEHPSY	PSYCHED
CDEHRRU	CHURRED
CDEHRSU	CRUSHED
CDEHSSU	DUCHESS
CDEHSTY	SCYTHED
CDEIIKR	DICKIER
CDEIIMR	DIMERIC

CDEIINS	INCISED
	INDICES
CDEIINT	INCITED
CDEIIST	DEISTIC
CDEIISU	SUICIDE
CDEIKLN	CLINKED
CDEIKLP	PICKLED
CDEIKLS	SICKLED
	SLICKED
CDEIKMS	MEDICKS
CDEIKNS	DICKENS
	SNICKED
CDEIKPR	PRICKED
CDEIKRR	DERRICK
CDEIKRS	DICKERS
CDEIKRT	TRICKED
CDEIKRU	DUCKIER
CDEIKRW	WRICKED
CDEIKST	STICKED
CDEIKSY	DICKEYS
CDEILLO	COLLIDE
CDEILMO	MELODIC
CDEILNU	INCLUDE
	NUCLIDE
CDEILOP	POLICED
CDEILPP	CLIPPED
CDEILPS	SPLICED
CDEILSU	SLUICED
CDEILTU	DUCTILE
CDEIMNO	DEMONIC
CDEIMOR	DORMICE
CDEIMOS	MEDICOS
CDEIMOT	DEMOTIC
CDEIMPR	CRIMPED
CDEIMPU	PUMICED
CDEIMSU	MISCUED
CDEINOS	SECONDI
CDEINOT	CTENOID
	D-NOTICE
	NOTICED
CDEINRS	CINDERS
	DISCERN
	RESCIND
CDEINRU	INDUCER
CDEINRY	CINDERY
CDEINSU	INCUDES
	INDUCES
CDEIOPT	PICOTED
CDEIOPZ	ZIP CODE
CDEIORT	CORDITE
CDEIORV	DIVORCE
CDEIPRS	CRISPED
CDEIPRT	PREDICT
CDEIPST	DEPICTS
CDEIRRU	CURRIED
CDEIRST	CREDITS
	DIRECTS
CDEIRSU	CRUISED
CDEIRTV	VERDICT
CDEISST	DISSECT
CDEISSY	ECDYSIS
CDEKKNO	KNOCKED
CDEKLNO	CLONKED
CDEKLOW	WEDLOCK
CDEKLPU	PLUCKED
CDEKMOS	SMOCKED
CDEKOOR	CROOKED
CDEKOPT	TOP DECK
CDEKORS	DOCKERS
CDEKOST	DOCKETS
	STOCKED

CDEKOTW	WET DOCK
CDEKRTU	TRUCKED
CDELLOU	COLLUDE
CDELLRY	DRY CELL
CDELLSU	SCULLED
CDELMPU	CLUMPED
CDELMSU	MUSCLED
CDELMTU	MULCTED
CDELNOO	CONDOLE
CDELNOY	CONDYLE
CDELOOR	COLORED
CDELORS	SCOLDER
CDELOST	COLDEST
CDELOSW	SCOWLED
CDELOTT	CLOTTED
CDELOTU	CLOUTED
CDELOUY	DOUCELY
CDELRSU	CURDLES
CDELRUY	CRUDELY
CDEMMNO	COMMEND
CDEMMOO	COMMODE
CDEMMSU	SCUMMED
CDEMNNO	CONDEMN
CDEMORU	DECORUM
CDEMPRU	CRUMPED
CDENNOO	CONDONE
CDENNOT	CONTEND
CDENOOR	CROONED
CDENOOS	SECONDO
CDENOPU	POUNCED
CDENORS	SCORNED
CDENORT	NET CORD
CDENORW	CROWNED
CDENOSS	SECONDS
CDENOTU	COUNTED
CDEOOPP	COPEPOD
CDEOOPS	SCOOPED
CDEOOPT	CO-OPTED
CDEOORR	CORRODE
CDEOORT	COTE DOR
CDEOORV	VOCODER
CDEOOST	SCOOTED
CDEOOTV	DOVECOT
CDEOPPR	CROPPED
CDEOPRU	PRODUCE
CDEORRS	CORDERS
	RECORDS
CDEORSS	CROSSED
CDEORSU	COURSED
	SCOURED
CDEORTU	COURTED
CDEOSSU	ESCUDOS
CDEOSTU	SCOUTED
CDEPRSU	SPRUCED
CDERSTU	CRUDEST
	CRUSTED
CDFHIOS	CODFISH
CDFIILU	FLUIDIC
CDGHIIN	CHIDING
CDGHOTU	GO DUTCH
CDGIKNO	DOCKING
CDGIKNU	DUCKING
CDGILNO	CODLING
CDGINNO	CONDIGN
CDGINOR	CORDING
CDGINTU	DUCTING
CDGLOOT	GOT COLD
CDHIINT	CHINDIT
CDHIIST	DISTICH
CDHILLY	CHILDLY
CDHILOS	COLDISH

CDHIOOR	CHOROID	CEEFSSU	FESCUES	CEEIPRS	PIERCES
CDHIORS	ORCHIDS	CEEGINR	GENERIC		PRECISE
CDHIPTY	DIPTYCH	CEEGINT	GENETIC		RECIPES
CDHLOOP	COP HOLD	CEEGINU	EUGENIC	CEEIPRT	RECEIPT
CDIIILP	LIPIDIC	CEEGKOS	GECKOES	CEEIPRU	EPICURE
CDIIIOT	IDIOTIC	CEEGLLO	COLLEGE	CEEIPSS	SPECIES
CDIILLY	IDYLLIC	CEEGLNT	NEGLECT	CEEIRRT	RECITER
CDIINOR	CRINOID	CEEGLOR	EL GRECO	CEEIRST	RECITES
CDIINOT	DICTION	CEEGLOU	ECLOGUE	CEEIRSV	SERVICE
CDIINST	INDICTS	CEEGNRY	REGENCY	CEEIRTX	EXCITER
CDIINWY	ICY WIND	CEEGORT	CORTEGE	CEEISSX	EXCISES
CDIKLNO	OLD NICK	CEEHILN	ELENCHI	CEEISTX	EXCITES
CDILLOO	COLLOID	CEEHILS	HELICES	CEEJORT	EJECTOR
CDILLUY	LUCIDLY		LICHEES	CEEJRST	REJECTS
CDIMMOU	MODICUM	CEEHILV	VEHICLE	CEEKLPS	SPECKLE
CDIMNOO	MONODIC	CEEHIMS	CHEMISE	CEEKOSY	SOCKEYE
CDIMSTU	DICTUMS	CEEHINS	CHINESE	CEEKPRS	PECKERS
CDINORS	NORDICS	CEEHIOR	CHEERIO	CEEKRRW	WRECKER
CDINORW	IN CROWD	CEEHIRT	ETHERIC	CEELLLU	CELLULE
CDINOSY	SYNODIC		HERETIC	CEELLNO	COLLEEN
CDINOTU	CONDUIT	CEEHKLR	HECKLER	CEELMNT	CLEMENT
CDINSTU	INDUCTS	CEEHKLS	HECKLES	CEELMOW	WELCOME
CDIOSTY	CYSTOID	CEEHKST	KETCHES	CEELNOS	ENCLOSE
CDIOTUV	OVIDUCT	CEEHLNO	ECHELON	CEELNRS	CRENELS
CDIRTUY	CRUDITY	CEEHLRS	LECHERS	CEELNRT	LECTERN
CDISSSU	DISCUSS	CEEHLRW	WELCHER	CEELNRU	LUCERNE
CDKNNOU	DUNNOCK	CEEHLRY	LECHERY	CEELORS	CREOLES
CDKNOSU	UNDOCKS	CEEHLSW	WELCHES	CEELORT	ELECTOR
CDKOPRS	DR. SPOCK	CEEHLSY	LYCHEES	CEELOSU	COULEES
CDLOOOT	TOO COLD	CEEHMRS	SCHEMER	CEELRSU	RECLUSE
CDLOOPY	LYCOPOD	CEEHMSS	SCHEMES	CEELRTU	LECTURE
CDLOOTU	OUT COLD	CEEHNRW	WENCHER	CEELRTY	ERECTLY
CDMNOOS	CONDOMS	CEEHNST	TENCHES	CEELSST	SELECTS
CDNOORS	CONDORS	CEEHNSW	WENCHES	CEELTTU	LETTUCE
	CORDONS	CEEHORS	COHERES	CEEMNRU	CERUMEN
CDNORWY	CRY DOWN	CEEHORT	TROCHEE	CEEMNRW	CREWMEN
CDNOTUW	CUT DOWN	CEEHPRS	PERCHES	CEEMNST	CEMENTS
CDOOOPT	OCTOPOD	CEEHPRU	CHEER UP	CEEMOPR	COMPEER
CDOORST	DOCTORS	CEEHQRU	CHEQUER		COMPERE
CDOOTUW	WOODCUT	CEEHQSU	CHEQUES	CEEMOPT	COMPETE
CDOPRTU	PRODUCT	CEEHRST	RETCHES	CEEMRRS	MERCERS
CDOSTUY	CUSTODY	CEEHRSU	EUCHRES	CEEMRRY	MERCERY
CEEEFLS	FLEECES	CEEHRSW	CHEWERS	CEENNOV	CONVENE
CEEEHLS	LEECHES	CEEHSSW	ESCHEWS	CEENOPT	POTENCE
CEEEHRR	CHEERER	CEEIJOR	REJOICE	CEENORS	ENCORES
CEEEHSS	CHEESES	CEEIKNT	NECKTIE	CEENPRT	PER CENT
CEEEINP	EPICENE	CEEILLM	MICELLE	CEENRSS	CENSERS
CEEEIRV	RECEIVE	CEEILNO	CINEOLE		SCREENS
CEEEKNW	EWE-NECK	CEEILNR	RECLINE	CEENRST	CENTERS
CEEELST	CELESTE	CEEILNS	LICENSE		CENTRES
CEEENSS	ESSENCE		SELENIC	CEENRSU	CENSURE
	SENESCE		SILENCE	CEENRSY	SCENERY
CEEEPRR	CREEPER	CEEILNU	LEUCINE	CEEOPTY	ECOTYPE
CEEERST	SECRETE	CEEILPS	ECLIPSE	CEEORRT	ERECTOR
CEEERTX	EXCRETE	CEEILRT	RETICLE	CEEORRV	RECOVER
CEEETUX	EXECUTE		TIERCEL	CEEPPRT	PERCEPT
CEEFFNO	OFFENCE	CEEILSS	ICELESS		PRECEPT
CEEFFOS	COFFEES	CEEILSV	VESICLE	CEEPPRU	CREEP UP
CEEFFST	EFFECTS	CEEIMNO	MIOCENE		PREPUCE
CEEFHLS	FLECHES	CEEIMNT	CENTIME	CEEPRSS	PRECESS
CEEFHRT	FETCHER	CEEIMRS	MERCIES	CEEPRST	RESPECT
CEEFHST	FETCHES	CEEIMST	EMETICS		SCEPTRE
CEEFILO	ICE FLOE	CEEINNS	INCENSE		SPECTRE
CEEFINN	FENCE IN	CEEINPR	CREEP IN	CEEPRTX	EXCERPT
CEEFIRR	FIERCER	CEEINRS	SINCERE	CEEPSTX	EXCEPTS
CEEFKLR	FRECKLE	CEEINRT	ENTERIC		EXPECTS
CEEFLRT	REFLECT	CEEINRV	CERVINE	CEERRSU	RESCUER
CEEFNNS	FENNECS	CEEINSV	EVINCES		SECURER
CEEFNOR	ENFORCE	CEEIOPT	PICOTEE	CEERRSW	SCREWER
CEEFPRT	PERFECT	CEEIORT	COTERIE	CEERSST	RESECTS
	PREFECT				SECRETS

CEERSSU	RESCUES	CEGILNY	GLYCINE	CEHKORS	CHOKERS
	SECURES	CEGIMNO	GENOMIC		SHOCKER
CEERSUX	EXCUSER	CEGINNS	CENSING	CEHKRSU	SHUCKER
CEERTTU	CURETTE	CEGINRS	CRINGES	CEHKSTY	SKETCHY
CEESSUX	EXCUSES	CEGINRW	CREWING	CEHLMSU	MULCHES
CEETTUV	CUVETTE	CEGIORT	ERGOTIC	CEHLNNU	CHUNNEL
CEFFIOR	OFFICER	CEGLNOO	COLOGNE	CEHLNRY	LYNCHER
CEFFIOS	COIFFES	CEGLOOY	ECOLOGY	CEHLNSU	LUNCHES
	OFFICES	CEGLOSU	GLUCOSE	CEHLNSY	LYNCHES
CEFFISU	SUFFICE	CEGNORS	CONGERS	CEHLNTY	LYNCHET
CEFFLSU	SCUFFLE	CEGNORY	CRYOGEN	CEHLORT	CHORTLE
CEFFMOO	COME OFF	CEGNOST	CONGEST	CEHLOST	CLOTHES
CEFFORS	COFFERS	CEGNRUY	URGENCY	CEHLPSS	SCHLEPS
	SCOFFER	CEGNSTY	CYGNETS	CEHLQSU	SQUELCH
CEFGINN	FENCING	CEGOORS	SCROOGE	CEHLRRU	LURCHER
CEFHILS	FILCHES	CEGORRS	GROCERS	CEHLRSU	LURCHES
CEFHILY	CHIEFLY	CEGORRY	GROCERY	CEHMNRU	MUNCHER
CEFHINS	FINCHES	CEGORSU	SCOURGE	CEHMNSU	MUNCHES
CEFHPTU	FETCH UP	CEHHIRS	CHERISH	CEHMOOR	MOOCHER
CEFIILT	FICTILE	CEHHIRT	HITCHER	CEHMOOS	MOOCHES
CEFIIOR	ORIFICE	CEHHIST	HITCHES	CEHMOOW	HOW COME?
CEFIITV	FICTIVE	CEHHNSU	HUNCHES	CEHMORS	CHROMES
CEFIKLR	FLICKER	CEHHSTU	HUTCHES	CEHNOOP	HEN COOP
CEFILNT	INFLECT	CEHIILS	CHILIES	CEHNORV	CHEVRON
CEFILRU	LUCIFER	CEHIIMN	CHIME IN	CEHNOSS	CHOSENS
CEFIMOR	COMFIER	CEHIINR	HIRCINE	CEHNOST	NOTCHES
CEFINNO	CONFINE	CEHIINT	THIN ICE	CEHNPRU	PUNCHER
CEFINOR	CONIFER	CEHIKNT	KITCHEN	CEHNPSU	PUNCHES
	FIR CONE		THE NICK	CEHNRTU	CHUNTER
	IN FORCE		THICKEN	CEHNSUU	EUNUCHS
CEFINST	INFECTS	CEHIKPS	PECKISH	CEHNTUY	CHUTNEY
CEFIPSY	SPECIFY	CEHIKRT	THICKER	CEHOOPS	POOCHES
CEFIRTY	CERTIFY	CEHIKTT	THICKET	CEHOORS	CHOOSER
	RECTIFY	CEHILNO	CHOLINE	CEHOORT	CHEROOT
CEFKLLO	ELF-LOCK		HELICON	CEHOOSS	CHOOSES
CEFKLOT	FETLOCK	CEHILNS	LICHENS	CEHOPPR	CHOPPER
CEFKLRY	FRECKLY	CEHILRV	CHERVIL	CEHOPRS	PORCHES
CEFLNOU	FLOUNCE	CEHILSS	CHISELS	CEHOPSU	POUCHES
CEFLNUY	FLUENCY	CEHIMNR	RICH MEN	CEHORST	HECTORS
CEFLOSS	FO'C'SLES	CEHIMNY	CHIMNEY		ROCHETS
CEFMORY	COMFREY	CEHIMOR	HOMERIC		TORCHES
CEFNOOR	FOR ONCE	CEHIMOS	ECHOISM		TROCHES
CEFNORS	CONFERS	CEHIMOZ	CHEZ MOI	CEHORSZ	SCHERZO
CEFNOSS	CONFESS	CEHIMRS	CHIMERS	CEHORTU	RETOUCH
CEFNOSU	CONFUSE	CEHIMST	CHEMIST		TOUCHER
CEFNOTU	CONFUTE	CEHINPR	PHRENIC	CEHORTW	WOTCHER
CEFOPRS	FORCEPS		PINCHER	CEHORUV	VOUCHER
CEFORRT	CROFTER	CEHINPS	PINCHES	CEHOSTU	TOUCHES
CEFORSS	FRESCOS	CEHINRT	CITHERN	CEHOSUV	VOUCHES
CEFOSSU	FOCUSES	CEHINRW	WINCHER	CEHOTUW	CHEW OUT
CEFRSUW	CURFEWS	CEHINST	ETHNICS	CEHPRSY	CYPHERS
CEFSSUU	FUCUSES	CEHINSU	ECHINUS	CEHPSSY	PSYCHES
CEGGHIR	CHIGGER	CEHINSW	WINCHES	CEHRRSU	CRUSHER
CEGGIOR	GEORGIC	CEHIOPS	HOSPICE	CEHRSSU	CRUSHES
CEGGPSU	EGG CUPS	CEHIORR	RICH ORE	CEHRSTT	STRETCH
	EGGCUPS	CEHIORS	HEROICS	CEHSSTY	SCYTHES
CEGHINO	ECHOING	CEHIOTV	CHEVIOT	CEIIJRU	JUICIER
CEGHINT	ETCHING	CEHIPPR	CHIPPER	CEIIKNR	ICE RINK
CEGHINW	CHEWING	CEHIPRS	CIPHERS	CEIIKNT	KINETIC
CEGHIOS	CHIGOES		SPHERIC	CEIIKQU	QUICKIE
CEGHIRT	GET RICH	CEHIPRT	PITCHER	CEIIKSS	SICKIES
CEGHLSU	GULCHES	CEHIPST	PITCHES	CEIIKST	EKISTIC
CEGIILN	CEILING	CEHIQSU	QUICHES		ICKIEST
CEGIINP	PIECING	CEHIRST	RICHEST	CEIILNN	INCLINE
CEGIKNN	NECKING	CEHIRSU	CUSHIER	CEIILPP	CLIPPIE
CEGIKNP	PECKING	CEHIRSZ	SCHERZI	CEIILST	ELICITS
CEGIKNR	RECKING	CEHISSU	CUISHES	CEIIMMT	MIMETIC
CEGIKST	GET SICK	CEHISTW	WITCHES	CEIIMNS	MENISCI
CEGILNR	CRINGLE	CEHITTY	THE CITY	CEIIMOT	MEIOTIC
CEGILNU	CLUEING	CEHKKRU	CHUKKER	CEIIMRT	TIM RICE
CEGILNW	CLEWING	CEHKLMO	HEMLOCK	CEIIMSS	SEISMIC

CEIIMST	SEMITIC	CEILOPS	POLICES	CEIORVY	VICEROY
CEIIMTT	TITMICE	CEILORS	RECOILS	CEIOSST	COSIEST
CEIINNO	CONIINE	CEILOSS	OSSICLE	CEIOSSV	VISCOSE
CEIINOR	ONEIRIC	CEILPPR	CLIPPER	CEIOSTT	SCOTTIE
CEIINOV	INVOICE		CRIPPLE	CEIOSTV	COSTIVE
CEIINPS	PISCINE	CEILPRS	SPLICER	CEIOSTX	COEXIST
CEIINRT	CITRINE	CEILPSS	SPLICES	CEIOSTY	SOCIETY
	INCITER	CEILPSU	SPICULE	CEIOSTZ	COZIEST
	NERITIC	CEILQSU	CLIQUES	CEIPRRS	CRISPER
CEIINSS	ICINESS	CEILQUY	CLIQUEY	CEIPRST	TRICEPS
	INCISES	CEILRRU	CURLIER	CEIPRSY	SPICERY
CEIINST	INCITES	CEILRSS	SLICERS	CEIPRTU	CUPRITE
CEIINSU	CUISINE	CEILRST	RELICTS		PICTURE
CEIINTZ	CITIZEN	CEILRSY	CLERISY	CEIPRXY	PYREXIC
CEIIPRS	SPICIER	CEILRTU	UTRICLE	CEIPSSS	SCEPSIS
CEIIRST	ERISTIC	CEILSSU	CELSIUS	CEIPSST	CESSPIT
CEIISSS	CISSIES		SLUICES	CEIPSTU	CUP TIES
CEIISVV	CIVVIES	CEIMMOS	COMMIES		CUP-TIES
CEIJNST	INJECTS	CEIMNOS	COMES IN	CEIRRRU	CURRIER
CEIJSTU	JUSTICE		INCOMES	CEIRRSU	CRUISER
CEIKKRS	KICKERS		MESONIC		CURRIES
CEIKLNR	CLINKER	CEIMNOT	CENTIMO	CEIRRTT	CRITTER
	CRINKLE		METONIC	CEIRRTU	RECRUIT
CEIKLNS	NICKELS		TONEMIC	CEIRRTX	RECTRIX
CEIKLPR	PRICKLE	CEIMNPU	MINCE UP	CEIRSSU	CRUISES
CEIKLPS	PICKLES	CEIMNTY	CITY MEN	CEIRSST	TRISECT
CEIKLPU	CUPLIKE	CEIMNYZ	ENZYMIC	CEIRSTU	ICTERUS
CEIKLRS	SLICKER	CEIMOST	COMES IT	CEIRSUV	CURSIVE
CEIKLRT	TRICKLE	CEIMOTT	TOTEMIC	CEISSSU	CUISSES
CEIKLRU	LUCKIER	CEIMPRR	CRIMPER	CEISSTU	CUTISES
CEIKLSS	SICKLES	CEIMPSU	PUMICES		ICTUSES
CEIKLST	TICKLES	CEIMRST	METRICS	CEJKOSY	JOCKEYS
CEIKMSY	MICKEYS	CEIMRSU	MURICES	CEJNORU	CONJURE
CEIKNOT	KETONIC	CEIMSSU	MISCUES	CEJOPRT	PROJECT
CEIKNQU	QUICKEN	CEINNOV	CONNIVE	CEKKLNU	KNUCKLE
CEIKNRS	NICKERS	CEINOOZ	NEOZOIC	CEKKNOR	KNOCKER
	SNICKER	CEINOPR	PORCINE	CEKKOPS	KOPECKS
CEIKNSS	SICKENS	CEINORR	CORNIER	CEKLLRY	CLERKLY
CEIKNST	SNICKET	CEINORS	COINERS	CEKLORS	LOCKERS
CEIKOOS	COOKIES		CRONIES	CEKLOST	LOCKETS
CEIKOTT	KETOTIC	CEINORV	CORVINE	CEKLPRU	PLUCKER
CEIKPRR	PRICKER	CEINOSS	CESSION	CEKLRTU	TRUCKLE
CEIKPRS	PICKERS		COSINES	CEKLSSU	SUCKLES
CEIKPRT	PRICKET	CEINOST	NOTICES	CEKMORY	MOCKERY
CEIKPST	PICKETS		SECTION	CEKMRSU	MUCKERS
	SKEPTIC	CEINOSV	NOVICES	CEKNOOV	CONVOKE
CEIKQRU	QUICKER	CEINOTT	TONETIC	CEKNORS	CONKERS
CEIKRST	RICKETS	CEINOTX	EXCITON		RECKONS
	STICKER	CEINPRS	CRISPEN	CEKNRWY	WRYNECK
	TICKERS		PINCERS	CEKOORS	COOKERS
CEIKRTY	RICKETY		PRINCES	CEKOORY	COOKERY
CEIKSST	SICKEST	CEINPRT	CREPT IN	CEKOPST	POCKETS
CEIKSTT	TICKETS	CEINPST	INCEPTS	CEKORRS	CORKERS
CEIKSTW	WICKETS		INSPECT		ROCKERS
CEILLOR	COLLIER	CEINQSU	QUINCES	CEKORRY	ROCKERY
CEILLOS	COLLIES	CEINRST	CISTERN	CEKORST	ROCKETS
CEILLST	CELLIST		CRETINS	CEKOSST	SOCKETS
CEILMOP	COMPILE	CEINRTT	CITTERN	CEKPRSU	PUCKERS
	POLEMIC	CEINSST	INSECTS	CEKRRTU	TRUCKER
CEILNNU	NUCLEIN	CEINSTY	CYSTINE	CEKRSSU	SUCKERS
CEILNOS	CLOSE IN	CEINTTX	EXTINCT	CEKRSTU	TUCKERS
	INCLOSE	CEIOOST	COOTIES	CELLNOO	COLONEL
CEILNOT	LECTION	CEIOPRS	COPIERS	CELLOST	COLLETS
CEILNOX	LEXICON	CEIOPST	POETICS	CELLOSU	OCELLUS
CEILNPS	PENCILS	CEIOPSU	PICEOUS	CELLOSY	CLOSELY
	SPLENIC	CEIORRS	CORRIES	CELLRSU	CULLERS
CEILNST	CLIENTS		CROSIER		SCULLER
	STENCIL	CEIORRU	COURIER	CELLRUY	CRUELLY
CEILNTU	CUTLINE	CEIORRZ	CROZIER	CELMNOO	MONOCLE
	TUNICLE	CEIORSW	COWRIES	CELMOOS	COELOMS
CEILOOS	COOLIES	CEIORTV	EVICTOR	CELMOPS	COMPELS

CELMOPX	COMPLEX	CENOORR	CORONER	CEPRSUW	SCREW UP
CELMPRU	CRUMPLE		CROONER	CEPSSTU	SUSPECT
CELMSSU	MUSCLES	CENOORT	CORONET	CERSSSU	CUSSERS
CELNNOU	NUCLEON	CENOPSU	POUNCES	CERSTTU	CUTTERS
CELNOOS	COLONES	CENOPSY	SYNCOPE		SCUTTER
	CONSOLE	CENOPTU	CUT OPEN	CFFGINU	CUFFING
CELNORS	CORNELS	CENOPTY	POTENCY	CFFHINO	CHIFFON
CELNOSU	COUNSEL	CENOQRU	CONQUER	CFFIKKO	KICK OFF
CELNOTU	NOCTULE	CENORRS	CORNERS		KICKOFF
CELNSUU	NUCLEUS		SCORNER	CFFIKOP	PICK OFF
CELOORS	COOLERS	CENORSS	CENSORS	CFFIKOT	TICK OFF
CELOOST	COOLEST	CENORST	CORNETS	CFFINOS	COFFINS
	LOCOEST	CENORTU	COUNTER	CFFLOOO	COOL OFF
	OCELOTS		RECOUNT	CFFOSTU	CUTS OFF
CELOPRU	COUPLER		TROUNCE		OFFCUTS
CELOPSU	CLOSE UP	CENORTV	CONVERT	CFFRSSU	SCRUFFS
	CLOSE-UP	CENORUV	UNCOVER	CFFRSUY	SCRUFFY
	COUPLES	CENOSSY	COYNESS	CFGINOR	FORCING
CELOPTU	COUPLET	CENOSTT	CONTEST	CFHIOSW	COWFISH
CELORST	CORSLET	CENOSTU	CONTUSE	CFIIKNY	FINICKY
	LECTORS	CENOSVY	CONVEYS	CFIILNT	INFLICT
CELORSU	CLOSURE	CENOTTX	CONTEXT	CFIINOT	FICTION
CELORSV	CLOVERS	CENRRTU	CURRENT	CFIKOSS	FOSSICK
CELORSW	SCOWLER	CENRSTU	ENCRUST	CFILORS	FROLICS
CELORTU	CLOTURE	CENRSUW	UNSCREW	CFIMNOR	CONFIRM
	COULTER	CENRTUY	CENTURY	CFIMOST	COMFITS
CELOSST	CLOSEST	CENSSTY	ENCYSTS	CFINOSU	IN FOCUS
	CLOSETS	CEOOPRS	COOPERS	CFISSTU	FUSTICS
CELOSSU	LOCUSES	CEOORST	SCOOTER	CFKLORU	FOR LUCK
CELOSSX	COXLESS	CEOOSTY	COYOTES	CFKNORU	UNFROCK
CELOTTU	CULOTTE		OOCYTES	CFKOTTU	FUTTOCK
CELPRSU	SCRUPLE	CEOPPRR	CROPPER	CFLLRUY	FULL CRY
CELPSUU	CUPULES	CEOPPRS	COPPERS	CFLMRUU	FULCRUM
CELPSUY	CLYPEUS	CEOPPRY	COPPERY	CFLNOUY	FLOUNCY
CELRRSU	CURLERS	CEOPRRT	PORRECT	CFLORWY	CRY WOLF
CELRSTU	CLUSTER	CEOPRRU	PROCURE	CFLPSUU	CUPFULS
	CUTLERS	CEOPRSS	CORPSES		CUPSFUL
CELRSUW	CURLEWS		PROCESS	CFMNOOR	CONFORM
CELRTTU	CLUTTER	CEOPRSU	RECOUPS	CFMOORT	COMFORT
CELRTUU	CULTURE	CEOPRTT	PROTECT	CFNORTU	FUNCTOR
CELRTUV	CULVERT	CEOPRUV	COVER UP	CFOSSUU	FUSCOUS
CELRTUY	CRUELTY		COVER-UP	CGGGINO	COGGING
	CUTLERY	CEOQRTU	CROQUET	CGHHOSU	CHOUGHS
CELSTTU	CUTLETS	CEORRSS	CROSSER	CGHIIMN	CHIMING
	SCUTTLE		SCORERS	CGHIINN	CHINING
CEMMNOT	COMMENT	CEORRST	RECTORS		INCHING
CEMMNOU	COMMUNE	CEORRSU	COURSER		NICHING
CEMMOTU	COMMUTE		SCOURER	CGHIINT	ITCHING
CEMNNOT	CONTEMN	CEORRSY	SORCERY	CGHIKNO	CHOKING
CEMNOOS	COME-ONS	CEORRTY	RECTORY		HOCKING
	COMES ON	CEORSSS	CROSSES	CGHILPY	GLYPHIC
CEMNOOY	ECONOMY	CEORSST	CORSETS	CGHINNO	CHIGNON
CEMNOSU	CONSUME		ESCORTS	CGHINOS	COSHING
CEMNRTU	CENTRUM		SCOTERS	CGHIORT	GOT RICH
CEMOOPS	COMPOSE		SECTORS	CGHIOST	GOTHICS
CEMOOPT	COMPOTE	CEORSSU	COURSES	CGHOPUU	COUGH UP
CEMOOST	COMES TO		SOURCES	CGHORUY	GROUCHY
CEMOOTU	COME OUT		SUCROSE	CGIIKKN	KICKING
	OUTCOME	CEORSTU	SCOUTER	CGIIKLN	LICKING
CEMOPSU	COMES UP	CEORSTV	COVERTS	CGIIKMM	GIMMICK
CEMOPTU	COMPUTE		VECTORS	CGIIKNN	NICKING
CEMOSTU	COSTUME	CEORTUU	COUTURE	CGIIKNP	PICKING
CEMPRTU	CRUMPET	CEOSSST	COSSETS	CGIIKNR	RICKING
CEMRRUY	MERCURY	CEOSSSU	SCOUSES	CGIIKNT	TICKING
CEMRSTU	RECTUMS	CEPPRRU	CRUPPER	CGIILNO	COILING
CENNOOT	CONNOTE	CEPPRSU	SCUPPER	CGIILNS	SLICING
CENNOST	CONSENT	CEPPRTU	CREPT UP	CGIIMNN	MINCING
CENNOTT	CONTENT	CEPRRSU	SPRUCER	CGIINNO	COINING
CENNOTV	CONVENT	CEPRSSU	PERCUSS	CGIINNW	WINCING
CENNRSU	SCUNNER		SPRUCES	CGIINOV	VOICING
		CEPRSSY	CYPRESS	CGIINPR	PRICING

CGIINPS	SPICING	CHINORS	CORNISH	CIKLLUY	LUCKILY
CGIINRT	TRICING	CHINOSU	CUSHION	CIKLMOW	MILK COW
CGIKLNO	LOCKING	CHINOTU	IN TOUCH	CIKLMPU	MILK CUP
CGIKMNO	MOCKING	CHINQSU	SQUINCH	CIKLNOS	LOCKS IN
CGIKNNO	CONKING	CHINRSU	URCHINS	CIKLNRY	CRINKLY
	NOCKING	CHINTYZ	CHINTZY	CIKLPRY	PRICKLY
CGIKNOO	COOKING	CHIOPRT	TROPHIC	CIKLQUY	QUICKLY
CGIKNOR	CORKING	CHIOPST	COP THIS	CIKMNSU	MUCKS IN
	ROCKING	CHIOPXY	HYPOXIC	CIKNOPS	PICKS ON
CGIKNOS	SOCKING	CHIORST	OSTRICH	CIKNOST	IN STOCK
CGIKNPU	KINGCUP	CHIOSSZ	SCHIZOS	CIKNPSU	UNPICKS
CGIKNRU	RUCKING	CHIPRRU	CHIRRUP	CIKNSSU	SUCKS IN
CGIKNSU	SUCKING	CHIPRRY	PYRRHIC	CIKNSTU	IN STUCK
CGIKNTU	TUCKING	CHIPSSY	PHYSICS		TUCKS IN
CGIKOST	GOT SICK	CHIRRSU	CURRISH	CIKOPRT	CORK TIP
CGILLNU	CULLING	CHIRSST	CHRISTS	CIKOPTU	PICK OUT
CGILNNO	CLING ON	CHITTWY	TWITCHY	CIKOSTT	STICK TO
	CLONING	CHKLOSY	SHYLOCK	CIKPPSU	PICKS UP
CGILNOO	COOLING	CHKMMOU	HUMMOCK		PICKUPS
CGILNOS	CLOSING	CHKMOOS	MOHOCKS	CIKPSTU	STICK UP
CGILNOW	COWLING	CHKOOPS	SOCK HOP		STICKUP
CGILNOY	CLOYING	CHLOOSS	SCHOOLS	OIKNOTY	TRICKSY
CGILNRU	CURLING	CHLOOWY	HOLY COW	CILLOOR	CRIOLLO
CGILOOO	OOLOGIC	CHLOPST	SPLOTCH	CILMOPY	OLYMPIC
CGILPTY	GLYPTIC	CHLOSUY	CHYLOUS	CILMSTU	CULTISM
CGIMNOS	COMINGS		SLOUCHY	CILNOPS	CLIP-ONS
CGINNNO	CONNING	CHMNOTU	NOT MUCH	CILNORY	CORNILY
CGINNNU	CUNNING	CHMOOSY	SMOOCHY	CILNOSU	UNCOILS
CGINNOP	PONCING	CHMOOTU	TOO MUCH	CILNOTU	LINO CUT
CGINNOR	CORNING	CHMORSY	CHRYSOM		LINOCUT
CGINNOS	CONSIGN	CHMOSUY	CHYMOUS	CILNPSU	SCULPIN
CGINOOP	COOPING	CHNNOSU	NONSUCH	CILNSTU	LINCTUS
CGINOPP	COPPING	CHNOOPS	PONCHOS	CILOOPT	CO-PILOT
CGINOPU	COUPING	CHNOOTU	TOUCH ON	CILOORU	COULOIR
CGINOPY	COPYING	CHNOTUU	UNCOUTH	CILOOSS	COLOSSI
CGINORS	SCORING	CHNPPUU	PUNCH UP	CILOOST	COOLS IT
CGINORW	CROWING		PUNCH-UP	CILOPRY	PYLORIC
CGINOST	GNOSTIC	CHOOPPS	COP SHOP	CILOPSU	COILS UP
CGINPPU	CUPPING	CHOORST	COHORTS	CILOPSW	COWSLIP
CGINRSU	CURSING	CHOPSSY	PSYCHOS	CILORST	LICTORS
CGINRSY	SCRYING	CHOPTUU	TOUCH UP	CILOSTU	OCULIST
CGINRUV	CURVING	CHILLT	ILLICIT	CILPRSY	CRISPLY
CGINSSU	CUSSING	CIIJLUY	JUICILY	CILPRTU	CULPRIT
CGINTTU	CUTTING	CIIKKLL	KILLICK	CILSTTU	CULTIST
CGIOTYZ	ZYGOTIC	CIIKNPT	NITPICK	CIMMOST	COMMITS
CGIRSTU	TUGRICS	CIIKPUW	WICKIUP	CIMNOOR	MORONIC
CGKLNOU	GUNLOCK	CIILLTY	LICITLY		OMICRON
CGLNNOU	CLUNG ON	CIILLVY	CIVILLY	CIMNORS	CRIMSON
CHHIORS	CHI-RHOS	CIILNOS	SILICON		MICRONS
CHIIKSS	SICKISH	CIILNOT	NILOTIC	CIMOORS	MORISCO
CHIILOT	THIOLIC	CIILNUV	UNCIVIL	CIMOOST	OSMOTIC
CHIILST	LITCHIS	CIILNVY	VINYLIC	CIMOOST	SITCOMS
CHIIMSU	ISCHIUM	CIILOOT	OOLITIC	CIMOSSY	MYCOSIS
CHIINPT	PITCH IN	CIILOPT	POLITIC	CIMOTYZ	ZYMOTIC
CHIIOPT	OPHITIC	CIILOST	COLITIS	CIMPRSS	SCRIMPS
CHIIPST	PICTISH		SOLICIT	CIMPRSY	SCRIMPY
CHIIRRS	SCIRRHI	CIILPSY	SPICILY	CIMSSTY	MYSTICS
CHIKLLO	HILLOCK	CIIMMRY	MIMICRY	CINNORU	UNICORN
CHIKLTY	THICKLY	CIIMOST	SOMITIC	CINNOSU	NUNCIOS
CHIKNOO	CHINOOK	CIIMOTT	MITOTIC	CINNOTU	COUNT IN
CHIKORY	HICKORY	CIIMSTV	VICTIMS		UNCTION
CHIKPSU	PUCKISH	CIINOOT	COITION	CINOOPS	COIN-OPS
CHIKSTY	KITSCHY	CIINORS	INCISOR		OPSONIC
CHILNSY	LYCHNIS	CIINOST	COINS IT	CINORRT	TRICORN
CHILOOS	COOLISH	CIIOSUV	VICIOUS	CINORST	CISTRON
CHILOST	COLTISH	CIIPRTY	PYRITIC		CITRONS
CHILSUY	CUSHILY	CIJNNOO	CONJOIN	CINORTU	RUCTION
CHIMORS	CHRISOM	CIKKOTU	KICK OUT	CINOSST	CONSIST
CHIMSSS	SCHISMS	CIKKPSU	KICKS UP		TOCSINS
CHINOOR	CHORION	CIKLLLU	ILL LUCK	CINOSSU	COUSINS
CHINOPS	PHONICS	CIKLLSY	SLICKLY	CINOSTU	SUCTION

CINOSUZ	ZINCOUS	CMOOORS	COMOROS	DDEEEMN	EMENDED
CINRSTU	INCRUST	CMOOPRT	COMPORT	DDEEENP	DEEP END
CIOOPRS	SCORPIO	CMOOPST	COMPOST	DDEEEPS	SPEEDED
CIOOPRT	PORTICO	CMORSTU	SCROTUM	DDEEERR	RED DEER
CIOOPSU	COPIOUS	CMORTUW	CUTWORM	DDEEESX	DESEXED
CIOPRST	TROPICS	CMOSSTU	CUSTOMS	DDEEFGL	FLEDGED
CIOPRTY	CYPRIOT	CMOSUVY	MUSCOVY	DDEEFII	DEIFIED
CIOPSTY	COPYIST	CMPRSSU	SCRUMPS		EDIFIED
CIORSSS	SCISSOR	CMPRSUY	SCRUMPY	DDEEFIL	DEFILED
CIORSTU	CITROUS	CNNOOTU	COUNT ON		FIELDED
CIORSTV	VICTORS	CNOOPPR	POPCORN	DDEEFIN	DEFINED
CIORSUU	CURIOUS	CNOOPSU	COUPONS	DDEEFNS	DEFENDS
CIORTVY	VICTORY		SOUPCON	DDEEFSU	DEFUSED
CIOSSSY	SYCOSIS	CNOORST	CONSORT	DDEEGIN	DEEDING
CIOSSUV	VISCOUS		CROTONS		DEIGNED
CIPRSST	SCRIPTS	CNOORTT	CONTORT	DDEEGIP	DIG DEEP
CIPRSSU	PRUSSIC	CNOORTU	CONTOUR	DDEEGLP	PLEDGED
CIPRTTY	TRYPTIC		CROUTON	DDEEGLS	SLEDGED
CIPRUVY	PYRUVIC	CNOOSTT	COTTONS	DDEEGLU	DELUGED
CIPSTTY	STYPTIC	CNOOSTY	TYCOONS	DDEEGPU	DUG DEEP
CIRSSTU	RUSTICS	CNOOSUU	NOCUOUS	DDEEGRR	DREDGER
CKKNNOO	KNOCK ON	CNOOSVY	CONVOYS	DDEEGRS	DREDGES
	KNOCK-ON	CNOOTTY	COTTONY	DDEEHLS	HEDDLES
CKKNOPU	KNOCK UP	CNOPTUU	COUNT UP	DDEEILW	WIELDED
CKLLMOU	MULLOCK	CNORTUY	COUNTRY	DDEEILY	YIELDED
CKLLOOP	POLLOCK	COOPPSU	COOPS UP	DDEEIMP	IMPEDED
CKLNOSU	UNLOCKS	COOPRRT	PROCTOR	DDEEIMS	DEMISED
CKLNOTU	LOCKNUT	COOPRTU	OUTCROP		MISDEED
CKLNUUY	UNLUCKY	COOPSTU	COP-OUTS	DDEEINT	ENDED IT
CKLOORW	ROWLOCK		OCTOPUS	DDEEINX	INDEXED
CKLOOTU	LOCK OUT	COOPTUY	COPY OUT	DDEEIRS	DERIDES
	LOCKOUT	COPRRTU	CORRUPT		DESIRED
CKLOPSU	LOCKS UP	COPRSTY	CRYPTOS		RESIDED
	LOCKUPS	COPRSUU	CUPROUS	DDEEIRV	DERIVED
CKLOPTU	POT LUCK	CORRSSU	CURSORS	DDEEIST	TEDDIES
	POTLUCK	CORRSUY	CURSORY	DDEEISV	DEVISED
CKLOTUU	LUCK OUT	CORSSST	ST. CROSS	DDEEITY	TIE-DYED
CKMOPSU	MOCK-UPS	COSTTUU	CUTOUTS	DDEELLU	DUELLED
CKNORSU	UNCORKS		CUTS OUT	DDEELLW	DWELLED
CKNSTUU	UNSTUCK	DDDEEGR	DREDGED	DDEELMR	MEDDLER
CKOOOTU	COOKOUT	DDDEEIR	DERIDED	DDEELMS	MEDDLES
CKOOPSU	COOKS UP	DDDEELS	SLEDDED	DDEELPR	PEDDLER
CKOPRSU	CORKS UP	DDDEELU	DELUDED	DDEELPS	PEDDLES
CKOPSTU	STOCK UP	DDDEENU	DENUDED	DDEELRS	SLEDDER
CKOSSTU	TUSSOCK	DDDEFLU	FUDDLED	DDEELRU	DELUDER
CKOSTTU	STUCK TO	DDDEGIR	GRIDDED	DDEELSU	DELUDES
CKPSTUU	STUCK UP	DDDEGLU	GUDDLED	DDEEMOT	DEMOTED
	STUCK-UP	DDDEGRU	DRUDGED	DDEENOT	DENOTED
CLLMOSU	MOLLUSC	DDDEHTU	THUDDED	DDEENOW	ENDOWED
CLLOOPS	COLLOPS	DDDEIIV	DIVIDED	DDEENPS	DEPENDS
	SCOLLOP	DDDEIKS	SKIDDED	DDEENPU	ENDED UP
CLLORSS	SCROLLS	DDDEILR	DIDDLER		UPENDED
CLLOSUU	LOCULUS		RIDDLED	DDEENRS	DRESDEN
CLMNOSU	COLUMNS	DDDEILS	DIDDLES		REDDENS
CLMOSUU	OSCULUM	DDDEILW	WIDDLED	DDEENRT	TRENDED
CLMSUUU	CUMULUS	DDDEIMU	MUDDIED	DDEENRU	ENDURED
CLNOORT	CONTROL	DDDEKNO	KEN DODD	DDEENSU	DENUDES
CLNOOSS	CONSOLS	DDDELOP	PLODDED	DDEEOPS	DEPOSED
CLNOSSU	CONSULS	DDDELOS	DODDLES	DDEEORR	ORDERED
CLNOSTU	CONSULT	DDDEOPR	PRODDED	DDEEOTV	DEVOTED
CLNRSUU	UNCURLS	DDDEORS	DODDERS	DDEEPTU	DEPUTED
CLOORSU	COLOURS	DDDEPSU	SPUDDED	DDEERSS	DRESSED
CLOOSTY	CYTOSOL	DDDESTU	STUDDED	DDEERST	REDDEST
CLORSSY	CROSSLY	DDDGIOO	DID GOOD		TEDDERS
CLORTUY	COURTLY	DDDIIRT	DID DIRT	DDEFIIN	DID FINE
CLOSSTU	LOCUSTS	DDDIMSU	DIDDUMS	DDEFILR	FIDDLER
CLPRSUU	CURLS UP	DDDINOW	DID DOWN	DDEFILS	FIDDLES
CLPSSTU	SCULPTS	DDDITUY	DID DUTY	DDEFIRT	DRIFTED
CMMNOOS	COMMONS	DDEEEGR	DEGREED	DDEFLOO	FLOODED
CMNOOOT	CON MOTO	DDEEELN	NEEDLED	DDEFLSU	FUDDLES
	MONOCOT	DDEEELT	DELETED	DDEFNOR	FRONDED

DDEFNOU	FOUNDED	DDEIOST	TODDIES	DDILRUY	RUDDILY
DDEGGRU	DRUGGED	DDEIOTT	DITTOED	DDIPRRY	DRIP DRY
	GRUDGED	DDEIOTU	DIED OUT		DRIP-DRY
DDEGIIR	GIDDIER	DDEIOWW	WIDOWED	DDMMSUU	DUMDUMS
DDEGILR	GRIDDLE	DDEIPRU	DRIED UP	DDOOPRU	DO PROUD
DDEGIMO	DEMIGOD		DRIED-UP	DEEEEWW	WEE-WEED
DDEGINT	TEDDING	DDEIRRU	RUDDIER	DEEEFLT	FLEETED
DDEGINW	WEDDING	DDEISSU	DISUSED	DEEEFNR	FREE END
DDEGINY	EDDYING	DDEISTU	STUDIED	DEEEFRS	FEEDERS
DDEGIOR	DODGIER	DDEJRSU	JUDDERS	DEEEFRV	FEVERED
DDEGLSU	GUDDLES	DDEKMOU	DUKEDOM	DEEEGLP	PLEDGEE
DDEGMOS	DODGEMS	DDELMOU	MOULDED	DEEEGMR	EMERGED
DDEGMSU	SMUDGED	DDELMRU	MUDDLER	DEEEGNR	GREENED
DDEGNOS	DOG ENDS	DDELMSU	MUDDLES		RENEGED
	DOG-ENDS	DDELNOS	NODDLES	DEEEGRS	DEGREES
	GODSEND	DDELOOR	DOODLER	DEEEGRT	GREETED
DDEGNOU	DUDGEON		DROOLED	DEEEGST	EGESTED
DDEGORS	DODGERS	DDELOOS	DOODLES	DEEEHLW	WHEEDLE
	GORSEDD	DDELOPR	PLODDER		WHEELED
DDEGOSS	GODDESS	DDELORT	TODDLER	DEEEHPT	THE DEEP
DDEGRRU	DRUDGER	DDELOST	TODDLES	DEEEHRS	SHEERED
DDEGRSU	DRUDGES	DDELPRU	PUDDLER	DEEEHST	SEETHED
DDEGRTU	TRUDGED	DDELPSU	PUDDLES		SHEETED
DDEHIRS	REDDISH	DDEMMRU	DRUMMED	DEEEHTT	TEETHED
DDEHIRY	HYDRIDE	DDEMNOT	ODDMENT	DEEEHWZ	WHEEZED
DDEHLSU	HUDDLES	DDENOPS	DESPOND	DEEEILS	LEE SIDE
DDEHNOU	HOUNDED	DDENOPU	POUNDED	DEEEILT	LEE TIDE
DDEHNRU	HUNDRED	DDENORT	TRODDEN	DEEEIPY	PIE-EYED
DDEHOST	THE ODDS	DDENORU	REDOUND	DEEEIRS	SEEDIER
DDEHRSU	SHUDDER		ROUNDED	DEEEIRW	WEEDIER
DDEIIKS	KIDDIES	DDENORW	DROWNED	DEEEISV	DEVISEE
DDEIIMS	MIDDIES	DDENOSS	ODDNESS	DEEEKLN	KNEELED
DDEIIMT	DID TIME	DDENOSU	SOUNDED	DEEEKLS	SLEEKED
DDEIINT	INDITED	DDENOUW	WOUNDED	DEEEKNW	WEEKEND
DDEIINV	DIVINED	DDENSSU	SUDDENS	DEEELNR	NEEDLER
DDEIIOS	IODIDES	DDEOOPR	DROOPED	DEEELNS	NEEDLES
	IODISED	DDEOORW	REDWOOD	DEEELPT	DEPLETE
DDEIIOX	DIOXIDE	DDEOOWY	DYEWOOD	DEEELRV	LEVERED
DDEIIOZ	IODIZED	DDEOPPR	DROPPED	DEEELST	DELETES
DDEIIRV	DIVIDER	DDEOPRR	PRODDER		SLEETED
DDEIISV	DIVIDES	DDEORSW	DROWSED		STEELED
DDEIIZZ	DIZZIED	DDEORVY	VERY ODD	DEEELSV	SLEEVED
DDEIKNR	KINDRED	DDERRSU	RUDDERS	DEEEMNR	EMENDER
DDEIKRS	SKIDDER	DDGGINO	DODGING	DEEEMNS	DEMESNE
DDEILLO	DOLLIED	DDGGOOO	GOOD DOG	DEEEMRS	REDEEMS
DDEILLR	DRILLED		GOOD GOD	DEEEMRT	METERED
DDEILLW	DID WELL	DDGIIKN	KIDDING	DEEENOP	ONE DEEP
DDEILMP	DIMPLED	DDGIILY	GIDDILY	DEEENPR	PREENED
DDEILMS	MIDDLES	DDGILOW	WILD DOG	DEEENPS	DEEPENS
DDEILNW	DWINDLE	DDGINNO	NODDING	DEEENPT	TEN DEEP
DDEILOT	DELTOID	DDGINOP	PODDING	DEEENQU	QUEENED
DDEILPS	PIDDLES	DDGINOS	SODDING	DEEENRS	SEEN RED
DDEILRR	RIDDLER	DDGINOW	WIND GOD		SNEERED
DDEILRS	RIDDLES	DDGINPU	PUDDING	DEEENRT	ENTERED
DDEILRT	TIDDLER	DDGLLOO	OLD GOLD	DEEENRW	RENEWED
DDEILSW	WIDDLES	DDGLOOR	LORD GOD	DEEENSZ	SNEEZED
DDEILTU	DILUTED	DDGLOOS	OLD DOGS	DEEENTT	DETENTE
	LUDDITE	DDGOOOW	DOGWOOD	DEEEORR	ROE DEER
DDEILTW	TWIDDLE	DDHIIKS	KIDDISH	DEEEOTV	DEVOTEE
DDEILTY	LYDDITE	DDHIISY	YIDDISH	DEEEPRS	SPEEDER
DDEIMMU	DUMMIED	DDHIKSU	KIDDUSH	DEEEPRT	PETERED
DDEIMNS	MIDDENS	DDHIORY	HYDROID	DEEEPST	DEEP SET
DDEIMRU	MUDDIER	DDHORSY	DRY-SHOD		DEEPEST
DDEIMSU	MUDDIES	DDHORUY	ROY HUDD		STEEPED
DDEINOS	NODDIES	DDIIKKS	DIK-DIKS	DEEEQRU	QUEERED
DDEINOW	DIE DOWN	DDIIKLS	SKID-LID	DEEERRV	REVERED
DDEINST	DISTEND	DDIILOP	DIPLOID	DEEERSS	SEEDERS
DDEIOOR	DO OR DIE	DDIKOOS	SKIDDOO	DEEERST	STEERED
DDEIORV	DID OVER	DDILMUY	MUDDILY	DEEERSV	DESERVE
	OVERDID	DDILNRS	DIRNDLS		SEVERED
DDEIORW	DOWDIER	DDILOWY	DOWDILY	DEEERSW	WEEDERS

DEEERTV	EVERTED	DEEGOSY	GEODESY	DEEIPRS	PRESIDE
DEEERTX	EXERTED	DEEGSSU	GUESSED	DEEIPRV	DEPRIVE
DEEESSX	DESEXES	DEEGSTU	GUESTED	DEEIPRX	EXPIRED
DEEETTV	VEDETTE	DEEHIKV	KHEDIVE	DEEIPSS	DESPISE
DEEETTW	TWEETED	DEEHINR	INHERED	DEEIPST	DESPITE
DEEFFIN	EFFENDI	DEEHIST	HEISTED	DEEIQRU	QUERIED
DEEFFOR	OFFERED	DEEHITV	THIEVED	DEEIQTU	QUIETED
DEEFFOT	TEED OFF	DEEHLLS	SHELLED	DEEIRRS	SERRIED
DEEFFSU	EFFUSED	DEEHLOT	THE DOLE	DEEIRRT	RETIRED
DEEFGIN	FEEDING	DEEHLPW	WHELPED	DEEIRRW	REWIRED
	FEIGNED	DEEHLSV	SHELVED		WEIRDER
DEEFGLS	FLEDGES	DEEHLSW	WELSHED	DEEIRSS	DESIRES
DEEFHLS	FLESHED	DEEHMUX	EXHUMED		RESIDES
DEEFHLU	HEEDFUL	DEEHNOT	HEN-TOED	DEEIRSU	RESIDUE
DEEFIIR	REIFIED	DEEHNOY	HONEYED	DEEIRSV	DERIVES
DEEFIIS	DEIFIES	DEEHORV	HOVERED		DIVERSE
	EDIFIES	DEEHPRS	SPHERED		REVISED
DEEFILR	DEFILER	DEEHRST	THE REDS	DEEIRTU	ERUDITE
	FIELDER	DEEHRSU	USHERED	DEEIRTV	RIVETED
DEEFILS	DEFILES	DEEHTTW	WHETTED	DEEIRVV	REVIVED
DEEFINR	DEFINER	DEEIINS	SINE DIE	DEEISSV	DEVISES
	REFINED	DEEIIRW	WEIRDIE	DEEISTW	DEWIEST
DEEFINS	DEFINES	DEEIIST	DEITIES	DEEISTX	EXISTED
DEEFINT	FEINTED	DEEIJLL	JELLIED	DEEISTY	TIE-DYES
DEEFIRR	FERRIED	DEEIJMM	JEMMIED	DEEJNOY	ENJOYED
DEEFIRS	DEFIERS	DEEIKLN	LIKENED	DEEKKRT	TREKKED
DEEFLLO	FEEL OLD	DEEIKMW	MIDWEEK	DEEKLLN	KNELLED
DEEFLLU	FELL DUE	DEEIKOV	DOVEKIE	DEEKORV	REVOKED
	FUELLED	DEEILLM	DE MILLE	DEELLMS	SMELLED
DEEFLLW	FED WELL	DEEILNR	RED LINE	DEELLPS	SPELLED
	WELL FED	DEEILNS	ENSILED	DEELLQU	QUELLED
DEEFLNS	FLENSED		LINSEED	DEELLRU	DUELLER
DEEFLNU	NEEDFUL	DEEILNV	LIVENED	DEELLRW	DWELLER
DEEFLOT	FEEDLOT	DEEILOS	OILSEED	DEELLRY	ELDERLY
DEEFMOR	FREEDOM	DEEILPR	REPLIED	DEELLSW	SWELLED
DEEFNRS	FENDERS	DEEILPS	SPIELED	DEELMOR	REMODEL
DEEFORV	OVERFED	DEEILRV	DELIVER	DEELMPU	DEPLUME
DEEFPRY	DEEP FRY		RELIVED	DEELMST	SMELTED
	DEEP-FRY		REVILED	DEELMSY	MEDLEYS
DEEFRSU	REFUSED	DEEILRW	WIELDER	DEELNRS	LENDERS
DEEFRTT	FRETTED	DEEILRY	YIELDER		SLENDER
DEEFRTU	REFUTED	DEEILSS	DIESELS	DEELNSS	ENDLESS
DEEFSSU	DEFUSES	DEEILSY	EYELIDS	DEELNST	NESTLED
DEEFSTT	DEFTEST		SEEDILY	DEELNSY	DENSELY
DEEGHIN	HEEDING	DEEIMNS	SIDEMEN	DEELOPP	PEOPLED
	NEIGHED	DEEIMPR	IMPEDER	DEELOPR	DEPLORE
DEEGHIW	WEIGHED	DEEIMPS	IMPEDES	DEELOPV	DEVELOP
DEEGHOW	HOGWEED	DEEIMPT	EMPTIED	DEELOPX	EXPLODE
DEEGILS	LEG SIDE	DEEIMRT	DEMERIT	DEELORU	URODELE
DEEGIMN	DEEMING		MERITED	DEELORW	LOWERED
DEEGINN	NEEDING	DEEIMSS	DEMISES	DEELOSU	DELOUSE
DEEGINR	REIGNED	DEEIMTT	EMITTED	DEELOVV	DEVOLVE
DEEGINS	SEEDING	DEEINNT	DENTINE	DEELPRU	PRELUDE
DEEGINW	WEEDING	DEEINNZ	DENIZEN	DEELPST	PESTLED
DEEGIOR	GEORDIE	DEEINPR	RED PINE	DEELRSV	DELVERS
DEEGIRV	DIVERGE		REPINED	DEELRSW	WELDERS
	GRIEVED	DEEINRS	DENIERS	DEELSTT	SETTLED
DEEGIST	EDGIEST		RESINED	DEELSTW	LEWDEST
DEEGLNS	LEGENDS	DEEINRW	RED WINE	DEELTUX	EXULTED
DEEGLNT	GENTLED	DEEINRX	INDEXER	DEEMMST	STEMMED
DEEGLPR	PLEDGER	DEEINST	DESTINE	DEEMNOY	MONEYED
DEEGLPS	PLEDGES	DEEINSV	ENDIVES	DEEMORV	REMOVED
DEEGLPT	PLEDGET	DEEINSX	INDEXES	DEEMOST	DEMOTES
DEEGLRS	LEDGERS	DEEINTT	DINETTE	DEEMOSY	MOSEYED
DEEGLSS	SLEDGES	DEEINTU	DETINUE	DEEMPTT	TEMPTED
DEEGLSU	DELUGES	DEEINTV	EVIDENT	DEEMRSU	RESUMED
DEEGNOR	GONE RED	DEEINWZ	WIZENED	DEENNOS	DONNEES
DEEGNRS	GENDERS	DEEIOPS	EPISODE	DEENNOT	NEED NOT
DEEGOOY	GOOD EYE	DEEIOPX	EPOXIDE		TENONED
DEEGORR	ROGERED		EPOXIED	DEENNPT	PENDENT
DEEGORS	GOES RED	DEEIPPT	PEPTIDE	DEENOPS	SPONDEE

DEENORS	ENDORSE	DEFFIOR	RIDE OFF	DEFMORS	DEFORMS
DEENOST	DENOTES	DEFFIOS	OFF SIDE		SERFDOM
DEENOSW	SEWED ON		OFFSIDE	DEFNOOR	DONE FOR
DEENPRS	SPENDER	DEFFIRS	DIFFERS	DEFNORS	SEND FOR
DEENPRT	PRETEND	DEFFISU	DIFFUSE	DEFNORT	FRONTED
DEENPRU	RUN DEEP	DEFFNOR	FORFEND	DEFNORU	FOUNDER
DEENPSX	EXPENDS	DEFFNOS	OFFENDS	DEFNORW	FROWNED
DEENRRS	RENDERS		SEND OFF	DEFNOST	FONDEST
DEENRSS	REDNESS		SEND-OFF	DEFNOSU	FONDUES
	SENDERS	DEFFNSU	SNUFFED	DEFNRSU	REFUNDS
DEENRST	TENDERS	DEFFOOR	RODE OFF	DEFOOPR	PROOFED
DEENRSU	ENDURES	DEFFORW	DREW OFF	DEFOOPS	SPOOFED
	ENSURED	DEFFRSU	DUFFERS	DEFOORS	DOES FOR
DEENRTU	DENTURE	DEFFSTU	DUFFEST	DEFORST	DEFROST
	TENURED		STUFFED		FROSTED
DEENRTW	WENT RED	DEFGGLO	FLOGGED		
DEENSST	DENSEST	DEFGINN	FENDING	DEGGGOO	GOOD EGG
DEENSTT	DETENTS	DEFGINR	FRINGED	DEGGHIN	HEDGING
DEENSTW	WEST END	DEFGINY	DEFYING	DEGGIKN	KEDGING
	WEST END	DEFGIOR	FIREDOG	DEGGILN	GELDING
DEENSTX	EXTENDS	DEFGIRS	FRIDGES	DEGGINS	EDGINGS
DEENSUX	UNSEXED	DEFGIRT	GRIFTED		SNIGGED
DEEOPPY	POP-EYED	DEFGIRU	FIGURED	DEGGINW	WEDGING
DEEOPRS	REPOSED	DEFGIST	FIDGETS	DEGGIOS	DOGGIES
DEEOPRW	POWERED	DEFGITY	FIDGETY	DEGGIRS	DIGGERS
DEEOPSS	DEPOSES	DEFGOOW	GOOD FEW	DEGGISW	SWIGGED
DEEOPST	TOP SEED	DEFHIST	SHIFTED	DEGGITW	TWIGGED
DEEOPSX	EXPOSED	DEFHLSU	FLUSHED	DEGGLOS	DOGLEGS
DEEOPTW	TWO DEEP	DEFHORT	FROTHED		SLOGGED
DEEOPXY	EPOXYED	DEFIILN	INFIDEL	DEGGLPU	PLUGGED
DEEORRR	REORDER		INFIELD	DEGGLSU	SLUGGED
DEEORRS	RED ROSE	DEFIIMS	FIDEISM	DEGGNOS	SNOGGED
	REREDOS	DEFIIMW	MIDWIFE	DEGGNOU	GUDGEON
DEEORRW	WORE RED	DEFIINU	UNIFIED	DEGGNSU	SNUGGED
DEEORST	OERSTED	DEFIINX	INFIXED	DEGGRRU	GRUDGER
	TEREDOS	DEFIIST	FIDEIST	DEGGRSU	GRUDGES
DEEORTW	TOWERED	DEFIKRS	FRISKED	DEGGRTU	DRUGGET
DEEORUV	OVERDUE	DEFILLR	FRILLED	DEGHHIT	THIGHED
DEEORXX	XEROXED	DEFILOO	FOLIOED	DEGHILN	HIND LEG
DEEOSTV	DEVOTES	DEFILPP	FLIPPED	DEGHILT	DELIGHT
DEEOTUW	WEED OUT	DEFILPU	UPFIELD		LIGHTED
DEEPPST	STEPPED	DEFILRT	FLIRTED	DEGHINR	HERDING
DEEPPSU	SPEED UP	DEFILTT	FLITTED	DEGHINW	WHINGED
	SPEED-UP	DEFILTY	FETIDLY	DEGHIRT	GIRTHED
DEEPRSS	DEPRESS	DEFILXY	FIXEDLY		RIGHTED
	PRESSED	DEFINOX	FIXED ON	DEGHIST	SIGHTED
DEEPRSU	PERUSED	DEFINRS	FINDERS	DEGHLOT	GET HOLD
DEEPRTU	ERUPTED		FRIENDS	DEGHNOT	THONGED
	REPUTED	DEFINSU	INFUSED	DEGHORU	ROUGHED
DEEPSTU	DEPUTES	DEFIOST	FOISTED	DEGHOST	GHOSTED
DEEQSTU	QUESTED	DEFIPRU	FRIED UP		THE DOGS
DEERRSS	DRESSER	DEFIPRY	PERFIDY		THE GODS
	REDRESS	DEFIPUX	FIXED UP	DEGHOSU	SOUGHED
DEERRUV	VERDURE	DEFIRRS	RED FIRS	DEGIILN	ELIDING
DEERSSS	DRESSES	DEFIRRT	DRIFTER	DEGIINR	DINGIER
DEERSST	DESERTS	DEFIRTT	FRITTED	DEGIINT	DIETING
	DESSERT	DEFIRTU	FRUITED		EDITING
	TRESSED	DEFKLNU	FLUNKED		IGNITED
DEERSTW	STREWED	DEFLLOT	FELT OLD	DEGIKLO	DOGLIKE
	WRESTED	DEFLLOU	DOLEFUL		GODLIKE
DEERSVW	SWERVED	DEFLMPU	FLUMPED	DEGILLR	GRILLED
DEERTTU	UTTERED	DEFLNOS	ENFOLDS	DEGILLU	GULLIED
DEERTUX	EXTRUDE		FONDLES	DEGILLY	GELIDLY
DEESSTT	DETESTS	DEFLNOT	TENFOLD	DEGILMN	MELDING
DEESTTT	STETTED	DEFLOOR	FLOORED	DEGILNN	LENDING
DEESTUW	DUE WEST	DEFLOPP	FLOPPED	DEGILNS	DINGLES
DEFFFLU	FLUFFED	DEFLORS	FOLDERS		SINGLED
DEFFHIW	WHIFFED	DEFLORU	FLOURED	DEGILNT	GLINTED
DEFFHLO	HELD OFF	DEFLOTU	FLOUTED	DEGILNU	ELUDING
DEFFIMO	FIEFDOM	DEFLPRU	PURFLED		INDULGE
DEFFINS	SNIFFED			DEGILNV	DELVING
				DEGILNW	WELDING

DEGILOR	GLORIED	DEGRSTU	TRUDGES	DEHPPUY	HYPED-UP
DEGILRS	GIRDLES	DEHHISW	WHISHED	DEIIKLS	DISLIKE
	GLIDERS	DEHHMPU	HUMPHED	DEIIKNR	DINKIER
DEGILRU	GUILDER	DEHHSSU	SHUSHED	DEIILLS	DILLIES
DEGILUV	DIVULGE	DEHIIPS	PIE DISH	DEIILMN	MIDLINE
DEGIMNN	MENDING	DEHIIRS	DISHIER	DEIILMP	IMPLIED
DEGIMST	MIDGETS	DEHIKRS	SHIRKED	DEIILMT	DELIMIT
DEGINNP	PENDING	DEHIKSW	WHISKED		LIMITED
DEGINNR	GRINNED	DEHILRW	WHIRLED	DEIILNV	LIVED IN
DEGINNS	ENDINGS	DEHILSS	SHIELDS	DEIILOS	DOILIES
DEGINNT	DENTING	DEHIMMS	SHIMMED		IDOLISE
	TENDING	DEHIMNU	INHUMED	DEIILOZ	IDOLIZE
DEGINNU	ENDUING	DEHIMOT	ETHMOID	DEIIMNX	MIXED IN
DEGINNV	VENDING	DEHINNS	SHINNED	DEIIMVW	DIM VIEW
DEGINNW	WENDING	DEHINNT	THIN END	DEIINOS	IONISED
DEGINNY	DENYING		THINNED	DEIINOT	EDITION
DEGINOR	ERODING	DEHINPT	IN DEPTH	DEIINOZ	IONIZED
	IGNORED		IN-DEPTH	DEIINRS	INSIDER
	NEGROID	DEHINRS	HINDERS	DEIINRT	NITRIDE
	REDOING	DEHINSW	WENDISH	DEIINRV	DIVINER
DEGINOS	DINGOES	DEHIOOS	HOODIES		DRIVE IN
DEGINOW	WIDGEON	DEHIOST	HOISTED		DRIVE-IN
DEGINRR	GRINDER	DEHIOSU	HIDEOUS	DEIINRW	WINDIER
DEGINRW	REDWING	DEHIOTU	HIDEOUT	DEIINSS	INSIDES
DEGINSS	DESIGNS	DEHIPPS	SHIPPED	DEIINST	INDITES
DEGINTW	GET WIND	DEHIPPW	WHIPPED	DEIINSV	DIVINES
DEGINUX	EXUDING	DEHIRRS	SHIRRED	DEIINTV	INVITED
DEGIOOS	GOODIES	DEHIRRU	HURRIED	DEIIORT	DIORITE
DEGIOPR	PODGIER	DEHIRST	DITHERS	DEIIOSS	IODISES
DEGIPPR	GRIPPED	DEHIRSV	DERVISH	DEIIOSX	OXIDISE
DEGIRRS	GIRDERS		SHRIVED	DEIIOSZ	IODIZES
DEGIRSS	DIGRESS	DEHIRTV	THRIVED	DEIIOXZ	OXIDIZE
DEGIRST	GETS RID	DEHIRTW	WRITHED	DEIIPRT	RIPTIDE
DEGIRTT	GRITTED	DEHIRTY	DITHERY	DEIIRRT	DIRTIER
DEGISST	DIGESTS	DEHISSW	SWEDISH	DEIIRST	TIDIERS
DEGLMOO	GLOOMED		SWISHED	DEIIRSV	DIVISER
DEGLNOU	LOUNGED	DEHISTW	WHISTED	DEIIRZZ	DIZZIER
DEGLNPU	PLUNGED	DEHIWZZ	WHIZZED	DEIISTT	DITTIES
DEGLNSU	GULDENS	DEHJNOO	JOHN DOE		TIDIEST
DEGLOPR	PLEDGOR	DEHLLOO	HOLLOED	DEIISTV	VISITED
DEGLOPS	SPLODGE	DEHLOOT	TOEHOLD	DEIISVV	DIVVIES
DEGLORS	LODGERS	DEHLORS	HOLDERS	DEIISZZ	DIZZIES
DEGLORW	GREW OLD	DEHLORT	THE LORD	DEIJLLO	JOLLIED
	GROWLED	DEHLORW	WHORLED	DEIJNOR	JOINDER
DEGLOSS	GLOSSED	DEHLOSS	SLOSHED	DEIJNOT	JOINTED
	GODLESS	DEHLOTU	HELD OUT	DEIJNRU	INJURED
DEGLOST	GETS OLD	DEHLRRU	HURDLER	DEIJORY	JOY RIDE
DEGLTTU	GLUTTED	DEHLRSU	HURDLES		JOYRIDE
DEGMNOO	GOOD MEN	DEHMOST	METHODS	DEIKLLS	SKILLED
DEGMOOR	GROOMED		THE MODS	DEIKLNS	KINDLES
DEGMSSU	SMUDGES	DEHMOTU	MOUTHED		SLINKED
DEGNNOU	DUNGEON	DEHMPTU	THUMPED	DEIKLNW	WINKLED
DEGNOPR	PRONGED	DEHNNSU	SHUNNED	DEIKLOR	RODLIKE
DEGNOPS	SPONGED	DEHNOOW	HOEDOWN	DEIKLRS	SKIRLED
DEGNORU	GO UNDER	DEHNORT	THORNED	DEIKLTT	KITTLED
	UNDERGO	DEHNORU	HOUNDER	DEIKMMS	SKIMMED
DEGNORW	WRONGED	DEHNOSY	HOYDENS	DEIKMPS	SKIMPED
DEGNOTU	TONGUED	DEHNOTZ	DOZENTH	DEIKMRS	SMIRKED
DEGNOTW	GET DOWN	DEHNRTU	THUNDER	DEIKNNS	SKINNED
DEGNRSU	GERUNDS	DEHNSTU	SHUNTED	DEIKNOS	DOESKIN
DEGNRTU	GRUNTED	DEHOOPT	PHOTOED	DEIKNOV	INVOKED
DEGOORV	GROOVED	DEHOOPW	WHOOPED	DEIKNPR	PRINKED
DEGOOST	STOOGED	DEHOOST	SOOTHED	DEIKNRR	DRINKER
DEGOPRU	GROUPED	DEHOOSW	WOOSHED	DEIKNRS	REDSKIN
DEGOPSY	PYE-DOGS	DEHOOTT	TOOTHED	DEIKNST	KINDEST
DEGORSS	GROSSED	DEHOPPS	SHOPPED	DEIKNSY	KIDNEYS
DEGORSU	DROGUES	DEHOPPW	WHOPPED	DEIKNTT	KNITTED
	GOURDES	DEHOPRT	THE DROP	DEIKPPS	SKIPPED
	GROUSED	DEHORST	SHORTED	DEIKRRS	SKIRRED
DEGORTU	GROUTED	DEHORTW	WORTHED	DEIKRST	SKIRTED
DEGRRTU	TRUDGER	DEHOSTU	SHOUTED		

DEIKRSU	DUIKERS	DEIMNRS	MINDERS	DEIOPST	DEPOSIT
	DUSKIER		REMINDS		POSITED
DEILLMU	ILLUMED	DEIMNSS	DIMNESS		TOPSIDE
DEILLNW	INDWELL	DEIMNTU	MINUTED	DEIOPSU	OEDIPUS
DEILLOS	DOLLIES	DEIMNUX	UNMIXED	DEIOPTV	PIVOTED
DEILLPS	SPILLED	DEIMOOR	MOIDORE	DEIORRW	WORDIER
DEILLQU	QUILLED		MOODIER		WORRIED
DEILLRT	TRILLED	DEIMOPS	IMPOSED	DEIORSS	DOSSIER
DEILLST	STILLED	DEIMOTT	OMITTED	DEIORST	EDITORS
DEILLSU	ILL-USED	DEIMOTV	VOMITED		STEROID
	SULLIED	DEIMPPR	PRIMPED		STORIED
DEILLSW	SWILLED	DEIMPRU	DUMPIER		TRIODES
DEILLTW	TWILLED		UMPIRED	DEIORSV	DEVISOR
DEILMMS	SLIMMED	DEIMPSU	MUD PIES		VISORED
DEILMOP	IMPLODE	DEIMPTU	IMPUTED		VOIDERS
DEILMOT	OLD TIME	DEIMPUX	MIXED UP	DEIORSW	DOWRIES
	OLD-TIME		MIXED-UP		ROWDIES
DEILMOY	MYELOID	DEIMSST	DEMISTS		WEIRDOS
DEILMPP	PIMPLED	DEIMSSU	MISUSED	DEIORTT	DOTTIER
DEILMPS	DIMPLES	DEIMSTY	STYMIED	DEIORTU	OUTRIDE
DEILMST	MILDEST	DEINNOS	NOSED IN		RIDE OUT
DEILMSW	MILDEWS	DEINNOT	INTONED	DEIORWW	WIDOWER
DEILMWY	MILDEWY	DEINNRS	DINNERS	DEIOSTU	DIES OUT
DEILNNS	LINDENS	DEINNRU	INURNED		OUTSIDE
DCILNOO	EIDOLON	DEINNST	INDENTS		TEDIOUS
DEILNOP	PILED ON		INTENDS	DEIOSTZ	DOZIEST
DEILNOR	RED LION	DEINNSU	DUNNIES	DEIOSUV	DEVIOUS
DEILNOW	LIE DOWN	DEINNTU	TUNED IN	DEIPPPU	PIPED UP
	LIE-DOWN		TUNED-IN	DEIPPQU	QUIPPED
DEILNPS	SPINDLE	DEINNTW	TWINNED	DEIPPRR	DRIPPER
	SPLINED	DEINOPT	POINTED	DEIPPRS	DIPPERS
DEILNPU	LINED UP	DEINOQU	ONE QUID	DEIPPRT	TRIPPED
DEILNRT	TENDRIL		QUOINED	DEIPPSU	DUPPIES
DEILNSW	SWINDLE	DEINORR	IN ORDER	DEIPRSS	SPIDERS
DEILNSY	SNIDELY	DEINORS	INDORSE	DEIPRST	SPIRTED
DEILNTU	DILUENT		ROSINED		STRIPED
DEILOPS	DESPOIL	DEINORT	TRIED ON	DEIPRSU	DRIES UP
	DIPOLES	DEINORV	DRIVE ON	DEIPRSY	SPIDERY
	SPOILED		DROVE IN	DEIPRWY	WIPE DRY
DEILOPT	PILOTED	DEINORW	DOWNIER	DEIPSSU	UPSIDES
DEILORS	SOLDIER	DEINOTU	DINE OUT	DEIPSTU	DISPUTE
DEILOTW	LOW TIDE	DEINOTW	TIE DOWN	DEIPSXY	PYXIDES
DEILOVW	LOW DIVE	DEINPPS	SNIPPED	DEIPTTU	PUTTIED
DEILPPS	SLIPPED	DEINPRT	PRINTED	DEIQRSU	SQUIRED
DEILPPU	PILED UP	DEINPST	STIPEND	DEIQRTU	QUIRTED
DEILPSS	DISPELS	DEINQTU	TEN QUID	DEIQTTU	QUITTED
DEILPTY	TEPIDLY	DEINRSU	INSURED	DEIQUZZ	QUIZZED
DEILPUV	LIVED UP	DEINRSW	REWINDS	DEIRRST	STIRRED
DEILQTU	QUILTED		WINDERS		STRIDER
DEILRSS	SLIDERS	DEINRTT	TRIDENT	DEIRRSV	DRIVERS
DEILRSV	DRIVELS	DEINRTU	INTRUDE	DEIRSST	STRIDES
DEILRSW	SWIRLED		UNTRIED	DEIRSTU	DUSTIER
DEILRTU	DILUTER	DEINRTX	DEXTRIN	DEIRSTV	DIVERTS
DEILRTW	TWIRLED	DEINRTY	TINDERY		STRIVED
DEILRTY	TIREDLY	DEINRWY	DRY WINE	DEISSST	DESISTS
DEILRVY	DEVILRY	DEINSST	DISSENT	DEISSSU	DISUSES
DEILRWY	WEIRDLY	DEINSSU	NIDUSES	DEISSTU	STUDIES
DEILRZZ	DRIZZLE	DEINSTT	DENTIST	DEISSTV	DIVESTS
DEILSTT	STILTED		STINTED	DEISTTW	TWISTED
DEILSTU	DILUTES	DEINSTW	WITS END	DEITTTW	TWITTED
DEILSTW	WILDEST	DEINSTY	DENSITY	DEJKLOO	OLD JOKE
DEIMMRS	DIMMERS		DESTINY	DEJOSTU	JOUSTED
DEIMMRT	TRIMMED	DEIOORW	WOODIER	DEKKLSU	SKULKED
DEIMMRU	IMMURED	DEIOPRS	PERIODS	DEKLLSU	SKULLED
DEIMMST	DIMMEST	DEIOPRT	DIOPTER	DEKLNOP	PLONKED
DEIMMSU	DUMMIES		DIOPTRE	DEKLNPU	PLUNKED
	MEDIUMS		PERIDOT	DEKLNRU	KNURLED
DEIMNNO	ONE MIND	DEIOPRV	PROVIDE	DEKNNRU	DRUNKEN
DEIMNNU	MINUEND	DEIOPSS	DISPOSE	DEKNOSY	DONKEYS
DEIMNOV	MOVED IN			DEKNOTT	KNOTTED
DEIMNPS	IMPENDS			DEKNOUY	UNYOKED

133

DEKNRRU	DRUNKER	DEMNOOR	DOORMEN	DEOOPST	STOOPED
DEKOOPS	SPOOKED	DEMNOOV	MOVED ON	DEOOPSW	SWOOPED
DEKORST	STROKED	DEMNOOW	WOODMEN	DEOORRT	TO ORDER
DELLNOW	DWELL ON	DEMNORT	MORDENT	DEOORST	ROOSTED
DELLOOW	WOOLLED	DEMNORU	MOURNED	DEOORSW	DO WORSE
DELLOPR	REDPOLL	DEMNOST	ENDMOST	DEOORTU	OUTRODE
DELLORR	DROLLER	DEMNOTU	DEMOUNT		RODE OUT
DELLORT	TROLLED		MOUNTED	DEOOSTU	OUTDOES
DELLSTU	DULLEST	DEMNSTU	DUSTMEN	DEOPPPR	PROPPED
DELMMSU	SLUMMED	DEMOORT	MOTORED	DEOPPRR	DROPPER
DELMNOS	DOLMENS	DEMOOSS	OSMOSED	DEOPPST	STOPPED
DELMORS	SMOLDER	DEMOPST	STOMPED	DEOPPSW	SWOPPED
DELMORU	MOULDER	DEMOPUV	MOVED UP	DEOPRRU	PROUDER
	REMOULD	DEMORRS	DORMERS	DEOPRST	DEPORTS
DELMOSU	MODULES	DEMORST	STORMED		RED TOPS
DELMOTT	MOTTLED	DEMOSTY	MODESTY		SPORTED
DELMOTU	MOULTED	DEMPRTU	TRUMPED	DEOPRSW	POWDERS
DELMOUV	VOLUMED	DEMPSTU	STUMPED	DEOPRWY	POWDERY
DELMPPU	PLUMPED	DEMRRSU	MURDERS	DEOPSST	DESPOTS
DELMPSU	SLUMPED	DEMSTTU	SMUTTED	DEOPSTT	SPOTTED
DELMTUY	MUTEDLY	DENNOOW	ONE DOWN	DEOPSTU	SPOUTED
DELNOOS	NOODLES	DENNOST	TENDONS	DEORRSV	DROVERS
DELNORS	RONDELS	DENNSTU	STUNNED	DEORRSW	REWORDS
DELNORU	ROUNDEL	DENOOPS	SNOOPED	DEORSSS	DOSSERS
DELNOSS	OLDNESS		SPOONED	DEORSSW	DOWSERS
DELNOSU	NODULES	DENOORR	ON ORDER		DROWSES
DELNOTW	DWELT ON	DENOORV	DROVE ON	DEORSTU	DETOURS
	LET DOWN	DENOORW	ONE WORD		DOUREST
	LETDOWN	DENOOST	DOES NOT	DEORSTW	WORSTED
DELNOTY	NOTEDLY	DENOOSW	SWOONED	DEORSTY	DESTROY
DELNPRU	PLUNDER	DENOOSZ	SNOOZED	DEORSUV	DEVOURS
DELNRTU	TRUNDLE	DENOOTU	DUOTONE	DEORTTT	TROTTED
DELNSSU	DULNESS		OUTDONE	DEORTTU	TUTORED
DELOOPR	OLD ROPE	DENOPRS	PONDERS	DEORTUW	DREW OUT
DELOOPS	POODLES		RESPOND	DEOSSYY	ODYSSEY
	SPOOLED	DENOPRT	PORTEND	DEOSTTU	TESTUDO
DELOOST	STOOLED	DENOPRU	POUNDER	DEOSTTW	SWOTTED
	TOLEDOS	DENOPUW	OWNED UP	DEOSTUU	DUTEOUS
DELOOTU	DOLE OUT	DENOPUX	EXPOUND	DEOSTUX	TUXEDOS
DELOPPP	PLOPPED	DENORRU	ROUNDER	DEPRRSU	SPURRED
DELOPPR	DOPPLER	DENORRW	DROWNER	DEPRRUY	PRUDERY
DELOPPS	SLOPPED		WORN RED	DEPRSSU	DRESS UP
DELOPPT	TOPPLED	DENORST	RODENTS	DEPRSTU	SPURTED
DELOPRS	POLDERS		SNORTED	DEPRSUU	PURSUED
DELOPRT	DROPLET	DENORSU	RESOUND		USURPED
	LET DROP		SOUNDER	DERSSTU	DUSTERS
DELOPRW	PROWLED		UNDOERS		TRUSSED
DELOPSY	DEPLOYS	DENORSV	VENDORS	DERSTTU	TRUSTED
DELOPTT	PLOTTED	DENORSW	DOWNERS	DERSTTY	TRYSTED
DELOPTU	LED UP TO		WONDERS	DERSTUU	SUTURED
DELORRY	ORDERLY	DENORUW	REWOUND	DFFGINO	DOFFING
DELORSS	RODLESS	DENORWW	NEW WORD	DFFHLOO	HOLD OFF
	SOLDERS	DENOSTU	SEND OUT	DFFIIMR	MIDRIFF
DELORST	OLDSTER		SNOUTED	DFFLOOS	SOLD OFF
DELORUV	LOUVRED	DENOSTW	SET DOWN	DFFLOOT	TOLD OFF
DELOSTT	DOTTLES	DENPRSU	SPURNED	DFFNOOS	NODS OFF
	SLOTTED	DENPRTU	PRUDENT	DFFOOPR	DROP OFF
DELOSTU	LOUDEST	DENPSSU	SEND-UPS		DROP-OFF
	TOUSLED		SENDS UP	DFFOTUY	OFF DUTY
DELOSYY	DOYLEYS		SUSPEND	DFGGINU	FUDGING
DELOSZZ	SOZZLED	DENPTUU	TUNED UP	DFGHIOS	DOGFISH
DELOTUV	VOLUTED	DENRRTU	TURN RED	DFGIINN	FINDING
DELPPRU	PURPLED	DENRSSU	SUNDERS	DFGIINY	DIGNIFY
DELPPSU	SUPPLED		UNDRESS	DFGILNO	FOLDING
DELPRSU	SLURPED	DENRSSY	DRYNESS	DFGINNU	FUNDING
DELPUZZ	PUZZLED	DENSTTU	STUDENT	DFGINOR	FORDING
DELRRSU	SLURRED		STUNTED	DFGINOU	FUNGOID
DELRSTU	LUSTRED	DEOOPPS	OPPOSED	DFGLOOY	OLD FOGY
	STRUDEL	DEOOPRS	SPOORED	DFGOOOR	FOR GOOD
DELSSTU	TUSSLED	DEOOPRT	TORPEDO		GOOD FOR
DEMMRRU	DRUMMER		TROOPED	DFHILSU	DISHFUL

DFHOOOT	HOT FOOD	DGILNOR	LORDING	DHMSTUU	MUD HUTS
DFILLUY	FLUIDLY	DGIMNOO	DOOMING	DHOOOOS	HOODOOS
DFILMNU	MINDFUL	DGIMNPU	DUMPING	DHOORST	HOT RODS
DFILNOP	PINFOLD	DGIMOPY	PYGMOID	DHOPRSU	PUSHROD
DFILNOS	INFOLDS	DGINNNO	DONNING	DHORSSU	SHROUDS
DFILOSX	SIXFOLD	DGINNNU	DUNNING	DHORSUY	HYDROUS
DFILTUU	DUTIFUL	DGINNOR	DRONING	DHORXYY	HYDROXY
DFINNSU	IN FUNDS	DGINNOU	UNDOING	DIIIMRU	IRIDIUM
DFINOTU	FIND OUT	DGINNOW	DOWNING	DIIINPS	INSIPID
DFKLLOO	OLD FOLK	DGINNUY	UNDYING	DIIJNOS	DISJOIN
DFLLOOO	OLD FOOL	DGINOPU	DOING UP	DIIKKNS	KIDSKIN
DFLNOSU	UNFOLDS	DGINORW	WORDING	DIIKNNR	DRINK IN
DFLOOTU	FOLDOUT	DGINOST	TIN GODS	DIILLNW	ILL WIND
DFLOOTW	TWOFOLD	DGINOSU	DOUSING	DIILMTY	TIMIDLY
DFLOPSU	FOLDS UP			DIILNWY	WINDILY
DFNORUY	FOUNDRY	DGINOSW	DOWSING	DIILRTY	DIRTILY
DGGGINO	DOGGING	DGINOTT	DOTTING	DIILSST	DISTILS
DGGIILN	GILDING	DGINOTW	GOT WIND	DIILVVY	VIVIDLY
	GLIDING	DGINSTU	DUSTING	DIILYZZ	DIZZILY
DGGIINU	GUIDING	DGIOOPT	GOOD TIP	DIIMSSS	DISMISS
DGGIJNU	JUDGING	DGIOPRY	PRODIGY	DIIMSTW	DIMWITS
DGGILNO	LODGING	DGIOSTW	GODWITS	DIINNSW	WINDS IN
DGGINNU	NUDGING	DGIQSUY	SQUIDGY	DIINORS	SORDINI
DGGNOSU	DUGONGS	DGISSTU	DISGUST	DIINQSU	QUIDS IN
	GUN DOGS	DGLNOOS	OLD SONG	DIIORSV	DIVISOR
	GUNDOGS	DGLNOUY	UNGODLY	DIIQSUX	SIX QUID
DGGOPSU	PUG DOGS	DGLOOPT	GOLD TOP	DIJOSTU	JUDOIST
DGHIINS	DISHING	DGLOORW	GROW OLD	DIKLSUY	DUSKILY
	HIDINGS	DGLOOST	LOST DOG	DIKNNOS	NONSKID
	SHINDIG	DGLOPSY	SPLODGY	DIKNNRU	DRUNK IN
DGHILNO	HOLDING	DGNOORS	DRONGOS	DIKNOOT	TOO KIND
DGHIOOS	GOODISH	DGNOORU	GO ROUND	DIKNPRU	DRINK UP
DGHIORT	DO RIGHT		GOOD RUN	DIKORSW	SKID ROW
DGHLOOT	GOT HOLD	DGNOORW	DO WRONG	DILLOSY	SOLIDLY
DGHOOST	HOT DOGS	DGNOOSS	GODSONS	DILLRUY	LURIDLY
DGHOOSW	DOG SHOW	DGNOOSW	GODOWNS	DILMNRU	DRUMLIN
	SHOW DOG	DGNOOTW	GOT DOWN	DILMOOY	MOODILY
DGHORTU	DROUGHT	DGNORSU	GROUNDS	DILMORS	MILORDS
DGHOTUY	DOUGHTY	DGOOOOT	TOO GOOD	DILMORU	OIL DRUM
DGIILNS	SIDLING	DGOOOPR	POOR DOG	DILMPUY	DUMPILY
	SLIDING	DGOOPST	TOP DOGS	DILMTUY	TUMIDLY
DGIILNW	WILDING	DGOORTY	GOOD TRY	DILNNSU	DUNLINS
DGIILNY	DINGILY	DGOOSTY	TOY DOGS	DILNPSY	SPINDLY
DGIILRY	RIGIDLY	DGOSTUU	DUGOUTS	DILNRUW	RUN WILD
DGIIMMN	DIMMING	DHHIOST	HOT DISH	DILOOPP	POP IDOL
DGIIMNN	MINDING	DHIILSW	WILDISH	DILOPST	POT LIDS
DGIIMNS	SMIDGIN	DHIIMNO	HOMINID	DILORST	LORDS IT
DGIIMOS	SIGMOID	DHIINRT	IN THIRD	DILORTU	DILUTOR
DGIINNN	DINNING	DHIIOPX	XIPHOID	DILORWY	ROWDILY
DGIINNO	DOING IN	DHIKRSU	KURDISH		WORDILY
DGIINNR	RINDING	DHILMUY	HUMIDLY	DILOSSU	SOLIDUS
DGIINNU	INDUING	DHILNOP	DOLPHIN	DILOSTY	STYLOID
DGIINNW	WINDING	DHILOST	DOLTISH	DILOTTY	DOTTILY
DGIINOS	INDIGOS	DHILRTY	THIRDLY	DILRYZZ	DRIZZLY
DGIINOT	DOING IT	DHIMOPS	DISH MOP	DILSTUY	DUSTILY
DGIINOV	VOIDING	DHIMORU	HUMIDOR	DIMMOST	MIDMOST
DGIINOX	DIGOXIN		RHODIUM	DIMNOOS	DOMINOS
DGIINPP	DIPPING	DHINNOS	DONNISH	DIMNOPU	IMPOUND
DGIINPR	PRIDING	DHINSSY	SHINDYS	DIMNOUY	MIND YOU
DGIINRS	RIDINGS	DHIOPTY	TYPHOID	DIMOPSU	PODIUMS
DGIINRV	DRIVING	DHIORTY	THYROID	DIMRUUV	DUUMVIR
DGIINSS	SIDINGS	DHIOSTU	DISH OUT	DIMSTUY	TIDY SUM
DGIINST	TIDINGS	DHKORSY	DROSHKY	DINNOPW	PIN DOWN
DGIINTY	DIGNITY	DHLLORU	ROD HULL	DINNOUW	WOUND IN
	TIDYING	DHLMOOU	HOODLUM	DINNSUW	UNWINDS
DGIKMNO	KINGDOM	DHLNOOS	HOLDS ON	DINOORS	INDOORS
DGIKNNU	DUNKING	DHLOOTU	HOLD OUT		SORDINO
DGILLNU	DULLING	DHLOPSU	HOLDS UP	DINOOST	STOOD IN
DGILLOR	OLD GIRL		HOLDUPS	DINOPRS	DROPS IN
DGILMNO	MOLDING		UPHOLDS	DINOPSU	DUPIONS
DGILNOP	GOLD PIN	DHMMRUU	HUMDRUM	DINORSW	IN WORDS

DINORWW	WINDROW	EEEFLRS	FEELERS	EEELSSY	EYELESS
DINOSSW	DISOWNS	EEEFLRT	FLEETER	EEELSTX	TELEXES
DINOSTW	SIT DOWN	EEEFLTY	LEFT EYE	EEELSTY	EYELETS
DINOSWW	WINDOWS	EEEFMNR	FREE MEN	EEELTTX	TELETEX
DINPRSY	SPIN-DRY		FREEMEN	EEEMRTX	EXTREME
DINPSTU	PUNDITS	EEEFNTT	TEN FEET	EEEMSST	ESTEEMS
DINPSUW	WINDS UP	EEEFORS	FORESEE	EEEMSTT	MEETEST
DINSSTU	NUDISTS	EEEFRRS	REEFERS	EEEMSTU	EMEUTES
DIOOPSS	ISOPODS	EEEFRRZ	FREEZER	EEENNTT	ENTENTE
DIOPRST	DISPORT	EEEFRST	SET FREE	EEENPRR	PREENER
	DROPS IT	EEEFRSZ	FREEZES	EEENPRT	TERPENE
	TRIPODS	EEEGILS	ELEGIES	EEENPST	STEEPEN
DIOQTUW	TWO QUID	EEEGILZ	ELEGIZE	EEENPSX	EXPENSE
DIORSTT	DISTORT	EEEGINP	EPIGENE	EEENRRS	SERENER
DIOSSTU	STUDIOS	EEEGIPR	PERIGEE		SNEERER
DIPRSTU	DISRUPT	EEEGLNT	GENTEEL	EEENRRT	REENTER
DJNNOOS	DONJONS	EEEGMRS	EMERGES	EEENRRW	RENEWER
DJNOOTW	JOT DOWN	EEEGNPR	EPERGNE	EEENRST	ENTREES
DKLLOOO	LOOK OLD	EEEGNRR	GREENER	EEENRSV	VENEERS
DKNPRUU	DRUNK UP		RENEGER	EEENRSZ	SNEEZER
DLLOOPS	DOLLOPS	EEEGNRS	RENEGES	EEENRTV	EVENTER
DLLOPSU	DOLLS UP	EEEGNRV	REVENGE	EEENRUV	REVENUE
DLLORWY	WORLDLY	EEEGNSS	GENESES	EEENSSZ	SNEEZES
DLMNOOO	OLD MOON	EEEGNTV	GET EVEN	EEENSTW	SWEETEN
DLMOSUU	MODULUS	EEEGRRT	GREETER	EEEORSV	OVERSEE
DLNOOWW	LOW DOWN	EEEGRSZ	GEEZERS		SEE OVER
	LOW-DOWN	EEEGRUX	EXERGUE	EEEORSY	EYESORE
	LOWDOWN	EEEHILW	WHEELIE	EEEPPRS	PEEPERS
DLNORUY	ROUNDLY	EEEHLLN	HELLENE	EEEPRSS	PEERESS
DLNOSUY	SOUNDLY	EEEHLOY	EYEHOLE	EEEPRST	STEEPER
DLOOPWY	PLYWOOD	EEEHLRW	WHEELER	EEEPRSW	SWEEPER
DLOOSTU	OUTSOLD	EEEHRRS	SHEERER		WEEPERS
	SOLD OUT	EEEHSST	SEETHES	EEEQRRU	QUEERER
	SOLD-OUT	EEEHSTT	ESTHETE	EEEQSUZ	SQUEEZE
DLOPRUY	PROUDLY	EEEHSWZ	WHEEZES	EEERRST	STEERER
DLOSTUW	WOULDST	EEEIKLL	EELLIKE	EEERRSV	RESERVE
DMNOOWW	MOW DOWN	EEEIKLY	EYELIKE		REVERES
DMORTUU	DRUM OUT	EEEIKLZ	EZEKIEL		REVERSE
DNNOORU	ROUND ON	EEEILRV	RELIEVE		SEVERER
DNNORUU	UNROUND	EEEILVY	EVIL EYE	EEERSTT	TEETERS
DNNORUW	RUN DOWN	EEEIMNS	ENEMIES	EEERSTW	SWEETER
	RUN-DOWN	EEEIMRT	EREMITE	EEERSVW	WEEVERS
	RUNDOWN	EEEINRT	TEENIER	EEERTTW	TWEETER
DNNOSUU	UNSOUND	EEEINRW	WEENIER	EEERTWY	YEW TREE
DNNOSUW	SUNDOWN	EEEIPST	EPEEIST	EEESSTT	SETTEES
DNNOUUW	UNWOUND	EEEIPSW	WEEPIES	EEFFFNO	ENFEOFF
DNOOPRS	DROPS ON	EEEIRRV	REVERIE	EEFFINT	FIFTEEN
DNOORTU	OROTUND	EEEIRST	EERIEST	EEFFKOP	KEEP OFF
DNOOTWW	TWO DOWN	EEEISTW	SWEETIE	EEFFKOW	WEEK OFF
DNOPRUU	ROUND UP	EEEISTY	EYETIES	EEFFLOP	PEEL OFF
	ROUNDUP	EEEKLNR	KNEELER	EEFFLOR	REEL OFF
DNOPTUW	PUT DOWN	EEEKLNS	SLEEKEN	EEFFNOS	SEEN OFF
	PUT-DOWN	EEEKLNX	KLEENEX	EEFFORR	FOR FREE
DNOPUUW	WOUND UP	EEEKLRS	SLEEKER		REOFFER
DOOOOSV	VOODOOS	EEEKMST	MEEKEST	EEFFOSS	SEES OFF
DOOORSU	ODOROUS	EEEKNOW	ONE WEEK	EEFFOST	TEES OFF
DOOORTU	OUTDOOR	EEEKNPT	KEEPNET		TOFFEES
DOOOSTT	STOOD TO	EEEKNST	KEENEST	EEFFSSU	EFFUSES
DOOPRSY	PROSODY	EEEKPRS	KEEPERS	EEFGILN	FEELING
DOOPRTU	DROP OUT	EEEKRSS	SEEKERS		FINE LEG
	DROPOUT	EEELMNT	ELEMENT	EEFGINR	FEIGNER
DOOPSTU	STOOD UP	EEELMRT	ELM TREE		FREEING
DPSSTUU	DUST-UPS	EEELNSV	ELEVENS		REEFING
EEEEFRR	REFEREE	EEELPRS	PEELERS	EEFGIRT	FIG TREE
EEEEGGS	GEE GEES		SLEEPER	EEFGLLT	LEFT LEG
	GEE-GEES	EEELPRT	REPLETE	EEFGLLU	GLEEFUL
EEEEGTX	EXEGETE	EEELPST	STEEPLE	EEFGLOR	FORELEG
EEEEPST	TEEPEES	EEELRTV	LEVERET	EEFGLOS	SOLFEGE
EEEESWW	WEE-WEES	EEELSSS	LESSEES	EEFGLOT	GOLF TEE
EEEFGRU	REFUGEE	EEELSST	LET'S SEE	EEFGRSU	REFUGES
EEEFILS	SEE LIFE	EEELSSV	SLEEVES	EEFHIRS	HEIFERS

EEFHIRT	FREE HIT	EEFRSSU	REFUSES	EEGNPTT	TENT PEG
	HEFTIER	EEFRSTT	FETTERS	EEGNPUX	EXPUNGE
EEFHISY	FISH-EYE	EEFRSTU	REFUTES	EEGNRSS	NEGRESS
EEFHITW	THE WIFE	EEFRVWY	VERY FEW	EEGNRST	REGENTS
EEFHLOT	FEEL HOT	EEFSSTU	FETUSES	EEGOPRT	PROTEGE
EEFHLRS	HERSELF	EEGGHTU	THUGGEE	EEGORTV	GET OVER
EEFHLSS	FLESHES	EEGGLPS	PEG LEGS	EEGOSSS	GESSOES
EEFHNRS	FRESHEN	EEGGNOR	ENGORGE	EEGRRSS	REGRESS
EEFHNST	THE FENS		GO GREEN	EEGRRST	REGRETS
EEFHORT	THEREOF	EEGGNST	NEST EGG	EEGRRSU	RESURGE
EEFHORW	WHEREOF	EEGHILN	HEELING	EEGRRSV	VERGERS
EEFHRRS	FRESHER	EEGHINY	HYGIENE	EEGRRUY	GRUYERE
	REFRESH	EEGHIOR	HERE I GO	EEGRSSU	GUESSER
EEFHRRU	FUEHRER	EEGHIRW	WEIGHER	EEGRSSY	GEYSERS
EEFHRST	FRESHET	EEGHLPT	GET HELP	EEGRSTT	GETTERS
EEFIIRS	REIFIES	EEGHMOT	GET HOME	EEGRSTU	GESTURE
EEFIKPT	KEEP FIT	EEGIJNR	JEERING	EEGSSSU	GUESSES
EEFILLL	FEEL ILL	EEGIKKN	KEEKING	EEGSSTT	GETS SET
EEFILRS	RELIEFS	EEGIKLN	KEELING	EEHHRTW	WHETHER
EEFILRT	FERTILE	EEGIKNN	KEENING	EEHIKLT	THE LIKE
EEFILST	FELSITE		KNEEING	EEHILMN	HEMLINE
	LEFTIES	EEGIKNP	KEEPING	EEHILNT	THE LINE
EEFIMNN	FINE MEN		PEEKING		THE NILE
EEFIMNR	FIREMEN	EEGIKNR	IN GREEK	EEHILPV	PEHLEVI
EEFIMNV	FIVE MEN		REEKING	EEHILST	SHELTIE
EEFINRR	REFINER	EEGILNP	PEELING	EEHILSX	HELIXES
EEFINRS	REFINES	EEGILNR	LEERING	EEHIMOT	HOME TIE
EEFINSS	FINESSE		REELING	EEHIMTT	THE TIME
EEFIRRS	FERRIES	EEGILNT	GENTILE	EEHINOR	HEROINE
EEFIRRT	FERRITE	EEGIMNR	REGIMEN	EEHINRS	INHERES
	FIR TREE	EEGIMNS	SEEMING	EEHINRT	NEITHER
EEFIRST	SET FIRE	EEGIMNT	MEETING		THEREIN
EEFIRSZ	FRIEZES		TEEMING	EEHINRW	WHEREIN
EEFISTV	FESTIVE	EEGIMRS	EMIGRES	EEHIORS	HEROISE
EEFISTX	SIX FEET		REGIMES	EEHIORZ	HEROIZE
EEFLLOS	FELLOES	EEGINNP	PEENING	EEHIPRT	PRITHEE
EEFLLRS	FELLERS	EEGINNR	IN GREEN	EEHIPSV	PEEVISH
EEFLLTY	FLEETLY	EEGINNS	ENGINES	EEHIPTT	EPITHET
EEFLNNS	FENNELS	EEGINNU	GENUINE	EEHIRSS	HEIRESS
EEFLNOS	FELONES		INGENUE	EEHIRST	THERE IS
	ONESELF	EEGINNV	EVENING	EEHISTV	THIEVES
EEFLNSS	FLENSES	EEGINOP	EPIGONE	EEHITTX	THE EXIT
EEFLNTW	NEW LEFT	EEGINPP	PEEPING	EEHKLOY	KEYHOLE
EEFLOTU	FEEL OUT	EEGINPR	PEERING	EEHLLMP	PHELLEM
EEFLRRU	FERRULE	EEGINPS	SEEPING	EEHLLOW	LOW HEEL
EEFLRSU	FERULES	EEGINPV	PEEVING	EEHLMST	HELMETS
	REFUELS	EEGINPW	WEEPING	EEHLOSW	WHO ELSE?
EEFLRUX	FLEXURE	EEGINRS	GREISEN	EEHLOSY	HOLY SEE
EEFLSTT	FETTLES	EEGINRT	INTEGER	EEHLRST	SHELTER
EEFLSUY	EYEFULS	EEGINRV	VEERING	EEHLRSW	WELSHER
EEFMNOR	FOREMEN	EEGINSS	GENESIS	EEHLRTU	THE RULE
EEFMNRT	FERMENT	EEGINTX	EXIGENT	EEHLSSV	SHELVES
EEFMOTT	MOFETTE	EEGIRRV	GRIEVER	EEHLSSW	WELSHES
EEFMPRU	PERFUME	EEGIRSV	GRIEVES	EEHLSTT	SHTETEL
EEFNRRU	RUN FREE	EEGISTV	VESTIGE	EEHMNOP	PHONEME
EEFNRRY	FERNERY	EEGLLSS	LEGLESS	EEHMORT	THEOREM
EEFNRTV	FERVENT	EEGLLTW	GET WELL	EEHMRUX	EXHUMER
EEFNSSW	FEWNESS	EEGLMMU	GEMMULE	EEHMSUX	EXHUMES
EEFNSSY	FEYNESS	EEGLMSU	LEGUMES	EEHNOPT	POTHEEN
EEFORRT	REFER TO	EEGLNOR	ERE LONG	EEHNORT	NOT HERE
EEFORRV	FOR EVER	EEGLNOZ	LOZENGE		THEREON
	FOREVER	EEGLNRT	GENTLER	EEHNORW	NOWHERE
EEFORTX	TREE FOX	EEGLNRY	GREENLY		WHEREON
EEFOTTU	FOUETTE	EEGLNST	GENTLES	EEHNPSW	NEPHEWS
EEFOTTW	TWO FEET	EEGLORV	LEG OVER	EEHNSTU	ENTHUSE
EEFPRRS	PREFERS	EEGLRST	ST.LEGER	EEHNSTV	SEVENTH
EEFPRSU	PERFUSE	EEGMNST	SEGMENT	EEHNSTW	THE NEWS
EEFRRST	FERRETS	EEGMRRS	MERGERS	EEHOOPW	WHOOPEE
EEFRRSU	REFUSER	EEGMRTU	GUM TREE	EEHOPPT	THE POPE
EEFRRTY	FERRETY	EEGNORS	NEGROES	EEHORRV	HOVERER
EEFRSST	FESTERS	EEGNOTV	GOT EVEN		

EEHORST	HETEROS	EEILRSU	LEISURE	EEINSTX	SIXTEEN
	SO THERE!	EEILRSV	RELIVES	EEINSTY	SYENITE
EEHORSU	REHOUSE		REVILES	EEINSTZ	SIZE TEN
EEHORTT	THERETO		SERVILE	EEIOPST	POETISE
EEHORTW	WHERETO	EEILSSS	SESSILE	EEIOPTZ	POETIZE
EEHORVW	HOWEVER	EEILSST	TIELESS	EEIORSV	EROSIVE
	WHOEVER	EEILSSU	ILEUSES	EEIOSTT	SEE TO IT
EEHOSTT	TEE SHOT	EEILSTV	LEVITES	EEIPPTT	PIPETTE
EEHOTTV	THE VOTE	EEILSUV	ELUSIVE	EEIPQRU	PERIQUE
EEHPPST	HEPPEST	EEILSVW	WEEVILS	EEIPRRS	REPRISE
EEHPRSS	SPHERES	EEILTTX	TEXTILE		RESPIRE
EEHPRTU	THREE UP	EEILVWY	WEEVILY	EEIPRST	RESPITE
EEHRRST	THREE RS	EEIMMNS	IMMENSE	EEIPRSX	EXPIRES
EEHRSTT	TETHERS	EEIMMRS	IMMERSE	EEIPRTT	PETTIER
EEHRSTW	WETHERS	EEIMNNN	NINE MEN	EEIPRVW	PREVIEW
EEHRTTW	WHETTER	EEIMNNO	NOMINEE	EEIPSTW	PEEWITS
EEHSTTW	THE WEST	EEIMNNT	EMINENT	EEIPSUZ	SEIZE UP
EEHSTUY	SHUT-EYE	EEIMNOT	ONE TIME	EEIQRRU	QUERIER
EEIILNX	IN EXILE		ONETIME		REQUIRE
EEIIMPR	RIEMPIE	EEIMNRS	ERMINES	EEIQRSU	ESQUIRE
EEIIMST	ITEMISE	EEIMNRW	WIREMEN		QUERIES
EEIIMTZ	ITEMIZE	EEIMNSS	MEISSEN	EEIQRTU	QUIETER
EEIINTV	INVITEE		NEMESIS		REQUITE
EEIJKRR	JERKIER		SIEMENS	EEIRRRT	TERRIER
EEIJLLS	JELLIES	EEIMNSW	WISE MEN	EEIRRST	ETRIERS
EEIJMMS	JEMMIES	EEIMOPT	EPITOME		RETIRES
EEIJRRS	JERRIES	EEIMOSS	MEIOSES		TERRIES
EEIJSTT	JETTIES	EEIMOTV	EMOTIVE	EEIRRSV	REVISER
EEIKLNT	NETLIKE	EEIMPRR	PREMIER	EEIRRSW	REWIRES
EEIKLPS	KELPIES	EEIMPRS	EMPIRES	EEIRRTV	RIVETER
EEIKLPT	PIKELET		EPIMERS	EEIRRTW	REWRITE
EEIKLST	SLEEKIT		PREMISE	EEIRRVV	REVIVER
EEIKNPS	KEEPS IN	EEIMPRT	EMPTIER	EEIRSSU	REISSUE
EEIKNPY	PINKEYE	EEIMPST	EMPTIES	EEIRSSV	REVISES
EEIKNSW	IN WEEKS	EEIMQRU	REQUIEM	EEIRSTT	TESTIER
EEIKPRR	PERKIER	EEIMRRR	MERRIER	EEIRSTV	RESTIVE
EEIKPRS	PESKIER	EEIMRRT	TRIREME	EEIRSUZ	SEIZURE
EEIKTTT	TEKTITE	EEIMRSS	MESSIER	EEIRSVV	REVIVES
EEILLNS	NELLIES	EEIMRST	METIERS	EEIRSVW	REVIEWS
EEILLPS	ELLIPSE	EEIMRTT	EMITTER		VIEWERS
EEILLRV	EVILLER		TERMITE	EEISSTX	SEXIEST
EEILLST	TELLIES	EEIMSST	SEMITES	EEJPRRU	PERJURE
EEILLSW	WELLIES	EEINNPS	PENNIES	EEJRSST	JESTERS
EEILMNO	ONE MILE	EEINNRT	INTERNE	EEJRSSY	JERSEYS
EEILMNV	EVIL MEN	EEINNST	INTENSE	EEKLLSY	SLEEKLY
EEILMRV	VERMEIL	EEINNTW	ENTWINE	EEKLLUU	UKULELE
EEILNNO	LEONINE	EEINNWW	NEW WINE	EEKLNNS	KENNELS
EEILNNT	LENIENT	EEINOPR	PIONEER	EEKLNOS	KEELSON
EEILNNV	ENLIVEN	EEINOPS	PEONIES	EEKLNRS	KERNELS
EEILNOV	EVIL ONE	EEINOSZ	SIZE ONE	EEKLOOS	LOOK SEE
EEILNPS	PENSILE	EEINPRR	REPINER	EEKLRST	KELTERS
	SLEEP IN		RIPENER		KESTREL
EEILNRS	LIERNES	EEINPRS	EREPSIN	EEKLSSY	KEYLESS
EEILNSS	ENSILES		REPINES	EEKLSTT	KETTLES
EEILNST	LISENTE	EEINPRT	PETRINE	EEKMMPU	KEEP MUM
	SETLINE	EEINPSS	PENISES	EEKMOVY	KEY MOVE
	TENSILE	EEINPSV	PENSIVE	EEKNOOT	TOO KEEN
EEILNTT	ENTITLE		VESPINE	EEKNOPS	KEEPS ON
EEILNTV	VEINLET	EEINQRU	ENQUIRE	EEKNOST	KETONES
EEILOPT	PETIOLE	EEINQTU	QUEEN IT	EEKNOTY	KEY NOTE
EEILORV	OVERLIE		QUIETEN		KEYNOTE
EEILOTZ	ZEOLITE	EEINRRT	RENTIER	EEKNPSU	KNEES UP
EEILPRS	REPLIES		TERRINE		KNEES-UP
	SPIELER	EEINRRV	VERNIER	EEKNSST	KNESSET
EEILPRT	PERLITE	EEINRST	ENTRIES	EEKNSTU	NETSUKE
	REPTILE	EEINRSV	INVERSE	EEKOPTU	KEEP OUT
EEILPRU	PUERILE	EEINRSW	WIENERS	EEKORRV	REVOKER
EEILPSS	PELISSE	EEINRTT	ENTER IT	EEKORSV	REVOKES
EEILPST	EPISTLE	EEINRTU	RETINUE	EEKOSTU	SEEK OUT
EEILRRV	REVILER		REUNITE	EEKPPSU	KEEPS UP
EEILRST	STERILE		UTERINE	EEKPRSU	PERUKES

EEKRSSW	SKEWERS	EELSTVV	VELVETS	EENSSTT	TENSEST
EEKRSSY	KERSEYS	EELSTVW	TWELVES	EENSSTW	WETNESS
EELLLVY	LEVELLY	EELSTWY	SWEETLY	EENSSUX	NEXUSES
EELLMOS	MOSELLE	EELTVVY	VELVETY		UNSEXES
EELLMRS	SMELLER	EEMMNOT	MEMENTO	EENSTTX	EXTENTS
EELLMTW	WELL MET	EEMNNOV	ENVENOM	EENSTVY	SEVENTY
EELLNOV	NOVELLE	EEMNOOS	SOMEONE	EEOPRRV	REPROVE
EELLPRS	RESPELL	EEMNORY	MONEYER	EEOPRSS	REPOSES
	SPELLER	EEMNOST	STONE ME!	EEOPRSX	EXPOSER
EELLPST	PELLETS	EEMNPTU	UMPTEEN	EEOPRTT	TREETOP
EELLQRU	QUELLER	EEMNSYZ	ENZYMES	EEOPSSU	ESPOUSE
EELLRSS	SELLERS	EEMOPRR	EMPEROR	EEOPSSX	EXPOSES
EELLRST	TELLERS	EEMOPRW	EMPOWER	EEOPSTU	SEEP OUT
EELLRSY	YELLERS	EEMOPST	METOPES		TOUPEES
EELLSSV	S LEVELS	EEMORRS	REMORSE	EEOPSTY	EYESPOT
EELLSTW	WELL SET	EEMORRT	REMOTER	EEORRST	RESTORE
EELMORW	EELWORM	EEMORRV	REMOVER	EEORRTW	REWROTE
EELMPST	PELMETS	EEMORST	METEORS	EEORSST	STEREOS
	TEMPLES	EEMORSV	REMOVES	EEORSTT	ROSETTE
EELMRST	SMELTER	EEMPPRT	PREEMPT	EEORSTV	OVERSET
EELMSTT	METTLES	EEMPRSS	EMPRESS	EEORSUV	OEUVRES
EELNOOV	ONE LOVE	EEMPRST	TEMPERS	EEORSVW	OVERSEW
EELNOPS	SLEEP ON	EEMPRSU	PRESUME	EEORSXX	XEROXES
EELNOPV	ENVELOP		SUPREME	EEOSSTU	SEES OUT
EELNOPY	POLYENE	EEMPRTT	TEMPTER	EEPPPRS	PEPPERS
EELNOSV	ELEVONS	EEMPRTU	PERMUTE	EEPPRSX	PERSPEX
	SLOVENE	EEMPSTT	TEMPEST	EEPPSST	STEPPES
EELNOTU	TOLUENE	EEMPSTU	SET EM UP	EEPPSUW	SWEEP UP
EELNPSY	SPLEENY	EEMPSTX	EXEMPTS	EEPQUUU	QUEUE UP
EELNRST	RELENTS	EEMRSSU	RESUMES	EEPRRSS	PRESSER
EELNRSU	UNREELS	EEMRSUX	MUREXES		REPRESS
EELNSSS	LESSENS	EENNORT	ENTERON	EEPRRSU	PERUSER
EELNSST	NESTLES	EENNOSS	NON ESSE	EEPRRTV	PERVERT
	NETLESS		ONENESS	EEPRSSS	PRESSES
EELNSTT	NETTLES	EENNOTY	NEOTENY	EEPRSST	PESTERS
EELNSTY	TENSELY	EENNPTU	NEPTUNE		PRESETS
EELNTTU	LUNETTE	EENNRST	TENNERS	EEPRSSU	PERUSES
EELOPPS	PEOPLES	EENNRUV	UNNERVE	EEPRSSV	VESPERS
EELOPRX	EXPLORE	EENNSST	SENNETS	EEPRSSW	SPEWERS
EELOPTU	EELPOUT	EENNSSU	UNSEENS	EEPRSSX	EXPRESS
EELORSV	RESOLVE	EENNSSW	NEWNESS	EEPRSTT	ST.PETER
EELORVV	REVOLVE	EENOPPT	PEPTONE	EEPRSTU	REPUTES
EELOSTT	TELEOST	EENOPRS	OPENERS	EEPRSTW	PEWTERS
EELOSVV	EVOLVES		REOPENS	EEPRSTX	EXPERTS
EELOTUV	EVOLUTE	EENOPST	ONE-STEP	EEPRSUV	SERVE UP
	VELOUTE		PENTOSE	EEPRTTX	PRETEXT
EELPPRX	PERPLEX		STEP ONE	EEPSSTT	SEPTETS
EELPRST	PETRELS	EENORSS	SENORES	EEPSTTU	PUTTEES
	PRESTEL	EENORTU	EN ROUTE	EEPSTTY	TYPESET
	SPELTER	EENOSTU	SEEN OUT	EEQRRUY	EQUERRY
EELPRSU	REPULSE	EENOSTW	SWEET ON	EEQRSTU	REQUEST
EELPRSY	YELPERS		TOWNEES	EEQSUXY	FXFOUYS
EELPRTZ	PRETZEL	EENOSVZ	EVZONES	EERRSSV	SERVERS
EELPRVY	REPLEVY	EENPRST	PRESENT	EERRSTU	URETERS
EELPSST	PESTLES		REPENTS	EERRSTV	REVERTS
EELPSTY	STEEPLY		SERPENT	EERRSVY	SERVERY
EELQRUY	QUEERLY	EENPRTV	PREVENT	EERRTTU	UTTERER
EELQSSU	SEQUELS	EENQSTU	SEQUENT	EERSSST	TRESSES
EELRRVY	REVELRY	EENRRST	RENTERS	EERSSTT	SETTERS
EELRSTT	LETTERS		STERNER		STREETS
	SETTLER	EENRRTY	REENTRY		TERSEST
	TRESTLE	EENRRUV	NERVURE	EERSSVW	SWERVES
EELRSTW	SWELTER	EENRSST	RESENTS	EERSTTU	TRUSTEE
	WELTERS	EENRSSU	ENSURES	EERSTTW	WETTERS
	WRESTLE	EENRSTT	TENTERS	EERSTUV	VESTURE
EELRSTY	TERSELY	EENRSTU	NEUTERS	EERTTUX	TEXTURE
EELRSTZ	SELTZER		TENURES	EESSTTX	SEXTETS
EELSSSU	USELESS		TUREENS	EESTTTW	WETTEST
EELSSSV	VESSELS	EENRSTW	WESTERN	EFFFIOR	FIRE OFF
EELSSSX	SEXLESS	EENRSTY	STYRENE	EFFFLLO	FELL OFF
EELSSTT	SETTLES	EENRTUV	VENTURE	EFFFLOT	LEFT OFF

EFFFLOW	FLEW OFF	EFGINRS	FINGERS	EFILORT	LOFTIER
EFFGNOO	GONE OFF		FRINGES		TREFOIL
EFFGOOS	GOES OFF	EFGINRU	GUNFIRE	EFILPPR	FLIPPER
EFFGORS	GOFFERS	EFGIOOR	GOOFIER	EFILPRS	PILFERS
EFFGOST	GETS OFF	EFGIORV	FORGIVE	EFILPTT	FELT TIP
EFFGRRU	GRUFFER	EFGIRRT	GRIFTER	EFILQUY	LIQUEFY
EFFHILW	WHIFFLE	EFGIRRU	FIGURER	EFILRRT	TRIFLER
EFFHIOV	HIVE OFF	EFGIRSU	FIGURES	EFILRST	FILTERS
EFFHIRS	SHERIFF	EFGLNSU	ENGULFS		TRIFLES
EFFHLSU	SHUFFLE	EFGLNTU	FULGENT	EFILRTT	FLITTER
EFFIIST	FIFTIES	EFGLORS	GOLFERS	EFILRZZ	FRIZZLE
EFFIKLS	SKIFFLE	EFGMNOR	FROGMEN	EFILSST	STIFLES
EFFILNO	OFF LINE	EFGNOOR	FORGONE	EFILSTT	LEFTIST
	OFF-LINE		GONE FOR	EFILSZZ	FIZZLES
EFFILNS	SNIFFLE	EFGOORS	FORGOES	EFIMMRU	FERMIUM
EFFILOR	FOR LIFE		GOES FOR	EFIMNOR	FERMION
EFFILRS	RIFFLES	EFGORRY	FORGERY	EFIMNTT	FITMENT
EFFILRY	FIREFLY	EFGORST	FORGETS	EFIMRST	FIRMEST
EFFIMOT	TIME OFF	EFGORXY	GREY FOX	EFINNOR	INFERNO
EFFINRS	SNIFFER	EFHIIRS	FISHIER	EFINNRU	FUNNIER
EFFINST	STIFFEN	EFHIJSW	JEWFISH	EFINNSU	FUNNIES
EFFIOPW	WIPE OFF	EFHILMS	FLEMISH	EFINOPR	PINE FOR
EFFIORT	FORFEIT		HIMSELF	EFINOSX	FIXES ON
EFFIRST	STIFFER	EFHILSS	SELFISH	EFINRST	SNIFTER
EFFKOPT	KEPT OFF	EFHILTY	HEFTILY	EFINRSU	INFUSER
EFFLLOR	FELL FOR	EFHINST	FISHNET	EFINSST	FITNESS
EFFLLOS	SELL OFF	EFHIORR	FOR HIRE		INFESTS
EFFLLOT	TELL OFF	EFHIORS	FISH ROE	EFINSSU	INFUSES
EFFLLOW	WELL OFF	EFHIRSY	FISHERY	EFIOOST	FOOTSIE
	WELL-OFF	EFHLLPU	HELPFUL	EFIORRT	ROTIFER
EFFLMRU	MUFFLER	EFHLLSY	FLESHLY	EFIORST	FORTIES
EFFLMSU	MUFFLES	EFHLMOY	FLY HOME	EFIOSST	SOFTIES
EFFLNSU	SNUFFLE	EFHLOOT	THE FOOL	EFIOSTX	FOXIEST
EFFLOST	LETS OFF	EFHLOOX	FOXHOLE	EFIPRSU	FRIES UP
EFFLOSU	SOUFFLE	EFHLOPU	HOPEFUL	EFIPRTY	PETRIFY
EFFLRSU	RUFFLES	EFHLOTT	FELT HOT	EFIPSUX	FIXES UP
EFFLRTU	FRETFUL	EFHLRSU	FLUSHER	EFIRRRU	FURRIER
	TRUFFLE	EFHLRSY	FRESHLY	EFIRRTT	FRITTER
EFFMOOV	MOVE OFF	EFHLSSU	FLUSHES	EFIRRTU	FRUITER
EFFNOOR	ON OFFER	EFHLSTY	THYSELF	EFIRRTY	TERRIFY
EFFNOST	SENT OFF	EFHLTTW	TWELFTH	EFIRSST	SIFTERS
EFFNOTW	WENT OFF	EFHNOTZ	THE FONZ	EFIRSSU	FISSURE
EFFNRSU	SNUFFER	EFHOORS	HOOFERS		FUSSIER
EFFOOPR	ROPE OFF	EFHRRTU	FURTHER	EFIRSTT	FITTERS
EFFOORT	TORE OFF	EFIIKLN	FINLIKE	EFIRSTU	SURFEIT
EFFOORW	WORE OFF	EFIILLS	FILLIES	EFIRSTW	SWIFTER
EFFOPRR	PROFFER	EFIILRY	FIERILY	EFIRSVY	VERSIFY
EFFOPRU	OFFER UP	EFIILSS	FISSILE	EFIRSZZ	FRIZZES
EFFOPSU	POUFFES	EFIIMRS	MISFIRE	EFIRTUV	FURTIVE
EFFORST	EFFORTS	EFIINRT	NIFTIER	EFIRTUX	FIXTURE
EFFOSST	OFFSETS	EFIINRU	UNIFIER	EFIRUZZ	FUZZIER
	SET-OFFS	EFIINSU	UNIFIES	EFISTTT	FITTEST
	SETS OFF	EFIINSX	INFIXES	EFISTTY	TESTIFY
EFFPRSU	PUFFERS	EFIKLNU	LIKE FUN	EFJLNUY	JUNE FLY
EFFRSSU	SUFFERS	EFIKLRU	FLUKIER	EFKLMNO	MENFOLK
EFFRSTU	STUFFER	EFIKNRU	FUNKIER	EFKNOPU	POKE FUN
EFFSSUU	SUFFUSE	EFIKPTT	KEPT FIT	EFLLOSW	FELLOWS
EFFSTTU	TUFFETS	EFILLLL	FELL ILL	EFLLOTU	FELL OUT
EFGGILP	EGG FLIP	EFILLLT	FELT ILL	EFLLRSU	FULLERS
EFGGIOR	FOGGIER	EFILLOS	FOLLIES	EFLLSTU	FULL SET
EFGHINT	HEFTING	EFILLOU	OIL FUEL		FULLEST
EFGHIRT	FIGHTER	EFILLRS	FILLERS	EFLLSTY	LETS FLY
	FREIGHT		REFILLS	EFLMOSU	FULSOME
EFGILLN	FELLING	EFILLST	FILLETS	EFLNNSU	FUNNELS
EFGILMN	FLEMING	EFILLTW	FIT WELL	EFLNORU	FLEURON
EFGILNT	FELTING	EFILMST	FILM SET	EFLNORY	FELONRY
EFGILNX	FLEXING		FILMSET	EFLNOTT	FLETTON
EFGILOR	LOG FIRE		LEFTISM	EFLNSSU	FULNESS
EFGIMNT	FIGMENT	EFILNOS	NO FLIES	EFLNTUU	TUNEFUL
EFGINNP	PFENNIG	EFILNOX	FLEXION	EFLOORV	FOR LOVE
EFGINOR	FOREIGN	EFILOPR	PROFILE	EFLOORY	FOOLERY

EFLOOST	FOOTLES	EGGIIPS	PIGGIES	EGHINRR	HERRING
EFLORST	FLORETS	EGGIJLS	JIGGLES	EGHINRT	THE RING
EFLORSU	OURSELF	EGGIJRS	JIGGERS	EGHINRW	WHINGER
EFLORSW	FLOWERS	EGGILLN	GELLING	EGHINSW	SHEWING
EFLORSX	FLEXORS	EGGILNR	NIGGLER		WHINGES
EFLORTU	FLOUTER	EGGILNS	NIGGLES	EGHINTT	TIGHTEN
EFLORVY	FLY OVER	EGGILRW	WIGGLER	EGHIORS	OGREISH
	FLYOVER		WRIGGLE	EGHIOTW	GO WHITE
	OVERFLY	EGGILSW	WIGGLES	EGHIPUW	WEIGH UP
EFLORWY	FLOWERY	EGGIMMN	GEMMING	EGHIRRT	RIGHTER
EFLOSSS	FLOSSES	EGGIMNR	MERGING	EGHIRSS	SIGHERS
EFLOSSW	SELF-SOW	EGGIMOS	MOGGIES	EGHIRSY	GREYISH
EFLOSTU	FOULEST	EGGIMRU	MUGGIER	EGHIRTT	TIGHTER
EFLOTTU	FELT OUT	EGGINNS	GINSENG	EGHISTW	WEIGHTS
	LEFT OUT	EGGINRS	GINGERS	EGHITWY	WEIGHTY
EFLPRSU	PURFLES		NIGGERS	EGHLLOU	LUGHOLE
EFLRSSU	FURLESS		SNIGGER	EGHLMPY	PHLEGMY
EFLRSTU	FLUSTER	EGGINRV	VERGING	EGHLNOR	LEGHORN
	RESTFUL	EGGINRY	GINGERY	EGHLNST	LENGTHS
EFLRTTU	FLUTTER		GREYING	EGHLNTY	LENGTHY
EFLSTUZ	ZESTFUL	EGGIORS	SOGGIER	EGHLOPT	GOT HELP
EFLSTWY	FLY WEST	EGGIPRY	PIGGERY	EGHMOOT	GOT HOME
EFMNOOT	FOOTMEN	EGGIRRS	RIGGERS	EGHMOSU	GUMSHOE
EFMNORU	FOUR MEN	EGGIRRT	TRIGGER	EGHMOSY	GYM SHOE
EFMNOST	FOMENTS	EGGIRSW	SWIGGER	EGHNORU	ROUGHEN
EFMNRTU	TURFMEN	EGGJLOS	JOGGLES	EGHINOTU	TOUGHEN
EFMOPRR	PERFORM	EGGJLRU	JUGGLER	EGHNRSU	HUNGERS
	PREFORM	EGGJLSU	JUGGLES	EGHOPRS	GOPHERS
EFMOPRT	POMFRET	EGGJORS	JOGGERS	EGHORRU	ROUGHER
EFMORRS	REFORMS	EGGKLOY	EGG YOLK	EGHORTU	TOUGHER
EFMRTUY	FURMETY	EGGLLNO	LONG LEG	EGHOSTT	GET SHOT
EFNOOOT	ONE FOOT	EGGLMSU	SMUGGLE		GHETTOS
EFNOOST	FESTOON	EGGLNSU	SNUGGLE	EGHRSSU	GUSHERS
EFNORRW	FROWNER	EGGLOOY	GEOLOGY	EGHRTUY	THEURGY
EFNORST	SENT FOR	EGGLORS	LOGGERS	EGIILLS	GILLIES
EFNORTU	FORTUNE		SLOGGER	EGIILNT	LIGNITE
	TEN FOUR	EGGLOST	TOGGLES	EGIILNV	VEILING
EFNORTW	FORWENT	EGGLOSW	WOGGLES	EGIILNX	EXILING
	WENT FOR	EGGLPRU	PLUGGER	EGIIMNP	IMPINGE
EFNORUZ	UNFROZE	EGGLRSU	GURGLES	EGIIMPS	PIGMIES
EFNOSST	SOFTENS		LUGGERS	EGIIMSV	MISGIVE
EFOOPRR	PROOFER		SLUGGER	EGIINNR	REINING
	REPROOF	EGGMRSU	SMUGGER	EGIINNS	INSIGNE
EFOOPRT	POOFTER	EGGNRSU	SNUGGER		SEINING
EFOORSW	WOOFERS	EGGNSTU	NUGGETS	EGIINNV	GIVEN IN
EFOORTV	VOTE FOR	EGGORST	GORGETS		VEINING
EFOOSTT	SET FOOT	EGGSSTU	SUGGEST	EGIINRT	IGNITER
EFOPPRY	FOPPERY	EGHHHIO	HEIGH-HO		TIERING
EFOPRSS	PROFESS	EGHHIST	EIGHTHS	EGIINST	IGNITES
EFOPRSU	PROFUSE		HEIGHTS	EGIINSV	GIVES IN
EFOPRUZ	FROZE UP		HIGHEST		SIEVING
EFORRSU	FERROUS	EGHIILL	GHILLIE	EGIINSZ	SEIZING
	FOR SURE	EGHIINT	NIGHTIE	EGIINVW	VIEWING
	FURORES		THINGIE	EGIIPRW	PERIWIG
EFORRUV	FERVOUR	EGHIINV	INVEIGH	EGIJKNR	JERKING
EFORSST	FORESTS	EGHIINW	WEIGH IN	EGIJLLN	JELLING
	FOSTERS		WEIGH-IN	EGIJLNS	JINGLES
EFOSSTT	SOFTEST	EGHIKNR	GHERKIN	EGIJNRW	J. R. EWING
EFPRTUY	PUTREFY	EGHIKNT	THE KING	EGIJNST	JESTING
EFPSTUY	STUPEFY	EGHILMN	HELMING	EGIJNTT	JETTING
EFRRSSU	SURFERS	EGHILNP	HELPING	EGIKNNN	KENNING
EFRSTUU	FUTURES	EGHILNS	ENGLISH	EGIKNOV	EVOKING
EGGGILN	LEGGING		SHINGLE	EGIKNPR	PERKING
EGGGILR	GIGGLER	EGHILNT	LIGHTEN	EGIKNSW	SKEWING
EGGGILS	GIGGLES	EGHILRT	LIGHTER	EGILLNO	GONE ILL
EGGGINP	PEGGING	EGHILSS	SLEIGHS	EGILLNS	SELLING
EGGGLOR	GOGGLER	EGHILST	SLEIGHT	EGILLNT	GILLNET
EGGGLOS	GOGGLES	EGHIMMN	HEMMING		TELLING
EGGGNOS	EGG NOGS	EGHIMNS	MESHING	EGILLNW	WELLING
EGGHHIT	GET HIGH	EGHINNU	UNHINGE	EGILLNY	YELLING
EGGHOST	HOGGETS	EGHINOS	SHOEING		

EGILLOS	GOES ILL	EGINNTT	NETTING
	GOLLIES		TENTING
EGILLRR	GRILLER	EGINNTV	VENTING
EGILLRS	GRILLES	EGINNVY	ENVYING
EGILLSU	GULLIES	EGINOPS	PIGEONS
	LIGULES	EGINORR	IGNORER
EGILMMN	LEMMING	EGINORS	IGNORES
EGILMMR	GLIMMER		REGIONS
EGILMNR	GREMLIN		SIGNORE
EGILMNS	MINGLES	EGINORT	NEGRITO
EGILMNT	MELTING	EGINORZ	ZEROING
EGILMNW	MEWLING	EGINOSU	IGNEOUS
EGILMPS	GLIMPSE	EGINOSW	WIGEONS
EGILMST	GIMLETS	EGINOTT	GET INTO
EGILNOP	ELOPING		GET IT ON
EGILNOS	LEGIONS	EGINOTV	VETOING
	LINGOES	EGINOUV	IN VOGUE
	SLOE GIN	EGINPPP	PEPPING
EGILNPT	PELTING	EGINPPS	PIGPENS
EGILNPY	YELPING	EGINPRS	SPRINGE
EGILNRS	LINGERS	EGINPRY	PREYING
	SLINGER	EGINPSW	SPEWING
EGILNRT	RINGLET	EGINPSY	ESPYING
EGILNRY	RELYING	EGINPTT	PETTING
EGILNSS	SINGLES	EGINPUV	GIVEN UP
EGILNST	GLISTEN	EGINPYY	EPIGYNY
	SINGLET	EGINQUU	QUEUING
	TINGLES	EGINRRS	RINGERS
EGILNSW	SLEWING	EGINRRW	WRINGER
EGILNTT	LETTING	EGINRSS	INGRESS
EGILNTU	ELUTING		RESIGNS
EGILNTW	WELTING		SIGNERS
	WINGLET	EGINRST	RESTING
EGILNVY	LEVYING	EGINRSU	REUSING
EGILOOS	OLOGIES	EGINRSV	SERVING
EGILORS	GLORIES	EGINRSW	SWINGER
EGILOTT	LET IT GO		WINGERS
EGILPST	PIGLETS	EGINRSY	SYRINGE
EGILRST	GLISTER	EGINRTT	GITTERN
	GRISTLE		RETTING
EGILRTT	GLITTER	EGINRVV	REVVING
EGILRZZ	GRIZZLE	EGINSST	INGESTS
EGILSSW	WIGLESS		SIGNETS
EGILSTU	UGLIEST	EGINSTT	SETTING
EGIMMRR	GRIMMER		TESTING
EGIMMRS	MEGRIMS	EGINSTV	VESTING
EGIMNOT	EMOTING	EGINSTW	STEWING
EGIMNOW	MEOWING		TWINGES
EGIMNPR	PERMING		WESTING
EGIMNPT	PIGMENT	EGINTTV	VETTING
	TEMPING	EGINTTW	WETTING
EGIMNRT	TERMING	EGIOPRS	PORGIES
EGIMNSS	MESSING	EGIOPRT	EGO TRIP
EGIMNUW	WINE GUM		EGO-TRIP
EGIMOST	EGOTISM	EGIOPRU	GROUPIE
EGIMPSY	PYGMIES	EGIORST	GOITRES
EGINNNP	PENNING		GORIEST
EGINNNY	YENNING	EGIORTV	VERTIGO
EGINNOP	OPENING	EGIOSST	EGOISTS
EGINNPU	PENGUIN		STOGIES
EGINNRR	GRINNER	EGIOSTT	EGOTIST
EGINNRT	RENTING	EGIOTUV	GIVE OUT
EGINNRU	ENURING	EGIPPRR	GRIPPER
EGINNRV	NERVING	EGIPPSU	GUPPIES
EGINNSS	ENSIGNS	EGIPRUU	GUIPURE
	SENSING	EGIPSSY	GYPSIES
EGINNST	NESTING	EGIPSUV	GIVES UP
	TENSING	EGIRSST	TIGRESS
EGINNSU	ENSUING	EGIRSTU	GUTSIER
	GUNNIES	EGISUWY	WISE GUY
		EGJLNSU	JUNGLES
EGKLORW	LEGWORK		
EGKRSYY	GREY SKY		
EGLLLPU	LEG-PULL		
EGLLOTW	GOT WELL		
EGLLOUY	YULE LOG		
EGLLSTU	GULLETS		
EGLMNOR	MONGREL		
EGLMOOR	LEGROOM		
EGLNNSU	GUNNELS		
EGLNOOW	GONE LOW		
EGLNOOY	ENOLOGY		
	NEOLOGY		
EGLNORU	LOUNGER		
EGLNOST	LONGEST		
EGLNOSU	LOUNGES		
EGLNPRU	PLUNGER		
EGLNPSU	PLUNGES		
EGLNSTU	GLUTENS		
EGLOOSW	GOES LOW		
EGLOPRS	PROLEGS		
EGLOPSS	GOSPELS		
EGLORRW	GROWLER		
EGLORSU	REGULOS		
EGLORSV	GROVELS		
EGLORSW	GLOWERS		
EGLOSSS	GLOSSES		
EGLOSTT	GET LOST		
EGLOSTW	TWO LEGS		
EGLPRSU	SPLURGE		
EGLRSUU	REGULUS		
EGLRUZZ	GUZZLER		
EGLSSTU	GUTLESS		
EGLSTUU	GLUTEUS		
	TELUGUS		
EGLSUZZ	GUZZLES		
EGMMORT	GROMMET		
EGMMRTU	GRUMMET		
EGMNORS	MONGERS		
EGMNOYZ	ZYMOGEN		
EGMNSTU	NUTMEGS		
EGMOORR	GROOMER		
EGMORSU	MORGUES		
EGMORTU	GOURMET		
EGNNORT	RONTGEN		
EGNNPTU	PUNGENT		
EGNNRSU	GUNNERS		
EGNNRUY	GUNNERY		
EGNNSTU	STEN GUN		
EGNNTUU	UNGUENT		
EGNOOTU	GONE OUT		
EGNOPRS	SPONGER		
EGNOPRY	PROGENY		
	PYROGEN		
EGNOPSS	SPONGES		
EGNORRW	WRONGER		
EGNORSS	ENGROSS		
EGNORSU	SURGEON		
EGNORSV	GOVERNS		
EGNORSY	GROYNES		
EGNORUY	YOUNGER		
EGNOSTU	TONGUES		
EGNRRTU	GRUNTER		
EGNRTTU	GRUTTEN		
EGOORRV	GROOVER		
EGOORSV	GROOVES		
EGOORTV	GOT OVER		
EGOOSST	STOOGES		
EGOOSTU	GOES OUT		
	OUTGOES		
EGOPRRU	GROUPER		
EGOPRUY	GUY ROPE		

EGOPSTU	PEGS OUT	EHIMNTY	THYMINE
EGORRSS	GROSSER	EHIMORS	HEROISM
EGORRSU	GROUSER		MOREISH
EGORRTU	GROUTER	EHIMORT	MOTHERI
EGORRUY	ROGUERY	EHIMORZ	RHIZOME
EGORSSS	GROSSES	EHIMPRW	WHIMPER
EGORSSU	GROUSES	EHIMPSU	HUMPIES
EGORSXY	SEX ORGY	EHIMRST	HERMITS
EGORTUW	GREW OUT	EHIMRSU	MUSHIER
	OUTGREW	EHIMRTT	THERMIT
EGOSTTU	GETS OUT	EHINNOP	PHONE IN
EGOSTYZ	ZYGOTES		PHONE-IN
EGPRSUU	UPSURGE	EHINNRT	THINNER
EGRRSUY	SURGERY	EHINOPR	PHONIER
EGRSTTU	GUTTERS	EHINOPV	HOP VINE
EGSSSTU	GUSSETS	EHINOPX	PHOENIX
EHHIKSS	SHEIKHS	EHINORS	INSHORE
EHHILLS	HELLISH	EHINOST	HISTONE
EHHIMOT	HIT HOME	EHINOSU	HEINOUS
EHHIRTT	THITHER	EHINPSS	HIPNESS
EHHIRTW	WHITHER	EHINRSS	SHINERS
EHHISSW	WHISHES		SHRINES
EHHNPSY	HYPHENS	EHINRSU	USHER IN
EHHSSSU	SHUSHES	EHINRSV	SHRIVEN
EHIINNS	HINNIES	EHINRSW	WHINERS
EHIINRS	SHINIER	EHINRTV	THRIVEN
EHIINRT	INHERIT	EHINRTW	THREW IN
EHIINTW	IN WHITE	EHINSTW	WHITENS
EHIIPPS	HIPPIES	EHINSTZ	ZENITHS
EHIIPRT	PITHIER	EHINTTU	HIT TUNE
EHIIRTW	WHITIER	EHIOPPS	PIE SHOP
EHIISST	SHIITES	EHIOPRS	ROSE HIP
EHIITTT	HITTITE	EHIORRT	HERITOR
EHIJLLO	JOE HILL	EHIORSS	HORSIES
EHIKLLT	THE KILL	EHIORST	SHORTIE
EHIKLST	THE SILK	EHIORSW	SHOWIER
EHIKNOS	HONKIES	EHIORSY	HOSIERY
EHIKNRT	RETHINK	EHIORTU	HIRE OUT
	THINKER	EHIOSTY	ISOHYET
EHIKRRS	SHIRKER	EHIPPRS	SHIPPER
EHIKRSS	SHRIEKS	EHIPPRW	WHIPPER
	SHRIKES	EHIPPST	HIPPEST
EHIKRSU	HUSKIER	EHIPPTW	WHIPPET
EHIKRSW	WHISKER	EHIPRST	HIPSTER
EHIKSST	THE KISS	EHIPRSW	WHISPER
EHIKSSU	HUSKIES	EHIPSTT	THE PITS
EHIKSWY	WHISKEY	EHIRRSU	HURRIES
EHILLNO	HELLION	EHIRRTV	THRIVER
EHILLTY	LITHELY	EHIRSSV	SHIVERS
EHILNOP	PINHOLE		SHRIVES
EHILNOT	HOT LINE	EHIRSSW	SWISHER
EHILOPT	HOPLITE		WISHERS
EHILOSS	ISOHELS	EHIRSTT	TITHERS
EHILOST	EOLITHS	EHIRSTU	HIRSUTE
	HOLIEST	EHIRSTV	THRIVES
	HOSTILE	EHIRSTW	WITHERS
EHILRRW	WHIRLER		WRITHES
EHILRST	SLITHER	EHIRSTZ	ZITHERS
EHILRSV	SHRIVEL	EHIRSVY	SHIVERY
EHILSTT	LETTISH	EHIRWZZ	WHIZZER
	LITHEST	EHISSSU	HUSSIES
	THISTLE	EHISSSW	SWISHES
EHILSTW	WHISTLE	EHISSTT	THEISTS
EHILTTW	WHITTLE	EHISSTU	HUSSITE
EHILTWY	WHITELY	EHISTTW	WETTISH
EHIMMRS	SHIMMER		WHITEST
EHIMNNT	THIN MEN	EHISTWY	WHITEYS
EHIMNOW	HOME WIN	EHISWZZ	WHIZZES
EHIMNRS	MENHIRS	EHKLPST	KLEPHTS
EHIMNRU	RHENIUM	EHKNOWW	KNEW HOW
EHIMNSU	INHUMES	EHKNRSU	HUNKERS

EHKOORS	HOOKERS
EHKORSS	KOSHERS
EHLLORS	HOLLERS
EHLMNOT	MENTHOL
EHLMPTU	THE LUMP
EHLNTYY	ETHYNYL
EHLOOPT	POT HOLE
	POTHOLE
	TOP HOLE
	TOP-HOLE
EHLOOST	LESOTHO
EHLOOTU	HOLE OUT
EHLOPTU	HELP OUT
EHLORST	HOLSTER
	HOSTLER
EHLORSW	HOWLERS
EHLORTY	HELOTRY
EHLOSSS	SLOSHES
EHLOSST	HOSTELS
EHLOSSV	SHOVELS
EHLPPSU	HELPS UP
EHLPRSU	PLUSHER
EHLPSSU	PLUSHES
EHLRSTU	HURTLES
	HUSTLER
EHLSSTU	HUSTLES
	LUSHEST
	SLEUTHS
EHLSTTU	SHUTTLE
EHMNOOR	HORMONE
	MOORHEN
EHMNOOT	THE MOON
EHMNORU	HOME RUN
EHMNOSW	SHOWMEN
EHMNPTY	NYMPHET
EHMNTTU	HUTMENT
EHMOOSW	SOMEHOW
EHMORST	MOTHERS
	SMOTHER
	THERMOS
EHMOSTT	THE MOST
EHMPRTU	THUMPER
EHMRSUU	HUMERUS
EHNNOPR	NEPHRON
EHNNOTW	NOW THEN
EHNNRSU	SHUNNER
EHNOOPR	NO-HOPER
EHNOORS	ONSHORE
EHNOORT	NO OTHER
EHNOORU	ONE HOUR
EHNOOTV	HOT OVEN
EHNOPPU	PHONE UP
EHNOPRY	HYPERON
EHNOPUY	EUPHONY
EHNORRY	HERONRY
EHNORSS	SENHORS
EHNORST	HORNETS
	SHORTEN
	THRONES
EHNORSU	UNHORSE
EHNOSST	HOTNESS
EHNOSTT	SHOTTEN
EHNOSTW	HOT NEWS
EHNOSTY	HONESTY
EHNRSTU	HUNTERS
	SHUNTER
EHNSSSY	SHYNESS
EHOOOPS	HOOPOES
EHOOPRU	OUR HOPE

EHOORST	HOOTERS	EIILSTU	UTILISE	EIJRSTT	JITTERS
	SHOOTER	EIILSTW	WILIEST	EIJRTTY	JITTERY
	SOOTHER	EIILTUZ	UTILIZE	EIJSSTU	JESUITS
EHOORSV	HOOVERS	EIIMMSS	MIMESIS	EIJSSUV	JUSSIVE
EHOOSST	SOOTHES	EIIMMST	MISTIME	EIKLLNW	INK WELL
EHOOSSW	WOOSHES	EIIMNNT	TIN MINE		INKWELL
EHOPPRS	HOPPERS	EIIMNRT	INTERIM	EIKLLRS	KILLERS
	SHOPPER		TERMINI	EIKLLST	SKILLET
EHOPPRT	PROPHET	EIIMNSX	MIXES IN	EIKLMMN	MILKMEN
EHOPPRW	WHOPPER	EIIMNTY	NIMIETY	EIKLMNN	LINKMEN
EHOPPST	PET SHOP	EIIMOSS	MEIOSIS	EIKLMNR	KREMLIN
EHOPRRY	ORPHREY	EIIMPRS	PISMIRE	EIKLNOO	ONE KILO
EHOPRST	POTHERS	EIIMPST	PIETISM	EIKLNOS	LIKE SON
	STROPHE	EIIMPSW	WIMPIES	EIKLNRW	WRINKLE
EHOPRSU	SHORE UP	EIIMPTY	IMPIETY	EIKLNST	TINKLES
EHOPRSW	REP SHOW	EIIMRST	MISTIER	EIKLNSV	KELVINS
EHOPSST	POSHEST	EIIMSSS	MISSIES	EIKLNSW	WINKLES
EHOPSSX	SEX SHOP	EIIMSSV	MISSIVE	EIKLNSY	SKYLINE
EHOPSTT	THE TOPS	EIINNNS	NINNIES	EIKLNTU	NUTLIKE
EHORRST	SHORTER	EIINNPS	PINNIES	EIKLNTW	TWINKLE
EHORRTW	THROWER	EIINNQU	QUININE	EIKLOTY	TOYLIKE
EHORSSV	SHOVERS	EIINNRT	TINNIER	EIKLPRY	PERKILY
EHORSSW	SHOWERS	EIINOPR	RIPIENO	EIKLRST	KILTERS
EHORSTU	SHOUTER	EIINORS	IONISER		KIRTLES
EHORSTX	EXHORTS		IRONIES	EIKLRSU	SULKIER
EHORSWY	SHOWERY		NOISIER	EIKLSTT	KITTLES
EHORTVY	VERY HOT	EIINORZ	IONIZER		SKITTLE
EHOSSST	HOSTESS	EIINOSS	IONISES	EIKMMRS	SKIMMER
EHOSTTT	HOTTEST	EIINOSZ	IONIZES	EIKMNNS	KINSMEN
EHPRSSU	PUSHERS	EIINPPR	NIPPIER	EIKMNOR	MONIKER
EHPRSYZ	ZEPHYRS	EIINPRS	INSPIRE	EIKMORS	IRKSOME
EHPRTUW	THREW UP	EIINPST	IN SPITE		SMOKIER
EHRSSTY	SHYSTER		TIE PINS	EIKMOSS	ESKIMOS
EHRSTTU	SHUTTER		TIEPINS	EIKMRRU	MURKIER
EHRSTTW	STREWTH	EIINQRU	INQUIRE	EIKMSST	MESS KIT
EIIILNT	LIE IN IT	EIINRTT	NITRITE	EIKNNOR	EINKORN
EIIINPR	RIPIENI	EIINRTV	INVITER	EIKNNRS	SKINNER
EIIKKNR	KINKIER	EIINRTW	WRITE IN	EIKNOPS	PINKOES
EIIKLLP	LIPLIKE	EIINSTT	TINIEST	EIKNORV	INVOKER
EIIKLRS	SILKIER	EIINSTU	UNITISE	EIKNORW	WONKIER
EIIKNPS	PINKIES	EIINSTV	INVITES	EIKNOSV	INVOKES
EIIKPRS	SPIKIER	EIINTUV	UNITIVE	EIKNPRR	PRINKER
EIIKSTT	KITTIES	EIINTUZ	UNITIZE	EIKNRSS	SINKERS
EIILLMM	MILLIME	EIIORSV	IVORIES	EIKNRST	STINKER
EIILLNV	VILLEIN	EIIPRST	TIPSIER		TINKERS
EIILLRS	SILLIER	EIIPRSV	PRIVIES	EIKNRTT	KNITTER
EIILLSW	WILLIES	EIIPSTT	PIETIST		TRINKET
EIILMPR	IMPERIL	EIIQUVV	QUI VIVE	EIKNSTT	KITTENS
EIILMPS	IMPLIES	EIIRSTW	WIRIEST	EIKOORS	ROOKIES
EIILMRS	SLIMIER	EIIRSVZ	VIZIERS	EIKOPPR	PORK PIE
EIILMRT	LIMITER	EIIRTTW	WITTIER		PORKPIE
EIILMSS	MISSILE	EIISSSS	SISSIES	EIKOSST	KETOSIS
	SIMILES	EIISSTX	SIXTIES	EIKPPRS	KIPPERS
EIILMST	ELITISM	EIISSXZ	SIZE SIX		SKIPPER
EIILMSU	MILIEUS	EIISTTT	TITTIES	EIKPSSS	SKEPSIS
EIILMUX	MILIEUX	EIISTZZ	TIZZIES	EIKRRST	SKIRTER
EIILNNS	IN LINES	EIJKLRY	JERKILY		STRIKER
EIILNOS	ELISION	EIJKNRS	JERKINS	EIKRSSS	KISSERS
	LIONISE	EIJKNSU	JUNKIES	EIKRSST	STRIKES
EIILNOV	OLIVINE	EIJLLOR	JOLLIER	EIKRSSV	SKIVERS
EIILNOZ	LIONIZE	EIJLLOS	JOLLIES	EIKRSTT	SKITTER
EIILNPR	IN PERIL	EIJLTTU	JULIETT	EILLLOS	LOLLIES
EIILNPS	SPLENII	EIJNNOS	ENJOINS	EILLLOW	OIL WELL
EIILNRS	INLIERS	EIJNORS	JOINERS	EILLMNO	ILL OMEN
EIILNRT	NITRILE		REJOINS	EILLMNU	MULLEIN
EIILNSV	LIVES IN	EIJNORT	JOINTER	EILLMOS	MOLLIES
EIILNTU	INUTILE	EIJNORY	JOINERY	EILLMOT	MELILOT
EIILOST	OILIEST	EIJNPRU	JUNIPER	EILLMOU	MOUILLE
EIILQSU	SILIQUE	EIJNRSU	INJURES	EILLMRS	MILLERS
EIILRSX	ELIXIRS	EIJNSTY	JITNEYS	EILLMST	MILLETS
EIILSTT	ELITIST	EIJPRTU	JUPITER	EILLMSU	ILLUMES

EILLNOS	NIELLOS
EILLNSS	ILLNESS
EILLNST	LENTILS
	LINTELS
EILLNTW	WENT ILL
EILLORW	LOWLIER
EILLOST	TOLLIES
EILLOSW	LIES LOW
EILLPPP	PEP PILL
EILLPRS	SPILLER
EILLPSS	LIPLESS
EILLPST	LET SLIP
EILLPSU	PILULES
EILLRRT	TRILLER
EILLRST	STILLER
	TILLERS
	TRELLIS
EILLRSW	SWILLER
	WILLERS
EILLSSU	ILL-USES
	SULLIES
EILLSTT	LITTLES
EILMMRS	SLIMMER
EILMNRS	MERLINS
EILMOPR	IMPLORE
EILMORR	LORIMER
EILMPPS	PIMPLES
EILMPPU	PLUM PIE
EILMPRS	PRELIMS
	SIMPLER
EILMPRU	LUMPIER
EILMPRY	PRIMELY
EILMPSS	SIMPLES
EILMPST	LIMPEST
	LIMPETS
EILMPSU	IMPULSE
EILMPSW	WIMPLES
EILMPSX	SIMPLEX
EILMPTY	EMPTILY
EILMRRY	MERRILY
EILMRSS	SMILERS
EILMRST	MILTERS
EILMRSU	MISRULE
EILMRSY	MISERLY
EILMSSY	MESSILY
EILMSUY	ELYSIUM
EILMSZZ	MIZZLES
EILMUUV	ELUVIUM
EILNNPU	PINNULE
EILNNST	LINNETS
EILNOOR	LOONIER
EILNOPS	EPSILON
	PILES ON
EILNOPT	TOP LINE
	TOP-LINE
EILNORR	LORINER
EILNORT	RETINOL
EILNOSS	INSOLES
	LESIONS
EILNOSU	ELUSION
EILNOTU	ELUTION
	LINE-OUT
	OUTLINE
EILNOTV	VIOLENT
EILNOTW	TOWLINE
	TWO-LINE
EILNOVV	INVOLVE
EILNPPS	NIPPLES
EILNPRS	PILSNER
EILNPRY	IN REPLY
EILNPSS	SPLINES

EILNPST	PINTLES
	SLEPT IN
EILNPSU	LINES UP
	LINE-UPS
	LINEUPS
	SPINULE
EILNPTY	INEPTLY
EILNPUV	LIVEN UP
	VULPINE
EILNRST	LINTERS
EILNRTY	INERTLY
EILNSSS	SINLESS
EILNSST	ENLISTS
	LISTENS
	TINSELS
EILNSSV	SNIVELS
EILNSTU	UTENSIL
EILNSTY	IN STYLE
EILNSUV	UNVEILS
EILOORS	ORIOLES
EILOOST	STOOLIE
EILOPRS	SPOILER
EILOPRT	POLITER
EILOPST	PIOLETS
	PISTOLE
EILOPSV	PLOSIVE
EILOPTX	EXPLOIT
EILORRS	LORRIES
EILORSS	LORISES
	RISSOLE
EILORST	LOITERS
	TOILERS
EILORSU	LOUSIER
EILORSW	LOW RISE
	LOW-RISE
EILORTT	TRIOLET
EILORTU	OUTLIER
EILOSTT	LITOTES
	TOILETS
EILOSTV	VIOLETS
EILOTUV	LIVE OUT
	OUTLIVE
EILPPRR	RIPPLER
EILPPRS	RIPPLES
	SLIPPER
EILPPRT	TIPPLER
EILPPST	STIPPLE
	TIPPLES
EILPPSU	PILES UP
	PILEUPS
EILPRST	LETS RIP
	TRIPLES
EILPRTT	TRIPLET
EILPRTX	TRIPLEX
EILPSSS	PLISSES
EILPSTT	SPITTLE
EILPSTU	STIPULE
EILPSUV	LIVES UP
EILPTTY	PETTILY
EILQRTU	QUILTER
EILQRUU	LIQUEUR
EILQTUY	QUIETLY
EILRRSU	SURLIER
EILRSSU	SILURES
EILRSSV	SILVERS
	SLIVERS
EILRSTT	LITTERS
	SLITTER
	TILTERS
EILRSTU	LUSTIER
EILRSVY	SILVERY

EILRSZZ	SIZZLER
EILRTTY	LITTERY
	TRITELY
EILRTUV	RIVULET
EILSSTW	WITLESS
EILSSTY	STYLISE
EILSSVW	SWIVELS
EILSSZZ	SIZZLES
EILSTTT	TITTLES
EILSTTV	VITTLES
EILSTTY	TESTILY
EILSTYZ	STYLIZE
EILSWZZ	SWIZZLE
EIMMMSU	MUMMIES
EIMMOPS	POMMIES
EIMMORS	MEMOIRS
EIMMOST	TOMMIES
EIMMPRR	PRIMMER
EIMMPRU	PREMIUM
EIMMRRT	TRIMMER
EIMMRSS	SIMMERS
EIMMRSU	IMMURES
EIMMRSW	SWIMMER
EIMMRUY	YUMMIER
EIMMSTU	TUMMIES
EIMNNOR	IRON MEN
EIMNNOT	MENTION
EIMNNOY	IN MONEY
EIMNOOS	MOONIES
	NOISOME
EIMNOOT	EMOTION
EIMNOPT	PIMENTO
EIMNOST	MOISTEN
EIMNOSV	MOVES IN
EIMNOSW	WINSOME
EIMNOTU	MOUNTIE
EIMNPTU	PINETUM
EIMNRST	ENTRISM
	MINSTER
EIMNSSU	MINUSES
EIMNSTT	MITTENS
	SMITTEN
EIMNSTU	MINUETS
	MINUTES
EIMNUZZ	MUEZZIN
EIMOORR	ROOMIER
EIMOPRS	IMPOSER
	PROMISE
	SEMIPRO
EIMOPRV	IMPROVE
EIMOPSS	IMPOSES
EIMORSS	ISOMERS
EIMORST	EROTISM
	MORTISE
EIMORTV	VOMITER
EIMOSTV	MOTIVES
EIMOSTZ	MESTIZO
EIMOSYZ	ISOZYME
EIMOTTU	TIME OUT
EIMOTTW	TWO-TIME
EIMPRRS	PRIMERS
EIMPRSS	IMPRESS
	SIMPERS
EIMPRST	PERMITS
EIMPRSU	UMPIRES
EIMPSST	MISSTEP
EIMPSTU	IMPETUS
	IMPUTES
	TIMES UP
EIMPSUX	MIXES UP

EIMRSST	MISTERS	EINPSST	IN STEPS	EIPQSTU	PIQUETS
	SMITERS		INSTEPS	EIPRRUV	UP RIVER
EIMRSSU	SURMISE		STEPS IN		UPRIVER
EIMRSTT	METRIST	EINPSSU	SUPINES	EIPRSST	PERSIST
EIMRSTU	MUSTIER	EINPSTU	PUNIEST		PRIESTS
EIMRTUX	MIXTURE	EINQRUY	ENQUIRY		SPRIEST
EIMSSSU	MISUSES	EINQSSU	SEQUINS		SPRITES
EIMSSTY	STYMIES	EINQSTU	INQUEST		STIRPES
EINNOPS	PENSION	EINQTTU	QUINTET		STRIPES
EINNOPT	ONE PINT	EINQTUU	UNQUIET	EIPRSSU	RISES UP
	PONTINE	EINRRSU	INSURER	EIPRSTT	TIPSTER
EINNOQU	QUINONE	EINRSST	INSERTS	EIPRSTY	PYRITES
EINNORT	INTONER		SINTERS	EIPRTUW	WRITE UP
EINNORU	REUNION	EINRSSU	INSURES		WRITE-UP
EINNORV	ENVIRON		SUNRISE	EIPRUVW	PURVIEW
EINNOSS	NOSES IN	EINRSTT	STINTER	EIPSSSU	PUSSIES
	SONNIES		TINTERS	EIPSTTU	PUTTIES
EINNOST	INTONES	EINRSTU	UNITERS	EIQRSSU	SQUIRES
	TENSION	EINRSTV	INVERTS	EIQRSUV	QUIVERS
EINNOSV	VENISON		STRIVEN	EIQRTTU	QUITTER
EINNOTT	TONTINE	EINRSTW	TWINERS	EIQRUZZ	QUIZZER
EINNOVW	WOVEN IN		WINTERS	EIQSTUU	QUIETUS
EINNPRS	SPINNER	EINRTTU	NUTTIER	EIQSUZZ	QUIZZES
EINNPSW	NEW PINS	EINRTTW	WRITTEN	EIRRRST	STIRRER
EINNPSY	SPINNEY	EINRTUV	VENTURI	EIRRSTU	RUSTIER
EINNPTU	NUT PINE	EINSSSU	SINUSES	EIRRSTV	STRIVER
EINNRSS	SINNERS	EINSSTV	INVESTS	EIRRSTW	WRITERS
EINNRST	INTERNS	EINSSTW	WITNESS	EIRSSST	RESISTS
	TINNERS	EINSSUW	SUNWISE		SISTERS
EINNRSU	SUNNIER	EINSTTW	TWIN SET	EIRSSTT	SITTERS
EINNRSW	WINNERS	EINSTUW	NEW SUIT	EIRSSTV	STRIVES
EINNRTV	VINTNER	EINTTUY	TENUITY	EIRSSUV	VIRUSES
EINNSST	SENNITS	EIOOPST	ISOTOPE	EIRSTTT	TITTERS
EINNSTT	INTENTS	EIOORST	SOOTIER	EIRSTTW	TWISTER
EINNSTU	SUNNITE	EIOORWZ	WOOZIER	EIRSTUV	VIRTUES
	TUNES IN	EIOPPPS	POPPIES	EIRSUVV	SURVIVE
	TUNNIES	EIOPPRS	SOPPIER	EIRTTTW	TWITTER
EINNSTV	INVENTS	EIOPPSS	POPSIES	EISSSTU	TISSUES
EINOORR	IRON ORE	EIOPPSY	YOPPIES	EISSSTX	SEXISTS
EINOORS	EROSION	EIOPRRT	PIERROT	EISSTUV	TUSSIVE
EINOOSZ	OZONISE	EIOPRST	RIPOSTE	EISSTUY	TISSUEY
EINOOZZ	OZONIZE	EIOPRSX	PROXIES	EJJMNUU	JEJUNUM
EINOPRT	POINTER	EIOPRTT	POTTIER	EJJMPTU	JUMP-JET
	PROTEIN	EIOPSST	POSTIES	EJKNRSU	JUNKERS
EINOPRW	IN POWER	EIOPSTT	POTTIES	EJKNSTU	JUNKETS
EINOPSS	SPINOSE		TIPTOES	EJLOSST	JOSTLES
EINOPST	PINTOES	EIOPSTU	PITEOUS	EJLOSSY	JOYLESS
	POINTES	EIOPTUW	WIPE OUT	EJMNOPU	ONE JUMP
EINOQUX	EQUINOX		WIPEOUT	EJMNRUY	JURYMEN
EINORRR	IN ERROR	EIOQSTU	QUITE SO	EJMNSTU	JUST MEN
EINORSS	SENIORS	EIORRRS	SORRIER	EJMPRSU	JUMPERS
EINORST	IN STORE	EIORRRW	WORRIER	EJNORUY	JOURNEY
	ORIENTS	EIORRST	ROISTER	EJOPPRT	PROPJET
	STONIER	EIORRSV	REVISOR	EJOPRUY	PURE JOY
	TRIES ON	EIORRSW	WORRIES	EJORSTT	JOTTERS
EINORSV	VERSION	EIORSST	ROSIEST	EJORSTU	JOUSTER
EINORSW	SWORE IN		SORTIES	EJPRRUY	PERJURY
EINORSZ	ZEROS IN		STORIES	EKKLRSU	SKULKER
EINORTU	ROUTINE	EIORSSU	SERIOUS	EKLNOOW	NEW LOOK
EINORTW	WROTE IN	EIORTTU	TIRE OUT	EKLNORS	SNORKEL
EINORVW	WIN OVER	EIOSSTV	SOVIETS	EKLNPRU	PLUNKER
EINOSSS	SESSION	EIOSTUZ	OUTSIZE	EKLOORS	LOOKERS
EINOSST	NOSIEST	EIOSTWZ	SIZE TWO	EKLOOTW	WET-LOOK
EINOSUV	ENVIOUS	EIPPPSU	PIPES UP	EKMMPTU	KEPT MUM
EINOTUW	WINE OUT		PUPPIES	EKMNORW	WORKMEN
EINPPRS	NIPPERS	EIPPRRT	TRIPPER	EKMNOSY	MONKEYS
	SNIPPER	EIPPRSS	SIPPERS	EKMNPTU	UNKEMPT
EINPPST	SNIPPET	EIPPRST	TIPPERS	EKMNRTU	TURKMEN
EINPRRT	PRINTER	EIPPRSZ	ZIPPERS	EKMORSS	SMOKERS
	REPRINT	EIPPSST	SIPPETS	EKMSSTU	MUSKETS
EINPRSU	RISEN UP	EIPPSTT	TIPPETS	EKNNOST	NEKTONS

EKNOORS	SNOOKER
EKNORTT	KNOTTER
EKNORTW	NETWORK
EKNORWY	NEW YORK
EKNOSUY	UNYOKES
EKNRTUY	TURNKEY
EKOOPRV	PROVOKE
EKOORRY	ROOKERY
EKOPPSU	SPOKE UP
EKOPRRS	PORKERS
EKOPSTY	KEY POST
	STOP KEY
EKOPTTU	KEPT OUT
EKORRST	STROKER
EKORRSW	REWORKS
	WORKERS
EKORRSY	YORKERS
EKORSST	STOKERS
	STROKES
FKRSSTU	TUSKERS
EKRSTUY	TURKEYS
ELLMOOR	MORELLO
ELLMPUU	PLUMULE
ELLMRSU	MULLERS
ELLMGTU	MULLETS
ELLNOOW	WOOLLEN
ELLNOPS	POLLENS
ELLNOOT	TELLS ON
ELLNOSW	SWOLLEN
ELLNRUW	RUN WELL
	WELL RUN
ELLNSUU	LUNULES
ELLOOSY	LOOSELY
ELLOPTU	POLLUTE
ELLORRS	ROLLERS
ELLORRT	TROLLER
ELLORTY	TROLLEY
ELLORVY	LOVERLY
ELLOSTU	OUTSELL
	SELL OUT
	SELL-OUT
ELLOSVY	VOLLEYS
ELLOSWY	YELLOWS
ELLOWYY	YELLOWY
ELLPSTU	PULLETS
ELLPSUW	SWELL UP
	WELLS UP
ELLPSUY	PULLEYS
ELMMOPS	POMMELS
ELMMORT	TROMMEL
ELMMOSS	MOSLEMS
ELMMPSU	PUMMELS
ELMMPTU	PLUMMET
ELMMRSU	SLUMMER
ELMNOOT	MOONLET
ELMNOPU	ONE LUMP
ELMNORS	MERLONS
ELMNOST	LOMENTS
ELMOORT	TREMOLO
ELMOPRY	POLYMER
ELMOPSU	PLUMOSE
ELMOPSY	EMPLOYS
ELMORSS	MORSELS
ELMOSST	MOLESTS
ELMOSTT	MOTTLES
ELMOSTY	MOTLEYS
ELMOSUU	EMULOUS
ELMOSUV	VOLUMES
ELMPPRU	PLUMPER
ELMPPSU	PEPLUMS
ELMPRSU	RUMPLES

ELMRUZZ	MUZZLER
ELMSSSU	MUSSELS
ELMSUZZ	MUZZLES
ELNNOSS	NELSONS
ELNNRSU	RUNNELS
ELNNSTU	TUNNELS
ELNOOSU	UNLOOSE
ELNOOTW	LOW NOTE
ELNOPRU	PLEURON
ELNOPRY	NO REPLY
	PRONELY
ELNOPST	LEPTONS
	SLEPT ON
ELNOPTU	OPULENT
ELNORTW	LOW RENT
ELNORTY	ELYTRON
ELNOSSS	LESSONS
	SONLESS
ELNOOOT	NET LOOO
ELNOSSV	SLOVENS
ELNOSSW	LOWNESS
ELNOSTV	SOLVENT
ELNOSZZ	NOZZLES
ELNOTVY	NOVELTY
ELNOTWW	WENT LOW
ELNRSSU	RUNLESS
ELNROTY	STERNLY
ELNSSSU	SUNLESS
ELNSSSY	SLYNESS
ELNSUZZ	NUZZLES
ELOOPRS	LOOPERS
ELOORST	RETOOLS
	ROOTLES
ELOORTT	ROOTLET
	TOOTLER
ELOOSST	LOOSEST
ELOOSTT	TOOTLES
ELOOSTU	LOSE OUT
ELOPPRS	PROPELS
ELOPPST	TOPPLES
ELOPPSU	SLOPE UP
ELOPRRW	PROWLER
ELOPRSU	LEPROUS
	PELORUS
ELOPRSV	PLOVERS
ELOPRSY	LEPROSY
ELOPRTT	PLOTTER
ELOPSST	TOPLESS
ELOPSTU	STOLE UP
	TUPELOS
ELORSSS	LESSORS
ELORSST	OSTLERS
ELORSSV	SOLVERS
ELORSTT	SETTLOR
ELORSTV	REVOLTS
ELORSTW	TROWELS
ELORSUV	LOUVRES
	VELOURS
ELORTTY	LOTTERY
ELORTUU	RULE OUT
ELORTVY	OVERTLY
ELOSSTU	LOTUSES
	SOLUTES
	TOUSLES
ELOSSTW	SLOWEST
ELOSSTY	SYSTOLE
ELOSTTU	LETS OUT
	OUTLETS
ELOSTUU	LUTEOUS
ELOSTUV	VOLUTES

ELPPRSU	PURPLES
	SUPPLER
ELPPSSU	SUPPLES
ELPRRSU	PURLERS
ELPRSTU	SPURTLE
ELPRUZZ	PUZZLER
ELPSTUU	PUSTULE
ELPSUZZ	PUZZLES
ELRRSTU	RUSTLER
ELRSSTU	LUSTRES
	RESULTS
	RUSTLES
	SUTLERS
ELRSSTY	STYLERS
ELRSTTU	TURTLES
ELRSUWZ	WURZELS
ELRTTUY	UTTERLY
ELRTUUV	VULTURE
ELSSSTU	TUSSLES
EMMMRUY	MUMMERY
EMMNOOR	MONOMER
EMMNOST	MOMENTS
EMMNOTU	OMENTUM
EMMNOTY	METONYM
EMMRRSU	RUMMERS
EMMRSSU	SUMMERS
EMMRSTU	RUMMEST
EMMRSUY	SUMMERY
EMMSSUU	MUSEUMS
EMNOOOW	NEW MOON
EMNNOSW	SNOWMEN
EMNOOPR	POOR MEN
EMNOOSV	MOVES ON
EMNOPST	POSTMEN
EMNOPSY	EPONYMS
EMNORRU	MOURNER
EMNORSS	SERMONS
EMNORST	MENTORS
	MONSTER
EMNORTT	TORMENT
EMNORTU	REMOUNT
EMNOSTY	ETYMONS
EMNRSTU	STERNUM
EMOOPRS	OOSPERM
EMOOPRT	PROMOTE
EMOORRS	ROOMERS
EMOOSTT	MOTTOES
EMOOSTW	TWOSOME
EMOOTUV	MOVE OUT
EMOPPST	MOPPETS
EMOPPTU	UP-TEMPO
EMOPRRS	ROMPERS
EMOPRSU	SUPREMO
EMOPSUV	MOVES UP
EMOQSSU	MOSQUES
EMORRST	TREMORS
EMORRSW	WORMERS
EMOSSSU	MOUSSES
EMPPTUU	PUT 'EM UP
EMPRSTU	STUMPER
EMPRTTU	TRUMPET
EMRSSTU	MUSTERS
	STUMERS
EMRSTTU	MUTTERS
EMRSTYY	MYSTERY
EMSSSTY	SYSTEMS
ENNNOPS	PENNONS
ENNOORZ	NONZERO
ENNORSU	NEURONS
ENNORSW	RENOWNS
ENNORTU	NEUTRON

ENNORTY	NO ENTRY	EOOPRTV	OVERTOP	EORTTTY	TOTTERY
ENNOSST	SONNETS	EOOPRTW	TOWROPE	EOSSTTU	OUTSETS
ENNOSTW	NEWTONS		TWO ROPE		SETS OUT
ENNOTWW	NEW TOWN	EOOORRST	ROOSTER	EPPPSTU	PUPPETS
ENNPSTU	PUNNETS		TOREROS	EPPRRUU	PURPURE
ENNRRSU	RUNNERS	EOORSTT	TOOTERS	EPPRSSU	PRESS UP
ENNRSTU	STUNNER	EOORTTU	TOO TRUE		PRESS-UP
ENOOPRS	SNOOPER	EOORTUW	OUTWORE		SUPPERS
ENOOPTT	TOP NOTE		WORE OUT	EPPSSTU	STEPS UP
ENOOPTU	OPEN OUT	EOOSSSU	OSSEOUS	EPPSTUW	SWEPT UP
ENOORSU	ONEROUS	EOOTTUV	OUTVOTE		UPSWEPT
ENOORSZ	SNOOZER		VOTE OUT	EPRRSSU	PURSERS
ENOORTW	NOTE-ROW	EOPPPRS	POPPERS	EPRRSUU	PURSUER
	TONE-ROW	EOPPPST	POPPETS		USURPER
ENOORVW	WON OVER	EOPPRRS	PROSPER	EPRRSUY	SPURREY
ENOOSST	SOONEST	EOPPRSS	OPPRESS	EPRRTUU	RUPTURE
ENOOSSZ	SNOOZES	EOPPRST	STOPPER	EPRSSTU	RESTS UP
ENOOSTU	NOSE OUT		TOPPERS	EPRSSTY	SPRYEST
ENOOSTW	TWO ONES	EOPPRSU	PURPOSE	EPRSSUU	PURSUES
ENOOTTW	TWO-TONE	EOPPRSY	PYROPES	EPRSTTU	PUTTERS
ENOPPSU	OPENS UP	EOPPSSU	SUPPOSE		SPUTTER
ENOPRSS	PERSONS	EOPRRST	PORTERS	EPRSUVY	PURVEYS
	PRESS ON		PRETORS	ERRSSUU	USURERS
ENOPRST	POSTERN		REPORTS	ERRSSUY	SURREYS
ENOPRTT	PORTENT	EOPRRTU	TROUPER	ERRSTTU	TURRETS
ENOPRTY	ENTROPY	EOPRRSU	POSEURS	ERSSSTU	RUSSETS
ENOPSST	STEPSON	EOPRRSW	PROWESS		TRUSSES
ENOPSTU	SET UPON	EOPRRSY	OSPREYS	ERSSTUU	SUTURES
ENOQSTU	QUONSET	EOPRRTT	POTTERS	ERSSUVY	SURVEYS
ENOQTUU	UNQUOTE		PROTEST	ERSTTTU	STUTTER
ENORRSS	SNORERS		SPOTTER	FFFGOOO	GOOF OFF
ENORRST	SNORTER	EOPRRTU	PETROUS	FFFILOT	LIFT OFF
ENORRTT	TORRENT		POSTURE		LIFT-OFF
ENORRUV	OVERRUN		POUTERS	FFGHINU	HUFFING
	RUN OVER		SPOUTER	FFGIIMN	MIFFING
	RUNOVER		TROUPES	FFGIINR	GRIFFIN
ENORSSS	SENSORS	EOPRSTX	EXPORTS	FFGIINT	TIFFING
ENORSST	TENSORS	EOPRTTY	POTTERY	FFGILNU	LUFFING
ENORSSY	SENSORY	EOPRTUV	PUT OVER	FFGIMNU	MUFFING
ENORSTU	TONSURE	EOPRTUW	WROTE UP	FFGINOR	GRIFFON
ENORSUV	NERVOUS	EOPRTVY	POVERTY		RING OFF
ENORTTU	RENT OUT	EOPSSSS	POSSESS	FFGINOS	SIGN OFF
ENORTUY	TOURNEY	EOPSSST	POSSETS		SIGN-OFF
ENOSSTT	STETSON	EOPSSSU	SPOUSES	FFGINPU	PUFFING
ENOSSTX	SEXTONS	EOPSSTX	SEXPOTS	FFGINRU	RUFFING
ENOSTTU	SENT OUT	EOPSTTU	STEP OUT	FFGLNOO	LONG OFF
	TEUTONS	EOPSTTW	STEP TWO	FFGLRUY	GRUFFLY
ENOSTUU	TENUOUS		TWO-STEP	FFGNORU	RUNG OFF
ENOTTUW	WENT OUT	EOQRSTU	ROQUETS	FFHHISU	HUFFISH
ENPPTTU	PUP TENT	EORRRST	TERRORS	FFHILSY	FISH FLY
ENPRSTU	PUNSTER	EORRSST	RESORTS	FFHILTY	FIFTHLY
	PUNTERS		ROSTERS	FFHILUY	HUFFILY
ENPSTUU	TUNES UP		SORTERS	FFHOOPS	HOPS OFF
ENRRSTU	RETURNS	EORRSTT	RETORTS	FFHOOST	SHOT OFF
	TURNERS		ROTTERS	FFHOOSW	SHOW OFF
ENRRSUU	UNSURER	EORRSTU	TROUSER		SHOW-OFF
ENRRSUY	NURSERY	EORRSZZ	ROZZERS	FFHOPSU	PUSH OFF
ENRRTUU	NURTURE	EORRTTT	TROTTER	FFHOSTU	SHUT OFF
ENRRTUY	TURNERY	EORRTTU	TORTURE		SHUTOFF
ENRSSTU	UNRESTS	EORSSST	TOSSERS	FFIKLLO	KILL OFF
ENRSSWY	WRYNESS	EORSSTU	OESTRUS	FFIKOPS	SKIP OFF
ENRSTTU	ENTRUST		OUSTERS	FFILLSU	FULFILS
	NUTTERS		SOUREST	FFILOPS	SLIP OFF
	TEST RUN		SOUTERS	FFILSTU	FISTFUL
ENSSSTU	SUNSETS	EORSSTY	OYSTERS	FFILSTY	STIFFLY
EOOOPRS	OOSPORE		STOREYS	FFIMNSU	MUFFINS
EOOPPRS	OPPOSER	EORSTTT	TOTTERS	FFINOPS	SPIN OFF
	PROPOSE	EORSTTU	STOUTER		SPIN-OFF
EOOPPSS	OPPOSES	EORSTTX	EXTORTS	FFINOPT	PONTIFF
EOOPRRT	TROOPER	EORSUVY	VOYEURS	FFINPSU	PUFFINS
EOOPRST	POOREST	EORSWWZ	WOWZERS	FFINSTU	SNUFF IT

FFIOPRS	RIP-OFFS	FGILNOW	FLOWING	FILLOTY	LOFTILY
	RIPS OFF		FOWLING	FILLPSU	FILLS UP
FFIOPSS	PISS OFF!		WOLFING	FILNNUY	FUNNILY
FFIOPST	TIP-OFFS	FGILNRU	FURLING	FILNORS	FLORINS
	TIPS OFF	FGILNTU	FLUTING	FILNOSW	INFLOWS
FFIORTY	FORTIFY	FGILNUX	FLUXING	FILORST	FLORIST
FFIOSST	SOFFITS	FGILOOY	GOOFILY	FILOSSS	FOSSILS
FFIQSUY	SQUIFFY	FGILORY	GLORIFY	FILPSTU	UPLIFTS
FFJMOPU	JUMP-OFF	FGIMNOR	FORMING	FILRSTY	FIRSTLY
FFKLORU	FORKFUL	FGINOOR	ROOFING	FILRYZZ	FRIZZLY
FFKLOSU	SUFFOLK	FGINOOT	FOOTING	FILSSUY	FUSSILY
FFKOOOT	TOOK OFF	FGINOOW	WOOFING	FILSTTU	FLUTIST
FFKOORW	WORK OFF	FGINRRU	FURRING	FILSTUW	WISTFUL
FFLLOPU	PULL OFF	FGINRSU	SURFING	FILSTUY	FUSTILY
FFLOSTY	FYLFOTS	FGINRTU	TURFING	FILSTWY	SWIFTLY
FFNOORT	TORN OFF	FGINSSU	FUSSING	FILUYZZ	FUZZILY
FFNOORW	WORN OFF	FGINTTU	TUFTING	FIMMMUY	MUMMIFY
FFNOPSU	SPUN OFF	FGIOORT	GO FOR IT	FIMNORS	INFORMS
FFNORSU	RUNOFFS	FGIORST	GO FIRST	FIMNORU	UNIFORM
	RUNS OFF	FGIORTW	FIGWORT	FIMORRT	TRIFORM
FFNORTU	TURN OFF	FGISTUU	FUGUIST	FIMORTY	MORTIFY
	TURNOFF	FGLNORU	FURLONG	FIMSTYY	MYSTIFY
FFOOPPS	POPS OFF	FGNOSUU	FUNGOUS	FINNORT	IN FRONT
FFOOPST	STOP OFF	FGNSUUY	FU-YUNGS	FINORSS	FRISSON
	STOP-OFF	FHIIMRS	FIRMISH	FINORST	FORINTS
FFOORTT	TROT OFF	FHIINNS	FINNISH	FINOSSU	FUSIONS
FFOOSST	TOSS OFF	FHIKNOT	THINK OF	FIOOTTU	OUT OF IT
FFOPSTU	PUTS OFF	FHILOOS	FOOLISH	FIOPRST	PROFITS
FGGGINO	FOGGING	FHILOSW	WOLFISH	FIORSUU	FURIOUS
FGGIINT	GIFTING	FHILSUW	WISHFUL	FIOSTTU	FITS OUT
FGGILNU	GULFING	FHINOST	ON SHIFT		OUTFITS
FGGILOY	FOGGILY	FHINRSU	FURNISH	FIRRSTY	STIR-FRY
FGGINOO	GOOFING	FHINSSU	SUNFISH	FKLNOOR	NORFOLK
FGGINOR	FORGING	FHIOOPR	HIP ROOF	FKLOOOR	LOOK FOR
FGHHILY	FLY HIGH	FHIOOST	HOOFS IT	FKOOORS	FORSOOK
FGHIINS	FISHING	FHIOPPS	FOPPISH	FKOORRW	WORK FOR
FGHIITT	FIGHT IT	FHIORRY	HORRIFY	FKOORTU	FORK OUT
FGHILST	FLIGHTS	FHIOSST	SOFTISH	FLLOOSW	FOLLOWS
FGHILTY	FLIGHTY	FHIOSTU	FISH OUT	FLLOOSY	FLY SOLO
FGHINOO	HOOFING	FHIRSTT	THRIFTS	FLLOSUU	SOULFUL
FGHINOT	FIGHT ON	FHIRTTY	THRIFTY	FLLOTUU	FULL OUT
FGHIRST	FRIGHTS	FHLRTUU	HURTFUL	FLLSTUU	LUSTFUL
FGHNOOR	FOGHORN	FHNOTUX	FOXHUNT	FLMMOUX	FLUMMOX
FGHOORT	GO FORTH	FHOOOTT	HOT FOOT	FLMNOOU	MOUFLON
FGIIKNN	KNIFING		HOTFOOT	FLMOOOT	TOMFOOL
FGIILLN	FILLING	FHOORST	SO FORTH	FLNOORR	FORLORN
FGIILMN	FILMING	FHOORSW	FOR SHOW	FLNRSUU	UNFURLS
FGIILNO	FOILING	FHOPRSU	PUSH FOR	FLOOTUW	OUTFLOW
FGIILNR	RIFLING	FHORSTU	FOURTHS	FLOPSTU	POTFULS
FGIILNS	FILINGS	FIIKNRS	FIRKINS	FLOPSTY	FLYPOST
FGIILNT	LIFTING	FIILLMO	MILFOIL	FLOPSUU	FOUL-UPS
FGIILNY	LIGNIFY	FIILLNS	FILLS IN		FOULS UP
FGIIMNR	FIRMING		INFILLS	FLOSUUV	FULVOUS
FGIINRS	FIRINGS	FIILLPS	FILLIPS	FLPRSUU	FURLS UP
FGIINRT	RIFTING	FIILNOT	TIN FOIL	FMRSTUU	FRUSTUM
FGIINST	FISTING		TINFOIL	FNOORSU	SUNROOF
	SIFTING	FIILPTU	PITIFUL	FNOPRTU	UP FRONT
FGIINSX	FIXINGS	FIIMSST	MISFITS	FNORSTY	Y-FRONTS
FGIINSY	SIGNIFY	FIINORT	IN FOR IT	FOOOPRT	ROOFTOP
FGIINTT	FITTING	FIINOSS	FISSION	FOOPSTT	SOFT TOP
FGIINZZ	FIZZING	FIINRST	FIRST IN	FOORSST	OF SORTS
	GIN FIZZ		IN FIRST	FOORTTX	FOX TROT
FGIKNNU	FUNKING	FIINRTY	NITRIFY		FOX-TROT
FGIKNOR	FORKING	FIIRTVY	VITRIFY		FOXTROT
FGILLNU	FULLING	FIJSTUY	JUSTIFY	FOOSTTY	SOFT TOY
FGILLOR	FIG ROLL	FIKLLSU	SKILFUL	FOPSSTU	FUSSPOT
FGILNOO	FOOLING	FIKLNSU	SKINFUL	FORRSUW	FURROWS
FGILNOT	LOFTING	FILLMOY	MOLLIFY	FORSSTW	FROWSTS
FGILNOU	FOULING	FILLNUY	NULLIFY	FORSTWY	FROWSTY
		FILLOTU	FILL OUT	FORTTUU	TURF OUT
			TOILFUL	GGGHINO	HOGGING

GGGHINU	HUGGING
GGGIIJN	JIGGING
GGGIINP	PIGGING
GGGIINR	RIGGING
GGGIINW	WIGGING
GGGIJNO	JOGGING
GGGIJNU	JUGGING
GGGILNO	LOGGING
GGGILNU	LUGGING
GGGIMNU	MUGGING
GGGINOR	GORGING
GGGINOT	TOGGING
GGGINOU	GOUGING
GGGINPU	PUGGING
GGGINTU	TUGGING
GGHHIOS	HOGGISH
GGHHIOT	GOT HIGH
GGHHINN	HINGING
GGHIINS	SIGHING
GGHIIPS	PIGGISH
GGHINSU	GUSHING
GGHIORT	GO RIGHT
GGIINNN	GINNING
GGIINNO	GOING IN
	INGOING
GGIINNP	PINGING
GGIINNR	GIRNING
	RINGING
GGIINNS	SIGNING
GGIINNT	TINGING
GGIINNW	WINGING
GGIINNZ	ZINGING
GGIINOT	GOING IT
GGIINPR	GRIPING
GGIINRT	GIRTING
	RINGGIT
GGIKNOZ	KING ZOG
GGILLNU	GULLING
GGILMUY	MUGGILY
GGILNNO	LONGING
GGILNNU	LUNGING
GGILNOS	GOSLING
GGILNOV	GLOVING
GGILNOW	GLOWING
GGILNPU	GULPING
GGILOOS	GIGOLOS
GGILOSY	SOGGILY
GGILRWY	WRIGGLY
GGIMMNU	GUMMING
GGIMNSU	MUGGINS
GGINNNU	GUNNING
GGINNOO	GOING ON
	ONGOING
GGINNOP	PONGING
GGINNOS	NIGNOGS
	NOGGINS
GGINOOS	GOOSING
GGINOOT	GOING TO
GGINOPR	GROPING
GGINOPU	GOING UP
GGINORS	GRINGOS
GGINORU	ROGUING
	ROUGING
GGINORW	GROWING
GGINPPY	GYPPING
GGINPRU	PURGING
GGINRST	G STRING
	G-STRING
GGINRSU	SURGING
GGINSTU	GUSTING
GGINTTU	GUTTING

GGLOOOS	GOOGOLS
GGNOORS	GORGONS
GGNOORW	GO WRONG
GHHIKSY	SKY-HIGH
GHHINRU	RUN HIGH
GHHINSU	HUSHING
GHHIPSU	HIGH-UPS
GHHORTU	THROUGH
GHHOTTU	THOUGHT
GHHSSTU	ST. HUGH'S
GHIIKRZ	KIRGHIZ
GHIILLN	HILLING
GHIILRS	GIRLISH
GHIINNS	SHINING
GHIINNT	HINTING
GHIINNW	WHINING
GHIINPT	PITHING
GHIINSS	HISSING
GHIINST	IN SIGHT
	INSIGHT
GHIINSW	WISHING
GHIINTT	TITHING
GHIINTW	WHITING
GHIKLNU	HULKING
GHIKNNO	HONKING
GHIKNOO	HOOKING
GHIKNST	KNIGHTS
GHIKNSU	HUSKING
GHILLNU	HULLING
GHILLTY	LIGHTLY
GHILNOS	LONGISH
GHILNOW	HOWLING
GHILNRU	HURLING
GHILNSY	SHINGLY
GHILNTY	NIGHTLY
GHILPST	PLIGHTS
GHILPTU	LIGHT UP
GHILRSY	SHY GIRL
GHILRTY	RIGHTLY
GHILSST	SLIGHTS
GHILSTY	SIGHTLY
GHILTTY	TIGHTLY
GHIMMNU	HUMMING
GHIMNNY	HYMNING
GHIMNOS	GNOMISH
GHIMNPU	HUMPING
GHIMNRY	RHYMING
GHIMRRT	MR.RIGHT
GHINNOP	PHONING
GHINNOS	NOSHING
GHINNOT	NOTHING
GHINNTU	HUNTING
GHINOOP	HOOPING
GHINOOS	SHOOING
GHINOOT	HOOTING
GHINOPP	HOPPING
GHINORS	HORSING
	SHORING
GHINORT	RIGHT ON
GHINORU	IN ROUGH
GHINORW	WHORING
GHINOST	HIT SONG
	HOSTING
	ON SIGHT
	SONG HIT
GHINOSU	HOUSING
GHINOSV	SHOVING
GHINOSW	SHOWING
GHINOTT	TONIGHT
GHINPSU	GUNSHIP
	PUSHING

GHINRSU	RUSHING
GHINSTU	UNSIGHT
GHIOPSZ	PHIZOGS
GHIORSU	ROGUISH
GHIORTU	ROUGH IT
GHIPRTU	UPRIGHT
GHIPTTU	UPTIGHT
GHIRSTW	WRIGHTS
GHLNOOP	LONG HOP
GHLOPSU	PLOUGHS
GHLORUY	ROUGHLY
GHLOSSU	SLOUGHS
GHLOSTY	GHOSTLY
GHLOTUY	TOUGHLY
GHMORSU	SORGHUM
GHNOORT	GO NORTH
GHNOPRY	GRYPHON
GHNORST	THRONGS
GHNOSSU	SHOGUNS
GHNOSTU	GUNSHOT
	NOUGHTS
	SHOTGUN
GHNOTUU	HUNG OUT
GHOORST	GO SHORT
GHOOSTT	GOT SHOT
GHOOSTU	GO SOUTH
GHOPRUU	ROUGH UP
GHORSTU	TROUGHS
GHORSTW	GROWTHS
GHORTUW	WROUGHT
GIIJKNN	JINKING
GIIJLNT	JILTING
GIIJNNO	JOINING
GIIKLLN	KILLING
GIIKLMN	MILKING
GIIKLNN	INKLING
	LINKING
GIIKNNP	KINGPIN
	PINK GIN
	PINKING
GIIKNNS	SINKING
GIIKNNW	WINKING
GIIKNPP	KIPPING
GIIKNPS	PIGSKIN
	SPIKING
GIIKNRS	RISKING
GIIKNSS	KISSING
GIIKNST	SKITING
GIIKNSV	SKIVING
	VIKINGS
GIIKNTT	KITTING
GIILLMN	MILLING
GIILLNO	GILLION
GIILLNT	LILTING
	TILLING
GIILLNW	WILLING
GIILMNP	LIMPING
GIILMNS	SLIMING
	SMILING
GIILMPR	PILGRIM
GIILNNS	LININGS
GIILNNY	LYING IN
	LYING-IN
GIILNOR	ROILING
GIILNOS	SOILING
GIILNOT	TOILING
GIILNPP	LIPPING
GIILNPS	LISPING
	SPILING
GIILNST	LISTING
	SILTING

GIILNSV	LIVINGS	GIKNNSU	SUN KING	GINNORS	SNORING
GIILNTT	TILTING	GIKNOOR	ROOKING	GINNOSS	SIGNS ON
	TITLING	GIKNOPS	SPOKING	GINNOST	STONING
GIILNTW	WILTING	GIKNORW	WORKING	GINNOSW	SNOWING
	WITLING	GIKNORY	YORKING	GINNPRU	PRUNING
GIILORS	OIL RIGS	GIKNOST	STOKING	GINNPTU	PUNTING
GIIMMNR	RIMMING	GIKNSTU	TUSKING	GINNRSU	NURSING
GIIMNNT	MINTING	GIKRSTU	TUGRIKS	GINNRTU	TURNING
GIIMNPR	PRIMING	GILLLNO	LOLLING	GINNTTU	NUTTING
GIIMNRT	MITRING	GILLLNU	LULLING	GINNTUW	WING NUT
GIIMNSS	MISSING	GILLMNU	MULLING	GINNTUY	UNTYING
GIIMNST	MISTING	GILLNOP	POLLING	GINOOPP	POOPING
	TIMINGS	GILLNOR	ROLLING	GINOORT	ROOTING
GIINNNP	PINNING	GILLNOT	TOLLING	GINOOST	SOOTING
GIINNNS	INN SIGN	GILLNPU	PULLING	GINOOTT	GOT INTO
	INNINGS	GILMNOO	LOOMING		GOT IT ON
	SINNING	GILMNOT	MOLTING		TOOTING
GIINNNT	TINNING	GILMNPU	LUMPING	GINOPPP	POPPING
GIINNNW	WINNING		PLUMING	GINOPPS	SOPPING
GIINNOP	OPINING	GILMPSY	GYM SLIP	GINOPPT	TOPPING
GIINNOR	IRONING		GYMSLIP	GINOPRT	PORTING
GIINNOS	NOISING	GILNNSU	UNSLING	GINOPRU	POURING
GIINNPP	NIPPING	GILNOOP	LOOPING	GINOPRV	PROVING
GIINNPS	SNIPING		POOLING	GINOPST	POSTING
GIINNRS	RINGS IN	GILNOOS	LOOGING	GINOPTT	POTTING
	RINSING		SOOLING	GINOPTU	POUTING
GIINNRU	INURING	GILNOOT	LOOTING	GINOQTU	QUOTING
	RUINING		TOOLING	GINORSS	GRISONS
GIINNSW	INSWING	GILNOPP	LOPPING		SIGNORS
GIINNTT	TINTING	GILNORU	LOURING	GINORST	SORTING
GIINNTU	UNITING	GILNOSV	SOLVING		STORING
GIINNTW	TWINING	GILNOSW	SING LOW	GINORSU	ROUSING
GIINNTY	TYING IN		SLOWING		SOURING
GIINOPR	PIG IRON	GILNOTT	LOTTING	GINORSV	ROVINGS
GIINOPS	POISING	GILNOWY	YOWLING	GINORTT	ROTTING
GIINORS	ORIGINS	GILNPPU	PULPING	GINORTU	RING OUT
	SIGNORI	GILNPRU	PURLING		ROUTING
GIINORT	IGNITOR	GILNPSU	PLUGS IN		TOURING
GIINPPP	PIPPING		PULSING	GINORTW	TROWING
GIINPPR	RIPPING	GILNPUY	LYING UP	GINOSST	TOSSING
GIINPPS	SIPPING	GILNRSU	RULINGS	GINOSSU	SOUSING
GIINPPT	TIPPING	GILNSTU	LUSTING	GINOSTU	OUSTING
GIINPPY	YIPPING	GILNSTY	STYLING		OUTINGS
GIINPPZ	ZIPPING	GILORTY	TRILOGY		SING OUT
GIINPQU	PIQUING	GILOSTT	GLOTTIS	GINOSTW	STOWING
GIINPRS	PRISING	GILRSTY	GRISTLY	GINOTTT	TOTTING
	SPIRING	GILRTUY	LITURGY	GINOTTU	TOUTING
GIINPRZ	PRIZING	GILRYZZ	GRIZZLY	GINPPPU	PUPPING
GIINPST	SPITING	GILSTUY	GUSTILY	GINPPSU	SUPPING
GIINPSW	SWIPING	GIMMMNU	MUMMING	GINPPTU	TUPPING
GIINPTT	PITTING	GIMMNSU	SUMMING	GINPRRU	PURRING
GIINPTY	PITYING	GIMNNOO	MOONING	GINPRSS	SPRINGS
GIINRSS	RISINGS	GIMNNOR	MORNING	GINPRSU	PURSING
GIINRSV	VIRGINS	GIMNOOR	MOORING		RINGS UP
GIINRTW	WRITING		ROOMING	GINPRSY	SPRINGY
GIINSSU	ISSUING	GIMNOOT	MOOTING		SPY RING
GIINSTT	SITTING	GIMNOOZ	ZOOMING	GINPSSU	SIGNS UP
GIINSTU	SUITING	GIMNOPP	MOPPING	GINPSTU	PIGNUTS
GIINSTW	SWING IT	GIMNOPR	ROMPING	GINPSUU	USING UP
GIINZZZ	ZIZZING	GIMNOPY	YOMPING	GINPSUW	UPSWING
GIJKLMU	MILK JUG	GIMNORW	WORMING	GINPSUZ	ZIP GUNS
GIJKNNU	JUNKING	GIMNOSU	MOUSING	GINPTTU	PUTTING
GIJLNOT	JOLTING	GIMNPPU	PUMPING	GINPTUY	TYING UP
GIJMNPU	JUMPING	GIMNPSU	IMPUGNS	GINRSST	STRINGS
GIJNOTT	JOTTING		SPUMING	GINRSTU	RUSTING
GIJNTTU	JUTTING	GIMNSSU	MUSINGS	GINRSTY	STRINGY
GIKLNOO	LOOKING		MUSSING	GINRTTU	RUTTING
GIKLNRU	LURKING	GINNNPU	PUNNING	GINSSSU	SUSSING
GIKLNSU	SULKING	GINNNRU	RUNNING	GINSSUX	SIX-GUNS
GIKMNOS	SMOKING	GINNNSU	SUNNING	GINSTUW	SWUNG IT
GIKNNOW	KNOWING	GINNOOS	NOOSING	GINTTTU	TUTTING

GIOPRRU	PRURIGO
GIOPSSS	GOSSIPS
GIOPSST	SPIGOTS
GIOPSSY	GOSSIPY
GIORRSU	RIGOURS
GIORSTU	RIGOUTS
	RIGS OUT
GIORSUV	VIGOURS
GLLMNOU	GUN MOLL
GLLOOPS	GOLLOPS
GLMNOOS	MONGOLS
GLMNOOT	LONG TOM
GLMORUW	LUGWORM
GLNNOOR	LORGNON
GLNNORU	LONG RUN
	LONG-RUN
GLNNSUU	UNSLUNG
GLNOOPR	PROLONG
GLNOOPY	POLYGON
GLNORWY	WRONGLY
GLNOSUW	SUNG LOW
GLNOTTU	GLUTTON
GLNPSUU	UNPLUGS
GLOOOYZ	ZOOLOGY
GLOORUY	UROLOGY
GLOOSSW	GO-SLOWS
GLOOSTT	GOT LOST
GLOPSTU	PUTLOGS
GLORSSY	GROSSLY
GMMPUUW	MUGWUMP
GMNNOOS	GNOMONS
GMNOORU	GUN ROOM
GMOOPRS	POGROMS
GMORTUW	MUGWORT
GMRUYYZ	ZYMURGY
GNNOORW	GROWN ON
GNOOPPS	POP SONG
GNOORSW	GROWS ON
GNOPPSU	POPGUNS
GNOPRTU	TOP RUNG
GNOPRUW	GROWN UP
	GROWN-UP
GNORSUV	GUVNORS
GNORTUU	RUNG OUT
GNOSTUU	SUNG OUT
GNOSTUY	TOY GUNS
GOORSTT	GROTTOS
GOORTUW	GROW OUT
	OUTGROW
GOPRSUW	GROWS UP
GPSSUUY	GUSSY UP
HHIISTW	WHITISH
HHINNSU	HUNNISH
HHIOSTT	HOTTISH
	SHIT HOT
HHMRSTY	RHYTHMS
HHOOSTT	HOTSHOT
HIIKMSS	SIKHISM
HIIKMUZ	MUZHIKI
HIIKNPS	KINSHIP
	PINKISH
HIILMTU	LITHIUM
HIILPTY	PITHILY
HIIMSST	MISHITS
HIINSSW	SWINISH
HIIOSTW	WHO IS IT?
HIIPSSW	WISPISH
HIISTWY	WHY IS IT?
HIKLMOT	HOT MILK
HIKLSUY	HUSKILY
HIKMNOS	MONKISH
HIKMSUZ	MUZHIKS
HIKNNOR	INKHORN
HIKNNOT	THINK ON
HIKNPTU	THINK UP
HIKNRSS	SHRINKS
HIKOOST	HOOKS IT
HIKRSTU	TURKISH
HILLNOR	RON HILL
HILLRSS	SHRILLS
HILLRST	THRILLS
HILLRSY	SHRILLY
HILMMOU	HOLMIUM
HILMPSU	LUMPISH
HILMSUY	MUSHILY
HILMTUU	THULIUM
HILNPST	PLINTHS
HILOOTT	OTOLITH
HILORSY	HORSILY
HILOSSW	SLOWISH
HILOSTU	LOUTISH
HILOSWY	SHOWILY
HILOTWW	WHITLOW
HILPSUY	PUSHILY
HILSSTY	STYLISH
HILSTTY	THISTLY
HILSTXY	SIXTHLY
HIMMOST	THOMISM
HIMOORS	MOORISH
HIMOPRS	ORPHISM
HIMOPSS	SOPHISM
HIMORTU	THORIUM
HIMOSTT	THOMIST
HIMOTTY	TIMOTHY
HIMPRSS	SHRIMPS
HIMPRSY	SHRIMPY
HIMPRTU	TRIUMPH
HIMSSTU	ISTHMUS
HINNOSW	SHOWN IN
HINOORZ	HORIZON
HINOOSS	SHOO-INS
HINOPSS	SIPHONS
	SONSHIP
HINORST	IN SHORT
HINORSU	IN HOURS
	NOURISH
HINORTW	THROW IN
	THROW-IN
HINOSSW	SHOWS IN
HINOTTU	THIN OUT
HINPSSU	UNSHIPS
HINRTTU	IN TRUTH
HINSTUW	WHITSUN
HIOOPRS	POORISH
HIOPPTW	WHIP TOP
HIOPRSW	WORSHIP
HIOPSST	SOPHIST
HIOPSTT	HOT TIPS
HIORSSU	SOURISH
HIORSTY	HISTORY
HIOSSTT	SOTTISH
HIOTTUW	WITHOUT
HIQSSUY	SQUISHY
HIRSSTT	T SHIRTS
	T-SHIRTS
	THIRSTS
HIRSTTU	RUTTISH
HIRSTTY	THIRSTY
HJNOSST	ST.JOHNS
HKKLOOZ	KOLKHOZ
HKNOOSU	UNHOOKS
HKNOOWW	KNOW HOW
	KNOW-HOW
HKOOOPT	POTHOOK
HKOOPSU	HOOKS UP
	HOOKUPS
	SHOOK UP
	SHOOK-UP
HKOORTW	HOT WORK
HKORSWY	WORKSHY
HLLOOSW	HOLLOWS
HLLPSUY	PLUSHLY
HLMNOTY	MONTHLY
HLNOORW	HORN OWL
HLOOVWY	HOLY VOW
HLORSTY	SHORTLY
HLPRSUU	SULPHUR
HMMNOOY	HOMONYM
HMNOPSY	NYMPHOS
HMOOSST	SMOOTHS
HMORSUU	HUMOURS
HNOOPST	PHOTONS
HNOOPTY	TYPHOON
HNOORSU	HONOURS
HNOPRTU	UP NORTH
HNOPSSU	NOSH-UPS
HNOPSSY	SYPHONS
HNOPSTY	PYTHONS
HNOPSUW	SHOWN UP
HNRTTUU	UNTRUTH
HOOPSTT	HOT SPOT
	POT SHOT
	POTSHOT
HOOPSTU	HOT SOUP
	SHOOT UP
HOOPSTY	TOY SHOP
HOORRRS	HORRORS
HOOSTTU	SHOT OUT
HOOSTUW	SHOW OUT
HOPRTTU	PRUTOTH
HOPRTUW	THROW UP
	UPTHROW
HOPSSSY	HYSSOPS
HOPSSTU	UPSHOTS
HOPSSUW	SHOWS UP
HOPSTUU	PUSH OUT
HOSSTVW	T V SHOWS
HOSTTUU	SHUT OUT
HPPSSUU	PUSH UPS
HPRRUUY	HURRY UP
HRSSTTU	THRUSTS
HRSSTUY	THYRSUS
IIJNNOS	JOINS IN
IIKKNOT	KON TIKI
IIKLLSY	SILKILY
IIKLNOS	OILSKIN
IIKLRSY	RISKILY
IIKMOST	MISKITO
IIKNNSS	SINKS IN
IIKNSSS	SISKINS
IILLLLW	ILL WILL
IILLLSY	SILLILY
IILLMNO	MILLION
IILLMSY	SLIMILY
IILLNOP	PILLION
IILLNOZ	ZILLION
IILMNOT	NO LIMIT
IILMSTU	STIMULI
IILMSTY	MISTILY
IILNNSU	INSULIN
IILNNTY	TINNILY
IILNORS	SIRLOIN

IILNOSV	VIOLINS	IKMNPPU	PUMPKIN	ILPPSTU	PULPITS
IILNOSY	NOISILY	IKMOOST	MISTOOK		SPLIT UP
IILNPPY	NIPPILY	IKMOSSU	KOUMISS	ILRSTUY	RUSTILY
IILNSST	INSTILS	IKNOOTY	IN TOKYO	ILSSTTY	STYLIST
IILORTV	VITRIOL	IKNORSW	WORK-INS	IMMOPTU	OPTIMUM
IILOSTV	VIOLIST		WORKS IN	IMMSSTU	SUMMITS
IILPPYZ	ZIPPILY	IKNPSTU	SPUTNIK	IMNNOSW	MINNOWS
IILPRVY	PRIVILY	IKOPSTU	SKIP OUT	IMNNSSU	SUNNISM
IILPSST	PISTILS	IKORSTY	YORKIST	IMNNSTU	MUNTINS
IILPSTY	TIPSILY	IKRSSSU	RUSSKIS	IMNOOPT	TOMPION
IILPSWY	WISPILY	IKSSTTT	ST.KITTS	IMNOORT	MONITOR
IILTTUY	UTILITY	ILLMNOU	MULLION	IMNOOST	MOTIONS
IILTTWY	WITTILY	ILLMOOT	LOMOTIL	IMNOOSU	OMINOUS
IIMMMNU	MINIMUM	ILLMPUY	LUMPILY	IMNOPRW	PINWORM
IIMNNOS	MINIONS	ILLMSUU	LIMULUS	IMOOPRX	PROXIMO
IIMNOSS	MISSION	ILLNORS	ROLLS IN	IMOOSSS	OSMOSIS
IIMNOSZ	ZIONISM	ILLNOTW	TILL NOW	IMOPRST	IMPORTS
IIMNPRT	IMPRINT		WILL NOT		TROPISM
IIMNTTY	TINY TIM	ILLNPSU	PULL-INS	IMOPRTU	PROTIUM
IIMOPSU	IMPIOUS		PULLS IN	IMOPSST	IMPOSTS
IIMOSST	MITOSIS	ILLNTUY	NULLITY	IMORRRS	MIRRORS
IIMOSTT	TITOISM	ILLOPRY	PILLORY	IMORSTU	TOURISM
IIMRTTU	TRITIUM	ILLOPSW	PILLOWS	IMORSTY	TORYISM
IIMRTUV	TRIVIUM	ILLOSUV	VILLOUS	IMOSSTU	MISS OUT
IINNOOP	OPINION	ILLOSUY	LOUSILY	IMOSTTT	TOMTITS
IINNOPS	PINIONS	ILLOSWW	WILLOWS	IMPSTUU	SUM IT UP
IINNPRT	IN PRINT	ILLOWWY	WILLOWY	IMQRSSU	SQUIRMS
IINNRSU	IN RUINS	ILLQSSU	SQUILLS	IMRSSTU	SISTRUM
IINORST	IRONIST	ILLRSUY	SURLILY		TRISMUS
IINORTT	INTROIT	ILLSTUY	LUSTILY	IMRTTUY	YTTRIUM
IINOSSV	VISIONS	ILMMSSU	MUSLIMS	INNOOPS	OPSONIN
IINOSTZ	ZIONIST	ILMNOOT	MOONLIT	INNOOPT	NO POINT
IINOTTU	TUITION	ILMNOSU	MOULINS	INNOOST	NOTIONS
IINPPPS	PIPPINS	ILMNPSU	IN LUMPS	INNORTU	RUN INTO
IINQRUY	INQUIRY	ILMOPPU	OIL PUMP	INNOSTU	NONSUIT
IINRTTY	TRINITY	ILMORTU	TURMOIL	INNOSWW	WINNOWS
IINSSST	INSISTS	ILMOSTY	MOISTLY	INNRSTU	IN TURNS
IINSTTU	INTUITS	ILMPSTU	LUMPS IT		TURNS IN
IINSTTW	NITWITS	ILMSTUY	MUSTILY	INOOPRT	PORTION
IIOPRSS	PISSOIR	ILMUYZZ	MUZZILY	INOOPSS	POISONS
IIORSTV	VISITOR	ILNNOPS	NONSLIP	INOOPST	OPTIONS
IIOSTTT	TITOIST	ILNNSUY	SUNNILY		POTIONS
IIPPSUU	PIUPIUS	ILNOOPS	PLOSION	INOORSS	ORISONS
IIPRSST	SPIRITS	ILNOOST	LOTIONS	INOORST	TORSION
IIPRIVY	PRIVITY	ILNOPRU	PURLOIN	INOORTU	IRON OUT
IJJSTUU	JU-JITSU	ILNOPSS	SLIP-ONS	INOOSUX	NOXIOUS
IJKLLOY	KILLJOY		SLIPS ON	INOPPST	TOP SPIN
IJKMOSU	MOUJIKS	ILNOPSU	UPSILON	INOPPTT	PINT POT
IJKMPSU	SKI JUMP	ILNORST	NOSTRIL	INOPPTY	PIT PONY
IJLLOTY	JOLLITY	ILNOSST	TONSILS	INOPRSS	PRISONS
IJLNOQU	JONQUIL	ILNOSTT	STILTON	INOPSST	IN SPOTS
IJLNOTY	JOINTLY	ILNOSTY	STONILY		PISTONS
IJMNPSU	JUMPS IN	ILNOSWY	SNOWILY	INOPSSU	POUSSIN
IJNORSU	JUNIORS	ILNPRSU	PURLINS		SPINOUS
IJRSSTU	JURISTS	ILNPSST	SPLINTS	INOPSTU	SPIN OUT
IKKSUUY	KIKUYUS	ILNSSTU	INSULTS	INOPSTW	TWO PINS
IKLLLOO	LOOK ILL	ILOOPRU	POUR OIL	INORRTU	RUN RIOT
IKLLOOT	TOOK ILL	ILOOPST	TOPSOIL	INORSTU	NITROUS
IKLLSUY	SULKILY	ILOOSST	SOLOIST	INORSUU	RUINOUS
IKLMNRU	MILK RUN	ILOOSTY	SOOTILY		URINOUS
IKLMOPS	MILKSOP	ILOOWYZ	WOOZILY	INORTTY	TRY IT ON
IKLMOSY	SMOKILY	ILOPPSY	SOPPILY	INOSSUU	SINUOUS
IKLMRUY	MURKILY	ILOPRRY	PRIORLY	INOTTTY	TINY TOT
IKLNOOS	LOOKS IN	ILOPRSY	PROSILY	INPRSST	SPRINTS
IKLNOOT	KILOTON	ILOPSST	PISTOLS	INPRSTU	TURNIPS
IKLNPSU	LINKS UP	ILOPSTU	SLIP OUT	INPRSTY	TRYPSIN
	LINKUPS	ILOPSUY	PIOUSLY	INQSSTU	SQUINTS
IKLNRWY	WRINKLY	ILOQRSU	LIQUORS	INQSTUY	SQUINTY
IKLNTWY	TWINKLY	ILOSSTU	ST.LOUIS	INRSTTU	INTRUST
IKLOOTT	TOOL KIT	ILPPSSU	SLIPS UP		TRUST IN
IKMNOOS	KIMONOS		SLIP-UPS	IOOPRSV	PROVISO

IOOPSTY	ISOTOPY
IOORSTT	RISOTTO
IOORSTU	RIOTOUS
IOPPSTT	PIT STOP
IOPRSTT	PROTIST
IOPRSTU	IT POURS
IOPSSTT	STOPS IT
IOPSTTU	SPIT OUT
IORRTTX	TORTRIX
IORSSTU	SUITORS
IORSTTU	TOURIST
IOSSTTU	SITS OUT
IOSTTUW	OUTWITS
IPPRSTU	TRIPS UP
IPPSSSU	PISS-UPS
IPRRSTU	IRRUPTS
	STIRRUP
IPRSSTU	PURISTS
	SPRUITS
	STIRS UP
IPRSTUU	PURSUIT
IPSSTTY	TYPISTS
IQRSSTU	SQUIRTS
JMNOPSU	JUMPS ON
JMOPTUU	JUMP OUT
JMPPSUU	JUMPS UP
JNOORSU	SOJOURN
JNOSTUW	JUST NOW
KLNOOOS	LOOKS ON
KLOOOST	LOOKS TO
KLOOOTU	LOOK OUT
	LOOKOUT
	OUTLOOK
KLOOPSU	LOOKS UP
KLRSTUU	KULTURS
KNNNOUW	UNKNOWN
KNNORSY	NYNORSK
KNOOOOY	YOKO ONO
KNOOPTT	TOPKNOT
KNOORSW	WORKS ON
KNOOUWY	YOU KNOW
KNOPRTY	KRYPTON
KOOOTTU	TOOK OUT
KOOPRTW	WORKTOP
KOORTUW	OUTWORK
	WORK OUT
	WORKOUT
KOOSTWW	KOWTOWS
KOPRSUW	WORKS UP
LLLOOOR	LOO ROLL
LLLOOPS	LOLLOPS
LLMOOPR	ROLLMOP
LLMPPUY	PLUMPLY
LLNOORS	ROLL-ONS
	ROLLS ON
LLNOPSU	PULL-ONS
	PULLS ON
LLNORSU	UNROLLS
LLOOPRT	ROLLTOP
	TROLLOP
LLOORTU	ROLL OUT
	ROLLOUT
LLOPRSU	ROLLS UP
	ROLL-UPS
LLOPTUU	PULL OUT
	PULLOUT
LLORSST	STROLLS
LLORSWY	L. S. LOWRY
LLPPSUU	PULLS UP
	PULL-UPS
LMMPSUU	LUMP SUM
LMNOOOS	SOLOMON
LMRSTUU	LUSTRUM
LMSTUUU	TUMULUS
LNNOOSY	ONLY SON
LNNOPSU	NONPLUS
LNRTUUY	UNTRULY
LOOOORS	OLOROSO
LOOOSTW	TOO SLOW
LOOSTTU	LOST OUT
LOPRSUY	PYLORUS
LOPRTUY	POULTRY
LOPSSUW	SLOWS UP
LOSTTUY	STOUTLY
LPRSSUU	SURPLUS
MMNOORS	MORMONS
MMNOSSU	SUMMONS
MMOOPPS	POM-POMS
MMOOSTT	TOM TOMS
	TOM-TOMS
MMOPSTY	SYMPTOM
MMRRSUU	MURMURS
MNNOOOS	MONSOON
MNNOSYY	SYNONYM
MNOOPTY	TOPONYM
MNOPRTU	NO TRUMP
	NO-TRUMP
MNOPTUU	MOUNT UP
MNORSTU	NOSTRUM
MNOSTTU	MUST NOT
	MUTTONS
MNOTTUY	MUTTONY
MOOPPSU	POMPOUS
MOOPSSU	OPOSSUM
MOOPSTT	TOPMOST
MOORRSW	MORROWS
MOPPRST	PROMPTS
MOPPTUU	PUMP OUT
MOPSSSU	POSSUMS
MOPSSUU	SPUMOUS
MOQRSUU	QUORUMS
MORRSTU	ROSTRUM
MORRSUU	RUMOURS
MORSTUU	TUMOURS
NNOOOPT	PONTOON
NNOOPRU	PRONOUN
NNOOPSS	SPONSON
NNOOPST	NONSTOP
NNORSTU	TURNS ON
NOOOOST	TOO SOON
NOOOSUZ	OZONOUS
NOOPRSS	SPONSOR
NOOPRST	PROTONS
NOOPTUW	OWN UP TO
NOORTUW	OUTWORN
	WORN OUT
	WORN-OUT
NOPPTUU	PUT UPON
	PUT-UPON
NOPSSTU	SUN SPOT
	SUNSPOT
	UNSTOPS
NOPSTUU	SPUN OUT
NORSTTU	ON TRUST
NORSTUU	OUTRUNS
	RUNS OUT
NORTTUU	TURN OUT
	TURNOUT
NPRSTUU	TURNS UP
	TURN-UPS
	UPTURNS
OOOOPRT	POTOROO
OOORTTU	ROOT OUT
OOPPSTT	TOP SPOT
OOPPSTU	POPS OUT
OOPRSTU	UPROOTS
OOPRSTV	PROVOST
OOPRTUU	POUR OUT
OOPSSTT	TOSSPOT
OOPSTTU	OUTPOST
	STOP OUT
OOPSWWW	POWWOWS
OORRSSW	SORROWS
OORSTTU	SORT OUT
	SORT-OUT
OORTTTU	TROT OUT
OOSTTWW	TWO TWOS
OPPPRSU	PROPS UP
OPPRRTU	PURPORT
OPPRSTU	SUPPORT
OPPRSTY	STROPPY
OPPSSTU	STOPS UP
OPRSSTU	SPROUTS
OPRSUUY	UP YOURS!
OPSSSTU	TOSS-UPS
OPSTTUU	OUTPUTS
	PUTS OUT
ORSTTUY	TRYOUTS
OSSSTUU	SUSS OUT
PRSSTUU	TRUSS UP

AAAAGGRR	AGAR-AGAR	AAACENRR	RAN A RACE	AAAEHNPV	HAVE A NAP
AAAAHMNY	MAHAYANA	AAACGLSW	SCALAWAG	AAAEHNRS	HAS AN EAR
AAAAKLRZ	KALA-AZAR	AAACGMNR	ARMAGNAC	AAAEIMRV	AVE MARIA
AAAAKNRW	ARAWAKAN	AAACHHST	HAS A CHAT	AAAEKLMW	MAKE A LAW
AAABBCHL	CABBALAH	AAACHIPS	APHASIAC	AAAEKLWY	LAY AWAKE
AAABBMRS	BAMBARAS	AAACHLLZ	CHALAZAL		LEAK AWAY
AAABCCLL	CALL A CAB	AAACHLSZ	CHALAZAS	AAAEKNPT	TAKE A NAP
AAABCCRT	BACCARAT	AAACILMN	MANIACAL	AAAEKTWY	TAKE AWAY
AAABCEKT	TAKE A CAB	AAACINTV	CAVATINA		TAKEAWAY
AAABCHIL	HAIL A CAB	AAACIRTX	ATARAXIC	AAAELLST	ALL AT SEA
AAABCHLS	CALABASH	AAACKMRT	TAMARACK	AAAFINPT	PANATELA
AAABCINT	ANABATIC	AAACLLPY	PAY A CALL	AAAEMTWY	AWAY TEAM
AAABCKWY	BACK AWAY	AAACLMNS	ALMANACS	AAAENPRV	PARAVANE
AAABCNRU	CARNAUBA	AAACLNST	CATALANS	AAAENPST	ANAPAEST
AAABCPRY	CAPYBARA	AAACNOSV	CASANOVA	AAAERTWY	TEARAWAY
AAABDHHL	HABDALAH	AAACNRSV	CARAVANS	AAAERWWY	WEAR AWAY
AAABDHHS	HAD A BASH	AAACNSTT	CANTATAS	AAAESTWY	EATS AWAY
AAABDHHT	HAD A BATH	AAACPRTT	ACT A PART	AAAFHLLS	HAS A FALL
AAABDHLL	HAD A BALL	AAACRSWY	CARAWAYS	AAAFHLMN	HALF A MAN
AAABDHST	HAD A STAB	AAACRTWY	CART AWAY	AAAFINST	FANTASIA
AAABDNNN	BANDANNA	AAACSTWY	CAST AWAY	AAAFINUV	AVIFAUNA
AAABDNR3	SARABAND		CASTAWAY	AAAFIRST	RATAFIAS
AAABEHNR	HABANERA			AAAFLLWY	FALL AWAY
AAABGRTU	RUTABAGA	AAADDEHT	HAD A DATE	AAAFPRRT	FAR APART
AAABHHSS	HAS A BASH	AAADDLLN	ALAN LADD	AAAGHNTY	YATAGHAN
AAABHHST	HAS A BATH	AAADEFHR	FAR AHEAD	AAAGINRR	AGRARIAN
AAABHLLS	HAS A BALL	AAADEFWY	FADE AWAY	AAAGLMMS	AMALGAMS
AAABHLMR	ALHAMBRA	AAADEHLM	HAD A MEAL	AAAGLMSY	MALAGASY
AAABHSST	HAS A STAB	AAADEHLS	HAD A SALE	AAAGLRST	ASTRAGAL
AAABILNN	ALBANIAN	AAADEHNR	HAD AN EAR	AAAGMMRY	GAMMA RAY
AAABINRS	ARABIANS		RAN AHEAD	AAAGMNRS	ANAGRAMS
AAABINRV	BAVARIAN	AAADEHST	HAS A DATE	AAAGNWWY	GNAW AWAY
AAABKPSS	BAASSKAP	AAADEHSW	SAW AHEAD	AAAGPRUY	PARAGUAY
AAABLLLN	ALAN BALL	AAADEHWY	WAY AHEAD	AAAHHPRS	PARASHAH
AAABLMOS	ABOMASAL	AAADELMS	ADAMS ALE	AAAHIINW	HAWAIIAN
AAABLMST	TAMBALAS		SALAAMED	AAAIIMNR	MAHARANI
AAABLOPR	PARABOLA	AAADELMW	MADE A LAW	AAAHIMRT	MATA HARI
AAACCELN	CALCANEA	AAADENTV	VANADATE	AAAHINNY	HINAYANA
AAACCEPR	CARAPACE	AAADFHLL	HAD A FALL	AAAHJLMT	TAJ MAHAL
AAACCLRS	CARACALS	AAADGGHH	HAGGADAH	AAAHKLRS	HAS A LARK
AAACCRTT	CATARACT	AAADHKLR	HAD A LARK	AAAHLNPS	HAS A PLAN
AAACDEHR	HAD A CARE	AAADHLMS	HAM SALAD	AAAHLPRY	ALPHA RAY
AAACDEHS	HAD A CASE	AAADHLNP	HAD A PLAN	AAAHLUWY	HAUL AWAY
AAACDHHT	HAD A CHAT	AAADHMNU	UM AND AAH	AAAHMMST	MAHATMAS
AAACDINN	CANADIAN	AAADHSWY	DASH AWAY	AAAHMNRT	AMARANTH
	IN CANADA	AAADIKKN	AKKADIAN	AAAHMRST	MARATHAS
AAACDINR	ARCADIAN	AAADLNTY	NATAL DAY	AAAHMRTT	MAHRATTA
AAACDINS	ACADIANS	AAADMNST	ADAMANTS	AAAHNOPR	ANAPHORA
AAACDMMS	MACADAMS	AAADMNSW	ASWAN DAM	AAAHSWWY	WASH AWAY
AAACDMNY	ADAMANCY	AAADMNTU	TAMANDUA	AAAHTTWY	THATAWAY
AAACDNNO	ANACONDA	AAADRWWY	AWAY DRAW	AAAIIMRT	TIA MARIA
AAACDNPR	PANDA CAR		DRAW AWAY	AAAIINPR	APIARIAN
AAACDNRS	SANDARAC	AAAEELMT	ATE A MEAL	AAAILLMR	MALARIAL
AAACDNYZ	ANZAC DAY		EAT A MEAL	AAAILLPT	PALATIAL
AAACDOTV	ADVOCAAT	AAAEFGHV	HAVE A FAG	AAAILMNR	MALARIAN
AAACEHLZ	CHALAZAE	AAAEFSTT	AT A FEAST	AAAILMSY	MALAYSIA
AAACEHNR	ARCHAEAN	AAAEGMWY	AWAY GAME	AAAILNST	ALSATIAN
AAACEHRS	HAS A CARE	AAAEGNPP	APPANAGE	AAAILSWY	SAIL AWAY
AAACEHSS	HAS A CASE	AAAEGNPS	APANAGES	AAAILTWY	TAIL AWAY
AAACELNT	ANALECTA	AAAEGVWY	GAVE AWAY	AAAIMMST	MIASMATA
AAACELRT	A LA CARTE	AAAEHLMS	HAS A MEAL	AAAINNTZ	TANZANIA
AAACENNP	PANACEAN	AAAEHLSS	HAS A SALE	AAAINOPR	PARANOIA
AAACENPS	PANACEAS	AAAEHMNT	ANATHEMA	AAAINQRU	AQUARIAN
		AAAEHNPS	ANAPHASE		

AAAIPSSV	PIASSAVA	AABCDESU	BAD CAUSE	AABCISSS	ABSCISSA
AAAIRRSV	RARA AVIS	AABCDHIT	ACID BATH	AABCISTX	TAXI CABS
AAAKLNPU	PAUL ANKA	AABCDHKN	BACKHAND		TAXICABS
AAAKLWWY	WALK AWAY		HAND BACK	AABCKKLT	TALK BACK
AAAKOSWY	SOAKAWAY	AABCDHKR	HARDBACK	AABCKKLW	WALK BACK
AAALLPRX	PARALLAX	AABCDHMT	BAD MATCH	AABCKLMN	BLACK MAN
AAALMNNV	NAVAL MAN	AABCDHPT	BAD PATCH	AABCKLNT	BLACK ANT
AAALNPRT	RATAPLAN	AABCDIKL	LAID BACK	AABCKLPS	BACKSLAP
AAALNRTT	TARLATAN		LAID-BACK	AABCKLPY	PLAY BACK
AAALPRTY	LAY A TRAP	AABCDIKP	PAID BACK		PLAYBACK
AAALPSSW	PASS A LAW	AABCDILL	BALLADIC	AABCKLRT	BLACK ART
AAALPWYY	PLAY AWAY	AABCDKRW	BACKWARD		BLACK RAT
AAALSTWY	SALT AWAY		DRAW BACK	AABCKNRS	CAB RANKS
AAAMNOPR	PANORAMA		DRAWBACK		SNACK BAR
AAAMNRST	RASTAMAN	AABCDKRY	BACK YARD	AABCKOOT	TOOK A CAB
AAAMOTTU	AUTOMATA	AABCDLNR	LAND CRAB	AABCKPSS	PASS BACK
AAAMRTTU	TRAUMATA	AABCDORT	BAD ACTOR	AABCKPSY	PAYS BACK
AAANTUUV	VANUAATU	AABCEENY	ABEYANCE	AABCKRRS	BARRACKS
AAAPQRTU	PARAQUAT	AABCEGKP	BACK PAGE	AABCKSTY	BACKSTAY
AAAPSSWY	PASS AWAY	AABCEGKV	GAVE BACK	AABCKSWY	SWAYBACK
AAASTWYY	STAY AWAY	AABCEGOT	CABOTAGE	AABCLNTY	BLATANCY
AABBCDRS	SCABBARD	AABCEHIR	HIRE A CAB	AABCORST	ACROBATS
AABBCEFY	BABY FACE	AABCEILM	AMICABLE	AABCOSTT	CATBOATS
AABBCEGS	CABBAGES	AABCEIRT	BACTERIA	AABCRSTT	ABSTRACT
AABBCEKR	BAREBACK	AABCEJNO	JACOBEAN	AABDDEEM	ADAM BEDE
AABBCEKT	BEAT BACK	AABCEKKT	TAKE BACK	AABDDEET	DEAD BEAT
AABBCERY	BABY CARE	AABCEKLM	CLAMBAKE		DEADBEAT
AABBCINR	BARBICAN	AABCEKLN	LEAN BACK	AABDDEGN	BANDAGED
AABBCIRR	BARBARIC	AABCEKLP	PACKABLE	AABDDEHL	BALD HEAD
AABBCRSY	BABY CARS	AABCEKLS	BLACK SEA	AABDDEHN	HEADBAND
AABBCTTY	TABBY CAT	AABCEKST	BACK SEAT	AABDDEIM	MADE A BID
AABBDHIT	BAD HABIT		BACK-SEAT	AABDDELL	DEAD BALL
AABBDHIU	ABU DHABI	AABCELLL	CALLABLE		DEAD-BALL
AABBDORS	BARBADOS	AABCELNR	BALANCER	AABDDEMR	BAD DREAM
AABBEGNS	BEANBAGS		BARNACLE	AABDDHNS	DAB HANDS
AABBEILL	BAILABLE	AABCELNS	BALANCES	AABDDINS	BAND AIDS
AABBEKLN	BANKABLE	AABCELRT	BRACTEAL		BAND-AIDS
AABBELLM	BLAMABLE	AABCELWY	CABLEWAY	AABDDLNS	BAD LANDS
AABBELLS	BASEBALL	AABCEORT	BOAT RACE		BADLANDS
AABBERWY	BABY WEAR	AABCERST	CABARETS	AABDDORS	BAD ROADS
AABBESWY	EBBS AWAY	AABCFHKL	HALFBACK	AABDDYYY	DAY BY DAY
AABBGGRS	GRAB BAGS	AABCFIIL	BIFACIAL	AABDEEHR	BARE HEAD
AABBHMRU	RHUM BABA	AABCFKLL	FALL BACK	AABDEELR	READABLE
AABBHSST	SABBATHS		FALLBACK	AABDEELT	DATEABLE
AABBIILL	BALI BALI	AABCFKST	FASTBACK	AABDEELV	EVADABLE
	BILABIAL	AABCFNOT	BACON FAT	AABDEEMT	MADE A BET
AABBILRT	BARBITAL	AABCGHKN	HANG BACK	AABDEFIR	BE AFRAID
AABBIRSU	BABIRUSA	AABCGKNR	RANG BACK	AABDEGIN	BADINAGE
AABBKLTY	BABY TALK	AABCHILR	BRACHIAL	AABDEGLR	GRADABLE
AABBKNOR	ROB A BANK	AABCHINR	BRANCHIA	AABDEGNR	BANDAGER
AABBLLMY	BLAMABLY	AABCHKKR	HARK BACK	AABDEGNS	BANDAGES
AABBMRSU	RUM BABAS	AABCHKLS	BACKLASH	AABDEHIT	HAD A BITE
AABCCEHK	BACKACHE	AABCHKSW	BACKWASH	AABDEHPS	BAD SHAPE
AABCCEKM	CAME BACK	AABCHLOO	COOLABAH	AABDEHRT	BAD HEART
AABCCELR	CABLE CAR	AABCIILS	BASILICA	AABDEIKM	MAKE A BID
AABCCHKT	BACKCHAT	AABCIKLT	TAILBACK	AABDEILR	LAID BARE
AABCCIMR	CARBAMIC	AABCILMS	BALSAMIC	AABDEILT	LAID A BET
AABCCKKP	BACKPACK		CABALISM	AABDEIMT	A BAD TIME
AABCCKLL	CALL BACK	AABCILMY	AMICABLY	AABDEIRS	ARABISED
AABCCKLP	BLACK CAP	AABCILNN	CANNIBAL	AABDEIRZ	ARABIZED
	BLACKCAP	AABCILNO	ANABOLIC	AABDEJLL	DJELLABA
AABCCKLT	BLACK CAT	AABCILST	BASALTIC	AABDEKRY	DAYBREAK
AABCCKLW	CLAW-BACK		CABALIST	AABDELLS	BALLADES
AABCCMOT	CATACOMB	AABCIMNR	CAMBRIAN	AABDELLU	LAUDABLE
AABCDEGR	BAD GRACE	AABCINNN	CANNABIN	AABDELMN	DAMNABLE
AABCDEHK	HEAD BACK	AABCINNR	CINNABAR	AABDELOR	ADORABLE
AABCDEIN	ABIDANCE	AABCINNS	CANNABIS	AABDELPP	BAD APPLE
AABCDEIT	ABDICATE	AABCINRS	CARIBANS	AABDELPR	DRAPABLE
AABCDEKT	BACKDATE	AABCINRT	BACTRIAN	AABDELPT	BALD PATE
AABCDELL	CABALLED	AABCIPSY	BASIC PAY	AABDELRT	TRADABLE
AABCDELN	BALANCED	AABCIRSS	BRASSICA	AABDELRY	READABLY

AABDEMOW	MADE A BOW
AABDENTU	UNABATED
AABDENUX	BANDEAUX
AABDEORS	SEABOARD
AABDESTT	BAD STATE
	BAD TASTE
AABDFHIT	BAD FAITH
AABDFIRY	BAD FAIRY
AABDGHNS	HANDBAGS
AABDGINR	ABRADING
AABDGNOV	VAGABOND
AABDGNSS	SAND BAGS
	SANDBAGS
AABDGOOR	GO ABOARD
	GO ABROAD
AABDGORR	GARBOARD
AABDGORS	GAS BOARD
AABDGOTU	GAD ABOUT
AABDHLLN	HANDBALL
AABDHLLR	HARD BALL
AABDHNST	HATBANDS
AABDIILS	BASIDIAL
AABDIKNR	BANK RAID
AABDIMRS	ADAMS RIB
AABDJLNO	I AND A JOB
AABDJNZZ	JAZZ BAND
AABDKMRS	BAD MARKS
AABDKNNS	SANDBANK
AABDLLUY	LAUDABLY
AABDLMNU	LABDANUM
AABDLMNY	DAMNABLY
AABDLORR	LABRADOR
	LARBOARD
AABDLORY	ADORABLY
	LABOR DAY
AABDLRSW	BRADAWLS
AABDMNNS	BANDSMAN
AABDNNTU	ABUNDANT
AABDNPSS	PASSBAND
AABDNRRY	BARNYARD
AABDNRSS	SANDBARS
AABDORSV	BRAVADOS
AABDORWW	DRAW A BOW
AABDORWY	BROADWAY
AABDRRSW	DRAWBARS
AABDRSST	BASTARDS
AABDRSTT	BAD START
AABDRSTY	BASTARDY
AABEEFLN	FLEABANE
AABEEGKR	BREAKAGE
AABEEHLT	HEATABLE
AABEEHTV	HAVE A BET
AABEEKMT	MAKE A BET
AABEEKRT	TEA BREAK
AABEEKTT	TAKE A BET
AABEELLS	SALEABLE
AABEELMN	AMENABLE
	NAMEABLE
AABEELMT	TAMEABLE
AABEELRS	ERASABLE
AABEELRT	RATEABLE
AABEELRW	WEARABLE
AABEELST	EATABLES
AABEELSV	SAVEABLE
AABEELTT	TEA TABLE
AABEENOR	ANAEROBE
AABEENTY	BAT AN EYE
AABEERST	BASE RATE
AABEFGLS	FLEABAGS
AABEFHKL	HALFBEAK
AABEFLMU	FLAMBEAU
AABEFORV	FAR ABOVE
AABEGGGS	BAGGAGES
AABEGHLN	HANGABLE
AABEGLLL	GLABELLA
AABEGLLM	BALL GAME
AABEGLRU	ARGUABLE
AABEGLRZ	GRAZABLE
AABEGMNY	MANGABEY
AABEGNOR	BARONAGE
AABEGORT	ABROGATE
AABEGOST	SABOTAGE
AABEGPPR	PAPER BAG
AABEGRRS	BARRAGES
AABEHIRR	HERBARIA
AABEHIST	HAS A BITE
AABEHJOV	HAVE A JOB
AABEHKLS	SHAKABLE
AABEHLPS	SHAPABLE
AABEHLPT	ALPHABET
AABEHLRS	SHARABLE
AABEHLSW	WASHABLE
AABEHMNO	OBEAHMAN
AABEHNSU	BEAU NASH
AABEHRTT	AT THE BAR
AABEIKRR	AIR BRAKE
AABEILLM	MAILABLE
AABEILLS	SAILABLE
AABEILMN	LIMA BEAN
AABEILRV	VARIABLE
AABEILST	SATIABLE
AABEILTV	ABLATIVE
AABEIRSS	AIR BASES
	ARABISES
AABEIRSV	ABRASIVE
AABEIRSZ	ARABIZES
AABEJKOT	TAKE A JOB
AABEJLLS	JELLABAS
AABEJNOZ	JOAN BAEZ
AABEKMOW	MAKE A BOW
AABEKNRT	BANK RATE
AABEKOTW	TAKE A BOW
AABEKSTU	TAKE A BUS
AABELLMT	MEAT BALL
AABELLNO	LOANABLE
AABELLOV	ABOVE ALL
AABELLPP	PALPABLE
AABELLPY	PLAYABLE
AABELLUV	VALUABLE
AABELMNY	AMENABLY
AABELMPP	MAPPABLE
AABELMST	LAMBASTE
AABELMTT	TABLEMAT
AABELNST	BALANTES
AABELORR	ARBOREAL
AABELPRS	PARABLES
AABELPSS	PASSABLE
AABELRST	ARBALEST
AABELRSY	LAYS BARE
AABELRTY	BETRAYAL
AABELSTT	STATABLE
AABELSTU	TABLEAUS
AABELSTY	LAYS A BET
AABELTTU	TABULATE
AABELTUX	TABLEAUX
AABELWWY	BLEW AWAY
AABEMNRV	BRAVE MAN
AABEMRRS	BEAR ARMS
AABENOSY	SOYA BEAN
	SOYA-BEAN
AABENRRT	ABERRANT
AABENRST	RATSBANE
AABENRUV	EVA BRAUN
AABEOPRV	ABOVE PAR
AABEORRT	ARBORETA
AABEOVWY	WAY ABOVE
AABERSTY	BETA RAYS
AABFILUX	FABLIAUX
AABFLLST	FAST BALL
AABFLTUY	BUY A FLAT
AABGGGNN	GANG BANG
	GANG-BANG
AABGGRRT	BRAGGART
AABGHKRS	SHAGBARK
AABGILMS	MAILBAGS
AABGILNT	ABLATING
AABGILRU	BULGARIA
AABGINRS	BARGAINS
AABGLNPS	SLAP-BANG
AABGLRUY	ARGUABLY
AABHHORU	BROUHAHA
AABHIIMP	AMPHIBIA
AABHILSU	HAIL A BUS
AABHILTU	HABITUAL
AABHINTT	HABITANT
AABHISST	BAHAISTS
AABHISTT	HABITATS
AABHKKKU	HABAKKUK
AABHMSTT	BATH MATS
AABHNOTU	AUTOBAHN
AABHOPST	BATH SOAP
AABHRSST	BRASS HAT
AABIITTW	WAIT A BIT
AABIJNPS	PANJABIS
AABIKLMS	KABALISM
AABIKLST	KABALIST
AABILLLY	LABIALLY
AABILLPY	PAY A BILL
AABILLRS	BARILLAS
AABILLST	BALLISTA
AABILMOT	MAIL BOAT
AABILMOW	AIM A BLOW
AABILNNU	BIANNUAL
AABILNOR	BARONIAL
AABILNOT	ABLATION
AABILNRU	BINAURAL
AABILNTY	BANALITY
AABILOST	SAILBOAT
AABILOWY	BOIL AWAY
AABILRVY	VARIABLY
AABIMMRS	MARIMBAS
AABIMNRU	MANUBRIA
AABIMORS	AMBROSIA
AABINORS	ABRASION
AABINRTZ	BARTIZAN
AABINSST	ABSTAINS
AABIOSSY	BIOASSAY
AABIRSST	ARABISTS
AABKLNNO	BANK LOAN
AABKOOSZ	BAZOOKAS
AABLLLPY	PLAY BALL
AABLLPPY	PALPABLY
AABLLSST	BALLASTS
AABLLSTU	BLASTULA
AABLLUVY	VALUABLY
AABLMMRY	MARY LAMB
AABLMNOR	ABNORMAL
AABLMNTU	AMBULANT
AABLNORW	BONAR LAW
AABLNSST	ST.ALBANS
AABLOTUY	LAY ABOUT
	LAYABOUT
AABLOWWY	BLOW AWAY

AABLPSSY	PASSABLY	AACDEEOR	AREA CODE	AACDLOSV	CALVADOS
AABMNRTU	RAMBUTAN	AACDEEPS	ESCAPADE	AACDLPRS	PLACARDS
AABMORSU	MARABOUS	AACDEFNN	FAN DANCE	AACDMMOR	CARDAMOM
AABMORTU	MARABOUT	AACDEGKP	PACKAGED	AACDMRSX	XMAS CARD
	TAMBOURA	AACDEGMR	CARD GAME	AACDNPPY	ANDY CAPP
AABMRRSS	MARS BARS	AACDEGRR	DRAG RACE	AACDOOSV	AVOCADOS
AABMRSTU	TAMBURAS	AACDEHHY	HEADACHY	AACDQRSU	SQUAD CAR
AABNNOSZ	BONANZAS	AACDEHIN	HACIENDA	AACEEFIT	FACETIAE
AABNORTU	RAN ABOUT	AACDEHLN	CHALDEAN	AACEEFLP	PALE FACE
AABNOSTW	BOTSWANA	AACDEHLU	HAD A CLUE		PALEFACE
AABORRRT	BARRATOR	AACDEHMR	DRACHMAE	AACEEFST	FACE EAST
AABOSTTU	SAT ABOUT	AACDEHRS	CHARADES	AACEEFSV	SAVE FACE
AABOSTUW	SAW ABOUT		HARD CASE	AACEEGLV	CLEAVAGE
AABRRRTY	BARRATRY	AACDEHRT	CATHEDRA	AACEEGPS	SPACE AGE
AACCCDIS	SACCADIC	AACDEHTT	ATTACHED	AACEEGRS	ACREAGES
AACCCHHU	CACHUCHA	AACDEIMN	MAENADIC	AACEEHRT	TRACHEAE
AACCCLOO	COCA COLA	AACDEINR	RADIANCE	AACEEIMT	EMACIATE
AACCCRUY	ACCURACY	AACDEJNT	ADJACENT	AACEEINN	ENCAENIA
AACCDDES	CASCADED	AACDEKTT	ATTACKED	AACEEKRT	TAKE CARE
AACCDEFR	FACE CARD	AACDELMN	MANACLED	AACEEKST	TEA CAKES
AACCDEIM	ACADEMIC	AACDELNR	CALENDAR	AACEELRT	LACERATE
AACCDELO	ACCOLADE	AACDELNS	CANDELAS	AACEELST	ESCALATE
AACCDENU	CADUCEAN	AACDELPT	PLACATED	AACEELTU	ACULEATE
AACCDESS	CASCADES	AACDELRY	CLEAR DAY	AACEEMNR	CAME NEAR
AACCDIRS	CARDIACS	AACDELTT	LACTATED	AACEEMNS	MAECENAS
AACCDOVY	ADVOCACY	AACDENOY	ONCE A DAY	AACEEMRT	CREAM TEA
AACCEENT	CETACEAN	AACDENPT	TAP DANCE		MACERATE
AACCEFKP	FACE PACK		TAP-DANCE		RACEMATE
	FACE-PACK	AACDENRV	ADVANCER	AACEEMST	CASEMATE
AACCEHIX	CACHEXIA	AACDENRW	WAR DANCE	AACEENRS	CESAREAN
AACCEILN	CALCANEI	AACDENSV	ADVANCES	AACEENTT	CATENATE
AACCEIRR	CERCARIA	AACDENSZ	CADENZAS	AACEEPSS	SEASCAPE
AACCEKRS	SACK RACE	AACDEORR	ROAD RACE	AACEEPSY	EASY PACE
AACCELLY	CAECALLY	AACDEOTV	ADVOCATE	AACEERSU	CAESURAE
	CALYCEAL	AACDEQUY	ADEQUACY	AACEERTU	ACUTE EAR
AACCERTU	ACCURATE	AACDERSV	CADAVERS	AACEESTT	ACETATES
AACCFILR	FARCICAL	AACDETTU	ACTUATED	AACEETUV	EVACUATE
AACCGILT	GALACTIC	AACDFHRT	HARD FACT	AACEETVX	EXCAVATE
AACCHINR	ANARCHIC	AACDGINR	CARDIGAN	AACEFFIN	AFFIANCE
AACCHISV	VISCACHA	AACDHHRS	HARD CASH	AACEFHHL	HALF EACH
AACCHIVZ	VIZCACHA	AACDHIMR	DRACHMAI	AACEFLNS	FLAN CASE
AACCHLLT	CATCHALL	AACDHINP	HANDICAP	AACEFLRT	FALCATER
AACCHLOR	CHARCOAL	AACDHINR	ARACHNID		FLAT RACE
AACCHLOT	CACHALOT	AACDHIPS	PAID CASH	AACEFPST	FAST PACE
AACCHMNO	COACHMAN	AACDHKRT	HARD TACK	AACEFRSS	FRACASES
AACCHRRS	CAR CRASH		HARDTACK	AACEFRST	FAST RACE
AACCIINV	VACCINIA	AACDHLOS	HAS A COLD	AACEFRTT	ARTEFACT
AACCIIST	SCIATICA	AACDHLOT	CATHODAL	AACEGILN	ANGELICA
AACCILMS	ACCLAIMS	AACDHLRY	CHARLADY	AACEGILT	GLACIATE
AACCILNV	VACCINAL	AACDHMRS	DRACHMAS	AACEGIRR	CARRIAGE
AACCILTT	TACTICAL	AACDHSTU	CUT A DASH	AACEGIRV	VICARAGE
AACCIORS	CARIOCAS	AACDIINS	ASCIDIAN	AACEGKPR	PACKAGER
AACCIPTY	CAPACITY	AACDILMT	DALMATIC	AACEGKPS	PACKAGES
AACCJORU	CARCAJOU	AACDILNO	DIACONAL	AACEGLNT	GLANCE AT
AACCLLST	CAT CALLS	AACDILNR	CARDINAL	AACEGLRR	LARGE CAR
	CATCALLS	AACDILNV	VANDALIC	AACEGMPR	CRAP GAME
AACCLRSU	CARACULS	AACDILOZ	ZODIACAL	AACEGNRS	CARNAGES
	SACCULAR	AACDILPS	CAPSIDAL	AACEGRSY	SAY GRACE
AACCOSTT	STACCATO	AACDILRS	RADICALS	AACEHILL	HELIACAL
	TOCCATAS	AACDIMRT	DRAMATIC	AACEHILN	ACHENIAL
AACDDELM	DEAD CALM	AACDINOR	ORCADIAN	AACEHIMR	CHIMAERA
AACDDENV	ADVANCED	AACDINRY	RADIANCY	AACEHIMT	HAEMATIC
AACDDETY	TEA CADDY	AACDIRSS	ASCARIDS	AACEHINS	CHINA SEA
AACDDHLO	HAD A COLD	AACDIRTY	CARYATID	AACEHINT	CHINA TEA
AACDDINS	CANDIDAS	AACDITUY	AUDACITY	AACEHIPT	HEPATICA
AACDEEHH	HEADACHE	AACDJKSW	JACKDAWS	AACEHIRR	HIRE A CAR
AACDEEHR	HEADRACE	AACDJQRU	JACQUARD	AACEHIRS	ARCHAISE
AACDEEHS	HEAD CASE	AACDKSSS	SAD SACKS	AACEHIRZ	ARCHAIZE
AACDEELN	LED AN ACE	AACDLNSS	SCANDALS	AACEHLRT	TRACHEAL
AACDEELS	ESCALADE	AACDLORS	CARLOADS	AACEHLRX	EXARCHAL
AACDEEMS	ACADEMES	AACDLORT	CARTLOAD	AACEHLSS	CASH SALE

AACEHLSU	HAS A CLUE
AACEHLTW	TEACH LAW
AACEHMST	SCHEMATA
AACEHRST	TRACHEAS
AACEHRTT	TEACH ART
AACEHSTT	ATTACHES
AACEHSTU	CHATEAUS
AACEHTUX	CHATEAUX
AACEILLM	CAMELLIA
AACEILLN	ALLIANCE
	CANAILLE
AACEILMN	CALAMINE
AACEILNS	CANALISE
AACEILNV	VALIANCE
AACEILNZ	CANALIZE
AACEILOP	ALOPECIA
AACEILRV	CAVALIER
AACEIMNR	AMERICAN
	CINERAMA
	IN CAMERA
AACEIMNS	AMNESIAC
AACEIMTT	CATAMITE
AACEINRS	CANARIES
	CESARIAN
AACEINRT	CARINATE
	CRANIATE
AACEINRV	VARIANCE
AACEINRW	WIN A RACE
AACEIPPS	PAPACIES
AACEIPRS	AIR SPACE
	AIRSPACE
AACEIPRT	AT A PRICE
AACEIRRS	AIR RACES
AACEITTV	ACTIVATE
	CAVITATE
AACEKKLW	CAKEWALK
AACEKNPS	PANCAKES
AACEKRTT	ATTACKER
AACEKTTU	TAKE A CUT
AACELLLR	ALL CLEAR
AACELLOT	ALLOCATE
AACELLTY	ALLEY CAT
AACELMNP	PLACEMAN
AACELMNS	MANACLES
AACELMOS	COAL SEAM
AACELMRS	CARAMELS
AACELMSS	CALM SEAS
AACELMST	CAME LAST
AACELNNU	CANNULAE
AACELNOP	AL CAPONE
AACELNPR	PARLANCE
AACELNPS	SCALEPAN
AACELNPT	PLACENTA
AACELNPY	ANYPLACE
AACELNST	ANALECTS
AACELNSV	VALANCES
AACELNTU	LACUNATE
	TENACULA
AACELORT	CARE A LOT
AACELOST	CATALOES
AACELPST	PLACATES
AACELPSU	SCAPULAE
AACELRST	LAST RACE
AACELRSU	CAESURAL
AACELRSV	CARAVELS
AACELRTY	ACRYLATE
AACELRWY	CLEARWAY
AACELSTT	LACTATES
AACELSTY	CATALYSE
AACEMNOR	ON CAMERA
AACEMNPS	SPACE MAN
	SPACEMAN
AACEMQSU	MACAQUES
AACEMRRS	ARMS RACE
AACEMRSS	MASSACRE
AACENORW	WON A RACE
AACENPRS	PANCREAS
AACENPSU	SAUCEPAN
AACENRRU	RUN A RACE
AACENRSS	SARACENS
AACENRSV	CANVASER
AACENRTT	REACTANT
AACENRTY	CATENARY
AACENSSV	CANVASES
AACENSTT	CAST A NET
	CASTANET
AACEORRW	ROW A RACE
AACERSST	CATSEARS
AACERSSU	CAESURAS
AACERSTT	CASTRATE
	TEA CARTS
AACESTTU	ACTUATES
AACESUWY	CAUSEWAY
AACFFRST	STAFF CAR
AACFHLPU	HALF A CUP
AACFHMST	CAMSHAFT
AACFIINR	IN AFRICA
AACFILLY	FACIALLY
AACFILNT	FINAL ACT
AACFINRS	AFRICANS
AACFINST	FANATICS
AACFIOPR	A FAIR COP
AACFIRRT	AIRCRAFT
AACFIRTT	ARTIFACT
AACFISST	FASCISTA
AACFISTT	ITS A FACT
AACFJKLP	FLAPJACK
AACFLPST	FLAT CAPS
AACFORTW	ACT OF WAR
AACFRSST	FAST CARS
AACGGINO	ANAGOGIC
AACGHIRS	CIGAR ASH
AACGHOPZ	GAZPACHO
AACGIIMN	MAGICIAN
AACGILNN	ANGLICAN
AACGILNO	ANALOGIC
	CALINAGO
AACGILNV	GALVANIC
AACGIMMT	MAGMATIC
AACGIMNN	MANGANIC
AACGIMNP	CAMPAIGN
AACGIMOP	APOGAMIC
AACGIMRS	SCIAGRAM
AACGIMUU	GUAIACUM
AACGINTV	VACATING
AACGIORR	AIR CARGO
AACGISTY	SAGACITY
AACGKNPU	PACK A GUN
AACGLLOR	LOCAL RAG
AACGLMOU	GLAUCOMA
AACGMNRS	CRAGSMAN
AACGNOSU	GUANACOS
AACGNRVY	VAGRANCY
AACHHKNU	CHANUKAH
AACHHTWY	HATCHWAY
AACHIINR	IN A CHAIR
AACHILLP	CALIPHAL
AACHILMT	THALAMIC
AACHILNP	CHAPLAIN
AACHILPS	CALIPASH
AACHILRV	ARCHIVAL
AACHIMNN	CHINAMAN
AACHIMNR	CHAIRMAN
AACHIMRR	ARMCHAIR
AACHIMRS	ARCHAISM
	CHARISMA
AACHINPT	AT A PINCH
AACHINRT	THRACIAN
AACHINSW	CHAIN SAW
AACHIPST	CHAPATIS
AACHIPTT	CHAPATTI
AACHIRST	ARCHAIST
	CITHARAS
AACHKSSW	HACKSAWS
AACHKSTY	HAYSTACK
AACHMNTW	WATCHMAN
AACHMORT	HAM ACTOR
	TRACHOMA
AACHMPRY	PHARMACY
AACHMRSS	CAR SMASH
AACHNORT	AT ANCHOR
AACHNRST	TRASH CAN
AACHNSTU	ACANTHUS
AACHOPPR	APPROACH
AACHPSSY	PAY CASH
AACHRSTY	HAY CARTS
AACHRSWY	ARCHWAYS
AACHRTUY	AUTARCHY
AACIILRV	VICARIAL
AACIINNP	IN A PANIC
AACIJLMO	MAJOLICA
AACIJNOP	JAPONICA
AACIKLLT	KILL A CAT
AACIKNST	SKIN A CAT
AACIKRTU	AUTARKIC
AACILLLY	LAICALLY
AACILLMR	LACRIMAL
AACILLMY	LAY CLAIM
AACILLPT	CAP IT ALL
AACILLPY	APICALLY
AACILLRY	RACIALLY
AACILMNT	CALAMINT
	CLAIMANT
AACILMPY	PAY CLAIM
AACILMTY	CALAMITY
AACILNOP	AL PACINO
AACILNRV	CARNIVAL
AACILNTT	ATLANTIC
AACILNTU	NAUTICAL
AACILNTY	ANALYTIC
AACILOTT	TAIL COAT
	TAILCOAT
AACILPST	APLASTIC
	CAPITALS
AACILPTU	CAPITULA
AACILPTY	ATYPICAL
AACILRRS	RAILCARS
AACILRTY	ALACRITY
AACILSTT	CAT'S-TAIL
	CATS TAIL
AACIMMRS	MARASMIC
AACIMNOR	MACARONI
AACIMNOT	ANATOMIC
AACIMORT	AROMATIC
AACINORS	OCARINAS
AACINORT	CROATIAN
	RAINCOAT
AACINOTV	VACATION
AACINPST	CAPTAINS
AACINQTU	ACQUAINT
AACINSTZ	STANZAIC
AACIPRST	ASPARTIC

AACIPRTY	RAPACITY	AADDEEHT	DEAD HEAT	AADEFHST	FATHEADS
AACIQSTU	AQUATICS		DEAD-HEAT	AADEFILR	FAIR DEAL
AACIRRTT	TARTARIC	AADDEERR	DEAR DEAR		FAIRLEAD
AACIRSTT	CASTRATI	AADDEESY	DEAD EASY	AADEFITX	FIX A DATE
AACJKOOR	JACKAROO	AADDEFHL	HALF DEAD	AADEFLLR	FALDERAL
AACJKRST	JACK TARS	AADDEFIS	DEAF-AIDS	AADEFLRY	DEFRAYAL
AACKKNPS	KNAPSACK	AADDEFLT	DEAD FLAT	AADEFMST	MADE FAST
AACKLOWY	LOCK AWAY	AADDEGRT	GRADATED	AADEFOTU	AUTO-DA-FE
AACKLSTW	CATWALKS	AADDEHHR	HARD HEAD	AADEFRTY	DAY AFTER
AACKMNRU	RAN AMUCK		HARDHEAD	AADEFSTY	FEAST DAY
AACKNRSS	RANSACKS	AADDEHLN	HEADLAND	AADEGGLS	EGG SALAD
AACKPRRS	CAR PARKS	AADDEHLT	DEAD HALT	AADEGHMR	HARD GAME
AACKTUWY	TUCK AWAY	AADDEHLU	HAD A DUEL	AADEGHNS	NAGS HEAD
AACLLLOW	LOCAL LAW	AADDEHMN	HANDMADE	AADEGHOT	GOT AHEAD
AACLLLST	LAST CALL	AADDEHRZ	HAZARDED	AADEGILL	LEGAL AID
AACLLMRS	SMALL CAR	AADDEIRT	RADIATED	AADEGINR	DRAINAGE
AACLLNRY	CARNALLY	AADDEIWY	DIED AWAY		GARDENIA
AACLLRRY	CAR RALLY	AADDELTU	ADULATED	AADEGITT	AGITATED
AACLLRSY	RASCALLY	AADDEMNT	MANDATED	AADEGITV	DIVAGATE
AACLLSUY	CASUALLY	AADDEMRU	MARAUDED	AADEGKRS	DARK AGES
	CAUSALLY	AADDEMRY	DAY DREAM	AADEGLMN	MAGDALEN
AACLLTUY	ACTUALLY		DAYDREAM	AADEGLSV	SALVAGED
AACLMNNS	CLANSMAN	AADDEORS	DEODARAS	AADEGMPR	RAMPAGED
AACLMSTY	STAY CALM	AADDERTW	ADD WATER	AADEGMRS	DAMAGERS
AACLNNOT	CANTONAL	AADDGHLN	GLAD HAND	AADEGNRR	ARRANGED
AACLNNOW	CANON LAW	AADDGNRU	GRADUAND	AADEGPRT	TRADE GAP
AACLNNSU	CANNULAS	AADDHHIL	LAH-DI-DAH	AADEGRRT	RAG TRADE
AACLNOPR	COPLANAR	AADDHIMN	HANDMAID	AADEGRST	GRADATES
AACLNRUY	LACUNARY	AADDHORR	HARD ROAD	AADEGRTU	GRADUATE
AACLNTVY	VACANTLY	AADDHORW	HAD A WORD	AADEGRTY	GREAT DAY
AACLORRU	ORACULAR	AADDHRSY	HARD DAYS	AADEGRWW	WAGED WAR
AACLORSU	CAROUSAL	AADDINPY	IN A PADDY	AADEGSSU	ASSUAGED
AACLORUV	VACUOLAR	AADDISST	DADAISTS	AADEHHOP	HAD A HOPE
AACLOSTT	CATTALOS	AADDKLRY	DARK LADY	AADEHILR	RAILHEAD
AACLPPRT	CLAPTRAP	AADDKRSY	DARK DAYS	AADEHIMT	MADE A HIT
AACLPRST	CALTRAPS	AADDLLNY	LANDLADY	AADEHIRR	DIARRHEA
AACLPRSU	CAPSULAR	AADDNRST	STANDARD	AADEHIWY	HIDE AWAY
	SCAPULAR	AADDOTYY	DAY TO DAY		HIDEAWAY
AACLPSSU	SCAPULAS		DAY-TO-DAY	AADEHKRT	TAKE HARD
AACLPSTY	PLAYACTS	AADDRSST	DASTARDS	AADEHLLO	HALLOAED
AACLPTTU	CATAPULT	AADEEEHS	SEE AHEAD	AADEHLMP	HEADLAMP
AACLRSST	ART CLASS	AADEEFIP	PAID A FEE	AADEHLNR	ANHEDRAL
AACLRSSW	CLASS WAR	AADEEFMS	MADE SAFE	AADEHLSU	HAS A DUEL
AACLRSUV	VASCULAR	AADEEFRS	DEAF EARS	AADEHMNS	HEADSMAN
AACLSTTY	CATALYST	AADEEGHT	GET AHEAD	AADEHMPR	HAD A PERM
AACLSTUY	CASUALTY	AADEEGHV	GAVE HEAD	AADEHMST	MASTHEAD
AACMMPRY	ARMY CAMP	AADEEGLT	GALEATED	AADEHNRU	RUN AHEAD
AACMNOOR	MACAROON	AADEEGMM	MADE GAME	AADEHRRW	HARDWARE
AACMNPRY	RAMPANCY	AADEEGNR	GADARENE	AADEHRSS	HARASSED
AACMNSTX	MANX CATS	AADEEGRV	AVERAGED	AADEHRST	HAD A REST
AACMORSS	SARCOMAS	AADEEILR	AIREDALE		HARD SEAT
AACMORTW	WARM COAT	AADEEKNP	NAKED APE		SAD HEART
AACMOSST	SAM COSTA	AADEEKNW	AWAKENED	AADEHRSW	WARHEADS
AACMPSTT	STAMP ACT	AADEELLM	MALE LEAD	AADEHRTY	DEATH RAY
AACMRRST	TRAMCARS	AADEELMR	DE LA MARE	AADEHSSY	SASHAYED
AACNPSST	CAPSTANS		MADE REAL	AADEHSTT	HAD TASTE
AACNRRSU	RUNS A CAR	AADEELNN	ANNEALED	AADEILMS	MALADIES
AACNRSTT	TRANSACT	AADEELPP	APPEALED	AADEILNT	DENTALIA
AACNRSTU	CURTANAS	AADEELRV	DE VALERA	AADEILPR	PRAEDIAL
AACORSTT	CASTRATO	AADEELRW	DELAWARE	AADEILPS	PALISADE
AACORTTU	ACTUATOR	AADEEMNT	EMANATED	AADEILRS	SALARIED
	AUTOCRAT	AADEEMRR	DEMERARA	AADEILRT	ARALDITE
AACPSSTW	CAT'S-PAWS	AADEEMST	SAME DATE	AADEILSS	ASSAILED
AACRSTTT	ATTRACTS		TEASMADE	AADEILSY	LAY ASIDE
AACRSTTY	STRAY CAT	AADEEMSY	MADE EASY	AADEILTU	AUDIT ALE
AACSTUWY	CUTS AWAY	AADEENTT	ANTEDATE	AADEILTV	VALIDATE
AADDDEEH	DEADHEAD	AADEEPPR	APPEARED	AADEIMNR	IN A DREAM
AADDDEHN	DEAD HAND	AADEEPPS	APPEASED		MARINADE
AADDDEIL	DID A DEAL	AADEEQTU	ADEQUATE	AADEIMNS	IDEAS MAN
AADDDGNR	GRANDDAD	AADEESTT	SET A DATE		SAID AMEN
AADDEEFL	DEAD LEAF	AADEETVX	EVADE TAX		

AADEIMNT	ANIMATED	AADGGLNN	GANGLAND	AADINOPS	DIAPASON
	DIAMANTE	AADGGLRS	GLAD RAGS	AADINPRS	SPANIARD
AADEIMPZ	DIAZEPAM		LAGGARDS	AADINRST	RADIANTS
AADEIMRV	MARAVEDI	AADGGNOP	PAGAN GOD	AADINRYY	RAINY DAY
AADEIMST	ADAMITES	AADGHINN	GANDHIAN	AADINSSS	SASSANID
AADEINTT	ATTAINED	AADGIINS	GAINSAID	AADIOPRS	DIASPORA
AADEIPRS	PARADISE	AADGILLR	GALLIARD	AADIORRT	RADIATOR
AADEIPSU	DIAPAUSE	AADGILMR	MADRIGAL	AADIOSSY	DO AS I SAY
AADEIPTV	ADAPTIVE	AADGILNO	DIAGONAL	AADIRRSY	DISARRAY
AADEIRST	RADIATES	AADGIMPR	PARADIGM	AADJNTTU	ADJUTANT
AADEIRSY	I DARE SAY!	AADGIMRS	DIAGRAMS	AADJNTUV	ADJUVANT
AADEIRWY	RIDE AWAY	AADGINPR	PARADING	AADJRTZZ	TRAD JAZZ
AADEISST	DIASTASE	AADGINPT	ADAPTING	AADKLMNR	LANDMARK
AADEISTT	SATIATED	AADGINRU	GUARDIAN	AADKLNPR	PARKLAND
AADEISWY	DIES AWAY	AADGINRW	AWARDING	AADKNRST	TANKARDS
AADEITVW	VIEWDATA	AADGLLSW	GADWALLS	AADKORWY	WORKADAY
AADEJNNP	JAPANNED	AADGLNRS	GARLANDS	AADLLMRS	MALLARDS
AADEKLLN	LAKELAND	AADGLOPR	PODAGRAL	AADLLMSS	SMALL ADS
AADEKMNN	NAKED MAN	AADGMNOR	DRAGOMAN	AADLLNOY	ANODALLY
AADEKMNR	MANDRAKE	AADGMNRS	GRANDMAS	AADLLORS	ALL ROADS
AADELLPP	APPALLED	AADGNPRS	GRANDPAS	AADLMNRY	LAND ARMY
AADELMNP	NAPALMED	AADGNRUV	VANGUARD	AADLMNSS	LANDMASS
AADELMNR	ALDERMAN	AADGNRUW	DRAW A GUN	AADLMNUU	LAUDANUM
AADELMNS	LEADSMAN	AADGOOSS	AS GOOD AS	AADLMPVY	DAVY LAMP
AADELMPT	DATE PALM	AADGOOWY	A GOOD WAY	AADLMR3T	SMART LAD
AADELMPY	MADE PLAY	AADHHMNU	HUM AND HA	AADLNRSY	LANYARDS
AADELMSW	MADE LAWS	AADHHNSW	WASH-HAND	AADLOPSY	PAYLOADS
AADELNRS	ADRENALS	AADHHOST	HAD A SHOT	AADLORST	LOADSTAR
AADELNSY	ANALYSED	AADHIKRR	DARK HAIR	AADLORTU	ADULATOR
AADELNYZ	ANALYZED	AADHILLR	HALLIARD	AADLPPSU	APPLAUDS
AADELPPT	PALPATED	AADHILNR	HANDRAIL	AADLSSTY	LAST DAYS
AADELPRY	PARLAYED	AADHILNT	THAILAND	AADMMNOW	MAD WOMAN
AADELSTU	ADULATES	AADHIMOR	RADIO HAM	AADMMNSU	MANDAMUS
AADEMMNR	DREAM MAN	AADHINPS	DAPHNIAS	AADMNNOS	MADONNAS
AADEMNOS	ADENOMAS	AADHINRR	HARD RAIN	AADMNORT	AT RANDOM
AADEMNPU	MADE A PUN	AADHIRTT	HARD AT IT	AADMOPRS	ROAD MAPS
AADEMNST	MANDATES	AADHKLOO	HAD A LOOK	AADMORRT	TRAMROAD
AADEMOVW	MADE A VOW	AADHKRST	HARD TASK	AADMORST	MATADORS
AADEMRRU	MARAUDER	AADHLLNS	ALL HANDS	AADMRRSY	YARDARMS
AADENOPR	ON PARADE	AADHLNOY	LAND AHOY	AADMRSWY	WARM DAYS
AADENRRT	NARRATED	AADHLPRY	PLAY HARD	AADMRSZZ	MAZZARDS
AADENRRW	DRAW NEAR	AADHLPSS	SLAPDASH	AADNOSUV	VANADOUS
AADENRSV	VERANDAS	AADHLRSY	HALYARDS	AADNOSWY	NOWADAYS
AADENSWY	SEND AWAY	AADHMNNY	HANDYMAN	AADNPRWY	DRAWN PAY
AADEORWY	RODE AWAY	AADHNRSS	HANSARDS	AADNPSTT	STAND PAT
AADEPRST	ADAPTERS	AADHNSSW	HANDSAWS	AADNPTUW	UP AT DAWN
AADEQRTU	QUADRATE	AADHORSW	HAS A WORD	AADNQRTU	QUADRANT
AADERRRW	REARWARD	AADHPPYY	HAPPY DAY	AADNQRUY	QUANDARY
AADERRSW	AWARDERS	AADIIMNN	INDIAMAN	AADNRVYY	NAVY YARD
AADERSTW	EASTWARD	AADIIRRS	AIR RAIDS	AADOPRST	ADAPTORS
AADERWWY	DREW AWAY	AADIKLLO	ALKALOID	AADORSWY	ROADWAYS
AADESSTT	AS STATED	AADIKLRY	KAILYARD	AADOSSTY	SAD TO SAY
AADFGLSY	FLAG DAYS	AADIKNQR	QINDARKA	AADPRSWY	DRAWS PAY
AADFGNNO	FANDANGO	AADILLOS	SALAD OIL	AADQRSTU	QUADRATS
AADFHHIT	HAD FAITH	AADILLRY	RADIALLY	AADRSTUY	SATURDAY
AADFHINR	FAIR HAND	AADILMNN	MAINLAND	AAEEFGLS	LEAFAGES
AADFHLSY	HALF DAYS	AADILMRS	ADMIRALS	AAEEFHVW	HAVE A FEW
AADFHMNR	FARM HAND	AADILNPR	PRANDIAL	AAEEFKMS	MAKE SAFE
	FARMHAND	AADILNPS	PALADINS	AAEEFLNW	A NEW LEAF
AADFIIMR	FAIR MAID	AADILORR	RAILROAD	AAEEFMST	MEAT SAFE
AADFILLT	LAID FLAT	AADILPPU	PAID PAUL	AAEEFPSY	PAYS A FEE
AADFILRY	FAIR LADY	AADILPRY	LAPIDARY	AAEEFRRS	SEAFARER
AADFINWY	FIND A WAY	AADILSWY	SLID AWAY	AAEEFRTT	AFTER TEA
AADFLLLN	LANDFALL	AADIMNNR	MANDARIN	AAEEFSST	SAFE SEAT
AADFLMNR	FARM LAND	AADIMNOR	MAIN ROAD	AAEEGGRT	GREAT AGE
AADFLOTX	TOADFLAX	AADIMNRT	TAMARIND	AAEEGILN	ALIENAGE
AADFLOWY	FOLDAWAY	AADIMNRY	DAIRYMAN	AAEEGKMM	MAKE GAME
AADFMRRY	FARMYARD	AADIMNUV	VANADIUM	AAEEGLRY	EARLY AGE
AADFNNOR	ANNA FORD	AADIMORS	DIORAMAS	AAEEGMMT	TEAM GAME
AADGGHRS	HAGGARDS	AADIMSTZ	SAMIZDAT	AAEEGMPR	AMPERAGE
AADGGIMN	DAMAGING	AADINOPR	PARANOID	AAEEGMSY	EASY GAME

AAEEGRRY	GREY AREA	AAEFIMRR	AIRFRAME	AAEGMNOW	WON A GAME
AAEEGRSV	AVERAGES	AAEFINNT	FAINEANT	AAEGMNRS	MANAGERS
AAEEGRTW	WAGE RATE	AAEFINPU	EPIFAUNA	AAEGMNRT	GREAT MAN
AAEEHHRR	HEAR HEAR	AAEFINPY	PAY A FINE	AAEGMNRV	GRAVAMEN
AAEEHRTW	WHEATEAR	AAEFIRRS	AIR FARES	AAEGMNST	MAGNATES
AAEEHSVY	HEAVY SEA		AIRFARES	AAEGMORR	AEROGRAM
AAEEHTVW	HEAT WAVE	AAEFIRTX	TAXI FARE	AAEGMPRS	RAMPAGES
AAEEIKLW	LIE AWAKE	AAEFIRWY	FIRE AWAY	AAEGMRRV	MARGRAVE
AAEEILNT	ALIENATE	AAEFKMST	MAKE FAST	AAEGMRSS	MASSAGER
AAEEJNPS	JAPANESE	AAEFKRST	ASK AFTER	AAEGMRSW	WAR GAMES
AAEEJNSV	JAVANESE	AAEFLLLT	LATE FALL	AAEGMSSS	MASSAGES
AAEEKLMR	MAKE REAL	AAEFLLRT	AFTER ALL	AAEGNOOR	NO-GO AREA
AAEEKLSV	ASK LEAVE	AAEFLLSW	WALL SAFE	AAEGNOWY	GONE AWAY
AAEEKMNS	NAMESAKE	AAEFLLWY	FELL AWAY	AAEGNPST	PAGEANTS
AAEEKMSY	MAKE EASY	AAEFLMOT	MEAT LOAF	AAEGNRRR	ARRANGER
AAEEKNRS	KANARESE	AAEFLMTT	FLATMATE	AAEGNRRS	ARRANGES
AAEEKNRW	AWAKENER	AAEFLNST	FAST LANE	AAEGNSTT	GETS A TAN
AAEEKPRT	PARAKEET	AAEFLPSY	PLAY SAFE		STAGNATE
AAEEKPTW	TAKE A PEW	AAEFLRTT	FLAT RATE	AAEGORRT	ARROGATE
AAEEKPWY	KEEP AWAY	AAEFLWWY	FLEW AWAY	AAEGORSY	YEARS AGO
AAEEKQSU	SEAQUAKE	AAEFNOTT	ATE NO FAT	AAEGORTT	AEGROTAT
AAEELLLM	LAMELLAE		EAT NO FAT	AAEGOSWY	GOES AWAY
AAEELLPS	PALE ALES	AAEFNRRT	RAN AFTER	AAEGPSSS	PASSAGES
AAEELLRS	REAL ALES	AAEFRRWY	WAYFARER	AAEGPSWY	PAY WAGES
AAEELMNT	LEAN MEAT	AAEFRTTX	AFTER TAX	AAEGRRTW	GREAT WAR
AAEELMST	EAT MEALS	AAEGGIOT	AGIOTAGE	AAEGRRVW	WAR GRAVE
AAEELNPS	SEAPLANE	AAEGGLNU	LANGUAGE	AAEGRSTT	REGATTAS
AAEELNSS	SEA-LANES	AAEGGLNY	LAY AN EGG	AAEGRSTZ	STARGAZE
AAEELORT	AREOLATE	AAEGGLOT	GET A GOAL	AAEGRSVY	SAVAGERY
AAEELPPR	APPEALER	AAEGGNOS	ANAGOGES	AAEGRSWW	WAGE WARS
AAEELPRY	LEAP YEAR	AAEGGNRY	GARGANEY		WAGES WAR
AAEELRTU	LAUREATE	AAEGGTUV	GAVE A TUG	AAEGSSSU	ASSUAGES
AAEELRTV	VALERATE	AAEGHLPS	SLAG HEAP		SAUSAGES
AAEELTUV	EVALUATE	AAEGHMRX	HEXAGRAM	AAEGSSTU	AT A GUESS
AAEELVWY	WAYLEAVE	AAEGHNRU	HARANGUE	AAEGSSTV	SAVAGEST
AAEEMMNS	SAME NAME	AAEGILLN	GALILEAN	AAEGSSTW	WASTAGES
AAEEMMTT	TEAM MATE	AAEGILNP	PELAGIAN	AAEGSTWY	GATEWAYS
AAEEMNNS	ANNAMESE	AAEGILNT	ALGINATE		GETS AWAY
AAEEMNRT	MAN-EATER	AAEGILSX	GALAXIES	AAEHHOPS	HAS A HOPE
AAEEMNST	EMANATES	AAEGILTT	TAILGATE	AAEHIKMT	MAKE A HIT
	MANATEES	AAEGIMNO	EGOMANIA	AAEHIKPV	HAVE A KIP
AAEEMSTY	EASY MEAT	AAEGIMNS	MAGNESIA	AAEHILNT	ANTHELIA
AAEENNNT	ANTENNAE	AAEGIMNW	WIN A GAME	AAEHILPR	PARHELIA
AAEENNRZ	NAZARENE	AAEGIMNZ	MAGAZINE	AAEHIMNT	HAEMATIN
AAEENRST	NEAR EAST	AAEGIMRR	MARRIAGE	AAEHINNT	ATHENIAN
AAEENRTT	ANTEATER	AAEGINPS	PAGANISE	AAEHINST	ASTHENIA
AAEENSTU	NAUSEATE	AAEGINPT	PAGINATE	AAEHIPRY	HAIRY APE
AAEEORRT	EAR TO EAR	AAEGINRT	AERATING	AAEHKMRY	HAYMAKER
AAEEPPRR	RAPPAREE	AAEGINTV	NAVIGATE	AAEHKMSY	MAKES HAY
AAEEPPRS	APPEASER	AAEGINTY	YET AGAIN	AAEHKSSW	SEA HAWKS
AAEEPPSS	APPEASES	AAEGIPTV	GAVE A TIP	AAEHKTTT	TAKE THAT
AAEEPRST	SEPARATE	AAEGIRSV	VAGARIES	AAEHLMSY	SEALYHAM
AAEERSTT	STEARATE	AAEGIRTX	EX GRATIA	AAEHLNOS	ON A LEASH
AAEERSTW	SEA WATER	AAEGISSS	ASSEGAIS	AAEHLNRT	ANTHERAL
AAEERVWY	VEER AWAY	AAEGISTT	AGITATES	AAEHLOSW	AS A WHOLE
AAEFFHLR	HALF FARE	AAEGIVWY	GIVE AWAY	AAEHLPUV	UPHEAVAL
AAEFFILS	FAILSAFE		GIVEAWAY	AAEHMOPR	AMPHORAE
AAEFFNRS	FANFARES	AAEGJOTV	GAVE A JOT	AAEHMORT	ATHEROMA
AAEFGGIV	GAVE A FIG	AAEGKLSS	GAS LEAKS	AAEHMPRS	HAS A PERM
AAEFGHRW	WHARFAGE	AAEGKRTU	GREAT AUK	AAEHMTTY	ATE MY HAT
AAEFGIMR	FAIR GAME	AAEGLLMW	WALL GAME		EAT MY HAT
AAEFGIRW	FAIR WAGE	AAEGLLPR	PELLAGRA	AAEHNPST	PHEASANT
AAEFGLLL	FLAGELLA	AAEGLMNS	GAMELANS	AAEHNTVX	TAX HAVEN
AAEFGLOT	FLOATAGE	AAEGLMSW	GAME LAWS	AAEHOPRT	OPERA HAT
AAEFGLPT	LEFT A GAP	AAEGLNOU	ANALOGUE	AAEHORVW	HAVE A ROW
AAEFHIMT	THE MAFIA	AAEGLNTW	LAW AGENT	AAEHPPRT	PAPER HAT
AAEFHITV	HAVE A FIT	AAEGLPST	LAST PAGE	AAEHRRSS	HARASSER
AAEFIILR	FILARIAE	AAEGLRSV	SALVAGER	AAEHRSSS	HARASSES
AAEFILRR	RAIL FARE	AAEGLSSV	LAS VEGAS	AAEHRSST	HAS A REST
AAEFILRY	LAY A FIRE		SALVAGES	AAEHRTVY	HAVE A TRY
AAEFILWY	FILE AWAY	AAEGLSVY	SAVAGELY	AAEHSSTT	HAS TASTE

AAEHTVXY	HEAVY TAX	AAEKLMPY	MAKE PLAY	AAELPPSU	APPLAUSE
AAEIILLN	NAIL A LIE	AAEKLMRW	LAWMAKER	AAELPQUY	EQUAL PAY
AAEIIPRS	APIARIES	AAEKLMRY	MALARKEY	AAELPRSV	PALAVERS
AAEIIRSV	AVIARIES	AAEKLMSW	MAKE LAWS	AAELPRSY	PARALYSE
AAEIKKMZ	KAMIKAZE	AAEKLNPR	PARK LANE	AAELPRUV	PAR VALUE
AAEIKLLL	ALL ALIKE	AAEKLNSW	SWAN LAKE	AAELPRYZ	PARALYZE
AAEIKLLN	ALKALINE	AAEKMNPU	MAKE A PUN	AAELPSTU	PLATEAUS
AAEIKLLS	ALKALIES	AAEKMOVW	MAKE A VOW	AAELPSTV	PALSTAVE
AAEIKLLV	LAVALIKE	AAEKMRRS	EARMARKS	AAELPTUX	PLATEAUX
AAEIKLMN	LIKE A MAN	AAEKMRSW	MAKES WAR	AAELRSTY	LAST YEAR
AAEIKMNT	TAKEN AIM	AAEKMRSY	EASY MARK	AAELRSTZ	LAZARETS
AAEIKMST	TAKES AIM	AAEKMSWY	MAKES WAY	AAELRUZZ	ZARZUELA
AAEIKPTT	TAKE A TIP	AAEKNPRT	PARTAKEN	AAELSSST	SALT SEAS
AAEIILLU	ALLELUIA	AAEKNRRR	REAR RANK	AAELSSTX	SALES TAX
AAEIILLMX	MAXILLAE	AAEKOTVW	TAKE A VOW	AAEMMMNRT	ARMAMENT
AAEIILLPP	PAPILLAE	AAEKPRRT	PARTAKER	AAEMMSTT	STEMMATA
AAEIILLRT	ARILLATE	AAEKPRTT	TAKE PART	AAEMNNOS	AS ONE MAN
AAEIILLRY	AERIALLY	AAEKPTWY	KEPT AWAY	AAEMNNOW	WON A NAME
AAEILMMN	MAIN MEAL	AAEKRSTW	RAW STEAK	AAEMNNOY	MANY A ONE
AAEILMNR	RAN A MILE	AAEKSSTT	SET A TASK	AAEMNOTZ	METAZOAN
AAEILMNT	LAMINATE	AAEKSSTY	EASY TASK	AAEMNPRS	PARMESAN
AAEILMNV	MAN ALIVE	AAELLLMR	LAMELLAR		SPARE MAN
AAEILMRT	MATERIAL	AAELLLMS	LAMELLAS		SPEARMAN
AAEILMSS	MALAISES	AAELLLNO	ALL ALONE	AAEMNPRT	NAME PART
AAEILNNN	LINNAEAN	AAELLLPR	PARALLEL	AAEMNRST	RASTAMEN
AAEILNPR	AIRPLANE	AAELLMPU	AMPULLAE	AAEMNRTW	WATERMAN
AAEILNPT	PALATINE	AAELLNNV	VAN ALLEN	AAEMNRTX	EXTRA MAN
AAEILNRS	AIR LANES	AAELLORV	ALVEOLAR	AAEMNSSY	SAYS AMEN
AAEILNRV	VALERIAN	AAELLPRT	PATELLAR	AAEMORTT	TERRA COTTA
AAEILNSS	NASALISE	AAELLPST	PATELLAS	AAEMOSTY	SOYA MEAT
	SEA SNAIL	AAELLRST	LATERALS	AAEMOTTU	AUTOMATE
AAEILNSZ	NASALIZE	AAELLSSW	AS WELL AS	AAEMOVWY	MOVE AWAY
AAEILNTT	LATINATE		SEA WALLS	AAEMPRSY	PAM AYRES
AAEILPRT	PARIETAL		SEAWALLS	AAEMPTTU	AMPUTATE
AAEILRRT	ARTERIAL	AAELLWWY	WELL AWAY	AAEMQSTU	SQUAMATE
AAEILRSS	SALARIES	AAELLWYY	ALLEYWAY	AAEMRRTU	ARMATURE
AAEILSTV	SALIVATE	AAELMMNO	MELANOMA	AAEMRSTU	AMATEURS
AAEILTVX	LAXATIVE	AAELMMSS	LAMMASES	AAENNNST	ANTENNAS
AAEIMNNR	ARMENIAN	AAELMNNV	NAVAL MEN	AAENNSTU	NAUSEANT
AAEIMNNT	ANNAMITE	AAELMNRT	MATERNAL	AAENNORRU	AUROREAN
AAEIMNNW	WIN A NAME	AAELMNSS	SALESMAN	AAENORTU	AERONAUT
AAEIMNPR	PEARMAIN	AAELMNST	LAST NAME	AAENPPRT	APPARENT
AAEIMNRT	MARINATE	AAELMNSY	SEAMANLY	AAENPSST	PEASANTS
AAEIMNST	ANIMATES	AAELMOSU	MAUSOLEA	AAENRRST	NARRATES
AAEIMNTZ	NIZAMATE	AAELMOTZ	METAZOAL	AAENRSTY	STAY NEAR
AAEIMOTX	TOXAEMIA	AAELMPPY	MAYAPPLE	AAENRSUW	UNAWARES
AAEIMPSY	PYAEMIAS	AAELMPTY	PLAYMATE	AAENSTWY	SENT AWAY
AAEINNRS	IN A SNARE	AAELMRSU	SLUM AREA	AAENTWWY	WENT AWAY
AAEINORT	AERATION	AAELMRSY	LAMASERY	AAEOPSTT	APOSTATE
AAEINORX	ANOREXIA	AAELMRTT	MALTREAT	AAEORRST	AERATORS
AAEINRRR	IN ARREAR	AAELMTWY	MELT AWAY	AAEORWWY	WORE AWAY
AAEINRST	ARTESIAN	AAELNNNT	ANTENNAL	AAEPPRRT	ART PAPER
	ERASTIAN	AAELNNOT	NEONATAL	AAEPPRST	PARAPETS
AAEINRSU	EURASIAN	AAELNNTU	ANNULATE	AAEPPRWX	WAX PAPER
AAEINSTT	ASTATINE	AAELNOPT	ON A PLATE	AAEPPSUY	PAY PAUSE
	IN A STATE	AAELNOSS	SEASONAL	AAEPRSSY	SEA SPRAY
	SANITATE	AAELNPRT	PARENTAL	AAEPRSTT	SET A TRAP
AAEINSTV	SANATIVE		PATERNAL		SET APART
AAEINSTW	IN A SWEAT		PRENATAL	AAEPRTTW	TAP WATER
AAEIPPRS	APPRAISE	AAELNPRW	WARPLANE	AAEPRTTY	TEA PARTY
AAEIPRST	ASPIRATE	AAELNPST	PLEASANT	AAEPRTXY	EXTRA PAY
	PARASITE	AAELNRSS	ARSENALS		PAY EXTRA
AAEIPRTZ	TRAPEZIA	AAELNRTX	RELAXANT		TAXPAYER
AAEIPWWY	WIPE AWAY	AAELNSST	SEALANTS	AAERRRSY	ARRAYERS
AAEIRRRT	TERRARIA	AAELNSSY	ANALYSES	AAERRSWY	WAR YEARS
AAEIRSVW	AIRWAVES	AAELNSWY	LANEWAYS	AAERRTTT	TARTRATE
AAEISSTT	SATIATES	AAELNSYZ	ANALYZES	AAERRTTW	WATER RAT
AAEJLMPP	APPLE JAM	AAELORTY	ALEATORY	AAERRWWY	WAR-WEARY
AAEJMNRY	MARY JANE	AAELOSTX	OXALATES	AAERSTTU	SATURATE
AAEKLLST	SALT LAKE	AAELPPRS	APPARELS	AAERSTTX	TAX RATES
AAEKLLTY	ALKYLATE	AAELPPST	PALPATES	AAERSTTY	TEA TRAYS

AAERTWWY	WATERWAY
AAFFIILX	AFFIXIAL
AAFFILRT	TAFFRAIL
AAFFINPR	PARAFFIN
AAFFINUX	FAUX-NAIF
AAFFLLLT	FALL FLAT
AAFFLSTU	AFFLATUS
AAFFMORR	FROM AFAR
AAFGHINS	AFGHANIS
AAFGILLP	FILL A GAP
AAFGLNRT	FLAGRANT
AAFGLNST	SANG FLAT
AAFGNRRT	FRAGRANT
AAFHHIST	HAS FAITH
AAFHIIRR	FAIR HAIR
AAFHILNS	IN A FLASH
AAFHLMST	HALF MAST
	HALF-MAST
AAFHLNOT	HALF A TON
AAFHLPST	HALF PAST
AAFHRSUU	HAUSFRAU
AAFIILLM	FAMILIAL
AAFIILLR	FILARIAL
AAFIILMR	FAMILIAR
AAFIINNT	IN A FAINT
AAFIKLLY	ALKALIFY
AAFILLNR	RAINFALL
AAFILLRS	ALLS FAIR
AAFILMST	FATALISM
AAFILNST	FANTAILS
AAFILNSU	ASIAN FLU
AAFILPRY	FAIR PLAY
	PLAY FAIR
AAFILSTT	FATALIST
AAFILTTY	FATALITY
AAFIMNOR	FORAMINA
AAFINNST	INFANTAS
AAFINORS	ON SAFARI
AAFINRRW	WARFARIN
AAFIPRST	PARFAITS
AAFIRSWY	FAIRWAYS
AAFJJMOR	JAR OF JAM
AAFKLORR	FOR A LARK
AAFKLSTT	FAST-TALK
AAFLLLST	LAST FALL
AAFLLNUY	FAUNALLY
AAFLLOVW	LAVA FLOW
AAFLLSTT	SALT FLAT
AAFLMNOW	MAN OF LAW
AAFLOTTU	TO A FAULT
AAFLSTWY	FLATWAYS
AAFMNORW	MAN OF WAR
	MAN-OF-WAR
AAFMNOTW	FAT WOMAN
AAFMNSST	FANTASMS
AAFNORTT	RAN TO FAT
AAFORUWY	FOUR AWAY
AAFPRSTT	FAT PARTS
AAGGGINR	GARAGING
AAGGIMNN	MANAGING
AAGGINRV	RAVAGING
AAGGINSV	SAVAGING
AAGGLNOT	TAG ALONG
AAGGLOST	TAGALOGS
AAGGNSWY	GANGWAYS
AAGGOOPP	PAGO PAGO
AAGHHINS	SHANGHAI
AAGHILNN	HANGNAIL
AAGHINPS	PAGANISH
AAGHINST	HIT A SNAG
AAGHKMNY	GYMKHANA

AAGHLNPY	ANAGLYPH
AAGHLSTU	LAUGHS AT
AAGHMNOY	HOGMANAY
	MAHOGANY
AAGHMRSS	MARSH GAS
AAGHRRTY	GARY HART
AAGIILMN	IMAGINAL
AAGIILNV	AVAILING
AAGIINTW	AWAITING
AAGIJRTU	GUJARATI
AAGIKLNR	KRAALING
AAGILLNY	ALLAYING
AAGILMNO	MAGNOLIA
AAGILMNR	ALARMING
	MARGINAL
AAGILNNS	ANGLIANS
AAGILOOP	APOLOGIA
AAGILSTT	SAGITTAL
AAGILSTW	WAGTAILS
AAGIMNNN	MANGANIN
AAGIMNPS	PAGANISM
AAGIMNSS	AMASSING
	GAS MAINS
AAGIMNSY	GYMNASIA
AAGIMPTU	PATAGIUM
AAGIMSTT	STIGMATA
AAGINRRS	ARRAIGNS
AAGINRRY	ARRAYING
AAGINRSU	GUARANIS
AAGINRTY	TRY AGAIN
AAGINSSU	GAUSSIAN
AAGINSSY	GAINSAYS
AAGINSTV	AVASTING
AAGINSWY	SIGN AWAY
AAGIORTT	AGITATOR
AAGIRSTV	GRAVITAS
AAGKMSSS	GAS MASKS
AAGKNOOR	KANGAROO
AAGKPRSY	GAY SPARK
AAGLLLNO	ALL ALONG
AAGLLMOY	ALLOGAMY
AAGLLNST	GALLANTS
AAGLLOWY	GALLOWAY
AAGLMPSS	GAS LAMPS
AAGLNNOR	RAN ALONG
AAGLNNUV	NAVAL GUN
AAGLNPST	GAS PLANT
AAGLNQUU	AQUALUNG
AAGLNRRU	GRANULAR
AAGLOSWY	SLOG AWAY
AAGLPSST	LAST GASP
AAGLPUWY	PLUG AWAY
AAGLRSTU	GASTRULA
AAGMMORT	GRAM ATOM
AAGMMRRS	GRAMMARS
AAGMNRST	TANGRAMS
AAGMOTUY	AUTOGAMY
AAGMOTYZ	ZYGOMATA
AAGNNSTT	STAGNANT
AAGNOPRS	PARAGONS
AAGNORRT	ARROGANT
	TARRAGON
AAGNRSTV	VAGRANTS
AAGNRTUY	GUARANTY
AAGNSTUU	AUGUSTAN
AAGOPPST	STOP A GAP
AAGORSSS	SARGASSO
AAGORSSU	SAGUAROS
AAGORSTY	GO ASTRAY
AAGPRTYY	GAY PARTY
AAGRRSUY	SUGAR RAY

AAHHKKNU	HANUKKAH
AAHHOPRS	PHARAOHS
AAHHOSST	HAS A SHOT
AAHIIKRR	HARA-KIRI
	HARI-KARI
AAHIINTT	TAHITIAN
AAHIJNRS	HARIJANS
AAHILLMN	MAIN HALL
AAHILMRY	HAIL MARY
AAHILNNT	INHALANT
AAHILNOT	HALATION
AAHILNSS	SALISHAN
AAHIMRST	MARATHIS
AAHINORT	HORATIAN
AAHINPRS	PIRANHAS
AAHINPRT	PARTHIAN
AAHINSST	ASHANTIS
AAHIPSXY	ASPHYXIA
AAHIRVWY	WAVY HAIR
AAHKLLMR	HALLMARK
AAHKLOOS	HAS A LOOK
AAHKMOTW	TOMAHAWK
AAHKMSSY	YASHMAKS
AAHKNORS	NOAHS ARK
AAHLLSWY	HALLWAYS
AAHLMRSS	MARSHALS
AAHLMSTU	THALAMUS
AAHLNPSU	PAUL NASH
AAHLNRSW	NARWHALS
AAHLNSTU	NAHUATLS
AAHMNNSU	HANUMANS
AAHMNORT	MARATHON
AAHMNPPY	HAPPY MAN
AAHMNPST	PHANTASM
AAHMRSWY	HARMS WAY
AAHNNOSS	HOSANNAS
AAHNOSTT	THANATOS
AAHNPSTY	PHANTASY
AAHOOSWY	SHOO AWAY
AAHOPRTU	AUTOHARP
AAHOSSWW	SAW A SHOW
AAHPRTTY	PARTY HAT
AAHPSTWY	PATHWAYS
AAHPSUWY	PUSH AWAY
AAHRSSTY	ASHTRAYS
AAHRSTTW	STRAW HAT
AAHRSUWY	RUSH AWAY
AAIILMNS	MAINSAIL
AAIILNRZ	ALIZARIN
AAIILNST	ITALIANS
AAIILNUX	UNIAXIAL
AAIILRTX	TRIAXIAL
AAIILTXY	AXIALITY
AAIIMNNT	MAINTAIN
AAIIMNRS	ARIANISM
AAIIMNTV	VITAMIN A
AAIINNRS	IRANIANS
AAIINOTV	AVIATION
AAIINPRR	RIPARIAN
AAIINRST	INTARSIA
AAIIORRT	AIR-TO-AIR
AAIIPRST	APIARIST
AAIISSTW	AS I SAW IT
AAIJNRYZ	JANIZARY
AAIKLNRS	SRI LANKA
AAIKMRST	TAMARISK
AAIKNPST	PAKISTAN
AAIKNRRS	RAN A RISK
AAIKNRTX	TAXI RANK
AAIKSSTW	SWASTIKA
AAILLLLN	ALL IN ALL

AAILLLUV	ALLUVIAL
AAILLMNT	MANTILLA
AAILLMNY	ANIMALLY
AAILLMSX	MAXILLAS
AAILLRXY	AXILLARY
AAILLSTW	SAW IT ALL
AAILMMRS	ALARMISM
AAILMNNP	PLAIN MAN
AAILMNOR	MANORIAL
	MORAINAL
AAILMNOS	MONA LISA
AAILMNRU	MANURIAL
AAILMNST	TALISMAN
AAILMNSV	MAIL VANS
AAILMORR	ARMORIAL
AAILMRST	ALARMIST
AAILMTTU	ULTIMATA
AAILNNOT	NATIONAL
AAILNNPT	PLANTAIN
AAILNNST	ANNALIST
AAILNOPS	PIANOLAS
	SALOPIAN
AAILNORS	ORINASAL
AAILNORT	NOTARIAL
	RATIONAL
AAILNOST	LAOTIANS
AAILNOTV	LAVATION
AAILNOTX	LAXATION
AAILNSSY	ANALYSIS
AAILNSTV	LATVIANS
AAILNSTY	NASALITY
AAILNTTY	NATALITY
AAILPRST	PARTIALS
	PATRIALS
AAILPSWY	SLIP AWAY
AAILRRSV	ARRIVALS
AAILRSTT	RATS TAIL
AAILRSTV	TRAVAILS
AAILRSVY	SALIVARY
AAILRSWY	RAILWAYS
AAILSSSW	WASSAILS
AAILSSTY	STAYSAIL
AAIMMNRR	ARM IN ARM
AAIMMNST	MAINMAST
AAIMMRSU	SAMARIUM
AAIMNNOR	ROMANIAN
AAIMNNRU	RUMANIAN
AAIMNORT	ANIMATOR
AAIMNORV	MORAVIAN
AAIMNPRT	MAIN PART
AAIMNPRZ	MARZIPAN
AAIMNRRT	TRIMARAN
AAIMNRST	TAMARINS
AAIMNSST	MANTISSA
	SATANISM
AAIMNSTU	AMIANTUS
AAIMNSTY	MAINSTAY
AAIMPRST	PASTRAMI
AAIMPRSU	MARSUPIA
AAIMQRUU	AQUARIUM
AAINNOST	SONATINA
AAINNOTT	NATATION
AAINNRTU	TURANIAN
AAINNWYY	IN ANY WAY
AAINOPRV	PAR AVION
AAINORRT	ROTARIAN
AAINOTTX	TAXATION
AAINPRST	ASPIRANT
	PARTISAN
AAINPRTW	WAR PAINT
AAINQRTU	QUATRAIN

AAINQTTU	AQUATINT
AAINRSST	ARTISANS
	TSARINAS
AAINRSSY	ASSYRIAN
AAINRSTV	VARIANTS
AAINRSTY	SANITARY
AAINSSSS	ASSASSIN
AAINSSTT	SATANIST
AAINSWWY	AWAY WINS
AAIORSTV	AVIATORS
AAIPRSTT	PARTITAS
AAIQRSTU	AQUARIST
AAIQRSUU	AQUARIUS
AAIQSSSU	QUASSIAS
AAIRSTTZ	TSARITZA
AAIRSTWY	STAIRWAY
AAISSTTV	ATAVISTS
AAJKLSWY	JAYWALKS
AAJMMORR	MARJORAM
AAJMORRW	MAJOR WAR
AAJMRSTT	JAM TARTS
AAKLLLTT	TALL TALK
AAKLLLTW	WALK TALL
AAKLLOTT	TALK A LOT
AAKLMNNS	KLANSMAN
AAKLMNST	MANS TALK
AAKLMRRX	KARL MARX
AAKLOORY	ROYAL OAK
AAKLOOWY	LOOK AWAY
AAKLORRY	ARK ROYAL
AAKLPSTW	WALK PAST
AAKLSWWY	WALKWAYS
AAKMMNRS	MARKSMAN
AAKMOSSU	MOUSSAKA
AAKMPRSS	PASS MARK
AAKMRSUZ	MAZURKAS
AAKNOOPT	TOOK A NAP
AAKNPRTT	TANK TRAP
AAKOOTWY	TOOK AWAY
AAKPRSWY	PARKWAYS
AALLLLMP	PALL MALL
AALLMMNS	SMALL MAN
AALLMNTY	TALLYMAN
AALLMNUY	MANUALLY
AALLMORW	MORAL LAW
AALLMORY	AMORALLY
AALLMPRU	AMPULLAR
AALLMSWY	SMALL WAY
AALLNNSY	SALLY ANN
AALLNNUY	ANNUALLY
AALLNOTT	NOT AT ALL
AALLNOTY	ATONALLY
AALLOORW	WALLAROO
AALLPRST	PLASTRAL
AALLRSST	ALL STARS
AALLRSTY	ASTRALLY
AALLRUVV	VALVULAR
AALMNORW	ROMAN LAW
AALMNTTU	TANTALUM
AALMNTUU	AUTUMNAL
AALNORSS	ALSO RANS
	ALSO-RANS
AALNOTTW	WANT A LOT
AALNPPSY	PLAY SNAP
AALNPSST	SALTPANS
AALNRRTY	ARRANTLY
AALNRSTU	NATURALS
AALNSSTU	SULTANAS
AALNSSTY	ANALYSTS
AALOPPRV	APPROVAL
AALOPRSS	PARASOLS

AALOPRST	PASTORAL
AALORTTW	TOTAL WAR
AALORTUV	VALUATOR
AALORTVY	LAVATORY
AALPPSUY	PAYS PAUL
AALPRSTY	LAY TRAPS
AALPSSSW	PASS LAWS
AALPSSTU	SPATULAS
AALRSTTW	STALWART
AALRSTUY	SALUTARY
AALSSSTU	ASSAULTS
AALSUUWY	USUAL WAY
AAMMNNOT	MAN TO MAN
	MAN-TO-MAN
AAMMNRST	SMART MAN
AAMMOTXY	MYXOMATA
AAMMRSSU	MARASMUS
AAMNPRST	MAN TRAPS
	MANTRAPS
AAMNPRTY	PARTY MAN
AAMNRSTW	STRAW MAN
AAMNRSTY	ARMY ANTS
AAMOPRRU	PARAMOUR
AAMORSSV	SAMOVARS
AAMORSTT	STROMATA
AAMPRRST	RAMPARTS
AAMRSSST	SMART ASS
AAMRSTWY	TRAMWAYS
AAMRTTTU	ART TATUM
AAMSSSTU	SATSUMAS
AANNOSST	ASSONANT
AANNRSTY	STANNARY
AANOOSSS	AS SOON AS
AANORRRT	NARRATOR
AANORWWY	WORN AWAY
AANPRSST	SPARTANS
AANRRSTW	WARRANTS
AANRRTWY	WARRANTY
AANRSTTU	SATURANT
AANRSUWY	RUNAWAYS
	RUNS AWAY
AANRTUWY	TURN AWAY
AAOPSSTY	APOSTASY
AAORSUVV	VAVASOUR
AAOSSTWY	TOSS AWAY
AAOSTWWY	STOW AWAY
	STOWAWAY
AAPRRSTT	STAR PART
AAPSTUWY	PUTS AWAY
AARRSSTW	STAR WARS
AARSSSTW	SAW STARS
AARSTTUY	STATUARY
ABBBEILR	BRIBABLE
ABBBELRS	BLABBERS
ABBBGILN	BABBLING
	BLABBING
ABBBMOSY	BOMB BAYS
ABBBOSYY	BABY BOYS
ABBCCKMO	BACKCOMB
ABBCDEKN	BEND BACK
ABBCEERU	BARBECUE
ABBCEGIR	CRIBBAGE
ABBCEHTU	BATH CUBE
ABBCEIKT	BACKBITE
ABBCEIRR	CRABBIER
ABBCEKNO	BACKBONE
ABBCEKNT	BENT BACK
ABBCEKNU	BUCKBEAN
ABBCEKST	BEST BACK
ABBCELRS	SCRABBLE
ABBCGINR	CRABBING

Code	Word	Code	Word	Code	Word
ABBCGINS	SCABBING	ABBGGINR	GRABBING	ABCDEKNU	UNBACKED
ABBCGIOR	GABBROIC	ABBGHRSU	HABSBURG	ABCDEKPU	BACKED UP
ABBCIILL	BIBLICAL	ABBGILRY	BABY GIRL	ABCDEKRW	DREW BACK
ABBCIINR	RABBINIC	ABBGINST	STABBING	ABCDELLY	CALLED BY
ABBCIKRT	BRICKBAT	ABBGINSW	SWABBING	ABCDELNO	BLANCOED
ABBCINOY	CABIN BOY	ABBGOOSU	BUGABOOS	ABCDELOO	CABOODLE
ABBCKLOW	BLOWBACK	ABBGOOTY	GO BY BOAT	ABCDEMPS	CAMP BEDS
ABBCKLOX	BLACK BOX	ABBHILSY	SHABBILY	ABCDENRU	UNBRACED
ABBCKSUY	BUYS BACK	ABBHNSTU	BATH BUNS	ABCDEORS	BROCADES
ABBCLOTU	BOAT CLUB	ABBHOSWY	BABY SHOW	ABCDERST	BEST CARD
ABBCMORS	CAR BOMBS	ABBILLSU	SILLABUB	ABCDFKLO	FOLD BACK
ABBDDEIL	AD-LIBBED	ABBILOST	BOBTAILS	ABCDGHOU	BAD COUGH
	BIDDABLE	ABBIMNOS	BAMBINOS	ABCDGKLO	BLACK DOG
ABBDDEST	BAD DEBTS	ABBINORT	RABBIT ON	ABCDHKLO	HOLD BACK
ABBDDILY	BIDDABLY	ABBIRSUU	SUBURBIA	ABCDHLOT	COLD BATH
ABBDDLOO	BAD BLOOD	ABBISSTY	BABY-SITS	ABCDIILO	DIABOLIC
ABBDEEER	BEEBREAD	ABBJMOOR	BOB MAJOR	ABCDIKLS	SLID BACK
ABBDEEJR	JABBERED	ABBKKNOO	BANKBOOK	ABCDILLR	BIRD CALL
ABBDEERT	RABBETED	ABBLLOSY	BALL BOYS		BIRDCALL
ABBDEILR	AD-LIBBER	ABBLLSUY	SYLLABUB	ABCDILOU	CUBOIDAL
ABBDEINR	BREAD BIN	ABBLOPRY	PROBABLY	ABCDILRS	BALDRICS
ABBDEIRT	RABBITED	ABBMMOOT	ATOM BOMB	ABCDKLOR	BLACK ROD
ABBDELNO	BONDABLE		ATOM-BOMB	ABCDKNOR	ROCK BAND
ABBDELRS	DABBLERS	ABBMOSST	BOMBASTS	ABCDKNOW	BACK DOWN
	DRABBLES	ABBMOSTU	BUMBOATS	ABCDKOOR	BACK DOOR
ABBDEORS	ABSORBED	ABBNRSTU	BRAN TUBS	ABCDKOPR	BACKDROP
ABBDERST	DRABBEST	ABBNRSUU	SUBURBAN		DROP BACK
ABBDFOOY	BABY FOOD	ABCCDHIK	DABCHICK	ABCDLLMO	COLD LAMB
ABBDGILN	DABBLING	ABCCEELP	PECCABLE	ABCDLLNU	CLUB LAND
ABBDGINS	BIG BANDS	ABCCEHNY	BY CHANCE	ABCDNOSS	ABSCONDS
ABBDHIRT	BIRD BATH	ABCCEIKL	BLACK ICE	ABCDOORS	CORDOBAS
	BIRDBATH	ABCCEILY	CELIBACY	ABCDOPRU	CUPBOARD
ABBDHOOY	BABYHOOD	ABCCEKMO	COME BACK	ABCDORTU	ABDUCTOR
ABBDIKSY	BABY KIDS		COMEBACK	ABCDORUY	OBDURACY
ABBDILNT	BLIND BAT	ABCCHNOO	CABOCHON	ABCEEEFK	BEEFCAKE
ABBDKOOS	BAD BOOKS	ABCCIKKK	KICK BACK	ABCEEHLM	BECHAMEL
ABBDLLOY	BABY DOLL		KICKBACK	ABCEEHLS	BLEACHES
ABBDLNOY	BOB DYLAN	ABCCILOR	CARBOLIC	ABCEEHLW	CHEWABLE
ABBDMORS	BOMBARDS	ABCCILOT	COBALTIC	ABCEEHRS	BREACHES
ABBDNORW	BROWBAND	ABCCINOR	CARBONIC	ABCEEIKR	BIKE RACE
ABBEEJRR	JABBERER	ABCCIORS	ASCORBIC	ABCEEILT	CELIBATE
ABBEENST	BE ABSENT	ABCCKSTU	CUTBACKS	ABCEEIMN	AMBIENCE
ABBEERTT	BARBETTE		CUTS BACK	ABCEEKKP	KEEP BACK
ABBEFILR	FLABBIER	ABCCOOST	TOBACCOS	ABCEEKLY	BLACK EYE
ABBEGIKR	BIG BREAK	ABCDDEOR	BROCADED	ABCEEKNR	BARE NECK
ABBEGNOS	BOGBEANS	ABCDDETU	ABDUCTED	ABCEELRR	CEREBRAL
ABBEGRSU	BUGBEARS	ABCDEEFK	FEEDBACK	ABCEEMRR	EMBRACER
ABBEHIRS	SHABBIER	ABCDEEHL	BLEACHED	ABCEEMRS	EMBRACES
ABBEHKOW	BOB HAWKE	ABCDEEHR	BREACHED	ABCEENSS	ABSENCES
ABBEHORT	BATH ROBE	ABCDEELM	BECALMED	ABCEFIIT	BEATIFIC
	BATHROBE	ABCDEELS	DEBACLES	ABCEFIKR	BACKFIRE
ABBEHRTU	BABE RUTH	ABCDEELU	EDUCABLE	ABCEFKLL	FELL BACK
ABBEIMWZ	ZIMBABWE	ABCDEEMR	CAMBERED	ABCEFKLT	LEFT BACK
ABBEIRRT	RABBITER		EMBRACED		LEFT-BACK
ABBEKLOO	BOOKABLE	ABCDEENO	OCEAN BED	ABCEFLSS	BASS CLEF
ABBELLRS	BARBELLS	ABCDEFLO	BOLD FACE	ABCEGHIN	BEACHING
ABBELMRS	BRAMBLES		BOLDFACE	ABCEGIKV	GIVE BACK
ABBELNRU	BURNABLE	ABCDEGIR	BIRD CAGE	ABCEGKLL	BLACKLEG
ABBELOPR	PROBABLE	ABCDEHKL	HELD BACK	ABCEGKLO	BLOCKAGE
ABBELORS	SORBABLE	ABCDEHLN	BLANCHED	ABCEGKNO	GONE BACK
ABBELORU	BELABOUR	ABCDEHNR	BRANCHED	ABCEGKOS	GOES BACK
ABBELOVY	BABY LOVE	ABCDEHOR	BROACHED	ABCEGKST	GETS BACK
ABBELQSU	SQUABBLE	ABCDEIIT	DIABETIC	ABCEGOSS	BOSCAGES
ABBELRSU	BARBULES	ABCDEIKN	BACKED IN	ABCEHHTU	BEACH HUT
ABBENORS	BASEBORN	ABCDEIKS	BACKSIDE	ABCEHITT	BATHETIC
ABBEORRS	ABSORBER	ABCDEIRS	ASCRIBED	ABCEHLNR	BLANCHER
ABBEORTW	BROWBEAT		CARBIDES	ABCEHLNS	BLANCHES
ABBERRRY	BARBERRY	ABCDEISS	ABSCISED	ABCEHLOR	BACHELOR
ABBERSSW	SWABBERS	ABCDEKLO	BLOCKADE	ABCEHLSU	CHASUBLE
ABBFILLY	FLABBILY	ABCDEKLV	BACKVELD	ABCEHMOT	HECATOMB
ABBGGILN	GABBLING	ABCDEKNS	SEND BACK	ABCEHMRS	CHAMBERS

Code	Word	Code	Word	Code	Word
ABCEHNRS	BRANCHES	ABCERRTU	CARBURET	ABCJLUZZ	JAZZ CLUB
ABCEHORS	BROACHES	ABCFFKOS	BACKS OFF	ABCKKLOO	LOOK BACK
ABCEHORU	BAROUCHE	ABCFHOTW	FOB WATCH	ABCKKOOT	TOOK BACK
ABCEHPUY	BUY CHEAP	ABCFIKLT	BACK LIFT	ABCKLLOR	ROLL BACK
ABCEIJOT	JACOBITE		BACKLIFT	ABCKLLOS	BALLOCKS
ABCEIKLS	LIES BACK	ABCFIKNS	FINBACKS	ABCKLLPU	PULL BACK
ABCEIKLT	BLACK TIE	ABCFILOS	BIFOCALS	ABCKLOPT	BLACKTOP
	BLACK-TIE	ABCFKLLU	FULL BACK		POT BLACK
ABCEIKWZ	ZWIEBACK		FULLBACK	ABCKLOTU	BLACK OUT
ABCEILLT	BALLETIC	ABCFKLLY	BLACKFLY		BLACKOUT
ABCEILMS	ALEMBICS	ABCFKLSY	FLYBACKS	ABCKLPSU	BLACKS UP
ABCEILNN	BINNACLE	ABCFKORU	BACK FOUR	ABCKMOOR	BACK ROOM
ABCEILOR	CABRIOLE	ABCFLNSU	FAN CLUBS		BACKROOM
ABCEILOS	SOCIABLE	ABCGHIMT	BIG MATCH	ABCKMOSS	MOSSBACK
ABCEINOS	BASE COIN	ABCGHKNU	HUNG BACK	ABCKMOST	BACKMOST
ABCEINRS	CARBINES	ABCGHKOS	HOGBACKS	ABCKNNOS	BANNOCKS
ABCEINST	CABINETS		HOGS BACK	ABCKNOOS	BACK SOON
ABCEINTU	INCUBATE		HOGSBACK	ABCKNRSU	RUNS BACK
ABCEIORS	AEROBICS	ABCGHNPU	PUNCH-BAG	ABCKNRTU	TURN BACK
ABCEIOST	ICE BOATS	ABCGIKLN	BLACKING	ABCKOPST	BACKSTOP
	ICEBOATS	ABCGIKNO	GO BACK IN	ABCKOSTU	BACKS OUT
ABCEIRSS	ASCRIBES	ABCGIKNR	RING BACK	ABCKPSTU	PUTS BACK
ABCEIRSW	CRABWISE	ABCGIKNS	BACKINGS	ABCKSSTU	SACKBUTS
ABCEIRTT	BRATTICE	ABCGILNO	LOG CABIN	ABCLLNOU	LOAN CLUB
ABCEIRTY	ACERBITY	ABCGIMOX	MAGIC BOX	ABCLLOOY	LOCAL BOY
ABCEISSS	ABSCISES	ABCGIORX	CIGAR BOX	ABCLLOPU	LOCAL PUB
ABCEJKLT	JET BLACK	ABCGKNRU	RUNG BACK	ABCLLOSY	CALL BOYS
	JET-BLACK	ABCHIKLS	BLACKISH		CALLBOYS
ABCEJLTY	ABJECTLY	ABCHIKRS	BRACKISH	ABCLLPUY	CULPABLY
ABCEKKPT	KEPT BACK	ABCHIKST	HITS BACK	ABCLMNSU	MANS CLUB
ABCEKLLO	LOCKABLE	ABCHILOO	COOLIBAH	ABCLNORY	CARBONYL
ABCEKLMN	BLACK MEN	ABCHIMOR	HAIR COMB	ABCLORXY	CARBOXYL
ABCEKLNS	BLACKENS	ABCHIMTU	A BIT MUCH	ABCLPRUW	PUB CRAWL
ABCEKLSS	BACKLESS	ABCHIOST	COHABITS	ABCLSSSU	SUBCLASS
ABCEKLST	BLACKEST	ABCHKMPU	HUMPBACK	ABCMOOPT	BOOT CAMP
ABCEKMOV	MOVE BACK	ABCHKOOS	CASH BOOK	ABCNNOYY	NANCY BOY
ABCEKNST	SENT BACK	ABCHKPSU	PUSH BACK	ABCNOUYY	BUOYANCY
ABCEKNTW	WENT BACK	ABCHLMOP	LAMB CHOP	ABCORRSS	CROSSBAR
ABCEKOOS	BOOKCASE	ABCIIMNS	MINI CABS	ABCORRSW	CROWBARS
	CASE BOOK		MINICABS	ABCORRSU	SCABROUS
	CASEBOOK	ABCIINSS	ABSCISIN	ABCRSTTU	SUBTRACT
ABCEKORS	SORE BACK	ABCIIORS	ISOBARIC	ABDDDEOY	DEAD BODY
ABCEKPST	BACK STEP	ABCIIRST	TRIBASIC	ABDDDGIY	BIG DADDY
	STEP BACK	ABCIISTY	BASICITY	ABDDDILY	DID BADLY
ABCEKRST	BRACKETS	ABCIITUX	BAUXITIC	ABDDEEEH	BEHEADED
ABCEKSST	SETBACKS	ABCIJNOS	JACOBINS	ABDDEEGG	DEBAGGED
	SETS BACK	ABCIKKLN	BLACK INK	ABDDEEGR	BADGERED
ABCEKSTW	WETBACKS	ABCIKLPS	SLIP BACK	ABDDEEHT	DEATH BED
ABCELLOS	CLOSABLE	ABCIKNPS	BACK SPIN		DEATHBED
ABCELLPU	CULPABLE		BACKSPIN	ABDDEEKR	DEBARKED
ABCELLSU	BULLACES	ABCIKNSW	WINS BACK	ABDDEERR	DEBARRED
ABCELMNY	LAMBENCY	ABCIKSST	SITS BACK	ABDDEEST	BEDSTEAD
ABCELMOS	CEMBALOS	ABCILLNY	BILLY CAN	ABDDEGIR	ABRIDGED
ABCELMRS	CLAMBERS	ABCILLSU	BACILLUS		BRIGADED
	SCRAMBLE	ABCILLSY	SYLLABIC	ABDDEHMO	HEBDOMAD
ABCELNOS	BLANCOES	ABCILMOO	COLOMBIA	ABDDEILS	DISABLED
ABCELOOT	BOOT LACE	ABCILNNV	VIN BLANC	ABDDEILU	BUDDLEIA
	BOOTLACE	ABCILNOR	CARBINOL	ABDDEINS	SIDEBAND
ABCELOPS	PLACEBOS	ABCILNPU	PUBLICAN	ABDDEINV	DIVAN BED
ABCELOST	OBSTACLE	ABCILOSY	SOCIABLY	ABDDELMO	MADE BOLD
ABCELOTU	BLUE COAT	ABCILRRU	RUBRICAL	ABDDELRS	BLADDERS
ABCELSSU	BASCULES	ABCILSTY	ICY BLAST	ABDDENOR	BORN DEAD
ABCEMNRU	CREAM BUN	ABCIMMSU	CAMBIUMS	ABDDENOU	ABOUNDED
ABCEMORS	CRAMBOES	ABCINORY	BARYONIC	ABDDEORS	ADSORBED
ABCEMOXY	MAX BOYCE	ABCIORSU	CARIBOUS	ABDDERRY	DRY BREAD
ABCENOSW	COWBANES	ABCIOSSU	SCABIOUS	ABDDERYY	DERBY DAY
ABCENRSU	UNBRACES	ABCIOSUV	BIVOUACS	ABDDGIOR	RABID DOG
ABCEOOSS	CABOOSES	ABCJJKOS	JACK JOBS	ABDDHNOY	DO BY HAND
ABCEOSUX	SAUCEBOX	ABCJKMPU	JUMP BACK	ABDDIKNU	DID A BUNK
ABCEOTUV	CUT ABOVE	ABCJKOOT	BOOTJACK	ABDDILRY	LADYBIRD
ABCEPSSU	SUBSPACE		JACKBOOT	ABDDINSS	DISBANDS

ABDDLLOS	ODDBALLS	
ABDDLOUZ	ZOLA BUDD	
ABDDOORU	BAD ODOUR	
ABDEEENR	ABERDEEN	
ABDEEERV	BEAVERED	
	BEREAVED	
ABDEEEST	BE SEATED	
ABDEEEYY	BEADY EYE	
ABDEEFLM	FLAMBEED	
ABDEEFLS	FEELS BAD	
ABDEEGGR	BEGGARED	
ABDEEHNO	BONEHEAD	
ABDEEHRT	BREATHED	
ABDEEHTT	BAD TEETH	
ABDEEILN	DENIABLE	
ABDEEILS	ABSEILED	
ABDEEILT	EDITABLE	
ABDEEILW	BEWAILED	
ABDEEINT	TEA IN BED	
ABDEEIST	BEADIEST	
	DIABETES	
ABDEEKMR	BEDMAKER	
	EMBARKED	
ABDEELLL	LABELLED	
ABDEELLW	WELDABLE	
ABDEELMM	EMBALMED	
ABDEELMN	MENDABLE	
ABDEELMS	BELDAMES	
ABDEELNV	VENDABLE	
ABDEELOR	LEEBOARD	
ABDEELRR	BARRELED	
ABDEEMNO	BEMOANED	
ABDEEMNS	BEAM ENDS	
	BEAM-ENDS	
ABDEEMST	BEDMATES	
ABDEENRT	BANTERED	
ABDEENRW	BE WARNED	
	NEW BREAD	
ABDEENRY	BARNEYED	
ABDEENRZ	BRAZENED	
ABDEENST	ABSENTED	
ABDEENTT	BATTENED	
ABDEEOTW	OWE A DEBT	
ABDEEPRS	SPARE BED	
ABDEEPSS	DEEP BASS	
ABDEERRT	BARTERED	
ABDEERRY	RYE BREAD	
ABDEERSS	DEBASERS	
ABDEERST	BREASTED	
	DEBATERS	
ABDEERTT	BATTERED	
ABDEERTY	BETRAYED	
ABDEFHLR	HALF-BRED	
ABDEFINO	BONA FIDE	
ABDEFLLO	FOLDABLE	
ABDEFLOR	FORDABLE	
ABDEGHIS	BIGHEADS	
ABDEGIIS	BIG IDEAS	
ABDEGILS	BIG DEALS	
ABDEGILU	GUIDABLE	
ABDEGIMR	GAME BIRD	
ABDEGIMX	MIXED BAG	
ABDEGINR	BEARDING	
	BREADING	
ABDEGINS	DEBASING	
ABDEGINT	DEBATING	
ABDEGIRR	ABRIDGER	
ABDEGIRS	ABRIDGES	
	BRIGADES	
ABDEGLNO	GONE BALD	
ABDEGLOS	GOES BALD	
ABDEGOOV	GOD ABOVE	
ABDEGOPR	PEGBOARD	
ABDEHILL	BILLHEAD	
ABDEHINS	BANISHED	
ABDEHKLU	BULKHEAD	
ABDEHLLU	BULLHEAD	
ABDEHLMS	SHAMBLED	
ABDEHLRS	HALBERDS	
ABDEHLRW	BLEW HARD	
ABDEHMSU	AMBUSHED	
ABDEHORR	ABHORRED	
ABDEHOSW	BOWHEADS	
ABDEHOTT	TO THE BAD	
ABDEHOTY	BODY HEAT	
ABDEHRST	BREADTHS	
ABDEHSSU	SUBHEADS	
ABDEIIRT	DIATRIBE	
ABDEILMN	MANDIBLE	
ABDEILNY	LAY IN BED	
ABDEILOV	VOIDABLE	
ABDEILPS	PIEBALDS	
ABDEILRT	LIBRATED	
ABDEILSS	DISABLES	
ABDEILTU	DUTIABLE	
ABDEIMOO	AMOEBOID	
ABDEIMRX	BAD MIXER	
ABDEIMST	BAD TIMES	
ABDEINNR	ENDBRAIN	
ABDEINOR	DEBONAIR	
ABDEINOT	OBTAINED	
ABDEINRS	BRANDIES	
ABDEINST	BANDIEST	
ABDEINSU	UNBIASED	
ABDEIOTV	OBVIATED	
ABDEIOTW	TIED A BOW	
ABDEIPST	BAPTISED	
ABDEIPTZ	BAPTIZED	
ABDEIRRR	RARE BIRD	
ABDEIRRS	BRAIDERS	
ABDEIRSS	SEABIRDS	
ABDEIRTV	VIBRATED	
ABDEISSU	DISABUSE	
ABDEISTW	BAWDIEST	
ABDEKLMO	MAKE BOLD	
ABDEKLRU	DARK BLUE	
ABDEKLSW	SKEWBALD	
ABDEKNNO	BANKED ON	
ABDEKNSU	SUNBAKED	
ABDEKORY	KEYBOARD	
ABDELLMS	BAD SMELL	
	SMELL BAD	
ABDELLNO	NO-BALLED	
ABDELLOR	BEADROLL	
ABDELLRS	RED BALLS	
ABDELNOZ	BLAZONED	
ABDELNSS	BALDNESS	
ABDELNST	BLANDEST	
ABDELNTW	WENT BALD	
ABDELORS	BAD LOSER	
ABDELORU	LABOURED	
ABDELOSV	ABSOLVED	
ABDELOTT	DO BATTLE	
ABDELOTU	BALED OUT	
ABDELRSU	DURABLES	
ABDEMNNS	BANDSMEN	
ABDEMNOS	ABDOMENS	
	BAD OMENS	
ABDEMNOY	BAD MONEY	
ABDEMOSV	BAD MOVES	
ABDEMRTU	DRUMBEAT	
ABDENNOS	NOSEBAND	
ABDENNPY	BAD PENNY	
ABDENNRW	BRAND NEW	
	BRAND-NEW	
	NEW BRAND	
ABDENORS	BROADENS	
ABDENORW	BEAR DOWN	
	RAWBONED	
ABDENOTW	BEAT DOWN	
	DOWN BEAT	
	DOWNBEAT	
ABDENRRS	BRANDERS	
ABDENRRU	UNBARRED	
ABDENRSS	DRABNESS	
ABDENRTU	TURBANED	
ABDENTTU	DEBUTANT	
ABDEOPRT	PROBATED	
ABDEORRS	BOARDERS	
ABDEORRW	WARDROBE	
ABDEORST	BROADEST	
ABDEORTU	OBDURATE	
ABDEORUX	BORDEAUX	
ABDEORWW	DREW A BOW	
ABDEPRSS	BAD PRESS	
ABDEPSST	BAD STEPS	
ABDEPSSY	PASSED BY	
ABDERSTW	BEDSTRAW	
ABDERSUY	BUYS DEAR	
ABDESSTY	BEST DAYS	
ABDFFLOY	BADLY OFF	
ABDFIILN	FINAL BID	
ABDFIIRS	BIDS FAIR	
ABDFIJNO	FIND A JOB	
ABDFILOT	TOLD A FIB	
ABDGHILT	BAD LIGHT	
ABDGHINT	BAD THING	
ABDGHIST	BAD SIGHT	
ABDGIINR	BRAIDING	
ABDGINNR	BRANDING	
ABDGINNY	BANDYING	
ABDGINOR	BOARDING	
ABDGINRS	BRIGANDS	
ABDGINSS	BAD SIGNS	
ABDGINST	DINGBATS	
ABDGINSW	WINDBAGS	
ABDGJOOO	A GOOD JOB	
ABDGLNOU	LOUD BANG	
ABDGLNOY	GO BY LAND	
ABDGLSUY	LADYBUGS	
ABDGOORY	GO BY ROAD	
ABDGOOUY	A GOOD BUY	
ABDHILLN	HANDBILL	
ABDHILNS	BLANDISH	
ABDHILOR	HARD-BOIL	
ABDHILOT	OLD HABIT	
ABDHINRS	BRANDISH	
ABDHIRTY	BIRTHDAY	
ABDHKNOO	HANDBOOK	
ABDHLNSU	BUSHLAND	
ABDHLORW	BLOW HARD	
	BLOWHARD	
	HARD BLOW	
ABDHMSTU	MUD BATHS	
ABDHNSSU	HUSBANDS	
ABDHOOTT	BAD TOOTH	
ABDIIJLR	JAIL BIRD	
	JAILBIRD	
ABDIILLR	BILLIARD	
ABDIIMNR	MIDBRAIN	
ABDIIMSU	BASIDIUM	
ABDIINOS	OBSIDIAN	
ABDIINTT	BANDITTI	

ABDIIRTY	RABIDITY	ABEEHQTU	BEQUEATH	ABEENPTU	BEATEN UP
ABDILMNN	BLIND MAN	ABEEHRRT	BREATHER	ABEENRRT	BANTERER
ABDILORW	WILD BOAR	ABEEHRST	BREATHES	ABEENRSS	BARENESS
ABDILOST	TABLOIDS	ABEEHRSV	BEHAVERS	ABEENSSS	BASENESS
ABDILRRY	RIBALDRY	ABEEHSTV	HAVE BETS	ABEEORRV	OVERBEAR
ABDILRZZ	BLIZZARD	ABEEHSTY	BY THE SEA	ABEEOSTU	SEE ABOUT
ABDINORY	ROBIN DAY		EYEBATHS	ABEEOVWW	WOVE A WEB
ABDINOTY	ANTIBODY	ABEEIKLT	BAKELITE	ABEERRRT	BARTERER
ABDINRTY	BANDITRY	ABEEIKRS	BAKERIES	ABEERRTV	VERTEBRA
ABDIPRSU	UPBRAIDS	ABEEILLR	RELIABLE	ABEERRTY	BETRAYER
ABDKOOSY	DAY BOOKS	ABEEILLV	LEVIABLE	ABEERSTT	ABETTERS
ABDLLORS	BOLLARDS	ABEEILNP	PLEBEIAN		BE AT REST
ABDLMORS	LOMBARDS	ABEEILNS	BASE LINE	ABEERSTY	BAY TREES
ABDMNNOS	BONDSMAN		BASELINE	ABEFFKOR	BREAK OFF
ABDMORST	BAD STORM	ABEEILNV	ENVIABLE		OFF BREAK
ABDMRSSU	BASS DRUM	ABEEILPX	EXPIABLE	ABEFFLRS	BAFFLERS
ABDNNORW	OWN-BRAND	ABEEILRR	BLEARIER	ABEFFOST	BEATS OFF
ABDNNOYY	DANNY BOY	ABEEILRT	LIBERATE	ABEEHLLU	HALF BLUE
ABDNOORR	BARN DOOR	ABEEILVW	VIEWABLE	ABEFHOOT	HOOFBEAT
ABDNOOST	NOT SO BAD	ABEEIMST	TIE-BEAMS	ABEFILLL	FALLIBLE
ABDNORSW	WAR BONDS	ABEEIMTT	BEAT TIME	ABEFILLR	FIREBALL
ABDNORUY	BOUNDARY	ABEEINNT	BEATEN IN	ABEFILLT	LIFTABLE
ABDNOSSY	SANDBOYS	ABEEIPRS	PRAISE BE		TELL A FIB
ABDNRSTU	BAD TURNS	ABEEISTU	BEAUTIES	ABEFILOT	LIFEBOAT
ABDNSSTY	STANDBYS	ABEEJMOR	JAMBOREE	ABEFILRS	FALSE RIB
	STANDS BY	ABEEJRST	SABRE JET	ABEFILSY	FEASIBLY
ABDOORTU	OUTBOARD	ABEEKLST	BLEAKEST	ABEFITUY	BEAUTIFY
ABDOOSSW	BASS WOOD	ABEEKMST	MAKE BETS	ABEFKLNT	LEFT BANK
ABDOPRST	BAD SPORT	ABEEKOOP	PEEKABOO	ABEFKLUY	BY A FLUKE
ABDOPRSU	BOARDS UP	ABEEKPSS	BESPEAKS	ABEFLLMU	BLAMEFUL
ABDORSST	BAD SORTS	ABEEKPST	KEEP TABS	ABEFLMOR	FORMABLE
ABDRSSTU	BUSTARDS	ABEEKRRS	BREAKERS	ABEFOORT	BAREFOOT
ABDRSUZZ	BUZZARDS	ABEEKSTT	TAKE BETS	ABEFORRS	FORBEARS
ABDSSUYY	BUSY DAYS	ABEELLLR	LABELLER	ABEFORTU	BEAUFORT
ABEEEFRT	BARE FEET	ABEELLLS	SELLABLE	ABEFRRUY	FEBRUARY
ABEEEGLV	BEG LEAVE	ABEELLMT	MELTABLE	ABEFRSSU	BUS FARES
ABEEEGRV	BEVERAGE	ABEELLPU	PALE BLUE	ABEGGHLU	HUGGABLE
ABEEELNS	LEBANESE	ABEELLSY	EYEBALLS	ABEGGILN	BEAGLING
ABEEELSV	LEAVES BE	ABEELMMR	EMBALMER	ABEGGIST	BAGGIEST
ABEEENST	ABSENTEE	ABEELMPR	PREAMBLE	ABEGGLRY	BEGGARLY
ABEEEOSV	SEE ABOVE	ABEELMSS	ASSEMBLE	ABEGGRRS	BRAGGERS
ABEEERSV	BEREAVES	ABEELMSW	EWE LAMBS	ABEGHINT	IN THE BAG
ABEEFILR	FEASIBLE	ABEELMTT	EMBATTLE	ABEGHINV	BEHAVING
ABEEFILT	FLEA BITE	ABEELNOP	BEANPOLE	ABEGHIRT	BIG HEART
	FLEABITE		OPENABLE	ABEGHNSS	SHEBANGS
ABEEFLLL	FELLABLE	ABEELNRT	RENTABLE	ABEGIKNR	BREAKING
ABEEFLLN	BEFALLEN	ABEELNTU	TUNEABLE	ABEGILLW	WAGE BILL
ABEEFLOS	BEEFALOS	ABEELOPR	OPERABLE	ABEGILNN	ENABLING
ABEEFLRT	BEAR LEFT	ABEELORS	EAR LOBES	ABEGILNO	BE IN GOAL
ABEEFLST	SALT BEEF		EARLOBES	ABEGILNR	BLEARING
ABEEFORR	FOREBEAR	ABEELRST	BLEATERS	ABEGILNS	BELGIANS
ABEEFRTU	TUBE FARE		STEEL BAR		BENGALIS
ABEEGHRS	HERBAGES	ABEELRSU	REUSABLE		SINGABLE
ABEEGIRV	VERBIAGE	ABEELRUW	WEAR BLUE	ABEGILNT	BLEATING
ABEEGKLR	LEG BREAK	ABEELSSS	BASELESS		TANGIBLE
ABEEGLRS	BARE LEGS	ABEELSST	BEATLESS	ABEGILNY	BELAYING
	BEAGLERS	ABEELSSU	SUBLEASE	ABEGILOT	OBLIGATE
ABEEGMTY	MEGABYTE	* ABEELSTT	SEAT BELT	ABEGILPP	BIG APPLE
ABEEGNRY	GREEN BAY		TESTABLE	ABEGIMNR	BREAMING
ABEEGSTV	GAVE BEST	ABEELSUX	SAXE BLUE	ABEGIMNS	BIG NAMES
ABEEGTTU	BAGUETTE	ABEELTTW	WETTABLE	ABEGIMNY	EMBAYING
ABEEHLLL	HEELBALL	ABEEMMNR	MEMBRANE	ABEGIMST	MEGABITS
ABEEHLLR	BEER HALL	ABEEMNRV	BRAVE MEN	ABEGINNO	ON A BINGE
	HAREBELL	ABEEMNST	BASEMENT	ABEGINOS	BEGONIAS
ABEEHLMO	LA BOHEME	ABEEMNTT	ABETMENT	ABEGINRS	BEARINGS
ABEEHMNO	OBEAHMEN	ABEEMSTT	BEST TEAM	ABEGINRT	BERATING
ABEEHNNS	HENBANES	ABEENNOT	NOTA BENE		REBATING
ABEEHNRY	HERNE BAY	ABEENNRT	BANNERET	ABEGINST	BEATINGS
ABEEHNSS	BANSHEES	ABEENNTU	UNBEATEN	ABEGINTT	ABETTING
	HAS-BEENS	ABEENNVY	NYE BEVAN		GNAT BITE
ABEEHNVY	BY HEAVEN!	ABEENORS	SEABORNE	ABEGIORY	YOGI BEAR

ABEGIPPR	BAGPIPER	ABEILMST	BALMIEST	ABEKOORR	RARE BOOK
ABEGIPPS	BAGPIPES	ABEILNNW	WINNABLE	ABEKOORY	YEAR BOOK
ABEGIRTY	TIGER BAY	ABEILNPS	BIPLANES		YEARBOOK
ABEGJORT	GREAT JOB	ABEILNPT	PIN TABLE	ABEKOOTT	TOOK A BET
ABEGJOST	GETS A JOB		PINTABLE	ABEKORTU	BREAK OUT
ABEGKMOO	GAMEBOOK	ABEILNSS	LESBIANS		BREAKOUT
ABEGKOSS	BOSKAGES	ABEILNTV	BIVALENT		OUTBREAK
ABEGLMRS	GAMBRELS	ABEILNVY	ENVIABLY	ABEKPRSU	BREAKS UP
ABEGLMUY	MEALYBUG	ABEILOTU	LIE ABOUT		BREAKUPS
ABEGLNOS	NOBLE GAS	ABEILPRT	PARTIBLE	ABEKPSTT	KEPT TABS
ABEGMNOY	BOGEYMAN	ABEILPST	EPIBLAST	ABEKRSTY	BASKETRY
ABEGMORT	BERGAMOT	ABEILRST	LIBRATES	ABELLLSY	SYLLABLE
ABEGMOST	STAGE MOB	ABEILRTW	WRITABLE	ABELLMPU	BLUE LAMP
ABEGMPSU	PUB GAMES	ABEILRYY	BIYEARLY	ABELLMRU	UMBRELLA
ABEGNOST	GO ABSENT	ABEILSTT	LEAST BIT	ABELLNST	NETBALLS
ABEGOPST	PEAT BOGS	ABEILSTU	SUITABLE	ABELLNSW	NEW BALLS
ABEGOPSY	PAGE BOYS	ABEILSUX	BISEXUAL	ABELLORT	BALLOTER
ABEGOTTU	GET ABOUT	ABEILSVV	BIVALVES	ABELLOSV	SOLVABLE
ABEGSSTY	BY STAGES	ABEIMNST	AMBIENTS	ABELLOTU	LOBULATE
ABEHIITX	EXHIBIT A	ABEIMRRU	BRUMAIRE	ABELLRVY	VERBALLY
ABEHIKLS	BLEAKISH	ABEIMRST	BARMIEST	ABELMNNO	NOBLEMAN
ABEHILNR	HIBERNAL	ABEIMRTV	AMBIVERT	ABELMNOZ	EMBLAZON
ABEHILTT	TITHABLE		VERBATIM	ABELMNTU	NEMBUTAL
ABEHIMMS	MEMSAHIB	ABEIMSSU	IAMBUSES	ABELMOSV	MOVABLES
ABEHIMNO	BOHEMIAN	ABEINORR	AIRBORNE	ABELMOTX	METAL BOX
ABEHINRS	BANISHER	ABEINORT	BARITONE	ABELMRRS	RAMBLERS
ABEHINRT	IN THE BAR		OBTAINER	ABELMRST	LAMBERTS
ABEHINSS	BANISHES	ABEINOST	BOTANISE	ABELMSSY	ASSEMBLY
ABEHINST	ABSINTHE		OBEISANT	ABELMSTW	LAMB STEW
ABEHIRST	HEBRAIST	ABEINOTT	A BIENTOT	ABELNNOR	BANNEROL
ABEHIRTW	BEAR WITH	ABEINOTZ	BOTANIZE	ABELNORT	NOBLE ART
ABEHISTU	HABITUES	ABEINPSW	SPIN A WEB	ABELNORW	BROWN ALE
ABEHKNST	THE BANKS	ABEINRST	BANISTER	ABELNORZ	BLAZONER
ABEHKRSU	HAUBERKS	ABEINRSU	URBANISE	ABELNOST	NOTABLES
ABEHLMSS	SHAMBLES	ABEINRSW	WINE BARS	ABELNOYZ	BONE LAZY
ABEHLRST	BLATHERS	ABEINRTU	URBANITE	ABELNRRY	BARRENLY
	HALBERTS	ABEINRUZ	URBANIZE	ABELNRTU	TURNABLE
ABEHLSVY	BY HALVES	ABEINSTT	TIBETANS	ABELNRUY	URBANELY
ABEHMNOR	HORNBEAM	ABEINTTU	INTUBATE	ABELNRYZ	BRAZENLY
ABEHMRTY	BY THE ARM	ABEIORRS	ARBORISE	ABELNSSU	BUS LANES
ABEHMSSU	AMBUSHES	ABEIORRZ	ARBORIZE	ABELNSTU	STALE BUN
ABEHNSTU	SUNBATHE	ABEIORTV	ABORTIVE		UNSTABLE
ABEHORRR	ABHORRER	ABEIOSTV	OBVIATES	ABELNSTY	ABSENTLY
ABEHORSY	BAY HORSE	ABEIOSTW	TIES A BOW	ABELNSUU	UNUSABLE
ABEHOSTX	HAT BOXES	ABEIPRRS	SPARE RIB	ABELNUVY	NAVY BLUE
ABEHOSXY	HAYBOXES		SPARERIB	ABELOPRT	PORTABLE
ABEHRSST	BRASHEST	ABEIPRST	BAPTISER	ABELOPRU	POURABLE
ABEHTWYY	BY THE WAY	ABEIPRTZ	BAPTIZER	ABELOPRW	BELOW PAR
ABEIILMT	IMITABLE	ABEIPSST	BAPTISES	ABELOPRY	OPERABLY
ABEIILNN	BIENNIAL	ABEIPSTZ	BAPTIZES	ABELOPTT	TABLE TOP
ABEIILPT	PITIABLE	ABEIRRRS	BARRIERS		TOP TABLE
ABEIILTV	LIVE BAIT	ABEIRRSS	BRASSIER	ABELOQTU	QUOTABLE
ABEIINRR	BRAINIER	ABEIRRST	ARBITERS	ABELORRU	LABOURER
ABEIINRS	IBERIANS	ABEIRRSZ	BRAZIERS	ABELORST	BLOATERS
ABEIJLNO	JOINABLE	ABEIRRVY	BREVIARY		SORTABLE
ABEIJLTU	JUBILATE	ABEIRSSU	AIR BUSES		STORABLE
ABEIJMRR	J.M.BARRIE		AIRBUSES	ABELORSV	ABSOLVER
ABEIKLNS	SINKABLE	ABEIRSTT	BIRETTAS	ABELOSSV	ABSOLVES
ABEIKLSS	KISSABLE	ABEIRSTV	VIBRATES	ABELOSTU	ABSOLUTE
ABEIKNRS	BEARSKIN	ABEIRSTY	BESTIARY		BALES OUT
	BREAKS IN		SYBARITE	ABELOSTW	BESTOWAL
ABEIKNST	BEATNIKS	ABEISTTT	BATTIEST	ABELPRTU	PUBERTAL
ABEILLLT	TILLABLE	ABEJLSUY	BLUE JAYS	ABELPSTU	BETA PLUS
ABEILLOS	ISOLABLE	ABEJMOOR	JEROBOAM	ABELRRSW	BRAWLERS
	LOBELIAS	ABEJNOSW	JAWBONES		WARBLERS
ABEILLOV	VIOLABLE	ABEKLNOW	KNOWABLE	ABELRSST	BLASTERS
ABEILLRS	LIBERALS	ABEKLNST	BLANKEST	ABELRSTT	BATTLERS
ABEILLRY	BLEARILY		BLANKETS	ABELRSTU	BALUSTER
	RELIABLY	ABEKLRSS	BARKLESS		BLUE STAR
ABEILLST	BASTILLE	ABEKMORT	TOM BAKER	ABELRTTU	REBUTTAL
ABEILMNT	BAILMENT	ABEKNNOT	BANK NOTE	ABELSSTT	STABLEST

ABELSTUU	SUBULATE	ABGHHILL	HIGH BALL	ABHLSSTU	SALTBUSH
ABELSTWY	BELTWAYS		HIGHBALL	ABHMNSUU	SUBHUMAN
ABEMMNOO	MOONBEAM	ABGHIINT	HABITING	ABHMOORT	BATHROOM
ABEMNORS	SOBER MAN	ABGHINWZ	WHIZ-BANG	ABHNORSS	BASS HORN
ABEMNOTU	UMBONATE	ABGHMORU	BROUGHAM	ABHNORTU	BOAR HUNT
ABEMNPRU	PENUMBRA	ABGHPRSU	HAPSBURG	ABHOORST	TARBOOSH
ABEMNSSU	SUNBEAMS	ABGIILNR	BRAILING	ABHOOSTW	BOAT SHOW
ABEMNTTU	ABUTMENT	ABGIIMST	BIGAMIST		SHOW BOAT
ABEMORRS	BORE ARMS	ABGIINNR	BRAINING	ABHOPPYY	HAPPY BOY
ABEMORST	BROMATES	ABGIINRS	BRAISING	ABHORRSU	HARBOURS
ABEMRSTY	STREAM BY	ABGIINSS	BIASSING	ABHOSTUY	HAUTBOYS
ABENOOPT	PAT BOONE	ABGIJNRU	ABJURING	ABHOSTWY	BOTH WAYS
ABENOPSU	SUBPOENA	ABGIKLNN	BLANKING	ABHSSTUW	WASH TUBS
ABENORSS	BARONESS	ABGIKLNU	BAULKING		WASHTUBS
ABENORST	BARONETS	ABGIKLST	TALKS BIG	ABIIIKRT	KIRIBATI
ABENORTT	BETATRON	ABGIKNNS	BANKINGS	ABIIKLSS	BASILISK
ABENOSST	BASS NOTE	ABGIKNOR	BANK GIRO	ABIILLMR	MILLIBAR
ABENOSSW	SAWBONES	ABGIKNRR	RINGBARK	ABIILLTY	LABILITY
ABENOSSY	SOYBEANS	ABGILLSS	GAS BILLS	ABIILMNU	BINOMIAL
ABENOSTY	BAYONETS	ABGILMNR	MARBLING	ABIILMNS	ALBINISM
ABENPSUW	SPUN A WEB		RAMBLING	ABIILNOT	LIBATION
ABENOSTU	BANQUETS	ABGILNRW	BRAWLING	ABIILNST	SIBILANT
ABENRTUY	BY NATURE		WARBLING	ABIILPTY	PITIABLY
ABEOPPRY	PAPERBOY	ABGILNST	BLASTING	ABIIMNOT	AMBITION
ABEOPRST	BE A SPORT		STABLING	ABIIMNTV	VITAMIN B
	PRODATES	ABGILNTT	BATTLING	ABIINRRX	BRIAN RIX
ABEORSST	ROASTERS	ABGILNTY	TANGIBLY	ABIIRSSV	VIRRISSA
ABEORSTT	ABETTORS	ABGILORW	BRIGALOW	ABIJLMPU	JUMP BAIL
ABEORSTU	BEARS OUT	ABGILORY	GO BY RAIL	ABIJLNRS	BRINJALS
	SABOTEUR	ABGIMOSU	BIGAMOUS	ABIJLNTU	JUBILANT
ABEORTTU	OBTURATE	ABGINNST	BANTINGS	ABIJNOST	BANJOIST
ABEOSSST	ASBESTOS	ABGINOOT	TABOOING	ABIJNPSU	PUNJABIS
ABEOSTTU	BEATS OUT	ABGINORT	ABORTING	ABIJOSWY	OJIBWAYS
	SET ABOUT	ABGINOST	BOASTING	ABIJSTTU	JUST A BIT
ABEPRSSY	PASSERBY	ABGINTTU	ABUTTING	ABIKLMNS	LAMBSKIN
ABEPRSTT	BEST PART	ABGIOTXY	GO BY TAXI	ABIKLMRS	MILK BARS
ABEPSSSY	BYPASSES	ABGIPRST	BIG PARTS	ABIKNNOT	BANK ON IT
	PASSES BY	ABGIRRSS	RIBGRASS	ABILLNPS	PINBALLS
ABEORSUU	ARQUEBUS	ABGKORSW	WORKBAGS	ABILLPSY	PAY BILLS
ABERSSTU	ABSTRUSE	ABGLLLOY	GLOBALLY	ABILLRTY	TRIBALLY
ABERSSWY	SWEARS BY	ABGLLORU	GLOBULAR	ABILLSSW	SAWBILLS
ABFFGILN	BAFFLING	ABGLMOPU	PLUMBAGO	ABILLSWX	WAXBILLS
ABFFIILS	BAILIFFS	ABGLNOOT	LONGBOAT	ABILLSWY	WAYBILLS
ABFFLLPU	PUFFBALL	ABGLNOUW	BUNGALOW	ABILMNSU	ALBUMINS
ABFFLOST	BLAST-OFF	ABGLORSU	GLABROUS	ABILNOOT	LOBATION
ABFFLOSU	BUFFALOS	ABGLOTUU	LUG ABOUT		OBLATION
ABFFNOTU	BOUFFANT	ABGLRRSU	BURGLARS	ABILNOTU	ABLUTION
ABFGGLOS	GOLF BAGS	ABGLRRUY	BURGLARY	ABILNRTU	TRIBUNAL
ABFGLLLO	GOLF BALL	ABGMORTY	GO BY TRAM	ABILNRWY	BRAWNILY
ABFGLLOO	GOOFBALL	ABGNOPRS	PROBANGS	ABILOPRS	PARBOILS
ABFGORUU	FAUBOURG	ABGNOSTU	GUNBOATS	ABILORST	ORBITALS
ABFHOOTT	FOOTBATH	ABGOOTTU	GOT ABOUT		STROBILA
ABFILLLY	FALLIBLY	ABGOPSST	POSTBAGS	ABILORSV	BOLIVARS
ABFILSTU	FABULIST	ABGOSTTU	TUG BOATS	ABILOSTU	BAILS OUT
ABFIMORS	FIBROMAS	ABGSTTUU	BUST A GUT	ABILRSSY	BRASSILY
ABFIRTTU	FRUIT BAT	ABHHIPST	HIP BATHS	ABILSTUY	SUITABLY
ABFLLOOT	FOOTBALL	ABHHOOPS	POOH-BAHS	ABIMPSST	BAPTISMS
ABFLLOST	SOFT BALL	ABHHOSTT	HOT BATHS	ABINOORT	ABORTION
	SOFTBALL	ABHHOSTU	SHABUOTH	ABINOPTX	PAINT BOX
ABFLOSTU	BOASTFUL	ABHIKLOR	KOHLRABI	ABINORRS	IRON BARS
ABFLOSUU	FABULOUS	ABHILNOS	HOBNAILS	ABINORSW	RAINBOWS
ABFLOTUY	FLY ABOUT	ABHILNOT	BIATHLON	ABINOSST	BASTIONS
ABFNORTU	TURBOFAN	ABHILOPS	BASOPHIL	ABINOSTT	BOTANIST
ABFORSTU	SURFBOAT	ABHIRRSU	AIRBRUSH	ABINRSTU	URBANIST
ABGGGINR	BRAGGING	ABHISTTZ	SITZ BATH	ABINRTUY	URBANITY
ABGGILMN	GAMBLING	ABHKOOOT	BOATHOOK	ABIORRST	RIB ROAST
ABGGILNR	GARBLING	ABHLLMOT	MOTH BALL	ABIORRTV	VIBRATOR
ABGGKOOS	GAG BOOKS		MOTHBALL	ABIORSTV	VIBRATOS
ABGGNOOT	TOBOGGAN	ABHLLNTU	HUNT BALL	ABIORTUY	OBITUARY
ABGGORSS	BOG GRASS	ABHLLOOY	BALLYHOO	ABIOSTTU	SIT ABOUT
		ABHLOSWW	WASHBOWL	ABIPRSTT	BIT PARTS

ABIPSSTT	BAPTISTS	ACCDEERT	ACCRETED	ACCEINRT	NEARCTIC
ABISSSST	BASSISTS	ACCDEESS	ACCESSED	ACCEINSV	VACCINES
ABJKOOOT	TOOK A JOB	ACCDEGIN	ACCEDING	ACCEIPRT	PRACTICE
ABKKMOOR	BOOK MARK	ACCDEHIK	CHIACKED	ACCEISTT	ECSTATIC
	BOOKMARK	ACCDEILN	CALCINED	ACCEKKOR	ROCK CAKE
ABKLOOSW	LAW BOOKS	ACCDEILY	DELICACY	ACCEKLNR	CRACKNEL
ABKLRSUW	BULWARKS	ACCDEINT	ACCIDENT	ACCEKLRS	CACKLERS
ABKNORTU	BURNT OAK	ACCDEIRT	ACCREDIT		CLACKERS
ABKNPRTU	BANKRUPT	ACCDEIST	CAST DICE		CRACKLES
ABKOOOTW	TOOK A BOW	ACCDEKOS	COCKADES	ACCEKNOR	CORN CAKE
ABKOOPSS	PASS BOOK	ACCDELSU	CUL-DE-SAC	ACCEKOPS	PEACOCKS
	PASSBOOK	ACCDEOST	ACCOSTED	ACCEKOSS	SEA-COCKS
ABKOOSTU	TOOK A BUS	ACCDERSU	ACCURSED	ACCEKRRS	CRACKERS
ABLLLOST	LOST BALL	ACCDESUU	CADUCEUS	ACCELMNY	CYCLAMEN
ABLLLOSW	SLOW BALL	ACCDHIOT	CATHODIC	ACCELNOS	CONCEALS
ABLLMOOR	BALLROOM	ACCDIIOT	ACIDOTIC	ACCELNOV	CONCLAVE
ABLLMOPW	BLOWLAMP	ACCDILTY	DACTYLIC	ACCELNRU	CARUNCLE
ABLLMOSY	SMALL BOY	ACCDINOR	CANCROID	ACCELNTU	CLEAN CUT
ABLLNOOS	BALLOONS		IN ACCORD		CLEAN-CUT
ABLLNOSW	SNOWBALL	ACCDIOOR	CORACOID	ACCELORS	CORACLES
ABLLOSTY	TALL BOYS	ACCDISTU	CUT A DISC	ACCELRSY	SCARCELY
	TALLBOYS	ACCDITUY	CADUCITY	ACCELRTU	CLEAR CUT
ABLLOSYZ	LAZY SLOB	ACCDOSUU	CADUCOUS		CLEAR-CUT
ABLLPSSU	BALLS-UPS	ACCEEFIN	NICE FACE	ACCELSSU	SACCULES
ABLLRTUY	BRUTALLY	ACCEEHLO	COCHLEAE	ACCELWYY	CYCLEWAY
ABLLSSUY	SYLLABUS	ACCEEILR	CELERIAC	ACCEMNOS	MECCANOS
ABLMNRUU	ALBURNUM	ACCEEIMR	ICE CREAM	ACCENNSY	NASCENCY
	LABURNUM	ACCEEKLN	NECKLACE	ACCENORT	ACCENTOR
ABLMOOPS	BOSOM PAL	ACCEELNR	CLARENCE	ACCENOST	COSECANT
ABLMOOST	TOMBOLAS	ACCEELOS	COALESCE	ACCEOPRT	ACCEPTOR
ABLNORSW	BARN OWLS	ACCEENNS	NASCENCE	ACCERSST	SCARCEST
ABLNORYZ	BLAZONRY	ACCEENST	ACESCENT	ACCERSSU	ACCUSERS
ABLNSTUY	UNSTABLY	ACCEERST	ACCRETES	ACCESSTU	CACTUSES
ABLOOSSS	BASS SOLO	ACCEESSS	ACCESSES	ACCESSUU	CAUCUSES
ABLOOSTW	SLOW BOAT	ACCEFFIY	EFFICACY	ACCFHKLO	HALF COCK
ABLOPRSU	SUBPOLAR	ACCEFILS	FASCICLE	ACCFHLTY	CATCHFLY
ABLOPRTY	PORTABLY	ACCEFLSU	FELUCCAS	ACCFLNOO	CONFOCAL
ABLOPSYY	PLAYBOYS	ACCEHIKP	CHICK-PEA	ACCFOORT	COFACTOR
ABLORSST	BORSTALS	ACCEHILM	ALCHEMIC	ACCGHINN	CHANCING
ABLOSTTU	SUBTOTAL		CHEMICAL	ACCGHINO	COACHING
ABLOSTUW	BAWLS OUT	ACCEHILP	CEPHALIC	ACCGHINT	CATCHING
ABLPRTUY	ABRUPTLY	ACCEHILS	CHALICES	ACCGIKLN	CACKLING
ABMOORRS	BARROOMS	ACCEHIMN	MECHANIC		CLACKING
ABMOOTTT	AT BOTTOM	ACCEHIMS	SACHEMIC	ACCGIKMR	GIMCRACK
ABMORSTU	TAMBOURS	ACCEHINO	ANECHOIC	ACCGIKNR	CRACKING
ABMORSTY	SMART BOY	ACCEHINR	CHANCIER	ACCGINRU	ACCRUING
ABNOORYZ	BRYOZOAN	ACCEHINS	CHICANES	ACCGINSU	ACCUSING
ABNOOSSS	BASSOONS	ACCEHINT	CHANCE IT	ACCHHITT	CHITCHAT
ABNORRTW	BROWN RAT	ACCEHIRT	CATCHIER	ACCHIIMS	CHIASMIC
ABNORTUU	RUN ABOUT	ACCEHLNS	CHANCELS	ACCHIIRT	RACHITIC
	RUNABOUT	ACCEHLOR	COCHLEAR	ACCHILNY	CHANCILY
ABOORSTW	ROWBOATS	ACCEHLOS	COCHLEAS	ACCHILOT	CATHOLIC
ABOOSTTW	TOW BOATS	ACCEHLOT	CATECHOL	ACCHINNO	CINCHONA
ABOPRSST	TOP BRASS	ACCEHMNO	COACHMEN	ACCHINPU	CAPUCHIN
ABOPTTUU	PUT ABOUT		COMANCHE		CHINA CUP
ABSSUWZZ	BUZZ SAWS	ACCEHNNO	CHACONNE	ACCHIORT	THORACIC
ACCCDIIO	COCCIDIA		NO CHANCE		TROCHAIC
ACCCEHIT	CACHETIC	ACCEHNOR	ENCROACH	ACCHIPTY	ICY PATCH
ACCCENPY	PECCANCY	ACCEHNRY	CHANCERY	ACCHKLOR	CHARLOCK
ACCCFIIL	CALCIFIC	ACCEHORS	COACHERS	ACCHKOSY	HAYCOCKS
ACCCHRTY	CATCHCRY	ACCEHRST	CATCHERS	ACCHLOPT	CLOTH CAP
ACCCIILT	CALCITIC	ACCEILLR	CLERICAL		CLOTH-CAP
ACCDDEEN	CADENCED	ACCEILLV	CLAVICLE	ACCHMPTU	CUP MATCH
ACCDDEKO	COCKADED	ACCEILNS	CALCINES	ACCHNOOR	CORONACH
ACCDDEOR	ACCORDED	ACCEILNT	CANTICLE	ACCHORVY	CRY HAVOC
ACCDDIIT	DIDACTIC	ACCEILOP	ALOPECIC	ACCHOSTW	CHOCTAWS
ACCDEEIK	ICED CAKE	ACCEILOS	CALICOES	ACCHOSTY	COSY CHAT
ACCDEENS	CADENCES	ACCEILRV	CERVICAL	ACCHOTTU	CATCH OUT
ACCDEENT	ACCENTED	ACCEILST	CALCITES	ACCHPSTU	CATCHUPS
ACCDEEPT	ACCEPTED	ACCEIMRS	CERAMICS	ACCHRSTY	SCRATCHY
ACCDEERS	ACCEDERS	ACCEINOT	ACETONIC	ACCIILLN	CLINICAL

ACCIILMT	CLIMATIC
ACCIILRT	CRITICAL
ACCIIMNN	CINNAMIC
ACCIINOT	ACONITIC
	CATIONIC
ACCIIOPT	OCCIPITA
ACCIIRTX	CICATRIX
ACCIKKNN	NICKNACK
ACCIKKRR	RICKRACK
ACCIKLOT	COCKTAIL
ACCILNOV	VOLCANIC
ACCILORS	CALORICS
ACCILORT	CORTICAL
ACCILRRU	CIRCULAR
ACCILRSY	ACRYLICS
ACCILSSS	CLASSICS
ACCIMNOS	MOCCASIN
ACCIMPSU	CAPSICUM
ACCINOOS	OCCASION
ACCINORT	NARCOTIC
ACCINOTY	CYANOTIC
ACCIOPST	SPICCATO
ACCIORST	ACROSTIC
	SOCRATIC
ACCIOSTU	ACOUSTIC
ACCIRSTY	SCARCITY
ACCISSTU	CAUCTIOS
ACCKKRSU	RUCKSACK
ACCKOOOT	COCKATOO
ACCKOPRT	CRACKPOT
ACCKORST	STOCK CAR
ACCKOSSS	CASSOCKS
	COSSACKS
ACCKPRSU	CRACKS UP
ACCLLSUU	CALCULUS
ACCLSSUU	SACCULUS
ACCMOPST	COMPACTS
ACCMOSTU	ACCUSTOM
ACCNOORS	RACCOONS
ACCNOPTU	OCCUPANT
ACCNORTT	CONTRACT
ACCNOSTT	CONTACTS
ACCNOSTU	ACCOUNTS
ACCOPSTY	COPY CATS
	COPYCATS
ACCORRTY	CARRYCOT
ACDDDEIT	ADDICTED
ACDDDEKU	DEAD DUCK
ACDDDETU	ADDUCTED
ACDDEEES	DECEASED
ACDDEEHT	DETACHED
ACDDEEIT	DEDICATE
ACDDEEIU	DECIDUAE
ACDDEELR	DECLARED
ACDDEEMP	DECAMPED
ACDDEENS	ASCENDED
ACDDEENT	DECADENT
	DECANTED
ACDDEERT	DEAD CERT
	REDACTED
ACDDEETU	EDUCATED
ACDDEHKN	DECKHAND
ACDDEILU	DECIDUAL
ACDDEINR	RIDDANCE
ACDDEITT	DICTATED
ACDDEKLO	DEADLOCK
ACDDEOPS	DECAPODS
ACDDEORR	CORRADED
ACDDERSU	CRUSADED
ACDDERTU	TRADUCED
ACDDESTU	CUTS DEAD

ACDDGILN	CLADDING
ACDDGINU	ADDUCING
ACDDHKOS	SHADDOCK
ACDDHRSU	CHUDDARS
ACDDIIOR	CARDIOID
ACDDILNY	CANDIDLY
ACDDIOPR	ACID DROP
ACDDIRSS	DISCARDS
ACDDKLNO	DOCKLAND
ACDDKOPS	PADDOCKS
ACDDKORY	DOCKYARD
ACDDLOSY	COLD DAYS
ACDDORTU	ADDUCTOR
ACDEEEFT	DEFECATE
ACDEEEKS	SEED CAKE
	SEEDCAKE
ACDEEEMR	REEDMACE
ACDEEENR	CAREENED
ACDEEERR	CAREERED
ACDEEERS	DECREASE
ACDEEESS	DECEASES
ACDEEFFT	AFFECTED
ACDEEFIN	DEFIANCE
ACDEEFPR	PREFACED
ACDEEFRS	DEFACERS
	RED FACES
ACDEEFTT	FACETTED
ACDEEGIM	DICE GAME
ACDEEGLY	DELEGACY
ACDEEHIN	ECHIDNAE
ACDEEHIV	ACHIEVED
ACDEEHLP	PLEACHED
ACDEEHLT	CHELATED
ACDEEHMR	DEMARCHE
ACDEEHNN	ENHANCED
ACDEEHNS	ENCASHED
	ENCHASED
ACDEEHPR	PREACHED
ACDEEHRS	SEARCHED
ACDEEHST	DETACHES
	SACHETED
ACDEEILT	DELICATE
ACDEEIMR	MEDICARE
ACDEEIMT	DECIMATE
	MEDICATE
ACDEEINN	DECENNIA
ACDEEINU	AUDIENCE
ACDEEINV	DEVIANCE
ACDEEJKT	JACKETED
ACDEEKNR	CANKERED
ACDEEKPT	TAPE DECK
ACDEEKRT	RACKETED
ACDEELLR	CELLARED
	RECALLED
ACDEELNR	CALENDER
ACDEELNS	CLEANSED
ACDEELPR	REPLACED
ACDEELRR	DECLARER
ACDEELRS	DECLARES
ACDEELRT	DECRETAL
ACDEELSS	DECLASSE
ACDEEMNO	CODE NAME
ACDEEMNP	ENCAMPED
ACDEEMOP	DEEP COMA
ACDEEMRS	SCREAMED
ACDEEMRT	CREMATED
ACDEENOT	ANECDOTE
ACDEENRT	CANTERED
	DECANTER
	RECANTED
ACDEENRZ	CREDENZA

ACDEENSV	VENDACES
ACDEEOPS	PEASECOD
ACDEEORT	DECORATE
ACDEEPPR	RECAPPED
ACDEEPRS	ESCARPED
ACDEEPRT	CARPETED
ACDEERRT	CRATERED
	RETRACED
	TERRACED
ACDEERSS	CARESSED
ACDEERSY	DECAYERS
ACDEESTU	EDUCATES
ACDEFGIN	DEFACING
ACDEFIIP	PACIFIED
ACDEFIKN	KIND FACE
ACDEFINN	FINANCED
ACDEFKLO	DOCK LEAF
ACDEFNOW	FACE DOWN
ACDEFORT	ACTED FOR
	FACTORED
ACDEFOTU	OUTFACED
ACDEFOTW	TWO-FACED
ACDEFRSU	SURFACED
ACDEGGRS	SCRAGGED
ACDEGIKM	MAGICKED
ACDEGIMR	DECIGRAM
ACDEGINU	GUIDANCE
ACDEGINY	DECAYING
ACDEGIRS	DISGRACE
ACDEGLLO	GOLD LACE
ACDEGNOS	DECAGONS
ACDEGNRS	SCRAG END
ACDEGOOS	GOOD CASE
ACDEGORS	CORDAGES
	DOG RACES
	GODS ACRE
ACDEHHTT	THATCHED
ACDEHIJK	HIJACKED
ACDEHILR	HERALDIC
ACDEHIMN	MACHINED
ACDEHINR	RED CHINA
ACDEHINS	CASHED IN
	ECHIDNAS
ACDEHIRR	HIRED CAR
ACDEHIRS	RACHIDES
ACDEHIRV	ARCHIVED
ACDEHKLS	SHACKLED
ACDEHKOO	HEAD COOK
ACDEHKRU	ARCHDUKE
ACDEHKSS	CASH DESK
ACDEHKTW	THWACKED
ACDEHLLU	DULL ACHE
ACDEHLNR	CHANDLER
ACDEHLNU	LAUNCHED
ACDEHLOO	COOL HEAD
ACDEHMRY	HAD MERCY
ACDEHNOR	ANCHORED
ACDEHNST	SNATCHED
	STANCHED
ACDEHORR	HARD CORE
	HARD-CORE
	HARDCORE
ACDEHORT	CHORDATE
ACDEHOST	CATHODES
ACDEHOTT	COT DEATH
	COT-DEATH
ACDEHOUV	AVOUCHED
ACDEHPRS	SCARPHED
ACDEHPST	DESPATCH
ACDEHRST	STARCHED
ACDEIILR	LIAR DICE

ACDEIILS	LAICISED	ACDELOVW	COLD WAVE	ACDHIRTT	THIRD ACT
ACDEIILT	CILIATED	ACDELPSU	SCALED UP	ACDHKLRU	HARD LUCK
ACDEIILZ	LAICIZED	ACDELRSW	ARC-WELDS	ACDHKORR	HARD ROCK
ACDEIINR	ACRIDINE		SCRAWLED		ROCK HARD
ACDEIINT	ACTINIDE	ACDELRSY	SACREDLY	ACDHLOPS	OLD CHAPS
	INDICATE	ACDELSWW	DEWCLAWS	ACDHMNTU	DUTCHMAN
ACDEIJNU	JAUNDICE	ACDEMMRS	SCRAMMED	ACDHNOSW	CASH DOWN
ACDEIKMN	MAIN DECK	ACDEMNOR	ROMANCED		COWHANDS
ACDEIKNP	PACKED IN	ACDEMNOW	CAME DOWN	ACDHNPSU	CUP HANDS
	PANICKED	ACDEMOPR	COMPARED	ACDHOPRS	POCHARDS
ACDEILLM	MEDALLIC	ACDEMORS	COMRADES	ACDHOPRY	HARD COPY
ACDEILLN	CALLED IN	ACDEMORT	DEMOCRAT	ACDHORRS	ORCHARDS
ACDEILLS	CEDILLAS	ACDEMSTU	MADE CUTS	ACDIIJLU	JUDICIAL
ACDEILLV	CAVILLED	ACDEMUUV	VACUUMED	ACDIILMS	DISCLAIM
ACDEILMS	DECIMALS	ACDENNNO	CANNONED	ACDIILNO	CONIDIAL
	DECLAIMS	ACDENNOR	ORDNANCE	ACDIILSU	SUICIDAL
	MEDICALS	ACDENNOT	CANTONED	ACDIILTY	DIALYTIC
ACDEILMX	CLIMAXED	ACDENOPR	ENDOCARP	ACDIIMNO	DAIMONIC
ACDEILNP	PANICLED	ACDENORT	DONT CARE		DOMINICA
ACDEILNY	LYCAENID	ACDENORY	CRAYONED	ACDIIMOR	DIORAMIC
ACDEILPS	DISPLACE	ACDENOSY	CYANOSED	ACDIIMOT	DIATOMIC
ACDEILPY	PLAY DICE	ACDENRTU	UNDERACT	ACDIINOT	DIATONIC
ACDEILRS	RADICLES	ACDENRVY	VERDANCY	ACDIINPR	PINDARIC
ACDEILRT	ARTICLED	ACDENSST	DESCANTS	ACDIIOSS	ACIDOSIS
ACDEILST	CITADELS	ACDEORRS	CORRADES	ACDIIRTY	ACRIDITY
	DIALECTS	ACDEORRT	REDACTOR	ACDIISST	SADISTIC
ACDEILTT	LATTICED	ACDEORST	RED COATS	ACDIKORT	DO A TRICK
ACDEIMNO	COMEDIAN		REDCOATS	ACDILLOU	CAUDILLO
	DEMONIAC	ACDEORSU	CAROUSED	ACDILLPY	PLACIDLY
ACDEIMNP	PANDEMIC	ACDEORTU	EDUCATOR	ACDILMTU	TALMUDIC
ACDEIMPT	IMPACTED	ACDEORTV	CARD VOTE	ACDILNOR	IRONCLAD
ACDEIMRT	TIME CARD		CAVORTED	ACDILNSY	SYNDICAL
ACDEINNR	CRANNIED	ACDEOTTU	ACTED OUT	ACDILORS	CORDIALS
ACDEINOP	CANOPIED	ACDEPPRS	SCRAPPED	ACDILSTW	WILD CATS
ACDEINOS	DIOCESAN	ACDEPRTU	CAPTURED		WILDCATS
ACDEINOT	ACTIONED	ACDEPRUV	CARVED UP	ACDIMNSU	SCANDIUM
ACDEINPT	PEDANTIC	ACDEQTUU	AQUEDUCT	ACDIMNSY	DYNAMICS
ACDEINSS	ACIDNESS	ACDERRTU	TRADUCER	ACDINNOY	ANODYNIC
ACDEINST	DISTANCE	ACDERSSU	CRUSADES	ACDINOPS	SPONDAIC
ACDEINTV	VEDANTIC		USED CARS	ACDINORS	SARDONIC
ACDEINVY	DEVIANCY	ACDERSTT	DETRACTS	ACDINORT	TORNADIC
ACDEIOSU	EDACIOUS	ACDERSTU	TRADUCES	ACDINORW	IN A CROWD
ACDEIPSS	SPADICES	ACDERTUY	READY CUT	ACDINSTY	DYNASTIC
ACDEIPSZ	CAPSIZED	ACDFFHNU	HANDCUFF	ACDIOPRS	PICADORS
ACDEIQRU	ACQUIRED	ACDFFIRT	DIFFRACT		SPORADIC
ACDEIRRT	DIRT RACE	ACDFFLOS	SCAFFOLD	ACDIORTT	DICTATOR
ACDEIRSS	SIDECARS	ACDFGOOT	ACT OF GOD	ACDIORWY	DAIRY COW
ACDEIRTT	TETRADIC	ACDFIILU	FIDUCIAL	ACDIPSUV	DAVIS CUP
ACDEISST	DIE-CASTS	ACDFRSTY	DRY FACTS	ACDIRSTT	DISTRACT
ACDEISTT	ACID TEST	ACDGHHIR	HIGH CARD	ACDIRSTU	AIR DUCTS
	DICTATES	ACDGHOOP	GOOD CHAP	ACDISSTX	TAX DISCS
ACDEJKPU	JACKED UP	ACDGHOTW	DOG WATCH	ACDISTUV	VIADUCTS
ACDEKLMU	LAME DUCK		DOGWATCH	ACDJNSTU	ADJUNCTS
ACDEKMMO	MADE MOCK		WATCHDOG	ACDKLLUY	LADY LUCK
ACDEKNPU	UNPACKED	ACDGIILO	DIALOGIC	ACDKLOPS	PADLOCKS
ACDEKOST	STOCKADE	ACDGILNN	CANDLING	ACDKLUYY	LUCKY DAY
ACDEKPPU	PACKED UP	ACDGILNR	CRADLING	ACDKMPSU	MUDPACKS
ACDELLMO	COLD MEAL	ACDGILNS	SCALDING	ACDLLTUY	DUTY CALL
ACDELLOR	CAROLLED	ACDGIMOT	DOGMATIC	ACDLMNOW	CALM DOWN
	COLLARED	ACDGKORT	DOG TRACK	ACDLNOPS	COLD SNAP
ACDELLOS	SO-CALLED	ACDGLNOO	GOLCONDA	ACDLNORS	CALDRONS
ACDELLOT	COLLATED	ACDGOOST	GOOD CAST	ACDLNORU	CAULDRON
ACDELLPU	CALLED UP	ACDGORST	DOG CARTS	ACDLNORY	CONDYLAR
ACDELMOR	MODEL CAR	ACDHHLNU	HAD LUNCH	ACDLNOST	SCOTLAND
ACDELMOT	COLD MEAT	ACDHIILS	CHILIADS	ACDLOORT	DOCTORAL
ACDELNOO	CANOODLE	ACDHIKNP	HANDPICK	ACDLORUY	CRY ALOUD
ACDELNOR	COLANDER	ACDHILPR	PILCHARD	ACDLORWY	COWARDLY
ACDELNPU	UNPLACED	ACDHINOR	HADRONIC	ACDLOSTU	COAL DUST
ACDELNRS	CANDLERS	ACDHINSW	SANDWICH	ACDMMNOO	COMMANDO
ACDELNRY	DRY CLEAN	ACDHIOPS	SCAPHOID	ACDMMNOS	COMMANDS
	DRY-CLEAN	ACDHIPST	DISPATCH		

Code	Word(s)
ACDMNORY	DORMANCY
	MORDANCY
ACDNOORV	CORDOVAN
ACDNOSTW	DOWNCAST
ACDOPRST	POSTCARD
ACDORSTW	TWO CARDS
ACDOSTTU	DUSTCOAT
ACDRSTTU	DUST CART
	DUSTCART
ACEEEFRR	CAREFREE
ACEEEGLN	ELEGANCE
ACEEEHMR	CAME HERE
ACEEEIPR	EARPIECE
ACEEEKPP	KEEP PACE
ACEEENPV	EVEN PACE
ACEEENSV	EVANESCE
ACEEERRT	RECREATE
ACEEERTT	ET CETERA
	ETCETERA
ACEEERTX	EXECRATE
ACEEESUV	EVACUEES
ACEEFFIN	CAFFEINE
ACEEFFLT	FACE LEFT
ACEEFINS	FIANCEES
ACEEFLOS	LOSE FACE
ACEEFLPU	PEACEFUL
ACEEFLSS	FACELESS
ACEEFNSW	NEW FACES
ACEEFPRR	PREFACER
ACEEFPRS	PREFACES
ACEEFPTY	TYPEFACE
ACEEFSTW	FACE WEST
ACEEGHNX	EXCHANGE
ACEEGHRR	HER GRACE
	RECHARGE
ACEEGILS	LEGACIES
ACEEGIMY	MAGIC EYE
ACEEGINS	AGENCIES
ACEEGIPS	SIEGE CAP
ACEEGIRS	GRAECISE
ACEEGIRZ	GRAECIZE
ACEEGKRW	WRECKAGE
ACEEGLRT	GET CLEAR
ACEEGNSV	SCAVENGE
ACEEGORV	COVERAGE
ACEEHHST	CHEETAHS
	THE CHASE
ACEEHIRV	ACHIEVER
ACEEHISV	ACHIEVES
ACEEHLOS	SHOELACE
ACEEHLPS	PLEACHES
ACEEHLST	CHELATES
ACEEHMMO	CAME HOME
ACEEHMNR	MENARCHE
ACEEHMRS	CASHMERE
	SEARCH ME!
ACEEHMST	MACHETES
ACEEHNNS	ENHANCES
ACEEHNOT	THE OCEAN
ACEEHNPS	CHEAPENS
ACEEHNRV	REVANCHE
ACEEHNSS	ENCASHES
	ENCHASES
ACEEHPRR	PREACHER
ACEEHPRS	PREACHES
ACEEHPST	CHEAPEST
ACEEHPTY	EYE PATCH
ACEEHRRS	RESEARCH
	SEARCHER
ACEEHRSS	SEARCHES
ACEEHRST	CHEATERS
	HECTARES
	TEACHERS
	THE RACES
ACEEHRTT	ACT THREE
	CATHETER
ACEEHSST	ESCHEATS
ACEEHSTX	CATHEXES
ACEEIKST	ICE-SKATE
ACEEILMR	MILE RACE
ACEEILNR	RELIANCE
ACEEILNS	SALIENCE
ACEEILPS	ESPECIAL
ACEEILST	ELEATICS
ACEEIMRS	RACEMISE
ACEEIMRZ	RACEMIZE
ACEEIMST	METICAES
ACEEINPS	SAPIENCE
ACEEINPT	PATIENCE
ACEEINRS	INCREASE
ACEEINRT	CREATINE
ACEEINST	CINEASTE
ACEEIRSU	CAUSERIE
ACEEIRSW	WISEACRE
ACEEIRTV	CREATIVE
	REACTIVE
ACEEIRTW	WATER ICE
ACEEISTV	VESICATE
ACEEKLMP	KEEP CALM
ACEEKLMR	MACKEREL
ACEEKNPS	KNEECAPS
ACEEKPPT	KEPT PACE
ACEELLNS	NACELLES
ACEELLNT	LANCELET
ACEELLOT	OCELLATE
ACEELLRR	CELLARER
ACEELMNP	PLACEMEN
ACEELNPT	PENTACLE
ACEELNRS	CLEANERS
	CLEANSER
ACEELNRU	CERULEAN
ACEELNSS	CLEANSES
ACEELNST	CLEANEST
ACEELNSU	NUCLEASE
ACEELNSV	ENCLAVES
ACEELNTT	TENTACLE
ACEELNTU	NUCLEATE
ACEELOPS	ESCALOPE
ACEELPRR	REPLACER
ACEELPRS	REPLACES
ACEELPTU	PECULATE
ACEELRRS	CLEARERS
ACEELRSS	CARELESS
ACEELRST	CLEAREST
ACEELRSU	CRUEL SEA
ACEELRSV	CLEAVERS
ACEELRTU	ULCERATE
ACEELRTX	EXCRETAL
ACEELSTT	TELECAST
ACEELSUY	EASY CLUE
ACEELSVX	EXCLAVES
ACEEMNPS	SPACE MEN
	SPACEMEN
ACEEMNST	CASEMENT
ACEEMNTX	CAME NEXT
ACEEMORS	RACEMOSE
ACEEMORV	CAME OVER
	OVERCAME
ACEEMOSY	EASY COME
ACEEMRRS	CREAMERS
	SCREAMER
ACEEMRRY	CREAMERY
ACEEMRST	CREMATES
ACEEMRTU	CAME TRUE
ACEENNPS	PENANCES
ACEENNRT	ENTRANCE
ACEENNST	CANTEENS
ACEENOPS	NO ESCAPE
ACEENORT	CAROTENE
ACEENRRT	RECREANT
ACEENRTT	ENTR'ACTE
ACEENRTX	NEXT RACE
ACEEPRSS	ESCAPERS
ACEEPSST	ESCAPEST
ACEEPSTT	SPECTATE
ACEERRSS	CARESSER
ACEERRST	CATERERS
	RETRACES
	TERRACES
ACEERRTU	CREATURE
ACEERSSS	CARESSES
ACEERSST	CERASTES
ACEERSTT	SAT ERECT
ACEERSTU	SECATEUR
ACEESSTT	CASETTES
	CASSETTE
	TEST CASE
ACEESSTY	CAT'S EYES
	CAT'S-EYES
ACEFFFOS	FACE-OFFS
ACEFFGIN	EFFACING
ACEFFILT	FACE LIFT
	FACE-LIFT
ACEFFLLU	FULL FACE
ACEFFLOR	CLEAR OFF
ACEFGIMR	GRIM FACE
ACEFGLMU	GLUM FACE
ACEFGLNO	LONG FACE
ACEFGLRU	GRACEFUL
ACEFGLUY	UGLY FACE
ACEFHIKS	FISH CAKE
ACEFHINP	FINE CHAP
ACEFHMRS	CHAMFERS
ACEFHORU	FAROUCHE
ACEFHSTT	THE FACTS
ACEFIIPR	PACIFIER
ACEFIIPS	PACIFIES
ACEFIIRT	ARTIFICE
ACEFIKLL	CALFLIKE
ACEFILLY	FACILELY
ACEFILOR	COAL FIRE
ACEFILOS	FOCALISE
ACEFILOZ	FOCALIZE
ACEFILRY	FIRECLAY
ACEFIMPR	CAMP FIRE
ACEFINNR	IN FRANCE
ACEFINNS	FINANCES
ACEFINOR	CAFE NOIR
ACEFINRS	FANCIERS
ACEFINRU	FACE RUIN
ACEFINSS	FASCINES
ACEFINST	FANCIEST
ACEFIORR	AIR FORCE
ACEFIOSS	FIASCOES
ACEFIRRT	CRAFTIER
ACEFLLOT	ALTO CLEF
ACEFLLOV	CALF LOVE
ACEFLMNO	FLAMENCO
ACEFLNNU	CLEAN FUN
ACEFLNOR	FALCONER
ACEFLNOT	CONFLATE
	FALCONET

Code	Word(s)	Code	Word(s)	Code	Word(s)
ACEFLORS	AL FRESCO / ALFRESCO	ACEGIOTT	COGITATE	ACEHIRSS	CASHIERS / RACHISES
ACEFLOST	LOST FACE	ACEGIPST	PIT CAGES	ACEHIRSV	ARCHIVES
ACEFLRUU	FURCULAE	ACEGJMRU	CREAM JUG	ACEHIRTT	CHATTIER
ACEFLSST	FACTLESS	ACEGKLRS	GRACKLES	ACEHIRTW	WITH CARE
ACEFMMOR	CAME FROM	ACEGKRTU	TRUCKAGE	ACEHISST	CHASTISE
ACEFNRSU	FURNACES	ACEGLLNO	COLLAGEN	ACEHISTX	CATHEXIS
ACEFOORT	FOOT RACE	ACEGLLOS	COLLAGES	ACEHKLSS	SHACKLES
ACEFOPTU	CUP OF TEA / FACE UP TO	ACEGLNOR	LONG ACRE / LONG RACE	ACEHKLTY	LATCHKEY
ACEFORST	FORECAST	ACEGLNOS	CONGEALS	ACEHKNSY	HACKNEYS
ACEFORSU	FOUR ACES	ACEGLNRS	CLANGERS	ACEHKOPS	CAKE SHOP
ACEFOSTU	OUTFACES	ACEGLOPS	GO PLACES	ACEHKOST	HOT CAKES / OAK CHEST
ACEFRRRY	CAR FERRY	ACEGLORT	GOT CLEAR	ACEHLLOO	COALHOLE
ACEFRRST	REFRACTS	ACEGLOSU	CAGOULES	ACEHLLSS	SHELLACS
ACEFRRSU	FARCEURS / SURFACER	ACEGMNRS	CRAGSMEN	ACEHLLST	HELLCATS
ACEFRRTU	FRACTURE	ACEGNNOY	CYANOGEN	ACEHLLSU	HALLUCES
ACEFRSSU	SURFACES	ACEGNOST	COGNATES	ACEHLNNS	CHANNELS
ACEFRSTU	FACTURES	ACEGNPSU	SPACE GUN	ACEHLNPT	PLANCHET
ACEGGIRR	CRAGGIER	ACEGORSS	CORSAGES / SOCAGERS	ACEHLNRU	LAUNCHER
ACEGHHIS	ACES HIGH	ACEGORST	ESCARGOT	ACEHLNSU	LAUNCHES
ACEGHILN	LEACHING	ACEGORTT	COTTAGER	ACEHLNTU	ATE LUNCH / EAT LUNCH
ACEGHILT	LICH-GATE	ACEGORTY	CATEGORY / GREY COAT	ACEHLORS	CHORALES
ACEGHINP	PEACHING	ACEGOSTT	COTTAGES	ACEHLORT	CHLORATE / TROCHLEA
ACEGHINR	IN CHARGE / REACHING	ACEGOTTY	COTTAGEY	ACEHLOST	CHOLATES
ACEGHINT	CHEATING / TEACHING	ACEHHILS	CHEHALIS	ACEHLPST	CHAPLETS
ACEGHIRS	HIS GRACE	ACEHHIPS	CHEAPISH	ACEHLRSS	CLASHERS
ACEGHJNO	JOHN CAGE	ACEHHIRT	THE CHAIR	ACEHLSST	SATCHELS
ACEGHLTY	LYCH-GATE	ACEHHLST	THE CLASH	ACEHLSTT	CHATTELS
ACEGHLUY	GAUCHELY	ACEHHMNN	HENCHMAN	ACEHLSTY	CHASTELY
ACEGHNNO	NO CHANGE	ACEHHNRT	ETHNARCH	ACEHMNRT	MERCHANT
ACEGHNOR	NO CHARGE	ACEHHNSU	HAUNCHES	ACEHMNSS	CHESSMAN
ACEGHNPU	CHANGE UP	ACEHHRSU	HACHURES	ACEHMNTW	WATCHMEN
ACEGHNRS	CHANGERS	ACEHHRTT	THATCHER	ACEHMORT	CHROMATE
ACEGHRRS	CHARGERS	ACEHHRTY	HATCHERY	ACEHMOST	CATS HOME
ACEGIINV	VICINAGE	ACEHHSTT	HATCHETS / THATCHES	ACEHMPRS	CHAMPERS
ACEGIKNR	CREAKING	ACEHIIRT	HIERATIC	ACEHMRRS	CHARMERS / MARCHERS
ACEGILLR	ALLERGIC / ILL GRACE	ACEHIJKR	HIJACKER	ACEHMRSY	CRY SHAME / HAS MERCY
ACEGILMU	MUCILAGE	ACEHIJNT	JACINTHE	ACEHMSTU	MUSTACHE
ACEGILNN	CLEANING / ENLACING	ACEHIKNW	WEAK CHIN	ACEHNNPT	PENCHANT
ACEGILNR	CLEARING	ACEHIKRT	THICK EAR	ACEHNNST	ENCHANTS
ACEGILNW	LACEWING	ACEHIKRW	WHACKIER	ACEHNOPR	CAPE HORN / CHAPERON
ACEGILPS	PELASGIC	ACEHILNT	ETHNICAL	ACEHNOPT	CENOTAPH
ACEGILRS	GLACIERS	ACEHILPR	PARHELIC	ACEHNORT	ANCHORET
ACEGIMNN	MENACING	ACEHILRS	CHARLIES	ACEHNPSU	PAUNCHES
ACEGIMNR	AMERCING / CREAMING / GERMANIC	ACEHILTT	ATHLETIC	ACEHNQUU	QUECHUAN
ACEGIMNT	MAGNETIC	ACEHIMMS	CHAMMIES	ACEHNRRS	RANCHERS
ACEGIMOX	EXOGAMIC	ACEHIMNN	CHINAMEN	ACEHNRSS	ARCHNESS
ACEGIMRR	GRIMACER	ACEHIMNR	CHAIRMEN	ACEHNRST	CHANTERS / SNATCHER / TRANCHES
ACEGIMRS	GRIMACES	ACEHIMNS	MACHINES	ACEHNSST	CHASTENS / SNATCHES / STANCHES
ACEGINNO	CANOEING	ACEHIMPT	EMPATHIC / EMPHATIC	ACEHNSTU	NAUTCHES
ACEGINNS	ENCASING	ACEHIMRS	RICH SEAM	ACEHOPRR	REPROACH
ACEGINNT	ENACTING	ACEHIMTT	THEMATIC	ACEHORST	THORACES
ACEGINOS	COINAGES	ACEHINNT	IN THE CAN	ACEHORTT	THEOCRAT
ACEGINOY	GYNOECIA	ACEHINOT	INCHOATE	ACEHORTU	OUTREACH / REACH OUT
ACEGINPR	CAPERING	ACEHINSS	ACHINESS / CASHES IN	ACEHOSSW	SHOW CASE / SHOWCASE
ACEGINPS	ESCAPING	ACEHINST	ASTHENIC / TEACH-INS	ACEHOSUV	AVOUCHES
ACEGINRS	CREASING	ACEHINTT	IN THE ACT	ACEHPRST	CHAPTERS
ACEGINRT	ARGENTIC / CATERING / CREATING / REACTING	ACEHIPRS	SERAPHIC	ACEHPRSU	PURCHASE
ACEGINSS	CAGINESS	ACEHIPRT	PHREATIC	ACEHQSUU	QUECHUAS
ACEGINTX	EXACTING	ACEHIPST	PASTICHE		
		ACEHIPTT	PATHETIC		
		ACEHIPTW	WHITECAP		
		ACEHIQSU	QUAICHES		
		ACEHIRRS	HIRE CARS		

ACEHRRST	CHARTERS	ACEILOVZ	VOCALIZE	ACEIOSSU	CAESIOUS
ACEHRRTT	TETRARCH	ACEILPPY	CLAY PIPE	ACEIOTVV	VOCATIVE
ACEHRSST	STARCHES		PIPE-CLAY	ACEIOVVV	VIVA VOCE
ACEHRSTT	CHATTERS	ACEILPRS	CALIPERS	ACEIPPRR	CRAPPIER
	RATCHETS		REPLICAS		PERICARP
ACEHRSTW	WATCHERS		SPIRACLE	ACEIPPRW	PRICE WAR
ACEHRTTY	TRACHYTE	ACEILPRT	PARTICLE	ACEIPRST	PRACTISE
ACEHSSTW	SWATCHES	ACEILPRU	PECULIAR	ACEIPSST	ESCAPIST
ACEIILSS	LAICISES	ACEILPSS	SLIPCASE	ACEIPSSU	AUSPICES
ACEIILST	SILICATE		SPECIALS	ACEIPSSZ	CAPSIZES
ACEIILSZ	LAICIZES	ACEILRSS	CLASSIER	ACEIQRSU	ACQUIRES
ACEIIMTU	MAIEUTIC	ACEILRST	ARTICLES	ACEIRRRS	CARRIERS
ACEIINRT	IN A TRICE		RECITALS	ACEIRRSU	CURARISE
ACEIINTV	INACTIVE	ACEILRSU	AURICLES	ACEIRRSW	AIR CREWS
ACEIIRRT	CRITERIA	ACEILRSV	CLAVIERS		AIRSCREW
ACEIISTV	CAVITIES		VISCERAL		WAR CRIES
ACEIJMST	MAJESTIC	ACEILRTV	VERTICAL	ACEIRRUZ	CURARIZE
ACEIKKST	TAKE SICK	ACEILRTY	LITERACY	ACEIRSST	SCARIEST
ACEIKLMR	MILK RACE	ACEILSST	SCALIEST	ACEIRSTT	CITRATES
ACEIKLRY	CREAKILY	ACEILSTT	LATTICES		ITS A CERT
ACEIKMNN	NICKNAME	ACEILTVY	ACTIVELY		SCATTIER
ACEIKMRV	MAVERICK	ACEIMMNP	PEMMICAN	ACEIRSTY	ICY STARE
ACEIKNRR	CRANKIER	ACEIMNRU	MANICURE	ACEIRSTZ	CRAZIEST
ACEIKNST	CAKE TINS	ACEIMNST	AMNESTIC	ACEIRTTU	URTICATE
ACEIKPSX	PICK AXES		SEMANTIC	ACEIRTTV	TRACTIVE
	PICKAXES	ACEIMNSX	MEXICANS	ACEIRTUV	CURATIVE
ACEIKQRU	QUICK EAR	ACEIMNSY	SYCAMINE	ACEIRTVY	VERACITY
ACEIKSTT	TACKIEST	ACEIMPSS	ESCAPISM	ACEIRTWY	ICY WATER
ACEIKSTW	WACKIEST	ACEIMPST	CAMP SITE	ACEISSTT	STATICES
ACEILLMR	MICELLAR	ACEIMRRV	RIVER CAM	ACEISSTU	SAUCIEST
	MILLRACE	ACEIMRRW	WAR CRIME		SUITCASE
ACEILLMT	CALL TIME	ACEIMRST	CERAMIST	ACEISTTT	CATTIEST
	METALLIC		MATRICES	ACEISTTU	EUSTATIC
ACEILLMY	MYCELIAL	ACEINNOS	CANONISE	ACEJLORS	CAJOLERS
ACEILLNT	CLIENTAL	ACEINNOT	ENACTION	ACEJLORY	CAJOLERY
ACEILLOS	LOCALISE	ACEINNOZ	CANONIZE	ACEJSSTU	JUST A SEC
ACEILLOZ	LOCALIZE	ACEINNPS	PINNACES	ACEKKMMO	MAKE MOCK
ACEILLPR	CALLIPER	ACEINNRS	CRANNIES	ACEKKMRU	MUCKRAKE
ACEILLPS	ALLSPICE	ACEINNST	ANCIENTS	ACEKKNRS	KNACKERS
ACEILLPY	EPICALLY		CANNIEST	ACEKKNRY	KNACKERY
ACEILLRV	CAVILLER		INSTANCE	ACEKLLOY	YALE LOCK
ACEILMMO	CAMOMILE	ACEINNSU	NUISANCE	ACEKLLRY	LAY CLERK
ACEILMMR	CLAMMIER	ACEINNTU	UNCINATE	ACEKLMPT	KEPT CALM
ACEILMNO	COAL MINE	ACEINOPR	APOCRINE	ACEKLMPU	PLUM CAKE
ACEILMNP	MANCIPLE	ACEINOPS	CANOPIES	ACEKLNSS	SLACKENS
ACEILMOS	CAMISOLE		CAPONISE	ACEKLPST	PLACKETS
ACEILMPS	MISPLACE	ACEINOPZ	CAPONIZE	ACEKLRST	TACKLERS
ACEILMRS	CLAIMERS	ACEINORR	RARE COIN	ACEKLRSU	CAULKERS
	MIRACLES	ACEINORS	SCENARIO	ACEKLRSY	CLEAR SKY
	RECLAIMS	ACEINORT	CREATION	ACEKLSST	SLACKEST
ACEILMRT	METRICAL		REACTION	ACEKMOOS	SAM COOKE
ACEILMRY	CREAMILY	ACEINORV	VERONICA	ACEKMRSS	SMACKERS
ACEILMST	CLEMATIS	ACEINOST	CANOEIST	ACEKMRSY	ASK MERCY
	CLIMATES	ACEINOTV	CONATIVE	ACEKMSTU	MAKE CUTS
ACEILMSX	CLIMAXES	ACEINOTX	EXACTION	ACEKNORT	ONE-TRACK
	EXCLAIMS	ACEINPSS	INSCAPES	ACEKNPRU	UNPACKER
ACEILNNP	PINNACLE	ACEINPTT	PITTANCE	ACEKNRRT	RACK-RENT
ACEILNOR	CAROLINE	ACEINPUY	PICAYUNE	ACEKOORT	TOOK CARE
ACEILNPS	PELICANS	ACEINRRU	CURARINE	ACEKORSW	CASEWORK
ACEILNRS	CARLINES	ACEINRRY	CINERARY	ACEKPSSY	SKYSCAPE
ACEILNRT	CLARINET	ACEINRSS	RACINESS	ACEKQRUY	QUACKERY
ACEILNRW	CLEAR WIN	ACEINRST	CANISTER	ACEKRRST	TRACKERS
ACEILNSU	LUNACIES		SCANTIER	ACELLLRU	CELLULAR
ACEILNSY	SALIENCY	ACEINRSW	WIN RACES	ACELLOPS	COLLAPSE
ACEILOPR	CAPRIOLE	ACEINRTT	INTERACT		ESCALLOP
ACEILORS	CALORIES	ACEINSTV	VESICANT	ACELLORV	CALL OVER
ACEILORT	EROTICAL	ACEINTTU	TUNICATE		COVER-ALL
	LORICATE	ACEINTTX	EXCITANT		OVERCALL
ACEILOST	SOCIETAL	ACEINTTY	TENACITY	ACELLOST	COLLATES
ACEILOSV	VOCALISE	ACEIOPRT	OPERATIC	ACELLOSW	COLESLAW
ACEILOTV	LOCATIVE	ACEIORSV	VARICOSE	ACELLOTU	LOCULATE

ACELLPSS	SCALPELS	ACEMPSSU	CAMPUSES	ACFFOSST	CASTOFFS
ACELLRSU	CURE-ALLS	ACENNNOU	ANNOUNCE		CASTS OFF
ACELLRTY	RECTALLY	ACENNOSS	CANONESS	ACFGINNY	FANCYING
ACELLSSU	CALLUSES	ACENNOTV	COVENANT	ACFGINPU	FACING UP
ACELLSTU	SCUTELLA	ACENNRSS	SCANNERS	ACFGINRS	SCARFING
ACELLSTW	ACTS WELL	ACENOPRY	PONY RACE	ACFGINRT	CRAFTING
ACELMNNS	CLANSMEN	ACENOPST	CAPSTONE	ACFGITUY	FUGACITY
ACELMNRU	CRUEL MAN		OPENCAST	ACFHHILN	HALF INCH
ACELMNSS	CALMNESS	ACENOPTW	CAPE TOWN		HALF-INCH
ACELMNSU	UNCLE SAM	ACENORRW	CAREWORN	ACFHHINW	HAWFINCH
ACELMORY	CLAYMORE	ACENORSS	COARSENS	ACFHILNO	FALCHION
ACELMOST	COME LAST		NARCOSES	ACFHILOS	COALFISH
ACELMSTU	CALUMETS	ACENORST	ANCESTOR	ACFHIRSW	CRAWFISH
	MUSCATEL	ACENORSU	NACREOUS	ACFHIRSY	CRAYFISH
ACELMTUU	CUMULATE	ACENORTU	COURANTE	ACFHISSU	FUCHSIAS
ACELNOTT	TOLTECAN		OUTRANCE	ACFHLOSW	CASH FLOW
ACELNOTU	CLEAN OUT	ACENOSSV	CAVESSON	ACFHLTUW	WATCHFUL
ACELNOTV	COVALENT	ACENOSTV	CENTAVOS	ACFIILTY	FACILITY
ACELNPSU	CLEANS UP	ACENPTTU	PUNCTATE	ACFIIMPS	PACIFISM
	CLEANUPS	ACENRSTT	RENT ACTS	ACFIIPST	PACIFIST
ACELNRVY	CRAVENLY		TRANSECT	ACFIISST	FASCISTI
ACELOPPT	TOP PLACE	ACENRSTU	CENTAURS	ACFIKLLS	FALL SICK
ACELOPPU	POPULACE		ETRUSCAN	ACFIKLNS	CALFSKIN
ACELOPRT	PECTORAL		RECUSANT	ACFILLSY	FISCALLY
ACELOPRU	OPERCULA	ACENRSTY	ANCESTRY	ACFILNPU	CUP FINAL
ACELOPST	POLE CATS	ACENRTTU	TRUNCATE	ACFILORT	TRIFOCAL
	POLECATS	ACENRTUY	CENTAURY	ACFILRTY	CRAFTILY
ACELOPSW	SLOW PACE	ACENSSTT	SCANTEST	ACFILSSY	CLASSIFY
ACELOPTU	COPULATE	ACENSSTU	NUTCASES	ACFIMNRU	FRANCIUM
ACELORSS	LACROSSE	ACENSSTW	NEWSCAST	ACFINORT	FRACTION
	SOLACERS	ACEOORTV	EVOCATOR	ACFINOST	FACTIONS
ACELORSU	CAROUSEL		OVERCOAT	ACFINRST	INFARCTS
ACELORSW	SLOW RACE	ACEOPPRS	COPPERAS	ACFINSTY	SANCTIFY
ACELORSY	COARSELY	ACEOPSTU	SPACE OUT	ACFIOPRY	FAIR COPY
ACELORTU	CLEAR OUT	ACEORRST	CREATORS	ACFIOSTU	FACTIOUS
ACELOSTU	OSCULATE		REACTORS	ACFIRSTT	FIRST ACT
ACELOSTY	ACOLYTES	ACEORRTU	EUROCRAT	ACFKLOPW	WOLF PACK
ACELPPRS	CLAPPERS	ACEORSST	COARSEST	ACFKOORR	ROOF RACK
ACELPRSS	CLASPERS		COASTERS	ACFKOSTT	FATSTOCK
	SCALPERS	ACEORSSU	CAROUSES	ACFLLMRU	CRAM-FULL
ACELPRST	SPECTRAL	ACEORSTV	OVERACTS	ACFLLORS	CALLS FOR
ACELPRSU	CLEARS UP		OVERCAST	ACFLMNOO	MOONCALF
	SPECULAR	ACEORSTW	EATS CROW	ACFLNORY	FALCONRY
ACELPSSU	CAPSULES	ACEORTUV	CARVE OUT	ACFLOOPS	FOOLS CAP
	SCALES UP	ACEOSSTU	SEA SCOUT		FOOLSCAP
ACELPTUY	EUCALYPT	ACEOSTTU	OUTCASTE	ACFLORSU	SCROFULA
ACELQRSU	LACQUERS	ACEOSTUU	AUTOCUES	ACFLRRUU	FURCULAR
ACELRRSW	CRAWLERS	ACEPPRSU	SCRAPE UP	ACFMOTTU	FACTOTUM
	SCRAWLER	ACEPRRSS	SCARPERS	ACFORSTU	FOUR ACTS
ACELRSSS	SCARLESS		SCRAPERS		FUR COATS
ACELRSSU	SECULARS	ACEPRSTU	CAPTURES	ACGGHINN	CHANGING
ACELRSTT	CLATTERS		PAST CURE	ACGGHINR	CHARGING
ACELRTTY	CLATTERY	ACEPRSUV	CARVES UPS	ACGGIINT	GIGANTIC
ACELSSTT	TACTLESS		CARVE-UPS	ACGGILNN	CLANGING
ACELSTTU	LATE CUTS	ACEPSTTY	TYPECAST		GLANCING
ACEMMRRS	CRAMMERS	ACERRSTT	RETRACTS	ACGGINNU	UNCAGING
ACEMNOOR	CAMEROON	ACERRSUV	VERRUCAS	ACGGINOR	GO RACING
	CON AMORE	ACERSSST	CRASSEST	ACGGLNOU	GLUCAGON
ACEMNOOS	CAME SOON	ACERSSTT	SCATTERS	ACGGLRSY	SCRAGGLY
ACEMNOPU	CAME UPON	ACERSTTX	EXTRACTS	ACGHHINT	HATCHING
ACEMNORR	ROMANCER	ACERTTUW	CUTWATER	ACGHIINN	CHAINING
ACEMNORS	ROMANCES	ACFFGHIN	CHAFFING	ACGHIINR	CHAIRING
ACEMNPSS	CAMPNESS	ACFFHMOR	MARCH OFF	ACGHIKLN	CHALKING
ACEMNPTY	EMPTY CAN	ACFFIILO	OFFICIAL	ACGHIKNW	WHACKING
ACEMNRUY	NUMERACY	ACFFILNU	FANCIFUL	ACGHILNS	CLASHING
ACEMOOST	COMATOSE	ACFFILST	AFFLICTS	ACGHILNT	LATCHING
ACEMOPRS	COMPARES	ACFFIRST	TRAFFICS	ACGHILNY	ACHINGLY
ACEMOPTU	CAME UP TO	ACFFKLOS	SLACK OFF	ACGHILOR	OLIGARCH
ACEMORSY	SYCAMORE	ACFFLLOS	CALLS OFF	ACGHILRT	ARC LIGHT
ACEMORTY	COMETARY	ACFFORRY	CARRY OFF	ACGHIMNP	CHAMPING
ACEMPRSS	SCAMPERS				

ACGHIMNR	CHARMING	ACGINOST	AGNOSTIC	ACHIOPRT	ATROPHIC
	MARCHING		COASTING	ACHIORST	ACTORISH
ACGHIMNT	MATCHING		COATINGS		CHARIOTS
ACGHINNR	RANCHING	ACGINPRS	SCARPING		HARICOTS
ACGHINNT	CHANTING		SCRAPING	ACHIRSTT	CHARTIST
ACGHINOP	POACHING	ACGINPSS	SPACINGS	ACHIRSTU	HAIR CUTS
ACGHINPP	CHAPPING	ACGINPTU	ACTING UP		HAIRCUTS
ACGHINPR	PARCHING	ACGINRRS	SCARRING	ACHISTTY	CHASTITY
ACGHINPT	NIGHT CAP	ACGINRRY	CARRYING	ACHKLOOR	ARCH LOOK
	NIGHTCAP	ACGINRSV	CARVINGS	ACHKLPSU	CHALKS UP
	PATCHING		CRAVINGS	ACHKMMOS	HAMMOCKS
ACGHINRR	CHARRING	ACGINSST	CASTINGS	ACHKMORS	SHAMROCK
ACGHINRS	CRASHING	ACGINSTT	SCATTING	ACHKOPSS	HOPSACKS
ACGHINRT	CHARTING	ACGIORST	ORGASTIC	ACHKOSSS	HASSOCKS
ACGHINST	SCATHING	ACGIORSU	GRACIOUS	ACHKPSSU	SHACKS UP
ACGHINSW	CHIN-WAGS	ACGJLNOU	CONJUGAL	ACHLLNWY	LYNCH LAW
ACGHINTT	CHATTING	ACGLMOUU	COAGULUM	ACHLLOOS	ALCOHOLS
ACGHINTW	WATCHING	ACGLNORU	CLANGOUR	ACHLLORY	CHORALLY
ACGHINTY	YACHTING	ACGLOSUU	GLAUCOUS	ACHLMOTZ	SCHMALTZ
ACGHIPRS	GRAPHICS	ACGLSSTU	CUT GLASS	ACHLNOSY	HALCYONS
ACGHITTU	CAUGHT IT	ACGMNOPS	CAMPONGS	ACHLOOST	AT SCHOOL
ACGHLLOR	GRALLOCH	ACGMOOPT	GO TO CAMP		HOT COALS
ACGHNOTU	CAUGHT ON	ACGNNOOT	CONTANGO	ACHLOPRT	CALTHROP
ACGHPTUU	CAUGHT UP	ACGNOOST	OCTAGONS	ACHLOPTT	POTLATCH
ACGIILMN	CLAIMING	ACGNORST	CONGRATS	ACHLORSS	SCHOLARS
ACGIILNO	LOGICIAN	ACGOORSS	GO ACROSS	ACHMNORS	MONARCHS
ACGIIMST	ITS MAGIC	ACGRSSTU	CUT GRASS	ACHMNORY	MONARCHY
ACGIINRT	GRANITIC	ACHHILPT	PHTHALIC	ACHMOSST	STOMACHS
ACGIJLNO	CAJOLING	ACHHILRU	RICH HAUL	ACHMOTTU	OUTMATCH
ACGIKKLO	GOAL KICK	ACHHINTW	WHINCHAT	ACHNNOSS	CHANSONS
ACGIKLMN	MACKLING	ACHHINTY	HYACINTH	ACHNPPSS	SCHNAPPS
ACGIKLNN	CLANKING	ACHHIWWY	WHICH WAY?	ACHNPSTU	SNATCH UP
ACGIKLNO	CLOAKING	ACHHLNSU	HAS LUNCH	ACHOOPPR	POOR CHAP
ACGIKLNS	SLACKING	ACHHNTTU	NUTHATCH	ACHOPRSY	CHARPOYS
ACGIKLNT	TACKLING	ACHHOSTW	CHAT SHOW	ACHOPSST	SPOT CASH
ACGIKLNU	CAULKING	ACHHPTUZ	CHUTZPAH	ACHOSSTW	CAT SHOWS
ACGIKLRY	GARLICKY	ACHIILMS	CHILIASM	ACHOTTUW	WATCH OUT
ACGIKMNS	SMACKING	ACHIILST	CHILIAST	ACIIILMN	INIMICAL
ACGIKNNR	CRANKING	ACHIIMNS	MISHNAIC	ACIIILNV	CIVILIAN
ACGIKNNS	SNACKING	ACHIIMRT	MITHRAIC	ACIIJKNT	JACK IT IN
ACGIKNOR	CROAKING	ACHIINNS	IN CHAINS	ACIIKNPT	PACK IT IN
ACGIKNQU	QUACKING	ACHIINPS	HISPANIC	ACIILLVW	CIVIL LAW
ACGIKNRT	TRACKING	ACHIINRT	TRICHINA	ACIILMNR	CRIMINAL
ACGIKNRW	WRACKING	ACHIIRST	RACHITIS	ACIILMPT	PALMITIC
ACGIKNSS	SACKINGS	ACHIJNST	JACINTHS	ACIILNPT	PLATINIC
ACGIKNST	STACKING	ACHIKKSW	KICKSHAW	ACIILRVW	CIVIL WAR
ACGILLLR	CALL GIRL	ACHIKQSU	QUACKISH	ACIIMNOR	MORAINIC
ACGILLNS	CALLINGS	ACHIKRSW	RICKSHAW	ACIIMNOS	SIMONIAC
ACGILMNP	CLAMPING	ACHIKRSY	HAY RICKS	ACIIMNOT	AMNIOTIC
ACGILMTU	GLUTAMIC		HAYRICKS	ACIIMNST	ACTINISM
ACGILNNU	UNLACING	ACHIKRTT	HAT TRICK	ACIIMNSU	MUSICIAN
ACGILNOS	SOLACING	ACHILLTY	CITY HALL	ACIIMNTU	ACTINIUM
ACGILNOT	LOCATING	ACHILMTY	MYTHICAL	ACIIMNTV	VITAMIN C
ACGILNPP	CLAPPING	ACHILNNS	CLANNISH	ACIIMNTY	INTIMACY
ACGILNPS	CLASPING	ACHILPSY	PHYSICAL	ACIIMRST	SCIMITAR
	SCALPING	ACHILPTY	PATCHILY	ACIIMSTT	MASTITIC
ACGILNRW	CRAWLING	ACHILRVY	CHIVALRY	ACIIMSTV	ACTIVISM
ACGILNSS	CLASSING	ACHILTTY	CHATTILY	ACIIMTUV	VIATICUM
ACGILNST	CASTLING	ACHIMMOS	MACHISMO	ACIINNOT	IN ACTION
ACGILRSU	SURGICAL	ACHIMMST	MISMATCH		INACTION
ACGIMMNR	CRAMMING	ACHIMNOP	CHAMPION	ACIINOPT	OPTICIAN
ACGIMNOS	COAMINGS	ACHIMNOR	HARMONIC	ACIINOSV	AVIONICS
ACGIMNPR	CRAMPING	ACHIMNOS	MOHICANS	ACIINOTT	CITATION
ACGIMNPS	SCAMPING	ACHIMNSU	INASMUCH	ACIINPSS	PISCINAS
ACGIMORS	ORGASMIC	ACHIMPSS	SCAMPISH	ACIIORST	AORISTIC
ACGINNNS	SCANNING	ACHIMRST	CHARTISM	ACIIORTV	VICTORIA
ACGINNPR	PRANCING	ACHINNSU	UNCHAINS	ACIIOSTT	TAOISTIC
ACGINNRU	UNCARING	ACHINOTT	THIN COAT	ACIIRSST	TRIASSIC
ACGINNST	SCANTING	ACHINRTU	RICH AUNT	ACIIRSTT	ARTISTIC
		ACHINSTT	THIN CATS	ACIISTTU	AUTISTIC
		ACHINSTY	SCYTHIAN	ACIISTTV	ACTIVIST

ACIITTVY	ACTIVITY	ACINNOST	CANONIST
ACIITVVY	VIVACITY		CONTAINS
ACIJKKPS	SKIPJACK		SANCTION
ACIJKLMR	JIM CLARK	ACINNOTU	CONTINUA
ACIJRSSU	JURASSIC	ACINNSTY	INSTANCY
ACIKLLST	SALT LICK	ACINOOTV	VOCATION
ACIKLNRY	CRANKILY	ACINOPRS	SCORPIAN
ACIKMNOT	MINK COAT	ACINOPST	CAPTIONS
ACIKNNPR	CRANKPIN	ACINOQUV	COQ AU VIN
ACIKPPTU	PACK IT UP	ACINORSS	NARCOSIS
ACIKPSSX	SIX-PACKS	ACINORST	CAST IRON
ACIKSSTT	STICKS AT		CAST-IRON
ACILLLNY	CLINALLY	ACINORTT	TRACTION
ACILLLOP	POLLICAL	ACINOSSS	CAISSONS
ACILLMMY	CLAMMILY	ACINOSSY	CYANOSIS
ACILLMOS	LOCALISM	ACINOSTU	AUCTIONS
ACILLNNO	LOCAL INN		CAUTIONS
ACILLNOO	COLONIAL	ACINOSTW	WAINSCOT
ACILLNOR	CARILLON	ACINOSWX	COXSWAIN
	IN COLLAR	ACINPQUY	PIQUANCY
ACILLNOS	SCALLION	ACINPSTY	SYNAPTIC
ACILLNUY	UNCIALLY	ACINRSTU	CURTAINS
ACILLORT	CLITORAL	ACINRTTU	TACITURN
ACILLORY	COLLYRIA	ACINSTTY	SANCTITY
ACILLOSY	SOCIALLY	ACINSTYY	SYNCYTIA
ACILLOTY	COITALLY	ACIOOPST	SCOTOPIA
	LOCALITY	ACIOPRST	APRICOTS
ACILLTWY	CITY WALL	ACIOPRTT	PROTATIC
ACILMNOP	COMPLAIN	ACIOPSST	POTASSIC
ACILMNOS	NO CLAIMS	ACIOPSSU	SPACIOUS
ACILMOPR	PROCLAIM	ACIOPSTU	CAPTIOUS
ACILMOSV	VOCALISM	ACIORRSS	CORSAIRS
ACILMSSU	MUSICALS	ACIORSSU	SCARIOUS
ACILMSTY	MYSTICAL	ACIORTTY	ATROCITY
ACILNOOT	LOCATION	ACIORTVY	VORACITY
ACILNOPT	PLATONIC	ACIOSTUU	CAUTIOUS
ACILNORS	CLARIONS	ACIPSSST	SPASTICS
ACILNORT	CONTRAIL	ACIRSSTY	SACRISTY
ACILNOSU	UNSOCIAL	ACISSTTU	CAT SUITS
ACILNOSV	SLAVONIC		CATSUITS
ACILNOUV	UNIVOCAL	ACJKKSSY	SKYJACKS
ACILNRSU	CISLUNAR	ACJKOPST	JACKPOTS
ACILNRUY	CULINARY	ACJKOSTW	TWO JACKS
ACILNSTY	SCANTILY	ACJMNSTU	MUNTJACS
ACILOORS	AIR-COOLS	ACKKLMSU	KALMUCKS
ACILOPRT	TROPICAL	ACKKMOPR	POCKMARK
ACILORTV	VORTICAL	ACKLLPSU	SKULLCAP
ACILOSTT	COAL TITS	ACKLMNUY	LUCKY MAN
ACILOSTV	VOCALIST	ACKLOOPW	WOOLPACK
ACILOTVY	VOCALITY	ACKLOORS	OARLOCKS
ACILPSST	PLASTICS	ACKLOOSW	WOOLSACK
ACILRSTU	CURTAILS	ACKLORST	ROCK SALT
ACILRTUV	CULTIVAR	ACKLORSW	WARLOCKS
ACILSTUV	VICTUALS	ACKMNOST	STOCKMAN
ACIMNNNO	CINNAMON	ACKMNRUU	RUN AMUCK
ACIMNOPR	MAIN CROP	ACKMOSTT	MATTOCKS
ACIMNORT	ROMANTIC	ACKOOTTU	TOOK A CUT
ACIMNORU	COUMARIN	ACKOPSTU	PACKS OUT
ACIMNORY	ACRIMONY	ACLLLLOR	ROLL CALL
ACIMNOST	MONASTIC	ACLLLNOY	CLONALLY
ACIMNPTY	TYMPANIC	ACLLMMOX	MALCOLM X
ACIMNRSU	CRANIUMS	ACLLNOPU	CALL UPON
ACIMNSTU	TSUNAMIC	ACLLOOPY	PLAY COOL
ACIMOSST	MASSICOT	ACLLOORT	COLLATOR
ACIMPPTU	CAMP IT UP	ACLLOOSS	COLOSSAL
ACIMRRSY	MISCARRY	ACLLOPSS	SCALLOPS
ACIMSSST	MISCASTS	ACLLOSSW	LOW CLASS
ACINNOOT	CONATION	ACLLOSTU	CALLS OUT
	NO ACTION	ACLLRTUU	CULTURAL
ACINNOSS	SCANSION	ACLMMNOU	COMMUNAL
		ACLMNORU	COLUMNAR

ACLMORSU	CLAMOURS
ACLMRSUU	MUSCULAR
ACLMSUUV	VASCULUM
ACLNOOST	COOLANTS
ACLNOOSV	VOLCANOS
ACLNOPSY	SYNCOPAL
ACLNORSU	CONSULAR
ACLNORSW	CORN LAWS
ACLNPSSU	UNCLASPS
ACLNPTUU	PUNCTUAL
ACLOOPRR	CORPORAL
ACLOPRRW	PROWL CAR
ACLOPRST	CALTROPS
ACLOPSSY	CALYPSOS
ACLORTUW	LAW COURT
ACLOSSTT	CAST LOTS
ACLOSSTU	OUTCLASS
ACLRSSTY	CRYSTALS
ACMMNOSY	SCAMMONY
ACMNOPRS	CRAMPONS
ACMNORSY	ACRONYMS
ACMNOSST	SCOTSMAN
ACMNSSTU	SANCTUMS
ACMOOSST	SCOTOMAS
ACMOPSTU	CAMPS OUT
ACMORSTW	WORMCAST
ACMORSTY	COSTMARY
ACMQSTUU	CUMQUATS
ACNNNORY	CANNONRY
ACNNOSTT	CONSTANT
ACNOORRY	CORONARY
ACNOORST	CARTOONS
ACNOPSSW	SNOWCAPS
ACNORRSY	CARRY-ONS
	CARRYONS
ACNORRTY	CONTRARY
ACNORSTT	CONTRAST
ACNORTTU	TURNCOAT
ACNPRSYY	SYNCARPY
ACNRRSTU	CURRANTS
ACOOPRST	POOR CAST
ACOOPSTT	TOPCOATS
ACOORSTU	TOURACOS
ACOPPRSY	PAY CORPS
ACOPRRST	CAR PORTS
	CARPORTS
ACOPRRTT	PROTRACT
ACOPRTUY	PAY COURT
ACOPSSTY	PAY COSTS
ACORRSTT	TRACTORS
ACORRSTU	CURATORS
ACORRTUY	CARRY OUT
	CARRYOUT
ACORSSTU	SURCOATS
ACORSTTY	CRYOSTAT
ACOSSTTU	CASTS OUT
ACPSSTUY	PUSSY CAT
	PUSSYCAT
ADDDDEEI	DID A DEED
ADDDEEEN	DEADENED
ADDDEEGR	DEGRADED
ADDDEEKR	DARK DEED
ADDDEELR	LADDERED
ADDDEEMN	DEMANDED
	MADDENED
ADDDEENS	DEAD ENDS
	SADDENED
ADDDEGJU	ADJUDGED
ADDDEHIR	DIED HARD
ADDDEMNU	ADDENDUM

Code	Word(s)
ADDDEOOW	DEAD WOOD / DEADWOOD
ADDDEOPR	DROP DEAD
ADDDEOST	ODD DATES
ADDDEPPU	PADDED UP
ADDEEEFN	DEAFENED
ADDEEEFT	DEFEATED
ADDEEEKN	DEAD KEEN
ADDEEEMN	DEMEANED
ADDEEENR	DEADENER / ENDEARED
ADDEEFIL	DEFILADE
ADDEEFLT	DEFLATED
ADDEEFRY	DEFRAYED
ADDEEGLN	DANEGELD
ADDEEGNR	DERANGED / GARDENED
ADDEEGOR	DOG-EARED
ADDEFGRR	DEGRADER / REGRADED
ADDEEGRS	DEGRADES
ADDEEGSS	DEGASSED
ADDEEGSW	SAW-EDGED
ADDEEHLR	HELD DEAR
ADDEEHLY	ALDEHYDE
ADDEEHNR	HARDENED
ADDEEHRS	REDHEADS
ADDEEHRT	THREADED
ADDEEILN	DEADLINE
ADDEEILR	DEADLIER / DERAILED
ADDEEILT	DETAILED
ADDEEIMT	MEDIATED
ADDEEINT	DETAINED
ADDEEIPR	DIAPERED
ADDEEISS	DISEASED
ADDEEIST	STEADIED
ADDEEITV	DEVIATED
ADDEEKNR	DARKENED
ADDEELLP	PEDALLED
ADDEELRT	TREADLED
ADDEELST	DESALTED
ADDEELUV	DEVALUED
ADDEEMNP	DAMPENED
ADDEEMNR	DAMNEDER / DEMANDER / REMANDED
ADDEENPP	APPENDED
ADDEENPR	PANDERED
ADDEENPX	EXPANDED
ADDEENRW	WANDERED
ADDEENSS	DEADNESS
ADDEENTT	ATTENDED
ADDEEPRT	DEPARTED / PREDATED
ADDEEPRV	DEPRAVED
ADDEERRT	RETARDED
ADDEERRW	REWARDED
ADDEERSU	DEAD SURE
ADDEERTV	ADVERTED
ADDEFFOR	AFFORDED
ADDEFILY	FIELD DAY
ADDEFLRU	DREADFUL
ADDEFOTU	FADED OUT
ADDEFRSU	DEFRAUDS
ADDEGINR	DREADING
ADDEGIOO	GOOD IDEA
ADDEGJSU	ADJUDGES
ADDEGLOO	GOOD DEAL
ADDEGMOO	MADE GOOD
ADDEGOSV	GAVE ODDS
ADDEGOTX	TAX DODGE
ADDEGPRU	UPGRADED
ADDEHHLR	HELD HARD
ADDEHILR	DIHEDRAL
ADDEHINN	HANDED IN
ADDEHINW	HEAD WIND / HEADWIND
ADDEHIRS	DIE-HARDS / DIES HARD
ADDEHIRY	DYED HAIR
ADDEHLOR	HOLD DEAR
ADDEHLOS	OLD HEADS
ADDEHMRU	DRUMHEAD
ADDEHNNU	UNHANDED
ADDEHORW	HEADWORD
ADDEHOST	DEAD SHOT / SHOT DEAD
ADDEHOSW	SHADOWED
ADDEHRTY	HYDRATED
ADDEIITV	ADDITIVE
ADDEIJNO	ADJOINED
ADDEIKRS	DARK SIDE
ADDEILOS	OLD IDEAS
ADDEILSY	DIALYSED
ADDEIMNN	IN DEMAND
ADDEIMRS	DISARMED
ADDEIMRV	DRIVE MAD
ADDEIMSY	DISMAYED
ADDEIMTT	ADMITTED
ADDEINOR	ORDAINED
ADDEINOS	ADENOIDS / ANODISED
ADDEINOZ	ANODIZED
ADDEINRT	TRADED IN
ADDEINST	DANDIEST
ADDEIOPR	PARODIED
ADDEIORS	ROADSIDE / SIDE ROAD
ADDEIORW	WIDE ROAD
ADDEIRST	DISRATED
ADDEISSU	DISSUADE
ADDEJSTU	ADJUSTED
ADDELMOS	DOLMADES
ADDELNNS	LANDS END
ADDELNOU	DUODENAL / UNLOADED
ADDELNPU	PUDENDAL
ADDELNSU	UNSADDLE
ADDELOOR	EL DORADO
ADDELOPU	LOADED UP
ADDELORS	SOLD DEAR
ADDELOSS	DEAD LOSS
ADDELOSW	DEAD SLOW
ADDELPSU	SADDLE UP
ADDELRSS	SADDLERS
ADDELRST	STRADDLE
ADDELRSW	DAWDLERS / WADDLERS
ADDELRSY	SADDLERY
ADDELRTW	TWADDLER
ADDELSST	STADDLES
ADDELSSW	SWADDLES
ADDELSTW	TWADDLES
ADDEMNNO	ON DEMAND
ADDEMNST	DAMNDEST
ADDEMORV	DROVE MAD
ADDEMOSY	DOMESDAY
ADDENNSU	SAND DUNE
ADDENOPR	PARDONED
ADDENORT	DARED NOT / TRADED ON
ADDENRST	STRANDED
ADDENRYY	YARN-DYED
ADDEOPST	STOP DEAD
ADDEOTTU	OUTDATED
ADDEPRSU	SUPERADD
ADDFFILO	DAFFODIL
ADDFFNRU	DANDRUFF
ADDFNORU	ROAD FUND
ADDGGORU	GUARD DOG
ADDGHNOO	GOOD HAND
ADDGHRRU	HARD DRUG
ADDGILNN	DANDLING
ADDGILNP	PADDLING
ADDGILNS	SADDLING
ADDGILNW	DAWDLING / WADDLING
ADDGINOT	ADDING TO
ADDGINPS	PADDINGS
ADDGINPU	ADDING UP
ADDGINWY	WADDYING
ADDGINYY	DYING DAY
ADDGLOOY	GOOD LADY
ADDGLORU	OLD GUARD
ADDGMRUU	MUDGUARD
ADDGNORW	DRAG DOWN
ADDGOOOR	GOOD ROAD
ADDGOOSY	GOOD DAYS
ADDHHLNO	HANDHOLD
ADDHHLOR	HOLD HARD
ADDHINSY	DANDYISH
ADDHIRTY	THIRD DAY
ADDHLNOS	OLD HANDS
ADDHNNOW	HAND DOWN
ADDHOORW	HARDWOOD
ADDHORRW	HARD WORD
ADDHORSW	HAD WORDS
ADDIIKMZ	ZADDIKIM
ADDIILLT	DID IT ALL
ADDIINOT	ADDITION
ADDIINSS	DISDAINS
ADDIKSTY	KATYDIDS
ADDILMNS	MIDLANDS
ADDILMOS	OLD MAIDS
ADDILNOW	LAID DOWN
ADDILOVW	DAVID LOW
ADDIMNOS	DIAMONDS
ADDIMNSY	DANDYISM
ADDINNOR	ORDINAND
ADDINORS	ANDROIDS
ADDINRWW	WINDWARD
ADDINWYY	WINDY DAY
ADDIORRT	DIRT ROAD
ADDIORSY	DORIS DAY
ADDIPTUY	DUTY PAID
ADDISSTV	ST.DAVIDS
ADDKNRRU	DRUNKARD
ADDLLNOR	LANDLORD
ADDLLRSU	DULLARDS
ADDLNNOW	DOWNLAND
ADDLNOOW	WOODLAND
ADDLORSY	LORDS DAY
ADDMNOPW	DAMP DOWN
ADDMOOSY	DOOMSDAY
ADDNORWW	DOWNWARD
ADDOPRUY	PROUD DAY
ADEEEFMR	MADE FREE
ADEEEFNY	FEDAYEEN
ADEEEFRT	FEDERATE
ADEEEGLT	DELEGATE
ADEEEGNR	RENEGADE
ADEEEHKT	TAKE HEED

ADEEEHSY	EYESHADE	ADEEGNSS	AGEDNESS	ADEEILRZ	REALIZED
ADEEEIMR	MERE IDEA	ADEEGORT	DEROGATE	ADEEILSS	IDEALESS
ADEEEINT	DETAINEE	ADEEGPRS	PRESAGED	ADEEIMMT	MADE TIME
ADEEEIUV	EAU DE VIE	ADEEGPRT	PARGETED	ADEEIMNR	REMAINED
	EAU-DE-VIE	ADEEGRSS	DRESSAGE	ADEEIMNS	IDEAS MEN
ADEEEKNY	NAKED EYE	ADEEGRTY	GET READY	ADEEIMNT	DEMENTIA
ADEEELNV	LEAVENED	ADEEGSTT	GESTATED	ADEEIMNX	EXAMINED
ADEEELPR	REPEALED	ADEEGSWY	EDGEWAYS	ADEEIMRR	DREAMIER
ADEEELRS	RELEASED	ADEEGTTZ	GAZETTED	ADEEIMRT	DIAMETER
ADEEELRV	REVEALED	ADEEHHRS	REHASHED	ADEEIMST	MEDIATES
ADEEELTV	ELEVATED	ADEEHHST	SHEATHED	ADEEIMTT	MEDITATE
ADEEEMMT	EMENDATE	ADEEHHTT	TED HEATH	ADEEINPT	NEAP TIDE
ADEEEMSY	MADE EYES	ADEEHILN	HEADLINE	ADEEINRS	NEAR SIDE
ADEEENNT	NEATENED	ADEEHILT	THE IDEAL		NEARSIDE
ADEEENRS	SERENADE	ADEEHIMT	THE MEDIA	ADEEINRT	DETAINER
ADEEENTT	EDENTATE	ADEEHIST	HEADIEST		RETAINED
ADEEENTV	EVEN DATE	ADEEHISV	ADHESIVE	ADEEINSW	NEW IDEAS
ADEEEPRS	RAPESEED	ADEEHISW	WISE HEAD	ADEEIPRR	REPAIRED
ADEEEPRT	REPEATED	ADEEHKNR	HANKERED	ADEEIPRS	AIRSPEED
ADEEEPSS	DEEP SEAS	ADEEHKWW	HAWKWEED	ADEEIPTX	EXPIATED
ADEEESSW	SEESAWED	ADEEHLLW	WELLHEAD	ADEEIRRR	DREARIER
ADEEFFOS	EASED OFF	ADEEHLRT	HALTERED	ADEEIRST	READIEST
ADEEFGNO	GONE DEAF		LATHERED		SERIATED
ADEEFGOS	GOES DEAF	ADEEHLSS	HEADLESS		STEADIER
ADEEFHNR	FREE HAND	ADEEHLST	THE DALES	ADEEIRTT	ITERATED
	FREEHAND	ADEEHLTW	THE WEALD	ADEEISSS	DISEASES
ADEEFHOR	FOREHEAD	ADEEHLTY	HEATEDLY	ADEEISST	EAST SIDE
ADEEFHRT	FATHERED	ADEEHMMO	HOMEMADE		SET ASIDE
ADEEFILN	ENFILADE	ADEEHMMR	HAMMERED		SET IDEAS
ADEEFILR	DEAR LIFE	ADEEHMNS	HEADSMEN	ADEEISTV	DEVIATES
ADEEFIRR	RAREFIED	ADEEHMPR	HAMPERED		SEDATIVE
ADEEFISS	SAFE SIDE	ADEEHNOV	HAVE DONE	ADEEKKPR	KEEP DARK
ADEEFLMS	SELF-MADE	ADEEHNRR	HARDENER	ADEEKMNN	NAKED MEN
ADEEFLOR	FREELOAD	ADEEHNRT	ADHERENT	ADEEKMRR	REMARKED
ADEEFLRR	DEFERRAL	ADEEHNSS	HAD SENSE	ADEEKMRT	MARKETED
ADEEFLRS	FEDERALS	ADEEHNST	HASTENED	ADEEKNPW	KNAPWEED
ADEEFLRT	FALTERED		THE ANDES	ADEEKNRR	DARKENER
ADEEFLST	DEFLATES	ADEEHNTT	AT THE END	ADEEKPRR	DEER PARK
ADEEFLSX	FLAXSEED	ADEEHORS	SORE HEAD	ADEEKQSU	SQUEAKED
ADEEFMNR	FREEDMAN		SOREHEAD	ADEEKRST	STREAKED
ADEEFMRS	DEFAMERS	ADEEHORV	OVERHEAD	ADEEKSWY	WEEKDAYS
ADEEFMTU	DEAF MUTE	ADEEHOTV	HEAVED TO	ADEELLMT	METALLED
	DEAF-MUTE	ADEEHPPU	HEAPED UP	ADEELLMU	MEDULLAE
ADEEFNOT	TONE DEAF	ADEEHPRS	RESHAPED	ADEELLMW	WELL MADE
	TONE-DEAF	ADEEHPTU	HEATED UP	ADEELLNP	PANELLED
ADEEFNSS	DEAFNESS	ADEEHPUV	UPHEAVED	ADEELLNY	LEADENLY
ADEEFNST	FASTENED	ADEEHRRT	THREADER	ADEELLPT	PETALLED
ADEEFNTT	FATTENED	ADEEHRST	HEADREST	ADEELLQU	EQUALLED
ADEEFNTW	WENT DEAF	ADEEHRTW	WREATHED	ADEELLRS	SELL DEAR
ADEEFRTU	FEATURED	ADEEHSST	HEADSETS	ADEELLRV	RAVELLED
ADEEGGHS	EGGHEADS	ADEEHVWY	HEAVY DEW	ADEELLRW	READ WELL
ADEEGHIV	GIVE HEAD	ADEEIILS	IDEALISE		WELL READ
ADEEGHRT	GATHERED	ADEEIILZ	IDEALIZE		WELL-READ
ADEEGINR	REGAINED	ADEEIJMR	JEREMIAD	ADEELLSS	ALLSEEDS
ADEEGIST	GET IDEAS	ADEEIKMR	MIKE READ		LEADLESS
ADEEGLLU	DE GAULLE	ADEEIKSW	WEAK SIDE	ADEELLTY	ELATEDLY
ADEEGLNR	ENLARGED	ADEEILLO	OEILLADE	ADEELLWY	WALLEYED
ADEEGLRW	LEW GRADE	ADEEILMN	LEAD MINE	ADEELMMR	MAL DE MER
ADEEGMNR	GENDARME	ADEEILMR	REMEDIAL	ADEELMNO	LEMONADE
ADEEGNNR	ENDANGER	ADEEILMV	MEDIEVAL	ADEELMNP	EMPLANED
ADEEGNOR	GRADE ONE	ADEEILNT	DATE LINE	ADEELMNR	ALDERMEN
ADEEGNOS	GO AND SEE		DATELINE	ADEELMNS	LEADSMEN
ADEEGNRR	GARDENER		DINE LATE	ADEELMNT	LAMENTED
	GARNERED		ENTAILED	ADEELMOV	MADE LOVE
ADEEGNRS	DERANGES	ADEEILNU	EAU-DE-NIL	ADEELMPR	RED MAPLE
	GRANDEES	ADEEILPP	LEAD PIPE	ADEELMRS	DEMERSAL
	GRENADES	ADEEILPS	PLEIADES	ADEELMTU	EMULATED
ADEEGNRU	DUNGAREE	ADEEILPT	DEPILATE	ADEELNNP	ENPLANED
	UNDER AGE	ADEEILRS	REALISED	ADEELNOR	OLEANDER
	UNDERAGE		SIDEREAL	ADEELNRT	ANTLERED
ADEEGNRV	ENGRAVED	ADEEILRT	RETAILED		

ADEELNRV	LAVENDER
ADEELNSV	ENSLAVED
ADEELNTT	TALENTED
ADEELOPR	LOP-EARED
ADEELOPS	PEDALOES
ADEELOPX	POLEAXED
ADEELOST	DESOLATE
ADEELPPR	RAPPELED
ADEELPRS	RELAPSED
ADEELPRT	PALTERED
ADEELPRY	PARLEYED
	REPLAYED
ADEELPST	PEDESTAL
ADEELPSU	SEALED UP
ADEELQSU	SQUEALED
ADEELRST	DESALTER
	TREADLES
ADEELRSV	SLAVERED
ADEELRSW	LEEWARDS
ADEELRSY	DELAYERS
ADEELRUV	REVALUED
ADEELSST	DATELESS
ADEELSTY	SEDATELY
ADEELSUV	DEVALUES
ADEEMMRY	YAMMERED
ADEEMMSS	MESDAMES
ADEEMNNR	MANNERED
ADEEMNOR	ONE ARMED
ADEEMNOT	NEMATODE
ADEEMNPR	DAMPENER
ADEEMNRS	MEANDERS
ADEEMNSS	SEEDSMAN
ADEEMNSW	MADE NEWS
ADEEMORT	MODERATE
ADEEMORV	MADE OVER
ADEEMOSY	SAMOYEDE
ADEEMPPR	PAMPERED
ADEEMPRT	TAMPERED
ADEEMPRV	REVAMPED
ADEEMPST	STAMPEDE
ADEEMRST	MASTERED
	STREAMED
ADEEMRSU	MADE SURE
	MEASURED
ADEEMRTT	MATTERED
ADEENNRS	ENSNARED
ADEENNRU	UNEARNED
ADEENNTT	TENANTED
ADEENOPS	ONE SPADE
ADEENOPT	OPEN DATE
ADEENORS	REASONED
ADEENOSS	SEASONED
ADEENOTT	DETONATE
ADEENPPR	ENDPAPER
ADEENPRT	PARENTED
ADEENPRX	EXPANDER
ADEENPRY	READY PEN
ADEENPTT	PATENTED
ADEENRRW	DREW NEAR
	WANDERER
ADEENRSS	DEARNESS
ADEENRSU	UNDERSEA
ADEENRSW	ANSWERED
ADEENRSY	YEAR-ENDS
ADEENRTT	ATTENDER
	NATTERED
ADEENRTU	DENATURE
ADEENSST	ASSENTED
ADEENSSU	DANSEUSE
	SUDANESE
ADEENSTU	UNSEATED

ADEENTTU	TAUTENED
ADEENTTV	VENDETTA
ADEEOPRT	OPERATED
ADEEOPST	ADOPTEES
ADEEORRT	ORDER TEA
ADEEORVW	OVERAWED
ADEEOSTU	EASED OUT
ADEEPPRR	PREPARED
ADEEPRRS	SPREADER
ADEEPRRU	REARED UP
ADEEPRRV	DEPRAVER
ADEEPRSS	ASPERSED
	REPASSED
ADEEPRST	PEDERAST
	PREDATES
ADEEPRSU	PERSUADE
ADEEPRSV	DEPRAVES
	PERVADES
ADEEPRTT	PATTERED
ADEEPSST	STAPEDES
ADEEPSWY	SPEEDWAY
ADEEQRUV	QUAVERED
ADEERRRW	REWARDER
ADEERRST	ARRESTED
	RETREADS
	SERRATED
ADEERRSW	WEARS RED
ADEERRVY	VERY DEAR
ADEERSST	ASSERTED
ADEERSTT	RESTATED
ADEERTTT	TATTERED
ADEERTTY	YATTERED
ADEERVYY	EVERY DAY
	EVERYDAY
ADEESSSS	ASSESSED
ADEESTTT	ATTESTED
ADEESTUX	EXUDATES
ADEFFGUW	GUFFAWED
ADEFFHOS	HEADS OFF
ADEFFIMR	AFFIRMED
ADEFFIRT	TARIFFED
ADEFFKOR	RAKED OFF
ADEFFLNS	SNAFFLED
ADEFFLOS	LEAD-OFFS
	LEADS OFF
ADEFFORS	READS OFF
ADEFFORT	TRADE OFF
	TRADE-OFF
ADEFFOSW	SAWED-OFF
ADEFGGOT	FAGGOTED
ADEFGIIS	GASIFIED
ADEFGILN	FINAGLED
ADEFGILO	FOLIAGED
ADEFGILS	GADFLIES
ADEFGIMN	DEFAMING
ADEFGIRU	ARGUFIED
ADEFGITU	FATIGUED
ADEFGLLO	GOLD LEAF
ADEFGLOS	FALSE GOD
ADEFGLOT	GATEFOLD
ADEFGOOW	A GOOD FEW
ADEFHILR	HARD LIFE
ADEFHIMS	FAMISHED
ADEFHLNT	LEFT HAND
	LEFT-HAND
ADEFHLST	HELD FAST
ADEFHLSU	USED HALF
ADEFHMOT	FATHOMED
ADEFHNOR	FOREHAND
ADEFHORS	HEADS FOR

ADEFHOST	SOFT HEAD
	SOFTHEAD
ADEFIILR	AIRFIELD
ADEFIIMR	RAMIFIED
ADEFIIRT	RATIFIED
ADEFILMN	INFLAMED
ADEFILNT	INFLATED
ADEFILNY	FINE LADY
ADEFILOT	FOLIATED
ADEFIMMR	MADE FIRM
ADEFIMPR	FIREDAMP
ADEFIMRT	FIRM DATE
ADEFINRR	INFRARED
ADEFINRU	FREUDIAN
ADEFINSY	FINE DAYS
ADEFINYZ	DENAZIFY
ADEFISTX	FIX DATES
ADEFISVY	FIVE DAYS
ADEFKOOT	TAKE FOOD
ADEFKORS	ASKED FOR
ADEFLLMO	OLD FLAME
ADEFLLOW	FALLOWED
ADEFLLSU	FALLS DUE
ADEFLLUY	FEUDALLY
ADEFLMRU	DREAMFUL
ADEFLNOR	FORELAND
ADEFLNTU	FLAUNTED
ADEFLOPR	DROP-LEAF
ADEFLORT	DEFLATOR
ADEFLPRS	FELDSPAR
ADEFLPRU	FLARED UP
ADEFLPSU	SPADEFUL
ADEFLRTW	LEFTWARD
ADEFLRZZ	FRAZZLED
ADEFLSTU	DEFAULTS
ADEFMPRU	FRAMED UP
ADEFNOPR	PROFANED
ADEFNSST	DAFTNESS
ADEFOOSS	SEAFOODS
ADEFORRW	FARROWED
ADEFORRY	READY FOR
ADEFORUV	FAVOURED
ADEFOSTU	FADE-OUTS
	FADES OUT
ADEFRRST	DRAFTERS
ADEFRRTU	FUR TRADE
ADEFSSTY	FAST DYES
ADEGGJLY	JAGGEDLY
ADEGGLRS	DRAGGLES
ADEGGLRY	RAGGEDLY
ADEGGMOO	GOOD GAME
ADEGGMOY	DEMAGOGY
ADEGGNPU	GANGED UP
ADEGGOOW	GOOD WAGE
ADEGGOPY	PEDAGOGY
ADEGGRTY	GADGETRY
ADEGHHOS	HOGSHEAD
ADEGHILO	DIG A HOLE
ADEGHILR	HEAD GIRL
ADEGHILT	ALIGHTED
ADEGHINR	ADHERING
ADEGHINS	HEADINGS
ADEGHLNO	HEADLONG
ADEGHLOS	GALOSHED
ADEGHLOU	DUG A HOLE
ADEGHLUY	UGLY HEAD
ADEGHNOR	GONE HARD
ADEGHORS	GOES HARD
ADEGHRTU	DAUGHTER
ADEGIIMN	IMAGINED
ADEGIINT	IDEATING

ADEGIITT	DIGITATE	ADEGOPRR	PROGRADE	ADEHNOPR	ORPHANED
ADEGIKNN	KNEADING	ADEGOPRT	PORTAGED	ADEHNOPT	PHONATED
ADEGIKOR	OAK RIDGE	ADEGORSW	DOWAGERS	ADEHNORT	NOT HEARD
ADEGILLP	PILLAGED	ADEGORTU	OUTRAGED	ADEHNORV	HAND OVER
ADEGILMN	MALIGNED	ADEGORTW	GRADE TWO		OVERHAND
ADEGILNO	AGED LION	ADEGORTY	GOT READY	ADEHNOSS	SANDSHOE
ADEGILNP	PLEADING	ADEGOSTY	GO STEADY	ADEHNPRS	SHARP END
ADEGILNR	DRAGLINE	ADEGPRSU	UPGRADES	ADEHNRSS	HARDNESS
ADEGILNS	DEALINGS	ADEGPSTU	UPSTAGED	ADEHNRSW	SWANHERD
ADEGILNY	DELAYING	ADEGRRST	DRAGSTER	ADEHNRTW	WENT HARD
ADEGILOU	DIALOGUE	ADEHHIPS	HEADSHIP	ADEHNSST	HANDSETS
ADEGILSS	GLISSADE	ADEHHOST	HOTHEADS	ADEHNSSU	SUNSHADE
ADEGIMNN	AMENDING	ADEHHRST	THRASHED	ADEHNSTU	THE SUDAN
ADEGIMNR	MARGINED	ADEHIITZ	THIAZIDE	ADEHNSUW	UNWASHED
ADEGIMOR	IDEOGRAM	ADEHIKLV	KHEDIVAL	ADEHNTTY	TENTH DAY
ADEGIMRT	MIGRATED	ADEHIKNS	SKINHEAD	ADEHOPSX	HEXAPODS
ADEGINNO	GAINED ON	ADEHILNR	HARD LINE	ADEHORRW	HARROWED
ADEGINNR	IN DANGER		HARD-LINE	ADEHORTT	THROATED
ADEGINNW	AWNINGED	ADEHILNU	HAULED IN	ADEHORTW	DEATH ROW
ADEGINOR	ORGANDIE	ADEHILSV	LAVISHED	ADEHOSTW	TWO HEADS
ADEGINOS	AGONISED	ADEHILTW	DEAL WITH	ADEHOTTY	TO THE DAY
	DIAGNOSE	ADEHIMNR	HIRED MAN	ADEHPPSU	SHAPED UP
	SAN DIEGO	ADEHIMRS	MISHEARD	ADEHPSUW	WASHED UP
ADEGINOZ	AGONIZED	ADEHIMRT	HARD TIME		WASHED-UP
ADEGINRS	READINGS	ADEHIMST	MEAT DISH	ADEHQSSU	SQUASHED
ADEGINRT	GRADIENT	ADEHINOS	ADHESION	ADEHRRVY	VERY HARD
ADEGINRY	READYING	ADEHINPS	DEANSHIP	ADEHRSTY	HYDRATES
ADEGINSS	ASSIGNED		PINHEADS	ADEHRTTW	THWARTED
ADEGINST	SEDATING	ADEHINPU	DAUPHINE	ADEIILMS	IDEALISM
	STEADING	ADEHINRT	THE NADIR		MILADIES
ADEGIOST	GODETIAS	ADEHINSS	SHANDIES	ADEIILNT	IN DETAIL
	GOT IDEAS	ADEHINST	HANDIEST	ADEIILST	IDEALIST
ADEGIRWY	RIDGEWAY	ADEHINSV	VANISHED	ADEIILTV	DILATIVE
ADEGISTU	GAUDIEST	ADEHINSW	SAID WHEN	ADEIILTY	IDEALITY
ADEGIUWY	GUIDEWAY	ADEHIPPY	DIE HAPPY	ADEIIMNN	INDIAMEN
ADEGJLUY	LAY JUDGE	ADEHIPRS	SEPHARDI	ADEIIMNR	MERIDIAN
ADEGKMOO	MAKE GOOD	ADEHIPST	PITHEADS	ADEIIMPR	IMPAIRED
ADEGKOPT	KEPT A DOG	ADEHIRSS	RADISHES	ADEIIMTT	IMITATED
ADEGKRRW	GREW DARK	ADEHIRST	HARDIEST	ADEIINOT	IDEATION
ADEGKRRY	DARK GREY	ADEHIRSV	RAVISHED		IODINATE
ADEGKRST	GETS DARK	ADEHISST	SHADIEST	ADEIINRT	DAINTIER
ADEGLLMO	GOLD LAME	ADEHISVW	HAD VIEWS	ADEIINST	DAINTIES
ADEGLLNO	LONG LEAD	ADEHKNRS	REDSHANK	ADEIIPRS	PRESIDIA
ADEGLLOP	GALLOPED	ADEHKORW	HEADWORK	ADEIITTV	VITIATED
ADEGLLOR	REAL GOLD	ADEHKPRY	HYDE PARK	ADEIITUV	AUDITIVE
ADEGLMOO	GOOD MEAL	ADEHLLOO	HALLOOED	ADEIJMSS	SID JAMES
ADEGLMOS	GLADSOME	ADEHLLOW	HALLOWED	ADEIJOSV	JOE DAVIS
	LAME DOGS	ADEHLLRS	HARD SELL	ADEIJRSU	JUDAISER
ADEGLMPU	PLUMAGED	ADEHLMNO	HOMELAND	ADEIJRUZ	JUDAIZER
ADEGLNPS	SPANGLED	ADEHLNRS	HANDLERS	ADEIKLLT	IDLE TALK
ADEGLNRS	DANGLERS	ADEHLNST	SHETLAND	ADEIKLLY	LADYLIKE
	GLANDERS	ADEHLOPS	ASPHODEL	ADEIKLNW	WALKED IN
ADEGLNSW	GLAD NEWS	ADEHLOST	LEAD SHOT	ADEIKLPV	KAPIL DEV
ADEGLORW	LOW GRADE	ADEHLPSS	SPLASHED	ADEIKLSW	SIDEWALK
	LOW-GRADE	ADEHLPSU	LASHED UP	ADEIKMNS	SAME KIND
ADEGMMRU	RUMMAGED	ADEHLRRY	HERALDRY	ADEIKMRT	TIDE MARK
ADEGMNOO	GOOD NAME	ADEHLSTY	HAD STYLE		TIDEMARK
ADEGMNOR	DRAGOMEN	ADEHLSWY	HELD SWAY	ADEILLMN	LAND MILE
ADEGMNOS	GOD'S NAME	ADEHMNNY	HANDYMEN	ADEILLMY	MEDIALLY
ADEGMNOY	ENDOGAMY	ADEHMNOR	DONE HARM	ADEILLNN	LAND-LINE
ADEGMORW	WORD GAME	ADEHMNOS	HANDSOME	ADEILLNT	END IT ALL
ADEGMOST	DOG TEAMS	ADEHMNOT	METHADON	ADEILLNW	WALLED IN
ADEGMPUZ	GAZUMPED	ADEHMNRS	HERDSMAN	ADEILLOT	TOLD A LIE
ADEGNNOR	ANDROGEN	ADEHMNRU	UNHARMED	ADEILLPR	PILLARED
ADEGNOPU	POUNDAGE	ADEHMOOR	HEADROOM	ADEILLPW	WELL PAID
ADEGNORT	DRAGONET	ADEHMORS	DOES HARM	ADEILLRS	DALLIERS
ADEGNRRU	GRANDEUR	ADEHMORW	HOME DRAW	ADEILLRV	RIVALLED
ADEGNRST	DRAGNETS		HOMEWARD	ADEILLSW	WELL SAID
	GRANDEST	ADEHMOST	HEADMOST	ADEILMMS	DILEMMAS
ADEGNRUW	DREW A GUN	ADEHMOSU	MADHOUSE	ADEILMNY	MAIDENLY
ADEGOOST	GOOD SEAT	ADEHNNOP	OPEN HAND	ADEILMPS	IMPLEADS

ADEILMRY	DREAMILY	ADEINNTU	INUNDATE	ADEISTTU	SITUATED
ADEILMSS	MISDEALS	ADEINNTW	WANTED IN	ADEITTTU	ATTITUDE
	MISLEADS	ADEINOOR	RADIO ONE	ADEJKNOS	JAN KODES
ADEILMST	MISDEALT	ADEINORT	RATIONED	ADEJKORS	SODA JERK
ADEILNNR	INLANDER	ADEINOSS	ADONISES	ADEJMMNO	JAMMED ON
ADEILNNS	ANNELIDS		ANODISES	ADEJMPTU	JUMPED AT
ADEILNNT	DENTINAL	ADEINOST	SEDATION	ADEJOPRY	JEOPARDY
ADEILNOP	PALINODE	ADEINOSZ	ANODIZES	ADEJRSTU	ADJUSTER
ADEILNPT	PANTILED	ADEINOTT	ANTIDOTE	ADEKKPRT	KEPT DARK
ADEILNRS	ISLANDER	ADEINOTV	DONATIVE	ADEKLMRY	MARKEDLY
ADEILNTV	DIVALENT	ADEINPPX	APPENDIX	ADEKLNOW	WALKED ON
ADEILOPS	SEPALOID	ADEINPRS	SPRAINED	ADEKLOOT	LOOKED AT
ADEILOPT	PETALOID	ADEINPRT	DIPTERAN	ADEKLPUW	WALKED UP
ADEILORS	DARIOLES		PAID RENT	ADEKMNSU	UNMASKED
ADEILORT	IDOLATER		RED PAINT	ADEKMORS	DARKSOME
	TAILORED	ADEINPRU	UNPAIRED	ADEKNNSS	DANKNESS
ADEILORV	OVERLAID	ADEINPSS	IN SPADES	ADEKNOTW	TAKE DOWN
ADEILORX	EXORDIAL		SAND PIES	ADEKNPTU	TANKED UP
ADEILOST	DIASTOLE	ADEINPSV	SPAVINED		TANKED-UP
	ISOLATED	ADEINRRS	SERRANID	ADEKNRSS	DARKNESS
ADEILOTV	DOVETAIL	ADEINRRW	DRAW REIN	ADEKNSVY	VANDYKES
	VIOLATED	ADEINRSS	ARIDNESS	ADEKOSTU	ASKED OUT
ADEILPPP	PEDIPALP		SARDINES	ADEKQSUW	SQUAWKED
ADEILPRU	EPIDURAL	ADEINRST	DETRAINS	ADELLMSU	MEDULLAS
ADEILPSS	PAID LESS		RANDIEST	ADELLNNU	ANNULLED
ADEILQTU	LIQUATED		STRAINED	ADELLNSS	LANDLESS
ADEILRRY	DREARILY		TRADE INS	ADELLNTY	DENTALLY
ADEILRSS	RED SAILS		TRADES IN	ADELLOPU	LOUD PEAL
ADEILRSU	RESIDUAL	ADEINRSU	DENARIUS	ADELLOPW	WALLOPED
ADEILRSY	DIALYSER	ADEINRSV	INVADERS	ADELLOTT	ALLOTTED
ADEILRTT	DETRITAL	ADEINRTT	NITRATED		TOTALLED
ADEILRVY	VARIEDLY	ADEINRTU	INDURATE	ADELLOWW	WALLOWED
ADEILSSY	DIALYSES		URINATED	ADELLPUW	WALLED UP
ADEILSTY	STEADILY	ADEINRTV	DRIVEN AT	ADELLQSU	SQUALLED
ADEILSUY	DAILY USE	ADEINRVY	VINEYARD	ADELLTUU	ULULATED
ADEILSVY	EVIL DAYS	ADEINSST	SANDIEST	ADELMNRS	MANDRELS
ADEILSXY	DYSLEXIA	ADEINSSV	AVIDNESS	ADELMORS	EARLDOMS
ADEILTTU	ALTITUDE	ADEINSTT	INSTATED	ADELMOSS	DAMOSELS
	LATITUDE	ADEINSTV	DEVIANTS	ADELMOSZ	DAMOZELS
ADEIMMNS	MISNAMED	ADEINSTW	EAST WIND	ADELMOTU	MODULATE
	SAME MIND	ADEIOPRS	PARODIES	ADELMOWX	WAX MODEL
ADEIMMRS	MERMAIDS	ADEIOPTV	ADOPTIVE	ADELMRRU	DEMURRAL
ADEIMNNT	IN TANDEM	ADEIORST	ASTEROID	ADELMSUY	AMUSEDLY
ADEIMNOP	DOPAMINE		RADIO SET	ADELNOPY	PLAYED ON
ADEIMNOT	ADMIT ONE	ADEIORSV	AVOIDERS	ADELNORU	UNLOADER
	DOMINATE	ADEIORTV	DEVIATOR	ADELNORV	OVERLAND
ADEIMNRS	IN DREAMS	ADEIPPRS	APPRISED		RONDAVEL
ADEIMNRT	TIRED MAN	ADEIPRSS	DESPAIRS	ADELNPRS	SPANDREL
ADEIMNRY	DAIRYMEN	ADEIPRST	TRAIPSED	ADELNPRU	UPLANDER
ADEIMNSS	SIDESMAN	ADEIPSTU	PUT ASIDE	ADELNRSS	SLANDERS
ADEIMNST	MEDIANTS	ADEIPTTU	APTITUDE	ADELNRSU	LAUNDERS
ADEIMNSU	MAUNDIES	ADEIPTUW	WAITED UP	ADELNRTY	ARDENTLY
ADEIMNSY	EASY MIND	ADEIQRRU	QUARRIED	ADELNRUY	UNDERLAY
ADEIMNTY	DYNAMITE	ADEIQSUY	QUAYSIDE	ADELNTUU	UNDULATE
ADEIMOPR	PAID MORE	ADEIRRSS	DEAR SIRS	ADELOORV	OVERLOAD
ADEIMORT	MEDIATOR	ADEIRRTW	TAWDRIER	ADELOPRS	LEOPARDS
ADEIMOSS	SESAMOID	ADEIRRWW	WIREDRAW	ADELOPST	TADPOLES
ADEIMOST	ATOMISED	ADEIRSST	DISASTER	ADELOPTU	LEAD UP TO
ADEIMOTZ	ATOMIZED		DISRATES	ADELORRV	ROD LAVER
ADEIMPRT	IMPARTED	ADEIRSSU	RADIUSES	ADELORSS	ROADLESS
ADEIMPTU	MADE IT UP	ADEIRSSV	ADVISERS		SEA-LORDS
ADEIMRRS	ADMIRERS	ADEIRSTT	EATS DIRT	ADELORST	LEOTARDS
ADEIMRSS	MISREADS		STRIATED		LODESTAR
	SIDE ARMS		TARDIEST	ADELORSU	ROULADES
ADEIMSST	MISDATES	ADEIRTTT	TITRATED	ADELORUY	YOUR DEAL
ADEINNOT	ANOINTED	ADEIRTUV	DURATIVE	ADELOSTU	LEADS OUT
	ANTINODE	ADEIRTWY	READY WIT	ADELOSTV	SOLVATED
ADEINNOV	DEVONIAN	ADEIRVWY	DRIVEWAY	ADELOTUV	OVULATED
ADEINNRT	AT DINNER	ADEISSST	ASSISTED	ADELOTUW	OUTLAWED
ADEINNSY	NINE DAYS	ADEISSTT	DISTASTE	ADELOVWY	AVOWEDLY
		ADEISSWY	SIDEWAYS	ADELPPRY	DAPPERLY

ADELPPUY	PLAYED UP	ADEOOPRR	POOR DEAR	ADFIMRSW	DWARFISM
ADELPRRU	LARRUPED	ADEOOPSS	APODOSES	ADFINORY	ON FRIDAY
ADELPRSW	SPRAWLED	ADEOORRT	TOREADOR	ADFINSWY	FIND WAYS
ADELPRTY	DRY PLATE	ADEOOTTT	TATTOOED	ADFIRSTY	FIRST DAY
ADELPSTU	PULSATED	ADEOPPRR	PEAR DROP	ADFLLLOU	FULL LOAD
ADELRSZZ	DAZZLERS	ADEOPPRV	APPROVED	ADFLLNOU	ALL FOUND
ADELRTUY	ADULTERY	ADEOPRRT	PARROTED	ADFLLNOW	DOWNFALL
ADELSTTY	STATELY		PREDATOR		FALL DOWN
ADEMMNOW	MAD WOMEN		PRORATED	ADFLMNOO	MAN OF OLD
ADEMMNOY	MAD MONEY		TEARDROP	ADFLMNOR	LANDFORM
ADEMMOOR	MADE ROOM	ADEOPRST	ADOPTERS	ADFLMOOS	MAD FOOLS
ADEMMSTU	SUMMATED	ADEOPRTT	TETRAPOD	ADFLMPSU	MUDFLAPS
ADEMNNNU	UNMANNED	ADEOPSTT	POSTDATE	ADFLMSTU	MUD FLATS
ADEMNNOR	ON REMAND	ADEOPTTU	UP TO DATE		MUDFLATS
ADEMNOOR	MAROONED		UP-TO-DATE	ADFLNOST	SOFT-LAND
ADEMNOPR	PARDON ME	ADEORRST	ROADSTER	ADFLORSU	FOULARDS
	POMANDER	ADEORRVW	OVERDRAW	ADFMRSTU	STUD FARM
ADEMNORS	RANSOMED	ADEORSST	ASSORTED	ADFNNOST	FONDANTS
ADEMNOSU	DONE A SUM	ADEORSTT	ROAD TEST	ADFNOORT	TO AND FRO
ADEMNOTU	AMOUNTED	ADEORSTU	READOUTS		TO-AND-FRO
ADEMNOUY	YOU AND ME	ADEORSTX	EXTRADOS	ADFNORST	STAND FOR
ADEMNPSS	DAMPNESS	ADEORSUV	SAVOURED	ADFOOPST	FOOTPADS
ADEMNRRU	UNDERARM	ADEOTUWY	OWE A DUTY	ADFOORTX	AT OXFORD
ADEMNRSU	MADE RUNS	ADEPPRST	STRAPPED	ADFORRSW	FORWARDS
	MAUNDERS	ADEPPSSU	PASSED UP	ADFORSUY	FOUR DAYS
ADEMOORT	MODERATO	ADEPRSTU	PASTURED	ADGGGINR	DRAGGING
ADEMOOSV	VAMOOSED	ADEPRTTU	TARTED UP	ADGGILNN	DANGLING
ADEMORRT	MORTARED	ADEPSTUY	STAYED UP	ADGGIMNO	GOING MAD
ADEMORRU	ARMOURED	ADEQSTTU	SQUATTED	ADGGINNU	GUNGA DIN
ADEMOSSU	DOES A SUM	ADERRSTT	REDSTART	ADGGINRS	NIGGARDS
ADEMOSSY	SAMOYEDS	ADERSSSU	ASSUREDS	ADGGINRU	GUARDING
ADEMPRST	RED STAMP	ADERSSTW	STEWARDS	ADGGLOOY	LAY DOGGO
ADEMPRUW	WARMED UP	ADERSSTY	REST DAYS	ADGGLRSU	SLUGGARD
ADEMRRSU	EARDRUMS	ADERSTWW	WESTWARD	ADGHHHIN	HIGH HAND
ADEMRRTY	MARTYRED	ADESSTUY	TUESDAYS	ADGHHILN	HIGHLAND
ADENNOPS	SENNA POD	ADFFGORU	OFF GUARD	ADGHHIOR	HIGH ROAD
ADENNOSY	ANODYNES	ADFFHIOT	HAD IT OFF		HIGHROAD
	YES AND NO	ADFFHITY	FIFTH DAY	ADGHHISY	HIGH DAYS
ADENNPST	PENDANTS	ADFFHNOS	HANDS OFF	ADGHILNN	HANDLING
ADENNTUW	UNWANTED	ADFFISST	DISTAFFS	ADGHILOS	HIDALGOS
ADENOOPR	OPEN ROAD	ADFFLOOS	OFF-LOADS	ADGHILTY	DAYLIGHT
ADENOORT	RATOONED	ADFFNNOO	OFF AND ON	ADGHINOR	HOARDING
ADENOORW	WANDEROO		ON AND OFF	ADGHINPR	HANDGRIP
ADENOPRR	PARDONER	ADFFNORW	DRAWN OFF	ADGHINRW	DRAW NIGH
ADENOPRS	OPERANDS	ADFFNOST	STAND OFF	ADGHIPRR	GRIP HARD
ADENOPRT	PRONATED		STAND-OFF	ADGHIPRS	DIGRAPHS
ADENOPRU	READ UP ON		STANDOFF	ADGHISST	SAD SIGHT
ADENOPSS	PASSED ON	ADFFOOST	FAST FOOD	ADGHKNOT	THANK GOD
ADENOPSY	DYSPNOEA	ADFFORSW	DRAWS OFF	ADGHLNNO	LONGHAND
ADENORRW	NARROWED		WARDS OFF	ADGHLOOU	GOOD HAUL
ADENORST	DARES NOT	ADFGGOYY	FOGGY DAY	ADGHNNOW	HANG DOWN
	TRADES ON	ADFGIINN	FADING IN	ADGHNNSU	HANDGUNS
	TREADS ON	ADFGIINR	INFRA DIG	ADGHNRTU	DRAG HUNT
ADENORTW	TEAR DOWN	ADFGINRT	DRAFTING	ADGHOORS	ROAD HOGS
ADENORUX	RONDEAUX	ADFGINRW	DWARFING	ADGHRSTU	DRAUGHTS
ADENORWW	WEAR DOWN	ADFGLNOW	FLAG DOWN	ADGHRTUY	DRAUGHTY
ADENOSTY	STEADY ON!	ADFGLOUW	GOD-AWFUL	ADGIILLN	DIALLING
ADENPPTU	UNTAPPED	ADFGMNOO	MAN OF GOD	ADGIILLO	GLADIOLI
ADENPRRS	PARDNERS	ADFGOORW	GOD OF WAR	ADGIILNO	GONIDIAL
ADENPRRU	UNDER PAR	ADFHIMNR	FIRM HAND	ADGIILNT	DILATING
ADENPRTY	PEDANTRY	ADFHIRSW	DWARFISH	ADGIILPY	PYGIDIAL
ADENQRSU	SQUANDER	ADFHISTY	DAY SHIFT	ADGIIMNR	ADMIRING
ADENRRSY	REYNARDS	ADFHLNSU	HANDFULS	ADGIINNR	DRAINING
ADENRSSU	DANSEURS		HANDSFUL	ADGIINNT	GIN AND IT
ADENRSTU	TRANSUDE	ADFHLOST	HOLD FAST	ADGIINNV	INVADING
ADENRSTW	ST.ANDREW		HOLDFAST	ADGIINOR	RADIOING
ADENRSTX	DEXTRANS	ADFIIILR	FILARIID	ADGIINOV	AVOIDING
ADENRSUY	DAY NURSE	ADFIIRST	FIRST AID	ADGIINRY	DAIRYING
ADENRSYY	YARN-DYES	ADFILLNW	WINDFALL	ADGIINSV	ADVISING
ADENRUWY	UNDER WAY	ADFILMNO	MANIFOLD	ADGIINTU	AUDITING
ADENSTUY	UNSTEADY	ADFIMRRT	DIRT FARM	ADGIJNRU	ADJURING

Code	Word	Code	Word	Code	Word
ADGIKLNR	DARKLING	ADHIMNOU	HUMANOID	ADIIPSTY	SAPIDITY
ADGIKMNO	MAKING DO	ADHIMNRT	THIRD MAN	ADIIPTVY	VAPIDITY
ADGILLNO	DOING ALL	ADHIMOPP	AMPHIPOD	ADIIRSST	DIARISTS
ADGILLNR	LAND GIRL	ADHINNOR	IRON HAND	ADIIRSTT	DISTRAIT
ADGILLNU	ALLUDING	ADHINNTY	NINTH DAY	ADIJKSTU	JUST A KID
ADGILLNW	WINDGALL		TINY HAND	ADIKKNRS	DARK SKIN
ADGILLNY	DALLYING	ADHINPSS	SHIN PADS	ADIKLLNS	ALL KINDS
ADGILMOR	MARIGOLD	ADHINPSU	DAUPHINS	ADIKLOOS	SOLID OAK
ADGILNNS	LANDINGS	ADHINPSW	HIND PAWS	ADIKNNST	INKSTAND
ADGILNOS	LOADINGS	ADHINSTU	DIANTHUS	ADIKNPSS	SKIDPANS
ADGILNOT	DOG LATIN	ADHINSTW	HAD TWINS	ADIKRSTU	DARK SUIT
ADGILNPP	DAPPLING	ADHIOPSS	SOAP DISH	ADILLLPY	PALLIDLY
ADGILNRS	DARLINGS	ADHIOTTU	HAD IT OUT	ADILLMMS	MILLDAMS
ADGILNRW	DRAWLING	ADHIPRSW	WARDSHIP	ADILLMNR	MANDRILL
ADGILNRY	DARINGLY	ADHIRTWW	WITHDRAW	ADILLMSY	DISMALLY
ADGILNZZ	DAZZLING	ADHISTXY	SIXTH DAY	ADILLNPS	LANDSLIP
ADGILOPR	PRODIGAL	ADHKLOOR	HARD LOOK	ADILLNPU	DULL PAIN
ADGILOST	DOGS TAIL	ADHKNORW	HANDWORK	ADILLOSW	DISALLOW
ADGILOTW	WILD GOAT	ADHKOORT	TOOK HARD	ADILLOSY	DISLOYAL
ADGILRVY	GRAVIDLY	ADHKORRW	HARD WORK	ADILLPSY	LILY PADS
ADGIMNNY	DYING MAN		WORK HARD	ADILLSTY	DISTALLY
ADGINNOR	ADORNING	ADHLLLOS	HOLDALLS	ADILMNNO	MANDOLIN
ADGINNOT	DONATING	ADHLLNOS	HOLLANDS	ADILMOPS	DIPLOMAS
ADGINNST	STANDING	ADHLLNOY	HOLY LAND	ADILMOPT	DIPLOMAT
ADGINNTU	DAUNTING	ADHLLPRU	PULL HARD	ADILMOPY	OLYMPIAD
ADGINOPT	ADOPTING	ADHLMORT	THRALDOM	ADILMOTY	MODALITY
ADGINORR	RING ROAD	ADHLNOOT	HAND TOOL	ADILNNOW	NAIL DOWN
ADGINORS	ROAD SIGN	ADHLNOTU	OLD HAUNT	ADILNNSU	DISANNUL
ADGINOTY	TOADYING	ADHLORRY	OLD HARRY	ADILNOOR	DOORNAIL
ADGINPTU	UPDATING	ADHLOSWY	HOLD SWAY	ADILNOOV	VINDALOO
ADGINRSW	DRAWINGS	ADHLOSYY	HOLY DAYS	ADILNORS	ORDINALS
ADGIRSZZ	GIZZARDS	ADHMNOOR	DO NO HARM	ADILNOTV	NOT VALID
ADGKMOOR	GOOD MARK	ADHMNPPU	HAND PUMP	ADILNRWY	INWARDLY
ADGKORRW	GROW DARK	ADHNOPRU	HARD UPON	ADILNSSU	SUN DIALS
ADGLLORS	RAG DOLLS	ADHNORSU	HONDURAS		SUNDIALS
ADGLNOOP	GOOD PLAN	ADHNOSTU	HAND-OUTS	ADILNSSW	WINDLASS
ADGLNOOR	LONG ROAD		HANDOUTS	ADILOOPR	POLAROID
ADGLNOOS	GONDOLAS		HANDS OUT	ADILOORT	TOROIDAL
ADGLNOSY	LONG DAYS		THOUSAND	ADILOPRS	SLIP ROAD
ADGLOOPR	DROP GOAL	ADHNOSTW	TWO HANDS	ADILOPRT	TRIPODAL
ADGLOOPS	GOOD PALS	ADHNOSWW	WASH DOWN	ADILOPSS	DISPOSAL
ADGLOOPY	GOOD PLAY	ADHNRRSU	RUNS HARD	ADILORSS	DORSALIS
ADGMNOOR	ROMAN GOD	ADHNRSTU	HARD NUTS	ADILORST	DILATORS
ADGMNOOY	GOOD MANY	ADHNRSTY	HYDRANTS	ADILORTY	ADROITLY
ADGMNORU	GOURMAND	ADHOORSW	ROAD SHOW		DILATORY
ADGMNRSU	GRAND SUM	ADHOPRST	HARD TOPS		IDOLATRY
ADGNNORS	GRANDSON		HARDTOPS	ADILOSST	SODALIST
ADGNOORS	DRAGOONS	ADHOPRSY	RHAPSODY	ADILOSTW	WILD OATS
	GADROONS	ADHOPSST	DASHPOTS	ADILOSTY	SODALITY
ADGNOORU	GO AROUND	ADHORRTY	HYDRATOR	ADILPSST	PLASTIDS
ADGNOORY	GOOD YARN	ADHORSSW	HAS WORDS	ADILPSSY	DISPLAYS
ADGNOSSS	SAD SONGS	ADHRSTUY	THURSDAY	ADILPSTU	PLAUDITS
ADGOOPRT	GOOD PART	ADIIIMNR	IN MID AIR	ADILRTTY	TILTYARD
ADGORSTU	DRAGS OUT	ADIIINRV	VIRIDIAN	ADILRTWY	TAWDRILY
ADGORSTY	STRAY DOG	ADIIIQRU	DAIQUIRI	ADIMMNOO	AMMONOID
ADHHINPW	WHIP HAND	ADIIKLMM	MILK MAID	ADIMMNOS	MONADISM
ADHHIPRS	HARDSHIP		MILKMAID		NOMADISM
ADHHIRST	HITS HARD	ADIILLMR	MILLIARD	ADIMMNSY	DYNAMISM
ADHHNORU	HOUR HAND	ADIILLUV	DILUVIAL	ADIMNNOT	DOMINANT
ADHHPRSU	PUSH HARD	ADIILNOT	DILATION	ADIMNRTY	DIRTY MAN
ADHIIMNS	MAIN DISH		LAID IT ON	ADIMNSTY	DYNAMIST
ADHIINNT	HAND IT IN	ADIILNSV	INVALIDS	ADIMOPRY	MYRIAPOD
ADHIINOP	OPHIDIAN	ADIILNTW	TAIL WIND	ADIMOSTY	TOADYISM
ADHIKNRS	HARD SKIN	ADIILNTY	DAINTILY	ADIMPRSY	PYRAMIDS
ADHILLOT	THALLOID	ADIILOPP	DIPLOPIA	ADIMSSST	DISMASTS
ADHILOPS	SHIPLOAD	ADIILSSY	DIALYSIS	ADIMSSTU	STADIUMS
ADHILOPY	HAPLOIDY	ADIILTVY	VALIDITY	ADINNOOT	DONATION
ADHILOSY	HOLIDAYS	ADIIMNTV	VITAMIN D	ADINNORS	ANDIRONS
ADHILPRT	THIRD LAP	ADIINOTU	AUDITION	ADINNOTU	IN AND OUT
ADHILPSY	LADYSHIP	ADIINRST	DISTRAIN	ADINNSST	STAND-INS
ADHIMNOS	ADMONISH	ADIIPRTY	RAPIDITY		STANDS IN

ADINOOPS	ISOPODAN
ADINOOPT	ADOPTION
ADINOORT	TANDOORI
ADINOOST	NOT AS I DO
ADINOPRS	PONIARDS
ADINORRY	ORDINARY
ADINORSS	SADIRONS
ADINORST	INTRADOS
ADINORSU	DINOSAUR
ADINORTU	DURATION
ADINOSTX	OXIDANTS
ADINPSST	SANDPITS
ADIOOPSS	APODOSIS
ADIOORTW	RADIO TWO
ADIOPPST	POST PAID
	POSTPAID
ADIOPRRS	AIRDROPS
ADIOPRST	PARODIST
	PORT SAID
ADIOPRTY	PODIATRY
ADIOPSTY	DYSTOPIA
ADIOQSUV	QUO VADIS?
ADIORRST	STAIR ROD
ADIORSST	SARODIST
ADIORSSV	ADVISORS
ADIORSTU	AUDITORS
ADIORSVY	ADVISORY
ADIORTUY	AUDITORY
ADIOSSVW	DISAVOWS
ADIPPSTU	PUTS PAID
ADIPRSTY	DAY TRIPS
ADIRRWYZ	WIZARDRY
ADIRSSXY	SIX YARDS
ADJNORSU	ADJOURNS
ADKLMRSU	MUDLARKS
ADKLNOTW	DONT WALK
	TALK DOWN
ADKLOOPT	POLKA DOT
	POLKA-DOT
ADKLOORW	WOODLARK
ADKMNORW	MARK DOWN
	MARKDOWN
ADKMOORR	DARK ROOM
	DARKROOM
ADKNNOSW	SANK DOWN
ADKOORRW	ROADWORK
ADKORSWY	DAYS WORK
ADKRSSWY	SKYWARDS
ADLLNORU	ALL ROUND
	ALL-ROUND
ADLLOORT	TOLLROAD
ADLLOPRS	POLLARDS
ADLLORSW	LAW LORDS
ADLLORSY	DORSALLY
ADLLOSST	OLD SALTS
ADLMMNOY	MY OLD MAN
ADLMNOOW	OLD WOMAN
ADLMNORY	RANDOMLY
ADLMOPSY	PSALMODY
ADLMORSU	OLD SARUM
ADLNNTUU	UNDULANT
ADLNOORW	LOANWORD
ADLNOOST	TOD SLOAN
ADLNOPSU	POUNDALS
ADLNOPSW	SLAP DOWN
ADLNOPWY	PLAY DOWN
ADLOPPSU	SOLD A PUP
ADLOPRST	LAST DROP
ADLOPRWY	WORD PLAY
	WORDPLAY

ADLORRSW	WAR LORDS
	WARLORDS
ADLORRWW	WORLD WAR
ADLORSTW	DRAW LOTS
	LAST WORD
ADLPRUWY	UPWARDLY
ADLSTUWY	STUDY LAW
ADMNNOOY	ON MONDAY
ADMNNORY	MONANDRY
ADMNNOSU	SOUND MAN
ADMNOOST	MASTODON
ADMNOOSW	WOODSMAN
ADMNOPRU	PROUD MAN
ADMNORST	MORDANTS
ADMNOSSU	OSMUNDAS
ADMOOPPP	POPPADOM
ADMOORRW	WARDROOM
ADMOORST	DOOR MATS
	DOORMATS
ADMRSTUY	MUSTARDY
ADNNORRU	RAN ROUND
ADNNORTY	DYNATRON
ADNNOSUY	ON SUNDAY
ADNOOQRU	QUADROON
ADNOORST	DONATORS
	TORNADOS
ADNOORTW	NOT A WORD
	ROAD TOWN
ADNOOSSS	SO-AND-SOS
ADNOOSVW	ADVOWSON
ADNOOTTY	NOT TODAY
ADNOPRUY	PAY ROUND
ADNOPSSW	PASS DOWN
ADNOQRSU	SQUADRON
ADNORSTU	ROTUNDAS
ADNORSTW	DR.WATSON
	SANDWORT
ADNORSUW	SAW ROUND
ADNORSXY	SARDONYX
ADNORTUW	DRAWN OUT
	UNTOWARD
ADNOSSTT	STANDS TO
ADNOSSTU	ASTOUNDS
ADNOSTTU	STAND OUT
ADNOSTWY	STAY DOWN
ADNPSSTU	DUST PANS
	DUSTPANS
	STANDS UP
ADOOPRRT	TRAP-DOOR
	TRAPDOOR
ADOOPSTT	STOOD PAT
ADOORSWY	DOORWAYS
ADOPPPYY	POPPY DAY
ADOPRSSW	PASSWORD
ADORSSTY	SAD STORY
ADORSTTU	DARTS OUT
ADORSTTY	DRY TOAST
ADORSTUW	DRAWS OUT
	OUTWARDS
ADORSTWY	TWO YARDS
ADRSSTTU	STARDUST
ADRSTTUY	STUDY ART
AEEEEGLY	EAGLE EYE
AEEEFFLS	FEEL SAFE
AEEEFKPS	KEEP SAFE
AEEEFLMR	FREE MEAL
AEEEFORS	FAEROESE
AEEEFRST	FREE SEAT
AEEEFRSV	SEA FEVER
AEEEGLRT	REGELATE
	RELEGATE

AEEEGLRV	LEVERAGE
AEEEGLST	LEGATEES
AEEEGNPR	PEA GREEN
AEEEGNRS	SEA GREEN
AEEEGNRT	GENERATE
	GREEN TEA
	TEENAGER
AEEEGPRS	PEERAGES
AEEEGRST	STEERAGE
AEEEGRSW	SEWERAGE
AEEEGTTV	VEGETATE
AEEEHLRT	ETHEREAL
AEEEHMPR	EPHEMERA
AEEEHNRR	NEAR HERE
AEEEHRRS	REHEARSE
AEEEHSTT	AESTHETE
AEEEIKLR	LAKE ERIE
AEEEIMNX	EXAMINEE
AEEEJNRY	JANE EYRE
AEEEKKPS	KEEPSAKE
AEEEKMSY	MAKE EYES
AEEELLSV	SEA LEVEL
AEEELMNR	ENAMELER
AEEELMRS	SEEM REAL
AEEELNPS	NEPALESE
AEEELNRV	VENEREAL
AEEELNSW	NEW LEASE
AEEELQSU	SEQUELAE
AEEELRRS	RELEASER
AEEELRRV	REVEALER
AEEELRSS	RELEASES
AEEELRTX	AXLETREE
AEEELSTV	ELEVATES
AEEEMMRT	METAMERE
AEEEMNST	EASEMENT
AEEEMPRT	PERMEATE
AEEENPTT	PATENTEE
AEEENRTV	ENERVATE
	VENERATE
AEEEPRRT	PEAR TREE
	REPARTEE
	REPEATER
AEEEPSTW	SWEET PEA
AEEERSST	TESSERAE
AEEESTTW	SWEET TEA
AEEFFINR	FINE FARE
AEEFFLLR	FREE FALL
	FREE-FALL
AEEFFLOV	LEAVE OFF
AEEFFLST	FELT SAFE
AEEFFLTT	FLAT FEET
	FLATFEET
AEEFFNRT	AFFERENT
AEEFFOSS	EASES OFF
AEEFGILN	FINE GAEL
AEEFGIPV	PAGE FIVE
AEEFGLSU	FUSELAGE
AEEFGPRS	GRAF SPEE
AEEFHILV	HAVE LIFE
AEEFHLLS	SELF-HEAL
AEEFHLST	SELF-HATE
AEEFHRST	FEATHERS
AEEFHRTY	FEATHERY
AEEFHRVY	HAY FEVER
AEEFHSTT	THE FATES
AEEFIKLL	LEAFLIKE
AEEFIKLT	TAKE LIFE
AEEFIKRR	FREAKIER
AEEFILLR	REAL LIFE
AEEFILNP	FEEL PAIN

AEEFILNV	LANE FIVE	AEEGIRST	GET A RISE	AEEHHRTY	HEATHERY
	VINE LEAF	AEEGIRSV	GAVE RISE	AEEHHSST	SHEATHES
AEEFILST	FEALTIES		GIVES EAR		THE ASHES
	LEAFIEST	AEEGJNRY	JANE GREY	AEEHHSTV	THE HAVES
AEEFILSY	EASY LIFE	AEEGKLLR	ALL GREEK	AEEHIJMR	JEREMIAH
AEEFILTW	LATE WIFE	AEEGKLOP	KEEP GOAL	AEEHINNV	IN HEAVEN
AEEFIMRS	SEEM FAIR	AEEGKRRT	GREEK ART	AEEHINST	IN THE SEA
AEEFINRV	IN A FEVER	AEEGKRWW	GREW WEAK	AEEHIPRS	PHARISEE
AEEFIPRT	PEAT FIRE	AEEGLLNR	ALLERGEN	AEEHIRRT	EARTHIER
AEEFIRRS	RAREFIES	AEEGLLOS	LOSE A LEG		HEARTIER
AEEFIRSS	FREESIAS	AEEGLLSZ	GAZELLES	AEEHIRST	HEARTIES
AEEFKPST	KEPT SAFE	AEEGLMNS	MELANGES	AEEHIRTW	WAIT HERE
AEEFLLRW	FAREWELL	AEEGLMOV	LOVE GAME	AEEHISST	ESTHESIA
AEEFLLSS	LEAFLESS	AEEGLMRT	TELEGRAM	AEEHISTT	HESITATE
AEEFLLST	LEAFLETS	AEEGLMRY	MEAGRELY	AEEHISTV	HEAVIEST
AEEFLLYZ	FEEL LAZY	AEEGLNNT	ENTANGLE	AEEHISTW	WHITE SEA
AEEFLMRW	FEEL WARM	AEEGLNOT	ELONGATE		WITH EASE
AEEFLMSS	SELFSAME	AEEGLNRS	ENLARGES	AEEHKLLU	KEELHAUL
AEEFLNRU	FUNEREAL		GENERALS	AEEHKMOT	TAKE-HOME
AEEFLORV	OVERLEAF	AEEGLNSV	EVANGELS	AEEHKNRS	HEARKENS
AEEFLPRY	FREE PLAY	AEEGLORT	ALTER EGO	AEEHLLRT	ALL THERE
AEEFLRRR	REFERRAL	AEEGLOSV	LEAVES GO		HEAR TELL
AEEFLRRT	FALTERER	AEEGLPRW	GREW PALE	AEEHLLSS	SEASHELL
AEEFLRSS	FEARLESS	AEEGLRSS	EELGRASS	AEEHLMNY	HYMENEAL
AEEFLSTW	FLEW EAST		GEARLESS	AEEHLMPT	HELPMATE
AEEFMNOR	FORENAME	AEEGLRSU	LEAGUERS	AEEHLNPT	ELEPHANT
AEEFMORS	FEARSOME	AEEGLRTU	REGULATE		THE PANEL
AEEFNRST	FASTENER	AEEGLSSW	WAGELESS	AEEHLNRT	LEATHERN
	FENESTRA	AEEGLSSY	EYEGLASS	AEEHLNST	ST.HELENA
AEEFNRTT	FATTENER		GLASS EYE	AEEHLNVY	HEAVENLY
AEEFNSSS	SAFENESS	AEEGLSTT	GET STALE	AEEHLORS	EAR HOLES
AEEFPRSS	FREE PASS	AEEGLTTU	TUTELAGE	AEEHLOSU	ALE HOUSE
AEEFRRST	FERRATES	AEEGMMOS	GAMESOME	AEEHLRRT	LATHERER
AEEFRSTU	FEATURES	AEEGMNNR	GREEN MAN	AEEHLRST	HALTERES
AEEFRSWY	FREEWAYS	AEEGMNOP	OPEN GAME		LEATHERS
AEEGGGLR	LARGE EGG	AEEGMNRT	GREAT MEN	AEEHLRTY	LEATHERY
AEEGGINR	AGREEING	AEEGMNSS	GAMENESS	AEEHLSST	HEATLESS
AEEGGIRV	AGGRIEVE	AEEGMOOT	OOGAMETE	AEEHLSTT	ATHLETES
AEEGGNNR	GANGRENE	AEEGMRRY	GREY MARE	AEEHMMOT	HOME TEAM
AEEGGPRU	PUGGAREE	AEEGMRST	GAMESTER	AEEHMMRR	HAMMERER
AEEGHHTU	THE HAGUE		GAS METER	AEEHMNOR	NEAR HOME
AEEGHILN	HEGELIAN	AEEGMSSS	MESSAGES	AEEHMPSS	EMPHASES
AEEGHIRT	HERITAGE	AEEGMSSU	MESSUAGE	AEEHMRTY	ERYTHEMA
AEEGHLLV	GAVE HELL	AEEGNOPT	OPEN GATE	AEEHNNVW	NEW HAVEN
AEEGHMMO	HOME GAME	AEEGNOST	GONE EAST	AEEHNOPR	EARPHONE
AEEGHMPR	GRAPHEME		STAGE ONE	AEEHNOPS	PHASE ONE
AEEGHNRS	SHAGREEN		STONE AGE	AEEHNORT	ONE HEART
AEEGHRRT	GATHERER	AEEGNOSY	GONE EASY	AEEHNOST	ON THE SEA
AEEGHRTV	THE GRAVE	AEEGNPTX	NEXT PAGE	AEEHNRST	HASTENER
AEEGHSTT	THE STAGE	AEEGNRRV	ENGRAVER	AEEHNRTT	THREATEN
AEEGILLS	LEGALISE	AEEGNRST	ESTRANGE	AEEHNRTU	URETHANE
AEEGILLZ	LEGALIZE		REAGENTS	AEEHNRTW	NEW HEART
AEEGILMS	MILEAGES		SERGEANT	AEEHNRWY	ANYWHERE
AEEGILNS	ENSILAGE	AEEGNRSV	AVENGERS	AEEHNSSS	HAS SENSE
AEEGILNT	GELATINE		ENGRAVES	AEEHNSSW	SHAWNEES
	LEGATINE	AEEGNSSS	SAGENESS	AEEHORRV	OVERHEAR
AEEGILNU	IN LEAGUE	AEEGNTVV	GAVE VENT	AEEHORSS	SEASHORE
AEEGILSY	LAY SIEGE	AEEGOORVV	GAVE OVER	AEEHORTV	OVERHEAT
AEEGILTV	LEVIGATE	AEEGOSST	GOES EAST	AEEHOSSW	SEE A SHOW
AEEGIMNT	GEMINATE	AEEGOSSY	GOES EASY	AEEHOSTU	TEAHOUSE
AEEGIMPS	GAME PIES	AEEGPRSS	PRESAGES	AEEHOSTV	HEAVES TO
AEEGIMRT	EMIGRATE	AEEGRRSW	WAGERERS	AEEHPRRS	RESHAPER
AEEGINNP	PAGE NINE	AEEGRSTT	GREATEST	AEEHPRSS	RESHAPES
AEEGINPR	PERIGEAN	AEEGSSTT	GESTATES	AEEHPRY	SHARP EYE
AEEGINRV	GIVEN EAR		STAGE SET	AEEHPRUV	UPHEAVER
AEEGINSS	ASSIGNEE	AEEGSTTZ	GAZETTES	AEEHPSTT	PET HATES
AEEGINSV	ENVISAGE	AEEHHIMN	NEHEMIAH	AEEHPSY	PAY SHEET
AEEGINTV	AGENTIVE	AEEHHNST	HEATHENS	AEEHPSUV	UPHEAVES
	NEGATIVE	AEEHHRSS	REHASHES	AEEHRRSS	SHEARERS
AEEGIPQU	EQUIPAGE	AEEHHRST	HEATHERS	AEEHRRTU	URETHRAE
AEEGIRRS	GREASIER	AEEHHRTT	THE EARTH		

AEEHRSST	ASH TREES	AEEIMSTY	EASY TIME	AEELLPTT	PLATELET
AEEHRSTT	THEATERS	AEEINNRR	INNER EAR	AEELLRTT	TALL TREE
	THEATRES	AEEINNSS	IN A SENSE	AEELLSTT	STELLATE
AEEHRSTW	THERE WAS	AEEINNTV	VENETIAN	AEELLSWY	WALLEYES
	WEATHERS	AEEINOPS	PAEONIES	AEELMNOT	LEMON TEA
	WREATHES	AEEINPRS	NAPERIES	AEELMNPS	EMPANELS
AEEHRSTY	STAY HERE	AEEINPRT	APERIENT		EMPLANES
AEEHRTVW	WHATEVER	AEEINRRT	RETAINER	AEELMNSS	LAMENESS
AEEIILLV	LIVE A LIE	AEEINRSS	AIR SENSE		MALENESS
AEEIISST	AS I SEE IT	AEEINRST	TRAINEES		NAMELESS
AEEIKLNW	WINE LAKE	AEEINRSU	UNEASIER		SALESMEN
AEEIKLRW	WEAKLIER	AEEINSSS	EASINESS	AEELMNTT	MANTELET
AEEIKLST	LEAKIEST	AEEINSTT	TETANISE	AEELMPRT	PALM TREE
AEEIKLSV	VASELIKE	AEEINSTV	NAIVETES	AEELMPRX	EXEMPLAR
AEEIKLVW	WAVELIKE	AEEINSVW	SINE WAVE	AEELMPRY	EMPYREAL
AEEIKMMT	MAKE TIME		WEAVES IN	AEELMPSX	EXAMPLES
AEEIKMTT	TAKE TIME	AEEINTTZ	TETANIZE	AEELMPTT	TEMPLATE
AEEIKPST	PEAKIEST	AEEIPPSU	EUPEPSIA	AEELMSSS	SEAMLESS
	STEAK PIE	AEEIPPTT	APPETITE	AEELMSTU	EMULATES
AEEIKPTT	KEEP AT IT	AEEIPRRR	REPAIRER	AEELNNPS	ENPLANES
AEEILLLT	TELL A LIE	AEEIPSTX	EXPIATES	AEELNNRT	LANNERET
AEEILLRT	LAETRILE	AEEIQRSU	QUEASIER	AEELNNSS	LEANNESS
AEEILLST	SEE IT ALL	AEEIRRST	ARTERIES	AEELNOPR	PERONEAL
AEEILMMN	MELAMINE	AEEIRRTX	REAR EXIT	AEELNOPT	ANTELOPE
AEEILMMT	MEALTIME	AEEIRRVW	REAR VIEW		OPEN LATE
AEEILMNS	MELANISE	AEEIRSST	SERIATES	AEELNORU	ALEURONE
AEEILMNZ	MELANIZE	AEEIRSTT	ITERATES	AEELNORV	LEAN OVER
AEEILMRS	MEASLIER		TREATIES	AEELNPSS	PALENESS
AEEILMRT	MATERIEL		TREATISE	AEELNRRS	LEARNERS
	REAL-TIME	AEEIRSTW	AS IT WERE	AEELNRSS	REALNESS
AEEILNPR	PERINEAL		SWEATIER	AEELNRST	ETERNALS
AEEILNPS	PENALISE		WEARIEST	AEELNRSV	ENSLAVER
AEEILNPZ	PENALIZE	AEEIRSVV	AVERSIVE	AEELNRSW	RENEWALS
AEEILNRT	ENTAILER	AEEISTTT	STEATITE	AEELNRTV	LEVANTER
	TREENAIL	AEEITUVX	EXUVIATE		RELEVANT
AEEILNSV	VASELINE	AEEJLNPT	JET PLANE	AEELNRTX	EXTERNAL
AEEILORT	AEROLITE	AEEJNRST	SERJEANT	AEELNSST	LAST SEEN
AEEILOTT	ETIOLATE	AEEJRSTW	SWEET JAR		LATENESS
AEEILPPP	APPLE PIE	AEEKLLST	SKELETAL		NET SALES
AEEILPRS	ESPALIER	AEEKLMMU	MAMELUKE	AEELNSSV	ENSLAVES
	PEARLIES	AEEKLMOV	MAKE LOVE	AEELNSTW	LATE NEWS
AEEILQSU	EQUALISE	AEEKLMRT	TELEMARK	AEELNSWY	WESLEYAN
AEEILQUZ	EQUALIZE	AEEKLSTW	LAST WEEK	AEELNTUV	EVENTUAL
AEEILRRT	RETAILER	AEEKLSTY	EYESTALK		NET VALUE
AEEILRSS	REALISES	AEEKMNSW	MAKE NEWS	AEELOPRV	LEAP OVER
AEEILRST	ATELIERS	AEEKMORV	MAKE OVER	AEELOPSX	POLEAXES
	EARLIEST	AEEKMPRW	KEEP WARM	AEELORST	OLEASTER
	REALTIES	AEEKMRST	MEERKATS		ROSE LATE
	RISE LATE	AEEKMRSU	MAKE SURE	AEELORSY	LEO SAYER
AEEILRSZ	REALIZES	AEEKMSSU	MAKES USE	AEELORTV	ELEVATOR
	SLEAZIER	AEEKNNNS	NANKEENS	AEELOTTT	TEETOTAL
AEEILRTT	LATERITE	AEEKNOTT	TAKE NOTE	AEELOTTW	TEA TOWEL
	LITERATE	AEEKNPSW	NEWSPEAK	AEELOTUV	LEAVE OUT
AEEILRTV	RELATIVE	AEEKNRSS	SNEAKERS	AEELPRRT	PALTERER
AEEILRVZ	VELARIZE	AEEKNRSW	WAKENERS	AEELPRSS	RELAPSES
AEEILSTV	LEAVES IT	AEEKNSSW	WEAKNESS	AEELPRST	PRELATES
AEEILTTV	LEVITATE	AEEKORRV	RAKE OVER	AEELPRSU	PLEASURE
AEEILTXX	TAX EXILE	AEEKORST	OAK TREES	AEELPSTT	PALETTES
AEEIMMNT	MEAN TIME	AEEKORTV	OVERTAKE	AEELQRSU	SQUEALER
	MEANTIME		TAKE OVER	AEELRRST	ALTERERS
AEEIMNRX	EXAMINER		TAKE-OVER	AEELRRSV	REVERSAL
AEEIMNSS	NEMESIAS		TAKEOVER	AEELRRTU	URETERAL
AEEIMNST	MATINEES	AEEKPRSS	SPEAKERS	AEELRSST	TEARLESS
AEEIMNSX	EXAMINES	AEEKQRSU	SQUEAKER	AEELRSTY	EASTERLY
AEEIMPST	MEAT PIES	AEEKRRST	STREAKER	AEELRSUV	REVALUES
AEEIMRST	EMIRATES	AEELLLPT	PELLETAL	AEELRSVY	AVERSELY
	STEAMIER	AEELLLTT	TELLTALE	AEELRTVY	VERY LATE
AEEIMSST	SEAMIEST	AEELLMNW	MEAN WELL	AEELSTTW	SWEATLET
AEEIMSTT	ESTIMATE	AEELLMYY	ALL MY EYE	AEELSTTY	LAYETTES
	MEATIEST	AEELLNOT	LET ALONE	AEELSTVW	WAVELETS
AEEIMSTV	SAVE TIME	AEELLNOV	ON A LEVEL	AEEMMPSY	EMPYEMAS

AEEMMRST	AMMETERS	AEENSTWY	WENT EASY	AEFFORST	AFFOREST
AEEMMSST	MESSMATE	AEEOPRRT	PERORATE		TEARS OFF
AEEMMNNOS	ANEMONES	AEEOPRST	OPERATES	AEFFORSW	WEARS OFF
AEEMMNNPS	PEN NAMES	AEEOPRSW	SEA POWER	AEFFOSTV	STAVE OFF
AEEMMNNRT	REMANENT	AEEOPRTT	OPERETTA	AEFFRSST	STAFFERS
AEEMMNNSS	MEANNESS	AEEORRTV	OVER RATE	AEFGGIIV	GIVE A FIG
AEEMMNORR	EARN MORE		OVERRATE	AEFGGMRS	FARM EGGS
AEEMMNPRS	SPEARMEN	AEEORSST	TEA ROSES	AEFGHINR	HANG FIRE
AEEMMNPRT	PERMEANT	AEEORSSV	OVERSEAS	AEFGHOVY	HEAVY FOG
AEEMMNPRY	EMPYREAN	AEEORSTU	SEA ROUTE	AEFGIIRS	GASIFIER
AEEMMNPST	PET NAMES	AEEORSTV	OVEREATS	AEFGIISS	GASIFIES
AEEMMNPTV	PAVEMENT	AEEORSVW	OVERAWES	AEFGIKNR	FREAKING
AEEMMNQUY	MAY QUEEN	AEEOSSTU	EASES OUT	AEFGILNR	FINAGLER
AEEMMNRTU	NUMERATE	AEEPPRRR	PREPARER	AEFGILNS	FINAGLES
AEEMMNRTV	AVERMENT	AEEPPRRS	PREPARES	AEFGILOS	FOLIAGES
AEEMMNRTW	WATERMEN	AEEPPRRT	PARTERRE	AEFGILTT	GET A LIFT
AEEMMNRTX	EXTRA MEN	AEEPPRRT	PATTERER	AEFGIMTU	FUMIGATE
AEEMMNRUV	MANEUVER	AEEPPRTU	APERTURE	AEFGINOR	GO IN FEAR
AEEMMNRVY	EVERY MAN	AEEPRSSS	ASPERSES	AEFGINST	FEASTING
	EVERYMAN		REPASSES	AEFGIRRT	RARE GIFT
AEEMMNSSS	SAMENESS	AEEPRSTU	UPAS TREE	AEFGIRRU	ARGUFIER
AEEMMNSST	TAMENESS	AEEPRSTZ	TRAPEZES	AEFGIRSS	GAS FIRES
AEEMORSU	MOUSE-EAR	AEEPRSYY	EASY PREY	AEFGIRST	FRIGATES
AEEMPRRT	TAMPERER	AEERRRST	ARRESTER	AEFGIRSU	ARGUFIES
AEEMPRTY	PETER MAY	AEERRSST	SERRATES	AEFGISTU	FATIGUES
AEEMPSTU	AMPUTEES	AEERRSSU	REASSURE	AEFGLLOP	FLAG POLE
AEEMQRSU	MARQUEES	AEERRSSW	SWEARERS	AEFGLMNU	FUGLEMAN
AEEMQTTU	MAQUETTE	AEERRSTT	RETREATS	AEFGLOPR	LEAPFROG
AEEMRRSS	SMEARERS		TREATERS	AEFGLRTU	GRATEFUL
AEEMRRST	STREAMER	AEERRSTU	TREASURE	AEFGMNRT	FRAGMENT
AEEMRRSST	MASSETER	AEERRSTV	TRAVERSE	AEFGNORT	FRONTAGE
	STEAMERS	AEERRSTW	SEWER RAT	AEFGNOST	GONE FAST
AEEMRSSU	MEASURES		WATERERS	AEFGNRTU	GREAT FUN
AEEMRSTT	TEAMSTER	AEERRSVW	WAVERERS	AEFGOPRU	PAGE FOUR
AEEMRSTY	MAY TREES	AEERSSST	SEE STARS	AEFGORTT	FROTTAGE
AEEMSSSU	MASSEUSE	AEERSSSY	ASSEYERS	AEFGOSST	GOES FAST
AEEMSSTU	MEATUSES	AEERSSTT	RESTATES	AEFHIKRS	FREAKISH
AEENNQTU	QUEEN ANT	AEERSSTW	SWEATERS	AEFHILLM	HALF MILE
AEENNRSS	ENSNARES	AEERSTTT	ATTESTER	AEFHILLN	FELLAHIN
	NEARNESS	AEERVWYY	EVERY WAY	AEFHILMT	HALF TIME
AEENNRTV	REVENANT	AEESSSSS	ASSESSES		HALFTIME
AEENNSSS	SANENESS	AEFFGIRS	GIRAFFES	AEFHILOX	FIX A HOLE
AEENNSST	NEATNESS	AEFFGOST	OFF STAGE	AEFHILRS	FLASHIER
AEENNTVY	ANY EVENT		OFFSTAGE	AEFHILSZ	HALF SIZE
AEENOPRS	OPEN EARS	AEFFGRSU	SUFFRAGE	AEFHIMSS	FAMISHES
	PERSONAE	AEFFHILL	HALF-LIFE	AEFHIRRS	FRESH AIR
AEENOPRT	TEAR OPEN	AEFFHKOS	SHAKE OFF	AEFHISTV	HAVE FITS
AEENOPRU	EUROPEAN	AEFFHLLT	LEFT HALF	AEFHLMRT	HALF TERM
AEENOPSS	OPEN SEAS		LEFT-HALF	AEFHLMSU	SHAMEFUL
AEENORRS	REASONER	AEFFILUV	EFFLUVIA	AEFHLNOT	HALFTONE
AEENORSS	SEASONER	AEFFIPRS	PIAFFERS	AEFHLNSS	HALFNESS
AEENORST	RESONATE	AEFFKMOS	MAKES OFF	AEFHLORY	HOLY FEAR
AEENORTV	RENOVATE	AEFFKNOS	SNEAK OFF	AEFHLRSS	FLASHERS
AEENORVW	OVENWARE	AEFFKNOT	TAKEN OFF	AEFHLRTY	FATHERLY
AEENOTTU	EATEN OUT	AEFFKORS	RAKES OFF	AEFHLSTT	FELT HATS
AEENPPRT	PETER PAN	AEFFKOST	TAKEOFFS	AEFHMMOR	HOME FARM
AEENPRUV	PARVENUE		TAKES OFF	AEFHMNRS	FRESHMAN
AEENRRSS	RARENESS	AEFFLLLT	FELL FLAT	AEFHMORS	FOR SHAME
AEENRRSW	ANSWERER	AEFFLLRU	FULL FARE	AEFHORSW	SHOW FEAR
AEENRRSY	YEARNERS	AEFFLLTT	LEFT FLAT	AEFHRSTT	FARTHEST
AEENRRVW	RAW NERVE	AEFFLNSS	SNAFFLES	AEFIILLN	NAIL FILE
AEENRRVY	VERY NEAR	AEFFLNTU	AFFLUENT	AEFIILMS	FAMILIES
AEENRSST	ASSENTER	AEFFLORU	FOUR-LEAF	AEFIILNS	FINALISE
	EARNESTS	AEFFLOSS	OFF SALES	AEFIILNZ	FINALIZE
AEENRSTT	ENTREATS		SEALS OFF	AEFIILRR	AIR RIFLE
AEENRSTV	VETERANS	AEFFLRSW	WAFFLERS	AEFIILRS	FAIR ISLE
AEENRSTY	TEN YEARS	AEFFMRSU	EARMUFFS	AEFIILRT	LIT A FIRE
AEENRTTY	ENTREATY	AEFFOOST	OFF TO SEA	AEFIIMRS	RAMIFIES
AEENRTXY	NEXT YEAR	AEFFOPRT	TAPER OFF	AEFIIMTX	FIX A TIME
AEENSSUV	NAEVUSES	AEFFOPRY	PAY OFFER	AEFIINNR	FINE RAIN
AEENSTTW	WENT EAST				

Code	Word	Code	Word	Code	Word
AEFIINRS	FINE AIRS / FRIESIAN	AEFKLLOT	FOLK TALE	AEFNOPRS	PROFANES
AEFIIPRT	APERITIF	AEFKLNRS	FLANKERS	AEFNORRW	FOREWARN
AEFIIRRS	FRIARIES	AEFKLNTU	FUEL TANK	AEFNORRY	YEARN FOR
AEFIIRST	RATIFIES	AEFKLOTU	FLAKE OUT	AEFNORST	SEAFRONT
AEFIITVX	FIXATIVE	AEFKMNSU	MAKES FUN	AEFNORVW	FAWN OVER
AEFIKLST	FLAKIEST	AEFKMOPR	PEAK FORM	AEFNPTTU	FATTEN UP
AEFIKLTY	FLY A KITE	AEFKMORS	MAKES FOR	AEFNRRST	TRANSFER
AEFIKMMR	MAKE FIRM	AEFKNORS	FORSAKEN	AEFNRRTU	RUN AFTER
AEFILLNN	FALLEN IN	AEFKNRST	FRANKEST	AEFNRRUY	FUNERARY
AEFILLST	LIES FLAT	AEFKOPRS	SPEAK FOR	AEFNSSST	FASTNESS
AEFILMNR	INFLAMER / RIFLEMAN	AEFKORSS	FORSAKES	AEFNSSTU	UNSAFEST
AEFILMNS	IN FLAMES / INFLAMES	AEFKORTU	FREAK OUT / FREAK-OUT	AEFNSTTW	WENT FAST
AEFILMNT	FILAMENT	AEFLLLMU	FULL MEAL	AEFOOPTT	POT OF TEA
AEFILMRY	ARMY LIFE	AEFLLLST	LETS FALL	AEFOORTW	FOOTWEAR
AEFILMSY	MAYFLIES	AEFLLNNS	FLANNELS	AEFOPRRT	FOREPART
AEFILNNR	INFERNAL	AEFLLNOX	FELL AN OX	AEFORRSW	FORSWEAR
AEFILNPS	LIFE SPAN	AEFLLORV	FALL OVER	AEFORSTW	SOFTWARE
AEFILNPT	FELT PAIN	AEFLLPRY	FALL PREY	AEFORSTY	FORESTAY
AEFILNRT	INFLATER	AEFLLPTU	PLATEFUL	AEFORTUY	AFTER YOU
AEFILNRU	FRAULEIN	AEFLLRUX	FLEXURAL	AEFOSSTT	SOFT SEAT
AEFILNST	INFLATES	AEFLLSSW	FLAWLESS	AEFRRSST	STRAFERS
AEFILOOR	AEROFOIL	AEFLLSTY	FESTALLY	AEFRSSTW	FRETSAWS
AEFILORS	FORESAIL	AEFLLTYZ	FELT LAZY	AEFRSTVY	VERY FAST
AEFILOST	FOLIATES	AEFLMNOW	MEN OF LAW	AEGGGINN	ENGAGING
AEFILPRX	PREFIXAL	AEFLMORU	FORMULAE / FUMAROLE	AEGGHHIR	HIGH GEAR
AEFILPST	FILE PAST / FLEA PITS / FLEAPITS / PAST LIFE	AEFLMOSS	FOAMLESS	AEGGHHIW	HIGH WAGE
		AEFLMRTW	FELT WARM	AEGGHIRS	SHAGGIER
AEFILPSV	FIVE LAPS	AEFLNORU	LANE FOUR	AEGGHISS	HAGGISES
AEFILPTT	LEFT A TIP	AEFLNOST	FLAT NOSE	AEGGHORU	ROUGHAGE
AEFILRST	FRAILEST	AEFLNOTT	FLAT NOTE	AEGGIINV	GINGIVAE
AEFILRSU	FAILURES	AEFLNOWY	ONLY A FEW	AEGGILLN	ALLEGING
AEFILRTT	FILTRATE	AEFLNRSU	FUNERALS	AEGGILLR	GRILLAGE
AEFILRTU	FILATURE	AEFLNSST	FLATNESS	AEGGILMN	GLEAMING
AEFILSSW	SAWFLIES	AEFLNSTT	FLATTENS	AEGGILNN	GLEANING
AEFILSTT	FLATTIES	AEFLOORS	SEA FLOOR	AEGGILNR	LARGE GIN / REGALING
AEFILSTU	FISTULAE	AEFLOPRY	FOREPLAY	AEGGILNT	GELATING
AEFILSTV	FESTIVAL	AEFLORST	FLOATERS	AEGGILNU	LEAGUING
AEFILSTW	FLATWISE	AEFLOSTT	FALSETTO	AEGGILOU	OIL GAUGE
AEFIMNST	MANIFEST	AEFLPPRS	FLAPPERS	AEGGINNR	ANGERING / ENRAGING
AEFIMNSW	WINS FAME	AEFLPPRY	FLY PAPER / FLYPAPER	AEGGINNT	NEGATING
AEFIMORT	FOR A TIME	AEFLPRSS	FELSPARS	AEGGINNV	AVENGING
AEFIMRRS	FIREARMS	AEFLPRSU	FLARE-UPS / FLARES UP	AEGGINOR	GEORGIAN
AEFIMSTT	FAST TIME			AEGGINOS	SEAGOING
AEFINNST	INFANTES	AEFLPRSY	PALFREYS	AEGGINRS	GEARINGS / GREASING
AEFINOPR	PINAFORE	AEFLRSSU	REFUSALS		
AEFINPSS	FINE PASS	AEFLRSTT	FLATTERS	AEGGINRW	WAGERING
AEFINRRS	REFRAINS	AEFLRSZZ	FRAZZLES	AEGGIOPR	ARPEGGIO
AEFINRRT	FAIR RENT	AEFLRTTU	AFLUTTER	AEGGIPRT	GET A GRIP
AEFINRRU	UNFAIRER	AEFLRTTY	FLAT TYRE / FLATTERY	AEGGISSW	SWAGGIES
AEFINRSS	FAIRNESS	AEFLSSTU	FLATUSES	AEGGITUV	GIVE A TUG
AEFINRST	FINE ARTS	AEFLSTTT	FLATTEST	AEGGLLMS	SMALL EGG
AEFINSTT	FAINTEST	AEFLSTTU	TASTEFUL	AEGGLMMY	GAMMY LEG
AEFINSTY	IN SAFETY	AEFLSTUW	WASTEFUL	AEGGLNOT	GET ALONG
AEFIPRRT	FIRETRAP	AEFMNORS	FORAMENS	AEGGLNPT	EGG PLANT / EGGPLANT
AEFIPRTV	TRAP FIVE	AEFMNORW	MEN OF WAR / MEN-OF-WAR		
AEFIPSTV	FIVE PAST			AEGGLORY	GARGOYLE
AEFIRRRS	FARRIERS	AEFMNOTW	FAT WOMEN	AEGGLRST	STRAGGLE
AEFIRRRY	FARRIERY	AEFMNRRY	FERRYMAN	AEGGLRSY	GREYLAGS
AEFIRRVY	VERY FAIR	AEFMORRS	FOREARMS	AEGGMMSU	MUGS GAME
AEFIRSTV	FIVE STAR / FIVE-STAR	AEFMORST	FOREMAST	AEGGMORT	MORTGAGE
		AEFMORVW	WAVE FORM / WAVEFORM	AEGGNRST	GANGSTER
AEFISTTT	FATTIEST / FIT STATE	AEFMOSTV	MOVE FAST	AEGGNRTY	GET ANGRY
		AEFMPRSU	FRAME-UPS / FRAMES UP	AEGGOPRU	AGE GROUP
AEFJKOOR	FOR A JOKE			AEGGRSST	STAGGERS
AEFJMOSX	JAMES FOX	AEFNNSTU	UNFASTEN	AEGGRSSW	SWAGGERS
AEFJSTUW	JUST A FEW	AEFNOPRR	PROFANER	AEGHHIRT	HIGH RATE
				AEGHHISS	HIGH SEAS
				AEGHILLS	SHIGELLA
				AEGHILLT	LIGHT ALE

AEGHILMT	MEGALITH
AEGHILNR	NARGHILE
AEGHILNT	ATHELING
AEGHILNX	EXHALING
AEGHILRT	LITHARGE
AEGHINNN	HENNAING
AEGHINRS	HEARINGS
	SHEARING
AEGHINRT	EARTHING
	GATHER IN
	HEARTING
AEGHINRV	HAVERING
AEGHINSV	SHEAVING
AEGHIPPR	EPIGRAPH
AEGHIPRT	GRAPHITE
AEGHIRRS	GHARRIES
AEGHIRRT	RIGHT EAR
AEGHIRRY	GREY HAIR
AEGHIRTT	GREAT HIT
AEGHLLOT	ALL THE GO
AEGHLNOS	HALOGENS
AEGHLNTT	AT LENGTH
AEGHLOPY	HYPOGEAL
AEGHLOSS	GALOSHES
AEGHLOSV	GO HALVES
AEGHLOSW	SHOW A LEG
AEGHLOTV	THE VOLGA
AEGHLRTU	LAUGHTER
AEGHLRTY	LETHARGY
AEGHMOPT	APOTHEGM
AEGHNNOR	HANGER-ON
AEGHNOPT	HEPTAGON
	PATHOGEN
AEGHNORV	HANG OVER
	HANGOVER
	OVERHANG
AEGHNOSX	HEXAGONS
AEGHNOTT	THE TANGO
AEGHOORS	GO ASHORE
AEGHORST	SHORTAGE
AEGHORSU	ROUGH SEA
AEGHORSV	ASH GROVE
AEGHOSST	HOSTAGES
AEGHPRTU	GATHER UP
AEGIIKLP	LIKE A PIG
AEGIILLU	AIGUILLE
AEGIILTT	LITIGATE
AEGIIMNN	GEMINIAN
AEGIIMNR	MIGRAINE
AEGIIMNS	IMAGINES
AEGIIMNT	GAIN TIME
AEGIIMTT	MITIGATE
AEGIINNR	ARGININE
AEGIINNT	EATING IN
AEGIINTT	EATING IT
AEGIIPTV	GIVE A TIP
AEGIIRRT	IRRIGATE
AEGIJOTV	GIVE A JOT
AEGIJRTU	GUJERATI
AEGIKLLO	LIKE A LOG
AEGIKLNR	KING LEAR
AEGIKLNS	LINKAGES
AEGIKLNW	WEAKLING
AEGIKLOT	GOATLIKE
AEGIKMNS	SKIN GAME
AEGIKNNS	SNEAKING
AEGIKNNW	WAKENING
AEGIKNPS	SPEAKING
AEGIKNRW	WREAKING
AEGIKNTW	TAKE WING
	TWEAKING

AEGIKSTW	GAWKIEST
AEGILLMS	LEGALISM
AEGILLNO	GOAL LINE
AEGILLNY	GENIALLY
AEGILLPR	PILLAGER
AEGILLPS	PILLAGES
AEGILLRV	VILLAGER
AEGILLST	LEGALIST
	STILLAGE
AEGILLSU	ILL-USAGE
AEGILLTU	LIGULATE
AEGILLTY	LEGALITY
AEGILMNR	GERMINAL
	MALINGER
AEGILMNS	GALENISM
AEGILMNT	LIGAMENT
AEGILMST	TIME LAGS
AEGILNNR	LEARNING
AEGILNNS	LEANINGS
AEGILNNW	WEANLING
AEGILNOR	REGIONAL
AEGILNOS	GASOLINE
AEGILNOT	GELATION
	LEGATION
AEGILNPR	PEARLING
AEGILNPS	ELAPSING
	PLEASING
AEGILNPT	PLEATING
AEGILNRS	ENGRAILS
	REALIGNS
AEGILNRT	ALERTING
	ALTERING
	INTEGRAL
	RELATING
	TRIANGLE
AEGILNRX	RELAXING
AEGILNRY	LAYERING
	RELAYING
	YEARLING
AEGILNSS	GLASSINE
AEGILNST	GENITALS
AEGILNSV	LEAVINGS
	SVENGALI
AEGILNTW	WANGLE IT
AEGILNTX	EXALTING
AEGILOPS	SPOILAGE
AEGILOPT	PILOTAGE
AEGILORS	SERAGLIO
AEGILPPS	SLIPPAGE
AEGILRSY	GREASILY
AEGILRSZ	GLAZIERS
AEGILRTU	LIGATURE
AEGILRTY	REGALITY
AEGILRVW	LAWGIVER
AEGILRYZ	GLAZIERY
AEGIMNNR	IN GERMAN
AEGIMNNS	MEANINGS
AEGIMNRR	REARMING
AEGIMNRS	SMEARING
AEGIMNRT	EMIGRANT
AEGIMNRU	GERANIUM
AEGIMNSS	GAMINESS
AEGIMNST	MANGIEST
	STEAMING
AEGIMNSV	MING VASE
	VEGANISM
AEGIMNSW	WIN GAMES
AEGIMPRS	EPIGRAMS
AEGIMQRU	QUAGMIRE
AEGIMQUZ	QUIZ GAME
AEGIMRRS	ARMIGERS

AEGIMRST	GEMARIST
	MIGRATES
AEGIMSSU	MISUSAGE
AEGINNNX	ANNEXING
AEGINNOS	ANGINOSE
AEGINNOT	NEGATION
AEGINNRS	EARNINGS
	ENGRAINS
	GRANNIES
AEGINNRV	RAVENING
AEGINNRY	YEARNING
AEGINNST	ANTIGENS
	GENTIANS
	NEAT GINS
	NET GAINS
AEGINNSU	SANGUINE
AEGINORS	IRON AGES
	ORGANISE
AEGINORT	IRON GATE
AEGINORZ	ORGANIZE
AEGINOSS	AGONISES
AEGINOSZ	AGONIZES
AEGINOTV	GAVE IN TO
	GO NATIVE
AEGINPPR	PAPERING
AEGINPRS	SPEARING
AEGINPRT	TAPERING
AEGINPSU	EASING UP
AEGINPTU	EATING UP
AEGINPTY	EGYPTIAN
AEGINQTU	EQUATING
AEGINRRS	EARRINGS
AEGINRRV	AVERRING
AEGINRSS	ASSIGNER
AEGINRST	ANGRIEST
	GANISTER
	GANTRIES
	INERT GAS
AEGINRTT	TREATING
AEGINRTV	AVERTING
	VINTAGER
AEGINRTW	WATERING
AEGINRVW	WAVERING
AEGINRVY	VINEGARY
AEGINRWY	WEARYING
AEGINSST	EASTINGS
	IN STAGES
AEGINSSY	ESSAYING
AEGINSTU	SAUTEING
AEGINSTV	VINTAGES
AEGINSTW	EAST WING
	SWEATING
AEGINVWY	GIVEN WAY
AEGIORSS	ARGOSIES
AEGIORST	GOT A RISE
AEGIORSV	VIRAGOES
AEGIOSTX	GEOTAXIS
AEGIPTUV	GAVE IT UP
AEGIRRSZ	GRAZIERS
AEGIRSUU	AUGURIES
AEGIRTTT	GREAT TIT
AEGIRTTW	GREAT WIT
AEGISSST	GASSIEST
AEGISVWY	GIVES WAY
AEGJORTY	GREAT JOY
AEGJRTUW	WATER JUG
AEGKLOPT	KEPT GOAL
AEGKORWW	GROW WEAK
AEGLLNNO	LONG LANE
AEGLLNOS	GALLEONS
AEGLLOPR	GALLOPER

AEGLLORS	ALLEGROS	AEGNOORS	OREGANOS	AEHINNTX	XANTHINE
AEGLLORY	ALLEGORY	AEGNOPRR	PARERGON	AEHINOPV	VAIN HOPE
AEGLLOST	LOST A LEG	AEGNORRY	ORANGERY	AEHINORT	ANTI-HERO
AEGLLOTT	TOLLGATE	AEGNORST	GO ASTERN		ON THE AIR
AEGLLRVY	GRAVELLY	AEGNORSW	WAGONERS	AEHINPPY	EPIPHANY
AEGLLSST	LAST LEGS	AEGNORTT	ON TARGET	AEHINPRT	PERIANTH
AEGLMNNO	MANGONEL	AEGNOSSV	GAS OVENS	AEHINPST	THESPIAN
AEGLMNTU	GUN METAL	AEGNOSSY	NOSEGAYS	AEHINRST	HAIR NETS
	GUNMETAL	AEGNOSTW	TEA GOWNS		THE RAINS
AEGLMPSU	PLUMAGES	AEGNOTTU	TOTE A GUN	AEHINRSV	VANISHER
AEGLMRSU	LARGE SUM	AEGNPPST	PEG PANTS	AEHINRTW	IN THE RAW
AEGLNNPT	PLANGENT	AEGNRRST	STRANGER		IN THE WAR
AEGLNNSY	LANG SYNE	AEGNRRTU	RANG TRUE	AEHINRTZ	HERTZIAN
AEGLNNTU	UNTANGLE	AEGNRTTU	GET A TURN	AEHINSSS	HESSIANS
AEGLNOOP	OPEN GOAL	AEGOPPST	STOPPAGE	AEHINSST	SHANTIES
AEGLNOOW	GONE AWOL	AEGOPRST	PORTAGES	AEHINSSV	VANISHES
AEGLNOST	TANGELOS	AEGOPSST	POSTAGES	AEHINSSZ	HAZINESS
AEGLNOVW	LONG WAVE	AEGOPSTT	GATEPOST	AEHINSTT	HESITANT
AEGLNPRS	GRAPNELS	AEGOPSTW	TWO PAGES	AEHINTTW	WHITE ANT
AEGLNPSS	SPANGLES	AEGORRTT	GARROTTE	AEHINTWY	IN THE WAY
AEGLNRRW	WRANGLER	AEGORSTU	OUTRAGES	AEHIOPRS	APHORISE
AEGLNRST	STRANGLE	AEGORSVY	VOYAGERS	AEHIOPRU	EUPHORIA
AEGLNRSU	GRANULES	AEGORUVW	WOVE A RUG	AEHIOPRZ	APHORIZE
	LASER GUN	AEGOSSTV	GAS STOVE	AEHIORST	HOARIEST
AEGLNRSW	WANGLERS	AEGOSTTV	GAVOTTES	AEHIORTU	THIOUREA
	WRANGLES	AEGOSTTW	STAGE TWO	AEHIPPRS	SAPPHIRE
AEGLNRSY	LARYNGES	AEGPSSTU	UPSTAGES	AEHIPPST	EPITAPHS
AEGLNRUY	GUNLAYER	AEGRRSSY	RYEGRASS	AEHIPRSS	PARISHES
AEGLNSTT	GANTLETS	AEGRSTTY	STRATEGY	AEHIRRRS	HARRIERS
AEGLNSUW	GUNWALES	AEHHILSS	SHEILAHS	AEHIRRST	TRASHIER
AEGLNTTU	GAUNTLET	AEHHRRST	THRASHER	AEHIRRSV	RAVISHER
AEGLNTUU	UNGULATE	AEHHRSST	HARSHEST	AEHIRRSY	AYRSHIRE
AEGLOOPU	APOLOGUE		THRASHES	AEHIRSSV	RAVISHES
AEGLOORY	AEROLOGY	AEHIIKLR	HAIRLIKE	AEHIRSTU	THESAURI
AEGLOOSW	GOES AWOL	AEHIILNR	HAIRLINE	AEHIRSTY	HYSTERIA
AEGLOPRS	PERGOLAS	AEHIILNW	IN A WHILE		THIS YEAR
AEGLOPRW	GROW PALE	AEHIIMNT	THIAMINE	AEHISSTT	ATHEISTS
AEGLORSW	LOW GEARS	AEHIIOPT	ETHIOPIA		HASTIEST
AEGLORTW	WATERLOG	AEHIIRSS	IRISH SEA		STAITHES
AEGLOSTT	GOT STALE	AEHIIRST	HAIRIEST	AEHISSTU	HIATUSES
AEGLOSTV	VOLTAGES	AEHIKMNR	KHMERIAN	AEHISSVW	HAS VIEWS
AEGLOSWW	LOW WAGES	AEHIKMST	MAKE HITS	AEHISSVY	YESHIVAS
AEGLPPRR	GRAPPLER	AEHIKSST	SHAKIEST	AEHJPRSW	JEWS HARP
AEGLPPRS	GRAPPLES	AEHIKSTT	TAKE THIS	AEHKMOPR	HOME PARK
AEGLPRSU	EAR PLUGS	AEHILMNY	HYMENIAL	AEHKNORT	THE KORAN
	EARPLUGS	AEHILMOS	HEMIOLAS	AEHKNPSU	SHAKEN UP
AEGLRRSU	REGULARS	AEHILMSW	LIMEWASH	AEHKNRST	THANKERS
AEGLRSTU	GESTURAL	AEHILNOP	APHELION	AEHKOPRU	PEAK HOUR
AEGMMRRU	RUMMAGER	AEHILNRS	INHALERS	AEHKOSTU	SHAKE OUT
AEGMMRSU	RUMMAGES	AEHILNTZ	ZENITHAL	AEHKPSSU	SHAKE-UPS
AEGMNNOT	MAGNETON	AEHILPRS	HARELIPS		SHAKES UP
AEGMNORV	MANGROVE	AEHILRSS	HAIRLESS	AEHLLLPY	PLAY HELL
AEGMNOST	MAGNETOS	AEHILRSU	HAULIERS	AEHLLLTY	LETHALLY
	MEGATONS	AEHILRSV	SHRIEVAL	AEHLLMSS	MESS HALL
	MONTAGES	AEHILRTT	THE TRIAL	AEHLMMNS	HELMSMAN
AEGMNRST	GARMENTS	AEHILRTY	EARTHILY	AEHLMNOS	MANHOLES
AEGMNRTU	ARGUMENT		HEARTILY	AEHLMNOT	METHANOL
AEGMNSTU	AUGMENTS	AEHILSSV	LAVISHES	AEHLMNSW	WELSHMAN
	MUTAGENS	AEHIMMNR	HAMMER IN	AEHLMNUY	HUMANELY
AEGMOOPR	POOR GAME	AEHIMNNU	INHUMANE	AEHLMORS	ARMHOLES
AEGMOORS	MOORAGES	AEHIMNSU	HUMANISE	AEHLMOST	HOT MEALS
AEGMOPRW	GAPEWORM	AEHIMNTW	WHITE MAN	AEHLMPPT	PAMPHLET
AEGMORSS	GOSSAMER	AEHIMNUZ	HUMANIZE	AEHLMRSS	HARMLESS
AEGMPRUZ	GAZUMPER	AEHIMPRS	SAMPHIRE	AEHLMRST	THERMALS
AEGMRRWW	GREW WARM		SERAPHIM	AEHLNPRS	SHRAPNEL
AEGMRSTW	GETS WARM	AEHIMPSS	EMPHASIS	AEHLNPTY	ENTHALPY
AEGNNOPT	PENTAGON		MISSHAPE	AEHLNRST	ENTHRALS
AEGNNOST	TONNAGES	AEHIMPST	SHIPMATE	AEHLNRTU	LUTHERAN
AEGNNPRT	PREGNANT	AEHIMRSS	MISHEARS	AEHLNTUZ	HAZEL NUT
AEGNNRTY	GANNETRY	AEHIMTTW	WHAT TIME?		HAZELNUT
AEGNNSTT	TANGENTS	AEHINNTV	IN THE VAN		

AEHLOPRT	PLETHORA	
AEHLOPST	LAST HOPE	
AEHLOPTT	HOT PLATE	
AEHLORST	RAT HOLES	
AEHLORSY	HOARSELY	
AEHLORTU	LATE HOUR	
AEHLORUV	HAUL OVER	
	OVERHAUL	
AEHLOSTW	LATE SHOW	
AEHLPPST	PAST HELP	
AEHLPRSS	SPLASHER	
AEHLPSSS	SPLASHES	
AEHLPSST	PATHLESS	
AEHLPSSU	LASHES UP	
AEHLPSTU	SULPHATE	
AEHLRRTU	URETHRAL	
AEHLRSSS	SLASHERS	
AEHLRSST	SLATHERS	
AEHLSSTY	HAS STYLE	
AEHLSTTY	STEALTHY	
AEHLSTUU	THE USUAL	
AEHLTTWZ	THE WALTZ	
AEHMMORS	RAMS HOME	
AEHMNOPT	ON THE MAP	
AEHMNORS	HORSEMAN	
	MENORAHS	
AEHMNOSU	HOUSEMAN	
ACHMNOTT	ON THE MAT	
AEHMNPPY	HAPPY MEN	
AEHMNPSY	SEA NYMPH	
AEHMNTUU	HUM A TUNE	
AEHMOPRT	METAPHOR	
AEHMOSTW	SOMEWHAT	
AEHMOSTY	STAY HOME	
AEHMRSSS	SMASHERS	
AEHMRSST	HAMSTERS	
AEHMRSSY	MYRA HESS	
AEHMSTTY	AMETHYST	
AEHMSUZZ	MEZUZAHS	
AEHNNOPT	PANTHEON	
AEHNNSUV	UNSHAVEN	
AEHNOPPY	PAY PHONE	
AEHNOPST	PHAETONS	
	PHONATES	
AEHNORST	NORTH SEA	
	SHERATON	
AEHNORTW	ON THE RAW	
AEHNOSTV	HAVE-NOTS	
AEHNOTWY	ON THE WAY	
AEHNPRSS	SHARPENS	
AEHNPRST	PANTHERS	
AEHNPRTY	HEN PARTY	
AEHNRSSS	RASHNESS	
AEHNRSTU	UNEARTHS	
AEHNRTTU	EARTHNUT	
AEHNSSWY	SAYS WHEN	
AEHNSTWW	WHATS NEW?	
AEHNTTWX	WHAT NEXT?	
AEHOOTTZ	AT THE ZOO	
AEHOPPRS	PROPHASE	
AEHOPPST	PAST HOPE	
AEHOPSST	TEA SHOPS	
AEHOPSTT	HEAT SPOT	
AEHOPSTU	PHASE OUT	
	PHASEOUT	
AEHOPSTW	PHASE TWO	
AEHOPTTT	AT THE TOP	
AEHOPTVY	TOP-HEAVY	
AEHORRRW	HARROWER	
AEHORRSW	WAR HORSE	
	WAR-HORSE	
AEHORSST	HOARSEST	
AEHORSSW	SAWHORSE	
AEHORSTT	RHEOSTAT	
AEHORSTU	SHARE OUT	
AEHORSTX	THORAXES	
AEHORSVW	WASH OVER	
AEHORTTW	HOT WATER	
	HOT-WATER	
AEHOSSTT	HOT SEATS	
AEHOSSTU	SOUTH SEA	
AEHPPSSU	SHAPES UP	
AEHPPSUV	HAVE PUPS	
AEHPRRSS	SHARPERS	
AEHPRSST	SHARPEST	
AEHPRSUW	WASHER-UP	
AEHPRSUX	HARUSPEX	
AEHPSSUW	WASHES UP	
AEHQSSSU	SQUASHES	
AEHRRSTU	URETHRAS	
AEHRRTTW	THWARTER	
AEHRSSTT	SHATTERS	
	THE STARS	
AEHRSSTV	HARVESTS	
AEHRSSTW	SWATHERS	
AEHSSTUX	EXHAUSTS	
AEIIINTT	INITIATE	
AEIIKLLT	TAILLIKE	
AEIIKNRS	KAISERIN	
AEIIKNTT	TAKE IT IN	
AEIILLRV	LIVE RAIL	
AEIILLTV	ILLATIVE	
AEIILMNN	MAIN LINE	
	MAINLINE	
AEIILMNS	ALIENISM	
AEIILMPR	IMPERIAL	
AEIILMSS	ISLAMISE	
AEIILMSZ	ISLAMIZE	
AEIILMTT	MILITATE	
AEIILNQU	AQUILINE	
AEIILNRR	AIRLINER	
AEIILNRS	AIR LINES	
	AIRLINES	
AEIILNRT	INERTIAL	
AEIILNST	ALIENIST	
	LATINISE	
	LITANIES	
AEIILNTZ	LATINIZE	
AEIILPPT	LIT A PIPE	
	TAILPIPE	
AEIILRSS	ISRAELIS	
AEIILRTT	LITERATI	
AEIILSTV	VITALISE	
AEIILTVZ	VITALIZE	
AEIIMMNT	MAIN ITEM	
AEIIMMRT	MARITIME	
AEIIMMSX	MAXIMISE	
AEIIMMXZ	MAXIMIZE	
AEIIMNTT	INTIMATE	
AEIIMNTU	MINUTIAE	
AEIIMNTV	VITAMIN E	
AEIIMPRR	IMPAIRER	
AEIIMRST	SERIATIM	
AEIIMSTT	IMITATES	
AEIINNRS	SIRENIAN	
AEIINNRT	TRIENNIA	
AEIINPRR	IN REPAIR	
AEIINRSS	AIRINESS	
AEIINSST	SANITISE	
AEIINSTV	VANITIES	
AEIINSTZ	SANITIZE	
AEIINSVV	INVASIVE	
AEIIPPRS	AIR PIPES	
AEIIPRRS	PRAIRIES	
AEIIPRST	PARITIES	
AEIIPRZZ	PIZZERIA	
AEIIRRST	RARITIES	
AEIIRRTT	IRRITATE	
AEIIRSST	SATIRISE	
AEIIRSTW	WISTERIA	
AEIIRSTZ	SATIRIZE	
AEIISTTV	VITIATES	
AEIISTVX	EXIT VISA	
AEIITTTV	TITIVATE	
AEIJKLMR	JIM LAKER	
AEIJLNSV	JAVELINS	
AEIJLOPS	JALOPIES	
AEIJLOSU	JALOUSIE	
AEIJMMST	JAMMIEST	
AEIJNRTU	JAUNTIER	
AEIJSTZZ	JAZZIEST	
AEIKKLNW	WEAK LINK	
AEIKKLST	TAKE SILK	
AEIKKMRT	KITE-MARK	
AEIKLLLW	WALL-LIKE	
AEIKLLMP	PALMLIKE	
AEIKLLNT	TAKEN ILL	
AEIKLLRS	REAL SILK	
AEIKLLST	SALTLIKE	
	TAKES ILL	
AEIKLNOV	NOVALIKE	
AEIKLNSS	SEALSKIN	
AEIKLNST	LANKIEST	
AEIKLOPT	LIKE A TOP	
AEIKLPSW	WASPLIKE	
AEIKLRST	STARLIKE	
AEIKMMRT	MARK TIME	
AEIKMNOS	ESKIMOAN	
AEIKMNRS	RAMEKINS	
AEIKMNST	MISTAKEN	
AEIKMPTU	MAKE IT UP	
AEIKMSST	MISTAKES	
AEIKNNSS	SNEAKS IN	
AEIKNOPY	PIANO KEY	
AEIKNOTT	TIE A KNOT	
AEIKNPSS	SEA PINKS	
AEIKNPST	SNAKE PIT	
AEIKNRSW	SWANKIER	
AEIKPRSS	APRES-SKI	
AEIKPTTT	KEPT AT IT	
AEIKPTTU	TAKE IT UP	
AEIKPTTY	TAKE PITY	
AEIKRSST	ASTERISK	
AEIKRSTW	WATER-SKI	
AEILLLMS	ALLELISM	
AEILLLNY	LINEALLY	
AEILLMNY	MENIALLY	
AEILLMSY	MESIALLY	
AEILLNNO	ALL IN ONE	
AEILLNRY	LINEARLY	
AEILLNSW	WELLSIAN	
AEILLNVY	VENIALLY	
AEILLOSS	LOESSIAL	
AEILLOTV	VOLATILE	
AEILLPST	PALLIEST	
	PASTILLE	
AEILLPSV	LIP SALVE	
AEILLQSU	SQUILLAE	
AEILLQTU	ALL QUIET	
AEILLRRY	RAILLERY	
AEILLRST	LITERALS	
AEILLRSY	SERIALLY	
AEILLRTT	ILL-TREAT	

AEILLSST	TAILLESS	AEILOSST	ISOLATES	AEIMPSTT	PAST TIME
AEILLSUV	ALLUSIVE	AEILOSTT	TOTALISE	AEIMQRSU	MARQUISE
AEILMMNS	MELANISM	AEILOSTV	VIOLATES	AEIMQSUU	ESQUIMAU
AEILMMOR	MEMORIAL	AEILOTTZ	TOTALIZE	AEIMRSST	ASTERISM
AEILMMOT	IMMOLATE	AEILPPPP	APPLE PIP	AEIMRSSY	EMISSARY
AEILMNNP	PLAIN MEN	AEILPPQU	APPLIQUE	AEIMRSTT	MISTREAT
AEILMNNS	LINESMAN	AEILPPRS	APPLIERS	AEIMRSTX	MATRIXES
AEILMNOS	SEMOLINA	AEILPRRS	REPRISAL	AEIMSSTT	ETATISMS
AEILMNPS	IMPANELS	AEILPRST	PILASTER		MISSTATE
	MANIPLES	AEILPRSV	PREVAILS	AEIMSSTZ	MESTIZAS
AEILMNRS	MARLINES	AEILPRXY	PYREXIAL	AEINNORT	ANOINTER
	MINERALS	AEILQRTU	QUARTILE	AEINNOSS	IN SEASON
AEILMNRT	TERMINAL		REQUITAL	AEINNOST	ESTONIAN
	TRAMLINE	AEILQSTU	LIQUATES		ETONIANS
AEILMNRU	RUN A MILE	AEILQSUY	QUEASILY	AEINNOTT	INTONATE
AEILMNST	AILMENTS	AEILQTUY	EQUALITY	AEINNOTV	INNOVATE
	ALIMENTS	AEILRRST	TRAILERS		VENATION
	MANLIEST	AEILRRTY	LITERARY	AEINNOWY	IN ONE WAY
	SALT MINE	AEILRSST	REALISTS	AEINNPRS	PANNIERS
AEILMOPR	PROEMIAL		SALTIRES	AEINNRST	ENTRAINS
AEILMORS	MORALISE	AEILRSVV	REVIVALS		TRANNIES
AEILMORZ	MORALIZE	AEILRTWY	WATERILY	AEINNSST	INSANEST
AEILMPRV	PRIMEVAL	AEILSSST	SETS SAIL	AEINNSSV	VAINNESS
AEILMPST	PALMIEST	AEILSSTT	SALTIEST	AEINNSSZ	ZANINESS
AEILMRTT	REMITTAL	AEILSTWY	SWEATILY	AEINNSUV	VENUSIAN
AEILMSTT	LAST TIME	AEILSTYY	YEASTILY	AEINOPPT	ANTIPOPE
AEILMSTU	SIMULATE	AEIMMNNT	IMMANENT	AEINOPRT	ATROPINE
AEILMSTY	STEAMILY	AEIMMNOT	AMMONITE	AEINOQTU	EQUATION
AEILMTTU	MUTILATE	AEIMMNSS	MISNAMES	AEINORRT	ANTERIOR
	ULTIMATE	AEIMMRRS	SMARMIER	AEINORRW	IRONWARE
AEILNNOS	SOLANINE	AEIMMRTU	IMMATURE	AEINORSS	SENSORIA
AEILNNRT	INTERNAL	AEIMNNNR	INNER MAN	AEINORST	NOTARIES
AEILNNSY	INSANELY	AEIMNNOT	NOMINATE		NOTARISE
AEILNNTY	INNATELY	AEIMNOPT	PTOMAINE		SENORITA
AEILNORS	AILERONS	AEIMNORS	MORAINES	AEINORSV	AVERSION
AEILNORT	ORIENTAL		ROMANIES	AEINORTZ	NOTARIZE
	RELATION		ROMANISE	AEINOSSV	EVASIONS
AEILNORV	OVERLAIN	AEIMNORT	MARONITE	AEINOSTT	EATS INTO
AEILNOSS	SEA LIONS	AEIMNORZ	ROMANIZE	AEINPPPS	PANPIPES
AEILNPRS	PRALINES	AEIMNOSW	WOMANISE	AEINPPRS	SNAPPIER
AEILNPRT	TRIPLANE	AEIMNOTT	AT NO TIME	AEINPRRT	TERRAPIN
AEILNPSS	PAINLESS	AEIMNOTZ	MONAZITE	AEINPRSS	PERSIANS
	SPANIELS	AEIMNOWZ	WOMANIZE	AEINPRST	PAINTERS
AEILNPST	PANTILES	AEIMNRRS	MARINERS		PANTRIES
	PLAINEST	AEIMNRSS	NEAR MISS		PERTAINS
AEILNPSX	AXLE PINS		SEMINARS	AEINPSTT	PATIENTS
	EXPLAINS	AEIMNRST	MINARETS	AEINPSTU	PETUNIAS
AEILNPTT	TIN-PLATE		STREAM IN		SUPINATE
	TINPLATE	AEIMNRSU	SUMERIAN	AEINPTTW	WET PAINT
AEILNRST	ENTRAILS		SURINAME	AEINPTTY	ANTITYPE
	LATRINES	AEIMNRSY	SEMINARY	AEINQSTU	ANTIQUES
	RATLINES	AEIMNRTT	MARTINET		QUANTISE
	RETINALS	AEIMNRTU	RUMINATE	AEINQTUZ	QUANTIZE
AEILNRTU	TENURIAL	AEIMNRTY	TYRAMINE	AEINRRST	RESTRAIN
AEILNRTV	INTERVAL	AEIMNSST	MATINESS		STRAINER
AEILNSST	SALIENTS		STEAMS IN		TRAINERS
AEILNSSZ	LAZINESS	AEIMOPSX	APOMIXES	AEINRRTW	INTERWAR
AEILNSTU	INSULATE	AEIMORST	AMORTISE	AEINRSST	ARTINESS
AEILNSUY	UNEASILY		ATOMISER		STAINERS
AEILNTVY	NATIVELY	AEIMORTZ	AMORTIZE	AEINRSSW	SWEARS IN
	VENALITY		ATOMIZER		WARINESS
AEILNUVV	UNIVALVE	AEIMOSST	ATOMISES	AEINRSTT	NITRATES
AEILNVWY	WAVY LINE	AEIMOSTZ	ATOMIZES		STRAITEN
AEILOPRS	POLARISE	AEIMOTTV	MOTIVATE		TRAIN SET
AEILOPRT	PETIOLAR	AEIMPRST	PRIMATES	AEINRSTU	URINATES
AEILOPRZ	POLARIZE	AEIMPRSV	VAMPIRES	AEINRSUZ	SUZERAIN
AEILOPST	SPOLIATE	AEIMPRTT	PART TIME	AEINRSZZ	SNAZZIER
AEILORSS	SOLARISE		PART-TIME	AEINSSTT	INSTATES
AEILORSV	VALORISE	AEIMPSSS	IMPASSES		NASTIEST
AEILORSZ	SOLARIZE	AEIMPSST	PASS TIME	AEINSSVW	WAVINESS
AEILORVZ	VALORIZE		PASTIMES	AEINSSWX	WAXINESS

Letters	Word(s)
AEINSSWY	EASY WINS
AEINSTTT	NATTIEST
AEINSTTV	TASTEVIN
AEINSUVV	VESUVIAN
AEIOPPST	APPOSITE
AEIOPRRT	PRIORATE
AEIOPRSV	VAPORISE
AEIOPRTX	EXPIATOR
AEIOPRVZ	VAPORIZE
AEIOPTTV	OPTATIVE
AEIOQSSU	SEQUOIAS
AEIORRSS	ROSARIES
AEIORRST	ROTARIES
AEIORRTU	AIR ROUTE
AEIORRUV	AU REVOIR
AEIORSSV	SAVORIES
AEIORSTV	VOTARIES
AEIORSTX	SEX RATIO
AEIORTTV	ROTATIVE
AEIPPRRU	UPPER AIR
AEIPPRSS	APPRISES
AEIPPSST	SAPPIEST
AEIPPSTZ	ZAPPIEST
AEIPQRTU	PRATIQUE
AEIPRRSS	ASPIRERS
AEIPRSST	PASTRIES
	PIASTRES
	SEA TRIPS
	TRAIPSES
AEIPRSSV	PARVISES
AEIPRSTV	PRIVATES
AEIPRSTW	WIRETAPS
AEIPRSTY	ASPERITY
AEIPRSVY	VESPIARY
AEIPRTTU	TEAR IT UP
AEIPRTUV	RAVE IT UP
AEIPSSSV	PASSIVES
AEIPTTUV	PUTATIVE
AEIQRRRU	QUARRIER
AEIQRRSU	QUARRIES
AEIRRRST	STARRIER
AEIRRTTY	TERTIARY
AEIRRTVY	RIVER TAY
AEIRSSTT	ARTISTES
	IS AT REST
AEIRSSXY	SIX YEARS
AEIRSTTT	RATTIEST
	TITRATES
AEIRSTVY	VESTIARY
AEISSSTY	ESSAYIST
AEISSTTT	TASTIEST
AEISSTTU	SITUATES
AEISSTVZ	VAST SIZE
AEISTTTT	TATTIEST
AEJKMORY	MAJOR KEY
AEJLNSTU	LAST JUNE
AEJLORWW	LOWER JAW
AEJLOSUY	JEALOUSY
AEJMSSST	ST.JAMESS
AEJNNNOS	ANN JONES
AEJPPRUW	UPPER JAW
AEKKMNOO	KAKEMONO
AEKLLMRW	MARK WELL
AEKLLOOP	LOOK PALE
AEKLLOTT	TAKE TOLL
AEKLMNNS	KLANSMEN
AEKLMRUW	LUKEWARM
AEKLMRUY	YARMULKE
AEKLNNSS	LANKNESS
AEKLNOSY	ANKYLOSE
AEKLOPRW	ROPEWALK
AEKLORTV	TALK OVER
AEKLORTW	WORK LATE
AEKLORVW	WALK OVER
	WALKOVER
AEKLOSTU	LEAKS OUT
AEKLPPST	PEP TALKS
AEKLPRRS	SPARKLER
AEKLPRSS	SPARKLES
AEKLQRUY	QUAKERLY
AEKLRSST	STALKERS
AEKMMNRS	MARKSMEN
AEKMMOOR	MAKE ROOM
AEKMNRST	TEN MARKS
AEKMNRSU	MAKE RUNS
AEKMOPTU	MAKE UP TO
AEKMORTW	TEAMWORK
	WORKMATE
AEKMOSTU	MAKES OUT
AEKMOSVW	MAKE VOWS
AEKMPRRV	VERKRAMP
AEKMPRTU	UP MARKET
	UP-MARKET
AEKMPRTW	KEPT WARM
AEKNNRSS	RANKNESS
AEKNOSST	ON SKATES
AEKNOSTU	SNEAK OUT
AEKNOTTU	TAKEN OUT
AEKNPRSS	SPANKERS
AEKNPSSU	SNEAKS UP
AEKOOPTW	TOOK A PEW
AEKOORTT	TAKE ROOT
AEKOPSTU	SPEAK OUT
AEKOPSTW	WEAK SPOT
AEKOSTTU	STAKE OUT
	STAKEOUT
	TAKES OUT
AEKOSTVW	TAKE VOWS
AEKPPSSU	SPEAKS UP
AEKPRRSS	SPARKERS
AEKPSSSY	PASS KEYS
	PASSKEYS
AEKPSSTU	UP STAKES
AEKQRSUW	SQUAWKER
AEKRRSST	STARKERS
AEKRRSTT	STAR TREK
AEKRSSTT	STARKEST
AEKRSUYZ	AZURE SKY
AELLLLST	TELLS ALL
AELLLLSW	ALLS WELL
AELLLNPW	PLAN WELL
AELLLPWY	PLAY WELL
AELLLSSW	WALL-LESS
AELLMMNS	SMALL MEN
AELLMNTY	MENTALLY
	TALLYMEN
AELLMORT	MARTELLO
AELLMSST	SMALLEST
AELLMSWX	MAXWELLS
AELLNOSV	NOVELLAS
AELLNOSW	SLOW LANE
AELLNPSS	PLANLESS
AELLNRUY	NEURALLY
AELLNRVY	VERNALLY
AELLNSST	TALLNESS
AELLNTTY	LATENTLY
AELLOPRW	WALLOPER
AELLORSS	ALL ROSES
	ROSELLAS
AELLORSV	OVERALLS
AELLORTT	ALLOTTER
AELLORWW	WALLOWER
AELLOSTV	LAST LOVE
AELLOSUV	ALVEOLUS
AELLQRSU	SQUALLER
AELLRTTY	LATTERLY
AELLRTVY	TREVALLY
AELLSTUU	ULULATES
AELLSTVY	VESTALLY
AELLSUXY	SEXUALLY
AELMMORW	MEALWORM
AELMMOSY	MYELOMAS
AELMMRST	TRAMMELS
AELMNNOT	NONMETAL
AELMNNOU	NOUMENAL
AELMNNRY	MANNERLY
AELMNOPS	NEOPLASM
	PLEONASM
AELMNORS	ALMONERS
AELMNOYY	YEOMANLY
AELMNPSW	NEW LAMPS
AELMNRSU	MENSURAL
	NUMERALS
AELMNSTT	MANTLETS
AELMOORS	SALE ROOM
	SALEROOM
AELMOPRR	PREMOLAR
AELMOPRT	TEMPORAL
AELMOPSU	AMPOULES
AELMOPSY	MAYPOLES
AELMOPTT	PALMETTO
AELMORSV	REMOVALS
AELMORSY	RAMOSELY
AELMORTU	EMULATOR
AELMOSSS	MOLASSES
AELMOSTT	MATELOTS
AELMOSTU	SOUL MATE
AELMOSTV	LAST MOVE
AELMPRRT	TRAMPLER
AELMPRSS	SAMPLERS
AELMPRST	TRAMPLES
AELMPRSY	LAMPREYS
AELMPSUX	AMPLEXUS
AELMRSTT	LAST TERM
	MARTLETS
AELMRSTY	MASTERLY
AELMRTUY	MATURELY
AELMSSSS	MASSLESS
AELMSUWY	MULEY SAW
AELNNOOP	NAPOLEON
AELNNOPP	OPEN PLAN
	OPEN-PLAN
AELNNORU	NEURONAL
AELNNRST	LANTERNS
AELNNRSU	UNLEARNS
AELNNRVY	VERA LYNN
AELNNSTU	ANNULETS
AELNOOPR	ON PAROLE
AELNOOPS	ON A SLOPE
AELNOPRS	PERSONAL
AELNORTT	TOLERANT
AELNORTY	ORNATELY
	TYROLEAN
AELNOSSV	OVALNESS
AELNOSTT	NOT LEAST
AELNOTWW	WENT AWOL
AELNPPSY	PLAY PENS
	PLAYPENS
AELNPRST	PLANTERS
	REPLANTS
AELNPRSU	PURSLANE
AELNPRTU	TURN PALE
AELNPSTX	EXPLANTS

AELNPTTU	PETULANT	AELRSTTU	LUSTRATE	AEMPRTYY	ARMY TYPE
AELNPTTY	PATENTLY	AELRSTUV	VAULTERS	AEMPSTTT	ATTEMPTS
AELNRRSS	SNARLERS	AELRSTWZ	WALTZERS	AEMQRSSU	MARQUESS
AELNRRTY	ERRANTLY	AELRTTUX	TEXTURAL	AEMRRSST	ARMRESTS
AELNRSST	SALTERNS	AELRTTUY	TUTELARY	AEMRRVWY	VERY WARM
AELNRSTT	SLATTERN	AELRTTWY	WAT TYLER	AEMRRWXY	WAX MERRY
AELNRSTU	NEUTRALS	AELRVYYZ	VERY LAZY	AEMRSSSU	MASSEURS
AELNRSUV	UNRAVELS	AELSTTUY	ASTUTELY	AEMRSSTT	MATTRESS
AELNRSXY	LARYNXES	AEMMNORY	MANY MORE		SMARTEST
AELNSSST	SALTNESS	AEMMNRST	SMART MEN	AENNNPST	PENNANTS
AELNTTUX	EXULTANT	AEMMOORT	ROOMMATE	AENNOORS	NO REASON
AELOORRS	ROSEOLAR	AEMMORST	MARMOSET	AENNORST	RESONANT
AELOORSS	AEROSOLS	AEMMRSST	STAMMERS	AENNORSW	NO ANSWER
AELOORTW	WATERLOO	AEMMSSTU	SUMMATES	AENNOSTU	TONNEAUS
AELOORTY	TOO EARLY	AEMNNOOR	ANN MOORE	AENNPRSS	SPANNERS
AELOPPPU	POPE PAUL	AEMNNORS	NORSEMAN	AENNRSTT	ENTRANTS
AELOPPRS	PROLAPSE	AEMNNORT	ORNAMENT	AENNRSWY	SWANNERY
AELOPPTU	POPULATE	AEMNNOWW	NEW WOMAN	AENNRTTY	TENANTRY
AELOPPXY	APOPLEXY	AEMNNPRU	PER ANNUM	AENNSSTT	ANTS NEST
AELOPQUY	OPAQUELY	AEMNNRST	REMNANTS	AENOOPST	TEASPOON
AELOPRST	POLE STAR	AEMNOORT	ANTEROOM	AENOPRSS	PERSONAS
	POLESTAR	AEMNOPRS	OPEN ARMS		RESPONSA
AELOPRSV	OVERLAPS	AEMNOPRW	MAN POWER	AENOPRST	OPERANTS
AELOPRTV	PORT VALE		MANPOWER		PRONATES
AELOPRTY	TOP LAYER	AEMNORRS	RANSOMER	AENOPRTT	PATENTOR
AELOPRVY	OVERPLAY	AEMNORST	ON STREAM	AENOPRWY	WEAPONRY
AELOPSST	APOSTLES		STOREMAN	AENOPSSS	PASSES ON
AELOPSSU	ESPOUSAL	AEMNORSU	ENAMOURS	AENOPSTT	ANTE-POST
AELOPSTU	PETALOUS	AEMNORSV	OVERMANS	AENOPSTV	SNAP VOTE
AELORRST	REALTORS	AEMNORTT	NO MATTER	AENOPSTY	STAY OPEN
	RELATORS	AEMNORTU	ROUTEMAN	AENOQRTU	ONE QUART
AELORRTV	ART LOVER	AEMNORTW	WANT MORE	AENORRRW	NARROWER
AELORSTV	LEVATORS	AEMNORTY	MONETARY	AENORSST	ASSENTOR
AELORSTW	LOW RATES	AEMNORYY	YEOMANRY		SENATORS
	SLOW RATE	AEMNOSSW	WOSSNAME	AENORSTX	TENOR SAX
AELORSVY	OVERLAYS	AEMNOSTU	SEAMOUNT	AENORSUV	RAVENOUS
AELORTWW	LOW WATER	AEMNPRSS	PRESSMAN	AENORTTY	ATTORNEY
AELORTYZ	ZEALOTRY	AEMNPRSU	SUPERMAN	AENOSSUU	NAUSEOUS
AELORUUX	ROULEAUX	AEMNPRTY	PARTY MEN	AENOSTTW	WASTE NOT
AELOSSTV	SOLVATES	AEMNPSTY	PAYMENTS	AENOSTTY	NOT AS YET
AELOSSVY	SAVELOYS	AEMNRSST	SMARTENS	AENOUUVX	NOUVEAUX
AELOSTUV	OVULATES	AEMNRSSU	SURNAMES	AENPPRSS	SNAPPERS
AELOSTUY	AUTOLYSE	AEMNRSSW	WARMNESS	AENPRRST	PARTNERS
AELPRRTT	PRATTLER	AEMNRSTU	MENSTRUA	AENPRSST	PASTERNS
AELPRSST	PLASTERS	AEMNRSTW	STRAW MEN		RAPTNESS
	PSALTERS	AEMNRSUY	ANEURYSM	AENPRSSW	SPAWNERS
	STAPLERS	AEMNRVYY	VERY MANY	AENPRSTT	PATTERNS
AELPRSSY	SPARSELY	AEMNSTUW	MUTE SWAN		TEN PARTS
AELPRSTT	PLATTERS	AEMOORST	TEAROOMS		TRANSEPT
	PRATTLES	AEMOORSW	WOOMERAS	AENPRSTY	PAYS RENT
	SPLATTER	AEMOOSSV	VAMOOSES	AENPRSUV	PARVENUS
AELPRSTY	PLASTERY	AEMOOSTT	TOMATOES	AENPSSSY	SYNAPSES
	PSALTERY	AEMOOSTU	AUTOSOME	AENPSSWW	SWAP NEWS
AELPSSSY	PAYS LESS	AEMOPPRS	PAMPEROS	AENQRRTU	QUARTERN
AELPSSTT	LAST STEP	AEMOPRSW	WAR POEMS	AENRRRTY	ERRANTRY
	LETS PAST	AEMOPRSY	PAYS MORE	AENRRSTT	TARTNESS
AELPSSTU	PULSATES	AEMOPRTW	TAPEWORM	AENRSSTU	SAUNTERS
	STEALS UP	AEMOPSST	PEAT MOSS	AENRSSTV	SERVANTS
AELQRRSU	QUARRELS	AEMORRRU	ARMOURER	AENRSTTU	TAUNTERS
AELQRSUY	SQUARELY	AEMORRST	REARMOST	AENRSTTW	NEW START
AELQSTUZ	QUETZALS	AEMORRSY	MARY ROSE	AENRSTUV	VAUNTERS
AELRRSTT	RATTLERS		ROSEMARY	AENRSTWY	STERNWAY
AELRRSTW	TRAWLERS	AEMORSSS	MORASSES	AENSSSTV	VASTNESS
AELRSSST	STARLESS	AEMORSST	MAESTROS	AENSSTTU	TAUTNESS
AELRSSTT	STARLETS	AEMORSSY	MAYORESS	AENSSTTX	SEXTANTS
	STARTLES	AEMORTTU	TAUTOMER	AEOOPPSS	PAPOOSES
AELRSSTU	SALUTERS	AEMOTTZZ	MOZZETTA	AEOOPRRT	OPERATOR
AELRSSTW	WASTRELS	AEMPRRST	TRAMPERS	AEOOPSTT	POTATOES
AELRSSUW	WALRUSES	AEMPRRSY	SPERMARY	AEOORTTT	TATTOOER
AELRSTTT	TARTLETS	AEMPRSST	STAMPERS	AEOORTTV	ROTOVATE
	TATTLERS	AEMPRSTU	UPSTREAM	AEOPPRSV	APPROVES

AEOPQSTU	OPAQUEST	AFFGIORT	GRAFFITO	AFGINRTU	FIGURANT
AEOPRRST	PRAETORS	AFFGLNRU	FAR-FLUNG	AFGLLOPY	PLAY GOLF
	PRORATES	AFFHILOT	HALF OF IT	AFGLLSSU	GLASSFUL
AEOPRSST	ESPARTOS	AFFHILST	FLAT FISH	AFGLLSUY	FALL GUYS
	PROTASES		FLATFISH	AFGLNNOO	GONFALON
	SEAPORTS	AFFHILTU	FAITHFUL	AFGLNSTU	SUNG FLAT
AEOPRSSV	OVERPASS	AFFHIOST	HAS IT OFF	AFGNNNOO	GONFANON
	PASS OVER	AFFHLLLU	HALF FULL	AFGNOORS	FOR A SONG
	PASSOVER	AFFIIJNY	IN A JIFFY	AFGOOORT	GO TOO FAR
AEOPRSTT	PROSTATE	AFFIINTY	AFFINITY	AFGOOSTU	OUT OF GAS
	TOP RATES	AFFILLMM	FLIMFLAM	AFGORTUW	TUG OF WAR
AEOPRSTU	APTEROUS	AFFILMNS	FILM FANS		TUG-OF-WAR
AEOPRSTW	WAR POETS	AFFILORT	TRAIL OFF	AFHHLORU	HALF HOUR
AEOPRSVW	SWAP OVER	AFFILOST	TAILS OFF	AFHIILSS	SAILFISH
AEOPRSVY	OVERPAYS	AFFILSUX	SUFFIXAL	AFHIKLPS	HIP FLASK
AEOPRSWW	POWER SAW	AFFIMSST	MASTIFFS	AFHIKNRS	FRANKISH
AEOPRSWY	ROPEWAYS	AFFINRSU	FUN FAIRS	AFHIKNST	FISH TANK
AEOPSTTU	PUT TO SEA		RUFFIANS	AFHILLST	THIS FALL
AEOQNSTU	EQUATONS	AFFIOPRS	PAIRS OFF	AFHILLST	FLASHILY
	QUAESTOR	AFFIPSTT	TIPSTAFF	AFHILNPT	HALF-PINT
AEORRRST	ARRESTOR	AFFJMPSU	JAM PUFFS	AFHILOSY	OAFISHLY
AEORRSST	ASSERTOR	AFFKLOSW	WALKS OFF	AFHILSTT	FLATTISH
	ASSORTER	AFFKMORS	MARKS OFF	AFHILSTW	HALF WITS
	ROASTERS	AFFKOPRS	SPARK OFF		HALF-WITS
AEORRTZZ	TERRAZZO	AFFLLLOU	FALL FOUL	AFHINOSS	FASHIONS
AEORSSSS	ASSESSOR	AFFLLOOT	FOOTFALL	AFHINSTU	TUNA FISH
AEORSSTT	TOASTERS	AFFLLORS	FALLS FOR	AFHIORST	SOFT HAIR
AEORSTTT	TESTATOR	AFFLOORT	FLAT ROOF	AFHIORTU	HIT A FOUR
AEORSTTU	OUTSTARE	AFFLOOTT	FLATFOOT	AFHIOTTW	WHAT OF IT?
AEORSTUW	OUTWEARS	AFFLOPSY	PLAY-OFFS	AFHIRSST	STARFISH
	WEARS OUT		PLAYS OFF	AFHISSWY	FISHWAYS
AEORSTVY	OVERSTAY	AFFMORRY	MARRY OFF	AFHKLNOT	HALF-KNOT
AEORSTWY	TWO YEARS	AFFNORSS	SAFFRONS	AFHKLNTU	THANKFUL
AEPPRRST	TRAPPERS	AFFNORST	AFFRONTS	AFHLMNOO	HALF MOON
AEPPRRSW	WRAPPERS	AFFNORSW	WARNS OFF		HALF-MOON
AEPPRSSW	SWAPPERS	AFFORSTT	START OFF	AFHLOSTY	HAY LOFTS
AEPPSSSU	PASSES UP	AFGGGILN	FLAGGING	AFHLRTUW	WRATHFUL
AEPQRSTU	PARQUETS	AFGGGINR	FRAGGING	AFHNNTUY	FUNNY HAT
AEPQRSUU	SQUARE UP	AFGGILNN	FLANGING	AFHNORRT	FAR NORTH
AEPRRSSY	SPRAYERS	AFGGINOR	FORAGING	AFHOOPTT	FOOTPATH
AEPRRSTU	RAPTURES		GOING FAR	AFHORSTU	FAR SOUTH
AEPRSSST	SPARSEST	AFGGINRT	GRAFTING	AFIIKNRS	FAIR SKIN
	TRESPASS	AFGHIINT	IN A FIGHT	AFIILLLY	FILIALLY
AEPRSSTT	SET TRAPS	AFGHILNS	FLASHING	AFIILNST	FINALIST
	SPATTERS	AFGHILNT	FANLIGHT		TAIL FINS
	TAPSTERS	AFGHILNW	WING HALF	AFIILNTY	FINALITY
AEPRSSTU	PASTURES	AFGHILPS	FLAGSHIP	AFIILORS	AIRFOILS
AEPRSTTY	TAPESTRY	AFGHINRT	FARTHING	AFIILRST	AIRLIFTS
AEPRSTUX	SUPERTAX	AFGHINST	SHAFTING	AFIINNOS	SAINFOIN
AEPRTTYY	ARTY TYPE	AFGHIOST	GOATFISH		SINFONIA
AEPRTUVY	PYRUVATE	AFGHLNSU	FLASH GUN	AFIINOTX	FIXATION
AEQRRSTU	QUARTERS		FLASHGUN	AFIINRSS	FRISIANS
AEQRSSTU	SQUAREST	AFGIILLN	FLAILING	AFIIORRT	TRIFORIA
AEQRSSTU	SQUAREST	AFGIILNS	FAILINGS	AFIKLNNR	FRANKLIN
AEQRSTTU	QUARTETS	AFGIINNT	FAINTING	AFIKMMNR	MINK FARM
	SQUATTER	AFGIINRS	FAIRINGS	AFIKORST	ASK FOR IT
AERRSSSU	ASSURERS	AFGIINTX	FIXATING	AFILLLLS	FALLS ILL
AERRSSTT	STARTERS	AFGIKLNN	FLANKING	AFILLLOT	FLOTILLA
AERRSTUY	TREASURY	AFGIKNNR	FRANKING	AFILLLSU	FULL SAIL
AERSSTTW	SWATTERS	AFGILMNO	FLAMINGO	AFILLPST	PITFALLS
AERSTTVY	TRAVESTY	AFGILNOT	FLOATING	AFILLTUY	FAULTILY
AESSTTTU	STATUTES	AFGILNPP	FLAPPING	AFILMNOR	FORMALIN
AFFFFIRR	RIFFRAFF	AFGILNST	FATLINGS		INFORMAL
AFFFLLOS	FALLS OFF		SING FLAT	AFILMRST	FILM STAR
AFFGHLOU	LAUGH OFF	AFGILNTT	FLATTING	AFILNORT	FLAT IRON
AFFGIINP	PIAFFING	AFGILOTT	GOT A LIFT		FLATIRON
AFFGIINX	AFFIXING	AFGIMNTU	FUMIGANT		INFLATOR
AFFGIIRT	GRAFFITI	AFGINNSU	SNAFUING	AFILNPPT	FLIPPANT
AFFGILNR	RAFFLING	AFGINORY	FORAYING	AFILNPST	FLAT SPIN
AFFGILNW	WAFFLING	AFGINPPR	FRAPPING	AFILNRTU	TRAINFUL
AFFGINQU	QUAFFING	AFGINRST	STRAFING	AFILNRUY	UNFAIRLY
AFFGINST	STAFFING				

AFILORSW	AIRFLOWS
AFILOSTX	FOXTAILS
AFILPRST	FIRST LAP
AFILSSTU	FISTULAS
AFILSTTU	FLAUTIST
AFIMMNOY	AMMONIFY
AFIMMORR	RAMIFORM
AFIMNOSU	INFAMOUS
AFIMNRST	FIRST MAN
AFIMORRV	VARIFORM
AFIMORSV	VASIFORM
AFINNOTU	FOUNTAIN
AFINNRTY	INFANTRY
AFINOPSY	SAPONIFY
AFINORRT	RAN FOR IT
AFINORUV	IN FAVOUR
AFINQTUY	QUANTIFY
AFINRSTX	TRANSFIX
AFINSSTU	FUSTIANS
AFIOPRSW	FAIR SWOP
AFIOPRTY	PAY FOR IT
AFIORSTW	WAITS FOR
AFIRSTTY	STRATIFY
AFISSTUV	FAUVISTS
AFKLNOTU	OUTFLANK
AFKORSTW	FAST WORK
AFLLLORY	FLORALLY
AFLLLUWY	LAWFULLY
AFLLMNUY	MANFULLY
AFLLMORY	FORMALLY
AFLLMRSY	SMALL FRY
	SMALL-FRY
AFLLNOSW	SNOWFALL
AFLLNUUW	UNLAWFUL
AFLLOPUY	FOUL PLAY
AFLLORSU	ALL FOURS
AFLLOSTU	FALLS OUT
	OUTFALLS
AFLLRTUY	ARTFULLY
AFLMNOPR	PLANFORM
AFLMOPRT	PLATFORM
AFLMORSU	FORMULAS
AFLMORTW	FLATWORM
AFLMOSUY	FAMOUSLY
AFLNORST	FRONTALS
AFLOOPTU	PAUL FOOT
AFLOPSTT	FLATTOPS
AFLORSUV	FLAVOURS
AFLPSSTY	FLYPASTS
AFMNNNUY	FUNNY MAN
AFMNNOOS	SON OF MAN
AFMNNORT	FRONT MAN
AFMNORST	FORMANTS
AFMOOPRR	PRO FORMA
AFMOORTZ	FROM A TO Z
AFMORRST	ART FORMS
AFMORSTU	FARMS OUT
AFMORSTX	TAX FORMS
AFNOORST	NOT SO FAR
AFNOPRTW	FRONT PAW
AFNORTTU	RUN TO FAT
AFOOPSST	SOFT SOAP
	SOFT-SOAP
AFOPRRTU	TRAP FOUR
AFOPRSTX	FOX TRAPS
AFORRSTU	FOUR STAR
	FOUR-STAR
AFPPPTUY	PUPPY FAT
AFPRRSUW	FUR WRAPS
AGGGHILN	HAGGLING
AGGGHINS	SHAGGING

AGGGILNN	GANGLING
AGGGILNR	GARGLING
AGGGILNS	LAGGINGS
AGGGILNW	WAGGLING
AGGGINNS	SNAGGING
AGGGINSW	SWAGGING
AGGHHINS	SANG HIGH
AGGHILNU	LAUGHING
AGGHILST	GASLIGHT
AGGHILSY	SHAGGILY
AGGHINNS	GNASHING
	HANGINGS
AGGHINNW	WHANGING
AGGHINPR	GRAPHING
AGGHNOSW	GANG SHOW
AGGIILNN	ALIGNING
AGGIILNT	LIGATING
AGGIILNV	GINGIVAL
AGGIINNR	GRAINING
AGGIJLNN	JANGLING
AGGILMNN	MANGLING
AGGILMNO	GLOAMING
AGGILNNO	GANGLION
AGGILNNS	SLANGING
AGGILNNT	TANGLING
AGGILNNW	WANGLING
AGGILNOT	GLOATING
AGGILNPU	PLAGUING
AGGILNPY	GAPINGLY
AGGILNRY	GRAYLING
AGGILNSS	GLASSING
AGGINNOP	GOING NAP
AGGINNOR	GROANING
AGGINNPR	PRANGING
AGGINNRT	GRANTING
AGGINNTW	TWANGING
AGGINORS	GO IN RAGS
AGGINOVY	VOYAGING
AGGINPRS	GRASPING
AGGINRSS	GAS RINGS
	GRASSING
AGGINRST	GRATINGS
AGGINRSU	SUGARING
AGGINRTY	GYRATING
AGGINRUU	AUGURING
AGGINSST	STAGINGS
AGGIOPRT	GOT A GRIP
AGGIRTUZ	ZIGGURAT
AGGLMOOR	LOGOGRAM
AGGLNOOT	GOT ALONG
AGGLOOOT	GO TO GAOL
AGGLRSTY	STRAGGLY
AGGNORTY	GOT ANGRY
AGHHIILT	HIGHTAIL
AGHHIIMS	AIMS HIGH
AGHHIKNR	HIGH RANK
	RANK HIGH
AGHHILLW	HIGH WALL
AGHHILPY	PLAY HIGH
AGHHIMSS	HIGH MASS
AGHHIRST	HIGH ARTS
AGHHISWY	HIGHWAYS
AGHHLOTU	ALTHOUGH
AGHIILNN	INHALING
AGHIIINRT	NIGHT AIR
AGHIINTV	HAVING IT
AGHIIPRR	HAIRGRIP
AGHIIRTT	AIRTIGHT
AGHIJMTT	JAM TIGHT
AGHIJNRT	NIGHTJAR
AGHIKNNT	THANKING

AGHILLNO	HALLOING
	HOLLAING
AGHILLNT	ALL NIGHT
AGHILLRT	ALL RIGHT
AGHILLRU	HULA GIRL
AGHILMTY	ALMIGHTY
AGHILNOO	HOOLIGAN
AGHILNOR	LONG HAIR
	LONG-HAIR
	LONGHAIR
AGHILNOS	SHOALING
AGHILNOT	LOATHING
AGHILNPS	PLASHING
AGHILNRS	RINGHALS
AGHILNSS	HASSLING
	LASHINGS
	SLASHING
AGHILNSU	LANGUISH
AGHILOST	GOLIATHS
AGHILRSY	GARISHLY
AGHIMMNS	SHAMMING
AGHIMMNW	WHAMMING
AGHIMNRT	RIGHT MAN
AGHIMNSS	SMASHING
AGHIMRRT	RIGHT ARM
AGHINNOV	HAVING ON
AGHINNTU	HAUNTING
AGHINNTY	ANYTHING
AGHINORS	ORANGISH
AGHINPRS	PHRASING
AGHINPRY	PHRYGIAN
AGHINPUV	HAVING UP
AGHINQSU	QUASHING
AGHINRRY	HARRYING
AGHINSST	HIT SNAGS
	STASHING
AGHINSSV	SHAVINGS
AGHINSTW	SWATHING
AGHIPRRT	TRIGRAPH
AGHIRSTT	STRAIGHT
AGHIRSTW	SAW RIGHT
AGHIRTWY	RIGHT WAY
AGHISTTT	SAT TIGHT
AGHKOSSW	GOSHAWKS
AGHLLNOU	LONG HAUL
	LONG-HAUL
AGHLMOOR	HOLOGRAM
AGHLMPSU	GALUMPHS
AGHLNOOP	HOP ALONG
AGHMNPSU	SPHAGNUM
AGHMOPRU	ROUGH MAP
AGHNNOOT	HANG ON TO
AGHNNSTU	SHANTUNG
AGHNOSTU	HANGOUTS
	HANGS OUT
AGHNSTTU	STAG HUNT
AGHNTTUU	UNTAUGHT
AGHOORTW	WORTH A GO
AGHORSTW	WARTHOGS
AGIIILNS	LIAISING
AGIIINNS	INSIGNIA
AGIIINRV	VIRGINIA
AGIIKMNT	MAKING IT
AGIIKNNS	ASKING IN
AGIIKNNT	TAKING IN
AGIIKNPR	KING PAIR
AGIIKNTT	TAKING IT
AGIILMNP	IMPALING
AGIILNNS	IN A SLING
AGIILNNU	INGUINAL
AGIILNOR	ORIGINAL

AGIILNOS	IS IN GOAL	AGILNNRS	SNARLING	AGINORST	ORGANIST
AGIILNOT	INTAGLIO	AGILNNST	SLANTING		ROASTING
	LIGATION	AGILNNUY	UNGAINLY	AGINORSU	AROUSING
AGIILNOX	GLOXINIA	AGILNOPR	PAROLING	AGINORTT	ROTATING
AGIILNPT	PLAITING	AGILNORT	TRIGONAL	AGINORTY	GYRATION
AGIILNQU	QUAILING	AGILNOSS	LASSOING		TORY GAIN
AGIILNRS	RAILINGS	AGILNOST	ANTILOGS	AGINOSST	AGONISTS
AGIILNRT	TRAILING	AGILNOTW	LONG WAIT	AGINOSSY	SAYING SO
AGIILNRV	VIRGINAL		WAGON-LIT	AGINOSTT	TOASTING
AGIILNTT	LITIGANT	AGILNPPS	SLAPPING	AGINPPRT	TRAPPING
AGIILNTV	VIGILANT	AGILNPPY	APPLYING	AGINPPRW	WRAPPING
AGIILPST	PIGTAILS	AGILNPSS	SAPLINGS	AGINPPSW	SWAPPING
AGIIMNOW	MIAOWING	AGILNPST	STAPLING	AGINPPTU	PUPATING
AGIIMNST	GIANTISM	AGILNPSW	LAPWINGS	AGINPPUY	PAYING UP
AGIINNPT	PAINTING	AGILNPSY	SPLAYING	AGINPRRS	SPARRING
AGIINNRS	INGRAINS	AGILNPTT	PLATTING	AGINPRRY	PARRYING
AGIINNRT	TRAINING	AGILNPUY	LAYING UP	AGINPRST	PARTINGS
AGIINNST	STAINING	AGILNRST	STARLING	AGINPRSY	SPRAYING
AGIINNTT	TAINTING	AGILNRSU	SINGULAR	AGINPRTU	UPRATING
AGIINORT	RIGATONI	AGILNRTT	RATTLING	AGINPRUV	RAVING UP
AGIINORT	RIGATONI	AGILNRTW	TRAWLING	AGINPSST	PASTINGS
AGIINPRS	ASPIRING	AGILNSTT	SLATTING	AGINPSUV	SAVING UP
	PRAISING	AGILNSTU	SALUTING	AGINQRSU	SQUARING
AGIINPRT	PIRATING	AGILNTTT	TATTLING	ACINNRST	STANNING
AGIINRRV	ARRIVING	AGILNTTW	WATTLING	AGINRRTY	TARRYING
AGIINRTT	ATTIRING	AGILNTUV	VAULTING	AGINRSSU	ASSURING
AGIJLOOT	GO TO JAIL	AGILNTUX	LUXATING	AGINRSTT	STARTING
AGIJNNTU	JAUNTING	AGILNTWZ	WALTZING	AGINRSTV	STARVING
AGIKLLRT	GIRL TALK	AGILNTXY	TAXINGLY	AGINRSTW	STRAWING
AGIKLMOR	KILOGRAM	AGILOOXY	AXIOLOGY	AGINRSTY	STINGRAY
AGIKLNNO	ALGONKIN	AGILORSS	GIRASOLS		STRAYING
AGIKLNNP	PLANKING	AGILSYYZ	SYZYGIAL	AGINSTTW	SWATTING
AGIKLNNR	RANKLING	AGIMMNNRS	SMARMING	AGINSTUU	IN AUGUST
AGIKLNST	STALKING	AGIMMNUX	MAXIM GUN	AGINSVVY	SAVVYING
AGIKMNNU	UNMAKING	AGIMMOSY	MISOGAMY	AGIOORTU	AUTOGIRO
AGIKMNPU	MAKING UP	AGIMMNRU	MANURING	AGIOPPRT	AGITPROP
AGIKMNRS	MARKINGS	AGIMNORS	ORGANISM	AGIOPRST	ROAST PIG
AGIKMRST	GRIM TASK	AGIMNORU	ORIGANUM	AGIRTTUY	GRATUITY
AGIKNNOT	TAKING ON	AGIMNORY	AGRIMONY	AGJNOORS	JARGOONS
AGIKNNPP	KNAPPING	AGIMNPRT	TRAMPING	AGKLLNOW	LONG WALK
AGIKNNPS	SPANKING	AGIMNPST	STAMPING	AGKMNOPS	KAMPONGS
AGIKNNSW	SWANKING	AGIMNPSW	SWAMPING	AGKORSSW	GASWORKS
AGIKNOST	GOATSKIN	AGIMNRRY	MARRYING	AGLLNOOS	GALLOONS
AGIKNOTT	TAKING TO	AGIMNRST	MIGRANTS	AGLLNOPY	LONG PLAY
AGIKNPRS	SPARKING		SMARTING	AGLLNORW	ALL WRONG
AGIKNPTU	TAKING UP	AGIMNRSW	SWARMING	AGLLNOST	LAST LONG
AGIKNPUW	WAKING UP	AGIMNRTU	MATURING		LONG LAST
AGILLLRT	TALL GIRL	AGIMNSSU	ASSUMING	AGLLOOTU	GO ALL OUT
AGILLMSU	GAULLISM	AGIMNSTT	MATTINGS	AGLLRUVY	VULGARLY
AGILLNOW	ALLOWING	AGIMORRT	MIGRATOR	AGLMNORS	LONG ARMS
AGILLNOY	ALLOYING	AGINNNOY	ANNOYING	AGLMOPYY	POLYGAMY
AGILLNPS	SPALLING	AGINNNPS	SPANNING	AGLNNOPS	LONG SPAN
AGILLNRU	ALLURING	AGINNNSW	SWANNING	AGLNNORU	RUN ALONG
AGILLNRY	RALLYING	AGINNOPT	POIGNANT	AGLNORSU	LANGUORS
AGILLNST	STALLING	AGINNORT	IGNORANT	AGLNOSWY	LONGWAYS
AGILLNSY	SALLYING	AGINNOTT	NOTATING	AGLOOPST	GOALPOST
	SIGNALLY	AGINNPPS	SNAPPING	AGLOPRTU	PORTUGAL
AGILLNTY	TALLYING	AGINNPSW	SPAWNING	AGLORSSY	GLOSSARY
AGILLOPT	GALLIPOT		WINGSPAN	AGLPSSSY	SPYGLASS
AGILLORS	GORILLAS	AGINNRSW	WARNINGS	AGLRTTUU	GUTTURAL
AGILLSSU	LUGSAILS	AGINNRSY	GRAYS INN	AGLSTUUY	AUGUSTLY
AGILLSSY	GLASSILY	AGINNTTU	ATTUNING	AGMMNOOR	MONOGRAM
AGILLSTU	GAULLIST		TAUNTING		NOMOGRAM
AGILMMNS	SLAMMING	AGINNTUV	VAUNTING	AGMMNOOY	MONOGAMY
AGILMNNT	MANTLING	AGINOORT	ROGATION	AGMMOORT	TOMOGRAM
AGILMNOO	MONGOLIA	AGINOPRU	IN A GROUP	AGMNNORW	WRONG MAN
AGILMNPS	SAMPLING	AGINORRS	GARRISON	AGMNNOUY	YOUNG MAN
AGILMNST	MALTINGS	AGINORRW	ARROWING	AGMNOORY	AGRONOMY
AGILNNNP	PLANNING	AGINORSS	ASSIGNOR	AGMNORST	ANGSTROM
AGILNNOP	PANGOLIN		SIGNORAS	AGMNSSTU	MUSTANGS
AGILNNOY	LAYING ON				
AGILNNPT	PLANTING				

AGMNSSTY	GYMNASTS	AHINRRUY	IN A HURRY	AIIKKSUY	SUKIYAKI
AGMOOOSU	OOGAMOUS	AHINRSVY	VARNISHY	AIIKLLMP	MILK PAIL
AGMOOSST	GO TO MASS	AHINSSTW	HAS TWINS	AIIKLNRR	LARRIKIN
AGMOPRRS	PROGRAMS	AHIOOPPT	PHOTOPIA	AIIKMNNN	MANNIKIN
AGMORRSW	RAGWORMS	AHIOPRSS	SHIP OARS	AIIKMNNS	MANIKINS
AGMORRWW	GROW WARM	AHIOPRST	APHORIST	AIIKNNST	INK STAIN
AGNNNOOS	NONAGONS	AHIORSSW	AIR SHOWS	AIIKNPTW	TIP A WINK
AGNNOSSW	SWAN SONG	AHIOSTTU	HAS IT OUT	AIILLNNV	VANILLIN
AGNOPRST	PART SONG	AHIPPSST	SAPPHIST	AIILLNOP	POLLINIA
	PART-SONG	AHIPRSST	HARPISTS	AIILLNSV	VILLAINS
AGNORSSW	WAR SONGS	AHIPRSSW	WARSHIPS	AIILLNVY	VILLAINY
AGNORTTU	GOT A TURN	AHIPRSTW	SHARP WIT	AIILLPRS	SPIRILLA
AGNORTUY	NUGATORY	AHIPRTTW	PART WITH	AIILMNPS	ALPINISM
AGNORWWY	WRONG WAY	AHIPSSWW	WHIPSAWS	AIILMNST	LATINISM
AGOORTUY	AUTOGYRO	AHIQRSSU	SQUARISH	AIILMNTT	MILITANT
AGOPPSST	STOPGAPS	AHIRSSTW	TRISHAWS	AIILMRST	MISTRIAL
AGORRTYY	GYRATORY	AHISSTTW	WHATSITS	AIILMRTY	MILITARY
AHHILPSW	WHIPLASH	AHKLMOOS	HOLM OAKS	AIILMSTV	VITALISM
AHHIMMSS	MISHMASH	AHKLOPST	TALK SHOP	AIILNOPV	PAVILION
AHHIMSST	SMASH HIT	AHKLOSTW	TALK SHOW	AIILNOSS	LIAISONS
AHHIOPSY	SHIP AHOY	AHKNNOST	NO THANKS	AIILNOSV	VISIONAL
AHHIPRSS	SHARPISH	AHKNOTUY	THANK YOU	AIILNPST	ALPINIST
AHHJNOTW	JOHN THAW		THANK-YOU		PINTAILS
AHHKMOTW	HAWKMOTH	AHLLMORS	HAM ROLLS		TAILSPIN
AHHKRSTU	KASHRUTH	AHLLNOST	SHALL NOT	AIILNRSU	SILURIAN
AHHLOOPU	HULA HOOP	AHLLNOTW	TOWN HALL	AIILNSTY	SALINITY
AHHMPRRU	HARRUMPH	AHLLORSU	ALL HOURS	AIILRSTT	TRIALIST
AHHNORTW	HAWTHORN	AHLLOSST	SHALLOTS	AIILSTTV	VITALIST
AHHOPRST	HAP'ORTHS	AHLLOSSW	SHALLOWS	AIILTTVY	VITALITY
AHHOSTTW	HOWS THAT?	AHLLOSTU	THALLOUS	AIIMNNOS	INSOMNIA
AHIIKLST	THAI SILK	AHLMMOPY	LYMPHOMA	AIIMNRST	MARTINIS
AHIIKMRS	KASHMIRI	AHLMNOOR	HORMONAL	AIIMNSST	ANIMISTS
AHIILNRW	IN A WHIRL	AHLMOPTY	POLYMATH	AIIMNSTV	VITAMINS
AHIILRTY	HILARITY	AHLNRTWY	THRAWNLY	AIIMNTTU	TITANIUM
AHIILSSW	SWAHILIS	AHLOPSTY	PLAY HOST	AIIMOPSX	APOMIXIS
AHIIMNOT	HIMATION	AHLORRTY	HARLOTRY	AIIMORTT	IMITATOR
AHIIMNRS	IRISHMAN	AHLORSTU	LAST HOUR	AIIMPRSS	PARSIISM
AHIIMNST	IAN SMITH	AHLORSWY	HOLY WARS	AIIMRUVV	VIVARIUM
	ISTHMIAN	AHMMMOST	MAMMOTHS	AIIMSSTT	MASTITIS
AHIIMOPX	AMPHIOXI	AHMNNORT	NORTHMAN	AIINNOSV	INVASION
AHIINPRS	HAIRPINS	AHMNNSTU	HUNTSMAN	AIINNQTU	QUINTAIN
AHIIPRSS	AIRSHIPS		MANHUNTS	AIINNSTY	INSANITY
AHIISSTX	HITS A SIX	AHMNOPST	PHANTOMS	AIINOSTV	ON A VISIT
AHIISTTW	WHAT IS IT?	AHMNORST	SHORT MAN	AIINPRSS	ASPIRINS
AHIKLRSY	RAKISHLY	AHMNORSU	MAN-HOURS	AIINPSST	PIANISTS
AHIKMSST	SHAKTISM	AHMNOSWY	SHY WOMAN	AIINRRTT	IRRITANT
AHIKPRSS	SPARKISH	AHMOOPSS	SHAMPOOS	AIINRSSU	IN RUSSIA
AHILLMSS	SMALLISH	AHMOORSW	WASHROOM	AIINSTTV	VISITANT
AHILLMTU	THALLIUM	AHMPSSSU	SMASH-UPS	AIINSTWY	IN ITS WAY
AHILLNST	ANTHILLS	AHMPSTYY	SYMPATHY	AIINTTVY	NATIVITY
AHILLSVY	LAVISHLY	AHMQSSUU	MUSQUASH	AIIORRST	SARTORII
AHILMQSU	QUALMISH	AHMRSSTU	RUSH MATS	AIIORSTV	OVARITIS
AHILOORT	LOTHARIO	AHNOOPRS	HARPOONS	AIIORTTV	VITIATOR
AHILOPST	HOSPITAL	AHNOORRY	HONORARY	AIIPRRST	AIRSTRIP
AHILPTWY	PLAY WITH	AHNOPPSW	PAWN SHOP	AIIRSSTT	SATIRIST
AHIMMNSU	HUMANISM		PAWNSHOP		SITARIST
AHIMNNOT	IN A MONTH	AHNOPSST	SNAPSHOT	AIJKKNOU	KINKAJOU
AHIMNOSW	WOMANISH	AHNORRST	RAN SHORT	AIJLLOVY	JOVIALLY
AHIMNSTU	HUMANIST	AHNORSSX	SAXHORNS	AIJLNOPT	LAP-JOINT
AHIMNTUY	HUMANITY	AHNOSTTW	WHATNOTS	AIJLNTUY	JAUNTILY
AHIMOPRS	APHORISM	AHNOSTWW	WONT WASH	AIJMORTY	MAJORITY
AHIMPPSS	SAPPHISM	AHOOSSTT	SHOOTS AT	AIJMPTTU	JUMP AT IT
AHIMPSTU	HAMS IT UP	AHOOSSTY	SOOTHSAY	AIJNOPPY	POPINJAY
AHIMRSST	SMARTISH	AHOOSTTT	HOT TOAST	AIJNORST	JANITORS
AHIMSTVZ	MITZVAHS	AHOOSTTW	SAWTOOTH	AIKLMMRW	WARM MILK
AHINNOPT	ANTIPHON	AHOPSTUW	SOUTH PAW	AIKLMWYY	MILKY WAY
AHINNORU	IN AN HOUR		SOUTHPAW	AIKLNOTW	WALK INTO
AHINOSST	ASTONISH	AHOSSTUW	WASHOUTS	AIKLOTTW	KILOWATT
AHINPPSS	SNAPPISH	AHPPSSTU	PUSH PAST	AIKLSSSY	SKYSAILS
AHINPRST	TRANSHIP	AIIILMST	MILITIAS	AIKMNORS	IRON MASK
AHINQSUV	VANQUISH	AIIILNST	INITIALS	AIKMNPRW	MINK WRAP

AIKNNOOS	NAINSOOK
AIKNOSTT	STOTINKA
AIKNRRSU	RUN A RISK
AIKNRSST	SANSKRIT
AIKOOPTT	TOOK A TIP
AILLLPSU	LAPILLUS
AILLLSTW	LAST WILL
AILLLSTY	LAY STILL
AILLMNOT	MONTILLA
AILLMOPS	OIL LAMPS
AILLMOTY	MOLALITY
AILLMRUY	ARUM LILY
AILLMSSW	SAW MILLS
	SAWMILLS
AILLMUUV	ALLUVIUM
AILLNOPP	PAPILLON
AILLNOST	STALLION
AILLNOSU	ALLUSION
AILLNOUV	ALLUVION
AILLNPSY	SPINALLY
AILLNPTY	PLIANTLY
AILLNSST	INSTALLS
AILLOPTT	TOP IT ALL
AILLORTT	LITTORAL
	TORTILLA
AILLOSTY	LOYALIST
AILLPRSY	SPIRALLY
AILLPSWY	SPILLWAY
AILLQSSU	SQUILLAS
AILLRTUY	RITUALLY
AILLSSSY	SILLY ASS
AILLSSTT	SAT STILL
AILLSUVY	VISUALLY
AILMMNOO	MONOMIAL
AILMMNUU	ALUMINUM
AILMMORS	MORALISM
AILMMORT	IMMORTAL
AILMNNOS	NOMINALS
AILMNOOP	PALOMINO
AILMNOOR	MONORAIL
AILMNOOT	MOTIONAL
AILMNOPY	OLYMPIAN
AILMNOSS	OSMANLIS
AILMNPST	IMPLANTS
AILMNPTU	PLATINUM
AILMNRUY	LUMINARY
AILMOORT	MOTORAIL
AILMOPRX	PROXIMAL
AILMORST	MORALIST
AILMORSU	SOLARIUM
AILMORSY	ROYALISM
AILMORTY	MOLARITY
	MORALITY
AILMOSTU	SOLATIUM
AILMPPSY	MISAPPLY
AILMPRSU	PRIMULAS
AILMRSST	MISTRALS
AILMRSTU	ALTRUISM
	MURALIST
	ULTRAISM
AILMRSTY	ARMY LIST
AILNNOOT	NOTIONAL
AILNNOSW	SON-IN-LAW
AILNNOTU	LUNATION
AILNOOPT	OPTIONAL
AILNOPRU	UNIPOLAR
AILNOPTY	PONY TAIL
	PONYTAIL
AILNOSTY	LAYS IT ON
AILNOSUV	AVULSION
AILNOSVY	SYNOVIAL
AILNOTTY	TONALITY
AILNOTUX	LUXATION
AILNPPSY	SNAPPILY
AILNPSTT	LAST PINT
AILNPSTU	NUPTIALS
AILNPSUU	NAUPLIUS
AILNQRTU	TRANQUIL
AILNQSTU	QUINTALS
AILNQTUY	QUAINTLY
AILNRRTU	TRIAL RUN
AILNRTTU	TURN TAIL
AILNSSTU	STUNSAIL
AILNSTUU	NAUTILUS
AILNSTVY	NAVY LIST
AILOORST	ISOLATOR
AILOORTV	VIOLATOR
AILOPRTY	POLARITY
AILOPSST	TOPSAILS
AILORSTT	ROTALIST
	SOLITARY
AILORTTU	TUTORIAL
AILOSTTU	TAILS OUT
AILOSTTW	TWO TAILS
AILOTTTY	TOTALITY
AILPPSST	SLIP PAST
AILPPSSY	PAY SLIPS
	PAYSLIPS
AILPRSTU	STIPULAR
AILPSSWY	SLIPWAYS
AILPSTUY	PLAY SUIT
	PLAYSUIT
AILRSSTY	TRYSAILS
AILRSTTU	ALTRUIST
	ULTRAIST
AILRSTTY	STRAITLY
AILRSUVV	SURVIVAL
AILSSSTV	SLAVISTS
AILSSTUW	LAW SUITS
	LAWSUITS
AIMMMNOU	AMMONIUM
AIMMMSUX	MAXIMUMS
AIMMNORS	ROMANISM
AIMMNORT	MORTMAIN
AIMMNSTU	MANUMITS
AIMNNNOU	UNION MAN
AIMNNOSS	MANSIONS
AIMNNOTU	MOUNTAIN
AIMNNOTY	ANTIMONY
	ANTINOMY
AIMNNRTU	RUMINANT
AIMNNTUU	IN AUTUMN
AIMNOPRS	RAMPIONS
AIMNORST	ROMANIST
AIMNORTU	MINOTAUR
AIMNORTY	MINATORY
AIMNOTTU	MUTATION
AIMNPRSU	UP IN ARMS
AIMNRSTT	TANTRISM
	TRANSMIT
AIMNRSTU	NATURISM
AIMNRSTV	VARMINTS
AIMNTTWY	WITTY MAN
AIMOPRSS	PROSAISM
AIMOPSST	IMPASTOS
AIMOPSSY	SYMPOSIA
AIMORRUV	VARIORUM
AIMORSST	AMORISTS
AIMOSSTT	ATOMISTS
AIMPPRSU	AIR PUMPS
AIMRSSTX	MARXISTS
AIMRTTUY	MATURITY
AIMSSTUY	I MUST SAY
AINNOOSW	IN A SWOON
AINNOOSX	OXONIANS
AINNOOTT	NOTATION
AINNORWY	IN NORWAY
AINNOTTU	NUTATION
AINNSSTT	INSTANTS
AINOOPTT	POTATION
AINOORST	ORATIONS
AINOORTT	ROTATION
AINOOSTT	OSTINATO
AINOOSTV	OVATIONS
AINOPPST	APPOINTS
AINOPPTT	PAINT POT
AINOPPTU	PUPATION
AINOPSSS	PASSIONS
AINOPSST	PASS IT ON
AINOPSTU	UTOPIANS
AINOPTTU	PAINT OUT
AINOPTTX	TAX POINT
AINOPTUW	WAIT UPON
AINORRTT	NITRATOR
AINORSST	ARSONIST
AINORSTT	STRONTIA
AINORTTY	TOY TRAIN
AINOSSTT	STATIONS
AINOOTTU	TITANOUS
AINPRRSS	PARSNIPS
AINPRSST	SPIRANTS
AINPRSSU	PRUSSIAN
AINPRSTU	PURITANS
AINPSSSY	SYNAPSIS
AINPSSTU	PUISSANT
AINQTTUY	QUANTITY
AINRSSSU	RUSSIANS
AINRSSTT	TRANSITS
AINRSTTT	TANTRIST
AINRSTTU	NATURIST
AINRTUXY	X-RAY UNIT
AINSSSTU	SUSTAINS
AIOOORRT	ORATORIO
AIOPRRST	AIRPORTS
AIOPRRTT	PORTRAIT
AIOPRSST	PROSAIST
	PROTASIS
AIOPRSTT	PATRIOTS
AIOPRSTW	TWO PAIRS
AIORRRSW	WARRIORS
AIORRRST	TRAITORS
AIORRTTT	TITRATOR
AIORSSUV	SAVIOURS
AIORSTTV	VOTARIST
AIOSSSTY	ISOSTASY
AIOSTTTU	SAT IT OUT
AIOSTTUW	SAW IT OUT
AIPPRSTT	TRAPPIST
AIPPRSTY	PAPISTRY
AIPPRTUW	WRAP IT UP
AIPRSSTU	UPSTAIRS
AIPRSSTY	SPARSITY
AIRRSTTY	ARTISTRY
AIRSSSTT	TSARISTS
AISSSTTT	STATISTS
AJLLMORS	JAM ROLLS
AJLLNOOS	AL JOLSON
AJLLSTUY	LAST JULY
AJLNORSU	JOURNALS
AKKLRSSY	SKYLARKS
AKKOORST	KOO STARK
AKLLNOSW	KNOW-ALLS
AKLLNPRU	PULL RANK

AKLMORSW	LOW MARKS	ALOPSSTT	LAST POST
AKLNNOPT	PLANKTON	ALOPSTUU	PATULOUS
AKLOPRST	SALT PORK	ALOPSTUY	OUTPLAYS
AKLOSTTU	TALKS OUT		PLAYS OUT
AKLOSTUW	WALKOUTS	ALOQRRSU	RORQUALS
	WALKS OUT	ALORSTTW	SALTWORT
AKLPRRSU	LARKSPUR	ALORTUWY	OUTLAWRY
AKMNORSU	RUNS AMOK	ALOSSTTU	OUTLASTS
AKMNORTU	TURKOMAN	ALPPSTUY	PLATYPUS
AKMOPRST	POSTMARK	ALPRSTUU	PUSTULAR
	TOP MARKS	AMMNOORT	MOTORMAN
AKMORSST	OSTMARKS	AMMNPTUY	TYMPANUM
AKMORSTU	MARKS OUT	AMNNOSTW	TOWNSMAN
AKMQSTUU	KUMQUATS	AMNNOSTY	ANTONYMS
AKMRSSTU	MUSK RATS	AMNNOTYY	ANTONYMY
	MUSKRATS	AMNNSTTU	STUNT MAN
AKNOPSTT	TANK TOPS	AMNOORST	MOONRATS
AKNORSTU	OUTRANKS	AMNOOSTT	OTTOMANS
AKOOOTVW	TOOK A VOW	AMNOOTUY	AUTONOMY
AKOOPRTT	TOOK PART	AMNOOTXY	TAXONOMY
AKORSWWX	WAXWORKS	AMNOSTTU	STOUT MAN
ALLLPRUY	PLURALLY	AMNRSTTU	TANTRUMS
ALLMMSSU	SMALL SUM	AMOOPRST	TAPROOMS
ALLMNORY	NORMALLY	AMOORSTT	TOO SMART
ALLMNPSU	PULLMANS	AMOORTWY	MOTORWAY
ALLMOOST	TOO SMALL	AMOOTTUY	AUTOTOMY
ALLMOPSX	SMALLPOX	AMOPRSTT	MOST PART
ALLMORTY	MORTALLY	AMOPRSXY	PAROXYSM
ALLMOSTW	TOM WALLS	AMOPSSTT	TOPMASTS
ALLMTUUY	MUTUALLY	AMOPSTTU	STAMP OUT
ALLNOOSW	WALLOONS	AMOQSSUU	SQUAMOUS
ALLOOPPY	PLAY POLO	AMORRTUY	MORTUARY
	PLAY POOL	AMORSTTU	OUTSMART
ALLOOPTT	ALL TO POT	ANNOSSTU	STANNOUS
ALLOOSTX	AXOLOTLS	ANNPRSUY	SPUN YARN
ALLOPRSY	PAYROLLS	ANOOPRSS	SOPRANOS
ALLOPSTY	POSTALLY	ANOOTUWY	NO WAY OUT
ALLORSST	ALL SORTS	ANOPRRSS	SPORRANS
ALLOSSWW	SWALLOWS	ANOSTTUW	WANTS OUT
ALLRUUVY	UVULARLY	ANPRSSTU	RUNS PAST
ALMNOOPS	LAMPOONS		SUN TRAPS
ALMNORTY	MATRONLY		SUNTRAPS
ALMNORYY	MYRNA LOY	ANRRSTTU	STAR TURN
ALMNPSSU	SUN LAMPS	ANRSSSUY	SUNS RAYS
	SUNLAMPS	AOOOPRTZ	PROTOZOA
ALMOSTTU	MULATTOS	AOOPPRSS	POOR PASS
	SUM TOTAL	AOOPRSTT	POT ROAST
	TOTAL SUM		POT-ROAST
ALNNOOPR	NONPOLAR	AOOPRSTW	SOAPWORT
ALNNOTWY	WANTONLY	AOOPRSUV	VAPOROUS
ALNOOPRT	ON PATROL	AOORRTTY	ROTATORY
ALNOOPST	PLATOONS	AOPPRSST	PASSPORT
ALNOOPYZ	POLYZOAN		POP STARS
ALNOORST	ORTOLANS	AOPRRSSW	SPARROWS
ALNOOSTU	NOT A SOUL	AOPRRSTY	PORTRAYS
ALNOPPTT	PLANT POT	AOPRSTTW	TWO PARTS
ALNOPRST	PLASTRON	AOPRTTWY	TWO-PARTY
ALNOPTTU	PLANT OUT	AORSTTTU	START OUT
ALNORRWY	NARROWLY	AORSTTYY	TRY TO SAY
ALNOTWWY	TAWNY OWL	AOSSTTUY	OUTSTAYS
ALNPPSTU	SUPPLANT	APRSSTTU	STARTS UP
ALNPRSSU	SNARL-UPS		UPSTARTS
ALOOPPRS	PROPOSAL	APSSTTUY	STAYS PUT
ALOOPRSW	POOR LAWS	BBBCEOWY	COBWEBBY
ALOORSUV	VALOROUS	BBBEILRU	BUBBLIER
ALOPPRYY	POLYPARY	BBBELPUU	BUBBLE UP
ALOPPSTY	STOP PLAY	BBBELRSU	BLUBBERS
ALOPPTUY	PLAY UP TO	BBBELRUY	BLUBBERY
ALOPRRSU	PARLOURS	BBBEOOTU	BOOB TUBE
ALOPRSTU	POSTURAL	BBBGILNO	BOBBLING
	PULSATOR	BBBGILNU	BUBBLING

BBBIITTY	BIT BY BIT
BBBMOUZZ	BUZZ BOMB
BBCCIKOS	BIBCOCKS
BBCDERSU	SCRUBBED
BBCEHIRU	CHUBBIER
BBCEILRS	SCRIBBLE
BBCEIRRS	CRIBBERS
BBCELORS	CLOBBERS
	COBBLERS
BBCERRSU	SCRUBBER
BBCGIINR	CRIBBING
BBCGILNO	COBBLING
BBCGILNU	CLUBBING
BBCHKSUU	BUSHBUCK
BBCKLOOU	BOOK CLUB
BBCLOSUY	BOYS CLUB
BBDDDIIY	BIDDY-BID
BBDDEEMO	DEMOBBED
BBDDEILR	DRIBBLED
BBDEEGIT	GIBBETED
BBDEEINT	BE IN DEBT
BBDEEMNU	BENUMBED
BBDEHORT	THROBBED
BBDEILRR	DRIBBLER
BBDEILRS	DRIBBLES
BBDEILRU	BLUE BIRD
	BLUEBIRD
BBDEIMOV	DIVE-BOMB
BBDEINRU	RUBBED IN
BBDEKNSU	BUNK BEDS
BBDELLMU	DUMBBELL
BBDENORU	RUBBED ON
BBDEPRUU	RUBBED UP
BBDGIILN	DIBBLING
BBDGINRU	DRUBBING
BBDGLOOO	OLD GOBBO
BBDIKMUY	DYBBUKIM
BBDILNOR	ROB BLIND
BBDLOOWY	BODY BLOW
BBDOSUYY	BUSYBODY
BBEEHILT	THE BIBLE
BBEEHTYY	BY THE BYE
BBEEIIRR	BERIBERI
BBEELLLU	BLUEBELL
BBEEOPPR	BEBOPPER
BBEESSUY	BUSY BEES
BBEFIMOR	FIRE BOMB
	FIREBOMB
BBEGILNP	PEBBLING
BBEGILST	GLIBBEST
BBEGIRRU	GRUBBIER
BBEGLOPU	GOBBLE UP
BBEGLORS	GOBBLERS
BBEGOTUY	GO BY TUBE
BBEHORRT	THROBBER
BBEILOST	BIBELOTS
BBEILQRU	QUIBBLER
BBEILQSU	QUIBBLES
BBEILRRY	BILBERRY
BBEIMMOT	TIME BOMB
BBEIMOST	BOMB SITE
	BOMBSITE
BBEIMRSU	BRUMBIES
BBEINOVY	BEVIN BOY
BBEIRSTU	STUBBIER
BBEISTTU	TUBBIEST
BBEKLOOU	BLUE BOOK
BBEKLOSS	BLESBOKS
BBEKNOOT	BONTEBOK
BBELLOSW	BOW BELLS

BBELLOSY	BELL BOYS	BCDEEMRU	CUMBERED	BCEILNRU	RUNCIBLE
	BELLBOYS	BCDEIKRR	BRICK RED	BCEILPRU	REPUBLIC
BBELLRUY	LUBBERLY		RED BRICK	BCEIMNOR	COMBINER
BBELORSS	SLOBBERS		REDBRICK	BCEIMNOS	COMBINES
BBELORSW	WOBBLERS	BCDEIKSS	SICKBEDS	BCEIMORS	MICROBES
BBELORSY	SLOBBERY	BCDEILRY	CREDIBLY	BCEINORU	BOUNCIER
BBENORSY	SNOBBERY	BCDEIMNO	COMBINED	BCEINOVX	BICONVEX
BBGGILNO	GOBBLING	BCDEKPUU	BUCKED UP	BCEIOOPS	BIOSCOPE
BBGGINRU	GRUBBING	BCDELLOW	BLEW COLD	BCEIORST	BISECTOR
BBGHILNO	HOBBLING	BCDELMRU	CRUMBLED	BCEIRRSS	SCRIBERS
BBGIIIMN	IMBIBING	BCDEMORY	CORYMBED	BCEJNOOT	NO OBJECT
BBGIIKLN	KIBBLING	BCDEORSU	OBSCURED	BCEJOORT	OBJECTOR
BBGIILNN	NIBBLING	BCDGIORW	BIG CROWD	BCEJSSTU	SUBJECTS
BBGIINRS	RIBBINGS	BCDIIKRT	TICKBIRD	BCEKLLNU	BULL NECK
BBGILLUY	BIG BULLY	BCDIIPSU	BICUSPID	BCEKLNUU	UNBUCKLE
BBGILMNU	BUMBLING	BCDIKLLU	DUCKBILL	BCEKLORS	BLOCKERS
BBGILNNO	NOBBLING	BCDIKMOY	MOBY DICK	BCEKLPUU	BUCKLE UP
BBGILNOW	WOBBLING	BCDINRUU	RUBICUND	BCEKLRSU	BUCKLERS
BBGILNOY	LOBBYING	BCDKLLOO	OLD BLOCK	BCEKORST	BROCKETS
BBGILNRU	BURBLING	BCDKOR3U	BURDOCKS	BCELLOSW	COWBELLS
BBGILRUY	GRUBBILY	BCDLLOOW	BLOW COLD	BCELMRSU	CRUMBLES
BBGINNSU	SNUBBING	BCEEEFIN	BENEFICE	BCELMSSU	SCUMBLES
BBGINOSW	SWOBBING	BCEEEHRS	BREECHES	BCENOPUU	BOUNCE UP
BBGINRSU	RUBBINGS	BCEEFLTU	CLUBFEET	BCENORSU	BOUNCERS
BBGINSTU	STUBBING	BCEEGINS	BIG SCENE	BCEOORST	OCTOBERS
BBHILOSS	SLOBBISH	BCEEGIRS	ICEBERGS	BCEOORSX	BOX SCORE
BBHINOSS	SNOBBISH	BCEEGLLU	GLEE CLUB	BCEOORTU	CUBE ROOT
BBHIOSTY	HOBBYIST	BCEEHHNT	THE BENCH	BCEORSSU	OBSCURES
BBHIRSUY	RUBBISHY	BCEEHKSU	BUCKSHEE	BCESSTTU	BEST CUTS
BBHRSSUU	SUBSHRUB	BCEEHLNS	BLENCHES	BCFGLLOU	GOLF CLUB
BBILOSTY	LOBBYIST	BCEEHNRS	BENCHERS	BCFIIORT	FIBROTIC
BBILOSUU	BIBULOUS	BCEEHQUY	BY CHEQUE	BCFILLMU	FILM CLUB
BBIMNOOR	BOB MINOR	BCEEIILM	IMBECILE	BCFILORY	FORCIBLY
BBIMNOSS	SNOBBISM	BCEEIKRR	BICKERER	BCFIMORU	CUBIFORM
BBLLOUYY	BULLYBOY	BCEEINOT	CENOBITE	BCFKLLOU	FOLK CLUB
BBNOORSU	BOURBONS	BCEEIOSX	ICEBOXES	BCFLOOTU	CLUBFOOT
BBNORSTU	STUBBORN	BCEELRTU	TUBERCLE	BCFLOSUW	WOLF CUBS
BBOOOSTY	BOOT BOYS	BCEEMNRU	ENCUMBER	BCFSSSUU	SUBFUSCS
BCCCIILY	BICYCLIC	BCEEMRRU	CEREBRUM	BCGHIINR	BIRCHING
BCCEEISU	ICE CUBES	BCEENORS	OBSCENER	BCGHIINT	BITCHING
BCCEHIRU	CHERUBIC	BCEFGHII	BIG CHIEF	BCGHINNU	BUNCHING
BCCEIIIS	CICISBEI	BCEFILOR	FORCIBLE	BCGHINOT	BOTCHING
BCCEIIOS	CICISBEO	BCEGHILN	BELCHING	BCGHINPU	BIG PUNCH
BCCEILRU	CRUCIBLE	BCEGHINN	BENCHING	BCGIIKNR	BRICKING
BCCEILRY	BYCLICER	BCEGIINO	BIOGENIC	BCGIIKST	BIG STICK
BCCEILSU	CUBICLES	BCEGIMNO	BECOMING	BCGIILMN	CLIMBING
BCCEILSY	BICYCLES	BCEGIORS	BIG SCORE	BCGIINRS	SCRIBING
BCCEMRUU	CUCUMBER	BCEGIRTU	TIGER CUB	BCGIKLNO	BLOCKING
BCCIIMOR	MICROBIC	BCEHIIRT	BITCHIER	BCGIKLNU	BUCKLING
BCCIISTU	CUBISTIC	BCEHILPU	BLUE CHIP	BCGILOPU	GO PUBLIC
BCCILOOR	BROCCOLI		BLUE-CHIP	BCGIMNOY	COMING BY
BCCIRTUU	CUCURBIT	BCEHIMRS	BESMIRCH	BCGIMNRU	CRUMBING
BCCMOOSX	COXCOMBS	BCEHIMRU	CHERUBIM	BCGINNOU	BOUNCING
BCCMSSUU	SUCCUMBS	BCEHINSY	BY INCHES	BCHIIKTT	BIT THICK
BCCNOORS	CORN COBS	BCEHIORS	BRIOCHES	BCHIILTY	BITCHILY
	CORNCOBS	BCEHIRST	BRITCHES	BCHIISSU	HIBISCUS
BCCOSTUU	CUB SCOUT	BCEHLOST	BLOTCHES	BCHINORR	BORN RICH
BCCSSUUU	SUCCUBUS	BCEHNOOT	ON THE COB	BCHIOORY	CHOIR BOY
BCDDEEEK	BEDECKED	BCEHNRSU	BRUNCHES		CHOIRBOY
BCDEEEMR	DECEMBER	BCEHOORS	BROOCHES	BCHIOPRS	PIBROCHS
BCDEEFLO	COLD BEEF	BCEHORRU	BROCHURE	BCHIRSTY	BY CHRIST!
BCDEEHLN	BLENCHED	BCEHORST	BOTCHERS	BCHJOSUY	CUSHY JOB
BCDEEIKR	BICKERED	BCEHRSTU	BUTCHERS	BCHKOSTU	BUCKSHOT
BCDEEILR	CREDIBLE	BCEHRTUY	BUTCHERY	BCHNORSU	BRONCHUS
BCDEEILS	DECIBELS	BCEIIKLN	ICEBLINK	BCHOOSSY	COSH BOYS
BCDEEILU	EDUCIBLE	BCEIIKRS	BRICKIES	BCIIILMU	UMBILICI
BCDEEIRS	DESCRIBE	BCEIILMS	MISCIBLE	BCIILLSY	SIBYLLIC
BCDEEIST	BISECTED	BCEIILNV	VINCIBLE	BCIILNPU	IN PUBLIC
BCDEEJOT	OBJECTED	BCEIINRS	INSCRIBE	BCIIMNOO	BIONOMIC
BCDEEKNO	BECKONED	BCEIKLMO	COMBLIKE	BCIIMORU	CIBORIUM
BCDEEKTU	BUCKETED	BCEILMRS	CLIMBERS	BCIISSTU	BISCUITS

BCIKKNSU	BUCKSKIN	BDDIILRW	WILD BIRD	BDEEMOSS	EMBOSSED
BCIKLOOT	BOOTLICK	BDDILORS	OLD BIRDS	BDEENORV	BEND OVER
BCILLPUY	PUBLICLY	BDDINORW	DID BROWN	BDEENPRS	PREBENDS
BCILMOSY	SYMBOLIC	BDEEEGIS	BESIEGED	BDEEOORR	BORDERER
BCILMPUY	MY PUBLIC	BDEEEILV	BELIEVED	BDEEOORS	RESORBED
BCILNOSU	LION CUBS	BDEEELLR	REBELLED	BDEEORSS	BEDSORES
BCILNOUY	BOUNCILY	BDEEELLV	BEVELLED	BDEEORST	BESTRODE
BCILSSUX	SIX CLUBS	BDEEELPU	DEEP BLUE	BDEEORSV	OBSERVED
BCIMOSUX	MUSIC BOX	BDEEELRS	BLEEDERS	BDEEORTT	DO BETTER
BCINOSSU	SUBSONIC	BDEEELUY	BLUE-EYED	BDEEORTU	OUTBREED
BCIOORST	ROBOTICS	BDEEERRT	RED BERET	BDEEOSSS	OBSESSED
BCJKMSUU	JUMBUCKS	BDEEERTT	BETTERED	BDEEOSSY	BOSS EYED
BCKKOOOO	COOKBOOK	BDEEFFRU	BUFFERED		BOSS-EYED
BCKLLOSU	BULLOCKS		REBUFFED	BDEEOSTT	BESOTTED
BCKLOOTU	BLOCK OUT	BDEEFFTU	BUFFETED		OBTESTED
BCKLOUYY	LUCKY BOY	BDEEFGGO	BEFOGGED	BDEEOSTW	BESTOWED
BCKOOOPY	COPY-BOOK	BDEEFINR	BEFRIEND	BDEEPRRU	PUREBRED
	COPYBOOK	BDEEFIRS	DEBRIEFS	BDEEPRUW	BREWED UP
BCKOSTTU	BUTTOCKS	BDEEFITT	BEFITTED	BDEERRWY	DEWBERRY
BCLMOOSU	COULOMBS	BDEEFOOR	FOREBODE	BDEERTTU	BUTTERED
BCLOORTU	CLUBROOT	BDEEFOOW	BEEFWOOD		REBUTTED
BCLOSTUW	TWO CLUBS	BDEEGGRU	BEGRUDGE	BDEESSTT	TEST-BEDS
BCMORSUU	CUMBROUS	BDEEGILN	BLEEDING	BDEFFOOT	OFF TO BED
BCMOSSTU	COMBUSTS	BDEEGILU	BEGUILED	BDEFIILR	BIRD LIFE
BCNOORWW	BROWN COW	BDEEGINR	BREEDING	BDEFIINR	FINE BIRD
BCOORSSW	CROSSBOW	BDEEGLNO	BELONGED	BDEFOOTU	OUT OF BED
BCOOSTTY	BOYCOTTS	BDEEGRSV	SVEDBERG	BDEGGIRS	BIRDS EGG
BCOOSTUY	BOY SCOUT	BDEEHIRT	THE BRIDE	BDEGHILT	BLIGHTED
BCORSTTU	OBSTRUCT	BDEEHLNO	BEHOLDEN	BDEGIINT	BETIDING
BCORSTUU	SCRUB OUT	BDEEHLOR	BEHOLDER		DEBITING
BDDDEEEM	EMBEDDED	BDEEHMOR	HOMEBRED	BDEGILNN	BLENDING
BDDDEEIM	IMBEDDED	BDEEHNST	THE BENDS	BDEGIORX	OXBRIDGE
BDDDEELO	BOLD DEED	BDEEHOOV	BEHOOVED	BDEGLNOU	BLUDGEON
BDDDEIRY	RED BIDDY	BDEEHORT	BOTHERED	BDEGLOSS	GOD BLESS
BDDEEESS	SEEDBEDS	BDEEHRTY	THE DERBY	BDEGNOOY	GO BEYOND
BDDEEFLU	BEFUDDLE	BDEEIILN	INEDIBLE	BDEGNPUU	BUNGED UP
BDDEEGGU	DEBUGGED		LIE IN BED	BDEGOORX	BOXER DOG
BDDEEGTU	BUDGETED	BDEEILLL	LIBELLED	BDEGOOSY	GOODBYES
BDDEEIIN	DIE IN BED	BDEEILLT	BILLETED	BDEHILNT	THE BLIND
BDDEEIMO	EMBODIED	BDEEILMR	MILD BEER	BDEHIMOR	HOMEBIRD
BDDEEINT	INDEBTED	BDEEILNN	BED LINEN	BDEHIRST	THE BIRDS
BDDEEINW	BINDWEED	BDEEILNO	BONE IDLE	BDEHMOOY	HOMEBODY
BDDEEIRS	BIRD SEED	BDEEILNV	VENDIBLE	BDEHNOST	BOTH ENDS
	BIRDSEED	BDEEILNY	BLIND EYE	BDEIIKLR	BIRDLIKE
BDDEEKNU	DEBUNKED	BDEEILOR	ERODIBLE	BDEIILMR	BIRDLIME
BDDEENRU	BURDENED	BDEEILOV	BODE EVIL	BDEIILTY	DEBILITY
BDDEEORR	BORDERED	BDEEILRW	BEWILDER	BDEIINST	IS IN DEBT
BDDEEORS	DESORBED	BDEEILSV	BEDEVILS	BDEIKNNU	BE UNKIND
BDDEGINY	DYING BED	BDEEIMOR	EMBODIER	BDEILLMU	BDELLIUM
BDDEILLO	BODED ILL	BDEEIMOS	EMBODIES	BDEILLOS	BODES ILL
BDDEILNR	BRINDLED	BDEEIMRT	TIMBERED	BDEILLOW	BILLOWED
BDDEILOO	BLOODIED	BDEEINOT	OBEDIENT	BDEILMNN	BLIND MEN
BDDEINNU	UNBIDDEN	BDEEIRST	BESTRIDE	BDEILMSU	SUBLIMED
BDDEINOR	DONE BIRD	BDEEIRSY	BIRD'S-EYE	BDEILNOY	BODY LINE
BDDEINRU	UNDERBID	BDEEISST	SIDE BETS		BODYLINE
BDDEIORS	DISROBED	BDEEKNRU	DEBUNKER	BDEILNRS	BLINDERS
	DOES BIRD	BDEELLMU	UMBELLED	BDEILNRU	UNBRIDLE
BDDEISSU	SUBSIDED	BDEELLOW	BELLOWED	BDEILNST	BLINDEST
BDDELOOR	BLOOD RED		BODE WELL	BDEILOOR	BLOODIER
	RED BLOOD	BDEELLRW	WELL-BRED	BDEILOOS	BLOODIES
BDDENNOW	BEND DOWN	BDEELMNO	EMBOLDEN	BDEILOPU	BOILED UP
BDDENOSW	BEDS DOWN	BDEELMRU	LUMBERED	BDEILORV	LOVEBIRD
BDDENOTU	OBTUNDED	BDEELNNO	ENNOBLED	BDEILRRY	LYRE BIRD
BDDEORTU	OBTRUDED	BDEELNRS	BLENDERS		LYREBIRD
BDDEOTYY	TEDDY BOY	BDEELORU	REDOUBLE	BDEILRSU	BUILDERS
BDDGILNO	BLIND DOG	BDEELPTU	BELTED UP	BDEIMORS	BROMIDES
BDDGIORS	BIRD DOGS	BDEELSST	DEBTLESS	BDEINOOS	NOBODIES
BDDGOOSY	DOGSBODY	BDEEMNOT	BODEMENT	BDEINOOW	WOODBINE
BDDHIIRY	DIHYBRID		ENTOMBED	BDEINORV	BIND OVER
BDDHIMSU	BUDDHISM	BDEEMNOY	BEYOND ME		OVENBIRD
BDDHISTU	BUDDHIST	BDEEMNRU	NUMBERED	BDEINOSU	BEDOUINS

BDEINSTW	TWIN BEDS	BDFLOTUU	DOUBTFUL	BEEEFLST	FEEBLEST
BDEINTTU	BUTTED IN	BDFORSUY	BODYSURF	BEEEFSTW	BEEF STEW
BDEIOORR	BROODIER	BDGGIINR	BRIDGING	BEEEGIRS	BESIEGER
BDEIORSS	DISROBES	BDGHOOUY	DOUGHBOY	BEEEGISS	BESIEGES
BDEIORSV	OVERBIDS	BDGIILNN	BLINDING	BEEEGRTT	BEGETTER
BDEIOSSY	DISOBEYS	BDGIILNR	BRIDLING	BEEEHISV	BEE HIVES
BDEIOSUX	SUBOXIDE	BDGIILNU	BUILDING		BEEHIVES
BDEIOSWY	WIDE BOYS	BDGIINNS	BINDINGS	BEEEHNOY	HONEY BEE
BDEIRSSU	DISBURSE	BDGILNNU	BUNDLING		HONEYBEE
BDEISSSU	SUBSIDES	BDGILNOO	BLOODING	BEEEILRV	BELIEVER
BDEISSTU	SUBEDITS	BDGILNOU	DOUBLING	BEEEILSV	BELIEVES
BDEKNOOS	BOOK ENDS	BDGINNOU	BOUNDING	BEEEINRZ	BREEZE IN
	BOOKENDS	BDGINOOR	BROODING	BEEEIRRZ	BREEZIER
BDEKOOPU	BOOKED UP	BDGINORS	BIRD SONG	BEEEJLSZ	JEZEBELS
BDELLOOR	BORDELLO		SONG BIRD	BEEELMNS	ENSEMBLE
BDELLOOT	LET BLOOD		SONGBIRD	BEEELMRS	RESEMBLE
BDELLOUZ	BULLDOZE	BDGINOTU	DOUBTING	BEEELMZZ	EMBEZZLE
BDELMOOU	BLUE MOOD	BDGINSUU	SUBDUING	BEEELOSW	SEE BELOW
BDELMOOV	BOLD MOVE	BDGIORSW	BIG WORDS	BEEELPRS	BLEEPERS
BDELMSTU	STUMBLED	BDGJOOOS	GOOD JOBS	BEEELSUY	BLUE EYES
BDELNNTU	BLUNT END	BDGKOOOO	GOOD BOOK	BEEEMMRR	REMEMBER
BDELNOOS	OLD BONES	BDGLLOSU	BULLDOGS	BEEENNSZ	BENZENES
BDELNOOW	NEW BLOOD	BDGNOOSW	BOGS DOWN	BEEERSTV	BEST EVER
BDELNOSS	BOLDNESS	BDGNRUUY	BURGUNDY	BEEFGOOR	GO BEFORE
BDELNOST	BLONDEST	BDGOOSUY	GOOD BUYS	BEEFHILS	FEEBLISH
BDELNOSW	BENDS LOW	BDHILNOS	BLONDISH	BEEFILLT	LIFE BELT
BDELNOTU	UNBOLTED	BDHIMOOR	RHOMBOID	BEEFILLX	FLEXIBLE
BBELNOWW	BLEW DOWN	BDHMOSUW	DUMB SHOW	BEEFILNU	UNBELIEF
BDELNRSU	BLUNDERS	BDIIJOTU	DJIBOUTI	BEEFILRS	BELFRIES
BDELOPTY	BOLD TYPE	BDIILORS	OILBIRDS	BEEFINST	BENEFITS
BDELOPUU	DOUBLE UP	BDIIMRUU	RUBIDIUM	BEEFIRSS	FRISBEES
BDELORSU	BOULDERS	BDIJORTY	DIRTY JOB	BEEFIRST	BRIEFEST
BDELOSTU	DOUBLETS	BDILLOOY	BLOODILY	BEEFLLTU	FELT BLUE
BDELTTUW	BUTT-WELD	BDILMORY	MORBIDLY	BEEFLORT	BORE LEFT
BDEMNNOS	BONDSMEN	BDILNNSU	SUNBLIND	BEEFNORR	BORN FREE
BDEMNSSU	DUMBNESS	BDILNOOW	BOIL DOWN		FREEBORN
BDEMOORS	BEDROOMS	BDILNPRU	PURBLIND	BEEGGORY	BY GEORGE
BDEMOOSY	SOMEBODY	BDILPSUU	BUILDS UP	BEEGGOSX	EGG BOXES
BDEMOOTT	BOTTOMED		BUILDUPS	BEEGHILW	BIG WHEEL
BDEMSSUU	SUBSUMED	BDILRTUY	TURBIDLY	BEEGIILL	ELIGIBLE
BDENNOTW	BENT DOWN	BDIMNORU	MORIBUND	BEEGILNP	BLEEPING
BDENNRUU	UNBURDEN	BDINNRUW	WINDBURN	BEEGILNT	BEETLING
BDENOORW	BORE DOWN	BDINOORS	BRIDOONS	BEEGILOS	OBLIGEES
BDENOOTW	BENTWOOD	BDINSSTU	DUSTBINS	BEEGILPS	BIG SLEEP
BDENORSU	BOUNDERS	BDIOORSU	BOUDOIRS	BEEGILRU	BEGUILER
	REBOUNDS	BDIORSTW	TWO BIRDS	BEEGILSU	BEGUILES
	SUBORNED	BDIRSSTU	DISTURBS	BEEGINNR	BEGINNER
BDENORSY	DRY BONES	BDKNOOOR	DOORKNOB	BEEGINRZ	BREEZING
BDENOSTU	SOUND BET	BDKOORWY	BODYWORK	BEEGINST	BEE STING
BDENOTTU	BUTTONED	BDKOOSTU	STUD BOOK	BEEGISTV	GIVE BEST
BDENSSTU	SUBTENDS		STUDBOOK	BEEGLOTW	GET BELOW
BDEOORRS	BROODERS	BDLNOOOU	DOUBLOON	BEEGMNOY	BOGEYMEN
BDEOORRW	BORROWED	BDLNOOWW	BLOW DOWN	BEEGMRSU	BEER MUGS
BDEOPSST	BED POSTS	BDLOOOST	OLD BOOTS		SUBMERGE
	BEDPOSTS	BDLOSTUW	DUST BOWL	BEEGNOTT	BEGOTTEN
BDEOPSTU	BUS DEPOT	BDNNORUW	BURN DOWN	BEEHINRT	THIN BEER
BDEOPTTU	PUT TO BED	BDNOOPTU	POT-BOUND	BEEHLLNT	HELL-BENT
BDEOPUUY	BUOYED UP	BDNOOSTU	NO DOUBTS	BEEHLOOR	BOREHOLE
BDEORRTU	OBTRUDER	BDNOOSUX	SOUND BOX	BEEHLRST	BLETHERS
BDEORRUW	BURROWED	BDNOOSWW	BOWS DOWN	BEEHLSTU	THE BLUES
BDEORSSU	ROSEBUDS	BDNORSUW	RUBS DOWN	BEEHNRRT	BRETHREN
BDEORSTU	OBTRUDES	BDORUWZZ	BUZZ WORD	BEEHOOSV	BEHOOVES
	REDOUBTS		BUZZWORD	BEEHOOTZ	THE BOOZE
BDEORSUY	RUDE BOYS	BEEEEFLN	ENFEEBLE	BEEIJLSU	JUBILEES
BDERSSUU	SUBDUERS	BEEEEFRR	FREE BEER	BEEIKLTU	TUBELIKE
BDFGNOOU	FOG BOUND	BEEEENQU	QUEEN BEE	BEEIKLWY	BIWEEKLY
	FOGBOUND	BEEEENRT	TEREBENE	BEEILLLR	LIBELLER
BDFIIITY	BIFIDITY	BEEEFIRS	FREEBIES	BEEILLNU	BLUE NILE
BDFIIORS	FIBROIDS	BEEEFIST	BEEFIEST	BEEILLTT	BELITTLE
BDFILLLO	BILLFOLD	BEEEFLLU	FEEL BLUE	BEEILNNS	BLENNIES
BDFILOST	TOLD FIBS			BEEILNOV	BE IN LOVE

BEEILNSS	SENSIBLE
BEEILNST	STEEL NIB
BEEILNSY	BYE-LINES
BEEILOPT	BE POLITE
BEEILOTV	LOVEBITE
BEEILRRT	TERRIBLE
BEEILRYZ	BREEZILY
BEEILSTT	LETS IT BE
BEEILSTU	BLUE TIES
BEEIMRTT	EMBITTER
BEEINNSV	BEN NEVIS
BEEINNSZ	BENZINES
BEEINOST	BETONIES
BEEINSTW	BEST WINE
BEEIRRTT	BITTERER
BEEIRTVY	EVERY BIT
BEEJKLOU	BLUE JOKE
BEEKMOPR	PEMBROKE
BEEKNOPS	BESPOKEN
BEEKNOST	BETOKENS
	STEENBOK
BEEKNSTW	KNEW BEST
BEEKPSUY	KEEP BUSY
BEEKRRSS	BERSERKS
BEELLNTT	BELL TENT
BEELLSST	BELTLESS
BEELLSUY	BULL'S-EYE
	BULLS EYE
BEELMNNO	NOBLEMEN
BEELMOVY	BE MY LOVE
BEELMRRT	TREMBLER
BEELMRRU	LUMBERER
BEELMRST	TREMBLES
BEELNNOS	ENNOBLES
BEELNOPW	BLEW OPEN
BEELNOSS	BONELESS
	NOBLESSE
BEELNSSU	BLUENESS
BEELNTTU	BETEL NUT
BEELOOST	OBSOLETE
BEELORUW	WORE BLUE
BEELORVW	BLEW OVER
BEELOSTV	BEST LOVE
BEELOSTY	EYEBOLTS
BEELRTTY	BY LETTER
BEELRTUU	TRUE BLUE
	TRUE-BLUE
BEELSSTU	TUBELESS
BEEMNOOR	BE NO MORE
BEEMNORS	SOBER MEN
BEEMNORV	NOVEMBER
BEEMNRRU	RENUMBER
BEEMORSS	EMBOSSER
BEEMOSSS	EMBOSSES
BEEMRSTU	BUM STEER
BEENNOOY	ONE BY ONE
BEENNOTU	NEON TUBE
BEENORTT	NO BETTER
BEENORTV	BENT OVER
	VERBOTEN
BEENRSTW	BESTREWN
BEENRTTU	BRUNETTE
BEENSTTX	NEXT BEST
BEEOORRT	ROOT BEER
BEEOORRV	OVERBORE
BEEOORTT	BEETROOT
BEEOPRRT	ROB PETER
BEEORRSU	BOURREES
BEEORRSV	OBSERVER
	OBVERSER

BEEORSSV	OBSERVES
	OBVERSES
BEEORSTU	TO BE SURE
	TUBEROSE
BEEORSWY	EYEBROWS
BEEOSSSS	OBSESSES
BEEQSSTU	BEQUESTS
BEEQSUUU	BUS QUEUE
BEERRTTU	REBUTTER
BEERSSTW	BESTREWS
BEERSSUV	SUBSERVE
BEERSTTU	BURETTES
BEERSTVY	VERY BEST
BEESTTTU	TEST TUBE
	TEST-TUBE
BEFFIOST	BITES OFF
BEFFKOOR	BROKE OFF
BEFGIILL	FILLIBEG
BEFGIILS	FILIBEGS
BEFGIINR	BRIEFING
BEFGILNU	FUNGIBLE
BEFGIRSU	FIREBUGS
BEFHILSU	BLUEFISH
BEFHIRSU	BUSH FIRE
BEFILLLU	FUEL BILL
BEFILLMU	BLUE FILM
BEFILLST	TELL FIBS
BEFILLXY	FLEXIBLY
BEFILMOR	FORELIMB
BEFILNOS	LOBE-FINS
BEFILOST	BOTFLIES
BEFILRST	FILBERTS
BEFILSTY	BY ITSELF
BEFINORS	BONFIRES
BEFKLNUU	BLUE FUNK
BEFLLLUU	FULL BLUE
BEFLLUUY	BELLYFUL
BEFLMSYY	BY MYSELF
BEFLORUW	FURBELOW
BEFNOORR	FORBORNE
BEFOOSTT	BEST FOOT
BEGGILOS	BOIL EGGS
BEGGIRTU	BUGGER IT!
BEGGNORW	BROWN EGG
BEGHIILP	PHILIBEG
BEGHILRT	BLIGHTER
BEGHINOV	BEHOVING
BEGHINRT	BERTHING
	BRIGHTEN
BEGHIOSU	BIG HOUSE
BEGHIRRT	BRIGHTER
BEGHITWY	BY WEIGHT
BEGHLNOU	BUNGHOLE
BEGHOSTU	BESOUGHT
BEGHRRSU	BURGHERS
BEGIILLY	ELIGIBLY
BEGIIMRT	BIG-TIMER
BEGIINOS	BIG NOISE
BEGIIPRZ	BIG PRIZE
BEGIKNRU	REBUKING
BEGILLLU	GULLIBLE
BEGILLNY	BELLYING
BEGILNNY	BENIGNLY
BEGILNOW	ELBOWING
BEGILNRT	TREBLING
BEGILNSS	BLESSING
	GLIBNESS
BEGILNST	BELTINGS
BEGIMNOY	BIG MONEY
BEGIMNRU	UMBERING
BEGIMNSU	BEMUSING

BEGINNOR	RINGBONE
BEGINORR	REBORING
BEGINORS	SOBERING
BEGINRRS	BRINGERS
BEGINRRY	BERRYING
BEGJNSUU	JUNE BUGS
BEGLLOSU	GLOBULES
BEGLMRRU	GRUMBLER
BEGLMRSU	GRUMBLES
BEGLOOST	BOOTLEGS
BEGLOOTW	GOT BELOW
BEGNNRSU	BREN GUNS
BEGNORSU	BURGEONS
BEGNOSTU	GONE BUST
BEGOSSTT	BEST TOGS
BEGOSSTU	GOES BUST
BEHIISTX	EXHIBITS
BEHIKNST	BETHINKS
BEHIKOSS	KIBOSHES
BEHIKPSU	PUSH-BIKE
BEHILLTY	BLITHELY
BEHILMRW	WHIMBREL
BEHILMST	THIMBLES
BEHILNPY	BIPHENYL
BEHILORR	HORRIBLE
BEHILORS	BOLSHIER
BEHILOSS	BOLSHIES
BEHILRTU	THURIBLE
BEHILTTZ	THE BLITZ
BEHIMNOO	BONHOMIE
BEHINNOS	SHIN BONE
	SHINBONE
BEHINOPS	HIPBONES
BEHINOSW	WISHBONE
BEHINOTX	IN THE BOX
BEHINRTW	NEW BIRTH
BEHINRTY	THE BRINY
BEHIORTT	BOTHER IT
BEHIORTW	BORE WITH
BEHISSTU	BUSHIEST
BEHJLNOU	BLUE JOHN
BEHJNOOT	ON THE JOB
	ON-THE-JOB
BEHLLOOT	BOLT HOLE
	BOLT-HOLE
BEHLLOOW	BLOWHOLE
BEHLLOPS	BELL HOPS
	BELLHOPS
BEHLMSTU	HUMBLEST
BEHLORST	BROTHELS
BEHNOOPX	PHONE BOX
BEHNOORT	NO BOTHER
BEHNORTX	THE BRONX
BEHOORST	THEORBOS
BEHOORSX	HORSEBOX
BEHOPRST	POTHERBS
BEHORRST	BROTHERS
BEHORSSU	ROSE BUSH
	ROSEBUSH
BEHORSTT	BETROTHS
BEIIKRTZ	KIBITZER
BEIILMMO	IMMOBILE
BEIILMOS	MOBILISE
BEIILMOZ	MOBILIZE
BEIILRST	TRILBIES
BEIILRTT	LIBRETTI
BEIIMNNU	BIENNIUM
BEIINNTT	BITTEN IN
BEIINOTT	BITE INTO
BEIIOPSS	BIOPSIES
BEIISTTT	BITTIEST

BEIKLNRS	BLINKERS	BEISSTTU	BEST SUIT	BENNNPUY	BUN PENNY
BEIKLOSS	OBELISKS		BUSTIEST	BENNOSSU	SNUB NOSE
BEIKLOTY	KILOBYTE	BEJKKOOO	JOKE BOOK	BENOORRV	OVERBORN
BEIKLSTU	BULKIEST	BEJORTTU	TURBOJET	BENOORTU	BORNE OUT
BEIKNNOR	BROKEN IN	BEKLNORY	BROKENLY	BENORRSU	SUBORNER
BEIKNOST	STEINBOK	BEKLOOST	BOOKLETS	BENORSSU	RUB NOSES
BEIKOSTX	BOX KITES	BEKNNORU	UNBROKEN	BENORSTW	BROWNEST
BEIKRSST	BRISKEST	BEKNOOOP	OPEN BOOK	BENOSSWY	NEWSBOYS
	BRISKETS	BEKNOOOT	NOTE BOOK	BENRRTUY	BY RETURN
BEILLMRY	LIMBERLY		NOTEBOOK	BENSSSUY	BUSYNESS
BEILLMSS	LIMBLESS	BEKNOORT	RENT BOOK	BENSTTUW	WENT BUST
	MESS BILL	BEKNOPRU	BROKEN UP	BEOOPSUZ	BOOZE-UPS
BEILLNTU	BULLETIN	BEKNOSTW	KNOW BEST	BEOORRRW	BORROWER
BEILLORS	BROLLIES	BEKOOORV	OVERBOOK	BEOORSST	BOOSTERS
BEILLRTU	TRUE BILL	BEKOORST	BOOKREST	BEOPRRSV	PROVERBS
BEILMMOS	EMBOLISM	BEKOORTU	BROKE OUT	BEOPRSSU	SOBERS UP
BEILMNOU	NOBELIUM	BEKOOSTT	TOOK BETS	BEOPRSSX	PRESS BOX
BEILMNRU	IN LUMBER	BEKOOTTX	TEXT BOOK	BEOQSTUU	BOUQUETS
	UNLIMBER		TEXTBOOK		
BEILMNST	NIMBLEST	BEKPSTUY	KEPT BUSY	BEORRRUW	BURROWER
BEILMORS	EMBROILS	BELLLLPU	BELLPULL	BEORSTUU	TUBEROUS
BEILMPRU	LIMBER UP	BELLNORW	WELLBORN	BEPRRSTU	PERTURBS
BEILMRSS	BRIMLESS	BELLOOSU	LOBULOSE	BEPRTTUU	BUTTER UP
BEILMSSU	SUBLIMES	BELLOPTY	POTBELLY	BERSSTTU	BUTTRESS
BEILNNTU	BUNTLINE	BELMNOOU	BLUE MOON	BERSSTUV	SUBVERTS
BEILNOPS	BONSPIEL	BELMOORS	BLOOMERS	BESSSUYY	BYSSUSES
BEILNOSW	BOWLINES	BELMOPRS	PROBLEMS	BFFFILMU	FILM BUFF
BEILNSSY	SENSIBLY	BELMORSY	SOMBRELY	BFFGILNU	BLUFFING
BEILNSTZ	BLINTZES	BELMOSST	TOMBLESS	BFFGINOR	BRING OFF
BEILOORV	BOIL OVER	BELMPRSU	PLUMBERS	BFFGISTU	BIG STUFF
BEILOPPW	BLOWPIPE	BELMRRUY	MULBERRY	BFFHORSU	BRUSH OFF
BEILOPSS	POSSIBLE	BELMRSSU	SLUMBERS		BRUSH-OFF
BEILORRS	BROILERS	BELMRSTU	STUMBLER	BFFINOTU	BIT OF FUN
BEILORST	STROBILE		TUMBLERS	BFFKNOSU	BUNKS OFF
BEILORSW	BLOWSIER		TUMBRELS	BFFLLOUY	BULLY OFF
BEILORTT	LIBRETTO	BELMSSTU	STUMBLES	BFFLNOOW	BLOWN OFF
BEILRRTT	BRITTLER	BELNOOPW	BLOW OPEN	BFFLOOSW	BLOWS OFF
BEILRRTY	TERRIBLY	BELNORUW	WORN BLUE	BFFMOPSU	BUMPS OFF
BEILRSST	BLISTERS	BELNOSUU	NEBULOUS	BFFNOOSU	BUFFOONS
	BRISTLES	BELNRTUU	TURN BLUE	BFFNOSUX	SNUFF BOX
BEILRSTU	BURLIEST	BELNSTTU	BLUNTEST		SNUFFBOX
BEILRSTY	BLISTERY	BELOOOSX	LOOSE BOX	BFFOSSTU	SOB STUFF
BEILRTTY	BITTERLY	BELOOPRS	BLOOPERS	BFGGHIIT	BIG FIGHT
BEILSTTU	BLUE TITS	BELOOPRT	BOLTROPE	BFGHINTU	BUN FIGHT
	SUBTITLE	BELOORSW	ROSE BOWL		BUN-FIGHT
BEILSTUU	BLUE SUIT	BELOORVW	BLOW OVER	BFGIILMS	BIG FILMS
BEIMMRSU	BRUMMIES		BOWL OVER	BFGILMNU	FUMBLING
BEIMNORY	IN EMBRYO	BELOOSST	BOOTLESS	BFGILNYY	FLYING BY
BEIMNSSU	NIMBUSES	BELOPTTU	BOTTLE UP	BFGLLORU	BULLFROG
BEIMOORS	RIBOSOME	BELORSST	BOLSTERS	BFGOOOTY	GO BY FOOT
BEIMORRV	BRIM OVER		LOBSTERS	BFHIISTY	BIT FISHY
BEIMORTY	BIOMETRY	BELORSTT	BLOTTERS	BFHILOSW	FISHBOWL
BEIMOSTY	SYMBIOTE		BOTTLERS	BFHLLSUU	BLUSHFUL
BEIMPSTU	BUMPIEST	BELORSTU	TROUBLES	BFIIORSS	FIBROSIS
BEIMSTUY	BUSY TIME	BELOSSUY	BLESS YOU	BFILLSSU	BLISSFUL
BEINNOST	BONNIEST	BELOSTUY	OBTUSELY	BFILNORU	FLOUR BIN
BEINNOSZ	BENZOINS	BELPRSUY	SUPERBLY	BFILOOST	SOFT-BOIL
BEINORSW	BROWNIES	BELRSSTU	BLUSTERS	BFLLNOWY	FLYBLOWN
BEINOSSX	BOXINESS	BELRSTUY	BLUSTERY	BFLLOOUW	FOUL BLOW
BEINOSTU	BOUNTIES	BELSSTTU	SUBTLEST	BFLLOSUW	BOWLFULS
BEINRSTT	BITTERNS	BELSTTUY	SUBTLETY	BGGGILNO	BOGGLING
BEINRSTU	TRIBUNES	BEMNNSSU	NUMBNESS	BGGIILNO	OBLIGING
	TURBINES	BEMNOORT	TROMBONE	BGGIILRS	BIG GIRLS
BEINSSSU	BUSINESS	BEMNOORW	NEW BROOM	BGGILNNU	BUNGLING
BEIOQTUU	BOUTIQUE	BEMOORRS	SOMBRERO	BGGILNRU	BURGLING
BEIORRST	ORBITERS	BEMOORST	REST ROOM	BGHHINOR	HIGHBORN
BEIORSTY	SOBRIETY	BEMOORTT	BOTTOMER	BGHHIORW	HIGHBROW
BEIOSSST	BOSSIEST	BEMOPTXY	EMPTY BOX	BGHHIOSY	HIGHBOYS
BEIQRSTU	BRIQUETS	BEMORSST	MOBSTERS	BGHIIKNT	THINK BIG
BEIRRSSU	BRUISERS	BEMSSSUU	SUBSUMES	BGHILMNU	HUMBLING
BEIRSTTU	TRIBUTES	BENNNOTY	TONY BENN	BGHILNSU	BLUSHING

Code	Word	Code	Word	Code	Word
BGHILRTY	BRIGHTLY	BHIIOPRT	PROHIBIT	BLNOOTUW	BLOWN OUT
BGHIMNTU	THUMBING	BHIKLLOO	BILLHOOK	BLOORSWW	LOWBROWS
BGHIMOTU	BIG MOUTH	BHILLNOR	HORNBILL	BLOOSTTU	BLOTS OUT
BGHINOTU	BOUGHT IN	BHILORRY	HORRIBLY	BLOOSTUW	BLOWOUTS
BGHINRSU	BRUSHING	BHILORTW	LOW BIRTH		BLOWS OUT
BGHIOPSY	GO BY SHIP	BHILOSYY	BOYISHLY		BOWLS OUT
BGHIOSST	BIG SHOTS	BHIMNORT	THROMBIN	BLOPSSTU	SUBPLOTS
BGHIRSTY	BY RIGHTS	BHINOORZ	B-HORIZON	BLORSTUY	ROBUSTLY
BGHJOOTU	TOUGH JOB	BHINORSW	BROWNISH	BLORTTUU	BLURT OUT
BGHMORSU	HOMBURGS	BHJLLNOU	JOHN BULL	BMNOOOTW	BOOM TOWN
BGHNNUUY	BUNNY HUG	BHKLOOOY	HOLY BOOK	BMNOORTW	TOM BROWN
BGHOORSU	BOROUGHS	BHKMNOOY	HYMN BOOK	BMNOOSSU	UNBOSOMS
BGHOPTUU	BOUGHT UP		HYMNBOOK	BMOOORSX	BOXROOMS
BGIIINNT	BITING IN	BHKNOOOR	HORNBOOK	BMOORSSS	MOSS BROS.
BGIIKLNN	BLINKING	BHKOOOPS	BOOK SHOP	BMOORTTY	BOTTOMRY
BGIILLNS	BILLINGS		BOOKSHOP	BNNOOSYY	SONNY BOY
BGIILNOR	BROILING			BNNORTUW	NUT-BROWN
BGIILNRS	BRISLING	BHLLNORU	BULLHORN	BNNOTTUU	UNBUTTON
BGIILNSS	SIBLINGS	BHLNOOTW	BLOWN HOT	BNNRSSUU	SUNBURNS
BGIILNTY	BITINGLY	BHLOOOTT	TOLBOOTH	BNNRSTUU	SUNBURNT
BGIIMMNR	BRIMMING	BHLOOSTW	BLOWS HOT	BNOOOSUY	SONOBUOY
BGIIMNRU	IMBRUING	BHMMOTTU	TOM THUMB	BNOPTTUU	BUTTON UP
BGIINNRS	BRINGS IN	BHMORSTU	THROMBUS	BNORSTUU	BURNS OUT
BGIINNUY	BUYING IN	BHMPSTUU	THUMBS UP	BNORTTUU	BURNT OUT
BGIINORT	ORBITING		THUMBS-UP	BNOSTUWY	BUSY TOWN
BGIINRSU	BRUISING	BHMRSSUU	BUM'S RUSH	BNRSSTUU	SUNBURST
BGIJLMNU	JUMBLING	BHNORSTY	BRYTHONS	BOOOPRSY	POOR BOYS
BGIKLNOT	KINGBOLT	BHOPRSUU	PUB HOURS	BOOPSSTY	POSTBOYS
BGIKNOOR	BROOKING	BIIKLOST	KILOBITS	BOORSSTY	SOB STORY
BGIKNOOS	BOOKINGS	BIILLNOS	BILLIONS	BOOTTWWY	TWO BY TWO
BGILLNOU	GLOBULIN	BIILMMPS	BLIMPISM	BOPRRTUY	RUBY PORT
BGILLNRU	BULLRING	BIILMOTY	MOBILITY	BOPSSSTU	BUS STOPS
BGILLNUY	BULLYING	BIILNOOV	OBLIVION		BUS-STOPS
BGILMMNU	MUMBLING	BIILNOTY	NOBILITY	BORSTTUU	BURST OUT
BGILMNOO	BLOOMING	BIILNTUY	NUBILITY		OUTBURST
BGILMNPU	PLUMBING	BIILORST	STROBILI		
BGILMNRU	RUMBLING	BIINRSTU	RUBS IT IN	CCCEEILT	ECLECTIC
BGILMNTU	TUMBLING	BIINSTTY	TINY BITS	CCCEGOSY	COCCYGES
BGILMOSU	GUMBOILS	BIIQTUUY	UBIQUITY	CCCEHIOS	CHOC-ICES
BGILNNTU	BLUNTING	BIIRSSTU	BURSITIS	CCCEOSXY	COCCYXES
BGILNORT	RINGBOLT	BIJNOSSU	SUBJOINS	CCCILLYY	CYCLICLY
BGILNORW	BRING LOW	BIKMNPSU	BUMPKINS	CCCILNOY	CYCLONIC
BGILNORY	BORINGLY	BIKOOUUZ	BOUZOUKI	CCCINSTU	SUCCINCT
BGILNOTT	BLOTTING	BILLNOOU	BOUILLON	CCCIOORS	SCIROCCO
	BOTTLING	BILMMPSU	PLUMBISM	CCCKOORW	COCKCROW
BGILNRRU	BLURRING	BILMOSTU	BOTULISM	CCCNOOST	CONCOCTS
BGILNSTU	BUSTLING	BILMRSTU	TUMBRILS	CCDDEENO	CONCEDED
BGILOORS	OBLIGORS	BILNORSU	BURNS OIL	CCDDEEOT	DECOCTED
BGINNORS	BRINGS ON	BILNORTU	BURNT OIL	CCDDELOU	OCCLUDED
BGINNORW	BROWNING	BILOPSSY	POSSIBLY	CCDDENOU	CONDUCED
BGINNORZ	BRONZING	BILORSST	BRISTOLS	CCDDKLOU	COLD DUCK
BGINOOST	BONGOIST	BILPRSUY	RUBY LIPS	CCDEEENR	CREDENCE
	BOOSTING	BIMNOPTU	BUMP INTO	CCDEEHLN	CLENCHED
BGINORST	BRINGS TO	BIMNOSTY	SYMBIONT	CCDEEIOP	CODPIECE
BGINORSW	BROWSING	BIMNRUUV	VIBURNUM	CCDEEKOY	COCKEYED
BGINORTU	BRING OUT	BINOSTWY	TWIN BOYS	CCDEELRY	RECYCLED
BGINPRSU	BRINGS UP	BINRSSTU	BURSTS IN	CCDEENOR	CONCEDER
BGINPUUY	BUYING UP	BINSSTUU	SUBUNITS	CCDEENOS	CONCEDES
BGINRSTU	BURSTING	BIOOPSTT	POST-OBIT	CCDEESSU	SUCCEEDS
BGIORSTY	BIG STORY	BIOPRSTW	BOWSPRIT	CCDEHILN	CLINCHED
BGJOSTUY	TOBY JUGS	BIORSSTT	BISTORTS	CCDEHLTU	CLUTCHED
BGKLOOOS	LOG BOOKS	BISSSSTU	SUBSISTS		DECLUTCH
	LOGBOOKS	BJOPPTUU	PUT-UP JOB	CCDEHNRU	CRUNCHED
BGKNOOOS	SONG BOOK	BKKOOORW	WORKBOOK	CCDEHORS	SCORCHED
BGLNOOSW	LONGBOWS	BKMOOORW	BOOKWORM	CCDEHORT	CROTCHED
BGLNOSUW	BLOWGUNS	BLLORSTY	STROLL BY	CCDEHORU	CROUCHED
BGLOORYY	BRYOLOGY	BLMOOOTY	LOBOTOMY	CCDEHOST	SCOTCHED
BGMOOSTU	GUMBOOTS	BLMOOSSS	BLOSSOMS	CCDEHSTU	SCUTCHED
BGNOOUYY	YOUNG BOY	BLMOOSSY	BLOSSOMY	CCDEIINO	COINCIDE
BHIIINST	INHIBITS	BLMOPSUU	PLUMBOUS	CCDEILSY	CYCLISED
BHIILMPS	BLIMPISH	BLNOORWW	BROWN OWL	CCDEILYZ	CYCLIZED
		BLNOOSUS	BLOUSONS	CCDEINOR	CORNICED

CCDEINOT	OCCIDENT	CCEHKPSU	CHECKS UP
CCDEIOPU	OCCUPIED		CHECKUPS
CCDEIPRU	CIDER CUP	CCEHLMOR	CROMLECH
CCDEKOPU	COCKED UP	CCEHLSTU	CLUTCHES
CCDELNOU	CONCLUDE	CCEHNRSU	CRUNCHES
CCDELORU	COLD CURE	CCEHORRS	SCORCHER
CCDELOSU	OCCLUDES	CCEHORSS	SCORCHES
CCDELOTU	OCCULTED	CCEHORST	CROCHETS
CCDENOOO	COCOONED		CROTCHES
CCDENOSU	CONDUCES	CCEHORSU	CROUCHES
CCDEORRU	OCCURRED	CCEHORTT	CROTCHET
CCDEOSTU	STUCCOED	CCEHOSST	SCOTCHES
CCDHIIOR	DICHROIC	CCEHRSTU	CRUTCHES
CCDIILNU	NUCLIDIC	CCEHSSTU	SCUTCHES
CCDIILOS	CODICILS	CCEIIKPS	ICE PICKS
CCDIIORT	DICROTIC	CCEIILNT	ENCLITIC
CCDILOSY	CYCLOIDS	CCEIILOR	LICORICE
CCDISSTU	CUT DISCS	CCEIILPT	ECLIPTIC
CCDKLOOR	OLD CROCK	CCEIILST	SCILICET
CCDKLOSU	CUCKOLDS	CCEIINOR	CICERONI
CCDKOOOW	WOODCOCK	CCEIKOST	COCKIEST
CCDNOORS	CONCORDS	CCEIKRST	CRICKETS
CCDNOSTU	CONDUCTS	CCEILMOO	COELOMIC
CCEEGINR	RECCEING	CCEILNUY	UNICYCLE
CCEEHKRS	CHECKERS	CCEILOSS	SCOLICES
CCEEHLNS	CLENCHES	CCEILRRS	CIRCLERS
CCEEHMOO	ECCE HOMO	CCEILRST	CIRCLETS
CCEEILNR	ENCIRCLE	CCEILRTY	TRICYCLE
CCEEILNS	LICENCES	CCEILRUU	CURLICUE
CCEEILPY	EPICYCLE	CCEILSSY	CYCLISES
CCEEILRT	ELECTRIC	CCEILSTU	CUTICLES
CCEEINOR	CICERONE	CCEILSYZ	CYCLIZES
CCEEINOV	CONCEIVE	CCEIMNOO	ECONOMIC
CCEEINSS	SCIENCES	CCEIMOST	COSMETIC
CCEEIORV	COERCIVE	CCEIMRRU	MERCURIC
CCEEIRSV	CERVICES	CCEINNOV	CONVINCE
	CREVICES	CCEINOOR	COERCION
CCEEITTU	EUTECTIC	CCEINORS	CONCISER
CCEEKLOR	COCKEREL		CORNICES
CCEEKNRW	CREW NECK	CCEINORT	CONCERTI
CCEELMNY	CLEMENCY		NECROTIC
CCEELRRY	RECYCLER	CCEINOST	CONCEITS
CCEELRSY	RECYCLES	CCEINOTT	TECTONIC
CCEEMMNO	COMMENCE	CCEINOTU	CUT NO ICE
CCEEMMOR	COMMERCE	CCEINPRT	PRECINCT
CCEENNOS	ENSCONCE	CCEINRTU	CINCTURE
CCEENORT	CONCRETE	CCEIOPPS	COPPICES
CCEENRST	CRESCENT	CCEIOPRR	RICE CROP
CCEFFHKO	CHECK OFF	CCEIOPRU	OCCUPIER
CCEFIIPS	SPECIFIC	CCEIOPSU	OCCUPIES
CCEFIRRU	CRUCIFER	CCEIOPTY	ECOTYPIC
CCEFLLOU	FLOCCULE	CCEIORST	CORTICES
CCEGHIKN	CHECKING	CCEIOTXY	EXOCYTIC
CCEGINOR	COERCING	CCEIPRTU	CUT PRICE
CCEHHRSU	CHURCHES		CUT-PRICE
CCEHIIMR	CHIMERIC		PRICE CUT
CCEHIKNS	CHECKS IN	CCEIPSST	SCEPTICS
	CHICKENS	CCEIRSSU	CIRCUSES
CCEHILNR	CLINCHER	CCEKLORS	CLOCKERS
CCEHILNS	CLINCHES	CCEKNOSY	COCKNEYS
CCEHILOR	CHOLERIC	CCEKORRY	CROCKERY
CCEHILOY	CHOICELY	CCEKORSU	COCKSURE
CCEHINOO	NO CHOICE	CCELLOST	COLLECTS
CCEHINOR	CORNICHE	CCELNOSY	CYCLONES
CCEHINOS	CONCHIES	CCELRUUY	CURLYCUE
CCEHINSS	CHICNESS	CCENNORS	CONCERNS
CCEHIORT	RICOCHET	CCENNOST	CONNECTS
CCEHIOST	CHOICEST	CCENOORT	CONCERTO
CCEHKLSU	CHUCKLES	CCENOPST	CONCEPTS
CCEHKOTU	CHECK OUT	CCENORST	CONCERTS
	CHECKOUT	CCENRRUY	CURRENCY
CCEORRST	CORRECTS		
CCEORSSU	CROCUSES		
CCEOSSTU	STUCCOES		
CCERSTUW	CREW CUTS		
CCESSSUU	CUSCUSES		
CCFIIRUX	CRUCIFIX		
CCFILLOU	FLOCCULI		
CCFILNOT	CONFLICT		
CCGHIINN	CINCHING		
CCGHIKNO	CHOCKING		
CCGHIKNU	CHUCKING		
CCGHINOU	COUCHING		
CCGIIKLN	CLICKING		
CCGIIKNR	CRICKING		
CCGIKLNO	CLOCKING		
CCGIKLNU	CLUCKING		
CCGIKNOR	CROCKING		
CCGINNOS	SCONCING		
CCHHIINN	CHIN-CHIN		
CCHHINOT	CHTHONIC		
CCHHLRUY	CHURCHLY		
CCHHOOPP	CHOP-CHOP		
CCHHOOWW	CHOW-CHOW		
CCHIINUZ	ZUCCHINI		
CCHIISTU	CUSHITIC		
CCHIKNSU	CHUCKS IN		
CCHIKCTU	CHUCKS IT		
CCHIPSSY	PSYCHICS		
CCHKOTUU	CHUCK OUT		
CCHKPSUU	CHUCKS UP		
CCIIKNPY	PICNICKY		
CCIILLRY	CYRILLIC		
CCIILORT	CLITORIC		
CCIIMNSY	CYNICISM		
CCIINOTY	CONICITY		
CCIIRSTU	CIRCUITS		
CCIIRTUY	CIRCUITY		
CCIKKOTT	TICKTOCK		
CCIKLNOS	CLOCKS IN		
CCIKLOSW	COWLICKS		
CCIKOPST	COCKPITS		
CCIKOPTU	COCK IT UP		
CCILLOPP	CLIP-CLOP		
CCILNOSU	COUNCILS		
CCILOOPS	PICCOLOS		
CCILOSSY	CYCLOSIS		
CCILSSTY	CYCLISTS		
CCINOSTV	CONVICTS		
CCIOOPST	SCOTOPIC		
CCIOORSS	SIROCCOS		
CCIOOTXY	OXYTOCIC		
CCIOPSTU	OCCIPUTS		
CCJNNOTU	CONJUNCT		
CCKLNOOS	CLOCKS ON		
CCKLOOTU	CLOCK OUT		
CCKOOPST	STOPCOCK		
CCLLOTUY	OCCULTLY		
CCMOOORS	MOROCCOS		
CCNOOSTU	COCONUTS		
CCOOSSUU	COUSCOUS		
CCORSSTU	CROSSCUT		
CCORSSUU	SUCCOURS		
CDDDEETU	DEDUCTED		
CDDEEEEX	EXCEEDED		
CDDEEEFT	DEFECTED		
CDDEEEIV	DECEIVED		
CDDEEEJT	DEJECTED		
CDDEEENT	DECEDENT		
CDDEEEPR	PRECEDED		
CDDEEETT	DETECTED		
CDDEEHIS	DEHISCED		

CDDEEHNR	DRENCHED
CDDEEIKR	DICKERED
CDDEEILN	DECLINED
CDDEEILP	PEDICLED
CDDEEIOV	DEVOICED
CDDEEIPT	DEPICTED
CDDEEIRS	DECIDERS
	DESCRIED
CDDEEIRT	CREDITED
	DIRECTED
CDDEEKOT	DOCKETED
CDDEEKUW	DUCKWEED
CDDEELSU	SECLUDED
CDDEELUX	EXCLUDED
CDDEELUY	DEUCEDLY
CDDEENOS	SECONDED
CDDEENSS	DESCENDS
CDDEEORR	RECORDED
CDDEEORS	DECODERS
CDDEFIIO	CODIFIED
CDDEFINO	CONFIDED
CDDEGIIN	DECIDING
CDDEGINO	DECODING
CDDEGINU	DEDUCING
CDDEHRSU	CHUDDERS
CDDEIINT	INDICTED
CDDEILLO	COLLIDED
CDDEILNU	INCLUDED
CDDEILRU	CUDDLIER
CDDEINTU	INDUCTED
CDDEIORT	DO CREDIT
CDDEIORV	DIVORCED
CDDELLOU	COLLUDED
CDDELNOO	CONDOLED
CDDELORS	CODDLERS
CDDELPUU	CUDDLE UP
CDDENNOO	CONDONED
CDDEOORR	CORRODED
CDDEOORT	DOCTORED
CDDEOORW	CODE WORD
CDDEOPRU	PRODUCED
CDDFLOOO	COLD FOOD
CDDGHILO	GODCHILD
CDDGILNO	CODDLING
CDDGILNU	CUDDLING
CDDGINSU	SCUDDING
CDDHILOS	CLODDISH
	COLD DISH
CDDHLOTU	OLD DUTCH
CDDIIIOS	DIDICOIS
CDDIIOSY	DIDICOYS
CDDIKLUW	WILD DUCK
CDDIKOPS	PIDDOCKS
CDDIKORT	ODD TRICK
CDDILNOW	COLD WIND
CDDIORSS	DISCORDS
CDDKNOPU	DUCK POND
CDDKORSU	RUDDOCKS
CDDKORSY	DRY DOCKS
CDDOOORW	CORD WOOD
	CORDWOOD
CDEEEFFT	EFFECTED
CDEEEFNS	DEFENCES
CDEEEHOR	REECHOED
CDEEEHRT	THE CREED
CDEEEHSW	ESCHEWED
CDEEEHTU	THE DEUCE
CDEEEINV	EVIDENCE
CDEEEIPY	PIECE-DYE
CDEEEIRV	DECEIVER
	RECEIVED
CDEEEISV	DECEIVES
CDEEEJRT	REJECTED
CDEEELLX	EXCELLED
CDEEELST	SELECTED
CDEEEMNT	CEMENTED
CDEEENRS	SCREENED
CDEEENRT	CENTERED
CDEEEPRS	PRECEDES
CDEEEPTX	EXCEPTED
	EXPECTED
CDEEERRS	DECREERS
CDEEERSS	RECESSED
	SECEDERS
CDEEERST	RESECTED
	SECRETED
CDEEERTX	EXCRETED
CDEEETUX	EXECUTED
CDEEFFOR	FORCE FED
	FORCE-FED
CDEEFHLT	FLETCHED
CDEEFIIS	EDIFICES
CDEEFINN	FENCED IN
CDEEFINT	INFECTED
CDEEFKLR	FRECKLED
CDEEFKOR	FOREDECK
CDEEFLLO	FEEL COLD
CDEEFLOT	COLD FEET
CDEEFLST	DEFLECTS
CDEEFNOR	ENFORCED
CDEEFORT	DEFECTOR
CDEEGIIR	REGICIDE
CDEEGINO	GENOCIDE
CDEEGINR	RECEDING
CDEEGINS	SECEDING
CDEEGIOS	GEODESIC
CDEEGIOT	GEODETIC
CDEEHINR	ENRICHED
CDEEHIPR	CIPHERED
	DECIPHER
CDEEHISS	DEHISCES
CDEEHKST	SKETCHED
CDEEHLSU	SCHEDULE
CDEEHNQU	QUENCHED
CDEEHNRS	DRENCHES
CDEEHNRT	TRENCHED
CDEEHNRW	WRENCHED
CDEEHNST	STENCHED
CDEEHORR	RED OCHRE
CDEEHORT	HECTORED
CDEEHPRY	CYPHERED
CDEEHRTW	WRETCHED
CDEEIILR	ERIC IDLE
CDEEIILT	ELICITED
CDEEIIMN	MEDICINE
CDEEIIMP	EPIDEMIC
CDEEIISV	DECISIVE
CDEEIITT	DIETETIC
CDEEIJNT	INJECTED
CDEEIJOR	REJOICED
CDEEIKNR	NICKERED
CDEEIKNS	SICKENED
CDEEIKPT	PICKETED
CDEEILNR	RECLINED
CDEEILNS	DECLINES
	LICENSED
	SILENCED
CDEEILOR	RECOILED
CDEEILPS	ECLIPSED
	PEDICELS
	PEDICLES
CDEEILRT	DERELICT
CDEEILSU	SELEUCID
CDEEIMNR	ENDERMIC
CDEEIMOR	MEDIOCRE
CDEEIMOS	COMEDIES
CDEEIMRV	DECEMVIR
CDEEINNS	INCENSED
CDEEINNT	INDECENT
CDEEINPT	INCEPTED
CDEEIORV	DIVORCEE
CDEEIOSV	DEVOICES
CDEEIPRS	PRECISED
CDEEIPRT	DECREPIT
	DEPICTER
CDEEIPRU	PEDICURE
CDEEIRRS	DECRIERS
CDEEIRRT	DIRECTER
	REDIRECT
CDEEIRSS	DESCRIES
CDEEIRST	DESERTIC
	DISCREET
	DISCRETE
CDEEIRSV	SERVICED
CDEEJKOY	JOCKEYED
CDEEKLPS	SPECKLED
CDEEKNOR	RECKONED
CDEEKOPT	POCKETED
CDEEKORT	ROCKETED
CDEEKOST	SOCKETED
CDEEKPRU	PUCKERED
CDEEKRSU	SUCKERED
CDEEKRTU	TUCKERED
CDEELLPU	CUPELLED
CDEELMOW	WELCOMED
CDEELNOS	ENCLOSED
CDEELNPU	PEDUNCLE
CDEELNTY	DECENTLY
CDEELOOW	LOCOWEED
CDEELOPU	DECOUPLE
CDEELOSS	CODELESS
CDEELOST	CLOSETED
CDEELPRU	PRECLUDE
CDEELRTU	LECTURED
CDEELRUX	EXCLUDER
CDEELSSU	SECLUDES
CDEELSUX	EXCLUDES
CDEEMOPR	COMPERED
CDEEMOPT	COMPETED
CDEEMORT	ECTODERM
CDEENNOS	CONDENSE
CDEENNOU	DENOUNCE
CDEENNOV	CONVENED
CDEENNPY	PENDENCY
CDEENNTY	TENDENCY
CDEENORR	CORNERED
CDEENORS	CENSORED
	SECONDER
CDEENOVY	CONVEYED
CDEENPRU	PRUDENCE
CDEENRSU	CENSURED
CDEENSST	DESCENTS
CDEENSTY	ENCYSTED
CDEEOPPS	SPEED COP
CDEEOPRS	PROCEEDS
CDEEOPRU	RECOUPED
CDEEORRR	RECORDER
CDEEORRU	CRUDE ORE
CDEEORST	CORSETED
	ESCORTED
CDEEORTT	DETECTOR
CDEEORTV	VECTORED

CDEEOSST	CESTODES	CDEIILNN	INCLINED
	COSSETED	CDEIILOT	IDIOLECT
CDEERRRU	RECURRED	CDEIILPS	DISCIPLE
CDEERRUV	RECURVED	CDEIILRU	RIDICULE
CDEERSSU	SEDUCERS	CDEIINNT	INCIDENT
CDEFFIOR	CRIED OFF	CDEIINOS	DECISION
CDEFFISU	SUFFICED	CDEIINOT	COINED IT
CDEFHILN	FLINCHED	CDEIINOV	INVOICED
CDEFHIMO	CHIEFDOM	CDEIINRT	IN CREDIT
CDEFIIOS	CODIFIES		INDICTER
CDEFIIST	DEFICITS		INDIRECT
CDEFILSW	W.C.FIELDS	CDEIINTY	CYTIDINE
CDEFINNO	CONFINED	CDEIIOPR	PERIODIC
CDEFINOS	CONFIDES	CDEIIOPS	EPISODIC
CDEFIORR	CRIED FOR	CDEIIOSU	DIECIOUS
CDEFKORS	DEFROCKS	CDEIIPPT	PEPTIDIC
CDEFLLOT	FELT COLD	CDEIIPRR	CIRRIPED
	LEFT COLD	CDEIIRTU	DIURETIC
CDEFLNOU	FLOUNCED	CDEIISSU	SUICIDES
CDEFLORY	FORCEDLY	CDEIKKPU	KICKED UP
CDEFNOSU	CONFUSED	CDEIKLNO	LOCKED IN
CDEFNOTU	CONFUTED	CDEIKLWY	WICKEDLY
CDEFOSSU	FOCUSSED	CDEIKMNU	MUCKED IN
CDEGGKSU	DUCKS EGG	CDEIKNOP	PICKED ON
CDEGIILO	GOIDELIC	CDEIKNPU	UNPICKED
CDEGIKNO	DECOKING	CDEIKNSU	SUCKED IN
CDEGINNO	ENCODING	CDEIKNTU	TUCKED IN
CDEGINNS	SCENDING	CDEIKPPU	PICKED UP
CDEGINOY	DECOYING	CDEIKRRS	DERRICKS
CDEGINRU	REDUCING	CDEIKSTU	DUCKIEST
CDEGINRY	DECRYING	CDEIKSTY	CITY DESK
CDEGINSU	SEDUCING	CDEILLOS	COLLIDES
CDEGINSY	DYSGENIC	CDEILLOY	DOCILELY
CDEGIORT	GO DIRECT	CDEILLPU	PELLUCID
CDEGLNOO	COLOGNED	CDEILMOP	COMPILED
CDEGLORW	GREW COLD		COMPLIED
CDEGLOST	GETS COLD	CDEILMRU	DULCIMER
CDEGORSU	SCOURGED	CDEILNOS	CLOSED IN
CDEHHOTU	DUTCH HOE		INCLOSED
CDEHIILO	HELICOID	CDEILNOU	UNCOILED
CDEHIILR	IDLE RICH	CDEILNOY	DO NICELY
CDEHIILS	CEILIDHS	CDEILNRY	CYLINDER
CDEHIIMN	CHIMED IN	CDEILNSU	INCLUDES
CDEHIIMO	HOMICIDE	CDEILOOT	COOLED IT
CDEHIINO	ECHINOID	CDEILOOW	WOODLICE
CDEHIIVV	CHIVVIED	CDEILOPU	COILED UP
CDEHILNR	CHILDREN	CDEILORU	CLOUDIER
CDEHILOR	CHLORIDE		CRUDE OIL
CDEHIMRS	SMIRCHED	CDEILORV	COD-LIVER
CDEHINST	SNITCHED	CDEILOSS	DISCLOSE
CDEHIOSW	COWHIDES	CDEILPPR	CRIPPLED
CDEHIOTY	THEODICY	CDEILRTY	DIRECTLY
CDEHISTT	STITCHED	CDEILSXY	DYSLEXIC
CDEHISTW	SWITCHED	CDEIMNPU	MINCED UP
CDEHITTW	TWITCHED	CDEIMOST	DOCETISM
CDEHKLSU	SHELDUCK		DOMESTIC
CDEHLOOS	SCHOOLED	CDEIMPRS	SCRIMPED
CDEHLOSU	SLOUCHED	CDEINNOS	IN SECOND
CDEHMNTU	DUTCHMEN	CDEINNOU	UNCOINED
CDEHMOOS	SMOOCHED	CDEINNOV	CONNIVED
CDEHNRSU	CHUNDERS	CDEINNOW	WIND-CONE
CDEHORSU	CHORUSED	CDEINORS	CONSIDER
CDEHORSW	COWHERDS	CDEINORT	CENTROID
CDEHOSSU	HOCUSSED		DOCTRINE
CDEHSSSU	SCHUSSED		ON CREDIT
CDEIIIOS	IDIOCIES	CDEINOST	D-NOTICES
CDEIIIRV	VIRICIDE	CDEINOTU	EDUCTION
CDEIIKKS	SIDEKICK	CDEINOUV	UNVOICED
CDEIIKMM	MIMICKED	CDEINPRS	PRESCIND
CDEIIKST	DICKIEST	CDEINRRU	INCURRED
CDEIILMO	DOMICILE		

CDEINRSS	DISCERNS		
	RESCINDS		
CDEIOPPT	COPPED IT		
CDEIOPST	DESPOTIC		
CDEIOPSZ	ZIP CODES		
CDEIOPTY	COPY-EDIT		
CDEIORRT	CREDITOR		
	DIRECTOR		
CDEIORSV	DISCOVER		
	DIVORCES		
CDEIORTU	CRIED OUT		
CDEIOSTT	DOCETIST		
CDEIPRST	PREDICTS		
	SCRIPTED		
CDEIPRTU	PICTURED		
CDEIRRSU	SCURRIED		
CDEIRSTU	CURTSIED		
CDEIRSTV	VERDICTS		
CDEISSST	DISSECTS		
CDEISSSU	DISCUSES		
CDEJNORU	CONJURED		
CDEKLNOU	UNLOCKED		
CDEKLOPU	LOCKED UP		
CDEKNOOV	CONVOKED		
CDEKNORU	UNCORKED		
CDEKOOPP	POOP DECK		
CDEKOOPU	COOKED UP		
CDEKOPRU	CORKED UP		
CDEKOSTW	WET DOCKS		
CDELLORS	SCROLLED		
CDELLOSU	COLLUDES		
CDELLOTU	CLOUDLET		
CDELLRSY	DRY CELLS		
CDELLTUY	DULCETLY		
CDELMNOO	MONOCLED		
CDELMNOU	COLUMNED		
CDELMPRU	CRUMPLED		
CDELNOOS	CONDOLES		
	CONSOLED		
CDELNOSS	COLDNESS		
CDELNOSY	SECONDLY		
CDELNRUU	UNCURLED		
CDELOORS	COLD SORE		
	OLD SCORE		
CDELOORU	COLOURED		
CDELOPSU	CLOSED UP		
CDELORSS	CORDLESS		
	SCOLDERS		
CDELORSU	CLOSURED		
CDELORVY	VERY COLD		
CDELPRSU	SCRUPLED		
CDELPRUU	CURLED UP		
CDELPSTU	SCULPTED		
CDELRSUY	CURSEDLY		
CDELRTUU	CULTURED		
CDELSSTU	DUCTLESS		
CDELSSUY	CUSSEDLY		
CDELSTTU	SCUTTLED		
CDEMMNOS	COMMENDS		
CDEMMNOU	COMMUNED		
CDEMMOOS	COMMODES		
CDEMMOTU	COMMUTED		
CDEMNNOS	CONDEMNS		
CDEMNOOW	COME DOWN		
	COMEDOWN		
CDEMNOSU	CONSUMED		
CDEMNOTU	DOCUMENT		
CDEMOOPS	COMPOSED		
CDEMOPTU	COMPUTED		
CDEMOSTU	COSTUMED		
CDEMPRSU	SCRUMPED		

Code	Word	Code	Word	Code	Word
CDENNOOR	CONDONER	CDIJNSTU	DISJUNCT	CEEEINNT	ENCEINTE
CDENNOOS	CONDONES	CDIKKOPR	DROP KICK	CEEEINOP	ONE PIECE
CDENNOOT	CONNOTED		DROP-KICK		ONE-PIECE
CDENNOST	CONTENDS		DROPKICK	CEEEIPRR	CREEPIER
CDENOORR	ON RECORD	CDIKLLMO	COLD MILK	CEEEIPRV	PERCEIVE
CDENOOTT	COTTONED	CDIKLORT	OLD TRICK	CEEEIPST	SET PIECE
CDENOOVY	CONVOYED	CDIKLPUY	LUCKY DIP	CEEEIRRV	RECEIVER
CDENORTU	TROUNCED	CDIKNOSW	WIND SOCK	CEEEIRSV	RECEIVES
CDENOSTU	CONTUSED		WIND-SOCK	CEEEIRSX	EXERCISE
CDENRTUU	UNDERCUT	CDIKORST	DO TRICKS	CEEEJRRT	REJECTER
CDEOOPPS	COPEPODS	CDILLOOS	COLLOIDS	CEEELLNR	CRENELLE
CDEOOPPU	COOPED UP	CDILLOUY	CLOUDILY	CEEELRRV	CLEVERER
CDEOOPST	POST CODE	CDILOOPZ	PODZOLIC	CEEELRTT	ELECTRET
	POSTCODE	CDILOORT	LORDOTIC	CEEEMNRT	CEREMENT
CDEOOORS	CORRODES	CDIMOORT	MICRODOT	CEEEMRTY	CEMETERY
CDEOORSU	DECOROUS	CDINORTU	INDUCTOR	CEEEMSUX	EXCUSE ME
CDEOORSV	VOCODERS	CDINOSTU	CONDUITS	CEEENNOS	SCENE ONE
CDEOOSTV	DOVECOTS		DISCOUNT	CEEENNPT	TEN PENCE
CDEOPRRU	PROCURED	CDIOOPRS	PROSODIC	CEEENNPW	NEW PENCE
	PRODUCER	CDIOORRR	CORRIDOR	CEEENNST	SENTENCE
CDEOPRSU	PRODUCES	CDIOPRSU	CUSPIDOR	CEEENPRS	PRESENCE
CDEOORRS	RED CROSS	CDIOSTUV	OVIDUCTS	CEEENPRT	PRETENCE
CDEPRRUY	RYDER CUP	CDJLNOUY	JOCUNDLY	CEEENQSU	SEQUENCE
CDERSTTU	DESTRUCT	CDKLLOOO	LOOK COLD	CEEENRRS	SCREENER
CDFHILOS	COLD FISH	CDKLOOPR	COLD PORK	CEEEPRRS	CREEPERS
CDFHIOOR	RICH FOOD	CDKNNOSU	DUNNOCKS	CEEERRTX	EXCRETER
CDFIILSU	FLUIDICS	CDKOOORW	CORKWOOD	CEEERSSS	RECESSES
CDFIKORS	DISFROCK	CDKOPSUU	DUCK SOUP	CEEERSST	SECRETES
CDFNNOOU	CONFOUND	CDLLOOUW	LOW CLOUD		SESTERCE
CDGHIINT	DITCHING	CDLMOOOR	COLD ROOM	CEEERSTX	EXCRETES
CDGHORUY	DRY COUGH	CDLNOOOW	COOL DOWN	CEEESSSX	EXCESSES
CDGIIKKN	KING DICK	CDLNOORY	OLD CRONY	CEEESTUX	EXECUTES
CDGIINNU	INDUCING	CDLNOOTU	COULD NOT	CEEFFINT	IN EFFECT
CDGIKLNU	DUCKLING	CDLNORTU	TURN COLD	CEEFFNOS	OFFENCES
CDGIKNOO	GOOD NICK	CDLOOPSY	LYCOPODS	CEEFFNOT	NO EFFECT
CDGILNOO	GOLD COIN	CDLOOSTW	COTSWOLD	CEEFFORT	EFFECTOR
CDGILNOS	SCOLDING	CDLOPRUW	WORLD CUP	CEEFGILN	FLEECING
CDGILNOU	CLOUDING	CDMNOOPU	COMPOUND	CEEFHIKR	KERCHIEF
CDGILNRU	CURDLING	CDMNORUU	CORUNDUM	CEEFHLRT	FLETCHER
CDGINORW	CROWDING	CDNOOORT	DOCTOR NO	CEEFHLRU	CHEERFUL
CDGKLOOU	GOOD LUCK	CDNOOPWY	COPY DOWN	CEEFHLST	FLETCHES
CDGKOOOO	GOOD COOK	CDNOSTUW	CUTS DOWN	CEEFIKKR	FREE KICK
CDGLOORW	GROW COLD	CDOOOPST	OCTOPODS	CEEFIKLS	FEEL SICK
CDGOOOPR	GOOD CROP	CDOORRUY	CORDUROY	CEEFIKOR	COKE FIRE
CDHHIILS	CHILDISH	CDOORTUW	CROWD OUT	CEEFILOS	ICE FLOES
CDHIINST	CHINDITS	CDOOSTUW	WOODCUTS	CEEFILRY	FIERCELY
CDHIIORT	HIDROTIC	CDOPRSTU	PRODUCTS	CEEFINNS	FENCES IN
CDHIIOSZ	SCHIZOID	CEEEEIPY	EYEPIECE	CEEFINRT	FRENETIC
CDHIISST	DISTICHS	CEEEELST	SELECTEE	CEEFIRST	FIERCEST
CDHILOTW	OLD WITCH	CEEEFHNT	THE FENCE	CEEFKLRS	FRECKLES
CDHIOORS	CHOROIDS	CEEEFNOR	CONFEREE	CEEFKLSS	FECKLESS
CDHIOPRW	WHIPCORD	CEEEGGMR	CREME EGG	CEEFLLLU	FUEL CELL
CDHIPSTY	DIPTYCHS	CEEEGIMN	EMCEEING	CEEFLNTU	FECULENT
CDHLOOPS	COPS HOLD	CEEEGITX	EXEGETIC	CEEFLRST	REFLECTS
CDHLOOPY	COPYHOLD	CEEEGMNR	MERGENCE	CEEFNORR	ENFORCER
CDHNOOPW	CHOP DOWN	CEEEHIKR	CHEEKIER	CEEFNORS	ENFORCES
CDHOORRU	UROCHORD	CEEEHIRR	CHEERIER	CEEFNRVY	FERVENCY
CDIIIORT	DIORITIC	CEEEHIST	CHEESE IT	CEEFOPRR	PERFORCE
CDIIKPST	DIPSTICK	CEEEHKOR	CHEROKEE	CEEFOPRT	PERFECTO
CDIILOPP	DIPLOPIC	CEEEHMOR	COME HERE	CEEFOPRY	FREE COPY
CDIILOTY	DOCILITY	CEEEHNNY	CHEYENNE	CEEFORSS	FRESCOES
CDIILSVY	VISCIDLY	CEEEHORS	REECHOES	CEEFORST	SCOT FREE
CDIILTUY	LUCIDITY	CEEEHPSS	SPEECHES		SCOT-FREE
CDIIMNOU	CONIDIUM	CEEEHRRS	CHEERERS	CEEFORSU	USE FORCE
CDIINORS	CRINOIDS	CEEEIJTV	EJECTIVE	CEEFPRST	PERFECTS
CDIINORT	INDICTOR	CEEEILNN	LENIENCE		PREFECTS
CDIINSTT	DISTINCT	CEEEILNS	LICENSEE	CEEGHIKN	CHEEKING
CDIINSWY	ICY WINDS	CEEEILNT	TELECINE	CEEGHILN	LEECHING
CDIIOPRT	DIOPTRIC	CEEEILRT	ERECTILE	CEEGHINP	CHEEPING
CDIIPTUY	CUPIDITY	CEEEILTV	ELECTIVE	CEEGHINR	CHEERING
CDIIRSTT	DISTRICT	CEEEIMNN	EMINENCE	CEEGHLOW	COGWHEEL

214

CEEGIJNT	EJECTING	CEEIKLPR	PICKEREL	CEEIRRSV	SERVICER
CEEGILNT	ELECTING	CEEIKNST	NECKTIES	CEEIRRSW	SCREWIER
CEEGINPR	CREEPING	CEEIKPRT	PICKETER	CEEIRRTU	URETERIC
CEEGINRT	ERECTING	CEEIKQUY	QUICK EYE	CEEIRSSV	SERVICES
CEEGINST	GENETICS	CEEILLLP	PELLICLE	CEEIRSTT	SIT ERECT
CEEGINSU	EUGENICS	CEEILLMS	MICELLES	CEEIRSTV	VERTICES
CEEGINXY	EXIGENCY	CEEILLNT	LENTICEL	CEEIRSVX	CERVIXES
CEEGLLOS	COLLEGES	CEEILMOR	COMELIER	CEEJORRT	REJECTOR
CEEGLNST	NEGLECTS	CEEILNNY	LENIENCY	CEEKLMRU	MERE LUCK
CEEGLOSU	ECLOGUES	CEEILNOP	PLIOCENE	CEEKLOOP	KEEP COOL
CEEGNNOR	CONGENER	CEEILNOS	CINEOLES	CEEKLPSS	SPECKLES
CEEGNORV	CONVERGE	CEEILNOT	ELECTION	CEEKLRSS	RECKLESS
CEEGORST	CORTEGES	CEEILNOV	VIOLENCE	CEEKNORR	RECKONER
CEEHHMNN	HENCHMEN	CEEILNRS	RECLINES	CEEKRRSW	WRECKERS
CEEHIKKL	LIKE HECK		SILENCER	CEELLLSU	CELLULES
CEEHIKLY	CHEEKILY	CEEILNSS	LICENSES	CEELLMOU	MOLECULE
CEEHILLN	CHENILLE		SILENCES	CEELLNOS	COLLEENS
	HELLENIC	CEEILPSS	ECLIPSES	CEELLPRU	CUPELLER
CEEHILRW	CLERIHEW	CEEILRST	RETICLES	CEELLRRU	CRUELLER
CEEHILRY	CHEERILY	CEEILRSV	VERSICLE	CEELLRVY	CLEVERLY
CEEHILSV	VEHICLES	CEEILRTU	RETICULE	CEELLSSU	CLUELESS
CEEHIMRT	HERMETIC	CEEILRTY	CELERITY	CEELMNRU	CRUEL MEN
CEEHIMSS	CHEMISES	CEEILSSV	VESICLES	CEELMOPT	COMPLETE
CEEHINPR	ENCIPHER	CEEILSTT	TESTICLE	CEELMORW	WELCOMER
CEEHINRR	ENRICHER	CEEIMMPY	EMPYEMIC	CEELMORW	WELCOMES
CEEHINRS	ENRICHES	CEEIMMRS	MESMERIC	CEELNOPU	OPULENCE
CEEHIOSV	COHESIVE	CEEIMNPS	SPECIMEN	CEELNORT	ELECTRON
CEEHIPRT	HERPETIC	CEEIMNSS	NICE MESS	CEELNOSS	ENCLOSES
CEEHIRRS	CHERRIES	CEEIMNST	CENTIMES	CEELNRST	LECTERNS
CEEHIRST	HERETICS	CEEIMOPP	EPIC POEM	CEELNRTY	RECENTLY
CEEHIRTT	TETCHIER	CEEIMORT	CORE TIME	CEELNSTU	ESCULENT
CEEHISTT	ESTHETIC		METEORIC	CEELORSS	SCLEROSE
CEEHKRST	SKETCHER	CEEINNOP	PINE CONE	CEELORST	CORSELET
CEEHKSST	SKETCHES		PINECONE		ELECTORS
CEEHLNOO	HOLOCENE	CEEINNOT	NEOTENIC		SELECTOR
CEEHLNOS	ECHELONS	CEEINNPZ	PINCE-NEZ	CEELORTV	COVERLET
CEEHLNSU	ELENCHUS	CEEINNSS	INCENSES	CEELOSST	CLOSE SET
CEEHLRSU	HERCULES		NICENESS	CEELOSSU	COLEUSES
CEEHLRSW	WELCHERS	CEEINNST	NESCIENT	CEELRRTU	LECTURER
CEEHMMOO	COME HOME	CEEINOOV	ONE VOICE	CEELRSSU	CURELESS
CEEHMNSS	CHESSMEN	CEEINORT	ERECTION		RECLUSES
CEEHMRSS	SCHEMERS		NEOTERIC	CEELRSSW	CREWLESS
CEEHNNRT	ENTRENCH	CEEINORX	EXOCRINE	CEELRSTU	LECTURES
CEEHNORT	COHERENT	CEEINOTV	EVECTION	CEELRSTY	SECRETLY
CEEHNQRU	QUENCHER	CEEINOTW	TWICE ONE	CEELRSUY	SECURELY
CEEHNQSU	QUENCHES	CEEINPRS	CREEPS IN	CEELSTTU	LETTUCES
CEEHNRRT	RETRENCH	CEEINPRT	NET PRICE	CEEMMNTU	CEMENTUM
	TRENCHER		TERPENIC	CEEMNOOR	ONCE MORE
CEEHNRST	TRENCHES	CEEINPST	PECTINES	CEEMNORW	NEWCOMER
CEEHNRSW	WENCHERS	CEEINPSX	SIX PENCE	CEEMNORY	CEREMONY
	WRENCHES	CEEINRST	IN SECRET	CEEMNOTX	COME NEXT
CEEHNSST	STENCHES	CEEINRSU	INSECURE	CEEMNOYZ	COENZYME
CEEHOPRY	CORYPHEE		SINECURE	CEEMOORV	COME OVER
CEEHORST	TROCHEES	CEEINRTT	RETICENT		OVERCOME
CEEHORVW	CHEW OVER	CEEINRTU	ENURETIC	CEEMOPRS	COMPEERS
CEEHPRSU	CHEERS UP	CEEINRVY	VERY NICE		COMPERES
CEEHQRSU	CHEQUERS	CEEINSSX	IN EXCESS	CEEMOPST	COMPETES
CEEHRSTW	WRETCHES	CEEINSTY	CYSTEINE	CEEMORTU	COME TRUE
CEEIIKLV	VICELIKE	CEEINTTW	TWICE TEN	CEENNOOU	ONE OUNCE
CEEIIMNP	MINCE PIE	CEEIOPPS	EPISCOPE	CEENNORT	CRETONNE
CEEIIMNT	NICE TIME	CEEIOPPT	EPIC POET	CEENNORU	RENOUNCE
CEEIIMPR	EPIMERIC	CEEIOPST	PICOTEES	CEENNOST	CENTONES
CEEIIMRT	EREMITIC	CEEIOPTW	TWO-PIECE	CEENNOSV	CONVENES
CEEIINPS	IN PIECES	CEEIORST	COTERIES	CEENNSTT	TEN CENTS
CEEIINST	NICETIES		ESOTERIC	CEENOORS	ONE SCORE
CEEIIPTU	CUTIE-PIE	CEEIORSX	EXORCISE	CEENOORV	ONCE OVER
CEEIJNOT	EJECTION	CEEIORTX	EXOTERIC		ONCE-OVER
CEEIJORR	REJOICER	CEEIPPTU	EUPEPTIC	CEENOPTW	TWO PENCE
CEEIJORS	REJOICES	CEEIPRSS	PRECISES		TWOPENCE
CEEIJRUV	VERJUICE	CEEIPRST	RECEIPTS	CEENORST	NO SECRET
CEEIKLNN	NECKLINE	CEEIPRSU	EPICURES		TEN SCORE

CEENORSV	CONSERVE	CEFIKLRS	FLICKERS	CEGIKLNO	KING COLE
	CONVERSE	CEFIKLRY	FLICKERY	CEGIKLNR	CLERKING
CEENORTT	TRECENTO	CEFIKLST	FELT SICK	CEGIKNNR	RINGNECK
CEENORVY	CONVEYER	CEFILLLO	FOLLICLE	CEGIKNOS	GONE SICK
CEENOSTW	SCENE TWO	CEFILMRU	MERCIFUL	CEGIKNPS	SPECKING
CEENOSUX	NO EXCUSE	CEFILMRW	FILM CREW	CEGIKNRW	WRECKING
CEENPPTU	TUPPENCE	CEFILNOT	FLECTION	CEGIKOSS	GOES SICK
CEENRRSU	CENSURER	CEFILNST	INFLECTS	CEGIKSST	GETS SICK
CEENRSSU	CENSURES	CEFILOST	CLOSE FIT	CEGILNRS	CRINGLES
CEENSSSU	CENSUSES	CEFILRSU	LUCIFERS	CEGILNRY	GLYCERIN
CEENSSTU	CUTENESS	CEFIMOST	COMFIEST	CEGILRSY	LYSERGIC
CEEOORST	CREOSOTE	CEFINNOR	CONFINER	CEGINNOR	ENCORING
CEEOPRRT	RECEPTOR	CEFINNOS	CONFINES	CEGINNRT	CENTRING
CEEOPRTU	CREEP OUT	CEFINORS	CONIFERS	CEGINNST	SCENTING
CEEOPSTY	ECOTYPES		FIR CONES	CEGINOPY	PYOGENIC
CEEOQTTU	COQUETTE		FORENSIC	CEGINORV	COVERING
CEEORRRS	SORCERER	CEFINORT	INFECTOR	CEGINORW	COWERING
CEEORRSU	RECOURSE	CEFINOTT	CONFETTI	CEGINOTV	COVETING
	RESOURCE	CEFIORRS	CRIES FOR		VIETCONG
CEEORRSV	RECOVERS	CEFIORTY	FEROCITY	CEGINOXY	OXYGENIC
CEEORRVY	RECOVERY	CEFKLLOS	ELF-LOCKS	CEGINRST	CRESTING
CEEORSSY	CROSS-EYE	CEFKLOOR	FORELOCK	CEGINRSU	RESCUING
CEEORSTX	CORTEXES	CEFKLOST	FETLOCKS		SECURING
CEEORTTV	CORVETTE	CEFKLPSY	FLYSPECK	CEGINRSW	SCREWING
CEEORTUX	EXECUTOR	CEFLNOSU	FLOUNCES	CEGINRSY	SYNERGIC
CEEOSSTX	TO EXCESS	CEFLNRUU	FURUNCLE	CEGINSUX	EXCUSING
CEEPPRST	PERCEPTS	CEFMMOOR	COME FROM	CEGINTTY	CITY GENT
	PRECEPTS	CEFMORSY	COMFREYS	CEGKLTUY	GET LUCKY
CEEPPRSU	CREEPS UP	CEFNOSSU	CONFUSES	CEGKSTTU	GET STUCK
CEEPRSST	RESPECTS	CEFNOSTU	CONFUTES	CEGLLORY	GLYCEROL
	SCEPTRES	CEFOORST	SOFT-CORE	CEGLNOTY	COGENTLY
	SPECTRES	CEFOORSU	OF COURSE	CEGMNNOO	COGNOMEN
CEEPRSTX	EXCERPTS	CEFOORTU	FORCE OUT	CEGMNTUU	UNCUT GEM
CEERRSSW	SCREWERS	CEFORRST	CROFTERS	CEGNNPUY	PUNGENCY
CEERRSTU	REST CURE	CEFORSTU	FRUCTOSE	CEGNORSS	CONGRESS
CEERSSTU	SECUREST	CEGGILOO	GEOLOGIC	CEGNORSU	SCROUNGE
CEERSSTW	SETSCREW	CEGGIORS	GEORGICS	CEGNORSY	CRYOGENS
CEERSTTU	CURETTES	CEGGKSSU	SUCK EGGS	CEGNOSST	CONGESTS
CEESTTUV	CUVETTES	CEGGLNOY	GLYCOGEN	CEGOORSS	SCROOGES
CEFFHKOO	CHOKE OFF	CEGHIINY	HYGIENIC	CEGORRSU	SCOURGER
CEFFIINO	IN OFFICE	CEGHIKLN	HECKLING	CEGORRST	GET CROSS
CEFFIORS	CRIES OFF	CEGHILNW	WELCHING	CEGORRSU	SCOURGES
	OFFICERS	CEGHILST	GLITCHES	CEHHOPTY	HYPOTHEC
CEFFIORU	COIFFEUR	CEGHIMNS	SCHEMING	CEHIILLR	CHILLIER
	COIFFURE	CEGHINNW	WENCHING	CEHIILLS	CHILLIES
CEFFISSU	SUFFICES	CEGHINOR	COHERING	CEHIILNT	LECITHIN
CEFFLORU	FORCEFUL	CEGHINPR	PERCHING	CEHIILOT	EOLITHIC
CEFFLSSU	CUFFLESS	CEGHINRT	RETCHING	CEHIIMRT	HERMITIC
	SCUFFLES	CEGHINRU	EUCHRING	CEHIINRV	RICH VEIN
CEFFMOOS	COMES OFF	CEGHINST	ETCHINGS	CEHIIOPT	ETHIOPIC
CEFFOORS	SCORE OFF	CEGHINSY	HYGENICS	CEHIIPPS	CHIPPIES
CEFFORSS	SCOFFERS	CEGHIRRW	GREW RICH	CEHIIPRR	CHIRPIER
CEFGHINT	FETCHING	CEGHIRST	GETS RICH	CEHIIRTT	TITCHIER
CEFGIKLN	FLECKING	CEGHIRTU	THEURGIC	CEHIISTT	THEISTIC
CEFHIIMS	MISCHIEF	CEGHNOOT	THE CONGO	CEHIISVV	CHIVVIES
CEFHIIRW	RICH WIFE	CEGHNORS	GROSCHEN	CEHIJKOR	RICH JOKE
CEFHILNS	FLINCHES	CEGHORSU	GROUCHES	CEHIKLMU	MUCH LIKE
CEFHILST	FLITCHES	CEGIIKNV	VICE KING	CEHIKLPT	KLEPHTIC
CEFHINNR	IN FRENCH	CEGIILNS	CEILINGS	CEHIKLSU	SUCH LIKE
CEFHINSU	FUCHSINE	CEGIINNT	ENTICING		SUCHLIKE
CEFHKOOR	FOREHOCK	CEGIINNV	EVINCING	CEHIKMOS	HOMESICK
CEFHLSTU	CHESTFUL	CEGIINOP	EPIGONIC	CEHIKNRU	CHUNKIER
CEFIILMP	EPIC FILM	CEGIINOS	ISOGENIC	CEHIKNST	KITCHENS
CEFIILNO	OLEFINIC	CEGIINPR	PIERCING	CEHIKSTT	THICKEST
CEFIILST	FELSITIC	CEGIINRT	RECITING		THICKETS
CEFIILTY	FELICITY	CEGIINRV	VICE RING		THICKSET
CEFIIORS	ORIFICES	CEGIINSS	GNEISSIC	CEHILMTY	METHYLIC
CEFIIRRT	FERRITIC	CEGIINSX	EXCISING	CEHILNOP	PHENOLIC
	TERRIFIC	CEGIINTV	EVICTING		PINOCHLE
CEFIKLLS	FELL SICK	CEGIINTX	EXCITING	CEHILNOR	CHLORINE
CEFIKLOR	FIRELOCK	CEGIIOST	EGOISTIC	CEHILNPY	PHENYLIC

CEHILNSS	CHINLESS	CEHNNOSU	NONESUCH	CEIISTWX	TWICE SIX
CEHILORT	CHLORITE	CEHNOOPS	HEN COOPS	CEIJKKOS	SICK JOKE
	CLOTHIER	CEHNOORS	SCHOONER	CEIJNORT	INJECTOR
CEHILTTY	TETCHILY	CEHNORSV	CHEVRONS	CEIJSSTU	JUSTICES
CEHIMMRU	CHUMMIER	CEHNORTW	THE CROWN	CEIKKLOR	ROCKLIKE
CEHIMNOP	PHONEMIC	CEHNOSUZ	CHEZ NOUS	CEIKKNRS	KNICKERS
CEHIMNOR	NICHROME	CEHNOTTU	THE COUNT	CEIKKORV	KICK OVER
CEHIMNOW	CHOW MEIN	CEHNRSTU	CHUNTERS	CEIKLNRS	CRINKLES
CEHIMNSY	CHIMNEYS	CEHNSTTU	CHESTNUT	CEIKLOSV	LOVESICK
CEHIMORT	CHROMITE	CEHOORSS	CHOOSERS	CEIKLPRS	PRICKLES
	TRICHOME	CEHOORST	CHEROOTS	CEIKLPRU	PLUCKIER
CEHIMPSU	CHIMES UP	CEHOORSU	OCHREOUS	CEIKLRSS	SLICKERS
CEHIMRSS	SMIRCHES	CEHOPPRS	CHOPPERS	CEIKLRST	STICKLER
CEHIMSST	CHEMISTS	CEHOPPRY	PROPHECY		STRICKLE
CEHINNRT	INTRENCH	CEHOPSUY	CHOP SUEY		TRICKLES
CEHINOOS	COHESION		CHOPSUEY	CEIKLSST	SLICKEST
CEHINOPT	PHONETIC	CEHORSSU	CHORUSES	CEIKLSTU	LUCKIEST
CEHINOPU	EUPHONIC	CEHORSSZ	SCHERZOS	CEIKMPPU	PICK-ME-UP
CEHINOSY	HYOSCINE	CEHORSTU	TOUCHERS	CEIKNNOT	NEKTONIC
CEHINPTU	IN THE CUP	CEHORSUV	VOUCHERS	CEIKNOPT	IN POCKET
CEHINRSS	RICHNESS	CEHOSTUW	CHEWS OUT	CEIKNOQU	QUICK ONE
CEHINRST	CHRISTEN	CEHPSSTU	PUTSCHES	CEIKNORT	ONE TRICK
	SNITCHER	CEHRRSSU	CRUSHERS	CEIKNORW	NICE WORK
CEHINRSW	WINCHERS	CEHRSTTY	STRETCHY	CEIKNOSU	QUICKENS
CEHINRTU	RUTHENIC	CEHSSSSU	SCHUSSES	CEIKNRSS	SNICKERS
CEHINSST	SNITCHES	CEIIILSV	CIVILISE	CEIKNRST	STRICKEN
CEHIOORS	CHOOSIER	CEIIILVZ	CIVILIZE	CEIKNRSY	SNICKERY
CEHIOPPR	CHOPPIER	CEIIINSV	INCISIVE	CEIKNRTW	NEW TRICK
CEHIOPRU	EUPHORIC	CEIIJSTU	JESUITIC	CEIKNSSS	SICKNESS
CEHIOPSS	HOSPICES		JUICIEST	CEIKNSST	SNICKETS
CEHIOPST	POSTICHE	CEIIKLMR	LIMERICK	CEIKNSTW	WENT SICK
CEHIOPTW	COPE WITH	CEIIKLRS	SICKLIER	CEIKORST	STOCKIER
CEHIORRT	RHETORIC	CEIIKNRS	ICE RINKS	CEIKORTV	TICK OVER
CEHIORTU	TOUCHIER	CEIIKNSS	KINESICS	CEIKPRST	PRICKETS
CEHIOSTV	CHEVIOTS	CEIIKNST	KINETICS	CEIKPSST	SKEPTICS
CEHIPRST	PITCHERS	CEIIKQSU	QUICKIES	CEIKQSTU	QUICKEST
CEHIRRVY	VERY RICH	CEIIKRRT	TRICKIER		QUICKSET
CEHIRSTT	STITCHER	CEIIKRST	STICKIER	CEIKRRTY	TRICKERY
CEHIRSTW	SWITCHER	CEIIKSST	EKISTICS	CEIKRSST	STICKERS
CEHIRSTY	HYSTERIC	CEIIKTTT	TEKTITIC	CEILLLOY	ICE LOLLY
CEHIRTTW	TWITCHER	CEIILLNO	LINOLEIC	CEILLNOU	NUCLEOLI
CEHIRTWY	WITCHERY	CEIILMNY	MYELINIC	CEILLOPS	POLLICES
CEHISSTT	STITCHES	CEIILMSY	ICY SMILE	CEILLORS	COLLIERS
CEHISSTU	CUSHIEST	CEIILNNP	IN PENCIL	CEILLORY	COLLIERY
CEHISSTW	SWITCHES		PENCIL IN	CEILLRTU	TELLURIC
CEHISTTW	TWITCHES	CEIILNNS	INCLINES	CEILLSST	CELLISTS
CEHISTWY	TWICE SHY	CEIILNOS	ISOCLINE	CEILMMUY	MYCELIUM
CEHKNPUY	KEY PUNCH		SILICONE	CEILMNOP	COMPLINE
	KEYPUNCH	CEIILOPS	POLICIES	CEILMOPR	COMPILER
CEHKORSS	SHOCKERS	CEIILORT	ELICITOR		COMPLIER
CEHKRSTU	HUCKSTER	CEIILOTZ	ZEOLITIC	CEILMOPS	COMPILES
CEHLLNOO	COLONEL H	CEIILPPS	CLIPPIES		COMPLIES
CEHLMSSU	MUCH LESS	CEIILPRT	PERLITIC		POLEMICS
CEHLNNOU	LUNCHEON	CEIILPTX	EXPLICIT	CEILMOSS	SOLECISM
CEHLNOSS	LOCH NESS	CEIILRTV	VERTICIL	CEILMOSU	COLISEUM
CEHLNOTU	UNCLOTHE	CEIILSSS	SCISSILE	CEILMRSU	CLUMSIER
CEHLNSTU	SET LUNCH	CEIIMORS	ISOMERIC	CEILNNSY	SYNCLINE
CEHLNSTY	LYNCHETS	CEIIMOST	SEMIOTIC	CEILNOOS	COLONIES
CEHLORRT	CHORTLER	CEIIMRRT	TRIMERIC		COLONISE
CEHLORST	CHORTLES	CEIIMSST	SEMITICS		ECLOSION
CEHLORSU	SLOUCHER	CEIINNOT	NICOTINE	CEILNOOZ	COLONIZE
CEHLOSSU	SLOUCHES	CEIINOSV	INVOICES	CEILNOPT	LEPTONIC
CEHLQSUY	SQUELCHY	CEIINOSX	EXCISION	CEILNOPY	POLYENIC
CEHLRRSU	LURCHERS	CEIINOTV	EVICTION	CEILNORV	IN CLOVER
CEHMMORU	MUCH MORE	CEIINRTU	NEURITIC	CEILNOSS	CLOSES IN
CEHMNSSU	MUCHNESS	CEIINSTY	SYENITIC		INCLOSES
CEHMOORS	SMOOCHER	CEIINSTZ	CITIZENS	CEILNOST	LECTIONS
CEHMOOSS	SMOOCHES	CEIIPRRS	CRISPIER	CEILNOSX	LEXICONS
CEHMORUV	OVERMUCH	CEIIPSST	SPICIEST	CEILNPRY	PRINCELY
CEHMRUVY	VERY MUCH	CEIIQRTU	CRITIQUE	CEILNRUV	CULVERIN
CEHNNOPU	PUNCHEON	CEIISTVV	VIVISECT	CEILNSST	STENCILS

CEILNSTU	CUTLINES
	TUNICLES
CEILOOVW	LOW VOICE
CEILOPRT	LEPROTIC
CEILOPRW	LOW PRICE
CEILOPTU	POULTICE
CEILOPTY	EPICOTYL
CEILORST	CLOISTER
	COSTLIER
CEILORTY	CRYOLITE
CEILOSSS	OSSICLES
CEILOSST	SOLSTICE
CEILOTVY	VELOCITY
CEILPPRS	CLIPPERS
	CRIPPLES
CEILPRSS	SPLICERS
CEILPRSU	SURPLICE
CEILPSSU	SPICULES
CEILRSTU	CURLIEST
	UTRICLES
CEIMMNNO	MNEMONIC
CEIMMNOU	MECONIUM
CEIMMRRU	CRUMMIER
CEIMNNOO	COME ON IN
CEIMNOPY	EPONYMIC
CEIMNORT	INTERCOM
CEIMNOST	CENTIMOS
CEIMNPSU	MINCES UP
CEIMNRST	CENTRISM
CEIMNSSU	MENISCUS
CEIMOOSZ	MESOZOIC
CEIMOPRS	COMPRISE
CEIMORSX	EXORCISM
CEIMPRRS	CRIMPERS
CEIMPRTU	PRIME CUT
CEIMRRTU	TURMERIC
CEIMSSTY	SYSTEMIC
CEINNNOT	INNOCENT
CEINNORU	NEURONIC
CEINNORV	CONNIVER
CEINNOSV	CONNIVES
CEINNOTU	CONTINUE
CEINOOTZ	ENZOOTIC
CEINOPRR	RIPE CORN
CEINOPRS	CONSPIRE
CEINOPRT	ENTROPIC
	INCEPTOR
CEINOPRV	PROVINCE
CEINORRS	RESORCIN
CEINORRT	TRICORNE
CEINORSS	NECROSIS
CEINORST	CORNIEST
CEINORTT	CONTRITE
CEINORTU	NEUROTIC
CEINORTV	CONTRIVE
CEINOSSS	CESSIONS
CEINOSST	SECTIONS
CEINOSTT	STENOTIC
CEINOSTU	COUNTIES
CEINOSTX	EXCITONS
CEINOSTY	CYTOSINE
CEINOTTU	TEUTONIC
CEINPRSS	CRISPENS
	PRINCESS
CEINPSST	INSPECTS
CEINRSST	CISTERNS
CEINRSTT	CENTRIST
CEINRTTU	INTERCUT
	TINCTURE
CEIOOPTV	CO-OPTIVE
CEIOPPRT	TOP PRICE

CEIOPRRU	CROUPIER
CEIOPRSU	PRECIOUS
CEIOPSSU	SPECIOUS
CEIORRSS	CROSIERS
CEIORRSU	COURIERS
CEIORRSZ	CROZIERS
CEIORRTU	COURTIER
CEIORRUZ	CRUZEIRO
CEIORSTU	CRIES OUT
	OUTCRIES
CEIORSTV	VORTICES
CEIORSTX	EXORCIST
CEIORSVY	VICEROYS
CEIORTTU	TOREUTIC
CEIOSSTT	SCOTTIES
CEIOSSTX	COEXISTS
CEIOTTWW	TWICE TWO
CEIPRRST	RESCRIPT
CEIPRSST	CRISPEST
CEIPRSTU	CREPITUS
	PICTURES
	PIECRUST
CEIPSSST	CESSPITS
CEIRRRSU	CURRIERS
CEIRRSSU	CRUISERS
	SCURRIES
CEIRRSTT	CRITTERS
	RESTRICT
	STRICTER
CEIRRSTU	CRUSTIER
	RECRUITS
CEIRSSTT	TRISECTS
CEIRSSTU	CITRUSES
	CURTSIES
	RICTUSES
CEIRSSUV	CURSIVES
CEIRSTUY	SECURITY
CEJLOOSY	JOCOSELY
CEJNORRU	CONJURER
CEJNORSU	CONJURES
CEJNOSTU	JUST ONCE
CEJNRTUU	JUNCTURE
CEJOPRST	PROJECTS
CEKKLNSU	KNUCKLES
CEKKNORS	KNOCKERS
CEKLLNOR	ROLL NECK
CEKLLOOV	LOVELOCK
CEKLMNUY	LUCKY MEN
CEKLNOOP	POLO NECK
CEKLOOPT	KEPT COOL
CEKLOORV	OVERLOCK
CEKLOPST	LOCKSTEP
CEKLRRTU	TRUCKLER
CEKLRSTU	TRUCKLES
CEKMNOST	STOCKMEN
CEKNNOOR	RECKON ON
CEKNOOSV	CONVOKES
CEKNOPRU	RECKON UP
CEKNOPST	PENSTOCK
CEKOORRS	ROCKROSE
CEKOORRW	CO-WORKER
CEKOPRST	SPROCKET
CEKORRTY	ROCKETRY
CEKRRSTU	TRUCKERS
CEKRSSUU	RUCKUSES
CELLNOOS	COLONELS
CELLNOSU	COUNSELL
CELLNTUY	LUCENTLY
CELLRSUY	SCULLERY
CELMNOOS	MONOCLES
CELMNOTU	UNCLE TOM

CELMOSYY	CYMOSELY
CELMPRSU	CRUMPLES
CELMPRTU	PLECTRUM
CELMPSUU	SPECULUM
CELNNOOY	ONCE ONLY
	ONLY ONCE
CELNNOSU	NUCLEONS
CELNOOSS	CONSOLES
	COOLNESS
CELNOPUU	UNCOUPLE
CELNORSU	CLOSE RUN
CELNORWY	CLOWNERY
CELNOSSU	COUNSELS
CELNOSTU	NOCTULES
CELNOSVY	SOLVENCY
CELNOVXY	CONVEXLY
CELOOPSS	CESSPOOL
CELOORSW	LOW SCORE
CELOOSTU	CUT LOOSE
CELOPRSU	COUPLERS
CELOPSSU	CLOSE-UPS
	CLOSES UP
CELOPSTU	COUPLETS
CELOPSUU	OPUSCULE
CELORSST	CORSLETS
CELORSSU	CLOSURES
CELORSSW	SCOWLERS
CELORSTU	CLOTURES
	COULTERS
CELORSUU	ULCEROUS
CELORSUW	SLOW CURE
CELORTVY	COVERTLY
CELOSSST	COSTLESS
CELOSTTU	CULOTTES
CELPRSSU	SCRUPLES
CELPRSUY	SPRUCELY
CELRSSTU	CLUSTERS
CELRSTTU	CLUTTERS
CELRSTUU	CULTURES
CELRSTUV	CULVERTS
CELRSTUY	CLUSTERY
CELSSTTU	SCUTTLES
CEMMNOOR	COMMONER
CEMMNOOS	CONSOMME
CEMMNOST	COMMENTS
CEMMNOSU	COMMUNES
CEMMORTU	COMMUTER
CEMMOSTU	COMMUTES
CEMNNOST	CONTEMNS
CEMNOOOS	COME SOON
CEMNOOPU	COME UPON
CEMNOOTY	MONOCYTE
CEMNOPTT	CONTEMPT
CEMNORSU	CONSUMER
	MUCRONES
CEMNOSST	SCOTSMEN
CEMNOSSU	CONSUMES
CEMNRSTU	CENTRUMS
CEMOOPRS	COMPOSER
CEMOOPSS	COMPOSES
CEMOOPTU	COME UP TO
CEMOOSTU	COMES OUT
	OUTCOMES
CEMOPRSS	COMPRESS
CEMOPRTU	COMPUTER
CEMOPSTU	COMPUTES
CEMORSTU	CUSTOMER
CEMOSSTU	COSTUMES
CEMOSTUY	COSTUMEY
CEMPRSTU	CRUMPETS
	SPECTRUM

CENNOOPR	CORN PONE	CERSSUUX	EXCURSUS	CGHILNNU	LUNCHING
CENNOOPU	POUNCE ON	CFFGHINU	CHUFFING	CGHILNNY	LYNCHING
CENNOORV	CONVENOR	CFFGIINO	COIFFING	CGHILNOT	CLOTHING
CENNOOST	CONNOTES	CFFGINOS	SCOFFING	CGHILNRU	LURCHING
CENNORTU	NOCTURNE	CFFGINSU	SCUFFING	CGHIMMNU	CHUMMING
CENNOSST	CONSENTS	CFFHIOPT	OFF PITCH	CGHIMMNU	MUNCHING
CENNOSTT	CONTENTS	CFFHOOTU	TOUCH OFF	CGHIMNOO	MOOCHING
CENNOSTV	CONVENTS	CFFIKKOS	KICKOFFS	CGHIMNOP	CHOMPING
CENNOTTU	COUNT TEN		KICKS OFF	CGHINNOS	CHIGNONS
CENOOPRT	ETON CROP	CFFIKOPS	PICKS OFF	CGHINNOT	NOTCHING
CENOOORRS	CORONERS	CFFIKOST	TICKS OFF	CGHINNPU	PUNCHING
	CROONERS	CFFIOTTU	CUT IT OFF	CGHINNRU	CHURNING
CENOOORST	CORONETS	CFFIRTUY	FRUCTIFY	CGHINOPP	CHOPPING
CENOOORSU	CORNEOUS	CFFKKNOO	KNOCK OFF	CGHINOPU	POUCHING
	ON COURSE	CFFLOOOS	COOLS OFF	CGHINOTU	TOUCHING
CENOPRSY	NECROPSY	CFFOORSS	CROSS OFF	CGHINOUV	VOUCHING
CENOPSTU	CUTS OPEN	CFGHIILN	FILCHING	CGHINPSY	PSYCHING
CENOQRSU	CONQUERS	CFGHIKOT	THICK FOG	CGHINRRU	CHURRING
CENOQSTU	CONQUEST	CFGIIKLN	FLICKING	CGHINRSU	CRUSHING
CENORRSS	SCORNERS	CFGIKLNO	FLOCKING	CGHINSTY	SCYTHING
CENORSSW	NEW CROSS	CFGINORT	CROFTING	CGHIORRW	GROW RICH
CENORSTU	CONSTRUE	CFHIIORR	HORRIFIC	CGHLLNOO	LOCH LONG
	COUNTERS	CFHIKLOR	RICH FOLK	CGHNOOSU	SOUCHONG
	RECOUNTS	CFHIKORS	ROCKFISH	CGHOPSUU	COUGHS UP
	TROUNCES	CFHILOOS	COOL FISH	CGIIILNT	LIGNITIC
CENORSTV	CONVERTS	CFHOORUV	VOUCH FOR	CGIIINNS	INCISING
CENORSUV	UNCOVERS	CFIIILSY	SILICIFY	CGIIINNT	INCITING
CENORSUY	CYNOSURE	CFIILNST	INFLICTS	CGIIKLNN	CLINKING
CENORTVY	COVENTRY	CFIILOPR	PROLIFIC	CGIIKLNP	PICKLING
CENOSSTT	CONTESTS	CFIINORT	FRICTION	CGIIKLNS	LICKINGS
CENOSSTU	CONTUSES	CFIINOST	FICTIONS		SICKLING
	COUNTESS	CFIKKORS	FOR KICKS		SLICKING
CENOSTTX	CONTEXTS	CFIKLLLU	FULL LICK	CGIIKLNT	TICKLING
CENPRTUU	PUNCTURE	CFIKOSSS	FOSSICKS	CGIIKMMS	GIMMICKS
CENRRSTU	CURRENTS	CFIMNORS	CONFIRMS	CGIIKMMY	GIMMICKY
CENRSSTU	CURTNESS	CFIMNORU	UNCIFORM	CGIIKNNS	SNICKING
	ENCRUSTS	CFINNOTU	FUNCTION	CGIIKNPR	PRICKING
CENRSSUW	UNSCREWS	CFIPRTUU	FRUIT CUP	CGIIKNPS	PICKINGS
CEOOPRST	TOP SCORE	CFIRSTTU	FIRST CUT	CGIIKNRT	TRICKING
CEOORRVW	CROW OVER	CFJOORYY	CRY OF JOY	CGIIKNRW	WRICKING
CEOORSST	SCOOTERS	CFKNORSU	UNFROCKS	CGIIKNST	STICKING
CEOORSTU	OUTSCORE	CFKOORST	SOFT ROCK	CGIILNOP	POLICING
CEOORSTW	TWO SCORE	CFKOSTTU	FUTTOCKS	CGIILNPP	CLIPPING
CEOOSTUV	COVETOUS	CFLMRSUU	FULCRUMS	CGIILNPS	SPLICING
CEOPPRRS	CROPPERS	CFLNORSU	SCORNFUL	CGIILNSU	SLUICING
CEOPPRST	PROSPECT	CFLOOPSU	SCOOPFUL	CGIILOST	LOGISTIC
CEOPRRRU	PROCURER	CFMNOORS	CONFORMS	CGIIMNNO	COMING IN
CEOPRRSU	PROCURES	CFMOORST	COMFORTS		INCOMING
CEOPRSTT	PROTECTS	CFNNOORT	CONFRONT	CGIIMNOT	COMING IT
CEOPRSUU	CUPREOUS	CFNORSTU	FUNCTORS	CGIIMNPR	CRIMPING
CEOPRSUV	COVER-UPS	CFOOORTW	CROWFOOT	CGIIMNPU	PUMICING
	COVERS UP	CFRSTUUU	USUFRUCT	CGIIMNSU	MISCUING
CEOPRTTU	CREPT OUT	CGGGHINU	CHUGGING	CGIINNOT	NOTICING
CEOPRTUW	POWER CUT	CGGGILNO	CLOGGING	CGIINOOS	ISOGONIC
CEOPRTUY	TRUE COPY	CGGHINOU	COUGHING	CGIINOPT	PICOTING
CEOQRTUY	COQUETRY	CGGIINNR	CRINGING	CGIINPRS	CRISPING
CEORRSSU	COURSERS	CGHHIIKK	HIGH KICK	CGIINRSU	CRUISING
	SCOURERS	CGHHIINT	HITCHING	CGIKKNNO	KNOCKING
CEORRSTY	CORSETRY	CGHHINNU	HUNCHING	CGIKLNNO	CLONKING
CEORSSST	CROSSEST	CGHHIOST	HIGH COST	CGIKLNOR	ROCKLING
CEORSSTU	SCOUTERS	CGHHIIKNO	HOICKING	CGIKLNPU	PLUCKING
CEORSTUY	COURTESY	CGHIILLN	CHILLING	CGIKLNSU	SUCKLING
CEPPRRSU	CRUPPERS	CGHIINNP	PINCHING	CGIKMNOS	SMOCKING
CEPPRSSU	SCUPPERS	CGHIINNW	WINCHING	CGIKNOOR	CROOKING
CEPPRSUU	SPRUCE UP	CGHIINPP	CHIPPING	CGIKNOST	STOCKING
CEPPRTUU	UPPER CUT	CGHIINPR	CHIRPING	CGIKNPSU	KINGCUPS
	UPPERCUT	CGHIINPT	PITCHING	CGIKNRTU	TRUCKING
CEPRSSTU	SPRUCEST	CGHIINRR	CHIRRING	CGILLNSU	SCULLING
CEPRSSUW	SCREWS UP	CGHIINTW	WITCHING	CGILMNPU	CLUMPING
CEPSSSTU	SUSPECTS	CGHIKNOS	SHOCKING	CGILMNSU	MUSCLING
CERSSTTU	SCUTTERS	CGHIKNSU	SHUCKING	CGILMNTU	MULCTING

CGILNNOS	CLINGS ON	CHILMMUY	CHUMMILY	CIIKQTUW	QUICK WIT
CGILNOOR	COLORING	CHILMOSU	SCHOLIUM	CIILLNOP	POLLINIC
CGILNOPU	COUPLING	CHILNNPY	LYNCHPIN	CIILMRSY	LYRICISM
CGILNOSW	SCOWLING	CHILNOOP	LOIN CHOP	CIILOOPT	POLITICO
CGILNOTT	CLOTTING	CHILNOOS	IN SCHOOL	CIILOPST	POLITICS
CGILNOTU	CLOUTING	CHILNOSW	CLOWNISH	CIILORST	CLITORIS
CGILNRSU	CURLINGS	CHILOOOZ	HOLOZOIC	CIILOSST	SOLICITS
CGILOOOZ	ZOOLOGIC	CHILOPTW	LOW PITCH	CIILRSTY	LYRICIST
CGILOORU	UROLOGIC	CHILOTUY	TOUCHILY	CIIMNOST	MONISTIC
CGIMMNSU	SCUMMING	CHILOTYY	HOLY CITY	CIIMOSST	STOICISM
CGIMNNOO	COMING ON	CHIMMORU	CHROMIUM	CIIMOSYZ	ISOZYMIC
	GNOMONIC	CHIMNORW	INCHWORM	CIINNNOO	NONIONIC
	ONCOMING	CHIMNOSU	INSOMUCH	CIINNSTT	INSTINCT
CGIMNOOT	COMING TO	CHIMOSTU	HOT MUSIC	CIINOOST	ISOTONIC
CGIMNOPU	COMING UP	CHINOOPT	PHOTONIC	CIINORSS	INCISORS
	UPCOMING	CHINOORS	ISOCHRON	CIINOSSS	SCISSION
CGIMNPRU	CRUMPING	CHINOORZ	C-HORIZON	CIINOTTY	TONICITY
CGINNNSU	CUNNINGS	CHINOPTY	HYPNOTIC	CIINPSTU	SINCIPUT
CGINNOOR	CROONING		PYTHONIC	CIIOOPST	ISOTOPIC
CGINNOPU	POUNCING	CHINORSU	IN CHORUS	CIIOQTUX	QUIXOTIC
CGINNORS	SCORNING	CHINOSSU	CUSHIONS	CIIOTTXY	TOXICITY
CGINNORW	CROWNING	CHINOSTW	SWITCH ON	CIIPRRTU	PRURITIC
CGINNOSS	CONSIGNS	CHINOSUY	CUSHIONY	CIIRSTTU	TRUISTIC
CGINNOTU	COUNTING	CHIOOPPT	PHOTOPIC	CIISSTTY	CYSTITIS
CGINOOPS	SCOOPING	CHIOORSU	ICHOROUS	CIJKLMUY	LUCKY JIM
CGINOOPT	CO-OPTING	CHIOPRST	STROPHIC	CIJKOSTY	JOYSTICK
CGINOOST	SCOOTING	CHIOSSTT	SCOTTISH	CIJNNOOS	CONJOINS
CGINOPPR	CROPPING	CHIPRRSU	CHIRRUPS	CIJNNOOT	CONJOINT
CGINORSS	CROSSING	CHIPRTTY	TRIPTYCH	CIJNNOTU	JUNCTION
CGINORSU	COURSING	CHIPSTTU	STITCH UP	CIJOOSTY	JOCOSITY
	SCOURING	CHIPSTUW	SWITCH UP	CIKKOOST	TOOK SICK
CGINORTU	COURTING	CHIRRSSU	SCIRRHUS	CIKKOPST	SPOT KICK
CGINOSTU	SCOUTING	CHKMMOSU	HUMMOCKS	CIKKOSTU	KICKS OUT
CGINPRSU	SPRUCING	CHKMMOUY	HUMMOCKY	CIKLLPUY	PLUCKILY
CGINRRUY	CURRYING	CHKOOPPR	PORK CHOP	CIKLMOSW	COWS MILK
CGINSTTU	CUTTINGS	CHKOPSTU	TUCK SHOP		MILK COWS
CGINSTUU	TUNGUSIC	CHLNOOOP	COLOPHON	CIKLNOST	LINSTOCK
CGKLNOSU	GUNLOCKS	CHLNOOSU	NO SLOUCH	CIKLNUWY	LUCKY WIN
CGKLOTUY	GOT LUCKY	CHLOORSU	CHLOROUS	CIKLOSTY	STOCKILY
CGKOSTTU	GOT STUCK	CHLOPSTY	SPLOTCHY	CIKLRSSU	KISS CURL
CGLMOOYY	MYCOLOGY	CHMMOORU	MUCH ROOM		KISS-CURL
CGLNOOOY	ONCOLOGY	CHMNORRU	CRUMHORN	CIKMOORS	SICK ROOM
CGLOOTYY	CYTOLOGY	CHMNPRUU	RUM PUNCH		SICKROOM
CGOORSST	GOT CROSS	CHMOORSU	CHROMOUS	CIKNNOOS	COONSKIN
CHHIIKST	THICKISH	CHNOOPTT	TOP NOTCH	CIKNNOST	NONSTICK
CHHIINPT	PINCH HIT		TOP-NOTCH	CIKOOQTU	TOO QUICK
CHHILRSU	CHURLISH	CHNOPRSU	SUN PORCH	CIKOPRST	CORK TIPS
CHHIMRTY	RHYTHMIC	CHNORTUU	CHURN OUT	CIKOPSTU	PICKS OUT
CHHIOPST	CHIP SHOT	CHNPPSUU	PUNCH-UPS	CIKORTYY	YORK CITY
CHHKOOPS	HOCK SHOP	CHOOPPSS	COP SHOPS	CIKOSSTT	STICKS TO
CHHLLOOY	HOLY LOCH	CHOPSSTU	COST-PUSH		STOCKIST
CHHLNOTU	HOT LUNCH	CHORRTUY	HOT CURRY	CIKOSTTU	STICK OUT
CHHNOPTU	HOT PUNCH	CHORSTTU	CUT SHORT	CIKPSSTU	STICKS UP
CHIIKLST	TICKLISH		SHORT CUT		STICKUPS
CHIILNNP	LINCHPIN	CIIILMPT	IMPLICIT		UP STICKS
CHIILORS	RICH SOIL	CIIILNOV	OLIVINIC	CILLMSUY	CLUMSILY
CHIILOST	HOLISTIC	CIIILTVY	CIVILITY	CILLNOOT	COTILLON
CHIILPRY	CHIRPILY	CIIINNOS	INCISION	CILLNOSU	SCULLION
CHIILQSU	CLIQUISH	CIIINNOT	COIN IT IN	CILLOORS	CRIOLLOS
CHIIMORZ	RHIZOMIC	CIIINOTY	IONICITY	CILMNOOU	INOCULUM
CHIIORST	HISTORIC	CIIINTVY	VICINITY	CILMNUUV	VINCULUM
	ORCHITIS	CIIJRSTU	JURISTIC	CILMOPSY	OLYMPICS
CHIKLLOS	HILLOCKS	CIIKKLLS	KILLICKS	CILNOORU	IN COLOUR
CHIKLLOY	HILLOCKY	CIIKLLOS	OIL SLICK	CILNOOST	COLONIST
CHIKLNUY	CHUNKILY	CIIKLPST	LIPSTICK	CILNOOTU	LOCUTION
CHIKLTUY	LUCKY HIT	CIIKLRTY	TRICKILY	CILNOPTU	PLUTONIC
CHIKMNPU	CHIPMUNK	CIIKLSST	SICK LIST	CILNOSTU	LINO CUTS
CHIKOPPS	PICK HOPS	CIIKLSTY	STICKILY		LINOCUTS
CHIKOPTY	KYPHOTIC	CIIKNPPR	PINPRICK	CILNPSSU	SCULPINS
CHILLOOT	OILCLOTH	CIIKNPST	STICK PIN	CILOOPST	CO-PILOTS
CHILLTUY	HULL CITY	CIIKPPTU	PICK IT UP	CILOORST	CORTISOL

CILOORSU	COULOIRS	CLLOOQUY	COLLOQUY	DDEEERSV	DESERVED
CILOPPRY	PROPYLIC	CLMMNOOY	COMMONLY	DDEEESTT	DETESTED
CILOPSSW	COWSLIPS	CLMOSSUU	OSCULUMS	DDEEEWYY	DEWY-EYED
CILOSSTU	OCULISTS	CLNOORST	CONTROLS	DDEEFFIR	DIFFERED
CILOSSTY	SYSTOLIC	CLNOSSTU	CONSULTS	DDEEFFNO	OFFENDED
CILOSSUU	LUSCIOUS	CLOOOPRT	PROTOCOL	DDEEFGGO	DEFOGGED
CILPRSTU	CULPRITS	CLOORTUV	COLOUR T.V.	DDEEFGIT	FIDGETED
CILRSTTY	STRICTLY	CLOOSSSU	COLOSSUS	DDEEFIPR	DRIP FEED
CILRSTUY	CRUSTILY	CLOPRSSY	CROSSPLY		DRIP-FEED
CILRSUVY	SCURVILY	CLOPRSTU	SCULPTOR	DDEEFLNO	ENFOLDED
CILSSTTU	CULTISTS	CLOPSSTU	COST-PLUS	DDEEFLOU	FOUL DEED
CIMMNNOO	IN COMMON	CMMMNOOU	UNCOMMON	DDEEFMOR	DEFORMED
CIMNOORS	OMICRONS	CMNOOOST	MONOCOTS	DDEEFNRU	REFUNDED
CIMNOOSW	IN MOSCOW	CMOOPRST	COMPORTS		UNDERFED
CIMNOOTT	TOM CONTI	CMOOPSST	COMPOSTS	DDEEGGIR	DRIED EGG
CIMNORSS	CRIMSONS	CMORSSTU	SCROTUMS	DDEEGINS	DESIGNED
CIMNOSTU	MISCOUNT	CMORSTUW	CUTWORMS	DDEEGIPS	DIGS DEEP
CIMNOSUY	SYCONIUM	CNNOOOTT	COTTON ON	DDEEGIRV	DIVERGED
CIMOORSS	MORISCOS	CNNOOSTU	COUNTS ON	DDEEGIST	DIGESTED
CIMOPPSU	POP MUSIC	CNOOOORT	OCTOROON	DDEEGOPS	GOD SPEED
CIMRRTUY	TIM CURRY	CNOOPSSU	SOUPCONS		GODSPEED
CINNOOVY	IN CONVOY	CNOORSST	CONSORTS	DDEEGOTW	TWO-EDGED
CINNORSU	UNICORNS	CNOORSSW	CROSS NOW	DDEEGRRS	DREDGERS
CINNOSTU	COUNTS IN	CNOORSTT	CONTORTS	DDEEHILS	SHIELDED
CINNQUUX	QUINCUNX	CNOORSTU	CONTOURS	DDEEHINR	HINDERED
CINOOOPT	CO-OPTION		CROUTONS	DDEEHIRT	DITHERED
CINOOOTZ	ZOONOTIC	CNOOTTUU	COUNT OUT	DDEEHNNO	HODDODEN
CINOOPRS	SCORPION	CNOPSTUU	COUNTS UP	DDEEILLV	DEVILLED
CINOOPRT	PROTONIC	CNOSTUUU	UNCTUOUS	DDEEILMW	MILDEWED
CINOOTXY	OXYTOCIN	COOOPPRR	POOR CROP	DDEEILRV	RED DEVIL
CINOPSTY	SYNOPTIC	COOOPRRT	ROOT CROP	DDEEILWY	WILD-EYED
CINORRST	TRICORNS	COOOPSTU	SCOOP OUT	DDEEIMNP	IMPENDED
CINORSST	CISTRONS	COOPRRST	PROCTORS	DDEEIMSS	MISDEEDS
CINORSTU	RUCTIONS	COOPRSTU	OUTCROPS	DDEEIMST	DEMISTED
CINOSSST	CONSISTS	COOPRSUU	CROUPOUS	DDEEIMTT	DEMITTED
CINOSTUV	VISCOUNT	COORSSTU	CROSS OUT	DDEEINNT	INDENTED
CINOTTUW	CUT IN TWO	COOSTTUU	SCOUT OUT		INTENDED
CINRSSTU	INCRUSTS	COPRRSTU	CORRUPTS	DDEEINOS	ONE-SIDED
CINRSTTU	INSTRUCT	DDDDEEOR	DODDERED	DDEEINRT	DENDRITE
CINRSTUY	SCRUTINY	DDDEEEFN	DEFENDED	DDEEINST	DESTINED
CIOOPRSS	SCORPIOS	DDDEEENP	DEPENDED	DDEEIPRS	PRESIDED
CIOOPRST	PORTICOS	DDDEEENR	REDDENED	DDEEIPRV	DEPRIVED
CIOPRSTY	CYPRIOTS	DDDEEGOO	GOOD DEED	DDEEIPSS	DESPISED
CIOPSSTY	COPYISTS	DDDEEHRS	SHREDDED	DDEEIRTV	DIVERTED
CIORSSSS	SCISSORS	DDDEEIKN	KIND DEED	DDEEISST	DESISTED
CIOTTTUU	CUT IT OUT	DDDEEJRU	JUDDERED	DDEEISTV	DIVESTED
CIPPRRUU	PURPURIC	DDDEEORR	DODDERER	DDEELLMO	MODELLED
CIQRSTUY	CRY QUITS	DDDEIINV	DIVIDEND	DDEELLOP	DEED POLL
CKKNNOOS	KNOCK-ONS	DDDEILTW	TWIDDLED	DDEELLOW	DOWELLED
	KNOCKS ON	DDDEINOW	DIED DOWN	DDEELLOY	YODELLED
CKKNOOTU	KNOCK OUT	DDDGIILN	DIDDLING	DDEELMPU	DEPLUMED
	KNOCKOUT	DDDIOPRU	DID PROUD	DDEELMRS	MEDDLERS
CKKNOPRU	PUNK ROCK	DDEEEEMR	REDEEMED	DDEELOPR	DEPLORED
CKKNOPSU	KNOCKS UP	DDEEEENP	DEEPENED	DDEELOPX	EXPLODED
CKLLOOOO	LOOK COOL	DDEEEFNR	DEFENDER	DDEELOPY	DEPLOYED
CKLNOSTU	LOCKNUTS	DDEEEFRR	DEFERRED	DDEELORS	SOLDERED
CKLOORSW	ROWLOCKS	DDEEEGLR	LEDGERED	DDEELOSU	DELOUSED
CKLOOSTU	LOCKOUTS	DDEEEHNU	UNHEEDED	DDEELOVV	DEVOLVED
	LOCKS OUT	DDEEEILV	EVIL DEED	DDEELPRS	PEDDLERS
CKLOSTUU	LUCKS OUT	DDEEEIMR	REMEDIED	DDEELPRU	PRELUDED
CKNOOOSY	COSY NOOK	DDEEEINR	DIRE NEED	DDEELRSS	SLEDDERS
CKOOOSTU	COOKOUTS	DDEEEIWY	WIDE-EYED	DDEELRSU	DELUDERS
CKOOPSTT	STOCK POT	DDEEELPT	DEPLETED	DDEEMNOR	ENDODERM
	STOCKPOT	DDEEELSS	DEEDLESS	DDEEMRRU	DEMURRED
CKOPSSTU	STOCKS UP	DDEEEMNT	DEMENTED		MURDERED
CKOSSSTU	TUSSOCKS	DDEEENPX	EXPENDED	DDEENNOT	END TO END
CKOSSTUY	TUSSOCKY	DDEEENRR	RENDERED	DDEENOPR	PONDERED
CKOSTTUU	STUCK OUT	DDEEENRT	TENDERED	DDEENOPW	DEEP DOWN
CKPRSTUU	STRUCK UP	DDEEENTX	EXTENDED		PONDWEED
CLLMOSSU	MOLLUSCS	DDEEERRT	DETERRED	DDEENORS	ENDORSED
CLLOOPSS	SCOLLOPS	DDEEERST	DESERTED	DDEENORW	WONDERED

DDEENRSU	SUNDERED	DDEILSTU	LUDDITES	DDGILNOT	TODDLING
DDEEOPRT	DEPORTED	DDEILSTW	TWIDDLES	DDGILNPU	PUDDLING
DDEEOPRW	POWDERED	DDEIMOSU	MEDUSOID	DDGILOSW	WILD DOGS
DDEEORRW	REWORDED	DDEIMRSU	SIDE DRUM	DDGIMNOO	GOOD MIND
DDEEORTU	DETOURED	DDEIMSTU	MUDDIEST	DDGIMNUY	MUDDYING
DDEEORUV	DEVOURED	DDEINORS	INDORSED	DDGINOPR	PRODDING
DDEERTUX	EXTRUDED	DDEINORT	DONE DIRT	DDGINORW	DID WRONG
DDEFFISU	DIFFUSED	DDEINOSW	DIES DOWN	DDGINPSU	PUDDINGS
DDEFIILM	MIDFIELD		DISENDOW		SPUDDING
DDEFIIMO	MODIFIED		DISOWNED	DDGINSTU	STUDDING
DDEFILNO	INFOLDED	DDEINOTU	DINED OUT	DDGIORTY	DIRTY DOG
DDEFLNOU	UNFOLDED	DDEINOTW	TIED DOWN	DDGLNOOS	LONG ODDS
DDEFLOPU	FOLDED UP	DDEINRST	STRIDDEN	DDGLOOOR	GOOD LORD
DDEGGINR	DREDGING	DDEINRTU	INTRUDED	DDGLOSTU	GOLD DUST
DDEGGIOU	GUIDE DOG	DDEINSST	DISTENDS	DDGMOOOO	GOOD MOOD
DDEGGLOY	DOGGEDLY	DDEIOORS	SIDE DOOR	DDGNOOOO	DO NO GOOD
DDEGGNOO	DOGGONED	DDEIOPRV	PROVIDED	DDGNOOPU	DOG POUND
DDEGHLOO	HELD GOOD	DDEIOPSS	DISPOSED	DDGOOORW	GOOD WORD
DDEGIINR	DERIDING	DDEIORRS	DISORDER	DDGOORSY	DRY GOODS
DDEGIIST	GIDDIEST	DDEIORST	DOES DIRT	DDHILOSY	SHODDILY
DDEGILMN	MEDDLING	DDEIORSW	DID WORSE	DDHILSUY	DUDISHLY
DDEGILNP	PEDDLING	DDEIORTU	DRIED OUT	DDHIORSY	HYDROIDS
DDEGILNS	SLEDDING	DDEIOSTW	DOWDIEST	DDHIOSWY	DOWDYISH
DDEGILNU	DELUDING	DDEIPRWY	WIPED DRY	DDHLLTUU	DULL THUD
	INDULGED	DDEIPSTU	DISPUTED	DDHLNOOW	HOLD DOWN
DDEGILOS	DISLODGE	DDEIRSTU	RUDDIEST	DDHOOTTY	HOT TODDY
DDEGILRS	GRIDDLES	DDEKMOSU	DUKEDOMS	DDIIKLSS	SKID-LIDS
DDEGILUV	DIVULGED	DDELLOPU	DOLLED UP	DDIILOPS	DIPLOIDS
DDEGIMOS	DEMIGODS	DDELNOSY	SODDENLY	DDIIMMUY	DIDYMIUM
DDEGINNU	DENUDING	DDELNSUY	SUDDENLY	DDIIMNTY	TIDY MIND
DDEGINSW	WEDDINGS	DDELOOTU	DOLED OUT	DDIIMRSU	SIDDURIM
DDEGIORT	DOG-TIRED	DDELOPTU	TODDLE UP	DDIIQTUY	QUIDDITY
DDEGIOSV	GIVE ODDS	DDELORSS	OLD DRESS	DDIKNORW	KIND WORD
DDEGLOPS	SPLODGED	DDELORST	TODDLERS	DDIKOOSS	SKIDDOOS
DDEGNOOO	DONE GOOD	DDEMNOST	ODDMENTS	DDILNOSW	SLID DOWN
DDEGNORU	GROUNDED	DDEMNOUU	DUODENUM	DDILOOPP	DIPLOPOD
	UNDERDOG	DDEMNPUU	PUDENDUM	DDILORSY	SORDIDLY
DDEGNOSS	GODSENDS	DDEMOOTU	OUTMODED	DDINNOWW	DOWN WIND
DDEGOOOR	DO-GOODER	DDENNOOW	DONE DOWN		DOWNWIND
DDEGOOOS	DOES GOOD	DDENNOSW	SEND DOWN		WIND DOWN
DDEGOOWW	WEDGWOOD	DDENOOSW	DOES DOWN	DDINOOOT	ODONTOID
DDEGOPTU	ODD GET-UP	DDENOPSS	DESPONDS	DDINOOWW	WOODWIND
DDEGRRUY	DRUDGERY	DDENORSU	REDOUNDS	DDLLOORW	OLD WORLD
DDEHIISS	SIDE DISH	DDENORSW	SEND WORD		OLD-WORLD
DDEHIORS	SHODDIER	DDENOTUY	DONE DUTY	DDLMORSU	DOLDRUMS
DDEHIOSS	SHODDIES	DDEOOOOV	VOODOOED	DDNOOPRW	DROP DOWN
DDEHIPSU	DISHED UP	DDEOORSW	REDWOODS	DDNOORTW	TROD DOWN
DDEHIRSY	HYDRIDES	DDEORRUW	RUDE WORD	DDNOSTUW	DUST DOWN
DDEHLNOW	HELD DOWN	DDEOSTUY	DOES DUTY	DEEEEFRR	REFEREED
DDEHNRSU	HUNDREDS	DDFGIILN	FIDDLING	DEEEEGKN	KEEN EDGE
DDEHOOOO	HOODOOED	DDFGILNU	FUDDLING	DEEEEGKR	KEDGEREE
DDEHOOSW	WOODSHED	DDFGOOOO	GOOD FOOD	DEEEEKNP	KNEE DEEP
DDEHORSU	SHROUDED	DDFLNOOW	FOLD DOWN		KNEE-DEEP
DDEHRSSU	SHUDDERS	DDGGILNU	GUDDLING	DEEEEMRR	REDEEMER
DDEIIKLS	DISLIKED	DDGGINNO	DINGDONG	DEEEEMST	ESTEEMED
DDEIILNR	DIELDRIN	DDGGINRU	DRUDGING	DEEEENRV	VENEERED
DDEIILOS	IDOLISED	DDGHIIRT	DID RIGHT	DEEEERTT	TEETERED
DDEIILOZ	IDOLIZED	DDGHILNU	HUDDLING	DEEEFGIN	FINE EDGE
DDEIILRT	TIDDLIER	DDGHINTU	THUDDING	DEEEFGOR	FORE-EDGE
DDEIINSW	SIDE WIND	DDGHIOST	ODD SIGHT	DEEEFIIX	IDEE FIXE
DDEIIOST	ODDITIES	DDGHLOOO	HOLD GOOD	DEEEFIPV	FIVE DEEP
DDEIIOSX	DIOXIDES	DDGHNOOU	HOUND DOG	DEEEFIRR	FREE RIDE
DDEIIOXZ	OXIDIZED	DDGIIINV	DIVIDING	DEEEFIRW	FIREWEED
DDEIIRSV	DIVIDERS	DDGIIKNS	SKIDDING	DEEEFLLW	FEED WELL
DDEIKRSS	SKIDDERS	DDGIILMN	MIDDLING	DEEEFLOS	FELO DE SE
DDEILMOP	IMPLODED	DDGIILNP	PIDDLING		FELO-DE-SE
DDEILNPS	SPLENDID	DDGIILNR	RIDDLING	DEEEFLRX	REFLEXED
DDEILNSW	DWINDLES	DDGIILNW	WIDDLING	DEEEFMNR	FREEDMEN
DDEILOPS	LOPSIDED	DDGILMNU	MUDDLING	DEEEFORV	OVERFEED
DDEILORT	LORDED IT	DDGILNOO	DOODLING	DEEEFIRRR	DEFERRER
DDEILRST	TIDDLERS	DDGILNOP	PLODDING		REFERRED

DEEEFRRT	FERRETED	DEEERRSV	RESERVED	DEEGHINT	THIN EDGE
DEEEFRST	FESTERED		REVERSED	DEEGHIPS	DEEP SIGH
DEEEFRTT	FETTERED	DEEERRTV	REVERTED	DEEGHITW	WEIGHTED
DEEEGIPR	PEDIGREE	DEEERSSV	DESERVES	DEEGHNRU	HUNGERED
DEEEGIRR	GREEDIER	DEEERSTW	WESTERED	DEEGHOPS	SHEEP DOG
DEEEGLPS	PLEDGEES	DEEERSTX	EXSERTED		SHEEPDOG
DEEEGNNR	ENGENDER	DEEERTTV	REVETTED	DEEGHORW	HEDGEROW
DEEEGNRV	REVENGED	DEEFFGOR	GOFFERED	DEEGHOTT	DOGTEETH
DEEEHITW	I THEE WED	DEEFFINS	EFFENDIS	DEEGILNN	NEEDLING
DEEEHLMT	HELMETED	DEEFFIRS	SERIFFED	DEEGILNP	IN PLEDGE
DEEEHLSS	HEEDLESS	DEEFFNOR	OFFENDER	DEEGILNR	LINGERED
DEEEHLSW	WHEEDLES	DEEFFRSU	SUFFERED	DEEGILNS	SEEDLING
DEEEHMNS	ENMESHED	DEEFGGIR	FRIED EGG	DEEGILNT	DELETING
DEEEHRTT	TETHERED	DEEFGGOR	DEFOGGER	DEEGILRV	LEG DRIVE
DEEEIKLS	SEEDLIKE	DEEFGINR	FINGERED	DEEGILRY	GREEDILY
DEEEILRV	RELIEVED	DEEFGLNU	ENGULFED	DEEGIMNN	EMENDING
DEEEIMRS	REMEDIES	DEEFGLOO	FEEL GOOD	DEEGIMRU	DEMIURGE
DEEEIMST	SEEDTIME	DEEFGLUW	GULFWEED	DEEGINRS	DESIGNER
DEEEINRR	REINDEER	DEEFGNOS	DENSE FOG		RESIGNED
DEEEINTV	EVENTIDE	DEEFHILT	THE FIELD	DEEGINSS	EDGINESS
DEEEIPRS	SPEEDIER	DEEFHINT	HIND FEET	DEEGINST	INGESTED
DEEEIPTX	EXPEDITE	DEEFHLOR	FREEHOLD	DEEGINSX	DESEXING
DEEEIRRR	DERRIERE	DEEFHORR	HEREFORD	DEEGIORS	GEORDIES
DEEEIRRV	RIVER DEE	DEEFIINT	DEFINITE	DEEGIRST	DIGESTER
DEEEIRVW	REVIEWED	DEEFIIRS	FIRESIDE	DEEGIRSV	DIVERGES
DEEEISST	SEEDIEST	DEEFIIRV	VERIFIED	DEEGIRTT	GET TIRED
DEEEISSV	DEVISEES	DEEFILLT	FILLETED	DEEGJPRU	PREJUDGE
DEEEISTW	WEEDIEST	DEEFILNX	INFLEXED	DEEGLNRY	LEGENDRY
DEEEJLLW	JEWELLED	DEEFILPR	PILFERED	DEEGLOOT	EDGE TOOL
DEEEKNSW	WEEKENDS	DEEFILRS	DEFILERS	DEEGLORT	GET OLDER
DEEEKOPW	POKEWEED		FIELDERS	DEEGLORW	GLOWERED
DEEEKRSW	SKEWERED	DEEFILRT	FILTERED	DEEGLPST	PLEDGETS
DEEELLLV	LEVELLED	DEEFILST	LEFT SIDE	DEEGNNOY	ENDOGENY
DEEELLPR	REPELLED	DEEFINNO	DONE FINE	DEEGNORV	GOVERNED
DEEELLPX	EXPELLED	DEEFINOS	DOES FINE	DEEGNPUX	EXPUNGED
DEEELNRT	RELENTED	DEEFINRR	INFERRED	DEEGOOST	GO TO SEED
DEEELNRU	UNREELED	DEEFINRS	DEFINERS	DEEGORVY	DOVE GREY
DEEELNSS	LESSENED	DEEFINRZ	FRENZIED	DEEGRSTU	GESTURED
	NEEDLESS	DEEFINSS	FINESSED	DEEGRTTU	GUTTERED
DEEELOSY	SLOE-EYED	DEEFINST	INFESTED	DEEHHNPY	HYPHENED
DEEELPST	DEPLETES	DEEFIPRX	PREFIXED	DEEHHPRS	SHEPHERD
DEEELRTT	LETTERED	DEEFIRRY	FIERY RED	DEEHHRST	THRESHED
DEEELRTW	WELTERED	DEEFIRTT	REFITTED	DEEHIKLR	HERDLIKE
DEEELSSS	SEEDLESS	DEEFLLOS	FEELS OLD	DEEHIKRS	SHRIEKED
DEEELSSW	WEEDLESS	DEEFLORW	DEFLOWER	DEEHIKSV	KHEDIVES
DEEEMNSS	SEEDSMEN		FLOWERED	DEEHILNW	NEW DELHI
DEEEMPRT	TEMPERED	DEEFLOST	FEEDLOTS	DEEHILRS	RELISHED
DEEEMPTX	EXEMPTED	DEEFLRUX	REFLUXED	DEEHILSV	DISHEVEL
DEEENOPR	REOPENED	DEEFMNOT	FOMENTED	DEEHILTV	THE DEVIL
DEEENOPT	DEEP NOTE	DEEFMORR	REFORMED	DEEHIMMN	HEMMED IN
	DEEP TONE	DEEFMORS	FREEDOMS	DEEHIMNR	HIRED MEN
DEEENORS	ENDORSEE	DEEFMPRU	PERFUMED	DEEHINNT	IN THE END
	SORE NEED	DEEFNOST	SOFTENED	DEEHINRR	HINDERER
DEEENPRT	REPENTED	DEEFNSST	DEFTNESS	DEEHINRT	IN THE RED
DEEENPRX	EXPENDER	DEEFOPRU	FOUR DEEP	DEEHINTW	WHITENED
DEEENPSS	DEEPNESS	DEEFORST	DEFOREST	DEEHIPPS	SHEEP-DIP
DEEENQRU	RED QUEEN		FORESTED	DEEHIPRS	PERISHED
DEEENRRT	TENDERER		FOSTERED	DEEHIRRT	DITHERER
DEEENRRV	REVEREND	DEEFORSX	RED FOXES	DEEHIRSV	SHIVERED
DEEENRST	RESENTED	DEEFPRSU	PERFUSED	DEEHIRTW	WITHERED
DEEENRTU	NEUTERED	DEEFRTUY	DUTY FREE	DEEHIRTY	HEREDITY
DEEENRTX	EXTENDER		DUTY-FREE	DEEHKNOS	KEESHOND
DEEEOPRT	DEPORTEE	DEEGGHHO	HEDGEHOG	DEEHKOOT	TOOK HEED
DEEEOSTV	DEVOTEES	DEEGGIJR	JIGGERED	DEEHKORS	KOSHERED
DEEEPPPR	PEPPERED		REJIGGED	DEEHLLOR	HOLLERED
DEEEPRSS	SPEEDERS	DEEGGILT	LEGGED IT	DEEHLNPS	SEND HELP
DEEEPRST	PESTERED	DEEGGKOR	GREEK GOD	DEEHLORV	HELD OVER
DEEEPRVY	VERY DEEP	DEEGGLOR	DOGGEREL	DEEHLPPU	HELPED UP
DEEEQSUZ	SQUEEZED	DEEGGNOR	ENGORGED	DEEHLRTU	HELD TRUE
DEEERRRV	VERDERER	DEEGHHOP	HEDGEHOG	DEEHLSTU	SLEUTHED
DEEERRST	DESERTER	DEEGHILS	SLEIGHED	DEEHMNOS	SEND HOME

DEEHMNRS	HERDSMEN	DEEIMMRS	IMMERSED	DEEIPSST	SIDESTEP
DEEHMORT	MOTHERED		SIMMERED	DEEIPSTU	DEPUTIES
DEEHNORT	DETHRONE	DEEIMNOR	DOMINEER		DEPUTISE
	THRENODE	DEEIMNOS	DEMONISE	DEEIPSUZ	SEIZED UP
DEEHNORW	DOWN HERE		SIMON DEE	DEEIPTUZ	DEPUTIZE
DEEHNOTT	TO THE END	DEEIMNOT	DONE TIME	DEEIQRRU	REQUIRED
DEEHNOWY	HONEYDEW	DEEIMNOZ	DEMONIZE	DEEIQRTU	REQUITED
DEEHNSTU	ENTHUSED	DEEIMNPT	PEDIMENT	DEEIQRUV	QUIVERED
DEEHOORV	HOOVERED	DEEIMNRR	REMINDER	DEEIQTUU	QUIETUDE
DEEHOPRT	POTHERED	DEEIMNRT	TIRED MEN	DEEIRRRV	RED RIVER
DEEHORSS	RED SHOES	DEEIMNSS	SIDESMEN	DEEIRRSS	DRESSIER
DEEHORSU	REHOUSED	DEEIMNST	SEDIMENT	DEEIRRST	DESTRIER
DEEHORSW	SHOWERED	DEEIMNSY	MINDS EYE	DEEIRRWW	WIREDREW
DEEHORTX	EXHORTED	DEEIMOST	DOES TIME	DEEIRSST	RESISTED
DEEHRRSW	SHREWDER	DEEIMPRS	PREMISED	DEEIRSSU	REISSUED
DEEIILNS	SIDE LINE		SIMPERED		RESIDUES
	SIDELINE	DEEIMRST	DEMERITS	DEEIRSSV	DISSEVER
DEEIILRV	LIVERIED		DEMISTER	DEEIRSTW	WEIRDEST
DEEIIMRZ	DIMERIZE	DEEIMRTT	REMITTED	DEEIRTTT	TITTERED
DEEIIMST	ITEMISED	DEEINNRT	INDENTER	DEEISSTW	WEST SIDE
DEEIIMTZ	ITEMIZED		INTERNED	DEEJKNTU	JUNKETED
DEEIINOS	DEIONISE	DEEINNSW	IN SWEDEN	DEEJPRRU	PERJURED
DEEIINOZ	DEIONIZE	DEEINNSZ	DENIZENS	DEEKKOOY	OKEYDOKE
DEEIIPRU	PRIE-DIEU	DEEINNTV	INVENTED	DEEKLLNY	NED KELLY
DEEIIRSS	DIERESIS	DEEINNTW	ENTWINED	DEEKMNOY	MONKEYED
DEEIIRST	SIDERITE	DEEINOPW	OPEN WIDE	DEEKNOPW	KEEP DOWN
DEEIIRSV	DERISIVE		WIDE OPEN	DEEKORRW	REWORKED
DEEIIRSW	WEIRDIES	DEEINORS	NO DESIRE	DEELLMOR	MODELLER
DEEIISSS	DISSEISE	DEEINORT	ORIENTED	DEELLNOR	ENROLLED
DEEIISSW	SIDEWISE	DEEINORV	DON REVIE		RONDELLE
DEEIIVWW	WIDE VIEW	DEEINORZ	ZEROED IN	DEELLNOW	DONE WELL
DEEIJNNO	ENJOINED	DEEINOSV	NOSE-DIVE		WELL DONE
DEEIJNOR	REJOINED	DEEINPRS	RED PINES		WELL-DONE
DEEIJRTT	JITTERED	DEEINPSS	DISPENSE	DEELLORY	YODELLER
DEEIKLLR	KILLDEER	DEEINQRU	ENQUIRED	DEELLOSW	DOES WELL
DEEIKLMW	MILKWEED	DEEINRRT	INTERRED	DEELLOTW	TOWELLED
DEEIKNPS	SKIN DEEP		TRENDIER	DEELLOTX	EXTOLLED
	SKIN-DEEP	DEEINRRW	DREW REIN	DEELLOVY	VOLLEYED
DEEIKNRT	TINKERED	DEEINRSS	DIRENESS	DEELLOWY	YELLOWED
DEEIKNTT	KITTENED	DEEINRST	INSERTED	DEELLRSU	DUELLERS
DEEIKOSV	DOVEKIES		RESIDENT	DEELLRSW	DWELLERS
DEEIKPPR	KIPPERED		SINTERED	DEELLSUW	WELL USED
DEEILLMP	IMPELLED		TRENDIES	DEELMNOO	MELODEON
DEEILLRT	TILLERED	DEEINRSV	VERSED IN	DEELMNOW	NEW MODEL
DEEILLST	LET SLIDE	DEEINRSW	RED WINES	DEELMOPY	EMPLOYED
DEEILMOS	MELODIES	DEEINRTU	REUNITED	DEELMORS	REMODELS
DEEILNOT	DELETION	DEEINRTV	INVERTED	DEELMOST	MOLESTED
DEEILNRS	RED LINES	DEEINRTW	WINTERED	DEELMPSU	DEPLUMES
DEEILNRU	UNDERLIE	DEEINSST	DESTINES	DEELMRUY	DEMURELY
DEEILNSS	IDLENESS	DEEINSSW	DEWINESS	DEELNOOS	LOOSE END
DEEILNST	ENLISTED		WIDENESS	DEELNOOV	LOVED ONE
	LISTENED	DEEINSTT	DINETTES	DEELNORS	ELDER SON
	TINSELED	DEEINSTV	INVESTED	DEELNORT	REDOLENT
DEEILNTT	ENTITLED	DEEIOPRX	PEROXIDE	DEELNRTY	TENDERLY
DEEILNUV	UNVEILED	DEEIOPSS	EPISODES	DEELNSSW	LEWDNESS
DEEILOPT	PETIOLED	DEEIOPST	POETISED	DEELNWWY	NEWLY WED
DEEILORT	DOLERITE	DEEIOPSX	EPOXIDES		NEWLYWED
	LOITERED	DEEIOPTZ	POETIZED	DEELNXYY	LYNX-EYED
DEEILPRR	RED PERIL	DEEIORRV	OVERRIDE	DEELOORT	RETOOLED
DEEILPSY	SPEEDILY		RIDE OVER	DEELOPRS	DEPLORES
DEEILRSU	LEISURED	DEEIORTV	TIDE OVER	DEELOPRX	EXPLODER
DEEILRSV	DELIVERS	DEEIOSTV	VIDEO SET		EXPLORED
	SILVERED	DEEIPPQU	EQUIPPED	DEELOPRY	REDEPLOY
	SLIVERED	DEEIPPST	PEPTIDES	DEELOPST	SEED PLOT
DEEILRSW	WIELDERS	DEEIPRRS	PRESIDER	DEELOPSV	DEVELOPS
DEEILRSY	YIELDERS		RESPIRED	DEELOPSW	LOW SPEED
DEEILRTT	LITTERED	DEEIPRSS	DESPISER	DEELOPSX	EXPLODES
DEEILRVY	DELIVERY		DISPERSE	DEELORRS	SOLDERER
DEEILSST	TIDELESS		PRESIDES	DEELORSV	RESOLVED
DEEILSUV	DELUSIVE	DEEIPRSV	DEPRIVES	DEELORTT	DOTTEREL
DEEIMMNS	ENDEMISM	DEEIPSSS	DESPISES	DEELORTV	REVOLTED

DEELORUV	LOUVERED	DEEORRVW	OVERDREW	DEFHLLOT	LEFT HOLD
DEELORVV	REVOLVED	DEEORSST	OERSTEDS	DEFHLOOS	SELFHOOD
DEELOSSU	DELOUSES	DEEORSTX	DEXTROSE	DEFHLOOT	THE FLOOD
DEELOSVV	DEVOLVES	DEEORSTY	STOREYED	DEFHNOOP	FOND HOPE
DEELPRRU	PRELUDER	DEEORTTT	TOTTERED	DEFIIILV	VILIFIED
DEELPRSU	PRELUDES	DEEORTTX	EXTORTED	DEFIIIVV	VIVIFIED
	REPULSED	DEEORTUV	DEVOUTER	DEFIILLN	FILLED IN
DEELPRTU	DRUPELET	DEEOSSUX	EXODUSES		INFILLED
DEELRSTU	DELUSTRE	DEEOSTUW	WEEDS OUT	DEFIILLP	FILLIPED
	RESULTED	DEEOSTUX	TUXEDOES	DEFIILLW	WILD LIFE
DEELRSTW	WRESTLED	DEEPPSSU	SPEEDS UP		WILDLIFE
DEEMMORS	MESODERM	DEEPQUUU	QUEUED UP	DEFIILMS	MISFILED
DEEMMRSU	SUMMERED	DEEPRSTU	RESTED UP	DEFIILNS	INFIDELS
DEEMNORY	NO REMEDY	DEEPRSUV	SERVED UP		INFIELDS
DEEMOORT	ODOMETER	DEEPRTTU	PUTTERED	DEFIILPS	FLIP SIDE
DEEMPRSU	PRESUMED	DEEPRUVV	REVVED UP	DEFIILRW	WILDFIRE
DEEMPRTU	PERMUTED	DEEPRUVY	PURVEYED	DEFIILSU	FLUIDISE
DEEMPSSU	MESSED UP	DEERRSSS	DRESSERS	DEFIILTY	FIDELITY
DEEMRRRU	DEMURRER	DEERRTTU	TURRETED	DEFIILUZ	FLUIDIZE
	MURDERER	DEERRTUX	EXTRUDER	DEFIIMNT	FIND TIME
DEEMRSTU	MUSTERED	DEERSSST	DESSERTS	DEFIIMOR	MODIFIER
DEEMRTTU	MUTTERED		STRESSED	DEFIIMOS	MODIFIES
DEENNOOZ	ONE DOZEN	DEERSTUX	EXTRUDES	DEFIIMRS	MISFIRED
DEENNOPT	DEPONENT	DEERSUVY	SURVEYED	DEFIINOT	NOTIFIED
DEENNORW	RENOWNED	DEERTTUX	TEXTURED	DEFIINTT	FITTED IN
DEENNOST	NEEDS NOT	DEFFFIOR	FIRED OFF	DEFIINTU	FINITUDE
DEENNOTZ	TEN DOZEN	DEFFHIOV	HIVED OFF	DEFIINTY	IDENTIFY
DEENNPRY	PENNY RED	DEFFILUV	FIVEFOLD	DEFIIOSS	OSSIFIED
DEENNRUV	UNNERVED	DEFFINOR	IN OFF RED	DEFIIPRU	PURIFIED
DEENNSSU	NUDENESS	DEFFIOPW	WIPED OFF	DEFIIPTY	TYPIFIED
DEENOORV	DONE OVER	DEFFIORS	RIDES OFF	DEFIIQUV	FIVE QUID
	OVERDONE	DEFFIORV	DRIVE OFF	DEFILLNU	UNFILLED
DEENOPPU	OPENED UP		OFF DRIVE	DEFILLPU	FILLED UP
DEENOPRR	PONDERER	DEFFIRSU	DIFFUSER	DEFILNNO	NINEFOLD
DEENOPSS	SPONDEES	DEFFISSU	DIFFUSES	DEFILNOW	FILE DOWN
DEENOPSW	DEEP SNOW	DEFFISUX	SUFFIXED	DEFILNRS	FLINDERS
DEENORRS	ENDORSER	DEFFLRTU	TRUFFLED	DEFILNRY	FRIENDLY
DEENORRW	WONDERER	DEFFMOOV	MOVED OFF	DEFILOPR	PROFILED
DEENORSS	ENDORSES	DEFFNORS	FORFENDS	DEFILORU	FLUORIDE
DEENORSU	SEE ROUND	DEFFNOSS	SEND-OFFS	DEFILOTU	OUTFIELD
DEENOSST	STENOSED		SENDS OFF	DEFILPTU	UPLIFTED
DEENOSWY	EYES DOWN	DEFFOOPR	ROPED OFF	DEFILRRU	FLURRIED
DEENPRSS	SPENDERS	DEFFOORR	ORDER OFF	DEFILRVY	FERVIDLY
DEENPRST	PRETENDS	DEFFOORV	DROVE OFF	DEFILRZZ	FRIZZLED
DEENPRSU	RUNS DEEP	DEFFSSUU	SUFFUSED	DEFIMNOR	INFORMED
DEENRRTU	RETURNED	DEFFSTUY	DYESTUFF	DEFIMNRY	MY FRIEND
DEENRSSU	RUDENESS	DEFGGILN	FLEDGING	DEFIMRRU	DRUMFIRE
DEENRSSW	NEW DRESS	DEFGHILT	FLIGHTED	DEFINOPR	PINED FOR
DEENRSTU	DENTURES	DEFGHIRT	FRIGHTED	DEFINOTT	FITTED ON
DEENRTUV	VENTURED	DEFGIILN	DEFILING	DEFINOVW	FIVE DOWN
DEEOORRV	OVERRODE		FIELDING	DEFINTTU	UNFITTED
	RODE OVER	DEFGIINN	DEFINING	DEFIOORW	FIREWOOD
DEEOORSV	DOES OVER	DEFGIINY	DEIFYING		WOOD FIRE
	OVERDOES		EDIFYING	DEFIOPRT	PROFITED
	OVERDOSE	DEFGILNO	FINE GOLD	DEFIOTXY	DETOXIFY
DEEOPPST	ESTOPPED	DEFGILOO	GOOD LIFE	DEFIPTTU	FITTED UP
	TOP SPEED	DEFGILOS	DOGS LIFE	DEFIRRST	DRIFTERS
DEEOPRRT	REPORTED	DEFGILTY	GIFTEDLY	DEFIRSSU	FISSURED
DEEOPRRV	REPROVED	DEFGILUW	WIDE GULF	DEFKNOPU	POKED FUN
DEEOPRRW	POWDERER	DEFGINSU	DEFUSING	DEFLLNOW	FELL DOWN
DEEOPRTT	POTTERED	DEFGIOOW	GOOD WIFE	DEFLLOOR	FOLDEROL
DEEOPRTX	EXPORTED	DEFGIORS	FIREDOGS	DEFLLOOW	FOLLOWED
DEEOPSSU	ESPOUSED	DEFGIORT	GET RID OF	DEFLMNOO	MEN OF OLD
DEEOQRTU	ROQUETED	DEFGLOOT	FELT GOOD	DEFLNORU	FLOUNDER
DEEORRRS	REORDERS	DEFGLOOY	OLD FOGEY	DEFLNRUU	UNFURLED
DEEORRRV	VERDEROR	DEFGMNOO	MEN OF GOD	DEFLOORT	FORETOLD
DEEORRSS	RED ROSES	DEFHIIMU	HUMIFIED	DEFLOORV	FOLD OVER
DEEORRST	RESORTED	DEFHIINS	FIENDISH		OVERFOLD
	RESTORED		FINISHED	DEFLOPUU	FOULED UP
DEEORRTT	RETORTED	DEFHIOOT	HOOFED IT	DEFLORTW	LEFT WORD
DEEORRUV	DEVOURER	DEFHIOOW	WIFEHOOD	DEFLPRUU	FURLED UP

DEFMNORU	UNFORMED	DEGIINNX	INDEXING	DEGKNRTU	GET DRUNK
DEFNNOSS	FONDNESS	DEGIINOS	GO INSIDE	DEGLLNOY	GOLDENLY
DEFNOOPS	SPOON FED		INDIGOES	DEGLLOOP	GOLLOPED
	SPOON-FED	DEGIINRS	DESIRING	DEGLNRTU	GRUNTLED
DEFNORRU	FRONDEUR		RESIDING	DEGLOOPY	PEDOLOGY
DEFNORSS	SENDS FOR		RINGSIDE	DEGLOORT	GOT OLDER
DEFNORSU	FOUNDERS	DEGIINRV	DERIVING	DEGLOORV	DOG LOVER
DEFOORRW	FOREWORD	DEGIINST	DINGIEST	DEGLOOUU	DUOLOGUE
DEFOORTV	VOTED FOR	DEGIINSV	DEVISING	DEGLOPRU	PURE GOLD
DEFORRUW	FURROWED	DEGIISSU	DISGUISE	DEGLOPSS	SPLODGES
DEFORSST	DEFROSTS	DEGIJMSU	MISJUDGE	DEGLPRSU	SPLURGED
DEFORSTW	FROWSTED	DEGIKLOV	KID GLOVE	DEGMNOOO	GOOD OMEN
DEFORSWW	FEW WORDS		KID-GLOVE	DEGMOOOS	SOME GOOD
DEGGHRSU	SHRUGGED	DEGILLNU	DUELLING	DEGMOOOV	GOOD MOVE
DEGGIINN	DEIGNING	DEGILLNW	DWELLING	DEGMRSSY	GYM DRESS
DEGGILNP	PLEDGING	DEGILMNO	GOLD MINE	DEGNNOOW	GONE DOWN
DEGGILNS	GELDINGS	DEGILMPS	GLIMPSED	DEGNNOSU	DUNGEONS
	SLEDGING	DEGILNOS	SIDELONG	DEGNOORS	DRONGOES
DEGGILNU	DELUGING	DEGILNOV	GOLD VEIN	DEGNOOSS	GOODNESS
DEGGILOO	LIE DOGGO	DEGILNOW	GONE WILD	DEGNOOSW	GOES DOWN
DEGGIMMT	M G MIDGET	DEGILNRU	INDULGER		GOOD NEWS
DEGGINOR	GOING RED	DEGILNSU	INDULGES	DEGNOPSU	PUG-NOSED
DEGGIORS	DISGORGE	DEGILOOY	IDEOLOGY	DEGNORSU	UNDERGOS
DEGGIPRS	SPRIGGED	DEGILORW	GOLD WIRE	DEGNORTU	GET ROUND
DEGGIPRU	RIGGED UP	DEGILOSW	GOES WILD	DEGNOSTW	GETS DOWN
DEGGLNSU	SNUGGLED	DEGILRSU	GUILDERS	DEGOOPTY	GOOD TYPE
DEGGLRUY	RUGGEDLY	DEGILRWW	GREW WILD	DEGOORVY	VERY GOOD
DEGGMPUU	MUGGED UP	DEGILRZZ	GRIZZLED	DEGRRSTU	TRUDGERS
DEGGNOSU	GUDGEONS	DEGILSUV	DIVULGES	DEHHILTW	HELD WITH
DEGGOPTU	TOGGED UP	DEGIMNNY	DYING MEN		WITHHELD
DEGGRSTU	DRUGGETS	DEGIMNOT	DEMOTING	DEHHIRTT	THE THIRD
DEGHHIIR	RIDE HIGH	DEGIMNPU	IMPUGNED	DEHHOOSW	WHOOSHED
DEGHHIIT	HIGH TIDE	DEGIMOOT	GOOD TIME	DEHHPSUU	HUSHED UP
DEGHHIIV	HIGH DIVE		GOOD-TIME	DEHIILSV	DEVILISH
DEGHHIOR	RODE HIGH	DEGINNNU	UNENDING	DEHIIMMS	SHIMMIED
DEGHIINS	DINGHIES	DEGINNOS	SIGNED ON	DEHIINNW	WHINNIED
DEGHIKNT	KNIGHTED	DEGINNOT	DENOTING	DEHIINSS	SHINDIES
DEGHILNS	HIND LEGS	DEGINNOW	ENDOWING	DEHIIOTT	THE IDIOT
	SHINGLED	DEGINNPS	SPENDING	DEHIISST	DISHIEST
DEGHILOS	DIG HOLES	DEGINNPU	ENDING UP		THIS SIDE
DEGHILPT	PLIGHTED		UPENDING	DEHIISTW	SIDE WITH
DEGHILRT	LIGHT RED	DEGINNRT	TRENDING	DEHIJMNO	DEMIJOHN
	RED LIGHT	DEGINNRU	ENDURING	DEHIKOOT	HOOKED IT
	RED-LIGHT	DEGINNSU	UNSIGNED	DEHILLRS	SHRILLED
DEGHILST	DELIGHTS	DEGINOOW	GOOD WINE	DEHILLRT	THRILLED
	SLIGHTED	DEGINOPS	DEPOSING	DEHILMOS	DEMOLISH
DEGHINNU	UNHINGED	DEGINORR	ORDERING	DEHILOPS	POLISHED
DEGHINRU	HIRED GUN	DEGINORV	RING DOVE	DEHILPSU	SULPHIDE
DEGHINRW	DREW NIGH		RINGDOVE	DEHILSTW	WHISTLED
DEGHLOPU	PLOUGHED	DEGINOSS	DOINGSES	DEHIMNOS	HEDONISM
DEGHLOST	GETS HOLD	DEGINOSW	WIDGEONS	DEHIMPRS	SHRIMPED
DEGHLOSU	SLOUGHED	DEGINOTV	DEVOTING	DEHINNOP	PHONED IN
DEGHMOOS	DOGS HOME	DEGINOUY	DIE YOUNG	DEHINOPP	HOPPED IN
DEGHNORT	THRONGED	DEGINPSU	SIGNED UP	DEHINOPS	SIPHONED
DEGHNORY	HYDROGEN	DEGINPTU	DEPUTING	DEHINORT	ONE THIRD
DEGHOOOP	GOOD HOPE	DEGINRRS	GRINDERS	DEHINOST	HEDONIST
DEGHOOST	THE GOODS	DEGINRSS	DRESSING	DEHINOSW	SHOWED IN
DEGHOOSU	DOGHOUSE	DEGINRST	STRINGED	DEHINOTW	DONE WITH
	HOUSE DOG	DEGINRSW	REDWINGS	DEHINPSU	PUNISHED
DEGIIIST	DIGITISE	DEGINRSY	SYRINGED	DEHINRSS	IN SHREDS
DEGIIITZ	DIGITIZE	DEGINSTW	GETS WIND	DEHINRSU	RUSHED IN
DEGIILNT	DILIGENT	DEGIOOVW	GOOD VIEW	DEHIOPPT	HOPPED IT
DEGIILNW	WIELDING	DEGIOPRR	PORRIDGE	DEHIOPRS	SPHEROID
DEGIILNY	YIELDING	DEGIOPSS	GOSSIPED	DEHIORTU	HIRED OUT
DEGIILTY	GELIDITY	DEGIOPST	PODGIEST	DEHIOSSW	SIDE SHOW
DEGIIMNP	IMPEDING	DEGIORRV	RIVER GOD		SIDESHOW
	IMPINGED	DEGIORST	STODGIER	DEHIOSTT	DOT THE I'S
DEGIIMNS	DEMISING	DEGIORTT	GOT TIRED	DEHIOSTU	HIDEOUTS
DEGIIMSU	MISGUIDE	DEGIRTTY	GET DIRTY	DEHIPSSU	DISHES UP
DEGIINNT	ENDING IT	DEGJKOOO	GOOD JOKE	DEHIOSSU	SQUISHED
	INDIGENT	DEGJMNTU	JUDGMENT	DEHIRRRW	WHIRRRED

DEHIRRST	RED SHIRT	DEIILORZ	IDOLIZER	DEILLSTU	DUELLIST
DEHIRSTT	THIRD SET	DEIILOSS	IDOLISES	DEILMNSS	MILDNESS
	THIRSTED	DEIILOSZ	IDOLIZES		MINDLESS
DEHIRTWW	WITHDREW	DEIILPSS	SIDESLIP	DEILMOOT	DOLOMITE
DEHKLNOU	ELK HOUND	DEIILSTU	UTILISED	DEILMOPR	IMPLORED
	ELKHOUND	DEIILTUV	DILUTIVE	DEILMOPS	IMPLODES
DEHKNOOU	UNHOOKED	DEIILTUZ	UTILIZED	DEILMORT	OLD TIMER
DEHKOOPU	HOOKED UP	DEIIMMRS	DIMERISM		OLD-TIMER
DEHLLOOW	HOLLOWED	DEIIMMST	MISTIMED	DEILMORU	MOULDIER
DEHLLOPY	PHYLLODE	DEIIMNOS	DOMINIES	DEILMOST	MELODIST
DEHLMOOR	LORD HOME	DEIIMSVW	MIDWIVES		OLD TIMES
DEHLNOOT	HELD ON TO	DEIINNOP	PINIONED	DEILMPTU	LUMPED IT
DEHLNOPW	HELP DOWN	DEIINNQU	NINE QUID	DEILMRSU	MISRULED
DEHLOOPT	POTHOLED	DEIINNRV	DRIVEN IN	DEILNNOS	LIONS DEN
DEHLOORV	HOLD OVER	DEIINORS	DERISION	DEILNNOT	INDOLENT
DEHLOOSS	OLD SHOES		RESINOID	DEILNOOS	EIDOLONS
DEHLOOST	TOEHOLDS	DEIINOST	EDITIONS		SOLENOID
	TOOLSHED		SEDITION	DEILNOSU	DELUSION
DEHLOOTT	DO THE LOT	DEIINPPW	WINDPIPE	DEILNOSW	LIES DOWN
DEHLOOTU	HOLED OUT	DEIINPRS	INSPIRED	DEILNOTU	OUTLINED
DEHLOPRU	UPHOLDER	DEIINPRT	INTREPID	DEILNOVV	INVOLVED
DEHLOPSS	SPLOSHED	DEIINPRY	PYRIDINE	DEILNOVW	LIVE DOWN
DEHLORST	THE LORDS	DEIINPSS	SIDESPIN	DEILNOWX	WILD OXEN
DEHLORSU	SHOULDER	DEIINQRU	INQUIRED	DEILNPRS	SPINDLER
DEHLORTU	HOLD TRUE	DEIINRSS	INSIDERS	DEILNPRU	UNDERLIP
DEHLORTW	THE WORLD	DEIINRST	DISINTER	DEILNPSS	SPINDLES
DEHLRSWY	SHREWDLY	DEIINRSV	DRIVES IN	DEILNPQT	3PLINTED
DEHMMRTU	THRUMMED	DEIINRTU	UNTIDIER	DEILNRST	TENDRILS
DEHMOORW	WHOREDOM	DEIINSST	INSISTED	DEILNRSW	SWINDLER
DEHMOOST	SMOOTHED		TIDINESS	DEILNSSW	SWINDLES
DEHMORUU	HUMOURED	DEIINSTU	DISUNITE		WILDNESS
DEHMRTUW	THREW MUD		UNITISED		WINDLESS
DEHNNOOT	ON THE NOD	DEIINSTW	WINDIEST	DEILNSTU	DILUENTS
DEHNNORT	NORTH END	DEIINTTU	INTUITED		INSULTED
DEHNOORU	HONOURED	DEIINTTY	IDENTITY		UNLISTED
DEHNOOSW	HOEDOWNS	DEIINTUZ	UNITIZED	DEILNTTU	UNTITLED
	HOSE DOWN	DEIIORSX	OXIDISER	DEILNTUY	UNITEDLY
DEHNOOTT	ON THE DOT	DEIIORXZ	OXIDIZER	DEILNTWW	WENT WILD
DEHNOPPU	PHONED UP	DEIIOSSX	OXIDISES	DEILNUWY	UNWIELDY
DEHNOPSU	PUSHED ON	DEIIOSXZ	OXIDIZES	DEILOOPW	WOODPILE
DEHNOPSY	SYPHONED	DEIIPRST	SPIRITED	DEILOPSS	DESPOILS
DEHNORSU	ENSHROUD	DEIIPTTY	TEPIDITY	DEILOQRU	LIQUORED
	UNHORSED	DEIIQSTU	DISQUIET	DEILORSS	SOLDIERS
DEHNORTU	DUE NORTH	DEIIRRVV	VIVERRID	DEILORSW	WILD ROSE
DEHNORTY	THRENODY	DEIIRSSU	DIURESIS	DEILORSY	SOLDIERY
DEHNOSTU	SOUTH END	DEIIRSTT	DIRTIEST	DEILOSSV	DISSOLVE
DEHNOSTW	THE DOWNS	DEIISTZZ	DIZZIEST	DEILOSTU	SOLITUDE
DEHNRSTU	THUNDERS	DEIJMNPU	JUMPED IN	DEILOSVW	LOW DIVES
DEHNRTUY	THUNDERY	DEIJNORS	JOINDERS	DEILOTUV	LIVED OUT
DEHOORTU	OUT-HEROD	DEIJORRY	JOYRIDER		OUTLIVED
DEHOOSSW	SWOOSHED	DEIJORSY	JOY RIDES	DEILPPSU	SUPPLIED
DEHOPRST	POTSHERD		JOYRIDES	DEILPRSS	DRIPLESS
DEHOPRSU	SHORED UP	DEIKLMRU	DRUMLIKE	DEILPTWY	WILD-TYPE
DEHOPSUW	SHOWED UP	DEIKLNOO	LOOKED IN	DEILRRSV	L DRIVERS
DEHORSTW	THE SWORD	DEIKLNPU	LINKED UP	DEILRSTU	DILUTERS
DEHOSTUU	DUE SOUTH	DEIKLNTW	TWINKLED	DEILRSZZ	DRIZZLES
DEHPPSUU	PUSHED UP	DEIKLSTU	DUSTLIKE	DEILRTVY	DEVILTRY
DEHPRSUU	RUSHED UP	DEIKNNRU	UNKINDER	DEILSSTY	STYLISED
DEIIIMST	DIMITIES	DEIKNNSS	KINDNESS	DEILSTWW	WILD WEST
DEIIISVV	DIVISIVE	DEIKNORU	IRON DUKE	DEILSTYZ	STYLIZED
DEIIJNNO	JOINED IN	DEIKNORW	WORKED IN	DEIMMNOS	DEMONISM
DEIIKLSS	DISLIKES	DEIKNRRS	DRINKERS	DEIMMOST	IMMODEST
DEIIKNST	DINKIEST	DEIKNRSS	REDSKINS	DEIMNNOP	OPEN MIND
DEIIKSVV	SKIVVIED	DEIKNRVY	VERY KIND	DEIMNNSU	MINUENDS
DEIILLMT	ILL-TIMED	DEIKSSTU	DUSKIEST	DEIMNOOS	DOMINOES
DEIILMRU	DELIRIUM	DEILLNOR	ROLLED IN		MONODIES
DEIILMST	DELIMITS	DEILLNPU	PULLED IN	DEIMNOOT	DEMOTION
DEIILNOS	LIONISED	DEILLNSW	INDWELLS		MOTIONED
DEIILNOZ	LIONIZED	DEILLOPW	PILLOWED	DEIMNOOX	MONOXIDE
DEIILNVY	DIVINELY	DEILLOST	TOLD LIES	DEIMNOPU	OPIUM DEN
DEIILORS	IDOLISER	DEILLOTW	DO IT WELL	DEIMNOTW	DOWNTIME

DEIMNPSS	MISSPEND	DEIOPSSS	DISPOSES
DEIMNPTU	IMPUDENT	DEIOPSST	DEPOSITS
DEIMNRTU	RUDIMENT	DEIOPTUW	WIPED OUT
DEIMNRTY	DIRTY MEN	DEIORRSW	DROWSIER
DEIMOORS	MOIDORES	DEIORRSY	DERISORY
DEIMOOST	MOODIEST	DEIORRTU	OUTRIDER
	SODOMITE	DEIORSSS	DOSSIERS
DEIMOPRS	PROMISED	DEIORSST	STEROIDS
DEIMOPRT	IMPORTED	DEIORSSU	DESIROUS
DEIMOPRV	IMPROVED	DEIORSSV	DEVISORS
DEIMORRR	MIRRORED	DEIORSTU	DRIES OUT
DEIMORSS	MESSIDOR		OUTRIDES
DEIMORST	MORTISED		OUTSIDER
DEIMORSU	DIMEROUS		RIDES OUT
DEIMORUX	EXORDIUM	DEIORSTW	WORDIEST
DEIMOTTW	TWO-TIMED	DEIORSWW	WIDOWERS
DEIMPSTU	DUMPIEST	DEIORTTU	TIRED OUT
DEIMQRSU	SQUIRMED		TRIED OUT
DEIMRSSU	SURMISED	DEIORTUV	DRIVE OUT
DEIMRSUU	RESIDUUM	DEIOSSTU	OUTSIDES
DEINNNOU	INNUENDO	DEIOSSTW	TWO SIDES
DEINNNPU	UNPINNED	DEIOSTTT	DOTTIEST
DEINNORV	DRIVEN ON	DEIOSTTU	USED TO IT
DEINNOSW	SNOWED IN	DEIPPPTU	TIPPED UP
DEINNOWW	WINNOWED	DEIPPRST	STRIPPED
DEINNPPU	PINNED UP	DEIPPSTU	SPED IT UP
DEINNPRU	UNDERPIN	DEIPRRST	RED STRIP
DEINNRTU	TURNED IN	DEIPRRTU	IRRUPTED
DEINNRTV	T.V.DINNER	DEIPRSTU	DISPUTER
DEINOOPS	POISONED	DEIPRSWY	WIPES DRY
DEINOOPT	OPTIONED	DEIPSSTU	DISPUTES
DEINOOTV	DEVOTION	DEIQRSTU	SQUIRTED
DEINOPPP	POPPED IN	DEIRRSST	STRIDERS
DEINOPPW	DOWNPIPE	DEIRRSTU	STURDIER
	PIPE DOWN	DEIRSSST	DISTRESS
DEINOPRY	PYRENOID	DEIRSTTU	DETRITUS
DEINOPSS	DOPINESS	DEIRSUVV	SURVIVED
DEINORSS	INDORSES	DEISSTTU	DUSTIEST
DEINORVW	OVERWIND	DEJKLLRY	DR.JEKYLL
DEINOSSV	VOIDNESS	DEJKLOOS	OLD JOKES
DEINOSSZ	DOZINESS	DEJMNOPU	JUMPED ON
DEINOSTU	DINES OUT	DEJMPPUU	JUMPED UP
DEINOSTW	DOWNIEST		JUMPED-UP
	TIES DOWN	DEJNOOSW	DOW JONES
DEINOSXZ	SIX DOZEN	DEKKORSW	DESK WORK
DEINOTUW	WINED OUT	DEKLNOOO	LOOKED ON
DEINPPUZ	UNZIPPED	DEKLOOOT	LOOKED TO
DEINPRST	SPRINTED	DEKLOOPU	LOOKED UP
DEINPSST	STIPENDS	DEKNOORW	WORKED ON
DEINQSTU	SQUINTED	DEKNOPTW	KEPT DOWN
DEINRRTU	INTRUDER	DEKNRSTU	DRUNKEST
DEINRSSU	INSUREDS	DEKOOPRV	PROVOKED
	SUNDRIES	DEKOOTWW	KOWTOWED
DEINRSTT	STRIDENT	DEKOPRUW	WORKED UP
	TRIDENTS	DELLLOOP	LOLLOPED
DEINRSTU	INTRUDES	DELLLOSW	SOLD WELL
DEINRSTX	DEXTRINS	DELLNOOR	ROLLED ON
DEINRSWY	DRY WINES	DELLNOPU	PULLED ON
DEINSSST	DISSENTS	DELLNORU	UNROLLED
DEINSSTT	DENTISTS	DELLNOSW	DWELLS ON
DEINSTUU	UNSUITED	DELLNSSU	DULLNESS
DEINSTWW	WEST WIND	DELLOOTW	WELL TO DO
DEIOOPRS	POOR SIDE		WELL-TO-DO
DEIOORTV	OVERDO IT	DELLOPRS	REDPOLLS
DEIOOSTW	WOODIEST	DELLOPRU	ROLLED UP
DEIOPRRV	PROVIDER	DELLOPTU	POLLUTED
DEIOPRST	DIOPTERS	DELLORRY	DROLLERY
	DIOPTRES	DELLORST	DROLLEST
	PORT SIDE		STROLLED
DEIOPRSV	DISPROVE	DELLOSTY	OLD STYLE
	PROVIDES	DELLPPUU	PULLED UP

DELMNOOW	OLD WOMEN
DELMNOOY	OLD MONEY
DELMNOTW	MELT DOWN
DELMNPUU	PENDULUM
DELMORSS	SMOLDERS
DELMORSU	MOULDERS
	REMOULDS
	SMOULDER
DELMOSTY	MODESTLY
DELNNOOR	LONDONER
DELNOOSU	UNLOOSED
DELNOOWY	WOODENLY
DELNORSU	ROUNDELS
DELNORWW	NEW WORLD
DELNOSSU	LOUDNESS
DELNOSTW	LETS DOWN
DELNOTWY	WONTEDLY
DELNPRSU	PLUNDERS
DELNRSTU	TRUNDLES
DELOORRV	OVERLORD
DELOORSS	DOORLESS
DELOORSV	OVERSOLD
DELOOSTU	DOLES OUT
DELOPPSU	SLOPED UP
DELOPRST	LETS DROP
DELOPSUW	SLOWED UP
DELORSST	OLDSTERS
DELORSSW	WORDLESS
DELORSTW	DREW LOTS
DELORSUY	DELUSORY
DELORTUU	RULED OUT
DELOSSUU	SEDULOUS
DELOTUVY	DEVOUTLY
DELRSSTU	STRUDELS
DELSSSSU	SUDSLESS
DELSSSTU	DUSTLESS
DEMMNOSU	SUMMONED
DEMMPSUU	SUMMED UP
DEMMRRSU	DRUMMERS
DEMMRRUU	MURMURED
DEMMRSTU	STRUMMED
DEMNNOSU	SOUND MEN
	WOODSMEN
DEMNOPRU	PROUD MEN
DEMNORST	MORDENTS
DEMNORSY	SYNDROME
DEMNOSTU	DEMOUNTS
	MUDSTONE
DEMOOPRT	PROMOTED
DEMOORSU	DORMOUSE
DEMOOTUV	MOVED OUT
DEMOPPPU	MOPPED UP
DEMOPPRT	PROMPTED
DEMORRUU	RUMOURED
DENNOOPR	PONDER ON
DENNOOPU	ONE POUND
DENNOORU	ONE ROUND
	ROUND ONE
DENNOORW	NO WONDER
DENNOOTW	NOTE DOWN
	TONE DOWN
DENNORTU	ROUND TEN
	TURNED ON
DENNOSTW	SENT DOWN
DENNOTUW	UNWONTED
DENNOTWW	WENT DOWN
DENOOOPR	OPEN DOOR
	OPEN-DOOR
DENOOORV	OVEN DOOR
DENOORSW	ONES WORD
DENOORTW	TORE DOWN

DENOORTX	NEXT DOOR	DFFOORUW	WOODRUFF	DGHIILMT	DIM LIGHT
	NEXT-DOOR	DFGGHIOT	DOG FIGHT	DGHIIMNT	MIDNIGHT
DENOORWW	WORE DOWN		DOGFIGHT	DGHIINPS	SPHINGID
DENOOSTU	NOSED OUT	DFGGIOST	GOD'S GIFT	DGHIINSS	SHINDIGS
DENOOTVW	VOTE DOWN	DFGHILOS	GOLDFISH	DGHILLNU	DUNGHILL
DENOOTWZ	TWO DOZEN	DFGIIIRY	RIGIDIFY	DGHILNOS	HOLDINGS
DENOPRSS	RESPONDS	DFGIILRY	FRIGIDLY	DGHILNOT	OLD THING
DENOPRST	PORTENDS	DFGIINNS	FINDINGS	DGHILNRU	HURDLING
DENOPRSU	POUNDERS	DFGIINRT	DRIFTING	DGHILOOR	GIRLHOOD
DENOPSTW	STEP DOWN	DFGILLOO	GOLD FOIL	DGHINNOU	HOUNDING
	STEP-DOWN	DFGILMNU	FLING MUD	DGHLORSU	GOLD RUSH
DENOPSUW	SNOWED UP	DFGILMOO	GOOD FILM	DGHNNOUW	HUNG DOWN
DENOPSUX	EXPOUNDS	DFGILMNO	FONDLING	DGHNOTUU	DOUGHNUT
DENORRSU	ROUNDERS	DFGILNOO	FLOODING	DGHOOOST	GOOD HOST
DENORRSY	SORRY END	DFGINNOU	FOUNDING		GOOD SHOT
DENORSSU	DOURNESS	DFGINOOR	DOING FOR		HOT GOODS
	RESOUNDS	DFGIOORT	GOT RID OF	DGHOOOSW	GOOD SHOW
	SOUNDERS	DFGKLOOO	GOOD FOLK	DGHOOOTT	DOGTOOTH
DENOROTU	TONSURED	DFGLMNUU	FLUNG MUD	DGHOOSSW	DOG SHOWS
DENORSTW	SENT WORD	DFGMOOOR	GOOD FORM		SHOW DOGS
DENORSTY	DRYSTONE	DFGNOOOS	SON OF GOD	DGHORRUY	ROUGH-DRY
DENORSWW	NEW WORDS	DFGORSTU	SOFT DRUG	DGHORSTU	DROUGHTS
DENORTUW	UNDERTOW	DFHIIMUY	HUMIDIFY	DGHORTUY	DROUGHTY
DENOSSTU	SENDS OUT	DFHILMOR	FIRM HOLD	DGIIINNT	INDITING
	SOUNDEST	DFHILSSU	DISHFULS	DGIIINNV	DIVINING
DENOSSTW	SETS DOWN	DFHINOPS	FISH POND	DGIIINOS	IODISING
DENOSTUY	ONES DUTY	DFHJNOOR	JOHN FORD	DGIIINOZ	IODIZING
DENPRTUU	TURNED UP	DFHLOOOT	FOOTHOLD	DGIIIRTY	RIGIDITY
	UPTURNED	DFHNOOUX	FOXHOUND	DGIIKLNN	KINDLING
DENPSSSU	SUSPENDS	DFIILLMO	FILM IDOL	DGIILLNR	DRILLING
DENRRSTU	TURNS RED	DFIILOSY	SOLIDIFY	DGIILMNP	DIMPLING
DENRRTUU	NURTURED	DFIILTUY	FLUIDITY	DGIILNTU	DILUTING
DENSSTTU	STUDENTS	DFILLORY	FLORIDLY	DGIIMNOU	GONIDIUM
DEOOORSW	ROSEWOOD	DFILLOWW	WILD FOWL	DGIIMNSS	SMIDGINS
DEOOPPRS	PROPOSED		WILDFOWL	DGIIMPUY	PYGIDIUM
DEOOPPRT	PTEROPOD	DFILNOPS	PINFOLDS	DGIINNOR	NONRIGID
DEOOPRRV	DROP OVER	DFILORTU	OLD FRUIT	DGIINORR	GRIDIRON
DEOOPRST	DOORSTEP	DFIMNOOR	FIND ROOM	DGIINOSX	DIGOXINS
	TORPEDOS	DFIMOOOR	IODOFORM	DGIINOWW	WIDOWING
DEOOPRTU	UPROOTED	DFINOSTU	FINDS OUT	DGIINPPR	DRIPPING
DEOOPWWW	POWWOWED	DFIOOPRS	DISPROOF	DGIINYZZ	DIZZYING
DEOORRSW	SORROWED	DFIOQRUU	FOUR QUID	DGIKMNOS	KINGDOMS
DEOORRTU	ORDER OUT	DFJKNOOU	JUNK FOOD	DGILLNOY	DOLLYING
DEOORTUV	DROVE OUT	DFKLLOOS	OLD FOLKS	DGILLOOW	GOOD WILL
DEOOTTUV	OUTVOTED	DFKOOOOT	TOOK FOOD		GOODWILL
DEOPPPTU	TOPPED UP	DFLLOOOS	OLD FOOLS	DGILLORS	OLD GIRLS
DEOPPRRS	DROPPERS	DFLMOOOU	FOUL MOOD	DGILLOSW	GODS WILL
DEOPPRST	STROPPED	DFLOOOSU	SOUL FOOD	DGILMNOU	MOULDING
DEOPPRSU	PURPOSED	DFLOOOTU	FLOOD OUT	DGILMNPU	DUMPLING
DEOPPSSU	SUPPOSED	DFLOOSTU	FOLDOUTS	DGILMNSU	SLING MUD
DEOPRRTU	PROTRUDE	DFMOORRW	WORD FORM	DGILMSUY	SMUDGILY
DEOPRSTU	POSTURED	DFNOOPRU	PROFOUND	DGILNOOR	DROOLING
	PROUDEST	DFNOORUW	FOUR DOWN	DGILNOPS	GOLD PINS
	SPROUTED	DFNOOTUU	FOUND OUT	DGILNOTY	DOTINGLY
DEOPSSTU	TOSSED UP	DFOOORST	STOOD FOR	DGILOOOS	GOOD SOIL
DEORRTTU	TORTURED	DFOOOSTW	SOFTWOOD	DGILORWW	GROW WILD
DEORRTUW	TRUE WORD	DGGGIINS	DIGGINGS	DGILOSTY	STODGILY
DEORSSTW	WORSTEDS	DGGGINRU	DRUGGING	DGILRTUY	TURGIDLY
DEORSSTY	DESTROYS		GRUDGING	DGIMMNRU	DRUMMING
DEORSTUX	DEXTROUS	DGGIILNR	GIRDLING	DGIMMNUY	DUMMYING
DEOSSSYY	ODYSSEYS	DGGIINNW	WINGDING	DGIMOORT	GOOD TRIM
DEOSSTTU	TESTUDOS	DGGIKNOO	GOOD KING	DGINNOPU	POUNDING
DEPRRTUU	RUPTURED	DGGILNOR	GOLD RING	DGINNORU	ROUNDING
DERSTTTU	STRUTTED	DGGILNOS	LODGINGS	DGINNORW	DROWNING
DFFHLOOS	HOLDS OFF	DGGILOOR	GOOD GIRL		RING DOWN
DFFLMPUU	PLUM DUFF	DGGIMNSU	SMUDGING	DGINNOSU	SOUNDING
DFFLOORU	FOURFOLD	DGGINOOS	GOOD SIGN	DGINNOUW	WOUNDING
DFFNOORU	ROUND OFF	DGGINRTU	TRUDGING	DGINOOPR	DROOPING
DFFNOOSU	SOUND OFF	DGGIRSTU	DRUGGIST	DGINOPPR	DROPPING
DFFOOOST	STOOD OFF	DGHHIINW	HIGH WIND	DGINORSW	DROWSING
DFFOOPRS	DROPS OFF	DGHIIINN	IN HIDING	DGINOTUY	DYING OUT

DGINRRWY	WRING DRY	DHNOSTUW	SHUT DOWN	DINRSTUY	INDUSTRY
DGINSTUY	STUDYING		SHUTDOWN	DIOPRSST	DISPORTS
DGIOOPST	GOOD TIPS	DHOOORTX	ORTHODOX	DIORSSTT	DISTORTS
DGIORTTY	GOT DIRTY	DHOPRSSU	PUSHRODS	DIOSSTUU	STUDIOUS
DGISSSTU	DISGUSTS	DIIILTVY	LIVIDITY	DIPRSSTU	DISRUPTS
DGKLOOOO	GOOD LOOK	DIIIMTTY	TIMIDITY	DIRSSTTU	DISTRUST
	LOOK GOOD	DIIINOSV	DIVISION	DJMNOPUW	JUMP DOWN
DGKNOOSW	GOD KNOWS	DIIINTVY	DIVINITY	DKLLORUW	DULL WORK
DGKNORTU	GOT DRUNK	DIIIPRST	DISPIRIT	DKLNOOOW	LOOK DOWN
DGKOOORW	GOOD WORK	DIIJNOSS	DISJOINS	DKNNOOTW	DONT KNOW
DGLLOORY	OLD GLORY	DIIJNOST	DISJOINT	DKNNOSUW	SUNK DOWN
DGLMNSUU	SLUNG MUD	DIIKKNSS	KIDSKINS	DKNOOOTW	TOOK DOWN
DGLNOORW	GROWN OLD	DIIKNNRS	DRINKS IN	DKOOORWW	WOODWORK
	LONG WORD	DIIKNSTY	SINK-TIDY	DKORSTUW	STUDWORK
DGLNOOSS	OLD SONGS	DIILLMNW	WINDMILL	DLLNOPUW	PULL DOWN
DGLNOPSU	SPUN GOLD	DIILLMPY	LIMPIDLY	DLMOORSU	DRUM SOLO
DGLNOPUW	GULP DOWN	DIILLQUY	LIQUIDLY	DLNOOSUW	LOW SOUND
DGLOOOXY	DOXOLOGY	DIILNOTU	DILUTION	DLNOOSWW	SLOW DOWN
DGLOOPST	GOLD TOPS	DIILNTUY	UNTIDILY	DLNOOTUW	WOULD NOT
DGLOORSW	GROWS OLD	DIILOSTY	SOLIDITY	DLNORTUY	ROTUNDLY
DGLOOSST	LOST DOGS	DIILQSUU	LIQUIDUS	DLOOORSU	DOLOROUS
DGNNORUW	RUNG DOWN	DIIMNNOO	DOMINION	DLOOPPUW	PULPWOOD
DGNOORSU	GOOD RUNS	DIIMNOPT	MIDPOINT		WOOD PULP
DGNOORTU	GOOD TURN	DIIMNSUU	INDUSIUM	DLOOPPYY	POLYPODY
	GOT ROUND	DIIMPUXY	PYXIDIUM	DLOORSTY	OLD STORY
DGNOOTUY	GO ON DUTY	DIIMTTUY	TUMIDITY	DMMNRUUY	DUMMY RUN
DGNRRUWY	WRUNG DRY	DIINNOSU	DISUNION	DMNNOOWW	MOWN DOWN
DGOOORST	GOOD SORT	DIINOOPS	IODOPSIN	DMNOOSWW	MOWS DOWN
DHHILOTW	HOLD WITH	DIINSTUY	DISUNITY	DMNORSUU	ROUND SUM
	WITHHOLD	DIIORSSV	DIVISORS	DMOOORWW	WOODWORM
DHIIIMNS	DIMINISH	DIKLNNUY	UNKINDLY		WORMWOOD
DHIIKWZZ	WHIZZ KID	DIKLNOSU	KIND SOUL	DMORSTUU	DRUMS OUT
DHIIMNOO	HOMINOID	DIKNNOSW	SINK DOWN	DNNOORSU	ROUNDS ON
DHIIMNOS	HOMINIDS	DIKNOTYY	DINKY TOY	DNNOORTW	TORN DOWN
DHIIMNSU	HINDUISM	DIKNPRSU	DRINKS UP	DNNOORWW	WORN DOWN
DHIIMPSS	MIDSHIPS	DIKRSTYY	DIRTY SKY	DNNOOTWW	DOWN TOWN
DHIIMTUY	HUMIDITY	DILLMNOP	MILL POND		DOWNTOWN
DHIIORSS	HIDROSIS		MILLPOND	DNNORRUU	RUN ROUND
DHIKNOOW	HOODWINK	DILLNOPY	LILY POND	DNNORSUU	UNROUNDS
DHIKNORT	HOT DRINK	DILLOSTY	STOLIDLY	DNNORSUW	RUNDOWNS
DHILLNOW	DOWNHILL	DILMORSU	OIL DRUMS		RUNS DOWN
DHILMOPY	LYMPHOID	DILNNNOO	IN LONDON	DNNORTUW	DOWNTURN
DHILMOSY	MODISHLY	DILNRSUW	RUNS WILD		TURN DOWN
DHILNOPS	DOLPHINS	DILOOPPS	POP IDOLS		TURNDOWN
DHILOPRS	LORDSHIP	DILOOPPY	POLYPOID	DNNOSSUW	SUNDOWNS
DHILOPSS	SLIPSHOD	DILOORSS	LORDOSIS	DNOOPPRU	PROPOUND
DHILORRY	HORRIDLY	DILOORSU	LOUIS DOR	DNOOPRSW	SNOWDROP
DHILRSYY	DRYISHLY	DILOOSUY	ODIOUSLY	DNOOPRUW	DOWNPOUR
DHIMNOST	HINDMOST	DILOPRTY	TORPIDLY	DNOORSUW	WONDROUS
DHIMOPSS	DISH MOPS	DILORRTY	TORRIDLY	DNOORTUW	DROWN OUT
DHIMORSU	HUMIDORS	DILORSTU	DILUTORS		ROUND TWO
DHINOTUW	WHODUNIT	DILORSWY	DROWSILY	DNOOSTUU	SOUND OUT
DHIOOPRZ	RHIZOPOD	DILPSTUY	STUPIDLY	DNOPRSUU	ROUNDS UP
DHIORRTW	THIRD ROW	DILRSTUY	STURDILY		ROUNDUPS
DHIORSTY	THYROIDS	DIMMNORY	MYRMIDON	DNOPSTUW	PUTS DOWN
DHJNOORY	JOHN DORY	DIMMNOTY	TO MY MIND	DNORRSUU	SURROUND
DHJOPRSU	JODHPURS	DIMNOOST	MONODIST	DOOOPRST	DOORPOST
DHKLOOOT	TOOK HOLD	DIMNOPSU	IMPOUNDS		DOORSTOP
DHKMNOOO	MONKHOOD	DIMNOSTU	DISMOUNT	DOOORSTU	OUTDOORS
DHLMOOSU	HOODLUMS	DIMNOSTW	TWO MINDS	DOOOSTTU	STOOD OUT
DHLNOOOT	HOLD ON TO	DIMNOSUW	UNWISDOM	DOOPRSTU	DROPOUTS
DHLNOOWW	HOWL DOWN	DIMOORTW	WOOD TRIM		DROPS OUT
DHLOOSTU	HOLDS OUT	DIMORSWY	ROWDYISM	DOORSTWW	TWO WORDS
DHLORXYY	HYDROXYL	DIMRSUUV	DUUMVIRS	EEEEFFLR	FEEL FREE
DHMORTUW	THROW MUD	DIMSSTUY	TIDY SUMS	EEEEFRRS	REFEREES
DHNNOTUW	HUNT DOWN	DINNOPSW	PINS DOWN	EEEEGQSU	SQUEEGEE
DHNOOSTW	SHOT DOWN	DINOOSTY	NODOSITY	EEEEGSSX	EXEGESES
DHNOOSWW	SHOW DOWN	DINOPRTY	DRYPOINT	EEEEGSTX	EXEGETES
	SHOWDOWN	DINORSUX	ROUND SIX	EEEEHTTY	EYETEETH
DHNOPSUW	PUSH DOWN	DINOSSTW	SITS DOWN	EEEEKLNV	EVEN KEEL
		DINPRTUY	PUNDITRY	EEEELLPX	EXPELLEE

EEEELMST	LET ME SEE	EEEHILTT	THE ELITE	EEEKNTWX	NEXT WEEK
EEEENRRV	VENEERER	EEEHINTY	IN THE EYE	EEELLLRV	LEVELLER
EEEEOTYY	EYE TO EYE	EEEHIRSS	HERESIES	EEELLNQU	QUENELLE
EEEFFILN	FEEL FINE	EEEHIRST	ETHERISE	EEELLPRX	EXPELLER
EEEFFITV	FIVE FEET	EEEHIRTZ	ETHERIZE	EEELLRRV	REVELLER
EEEFFLRT	FELT FREE	EEEHLLNS	HELLENES	EEELMNST	ELEMENTS
EEEFFLTT	LEFT FEET	EEEHLLSS	HEELLESS	EEELMOPY	EMPLOYEE
EEEFFLTY	EFFETELY	EEEHLMPT	HELPMEET	EEELMOTT	OMELETTE
EEEFFNRT	EFFERENT	EEEHLNOW	ONE WHEEL	EEELMRST	ELM TREES
EEEFFORT	FOREFEET	EEEHLNTV	ELEVENTH	EEELMRTU	MULETEER
EEEFFRVW	FEVERFEW	EEEHLNTY	ETHYLENE	EEELNOPV	ENVELOPE
EEEFGRSU	REFUGEES	EEEHLOPP	PEEPHOLE	EEELNRSW	NEWSREEL
EEEFHLTT	THE FLEET	EEEHLORS	LEE SHORE	EEELNRSY	SERENELY
EEEFHMOR	HOME FREE	EEEHLORV	HEEL OVER	EEELNRTY	TERYLENE
EEEFIKLL	FEEL LIKE	EEEHLOSY	EYEHOLES	EEELPRSS	PEERLESS
EEEFIKNP	KEEP FINE	EEEHLRSW	WHEELERS		SLEEPERS
EEEFILNS	SEEN LIFE	EEEHMNRT	THREE MEN	EEELPSST	STEEPLES
EEEFILPR	LIFE PEER	EEEHMNSS	ENMESHES	EEELPTTY	TELETYPE
EEEFILSS	SEES LIFE	EEEHMNTV	VEHEMENT	EEELRSST	TREELESS
EEEFIMRT	FREE TIME	EEEHMNTY	THE ENEMY	EEELRSTV	LEVERETS
EEEFINNT	NINE FEET	EEEHNNQU	HENEQUEN	EEELRSVY	SEVERELY
EEEFINRR	FREE REIN	EEEHNQTU	THE QUEEN	EEELTTTX	TELETEXT
EEEFKLPT	KEEP LEFT	EEEHNRVW	WHENEVER	EEEMNNSV	SEVEN MEN
EEEFLLLW	FEEL WELL	EEEHORRV	OVER HERE	EEEMNNTT	TENEMENT
EEEFLMOS	FEME SOLE	EEEHRRVW	WHEREVER	EEEMNORT	ONE METRE
EEEFLORS	FEEL SORE	EEEHRSST	SHEEREST	EEEMNORV	EVEN MORE
EEEFLORV	FREE LOVE	EEEHSSTT	ESTHETES	EEEMNORZ	MEZEREON
EEEFLRSU	FEEL SURE	EEEHSTTW	THE SWEET	EEEMORRV	EVERMORE
EEEFLRSX	REFLEXES		WET SHEET	EEEMPRRT	TEMPERER
EEEFLRTV	VEER LEFT	EEEIKLRT	TREELIKE	EEEMRRTX	EXTREMER
EEEFLSTT	FLEETEST	EEEIKLSW	WEEKLIES	EEEMRSST	SEMESTER
EEEFLSTY	EYES LEFT	EEEIKMPT	KEEP TIME	EEEMRSTX	EXTREMES
EEEFNORS	FORESEEN	EEEIKNPS	PEKINESE	EEENNOPR	NEOPRENE
EEEFNRRT	REFERENT	EEEILLRV	REVEILLE	EEENNOPY	OPEN EYES
	RENT FREE	EEEILNPR	PELERINE	EEENORSV	ONE VERSE
EEEFNRTT	ENFETTER	EEEILNRT	TREE LINE		OVERSEEN
EEEFNRTY	ENTRY FEE	EEEILNRY	EYELINER		SEEN OVER
EEEFNRUZ	UNFREEZE	EEEILNST	SELENITE	EEENORVY	EVERY ONE
EEEFORRS	FORESEER	EEEILPRS	SLEEPIER		EVERYONE
EEEFORSS	FORESEES	EEEILRST	STEELIER	EEENPRRT	REPENTER
EEEFORST	SORE FEET	EEEILRSV	RELIEVES	EEENPSST	STEEPENS
EEEFORTV	FREE VOTE	EEEILSTV	TELEVISE	EEENPSSX	EXPENSES
EEEFPRUZ	FREEZE UP	EEEIMNRU	MEUNIERE	EEENRRSS	SNEERERS
	FREEZE-UP	EEEIMNTV	EVEN TIME	EEENRRTV	REVERENT
EEEFRRRT	FERRETER	EEEIMPRR	PREMIERE	EEENRSST	SERENEST
EEEFRRSZ	FREEZERS	EEEIMRRS	MISERERE	EEENRSSZ	SNEEZERS
EEEFRSST	SETS FREE	EEEIMRST	EREMITES	EEENRSUV	REVENUES
EEEFRSTW	FREE WEST	EEEINNNT	NINETEEN	EEENSSTW	SWEETENS
EEEGGILN	NEGLIGEE	EEEINNRT	INTERNEE		TWEENESS
EEEGGLPY	PEGGY LEE	EEEINPRT	PINE TREE	EEEORRSV	OVERSEER
EEEGHINT	EIGHTEEN	EEEINRSS	EERINESS	EEEORSSV	OVERSEES
EEEGHORS	HERE GOES	EEEINRST	TEENSIER		SEES OVER
EEEGHORW	HERE WE GO	EEEINRTZ	ETERNIZE	EEEORSSY	EYESORES
EEEGHRTT	GET THERE	EEEINSTT	TEENIEST		SORE EYES
EEEGINNR	ENGINEER	EEEINSTW	WEENIEST	EEEPRRSV	PERVERSE
EEEGINRS	ENERGIES	EEEIPRRV	REPRIEVE		PRESERVE
	ENERGISE	EEEIRRSV	REVERIES	EEEPRRTW	PEWTERER
EEEGINRT	GREEN TIE	EEEIRRTV	RETRIEVE	EEEPRSSW	SWEEPERS
EEEGINRZ	ENERGIZE	EEEIRRVW	REVIEWER	EEEPSSTT	STEEPEST
EEEGISSX	EXEGESIS	EEEISSTW	SWEETIES	EEEQRSTU	QUEEREST
EEEGISTV	EGESTIVE	EEEJLLRW	JEWELLER	EEEQRSUZ	SQUEEZER
EEEGMNOS	MONGEESE	EEEKLLPW	KEEP WELL	EEEQSSUZ	SQUEEZES
EEEGMNRT	EMERGENT	EEEKLLSS	KEELLESS	EEERRRSV	REVERSER
EEEGMORT	GEOMETER	EEEKLORV	KEEL OVER	EEERRSST	STEERERS
EEEGNPRS	EPERGNES	EEEKLSST	SLEEKEST	EEERRSSV	RESERVES
EEEGNRRV	REVENGER	EEEKMNSS	MEEKNESS		REVERSES
EEEGNRRY	GREENERY	EEEKNNSS	KEENNESS	EEERRSTT	STREETER
EEEGNRSV	REVENGES	EEEKNOPP	KEEP OPEN	EEERSSTV	SEVEREST
EEEGNSTV	GETS EVEN	EEEKNPST	KEEPNETS		
EEEGRSUX	EXERGUES	EEEKNRVY	VERY KEEN		
EEEHILSW	WHEELIES	EEEKNSTW	TEN WEEKS		

231

EEERSTTW	TWEETERS	EEFIIRTX	FIRE EXIT
EEERSTVX	VERTEXES	EEFIISVZ	SIZE FIVE
EEERSTWY	YEW TREES	EEFIKLLT	FELT LIKE
EEERSTWZ	TWEEZERS	EEFIKLMR	FREE MILK
EEERSVYY	VERY EYES	EEFIKLNR	FERNLIKE
EEESSTTW	SWEETEST	EEFIKNNP	PENKNIFE
EEFFFNOS	ENFEOFFS	EEFIKNPT	KEPT FINE
EEFFGIIS	EFFIGIES	EEFIKPST	KEEPS FIT
EEFFGIRT	FREE GIFT	EEFILLLS	FEELS ILL
EEFFHORS	SHEER OFF	EEFILLNY	FELINELY
EEFFILNT	FELT FINE	EEFILLRW	FREE WILL
EEFFINST	FIFTEENS	EEFILLSS	LIFELESS
EEFFISUV	EFFUSIVE	EEFILMNR	RIFLEMEN
EEFFKOPS	KEEPS OFF	EEFILNOS	FELONIES
EEFFKOSW	WEEKS OFF	EEFILPRR	PILFERER
EEFFLLOV	LEVEL OFF	EEFILRSS	FIRELESS
EEFFLMOR	FLEE FROM	EEFILSSW	WIFELESS
EEFFLNTU	EFFLUENT	EEFIMNSS	FINE MESS
EEFFLOPS	PEELS OFF	EEFIMSTU	TIME FUSE
	SLEEP OFF	EEFINNSS	FINENESS
EEFFLORS	REELS OFF	EEFINOPR	OPEN FIRE
EEFFLORW	FREE FLOW	EEFINOSV	FIVE ONES
EEFFLSUX	EFFLUXES	EEFINRRY	REFINERY
EEFFORRS	REOFFERS	EEFINRSZ	FRENZIES
EEFFORTU	FOUR FEET	EEFINSSS	FINESSES
EEFFRRSU	SUFFERER	EEFIPRSX	PREFIXES
EEFGGHRS	FRESH EGG	EEFIRRST	FERRITES
EEFGHRST	GET FRESH		FIR TREES
EEFGIILR	FILIGREE	EEFIRRSU	SUREFIRE
EEFGILNS	FEELINGS	EEFIRSST	SETS FIRE
EEFGILNT	FLEETING	EEFIRSTT	FIRST TEE
EEFGINNP	PFENNIGE	EEFIRSTY	ESTERIFY
EEFGINRV	FEVERING	EEFIRSUW	FUSE WIRE
EEFGIRST	FIG TREES	EEFISSTV	FIVE SETS
EEFGLMNU	FUGLEMEN	EEFKNORT	REEF KNOT
EEFGLNRY	GREENFLY	EEFKNORW	FOREKNEW
EEFGLNUV	VENGEFUL	EEFKOPRS	FOR KEEPS
EEFGLORS	FORELEGS	EEFLLLTW	FELT WELL
EEFGLOST	GOLF TEES	EEFLLNSS	FELLNESS
EEFGNOOR	FOREGONE	EEFLLORT	FORETELL
EEFGOORS	FOREGOES	EEFLLORV	FELL OVER
EEFGOORT	FREE TO GO	EEFLLOSV	SELF-LOVE
EEFHILMO	HOME LIFE	EEFLLPRY	FELL PREY
EEFHIRSV	FEVERISH	EEFLLRXY	REFLEXLY
EEFHISST	FETISHES	EEFLLSSS	SELFLESS
EEFHISTT	HEFTIEST	EEFLNNOT	NONE LEFT
EEFHLLPS	SELF HELP	EEFLNTUV	EVENTFUL
	SELF-HELP	EEFLOPTU	FEEL UP TO
EEFHLLWY	FLYWHEEL	EEFLORRW	FLOWERER
EEFHLMOT	LEFT HOME	EEFLORST	FELT SORE
EEFHLMOW	FLEW HOME	EEFLORTV	LEFT OVER
EEFHLOST	FEELS HOT		LEFTOVER
EEFHNRSS	FRESHENS	EEFLORVW	FLEW OVER
EEFHORRT	THEREFOR		OVERFLEW
EEFHRRSS	FRESHERS	EEFLORWW	WEREWOLF
EEFHRSST	FRESHEST	EEFLOSTU	FEELS OUT
	FRESHETS	EEFLRRSU	FERRULES
EEFIIKLL	LIFELIKE	EEFLRSTU	FELT SURE
EEFIIKLW	WIFELIKE	EEFLRSUX	FLEXURES
EEFIILLN	LIFELINE		REFLUXES
EEFIILMT	LIFETIME	EEFLSTWW	FLEW WEST
EEFIILNR	IN RELIEF	EEFMNORT	FOMENTER
EEFIILSZ	LIFE-SIZE	EEFMNRST	FERMENTS
EEFIIMNN	FEMININE	EEFMORRR	REFORMER
EEFIIMNS	FEMINISE	EEFMOSTT	MOFETTES
EEFIIMNT	FINE TIME	EEFMPRRU	PERFUMER
EEFIIMNZ	FEMINIZE	EEFMPRSU	PERFUMES
EEFIINRS	FINERIES	EEFNORST	SOFTENER
EEFIINVW	FINE VIEW	EEFNORTU	FOURTEEN
EEFIIRRV	VERIFIER	EEFNORTW	FOREWENT
EEFIIRSV	VERIFIES	EEFNQRTU	FREQUENT

EEFNRRSU	RUNS FREE
EEFNRTTU	UNFETTER
EEFOORRT	ROOFTREE
EEFOPRRT	FREE PORT
EEFOPRST	POST FREE
	POST-FREE
EEFORRST	FORESTER
	FOSTERER
	REFERS TO
EEFOSSTU	FOETUSES
EEFOSTTU	FOUETTES
EEFPRSSU	PERFUSES
EEGGGOOS	GOOSE EGG
EEGGHITW	EGG WHITE
	WHITE EGG
EEGGHLLS	EGGSHELL
EEGGHNSS	HENS EGGS
EEGGIMNR	EMERGING
EEGGIMRT	EGG TIMER
EEGGINNR	GREENING
	RENEGING
EEGGINRT	GREETING
EEGGINST	EGESTING
EEGGINSU	SIEGE GUN
EEGGNORS	ENGORGES
EEGGNORY	GONE GREY
EEGGNSST	NEST EGGS
EEGGORST	ST.GEORGE
EEGGORSY	GOES GREY
EEGGORTT	GO-GETTER
EEGGPRRS	PREGGERS
EEGHHIKN	KNEE HIGH
	KNEE-HIGH
EEGHHINT	HEIGHTEN
EEGHIIST	EIGHTIES
EEGHILLV	GIVE HELL
EEGHILNW	WHEELING
EEGHIMNT	EIGHT MEN
EEGHINRS	GREENISH
	SHEERING
	SIGN HERE
EEGHINST	SEETHING
	SHEETING
EEGHINTT	TEETHING
EEGHINWZ	WHEEZING
EEGHIRST	SEE RIGHT
EEGHIRSW	WEIGHERS
EEGHIRTY	RIGHT EYE
EEGHISTY	EYESIGHT
EEGHISUZ	HUGE SIZE
EEGHKOTT	GET THE O.K.
EEGHLNNT	LENGTHEN
EEGHLPST	GETS HELP
EEGHMNOO	GONE HOME
EEGHMNOY	HEGEMONY
EEGHMOOS	GOES HOME
EEGHMOST	GETS HOME
EEGHNOPS	PHOSGENE
EEGHNOPY	HYPOGENE
EEGHNSSU	HUGENESS
EEGHORTT	GOT THERE
	TOGETHER
EEGHOSTT	GHETTOES
EEGIILNR	LINGERIE
EEGIILNV	INVEIGLE
EEGIINNS	SEEING IN
EEGIINTV	GENITIVE
EEGIIRSV	GIVE RISE
EEGIKLNS	SLEEKING
EEGIKNNR	GREEN INK
EEGIKNPS	KEEPINGS

EEGILNPS	PEELINGS	EEGNOORV	GONE OVER	EEHIORST	THEORIES
	SLEEPING	EEGNOPTY	GENOTYPE		THEORISE
EEGILNRR	LINGERER	EEGNORSU	GENEROUS	EEHIORTZ	THEORIZE
EEGILNRV	LEVERING	EEGNOSTW	GONE WEST	EEHIPPTY	EPIPHYTE
EEGILNST	SLEETING	EEGNOTYZ	ZYGOTENE	EEHIPRRS	PERISHER
	STEELING	EEGNPRTY	PEER GYNT	EEHIPRSS	PERISHES
EEGILNSV	SLEEVING	EEGNPRUX	EXPUNGER	EEHIPSST	STEEPISH
EEGILOPU	EPILOGUE	EEGNPSTT	TENT PEGS	EEHIPSTT	EPITHETS
EEGILOSU	EULOGIES	EEGNPSUX	EXPUNGES	EEHIQRSU	QUEERISH
	EULOGISE	EEGNRSSY	GREYNESS	EEHIRRSS	SHERRIES
EEGILOUZ	EULOGIZE	EEGNRSUY	GUERNSEY	EEHIRRSW	WHERRIES
EEGILRTV	VERLIGTE	EEGNRTWY	WENT GREY	EEHIRTVY	THIEVERY
EEGIMNNS	MENINGES	EEGOORSV	GOES OVER	EEHISSST	ESTHESIS
EEGIMNRS	REGIMENS	EEGOORVW	OVER WE GO	EEHISSTW	SWEETISH
EEGIMNRT	METERING	EEGOPRST	PROTEGES	EEHJKORT	THE JOKER
	REGIMENT	EEGOPRSU	SUPEREGO	EEHJLNOP	JOHN PEEL
EEGIMNRU	MERINGUE	EEGORRVW	OVERGREW	EEHKLOOR	LOOK HERE
EEGIMNST	MEETINGS	EEGORSTV	GETS OVER	EEHKLOSY	KEYHOLES
EEGINNPR	PREENING	EEGORSTW	GET WORSE	EEHKLOWY	HOLY WEEK
EEGINNQU	QUEENING	EEGOSSTW	GOES WEST	EEHKMOST	THE SMOKE
EEGINNRS	SNEERING	EEGPSTTU	GET UPSET	EEHKOPPS	KEEP SHOP
EEGINNRT	ENTERING	EEGRSSTU	GESTURES	EEHLLOSW	LOW HEELS
EEGINNRW	RENEWING	EEHHIKST	THE SHEIK	EEHLLPSS	HELPLESS
EEGINNRY	ENGINERY	EEHHINRT	THE RHINE	EEHLMMNS	HELMSMEN
EEGINNSU	INGENUES	EEHHIPSS	SHEEPISH	EEHLMNSW	WELSHMEN
	UNSEEING	EEHHIRST	ETHERISH	EEHLMORU	HOME RULE
EEGINNSV	EVENINGS	EEHHIRTW	HEREWITH	EEHLMOSS	HOMELESS
EEGINNSZ	SNEEZING	EEHHLLLO	HELL HOLE	EEHLNOSW	ON WHEELS
EEGINNTV	EVENTING	EEHHLMOP	HOME HELP	EEHLNPST	SENT HELP
EEGINOPS	EPIGONES	EEHHLSTW	THE WELSH	EEHLNSST	ST.HELENS
EEGINOST	EGESTION	EEHHNOSU	HEN HOUSE	EEHLOOPS	LOSE HOPE
	SEEING TO	EEHHNTTT	THE TENTH	EEHLOPSS	HOPELESS
EEGINPRT	PETERING	EEHHORST	THE SHORE	EEHLORST	THE LOSER
EEGINPST	STEEPING	EEHHORSW	HERES HOW	EEHLOTUW	WHEEL OUT
EEGINPSW	SWEEPING	EEHHORTT	THE OTHER	EEHLPRSU	SPHERULE
EEGINQRU	QUEERING	EEHHRRST	THRESHER	EEHLRSST	SHELTERS
EEGINQUU	QUEUEING	EEHHRSST	THRESHES	EEHLRSSW	WELSHERS
EEGINRRS	RESIGNER	EEHIILTW	WHITE LIE	EEHLRSTU	THE RULES
EEGINRRV	REVERING	EEHIITTW	WHITE TIE	EEHMMOPR	MORPHEME
EEGINRST	INTEGERS		WHITE-TIE	EEHMMORT	OHMMETER
	STEERING	EEHIKLLL	LIKE HELL	EEHMMOST	THE SOMME
EEGINRSU	SEIGNEUR	EEHIKLMO	HOMELIKE	EEHMNORS	HORSEMEN
EEGINRSV	SEVERING	EEHIKSTW	THIS WEEK	EEHMNOST	SENT HOME
EEGINRTV	EVERTING	EEHIKTWW	WHIT WEEK	EEHMNOSU	HOUSEMEN
EEGINRTX	EXERTING	EEHILMNS	HEMLINES	EEHMNOSW	HOME NEWS
EEGINSSU	GENIUSES	EEHILMOR	HOMELIER	EEHMNOTW	WENT HOME
EEGINSTW	SWEETING	EEHILNOP	ENOPHILE	EEHMOOPS	SOME HOPE
EEGINTTV	VIGNETTE	EEHILNOR	IRON HEEL	EEHMORST	REST HOME
EEGINTTW	TWEETING	EEHILNPW	PINWHEEL		THEOREMS
EEGINTVV	GIVE VENT	EEHILORS	SOLE HEIR	EEHMORVW	WHOMEVER
EEGIORVV	GIVE OVER	EEHILORT	HOTELIER	EEHMSSTU	THE MUSES
EEGIPRST	PRESTIGE	EEHILRSS	HEIRLESS	EEHNNORT	ENTHRONE
EEGIRRST	REGISTER		RELISHES	EEHNNOTT	ONE TENTH
EEGIRSTT	GRISETTE	EEHILRST	ST.HELIER	EEHNOORS	ONE-HORSE
EEGISSTV	VESTIGES	EEHILSST	SHELTIES	EEHNOPRU	HEREUPON
EEGKNRRU	GREEK URN	EEHILWYZ	WHEEZILY	EEHNOPRY	PHONEYER
EEGLLNOW	GONE WELL	EEHIMNTW	WHITE MEN	EEHNOPTY	NEOPHYTE
EEGLLOSW	GOES WELL	EEHIMOST	HOME TIES	EEHNORSS	SENHORES
EEGLLSTW	GETS WELL	EEHIMRST	ERETHISM	EEHNORTT	NOT THERE
EEGLMMSU	GEMMULES	EEHIMRSW	WIRE MESH	EEHNORTU	HEREUNTO
EEGLNNOO	ON ONE LEG	EEHIMRTT	THERMITE	EEHNORTW	THERE NOW
EEGLNOSZ	LOZENGES	EEHIMSTT	THE TIMES	EEHNOSSW	NEW SHOES
EEGLNSTT	GENTLEST	EEHINNRS	ENSHRINE	EEHNOSTT	ON THE SET
EEGLORSV	LEGS OVER	EEHINNRT	INHERENT	EEHNOSUW	NEW HOUSE
EEGMNOST	GEMSTONE	EEHINNTT	IN THE NET	EEHNSSTU	ENTHUSES
EEGMNSST	SEGMENTS	EEHINPRT	NEPHRITE	EEHNSSTV	SEVENTHS
EEGMNTTU	TEGUMENT		TREPHINE	EEHOORSV	OVERSHOE
EEGMORSU	GRUESOME	EEHINRTT	THIRTEEN	EEHOOTTY	EYETOOTH
EEGMORTY	GEOMETRY	EEHINRTW	WHITENER	EEHOPPSW	PEEP SHOW
EEGNNORT	ROENTGEN	EEHIOPPS	HOSEPIPE	EEHOPRST	STOP HERE
EEGNNOSV	EVENSONG	EEHIORRT	EITHER-OR		THE ROPES

EEHOPRTU	UP TO HERE	EEILMNOP	LEMON PIE	EEIMRRTT	REMITTER
EEHORRTX	EXHORTER	EEILMNOV	EVIL OMEN		TRIMETER
EEHORSSU	REHOUSES	EEILMNST	TEN MILES	EEIMRSTT	EMITTERS
EEHORSUW	WEE HOURS	EEILMNSU	SELENIUM		TERMITES
EEHORTTW	THE TOWER	EEILMOPS	POLEMISE	EEIMRSTU	EMERITUS
EEHOSSTT	TEE SHOTS	EEILMOPZ	POLEMIZE	EEIMRTTY	TEMERITY
EEHPRSST	THE PRESS	EEILMOST	LOSE TIME	EEIMSSST	MESSIEST
EEHPRSSU	HESPERUS	EEILMSST	SET SMILE	EEINNNOT	ONE IN TEN
EEHRSTTW	WHETTERS		TIMELESS	EEINNPTT	PENITENT
EEIIKLLR	LIKELIER	EEILMSUV	EMULSIVE	EEINNRST	INTERNES
EEIIKLRW	WIRELIKE	EEILNNST	SENTINEL	EEINNRTV	REINVENT
EEIIKLSW	LIKEWISE	EEILNNSV	ENLIVENS	EEINNSTT	SENTIENT
EEIIKNPT	KEEP IT IN	EEILNOPR	LEPORINE	EEINNSTW	ENTWINES
EEIILLRV	LIVELIER	EEILNORT	ONE LITRE	EEINOPRS	IN REPOSE
EEIILLTT	LET IT LIE	EEILNPPZ	ZEPPELIN		ISOPRENE
EEIILNNT	LENINITE	EEILNPRU	PERILUNE		PIONEERS
EEIILNPP	PIPELINE	EEILNPRV	REPLEVIN	EEINOPRU	IN EUROPE
EEIILNTV	LENITIVE	EEILNPSS	SLEEPS IN	EEINORSV	EVERSION
EEIILNTX	EXIT LINE	EEILNQUY	EQUINELY	EEINORTX	EXERTION
EEIILRSV	LIVERIES	EEILNRST	LISTENER	EEINOSTT	NOISETTE
EEIILRVW	LIVE WIRE	EEILNRTY	ENTIRELY		SEEN TO IT
EEIILSTW	LEWISITE	EEILNSST	SETLINES	EEINPRSS	RIPENESS
EEIIMNST	ENMITIES	EEILNSSV	EVILNESS	EEINPRTX	INEXPERT
EEIIMOST	MOIETIES		VILENESS	EEINQRSU	ENQUIRES
EEIIMPRS	RIEMPIES	EEILNSTT	ENTITLES	EEINQSTU	QUEENS IT
EEIIMRSS	MISERIES		SETTLE IN		QUIETENS
EEIIMSST	ITEMISES	EEILNSTV	VEINLETS	EEINRRST	INSERTER
EEIIMSSV	EMISSIVE	EEILOPST	PETIOLES		RENTIERS
EEIIMSTZ	ITEMIZES	EEILORRT	LOITERER	EEINRRSU	REINSURE
EEIINNST	NINETIES	EEILORSV	OVERLIES	EEINRRTV	INVERTER
EEIINNSZ	SIZE NINE	EEILOTTT	TOILETTE	EEINRSST	SENTRIES
EEIINRRV	RIVERINE	EEILPPSY	EPILEPSY	EEINRSSU	ENURESIS
EEIINRSS	IN SERIES	EEILPRSS	SPIELERS	EEINRSSV	INVERSES
EEIINSTT	ENTITIES	EEILPRST	REPTILES	EEINRSTT	ENTERS IT
EEIINSTV	INVITEES	EEILPSSS	PELISSES		INTEREST
EEIIPRSX	EXPIRIES	EEILPSST	EPISTLES	EEINRSTU	ESURIENT
EEIIQSTU	EQUITIES	EEILPSSV	PELVISES		RETINUES
EEIJKRST	JERKIEST	EEILRRSV	SILVERER		REUNITES
EEIJLNNU	JULIENNE	EEILRSST	TIRELESS	EEINRSTV	REINVEST
EEIJLNUV	JUVENILE	EEILRSSU	LEISURES	EEINRSTX	INTERSEX
EEIKLNSS	LIKENESS	EEILRSSW	WIRELESS	EEINRSTY	SERENITY
EEIKLORS	ROSELIKE	EEILSSVW	VIEWLESS	EEINRSUV	UNIVERSE
EEIKLORT	LORIKEET	EEILSTTX	TEXTILES	EEINRTTY	ENTIRETY
EEIKLPST	PIKELETS	EEIMMORS	MEMORIES		ETERNITY
	SPIKELET		MEMORISE	EEINSSSW	WISENESS
	STEPLIKE	EEIMMORT	MORE TIME	EEINSSSX	SEXINESS
EEIKLSTV	VESTLIKE	EEIMMOST	SOMETIME	EEINSSTX	SIXTEENS
EEIKMPTT	KEPT TIME	EEIMMRSS	IMMERSES	EEINSSUW	NEW ISSUE
EEIKNORS	KEROSINE	EEIMMRST	MERISTEM	EEINSTTW	TWENTIES
EEIKNRRT	TINKERER	EEIMMRTT	TERM TIME	EEINSTTX	EXISTENT
EEIKPPTU	KEEP IT UP	EEIMNNOS	NOMINEES	EEIOPRRT	PORTIERE
EEIKPRST	PERKIEST	EEIMNORV	VOMERINE	EEIOPRRV	OVERRIPE
EEIKPSST	PESKIEST	EEIMNOST	SEMITONE	EEIOPRST	POETISER
EEIKRRSS	SKERRIES	EEIMNOTZ	TIME ZONE	EEIOPRTZ	POETIZER
EEIKSSUY	KEY ISSUE	EEIMNPRU	PERINEUM	EEIOPSST	POETISES
EEIKSSWX	SIX WEEKS	EEIMNRTU	MUTINEER	EEIOPSTZ	POETIZES
EEILLLST	TELL LIES	EEIMNSTT	TEN TIMES	EEIORRRS	ORRERIES
EEILLLVW	LIVE WELL	EEIMNSTW	NEWS ITEM	EEIORRTX	EXTERIOR
EEILLMPR	IMPELLER	EEIMNTTX	NEXT TIME	EEIORSVZ	OVERSIZE
EEILLMRS	SMELLIER	EEIMOPRS	PROMISEE	EEIORVVW	OVERVIEW
EEILLMTT	LITTLE ME	EEIMORST	TIRESOME	EEIOSSTT	SEES TO IT
EEILLNOR	LONELIER	EEIMORTV	OVERTIME	EEIOSTTU	SEE IT OUT
EEILLORV	LOVELIER	EEIMOSVW	WISE MOVE	EEIPPRRS	PERSPIRE
EEILLOSV	LOVELIES	EEIMPRRS	PREMIERS	EEIPPSTT	PIPETTES
EEILLPSS	ELLIPSES		SIMPERER	EEIPRRSS	REPRISES
EEILLPSY	SLEEPILY	EEIMPRSS	PREMISES		RESPIRES
EEILLSTV	EVILLEST	EEIMPSTT	EMPTIEST	EEIPRRST	ST.PIERRE
EEILLTVY	VELLEITY	EEIMQRSU	REQUIEMS	EEIPRRTT	PRETTIER
EEILLVWY	WEEVILLY	EEIMQSTU	MESQUITE	EEIPRSST	RESPITES
EEILMNNS	LINESMEN	EEIMRRST	MERRIEST	EEIPRSTT	PRETTIES
	NINE ELMS			EEIPRSTX	PREEXIST

EEIPRSVW	PREVIEWS	EELMNSUY	UNSEEMLY	EEMNORST	STOREMEN
EEIPRTUV	ERUPTIVE	EELMOOPV	LOVE POEM	EEMNORSY	MONEYERS
EEIPSSTW	STEPWISE	EELMOPRY	EMPLOYER	EEMNORTU	ROUTEMEN
EEIPSSUZ	SEIZES UP	EELMORST	MOLESTER	EEMNOTVX	NEXT MOVE
EEIPSTTT	PETTIEST	EELMORSW	EELWORMS	EEMNPRSS	PRESSMEN
EEIPSTYZ	TYPE SIZE	EELMORTY	REMOTELY	EEMNPRSU	SUPERMEN
EEIQRRSU	REQUIRES	EELMPRTU	PLUM TREE	EEMNPSYY	ENEMY SPY
EEIQRSSU	ESQUIRES	EELMRSST	SMELTERS	EEMNSSTU	MUTENESS
EEIQRSTU	REQUITES		TERMLESS		TENESMUS
EEIQSTTU	QUIETEST	EELMRSTY	SMELTERY	EEMNSTTV	VESTMENT
EEIRRRST	TERRIERS	EELMSSST	STEMLESS	EEMOORRV	MOREOVER
EEIRRRTW	REWRITER	EELNNOSS	LONENESS	EEMOORVV	MOVE OVER
EEIRRSST	RESISTER	EELNNOVW	NEW NOVEL	EEMOPRRS	EMPERORS
EEIRRSTW	REWRITES	EELNNUVY	UNEVENLY		PREMORSE
EEIRRVWY	RIVER WYE	EELNOPSS	SLEEPS ON	EEMOPRSW	EMPOWERS
EEIRSSSU	REISSUES	EELNOPSV	ENVELOPS	EEMOQRSU	MORESQUE
EEIRSSTV	VESTRIES	EELNOQTU	ELOQUENT	EEMOQTTU	MOQUETTE
EEIRSSUZ	SEIZURES	EELNORST	ENTRESOL	EEMORSTT	REMOTEST
EEIRSTVY	SEVERITY	EELNOSSS	SOLENESS	EEMOTTTU	TEE-TOTUM
EEISSTTT	TESTIEST	EELNOSST	TONELESS	EEMPPRST	PREEMPTS
EEJJLNUY	JEJUNELY	EELNOSSV	SLOVENES	EEMPRRSU	PRESUMER
EEJKNRTU	JUNKETER	EELNOSTT	SETTLE ON	EEMPRSSU	PRESUMES
EEJNNTUX	NEXT JUNE	EELNOTVV	ON VELVET	EEMPRSTU	PERMUTES
EEJPRRRU	PERJURER	EELNSSSW	NEWSLESS	EEMPSSSU	MESSES UP
EEJPRRSU	PERJURES	EELNSSTT	TENTLESS	EEMPSSTT	TEMPESTS
EEKKORSW	SEEK WORK	EELNSSTU	TUNELESS	EEMPSSTU	SETS 'EM UP
EEKLLNWW	KNEW WELL	EELNOOTV	VENTLESS	EEMRRTTU	MUTTERER
EEKLLPTW	KEPT WELL	EELNSTTU	LUNETTES	EENNNOPY	ONE PENNY
EEKLLSUU	UKULELES		UNSETTLE	EENNNOSS	NONSENSE
EEKLNOST	SKELETON	EELNSTWY	NEW STYLE	EENNNOTV	NONEVENT
EEKLNOSV	VELSKOEN	EELOOSST	SET LOOSE	EENNNPWY	NEW PENNY
EEKLRSST	KESTRELS	EELOPPSS	PEPLOSES	EENNOOOT	ONE-TO-ONE
EEKMMPSU	KEEPS MUM	EELOPPST	ESTOPPEL	EENNOOPT	OPEN NOTE
EEKMOSVY	KEY MOVES	EELOPRRX	EXPLORER	EENNOORW	ONE OWNER
EEKNOPPT	KEPT OPEN	EELOPRSX	EXPLORES	EENNOOTT	TEN TO ONE
EEKNOSTY	KEY NOTES	EELOPRTT	TELEPORT	EENNOPSS	OPENNESS
	KEYNOTES	EELOPSTU	SLEEP OUT	EENNORWW	NEW OWNER
	KEYSTONE	EELORRSV	RESOLVER	EENNOTTT	TEN TO TEN
EEKNSSSW	SKEWNESS	EELORRTV	REVOLTER	EENNRSUV	UNNERVES
EEKNSSTU	NETSUKES	EELORRUV	OVERRULE	EENOOPRT	TORE OPEN
EEKOPSTU	KEEPS OUT	EELORRVV	REVOLVER	EENOOPTV	OPEN VOTE
EEKOSSTU	SEEKS OUT	EELORSSV	RESOLVES	EENOORST	OESTRONE
EEKOSTWW	TWO WEEKS	EELORSTU	RESOLUTE	EENOORTV	OVERTONE
EELLLLMP	PELL-MELL	EELORSVV	REVOLVES	EENOPRSS	RESPONSE
EELLLLSW	SELL WELL	EELORTTU	ROULETTE	EENOPRTT	ENTREPOT
EELLLLWW	WELL WELL	EELORTUV	REVOLUTE	EENOPRXY	PYROXENE
EELLLOVW	LOW-LEVEL		TRUE LOVE	EENORRTT	ROTTENER
EELLMORW	MELLOWER		TRUELOVE	EENORSSS	SORENESS
EELLMRSS	SMELLERS	EELOSSTV	VOTELESS	EENORSSU	NEUROSES
EELLNOTW	NOTE WELL	EELOSTUV	EVOLUTES	EENORSTX	EXTENSOR
EELLNOUV	NOUVELLE	EELPRSSU	REPULSES	EENORSVW	OVERSEWN
EELLNSSS	LENSLESS	EELPRSTZ	PRETZELS	EENORTVW	WENT OVER
EELLNSSW	WELLNESS	EELPRTXY	EXPERTLY	EENOSSST	STENOSES
EELLNTWW	WENT WELL	EELPSSUX	PLEXUSES	EENPPRTU	UPPER TEN
EELLOOST	LET LOOSE	EELPSTTU	SETTLE UP	EENPRSST	PERTNESS
EELLOPTV	TOP LEVEL	EELPSTUX	SEXTUPLE		PRESENTS
	TOP-LEVEL	EELRRSTW	WRESTLER		SERPENTS
EELLORSV	OVERSELL	EELRSSST	RESTLESS	EENPRSSU	PURENESS
EELLORTX	EXTOLLER	EELRSSTT	SETTLERS	EENPRSTV	PREVENTS
EELLORVW	WELL OVER		TRESTLES	EENPSSSU	SUSPENSE
EELLORVY	VOLLEYER	EELRSSTW	SWELTERS	EENPSTTX	NEXT STEP
EELLORWY	YELLOWER		WRESTLES	EENRRRTU	RETURNER
EELLOSSV	LOVELESS	EELRSTWY	WESTERLY	EENRRSUV	NERVURES
EELLOTUV	LEVEL OUT	EEMMNOST	MEMENTOS	EENRSSSU	SURENESS
EELLPRSS	RESPELLS	EEMMNOTV	MOVEMENT	EENRSSTT	STERNEST
	SPELLERS	EEMMNRRY	MERRY MEN	EENRSSTW	WESTERNS
EELLPSTW	WET SPELL	EEMMOORS	SOME MORE	EENRSTUV	VENTURES
EELLRVWY	VERY WELL	EEMMNNORS	NORSEMEN	EENRSTUW	WET NURSE
EELMMPUX	EXEMPLUM	EEMMNOSV	ENVENOMS		WET-NURSE
EELMNOOS	LONESOME	EEMNOOPT	TONE POEM	EENSTTWW	WENT WEST
EELMNORS	SOLEMNER	EEMNOOWY	OWE MONEY	EEOOOTTT	TOE TO TOE

EEOOPRRV	PORE OVER
EEOOPSTT	TOO STEEP
EEOPRRRT	REPORTER
EEOPRRRV	REPROVER
EEOPRRSV	REPROVES
EEOPRRTX	EXPORTER
EEOPRSSS	ESPRESSO
EEOPRSSU	ESPOUSER
	REPOUSSE
EEOPRSTT	TREE TOPS
	TREETOPS
EEOPRSTV	OVERSTEP
	STEP OVER
EEOPRSUX	EXPOSURE
EEOPRTTU	PETER OUT
EEOPSSSU	ESPOUSES
EEOPSSTU	SEEPS OUT
EEOPSSTY	EYESPOTS
EEOPSTUW	SWEEP OUT
EEORRRST	RESTORER
	RETRORSE
EEORRSST	RESTORES
EEORRTTX	EXTORTER
EEORRTUV	OVERTURE
	TROUVERE
EEORSSTT	ROSETTES
	SET STORE
EEORSSTV	OVERSETS
EEORSSVW	OVERSEWS
EEORSTUV	SERVE OUT
EEORSTVX	VORTEXES
EEPPSSUW	SWEEPS UP
EEPQSUUU	QUEUES UP
EEPRRSSU	PRESSURE
EEPRRSTV	PERVERTS
EEPRSSTT	ST.PETERS
EEPRSSUV	SERVES UP
EEPRSTTU	UPSETTER
EEPRSTTX	PRETEXTS
EEPSSTTY	TYPESETS
EEQRSSTU	REQUESTS
EERRSTTU	UTTERERS
EERRTUVY	VERY TRUE
EERSSSST	STRESSES
EERSSTTU	TRUSTEES
EERSSTUU	UTERUSES
EERSSTUV	VESTURES
EERSTTTU	UTTEREST
EERSTTUX	TEXTURES
EFFFILOS	FLIES OFF
EFFFILRU	FLUFFIER
EFFFIORS	FIRES OFF
EFFGHOOT	OFF THE GO
EFFGILST	STIFF LEG
EFFGINOR	OFFERING
EFFGINSU	EFFUSING
EFFGRSTU	GRUFFEST
EFFHHITT	THE FIFTH
EFFHIILS	FILEFISH
EFFHIISW	FISHWIFE
EFFHIITT	FIFTIETH
EFFHILRW	WHIFFLER
EFFHILSW	WHIFFLES
EFFHINOT	ONE FIFTH
EFFHIOSV	HIVES OFF
EFFHIOTW	OFF-WHITE
EFFHIRSS	SHERIFFS
EFFHISTT	FIFTH SET
EFFHLRSU	SHUFFLER
EFFHLSSU	SHUFFLES
EFFHOORS	OFFSHORE

EFFHOOSV	SHOVE OFF
EFFHORTW	THREW OFF
EFFILLLU	FULL LIFE
EFFILNRS	SNIFFLER
EFFILNSS	SNIFFLES
EFFILRSU	SIFFLEUR
EFFIMNOR	FINE FORM
EFFINOSU	EFFUSION
EFFINRSS	SNIFFERS
EFFIOPSW	WIPES OFF
EFFIORST	FORFEITS
EFFIORTW	WRITE OFF
	WRITE-OFF
EFFIRSTU	STUFFIER
EFFISSTT	STIFFEST
EFFISSUX	SUFFIXES
EFFLLLOU	FELL FOUL
EFFLLOSS	SELLS OFF
EFFLLOST	TELLS OFF
EFFLMPUU	MUFFLE UP
EFFLMRSU	MUFFLERS
EFFLNRSU	SNUFFLER
EFFLNSSU	SNUFFLES
EFFLOOPS	SLOPE OFF
EFFLOOTT	LEFT FOOT
EFFLOPST	SLEPT OFF
EFFLOSSU	SOUFFLES
EFFLRSTU	TRUFFLES
EFFMOOSV	MOVES OFF
EFFNOORT	NO EFFORT
EFFNRSSU	SNUFFERS
EFFOOORT	FOREFOOT
EFFOOPRS	ROPES OFF
EFFOORSW	WORSE OFF
	WORSE-OFF
EFFOORTW	WROTE OFF
EFFOPRRS	PROFFERS
EFFOPRSU	OFFERS UP
EFFRSSTU	STUFFERS
EFFSSSUU	SUFFUSES
EFGGIINN	FEIGNING
EFGGILPS	EGG FLIPS
EFGGIOST	FOGGIEST
EFGHHIIL	HIGH LIFE
EFGHHILW	FLEW HIGH
EFGHILNS	FLESHING
EFGHINRT	FRIGHTEN
EFGHINRU	HUNG FIRE
EFGHIOSY	FOGEYISH
EFGHIRST	FIGHTERS
	FREIGHTS
EFGHORST	GOT FRESH
EFGIINNR	INFRINGE
	REFINING
EFGIINRU	FIGURINE
EFGIINRY	REIFYING
EFGIITUV	FUGITIVE
EFGILLNO	LIFELONG
	LONG LIFE
	LONG-LIFE
EFGILLNU	FUELLING
EFGILLUU	GUILEFUL
EFGILMNS	FLEMINGS
EFGILNNS	FLENSING
EFGILNST	FELTINGS
EFGILNTT	FETTLING
EFGILNTW	LEFT WING
	LEFT-WING
EFGILORS	LOG FIRES
EFGILPRU	FIRE-PLUG
EFGIMNST	FIGMENTS

EFGIMOSY	FOGEYISM
EFGINNPS	PFENNIGS
EFGINORV	FORGIVEN
EFGINRRY	FERRYING
EFGINRSU	REFUSING
EFGINRTT	FRETTING
EFGINRTU	REFUTING
EFGIOOST	GOOFIEST
EFGIOPTT	PETTIFOG
EFGIORRV	FORGIVER
EFGIORSV	FORGIVES
EFGIORTT	FORGET IT
EFGLOOVX	FOXGLOVE
EFGLORSU	FOUR LEGS
EFGNSSUU	FUNGUSES
EFGOOPRR	GROPE FOR
EFHIIKLS	FISHLIKE
EFHIILRT	FILTHIER
EFHIIMSU	HUMIFIES
EFHIINRS	FINISHER
EFHIINSS	FINISHES
EFHIIPPS	PIPEFISH
EFHIIRST	SHIFTIER
EFHIISST	FISHIEST
EFHILLSY	ELFISHLY
EFHILOSX	FIX HOLES
EFHILSSS	FISHLESS
EFHILTWY	WHITEFLY
EFHIMOPR	FIRM HOPE
EFHINSST	FISHNETS
EFHIORRT	FROTHIER
EFHIORSV	OVERFISH
EFHIORTT	FORTIETH
EFHIPRSU	FURPHIES
EFHIRSTT	THE FIRST
EFHKLOOR	FOLK HERO
EFHKLOOT	LEFT HOOK
EFHLOOSX	FOXHOLES
EFHLOPST	FLESH POT
	FLESHPOT
EFHLOPSU	HOPEFULS
EFHLORSY	HORSEFLY
EFHLORVY	HOVERFLY
EFHLOSUU	HOUSEFUL
EFHLOSUY	HOUSE FLY
	HOUSEFLY
EFHLSTTW	TWELFTHS
EFHNORTT	THE FRONT
EFHOORST	THOSE FOR
EFHOORSW	FORESHOW
EFHOOSST	SOFT-SHOE
EFHOPRST	FRESH POT
EFHORSTT	SET FORTH
EFHRRSTU	FURTHERS
EFHRSTTU	FURTHEST
EFIIILRV	VILIFIER
EFIIILSV	VILIFIES
EFIIINNT	INFINITE
EFIIIRVV	VIVIFIER
EFIIISTX	FIXITIES
EFIIISVV	VIVIFIES
EFIIKRRS	FIRE RISK
	FRISKIER
EFIILMNR	FIRM LINE
EFIILMRS	FLIMSIER
EFIILMSS	FLIMSIES
EFIILNRT	FILTER IN
EFIILNTY	FELINITY
	FINITELY
EFIILOQU	FILIOQUE
EFIILRSU	FUSILIER

236

Code	Word	Code	Word	Code	Word
EFIIMMNS	FEMINISM	EFINNORS	INFERNOS	EFLOPTTU	FELT UP TO
EFIIMNST	FEMINIST	EFINNPSU	FINESPUN	EFLORSTU	FUR STOLE
EFIIMRSS	MISFIRES	EFINNSTU	FUNNIEST	EFLORSUY	YOURSELF
EFIIMSTX	FIX TIMES	EFINOOSX	SIX OF ONE	EFLORSVY	FLYOVERS
EFIINNNS	SINN FEIN	EFINOPRS	PINES FOR	EFLOSSSW	SELF-SOWS
EFIINNOS	SINFONIE	EFINOPRU	FIRE UPON	EFLRSSTU	FLUSTERS
EFIINORR	INFERIOR	EFINOPTX	PONTIFEX	EFLRSTTU	FLUTTERS
EFIINORT	NOTIFIER	EFINORRT	FRONTIER	EFLRSTUU	FRUSTULE
EFIINOST	NOTIFIES	EFINOSSX	FOXINESS	EFLRTTUY	FLUTTERY
EFIINPSX	SPINIFEX	EFINRSST	SNIFTERS	EFMNNNUY	FUNNY MEN
EFIINRRT	FERRITIN	EFINRTUU	IN FUTURE	EFMNNORT	FRONT MEN
EFIINRSU	UNIFIERS	EFIORRST	FROSTIER	EFMNRTUY	FRUMENTY
EFIINSTT	NIFTIEST		ROTIFERS	EFMOORST	FOREMOST
EFIIOSSS	OSSIFIES	EFIORRSW	FROWSIER	EFMOORSU	FOURSOME
EFIIPRRU	PURIFIER	EFIORRTT	RETROFIT	EFMOPRRS	PERFORMS
EFIIPRST	SPITFIRE	EFIORSUZ	SIZE FOUR		PREFORMS
EFIIPRSU	PURIFIES	EFIOSSTX	SET OF SIX	EFNNOOOR	FORENOON
EFIIPRTU	FRUIT PIE	EFIPPRRY	FRIPPERY	EFNNOOTT	NOT OFTEN
FFIIPRYX	PRIX FIVE	EFIPRTTY	PRETTIFY	EFNNORUZ	UNFROZEN
ErIIPGTY	TYPIFIES	EFIRRRSU	FURRIERS	EFNOOOTT	FOOTNOTE
EFIIRRTU	FRUITIER	EFIRRSTT	FRITTERS	EFNOOSST	FESTOONS
EFIKLLOW	WOLFLIKE	EFIRRSTU	FRUITERS	EFNOPRUZ	FROZEN UP
EFIKLNSU	FLUNKIES	EFIRSSSU	FISSURES	EFNOPSTU	SOFTEN UP
EFIKLOOR	ROOFLIKE	EFIRSSTT	FIRST SET	EFNORSTU	FORTUNES
EFIKLOOT	TOOK LIFE	EFIRSSTU	SURFEITS		FOUR TENS
EFIKLORW	LIFE WORK	EFIRSTUX	FIXTURES	EFNOSSST	SOFTNESS
	LIFEWORK	EFISSSTU	FUSSIEST	EFOOORST	FOOTSORE
EFIKLRUY	LIKE FURY	EFISSTTW	SWIFTEST		SORE FOOT
EFIKLSTU	FLUKIEST	EFISTUZZ	FUZZIEST	EFOOPRRS	REPROOFS
EFIKNORS	FORESKIN	EFKLLOOR	FOLK LORE	EFOOPRST	POOFTERS
EFIKNSTU	FUNKIEST		FOLKLORE	EFOOPSTT	FOOTSTEP
EFIKORRW	FIREWORK	EFKLLOOT	LOOK LEFT	EFOORSTV	VOTES FOR
EFILLLSW	SELF-WILL	EFKLORTW	LEFT WORK	EFOORTUZ	FROZE OUT
EFILLMTU	FULL TIME	EFKNOORW	FOREKNOW	EFOOSSTT	SETS FOOT
	FULL-TIME	EFKNOPSU	POKES FUN	EFOOSTUU	OUT OF USE
EFILLNRU	FULL REIN	EFKOOPRS	SPOKE FOR	EFORRSST	FORTRESS
EFILLSTW	FITS WELL	EFKOOTUY	OUT OF KEY	EFORRSTY	FORESTRY
EFILLSUZ	FULL SIZE	EFKORRTW	FRETWORK	EFORRSUV	FERVOURS
EFILLTUY	FUTILELY	EFLLLLUW	FULL WELL	EFORRSTU	FOUR SETS
EFILMNOY	ON MY LIFE	EFLLLPTU	FULL PELT	EFORSTVY	VERY SOFT
EFILMSST	FILM SETS	EFLLMRTU	FULL-TERM	EGGGILNS	LEGGINGS
EFILMSUY	EMULSIFY	EFLLNOOW	LONE WOLF	EGGGINOT	GET GOING
EFILNNTU	INFLUENT	EFLLNSSU	FULLNESS	EGGGIORR	GROGGIER
EFILNORU	FLUORINE	EFLLNTUY	FLUENTLY	EGGGOOSU	GOOSEGOG
EFILNORW	IN FLOWER	EFLLOORW	FOLLOWER	EGGHHINO	GONE HIGH
EFILNOSX	FLEXIONS	EFLLOOSW	FLEW SOLO	EGGHHIOS	GOES HIGH
EFILNSUX	INFLUXES	EFLLOUWY	WOEFULLY	EGGHHIST	GETS HIGH
EFILOORT	TILE ROOF	EFLLRUUY	RUEFULLY	EGGHIINN	NEIGHING
EFILOOSZ	FLOOZIES	EFLLRUVY	VERY FULL	EGGHIINW	WEIGHING
EFILOPPR	FLOPPIER	EFLLSUUY	USEFULLY	EGGHILRT	RIGHT LEG
EFILOPRR	PROFILER	EFLMMRUY	FLUMMERY	EGGHIRTT	GET RIGHT
EFILOPRS	PROFILES	EFLMNOTY	ON MY LEFT	EGGHIRWY	WHIGGERY
EFILORTU	FLUORITE	EFLMNRUU	FRENULUM	EGGHORTU	GET ROUGH
EFILOSTT	LOFTIEST	EFLMOORS	LOSE FORM	EGGHOTTU	GET TOUGH
EFILOSTW	LOTS WIFE	EFLMOORT	LEFT ROOM	EGGHRTUY	THUGGERY
EFILPPRS	FLIPPERS	EFLMORRY	FORMERLY	EGGIINNR	REIGNING
EFILPRTU	UPLIFTER	EFLMORSS	FORMLESS	EGGIINNS	SINGEING
EFILPSTT	FELT TIPS	EFLNORSU	FLEURONS	EGGIINNT	TINGEING
EFILPSTU	SPITEFUL	EFLNORYZ	FROZENLY	EGGIINRV	GRIEVING
EFILPSTY	SELF-PITY	EFLNOSSU	FOULNESS	EGGIKNOS	GINGKOES
EFILRRST	TRIFLERS	EFLNOSSW	SELF-SOWN		GINKGOES
EFILRRSU	FLURRIES	EFLNOSTT	FLETTONS	EGGILNNT	GENTLING
EFILRSTT	FLITTERS	EFLNRTTU	LEFT TURN	EGGILNRY	GINGERLY
EFILRSZZ	FRIZZLES		TURN LEFT	EGGILOOS	GOOGLIES
EFIMNORR	INFORMER	EFLOORSS	ROOFLESS	EGGILOSU	SQUIGGLE
	RENIFORM	EFLOORTU	FOOTRULE	EGGILRRW	WRIGGLER
EFIMNORS	FERMIONS	EFLOORVW	FLOW OVER	EGGILRSW	WIGGLERS
EFIMNRSS	FIRMNESS		OVERFLOW		WRIGGLES
EFIMNSTT	FITMENTS	EFLOOSST	FOOTLESS	EGGIMSTU	MUGGIEST
EFIMORRT	RETIFORM	EFLOPRUW	POWERFUL	EGGINORR	ROGERING
EFIMOSST	SEMISOFT	EFLOPSTW	FOWL PEST	EGGINORU	ROGUEING

EGGINPRU	GINGER UP	EGHINORV	HOVERING	EGIINRRT	RETIRING
EGGINRSS	SNIGGERS	EGHINOTW	GONE WITH	EGIINRRW	REWIRING
EGGINSSU	GUESSING	EGHINPRS	SPHERING	EGIINRST	STINGIER
EGGINSTU	GUESTING	EGHINPSS	SPHINGES	EGIINRSV	REVISING
EGGIOSST	SOGGIEST	EGHINRRS	HERRINGS	EGIINRTU	INTRIGUE
EGGIPRRY	PRIGGERY	EGHINRRU	HUNGRIER	EGIINRTV	RIVETING
EGGIRRST	TRIGGERS	EGHINRSU	USHERING	EGIINRVV	REVIVING
EGGIRSSW	SWIGGERS	EGHINRSW	WHINGERS	EGIINSTX	EXISTING
EGGJLRSU	JUGGLERS	EGHINSTT	THE STING		EXIT SIGN
EGGJLRUY	JUGGLERY		TIGHTENS	EGIIPRSW	PERIWIGS
EGGKLOSY	EGG YOLKS	EGHINTTW	WHETTING	EGIIPSST	PIG STIES
EGGLLNOS	LONG LEGS	EGHIOSTW	GOES WITH		PIGSTIES
	LONGLEGS	EGHIOTUW	OUTWEIGH	EGIIPSTV	GIVE TIPS
EGGLMRSU	SMUGGLER	EGHIPSUW	WEIGHS UP	EGIIPTUV	GIVE IT UP
EGGLMSSU	SMUGGLES	EGHIRSTT	SET RIGHT	EGIIRRTT	GRITTIER
EGGLNNOO	LONG GONE	EGHISTTT	TIGHTEST	EGIITUXY	EXIGUITY
EGGLNSSU	SNUGGLES	EGHKOOTT	GOT THE O.K.	EGIJLLNY	JELLYING
EGGLORSS	SLOGGERS	EGHLLNUW	WELL-HUNG	EGIJMMNY	JEMMYING
EGGLRSSU	SLUGGERS	EGHLLOOT	GO TO HELL	EGIJNNOY	ENJOYING
EGGLRSTU	STRUGGLE	EGHLLOSU	LUGHOLES	EGIKKNRT	TREKKING
EGGMSSTU	SMUGGEST	EGHLMNOO	LONG HOME	EGIKLLNN	KNELLING
EGGNOOPS	EGG SPOON	EGHLNORS	LEGHORNS	EGIKNORV	REVOKING
EGGNORTW	GET WRONG	EGHLOORY	RHEOLOGY	EGILLMNS	SMELLING
EGGNRSUY	SNUGGERY	EGHLOOSS	GOLOSHES	EGILLNNO	LONG LINE
EGGNSSTU	SNUGGEST	EGHLOOTY	ETHOLOGY	EGILLNOR	NEGRILLO
EGGOORSU	GORGEOUS		THEOLOGY	EGILLNOV	LIVELONG
EGGSSSTU	SUGGESTS	EGHLOPRU	PLOUGHER	EGILLNPS	SPELLING
EGHHHIOP	HIGH HOPE	EGHLORST	SHORT LEG	EGILLNQU	QUELLING
EGHHIIMT	HIGH TIME	EGHMNOOY	HOMOGENY	EGILLNSW	SWELLING
EGHHIIRS	HIGH RISE	EGHMOORT	THE GROOM	EGILMMNS	LEMMINGS
	HIGH-RISE	EGHMOSSU	GUMSHOES	EGILMMRS	GLIMMERS
EGHHIIRW	HIGH WIRE	EGHMOSSY	GYM SHOES	EGILMNOT	LONG TIME
EGHHINOT	HIGH NOTE	EGHNOOTY	THEOGONY	EGILMNRS	GREMLINS
EGHHINRT	HIGH RENT	EGHNOPTU	GONE PHUT	EGILMNST	SMELTING
EGHHINSS	HIGHNESS	EGHNORSU	ROUGHENS	EGILMOOR	GLOOMIER
EGHHINTT	THE THING	EGHNORUV	HUNG OVER		OLIGOMER
EGHHINTW	WENT HIGH		OVERHUNG	EGILMPSS	GLIMPSES
EGHHIPRU	HIGHER UP	EGHNOSTU	TOUGHENS	EGILNNOR	LINGER ON
	HIGHER-UP	EGHNRSTT	STRENGTH	EGILNNPU	PLUNGE IN
EGHHIRVY	VERY HIGH	EGHOPSTU	GOES PHUT	EGILNNST	NESTLING
EGHHLOOW	WHOLE HOG	EGHORSTU	ROUGHEST	EGILNNTT	NETTLING
EGHHORUW	ROUGH-HEW	EGHOSSUW	GUESS WHO	EGILNOPP	PEOPLING
EGHIILLS	GHILLIES	EGHOSTTU	TOUGHEST	EGILNORW	LOWERING
EGHIILNR	HIRELING	EGIIKLNN	LIKENING	EGILNOSW	LONGWISE
EGHIILNS	SHIELING	EGIIKLNR	RINGLIKE	EGILNOVV	EVOLVING
EGHIIMRT	MIGHTIER	EGIIKLNW	WINGLIKE	EGILNOVW	LONG VIEW
EGHIINNR	INHERING	EGIIKNSZ	KING SIZE	EGILNPRY	REPLYING
EGHIINST	HEISTING		KING-SIZE	EGILNPST	PESTLING
	NIGHTIES	EGIILNNS	ENSILING	EGILNRSS	SLINGERS
	THINGIES	EGIILNNV	LIVENING	EGILNRST	RINGLETS
EGHIINSV	INVEIGHS	EGIILNOR	RELIGION		STERLING
EGHIINSW	WEIGH-INS	EGIILNPS	SPIELING	EGILNSST	GLISTENS
	WEIGHS IN	EGIILNRS	RIESLING		SINGLETS
EGHIINTV	THIEVING	EGIILNRV	RELIVING	EGILNSSU	UGLINESS
EGHIIRST	TIGERISH		REVILING	EGILNSSW	WINGLESS
EGHIKNRS	GHERKINS	EGIILRRS	GRISLIER	EGILNSTT	LETTINGS
EGHILLNS	SHELLING	EGIILRTU	GUILTIER		SETTLING
EGHILLNW	WELL-NIGH	EGIIMNPS	IMPINGES	EGILNSUW	LEWIS GUN
EGHILNPS	HELPINGS	EGIIMNRT	MERITING	EGILNTUX	EXULTING
EGHILNPW	WHELPING	EGIIMNSV	MISGIVEN	EGILOOTY	ETIOLOGY
EGHILNSS	SHINGLES	EGIIMNTT	EMITTING	EGILORSS	GLOSSIER
EGHILNST	LIGHTENS	EGIIMOPT	IMPETIGO	EGILOSSS	GLOSSIES
EGHILNSV	SHELVING	EGIIMRVW	GRIM VIEW	EGILOSTT	LETS IT GO
EGHILNSW	WELSHING	EGIIMSSV	MISGIVES	EGILOSTU	EULOGIST
EGHILNTW	NEW LIGHT	EGIINNPR	REPINING	EGILRSST	GLISTERS
EGHILRST	LIGHTERS	EGIINNRS	RESINING		GRISTLES
	SLIGHTER	EGIINNWZ	WIZENING	EGILRSTT	GLITTERS
EGHILSTT	LIGHTEST	EGIINOPR	PEIGNOIR	EGILRSZZ	GRIZZLES
EGHIMNUX	EXHUMING	EGIINOTV	GIVE IN TO	EGILRTTY	GLITTERY
EGHINNOT	ONE-NIGHT	EGIINPRX	EXPIRING	EGIMMNST	STEMMING
EGHINNSU	UNHINGES	EGIINQTU	QUIETING	EGIMMRST	GRIMMEST

EGIMNORV	REMOVING	EGLLLPSU	LEG-PULLS	EGOPRRSS	PROGRESS
EGIMNOSY	MOSEYING	EGLLMORW	GROMWELL	EGOPRRSU	GROUPERS
EGIMNPRU	IMPUGNER	EGLLOOWY	GO YELLOW	EGOPRSUY	GUY ROPES
EGIMNPST	PIGMENTS	EGLLOSUY	YULE LOGS	EGOPSSUY	GYPSEOUS
EGIMNPTT	TEMPTING	EGLMNORS	MONGRELS	EGOPSTTU	GOT UPSET
EGIMNPTY	EMPTYING	EGLMNORT	LONG TERM	EGORSSST	GROSSEST
EGIMNRSS	GRIMNESS		LONG-TERM	EHHIIPRS	HEIRSHIP
EGIMNRSU	RESUMING	EGLMNSSU	GLUMNESS	EHHIIRST	THE IRISH
EGIMNSUW	WINE GUMS	EGLMORSS	GORMLESS	EHHIISTV	THIEVISH
EGIMOOTT	TIME TO GO	EGLMOSSS	SMOGLESS	EHHILMNT	HELMINTH
EGIMORST	ERGOTISM	EGLMPSTU	LEG STUMP	EHHIMOST	HITS HOME
EGIMPRRU	GRUMPIER	EGLNNOOR	LONGERON	EHHIORTT	HITHERTO
EGINNNOS	NEON SIGN		NO LONGER	EHHIOTTW	WHITE HOT
EGINNNOT	TENONING	EGLNNOOS	LONG NOSE		WHITE-HOT
EGINNOPS	OPENINGS	EGLNNOSS	LONGNESS	EHHIRSSW	SHREWISH
EGINNORT	NITROGEN	EGLNOOOY	OENOLOGY	EHHNOOPT	ON THE HOP
EGINNOSW	SEWING ON	EGLNOOPR	LONG ROPE	EHHNOORS	SHOE-HORN
EGINNPSU	PENGUINS	EGLNOOPY	PENOLOGY		SHOEHORN
EGINNRRU	UNERRING	EGLNOORV	OVERLONG	EHHNORTT	THE NORTH
EGINNRSU	ENSURING	EGLNOOSV	LOVE SONG	EHHOOPSS	SHOE SHOP
EGINNSUX	UNSEXING	EGLNOOSW	GONE SLOW	EHHOOSSW	WHOOSHES
EGINOPRS	REPOSING	EGLNORST	LONG REST	EHHOOSTU	HOTHOUSE
	SPONGIER	EGLNORUU	LONGUEUR	EHHOSTTU	THE SOUTH
EGINOPRW	POWERING	EGLNPRSU	PLUNGERS	EHHOSTUV	SHEVUOTH
EGINOPSX	EXPOSING	EGLNRTUY	URGENTLY	EHHPSSUU	HUSHES UP
EGINORST	NEGRITOS	EGLOOPRU	PROLOGUE	EHHRSSTU	THRUSHES
EGINORTW	TOWERING	EGLOOPTY	LOGOTYPE	EHIIPSX	PIXIEISH
EGINORUV	VIN ROUGE	EGLOORSY	SEROLOGY	EHIIKLPW	WHIPLIKE
EGINORXX	XEROXING	EGLOOSSW	GOES SLOW	EHIIKLRS	IRISH ELK
EGINOSTT	GETS INTO	EGLOOSXY	SEXOLOGY	EHIIKSSW	WHISKIES
	GETS IT ON	EGLORRSW	GROWLERS	EHIILMOS	HOMILIES
EGINOTUV	GIVEN OUT	EGLORSUY	RUGOSELY	EHIILMTT	THE LIMIT
EGINPPST	STEPPING	EGLOSSTT	GETS LOST	EHIILRSV	LIVERISH
EGINPRSS	PRESSING	EGLPRSSU	SPLURGES	EHIIMMSS	SHIMMIES
	SPRINGES	EGMMNOOR	MONOGERM	EHIIMNRS	IRISHMEN
EGINPRSU	PERUSING	EGMMORST	GROMMETS	EHIIMNTT	THIN TIME
EGINPRTU	ERUPTING	EGMMRSTU	GRUMMETS	EHIIMSST	SMITHIES
	REPUTING	EGMNNOOY	MONOGENY	EHIIMSTT	THIS TIME
EGINPRYY	PERIGYNY	EGMNNORW	GROWN MEN	EHIINNOS	INHESION
EGINQRUY	QUERYING		WRONG MEN	EHIINNSW	WHINNIES
EGINQSTU	QUESTING	EGMNNOUY	YOUNG MEN	EHIINRST	INHERITS
EGINRRST	STRINGER	EGMNOOOS	MONGOOSE	EHIINSST	SHINIEST
EGINRRSW	WRINGERS	EGMNSSSU	SMUGNESS	EHIINSVX	VIXENISH
EGINRRTU	RING TRUE	EGMORSTU	GOURMETS	EHIIPRSV	VIPERISH
EGINRSSV	SERVINGS	EGNNOOTY	ONTOGENY	EHIIPSTT	PITHIEST
EGINRSSW	SWINGERS	EGNNORST	RONTGENS	EHIIRRST	SHIRTIER
EGINRSSY	SYRINGES	EGNNSSSU	SNUGNESS	EHIIRSTT	THIRTIES
EGINRSTT	GITTERNS	EGNNSSTU	STEN GUNS	EHIISSTT	STITHIES
EGINRSTW	WRESTING	EGNNSTTU	TUNGSTEN	EHIISSTX	HIT SIXES
EGINRSVW	SWERVING	EGNOOPTT	GET ON TOP	EHIISTTT	HITTITES
EGINRTTU	UTTERING	EGNOORRV	GOVERNOR	EHIISTTW	WHITIEST
EGINSSTT	SETTINGS	EGNOORSS	ONE GROSS	EHIISTTX	SIXTIETH
EGINSTTT	STETTING	EGNOOTUX	OX TONGUE	EHIJNNOS	JOHNNIES
EGINSTWW	WEST WING		OXTONGUE	EHIKKNST	THE KINKS
EGIOORRV	GROOVIER	EGNOPRSS	SPONGERS	EHIKLNOR	HORNLIKE
EGIOOSST	SO IT GOES	EGNOPRSY	PYROGENS	EHIKMNST	METHINKS
EGIOPRSS	GOSSIPER	EGNORRST	STRONGER	EHIKNRRS	SHRINKER
EGIOPRST	EGO TRIPS	EGNORRSW	WRONGERS	EHIKNRST	RETHINKS
EGIOPRSU	GROUPIES	EGNORSST	SONGSTER	EHIKRRSS	SHIRKERS
EGIORRTT	GROTTIER		TEN GROSS	EHIKRSSW	WHISKERS
EGIORSST	STRIGOSE	EGNORSSU	SURGEONS	EHIKRSWY	WHISKERY
EGIORSUV	GRIEVOUS	EGNORSTU	STURGEON	EHIKSSTU	HUSKIEST
EGIOSSTT	EGOTISTS	EGNORSTY	SENTRY-GO	EHIKSSWY	WHISKEYS
EGIOSTUV	GIVES OUT	EGNOSTUY	YOUNGEST	EHILLLMO	MOLEHILL
EGIOSUUX	EXIGUOUS	EGNRRTUU	RUNG TRUE	EHILLNOS	HELLIONS
EGIRRSTY	REGISTRY	EGNRRTUY	TURN GREY	EHILLNTT	TILL THEN
EGIRSTUY	GREY SUIT	EGNSSTUU	TUNGUSES	EHILLRRS	SHRILLER
EGISSTTU	GUTSIEST	EGOOPPRU	PROROGUE	EHILLRRT	THRILLER
EGISSUWY	WISE GUYS	EGOORRVW	OVERGROW	EHILMMST	MEL SMITH
EGJLNORU	JONGLEUR	EGOORSTT	GROTTOES	EHILMNOP	PHILEMON
EGJNOSTU	JUST GONE	EGOORSTW	GOT WORSE	EHILMOOR	HEIRLOOM

EHILMRSU	MULISHER
EHILMSSY	SHY SMILE
EHILNORU	UNHOLIER
EHILNOSS	HOLINESS
EHILNOST	HOLSTEIN
	HOT LINES
EHILNOTX	XENOLITH
EHILOPRS	POLISHER
EHILOPRT	HELIPORT
EHILOPSS	POLISHES
EHILOPST	HOPLITES
	ISOPLETH
EHILORTY	RHYOLITE
EHILORUV	EVIL HOUR
EHILOSVW	LIVE SHOW
EHILOTVW	WITH LOVE
EHILPRST	PHILTRES
EHILPSTU	SULPHITE
EHILRRSW	WHIRLERS
EHILRSST	SLITHERS
EHILRSSV	SHRIVELS
EHILRSTW	WHISTLER
EHILRSTY	SLITHERY
EHILRTTW	WHITTLER
EHILSSTT	THISTLES
EHILSSTW	WHISTLES
EHILSTTW	WHITTLES
EHIMMNUY	HYMENIUM
EHIMMRSS	SHIMMERS
EHIMMRSY	SHIMMERY
EHIMNOPR	MORPHINE
EHIMNORT	THERMION
EHIMNOST	MINE HOST
EHIMNOSW	HOME WINS
EHIMNPST	SHIPMENT
EHIMOOST	SMOOTHIE
EHIMORST	ISOTHERM
EHIMORSZ	RHIZOMES
EHIMPRSW	WHIMPERS
EHIMPSUU	EUPHUISM
EHIMRSTT	THERMITS
EHIMRSTY	SMITHERY
EHIMSSTU	MUSHIEST
EHINNNOT	ONE NINTH
EHINNOPS	PHONE-INS
	PHONES IN
EHINNOTW	NONWHITE
EHINNSST	THINNESS
EHINNSSU	SUNSHINE
EHINNSTT	THINNEST
EHINNSTU	IN THE SUN
EHINOPPR	HORNPIPE
EHINOPST	PHONIEST
EHINOPSW	WINE SHOP
EHINOPTT	THE POINT
EHINORRT	THORNIER
EHINORTY	IN THEORY
EHINOSST	HISTONES
EHINOSTU	OUTSHINE
EHINOSTX	ONE SIXTH
EHINPRSU	PUNISHER
EHINPSSU	PUNISHES
EHINPSSX	SPHINXES
EHINRSSU	INRUSHES
	RUSHES IN
	USHERS IN
EHINTTWW	WENT WITH
EHIOOPST	ISOPHOTE
EHIOORTT	TOOTHIER
EHIOPPSS	PIE SHOPS
EHIOPPSU	EOHIPPUS
EHIOPRSS	ROSE HIPS
EHIOPRST	TROPHIES
EHIORRST	HERITORS
EHIORRTW	WORTHIER
EHIORSST	SHORTIES
EHIORSTU	HIRES OUT
EHIORSTW	WORTHIES
EHIORTWZ	HOWITZER
EHIOSSTW	SHOWIEST
EHIOSSTY	ISOHYETS
EHIOTTUW	WHITEOUT
EHIPPRSS	SHIPPERS
EHIPPRSW	WHIPPERS
EHIPPSTW	WHIPPETS
EHIPQSUY	PHYSIQUE
EHIPRSST	HIPSTERS
EHIPRSSW	WHISPERS
EHIPSTUU	EUPHUIST
EHIQSSSU	SQUISHES
EHIRRSTV	THRIVERS
EHIRSWZZ	WHIZZERS
EHISSSTU	HUSSITES
EHISTTTW	THE TWIST
EHJNOOPP	POPE JOHN
EHJNSTTU	JUST THEN
EHJOPSST	ST.JOSEPH
EHKLNOOT	KNOTHOLE
EHKMOORW	HOMEWORK
EHKNNRSU	SHRUNKEN
EHKOPPST	KEPT SHOP
EHKORSTW	THE WORKS
EHLLNSTU	NUTSHELL
EHLLOOOP	LOOPHOLE
EHLLOOTW	WHOLE LOT
EHLLOPST	HOT SPELL
EHLLOSTU	SHELL OUT
EHLMOORW	WORMHOLE
EHLMORTY	MOTHERLY
EHLNOOPY	ONLY HOPE
EHLNORSS	HORNLESS
EHLNOSTY	HONESTLY
	ON THE SLY
EHLOOPRT	PORTHOLE
	POTHOLER
EHLOOPST	LOST HOPE
	POT HOLES
	POTHOLES
	THE POOLS
EHLOOSTU	HOLES OUT
EHLOPSSS	SPLOSHES
EHLOPSTU	HELPS OUT
EHLORSST	HOLSTERS
	HOSTLERS
EHLORSTT	THROSTLE
EHLORSTY	HOSTELRY
EHLORTTT	THROTTLE
EHLPSSTU	PLUSHEST
EHLRSSTU	RUTHLESS
EHLRSTTU	SHUTTLER
EHLSSTTU	SHUTTLES
EHMMOOPR	ROMP HOME
EHMNNOOT	ONE MONTH
EHMNNORT	NORTHMEN
EHMNNSTU	HUNTSMEN
EHMNNTUY	HYMN TUNE
EHMNOORS	HORMONES
	MOORHENS
EHMNOOST	SMOOTHEN
EHMNOOTW	HOME TOWN
EHMNOOTY	HOT MONEY
EHMNOPRT	PER MONTH
EHMNOPSU	HOMESPUN
EHMNORSU	HOME RUNS
EHMNOSWY	SHY WOMEN
EHMNPSTY	NYMPHETS
EHMNSTTU	HUTMENTS
EHMNSTUU	HUM TUNES
EHMOOPST	STOP HOME
EHMOORST	SMOOTHER
	THE MOORS
EHMORSST	SMOTHERS
EHMORSTY	SMOTHERY
EHMORTUV	VERMOUTH
EHMPRSTU	THUMPERS
EHNNOPRS	NEPHRONS
EHNNORRT	NORTHERN
EHNNORTU	ON THE RUN
EHNNRSSU	SHUNNERS
EHNOOPPS	OPEN SHOP
EHNOOPRS	NO-HOPERS
EHNOOPTT	ON THE TOP
EHNOOPTY	HONEY POT
EHNOORST	NO OTHERS
	ONE SHORT
	SHORT ONE
EHNOOSSW	SNOWSHOE
EHNOOSTU	OUTSHONE
EHNOOSTV	HOT OVENS
EHNOPPSU	PHONES UP
EHNOPRSY	HYPERONS
EHNOPSSU	PUSHES ON
EHNOPSSY	HYPNOSES
EHNORSST	SHORTENS
EHNORSSU	ONRUSHES
	UNHORSES
EHNORSTU	SOUTHERN
	TEN HOURS
EHNORSTY	HYSTERON
EHNORTTW	TENTH ROW
EHNOSTUU	NUTHOUSE
EHNOSTWX	WHOS NEXT?
EHNPTTUW	WENT PHUT
EHNRSSTU	SHUNTERS
EHOOPRSU	OUR HOPES
EHOOPRTY	ORTHOEPY
EHOOPSTU	HOUSETOP
EHOOPTTT	TO THE TOP
EHOOPTYZ	ZOOPHYTE
EHOORRUZ	ZERO HOUR
EHOORSST	SHOOTERS
	SOOTHERS
EHOORSTV	OVERSHOT
EHOORSVW	SHOW OVER
EHOOSSSW	SWOOSHES
EHOOSTTV	HOT STOVE
EHOOSTUU	OUTHOUSE
EHOPPRSS	SHOPPERS
EHOPPRST	PROPHETS
EHOPPRSW	WHOPPERS
EHOPPRSY	PROPHESY
EHOPPSST	PET SHOPS
EHOPRSSU	SHORES UP
EHOPRSSW	REP SHOWS
EHOPRSUV	PUSH OVER
	PUSHOVER
EHOPRTUY	EUTROPHY
EHOPSSSX	SEX SHOPS
EHORRSTW	THROWERS
EHORSSTT	SHORTEST
EHORSSTU	SHOUTERS
	SURE SHOT
EHORSTTW	THE WORST

EHORSTUU	USHER OUT	EIIMMSST	MISTIMES
EHORTTUW	THREW OUT		SEMITISM
EHPPSSUU	PUSHES UP	EIIMNNOT	IN NO TIME
EHPRSSTU	THE SPURS	EIIMNNRT	TIN MINER
EHPRSSUU	RUSHES UP	EIIMNNST	TIN MINES
EHRRSTTU	THRUSTER	EIIMNOPT	PIMIENTO
EHRSSSTY	SHYSTERS	EIIMNOSS	EMISSION
EHRSSTTU	SHUTTERS	EIIMNRST	MINISTER
EIIILNST	LIES IN IT	EIIMNRSV	MINIVERS
EIIIMMNS	MINIMISE	EIIMNRTT	INTERMIT
EIIIMMNZ	MINIMIZE	EIIMNSTU	MUTINIES
EIIJNRSU	INJURIES	EIIMNVWY	IN MY VIEW
EIIKKNOP	KIP KEINO	EIIMOPRX	MIREPOIX
EIIKKNST	KINKIEST	EIIMOPST	OPTIMISE
EIIKLLMT	KILL TIME	EIIMOPTZ	OPTIMIZE
EIIKLNRS	SLINKIER	EIIMPRSS	PISMIRES
EIIKLPSW	WISPLIKE	EIIMPSTU	TIME IS UP
EIIKLSST	SILKIEST	EIIMOSTU	QUIETISM
EIIKMPRS	SKIMPIER	EIIMSSSV	MISSIVES
EIIKNNRS	SKINNIER	EIIMSSTT	MISTIEST
EIIKNPTT	KEPT IT IN	EIIMSSTX	SIX TIMES
EIIKPSST	SPIKIEST	EIINNOSU	UNIONISE
EIIKSSVV	SKIVVIES	EIINNOSV	ENVISION
EIILLLST	LIE STILL	EIINNOSW	IN NO WISE
EIILLLVY	LIVELILY	EIINNOSX	ONE IN SIX
EIILLMMS	MILLIMES	EIINNOUZ	UNIONIZE
EIILLMNR	MILLINER	EIINNRTW	IN WINTER
EIILLMNU	ILLUMINE	EIINNSST	TININESS
EIILLNSV	VILLEINS	EIINNSTT	TINNIEST
EIILLNTV	VITELLIN	EIINOPRS	RIPIENOS
EIILLOOV	OLIVE OIL	EIINOPTT	PETITION
EIILLPSS	ELLIPSIS	EIINORRT	INTERIOR
EIILLSST	SILLIEST	EIINORSV	REVISION
EIILMNNS	LENINISM	EIINOSST	NOISIEST
EIILMNNT	LINIMENT	EIINPPST	NIPPIEST
EIILMOPT	IMPOLITE	EIINPRRS	INSPIRER
EIILMPRS	IMPERILS	EIINPRSS	INSPIRES
EIILMSSS	MISSILES	EIINPRST	PRISTINE
EIILMSST	SLIMIEST	EIINPSTZ	PINT SIZE
EIILMSSX	SIX MILES		PINT-SIZE
EIILMSTY	MYELITIS	EIINPTUV	PUNITIVE
EIILNNOT	INTO LINE	EIINQRRU	INQUIRER
EIILNNST	LENINIST	EIINQRSU	INQUIRES
	LISTEN IN	EIINQTUY	INEQUITY
EIILNOPT	PILE IT ON	EIINRRTW	WINTRIER
EIILNORS	LIONISER	EIINRSST	SINISTER
EIILNORZ	LIONIZER	EIINRSSW	WIRINESS
EIILNOSS	ELISIONS	EIINRSTT	NITRITES
	LIONISES	EIINRSTU	NEURITIS
	OILINESS	EIINRSTW	WRITES IN
EIILNOSV	IS IN LOVE	EIINSSTU	UNITISES
EIILNOSZ	LIONIZES	EIINSTUZ	UNITIZES
EIILNSSW	WILINESS	EIIOPRRS	PRIORIES
EIILNSTW	WINE LIST	EIIOPSTV	POSITIVE
EIILNSTY	SENILITY	EIIPRRST	STRIPIER
EIILNTTU	INTITULE	EIIPRRTW	TRIP WIRE
EIILOPPS	OIL PIPES	EIIPSSTT	STIPITES
EIILOTVV	VOLITIVE		TIPSIEST
EIILPPRS	SLIPPIER	EIIQSTTU	QUIETIST
EIILPRTT	LET IT RIP	EIISTTTW	WITTIEST
EIILPSST	PITILESS	EIJLLOST	JOLLIEST
EIILPSTY	PYELITIS	EIJLOOSU	JOE LOUIS
EIILPTUV	LIVE IT UP	EIJNORST	JOINTERS
EIILRSTU	UTILISER	EIJNORTU	JOINTURE
EIILRTUZ	UTILIZER	EIJNOSTT	JETTISON
EIILSSTU	UTILISES	EIJNPRSU	JUNIPERS
EIILSTUZ	UTILIZES	EIJRSTUY	JESUITRY
EIIMMNNT	IMMINENT	EIKKLLOO	LOOK LIKE
EIIMMNSU	IMMUNISE	EIKKLSTU	TUSKLIKE
EIIMMNUZ	IMMUNIZE	EIKLLMPU	PLUMLIKE
EIIMMPRU	IMPERIUM		
		EIKLLNSW	INK WELLS
			INKWELLS
		EIKLLNTW	WELL-KNIT
		EIKLLNUY	UNLIKELY
		EIKLLORV	OVERKILL
		EIKLLOSS	SKOLLIES
		EIKLLSST	SKILLETS
		EIKLMNOO	MOONLIKE
		EIKLMORW	WORMLIKE
		EIKLMOSS	MOSSLIKE
		EIKLNOST	TEN KILOS
		EIKLNPRS	SPRINKLE
		EIKLNRSW	WRINKLES
		EIKLNRTW	TWINKLER
		EIKLNSSS	SKINLESS
		EIKLNSSY	SKYLINES
		EIKLNSTW	TWINKLES
		EIKLOORT	ROOTLIKE
		EIKLOPSS	SKI SLOPE
		EIKLPRSU	PURE SILK
		EIKLSSTT	SKITTLES
		EIKLSSTU	SULKIEST
		EIKMMRSS	SKIMMERS
		EIKMNORS	MONIKERS
		EIKMNORY	MINOR KEY
		EIKMNOST	TOKENISM
		EIKMOOTT	TOOK TIME
		EIKMORSV	SKIM OVER
		EIKMOSST	SMOKIEST
		EIKMRSTU	MURKIEST
		EIKMSSST	MESS KITS
		EIKNNPSS	PINKNESS
		EIKNNRSS	SKINNERS
		EIKNOPRS	ROSE PINK
		EIKNOPSS	POKINESS
		EIKNOPTY	KEY POINT
		EIKNORST	ON STRIKE
		EIKNORTT	KNOTTIER
		EIKNOSTT	TIE KNOTS
		EIKNOSTW	WONKIEST
		EIKNPRTU	TURNPIKE
		EIKNRSST	STINKERS
		EIKNRSTT	KNITTERS
			TRINKETS
		EIKOOPRS	SPOOKIER
		EIKOPPRS	PORK PIES
		EIKOPRSV	SKIP OVER
		EIKPPRSS	SKIPPERS
		EIKPPTTU	KEPT IT UP
		EIKPRSTU	STRIKE UP
		EIKRRSST	STRIKERS
		EIKRSSTT	SKITTERS
		EILLLNOY	LONELILY
		EILLLOSW	OIL WELLS
		EILLLOVY	LOVELILY
		EILLLSSW	WILL-LESS
		EILLMNOS	ILL OMENS
		EILLMNOU	LINOLEUM
		EILLMOTT	LITTLE MO
		EILLMPSS	MISSPELL
		EILLMPTU	MULTIPLE
		EILLMUVX	VEXILLUM
		EILLNOWY	IN YELLOW
		EILLNPQU	QUILL PEN
		EILLNPST	ILL SPENT
		EILLNPUW	WELL UP IN
		EILLNSTY	SILENTLY
		EILLOORW	WOOLLIER
		EILLOOSW	WOOLLIES
		EILLOOVY	OLIVE OYL
		EILLOPRW	LOWER LIP

Code	Word	Code	Word	Code	Word
EILLOPTY	POLITELY	EILNPSUY	SUPINELY	EIMNNOST	MENTIONS
EILLOSSS	SOILLESS	EILNQUUY	UNIQUELY	EIMNNOSU	MINUS ONE
EILLOSTW	LOWLIEST	EILNRRUU	UNRULIER	EIMNNOTT	OINTMENT
EILLPPPS	PEP PILLS	EILNRTUU	UNIT RULE	EIMNNOWY	WIN MONEY
EILLPRSS	SPILLERS	EILNRTUV	VIRULENT	EIMNNSTU	MINUS TEN
EILLPSST	LETS SLIP	EILNSSTU	UTENSILS	EIMNOOPS	EMPOISON
EILLRRST	TRILLERS	EILNSTTU	LUTENIST	EIMNOORS	IS NO MORE
EILLRSSW	SWILLERS	EILNSUWY	UNWISELY	EIMNOORV	OMNIVORE
EILLSSST	LISTLESS	EILOORST	OESTRIOL	EIMNOOST	EMOTIONS
	SLITLESS	EILOOSST	STOOLIES	EIMNOPRT	ORPIMENT
EILLSSTT	STILLEST	EILOOSTV	OIL STOVE	EIMNOPST	NEPOTISM
EILLSTUV	VITELLUS	EILOOSTY	OTIOSELY		PIMENTOS
EILMMPRU	PLUMMIER	EILOOUVY	I LOVE YOU	EIMNOPTT	IMPOTENT
EILMMRSS	SLIMMERS	EILOPPRS	SLOPPIER	EIMNORSU	MONSIEUR
EILMMSST	SLIMMEST	EILOPRRT	PORTLIER	EIMNORTW	TIMEWORN
EILMNOSU	EMULSION	EILOPRSS	SPOILERS	EIMNORTY	ENORMITY
EILMNPSS	LIMPNESS	EILOPRSU	PERILOUS	EIMNOSTU	MOUNTIES
EILMNRST	MINSTREL	EILOPSST	PISTOLES	EIMNPRSS	PRIMNESS
EILMNRSU	RUN MILES	EILOPSTT	POLITEST	EIMNPSST	MISSPENT
EILMNSSS	SLIMNESS	EILOPSTX	EXPLOITS	EIMNPTTY	EMPTY TIN
EILMNTUY	MINUTELY	EILOPTUV	LIVE UP TO	EIMNRRST	ST.MIRREN
	UNTIMELY	EILORRTU	ULTERIOR	EIMNRSST	MINSTERS
EILMOOST	TOILSOME	EILORSSS	RISSOLES		TRIMNESS
EILMOPRS	IMPLORES	EILORSTU	OUTLIERS	EIMNRSTU	TERMINUS
EILMOPST	MILEPOST	EILORTTY	TOILETRY	EIMNRSTY	ENTRYISM
	POLEMIST	EILOSSTT	LOUSIEST	EIMNSUZZ	MUEZZINS
EILMORRS	LORIMERS	EILOSTTT	STILETTO	EIMNTTWY	WITTY MEN
EILMOSTT	LOST TIME	EILOSTUV	LIVES OUT	EIMOORST	MOTORISE
EILMOSTU	MILES OUT		OUTLIVES		ROOMIEST
EILMOSTW	SLOW TIME	EILOSTVW	TWO EVILS	EIMOORTZ	MOTORIZE
	TWO MILES	EILOTVVY	VOTIVELY	EIMOPPRR	IMPROPER
EILMPPSU	PLUM PIES	EILPPPRU	UPPER LIP	EIMOPRRS	PRIMROSE
EILMPRUY	IMPURELY	EILPPRSS	SLIPPERS	EIMOPRRT	IMPORTER
EILMPSST	MISSPELT	EILPPRST	STIPPLER	EIMOPRRV	IMPROVER
	SIMPLEST		TIPPLERS	EIMOPRSS	PROMISES
EILMPSSU	IMPULSES	EILPPRSU	SUPPLIER		SEMIPROS
EILMPSTU	LUMPIEST	EILPPRSY	SLIPPERY	EIMOPRSV	IMPROVES
EILMRSSU	MISRULES	EILPPSST	STIPPLES	EIMOPRUU	EUROPIUM
EILMRSSY	REMISSLY	EILPPSSU	SUPPLIES	EIMOQSTU	MISQUOTE
EILMRSWY	WRY SMILE	EILPRSTT	SPLITTER	EIMORRST	STORMIER
EILMSSUY	ELYSIUMS		TRIPLETS	EIMORRWW	WIREWORM
EILMTTUU	LUTETIUM	EILPRSTY	PRIESTLY	EIMORSST	MORTISES
EILNNOST	INSOLENT	EILPRSUU	PURLIEUS	EIMORSTU	MOISTURE
EILNNOSW	SNOW LINE	EILPRSUY	PLEURISY		OUR TIMES
EILNNPSU	PINNULES	EILPRTTY	PRETTILY	EIMORSTV	VOMITERS
EILNNTTY	INTENTLY	EILPSSTU	STIPULES	EIMORTTW	TWO TIMER
EILNOOPS	POLONIES	EILQRRSU	SQUIRREL		TWO-TIMER
EILNOOST	LOONIEST	EILQRSUU	LIQUEURS	EIMOSSTZ	MESTIZOS
	OILSTONE	EILRRSTU	SULTRIER	EIMOSTTT	TOTEMIST
EILNOPRT	INTERPOL	EILRSSTT	SLITTERS	EIMOSTTU	TIME-OUTS
	TOP LINER	EILRSSTU	SURLIEST		TITMOUSE
	TOP-LINER	EILRSSTY	SISTERLY	EIMOSTTW	TWO TIMES
EILNOPST	SLIT OPEN	EILRSSZZ	SIZZLERS		TWO-TIMES
EILNOPTY	LINOTYPE	EILRSTUV	RIVULETS	EIMPRSSU	PRIMUSES
EILNORRS	LORINERS	EILRSUUX	LUXURIES	EIMPRSTU	STUMPIER
EILNORRU	IRON RULE	EILSSSTY	STYLISES	EIMPSSST	MISSTEPS
EILNORTV	IN REVOLT	EILSSSTU	LUSTIEST	EIMPSSTU	MESS IT UP
EILNORVV	INVOLVER	EILSSTYZ	STYLIZES	EIMQRRSU	SQUIRMER
EILNOSTU	LINE-OUTS	EIMMNNTU	MUNIMENT	EIMQSTUY	MYSTIQUE
	OUTLINES	EIMMNORS	MISNOMER	EIMRRSSU	SURMISER
EILNOSTV	NOVELIST	EIMMNRSU	IN SUMMER	EIMRSSST	MISTRESS
EILNOSTW	TOWLINES	EIMMOPRU	EMPORIUM	EIMRSSSU	SURMISES
EILNOSUV	EVULSION	EIMMOSTT	TOTEMISM	EIMRSTUX	MIXTURES
EILNOSVV	INVOLVES	EIMMPRST	PRIMMEST	EIMSSSSU	MISSUSES
EILNOTUV	INVOLUTE	EIMMPRSU	PREMIUMS	EINNOOPT	ONE POINT
EILNPRSS	PILSNERS	EIMMRRST	TRIMMERS	EINNOOTW	ONE IN TWO
EILNPRST	SPLINTER	EIMMRSSW	SWIMMERS		TWO IN ONE
EILNPSSS	SPINLESS	EIMMRSTT	TRIMMEST	EINNOPRS	IN PERSON
EILNPSSU	SPINULES	EIMMSTUY	YUMMIEST	EINNOPSS	PENSIONS
	SPLENIUS	EIMNNNOU	UNION MEN	EINNORSS	IRONNESS
EILNPSUV	LIVENS UP	EIMNNOPY	PIN MONEY	EINNORSU	REUNIONS

Code	Word	Code	Word	Code	Word
EINNORSV	ENVIRONS	EINRSSSU	SUNRISES	EJOPPRST	PROPJETS
EINNORTU	NEUTRINO	EINRSSTT	STINTERS	EKKLRSSU	SKULKERS
EINNORTV	INVENTOR	EINRSSXY	SYRINXES	EKLLLOOW	LOOK WELL
EINNORWW	WINNOWER	EINSSTTW	TWIN SETS	EKLLNOWW	KNOW WELL
EINNOSSS	NOSINESS	EINSSTUW	NEW SUITS	EKLLORWW	WORK WELL
EINNOSST	TENSIONS	EINSTTTU	NUTTIEST	EKLNOOOR	ONLOOKER
EINNOSTT	TINSTONE	EIOOPPRS	PORPOISE	EKLNORSS	SNORKELS
EINNPRSS	SPINNERS	EIOOPPST	OPPOSITE	EKLOOORV	LOOK OVER
EINNPSSU	PUNINESS	EIOOPRVW	POOR VIEW		LOOKOVER
EINNPSSY	SPINNEYS	EIOOPSST	ISOTOPES		OVERLOOK
EINNPSTU	NUT PINES	EIOORSTT	TORTOISE	EKLOOPSW	SLOW POKE
EINNRSTV	VINTNERS	EIOOSSTT	SOOTIEST		SLOWPOKE
EINNRTTU	NUTRIENT		TOOTSIES	EKLORSSW	WORKLESS
EINNSSTU	SUNNIEST	EIOOSTWZ	WOOZIEST	EKMNOSUX	MUSK-OXEN
	SUNNITES	EIOPPPSU	POPE PIUS	EKMOOSTU	SMOKE OUT
EINOOPRS	POISONER	EIOPPRTZ	TOP PRIZE	EKMOPRTW	TEMP WORK
EINOOPTT	ON TIP-TOE	EIOPPSST	SOPPIEST	EKMORSSU	MUSK ROSE
	ON TIPTOE	EIOPRRSS	PRIORESS	EKMRSTUY	MUSKETRY
EINOORSS	EROSIONS	EIOPRRST	PIERROTS	EKNNOPSU	UNSPOKEN
EINOORST	SNOOTIER		SPORTIER	EKNOOOTT	TOOK NOTE
EINOOSTX	SIX TO ONE	EIOPRRSU	SUPERIOR	EKNOOPRW	OPENWORK
EINOPRRS	PRISONER	EIOPRRTV	TRIP OVER	EKNOORSS	SNOOKERS
EINOPRSS	ROPINESS	EIOPRSST	RIPOSTES	EKNOPRTY	PONY TREK
EINOPRST	POINTERS	EIOPRSTV	SPORTIVE	EKNORSTW	NETWORKS
	PROTEINS	EIOPRSUV	PERVIOUS	EKNRSTUY	TURNKEYS
EINOPRSU	PRUINOSE		PREVIOUS	EKOOORTV	OVERTOOK
EINOPRTU	ERUPTION		VIPEROUS		TOOK OVEN
EINOPRTW	PORT WINE	EIOPRTTU	TORE IT UP	EKOOPRSV	PROVOKES
EINOPSTT	NEPOTIST	EIOPSTTT	POTTIEST	EKOOPSTU	SPOKE OUT
	SET POINT	EIOPSTUW	WIPEOUTS	EKOORRVW	OVERWORK
	STEP INTO		WIPES OUT		WORK OVER
	STEP ON IT	EIORRRSW	WORRIERS	EKOPRSTU	UPSTROKE
EINOQSTU	IN QUOTES	EIORRRTU	ROTURIER	EKOPSSTY	KEY POSTS
	QUESTION	EIORRSST	RESISTOR		STOP KEYS
EINOQTTU	NOT QUITE		ROISTERS	EKORRSST	STROKERS
	QUOTIENT		SORRIEST	ELLLMOWY	MELLOWLY
EINORRRT	IN TERROR	EIORSTTU	TIRES OUT	ELLLNSUY	SULLENLY
EINORSSS	ROSINESS		TRIES OUT	ELLMNOSY	SOLEMNLY
EINORSSU	NEUROSIS	EIORSTUV	VITREOUS	ELLMOORS	MORELLOS
	RESINOUS	EIORTTUW	WRITE OUT	ELLMPSUU	PLUMULES
EINORSSV	VERSIONS	EIOSTVWW	TWO WIVES	ELLNOORV	LOVELORN
EINORSTT	SNOTTIER	EIPPRRST	STRIPPER	ELLNOOSW	WOOLLENS
EINORSTU	RINSE OUT		TRIPPERS	ELLNORRT	RENT ROLL
	ROUTINES	EIPQRSTU	QUIPSTER	ELLNORWW	WELL WORN
EINORSTV	INVESTOR	EIPRRRSU	SPURRIER		WELL-WORN
EINORSTY	TYROSINE	EIPRRSSU	SPURRIES	ELLNOSVY	SLOVENLY
EINORSUV	SOUVENIR		SURPRISE	ELLNOUVY	UNLOVELY
EINORSVW	WINS OVER	EIPRSSST	PERSISTS	ELLNRSUW	RUNS WELL
EINORTTU	RITENUTO	EIPRSSTT	TIPSTERS	ELLOORRV	ROLL OVER
EINOSSSS	SESSIONS	EIPRSTUW	WRITES UP	ELLOOSTV	LOST LOVE
EINOSSST	STENOSIS		WRITE-UPS	ELLOPRST	POLLSTER
EINOSSTT	STONIEST	EIPRSUVW	PURVIEWS	ELLOPRTU	POLLUTER
EINOSTTU	ETON SUIT	EIPRSVVY	SPIVVERY	ELLOPRUV	PULL OVER
EINOSTTX	TEN TO SIX	EIQRSTTU	QUITTERS		PULLOVER
EINOSTUW	WINES OUT	EIRRRSST	STIRRERS	ELLOPSST	PLOTLESS
EINOSTVY	VENOSITY	EIRRSSTV	STRIVERS	ELLOPSTU	POLLUTES
EINPPRRT	PREPRINT	EIRRSTTU	TRUSTIER		SPELL OUT
EINPPRSS	SNIPPERS	EIRSSTTU	RUSTIEST	ELLORRST	STROLLER
EINPPSST	SNIPPETS		TRUSTIES		TROLLERS
EINPPSTY	SNIPPETY	EIRSSTTW	TWISTERS	ELLORSTY	TROLLEYS
EINPRRST	PRINTERS	EIRSSUVV	SURVIVES	ELLOSSSU	SOULLESS
	REPRINTS	EIRSTTTW	TWITTERS	ELLOSSTU	OUTSELLS
	SPRINTER	EJJMPSTU	JUMP-JETS		SELL-OUTS
EINPRRTU	PRURIENT	EJLMOPPU	POLE JUMP		SELLS OUT
EINPRSST	SPINSTER	EJLNTUXY	NEXT JULY	ELLOSTUW	SWELL OUT
EINQRSTU	SQUINTER	EJMNOOST	TOM JONES	ELLPPSUY	SUPPLELY
EINQRTTU	QUIT RENT	EJMOPRUV	JUMP OVER	ELLPSSUW	SWELLS UP
	QUITRENT	EJMOSTTU	MOT JUSTE	ELMMORST	TROMMELS
EINQSSTU	INQUESTS	EJNOOORT	JOE ORTON	ELMMOSUX	LUMMOXES
EINQSTTU	QUINTETS	EJNORSUY	JOURNEYS	ELMMPSTU	PLUMMETS
EINRRSSU	INSURERS	EJNSSSTU	JUSTNESS	ELMMRSSU	SLUMMERS

ELMNOOOP	MONOPOLE	EMNOORSW	NEWS ROOM	ENPRSSTU	PUNSTERS
ELMNOOSS	MOONLESS		NEWSROOM	ENRRSTUU	NURTURES
ELMNOOSZ	ZOOM LENS	EMNOOSUV	VENOMOUS	ENRSSTTU	ENTRUSTS
ELMOOORV	LOOM OVER	EMNORSST	MONSTERS		TEST RUNS
ELMOORST	TREMOLOS	EMNORSTT	TORMENTS	ENRSSTUU	UNSUREST
ELMOORSY	MOROSELY	EMNORSTU	REMOUNTS	EOOOOPRS	OOSPORES
ELMOOSSY	LYSOSOME	EMNORSUU	NUMEROUS	EOOOOPRSZ	ZOOSPORE
ELMOPRSY	POLYMERS	EMNOSTTU	STOUT MEN	EOOOPTTT	TOP TO TOE
ELMOPSYY	POLYSEMY	EMNOSUUY	EUONYMUS	EOOPPRRS	PROPOSER
ELMOSYYZ	LYSOZYME	EMNRSSTU	STERNUMS	EOOPPRSS	OPPOSERS
ELMPPSTU	PLUMPEST	EMOOPRRT	PROMOTER		PROPOSES
ELNNOOSU	UNLOOSEN	EMOOPRST	PROMOTES	EOOPPRRST	TROOPERS
ELNOOPSU	LOOSEN UP	EMOORRST	REST ROOM	EOOPPRRTU	UPROOTER
ELNOOSSU	UNLOOSES	EMOORUVY	YOUR MOVE	EOOPRRVY	VERY POOR
ELNOPRUY	RELY UPON	EMOOSSTW	TWOSOMES	EOOPRSTV	OVERTOPS
ELNOPSTU	PLEUSTON	EMOOSTUV	MOVES OUT		STOP OVER
	STOLEN UP	EMOPPRRT	PROMPTER		STOPOVER
ELNOPTTY	POTENTLY	EMOPRSSU	SUPREMOS	EOOPRSTW	TOW ROPES
ELNORSTU	TURNSOLE	EMORSSTU	STRUMOSE		TOWROPES
ELNORSTW	LOW RENTS	EMPRRTUY	TRUMPERY	EOOPRSVW	SWOP OVER
ELNORTTY	ROTTENLY	EMPRSSTU	STUMPERS	EOORRRSW	SORROWER
ELNOSSSW	SLOWNESS	EMPRSSUU	RUMPUSES	EOORRSST	ROOSTERS
	SNOWLESS	EMPRSTTU	STRUMPET	EOORSSTU	OESTROUS
ELNOSSTV	SOLVENTS		TRUMPETS	EOORTTUW	WROTE OUT
ELNOSTWW	WENT SLOW	ENNOOPPT	OPPONENT	EOORTTVY	TORY VOTE
ELNOSUVY	VENOUSLY	ENNOOPRT	TORN OPEN		VOTE TORY
ELNPRTUU	PURULENT	ENNOOPTW	OPEN TOWN	EOOSTTUV	OUTVOTES
ELOOPRSV	SLOP OVER	ENNOPRSU	UNPERSON	EOPPRRSS	PROSPERS
ELOOPRUW	PURE WOOL	ENNOPTWY	TWOPENNY	EOPPRRTY	PROPERTY
ELOORSST	ROOTLESS	ENNORRTU	NO RETURN	EOPPRSST	STOPPERS
ELOORSTT	TOOTLERS	ENNORSTU	NEUTRONS	EOPPRSSU	PURPOSES
ELOOSSTU	LOSES OUT	ENNOSTWW	NEW TOWNS	EOPPSSSU	SUPPOSES
ELOPPRRY	PROPERLY	ENNPPTUY	TUPPENNY	EOPRRSST	PORTRESS
ELOPPSSU	SLOPES UP	ENNPRRUU	RUNNER-UP	EOPRRSTU	POSTURER
ELOPRSUV	OVERPLUS	ENNRSSTU	STUNNERS		TROUPERS
ELOPRSYY	PYROLYSE	ENOOOORTW	ONE OR TWO	EOPRRUVY	PURVEYOR
ELOPRUYZ	RUY LOPEZ	ENOOOSSZ	ZOONOSES	EOPRSSTT	PROTESTS
ELOPSSST	SPOTLESS	ENOOOTTW	TWO TO ONE		SPOTTERS
ELOPSTTU	SLEPT OUT	ENOOPPST	POSTPONE	EOPRSSTU	POSTURES
	SPELT OUT	ENOOPRSS	POORNESS		SPOUTERS
ELORSSTT	SETTLORS		SNOOPERS	EOPRSTUV	PUTS OVER
ELORSTUU	RULES OUT	ENOOPSTT	TOP NOTES	EOPSSSTU	TOSSES UP
ELORSTUY	UROSTYLE	ENOOPSTU	OPENS OUT	EOPSSTTU	STEPS OUT
ELORSVWY	VERY SLOW	ENOORSSZ	SNOOZERS	EOPSTTUU	PUT TO USE
ELPPSSTU	SUPPLEST	ENOORSTW	TONE-ROWS	EOPSTTUW	SWEPT OUT
ELPRSSTU	SPURTLES	ENOORSVY	VERY SOON	EORRRTTU	TORTURER
ELPRSTTU	SPLUTTER	ENOOSSTU	NOSES OUT	EORRSSST	STRESSOR
ELPSSTUU	PUSTULES	ENOOTTTW	TEN TO TWO	EORRSSTU	TROUSERS
ELRRSSTU	RUSTLERS	ENOPPRUY	PREY UPON	EORRSTTT	TROTTERS
ELRSTUUV	VULTURES	ENOPRSST	POSTERNS	EORRSTTU	TORTURES
ELSSSTUY	STYLUSES	ENOPRSTT	PORTENTS	EORRSUVY	SURVEYOR
EMMMNOTU	MOMENTUM	ENOPSSST	STEPSONS	EOSSTTTU	STOUTEST
EMMNNOTU	MONUMENT	ENOPSSSY	SYNOPSES	EPPPRTUY	PUPPETRY
EMMNOORS	MEN'S ROOM	ENOPSSTU	SETS UPON	EPPRSSSU	PRESS-UPS
EMMNOORT	MOTORMEN	ENOPSSWW	SWOP NEWS		SUPPRESS
EMMNORSU	SUMMONER	ENORRSST	SNORTERS	EPRRSSUU	PURSUERS
EMMNOSTU	OMENTUMS	ENORRSTT	TORRENTS		USURPERS
EMMNOSTY	METONYMS	ENORRSUV	OVERRUNS	EPRRSSUY	SPURREYS
EMMNOTTU	TOMENTUM		RUNS OVER	EPRRSTUU	RUPTURES
EMMNOTYY	METONYMY	ENORRTUV	OVERTURN	EPRSSTTU	SPUTTERS
EMMRRRUU	MURMURER		TURN OVER	ERRSTTTU	STRUTTER
EMMRRSTU	STRUMMER		TURNOVER	ERSSTTTU	STUTTERS
EMMRSTYY	SYMMETRY	ENORSSSU	SOURNESS	FFFGHIOT	FIGHT OFF
EMNNNOOU	NOUMENON	ENORSSTU	TONSURES	FFFGILNO	FLING OFF
EMNNOOOT	MONOTONE	ENORSTTU	RENTS OUT	FFFGILNU	FLUFFING
EMNNOOWY	WON MONEY	ENORSTUY	TOURNEYS	FFFGLNOU	FLUNG OFF
EMNNOSTW	TOWNSMEN	ENOSSSTT	STETSONS	FFFGOOOS	GOOFS OFF
EMNNSTTU	STUNT MEN	ENOSSSUU	SENSUOUS	FFFILOST	LIFTS OFF
EMNOOPRS	MON REPOS	ENOTTTWY	TWENTY TO	FFFIORST	FIRST OFF
EMNOOPTY	MONOTYPE	ENPRSSSY	SPRYNESS	FFFLNOOW	FLOWN OFF
EMNOORSU	ENORMOUS			FFFLOTUU	FLUFF OUT

FFGGINOO	GOING OFF
FFGHIINW	WHIFFING
FFGHINOT	NIGHT OFF
FFGHIORS	FROGFISH
FFGHIORT	FIGHT FOR
	RIGHT OFF
FFGHORSU	SHRUG OFF
FFGIILNP	PIFFLING
FFGIILNR	RIFFLING
FFGIINNS	SNIFFING
FFGIINPS	SPIFFING
FFGIINRS	GRIFFINS
FFGILMNU	MUFFLING
FFGILNRU	RUFFLING
FFGINNSU	SNUFFING
FFGINORS	GRIFFONS
	RINGS OFF
FFGINOSS	SIGNS OFF
FFGINSTU	STUFFING
FFGLLOOU	FULL OF GO
FFHIIOTT	HIT IT OFF
FFHIISST	STIFFISH
FFHIKORS	FISH FORK
FFHIKOSW	WHISK OFF
FFHILOSW	WOLFFISH
FFHILOSY	OFFISHLY
FFHIORTW	FIFTH ROW
FFHKOOOS	SHOOK OFF
FFHNOOSW	SHOWN OFF
FFHOOOST	OFFSHOOT
	SHOOT OFF
FFHOORTW	THROW OFF
FFHOOSSW	SHOW-OFFS
	SHOWS OFF
FFHORRUY	HURRY OFF
FFHOSSTU	SHUTOFFS
	SHUTS OFF
FFHOSTTU	HOT STUFF
FFHILNSY	SNIFFILY
FFIKLLOS	KILLS OFF
FFIKLORT	FORKLIFT
FFIKOPSS	SKIPS OFF
FFILLOPP	FLIP-FLOP
FFILLTUY	FITFULLY
FFILOPSS	SLIPS OFF
FFILRTUU	FRUITFUL
FFILSSTU	FISTFULS
FFILSTUY	STUFFILY
FFIMORSU	FUSIFORM
FFINOPRT	OFFPRINT
FFINOPSS	SPIN-OFFS
	SPINS OFF
FFINOPST	PONTIFFS
FFINSSTU	SNUFFS IT
FFIOPRST	STRIP OFF
FFIOPTTY	TOP FIFTY
FFJMOPSU	JUMP-OFFS
FFKLOSSU	SUFFOLKS
FFKOORSW	WORKS OFF
FFLLOPSU	PULLS OFF
FFMOPSTU	OFF STUMP
FFNORSTU	TURNOFFS
	TURNS OFF
FFNOSTUU	SNUFF OUT
FFOOOPRT	TROOP OFF
FFOOPSST	STOP-OFFS
	STOPS OFF
FFOORRUU	FROUFROU
FFOORSTT	TROTS OFF
FGGGILNO	FLOGGING
FGGHIINT	FIGHTING

FGGHINTU	GUN FIGHT
FGGIILNN	FLINGING
FGGIINNR	FRINGING
FGGIINRT	GRIFTING
FGGIINRU	FIGURING
FGGINOOR	FORGOING
	GOING FOR
FGHHISTY	FIGHT SHY
FGHIIKNS	KINGFISH
FGHIILNT	IN FLIGHT
	IN-FLIGHT
FGHIINST	IN FIGHTS
	SHIFTING
FGHIISTT	FIGHTS IT
FGHIITTT	TIGHT FIT
FGHILNSU	FLUSHING
	LUNGFISH
FGHILRTU	RIGHTFUL
FGHINORT	FROTHING
FGHINOST	FIGHTS ON
FGHIOPST	GIFT SHOP
FGHIOTTU	FOUGHT IT
FGHLORUU	FURLOUGH
FGHNOORS	FOGHORNS
FGHNOOTU	FOUGHT ON
FGIIINNX	INFIXING
FGIIKNRS	FRISKING
FGIILLNR	FRILLING
FGIILLNS	FILLINGS
FGIILNOO	FOLIOING
FGIILNPP	FLIPPING
FGIILNRT	FLIRTING
	TRIFLING
FGIILNST	STIFLING
FGIILNTT	FLITTING
FGIILNZZ	FIZZLING
FGIIMPRR	FIRM GRIP
FGIINNOP	NIP OF GIN
FGIINNOX	FIXING ON
FGIINNSU	INFUSING
FGIINNUY	UNIFYING
FGIINOST	FOISTING
FGIINPUX	FIXING UP
FGIINRTT	FRITTING
FGIINRTU	FRUITING
FGIINSTT	FITTINGS
FGIKLNNU	FLUNKING
FGILLORS	FIG ROLLS
FGILMNPU	FLUMPING
FGILNOOR	FLOORING
FGILNOOT	FOOTLING
FGILNOPP	FLOPPING
FGILNORU	FLOURING
FGILNOTU	FLING OUT
	FLOUTING
FGILNPRU	PURFLING
FGIMRTUU	FRUIT GUM
FGINNORT	FRONTING
FGINNORW	FROWNING
FGINOOPR	PROOFING
FGINOOPS	SPOOFING
FGINORST	FROSTING
FGINPRUY	FRYING UP
FGIOORTT	FORGOT IT
FGKLNOOS	FOLK SONG
FGLNORSU	FURLONGS
FGLNORUW	WRONGFUL
FGLNOTUU	FLUNG OUT
FGLOOOST	FOOTSLOG
FGNOOOOT	GO ON FOOT
FHHIKOOS	FISHHOOK

FHHIOPSS	FISH SHOP
FHHLOSTU	HOT FLUSH
FHHOORST	SHOFROTH
FHIILLTY	FILTHILY
FHIILSTY	SHIFTILY
FHIINPSU	FINISH UP
FHIKMNOS	MONKFISH
FHIKNOST	THINKS OF
FHILLOOT	FOOTHILL
FHILLORT	HILLFORT
FHILMOSW	FILM SHOW
FHILMRTU	MIRTHFUL
FHILOPST	SHOPLIFT
FHILORSU	FLOURISH
FHILORTY	FROTHILY
FHIMNOOS	MOONFISH
FHIMPRSU	FRUMPISH
FHINORTU	IN FOURTH
FHIOOPTT	PHOTO-FIT
FHIORSTU	HIT FOURS
FHLLOSTU	SLOTHFUL
FHLMOTUU	MOUTHFUL
FHLNORTY	FLY NORTH
FHLORTUY	FOURTHLY
FHLOSTUU	FLUSH OUT
FHLOSTUY	FLY SOUTH
FHLOTUUY	YOUTHFUL
FHLRTTUU	TRUTHFUL
FHNOSTUX	FOX HUNTS
FHOOORST	FORSOOTH
FHOOOSTT	HOTFOOTS
FHOORRST	FOR SHORT
FIIILNOP	FILIPINO
FIIINNTY	INFINITY
FIILLMOS	MILFOILS
FIILLMSY	FLIMSILY
FIILMNRY	INFIRMLY
FIILMPSY	SIMPLIFY
FIILRTUY	FRUITILY
FIILTTUY	FUTILITY
FIIMOPRS	PISIFORM
FIINNOSU	INFUSION
FIINOPRT	IN PROFIT
FIINORST	IRON FIST
FIINORTU	FRUITION
FIINOSSS	FISSIONS
FIKKLNOS	KINSFOLK
FIKLLOSY	FOLKSILY
FIKLNSSU	SKINFULS
FIKNOSST	SOFT SKIN
FILLLTTU	FULL TILT
FILLLUWY	WILFULLY
FILLNSUY	SINFULLY
FILLOPPY	FLOPPILY
FILLOSTU	FILLS OUT
FILNOSUX	FLUXIONS
FILOOOTU	OUT OF OIL
FILOPTUU	FOUL IT UP
FILORSST	FLORISTS
FILORSTY	FROSTILY
FILSSTTU	FLUTISTS
FILSTTUY	STULTIFY
FIMNORSU	UNIFORMS
FIMORTUY	FUMITORY
FIMRSTUU	FUTURISM
FINOORTW	NOW FOR IT
FINORRTU	RUN FOR IT
FINORSSS	FRISSONS
FIORRSTW	FIRST ROW
FIORRTTY	TRY FOR IT
FIORSTTU	FIRST OUT

FIPRSTTU	PUT FIRST	GGHIINST	SIGHTING	GHHIILST	LIGHTISH
FIRSTTUU	FUTURIST	GGHIIPRS	PRIGGISH	GHHIINSW	WHISHING
FIRTTUUY	FUTURITY	GGHILSSU	SLUGGISH	GHHIJMPU	HIGH JUMP
FJLLOUYY	JOYFULLY	GGHINORU	ROUGHING	GHHILOSU	GHOULISH
FKLOOOPR	POOR FOLK	GGHINOST	GHOSTING	GHHIMNPU	HUMPHING
FKMOORRW	FORMWORK	GGHINOSU	SOUGHING	GHHINNOO	HIGH NOON
FKNOORTX	FORT KNOX	GGHIORTT	GOT RIGHT	GHHINOTT	HOT NIGHT
FKOOORTW	FOOTWORK	GGHKNNOO	HONG KONG	GHHINRSU	RUNS HIGH
FKOORRSW	WORKS FOR	GGHNORUY	GO HUNGRY	GHHINSSU	SHUSHING
FKOORSTU	FORKS OUT	GGHOORTU	GOT ROUGH	GHHINSTY	SHY THING
FLLMNOOU	FULL MOON	GGHOOTTU	GOT TOUGH	GHHIOPST	HIGH SPOT
FLLNOOOW	FOLLOW ON	GGHOTUUY	TOUGH GUY		HIGHSPOT
	FOLLOW-ON	GGIIINNT	IGNITING	GHHIORSU	ROUGHISH
FLLOOPUW	FOLLOW UP	GGIIINNV	GIVING IN	GHHOORTU	THOROUGH
	FOLLOW-UP	GGIIJLNN	JINGLING	GHHOSTTU	THOUGHTS
FLLOPSTU	FULL STOP	GGIILLNO	GOING ILL	GHIIIJRS	IRISH JIG
FLLOSSTU	FULL TOSS	GGIILLNR	GRILLING	GHIIKNNT	THINKING
FLMNOOSU	MOUFLONS	GGIILMNN	MINGLING	GHIIKNPS	KINGSHIP
FLMNORUU	MOURNFUL	GGIILNNS	GIN SLING	GHIIKNRS	SHIRKING
FLMOOOST	TOMFOOLS		SINGLING	GHIIKNSW	WHISKING
FLMOORST	LOST FORM	GGIILNNT	GLINTING	GHIILLNS	SHILLING
FLNOOPSU	SPOONFUL		TINGLING	GHIILMTY	MIGHTILY
FLOOOPRT	TOP FLOOR	GGIINNNR	GRINNING	GHIILNRW	WHIRLING
FLOOSTUW	OUTFLOWS	GGIINNOR	IGNORING	GHIILTTW	TWILIGHT
FLRSTTUU	TRUSTFUL	GGIINNSS	SING SING	GHIIMMNS	SHIMMING
FMNOORRU	MOURN FOR	GGIINNSW	SWINGING	GHIIMNNU	INHUMING
FMOOOPRR	POOR FORM	GGIINNTW	TWINGING	GHIIMRST	RIGHTISM
FMOORTTU	TOT OF RUM	GGIINPPR	GRIPPING	GHIINNNS	SHINNING
FMRSSTUU	FRUSTUMS	GGIINPUV	GIVING UP	GHIINNNT	THINNING
FNOORRSW	FORSWORN	GGIINRST	RINGGITS	GHIINOST	HOISTING
FNOORRTW	FRONT ROW	GGIINRTT	GRITTING	GHIINPPS	SHIPPING
FNOORSSU	SUNROOFS	GGIIRRSS	GRIS-GRIS	GHIINPPW	WHIPPING
FNORRSUU	FOUR RUNS	GGIKKNNO	KING KONG	GHIINRRS	SHIRRING
FNORSTTU	TURN SOFT	GGILLNUY	GULLYING	GHIINRST	SHIRTING
FOOOPRST	ROOFTOPS	GGILLOOW	GOLLIWOG	GHIINRTW	WRITHING
FOOPRSTU	FOUR TOPS	GGILMNOO	GLOOMING	GHIINSST	INSIGHTS
FOOPRTTY	TOP FORTY	GGILNNOS	LONGINGS	GHIINSSW	SWISHING
FOOPSSTT	SOFT SPOT	GGILNNOU	LOUNGING	GHIINSTW	WHISTING
	SOFT TOPS	GGILNNPU	PLUNGING		WHITINGS
FOORSTTX	FOX-TROTS	GGILNOOW	GOING LOW	GHIINWZZ	WHIZZING
FOORSTUW	FOUR TWOS	GGILNORW	GROWLING	GHIIOSTV	VISIGOTH
FOOSSTTY	SOFT TOYS	GGILNORY	GLORYING	GHIIRSTT	RIGHTIST
FOPSSSTU	FUSSPOTS	GGILNOSS	GLOSSING	GHIISTTT	SIT TIGHT
FORSTTUU	TURFS OUT		GOSLINGS	GHIJKNNO	KING JOHN
GGGGIILN	GIGGLING	GGILNTTU	GLUTTING	GHIKLNTY	KNIGHTLY
GGGGILNO	GOGGLING	GGILNUZZ	GUZZLING	GHIKLSTY	SKYLIGHT
GGGIIJLN	JIGGLING	GGILQSUY	SQUIGGLY	GHIKNSTY	NIGHT SKY
GGGIILNN	NIGGLING	GGIMNOOR	GROOMING	GHILLNOO	HOLLOING
GGGIILNW	WIGGLING	GGINNOOS	GOINGS ON	GHILLOPU	GO UPHILL
GGGIINNS	SNIGGING		GOINGS-ON	GHILLSTY	SLIGHTLY
GGGIINSW	SWIGGING	GGINNOOW	GOING NOW	GHILNOPS	LONGSHIP
GGGIINTW	TWIGGING	GGINNOPP	PING-PONG	GHILNOSS	SLOSHING
GGGIJLNO	JOGGLING	GGINNOPR	PRONGING	GHILNOTW	NIGHT OWL
GGGIJLNU	JUGGLING	GGINNOPS	SPONGING	GHILNRUY	HUNGRILY
GGGILNOS	SLOGGING	GGINNORW	WRONGING	GHILNSTU	HUSTLING
GGGILNOT	TOGGLING	GGINNOSS	SINGSONG		SUNLIGHT
GGGILNPU	PLUGGING	GGINNOTU	TONGUING	GHILOPRS	SHOP GIRL
GGGILNRU	GURGLING	GGINNRTU	GRUNTING	GHILOPSS	SHIPS LOG
GGGILNSU	SLUGGING	GGINOORV	GROOVING	GHILORSW	SHOW GIRL
GGGILORY	GROGGILY	GGINOOST	STOOGING		SHOWGIRL
GGGINNOS	SNOGGING	GGINOOTU	GOING OUT	GHILPSTU	LIGHTS UP
GGGINNSU	SNUGGING		OUTGOING	GHILRSSY	SHY GIRLS
GGGINOOT	GOT GOING	GGINOPRU	GROUPING	GHIMNOTU	MOUTHING
GGHHIINS	SING HIGH	GGINORSS	GROSSING	GHIMNPTU	THUMPING
GGHHIISW	WHIGGISH	GGINORSU	GROUSING	GHIMNSTU	GUNSMITH
GGHHINSU	SUNG HIGH	GGINORTU	GROUTING	GHINNNSU	SHUNNING
GGHHISTU	THUGGISH	GGINRSST	G STRINGS	GHINNORT	NORTHING
GGHIILNT	LIGHTING		G-STRINGS	GHINNOST	NOTHINGS
GGHIIMSW	WHIGGISM	GGLLPUUY	PLUG UGLY	GHINNSTU	SHUNTING
GGHIINRT	GIRTHING	GGNOORST	GO STRONG	GHINOOPT	PHOTOING
	RIGHTING	GGNOORTW	GOT WRONG	GHINOOPW	WHOOPING

GHINOOST	SHOOTING	GIIKNNTT	KNITTING	GIINOPRR	IRON GRIP
	SOOTHING	GIIKNPPS	SKIPPING	GIINOPST	POSITING
GHINOOSW	WOOSHING	GIIKNRRS	SKIRRING	GIINOPTV	PIVOTING
GHINOOTT	TOOTHING	GIIKNRST	SKIRTING	GIINPPPU	PIPING UP
GHINOPPS	SHOPPING	GIILLMNU	ILLUMING	GIINPPQU	QUIPPING
GHINOPPW	WHOPPING	GIILLNOR	GRILLION	GIINPPRT	TRIPPING
GHINORST	SHORTING	GIILLNOS	GILLIONS	GIINPRST	SPIRTING
GHINORTW	INGROWTH	GIILLNQU	QUILLING	GIINPRSU	RISING UP
	RIGHT NOW	GIILLNRT	TRILLING		UPRISING
	WORTHING	GIILLNST	STILLING	GIINPSTT	SPITTING
GHINOSST	SONG HITS	GIILLNSU	ILL-USING	GIINQRSU	SQUIRING
GHINOSSW	SHOWINGS	GIILLNSW	SWILLING	GIINQRTU	QUIRTING
GHINOSTU	SHOUTING	GIILLPSW	PIG SWILL	GIINQUZZ	QUIZZING
	SOUTHING	GIILLTUY	GUILTILY	GIINRRST	STIRRING
GHINOSUY	YOUNGISH	GIILMMNS	SLIMMING	GIINRSTW	WRITINGS
GHINOTTU	NIGHT OUT	GIILMNPW	WIMPLING	GIINSSTT	SITTINGS
GHINPSSU	GUNSHIPS	GIILMNPY	IMPLYING	GIINSSTU	SUITINGS
GHINRRUY	HURRYING	GIILMNZZ	MIZZLING	GIINSSTW	SWINGS IT
GHINSSTII	HISTINGS	GIILMPRS	PII GRIMS	GIINSTTW	TWISTING
	UNSIGHTS	GIILMPSU	PUGILISM	GIINTTTW	TWITTING
GHIOORTT	TOO RIGHT!	GIILNNOP	PILING ON	GIJKLMSU	MILK JUGS
GHIORSTU	ROUGHS IT	GIILNNPU	LINING UP	GIJKLNOY	JOKINGLY
GHIORTTU	OUTRIGHT	GIILNOPT	PILOTING	GIJLLNOY	JOLLYING
	RIGHT OUT	GIILNPPR	RIPPLING	GIJLNOST	JOSTLING
GHIPRSTU	UPRIGHTS	GIILNPPS	LIPPINGS	GIJNOSTU	JOUSTING
GHIPRTTU	PUT RIGHT		SLIPPING	GIKKLNSU	SKULKING
GHJNRUUY	HUNG JURY	GIILNPPT	TIPPLING	GIKLMOOR	LOOK GRIM
GHLMOOOY	HOMOLOGY	GIILNPPU	PILING UP	GIKLNNOP	PLONKING
GHLNNOOR	LONGHORN	GIILNPRT	TRIPLING	GIKLNNPU	PLUNKING
GHLNOOST	LONG SHOT	GIILNPUV	LIVING UP	GIKLNOSW	SILK GOWN
GHLOOORY	HOROLOGY	GIILNQSU	QUISLING	GIKNNOTT	KNOTTING
GHNNOOTU	HUNG ON TO	GIILNQTU	QUILTING	GIKNNOUY	UNYOKING
GHNOOOSW	GOON SHOW	GIILNRSW	SWIRLING	GIKNOOPS	SPOOKING
GHNOPRSY	GRYPHONS	GIILNRTW	TWIRLING	GIKNOOTW	TOOK WING
GHNOPYYY	HYPOGYNY	GIILNSST	LISTINGS	GIKNOPST	KING POST
GHNOSSTU	GUNSHOTS	GIILNSTU	LINGUIST	GIKNORST	STROKING
	SHOTGUNS	GIILNSTY	STINGILY	GIKNORSW	WORKINGS
GHNOTTUU	TOUGH NUT	GIILNSZZ	SIZZLING	GIKNOSTW	TWO KINGS
GHOORTUU	ROUGH OUT	GIILPSTU	PUGILIST	GILLMOOY	GLOOMILY
GHOORTUY	YOGHOURT	GIILRTTY	GRITTILY	GILLNORT	TROLLING
GHOPRSUU	ROUGHS UP	GIIMMNRT	TRIMMING	GILLNOST	LONG LIST
GHOPRTUW	UPGROWTH	GIIMMNRU	IMMURING	GILLNOVY	LOVINGLY
GHOSSTUW	SHOW GUTS	GIIMMNSW	SWIMMING	GILLNOWY	LOW-LYING
GIIILMNT	LIMITING	GIIMMNOV	MOVING IN		LYING LOW
GIIILNNV	LIVING IN	GIIMMNOY	IGNOMINY	GILLNPRU	RING PULL
GIIIMNNX	MIXING IN	GIIMMNTU	MINUTING		RING-PULL
GIIINNOS	IONISING	GIIMNOPS	IMPOSING	GILLNSUY	SULLYING
GIIINNOT	IGNITION	GIIMNOTT	OMITTING	GILLOOPW	POLLIWOG
GIIINNOZ	IONIZING	GIIMNOTV	VOMITING	GILLOSSY	GLOSSILY
GIIINNTV	INVITING	GIIMNPPR	PRIMPING	GILMMNSU	SLUMMING
GIIINSTV	VISITING	GIIMNPRS	PRIMINGS	GILMNOTT	MOTTLING
GIIJMNOS	JINGOISM	GIIMNPRU	UMPIRING	GILMNOTU	MOULTING
GIIJNNOT	JOINTING	GIIMNPTU	IMPUTING	GILMNOVY	MOVINGLY
GIIJNNRU	INJURING	GIIMNPUX	MIXING UP	GILMNPPU	PLUMPING
GIIJNOST	JINGOIST	GIIMNSSU	MISUSING	GILMNPRU	RUMPLING
GIIKKLNP	KINGKLIP	GIINNNOS	NOSING IN	GILMNPSU	SLUMPING
GIIKLLNS	KILLINGS	GIINNNOT	INTONING	GILMNSUY	MUSINGLY
GIIKLNNS	INKLINGS	GIINNNPS	SPINNING	GILMNUZZ	MUZZLING
GIIKLNNT	TINKLING	GIINNNRU	INURNING	GILMOOSY	MISOLOGY
GIIKLNNW	WINKLING	GIINNNSS	INN SIGNS	GILMPRUY	GRUMPILY
GIIKLNRS	SKIRLING	GIINNNSW	WINNINGS	GILMPSSY	GYM SLIPS
GIIKLNTT	KITTLING	GIINNNTU	TUNING IN		GYMSLIPS
GIIKMMNS	SKIMMING	GIINNNTW	TWINNING	GILNNORU	IRON LUNG
GIIKMNPS	SKIMPING	GIINNOPT	POINTING	GILNNRSU	NURSLING
GIIKMNRS	SMIRKING	GIINNOQU	QUOINING	GILNNSSU	UNSLINGS
GIIKNNNS	SKINNING	GIINNORS	ROSINING	GILNNUZZ	NUZZLING
GIIKNNOV	INVOKING	GIINNPPS	SNIPPING	GILNOOPS	SPOOLING
GIIKNNPR	PRINKING	GIINNPRS	IN SPRING	GILNOORT	ROOTLING
GIIKNNPS	KINGPINS	GIINNPRT	PRINTING	GILNOOST	STOOLING
	PINK GINS	GIINNSSW	INSWINGS	GILNOOSY	SINOLOGY
GIIKNNST	STINKING	GIINNSTT	STINTING	GILNOOTT	TOOTLING

GILNOPPP	PLOPPING	GINOPSST	POSTINGS	GNPPRSUU	SPRUNG UP
GILNOPPS	SLOPPING		SIGNPOST	GNPRSTUU	STRUNG UP
GILNOPPT	TOPPLING	GINOPSTT	SPOTTING		STRUNG-UP
GILNOPRW	PROWLING	GINOPSTU	SPOUTING	GOOPPPRU	POP GROUP
GILNOPTT	PLOTTING	GINORRWY	WORRYING	GOORSSTW	TWO GROSS
GILNOSSW	SINGS LOW	GINORSTU	RINGS OUT	GOORSTUW	GROWS OUT
GILNOSTT	SLOTTING	GINORSTW	WORSTING		OUTGROWS
GILNOSTU	SLING OUT	GINORTTT	TROTTING	HHHHSSUU	HUSH-HUSH
	TOUSLING	GINORTTU	TUTORING	HHIINNST	THINNISH
GILNOSWW	SWING LOW	GINORTUW	WRING OUT	HHIIPSST	PHTHISIS
GILNOTUY	OUTLYING	GINOSSTU	SINGS OUT	HHJNORTU	JOHN HURT
GILNPPRU	PURPLING	GINOSTTW	SWOTTING	HHOOOOPP	POOH-POOH
GILNPPSU	SUPPLING	GINOSTUW	OUTSWING	HHOOPPRS	PHOSPHOR
GILNPRSU	SLURPING	GINPPRSU	SPRING UP	HHOOSSTT	HOTSHOTS
GILNPSSU	PLUS SIGN	GINPRRSU	SPURRING	HHORRSUU	RUSH HOUR
GILNPUZZ	PUZZLING	GINPRSSY	SPY RINGS	HIIILMNS	NIHILISM
GILNRRSU	SLURRING	GINPRSTU	SPURTING	HIIILNST	NIHILIST
GILNRSTU	LUSTRING		STRING UP	HIIINRST	RHINITIS
	RUSTLING	GINPRSUU	PURSUING	HIIISSTT	THIS IS IT
GILNRTYY	TRYINGLY		USURPING	HIIKMRSS	SKIRMISH
GILNSSTU	TUSSLING	GINPSSUW	UPSWINGS	HIIKNNST	THIN SKIN
GILOOOST	OOLOGIST	GINPTTUY	PUTTYING	HIIKSSTT	SKITTISH
GILOOPRR	POOR GIRL	GINRSSTU	TRUSSING	HIILLLLM	MILL HILL
GILOORSU	GLORIOUS	GINRSTTU	TRUSTING	HIILMPSY	IMPISHLY
GILOORVY	VIROLOGY	GINRSTTY	TRYSTING	HIILMTUY	HUMILITY
GILOOSSS	ISOGLOSS	GINRSTUU	SUTURING	HIILPSSY	SYPHILIS
GILORTTY	GROTTILY	GIOORRSU	RIGOROUS	HIIMNSTT	TINSMITH
GIMMNRUY	GIN RUMMY	GIOORSUV	VIGOROUS	HIINPSTW	TWINSHIP
GIMNNOOV	MOVING ON	GIOPRRSU	PRURIGOS	HIKLOSST	SHOT SILK
GIMNNORS	MORNINGS	GIOPRSSY	GOSSIPRY	HIKNNORS	INKHORNS
GIMNNORU	MOURNING	GIORSSSX	SIX GROSS	HIKNNOST	THINKS ON
GIMNNOTU	MOUNTING	GIORSTUY	RUGOSITY	HIKNOTTU	THINK OUT
GIMNOORS	MOORINGS	GJLMNOPU	LONG JUMP	HIKNPSTU	THINKS UP
GIMNOORT	MOTORING	GKLLOOUY	UGLY LOOK	HIKOOPSS	SPOOKISH
GIMNOOSS	OSMOSING	GKOOORTW	GO TO WORK	HIKOPSSY	KYPHOSIS
GIMNOPST	STOMPING	GLLMNOSU	GUN MOLLS	HILLMSUY	MULISHLY
GIMNOPTU	GUMPTION	GLLNOOST	LONG LOST	HILLOSWY	OWLISHLY
GIMNOPUV	MOVING UP	GLLOOPTY	POLYGLOT	HILMNOOT	MONOLITH
GIMNORRW	RINGWORM	GLMNOOOR	LONG ROOM	HILMPPSU	PLUMPISH
GIMNORST	STORMING	GLMOOOPY	POMOLOGY	HILOOSTT	OTOLITHS
GIMNOSYY	MISOGYNY	GLMOORWW	GLOW WORM	HILOOTTY	TOOTHILY
GIMNPRTU	TRUMPING		GLOWWORM	HILOPPSU	POLISH UP
GIMNPSTU	STUMPING	GLMOOYYZ	ZYMOLOGY	HILOPPSY	POPISHLY
GIMNSTTU	SMUTTING	GLMORSUW	LUGWORMS	HILORTWY	HOLY WRIT
GINNNSTU	STUNNING	GLNNOORS	LORGNONS		WORTHILY
GINNOOPS	SNOOPING	GLNOOOSY	NOSOLOGY	HILPPRSU	PURPLISH
	SPOONING	GLNOOOTY	ONTOLOGY	HILPPSUY	UPPISHLY
GINNOOSW	SWOONING	GLNOOPRS	PROLONGS	HILSSTTU	SLUTTISH
GINNOOSZ	SNOOZING	GLNOOPST	LONG STOP	HIMNNOST	IN MONTHS
GINNOPTU	GUNPOINT	GLNOOPSY	POLYGONS	HIMNORRS	HORN-RIMS
GINNOPUW	OWNING UP	GLNOPYYY	POLYGYNY	HIMOOPRS	ISOMORPH
GINNORST	SNORTING	GLNORSTY	STRONGLY	HIMOPRSW	SHIPWORM
GINNORTY	TRYING ON	GLNOSTTU	GLUTTONS	HIMOPSSS	SOPHISMS
GINNPRSU	SPURNING	GLNOSTUU	SLUNG OUT	HIMORSTU	HUMORIST
GINNPTUU	TUNING UP	GLNOSUWW	SWUNG LOW	HIMOSSTT	THOMISTS
GINNRSTU	TURNINGS	GLNOTTUY	GLUTTONY	HIMOTTVZ	MITZVOTH
	UNSTRING	GLOOOPTY	TOPOLOGY	HIMPRSTU	TRIUMPHS
GINNSTTU	STUNTING	GLOOPTYY	TYPOLOGY	HINNORTW	THROWN IN
GINNSTUW	WING NUTS	GLOORSWY	ROSY GLOW	HINNSSUY	SUNSHINY
GINOOPPS	OPPOSING	GMMNOTUY	TOMMY GUN	HINOORRR	IN HORROR
GINOOPRS	SPOORING	GMMPSUUW	MUGWUMPS	HINOORST	IRON SHOT
GINOOPRT	TROOPING	GMNNOOYY	MONOGYNY	HINOORSZ	HORIZONS
GINOOPST	STOOPING	GNNRSTUU	UNSTRUNG	HINOPSSY	HYPNOSIS
GINOOPSW	SWOOPING	GNOOOPTT	GOT ON TOP	HINOPSTW	TOWNSHIP
GINOORST	ROOSTING	GNOOOTTW	GO TO TOWN	HINORSST	IN SHORTS
GINOPPPR	PROPPING	GNOOOTUY	TOO YOUNG	HINORSTU	RUSH INTO
GINOPPST	STOPPING	GNOOPPSS	POP SONGS	HINORSTW	THROW-INS
GINOPPSW	SWOPPING	GNOORTUW	GROWN OUT		THROWS IN
GINOPRST	SPORTING		OUTGROWN	HINOSSTU	SNOUTISH
GINOPRSU	IN GROUPS	GNOPRSUW	GROWN-UPS	HINOSTTU	THINS OUT
		GNORTUUW	WRUNG OUT	HIOPPSTW	WHIP TOPS

HIOPRSSW	WORSHIPS	IIKLMPSY	SKIMPILY	IJLNOQSU	JONQUILS
HIOPSSST	SOPHISTS	IIKLNOSS	OILSKINS	IJLRSTUY	JURY LIST
HIOPSTWY	SHOW PITY	IIKLNPPS	PINK SLIP	IJMNNSUY	SUNNY JIM
HIOQSUWZ	QUIZ SHOW	IIKLOSSX	SIX KILOS	IJMNOPTU	JUMP INTO
HIORSSUX	SIX HOURS	IIKNNSTU	SINK UNIT	IJMOPTTU	JUMP TO IT
HIOSSTTU	STOUTISH	IIKNOOTT	TOOK IT IN	IJMPSTUU	JUMP SUIT
HJKNNOOX	JOHN KNOX	IIKNOSTT	STOTINKI		JUMPSUIT
HJKNOPSU	JUNK SHOP	IILLMNOS	MILLIONS	IJMSSSTU	JUST MISS
HJNOOOPR	POOR JOHN	IILLNOPS	PILLIONS	IKKLNOSY	KOLINSKY
HKKLOOYZ	KOLKHOZY	IILLNORT	TRILLION	IKKLOOST	TOOK SILK
HKLOORTU	LOOK HURT	IILLNORW	IRON WILL	IKLMOPSS	MILKSOPS
HKMOOORW	HOOKWORM	IILLNOSU	ILLUSION	IKLMORSU	SOUR MILK
HKNOOSWW	KNOWS HOW	IILLNOSZ	ZILLIONS	IKLMORSW	SILKWORM
HKOOOPST	POTHOOKS	IILLSSTT	SIT STILL	IKLMORTW	MILKWORT
HKOOOSTU	SHOOK OUT	IILMNOST	NO LIMITS	IKLNOOOT	LOOK INTO
HKOOPRSW	WORKSHOP	IILMOTTY	MOTILITY	IKLNOOST	KILOTONS
HLLLOOWY	HOLLOWLY	IILNOOTV	VOLITION	IKLNOPST	SLIP KNOT
HLLPPSUU	PUSH-PULL	IILNOPST	SLIP INTO		SLIPKNOT
HLMOOSTY	SMOOTHLY	IILNORSS	SIRLOINS	IKLNPSSU	SPUN SILK
HLNOORSW	HORN OWLS	IILNPPST	SPLIT PIN	IKLOOPTU	LOOK IT UP
HLOOORST	SHOT POOL	IILNRTWY	WINTRILY	IKLOOSTT	TOOL KITS
HLOOOPSW	WOOL SHOP	IILNTYZZ	TIN LIZZY	IKLOOSTW	TWO KILOS
HLOOSVWY	HOLY VOWS	IILOPSTY	PILOSITY	IKLOPSTY	SKY PILOT
HLPRSSUU	SULPHURS	IILPRSSY	PRISSILY	IKMNPPSU	PUMPKINS
HMMNOOSY	HOMONYMS	IILRSTWY	WRISTILY	IKNOOPPS	SPION KOP
HMMNOOYY	HOMONYMY	IIMMMNSU	MINIMUMS	IKNPSSTU	SPUTNIKS
HMMOORSU	MUSHROOM	IIMMNTUY	IMMUNITY	IKNRRSSU	RUN RISKS
HMNOPSYY	SYMPHONY	IIMMOPST	OPTIMISM	IKOOPRRS	POOR RISK
HMOOORSW	SHOWROOM	IIMNNOOT	IN MOTION	IKOOPTTU	TOOK IT UP
HMOORSUU	HUMOROUS	IIMNNOSU	UNIONISM	IKOOPTTY	TOOK PITY
HNOOOSTT	NOT SO HOT	IIMNNOTU	MUNITION	IKOPSSTU	SKIPS OUT
HNOOPRSW	SHOPWORN	IIMNNTUY	IN MUTINY	IKORSSTU	KURTOSIS
HNOOPSTY	TYPHOONS	IIMNOOSS	OMISSION	IKORSTTU	OUTSKIRT
HNOORSTT	SHORT TON	IIMNOPRS	IMPRISON	ILLLLORT	TILL ROLL
HNOOSTUW	SHOWN OUT	IIMNORTT	INTROMIT	ILLLMOPS	PLIMSOLL
HNOPRTUW	THROWN UP	IIMNORTY	MINORITY	ILLLOOPP	LOLLIPOP
HNORRSTU	RUN SHORT	IIMNOSSS	MISSIONS	ILLLOOWY	WOOLLILY
	SHORT RUN	IIMNPRST	IMPRINTS	ILLMMRSS	MRS.MILLS
HNORTUWY	UNWORTHY		MISPRINT	ILLMNOSU	MULLIONS
HOOOPRST	POOR SHOT	IIMNPTUY	IMPUNITY	ILLMPTUY	MULTIPLY
HOOOPRSW	POOR SHOW	IIMNRSTY	MINISTRY	ILLNOPSY	LILY PONS
HOOOSTTU	SHOOT OUT	IIMOPSTT	OPTIMIST	ILLOPPSY	SLOPPILY
	SHOOT-OUT	IIMOTTVY	MOTIVITY	ILLOPRXY	PROLIXLY
HOOOSTTW	TWO HOOTS	IIMPRTUY	IMPURITY	ILLORSUY	ILLUSORY
HOOPSSTT	HOT SPOTS	IIMRRTUV	TRIUMVIR	ILLRSTUY	SULTRILY
	POT SHOTS	IIMSSTUW	SWIM SUIT	ILMNOOPU	POLONIUM
	POTSHOTS		SWIMSUIT	ILMNOSUU	LUMINOUS
HOOPSSTU	SHOOTS UP	IINNOOPS	OPINIONS	ILMOOORT	MOTOR OIL
HOOPSSTY	TOY SHOPS	IINNOPPT	PINPOINT	ILMOPPSU	OIL PUMPS
HOORSTUW	TWO HOURS	IINNOPRS	IN PRISON		POPULISM
HOORTTUW	THROW OUT	IINNOSTU	UNIONIST	ILMORSTU	TURMOILS
HOOSSTUW	SHOWS OUT	IINNRTTU	TURN IT IN	ILMORSTY	STORMILY
HOOSTTUU	SHOUT OUT	IINNSTTU	TINNITUS	ILMSSTUU	STIMULUS
HOPPRRYY	PORPHYRY	IINOOPST	POSITION	ILMSTTUY	SMUTTILY
HOPRSTUW	THROWS UP	IINOPTTW	TIP TO WIN	ILNNOTUW	UNTIL NOW
HORRSTTU	THRUSTOR	IINORSST	IRONISTS	ILNOOPSS	PLOSIONS
HORRTUUY	HURRY OUT	IINORSTT	INTROITS	ILNOOPSW	POOLS WIN
HORRWWYY	WHY WORRY?	IINOSSTZ	ZIONISTS	ILNOOSTU	SOLUTION
HOSSTTUU	SHUTS OUT	IINOSTVY	VINOSITY	ILNOOSTY	SNOOTILY
HPRSTTUU	UPTHRUST	IINPSSTX	SIX PINTS	ILNOOTUV	VOLUTION
IIILLMNP	MINIPILL	IIOOPSTV	OVIPOSIT	ILNOPRSU	PURLOINS
IIILMRSV	VIRILISM	IIOOQRSU	IROQUOIS	ILNOPSTU	UNSPOILT
IIILNOPP	PILIPINO	IIOPRRTY	PRIORITY	ILNORSST	NOSTRILS
IIILRTVY	VIRILITY	IIOPRSSS	PISSOIRS	ILNOSSTT	ON STILTS
IIIMMPRS	IMPRIMIS	IIORSSTV	VISITORS	ILNOSUVY	VINOUSLY
IIINPRST	IN SPIRIT	IIORSTUV	VIRTUOSI	ILNRUUXY	IN LUXURY
	INSPIRIT	IIOSTTTU	SIT IT OUT	ILOOOPRS	POOR SOIL
IIINQTUY	INIQUITY	IIPRSTTU	STIR IT UP	ILOOPPRS	PROPOLIS
IIJJSTUU	JIU-JITSU	IJKLLOSY	KILLJOYS	ILOOPRSU	POURS OIL
IIKLLNOS	SKILLION	IJKMPSSU	SKI JUMPS	ILOOSSST	SOLOISTS
IIKLLNSY	SLINKILY	IJLNOOTW	LOW JOINT	ILOPPSTU	POPULIST

ILOPRSTY	SPORTILY	IORSSTTU	TOURISTS	MNOOPTYY	TOPONYMY
ILOPSSTU	SLIPS OUT	IORSSUUU	USURIOUS	MNOPRSTU	NO TRUMPS
ILOPSTTY	SPOTTILY	IORSTTUY	TOURISTY		NO-TRUMPS
ILPPSSTU	SPLITS UP	IORSTUUV	VIRTUOUS	MNOPSTUU	MOUNTS UP
ILRSTTUY	TRUSTILY	IORTTTUY	TRY IT OUT	MNORSSTU	NOSTRUMS
ILSSSTTY	STYLISTS	IPRRRSTU	STIRRUPS	MNORSTUU	SURMOUNT
IMMNOORS	MORONISM	IPRRSTUU	PRURITUS	MOOORRTW	TOMORROW
IMMOPSTU	OPTIMUMS	IPRSSTUU	PURSUITS	MOORSTUU	TUMOROUS
IMNNOSUU	NUMINOUS	JLNOSTUY	ONLY JUST	MOPPSTUU	PUMPS OUT
IMNOORST	MONITORS	JLNSTUUY	UNJUSTLY	MORRSSTU	ROSTRUMS
IMNOORTY	MONITORY	JLOOSUYY	JOYOUSLY	NNOOOPST	PONTOONS
IMNOPRSW	PINWORMS	JMOPSTUU	JUMPS OUT		SPONTOON
IMNOSTUU	MUTINOUS	JNNOORRU	NONJUROR	NNOOPRSU	PRONOUNS
IMNOSTUW	MINUS TWO	JNOORSSU	SOJOURNS	NNOOPSSS	SPONSONS
IMOOPRRS	PROMISOR	KLLMNSUU	NUMSKULL	NNOPRTUU	TURN UPON
IMOOPRST	IMPOSTOR	KLLOOOTT	TOOK TOLL	NOOORSSU	SONOROUS
IMOOQSTU	MOSQUITO	KLMMOOOS	KOMSOMOL	NOOPRSSS	SPONSORS
IMOORSTT	MOTORIST	KLNOOOPU	LOOK UPON	NOOPSTUW	OWNS UP TO
IMOORSTU	TIMOROUS	KLNORSTY	KLYSTRON	NOPSSSTU	SUN SPOTS
IMOORTVY	VOMITORY	KLOOOPTU	LOOK UP TO		SUNSPOTS
IMORSTTZ	ST.MORITZ	KLOOOSTU	LOOKOUTS	NORRSTUU	TURN SOUR
IMPSSTUU	SUMS IT UP		LOOKS OUT	NORRTUUY	YOUR TURN
IMRSSSTU	SISTRUMS	KLOOPRSY	LOOK SPRY	NORSTTUU	TURNS OUT
IMRSSTTU	MISTRUST	KMOOORRW	WORKROOM	OOOOPRST	POTOROOS
INNNNOOU	NONUNION	KNNNOSUW	UNKNOWNS	OOOPRTTU	TROOP OUT
INNNORTU	TRUNNION	KNOOPSTT	TOPKNOTS	OOORSTTU	ROOTS OUT
INNOOOPT	NO OPTION	KOOOORTT	TOOK ROOT	OOPRSSTV	PROVOSTS
INNOOPST	NO POINTS	KOOOPRRW	POOR WORK	OOPRSTUU	POURS OUT
INNORSTU	RUNS INTO	KOOOSTVW	TOOK VOWS	OOPSSSTT	TOSSPOTS
INNORTTU	TURN INTO	KOOPRSTW	STOP WORK	OOPSSTTU	OUTPOSTS
	TURN IT ON		WORKTOPS		STOPS OUT
INNOTTWW	TWIN TOWN	KOORSTUW	OUTWORKS	OORSSTTU	SORT-OUTS
INOOOSSZ	ZOONOSIS		WORKOUTS		SORTS OUT
INOOPRST	PORTIONS		WORKS OUT	OORSTTTU	TROTS OUT
	POSITRON	LLLOOORS	LOO ROLLS	OORSTTUU	TORTUOUS
	SORPTION	LLMOOPRS	ROLLMOPS	OPPRRSTU	PURPORTS
INOOPSTT	SPITTOON	LLNOORST	STROLL ON!	OPPRSSTU	SUPPORTS
INOOPTTU	OUTPOINT	LLOOPRST	TROLLOPS	OPRSSSUU	SOURPUSS
	POINT OUT	LLOOPRTY	TROLLOPY	OPSTTTUW	TWO PUTTS
INOORSTU	IRONS OUT	LLOOPRYY	ROLY-POLY		
INOORSTY	SONORITY	LLOORSTU	ROLLS OUT		
INOOTTUW	OUT TO WIN	LLOOSSTU	LOST SOUL		
INOPPSTT	PINT POTS	LLOPSTUU	PULLOUTS		
INOPRTTU	PRINTOUT		PULLS OUT		
	TORN IT UP	LLOSUUVV	VOLVULUS		
INOPSSSU	POUSSINS	LMMPSSUU	LUMP SUMS		
INOPSSSY	SYNOPSIS	LMNOOOPY	MONOPOLY		
INOPSSTU	SPINS OUT	LMOOOOPR	POOL ROOM		
INOPSTTW	TWO PINTS	LMOOOORT	TOOLROOM		
INORRSTU	RUNS RIOT	LMOORSWW	SLOWWORM		
INOSTTTY	TINY TOTS	LMOPPRTY	PROMPTLY		
INPRSTTU	TURNSPIT	LMOPSTUW	TWO LUMPS		
INPRTTUU	TURN IT UP	LMRSSTUU	LUSTRUMS		
INRSSTTU	INTRUSTS	LNOOOPPY	POLO PONY		
	TRUSTS IN	LNOOOPRT	POLTROON		
IOOPRSSV	PROVISOS	LNOOSWWY	SNOWY OWL		
IOOPRSTY	ISOTROPY	LOOOORSS	OLOROSOS		
	POROSITY	LOOOPRSU	POOR SOUL		
IOORRSTY	SORORITY	LOOPPSUU	POPULOUS		
IOORSSTT	RISOTTOS	LOOPPSUY	POLYPOUS		
IOORSSUV	VOUSSOIR	LOOPRSUY	POROUSLY		
IOORSTTU	TORTIOUS	LORSSTUU	LUSTROUS		
IOORSTUV	VIRTUOSO	MMNOPSUU	SUMMON UP		
IOORSUUX	UXORIOUS	MMOORTTY	TOMMYROT		
IOOSTTUZ	ZOOT SUIT	MMOPSSTY	SYMPTOMS		
IOPPSSTT	PIT STOPS	MNNOOOSS	MONSOONS		
IOPRSSTT	PROTISTS	MNNOOOTY	MONOTONY		
IOPRSSUU	SPURIOUS	MNNOSSYY	SYNONYMS		
IOPRSTTU	OUTSTRIP	MNNOSYYY	SYNONYMY		
IOPSSTTU	SPITS OUT	MNOOORXY	OXYMORON		
IORRSUVV	SURVIVOR	MNOOPSTY	TOPONYMS		

AAAABCLLV	BALACLAVA	AAABLOPRS	PARABOLAS
AAAABIKLL	BALALAIKA	AAACCCHHH	CHA CHA CHA
AAAACCHMT	TACAMAHAC	AAACCDELV	CAVALCADE
AAAACIRRU	ARAUCARIA	AAACCDHKR	HAD A CRACK
AAAACMNRT	CATAMARAN	AAACCEPRS	CARAPACES
AAAADILLM	DALAI LAMA	AAACCHKRS	HAS A CRACK
AAAAHHJMR	MAHARAJAH	AAACCINSU	CAUCASIAN
AAAAHMNPT	PANAMA HAT	AAACCIRTT	ATARACTIC
AAAAKNRSW	ARAWAKANS	AAACCRSTT	CATARACTS
AAAALLMMY	MALAYALAM	AAACDDELR	DEAL A CARD
AAABBDELR	ABRADABLE	AAACDEEFM	MADE A FACE
AAABBGINN	BIG BANANA	AAACDEEHR	RACE AHEAD
AAABBINRR	BARBARIAN	AAACDEEKM	MADE A CAKE
AAABCCEMN	MACCABEAN	AAACDEELN	LEAD AN ACE
AAABCCHLN	BACCHANAL	AAACDEKRT	TAKE A CARD
AAABCCHNR	CHARABANC	AAACDELLM	MADE A CALL
AAABCCLLS	CALLS A CAB	AAACDEMNR	CARE A DAMN
AAABCDIIT	ADIABATIC	AAACDENRR	CARE A DARN
AAABCDRRU	BARRACUDA	AAACDENRW	DRAW AN ACE
AAABCEEKK	BAKE A CAKE	AAACDHKNS	HAD A SNACK
AAABCEKKT	TAKE ABACK	AAACDILLP	PAID A CALL
AAABCEKNT	TAKEN A CAB	AAACDILNR	CALANDRIA
AAABCEKST	TAKES A CAB	AAACDINNS	CANADIANS
AAABCELTU	ACETABULA	AAACDLPRY	PLAY A CARD
AAABCEMRT	CARBAMATE	AAACDNNOS	ANACONDAS
AAABCESSY	EASY AS A B C	AAACDNPRS	PANDA CARS
AAABCGIKN	BACK AGAIN	AAACDNRSS	CASSANDRA
AAABCHILS	HAILS A CAB	AAACEEFKM	MAKE A FACE
AAABCHNNR	ANABRANCH	AAACEEHRV	HAVE A CARE
AAABCIKTT	KATABATIC	AAACEEHSV	HAVE A CASE
AAABCKSWY	BACKS AWAY	AAACEEKKM	MAKE A CAKE
AAABDELPT	ADAPTABLE	AAACEENRS	CAESAREAN
AAABDELRV	LAVA BREAD	AAACEGLNT	AT A GLANCE
AAABDELRW	AWARDABLE	AAACEHHTV	HAVE A CHAT
AAABDILLS	SABADILLA	AAACEHLNV	AVALANCHE
AAABDINWY	IN A BAD WAY	AAACEHSWY	CHASE AWAY
AAABDLLOR	ALL ABOARD	AAACEIMPR	PARAMECIA
	ALL ABROAD	AAACEINOR	OCEANARIA
AAABDNNNS	BANDANNAS	AAACEINRS	CAESARIAN
AAABEFKLO	BAKE A LOAF	AAACEJMNS	JAMES CAAN
AAABEHHSV	HAVE A BASH	AAACEKLLM	MAKE A CALL
AAABEHHTV	HAVE A BATH	AAACEKLLT	TAKE A CALL
AAABEHKTT	TAKE A BATH	AAACELLPP	A CAPPELLA
AAABEHLLV	HAVE A BALL	AAACELNPY	PLAY AN ACE
AAABEHNRS	HABANERAS	AAACELNWY	CLEAN AWAY
AAABEHPTT	BEAT A PATH	AAACELRWY	CLEAR AWAY
AAABEHSTV	HAVE A STAB	AAACEMMNR	CAMERAMAN
AAABEILLV	AVAILABLE	AAACEMPRT	CAME APART
AAABEKLOR	KOALA BEAR	AAACENRTT	AT A CANTER
AAABEKRWY	BREAK AWAY	AAACFILNT	FANATICAL
	BREAKAWAY	AAACGILLN	CALL AGAIN
AAABELLPT	PALATABLE	AAACGIMWY	MAGIC AWAY
AAABELNST	ALAN BATES	AAACGINRU	NICARAGUA
AAABELNSV	NAVAL BASE	AAACGKSTT	GAS ATTACK
AAABELRST	ALABASTER	AAACGLMNO	ALMA COGAN
AAABGLWYY	GALWAY BAY	AAACGLSSW	SCALAWAGS
AAABGRSTU	RUTABAGAS	AAACGMNRS	ARMAGNACS
AAABHNSTU	SAUNA BATH	AAACGNORT	ANGORA CAT
AAABILLVY	AVAILABLY	AAACHIMST	CHIASMATA
AAABILNNO	BANANA OIL	AAACHINPS	ANAPHASIC
AAABILNNS	ALBANIANS	AAACHKNSS	HAS A SNACK
AAABINRSV	BAVARIANS	AAACHLLLT	CALL A HALT
AAABLLPTY	PALATABLY	AAACHLNRT	CHARLATAN

AAACHLPRR	CHAPARRAL	AAADHITWY	HAD IT AWAY
AAACHLRRT	CATARRHAL	AAADHLLSY	HAS ALL DAY
AAACHMRWY	MARCH AWAY	AAADHLMSS	HAM SALADS
AAACHMTWY	AWAY MATCH	AAADHPRTY	HAD A PARTY
AAACIIRSS	ACARIASIS	AAADIKKNS	AKKADIANS
AAACILLTX	CALL A TAXI	AAADILLNP	PALLADIAN
AAACILNPT	APLANATIC	AAADILMNT	DALMATIAN
AAACILRTU	ACTUARIAL	AAADILPRT	LAID A TRAP
AAACINOPR	PARANOIAC	AAADIMNRX	MAX ADRIAN
AAACINOTT	CATATONIA	AAADINRWY	DRAIN AWAY
AAACIRSTX	ATARAXICS	AAADJNNPR	PANJANDRA
AAACLLLMR	ALARM CALL	AAADLMNTY	ADAMANTLY
AAACLLPSY	PAYS A CALL	AAADLNNSY	ANALYSAND
AAACLMNPU	CAMPANULA	AAADLORST	ROAD ATLAS
AAACMORST	SARCOMATA	AAADNPUWY	UP AND AWAY
AAACNOSSV	CASANOVAS	AAADNRWWY	DRAWN AWAY
AAACPRSTT	ACTS A PART	AAADNSTWY	STAND AWAY
AAACRRWYY	CARRY AWAY	AAADPRRTW	DRAW APART
AAACRSTWY	CARTS AWAY	AAADRSWWY	AWAY DRAWS
AAACSSTWY	CASTAWAYS		DRAWS AWAY
	CASTS AWAY	AAAEEEGNS	AEGEAN SEA
AAADDDEEH	DEAD AHEAD	AAAEEGLPV	LEAVE A GAP
AAADDEELM	MADE A DEAL	AAAEEGLRR	LARGE AREA
AAADDEEMT	MADE A DATE	AAAEEGNRW	EARN A WAGE
AAADDEFWY	FADED AWAY	AAAEEGRRR	ARREARAGE
AAADDEGNY	DAY AND AGE	AAAEEHLMV	HAVE A MEAL
AAADDEHIN	HAD AN IDEA	AAAEEHLSV	HAVE A SALE
AAADDEHLN	LAND AHEAD	AAAEEHNRV	HAVE AN EAR
AAADDEHMR	HAD A DREAM	AAAEEHSTV	HAVE A SEAT
AAADDEMMR	DEAR MADAM	AAAEEKLMM	MAKE A MEAL
AAADDHLLY	HAD ALL DAY	AAAEEKLMS	MAKE A SALE
AAADDHMRY	HAMADRYAD	AAAEEKMMN	MAKE A NAME
AAADDLMOS	OLD AS ADAM	AAAEEKSTT	TAKE A SEAT
AAADDLSSY	SALAD DAYS	AAAEELMST	EATS A MEAL
AAADEEGLV	GAVE A LEAD	AAAEEMNNR	EARN A NAME
AAADEEHLP	LEAP AHEAD	AAAEENTWY	EATEN AWAY
AAADEEHTV	HAVE A DATE	AAAEFHKLW	HALF AWAKE
AAADEEKLM	MAKE A DEAL	AAAEFHLLV	HAVE A FALL
AAADEEKMT	MAKE A DATE	AAAEFKLLT	TAKE A FALL
AAADEELMM	MADE A MEAL	AAAEGGRTV	AGGRAVATE
AAADEELMS	MADE A SALE	AAAEGILNS	ANALGESIA
AAADEEMMN	MADE A NAME	AAAEGIMNS	SAME AGAIN
AAADEFSWY	FADES AWAY	AAAEGKLTV	GAVE A TALK
AAADEGHNV	GAVE A HAND	AAAEGLMPY	PLAY A GAME
AAADEGMNV	GAVE A DAMN	AAAEGLMTU	GUATEMALA
AAADEGMRW	WAR DAMAGE	AAAEGLNNT	AT AN ANGLE
AAADEGNRV	GAVE A DARN	AAAEGLNPR	RANG A PEAL
AAADEGNTV	ADVANTAGE	AAAEGLRWY	LAY A WAGER
AAADEHHMS	MADE A HASH	AAAEGMSWY	AWAY GAMES
AAADEHINS	HAS AN IDEA	AAAEGNPPS	APPANAGES
AAADEHKNT	TAKE A HAND	AAAEHHKMS	MAKE A HASH
AAADEHLNP	PLAN AHEAD	AAAEHKLRV	HAVE A LARK
AAADEHMRS	HAS A DREAM	AAAEHLNPV	HAVE A PLAN
AAADEHMRT	THE ARMADA	AAAEHLORW	WEAR A HALO
AAADEHRTV	THERAVADA	AAAEHMMOT	HAEMATOMA
AAADEHSTY	STAY AHEAD	AAAEHNPSS	ANAPHASES
AAADEKMMR	MADE A MARK	AAAEIKLNW	LAIN AWAKE
AAADELLMR	ALL A DREAM	AAAEIKTTX	TAKE A TAXI
AAADELMMR	MARMALADE	AAAEIQTUV	AQUA VITAE
AAADELMPY	MADE A PLAY	AAAEJMNRT	JEAN MARAT
AAADELPPY	APPLE A DAY	AAAEKKLTW	TAKE A WALK
AAADEMNOT	ADENOMATA	AAAEKKMMR	MAKE A MARK
AAADEMNSU	AD NAUSEAM	AAAEKLMPY	MAKE A PLAY
AAADEMPSS	MADE A PASS	AAAEKLMSW	MAKES A LAW
AAADENNYY	YEA AND NAY	AAAEKLNSY	LAKE NYASA
AAADENVWW	WAVE A WAND	AAAEKLSWY	LEAKS AWAY
AAADEOPTZ	ZAPATEADO	AAAEKMPSS	MAKE A PASS
AAADFHIMT	ADAM FAITH	AAAEKMRSW	WEAR A MASK
AAADFHLRY	HALF A YARD	AAAEKNNPT	TAKEN A NAP
AAADGLMNR	GRAND LAMA	AAAEKNPST	TAKES A NAP
AAADHHPRZ	HAPHAZARD	AAAEKNSWY	SNEAK AWAY

252

AAAEKNTWY	TAKEN AWAY	AAAINNSSS	SASSANIAN
AAAEKPRTT	TAKE A PART	AAAINORST	SANATORIA
	TAKE APART	AAAINPPWY	APPIAN WAY
AAAEKSTWY	STAY AWAKE	AAAINRRTT	TARTARIAN
	TAKEAWAYS	AAAIPRSTX	PARATAXIS
	TAKES AWAY	AAAKLNNRV	NAVAL RANK
AAAELMMRT	ALMA MATER	AAAKLSWWY	WALKS AWAY
AAAELNNTT	ANTENATAL	AAAKOSSWY	SOAKAWAYS
AAAELNPQU	AQUAPLANE	AAALLLPTY	PALATALLY
AAAELNPST	PANATELAS	AAALLMPSS	LAS PALMAS
AAAELSTWY	STEAL AWAY	AAALNPRST	RATAPLANS
AAAELSVWY	SLAVE AWAY	AAALNRTTU	TARANTULA
AAAEMSTWY	AWAY TEAMS	AAALOOPPS	APPALOOSA
AAAENPRSV	PARAVANES	AAALPPRTY	PLAY A PART
AAAENRTTY	AT ANY RATE	AAALPRSTY	LAYS A TRAP
AAAEPRRTT	TEAR APART	AAALPSWYY	PLAYS AWAY
AAAERSTWY	TEARAWAYS	AAALSSTWY	SALTS AWAY
AAAERSWWY	WEARS AWAY	AAAMMMNRST	MAN-AT-ARMS
AAAESTWWY	WASTE AWAY	AAAMNOPRS	PANORAMAS
AAAFFHLLO	HALF A LOAF	AAAPPRSTU	APPARATUS
AAAFGIPST	FAT AS A PIG	AAAPRSTTY	STAY APART
AAAFIKNRS	AFRIKAANS	AAARRSTTW	START A WAR
AAAFILMNT	ANIMAL FAT	AAASSTWYY	STAYS AWAY
AAAFILNUV	AVIFAUNAL	AABBCCIRR	BRIC-A-BRAC
AAAFINSST	FANTASIAS	AABBCDEIL	ABDICABLE
AAAFLLPRT	FALL APART	AABBCDKOR	BACKBOARD
AAAFLLSWY	FALLS AWAY		BROAD BACK
AAAFLORST	SOLFATARA	AABBCDORS	SCABBARDS
AAAFRSSSS	SASSAFRAS	AABBCEHLL	BEACH BALL
AAAGGINNR	RANG AGAIN	AABBCEINR	CARIBBEAN
AAAGHLUWY	LAUGH AWAY	AABBCEKKR	BREAK BACK
AAAGHPPRR	PARAGRAPH	AABBCEKLR	BLACK BEAR
AAAGILMNS	SALAAMING	AABBCEKST	BEATS BACK
AAAGILNST	GALATIANS	AABBCINRS	BARBICANS
AAAGILRST	ASTRAGALI	AABBCKLLL	BLACKBALL
AAAGIMNRV	GRAVAMINA	AABBCSTTY	TABBY CATS
AAAGINNRU	GUARANIAN	AABBDDJOO	DO A BAD JOB
AAAGINRRS	AGRARIANS	AABBDEEKR	BAKE BREAD
AAAGLLOPT	AT A GALLOP	AABBDEELT	DEBATABLE
AAAGLRSST	ASTRAGALS	AABBDEEWY	EBBED AWAY
AAAGMMRSY	GAMMA RAYS	AABBDEMMO	MADE A BOMB
AAAGNSWWY	GNAWS AWAY	AABBDEMOR	BROAD BEAM
AAAGPRSSU	ASPARAGUS	AABBDENOR	BROAD BEAN
AAAHIILTX	HAIL A TAXI	AABBDEORS	BASEBOARD
AAAHIINSW	HAWAIIANS	AABBDGNRY	BABY GRAND
AAAHIMNRS	MAHARANIS	AABBDHIST	BAD HABITS
AAAHINSVV	VAISHNAVA	AABBDNRSS	BRASS BAND
AAAHISTWY	HAS IT AWAY	AABBDORSU	BOARD A BUS
AAAHKNRST	ASTRAKHAN	AABBEEKLR	BREAKABLE
AAAHLLOTY	AYATOLLAH	AABBEHILT	HABITABLE
AAAHLNNTU	NAHUATLAN	AABBEINRT	RABBINATE
AAAHLPRSY	ALPHA RAYS	AABBEIRRS	BARBARISE
AAAHLSUWY	HAULS AWAY	AABBEIRRZ	BARBARIZE
AAAHMNNTT	MANHATTAN	AABBEIRST	TAR BABIES
AAAHMNRST	AMARANTHS	AABBEKMMO	MAKE A BOMB
AAAHMNRTT	HARMATTAN	AABBELLSS	BASEBALLS
AAAHMRSTT	MAHRATTAS	AABBELOTW	AT A LOW EBB
AAAHPRSTY	HAS A PARTY	AABBEMNOR	EARN A BOMB
AAAIJMNRU	MARIJUANA	AABBERTWY	WATER BABY
AAAILMMMN	MAMMALIAN	AABBFFINY	BAFFIN BAY
AAAILNNOT	ANATOLIAN	AABBHILTY	HABITABLY
AAAILNNPR	PLANARIAN	AABBHIMST	SHABBATIM
AAAILNSST	ALSATIANS	AABBHMRSU	RHUM BABAS
	ASSAILANT	AABBIILLS	BILABIALS
AAAILPPRS	APPRAISAL	AABBIMRRS	BARBARISM
AAAILRSTU	AUSTRALIA	AABBIRRTY	BARBARITY
AAAILSSWY	SAILS AWAY	AABBIRSSU	BABIRUSAS
AAAILSTWY	TAILS AWAY		BABIRUSSA
AAAIMNNOZ	AMAZONIAN	AABBKNORS	ROBS A BANK
AAAIMNORT	INAMORATA	AABBMOSWY	BOMBS AWAY
AAAIMNRST	SAMARITAN	AABBNOTYY	BOTANY BAY

AABBNRTYY	BANTRY BAY	AABCDLOPR	CLAPBOARD
AABBORRSU	BARBAROUS	AABCDNNUY	ABUNDANCY
AABCCEEMS	MACCABEES	AABCDNOOR	CARBONADO
AABCCEHKS	BACKACHES	AABCDORST	BAD ACTORS
AABCCEHLT	CATCHABLE		BROADCAST
AABCCEHNT	BACCHANTE	AABCEEELP	PEACEABLE
AABCCEKLL	BLACK LACE	AABCEEEPT	BE AT PEACE
AABCCEKLM	CAMELBACK	AABCEEFRV	BRAVE FACE
AABCCEKPS	BACKSPACE	AABCEEHLR	REACHABLE
AABCCELRS	CABLE CARS	AABCEEHLT	TEACHABLE
AABCCELRU	ACCRUABLE	AABCEEHRW	BEACH WEAR
AABCCENOO	COCOA BEAN	AABCEEKKS	BAKE CAKES
AABCCHHKT	HATCHBACK	AABCEELLN	CLEANABLE
AABCCHKKU	HUCKABACK	AABCEELLP	PLACEABLE
AABCCHSTU	CATCH A BUS	AABCEELLR	CLEARABLE
AABCCIKKP	PICKABACK	AABCEELLV	CLEAVABLE
AABCCIKRR	CRACK A RIB	AABCEELPS	ESCAPABLE
AABCCILMY	BY ACCLAIM	AABCEELPT	PLACE A BET
AABCCILOT	CATABOLIC	AABCEELPY	PEACEABLY
AABCCIORT	ACROBATIC	AABCEELRS	CALABRESE
AABCCJKKL	BLACK JACK	AABCEELRT	TRACEABLE
	BLACKJACK	AABCEELTX	EXACTABLE
AABCCKKPS	BACKPACKS	AABCEENRR	ABERRANCE
AABCCKKRT	BACKTRACK	AABCEENSY	ABEYANCES
AABCCKLLO	COAL BLACK	AABCEERTT	BRACTEATE
AABCCKLLS	CALLS BACK	AABCEFILN	FANCIABLE
AABCCKLPS	BLACKCAPS	AABCEFIRT	FABRICATE
AABCCKLST	BLACK CATS	AABCEFOTU	ABOUT FACE
AABCCMOST	CATACOMBS		ABOUT-FACE
AABCDDEFL	BALD-FACED	AABCEFRST	BARE FACTS
AABCDDEIT	ABDICATED	AABCEGILR	ALGEBRAIC
AABCDDEIV	BAD ADVICE	AABCEGISW	BASIC WAGE
AABCDDEKT	BACKDATED	AABCEGKPS	BACK PAGES
AABCDDENN	DANCE BAND	AABCEGKST	BACK STAGE
AABCDDORR	CARDBOARD		BACKSTAGE
AABCDEEFR	BAREFACED	AABCEGLMR	CABLEGRAM
AABCDEEHH	BEACHHEAD	AABCEGPRT	CARPET BAG
AABCDEELN	DANCEABLE		CARPETBAG
AABCDEHIR	HIRED A CAB	AABCEHHLT	HATCHABLE
AABCDEHKL	BLACKHEAD	AABCEHINR	BRANCHIAE
AABCDEHKS	HEADS BACK	AABCEHIRS	HIRES A CAB
AABCDEILL	CABLE-LAID	AABCEHIRT	BRACHIATE
AABCDEILN	ALICE BAND	AABCEHKLW	WHALEBACK
AABCDEIMR	CARBAMIDE	AABCEHKTT	AT THE BACK
AABCDEIRR	BARRICADE	AABCEHLMP	PALM BEACH
AABCDEIST	ABDICATES	AABCEHLTY	TEACHABLY
AABCDEKLP	BACKPEDAL	AABCEIIRS	ARABICISE
AABCDEKRR	BARRACKED	AABCEIIRZ	ARABICIZE
AABCDEKST	BACKDATES	AABCEILLM	CLAIMABLE
AABCDELNR	BARNACLED	AABCEILMN	IMBALANCE
AABCDELRT	CARD TABLE	AABCEILMR	BICAMERAL
AABCDEMSU	AMBUSCADE	AABCEILNP	INCAPABLE
AABCDENNR	BARN DANCE	AABCEILNT	CANTABILE
AABCDENNU	ABUNDANCE	AABCEILRT	BACTERIAL
AABCDEPRS	BAD SCRAPE		CALIBRATE
AABCDFLST	BALD FACTS	AABCEILST	BALTIC SEA
AABCDHKNS	BACKHANDS	AABCEINOR	ANAEROBIC
	HANDS BACK	AABCEINRR	CARABINER
AABCDHKRS	HARDBACKS	AABCEIORT	AEROBATIC
AABCDHLPT	BALD PATCH	AABCEISSS	ABSCISSAE
AABCDIMNO	CAMBODIAN	AABCEKKNT	TAKEN BACK
AABCDIORT	ABDICATOR	AABCEKKST	TAKES BACK
AABCDKLMP	BLACKDAMP	AABCEKLLY	BACK ALLEY
AABCDKNRW	DRAWN BACK	AABCEKLMS	CLAMBAKES
AABCDKNST	STAND BACK	AABCEKLNS	LEANS BACK
AABCDKRSW	BACKWARDS	AABCEKLNT	LEANT BACK
	DRAWBACKS	AABCEKLRW	WEAR BLACK
	DRAWS BACK	AABCEKLST	STACKABLE
AABCDKRSY	BACK YARDS	AABCEKMPR	BREAK CAMP
AABCDLNRS	LAND CRABS	AABCEKPPR	PAPER BACK
AABCDLOOR	COAL BOARD		PAPERBACK

AABCEKRRR	BARRACKER	AABCKLPSS	BACKSLAPS
AABCEKRTW	BACK WATER	AABCKLPSY	PLAYBACKS
	BACKWATER		PLAYS BACK
AABCEKSST	BACK SEATS	AABCKLRST	BLACK ARTS
AABCELLLO	ALLOCABLE		BLACK RATS
AABCELLOR	CABALLERO	AABCKNRSS	SNACK BARS
AABCELLOT	LOCATABLE	AABCKRSST	BRASS TACK
AABCELMNU	AMBULANCE	AABCKSSTY	BACKSTAYS
AABCELNNO	ON BALANCE	AABCLMNOR	MARC BOLAN
AABCELNNU	UNBALANCE	AABCLRTTY	TRACTABLY
AABCELNPU	BALANCE UP	AABCMNOTT	COMBATANT
AABCELNRS	BALANCERS	AABCOSTTU	CAST ABOUT
	BARNACLES	AABCRSSTT	ABSTRACTS
AABCELOOS	CALABOOSE	AABDDEEST	DEADBEATS
AABCELORR	BARCAROLE	AABDDEGLS	SADDLEBAG
AABCELPPR	CRAB APPLE	AABDDEHLS	BALD HEADS
AABCELRTT	TRACTABLE	AABDDEHNS	HEADBANDS
AABCELRTU	TRABECULA	AABDDEHOR	HEADBOARD
AABCELSWY	CABLEWAYS	AABDDEMRS	BAD DREAMS
AABCEMORX	BOX CAMERA	AABDDHORR	HARDBOARD
AABCEMOTU	CAME ABOUT	AABDDHORS	DASHBOARD
AABCENORT	CARBONATE	AABDDNNST	BANDSTAND
AABCENRRY	ABERRANCY	AABDDORRT	DARTBOARD
AABCEORST	ASCORBATE	AABDEEGLL	BALD EAGLE
	BOAT RACES	AABDEEHRS	BARE HEADS
AABCEOTUV	A CUT ABOVE	AABDEEKLN	KNEADABLE
AABCFHKLS	FLASHBACK	AABDEELLP	PLEADABLE
	HALFBACKS	AABDEELPR	DRAPEABLE
AABCFKLLS	FALLS BACK	AABDEELRT	TRADEABLE
AABCFKSST	FASTBACKS	AABDDEENRT	NEAT BEARD
AABCGHKNS	HANGS BACK	AABDEFHKL	HALF-BAKED
AABCGILLN	CABALLING	AABDEFLOR	BROADLEAF
AABCGILNN	BALANCING	AABDEFLRT	DRAFTABLE
AABCGIMRU	GUM ARABIC	AABDEGINR	BARGAINED
AABCGKLNS	BACK SLANG		GABARDINE
AABCGRRSS	CRAB GRASS	AABDEGMOR	BOARD GAME
	CRABGRASS	AABDEGNRS	BANDAGERS
AABCHHIRT	BATH CHAIR	AABDEGORT	ABROGATED
AABCHIKLR	BLACK HAIR	AABDEGOST	SABOTAGED
AABCHILNR	BRANCHIAL	AABDEHHLT	BAD HEALTH
AABCHIMNR	BRAHMANIC	AABDEHKNR	HAND BRAKE
AABCHLOOS	COOLABAHS	AABDEHLNR	HANDLEBAR
AABCHMNOS	HANSOM CAB	AABDEHLTY	HELD AT BAY
AABCHPSYY	PAY BY CASH	AABDEHNRS	BARE HANDS
AABCIILNS	BASILICAN	AABDEHNSU	UNABASHED
AABCIILSS	BASILICAS	AABDEIKMS	MAKES A BID
AABCIINOT	ANABIOTIC	AABDEILLT	DILATABLE
AABCIKLLM	BLACKMAIL	AABDEILMR	ADMIRABLE
AABCIKLST	TAILBACKS	AABDEILOV	AVOIDABLE
AABCILLRY	BACILLARY	AABDEILRV	ADVERBIAL
AABCILLSY	BASICALLY	AABDEILSV	ADVISABLE
AABCILNNS	CANNIBALS	AABDEILTU	AUDITABLE
AABCILNOT	BOTANICAL	AABDEINST	ABSTAINED
AABCILNPY	INCAPABLY		BASTINADE
AABCILNTU	TUBAL CAIN	AABDEJLLS	DJELLABAS
AABCILOPR	PARABOLIC	AABDEKMOO	MADE A BOOK
AABCILSST	CABALISTS	AABDEKOOR	READ A BOOK
AABCINNOR	CARBANION	AABDELLNT	TABLELAND
AABCIRSSS	BRASSICAS	AABDELLOW	DEAL A BLOW
AABCISSSS	ABSCISSAS	AABDELLST	BALLASTED
AABCKKLMR	BLACK MARK	AABDELMST	LAMBASTED
AABCKKLST	TALKS BACK	AABDELOPT	ADOPTABLE
AABCKKLSW	WALKS BACK	AABDELPPS	BAD APPLES
AABCKKOOT	TOOK ABACK	AABDELPRY	BAD PLAYER
AABCKLLLS	ALL BLACKS	AABDELPST	BALD PATES
AABCKLLMP	LAMPBLACK	AABDELTTU	TABULATED
AABCKLLOP	BLACK OPAL	AABDELTWY	TWAYBLADE
AABCKLMSS	BLACK MASS	AABDEMNNR	BRAND NAME
AABCKLNPW	BLACK PAWN		NAME BRAND
AABCKLNST	BLACK ANTS	AABDEMORT	DREAMBOAT
AABCKLNSW	BLACK SWAN	AABDEMRST	BAD MASTER

AABDEMRTU	ADUMBRATE	AABEEIKTT	TAKE A BITE
AABDENSTW	SWEATBAND	AABEEILLN	ALIENABLE
AABDFHLOR	HALF-BOARD	AABEEINRS	BEARNAISE
AABDFILOT	BIT OF A LAD	AABEEKLPS	SPEAKABLE
AABDGGINN	BANDAGING	AABEEKMST	MAKES A BET
AABDGIILR	GARIBALDI	AABEEKNTT	TAKEN A BET
AABDGLORT	OLD RATBAG	AABEEKPTY	KEEP AT BAY
AABDGNNOW	BANDWAGON	AABEEKRST	TEA BREAKS
AABDGNOSV	VAGABONDS	AABEEKSTT	TAKES A BET
AABDGOSTU	GADS ABOUT	AABEELLLM	MALLEABLE
AABDHINNS	HAND BASIN	AABEELLNR	LEARNABLE
AABDHLLNS	HANDBALLS	AABEELLRT	ALTERABLE
AABDHLLRS	HARD BALLS		RELATABLE
AABDHLOTY	HOLD AT BAY	AABEELMRS	LASER BEAM
AABDHORSW	WASHBOARD	AABEELMST	BASE METAL
AABDIILLP	PAID A BILL	AABEELNTU	UNEATABLE
AABDIJNOR	JABORANDI	AABEELORT	ELABORATE
AABDIKNRS	BANK RAIDS	AABEELPRR	REPARABLE
AABDILMNO	ABDOMINAL	AABEELPRS	SEPARABLE
AABDILMRY	ADMIRABLY	AABEELPRY	REPAYABLE
AABDILNST	STAND BAIL	AABEELRTT	TREATABLE
AABDILORS	BAD SAILOR	AABEELRTW	TABLEWARE
	SAILBOARD	AABEELSTT	SEA BATTLE
AABDILORT	TAILBOARD		STATEABLE
AABDILOTU	LAID ABOUT		TEA TABLES
AABDILOVY	AVOIDABLY	AABEELSVY	BAY LEAVES
AABDILSVY	ADVISABLY	AABEELTTX	BATTLE-AXE
AABDINNRT	TRAINBAND	AABEEMNSY	BE A YES-MAN
AABDINOST	BASTINADO	AABEENORS	ANAEROBES
AABDINPRT	IN BAD PART	AABEENSTY	BATS AN EYE
AABDINSTW	WAISTBAND	AABEEQRSU	ARABESQUE
AABDJLNOS	LANDS A JOB	AABEERTTX	TAX REBATE
AABDJNSZZ	JAZZ BANDS	AABEFFILX	AFFIXABLE
AABDKLORW	BOARDWALK	AABEFGILT	FATIGABLE
AABDKNNSS	SANDBANKS	AABEFHLOY	BALE OF HAY
AABDLLNOW	LAND A BLOW	AABEFIIKL	FAKE ALIBI
AABDLLORW	WALLBOARD	AABEFILSS	ALFIE BASS
AABDLLOSW	SALAD BOWL	AABEFKRST	BREAKFAST
AABDLNSST	SANDBLAST	AABEFLLMM	FLAMMABLE
AABDLNTWY	WANT BADLY	AABEFLMSU	FLAMBEAUS
AABDLOOSW	BALSA WOOD	AABEFLMUX	FLAMBEAUX
AABDLORRS	LABRADORS	AABEFLTTU	BE AT FAULT
AABDLORUY	LABOUR DAY	AABEGGLUY	GAUGEABLY
AABDLRSTY	BASTARDLY	AABEGHIMT	THE GAMBIA
AABDMNNOY	MAN AND BOY	AABEGHLLU	LAUGHABLE
AABDMORRU	BURMA ROAD	AABEGILNV	NAVIGABLE
AABDNORWW	DRAWN A BOW	AABEGINRR	BARGAINER
AABDNPSSS	PASSBANDS	AABEGKLNP	BLANK PAGE
AABDNRRSY	BARNYARDS	AABEGLLLR	GLABELLAR
AABDORRST	STARBOARD	AABEGLLMS	BALL GAMES
AABDORSWW	DRAWS A BOW	AABEGLLNR	RANG A BELL
AABDORSWY	BROADWAYS	AABEGLNRT	GRANTABLE
AABEEEGLR	AGREEABLE	AABEGLPRS	GRASPABLE
AABEEEVWW	WEAVE A WEB	AABEGMNRT	BAR MAGNET
AABEEFGNO	BE OF AN AGE	AABEGMNSY	MANGABEYS
AABEEFNST	BEANFEAST	AABEGORST	ABROGATES
AABEEGGLU	GAUGEABLE	AABEGOSST	SABOTAGES
AABEEGKLR	BREAK A LEG	AABEGPPRS	PAPER BAGS
AABEEGKRS	BREAKAGES	AABEHHITW	WAHHABITE
AABEEGLLL	GLABELLAE	AABEHITTU	HABITUATE
AABEEGLLN	GLEANABLE	AABEHLLLT	HALL TABLE
AABEEGLLT	BAGATELLE	AABEHLOTW	WHALEBOAT
AABEEGLNN	BE AN ANGEL	AABEHLPST	ALPHABETS
AABEEGLRY	AGREEABLY	AABEHORRS	ARAB HORSE
AABEEGRRT	GREAT BEAR	AABEHORTU	HEAR ABOUT
AABEEHITV	HAVE A BITE	AABEHORSU	SHABRAQUE
AABEEHKLS	SHAKEABLE	AABEHRTTW	BATH WATER
AABEEHLPS	SHAPEABLE	AABEHRTWY	BAR THE WAY
AABEEHLRS	SHAREABLE	AABEIILLS	LABIALISE
AABEEHPSU	HEAP ABUSE	AABEIILLZ	LABIALIZE
AABEEHRTT	HEARTBEAT	AABEIILRS	RAISE BAIL

AABEIIMNR	BAIN-MARIE	AABEORTTU	TEAR ABOUT
AABEIIRTU	AUBRIETIA	AABERSTUY	BURY AT SEA
AABEIJKLR	BREAK JAIL	AABFIIMNS	FABIANISM
	JAILBREAK	AABFIMORT	FIBROMATA
AABEIKLLM	LIKE A LAMB	AABFLLOTU	FALL ABOUT
AABEIKLNS	BALKANISE	AABFLLOTW	FATAL BLOW
AABEIKLNZ	BALKANIZE	AABFLLSST	FAST BALLS
AABEIKNRR	KARABINER	AABFLSTUY	BUYS A FLAT
AABEIKRRS	AIR BRAKES	AABFOOPRS	BAR OF SOAP
AABEILLNR	BALLERINA	AABGGGNNS	GANG BANGS
AABEILLRT	BILATERAL		GANG-BANGS
AABEILLST	BALLISTAE	AABGGRRST	BRAGGARTS
AABEILLSW	WALLABIES	AABGGRRYY	ARGY-BARGY
AABEILMNR	LAMEBRAIN	AABGHINTW	WITH A BANG
AABEILMNS	LIMA BEANS	AABGHLLUY	LAUGHABLY
AABEILMSY	BY SEA MAIL	AABGHNOTU	HANG ABOUT
AABEILNRT	TRAINABLE	AABGHOPRR	BAROGRAPH
AABEILNST	STAINABLE	AABGIINRS	ARABISING
AABEILRSV	VARIABLES	AABGIINRZ	ARABIZING
AABEILRTT	AIR BATTLE	AABGIINWY	IN A BIG WAY
AABEILSTV	ABLATIVES	AABGILNRU	BULGARIAN
AABEIMNOT	ABOMINATE	AABGILNVY	NAVIGABLY
AABEINOSS	ANABIOSES	AABGILRRT	GIBRALTAR
AABEINRST	ABSTAINER	AABGINNOR	BORN AGAIN
AABEINRVW	BRAIN WAVE		BORN-AGAIN
AABEIRRTT	ARBITRATE	AABGINRWY	BRING AWAY
AABEIRSSV	ABRASIVES	AABGINTVY	VANITY BAG
AABEJKNOT	TAKEN A JOB	AABGLLORW	GLOBAL WAR
AABEJKOST	TAKES A JOB	AABGORTVY	GRAVY BOAT
AABEKKMOO	MAKE A BOOK	AABHHIMSW	WAHHABISM
AABEKLLTT	TABLE TALK	AABHIILRZ	BILHARZIA
AABEKMOSW	MAKES A BOW	AABHIIMNP	AMPHIBIAN
AABEKNOTW	TAKEN A BOW	AABHILSSU	HAILS A BUS
AABEKNRST	BANK RATES	AABHIMNOT	IAN BOTHAM
AABEKNRTU	BREAK A NUT	AABHINRSW	BRAINWASH
AABEKNSTU	TAKEN A BUS	AABHINSSW	WASHBASIN
AABEKOOST	BOOK A SEAT	AABHINSTT	HABITANTS
AABEKORWY	BROKE AWAY	AABHKKLNU	KUBLA KHAN
AABEKOSTW	TAKES A BOW	AABHKOOTT	TOOK A BATH
AABEKPTTY	KEPT AT BAY	AABHLSSTT	BATH SALTS
AABEKSSTU	TAKES A BUS	AABHMNORT	ROMAN BATH
AABELLLMR	ALARM BELL	AABHNOSTU	AUTOBAHNS
AABELLLOW	ALLOWABLE	AABHOTTUW	WHAT ABOUT
AABELLLPS	SPALLABLE	AABHRSSST	BRASS HATS
AABELLMPT	TABLE LAMP	AABHRSUWY	BRUSH AWAY
AABELLMST	MEAT BALLS	AABIILMRY	BY AIR MAIL
AABELLNPT	PLANTABLE	AABIILNRR	LIBRARIAN
AABELLPPR	PALPEBRAL	AABIILRTY	ARABILITY
AABELLRTY	ALTERABLY	AABIINNRT	BRITANNIA
AABELLSTT	TABLE SALT	AABIINOSS	ANABIOSIS
AABELLSTU	BLASTULAE	AABIISTTW	WAITS A BIT
AABELLSUV	VALUABLES	AABILLLOW	ALLOW BAIL
AABELMSST	LAMBASTES	AABILLMST	LAMB'S TAIL
AABELMSSU	ASSUMABLE	AABILLPSY	PAYS A BILL
AABELMSTT	TABLEMATS	AABILMNOS	ANABOLISM
AABELOPRR	POLAR BEAR	AABILMOPY	AMBLYOPIA
AABELOPTU	LEAP ABOUT	AABILMORS	AMBROSIAL
AABELORST	ASTROLABE	AABILMOST	MAIL BOATS
AABELORTT	ROTATABLE	AABILMOSW	AIMS A BLOW
AABELPRSY	SEPARABLY	AABILMPST	BAPTISMAL
AABELPRYY	PLAY BY EAR	AABILNORT	BARITONAL
AABELRRRT	TAR BARREL	AABILNOST	ABLATIONS
AABELRSST	ARBALESTS	AABILNOTT	BATTALION
AABELRSTY	BETRAYALS	AABILNOTU	LAIN ABOUT
AABELRTTU	TABLATURE	AABILOSST	SAILBOATS
AABELSTTU	TABULATES	AABILOSWY	BOILS AWAY
AABEMOSTT	STEAMBOAT	AABILRRTW	TRIBAL WAR
AABEMRRSS	BEARS ARMS	AABINORSS	ABRASIONS
	EMBARRASS	AABINORTT	BOAT TRAIN
AABENOSSY	SOYA BEANS	AABINOSTV	VAIN BOAST
AABEOORSV	SOAR ABOVE	AABINOSTW	BOATSWAIN

AABINRSTZ	BARTIZANS	AACCEINSV	VACANCIES
AABIOSSSY	BIOASSAYS	AACCEINTV	VACCINATE
AABIRRRTY	ARBITRARY	AACCEKNRS	CRANKCASE
AABKLLLNW	BLANK WALL	AACCEKRRT	RACE TRACK
AABKLNNOS	BANK LOANS	AACCEKRSS	SACK RACES
AABKLNTUV	BANK VAULT	AACCELLTU	CALCULATE
AABKLORTU	LARK ABOUT	AACCELMNU	CALCANEUM
AABKLOTTU	TALK ABOUT	AACCELMTY	CYCLAMATE
AABKLOTUW	WALK ABOUT	AACCELNSU	CALCANEUS
	WALKABOUT	AACCELNTU	ACCENTUAL
AABLLLPPU	PAPAL BULL	AACCELOTY	ACETYL-COA
AABLLLPSY	PLAYS BALL	AACCELSTU	SACCULATE
AABLLMSYY	ABYSMALLY	AACCEORTT	COARCTATE
AABLLNTTY	BLATANTLY	AACCEPRTU	CUT A CAPER
AABLLRSTU	BLASTULAR	AACCERSSS	CARCASSES
AABLLRTUY	TABULARLY	AACCERSSY	ACCESSARY
AABLLSSTU	BLASTULAS	AACCERSTU	CRUSTACEA
AABLMNORY	MYROBALAN	AACCFIKRR	FAIR CRACK
AABLMORST	ROAST LAMB	AACCGINRR	RACING CAR
AABLMSSUY	ASSUMABLY	AACCGKORT	GOT A CRACK
AABLNOORS	SALOON BAR	AACCHILNY	CHINA CLAY
AABLNOWWY	BLOWN AWAY	AACCHINRS	SACCHARIN
AABLOPTUY	PLAY ABOUT	AACCHIRTT	CATHARTIC
AABLORSST	ALBATROSS	AACCHIRTU	AUTARCHIC
AABLORTTU	TABULATOR	AACCHLOST	CACHALOTS
AABLOSTUY	LAYABOUTS	AACCIILNV	VACCINIAL
	LAYS ABOUT	AACCIINTT	TACTICIAN
AABMNRSTU	RAMBUTANS	AACCILLSS	CLASSICAL
AABMORSTU	MARABOUTS	AACCILNNO	CANONICAL
	TAMBOURAS	AACCILPRT	PRACTICAL
AABNNSTTU	BANTUSTAN	AACCILTTY	CATALYTIC
AABNOOSSV	BOSSA NOVA	AACCIMNOR	CARCINOMA
AABORRRST	BARRATORS		MACARONIC
AABRSSTTU	SUBSTRATA	AACCIMNTT	TIC-TAC MAN
AACCDDEIR	CADDIE CAR	AACCINOTT	CATATONIC
AACCDDINY	CANDIDACY	AACCINPTY	CAPTAINCY
AACCDEFRS	FACE CARDS	AACCINRTT	ANTARCTIC
AACCDEILM	ACCLAIMED	AACCIOPRT	CAPACITOR
AACCDEIMS	ACADEMICS	AACCIOPSU	CAPACIOUS
AACCDEJNY	ADJACENCY	AACCIORST	COSTA RICA
AACCDELOS	ACCOLADES	AACCIRSST	SARCASTIC
AACCDGINS	CASCADING	AACCKMNRS	CRACKSMAN
AACCDHLRU	ARCHDUCAL	AACCKNRTU	CRACK A NUT
AACCDIINR	CIRCADIAN	AACCLLLLO	LOCAL CALL
AACCDIOSU	CAUCASOID	AACCLMSTY	CATACLYSM
AACCDNORT	ACCORDANT	AACCMNNOPY	ACCOMPANY
AACCEEFMR	FACE CREAM	AACCORTUY	AUTOCRACY
AACCEEKMR	CREAM CAKE	AACCOSSTT	STACCATOS
AACCEELMN	CAME CLEAN	AACDDEELN	LED A DANCE
AACCEELNR	CLEARANCE	AACDDEHMR	DEAD MARCH
AACCEELRS	CLEAR CASE	AACDDEINT	CANDIDATE
AACCEENRT	REACTANCE	AACDDELOP	DECAPODAL
AACCEEPRS	SPACE RACE	AACDDELPR	PLACARDED
AACCEFFST	FACE FACTS	AACDDELRS	DEAL CARDS
AACCEFHNT	FAT CHANCE	AACDDENOP	DECAPODAN
AACCEFHST	SAFE CATCH	AACDDENPT	TAP DANCED
AACCEFKPS	FACE PACKS	AACDDEOTV	ADVOCATED
	FACE-PACKS	AACDDGNOT	CAT AND DOG
AACCEGKRT	GET A CRACK	AACDDHOTU	ADD A TOUCH
AACCEHINR	CANE CHAIR	AACDDIIST	DADAISTIC
AACCEHJKP	CHEAP JACK	AACDDILLO	CLADODIAL
	CHEAP-JACK	AACDEEEFT	DEFAECATE
AACCEHRRT	CHARACTER	AACDEEEMP	MADE PEACE
AACCEHRTY	YACHT RACE	AACDEEFHT	FACE DEATH
AACCEHSTW	WATCH-CASE	AACDEEFMS	MADE FACES
AACCEHSTY	EASY CATCH	AACDEEFST	FACED EAST
AACCEILMR	ACCLAIMER	AACDEEFSV	SAVED FACE
AACCEILMT	ACCLIMATE	AACDEEHHS	HEADACHES
AACCEILRR	CERCARIAL	AACDEEHLR	CLEAR HEAD
AACCEINNR	CANCERIAN	AACDEEHSS	HEAD CASES
AACCEINRS	SARACENIC	AACDEEIMS	ACADEMIES

AACDEEIMT	EMACIATED	AACDELNPS	LANDSCAPE
AACDEEIRT	ERADICATE	AACDELNRS	CALENDARS
AACDEEKPP	PEAKED CAP	AACDELNRT	DECLARANT
AACDEELLR	CLEAR LEAD	AACDELNST	LAST DANCE
AACDEELMR	MADE CLEAR	AACDELNWX	WAX CANDLE
AACDEELRS	ESCALADER	AACDELORR	CLEAR ROAD
AACDEELRT	LACERATED	AACDELORT	CARED A LOT
AACDEELSS	ESCALADES	AACDELPTY	PLAYACTED
AACDEELST	ESCALATED	AACDELRSY	CLEAR DAYS
AACDEEMNS	DAMASCENE	AACDELSTY	CATALYSED
AACDEEMRT	DEMARCATE	AACDEMRSS	MASSACRED
	MACERATE	AACDEMRTY	ARMY CADET
AACDEENRW	DREW AN ACE	AACDENNNO	CANNONADE
AACDEENTT	CATENATED	AACDENNST	ASCENDANT
AACDEEPSS	ESCAPADES	AACDENORR	CARRONADE
AACDEETUV	EVACUATED	AACDENPRT	TAP DANCER
AACDEETVX	EXCAVATED	AACDENPST	TAP DANCES
AACDEFFIN	AFFIANCED	AACDENRSV	ADVANCERS
AACDEFFIR	FAIRFACED	AACDENRSW	WAR DANCES
AACDEFHLS	CALFS HEAD	AACDEOOSV	AVOCADOES
AACDEFIST	FASCIATED	AACDEORRS	ROAD RACES
AACDEFNNR	FAN DANCER	AACDEORRV	DROVE A CAR
AACDEGIJN	DANCE A JIG	AACDEOSTV	ADVOCATES
AACDEGILT	GLACIATED	AACDERSTT	CASTRATED
AACDEGIRS	SAID GRACE	AACDERTTT	ATTRACTED
AACDEGMRS	CARD GAMES	AACDFHNRT	HANDCRAFT
AACDEGRRS	DRAG RACES	AACDFHRST	HARD FACTS
AACDEHILN	ENCHILADA	AACDGIMNW	MAGIC WAND
AACDEHINS	HACIENDAS	AACDGINNV	ADVANCING
AACDEHIRR	HIRED A CAR	AACDGINRS	CARDIGANS
AACDEHLLN	DANCE HALL	AACDHHKOS	HAD A SHOCK
AACDEHLLS	CALL HEADS	AACDHINNP	CAP IN HAND
AACDEHLNR	REACH LAND	AACDHINOR	ARACHNOID
AACDEHLNS	CHALDEANS	AACDHINPS	HANDICAPS
AACDEHLOV	HAVE A COLD	AACDHINRS	ARACHNIDS
AACDEHLRT	CATHEDRAL	AACDHLNPS	CLAP HANDS
AACDEHMNR	HAND CREAM	AACDHLNPU	LAUNCH PAD
AACDEHNRR	DAN ARCHER	AACDHLNRS	CRASH-LAND
AACDEHORT	OCTAHEDRA	AACDHMPPT	DAMP PATCH
AACDEHRSS	HARD CASES	AACDHPRRS	CARDSHARP
AACDEHRSU	HARD SAUCE	AACDHSSTU	CUTS A DASH
AACDEHRSY	READY CASH	AACDIILLM	LAID CLAIM
AACDEIIPR	EPICARDIA	AACDIIMNO	AMINO ACID
AACDEIKSV	ASK ADVICE	AACDIINSS	ASCIDIANS
AACDEILLN	DALLIANCE	AACDIISTT	DIASTATIC
AACDEILLT	DIALECTAL	AACDILLRU	CUADRILLA
AACDEILNO	LAODICEAN	AACDILLRY	RADICALLY
AACDEILNS	CANALISED	AACDILMNY	DYNAMICAL
AACDEILNT	CADENTIAL	AACDILMST	DALMATICS
AACDEILNZ	CANALIZED	AACDILNRS	CARDINALS
AACDEILTU	ACIDULATE	AACDILRRU	RADICULAR
AACDEIMNY	CYANAMIDE	AACDIMRST	DRAMATICS
AACDEINNV	IN ADVANCE	AACDINNOR	DRACONIAN
AACDEINOR	ANDROECIA	AACDINORS	ORCADIANS
AACDEINOT	DIACONATE	AACDIOSUU	AUDACIOUS
AACDEINOV	AVOIDANCE	AACDIQRTU	QUADRATIC
AACDEINPT	CAPTAINED	AACDIRSSY	DYSCRASIA
AACDEIRRV	DRIVE A CAR	AACDIRSTY	CARYATIDS
AACDEIRSS	ASCARIDES	AACDJNTUY	ADJUTANCY
AACDEISST	CAST ASIDE	AACDKOORT	TOOK A CARD
AACDEITTV	ACTIVATED	AACDLORST	CARTLOADS
	CAVITATED	AACDLPRSY	PLAY CARDS
AACDEITWY	TWICE A DAY	AACDMMORS	CARDAMOMS
AACDEJKMP	JAM-PACKED	AACDMRSSX	XMAS CARDS
AACDEJORT	CARED A JOT	AACDOORTV	ADVOCATOR
AACDEKNRS	RANSACKED	AACDPRRSY	SCRAPYARD
AACDEKNST	CAKE STAND	AACDQRSSU	SQUAD CARS
AACDEKPRR	PARKED CAR	AACEEEKMP	MAKE PEACE
AACDELLOT	ALLOCATED	AACEEFGLN	ANGEL FACE
AACDELMNS	CANDLEMAS	AACEEFGMO	CAME OF AGE
AACDELNOT	ANECDOTAL	AACEEFHPR	CHEAP FARE

AACEEFIRT	CAFETERIA	AACEFGLNR	FLAGRANCE
AACEEFKMS	MAKE FACES	AACEFGNRR	FRAGRANCE
AACEEFLPS	PALEFACES	AACEFGOPR	FORAGE CAP
	SAFE PLACE	AACEFGORT	FACTORAGE
AACEEFLPT	FACEPLATE	AACEFHLST	HALF-CASTE
AACEEFLUV	FACE VALUE	AACEFIKRY	FAIRY CAKE
AACEEFRRT	AFTERCARE	AACEFILLS	FALLACIES
AACEEFRSV	FACE-SAVER	AACEFINST	FANTACISE
AACEEFRTX	EXACT FARE		FASCINATE
AACEEFSST	FACES EAST	AACEFLLPU	PULL A FACE
AACEEFSSV	SAVES FACE	AACEFLNPU	FUN PALACE
AACEEGHSV	GAVE CHASE	AACEFLNSS	FLAN CASES
AACEEGILL	ELEGIACAL	AACEFLORY	CAFE ROYAL
AACEEGKNO	GENOA CAKE	AACEFLRST	FLAT RACES
AACEEGLLR	CELLARAGE	AACEFLSTT	FALCATEST
AACEEGLPV	GAVE PLACE	AACEFLTTT	FAT CATTLE
AACEEGLSV	CLEAVAGES	AACEFRSST	FAST RACES
AACEEGLSW	WAGE SCALE	AACEFRSTT	ARTEFACTS
AACEEGNRR	CARRAGEEN	AACEGHLLN	ALL CHANGE
AACEEGPSS	GAS ESCAPE	AACEGHLNR	ARCHANGEL
AACEEGRRT	GREAT CARE	AACEGHMNP	CHAMPAGNE
AACEEHHRT	HEARTACHE	AACEGHNOR	ANCHORAGE
AACEEHLNP	ENCEPHALA		ON A CHARGE
AACEEHLUV	HAVE A CLUE	AACEGHRST	GATE-CRASH
AACEEHPRT	CHEAP RATE	AACEGHRTX	TAX CHARGE
AACEEHRTT	TRACHEATE	AACEGILLN	ANGELICAL
AACEEHRTX	EXARCHATE		GALENICAL
AACEEILMV	CAME ALIVE	AACEGILMW	WAGE CLAIM
AACEEILNR	ALIEN RACE	AACEGILNS	ANALGESIC
AACEEIMST	EMACIATES		ANGELICAS
AACEEJKPT	PEA JACKET	AACEGILNT	ANALGETIC
AACEEJLTU	EJACULATE	AACEGILRT	CARTILAGE
AACEEKKMS	MAKE CAKES	AACEGILST	GLACIATES
AACEEKLMR	MAKE CLEAR	AACEGIMNO	COME AGAIN
AACEEKLPT	TAKE PLACE		EGOMANIAC
AACEEKLRY	LAYER CAKE	AACEGIMOT	ATOMIC AGE
AACEEKLST	STALE CAKE	AACEGINNO	ONCE AGAIN
AACEEKMPR	PACEMAKER	AACEGIRRS	CARRIAGES
AACEEKNRT	TAKEN CARE	AACEGIRSV	VICARAGES
AACEEKRRT	CARETAKER	AACEGISTT	CASTIGATE
AACEEKRST	TAKES CARE	AACEGLMNO	CAME ALONG
AACEELMNP	PLACE NAME	AACEGLOST	GALACTOSE
	PLACE-NAME	AACEGLOTU	CATALOGUE
AACEELMPS	SAME PLACE		COAGULATE
AACEELMRR	REAL CREAM	AACEGLRRS	LARGE CARS
AACEELMRY	CAME EARLY	AACEGLSSS	GLASS CASE
AACEELNNO	OCEAN LANE	AACEGMPRS	CRAP GAMES
AACEELNPT	PLACENTAE	AACEGNORR	ARROGANCE
AACEELPRT	PARACLETE	AACEGNOST	OCTANE GAS
AACEELRRY	RELAY RACE	AACEGNRSU	CANE SUGAR
AACEELRST	LACERATES		SUGAR CANE
AACEELSST	ESCALATES		SUGARCANE
AACEEMMNR	CAMERAMEN	AACEGOPST	SCAPEGOAT
AACEEMNNY	MYCENAEAN	AACEGORTT	GREAT COAT
AACEEMRST	CREAM TEAS		GREATCOAT
	MACERATES	AACEGRSSY	SAYS GRACE
AACEEMSST	CASEMATES	AACEHHIRZ	ZECHARIAH
AACEENORY	ONCE A YEAR	AACEHHMRR	MARCH HARE
AACEENOVW	OCEAN WAVE	AACEHIIMS	ISCHAEMIA
AACEENRSS	CESAREANS	AACEHILLO	ECHOLALIA
AACEENSTT	CATENATES	AACEHILMT	MALACHITE
AACEENSTY	CAST AN EYE	AACEHILNS	SELACHIAN
AACEEOPRS	AEROSPACE	AACEHILNT	CHATELAIN
AACEEPSSS	SEASCAPES	AACEHILNU	ACHEULIAN
AACEEPSSV	SAVE SPACE	AACEHILPT	CALIPHATE
AACEERSTT	ESTATE CAR	AACEHIMNT	MACHINATE
AACEERSTU	ACUTE EARS	AACEHIMRR	HAIR CREAM
AACEESTUV	EVACUATES	AACEHINRW	CHINAWARE
AACEESTVX	EXCAVATES	AACEHINST	HANSEATIC
AACEFFINS	AFFIANCES	AACEHIPST	CHAPATIES
AACEFFIRT	AFFRICATE	AACEHIPTT	APATHETIC

AACEHIRRS	HIRES A CAR	AACEISTUV	CAUSATIVE
AACEHIRSY	EASY CHAIR	AACEJKSSS	JACKASSES
AACEHKMOR	HACKAMORE	AACEJORST	CARES A JOT
AACEHKMPU	KAMPUCHEA	AACEKKLSW	CAKEWALKS
AACEHKRSV	HAVERSACK	AACEKLLMS	MAKE CALLS
AACEHLLLR	CLARE HALL	AACEKLMOO	COOK A MEAL
AACEHLNSW	WASH CLEAN	AACEKLPRT	PLATE RACK
AACEHLRTT	CLATHRATE	AACEKLPSW	SPACE WALK
AACEHLSSS	CASH SALES	AACEKMRTT	TRACK TEAM
AACEHMNRU	HUMAN RACE	AACEKNRRS	RANSACKER
AACEHMRSY	CAMERA SHY	AACEKNTTU	TAKEN A CAT
	EASY CHARM	AACEKOPTY	TAKE A COPY
AACEHNRRT	RAN THE CAR	AACEKPPRR	PAPER RACK
AACEHNSSS	SASSENACH	AACEKPPTY	PAY-PACKET
AACEHOORT	CARE A HOOT	AACEKRSTT	ATTACKERS
AACEHPRSS	SPARE CASH	AACEKSTTU	TAKES A CUT
AACEHPRTU	PARACHUTE	AACELLLRY	EARLY CALL
AACEHRSST	CATHARSES	AACELLNOT	ALL AT ONCE
AACEHRSSW	CAR WASHES	AACELLNOW	ALLOWANCE
AACEIILNT	LACINIATE	AACELLNPT	PLACENTAL
AACEIIMNR	IN AMERICA	AACELLNST	CASTELLAN
AACEIINRR	CINERARIA	AACELLOST	ALLOCATES
AACEIIRTV	VICARIATE	AACELLPST	LAST PLACE
AACEIKLNP	PLAIN CAKE	AACELLSTY	ALLEY CATS
AACEIKMPT	PICK A TEAM	AACELLTVY	CLAVATELY
AACEIKPRS	ASK A PRICE	AACELMNNT	CATTLEMAN
AACEILLMS	CAMELLIAS	AACELMOOT	COELOMATA
AACEILLNS	ALLIANCES	AACELMPRW	WARM PLACE
AACEILLRV	VARICELLA	AACELMRST	SMART ALEC
AACEILLTV	VACILLATE		SMART-ALEC
AACEILMNN	ALEMANNIC	AACELNNTU	CANNULATE
AACEILMNP	CAMPANILE	AACELNPSS	SCALEPANS
AACEILMPS	ECLAMPSIA	AACELNPST	PLACENTAS
AACEILMTV	CALMATIVE	AACELNRST	ANCESTRAL
AACEILNNR	CARNELIAN		LANCASTER
AACEILNPP	APPLIANCE	AACELNSUZ	SUEZ CANAL
AACEILNPS	SNAIL PACE	AACELORST	CARES A LOT
AACEILNPT	ANALEPTIC		ESCALATOR
AACEILNRS	ARSENICAL	AACELOSTT	CATTALOES
AACEILNSS	CANALISES	AACELOTUV	AUTOCLAVE
AACEILNSZ	CANALIZES		VACUOLATE
AACEILORT	ALEATORIC	AACELPPRT	APPLE CART
AACEILPTV	PLACATIVE	AACELPSTU	ASPECTUAL
AACEILRSV	CALVARIES		CAPSULATE
	CAVALIERS	AACELPSTY	CATALEPSY
	CAVALRIES	AACELPTXY	CATAPLEXY
AACEILTUZ	ACTUALIZE	AACELRRTU	CREATURAL
AACEIMNRS	AMERICANS	AACELRSTY	ACRYLATES
AACEIMNTU	ACUMINATE	AACELRTUW	CATERWAUL
AACEIMRST	MARCASITE	AACELRTUY	ARCUATELY
AACEIMSTT	CATAMITES		YER ACTUAL
	MASTICATE	AACELSSTY	CATALYSES
AACEINNRT	IN A CANTER	AACEMNPRT	MERCAPTAN
	IN A TRANCE	AACEMNRST	SACRAMENT
	INCARNATE	AACEMOPRT	COME APART
AACEINNSY	IN ANY CASE	AACEMORRT	MACERATOR
AACEINPRS	IN A SCRAPE	AACEMPRST	SMART PACE
AACEINPSU	CAUSE PAIN	AACEMRRSS	MASSACRER
AACEINRST	ASCERTAIN	AACEMRSSS	MASSACRES
	CARTESIAN	AACENNNOY	ANNOYANCE
	CRANIATES	AACENNOSS	ASSONANCE
	SECTARIAN	AACENPSSU	SAUCEPANS
AACEINRSW	WINS A RACE	AACENRRSU	RUNS A RACE
AACEIOSST	ASSOCIATE	AACENRSSU	ANACRUSES
AACEIPPRT	PER CAPITA		ASSURANCE
AACEIPRSS	AIRSPACES	AACENRSSV	CANVASERS
AACEIPTTV	CAPTIVATE		CANVASSER
AACEIRSST	STAIRCASE	AACENRSTT	REACTANTS
AACEIRSTU	ACTUARIES	AACENSSSV	CANVASSES
AACEISTTV	ACTIVATES	AACENSSTT	CASTANETS
	CAVITATES		CASTS A NET

AACEOPRSY	PAY A SCORE	AACHILMTT	LIT A MATCH
AACEORRSW	ROWS A RACE	AACHILNPS	CHAPLAINS
AACEORTVX	EXCAVATOR		SHIP CANAL
AACEOSSTT	EAST COAST	AACHILOPR	PAROCHIAL
AACEOSTTV	CAST A VOTE	AACHILOPT	CHIPOLATA
AACERSSTT	CASTRATES	AACHILORS	CHAROLAIS
AACESSUWY	CAUSEWAYS	AACHILPST	ASPHALTIC
AACFFRSST	STAFF CARS	AACHILSST	THALASSIC
AACFGLNRY	FLAGRANCY	AACHIMNOR	HARMONICA
AACFHIKLT	HALF A TICK	AACHIMNRS	ANARCHISM
	LACK FAITH	AACHIMNTW	WIN A MATCH
AACFHKLRT	HALF-TRACK	AACHIMRRS	ARMCHAIRS
AACFHMSST	CAMSHAFTS	AACHIMRRT	MATRIARCH
AACFIILNN	FINANCIAL	AACHIMRSS	ARCHAISMS
AACFILMRY	FAMILY CAR	AACHIMRST	CATHARISM
AACFILMST	CAST A FILM	AACHIMSTT	ASTHMATIC
AACFILMTY	CAT FAMILY	AACHINOPR	ANAPHORIC
AACFILNOT	FACTIONAL		PHARAONIC
AACFILNPT	PLAIN FACT	AACHINORT	TOCHARIAN
AACFILORT	FACTORIAL	AACHINPSY	PAY IN CASH
AACFILOTT	FAIL TO ACT	AACHINRST	ANARCHIST
AACFILRTY	ACT FAIRLY		CANTHARIS
AACFINSTT	FANTASTIC		THRACIANS
AACFIRSTT	ARTIFACTS	AACHINSSW	CHAIN SAWS
AACFJKLPS	FLAPJACKS	AACHIPRRT	PATRIARCH
AACFJNOOR	JOAN OF ARC	AACHIPSTT	CHAPATTIS
AACFLLTUW	LAWFUL ACT	AACHIRSST	CATHARSIS
AACFLLTUY	FACTUALLY	AACHKSSTY	HAYSTACKS
AACFLOPSW	SCAPA FLOW	AACHLLMRY	LACHRYMAL
AACFMNRST	CRAFTSMAN	AACHLMNOR	MONARCHAL
AACFORSTW	ACTS OF WAR	AACHLMPTY	MATCH PLAY
AACGGHINN	CHAIN GANG	AACHLMRST	LAST MARCH
AACGGIKNP	PACKAGING	AACHLMRSY	MARSHALCY
AACGGIMNT	GAMING ACT	AACHLOPVY	PLAY HAVOC
AACGGNRYZ	CRAZY GANG	AACHMNNOR	ANCHORMAN
AACGHIMNP	CHAMPAIGN	AACHMNORW	CHARWOMAN
AACGHINTT	ATTACHING	AACHMNOTW	WON A MATCH
AACGIIMNS	MAGICIANS	AACHMNSTY	YACHTSMAN
AACGIKNTT	ATTACKING	AACHMORST	HAM ACTORS
AACGILLLY	GLACIALLY	AACHMPRST	MARCH PAST
AACGILLMY	MAGICALLY	AACHNOTTY	CHATOYANT
AACGILLOS	SCAGLIOLA	AACHNRSST	TRASH CANS
AACGILLRT	LARGACTIL	AACHOOPTT	CAP A TOOTH
AACGILMMP	MAGIC LAMP	AACHOPPRY	APOCRYPHA
AACGILMNN	MANACLING	AACHOSSTT	ACT AS HOST
AACGILMNT	GIANT CLAM	AACHOSSTW	CAST A SHOW
AACGILNPT	PLACATING	AACHQSSTU	SASQUATCH
AACGILNTT	LACTATING	AACIIKTTW	WAIT A TICK
AACGIMNNR	RACING MAN	AACIILLRT	ALTRICIAL
AACGIMNPS	CAMPAIGNS	AACIILMNP	CAMPANILI
AACGIMPRT	PRAGMATIC	AACIILMRS	RACIALISM
AACGIMSUU	GUAIACUMS	AACIILMST	LAMAISTIC
AACGINPST	SIGN A PACT	AACIILNST	CASTILIAN
AACGINSTW	SWING A CAT	AACIILPRT	PIRATICAL
AACGINTTU	ACTUATING	AACIILRST	RACIALIST
AACGIOSSU	SAGACIOUS		SATIRICAL
AACGKNPSU	PACKS A GUN	AACIIMMST	MIASMATIC
AACGLLSWY	SCALLYWAG	AACIIMOTX	AXIOMATIC
AACGLNOOT	OCTAGONAL	AACIINNOP	POINCIANA
AACGLNOTU	COAGULANT	AACIINPRT	PATRICIAN
AACGMORRT	CARTOGRAM	AACIIPRST	PARASITIC
AACGNNSTY	STAGNANCY	AACIIRRTU	URTICARIA
AACGNRRTY	CARY GRANT	AACIISTTV	ATAVISTIC
AACGNRRUY	CARRY A GUN	AACIKLLST	KILLS A CAT
AACHHHIUU	CHIHUAHUA	AACILLLST	CALL TAILS
AACHHKOSS	HAS A SHOCK	AACILLMNY	MANICALLY
AACHHSTWY	HATCHWAYS	AACILLMSY	LAYS CLAIM
AACHIILMN	CHAIN MAIL	AACILLNOT	ALL ACTION
AACHIILPT	ALIPHATIC		ALLANTOIC
AACHIIPRS	PHARISAIC	AACILLNRY	ANCILLARY
AACHIIRRV	CHARIVARI	AACILLOXY	COAXIALLY

AACILLPRY	CAPILLARY
AACILLPST	CAPS IT ALL
AACILMNST	CALAMINTS
	CLAIMANTS
AACILMOSW	MOSAIC LAW
AACILMPST	PLASMATIC
AACILMPSY	PAY CLAIMS
AACILMRSU	SIMULACRA
AACILNOPT	PLACATION
AACILNOTT	LACTATION
AACILNOTV	CLAVATION
AACILNPPT	APPLICANT
AACILNRSV	CARNIVALS
AACILNRTY	CARNALITY
AACILNRUV	NAVICULAR
AACILOSSU	SALACIOUS
AACILOSTT	COAT TAILS
	TAIL COATS
	TAIL COATS
AACILPRTU	CAPITULAR
AACILPRTY	PARALYTIC
AACILOTTU	ACQUITTAL
AACILRRTU	ARTICULAR
AACILRRUU	AURICULAR
AACILSSTY	CATALYSIS
AACILSTTT	ATTIC SALT
AACILSTUY	CAUSALITY
AACILTTUY	ACTUALITY
AACIMNNNU	MANCUNIAN
AACIMNOPR	PANORAMIC
AACIMNORS	MACARONIS
AACIMNUUV	IN A VACUUM
AACIMORST	AROMATICS
AACIMORTU	AMAUROTIC
AACIMORTW	ATOMIC WAR
AACIMOTTU	AUTOMATIC
AACIMRTTU	TRAUMATIC
AACINNORT	CARNATION
AACINOOTV	AVOCATION
AACINOPRS	CAPARISON
AACINORST	CROATIANS
	RAINCOATS
AACINOSTU	CAUSATION
AACINOSTV	VACATIONS
AACINOTTU	ACTUATION
AACINQSTU	ACQUAINTS
AACINRSST	SACRISTAN
AACINRSSU	ANACRUSIS
AACIOPRSU	RAPACIOUS
AACIORTTV	ACTIVATOR
AACIOSTTW	WAISTCOAT
AACJKOORS	JACKAROOS
AACJKPRST	JACK SPRAT
AACKKNPSS	KNAPSACKS
AACKLLOOT	TOOK A CALL
AACKLMNPX	MAX PLANCK
AACKLOOST	CAST A LOOK
AACKLOSWY	LOCKS AWAY
AACKORSTT	TOAST RACK
AACKSTUWY	TUCKS AWAY
AACLLLOSW	LOCAL LAWS
AACLLMRSS	SMALL CARS
AACLLNOPY	PAY ON CALL
AACLLOORT	ALLOCATOR
AACLLOSTY	COASTALLY
AACLLRSTU	CLAUSTRAL
AACLLTTUY	TACTUALLY
AACLMSSTY	STAYS CALM
AACLNOORS	SALOON CAR
AACLNOPTU	CANTALOUP
AACLNOTTV	VACANT LOT

AACLNRUUV	AVUNCULAR
AACLOPRRR	PARLOR CAR
AACLOPRRT	PATROL CAR
AACLOPRTY	PLACATORY
AACLORSSU	CAROUSALS
AACLPRSSU	SCAPULARS
AACLPSTTU	CATAPULTS
AACLRRTUY	CARTULARY
AACMMNOPR	ROMAN CAMP
AACMMPRSY	ARMY CAMPS
AACMNOORS	MACAROONS
AACMNOTTU	CATAMOUNT
AACMOOSTT	SCOTOMATA
AACMORSTW	WARM COATS
AACMRRRSY	CARRY ARMS
AACNORRSS	RAN ACROSS
AACNOSTTY	AT ANY COST
AACNPRSST	ST.PANCRAS
AACNQSTUY	QANTOOT
AACNRSTUZ	SANTA CRUZ
AACORRRTW	RAW CARROT
AACORRSTT	STAR ACTOR
AACORRTTT	ATTRACTOR
AACORSSWY	CASSOWARY
AACORSTTU	ACTUATORS
	AUTOCRATS
AACRSSTTY	STRAY CATS
AADDDEEHS	DEADHEADS
AADDDGNRS	GRANDDADS
AADDDMMNU	MUM AND DAD
AADDEEFHT	FATHEADED
AADDEEGHN	HAD AN EDGE
AADDEEHIT	DIE A DEATH
AADDEELNO	DONE A DEAL
AADDEELOS	DOES A DEAL
AADDEEMNT	MADE A DENT
AADDEEMRY	MADE READY
	READY MADE
	READY-MADE
AADDEENTT	ANTEDATED
AADDEERTW	DEAD WATER
AADDEETVX	EVADED TAX
AADDEFINT	DEAD FAINT
AADDEGITV	DIVAGATED
AADDEGLNR	GARLANDED
AADDEGLOO	A GOOD DEAL
AADDEGMNU	UNDAMAGED
AADDEGRTU	GRADUATED
AADDEHHMN	HAM-HANDED
AADDEHHRS	HARDHEADS
AADDEHIMT	HAD IT MADE
AADDEHINO	HAD NO IDEA
AADDEHLNN	LEND A HAND
AADDEHLNS	HEADLANDS
AADDEHLSY	SHADY DEAL
AADDEHSYY	HEADY DAYS
AADDEIILS	LAID ASIDE
AADDEILNO	ADENOIDAL
AADDEILPS	PALISADED
AADDEILSY	LADIES DAY
AADDEILTV	VALIDATED
AADDEIMNR	MARINADED
AADDEINRW	EDWARDIAN
AADDEKLNY	NAKED LADY
AADDEKOSS	DO AS ASKED
AADDELMNR	DREAMLAND
AADDELORU	READ ALOUD
AADDELPPU	APPLAUDED
AADDELRST	ASTRADDLE
AADDEMNNT	DEMANDANT
AADDEMNTX	TAX DEMAND

AADDEMRSY	DAY DREAMS	AADEELMRU	MADE A RULE
	DAYDREAMS	AADEELNNR	LEND AN EAR
AADDEOPRV	PAVED ROAD	AADEELNPS	ESPLANADE
AADDERSTW	ADDS WATER	AADEELRRT	ART DEALER
AADDGNRSU	GRADUANDS	AADEELRRW	WAR LEADER
AADDHHINN	HAD IN HAND	AADEELRST	TARSEALED
AADDHIKNR	HAD A DRINK	AADEELRSW	DELAWARES
AADDHIMNS	HANDMAIDS	AADEELRTT	LATER DATE
AADDHLLOR	ROALD DAHL	AADEELTUV	EVALUATED
AADDHNNST	HANDSTAND	AADEEMMOV	MADE A MOVE
AADDHORRS	HARD ROADS	AADEEMMSS	MADE A MESS
AADDIIMRY	DAIRY MAID	AADEEMNOT	MADE A NOTE
AADDIINRV	DRAVIDIAN	AADEEMNRT	TRADE NAME
AADDILMSY	LADYS MAID	AADEEMRTW	MADE WATER
AADDINORS	DIANA DORS	AADEEMSST	TEASMADES
AADDLRSTY	DASTARDLY	AADEEMSVW	MADE WAVES
AADDNNPYY	ANDY PANDY	AADEENSTT	ANTEDATES
AADDNRSST	STANDARDS	AADEENSTU	NAUSEATED
AADEEEHKP	KEEP AHEAD	AADEEPPRT	PARAPETED
AADEEEHNS	SEEN AHEAD	AADEEPRST	SEPARATED
AADEEEHSS	SEES AHEAD	AADEERSTY	EASTER DAY
AADEEEKPT	KEEP A DATE	AADEESSTT	SETS A DATE
AADEEFILS	FALSE IDEA	AADEESTTV	DEVASTATE
AADEEFIMR	MADE A FIRE	AADEESTVX	EVADES TAX
AADEEGHMT	MEGADEATH	AADEFFILR	FAR AFIELD
AADEEGHNO	GONE AHEAD	AADEFGIMT	MADE A GIFT
AADEEGHNS	HAS AN EDGE	AADEFGRSU	SAFEGUARD
AADEEGHOS	GOES AHEAD	AADEFHNOR	HAD NO FEAR
AADEEGHST	GETS AHEAD	AADEFHNSS	SAFE HANDS
AADEEGILV	GIVE A LEAD	AADEFIILR	LAID A FIRE
AADEEGINT	GET AN IDEA	AADEFIINP	PAID A FINE
AADEEGIRT	GREAT IDEA	AADEFILRS	FAIRLEADS
AADEEGIUV	VAGUE IDEA	AADEFILWY	FILED AWAY
AADEEGLLR	ALL AGREED	AADEFINST	FANTASIED
AADEEGLRT	GREAT DEAL	AADEFIORS	AFORESAID
AADEEGNPP	APPENDAGE	AADEFIRRT	FAIR TRADE
AADEEGNRT	GREAT DANE		TRADE FAIR
	TEA GARDEN	AADEFIRWY	FIRED AWAY
AADEEHHRX	HEXAHEDRA	AADEFJNNO	JANE FONDA
AADEEHKPT	KEPT AHEAD	AADEFKRRT	AFTER DARK
AADEEHLLS	HELD A SALE	AADEFLLRS	FALDERALS
AADEEHLLW	WELL AHEAD	AADEFLLUW	FEUDAL LAW
AADEEHLMO	MADE A HOLE	AADEFLNOR	FARANDOLE
AADEEHLUV	HAVE A DUEL	AADEFLORY	YARD OF ALE
AADEEHMST	MADE HASTE	AADEFLOST	FATAL DOSE
AADEEHNTW	WENT AHEAD	AADEFLTUX	FEUDAL TAX
AADEEHPRS	SPEARHEAD	AADEFMRST	FARMSTEAD
AADEEHRRT	DEAR HEART	AADEFOSTU	AUTOS-DA-FE
AADEEHRST	SHED A TEAR	AADEFSSTT	STEADFAST
AADEEHRTT	DEATH RATE	AADEFSSTY	FEAST DAYS
AADEEHRTW	HEADWATER	AADEGGHMN	HAM AND EGG
AADEEIKST	TAKE ASIDE	AADEGGILN	LAID AN EGG
AADEEIKTV	TAKE A DIVE	AADEGGIRV	DIG A GRAVE
AADEEIKWW	WIDE AWAKE	AADEGGLSS	EGG SALADS
	WIDE-AWAKE	AADEGGOSV	SAVAGE DOG
AADEEILMP	MADE A PILE	AADEGGRUV	DUG A GRAVE
AADEEILMV	MEDIAEVAL	AADEGHINV	GIVE A HAND
AADEEILNT	ALIENATED	AADEGHLTU	LAUGHED AT
AADEEILRS	AIREDALES	AADEGHMRS	HARD GAMES
AADEEILST	LEAST IDEA	AADEGHNOO	GO AHEAD ON
	TEA LADIES	AADEGHNRU	HARANGUED
AADEEJKMO	MADE A JOKE	AADEGHNRY	HYDRANGEA
AADEEJMNS	JAMES DEAN	AADEGHNST	STAGE HAND
AADEEKMNT	MAKE A DENT		STAGEHAND
AADEEKMRR	EARMARKED	AADEGHSSU	HAD A GUESS
AADEEKMRY	MAKE READY	AADEGIIRT	DEI GRATIA
	MAKEREADY	AADEGIKPR	GIDEA PARK
AADEEKNPS	NAKED APES	AADEGILTT	TAILGATED
AADEEKPTT	KEPT A DATE	AADEGILWY	GLIDE AWAY
AADEELLMN	ALLEMANDE	AADEGIMNS	MADE A SIGN
AADEELLNV	DAVE ALLEN	AADEGIMNT	DIAMAGNET

AADEGIMNV	GIVE A DAMN	AADEIINST	EAST INDIA
AADEGINOT	GOT AN IDEA	AADEIIRRT	IRRADIATE
AADEGINPT	PAGINATED	AADEIKLLLM	MADE A KILL
AADEGINRR	ARRAIGNED	AADEILLMW	MADE A WILL
AADEGINRS	GARDENIAS	AADEILLPT	PALLIATED
AADEGINRT	TRAGEDIAN	AADEILMNN	ALMANDINE
AADEGINRV	GIVE A DARN	AADEILMNP	MADE PLAIN
AADEGINTV	NAVIGATED	AADEILMNS	LADIES MAN
AADEGIPRS	DISPARAGE	AADEILMNT	LAMINATED
AADEGIPSW	PAID WAGES	AADEILMPS	MADE A SLIP
AADEGISTV	DIVAGATES	AADEILMRT	DIAMETRAL
AADEGKRTU	TAKE A DRUG	AADEILMST	MADE A LIST
AADEGLMNS	MAGDALENS	AADEILNNN	ANNELIDAN
AADEGLNNT	LAND AGENT	AADEILNNR	ADRENALIN
AADEGMNRW	DRAWN GAME	AADEILNNS	INLAND SEA
AADEGNSTT	STAGNATED	AADEILNRW	DRAW A LINE
AADEGORRT	ARROGATED	AADEILNSS	NASALISED
AADEGRRRU	REARGUARD	AADEILNSV	VANDALISE
AADEGRRVY	GRAVEYARD	AADEILNSZ	NASALIZED
AADEGRSTU	GRADUATES	AADEILNVZ	VANDALIZE
AADEGRSTY	GREAT DAYS	AADEILPSS	PALISADES
AADEGRSTZ	STARGAZED	AADEILRTV	TRAVAILED
AADEHHKNS	HANDSHAKE	AADEILRTY	RADIATELY
AADEHHNVY	HEAVY HAND	AADEILRVW	DRAW A VEIL
AADEHHOST	SHOT AHEAD	AADEILSST	LEAST SAID
AADEHHRRT	HARD HEART	AADEILSSY	LAYS ASIDE
AADEHILRS	RAILHEADS	AADEILSTV	SALIVATED
AADEHIMST	HAS IT MADE		VALIDATES
AADEHIMSW	MADE A WISH	AADEILSTW	LAID WASTE
AADEHINOS	HAS NO IDEA	AADEILSTY	DIALYSATE
AADEHIORR	DIARRHOEA	AADEILSWY	SLIDE AWAY
AADEHIPRT	APARTHEID	AADEILTVW	TIDAL WAVE
	HIT PARADE	AADEIMMNT	MADE A MINT
AADEHISWY	HIDEAWAYS	AADEIMMSS	MASS MEDIA
	HIDES AWAY	AADEIMNOR	MAINE ROAD
AADEHJMPU	JUMP AHEAD	AADEIMNRS	MARINADES
AADEHKLOO	LOOK AHEAD	AADEIMNRT	MARINATED
AADEHKMOS	HAD A SMOKE	AADEIMNST	DIAMANTES
AADEHKMST	DEATH MASK	AADEIMNSW	ADAMS WINE
AADEHKNRT	TAKEN HARD	AADEIMPTY	MADE IT PAY
AADEHKRST	TAKES HARD	AADEIMRST	DRAMATISE
AADEHLLMS	MAD AS HELL	AADEIMRTZ	DRAMATIZE
	SMALL HEAD	AADEINRST	STERADIAN
AADEHLLOS	HOLD A SALE	AADEINRTT	ATTAINDER
AADEHLLPU	PULL AHEAD	AADEIPPRS	APPRAISED
AADEHLLST	HEADSTALL		DISAPPEAR
AADEHLLTY	ALL THE DAY	AADEIPRRT	RAPID RATE
AADEHLMNN	MANHANDLE	AADEIPRST	ASPIRATED
AADEHLMPS	HEADLAMPS		DISPARATE
	LAMP SHADE	AADEIPRTW	WIDE APART
	LAMPSHADE	AADEIPRTX	PAID EXTRA
AADEHLMSY	ASHAMEDLY	AADEIPWWY	WIPED AWAY
AADEHLNNP	PANHANDLE	AADEIRSTW	ARID WASTE
AADEHLNNT	LENT A HAND	AADEIRSWY	RIDES AWAY
AADEHLNRT	HEARTLAND	AADEIRVWY	DRIVE AWAY
AADEHLOVY	HEAVY LOAD	AADEJKLWY	JAYWALKED
AADEHMNSU	UNASHAMED	AADEKLLTY	ALKYLATED
AADEHMOSW	MADE A SHOW	AADEKMMNR	MARKED MAN
AADEHMRTT	MAD HATTER	AADEKMMNS	MASKED MAN
AADEHMSST	MASTHEADS	AADEKMRRT	TRADE MARK
AADEHNRSU	RUNS AHEAD		TRADEMARK
AADEHORRW	ARROWHEAD	AADEKMRTY	MARKET DAY
AADEHORVW	HAVE A WORD	AADEKNNYY	DANNY KAYE
AADEHPRST	HARD-PASTE	AADEKNOTV	NEAT VODKA
AADEHPRTT	DEATH TRAP	AADEKOPRT	TAKE A DROP
AADEHRRTW	EARTHWARD	AADELLMPY	MEDAL PLAY
	HARD WATER	AADELLNNO	ONE AND ALL
AADEHRSST	HARD SEATS	AADELLNPR	LAPLANDER
AADEHRSTT	HEAD START	AADELLNRY	ADRENALLY
AADEHRSTY	DEATH RAYS	AADELLNTU	LANDAULET
AADEIINNT	INDIAN TEA	AADELLOTT	TOLD A TALE

AADELLSSY	SALESLADY	AADFLLLNS	LANDFALLS
AADELMMOR	MELODRAMA	AADFMNRST	DRAFTSMAN
AADELMNOR	EALDORMAN	AADFMRRSY	FARMYARDS
AADELMNPS	MADE PLANS	AADFNOUWY	FOUND A WAY
AADELMORT	ROAD METAL	AADFNSSTT	STAND FAST
AADELMORV	AD VALOREM	AADFOORUV	DO A FAVOUR
AADELMOSS	MADE A LOSS	AADFRRSTW	DWARF STAR
AADELMPST	DATE PALMS	AADGGHLRY	HAGGARDLY
AADELNNPS	AS PLANNED	AADGGIINR	DIANA RIGG
AADELNRRU	RURAL DEAN	AADGGINRT	GRADATING
AADELNSTW	WASTE LAND	AADGGLLRY	LAGGARDLY
	WASTELAND	AADGGLNNS	GANGLANDS
AADELPPRU	APPLAUDER	AADGGNOPS	PAGAN GODS
AADELPRTW	DRAWPLATE	AADGHIMPR	DIAPHRAGM
AADELPRTY	LED A PARTY	AADGHINRZ	HAZARDING
	PLY A TRADE	AADGHIOPR	PARIAH DOG
AADELPRYY	PAY DEARLY	AADGIINOT	DO IT AGAIN
AADELRSTY	LED ASTRAY	AADGIINRT	RADIATING
AADELRSYY	EARLY DAYS	AADGILLRS	GALLIARDS
AADELRTTY	LATTER DAY	AADGILMNY	AMYGDALIN
	LATTER-DAY	AADGILMRS	MADRIGALS
AADELSSTU	ASSAULTED	AADGILNOS	DIAGONALS
AADEMMNOR	MEMORANDA	AADGILNTU	ADULATING
AADEMNNTW	WANTED MAN	AADGILORT	GLADIATOR
AADEMNPRS	AMPERSAND	AADGILRRU	GUARDRAIL
AADEMNPTU	UP AND AT EM	AADGIMNNT	MANDATING
AADEMNRST	TRADESMAN	AADGIMNRU	MARAUDING
AADEMOTTU	AUTOMATED	AADGIMNRV	RAVING MAD
AADEMOVVWY	MOVED AWAY	AADGIMORR	RADIOGRAM
AADEMPSTT	DATE STAMP	AADGIMPRS	PARADIGMS
	DATESTAMP	AADGIMRRS	MARDI GRAS
AADEMPTTU	AMPUTATED	AADGINORT	GRADATION
AADEMRSTT	DARTS TEAM	AADGINRSU	GUARDIANS
AADENNOTT	ANNOTATED	AADGINWYY	DYING AWAY
AADENNPPT	APPENDANT	AADGLLNRU	GLANDULAR
AADENNRRW	DRAWN NEAR	AADGLLOPR	DOLLAR GAP
AADENNTTT	ATTENDANT	AADGLLRUY	GRADUALLY
AADENPPRS	SANDPAPER	AADGLMNRS	GRAND SLAM
AADENPPST	SNAPPED AT	AADGLNRSS	GRASSLAND
AADENRRSW	DRAWS NEAR	AADGMNOOY	A GOOD MANY
AADENRRTT	RETARDANT	AADGMNORS	DRAGOMANS
AADENRRTW	WARRANTED	AADGMNRSU	GUARDSMAN
AADENSSTY	STAND EASY	AADGNNRTU	GRANDAUNT
AADENSSWY	SENDS AWAY	AADGNNRUW	DRAWN A GUN
AADEOPRSX	PARADOXES	AADGNRSUV	GUARDS VAN
AADEORSTW	SODA WATER		VANGUARDS
AADEORVVWY	DROVE AWAY	AADGNRSUW	DRAWS A GUN
AADEPRRTW	DREW APART	AADGORRTU	GRADUATOR
AADEQRSTU	QUADRATES	AADHHINNS	HAS IN HAND
AADERRRSW	REARWARDS	AADHHMNNU	HUMAN HAND
AADERRSVY	ADVERSARY	AADHHMNUW	HUM AND HAW
AADERRTWW	DRAW WATER	AADHIKNRS	HAS A DRINK
AADERSSTW	EASTWARDS	AADHIKRRS	DARK HAIRS
AADERSTTU	SATURATED	AADHILLRS	HALLIARDS
AADFFIITV	AFFIDAVIT	AADHILNRS	HANDRAILS
AADFFILNT	FIND A FLAT	AADHILRST	TAHSILDAR
AADFGHHIT	HAD A FIGHT	AADHIMMST	ADAM SMITH
AADFGHRRT	HARD GRAFT	AADHIMORS	RADIO HAMS
AADFGNNOS	FANDANGOS	AADHINPSU	UPANISHAD
AADFHHLRY	HALF-HARDY	AADHINRRS	HARRIDANS
AADFHILMN	HALF A MIND	AADHIPSSY	DYSPHASIA
AADFHILNT	LIFT A HAND	AADHJMNOS	JOHN ADAMS
AADFHILQU	HALF A QUID	AADHKNOOT	TOOK A HAND
AADFHMNRS	FARM HANDS	AADHKRSST	HARD TASKS
	FARMHANDS	AADHLLNST	HALLSTAND
AADFILNRY	FAIRYLAND	AADHLMQSU	HAD QUALMS
AADFIMNRY	MAN FRIDAY	AADHLNRYY	HARDLY ANY
AADFIMRRY	DAIRY FARM	AADHLPRSY	PLAYS HARD
AADFINSWY	FINDS A WAY	AADHMNNSY	MANY HANDS
AADFIRTWY	DRIFT AWAY	AADHMNRSW	WARM HANDS
AADFKLLNS	FALKLANDS	AADHNSSTW	WASHSTAND

AADHOPRRT	HARD APORT	AADLORTUY	ADULATORY
AADHORSTY	HARD TO SAY		LAUDATORY
AADHORSUZ	HAZARDOUS	AADLPRSTY	PLAY DARTS
AADHPPSYY	HAPPY DAYS	AADLRWWYY	WAYWARDLY
AADIIKLNU	NIKI LAUDA	AADMNOORR	ROMAN ROAD
AADIILLMY	DAILY MAIL	AADMNORTY	DAMNATORY
AADIILSUV	VISUAL AID		MANDATORY
AADIIMMOT	OMMATIDIA	AADNNORRU	RAN AROUND
AADIINNRS	SARDINIAN	AADNNOWYY	ANY DAY NOW
AADIINNRW	DARWINIAN	AADNOORRS	AARONS ROD
AADIINORT	RADIATION	AADNORSTU	SAT AROUND
AADIIORTU	AUDITORIA	AADNPSSTT	STANDS PAT
AADIKLLOS	ALKALOIDS	AADNQRSTU	QUADRANTS
AADILLMOR	ARMADILLO	AADNRSVYY	NAVY YARDS
AADILLMPU	PALLADIUM	AADOOSTWY	STOOD AWAY
AADILLOPS	SAPODILLA	AADOPPRST	STRAPPADO
AADILMNSV	VANDALISM	AADRSSTUY	SATURDAYS
AADILMOPS	PLASMODIA	AAEEEKLTV	TAKE LEAVE
AADILMORT	MALADROIT	AAEEEKPPT	TAKE A PEEP
AADILMPRY	PYRAMIDAL	AAEEELPPV	EYE APPEAL
AADILMRTY	ADMIRALTY	AAEEELSTV	TEA LEAVES
AADILMTUU	MUTUAL AID	AAEEESSTT	SET AT EASE
AADILNNOT	ANTINODAL	AAEEFGMRT	GREAT FAME
AADILNOPT	ANTIPODAL	AAEEFGRST	FARE STAGE
AADILNORU	RADIO-ULNA	AAEEFGRTT	GREAT FEAT
AADILNOTT	ANTIDOTAL	AAEEFHLNY	HALF AN EYE
AADILNOTU	ADULATION	AAEEFHNRT	FAN HEATER
AADILNRTY	RADIANTLY	AAEEFIKLL	LIKE A LEAF
AADILNSWZ	SWAZILAND	AAEEFIKMR	MAKE A FIRE
AADILOPRY	RADIO PLAY	AAEEFIRRS	FREE AS AIR
AADILORRS	RAILROADS	AAEEFKMSS	MAKES SAFE
AADILOSVW	DISAVOWAL	AAEEFKRTT	TAKE AFTER
AADILPSSY	DYSPLASIA	AAEEFLLMP	MAPLE LEAF
AADILRSTY	DAILY STAR	AAEEFLMNS	FALSE NAME
AADIMNNOT	DAMNATION	AAEEFLNNU	ANNUAL FEE
AADIMNNRS	MANDARINS	AAEEFMSST	MEAT SAFES
AADIMNORS	MAIN ROADS	AAEEFPRTT	FEET APART
AADIMNRST	TAMARINDS	AAEEFRRSS	SEAFARERS
AADIMORST	RADIO MAST	AAEEFSSST	SAFE SEATS
AADIMRSTT	DRAMATIST	AAEEGGGRT	AGGREGATE
AADINNORY	INDO ARYAN	AAEEGHKLS	SHAKE A LEG
AADINNRSU	SUN AND AIR	AAEEGHRST	GAS HEATER
AADINOORT	ADORATION	AAEEGIRTV	VARIEGATE
AADINOPSS	DIAPASONS	AAEEGKMMS	MAKES GAME
AADINORSS	DIANA ROSS	AAEEGLMNP	PANEL GAME
AADINPRSS	SPANIARDS	AAEEGLMNT	MENTAL AGE
AADINRSYY	RAINY DAYS	AAEEGLMOS	LOSE A GAME
AADINSSTY	SAINTS DAY	AAEEGLRST	GREAT SEAL
AADIORRST	RADIATORS	AAEEGLRSW	REAL WAGES
	RADIO STAR	AAEEGLRVY	AVERAGELY
AADIPSSUY	UPSADAISY	AAEEGLSTT	LATE STAGE
AADIRRSSY	DISARRAYS	AAEEGMMST	TEAM GAMES
AADJMMNOS	DAMSON JAM	AAEEGMNNS	MANGANESE
AADJMOORR	MAJOR ROAD	AAEEGMNRT	GREAT NAME
AADJNSTTU	ADJUTANTS	AAEEGMNST	STAGE NAME
AADJNSTUV	ADJUVANTS	AAEEGMSSY	EASY GAMES
AADKLMNRS	LANDMARKS	AAEEGNORV	ON AVERAGE
AADKLRWWY	AWKWARDLY	AAEEGNPRT	PARENTAGE
AADLLNORU	ALL AROUND	AAEEGNRSW	EARN WAGES
	ALL-AROUND	AAEEGNRTU	GUARANTEE
AADLLNSTT	STAND TALL	AAEEGORTV	GAVE EAR TO
AADLLOPSU	PALLADOUS	AAEEGOSVY	SEA VOYAGE
AADLMPSVY	DAVY LAMPS	AAEEGPRSS	REPASSAGE
AADLMPSYY	PALMY DAYS	AAEEGPSSU	USE AS A PEG
AADLMRSST	SMART LADS	AAEEGPSUV	GAVE PAUSE
AADLNORUY	LAY AROUND	AAEEGPSUW	WAGE PAUSE
AADLNSSTT	LAST STAND	AAEEGRRSS	RARE GASES
AADLOORRY	ROYAL ROAD	AAEEGRSTW	WAGE RATES
AADLOPRUY	PRAY ALOUD	AAEEGRUVW	WEAVE A RUG
AADLORSTU	ADULATORS	AAEEHHOPV	HAVE A HOPE
AADLORSTY	LADY ASTOR	AAEEHIMTT	HAEMATITE

AAEEHINRT	IN THE AREA	AAEELLLMT	LAMELLATE
AAEEHISST	AESTHESIA	AAEELLLTT	TELL A TALE
AAEEHKLMO	MAKE A HOLE	AAEELLPPT	APPELLATE
AAEEHKMST	MAKE HASTE	AAEELLPSY	LAY ASLEEP
AAEEHKPST	TAKE SHAPE	AAEELLQRU	AQUARELLE
AAEEHKPTT	AT THE PEAK	AAEELMNPT	NAMEPLATE
AAEEHKRTT	TAKE HEART	AAEELMRTY	RELAY TEAM
AAEEHKRTW	WEAK HEART	AAEELMSST	SALES TEAM
AAEEHLMSV	HAVE MEALS	AAEELMSTT	STALEMATE
AAEEHLMTW	WHALE MEAT	AAEELNNOT	ATE NO LEAN
AAEEHLMVY	HEAVY MEAL		EAT NO LEAN
AAEEHLRRS	REHEARSAL	AAEELNNRT	LENT AN EAR
AAEEHMNTU	ATHENAEUM	AAEELNOPR	AEROPLANE
AAEEHMNTX	EXANTHEMA	AAEELNORS	LOSE AN EAR
AAEEHMOTT	ATE AT HOME	AAEELNPSS	SEAPLANES
	EAT AT HOME	AAEELNRSY	LEAN YEARS
AAEEHMPRV	HAVE A PERM	AAEELNRTT	ALTERNATE
AAEEHMPST	METAPHASE	AAEELPPSX	SEX APPEAL
AAEEHRRRT	RARE-EARTH	AAEELPRSY	LEAP YEARS
AAEEHRRTT	AT THE REAR	AAEELPSSY	SAY PLEASE
AAEEHRSTV	HAVE A REST	AAEELRSTU	LAUREATES
AAEEHRSTW	WHEATEARS	AAEELRTTX	LATE EXTRA
AAEEHSSVY	HEAVY SEAS	AAEELSTUV	EVALUATES
AAEEHSTTV	HAVE TASTE	AAEEMMNNS	NAME NAMES
AAEEIKLMP	MAKE A PILE	AAEEMMNTZ	AMAZEMENT
AAEEIKLMT	TAKE A MILE	AAEEMMPTY	EMPYEMATA
AAEEIKLMU	LEUKAEMIA	AAEEMMSTT	TEAM MATES
AAEEIKLSW	LIES AWAKE	AAEEMNNSS	ANAMNESES
AAEEIKRST	TAKE A RISE	AAEEMNOTT	ATE NO MEAT
AAEEIKTVW	TAKE A VIEW		EAT NO MEAT
AAEEILLMN	EL ALAMEIN	AAEEMNRST	MAN-EATERS
AAEEILLST	ILL AT EASE	AAEEMPRRT	PARAMETER
AAEEILLTV	ALLEVIATE	AAEEMPSTT	MEAT PASTE
AAEEILPTV	LEAVE A TIP	AAEENNRSZ	NAZARENES
AAEEILRTT	RETALIATE	AAEENRRTW	WARRANTEE
AAEEIMNTV	EMANATIVE	AAEENRSSW	AWARENESS
AAEEIMNTX	EXANIMATE	AAEENRSTT	ANTEATERS
AAEEIPSSY	EASY AS PIE	AAEENSSTU	NAUSEATES
AAEEIPTTX	EXPATIATE	AAEENTTTU	ATTENUATE
AAEEISTTV	AESTIVATE	AAEEOPRTV	EVAPORATE
AAEEJKKMO	MAKE A JOKE	AAEEPPRRS	RAPPAREES
AAEEKLMRS	MAKES REAL	AAEEPPRSS	APPEASERS
AAEEKLMRU	MAKE A RULE	AAEEPRRTY	RATEPAYER
AAEEKLMSS	MAKE SALES	AAEEPRSST	SEPARATES
AAEEKLNSW	ALAN WEEKS	AAEEPSTTU	PUT AT EASE
AAEEKLOSV	OAK LEAVES	AAEEPSWWY	SWEEP AWAY
AAEEKLRWY	WAKE EARLY	AAEERRRTT	RARE TREAT
AAEEKLSSV	ASKS LEAVE	AAEERRTTW	WATER RATE
AAEEKMMOV	MAKE A MOVE	AAEERSTTT	TEA TASTER
AAEEKMMSS	MAKE A MESS	AAEERSTTX	EXTRA SEAT
AAEEKMNOT	MAKE A NOTE	AAEERSVWY	VEERS AWAY
AAEEKMNSS	NAMESAKES	AAEESTTTX	ESTATE TAX
AAEEKMRTW	MAKE WATER	AAEFFIILT	AFFILIATE
AAEEKMSSY	MAKES EASY	AAEFGIKMT	MAKE A GIFT
AAEEKMSVW	MAKE WAVES	AAEFGILTV	GAVE A LIFT
AAEEKNOTT	TAKE A NOTE	AAEFGINRS	SEAFARING
AAEEKNPTW	TAKEN A PEW	AAEFGIRSW	FAIR WAGES
	WAPENTAKE	AAEFGIRSX	SAXIFRAGE
AAEEKNRSW	AWAKENERS	AAEFGKMOS	SMOKE A FAG
AAEEKOTTV	TAKE A VOTE	AAEFGLLLR	FLAGELLAR
AAEEKPPRT	KEEP APART	AAEFGLLOR	LARGE LOAF
AAEEKPRRT	PARRAKEET	AAEFGLLRT	LARGE FLAT
AAEEKPRST	PARAKEETS	AAEFGLLUW	LAWFUL AGE
AAEEKPSSY	SPEAKEASY	AAEFGLNRS	RANG FALSE
AAEEKPSTW	TAKES A PEW	AAEFGLRVW	FLAG-WAVER
AAEEKPSWY	KEEPS AWAY	AAEFGORRS	FARRAGOES
AAEEKQSSU	SEAQUAKES	AAEFHHITV	HAVE FAITH
AAEEKRRST	RARE STEAK	AAEFHHLRS	HALF SHARE
AAEEKRSTT	TAKE A REST	AAEFHILNT	FINAL HEAT
AAEEKSTTT	TAKE A TEST	AAEFHILTW	WHAT A LIFE!
AAEEKSTTW	WEAK STATE	AAEFHIRRS	FAIR SHARE

AAEFHLLVY	HEAVY FALL	AAEGHMOPY	PAY HOMAGE
AAEFHLOST	FALSE OATH	AAEGHMRSX	HEXAGRAMS
AAEFHLPRT	FLARE PATH	AAEGHNOPR	ORPHANAGE
AAEFHLRTT	FLAT EARTH	AAEGHNRSU	HARANGUES
AAEFHMRTT	AFTERMATH	AAEGHOOTV	GAVE A HOOT
AAEFHNORS	HAS NO FEAR	AAEGHRTWY	GATHER WAY
AAEFIKNRR	AFRIKANER	AAEGHSSSU	HAS A GUESS
AAEFILMRR	FIRE ALARM	AAEGIILNT	GENITALIA
AAEFILNPU	EPIFAUNAL	AAEGIILNV	LIVE AGAIN
AAEFILNRY	FINAL YEAR	AAEGIILQU	AQUILEGIA
AAEFILRRS	RAIL FARES	AAEGIKLTV	GIVE A TALK
AAEFILRSY	LAYS A FIRE	AAEGIKMNS	MAKE A SIGN
AAEFILRTY	FAIRY TALE	AAEGIKNNW	AWAKENING
	FAIRY-TALE	AAEGIKPRT	TAKE A GRIP
AAEFILRUV	FAIR VALUE	AAEGILMRR	ARMIGERAL
AAEFILSWY	FILES AWAY	AAEGILMRT	TRIAL GAME
	FLIES AWAY	AAEGILNNN	ANNEALING
AAEFIMMNR	MAINFRAME	AAEGILNNT	GALANTINE
AAEFINNRS	SAFRANINE		IN A TANGLE
AAEFINPSY	PAYS A FINE	AAEGILNOS	ANALOGIES
AAEFINRRT	TRAIN FARE		ANALOGISE
AAEFINSST	FANTASIES	AAEGILNOZ	ANALOGIZE
AAEFINSTZ	FANTASIZE	AAEGILNPP	APPEALING
AAEFINTTU	INFATUATE	AAEGILNPR	RING A PEAL
AAEFINOTX	TAXI FARES	AAEGILNPS	PELAGIANS
AAEFIRSWY	FIRES AWAY		PELASGIAN
AAEFKLLST	LEAFSTALK	AAEGILNRU	NEURALGIA
AAEFKLMRT	LEFT A MARK	AAEGILNSV	GALVANISE
AAEFKMSST	MAKES FAST	AAEGILNVZ	GALVANIZE
AAEFKMSSU	MAKE A FUSS	AAEGILSTT	TAILGATES
AAEFKNNNR	ANNE FRANK	AAEGIMMNS	MISMANAGE
AAEFKRSST	ASKS AFTER	AAEGIMNNS	MAGNESIAN
AAEFLLLRY	EARLY FALL	AAEGIMNNT	EMANATING
AAEFLLOST	STALE LOAF		MAN-EATING
AAEFLLPRT	FELL APART	AAEGIMNRR	MARGARINE
AAEFLLPSY	PLAY FALSE	AAEGIMNSW	WINS A GAME
AAEFLLRTW	WATERFALL	AAEGIMNSZ	MAGAZINES
AAEFLLSSW	WALL SAFES	AAEGIMRRS	MARRIAGES
AAEFLLTTW	FAT WALLET	AAEGIMSSV	GAVE A MISS
AAEFLMOOR	ALFA ROMEO	AAEGINNRT	ARGENTINA
AAEFLMOTV	FATAL MOVE	AAEGINNRW	WAGNERIAN
AAEFLMRSY	ALF RAMSEY	AAEGINORV	OVER AGAIN
AAEFLMSTT	FLATMATES	AAEGINPPR	APPEARING
AAEFLNRRT	FRATERNAL	AAEGINPPS	APPEASING
AAEFLNRST	LEARN FAST	AAEGINPRT	GREAT PAIN
AAEFLNRTT	RENT A FLAT	AAEGINPST	PAGINATES
AAEFLPSSY	PLAYS SAFE	AAEGINRRS	GRANARIES
AAEFMRSTT	STATE FARM	AAEGINRSU	GUARANIES
AAEFNOSTT	EATS NO FAT	AAEGINRSY	GAINSAYER
AAEFRRSWY	WAYFARERS	AAEGINSTV	NAVIGATES
AAEGGILLN	GALINGALE	AAEGINVWY	GIVEN AWAY
AAEGGIMMY	MAGGIE MAY	AAEGIRTTV	GRAVITATE
AAEGGINRT	GREAT GAIN	AAEGISTTT	SAGITTATE
AAEGGINRV	AVERAGING	AAEGISVWY	GIVES AWAY
	GAVE A RING	AAEGKRSTU	GREAT AUKS
AAEGGINSV	GAVE A SIGN	AAEGLLMMS	SMALL GAME
AAEGGIOTV	GAVE IT A GO	AAEGLLNRY	LARYNGEAL
AAEGGLLNO	GALLONAGE	AAEGLMNST	GAS MANTLE
AAEGGLNSU	LANGUAGES	AAEGLMOST	LOST A GAME
AAEGGLNSY	LAYS AN EGG	AAEGLMPSY	PLAY GAMES
AAEGGLORT	GREAT GOAL	AAEGLMRRY	LARGE ARMY
AAEGGLOST	GETS A GOAL	AAEGLMTTU	GLUTAMATE
AAEGGNRSY	GARGANEYS	AAEGLNORT	TEAR ALONG
AAEGHHNVY	HANG HEAVY	AAEGLNOSU	ANALOGUES
AAEGHIMNO	HOME AGAIN	AAEGLNPRU	RUNG A PEAL
AAEGHINTV	GAVE A HINT	AAEGLNRTU	GRANULATE
AAEGHLLRT	GREAT HALL	AAEGLNSTW	LAW AGENTS
AAEGHLNOX	HEXAGONAL	AAEGLPRST	LEGS APART
AAEGHLNPR	PHALANGER	AAEGLPRTU	GREAT PAUL
AAEGHLNPS	PHALANGES	AAEGLPSST	LAST PAGES
AAEGHLPSS	SLAG HEAPS	AAEGLPSTY	STAGE PLAY

AAEGLRSSV	SALVAGERS	AAEHNSTVX	TAX HAVENS
AAEGLRSSW	GLASSWARE	AAEHOPRST	OPERA HATS
AAEGLRSTU	GASTRULAE	AAEHPPRST	PAPER HATS
AAEGLRSWY	LAY WAGERS	AAEHPRRSS	SHARP EARS
AAEGLSSSV	GLASS VASE	AAEHRTWWY	THREW AWAY
AAEGLSSTT	LAST STAGE	AAEHSSTYY	AS THEY SAY
AAEGMNNOR	ORANGEMAN	AAEIIKNRT	AIR INTAKE
AAEGMNPRT	PENTAGRAM	AAEIILLNS	NAILS A LIE
AAEGMNRTT	TERMAGANT	AAEIILMNS	ANIMALISE
AAEGMNRTY	GREAT MANY	AAEIILMNZ	ANIMALIZE
AAEGMORRS	AEROGRAMS	AAEIILMRT	LATIMERIA
AAEGMPRTY	PARTY GAME	AAEIILNRT	INTER ALIA
AAEGMRRSV	MARGRAVES	AAEIILPTX	EPITAXIAL
AAEGMRSTT	STRATAGEM	AAEIIMNNT	INANIMATE
AAEGNOPRS	PARSONAGE	AAEIIMRST	ARTEMISIA
AAEGNOPRT	PATRONAGE	AAEIINNPR	NAPIERIAN
AAEGNPRTY	PAGEANTRY	AAEIINSTT	INSATIATE
AAEGNRRRS	ARRANGERS	AAEIJLNNP	PLAIN JANE
AAEGNRTTU	GREAT AUNT	AAEIKKLLM	MAKE A KILL
	GREAT-AUNT	AAEIKKRST	TAKE A RISK
AAEGNRTUV	GAVE A TURN	AAEIKLLMW	MAKE A WILL
AAEGNSSTT	STAGNATES	AAEIKLLPT	TAKE A PILL
AAEGOPPRT	PROPAGATE	AAEIKLMNP	MAKE PLAIN
AAEGORRST	ARROGATES	AAEIKLMPS	MAKE A SLIP
AAEGPRRTW	GREW APART	AAEIKLMST	MAKE A LIST
AAEGPRSTU	PASTURAGE	AAEIKLTTV	TALKATIVE
AAEGPSSWY	PAYS WAGES	AAEIKMMNT	MAKE A MINT
AAEGRRSTZ	STAR GAZER	AAEIKMPTY	MAKE IT PAY
	STARGAZER	AAEIKMSST	TAKE AMISS
AAEGRRSVW	WAR GRAVES	AAEIKNPST	TAKE PAINS
AAEGRSSTZ	STARGAZES	AAEIKNPTT	TAKEN A TIP
AAEGRSTTT	GET A START	AAEIKPRTT	TAKE A TRIP
AAEHHINPZ	ZEPHANIAH	AAEIKPSTT	TAKES A TIP
AAEHHLNOT	HALOTHANE	AAEILLMMT	MAMILLATE
AAEHHOSTV	HAVE A SHOT	AAEILLNPS	SAILPLANE
AAEHIKKLW	LIKE A HAWK	AAEILLNPT	TAILPLANE
AAEHIKMST	MAKES A HIT	AAEILLPPT	PAPILLATE
AAEHIKMSW	MAKE A WISH	AAEILLPSS	PAILLASSE
AAEHIKNSZ	ASHKENAZI		PALLIASSE
AAEHIKNTT	TAKE A HINT	AAEILLPST	PALLIATES
AAEHILNRT	IN A LATHER	AAEILMMNS	MAIN MEALS
AAEHILNTV	LEVIATHAN	AAEILMMST	MELISMATA
AAEHILSTV	SHAVETAIL	AAEILMNOS	ANOMALIES
AAEHIMNTT	AT THE MAIN	AAEILMNST	LAMINATES
AAEHINNST	ATHENIANS	AAEILMNTU	ALUMINATE
AAEHINRVY	HEAVY RAIN	AAEILMNTY	ANIMATELY
AAEHINSST	ASTHENIAS	AAEILMPRV	PRIMAEVAL
AAEHIPRSY	HAIRY APES	AAEILMPTT	PALMITATE
AAEHKLOOV	HAVE A LOOK	AAEILMRST	MATERIALS
AAEHKMOSS	HAS A SMOKE	AAEILMSWY	MILES AWAY
AAEHKMOSW	MAKE A SHOW	AAEILNORT	ALIENATOR
AAEHKMRSY	HAYMAKERS		RATIONALE
AAEHKNTVY	HEAVY TANK	AAEILNPRS	AIRPLANES
AAEHKOSTT	TAKE A SHOT	AAEILNPRT	PERINATAL
AAEHKSTWY	ASK THE WAY	AAEILNPST	PALATINES
AAEHLLSTU	HAUSTELLA	AAEILNSSS	NASALISES
AAEHLLTWY	ALL THE WAY		SEA SNAILS
AAEHLNPSV	HAVE PLANS	AAEILNSSZ	NASALIZES
AAEHLNPSX	PHALANXES	AAEILNSTT	TANTALISE
AAEHLOORW	WORE A HALO	AAEILNTTT	TANTALITE
AAEHLOPPR	PHALAROPE	AAEILNTTZ	TANTALIZE
AAEHLPSUV	UPHEAVALS	AAEILPPTT	PALPITATE
AAEHLSTTY	HASTATELY	AAEILPRTV	LIVE APART
AAEHLTTWX	WEALTH TAX	AAEILRRTV	AIR TRAVEL
AAEHMNOTZ	THE AMAZON	AAEILRSSW	WASSAILER
AAEHMNPPY	HAPPY MEAN	AAEILSSTV	SALIVATES
AAEHMRRTW	WARM HEART	AAEILSTVX	LAXATIVES
AAEHMRSTU	SHAMATEUR	AAEILSTVY	STAY ALIVE
AAEHNORRS	RAN ASHORE	AAEIMMNOT	AMMONIATE
AAEHNPSST	PHEASANTS	AAEIMMNTY	MANY A TIME
AAEHNSSTY	SEA SHANTY	AAEIMNNOT	EMANATION

AAEIMNNRS	ARMENIANS	AAELLLRTY	LATERALLY
AAEIMNNRT	EARN A MINT	AAELLMPTY	PALMATELY
AAEIMNNSS	ANAMNESIS	AAELLMRST	SMELL A RAT
AAEIMNNSW	WINS A NAME	AAELLNNOT	NONE AT ALL
AAEIMNOST	ANATOMIES	AAELLNPPT	APPELLANT
	ANATOMISE	AAELLORSY	ROYAL SEAL
AAEIMNOTZ	ANATOMIZE	AAELLPPRW	WALLPAPER
AAEIMNPRS	PEARMAINS	AAELLQRSU	ALL SQUARE
AAEIMNRST	MARINATES	AAELLSUXY	ASEXUALLY
AAEIMNRTW	WATER MAIN	AAELLSWYY	ALLEYWAYS
AAEIMNSTT	STAMINATE	AAELMMNOS	MELANOMAS
AAEIMNTTY	AT ANY TIME	AAELMMORR	MARMOREAL
AAEIMORST	AROMATISE	AAELMNORS	¶LOSE AN ARM
AAEIMORTZ	AROMATIZE	AAELMPPSY	MAYAPPLES
AAEIMPRST	SPERMATIA	AAELMPSTY	PLAYMATES
AAEIMRRSS	ARMS RAISE	AAELMRSSU	SLUM AREAS
AAEINPPRT	APPERTAIN	AAELMRSTT	MALTREATS
AAEINRRRS	IN ARREARS	AAELMSTWY	MELTS AWAY
AAEINRRTV	NARRATIVE	AAELNNOST	NASAL TONE
AAEINRRTW	RAINWATER	AAELNORST	LOST AN EAR
AAEINRSSU	EURASIANS	AAELNPRSW	WARPLANES
AAEINSTVX	VEX A SAINT	AAELNPRTY	PLANETARY
AAEIPPRRS	APPRAISER	AAELNPSTT	PANTALETS
AAEIPPRSS	APPRAISES	AAELNPTUY	PLAY A TUNE
AAEIPRSST	ASPIRATES	AAELNPTVY	NAVAL TYPE
	PARASITES	AAELNRRUY	LUNAR YEAR
AAEIPSSTV	PASSIVATE	AAELNRSTT	TRANSLATE
AAEIPSWWY	WIPES AWAY	AAELNSTTU	SULTANATE
AAEJKLOPY	PLAY A JOKE	AAELOPRST	PASTORALE
AAEJKLRWY	JAYWALKER	AAELOPSTU	APETALOUS
AAEJMSTTW	JAMES WATT	AAELORRSY	SOLAR YEAR
AAEJQRSUW	SQUARE JAW	AAELORSTV	ROAST VEAL
AAEKKLOOT	TAKE A LOOK	AAELORSTY	ROYAL SEAT
AAEKLLNSW	SANK A WELL	AAELORTTZ	LAZARETTO
AAEKLLSST	SALES TALK	AAELORTUV	EVALUATOR
	SALT LAKES	AAELOSSTT	LOST AT SEA
AAEKLLSTY	ALKYLATES	AAELOSTWY	STOLE AWAY
AAEKLMNPS	MAKE PLANS	AAELPPRTT	APPLE TART
AAEKLMOSS	MAKE A LOSS	AAELPRSSY	PARALYSES
AAEKLMPRT	PLATE-MARK	AAELPSSTT	STEAL PAST
AAEKLMPSY	MAKES PLAY	AAELPSSTV	PALSTAVES
AAEKLMRSW	LAWMAKERS	AAELPSTTU	SPATULATE
AAEKLMSSW	MAKES LAWS	AAELRRSTV	TRAVERSAL
AAEKLNQRU	EQUAL RANK	AAELRSSTU	AS A RESULT
AAEKLOPST	STOP A LEAK		ASSAULTER
AAEKMMNPU	MAKE-UP MAN		SALERATUS
AAEKMMORR	MAKE OR MAR	AAELRSTTT	LATE START
AAEKMNOWW	WEAK WOMAN	AAELRSTTW	SALT WATER
AAEKMNPSU	MAKES A PUN		SALTWATER
AAEKMOORT	TAKE A ROOM	AAELRSTTY	LAY AT REST
AAEKMORSW	WORE A MASK	AAELSSTWY	LAYS WASTE
AAEKMOSVW	MAKES A VOW		LEASTWAYS
AAEKMRRTW	WATERMARK	AAEMMNRST	ARMAMENTS
AAEKMRSSY	EASY MARKS		MEN-AT-ARMS
AAEKNORRW	KOREAN WAR	AAEMNOSTY	MEAN TO SAY
AAEKNOTVW	TAKEN A VOW	AAEMNPRST	NAME PARTS
AAEKNPRTT	TAKEN PART	AAEMNPRTT	APARTMENT
AAEKNPSST	SNEAK PAST	AAEMNQRSU	MARQUESAN
AAEKNRSTY	ANY TAKERS?	AAEMNRSYY	MANY YEARS
AAEKNRTTU	TAKE A TURN	AAEMNSSTT	STATESMAN
AAEKNRTTW	WATER TANK	AAEMORSSU	AMAUROSES
AAEKOOSTT	TOOK A SEAT	AAEMORSTT	ROAST MEAT
AAEKORSTT	AT A STROKE	AAEMOSTTU	AUTOMATES
AAEKOSTVW	TAKES A VOW	AAEMOSVWY	MOVES AWAY
AAEKPPRTT	KEPT APART	AAEMPRRST	RARE STAMP
AAEKPRSTT	TAKES PART	AAEMPRSTY	PAYMASTER
AAEKRSSTW	RAW STEAKS	AAEMPSTTU	AMPUTATES
AAEKSSSTT	SETS A TASK	AAEMRRSTT	ART MASTER
AAEKSSSTY	EASY TASKS	AAEMRRSTU	ARMATURES
AAELLLNRY	NEARLY ALL	AAEMRRTWW	WARM WATER
AAELLLPRS	PARALLELS	AAENNOSTT	ANNOTATES

AAENNPSST	EN PASSANT	AAFKMMNOR	MAN OF MARK
AAENORSSW	SAW REASON	AAFKMNNOR	MAN OF RANK
AAENORSTU	AERONAUTS	AAFLLLMOS	SMALL LOAF
AAENPRSTY	PEASANTRY	AAFLLLMST	SMALL FLAT
AAENRRRTW	WARRANTER	AAFLLLOST	LAST OF ALL
AAENRSTTW	START ANEW	AAFLLLOWY	LAY FALLOW
AAEOOPPRS	SOAP OPERA	AAFLLSSTT	SALT FLATS
AAEOPRRST	SEPARATOR	AAFLNOWWY	FLOWN AWAY
AAEOPRRTT	TORE APART	AAFMMNOSU	FAMOUS MAN
AAEOPRSTT	PASTORATE	AAFMNOSTW	FAST WOMAN
AAEOPSSTT	APOSTATES	AAFMOPRRT	APART FROM
AAEORSTWY	STORE AWAY	AAFMORRTW	MARROWFAT
AAEPPRRST	SPARE PART	AAFNORRTY	ROTARY FAN
AAEPRSSTT	SETS A TRAP	AAFORRSTT	FOR A START
	SETS APART	AAGGHILNT	GALA NIGHT
AAEPRSSTW	PASS WATER	AAGGHINOV	HAVING A GO
AAEPRSTXY	PAYS EXTRA	AAGGIINNR	RING AGAIN
	TAXPAYERS	AAGGIINTT	AGITATING
AAEPRTTWY	WYATT EARP	AAGGILNSV	SALVAGING
AAEPSTWWY	SWEPT AWAY	AAGGIMNPR	RAMPAGING
AAERRSTTW	WATER RATS	AAGGIMNRW	WARGAMING
AAERSSTTU	SATURATES	AAGGINNRR	ARRANGING
AAERSSTTW	WAS AT REST	AAGGINNRU	RUNG AGAIN
AAERSTWWY	WATERWAYS	AAGGINOST	GO AGAINST
AAFFGNRSU	SUFFRAGAN	AAGGINOWY	GOING AWAY
AAFFIIRRS	FAIRS FAIR	AAGGINRWW	WAGING WAR
AAFFINPRS	PARAFFINS	AAGGINSSU	ASSUAGING
AAFFINSUX	FAUX-NAIFS	AAGGKLNNP	GANGPLANK
AAFFLLLST	FALLS FLAT	AAGGLNOST	TAGS ALONG
AAFFLLMNO	FALL OF MAN	AAGGLNOSY	SYNAGOGAL
AAFGHHIST	HAS A FIGHT	AAGGNNOSS	SANG A SONG
AAFGHILNS	HAS A FLING	AAGHHILRT	HIGH ALTAR
AAFGHLORU	FOR A LAUGH	AAGHHINSS	SHANGHAIS
AAFGHLOWY	GO HALF-WAY	AAGHIKMNY	HAYMAKING
AAFGILLNO	ALL IN A FOG		MAKING HAY
AAFGILLPS	FILLS A GAP	AAGHILLNO	HALLOAING
AAFGILNRS	FRANGLAIS	AAGHILLNT	HANG IT ALL
AAFGILNST	FALANGIST	AAGHILNNS	HANGNAILS
AAFGILNWY	FLING AWAY	AAGHILNRS	SHANGRI LA
AAFGLLORT	ALLOGRAFT		SHANGRI-LA
AAFGLNUWY	FLUNG AWAY	AAGHINNRU	HUNGARIAN
AAFGLORSU	LOAF SUGAR	AAGHINRSS	HARASSING
AAFGORTTU	AUTOGRAFT	AAGHINSST	HITS A SNAG
AAFHHNNUY	FUNNY HA-HA	AAGHINSSY	SASHAYING
AAFHIINRS	SHARIFIAN	AAGHIORST	GOATS HAIR
AAFHIKLLO	HALF A KILO	AAGHIRTWY	RIGHT AWAY
AAFHILNPT	HALF A PINT	AAGHLLSTU	LAST LAUGH
AAFHLLPRS	SHARP FALL	AAGHLNPSY	ANAGLYPHS
AAFHLNOPY	ON HALF PAY	AAGHLTTUW	TAUGHT LAW
AAFHLPUWY	HALF WAY UP	AAGHNPRST	STRAPHANG
AAFHLSTTT	THATS FLAT	AAGHOPRTU	AUTOGRAPH
AAFHRSSUU	HAUSFRAUS	AAGHRTTTU	TAUGHT ART
AAFIILMRS	FAMILIARS	AAGIIKMNT	TAKING AIM
AAFIILRRT	FAIR TRIAL	AAGIILNSS	ASSAILING
AAFIIRRYY	AIRY-FAIRY	AAGIIMNNT	ANIMATING
AAFILLNOP	FALLOPIAN	AAGIIMNRY	IMAGINARY
AAFILMMNY	FAMILY MAN	AAGIINNTT	ATTAINING
AAFILMNOR	FORAMINAL	AAGIINOTT	AGITATION
AAFILMWYY	FAMILY WAY	AAGIINSTT	SATIATING
AAFILNOOV	OF NO AVAIL	AAGIJNNNP	JAPANNING
AAFILNOTX	AFLATOXIN	AAGIKLMNW	LAWMAKING
AAFILOPTY	FAIL TO PAY	AAGIKLNNO	ALGONKIAN
AAFILPRSY	PLAYS FAIR	AAGIKMNRW	MAKING WAR
AAFILSSTT	FATALISTS	AAGIKMNWY	MAKING WAY
AAFIMORRW	MIA FARROW	AAGILLNOS	SAIL ALONG
AAFINRSTT	FAST TRAIN	AAGILLNPP	APPALLING
AAFINSSTT	FANTASIST	AAGILLNTV	GALLIVANT
AAFIOPRTT	AT A PROFIT	AAGILLORT	ALLIGATOR
AAFJJMORS	JARS OF JAM	AAGILMNNP	NAPALMING
AAFKLLOOT	TOOK A FALL	AAGILMNNS	SIGNALMAN
AAFKLSSTT	FAST-TALKS	AAGILMNNT	MALIGNANT

AAGILMNOS	MAGNOLIAS	AAHIMNOPY	HYPOMANIA
AAGILMNRS	MARGINALS	AAHIMNSST	SHAMANIST
AAGILMNSV	GALVANISM	AAHIMNSTU	AMIANTHUS
AAGILMNYZ	AMAZINGLY	AAHINOORR	HONORARIA
AAGILMRST	MAGISTRAL	AAHINOPRT	PARATHION
AAGILNNSY	ANALYSING	AAHINORRV	HARROVIAN
AAGILNNYZ	ANALYZING	AAHINPPRS	SHARP PAIN
AAGILNOST	ANALOGIST	AAHINPTTY	ANTIPATHY
	NOSTALGIA	AAHINRRTU	TURN A HAIR
AAGILNOSW	WAS IN GOAL	AAHIPPPRY	HAPPY PAIR
AAGILNPPT	PALPATING	AAHIPTTWY	WHAT A PITY!
AAGILNPRY	PARLAYING	AAHISTTWW	WHAT WAS IT?
AAGILNRUU	INAUGURAL	AAHKLLMRS	HALLMARKS
AAGILNRUV	VULGARIAN	AAHKMOSTW	TOMAHAWKS
AAGILNWYY	WAYLAYING	AAHLLOPTY	ALLOPATHY
AAGIMNPRT	PTARMIGAN	AAHLLPPSU	ALPHA PLUS
AAGINNRRT	NARRATING	AAHLLPRSY	PHRASALLY
AAGINNRTU	TURN AGAIN	AAHLMNNTU	LANTHANUM
AAGINOPRS	SPORANGIA	AAHIMPSTU	ASPHALTUM
AAGINORTV	NAVIGATOR	AAHLMQSSU	HAS QUALMS
AAGINPSTU	UP AGAINST	AAHLNOORW	WORN A HALO
AAGINPTXY	TAXPAYING	AAHLPPPSY	SLAPHAPPY
AAGINSSWY	SIGNS AWAY	AAHMNORST	MARATHONS
AAGIORSTT	AGITATORS	AAHMNOSWW	WASHWOMAN
AAGIORSUV	VAGARIOUS	AAHMNOUVX	VOX HUMANA
AAGIPRSTZ	GAZA STRIP	AAHMNPSST	PHANTASMS
AAGKLLNOW	WALK ALONG	AAHMOPRRX	HARPO MARX
AAGKNOOR3	KANGAROOS	AAHNNOOTZ	ANTHOZOAN
AAGLLLNTY	GALLANTLY	AAHNPPRSY	NAPPY RASH
AAGLLNOPY	PLAY ALONG	AAHOOSSWY	SHOOS AWAY
AAGLLNRTY	GALLANTRY	AAHOPRSTU	AUTOHARPS
AAGLLNRUY	ANGULARLY	AAHORTWWY	THROW AWAY
AAGLLOSWY	GALLOWAYS		THROWAWAY
AAGLNNSUV	NAVAL GUNS	AAHRRUWYY	HURRY AWAY
AAGLNOOSU	ANALOGOUS	AAHRSSTTW	STRAW HATS
AAGLNOPSS	PASS ALONG	AAIIILNNT	IN ITALIAN
AAGLNOSTT	LAST TANGO	AAIIKNNRU	UKRAINIAN
AAGLNPSST	GAS PLANTS	AAIIKNPST	PAKISTANI
AAGLNQSUU	AQUALUNGS	AAIILLMNO	ANIMAL OIL
AAGLNRTVY	VAGRANTLY	AAIILLNNV	ALL IN VAIN
AAGLOSSWY	SLOGS AWAY	AAIILMMNS	ANIMALISM
AAGLPSUWY	PLUGS AWAY	AAIILMNRT	MAIL TRAIN
AAGLRRSTU	GASTRULAR	AAIILMNST	ANIMALIST
AAGLRSSTU	GASTRULAS	AAIILMNTY	ANIMALITY
AAGMMORST	GRAM ATOMS	AAIILMPRT	IMPARTIAL
AAGMNNOSU	MANGANOUS		PRIMATIAL
AAGMNNOORT	ROMAN TOGA	AAIILNTWY	LAY IN WAIT
AAGMOOPSU	APOGAMOUS	AAIILRUXY	AUXILIARY
AAGMRSSSU	SARGASSUM	AAIIMNNOT	ANIMATION
AAGNNNOTY	NANNY GOAT	AAIIMNNST	MAINTAINS
AAGNNORTU	ORANGUTAN	AAIIMNORS	ASIA MINOR
AAGNORRTU	GUARANTOR	AAIIMPPRR	PRIMIPARA
AAGNORSTU	ANGOSTURA	AAIINNRTU	UNITARIAN
AAGOPPSST	STOPS A GAP	AAIINNRTV	INVARIANT
AAGOPRRTW	GROW APART	AAIINORTV	VARIATION
AAGORSSSS	SARGASSOS	AAIINOSTT	SATIATION
AAGORSTTT	GOT A START	AAIINPRRU	RIPUARIAN
AAGPRSTTY	STAG PARTY	AAIINRSTU	IN AUSTRIA
AAHHIIMRS	MAHARISHI	AAIIPRSST	APIARISTS
AAHHSTTTT	THATS THAT	AAIIPSTVY	PAY A VISIT
AAHHSTTWW	WHATS WHAT	AAIJNNOST	SAINT JOAN
AAHIILPSS	SAIL A SHIP	AAIJNNRUY	IN JANUARY
AAHIINSTT	TAHITIANS	AAIJNRSSY	JANISSARY
AAHIKRSTY	KSHATRIYA	AAIJRSSTW	SWARAJIST
AAHILMNOT	MALATHION	AAIKLLMRY	RIK MAYALL
AAHILMTUZ	AZIMUTHAL	AAIKLLNPT	PLAIN TALK
AAHILNNST	INITALANTS	AAIKLLOSS	ALKALOSIS
AAHILNOST	HALATIONS	AAIKLLPRV	VILLA PARK
AAHILORST	SAILOR HAT	AAIKLNORW	WALK ON AIR
AAHILORTU	AUTHORIAL	AAIKLNOSV	SLOVAKIAN
AAHIMMNSS	SHAMANISM	AAIKLNSWY	SLINK AWAY

AAIKMNRST	SAINT MARK	AAIMNOPRY	PYROMANIA
AAIKMNRTW	MARK TWAIN	AAIMNORST	ANIMATORS
AAIKMRSST	TAMARISKS	AAIMNORSV	MORAVIANS
AAIKOOTTX	TOOK A TAXI	AAIMNOSTT	ANATOMIST
AAIKSSSTW	SWASTIKAS	AAIMNPRST	MAIN PARTS
AAILLMMRY	MAMILLARY	AAIMNPTTT	MATT PAINT
AAILLMMXY	MAXIMALLY	AAIMNRRST	TRIMARANS
AAILLMNST	MANTILLAS	AAIMNRSTT	TARANTISM
AAILLMOPP	PAPILLOMA	AAIMORSSU	AMAUROSIS
AAILLMORY	ROYAL MAIL	AAIMQRSUU	AQUARIUMS
AAILLMRRY	ARMILLARY	AAINNNTTU	ANNUITANT
AAILLMRSY	AMARYLLIS	AAINNORRT	NARRATION
AAILLMRTY	MARITALLY	AAINNPRSY	SPIN A YARN
	MARTIALLY	AAINNRSTU	SATURNIAN
AAILLMRXY	MAXILLARY	AAINOORRT	ORATORIAN
AAILLNOST	ALLANTOIS	AAINOPSTT	ANTIPASTO
AAILLNPRU	NULLIPARA	AAINORRST	ROTARIANS
AAILLNSST	ALL SAINTS	AAINPRSST	ASPIRANTS
AAILLNTVY	VALIANTLY		PARTISANS
AAILLOPRT	PALLIATOR	AAINPRTYZ	NAZI PARTY
AAILLPPRY	PAPILLARY	AAINQRSTU	QUATRAINS
AAILLPRST	LAST APRIL	AAINQRTUY	ANTIQUARY
AAILLPRTY	PARTIALLY	AAINQSTTU	AQUATINTS
AAILLPSTY	SPATIALLY	AAINRSSSY	ASSYRIANS
AAILMMORS	AMORALISM	AAINRSTTY	TRY A SAINT
AAILMMRSS	ALARMISMS	AAINSSSSS	ASSASSINS
AAILMMTUU	MUTUAL AIM	AAINSSSTT	ASSISTANT
AAILMNNST	LAST MAN IN		SATANISTS
AAILMNOPT	PALMATION	AAIOPPRRT	PRO PATRIA
AAILMNOST	ATONALISM	AAIOPRRST	ASPIRATOR
AAILMNPSY	MANY A SLIP	AAIORRTTT	TRATTORIA
AAILMNSST	TALISMANS	AAIPPRSSU	PARI PASSU
AAILMNTTU	MATUTINAL	AAIPSSTWW	WASP WAIST
AAILMORSU	MALARIOUS	AAIRSSTTZ	TSARITZAS
AAILMORTY	AMORALITY	AAJMOPRRT	MAJOR PART
AAILMPRSU	MARSUPIAL	AAJMORRSU	URSA MAJOR
AAILMRSST	ALARMISTS	AAJMORRSW	MAJOR WARS
AAILNNOST	NATIONALS	AAJNORRTW	TROJAN WAR
	SANTOLINA	AAKKLOOTW	TOOK A WALK
AAILNNOSV	SLAVONIAN	AAKLLLMST	SMALL TALK
AAILNNPQU	PALANQUIN	AAKLLLSTW	WALKS TALL
AAILNNSST	ANNALISTS	AAKLLOSTT	TALKS A LOT
AAILNOOTV	TO NO AVAIL	AAKLMRSTW	SMART WALK
AAILNOPPT	PALPATION	AAKLNSUWY	SLUNK AWAY
AAILNOPSS	PASSIONAL	AAKLOOSWY	LOOKS AWAY
	SALOPIANS	AAKLOPRRY	ROYAL PARK
AAILNOPUW	PAULOWNIA	AAKLPSSTW	WALKS PAST
AAILNORRV	ON ARRIVAL	AAKMNORSW	WORN A MASK
AAILNORST	RATIONALS	AAKMPRSSS	PASS MARKS
AAILNOSTT	ATONALIST	AAKNPRSTT	TANK TRAPS
AAILNOSTV	LAVATIONS	AAKNPSTTU	SANK A PUTT
	SALVATION	AAKOOPRTT	TOOK A PART
AAILNOTTY	ATONALITY		TOOK APART
AAILNOTUV	VALUATION	AALLLMMSS	SMALL SLAM
AAILNPPTT	PALPITANT	AALLLMOST	ALMOST ALL
AAILNPRTU	TARPAULIN	AALLMMRSS	SMALL ARMS
AAILNPRTY	PLANARITY	AALLMNORW	ROMAN WALL
AAILNPSTU	SAINT PAUL	AALLMNOTW	TALL WOMAN
AAILNRSTT	LAST TRAIN	AALLMORSW	MORAL LAWS
AAILOPRRT	RAPTORIAL	AALLMPRST	SMALL PART
AAILORRST	SARTORIAL	AALLNNOPY	POLLYANNA
AAILPRSSY	PARALYSIS	AALLNNRUY	ANNULARLY
AAILPRTTV	VITAL PART	AALLNRTUY	NATURALLY
AAILPSSWY	SLIPS AWAY	AALLNSTUY	AUNT SALLY
AAILSSSTY	STAYSAILS	AALLOORSW	WALLAROOS
AAIMMNNOO	MONOMANIA	AALLORSWY	LOW SALARY
AAIMMNRST	MARTINMAS	AALLORTUW	ALL-OUT WAR
AAIMNNORS	ROMANIANS	AALLPPRTU	PULL APART
	SAN MARINO	AALLPRTWY	PARTY WALL
AAIMNNORU	ROUMANIAN	AALLSTTWZ	LAST WALTZ
AAIMNNRSU	RUMANIANS	AALMNOOSU	ANOMALOUS

AALMNOPRT	PATROLMAN	ABBCEKLLU	BLUE-BLACK
AALMNORST	LOST AN ARM	ABBCEKLSS	BLACK BESS
AALMNORSW	ROMAN LAWS	ABBCEKNOS	BACKBONES
AALMNPRTY	RAMPANTLY	ABBCEKNSU	BUCKBEANS
AALMOOSTU	AUTOSOMAL	ABBCELRRS	SCRABBLER
AALMORRSY	ROYAL ARMS	ABBCELRSS	SCRABBLES
AALMORSTT	STROMATAL	ABBCGIKNR	BRING BACK
AALMORTYY	MAYORALTY	ABBCHJKOS	JACK HOBBS
AALNNOOPT	PANTALOON	ABBCIKRST	BRICKBATS
AALNNOTUV	ANOVULANT	ABBCILPRU	PUBLIC BAR
AALNNRTUU	UNNATURAL	ABBCIMOST	BOMBASTIC
AALNOOPZZ	POZZOLANA	ABBCINOSY	CABIN BOYS
AALNOPSTT	POSTNATAL	ABBCKKLOO	BLACK BOOK
AALNORVYY	ROYAL NAVY	ABBCKLOOT	BOOTBLACK
AALNOSTTW	WANTS A LOT	ABBCKLOSW	BLOWBACKS
AALNPPSSY	PLAYS SNAP	ABBCLOSTU	BOAT CLUBS
AALNSSTWY	SLANTWAYS	ABBCMOOST	COST A BOMB
AALOPPRSV	APPROVALS	ABBDDEMOR	BOMBARDED
AALOPRRTY	PORTRAYAL	ABBDEELRU	BLUEBEARD
AALOPRSST	PASTORALS	ABBDEILOT	BOBTAILED
AALORSTUV	VALUATORS	ABBDEILRT	BIRD TABLE
AALRSSTTW	LAST STRAW	ABBDEINRS	BREAD BINS
	STALWARTS	ABBDEIRTW	BARBED WIT
AAMMNNOSW	WOMANS MAN	ABBDELORU	DOUBLE BAR
AAMMNORRY	ROMAN ARMY	ADDDCLOTU	DOUBTABLE
AAMNOOTTU	AUTOMATON	ABBDENOSX	BANDBOXES
AAMNOPRSY	PAY RANSOM	ABBDGIILN	AD-LIBBING
AAMNOPRTU	PARAMOUNT	ADDDGILNR	DRABBLING
AAMNPRSTY	MANY PARTS	ABBDGILNS	DABBLINGS
AAMOORTTW	RAW TOMATO	ABBDHIRST	BIRD BATHS
AAMOPRRSU	PARAMOURS		BIRDBATHS
AAMOPRTTU	AMPUTATOR	ABBDHLOOT	BLOOD BATH
AAMORRSTY	MARY ASTOR		BLOODBATH
AANNOORTT	ANNOTATOR	ABBDIINRR	BIRD BRAIN
AANNORTWW	WAR ON WANT		BIRDBRAIN
AANNPRSUY	SPUN A YARN	ABBDILLOR	BILLBOARD
AANOPRRTT	TORN APART	ABBDILNST	BLIND BATS
AANORRRST	NARRATORS	ABBDKLNOO	BLOOD BANK
AANORRRTW	WARRANTOR	ABBDLLOSY	BABY DOLLS
AANORSTTU	ASTRONAUT	ABBDMOOPR	DROP A BOMB
AANPRSSSU	PARNASSUS	ABBDNORSW	BROWBANDS
AANRSTUWY	TURNS AWAY	ABBEELRRY	BLAEBERRY
AAORRSTTU	SATURATOR	ABBEEENORS	BARE BONES
AAORRSTTW	START A ROW	ABBEERSTT	BARBETTES
AAOSSTWWY	STOWAWAYS	ABBEFILST	FLABBIEST
	STOWS AWAY	ABBEGHIRT	BIG BERTHA
AAPRRSSTT	STAR PARTS	ABBEGIJNR	JABBERING
ABBBCELLU	CLUBBABLE	ABBEGIKRS	BIG BREAKS
ABBBCELRU	BUBBLE CAR	ABBEGINRT	RABBETING
ABBBDEELR	BLABBERED	ABBEGMNOO	GONE A BOMB
ABBCCEHKN	BACK BENCH	ABBEGMOOS	GOES A BOMB
ABBCCEHMO	BEACHCOMB	ABBEHISST	SHABBIEST
ABBCCKKLU	BLACKBUCK	ABBEHORST	BATH ROBES
ABBCCKMOS	BACKCOMBS		BATHROBES
ABBCDEERU	BARBECUED	ABBEIIPRT	RABBIT PIE
ABBCDEFNO	CONFABBED	ABBEIKLMO	LIKE A BOMB
ABBCDEKNS	BENDS BACK	ABBEILNNY	BABY LINEN
ABBCDELRY	CRABBEDLY	ABBEIMNOZ	BOMBAZINE
ABBCDKORU	BUCKBOARD	ABBEINORT	BARBITONE
ABBCEERRU	BARBECUER	ABBEJLLYY	JELLY BABY
ABBCEERSU	BARBECUES	ABBELMOOZ	BAMBOOZLE
ABBCEHOSY	BEACH BOYS	ABBELMORY	BOB MARLEY
ABBCEHSTU	BATH CUBES	ABBELOPRS	PROBABLES
ABBCEIKRT	BACKBITER	ABBELORSU	BELABOURS
ABBCEIKST	BACKBITES	ABBELOSTY	STABLE BOY
ABBCEILLM	CLIMBABLE	ABBELORSU	SQUABBLER
ABBCEIRST	CRABBIEST	ABBELOSSU	SQUABBLES
ABBCEIRSY	CRY BABIES	ABBEMNOTW	WENT A BOMB
	CRYBABIES	ABBENORRW	BROWN BEAR
ABBCEKKOR	BROKE BACK	ABBENORST	ABSORBENT
ABBCEKLLT	BLACK BELT	ABBENORUY	BURY A BONE

ABBEORSTW	BROWBEATS	ABCDEEKLN	BLACKENED
ABBFHLLSU	FLASH BULB	ABCDEEKLY	BLACK-EYED
	FLASHBULB	ABCDEEKRT	BRACKETED
ABBGHRSSU	HABSBURGS	ABCDEELMR	CLAMBERED
ABBGIILOT	OBBLIGATI	ABCDEEMOT	CAME TO BED
ABBGIINRT	RABBITING	ABCDEESSS	ABSCESSED
ABBGILLNO	BILLABONG	ABCDEESUX	BAD EXCUSE
ABBGILMNR	BRAMBLING	ABCDEFFKO	BACKED OFF
ABBGILOOT	OBBLIGATO	ABCDEFIKR	BACKFIRED
ABBGILRSY	BABY GIRLS	ABCDEGIRS	BIRD CAGES
ABBGINORS	ABSORBING	ABCDEHIOT	COHABITED
ABBGLLRUY	RUGBY BALL	ABCDEHKLO	BLOCKHEAD
ABBHINOOS	BABOONISH	ABCDEIIST	DIABETICS
ABBHIORRS	BOB HARRIS	ABCDEIKLS	BACKSLIDE
ABBHOSSWY	BABY SHOWS		BLACK SIDE
ABBINORST	RABBITS ON		SLIDE BACK
ABBKKNOOS	BANKBOOKS	ABCDEIKRS	DISC BRAKE
ABBKLLOTY	LOBBY TALK	ABCDEIKRU	RUDBECKIA
ABBKNORSS	BRASS KNOB	ABCDEIKSS	BACKSIDES
ABBLLOOTX	BALLOT BOX	ABCDEILNO	BALCONIED
ABBMMOOST	ATOM BOMBS	ABCDEINTU	INCUBATED
	ATOM-BOMBS	ABCDEIRRV	CAB DRIVER
ABBMSTTUY	MATT BUSBY	ABCDEKLOR	BLOCKADER
ABBNSSTUU	UNA STUBBS	ABCDEKLOS	BLOCKADES
ABBOOPRTY	BOOBY TRAP	ABCDEKLPU	BLACKED UP
	BOOBY-TRAP	ABCDEKMOV	MOVED BACK
ABBOORRWY	BARROW BOY	ABCDEKNSS	SENDS BACK
ABCCCEFIO	BECCAFICO	ABCDEKOTU	BACKED OUT
ABCCCKKLO	BLACKCOCK	ABCDELMRS	SCRAMBLED
ABCCDHIKS	DABCHICKS	ABCDELOTU	DOUBLE ACT
ABCCDIRUY	CUBIC YARD	ABCDEMOTT	COMBATTED
ABCCDKKSU	DUCKS BACK	ABCDENORR	CORN BREAD
ABCCEEHKL	CHECKABLE	ABCDENORS	ABSCONDER
ABCCEENRU	BUCCANEER	ABCDENOSU	SUBDEACON
ABCCEGHIN	BIG CHANCE	ABCDERSST	BEST CARDS
ABCCEHKKO	CHOKE BACK	ABCDFKLOS	FOLDS BACK
ABCCEHNNO	BON CHANCE	ABCDGINTU	ABDUCTING
ABCCEIIST	SCABIETIC	ABCDGKLLO	BLACK GOLD
ABCCEINOV	BICONCAVE	ABCDGKLOS	BLACK DOGS
ABCCEINRW	CABIN CREW	ABCDHILMR	HARD CLIMB
ABCCEKMOS	COMEBACKS	ABCDHIOPR	CHIPBOARD
	COMES BACK	ABCDHKLOS	HOLDS BACK
ABCCEKORV	BACK COVER	ABCDHLOST	COLD BATHS
ABCCELNRU	CARBUNCLE	ABCDIKRRY	BRICKYARD
ABCCGHOOY	GO BY COACH	ABCDILLRS	BIRD CALLS
ABCCHHKNU	HUNCHBACK		BIRDCALLS
ABCCHKLOT	BACKCLOTH	ABCDILMOR	LOMBARDIC
ABCCHLTUY	YACHT CLUB	ABCDILOPR	CLIPBOARD
ABCCHNOOS	CABOCHONS	ABCDINNOR	BACON RIND
ABCCIKKKS	KICKBACKS	ABCDINOOT	BANDICOOT
	KICKS BACK	ABCDINOTU	ABDUCTION
ABCCILLUY	CUBICALLY	ABCDKLMOO	BLACK MOOD
ABCCIRSTU	SUBARCTIC	ABCDKLOOR	ROAD BLOCK
ABCCKKKNO	KNOCK BACK		ROADBLOCK
ABCCMOORY	MOBOCRACY	ABCDKNORS	ROCK BANDS
ABCDDEEHU	DEBAUCHED	ABCDKNOSW	BACKS DOWN
ABCDDEEIL	DECIDABLE	ABCDKOORS	BACK DOORS
ABCDDEIRT	BAD CREDIT	ABCDKOOST	STOOD BACK
ABCDDEKLO	BLOCKADED	ABCDKOOSW	BACKWOODS
ABCDDENOS	ABSCONDED	ABCDKOPRS	BACKDROPS
	BAD SECOND		DROPS BACK
ABCDDEORR	BAD RECORD	ABCDKORSW	BACKSWORD
ABCDDKORU	DUCKBOARD	ABCDLLOST	COLD BLAST
ABCDEEEHU	DEBAUCHEE	ABCDMMNOY	BY COMMAND
ABCDEEEMU	BECAME DUE	ABCDNOOXX	BOX AND COX
ABCDEEFKS	FEEDBACKS	ABCDOPRSU	CUPBOARDS
ABCDEEHMR	CHAMBERED	ABCDORSTU	ABDUCTORS
ABCDEEHRU	DEBAUCHER	ABCDOSTTU	CAST DOUBT
ABCDEEHSU	DEBAUCHES	ABCEEEJLT	EJECTABLE
ABCDEEILM	MEDICABLE	ABCEEELLR	CEREBELLA
ABCDEEINS	BASIC NEED		

ABCEEELRT	CELEBRATE	ABCEHKLST	THE BLACKS
	ERECTABLE	ABCEHKMNR	BENCHMARK
ABCEEELRX	EXECRABLE	ABCEHKNPR	PARK BENCH
ABCEEEMNO	BECAME ONE	ABCEHKORS	HORSEBACK
ABCEEEOST	CEASE TO BE	ABCEHKRTW	THREW BACK
ABCEEERRT	CEREBRATE	ABCEHKTUW	BUCKWHEAT
ABCEEFFOR	COFFEE BAR	ABCEHLNRS	BLANCHERS
ABCEEFIRS	BRIEFCASE	ABCEHLNRT	BRANCHLET
ABCEEFLRU	BE CAREFUL	ABCEHLORS	BACHELORS
ABCEEFNOR	CAN OF BEER	ABCEHLOTU	TOUCHABLE
ABCEEGKNR	GREENBACK	ABCEHLRSU	CRUSHABLE
ABCEEHKLW	BACK WHEEL	ABCEHLSSU	CHASUBLES
ABCEEHKTT	BACK TEETH	ABCEHMNOR	BON MARCHE
ABCEEHLLY	BELLYACHE	ABCEHMOST	HECATOMBS
ABCEEHLNU	CUBAN HEEL	ABCEHOQRU	QUEBRACHO
ABCEEIKRS	BIKE RACES	ABCEHORSU	BAROUCHES
ABCEEIILLS	LIBEL CASE	ABCEHOSSX	CASH BOXES
	SLICEABLE	ABCEHPSUY	BUYS CHEAP
ABCEEILST	CELIBATES	ABCEIILNS	SIBILANCE
ABCEEILSX	EXCISABLE	ABCEIIMRT	IMBRICATE
ABCEEILTX	EXCITABLE	ABCEIJLNU	JUBILANCE
ABCEEIMNS	AMBIENCES	ABCEIJNOT	ABJECTION
ABCEEIMRV	EMBRACIVE	ABCEIJOST	JACOBITES
ABCEEINOS	OBEISANCE	ABCEIKKLR	ACKER BILK
ABCEEINRT	BE CERTAIN	ABCEIKLST	BLACK TIES
ABCEEKKNR	BREAKNECK	ABCEIKRTW	WRITE BACK
ABCEEKKPS	KEEPS BACK	ABCEILLLN	CLEAN BILL
ABCEEKLNR	BLACKENER	ABCEILLNR	BRAIN CELL
ABCEEKLSY	BLACK EYES	ABCEILMOT	METABOLIC
ABCEEKPSW	SWEEPBACK	ABCEILMSY	EASY CLIMB
ABCEELLOS	CLOSEABLE	ABCEILNNS	BINNACLES
ABCEELMNS	SEMBLANCE	ABCEILNNU	INCUNABLE
ABCEELMRR	CLAMBERER	ABCEILNOS	BALCONIES
ABCEELNRT	CELEBRANT	ABCEILNRU	INCURABLE
ABCEELORT	BRACTEOLE	ABCEILORS	CABRIOLES
ABCEELORV	REVOCABLE	ABCEILORT	CABRIOLET
ABCEELRST	BRACELETS	ABCEILRTU	LUBRICATE
ABCEELRXY	EXECRABLY	ABCEIMOTV	COMBATIVE
ABCEELSUX	EXCUSABLE	ABCEIMRTU	BACTERIUM
ABCEEMMRT	CAMEMBERT	ABCEIMSTU	BEAT MUSIC
ABCEEOSSU	SEBACEOUS	ABCEINORS	CARBONISE
ABCEESSSS	ABSCESSES	ABCEINORZ	CARBONIZE
ABCEFHLSU	FLASHCUBE	ABCEINOSS	BASE COINS
ABCEFIKRS	BACKFIRES	ABCEINSTU	INCUBATES
	FIREBACKS	ABCEIOSSV	BASS VOICE
ABCEFIRTU	BIFURCATE	ABCEIRRTU	RUBRICATE
ABCEFKLST	LEFT-BACKS	ABCEIRSTT	BRATTICES
ABCEFORST	SOBER FACT	ABCEJKNNY	JACK BENNY
ABCEFOSTU	OBFUSCATE	ABCEJNSTU	SUBJACENT
ABCEGHILN	BLEACHING	ABCEKKLNR	BANK CLERK
ABCEGHINR	BREACHING	ABCEKLNSS	BLACKNESS
ABCEGHLNO	LONG BEACH	ABCEKLORW	WORE BLACK
ABCEGIKNV	GIVEN BACK	ABCEKLPRU	PARBUCKLE
ABCEGIKSV	GIVES BACK	ABCEKLSTU	CLUB STEAK
ABCEGILMN	BECALMING	ABCEKMOPR	BROKE CAMP
ABCEGIMNR	CAMBERING	ABCEKOOSS	BOOKCASES
	EMBRACING		CASE BOOKS
ABCEGKLLS	BLACKLEGS		CASEBOOKS
ABCEGKLOS	BLOCKAGES	ABCEKORTW	WROTE BACK
ABCEGLLLU	BUGLE CALL	ABCEKPSST	BACK STEPS
ABCEGMNOU	BUNCO GAME		STEPS BACK
ABCEGNORY	GONE BY CAR	ABCEKPSTW	SWEPT-BACK
ABCEGORSY	GOES BY CAR	ABCEKRTUW	WATERBUCK
ABCEGRSUU	CUBE SUGAR	ABCELLNOW	CLEAN BLOW
ABCEHHSTU	BEACH HUTS	ABCELLOSX	CALL BOXES
ABCEHILTT	THE BALTIC	ABCELLRSW	SCREWBALL
ABCEHINNO	BONE CHINA	ABCELLSTU	SLATE CLUB
ABCEHINOT	AITCHBONE	ABCELMOOR	ROCAMBOLE
ABCEHINRT	BRECHTIAN	ABCELMRSS	SCRAMBLES
ABCEHINST	BEST CHINA	ABCELNOST	CONSTABLE
ABCEHKLLO	BLACK HOLE	ABCELNOTU	COUNTABLE

ABCELOOST	BOOT LACES	ABCIILLST	BALLISTIC
	BOOTLACES	ABCIILMOR	MICROBIAL
ABCELOSST	OBSTACLES	ABCIILNSY	SIBILANCY
ABCELOSTT	ECTOBLAST	ABCIILRSY	IRASCIBLY
ABCELOSTU	BLUE COATS	ABCIINNRT	BRITANNIC
ABCELPSUY	BUSY PLACE	ABCIIRSTY	SYBARITIC
ABCELRTUU	LUCUBRATE	ABCIKLLRW	BRICK WALL
ABCELSUXY	EXCUSABLY	ABCIKLLST	BLACK LIST
ABCEMNRSU	CREAM BUNS		BLACKLIST
ABCEMOOTU	COME ABOUT	ABCIKLPSS	SLIPS BACK
ABCEMPRRU	BUMPER CAR	ABCIKLSTU	BLACK SUIT
ABCEMRSTU	CUB MASTER	ABCILLNSY	BILLY CANS
ABCENORTY	BARONETCY	ABCILMOPY	AMBLYOPIC
ABCENRRRY	CRANBERRY	ABCILMSTY	CYMBALIST
ABCENRTWY	WENT BY CAR	ABCILNNOU	CONNUBIAL
ABCENSSTU	SUBSTANCE	ABCILNORU	BINOCULAR
ABCERRSTU	CARBURETS	ABCILNPSU	PUBLICANS
ABCFFHNOR	BRANCH OFF	ABCILNRTU	LUBRICANT
ABCFGHIKT	FIGHT BACK	ABCILORRU	ORBICULAR
	FIGHTBACK	ABCILSSTY	ICY BLASTS
ABCFHIKLS	BLACKFISH	ABCIMNOOS	MONOBASIC
ABCFHRSTU	BUSHCRAFT	ABCIMNORU	CARBONIUM
ABCFKLLSU	FULLBACKS	ABCIMOSTU	SUBATOMIC
ABCFKOOTU	BACK OUT OF	ABCINORTU	INCUBATOR
ABCGGIKNO	GOING BACK	ABCINOTUY	BY AUCTION
ABCGGIKPY	PIGGYBACK	ABCJKMPSU	JUMPS BACK
ABCGHIKRT	RIGHT BACK	ABCJKOOST	BOOTJACKS
	RIGHT-BACK		JACKBOOTS
ABCGHIKST	BACKSIGHT	ABCJLSUZZ	JAZZ CLUBS
ABCGHILNN	BLANCHING	ABCKKLLOO	BLACK LOOK
ABCGHINNR	BRANCHING		LOOK BLACK
ABCGHINOR	BROACHING	ABCKKLOOR	BLACK ROOK
ABCGHKOSS	HOGSBACKS	ABCKKLOOS	LOOKS BACK
ABCGHNPSU	PUNCH-BAGS	ABCKLLORS	ROLLS BACK
ABCGIIKNN	BACKING IN	ABCKLLPSU	PULLS BACK
ABCGIINRS	ASCRIBING	ABCKLNORW	WORN BLACK
ABCGIINSS	ABSCISING	ABCKLNRTU	TURN BLACK
ABCGIKKLN	BLACK KING	ABCKLOPST	BLACK SPOT
ABCGIKLNS	BLACKINGS		BLACKTOPS
	SLINGBACK	ABCKLOSTU	BLACKOUTS
ABCGIKLNY	LYING BACK		BLACKS OUT
ABCGIKNOR	KING COBRA	ABCKMOORS	BACK ROOMS
ABCGIKNPU	BACKING UP	ABCKMOSSS	MOSSBACKS
ABCGIKNRS	RINGS BACK	ABCKMOTUU	MUCK ABOUT
ABCGIKNSW	BACKSWING	ABCKNRSTU	TURNS BACK
	SWING BACK	ABCKOOPRS	SCRAPBOOK
ABCGILLNY	CALLING BY	ABCKOPSST	BACKSTOPS
ABCGILNNO	BLANCOING	ABCLLOOSY	LOCAL BOYS
ABCGILNOS	LOG CABINS	ABCLLOPSU	LOCAL PUBS
ABCGINNRU	UNBRACING	ABCLMNNOT	MONT BLANC
ABCGIRTTU	CIGAR BUTT	ABCLMRRUY	LAMB CURRY
ABCGKNSUW	SWUNG BACK	ABCLNOWYY	COLWYN BAY
ABCGKOOTU	GO BACK OUT	ABCLOORRU	COLOUR BAR
ABCHIIKTT	A BIT THICK	ABCLOOSTU	COBALTOUS
ABCHIILLN	CHILBLAIN	ABCLPRSUW	PUB CRAWLS
ABCHIKKNT	THINK BACK	ABCMOSSUU	SUBMUCOSA
ABCHILMOS	SHAMBOLIC	ABCNNOSYY	NANCY BOYS
ABCHILNOR	BRONCHIAL	ABCORRSSS	CROSSBARS
ABCHILOOS	COOLIBAHS	ABCRSSTTU	SUBTRACTS
ABCHIMORS	HAIR COMBS	ABDDDEINS	DISBANDED
ABCHJNOOT	JOHN CABOT	ABDDDHINY	DID BY HAND
ABCHKMTTU	THUMB TACK	ABDDEEERV	BRAVE DEED
	THUMBTACK	ABDDEEGHI	BIGHEADED
ABCHKOOSS	CASH BOOKS	ABDDEEHOW	BOWED HEAD
ABCHKORTW	THROW BACK	ABDDEEHST	DEATHBEDS
	THROWBACK	ABDDEEINR	READ IN BED
ABCHKRRUY	HURRY BACK	ABDDEEISV	BE ADVISED
ABCHLMOPS	LAMB CHOPS	ABDDEENOR	BROADENED
ABCHNORTU	BRANCH OUT	ABDDEEORS	DEAD SOBER
ABCIIKLW	BAILIWICK	ABDDEEOTW	OWED A DEBT
ABCIILLMU	UMBILICAL	ABDDEEPRS	BEDSPREAD

ABDDEERTY	TEDDY BEAR	ABDEEKMRS	BEDMAKERS
ABDDEESST	BEDSTEADS	ABDEELLPS	SPEEDBALL
ABDDEGIMN	BIG DEMAND	ABDEELLRR	BARRELLED
ABDDEGINS	BAD DESIGN	ABDEELLTY	BELATEDLY
ABDDEGTUY	BUDGET DAY	ABDEELMTT	EMBATTLED
ABDDEHMOS	HEBDOMADS	ABDEELNOR	BANDEROLE
ABDDEHNSU	HUSBANDED	ABDEELNPR	PREBENDAL
ABDDEIILV	DIVIDABLE	ABDEELNPS	SPENDABLE
ABDDEILNT	BLIND DATE	ABDEELNRU	ENDURABLE
ABDDEILTT	DID BATTLE	ABDEELNST	STEEL BAND
ABDDEINSS	SIDEBANDS	ABDEELORS	LEEBOARDS
ABDDEINSV	DIVAN BEDS	ABDEELRSS	BEARDLESS
ABDDEIORS	BROADSIDE	ABDEELSSU	SUBLEASED
	SIDEBOARD	ABDEEMNRT	DEBARMENT
ABDDEIPRU	UPBRAIDED	ABDEEMPRT	BAD TEMPER
ABDDEIRRS	DISBARRED	ABDEEMRSY	EMBER DAYS
ABDDEIRRV	BAD DRIVER	ABDEENOTY	BAYONETED
ABDDEISSU	DISABUSED	ABDEENQTU	BANQUETED
ABDDELNOY	BADLY DONE	ABDEENRRT	BARTENDER
	DONE DADLY	ADDCENTTU	DEBUTANTE
ABDDELOSW	SADDLEBOW	ABDEEORRU	BORDEREAU
ABDDELOSY	DOES BADLY	ABDEEOSTW	OWES A DEBT
ABDDEOPRU	BOARDED UP	ABDEEPRSS	SPARE BEDS
ABDDGILOR	GOLD BRAID	ABDEERRST	REDBREAST
ABDDGIORS	RABID DOGS	ABDEFFGLU	DUFFLE BAG
ABDDGORUY	BODYGUARD	ABDEFHINR	FAR BEHIND
ABDDHINTW	BANDWIDTH	ABDEFINOS	BONA FIDES
ABDDHOSTU	HAD DOUBTS	ABDEFINRR	FIREBRAND
ABDDILNNS	SAND-BLIND	ABDEFLTUY	BY DEFAULT
ABDDILRSY	LADYBIRDS	ABDEFNOOR	BAD FOR ONE
ABDDIMNOR	BROAD MIND	ABDEFNORY	FAR BEYOND
ABDDJMNOO	ODD JOB MAN	ABDEGGGIN	DEBAGGING
ABDDLOORW	DRAW BLOOD	ABDEGGGIO	DOGGIE BAG
ABDDOORSU	BAD ODOURS	ABDEGGINR	BADGERING
ABDEEEGLL	DELEGABLE	ABDEGHHTU	HAD THE BUG
ABDEEELMN	EMENDABLE	ABDEGHILN	LAG BEHIND
ABDEEELNR	BRENDA LEE	ABDEGIIMT	MADE IT BIG
ABDEEELRT	DETERABLE	ABDEGIIRR	BRIGADIER
ABDEEENRS	ABERDEENS	ABDEGIKLT	TALKED BIG
ABDEEESYY	BEADY EYES	ABDEGIKNR	DEBARKING
ABDEEFHLR	HALF BREED	ABDEGILNO	NO BIG DEAL
	HALF-BREED	ABDEGILOT	OBLIGATED
ABDEEFIIT	BEATIFIED	ABDEGIMRS	GAME BIRDS
ABDEEFILN	DEFINABLE	ABDEGINRR	DEBARRING
ABDEEFORR	FREE BOARD	ABDEGIRRS	ABRIDGERS
	FREEBOARD	ABDEGIRTY	TAY BRIDGE
ABDEEFORY	DAY BEFORE	ABDEGKOOR	GOOD BREAK
ABDEEFRST	BREAST-FED	ABDEGKOST	DOG BASKET
ABDEEGGLR	BEDRAGGLE	ABDEGLNOR	LONG BEARD
ABDEEGHIN	BEHEADING		OLD BANGER
ABDEEGINR	GABERDINE	ABDEGLNOU	GO A BUNDLE
ABDEEGORR	GARDEROBE	ABDEGLNOY	GONE BADLY
ABDEEGRRY	GREYBEARD	ABDEGLNSY	BANDY LEGS
ABDEEGRST	BEST GRADE	ABDEGLOOT	GOOD TABLE
ABDEEHIRT	AIR THE BED	ABDEGLOOV	GAVE BLOOD
ABDEEHNOS	BONEHEADS	ABDEGLOSY	GOES BADLY
ABDEEHNTU	THE DANUBE	ABDEGNOPR	BEG PARDON
ABDEEHRSW	SHEWBREAD	ABDEGOPRS	PEGBOARDS
ABDEEIIKR	RIDE A BIKE	ABDEGRTUY	BUDGETARY
ABDEEIILR	DIABLERIE	ABDEHILLN	ALL BEHIND
ABDEEIKOR	RODE A BIKE	ABDEHILLS	BILLHEADS
ABDEEILNR	BREAD LINE	ABDEHILMO	BOILED HAM
	BREADLINE	ABDEHILNO	HOBNAILED
ABDEEILRS	DESIRABLE	ABDEHILOS	ABOLISHED
ABDEEILRT	LIBERATED	ABDEHINWY	WAY BEHIND
ABDEEILRV	DERIVABLE	ABDEHKLSU	BULKHEADS
ABDEEILSV	DEVISABLE	ABDEHLLSU	BULLHEADS
ABDEEINTU	BUTADIENE	ABDEHLNOS	ASH BLONDE
ABDEEIRVW	BAD REVIEW	ABDEHLOTW	DEATH BLOW
ABDEEITTU	BEATITUDE		DEATHBLOW
ABDEEKLNT	BLANKETED	ABDEHNPRS	SHARP BEND

ABDEHNSTU	SUNBATHED	ABDELOPUY	DOUBLE PAY
ABDEHORRU	HARBOURED		PAY DOUBLE
ABDEHORST	THE BOARDS	ABDELORSS	BAD LOSERS
	THE BROADS	ABDELORUV	BOULEVARD
ABDEHORSW	SHOWBREAD	ABDELOSUW	SAW DOUBLE
ABDEHRTYY	BY THE YARD	ABDELOTUW	BAWLED OUT
ABDEIIKLR	LIKE A BIRD	ABDEMMORY	BAD MEMORY
ABDEIILNU	INAUDIBLE	ABDEMOORR	BROOD MARE
ABDEIILNV	DIVINABLE	ABDEMORTU	TAMBOURED
ABDEIILOZ	DIABOLIZE	ABDEMORYY	MY DEAR BOY
ABDEIIRST	DIATRIBES	ABDEMRSTU	DRUMBEATS
ABDEIKLNR	DRINKABLE	ABDENNOSS	NOSEBANDS
ABDEIKLOR	BOARDLIKE	ABDENNRSW	NEW BRANDS
ABDEIKMRS	DISEMBARK	ABDENNRTU	TURBANNED
ABDEIKNRW	BREAK WIND	ABDENORRY	ERRAND BOY
	WINDBREAK	ABDENORST	ADSORBENT
ABDEILLLR	DRILLABLE	ABDENORSW	BEARS DOWN
ABDEILLOY	OLD BAILEY	ABDENOSTW	BEATS DOWN
ABDEILMNS	MANDIBLES		DOWNBEATS
ABDEILMOR	BROMELIAD	ABDENRRST	ST.BERNARD
ABDEILNOR	BANDOLIER	ABDENRSTY	BYSTANDER
ABDEILOPR	PARBOILED	ABDENSTTU	DEBUTANTS
ABDEILORV	OLIVE DRAB	ABDEOORRV	OVERBOARD
ABDEILOST	IDLE BOAST	ABDEOPRRT	BAD REPORT
ABDEILOTU	BAILED OUT	ABDEORRSW	WARDROBES
ABDEILRRY	EARLY BIRD	ABDEORSUV	DROVE A BUS
ABDEILRSY	DESIRABLY	ABDEORTTU	OBTURATED
ABDEILRWY	BRIDLEWAY	ABDEPRTTY	PRETTY BAD
ABDEILSTW	WILD BEAST	ABDFGLMOO	LAMB OF GOD
ABDEILSUW	WILD ABUSE	ABDFHLNOU	HALF-BOUND
ABDEIMRSX	BAD MIXERS	ABDFIJNOS	FINDS A JOB
ABDEINNTT	BAD INTENT	ABDFIMNOR	IN BAD FORM
ABDEINOST	BOTANISED	ABDFJNOOU	FOUND A JOB
ABDEINOTZ	BOTANIZED	ABDFLLORU	FULL BOARD
ABDEINRSS	RABIDNESS	ABDFLOOWY	BODY OF LAW
ABDEINRSU	URBANISED	ABDFOOORT	FOOTBOARD
ABDEINRUZ	URBANIZED	ABDFORRSU	SURFBOARD
ABDEINSSW	BAWDINESS	ABDGGIINR	ABRIDGING
ABDEINSTW	WAS IN DEBT		BRIGADING
ABDEINSTY	STAY IN BED	ABDGGILNO	GOING BALD
ABDEIORRS	ARBORISED	ABDGHILRT	BRIGHT LAD
ABDEIORRZ	ARBORIZED	ABDGHINST	BAD THINGS
ABDEIORVW	BROAD VIEW	ABDGHIOOT	GOOD HABIT
ABDEIPRRU	UPBRAIDER	ABDGHIRTU	DRUG HABIT
ABDEIRRRS	RARE BIRDS	ABDGIILNS	DISABLING
ABDEIRSUV	DRIVE A BUS	ABDGIILNY	ABIDINGLY
ABDEISSSU	DISABUSES	ABDGIIMNT	BAD TIMING
ABDEJMNOS	JAMES BOND	ABDGINNOU	ABOUNDING
ABDEJORTT	OBJET DART	ABDGINNSW	SWING BAND
ABDEKLMOS	MAKES BOLD	ABDGINORR	BROAD GRIN
ABDEKLRSU	DARK BLUES	ABDGINORS	ADSORBING
ABDEKMRRU	BRAKE DRUM		SIGNBOARD
ABDEKNNOU	DONE A BUNK	ABDGINOXY	BOXING DAY
ABDEKNORW	BREAK DOWN	ABDGLNOSU	LOUD BANGS
	BREAKDOWN	ABDGNOOOR	GO ON BOARD
ABDEKNOSU	DOES A BUNK	ABDHHNOST	BOTH HANDS
ABDEKOORS	READ BOOKS	ABDHIINNR	HINDBRAIN
ABDEKOORT	BOOK TRADE	ABDHIJNNO	JOB IN HAND
ABDEKORSY	KEYBOARDS	ABDHILLNS	HANDBILLS
ABDELLLNY	BELLY-LAND	ABDHILNOR	BLOND HAIR
ABDELLLSY	SYLLABLED	ABDHILORS	HARD-BOILS
ABDELLMSS	BAD SMELLS	ABDHILOST	OLD HABITS
	SMELLS BAD	ABDHIMRTY	DITHYRAMB
ABDELLNOO	BALLOONED	ABDHINORT	BROAD HINT
ABDELLNOY	NOBLE LADY	ABDHIOPRS	SHIPBOARD
ABDELLORR	BREAD ROLL	ABDHIRSTY	BIRTHDAYS
ABDELNNSS	BLANDNESS	ABDHKNOOS	HANDBOOKS
ABDELNOSU	SOUNDABLE	ABDHLNORW	BLOWN HARD
ABDELNRUY	ENDURABLY	ABDHLNSUY	HUSBANDLY
ABDELNTWY	WENT BADLY		
ABDELOORV	LORD ABOVE		

ABDHLORSW	BLOWHARDS	ABEEELNRV	VENERABLE
	BLOWS HARD	ABEEELNRW	RENEWABLE
	HARD BLOWS	ABEEELOST	ABLE TO SEE
ABDHLRTTU	BALD TRUTH	ABEEELRST	STEERABLE
ABDHLRTUY	BADLY HURT	ABEEELRSV	SEVERABLE
ABDHMNSUY	MY HUSBAND	ABEEENSST	ABSENTEES
ABDHNOSUY	HUDSON BAY	ABEEERRTV	VERTEBRAE
ABDHNRSUY	HUSBANDRY	ABEEFFILN	INEFFABLE
ABDHOOSWX	SHADOW-BOX	ABEEFFNOT	BEATEN OFF
ABDHOSSTU	HAS DOUBTS	ABEEFGLOR	FORGEABLE
ABDIIILLN	LIBIDINAL	ABEEFIIST	BEATIFIES
ABDIIJLRS	JAILBIRDS	ABEEFIKRR	FIREBREAK
ABDIILLRS	BILLIARDS	ABEEFILNR	INFERABLE
ABDIILMOS	DIABOLISM	ABEEFILRS	BAS RELIEF
ABDIILOST	DIABOLIST		BAS-RELIEF
ABDIKLMNN	BLANK MIND	ABEEFILST	FLEA BITES
ABDIKNRUY	BUY A DRINK		FLEABITES
ABDILLLOS	SOLID BALL	ABEEFLRST	BEARS LEFT
ABDILLMOR	MILLBOARD	ABEEFLRSU	REFUSABLE
ABDILOOST	STOOD BAIL	ABEEFLRTU	REFUTABLE
ABDILORSW	WILD BOARS	ABEEFLSSU	SELF-ABUSE
ABDILRSZZ	BLIZZARDS	ABEEFORST	ROAST BEEF
ABDILRYZZ	BLIZZARDY	ABEEFORTX	BEFORE TAX
ABDIMNNOT	BADMINTON	ABEEFRRTT	FAR BETTER
ABDIMPQSU	DAMP SQUIB	ABEEFRSTU	TUBE FARES
ABDIMRSSU	ABSURDISM	ABEEGHILW	WEIGHABLE
ABDINOWWY	BAY WINDOW	ABEEGHNOR	HABERGEON
ABDINRSTW	WRISTBAND	ABEEGIINV	LEAVING BE
ABDIOOSTT	ITS TOO BAD	ABEEGINRU	AUBERGINE
ABDIRSSTU	ABSURDIST	ABEEGINRV	BEAVERING
ABDIRSTUY	ABSURDITY	ABEEGKLOR	BROKE A LEG
ABDJMOPRU	BROAD JUMP	ABEEGKLRS	LEG BREAKS
ABDKLNORW	WORLD BANK	ABEEGKORR	BROKERAGE
ABDKNORRW	DARK BROWN	ABEEGLLNU	BLUE ANGEL
ABDLLNOSW	LAND BLOWS	ABEEGLLNW	BEGAN WELL
ABDLMOOOR	BROADLOOM	ABEEGLNOR	LARGE BONE
ABDMMNOSU	OMBUDSMAN	ABEEGLOPR	PORBEAGLE
ABDMNNOOW	BONDWOMAN	ABEEGLRSS	BEER GLASS
ABDMNORUU	BUM AROUND	ABEEGLTVY	VEGETABLY
ABDMOOORR	BOARD ROOM	ABEEGMORS	EMBARGOES
	BOARDROOM	ABEEGMSTY	MEGABYTES
ABDMORSST	BAD STORMS	ABEEGNOOV	GONE ABOVE
ABDMRSSSU	BASS DRUMS	ABEEGNORZ	BRONZE AGE
ABDNOOOTT	NOT TOO BAD	ABEEGNOSY	GONE BY SEA
ABDNOORRS	BARN DOORS	ABEEGNRSW	GREW BEANS
ABDNORUUY	BUY A ROUND	ABEEGOOSV	GOES ABOVE
ABDNOSTUW	STAB WOUND	ABEEGORSX	GEARBOXES
ABDOPRSST	BAD SPORTS	ABEEGOSSY	GOES BY SEA
ABEEEEFRT	BEEFEATER	ABEEGRSTU	BEET SUGAR
ABEEEERSZ	SEA BREEZE		SUGAR BEET
ABEEEFGNO	BEEN OF AGE	ABEEGSTTU	BAGUETTES
ABEEEFKST	BEEFSTEAK	ABEEHHKSS	BAKSHEESH
ABEEEFLRR	REFERABLE	ABEEHILRT	HERITABLE
ABEEEFORT	BEFORE TEA	ABEEHIMSV	MISBEHAVE
ABEEEGGRT	EGG BEATER	ABEEHIMTW	WHITEBEAM
ABEEEGLRR	LAGER BEER	ABEEHINRT	BREATHE IN
	LARGE BEER		HIBERNATE
ABEEEGLRU	BELEAGUER	ABEEHIRRT	BREATHIER
ABEEEGLSV	BEGS LEAVE	ABEEHIRTW	WHITE BEAR
ABEEEGLTV	VEGETABLE	ABEEHKORS	BRAKE SHOE
ABEEEGNNR	GREEN BEAN	ABEEHKOSU	BAKEHOUSE
ABEEEGNOS	BE ONES AGE	ABEEHLLRS	BEER HALLS
ABEEEGRSV	BEVERAGES		HAREBELLS
ABEEEGSTU	BEAU GESTE	ABEEHLLUW	BLUE WHALE
ABEEEHLSW	WHEELBASE	ABEEHLMPS	BLASPHEME
ABEEEKNRS	BARE KNEES	ABEEHLNOW	WHALEBONE
ABEEEKNRV	BREAK EVEN	ABEEHLOOR	BORE A HOLE
	BREAK EVEN	ABEEHLRRT	BLATHERER
ABEEEKPRR	BARKEEPER	ABEEHMNOT	ON THE BEAM
ABEEELMPR	PERMEABLE	ABEEHNORS	HORSEBEAN
ABEEELNRT	ENTERABLE	ABEEHNOTT	ON THE BEAT

ABEEHQSTU	BEQUEATHS	ABEELRUUZ	AZURE BLUE
ABEEHRRST	BREATHERS	ABEELSSSU	SUBLEASES
ABEEHSTTT	AT THE BEST	ABEELSSTT	SEAT BELTS
ABEEIINRT	INEBRIATE	ABEELSTUV	BEST VALUE
ABEEIKNNR	KEEN BRAIN	ABEEMMNRS	MEMBRANES
ABEEIKNST	SNAKE BITE	ABEEMMNTY	EMBAYMENT
ABEEILMRS	MISERABLE	ABEEMNPRU	PENUMBRAE
ABEEILMST	ESTIMABLE	ABEEMNRTT	BETTER MAN
ABEEILMTT	TIMETABLE	ABEEMNSST	BASEMENTS
ABEEILNPS	PLEBEIANS	ABEEMORRT	BAROMETER
ABEEILNSS	BASELINES	ABEEMRRSU	EMBRASURE
ABEEILNTW	TABLE WINE	ABEENNRST	BANNERETS
ABEEILQTU	EQUITABLE	ABEENNRTW	NEW BARNET
ABEEILRST	BEASTLIER	ABEENOPRT	BEER ON TAP
	BLEARIEST	ABEENOSTU	SEEN ABOUT
	LIBERATES	ABEENOTTU	BEATEN OUT
ABEEILRSV	REVISABLE	ABEENOTVW	WENT ABOVE
	VERBALISE	ABEENOVWW	WOVEN A WEB
ABEEILRTT	BITTER ALE	ABEENQRTU	BANQUETER
ABEEILRTV	VERITABLE	ABEENQTTU	BANQUETTE
ABEEILRVV	REVIVABLE	ABEENRRST	BANTERERS
ABEEILRVZ	VERBALIZE	ABEENSTWY	WENT BY SEA
ABEEIMSSS	EMBASSIES	ABEEOORSV	ROSE ABOVE
ABEEIMSTT	BEATS TIME	ABEEOORVZ	ABOVE ZERO
ABEEIORSV	RISE ABOVE	ABEEOPRRT	REPROBATE
ABEEIOTTT	BITE TO EAT	ABEEORRSV	OVERBEARS
ABEEIPSTT	A BIT STEEP	ABEEOSSTU	SEES ABOUT
ABEEIRRSS	BRASSERIE	ABEEOSTUU	BEAUTEOUS
	BRASSIERE	ABEEPRSTT	BESPATTER
ABEEIRSTT	BATTERIES	ABEEPRTTY	BETTER PAY
ABEEJLNOY	ENJOYABLE	ABEERRRST	BARTERERS
ABEEJLNSU	BLUE JEANS	ABEERRSTV	VERTEBRAS
ABEEJMORS	JAMBOREES	ABEERRSTY	BETRAYERS
ABEEJRSST	SABRE JETS	ABEFFILNY	INEFFABLY
ABEEKLNSS	BLEAKNESS	ABEFFKORS	BREAKS OFF
ABEEKLORV	REVOKABLE		OFF BREAKS
ABEEKLRSS	BRAKELESS	ABEFFLOSU	BUFFALOES
ABEEKNOPR	BREAK OPEN	ABEFGLLMO	LEG OF LAMB
ABEEKNOST	ONE BASKET	ABEFGLOOR	GABLE ROOF
ABEEKNSTT	TAKEN BETS	ABEFHILST	TABLE FISH
ABEEKOOPS	PEEKABOOS	ABEFHLSTU	FLASHTUBE
ABEEKPSST	KEEPS TABS	ABEFHOOST	HOOFBEATS
ABEEKSSTT	TAKES BETS	ABEFIILNU	UNIFIABLE
ABEELLMRS	SMALL BEER	ABEFIIMRT	FIMBRIATE
ABEELLMSS	BLAMELESS	ABEFILLLN	FINAL BELL
ABEELLMTU	UMBELLATE	ABEFILLRS	FIREBALLS
ABEELLORT	TOLERABLE	ABEFILLRT	FILTRABLE
ABEELLOVV	EVOLVABLE	ABEFILLST	TELLS A FIB
ABEELLOVW	WELL ABOVE	ABEFILOST	LIFEBOATS
ABEELMMOR	MEMORABLE	ABEFILTUU	BEAUTIFUL
ABEELMNRU	NUMERABLE	ABEFINORR	FOREBRAIN
ABEELMORV	REMOVABLE	ABEFIRRTU	BEAR FRUIT
ABEELMPRS	PREAMBLES	ABEFIRSST	BARE FISTS
ABEELMPRT	TEMPLE BAR		FIRST BASE
ABEELMPRY	PERMEABLY	ABEFKLORT	FLAT BROKE
ABEELMPTT	TEMPTABLE	ABEFKLSTU	BASKETFUL
ABEELMRRY	REBEL ARMY	ABEFLLLTU	FULL TABLE
ABEELMRSS	ASSEMBLER	ABEFLLLUY	BALEFULLY
ABEELMSSS	ASSEMBLES	ABEFLLOST	BEST OF ALL
ABEELMSTT	EMBATTLES	ABEFLLOTU	FELL ABOUT
ABEELMTTU	METAL TUBE	ABEFLLOTY	ABLE TO FLY
ABEELMTWY	AT WEMBLEY	ABEFLNOSW	WOLFSBANE
ABEELNNTU	UNTENABLE	ABEFLOTUW	FLEW ABOUT
ABEELNOPS	BEANPOLES	ABEFLRTUY	REFUTABLY
ABEELNRVY	VENERABLY	ABEFMOORV	FROM ABOVE
ABEELNRWY	RENEWABLY	ABEFOORRT	FERRYBOAT
ABEELPRTU	REPUTABLE	ABEFORRTY	BUTTERFAT
ABEELRRTV	VERTEBRAL	ABEFRTTTU	BEGGARING
ABEELRSUW	WEARS BLUE	ABEGGGINR	BOIL AN EGG
ABEELRTTU	UTTERABLE	ABEGGILNO	BAGGINESS
ABEELRTUW	BLUE WATER	ABEGGINSS	BUGGER ALL
		ABEGGLLRU	

ABEGGNOPS	SPONGE BAG	ABEGNORSW	GROW BEANS
ABEGHHILT	HIGH TABLE	ABEGNOSTU	GET ON A BUS
ABEGHHIOV	HIGH ABOVE	ABEGOOSTU	GOES ABOUT
ABEGHHSTU	HAS THE BUG	ABEGOPRTU	BEAT GROUP
ABEGHINRR	HARBINGER	ABEGORTWY	GO BY WATER
ABEGHINRT	BREATHING	ABEGOSTTU	GETS ABOUT
ABEGHIRRT	BEAR RIGHT	ABEHHINTT	IN THE BATH
ABEGHIRTV	GAVE BIRTH	ABEHHIRTT	HIT THE BAR
ABEGHLOTT	BAG THE LOT	ABEHHOSTU	BATHHOUSE
ABEGHMRRU	HAMBURGER	ABEHIINNR	HIBERNIAN
ABEGHRSSU	SAGEBRUSH	ABEHIITTW	WHITEBAIT
ABEGIIKMT	MAKE IT BIG	ABEHIKLNT	THINKABLE
ABEGIILLT	LITIGABLE	ABEHILLLY	BILL HALEY
ABEGIILNS	ABSEILING	ABEHILMOP	AMPHIBOLE
ABEGIILNT	IGNITABLE	ABEHILMSU	BASIL HUME
ABEGIILNW	BEWAILING	ABEHILNOT	THE ALBION
ABEGIINNT	BEATING IN	ABEHILOPS	BASOPHILE
ABEGIINOR	ABORIGINE	ABEHILORS	ABOLISHER
ABEGIKLRT	BIG TALKER	ABEHILOSS	ABOLISHES
ABEGIKMNR	EMBARKING	ABEHILPPS	SHIPPABLE
ABEGILLLN	LABELLING	ABEHILRST	HERBALIST
ABEGILLLR	LARGE BILL	ABEHILRSY	BEARISHLY
ABEGILLNR	RING A BELL	ABEHILRTY	BREATHILY
ABEGILLOS	GLOBALISE	ABEHILSST	ESTABLISH
ABEGILLOZ	GLOBALIZE	ABEHIMMSS	MEMSAHIBS
ABEGILLSW	WAGE BILLS	ABEHIMNOS	BOHEMIANS
ABEGILMMN	EMBALMING	ABEHIMRRU	HERBARIUM
ADEGILNOR	IGNORABLE	ABEHINRSS	BANISHERS
ABEGILNSW	SWINGABLE	ABEHINRTT	TITHE BARN
ABEGILOST	OBLIGATES	ABEHIORUV	BEHAVIOUR
ABEGIMNNO	BEMOANING	ABEHIRRTT	BIRTH RATE
ABEGIMRRS	AMBERGRIS		BIRTHRATE
ABEGINNNT	BENIGNANT	ABEHIRSST	HEBRAISTS
ABEGINNRT	BANTERING	ABEHIRSTW	BEARS WITH
ABEGINNRY	BARNEYING	ABEHLLNOT	ON THE BALL
ABEGINNRZ	BRAZENING	ABEHLMPSY	BLASPHEMY
ABEGINNST	ABSENTING	ABEHLNORU	BURN A HOLE
ABEGINNTT	BATTENING	ABEHLOPRY	HYPERBOLA
ABEGINORT	BARGE INTO	ABEHLORTT	BETROTHAL
ABEGINORY	GONE BY AIR	ABEHLORTW	BOWLER HAT
ABEGINPRU	BEARING UP	ABEHLOTTW	BATH TOWEL
ABEGINPTU	BEATING UP	ABEHLOVWY	HEAVY BLOW
ABEGINRRT	BARTERING	ABEHLRSUU	HURL ABUSE
ABEGINRST	BREASTING	ABEHMNORS	HORNBEAMS
ABEGINRTT	BATTERING	ABEHNORRT	ABHORRENT
ABEGINRTY	BETRAYING	ABEHNRRTU	HEARTBURN
ABEGINSST	BEASTINGS	ABEHNRSSS	BRASHNESS
ABEGINSTT	GNAT BITES	ABEHNSSTU	SUNBATHES
ABEGIORSY	GOES BY AIR	ABEHOOSTU	BOATHOUSE
ABEGIPPRS	BAGPIPERS		HOUSE BOAT
ABEGJSTUU	SUBJUGATE		HOUSEBOAT
ABEGKMOOS	GAMEBOOKS	ABEHOPRTY	THORPE BAY
ABEGKNORW	BEGAN WORK	ABEHORSSY	BAY HORSES
ABEGKRSTU	GRUBSTAKE	ABEHOSUUY	BUY A HOUSE
ABEGLLNRU	RUNG A BELL	ABEHQRSUU	HARQUEBUS
ABEGLMSUY	MEALYBUGS	ABEHRRTTU	BARE TRUTH
ABEGLNOPY	GO BY PLANE	ABEHRSSUY	BUY SHARES
ABEGLNORU	LOUNGE BAR	ABEIIILST	ABILITIES
ABEGLNTTU	GUN BATTLE	ABEIILLLR	ILLIBERAL
ABEGLOPRU	GROUPABLE	ABEIILLMT	LIMITABLE
ABEGLORTW	GREAT BLOW	ABEIILNOS	IONISABLE
ABEGLRSSU	BLUEGRASS	ABEIILNOZ	IONIZABLE
ABEGLSSTU	GLASS TUBE	ABEIILRRS	LIBRARIES
ABEGMMMRU	BRUMMAGEM	ABEIILRRT	IRRITABLE
ABEGMNOOR	BOOMERANG	ABEIILRTV	VIBRATILE
ABEGMNOSY	MONEYBAGS	ABEIILSST	STABILISE
ABEGMORST	BERGAMOTS	ABEIILSTV	VISITABLE
ABEGMOSST	STAGE MOBS	ABEIILSTZ	STABILIZE
ABEGMRTUY	RUGBY TEAM	ABEIINNRT	INEBRIANT
ABEGNOOTU	GONE ABOUT	ABEIINOTW	TIE IN A BOW
ABEGNOOVY	BON VOYAGE	ABEIINRST	BRAINIEST

ABEIIPPRR	BRIAR PIPE	ABEINRSTU	URBANITES
ABEIIPRTT	BIPARTITE	ABEINRSTW	BRAWNIEST
ABEIIRSSV	VIBRISSAE	ABEINRSUZ	URBANIZES
ABEIIRTVV	VIBRATIVE	ABEINRTTU	TRIBUNATE
ABEIJKLOR	BROKE JAIL		TUBE TRAIN
ABEIJLSTU	JUBILATES		TURBINATE
ABEIJOPRR	REPAIR JOB	ABEINRTWY	WENT BY AIR
ABEIKLSSW	BLEW A KISS	ABEINSSTT	BATTINESS
ABEIKNNRU	IN A BUNKER	ABEIOPRTV	PROBATIVE
ABEIKNORW	WAKE-ROBIN	ABEIORRSS	ARBORISES
ABEIKNRRV	RIVER BANK	ABEIORRSZ	ARBORIZES
ABEIKNRSS	BEARSKINS	ABEIORRTV	RIVER BOAT
ABEIKOOTT	TOOK A BITE	ABEIPRRSS	SPARE RIBS
ABEIKPRTU	BREAK IT UP		SPARERIBS
ABEILLLPS	SPILLABLE	ABEIPRRST	STRIP BARE
ABEILLLRY	LIBERALLY	ABEIPRSST	BAPTISERS
ABEILLLSU	LULLABIES	ABEIPRSTZ	BAPTIZERS
ABEILLMOS	LOSE A LIMB	ABEIRRRST	BARRISTER
ABEILLOPS	SPOILABLE	ABEIRRSSU	BURSARIES
ABEILLPPR	PAPER BILL	ABEIRSSST	BRASSIEST
ABEILLPSU	PLAUSIBLE	ABEIRSTWY	SWEAR BY IT
ABEILLRTW	WATER BILL	ABEIRTTTU	ATTRIBUTE
ABEILLSTY	BESTIALLY	ABEJLNOYY	ENJOYABLY
ABEILMMOV	IMMOVABLE	ABEJMOORS	JEROBOAMS
ABEILMMSW	SWIMMABLE	ABEKKMOOR	BOOKMAKER
ABEILMMTU	IMMUTABLE	ABEKLLNNY	KENNY BALL
ABEILMNSS	BALMINESS	ABEKLNNSS	BLANKNESS
ABEILMOSX	MAILBOXES	ABEKLOOPT	BOOKPLATE
ABEILMPTU	IMPUTABLE	ABEKLOOUV	BOOK VALUE
ABEILMRSV	VERBALISM	ABEKLOOWX	OX-BOW LAKE
ABEILMRSY	MISERABLY	ABEKLORTW	WORK TABLE
ABEILMSTU	SUBLIMATE		WORKTABLE
ABEILNPRT	PRINTABLE	ABEKMNNOR	BROKEN MAN
ABEILNPST	PIN TABLES	ABEKMNORR	BROKEN ARM
	PINTABLES	ABEKNNOST	BANK NOTES
ABEILNPSU	SUBALPINE	ABEKNOOOP	OPEN A BOOK
ABEILNPTU	BLUE PAINT	ABEKNORTU	BROKE A NUT
ABEILNRSS	BRAINLESS	ABEKOORRS	RARE BOOKS
ABEILNRSU	INSURABLE	ABEKOORSY	YEAR BOOKS
ABEILNRUV	BURN ALIVE		YEARBOOKS
ABEILOPTV	PIVOTABLE	ABEKOOSST	BOOK SEATS
ABEILORRT	LIBERATOR	ABEKORSTU	BREAKOUTS
ABEILORST	STROBILAE		BREAKS OUT
ABEILORSV	BOLIVARES		OUTBREAKS
ABEILORTU	LABOURITE	ABELLLOOS	LOOSE BALL
ABEILORTW	BOIL WATER	ABELLLSSY	SYLLABLES
ABEILOSTU	LIES ABOUT	ABELLMNTY	LAMBENTLY
ABEILPRTY	BIT PLAYER	ABELLMORS	SMALL BORE
ABEILQTUY	EQUITABLY		SMALL-BORE
ABEILRRYZ	BIZARRELY	ABELLMRSU	UMBRELLAS
ABEILRSTU	BRUTALISE	ABELLNOOR	BALLOONER
ABEILRTTY	AT LIBERTY	ABELLNOTU	ALL BUT ONE
ABEILRTUZ	BRUTALIZE	ABELLORST	BALLOTERS
ABEILRTVY	VERITABLY	ABELLORTY	TOLERABLY
ABEILRUVY	BURY ALIVE	ABELLORUY	ROYAL BLUE
ABEILSUVY	ABUSIVELY	ABELLOSWY	BOYLES LAW
ABEIMMNRT	TIMBERMAN	ABELMMORY	MEMORABLY
ABEIMNRST	TRIBESMAN	ABELMNOSZ	EMBLAZONS
ABEIMNRSU	SUBMARINE	ABELMNPRU	PENUMBRAL
ABEIMOTTU	ABOUT TIME	ABELMORVY	REMOVABLY
ABEIMRSTV	AMBIVERTS	ABELMOSST	MESOBLAST
ABEINNRST	BANNISTER	ABELMPSTU	BLUE STAMP
ABEINNSTT	ABSTINENT	ABELMSSTW	LAMB STEWS
ABEINNTYZ	BYZANTINE	ABELNNORS	BANNEROLS
ABEINORST	BARITONES	ABELNORST	NOBLE ARTS
ABEINOSST	BOTANISES	ABELNORSZ	BLAZONERS
ABEINOSTT	OBSTINATE	ABELNOSUV	SNOB VALUE
ABEINOSTZ	BOTANIZES	ABELNOSYZ	LAZY BONES
ABEINPSSW	SPINS A WEB		LAZYBONES
ABEINRSST	BANISTERS	ABELNRSTU	SUBALTERN
ABEINRSSU	URBANISES		UNSTABLER

ABELNRTTU	TURNTABLE	ABFLOOOTU	FOOL ABOUT
ABELNSSTU	STALE BUNS	ABFNORSTU	TURBOFANS
ABELOOPPS	OPPOSABLE	ABFORSSTU	SURFBOATS
ABELOPPST	STOPPABLE	ABGGIIMNR	BIG MARGIN
ABELOPRST	PORTABLES	ABGGIKNPY	PIGGY BANK
ABELOPSTT	SPOTTABLE	ABGGINRST	STRING BAG
ABELOQRUY	BAROQUELY	ABGGINRUU	BUG IN A RUG
ABELORRSU	LABOURERS	ABGGNOOST	TOBOGGANS
ABELORSSV	ABSOLVERS	ABGHHILLS	HIGH BALLS
ABELOSSTU	ABSOLUTES		HIGHBALLS
ABELPRTUY	REPUTABLY	ABGHIINNS	BANISHING
ABELRSSTU	BALUSTERS	ABGHIKNRT	RIGHT BANK
ABELRSTTU	TRUSTABLE	ABGHILLNO	BINGO HALL
ABELRSUYY	AYLESBURY	ABGHILMNS	SHAMBLING
ABEMMNOOS	MOONBEAMS	ABGHIMNSU	AMBUSHING
ABEMMNOSY	BY NO MEANS	ABGHINORR	ABHORRING
ABEMNORST	MRS.BEATON	ABGHINSWZ	WHIZ-BANGS
ABEMNORSW	SAM BROWNE	ABGHIOPRY	BIOGRAPHY
ABEMNPRSU	PENUMBRAS	ABGHMORSU	BROUGHAMS
ABEMNSTTU	ABUTMENTS	ABGHNOTUU	HUNG ABOUT
ABEMOOPRR	BROOMRAPE	ABGHPRSSU	HAPSBURGS
ABEMOOTUV	MOVE ABOUT	ABGIIKNNT	BAKING TIN
ABEMORRTU	ARBORETUM	ABGIILLNU	BILINGUAL
	TAMBOURER	ABGIILNRT	LIBRATING
ABEMORRTY	BAROMETRY	ABGIIMSST	BIGAMISTS
ABEMOSSTU	MESS ABOUT	ABGIIMTUY	AMBIGUITY
ABEMRSSTY	STREAMS BY	ABGIINNOT	OBTAINING
ABENNSTTU	SUBTENANT	ABGIINOTV	OBVIATING
ABENOPSSU	SUBPOENAS	ABGIINPST	BAPTISING
ABENORSTT	BETATRONS	ABGIINPTZ	BAPTIZING
ABENORSTV	OBSERVANT	ABGIINRTV	VIBRATING
ABENORTUZ	BRAZEN OUT	ABGIKNNNO	BANKING ON
ABENOSSST	BASS NOTES	ABGIKNRRS	RINGBARKS
ABENOTTUW	WENT ABOUT	ABGILLNNO	NO-BALLING
ABEOOPSSX	SOAP BOXES	ABGILLNOT	BALLOTING
	SOAPBOXES	ABGILLOTY	BILLY GOAT
ABEOORRST	BARE TORSO	ABGILNNOZ	BLAZONING
ABEOORRSU	ARBOREOUS	ABGILNOPY	PLAY BINGO
ABEOORTTU	TORE ABOUT	ABGILNORU	LABOURING
ABEOPPRSY	PAPERBOYS	ABGILNOSV	ABSOLVING
ABEOPRRSY	SOAPBERRY	ABGILNOSX	SIGNAL BOX
ABEORSSTU	SABOTEURS		SIGNALBOX
ABEORSSTY	STAY SOBER	ABGILNOTU	BALING OUT
ABEORSTTU	OBTURATES	ABGILORSW	BRIGALOWS
ABEOSSTTU	SETS ABOUT	ABGIMOSUU	AMBIGUOUS
ABEPRRRSY	RASPBERRY	ABGINNRRU	UNBARRING
ABEPRSSSY	PASSERSBY	ABGINOPRT	PROBATING
ABEPRSSTT	BEST PARTS	ABGINORTY	GO BY TRAIN
ABERSSTTU	SUBSTRATE	ABGINOTWY	TYING A BOW
ABFFLLPSU	PUFFBALLS	ABGINPSSY	BYPASSING
ABFFLOSST	BLAST-OFFS		PASSING BY
ABFGIOORT	FAR TOO BIG	ABGLLNOOW	BOWL ALONG
ABFGLLLOS	GOLF BALLS	ABGLMNOOS	BOOMSLANG
ABFGLLOOS	GOOFBALLS	ABGLNOOST	LONGBOATS
ABFHLLSUY	BASHFULLY	ABGLNOSUW	BUNGALOWS
ABFHOOSTT	FOOTBATHS	ABGLORSUW	SUGAR BOWL
ABFIILLRR	FIBRILLAR	ABGLOSTUU	LUGS ABOUT
ABFIILLRY	BIFILARLY	ABGLPRUYY	PLAY RUGBY
ABFIILOTT	BIT OF TAIL	ABGNOOSTU	GOT ON A BUS
ABFIIMRSS	FIRM BASIS	ABGSSTTUU	BUSTS A GUT
ABFILLNOW	FINAL BLOW	ABHHILOTT	BATHOLITH
ABFILLSYY	SYLLABIFY	ABHHIRRSU	HAIRBRUSH
ABFILOTTU	FLIT ABOUT	ABHIKLLSW	HAWKSBILL
ABFILSSTU	FABULISTS	ABHIKMRRT	BIRTH MARK
ABFIRSTTU	FRUIT BATS		BIRTHMARK
ABFJOOOTU	OUT OF A JOB	ABHILMNTU	THUMBNAIL
ABFLLLSTU	FULL BLAST	ABHILNOST	BIATHLONS
ABFLLOOST	FOOTBALLS	ABHILNRTY	LABYRINTH
ABFLLOSST	SOFTBALLS	ABHILOPSS	BASOPHILS
ABFLMOORW	FORMAL BOW	ABHILOTTU	ALI BHUTTO
ABFLNOORW	BROWN LOAF	ABHILRTTY	TRILBY HAT

ABHINNSTU	NUNS HABIT	ABILOORSY	SAILOR BOY
ABHINORRU	IN HARBOUR	ABILORRST	STROBILAR
ABHINORRW	BROWN HAIR	ABILORRTY	LIBRATORY
ABHISSTTZ	SITZ BATHS	ABILPPTUU	PUT UP BAIL
ABHJNORRY	BARRY JOHN	ABILRSTUY	SALUBRITY
ABHKNOSTU	SOUTH BANK	ABILRTTUY	BRUTALITY
ABHKOOOST	BOATHOOKS	ABIMMNRUU	MANUBRIUM
ABHLLMOST	MOTH BALLS	ABINNOTVV	BON VIVANT
	MOTHBALLS	ABINOOPRT	PROBATION
ABHLLMSTU	ALL THUMBS	ABINOORST	ABORTIONS
ABHLLOOSY	BALLYHOOS	ABINOOSTT	BOTANISTS
ABHLMNORS	SHORN LAMB	ABINRSSTU	URBANISTS
ABHLOPRSW	SHARP BLOW	ABIORRSTV	VIBRATORS
ABHLOPSTY	HYPOBLAST	ABIORRTVY	VIBRATORY
ABHLOSSWW	WASHBOWLS	ABIOSSTTU	SITS ABOUT
ABHMOORST	BATHROOMS	ABIRRTTUY	TRIBUTARY
ABHNOOPRY	ORPHAN BOY	ABJMOPTUU	JUMP ABOUT
ABHNORSSS	BASS HORNS	ABJOSTTUU	JUST ABOUT
ABHOOSSTW	BOAT SHOWS	ABKKLLNOO	BLANK LOOK
	SHOW BOATS	ABKKMOORS	BOOK MARKS
ABHOPPSYY	HAPPY BOYS		BOOKMARKS
ABHORSTUU	RUSH ABOUT	ABKLLOOST	BOOKSTALL
ABHPRSSTU	BRUSH PAST	ABKMOOOOR	BOOK A ROOM
ABIIILNTY	INABILITY	ABKNPRSTU	BANKRUPTS
ABIIILTVY	VIABILITY	ABKOOPSSS	PASS BOOKS
ABIIINNRT	IN BRITAIN		PASSBOOKS
ABIIKLSSS	BASILISKS	ABLLLOOST	STOOLBALL
ABIIILLRY	BILLY LIAR	ABLLLOSSW	SLOW BALLS
ABIILLMRS	MILLIBARS	ABLLMOOSW	LAMBS WOOL
ABIIILLNRT	BRILLIANT	ABLLMOPSW	BLOWLAMPS
ABIILMNNO	BINOMINAL	ABLLMOSSY	SMALL BOYS
ABIILMNOS	BINOMIALS	ABLLNOSSW	SNOWBALLS
ABIILMRST	TRIBALISM	ABLLOPSWY	PLAY BOWLS
ABIILNOOT	ABOLITION	ABLLOSSYZ	LAZY SLOBS
ABIILNORT	LIBRATION	ABLLRTUUY	TUBULARLY
ABIILNOST	LIBATIONS	ABLMNORSU	SUBNORMAL
ABIILRRTY	IRRITABLY	ABLMNRSUU	LABURNUMS
ABIILSTTY	STABILITY	ABLMOOPSS	BOSOM PALS
ABIILSTUY	SUABILITY	ABLNNOSSY	BONNY LASS
	USABILITY	ABLNOTUYY	BUOYANTLY
ABIIMNOST	AMBITIONS	ABLNRSUUY	SUBLUNARY
ABIIMOSTU	AMBITIOUS	ABLOOSSTW	SLOW BOATS
ABIINOOTV	OBVIATION	ABLOSSTTU	SUBTOTALS
ABIINORTV	VIBRATION	ABMNOOOTU	MOON ABOUT
ABIJLMPSU	JUMPS BAIL	ABMNORRST	BARNSTORM
ABIJNOSST	BANJOISTS	ABMOOORTT	MOTOR BOAT
ABIKKLRSW	BRISK WALK		MOTORBOAT
ABIKLOSSW	BLOW A KISS	ABMOORSTY	ARMY BOOTS
ABIKNNOST	BANKS ON IT	ABMORSSTY	SMART BOYS
ABIKOPRRX	IBROX PARK	ABNOOORSYZ	BRYOZOANS
ABILLMOST	LOST A LIMB	ABNOORTTU	TORN ABOUT
ABILLNOPT	BALL POINT	ABNORRSTW	BROWN RATS
	BALLPOINT	ABNORSTUU	RUNABOUTS
ABILLOPRX	PILLAR BOX		RUNS ABOUT
	PILLAR-BOX	ABNORTTUU	ABOUT TURN
ABILLORRZ	RAZORBILL		ABOUT-TURN
ABILLPSUY	PLAUSIBLY		TURN ABOUT
ABILMMOVY	IMMOVABLY		TURNABOUT
ABILMMTUY	IMMUTABLY	ABOORRTTU	OBTURATOR
ABILMOORS	RIBOSOMAL	ABOOSSTTU	TOSS ABOUT
ABILNOOST	LOBATIONS	ABOPSTTUU	PUTS ABOUT
	OBLATIONS	ABORSSSTW	STRAW BOSS
ABILNOOTU	OUT ON BAIL	ACCCDEEEN	ACCEDENCE
ABILNOPSS	SLOP BASIN	ACCCDEEIN	ACCIDENCE
ABILNORST	IN BORSTAL	ACCCDHLOT	CATCH COLD
ABILNOSTU	ABLUTIONS	ACCCDKLOR	CLOCK CARD
ABILNRSTU	RUB SALT IN	ACCCEEENS	ACESCENCE
	TRIBUNALS	ACCCEELRY	CYCLE RACE
ABILNRTUZ	BRAZIL NUT	ACCCEGLOY	COCCYGEAL
ABILNRTVY	VIBRANTLY	ACCCEHITT	CATHECTIC
ABILOORSU	LABORIOUS	ACCCEIIRT	CICATRICE

ACCCHKOOR	COCKROACH
ACCCIILLY	ALICYCLIC
ACCCIILMT	CLIMACTIC
ACCCIRSTU	CIRCUS ACT
ACCCNOPUY	OCCUPANCY
ACCDDEEEN	DECADENCE
ACCDDEILS	DISCALCED
ACCDEEIKS	ICED CAKES
ACCDEEIST	DESICCATE
ACCDEELLN	CANCELLED
ACCDEELNO	CONCEALED
ACCDEELOS	COALESCED
ACCDEFIIL	CALCIFIED
ACCDEFILS	FASCICLED
ACCDEFILY	DECALCIFY
ACCDEGLNO	CLOG DANCE
ACCDEHIKR	DECK CHAIR
ACCDEHILR	CHILD CARE
ACCDEHINT	CHANCED IT
ACCDEHKOT	COCKED HAT
ACCDEHRST	SCRATCHED
ACCDEIILN	ICELANDIC
ACCDEILOS	COLD AS ICE
ACCDEINOT	ANECDOTIC
ACCDEINST	ACCIDENTS
	DESICCANT
ACCDEIORW	COWARDICE
ACCDEIRST	ACCREDITS
ACCDEISST	CASTS DICE
ACCDEKPRU	CRACKED UP
ACCDELMOR	COLD CREAM
ACCDELSSU	CUL-DE-SACS
	CULS-DE-SAC
ACCDEMNOO	CACODEMON
ACCDEMOPT	COMPACTED
ACCDEMORY	DEMOCRACY
ACCDENOST	SECOND ACT
ACCDENOTT	CONTACTED
ACCDENOTU	ACCOUNTED
ACCDENPSU	DUNCES CAP
ACCDEORRS	SCORE CARD
ACCDEORSW	SACRED COW
ACCDFILLY	FLACCIDLY
ACCDGHOOT	GOOD CATCH
ACCDGINOR	ACCORDING
ACCDHHLOT	CATCH HOLD
ACCDHHRUY	ARCHDUCHY
ACCDHINOR	CHANCROID
ACCDHNPRU	CARD PUNCH
	PUNCH CARD
ACCDHORTW	CATCHWORD
ACCDIIIRT	DIACRITIC
ACCDIIOPT	APODICTIC
ACCDIKRRT	CARD TRICK
ACCDILLOY	CYCLOIDAL
ACCDINOOR	ACCORDION
ACCDISSTU	CUTS A DISC
ACCDKLNOS	COLD SNACK
ACCDKNORW	CRACKDOWN
ACCDNOORT	CONCORDAT
ACCDORRTU	COURT CARD
ACCEEFINS	NICE FACES
ACCEEGLMY	MEGACYCLE
ACCEEHIST	CATECHISE
ACCEEHITZ	CATECHIZE
ACCEEHKMT	CHECK MATE
	CHECKMATE
ACCEEHNNO	ONE CHANCE
ACCEEHNPR	PERCHANCE
ACCEEIPRS	PECCARIES
ACCEEIQSU	ACQUIESCE

ACCEEIRTV	ACCRETIVE
ACCEEKLNS	NECKLACES
ACCEELLNR	CANCELLER
ACCEELLOR	CLEARCOLE
ACCEELMNO	COME CLEAN
ACCEELMOS	CAME CLOSE
ACCEELNOR	CONCEALER
ACCEELORS	CLOSE RACE
ACCEELOSS	COALESCES
ACCEELPST	SPECTACLE
ACCEEOSTU	CETACEOUS
ACCEERRUV	VERRUCCAE
ACCEFFHNO	OFF CHANCE
	OFF-CHANCE
ACCEFFIIN	CAFFEINIC
ACCEFHLOT	FACECLOTH
ACCEFIILS	CALCIFIES
ACCEFIIRS	SACRIFICE
ACCEFILSS	FASCICLES
ACCEFILSU	FASCICULE
ACCEGINNT	ACCENTING
ACCEGINPT	ACCEPTING
ACCEGINRT	ACCRETING
ACCEGINSS	ACCESSING
ACCEGIOTT	GEOTACTIC
ACCEHIKNR	RAIN CHECK
ACCEHIKPS	CHICK-PEAS
ACCEHILMS	CHEMICALS
ACCEHILNO	COCHINEAL
ACCEHILNT	TECHNICAL
ACCEHILOR	CHOLERAIC
ACCEHIMNS	MECHANICS
	MISCHANCE
ACCEHIMST	CATECHISM
	SCHEMATIC
ACCEHINRY	CHICANERY
ACCEHINST	CHANCES IT
	CHANCIEST
ACCEHIPRS	CASH PRICE
ACCEHIRTT	ARCHITECT
	THE ARCTIC
ACCEHISTT	CATCHES IT
	CATCHIEST
	CATECHIST
ACCEHJKKT	JACK KETCH
ACCEHLOOT	CHOCOLATE
ACCEHMNOS	COMANCHES
ACCEHMNTT	CATCHMENT
ACCEHMPSU	MUCH SPACE
ACCEHNOST	CATCHES ON
ACCEHORTU	CARTOUCHE
ACCEHORTY	THEOCRACY
ACCEHPSTU	CATCHES UP
ACCEHRRST	SCRATCHER
ACCEHRSST	SCRATCHES
ACCEIILNR	IN A CIRCLE
ACCEIILSV	CIVIL CASE
ACCEIIMNT	CINEMATIC
ACCEIINRT	CIRCINATE
ACCEIIPRT	ACCIPITER
ACCEIIRST	CICATRISE
ACCEIIRTZ	CICATRIZE
ACCEIISTV	SICCATIVE
ACCEIKKLP	PLACEKICK
ACCEIKLNP	PICK CLEAN
ACCEIKLOT	COCKATIEL
ACCEIKRSW	WISECRACK
ACCEILLSV	CLAVICLES
ACCEILMPT	ECLAMPTIC
ACCEILNST	CANTICLES
ACCEILNTU	INCULCATE

ACCEILOPR	POLICE CAR	ACCHINPSU	CAPUCHINS
	PRECOCIAL		CHINA CUPS
ACCEILPST	SCEPTICAL	ACCHIOPRT	COACH TRIP
ACCEILRTU	CIRCULATE	ACCHIRTTY	TRACHYTIC
ACCEIMNTT	TIC-TAC MEN	ACCHJKLNY	JACK LYNCH
ACCEIMOSU	MICACEOUS	ACCHKLMOT	MATCHLOCK
ACCEIMSSU	MUSIC CASE	ACCHKLOST	SACKCLOTH
ACCEINORT	ACCRETION	ACCHKLPUY	LUCKY CHAP
	ANORECTIC	ACCHKOOOP	COCK-A-HOOP
ACCEINOSS	ACCESSION	ACCHKOORW	COACHWORK
ACCEINSTU	ENCAUSTIC	ACCHLOOPS	SCHOOL CAP
ACCEIORTT	CORTICATE	ACCHLOOSW	SLOW COACH
ACCEIOTTT	TIC TAC TOE		SLOWCOACH
ACCEIPRST	PRACTICES	ACCHLOPST	CLOTH CAPS
ACCEKKORS	ROCK CAKES	ACCHNOOPY	CACOPHONY
ACCEKLNRS	CRACKNELS	ACCHNORSU	CHANCROUS
ACCEKMNRS	CRACKSMEN	ACCHOORTU	COACH TOUR
ACCEKNOPR	CRACK OPEN	ACCHOSSTU	SUCCOTASH
ACCEKNORR	CORNCRAKE	ACCHOSSTY	COSY CHATS
ACCELLLOS	CLOSE CALL	ACCIIILNN	CLINICIAN
ACCELLOOT	COLLOCATE	ACCIILLVY	CIVICALLY
ACCELMNSY	CYCLAMENS	ACCIILNOR	CONCILIAR
ACCELMORY	REAL MCCOY	ACCIILOPT	OCCIPITAL
ACCELNOSV	CONCLAVES	ACCIILRTU	CIRCUITAL
ACCELNOTU	CANCEL OUT	ACCIILTVY	ACCLIVITY
ACCELNOVY	CONCAVELY	ACCIIMNOS	COCAINISM
	COVALENCY	ACCIIMOPT	APOMICTIC
ACCELNPTY	PECCANTLY	ACCIINOOZ	CAINOZOIC
ACCELPRTU	CLARET CUP	ACCIIRRTT	ART CRITIC
ACCELSWYY	CYCLEWAYS	ACCIISSTU	CASUISTIC
ACCENORST	ACCENTORS	ACCIKKLOP	PICK A LOCK
ACCENORSU	CANCEROUS	ACCIKKNNS	NICKNACKS
ACCENOSST	COSECANTS	ACCIKLOST	COCKTAILS
ACCENRSUY	RECUSANCY	ACCILLMOY	COMICALLY
ACCEOPRST	ACCEPTORS	ACCILLNOY	CONICALLY
ACCEOPTXY	EXACT COPY	ACCILLNYY	CYNICALLY
ACCEORRSW	SCARECROW	ACCILLRUY	CRUCIALLY
ACCEORSSY	ACCESSORY	ACCILMOPS	ACCOMPLIS
ACCEORSTU	CORUSCATE	ACCILMOPY	COMIC PLAY
	COURT CASE	ACCILRRSU	CIRCULARS
ACCEPRSTU	CUT CAPERS	ACCILRRUU	CURRICULA
ACCFFHHIN	CHAFFINCH	ACCILRTUU	CUTICULAR
ACCFHHIST	CATCH FISH	ACCIMNORY	ACRONYMIC
ACCFIILOR	CALORIFIC	ACCIMNOSS	MOCCASINS
ACCFIILSU	FASCICULI	ACCIMORSY	COSMIC RAY
ACCFIISST	FASCISTIC	ACCIMORTY	TIMOCRACY
ACCFIITTY	FACTICITY	ACCIMPSSU	CAPSICUMS
ACCFINNOU	CONFUCIAN	ACCINNOTT	IN CONTACT
ACCFKOORT	FROCK COAT	ACCINOOSS	OCCASIONS
ACCFOORST	COFACTORS	ACCINOPRR	CAPRICORN
ACCGHIIKN	CHIACKING	ACCINORST	NARCOTICS
ACCGIILNN	CALCINING	ACCINOTVY	CONCAVITY
ACCGIKLNR	CRACKLING	ACCINSTTY	SYNTACTIC
ACCGIKMRS	GIMCRACKS	ACCIOPRTT	CATOPTRIC
ACCGINOST	ACCOSTING	ACCIOPSST	SPICCATOS
ACCHHMNRU	CHURCHMAN	ACCIORSST	ACROSTICS
ACCHIILNN	IN A CLINCH	ACCIOSSTU	ACOUSTICS
ACCHIILRV	CHIVALRIC	ACCKKRSSU	RUCKSACKS
ACCHIINST	ITS A CINCH	ACCKOOOST	COCKATOOS
ACCHIKOTT	THICK COAT	ACCKOPRST	CRACKPOTS
ACCHILLOO	ALCOHOLIC	ACCKOPSTU	SCOUT PACK
ACCHILLOT	LACCOLITH	ACCKORSST	STOCK CARS
ACCHILORT	HOLARCTIC	ACCLLOSUU	CALCULOUS
ACCHILOST	CATHOLICS	ACCLMOPTY	COMPACTLY
ACCHIMNOR	MONARCHIC	ACCMMOORS	MACROCOSM
ACCHIMOPR	CAMPHORIC	ACCMNOTUY	CONTUMACY
ACCHIMORT	CHROMATIC	ACCMOOPRT	COMPACTOR
ACCHIMORX	CHICO MARX	ACCMOSSTU	ACCUSTOMS
ACCHIMOST	STOMACHIC	ACCNNOOTU	NO ACCOUNT
ACCHIMPPT	PITCH CAMP		ON ACCOUNT

ACCNNOSTY	CANNY SCOT	ACDEEERTU	REEDUCATE
	CONSTANCY	ACDEEERTX	EXECRATED
ACCNOPSTU	OCCUPANTS	ACDEEFFLT	FACED LEFT
ACCNORSTT	CONTRACTS	ACDEEFHMR	CHAMFERED
ACCORRSTY	CARRYCOTS	ACDEEFHTT	FED THE CAT
ACCORSSTU	CUT ACROSS	ACDEEFHWY	WHEY-FACED
ACDDDEEIT	DEDICATED	ACDEEFIIT	ACETIFIED
ACDDDEIRS	DISCARDED	ACDEEFINP	FIND PEACE
ACDDDEKSU	DEAD DUCKS	ACDEEFNTU	FECUNDATE
ACDDEEEFT	DEFECATED	ACDEEFRRT	REFRACTED
ACDDEEEIT	DEDICATEE	ACDEEFSTW	FACED WEST
ACDDEEENW	NEW DECADE	ACDEEGHNX	EXCHANGED
ACDDEEERS	DECREASED	ACDEEGHRR	RECHARGED
ACDDEEILM	DECLAIMED	ACDEEGIMS	DICE GAMES
ACDDEEIMT	DECIMATED	ACDEEGIRS	GRAECISED
	MEDICATED	ACDEEGIRZ	GRAECIZED
ACDDEEIST	DEDICATES	ACDEEGKMS	DECK GAMES
ACDDEELRW	ARC-WELDED	ACDEEGLLO	LEGAL CODE
ACDDEELWW	DEWCLAWED	ACDEEGLNO	CONGEALED
ACDDEENST	DECOANTED	ACDEEGLOU	DECALOGUE
ACDDEEORT	DECORATED	ACDEEGNSV	SCAVENGED
ACDDEERST	DEAD CERTS	ACDEEGOPU	DECOUPAGE
ACDDEERTT	DETRACTED	ACDEEHIMP	IMPEACHED
ACDDEFIII	ACIDIFIED	ACDEEHIRS	CASHIERED
ACDDEGIRS	DISGRACED	ACDEEHKNY	HACKNEYED
ACDDEGMOR	DODGEM CAR	ACDEEHLLT	DEATH CELL
ACDDEGNOQ	DODECAGON	ACDEEHLPT	CHAPLETED
ACDDEHILY	ALDEHYDIC	ACDEEHMMS	MAD SCHEME
ACDDEHKNS	DECKHANDS	ACDEEHNNT	ENCHANTED
ACDDEHNRU	DUDE RANCH	ACDEEHNST	CHASTENED
ACDDEIINT	INDICATED	ACDEEHPSY	SPEECH DAY
ACDDEIITV	ADDICTIVE	ACDEEHRRT	CHARTERED
ACDDEIJNU	JAUNDICED	ACDEEHRTT	CHATTERED
ACDDEILPS	DISPLACED	ACDEEIIRT	DIAERETIC
ACDDEINRX	CARD INDEX	ACDEEIJTV	ADJECTIVE
	CARD-INDEX	ACDEEILMR	DECLAIMER
ACDDEINST	DISTANCED		RECLAIMED
ACDDEIORT	DEDICATOR	ACDEEILMX	EXCLAIMED
ACDDEITUV	ADDUCTIVE	ACDEEILNN	CELANDINE
ACDDEKOST	DEAD STOCK		DECENNIAL
	STOCKADED	ACDEEILNR	ICELANDER
ACDDELNOO	CANOODLED	ACDEEILNU	EUCLIDEAN
ACDDEMMNO	COMMANDED	ACDEEILPR	CALIPERED
ACDDENOSY	SECOND DAY	ACDEEILRT	DECALITRE
ACDDGIINT	ADDICTING	ACDEEILTU	ELUCIDATE
ACDDGINTU	ADDUCTING	ACDEEIMNO	MACEDOINE
ACDDHHNSU	DACHSHUND	ACDEEIMNP	IMPEDANCE
ACDDHKOSS	SHADDOCKS	ACDEEIMST	DECIMATES
ACDDHLNOS	COLD HANDS		MEDICATES
ACDDIIKRT	DID A TRICK	ACDEEINRS	INCREASED
ACDDIILRU	DRUIDICAL	ACDEEINSU	AUDIENCES
ACDDIINOT	ADDICTION	ACDEEIPRT	PREDICATE
ACDDINOTU	ADDUCTION	ACDEEIRRT	TRACERIED
ACDDIOPRS	ACID DROPS	ACDEEIRTW	ICED WATER
ACDDKLORU	DARK CLOUD	ACDEEISTV	VESICATED
ACDDKORSY	DOCKYARDS	ACDEEITUV	EDUCATIVE
ACDDLOORU	ADD COLOUR	ACDEEITVV	ADVECTIVE
ACDDNOORR	DONOR CARD	ACDEEKKNR	KNACKERED
ACDDORSTU	ADDUCTORS	ACDEEKLNS	SLACKENED
ACDEEEFST	DEFECATES	ACDEEKPST	TAPE DECKS
ACDEEEHIP	HEADPIECE	ACDEELLOT	OCELLATED
ACDEEEHNP	CHEAPENED	ACDEELLOV	LEAVE COLD
ACDEEEHNR	ADHERENCE	ACDEELLPR	PARCELLED
ACDEEEHST	ESCHEATED	ACDEELLTW	ACTED WELL
ACDEEEKSS	SEED CAKES	ACDEELNOP	PENAL CODE
ACDEEEPRT	DEPRECATE	ACDEELNPU	CLEANED UP
ACDEEEPRV	CAPE VERDE	ACDEELNRS	CALENDERS
ACDEEERRT	CEDAR TREE	ACDEELNTT	TENTACLED
	RECREATED	ACDEELNTU	NUCLEATED
ACDEEERSS	DECREASES	ACDEELORR	CAROL REED
ACDEEERST	DESECRATE	ACDEELPRU	CLEARED UP

289

ACDEELPTU	PECULATED	ACDEGILNO	GENOCIDAL
ACDEELQRU	LACQUERED	ACDEGILNR	DECLARING
ACDEELRRS	DECLARERS	ACDEGIMNP	DECAMPING
ACDEELRRW	ARC WELDER	ACDEGIMRS	DECIGRAMS
ACDEELRST	DECRETALS	ACDEGINNS	ASCENDING
ACDEELRSW	LEADSCREW	ACDEGINNT	DECANTING
ACDEELRTT	CLATTERED	ACDEGINRT	REDACTING
ACDEELRTU	ULCERATED	ACDEGINRY	DYING RACE
ACDEEMMUV	VADE MECUM	ACDEGINTU	EDUCATING
ACDEEMNOS	CODE NAMES	ACDEGIOTT	COGITATED
ACDEEMNRU	CAME UNDER	ACDEGIRRT	CARTRIDGE
ACDEEMPRS	SCAMPERED	ACDEGIRSS	DISGRACES
ACDEENNOP	DO PENANCE	ACDEGJPSU	JUDGES CAP
ACDEENNRT	ENTRANCED	ACDEGLNPU	GLANCED UP
ACDEENNRU	ENDURANCE	ACDEGMNOO	COME AND GO
ACDEENNTU	DANCE TUNE	ACDEGNRSS	SCRAG ENDS
ACDEENORS	COARSENED	ACDEGOOSU	GOOD CAUSE
ACDEENOSS	DEACONESS	ACDEHHIKT	THICK HEAD
ACDEENOST	ANECDOTES		THICKHEAD
ACDEENPST	DANCE STEP	ACDEHIIRS	DIARCHIES
	STEP DANCE	ACDEHIITT	DIATHETIC
ACDEENRSS	CARD SENSE	ACDEHIMRT	CAME THIRD
ACDEENRST	DECANTERS	ACDEHINNR	HINDRANCE
ACDEENRTY	DAY CENTRE	ACDEHINNU	UNCHAINED
ACDEEOPSS	PEASECODS	ACDEHINSV	CAVENDISH
ACDEEORST	DECORATES	ACDEHIPRS	SEPHARDIC
ACDEEORTV	OVERACTED	ACDEHIPRT	DIRT CHEAP
ACDEEPRRS	SCARPERED	ACDEHIPST	CADETSHIP
ACDEEPRRT	RED CARPET	ACDEHIRRS	HIRED CARS
	RED-CARPET	ACDEHIRST	CRASH DIET
ACDEEPSTT	SPECTATED	ACDEHIRSV	CRASH-DIVE
ACDEERRTT	RETRACTED		CRASHDIVE
ACDEERSTT	SCATTERED	ACDEHIRSY	DYARCHIES
ACDEERTTX	EXTRACTED	ACDEHISST	CHASTISED
ACDEESSTU	DECUSSATE	ACDEHKLPU	CHALKED UP
ACDEFFILT	AFFLICTED	ACDEHKMOP	CHOKEDAMP
ACDEFFIST	DISAFFECT	ACDEHKOST	HEADSTOCK
ACDEFFLLO	CALLED OFF	ACDEHKPST	SKETCH PAD
ACDEFFMOR	COFFERDAM	ACDEHKPSU	SHACKED UP
ACDEFIIIR	ACIDIFIER	ACDEHKRSU	ARCHDUKES
ACDEFIIIS	ACIDIFIES	ACDEHKSSS	CASH DESKS
ACDEFIILR	CLARIFIED	ACDEHLNOR	CHLORDANE
ACDEFIIRS	SCARIFIED	ACDEHLNOT	DECATHLON
ACDEFIKNS	KIND FACES	ACDEHLNRS	CHANDLERS
ACDEFILLO	COAL FIELD	ACDEHLNRY	CHANDLERY
	COALFIELD	ACDEHLNTU	LUNCH DATE
ACDEFILNY	IDLE FANCY		UNLATCHED
ACDEFILOS	FOCALISED	ACDEHLORT	COLD HEART
ACDEFILOZ	FOCALIZED	ACDEHLOVY	HEAVY COLD
ACDEFINRT	INFARCTED	ACDEHMOST	STOMACHED
ACDEFINRU	FACED RUIN	ACDEHMPRY	PACHYDERM
ACDEFIRSV	FIVE CARDS	ACDEHMPTU	MATCHED UP
ACDEFKLNO	FOLK DANCE	ACDEHNORW	REACH DOWN
ACDEFLLOR	CALLED FOR	ACDEHNOTU	HEAD COUNT
ACDEFLMOR	COLD FRAME	ACDEHNRUY	HUE AND CRY
ACDEFLNOR	FORCE-LAND	ACDEHNSTU	STAUNCHED
	LAND FORCE		UNSCATHED
ACDEFLNOT	CONFLATED	ACDEHORRV	HARD COVER
ACDEFLOOW	CODE OF LAW	ACDEHORSS	CROSSHEAD
ACDEFNORU	ROUND FACE	ACDEHORST	CHORDATES
ACDEFOPTU	FACED UP TO	ACDEHOSTT	COT DEATHS
ACDEFRRTU	FRACTURED		COT-DEATHS
ACDEGGIMO	DEMAGOGIC	ACDEHPPTU	PATCHED UP
ACDEGGIOP	PEDAGOGIC	ACDEHPRSU	PURCHASED
ACDEGGOOR	GOOD GRACE	ACDEHTTVW	WATCHED T.V.
ACDEGHINR	CHAGRINED	ACDEIIINT	DIETICIAN
ACDEGHINT	DETACHING	ACDEIILMN	MEDICINAL
ACDEGHIRS	DISCHARGE	ACDEIILNT	IDENTICAL
ACDEGHNNU	UNCHANGED	ACDEIILNX	INDEXICAL
ACDEGHNPU	CHANGED UP	ACDEIILRV	LARVICIDE
ACDEGIILR	REGICIDAL		VERIDICAL

ACDEIILTW	TWICE-LAID	ACDEIRRSU	CURARISED
ACDEIIMMY	IMMEDIACY	ACDEIRRUZ	CURARIZED
ACDEIIMNR	AMERINDIC	ACDEIRTTU	URTICATED
ACDEIIMRT	DIAMETRIC	ACDEIRTTX	DIRECT TAX
	MATRICIDE	ACDEJKKSY	SKYJACKED
ACDEIINST	INDICATES	ACDEKKMRU	MUCKRAKED
ACDEIINTV	VINDICATE	ACDEKNOPU	POUND CAKE
ACDEIIOPR	APERIODIC	ACDEKOPTU	PACKED OUT
ACDEIIPRR	PARRICIDE	ACDEKOSST	STOCKADES
ACDEIIPRT	PATRICIDE	ACDELLMOS	COLD MEALS
ACDEIISST	DIE IS CAST	ACDELLOPS	COLLAPSED
ACDEIKMNW	WICKED MAN		SCALLOPED
ACDEIKRST	SIDETRACK	ACDELLORR	CORRALLED
ACDEIKSTY	DICKY SEAT	ACDELLOTU	CALLED OUT
ACDEILLMY	DECIMALLY	ACDELMOOR	MORAL CODE
	MEDICALLY	ACDELMORS	MODEL CARS
ACDEILLOS	LOCALISED	ACDELMORU	CLAMOURED
ACDEILLOZ	LOCALIZED	ACDELMORY	COMRADELY
ACDEILMNR	CLEAR MIND	ACDELMTUU	CUMULATED
ACDEILMNU	UNCLAIMED	ACDELNNOO	COLONNADE
ACDEILMPS	MISPLACED	ACDELNOOS	CANOODLES
ACDEILMST	METAL DISC	ACDELNOOW	LANCEWOOD
ACDEILNNP	PINNACLED	ACDELNOPS	SECOND LAP
ACDEILNSW	WIND SCALE	ACDELNORS	COLANDERS
ACDEILOQR	AIR-COOLED	ACDELNOGW	SCALE DOWN
ACDEILORT	LORICATED	ACDELNPSU	UNCLASPED
ACDEILOST	DISLOCATE	ACDELNRSY	DRY CLEANS
ACDEILOSV	VOCALISED		DRY-CLEANS
ACDEILOVZ	VOCALIZED	ACDELOPRR	LAP RECORD
ACDEILPSS	DISPLACES	ACDELOPTU	COPULATED
ACDEILPSY	PLAYS DICE	ACDELORTW	COLD WATER
ACDEILPTU	DUPLICATE	ACDELORTY	CORDATELY
ACDEILRTU	CURTAILED	ACDELOSTU	OSCULATED
ACDEILSWY	C.DAY LEWIS	ACDELOSTW	COLD SWEAT
ACDEIMMSU	MADE MUSIC	ACDELPRSY	CLEPSYDRA
ACDEIMNNO	DOMINANCE	ACDEMMNOR	COMMANDER
ACDEIMNNT	MENDICANT	ACDEMNNOS	SECOND MAN
ACDEIMNOP	COMPENDIA	ACDEMNORU	CAME ROUND
ACDEIMNOS	COMEDIANS	ACDEMOORT	MOTORCADE
	DEMONIACS	ACDEMOPSS	COMPASSED
ACDEIMNOV	VIC DAMONE	ACDEMOPTU	CAMPED OUT
ACDEIMNRU	MANICURED	ACDEMORST	DEMOCRATS
ACDEIMNSU	MUSCADINE	ACDENNNOU	ANNOUNCED
ACDEIMNTY	MENDACITY	ACDENNRRT	TRANSCEND
ACDEIMOSY	SAMOYEDIC	ACDENOPST	SPOT DANCE
ACDEIMRST	TIME CARDS	ACDENORRY	RED CRAYON
ACDEIMRSU	READ MUSIC	ACDENORSY	SECONDARY
ACDEINNOR	ORDINANCE	ACDENORTU	UNDERCOAT
ACDEINNOS	CANONISED	ACDENRRTY	ENTRY CARD
	IN A SECOND	ACDENRSTU	UNDERACTS
ACDEINNOT	CONTAINED	ACDENRTTU	REDUCTANT
ACDEINNOZ	CANONIZED		TRUNCATED
ACDEINNST	INSTANCED	ACDEOORRT	DECORATOR
ACDEINOPS	CAPONISED	ACDEOORTT	DOCTORATE
ACDEINOPZ	CAPONIZED	ACDEOPSTU	SPACED OUT
ACDEINORR	CARRIED ON		SPACED-OUT
	CORIANDER	ACDEOPTTU	COUP DETAT
ACDEINORT	REDACTION	ACDEORRRW	WAR RECORD
ACDEINOSS	DIOCESANS	ACDEORRSW	SCORE DRAW
ACDEINOTU	AUCTIONED	ACDEORRTT	DETRACTOR
	CAUTIONED	ACDEORSST	DRESS COAT
	EDUCATION	ACDEORSTV	CARD VOTES
ACDEINOTV	ADVECTION	ACDEORTUV	CARVED OUT
ACDEINRSS	ACRIDNESS	ACDEPPRSU	SCRAPED UP
ACDEINRTU	CURTAINED	ACDEQSTUU	AQUEDUCTS
ACDEINSST	DISTANCES	ACDERRSTU	TRADUCERS
ACDEINSTY	SYNDICATE	ACDFFHNSU	HANDCUFFS
ACDEIPRST	PRACTISED	ACDFFIRST	DIFFRACTS
ACDEIQSUV	VICE SQUAD	ACDFFLOSS	SCAFFOLDS
ACDEIQTTU	ACQUITTED	ACDFGOOST	ACTS OF GOD
ACDEIRRRV	CAR DRIVER	ACDFIIRUY	FIDUCIARY

ACDFINNOT	CONFIDANT	ACDIINOTT	DICTATION
ACDFIRTTU	CUT ADRIFT	ACDIINPRS	PINDARICS
ACDFLLLUY	FULLY CLAD	ACDIINRTY	RANCIDITY
ACDFNTTUY	CANDYTUFT	ACDIIOPRT	PODIATRIC
ACDFOORTW	WOODCRAFT	ACDIKKNST	KICKSTAND
ACDFORRSU	FOUR CARDS	ACDIKLLPR	PACK DRILL
ACDGGINNO	GO DANCING	ACDIKLNTY	KINDLY ACT
ACDGGINOR	DOG RACING	ACDIKNQSU	QUICKSAND
ACDGHHIRS	HIGH CARDS	ACDIKRRTT	DIRT TRACK
ACDGHIIPR	DIGRAPHIC	ACDIKRSTY	YARDSTICK
ACDGHILNO	GOLD CHAIN	ACDILLLOO	COLLOIDAL
ACDGHLOTW	GOLD WATCH	ACDILLOOR	CORALLOID
ACDGHMOOT	GOOD MATCH	ACDILLORY	CORDIALLY
ACDGHOOPS	GOOD CHAPS	ACDILLOSU	CAUDILLOS
ACDGHOOPT	GOOD PATCH	ACDILMNOO	MONODICAL
ACDGHOSTW	WATCHDOGS	ACDILMOPY	DIPLOMACY
ACDGIINNR	DINING CAR	ACDILNORS	IRONCLADS
ACDGIINPR	RIDING CAP	ACDILNORT	DOCTRINAL
ACDGIINTT	DICTATING	ACDILNORU	RAIN CLOUD
ACDGIIRST	DIGASTRIC	ACDILNPPU	CUP AND LIP
ACDGIMORW	MAGIC WORD	ACDILOPRS	DROPSICAL
ACDGIMOST	DOGMATICS	ACDILOSTU	CUSTODIAL
ACDGINORR	CORRADING	ACDILOSUU	ACIDULOUS
ACDGINRSU	CRUSADING	ACDILOTUV	OVIDUCTAL
ACDGINRTU	TRADUCING	ACDIMMNNO	IN COMMAND
ACDGKORST	DOG TRACKS	ACDIMOPSS	SPASMODIC
ACDGLLOOR	DOG COLLAR	ACDIMORTY	MORDACITY
ACDGLOOSS	GOOD CLASS	ACDINNOOT	ANTICODON
ACDGLOOST	GOLD COAST	ACDINNORU	UNION CARD
ACDGOOORT	GOOD ACTOR	ACDINOORW	COIN A WORD
ACDHIILMO	HOMICIDAL	ACDINORWW	CAR WINDOW
ACDHIILOP	ACIDOPHIL	ACDINOSTU	CUSTODIAN
ACDHIIMRS	MIDRASHIC	ACDIOPSST	PAID COSTS
ACDHIKNPS	HANDPICKS	ACDIORSTT	DICTATORS
ACDHIKPRT	PITCH DARK	ACDIORSWY	DAIRY COWS
ACDHILLNO	CHINA DOLL	ACDIRSSTT	DISTRACTS
ACDHILPRS	PILCHARDS	ACDJLNTUY	ADJUNCTLY
ACDHILRST	CHILD STAR	ACDJOORTU	COADJUTOR
ACDHILRSY	CHRYSALID	ACDKLRUWY	LUCKY DRAW
ACDHILRUY	HYDRAULIC	ACDKNORTW	TRACK DOWN
ACDHILSTT	LAST DITCH	ACDKORSTU	ROAST DUCK
	LAST-DITCH	ACDKORSTY	STOCKYARD
ACDHIMORT	CHROMATID	ACDLLNORU	LORD LUCAN
ACDHINNOW	CHAIN DOWN	ACDLLSTUY	DUTY CALLS
ACDHIOPRS	RHAPSODIC	ACDLMNOOY	CONDYLOMA
ACDHIOPSS	SCAPHOIDS	ACDLMNOPW	CLAMP DOWN
ACDHIPSSY	DYSPHASIC		CLAMP-DOWN
ACDHKKNOR	HARD KNOCK	ACDLMNOSW	CALMS DOWN
ACDHLOOSY	DAY SCHOOL	ACDLNNORW	CROWN LAND
ACDHMOOTW	MATCHWOOD	ACDLNOORS	DON CARLOS
ACDHNORRU	ROUND ARCH	ACDLNOPSS	COLD SNAPS
ACDHNORSW	CRASH DOWN	ACDLNORSU	CAULDRONS
ACDHNPSSU	CUPS HANDS	ACDMMNOOS	COMMANDOS
ACDHOOPPS	SCAPHOPOD	ACDMMNORU	COMMUNARD
ACDHORRTU	HARD COURT	ACDMOOSUV	MUSCOVADO
ACDHORTWW	WATCHWORD	ACDMPRRTU	TRUMP CARD
ACDIIILRV	VIRICIDAL	ACDNNRTUU	CUT AND RUN
ACDIIIMOT	IDIOMATIC	ACDNOOOPT	OCTOPODAN
ACDIIJLRU	JURIDICAL	ACDOORRSS	CROSSROAD
ACDIIJRUY	JUDICIARY	ACDOPRSST	POSTCARDS
ACDIILLMW	WILD CLAIM	ACDORRTUY	COURTYARD
ACDIILMNO	DOMINICAL	ACDOSSTTU	DUSTCOATS
ACDIILMSS	DISCLAIMS	ACDRSSTTU	DUST CARTS
ACDIILOST	DIASTOLIC		DUSTCARTS
ACDIILPSS	SLIP A DISC	ACEEEEKPS	SEEK PEACE
ACDIILPTY	PLACIDITY	ACEEEFHRS	SEARCH FEE
ACDIILSUU	I,CLAUDIUS	ACEEEFIRS	CEASE FIRE
ACDIIMNNO	DOMINICAN		CEASE-FIRE
ACDIIMRTY	MYDRIATIC	ACEEEFLNR	FREE-LANCE
ACDIINORT	INDICATOR		FREELANCE
ACDIINOSY	DIONYSIAC	ACEEEFPRS	FREE SPACE

ACEEEGHIT	THE ICE AGE	ACEEGIRTT	CIGARETTE
ACEEEGHPR	REPECHAGE	ACEEGKRWY	GREYWACKE
ACEEEGNNV	VENGEANCE	ACEEGLLOT	AT COLLEGE
ACEEEHPRT	PEACH TREE	ACEEGLLOU	COLLEAGUE
ACEEEHRST	THREE ACES	ACEEGLMOS	CLOSE GAME
ACEEEHSSY	SAY CHEESE	ACEEGLNRT	RECTANGLE
ACEEEILMP	PIECEMEAL	ACEEGLPUU	LEAGUE CUP
ACEEEIMPT	PEACETIME	ACEEGLRSS	GRACELESS
ACEEEIPPP	PEACE PIPE	ACEEGLRST	GETS CLEAR
ACEEEIPRS	EARPIECES	ACEEGNORT	GRACE NOTE
ACEEEIPRT	PIECE RATE	ACEEGNORU	ENCOURAGE
ACEEEJLSW	JEWEL CASE	ACEEGNRSV	SCAVENGER
ACEEEKLPR	KEEP CLEAR	ACEEGNSSV	SCAVENGES
ACEEEKNOW	ONCE A WEEK	ACEEGNSSY	CAGEYNESS
ACEEEKPPS	KEEPS PACE	ACEEGOOPR	COOPERAGE
ACEEEKRRT	RACKETEER	ACEEGRTTU	CURETTAGE
ACEEELNRV	RELEVANCE	ACEEHHMOR	REACH HOME
ACEEELNTU	ENUCLEATE	ACEEHIIPR	HAIRPIECE
ACEEELNTY	ACETYLENE	ACEEHILMS	ALCHEMIES
ACEEELSSS	CEASELESS	ACEEHILRT	HERETICAL
ACEEEMNNR	REMANENCE	ACEEHILRV	CHEVALIER
ACEEEMNPR	PERMEANCE	ACEEHIMNS	MECHANISE
ACEEENRSV	SEVERANCE	ACEEHIMNT	THE CINEMA
ACEEERRST	RECREATES	ACEEHIMNZ	MECHANIZE
ACEEERSTT	ETCETERAS	ACEEHIMPS	IMPEACHES
ACEEERSTX	EXECRATES	ACEEHIMRT	THE CRIMEA
ACEEFFHRU	RECHAUFFE	ACEEHINPW	CHEAP WINE
ACEEFFITV	AFFECTIVE	ACEEHINRT	IN THE RACE
ACEEFFLNU	AFFLUENCE	ACEEHINST	HESITANCE
ACEEFFLST	FACES LEFT	ACEEHIRSV	ACHIEVERS
ACEEFFLTU	EFFECTUAL	ACEEHISTT	AESTHETIC
ACEEFFNRY	FANCY FREE	ACEEHKMNT	KEEN MATCH
	FANCY FREE	ACEEHKPTW	KEEP WATCH
ACEEFGLOR	GALE FORCE	ACEEHLMNO	CHAMELEON
ACEEFGMOO	COME OF AGE	ACEEHLMPV	CHAMPLEVE
ACEEFHINT	IN THE FACE	ACEEHLNRU	HERCULEAN
ACEEFIIRT	ACETIFIER	ACEEHLNSS	SENESCHAL
ACEEFIIST	ACETIFIES	ACEEHLORT	TROCHLEAE
ACEEFILPR	FIREPLACE	ACEEHLOSS	SHOELACES
ACEEFINRT	INTERFACE	ACEEHLRTW	CARTWHEEL
ACEEFIRSS	FRICASSEE	ACEEHMNRY	ARCH ENEMY
ACEEFKOPR	POKER FACE	ACEEHMOTY	HAEMOCYTE
ACEEFLORR	CORAL REEF	ACEEHMRVY	HAVE MERCY
ACEEFLOSS	LOSES FACE	ACEEHNNRT	ENCHANTER
ACEEFLOTV	VOLTE FACE	ACEEHNPSS	CHEAPNESS
	VOLTE-FACE	ACEEHNPTY	PACHYTENE
ACEEFLOTW	FACE TOWEL	ACEEHNRST	CHASTENER
ACEEFLRTU	CRUEL FATE	ACEEHNRTT	ENTRECHAT
ACEEFMORT	FORCEMEAT	ACEEHNSTU	CHANTEUSE
ACEEFNORW	CAFE OWNER	ACEEHORRS	HORSE RACE
ACEEFPSTY	TYPEFACES	ACEEHORRV	OVERREACH
ACEEFSSTW	FACES WEST	ACEEHPRTY	ARCHETYPE
ACEEGGLLN	LEG GLANCE	ACEEHPRVY	VERY CHEAP
ACEEGHHNT	THE CHANGE	ACEEHRRRT	CHARTERER
ACEEGHIRU	GAUCHERIE	ACEEHRRTT	CHATTERER
ACEEGHISV	GIVE CHASE	ACEEHRRTY	TREACHERY
ACEEGHLLN	CHALLENGE	ACEEHRSTT	CATHETERS
ACEEGHNRX	EXCHANGER		THREE ACTS
ACEEGHNSX	EXCHANGES	ACEEIILPT	TAILPIECE
ACEEGHRRS	RECHARGES	ACEEIJQRU	JACQUERIE
ACEEGILNS	CINGALESE	ACEEIKLSV	SICK LEAVE
ACEEGILNT	CLIENTAGE	ACEEIKOVW	WEAK VOICE
ACEEGILPV	GIVE PLACE	ACEEIKSST	ICE SKATES
ACEEGILRS	SACRILEGE	ACEEILLNO	CLEO LAINE
ACEEGILRV	VICEREGAL	ACEEILLRT	LILAC TREE
ACEEGINNR	CAREENING	ACEEILLST	CELESTIAL
ACEEGINRR	CAREERING	ACEEILMNS	MESCALINE
ACEEGINRV	GRIEVANCE	ACEEILMOV	COME ALIVE
ACEEGIOVV	GAVE VOICE		MALE VOICE
ACEEGIRSS	GRAECISES	ACEEILMRT	CARMELITE
ACEEGIRSZ	GRAECIZES	ACEEILMRX	EXCLAIMER

ACEEILNPR	PERCALINE	ACEELNSTT	TENTACLES
ACEEILNPW	WIPE CLEAN	ACEELNSTU	NUCLEATES
	WIPE-CLEAN	ACEELNTUX	EXULTANCE
ACEEILNRT	INTERLACE	ACEELNTUY	CUNEATELY
ACEEILPRS	SALE PRICE	ACEELOPRT	PERCOLATE
ACEEILPRT	REPLICATE	ACEELOPSS	ESCALOPES
ACEEILPTX	EXPLICATE	ACEELORRT	CORRELATE
ACEEILRVW	CLEAR VIEW	ACEELORSS	CASSEROLE
ACEEILSTV	CEST LA VIE	ACEELORSW	LOWER CASE
ACEEIMMNN	IMMANENCE		LOWER-CASE
ACEEIMMNT	MINCEMEAT	ACEELORTU	URCEOLATE
ACEEIMMRT	METAMERIC	ACEELOSST	LOSE CASTE
ACEEIMNSX	EXCISEMAN	ACEELPSSS	SPACELESS
ACEEIMPRT	IMPRECATE	ACEELPSTU	PECULATES
ACEEIMPST	SPACE-TIME		SPECULATE
ACEEIMRRS	CAREERISM	ACEELPTUX	EXCULPATE
ACEEIMRST	MISCREATE	ACEELQRRU	LACQUERER
ACEEIMRTT	METRICATE	ACEELRRTT	CLATTERER
ACEEIMRVW	CRIME WAVE	ACEELRSSU	CRUEL SEAS
ACEEIMTTX	EXACT TIME	ACEELRSTU	ULCERATES
ACEEINNRS	CANNERIES	ACEELSSSU	CAUSELESS
ACEEINNRT	NECTARINE	ACEELSSTT	TELECASTS
ACEEINNTU	ENUNCIATE	ACEELSSUY	EASY CLUES
ACEEINPRU	EPICUREAN	ACEEMMNPY	ENEMY CAMP
ACEEINPTT	PECTINATE	ACEEMMNTT	ENACTMENT
ACEEINRSS	INCREASES	ACEEMNORS	COMES NEAR
ACEEIORTX	EXCORIATE	ACEEMNRRY	MERCENARY
ACEEIOSSS	ECOSSAISE	ACEEMNSST	CASEMENTS
ACEEIOSST	TEA COSIES	ACEEMORTT	OCTAMETER
ACEEIOTVV	EVOCATIVE	ACEEMRRSS	SCREAMERS
ACEEIPPRR	RICE PAPER	ACEEMRSTV	STEVE CRAM
ACEEIPRTT	CREPITATE	ACEEMRSTY	MERCY SEAT
ACEEIPRTV	PRECATIVE	ACEENNOPR	CAN OPENER
ACEEIRRST	CAREERIST	ACEENNORS	RESONANCE
ACEEIRSSU	SEA CRUISE	ACEENNOST	CANTONESE
ACEEIRSSW	WISEACRES	ACEENNRST	ENTRANCES
ACEEIRSTT	CATTERIES		RENASCENT
ACEEIRSTU	CAUTERIES	ACEENNRTY	CENTENARY
	CAUTERISE	ACEENOOTV	ONE OCTAVE
ACEEIRSVV	VICE VERSA	ACEENOPPS	OPEN SPACE
ACEEIRTTX	EXTRICATE	ACEENORST	CAROTENES
ACEEIRTUZ	CAUTERIZE	ACEENORTW	EATEN CROW
ACEEISSST	ECSTASIES	ACEENPRRT	CARPENTER
ACEEISSTV	VESICATES	ACEENPTTX	EXPECTANT
ACEEKKPRT	KEEP TRACK	ACEENRSSS	ANCRESSES
ACEEKLMNO	LEMON CAKE	ACEENRSSY	NECESSARY
ACEEKLMPS	KEEPS CALM	ACEENRSTT	ENTR'ACTES
ACEEKLNSS	LACK SENSE	ACEENRTTU	UTTERANCE
ACEEKLPRT	KEPT CLEAR	ACEENSSTU	ACUTENESS
ACEEKORTV	TAKE COVER	ACEENSSTX	EXACTNESS
ACEELLNST	LANCELETS	ACEENSUXY	ANY EXCUSE
ACEELLORT	ELECTORAL	ACEENTTUX	EXECUTANT
ACEELLRRS	CELLARERS	ACEEOOPRT	COOPERATE
ACEELLSSS	SCALELESS	ACEEOPRRT	PROCREATE
ACEELMNPT	PLACEMENT	ACEEORRTT	RECTORATE
ACEELMNRV	CLEVER MAN	ACEEORRTV	OVERREACT
ACEELMNTT	CATTLEMEN	ACEEORRTX	EXECRATOR
ACEELMOOS	CAME LOOSE	ACEEORTUY	EUCARYOTE
ACEELMOOT	COELOMATE	ACEEOSSTU	SETACEOUS
ACEELMOPS	SOMEPLACE	ACEEPPRSU	UPPER CASE
ACEELMORY	COME EARLY		UPPER-CASE
ACEELNNSS	CLEANNESS	ACEEPRRTU	RECAPTURE
ACEELNORT	TOLERANCE	ACEEPSSTT	SPECTATES
ACEELNOTY	CEYLON TEA	ACEERRSSS	CARESSERS
ACEELNPST	PENTACLES	ACEERRSTT	SCATTERER
ACEELNPTU	PETULANCE		SECRET ART
ACEELNRSS	CLEANSERS		STREETCAR
	CLEARNESS	ACEERRSTU	CREATURES
ACEELNRTW	LAW CENTRE	ACEERRSTY	SECRETARY
ACEELNRVY	RELEVANCY	ACEERSSSV	CREVASSES
ACEELNSST	LAST SCENE	ACEERSSTU	SECATEURS

ACEESSSTT	CASSETTES	ACEFIRSTT	CRAFTIEST
	TEST CASES	ACEFKORST	TASK FORCE
ACEFFGINT	AFFECTING	ACEFLLLSU	FULL-SCALE
ACEFFGLNO	GLANCE OFF	ACEFLLPSU	PULL FACES
ACEFFHRUU	CHAUFFEUR	ACEFLLRUY	CAREFULLY
ACEFFIIOT	OFFICIATE	ACEFLMNOS	FLAMENCOS
ACEFFILST	FACE LIFTS	ACEFLNORR	CONFERRAL
	FACE-LIFTS	ACEFLNORS	FALCONERS
ACEFFINOT	AFFECTION	ACEFLNOST	CONFLATES
ACEFFIOPY	PAY OFFICE		FALCONETS
ACEFFIORW	WAR OFFICE	ACEFLOOTV	ACT OF LOVE
ACEFFLNUY	AFFLUENCY	ACEFLTTUU	FLUCTUATE
ACEFFLORS	CLEARS OFF	ACEFMNRST	CRAFTSMEN
ACEFFMPRU	CREAM PUFF	ACEFNOORR	EAR OF CORN
ACEFFNNUY	FUNNY FACE	ACEFNORRR	FAR CORNER
ACEFFOPRS	SCRAPE OFF	ACEFOORST	FOOT RACES
ACEFFOSTU	SUFFOCATE	ACEFOPSTU	CUPS OF TEA
ACEFGHIRT	FACE RIGHT		FACES UP TO
ACEFGHLNU	CHANGEFUL	ACEFORRRT	REFRACTOR
ACEFGIMRS	GRIM FACES	ACEFORRRU	CARREFOUR
ACEFGINPR	PREFACING	ACEFORSST	FORECASTS
ACEFGLMSU	GLUM FACES	ACEFOSTUU	TUFACEOUS
ACEFGLNOR	GERFALCON	ACEFRRSSU	SURFACERS
ACEFGLNOS	LONG FACES	ACEFRRSTU	FRACTURES
ACEFGLSUY	UGLY FACES	ACEGGINRT	GINGER CAT
ACEFHIINT	CHIEFTAIN	ACEGGIRRS	SCRAGGIER
ACEFHIKSS	FISH CAKES	ACEGGIRST	CRAGGIEST
ACEFHILPR	HALF PRICE	ACEGHHIST	HIGH CASTE
ACEFHINPS	FINE CHAPS	ACEGHIINV	ACHIEVING
ACEFHINRS	FRANCHISE	ACEGHILLT	GET A CHILL
ACEFHIPRT	CHIEF PART	ACEGHILNP	PLEACHING
ACEFHIRTU	FAITH CURE	ACEGHILNT	CHELATING
ACEFHLNOU	HALF OUNCE	ACEGHILRT	LETHARGIC
ACEFHMNNR	FRENCHMAN	ACEGHILST	LICH-GATES
ACEFHMORT	CAME FORTH	ACEGHIMPR	GRAPHEMIC
ACEFHNORT	FACE NORTH	ACEGHIMRT	CAME RIGHT
	NORTH FACE	ACEGHINNN	ENHANCING
ACEFHORRS	SEARCH FOR	ACEGHINNS	ENCASHING
ACEFHOSTU	FACE SOUTH		ENCHASING
ACEFHOSUV	VOUCHSAFE	ACEGHINPR	PREACHING
ACEFIILMS	FACSIMILE	ACEGHINRS	SEARCHING
ACEFIILRR	CLARIFIER	ACEGHINSS	CHASSEING
ACEFIILRS	CLARIFIES	ACEGHINST	TEACHINGS
ACEFIINNR	FINANCIER	ACEGHKOST	GET A SHOCK
ACEFIIPRR	FAIR PRICE	ACEGHLNOR	LONG REACH
ACEFIIPRX	FIX A PRICE	ACEGHLOOS	SCHOOL AGE
ACEFIIRRS	SCARIFIER	ACEGHLSTY	LYCH-GATES
ACEFIIRRT	ARTIFICER	ACEGHMNOS	CHEONGSAM
ACEFIIRSS	SCARIFIES	ACEGHNORS	NO CHARGES
ACEFIIRST	ARTIFICES		ON CHARGES
ACEFIIRTV	FRICATIVE	ACEGHNPSU	CHANGES UP
ACEFIITTV	FACTITIVE	ACEGHOPTY	PHAGOCYTE
ACEFIJKKN	JACKKNIFE	ACEGHORRU	ARCH ROGUE
ACEFIKRTU	FRUIT CAKE	ACEGHRRSU	SURCHARGE
ACEFILNOS	FALSE COIN	ACEGIIKLM	LIKE MAGIC
ACEFILORT	FORTALICE	ACEGIILLS	GALLICISE
ACEFILOSS	FOCALISES	ACEGIILLZ	GALLICIZE
ACEFILOSZ	FOCALIZES	ACEGIILNS	ANGLICISE
ACEFILOTV	OLFACTIVE	ACEGIILNV	VIGILANCE
ACEFILSTU	FACULTIES	ACEGIILNZ	ANGLICIZE
ACEFIMNOR	MAIN FORCE	ACEGIIMNT	ENIGMATIC
ACEFIMPRS	CAMP FIRES	ACEGIINNT	ANTIGENIC
ACEFIMRST	CAME FIRST	ACEGIIRRT	GERIATRIC
ACEFINORT	FORNICATE	ACEGIJKNT	JACKETING
ACEFINRSU	FACES RUIN	ACEGIKNNR	CANKERING
ACEFINTTV	VENTIFACT	ACEGIKNRT	RACKETING
ACEFIORST	FACTORIES	ACEGIKSTV	GAVE STICK
	FACTORISE	ACEGILLLO	COLLEGIAL
ACEFIORTZ	FACTORIZE	ACEGILLNO	COLLEGIAN
ACEFIOSTU	FACETIOUS	ACEGILLNR	CELLARING
ACEFIRRST	FIRST RACE		RECALLING

ACEGILLNY	GENICALLY	ACEHIKORT	ARTICHOKE
ACEGILNNO	CONGENIAL	ACEHIKRST	HEARTSICK
ACEGILNNS	CLEANSING	ACEHIKSTW	WHACKIEST
ACEGILNOS	LIONS CAGE	ACEHILLLY	HELICALLY
ACEGILNPR	REPLACING	ACEHILLNT	CAT IN HELL
ACEGILNRS	CLEARINGS	ACEHILLTY	ETHICALLY
ACEGILNRU	NEURALGIC	ACEHILMMO	CHAMOMILE
ACEGILRTU	CURTILAGE	ACEHILMOR	LOCH MARIE
	GRATICULE		MALE CHOIR
ACEGILRTY	LARGE CITY	ACEHILMST	ALCHEMIST
ACEGIMMNR	ENGRAMMIC		ST.MICHAEL
ACEGIMMRS	SCRIMMAGE	ACEHILNOT	CHELATION
ACEGIMNNP	ENCAMPING	ACEHILNOU	CHOU EN-LAI
ACEGIMNRS	GERMANICS	ACEHILNTU	UNETHICAL
	SCREAMING	ACEHILNTY	THYLACINE
ACEGIMNRT	CENTIGRAM	ACEHILPRS	SPHERICAL
	CREMATING	ACEHILRUV	VEHICULAR
ACEGIMNTU	MUTAGENIC	ACEHILSTT	ATHLETICS
ACEGIMPRU	PURE MAGIC	ACEHIMMNS	MECHANISM
ACEGINNOR	IGNORANCE	ACEHIMNRY	MACHINERY
ACEGINNRT	CANTERING	ACEHIMNST	MECHANIST
	RECANTING	ACEHIMRSS	RICH SEAMS
ACEGINNSU	UNCEASING	ACEHIMRTU	RHEUMATIC
ACEGINPPR	RECAPPING	ACEHINORS	CHINA ROSE
ACEGINPRS	ESCARPING	ACEHINORT	ANCHORITE
ACEGINPRT	CARPETING	ACEHINOSV	ANCHOVIES
ACEGINPRY	PANEGYRIC	ACEHINPST	CATHEPSIN
ACEGINRRT	CRATERING	ACEHINRRU	HURRICANE
	RETRACING	ACEHINRSS	CHARINESS
	TERRACING	ACEHINRST	CHANTRIES
ACEGINRSS	CARESSING	ACEHINRSU	SEA URCHIN
ACEGINRST	RACING SET	ACEHINRTT	IN THE CART
ACEGIOPRR	PAREGORIC	ACEHINSTY	HESITANCY
ACEGIOSTT	COGITATES	ACEHINTTU	AUTHENTIC
ACEGIRSTT	STRATEGIC	ACEHIOPRY	CORYPHAEI
ACEGJMRSU	CREAM JUGS	ACEHIORST	SCORE A HIT
ACEGJNOTU	CONJUGATE	ACEHIPPSS	SPACE SHIP
ACEGKOORS	GAS COOKER		SPACESHIP
ACEGLMNOO	COME ALONG	ACEHIPRSZ	CASH PRIZE
ACEGLMNRY	CLERGYMAN	ACEHIPRTW	WHAT PRICE
ACEGLNNPY	PLANGENCY	ACEHIPSST	PASTICHES
ACEGLNORS	LONG RACES	ACEHIPSTW	WHITECAPS
ACEGLNOTY	COGNATELY	ACEHIORSU	CHI-SQUARE
ACEGLNPSU	GLANCES UP	ACEHIRRST	STARCHIER
ACEGMMRSU	SCRUMMAGE	ACEHIRSST	CHASTISER
ACEGNNOTT	COTANGENT	ACEHIRSTU	EUCHARIST
ACEGNNPRY	PREGNANCY	ACEHISSST	CHASTISES
ACEGNORYZ	GONE CRAZY	ACEHISTTT	CHATTIEST
ACEGNPSSU	SPACE GUNS	ACEHKLNSU	UNSHACKLE
ACEGORRTU	CORRUGATE	ACEHKLNTU	TAKE LUNCH
ACEGORRUY	YOUR GRACE	ACEHKLSTY	LATCHKEYS
ACEGORSST	ESCARGOTS	ACEHKMPST	SKETCH MAP
	GET ACROSS	ACEHKNORT	ON THE RACK
ACEGORSTT	COTTAGERS	ACEHKOPRS	PACKHORSE
ACEGORSTY	GREY COATS	ACEHKOPSS	CAKE SHOPS
ACEGORSYZ	GOES CRAZY	ACEHKORST	SHORTCAKE
ACEHHIRRY	HIERARCHY	ACEHKORVY	HEAVY ROCK
ACEHHLNUV	HAVE LUNCH	ACEHKOSST	OAK CHESTS
ACEHHLSTT	SHTETLACH	ACEHKOSVW	SHOCK WAVE
ACEHHMMOT	HOME MATCH	ACEHKPTTW	KEPT WATCH
ACEHHMNTT	HATCHMENT	ACEHLLLOR	CHLORELLA
ACEHHMRTW	WEHRMACHT	ACEHLLNOP	PHONE CALL
ACEHHNRTY	ETHNARCHY	ACEHLLNTU	LATE LUNCH
ACEHHOOTT	TOOTHACHE	ACEHLLOOS	COALHOLES
ACEHHPRTY	HEPTARCHY	ACEHLLOPY	EPOCHALLY
ACEHHRSTT	THATCHERS		HOLY PLACE
ACEHIINPP	EPIPHANIC	ACEHLMOTV	LOVE MATCH
ACEHIINRT	TRICHINAE	ACEHLMRSS	CHARMLESS
ACEHIIRST	CHARITIES	ACEHLMRTU	MUCH LATER
ACEHIISTT	ATHEISTIC	ACEHLMSST	MATCHLESS
ACEHIJNST	JACINTHES	ACEHLNNOY	LON CHANEY

296

ACEHLNPST	PLANCHETS	ACEIILORT	AEROLITIC
ACEHLNRSU	LAUNCHERS	ACEIILOSS	SOCIALISE
ACEHLNSTU	EATS LUNCH	ACEIILOST	SOCIALITE
	UNLATCHES	ACEIILOSZ	SOCIALIZE
ACEHLOOSS	LOOSE CASH	ACEIILRRT	CRITERIAL
ACEHLOPSW	SHOWPLACE	ACEIILRST	REALISTIC
ACEHLORRT	TROCHLEAR	ACEIILRTT	LATERITIC
ACEHLORST	CHLORATES		TRITICALE
	CLOTH EARS	ACEIILSST	SILICATES
	TROCHLEAS	ACEIIMMRU	AMERICIUM
ACEHLORSU	HOUSECARL	ACEIIMNRT	CRIMINATE
ACEHLPSSY	PLAY CHESS	ACEIIMNSS	MESSIANIC
ACEHMMTUY	TUMMY ACHE	ACEIIMPRS	PRIMACIES
ACEHMNNOR	ANCHORMEN	ACEIIMPTV	IMPACTIVE
ACEHMNORW	CHARWOMEN	ACEIIMRST	ARMISTICE
ACEHMNPRT	PARCHMENT	ACEIINRTT	INTRICATE
ACEHMNRST	MERCHANTS	ACEIIPRSS	PISCARIES
ACEHMNRTX	NEXT MARCH	ACEIIPRSV	PRIVACIES
ACEHMNSTY	YACHTSMEN	ACEIIPSTT	EPISTATIC
ACEHMORST	CAME SHORT	ACEIISTTT	STEATITIC
	CHROMATES	ACEIJKNPS	JACKSNIPE
	STOMACHER	ACEIKKNST	TAKEN SICK
ACEHMOSTU	MOUSTACHE	ACEIKKSST	TAKES SICK
ACEHMPRTY	CHAMPERTY	ACEIKLMQU	QUICK MEAL
ACEHMPSTU	MATCHES UP	ACEIKLNRS	SLACK REIN
ACEHMRSST	CASH TERMS	ACEIKLNSY	ASK NICELY
ACEHMSSTU	MUSTACHES	ACEIKLOPS	LACK POISE
ACEHMSTTT	TEST MATCH	ACEIKLPST	SKEPTICAL
ACEHNNPST	PENCHANTS	ACEIKLQSU	QUICK SALE
ACEHNNRTT	TRENCHANT	ACEIKMMSU	MAKE MUSIC
ACEHNOPRS	CHAPERONS	ACEIKMNNS	NICKNAMES
ACEHNOPST	CENOTAPHS	ACEIKMNRT	MEAN TRICK
ACEHNORST	ANCHORETS	ACEIKMRRY	ICY REMARK
ACEHNORTT	ON THE CART	ACEIKMRSV	MAVERICKS
ACEHNOSTT	STONECHAT	ACEIKNOQU	A QUICK ONE
ACEHNPPTU	PUNCH TAPE	ACEIKNRST	CRANKIEST
ACEHNRRTU	RUN THE CAR	ACEIKNRTT	NEAT TRICK
ACEHNRSST	SNATCHERS	ACEIKNSST	TACKINESS
ACEHNRSTU	STAUNCHER	ACEIKNSSW	WACKINESS
ACEHNRSUZ	SCHNAUZER	ACEIKOPRT	AIR POCKET
ACEHNSSTU	STAUNCHES	ACEIKPSTY	TIPSY CAKE
ACEHNSTUW	CASHEW NUT	ACEILLLXY	LEXICALLY
ACEHOOSTU	HOUSECOAT	ACEILLMOP	POLEMICAL
ACEHOPPSY	CHOPPY SEA	ACEILLMOT	COLLIMATE
ACEHOPRRS	SHARECROP		LOCAL TIME
ACEHOPSST	CHASSEPOT	ACEILLMRS	MILLRACES
ACEHORRST	ORCHESTRA	ACEILLMST	CALLS TIME
ACEHORSTU	SEARCH OUT	ACEILLNOR	COLLINEAR
ACEHORTVW	WATCH OVER		CORALLINE
ACEHOSSSW	SHOW CASES	ACEILLOSS	LOCALISES
	SHOWCASES	ACEILLOST	OSCILLATE
ACEHOSTUY	EASY TOUCH	ACEILLOSZ	LOCALIZES
ACEHOSTVY	HEAVY COST	ACEILLPRS	CALLIPERS
ACEHPPSTU	PATCHES UP	ACEILLPSY	SPECIALLY
ACEHPRRSU	PURCHASER	ACEILLPTY	PLICATELY
	URSPRACHE	ACEILLRSV	CAVILLERS
ACEHPRSSU	PURCHASES	ACEILLTTY	TACTILELY
ACEHPSTTY	PETTY CASH	ACEILMMOS	CAMOMILES
ACEHRRSTT	TETRARCHS	ACEILMMST	CLAMMIEST
ACEHSTTVW	WATCHES T.V.	ACEILMNNU	LUMINANCE
ACEIIILST	ITALICISE	ACEILMNOP	POLICEMAN
ACEIIILTZ	ITALICIZE	ACEILMNOR	COAL MINER
ACEIIKLNP	IN A PICKLE	ACEILMNOT	MELANOTIC
ACEIILLMT	LILAC TIME	ACEILMNPS	MANCIPLES
ACEIILLTV	LEVITICAL	ACEILMNRU	NUMERICAL
ACEIILMPR	EMPIRICAL	ACEILMNSU	CALUMNIES
ACEIILMPT	IMPLICATE		MASCULINE
ACEIILNNT	ANTICLINE	ACEILMNTU	CULMINATE
ACEIILNNV	VICENNIAL	ACEILMOPT	PTOLEMAIC
ACEIILNPS	CISALPINE	ACEILMOSS	CAMISOLES
ACEIILNST	INELASTIC		COSEISMAL

ACEILMPSS	MISPLACES	ACEIMRRSW	WAR CRIMES
ACEILMRRU	MERCURIAL	ACEIMRSST	CERAMISTS
ACEILNNOR	ALIEN CORN	ACEIMRTTU	MICTURATE
	CORNELIAN	ACEINNNRU	UNCANNIER
ACEILNNPS	PINNACLES	ACEINNNSS	CANNINESS
ACEILNNTY	ANCIENTLY	ACEINNORR	IN A CORNER
ACEILNOPR	PORCELAIN	ACEINNORT	CONTAINER
ACEILNOPV	POLICE VAN		CRENATION
ACEILNORS	CENSORIAL	ACEINNOSS	ASCENSION
ACEILNORT	REAL TONIC		CANONISES
ACEILNORU	ALEURONIC	ACEINNOSZ	CANONIZES
ACEILNOST	COASTLINE	ACEINNRST	CANNISTER
	SECTIONAL	ACEINNRSU	INSURANCE
ACEILNOTU	INOCULATE	ACEINNRTU	RUNCINATE
ACEILNPTU	INCULPATE		UNCERTAIN
ACEILNPTZ	ZINC PLATE	ACEINNSST	INCESSANT
ACEILNRST	CLARINETS		INSTANCES
ACEILNRSW	CLEAR WINS	ACEINNSSU	NUISANCES
ACEILNRTY	CERTAINLY	ACEINOOTV	EVOCATION
ACEILNSSS	SCALINESS	ACEINOPSS	CAPONISES
ACEILNSUV	VULCANISE	ACEINOPSZ	CAPONIZES
ACEILNTXY	INEXACTLY	ACEINORRS	CARRIES ON
ACEILNUVZ	VULCANIZE		RARE COINS
ACEILOPPS	EPISCOPAL	ACEINORRV	CARNIVORE
ACEILOPRS	CAPRIOLES	ACEINORSS	SCENARIOS
ACEILOQUV	EQUIVOCAL	ACEINORST	CREATIONS
ACEILORRT	RECTORIAL		NARCOTISE
ACEILORST	SCLEROTIA		REACTIONS
	SECTORIAL	ACEINORTZ	NARCOTIZE
ACEILORSV	VOCALISER	ACEINOSST	CANOEISTS
ACEILORTV	VECTORIAL		CESSATION
ACEILORVZ	VOCALIZER	ACEINOSTU	TENACIOUS
ACEILOSSV	VOCALISES	ACEINOSTX	EXACTIONS
ACEILOSVZ	VOCALIZES	ACEINOSUV	VINACEOUS
ACEILOTVY	COEVALITY	ACEINPRUY	PECUNIARY
ACEILPPPR	PAPER CLIP	ACEINPSSU	PUISSANCE
ACEILPPSY	CLAY PIPES	ACEINPSTT	PITTANCES
	PIPE-CLAYS	ACEINQTTU	QUITTANCE
ACEILPRSS	SPIRACLES	ACEINRSST	CANISTERS
ACEILPRST	PARTICLES	ACEINRSSZ	CRAZINESS
ACEILPRSU	PECULIARS	ACEINRSTT	INTERACTS
ACEILPSSU	CAPSULISE	ACEINRSTY	INSECTARY
ACEILPSTU	SPICULATE	ACEINRTTY	CERTAINTY
ACEILPSTY	SPECIALTY	ACEINSSSU	SAUCINESS
ACEILPSUZ	CAPSULIZE	ACEINSSTT	CATTINESS
ACEILPTUY	EUCALYPTI		SCANTIEST
ACEILRRTU	CURTAILER	ACEINSSTY	IN ECSTASY
ACEILRSSZ	CARL ZEISS	ACEINSTTU	TUNICATES
ACEILRSUV	VESICULAR	ACEINSTTY	INTESTACY
ACEILRTUV	LUCRATIVE	ACEIOPRTT	POETIC ART
ACEILSSST	CLASSIEST	ACEIOPTTT	PETTICOAT
ACEILSTWY	ACT WISELY	ACEIORRST	RACE RIOTS
ACEILSUWY	SLUICEWAY	ACEIORRSV	CORRASIVE
ACEILTTUV	CULTIVATE	ACEIORSST	OSTRACISE
ACEIMNNRY	ICY MANNER	ACEIORSTT	CASTROITE
ACEIMNOPS	COMPANIES	ACEIORSTZ	OSTRACIZE
ACEIMNORT	CREMATION	ACEIORSUV	VERACIOUS
ACEIMNOST	ENCOMIAST	ACEIOSTVV	VOCATIVES
ACEIMNOTX	INCOME TAX	ACEIPPRRS	SCRAPPIER
ACEIMNPTU	PNEUMATIC	ACEIPPRST	CRAPPIEST
ACEIMNRST	MISCREANT	ACEIPRRST	PRACTISER
ACEIMNRSU	MANICURES	ACEIPRRSW	PRICE WARS
	MUSCARINE	ACEIPRSST	PRACTISES
ACEIMNSST	SEMANTICS	ACEIPSSST	ESCAPISTS
ACEIMNSTU	MINT SAUCE	ACEIPSSTU	SPACE SUIT
ACEIMNTYZ	ENZYMATIC	ACEIQRTTU	ACQUITTER
ACEIMOPRT	PREATOMIC	ACEIRRSSU	CURARISES
ACEIMORST	MASORETIC	ACEIRRSSW	AIRSCREWS
ACEIMORVW	MICROWAVE	ACEIRRSUZ	CURARIZES
ACEIMPRST	SPERMATIC	ACEIRSSSU	CUIRASSES
ACEIMPSST	CAMP SITES	ACEIRSSTY	ICY STARES

ACEIRSTTU	RUSTICATE	ACELOORTW	COOL WATER
	URTICATES		WATER-COOL
ACEISSSTU	SUITCASES	ACELOOSST	CAST LOOSE
ACEISSTTT	SCATTIEST	ACELOPRRU	OPERCULAR
ACEISTTTY	CITY STATE	ACELOPRSU	CLEAR SOUP
	CITY-STATE	ACELOPRTU	PECULATOR
ACEJJKNOS	JACK JONES	ACELOPSSY	CALYPSOES
ACEJKKMOS	SMOKEJACK	ACELOPSTU	COPULATES
ACEJKKRSY	SKYJACKER	ACELORRSU	CARROUSEL
ACEJKMOOS	JAMES COOK	ACELORRSSU	CAROUSELS
ACEJLMPRU	JUMP CLEAR	ACELORRSSW	SLOW RACES
ACEJLMSUU	MAJUSCULE	ACELORSTU	CLEARS OUT
ACEJSSTUU	JUST CAUSE	ACELORSTY	ROY CASTLE
ACEKKLNRT	CLARK KENT	ACELOSSTU	CASSOULET
ACEKKMMOS	MAKES MOCK		LOST CAUSE
ACEKKMRRU	MUCKRAKER		OSCULATES
ACEKKMRSU	MUCKRAKES	ACELOSSTY	STAY CLOSE
ACEKKOSTT	TAKE STOCK	ACELOSTXY	EXACTLY SO
ACEKKPRTT	KEPT TRACK	ACELPPRRU	CURLPAPER
ACEKLLOSY	YALE LOCKS	ACELPSTUY	EUCALYPTS
ACEKLLRSY	LAY CLERKS	ACELRRSSW	SCRAWLERS
ACEKLMNOY	LACK MONEY	ACELRSTYY	RACY STYLE
ACEKLMOOO	COOK MEALS	ACELSSSTU	CUTLASSES
ACEKLMPSU	PLUM CAKES	ACEMNOORU	COUMARONE
ACEKLNSSS	SLACKNESS	ACEMNOPSS	ENCOMPASS
ACEKLOOPT	TOOK PLACE	ACEMNORRS	ROMANCERS
ACEKLOPRS	SLACK ROPE	ACEMNORTU	MUCRONATE
ACEKLORST	LOSE TRACK	ACEMNPSTY	EMPTY CANS
ACEKLPRUW	WALKER CUP	ACEMOORRT	MOTOR RACE
ACEKLRSST	TRACKLESS	ACEMOPSSS	COMPASSES
ACEKMNORT	ROCKET MAN	ACEMORRSU	SOUR CREAM
ACEKMPSTY	EMPTY SACK	ACEMORSSY	SYCAMORES
ACEKMRRSY	ASKS MERCY	ACEMORSTU	SCREAM OUT
ACEKMSSTU	MAKES CUTS	ACEMOSTVY	VASECTOMY
ACEKNORSU	CANKEROUS	ACEMPPSTU	SET UP CAMP
ACEKNPRSU	UNPACKERS	ACEMPRSUY	SUPREMACY
ACEKOPPRW	POWER PACK	ACEMRRTUY	MEAT CURRY
ACEKORSSW	CASEWORKS	ACENNNORU	ANNOUNCER
ACEKPSSSY	SKYSCAPES	ACENNNOSU	ANNOUNCES
ACEKRSTUW	AWESTRUCK	ACENNOSTV	COVENANTS
ACELLLORS	SOLAR CELL	ACENNSSST	SCANTNESS
ACELLMORS	ALL COMERS	ACENOORSS	ONE ACROSS
ACELLMORU	MOLECULAR	ACENOPRRT	COPARTNER
ACELLNORU	NUCLEOLAR	ACENOPRSY	PONY RACES
ACELLNOSW	LOCAL NEWS	ACENOPSST	CAPSTONES
ACELLNRTY	CENTRALLY	ACENOPSTW	TOWNSCAPE
ACELLOORT	COROLLATE	ACENOPSTY	SYNCOPATE
ACELLOPSS	COLLAPSES	ACENORRSU	SCORE A RUN
	ESCALLOPS	ACENORRTU	RACONTEUR
ACELLORSV	CALLS OVER	ACENORSST	ANCESTORS
	OVERCALLS	ACENORSTU	COURANTES
ACELLRSTU	SCUTELLAR		COURTESAN
ACELLRSUY	SECULARLY		NECTAROUS
ACELLSSSS	CLASSLESS	ACENORSUV	CAVERNOUS
ACELMMNOS	COMMENSAL	ACENOSTTU	EN TOUT CAS
ACELMNTUU	TENACULUM	ACENOSTUU	CUTANEOUS
ACELMOPST	ECTOPLASM	ACENPRRTY	CARPENTRY
ACELMORSY	CLAYMORES	ACENPRSUU	PURSUANCE
ACELMOSST	COMES LAST	ACENPTTUU	PUNCTUATE
ACELMSSTU	MUSCATELS	ACENRRSTU	CRESTA RUN
ACELNNOTY	CONNATELY	ACENRSSSS	CRASSNESS
ACELNOOSV	VOLCANOES	ACENRSSTT	TRANSECTS
ACELNOPRT	PETROL CAN	ACENRSSTU	ETRUSCANS
ACELNOPRV	PROVENCAL	ACENRSTTU	TRUNCATES
ACELNORTU	NUCLEATOR	ACENRTWYZ	WENT CRAZY
ACELNOSTU	CLEANS OUT	ACENSSSTW	NEWSCASTS
	CONSULATE	ACEOOPRRT	CORPORATE
ACELNPRTU	CRAPULENT	ACEOORSSU	ROSACEOUS
ACELNRTTU	RELUCTANT	ACEOORSTU	ROOT CAUSE
ACELNTUXY	EXULTANCY	ACEOORSTV	OVERCOATS
ACELOOPRR	CORPOREAL	ACEOPRRTY	PRECATORY

ACEOPRSSY	CARYOPSES	ACFILORST	TRIFOCALS
ACEOPRSTT	SPECTATOR	ACFIMORRY	FORMICARY
ACEOPSSTU	SPACES OUT	ACFINORST	FRACTIONS
ACEORRRTT	RETRACTOR	ACFINRSST	ST.FRANCIS
ACEORRRVY	CARRY OVER	ACFIOOPST	IPSO FACTO
ACEORRSTU	EUROCRATS	ACFIORSTT	FIRST COAT
ACEORRSTY	SCORE A TRY	ACFIORSTU	FRACTIOUS
ACEORRTTX	EXTRACTOR	ACFJKORST	JACK FROST
ACEORSTUV	CARVES OUT	ACFJKORSU	FOUR JACKS
ACEOSSSTU	SEA SCOUTS	ACFJNSTUY	JUST FANCY
ACEOSSTTU	OUTCASTES	ACFKLOPSW	WOLF PACKS
ACEOSSTTV	CAST VOTES	ACFKNORWY	FANCYWORK
ACEOSSTTW	WEST COAST	ACFKOORRS	ROOF RACKS
ACEPPRSSU	SCRAPES UP	ACFKSSTTU	STUCK FAST
ACEPSSTTY	TYPECASTS	ACFLLORRU	FUR COLLAR
ACEQRSTUU	SQUARE CUT	ACFLLTTUY	TACTFULLY
ACERRTUUV	CURVATURE	ACFLMNOOR	CONFORMAL
ACERSTTUW	CUTWATERS	ACFLMOORY	MYCOFLORA
ACFFIILNO	OFFICINAL	ACFLNOOOT	TON OF COAL
ACFFIILOS	OFFICIALS	ACFLNTTUU	FLUCTUANT
ACFFIINOT	OFFICIANT	ACFLOORTY	OLFACTORY
ACFFIINRT	IN TRAFFIC	ACFMOSTTU	FACTOTUMS
ACFFILLOT	CALL IT OFF	ACGGGINRS	SCRAGGING
ACFFILMOR	FALCIFORM	ACGGIIKMN	MAGICKING
ACFFKLOSS	SLACKS OFF	ACGGIIMNR	MAGIC RING
ACFFLOOST	CALF'S-FOOT	ACGGIIMNS	MAGIC SIGN
ACFFORTXY	CRAFTY FOX	ACGHHIIR	HIGH CHAIR
ACFGHMORR	FROGMARCH	ACGHHILNT	HATCHLING
ACFGIINNN	FINANCING	ACGHHILSS	HIGH-CLASS
ACFGIINPY	PACIFYING	ACGHHINTT	THATCHING
ACFGIKNRT	KINGCRAFT	ACGHIIJKN	HIJACKING
ACFGINORT	ACTING FOR	ACGHIIMNN	MACHINING
	FACTORING	ACGHIINNS	CASHING IN
ACFGINOTU	OUTFACING	ACGHIINRV	ARCHIVING
ACFGINRSU	SURFACING	ACGHIIPRT	GRAPHITIC
ACFGIOSUU	FUGACIOUS	ACGHIKLNS	SHACKLING
ACFGLNORY	GYRFALCON	ACGHIKNTW	THWACKING
ACFHHHILT	HALF HITCH	ACGHIKRTT	RIGHT TACK
ACFHIILMN	FILM CHAIN	ACGHILLOT	GOT A CHILL
ACFHILNOS	FALCHIONS	ACGHILNNO	LONG-CHAIN
ACFHILNTU	CUT IN HALF	ACGHILNNU	LAUNCHING
ACFHKORST	ROCKSHAFT	ACGHILORS	OLIGARCHS
ACFHLLORT	CALL FORTH	ACGHILORY	OLIGARCHY
ACFHLMRSU	SCRUM HALF	ACGHILRST	ARC LIGHTS
	SCRUM-HALF	ACGHINNOR	ANCHORING
ACFHLNORW	HALF CROWN	ACGHINNST	SNATCHING
ACFHLORTU	HALF-COURT		STANCHING
ACFHLORTW	FLOWCHART	ACGHINOUV	AVOUCHING
ACFHMORSU	FORASMUCH	ACGHINPRS	SCARPHING
ACFIIILOR	ORIFICIAL	ACGHINPST	NIGHT CAPS
ACFIILLNY	FINICALLY		NIGHTCAPS
ACFIILNOP	FLIP A COIN	ACGHINRST	STARCHING
ACFIILRSU	SURFICIAL	ACGHIOPRS	CARGO SHIP
ACFIINNNY	IN INFANCY	ACGHKLLNO	LONG CHALK
ACFIINSTU	FAUNISTIC	ACGHKOOST	GOT A SHOCK
ACFIIPSST	PACIFISTS	ACGHLMNOR	LONG MARCH
ACFIKLLSS	FALLS SICK	ACGHORSTU	ROUGH CAST
ACFIKLRSS	SILK SCARF		ROUGHCAST
ACFIKNRSS	SCARFSKIN	ACGHOTTUU	CAUGHT OUT
ACFIKRRTU	FRIAR TUCK	ACGIIILNS	LAICISING
ACFIKSSTT	STICK FAST	ACGIIILNZ	LAICIZING
ACFILMORT	FILM ACTOR	ACGIIIMST	IMAGISTIC
ACFILMORU	FORMULAIC	ACGIIKNNP	PACKING IN
	FUMAROLIC		PANICKING
ACFILMORV	CLAVIFORM	ACGIILLLO	ILLOGICAL
ACFILNNOR	FRANCOLIN	ACGIILLMS	GALLICISM
ACFILNOOT	OLFACTION	ACGIILLNN	CALLING IN
ACFILNPPY	FLIPPANCY	ACGIILLNV	CAVILLING
ACFILNPSU	CUP FINALS	ACGIILLOR	CIGARILLO
ACFILNRTY	FRANTICLY	ACGIILMNS	ANGLICISM
ACFILNRUU	FUNICULAR	ACGIILMNX	CLIMAXING

ACGIILNOS	GASOLINIC	ACHHINSTW	WHINCHATS
ACGIILNST	ANGLICIST	ACHHINSTY	HYACINTHS
ACGIILRTY	GRACILITY	ACHHIPRSU	PUSHCHAIR
ACGIIMNPT	IMPACTING	ACHHLOSTU	SLOUCH HAT
ACGIIMSTT	STIGMATIC	ACHHLOSTW	WASH CLOTH
ACGIINNOR	INORGANIC		WASHCLOTH
ACGIINNOT	ACTIONING	ACHHOSSTW	CHAT SHOWS
ACGIINOST	AGONISTIC	ACHIILMSW	WHIMSICAL
ACGIINPSZ	CAPSIZING	ACHIILNRT	TRICHINAL
ACGIINQRU	ACQUIRING	ACHIILOTT	HALITOTIC
ACGIIORST	ORGIASTIC	ACHIILRTY	CHIRALITY
ACGIJKNPU	JACKING UP	ACHIILSST	CHILIASTS
ACGIKKLOS	GOAL KICKS	ACHIIMNST	MACHINIST
ACGIKNNPU	UNPACKING	ACHIINORT	HAIR TONIC
ACGIKNPPU	PACKING UP	ACHIINPSY	PHYSICIAN
ACGIILLOY	LOGICALLY	ACHIINRST	CHRISTIAN
ACGILLLRS	CALL GIRLS		TRICHINAS
ACGILLNOR	CAROLLING	ACHIIOPST	PISTACHIO
	COLLARING	ACHIIPRSV	VICARSHIP
ACGILLNOT	COLLATING	ACHIIRRTT	ARTHRITIC
ACGILLNPU	CALLING UP	ACHIIRSTV	ARCHIVIST
ACGILLOOO	OOLOGICAL	ACHIISTWY	YAHWISTIC
ACGILLOST	COLLAGIST	ACHIKKSSW	KICKSHAWS
ACGILNNST	SCANTLING	ACHIKLMST	MAHLSTICK
ACGILNOST	NOSTALGIC	ACHIKLPTU	CHALK IT UP
ACGILNPSU	SCALING UP	ACHIKRSSW	RICKSHAWS
ACGILNRSW	SCRAWLING	ACHIKRSTT	HAT TRICKS
ACGILTTUY	GUILTY ACT	ACHILLMOY	OHMICALLY
ACGIMMNOO	MONOGAMIC	ACHILLMSU	MUSIC HALL
ACGIMMNRS	SCRAMMING	ACHILLNPU	LUNCH PAIL
ACGIMNNOO	COGNOMINA	ACHILLNTY	CHANTILLY
ACGIMNNOR	ROMANCING	ACHILLOST	SAILCLOTH
ACGIMNOOR	AGRONOMIC	ACHILMPTY	ITCHY PALM
ACGIMNOPR	COMPARING		LYMPHATIC
ACGIMNORR	CAIRNGORM	ACHILNRUY	RAUNCHILY
ACGIMNSTY	GYMNASTIC	ACHILOPTU	PATCHOULI
	NYSTAGMIC	ACHILOSST	SCHOLIAST
ACGIMNUUV	VACUUMING	ACHILRRUY	CURLY HAIR
ACGIMOTYZ	ZYGOMATIC	ACHILRSSY	CHRYSALIS
ACGINNNNO	CANNONING	ACHILRSTY	STARCHILY
ACGINNNOT	CANTONING	ACHIMMOSS	MASOCHISM
ACGINNOOT	COGNATION	ACHIMNOPS	CHAMPIONS
	CONTAGION	ACHIMNOPY	HYPOMANIC
ACGINNOPY	POIGNANCY	ACHIMNORS	HARMONICS
ACGINNORY	CRAYONING	ACHIMNORT	CHROMATIN
ACGINNOST	COGNISANT	ACHIMNORW	RICH WOMAN
ACGINNOTZ	COGNIZANT	ACHIMNSTW	SWITCHMAN
ACGINORSU	CAROUSING	ACHIMOSST	MASOCHIST
ACGINORTV	CAVORTING	ACHIMOSTU	MUSTACHIO
ACGINOSST	AGNOSTICS	ACHIMRSST	CHRISTMAS
ACGINOTTU	ACTING OUT	ACHIMRSSW	SCRIMSHAW
ACGINPPRS	SCRAPPING	ACHINNOST	STANCHION
ACGINPRTU	CAPTURING	ACHINNOTW	CHINATOWN
ACGINPRUV	CARVING UP	ACHINOOST	IN CAHOOTS
ACGINPTUY	PUGNACITY	ACHINRSTU	RICH AUNTS
ACGJNNOTU	CONJUGANT	ACHINSSTY	SCYTHIANS
ACGKNORTW	WRONG TACK	ACHIOPPRS	PROPHASIC
ACGLMOSUU	COAGULUMS	ACHIOPRRZ	RHIZOCARP
ACGLNORSU	CLANGOURS	ACHIPPTTU	PATCH IT UP
ACGLOOSTY	SCATOLOGY	ACHIRSSTT	CHARTISTS
ACGMNNOOR	CRO-MAGNON	ACHKMORSS	SHAMROCKS
ACGMOPRTY	CRYPTOGAM	ACHKMORTU	TOUCHMARK
ACGNNOOST	CONTANGOS	ACHKOPRTW	PATCHWORK
ACGOORSST	GOT ACROSS	ACHLLOOPT	PHOTOCALL
ACGRSSSTU	CUTS GRASS	ACHLLOOSW	LAW SCHOOL
ACHHIIKRT	THICK HAIR	ACHLLORSY	SCHOLARLY
ACHHILORT	HAIRCLOTH	ACHLMORSW	SLOW MARCH
ACHHILRSU	RICH HAULS	ACHLMOSTW	SLOW MATCH
ACHHILSTW	CLASH WITH	ACHLMSTYZ	SCHMALTZY
ACHHINNOT	CHTHONIAN	ACHLNSSSU	ANSCHLUSS
ACHHINOPS	CHINA SHOP	ACHLNSTUY	STAUNCHLY

ACHLOORST	ART SCHOOL	ACIIOPRST	PSORIATIC
ACHLOOSTU	HOLOCAUST	ACIIOPRTT	PATRIOTIC
ACHLOPRST	CALTHROPS	ACIIOPTZZ	PIZZICATO
ACHMOOPRT	POOR MATCH	ACIIORSUV	VICARIOUS
ACHNOPSTY	SYCOPHANT	ACIIOSSTT	ISOSTATIC
ACHOOPPRS	POOR CHAPS	ACIIOSUVV	VIVACIOUS
ACHOOTTTU	CUT A TOOTH	ACIIPRSTT	PATRISTIC
ACHOPSTTW	STOP WATCH	ACIIPTTVY	CAPTIVITY
	STOPWATCH	ACIISSTTT	STATISTIC
ACHOPSTUY	HYPOCAUST	ACIJKKPSS	SKIPJACKS
ACHORTTTU	CUTTHROAT	ACIJKNNOU	UNION JACK
ACIIILNOT	CILIATION	ACIJKSTTU	JUST A TICK
ACIIILNRT	TRICLINIA	ACIJLMSTU	JUST CLAIM
ACIIILNST	IN ITALICS	ACIJMSUZZ	JAZZ MUSIC
ACIIILNSV	CIVILIANS	ACIKKNNOT	ANTIKNOCK
ACIIIMNST	ANIMISTIC	ACIKKRSTT	KICK-START
ACIIINPST	PIANISTIC	ACIKLMORT	MOCK TRIAL
	SINCIPITA	ACIKLMSTU	MAULSTICK
ACIIIPTZZ	PIZZICATI	ACIKLNOOP	PLAIN COOK
ACIIJKNST	JACKS IT IN	ACIKLNOTY	ANKYLOTIC
ACIIKNPST	PACKS IT IN	ACIKLOSTT	TAILSTOCK
ACIIKNRTW	WIN A TRICK	ACIKLPSSS	SKIP CLASS
ACIIKSTTT	STICK AT IT	ACIKLPSST	SLAPSTICK
ACIILLNOS	ISOCLINAL	ACIKMNOST	MINK COATS
ACIILLNST	SCINTILLA	ACIKNNPRS	CRANKPINS
ACIILLOPT	POLITICAL	ACIKNORTW	WON A TRICK
ACIILMNPU	MUNICIPAL	ACIKPPSTU	PACKS IT UP
ACIILMNRS	CRIMINALS	ACIKPRSTT	ST.PATRICK
ACIILMNSV	CALVINISM	ACIKRSTTU	TRACK SUIT
ACIILMNTY	MILITANCY	ACIKSTTTU	STUCK AT IT
ACIILMOSS	SOCIALISM	ACILLLRYY	LYRICALLY
ACIILMOSU	MALICIOUS	ACILLLTYY	LYTICALLY
ACIILMQTU	QUITCLAIM	ACILLMNOS	SMALL COIN
ACIILNOOT	COALITION	ACILLMSUY	MUSICALLY
	COITIONAL	ACILLNNOS	LOCAL INNS
ACIILNOPT	PLICATION	ACILLNNSY	SYNCLINAL
ACIILNOVV	CONVIVIAL	ACILLNOOS	COLONIALS
ACIILNOVY	INVIOLACY	ACILLNOOT	COLLATION
ACIILNPPR	PRINCIPAL	ACILLNOSY	SONICALLY
ACIILNSTV	CALVINIST	ACILLNOTY	TONICALLY
ACIILOPRT	PICTORIAL	ACILLOOQU	COLLOQUIA
ACIILOSST	SOCIALIST	ACILLOPTY	OPTICALLY
ACIILOSTY	SOCIALITY		TOPICALLY
ACIILQUZZ	QUIZZICAL	ACILLORST	CLOISTRAL
ACIILRSVW	CIVIL WARS	ACILLOSTY	CALLOSITY
ACIILSSTV	SLAVICIST		STOICALLY
ACIILTTTY	TACTILITY	ACILLPTYY	TYPICALLY
ACIIMMNOT	AMMONITIC	ACILLSTWY	CITY WALLS
ACIIMMOSS	MOSAICISM	ACILMMOTT	COMMITTAL
ACIIMNNOS	INSOMNIAC	ACILMNNTU	CULMINANT
ACIIMNOPT	IMPACTION	ACILMNOPS	COMPLAINS
ACIIMNORT	MORTICIAN	ACILMNOPT	COMPLAINT
ACIIMNOSU	MINACIOUS		COMPLIANT
ACIIMNSSU	MUSICIANS	ACILMOPRS	PROCLAIMS
ACIIMORST	AMORISTIC	ACILMPTUU	CAPITULUM
ACIIMORTT	TRIATOMIC	ACILNNNUY	UNCANNILY
ACIIMOSST	MOSAICIST	ACILNNOTU	CONTINUAL
ACIIMOSTT	ATOMISTIC	ACILNNRUU	RANUNCULI
ACIIMOTTY	ATOMICITY	ACILNOOST	LOCATIONS
ACIIMPRST	PRISMATIC	ACILNOPRT	PROLACTIN
ACIIMRSST	SCIMITARS	ACILNORST	CONTRAILS
ACIIMRTVW	WAR VICTIM	ACILNOSSV	SLAVONICS
ACIIMSTUV	VIATICUMS	ACILNOSTU	SUCTIONAL
ACIINNOPS	SPIN A COIN	ACILNSTYY	SYNCYTIAL
ACIINNOST	ONANISTIC	ACILOOPRS	ACROPOLIS
ACIINOPST	OPTICIANS	ACILOOPST	APOSTOLIC
ACIINORTV	VICTORIAN	ACILOORST	CASTOR OIL
ACIINOSTT	CITATIONS	ACILOQTUY	LOQUACITY
ACIINOTTX	ANTITOXIC	ACILORRSU	CURSORIAL
ACIINOTTY	ATONICITY	ACILORSSU	OSSICULAR
ACIINPRST	PITCAIRNS	ACILORSTU	SUCTORIAL

ACILOSSTV	VOCALISTS	ACLMOPRTU	PALM COURT
ACILOTTUY	AUTOLYTIC	ACLMOPSTY	CYTOPLASM
ACILRRTUU	UTRICULAR	ACLNNORTU	NOCTURNAL
ACILRSTUV	CULTIVARS	ACLNOORTT	CONTRALTO
ACILSSTTY	SYSTALTIC	ACLNOORTU	COLOURANT
ACIMMNOOT	MONATOMIC	ACLOOPRRS	CORPORALS
ACIMMORSS	COMMISSAR	ACLOORSTY	ROYAL SCOT
ACIMNNOOP	COMPANION	ACLOORUWY	COLOURWAY
ACIMNNOOR	ROMAN COIN	ACLOOSTTT	TOTAL COST
ACIMNNOPY	IN COMPANY	ACLOPRRSW	PROWL CARS
ACIMNOOST	ONOMASTIC	ACLOPRSUU	CRAPULOUS
ACIMNOOTU	AUTONOMIC	ACLOPRTTU	PLUTOCRAT
ACIMNOOTX	TAXONOMIC	ACLORSTUW	LAW COURTS
ACIMNOPRS	MAIN CROPS	ACLORSUUY	RAUCOUSLY
ACIMNORST	ROMANTICS	ACLOSSSTT	CASTS LOTS
ACIMNTTUY	MUTINY ACT	ACLOSUUVY	VACUOUSLY
ACIMOOTTU	AUTOTOMIC	ACMMMNNOO	COMMON MAN
ACIMORSST	CASTROISM	ACMNOORRT	CORMORANT
	OSTRACISM	ACMNOOSTU	COSMONAUT
ACIMORSTT	STROMATIC	ACMNORSTU	SANCTORUM
ACIMPPSTU	CAMPS IT UP	ACMOPRRSY	ARMY CORPS
ACINNOPSU	SPUN A COIN	ACMORSSTW	WORMCASTS
ACINNORST	CONSTRAIN	ACMORSTUY	CUSTOMARY
	TRANSONIC	ACNNNOOST	CONSONANT
ACINNOSST	CANONISTS	ACNNOSSTT	CONSTANTS
	SANCTIONS	ACNOOPRST	CORPOSANT
ACINOORRS	CORRASION	ACNOORRSU	RANCOROUS
ACINOORST	CONSORTIA	ACNORRSSU	RUN ACROSS
ACINOOSST	TOSS A COIN	ACNORSSTT	CONTRASTS
ACINOOSTV	VOCATIONS	ACNORSTTU	TURNCOATS
ACINOPRRS	SCRAP IRON	ACOORSSTU	AUTOCROSS
ACINORSST	CROISSANT	ACOPRRSST	SPORTS CAR
ACINOSSTW	WAINSCOTS	ACOPRRSTT	PROTRACTS
ACINOSSWX	COXSWAINS	ACOPRSSTU	PUT ACROSS
ACINPRSUW	PUNIC WARS	ACOPSSSTY	PAYS COSTS
ACINPRTUU	CURTAIN UP	ACORRSTUY	CARRYOUTS
ACINRSSSU	NARCISSUS	ACORSSSWY	CROSSWAYS
ACIOORSUV	VORACIOUS	ACORSSTTY	CRYOSTATS
ACIOPRSSY	CARYOPSIS	ACPSSSTUY	PUSSY CATS
ACIOPRSTY	PISCATORY		PUSSYCATS
ACIRSSTUY	CASUISTRY	ADDDEEEHR	REDHEADED
ACJKOPRST	JOCKSTRAP	ADDDEEENO	DONE A DEED
ACJLLORUY	JOCULARLY	ADDDEEEOS	DOES A DEED
ACKKMOPRS	POCKMARKS	ADDDEEFIL	DEFILADED
ACKLLNRTU	TRUNK CALL	ADDDEEFRU	DEFRAUDED
ACKLLPSSU	SKULLCAPS	ADDDEEGGL	ADDLED EGG
ACKLMOOOR	CLOAKROOM	ADDDEEHNR	RED-HANDED
ACKLNOPRT	ROCK PLANT	ADDDEEIRT	DEAD TIRED
ACKLORSST	CROSS-TALK	ADDDEEKLS	SKEDADDLE
ACKLORSTT	LOST TRACK	ADDDEEKRS	DARK DEEDS
ACKLRSTUY	LUCKY STAR	ADDDEENUY	DUANE EDDY
ACKMNRSUU	RUNS AMUCK	ADDDEERSS	ADDRESSED
ACKNOPRST	TANK CORPS	ADDDEFIIN	DANDIFIED
ACKOOOPTY	TOOK A COPY	ADDDEGLOP	DOG-PADDLE
ACKOPRSTT	STOCK PART	ADDDEGMNO	GODDAMNED
ACKRSTTUY	CUTTY SARK	ADDDEIINS	DISDAINED
ACLLLLORS	ROLL CALLS	ADDDEISSU	DISSUADED
ACLLLOSUY	CALLOUSLY	ADDDEKNRU	DEAD DRUNK
ACLLMNOSU	MOLLUSCAN	ADDDELNSU	UNSADDLED
ACLLNOORY	CORONALLY	ADDDELPSU	SADDLED UP
ACLLNOPSU	CALLS UPON	ADDDEOPRS	DROPS DEAD
ACLLOOPSY	PLAYS COOL	ADDEEEFRT	FEDERATED
ACLLOORRY	COROLLARY	ADDEEEGGH	EGGHEADED
ACLLOORST	COLLATORS	ADDEEEGLT	DELEGATED
	COLOSTRAL	ADDEEEGRT	GREAT DEED
ACLMMNOOW	COMMON LAW	ADDEEEGRY	DEGREE-DAY
	COMMON-LAW	ADDEEELLV	DEAD LEVEL
ACLMNOORU	MONOCULAR	ADDEEELPS	DEAD SLEEP
ACLMOOOPR	MARCO POLO	ADDEEEMNR	MEANDERED
ACLMOORSS	CLASSROOM	ADDEEEMNT	EMENDATED
ACLMOORSU	CLAMOROUS	ADDEEENRS	SERENADED

ADDEEEPRT	DEPREDATE	ADDEFFORT	TRADED OFF
ADDEEERRT	RETREADED	ADDEFFORW	WARDED OFF
ADDEEERSS	ADDRESSEE	ADDEFIIMN	DAMNIFIED
ADDEEFFHO	HEADED OFF	ADDEFIINS	DANDIFIES
ADDEEFHOR	HEADED FOR	ADDEFILTX	TAX FIDDLE
ADDEEFIIX	FIXED IDEA	ADDEFORRW	FORWARDED
ADDEEFILN	ENFILADED	ADDEFORWX	EDWARD FOX
ADDEEFILS	DEFILADES	ADDEGGINR	DEGRADING
ADDEEFLTU	DEFAULTED	ADDEGGOOR	GOOD GRADE
ADDEEFNNT	DEFENDANT	ADDEGGOOT	DOG ATE DOG
ADDEEFRRU	DEFRAUDER		DOG EAT DOG
ADDEEGHIP	PIGHEADED		DOG-EAT-DOG
ADDEEGILM	MIDDLE AGE	ADDEGGPRU	DRAGGED UP
ADDEEGINN	DEADENING	ADDEGHILT	DEADLIGHT
ADDEEGINR	ANDRE GIDE	ADDEGHIRT	DEAD RIGHT
ADDEEGIRS	DISAGREED	ADDEGILNR	LADDERING
ADDEEGLNR	GLANDERED	ADDEGILSS	GLISSADED
ADDEEGORT	DEROGATED	ADDEGIMNN	DEMANDING
ADDEEGRRS	DEGRADERS		MADDENING
ADDEEGSSU	DEGAUSSED	ADDEGINNS	SAD ENDING
ADDEEHHOT	HOTHEADED		SADDENING
ADDEEHINP	PINHEADED	ADDEGINOS	DIAGNOSED
ADDEEHORS	DEAD HORSE	ADDEGIOOS	GOOD IDEAS
ADDEEHOTW	TOWHEADED	ADDEGIRRS	DISREGARD
ADDEEHRSS	HEADDRESS	ADDEGKNRU	GRAND DUKE
ADDEEHRTY	DEHYDRATE	ADDEGLLMO	GOLD MEDAL
ADDEEIILS	IDEALISED	ADDEGLNOU	LOADED GUN
ADDEEIILZ	IDEALIZED	ADDEGLORR	LORD GRADE
ADDEEILMP	IMPLEADED	ADDEGLRUY	GUARDEDLY
ADDEEILNS	DEADLINES	ADDEGNOOR	DRAGOONED
ADDEEILNT	DINED LATE	ADDEGNORR	RED DRAGON
ADDEEILOX	LEAD OXIDE	ADDEGNORW	DOWNGRADE
ADDEEILPT	DEPILATED	ADDEGNRRU	UNDERGRAD
ADDEEILRV	DAREDEVIL	ADDEGNRUU	UNGUARDED
ADDEEILST	DEADLIEST	ADDEGOOST	GOOD STEAD
ADDEEIMTT	MEDITATED	ADDEGOSTX	TAX DODGES
ADDEEINRT	DETRAINED	ADDEGRRSU	RED GUARDS
ADDEEIPRS	DESPAIRED	ADDEHHINR	HIRED HAND
	DRIED PEAS	ADDEHHLNS	HELD HANDS
ADDEEIQTU	DEAD QUIET	ADDEHILNS	IDLE HANDS
ADDEELNPS	LAND SPEED	ADDEHILNU	IN A HUDDLE
ADDEELNRS	SLANDERED	ADDEHILNY	LAY HIDDEN
ADDEELNRU	LAUNDERED	ADDEHILOY	HOLIDAYED
ADDEELOST	DESOLATED	ADDEHILRS	DIHEDRALS
ADDEELPPW	DEWLAPPED	ADDEHINNR	HAD DINNER
ADDEEMNRS	DEMANDERS	ADDEHINRY	ANHYDRIDE
ADDEEMNRU	MAUNDERED	ADDEHINSW	HEAD WINDS
	UNDREAMED		HEADWINDS
ADDEEMNST	DAMNEDEST	ADDEHINSY	HENDIADYS
ADDEEMORT	MODERATED	ADDEHIPPY	DIED HAPPY
ADDEEMPST	STAMPEDED	ADDEHIRRT	TRIED HARD
ADDEENNPT	DEPENDANT	ADDEHIRRV	DRIVE HARD
ADDEENOST	STONE DEAD	ADDEHIRRY	DAIRY HERD
ADDEENOTT	DETONATED	ADDEHLORS	HOLDS DEAR
ADDEENRST	DARNEDEST	ADDEHNNRU	UNDERHAND
ADDEENRTU	DENATURED	ADDEHNORS	HARD-NOSED
ADDEENSST	DATEDNESS	ADDEHNORU	ROUND HEAD
ADDEENSSZ	DAZEDNESS		ROUNDHEAD
ADDEENSWY	WEDNESDAY	ADDEHNOTU	HANDED OUT
ADDEEOPRS	DESPERADO	ADDEHNOTW	TWO-HANDED
ADDEEORRS	AS ORDERED	ADDEHOOST	SHOOT DEAD
ADDEEPRSU	PERSUADED	ADDEHOOTT	DO TO DEATH
ADDEEPSUX	PAS DE DEUX	ADDEHORRV	DROVE HARD
ADDEERRSS	ADDRESSER	ADDEHORSW	HEADWORDS
ADDEERRUW	DUE REWARD	ADDEHOSTU	DASHED OUT
ADDEERSSS	ADDRESSES	ADDEHOSVY	HEAVY ODDS
ADDEERSTW	STEWARDED	ADDEHTTUY	DEATH DUTY
ADDEFFHNO	HANDED OFF	ADDEIILNV	INVALIDED
	OFFHANDED	ADDEIILNX	DIXIELAND
ADDEFFHOS	DASHED OFF	ADDEIINNR	RED INDIAN
ADDEFFLOO	OFF-LOADED	ADDEIINVV	DAVID VINE

ADDEIISTV	ADDITIVES	ADDFGHNOO	HAND OF GOD
ADDEIKLRR	DR.KILDARE	ADDFLNNOO	LAND OF NOD
ADDEILLNS	LANDSLIDE	ADDFLOOSY	DAYS OF OLD
ADDEILLOS	OLD LADIES	ADDFMOOOY	DAY OF DOOM
ADDEILLTY	DILATEDLY	ADDGGIJNU	ADJUDGING
ADDEILMMN	MIDDLEMAN	ADDGGIOTY	GIDDY GOAT
ADDEILMNU	IN A MUDDLE	ADDGGORSU	GUARD DOGS
ADDEILMWY	MIDDLE WAY	ADDGHINRR	HARD GRIND
ADDEILNNO	DANDELION	ADDGHINRY	DYING HARD
ADDEILNQU	LEND A QUID	ADDGHLOOR	HOARD GOLD
ADDEILNRU	UNDERLAID	ADDGHNOOS	GOOD HANDS
ADDEILNST	STAND IDLE	ADDGHRRSU	HARD DRUGS
ADDEILNSY	DEADLY SIN	ADDGILNSW	SWADDLING
ADDEILPSY	DISPLAYED	ADDGILNTW	TWADDLING
ADDEILSVY	ADVISEDLY	ADDGINPPU	PADDING UP
ADDEIMNOT	DEMANTOID	ADDGMRSUU	MUDGUARDS
	DOMINATED	ADDGNORSW	DRAGS DOWN
		ADDGOOORS	GOOD ROADS
ADDEIMNRV	DRIVEN MAD	ADDGQRSUU	DRUG SQUAD
ADDEIMNSY	MANY SIDED	ADDGRTUUY	GUARD DUTY
ADDEIMNTY	DYNAMITED	ADDHHINRT	THIRDHAND
ADDEIMRSV	DRIVES MAD	ADDHHLNOS	HANDHOLDS
ADDEIMSST	DISMASTED		HOLD HANDS
ADDEINNTU	INUNDATED	ADDHHLORS	HOLDS HARD
ADDEINOSY	DAY IS DONE	ADDHIIMNN	HAD IN MIND
ADDEINOVW	DAVID OWEN	ADDHIITTT	THAT DID IT!
ADDEINPRU	UNDERPAID	ADDHIMNOR	DID NO HARM
ADDEINRTU	INDURATED	ADDHLOOTU	ADULTHOOD
ADDEINRTW	TRADE WIND	ADDHNNORU	HAND ROUND
ADDEINSUV	UNADVISED	ADDHNNOSW	HANDS DOWN
ADDEIORSS	ROADSIDES	ADDHORRSW	HARD WORDS
	SIDE ROADS	ADDHRSTUY	STUDY HARD
ADDEIORSW	WIDE ROADS	ADDIIKMTZ	TZADDIKIM
ADDEIOSVW	DISAVOWED	ADDIINOST	ADDITIONS
ADDEIQSSU	SQUADDIES	ADDILLORR	ROAD DRILL
ADDEIRSSW	SIDEWARDS	ADDILOSUV	DAVID SOUL
ADDEISSSU	DISSUADES	ADDIMNSUY	MID-DAY SUN
ADDEJNORU	ADJOURNED	ADDINNORS	ORDINANDS
ADDEKRRSS	DARK DRESS	ADDINORSU	DIANDROUS
ADDELLOPR	POLLARDED	ADDINSWYY	WINDY DAYS
ADDELLOPU	LOUD PEDAL	ADDIORRST	DIRT ROADS
ADDELMOTU	MODULATED	ADDKNRRSU	DRUNKARDS
ADDELNNOW	OLD AND NEW	ADDLLNORS	LANDLORDS
ADDELNOSY	OLDEN DAYS	ADDLNNORY	ON DRY LAND
ADDELNOTU	NODULATED	ADDLNNOSW	DOWNLANDS
ADDELNSSU	UNSADDLES	ADDLNOOSW	WOODLANDS
ADDELNTUU	UNDULATED	ADDMNOOTU	ODD MAN OUT
ADDELPSSU	SADDLES UP	ADDMNOPSW	DAMPS DOWN
ADDELRRST	STRADDLER	ADDNNOPUW	UP AND DOWN
ADDELRSST	STRADDLES		UP-AND-DOWN
ADDELRSTW	TWADDLERS	ADDNNOSTW	STAND DOWN
ADDEMORRY	DROMEDARY	ADDNORSWW	DOWNWARDS
ADDENNORU	UNADORNED	ADDOPRSUY	PROUD DAYS
ADDENNOSY	DAYS ON END	ADDRSSTUY	DRY AS DUST
ADDENNRTU	REDUNDANT		DRYASDUST
ADDENNSSU	SAND DUNES	ADEEEEFLN	FEEL A NEED
ADDENNTUU	UNDAUNTED	ADEEEERST	SEEDEATER
ADDENOORT	DEODORANT	ADEEEFHRT	FEATHERED
ADDENOPTU	UNADOPTED	ADEEEFLNT	FELT A NEED
ADDENORTW	TREAD DOWN	ADEEEFNRR	REFERENDA
ADDENOSTU	ASTOUNDED	ADEEEFRRT	FREE TRADE
ADDENRSTU	TRANSUDED	ADEEEFRST	FEDERATES
ADDEOPSST	STOPS DEAD	ADEEEGGNT	GET AN EDGE
ADDEOPSTT	POSTDATED	ADEEEGJNR	JADE GREEN
ADDEORTTU	DARTED OUT	ADEEEGLRT	RELEGATED
ADDEOSSTT	SET AT ODDS	ADEEEGLST	DELEGATES
ADDEOTUWY	OWED A DUTY	ADEEEGNRS	RENEGADES
ADDEPQRUU	QUADRUPED	ADEEEGNRT	GENERATED
ADDEPRSSU	SUPERADDS		TENDER AGE
ADDFFILOS	DAFFODILS	ADEEEGORT	TO A DEGREE
ADDFFNRUY	DANDRUFFY	ADEEEGTTV	VEGETATED

ADEEEHKNR	HEARKENED	ADEEFNOST	STONE DEAF
ADEEEHKNT	TAKEN HEED	ADEEGGINS	DISENGAGE
ADEEEHKST	TAKES HEED	ADEEGGIRV	AGGRIEVED
ADEEEHLLV	LEVEL HEAD	ADEEGGIUW	WIDE GAUGE
ADEEEHLRT	LEATHERED	ADEEGGLNO	GOLDEN AGE
ADEEEHNRT	HEARTENED	ADEEGGMOU	DEMAGOGUE
ADEEEHRRS	REHEARSED	ADEEGGNNR	GANGRENED
ADEEEHRST	THE RED SEA	ADEEGGNOT	GOT AN EDGE
ADEEEHRTW	WEATHERED	ADEEGGOPU	PEDAGOGUE
ADEEEHSSY	EYESHADES	ADEEGGRST	STAGGERED
ADEEEILNT	DELINEATE	ADEEGGRSW	SWAGGERED
ADEEEINST	DETAINEES	ADEEGHINV	GIVEN HEAD
ADEEEIRSS	DIAERESES	ADEEGHISV	GIVES HEAD
ADEEEIUVX	EAUX-DE-VIE	ADEEGHPRS	SHARP EDGE
ADEEEKKNW	WEAK-KNEED	ADEEGIILS	LAID SIEGE
ADEEEKLNP	ANKLE DEEP	ADEEGILLR	GALLERIED
ADEEEKNSW	SNAKEWEED	ADEEGILNR	ENGRAILED
ADEEELLMN	ENAMELLED		REALIGNED
ADEEELLNS	LEASE LEND	ADEEGILNW	WIDE ANGLE
	LEND-LEASE		WIDE-ANGLE
ADEEELLST	TEASELLED	ADEEGILTV	LEVIGATED
ADEEELNRW	NEW DEALER	ADEEGIMNN	DEMEANING
ADEEELPRS	SEED PEARL	ADEEGIMNT	GEMINATED
ADEEEMNSS	MADE SENSE	ADEEGIMOV	VIDEO GAME
ADEEEMNST	EMENDATES	ADEEGIMRT	EMIGRATED
ADEEEMPRT	PERMEATED	ADEEGINNR	ENDEARING
ADEEENRRS	SERENADER		ENGRAINED
ADEEENRRW	NEW READER		GRENADINE
ADEEENRSS	SERENADES	ADEEGINPS	GAIN SPEED
ADEEENRST	EAST ENDER	ADEEGINRR	GRENADIER
ADEEENRTT	ENTREATED	ADEEGINRT	DENIGRATE
ADEEENRTV	ENERVATED	ADEEGINRW	WIDE RANGE
	VENERATED	ADEEGINST	DESIGNATE
ADEEENSTT	EDENTATES	ADEEGINSV	ENVISAGED
ADEEENSTV	EVEN DATES	ADEEGINTV	NEGATIVED
ADEEEPRST	DESPERATE	ADEEGIRSS	DISAGREES
ADEEEPRTW	DEEP WATER	ADEEGIRST	TRAGEDIES
ADEEERRSV	READ VERSE	ADEEGISST	GETS IDEAS
ADEEERRTT	RETREATED	ADEEGIUVW	WAVEGUIDE
ADEEERTTU	DEUTERATE	ADEEGKNRR	DARK GREEN
ADEEERTWW	WATERWEED	ADEEGKOPS	KEEPS A DOG
ADEEFFILR	FIELDFARE	ADEEGKPRU	KEEP GUARD
ADEEFFIOR	DIE OF FEAR	ADEEGLLLY	ALLEGEDLY
ADEEFFLOS	SEALED OFF	ADEEGLLNO	ALL ON EDGE
ADEEFGILM	FIELD GAME	ADEEGLLRV	GRAVELLED
ADEEFGINN	DEAFENING	ADEEGLNNR	ENGLANDER
ADEEFGINT	DEFEATING	ADEEGLNOR	LONG-EARED
ADEEFHIRS	FRESH IDEA	ADEEGLNOT	ELONGATED
ADEEFHLPS	HALF SPEED	ADEEGLNRY	LEGENDARY
ADEEFHORS	FOREHEADS	ADEEGLOPS	PLEASE GOD!
ADEEFIILW	IDEAL WIFE	ADEEGLRSS	GRADELESS
ADEEFIISV	FIVE A SIDE	ADEEGLRTU	REGULATED
ADEEFILLN	FILL A NEED	ADEEGMNRR	GERMANDER
ADEEFILNS	ENFILADES	ADEEGMNRS	GENDARMES
ADEEFILOT	DEFOLIATE	ADEEGMNTU	AUGMENTED
ADEEFILSU	FEUDALISE	ADEEGNNRS	ENDANGERS
ADEEFILUZ	FEUDALIZE		GREENSAND
ADEEFIMST	DEFEATISM	ADEEGNORR	REED ORGAN
ADEEFINRR	REFRAINED	ADEEGNRRS	GARDENERS
ADEEFIRTX	FIXED RATE	ADEEGNRST	ESTRANGED
ADEEFISTT	DEFEATIST	ADEEGNRSU	DUNGAREES
ADEEFLLRY	FEDERALLY	ADEEGORST	DEROGATES
ADEEFLNTT	FLATTENED	ADEEGRSSU	DEGAUSSER
ADEEFLORS	FREELOADS	ADEEGRSTY	GETS READY
ADEEFLRTT	FLATTERED	ADEEGSSSU	DEGAUSSES
ADEEFLRTU	DEFAULTER	ADEEHHITW	WHITEHEAD
ADEEFLSSX	FLAXSEEDS	ADEEHHNOP	HEADPHONE
ADEEFMNSU	MEND A FUSE	ADEEHHNOT	ON THE HEAD
ADEEFMORR	FOREARMED	ADEEHIISV	HEAVISIDE
ADEEFMSTU	DEAF MUTES	ADEEHILMO	IDEAL HOME
	DEAF-MUTES	ADEEHILNS	HEADLINES

ADEEHILNT	IN THE LEAD	ADEEILMNS	LEAD MINES
ADEEHILVW	HELD A VIEW		MELANISED
ADEEHINRT	HERNIATED	ADEEILMNT	DEMENTIAL
ADEEHINSS	HEADINESS	ADEEILMNZ	MELANIZED
ADEEHISST	DIATHESES	ADEEILMPR	EPIDERMAL
ADEEHISSV	ADHESIVES	ADEEILMTY	MEDIATELY
ADEEHISSW	WISE HEADS	ADEEILNOR	RIDE ALONE
ADEEHISTT	AT THE SIDE	ADEEILNPS	PENALISED
	HESITATED	ADEEILNPX	EXPLAINED
ADEEHKLRS	SHELDRAKE	ADEEILNPZ	PENALIZED
ADEEHLLOS	LEASEHOLD	ADEEILNRT	TAILENDER
ADEEHLLOV	LEAVE HOLD	ADEEILNRW	DREW A LINE
ADEEHLLRT	HEARD TELL	ADEEILNRY	DINE EARLY
ADEEHLLSW	WELLHEADS	ADEEILNST	DATELINES
ADEEHLMOW	MADE WHOLE		DINES LATE
ADEEHLNSU	UNLEASHED	ADEEILNTZ	DENTALIZE
ADEEHLNTV	LED THE VAN	ADEEILOTT	ETIOLATED
ADEEHLRST	HARD STEEL	ADEEILPPS	LEAD PIPES
ADEEHLRTW	HELD WATER	ADEEILPRR	LIP READER
ADEEHLSST	DEATHLESS		LIP-READER
ADEEHLTWY	LED THE WAY	ADEEILPRV	PREVAILED
ADEEHMNOT	METHADONE	ADEEILPSS	DISPLEASE
ADEEHMORT	HOME TRADE	ADEEILPST	DEPILATES
ADEEHMOST	HOMESTEAD	ADEEILQSU	EQUALISED
ADEEHNOST	HEADSTONE	ADEEILQUZ	EQUALIZED
ADEEHNPPR	APPREHEND	ADEEILRVW	DREW A VEIL
ADEEHNPRS	SHARPENED	ADEEILTTV	LEVITATED
ADEEHNRSS	HARNESSED	ADEEIMMRT	DREAMTIME
ADEEHNRST	ADHERENTS	ADEEIMNRR	REMAINDER
ADEEHNRTU	UNEARTHED	ADEEIMNST	STEAMED IN
ADEEHOOTT	HEAD TO TOE	ADEEIMPPR	PIPE DREAM
ADEEHORRV	OVERHEARD	ADEEIMPRY	EMPIRE DAY
ADEEHORSS	SOREHEADS	ADEEIMRST	DIAMETERS
ADEEHORST	HARD TO SEE		DREAMIEST
ADEEHORSV	OVERHEADS	ADEEIMSST	DEMITASSE
ADEEHORTY	HERE TODAY	ADEEIMSSY	SEAMY SIDE
ADEEHOSWY	EYE SHADOW	ADEEIMSTT	ESTIMATED
ADEEHRRST	THREADERS		MEDITATES
ADEEHRRTY	REHYDRATE	ADEEIMSTV	SAVED TIME
ADEEHRSST	HEADRESTS	ADEEINNOS	ADENOSINE
	SHED TEARS	ADEEINNRT	ATE DINNER
ADEEHRSTT	SHATTERED		EAT DINNER
ADEEHRSTV	HARVESTED		ENTRAINED
ADEEHRSTW	WATERSHED	ADEEINPRT	PERTAINED
ADEEHRSTY	SHADY TREE	ADEEINPST	NEAP TIDES
	THREE DAYS	ADEEINRSS	NEARSIDES
ADEEHRTUY	RUE THE DAY		READINESS
ADEEHSSTY	THESE DAYS	ADEEINRST	DETAINERS
ADEEHSTUX	EXHAUSTED	ADEEINRSW	SEND A WIRE
ADEEIILLV	LIVED A LIE	ADEEINRTT	EATEN DIRT
ADEEIILMT	IDEAL TIME	ADEEINSTT	TETANISED
ADEEIILRS	IDEALISER	ADEEINTTZ	TETANIZED
ADEEIILRZ	IDEALIZER	ADEEIOPTV	VIDEOTAPE
ADEEIILSS	IDEALISES	ADEEIPRRS	DRAPERIES
ADEEIILSZ	IDEALIZES	ADEEIPRTU	REPUDIATE
ADEEIIMMT	IMMEDIATE	ADEEIPSST	STEP ASIDE
ADEEIIMTV	MEDIATIVE	ADEEIPSTW	WAIST-DEEP
ADEEIIPRS	RAISED PIE	ADEEIQRTU	QUIET READ
ADEEIIRSS	DIAERESIS	ADEEIRRST	DREARIEST
ADEEIJMRS	JEREMIADS	ADEEIRRSY	EASY RIDER
ADEEIKLMR	DREAMLIKE	ADEEIRSST	STEADIERS
ADEEIKNNS	SNEAKED IN	ADEEIRSTV	ADVERTISE
ADEEIKPRT	TAKE PRIDE	ADEEIRSTW	WATERSIDE
ADEEIKSST	TAKE SIDES	ADEEIRTTW	TIDEWATER
ADEEILLOS	OEILLADES	ADEEIRTTX	EXTRADITE
ADEEILLSS	IDEALLESS	ADEEISSST	SETS ASIDE
ADEEILLSW	SWELL IDEA	ADEEISSTT	STATESIDE
ADEEILLSY	EASILY LED		STEADIEST
ADEEILMNN	MENDELIAN	ADEEISSTV	SEDATIVES
ADEEILMNP	IMPANELED	ADEEITUVX	EXUVIATED
		ADEEJLNRY	LEYDEN JAR

ADEEJRSTU	JUDAS TREE	ADEEMOSTU	EDEMATOUS
ADEEKKPRS	KEEPS DARK	ADEEMPSST	STAMPEDES
ADEEKLOTU	LEAKED OUT	ADEEMPSTU	STEAMED UP
ADEEKLSTY	STALK-EYED	ADEEMPTTT	ATTEMPTED
ADEEKNNSS	NAKEDNESS	ADEENNPRT	TREPANNED
ADEEKNPSU	SNEAKED UP	ADEENORSS	ROAD SENSE
ADEEKNRRS	DARKENERS	ADEENORST	RAN TO SEED
ADEEKNRTU	UNDERTAKE		RESONATED
ADEEKORRV	RAKED OVER	ADEENORTV	RENOVATED
ADEEKOTWY	TODAY WEEK	ADEENORUV	ENDEAVOUR
ADEEKPRRS	DEER PARKS	ADEENOSSW	SOWN A SEED
ADEELLMMO	MALE MODEL	ADEENOSTT	DETONATES
ADEELLMRV	MARVELLED	ADEENPPRS	ENDPAPERS
ADEELLNRY	LEARNEDLY	ADEENPPRT	ENTRAPPED
ADEELLRSS	SELLS DEAR	ADEENPRRT	PARTNERED
ADEELLRSW	READS WELL	ADEENPRSX	EXPANDERS
ADEELLRTV	TRAVELLED	ADEENPRTT	PATTERNED
ADEELLRVW	DRAW LEVEL	ADEENPSST	ADEPTNESS
ADEELLRXY	RELAXEDLY	ADEENRRSW	WANDERERS
ADEELLTXY	EXALTEDLY	ADEENRRTU	UNDERRATE
ADEELMNOR	EALDORMEN	ADEENRRUW	UNDERWEAR
ADEELMPRS	RED MAPLES	ADEENRSTT	ATTENDERS
ADEELMRSS	DREAMLESS	ADEENRSTU	DENATURES
ADEELNNRU	UNLEARNED		SAUNTERED
ADEELNOOR	RODE ALONE	ADEENRSTY	SEDENTARY
ADEELNORS	OLEANDERS	ADEENRTUV	ADVENTURE
ADEELNORV	OVERLADEN	ADEENSSSU	DANSEUSES
ADEELNPRT	RED PLANET	ADEENSSVY	SEVEN DAYS
	REPLANTED	ADEENSTTV	VENDETTAS
ADEELNPTX	EXPLANTED	ADEEOPRSV	EAVESDROP
ADEELNRRS	SLANDERER	ADEEOPRVY	OVERPAYED
ADEELNRRU	LAUNDERER	ADEEORRST	ORDERS TEA
ADEELNRSU	UNDER SEAL	ADEEORRTV	OVERRATED
	UNDERSEAL	ADEEORRTZ	ZERO RATED
ADEELNRTU	UNALTERED	ADEEORTVX	OVERTAXED
	UNRELATED	ADEEPPRSS	APPRESSED
ADEELNSSW	WALDENSES	ADEEPPRST	SPEED TRAP
ADEELNTTY	DENTATELY	ADEEPQRTU	PARQUETED
ADEELORTT	TOLERATED	ADEEPRRSS	SPREADERS
ADEELORVW	LEAVE WORD	ADEEPRRSU	PERSUADER
ADEELOSST	DESOLATES	ADEEPRRSV	DEPRAVERS
ADEELPRST	PLASTERED	ADEEPRRTU	DEPARTURE
ADEELPRSU	PLEASURED	ADEEPRSST	PEDERASTS
ADEELPSST	PEDESTALS		PRESS DATE
ADEELRRTU	ADULTERER	ADEEPRSSU	PERSUADES
ADEELRSST	DESALTERS	ADEEPRSTT	SPATTERED
	TREADLESS	ADEEPRSTY	PEDERASTY
ADEELRSTY	STEELYARD	ADEEQRRSU	RED SQUARE
ADEELRSVY	ADVERSELY	ADEEQRRTU	QUARTERED
ADEEMMNNT	AMENDMENT	ADEERRSSU	REASSURED
ADEEMMNOY	MADE MONEY	ADEERRSTT	DESERT RAT
ADEEMMOXY	MYXOEDEMA	ADEERRSTU	TREASURED
ADEEMMRRY	MADE MERRY	ADEERRSTV	TRAVERSED
ADEEMMRST	MADE TERMS	ADEERRTWW	DREW WATER
	STAMMERED	ADEERSTYY	YESTERDAY
ADEEMNOPR	PROMENADE	ADEFFGOOR	FEAR OF GOD
ADEEMNORT	EMENDATOR	ADEFFHOSS	DASHES OFF
	NOTRE DAME	ADEFFIILS	FALSIFIED
ADEEMNORU	DEMEANOUR	ADEFFIINW	FIND A WIFE
	ENAMOURED	ADEFFILOT	TAILED OFF
ADEEMNOST	NEMATODES	ADEFFIOPR	PAIRED OFF
ADEEMNRRU	MAUNDERER	ADEFFKLOW	WALKED OFF
ADEEMNRST	SMARTENED	ADEFFKMOR	MARKED OFF
	TRADESMEN	ADEFFKOSY	OFFAS DYKE
ADEEMNSSS	MADNESSES	ADEFFLOPY	PLAYED OFF
ADEEMOORR	AERODROME	ADEFFMNOU	MADE FUN OF
ADEEMOPRR	MADREPORE	ADEFFNORT	AFFRONTED
ADEEMORST	MODERATES	ADEFFNORW	WANDER OFF
ADEEMORSW	MADE WORSE		WARNED OFF
ADEEMORTT	TREMATODE	ADEFFOPSS	PASSED OFF
ADEEMOSSY	SAMOYEDES		

ADEFFORST	TRADE-OFFS	ADEFKOOST	TAKES FOOD
	TRADES OFF	ADEFKRSTU	AFTER DUSK
ADEFFOSTV	STAVED OFF	ADEFLLMOS	OLD FLAMES
ADEFGGINO	GOING DEAF	ADEFLLMOU	LEAF MOULD
ADEFGGOTU	FAGGED OUT	ADEFLLMSY	DAMSELFLY
ADEFGHORT	GODFATHER	ADEFLLNRU	FALL UNDER
ADEFGIILT	IDEAL GIFT	ADEFLMMOR	MALFORMED
ADEFGIIMN	MAGNIFIED	ADEFLNOOT	TON OF LEAD
ADEFGIIRT	GRATIFIED	ADEFLNORS	FORELANDS
ADEFGIJRU	FAIR JUDGE	ADEFLOOUV	FOOD VALUE
ADEFGILNT	DEFLATING	ADEFLOPST	SOFT PEDAL
ADEFGILOS	A DOGS LIFE		SOFT-PEDAL
ADEFGILRU	LIFEGUARD	ADEFLORST	DEFLATORS
ADEFGIMNT	GIFTED MAN	ADEFLORUV	FLAVOURED
ADEFGIMTU	FUMIGATED	ADEFLPRSS	FELDSPARS
ADEFGINRY	DEFRAYING	ADEFLRSTW	LEFTWARDS
ADEFGIRRU	FIREGUARD	ADEFMNNTU	FUNDAMENT
ADEFGLNRU	GARDENFUL	ADEFMNRST	DRAFTSMEN
ADEFGLOOT	FLOOD GATE	ADEFMOORR	DOOR FRAME
	FLOODGATE		DOORFRAME
ADEFGLOSS	FALSE GODS	ADEFMORTU	FARMED OUT
ADEFGLRRU	REGARDFUL	ADEFMOSTV	MOVED FAST
ADEFHIIPT	EDITH PIAF	ADEFNRSSW	DWARFNESS
ADEFHIMNO	FIND A HOME	ADEFOOPRR	PROOFREAD
ADEFHIMST	HAM-FISTED	ADEFOOPRT	DROP OF TEA
	MADE SHIFT	ADEFOORTX	EXTRA FOOD
ADEFHINOS	FASHIONED	ADEFOOTTU	OUT OF DATE
ADEFHIRST	HEAD FIRST		OUT-OF-DATE
	HEADFIRST	ADEFOPRSS	PASSED FOR
ADEFHLLOT	HELD ALOFT	ADEFORRRW	FORWARDER
ADEFHLOOS	FALSEHOOD	ADEFORRTV	OVERDRAFT
ADEFHNORS	FOREHANDS	ADEFORRTW	AFTERWORD
ADEFHNORU	UNHEARD OF	ADEFORSTY	DAY OF REST
	UNHEARD-OF	ADEFORTUY	FEUDATORY
ADEFHORRZ	FROZE HARD	ADEFRRRTU	FUR TRADER
ADEFIILMP	AMPLIFIED	ADEGGGIWW	WIGWAGGED
ADEFIILNS	FINALISED	ADEGGGIZZ	ZIGZAGGED
ADEFIILNZ	FINALIZED	ADEGGHHIR	HIGH GRADE
ADEFIILQU	QUALIFIED		HIGH-GRADE
ADEFIILRS	AIRFIELDS	ADEGGHILN	HANG-GLIDE
ADEFIIMNS	DAMNIFIES	ADEGGIMOO	GOOD IMAGE
ADEFIIPRR	RAPID FIRE	ADEGGIMOS	GODS IMAGE
	RAPID-FIRE	ADEGGINNR	GARDENING
ADEFIIRST	FIRST IDEA	ADEGGINRR	REGARDING
ADEFIISST	SATISFIED	ADEGGINSS	DEGASSING
ADEFIKLRW	DWARFLIKE	ADEGGINUW	WIND GAUGE
ADEFILLOS	FALSE IDOL	ADEGGLNOO	GOOD ANGEL
ADEFILLSU	FUSILLADE	ADEGGLORY	GARGOYLED
ADEFILMNS	FIELDSMAN	ADEGGMOOS	GOOD GAMES
ADEFILMRY	FIELD ARMY	ADEGGMORT	MORTGAGED
ADEFILMSU	FEUDALISM	ADEGGOOSU	GOOD USAGE
ADEFILNOT	DEFLATION	ADEGGOOSW	GOOD WAGES
	DEFOLIANT	ADEGHHIIM	AIMED HIGH
ADEFILNSS	SAND FLIES	ADEGHHILT	HEADLIGHT
ADEFILNTY	DEFIANTLY	ADEGHHITY	EIGHTH DAY
ADEFILORT	FLORIATED	ADEGHHNOU	HAD ENOUGH
ADEFILPST	FILED PAST	ADEGHHOSS	HOGSHEADS
ADEFILRST	FIRST LEAD	ADEGHIIRT	RIGHT IDEA
ADEFILRTT	FILTRATED	ADEGHIKNS	KINGS HEAD
ADEFILSTU	FEUDALIST	ADEGHILMT	MADE LIGHT
ADEFILTUY	FEUDALITY	ADEGHILOS	DIGS A HOLE
ADEFIMOTY	TIME OF DAY	ADEGHIMRT	GRIM DEATH
ADEFIMRST	FIRM DATES	ADEGHIMTT	MADE TIGHT
ADEFINSTW	DEAN SWIFT	ADEGHINNR	HARDENING
ADEFIORTW	WAITED FOR	ADEGHINRS	GARNISHED
ADEFIRSTX	FIXED STAR	ADEGHINRT	THREADING
ADEFIRSVY	FIVE YARDS	ADEGHINSU	ANGUISHED
ADEFISWXY	FIXED WAYS	ADEGHIOPR	IDEOGRAPH
ADEFKLOTU	FLAKED OUT	ADEGHIORU	ROUGH IDEA
ADEFKNOOT	TAKEN FOOD	ADEGHIPRT	THIRD PAGE
ADEFKNORR	FRED KARNO	ADEGHIRRT	THIRD GEAR

ADEGHIRST	SIGHT-READ
ADEGHISTY	EIGHT DAYS
ADEGHLMPU	GALUMPHED
ADEGHLORS	GASHOLDER
ADEGHMORU	HOME GUARD
ADEGHNNOS	OGDEN NASH
ADEGHOOPS	GOOD SHAPE
ADEGHOORT	GOOD EARTH
	GOOD HEART
ADEGHORTT	HARD TO GET
ADEGHOSTT	AT THE DOGS
ADEGHRSTU	DAUGHTERS
ADEGIILMN	AGILE MIND
ADEGIILNN	DEALING IN
	LEADING IN
ADEGIILNR	DERAILING
ADEGIILNT	DETAILING
ADEGIILPT	PIGTAILED
ADEGIILTT	LITIGATED
ADEGIIMNT	MEDIATING
ADEGIIMTT	MITIGATED
ADEGIINNR	INGRAINED
ADEGIINNT	DETAINING
ADEGIINPR	DIAPERING
ADEGIINTV	DEVIATING
ADEGIIRRT	IRRIGATED
ADEGIKLNV	GAVELKIND
ADEGIKNNR	DARKENING
ADEGILLNP	PEDALLING
ADEGILLNS	SIGNALLED
ADEGILMOR	GOLDA MEIR
ADEGILMRR	DREAM GIRL
ADEGILNNN	IN ENGLAND
ADEGILNNO	END IN GAOL
	LEADING ON
ADEGILNNU	UNALIGNED
ADEGILNOR	GIRANDOLE
ADEGILNOS	AGED LIONS
	ALONGSIDE
ADEGILNPS	PLEADINGS
ADEGILNPU	LEADING UP
ADEGILNRS	DRAGLINES
ADEGILNRT	TREADLING
ADEGILNST	DESALTING
ADEGILNTW	WANGLED IT
ADEGILNUV	DEVALUING
ADEGILORV	GORE VIDAL
ADEGILOSU	DIALOGUES
ADEGILSSS	GLISSADES
ADEGIMNNP	DAMPENING
ADEGIMNNR	REMANDING
ADEGIMNRT	GRAND TIME
	GREAT MIND
ADEGIMNTU	MAGNITUDE
ADEGIMORS	IDEOGRAMS
ADEGIMOTZ	DOGMATIZE
ADEGINNPP	APPENDING
ADEGINNPR	PANDERING
ADEGINNPX	EXPANDING
ADEGINNRT	INTEGRAND
ADEGINNRW	WANDERING
ADEGINNTT	ATTENDING
ADEGINOOT	GO ON A DIET
ADEGINORR	RIO GRANDE
ADEGINORS	GRANDIOSE
	ORGANISED
ADEGINORW	WRONG IDEA
ADEGINORZ	ORGANIZED
ADEGINOSS	DIAGNOSES
ADEGINOUY	YOUNG IDEA

ADEGINPRT	DEPARTING
	PREDATING
ADEGINPRU	READING UP
ADEGINPRV	DEPRAVING
	PERVADING
ADEGINRRT	RETARDING
ADEGINRRW	REWARDING
ADEGINRST	GRADIENTS
ADEGINRTV	ADVERTING
ADEGINSSU	GAUDINESS
ADEGINSTY	STEADYING
ADEGIPRRT	PARTRIDGE
ADEGIRSWY	RIDGEWAYS
ADEGIRTTU	GRATITUDE
ADEGISUWY	GUIDEWAYS
ADEGJLSUY	LAY JUDGES
ADEGKMOOS	MAKES GOOD
ADEGKPRTU	KEPT GUARD
ADEGKRSTU	TAKE DRUGS
ADEGLLNOO	GALLOONED
ADEGLLNOY	LONG DELAY
ADEGLLNSS	GLANDLESS
ADEGLLOPT	GOLD PLATE
ADEGLMOOS	GOOD MEALS
ADEGLNNTU	UNTANGLED
ADEGLNRST	STRANGLED
ADEGLNSTU	ANGEL DUST
ADEGLOOUV	GOOD VALUE
ADEGLORST	OLD STAGER
ADEGLRSST	LAST DREGS
ADEGMNNOO	ONE-MAN DOG
ADEGMNOOS	GOOD NAMES
ADEGMNORU	ROUND GAME
ADEGMNRSU	GUARDSMEN
ADEGMORSW	WORD GAMES
ADEGNNORW	DOWNRANGE
ADEGNNRSS	GRANDNESS
ADEGNOORS	GOOSANDER
ADEGNOOSW	GOOD AS NEW
ADEGNOPRT	GODPARENT
ADEGNOPSU	POUNDAGES
ADEGNORST	DRAGONETS
ADEGNORSU	DANGEROUS
ADEGNORTU	GET AROUND
ADEGNOSTW	DOWN STAGE
	DOWNSTAGE
ADEGNOTTU	TOTED A GUN
ADEGOOOTT	GOOD TO EAT
ADEGOORST	STAGE DOOR
ADEGOORTY	READY TO GO
ADEGOOSST	GOOD SEATS
ADEGOOSTT	GOOD STATE
	GOOD TASTE
ADEGORRTT	GARROTTED
ADEGRRSST	DRAGSTERS
ADEHHISTW	DEATH WISH
ADEHHNOOP	HAD NO HOPE
ADEHHORST	SHORT HEAD
ADEHIIKLV	KHEDIVIAL
ADEHIILRS	HAIR-SLIDE
ADEHIINSW	HEADS I WIN
ADEHIINVW	HAD IN VIEW
ADEHIISST	DIATHESIS
ADEHIKMOT	THE MIKADO
ADEHIKNPS	HANDSPIKE
ADEHIKNRT	IN THE DARK
	KIND HEART
ADEHIKNSS	SKINHEADS
ADEHILLPY	DAILY HELP
ADEHILMNS	MISHANDLE
ADEHILNPR	PHILANDER

ADEHILNPS	PLANISHED	ADEHNNOPS	OPEN HANDS
ADEHILNRR	HARD-LINER	ADEHNNOVW	HANDWOVEN
ADEHILNRS	HARD LINES	ADEHNOORT	ON THE ROAD
ADEHILOVW	HOLD A VIEW	ADEHNORSV	HANDS OVER
ADEHILRTZ	THE LIZARD	ADEHNORTU	UNDER OATH
ADEHILSTW	DEALS WITH	ADEHNOSSS	SANDSHOES
ADEHILTTW	DEALT WITH	ADEHNOTWY	WON THE DAY
ADEHILTWY	WHITE LADY	ADEHNPPRU	UPPER HAND
ADEHIMNOR	RHODAMINE	ADEHNRSSW	SWANHERDS
ADEHIMNOT	HAD NO TIME	ADEHNRSTT	THE STRAND
ADEHIMNSU	HUMANISED	ADEHNSSSU	SUNSHADES
ADEHIMNUZ	HUMANIZED	ADEHOORSU	ROADHOUSE
ADEHIMOSU	HOUSEMAID	ADEHOORTT	AT THE DOOR
ADEHIMOTT	MADE IT HOT	ADEHOORTW	HEARTWOOD
ADEHIMPRS	SEPHARDIM	ADEHOOSTT	STATEHOOD
ADEHIMPSS	MISSHAPED	ADEHOPSTU	PHASED OUT
ADEHIMRST	HARD TIMES	ADEHORRSY	DRAY HORSE
ADEHIMRTT	THIRD MATE		DRAYHORSE
	THIRD TEAM	ADEHORRTW	HOT DRAWER
ADEHIMRTY	DIATHERMY	ADEHORSTU	SHARED OUT
ADEHINNRS	HAS DINNER	ADEHQRSVW	HAVE WORDS
	SANHEDRIN	ADEHOSSTU	DASHES OUT
ADEHINNSS	HANDINESS	ADEHOSTUW	WASHED OUT
ADEHINORT	IN THE ROAD		WASHED-OUT
ADEHINOSS	ADHESIONS	ADEHPRRSS	PRESS HARD
ADEHINPSU	DAUPHINES	ADEHRRRTY	TRY HARDER
ADEHINRSS	HARDINESS	ADEHTUVYY	HEAVY-DUTY
ADEHINRST	TARNISHED	ADEIIINTT	DIETITIAN
ADEHINRSV	VARNISHED		INITIATED
ADEHINRTU	HUNTED AIR	ADEIIJLNN	END IN JAIL
ADEHINRYZ	HYDRAZINE	ADEIILMNN	MAINLINED
ADEHINSSS	SHADINESS	ADEIILMOZ	IMIDAZOLE
ADEHINTWY	WIN THE DAY	ADEIILMTT	MILITATED
ADEHIOPRS	APHORISED	ADEIILNNR	IN IRELAND
ADEHIOPRT	ATROPHIED	ADEIILNSS	DAILINESS
ADEHIOPRZ	APHORIZED	ADEIILNST	DISENTAIL
ADEHIORSW	SHADOWIER		LATINISED
ADEHIPPSY	DIES HAPPY	ADEIILNTZ	LATINIZED
ADEHIPSSU	PUSH ASIDE	ADEIILORT	EDITORIAL
ADEHIRRST	TRIES HARD	ADEIILPTX	PIXILATED
ADEHIRRTT	THIRD RATE	ADEIILQTU	LIQUIDATE
	THIRD-RATE	ADEIILRTY	DIETARILY
ADEHIRRTY	THIRD YEAR	ADEIILSST	IDEALISTS
ADEHIRSTW	DISH WATER	ADEIILSTV	VITALISED
	DISHWATER	ADEIILTVZ	VITALIZED
ADEHKLNOT	TAKEN HOLD	ADEIIMMSX	MAXIMISED
ADEHKLOST	TAKES HOLD	ADEIIMMXZ	MAXIMIZED
ADEHKMMOS	SMOKED HAM	ADEIIMNOT	MEDIATION
ADEHKNOSW	SHAKE DOWN	ADEIIMNRS	MERIDIANS
	SHAKEDOWN	ADEIIMNTT	INTIMATED
ADEHKNRSS	REDSHANKS	ADEIIMOTT	DIATOMITE
ADEHKORRS	DARK HORSE	ADEIIMSSV	ADMISSIVE
ADEHLLOSW	SHALLOWED	ADEIINNOS	INDONESIA
ADEHLMNOS	HOMELANDS	ADEIINOTV	DEVIATION
ADEHLNOTW	HAND TOWEL	ADEIINPPR	DRAINPIPE
ADEHLNSST	SHETLANDS	ADEIINPRS	IN DESPAIR
ADEHLOPRY	POLYHEDRA	ADEIINSST	SANITISED
ADEHLOPSS	ASPHODELS	ADEIINSTT	DAINTIEST
ADEHLORTW	HOLD WATER	ADEIINSTZ	SANITIZED
ADEHLOSTU	LASHED OUT	ADEIIOTVX	OXIDATIVE
ADEHLOSTW	SLOW DEATH	ADEIIPRRS	DISREPAIR
ADEHLOTWY	THE OLD WAY	ADEIIPRSS	DISPRAISE
ADEHMNORS	HANDSOMER	ADEIIPSST	DISSIPATE
ADEHMNORY	HARD MONEY	ADEIIRRTT	IRRITATED
ADEHMNSTU	THEM-AND-US	ADEIIRSST	SATIRISED
ADEHMOOPS	SHAMPOOED	ADEIIRSTZ	SATIRIZED
ADEHMORSW	HOME DRAWS	ADEIIRTTT	TRITIATED
	HOMEWARDS	ADEIITTTV	TITIVATED
ADEHMOSSU	MADHOUSES	ADEIJLSTU	JUST IDEAL
ADEHMPSSU	SMASHED UP	ADEIJMMNY	JIMMY DEAN
ADEHNNNOO	ON ONE HAND	ADEIJSTUV	ADJUSTIVE

ADEIKLLLY	LIKELY LAD	ADEILORVZ	VALORIZED
ADEIKLLTU	ADULTLIKE	ADEILOSST	DIASTOLES
ADEIKLOST	SOLID TEAK	ADEILOSTT	TOTALISED
ADEIKLSSW	SIDEWALKS	ADEILOSTV	DOVETAILS
ADEIKMORS	KAISERDOM	ADEILOTTU	TAILED OUT
ADEIKMRST	TIDE MARKS	ADEILOTTZ	TOTALIZED
	TIDEMARKS	ADEILPPPS	PEDIPALPS
ADEIKNNNP	PEN AND INK	ADEILPPRY	REPLY PAID
ADEIKNNRT	NEAT DRINK	ADEILPRSS	DISPERSAL
ADEIKNNRW	DRANK WINE	ADEILPTTU	PLATITUDE
ADEIKNOTT	TIED A KNOT	ADEILRSSU	RESIDUALS
ADEIKNPPR	KIDNAPPER	ADEILSSTU	LASSITUDE
ADEIKNPRS	SPIKENARD	ADEILSTTU	ALTITUDES
ADEIKOOST	TOOK ASIDE		LATITUDES
ADEIKOOTV	TOOK A DIVE	ADEIMMNNO	MONIED MAN
ADEILLMNO	MEDALLION	ADEIMMRST	MIDSTREAM
ADEILLMNS	LAND MILES	ADEIMNNOT	NOMINATED
ADEILLMOS	SOLID MEAL	ADEIMNORS	RANDOMISE
ADEILLMOT	METALLOID		ROMANISED
ADEILLMRT	TREADMILL	ADEIMNORZ	RANDOMIZE
ADEILLMST	MEDALLIST		ROMANIZED
ADEILLNNS	LAND-LINES	ADEIMNOST	ADMITS ONE
ADEILLNOT	DONE IT ALL		DOMINATES
ADEILLNST	ENDS IT ALL	ADEIMNOSW	WOMANISED
	INSTALLED	ADEIMNOWZ	WOMANIZED
ADEILLOST	DOES IT ALL	ADEIMNPRR	REPRIMAND
ADEILLPRS	SPIRALLED	ADEIMNRRU	UNMARRIED
ADEILLPRU	PRELUDIAL	ADEIMNRSU	NURSEMAID
ADEILLPSU	PULL ASIDE	ADEIMNRTU	RUMINATED
ADEILLQRU	QUADRILLE	ADEIMNRTY	DYNAMITER
ADEILMMOT	IMMOLATED	ADEIMNSTV	ADVENTISM
ADEILMNPT	IMPLANTED		VEDANTISM
ADEILMNRT	ALERT MIND	ADEIMNSTY	DYNAMITES
ADEILMNST	DISMANTLE	ADEIMOPST	IMPASTOED
ADEILMNTU	DENTALIUM	ADEIMORST	AMORTISED
ADEILMOPT	DIPLOMATE	ADEIMORTT	MEDITATOR
ADEILMOPY	POLYAMIDE	ADEIMORTY	MEDIATORY
ADEILMORR	MAIL ORDER	ADEIMORTZ	AMORTIZED
	MAIL-ORDER	ADEIMOTTV	MOTIVATED
ADEILMORS	MORALISED	ADEIMPRST	SPERMATID
ADEILMORZ	MORALIZED	ADEIMRRSY	MY DEAR SIR
ADEILMOST	OLD AS TIME	ADEIMRRUU	DU MAURIER
ADEILMPTU	AMPLITUDE	ADEIMRTUX	ADMIXTURE
ADEILMSTU	SIMULATED	ADEIMSSTT	MISSTATED
ADEILMTTU	MUTILATED	ADEINNNTT	INTENDANT
ADEILNNRS	INLANDERS	ADEINNOPR	OPEN DRAIN
ADEILNNRU	UNDERLAIN	ADEINNOSX	ONE AND SIX
ADEILNOPP	PANOPLIED	ADEINNOSY	IN ONE'S DAY
ADEILNOPR	DROP A LINE	ADEINNOTT	DENTATION
ADEILNOPS	PALINODES		INTONATED
ADEILNOPT	PLANETOID	ADEINNOTV	INNOVATED
ADEILNORU	LIE AROUND	ADEINNRRW	DRAWN REIN
ADEILNOTU	LENT A QUID	ADEINNSSS	SANDINESS
ADEILNRRT	INTERLARD	ADEINNSTU	INUNDATES
ADEILNRSS	ISLANDERS	ADEINOPPT	APPOINTED
ADEILNRSU	LAUNDRIES	ADEINOPRR	PREORDAIN
	UNDER SAIL	ADEINOPRT	PREDATION
ADEILNRTU	UITLANDER	ADEINOPST	ANTIPODES
ADEILNSSV	VALIDNESS	ADEINOPTU	PIANO DUET
ADEILNSTU	INSULATED	ADEINORRS	SERRANOID
ADEILNSWY	DAILY NEWS	ADEINORST	NOTARISED
ADEILOPRS	POLARISED		ORDINATES
ADEILOPRW	LOWER-PAID	ADEINORTZ	NOTARIZED
ADEILOPRZ	POLARIZED	ADEINOSTT	ANTIDOTES
ADEILOPST	SPOLIATED	ADEINOSTV	DONATIVES
ADEILOQSU	ODALISQUE	ADEINOTUX	EXUDATION
ADEILORSS	SOLARISED	ADEINPPRS	SANDPIPER
ADEILORST	IDOLATERS	ADEINPPST	STANDPIPE
	STEROIDAL	ADEINPRSS	RAPIDNESS
ADEILORSV	VALORISED	ADEINPRST	DIPTERANS
ADEILORSZ	SOLARIZED	ADEINPSSV	VAPIDNESS

ADEINPSTU	SUPINATED	ADELLOSWW	SWALLOWED
ADEINQSTU	QUANTISED	ADELLOVYY	LOVELY DAY
ADEINQTUZ	QUANTIZED	ADELLRTXY	DEXTRALLY
ADEINRRSW	DRAWS REIN	ADELMNNUY	MUNDANELY
ADEINRRVV	VAN DRIVER	ADELMNOOP	LAMPOONED
ADEINRRWW	WIREDRAWN	ADELMNOPS	ENDOPLASM
ADEINRSST	TARDINESS	ADELMORST	OLD MASTER
ADEINRSTU	TURN ASIDE	ADELMOSTU	MODULATES
ADEINRSVY	VINEYARDS	ADELMOSWX	WAX MODELS
ADEINRTUY	AYR UNITED	ADELMPRTU	LED A TRUMP
ADEINSSST	STAIDNESS	ADELNNNPU	UNPLANNED
ADEINSSTU	SUSTAINED	ADELNOOPR	DOOR PANEL
ADEINSSTY	DYNASTIES	ADELNOOST	LOADSTONE
ADEINSTTV	ADVENTIST	ADELNORRV	LAND ROVER
	VEDANTIST	ADELNORSU	UNLOADERS
ADEIOPRSV	VAPORISED	ADELNORSV	RONDAVELS
ADEIOPRTZ	TRAPEZOID	ADELNORUY	ROUNDELAY
ADEIOPRVZ	VAPORIZED	ADELNOSSW	LES DAWSON
ADEIORRTT	ART EDITOR	ADELNPRSU	UPLANDERS
ADEIORSST	ASTEROIDS	ADELNPRUY	UNDERPLAY
	RADIO SETS	ADELNRRUY	DRURY LANE
ADEIORSTT	STORIATED	ADELNRSSU	LAUNDRESS
ADEIORSTV	DEVIATORS	ADELNRSUY	UNDERLAYS
ADEIORTVY	DEVIATORY	ADELNRTVY	VERDANTLY
ADEIOSSST	TOSS ASIDE	ADELNSSTU	ADULTNESS
ADEIPPSSY	DYSPEPSIA		DAUNTLESS
ADEIPRRWZ	PRIZE DRAW	ADELNSTUU	UNDULATES
ADEIPRSTU	DRAPE SUIT	ADELOORST	DESOLATOR
ADEIPRSTV	DRIVE PAST	ADELOORSV	OVERLOADS
ADEIPRTUV	RAVED IT UP	ADELOORTW	WOOL TRADE
ADEIPRTVY	DEPRAVITY	ADELOPPTU	POPULATED
ADEIPSSSX	SIX SPADES	ADELOPSTU	LEADS UP TO
ADEIPSSTU	PUTS ASIDE	ADELOPTUY	OUTPLAYED
ADEIPSTTU	APTITUDES		PLAYED OUT
ADEIQSSUY	QUAYSIDES	ADELORRST	LAST ORDER
ADEIRRSSU	RED RUSSIA	ADELOSTTU	OUTLASTED
ADEIRRSUY	RESIDUARY	ADELPQRUU	QUADRUPLE
ADEIRRSWW	WIREDRAWS	ADELPRSTY	DRY PLATES
ADEIRSSST	DISASTERS	ADELRSSUY	ASSUREDLY
ADEIRSTTW	TAWDRIEST	ADELRSTTU	LUSTRATED
ADEIRSTVY	ADVERSITY	ADEMMRSUY	SUMMER DAY
ADEIRSVWY	DRIVEWAYS	ADEMNNORT	ADORNMENT
ADEISSSTT	DISTASTES	ADEMNNOUW	NUDE WOMAN
ADEISTTTU	ATTITUDES	ADEMNOPRS	POMANDERS
ADEJNOSVY	DAVY JONES	ADEMNORRT	MODERN ART
ADEJRSSTU	ADJUSTERS	ADEMNORWY	DRAW MONEY
ADEKKLRSY	SKYLARKED	ADEMNOSTU	NOT AMUSED
ADEKLNOSY	ANKYLOSED	ADEMNRRSU	UNDER ARMS
ADEKLOTTU	TALKED OUT		UNDERARMS
ADEKLOTUW	WALKED OUT	ADEMOORRT	MODERATOR
ADEKMNNOW	MADE KNOWN	ADEMOPPTU	MAPPED OUT
ADEKMORTU	MARKED OUT	ADEMOPRST	ARMS DEPOT
ADEKNNOTW	TAKEN DOWN		MADE SPORT
ADEKNOPUW	WEAK POUND	ADEMORRRS	ORDER ARMS
ADEKNORTU	OUTRANKED	ADEMPRRRU	MURDER RAP
ADEKNOSTW	TAKES DOWN	ADEMPRSST	RED STAMPS
ADEKOPRSW	SPADE WORK	ADENNOOTW	ONE AND TWO
	SPADEWORK	ADENNOPSS	SENNA PODS
ADEKOSTTU	STAKED OUT	ADENNOSST	NOD ASSENT
ADELLLOWY	ALLOWEDLY		SANDSTONE
ADELLMRUY	MEDULLARY	ADENNOTTW	NOT WANTED
ADELLNOOR	ONE DOLLAR	ADENNSSTW	NEWSSTAND
ADELLNORW	LOWLANDER	ADENOOOPR	OPEN A DOOR
ADELLOORW	LOW-LOADER	ADENOORST	TORNADOES
ADELLOPPR	PAPER DOLL	ADENOORSW	WANDEROOS
ADELLOPRT	PATROLLED	ADENOORTT	DETONATOR
ADELLOPSU	LOUD PEALS	ADENOPRRS	PARDONERS
	SOUP LADLE	ADENOPRSU	READS UP ON
ADELLORRT	TALL ORDER	ADENOPRTV	DAVENPORT
ADELLORRW	REAL WORLD	ADENOPRUV	UP AND OVER
ADELLOSTT	TOLD TALES	ADENOPRUZ	EZRA POUND

ADENORRUY	YEAR-ROUND	ADFGOORSW	DOGS OF WAR
ADENORRVW	OVERDRAWN	ADFHIMNRS	FIRM HANDS
ADENORSSY	DRY SEASON	ADFHINRST	FIRST HAND
ADENORSTV	STAND OVER		FIRSTHAND
	STANDOVER	ADFHIRRTU	HARD FRUIT
ADENORSTW	STARE DOWN	ADFHISSTY	DAY SHIFTS
	TEARS DOWN	ADFHKLNRU	HALF DRUNK
ADENORSWW	WEARS DOWN	ADFHLLOOT	HOLD ALOFT
ADENORTUW	WANDER OUT	ADFHLNOPU	HALF POUND
ADENOSTUY	ON TUESDAY	ADFHLNORU	HALF-ROUND
ADENOSUVW	SOUND WAVE	ADFHLOORY	FOOLHARDY
ADENOTTUW	WANTED OUT	ADFHLOSST	HOLDS FAST
ADENPPRUW	UNWRAPPED	ADFHNOOTU	OUT OF HAND
ADENPRRTU	UNDERPART	ADFHORRST	HARD FROST
ADENPRSSU	UNDERPASS	ADFHORRTW	DRAW FORTH
ADENQRSSU	SQUANDERS	ADFHORTUY	FOURTH DAY
ADENRRTUY	DAY-RETURN	ADFIILNNN	IN FINLAND
ADENRSSTU	TRANSUDES	ADFIINRSW	FAIR WINDS
ADENRSSTW	ST.ANDREWS	ADFIIOPRT	PAID FOR IT
ADENRSSUY	DAY NURSES	ADFILLMOY	OLD FAMILY
ADEOOPRRS	POOR DEARS	ADFILLNSW	WINDFALLS
ADEOOORRST	TOREADORS	ADFILLOTW	TIDAL FLOW
ADEOOOSSTY	STOOD EASY	ADFILLPUY	FULLY PAID
ADEOPPRRS	PEAR DROPS	ADFILMNOS	MANIFOLDS
ADEOPRRST	PREDATORS	ADFILNOOP	PLAIN FOOD
	TEARDROPS	ADFILNORS	DORSAL FIN
ADEOPRRTW	TOP DRAWER	ADFILNORW	FINAL WORD
	TOP-DRAWER	ADFILORRW	WORLD FAIR
ADEOPRRTY	PORTRAYED	ADFILRSTY	FIRST LADY
	PREDATORY	ADFIMNRST	FIRM STAND
ADEOPRSTT	TETRAPODS		STAND FIRM
ADEOPRSTU	SPREAD OUT	ADFIMRRST	DIRT FARMS
ADEOPRSTV	DROVE PAST	ADFINORSZ	SFORZANDI
ADEOPSSTT	POSTDATES	ADFIOORRU	RADIO FOUR
ADEOPSSTU	PASSED OUT	ADFIORRSW	FAIR WORDS
ADEOPSSTW	TWO SPADES	ADFIORSUV	DISFAVOUR
ADEORRSST	ROADSTERS	ADFIRSSTY	FIRST DAYS
ADEORRSVW	OVERDRAWS	ADFLLNOSW	DOWNFALLS
ADEORRSWW	SWEAR WORD		FALLS DOWN
ADEORRTTW	TROD WATER	ADFLLOOST	FALDSTOOL
ADEORSSTT	ROAD TESTS	ADFLNNUYY	FUNNY LADY
ADEORSTTU	OUTSTARED	ADFLNOOTW	FLOAT DOWN
ADEOSTTUY	OUTSTAYED	ADFLNOSST	SOFT-LANDS
ADEOSTUWY	OWES A DUTY	ADFLORRWY	FORWARDLY
ADEPPPRUW	WRAPPED UP		FROWARDLY
ADEPQRSUU	SQUARED UP	ADFMOOPPR	DAMP-PROOF
ADEPRSSSU	SURPASSED	ADFMRSSTU	STUD FARMS
ADEPRSTTU	STARTED UP	ADFNOORSZ	SFORZANDO
ADEPSTTUY	STAYED PUT	ADFNORSST	STANDS FOR
ADERRSSTT	REDSTARTS	ADFOOORSUV	DO FAVOURS
ADERSSTWW	WESTWARDS	ADFOOSSTT	STOOD FAST
ADFFGINOR	AFFORDING	ADFORRSUY	FOUR YARDS
ADFFHRSTU	HARD STUFF	ADFORSTYY	FORTY DAYS
ADFFIIMRS	DISAFFIRM	ADGGGHOSY	SHAGGY DOG
ADFFILNTU	FIND FAULT	ADGGGILNR	DRAGGLING
ADFFNOSST	STAND-OFFS	ADGGHINOR	GOING HARD
	STANDOFFS		HARD GOING
	STANDS OFF	ADGGILNRY	NIGGARDLY
ADFGGLOOT	OLD FAGGOT	ADGGINPRU	UPGRADING
ADFGGOSYY	FOGGY DAYS	ADGGLRSSU	SLUGGARDS
ADFGHHIRT	HARD FIGHT	ADGGNOORU	GO AGROUND
ADFGHIOOT	GOOD FAITH	ADGHHILNS	HIGHLANDS
ADFGILMOY	DOG FAMILY	ADGHHINRT	RIGHT HAND
ADFGINORS	SANGFROID		RIGHT-HAND
ADFGINOTU	FADING OUT	ADGHHIORS	HIGH ROADS
ADFGIOOPR	GO FOR A DIP		HIGHROADS
ADFGIOORY	GOOD FAIRY	ADGHIINNN	HANDING IN
ADFGLNORY	DRAGONFLY	ADGHIINRT	RIDING HAT
ADFGLNOSW	FLAGS DOWN	ADGHIKNRT	DARK NIGHT
ADFGLOOTU	GOOD FAULT	ADGHILLLU	GUILDHALL
ADFGOORRW	GO FORWARD	ADGHILNNS	HANDLINGS

ADGHILNST	SIGHT LAND	ADGINNOPR	PARDONING
ADGHILPST	SAD PLIGHT	ADGINNORT	DARING NOT
ADGHILSSS	GLASS DISH		TRADING ON
ADGHIMNOR	DOING HARM	ADGINNORW	DRAWING ON
ADGHIMNRS	MRS. GANDHI	ADGINNRST	STRANDING
ADGHINNNU	UNHANDING	ADGINNSST	STANDINGS
ADGHINNRW	DRAWN NIGH	ADGINOPRY	PARODYING
ADGHINORS	DRAGONISH	ADGINORRS	RING ROADS
	HOARDINGS	ADGINORRU	IRON GUARD
ADGHINOSW	SHADOWING	ADGINORSS	ROAD SIGNS
ADGHINPRS	HANDGRIPS	ADGINPRRX	GRAND PRIX
ADGHINRSW	DRAWS NIGH	ADGINPRSY	DAYSPRING
ADGHINRTU	INDRAUGHT	ADGINPRUW	DRAWING UP
ADGHINRTY	HYDRATING	ADGJNRRUY	GRAND JURY
ADGHIORRT	RIGHT ROAD	ADGKLNOOO	GO AND LOOK
ADGHIPRRS	GRIPS HARD	ADGKMOORS	GOOD MARKS
ADGHIRRTW	RIGHTWARD	ADGKNORRW	GROWN DARK
ADGHIRTTW	DRAW TIGHT	ADGKNRRTU	GRAND TURK
ADGHLLOUU	LOUD LAUGH	ADGKOORTU	TOOK A DRUG
ADGHNNOSW	HANGS DOWN	ADGKORRSW	GROWS DARK
ADGHNORTU	ON DRAUGHT	ADGLLNOOP	PLOD ALONG
ADGHOORRU	ROUGH ROAD	ADGLMOOYY	GLOOMY DAY
ADGHPRTUU	UPDRAUGHT	ADGLNOOPS	GOOD PLANS
ADGIIILST	DIGITALIS	ADGLNOORS	LONG ROADS
ADGIIJNNO	ADJOINING	ADGLNORSW	SLANG WORD
ADGIIKMNS	KING MIDAS	ADGLNOUYY	YOUNG LADY
ADGIILLTY	DIGITALLY	ADGLOOPRS	DROP GOALS
ADGIILNSS	GLISSANDI	ADGMNOOOW	GOOD WOMAN
ADGIILNSY	DIALYSING	ADGMNOORS	ROMAN GODS
ADGIILOST	DIALOGIST	ADGMNORSU	GOURMANDS
ADGIIMNRS	DISARMING	ADGMOORRU	GUARD ROOM
ADGIIMNST	MISDATING		GUARDROOM
ADGIIMNSY	DISMAYING	ADGNNNOOO	GO ON AND ON
ADGIIMNTT	ADMITTING	ADGNNORRU	RANG ROUND
ADGIINNNT	INDIGNANT	ADGNNORSS	GRANDSONS
ADGIINNOR	ORDAINING	ADGNNORYY	ANDROGYNY
ADGIINNOS	ANODISING	ADGNOORRW	WRONG ROAD
ADGIINNOZ	ANODIZING	ADGNOORTU	GOT AROUND
ADGIINNRT	TRADING IN	ADGNORRTU	GRAND TOUR
ADGIINNRW	DRAWING IN	ADGOOPRST	GASTROPOD
ADGIINORT	GRANITOID		GOOD PARTS
ADGIINOSS	DIAGNOSIS	ADGOORSTT	GOOD START
ADGIINRST	DISRATING	ADGOORSTW	GO TOWARDS
ADGIINRSY	DAIRYINGS	ADGORSSTY	STRAY DOGS
ADGIINRTV	DRIVING AT	ADHHIKNRT	THINK HARD
ADGIINRTY	DIGNITARY	ADHHIORRT	THORA HIRD
ADGIIRTVY	GRAVIDITY	ADHHIPRSS	HARDSHIPS
ADGIJNSTU	ADJUSTING	ADHHNORST	SHORTHAND
ADGIKNORS	KINGS ROAD	ADHHNOWWY	HOW AND WHY
ADGILLNRS	LAND GIRLS	ADHHORRSW	HARSH WORD
ADGILLNSW	WINDGALLS	ADHIIMMRS	MIDRASHIM
ADGILLNUY	LANGUIDLY	ADHIIMNNS	HAS IN MIND
ADGILLOSU	GLADIOLUS	ADHIIMPSS	AMIDSHIPS
ADGILMNNY	DAMNINGLY	ADHIINNST	HANDS IT IN
ADGILMNRY	MY DARLING	ADHIJNNOS	JOIN HANDS
ADGILMNSU	GUILDSMAN	ADHIKMNNU	HUMANKIND
ADGILMORS	MARIGOLDS	ADHIKNORW	HANDIWORK
ADGILNNOU	UNLOADING	ADHILNOOY	ON HOLIDAY
ADGILNOPT	GOLD PAINT	ADHILOPSS	SHIPLOADS
ADGILNOPU	LOADING UP	ADHILPSSY	LADYSHIPS
ADGILNOSS	GLISSANDO	ADHIMOPPS	AMPHIPODS
ADGILNOSY	OLD SAYING	ADHINNORS	IRON HANDS
ADGILOORY	RADIOLOGY	ADHINNPTU	PUT IN HAND
ADGILOOUY	AUDIOLOGY	ADHINNRTU	HIT AND RUN
ADGILOPRS	PRODIGALS		HIT-AND-RUN
ADGILOSTW	WILD GOATS	ADHINNSTY	TINY HANDS
ADGILRSSW	WILD GRASS	ADHINOOST	SAINTHOOD
ADGIMMOST	DOGMATISM	ADHINOPRT	DROP A HINT
ADGIMNOSU	DOING A SUM	ADHINORTY	HYDRATION
ADGIMOSTT	DOGMATIST	ADHINOTTU	HAND IT OUT
ADGINNOOU	IGUANODON	ADHINRTWW	WITHDRAWN

ADHINSTTW	WITHSTAND	ADILLOSSW	DISALLOWS
ADHIOPRSY	DYSPHORIA	ADILLQSUY	SQUALIDLY
ADHIOSTTY	TO THIS DAY	ADILMMSTU	TALMUDISM
ADHIPRRTT	THIRD PART	ADILMNNOS	MANDOLINS
ADHIRSTWW	WITHDRAWS	ADILMNOOS	SALMONOID
ADHISTWWY	WIDTHWAYS	ADILMNRUU	DURALUMIN
ADHKLOORS	HARD LOOKS	ADILMOPST	DIPLOMATS
ADHKNOOSY	SHADY NOOK	ADILMOPSY	OLYMPIADS
ADHKNORSW	HANDWORKS		SYMPODIAL
ADHKORRSW	WORKS HARD	ADILMOSSS	SOLID MASS
ADHLLMORT	THRALLDOM	ADILMSTTU	TALMUDIST
ADHLLPRSU	PULLS HARD	ADILNNOSW	NAILS DOWN
ADHLNNORT	NORTHLAND	ADILNNSSU	DISANNULS
ADHLNOOST	HAND TOOLS	ADILNOORS	DOORNAILS
ADHLNOOWY	ANY OLD HOW	ADILNOOSV	VINDALOOS
ADHLNOSTU	OLD HAUNTS	ADILNOPSY	ON DISPLAY
ADHLOSSWY	HOLDS SWAY	ADILNORSU	SAIL ROUND
ADHMNOOOW	WOMANHOOD	ADILNSTTY	DISTANTLY
ADHMNPPSU	HAND PUMPS	ADILOOPRS	POLAROIDS
ADHNNRSTU	HANDS TURN	ADILOPSSS	DISPOSALS
ADHNOORTU	ROUND OATH	ADILORSTW	SWORDTAIL
ADHNOORYZ	HYDROZOAN	ADILOSSST	SODALISTS
ADHNORRTW	NORTHWARD	ADILPRSTU	LURID PAST
ADHNORSUY	ANHYDROUS	ADILPRTWY	WILD PARTY
ADHNOSSTU	THOUSANDS	ADIMMNOOS	AMMONOIDS
ADHOOPRRT	ARTHROPOD	ADIMNNOST	DOMINANTS
ADHOORSSW	ROAD SHOWS	ADIMNOORR	MINOR ROAD
ADHORSTUW	SOUTHWARD	ADIMNOORT	DOMINATOR
ADHORSTWY	HASTY WORD	ADIMNPSTU	STUPID MAN
ADHRSSTUY	THURSDAYS	ADIMOPRSY	MYRIAPODS
ADIIIKNNN	INDIAN INK	ADINNOOST	DONATIONS
ADIIILQRU	LIQUID AIR	ADINNORTW	DOWN TRAIN
ADIIIQRSU	DAIQUIRIS	ADINNOSST	DISSONANT
ADIIKLMMS	MILK MAIDS	ADINNPRTU	TIP AND RUN
	MILKMAIDS	ADINOORRT	TROD ON AIR
ADIIKMNRX	MIX A DRINK	ADINOOSTW	SATINWOOD
ADIIKNNPY	PAY IN KIND	ADINOPSTY	DYSTOPIAN
ADIILLMRS	MILLIARDS	ADINORSSU	DINOSAURS
ADIILLNVY	INVALIDLY	ADINORSTU	DURATIONS
ADIILMSSS	DISMISSAL		SIT AROUND
ADIILNSTW	TAIL WINDS	ADINOSTWX	TWO AND SIX
ADIIMNOSS	ADMISSION	ADINPSTTU	DISPUTANT
ADIIMNOUZ	DIAZONIUM	ADIOPPTTU	PUT PAID TO
ADIIMNRSW	DARWINISM	ADIOPRSTT	DO ITS PART
ADIIMOPRR	PRIMORDIA	ADIOQRSTU	RIOT SQUAD
ADIIMRSSY	MYDRIASIS	ADIORRSST	STAIR RODS
ADIINNOSY	DIONYSIAN	ADIORSSST	SARODISTS
ADIINOOTX	OXIDATION	ADIOSSSUU	ASSIDUOUS
ADIINOQTU	QUOTIDIAN	ADIPSSUYY	UPSYDAISY
ADIINORTT	TRADITION	ADJMMOOOR	MAJOR DOMO
ADIINOSST	SOI-DISANT		MAJORDOMO
ADIINOSTU	AUDITIONS	ADJMMORRU	DRUM MAJOR
ADIINRSST	DISTRAINS	ADJOPRSTU	JUST A DROP
ADIINRSTT	DISTRAINT	ADKLNOORW	LOOK DRAWN
ADIINRSTU	SATURNIID	ADKLNORTU	TALK ROUND
ADIINRSTW	DARWINIST	ADKLNOSTW	TALKS DOWN
ADIIOPSTY	ADIPOSITY	ADKLOOPST	POLKA DOTS
ADIIOSTUY	YOU SAID IT	ADKLOORSW	WOODLARKS
ADIIPRSTY	DISPARITY	ADKMNORSW	MARKDOWNS
ADIISSTUY	ASSIDUITY		MARKS DOWN
ADIJKSSSU	JUDAS KISS	ADKMOORRS	DARKROOMS
ADIJMOPSU	POUJADISM	ADKNORRTU	TRUNK ROAD
ADIJOPSTU	POUJADIST	ADKNORRWW	DRAWNWORK
ADIKLORWY	DAILY WORK	ADKOOOPRT	TOOK A DROP
ADIKMNNOW	WOMANKIND	ADKOORRSW	ROAD WORKS
ADIKNNSST	INKSTANDS		ROADWORKS
ADILLMMNS	SMALL MIND	ADLLMNOPS	SMALL POND
ADILLMNRS	MANDRILLS	ADLLMOORS	SMALL DOOR
ADILLNPSS	LANDSLIPS	ADLLMOPRS	DOLLS PRAM
ADILLNPSU	DULL PAINS	ADLLMORUY	MODULARLY
ADILLNRUY	DIURNALLY	ADLLOORST	TOLLROADS

ADLLOOSTT	STOOD TALL	AEEEFIRRT	FIRE EATER
ADLMNORTY	MORDANTLY		FIRE-EATER
ADLMOORRY	LORD MAYOR	AEEEFKMRS	MAKES FREE
ADLMOORTU	MODULATOR	AEEEFKPSS	KEEPS SAFE
ADLMORTUY	MORAL DUTY	AEEEFKRST	SEEK AFTER
ADLNOORSW	LOANWORDS	AEEEFLMRS	FREE MEALS
ADLNOPRYY	POLYANDRY	AEEEFLMSX	FEMALE SEX
ADLNOPSSW	SLAPS DOWN	AEEEFNRRV	NEVER FEAR
ADLNOPSWY	PLAYS DOWN	AEEEFNRST	FENESTRAE
ADLNORSTU	LAST ROUND	AEEEFPRYZ	PAY FREEZE
ADLNORSTW	DRAWN LOTS	AEEEFRRTV	EVER AFTER
ADLOOOSTT	TOADSTOOL	AEEEFRSST	FREE SEATS
ADLOPRSWY	SWORDPLAY	AEEEGGGNR	GREENGAGE
ADLORRSWW	WORLD WARS	AEEEGGRST	EASTER EGG
ADLORSSTW	DRAWS LOTS		SEGREGATE
	LAST WORDS	AEEEGHJTT	THE JET AGE
ADLORSUUY	ARDUOUSLY	AEEEGHLST	THE EAGLES
ADLORTUWY	OUTWARDLY	AEEEGHPRT	PAGE THREE
ADLPQRUUY	QUADRUPLY	AEEEGIMNR	MENAGERIE
ADMMNOOPW	MOP AND MOW	AEEEGLNPR	PALE GREEN
ADMMORRTY	MARTYRDOM	AEEEGLRRV	GEAR LEVER
ADMNNORSU	ROUNDSMAN	AEEEGLRST	RELEGATES
ADMNOOSST	MASTODONS	AEEEGMNRT	AGREEMENT
ADMNOOSTT	MASTODONT	AEEEGNPRS	GREEN PEAS
ADMNOPSTW	STAMP DOWN	AEEEGNPSV	PAGE SEVEN
ADMNORSST	SANDSTORM	AEEEGNRSS	EAGERNESS
ADMNORSSW	SWORDSMAN	AEEEGNRST	GENERATES
ADMNORSWY	MANY WORDS		TEENAGERS
ADMOOPPPS	POPPADOMS	AEEEGNSSV	SEVEN AGES
ADMOOPPRU	POMPADOUR	AEEEGRTTZ	GAZETTEER
ADMOOPRTY	PARTY MOOD	AEEEGSTTV	VEGETATES
ADMOORRSW	WARDROOMS	AEEEHLMOV	LEAVE HOME
ADMORRTUY	MARY TUDOR	AEEEHLMPR	EPHEMERAL
ADMPSTTUY	STAMP DUTY	AEEEHLNRT	LANE THREE
ADNNOOSTU	NOT A SOUND	AEEEHLRRW	REAR WHEEL
ADNNORRUU	RUN AROUND	AEEEHLSSY	EYELASHES
	RUNAROUND	AEEEHLSYZ	HAZEL EYES
ADNNORSTY	DYNATRONS	AEEEHMRTX	HEXAMETER
ADNNOSSUY	ON SUNDAYS	AEEEHNSST	EAST SHEEN
ADNNOSSWW	SWANSDOWN	AEEEHNSSV	HAVE SENSE
ADNNSSUYY	SUNNY DAYS	AEEEHNSTT	THE SENATE
ADNOOOQRSU	QUADROONS	AEEEHRRRS	REHEARSER
ADNOOTTUU	OUT AND OUT	AEEEHRRSS	REHEARSES
	OUT-AND-OUT	AEEEHSSTT	AESTHETES
ADNOOTTWW	TWO AND TWO	AEEEIKLPV	KEEP ALIVE
ADNOPRRUW	WRAP ROUND	AEEEILLPS	LIE ASLEEP
ADNOPRSSU	PASS ROUND	AEEEIRRTT	REITERATE
ADNOPRSTW	STRAP DOWN	AEEEKKPSS	KEEPSAKES
ADNOPRSUY	PAY ROUNDS	AEEEKKSWW	WAKES WEEK
ADNOPRTWY	PARTY DOWN	AEEEKLTTT	TEA KETTLE
ADNOPSTTU	STAND UP TO	AEEEKMNSS	MAKE SENSE
ADNOOQRSSU	SQUADRONS	AEEEKMPUY	EYE MAKE-UP
ADNORSSTW	SANDWORTS	AEEEKMRRT	MARKETEER
ADNORSTWY	NASTY WORD	AEEEKMSSY	MAKES EYES
ADNOSSTTU	STANDS OUT	AEEEKRSWX	WEAKER SEX
ADNOSSTWY	STAYS DOWN	AEEELLMNT	ELEMENTAL
ADOOPRRST	TRAPDOORS	AEEELMPRT	MAPLE TREE
ADOPRSSSW	PASSWORDS	AEEELMRSS	SEEMS REAL
ADOPRSSTY	SPORTS DAY	AEEELNOPV	LEAVE OPEN
AEEEEGLSY	EAGLE EYES	AEEELNOPW	WEEP ALONE
AEEEETTTT	TETE-A-TETE	AEEELNOSY	LOSE AN EYE
AEEEFFLSS	FEELS SAFE	AEEELNPRT	PLANE TREE
AEEEFGLRT	FEEL GREAT	AEEELNSVW	NEW LEAVES
AEEEFGNRR	FREE RANGE	AEEELNUVZ	VENEZUELA
	FREE-RANGE	AEEELORVV	LEAVE OVER
AEEEFGNRT	FREE AGENT	AEEELPPRT	APPLE TREE
AEEEFHLLN	FELLAHEEN	AEEELPSSY	YES PLEASE
AEEEFHLMS	FEEL SHAME	AEEELPTTU	EPAULETTE
AEEEFHRRT	HEREAFTER	AEEELRSTX	AXLETREES
AEEEFHRTV	FEVER HEAT	AEEEMMRST	METAMERES
		AEEEMNNRT	NEMERTEAN

AEEEMNRTU	ENUMERATE	AEEFILNSS	LEAFINESS
AEEEMNSST	EASEMENTS	AEEFILOST	FAIL TO SEE
AEEEMNTTV	TEAM EVENT	AEEFILOTX	EXFOLIATE
AEEEMPRST	PERMEATES	AEEFILRRT	FREE TRIAL
AEEEMPRTT	TEMPERATE	AEEFILRSV	LIFESAVER
AEEEMSTTW	SWEETMEAT	AEEFILRTX	TAX RELIEF
AEEENNNQU	QUEEN ANNE	AEEFILSST	FLIES EAST
AEEENORSS	SEE REASON	AEEFIMRSS	SEEMS FAIR
AEEENORTV	OVEREATEN	AEEFIMRTT	AFTER TIME
AEEENORTX	EXONERATE	AEEFIPRST	PEAT FIRES
AEEENPRTT	PENETRATE	AEEFIQTUW	QUITE A FEW
AEEENPSTT	PATENTEES	AEEFIRRTW	FIREWATER
AEEENRRST	EASTERNER	AEEFIRSVY	FIVE YEARS
AEEENRRTV	RARE EVENT	AEEFKLPRT	PETER FALK
AEEENRSTV	ENERVATES	AEEFLLLMS	FEEL SMALL
	VENERATES	AEEFLLMSS	FLAMELESS
AEEENSSSV	SEVEN SEAS	AEEFLLMST	SMALL FEET
AEEENTTUV	EVENTUATE	AEEFLLNOT	LEFT ALONE
AEEENTTUX	EXTENUATE	AEEFLLOOS	LOOSE-LEAF
AEEEOSSTY	EASY TO SEE	AEEFLLRSW	FAREWELLS
AEEEPRRST	PEAR TREES	AEEFLLRTY	LEFT EARLY
	REPARTEES	AEEFLLSUY	EASEFULLY
	REPEATERS	AEEFLLSVY	FLYLEAVES
AEEEPSSTW	SWEET PEAS	AEEFLLSYZ	FEELS LAZY
AEEERRRTT	RETREATER	AEEFLMOSV	FALSE MOVE
AEEERRVYY	EVERY YEAR	AEEFLMRSW	FEELS WARM
AEEFFILNT	FEEL FAINT	AEEFLNOST	FALSE NOTE
AEEFFILRT	AFTERLIFE	AEEFLNOTT	LEFT A NOTE
AEEFFLLOO	FEEL A FOOL	AEEFLNRST	FENESTRAL
AEEFFLLRS	FREE-FALLS	AEEFLNRTT	FLATTENER
AEEFFLLUW	FEEL AWFUL	AEEFLNSSS	FALSENESS
AEEFFLOSV	LEAVES OFF	AEEFLOOTW	TALE OF WOE
AEEFFNORR	NEAR OFFER	AEEFLRRTT	FLATTERER
AEEFFORTX	FREE OF TAX	AEEFMNORS	FORENAMES
AEEFGGLNR	GREEN FLAG		FREEMASON
AEEFGILMS	SELF-IMAGE	AEEFMPTTT	TEMPT FATE
AEEFGILPR	PILFERAGE	AEEFNORSZ	FROZEN SEA
AEEFGILRT	GREAT LIFE	AEEFNRSST	FASTENERS
AEEFGILSV	FIG LEAVES	AEEFNRTTW	WENT AFTER
AEEFGINRS	FARSEEING	AEEFNSTTY	SAFETY NET
AEEFGIRRT	GREAT FIRE	AEEFOPRRT	PERFORATE
AEEFGLLOT	FLAGEOLET	AEEFORSTT	FORETASTE
AEEFGLNRY	FEEL ANGRY	AEEGGGLRS	LARGE EGGS
AEEFGLRTT	FELT GREAT	AEEGGHIPT	PAGE EIGHT
AEEFGLSSU	FUSELAGES	AEEGGHNST	THE GANGES
AEEFGLSTT	STAGE LEFT	AEEGGILNR	GINGER ALE
AEEFGNORT	GONE AFTER	AEEGGINNS	GAS ENGINE
AEEFGORST	FOSTERAGE	AEEGGIRSV	AGGRIEVES
	GOES AFTER	AEEGGIRSW	WAGGERIES
AEEFGRTTT	GET FATTER	AEEGGLNOY	GENEALOGY
AEEFHIKPT	KEEP FAITH	AEEGGMORT	MORTGAGEE
AEEFHINST	IN THE SAFE	AEEGGPRSU	PUGGAREES
AEEFHINVY	HEAVY FINE	AEEGGRRST	STAGGERER
AEEFHIRVY	HEAVY FIRE	AEEGGRRSW	SWAGGERER
AEEFHISTT	SET A THIEF	AEEGHILLR	LEGAL HEIR
AEEFHLLSS	SELF-HEALS	AEEGHILLS	SHIGELLAE
AEEFHLMST	FELT SHAME	AEEGHIMRT	HERMITAGE
AEEFHLOPS	FALSE HOPE	AEEGHINNU	GUINEA HEN
AEEFHLPPY	FEEL HAPPY	AEEGHINRR	REHEARING
AEEFHLRTT	HEARTFELT	AEEGHINRS	GARNISHEE
AEEFHMPRS	SHEEP FARM	AEEGHIRST	HERITAGES
AEEFHMRST	FRESH MEAT	AEEGHIRTW	AGREE WITH
AEEFIKLNT	TAKEN LIFE	AEEGHKOTV	GAVE THE O.K.
AEEFIKLST	TAKES LIFE	AEEGHLPRT	GREAT HELP
AEEFIKLTW	FLEW A KITE		TELEGRAPH
AEEFIKRST	FREAKIEST	AEEGHLPTU	THE PLAGUE
AEEFILLRY	EARLY LIFE	AEEGHMMOS	HOME GAMES
AEEFILMPR	RELIEF MAP	AEEGHMNOP	MEGAPHONE
AEEFILNOP	OPEN A FILE	AEEGHMNOT	ON THE GAME
AEEFILNPS	FEELS PAIN	AEEGHMPRS	GRAPHEMES
AEEFILNRT	INTERLEAF	AEEGHMRTW	WHEAT GERM

AEEGHMRTZ	MEGAHERTZ	AEEGLNNPT	PENTANGLE
AEEGHORTT	GET TO HEAR	AEEGLNNRT	ENTANGLER
AEEGHOSST	SEE A GHOST	AEEGLNNST	ENTANGLES
AEEGHOSTU	GATEHOUSE	AEEGLNOST	ELONGATES
AEEGIIMRS	IMAGERIES		SOLE AGENT
AEEGIKPPR	KEEP A GRIP	AEEGLNRSS	ANGERLESS
AEEGILLRS	ALLERGIES		LARGENESS
	GALLERIES	AEEGLNSTT	GESTALTEN
AEEGILLST	LEGISLATE	AEEGLPTTU	GET UP LATE
AEEGILLVW	LEGAL VIEW	AEEGLQRSU	SQUARE LEG
AEEGILMNN	MENINGEAL	AEEGLRSTU	REGULATES
AEEGILNNR	IN GENERAL	AEEGLRSTW	GREW STALE
AEEGILNNT	EGLANTINE	AEEGLRSVY	GAY REVELS
	INELEGANT	AEEGLSSTT	GETS STALE
AEEGILNNV	LEAVENING	AEEGMNNOR	ORANGEMEN
AEEGILNPR	REPEALING	AEEGMNOTY	GATE MONEY
AEEGILNRS	RELEASING	AEEGMNRRS	MERGANSER
AEEGILNRV	REVEALING	AEEGMNRTU	AUGMENTER
AEEGILNSS	ENSILAGES	AEEGMOOST	OOGAMETES
AEEGILNTV	ELEVATING	AEEGMOPRW	POWER GAME
AEEGILPTT	TITLE PAGE	AEEGMORST	GASOMETER
AEEGILRSZ	LARGE SIZE	AEEGMRRSY	GREY MARES
AEEGILRTU	GAULEITER	AEEGMRSST	GAMESTERS
AEEGILSSY	LAYS SIEGE		GAS METERS
AEEGILGTV	LEVIGATES	AEEGMRSTV	GAVE TERMS
AEEGILUVY	IVY LEAGUE	AEEGMSSSU	MESSUAGES
AEEGIMNRT	GERMINATE	AEEGNNSTW	NEWSAGENT
AEEGIMNST	GEMINATES	AEEGNOOST	GONE TO SEA
	MAGNESITE	AEEGNOPRS	GONE SPARE
	MAGNETISE		PERSONAGE
AEEGIMNTT	MAGNETITE	AEEGNOPRT	OPEN GRATE
AEEGIMNTZ	MAGNETIZE	AEEGNOPRV	OPEN GRAVE
AEEGIMOSX	EXOGAMIES	AEEGNOPST	OPEN GATES
AEEGIMPTT	PEGMATITE	AEEGNORRT	GENERATOR
AEEGIMRST	EMIGRATES	AEEGNORTT	TERATOGEN
AEEGINNNT	NEATENING	AEEGNORTU	ENTOURAGE
AEEGINNRT	ARGENTINE	AEEGNOSST	STONE AGES
	TANGERINE	AEEGNOTTW	WAGONETTE
AEEGINNUW	NEW GUINEA	AEEGNOTXY	OXYGENATE
AEEGINOPS	ESPIONAGE	AEEGNPRSS	PASSENGER
AEEGINOTT	NEGOTIATE	AEEGNRRST	ESTRANGER
AEEGINPRT	REPEATING	AEEGNRSST	ESTRANGES
AEEGINPRV	GRAPEVINE		GREATNESS
AEEGINRTT	INTEGRATE		SERGEANTS
AEEGINSSS	ASSIGNEES	AEEGNRSSV	GRAVENESS
AEEGINSSV	ENVISAGES	AEEGNRSTW	GREAT NEWS
AEEGINSSW	SEESAWING	AEEGNRSVW	GRAVE NEWS
AEEGINSTV	NEGATIVES	AEEGNRTUY	GENE AUTRY
AEEGIORTV	GIVE EAR TO	AEEGNSSUV	VAGUENESS
AEEGIPQSU	EQUIPAGES	AEEGOOSST	GOES TO SEA
AEEGIPSUV	GIVE PAUSE	AEEGOPRRT	PORTERAGE
AEEGIRSST	GETS A RISE		REPORTAGE
	GREASIEST	AEEGOPRSS	GOES SPARE
AEEGKLOPS	KEEPS GOAL	AEEGPQRSU	SQUARE PEG
AEEGKLPRY	GREEK PLAY	AEEGPRTUX	EXPURGATE
AEEGKNPRR	GREEN PARK	AEEGRRWWY	GREW WEARY
AEEGLLMRT	LEGAL TERM	AEEGSSSTT	STAGE SETS
AEEGLLNOR	ORGANELLE	AEEHHIKLT	HEATHLIKE
AEEGLLNOS	LONG LEASE	AEEHHILRT	HEALTHIER
AEEGLLNRS	ALLERGENS	AEEHHIPRU	URIAH HEEP
AEEGLLNRY	GENERALLY	AEEHHITTW	WHITE HEAT
AEEGLLNTY	ELEGANTLY	AEEHHKSST	THE SHAKES
AEEGLLOSS	LOSES A LEG	AEEHHLMTT	AT THE HELM
AEEGLLSSY	AGELESSLY	AEEHHLOSW	HAWSEHOLE
AEEGLMNNT	GENTLEMAN	AEEHHLSST	HEATHLESS
AEEGLMNRY	GERMANELY	AEEHHMSTT	THE THAMES
AEEGLMNST	SEGMENTAL	AEEHHNPTY	HYPHENATE
AEEGLMOSS	LOSE GAMES	AEEHHNSTU	UNSHEATHE
AEEGLMOSV	LOVE GAMES	AEEHHOPSV	HAVE HOPES
AEEGLMRRW	LEG-WARMER	AEEHHORTY	AHOY THERE
AEEGLMRST	TELEGRAMS	AEEHIILPR	PERIHELIA

AEEHIILPT	EPITHELIA	AEEHLPSSS	SHAPELESS
AEEHIJMRS	JEREMIAHS	AEEHLPTTY	TELEPATHY
AEEHIKLRT	EARTHLIKE	AEEHLRSST	HEARTLESS
AEEHIKNTW	IN THE WAKE	AEEHLRTTT	THE LATTER
AEEHIKRST	THE KAISER		THE TATLER
AEEHILLRS	RAISE HELL	AEEHLRTWY	WEATHERLY
AEEHILLST	THE ALLIES	AEEHLSTTT	THE LATEST
AEEHILMNW	MEANWHILE	AEEHLSTVY	HAVE STYLE
AEEHILNSS	SINHALESE	AEEHMMORT	HAMMERTOE
AEEHILNTV	HELVETIAN	AEEHMMPSY	EMPHYSEMA
AEEHILORT	OIL HEATER	AEEHMNNOP	PHENOMENA
AEEHILPRS	SHAPELIER	AEEHMNOSU	HOUSE NAME
AEEHIMMNT	MAIN THEME	AEEHMNOTT	MOTH-EATEN
AEEHIMNTT	IN THE TEAM	AEEHMOPRS	SEMAPHORE
AEEHIMPSS	EMPHASISE	AEEHMORST	MORE HASTE
AEEHIMPST	EMPATHIES	AEEHMPRST	PETERSHAM
AEEHIMPSZ	EMPHASIZE	AEEHMRSTT	THE MASTER
AEEHIMPTZ	EMPATHIZE	AEEHMSSST	THE MASSES
AEEHIMRST	HETAERISM	AEEHNNOTW	ON THE WANE
AEEHIMTTT	AT THE TIME	AEEHNOPRS	EARPHONES
AEEHIMTTW	WHITE MEAT	AEEHNOPRT	OPEN HEART
AEEHINNPS	HA'PENNIES		OPEN-HEART
AEEHINPRS	HESPERIAN	AEEHNOSSW	SEEN A SHOW
AEEHINPSS	EPHESIANS	AEEHNPRRS	SHARPENER
AEEHINRRT	IN THE REAR	AEEHNPTTU	UP THE ANTE
AEEHINRTU	EUTHERIAN	AEEHNRSSS	HARNESSES
AEEHINRTV	HIT A NERVE	AEEHNRSTT	THREATENS
AEEHINSSV	HEAVINESS	AEEHNRSTX	NARTHEXES
AEEHINSTT	IN THE EAST	AEEHNRTTT	TENTH-RATE
AEEHINVVW	HEAVY WINE	AEEHNRTTY	HENRY TATE
AEEHIPRSS	PHARISEES	AEEHORRST	HEARTSORE
AEEHIPRST	THERAPIES	AEEHORRSV	OVERHEARS
AEEHIRRTW	EARTH WIRE	AEEHORRSW	WAR HEROES
AEEHIRSTT	EARTHIEST	AEEHORSSS	SEASHORES
	HEARTIEST	AEEHORSTV	OVERHEATS
	HESITATER	AEEHORSTZ	THE AZORES
AEEHIRTTW	WAIT THERE	AEEHORSUW	WAREHOUSE
AEEHIRTWW	WEAR WHITE	AEEHOSSSW	SEES A SHOW
AEEHIRTWY	EITHER WAY	AEEHOSSTU	TEAHOUSES
AEEHISSTT	HESITATES	AEEHOSTTT	TO THE EAST
AEEHISVVW	HAVE VIEWS	AEEHPPRST	THE PAPERS
AEEHJNORS	JANE SHORE	AEEHPRRTT	TRAP THREE
AEEHKLLSU	KEELHAULS	AEEHPRSST	SET PHRASE
AEEHKLMOW	MAKE WHOLE	AEEHPRSSY	SHARP EYES
AEEHKMNOT	ON THE MAKE	AEEHPRSTU	SUPERHEAT
AEEHKMORS	SHOEMAKER	AEEHPRSUV	UPHEAVERS
AEEHKMRTT	THE MARKET	AEEHPSSTY	PAY SHEETS
AEEHLLMNS	HELL'S NAME	AEEHRRSTT	THREE STAR
AEEHLLMOW	WHOLEMEAL	AEEHRRSTV	HARVESTER
AEEHLLNOW	HALLOWEEN	AEEHRSSTY	STAYS HERE
AEEHLLOSW	WHOLESALE	AEEHRSTUX	EXHAUSTER
AEEHLLPSS	SHELL PEAS	AEEHSSTTT	THE STATES
AEEHLLRST	HEARS TELL	AEEIILLSV	LIVES A LIE
AEEHLLSSS	SEASHELLS	AEEIILMNT	ELIMINATE
AEEHLMMNT	EMMENTHAL	AEEIILQRU	RELIQUIAE
AEEHLMNSW	WHEELSMAN	AEEIILRSS	SERIALISE
AEEHLMOSY	HAEMOLYSE	AEEIILRST	ISRAELITE
AEEHLMPST	HELPMATES		REALITIES
AEEHLMSSS	SHAMELESS	AEEIILRSZ	SERIALIZE
AEEHLMTTY	METHYLATE	AEEIIMNST	AMENITIES
AEEHLNNOR	LENA HORNE	AEEIINRTT	ITINERATE
AEEHLNOPS	ANOPHELES	AEEIINSTV	NAIVETIES
AEEHLNPST	ELEPHANTS	AEEIINSTX	ANXIETIES
AEEHLNSSU	UNLEASHES	AEEIIRSTV	VARIETIES
AEEHLNTTV	THE LEVANT	AEEIIRTTV	ITERATIVE
AEEHLOPST	TELOPHASE	AEEIIRTVZ	VIZIERATE
AEEHLORST	LOSE HEART	AEEIJMSST	MAJESTIES
AEEHLORTW	WATER HOLE	AEEIKKLNS	SNAKELIKE
AEEHLOSSU	ALE HOUSES	AEEIKLLMU	LIKE A MULE
AEEHLPRST	THREE LAPS	AEEIKLLPT	PETALLIKE
AEEHLPRTX	EXTRA HELP		PLATELIKE

AEEIKLLST	SLATELIKE	AEEILQSUZ	EQUALIZES
AEEIKLMPS	MAKE PILES	AEEILRRST	LATE RISER
AEEIKLNNP	LENIN PEAK	AEEILRRSY	RISE EARLY
AEEIKLNPR	KEPLERIAN	AEEILRRTT	AIR LETTER
AEEIKLNSS	LEAKINESS	AEEILRRTV	RETRIEVAL
AEEIKLPTV	KEPT ALIVE	AEEILRSST	RISES LATE
AEEIKLRTW	LIKE WATER	AEEILRSTT	LIE AT REST
AEEIKLSTW	WEAKLIEST		LITERATES
AEEIKMMST	MAKES TIME		STATELIER
AEEIKMNTT	TAKEN TIME	AEEILRSTU	AT LEISURE
	TIME TAKEN	AEEILRSTV	RELATIVES
AEEIKMSTT	TAKES TIME		VERSATILE
AEEIKNNSY	KEYNESIAN	AEEILRTTU	ELUTRIATE
AEEIKNRRS	INK ERASER	AEEILSSTZ	SLEAZIEST
AEEIKPSST	STEAK PIES	AEEILSSUX	SEXUALISE
AEEIKPSTT	KEEPS AT IT	AEEILSTTV	LEVITATES
AEEIKSSTU	TAKE ISSUE	AEEILSUXZ	SEXUALIZE
AEEILLLST	TELLS A LIE	AEEILSVVY	EVASIVELY
AEEILLMOZ	EMILE ZOLA	AEEIMMNST	MEANTIMES
AEEILLMST	METALLISE	AEEIMNNOT	MATE IN ONE
AEEILLMTZ	METALLIZE	AEEIMNNTV	MAIN EVENT
AEEILLNOT	LINOLEATE	AEEIMNNZZ	MEZZANINE
AEEILLNST	SEEN IT ALL	AEEIMNOTT	AT ONE TIME
AEEILLPST	PALLETISE	AEEIMNPRT	IN A TEMPER
AEEILLPTT	PALLETTE	AEEIMNRSW	MAIN SEWER
AEEILLPTZ	PALLETIZE	AEEIMNRSX	EXAMINERS
AEEILLSSS	AISLELESS	AEEIMNRTT	TERMINATE
AEEILLOST	SEES IT ALL	AEEIMNSSS	SEAMINESS
AEEILLSTT	SATELLITE	AEEIMNSST	AMNESTIES
AEEILMMST	MEALTIMES		MEATINESS
	SEMIMETAL	AEEIMNSTT	ESTAMINET
AEEILMNNT	LINEAMENT	AEEIMORRS	ROSE MARIE
AEEILMNRY	MINELAYER	AEEIMORSW	WEARISOME
AEEILMNSS	MELANISES	AEEIMOTTT	TIME TO EAT
AEEILMNST	ENAMELIST	AEEIMPRST	SPARE TIME
AEEILMNSZ	MELANIZES	AEEIMRTTX	EXTRA TIME
AEEILMORT	MELIORATE		TAXIMETER
AEEILMPST	TIME-LAPSE	AEEIMSSTT	ESTIMATES
AEEILMRTT	ALTIMETER		STEAMIEST
AEEILMRTW	LIMEWATER	AEEIMSSTV	SAVES TIME
AEEILMSST	MEASLIEST	AEEIMSTTW	WASTE TIME
AEEILMTUV	EMULATIVE	AEEIMSTVW	EMIT WAVES
AEEILNNPP	PENEPLAIN	AEEINNNSS	INANENESS
AEEILNNPR	PERENNIAL	AEEINNOTT	EATEN INTO
AEEILNNTV	VALENTINE	AEEINNRST	IN EARNEST
AEEILNOTV	ELEVATION		TANNERIES
AEEILNPPP	PINEAPPLE	AEEINNRSY	NINE YEARS
AEEILNPRX	EXPLAINER	AEEINNRTT	ENTERTAIN
AEEILNPSS	PENALISES	AEEINNRTV	INNERVATE
AEEILNPST	PENALTIES	AEEINNSST	INSENSATE
AEEILNPSX	EXPANSILE	AEEINNSSV	NAIVENESS
AEEILNPSZ	PENALIZES		SAVES NINE
AEEILNRSS	EARLINESS	AEEINNSTT	SENTENTIA
AEEILNRST	RISEN LATE	AEEINOPPT	APPOINTEE
AEEILNRSV	VERNALISE	AEEINOPRT	PERITONEA
AEEILNRTW	WATERLINE	AEEINORTT	ORIENTATE
AEEILNRVZ	VERNALIZE	AEEINPRSS	PASSERINE
AEEILNSST	ESSENTIAL	AEEINPRST	APERIENTS
AEEILNSSV	ALIVENESS	AEEINPSVX	EXPANSIVE
AEEILNTTV	VENTILATE	AEEINQRTU	QUITE NEAR
AEEILOPTT	PETIOLATE	AEEINRRTT	IN RETREAT
AEEILORRT	ARTERIOLE	AEEINRRTV	VERATRINE
AEEILORST	AEROLITES	AEEINRSST	IRATENESS
AEEILOSTT	ETIOLATES	AEEINRSSW	WEARINESS
AEEILPPPR	RIPE APPLE	AEEINRSTT	REINSTATE
AEEILPPPS	APPLE PIES	AEEINRSTU	ESTUARINE
AEEILPRSS	ESPALIERS	AEEINRSTV	INVERTASE
	PLEASE SIR	AEEINRSTW	SENT A WIRE
AEEILQRSU	EQUALISER	AEEINRSTY	EYE STRAIN
AEEILQRUZ	EQUALIZER	AEEINSSTT	TETANISES
AEEILQSSU	EQUALISES	AEEINSSTU	UNEASIEST

AEEINSSVW	SINE WAVES	AEEKPSSTT	TAKE STEPS
AEEINSTTT	INTESTATE	AEEKQRSSU	SQUEAKERS
AEEINSTTZ	TETANIZES	AEEKRRSST	STREAKERS
AEEINTTTV	ATTENTIVE	AEEKSSTTT	TAKE TESTS
	TENTATIVE	AEELLLSTT	TELL TALES
AEEIOPRTV	OPERATIVE		TELLTALES
AEEIPPRST	APPETISER	AEELLMNSW	MEANS WELL
AEEIPPRSU	PAUPERISE	AEELLMNTW	MEANT WELL
AEEIPPRTZ	APPETIZER		WELL-MEANT
AEEIPPRUZ	PAUPERIZE	AEELLNOST	LETS ALONE
AEEIPPSTT	APPETITES	AEELLNRTY	ETERNALLY
AEEIPRRTV	PRIVATEER	AEELLOPPV	LOVE APPLE
AEEIPRSSS	PESSARIES	AEELLOPST	SELLOTAPE
AEEIPRSVV	PERVASIVE		SOLEPLATE
AEEIPRTTX	EXTIRPATE	AEELLOSUV	LAEVULOSE
AEEIPSSST	EPISTASES	AEELLPSST	PLEATLESS
AEEIPSSTX	EPISTAXES	AEELLPSTT	PLATELETS
AEEIQSSTU	QUEASIEST	AEELLRRTV	TRAVELLER
AEEIRRSTV	EAST RIVER	AEELLRSTT	TALL TREES
AEEIRSSTT	SESTERTIA	AEELLRSVY	SEVERALLY
	TREATISES	AEELLRTTW	TREAT WELL
AEEIRSSTU	ESTUARIES	AEELLRTWX	EXTRA WELL
AEEIRSSTV	ASSERTIVE	AEELLSSUV	VALUELESS
AEEISSTTW	SWEATIEST	AEELLSSVV	VALVELESS
AEEISTUVX	EXUVIATES	AEELLSUWY	SUE LAWLEY
AEEJKKMOS	MAKE JOKES	AEELMNORY	REAL MONEY
AEEJLLMTY	MEAT JELLY	AEELMNPSS	AMPLENESS
AEEJLMORS	LEE MAJORS	AEELMNRSU	MALE NURSE
AEEJLNPST	JET PLANES	AEELMNSTT	MANTELETS
AEEJMORTT	MAJORETTE	AEELMOORV	LEAVE ROOM
AEEJNRSST	SERJEANTS	AEELMORST	ELASTOMER
AEEJRSSTW	SWEET JARS	AEELMOSWY	AWESOMELY
AEEKLLPSW	SLEEPWALK	AEELMPRST	PALM TREES
	SPEAK WELL	AEELMPRSX	EXEMPLARS
AEEKLMMSU	MAMELUKES	AEELMPRXY	EXEMPLARY
AEEKLMOSV	MAKES LOVE	AEELMPSTT	TEMPLATES
AEEKLMRSU	MAKE RULES	AEELMRTTW	MELTWATER
AEEKLNSST	TALK SENSE	AEELNNOSS	ALONENESS
AEEKLOOTV	TOOK LEAVE	AEELNNRST	LANNERETS
AEEKLOPST	LAKE POETS	AEELNOPST	ANTELOPES
AEEKLORVW	LEAVE WORK		OPENS LATE
AEEKLORWY	WOKE EARLY	AEELNOQSU	ONES EQUAL
AEEKLSSTY	EYESTALKS	AEELNORSV	LEANS OVER
AEEKLSTTW	SWEET TALK	AEELNORTV	LEANT OVER
	SWEET-TALK	AEELNOSTY	LOST AN EYE
AEEKMMNOY	MAKE MONEY	AEELNOSYY	LAY EYES ON
AEEKMMOSV	MAKE MOVES	AEELNPRTV	PREVALENT
AEEKMMRRY	MAKE MERRY	AEELNRSST	ALERTNESS
AEEKMMRST	MAKE TERMS	AEELNRSTV	LEVANTERS
AEEKMNOST	MAKE NOTES	AEELNRSTX	EXTERNALS
AEEKMNSSW	MAKES NEWS	AEELNRSTY	EARNESTLY
AEEKMORSV	MAKES OVER	AEELNRTTV	TERVALENT
AEEKMORSW	MAKE WORSE	AEELNRTTY	LATE ENTRY
AEEKMPRRS	MR.SPEAKER		TERNATELY
AEEKMPRSW	KEEPS WARM	AEELNSSST	STALENESS
AEEKMRSSU	MAKES SURE	AEELNSSTW	STALE NEWS
AEEKMRSTY	MASTER KEY	AEELNSSTY	SENSATELY
AEEKNNOTT	TAKEN NOTE	AEELNSTTV	LAST EVENT
AEEKNNPST	KNEE PANTS	AEELOPRST	ROSE PETAL
AEEKNORTV	OVERTAKEN	AEELOPRSV	LEAPS OVER
	TAKEN OVER	AEELOPRTV	LEAPT OVER
AEEKNOSTT	TAKE NOTES	AEELORSST	OLEASTERS
	TAKES NOTE	AEELORSTT	TOLERATES
AEEKNSSSW	ASKEWNESS	AEELORSTV	ELEVATORS
AEEKOOPPT	TOOK A PEEP	AEELORSTY	ROSEATELY
AEEKORRSV	RAKES OVER	AEELOSTTW	TEA TOWELS
AEEKORSTV	OVERTAKES	AEELOSTUV	LEAVES OUT
	SKATE OVER	AEELPPRRU	PUERPERAL
	TAKEOVERS	AEELPPRTU	PERPETUAL
	TAKES OVER	AEELPRRST	PLASTERER
AEEKORTUY	EUKARYOTE	AEELPRSSU	PLEASURES

AEELPRSTT	SALTPETER	AEENOSSTW	WET SEASON
	SALTPETRE	AEENOSTTW	WENT TO SEA
AEELQRSSU	SQUEALERS	AEENPPRSW	NEWSPAPER
AEELQSTUZ	QUETZALES	AEENPRRTU	ENRAPTURE
AEELRRSSV	REVERSALS	AEENPRSSS	SPARENESS
AEELRSSTV	LAST VERSE	AEENPRSTT	AT PRESENT
AEELRSSTW	WATERLESS	AEENPRSTW	WENT SPARE
AEELRSTUY	AUSTERELY	AEENPSSTT	PAST TENSE
AEELRSTVY	SEVERALTY	AEENRRSSW	ANSWERERS
AEELRTUUV	TRUE VALUE	AEENRRSTU	SAUNTERER
AEELSSSTT	STATELESS	AEENRRSVW	RAW NERVES
	TASTELESS	AEENRSSST	ASSENTERS
AEELSSTTW	SWEATLETS		SEEN STARS
AEELSSTWW	WEST WALES	AEENRSSTU	SAUTERNES
AEEMMMNORT	MANOMETER	AEENSSSTT	NET ASSETS
AEEMMMNSTU	AMUSEMENT	AEEOOPRTZ	AZEOTROPE
AEEMMRRST	STAMMERER	AEEOPPRRV	PAPER OVER
AEEMMSSST	MESSMATES	AEEOPPRSU	PEA-SOUPER
AEEMNNORY	EARN MONEY	AEEOPRSSW	SEA POWERS
AEEMNNOTT	ATONEMENT	AEEOPRSTT	OPERETTAS
AEEMNNPRT	PERMANENT		POETASTER
AEEMNOPRT	TREPONEMA	AEEOPRVVW	WAVE POWER
AEEMNOPST	STEAM OPEN	AEEOORRSTV	OVERRATES
AEEMNOPSU	MENOPAUSE	AEEOORRSTW	ROSE WATER
AEEMNOPYZ	APOENZYME	AEEORSSTU	SEA ROUTES
AEEMNORRS	EARNS MORE	AEEORSTTV	OVERSTATE
AEEMNORTW	WORM-EATEN	AEEORSTVX	OVERTAXES
AEEMNORUV	MANOEUVRE	AEEPPRSTT	TEST PAPER
AEEMNOSVY	SAVE MONEY	AEEPPSSTW	SWEEP PAST
AEEMNOSYY	EASY MONEY	AEEPRRSTU	APERTURES
AEEMNPRTY	REPAYMENT	AEEPRRSTY	SPARE TYRE
AEEMNPSTV	PAVEMENTS	AEEPRRTUW	PURE WATER
AEEMNQRUY	QUEEN MARY	AEEPRSSTU	UPAS TREES
AEEMNRSST	MARES NEST	AEEQRSSTU	SET SQUARE
	STEERSMAN	AEERRRSST	ARRESTERS
AEEMNRSTV	AVERMENTS	AEERRRSTU	TREASURER
AEEMNRSUV	MANEUVERS	AEERRRSTV	TRAVERSER
AEEMNRTTT	TREATMENT	AEERRSSSU	REASSURES
AEEMNSSTT	MEANS TEST	AEERRSSTU	TREASURES
	STATESMEN	AEERRSSTV	TRAVERSES
AEEMNSSTY	MATEYNESS	AEERRSSTW	SEWER RATS
AEEMNSTTT	STATEMENT	AEERRTTVX	EXTRAVERT
	TESTAMENT	AEERSSSST	SEES STARS
AEEMOPRST	TOM PEARSE	AEERSSTTT	ATTESTERS
AEEMPRRST	TAMPERERS		SET AT REST
AEEMPRRTU	PREMATURE	AEESTTTTU	STATUETTE
AEEMPRSTT	STREET MAP	AEFFFIORR	FAIR OFFER
AEEMPSTTY	EMPTY SEAT	AEFFFLTUW	LUFTWAFFE
AEEMQSTTU	MAQUETTES	AEFFGINOS	EASING OFF
AEEMRRSST	STREAMERS	AEFFGIORT	FIT OF RAGE
AEEMRSSTT	TEAMSTERS	AEFFGIWXY	WAX EFFIGY
AEEMRSSTY	EASY TERMS	AEFFGORTT	OFF TARGET
AEEMSSSSU	MASSEUSES	AEFFHIORT	OFF THE AIR
AEENNNPTY	TEN A PENNY	AEFFHIOTV	HAVE IT OFF
AEENNPRTT	REPENTANT	AEFFHKNOS	SHAKEN OFF
AEENNRRTT	REENTRANT	AEFFHKOSS	SHAKES OFF
AEENNRSTV	REVENANTS	AEFFHLORS	FRESH LOAF
AEENNSTTW	NEWS AT TEN	AEFFHMOPT	OFF THE MAP
AEENOPPRT	NOTE PAPER	AEFFIILRS	FALSIFIER
AEENOPRST	ESPERANTO	AEFFIILSS	FALSIFIES
	PERSONATE	AEFFIKPST	PIKESTAFF
	TEARS OPEN	AEFFILNTT	FELT FAINT
AEENOPRSU	EUROPEANS	AEFFILOWY	WAY OF LIFE
AEENOPTTT	POTENTATE	AEFFIMNTX	AFFIXMENT
AEENOQRSU	SQUARE ONE	AEFFIRTUX	AFFIXTURE
AEENORRTV	VENERATOR	AEFFKLLNT	LEFT FLANK
AEENORRTW	ROWAN TREE	AEFFKMNOU	MAKE FUN OF
AEENORSSS	SEASONERS	AEFFKNOSS	SNEAKS OFF
AEENORSST	RESONATES	AEFFKNSTU	TAKE SNUFF
AEENORSTV	RENOVATES	AEFFLLOOT	FELT A FOOL
AEENORSTW	STONEWARE	AEFFLLRSU	FULL FARES

323

AEFFLLRUY	FEARFULLY
AEFFLLTUW	FELT AWFUL
AEFFLLTUY	FATEFULLY
AEFFLORST	LAST OFFER
AEFFLORSW	SAFFLOWER
AEFFLORTT	RATTLE OFF
AEFFNOOSS	OFF SEASON
	OFF-SEASON
AEFFNORSY	ANY OFFERS?
AEFFOORTW	FAR TOO FEW
AEFFOPRST	TAPERS OFF
AEFFOPRSY	PAY OFFERS
AEFFOPSSS	PASSES OFF
AEFFOOQRSU	SQUARE OFF
AEFFORRTW	WAR EFFORT
AEFFORSST	AFFORESTS
AEFFOSSTV	STAVES OFF
AEFFRSTUX	SUFFER TAX
AEFGGIINV	GIVEN A FIG
AEFGGIISV	GIVES A FIG
AEFGHILNS	ANGEL FISH
	ANGELFISH
AEFGHILST	SAFELIGHT
AEFGHILTW	WHITE FLAG
AEFGHINRS	HANGS FIRE
AEFGHINRT	FATHERING
AEFGHINST	NIGHT SAFE
AEFGHIRST	GEAR SHIFT
	GEARSHIFT
	SHIFT GEAR
AEFGHNORU	FAR ENOUGH
AEFGHORRT	FORGATHER
AEFGHORTV	GAVE FORTH
AEFGIILTV	GIVE A LIFT
AEFGIIMNR	MAGNIFIER
AEFGIIMNS	MAGNIFIES
AEFGIINNR	FINE GRAIN
AEFGIIRST	GRATIFIES
AEFGILNRS	RING FALSE
AEFGILNRT	FALTERING
AEFGILSTT	GETS A LIFT
AEFGIMSTU	FUMIGATES
AEFGINNST	FASTENING
AEFGINNTT	FATTENING
AEFGINRRY	RAREFYING
AEFGINRTU	FEATURING
AEFGIOORS	GOOSE FAIR
AEFGIORSS	OSSIFRAGE
AEFGIPRST	FIRST PAGE
AEFGIRRST	FIRST GEAR
	RARE GIFTS
AEFGIRRSU	ARGUFIERS
AEFGIRSTT	GAS FITTER
	GET A FIRST
AEFGIRUWX	WAX FIGURE
AEFGKSUWY	GUY FAWKES
AEFGLLLMU	FLAGELLUM
AEFGLLOPS	FLAG POLES
AEFGLNORT	LONG AFTER
AEFGLNRSU	RUNG FALSE
AEFGLNRTY	FELT ANGRY
AEFGLOPRS	LEAPFROGS
AEFGLORTW	AFTERGLOW
AEFGMNRST	FRAGMENTS
AEFGMORRT	GREAT FORM
AEFGNOPRT	FRONT PAGE
	FRONT-PAGE
AEFGNORST	FRONTAGES
AEFGNORTX	XENOGRAFT
AEFGOOPPR	PAGE PROOF
AEFGOORTU	OUT OF GEAR

AEFGOPRSU	FOUR PAGES
AEFGORTTT	GOT FATTER
AEFHHISST	SHEATFISH
AEFHHLLTU	HEALTHFUL
AEFHHLORT	OTHER HALF
AEFHIIKLS	LIKE A FISH
AEFHIKMST	MAKE SHIFT
	MAKESHIFT
AEFHIKPTT	KEPT FAITH
AEFHIKSST	FISH STEAK
AEFHILLNT	IN THE FALL
AEFHILLSV	HALF-LIVES
AEFHILMNU	HUMAN LIFE
AEFHILNOP	FINAL HOPE
AEFHILORW	FOR A WHILE
AEFHILOST	LOSE FAITH
AEFHILOTW	WHITE LOAF
AEFHILPPY	HAPPY LIFE
AEFHILPST	FISHPLATE
AEFHILSST	FAITHLESS
	FLASHIEST
AEFHILSTT	LATE SHIFT
	THATS LIFE
AEFHILSTY	FISHY TALE
AEFHIMNRS	FISHERMAN
AEFHIMNST	MINE SHAFT
AEFHINOPT	FAINT HOPE
AEFHINORS	FASHIONER
AEFHINRTY	IN THE FRAY
AEFHIORRS	HORSE FAIR
AEFHIORST	FIRE A SHOT
	HOT AS FIRE
AEFHIPRSS	SPEARFISH
AEFHIPSST	FISH PASTE
AEFHIRSTT	FIRST HEAT
AEFHIRTTW	THREW A FIT
AEFHLLTUY	HATEFULLY
AEFHLMPTY	HALF EMPTY
AEFHLNNPY	HALFPENNY
AEFHLNOST	HALFTONES
AEFHLNOTT	ON THE FLAT
AEFHLNSSW	NEWS FLASH
AEFHLORSV	FLASHOVER
AEFHLPPTY	FELT HAPPY
AEFHMMORS	HOME FARMS
AEFHMNOOT	ONE FATHOM
AEFHMNORT	ON THE FARM
AEFHMORRS	FARM HORSE
AEFHMORSU	FARMHOUSE
AEFHNORSW	SHOWN FEAR
AEFHOOPRT	HEATPROOF
AEFHOOPRY	RAY OF HOPE
AEFHORSSW	SHOWS FEAR
AEFHORSTT	SOFT HEART
AEFIIKLRY	FAIRYLIKE
AEFIILLNS	NAIL FILES
AEFIILMNS	SEMIFINAL
AEFIILMPR	AMPLIFIER
AEFIILMPS	AMPLIFIES
AEFIILNNT	FAINT LINE
	INFANTILE
AEFIILNSS	FINALISES
AEFIILNSZ	FINALIZES
AEFIILNTX	FINAL EXIT
AEFIILQRU	QUALIFIER
AEFIILQSU	QUALIFIES
AEFIILRRS	AIR RIFLES
AEFIILRST	FRAILTIES
AEFIILSSS	SALSIFIES
AEFIILSTU	FILE A SUIT
AEFIIMNNS	FENIANISM

AEFIINRTU	INFURIATE	AEFKLOORT	LOOK AFTER
AEFIIPRST	APERITIFS	AEFKLORSW	FALSEWORK
AEFIISSST	SATISFIES	AEFKLOSTU	FLAKES OUT
AEFIISTVX	FIXATIVES	AEFKMMNOR	MEN OF MARK
AEFIKLLOO	LIKE A FOOL	AEFKMNNOR	MEN OF RANK
AEFIKLNSS	FLAKINESS	AEFKMORRW	FRAMEWORK
AEFIKMMNP	MEIN KAMPF	AEFKNNRSS	FRANKNESS
AEFIKMMRS	MAKES FIRM	AEFKNOPTU	POKE FUN AT
AEFIKMRSV	FIVE MARKS	AEFKOORTT	TOOK AFTER
AEFIKOOTW	TOOK A WIFE	AEFKOPRSS	SPEAKS FOR
AEFILLLOW	LIE FALLOW	AEFKORSTU	FREAK-OUTS
AEFILLLTW	LEFT A WILL		FREAKS OUT
AEFILLNPT	PLANT LIFE	AEFLLLMST	FELT SMALL
AEFILMNOR	FORM A LINE	AEFLLLMSU	FULL MEALS
AEFILMNOS	ISLE OF MAN	AEFLLLNNY	FLANNELLY
AEFILMNOV	FINAL MOVE	AEFLLLUUV	FULL VALUE
AEFILMNST	FILAMENTS	AEFLLMSTU	FULL STEAM
AEFILMNTU	FULMINATE	AEFLLNOOR	ALL FOR ONE
AEFILMORS	FORMALISE		ONE FOR ALL
AEFILMORZ	FORMALIZE	AEFLLNOSX	FELLS AN OX
AEFILMPWY	FAMILY PEW	AEFLLNOTU	FALLEN OUT
AEFILMRTX	FILM EXTRA	AEFLLNTTU	FLATULENT
AEFILNNUZ	INFLUENZA	AEFLLORST	FORESTALL
AEFILNORT	REFLATION	AEFLLORSV	FALLS OVER
AEFILNPST	FINAL STEP	AEFLLORUW	RULE OF LAW
AEFILNRSS	FRAILNESS	AEFLLOTTT	FLAT TO LET
AEFILNRSU	FRAULEINS	AEFLLPRSY	FALLS PREY
AEFILNRWY	FAIRLY NEW	AEFLLPSTU	PLATEFULS
AEFILNSTT	FINAL TEST	AEFLLRTUY	TEARFULLY
AEFILOORS	AEROFOILS	AEFLLSSTU	FAULTLESS
AEFILOPRR	PORIFERAL	AEFLMNRUU	FRAENULUM
AEFILORSS	FORESAILS	AEFLMOOST	FOOLS MATE
AEFILPSST	FILES PAST	AEFLMORRW	LAW REFORM
AEFILRSTT	FILTRATES	AEFLMORSU	FUMAROLES
AEFILRSTU	FILATURES	AEFLMORTU	FORMULATE
AEFILSSTV	FESTIVALS	AEFLMORWY	MAYFLOWER
AEFIMMNRT	FIRMAMENT	AEFLMRSTU	MASTERFUL
AEFIMNNOW	FINE WOMAN	AEFLNOOSS	ALOOFNESS
AEFIMNORR	IRON FRAME	AEFLNOPRY	PROFANELY
AEFIMNOSS	FOAMINESS	AEFLNORTX	FRONT AXLE
AEFIMNOST	MANIFESTO	AEFLNOSTT	FLAT NOTES
AEFIMNRST	FIRST NAME		LAST OF TEN
AEFIMNSST	MANIFESTS	AEFLNOSTW	FLOWN EAST
AEFIMORSS	MISFEASOR	AEFLNSSUW	AWFULNESS
AEFIMORTV	FORMATIVE	AEFLOOPTT	FOOTPLATE
AEFIMORTW	TIME OF WAR	AEFLOORST	SLATE ROOF
	WAIT FOR ME	AEFLOORVW	LOVE OF WAR
AEFIMRSTT	FIRST MATE	AEFLOPRSU	UP FOR SALE
	FIRST TEAM	AEFLOPSTT	PETAL SOFT
AEFIMSSTT	FAST TIMES	AEFLORSTW	FOREST LAW
AEFINNRYZ	IN A FRENZY	AEFLORTWW	WATER FOWL
AEFINNSST	FAINTNESS		WATERFOWL
AEFINOPRR	PORIFERAN	AEFLOSSTT	FALSETTOS
AEFINOPRS	PINAFORES	AEFLPPRSY	FLYPAPERS
AEFINORSU	NEFARIOUS	AEFLPRRUY	PRAYERFUL
AEFINPRSY	FINE SPRAY	AEFLRSTTY	FLAT TYRES
AEFINPSTY	SAFETY PIN	AEFMMNOSU	FAMOUS MEN
AEFINRRST	FAIR RENTS	AEFMNNOOT	MAN OF NOTE
AEFINRSSS	SANS SERIF	AEFMNNOOY	ONE OF MANY
AEFINRSTU	UNFAIREST	AEFMNOORW	FOREWOMAN
AEFINSSTT	FATTINESS	AEFMNOSTW	FAST WOMEN
AEFIORTUV	FAVOURITE	AEFMORSST	FOREMASTS
AEFIPRRST	FIRETRAPS	AEFMORSTT	AFTERMOST
AEFIRRSTT	FIRST RATE	AEFMORSVW	WAVE FORMS
	FIRST-RATE		WAVEFORMS
AEFIRRSTY	FIRST YEAR	AEFMOSSTV	MOVES FAST
AEFIRSSTY	EASY FIRST	AEFNNOORT	AFTER NOON
AEFKLLOST	FOLK TALES		AFTERNOON
AEFKLLUWY	WAKEFULLY	AEFNNSSTU	UNFASTENS
AEFKLNOSW	SNOWFLAKE	AEFNOORST	SOON AFTER
AEFKLNSTU	FUEL TANKS	AEFNORRSW	FOREWARNS

325

AEFNORRSY	YEARNS FOR	AEGGLRRST	STRAGGLER
AEFNORSTT	FRONT SEAT	AEGGLRSST	STRAGGLES
AEFNORSVW	FAWNS OVER	AEGGMORST	MORTGAGES
AEFNORTTU	FORTUNATE	AEGGNOSUY	SYNAGOGUE
AEFNPSTTU	FATTENS UP	AEGGNPRSS	PRESS GANG
AEFNRRSST	TRANSFERS		PRESS-GANG
AEFNRRSTU	RUNS AFTER	AEGGNRRWY	GREW ANGRY
AEFNRSSTU	TRANSFUSE	AEGGNRSST	GANGSTERS
AEFOOPSTT	POTS OF TEA	AEGGNRSTU	GREAT GUNS
AEFOORTTW	TEA FOR TWO	AEGGNRSTY	GETS ANGRY
	TWO FOR TEA	AEGGOPRSU	AGE GROUPS
AEFOPRRST	FOREPARTS	AEGGORRSS	AGGRESSOR
AEFOPRRTY	PREFATORY	AEGHHILUV	HIGH VALUE
AEFOPRSSS	PASSES FOR	AEGHHINRS	REHASHING
AEFOPSSTT	SOFT-PASTE	AEGHHINST	SHEATHING
AEFORRSSW	FORSWEARS	AEGHHIPRY	HIGHER PAY
AEFORRSUY	FOUR YEARS	AEGHHIRST	HIGH RATES
AEFORSSTY	FORESTAYS	AEGHHIRTU	HAUGHTIER
AEFORSTTW	SOFT WATER	AEGHHIRTW	HIGH WATER
AEFOSSSTT	SOFT SEATS		HIGH-WATER
AEFRRSTTU	FRUSTRATE	AEGHHNOSU	HAS ENOUGH
AEGGHHIRS	HIGH GEARS	AEGHHNUVY	HUNG HEAVY
AEGGHHISW	HIGH WAGES	AEGHIINTV	GIVE A HINT
AEGGHINRT	GATHERING	AEGHIKLMT	MAKE LIGHT
AEGGHIRTZ	GIGAHERTZ	AEGHIKMTT	MAKE TIGHT
AEGGHISST	SHAGGIEST	AEGHIKNNR	HANKERING
AEGGHMORU	ROUGH GAME	AEGHIKNRS	SHRINKAGE
AEGGHOPRY	GEOGRAPHY	AEGHILLMT	LIGHT MEAL
AEGGIINNR	REGAINING	AEGHILLSS	SHIGELLAS
AEGGIINPU	GUINEA PIG	AEGHILMST	MEGALITHS
AEGGIINRV	GIVE A RING	AEGHILNRS	NARGHILES
	GIVING EAR		SHEARLING
AEGGIINSV	GIVE A SIGN	AEGHILNRT	EARTHLING
AEGGIIOTV	GIVE IT A GO		HALTERING
AEGGILNNR	ENLARGING		LATHERING
AEGGILNNS	GLEANINGS		REAL THING
AEGGILNOV	LEAVING GO	AEGHILNST	ATHELINGS
AEGGILNRS	LARGE GINS	AEGHILNTT	LATE NIGHT
AEGGILOSU	OIL GAUGES	AEGHILRRT	REAR LIGHT
AEGGINNOR	ORANGE GIN	AEGHILRTY	LIGHT YEAR
AEGGINNRR	GARNERING		LIGHT-YEAR
AEGGINNRV	ENGRAVING	AEGHILSTT	LIT THE GAS
AEGGINORR	GREGORIAN		SET ALIGHT
AEGGINORS	GEORGIANS	AEGHILTVW	LIGHT WAVE
AEGGINORT	GOING RATE	AEGHIMMNR	HAMMERING
AEGGINOST	GOING EAST	AEGHIMNPR	HAMPERING
AEGGINOSY	EASY GOING	AEGHIMNRT	NIGHTMARE
	EASYGOING	AEGHIMNST	SAME THING
	GOING EASY	AEGHIMPRT	TEPHIGRAM
AEGGINOTV	VOTING AGE	AEGHINNPP	HAPPENING
AEGGINPRS	PRESAGING	AEGHINNRT	NEAR THING
AEGGINPRT	PARGETING	AEGHINNST	HASTENING
AEGGINRST	STAGGER IN	AEGHINOTV	HEAVING TO
AEGGINSTT	GESTATING	AEGHINPPU	HEAPING UP
AEGGINTTT	GETTING AT	AEGHINPRS	RESHAPING
AEGGINTTZ	GAZETTING	AEGHINPTU	HEATING UP
AEGGINTUV	GIVEN A TUG	AEGHINPUV	UPHEAVING
AEGGIOPRS	ARPEGGIOS	AEGHINRSS	GARNISHES
AEGGIPRST	GETS A GRIP	AEGHINRST	GATHERS IN
AEGGIRRTW	GAG WRITER		NEAR SIGHT
AEGGISTUV	GIVES A TUG	AEGHINRTU	NAUGHTIER
AEGGLLMSS	SMALL EGGS	AEGHINRTW	WREATHING
AEGGLNNOO	GONE ALONG	AEGHINSTY	EASY THING
AEGGLNNOR	LONG RANGE	AEGHINSVX	HAVING SEX
	LONG-RANGE	AEGHIOOPS	OESOPHAGI
AEGGLNOOS	GOES ALONG	AEGHIOOTV	GIVE A HOOT
AEGGLNOST	GETS ALONG	AEGHIORWY	GO HAYWIRE
AEGGLNPST	EGG PLANTS	AEGHIPPRS	EPIGRAPHS
	EGGPLANTS	AEGHIPPRY	EPIGRAPHY
AEGGLNRRY	GLENGARRY	AEGHIPRRS	SERIGRAPH
AEGGLORSY	GARGOYLES	AEGHIPSTT	SPAGHETTI

AEGHIRRSY	GREY HAIRS	AEGIJNORS	JARGONISE
AEGHISTVW	WHAT GIVES?	AEGIJNORZ	JARGONIZE
AEGHKLOOS	SHOOK A LEG	AEGIJNOTV	GIVEN A JOT
AEGHLLNOP	HELP ALONG	AEGIJOSTV	GIVES A JOT
AEGHLNOOS	HANG LOOSE	AEGIKKMNR	KINGMAKER
AEGHLNOSW	SHOWN A LEG	AEGIKLNSW	WEAKLINGS
AEGHLNRTU	HEART-LUNG	AEGIKLRSS	GRASSLIKE
AEGHLOOPR	OLEOGRAPH	AEGIKMNRR	REMARKING
AEGHLORTT	LARGHETTO	AEGIKMNRT	MARKETING
AEGHLORUV	LAUGH OVER	AEGIKMNSS	MAKE SIGNS
AEGHLOSSU	GOULASHES	AEGIKMNSU	MAKING USE
AEGHLOSSW	SHOWS A LEG	AEGIKNNTW	TAKEN WING
AEGHLRSTU	SLAUGHTER	AEGIKNQSU	SQUEAKING
AEGHMOPST	APOTHEGMS	AEGIKNRST	STREAKING
AEGHMOTTU	TOUGH MEAT	AEGIKNSTW	TAKE WINGS
AEGHNNORS	HANGERS-ON		TAKES WING
AEGHNOPST	HEPTAGONS	AEGIKPPRT	KEPT A GRIP
	PATHOGENS	AEGILLLLY	ILLEGALLY
AEGHNORSV	HANGOVERS	AEGILLLNU	GALLINULE
	HANGS OVER	AEGILLNNP	PANELLING
	OVERHANGS	AEGILLNQU	EQUALLING
AEGHNOSTU	SHOGUNATE	AEGILLNRS	SIGNALLER
AEGHNPRSY	PHARYNGES	AEGILLNRV	RAVELLING
AEGHNSUVY	HEAVY GUNS	AEGILLNTY	GENITALLY
AEGHOORTT	GO TO EARTH	AEGILLPPU	PUPILLAGE
	GOT TO HEAR	AEGILLPSX	PLEXIGLAS
AEGHOPRST	GRAPESHOT	AEGILLRRU	GUERRILLA
AEGHORSST	SHORTAGES	AEGILLRSS	SALESGIRL
AEGHORSSU	ROUGH SEAS	AEGILLRSV	VILLAGERS
AEGHORSSV	ASH GROVES	AEGILMNNP	EMPLANING
AEGHOSSTW	STAGE SHOW	AEGILMNNS	SIGNAL MEN
AEGHPRSTU	GATHERS UP		SINGLE MAN
AEGIIKKLN	LIKE A KING	AEGILMNNT	ALIGNMENT
AEGIIKLNT	GIANTLIKE		LAMENTING
AEGIILLNN	LILANGENI	AEGILMNNY	MEANINGLY
AEGIILMSV	VIGESIMAL	AEGILMNRS	MALINGERS
AEGIILNNT	ENTAILING	AEGILMNRT	METAL RING
AEGIILNRS	REALISING	AEGILMNST	LIGAMENTS
AEGIILNRT	RETAILING	AEGILMNTU	EMULATING
AEGIILNRZ	REALIZING		GLUTAMINE
AEGIILNSS	SIGNALISE	AEGILMORR	RIGMAROLE
AEGIILNSZ	SIGNALIZE	AEGILMORS	GLAMORISE
AEGIILNTV	GENITIVAL	AEGILMORZ	GLAMORIZE
	LEAVING IT	AEGILMRSV	ALMSGIVER
	VIGILANTE	AEGILNNNP	ENPLANING
AEGIILNTY	GENIALITY	AEGILNNSV	ENSLAVING
AEGIILSTT	LITIGATES	AEGILNNSW	WEANLINGS
AEGIILSTV	VESTIGIAL	AEGILNOOT	GO IT ALONE
AEGIIMMRT	IMMIGRATE	AEGILNOPX	POLEAXING
AEGIIMNNR	REMAINING	AEGILNORU	NEUROGLIA
AEGIIMNNX	EXAMINING	AEGILNORY	LEGIONARY
AEGIIMNRS	MIGRAINES	AEGILNOST	GELATIONS
AEGIIMNST	GAINS TIME		LEGATIONS
AEGIIMSSV	GIVE A MISS	AEGILNPPR	RAPPELING
AEGIIMSTT	MITIGATES	AEGILNPPU	LEAPING UP
AEGIINNOS	IN AGONIES	AEGILNPRS	RELAPSING
AEGIINNRT	RETAINING	AEGILNPRT	PALTERING
AEGIINNRW	WEARING IN	AEGILNPRY	PARLEYING
AEGIINNVW	WEAVING IN		REPLAYING
AEGIINORT	ORIGINATE	AEGILNPSS	SALPINGES
AEGIINPRR	REPAIRING	AEGILNPSU	SEALING UP
AEGIINPRW	WIGAN PIER	AEGILNQSU	SQUEALING
AEGIINPTV	GIVEN A TIP	AEGILNRST	INTEGRALS
AEGIINPTX	EXPIATING		TRIANGLES
AEGIINRST	SERIATING	AEGILNRSV	SLAVERING
AEGIINRTT	ITERATING	AEGILNRSY	SEARINGLY
AEGIINSTT	INSTIGATE		YEARLINGS
AEGIINSTZ	GIANT SIZE	AEGILNRUV	REVALUING
AEGIIPSTV	GIVES A TIP	AEGILNRWY	WEARINGLY
AEGIIRRST	IRRIGATES	AEGILNSSV	SVENGALIS
AEGIJKMNS	KING JAMES		

AEGILNSSW	WINE GLASS	AEGINORVW	OVERAWING
	WINEGLASS	AEGINOSTT	GESTATION
AEGILNSTW	WANGLES IT	AEGINOSTU	EASING OUT
AEGILNSTY	TEASINGLY	AEGINOTTU	EATING OUT
AEGILOOPS	APOLOGIES	AEGINPPRR	PREPARING
	APOLOGISE	AEGINPRRU	REARING UP
AEGILOOPZ	APOLOGIZE	AEGINPRSS	ASPERSING
AEGILOOTY	AETIOLOGY		REPASSING
AEGILORSS	SERAGLIOS	AEGINPRTT	PATTERING
AEGILPRSS	PIER GLASS	AEGINPRTU	PUT IN GEAR
AEGILPRTV	GRAVEL PIT		TEARING UP
AEGILRRRU	IRREGULAR	AEGINPSTY	EGYPTIANS
AEGILRSTU	LIGATURES	AEGINQRUV	QUAVERING
AEGILRSUV	VULGARISE	AEGINRRST	ARRESTING
AEGILRSVW	LAWGIVERS		SERRATING
AEGILRUVZ	VULGARIZE	AEGINRRTU	GARNITURE
AEGIMMNOT	GEMMATION	AEGINRSSS	ASSIGNERS
AEGIMMNRU	GERMANIUM	AEGINRSST	ASSERTING
AEGIMMNRY	YAMMERING	AEGINRSTT	RESTATING
AEGIMMNST	MAGNETISM	AEGINRSTU	SIGNATURE
AEGIMMNSU	MAGNESIUM	AEGINRSTV	VINTAGERS
AEGIMNNNO	NO MEANING	AEGINRTTY	YATTERING
AEGIMNNRY	IN GERMANY	AEGINRTUV	GIVE A TURN
AEGIMNOPT	GAME POINT	AEGINSSSS	ASSESSING
AEGIMNORS	ORANGEISM		GASSINESS
AEGIMNORT	MORGANITE	AEGINSSST	STAGINESS
AEGIMNPPR	PAMPERING	AEGINSSUZ	GAUZINESS
AEGIMNPRT	TAMPERING	AEGINSTTT	ATTESTING
AEGIMNPRV	REVAMPING	AEGIPRTTY	GREAT PITY
AEGIMNRST	EMIGRANTS	AEGIPRTUV	PURGATIVE
	GERMANIST	AEGIRRRST	REGISTRAR
	MASTERING	AEGIRSTTT	GREAT TITS
	STREAMING	AEGJLLNUW	JUNGLE LAW
AEGIMNRSU	GERANIUMS	AEGJMNOPS	JAM SPONGE
	MEASURING	AEGJRSTUW	WATER JUGS
AEGIMNRTT	MATTERING	AEGKNORWW	GROWN WEAK
AEGIMNSSV	MING VASES	AEGKORRTW	GREAT WORK
AEGIMNRSU	QUAGMIRES	AEGKORSWW	GROWS WEAK
AEGIMQSUZ	QUIZ GAMES	AEGLLMOOR	LOOM LARGE
AEGIMRTVY	GRAVIMETY	AEGLLNNOO	ONE GALLON
AEGIMSSSU	MISUSAGES	AEGLLNNOT	TEN-GALLON
AEGINNNRS	ENSNARING	AEGLLNOPW	ALPENGLOW
AEGINNNTT	TENANTING	AEGLLNOST	GALLSTONE
AEGINNORS	REASONING		LOST ANGEL
AEGINNORW	NORWEGIAN	AEGLLOSTT	TOLLGATES
	WEARING ON	AEGLLRRUY	REGULARLY
AEGINNORZ	ORGANZINE	AEGLLRUUW	AUGUR WELL
AEGINNOSS	SEASONING	AEGLLSSSS	GLASSLESS
AEGINNOSU	GUANOSINE	AEGLMNNOS	MANGONELS
AEGINNOTT	NEGOTIANT	AEGLMNOOV	MOVE ALONG
AEGINNPRT	PARENTING	AEGLMNORW	LOW GERMAN
AEGINNPTT	PATENTING	AEGLMOORR	LARGE ROOM
AEGINNRSS	ANGRINESS	AEGLMRSSU	LARGE SUMS
	RANGINESS	AEGLNNOTW	WENT ALONG
AEGINNRSW	ANSWERING	AEGLNNSTU	UNTANGLES
AEGINNRTT	NATTERING	AEGLNOOPS	OPEN GOALS
AEGINNSST	ASSENTING	AEGLNOORT	TORE ALONG
AEGINNSTU	UNSEATING	AEGLNOPRW	GROWN PALE
AEGINNTTU	TAUTENING	AEGLNOPRY	GYROPLANE
AEGINOORV	IN A GROOVE	AEGLNORST	STRONG ALE
AEGINOPPR	ORANGE PIP	AEGLNORTW	LARGE TOWN
	PIPE ORGAN	AEGLNRRST	STRANGLER
AEGINOPRS	SINGAPORE	AEGLNRRSW	WRANGLERS
AEGINOPRT	IN TOP GEAR	AEGLNRSST	STRANGLES
	OPERATING	AEGLNRSSU	LASER GUNS
AEGINOPRW	GAIN POWER	AEGLNRSTY	STRANGELY
AEGINORRS	ORGANISER	AEGLNRSUY	GUNLAYERS
AEGINORRZ	ORGANIZER	AEGLNSTTU	GAUNTLETS
AEGINORSS	ORGANISES	AEGLNSTUU	UNGULATES
AEGINORST	IRON GATES	AEGLOOPSU	APOLOGUES
AEGINORSZ	ORGANIZES	AEGLOORTV	GLOAT OVER

AEGLOPRRT	LARGE PORT	AEHIILMNT	IN THE MAIL
AEGLOPRSW	GROWS PALE	AEHIILMTU	HUMILIATE
AEGLOPTTU	GOT UP LATE	AEHIILNRS	HAIRLINES
AEGLORRTU	REGULATOR	AEHIILNRT	HITLERIAN
AEGLORSST	GREAT LOSS	AEHIIMNNT	IN THE MAIN
AEGLORSTW	GROW STALE	AEHIINNRT	IN THE RAIN
	WATERLOGS	AEHIINOPT	ETHIOPIAN
AEGLORTTY	TETRALOGY	AEHIINRSS	HAIRINESS
AEGMMOORS	GAMES ROOM	AEHIINSVW	HAS IN VIEW
AEGMMOPRR	PROGRAMME	AEHIIPSTT	HEPATITIS
AEGMMNNORT	MAGNETRON	AEHIJNNNO	JOHANNINE
AEGMNNORW	WRONG NAME	AEHIKKLMS	MILK SHAKE
AEGMNNOST	MAGNETONS	AEHIKLOST	LIKE A SHOT
AEGMNORRW	WARMONGER	AEHIKMOTT	MAKE IT HOT
AEGMNORSV	MANGROVES	AEHIKMRSS	SHAKERISM
AEGMNORTU	AUGMENTOR	AEHIKNPRT	IN THE PARK
AEGMNPRSY	GERMAN SPY	AEHIKNSSS	SHAKINESS
AEGMNRSTU	ARGUMENTS	AEHIKNTTW	TAKEN WITH
AEGMOOPRS	POOR GAMES	AFHIKORSU	QUAKERISH
AEGMOOSUX	EXOGAMOUS	AEHILLPTY	PHILATELY
AEGMORSSY	GOSSAMERY	AEHILLTTY	LETHALITY
AEGMPRSSU	GRAMPUSES	AEHILLTWY	WEALTHILY
AEGNNOPST	PENTAGONS	AEHILMRRY	HARRY LIME
AEGNNPRTU	REPUGNANT	AEHILNNOT	ANTHELION
AEGNNSSTU	GAUNTNESS		ON THE NAIL
AEGNOORTW	GONE TO WAR	AEHILNOPR	PARHELION
AEGNOOSWY	GO ONES WAY	AEHILNORT	LION HEART
AEGNORSTT	STRONG TEA	AEHILNOST	HAILSTONE
AEGNORSTU	ARGENTOUS		SHOT A LINE
AEGNORUVW	WOVEN A RUG	AEHILNPRS	PLANISHER
AEGNOSTTU	TOTES A GUN	AEHILNPSS	PLANISHES
AEGNRRSST	STRANGERS	AEHILNQRU	HARLEQUIN
AEGNRSSTT	STRANGEST	AEHILNRTY	THIN-LAYER
AEGNRSTTU	GETS A TURN	AEHILORST	HORSETAIL
AEGOORSTW	GOES TO WAR	AEHILOSTT	HELIOSTAT
AEGOOSTTW	GO TO WASTE	AEHILOSTY	ISOHYETAL
AEGOPPSST	STOPPAGES	AEHILOSVY	HEAVY SOIL
AEGOPSSTT	GATEPOSTS	AEHILRSTV	THE RIVALS
AEGORRRTT	GARROTTER	AEHILRSTY	HAIRSTYLE
AEGORRSTT	GARROTTES	AEHILTTWY	LIT THE WAY
AEGORRSTU	SURROGATE	AEHIMMNRS	HAMMERS IN
AEGORRWWY	GROW WEARY	AEHIMMNSS	HAMMINESS
AEGORSSTU	STEGOSAUR	AEHIMNORS	HARMONIES
AEGOSSSTV	GAS STOVES		HARMONISE
AEGRSSTTU	GUEST STAR	AEHIMNORZ	HARMONIZE
AEHHHITTY	HIT THE HAY	AEHIMNOST	HAS NO TIME
AEHHHOSSU	HASH HOUSE	AEHIMNPSS	MISSHAPEN
AEHHIIRTW	WHITE HAIR	AEHIMNPST	PANTHEISM
AEHHILLLT	ILL HEALTH	AEHIMNRSY	HYMNARIES
AEHHILLTW	WHITEHALL	AEHIMNRTY	IN THE ARMY
AEHHILLTY	HEALTHILY	AEHIMNSST	IN THE MASS
AEHHINPST	THANESHIP	AEHIMNSSU	HUMANISES
AEHHINSTW	IN THE WASH	AEHIMNSUZ	HUMANIZES
AEHHIORRS	HORSEHAIR	AEHIMOSTT	SIT AT HOME
AEHHIPPSS	SHIPSHAPE	AEHIMPRSS	SAMPHIRES
AEHHISTWW	WHITEWASH	AEHIMPSSS	MISSHAPES
AEHHKOOSV	SHAVEHOOK	AEHIMPSST	SHIPMATES
AEHHLLNRY	HENRY HALL		SHIPS MATE
AEHHLLOST	HOT AS HELL		STEAMSHIP
AEHHLNTUY	UNHEALTHY	AEHIMQSSU	SQUEAMISH
AEHHLOSTV	SHOVEL HAT	AEHIMSTVY	HEAVY MIST
AEHHLPRSW	WELSH HARP	AEHINNRSS	IN HARNESS
AEHHMOPPY	HAPPY HOME	AEHINNTVY	IN THE NAVY
AEHHNOOPS	HAS NO HOPE	AEHINOPSV	VAIN HOPES
AEHHNORST	HARSH NOTE	AEHINORSS	HOARINESS
	HARSH TONE	AEHINORST	ANTI-HEROS
AEHHNRSSS	HARSHNESS		SENHORITA
AEHHOPPST	PHOSPHATE	AEHINPPRU	UNHAPPIER
AEHHOSSUW	WASHHOUSE	AEHINPSSS	APISHNESS
AEHHRRSST	THRASHERS	AEHINPSST	THESPIANS
AEHIIKLTT	I LIKE THAT!	AEHINPSSY	SISYPHEAN

AEHINPSTT	IN THE PAST	AEHLOPPSY	POLYPHASE
	PANTHEIST	AEHLOPRSY	HORSE PLAY
AEHINPTWW	WHITE PAWN		HORSEPLAY
AEHINRRSV	VARNISHER	AEHLOPSTT	HOT PLATES
AEHINRSST	TARNISHES	AEHLOPSUY	PLAYHOUSE
AEHINRSSV	VANISHERS	AEHLORRUY	EARLY HOUR
	VARNISHES	AEHLORSTT	LOST HEART
AEHINRSTW	IN THE WARS	AEHLORSTU	HOURS LATE
AEHINRTWW	WIN THE WAR		LATE HOURS
AEHINSSST	HASTINESS	AEHLORSUV	HAULS OVER
AEHINSSSW	WASHINESS		OVERHAULS
AEHINSSTT	THE SAINTS	AEHLORTWY	HOLY WATER
AEHINSTTW	WHITE ANTS	AEHLOSSTU	LASHES OUT
AEHINSTVW	HAVE TWINS	AEHLOSSVY	HEAVY LOSS
AEHIOPPRY	HYPEROPIA	AEHLOSTTT	TO THE LAST
AEHIOPRSS	APHORISES	AEHLPRSSS	SPLASHERS
AEHIOPRST	ATROPHIES	AEHLRRTTU	REAL TRUTH
AEHIOPRSZ	APHORIZES	AEHMMORTU	HAMMER OUT
AEHIORRTT	THROATIER	AEHMNNOST	HONEST MAN
AEHIORSTU	AUTHORISE	AEHMNNSSU	HUMANNESS
AEHIORTTV	HORTATIVE	AEHMNOOTT	NOT AT HOME
AEHIORTUZ	AUTHORIZE	AEHMNOPPY	HAPPY OMEN
AEHIOTTUV	HAVE IT OUT	AEHMNOSWW	WASHWOMEN
AEHIPPRSS	SAPPHIRES	AEHMNPSSY	SEA NYMPHS
AEHIPRRSS	SHARP RISE	AEHMNSTUU	HUMS A TUNE
AEHIPRRST	PHRATRIES	AEHMNTTUU	THE AUTUMN
AEHIPRSTT	THERAPIST	AEHMOOSST	SMOOTH SEA
AEHIRRSSY	AYRSHIRES	AEHMOPPRT	TOP-HAMPER
AEHIRRSTW	SWARTHIER	AEHMOPRST	METAPHORS
AEHIRSSTT	TRASHIEST	AEHMORRTW	EARTHWORM
AEHIRSSTX	SIX HEARTS	AEHMOSSTY	STAYS HOME
AEHIRSTTW	WHITE STAR	AEHMOSTTT	AT THE MOST
AEHJKNOST	JOHN KEATS	AEHMPRSTU	PURE MATHS
AEHJLLRRY	JERRY HALL	AEHMPSSSU	SMASHES UP
AEHJMNSTU	JAMES HUNT	AEHMSSTTY	AMETHYSTS
AEHJNNOWY	JOHN WAYNE	AEHMSTTTW	ST.MATTHEW
AEHKLNORU	LAKE HURON	AEHNOOPPS	OPEN A SHOP
AEHKLNSST	THANKLESS	AEHNOOPRR	HARPOONER
AEHKMNORT	ON THE MARK	AEHNOOPSX	SAXOPHONE
AEHKNORSW	NO HAWKERS	AEHNOOSST	HOT SEASON
AEHKNOSTU	SHAKEN OUT	AEHNOOSUW	OWN A HOUSE
AEHKOOPST	TOOK SHAPE	AEHNOPPSY	PAY PHONES
AEHKOORTT	TOOK HEART	AEHNOPRST	SHARP NOTE
AEHKOPRSU	PEAK HOURS	AEHNOPRWY	PHONEY WAR
AEHKORRTW	EARTHWORK	AEHNORRSU	RUN ASHORE
AEHKORVWY	HEAVY WORK	AEHNORSTT	NORTHEAST
AEHKOSSTU	SHAKES OUT	AEHNORSWY	REASON WHY
AEHKOSSTW	TWO SHAKES	AEHNORTWW	WON THE WAR
AEHLLLMOS	SMALL HOLE	AEHNOSVWY	HEAVY SNOW
AEHLLLPSY	PLAYS HELL	AEHNPRSSS	SHARPNESS
AEHLLMRTY	THERMALLY	AEHNPRSXY	PHARYNXES
AEHLLNOOP	ALLOPHONE	AEHNRSTTU	EARTHNUTS
AEHLLNOTW	ON THE WALL	AEHOOPPRS	POOR SHAPE
AEHLLOPTY	HELL TO PAY	AEHOOPRRY	PYORRHOEA
AEHLLOPVY	HEAVY POLL	AEHOOPSTT	OSTEOPATH
AEHLLORSW	SHALLOWER	AEHOORUWY	HOW ARE YOU?
AEHLLPSSU	PHALLUSES		WHO ARE YOU?
AEHLLPSSY	HAPLESSLY	AEHOOSSTU	OAST HOUSE
AEHLLPTUW	UP THE WALL	AEHOPSSTT	HEAT SPOTS
AEHLLSSTU	THALLUSES		POSTHASTE
AEHLMOOST	LOATHSOME	AEHOPSSTU	PHASES OUT
AEHLMOSSU	ALMS HOUSE	AEHOPSSTW	SWEATSHOP
	ALMSHOUSE	AEHOPSTTT	AT THE POST
AEHLMPPST	PAMPHLETS	AEHORRSSW	WAR HORSES
AEHLNNOPR	ALPENHORN	AEHORRSSW	SAWHORSES
AEHLNOPSU	HOUSE PLAN	AEHORSSTT	RHEOSTATS
AEHLNOPTT	PENTOTHAL	AEHORSSTU	SHARES OUT
AEHLNRSTU	LUTHERANS	AEHORSTTW	TWO HEARTS
AEHLNRTUY	UNEARTHLY	AEHORSTTW	SHORT WAVE
AEHLNSTUZ	HAZEL NUTS		SHORTWAVE
	HAZELNUTS	AEHORSTWY	SEAWORTHY

AEHOSSSTU	SOUTH SEAS	AEIIMPSSV	IMPASSIVE
AEHOSSTTU	SOUTHEAST	AEIINNNTV	ANTIVENIN
AEHOSSTUW	WASHES OUT	AEIINNPTT	INPATIENT
AEHOTTUWY	THE WAY OUT	AEIINNRSS	SIRENIANS
AEHPRSSUW	WASHERS-UP	AEIINNRTT	ITINERANT
AEHRRSTTW	THWARTERS	AEIINNSTU	ANNUITIES
AEHRSSTUU	THESAURUS		INSINUATE
AEIIILNTW	LIE IN WAIT	AEIINOPTX	EXPIATION
AEIIILRVZ	VIZIERIAL	AEIINORTT	ITERATION
AEIIILTVX	LIXIVIATE	AEIINOTTV	NOVITIATE
AEIIIMTTV	IMITATIVE	AEIINPRTV	IN PRIVATE
AEIIINSTT	INITIATES	AEIINPRWZ	WIN A PRIZE
AEIIJLNUV	JUVENILIA	AEIINRRTY	ITINERARY
AEIIKKTTW	KITTIWAKE	AEIINSSST	SANITISES
AEIIKLLNS	SNAILLIKE	AEIINSSTZ	SANITIZES
AEIIKLNST	SAINTLIKE	AEIINTTVW	NATIVE WIT
AEIIKNNTT	TAKEN IT IN	AEIIPRRTW	RAPIER WIT
AEIIKNRSS	KAISERINS	AEIIPRSTV	PRIVATISE
AEIIKNSTT	TAKES IT IN	AEIIPRSZZ	PIZZERIAS
AEIIKRRVW	RIVER KWAI	AEIIPRTTV	PARTITIVE
AEIILLMNN	MILLENNIA	AEIIPRTVV	PRIVATIVE
AEIILLMSY	MAY LILIES	AEIIPRTVZ	PRIVATIZE
AEIILLNTY	LINEALITY	AEIIPSSST	EPISTASIS
AEIILLRSV	LIVE RAILS	AEIIPSSTX	EPISTAXIS
AEIILLTTT	TITILLATE	AEIIPRSTT	STIPITATE
AEIILMNNR	MAINLINER	AEIIRRSTT	IRRITATES
AEIILMNNS	MAIN LINES	AEIIRSSST	SATIRISES
	MAINLINES	AEIIRSSTV	VARSITIES
AEIILMNOS	AI IMONIES	AEIIRSSTZ	SATIRIZES
AEIILMNSU	ALUMINISE	AEIISTTTV	TITIVATES
AEIILMNUZ	ALUMINIZE	AEIITTTTV	TITTIVATE
AEIILMPRS	IMPERIALS	AEIJLMRST	JIM SLATER
AEIILMRSS	SERIALISM	AEIJLOSSU	JALOUSIES
AEIILMSTT	MILITATES	AEIJMOPPR	PIPE MAJOR
AEIILNNOT	LINEATION	AEIJNORTU	JUNIORATE
AEIILNNRT	TRIENNIAL	AEIJNSTTU	JAUNTIEST
AEIILNNSY	ASININELY	AEIKKLLOO	LOOK ALIKE
AEIILNOPT	EPILATION		LOOK-ALIKE
AEIILNORV	LIVE ON AIR	AEIKKLNST	TAKEN SILK
AEIILNOTV	INVIOLATE	AEIKKLNSW	WEAK LINKS
AEIILNPRT	REPTILIAN	AEIKKLSST	TAKES SILK
AEIILNPST	PLATINISE	AEIKKMRST	KITE-MARKS
AEIILNPTV	PLAINTIVE	AEIKKNNSS	SNAKESKIN
AEIILNPTZ	PLATINIZE	AEIKKRSST	TAKE RISKS
AEIILNRRS	AIRLINERS	AEIKLLNPT	PLANTLIKE
AEIILNRRT	TRILINEAR	AEIKLLNSW	SINK A WELL
AEIILNRTY	IN REALITY	AEIKLLNTW	KNEW IT ALL
	LINEARITY	AEIKLLOOV	LOOK ALIVE
AEIILNSST	ALIENISTS	AEIKLLPST	TAKE PILLS
	LATINISES	AEIKLLTTU	LITTLE AUK
AEIILNSTW	WAISTLINE	AEIKLMNOW	WOMANLIKE
AEIILNSTZ	LATINIZES	AEIKLMPSS	MAKE SLIPS
AEIILNSWY	WIN EASILY	AEIKLNNSS	LANKINESS
AEIILORST	SOLITAIRE	AEIKLNOOT	TAKE ON OIL
AEIILOTVV	VIOLATIVE	AEIKLNORT	OIL TANKER
AEIILQSTU	QUALITIES	AEIKLNOST	LIKE AS NOT
AEIILRSST	SERIALIST	AEIKLNSSS	SEALSKINS
AEIILRSTU	RITUALISE	AEIKLNSTU	SAINT LUKE
AEIILRTUZ	RITUALIZE	AEIKLPRTT	TALK TRIPE
AEIILSSTV	VITALISES	AEIKLRSTY	STREAKILY
AEIILSSUV	VISUALISE	AEIKMMRST	MARKS TIME
AEIILSTVZ	VITALIZES	AEIKMNOST	NO MISTAKE
AEIILSUVZ	VISUALIZE	AEIKMPSTU	MAKES IT UP
AEIIMMSSX	MAXIMISES	AEIKMPTTY	TAKE MY TIP
AEIIMMSXZ	MAXIMIZES	AEIKMQRSU	QUAKERISM
AEIIMNNTU	IN A MINUTE	AEIKNNPRS	SPINNAKER
AEIIMNPTT	IMPATIENT	AEIKNOPSY	PIANO KEYS
AEIIMNRTU	MINIATURE	AEIKNOPTW	WEAK POINT
AEIIMNSSU	MAIN ISSUE	AEIKNOSTT	TIES A KNOT
AEIIMNSTT	INTIMATES	AEIKNPSST	SNAKE PITS
AEIIMPRRS	PRIMARIES	AEIKNPTTU	TAKEN IT UP

AEIKNPTTY	TAKEN PITY	AEILMORRZ	MORALIZER
AEIKNSSTW	SWANKIEST	AEILMORSS	MORALISES
AEIKOORST	TOOK A RISE	AEILMORST	SOLAR TIME
AEIKOOTVW	TOOK A VIEW	AEILMORSZ	MORALIZES
AEIKOQTUY	QUITE OKAY	AEILMORVW	MORAL VIEW
AEIKOTTTU	TAKE IT OUT	AEILMRSTT	REMITTALS
AEIKPPQSU	PIP-SQUEAK	AEILMRTTY	ALTIMETRY
AEIKPRSTY	STRIKE PAY	AEILMSSTU	SIMULATES
AEIKPSTTU	TAKES IT UP	AEILMSSVY	MASSIVELY
AEIKPSTTY	TAKES PITY	AEILMSTTU	MUTILATES
AEIKRSSST	ASTERISKS		STIMULATE
AEILLLLSW	ALL IS WELL		ULTIMATES
AEILLLRTY	LITERALLY	AEILMSTUU	MUTUALISE
AEILLMMRX	MAX MILLER	AEILMTTWZ	WALTZ TIME
AEILLMMST	SMALL-TIME	AEILNNOPR	NONPAREIL
AEILLMNNO	MEAN NO ILL	AEILNNOST	TENSIONAL
AEILLMNRU	MULLERIAN	AEILNNOSV	SLOVENIAN
AEILLMNRY	MILLENARY	AEILNNPSS	PLAINNESS
AEILLMNSY	SEMINALLY	AEILNNPSU	PENINSULA
AEILLMNTT	LITTLE MAN	AEILNNPTU	PINNULATE
AEILLMORY	ROYAL MILE	AEILNNPTY	PINNATELY
AEILLMPPR	PAPER MILL	AEILNNRTU	IN NEUTRAL
AEILLMSSY	AIMLESSLY	AEILNNTUV	UNIVALENT
AEILLMSSZ	SMALL SIZE	AEILNOOPS	POLONAISE
AEILLNOPT	POLLINATE	AEILNOORS	EROSIONAL
AEILLNORY	ROYAL LINE	AEILNOPSY	POLYNESIA
AEILLNPST	PANELLIST	AEILNOPTT	POTENTIAL
AEILLNPTT	PETILLANT	AEILNORSS	SENSORIAL
AEILLNRST	INSTALLER	AEILNORST	ORIENTALS
AEILLNRTU	TELLURIAN		RELATIONS
AEILLNRTY	RELIANTLY	AEILNORSV	VERSIONAL
AEILLNSTY	SALIENTLY	AEILNOSSS	SESSIONAL
AEILLOPPS	PAPILLOSE	AEILNOSVW	WAS IN LOVE
AEILLOPPT	POPLITEAL	AEILNOSWY	WON EASILY
AEILLORTV	VITAL ROLE	AEILNPRST	TRIPLANES
AEILLOSTV	VOLATILES	AEILNPRTX	NEXT APRIL
AEILLPRSU	PLURALISE	AEILNPRTY	INTERPLAY
AEILLPRUZ	PLURALIZE		PAINTERLY
AEILLPSST	PASTILLES		PARTY LINE
AEILLPSTU	PULSATILE	AEILNPSTT	TINPLATES
AEILLRRTY	ARTILLERY	AEILNPSTY	SAPIENTLY
AEILLRSST	TRAILLESS	AEILNPTTX	PLAINTEXT
AEILLRSTT	ILL-TREATS	AEILNPTTY	PATIENTLY
AEILLRSTW	STAIRWELL	AEILNRSTT	STERILANT
AEILLRTWY	WATER LILY	AEILNRSTV	INTERVALS
AEILLRVXY	VEXILLARY	AEILNRSUV	UNIVERSAL
AEILLSTTY	SAY LITTLE	AEILNRSVY	IN SLAVERY
AEILMMNST	MENTALISM	AEILNRTTV	TRIVALENT
AEILMMNSY	MANY MILES	AEILNSSST	SALTINESS
AEILMMORS	MEMORIALS		STAINLESS
AEILMMOST	IMMOLATES	AEILNSSTT	TAINTLESS
AEILMNNOS	LIONS MANE	AEILNSSTU	INSULATES
AEILMNNOT	MELATONIN	AEILNSSTW	SLANTWISE
AEILMNNSS	MANLINESS	AEILNSTUY	SINUATELY
AEILMNOOT	EMOTIONAL	AEILNSUUX	UNISEXUAL
AEILMNORS	NORMALISE	AEILNSVWY	WAVY LINES
AEILMNORT	LION TAMER	AEILOPRSS	POLARISES
AEILMNORZ	NORMALIZE	AEILOPRSZ	POLARIZES
AEILMNOSS	MELANOSIS	AEILOPSST	SPOLIATES
AEILMNOTU	EMULATION	AEILORSSS	SOLARISES
AEILMNPRT	IMPLANTER	AEILORSSV	VALORISES
AEILMNRST	TERMINALS	AEILORSSZ	SOLARIZES
	TRAMLINES	AEILORSTT	TOTALISER
AEILMNRSU	RUNS A MILE	AEILORSTY	ROYALTIES
	SEMILUNAR	AEILORSVW	SAVILE ROW
AEILMNRTU	MULE TRAIN	AEILORSVZ	VALORIZES
AEILMNRVY	LIVERYMAN	AEILORTTZ	TOTALIZER
AEILMNSST	SALT MINES	AEILOSSTT	TOTALISES
AEILMNSTT	MENTALIST	AEILOSTTZ	TOTALIZES
AEILMNTTY	MENTALITY	AEILPPPPS	APPLE PIPS
AEILMORRS	MORALISER	AEILPPRTU	PREPUTIAL

AEILPRRSS	REPRISALS	AEIMQRSSU	MARQUISES
AEILPRSST	PILASTERS	AEIMQSUUX	ESQUIMAUX
AEILPRSVY	PRIVY SEAL	AEIMRRRTU	TERRARIUM
AEILPRTVY	PRIVATELY	AEIMRRSTY	MARTYRISE
AEILPSSVY	PASSIVELY	AEIMRRTYZ	MARTYRIZE
AEILPSTTU	SIT UP LATE	AEIMRSSST	ASTERISMS
	STIPULATE	AEIMRSSTT	MISTREATS
AEILQRRUY	RELIQUARY	AEIMRSSUY	ARMY ISSUE
AEILQRSTU	QUARTILES	AEIMSSSTT	MISSTATES
AEILRRSTV	SALT RIVER	AEINNNOTW	NEWTONIAN
AEILRSSTT	LAST RITES	AEINNNPTU	NEPTUNIAN
AEILRTUUX	LUXURIATE	AEINNOPSX	EXPANSION
AEILSSSTV	VISTALESS	AEINNORST	ANOINTERS
AEILSTUXY	SEXUALITY		NESTORIAN
AEIMMNNOT	IN A MOMENT	AEINNORTV	VERNATION
AEIMMNNRS	MANNERISM	AEINNOSST	ESTONIANS
AEIMMNNTU	MINUTE MAN		SENSATION
	MINUTEMAN	AEINNOSTT	INTONATES
AEIMMNOPT	PANTOMIME	AEINNOSTV	INNOVATES
AEIMMNOST	AMMONITES	AEINNOSWY	IN ONES WAY
AEIMMNSTY	MANY TIMES	AEINNOTTT	ATTENTION
AEIMMRSST	SMARMIEST	AEINNPSST	INAPTNESS
AEIMMRSSU	SUMMARIES	AEINNPSXY	SIX A PENNY
	SUMMARISE	AEINNRSTT	TRANSIENT
AEIMMRSUZ	SUMMARIZE	AEINNRSTU	SATURNINE
AEIMNNNQU	MANNEQUIN	AEINNRSTY	TYRANNIES
AEIMNNNTX	NEXT MAN IN		TYRANNISE
AEIMNNOPU	PNEUMONIA	AEINNRTTX	NEXT TRAIN
AEIMNNOST	NOMINATES	AEINNRTYZ	TYRANNIZE
AEIMNNOTT	MENTATION	AEINNSSST	NASTINESS
AEIMNNRST	MANNERIST	AEINNSSTT	NATTINESS
AEIMNOOTZ	ZOO INMATE	AEINNSSTW	TAWNINESS
AEIMNOPRT	PROTAMINE	AEINOOPRT	OPERATION
AEIMNORSS	ROMANISES	AEINOPRRT	PRETORIAN
AEIMNORST	MARONITES	AEINOPRSS	ASPERSION
	STEAM IRON	AEINOPRST	PATRONISE
AEIMNORSW	WOMANISER	AEINOPRSV	PERVASION
AEIMNORSZ	ROMANIZES	AEINOPRTV	PAINT OVER
AEIMNORTV	NORMATIVE	AEINOPRTZ	PATRONIZE
AEIMNORWZ	WOMANIZER	AEINOPRWZ	WON A PRIZE
AEIMNOSSW	WOMANISES	AEINOPSSS	SOAPINESS
AEIMNOSWY	IN SOME WAY	AEINOQSTU	EQUATIONS
AEIMNOSWZ	WOMANIZES	AEINORRST	SERRATION
AEIMNOTTW	MATE IN TWO	AEINORRTV	OVERTRAIN
AEIMNOTUY	YOU NAME IT	AEINORRVV	RIVER AVON
AEIMNPRST	SPEARMINT	AEINORSST	ASSERTION
AEIMNRSST	INERT MASS		NOTARISES
	STREAMS IN		SENORITAS
AEIMNRSSU	SUMERIANS	AEINORSSU	ARSENIOUS
AEIMNRSTT	MARTINETS	AEINORSSV	AVERSIONS
AEIMNRSTU	ANTISERUM	AEINORSTT	STATIONER
	RUMINATES	AEINORSTZ	NOTARIZES
AEIMNRSTX	AXMINSTER	AEINORTTW	TEAR IN TWO
AEIMNRTTY	MATERNITY	AEINOSTVX	VEXATIONS
AEIMOPRRT	IMPERATOR	AEINPPSSS	SAPPINESS
AEIMOPRTX	PROXIMATE	AEINPPSST	SNAPPIEST
AEIMOPTTY	TIME TO PAY	AEINPRRST	TERRAPINS
AEIMORRSU	ARMOURIES		TRANSPIRE
AEIMORSST	AMORTISES	AEINPRTTY	PATERNITY
	ATOMISERS	AEINPSSST	PASTINESS
AEIMORSTT	ESTIMATOR	AEINPSTTY	ANTITYPES
AEIMORSTV	MOVIE STAR	AEINQRSTU	QUANTISER
AEIMORSTZ	AMORTIZES	AEINQRTUZ	QUANTIZER
	ATOMIZERS	AEINQSSTU	QUANTISES
AEIMOSTTV	MOTIVATES	AEINQSTTU	QUAINTEST
AEIMPPRSU	PAUPERISM	AEINQSTUZ	QUANTIZES
AEIMPRRTT	PART TIMER	AEINRRSST	RESTRAINS
AEIMPRSST	TEAM STRIP		STRAINERS
AEIMPRTUZ	TRAPEZIUM	AEINRRSTT	RESTRAINT
AEIMPSSTT	TIMES PAST		
AEIMPSTUW	TIME WAS UP		

AEINRSSTT	RESISTANT	AEKMNOPTW	KEPT WOMAN
	STRAITENS	AEKMNORTW	MEN AT WORK
	TARTINESS	AEKMNPTTY	EMPTY TANK
	TRAIN SETS	AEKMNRSSU	MAKES RUNS
AEINRSSTU	SUSTAINER	AEKMOPRST	MAKE SPORT
AEINRSTTT	IN TATTERS	AEKMOPSTU	MAKES UP TO
AEINRSTVY	ENTRY VISA	AEKMORSTW	WORKMATES
AEINSSSTT	TASTINESS	AEKMPRRSS	PRESSMARK
AEINSSTTV	TASTEVINS	AEKMPRSTU	RUMP STEAK
AEINSSTZZ	SNAZZIEST	AEKNNOPSU	SNEAK UP ON
AEIOORRST	ORATORIES	AEKNOOOTT	TOOK A NOTE
AEIOPRRSV	VAPORISER	AEKNOORST	SNAKEROOT
AEIOPRRVZ	VAPORIZER	AEKNOORTT	TAKEN ROOT
AEIOPRSSV	VAPORISES	AEKNORRTW	WORKER ANT
AEIOPRSVZ	VAPORIZES	AEKNOSSTU	SNEAKS OUT
AEIOPRTXY	EXPIATORY	AEKNOSTVW	TAKEN VOWS
AEIOPSSTU	AUTOPSIES		TWO KNAVES
AEIORRSTU	AIR ROUTES	AEKNPRRST	PRANKSTER
AEIORRTTT	TRATTORIE	AEKNRSSST	STARKNESS
AEIORSSSU	OSSUARIES	AEKNRSTTU	TAKE TURNS
AEIORSSTV	TRAVOISES	AEKOOOTTV	TOOK A VOTE
AEIORSSUV	SAVOURIES	AEKOOPSST	SO TO SPEAK
AEIOSTUVX	VEXATIOUS	AEKOORSTT	TAKES ROOT
AEIPPRSTU	PERIPATUS		TOOK A REST
AEIPRSTTU	TEARS IT UP	AEKOOSTTT	TOOK A TEST
AEIPRSTUV	RAVES IT UP	AEKOPPRRW	PAPER WORK
AEIPSSTTV	TIPSTAVES		PAPERWORK
AEIQRTTUZ	QUARTZITE	AEKOPRTYY	KARYOTYPE
AEIRRSSTT	STARRIEST	AEKOPSSTU	SPEAKS OUT
AEIRRTTTU	TRITURATE	AEKOPSSTW	WEAK SPOTS
AEIRSSTTU	TESSITURA	AEKORRTWX	EXTRA WORK
AEIRSTTUY	AUSTERITY	AEKORSTTU	STREAK OUT
AEISSSSTY	ESSAYISTS	AEKOSSTTU	STAKEOUTS
AEJKLOPSY	PLAY JOKES		STAKES OUT
AEJKMORSY	MAJOR KEYS	AEKOSSTVW	TAKES VOWS
AEJLLOSUY	JEALOUSLY	AEKQRSSUW	SQUAWKERS
AEJLMOORR	MAJOR ROLE	AELLLNPSW	PLANS WELL
AEJLNOPSU	PAUL JONES	AELLLPSWY	PLAYS WELL
AEJMOOPRT	MAJOR POET	AELLLPTUU	PULLULATE
AEJMPRTUW	WATER JUMP	AELLLSSWY	LAWLESSLY
AEJNNOPRU	JUAN PERON	AELLMNOTT	ALLOTMENT
AEJOPSTUX	JUXTAPOSE	AELLMNRUY	NUMERALLY
AEKKLRRSY	SKYLARKER	AELLMNSSS	SMALLNESS
AEKKMNNOW	MAKE KNOWN	AELLMOORW	LOW MORALE
AEKKMNOOS	KAKEMONOS	AELLMOPRY	PERMALLOY
AEKLLMRSW	MARKS WELL	AELLMORST	MARTELLOS
AEKLLNOTT	TAKEN TOLL	AELLMPRSW	WARM SPELL
AEKLLNSUW	SUNK A WELL	AELLMRRWY	MARRY WELL
AEKLLOOPS	LOOKS PALE	AELLNOOPT	OPEN TO ALL
AEKLLOOST	LOOSE TALK	AELLNOSTW	STONE WALL
AEKLLOSTT	TAKES TOLL		STONEWALL
AEKLLSSST	STALKLESS	AELLNQUUY	UNEQUALLY
AEKLMNOTY	TALK MONEY	AELLNRTUY	NEUTRALLY
AEKLMOORT	TOOLMAKER	AELLNRTVY	VENTRALLY
AEKLMOOSS	LOOK A MESS	AELLNSSUY	SENSUALLY
AEKLMORTW	METALWORK	AELLOOPRT	ALLOTROPE
AEKLMPTTY	EMPTY TALK	AELLOPRRT	PATROLLER
AEKLNNOWW	KNEW NO LAW	AELLOPRSW	WALLOPERS
AEKLNOPRW	PENAL WORK	AELLOPTUV	POLE VAULT
AEKLNOSSY	ANKYLOSES		POLE-VAULT
AEKLOORWY	LOOK WEARY	AELLORRST	ROSTELLAR
AEKLOPPRY	PLAY POKER	AELLORSTT	ALLOTTERS
AEKLOPRSW	ROPEWALKS	AELLORSWW	SWALLOWER
AEKLORSTV	TALKS OVER	AELLOSUYZ	ZEALOUSLY
AEKLORSTW	WORKS LATE	AELLQRSSU	SQUALLERS
AEKLORSVW	WALKOVERS	AELLRSSTY	ARTLESSLY
	WALKS OVER	AELLRSTTW	START WELL
AEKLPRRSS	SPARKLERS	AELLSSTTU	ST.AUSTELL
AEKMMOORS	MAKES ROOM	AELLTTUXY	TEXTUALLY
AEKMNOOQU	MOONQUAKE	AELMMOOPR	AMPLE ROOM
AEKMNOPSS	SPOKESMAN	AELMMORST	MAELSTROM

AELMMORSW	MEALWORMS	AELPRSSTT	SPLATTERS
AELMMOSUU	MAUSOLEUM	AELPRSTUY	LET US PRAY
AELMNNNTU	ANNULMENT	AELQRRTUY	QUARTERLY
AELMNNOOP	MONOPLANE	AELRSSTTU	LUSTRATES
AELMNNOST	NONMETALS	AEMMNNOTY	ANY MOMENT
AELMNOOPR	LAMPOONER	AEMMNORTY	MANOMETRY
AELMNOORT	MORAL TONE		MOMENTARY
AELMNOORY	MONOLAYER	AEMMOORST	ROOMMATES
AELMNOPRT	PATROLMEN	AEMMORSST	MARMOSETS
	TRAMPLE ON	AEMMRSTUU	ART MUSEUM
AELMNOPTU	PULMONATE	AEMMRSTYY	ASYMMETRY
AELMNORWW	LAWN MOWER	AEMMRSUUW	WAR MUSEUM
AELMNOSSW	WOMANLESS	AEMNNNORS	NO MANNERS
AELMNRRUY	LEN MURRAY	AEMNNOORS	ROMAN NOSE
AELMNRSTU	MENSTRUAL	AEMNNORST	ORNAMENTS
	ULSTERMAN	AEMNNOTTU	MOUNT ETNA
AELMNRTTU	TREMULANT		NET AMOUNT
AELMOORSS	SALE ROOMS	AEMNOORST	ANTEROOMS
	SALEROOMS	AEMNOORSW	WAS NO MORE
AELMOPRRS	PREMOLARS	AEMNOORSY	SAY NO MORE
AELMOPRSS	SLOPE ARMS	AEMNOPPRR	PROPER MAN
AELMOPSTT	PALMETTOS	AEMNOPRTY	ROMAN TYPE
AELMORRSW	ARMS LOWER	AEMNOPRUW	PURE WOMAN
AELMORSTU	EMULATORS	AEMNORRTU	NUMERATOR
AELMOSSTU	SOUL MATES	AEMNORRYY	ROMANY RYE
AELMOSSTV	LAST MOVES	AEMNORSTW	WANTS MORE
AELMOSTTU	MULATTOES	AEMNORSTY	MONASTERY
AELMPRRST	TRAMPLERS	AEMNOSSSV	MOSS EVANS
AELNNOOPS	NAPOLEONS	AEMNOSSSW	WOSSNAMES
AELNNOPTY	ON PENALTY	AEMNPRSTU	SMARTEN UP
AELNNPSTY	LAST PENNY	AEMNRSSST	SMARTNESS
AELNNSSUU	ANNULUSES	AEMNRSTTU	TRANSMUTE
AELNOOSTT	STOLONATE	AEMNSSSTY	NASTY MESS
AELNOPSTU	PUT ON SALE	AEMNSSTUW	MUTE SWANS
	STEAL UP ON	AEMOOPRRS	SPARE ROOM
AELNORSST	ART LESSON	AEMOORRTX	EXTRA ROOM
AELNORSTU	SOLUTREAN	AEMOORSTT	STATEROOM
AELNOTUVV	VOL-AU-VENT	AEMOOSSTU	AUTOSOMES
AELNPRSTU	TURNS PALE	AEMOOSTUY	SAME TO YOU
AELNPSTUY	PLAY TUNES	AEMOPRRTY	TEMPORARY
AELNRRUVY	VULNERARY	AEMOPRSTU	MOUSE TRAP
AELNRSSTT	SLATTERNS		MOUSETRAP
AELNRSTTU	RESULTANT	AEMOPRSTW	TAPEWORMS
AELNSSSUU	USUALNESS	AEMOPSTTY	ASYMPTOTE
AELNTTUWZ	WALTZ TUNE	AEMORRRSU	ARMOURERS
AELOOPRTW	WATER POLO	AEMORRSVW	SWARM OVER
AELOOPRUV	POOR VALUE	AEMORSSTY	STORMY SEA
AELOORRTT	TOLERATOR	AEMORSTTU	STREAM OUT
AELOORSTW	WATERLOOS	AEMORSTWY	TOM SAWYER
AELOOSTVW	TWO LOAVES	AEMOSTTZZ	MOZZETTAS
AELOPPRSS	PROLAPSES	AEMPRSSTY	MASTER SPY
AELOPPSTU	POPULATES	AEMPRSTYY	ARMY TYPES
	SOUP PLATE	AEMPRSUVY	SURVEY MAP
AELOPRRST	REAL SPORT	AEMQRRTUY	MARQUETRY
AELOPRRTW	LAW REPORT	AENNOORSS	NO REASONS
	PEARLWORT	AENNOOSWY	ON ONES WAY
AELOPRSSY	LOSER PAYS	AENNOPTWY	TWO A PENNY
AELOPRSTU	SPORULATE	AENNORSSW	NO ANSWERS
AELOPRSTY	POST EARLY	AENNPSSTU	UNAPTNESS
AELOPRSVY	OVERPLAYS	AENNSSTUY	SUN YAT SEN
AELOPRTTX	PETROL TAX	AENOOPSST	SOAPSTONE
AELOPSSSU	ESPOUSALS		TEASPOONS
AELOPSSTT	STOLE PAST	AENOOPTTW	NEW POTATO
AELOPSTTU	POSTULATE	AENOORRST	RESONATOR
AELOQSUUY	AQUEOUSLY	AENOORRTV	RENOVATOR
AELORRSTV	ART LOVERS	AENOPPTTU	PUT ON TAPE
AELORSSTW	SLOW RATES	AENOPRSST	TRANSPOSE
AELORSSTY	LOST YEARS	AENOPRSUV	SUPERNOVA
AELORSTTY	LAY TO REST	AENOPSSTV	SNAP VOTES
AELORTUVV	VAULT OVER	AENOPSSTY	STAYS OPEN
AELPRSSSW	PRESS LAWS	AENOQRRTU	NO QUARTER

AENORRSTW	NARROWEST	AFFIKLORY	FAIRY FOLK
AENORRTWW	WATERWORN	AFFILLMMS	FLIMFLAMS
AENORSSST	ASSENTORS	AFFILLORT	FALL FOR IT
AENORSSTU	ANOESTRUS	AFFILNRUY	RUFFIANLY
AENORSTTY	ATTORNEYS	AFFILORST	TRAILS OFF
AENORTTWW	WENT TO WAR	AFFIMMNNU	MUFFIN MAN
AENPRSSTT	TRANSEPTS	AFFIMORRT	FAR FROM IT
AENPSSSTW	WASPS NEST	AFFIOPRTT	FAT PROFIT
AENPSSSWW	SWAPS NEWS	AFFKOPRSS	SPARKS OFF
AENQRRSTU	QUARTERNS	AFFLLLOSU	FALLS FOUL
AENQSSSTU	SQUATNESS	AFFLLOORT	ROLL OF FAT
AENRRTTUX	TAX RETURN	AFFLLOOST	FOOTFALLS
AEOOPRRST	OPERATORS	AFFLOORST	FLAT ROOFS
AEOOPRSTT	POOR TASTE	AFFLOOTTU	FOOT FAULT
AEOORRTWY	YEAR OR TWO	AFFMNNRUY	FUNNY FARM
AEOORSTTT	TATTOOERS	AFFMOORST	STAFF ROOM
AEOORTTUU	AUTOROUTE	AFFORSSTT	STARTS OFF
AEOPPRRWY	PROPER WAY	AFGGGINOT	FAGGOTING
AEOPRRRTY	PORTRAYER	AFGGIILNN	FINAGLING
AEOPRRSTT	PROSTRATE	AFGGIINSY	GASIFYING
AEOPRRSTU	PTEROSAUR	AFGGIINTU	FATIGUING
AEOPRSSTT	PROSTATES	AFGGINRUY	ARGUFYING
AEOPRSSVW	SWAPS OVER	AFGGJOOOR	GO FOR A JOG
AEOPRSSWW	POWER SAWS	AFGGLOOOR	GO FOR GOAL
AEOPSSSTU	PASSES OUT	AFGHHILLT	HALF LIGHT
AEOPSSTTU	PUTS TO SEA		HALF-LIGHT
AEOQRRTTU	QUARTER TO	AFGHHILRT	RIGHT HALF
AEOQRSSTU	QUAESTORS		RIGHT-HALF
AEOQRSTUZ	QUARTZOSE	AFGHHIMST	SHAM FIGHT
AEORRRSST	ARRESTORS	AFGHIIMNS	FAMISHING
AEORRSSST	ASSERTORS	AFGHIINTW	WIN A FIGHT
	ASSORTERS	AFGHILLNT	NIGHTFALL
AEORSSSSS	ASSESSORS	AFGHILNSS	FLASHINGS
AEORSSTTT	TESTATORS	AFGHILNST	FANLIGHTS
AEORSSTTU	OUTSTARES	AFGHILPSS	FLAGSHIPS
	SOUR TASTE	AFGHIMNOT	FATHOMING
AEORSSTUU	TROUSSEAU	AFGHINNUV	HAVING FUN
AEORSSTVY	OVERSTAYS	AFGHINOTW	WON A FIGHT
AEORSTTUV	STARVE OUT	AFGHINRST	FARTHINGS
AEORSTTVW	STRAW VOTE	AFGHLNSSU	FLASH GUNS
AEORSTTVY	TRY TO SAVE		FLASHGUNS
AEPPRSSUY	PAPYRUSES	AFGHMOORT	HOMOGRAFT
AEPPRSTUU	SUPPURATE	AFGIIKNRY	FAIRY KING
AEPPSSTTW	SWEPT PAST	AFGIILLNN	FALLING IN
AEPQRRTUY	PARQUETRY	AFGIILLNY	FAILINGLY
AEPQRSSUU	SQUARES UP	AFGIILMNN	INFLAMING
AEPRSSSSU	SURPASSES	AFGIILNNT	INFLATING
AEPRSTTTY	SAT PRETTY	AFGIILNNU	UNFAILING
AEPRSTTYY	ARTY TYPES	AFGIILNOT	FOLIATING
AEQRSSTTU	SQUATTERS	AFGIILRTY	FRAGILITY
AFFFNOORT	NOT FAR OFF	AFGIIMNRY	RAMIFYING
AFFGGINUW	GUFFAWING	AFGIINRRY	FAIRY RING
AFFGHIIRT	FAIR FIGHT	AFGIINRTY	RATIFYING
	FIGHT FAIR	AFGIKMNNU	MAKING FUN
AFFGHLOSU	LAUGHS OFF	AFGIKMNOR	MAKING FOR
AFFGIIMNR	AFFIRMING	AFGIKNORS	ASKING FOR
AFFGIINRT	TARIFFING	AFGIKNRST	SKIN GRAFT
AFFGIIRST	SGRAFFITI	AFGILLMNY	FLAMINGLY
AFFGIKMNO	MAKING OFF	AFGILLNOW	FALLOWING
AFFGIKNOR	RAKING OFF	AFGILLNST	LAST FLING
AFFGIKNOT	TAKING OFF	AFGILLNTY	LYING FLAT
AFFGILNNS	SNAFFLING	AFGILLNUY	GAINFULLY
AFFGILNOY	LAYING OFF	AFGILMNOS	FLAMINGOS
AFFGINOPY	PAYING OFF	AFGILNNOU	UNION FLAG
AFFGIORST	SGRAFFITO	AFGILNNTU	FLAUNTING
AFFGLLOOP	GALLOP OFF	AFGILNNWY	FAWNINGLY
AFFHIIMRT	FIRM FAITH	AFGILNPRU	FLARING UP
AFFHILRST	FIRST HALF	AFGILNRTZ	FRITZ LANG
AFFHILRSY	RAFFISHLY	AFGILNRZZ	FRAZZLING
AFFHILSTU	FAITHFULS	AFGILNSST	SINGS FLAT
AFFIILNPT	PLAINTIFF	AFGILRTUY	FRUGALITY

AFGIMNPRU	FRAMING UP	AFILNORST	FLAT IRONS
AFGIMORTU	FUMIGATOR		FLATIRONS
AFGINNOPR	PROFANING	AFILOORSS	FOSSORIAL
AFGINNPRY	FRYING PAN	AFILSSTTU	FLAUTISTS
AFGINOPRY	PAYING FOR	AFIMNNOOR	MAN OF IRON
AFGINORRW	FARROWING	AFIMNNORT	INFORMANT
AFGINORUV	FAVOURING	AFIMNOORT	FORMATION
AFGINRSTU	FIGURANTS	AFINNOSTU	FOUNTAINS
AFGIORSTT	GOT A FIRST	AFINOOPRR	RAINPROOF
AFGLLOPSY	PLAYS GOLF	AFINOPRTY	PROFANITY
AFGLNNOOS	GONFALONS	AFINORUVW	WIN FAVOUR
AFGLNOORT	ORGAN LOFT	AFIOPRRSU	FOUR PAIRS
AFGLOOTTU	GO FLAT OUT	AFIOPRSSW	FAIR SWOPS
AFGNNNOOS	GONFANONS	AFIOPRSTY	PAYS FOR IT
AFGNNOOSU	SON OF A GUN	AFIORTTTT	TIT FOR TAT
AFGNOORRU	GO FOR A RUN	AFIPRRSTT	FIRST PART
AFGNOPRSW	FROGSPAWN	AFIRRTTTU	FRUIT TART
AFGORSTUW	TUGS OF WAR	AFJMOOPST	POTS OF JAM
	TUGS-OF-WAR	AFKLLMRSU	FULL MARKS
AFHHLRTTU	HALF TRUTH	AFKLLOOOO	LOOK A FOOL
	HALF-TRUTH	AFKLNOSTU	OUTFLANKS
AFHIILRSY	FAIRISHLY	AFKLPRSSY	SPARKS FLY
AFHIINNOS	IN FASHION	AFKOORRTW	WORK OF ART
AFHIKLOTT	OF THAT ILK	AFLLLPUYY	PLAYFULLY
AFHIKLPSS	HIP FLASKS	AFLLMOOPR	FLOOR LAMP
AFHIKNSST	FISH TANKS	AFLLMOOST	MOST OF ALL
AFHIIKNSTT	THINK FAST	AFLLNOOPR	FLOOR PLAN
AFHILLMSS	SMALL FISH	AFLLNORTY	FRONTALLY
AFHILLNNY	FANNY HILL	AFLLNOSSW	SNOWFALLS
AFHILNPST	HALF-PINTS	AFLLOQTUU	FULL QUOTA
AFHILOSTT	LOST FAITH	AFLLORSUW	FOUR WALLS
AFHIORSTU	HITS A FOUR	AFLMOPRST	PLATFORMS
AFHIORSTY	FORSYTHIA	AFLMORRUY	FORMULARY
AFHIORTTW	THROW A FIT	AFLMORSTW	FLATWORMS
AFHKLNOST	HALF-KNOTS	AFLMORSTY	FLY TO ARMS
AFHLLMRUY	HARMFULLY	AFLOOPSTY	SPLAYFOOT
AFHLLORST	FALL SHORT	AFLOORRUV	FOR VALOUR
	SHORTFALL	AFLOOSTTW	LAST OF TWO
AFHLMNOOS	HALF-MOONS	AFLOPRRSU	FLUORSPAR
AFHNNSTUY	FUNNY HATS	AFLORTUUY	YOUR FAULT
AFHOOPSTT	FOOTPATHS	AFLOSTUUY	FATUOUSLY
AFHOORRST	HOARFROST	AFMNORRST	TRANSFORM
AFIIILNOT	FILIATION	AFMNORRTW	WARM FRONT
AFIILMRRV	RIVAL FIRM	AFMOPRRTY	FOR MY PART
AFIILNNOT	INFLATION	AFNOOORTT	NOT TOO FAR
AFIILNOOT	FOLIATION	AFNOORUVW	WON FAVOUR
AFIILNOSS	FISSIONAL	AFNOOSSTT	NOT SO FAST
AFIILNOTW	FAIL TO WIN	AFNOPRSTW	FRONT PAWS
AFIILNSST	FINALISTS	AFNORSTTU	RUNS TO FAT
AFIIMNRRY	INFIRMARY	AFOOPSSST	SOFT-SOAPS
AFIINNOSS	SINFONIAS	AFOPRRSTU	FOUR PARTS
AFIINOSTX	FIXATIONS	AFORRSTTU	ASTROTURF
AFIIORTTW	WAIT FOR IT	AGGGILNNY	NAGGINGLY
AFIKLLMOT	MILK FLOAT	AGGGINNPU	GANGING UP
AFIKLNNRS	FRANKLINS	AGGHILSWY	WAGGISHLY
AFIKMNRRU	FRANK MUIR	AGGHINNNO	HANGING ON
AFIKORSST	ASKS FOR IT	AGGHINNPU	HANGING UP
AFILLLOST	FLOTILLAS	AGGHLOOPR	LOGOGRAPH
AFILLLUWY	WAILFULLY	AGGHNOSSW	GANG SHOWS
AFILLNOUX	FLUXIONAL	AGGIIIMNN	IMAGINING
AFILLNPUY	PAINFULLY	AGGIILLNP	PILLAGING
	PAY IN FULL	AGGIILMNN	MALIGNING
AFILLOOPR	APRIL FOOL	AGGIILNOS	GO SAILING
AFILLOPST	FILL A POST	AGGIIMNNR	MARGINING
AFILMMORS	FORMALISM	AGGIIMNRT	MIGRATING
AFILMNNTU	FULMINANT	AGGIIMNST	GIGANTISM
AFILMORST	FORMALIST	AGGIINNNO	GAINING ON
AFILMORTY	FORMALITY	AGGIINNOS	AGONISING
AFILMORWY	FAMILY ROW	AGGIINNOZ	AGONIZING
AFILMRSST	FILM STARS	AGGIINNSS	ASSIGNING
AFILNOOTT	FLOTATION	AGGIINVWY	GIVING WAY

337

AGGIKNOST	GO SKATING	**AGHIMNRST**	HAMSTRING
AGGILLLNY	GALLINGLY	**AGHIMNRTW**	WARM NIGHT
AGGILLNOP	GALLOPING	**AGHIMORST**	HISTOGRAM
AGGILLNRY	GLARINGLY	**AGHINNOPR**	ORPHANING
AGGILMNOS	GLOAMINGS	**AGHINNOPT**	PHONATING
AGGILNNOS	GANGLIONS	**AGHINNOTV**	HAVING NOT
AGGILNNPS	SPANGLING	**AGHINORRW**	HARROWING
AGGILNNRW	WRANGLING	**AGHINOSSW**	SHOW A SIGN
AGGILNOOW	GOING AWOL	**AGHINOTUV**	HAVING OUT
AGGILNPPR	GRAPPLING	**AGHINPPSU**	SHAPING UP
AGGIMMNRU	RUMMAGING	**AGHINPRSS**	PHRASINGS
AGGIMNPUZ	GAZUMPING	**AGHINPRSY**	PHRYGIANS
AGGINNOOR	GORGONIAN	**AGHINPSUW**	WASHING UP
AGGINNOSS	SING A SONG		WASHING-UP
AGGINOPRT	PORTAGING	**AGHINQSSU**	SQUASHING
AGGINORRS	GROSGRAIN	**AGHINRTTW**	THWARTING
AGGINORTU	OUTRAGING	**AGHINSSTW**	SAW THINGS
AGGINPSTU	UPSTAGING	**AGHIPRRST**	TRIGRAPHS
AGGLMOORS	LOGOGRAMS	**AGHIRSSTT**	STRAIGHTS
AGGLNORSS	LONG GRASS	**AGHIRSTUW**	WITH SUGAR
AGGMOORRT	MORTGAGOR	**AGHLLOOPY**	HAPLOLOGY
AGGNNOSSU	SUNG A SONG	**AGHLMNOPU**	PLOUGHMAN
AGGNORRWY	GROW ANGRY	**AGHLMOOPR**	LAGOMORPH
AGHHIILRT	LIGHT HAIR	**AGHLMOORS**	HOLOGRAMS
AGHHIILST	HIGHTAILS	**AGHLMOOTU**	GOALMOUTH
AGHHIISTW	WAIST HIGH	**AGHLNOOPS**	HOPS ALONG
	WAIST-HIGH	**AGHLNOOTY**	ANTHOLOGY
AGHHIKMRS	HIGH MARKS	**AGHLNOPRU**	ROUGH PLAN
AGHHIKNRS	RANKS HIGH	**AGHLNOSTU**	ONSLAUGHT
AGHHIKNTW	NIGHT HAWK	**AGHLOOPTY**	PATHOLOGY
	NIGHTHAWK	**AGHLOPPRY**	POLYGRAPH
AGHHILLSW	HIGH WALLS	**AGHLOPPYY**	POLYPHAGY
AGHHILPSY	PLAYS HIGH	**AGHLOPRUY**	PLAY ROUGH
AGHHILTUY	HAUGHTILY		ROUGH PLAY
AGHHINRST	THRASHING	**AGHLOPRXY**	XYLOGRAPH
AGHHLOOPR	HOLOGRAPH	**AGHLORSSU**	HOURGLASS
AGHHMOOPR	HOMOGRAPH	**AGHMNNRUY**	HUNGRY MAN
AGHIILNNU	HAULING IN	**AGHMNOOPR**	MONOGRAPH
AGHIILNRT	LIGHT RAIN		PHONOGRAM
AGHIILNSV	LAVISHING	**AGHMNRSTU**	HAMSTRUNG
AGHIIMNNT	MAIN THING	**AGHNNOOST**	HANGS ON TO
AGHIINNSV	VANISHING	**AGHNOPTUU**	PUTONGHUA
AGHIINRSV	RAVISHING	**AGHNSSTTU**	STAG HUNTS
AGHIIPRRS	HAIRGRIPS	**AGHOOOSTW**	GO TO A SHOW
AGHIJNRST	NIGHTJARS	**AGHOOPRRY**	OROGRAPHY
AGHIKLNTT	LIGHT TANK	**AGIIIMNPR**	IMPAIRING
AGHIKLSWY	GAWKISHLY	**AGIIIMNTT**	IMITATING
AGHIKNPSU	SHAKING UP	**AGIIINNSS**	INSIGNIAS
AGHIKNRRY	KING HARRY	**AGIIINNTW**	IN WAITING
AGHILLMPT	LIGHT LAMP	**AGIIINRRS**	RISING AIR
AGHILLNOO	HALLOOING	**AGIIINSTV**	VAGINITIS
AGHILLNOW	HALLOWING	**AGIIINTTV**	VITIATING
AGHILLNST	ALL THINGS	**AGIIKLLNT**	TAKING ILL
AGHILLNTY	HALTINGLY	**AGIIKLMNR**	GRIMALKIN
AGHILLORY	HOLY GRAIL	**AGIIKLNNW**	WALKING IN
AGHILLRSU	HULA GIRLS	**AGIILLMMR**	MILLIGRAM
AGHILLSTT	LAST LIGHT	**AGIILLNNW**	WALLING IN
AGHILMORT	ALGORITHM	**AGIILLNPR**	PILLARING
	LOGARITHM	**AGIILLNRV**	RIVALLING
AGHILNOOS	HOOLIGANS	**AGIILNNWZ**	ZWINGLIAN
AGHILNORS	LONG HAIRS	**AGIILNORS**	ORIGINALS
	LONGHAIRS	**AGIILNORT**	TAILORING
AGHILNORT	GRANOLITH	**AGIILNOST**	INTAGLIOS
AGHILNPSS	SPLASHING		ISOLATING
AGHILNPSU	LASHING UP	**AGIILNOSX**	GLOXINIAS
AGHILNPTY	PLAYTHING	**AGIILNOTV**	VIOLATING
AGHILNSTT	LAST NIGHT	**AGIILNOVY**	IAN OGILVY
	LAST THING	**AGIILNQTU**	LIQUATING
AGHILNTUY	NAUGHTILY	**AGIILNRSV**	VIRGINALS
AGHILPPRY	HAPPY GIRL	**AGIILNSSS**	ISINGLASS
AGHIMMNTY	MIGHTY MAN	**AGIIMMNNS**	MISNAMING

AGIIMMNRT	IMMIGRANT	AGILNNRTY	RANTINGLY
AGIIMNORT	MIGRATION	AGILNNRWY	WARNINGLY
AGIIMNOST	ATOMISING	AGILNNWYY	YAWNINGLY
AGIIMNOTZ	ATOMIZING	AGILNORVY	VAIN GLORY
AGIIMNPRT	IMPARTING		VAINGLORY
AGIINNNOT	ANOINTING	AGILNOSTV	SOLVATING
AGIINNNTW	WANTING IN	AGILNOSTW	WAGON-LITS
AGIINNORS	SIGNORINA	AGILNOTUV	OVULATING
AGIINNORT	RATIONING	AGILNOTUW	OUTLAWING
AGIINNOTW	NO WAITING	AGILNOTUY	LAYING OUT
AGIINNPRS	SPRAINING	AGILNPPUY	PLAYING UP
AGIINNPSS	IN PASSING	AGILNPRRU	LARRUPING
AGIINNPST	PAINTINGS	AGILNPRSW	SPRAWLING
AGIINNRST	STRAINING	AGILNPRSY	RASPINGLY
AGIINNRTT	NITRATING		SPARINGLY
AGIINNRTU	URINATING	AGILNPRTT	PRATTLING
AGIINNSTT	INSTATING	AGILNPRTY	PRATINGLY
AGIINPPRS	APPRISING	AGILNPSTU	PULSATING
AGIINPRST	TRAIPSING	AGILNRSST	STARLINGS
AGIINPTUW	WAITING UP	AGILNRSSU	SINGULARS
AGIINRTTT	TITRATING	AGILNRSTT	STARTLING
AGIINSSST	ASSISTING	AGILNRVYY	VARYINGLY
AGIINSTTU	SITUATING	AGILNSSUY	UGLY AS SIN
AGIIORRRT	IRRIGATOR	AGILNSTWY	WASTINGLY
AGIIRSTTU	GUITARIST	AGILOOPST	APOLOGIST
AGIJLNRRY	JARRINGLY	AGILOPRUY	UROPYGIAL
AGIJMMNNO	JAMMING ON	AGILRRTUY	GARRULITY
AGIJMNPTU	JUMPING AT	AGILRTUVY	VULGARITY
AGIKLMORS	KILOGRAMS	AGIMMNSTU	SUMMATING
AGIKLMOST	GOATS MILK	AGIMMNSUX	MAXIM GUNS
AGIKLNNOS	ALGONKINS	AGIMMNSUY	GYMNASIUM
AGIKLNNOW	WALKING ON	AGIMNNNNU	UNMANNING
AGIKLNOOT	LOOKING AT	AGIMNNOOR	MAROONING
AGIKLNOTT	TALKING-TO	AGIMNNORS	RANSOMING
AGIKLNPRS	SPARKLING	AGIMNNOTU	AMOUNTING
AGIKLNPUW	WALKING UP	AGIMNOOSV	VAMOOSING
AGIKMNNSU	UNMASKING	AGIMNORRT	MORTARING
AGIKMNOTU	MAKING OUT	AGIMNORSS	ORGANISMS
AGIKMNRSS	KINGS ARMS	AGIMNORSU	IGNORAMUS
AGIKMRSST	GRIM TASKS	AGIMNPRUW	WARMING UP
AGIKNNOPR	NO PARKING	AGIMNRRTY	MARTYRING
AGIKNNPSW	KINGS PAWN	AGIMORRTY	MIGRATORY
AGIKNOSST	GOATSKINS	AGINNNORW	NO WARNING
AGIKNOSTU	ASKING OUT	AGINNNRTU	RUNNING AT
AGIKNOTTU	TAKING OUT	AGINNOORT	RATOONING
AGIKNQSUW	SQUAWKING	AGINNOPRT	PRONATING
AGIKOOPRT	TOOK A GRIP	AGINNOPSS	PASSING ON
AGILLLMRS	SMALL GIRL	AGINNORRW	NARROWING
AGILLLNUY	LINGUALLY	AGINNORST	ON A STRING
AGILLLRST	TALL GIRLS	AGINNPRSU	UNSPARING
AGILLMNSS	SING SMALL	AGINNRTTU	TRUANTING
AGILLNNNU	ANNULLING	AGINNRUVY	UNVARYING
AGILLNOPW	WALLOPING	AGINOOPSS	POISON GAS
AGILLNORT	LONG TRIAL	AGINOORRT	RARIN' TO GO
AGILLNOTT	ALLOTTING	AGINOOTTT	TATTOOING
AGILLNOWW	WALLOWING	AGINOPPRV	APPROVING
AGILLNPUW	WALLING UP	AGINOPRRT	PARROTING
AGILLNQSU	SQUALLING		PRORATING
AGILLNSTY	LASTINGLY	AGINOPRTU	PURGATION
AGILLNTUU	ULULATING	AGINOPRUV	VAPOURING
AGILLOPST	GALLIPOTS	AGINOPTUY	PAYING OUT
AGILMNNOO	MONGOLIAN	AGINORRSS	GARRISONS
AGILMNPRT	TRAMPLING	AGINORSSS	ASSIGNORS
AGILMNSUY	AMUSINGLY	AGINORSST	ASSORTING
AGILMNTUY	GUILTY MAN	AGINORSTY	SIGNATORY
AGILMRRST	SMART GIRL		TORY GAINS
AGILMRSUV	VULGARISM	AGINORSUV	SAVOURING
AGILNNOPS	PANGOLINS	AGINOSTTU	GUSTATION
	PLAINSONG	AGINPPRST	STRAPPING
AGILNNOPY	PLAYING ON		TRAPPINGS
AGILNNOQU	ALGONQUIN	AGINPPRSW	WRAPPINGS

AGINPPSSU	PASSING UP	AHIILLTWW	WITH A WILL
AGINPRSTU	PASTURING	AHIILORSU	HILARIOUS
AGINPRTTU	TARTING UP	AHIILOSST	HALITOSIS
AGINPSSTW	WASP STING		HOIST SAIL
AGINPSTUY	STAYING UP	AHIIMMRST	MITHRAISM
AGINQRRUY	QUARRYING	AHIIMNOST	HIMATIONS
AGINQSTTU	SQUATTING	AHIIMRSTT	MITHRAIST
AGINRSSTY	STINGRAYS	AHIINNPSS	IN SPANISH
AGIOORSTU	AUTOGIROS	AHIINORST	HISTORIAN
AGIOPRRSY	SPIROGYRA	AHIINSTWY	THIS WAY IN
AGJKNORRU	KURRAJONG	AHIIRRSTT	ARTHRITIS
AGKLLNOSW	LONG WALKS	AHIISSTTW	THIS WAS IT
AGKLNOORY	ANGRY LOOK	AHIJMNNNO	JOHN INMAN
AGKLPPRSU	SPARK PLUG	AHIJNNOST	IAN ST. JOHN
AGKNORSST	KNOTGRASS		SAINT JOHN
AGLLLNOOR	ROLL ALONG	AHIKKNRSS	SHARKSKIN
AGLLNOOPY	POLYGONAL	AHIKLMSWY	MAWKISHLY
AGLLNOSST	LASTS LONG	AHIKLNSVY	KNAVISHLY
AGLMOORSU	GLAMOROUS	AHIKNOOTT	TOOK A HINT
AGLMPRSUU	LUMP SUGAR	AHIKNOTWW	I KNOW WHAT
	SUGAR LUMP	AHILLMMSU	MULLAHISM
	SUGAR PLUM	AHILLOPSV	SLAVOPHIL
	SUGARPLUM	AHILLOSSW	SALLOWISH
AGLNNOORT	TORN ALONG	AHILLRTTY	THIRTY ALL
AGLNNOPST	LONG PANTS	AHILLSSVY	SLAVISHLY
AGLNNORSU	RUNS ALONG	AHILMNNSY	MANNISHLY
AGLNOPUUY	PAUL YOUNG	AHILMNNUY	INHUMANLY
AGLOOPRUU	LOUP-GAROU	AHILMPRTU	TRIUMPHAL
AGLOOPSST	GOALPOSTS	AHILNOORZ	HORIZONAL
AGLOORSTY	ASTROLOGY	AHILNOPTY	POLYANTHI
AGLOOTTUY	TAUTOLOGY	AHILNPPUY	UNHAPPILY
AGLOPPRUY	PLAY GROUP	AHILOOPST	ISOPHOTAL
	PLAYGROUP	AHILOORST	LOTHARIOS
AGLOPRSST	GRASS PLOT	AHILOPSST	HOSPITALS
AGLOPRSTY	PAST GLORY	AHILORTTY	THROATILY
AGLORRSUU	GARRULOUS	AHILPSSWY	WASPISHLY
AGLORSSTW	GLASSWORT	AHILPSTWY	PLAY WHIST
AGMMNOORS	MONOGRAMS		PLAYS WITH
	NOMOGRAMS	AHILQSSUY	SQUASHILY
AGMMOSTUU	GUMMATOUS	AHILRSTTY	TARTISHLY
AGMNNORST	STRONG MAN	AHIMMNORU	HARMONIUM
AGMNNORRY	ROMAN ORGY	AHIMNNORY	IN HARMONY
AGMNORRST	STRONG ARM	AHIMNORST	HARMONIST
	STRONGARM	AHIMOPRSS	APHORISMS
AGMNORRWW	GROWN WARM	AHIMOPSUX	AMPHIOXUS
AGMNORSST	ANGSTROMS	AHIMORTWY	WORTHY AIM
AGMNSSTUY	NYSTAGMUS	AHINNOOPT	PHONATION
AGMORRSWW	GROWS WARM	AHINNOPST	ANTIPHONS
AGNOOPRST	ORGAN STOP	AHINNOPTY	ANTIPHONY
AGNOPRSST	PART-SONGS	AHINPRSST	TRANSHIPS
AGNORSTWX	WAX STRONG		TRANSSHIP
AGNOSTUYY	STAY YOUNG	AHIOPPRRY	PORPHYRIA
AGNRRSTUY	STRANGURY	AHIOPRSST	APHORISTS
AGOORSTTT	START TO GO	AHIOPSTXY	HYPOTAXIS
AGOORSTUY	AUTOGYROS	AHIORRTWY	AIRWORTHY
AGOPRRTUY	PURGATORY	AHIORTTUY	AUTHORITY
AGORSTTUY	GUSTATORY	AHIOSSUWY	AS YOU WISH
AHHIIRRST	HAIR SHIRT	AHIPPRTWY	PARTY WHIP
AHHIKLSWY	HAWKISHLY	AHIPPSSST	SAPPHISTS
AHHIMSSST	SMASH HITS	AHIPRSTTW	PARTS WITH
AHHIORRST	SHORT HAIR	AHIPSTUWY	THIS WAY UP
AHHKMOSTW	HAWKMOTHS	AHIRSTTTW	START WITH
AHHLOOPSU	HULA HOOPS	AHKLOOPPY	LOOK HAPPY
AHHMOPRTU	MOUTH HARP	AHKLOOPRS	LOOK SHARP
AHHMPRRSU	HARRUMPHS	AHKLOPSST	TALKS SHOP
AHHNORRST	HARTSHORN	AHKLORSTW	SHORT WALK
AHHNORSTW	HAWTHORNS	AHKLOSSTW	TALK SHOWS
AHHOPPRUY	HAPPY HOUR	AHKNOSTUY	THANK-YOUS
AHHORSTTU	THRASH OUT	AHKOOOSTT	TOOK A SHOT
AHIIKMRSS	KASHMIRIS	AHLLLOSWY	SHALLOWLY
AHIILLMTT	TALLITHIM	AHLLMOOPR	ALLOMORPH

AHLMMOPSY	LYMPHOMAS	**AIILSSTTV**	VITALISTS
AHLMNNOUY	ONLY HUMAN	**AIIMMPRSV**	VAMPIRISM
AHLMNOSTT	LAST MONTH	**AIIMNNTUY**	UNANIMITY
AHLMNOSUU	HUMAN SOUL	**AIIMNOPSS**	IMPASSION
AHLMOPSTY	POLYMATHS	**AIIMNOSTY**	ANIMOSITY
AHLMOPTYY	POLYMATHY	**AIIMNPSTT**	TIMPANIST
AHLOORTTW	WORTH A LOT	**AIIMRSTTW**	TRIM WAIST
AHLOPSSTY	PLAYS HOST	**AIIMRSTUU**	MAURITIUS
AHLORSSTU	LAST HOURS	**AIIMRSUVV**	VIVARIUMS
AHMOOPRSU	AMORPHOUS	**AIINNNOPT**	PINNATION
AHMOORSSW	WASHROOMS	**AIINNOPTW**	WIN A POINT
AHMOPRTTU	MOUTHPART	**AIINNORTT**	NITRATION
AHNOOPTTU	PUT ON OATH	**AIINNORTU**	RUINATION
AHNOPPSSW	PAWNSHOPS		URINATION
AHNOPRSST	SHORT SPAN	**AIINNOSSV**	INVASIONS
AHNOPSSST	SNAPSHOTS	**AIINNOTTX**	ANTITOXIN
AHNORRSTT	NORTH STAR	**AIINNQSTU**	QUINTAINS
AHOOOPTTT	HOT POTATO	**AIINNRSSU**	IN RUSSIAN
AHOOPRRTX	PROTHORAX	**AIINNRSTT**	IN TRANSIT
AHOOPRTTU	AUTOTROPH	**AIINNRTVY**	TRY IN VAIN
AHOOPRTUX	AUXOTROPH	**AIINOOQRU**	IROQUOIAN
AHOOPSTTT	PHOTOSTAT	**AIINOPRTT**	PARTITION
AHOOSSSTY	SOOTHSAYS	**AIINOPRTV**	PRIVATION
AHOPSSTUW	SOUTHPAWS	**AIINORSTT**	STRIATION
AHORRTTWY	WORTH A TRY	**AIINORSVY**	VISIONARY
AHORSSTTY	SHORT STAY	**AIINORTTT**	ATTRITION
AIIILLNTY	INITIALLY		TITRATION
AIIILMNST	LAMINITIS	**AIINOSTTU**	SITUATION
AIIIMNOTT	IMITATION	**AIINQTTUY**	ANTIQUITY
AIIINNNOT	INANITION	**AIINRRSTT**	IRRITANTS
AIIINNSTY	ASININITY	**AIINSSTTV**	VISITANTS
AIIINORTT	INITIATOR	**AIIOPRRTY**	APRIORITY
AIIJLNPTU	PUT IN JAIL	**AIIOPRSSS**	PSORIASIS
AIIJLOTVY	JOVIALITY	**AIIOPRSTT**	PAROTITIS
AIIKLLMOT	AIM TO KILL	**AIIOPRTVY**	OVIPARITY
AIIKLLMPS	MILK PAILS	**AIIORSTTV**	VITIATORS
AIIKLNRRS	LARRIKINS	**AIIPRRSST**	AIRSTRIPS
AIIKMNNNS	MANNIKINS	**AIIPRTTUY**	PITUITARY
AIIKNNSST	INK STAINS	**AIIPSSTVY**	PASSIVITY
AIIKNPSTW	TIPS A WINK	**AIIRSSSTT**	SATIRISTS
AIILLLNST	LAIN STILL		SITARISTS
AIILLMMNY	MINIMALLY	**AIJKKNOSU**	KINKAJOUS
AIILLMRSY	SIMILARLY	**AIJLRRTUY**	TRIAL JURY
AIILLNOST	LIONS TAIL	**AIJMORSTU**	MAJOR SUIT
AIILLRTVY	TRIVIALLY	**AIJMPSTTU**	JUMPS AT IT
AIILMMNUU	ALUMINIUM	**AIJNOPPSY**	POPINJAYS
AIILMNORT	TRINOMIAL	**AIKKOORST**	TOOK A RISK
AIILMNSST	LATINISMS	**AIKLLLSTY**	SILLY TALK
	STALINISM	**AIKLLLSWY**	SILLY WALK
AIILMPRRY	PRIMARILY	**AIKLLNOTW**	KNOW IT ALL
AIILMPRTY	PRIMALITY		KNOW-IT-ALL
AIILMRSST	MISTRIALS	**AIKLLOOPT**	TOOK A PILL
AIILMRSTU	RITUALISM	**AIKLNOSSY**	ANKYLOSIS
AIILMSSTW	SLIM WAIST	**AIKLNOSTW**	WALKS INTO
AIILNNPST	IN A SPLINT	**AIKLOSTTW**	KILOWATTS
AIILNOOST	ISOLATION	**AIKLOTTTU**	TALK IT OUT
AIILNOOTV	VIOLATION	**AIKMNNPRSW**	MINK WRAPS
AIILNOPST	OIL PAINTS	**AIKMOOSST**	TOOK AMISS
AIILNOPSV	PAVILIONS	**AIKMPRSTZ**	MARK SPITZ
AIILNOQTU	LIQUATION	**AIKNOOOPS**	POISON OAK
AIILNOSTT	SILTATION	**AIKNOOPST**	TOOK PAINS
AIILNOTTU	TUITIONAL	**AIKNOPRTW**	PAINTWORK
AIILNPRST	TRIAL SPIN	**AIKNPSTTU**	SINK A PUTT
AIILNPSST	ALPINISTS	**AIKNRRSSU**	RUNS A RISK
AIILNRSST	SINISTRAL	**AIKOOPRTT**	TOOK A TRIP
AIILNRTUY	UNITARILY	**AILLLOSST**	ALL IS LOST
AIILNSSTT	STALINIST	**AILLMMORY**	IMMORALLY
AIILPRSST	SPRITSAIL	**AILLMNNOY**	NOMINALLY
AIILPRSTU	SPIRITUAL	**AILLMOPTY**	OPTIMALLY
AIILRSSTT	TRIALISTS	**AILLMPRSU**	PLURALISM
AIILRSTTU	RITUALIST	**AILLMSUUV**	ALLUVIUMS

AILLNOPPS	PAPILLONS	AILOOPTTT	TOP TO TAIL
AILLNORST	TONSILLAR	AILOOPTTU	AUTOPILOT
AILLNORSU	LUNISOLAR	AILOORSTV	VIOLATORS
AILLNOSST	STALLIONS	AILOORSUV	VARIOLOUS
AILLNOSSU	ALLUSIONS	AILORSSTY	ROYALISTS
AILLNOTUU	ULULATION	AILORSTTU	TUTORIALS
AILLNRSUY	INSULARLY	AILORSUVY	VARIOUSLY
AILLOPSTT	TOPS IT ALL	AILOSSTUY	AUTOLYSIS
AILLOPTVY	PIVOTALLY	AILPPRSTU	STAR PUPIL
AILLOQRUW	LIQUOR LAW	AILPPSSST	SLIPS PAST
AILLORSTT	LITTORALS	AILPSSSSW	SWISS ALPS
AILLORTYZ	LIZ TAYLOR	AILPSSTUY	PLAYSUITS
AILLOSSTY	LOYALISTS	AILRSSTTU	ALTRUISTS
AILLPPRUY	PUPILLARY	AILRSSUVV	SURVIVALS
AILLPRSTU	PLURALIST	AIMMNORTY	MATRIMONY
AILLPRTUY	PLURALITY	AIMMNOSTU	SUMMATION
AILLPSSTT	PIT STALLS	AIMMPRSUU	MARSUPIUM
AILLRTTUY	TITULARLY	AIMNNOORT	NOMINATOR
AILLRTUVY	VIRTUALLY	AIMNNOPST	POINTSMAN
AILLSSTTY	STAY STILL	AIMNNOSTU	MOUNTAINS
AILMMNOOS	MONOMIALS	AIMNNOSUU	UNANIMOUS
AILMMOORT	IMMOLATOR	AIMNNOTYY	ANONYMITY
AILMMORST	IMMORTALS	AIMNNRSTU	RUMINANTS
AILMMRSUY	SUMMARILY	AIMNNSTUY	NUTS IN MAY
AILMMSTUU	MUTUALISM	AIMNOPRRT	MINOR PART
AILMMTTUU	ULTIMATUM	AIMNOPRSY	PARSIMONY
AILMNOOPS	PALOMINOS	AIMNOPRTT	IMPORTANT
AILMNOORS	MONORAILS	AIMNOPRTY	PATRIMONY
AILMNOPST	PLATONISM	AIMNORRSU	URSA MINOR
AILMNOPSU	PAUL SIMON	AIMNORRTU	RUM RATION
AILMNOPSY	AMYLOPSIN		RUMINATOR
	OLYMPIANS	AIMNORSST	ROMANISTS
AILMNORST	MORTAL SIN	AIMNORSTU	MINOTAURS
AILMNORTY	NORMALITY	AIMNOSSSY	SIMON SAYS
	ROYAL MINT	AIMNOSTTU	MUTATIONS
AILMNOSUU	ALUMINOUS	AIMNRSSTT	TRANSMITS
AILMNSTTU	STIMULANT	AIMOOPRST	PROSTOMIA
AILMOORST	MOTORAILS	AIMOPSSTU	POTASSIUM
AILMORSST	MORALISTS	AIMRSSTTU	SMART SUIT
AILMORSSU	SOLARIUMS	AINNOOPRS	SOPRANINO
AILMORSTU	SIMULATOR	AINNOOPRT	PRONATION
AILMORTTU	MUTILATOR	AINNOOPTW	WON A POINT
AILMORTTY	MORTALITY	AINNOORTV	INNOVATOR
AILMPRSTY	PALMISTRY	AINNOOSTT	NOTATIONS
AILMSTTUU	MUTUALIST	AINNORRWW	NARROW WIN
AILMTTUUY	MUTUALITY	AINNOSTTU	NUTATIONS
AILNNOPTU	PLUTONIAN	AINOOPPRT	APPORTION
AILNNOSSW	SONS-IN-LAW	AINOOPRRT	PRORATION
AILNNOSTU	LUNATIONS	AINOOPRST	RAT POISON
AILNNSTTY	INSTANTLY	AINOOPSTT	POTATIONS
AILNOOOPS	PIANO SOLO	AINOOQTTU	QUOTATION
AILNOORST	TONSORIAL	AINOORSTT	ROTATIONS
	TORSIONAL	AINOORTTU	RATION OUT
AILNOOSTV	SOLVATION	AINOOSSTT	OSTINATOS
AILNOOTUV	OVULATION	AINOPPSTT	PAINT POTS
AILNOPSTT	PLATONIST	AINOPRSTT	PROTISTAN
AILNOPSTU	PLATINOUS	AINOPRSTU	IN A STUPOR
	PULSATION		PUT ON AIRS
AILNOPSTY	PONY TAILS	AINOPRSUU	UNIPAROUS
	PONYTAILS	AINOPSTTU	PAINTS OUT
AILNOPTWY	PLAY TO WIN	AINOPSTUW	WAITS UPON
AILNORSTU	INSULATOR	AINORSTTY	TOY TRAINS
AILNORSTW	SLOW TRAIN	AINRSTTTU	ANTITRUST
AILNOSSUV	AVULSIONS	AIOOORRST	ORATORIOS
AILNOSUXY	ANXIOUSLY	AIOOPRSUV	OVIPAROUS
AILNPPSTU	SUPPLIANT	AIOOSTTTT	TATTOOIST
AILNPQTUY	PIQUANTLY	AIOPPRSTT	POP ARTIST
AILNRRSTU	TRIAL RUNS	AIOPRRSTT	PORTRAITS
AILNRSTTU	TURNS TAIL	AIOPRSSST	PROSAISTS
AILNRTUUX	LUXURIANT	AIOPSTTTU	SPAT IT OUT
AILOOPRST	SPOLIATOR	AIORRSSTU	SARTORIUS

AIORRSTTT	TITRATORS	AMNNOOSUY	ANONYMOUS
AIORSSTTV	VOTARISTS	AMNOOOPRW	POOR WOMAN
AIPPRSSTT	TRAPPISTS	AMNOORSTY	ASTRONOMY
AIPPRSTUW	WRAPS IT UP	AMNOPRSST	SPORTSMAN
AJKMOORRW	MAJOR WORK	AMOOOORSTV	VASOMOTOR
AKKLOOOOT	TOOK A LOOK	AMOORSTWY	MOTORWAYS
AKLLNPRSU	PULLS RANK	AMOPRSSXY	PAROXYSMS
AKLMOORST	LOOK SMART	AMORSSTTU	STAMPS OUT
AKLNNOOWW	KNOW NO LAW	AMORSSTTU	OUTSMARTS
AKLNOOTUW	WALK OUT ON	AMPRSTUUY	SUMPTUARY
AKMNORSTU	TURKOMANS	ANNORSTUY	TYRANNOUS
AKMOOOORT	TOOK A ROOM	ANNRSTTUY	TURN NASTY
AKMOPRSST	POSTMARKS	ANOOOPRSZ	SPOROZOAN
AKNOOPRSW	ROOKS PAWN	ANOOOOPRTZ	PROTOZOAN
AKNOORTTU	TOOK A TURN	ANOPRRSTT	TRANSPORT
AKNORSTWY	NASTY WORK	ANOPRTTWY	TAWNY PORT
AKNPSTTUU	SUNK A PUTT	ANORSUUVY	UNSAVOURY
AKOOPRRST	ROAST PORK	ANRRSSTTU	STAR TURNS
AKOPRRTWY	WORK PARTY	AOOOORRTW	ARROWROOT
AKORRSTTW	START WORK	AOOORRTTV	ROTOVATOR
AKRRSSTYY	STARRY SKY	AOOPRRSTT	POOR START
ALLLNNSUY	SALLY LUNN	AOOPRSTTU	AUTOSPORT
ALLMMOORS	SMALL ROOM	AOPPRSSST	PASSPORTS
ALLMMSSSU	SMALL SUMS	AOPRRSTTW	WORST PART
ALLMNOSTW	SMALL TOWN	AOPRRSTUU	RAPTUROUS
ALLMOOSSY	LYSOSOMAL	AOPRRTTYY	TORY PARTY
ALLNOOPTY	POLYTONAL	AOQRSTTUW	TWO QUARTS
ALLNOPTTU	POLLUTANT	AOQSSTTUU	STATUS QUO
ALLNSUUUY	UNUSUALLY	AORSSTTTU	STARTS OUT
ALLOOPPSY	PLAYS POLO	AORSTTTUY	STATUTORY
	PLAYS POOL	BBBCDEEOW	COBWEBBED
ALLOOPRTY	ALLOTROPY	BBBDEELRU	BLUBBERED
ALLOPPRUY	POPULARLY	BBBDEHNOO	HOBNOBBED
ALLOPRSTW	STRAW POLL	BBBDEIKOS	SKIBOBBED
ALLOPSUWW	SWALLOW UP	BBBDELPUU	BUBBLED UP
ALLORSTTY	TALL STORY	BBBEEELMU	BUMBLE BEE
ALLOSTWWZ	SLOW WALTZ		BUMBLEBEE
ALLRSTUUY	SUTURALLY	BBBEEILLT	BIBLE BELT
ALMMNSSUU	MUSSULMAN	BBBEGLMUU	BUBBLE GUM
ALMMPRUYY	PLAY RUMMY	BBBEIKORS	SKIBOBBER
ALMNNOOOS	MONSOONAL	BBBEILSTU	BUBBLIEST
ALMNOPRUY	PULMONARY	BBBELPSUU	BUBBLES UP
ALMOORSUY	AMOROUSLY	BBBEOOSTU	BOOB TUBES
ALMOPPSST	LAMP POSTS	BBBMOSUZZ	BUZZ BOMBS
ALNOOPSST	SALT SPOON	BBCDEELOR	CLOBBERED
ALNOOPSTT	TONOPLAST	BBCDHLTUU	DUTCH BULB
ALNOOPSYZ	POLYZOANS	BBCEHLOUY	CUBBY HOLE
ALNOPPRUU	UNPOPULAR	BBCEILRRS	SCRIBBLER
ALNOPPSTT	PLANT POTS	BBCEILRSS	SCRIBBLES
	POT PLANTS	BBCEIRSSU	SUBSCRIBE
ALNOPRSST	PLASTRONS	BBCERRSSU	SCRUBBERS
ALNOPSTTU	PLANTS OUT	BBCGINRSU	SCRUBBING
	POSTULANT	BBCHKSSUU	BUSHBUCKS
ALNORTUVY	VOLUNTARY	BBCIIILMS	BIBLICISM
ALNOSTWWY	TAWNY OWLS	BBCIIILST	BIBLICIST
ALNPPSSTU	SUPPLANTS	BBCKLOOSU	BOOK CLUBS
ALNPSTTUU	PUSTULANT	BBCLOSSUY	BOYS CLUBS
ALOOOPRTZ	PROTOZOAL	BBDDDIISY	BIDDY-BIDS
ALOOPPRSS	PROPOSALS	BBDDEELOU	DOUBLE BED
ALOORRTUY	ROYAL TOUR	BBDDEESYY	BEDDY-BYES
ALOORTUVY	OVULATORY	BBDDILLUY	BILLY BUDD
ALOPPSSTY	STOPS PLAY	BBDEEIORT	BRIDE TO BE
ALOPPSTUY	PLAYS UP TO	BBDEELORS	SLOBBERED
ALOPRSSTU	PULSATORS	BBDEFFFOO	FOBBED OFF
ALOPRSTUY	PULSATORY	BBDEFGLOO	BOB GELDOF
ALORSSTTW	SALTWORTS	BBDEGIMNO	DEMOBBING
	SLOW START	BBDEGLOPU	GOBBLED UP
ALOSSTTUW	LOW STATUS	BBDEHIRSU	RUBBISHED
AMMNNOOSY	MANY MOONS	BBDEILRSU	BLUE BIRDS
AMMNOORTT	MATT MONRO		BLUEBIRDS
AMMNPSTUY	TYMPANUMS	BBDEIMOSV	DIVE-BOMBS

BBDEINORR	RED RIBBON	BBILLMMOS	MILLS BOMB
BBDELLMSU	DUMBBELLS	BBILNOOSW	BOB WILSON
BBDELLOOU	BLUE BLOOD	BBLLOSUUY	BULBOUSLY
BBDEORTUU	RUBBED OUT	BBLLOSUYY	BULLYBOYS
BBDGIILNR	DRIBBLING	BCCCHIINU	CUBIC INCH
BBDILNORS	ROBS BLIND	BCCDEHKOY	BODY CHECK
BBDLOOSWY	BODY BLOWS	BCCDEMSUU	SUCCUMBED
BBDMOOPRS	DROP BOMBS	BCCEEFITU	CUBIC FEET
BBEEEHLMU	HUMBLE-BEE	BCCEEILOR	COERCIBLE
BBEEEHSTT	BE THE BEST	BCCEHIKNP	PINCHBECK
BBEEEINRR	BERBERINE	BCCEHLSSU	CHESS CLUB
BBEEFFIOR	RIB OF BEEF	BCCEIIILM	IMBECILIC
BBEEFIORT	TO BE BRIEF	BCCEIINOT	CENOBITIC
BBEEFLLUY	BULLY BEEF	BCCEILRSU	CRUCIBLES
BBEEIORRS	ROBBERIES	BCCEILRSY	BICYCLERS
BBEEIRRSU	RUBBERISE	BCCEINNOU	CONCUBINE
BBEEIRRUZ	RUBBERIZE	BCCEMRSUU	CUCUMBERS
BBEELLLSU	BLUEBELLS	BCCFIOOTU	CUBIC FOOT
BBEELORRS	SLOBBERER	BCCGIILNY	BICYCLING
BBEELRRUY	BLUEBERRY	BCCIILSTY	BICYCLIST
BBEFIMORS	FIRE BOMBS	BCCIKMOOO	COMIC BOOK
	FIREBOMBS	BCCIKNOOR	COCK ROBIN
BBEGGIINR	GIBBERING	BCCIMNOOR	BORN COMIC
BBEGGIINT	GIBBETING	BCCIORSTU	SCORBUTIC
BBEGHIIRS	GIBBERISH	BCCIRSTUU	CUCURBITS
BBEGHILOS	BOBSLEIGH	BCCMORRUY	CURRYCOMB
BBEGIMNNU	BENUMBING	BCCOSSTUU	CUB SCOUTS
BBEGIRSTU	GRUBBIEST	BCDDEEHOU	DEBOUCHED
BBEGLOPSU	GOBBLES UP	BCDDEEILU	DEDUCIBLE
BBEGNOSUY	GONE BY BUS	BCDDEEIRS	DESCRIBED
BBEGOSSUY	GOES BY BUS	BCDDEIORR	RECORD BID
BBEHILLOY	HOLY BIBLE	BCDDLLOOO	COLD BLOOD
BBEHIRSSU	RUBBISHES	BCDEEEEHS	BESEECHED
BBEHKOOTY	BY THE BOOK	BCDEEEINO	OBEDIENCE
BBEHLLMOS	BOMBSHELL	BCDEEEMOU	BECOME DUE
BBEHRRSUY	SHRUBBERY	BCDEEGIKN	BEDECKING
BBEIKNORR	BROKEN RIB	BCDEEHIIR	HERBICIDE
BBEIMMOST	TIME BOMBS	BCDEEHITW	BEWITCHED
BBEIMOSST	BOMB SITES	BCDEEHOSU	DEBOUCHES
	BOMBSITES	BCDEEHRTU	BUTCHERED
BBEINOSVY	BEVIN BOYS	BCDEEILRU	REDUCIBLE
BBEINSSTU	TUBBINESS	BCDEEIRSS	DESCRIBES
BBEISSTTU	STUBBIEST	BCDEEIRSU	RESCUE BID
BBEKMMOOS	SMOKE BOMB	BCDEEJSTU	SUBJECTED
BBEKNOOST	BONTEBOKS	BCDEEKLOW	BELOW DECK
BBELNORTW	BROWN BELT	BCDEELLOR	CORBELLED
BBEMNORUX	BOX NUMBER	BCDEELRTU	TUBERCLED
BBEMNRSUY	BY NUMBERS	BCDEEMNTU	DECUMBENT
BBENORSSW	BROWN BESS	BCDEEMOOT	COME TO BED
BBENSTUWY	WENT BY BUS	BCDEFKORU	BUCKED FOR
BBEOORVVY	BOVVER BOY	BCDEHIPTU	BITCHED UP
BBERRTTUU	BUTTERBUR	BCDEIILMN	BLIND MICE
BBGHILLTU	LIGHT BULB	BCDEIILNU	INDUCIBLE
BBGHILNOO	HOBGOBLIN	BCDEIINRS	INSCRIBED
BBGHIMOST	BOMBSIGHT	BCDEIJSUU	SUB JUDICE
BBGHINORT	THROBBING	BCDEIKOWY	WICKED BOY
BBGHIORTY	BRIGHT BOY	BCDEIKRRS	RED BRICKS
BBGIILNQU	QUIBBLING		REDBRICKS
BBGIINNRU	RUBBING IN	BCDEKLNUU	UNBUCKLED
BBGIIOOTT	TITO GOBBI	BCDEKLPUU	BUCKLED UP
BBGIIOSTY	GIBBOSITY	BCDELOORS	COLD SOBER
BBGILOSUY	GIBBOUSLY	BCDEMOSTU	COMBUSTED
BBGINNORU	RUBBING ON	BCDENOPUU	BOUNCED UP
BBGINPRUU	RUBBING UP	BCDEOOTTY	BOYCOTTED
BBGJNOORR	BJORN BORG	BCDEORRSS	CROSSBRED
BBIIILNRU	BILIRUBIN	BCDGIKLOR	GOLD BRICK
BBIIKMTUZ	KIBBUTZIM		GOLDBRICK
BBIILLOSW	BOB WILLIS	BCDGIORSW	BIG CROWDS
BBIKLNUUY	BUY IN BULK	BCDIIKRST	TICKBIRDS
BBIKMNOST	STINK BOMB	BCDIIMMUY	CYMBIDIUM
	STINK-BOMB	BCDIIPSSU	BICUSPIDS

344

BCDIKLLSU	DUCKBILLS	BCEHIPSSU	SPICEBUSH
BCDILMNOW	CLIMB DOWN	BCEHIPSTU	BITCHES UP
	CLIMB-DOWN	BCEHKLLOO	BLOCK HOLE
BCDIMOORS	SCOMBROID	BCEHKNORW	WORK BENCH
BCDIOPSUW	CUPIDS BOW		WORKBENCH
BCDKLOOOW	WOOD-BLOCK	BCEHKOSUU	BUCK HOUSE
	WOODBLOCK	BCEHMNOOY	HONEYCOMB
BCDKNOORU	ROCKBOUND	BCEHMOORS	CHEMOSORB
BCDLLNOOW	BLOWN COLD	BCEHORRSU	BROCHURES
BCDLLOOOT	BLOOD CLOT	BCEIILPSU	PUBLICISE
BCDLLOOSW	BLOWS COLD	BCEIILPUZ	PUBLICIZE
BCDNORSUW	SCRUB DOWN	BCEIIMORT	BIOMETRIC
BCDOPRTUY	BY-PRODUCT	BCEIINOST	BISECTION
BCEEEEHRT	BEECH TREE	BCEIINRRS	INSCRIBER
BCEEEEHSS	BESEECHES	BCEIINRSS	INSCRIBES
BCEEEGHIS	BIG CHEESE	BCEIIOPRT	PREBIOTIC
BCEEEHKNO	CHEEKBONE	BCEIJLOPU	JOE PUBLIC
BCEEEMNOO	BECOME ONE	BCEIJNOOT	OBJECTION
BCEEERSSU	BERCEUSES	BCEIKSTTU	BUS TICKET
BCEEFRRUY	BEEF CURRY	BCEILMNOU	COLUMBINE
BCEEGINSS	BIG SCENES	BCEILMORV	CLIMB OVER
BCEEGLLSU	GLEE CLUBS	BCEILMORY	COR BLIMEY
BCEEHIRRT	BIRCH TREE	BCEILNOOT	BOLECTION
BCEEHISTW	BEWITCHES	BCEILNORU	COLUBRINE
BCEEHKTTU	BUCK TEETH	BCEILPRSU	REPUBLICS
BCEEHORTT	BROCHETTE	BCEILPSTU	PUBLICEST
BCEEHRRTU	BUTCHERER	BCEIMNNTU	INCUMBENT
BCEEHRTTU	TREBUCHET	BCEIMNORS	COMBINERS
BCEEIILMS	IMBECILES	BCEIMNORY	EMBRYONIC
BCEEIILNV	EVINCIBLE	BCEINOORT	IN OCTOBER
BCEEIJOTV	OBJECTIVE	BCEINOOSX	COIN BOXES
BCEEIKRRS	BICKERERS		COIN-BOXES
BCEEILPUY	PUBLIC EYE	BCEINOSTU	BOUNCIEST
BCEEILRTY	CELEBRITY	BCEINOSTY	OBSCENITY
BCEEINOOT	COENOBITE	BCEINSSUU	INCUBUSES
BCEEIOQSU	QUEBECOIS	BCEIOPRRS	PROSCRIBE
BCEEIPRRS	PRESCRIBE	BCEIORSST	BISECTORS
BCEEJNORT	JOB CENTRE	BCEIORSTT	OBSTETRIC
BCEEJORSU	SECURE JOB	BCEJOORST	OBJECTORS
BCEELNOSY	OBSCENELY	BCEKLNSUU	UNBUCKLES
BCEELORVX	BOX CLEVER	BCEKLOOTV	BLOCK VOTE
BCEELRSTU	TUBERCLES	BCEKLOSSU	BLUE SOCKS
BCEEMNRSU	ENCUMBERS	BCEKLPSUU	BUCKLES UP
BCEEMNRTU	RECUMBENT	BCEKOOORV	BOOK COVER
BCEEMRRSU	CEREBRUMS	BCEKOSTUX	TUCK BOXES
BCEENOSST	OBSCENEST	BCELLORUW	CRUEL BLOW
BCEENPSTU	PUBESCENT	BCELMOOTY	LOBECTOMY
BCEEFFIJOO	OFFICE JOB	BCELOOSSU	LOBSCOUSE
BCEFFIOOX	BOX OFFICE	BCELOOSTW	BELOW COST
BCEFFIOOY	OFFICE BOY	BCELOORSTW	SCREW-BOLT
BCEFFLOUV	BLUFF COVE	BCELORSUY	OBSCURELY
BCEFIIKRR	FIREBRICK	BCELPRSSU	PRESS CLUB
BCEFIJOTY	OBJECTIFY	BCEMOORSY	CORYMBOSE
BCEFILSUV	FIVE CLUBS	BCENNOSTY	BY CONSENT
BCEFKLTUU	BUCKETFUL	BCENOPSUU	BOUNCES UP
BCEGHILNN	BLENCHING	BCEOORSTU	CUBE ROOTS
BCEGIIIST	BIG CITIES	BCEOORTTY	BOYCOTTER
BCEGIIKNR	BICKERING	BCEORRRWY	CROWBERRY
BCEGIINST	BISECTING	BCEPRTTUU	BUTTERCUP
BCEGIJNOT	OBJECTING	BCFGLLOSU	GOLF CLUBS
BCEGIKNNO	BECKONING	BCFHILLNU	BULLFINCH
BCEGIKNTU	BUCKETING	BCFIKLOTU	BIT OF LUCK
BCEGIMNRU	CUMBERING	BCFILLMSU	FILM CLUBS
BCEGIORSS	BIG SCORES	BCFKLLOSU	FOLK CLUBS
BCEGIRSTU	TIGER CUBS	BCFLORSUU	FOUR CLUBS
BCEGRRSUW	GRUB-SCREW	BCGHILNTU	NIGHT CLUB
BCEHIISTT	BITCHIEST		NIGHTCLUB
BCEHILNTU	IN THE CLUB	BCGIIKSST	BIG STICKS
BCEHILPSU	BLUE CHIPS	BCGIIMNNO	COMBINING
BCEHILPTU	THE PUBLIC	BCGIKLNSU	BUCKLINGS
BCEHIMORS	CHEMISORB	BCGIKNPUU	BUCKING UP

BCGILLRSU	GIRLS CLUB	BDDEFINOR	FORBIDDEN
BCGILMNRU	CRUMBLING	BDDEFIORR	FORBIDDER
BCGILMNSU	SCUMBLING	BDDEFLOOU	BLOOD FEUD
BCGINORSU	OBSCURING	BDDEGIIMN	IMBEDDING
BCHIIMSTU	BISMUTHIC	BDDEGLOOU	DOODLEBUG
BCHIIOPRS	BISHOPRIC	BDDEHINOU	HIDEBOUND
BCHIIRSTU	HUBRISTIC	BDDEHLOOS	BLOODSHED
BCHILLOTY	BLOTCHILY		SHED BLOOD
BCHILOOPY	LYOPHOBIC	BDDEIILLO	BILL ODDIE
BCHINORTY	BRYTHONIC	BDDEIILNS	BLIND SIDE
BCHIOORSY	CHOIR BOYS	BDDEIISUV	SUBDIVIDE
	CHOIRBOYS	BDDEILNRU	UNBRIDLED
BCHJOSSUY	CUSHY JOBS	BDDEILORW	BLOW-DRIED
BCHKNORTU	BUCKTHORN	BDDEIMOSY	DISEMBODY
BCHKOOTTU	BUCKTOOTH	BDDEINRSU	DISBURDEN
BCHLNOPUW	PUNCH BOWL		UNDERBIDS
BCHLOOOSY	SCHOOLBOY	BDDEIRSSU	DISBURSED
BCHLOORTW	BLOWTORCH	BDDEIRSTU	DISTURBED
BCHLOTUUY	YOUTH CLUB	BDDEJMNOO	ODD JOB MEN
BCHMOOOTT	TOOTHCOMB	BDDELLOUZ	BULLDOZED
BCIIKRTTY	TRICKY BIT	BDDELOORW	DREW BLOOD
BCIILMSUU	UMBILICUS	BDDELOPUU	DOUBLED UP
BCIILPSTU	PUBLICIST	BDDELORRY	LORD DERBY
BCIILPTUY	PUBLICITY	BDDELSUUY	SUBDUEDLY
BCIILRTUY	LUBRICITY	BDDEMNORU	ODD NUMBER
BCIIMMNOR	BORN MIMIC	BDDENNOOT	DO NOT BEND
BCIIMNOOS	BIONOMICS	BDDENNOSW	BENDS DOWN
BCIIMOSTY	SYMBIOTIC	BDDENNOUU	UNBOUNDED
BCIJKORTY	TRICKY JOB	BDDENOOST	ODDS-ON BET
BCIKKORRW	BRICKWORK	BDDENOOWW	BOWED DOWN
BCIKLOOST	BOOTLICKS	BDDENORUY	UNDERBODY
BCIKNOTUY	BUY ON TICK	BDDENOTUU	UNDOUBTED
BCILLORSS	CROSSBILL	BDDEOPPRY	DROPPED BY
BCILMMOUU	COLUMBIUM	BDDEOSTYY	TEDDY BOYS
BCILORSUU	LUBRICOUS	BDDFGIOOR	GOD FORBID
BCILPRSTU	STRIP CLUB	BDDFILLNO	BLINDFOLD
BCIMNOOOS	SONIC BOOM	BDDFMNOUU	DUMBFOUND
BCIOOPRSS	PROBOSCIS	BDDGIINOR	DOING BIRD
BCIORSTUY	OBSCURITY	BDDGIINPU	BIDDING UP
BCIPRSSTU	SUBSCRIPT	BDDGILNOS	BLIND DOGS
BCKKOOOOS	COOKBOOKS	BDDHIIRSY	DIHYBRIDS
BCKLOOSTU	BLOCKS OUT	BDDHISSTU	BUDDHISTS
BCKLOSUYY	LUCKY BOYS	BDDIILRSW	WILD BIRDS
BCKNORRTU	BURNT CORK	BDDILLORY	DOLLY BIRD
BCKOOOPSY	COPYBOOKS	BDDILOOSY	SOLID BODY
BCNOORSWW	BROWN COWS	BDDNOOSUY	SOUND BODY
BCOORSSSW	CROSSBOWS	BDDNOTUUY	DUTY BOUND
BCOOSSTUY	BOY SCOUTS	BDDOOORUY	BODY ODOUR
BCORSSTTU	OBSTRUCTS	BDEEEEFLN	ENFEEBLED
BCORSSTUU	SCRUBS OUT	BDEEEELRV	BELVEDERE
BDDDDEISU	DISBUDDED	BDEEEESTT	BEDSETTEE
BDDDEEIIN	DIED IN BED	BDEEEGRSY	BY DEGREES
BDDDEEINR	BEDRIDDEN	BDEEEHLRT	BLETHERED
BDDDEELOS	BOLD DEEDS	BDEEEINRR	INBREEDER
BDDDEEOTU	BEDDED OUT	BDEEEINRZ	BREEZED IN
BDDDEILOY	BO DIDDLEY	BDEEEIOTW	WOE BETIDE
BDDEEEFIR	DEBRIEFED	BDEEEKNNS	KNEES BEND
BDDEEEOSX	DEED BOXES	BDEEEKNOT	BETOKENED
BDDEEFLSU	BEFUDDLES	BDEEELNOS	NOSEBLEED
BDDEEFOOR	FOREBODED	BDEEELOSU	SEE DOUBLE
BDDEEGGRU	BEGRUDGED	BDEEELPSU	DEEP BLUES
BDDEEGIMN	EMBEDDING	BDEEENRTU	DEBENTURE
BDDEEIINS	DIES IN BED	BDEEERRST	RED BERETS
BDDEEINSW	BINDWEEDS	BDEEERSTW	BESTREWED
BDDEEIOSY	DISOBEYED	BDEEERTTV	BREVETTED
BDDEEIRTT	DID BETTER	BDEEFIILS	DISBELIEF
BDDEEISTU	SUBEDITED	BDEEFINRS	BE FRIENDS
BDDEELNRU	BLUNDERED		BEFRIENDS
BDDEENORU	REBOUNDED	BDEEFLLOW	BEDFELLOW
BDDEENRRU	UNDERBRED	BDEEFLORW	FLOWER BED
BDDEENSTU	SUBTENDED	BDEEFLOTT	BOTTLE-FED

BDEEFOORR	FOREBODER	BDEEORRRS	BORDERERS
BDEEFOORS	FOREBODES	BDEEORSTY	OYSTER BED
BDEEFOOSW	BEEFWOODS	BDEEORVYY	EVERYBODY
BDEEFOOTW	WEB-FOOTED	BDEEPRRTU	PERTURBED
BDEEGGILO	BOILED EGG	BDEERSSST	BEST DRESS
BDEEGGLOU	DOUBLE EGG	BDEERSSUV	SUBSERVED
BDEEGGLOW	BOWLEGGED	BDEERSTUV	SUBVERTED
BDEEGGRRU	BEGRUDGER	BDEFFKNOU	BUNKED OFF
BDEEGGRSU	BEGRUDGES	BDEFFLORU	OLD BUFFER
BDEEGHINT	BENIGHTED	BDEFFMOPU	BUMPED OFF
	GET BEHIND	BDEFHIRSU	FURBISHED
BDEEGHTTU	THE BUDGET	BDEFIINRS	FINE BIRDS
BDEEGIKRW	KEW BRIDGE	BDEFILLOO	LIFE BLOOD
BDEEGILNS	SINGLE BED		LIFEBLOOD
BDEEGINRS	BREEDINGS	BDEFINORY	BOY FRIEND
BDEEGLNTU	BLUNT EDGE		BOYFRIEND
BDEEGMRSU	SUBMERGED	BDEFLOSTU	SELF-DOUBT
BDEEGNOOT	GONE TO BED	BDEFMNOOY	BODY OF MEN
BDEEGNORU	BURGEONED	BDEFOOTTU	OUT OF DEBT
BDEEGOOOT	GOES TO BED	BDEGGGINU	DEBUGGING
BDEEGRSSV	SVEDBERGS	BDEGGHMUU	HUMBUGGED
BDEEHIITX	EXHIBITED	BDEGGINTU	BUDGETING
BDEEHILMS	BLEMISHED	BDEGGIRSS	BIRD'S EGGS
BDEEHILTW	BLED WHITE	BDEGHILSU	SHIELDBUG
BDEEHIRTW	WIDE BERTH	BDEGHINOT	GOT BEHIND
BDEEHLORS	BEHOLDERS	BDEGHIRRT	BRIGHT RED
BDEEHORTT	BETROTHED	BDEGIIILR	DIRIGIBLE
BDEEIIKRS	RIDE BIKES	BDEGIIINR	BIRDIEING
BDEEIILLN	INDELIBLE	BDEGIILOS	DISOBLIGE
BDEEIILNS	LIES IN BED	BDEGIIPPR	BIG DIPPER
BDEEIISTU	DUBIETIES	BDEGIKLOO	LOOKED BIG
BDEEIKLNR	BLINKERED	BDEGIKNNU	DEBUNKING
BDEEIKNRR	DRINK BEER	BDEGIKOOU	GUIDE BOOK
BDEEILMOR	EMBROILED		GUIDEBOOK
BDEEILMRS	MILD BEERS	BDEGILNOU	DOUBLE GIN
BDEEILMSS	DISSEMBLE	BDEGILOOV	GIVE BLOOD
BDEEILOSV	BODES EVIL	BDEGILORW	LOW BRIDGE
BDEEILRRY	BERYL REID	BDEGILOTY	BIGOTEDLY
BDEEILRST	BLISTERED	BDEGIMNOY	EMBODYING
BDEEILRSW	BEWILDERS	BDEGINNNU	UNBENDING
BDEEIMMRS	DISMEMBER	BDEGINNOR	RINGBONED
BDEEIMORR	EMBROIDER	BDEGINNRU	BURDENING
BDEEINNOZ	BENZENOID	BDEGINORR	BORDERING
BDEEINRRT	INTERBRED	BDEGINORS	DESORBING
BDEEINRTT	BITTER END	BDEGINPRS	BEDSPRING
BDEEIPRSW	SPIDERWEB	BDEGIORRX	BOX GIRDER
BDEEIRRST	BESTIRRED		BOX-GIRDER
BDEEIRSST	BESTRIDES	BDEGKLOOO	GOOD BLOKE
BDEEIRSSU	SUBERISED	BDEGLNOOY	GOLDEN BOY
BDEEIRSSY	BIRD'S-EYES	BDEGLNOSU	BLUDGEONS
BDEEIRSTT	BED-SITTER	BDEGOORSX	BOXER DOGS
BDEEIRSUZ	SUBERIZED	BDEHIIINT	INHIBITED
BDEEKNRRU	DRUNK BEER	BDEHIIRSY	HYBRIDISE
BDEEKNRSU	DEBUNKERS	BDEHIIRYZ	HYBRIDIZE
BDEELLOSW	BODES WELL	BDEHILPSU	PUBLISHED
BDEELLSSY	BLESSEDLY	BDEHIMORS	HOMEBIRDS
BDEELMNOS	EMBOLDENS	BDEHINRSU	BURNISHED
BDEELMRSU	SLUMBERED	BDEHIOSST	BOTH SIDES
BDEELMSUY	BEMUSEDLY	BDEHMNOOU	HOMEBOUND
BDEELNOOU	DOUBLE ONE	BDEHNOORY	BROODY HEN
BDEELNOTU	DOUBLE TEN	BDEHNRTUY	BY THUNDER
BDEELNRRU	BLUNDERER	BDEHPRSUU	BRUSHED UP
BDEELORST	BOLSTERED	BDEIIILSV	DIVISIBLE
BDEELORSU	REDOUBLES	BDEIIILTY	EDIBILITY
BDEELRSTU	BLUSTERED	BDEIIJNOS	INSIDE JOB
BDEEMRSSU	SUBMERSED	BDEIIILNY	INDELIBLY
BDEENNOOY	BEYOND ONE	BDEIIIMOS	MOBILISED
BDEENORSV	BENDS OVER	BDEIILMOZ	MOBILIZED
BDEENOTTW	WENT TO BED	BDEIILRRV	LIVER BIRD
BDEENPRTU	BE PRUDENT	BDEIISSSU	SUBSIDIES
BDEEOPRSU	SOBERED UP		SUBSIDISE

BDEIISSUZ	SUBSIDIZE	BDEOPSTTU	PUTS TO BED
BDEIJNOSU	SUBJOINED	BDFILLLOS	BILLFOLDS
BDEIKLLRR	KERB DRILL	BDFIOORST	BIRDS-FOOT
BDEIKNORW	BROKE WIND	BDFLNOORT	BOLD FRONT
BDEILLNOO	BLOODLINE	BDFLOOORU	FOULBROOD
BDEILMOOR	DORMOBILE	BDFORSSUY	BODYSURFS
BDEILNNSS	BLINDNESS	BDGGINOOW	GO DOWN BIG
BDEILNRSU	UNBRIDLES	BDGHOOSUY	DOUGHBOYS
BDEILOOST	BLOODIEST	BDGIILLNO	BODING ILL
BDEILORRW	BLOW-DRIER	BDGIILNSU	BUILDINGS
BDEILORSV	LOVEBIRDS	BDGIINNNU	UNBINDING
BDEILORSW	BLOW-DRIES	BDGIINNPU	BINDING UP
BDEILORUV	OVERBUILD	BDGIINORS	DISROBING
BDEILOSUX	DOUBLE SIX	BDGIINSSU	SUBSIDING
BDEILRRSY	LYRE BIRDS	BDGILNOOY	BLOODYING
	LYREBIRDS	BDGINNORW	BRING DOWN
BDEIMOSTU	DEMOB SUIT	BDGINNOTU	OBTUNDING
BDEIMSTTU	SUBMITTED	BDGINORRW	BRING WORD
BDEINOOST	DO ONES BIT	BDGINORSS	BIRD SONGS
BDEINOPST	STOP IN BED		SONG BIRDS
BDEINORSV	BINDS OVER		SONGBIRDS
	OVENBIRDS	BDGINORTU	OBTRUDING
BDEINORTX	TINDER BOX	BDGINORUY	YOUNG BIRD
	TINDERBOX	BDGKOOOOS	GOOD BOOKS
BDEINRSST	BIRDS NEST	BDHIIMRSY	HYBRIDISM
BDEINRSSU	SIDEBURNS	BDHIIRSTY	HYBRIDIST
BDEIOORST	BROODIEST	BDHIIRTYY	HYBRIDITY
BDEIORSTU	SUBEDITOR	BDHILNOOT	THIN BLOOD
BDEIRRSSU	DISBURSER	BDHIMOORS	RHOMBOIDS
BDEIRRSUV	BUS DRIVER	BDHINOOOR	ROBIN HOOD
BDEIRSSSU	DISBURSES	BDHLOOOST	BLOODSHOT
BDEISSSTU	SUBSISTED	BDHMOSSUW	DUMB SHOWS
BDEKNOORW	BROKE DOWN	BDHNORSUW	BRUSH DOWN
BDEKOOORR	ORDER BOOK	BDHOORSUW	BRUSHWOOD
BDELLNOOR	NOBLE LORD	BDIILLMSU	SLIM BUILD
BDELLOORS	BORDELLOS	BDIIMORTY	MORBIDITY
BDELLOOSS	BLOODLESS	BDIIRTTUY	TURBIDITY
BDELLOOST	LETS BLOOD	BDIJORSTY	DIRTY JOBS
BDELLORUZ	BULLDOZER	BDIKNRSUY	BUY DRINKS
BDELLOSUZ	BULLDOZES	BDIKOORTY	DIRTY BOOK
BDELMNNOO	BEN LOMOND	BDILMNORW	BLINDWORM
BDELMNPUU	UNPLUMBED	BDILNNOSW	SNOW-BLIND
BDELMOOSS	BLOSSOMED	BDILNNOWW	WINDBLOWN
BDELMOOSV	BOLD MOVES	BDILNNSSU	SUNBLINDS
BDELMRTUY	TUMBLE-DRY	BDILNOOSW	BOILS DOWN
BDELNOOWW	DOWN BELOW	BDILNOPRT	BOLD PRINT
BDELNOSSU	BOUNDLESS	BDILNOPST	BLIND SPOT
BDELOOPRU	PUREBLOOD	BDILOSUUY	DUBIOUSLY
BDELOOPTU	DOUBLE TOP	BDINNOORU	IRONBOUND
BDELOOPTY	BLOOD TYPE	BDINNOOTU	IN NO DOUBT
BDELOOSTT	BLOOD TEST	BDINNRTUW	WINDBURNT
BDELOOSTY	OLDEST BOY	BDINOOWWW	BOW WINDOW
BDELOOTUW	BOWLED OUT	BDINOOWWX	WINDOW BOX
	DOUBLE TWO	BDIOPSTUY	STUPID BOY
BDELOPSUU	DOUBLES UP	BDKNOOORS	DOORKNOBS
BDELOPTTU	BOTTLED UP	BDLLOOSTU	BLOOD LUST
BDELOSSTU	DOUBTLESS	BDLMOOORW	BLOODWORM
BDEMMNNOSU	OMBUDSMEN	BDLNNOOSU	LONDON BUS
BDEMNNOOW	BONDWOMEN	BDLNNOOWW	BLOWN DOWN
BDEMNOOSU	UNBOSOMED	BDLNOOOSU	DOUBLOONS
BDENNOORW	DONE BROWN	BDLNOORRY	LORD BYRON
BDENNOOST	BONDSTONE	BDLNOOSWW	BLOWS DOWN
BDENNOSSU	SNUB-NOSED	BDNNOOSUW	SNOWBOUND
BDENNRSUU	SUNBURNED	BDNNORSUW	BURNS DOWN
	UNBURDENS	BDNNORTUW	BURNT DOWN
BDENOOOWX	WOODEN BOX	BDORSUWZZ	BUZZ WORDS
BDENOORSW	DOES BROWN		BUZZWORDS
BDENOORUV	BOUND OVER	BEEEEFLNS	ENFEEBLES
BDENOORWY	BOY WONDER	BEEEEILMV	BELIEVE ME
BDENORTUU	BURNED OUT	BEEEEKNSS	BEE'S KNEES
BDEOPSSTU	BUS DEPOTS	BEEEENQSU	QUEEN BEES

BEEEFFLOT	BEETLE OFF	**BEEGILLNW**	BEGIN WELL
BEEEFGLOR	LEG BEFORE		WELL-BEING
BEEEFIMPR	PRIME BEEF	**BEEGILNTT**	LETTING BE
BEEEFLLSU	FEELS BLUE	**BEEGILRSU**	BEGUILERS
BEEEFLNOS	BE ONESELF	**BEEGINNRS**	BEGINNERS
BEEEGIRSS	BESIEGERS	**BEEGINRTT**	BETTERING
BEEEGLNRT	GREEN BELT	**BEEGINSST**	BEE STINGS
BEEEGLNRU	BLUE-GREEN		BEESTINGS
BEEEGNOOW	WOEBEGONE	**BEEGINSTT**	BESETTING
BEEEGNOTW	GO BETWEEN	**BEEGINSTV**	GIVEN BEST
	GO-BETWEEN	**BEEGISSTV**	GIVES BEST
BEEEGRSTT	BEGETTERS	**BEEGJNORU**	JOE BUGNER
BEEEGRTTT	GET BETTER	**BEEGKLNOR**	BROKEN LEG
BEEEHLLOR	HELLEBORE	**BEEGKNOOR**	GONE BROKE
BEEEHLORW	HERE BELOW	**BEEGKOORS**	GOES BROKE
BEEEHNOSY	HONEY BEES	**BEEGKORRS**	GO BERSERK
	HONEYBEES	**BEEGLLNUW**	BEGUN WELL
BEEEILMNT	BELEMNITE		WELL BEGUN
BEEEILRSV	BELIEVERS	**BEEGLNOOW**	GONE BELOW
	EVERSIBLE	**BEEGLOOSW**	GOES BELOW
BEEEIMRSV	SEMIBREVE	**BEEGLOSTW**	GETS BELOW
BEEEINNTW	IN BETWEEN	**BEEGMRSSU**	SUBMERGES
	IN-BETWEEN	**BEEGMSTUY**	BE MY GUEST
BEEEINORT	BETE NOIRE	**BEEGORTTT**	GOT BETTER
BEEEINRSZ	BREEZES IN	**BEEGRSSSU**	DUNGEOGEO
BEEEIRRSW	BREWERIES	**BEEHILLMS**	EMBELLISH
BEEEIRSTZ	BREEZIEST	**BEEHILMPU**	HUMBLE PIE
BEEEKOPRS	KEEP SOBER	**BEEHILMSS**	BLEMISHES
BEEEKORRW	WORKER BEE	**BEEHILTTW**	WHITE BELT
BEEEKRRRS	BERSERKER	**BEEHINRTT**	TEREBINTH
BEEELLSTU	STEEL BLUE	**BEEHIOPRS**	BIOSPHERE
BEEELLSTV	LEVEL BEST	**BEEHIORRV**	HERBIVORE
BEEELMNSS	ENSEMBLES	**BEEHLOORS**	BORE HOLES
BEEELMRSS	RESEMBLES		BOREHOLES
BEEELMRZZ	EMBEZZLER	**BEEHLOPRY**	HYPERBOLE
BEEELMSZZ	EMBEZZLES	**BEEHNNOOT**	ON THE BONE
BEEELPRTU	BLUE PETER	**BEEHNOOPX**	XENOPHOBE
BEEEMMNRW	NEW MEMBER	**BEEHNOOTT**	TO THE BONE
BEEEMMRRS	REMEMBERS	**BEEIILNRT**	LIBERTINE
BEEEMNORY	BEER MONEY	**BEEIILRST**	LIBERTIES
BEEEMNSTT	BESETMENT	**BEEIINRTY**	INEBRIETY
BEEEMPRST	SEPTEMBER	**BEEIKLMRU**	BERKELIUM
BEEENORTT	ONE BETTER	**BEEIKLRRY**	BERRYLIKE
BEEENOSTW	BE SWEET ON	**BEEIKLSSU**	BLUE SKIES
BEEENPRST	BE PRESENT	**BEEILLNOR**	REBELLION
BEEENOSSU	QUEEN BESS	**BEEILLNTU**	EBULLIENT
BEEENSTUW	BETWEEN US	**BEEILLRTT**	BELITTLER
BEEFFGIRU	FEBRIFUGE	**BEEILLRTU**	RUBELLITE
BEEFFORTT	BETTER OFF	**BEEILLSTT**	BELITTLES
BEEFHLRSY	BY HERSELF	**BEEILNRSU**	BLUE RINSE
BEEFILLST	LIFE BELTS	**BEEILNSST**	STEEL NIBS
BEEFILOSW	WEB OF LIES	**BEEILOSTV**	LOVEBITES
BEEFINRSS	BRIEFNESS	**BEEILOTTU**	OUBLIETTE
BEEFINRSU	REFUSE BIN	**BEEILPRST**	BEL ESPRIT
BEEFIORSX	FIREBOXES	**BEEILPRTU**	ERUPTIBLE
BEEFISTUX	TUBIFEXES	**BEEILRRRT**	TERRIBLER
BEEFLLOTW	LEFT ELBOW	**BEEILRRSV**	VERS LIBRE
BEEFLNOSY	BY ONESELF	**BEEILSTUV**	VESTIBULE
BEEFNOORW	BEFORE NOW	**BEEIMMNRT**	TIMBERMEN
BEEFOSSUX	FUSE BOXES	**BEEIMNRST**	TRIBESMEN
BEEGGHTTU	GET THE BUG	**BEEIMRRSU**	REIMBURSE
BEEGGIINS	BESIEGING	**BEEIMRSTT**	EMBITTERS
BEEGGOORY	BOY GEORGE	**BEEINNOTT**	BENTONITE
BEEGHILSW	BIG WHEELS	**BEEINNRTU**	INNER TUBE
BEEGHINOT	THE BIG ONE	**BEEINSSTW**	BEST WINES
BEEGHIRTY	EYEBRIGHT	**BEEIOQSSU**	OBSEQUIES
BEEGIILLL	ILLEGIBLE	**BEEIORSSU**	BE SERIOUS
BEEGIILNV	BELIEVING	**BEEIOSSSV**	OBSESSIVE
BEEGIIMNT	TIME BEING	**BEEIQRTTU**	BRIQUETTE
BEEGILLNR	REBELLING	**BEEIRSTTT**	BITTEREST
BEEGILLNV	BEVELLING	**BEEIRSTTU**	BUTTERIES

BEEJKLOSU	BLUE JOKES
BEEJKOSUX	JUKE BOXES
	JUKEBOXES
BEEKKOOPS	KEEP BOOKS
BEEKLRRUY	KERRY BLUE
BEEKNOOPR	BROKE OPEN
BEEKNORST	KERBSTONE
BEEKNORTW	WENT BROKE
BEEKNOSST	STEENBOKS
BEEKOPRST	KEPT SOBER
BEEKPSSUY	KEEPS BUSY
BEELLLOWW	WELL BELOW
BEELLNSTT	BELL TENTS
BEELLORTW	BELL TOWER
BEELLOSSW	BOWELLESS
BEELLSSUY	BULL'S-EYES
BEELMOORT	BOLOMETER
BEELMRRST	TREMBLERS
BEELMRRSU	SLUMBERER
BEELNNOSS	NOBLENESS
BEELNOTWW	WENT BELOW
BEELNSTTU	BETEL NUTS
BEELOORWZ	BELOW ZERO
BEELORRST	BOLSTERER
BEELORSVY	OBVERSELY
	VERBOSELY
BEELORTTX	LETTER BOX
BEELOSSTU	BOLETUSES
BEELQRSUU	BURLESQUE
BEELRRSTU	BLUSTERER
BEEMNNORU	NUMBER ONE
BEEMNNRTU	NUMBER TEN
BEEMNORST	MRS. BEETON
BEEMNORSV	NOVEMBERS
BEEMNNRSU	RENUMBERS
BEEMRRSSU	BRESSUMER
BEEMRSSTU	BUM STEERS
BEENNOSTU	NEON TUBES
BEENOORRV	OVERBORNE
BEENORSSS	SOBERNESS
BEENORSWY	BROWN EYES
BEENRSTTU	BRUNETTES
BEEOORSTT	BEETROOTS
BEEOPRRST	ROBS PETER
BEEORRSSV	OBSERVERS
BEEORSTTU	SOUBRETTE
BEEORSTTW	BOW STREET
BEEPRRSTY	PRESBYTER
BEEQRSTUY	BY REQUEST
BEEQSSUUU	BUS QUEUES
BEERRSTTU	REBUTTERS
BEERSSSUV	SUBSERVES
BEERTTTUU	ET TU BRUTE
BEESSTTTU	TEST TUBES
BEFFGGORU	BUGGER OFF
BEFFGINRU	BUFFERING
	REBUFFING
BEFFGINTU	BUFFETING
BEFFGIORT	BIG EFFORT
BEFFHINTU	IN THE BUFF
BEFFINOTT	BITTEN OFF
BEFFIORST	BORE STIFF
BEFFKNOOR	BROKEN OFF
BEFFLMOTU	TUMBLE OFF
BEFFLNSSU	BLUFFNESS
BEFGGGINO	BEFOGGING
BEFGHILOS	GLOBEFISH
BEFGIILLS	FILLIBEGS
BEFGIINRS	BRIEFINGS
BEFGIINTT	BEFITTING
BEFGILNSU	FUNGIBLES

BEFGIOOUY	I BEG OF YOU
BEFGIOSTX	GIFT BOXES
BEFHILMSY	BY HIMSELF
BEFHIRRSU	BRUSHFIRE
	FURBISHER
	REFURBISH
BEFHIRSSU	BUSH FIRES
	FURBISHES
BEFIILNSU	INFUSIBLE
BEFILLLSU	FUEL BILLS
BEFILLMSU	BLUE FILMS
BEFILLOSW	BLOWFLIES
BEFILLSST	TELLS FIBS
BEFILMORS	FORELIMBS
BEFIORRTU	BORE FRUIT
BEFIORSTT	FROSTBITE
BEFIOTVWY	FIVE BY TWO
	TWO BY FIVE
BEFLLOTTU	BOTTLEFUL
BEFLMOORW	FROM BELOW
BEFLORSUW	FURBELOWS
BEFLRTTUY	BUTTERFLY
BEFNNNOUY	FUNNY BONE
BEGGGGINO	GO BEGGING
BEGGGLOOX	GOGGLE BOX
	GOGGLE-BOX
BEGGHOTTU	GOT THE BUG
BEGGIILNU	BEGUILING
BEGGIIINNN	BEGINNING
BEGGILNNO	BELONGING
BEGGINTTY	GETTING BY
BEGGIOORV	GO OVER BIG
BEGGJLOOS	JOE BLOGGS
BEGGNORSW	BROWN EGGS
BEGHHINOT	THIGHBONE
BEGHHOTTU	BETHOUGHT
BEGHIILPS	PHILIBEGS
BEGHIIRTT	BIG HITTER
BEGHIIRTV	GIVE BIRTH
BEGHILLTU	LIGHT BLUE
BEGHILRST	BLIGHTERS
BEGHIMNOR	BRING HOME
BEGHINOOV	BEHOOVING
BEGHINORT	BOTHERING
BEGHINORU	NEIGHBOUR
BEGHINRST	BRIGHTENS
BEGHINSTT	BEST THING
BEGHIOPTT	THE BIG TOP
BEGHIORRT	BORE RIGHT
BEGHIOSSU	BIG HOUSES
BEGHIRSTT	BRIGHTEST
BEGHLNORU	BUGLE HORN
BEGHLNOSU	BUNGHOLES
BEGIIILNT	IGNITIBLE
BEGIILLLN	LIBELLING
BEGIILLLY	ILLEGIBLY
BEGIILLNT	BILLETING
BEGIILMNU	IN BELGIUM
BEGIILOOS	BIOLOGIES
BEGIIMNRT	TIMBERING
BEGIIMRST	BIG-TIMERS
	MISTER BIG
BEGIINNTY	BENIGNITY
BEGIIPRSZ	BIG PRIZES
BEGIJRTTU	JITTERBUG
BEGIKNNRU	BUNKERING
BEGIKNORW	BEGIN WORK
BEGILLNOW	BELLOWING
BEGILLNRS	RING BELLS
BEGILMNOS	MEL GIBSON
BEGILMNRT	TREMBLING

BEGILMNRU	LUMBERING
BEGILMORY	GOR BLIMEY!
	GORBLIMEY
BEGILNNNO	ENNOBLING
BEGILNOST	LOSING BET
BEGILNOSW	SIGN BELOW
BEGILNPTU	BELTING UP
BEGILNSSS	BLESSINGS
BEGILRSTW	W.S.GILBERT
BEGILRTTU	LITTER BUG
	LITTERBUG
BEGIMNNOT	ENTOMBING
BEGIMNNRU	NUMBERING
BEGINNORS	RINGBONES
BEGINORRS	RESORBING
BEGINORRV	BRING OVER
BEGINORSV	OBSERVING
BEGINOSSS	OBSESSING
BEGINOSTT	OBTESTING
BEGINOSTW	BESTOWING
BEGINPRUW	BREWING UP
BEGINRTTU	BUTTERING
	REBUTTING
BEGIOORSU	BOURGEOIS
BEGIPRTTY	PRETTY BIG
BEGKNORUW	BEGUN WORK
BEGLMRUUX	LUXEMBURG
BEGLNOCCU	BLUES SONG
BEGLNRTUY	RUB GENTLY
BEGLRTUUY	UGLY BRUTE
BEGNOSSSU	BOGUSNESS
BEHHIKOST	THE KIBOSH
BEHHINSTU	IN THE BUSH
BEHHORSSU	SHOE BRUSH
BEHHORTUY	BY THE HOUR
BEHIILPST	PHLEBITIS
BEHIIORTX	EXHIBITOR
BEHIIRRST	BRITISHER
BEHIIRSTT	BITTERISH
BEHIKLOSV	BOLSHEVIK
BEHIKNOOT	IN THE BOOK
BEHIKPSSU	PUSH BIKES
BEHILLLOT	HOTEL BILL
BEHILLNNY	BENNY HILL
BEHILLNOP	PHONE BILL
BEHILLPSS	SHIPS BELL
BEHILNOOT	ON THE BOIL
BEHILOOTT	TO THE BOIL
BEHILOSST	BOLSHIEST
BEHILPRSU	PUBLISHER
BEHILPSSU	PUBLISHES
BEHILRSTU	BLUE SHIRT
BEHIMORTT	TO THE BRIM
BEHINNOSS	SHIN BONES
	SHINBONES
BEHINOSSW	WISHBONES
BEHINRSSU	BURNISHES
BEHINSSSU	BUSHINESS
BEHKNOOOP	PHONE BOOK
BEHLLOOST	BOLT HOLES
	BOLT-HOLES
BEHLLOOSW	BLOWHOLES
BEHLNORSU	BURN HOLES
BEHLORRTY	BROTHERLY
BEHLRSSUU	BULRUSHES
BEHMNORTU	HOT NUMBER
BEHMORSSU	RHOMBUSES
BEHMORSTU	SORE THUMB
BEHNORSTU	BUHRSTONE
BEHNOTTUY	THE BOUNTY
BEHOPRTYY	BRYOPHYTE

BEHORRSUV	BRUSH OVER
BEHPRSSUU	BRUSHES UP
BEIIILNSV	INVISIBLE
BEIIKLLSS	BILL SIKES
BEIIKRSTZ	KIBITZERS
BEIILLLST	LIBELLIST
BEIILLNSY	SIBYLLINE
BEIILLSTU	LIBEL SUIT
BEIILLTTT	LITTLE BIT
BEIILMOSS	MOBILISES
	OMISSIBLE
BEIILMOSZ	MOBILIZES
BEIILNRTT	LITTER BIN
BEIILORTT	TRILOBITE
BEIIMNNSU	BIENNIUMS
BEIIMNSSU	MINIBUSES
BEIINNRSS	BRININESS
BEIINOSTT	BITES INTO
BEIJLLLOY	BILLY JOEL
BEIKLNOTT	INK BOTTLE
BEIKLNSSU	BULKINESS
BEIKLOOTT	BOOK TITLE
BEIKLOSTY	KILOBYTES
BEIKMOORT	MOTOR BIKE
BEIKNOSST	STEINBOKS
BEIKNRSSS	BRISKNESS
BEIKOPRTU	BROKE IT UP
BEIKRSSTU	BUS STRIKE
BEILLLOSU	LIBELLOUS
BEILLLTUW	WELL-BUILT
BEILLMNPU	PLUMB LINE
BEILLMORW	LOWER LIMB
BEILLMRUY	BERYLLIUM
BEILLMSUY	SUBLIMELY
BEILLNOSU	INSOLUBLE
BEILLNSTU	BULLETINS
BEILLOPSX	PILL BOXES
	PILLBOXES
BEILLOQUY	OBLIQUELY
BEILLOTTY	LITTLE BOY
BEILLPRUZ	PRIZE BULL
BEILMMOSS	EMBOLISMS
BEILMNOSW	WOMENS LIB
BEILMNRSU	UNLIMBERS
BEILMOSSY	SYMBOLISE
BEILMOSYZ	SYMBOLIZE
BEILMPPRU	UPPER LIMB
BEILMPRSU	LIMBERS UP
BEILNNSTU	BUNTLINES
BEILNOPSS	BONSPIELS
BEILNORTU	IN TROUBLE
BEILNPRTU	BLUEPRINT
BEILNRSSU	BURLINESS
BEILOOPRT	POT BOILER
	POTBOILER
BEILOORSV	BOILS OVER
BEILOPPSW	BLOWPIPES
BEILOPSSS	POSSIBLES
BEILORSTT	LIBRETTOS
	LOST TRIBE
BEILORTUV	OVERBUILT
BEILOSSTW	BLOWSIEST
BEILPRSTU	BLUE STRIP
BEILRSTTT	BRITTLEST
BEILSSTTU	SUBTITLES
BEIMNORST	BRIMSTONE
BEIMNOSSU	OMNIBUSES
BEIMNPSSU	BUMPINESS
BEIMNRSUX	NUMBER SIX
BEIMOORSS	RIBOSOMES
BEIMORRSV	BRIMS OVER

BEIMOSSSY	SYMBIOSES	BENOOSTUU	BOUNTEOUS
BEIMRTTUY	YTTERBIUM	BENOPRSTU	BURST OPEN
BEINOORSY	SENIOR BOY	BENORRSSU	SUBORNERS
BEINOOSSS	OBSESSION	BENORRSWY	SNOWBERRY
BEINORUVV	BON VIVEUR	BENORSSSU	RUBS NOSES
BEINOSSSS	BOSSINESS	BENORSSUU	BURNOUSES
BEINRRSUU	RUS IN URBE	BENORSTXY	SENTRY BOX
BEIOQRSTU	SOBRIQUET	BENRTTTUU	BUTTERNUT
BEIOQSTUU	BOUTIQUES	BEOOPSSTX	POSTBOXES
BEIORSSST	SOB SISTER	BEOORRRSW	BORROWERS
BEIORSTUV	OBTRUSIVE	BEOPRTTYY	PRETTY BOY
BEIORSTVY	VERBOSITY	BEORRRSUW	BURROWERS
BEIORSTWY	SWORE BY IT	BEPRSTTUU	BUTTERS UP
BEIPPRSTU	BURST PIPE	BERRSTTUY	BURST TYRE
BEJKKOOOS	JOKE BOOKS	BFFFILMSU	FILM BUFFS
BEJNNNOOS	BEN JONSON	BFFGHOOTU	BOUGHT OFF
BEJORSTTU	TURBOJETS	BFFGIINOT	BITING OFF
BEKKNOOOT	BOOK TOKEN	BFFGINORS	BRINGS OFF
BEKKOOPST	KEPT BOOKS	BFFGINOUY	BUYING OFF
BEKLMOORS	MEL BROOKS	BFFHORSSU	BRUSH-OFFS
BEKLOOORV	BOOK LOVER	BFGGHIIST	BIG FIGHTS
BEKNNNOUW	UNBEKNOWN	BFGHILLTU	BULL FIGHT
BEKNNOSTW	KNOWN BEST		BULLFIGHT
BEKNOOOPS	OPEN BOOKS	BFGHINSTU	BUN FIGHTS
BEKNOOOST	NOTE BOOKS		BUN-FIGHTS
	NOTEBOOKS	BFGIIOPRT	BIG PROFIT
BEKNOORST	RENT BOOKS	BFGLLORSU	BULLFROGS
BEKNOORTU	BROKEN OUT	BFHILOSSW	FISHBOWLS
BEKNOTTUY	KEYBUTTON	BFIILMORY	MYOFIBRIL
BEKOOORSV	OVERBOOKS	BFIINORSU	FIBRINOUS
BEKOORSST	BOOKRESTS	BFIKOORST	FIRST BOOK
BEKOORSWX	WORKBOXES	BFILLRUYY	BILLY FURY
BEKOOSTTX	TEXT BOOKS	BFILNORSU	FLOUR BINS
	TEXTBOOKS	BFILNOTUU	BOUNTIFUL
BELLLLPSU	BELLPULLS	BFILOOSST	SOFT-BOILS
BELMNOOPR	NO PROBLEM	BFILORSTW	FIRST BLOW
BELMNORUW	LOW NUMBER	BFILORSUY	FIBROUSLY
BELMOOORW	ELBOW ROOM	BFILORTUW	FRUIT BOWL
	ELBOWROOM	BFINORRST	FIRST BORN
BELMOPSUU	PLUMBEOUS		FIRSTBORN
BELMORTTU	RUM BOTTLE	BFIORSSTU	IFS OR BUTS
BELMOSSXY	SEX SYMBOL	BFIOSTTTU	FIT TO BUST
BELMOTTUU	TUMBLE OUT	BFJKOOORW	JOB OF WORK
BELMRSSTU	STUMBLERS	BFLLLMOOU	FULL BLOOM
BELNNOOPW	BLOWN OPEN	BFLLLNOUW	FULL-BLOWN
BELNNSSTU	BLUNTNESS	BFLLOOSUW	FOUL BLOWS
BELNOOPSW	BLOWS OPEN	BFOORTUWY	FOUR BY TWO
BELNOORTU	NO TROUBLE		TWO BY FOUR
BELNOORVW	BLOWN OVER	BGGHIILNT	BLIGHTING
	OVERBLOWN	BGGILMNRU	GRUMBLING
BELNRSTUU	TURNS BLUE	BGGINNPUU	BUNGING UP
BELNRTTUU	TURBULENT	BGGINOSTU	GOING BUST
BELOOOSTX	TOOL BOXES	BGHHHIIRT	HIGH BIRTH
	TOOLBOXES	BGHHIOOST	HIGH BOOTS
BELOOPRST	BOLTROPES	BGHIIKNST	THINKS BIG
BELOORSSW	ROSE BOWLS	BGHIILLRT	BIG THRILL
BELOORSVW	BLOWS OVER	BGHIMOSTU	BIG MOUTHS
	BOWLS OVER	BGHINORTU	BROUGHT IN
BELOPRSTU	BOLSTER UP	BGHJOOSTU	TOUGH JOBS
BELOPSTTU	BOTTLES UP	BGHNNSUUY	BUNNY HUGS
BELQRSUUY	BRUSQUELY	BGHNOORTU	BROUGHT ON
BEMNOORST	TROMBONES	BGHOORTTU	BROUGHT TO
BEMNOORSW	NEW BROOMS	BGHOOTTUU	BOUGHT OUT
BEMNOOSTT	TOMBSTONE	BGHOPRTUU	BROUGHT UP
BEMNORTUU	OUTNUMBER	BGIIINTTW	BITING WIT
BEMNORTUW	NUMBER TWO	BGIIJNORT	TIRING JOB
BEMNOSSUX	BUXOMNESS	BGIIKPRRY	KIRBY GRIP
BEMOORRSS	SOMBREROS	BGIILLNOW	BILLOWING
BEMOORSTT	BOTTOMERS	BGIILMNSU	SUBLIMING
BENNNOSTU	SUN BONNET	BGIILMOOR	IMBROGLIO
	SUNBONNET	BGIILNOPU	BOILING UP

BGIILNOTW	BLOWING IT	BIILOOSUV	OBLIVIOUS
BGIILNRSS	BRISLINGS	BIILOQTUY	OBLIQUITY
BGIILNRST	BRISTLING	BIIMOPRTY	IMPROBITY
BGIILOOST	BIOLOGIST	BIIMOSSSY	SYMBIOSIS
BGIINNTTU	BUTTING IN	BIISSTTYY	ITSY-BITSY
BGIINPRTU	BRING IT UP	BIKLNNOSW	SNOWBLINK
BGIKLNOST	KINGBOLTS	BIKOOSUUZ	BOUZOUKIS
BGIKNOOPU	BOOKING UP	BILLNOOPS	SPOONBILL
BGIKNOPRS	SPRINGBOK	BILLNORST	STILLBORN
BGIILNRSU	BULLRINGS	BILLNOSUY	INSOLUBLY
BGILMNNUY	NUMBINGLY	BILMMOSSY	SYMBOLISM
BGILMNOOY	MYOGLOBIN	BILMNOOSS	IN BLOSSOM
BGILMNSTU	STUMBLING	BILMOSSTY	SYMBOLIST
BGILNNOTU	UNBOLTING	BILOOPRTU	POLITBURO
BGILNNRUY	BUNNY GIRL	BILOOSUVY	OBVIOUSLY
	BURNINGLY	BILORSSTU	STROBILUS
BGILNOPUW	BLOWING UP	BIMNOPSTU	BUMPS INTO
BGILNORST	RINGBOLTS	BIMNOSSTY	SYMBIONTS
BGILNORSW	BRINGS LOW	BIMOPSTUU	BUMPTIOUS
BGILNORTU	TROUBLING	BINNOOSSU	UNION BOSS
BGILOORTY	TRIBOLOGY	BINOOOSUX	OBNOXIOUS
BGIMNOOTT	BOTTOMING	BINOORSTU	OBTRUSION
BGIMNSSUU	SUBSUMING	BINORSTUW	BROWN SUIT
BGINNORSU	SUBORNING	BINORSTWY	SWORN BY IT
BGINNORTU	BINTURONG	BIOPRSSTW	BOWSPRITS
BGINNOTTU	BUTTONING	BJRRTUYYY	TRY BY JURY
BGINOORRW	BORROWING	BKKOOORSW	WORKBOOKS
BGINOOSST	BONGOISTS	BKLLMNSUU	NUMBSKULL
BGINOPUUY	BUOYING UP	BKMOOOORS	BOOK ROOMS
BGINORRUW	BURROWING	BKMOOORSW	BOOKWORMS
BGINORSTU	BRINGS OUT	BKOOORSTY	STORY BOOK
BGINOTUUY	BUYING OUT		STORYBOOK
BGINPSTUU	BUSTING UP	BLLLOOSUW	BULLSWOOL
BGINPTTUY	PUTTING BY	BLLORSSTY	STROLLS BY
BGKNOOOSS	SONG BOOKS	BLMORSSUU	SLUMBROUS
BGLMOOSYY	SYMBOLOGY	BLNOORSWW	BROWN OWLS
BGNOORSTX	STRONG BOX	BLOORSTUU	TROUBLOUS
	STRONGBOX	BLORSTTUU	BLURTS OUT
BGNOOSUYY	YOUNG BOYS	BMNOOOSTW	BOOM TOWNS
BHHIMORTY	BIORHYTHM	BMOOOTTTU	BOTTOM OUT
BHHIRSSTU	BUSH SHIRT	BMOOPPRTX	PROMPT BOX
BHHLLOSUY	HOLLY BUSH	BMOOPSTTU	BOTTOMS UP
BHHNORSTU	THORNBUSH	BNNORRTUW	TURN BROWN
BHIIINORT	INHIBITOR	BNNOSTTUU	UNBUTTONS
BHIILLLLY	HILLBILLY	BNOPSTTUU	BUTTONS UP
BHIILLNOT	BILLIONTH	BNOSSTUWY	BUSY TOWNS
BHIILLRSU	IRISH BULL	BNRSSSTUU	SUNBURSTS
BHIIOPRST	PROHIBITS	BOOPPRRTU	TURBOPROP
BHIKLLOOS	BILLHOOKS	BORSSTTUU	BURSTS OUT
BHIKLOOSY	BOOKISHLY		OUTBURSTS
BHILLNORS	HORNBILLS	CCCDENOOT	CONCOCTED
BHILLSSTU	BULLSHITS	CCCDIIMOU	COCCIDIUM
BHILMNOTY	BIMONTHLY	CCCEEILST	ECLECTICS
BHILRSTUY	BRUTISHLY	CCCEEINRT	ECCENTRIC
BHIMOOSTY	TOMBOYISH	CCCEIILPY	EPICYCLIC
BHIORRSST	SHORT RIBS	CCCENOORT	CONCOCTER
BHJNNOORW	JOHN BROWN	CCCGINOOO	GONOCOCCI
BHKMNOOSY	HYMN BOOKS	CCCHILMOU	COLCHICUM
	HYMNBOOKS	CCCIMOSTU	COMIC CUTS
BHKOOOPSS	BOOK SHOPS	CCDDEEESU	SUCCEEDED
	BOOKSHOPS	CCDDEIINO	COINCIDED
BHKORRSUW	BRUSHWORK	CCDDEKLOU	CUCKOLDED
BHLLNORSU	BULLHORNS	CCDDEKOUY	DECOY DUCK
BHLLOOOTT	TOLLBOOTH	CCDDELNOU	CONCLUDED
BHLOOOSTT	TOLBOOTHS	CCDDENOTU	CONDUCTED
BHMPSSTUU	THUMBS-UPS	CCDEEEHKR	CHECKERED
BHNOORSTW	SNOW-BROTH	CCDEEEHRS	SCREECHED
BIIILNSVY	INVISIBLY	CCDEEENRS	CREDENCES
BIILLOSUY	BILIOUSLY	CCDEEERSU	SUCCEEDER
BIILMSTUY	SUBLIMITY	CCDEEHIKN	CHECKED IN
BIILNOOVW	VIOLIN BOW	CCDEEHIKW	CHICKWEED

CCDEEHKNU	UNCHECKED	CCEEHLORT	CERECLOTH
CCDEEHKPU	CHECKED UP	CCEEHNORY	COHERENCY
CCDEEHORT	CROCHETED	CCEEHORRT	CROCHETER
CCDEEIINN	INCIDENCE	CCEEHOTTU	COUCHETTE
CCDEEILNR	ENCIRCLED	CCEEIIPPR	PRECIPICE
CCDEEINNY	INDECENCY	CCEEIKRRT	CRICKETER
CCDEEINOT	CONCEITED	CCEEILNOR	RECONCILE
CCDEEINOV	CONCEIVED	CCEEILNRS	ENCIRCLES
CCDEEIOPR	PRICE CODE	CCEEILNTV	T.V.LICENCE
CCDEEIOPS	CODPIECES	CCEEILPRY	PERICYCLE
CCDEELLOT	COLLECTED	CCEEILPSY	EPICYCLES
CCDEEMMNO	COMMENCED	CCEEILRST	ELECTRICS
CCDEENNOR	CONCERNED	CCEEINNNO	INNOCENCE
CCDEENNOS	ENSCONCED	CCEEINORT	ICE CORNET
CCDEENNOT	CONNECTED	CCEEINORV	CONCEIVER
CCDEENORS	CONCEDERS	CCEEINOSV	CONCEIVES
	CRESCENDO	CCEEIRRST	RECTRICES
CCDEENORT	CONCERTED	CCEEKLORS	COCKERELS
	CONCRETED	CCEELLORT	RECOLLECT
CCDEEORRT	CORRECTED	CCEELMOOS	COME CLOSE
CCDEFIIRU	CRUCIFIED	CCEELOTUY	LEUCOCYTE
CCDEGINNO	CONCEDING	CCEEMMNOS	COMMENCES
CCDEGINOT	DECOCTING	CCEENNORT	CONNECTER
CCDEHIKNU	CHUCKED IN	CCEENNOSS	ENSCONCES
CCDEHIKTU	CHUCKED IT	CCEENOOTY	COENOCYTE
CCDEHIPPU	HICCUPPED	CCEENORST	CONCRETES
CCDEHKPUU	CHUCKED UP	CCEENRSST	CRESCENTS
CCDEHNRSU	SCRUNCHED	CCEEORRRT	CORRECTER
CCDEIIKNP	PICNICKED	CCEESSSSU	SUCCESSES
CCDEIILOV	CIVIL CODE	CCEFFHKOS	CHECKS OFF
CCDEIIINOS	COINCIDES	CCEFFIIIL	FELICIFIC
CCDEIKLNO	CLOCKED IN	CCEFHIKOO	CHIEF COOK
CCDEILOOR	CROCODILE	CCEFIIPSS	SPECIFICS
CCDEILRTY	TRICYCLED	CCEFIIRSU	CRUCIFIES
CCDEINNOV	CONVINCED	CCEFIRRSU	CRUCIFERS
CCDEINOOT	DECOCTION	CCEFKNOYY	COCKNEYFY
CCDEINOST	OCCIDENTS	CCEFLLOSU	FLOCCULES
CCDEINOTV	CONVICTED	CCEGGHOST	SCOTCH EGG
CCDEINOUV	CONDUCIVE	CCEGHILNN	CLENCHING
CCDEKLNOO	CLOCKED ON	CCEGILNRY	RECYCLING
CCDEKLORU	CUCKOLDER		RING CYCLE
CCDELNOSU	CONCLUDES	CCEGINNOO	ONCOGENIC
CCDELNOTU	OCCLUDENT	CCEGINORY	CRYOGENIC
CCDENORRU	CONCURRED	CCEGLNOSY	SONG CYCLE
CCDENOSSU	CONCUSSED	CCEHHMNRU	CHURCHMEN
CCDEORSUU	SUCCOURED	CCEHIILRS	SCHLIERIC
CCDGILNOU	OCCLUDING	CCEHIKLST	CHECKLIST
CCDGINNOU	CONDUCING	CCEHIKNNO	NO CHICKEN
CCDHKOOUW	WOODCHUCK	CCEHILNOR	CHRONICLE
CCDHLLNOU	COLD LUNCH	CCEHILNRS	CLINCHERS
CCDIIOORT	CORTICOID	CCEHILNRU	RICH UNCLE
CCDIITUVY	CIVIC DUTY	CCEHINORR	CHRONICER
CCDKKLNOO	KNOCK COLD	CCEHINORS	CORNICHES
CCDKLOORS	OLD CROCKS	CCEHINRRU	CRUNCHIER
CCDKLORUY	CUCKOLDRY	CCEHIORST	RICOCHETS
CCDKOOOSW	WOODCOCKS	CCEHKMOOR	CHECKROOM
CCDNOORTU	CONDUCTOR	CCEHKOPST	SPOT CHECK
CCEEEFLNU	FECULENCE		SPOT-CHECK
CCEEEHHRR	RECHERCHE	CCEHKOSTU	CHECKOUTS
CCEEEHNOR	COHERENCE		CHECKS OUT
CCEEEHRRS	SCREECHER	CCEHLOTTU	THE OCCULT
CCEEEHRSS	SCREECHES	CCEHNRSSU	SCRUNCHES
CCEEEINNS	NESCIENCE	CCEHORRSS	SCORCHERS
CCEEEINRT	RETICENCE	CCEHORSTT	CROTCHETS
CCEEFFOPU	COFFEE CUP	CCEHORTTY	CROTCHETY
CCEEFILLY	LIFE CYCLE	CCEHOTTUZ	ZUCCHETTO
CCEEGINOR	CONCIERGE	CCEIIIPRT	EPICRITIC
CCEEHIKMT	TIME CHECK	CCEIIIRST	CRITICISE
CCEEHIKNR	CHECKREIN	CCEIIIRTZ	CRITICIZE
CCEEHIKOY	ICE HOCKEY	CCEIIKNPR	PICNICKER
CCEEHIKORV	CHECK OVER	CCEIILNRS	IN CIRCLES

CCEIILPST	ECLIPTICS	CCGILMOOY	MYCOLOGIC
CCEIILSTT	CELTICIST	CCGILNOOO	ONCOLOGIC
CCEIINOTX	EXCITONIC	CCGILNOTU	OCCULTING
CCEIKKLLO	CLOCKLIKE	CCGILOOTY	CYTOLOGIC
CCEIKLLOY	KILOCYCLE	CCGINNOOO	COCOONING
CCEIKLOSW	CLOCKWISE	CCGINOPUY	OCCUPYING
CCEIKNOSS	COCKINESS	CCGINORRU	OCCURRING
CCEILNNOU	NUCLEONIC	CCGINOSTU	STUCCOING
CCEILNOSY	CONCISELY	CCHHLORUW	LOW CHURCH
CCEILNSUY	UNICYCLES	CCHHMOPPU	CHUMP CHOP
CCEILORST	SCLEROTIC	CCHHOOPST	HOPSCOTCH
CCEILOSUV	OCCLUSIVE	CCHHOOSWW	CHOW-CHOWS
CCEILRSTY	TRICYCLES	CCHIIKNTU	CHUCK IT IN
CCEILRSUU	CURLICUES	CCHIIMORT	TRICHOMIC
CCEIMNOOS	ECONOMICS	CCHIINOOR	CHORIONIC
CCEIMOSST	COSMETICS	CCHIINSUZ	ZUCCHINIS
CCEINNNOY	INNOCENCY	CCHIIORRT	CIRRHOTIC
CCEINNORT	IN CONCERT	CCHIKOPST	CHOPSTICK
CCEINNOSV	CONVINCES	CCHILOORT	CHLOROTIC
CCEINORRT	INCORRECT	CCHINRTUU	URCHIN CUT
CCEINOSST	CONCISEST	CCHIOPSTY	PSYCHOTIC
CCEINOSTT	TECTONICS	CCHKOSTUU	CHUCKS OUT
CCEINOSTU	CUTS NO ICE	CCHLOORUW	CROUCH LOW
CCEINPRST	PRECINCTS	CCIIILNOS	ISOCLINIC
CCFINRSTU	CINCTURES	CCIIILNRT	TRICLINIC
CCEINRSTY	SYNCRETIC	CCIIILOST	SILICOTIC
CCEIOPRRS	RICE CROPS	CCIIIMRST	CRITICISM
CCEIOPRST	COST PRICE	CCIIINNOT	NICOTINIC
CCEIOPRTY	PRECOCITY	CCIIINOTY	ICONICITY
CCEIPRSTU	PRICE CUTS	CCIILNNOU	IN COUNCIL
CCEKKNNOO	KNOCK ONCE	CCIILNOTY	CLONICITY
CCEKLNOOO	ONE O CLOCK	CCIILOOST	SCOLIOTIC
CCEKLNOOT	TEN O CLOCK	CCIILOPRT	PROCLITIC
CCEKORRSW	CORKSCREW	CCIINNOOS	CONCISION
CCELLNOOY	COLONELCY	CCIINOPTY	PINOCYTIC
CCELLOORT	COLLECTOR	CCIINORST	CISTRONIC
CCELNSTUU	SUCCULENT	CCIIRRTUY	CIRCUITRY
CCELOOPRS	CLOSE CROP	CCIKKLOPS	PICK LOCKS
CCELOPRSU	CORPUSCLE	CCIKLOOSX	SIX O CLOCK
CCELORRTY	CORRECTLY	CCIKMORSU	ROCK MUSIC
CCELORTUY	CYCLE TOUR	CCIKOPSTU	COCKS IT UP
CCELRSUUY	CURLYCUES	CCILLOPPS	CLIP-CLOPS
CCENNNORU	UNCONCERN	CCILMOSTU	OCCULTISM
CCENNOORT	CONNECTOR	CCILNOORU	COUNCILOR
CCENOORST	CONCERTOS	CCILNOOSU	OCCLUSION
CCENOORSU	CONCOURSE	CCILOSTTU	OCCULTIST
CCENOORTV	CONVECTOR	CCIMMOORS	MICROCOSM
CCENOPSTU	CONCEPTUS	CCIMNOOTY	MONOCYTIC
CCENOSSSU	CONCUSSES	CCIMOOPRY	MICROCOPY
CCEOORRRT	CORRECTOR	CCINOOSSU	CONSCIOUS
CCEOPPRUY	PREOCCUPY	CCINOPRST	CONSCRIPT
CCEORSSSU	SUCCESSOR	CCINORSTT	CONSTRICT
CCFGHIKOT	COCKFIGHT	CCIOOTTXY	CYTOTOXIC
CCFGKLLOO	CLOCK GOLF	CCKKLOORW	CLOCKWORK
CCFHIORST	SCOTCH FIR	CCKLOOOTW	TWO O CLOCK
CCFILNOST	CONFLICTS	CCKLOOSTU	CLOCKS OUT
CCFIMORRU	CRUCIFORM	CCKNOORRW	CROWN CORK
CCFLLOSUU	FLOCCULUS	CCKOOPPPY	POPPYCOCK
CCGHHINRU	CHURCHING	CCKOOPSST	STOPCOCKS
CCGHIILNN	CLINCHING	CCLNOORTY	CYCLOTRON
CCGHIKLNU	CHUCKLING	CCNORSTTU	CONSTRUCT
CCGHILNTU	CLUTCHING	CCORSSSTU	CROSSCUTS
CCGHILOOP	CHOP LOGIC	CDDDEEENS	DESCENDED
CCGHINNRU	CRUNCHING	CDDDEEILY	DECIDEDLY
CCGHINORS	SCORCHING	CDDDEEINU	UNDECIDED
CCGHINORU	CROUCHING	CDDDEIIRT	DID CREDIT
CCGHINOST	SCOTCHING	CDDDELPUU	CUDDLED UP
CCGHINSTU	SCUTCHING	CDDEEEFLT	DEFLECTED
CCGIILNSY	CYCLISING	CDDEEEINV	EVIDENCED
CCGIILNYZ	CYCLIZING	CDDEEEIPY	PIECE-DYED
CCGIKNOPU	COCKING UP	CDDEEENST	DECEDENTS

CDDEEEEOPR	PROCEEDED	CDEEEHKRS	RED CHEEKS
CDDEEEESTU	DEUCEDEST	CDEEEHPRU	CHEERED UP
CDDEEFKOR	DEFROCKED	CDEEEHQRU	CHEQUERED
CDDEEFOSU	DEFOCUSED	CDEEEIMRT	DECIMETRE
CDDEEGLLU	CUDGELLED	CDEEEINPT	CENTIPEDE
CDDEEHLSU	SCHEDULED	CDEEEINRS	RESIDENCE
CDDEEHNRU	CHUNDERED	CDEEEINRT	INTERCEDE
CDDEEHQUU	DUD CHEQUE	CDEEEINSV	EVIDENCES
CDDEEIKRU	EIDER DUCK	CDEEEINUV	UNDECEIVE
CDDEEINRS	DISCERNED	CDEEEIOPV	DEEP VOICE
	RESCINDED	CDEEEIPRT	RECEIPTED
CDDEEIPRT	PREDICTED	CDEEEIPRV	PERCEIVED
CDDEEISST	DISSECTED	CDEEEIPSY	PIECE-DYES
CDDEEITUV	DEDUCTIVE	CDEEEIPTV	DECEPTIVE
CDDEELNPU	PEDUNCLED	CDEEEIRSV	DECEIVERS
CDDEELOPU	DECOUPLED	CDEEEIRSX	EXERCISED
CDDEELPRU	PRECLUDED	CDEEEITTV	DETECTIVE
CDDEEMMNO	COMMENDED	CDEEELLOT	DECOLLETE
CDDEEMNNO	CONDEMNED	CDEEELNOR	REDOLENCE
CDDEENNOS	CONDENSED	CDEEELORT	ELECTRODE
CDDEENNOT	CONTENDED	CDEEENPRT	PRECEDENT
CDDEENNOU	DENOUNCED	CDEEENQSU	SEQUENCED
CDDEGINTU	DEDUCTING	CDEEEOORRV	RECOVERED
CDDEGIOTY	DODGE CITY	CDEEEPRSS	PRECESSED
CDDEGLOOR	OLD CODGER	CDEEEPRST	RESPECTED
CDDEHIJNU	JUDI DENCH	CDEEEPRTX	EXCERPTED
CDDEIIKNR	ICED DRINK	CDEEFFIOR	OFFICERED
CDDEIILMO	DOMICILED	CDEEFGINT	DEFECTING
CDDEIILNY	DID NICELY	CDEEFHPTU	FETCHED UP
CDDEIILRU	RIDICULED	CDEEFIILR	RICE FIELD
CDDEIINRT	DENDRITIC	CDEEFIINT	DEFICIENT
CDDEIIOSV	VIDEODISC	CDEEFIIPS	SPECIFIED
CDDEIIRST	DISCREDIT	CDEEFIIRR	FRIED RICE
CDDEILOSS	DISCLOSED	CDEEFIIRT	CERTIFIED
CDDEILSTU	CUDDLIEST		RECTIFIED
CDDEIMMOU	DUODECIMO	CDEEFIKLR	FLICKERED
CDDEINORW	CRIED DOWN	CDEEFILNT	INFLECTED
CDDEINOTU	DEDUCTION	CDEEFILTU	DECEITFUL
CDDEIOSUU	DECIDUOUS	CDEEFINOT	DEFECTION
CDDEISSSU	DISCUSSED	CDEEFINOV	DEN OF VICE
CDDELOOPU	ODD COUPLE	CDEEFKORS	FOREDECKS
CDDELOORR	OLD RECORD	CDEEFKOST	FEEDSTOCK
CDDELPSUU	CUDDLES UP	CDEEFLLOS	FEELS COLD
CDDEOORSW	CODE WORDS	CDEEFLORT	DEFLECTOR
CDDGIKNUY	DYING DUCK	CDEEFLRUU	FLUE-CURED
CDDHHILOO	CHILDHOOD	CDEEFNORR	CONFERRED
CDDHIIORY	HYDRIODIC	CDEEFNOSS	CONFESSED
CDDHOORTU	DUTCH DOOR	CDEEFORST	DEFECTORS
CDDIIKRTY	DIRTY DICK	CDEEFORSU	USED FORCE
CDDIILMNU	LUCID MIND	CDEEFOSSU	DEFOCUSES
CDDIKLNOR	COLD DRINK	CDEEGHIKT	THICK EDGE
CDDIKLSUW	WILD DUCKS	CDEEGHOOR	GOOD CHEER
CDDIKNORY	IN DRY DOCK	CDEEGIILN	DILIGENCE
CDDILNOOY	CONDYLOID	CDEEGIIMR	GERMICIDE
CDDILNOSW	COLD WINDS	CDEEGIINN	INDIGENCE
CDDKNOPSU	DUCK PONDS	CDEEGIINT	DIGENETIC
CDDLOTUYY	CUDDLY TOY	CDEEGIINV	DECEIVING
CDEEEEFNR	DEFERENCE	CDEEGIIRS	REGICIDES
CDEEEEHRS	RED CHEESE	CDEEGILOP	GOLD PIECE
CDEEEEKNW	EWE-NECKED	CDEEGILRY	GLYCERIDE
CDEEEFFOR	FORCE FEED	CDEEGINOR	ENDOERGIC
	FORCE-FEED	CDEEGINOS	GENOCIDES
CDEEEFINN	IN DEFENCE	CDEEGINPR	PRECEDING
CDEEEFITV	DEFECTIVE	CDEEGINTT	DETECTING
CDEEEFLRT	REFLECTED	CDEEGKNOR	DOCK GREEN
CDEEEFNNO	NO DEFENCE	CDEEGNORV	CONVERGED
CDEEEFPRT	PERFECTED	CDEEGNOST	CONGESTED
CDEEEGINR	DECREEING	CDEEGORSU	RESCUE DOG
CDEEEGINX	EXCEEDING	CDEEHHIRS	CHERISHED
CDEEEGLNT	NEGLECTED	CDEEHIKRS	SHICKERED
CDEEEHKNP	HENPECKED	CDEEHILLS	CHISELLED

CDEEHINST	DEHISCENT	CDEEJOPRT	PROJECTED
CDEEHIPRS	DECIPHERS	CDEEKKLRS	DESK CLERK
CDEEHKOSS	DECK SHOES	CDEEKLNOW	LOW-NECKED
CDEEHKOSU	DECKHOUSE	CDEEKLORW	LOWER DECK
CDEEHLLOS	HELD CLOSE	CDEEKPPRU	UPPER DECK
CDEEHLORU	LOUD CHEER	CDEELLMOP	COMPELLED
CDEEHLORY	HYDROCELE	CDEELLNRU	CULLENDER
CDEEHLQSU	SQUELCHED	CDEELLOST	COLD STEEL
CDEEHLRSU	SCHEDULER	CDEELMNTU	DEMULCENT
CDEEHLSSU	SCHEDULES	CDEELMOPT	COMPLETED
CDEEHNOST	THE SECOND	CDEELNPSU	PEDUNCLES
CDEEHNRTU	CHUNTERED	CDEELOPSU	DECOUPLES
CDEEHORTU	RETOUCHED	CDEELPRSU	PRECLUDES
CDEEHOTUW	CHEWED OUT	CDEELRSTU	CLUSTERED
CDEEHRRRY	CHERRY RED	CDEELRTTU	CLUTTERED
CDEEHRSTT	STRETCHED	CDEEMMNOR	RECOMMEND
CDEEHSSSU	DUCHESSES	CDEEMMNOT	COMMENTED
CDEEIIKLW	WICKED LIE	CDEEMNNOT	CONTEMNED
CDEEIILRT	DECILITRE	CDEEMNOOS	COMEDONES
CDEEIILTV	VIDELICET	CDEEMNORU	COME UNDER
CDEEIIMNS	MEDICINES	CDEEMOOPS	DECOMPOSE
CDEEIIMPR	EPIDERMIC	CDEEMOORS	MORSE CODE
CDEEIIMPS	EPIDEMICS	CDEEMORST	ECTODERMS
CDEEIIPRR	CIRRIPEDE	CDEENNOOS	ONE SECOND
CDEEIIPST	PESTICIDE	CDEENNORS	CONDENSER
CDEEIIRTV	DIRECTIVE	CDEENNORT	CONTENDER
CDEEIISTT	DIETETICS	CDEENNORU	DENOUNCER
CDEEIJNOT	DEJECTION		RENOUNCED
CDEEIJPRU	PREJUDICE	CDEENNOSS	CONDENSES
CDEEIKMNP	PICKED MEN	CDEENNOST	CONSENTED
CDEEIKMRY	DICK EMERY	CDEENNOSU	DENOUNCES
CDEEIKNOW	WICKED ONE	CDEENNOTT	CONTENTED
CDEEIKNQU	QUICKENED	CDEENNRSU	SCUNNERED
CDEEIKNRS	SNICKERED	CDEENOOPS	ENDOSCOPE
CDEEIKOPR	POKER DICE	CDEENOQRU	CONQUERED
CDEEILLNP	PENCILLED	CDEENORRW	NEW RECORD
CDEEILNNO	INDOLENCE	CDEENORSS	SECONDERS
CDEEILNPR	RED PENCIL	CDEENORSV	CONSERVED
CDEEILRST	DERELICTS		CONVERSED
CDEEILTXY	EXCITEDLY	CDEENORTU	COUNTERED
CDEEIMNNU	DECENNIUM		RECOUNTED
CDEEIMNPU	IMPUDENCE	CDEENORTV	CONVERTED
CDEEIMRSV	DECEMVIRS	CDEENORUV	UNCOVERED
CDEEINNOR	ENDOCRINE	CDEENOSST	SECOND SET
CDEEINOPT	DECEPTION	CDEENOSTT	CONTESTED
CDEEINORT	RECONDITE	CDEENPRSU	PRUDENCES
CDEEINOST	SECTIONED	CDEENRSSU	CRUDENESS
CDEEINOTT	DETECTION	CDEENRSTU	ENCRUSTED
CDEEINOTU	DUE NOTICE	CDEENRSUW	UNSCREWED
CDEEINPRS	CRISPENED	CDEEOORST	CREOSOTED
CDEEINPST	INSPECTED	CDEEOORTY	EYE DOCTOR
CDEEINRRS	DISCERNER	CDEEOPPSS	SPEED COPS
	RESCINDER	CDEEOPRRR	PRERECORD
CDEEINRST	STRIDENCE	CDEEOPRRU	PROCEDURE
CDEEINRSY	RESIDENCY		REPRODUCE
CDEEIOPSW	WIDE SCOPE	CDEEOPRSS	PROCESSED
CDEEIORSV	DIVORCEES	CDEEOPRTT	PROTECTED
CDEEIORSX	EXORCISED	CDEEOPRUV	COVERED UP
CDEEIOSTX	COEXISTED	CDEEORRRS	RECORDERS
CDEEIOTTU	EUTECTOID	CDEEORRTY	DECRETORY
CDEEIPRST	DEPICTERS	CDEEORSSY	CROSS-EYED
CDEEIPRSU	PEDICURES	CDEEORSTT	DETECTORS
CDEEIRRST	REDIRECTS	CDEEPPRSU	SCUPPERED
CDEEIRRTU	RECRUITED	CDEEPRSSU	PERCUSSED
CDEEIRSTT	DIRECTEST	CDEEPRSUW	SCREWED UP
	TRISECTED	CDEEPSSTU	SUSPECTED
CDEEIRTTU	CERTITUDE	CDEERSTTU	SCUTTERED
	RECTITUDE	CDEESSSTU	CUSSEDEST
CDEEIRTUV	REDUCTIVE	CDEFFHKOO	CHOKED OFF
CDEEISTUV	SEDUCTIVE	CDEFFIKKO	KICKED OFF
CDEEJKORU	CRUDE JOKE	CDEFFIKOP	PICKED OFF

CDEFFIKOT	TICKED OFF	CDEHINOUU	EUNUCHOID
CDEFFIORU	COIFFURED	CDEHIOPTW	COPED WITH
CDEFFLOOO	COOLED OFF	CDEHIPRRU	CHIRRUPED
CDEFFOORS	SCORED OFF	CDEHKLSSU	SHELDUCKS
CDEFGIINU	FUNGICIDE	CDEHKNOOW	CHOKE DOWN
CDEFHITUW	DUTCH WIFE	CDEHLLOOS	HOLD CLOSE
CDEFIIIST	FIDEISTIC	CDEHLNORU	CHONDRULE
CDEFIILNT	INFLICTED	CDEHLNOTU	UNCLOTHED
CDEFIINST	DISINFECT	CDEHLOPST	SPLOTCHED
CDEFIKLOR	FROLICKED	CDEHLORTU	HELD COURT
CDEFIKOSS	FOSSICKED	CDEHMMOUV	MUCH MOVED
CDEFILLOT	COD FILLET	CDEHNOOTU	TOUCHED ON
CDEFILORW	CRIED WOLF	CDEHNOTUU	UNTOUCHED
CDEFIMNOR	CONFIRMED	CDEHNOTUV	DUTCH OVEN
CDEFINNOT	CONFIDENT	CDEHNTTUW	WENT DUTCH
CDEFINTUY	FECUNDITY	CDEHOPTUU	TOUCHED UP
CDEFKNORU	UNFROCKED	CDEHPPSUY	PSYCHED UP
CDEFMNOOR	CONFORMED	CDEIIILSV	CIVILISED
CDEFMOORT	COMFORTED	CDEIIILVZ	CIVILIZED
CDEFOORTU	FORCED OUT	CDEIIIRST	SIDERITIC
CDEGGKSSU	DUCKS EGGS	CDEIIKKSS	SIDEKICKS
CDEGHIINS	DEHISCING	CDEIIKMTW	MID-WICKET
CDEGHINNR	DRENCHING	CDEIILMOS	DOMICILES
CDEGHNOTU	GONE DUTCH	CDEIILORT	DOLERITIC
CDEGHOPUU	COUGHED UP	CDEIILOST	IDIOLECTS
CDEGHOSTU	GOES DUTCH		SOLICITED
CDEGIIKNR	DICKERING	CDEIILOSU	DELICIOUS
CDEGIILNN	DECLINING	CDEIILPSS	DISCIPLES
CDEGIILOO	IDEOLOGIC	CDEIILRSU	RIDICULES
CDEGIIMRU	DEMIURGIC	CDEIILTVY	DECLIVITY
CDEGIINOV	DEVOICING	CDEIIMNTY	MENDICITY
CDEGIINPT	DEPICTING	CDEIIMRST	MISDIRECT
CDEGIINRT	CREDITING	CDEIINNST	INCIDENTS
	DIRECTING	CDEIINOPT	DEPICTION
CDEGIKNOT	DOCKETING	CDEIINORT	DIRECTION
CDEGILNSU	SECLUDING	CDEIINOSS	DECISIONS
CDEGILNUX	EXCLUDING	CDEIINRTT	INTERDICT
CDEGILOOP	PEDOLOGIC	CDEIINTUV	INDUCTIVE
	POLICE DOG	CDEIIOOSU	DIOECIOUS
CDEGILOPR	GOLD PRICE	CDEIIOPRX	PEROXIDIC
CDEGILOSU	GLUCOSIDE	CDEIIPRRS	CIRRIPEDS
CDEGILOSY	GLYCOSIDE	CDEIIRRTX	DIRECTRIX
CDEGINNOS	CONSIGNED	CDEIIRSTU	DIURETICS
	SECONDING	CDEIJNNOO	CONJOINED
CDEGINORR	RECORDING	CDEIJOSTU	DO JUSTICE
CDEGINRSY	DESCRYING	CDEIKKOTU	KICKED OUT
CDEGINSSY	DYSGENICS	CDEIKLRST	STRICKLED
CDEGIOOOV	GOOD VOICE	CDEIKNSTY	STICKY END
CDEGIOOPR	GOOD PRICE	CDEIKOPTU	PICKED OUT
CDEGLORST	GOLDCREST	CDEILLLOU	CELLULOID
CDEGLORUY	GREY CLOUD	CDEILLLOY	ICED LOLLY
CDEGNORSU	SCROUNGED	CDEILLPRU	CURLED LIP
CDEGOOORS	GOOD SCORE	CDEILMRSU	DULCIMERS
CDEHIIKLL	CHILDLIKE	CDEILNNOU	CLOUD NINE
CDEHIILNO	LICHENOID	CDEILNOOS	COLONISED
CDEHIIMOS	HOMICIDES	CDEILNOOZ	COLONIZED
CDEHIINOS	ECHINOIDS	CDEILNRSY	CYLINDERS
CDEHIINPT	PITCHED IN	CDEILNSSU	LUCIDNESS
CDEHIIRTT	DIRECT HIT	CDEILOOUV	LOUD VOICE
CDEHIKNOT	IN THE DOCK	CDEILOPTU	POULTICED
CDEHIKPSY	PHYSICKED	CDEILORSS	DISCLOSER
CDEHILLOV	LOVE CHILD	CDEILOSSS	DISCLOSES
CDEHILLSS	CHILDLESS	CDEILOSTU	CLOUDIEST
CDEHILNOT	IN THE COLD	CDEILOTTW	TWICE-TOLD
CDEHILORS	CHLORIDES	CDEILRTUY	CREDULITY
CDEHILOTV	THE OLD VIC	CDEIMMNOO	INCOMMODE
CDEHILPST	STEPCHILD	CDEIMMOTT	COMMITTED
CDEHIMORT	COME THIRD	CDEIMNNOT	CONDIMENT
CDEHINORT	CHONDRITE	CDEIMNOPR	PRINCEDOM
	THRENODIC	CDEIMNORS	CRIMSONED
CDEHINOSU	CUSHIONED	CDEIMNORU	INDECORUM

CDEIMOPRS	COMPRISED
CDEIMOSST	DOMESTICS
CDEINNOSS	IN SECONDS
CDEINNOSW	WIND-CONES
CDEINNOTU	CONTINUED
	COUNTED IN
CDEINOPRS	CONSPIRED
CDEINOPSY	DYSPNOEIC
CDEINORSS	CONSIDERS
CDEINORST	CENTROIDS
	DOCTRINES
CDEINORSW	CRIES DOWN
CDEINORTU	INTRODUCE
	REDUCTION
CDEINORTV	CONTRIVED
CDEINOSST	CONSISTED
CDEINOSTU	SEDUCTION
CDEINPRSS	PRESCINDS
CDEINRSTU	INCRUSTED
CDEINRSTY	STRIDENCY
CDEINRTTU	TINCTURED
CDEIOOPTU	COPIED OUT
CDEIOPRRT	PREDICTOR
CDEIOPSTY	COPY-EDITS
CDEIORRST	CREDITORS
	DIRECTORS
	RECORDIST
CDEIORRTY	DIRECTORY
CDEIORSSS	SCISSORED
CDEIORSST	DISSECTOR
CDEIORSSU	DISCOURSE
CDEIORSSV	DISCOVERS
CDEIORSVY	DISCOVERY
CDEIPPSTY	DYSPEPTIC
CDEISSSSU	DISCUSSES
CDEKKNNOO	KNOCKED ON
CDEKKNOPU	KNOCKED UP
CDEKLOOPR	ORLOP DECK
CDEKLOORY	CROOKEDLY
CDEKLOOTU	LOCKED OUT
CDEKLOTUU	LUCKED OUT
CDEKNNORU	ROUND NECK
CDEKOPSTU	STOCKED UP
CDELLLOPS	COLD SPELL
CDELLOOPU	OLD COUPLE
CDELLOSSU	CLOUDLESS
CDELMNORU	LEMON CURD
CDELMOOWY	LOW COMEDY
CDELNOOST	STONE COLD
CDELNOOSW	CLOSE DOWN
	CLOSEDOWN
CDELNOOTY	COTYLEDON
CDELNOPUU	UNCOUPLED
CDELNORSU	SCOUNDREL
CDELNOSTU	CONSULTED
CDELNOSUV	CONVULSED
CDELOOPTU	POODLE CUT
CDELOORSS	COLD SORES
	OLD SCORES
CDELOORSU	COLOUREDS
CDELOORUV	CLOUD OVER
	OVERCLOUD
CDELORSUU	CREDULOUS
CDEMMNNOO	COMMON END
CDEMMOOOR	COMMODORE
CDEMNOORU	COME ROUND
CDEMNOOSW	COMEDOWNS
	COMES DOWN
CDEMNOSTU	DOCUMENTS
CDEMOOPRT	COMPORTED
CDEMOOPST	COMPOSTED

CDEMORRSU	RECORD SUM
CDENNOOPU	POUNCED ON
CDENNOORS	CONDONERS
CDENNOOTU	COUNTED ON
CDENNORUW	UNCROWNED
CDENNOTUU	UNCOUNTED
CDENOOPRS	DROP SCONE
CDENOOPSY	ENDOSCOPY
CDENOORST	CONSORTED
CDENOORSW	SECOND ROW
CDENOORTT	CONTORTED
CDENOORTU	CONTOURED
CDENOPTUU	COUNTED UP
CDENORSTU	CONSTRUED
CDENORSTY	SECOND TRY
CDENOR3WW	SCREW DOWN
CDENPRTUU	PUNCTURED
CDENRSTUU	UNDERCUTS
CDEOOPPRR	POP RECORD
CDEOOPSST	POSTCODES
CDEOORRVW	OVERCROWD
CDEOORSTU	OUTSCORED
CDEOPRRSU	PRODUCERS
CDEOPRRTU	CORRUPTED
CDEORSTUV	DUST COVER
	DUSTCOVER
CDEPPRSUU	SPRUCED UP
CDERSSTTU	DESTRUCTS
CDFFIILTU	DIFFICULT
CDFFNOOOR	CORDON OFF
CDFGHILNO	GOLDFINCH
CDFGIINNO	CONFIDING
CDFGIINOY	CODIFYING
CDFHINOTU	FIND TOUCH
CDFHIOORS	RICH FOODS
CDFHLOOOP	COP HOLD OF
CDFIIMOST	DISCOMFIT
CDFIIORSU	SUDORIFIC
CDFIKLNUY	LUCKY FIND
CDFIKORSS	DISFROCKS
CDFLNOORT	COLD FRONT
CDFNNOOSU	CONFOUNDS
CDGHHILOU	HIGH CLOUD
CDGHIILNY	CHIDINGLY
CDGHILLOT	COLD LIGHT
CDGHILNOT	COLD NIGHT
CDGHLNOOU	GOOD LUNCH
CDGHOOPRU	COUGH DROP
CDGIIINNT	INDICTING
CDGIILLNO	COLLIDING
CDGIILNNU	INCLUDING
CDGIINNTU	INDUCTING
CDGIINORV	DIVORCING
CDGIIOTYZ	DIZYGOTIC
CDGIKLNSU	DUCKLINGS
CDGIKNNOU	UNDOCKING
CDGILLNOU	COLLUDING
CDGILNNOO	CONDOLING
CDGILNNOY	CONDIGNLY
CDGILNOOS	GOLD COINS
CDGIMOOSU	GOOD MUSIC
CDGINNNOO	CONDONING
CDGINOOOT	GOOD TONIC
CDGINOORR	CORRODING
CDGINOORT	DOCTORING
CDGINOPRU	PRODUCING
CDGKOOOOS	GOOD COOKS
CDGLNOORW	GROWN COLD
CDGLOORSW	GROWS COLD
CDGLORUWY	UGLY CROWD
CDGOOOPRS	GOOD CROPS

CDHHILOST	DISH CLOTH	CDLMOOORS	COLD ROOMS
	DISHCLOTH	CDLMOOSTU	OLD CUSTOM
CDHIILLNW	WINDCHILL	CDLNOOOSW	COOLS DOWN
CDHIIMOPR	DIMORPHIC	CDLNORSTU	TURNS COLD
CDHIIMORS	DICHROISM	CDLOOSSTW	COTSWOLDS
CDHIIORWW	RICH WIDOW	CDMNNORUU	CONUNDRUM
CDHIKLOOS	SCHOOL KID	CDMNOOPSU	COMPOUNDS
	SCHOOLKID	CDMNORSUW	SCRUM DOWN
CDHILLNOY	ONLY CHILD	CDNNOOTUW	COUNT DOWN
CDHILOOPR	POOR CHILD		COUNTDOWN
CDHILOSTU	DISH CLOUT	CDOOORRSSW	CROSSWORD
CDHILOSTY	CHILDS TOY	CDOORRSUY	CORDUROYS
CDHIMOOTY	DICHOTOMY	CDOORRSTUW	CROWDS OUT
CDHIOOPRY	CHIROPODY	CEEEEFNRR	REFERENCE
CDHIOPRSW	WHIPCORDS	CEEEEGMNR	EMERGENCE
CDHIOPRSY	DYSPHORIC	CEEEEHMNV	VEHEMENCE
CDHLLOOOS	OLD SCHOOL	CEEEEIPSY	EYEPIECES
CDHLOORST	LOST CHORD	CEEEELSST	SELECTEES
CDHLOORTU	HOLD COURT	CEEEENRRV	REVERENCE
CDHMNOOOR	MONOCHORD	CEEEFFITV	EFFECTIVE
CDHNOOORT	NOTOCHORD	CEEEFFLNU	EFFLUENCE
CDHNOOPSW	CHOPS DOWN	CEEEFHLTT	FLECHETTE
CDHNOOTUW	TOUCH DOWN	CEEEFINNR	INFERENCE
	TOUCHDOWN	CEEEFINPV	FIVE PENCE
CDHOOORTW	DOCTOR WHO	CEEEFINRW	WIRE FENCE
CDHOOOTUW	TOUCH WOOD	CEEEFLNSS	FENCELESS
	TOUCHWOOD	CEEEFLSTW	SELECT FEW
CDIIISTVY	VISCIDITY	CEEEFNORS	CONFEREES
CDIIJOSUU	JUDICIOUS	CEEEFPRRT	PERFECTER
CDIIKPSST	DIPSTICKS	CEEEGGMRS	CREME EGGS
CDIILMOOT	DOLOMITIC	CEEEGINRS	REGENCIES
CDIILPTUY	DUPLICITY	CEEEGINRT	ENERGETIC
CDIILTTUY	DUCTILITY	CEEEGLNOR	CONGER EEL
CDIIMORST	DICROTISM	CEEEGLNRT	NEGLECTER
CDIINNOOT	CONDITION	CEEEGMNRY	EMERGENCY
CDIINNOTU	INDUCTION	CEEEHIKST	CHEEKIEST
CDIINTWYY	WINDY CITY	CEEEHILRS	LECHERIES
CDIIOOPRS	SCORPIOID	CEEEHILST	SCHEELITE
CDIIORRTT	TORTRICID	CEEEHINNR	INHERENCE
CDIIPRSTU	TRICUSPID	CEEEHIRST	CHEERIEST
CDIIRSSTT	DISTRICTS	CEEEHKORS	CHEROKEES
CDIJNOTUY	JOCUNDITY	CEEEHLRSS	CHEERLESS
CDIJNSSTU	DISJUNCTS	CEEEHMORS	COMES HERE
CDIKKOPRS	DROP KICKS	CEEEHNNSY	CHEYENNES
	DROPKICKS	CEEEHOPRS	ECOSPHERE
CDIKLNOOR	COOL DRINK	CEEEHOPST	SHEEPCOTE
CDIKLORST	OLD TRICKS	CEEEHPRST	THE CREEPS
CDIKMRSTU	DRUMSTICK	CEEEHPSST	SET SPEECH
CDIKNOSSW	WIND SOCKS	CEEEHQRUX	EXCHEQUER
	WIND-SOCKS	CEEEIIMPT	TIMEPIECE
CDIKOQRUW	QUICK WORD	CEEEIINRV	VICEREINE
CDILLNOOO	COLLODION	CEEEIKNOP	KEEP ON ICE
CDILMOSUU	LOUD MUSIC	CEEEIKNPR	KEEN PRICE
CDILMRRUY	MILD CURRY	CEEEILLNT	CLIENTELE
CDILOORSU	DISCOLOUR	CEEEILNPS	NICE SLEEP
CDILORSUU	LUDICROUS	CEEEILNSS	LICENSEES
CDIMMOOTY	COMMODITY	CEEEILSTV	SELECTIVE
CDIMOORST	MICRODOTS	CEEEIMNNS	EMINENCES
CDINORSSW	CROSS WIND	CEEEIMNSX	EXCISEMEN
	CROSSWIND	CEEEIMNTT	CEMENTITE
CDINORSTU	INDUCTORS	CEEEIMRRS	MERCERISE
CDINOSSTU	DISCOUNTS	CEEEIMRRZ	MERCERIZE
CDINOSTUY	IN CUSTODY	CEEEINNNP	NINE PENCE
CDIOORRRS	CORRIDORS	CEEEINNPT	PENITENCE
CDIOPRSSU	CUSPIDORS	CEEEINNSS	IN ESSENCE
CDKKLNOOU	LOUD KNOCK	CEEEINNST	ENCEINTES
CDKKNNOOW	KNOCK DOWN		SENTIENCE
	KNOCKDOWN	CEEEINOPS	NOSEPIECE
CDKLLOOOS	LOOKS COLD	CEEEINOST	NICE TO SEE
CDKLOSUYY	CLOUDY SKY	CEEEINPRT	EPICENTRE
CDKMOORTU	MOCK TUDOR	CEEEINRSU	ESURIENCE

CEEEINRSV	EVER SINCE	CEEFIIRST	CERTIFIES
CEEEINSTX	EXISTENCE		RECTIFIES
CEEEIPRRV	PERCEIVER	CEEFIITVW	TWICE FIVE
CEEEIPRST	CREEPIEST	CEEFIKKRS	FREE KICKS
CEEEIPRSV	EPIC VERSE	CEEFIKLSS	FEELS SICK
	PERCEIVES	CEEFIKORS	COKE FIRES
CEEEIPRTV	RECEPTIVE	CEEFILNNU	INFLUENCE
CEEEIPSST	SET PIECES	CEEFILRTY	ELECTRIFY
CEEEIPSTT	TEST PIECE	CEEFIMPRT	IMPERFECT
CEEEIRRSV	RECEIVERS	CEEFINORR	REINFORCE
CEEEIRRSX	EXERCISER	CEEFINORT	REFECTION
CEEEIRSSV	RECESSIVE	CEEFIORSV	FIVE SCORE
CEEEIRSSX	EXERCISES	CEEFIRRST	FIRECREST
CEEEIRSTV	SECRETIVE	CEEFKNNSU	SUNK FENCE
CEEEISSVX	EXCESSIVE	CEEFLLLSU	FUEL CELLS
CEEEITUVX	EXECUTIVE	CEEFLNORT	TENOR CLEF
CEEEKLOPS	KEEP CLOSE	CEEFLOORS	FORECLOSE
CEEEKOPRS	KEEP SCORE	CEEFLORRT	REFLECTOR
CEEEKORRT	ROCKETEER	CEEFLORSU	FLUORESCE
CEEEKOSWW	COWES WEEK	CEEFLPRTY	PERFECTLY
CEEELLNRS	CRENELLES	CEEFNOOPR	FORCE OPEN
CEEELLNTX	EXCELLENT	CEEFNOPRU	FOUR PENCE
CEEELNOQU	ELOQUENCE		FOURPENCE
CEEELNOSV	LOVE SCENE	CEEFNORRR	CONFERRER
CEEELOPST	TELESCOPE	CEEFNORSU	SCENE FOUR
CEEELRSTV	CLEVEREST	CEEFNOSSS	CONFESSES
CEEEMNRTX	EXCREMENT	CEEFNORUY	FREQUENCY
CEEENNSST	SENESCENT	CEEFNRSTU	RUFESCENT
	SENTENCES	CEEFOPRST	PERFECTOS
CEEENORSV	EVEN SCORE	CEEFORRTY	REFECTORY
CEEENORTT	ENTRECOTE	CEEFORSSU	USES FORCE
CEEENPRSS	PRESENCES	CEEFORSTW	CROW'S-FEET
CEEENPRST	PRETENCES		CROWS FEET
CEEENQRSU	SEQUENCER	CEEGHINOR	REECHOING
CEEENQSSU	SEQUENCES	CEEGHINSW	ESCHEWING
CEEENRRSS	SCREENERS	CEEGHLOSW	COGWHEELS
CEEENRSST	ERECTNESS	CEEGHLRTY	THE CLERGY
CEEEOQRUV	QUEER COVE	CEEGIINRV	RECEIVING
CEEEPRRST	RESPECTER	CEEGIIOVV	GIVE VOICE
CEEEPRRTX	EXCERPTER	CEEGIJNRT	REJECTING
CEEEPRSSS	PRECESSES	CEEGIKNRS	GREENSICK
CEEEPRSTU	PERSECUTE	CEEGILLNX	EXCELLING
CEEERSSST	SESTERCES	CEEGILNOO	OLIGOCENE
CEEFFFORT	FOR EFFECT	CEEGILNRY	GLYCERINE
CEEFFGINT	EFFECTING	CEEGILNST	SELECTING
CEEFFIINT	EFFICIENT	CEEGILOOS	ECOLOGIES
CEEFFILLT	ILL EFFECT	CEEGIMNNT	CEMENTING
CEEFFILOR	LIFE FORCE	CEEGIMORT	GEOMETRIC
	LIFE-FORCE	CEEGINNOS	CONSIGNEE
CEEFFIOSU	COIFFEUSE	CEEGINNRS	SCREENING
CEEFFNORS	OFFSCREEN	CEEGINNRT	CENTERING
CEEFFNORT	OFF CENTRE	CEEGINOOT	OOGENETIC
CEEFFOOPT	COFFEE POT	CEEGINORS	RECOGNISE
CEEFFORST	EFFECTORS	CEEGINORZ	RECOGNIZE
CEEFGINNR	RING FENCE	CEEGINPTX	EXCEPTING
CEEFGLNTU	GENUFLECT		EXPECTING
CEEFHHNRT	THE FRENCH	CEEGINRSS	RECESSING
CEEFHIKRS	KERCHIEFS	CEEGINRST	RESECTING
CEEFHIPSY	SPEECHIFY		SECRETING
CEEFHLNRU	FREE LUNCH	CEEGINRTX	EXCRETING
CEEFHLRST	FLETCHERS	CEEGINTUX	EXECUTING
CEEFHMNNR	FRENCHMEN	CEEGIORRS	GROCERIES
CEEFHNOSW	CHOSEN FEW	CEEGKNOOS	GOOSENECK
CEEFHORST	THE FORCES	CEEGLMNRY	CLERGYMEN
CEEFHPSTU	FETCHES UP	CEEGLRTTU	LEG CUTTER
CEEFIINOV	FINE VOICE	CEEGNNORS	CONGENERS
CEEFIIPRS	SPECIFIER	CEEGNORSV	CONVERGES
CEEFIIPSS	SPECIFIES	CEEGORTTU	COURGETTE
CEEFIIRRT	CERTIFIER	CEEHHIRSS	CHERISHES
	RECTIFIER	CEEHHIRVW	WHICHEVER
		CEEHHOPST	HOPE CHEST

CEEHIILPR	PERIHELIC	CEEIKOPRW	PIECE WORK
CEEHIIMTW	WHITE MICE		PIECEWORK
CEEHIIPTT	EPITHETIC		WORKPIECE
CEEHIKNNT	IN THE NECK	CEEIKORRS	ROCKERIES
CEEHIKNRT	THICKENER	CEEIKRSSY	ERIC SYKES
CEEHIKRST	SKETCHIER	CEEILLLPS	PELLICLES
CEEHIKTTT	THE TICKET	CEEILLLTU	CELLULITE
CEEHILLRS	CHISELLER	CEEILLNPR	PENCILLER
CEEHILNRS	SCHLIEREN	CEEILLNST	LENTICELS
CEEHILNTY	ETHYLENIC	CEEILLNTT	INTELLECT
CEEHILOPT	THE POLICE	CEEILMNNT	INCLEMENT
CEEHILRSV	CLEVERISH	CEEILMNOP	POLICEMEN
CEEHILRSW	CLERIHEWS	CEEILMNOW	WELCOME IN
CEEHIMRSW	SHREWMICE	CEEILMNPR	CRIMPLENE
CEEHINPRS	ENCIPHERS	CEEILMNSU	LUMINESCE
CEEHINPRT	PHRENETIC	CEEILMOST	COMELIEST
	THE PRINCE	CEEILMRSS	MERCILESS
CEEHINQTU	TECHNIQUE	CEEILNNOS	INSOLENCE
CEEHINRVY	EVERY INCH	CEEILNORT	CENTRIOLE
CEEHIOPSW	SHOWPIECE	CEEILNOST	SELECTION
CEEHIORTT	HETEROTIC	CEEILNPST	SPLENETIC
CEEHIPRRY	CHERRY PIE	CEEILNRSS	SILENCERS
CEEHISSTT	ESTHETICS	CEEILNRSY	SINCERELY
CEEHISTTT	TETCHIEST	CEEILNRTV	VENTRICLE
CEEHKRSST	SKETCHERS	CEEILNRUV	VIRULENCE
CEEHLORSU	LECHEROUS	CEEILOSSS	ISOSCELES
CEEHLPRSU	SEPULCHER	CEEILOSSV	VOICELESS
	SEPULCHRE	CEEILPRSS	PRICELESS
CEEHLQSSU	SQUELCHES	CEEILPRSY	PRECISELY
CEEHMMOOS	COMES HOME	CEEILRSTU	CRUELTIES
CEEHMNORZ	CHERNOZEM		RETICULES
CEEHNOPRR	PERCHERON	CEEILRSUV	RECLUSIVE
CEEHNRRST	TRENCHERS	CEEILSSTT	TESTICLES
CEEHOORTT	TO THE CORE	CEEILSSUV	SECLUSIVE
CEEHOPRSY	CORYPHEES	CEEILSUVX	EXCLUSIVE
CEEHORRTU	RETOUCHER	CEEIMMNSU	ECUMENISM
CEEHORSTU	RETOUCHES	CEEIMMOTT	COMMITTEE
CEEHORSVW	CHEWS OVER	CEEIMNNOT	NET INCOME
CEEHRRSTT	STRETCHER	CEEIMNNRT	INCREMENT
CEEHRSSTT	STRETCHES	CEEIMNOOS	ECONOMIES
CEEHSSSST	CHESS SETS		ECONOMISE
CEEIIJLMU	LIME JUICE	CEEIMNOOZ	ECONOMIZE
CEEIILNNS	IN SILENCE	CEEIMNOPT	IMPOTENCE
CEEIILPPT	EPILEPTIC	CEEIMNOST	CENTESIMO
CEEIIMMNN	IMMINENCE	CEEIMNOWX	NEW MEXICO
CEEIIMNPS	MINCE PIES	CEEIMNPSS	SPECIMENS
CEEIIMNRS	REMINISCE	CEEIMNSTU	ECUMENIST
CEEIIMPST	EPISTEMIC		INTUMESCE
CEEIINNRS	INSINCERE	CEEIMOPPS	EPIC POEMS
CEEIINNTV	INCENTIVE	CEEINNOPS	PINE CONES
CEEIINNTW	TWICE NINE		PINECONES
CEEIINPRT	RECIPIENT	CEEINNORS	RECENSION
CEEIINPTV	INCEPTIVE	CEEINOPRT	RECEPTION
CEEIINRSV	IN SERVICE	CEEINOPTX	EXCEPTION
	IN-SERVICE	CEEINORSS	RECESSION
CEEIINTVV	INVECTIVE	CEEINORST	ERECTIONS
CEEIIOPST	POETICISE		NECROTISE
CEEIIOPTZ	POETICIZE		RESECTION
CEEIIORTZ	EROTICIZE		SECRETION
CEEIIOSST	SOCIETIES	CEEINORTX	EXCRETION
CEEIIPRRS	PRICE RISE	CEEINORTZ	NECROTIZE
CEEIJLSSU	JUICELESS	CEEINOSSS	SECESSION
CEEIJNORT	REJECTION	CEEINOTUX	EXECUTION
CEEIJNRTT	INTERJECT	CEEINPRRU	PRURIENCE
CEEIKLNNS	NECKLINES	CEEINPRST	IN RESPECT
CEEIKLRSW	SCREWLIKE		NET PRICES
CEEIKMORS	MOCKERIES		PRESCIENT
CEEIKNOPT	KEPT ON ICE	CEEINPRTT	INTERCEPT
CEEIKNOTW	ONE WICKET	CEEINQSTU	QUIESCENT
CEEIKNQRU	QUICKENER	CEEINRRSV	SCRIVENER
CEEIKNRRS	SNICKERER	CEEINRSSU	SINECURES

CEEINRSTT	INTERSECT	CEENNORSU	RENOUNCES
CEEINRSTU	CENTURIES	CEENNORTU	ENCOUNTER
CEEINRSTV	VIRESCENT	CEENNOSSW	SNOW SCENE
CEEINRSUY	ESURIENCY	CEENNOSTU	TEN OUNCES
CEEINSSTY	NECESSITY	CEENOOPST	COPESTONE
CEEIOORTZ	OZOCERITE	CEENOPRRT	PRECENTOR
CEEIOORVV	VOICE OVER	CEENOPSTT	PENTECOST
	VOICE-OVER	CEENORRSV	CONSERVER
CEEIOPPRS	PERISCOPE	CEENORRTV	CONVERTER
CEEIOPPSS	EPISCOPES	CEENORSST	NO SECRETS
CEEIOPPST	EPIC POETS	CEENORSSV	CONSERVES
CEEIORRST	RECTORIES		CONVERSES
CEEIORRSX	EXORCISER	CEENORSTT	CONTESTER
CEEIORSSU	SERICEOUS		TRECENTOS
CEEIORSSX	EXORCISES	CEENORSTW	SWEET CORN
CEEIORTVW	TWICE OVER	CEENORSVY	CONVEYERS
CEEIPRRWZ	PRIZE CREW	CEENOSSUX	NO EXCUSES
CEEIRRRTU	RECRUITER	CEENRRRTU	RECURRENT
CEEIRRSSV	SERVICERS	CEENRRSSU	CENSURERS
CEEIRRSUV	RECURSIVE	CEEOORSST	CREOSOTES
CEEIRSSTT	SITS ERECT	CEEOOSTXY	EXOCYTOSE
CEEIRSSTW	SCREWIEST	CEEOPPRRT	PRECEPTOR
CEEIRSUVX	EXCURSIVE	CEEOPRRST	RECEPTORS
CEEJORSWY	JERSEY COW	CEEOPRRTX	EXCERPTOR
CEEKKKNNO	KNOCK-KNEE	CEEOPRSSS	PROCESSES
CEEKKOPST	KEEP STOCK	CEEOPRSTT	TOP SECRET
CEEKLMNOR	LEO MCKERN	CEEPRSTU	GREEPS OUT
CEEKLOOPS	KEEPS COOL		PROSECUTE
CEEKLOPST	KEPT CLOSE	CEEOQRTTU	CROQUETTE
CEEKNOPTU	KEEP COUNT	CEEOQSTTU	COQUETTES
CEEKOOPRT	PETER COOK	CEEORRRSS	SORCERERS
CEEKOPRST	KEPT SCORE	CEEORRSSU	RESOURCES
CEELLLOSU	CELLULOSE	CEEORRSTY	SECRETORY
CEELLMNTY	CLEMENTLY	CEEORRSUV	VERRUCOSE
CEELLMOSU	MOLECULES	CEEORRTXY	EXCRETORY
CEELLMOWY	WELCOMELY	CEEORSSSY	CROSS EYES
CEELLORTU	COURTELLE	CEEORSSTT	TEST SCORE
CEELLRSTU	CRUELLEST	CEEORSSTU	SET COURSE
CEELMNOUW	UNWELCOME	CEEORSTTV	CORVETTES
CEELMOOOS	COME LOOSE	CEEORSTUX	EXECUTORS
CEELMOPRT	COMPLETER	CEEORTUXY	EXECUTORY
CEELMOPST	COMPLETES	CEEPRSSSU	PERCUSSES
CEELMOPSX	COMPLEXES	CEEPRSSSY	CYPRESSES
CEELMORSW	WELCOMERS	CEERRRSTU	RESURRECT
CEELNORST	ELECTRONS	CEFFFFLUU	CUFFUFFLE
CEELNORSU	ENCLOSURE	CEFFHKOOS	CHOKES OFF
CEELNOSSS	CLOSENESS	CEFFIIOOX	EX OFFICIO
CEELNPRUU	PURULENCE	CEFFIKNST	STIFF NECK
CEELNRSSU	CRUELNESS	CEFFIMOOT	COME OFF IT
CEELNSSST	SCENTLESS	CEFFIORSU	COIFFEURS
CEELNSSUU	NUCLEUSES		COIFFURES
CEELOORTV	TOO CLEVER	CEFFIRRSU	SCRUFFIER
CEELOOSTV	CLOSE VOTE	CEFFOORSS	SCORES OFF
CEELORSST	CORSELETS	CEFFOORSU	OFF COURSE
	SELECTORS	CEFFORTTU	OFF CUTTER
CEELORSTV	COVERLETS	CEFGHILNT	FLETCHING
CEELRRSTU	LECTURERS	CEFGIINNN	FENCING IN
CEELRSSST	CRESTLESS	CEFGIINNT	INFECTING
CEEMNNORT	CONTEMNER	CEFGIKLNR	FRECKLING
CEEMNOPTT	COMPETENT	CEFGINNOR	ENFORCING
CEEMNORSW	NEWCOMERS	CEFHHIIPS	CHIEFSHIP
CEEMNOSTX	COMES NEXT	CEFHHIIPW	CHIEF WHIP
CEEMNOSYZ	COENZYMES	CEFHIILSS	FISH SLICE
CEEMNSTTU	TUMESCENT	CEFHIIMSS	MISCHIEFS
CEEMOORSV	COMES OVER	CEFHIKLST	THE FLICKS
	OVERCOMES	CEFHILNOT	FINE CLOTH
CEEMOOTTY	YET TO COME	CEFHINOTU	FINE TOUCH
CEEMORSTU	COMES TRUE	CEFHKOORS	FOREHOCKS
CEEMOSSTY	ECOSYSTEM	CEFHMOORT	COME FORTH
CEENNORRU	RENOUNCER	CEFIIILLV	CIVIL LIFE
CEENNORST	CONSENTER		

CEFIIKQRU	QUICK FIRE	CEGIIJNOR	REJOICING
	QUICKFIRE	CEGIIKNNR	NICKERING
CEFIILMPS	EPIC FILMS	CEGIIKNNS	SICKENING
CEFIILNRT	INFLICTER	CEGIIKNPT	PICKETING
CEFIILNRU	LUCIFERIN	CEGIIKSTV	GIVE STICK
CEFIILTVY	FICTIVELY	CEGIILNNR	RECLINING
CEFIIMNOR	FERMIONIC	CEGIILNNS	LICENSING
CEFIIMPRR	FIRM PRICE		SILENCING
CEFIINNOT	INFECTION	CEGIILNOR	RECOILING
CEFIINTTU	CUT IT FINE	CEGIILNPS	ECLIPSING
CEFIIPRSX	FIX PRICES	CEGIILOOT	ETIOLOGIC
CEFIKLORS	FIRELOCKS	CEGIINNNS	INCENSING
CEFIKORSS	FOSSICKER	CEGIINNPT	INCEPTING
CEFIKRRTU	FIRE TRUCK	CEGIINOTV	COGNITIVE
CEFILLLOS	FOLLICLES	CEGIINOTX	TOXIGENIC
CEFILLPRU	FULL PRICE	CEGIINPRR	PRICE RING
CEFILMORU	FOUL CRIME		PRICE-RING
CEFILNOST	FLECTIONS	CEGIINPRS	PRECISING
CEFILORSW	CRIES WOLF	CEGIINRSV	SERVICING
CEFIMNORU	CUNEIFORM	CEGIIOSTT	EGOTISTIC
CEFIMORST	COME FIRST	CEGIJKNOY	JOCKEYING
	FIRST COME	CEGIKLNPS	SPECKLING
CEFINNORS	CONFINERS	CEGIKNNOR	RECKONING
CEFINOORT	CONFITEOR	CEGIKNOPT	POCKETING
CEFIOORSU	FEROCIOUS	CEGIKNORT	ROCKETING
CEFIOOSTV	SOFT VOICE	CEGIKNOST	SOCKETING
CEFIORRSS	CROSS FIRE	CEGIKNPRU	PUCKERING
	CROSSFIRE	CEGIKNRSU	SUCKERING
CEFIORTUW	TWICE FOUR	CEGIKNRTU	TUCKERING
CEFKLOORS	FORELOCKS	CEGILLNPU	CUPELLING
CEFKLOPTU	POCKETFUL	CEGILMMNO	COMMINGLE
CEFKLPSSY	FLYSPECKS	CEGILMNOW	WELCOMING
CEFKNOOOT	TON OF COKE	CEGILNNOS	ENCLOSING
CEFKOORRW	WORK FORCE		LONG SINCE
	WORKFORCE	CEGILNOST	CLOSETING
CEFLLOPSU	FULL SCOPE	CEGILNRSU	SURCINGLE
CEFLLORSU	FULL SCORE	CEGILNRTU	LECTURING
CEFLLORUV	FULL COVER	CEGILOOST	ECOLOGIST
CEFLNNOTU	CONFLUENT	CEGILORRV	COVER GIRL
CEFLNRSUU	FURUNCLES	CEGIMNOOR	ERGONOMIC
CEFMMOORS	COMES FROM	CEGIMNOPR	COMPERING
CEFMNOORR	CONFORMER	CEGIMNOPT	COMPETING
CEFMOORRT	COMFORTER	CEGIMNOUY	GYNOECIUM
CEFNOORSS	CONFESSOR	CEGIMNOYZ	ZYMOGENIC
CEFOORRSU	FOUR SCORE	CEGINNNOV	CONVENING
	FOURSCORE	CEGINNORR	CORNERING
CEFOORRTU	FORECOURT	CEGINNORS	CENSORING
CEFOORSTU	FORCES OUT	CEGINNOVY	CONVEYING
CEFOORSTV	SOFT-COVER	CEGINNRSU	CENSURING
CEGGINNOO	GOING ONCE	CEGINNSTY	ENCYSTING
CEGGKSSSU	SUCKS EGGS	CEGINOPRU	RECOUPING
CEGHHIIOV	HIGH VOICE	CEGINOPRY	PYROGENIC
CEGHHIIPR	HIGH PRICE	CEGINOPTY	GENOTYPIC
CEGHHIORS	HIGH SCORE	CEGINORST	CORSETING
CEGHIINNR	ENRICHING		ESCORTING
CEGHIINPR	CIPHERING	CEGINORSV	COVERINGS
CEGHIIOST	GOTHICISE	CEGINORTV	VECTORING
CEGHIIOTZ	GOTHICIZE	CEGINOSST	COSSETING
CEGHIKNST	SKETCHING	CEGINOTYZ	ENZYGOTIC
CEGHILNTV	VETCHLING	CEGINRRRU	RECURRING
CEGHIMORT	COME RIGHT	CEGINSTTY	CITY GENTS
CEGHINNQU	QUENCHING	CEGIOOPRT	GEOTROPIC
CEGHINNRT	TRENCHING	CEGKLSTUY	GETS LUCKY
CEGHINNRW	WRENCHING	CEGKORSSY	GREY SOCKS
CEGHINNST	STENCHING	CEGKSSTTU	GETS STUCK
CEGHINOOT	THEOGONIC	CEGLNOORY	NECROLOGY
CEGHINORT	HECTORING	CEGMNNOOS	COGNOMENS
CEGHINPRY	CYPHERING	CEGMNSTUU	UNCUT GEMS
CEGHKNORU	ROUGHNECK	CEGNNORTU	CONGRUENT
CEGIIILNT	ELICITING	CEGNORRSU	SCROUNGER
CEGIIJNNT	INJECTING	CEGNORSSU	SCROUNGES

CEGOOPRSY	GYROSCOPE	CEHIOPPST	CHOPPIEST
CEGORRSSU	SCOURGERS	CEHIOPRRT	CHIROPTER
CEGORSSST	GETS CROSS	CEHIOPRTT	PROTHETIC
CEGORSTUU	GUT COURSE	CEHIOPRTU	EUTROPHIC
CEHHHIIKT	HITCH HIKE	CEHIOPRTV	OVERPITCH
	HITCHHIKE	CEHIOPRTY	HYPOCRITE
CEHHIIMST	HEMISTICH	CEHIOPSST	POSTICHES
CEHHIMSTT	HEMSTITCH	CEHIOPSTW	COPES WITH
CEHHINNOT	ON THE CHIN	CEHIORRSS	CIRRHOSES
CEHHLOOTU	TOUCHHOLE	CEHIORRST	CHORISTER
CEHHOOPSU	CHOP HOUSE	CEHIORSST	OSTRICHES
	CHOPHOUSE	CEHIORSUV	ECHOVIRUS
CEHIIKLTW	WITCHLIKE	CEHIOSSST	SCHISTOSE
CEHIIKNNT	IN THE NICK	CEHIOSTTU	TOUCHIEST
CEHIIKTTW	HIT WICKET	CEHIRSSTT	STITCHERS
CEHIILLST	CHILLIEST	CEHIRSSTW	SWITCHERS
CEHIILMOT	HOMILETIC	CEHIRSSTY	HYSTERICS
CEHIILNOT	NEOLITHIC	CEHIRSTTW	TWITCHERS
CEHIILNST	THIN SLICE	CEHITTTWY	WITCHETTY
CEHIIMSTY	MYTHICISE	CEHJKLNOO	JOHN LOCKE
CEHIIMTYZ	MYTHICIZE	CEHKLNORS	SCHNORKEL
CEHIINNOT	ON THIN ICE	CEHKOOOSU	COOKHOUSE
CEHIINPPT	PITCH PINE	CEHKOSSTT	THE STOCKS
CEHIINPRT	NEPHRITIC	CEHKRSSTU	HUCKSTERS
CEHIINPST	PITCHES IN	CEHLLOOPT	PHOTOCELL
CEHIINRSV	RICH VEINS	CEHLNNOSU	LUNCHEONS
CEHIINSST	ITCHINESS	CEHLNOOSW	NEW SCHOOL
CEHIINTTY	ETHNICITY	CEHLNOSTU	UNCLOTHES
	IN THE CITY	CEHLOOPRS	PRESCHOOL
CEHIIPPTY	EPIPHYTIC	CEHLOOSTT	TOOL CHEST
CEHIIPRST	CHIRPIEST	CEHLOOSTU	LOSE TOUCH
CEHIIRSTU	HEURISTIC	CEHLOPSST	SPLOTCHES
CEHIISTTT	TITCHIEST	CEHLORRST	CHORTLERS
CEHIITTWY	WHITE CITY	CEHLORSSU	SLOUCHERS
CEHIKLOPS	PICK HOLES	CEHMOOPRT	ECTOMORPH
CEHIKLPRS	CLERKSHIP	CEHMOORSS	SMOOCHERS
CEHIKNOST	ON THE SICK	CEHMOORST	COME SHORT
CEHIKNSST	THICKNESS	CEHMORSUW	MUCH WORSE
CEHIKNSTU	CHUNKIEST	CEHMORSWY	SHOW MERCY
CEHIKOPPR	HOP PICKER	CEHNNOPSU	PUNCHEONS
CEHIKPRSW	SHIPWRECK	CEHNNORTU	TRUNCHEON
CEHIKSSTT	THE STICKS	CEHNOORSS	SCHOONERS
CEHILLNSS	CHILLNESS	CEHNOOSTU	TOUCHES ON
CEHILMNTU	LUNCH TIME	CEHNOPTUW	WON THE CUP
CEHILNNPU	PUNCH LINE	CEHNSSTTU	CHESTNUTS
CEHILNOSU	LICHENOUS	CEHOOOPRS	HOROSCOPE
CEHILNOTU	TOUCH LINE	CEHOPSSSY	PSYCHOSES
	TOUCHLINE	CEHOPSTUU	TOUCHES UP
CEHILNSTZ	SCHNITZEL	CEHOPSTUY	PSYCHE OUT
CEHILOOST	SCHOOL TIE	CEHOPTTUY	TOUCH TYPE
CEHILOPRT	PLETHORIC		TOUCH-TYPE
CEHILORST	CLOTHIERS	CEHOSSTTU	THE SCOUTS
CEHIMMOPR	MORPHEMIC	CEHPRSTTU	STRETCH UP
CEHIMMSTU	CHUMMIEST	CEIIILRSV	CIVILISER
CEHIMNNOU	ICHNEUMON	CEIIILRVZ	CIVILIZER
CEHIMNOPS	PHONEMICS	CEIIILSSV	CIVILISES
CEHIMNSTW	SWITCHMEN	CEIIILSVZ	CIVILIZES
CEHIMNSUU	EUNUCHISM	CEIIIMSTV	VICTIMISE
CEHIMRSTY	CHEMISTRY	CEIIIMTVZ	VICTIMIZE
CEHINOPST	PHONETICS	CEIIINNPT	INCIPIENT
CEHINPRST	SPHINCTER	CEIIIPSTT	PIETISTIC
CEHINPTUW	WIN THE CUP	CEIIJNNOT	INJECTION
CEHINQSSU	SQUINCHES	CEIIJNSSU	JUICINESS
CEHINRSST	CHRISTENS	CEIIJNSTU	INJUSTICE
	SNITCHERS	CEIIKLMQU	QUICKLIME
CEHINSSSU	CUSHINESS	CEIIKLMRS	LIMERICKS
CEHINSTTY	SYNTHETIC	CEIIKLPRR	PRICKLIER
CEHIOOPRT	ORTHOEPIC	CEIIKLSST	SICKLIEST
CEHIOOSST	CHOOSIEST	CEIIKMQTU	QUICK TIME
CEHIOPPRT	PROPHETIC	CEIIKRRST	TRICKSIER
CEHIOPPRY	HYPEROPIC	CEIIKRSTT	TRICKIEST

CEIIKSSTT	STICKIEST	CEIKQRUVY	VERY QUICK
CEIILLNNO	LINOLENIC	CEIKRRSTT	TRICKSTER
CEIILMNSU	MINISCULE	CEILLOSUV	COLLUSIVE
CEIILMSSY	ICY SMILES	CEILLPSTY	SYLLEPTIC
CEIILNNOR	CRINOLINE	CEILMNNOO	MONOCLINE
CEIILNNPS	PENCILS IN	CEILMNOOS	SEMICOLON
CEIILNOSS	ISOCLINES	CEILMNOOW	LOW INCOME
CEIILNPPR	PRINCIPLE	CEILMNOTU	MONTICULE
CEIILNSUV	INCLUSIVE	CEILMNSUU	MINUSCULE
CEIILNTYZ	CITIZENLY	CEILMOPRS	COMPILERS
CEIILOQRU	LIQUORICE		COMPLIERS
CEIILOSSU	SILICEOUS	CEILMOPRY	LYRIC POEM
CEIILPRST	LIST PRICE		MICROPYLE
	PRICE LIST		POLYMERIC
CEIILPRTU	PLEURITIC	CEILMRTUU	RETICULUM
CEIILSTUV	LEVITICUS	CEILMSSTU	CLUMSIEST
CEIIMNOST	SEMITONIC	CEILNNOOS	CLOISONNE
CEIIMNRST	CRETINISM	CEILNOOPR	NECROPOLI
CEIIMNSST	SCIENTISM	CEILNOORS	COLONISER
CEIIMOPST	POETICISM	CEILNOORZ	COLONIZER
CEIIMORST	EROTICISM	CEILNOOSS	COLONISES
	ISOMETRIC	CEILNOOSZ	COLONIZES
CEIIMOSST	SEMIOTICS	CEILNOOTU	ELOCUTION
CEIIMOSTX	EXOTICISM	CEILNORSU	INCLOSURE
CEIIMPPSU	PIPE MUSIC		RECLUSION
CEIIMPRSU	EPICURISM	CEILNORUV	INVOLUCRE
CEIINNOPT	INCEPTION	CEILNOSSU	SECLUSION
CEIINNRTY	INNER-CITY	CEILNOSUX	EXCLUSION
CEIINOPRS	PRECISION	CEILNRSSU	CURLINESS
CEIINORRT	CRITERION	CEILNRSUV	CULVERINS
CEIINOSTY	IN SOCIETY	CEILNSSTU	LINCTUSES
CEIINPSSS	SPICINESS	CEILOOPRT	COPROLITE
CEIINRSTX	EXTRINSIC	CEILOOSSS	SCOLIOSES
CEIINRSTY	SINCERITY	CEILOOSVW	LOW VOICES
CEIINRSUV	INCURSIVE	CEILOPPRT	PROLEPTIC
CEIINRTTY	INTERCITY	CEILOPRSV	SLIP COVER
CEIINRTYZ	CITIZENRY	CEILOPRSW	LOW PRICES
CEIINSSTT	SCIENTIST	CEILOPRTY	LYRIC POET
CEIIOOPTZ	EPIZOOTIC	CEILOPSTU	POULTICES
CEIIORSTT	EROTICIST	CEILORSSS	SCLEROSIS
CEIIORSTV	VICTORIES	CEILORSST	CLOISTERS
CEIIPRSST	CRISPIEST	CEILOSSST	SOLSTICES
CEIIQRSTU	CRITIQUES	CEILOSSTT	COSTLIEST
CEIISSTVV	VIVISECTS	CEILOSTVY	COSTIVELY
CEIJKKOSS	SICK JOKES	CEILPRSSU	SURPLICES
CEIJNORTT	INTROJECT	CEILPRSUV	SILVER CUP
CEIKKORSV	KICKS OVER	CEILRSUVY	CURSIVELY
CEIKLNORT	INTERLOCK	CEIMMNNOS	MNEMONICS
CEIKLNOST	CLOSE-KNIT	CEIMMNOOR	MONOMERIC
CEIKLNRUU	UNLUCKIER	CEIMMNOOS	MONOECISM
CEIKLNSSS	SLICKNESS	CEIMMNOSU	COMMUNISE
CEIKLNSSU	LUCKINESS		ENCOMIUMS
CEIKLOPST	STOCKPILE	CEIMMNOTU	COMMINUTE
CEIKLOSTV	LIVESTOCK	CEIMMNOUZ	COMMUNIZE
CEIKLPSTU	PLUCKIEST	CEIMMOORS	MICROSOME
CEIKLRSST	STICKLERS	CEIMMOORT	MICROTOME
	STRICKLES	CEIMMRSTU	CRUMMIEST
CEIKMPPSU	PICK-ME-UPS	CEIMNNOOY	COIN MONEY
CEIKMPSTU	STICK EM UP	CEIMNNOPU	PNEUMONIC
CEIKNORSS	ROCKINESS	CEIMNNORT	COMINTERN
CEIKNOSTT	STOCKINET	CEIMNOORT	MICROTONE
CEIKNQSSU	QUICKNESS	CEIMNOOST	ECONOMIST
CEIKNRSTT	TEN TRICKS	CEIMNOOSU	MONECIOUS
CEIKNRSTW	NEW TRICKS	CEIMNOPTY	IMPOTENCY
CEIKOPRRT	ROPE TRICK	CEIMNORST	INTERCOMS
CEIKORRTV	OVERTRICK	CEIMNORTT	METRIC TON
CEIKORSTV	TICKS OVER	CEIMNOSTU	IN COSTUME
CEIKOSSTT	STOCKIEST	CEIMOOPST	COMPOSITE
CEIKOSSTZ	STOCK SIZE	CEIMOORSS	MORISCOES
CEIKOSTTY	STOKE CITY	CEIMOOSTX	EXOSMOTIC
CEIKPQSTU	QUICKSTEP	CEIMOPRSS	COMPRISES

CEIMOPRST	PRIME COST
CEIMOPSUU	PUMICEOUS
CEIMORSTU	COSTUMIER
CEIMOSSTU	CUSTOMISE
CEIMOSTUV	MUSCOVITE
CEIMOSTUZ	CUSTOMIZE
CEINNNOST	INNOCENTS'
CEINNNOTT	CONTINENT
CEINNORSS	CORNINESS
CEINNORSV	CONNIVERS
CEINNORTU	CENTURION
	CONTINUER
CEINNOSTU	CONTINUES
CEINNPRUW	CUP WINNER
CEINNSTTV	ST.VINCENT
CEINOORST	CORTISONE
CEINOPPRS	IN COPPERS
CEINOPPRU	PORCUPINE
CEINOPRRT	INTERCROP
CEINOPRSS	CONSPIRES
CEINOPRST	INSPECTOR
CEINOPRSV	PROVINCES
CEINOPSST	SCOTS PINE
CEINORRST	TRICORNES
CEINORRSU	RECURSION
CEINORRTV	CONTRIVER
CEINORRTW	TOWN CRIER
CEINORSTT	CORNETIST
CEINORSTU	COUNTRIES
	CRETINOUS
	NEUROTICS
CEINORSTV	CONTRIVES
CEINORSUX	EXCURSION
CEINORTTU	TURN TO ICE
CEINOSSUX	SIX OUNCES
CEINOSTTU	TEUTONICS
CEINOTVXY	CONVEXITY
CEINPRSSS	CRISPNESS
CEINRSSTT	CENTRISTS
CEINRSTTU	INTERCUTS
	TINCTURES
CEINRSTWW	TWIN SCREW
CEIOOPRST	PORTICOES
CEIOOPSTW	TWO COPIES
CEIOORRSV	CORROSIVE
CEIOORSTV	VORTICOSE
CEIOOSSTX	TOXICOSES
CEIOPRRSU	CROUPIERS
CEIORRSTT	TRISECTOR
CEIORRSTU	COURTIERS
CEIORRSUU	CURIOUSER
CEIORRSUZ	CRUZEIROS
CEIORRTUU	COUTURIER
CEIORSSSW	CROSSWISE
CEIORSTTU	TOREUTICS
CEIPPRRST	PRESCRIPT
CEIPRRSST	RESCRIPTS
CEIPRRSTU	SCRIPTURE
CEIPRSSTU	PIECRUSTS
CEIRRSSTT	RESTRICTS
CEIRRSTTU	STRICTURE
CEIRSSTTT	STRICTEST
CEIRSSTTU	CRUSTIEST
CEJKNOORY	CORNY JOKE
CEJNOPRUU	CONJURE UP
CEJNORRSU	CONJURERS
CEJNRSTUU	JUNCTURES
CEJOOPRRT	PROJECTOR
CEKKNOORV	KNOCK OVER
CEKKOPSTT	KEPT STOCK
CEKKORSTY	SKYROCKET

CEKLLOOOS	CLOSE LOOK
CEKLLOOSV	LOVELOCKS
CEKLMNOUY	LUCKY OMEN
CEKLMOUVY	LUCKY MOVE
CEKLNORTW	TOWN CLERK
CEKLORSUW	WORSE LUCK
CEKLRRSTU	TRUCKLERS
CEKNNOORS	RECKONS ON
CEKNOPRSU	RECKONS UP
CEKNOPSST	PENSTOCKS
CEKNOPTTU	KEPT COUNT
CEKOOORTV	TOOK COVER
CEKOORRSS	ROCKROSES
CEKOORRSW	CO-WORKERS
CEKOPRSST	SPROCKETS
CEKORSSSY	CROSS KEYS
CELLMOPXY	COMPLEXLY
CELLMSTUU	SCUTELLUM
CELLNOSUU	NUCLEOLUS
CELMNOTUY	CONTUMELY
CELMOOPRY	COPOLYMER
CELMOOSSU	COLOSSEUM
CELMOOTUY	LEUCOTOMY
CELMOPRUU	OPERCULUM
CELMPPRUU	CRUMPLE UP
CELMPRSTU	PLECTRUMS
CELMPSSUU	SPECULUMS
CELNOORSU	COUNSELOR
CELNOOSTU	LOSE COUNT
CELNOOTUV	CONVOLUTE
CELNOPRTU	CORPULENT
CELNOPRUU	UNCOUPLER
CELNOPSUU	UNCOUPLES
CELNORSTU	CONSULTER
CELNOSSTU	COUNTLESS
CELNOSSUV	CONVULSES
CELNRRTUY	CURRENTLY
CELNRTTUU	TRUCULENT
CELOOPRSU	SUPERCOOL
CELOOPSSS	CESSPOOLS
CELOORSSW	LOW SCORES
CELOOSSTU	CUTS LOOSE
CELPRRTUY	CURT REPLY
CELPRSTUU	SCULPTURE
CEMMNNOOT	NO COMMENT
CEMMNOORS	COMMONERS
CEMMNOOST	COMMONEST
CEMMORSTU	COMMUTERS
CEMNNOOPT	COMPONENT
CEMNNOORT	CONTEMNOR
CEMNOOOQU	MONOCOQUE
CEMNOOOSS	COMES SOON
CEMNOOPSU	COMES UPON
CEMNOORRY	CRY NO MORE
CEMNOORST	STORM CONE
CEMNORSSU	CONSUMERS
CEMOOPRRY	PERRY COMO
CEMOOPRSS	COMPOSERS
CEMOOPRST	COMPOSTER
CEMOOPRSU	COMPOSURE
CEMOOPSTU	COMES UP TO
CEMOPRSTU	COMPUTERS
CEMORRSUU	MERCUROUS
CEMORSSTU	CUSTOMERS
CEMPRSSTU	SPECTRUMS
CENNOOPSU	POUNCES ON
CENNOORSV	CONVENORS
CENNOOSTT	NO CONTEST
CENNORSTU	NOCTURNES
CENNOSSSU	CONSENSUS
CENNOSTTU	COUNTS TEN

CENOOPRST	STONECROP
CENOOPRTU	OPEN COURT
CENOOQRRU	CONQUEROR
CENOORTUY	TROY OUNCE
CENOORTYY	TYCOONERY
CENOOSTUW	TWO OUNCES
CENOQSSTU	CONQUESTS
CENORSSSS	CROSSNESS
CENORSSTU	CONSTRUES
CENORSSTW	CROWS NEST
CENORSSUY	CYNOSURES
CENPRSTUU	PUNCTURES
CEOOOSTTV	SOTTO VOCE
CEOOPRRSS	PROCESSOR
CEOOPRRTT	PROTECTOR
CEOOPRSST	TOP SCORES
CEOOPSSTU	OCTOPUSES
CEOORRSSV	CROSS OVER
CEOORRSVW	CROWS OVER
CEOORSSTU	OUTSCORES
CEOORSTUU	COURTEOUS
CEOPPRSST	PROSPECTS
CEOPRRRSU	PRECURSOR
	PROCURERS
CEOPRRRTU	CORRUPTER
CEOPRSTUW	POWER CUTS
CEORSSSTT	TESTCROSS
CEPPRSSUU	SPRUCES UP
CEPPRSTUU	UPPERCUTS
CERRSTTUU	STRUCTURE
CFFGIINSU	SUFFICING
CFFGILNSU	SCUFFLING
CFFGIMNOO	COMING OFF
CFFGINORY	CRYING OFF
CFFHIOSTW	SWITCH OFF
CFFIIOOSU	OFFICIOUS
CFFIKLNSU	CUFF LINKS
CFFIOSTTU	CUTS IT OFF
CFFKKNOOS	KNOCKS OFF
CFFKORSTU	STRUCK OFF
CFFLOOORU	OFF COLOUR
	OFF-COLOUR
CFGHIILNN	FLINCHING
CFGIIIKNN	FINICKING
CFGIINNNO	CONFINING
CFGILNNOU	FLOUNCING
CFGINNOSU	CONFUSING
CFGINNOTU	CONFUTING
CFGINORRY	CRYING FOR
CFGINOSSU	FOCUSSING
CFHIINOOR	HONORIFIC
CFHIKLORS	RICH FOLKS
CFHIKOPRT	PITCHFORK
CFHIKOSST	STOCKFISH
CFHOOSTTU	SOFT TOUCH
CFIIKPRTU	PICK FRUIT
CFIILMMOR	MICROFILM
CFIILNORT	INFLICTOR
CFIINORST	FRICTIONS
CFIIOOPRS	SOPORIFIC
CFIKLLNOT	FLINTLOCK
CFIKLLOOR	FOLKLORIC
CFIKLMOPU	CUP OF MILK
CFIKLMOSU	FOLK MUSIC
CFILLNRUY	IN FULL CRY
CFILOORTU	FLUOROTIC
CFIMMNOOR	COMINFORM
CFIMNOORT	IN COMFORT
CFIMOSSTU	SOFT MUSIC
CFINNOOSU	CONFUSION
CFINNOSTU	FUNCTIONS

CFIOPRSTY	FIRST COPY
CFIORSSTT	FIRST COST
CFIPRSTUU	FRUIT CUPS
CFJOORRYY	CRY FOR JOY
CFKLNORUU	RUN OF LUCK
CFKLOOTUU	OUT OF LUCK
CFLLOORUU	COLOURFUL
CFLNOORRU	CORNFLOUR
CFLOOOSTT	COLTSFOOT
CFNNOORST	CONFRONTS
CFOOOPPRY	PROOF COPY
CFOOORSTW	CROW'S-FOOT
	CROWFOOTS
CGHNOORST	TORCH SONG
CGHOOPRUY	ROUGH COPY
CGIIIKMMN	MIMICKING
CGIIIKNNP	PINK ICING
CGIIILNNN	INCLINING
CGIIINNOT	COINING IT
CGIIINNOV	INVOICING
CGIIKKNPU	KICKING UP
CGIIKLNNO	LOCKING IN
CGIIKLNNR	CRINKLING
CGIIKLNPR	PRICKLING
CGIIKLNRT	TRICKLING
CGIIKMMRY	GIMMICKRY
CGIIKMNNU	MUCKING IN
CGIIKNNOP	PICKING ON
CGIIKNNPU	UNPICKING
CGIIKNNSU	SUCKING IN
CGIIKNNTU	TUCKING IN
CGIIKNPPU	PICKING UP
CGIILMNNY	MINCINGLY
CGIILMNOP	COMPILING
CGIILNNOS	CLOSING IN
	INCLOSING
CGIILNNOU	UNCOILING
CGIILNOOT	COOLING IT
CGIILNOPU	COILING UP
CGIILNPPR	CRIPPLING
CGIILNPPS	CLIPPINGS
CGIILOORV	VIROLOGIC
CGIILOSST	LOGISTICS
CGIIMNNPU	MINCING UP
CGIIMNPRS	SCRIMPING
CGIINNNOV	CONNIVING
CGIINNOOT	COGNITION
	INCOGNITO
CGIINNRRU	INCURRING
CGIINNTTU	CUTTING IN
CGIINOPPT	COPPING IT
CGIINPRST	SCRIPTING
CGIINPRTU	PICTURING
CGIINTTTU	CUTTING IT
CGIJNNORU	CONJURING
CGIKKLNNU	KNUCKLING
CGIKLLRUY	LUCKY GIRL
CGIKLMNOY	MOCKINGLY
CGIKLNNOU	UNLOCKING
CGIKLNOPU	LOCKING UP
CGIKLNRTU	TRUCKLING
CGIKLNSSU	SUCKLINGS
CGIKNNOOV	CONVOKING
CGIKNNORU	UNCORKING
CGIKNOOPU	COOKING UP
CGIKNOPRU	CORKING UP
CGIKNOSST	STOCKINGS
CGIKOOPST	POGO STICK
CGILLNOYY	CLOYINGLY
CGILMNOPY	COMPLYING
CGILMNPRU	CRUMPLING

CGILNNNUY	CUNNINGLY	CHIIPSSTY	PHYSICIST
CGILNNOOR	LONGICORN	CHIKLMNPU	MILK PUNCH
CGILNNOOS	CONSOLING	CHIKLMNRU	MILK CHURN
CGILNNRUU	UNCURLING	CHIKLMOST	LOCKSMITH
CGILNOOOS	NOSOLOGIC	CHIKLSTUY	LUCKY HITS
CGILNOOOY	ICONOLOGY	CHIKMNPSU	CHIPMUNKS
CGILNOORU	COLOURING	CHIKNOSTW	THICK SNOW
CGILNOPSU	CLOSING UP	CHIKOOPTT	TOOTHPICK
	COUPLINGS	CHIKOPSTU	THICK SOUP
CGILNOPUV	LOVING CUP	CHIKOPSTW	WHIPSTOCK
CGILNORSU	CLOSURING	CHILLNOOT	LOINCLOTH
CGILNPRSU	SCRUPLING	CHILLOSTY	COLTISHLY
CGILNPRUU	CURLING UP	CHILLRRSY	SHRILL CRY
CGILNPSTU	SCULPTING	CHILMNOUU	HOMUNCULI
CGILNRTUU	CULTURING	CHILMOSSU	SCHOLIUMS
CGILNSTTU	SCUTTLING	CHILNNPSY	LYNCHPINS
CGILNTTUY	CUTTINGLY	CHILNOOPS	LOIN CHOPS
CGILOOOSY	SOCIOLOGY	CHILNOPSU	SULPHONIC
CGILOORTU	GIRL SCOUT	CHILOORSS	CHLOROSIS
CGIMMNNOU	COMMUNING	CHILORTUY	ULOTRICHY
CGIMMNOTU	COMMUTING	CHILPRSUU	SULPHURIC
CGIMNNOSU	CONSUMING	CHILRRSUY	CURRISHLY
CGIMNOOPS	COMPOSING	CHIMMNOOY	HOMONYMIC
CGIMNOOTU	COMING OUT	CHIMNOPSY	SYMPHONIC
CGIMNOPTU	COMPUTING	CHIMNORSW	INCHWORMS
CGIMNOSTU	COSTUMING	CHIMOPSSU	MUSIC SHOP
CGIMNPRSU	SCRUMPING	CHINOOPTY	HYPOTONIC
CGINNNOOT	CONNOTING	CHINOOTTU	INTO TOUCH
CGINNOORS	CONSIGNOR	CHIOOPRSU	CURIO SHOP
CGINNOOTT	COTTON GIN	CHIOOPTYZ	ZOOPHYTIC
	COTTONING	CHIOPRSTU	COURTSHIP
CGINNOOVY	CONVOYING	CHIOPRSYY	HYPOCRISY
CGINNORTU	TROUNCING	CHIOPSSSY	PSYCHOSIS
CGINNOSTU	CONTUSING	CHIORRSSU	SCIRRHOUS
CGINOOPPU	COOPING UP	CHIPRSTTY	TRIPTYCHS
CGINOPRRU	PROCURING	CHJNORRUY	JOHN CURRY
CGINORSSS	CROSSINGS	CHKLNOORS	LOCK HORNS
CGINORTUY	CONGRUITY	CHKLNOOTU	TOOK LUNCH
	CRYING OUT	CHKLOSTUY	LUCKY SHOT
CGINPTTUU	CUTTING UP	CHKOOPPRS	PORK CHOPS
CGINRRSUY	SCURRYING	CHKOPSSTU	TUCK SHOPS
CGINRSTUY	CURTSYING	CHLNOOOPS	COLOPHONS
CGKLNOOSS	LONG SOCKS	CHLNOOOPY	COLOPHONY
CGKOOPRRU	ROCK GROUP	CHLNOTUUY	UNCOUTHLY
CGLMOOOSY	COSMOLOGY	CHLOOPTYY	HYPOCOTYL
CGMNOOOSY	COSMOGONY	CHLOOSTTU	LOST TOUCH
CGNNOOTTU	GUN COTTON	CHMNORRSU	CRUMHORNS
	GUNCOTTON	CHNNORSYY	SYNCHRONY
CGNOORSUU	CONGRUOUS	CHNOOPTUU	TOUCH UPON
CHHHIIMNO	HO CHI MINH	CHNORSTUU	CHURNS OUT
CHHINTTUW	WITCH HUNT	CHOOOPPTY	PHOTOCOPY
	WITCH-HUNT	CHORSSTTU	CUTS SHORT
CHHIOPSST	CHIP SHOTS		SHORT CUTS
CHHKLLOOY	HOLLYHOCK		SHORTCUTS
CHHKOOPSS	HOCK SHOPS	CIIILLLTY	ILLICITLY
CHHLNORUU	LUNCH HOUR	CIIILLSTV	CIVIL LIST
CHIIILPPP	PHILIPPIC	CIIILMOPT	IMPOLITIC
CHIIKKNST	THICK SKIN	CIIILORSS	OIL CRISIS
CHIIKMSTT	THICK MIST	CIIILORTV	VITRIOLIC
CHIILLOPY	LYOPHILIC	CIIILOSSS	SILICOSIS
CHIILMORT	MICROLITH	CIIILSTUV	CIVIL SUIT
CHIILNNPS	LINCHPINS	CIIIMSTTW	WITTICISM
CHIILOOTT	OTOLITHIC	CIIINNOSS	INCISIONS
CHIILORTY	RHYOLITIC	CIIINNOST	COINS IT IN
CHIILTTWY	TWITCHILY	CIIINNRST	INTRINSIC
CHIIMNOPR	MORPHINIC	CIIJLNOPT	CLIP JOINT
CHIIMOSTT	THOMISTIC	CIIKLLOSS	OIL SLICKS
CHIINOPTT	PITCH INTO	CIIKLPSST	LIPSTICKS
CHIINOSTU	CHITINOUS	CIIKNOSTT	STICK IT ON
CHIIOPSST	SOPHISTIC	CIIKNPPRS	PINPRICKS
CHIIORRSS	CIRRHOSIS	CIIKNPSST	STICK PINS

CIIKNRSTW	WIN TRICKS
CIIKOSTTT	STICK TO IT
CIIKPPSTU	PICKS IT UP
CIIKRSSTX	SIX TRICKS
CIILLNOOS	COLLISION
CIILLNOOT	COTILLION
CIILLNUVY	UNCIVILLY
CIILMRSSY	LYRICISMS
CIILNNOSU	INCLUSION
CIILNOPTU	PUNCTILIO
CIILOOPST	POLITICOS
CIILOORST	SOLICITOR
CIILOOSSS	SCOLIOSIS
CIILOSUVY	VICIOUSLY
CIILSSTTY	STYLISTIC
CIIMMSSTY	MYSTICISM
CIIMNORUZ	ZIRCONIUM
CIIMORSTV	VORTICISM
CIINNOORT	IRON TONIC
CIINNORSU	INCURSION
CIINNSSTT	INSTINCTS
CIINOOPPR	PROPIONIC
CIINOOPRT	INOTROPIC
CIINOPSSU	SUSPICION
CIINORSUU	INCURIOUS
CIINOSSSS	SCISSIONS
CIINPSSTU	SINCIPUTS
CIIOOPRST	ISOTROPIC
CIIOOSSTX	TOXICOSIS
CIIORSTTV	VORTICIST
CIIORSTUV	VIRTUOSIC
CIIORSTUY	CURIOSITY
CIIORTTVY	VORTICITY
CIIOSSTVY	VISCOSITY
CIIRSTTUY	RUSTICITY
CIJKOSSTY	JOYSTICKS
CIJNNOSTU	JUNCTIONS
CIKKOPSST	SPOT KICKS
CIKKOQRUW	QUICK WORK
CIKLLNUUY	UNLUCKILY
CIKLNORSS	CROSS-LINK
CIKLNOSST	LINSTOCKS
CIKLNSUWY	LUCKY WINS
CIKLORSTU	STRUCK OIL
CIKLOSSTT	STOCK LIST
CIKLRSSSU	KISS-CURLS
CIKMOORSS	SICKROOMS
CIKNNOOSS	COONSKINS
CIKNOSTTU	STUCK IT ON
CIKORRSWY	WORRY SICK
CIKORSTTW	TWO TRICKS
CIKOSSSTT	STOCKISTS
CIKOSSTTU	STICKS OUT
CIKOSTTTU	STUCK TO IT
CILLMORUY	COLLYRIUM
CILLNOOSU	COLLUSION
CILLNOSSU	SCULLIONS
CILLOOORU	OIL COLOUR
CILMNOSTU	COLUMNIST
CILMNSUUV	VINCULUMS
CILMOSSUU	SOUL MUSIC
CILMOSSUW	SLOW MUSIC
CILNNOORT	IN CONTROL
CILNOOOTY	OIL TYCOON
CILNOOSST	COLONISTS
CILNOOSTU	LOCUTIONS
CILOOPSUY	COPIOUSLY
CILOORRTU	TRICOLOUR
CILOORSTU	COLOURIST
CILOPRTYY	PYROLYTIC
CILORRSUY	CURSORILY
CILORSUUY	CURIOUSLY
CILOSSUVY	VISCOUSLY
CIMMMNOSU	COMMUNISM
CIMMNNOOU	COMMUNION
CIMMNOOOT	COMMOTION
CIMMNOSTU	COMMUNIST
CIMMNOTUY	COMMUNITY
CIMMOORSU	MUSIC ROOM
CIMMNOOOT	MONOTONIC
CIMNNOSYY	SYNONYMIC
CIMNNOTUU	CONTINUUM
CIMNOOPTY	TOPONYMIC
CIMNOOTXY	MYCOTOXIN
CIMNOSSTU	MISCOUNTS
CIMNSTUYY	SYNCYTIUM
CIMORSUXY	ROXY MUSIC
CIMPRSSTU	PRIMS CUTS
CINNOOSTU	CONTINUOS
	CONTUSION
CINNOOSUU	INNOCUOUS
CINNOOTTU	COUNT ON IT
CINOOORRS	CORROSION
CINOOPRSS	SCORPIONS
CINOORRSS	IRON CROSS
CINOOSSST	TOSS COINS
CINOOTTXY	CYTOTOXIN
CINOSSTUV	VISCOUNTS
CINOSTTUW	CUTS IN TWO
CINOSTUVY	VISCOUNTY
CINRSSTTU	INSTRUCTS
CIOOOPRRT	PORTO RICO
CIOOOPRTZ	PROTOZOIC
CIOPPRRST	STRIP-CROP
CIOSTTTUU	CUTS IT OUT
CKKNOOSTU	KNOCKOUTS
	KNOCKS OUT
CKKOOOSTT	TOOK STOCK
CKLLNOORR	ROCK N ROLL
CKLLOOOOS	LOOKS COOL
CKLMNOOSW	MONKS COWL
CKNOOOSSY	COSY NOOKS
CKOOORSTT	ROOTSTOCK
CKOOPSSTT	STOCKPOTS
CKOPRSTTU	TRUCK STOP
CKORSTTUU	STRUCK OUT
CLMMNOOOT	COMMON LOT
CLMOOOORT	LOCOMOTOR
CLMOOOSTY	COLOSTOMY
CLMOORSTU	COLOSTRUM
CLNOOPRSU	PROCONSUL
CLNOOSTTU	LOST COUNT
CLNOOSUUY	NOCUOUSLY
CLOOOPRST	PROTOCOLS
CLOPRRTUY	CORRUPTLY
CLOPRSSTU	SCULPTORS
CMOOORSST	MOTO-CROSS
CNNOOOSTT	COTTONS ON
CNNOOPTUU	COUNT UPON
CNOOOORST	OCTOROONS
CNOOSTTUU	COUNTS OUT
CNOPRTUUY	UP-COUNTRY
COOOPPRRS	POOR CROPS
COOOPRRST	ROOT CROPS
COOOPSSTU	SCOOPS OUT
COOPRRRTU	CORRUPTOR
COOPRSSTY	SPOROCYST
COOSSTTUU	SCOUTS OUT
DDDDEEIIK	EDDIE KIDD
DDDEEEHOT	DO THE DEED
DDDEEGOOS	GOOD DEEDS
DDDEEHRSU	SHUDDERED

DDDEEIKNS	KIND DEEDS	DDEEIISSS	DISSEISED
DDDEEINST	DISTENDED	DDEEILLNW	INDWELLED
DDDEEIRTY	DIRTY DEED	DDEEILLPS	DISPELLED
DDDEENNSU	SUDDEN END	DDEEILLRV	DRIVELLED
DDDEENORU	REDOUNDED	DDEEILMMN	MIDDLEMEN
DDDEFFNOO	NODDED OFF	DDEEILNRT	TENDRILED
DDDEFIOSX	FIXED ODDS	DDEEILOPS	DESPOILED
DDDEGILOS	DISLODGED	DDEEILORS	SOLDIERED
DDDEGINOR	DODDERING	DDEEILRSV	RED DEVILS
DDDEIINSV	DIVIDENDS	DDEEIMMOS	SEMIDOMED
DDDEIINUV	UNDIVIDED	DDEEIMNOS	DEMONISED
DDDEIIPRR	DRIP-DRIED	DDEEIMNOZ	DEMONIZED
DDDEIKOOS	SKIDDOOED	DDEEINNST	INTENDEDS
DDDELOPTU	TODDLED UP	DDEEINORW	EIDERDOWN
DDDGINOOO	DID NO GOOD	DDEEINPSS	DISPENSED
DDDMNOPUY	MUDDY POND	DDEEINRSU	UNDERSIDE
DDEEEEKNW	WEEKENDED	DDEEINSSS	SIDEDNESS
DDEEEFILP	DEEP FIELD	DDEEINSST	DISSENTED
DDEEEFIPR	DEEP-FRIED	DDEEIOORS	DEODORISE
DDEEEFNRS	DEFENDERS	DDEEIOORZ	DEODORIZE
DDEEEFNRU	UNDERFEED	DDEEIOPRX	PEROXIDED
DDEEEGIPR	PEDIGREED	DDEEIOPST	DEPOSITED
DDEEEILHV	DELIVERED	DDEEIORTV	TIDED OVER
DDEEEILSV	EVIL DEEDS	DDEEIPRRS	RED SPIDER
DDEEEILTT	TITLE DEED	DDEEIPRSS	DISPERSED
DDEEEINRX	DEXEDRINE	DDEEIPSTU	DEPUTISED
DDEEEIPTX	EXPEDITED	DDEEIPTUZ	DEPUTIZED
DDEEELOPV	DEVELOPED	DDEELMORS	SMOLDERED
DDEEENNOP	OPEN-ENDED	DDEELMORU	MOULDERED
DDEEENNOT	NEEDED NOT		REMOULDED
DDEEENNPT	DEPENDENT	DDEELNPRU	PLUNDERED
DDEEENPRT	PRETENDED	DDEELOTVY	DEVOTEDLY
DDEEEORRR	REORDERED	DDEELRSTU	DELUSTRED
DDEEEOTUW	WEEDED OUT	DDEEMNOTU	DEMOUNTED
DDEEEPRSS	DEPRESSED	DDEENNORU	UNDERDONE
DDEEERRSS	REDRESSED	DDEENOORV	ODD OR EVEN
DDEEERTTX	TED DEXTER	DDEENOPRS	RESPONDED
DDEEESTUU	DESUETUDE	DDEENOPRT	PORTENDED
DDEEFGHOT	FED THE DOG	DDEENOPUX	EXPOUNDED
DDEEFGILY	FEEL GIDDY	DDEENORSU	RESOUNDED
DDEEFGINN	DEFENDING	DDEENPSSU	SUSPENDED
DDEEFGLNU	UNFLEDGED	DDEENRRTU	TURNED RED
DDEEFIILW	WIDE FIELD	DDEENRSSU	UNDRESSED
DDEEFINOP	DOPE FIEND	DDEEOOPRT	TORPEDOED
DDEEFIPRS	DRIP-FEEDS	DDEEOORSV	OVERDOSED
DDEEFLOSU	FOUL DEEDS	DDEEORSTY	DESTROYED
DDEEFNORU	FOUNDERED	DDEEPRSSU	DRESSED UP
DDEEFORST	DEFROSTED	DDEERRSTU	RED DUSTER
DDEEGGILT	GILT EDGED	DDEERSTTU	TRUST DEED
	GILT-EDGED	DDEFFIINT	DIFFIDENT
DDEEGGIRS	DRIED EGGS	DDEFFINOR	RIDDEN OFF
DDEEGHILT	DELIGHTED	DDEFFIOOR	FRIED FOOD
DDEEGINNP	DEPENDING	DDEFFLOOT	TODDLE OFF
DDEEGINNR	REDDENING	DDEFGIIIN	DIGNIFIED
DDEEGIRSS	DIGRESSED	DDEFGIIRS	DRIED FIGS
DDEEGJPRU	PREJUDGED	DDEFGILTY	FELT GIDDY
DDEEGLOOT	EDGED TOOL	DDEFGINRU	DRUG FIEND
DDEEGOOPS	GOOD SPEED	DDEFIILSU	FLUIDISED
DDEEGOSSS	GODDESSES	DDEFIILUZ	FLUIDIZED
DDEEHIILN	LIE HIDDEN	DDEFILNOR	OLD FRIEND
DDEEHNORT	DETHRONED	DDEFILNOW	DOWNFIELD
DDEEHNORU	DEERHOUND		FILED DOWN
DDEEHNRTU	THUNDERED	DDEFILOOT	FLOOD TIDE
DDEEHRRSS	SHREDDERS	DDEFINSTU	SUDDEN FIT
DDEEIILMT	DELIMITED	DDEFNNOUU	UNFOUNDED
DDEEIIMRS	DIMERISED	DDEGGIORS	DISGORGED
DDEEIIMRZ	DIMERIZED	DDEGGIOSU	GUIDE DOGS
DDEEIINOS	DEIONISED	DDEGGJOOU	GOOD JUDGE
DDEEIINOZ	DEIONIZED	DDEGHINRS	SHREDDING
DDEEIINRV	I NEVER DID!	DDEGIIIST	DIGITISED
DDEEIIPPT	DIPEPTIDE	DDEGIIITZ	DIGITIZED

DDEGIIMSU	MISGUIDED
DDEGIINSS	GIDDINESS
DDEGIISSU	DISGUISED
DDEGIJMSU	MISJUDGED
DDEGIJNRU	JUDDERING
DDEGILOOY	GOOD YIELD
DDEGILOSS	DISLODGES
DDEGINORR	DERRING-DO
DDEGINOSV	GIVEN ODDS
DDEGINOUY	DIED YOUNG
DDEGIOSSV	GIVES ODDS
DDEGISSTU	DISGUSTED
DDEGLNOOR	GOLDEN ROD
	GOLDENROD
DDEGNORSU	UNDERDOGS
DDEGOOORS	DO-GOODERS
DDEHHNRTU	HUNDREDTH
DDEHIIRST	THIRD SIDE
DDEHIIRSY	YIDDISHER
DDEHIISTW	SIDED WITH
DDEHILNSU	IN HUDDLES
DDEHIORXY	HYDROXIDE
DDEHIOSST	SHODDIEST
DDEHIOSTU	DISHED OUT
DDEHLMOOT	OLD METHOD
DDEHNOOSW	HOSED DOWN
DDEHOOSSW	WOODSHEDS
DDEIIJNOS	DISJOINED
DDEIIKLMR	DRIED MILK
DDEIILLST	DISTILLED
DDEIILLTW	DID IT WELL
DDEIILSTT	TIDDLIEST
DDEIIMSSS	DISMISSED
DDEIIMTTW	DIM-WITTED
DDEIINPRS	SPIN-DRIED
DDEIINSST	DISSIDENT
DDEIINSSW	SIDE WINDS
DDEIINSTU	DISUNITED
DDEIIORTV	OVERDID IT
DDEIIPRRS	DRIP-DRIES
DDEILNOSW	SLIDE DOWN
DDEILNOVW	LIVED DOWN
DDEILOOST	STOOD IDLE
DDEILORWW	WIDE WORLD
	WORLDWIDE
DDEILSTUY	STUDIEDLY
DDEIMMRUY	MEDIUM DRY
DDEIMNOPU	IMPOUNDED
DDEIMNSSU	MUDDINESS
DDEIMRSSU	SIDE DRUMS
DDEINOPPR	DROPPED IN
DDEINOPPW	PIPED DOWN
DDEINORTU	OUTRIDDEN
	RIDDEN OUT
DDEINOSSW	DISENDOWS
	DOWDINESS
DDEINRSSU	RUDDINESS
DDEINSTUU	UNSTUDIED
DDEIOORSS	SIDE DOORS
DDEIOPPRT	DROPPED IT
DDEIOPRST	DISPORTED
DDEIOPRSV	DISPROVED
DDEIORRSS	DISORDERS
DDEIORSTT	DISTORTED
DDEIPRSTU	DISRUPTED
DDEKLLOOO	LOOKED OLD
DDELNORSU	UNDERSOLD
DDELNORSW	WORLDS END
DDELOPSTU	TODDLES UP
DDEMMNOOT	ODD MOMENT
DDEMNOOWW	MOWED DOWN

DDEMNOSUU	DUODENUMS
DDENNOOOW	DO ONE DOWN
DDENNOORU	ROUNDED ON
DDENNOOTW	NOTED DOWN
	TONED DOWN
DDENNORUU	UNROUNDED
DDENNORUW	DOWN UNDER
DDENNOSSW	SENDS DOWN
DDENOOPPR	DROPPED ON
DDENOOPRS	ODD PERSON
DDENOOPRU	DONE PROUD
DDENOORSW	DO WONDERS
DDENOOTVW	VOTED DOWN
DDENOPRUU	ROUNDED UP
DDENORSSW	DRESS DOWN
	SENDS WORD
DDEOOPPSU	PSEUDOPOD
DDEOOPRSU	DOES PROUD
DDEOOQSTU	QUOTE ODDS
DDEOPRRTU	PROTRUDED
DDEORRSUW	RUDE WORDS
DDFILOOOS	SOLID FOOD
DDFINORSW	FIND WORDS
DDFIOORTW	DRIFTWOOD
DDFLNOOSW	FOLDS DOWN
DDFNOOORX	OXFORD DON
DDGGINNOS	DINGDONGS
DDGGINOOO	DOING GOOD
DDGHLOOOS	HOLDS GOOD
DDGHNOOSU	HOUND DOGS
DDGIIKLNY	KIDDINGLY
DDGIIKNNO	NO KIDDING
DDGIILMNS	MIDDLINGS
DDGIILNNW	DWINDLING
DDGIILNTW	TWIDDLING
DDGIINORT	DOING DIRT
DDGIKNOOR	GOOD DRINK
DDGILLOOS	SOLID GOLD
DDGINNOOW	DOING DOWN
DDGINNORW	GRIND DOWN
DDGINNOWY	DYING DOWN
DDGINOTUY	DOING DUTY
DDGIORSTY	DIRTY DOGS
DDGNOOPSU	DOG POUNDS
DDGOOOORU	GOOD ODOUR
DDGOOORSW	GOOD WORDS
DDHIOOOWW	WIDOWHOOD
DDHLNOOSW	HOLDS DOWN
DDHNNOOUW	HOUND DOWN
DDHOORSST	SHORT ODDS
DDIIIKKNW	KIDDIWINK
DDIKNORSW	KIND WORDS
DDILOOPPS	DIPLOPODS
DDIMNNOSU	SOUND MIND
DDIMNOOUY	DO YOU MIND?
DDINNOSWW	WINDS DOWN
DDIORRTWY	DIRTY WORD
DDLNOOSUU	LOUD SOUND
DDNNOOUWW	WOUND DOWN
DDNOOOSTW	STOOD DOWN
DDNOOPRSW	DROPS DOWN
DDNOSSTUW	DUSTS DOWN
DEEEEGNOR	ONE DEGREE
DEEEEGNPR	DEEP GREEN
DEEEEGNRY	GREEN-EYED
DEEEEGQSU	SQUEEGEED
DEEEEHPRT	THREE DEEP
DEEEEKNRW	WEEKENDER
DEEEELPPS	DEEP SLEEP
DEEEEMRRS	REDEEMERS
DEEEENPST	STEEPENED

DEEEENSTW	SWEETENED	DEEEIPRRV	DEEP RIVER
DEEEFFFNO	ENFEOFFED		REPRIEVED
DEEEFFLOP	PEELED OFF	DEEEIPRTX	EXPEDITER
DEEEFFLOR	REELED OFF	DEEEIPRVW	PREVIEWED
DEEEFFORR	REOFFERED	DEEEIPSST	SPEEDIEST
DEEEFGIKN	KNIFE EDGE	DEEEIPSTX	EXPEDITES
	KNIFE-EDGE	DEEEIPSWW	WIDE SWEEP
DEEEFGORS	FORE-EDGES	DEEEIRRRS	DERRIERES
DEEEFHNRS	FRESHENED	DEEEIRRTV	RETRIEVED
DEEEFHRRS	REFRESHED	DEEEIRSTY	TIRED EYES
DEEEFILRT	FEEL TIRED	DEEEIRSVY	EVERY SIDE
DEEEFINSV	DEFENSIVE	DEEEIRUZZ	ZUIDER ZEE
DEEEFIPRS	DEEP-FRIES	DEEEKLLNN	KENNELLED
DEEEFIRRS	FREE RIDES	DEEEKLMOS	SMOKED EEL
DEEEFLLRU	REFUELLED	DEEEKNPRU	KEEP UNDER
DEEEFLLSW	FEEDS WELL	DEEEKOPRR	KEEP ORDER
DEEEFMNRT	DEFERMENT	DEEELLPRS	RESPELLED
	FERMENTED	DEEELLPSW	SPEEDWELL
DEEEFMNRV	FRED EMINEV	DEEELLRVW	DREW LEVEL
DEEEFOPRZ	DEEP-FROZE	DEEELNOPS	EDSON PELE
DEEEFORSV	OVERFEEDS	DEEELNOPV	ENVELOPED
DEEEFPRRR	PREFERRED	DEEELOPRV	DEVELOPER
DEEEFPRRY	DEEP-FRYER		REDEVELOP
DEEEFRRRS	DEFERRERS	DEEELPPRX	PERPLEXED
DEEEFRRYZ	FREEZE-DRY	DEEELPSSS	LESS SPEED
DEEEGHNOT	ON THE EDGE	DEEELRRTT	RED LETTER
DEEEGHNRT	NTH DEGREE		RED-LETTER
DEEEGHOTT	TO THE EDGE	DEEELRSTW	SWELTERED
DEEEGIMNR	REDEEMING	DEEEMNNOV	ENVENOMED
DEEEGINNP	DEEPENING	DEEEMNRTT	DETERMENT
DEEEGINRS	ENERGISED	DEEEMOPRT	PEDOMETER
	SEEING RED	DEEEMOPRW	EMPOWERED
DEEEGINRZ	ENERGIZED	DEEEMPPRT	PREEMPTED
DEEEGIPRS	PEDIGREES	DEEENNSSS	DENSENESS
DEEEGIRST	GREEDIEST	DEEENOPST	DEEP NOTES
DEEEGKLNT	KENTLEDGE		DEEP TONES
DEEEGLNOY	GOLDENEYE	DEEENPRRT	PRETENDER
DEEEGMNST	SEGMENTED	DEEENPRST	PRESENTED
DEEEGNNRS	ENGENDERS	DEEENPRTV	PREVENTED
DEEEGNOST	SET ON EDGE	DEEENRRST	TENDERERS
DEEEGNRTT	DETERGENT	DEEENRRSV	REVERENDS
DEEEGORTU	OUTER EDGE	DEEENRRTT	DETERRENT
DEEEGRRSS	REGRESSED	DEEENRSTT	TENDEREST
DEEEGRRTT	REGRETTED	DEEENRSTX	EXTENDERS
DEEEHINPR	EPHEDRINE	DEEENRSUV	NEVER USED
DEEEHIRST	ETHERISED	DEEEOPRST	DEPORTEES
DEEEHIRTZ	ETHERIZED	DEEEOPSTU	SEEPED OUT
DEEEHISTT	DIET SHEET	DEEEORRSS	REREDOSES
DEEEHLRST	SHELTERED	DEEEORSTV	STEVEDORE
DEEEHNPRR	REPREHEND	DEEEORSVW	OVERSEWED
DEEEHNRRU	HEREUNDER	DEEEORSVX	OVERSEXED
DEEEHRSTT	THE DESERT	DEEEPPPRR	RED PEPPER
DEEEILLMP	MILLEPEDE	DEEEPPRSS	DEREPRESS
DEEEILNNV	ENLIVENED		REPRESSED
DEEEILNRW	ELDER WINE	DEEEPRRSV	PRESERVED
DEEEILRRV	DELIVERER	DEEEPRRTV	PERVERTED
DEEEILSSW	EDELWEISS	DEEEPRSSS	DEPRESSES
DEEEILSTV	TELEVISED	DEEEPRSST	SPEEDSTER
DEEEIMNRT	DETERMINE	DEEEPRSSU	SUPERSEDE
DEEEIMNSU	EUMENIDES	DEEEPRSSX	EXPRESSED
DEEEINNSS	NEEDINESS	DEEEQRSTU	REQUESTED
DEEEINOPR	PIONEERED	DEEERRRSV	VERDERERS
DEEEINPTX	EXPEDIENT	DEEERRSSS	REDRESSES
DEEEINQTU	QUEENED IT	DEEERRSST	DESERTERS
	QUIETENED	DEEERRSTT	RED SETTER
DEEEINRST	TENDERISE	DEEEFFILLT	LEFT FIELD
	TEREDINES	DEEFFINRT	DIFFERENT
DEEEINRTT	ENTERED IT	DEEFFIORT	FORFEITED
DEEEINRTZ	TENDERIZE	DEEFFIRRY	FIERY FRED
DEEEINSSS	SEEDINESS	DEEFFOPRR	PROFFERED
DEEEINSSW	WEEDINESS	DEEFFOPRU	OFFERED UP

DEEFGGIRS	FRIED EGGS	DEEGGHHOS	HEDGEHOGS
DEEFGGORS	DEFOGGERS	DEEGGHORU	ROUGH EDGE
DEEFGHIRT	FREIGHTED	DEEGGILNR	LEDGERING
DEEFGIILR	FILIGREED	DEEGGINRS	SNIGGERED
DEEFGINRR	DEFERRING	DEEGGIPRY	GREEDY PIG
DEEFGJORU	FOREJUDGE	DEEGGIRRT	TRIGGERED
DEEFGLOOS	FEELS GOOD	DEEGGKORS	GREEK GODS
DEEFGLORV	GOLD FEVER	DEEGGNOSZ	DOZEN EGGS
DEEFHLLUY	HEEDFULLY	DEEGGOPTU	PEGGED OUT
DEEFHLOPS	SHEEPFOLD	DEEGGSSTU	SUGGESTED
DEEFHLORS	FREEHOLDS	DEEGHHIPS	HIGH SPEED
DEEFHLORT	THREEFOLD		HIGH-SPEED
DEEFHORRS	HEREFORDS	DEEGHHOPS	HEDGEHOPS
DEEFHRRTU	FURTHERED	DEEGHIINV	INVEIGHED
DEEFIILNR	INFIELDER	DEEGHIINW	WEIGHED IN
DEEFIILQU	LIQUEFIED	DEEGHILNT	LIGHTENED
DEEFIIMNS	FEMINISED	DEEGHILNW	WHEEDLING
DEEFIIMNZ	FEMINIZED	DEEGHILRT	DELIGHTER
DEEFIIMTX	FIXED TIME		LIGHTERED
DEEFIIPRS	PERFIDIES	DEEGHINTT	TIGHTENED
DEEFIIPRT	PETRIFIED	DEEGHIPSS	DEEP SIGHS
DEEFIIRRT	TERRIFIED	DEEGHIPUW	WEIGHED UP
DEEFIIRSS	FIRESIDES	DEEGHLMOP	HELP ME GOD
DEEFIIRSV	VERSIFIED	DEEGHNORU	ROUGHENED
DEEFIISTT	TESTIFIED	DEEGHNOTU	TOUGHENED
DEEFIKNRR	FREE DRINK	DEEGHOPSS	SHEEP DOGS
DEEFILMNS	FIELDSMEN		SHEEPDOGS
DEEFILMOW	MODEL WIFE	DEEGHORSW	HEDGEROWS
DEEFILNOP	OPEN FIELD	DEEGIILNU	GUIDELINE
DEEFILOTT	LEFT TO DIE	DEEGIINSS	DIGENESIS
DEEFILRSV	SELF-DRIVE	DEEGIINTY	TIE-DYEING
DEEFILRTT	FELT TIRED	DEEGIISTV	DIGESTIVE
	FLITTERED	DEEGIKLLT	GET KILLED
DEEFILSTT	FIELD TEST	DEEGIKNPS	SPEED KING
DEEFIMNOT	END OF TIME	DEEGILMMR	GLIMMERED
DEEFIMRSU	FRUSEMIDE	DEEGILMOR	OLD REGIME
DEEFINNPR	PEN FRIEND	DEEGILNOU	EUGLENOID
	PEN-FRIEND	DEEGILNPT	DEPLETING
DEEFINNRW	NEW FRIEND	DEEGILNSS	SEEDLINGS
DEEFINOVZ	FIVE DOZEN	DEEGILNST	GLISTENED
DEEFINRRU	UNDER FIRE	DEEGILOOU	IDEOLOGUE
DEEFINSST	FETIDNESS	DEEGILOPR	RIDGEPOLE
DEEFINSSX	FIXEDNESS	DEEGILOSU	EULOGISED
DEEFIPRRV	PERFERVID	DEEGILOUZ	EULOGIZED
DEEFIPRTU	PUTREFIED	DEEGILRST	GLISTERED
DEEFIPSTU	STUPEFIED	DEEGILRSV	LEG DRIVES
DEEFIRSTU	SURFEITED	DEEGILRTT	GLITTERED
DEEFKLNRU	FEEL DRUNK	DEEGIMNPT	PIGMENTED
DEEFLLNNU	FUNNELLED	DEEGIMNRY	REMEDYING
DEEFLLNRU	FELL UNDER	DEEGIMORT	GEOMETRID
DEEFLLPSU	FULL SPEED	DEEGIMRSU	DEMIURGES
DEEFLNOSV	SEVENFOLD	DEEGINNPX	EXPENDING
DEEFLNRTU	UNDERFELT	DEEGINNRR	RENDERING
DEEFLORRW	FREE WORLD	DEEGINNRS	RED ENSIGN
	RED FLOWER	DEEGINNRT	TENDERING
DEEFLORSW	DEFLOWERS	DEEGINNTX	EXTENDING
DEEFLOSSW	SELF-SOWED	DEEGINORT	REDINGOTE
DEEFLRSTU	FLUSTERED	DEEGINRRR	DERRINGER
DEEFLRTTU	FLUTTERED	DEEGINRRT	DETERRING
DEEFMNORT	END OF TERM	DEEGINRSS	DESIGNERS
DEEFMOPRR	PERFORMED	DEEGINRST	DESERTING
	PREFORMED	DEEGINRSV	DESERVING
DEEFNOOPS	SPOON FEED	DEEGINRTU	NEGRITUDE
	SPOON-FEED	DEEGINRTV	DIVERGENT
DEEFNOOST	FESTOONED	DEEGINRUV	GERUNDIVE
DEEFOPRSS	PROFESSED	DEEGINSTT	DETESTING
DEEFORRST	DEFROSTER	DEEGIOPRU	GUIDE ROPE
DEEFORSST	DEFORESTS	DEEGIOSST	GEODESIST
DEEFPRRRY	FRED PERRY	DEEGIPRST	PREDIGEST
DEEFRSTUY	DUTY FREES	DEEGIRRTW	GREW TIRED
DEEGGGLNO	GOLDEN EGG	DEEGIRRUU	DE RIGUEUR

DEEGIRSSS	DIGRESSES	DEEHNORTW	DOWN THERE
DEEGIRSST	DIGESTERS		THREE DOWN
DEEGIRSTT	GETS TIRED	DEEHNRRTU	THUNDERER
DEEGJPRRU	PREJUDGER	DEEHOORTX	HETERODOX
DEEGJPRSU	PREJUDGES	DEEHOPRRS	SHEER DROP
DEEGKLNNO	DOG KENNEL	DEEHOPRTT	POT THE RED
DEEGKLNOW	KNOWLEDGE	DEEHOPSTU	DEEP SOUTH
DEEGKOPRW	POWDER KEG	DEEHRSSTW	SHREWDEST
DEEGLLORV	GROVELLED	DEEHRSTTU	SHUTTERED
DEEGLNOOW	WOODEN LEG	DEEHSSTTU	DUSTSHEET
DEEGLOOST	EDGE TOOLS	DEEIILLMP	MILLIPEDE
DEEGLORRW	GREW OLDER	DEEIILLOS	DIESEL OIL
DEEGLORST	GETS OLDER	DEEIILNSS	SIDE LINES
DEEGNNORU	GONE UNDER		SIDELINES
	UNDERGONE	DEEIILORV	LIVE OR DIE
DEEGNOORW	GREENWOOD	DEEIILRSV	DEVILRIES
	WOOD GREEN	DEEIIMNTU	IN DUE TIME
DEEGNOOSS	GOOD SENSE	DEEIIMOTT	TIME TO DIE
DEEGNORSS	ENGROSSED	DEEIIMPRS	EPIDERMIS
DEEGNORSU	GOES UNDER	DEEIIMRSS	DIMERISES
DEEGOOOST	GOOD TO SEE	DEEIIMRSZ	DIMERIZES
DEEGORRST	TED ROGERS	DEEIINNVW	END IN VIEW
DEEGORRSU	RED GROUSE	DEEIINOSS	DEIONISES
DEEHHILOY	HIDEY-HOLE	DEEIINOST	EDITIONES
DEEHHILPR	HIRED HELP	DEEIINOSZ	DEIONIZES
DEEHHPRSS	SHEPHERDS	DEEIINSST	DESTINIES
DEEHIINPT	PETHIDINE	DEEIIOPSX	EPOXIDISE
DEEHIINRT	INHERITED	DEEIIOPXZ	EPOXIDIZE
DEEHIIPSS	PIE DISHES	DEEIIPPPR	PIED PIPER
DEEHIKRSW	WHISKERED	DEEIIPRUX	PRIE-DIEUX
DEEHILPRS	ELDERSHIP	DEEIIPSSW	SIDESWIPE
DEEHILRST	SLITHERED	DEEIISSSS	DISSEISES
DEEHILSSV	DISHEVELS	DEEIISSSU	SIDE ISSUE
DEEHIMMRS	SHIMMERED	DEEIJNORR	REJOINDER
DEEHIMORV	DRIVE HOME	DEEIKLLRS	KILLDEERS
DEEHIMOST	METHODISE	DEEIKLMWY	MIDWEEKLY
DEEHIMOTZ	METHODIZE	DEEIKLNSX	SEX-LINKED
DEEHIMPRW	WHIMPERED	DEEIKNSTW	STINKWEED
DEEHINNRS	ENSHRINED	DEEIKPPRS	SKIPPERED
DEEHINNTU	IN THE NUDE	DEEIKRSTT	SKITTERED
DEEHINORT	DINOTHERE	DEEILLLNW	WELL-LINED
DEEHINOST	ON THE SIDE	DEEILLLOW	WELL OILED
DEEHINPRT	TREPHINED		WELL-OILED
DEEHINRSU	USHERED IN	DEEILLLVW	LIVED WELL
DEEHINRSW	SWINEHERD	DEEILLMST	MILD STEEL
DEEHIOOPT	HOPE TO DIE	DEEILLMTW	WELL-TIMED
DEEHIORST	OTHER SIDE	DEEILLNRW	INDWELLER
	THEORISED	DEEILLNST	TINSELLED
DEEHIORTZ	THEORIZED	DEEILLNSV	SNIVELLED
DEEHIOSTT	TO THE SIDE	DEEILLRRV	DRIVELLER
DEEHIOSTU	TIED HOUSE	DEEILLRST	TRELLISED
DEEHIPRSW	WHISPERED	DEEILLRSU	SLIDE RULE
DEEHIQRTU	THREE QUID	DEEILLRTU	TELLURIDE
DEEHIRSSV	DERVISHES	DEEILLRTW	WELL-TRIED
DEEHISSTW	SWEET DISH	DEEILLSST	LETS SLIDE
DEEHKNOSS	KEESHONDS	DEEILLSVW	SWIVELLED
DEEHLLOSV	SHOVELLED	DEEILMMNS	MENDELISM
DEEHLNOOT	ON THE DOLE	DEEILMNOV	DIME NOVEL
DEEHLNOPR	PENHOLDER	DEEILMNTV	DEVILMENT
DEEHLNPSS	SENDS HELP	DEEILMOPS	POLEMISED
DEEHLOPTU	HELPED OUT	DEEILMOPZ	POLEMIZED
DEEHMNNOT	ON THE MEND	DEEILNNRU	UNDERLINE
DEEHMNORT	DEN MOTHER	DEEILNOPT	DEPLETION
DEEHMNOSS	SENDS HOME		DIPLOTENE
DEEHMNOTW	NEW METHOD	DEEILNOST	DELETIONS
DEEHMOORV	DROVE HOME	DEEILNPTU	PLENITUDE
DEEHMORST	SMOTHERED	DEEILNPUV	LIVENED UP
DEEHNNORT	ENTHRONED	DEEILNRTU	INTERLUDE
DEEHNOPTY	ENDOPHYTE	DEEILNSTT	SETTLED IN
DEEHNORST	DETHRONES	DEEILNTVY	EVIDENTLY
	SHORTENED	DEEILOPRS	DESPOILER

DEEILOPTX	EXPLOITED	DEEIPRSTU	DISREPUTE
DEEILORRS	ORDERLIES	DEEIPSSST	SIDESTEPS
DEEILRSVY	DIVERSELY	DEEIPSSTU	DEPUTISES
DEEILRTUY	ERUDITELY	DEEIPSTUZ	DEPUTIZES
DEEIMMORS	MEMORISED	DEEIRRSST	DESTRIERS
DEEIMMORZ	MEMORIZED	DEEIRSSST	DRESSIEST
DEEIMMOSS	SEMIDOMES	DEEIRSSSV	DISSEVERS
DEEIMNNOT	MENTIONED	DEEIRSTTV	TEST DRIVE
DEEIMNNRU	UNDERMINE		TEST-DRIVE
DEEIMNNRV	NEVER MIND	DEEIRSTUV	SERVITUDE
DEEIMNORS	DOMINEERS	DEEIRTTTW	TWITTERED
	MODERNISE	DEEIRTTXY	DEXTERITY
DEEIMNORZ	MODERNIZE	DEEISTTTU	DESTITUTE
DEEIMNOSS	DEMONISES	DEEISTTUW	TWEED SUIT
DEEIMNOSZ	DEMONIZES	DEEJOORVY	OVERJOYED
DEEIMNPST	PEDIMENTS	DEEKLNNOW	KNEEL DOWN
	SPEND TIME	DEEKMOOPS	SMOKE DOPE
DEEIMNRTT	DETRIMENT	DEEKNOORS	SNOOKERED
DEEIMNRTU	UNMERITED	DEEKNOPSW	KEEPS DOWN
DEEIMOORT	METEOROID	DEEKNORTW	NETWORKED
DEEIMORST	DIME STORE	DEEKNPRTU	KEPT UNDER
	DOSIMETER	DEEKOPRRT	KEPT ORDER
DEEIMORSX	EXODERMIS	DEELLMMOP	POMMELLED
DEEIMPRSS	IMPRESSED	DEELLMMPU	PUMMELLED
DEEIMPRST	DISTEMPER	DEELLMRTU	RED MULLET
DEEIMPRTT	PERMITTED	DEELLNNTU	TUNNELLED
DEEIMRTUU	DEUTERIUM	DEELLNORS	RONDELLES
DEEINNOOS	ON ONE SIDE	DEELLNOTW	NOTED WELL
DEEINNOPS	PENSIONED	DEELLNRSU	UNDERSELL
DEEINNORT	INTERNODE	DEELLNRSY	SLENDERLY
DEEINNORV	ENVIRONED	DEELLNSSY	ENDLESSLY
DEEINNOST	TENSIONED	DEELLOOPP	OLD PEOPLE
DEEINNOTT	DETENTION	DEELLOPPR	PROPELLED
DEEINNRST	DINNER SET	DEELLORSY	YODELLERS
DEEINNRTU	INDENTURE	DEELLORTW	TROWELLED
DEEINNSSS	SNIDENESS	DEELLPSUW	SWELLED UP
DEEINOOST	TO ONE SIDE	DEELLRSSW	DRESS WELL
DEEINOPRT	TERPENOID	DEELMMPTU	PLUMMETED
DEEINOPSW	OPENS WIDE	DEELMNNOY	LEND MONEY
DEEINOPTX	PENTOXIDE	DEELMNOOS	MELODEONS
DEEINORST	DESERTION	DEELMNOSW	NEW MODELS
DEEINPPST	STEPPED IN	DEELNNPST	SPLENDENT
DEEINPRSS	DISPENSER	DEELNOOSS	LOOSE ENDS
DEEINPRST	PRESIDENT	DEELNOOST	LODESTONE
DEEINPSSS	DISPENSES	DEELNOOSV	LOVED ONES
DEEINPSST	TEPIDNESS	DEELNOSST	ELDEST SON
DEEINQSUV	SEVEN QUID	DEELNOSTT	SETTLED ON
DEEINRRSU	REINSURED	DEELNPRRU	PLUNDERER
DEEINRSST	DISSENTER	DEELNSTTU	UNSETTLED
	RESIDENTS	DEELNSWWY	NEWLYWEDS
	TIREDNESS	DEELOORSV	DOVER SOLE
DEEINRSSW	WEIRDNESS	DEELOPRSY	REDEPLOYS
DEEINRSTT	TRENDIEST	DEELOPSST	SEED PLOTS
DEEINSSTW	WITNESSED	DEELOPSSW	LOW SPEEDS
DEEIOPRSX	PEROXIDES	DEELORRSS	SOLDERERS
DEEIOPRVW	POWER DIVE	DEELORRUV	OVERRULED
	POWER-DIVE	DEELORSTT	DOTTERELS
DEEIORRRV	OVER-RIDER		OLD STREET
DEEIORRST	ROISTERED	DEELORTUV	REVOLUTED
DEEIORRSV	OVERRIDES	DEELPRRUY	RUDE REPLY
	RIDES OVER	DEELPRSTU	DRUPELETS
DEEIORRVV	OVERDRIVE	DEELPRTUY	REPUTEDLY
DEEIORSTU	SURE TO DIE	DEELPSTTU	SETTLED UP
DEEIORSTV	TIDES OVER	DEELPSTUX	SEXTUPLED
DEEIOSSTV	VIDEO SETS	DEELRSSTU	DELUSTRES
DEEIPPRRS	PERSPIRED	DEEMNNOTW	ENDOWMENT
DEEIPPSTU	SPEED IT UP	DEEMNOOWY	OWED MONEY
DEEIPRRSS	DISPERSER	DEEMNOPRS	ENDOSPERM
DEEIPRSSS	DESPISERS	DEEMNOPSU	SPODUMENE
	DISPERSES	DEEMNORTT	TORMENTED
DEEIPRSST	PERSISTED	DEEMNORTU	REMOUNTED

DEEMNORWY	DREW MONEY	DEFFGIOOR	GOD OF FIRE
DEEMNSSTU	NEEDS MUST	DEFFGOOOR	GOOD OFFER
DEEMOORST	ODOMETERS	DEFFHIIRS	FRIED FISH
DEEMOORVV	MOVED OVER	DEFFHIOPP	HOPPED OFF
DEEMORRSW	MERE WORDS	DEFFHOORS	FRESH FOOD
DEEMPRTTU	TRUMPETED	DEFFHOOSV	SHOVED OFF
DEEMRRRSU	DEMURRERS	DEFFHOOSW	SHOWED OFF
	MURDERERS	DEFFHOPSU	PUSHED OFF
DEEMRRSSU	MURDERESS	DEFFIIORT	FORTIFIED
DEENNOPST	DEPONENTS	DEFFIISUV	DIFFUSIVE
DEENNORSU	SEEN ROUND	DEFFIKLLO	KILLED OFF
DEENNORTU	UNDERTONE	DEFFILLLU	FULFILLED
DEENNOSST	NOTEDNESS	DEFFILNOU	FOUL FIEND
DEENNPRSY	PENNY REDS	DEFFILSUY	DIFFUSELY
DEENNRTUW	UNDERWENT	DEFFINORV	DRIVEN OFF
	WENT UNDER	DEFFINSTU	SNUFFED IT
DEENOOPRR	OPEN ORDER	DEFFIOPPR	RIPPED OFF
DEENOOPRS	ENDOSPORE	DEFFIOPPT	TIPPED OFF
DEENOOPTU	OPENED OUT	DEFFIOPSS	PISSED OFF
DEENOORSW	DONE WORSE	DEFFIORSV	DRIVES OFF
DEENOPRRS	RESPONDER		OFF DRIVES
DEENOPRRV	PROVENDER	DEFFIRSSU	DIFFUSERS
DEENOPRSS	PRESSED ON	DEFFKOORW	WORKED OFF
DEENOPRSV	OVERSPEND	DEFFLLOPU	PULLED OFF
DEENOPRUX	EXPOUNDER	DEFFLMPUU	MUFFLED UP
DEENOPSWW	SWEEP DOWN	DEFFLNRUU	UNRUFFLED
DEENORRSW	WONDERERS	DEFFLOOPS	SLOPED OFF
DEENORRUV	VEER ROUND	DEFFNORTU	TURNED OFF
DEENORSSU	SEES ROUND	DEFFOOPPP	POPPED OFF
DEENORSTU	RUN TO SEED	DEFFOORRS	ORDERS OFF
DEENORTTU	RENTED OUT	DEFFOOSST	TOSSED OFF
DEENORTUY	TOURNEYED	DEFGGGINO	DEFOGGING
DEENPRSSU	SUSPENDER	DEFGGIINT	FIDGETING
DEENRRRSU	SURRENDER	DEFGGILLN	FLEDGLING
DEENRSSSU	UNDRESSES	DEFGGIOOR	GOOD GRIEF
DEENRSTTU	ENTRUSTED	DEFGHILOT	EIGHTFOLD
DEENRSTUW	WET NURSED	DEFGIIILN	LIGNIFIED
	WET-NURSED	DEFGIIINS	DIGNIFIES
DEENRSTYY	DYSENTERY		SIGNIFIED
DEEOOPRRV	PORED OVER	DEFGIILOR	GLORIFIED
DEEOOPRST	TORPEDOES	DEFGIINNO	DOING FINE
DEEOORSSV	OVERDOSES	DEFGIINNR	INFRINGED
DEEOORSSW	DOES WORSE	DEFGIINRX	FIXED GRIN
DEEOPPRRS	PROSPERED	DEFGIIRSU	DISFIGURE
DEEOPPRSS	OPPRESSED	DEFGILNNO	ENFOLDING
DEEOPPRST	STOPPERED	DEFGILOOS	OLD FOGIES
DEEOPRRSS	DEPRESSOR	DEFGIMNOR	DEFORMING
DEEOPRSTT	PROTESTED	DEFGINNRU	REFUNDING
DEEOPSSSS	POSSESSED	DEFGINOOW	GOD OF WINE
DEEORRRSV	VERDERORS	DEFGINOTW	GET WIND OF
DEEORRSSV	OVERDRESS	DEFGIORST	GETS RID OF
DEEORRSTX	DEXTRORSE	DEFGLOOOV	GOD OF LOVE
DEEORRSTY	DESTROYER		LOVE OF GOD
DEEORRSUV	DEVOURERS	DEFGLOOSY	OLD FOGEYS
DEEORRVWY	EVERY WORD	DEFGOOPRR	DROP-FORGE
DEEORSSTX	DEXTROSES		GROPED FOR
DEEORSTTV	TEST-DROVE	DEFHHLORT	HELD FORTH
DEEORSTUV	SERVED OUT	DEFHIILSV	DEVIL FISH
DEEORSTUX	DEXTEROUS		DEVILFISH
DEEOSTTUV	DEVOUTEST	DEFHIIORR	HORRIFIED
DEEPPPSTU	STEPPED UP	DEFHILNOT	IN THE FOLD
DEEPPRSSU	PRESSED UP	DEFHIMNOS	FIND HOMES
DEEPRRSSU	PRESSURED	DEFHINRSU	FURNISHED
DEEPRSSSU	DRESSES UP	DEFHINRSW	FRESH WIND
DEEPRSTTU	SPUTTERED	DEFHIOSTU	FISHED OUT
DEERSTTTU	STUTTERED	DEFHLOOOW	WHOLEFOOD
DEFFFGOOO	GOOFED OFF	DEFHNOOPS	FOND HOPES
DEFFFILOT	LIFTED OFF	DEFHNORRY	HENRY FORD
DEFFGIINR	DIFFERING	DEFHNORST	SEND FORTH
DEFFGINNO	OFFENDING	DEFHOOOTT	HOTFOOTED
DEFFGINOS	SIGNED OFF	DEFHOPRSU	PUSHED FOR

377

DEFHORRTW	DREW FORTH	DEGGIILRU	GIRL GUIDE
DEFIIINRT	NITRIFIED	DEGGIINNS	DESIGNING
DEFIIIRTV	VITRIFIED	DEGGIINRV	DIVERGING
DEFIIJSTU	JUSTIFIED	DEGGIINST	DIGESTING
DEFIILLMO	MOLLIFIED	DEGGILNPU	PLUGGED IN
DEFIILLNU	NULLIFIED	DEGGILOOS	LIES DOGGO
DEFIILLRR	FIRE DRILL	DEGGILQSU	SQUIGGLED
DEFIILMSS	MISFIELDS	DEGGINRRY	DRY GINGER
DEFIILMSU	SEMIFLUID	DEGGIORSS	DISGORGES
DEFIILRSU	FLUIDISER	DEGGIORTU	RIGGED OUT
DEFIILRUZ	FLUIDIZER	DEGGLNPUU	UNPLUGGED
DEFIILSSU	FLUIDISES	DEGGOOSSU	GOOD GUESS
DEFIILSUZ	FLUIDIZES	DEGHHIIRS	RIDES HIGH
DEFIIMMMU	MUMMIFIED	DEGHHIIST	HIGH TIDES
DEFIIMNNY	INDEMNIFY	DEGHHIISV	HIGH DIVES
DEFIIMNST	FINDS TIME	DEGHHILST	SHED LIGHT
DEFIIMORS	MODIFIERS	DEGHHILTT	HELD TIGHT
DEFIIMORT	MORTIFIED	DEGHHINOT	HIGH-TONED
DEFIIMRWY	MIDWIFERY	DEGHHIRTU	HIRED THUG
DEFIIMSTY	MYSTIFIED	DEGHIILNS	SHIELDING
DEFIINRTY	DENITRIFY	DEGHIILST	LIGHT SIDE
DEFIINSST	DISINFEST		SIDELIGHT
DEFIINSVW	FIND WIVES	DEGHIILTT	LIGHT DIET
DEFIIRSVY	DIVERSIFY	DEGHIINNR	HINDERING
DEFIKLORW	FIELD WORK	DEGHIINRT	DITHERING
	FIELDWORK	DEGHIIQTU	EIGHT QUID
DEFILLOSU	SOLID FUEL	DEGHIIRST	RIGHT SIDE
DEFILLOTU	FILLED OUT	DEGHIJPSU	JUDGESHIP
DEFILNOSW	FILES DOWN	DEGHIKLOU	DOUGHLIKE
DEFILNSSU	FLUIDNESS	DEGHILOTW	WHITE GOLD
DEFILORSU	FLUORIDES	DEGHILRST	RED LIGHTS
DEFILSTUY	LIFE STUDY	DEGHIMNRU	HUMDINGER
DEFIMNNOO	OF ONE MIND	DEGHINNOT	DONE THING
DEFIMNORU	UNIFORMED	DEGHINORT	DONE RIGHT
DEFIMNOTU	FOUND TIME	DEGHINOST	IN THE GODS
DEFIMOORX	FOOD MIXER	DEGHINOWW	WEIGH DOWN
DEFIMORTY	DEFORMITY	DEGHINRSU	HIRED GUNS
DEFIMSTYY	DEMYSTIFY	DEGHINSTU	UNSIGHTED
DEFINOPRU	FIRED UPON	DEGHIORRU	RIDE ROUGH
DEFINORSU	FOUNDRIES		ROUGH RIDE
DEFINORSW	FINE WORDS	DEGHIORST	DOES RIGHT
DEFINORUV	ROUND FIVE	DEGHIORTU	DOUGHTIER
DEFIOORSW	WOOD FIRES		ROUGHED IT
DEFIORSSU	FOUR SIDES	DEGHIRTTW	DREW TIGHT
DEFIORTTU	FORTITUDE	DEGHLOPSU	GOD HELP US
DEFIOTTTU	FITTED OUT	DEGHMOORT	GODMOTHER
	OUTFITTED	DEGHNNRUU	UNDERHUNG
DEFKLNOOW	KNEW OF OLD	DEGHNORUY	GREYHOUND
DEFKLNRTU	FELT DRUNK	DEGHOOOPT	HOPE TO GOD
DEFKLOOOR	LOOKED FOR	DEGHOOOSU	GOOD HOUSE
DEFKOORRW	WORKED FOR	DEGHOOOTT	TO THE GOOD
DEFKOORTU	FORKED OUT	DEGHOORRU	RODE ROUGH
DEFLLLOOW	OLD FELLOW	DEGHOOSSU	HOUSE DOGS
DEFLLLOUY	DOLEFULLY	DEGHOPRUU	ROUGHED UP
DEFLLNOUW	WELL-FOUND	DEGIIIMRS	DIRIGISME
DEFLLOORS	FOLDEROLS		SEMIRIGID
DEFLLRSSU	FULL DRESS	DEGIIINPS	PIDGINISE
	FULL-DRESS	DEGIIINPZ	PIDGINIZE
DEFLMMOUX	FLUMMOXED	DEGIIINST	DIGNITIES
DEFLNORSU	FLOUNDERS	DEGIIIRST	DIGITISER
DEFLNORUW	WONDERFUL		DIRIGISTE
DEFLOORSV	FOLDS OVER	DEGIIIRTZ	DIGITIZER
	OVERFOLDS	DEGIIISST	DIGITISES
DEFMOORRR	ORDER FORM	DEGIIISTZ	DIGITIZES
DEFNOORTU	UNDERFOOT	DEGIILLNV	DEVILLING
DEFNOORUZ	FOUR DOZEN	DEGIILMNW	MILDEWING
DEFNORRSU	FRONDEURS	DEGIIMNNP	IMPENDING
DEFOOORST	FOOD STORE	DEGIIMNNR	REMINDING
DEFOORRSW	FOREWORDS	DEGIIMNOT	DOING TIME
DEFORTTUU	TURFED OUT	DEGIIMNST	DEMISTING
DEGGHILNY	HEDGINGLY	DEGIIMNTT	DEMITTING

DEGIIMSSU	MISGUIDES	DEGINORSV	RING DOVES
DEGIINNNT	INDENTING		RINGDOVES
	INTENDING	DEGINORSW	WRONG SIDE
DEGIINNSS	DINGINESS	DEGINORTU	DETOURING
DEGIINNST	DESTINING	DEGINORUV	DEVOURING
DEGIINOSS	GNEISSOID	DEGINOSUY	DIES YOUNG
DEGIINOST	DIGESTION	DEGINOTTW	GET IT DOWN
DEGIINPRS	PRESIDING	DEGINOTWW	TWO-WINGED
DEGIINPRV	DEPRIVING	DEGINPSSU	PUDGINESS
DEGIINPSS	DESPISING	DEGINRSSS	DRESSINGS
DEGIINRSS	RIGIDNESS	DEGINRTUX	EXTRUDING
DEGIINRTU	INTRIGUED	DEGIOOQTU	QUITE GOOD
	NIGRITUDE	DEGIOORST	GOOD TRIES
DEGIINRTV	DIVERTING	DEGIOOSTU	GO OUTSIDE
DEGIINSST	DESISTING	DEGIOPRTY	PTERYGOID
DEGIINSTU	DISTINGUE	DEGIOPSTU	GUIDEPOST
DEGIINSTV	DIVESTING	DEGIORRTW	GROW TIRED
DEGIIOPRS	PRODIGIES	DEGIOSSTT	STODGIEST
DEGIIRRSV	VERDIGRIS	DEGIPSSUU	GUSSIED UP
DEGIISSSU	DISGUISES	DEGIRSTTY	GETS DIRTY
DEGIJMSSU	MISJUDGES	DEGJKOOOS	GOOD JOKES
DEGIKLLOT	GOT KILLED	DEGJMNSTU	JUDGMENTS
DEGIKLOGV	KID GLOVES	DEGJOOPRU	POOR JUDGE
DEGIKMOOS	ESKIMO DOG	DEGKNRSTU	GETS DRUNK
DEGILLMNO	MODELLING	DEGLLOOWY	YELLOW DOG
DEGILLMOR	MODEL GIRL	DEGLMOOVY	LOVE MY DOG
DEGILLNOV	LONG-LIVED	DEGLNNOOZ	LONG DOZEN
DEGILLNOW	DOING WELL	DEGLNOOPR	PROLONGED
	DOWELLING	DEGLNORSS	LONG DRESS
DEGILLNOY	YODELLING	DEGLNORSU	GROUNDSEL
DEGILLNSW	DWELLINGS	DEGLOOORS	GOOD LOSER
DEGILLOTT	LITTLE DOG	DEGLOORRW	GROW OLDER
DEGILMNOR	GOLD MINER	DEGLOORSV	DOG LOVERS
DEGILMNOS	GOLD MINES	DEGLOOSUU	DUOLOGUES
DEGILMNPU	DEPLUMING	DEGMNOOOS	GOOD OMENS
DEGILMNSU	GUILDSMEN	DEGMNOOOY	GOOD MONEY
DEGILNNPU	PLUNGED IN	DEGMOOOSV	GOOD MOVES
DEGILNNRU	UNDERLING	DEGNNOORU	GONE ROUND
DEGILNNSW	LEND WINGS	DEGNNOORW	DONE WRONG
DEGILNNTU	INDULGENT	DEGNNORUW	NEW GROUND
DEGILNOOR	GONDOLIER	DEGNOORRW	WRONGDOER
DEGILNOPR	DEPLORING	DEGNOORSU	GOES ROUND
DEGILNOPX	EXPLODING	DEGNOORSW	DOES WRONG
DEGILNOPY	DEPLOYING	DEGNOPRUW	GUNPOWDER
DEGILNORS	SOLDERING	DEGNORSTU	GETS ROUND
DEGILNORV	LONG DRIVE	DEGOOPRRU	PROROGUED
DEGILNOSS	GODLINESS	DEGOOPSTY	GOOD TYPES
DEGILNOSU	DELOUSING	DEGORRSTU	DRUGSTORE
DEGILNOTU	LONGITUDE	DEHHIKMOS	SHEIKHDOM
DEGILNOVV	DEVOLVING	DEHHILORT	THIRD HOLE
DEGILNPRU	PRELUDING	DEHHINOSY	HOYDENISH
DEGILOORV	GOOD LIVER	DEHHIOPPS	PHOSPHIDE
DEGILOOSW	WILD GOOSE	DEHHIOSST	HOT DISHES
	WILD-GOOSE	DEHHLLNOU	HELLHOUND
DEGILOSTT	GLOTTIDES	DEHHLOOSU	HOUSEHOLD
DEGILSSUW	WILD GUESS	DEHHLORST	THRESHOLD
DEGIMNRRU	DEMURRING	DEHHNOORU	HOREHOUND
	MURDERING	DEHIIINST	HISTIDINE
DEGIMOORX	GOOD MIXER	DEHIIMNNT	IN THE MIND
DEGIMOOST	GOOD TIMES	DEHIIMNTY	THYMIDINE
DEGINNOPR	PONDERING	DEHIIMOPP	HIPPIEDOM
DEGINNORS	ENDORSING	DEHIIMRTT	THIRD TIME
DEGINNORW	WONDERING	DEHIINNTW	IN THE WIND
DEGINNPSU	SENDING UP	DEHIIPRST	PETRI DISH
DEGINNRSU	SUNDERING	DEHIIPRTW	WITH PRIDE
DEGINNRUW	UNDERWING	DEHIISSTW	SIDES WITH
DEGINOORV	DOING OVER	DEHIISTWW	WIDTHWISE
DEGINOOSW	GOOD WINES	DEHIJMNOS	DEMIJOHNS
DEGINOPRT	DEPORTING	DEHIKORSS	DROSHKIES
DEGINOPRW	POWDERING	DEHILLLST	HELD STILL
DEGINORRW	REWORDING	DEHILNOWY	WILD HONEY

DEHILOORT	RHODOLITE	DEIIIKNTT	IDENTIKIT
DEHILORRT	LORD REITH	DEIIILQSU	LIQUIDISE
DEHILORSW	WILD HORSE	DEIIILQUZ	LIQUIDIZE
DEHILOSTW	DISH TOWEL	DEIIIMMNS	MINIMISED
DEHILOSUY	HIDEOUSLY	DEIIIMMNZ	MINIMIZED
DEHILOSVW	HOLD VIEWS	DEIIINSSS	DISSEISIN
DEHILRRUY	HURRIEDLY	DEIIKKLNR	KILDERKIN
DEHIMMOST	METHODISM	DEIIKLLOS	OILED SILK
DEHIMNOOT	IN THE MOOD	DEIIKNNRW	DRINK WINE
DEHIMORRT	THERMIDOR	DEIIKNRSV	SKIN DIVER
DEHIMOSTT	METHODIST	DEIIKRSST	KID SISTER
DEHIMPRTU	TRIUMPHED	DEIILLMNU	ILLUMINED
DEHIMRRTT	THIRD TERM	DEIILLMTY	LIMITEDLY
DEHINNORT	HOT DINNER	DEIILLNST	INSTILLED
DEHINOORT	RHODONITE	DEIILLOPR	PILLORIED
DEHINOPSS	SPHENOIDS	DEIILLOPS	ELLIPSOID
DEHINORST	NORTH SIDE	DEIILLRST	DISTILLER
DEHINORSU	NOURISHED	DEIILMNTU	UNLIMITED
DEHINORVW	WINDHOVER	DEIILMOSS	SEMISOLID
DEHINOSST	DISHONEST	DEIILNOPT	PILED IT ON
	HEDONISTS	DEIILNPRS	SPINDLIER
DEHINOSTU	OUTSHINED	DEIILNSSV	LIVIDNESS
DEHINPPSU	UNSHIPPED	DEIILNTTU	INTITULED
DEHINRRUU	UNHURRIED	DEIILORSU	DELIRIOUS
DEHIOOTWW	WHITEWOOD	DEIILPSSS	SIDESLIPS
DEHIOPPST	DEPOT SHIP	DEIILPTUV	LIVED IT UP
DEHIOPRSS	SPHEROIDS	DEIIMNNOS	DIMENSION
DEHIORTUY	EUTHYROID	DEIIMNNTY	INDEMNITY
DEHIOSSSW	SIDE SHOWS	DEIIMNOSS	DEMISSION
	SIDESHOWS	DEIIMNPRT	IMPRINTED
DEHIOSSTT	DOTS THE I'S	DEIIMNRTW	MIDWINTER
DEHIOSSTU	DISHES OUT	DEIIMNSST	TIMIDNESS
	SOUTH SIDE	DEIIMPRSU	PRESIDIUM
DEHIPRRUU	HURRIED UP	DEIIMSSSS	DISMISSES
DEHIRSTTT	THIRD TEST	DEIINNNOT	INDENTION
DEHJNNNOO	JOHN DONNE	DEIINNORT	RENDITION
DEHKLNOSU	ELK HOUNDS	DEIINNOSU	UNIONISED
	ELKHOUNDS	DEIINNOTT	DENTITION
DEHKLOOST	STOKEHOLD	DEIINNOUZ	UNIONIZED
DEHLLOOOP	LOOPHOLED	DEIINNSSW	WINDINESS
DEHLLOPSY	PHYLLODES	DEIINNTUV	UNINVITED
DEHLMNOPY	ENDOLYMPH	DEIINOORX	IRON OXIDE
DEHLNOORU	ROUND HOLE	DEIINOPRT	PERDITION
DEHLNOPSW	HELPS DOWN	DEIINOPSS	INDISPOSE
DEHLOORSV	HOLDS OVER	DEIINORST	DISORIENT
DEHLOOSST	TOOLSHEDS	DEIINORSV	DIVERSION
DEHLOPRSU	UPHOLDERS	DEIINORTT	DETRITION
DEHLORSSU	SHOULDERS		TRIED IT ON
DEHLORSTU	HOLDS TRUE	DEIINORTU	ERUDITION
DEHLORSYY	HYDROLYSE	DEIINOSTU	INSIDE OUT
DEHLORYYZ	HYDROLYZE	DEIINPPSW	WINDPIPES
DEHLOSSTU	SHOULDEST	DEIINPRRS	SPIN DRIER
DEHLPRSUU	SULPHURED		SPIN-DRIER
DEHMNOOPR	ENDOMORPH	DEIINPRSS	SPIN-DRIES
DEHNNOOPS	SPHENODON	DEIINPSTU	IN DISPUTE
DEHNOORWY	HENRY WOOD	DEIINRSST	DIRTINESS
DEHNOOSSW	HOSES DOWN		DISINTERS
DEHNOOTTW	DO THE TOWN	DEIINSSTU	DISUNITES
DEHNORSSU	ENSHROUDS	DEIINSSVV	VIVIDNESS
DEHNORSTU	UNDERSHOT	DEIINSSZZ	DIZZINESS
DEHNORTWW	THREW DOWN	DEIINSTTU	UNTIDIEST
DEHNORWWY	WONDER WHY	DEIINTTTW	NIT-WITTED
DEHOORSTU	OUT-HERODS	DEIIORTTU	RIDE IT OUT
DEHOOSSSU	DOSS HOUSE	DEIIOSSTU	SEDITIOUS
	DOSSHOUSE	DEIIOSSTU	DISQUIETS
DEHOOSTUW	SHOWED OUT	DEIIRSTVY	DIVERSITY
DEHOPRSST	POTSHERDS	DEIJKORTY	DIRTY JOKE
DEHOPSTUU	PUSHED OUT	DEIJLNNNY	JENNY LIND
DEHORSSTU	STUD HORSE	DEIJLNOTY	JOINTEDLY
	STUDHORSE	DEIKLLNSU	UNSKILLED
DEHRRRSYY	DRY SHERRY	DEIKLOORT	LOOK TIRED

DEIKLORSW	SWORDLIKE	DEIMOOSST	SODOMITES
DEIKMNNOW	WOMENKIND	DEIMOPSST	DESPOTISM
DEIKNNRUW	DRUNK WINE	DEIMOQSTU	MISQUOTED
DEIKNNSTU	UNKINDEST	DEIMORSTY	DOSIMETRY
DEIKNSSSU	DUSKINESS	DEIMORSUX	EXORDIUMS
DEIKOOPRT	TOOK PRIDE	DEIMOSSTU	MISSED OUT
DEIKOOSST	TOOK SIDES	DEINNNOOW	DOWN IN ONE
DEILLNOOT	TOLD NO LIE	DEINNNORU	ROUND NINE
DEILLORRW	WORLDLIER	DEINNNOSU	INNUENDOS
DEILLORSY	SOLDIERLY	DEINNOORW	IN ONE WORD
DEILLSTTY	STILTEDLY	DEINNOSTU	TENDINOUS
	SYD LITTLE	DEINNPRSU	UNDERPINS
DEILMOOST	DOLOMITES		UNDERSPIN
DEILMOOSU	MELODIOUS	DEINNSSUY	SUNNY SIDE
DEILMORST	OLD TIMERS	DEINOOPRT	PORTIONED
	OLD-TIMERS	DEINOOPST	NO DEPOSIT
DEILMOSST	MELODISTS		ON DEPOSIT
DEILMOSTU	MOULDIEST	DEINOORTU	IRONED OUT
DEILMTTUU	MULTITUDE	DEINOOSST	DOT ONE'S I'S
DEILNOORS	SOLDIER ON	DEINOOSSW	WOODINESS
DEILNOOSS	SOLENOIDS	DEINOOSTV	DEVOTIONS
DEILNOOSU	LOUD NOISE	DEINOPPSW	DOWNPIPES
DEILNOPPS	SLIPPED ON		PIPES DOWN
DEILNOPRU	PURLOINED	DEINOPRST	DRIPSTONE
DEILNOPSU	UNSPOILED	DEINOPRTV	PROVIDENT
DEILNOPTY	POINTEDLY	DEINOPRWW	WIND POWER
DEILNOSSS	SOLIDNESS	DEINORRVW	DOWN RIVER
DEILNOSSU	DELUSIONS	DEINORSSW	ROWDINESS
DEILNOSVW	DEVILS OWN		WORDINESS
	LIVES DOWN	DEINORSTU	RINSED OUT
DEILNOTUV	INVOLUTED	DEINORSVW	OVERWINDS
DEILNPRSS	SPINDLERS	DEINORTUV	DRIVEN OUT
DEILNRSSU	LURIDNESS	DEINORTWW	WRITE DOWN
DEILNRSSW	SWINDLERS		WRITE-DOWN
DEILOOPRU	POURED OIL	DEINOSSTT	DOTTINESS
DEILOOPRV	POOR DEVIL	DEINPSTWW	WINDSWEPT
DEILOOPRY	POOR YIELD	DEINRRSTU	INTRUDERS
DEILOOPSS	PODSOLISE	DEINRSTTU	INTRUSTED
DEILOOPSW	WOODPILES		TRUSTED IN
DEILOOPSZ	PODZOLISE	DEINRSTTY	DENTISTRY
DEILOOPZZ	PODZOLIZE	DEINSSSTU	DUSTINESS
DEILOPTUV	LIVED UP TO	DEIOOPRSS	POOR SIDES
DEILORRWY	WORRIEDLY	DEIOOPRST	DEPOSITOR
DEILORSSV	DISSOLVER	DEIOORTTU	RODE IT OUT
DEILORSSW	WILD ROSES	DEIOPPSTT	STOPPED IT
DEILORSTY	IDLE STORY	DEIOPRRSV	PROVIDERS
	SOLID TYRE	DEIOPRSSV	DISPROVES
DEILOSSSV	DISSOLVES	DEIOPRSTU	DIPTEROUS
DEILOSSTU	DISSOLUTE	DEIOQRTUW	QUIET WORD
DEILOSTUY	TEDIOUSLY	DEIORRSTU	OUTRIDERS
DEILOSUVY	DEVIOUSLY	DEIORSSTU	OUTSIDERS
DEILPPPSU	SLIPPED UP	DEIORSTTU	STRIDE OUT
DEIMMMORY	DIM MEMORY	DEIORSTUV	DRIVES OUT
DEIMMMRSU	MIDSUMMER	DEIOTTTUW	OUTWITTED
DEIMMNORS	MODERNISM	DEIPPPRTU	TRIPPED UP
DEIMMNOUY	NEODYMIUM	DEIPRRSSU	SURPRISED
DEIMMOSTY	IMMODESTY	DEIPRRSTU	STIRRED UP
DEIMNNOPS	OPEN MINDS	DEIPRTTUU	TURPITUDE
DEIMNOORT	MONITORED	DEIRSSSTU	DRESS SUIT
DEIMNOOSS	MOODINESS	DEIRSSTTU	STURDIEST
DEIMNOOST	DEMOTIONS	DEJKMNORU	JUNKERDOM
DEIMNOPSU	OPIUM DENS	DEJMOPTUU	JUMPED OUT
DEIMNORST	MODERNIST	DEJNOORSU	SOJOURNED
DEIMNORTY	MODERNITY	DEKLNNOTW	KNELT DOWN
DEIMNPRTU	IMPRUDENT	DEKLNNRUY	DRUNKENLY
DEIMNPSSS	MISSPENDS	DEKLOOOTU	LOOKED OUT
DEIMNPSSU	DUMPINESS	DEKMOOSTU	SMOKED OUT
DEIMNRSTU	RUDIMENTS	DEKNOORTU	UNDERTOOK
DEIMNSTUX	MIXED NUTS	DEKOORTUW	WORKED OUT
DEIMOORST	MOTORISED	DEKOPRSTU	STUD POKER
DEIMOORTZ	MOTORIZED	DELLNOPUW	DWELL UPON

DELLNORSS	DROLLNESS	DEOOORTTU	ROOTED OUT
DELLOORTU	ROLLED OUT	DEOOPPPTU	POPPED OUT
DELLOPTUU	PULLED OUT	DEOOPPRST	PTEROPODS
DELLOSSTY	OLD STYLES	DEOOPRRSV	DROPS OVER
DELMNOSTW	MELTS DOWN	DEOOPRSST	DOORSTEPS
DELMNPSUU	PENDULUMS	DEOOPRTUU	POURED OUT
DELMOOORX	LOXODROME	DEOORRSTU	ORDERS OUT
DELMORSSU	SMOULDERS		TUDOR ROSE
DELMPRSTU	LED TRUMPS	DEOORSTTU	SORTED OUT
DELNNNOOW	NEW LONDON		STRODE OUT
DELNNOOOT	TOLD NO ONE	DEOORTTVY	VOTED TORY
DELNNOORS	LONDONERS	DEOPPPPRU	PROPPED UP
DELNOOPSW	SLOPE DOWN	DEOPPPSTU	STOPPED UP
DELNOORWW	LOWER DOWN	DEOPPRRTU	PURPORTED
DELNOOSST	OLDEST SON	DEOPPRSTU	SUPPORTED
DELNOPRSU	SPLENDOUR	DEOPRRSTU	PROTRUDES
DELNOPRTU	UNDERPLOT	DEORRSTUW	TRUE WORDS
DELNOPSUU	PENDULOUS	DEOSSSTUU	SUSSED OUT
DELNOPTUW	DWELT UPON	DEPRSSSTU	PRESS-STUD
DELNORTWX	NEXT WORLD	DEPRSSTUU	TRUSSED UP
DELNOSSSU	SOUNDLESS	DFFFILOTY	FIFTYFOLD
DELNPRTUY	PRUDENTLY	DFFFOOSTU	FOODSTUFF
DELOOOPTY	TOY POODLE	DFFGIINOR	RIDING OFF
DELOOOSUW	WOODLOUSE	DFFGIINSU	DIFFUSING
DELOORRSV	OVERLORDS	DFFGOOSTU	GOOD STUFF
DELOORSSU	ODOURLESS	DFFGOOTUY	GO OFF DUTY
DELOPRSYY	PYROLYSED	DFFIINOSU	DIFFUSION
DELORSTUY	DESULTORY	DFFIINSTW	STIFF WIND
DEMMNOSSU	SUMMONSED	DFFIIQTUY	FIFTY QUID
DEMMRRSUY	DRY SUMMER	DFFIKSSTU	KIDS STUFF
DEMNNOOWY	MONEY DOWN	DFFINOTUW	FUND OF WIT
DEMNNORSU	ROUNDSMEN	DFFLLLOOU	FULL FLOOD
DEMNOORUV	MOVE ROUND	DFFLOORTY	FORTYFOLD
DEMNOPSUY	PSEUDONYM	DFFNOORSU	ROUNDS OFF
DEMNOPTUU	MOUNTED UP	DFFNOOSSU	SOUNDS OFF
DEMNORRTU	TENOR DRUM	DFGGHIOOT	GOOD FIGHT
DEMNORSSW	SWORDSMEN	DFGGHIOST	DOG FIGHTS
DEMNORSSY	SYNDROMES		DOGFIGHTS
DEMOPPTUU	PUMPED OUT	DFGGOOOOR	GO FOR GOOD
DEMORRSUU	MURDEROUS	DFGIIIRTY	FRIGIDITY
DENNOOOST	ON ONE'S TOD	DFGIILNNO	INFOLDING
DENNOOPRS	PONDERS ON	DFGIIMNOY	MODIFYING
DENNOOPTU	POUND NOTE	DFGILLOOW	WILL OF GOD
DENNOOPUW	OPEN WOUND	DFGILMOOS	GOOD FILMS
DENNOOSTU	DO ONE'S NUT	DFGILNNOU	FOUNDLING
DENNOOSTW	NOTES DOWN		UNFOLDING
	TONES DOWN	DFGILNNOW	FLING DOWN
DENNOPSTU	TEN POUNDS	DFGILNOPU	FOLDING UP
DENNORSSU	ROUNDNESS	DFGILOOST	GOODS LIFT
DENNORSTU	TEN ROUNDS	DFGILOOWW	GOLF WIDOW
DENNORTUW	WENT ROUND	DFGINOOTW	GOT WIND OF
DENNOSSSU	SOUNDNESS	DFGKLOOOS	GOOD FOLKS
DENOOOPRS	OPEN DOORS	DFGLLOOOS	FOOLS GOLD
DENOOPPST	POSTPONED	DFGLNNOOO	LONDON FOG
DENOOPPSU	UNOPPOSED	DFGLNNOUW	FLUNG DOWN
DENOOPRSS	SPONSORED	DFGLNOOOT	TON OF GOLD
DENOOPRSU	PONDEROUS	DFGLOOOOT	LOT OF GOOD
DENOOPTUW	OWNED UP TO	DFGLOOOOW	LOG OF WOOD
DENOORSTU	TOURNEDOS	DFGOOOSST	SOFT GOODS
DENOORTUW	OWEN TUDOR	DFGORSSTU	SOFT DRUGS
DENOORTWW	WROTE DOWN	DFHHLOORT	HOLD FORTH
DENOORUVW	OVERWOUND	DFHIIRSTU	FRUIT DISH
DENOOSTVW	VOTES DOWN	DFHILOORY	HYDROFOIL
DENOPPSTU	UNSTOPPED	DFHIMORRT	THIRD FORM
DENOPRSSW	PRESS DOWN	DFHINOPSS	FISH PONDS
DENOPSSTW	STEPS DOWN	DFHIORSSW	SWORDFISH
DENOPSTTU	UNSPOTTED	DFHLNOOUW	WOLFHOUND
DENOPSTWW	SWEPT DOWN	DFHLNSSUU	SLUSH FUND
DENORTTUU	TURNED OUT	DFHLOOOST	FOOTHOLDS
	UNTUTORED	DFHNOOSUX	FOXHOUNDS
DEOOORSTV	STOOD OVER	DFIILLMOS	FILM IDOLS

DFIILORTY	FLORIDITY	DGHLOOOTT	GOLD TOOTH
DFIINPRST	SPINDRIFT	DGHLOORYY	HYDROLOGY
DFIKNORST	SOFT DRINK	DGHNOSTUU	DOUGHNUTS
DFILLMNUY	MINDFULLY	DGHOOORSU	GOOD HOURS
DFILLTUUY	DUTIFULLY	DGHOOOSTT	DOGSTOOTH
DFILMNNUU	UNMINDFUL	DGHOORSUU	SOURDOUGH
DFILORRST	FIRST LORD	DGHORSTTU	GODS THRUST
DFILOSTXY	SIXTYFOLD	DGHRRTTUU	TRUTH DRUG
DFIMNOORS	FINDS ROOM	DGIIIKLNS	DISLIKING
DFIMNOOTU	OUT OF MIND	DGIIILNOS	IDOLISING
DFIMOORST	STOOD FIRM	DGIIILNOZ	IDOLIZING
DFINOOORR	ROD OF IRON	DGIIINNNW	WINDING IN
DFINORSTW	SNOWDRIFT	DGIIINNRV	DRIVING IN
DFINORSUW	FOUR WINDS	DGIIINNTY	INDIGNITY
DFIOOPRSS	DISPROOFS	DGIIINOSX	OXIDISING
DFIOOPRTT	FIT TO DROP	DGIIINOTX	DIGITOXIN
DFIOORRTW	WORD FOR IT	DGIIINOXZ	OXIDIZING
DFIOQRTUY	FORTY QUID	DGIIJNORY	JOYRIDING
DFIORRSTW	FIRST WORD	DGIIKNSVY	SKYDIVING
DFIRSTTUY	DUTY FIRST	DGIILMNOP	IMPLODING
DFKLNOOOW	KNOW OF OLD	DGIILNNPS	SPINDLING
DFLOOOSTU	FLOODS OUT	DGIILNNSW	SWINDLING
DFLOORRSW	FOR WORLDS	DGIILNNWY	WINDINGLY
DFMNOOORU	FOUND ROOM	DGIILNORT	LORDING IT
DFMOORRSW	WORD FORMS	DGIILNRZZ	DRIZZLING
DFMORSTUY	STUDY FORM	DGIINNNUW	UNWINDING
DFNOOOORT	FRONT DOOR	DGIINNORS	INDORSING
DFNOORRUU	ROUND FOUR	DGIINNORV	DRIVING ON
DFNORSTTU	FRONT STUD	DGIINNOSW	DISOWNING
DFNRSTTUU	TRUST FUND	DGIINNOTU	DINING OUT
DFOORSSTW	SOFT WORDS	DGIINNPUW	WINDING UP
DGGGINOOO	GOOD GOING	DGIINNRTU	INTRUDING
DGGHILOOT	GOOD LIGHT	DGIINOPRV	PROVIDING
DGGHINOOT	GOOD THING	DGIINOPSS	DISPOSING
DGGHIOORT	RIGHT GOOD	DGIINORRS	GRIDIRONS
DGGHIOOST	GOOD SIGHT	DGIINORTU	RIDING OUT
DGGIILNNU	INDULGING	DGIINPRWY	WIPING DRY
DGGIILNOW	GOING WILD	DGIINPSTU	DISPUTING
DGGIILNUV	DIVULGING	DGIINSSTU	IN DISGUST
DGGILNOOT	GOLD INGOT	DGIIRTTUY	TURGIDITY
DGGILNOPS	SPLODGING	DGIJMNOOR	JO GRIMOND
DGGILNORS	GOLD RINGS	DGIKLNNOR	LONG DRINK
DGGILOORS	GOOD GIRLS	DGILLNOPU	DOLLING UP
DGGINNOOW	GOING DOWN	DGILLNORW	WORLDLING
DGGINNORU	GROUNDING	DGILLOOOR	GOOD OR ILL
DGGINOOSS	GOOD SIGNS	DGILLOOSW	GOODWILLS
DGGINOOTY	DYING TO GO	DGILMNOOO	MONGOLOID
DGGIRSSTU	DRUGGISTS	DGILMNOSU	MOULDINGS
DGHHIINST	HINDSIGHT	DGILMNPSU	DUMPLINGS
DGHHIINSW	HIGH WINDS	DGILMNSSU	SLINGS MUD
DGHHILOTT	HOLD TIGHT	DGILNNORY	DRONINGLY
DGHHINOPT	DIPHTHONG	DGILNNOWY	LYING DOWN
DGHHOORSU	ROUGHSHOD	DGILNNRTU	TRUNDLING
DGHIILPSU	GUILDSHIP	DGILNOOTU	DOLING OUT
DGHIIMNRT	RIGHT MIND	DGILNORWW	GROWN WILD
DGHIINPSS	SPHINGIDS	DGIMNRSUY	GRUNDYISM
DGHIINPSU	DISHING UP	DGINNNORY	NONDRYING
DGHIINSWY	DYING WISH	DGINNORRU	RING ROUND
DGHILLNSU	DUNGHILLS	DGINNORSW	RINGS DOWN
DGHILMOST	GOLDSMITH	DGINNOSSU	SOUNDINGS
DGHILNNOO	HOLDING ON	DGINNOTWY	TYING DOWN
DGHILNOPU	HOLDING UP	DGINOOOOV	VOODOOING
DGHILNOST	OLD THINGS	DGINOOOPT	GOOD POINT
DGHILOTUY	DOUGHTILY	DGINOOORS	GO INDOORS
DGHINNOOT	DO NOTHING	DGINOORSW	SWING DOOR
DGHINOOOO	HOODOOING	DGINOOTTW	GOT IT DOWN
DGHINORSU	SHROUDING	DGINOPPRS	DROPPINGS
DGHINORTW	DOWNRIGHT	DGINORTUY	DRYING OUT
	RIGHT DOWN	DGINRRSWY	WRINGS DRY
DGHINTTUY	NIGHT DUTY	DGJLLOOOY	JOLLY GOOD
DGHIORRTW	RIGHT WORD		

DGKLOOOOS	GOOD LOOKS
	LOOKS GOOD
DGKOOOORSW	GOOD WORKS
DGKOORSTU	TOOK DRUGS
DGLNOORSW	LONG WORDS
DGLNOORUW	LOW GROUND
DGLNOPSUW	GULPS DOWN
DGMNRRSUY	MRS.GRUNDY
DGNNOORSU	NO GROUNDS
DGNNORRUU	RUNG ROUND
DGNNORTUU	GROUND NUT
	GROUNDNUT
DGNOOOOST	NOT SO GOOD
DGNOORSTU	GOOD TURNS
DGOOOPRST	GOOD SPORT
DGOOOORSST	GOOD SORTS
DGOOOORSTY	GOOD STORY
DGOOPSTTY	SPOTTY DOG
DHHILOSTW	HOLDS WITH
	WITHHOLDS
DHIIIPSTY	HISPIDITY
DHIIKSWZZ	WHIZZ KIDS
DHIILNRWW	WHIRLWIND
DHIILPRST	THIRD SLIP
DHIINNNRY	NINHYDRIN
DHIKNOOSW	HOODWINKS
DHIKNORST	HOT DRINKS
DHILLLOST	HOLD STILL
DHILLLOSY	DOLLISHLY
DHILLOSTY	DOLTISHLY
DHILNNOSY	DONNISHLY
DHILOPRSS	LORDSHIPS
DHILPRSUY	PRUDISHLY
DHIMNORUY	HYDRONIUM
DHIMOOOOS	HOODOOISM
DHINNORTW	NORTH WIND
DHINOOPRS	RHODOPSIN
DHINOORSU	DISHONOUR
DHINOPRST	DROP HINTS
DHINOPRUW	WHIP ROUND
	WHIP-ROUND
DHINOSTUW	SOUTH WIND
	WHODUNITS
DHIOOPRSZ	RHIZOPODS
DHIOOSTTW	WITHSTOOD
DHIOOTTUW	DO WITHOUT
DHIORSTTW	TWO THIRDS
DHJOORTUW	JUDO THROW
DHKMNOOOS	MONKSHOOD
DHKNOOOSW	SHOOK DOWN
DHKNORUYY	HUNKY-DORY
DHLLOOOWY	HOLLYWOOD
DHLLOOPPY	PHYLLOPOD
DHLMOOTUU	LOUD MOUTH
	LOUDMOUTH
DHLNOOOST	HOLDS ON TO
DHLNOORRT	LORD NORTH
DHLNOOSWW	HOWLS DOWN
DHLOORSST	SOLD SHORT
DHLORSXYY	HYDROXYLS
DHMNOOPWY	WOOD NYMPH
DHMNORTUW	THROWN MUD
DHMORRUUY	DRY HUMOUR
DHNNOSTUW	HUNTS DOWN
DHNOOOSTW	SHOOT DOWN
DHNOORSTU	ROUND SHOT
DHNOORSUW	SHOW ROUND
DHNOORTWW	THROW DOWN
DHNOOSSWW	SHOWDOWNS

DHNOOSTUW	DOWN SOUTH
	SHOUT DOWN
	SOUTHDOWN
DHNORRUWY	HURRY DOWN
DHNOSSTUW	SHUTDOWNS
	SHUTS DOWN
DHOOOORTXY	ORTHODOXY
DHOOPRRST	DROP SHORT
DHOORRSTW	SHORT WORD
DHOPRSTYY	DYSTROPHY
DIIIKLNPV	LIVID PINK
DIIILMPTY	LIMPIDITY
DIIILNPSY	INSIPIDLY
DIIILQTUY	LIQUIDITY
DIIINOSSU	INSIDIOUS
DIIINOSSV	DIVISIONS
DIIINOSUV	INVIDIOUS
DIIIPRSST	DISPIRITS
DIIJNOSST	DISJOINTS
DIIKKLMNR	MILK DRINK
DIIKMNRSX	MIX DRINKS
DIILLMNSW	WINDMILLS
DIILOSTTY	STOLIDITY
DIIMMNNOOS	DOMINIONS
DIIMNNPTU	PUT IN MIND
DIIMNOPST	MIDPOINTS
DIIMORSSY	DIMISSORY
DIINNOSSU	DISUNIONS
DIIOPRTTY	TORPIDITY
DIIORRTTY	TORRIDITY
DIIPRTTUY	PUTRIDITY
DIIPSTTUY	STUPIDITY
DIJNOOTTW	JOT IT DOWN
DIKLMNORU	MILK ROUND
DIKLNOSSU	KIND SOULS
DIKLOORTY	DIRTY LOOK
DIKNNOSSW	SINKS DOWN
DIKNOOSTW	STINKWOOD
DIKNOSTYY	DINKY TOYS
DIKORRTWY	DIRTY WORK
DILLMNOPS	MILL PONDS
	MILLPONDS
DILLNOPSY	LILY PONDS
DILLOOPPY	POLYPLOID
DILNOQTUW	DOWN QUILT
DILOOPRTY	DIRTY POOL
DILOOPTUW	TULIPWOOD
DIMMNORSY	MYRMIDONS
DIMNOSSTU	DISMOUNTS
DIMOOOOSV	VOODOOISM
DIMOORRTY	DORMITORY
DINNOPRSU	SPIN ROUND
DINOOPRST	PISTON ROD
DINOPRRTU	ROUND TRIP
DINOPSSUX	SIX POUNDS
DINOPTTUW	PUT IT DOWN
DINOPTTUY	POINT DUTY
	POINT-DUTY
DINORTTUY	ROTUNDITY
DIOOPRSST	PROSODIST
DIRSSSTTU	DISTRUSTS
DJMNOPSUW	JUMPS DOWN
DKLNOOORU	LOOK ROUND
DKLNOOOSW	LOOKS DOWN
DKLNOORSW	LORD KNOWS!
DKORSTUWY	WORK STUDY
DLLNOPSUW	PULLS DOWN
DLLNORUWY	UNWORLDLY
DLLOORSTW	LOST WORLD
DLNNOOOOZ	LONDON ZOO
DLNNOSUUY	UNSOUNDLY

DLNOOOSTW	DOWN TOOLS	EEEFIKNPS	KEEPS FINE
DLNOOSSUW	LOW SOUNDS	EEEFIKSVW	FIVE WEEKS
DLNOOSSWW	SLOWS DOWN	EEEFILMPS	FEE SIMPLE
DLOOORSUY	ODOROUSLY	EEEFILPRS	LIFE PEERS
DLOOOSTUY	TOLD YOU SO	EEEFILRRV	FREE-LIVER
DLOOPPSUW	PULPWOODS	EEEFILRVX	REFLEXIVE
DLOORRTUW	WORLD TOUR	EEEFIMNRY	ENEMY FIRE
DMMNRSUUY	DUMMY RUNS	EEEFINRRS	FERNERIES
DMNOORRUW	ROUNDWORM	EEEFINRRT	INTERFERE
DMNORSSUU	ROUND SUMS	EEEFLLLSW	FEELS WELL
DMOOOORRST	STORM DOOR	EEEFLNSST	FLEETNESS
DMORSSTTU	DUST STORM	EEEFLORSS	FEELS SORE
DNNOPRSUU	SPUN ROUND	EEEFLRSSU	FEELS SURE
DNNORRSUU	RUNS ROUND	EEEFLRSTV	VEERS LEFT
DNNORRTUU	TURN ROUND	EEEFLRSTY	FREE STYLE
	TURNROUND		FREESTYLE
DNNORSTUW	DOWNTURNS	EEEFMNRRT	FERMENTER
	TURNS DOWN	EEEFNORST	FREESTONE
DNOOOPSTW	STOOP DOWN	EEEFNRRST	REFERENTS
DNOOOPSWW	SWOOP DOWN	EEEFNRRTY	FREE ENTRY
DNOOPPRSU	PROPOUNDS	EEEFNRSTT	ENFETTERS
DNOOPRSSW	SNOWDROPS	EEEFNRSTY	ENTRY FEES
DNOOPRSUW	DOWNPOURS	EEEFNRSUZ	UNFREEZES
DNOOPSTUW	TWO POUNDS	EEEFORSTV	FREE VOTES
DNOORRTUU	ROUND TOUR	EEEFORSTX	TREE FOXES
DNOORRTWY	DONT WORRY	EEEFORTUZ	FREEZE OUT
DNOORSTUW	DROWNS OUT	EEEFPRRRR	PREFERRER
	TWO ROUNDS	EEEFPRRSS	FREE PRESS
DNOORTUWW	WOUNDWORT	EEEFPRSUZ	FREEZE-UPS
DNOOSSTUU	SOUNDS OUT		FREEZES UP
DNORRSSUU	SURROUNDS	EEEGGILNS	NEGLIGEES
DOOOPRSST	DOORPOSTS	EEEGGNNOR	GONE GREEN
	DOORSTOPS	EEEGGNORS	GOES GREEN
DOOOPSTTU	STOOD UP TO	EEEGGORTT	GEORGETTE
EEEEFFLRS	FEELS FREE	EEEGHINST	EIGHTEENS
EEEEFHLRW	FREE WHEEL	EEEGHLRSS	SHEERLEGS
	FREEWHEEL	EEEGHRSTT	GETS THERE
EEEEFHRTT	THREE FEET	EEEGIJNNT	JET ENGINE
EEEEFNSTV	SEVEN FEET	EEEGIKNPS	PEKINGESE
EEEEFRRSV	FREE VERSE	EEEGILLNR	LEGER LINE
EEEEGINWW	WEE-WEEING	EEEGILMNR	LIME GREEN
EEEEGNRRV	EVERGREEN	EEEGILNNR	GREEN LINE
EEEEGNRSY	GREEN EYES		NILE GREEN
EEEEGQSSU	SQUEEGEES	EEEGIMNRW	NEW REGIME
EEEEHLRSW	ELSEWHERE	EEEGIMNST	ESTEEMING
	WHERE ELSE?	EEEGINNRS	ENGINEERS
EEEEHMTTY	MET THE EYE	EEEGINNRV	VENEERING
EEEEHQRUU	QUEUE HERE	EEEGINPRR	PEREGRINE
EEEEKRVWY	EVERY WEEK	EEEGINRRS	ENERGISER
EEEELMNNV	ELEVEN MEN	EEEGINRRZ	ENERGIZER
EEEELMRTT	TELEMETER	EEEGINRSS	ENERGISES
EEEELNSSV	ELEVENSES	EEEGINRSZ	ENERGIZES
EEEELNTVV	VELVETEEN	EEEGINRTT	TEETERING
EEEENNSTV	SEVENTEEN	EEEGIRSTY	TIGER'S-EYE
EEEENOPRY	EYE-OPENER	EEEGLLNTY	GENTEELLY
EEEENRRSV	VENEERERS	EEEGLMNNT	GENTLEMEN
EEEENRSTW	SWEETENER	EEEGLNSTX	GENTLE SEX
EEEEPRRSV	PERSEVERE	EEEGLRSTY	STEEL GREY
EEEEPRSSS	PEERESSES	EEEGMNRSS	MESSENGER
EEEFFFORR	FREE OFFER	EEEGMORRT	ERGOMETER
EEEFFILNS	FEELS FINE	EEEGMORST	GEOMETERS
EEEFGHITT	EIGHT FEET	EEEGNNRSS	GREENNESS
EEEFGIKRR	GREEK FIRE	EEEGNNRTW	WENT GREEN
EEEFGKNRU	FENUGREEK	EEEGNNRWY	NEW ENERGY
EEEFHKPRS	KEEP FRESH	EEEGNOOST	GONE TO SEE
EEEFHORRT	THEREFORE	EEEGNRSSS	NEGRESSES
EEEFHORRW	WHEREFORE	EEEGOOSST	GOES TO SEE
EEEFHORSU	FREE HOUSE	EEEGRRSSS	REGRESSES
EEEFHRRRS	REFRESHER	EEEHIKLPS	LIKE SHEEP
EEEFHRRSS	REFRESHES	EEEHILLNS	HELLENISE
EEEFIKLLS	FEELS LIKE	EEEHILLNZ	HELLENIZE

EEEHIMPRS	EPHEMERIS	EEEINSSVZ	SIZE SEVEN
EEEHIMPRT	THE EMPIRE	EEEINSTVX	EXTENSIVE
EEEHIMPSU	EUPHEMISE	EEEINSTWW	SWEET WINE
EEEHIMPUZ	EUPHEMIZE	EEEIPRRSV	REPRIEVES
EEEHIRRST	ETHERISER	EEEIPRRTT	PRETERITE
EEEHIRRTZ	ETHERIZER	EEEIPRSTX	EXPERTISE
EEEHIRSSS	HEIRESSES	EEEIQRRSU	EQUERRIES
EEEHIRSST	ETHERISES	EEEIQTTTU	ETIQUETTE
EEEHIRSTZ	ETHERIZES	EEEIRRRTV	RETRIEVER
	SIZE THREE	EEEIRRSTV	RETRIEVES
EEEHIRTVW	THE REVIEW	EEEIRRSVW	REVIEWERS
EEEHKLOSU	HOUSELEEK	EEEIRSTTV	SERVIETTE
EEEHKOPSU	KEEP HOUSE	EEEJKNRTU	JUNKETEER
EEEHLLSSW	WHEELLESS	EEEJLLRSW	JEWELLERS
EEEHLMNSW	WHEELSMEN	EEEJLLRWY	JEWELLERY
EEEHLMNTY	METHYLENE	EEEJNRSWY	NEW JERSEY
EEEHLMPST	HELPMEETS	EEEJRSTTT	JETSETTER
EEEHLNOPT	TELEPHONE	EEEKLLPSW	KEEPS WELL
EEEHLOPPS	PEEPHOLES	EEEKLLSYY	KELLYS EYE
EEEHLOPPT	THE PEOPLE	EEEKLNSSS	SLEEKNESS
EEEHLORSV	HEELS OVER	EEEKLORSV	KEELS OVER
EEEHMNOPR	EPHEMERON	EEEKMRSTU	MUSKETEER
EEEHMORST	THREESOME	EEEKNOPPS	KEEPS OPEN
EEEHMORSW	SOMEWHERE	EEELLLPSW	SLEEP WELL
EEEHNNSTU	THE UNSEEN	EEELLLRSV	LEVELLERS
EEEHNRSTT	THREE TENS	EEELLMNOP	LEMON PEEL
EEEHNRSTV	THE SEVERN	EEELLNPRT	REPELLENT
EEEHNSSTW	NEWS SHEET	EEELLNQSU	QUENELLES
EEEHOPRSX	EXOSPHERE	EEELLNSSV	LEVELNESS
EEEHORRTV	OVER THERE	EEELLNSTW	SWEET NELL
EEEHPRSTT	STEP THREE	EEELLOPSS	LOSE SLEEP
EEEHRSSTT	THREE SETS	EEELLPSSS	SLEEPLESS
EEEHSSTTW	WET SHEETS	EEELLRRSV	REVELLERS
EEEIINRSW	ERNIE WISE	EEELLRSVW	SERVE WELL
EEEIJMRSV	JIM REEVES	EEELMNOPT	ELOPEMENT
EEEIKMPST	KEEPS TIME	EEELMNORT	LEMON TREE
EEEIKNNPR	INNKEEPER	EEELMNTVW	TWELVE MEN
EEEIKNNSW	NINE WEEKS	EEELMOPSY	EMPLOYEES
EEEIKPQTU	KEEP QUIET	EEELMOSTT	OMELETTES
EEEIILLPST	PELLETISE	EEELMRSTU	MULETEERS
EEEIILLPTZ	PELLETIZE	EEELMRTTY	TELEMETRY
EEEIILNOSV	SEE NO EVIL	EEELMRTXY	EXTREMELY
EEEIILNPRS	PELERINES	EEELNNOOS	NO ONE ELSE
EEEIILORTV	OLIVE TREE	EEELNOPSV	ENVELOPES
EEEIILPSST	SLEEPIEST	EEELNOTTV	NOVELETTE
EEEIILPTVX	EXPLETIVE	EEELNRSSV	NERVELESS
EEEIILRRSV	REVELRIES	EEELNRSSW	NEWSREELS
EEEIILSSTT	STEELIEST	EEELNSSSS	SENSELESS
EEEIILSSTV	TELEVISES	EEELNSSTV	EVENTLESS
EEEIIMMRSS	MESMERISE	EEELOPRSV	OVERSLEEP
EEEIIMMRSZ	MESMERIZE	EEELOSTVW	SWEET LOVE
EEEIIMNNRT	NEMERTINE	EEELPPRSX	PERPLEXES
EEEIIMORTT	METEORITE	EEELPSTTY	TELETYPES
EEEIIMPRRS	PREMIERES	EEELRRSVY	REVERSELY
EEEIIMPRRT	PERIMETER	EEELRRTVY	TYRE LEVER
EEEIIMRRSS	MISERERES	EEEMMNOST	MEMENTOES
EEEIIMRSTV	SERVE TIME	EEEMMNOVY	EVEN MONEY
EEEIIMRTVY	EVERY TIME	EEEMMNNSTT	TENEMENTS
EEEIINNNST	NINETEENS	EEEMNORRV	NEVER MORE
EEEIINNRTV	INTERVENE		NEVERMORE
EEEIINORRT	ORIENTEER	EEEMNRSST	STEERSMEN
EEEIINPRRS	RESERPINE	EEEMNRSTT	ENTREMETS
EEEIINPRST	PINE TREES		TEN METRES
EEEIINPSVX	EXPENSIVE	EEEMNRSTY	MESENTERY
EEEIINQSUZ	SQUEEZE IN	EEEMNRTTV	REVETMENT
EEEIINRRST	REENTRIES	EEEMOPRTX	EXTEMPORE
EEEIINRRSV	IN RESERVE	EEEMPRRST	TEMPERERS
	IN REVERSE	EEEMPRSSS	EMPRESSES
EEEIINRTTV	RETENTIVE	EEEMRSSST	SEMESTERS
EEEIINSSTT	TEENSIEST	EEEMRSTTX	EXTREMEST
EEEIINSSTV	SEVENTIES	EEENNORST	SONNETEER

EEEENNSSST	TENSENESS	EEFGINRRT	FERRETING
EEEENOPRSW	OPEN SEWER	EEFGINRST	FESTERING
EEEENOSSTY	SET EYES ON	EEFGINRTT	FETTERING
EEEENOSTTW	WENT TO SEE	EEFGIORRS	FORGERIES
EEEENPRRST	PRESENTER	EEFGIPRRU	PREFIGURE
	REPRESENT	EEFGLLLUY	GLEEFULLY
EEEENPRRTV	PREVENTER	EEFGLNRTU	REFULGENT
EEEENPRSUV	SUPERVENE	EEFGLRRTU	REGRETFUL
EEEENPSSST	STEEPNESS	EEFGORRTT	FORGETTER
EEEENPSTUW	SWEETEN UP	EEFGORSTV	SOFT VERGE
EEEENQRSSU	QUEERNESS	EEFGORSXY	GREY FOXES
EEEENRRSTW	WESTERNER	EEFHIINRT	IN THE FIRE
EEEENRSSST	TERSENESS	EEFHIIRSS	FISHERIES
EEEENSSSTW	SWEETNESS	EEFHILMOS	FLIES HOME
EEEEOORSTV	TOO SEVERE	EEFHILOTT	TO THE LIFE
EEEEORRSSV	OVERSEERS	EEFHIMNRS	FISHERMEN
EEEEORRSTV	OVERSTEER	EEFHIMORS	HOME FIRES
EEEEORRTVV	TREVOR EVE	EEFHINPRY	HYPERFINE
EEEEPPPRTU	PUPPETEER	EEFHINSST	HEFTINESS
EEEEPRRRSV	PRESERVER	EEFHIOSUW	HOUSEWIFE
EEEEPRRRTV	PERVERTER	EEFHIQRSU	QUEER FISH
EEEEPRRSSS	REPRESSES	EEFHKNRSU	SHEER FUNK
EEEEPRRSSV	PRESERVES	EEFHIKPRST	KEPT FRESH
EEEEPRRSSX	EXPRESSER	EEFHLLSWY	FLYWHEELS
EEEEPRRSTW	PEWTERERS	EEFHLNOTT	ON THE LEFT
EEEEPRSSSX	EXPRESSES	EEFHLORUW	FOUR-WHEEL
EEEEPRSTTW	PETER WEST	EEFHLOTTT	TO THE LEFT
EEEEPRSTVY	VERY STEEP	EEFHMORRT	THE FORMER
EEEEQRSSTU	SEQUESTER	EEFHMORRW	WHEREFROM
EEEEQRSSUZ	SQUEEZERS	EEFHNPRSU	FRESHEN UP
EEEFRSTVWY	VERY SWEET	EEFHNRSSS	FRESHNESS
EEEFFFKLRU	KERFUFFLE	EEFHOORRS	FORESHORE
EEEFFFMNOT	FEOFFMENT	EEFHOORTT	TO THE FORE
EEEFFFOORT	FOR TOFFEE	EEFHRRRTU	FURTHERER
EEEFFGHIRT	FREE FIGHT	EEFHRTTUU	THE FUTURE
EEEFFGHOPT	OFF THE PEG	EEFIIKKLN	KNIFELIKE
	OFF-THE-PEG	EEFIILLNS	LIFELINES
EEEFFGINOS	SEEING OFF	EEFIILMST	LIFETIMES
EEEFFGINOT	TEEING OFF		TIME FLIES
EEEFFGIRST	FREE GIFTS	EEFIILMSV	FIVE MILES
EEEFFGLNTU	EFFULGENT	EEFIILMTX	FLEXITIME
EEEFFHILLS	SHELF-LIFE	EEFIILNRT	INFERTILE
EEEFFHINTT	FIFTEENTH		INTERFILE
EEEFFHLRSU	RESHUFFLE	EEFIILQRU	LIQUEFIER
EEEFFHORSS	SHEERS OFF	EEFIILQSU	LIQUEFIES
EEEFFHORTY	THEYRE OFF!	EEFIILQTU	QUIET LIFE
EEEFFIILRR	RIFLE FIRE	EEFIILRST	FERTILISE
EEEFFIILRS	FIREFLIES	EEFIILRTZ	FERTILIZE
EEEFFINOSV	OFFENSIVE	EEFIIMNSS	FEMINISES
EEEFFINRST	STIFFENER	EEFIIMNSZ	FEMINIZES
EEEFFIRSTT	FEET FIRST	EEFIIMSTV	FIVE TIMES
EEEFFLLOSV	LEVELS OFF	EEFIINNOV	FIVE IN ONE
EEEFFLNNUY	FEEL FUNNY		ONE IN FIVE
EEEFFLNSTU	EFFLUENTS	EEFIINRSS	FIERINESS
EEEFFLOPSS	SLEEPS OFF	EEFIIPRST	PETRIFIES
EEEFFRRSSU	SUFFERERS	EEFIIRRST	TERRIFIES
EEEFGGHRSS	FRESH EGGS	EEFIIRRSV	VERIFIERS
EEEFGGIKRT	GREEK GIFT		VERSIFIER
EEEFGHHIRV	HIGH FEVER	EEFIIRSSV	VERSIFIES
EEEFGHIKNT	KEEN FIGHT	EEFIIRSTT	TESTIFIER
EEEFGHILRT	FEEL RIGHT	EEFIISSTT	TESTIFIES
EEEFGHIRRT	FREIGHTER	EEFIJLNOY	ENJOY LIFE
EEEFGHRSST	GETS FRESH	EEFIJLNSU	JUNE FLIES
EEEFGIILRS	FILIGREES	EEFILLLSY	FEEL SILLY
EEEFGILLNY	FEELINGLY	EEFILLORW	LOW RELIEF
EEEFGILMNY	MY FEELING	EEFILLOSY	ISLE OF ELY
EEEFGILNNU	UNFEELING	EEFILLRTY	FERTILELY
EEEFGILRSS	GRIEFLESS	EEFILLSTY	LIFE STYLE
EEEFGINORR	FOREIGNER		LIFE-STYLE
EEEFGINORU	FIGURE ONE	EEFILMPXY	EXEMPLIFY
EEEFGINRRR	REFERRING	EEFILNNRS	INNER SELF

EEFILNORS	FELONRIES	EEGGIKNOP	KEEP GOING
EEFILNSTY	FINE STYLE	EEGGILNNT	NEGLIGENT
EEFILORSV	FLIES OVER	EEGGILOOS	GEOLOGISE
	OVERFLIES	EEGGILOOZ	GEOLOGIZE
EEFILSSTW	FLIES WEST	EEGGIMRST	EGG TIMERS
EEFILSTVY	FESTIVELY	EEGGINNRV	REVENGING
EEFIMNNOW	FINE WOMEN	EEGGINRRS	SNIGGERER
EEFIMSSTU	TIME FUSES	EEGGINRST	GREETINGS
EEFINOOTV	FIVE TO ONE	EEGGINSSU	SIEGE GUNS
EEFINOPRS	OPENS FIRE	EEGGIORSU	EGREGIOUS
EEFINORST	FIRESTONE	EEGGNORTT	ROTTEN EGG
	SET ON FIRE	EEGGOORSY	GREY GOOSE
EEFINOTTV	FIVE TO TEN	EEGGORSST	ST. GEORGE'S
	TEN TO FIVE	EEGGORSTT	GO-GETTERS
EEFINPRSU	SUPERFINE	EEGGRSSTU	SUGGESTER
EEFINRSTT	IN FETTERS	EEGHHHILS	HIGH HEELS
EEFINRSTU	INTERFUSE	EEGHHIITT	EIGHTIETH
EEFIOPPRS	FOPPERIES	EEGHHILLV	HIGH LEVEL
EEFIOPRRT	PROFITEER		HIGH-LEVEL
EEFIOPRRW	FIRE POWER	EEGHHINOT	ONE EIGHTH
	FIREPOWER	EEGHHINST	HEIGHTENS
EEFIORSTT	SET FIRE TO	EEGHIIRTW	WEIGHTIER
EEFIPRSTU	PUTREFIES	EEGHIISTZ	SIZE EIGHT
EEFIPRSUV	PERFUSIVE	EEGHIKNTW	WEEKNIGHT
EEFIPSSTU	STUPEFIES	EEGHIKOTV	GIVE THE O.K.
EEFIRRRTU	FRUITERER	EEGHIKPRT	KEEP RIGHT
EEFIRRSTU	SURFEITER	EEGHIKPST	KEEP SIGHT
EEFIRRTTU	FRUIT TREE	EEGHILLNR	GREEN HILL
EEFIRSSUW	FUSE WIRES	EEGHILLNV	GIVEN HELL
EEFJMORRW	REFORM JEW	EEGHILLSV	GIVES HELL
EEFKNOORT	FORETOKEN	EEGHILMNT	METHEGLIN
EEFKNORST	REEF KNOTS	EEGHILNNT	ENLIGHTEN
EEFKORSUW	FOUR WEEKS	EEGHILNRT	LIGHTENER
EEFLLNPSU	SPLEENFUL	EEGHIMNNS	ENMESHING
EEFLLORST	FORETELLS	EEGHIMOST	EIGHTSOME
EEFLNRSTU	RESENTFUL	EEGHINOTW	GONE WHITE
EEFLNRTVY	FERVENTLY	EEGHINRST	SEEN RIGHT
EEFLOPRSU	REPOSEFUL	EEGHINRTT	TETHERING
EEFLOPSTU	FEELS UP TO		TIGHTENER
EEFLORRSY	FEEL SORRY	EEGHINSST	SEE THINGS
EEFLORRTX	RETROFLEX	EEGHINTTW	NET WEIGHT
EEFLORSTV	LEFTOVERS	EEGHIOSTW	GOES WHITE
EEFLRRSSY	LESSER FRY	EEGHIPPTT	GET THE PIP
EEFLRRTTU	FLUTTERER	EEGHIRRTV	VEER RIGHT
EEFLSSTTY	TSETSE FLY	EEGHIRSST	SEES RIGHT
EEFMNNOOT	MEN OF NOTE		SIGHTSEER
EEFMNOORW	FOREWOMEN	EEGHIRSTY	EYES RIGHT
EEFMOPRRR	PERFORMER	EEGHKMRTY	GREEK MYTH
EEFMORRRS	REFORMERS	EEGHKOSTT	GETS THE O.K.
EEFMORRST	E.M.FORSTER	EEGHLLNOP	PHELLOGEN
EEFMORRSV	VERSE FORM	EEGHLNNOT	ONE LENGTH
EEFMPRRUY	PERFUMERY	EEGHLNNST	LENGTHENS
EEFNOOOTW	ONE TOO FEW	EEGHLOPST	THE GOSPEL
EEFNORRST	FOURTEENS	EEGHLORTY	LEG THEORY
EEFNORSTW	NEW FOREST	EEGHMNOST	THEME SONG
EEFNORSTY	EYES FRONT	EEGHMORTU	THE MORGUE
EEFNORTVY	VERY OFTEN	EEGHNNORR	GREENHORN
EEFNQRSTU	FREQUENTS	EEGHNOSST	SONG SHEET
EEFNRSTTU	UNFETTERS	EEGHNRTTY	THE GENTRY
EEFOORRST	ROOFTREES	EEGHORRSY	GREY HORSE
EEFOORRVZ	FROZE OVER	EEGHOSSST	SEE GHOSTS
EEFOPRRST	FREE PORTS	EEGIIKLPV	KEEP VIGIL
EEFOPRSSS	PROFESSES	EEGIIKLRT	TIGERLIKE
EEFORRSST	FORESTERS	EEGIIKNNP	IN KEEPING
EEFORRTTU	FERRET OUT		KEEPING IN
EEGGGOOSS	GOOSE EGGS	EEGIILNNT	GET IN LINE
EEGGHISTW	EGG WHITES	EEGIILNRV	RELIEVING
	WHITE EGGS	EEGIILNSV	INVEIGLES
EEGGHLLSS	EGGSHELLS	EEGIILORS	RELIGIOSE
EEGGIILNT	GELIGNITE	EEGIILPRV	PRIVILEGE
EEGGIIPRS	PIGGERIES	EEGIIMNTV	GIVEN TIME

EEGIINOPP	PIGEON PIE	EEGIRSSST	TIGRESSES
EEGIINRSV	GIVEN RISE	EEGIRSSTT	GRISETTES
EEGIINRVW	REVIEWING	EEGKNRRSU	GREEK URNS
EEGIINSTV	INGESTIVE	EEGLLMORU	GLOMERULE
EEGIIRSSV	GIVES RISE	EEGLLNOPS	LONG SLEEP
EEGIISTTZ	ZEITGEIST	EEGLLNOTW	GET ON WELL
EEGIJLNRY	JEERINGLY	EEGLLOOTY	TELEOLOGY
EEGIKNNOP	KEEPING ON	EEGLLORRV	GROVELLER
EEGIKNPPU	KEEPING UP	EEGLNORTT	LORGNETTE
EEGIKNRSW	SKEWERING	EEGLOOPST	GO TO SLEEP
EEGIKRSSY	GREY SKIES	EEGMNOORR	GREENROOM
EEGILLLNV	LEVELLING	EEGMNORSS	MOSS GREEN
EEGILLNPR	REPELLING	EEGMNOSST	GEMSTONES
EEGILLNPX	EXPELLING	EEGNNORST	ROENTGENS
EEGILLNRV	REVELLING	EEGNNRRTU	TURN GREEN
EEGILLSSU	GUILELESS	EEGNOORST	OESTROGEN
EEGILMNSY	SEEMINGLY	EEGNOORSU	EROGENOUS
EEGILMORV	LIME GROVE	EEGNOOSUX	EXOGENOUS
EEGILMRSY	LYME REGIS	EEGNOPSTW	WET SPONGE
EEGILNNRT	RELENTING	EEGNOPSTY	GENOTYPES
EEGILNNRU	UNREELING	EEGNORRSS	ENGROSSER
EEGILNNSS	LESSENING	EEGNORRST	NO REGRETS
EEGILNNUY	GENUINELY	EEGNORRTW	WRONG TREE
EEGILNRTT	LETTERING	EEGNORSSS	ENGROSSES
EEGILNRTW	WELTERING	EEGNORSSV	GOVERNESS
EEGILNRVY	VEERINGLY	EEGNOSSTW	SWEET SONG
EEGILNTXY	EXIGENTLY	EEGNRRSTU	RESURGENT
EEGILOPSU	EPILOGUES	EEGNRSSUY	GUERNSEYS
EEGILORSU	EULOGISER	EEGOOPSST	GOOSE-STEP
EEGILORUZ	EULOGIZER	EEGOPRSSU	SUPEREGOS
EEGILOSSU	EULOGISES	EEGOQRSTU	GROTESQUE
EEGILOSUZ	EULOGIZES	EEGORSSTW	GETS WORSE
EEGILPRST	STEEL GRIP	EEGPSSTTU	GETS UPSET
EEGIMNPRT	TEMPERING	EEHHILOTW	WHITE HOLE
EEGIMNPTX	EXEMPTING	EEHHIMNOT	IN THE HOME
EEGIMNRST	REGIMENTS	EEHHINTTZ	THE ZENITH
EEGIMNRSU	MERINGUES	EEHHIOPTW	WHITE HOPE
EEGIMRSTV	GIVE TERMS	EEHHIRTTW	THEREWITH
EEGINNOPR	REOPENING	EEHHIRTWW	WHEREWITH
EEGINNPRT	REPENTING	EEHHISTTW	THE WHITES
EEGINNRST	RESENTING	EEHHLLLOS	HELLHOLES
EEGINNRSU	GUNNERIES	EEHHLMOPS	HOME HELPS
EEGINNRTU	NEUTERING	EEHHMNORT	MOTHER HEN
EEGINNTVV	GIVEN VENT	EEHHNOPPS	PHOSPHENE
EEGINOOSS	OOGENESIS	EEHHNOSSU	HEN HOUSES
EEGINORSS	EGRESSION	EEHHOORSS	HORSESHOE
EEGINORST	NEGRITOES	EEHHRRSST	THRESHERS
EEGINORSV	SOVEREIGN	EEHIILNTW	WHITE LINE
EEGINORVV	GIVEN OVER		WHITE NILE
EEGINORVY	ROVING EYE	EEHIILRTT	HITLERITE
EEGINOSSS	GNEISSOSE	EEHIILSTW	WHITE LIES
EEGINOSTU	SEEING OUT	EEHIINNRW	RHINE WINE
EEGINOTTU	TONGUE-TIE	EEHIINNTT	NINETIETH
EEGINPPPR	PEPPERING	EEHIINNTV	IN THE VEIN
EEGINPRST	PESTERING	EEHIINPTW	WHITE PINE
EEGINPSSW	SWEEPINGS	EEHIINTWW	WHITE WINE
EEGINQSUZ	SQUEEZING	EEHIIRSSY	IRISH EYES
EEGINRRSV	RESERVING	EEHIIRSTT	THERE IT IS
	REVERSING	EEHIIRSTW	WHERE IS IT?
EEGINRRTV	REVERTING	EEHIISTTW	WHITE TIES
EEGINRSSU	SEIGNEURS	EEHIKLMTT	MILK TEETH
EEGINRSTW	WESTERING	EEHIKLRSS	SHEER SILK
EEGINRSUY	SEIGNEURY	EEHIKMNSV	MENSHEVIK
EEGINRTTV	REVETTING	EEHIKNPSS	SHEEPSKIN
EEGINSTVV	GIVES VENT	EEHIKNRRT	RETHINKER
EEGIORRSU	ROGUERIES	EEHILLMNS	HELLENISM
EEGIORSSX	SEX ORGIES	EEHILLNST	HELLENIST
EEGIORSVV	GIVES OVER	EEHILLPST	STEEP HILL
EEGIRRSST	REGISTERS	EEHILLRST	STILL HERE
EEGIRRSSU	REGISSEUR	EEHILMNTT	TIN HELMET
	SURGERIES	EEHILMOST	HOMELIEST

EEHILMOTW	WHOLE-TIME	EEHLMOOSW	WHOLESOME
EEHILNNOO	HOLE IN ONE	EEHLMORVW	OVERWHELM
EEHILNNOS	NINE HOLES	EEHLMOSZZ	SHEMOZZLE
EEHILNNOT	ON THE LINE	EEHLMRSSY	RHYMELESS
EEHILNOOP	OENOPHILE	EEHLNOPTY	POLYTHENE
EEHILNOPS	ENOPHILES		TELEPHONY
EEHILNPRS	REPLENISH	EEHLNOSSW	WHOLENESS
EEHILNPSW	PINWHEELS	EEHLNOSTT	THE SOLENT
EEHILNPTU	UP THE LINE	EEHLOOPSS	LOSES HOPE
EEHILNSST	LITHENESS	EEHLOOPTT	TELEPHOTO
EEHILOPRX	XEROPHILE	EEHLOPPSY	SHY PEOPLE
EEHILORST	HOTELIERS	EEHLOPPTU	UP THE POLE
EEHILPSVY	PEEVISHLY	EEHLOPSST	LOST SHEEP
EEHILRSTW	ERSTWHILE	EEHLORTUV	THE LOUVRE
EEHILSSWX	SIX WHEELS	EEHLOSSSU	HOUSELESS
EEHIMMPSU	EUPHEMISM	EEHLOSTUW	WHEELS OUT
EEHIMMRST	HERMETISM	EEHLOSTWW	TWO WHEELS
EEHIMNTTT	TENTH TIME	EEHLPRSSU	SPHERULES
EEHIMORTW	WRITE HOME	EEHMMOPRS	MORPHEMES
EEHIMOSTV	THE MOVIES	EEHMMORST	OHMMETERS
EEHIMPRTU	THE UMPIRE	EEHMMRSTU	THE SUMMER
EEHIMRSTT	HERMETIST	EEHMNNOTU	ON THE MENU
EEHINNOPT	IN THE OPEN	EEHMNOOPR	PHEROMONE
EEHINNORT	THREONINE	EEHMNOOTV	ON THE MOVE
EEHINNOTV	IN THE OVEN	EEHMNORTY	HETERONYM
EEHINNRSS	ENSHRINES	EEHMNPTTU	UMPTEENTH
EEHINNRTW	THE WINNER	EEHMOOPSS	SOME HOPES
EEHINNSTW	IN THE NEWS	EEHMOORTW	WROTE HOME
EEHINOPRT	ON THE PIER	EEHMOOSUV	MOVE HOUSE
EEHINOPSU	EUPHONIES	EEHMOPRSS	PRESS HOME
	EUPHONISE	EEHMOPRTT	HOT TEMPER
EEHINOPSX	PHOENIXES	EEHMOPSTU	SET UP HOME
EEHINOPUZ	EUPHONIZE	EEHMOPSTY	MESOPHYTE
EEHINOPVW	VIEWPHONE	EEHMORSST	REST HOMES
EEHINORRS	HERONRIES		THERMOSES
EEHINORRT	THREE IRON	EEHMPSTTU	SET THEM UP
EEHINORTT	THE ORIENT	EEHMRRSTY	RHYMESTER
EEHINORTW	WHEREINTO	EEHNNOORT	NONE OTHER
EEHINPRST	TREPHINES	EEHNNOOST	ON THE NOSE
EEHINRTTW	THE WINTER	EEHNNORST	ENTHRONES
EEHINSSTW	WHITENESS	EEHNOOPSU	OPEN HOUSE
EEHINSTTW	IN THE WEST	EEHNOPPTY	PHENOTYPE
EEHINSTTX	SIXTEENTH	EEHNOPRTU	THEREUPON
EEHINTTTW	TWENTIETH	EEHNOPRTW	THREW OPEN
EEHINTTWW	WENT WHITE	EEHNOPRUW	WHEREUPON
EEHIOPPSS	HOSEPIPES	EEHNOPSTU	PENTHOUSE
EEHIORRST	THEORISER	EEHNOPSTY	NEOPHYTES
EEHIORRTZ	THEORIZER		PHONEYEST
EEHIORSST	HETEROSIS	EEHNORSST	OTHERNESS
	THEORISES	EEHNORTUW	WHEREUNTO
EEHIORSTT	THE TORIES	EEHNORTWY	NEW THEORY
EEHIORSTW	OTHERWISE	EEHNOSSTT	THE STONES
	WHITE ROSE	EEHNOSSUW	NEW HOUSES
EEHIORSTZ	THEORIZES	EEHNOSTTW	WHETSTONE
EEHIORTWW	WORE WHITE	EEHNOTTTU	TO THE TUNE
EEHIPPRRY	PERIPHERY	EEHNPSSTT	ST.STEPHEN
EEHIPPSSY	EPIPHYSES	EEHNSSSTY	SYNTHESES
EEHIPPSTY	EPIPHYTES	EEHOOPPST	POOP SHEET
EEHIPRRSS	PERISHERS	EEHOORSSV	OVERSHOES
EEHIPRRSW	WHISPERER	EEHOORSVW	WHOSOEVER
EEHIPRTUW	PURE WHITE	EEHOPPPRT	HOT PEPPER
EEHJNOOST	HONEST JOE	EEHOPPSSW	PEEP SHOWS
EEHKLOORT	LOOK THERE	EEHOPRSST	PROTHESES
EEHKLOOST	STOKEHOLE	EEHOPRSTY	HEY PRESTO
EEHKOPPSS	KEEPS SHOP	EEHOPRTTY	PET THEORY
EEHKOPSTU	KEPT HOUSE	EEHOPRTXY	XEROPHYTE
EEHLLMRRY	MERRY HELL	EEHOPSSTW	SWEET SHOP
EEHLLORST	HOSTELLER	EEHORRTVW	OVERTHREW
EEHLLORSV	SHOVELLER		THREW OVER
EEHLMNSTU	SUN HELMET	EEHORRUVY	EVERY HOUR
EEHLMOORV	HOME LOVER	EEHORSSTU	HERE'S TO US

EEHORSTTW	THREE TWOS	EEILLMSST	SMELLIEST
EEHOSSSST	HOSTESSES	EEILLMSTW	SWELL TIME
EEHOSTTTW	TO THE WEST	EEILLNNTY	LENIENTLY
EEIIIMPST	IMPIETIES	EEILLNOST	LONELIEST
EEIIJSTUZ	JESUITIZE	EEILLNOTT	LITTLE ONE
EEIIKLLST	LIKELIEST	EEILLNRSS	LINERLESS
EEIIKNPST	KEEPS IT IN	EEILLNRSV	SNIVELLER
EEIIILLNTV	VITELLINE	EEILLNSSS	ILLNESSES
EEIIILLSTT	LETS IT LIE	EEILLOOST	LOOSE TILE
EEIIILLSTV	LIVELIEST	EEILLORTT	TITLE ROLE
EEIILMNNS	NINE MILES	EEILLOSTV	LOVELIEST
EEIILNNRT	INTERLINE	EEILLOTTT	LITTLE TOE
EEIILNNSV	NINE LIVES	EEILLPRTU	ILL REPUTE
EEIILNPPS	PIPELINES	EEILLQTUW	QUITE WELL
EEIILNRRV	RIVER NILE	EEILLRSST	TRELLISES
EEIILNRST	RESILIENT	EEILLRSTY	STERILELY
EEIILNSTU	LUTEINISE	EEILLRSUY	LEISURELY
EEIILNTUZ	LUTEINIZE	EEILLRSVY	SERVILELY
EEIILRSST	STERILISE	EEILLRTWW	WRITE WELL
EEIILNOTZ	STERILIZE	EEILLSUVY	ELUSIVELY
EEIILRSVW	LIVE WIRES	EEILMMNPT	IMPLEMENT
EEIIMNNST	NINE TIMES	EEILMMNSY	IMMENSELY
EEIIMOPST	EPITOMISE	EEILMMORS	SOMMELIER
EEIIMOPTZ	EPITOMIZE	EEILMMORT	MILOMETER
EEIIMORSS	ISOMERISE	EEILMNNTY	EMINENTLY
EEIIMORSZ	ISOMERIZE	EEILMNOSS	SOLEMNISE
EEIINNNNO	ONE IN NINE	EEILMNOST	LIMESTONE
EEIINNSTT	INTESTINE		MILESTONE
EEIINNSTV	INTENSIVE	EEILMNOSV	EVIL OMENS
EEIINNTVV	INVENTIVE	EEILMNOSZ	SOLEMNIZE
EEIINQRSU	ENQUIRIES	EEILMNPPR	PIMPERNEL
EEIINRSTT	ENTERITIS	EEILMNRVY	LIVERYMEN
EEIINRSTW	WINTERISE	EEILMOPSS	POLEMISES
EEIINRSVV	INVERSIVE	EEILMOPSZ	POLEMIZES
EEIINRTVW	INTERVIEW	EEILMORTT	TREMOLITE
EEIINRTWZ	WINTERIZE	EEILMOSST	LOSES TIME
EEIINSSST	SENSITISE	EEILMOSTT	MISTLETOE
EEIINSSTV	SENSITIVE	EEILMOSVW	SEMIVOWEL
EEIINSSTZ	SENSITIZE	EEILMOTVY	EMOTIVELY
EEIIOPQSU	EQUIPOISE	EEILMSSST	SET SMILES
EEIIQRSTU	REQUISITE	EEILNNPSS	PENNILESS
EEIIQSTUX	EXQUISITE	EEILNNSST	SENTINELS
EEIIRSSTT	SESTERTII	EEILNNSTY	INTENSELY
EEIIRSSTV	RESISTIVE	EEILNOORS	LOOSE REIN
EEIJKNNOT	KNEE JOINT		OLEORESIN
EEIJKNRSS	JERKINESS	EEILNOOTY	EYE LOTION
EEIJLNSUV	JUVENILES	EEILNOPRT	INTERLOPE
EEIJOSTVW	SOVIET JEW		REPLETION
EEIKKLMOS	SMOKELIKE	EEILNOPST	SLEEP ON IT
EEIKLLPST	KEEP STILL	EEILNORVW	WOLVERINE
EEIKLMORT	KILOMETRE	EEILNOSSS	NOISELESS
EEIKLORST	LORIKEETS	EEILNOSTV	NOVELTIES
EEIKLORTW	TOWERLIKE	EEILNPPSZ	ZEPPELINS
EEIKLPSST	SPIKELETS	EEILNPSSS	SPINELESS
EEIKLRTWY	TRIWEEKLY	EEILNPSTT	PESTILENT
EEIKNNPSV	PENKNIVES	EEILNPSVY	PENSIVELY
EEIKNPRSS	PERKINESS	EEILNRSST	LISTENERS
EEIKNRRST	TINKERERS	EEILNRSTT	TEN LITRES
EEIKNSTTX	SEX KITTEN	EEILNRSVY	INVERSELY
EEIKOORRS	ROOKERIES	EEILOPRST	PISTOLEER
EEIKOPTTU	KEEP IT OUT	EEILOPRTX	EXPLOITER
EEIKPPSTU	KEEPS IT UP	EEILOPSVX	EXPLOSIVE
EEIKPQTTU	KEPT QUIET	EEILORSTT	LOTTERIES
EEIKSSSUY	KEY ISSUES	EEILOSTTT	TOILETTES
EEIILLLMST	STEEL MILL	EEILPRSTY	PERISTYLE
EEIILLLNOT	TELL NO LIE	EEILPRSUV	PRELUSIVE
EEIILLLSST	TELLS LIES		PULVERISE
EEIILLLSVW	LIVES WELL		REPULSIVE
EEIILLMNOT	EMOLLIENT	EEILPRTTU	TULIP TREE
EEIILLMOPR	MILLEPORE	EEILPRUVZ	PULVERIZE
EEIILLMPRS	IMPELLERS	EEILPSUVX	EXPULSIVE

EEILRSTVY	RESTIVELY
EEILRSUVV	REVULSIVE
EEILSSSSU	ISSUELESS
EEIMMMRSS	MESMERISM
EEIMMNNTU	MINUTEMEN
EEIMMNRRT	MERRIMENT
EEIMMNRTT	REMITMENT
EEIMMORSS	MEMORISES
EEIMMORSZ	MEMORIZES
EEIMMOSST	SOMETIMES
EEIMMRRSU	SUMMERIER
EEIMMRSST	MESMERIST
EEIMMRSTW	SWIMMERET
EEIMMRSTX	EXTREMISM
EEIMNNNOT	MENNONITE
EEIMNNOOV	IN ONE MOVE
EEIMNNOTU	ONE MINUTE
EEIMNNRTT	INTERMENT
EEIMNNRTU	INUREMENT
EEIMNNSTT	SENTIMENT
EEIMNOPTX	EXEMPTION
EEIMNORSS	SERMONISE
EEIMNORSZ	SERMONIZE
EEIMNOSST	SEMITONES
EEIMNOSTZ	TIME ZONES
EEIMNOSYZ	ISOENZYME
EEIMNPQTU	EQUIPMENT
EEIMNPRSS	PRIMENESS
EEIMNPSST	EMPTINESS
EEIMNPSTT	SPENT TIME
EEIMNRRSS	MERRINESS
EEIMNRSTU	MUTINEERS
EEIMNRTTT	REMITTENT
EEIMNSSSS	MESSINESS
EEIMNSSTW	NEWS ITEMS
EEIMOPRSS	PROMISEES
EEIMOPRST	TEMPORISE
EEIMOPRTZ	TEMPORIZE
EEIMOSSST	SO IT SEEMS
EEIMOSSVW	WISE MOVES
EEIMPRRSS	SIMPERERS
EEIMPRRTT	PERMITTER
EEIMPRSSS	IMPRESSES
EEIMQSSTU	MESQUITES
EEIMRRSTT	TRIMESTER
	TRIMETERS
EEIMRSSSU	MESSIEURS
EEIMRSSTX	SIX METRES
EEIMRSSTY	MYSTERIES
EEIMRSTTX	EXTREMIST
EEIMRTTXY	EXTREMITY
EEIMSSSTY	SYSTEMISE
EEIMSSTYZ	SYSTEMIZE
EEINNNOOT	NINE TO ONE
EEINNNORT	NINE OR TEN
EEINNNOTT	TEN TO NINE
EEINNNRSU	NUNNERIES
EEINNNSTT	TENNIS NET
EEINNOPPS	NIPPONESE
EEINNOPRS	PENSIONER
EEINNOPRT	TIN OPENER
EEINNORST	TENSIONER
EEINNORTT	ENTER INTO
	RETENTION
EEINNOSTX	EXTENSION
EEINNPRST	SPINNERET
EEINNPRTT	PERTINENT
EEINNPSST	INEPTNESS
EEINNPSTT	PENITENTS
EEINNPSWY	PENNY WISE
	PENNY-WISE
EEINNRSST	INERTNESS
EEINNRSSV	NERVINESS
EEINNRSTV	REINVENTS
EEINNSSSW	NEWSINESS
EEINOPPST	PEPTONISE
EEINOPPTZ	PEPTONIZE
EEINOPRSS	ISOPRENES
EEINOPRST	INTERPOSE
	ONE STRIPE
EEINOPSUZ	SEIZE UPON
EEINOQSUX	EQUINOXES
EEINORRSV	REVERSION
EEINORTVW	INTERWOVE
EEINOSSTT	NOISETTES
EEINOSSTV	OSTENSIVE
EEINOSTTU	SEEN IT OUT
EEINPPPSS	PEPPINESS
EEINPRRTT	INTERPRET
EEINPSSTT	PETTINESS
EEINQSSTU	QUIETNESS
EEINRRRSU	REINSURER
EEINRRSSU	NURSERIES
	REINSURES
EEINRRSTV	INVERTERS
EEINRRTTW	REWRITTEN
EEINRSSTT	INTERESTS
	TRITENESS
EEINRSSTV	REINVESTS
EEINSSSTT	TESTINESS
EEINSSSTW	WITNESSES
EEINSSSUW	NEW ISSUES
EEINSSTUX	NEXT ISSUE
EEIOPPSTV	STOVEPIPE
EEIOPRRST	PORTIERES
EEIOPRSTT	POTTERIES
EEIOPRTTU	PIROUETTE
EEIOPSTTT	PETTITOES
EEIOQQUUV	EQUIVOQUE
EEIORRRST	ROISTERER
	TERRORISE
EEIORRRSV	RESERVOIR
EEIORRRTZ	TERRORIZE
EEIORRSTX	EXTERIORS
EEIORRSUV	RIVER OUSE
EEIORRTVW	OVERWRITE
EEIORSSUV	OVERISSUE
EEIORSVVW	OVERVIEWS
EEIORTTVX	EXTORTIVE
EEIOSSTTU	SEES IT OUT
EEIPPRSSS	PERSPIRES
EEIPPRSTU	PURE SPITE
EEIPRRSST	PERSISTER
EEIPRSSST	PRIESTESS
EEIPRSSUV	SUPERVISE
EEIPRSTTT	PRETTIEST
EEIPRTTWY	TYPEWRITE
EEIQRSTUU	QUITE SURE
EEIQSSTUU	QUIETUSES
EEIRRSSST	RESISTERS
EEIRRSSTV	RESERVIST
EEIRSTUVX	EXTRUSIVE
EEJMNNOTY	ENJOYMENT
EEJMPQUUU	QUEUE-JUMP
EEJNNNRWY	JENNY WREN
EEJNOQSUU	JUNOESQUE
EEJNORRUY	JOURNEYER
EEJPSSTUW	JESUS WEPT
EEKKORRWY	KEY WORKER
EEKKORSSW	SEEKS WORK
EEKLLOPSW	SPOKE WELL
EEKLMOSSS	SMOKELESS

EEKLNOOTV	LOVE TOKEN	EELOPRSSW	POWERLESS
EEKLNORRS	SNORKELER	EELOPRSTT	TELEPORTS
EEKLNOSST	SKELETONS	EELOPRSTV	OVERSLEPT
EEKLNPRSU	SPELUNKER	EELOPRSTY	POLYESTER
EEKMMNOTY	KEY MOMENT		PROSELYTE
EEKMNOPSS	SPOKESMEN	EELOPSSTU	SLEEPS OUT
EEKNOORST	ONE STROKE	EELORRRSS	ERRORLESS
EEKNOOTTV	TOKEN VOTE	EELORRSUV	OVERRULES
EEKNORRWY	NEW YORKER	EELORRSVV	REVOLVERS
EEKNOSSTY	KEYSTONES	EELORSSUV	OURSELVES
EEKOORTWW	WEEK OR TWO	EELORSTUV	REVOLUTES
EELLLLSSW	SELLS WELL		TRUELOVES
EELLLPSTW	SLEPT WELL	EELPRSSXY	EXPRESSLY
EELLMNOOS	LEMON SOLE	EELPRSTUU	SEPULTURE
EELLMOSTW	MELLOWEST	EELPSSTTU	SETTLES UP
EELLNNOOT	TELL NO ONE	EELPSSTUX	SEXTUPLES
EELLNOPRT	PORT ELLEN	EELPSTTUX	SEXTUPLET
EELLNOSTW	NOTES WELL	EEMMNNOOT	ONE MOMENT
EELLNPSTW	WELL SPENT	EEMMNNOORT	METRONOME
EELLOOSST	LETS LOOSE		MONOTREME
EELLOOSTW	STEEL WOOL	EEMMNOORY	MORE MONEY
EELLOPPRR	PROPELLER	EEMMNOSTV	MOVEMENTS
EELLOPSST	LOST SLEEP	EEMMOORST	OSMOMETER
EELLORSSV	OVERSELLS	EEMMRSTUW	WET SUMMER
EELLORSVY	VOLLEYERS	EEMNOOPST	TONE POEMS
EELLORTWW	WROTE WELL	EEMNOORTT	TONOMETER
EELLOSTUV	LEVELS OUT	EEMNOOSTT	TOMENTOSE
EELLOSTWY	YELLOWEST	EEMNOOSWY	OWES MONEY
EELLPSSSY	SYLLEPSES	EEMNOPRYZ	PROENZYME
EELLPSSTW	WET SPELLS	EEMNORRTT	TORMENTER
EELLPSTUW	WELL SET UP	EEMNOSTVX	NEXT MOVES
EELLSSSTY	STYLELESS	EEMNRRTUY	MERRY TUNE
EELLSSSUY	USELESSLY	EEMNSSTTV	VESTMENTS
EELMMNOTU	EMOLUMENT	EEMOOPPRS	PROSE POEM
EELMMNNORT	ENROLMENT	EEMOORSVV	MOVES OVER
EELMNNOTY	LENT MONEY	EEMOPPRRT	PREEMPTOR
EELMNOOSY	LOSE MONEY	EEMOPRRTY	PYROMETER
EELMNOOUV	VOLUME ONE	EEMORSTTW	TWO METRES
EELMNOSST	SOLEMNEST	EEMPRRTTU	TRUMPETER
EELMNOTTX	EXTOLMENT	EEMPRSSTT	TEMPTRESS
EELMNOTUV	VOLUME TEN	EEMPRSTTU	TREE STUMP
EELMNRSTU	ULSTERMEN	EENNNOSTV	NONEVENTS
EELMOOPSV	LOVE POEMS	EENNOPRSS	PRONENESS
EELMOOPTT	TOTEM POLE	EENNOPSTX	EXPONENTS
EELMOPRTU	PETROLEUM	EENNOTTWY	TWENTY-ONE
EELMORTTV	VOLTMETER	EENNRSSST	STERNNESS
EELMPRSTU	PLUM TREES	EENOORRSU	ERRONEOUS
EELMPRSUY	SUPREMELY	EENOORSTV	OVERTONES
EELNNOOSS	LESSON ONE	EENOPPRSU	OPEN PURSE
EELNNOPRS	PERSONNEL	EENOPRSSS	PRESSES ON
EELNNOSST	LESSON TEN		RESPONSES
EELNNOSVW	NEW NOVELS	EENOPRSTT	ENTREPOTS
EELNOORSW	SOLE OWNER	EENOPRSTV	NEVER STOP
EELNOOSSS	LOOSENESS		OVERSPENT
EELNOPPRY	PROPYLENE	EENOPRSXY	PYROXENES
EELNOPSTU	PLENTEOUS	EENOPSTTY	STENOTYPE
EELNORSST	ENTRESOLS	EENOQSTUW	TWO QUEENS
EELNORSTV	RESOLVENT	EENORSSTX	EXTENSORS
EELNORTUV	VOLUNTEER	EENORSTTT	ROTTENEST
EELNOSSST	NET LOSSES	EENRSSTUW	WET NURSES
EELNOSSTT	SETTLES ON		WET-NURSES
EELNPRSTY	PRESENTLY	EEOOPRRSV	PORES OVER
EELNRSTTU	NET RESULT	EEOOPRRVW	OVERPOWER
EELNSSTTU	UNSETTLES	EEOORRTVW	OVERWROTE
EELNSSTWY	NEW STYLES	EEOOSSSTX	EXOSTOSES
EELOOPPPT	TOP PEOPLE	EEOPPPPRT	PEPPER POT
EELOOSSST	SETS LOOSE	EEOPPRSSS	OPPRESSES
EELOPPRSS	PROLEPSES	EEOPPRSSU	SUPERPOSE
EELOPRRSX	EXPLORERS	EEOPPRTTW	PEWTER POT
EELOPRRTU	POULTERER	EEOPRRRSS	REPRESSOR
EELOPRSSU	PELORUSES	EEOPRRRST	REPORTERS

EEOPRRRTY	REPERTORY	EFFIORSTW	WRITE-OFFS
EEOPRRSTT	PROTESTER		WRITES OFF
EEOPRRSTX	EXPORTERS	EFFIORSUV	FOUR FIVES
EEOPRRTUV	PROVE TRUE	EFFIORTVY	FORTY-FIVE
EEOPRSSSS	ESPRESSOS		OVER FIFTY
	REPOSSESS	EFFISSTTT	STIFF TEST
EEOPRSSTV	OVERSTEPS	EFFISSTTU	STUFFIEST
	STEPS OVER	EFFISSUUV	SUFFUSIVE
EEOPRSSUX	EXPOSURES	EFFLLOOUW	FULL OF WOE
EEOPRSTTU	PETERS OUT	EFFLLOPPU	FULL OF PEP
EEOPRTTWY	TYPEWROTE	EFFLLRTUY	FRETFULLY
EEOPSSSSS	POSSESSES	EFFLMPSUU	MUFFLES UP
EEOPSSTUW	SWEEPS OUT	EFFLNNTUY	FELT FUNNY
EEORRSSTU	RETROUSSE	EFFLNRSSU	SNUFFLERS
EEORRSTTX	EXTORTERS	EFFLOOPSS	SLOPES OFF
EEORRSTUV	OVERTURES	EFFMMNOOT	OFF MOMENT
	TROUVERES	EFFNOORRT	FOREFRONT
EEORRTTVX	EXTROVERT	EFFOORRTY	OFFERTORY
EEORSSSTT	SETS STORE	EFFOORSTU	SET OF FOUR
EEORSSTUV	SERVES OUT	EFFOOSSST	TOSSES OFF
EEORSSTUW	SOU'WESTER	EFFORSTUV	OVERSTUFF
EEORSSTVW	TWO VERSES	EFGGIINNR	FINGERING
EEPPRSSSU	PRESSES UP	EFGGILNNU	ENGULFING
EEPRRSSST	PRESTRESS	EFGGILOOS	SOLFEGGIO
EEPRRSSSU	PRESSURES	EFGGINOOR	FOREGOING
EEPRRSTTU	SPUTTERER	EFGGINOSS	FOGGINESS
EEPRSSTTU	UPSETTERS	EFGHHIILR	HIGH FLIER
EERRSTTTU	STUTTERER		HIGH-FLIER
EFFFIILSTU	FLUFFIEST	EFGHHIILS	FLIES HIGH
EFFFIMORR	FIRM OFFER	EFGHIILNT	NIGHT LIFE
EFFFLORTU	EFFORTFUL		NIGHTLIFE
EFFGGINOR	GOFFERING	EFGHIILRT	FIRELIGHT
EFFGHIIRT	FIGHT FIRE		FLIGHTIER
	FIREFIGHT	EFGHIINRT	INFIGHTER
EFFGHNOTU	GEOFF HUNT	EFGHIJLTT	JET FLIGHT
EFFGILNSU	GLUE-SNIFF	EFGHILNSS	FLESHINGS
	SNIFF GLUE	EFGHILRTT	FELT RIGHT
EFFGILSST	STIFF LEGS	EFGHILTWY	FLYWEIGHT
EFFGINORS	OFFERINGS	EFGHINRST	FRIGHTENS
EFFGINRSU	SUFFERING	EFGHIORST	FORESIGHT
EFFGLORTU	FORGETFUL		GIFT HORSE
EFFGNOOPS	SPONGE OFF	EFGHIORTV	GIVE FORTH
EFFGNRSSU	GRUFFNESS	EFGHLOOPR	GO FOR HELP
EFFHHIRSS	FRESH FISH	EFGHNOORT	GONE FORTH
EFFHIIKNS	FISH KNIFE	EFGHOORST	GOES FORTH
EFFHIILSS	FISH FLIES	EFGHORRTU	GO FURTHER
EFFHIIMTT	FIFTH TIME	EFGIIILNS	LIGNIFIES
EFFHIKSWW	SKEW-WHIFF	EFGIIINRS	SIGNIFIER
EFFHILRSW	WHIFFLERS	EFGIIINSS	SIGNIFIES
EFFHINSSU	HUFFINESS	EFGIILLNT	FILLETING
EFFHISTTT	FIFTH TEST	EFGIILNPR	PILFERING
EFFHLRSSU	SHUFFLERS	EFGIILNRT	FILTERING
EFFHOOSSV	SHOVES OFF	EFGIILORR	GLORIFIER
EFFHOPSSU	PUSHES OFF	EFGIILORS	GLORIFIES
EFFIILNOS	LIFE OF SIN	EFGIINNRR	INFERRING
EFFIIORRT	FORTIFIER	EFGIINNRS	INFRINGES
EFFIIORST	FORTIFIES	EFGIINNSS	FINESSING
EFFIIORSU	SQUIFFIER	EFGIINNST	INFESTING
EFFIKORST	STRIKE OFF	EFGIINPRT	FINGERTIP
EFFILLLRU	FULFILLER	EFGIINPRX	PREFIXING
EFFILLORT	FELL FOR IT	EFGIINRSU	FIGURINES
EFFILMUUV	EFFLUVIUM	EFGIINRTT	REFITTING
EFFILNOUX	EFFLUXION	EFGIINRVY	VERIFYING
EFFILNRSS	SNIFFLERS	EFGIIRSUX	FIGURE SIX
EFFIMOORV	FOVEIFORM	EFGIISTUV	FUGITIVES
EFFINOSSU	EFFUSIONS	EFGIKNOTT	GIFT TOKEN
EFFINPSSU	PUFFINESS	EFGILNORW	FLOWERING
EFFINSSST	STIFFNESS	EFGILNRUX	REFLUXING
EFFIOOPRR	FIREPROOF	EFGILNSTW	LEFT-WINGS
EFFIORSTU	FIT FOR USE	EFGILPRSU	FIRE-PLUGS
		EFGILRTUU	FULGURITE

EFGIMNNOT	FOMENTING	EFHLLORST	FELL SHORT
EFGIMNORR	REFORMING	EFHLLOSST	SOFT-SHELL
EFGIMNPRU	PERFUMING	EFHLLOSUU	FULL HOUSE
EFGINNOOR	GONE IN FOR		HOUSE FULL
EFGINNOST	SOFTENING	EFHLLOSUV	SHOVELFUL
EFGINNOTW	FIG NEWTON	EFHLLOTTU	TO THE FULL
EFGINOORS	GOES IN FOR	EFHLLTTWY	TWELFTHLY
EFGINOORT	GONE FOR IT	EFHLMNOOW	FLOWN HOME
EFGINOOSS	GOOFINESS	EFHLNORTW	FLEW NORTH
EFGINORST	FORESTING	EFHLNSSSU	FLUSHNESS
	FOSTERING	EFHLOPSST	FLESH POTS
	GONE FIRST		FLESHPOTS
EFGINPRSU	PERFUSING	EFHLOSTUW	FLEW SOUTH
EFGIOORST	GOES FOR IT	EFHMNOORT	HOME FRONT
EFGIOPSTT	PETTIFOGS	EFHNOOORT	ON THE ROOF
EFGIORRUV	FRUGIVORE	EFHNOORSW	FORESHOWN
EFGIORSST	GOES FIRST	EFHNOORTU	ONE FOURTH
EFGIORSSV	FIVE GROSS	EFHNORRTU	FURTHER ON
EFGIORSTT	FORGETS IT		NO FURTHER
EFGIONTUU	FIGURE OUT	EFHNORSTT	SENT FORTH
EFGIORTUW	FIGURE TWO	EFHNORTTW	WENT FORTH
EFGIRRTUW	GREW FRUIT	EFHNORTUX	FOXHUNTER
EFGKLOOPR	LEG OF PORK	EFHOORSSW	FORESHOWS
EFGLLLNTUY	FULGENTLY	EFHOPRSSU	PUSHES FOR
EFGLOOSVX	FOXGLOVES	EFHORSSTT	SETS FORTH
EFGLOOTUV	TUG OF LOVE	EFHORSTTU	FOURTH SET
EFGLORSUV	FUR GLOVES	EFHPRRTUU	FURTHER UP
EFGMOOPRR	GERMPROOF	EFIIILRSV	VILIFIERS
EFGNOORTT	FORGOTTEN	EFIIINNST	INFINITES
EFGOOOOST	GOOSEFOOT	EFIIINRST	NITRIFIES
EFGOOPRRS	GROPES FOR	EFIIIRSTV	VITRIFIES
EFHHIINST	THE FINISH	EFIIIRSVV	VIVIFIERS
EFHHIISTW	WHITEFISH	EFIIJRSTU	JUSTIFIER
EFHHILLSS	SHELLFISH	EFIIJSSTU	JUSTIFIES
EFHHNOOOT	ON THE HOOF	EFIIKLLNT	FLINTLIKE
EFHIILNTT	IN THE LIFT	EFIIKLOSV	FIVE KILOS
EFHIILSTT	FILTHIEST	EFIIKRSST	FRISKIEST
EFHIIMOOT	FETISHISM	EFIILLLST	STILL LIFE
EFHIINRSS	FINISHERS	EFIILLMOS	MOLLIFIES
EFHIIORRS	HORRIFIES	EFIILLNSU	NULLIFIES
EFHIIRRSV	RIVER FISH	EFIILMNSS	FILMINESS
EFHIISSTT	FETISHIST	EFIILMSST	FLIMSIEST
	SHIFTIEST	EFIILNOPR	IN PROFILE
EFHIISSVW	FISHWIVES	EFIILNRST	FILTERS IN
EFHIJLLSY	JELLYFISH		FIRST LINE
EFHIKLMRS	FRESH MILK	EFIILOSSS	FOSSILISE
EFHIKLNPS	FLESH PINK	EFIILOSSZ	FOSSILIZE
EFHILLPRU	FILL HER UP	EFIILPRTT	FILTER TIP
EFHILLSSY	SELFISHLY	EFIILRRSV	SILVER FIR
EFHILNOTT	IN THE LOFT	EFIILRSSU	FUSILIERS
EFHILNSSU	UNSELFISH	EFIILRTTY	FERTILITY
EFHILNSTT	FLESH TINT	EFIIMMMSU	MUMMIFIES
EFHILORST	RIFLE SHOT	EFIIMNSST	FEMINISTS
	SHORT LIFE	EFIIMORST	MORTIFIES
EFHILSSST	SHIFTLESS	EFIIMRSTT	FIRST TIME
EFHIMOPRS	FIRM HOPES	EFIIMRSTY	MYSTIFIER
EFHIMORST	FIRST HOME	EFIIMSSTY	MYSTIFIES
EFHINRRSU	FURNISHER	EFIINNOPT	FINE POINT
EFHINRSSU	FURNISHES	EFIINNSTY	INTENSIFY
EFHIOPSTT	STOP THIEF!	EFIINORRS	FIRE IRONS
EFHIORSST	FIRE SHOTS	EFIINPSTV	FIVE PINTS
EFHIORSTT	FROTHIEST	EFIIORSVX	FIVE OR SIX
EFHIORSUV	FIVE HOURS	EFIIOSTVX	FIVE TO SIX
EFHIOSSTU	FISHES OUT	EFIIPRRTU	RIPE FRUIT
EFHIRSSTT	THE FIRSTS	EFIIPRSST	SPITFIRES
EFHKLOORS	LOOK FRESH	EFIIPRSTU	FRUIT PIES
EFHKLOOST	LEFT HOOKS	EFIIRSTTU	FRUITIEST
EFHLLLPUY	HELPFULLY	EFIISTTVY	FESTIVITY
EFHLLNPUU	UNHELPFUL	EFIKLORSW	LIFES WORK
EFHLLOPUY	HOPEFULLY	EFIKNNOTX	NEXT OF KIN
EFHLLORRS	FRESH ROLL	EFIKNNSSU	FUNKINESS

EFIKNORSS	FORESKINS	EFKNNOORW	FOREKNOWN
EFIKORRSW	FIREWORKS	EFKNOOPRS	SPOKEN FOR
EFILLLSSW	SELF-WILLS	EFKNOORSW	FOREKNOWS
EFILLLSTY	FELT SILLY	EFLLLMOSU	FOUL SMELL
EFILLNPTU	PLENTIFUL	EFLLLOOWW	LOW FELLOW
EFILLOOSS	FLIES SOLO	EFLLMORUW	RUM FELLOW
EFILLOTTX	LITTLE FOX	EFLLMOSUY	FULSOMELY
EFILLPRUY	FULLY RIPE	EFLLNTUUY	TUNEFULLY
EFILLQTUU	QUITE FULL	EFLLOORSW	FOLLOWERS
EFILMNORS	FORM LINES	EFLLPRSUU	FULL PURSE
EFILMNOSY	SOLEMNIFY	EFLLRSTUY	RESTFULLY
EFILMOPRX	PLEXIFORM	EFLMMOSUX	FLUMMOXES
EFILMORSU	FOUR MILES	EFLMOORRW	LOWER FORM
EFILNNORT	FRONT LINE	EFLMOORSS	LOSES FORM
	FRONT-LINE	EFLNOOOPR	OPEN FLOOR
EFILNNSTU	INFLUENTS	EFLNOORSW	NO FLOWERS
EFILNOOSU	FELONIOUS	EFLNOORVW	FLOWN OVER
EFILNOOTU	OUT OF LINE		OVERFLOWN
EFILNOSST	LOFTINESS	EFLNORSUW	SUNFLOWER
EFILOORST	TILE ROOFS	EFLNOSTWW	FLOWN WEST
EFILOPPST	FLOPPIEST	EFLNRSTTU	TURNS LEFT
EFILORSTV	FIRST LOVE	EFLOOOOST	FOOTLOOSE
EFILORSTY	LIFE STORY	EFLOOOTUV	OUT OF LOVE
EFILORSVX	SILVER FOX	EFLOOPRTW	FLOWERPOT
EFILOTUZZ	FIZZLE OUT	EFLOORSTU	FOOTRULES
EFILPRSTU	UPLIFTERS	EFLOORSVW	FLOWS OVER
EFILPSTUU	USEFUL TIP		OVERFLOWS
EFILRRSTU	FIRST RULE	EFLOORTTT	LEFT TO ROT
EFILRSSTU	FRUITLESS	EFLOORTVY	FORTY LOVE
EFILRTUVY	FURTIVELY		LOVE FORTY
EFIMMORRS	REFORMISM	EFLOPRSUY	PROFUSELY
EFIMMORRV	VERMIFORM	EFLORRSTY	FELT SORRY
EFIMNNTUY	FUNNY TIME	EFLORSSTU	FUR STOLES
EFIMNORRS	INFORMERS	EFLRSSSTU	STRESSFUL
EFIMOOTTU	OUT OF TIME	EFLRSSTUU	FRUSTULES
EFIMORRST	REFORMIST	EFMNORRTY	ENTRY FORM
EFIMORSTU	FOUR TIMES	EFMOORSSU	FOURSOMES
EFIMORSTV	FIRST MOVE	EFNNOPRUY	FOURPENNY
EFIMRRSTT	FIRST TERM	EFNOOORTU	FOUR TO ONE
EFINNNSSU	FUNNINESS	EFNOOOSTT	FOOTNOTES
EFINNOORU	FOUR IN ONE		SET ON FOOT
	ONE IN FOUR	EFNOORSST	FOSTER SON
EFINNORSU	FOUR NINES	EFNOORSSW	SWORN FOES
EFINNORTW	WENT IN FOR	EFNOORTTU	TEN TO FOUR
EFINNSSTU	UNFITNESS	EFNOORTUZ	FROZEN OUT
EFINOPRST	FINE SPORT	EFNOOTTUU	OUT OF TUNE
	FIT PERSON	EFNOPRSTT	FRONT STEP
EFINOPRSU	FIRES UPON	EFNOPSSTU	SOFTENS UP
	PERFUSION	EFOOOPRRV	OVERPROOF
EFINOPRSY	PERSONIFY	EFOOOPRRSS	PROFESSOR
EFINOPRTT	NET PROFIT	EFOOPRRTX	FOR EXPORT
EFINORRST	FRONTIERS	EFOOPSSTT	FOOTSTEPS
EFINORTTW	WENT FOR IT	EFOOPSTTU	OUT OF STEP
EFINORTVW	FRONT VIEW	EFOOQRRTU	ROQUEFORT
EFINRRTUU	FURNITURE	EFOORRTVY	OVER FORTY
EFINRSTTW	WENT FIRST	EFOORTTUU	OUT OF TRUE
EFINSSSSU	FUSSINESS	EGGGIIJNR	REJIGGING
EFINSSSTU	FUSTINESS	EGGGIILNT	LEGGING IT
EFINSSSTW	SWIFTNESS	EGGGINNOR	ENGORGING
EFINSSUZZ	FUZZINESS	EGGGINORY	GOING GREY
EFIOOTTVW	FIVE TO TWO	EGGGINOST	GETS GOING
EFIOPRTTU	PETIT FOUR	EGGGINOTT	GO-GETTING
EFIORRSTT	RETROFITS	EGGGIORST	GROGGIEST
EFIORSSTT	FROSTIEST	EGGGOOOSS	GOOSEGOGS
EFIORSSTW	FROWSIEST	EGGHIILNS	SLEIGHING
EFIORSSUX	FOUR SIXES	EGGHIINTW	WEIGHTING
EFIORTTTU	OUTFITTER	EGGHILRTY	LIGHT GREY
EFIPRSSTT	FIRST STEP	EGGHIMNOO	GOING HOME
EFIRSSTTT	FIRST TEST	EGGHINNRU	HUNGERING
EFJKNNOUY	FUNNY JOKE	EGGHINORT	GONE RIGHT
EFKLMNOOW	WOMENFOLK	EGGHIORST	GOES RIGHT

EGGHIRSTT	GETS RIGHT	EGHIILNTW	LIGHT WINE
EGGHORSTU	GETS ROUGH	EGHIILTWY	WEIGHTILY
EGGHOSTTU	GETS TOUGH	EGHIIMMNN	HEMMING IN
EGGIILNNR	LINGERING	EGHIIMNTT	NIGHT TIME
EGGIINNRS	RESIGNING	EGHIIMRTT	RIGHT TIME
EGGIINNST	INGESTING	EGHIIMSTT	MIGHTIEST
EGGIINNSW	SWINGEING	EGHIINNTW	WHITENING
EGGIINNTT	GETTING IN	EGHIINPRS	PERISHING
EGGIINNTW	TWINGEING	EGHIINPRT	IN THE GRIP
EGGIINSSV	GIVE SIGNS	EGHIINRSV	SHIVERING
EGGIINTTT	GETTING IT	EGHIINRTT	TIGHT REIN
EGGIKNOPT	KEPT GOING	EGHIINRTW	WITHERING
EGGILLNOW	GOING WELL	EGHIINSTV	GIVE HINTS
EGGILLNRU	GRUELLING	EGHIINSTY	HYGIENIST
EGGILMNSU	SMUGGLE IN	EGHIIRSTZ	RIGHT SIZE
EGGILNNOR	LONG REIGN	EGHIITTTW	GET WITH IT
EGGILNORW	GLOWERING	EGHIKLOST	GHOSTLIKE
EGGILNOTT	LETTING GO	EGHIKNNRY	KING HENRY
EGGILOOST	GEOLOGIST	EGHIKNORS	KOSHERING
EGGILOSSU	EGUIGGLES	EGHIKPSTT	KEPT SIGHT
EGGILRR3W	WRIGGLERS	EGHILLNOR	HOLLERING
EGGIMNORT	GINGER TOM	EGHILLNOW	LONG WHILE
EGGIMNOTV	GET MOVING	EGHILLSST	LIGHTLESS
EGGIMNSSU	MUGGINESS	EGHILNNOT	NEON LIGHT
EGGINNORV	GOVERNING	EGHILNPPU	HELPING UP
EGGINNOTT	GETTING ON	EGHILNRTU	THIN GRUEL
EGGINNPUX	EXPUNGING	EGHILNSST	LIGHTNESS
EGGINNRTU	GINGER NUT	EGHILNSTU	SLEUTHING
EGGINOORT	GOITROGEN	EGHILORUV	LIVE ROUGH
EGGINOORV	GOING OVER	EGHILOSST	LOSE SIGHT
	GOING-OVER	EGHILRTTU	TRUE LIGHT
EGGINOPPR	GINGER POP	EGHILRTVY	VERY LIGHT
EGGINORTY	TONY GREIG	EGHILSSST	SIGHTLESS
EGGINUSSS	SOGGINESS	EGHILSSTT	SLIGHTEST
EGGINOSTW	GOING WEST	EGHILTTUY	THE GUILTY
EGGINPRSU	GINGERS UP	EGHIMNORT	MOTHERING
EGGINPTTU	GETTING UP	EGHIMNOST	SOMETHING
EGGINRSTU	GESTURING	EGHIMORTT	TIGER MOTH
EGGINRTTU	GUTTERING	EGHIMORTU	ROUGH TIME
EGGIORRTU	OUTRIGGER	EGHIMORTV	RIGHT MOVE
EGGLMRSSU	SMUGGLERS	EGHIMPPSU	PEMPHIGUS
EGGLNPSUU	SNUGGLE UP	EGHINNOTW	ON THE WING
EGGLRRSTU	STRUGGLER	EGHINNSTU	ENTHUSING
EGGLRSSTU	STRUGGLES	EGHINOORV	HOOVERING
EGGNNOORW	GONE WRONG	EGHINOPRT	POTHERING
EGGNOOPSS	EGG SPOONS	EGHINORSU	REHOUSING
EGGNOORSW	GOES WRONG	EGHINORSW	SHOWERING
EGGNORSTW	GETS WRONG	EGHINORTT	RIGHT NOTE
EGHHIIOPS	HIGH HOPES	EGHINORTV	OVERNIGHT
EGHHHIORS	HIGH HORSE	EGHINORTX	EXHORTING
EGHHIIRSW	HIGH WIRES	EGHINOTTW	TON WEIGHT
EGHHIMTTY	THE MIGHTY	EGHINPRST	THE SPRING
EGHHINNPY	HYPHENING	EGHINPTTU	TIGHTEN UP
EGHHINOST	HIGH NOTES	EGHINRSST	RIGHTNESS
EGHHINRST	HIGH RENTS	EGHINRSTU	HUNGRIEST
	THRESHING		SURE THING
EGHHIORTW	HIGH TOWER	EGHINRTTW	WENT RIGHT
EGHHIPRSU	HIGHER-UPS	EGHINSSTT	TIGHTNESS
EGHHLOOTT	HOG THE LOT	EGHIOOSTW	HOW GOES IT?
EGHHLOPTU	THE PLOUGH	EGHIOPPTT	GOT THE PIP
EGHHMOTTU	METHOUGHT	EGHIOPRTT	TIGHTROPE
EGHHNORUW	ROUGH-HEWN	EGHIORSTU	RIGHTEOUS
EGHHORSUW	ROUGH-HEWS	EGHIORSTV	OVERSIGHT
EGHHORTTU	RETHOUGHT	EGHIOSTUW	OUTWEIGHS
EGHIIKNRS	SHRIEKING	EGHIRRSTY	GREY SHIRT
EGHIIKNTW	WHITE KING	EGHIRSSTT	SETS RIGHT
EGHIILLMT	LIMELIGHT	EGHIRSTTU	THEURGIST
EGHIILNNS	IN ENGLISH	EGHJLNNNO	JOHN GLENN
EGHIILNRS	HIRELINGS	EGHLLOORY	GLORY HOLE
	RELISHING	EGHLMNOPU	PLOUGHMEN
EGHIILNRT	RIGHT LINE	EGHLMOOOU	HOMOLOGUE

397

EGHLNOOSU	HUNG LOOSE	EGIINNRSW	INSWINGER
EGHLNOOTY	ETHNOLOGY	EGIINNRTU	REUNITING
EGHLNOPYY	PHYLOGENY	EGIINNRTV	INVERTING
EGHLOOORR	HOROLOGER	EGIINNRTW	WINTERING
EGHLORSST	SHORT LEGS	EGIINNSTT	SETTING IN
EGHMNOORW	HOME GROWN	EGIINNSTV	INVESTING
	HOMEGROWN	EGIINNTUY	INGENUITY
EGHNNOORT	GONE NORTH	EGIINOPRS	PEIGNOIRS
EGHNOORST	GOES NORTH	EGIINOPST	POETISING
	GONE SHORT	EGIINOPTT	TIPTOEING
EGHNOORTU	ROUGH NOTE	EGIINOPTZ	POETIZING
EGHNOOSTU	GONE SOUTH	EGIINOSTV	GIVES IN TO
EGHNOPTUU	TOUGHEN UP	EGIINPPQU	EQUIPPING
EGHNORSSU	ROUGHNESS	EGIINPRRS	RESPIRING
EGHNOSSTU	TOUGHNESS		SPRINGIER
EGHNRSSTT	STRENGTHS	EGIINPRRZ	PRIZE RING
EGHOORSST	GOES SHORT	EGIINPSUZ	SEIZING UP
EGHOOSSTU	GOES SOUTH	EGIINPTUV	GIVEN IT UP
EGIIIMNST	ITEMISING	EGIINQRRU	REQUIRING
EGIIIMNTZ	ITEMIZING	EGIINQRTU	REQUITING
EGIIINPRX	PIXIE RING	EGIINQRUV	QUIVERING
EGIIJNNNO	ENJOINING	EGIINRRST	STRINGIER
EGIIJNNOR	REJOINING	EGIINRRTU	INTRIGUER
EGIIJNRTT	JITTERING	EGIINRRTW	REWRITING
EGIIKLPTV	KEPT VIGIL	EGIINRSST	RESISTING
EGIIKNNRT	TINKERING	EGIINRSSU	REISSUING
EGIIKNNTT	KITTENING	EGIINRSTU	INTRIGUES
EGIIKNPPR	KIPPERING	EGIINRTTT	TITTERING
EGIILLMNP	IMPELLING	EGIINRTTY	INTEGRITY
EGIILLNRT	TILLERING	EGIINSSTT	STINGIEST
EGIILLRTY	TIGER LILY	EGIINSSTX	EXIT SIGNS
EGIILMMRS	GRIM SMILE	EGIIRSTTT	GRITTIEST
EGIILNNOT	GOT IN LINE	EGIJKNNTU	JUNKETING
EGIILNNST	ENLISTING	EGIJNPRRU	PERJURING
	LISTENING	EGIKLNNOO	INGLE NOOK
EGIILNNTT	ENTITLING		INGLENOOK
	LETTING IN	EGIKMNNOY	MONKEYING
EGIILNNUV	UNVEILING	EGIKMNORS	SMOKE RING
EGIILNORS	RELIGIONS	EGIKNORRW	REWORKING
EGIILNORT	LOITERING	EGILLLNTY	TELLINGLY
EGIILNRSV	SILVERING	EGILLMNTY	MELTINGLY
	SLIVERING	EGILLMORU	GLOMERULI
EGIILNRTT	LITTERING	EGILLMOTU	GUILLEMOT
EGIILNTTY	GENTILITY	EGILLNNOR	ENROLLING
EGIILORST	TRILOGIES	EGILLNNOS	LONG LINES
EGIILORSU	RELIGIOUS	EGILLNNOT	NO TELLING
EGIILRSST	GRISLIEST		TELLING ON
EGIILRSTU	LITURGIES	EGILLNORS	NEGRILLOS
EGIILRSZZ	GRIZZLIES	EGILLNOTT	ILL-GOTTEN
EGIILSTTU	GUILTIEST	EGILLNOTW	TOWELLING
EGIIMMNRS	IMMERSING	EGILLNOTX	EXTOLLING
	SIMMERING	EGILLNOVY	VOLLEYING
EGIIMNOPS	EPIGONISM	EGILLNOWY	YELLOWING
EGIIMNPRS	PREMISING	EGILLNPSS	SPELLINGS
	SIMPERING	EGILLNPUW	WELLING UP
EGIIMNRSS	GRIMINESS	EGILLNSSW	SWELLINGS
EGIIMNRTT	REMITTING	EGILLOSSY	SYLLOGISE
EGIIMOPST	IMPETIGOS	EGILLOSYZ	SYLLOGIZE
EGIINNNRT	INTERNING	EGILMNOOS	NEOLOGISM
EGIINNNTV	INVENTING	EGILMNOPY	EMPLOYING
EGIINNNTW	ENTWINING	EGILMNOST	MOLESTING
EGIINNORS	SIGNORINE	EGILMOOST	GLOOMIEST
EGIINNORT	ORIENTING	EGILMOOSY	SEMIOLOGY
EGIINNORZ	ZEROING IN	EGILNNORS	LINGERS ON
EGIINNOST	INGESTION	EGILNNOST	SINGLETON
EGIINNOSU	INGENIOUS	EGILNNOTT	LETTING ON
EGIINNOTV	GIVEN IN TO	EGILNNOUY	NEIL YOUNG
EGIINNQRU	ENQUIRING	EGILNNPSU	PLUNGES IN
EGIINNRRT	INTERRING	EGILNNSST	NESTLINGS
EGIINNRST	INSERTING	EGILNNSTW	LENT WINGS
	SINTERING	EGILNNVYY	ENVYINGLY

EGILNOORT	RETOOLING	EGINRSUVY	SURVEYING
EGILNOOST	ENOLOGIST	EGINRTTUX	TEXTURING
EGILNOOSU	SINOLOGUE	EGINSSSTU	GUSTINESS
EGILNOPRX	EXPLORING		GUTSINESS
EGILNORSV	RESOLVING	EGIOORSTV	GROOVIEST
EGILNORTV	REVOLTING	EGIORSTTT	GROTTIEST
EGILNORVV	REVOLVING	EGIPSSSUU	GUSSIES UP
EGILNOSTT	SONG TITLE	EGJLNORSU	JONGLEURS
EGILNOSTU	SINGLE OUT	EGKNOOTTW	GET TO KNOW
EGILNOTVY	LONGEVITY	EGKORSSUW	GUESSWORK
EGILNPRSU	REPULSING	EGLLLNOPS	LONG SPELL
EGILNPTTU	LETTING UP	EGLLMNORY	MONGRELLY
EGILNRSTU	RESULTING	EGLLNOOTW	GOT ON WELL
EGILNRSTW	WRESTLING	EGLLNOOVW	LONG VOWEL
EGILNSSST	STINGLESS	EGLMNOOOU	MONOLOGUE
EGILOQTUY	GO QUIETLY	EGLMOOTYY	ETYMOLOGY
EGILOSSST	GLOSSIEST	EGLNNOORS	LONGERONS
EGIMMNRSU	SUMMERING	EGLNNOSUU	SUN LOUNGE
EGIMMNNOSS	NO MESSING		SUNLOUNGE
EGIMNORSV	MISGOVERN	EGLNOOPRR	PROLONGER
EGIMNORTW	WRONG TIME	EGLNOOPRS	LONG ROPES
EGIMNPRSU	PRESUMING	EGLNOORUY	NEUROLOGY
EGIMNPRTU	PERMUTING	EGLNOOSSV	LOVE SONGS
EGIMNPSSU	MESSING UP	EGLNOOSTW	ON TWO LEGS
EGIMNRSSY	SYNERGISM	EGLNOOUVY	YOUNG LOVE
EGIMNRSTU	MUSTERING	EGLNOPRSU	LONG PURSE
EGIMNRTTU	MUTTERING	EGLNORSUU	LONGUEURS
EGIMPRSTU	GRUMPIEST	EGLNOSTUU	GLUTENOUS
EGINNNOSS	NEON SIGNS	EGLOOPRSU	PROLOGUES
EGINNNRUV	UNNERVING	EGLOOPRTY	PETROLOGY
EGINNOPPU	OPENING UP	EGLOOPSTY	LOGOTYPES
EGINNOSTT	SETTING ON	EGLOORSSV	GLOSS OVER
EGINNOSUU	INGENUOUS	EGMNOORVW	WRONG MOVE
EGINNRRTU	RETURNING	EGMOORSTU	GUEST ROOM
EGINNRSTT	STRINGENT	EGNNNRRUU	GUN RUNNER
EGINNRSTU	INSURGENT		GUNRUNNER
EGINNRTUV	VENTURING	EGNNOORTW	WRONG NOTE
EGINNTTUV	VINGT ET UN	EGNNORSSW	WRONGNESS
	VINGT-ET-UN	EGNNORTWW	WENT WRONG
EGINOOPSU	EPIGONOUS	EGNNOSSUY	YOUNGNESS
EGINOOPPRS	POP SINGER	EGNOOOPTT	GONE TO POT
EGINOPPST	ESTOPPING	EGNOOOSSW	SNOW GOOSE
EGINOPRRR	PORRINGER	EGNOOPRSS	PROGNOSES
EGINOPRRT	REPORTING	EGNOOPSTT	GETS ON TOP
EGINOPRRV	REPROVING	EGNOORRSV	GOVERNORS
EGINOPRST	PROGESTIN	EGNOORRWW	OVERGROWN
EGINOPRTT	POTTERING	EGNORSSSS	GROSSNESS
EGINOPRTX	EXPORTING	EGNORSSST	SONGSTERS
EGINOPSST	SPONGIEST	EGNORSSTT	STRONGEST
EGINOPSSU	ESPOUSING	EGNORSSTU	STURGEONS
EGINOPSUY	EPIGYNOUS	EGNORSTUY	YOUNGSTER
EGINOQRTU	ROQUETING	EGNRRSTUY	TURNS GREY
EGINORRST	RESORTING	EGNRRTTUU	GUN TURRET
	RESTORING	EGOOOPSTT	GOES TO POT
EGINORRTT	RETORTING	EGOOPRRSU	PROROGUES
EGINORTTT	TOTTERING	EGOOPRSST	GO TO PRESS
EGINORTTX	EXTORTING	EGOOPRSYZ	ZYGOSPORE
EGINORVWW	WRONG VIEW	EGOORRRSY	ROY ROGERS
EGINOSTTT	SETTING TO	EGOORRSVW	OVERGROWS
EGINPRSSS	PRESSINGS	EHHIIRTTT	THIRTIETH
EGINPRSTU	RESTING UP	EHHILLLSY	HELLISHLY
EGINPRSUV	SERVING UP	EHHILLNST	THIN SHELL
EGINPRTTU	PUTTERING	EHHILLPTU	UP THE HILL
EGINPRUVV	REVVING UP	EHHILMNST	HELMINTHS
EGINPRUVY	PURVEYING	EHHILNOTT	THE HILTON
EGINPSTTU	SETTING UP	EHHILOTTT	TO THE HILT
EGINPSTWW	SWEPT-WING	EHHINNTTU	IN THE HUNT
EGINRRSST	STRINGERS	EHHINPSTX	THE SPHINX
EGINRRSTU	RINGS TRUE	EHHIOPRSW	HORSEWHIP
EGINRSSST	STRESSING	EHHIORSST	HORSESHIT
EGINRSSTY	SYNERGIST	EHHIOSTVY	YESHIVOTH

EHHMNNOPP	PHNOM PENH
EHHMNOOOP	HOMOPHONE
EHHMNOSUY	HUSH MONEY
EHHMORRUY	HURRY HOME
EHHMORTTU	HOME TRUTH
EHHNOORSS	SHOE-HORNS
	SHOEHORNS
EHHNOORTU	ON THE HOUR
EHHOOPSSS	SHOE SHOPS
EHHOOPSTY	THEOSOPHY
EHHOORSSW	HORSE SHOW
EHHOORSTW	HOT SHOWER
EHHOOSSTU	HOTHOUSES
EHIIJNORT	JOINT HEIR
EHIIKLRSS	IRISH ELKS
EHIIKNNPT	IN THE PINK
EHIIKNNST	IN THE SINK
EHIIKNSTT	KITTENISH
EHIILLNTT	IN THE TILL
EHIILLTWY	LILY-WHITE
EHIILMRST	HITLERISM
EHIIMMRST	HERMITISM
EHIIMNORS	HEROINISM
EHIIMNSTW	IN THE SWIM
EHIINNOSS	INHESIONS
EHIINNSSS	SHININESS
EHIINORRT	INHERITOR
EHIINPPRW	WHIPPER-IN
EHIINPRST	NEPHRITIS
EHIINPSST	PITHINESS
EHIIORSST	HISTORIES
EHIIPPSSY	EPIPHYSIS
EHIIQRSSU	SQUISHIER
EHIIRRSTT	THIRSTIER
EHIIRSSTT	SHIRTIEST
EHIIRSSTW	IRISH STEW
EHIIRSTTZ	ZITHERIST
EHIISTTUW	WHITE SUIT
EHIJMNNOS	JIM HENSON
EHIKLLPSY	SYLPHLIKE
EHIKLMOTU	MOUTHLIKE
EHIKLOOTT	TOOTHLIKE
EHIKLORTZ	KILOHERTZ
EHIKNNOTW	IN THE KNOW
EHIKNORTV	THINK OVER
EHIKNPRRS	PRESHRINK
EHIKNRRSS	SHRINKERS
EHIKNSSSU	HUSKINESS
EHIKOORTW	WHITE ROOK
EHIKORRSY	YORKSHIRE
EHIKORSTU	SHRIEK OUT
EHIKRSWYY	RYE WHISKY
EHILLLMOS	MOLEHILLS
EHILLNOPT	ON THE PILL
EHILLNORT	ROT IN HELL
EHILLORTW	TOWER HILL
EHILLOSTY	HOSTILELY
EHILLOSWY	YELLOWISH
EHILLRRST	THRILLERS
EHILLRSST	SHRILLEST
EHILMNOST	MONTHLIES
EHILMOORS	HEIRLOOMS
EHILMOTWY	HOMELY WIT
EHILMPPRY	PERILYMPH
EHILMRSST	MIRTHLESS
EHILMSSSY	SHY SMILES
EHILMSSTU	MULISHEST
EHILNNTTU	UNTIL THEN
EHILNOOPT	LITHOPONE
EHILNOOST	LINE SHOOT
EHILNOSTT	ON THE LIST

EHILNOSTU	UNHOLIEST
EHILNOSTX	XENOLITHS
EHILNOSUY	HEINOUSLY
EHILOPRST	HELIPORTS
EHILOPRXY	XEROPHILY
EHILOPSST	ISOPLETHS
	THE SPOILS
EHILOSSVW	LIVE SHOWS
EHILPRRSU	RULERSHIP
EHILPRSUV	SHRIVEL UP
EHILPSSTT	THE SPLITS
EHILRSSTW	WHISTLERS
EHILRSTTW	WHITTLERS
EHIMNNOOS	MOONSHINE
EHIMNNOOT	IN THE MOON
EHIMNOORT	IN THE ROOM
EHIMNOPUU	EUPHONIUM
EHIMNORST	THERMIONS
EHIMNPSST	SHIPMENTS
EHIMNRTUU	RUTHENIUM
EHIMNSSSU	MUSHINESS
EHIMOOSST	SMOOTHIES
EHIMORSST	ISOTHERMS
EHIMORSTT	SHORT TIME
EHIMORTTW	MOTHER WIT
EHIMPSSUU	EUPHUISMS
EHIMSSSTU	ISTHMUSES
EHINNOPTY	PYTHONINE
EHINNORSU	NINE HOURS
EHINNOSTW	IN THE SNOW
	NONWHITES
	WHINSTONE
EHINNSSTU	NISSEN HUT
EHINOOOPR	IONOPHORE
EHINOORRS	IRON HORSE
EHINOPPRS	HORNPIPES
EHINOPRST	OPEN SHIRT
EHINOPRSW	OWNERSHIP
	SHIPOWNER
EHINOPSSW	WINE SHOPS
EHINOPSTT	IN THE POST
EHINOPSTU	IN THE SOUP
EHINOPSTY	HYPNOTISE
EHINOPTYZ	HYPNOTIZE
EHINORRSU	NOURISHER
EHINORSSS	HORSINESS
EHINORSSU	NOURISHES
EHINORSTT	THORNIEST
EHINORTWW	WORN WHITE
EHINORTXY	THYROXINE
EHINOSSSW	SHOWINESS
EHINOSSTU	OUTSHINES
EHINOSTWW	SNOW WHITE
	SNOW-WHITE
EHINPRRTY	PYRETHRIN
EHINPSSSU	PUSHINESS
EHINRTTUW	TURN WHITE
EHINSSSTY	SYNTHESIS
EHINSSTTX	SIX TENTHS
EHIOOPPSU	PIOUS HOPE
EHIOOSTTT	TOOTHIEST
EHIOPRSST	PROTHESIS
EHIOPRTTW	WHITE PORT
EHIOPSTTW	WHITE SPOT
EHIORSSTT	THEORISTS
EHIORSTTW	WORTHIEST
EHIORSTVW	SHORT VIEW
EHIORSTWZ	HOWITZERS
EHIOSTTUW	WHITEOUTS
EHIPQSSUY	PHYSIQUES
EHIPRRSUU	HURRIES UP

EHIPRSTTY	PRETTYISH	EHNOOPRTW	THROW OPEN
EHISSTTTX	SIXTH TEST	EHNOOPSTT	ON THE SPOT
EHJLLNOSW	JOHN WELLS	EHNOOPSTY	HONEY POTS
EHJLNNOOT	ELTON JOHN	EHNOORSVW	SHOWN OVER
EHKKLOOSZ	KOLKHOZES	EHNOORTTT	ON THE TROT
EHKLMOOSY	HOLY SMOKE	EHNOOSSSW	SNOWSHOES
EHKLNOOST	KNOTHOLES	EHNOOSTUW	TOWN HOUSE
EHKNPRRSU	PRESHRUNK	EHNOOSTUZ	SOUTH ZONE
EHKOORRSW	WORK HORSE	EHNOOTTTT	HOTTENTOT
EHKOORSUW	HOUSEWORK	EHNOPRSSY	SHY PERSON
	WORKHOUSE	EHNOPRTTU	POT HUNTER
EHLLMOPSY	MESOPHYLL		POTHUNTER
EHLLNSSTU	NUTSHELLS	EHNOPSSTY	PYTHONESS
EHLLOOOPS	LOOPHOLES	EHNORSSST	SHORTNESS
EHLLOOSTU	TOLLHOUSE	EHNORSTTW	NORTHWEST
EHLLOPSST	HOT SPELLS		WENT SHORT
EHLLORSST	SELL SHORT	EHNOSTTTW	TWO TENTHS
EHLLOSSTU	SHELLS OUT	EHNOSTTUW	WENT SOUTH
EHLMOOORT	HOTEL ROOM	EHOOOPRSU	POORHOUSE
EHLMOORSW	WORMHOLES	EHOOORSTV	OVERSHOOT
EHLMOOSSY	HOLY MOSES	EHOOPRRTV	HOVERPORT
EHLNNOTTU	LEN HUTTON	EHOOPRSST	POST-HORSE
EHLNOOPRT	NORTH POLE	EHOOPSSTU	HOUSETOPS
EHLNOOSTY	HOLYSTONE	EHOORRTVW	OVERTHROW
EHLNORRTY	NORTHERLY		THROW OVER
EHLNORSST	THORNLESS	EHOORSSVW	SHOWS OVER
EHLNPSSSU	PLUSHNESS	EHOOSSTTV	HOT STOVES
EHLOOPRST	PORTHOLES	EHOOSSTUU	HOTHOUSES
	POTHOLERS	EHOPRSSSW	PRESS SHOW
EHLOOPSTT	SHOP TO LET	EHOPRSSTT	SHORT STEP
EHLOOPSTU	SOUTH POLE	EHOPRSSUV	PUSHOVERS
EHLOOPSTY	PHOTOLYSE	EHOPSSTUU	PUSHES OUT
EHLOOSSTT	TOOTHLESS	EHORRSSTT	SHORT REST
EHLOPRSTU	UPHOLSTER	EHORRSTTW	THROWSTER
EHLOPRTTY	TRY TO HELP	EHORRTTUW	TRUE NORTH
EHLORRTTT	THROTTLER	EHORSSTUU	USHERS OUT
EHLORSSTT	THROSTLES	EHOSSTTUW	SOUTHWEST
EHLORSSTW	WORTHLESS	EHRRSSTTU	THRUSTERS
EHLORSTTT	THROTTLES	EIIILLMNT	LIMIT LINE
EHLORSTUY	SOUTHERLY	EIIILMMTT	TIME LIMIT
EHLOSSTWY	SHOW STYLE	EIIILNNQU	INQUILINE
EHLPRSTUU	SULPHURET	EIIILNNSV	LIVE IN SIN
EHLRSSTTU	SHUTTLERS	EIIILNTZZ	TIN LIZZIE
EHMMOOPRS	MESOMORPH	EIIILSTTU	UTILITIES
	ROMPS HOME	EIIIMMNRS	MINIMISER
EHMMORSTU	HOT SUMMER	EIIIMMNRZ	MINIMIZER
EHMMNOOOT	ON THE MOON	EIIIMMNSS	MINIMISES
EHMMNOOOY	HONEYMOON	EIIIMMNSZ	MINIMIZES
EHMMNOSTT	TEN MONTHS	EIIIMPRTV	PRIMITIVE
EHMMNOTTX	NEXT MONTH	EIIINQRSU	INQUIRIES
EHMMNNSTUY	HYMN TUNES	EIIINTTUV	INTUITIVE
EHMNOOPTU	OPEN MOUTH	EIIJMSSTU	JESUITISM
EHMNOOSST	SMOOTHENS	EIIJNOSSU	JOIN ISSUE
EHMOOOPRS	SOPHOMORE	EIIJQRTUY	JEQUIRITY
EHMOOORSU	HOUSE ROOM	EIIKKLNST	LIKE STINK
EHMOOOSTT	TOOTHSOME	EIIKKNNSS	KINKINESS
EHMOOPRST	SHORT POEM	EIIKLLMST	KILLS TIME
EHMOOPSST	STOPS HOME	EIIKLMNSS	MILKINESS
EHMOOSSTT	SMOOTHEST	EIIKLNNOS	NINE KILOS
EHMOPSTWY	EMPTY SHOW	EIIKLNRSW	WRINKLIES
EHMORRSTT	SHORT TERM	EIIKLNSSS	SILKINESS
	SHORT-TERM	EIIKLNSST	SLINKIEST
EHMPPTTUU	PUT THEM UP	EIIKLORST	OIL STRIKE
EHMPRRTUY	PYRETHRUM		STRIKE OIL
EHMPSSSYY	SYMPHYSES	EIIKMPSST	SKIMPIEST
EHNNOORRT	TENOR HORN	EIIKNNSST	SKINNIEST
EHNNOORTZ	NORTH ZONE	EIIKNRSSS	RISKINESS
EHNNOOTTW	ON THE TOWN	EIILLLSST	LIES STILL
EHNNORTTU	ON THE TURN	EIILLMNRS	MILLINERS
EHNNORTTW	WENT NORTH	EIILLMNRY	MILLINERY
EHNOOPPSS	OPENS SHOP	EIILLMNSU	ILLUMINES

EIILLMSST	LIMITLESS
EIILLNSSS	SILLINESS
EIILLNSTW	STILL WINE
EIILLOPRS	PILLORIES
EIILLORWW	WILLOWIER
EIILMNNST	LINIMENTS
EIILMNORV	VERMILION
EIILMNOSU	LIMOUSINE
EIILMNSSS	SLIMINESS
EIILMOPSV	IMPLOSIVE
EIILMOTTV	LEITMOTIV
EIILMPRSU	PUERILISM
EIILMPSUV	IMPULSIVE
EIILMRSSY	MISSILERY
EIILNNOTU	IN OUTLINE
EIILNNSST	LISTENS IN
EIILNOPST	PILES IT ON
EIILNSTTU	INTITULES
EIILNSTTY	TENSILITY
EIILPPSST	SLIPPIEST
EIILPRSTT	LETS IT RIP
EIILPRSTU	SPIRITUEL
EIILPRSTZ	PRIZE LIST
EIILPRTUY	PUERILITY
EIILPSTUV	LIVES IT UP
EIILRSSTU	UTILISERS
EIILRSSTX	SIX LITRES
EIILRSTTY	STERILITY
EIILRSTUZ	UTILIZERS
EIILRSTVY	SERVILITY
EIILSSSTY	SESSILITY
EIIMMNORS	IMMERSION
EIIMMNORT	MINI METRO
EIIMMNSTY	IMMENSITY
EIIMMORSS	ISOMERISM
EIIMMORST	MEMOIRIST
EIIMMPSSS	PESSIMISM
EIIMMNOTT	NOT IN TIME
EIIMNNRST	TIN MINERS
EIIMNNRTU	TRIENNIUM
EIIMNNSTU	IN MINUTES
EIIMNOPST	PIMIENTOS
EIIMNORSS	MISSIONER
	REMISSION
EIIMNOSSS	EMISSIONS
EIIMNPRST	STRIP-MINE
EIIMNRSST	MINISTERS
EIIMNRSTT	INTERMITS
EIIMNSSST	MISTINESS
EIIMOPRSU	IMPERIOUS
EIIMOPRSV	IMPROVISE
EIIMOSSTV	SOVIETISM
EIIMOTTVY	EMOTIVITY
EIIMPSSST	PESSIMIST
EIINNNOST	INTENSION
EIINNNOTT	INTENTION
EIINNNOTV	INVENTION
EIINNNSST	TINNINESS
EIINNORST	INSERTION
EIINNOSSS	IN SESSION
	NOISINESS
EIINNOSSU	UNIONISES
EIINNOSSV	ENVISIONS
EIINNOSUZ	UNIONIZES
EIINNPPSS	NIPPINESS
EIINNPSSS	SPININESS
EIINNRTTW	WRITTEN IN
EIINNSSTT	INSISTENT
EIINNSTTY	INTENSITY
EIINNSTXY	SIXTY-NINE
EIINOPPST	PIT PONIES

EIINOPRSV	PREVISION
EIINOPSTT	PETITIONS
EIINOPTVW	VIEWPOINT
EIINORRST	INTERIORS
EIINORSSV	REVISIONS
EIINORSTT	TRIES IT ON
EIINORSTY	SENIORITY
EIINPPRST	PINSTRIPE
EIINPRSWZ	WIN PRIZES
EIINPSSST	TIPSINESS
EIINRSSTU	SIREN SUIT
EIINRSSTZ	RITZINESS
EIINRSTTW	WINTRIEST
EIINRSTUV	INTRUSIVE
EIINRTTUV	NUTRITIVE
EIINSSTTW	WITTINESS
EIINSTTTU	INSTITUTE
EIIOPSSTV	POSITIVES
EIIPRRRTV	RIVER TRIP
EIIPRRSTW	TRIP WIRES
EIIPRRTUV	IRRUPTIVE
EIIPRSSTT	STRIPIEST
EIJKLNORT	J.R.TOLKIEN
EIJKMNRSU	JUNKERISM
EIJLLNOSS	JOLLINESS
EIJLMNPTU	MINT JULEP
EIJMNPSSU	JUMPINESS
EIJNORSTU	JOINTURES
EIJNOSSTT	JETTISONS
EIKKLLOOS	LOOKS LIKE
EIKKNOOSS	KOOKINESS
EIKLLLSSS	SKILL-LESS
EIKLLNOTY	NOT LIKELY
EIKLLORSV	OVERKILLS
EIKLLPSTT	KEPT STILL
EIKLLRTUW	KURT WEILL
EIKLMNOST	MINK STOLE
EIKLMORSY	IRKSOMELY
EIKLNNRTU	TRUNK LINE
EIKLNOTUW	WINKLE OUT
EIKLNPRRS	SPRINKLER
EIKLNPRSS	SPRINKLES
EIKLNRSTW	TWINKLERS
EIKLNSSSU	SULKINESS
EIKLOPSSS	SKI SLOPES
EIKLPRSSU	SILK PURSE
EIKMNOPSU	UP IN SMOKE
EIKMNORSY	MINOR KEYS
EIKMNOSSS	SMOKINESS
EIKMNRSSU	MURKINESS
EIKMOPPRR	PRIME PORK
EIKMORSSV	SKIMS OVER
EIKNNORWY	IN NEW YORK
EIKNOPSTY	KEY POINTS
EIKNORSTU	OUTER SKIN
EIKNOSTTT	KNOTTIEST
EIKNPRSTU	TURNPIKES
EIKNRRTTY	TRINKETRY
EIKOOPSST	SPOOKIEST
EIKOOSSTU	TOOK ISSUE
EIKOPRRTW	PIT WORKER
EIKOPRSSV	SKIPS OVER
EIKOPTTTU	KEPT IT OUT
EIKORSTTU	STRIKE OUT
EIKPRSSTU	STRIKES UP
EILLMNOST	MILLSTONE
EILLMORST	STILL MORE
EILLMPSSS	MISSPELLS
EILLMPSTU	MULTIPLES
EILLMPTUX	MULTIPLEX
EILLMRTUU	TELLURIUM

EILLNOSSW	LOWLINESS	EILOPRSTT	PORTLIEST
EILLNOTVY	VIOLENTLY	EILOPSTTT	TEST PILOT
EILLNPQSU	QUILL PENS	EILOPSTTV	SPLIT VOTE
EILLNSSST	STILLNESS	EILOPSTUV	LIVES UP TO
EILLNSSSY	SINLESSLY	EILOPSTUY	PITEOUSLY
EILLOOSTW	WOOLLIEST	EILORRTVW	LIVERWORT
EILLOOTTT	TOO LITTLE	EILORSSSV	VISORLESS
EILLOPRRT	ILL REPORT	EILORSSUY	SERIOUSLY
EILLOPRSV	OVERSPILL	EILORSTTW	TWO LITRES
	SPILL OVER	EILOSSTTT	STILETTOS
EILLOPRTY	PELLITORY	EILPPRSSU	SUPPLIERS
EILLOPRWW	WILLPOWER	EILPRSSTT	SPLITTERS
EILLOPSST	PILOTLESS	EILQRRSSU	SQUIRRELS
EILLOPTUV	POLLUTIVE	EILRSSTTU	SULTRIEST
EILLPRSUW	PULL WIRES	EIMMNNOST	IN MOMENTS
EILLPSSSY	SYLLEPSIS	EIMMNNSTU	MUNIMENTS
EILMMPSSU	SIMPLE SUM	EIMMNOPRS	PERSIMMON
EILMMPSTU	PLUMMIEST	EIMMNORSS	MISNOMERS
EILMNOORR	MINOR ROLE	EIMMOPRSU	EMPORIUMS
EILMNOOSY	NOISOMELY	EIMNNOORR	INNER ROOM
EILMNOPST	SIMPLETON	EIMNNOPRT	PROMINENT
EILMNOPSU	ON IMPULSE	EIMNNOPST	POINTSMEN
EILMNORTT	TORMENTIL	EIMNNORST	INNERMOST
EILMNOSSU	EMULSIONS	EIMNNORTT	IN TORMENT
EILMNOSTY	SOLEMNITY	EIMNNOSTT	OINTMENTS
EILMNOSWY	WINSOMELY	EIMNNOSWY	WINS MONEY
EILMNPSSU	LUMPINESS	EIMNNPTUU	NEPTUNIUM
EILMNRSST	MINSTRELS	EIMNNRTTU	NUTRIMENT
EILMOPSST	MILEPOSTS	EIMNOOPRT	MINOR POET
EILMOSSTW	SLOW TIMES	EIMNOOPSS	EMPOISONS
EILMRSSWY	WRY SMILES	EIMNOORRV	MOON RIVER
EILNNOOPT	ON TOP LINE	EIMNOORSS	ROOMINESS
EILNNOOSS	LOONINESS	EIMNOPRTU	IMPORTUNE
EILNNOSTV	INSOLVENT	EIMNORRTW	WORRIMENT
EILNOOPSX	EXPLOSION	EIMNORSSU	SENSORIUM
EILNOORSW	WIN OR LOSE	EIMNORSUV	VERMINOUS
EILNOOTUV	EVOLUTION	EIMNOSSST	MOISTNESS
EILNOPPST	SPLIT OPEN	EIMNOSTTY	TESTIMONY
EILNOPRST	TOP LINERS	EIMNOTTZZ	MEZZOTINT
EILNOPRSU	REPULSION	EIMNPSTTY	EMPTY TINS
EILNOPSST	POINTLESS	EIMNSSSTU	MUSTINESS
	SLITS OPEN	EIMNSSUZZ	MUZZINESS
EILNOPSSU	SPINULOSE	EIMOOPRTV	PROMOTIVE
EILNOPSSY	SPINOSELY	EIMOORRSW	WORRISOME
EILNOPSTT	SLEPT ON IT	EIMOORSST	MOTORISES
EILNOPSUX	EXPULSION	EIMOORSSU	ISOMEROUS
EILNORSTY	STORY LINE	EIMOORSTZ	MOTORIZES
EILNORSUV	REVULSION	EIMOOSSSX	EXOSMOSIS
EILNORTUY	ROUTINELY	EIMOPRRSS	PRIMROSES
EILNOSSSU	LOUSINESS	EIMOPRRST	MISREPORT
EILNOSSTT	LISTENS TO	EIMOPRRSV	IMPROVERS
	SILTSTONE	EIMOPRSTU	IMPOSTURE
EILNOSSTV	NOVELISTS	EIMOPSTUU	IMPETUOUS
EILNOSSUV	EVULSIONS	EIMOQSSTU	MISQUOTES
EILNOSTUV	INVOLUTES	EIMORRRST	TERRORISM
EILNOSUVY	ENVIOUSLY	EIMORSSTT	STORMIEST
EILNPPSSU	PULPINESS	EIMORSTTW	TWO-TIMERS
EILNPQTUU	QUINTUPLE	EIMORSUVY	VOYEURISM
EILNPRSST	SPLINTERS	EIMOSSSTU	MISSES OUT
EILNPRSTY	SPLINTERY	EIMOSSTTT	TOTEMISTS
EILNQTUUY	UNQUIETLY	EIMPSSTTU	STUMPIEST
EILNRRSUV	SILVER URN	EIMOQSTUY	MYSTIQUES
EILNRSSSU	SURLINESS	EIMRRSSSU	SURMISERS
EILNRSTTU	TURNSTILE	EINNNORWW	WIN RENOWN
EILNRSTUU	UNRULIEST	EINNNOTTY	NONENTITY
EILNRTUUV	VULTURINE	EINNNSSSU	SUNNINESS
EILNSSSTU	LUSTINESS	EINNOOPPS	POISON PEN
EILNSSTTU	LUTENISTS		POISON-PEN
EILOOSSTV	OIL STOVES	EINNOOPRT	PRENOTION
EILOPPRSS	PROLEPSIS	EINNOORST	IRONSTONE
EILOPPSST	SLOPPIEST		SEROTONIN

EINNOPSTT	TEN POINTS	EIORRRSTU	ROTURIERS
EINNORSTU	NEUTRINOS	EIORRRTTY	TERRITORY
EINNORSWW	WINNOWERS	EIORRSSST	RESISTORS
EINNORTVY	INVENTORY	EIORSTTUW	WRITES OUT
EINNOSSST	STONINESS	EIORSTVXY	OVER SIXTY
EINNOSSSW	SNOWINESS	EIPPPRSST	STRIPPERS
EINNPRSTW	NEWSPRINT	EIPRRRSSU	SPURRIERS
EINNRSTTU	NUTRIENTS		SURPRISER
EINNRTTUW	UNWRITTEN	EIPRRSSSU	SURPRISES
EINNSSTTU	NUTTINESS	EIPRSSSTU	PERTUSSIS
EINOOPRST	SORE POINT	EIPRSTTTY	SIT PRETTY
EINOORTTW	TORE IN TWO	EIRRSTVXY	RIVER STYX
EINOORTTX	EXTORTION	EIRSSTTTU	TRUSTIEST
EINOORTTY	NOTORIETY	EJLLLLORY	JELLY ROLL
EINOOSSST	SOOTINESS	EJLLLLOWY	JOLLY WELL
EINOOSSTT	SNOOTIEST	EJLLOSSYY	JOYLESSLY
EINOOSSWZ	WOOZINESS	EJLMOPPSU	POLE JUMPS
EINOPPSSS	SOPPINESS	EJLOOPPSY	SLOPPY JOE
EINOPRRSS	PRISONERS	EJMOPRSUV	JUMPS OVER
EINOPRRTV	OVERPRINT	EJNNOOOTT	NOT ONE JOT
EINOPRSTT	IN PROTEST	EJNOORRSU	SOJOURNER
EINOPRSTU	ERUPTIONS	EJPRTTUYY	PETTY JURY
EINOPRSUU	PENURIOUS	EKKOOPRRW	POKERWORK
EINOPSSSU	PIOUSNESS	EKLLLOOSW	LOOKS WELL
EINOPSSTT	STEPS INTO	EKLLNNOWW	KNOWN WELL
	STEPS ON IT		WELL-KNOWN
EINOPSTTW	WEST POINT	EKLLNOSWW	KNOWS WELL
EINOQSSTU	QUESTIONS	EKLLORSWW	WORKS WELL
EINOQSTTU	QUOTIENTS	EKLMMNOSU	MUSKMELON
EINOQTTUW	QUIET TOWN	EKLNOOORS	ONLOOKERS
EINORRSSS	SORRINESS	EKLOOORSV	LOOKS OVER
EINORRTTV	INTROVERT		OVERLOOKS
EINORSSTU	RINSES OUT	EKLOOORSW	WORK LOOSE
EINORSSTV	INVESTORS	EKLOOPSSW	SLOWPOKES
EINORSSUV	SOUVENIRS	EKMNNOTUY	MONKEY NUT
EINORSTTU	RITENUTOS	EKMOOSSTU	SMOKES OUT
EINORSTUW	SURE TO WIN	EKMORSSSU	MUSK ROSES
EINORSTUX	EXTRUSION	EKNOOOSTT	TOOK NOTES
EINORSTVY	NERVOSITY	EKNOOPSTU	OUTSPOKEN
EINOSSTTT	SNOTTIEST		SPOKEN OUT
EINOSSTTU	ETON SUITS	EKNOORSST	ROOKS NEST
EINPPPRRST	PREPRINTS	EKNOORSTW	STONEWORK
EINPRRSST	SPRINTERS	EKNOPRSTY	PONY TREKS
EINPRRTTU	INTERRUPT	EKNORSSTU	SUNSTROKE
EINPRSSST	SPINSTERS	EKOOPSSTT	TOOK STEPS
EINPRSSSU	PURSINESS	EKOORRSVW	OVERWORKS
EINPRTTUW	WRITTEN UP		WORKS OVER
EINQRSSTU	SQUINTERS	EKOORRTUW	OUTWORKER
EINQRSTTU	QUITRENTS	EKOORSTTW	SET TO WORK
EINRRTTUU	UTTER RUIN		TWO STROKE
EINRSSSTU	RUSTINESS		TWO-STROKE
EIOOPPRSS	PORPOISES	EKOPRSSTU	UPSTROKES
EIOOPPSST	OPPOSITES	ELLMNOORT	MELLOTRON
EIOOPRRST	POSTERIOR	ELLMOPSUU	PLUMULOSE
EIOOPRSSV	PROVISOES	ELLMOPSUY	PLUMOSELY
EIOOPRSTX	EXPOSITOR	ELLMORSTU	ROSTELLUM
EIOORSSTT	TORTOISES	ELLMOSUUY	EMULOUSLY
EIOOSSSTX	EXOSTOSIS	ELLNOPSUW	SWOLLEN UP
EIOOSSTTV	OVOTESTIS	ELLNOPTUY	OPULENTLY
EIOPPPRST	STROPPIER	ELLNOSTVY	SOLVENTLY
EIOPPRRTY	PROPRIETY	ELLOORRSV	ROLLS OVER
EIOPPRSTZ	SPOT PRIZE	ELLOOSSTV	LOST LOVES
EIOPPRSUV	PURPOSIVE	ELLOPRSST	POLLSTERS
EIOPRRSSU	SUPERIORS	ELLOPRSUV	PULLOVERS
EIOPRRSTV	TRIPS OVER		PULLS OVER
EIOPRSSTT	SPORTIEST	ELLOPSSTU	SPELLS OUT
EIOPRSTTY	POSTERITY	ELLOPSSUW	SLOW PULSE
EIOPRTTUV	PUT IT OVER	ELLORRSST	STROLLERS
EIOPSSTTT	SPOTTIEST	ELLORSTUU	TELLUROUS
EIOQRSTUU	TURQUOISE	ELLOSSTUW	SWELLS OUT
EIORRRSTT	TERRORIST	ELMMNSSUU	MUSSULMEN

ELMNNOOST	SOMNOLENT	ENNOPPSTY	PENNY POST
ELMNOOSTY	LOST MONEY	ENNOPRSSU	UNPERSONS
ELMNOOSVW	SOLEMN VOW	ENNOPRTWY	PENNYWORT
ELMNPPSSU	PLUMPNESS	ENNORSTTU	TURNSTONE
ELMOOORSV	LOOMS OVER	ENNPRRSUU	RUNNERS-UP
ELMOOORTT	ROOM TO LET	ENOOPPRST	POSTPONER
ELMOOPSTW	SLOW TEMPO		TOP PERSON
ELMOORSST	MOTORLESS	ENOOPPRSU	ON PURPOSE
ELMOORSTW	LOWERMOST	ENOOPPRTU	OPPORTUNE
ELMOOTUVW	VOLUME TWO	ENOOPPSST	POSTPONES
ELMORSTUU	TREMULOUS	ENOOPTTTW	WENT TO POT
ELNNOOSSU	UNLOOSENS	ENOORRTTW	ROTTEN ROW
ELNOOPRSW	LOW PERSON	ENOORSSTU	SOUR NOTES
ELNOOPSSU	LOOSENS UP	ENOORSSWY	ROSS ON WYE
ELNOOPSTU	STOLE UP ON	ENOORSTTW	STONEWORT
ELNOORSTU	TURN LOOSE	ENOOSSTTU	SOSTENUTO
ELNOORSUY	ONEROUSLY	ENOPPRSUY	PREYS UPON
ELNOOSSTW	LESSON TWO	ENOPRSSTT	STERNPOST
ELNORRTUW	LOW RETURN	ENOPSSSWW	SWOPS NEWS
ELNORSUVY	NERVOUSLY	ENOPSTTVY	STENOTYPY
ELNOSTUUY	TENUOUSLY	ENOPTTTWY	TOP TWENTY
ELOOPRSSV	SLOPS OVER	ENORRSTUV	OVERTURNS
ELOORSTUW	LOUSEWORT		TURNS OVER
ELOORSTY	LOVE STORY	ENORSSTUU	STRENUOUS
ELOORSVVW	LOVERS VOW	ENORSTUUV	VENTUROUS
ELOPPPUVY	PUPPY LOVE	ENOSSSTTU	STOUTNESS
ELOPPRSUY	PURPOSELY	ENOTTTWWY	TWENTY-TWO
ELOPRSSYY	PYROLYSES	EOOORTUVY	OVER TO YOU
ELOQRSUUU	QUERULOUS	FOOPPRRSS	OPPRESSOR
ELPRSSSUU	SURPLUSES	EOOPPRTTY	PROTOTYPE
ELPRSSTTU	SPLUTTERS	EOOPPSSSU	SUPPOSE SO
ELPRSTTUY	SPLUTTERY	EOOPRRSTT	PROTESTOR
EMMNNOSTU	MONUMENTS	EOOPRRSTU	UPROOTERS
EMMNOOSTU	MOMENTOUS	EOOPRSSSS	POSSESSOR
EMMNORSSU	SUMMONERS	EOOPRSSTV	STOPOVERS
EMMNOSSSU	SUMMONSES		STOPS OVER
EMMNRSTUU	MENSTRUUM	EOOPRSSVW	SWOPS OVER
EMMOOPRTY	EMPTY ROOM	EOOPRSTTY	TOP STOREY
EMMOORSTY	OSMOMETRY	EOORRRSSW	SORROWERS
EMMRRSSTU	STRUMMERS	EOORRTTVY	TORY VOTER
EMNNOOOST	MONOTONES	EOORSTTVY	TORY VOTES
	MOONSTONE		VOTES TORY
EMNNRRRUU	RUM RUNNER	EOPPRRSTU	SUPPORTER
EMNOOPSTY	MONOTYPES	EOPPRSSST	STOP PRESS
EMNOOPSUY	EPONYMOUS	EOPRRSUVY	PURVEYORS
EMNOORRTT	TORMENTOR	EOPSSTTUU	PUTS TO USE
EMNOORSSW	NEWS ROOMS	EORRRSTTU	TORTURERS
	NEWSROOMS	EORRSSSST	STRESSORS
EMNOORTTY	TONOMETRY	EORRSSUVY	SURVEYORS
EMNOORTWY	MONEYWORT	EORRSTTUY	TRUE STORY
EMNOOSTUW	TOWN MOUSE	EORRSTVWY	VERY WORST
EMNOPRSST	SPORTSMEN	EOSSSSTUU	SUSSES OUT
EMNOPRSSU	RESPONSUM	EPRSSSTUU	TRUSSES UP
EMNORSSTT	STERNMOST	ERRSSTTTU	STRUTTERS
EMOOORRST	STOREROOM	FFFGHIOST	FIGHTS OFF
EMOOPRTTY	OPTOMETRY	FFFGHOOTU	FOUGHT OFF
EMOORRSST	REST ROOMS	FFFGIINOR	FIRING OFF
EMOORSTTU	OUTERMOST	FFFGILNOS	FLINGS OFF
EMOPPRSTU	UPPERMOST	FFFGILNOY	FLYING OFF
EMOPRRTUV	OVERTRUMP	FFFHIINOS	FINISH OFF
EMOPRRTYY	PYROMETRY	FFFHIMORT	FIFTH FORM
EMORSTTTU	UTTERMOST	FFFLLNOUU	FULL OF FUN
EMPRSSTTU	STRUMPETS	FFFLOSTUU	FLUFFS OUT
ENNNOOOSW	ON ONES OWN	FFGHIILNW	WHIFFLING
ENNNOORWW	WON RENOWN	FFGHIINOV	HIVING OFF
ENNNORSSU	ON RUNNERS	FFGHILNSU	SHUFFLING
ENNNORSUY	RUNNY NOSE	FFGHILRTU	FRIGHTFUL
ENNOOPPRT	PROPONENT	FFGHIORST	FIGHTS FOR
ENNOOPPST	OPPONENTS	FFGHOORTU	FOUGHT FOR
ENNOOPRTV	NOT PROVEN	FFGHORSSU	SHRUGS OFF
		FFGIILNNS	SNIFFLING

FFGIINOPW	WIPING OFF
FFGIINSUX	SUFFIXING
FFGILNNSU	SNUFFLING
FFGILNOXY	FLYING FOX
FFGIMNOOV	MOVING OFF
FFGINOOPR	ROPING OFF
FFGINOPRS	OFFSPRING
FFGINSSUU	SUFFUSING
FFHIIOSTT	HITS IT OFF
FFHIKORSS	FISH FORKS
FFHIKOSSW	WHISKS OFF
FFHILOOPS	POLISH OFF
FFHIOSTTW	TWO FIFTHS
FFHNOORTW	THROWN OFF
FFHOOOSST	OFFSHOOTS
	SHOOTS OFF
FFIILMOST	OFF LIMITS
FFIKLORST	FORKLIFTS
FFILLOPPS	FLIP-FLOPS
FFILLOPTU	PULL IT OFF
FFILMNNUY	FUNNY FILM
FFIMORRST	FIRST FORM
FFINNOORT	IN FRONT OF
FFINOPRST	OFFPRINTS
FFINORTTU	TURN IT OFF
FFINOSSUU	SUFFUSION
FFIOORSTT	FIRST FOOT
	FIRSTFOOT
FFIOPRSST	STRIPS OFF
FFIORSTTU	SOFT FRUIT
FFJLLOOUY	FULL OF JOY
FFKNOOSTU	TOOK SNUFF
FFKOOORTW	OFF TO WORK
FFLNOOSTU	LOTS OF FUN
FFLOOOOPR	FOOLPROOF
FFMOOORTU	OUT OF FORM
FFMOORRSU	FORM FOURS
FFNOPSTUU	UP TO SNUFF
FFNOSSTUU	SNUFFS OUT
FFOOOPRST	TROOPS OFF
FFOORRSUU	FOUR FOURS
FGGHIILNT	FLIGHTING
FGGHIINOS	GO FISHING
FGGHIINRT	FRIGHTING
FGGHINSTU	GUN FIGHTS
FGGIIMNOR	FIRM GOING
FGGIIINORV	FORGIVING
FGGINOOST	SOFT GOING
FGHHIITTW	FIGHT WITH
FGHHILNOW	FLOWN HIGH
	HIGH-FLOWN
FGHHILOOR	HIGH FLOOR
FGHHIOSTW	SHOW FIGHT
FGHHISSTY	FIGHTS SHY
FGHHOOTTU	THOUGHT OF
FGHHOSTUY	FOUGHT SHY
FGHIIINNS	FINISHING
FGHIIILLTY	FLIGHTILY
FGHIIMNUY	HUMIFYING
FGHIINNOS	NO FISHING
FGHIINOOT	HOOFING IT
FGHIINSTW	WIN FIGHTS
FGHILOORT	RIGHT FOOL
FGHILOPTT	TOP-FLIGHT
FGHILOSTT	SOFT LIGHT
FGHINORTT	FORTNIGHT
FGHIOORTT	RIGHT FOOT
FGHIOPSST	GIFT SHOPS
FGHLORSUU	FURLOUGHS
FGIIILLNN	FILLING IN
	INFILLING
FGIIILLNP	FILLIPING
FGIIILNVY	VILIFYING
FGIIIMNRS	MISFIRING
FGIIINNTT	FITTING IN
FGIIINVVY	VIVIFYING
FGIILLNPU	FILLING UP
FGIILNNRU	FUR LINING
FGIILNOPR	PROFILING
FGIILNPTU	UPLIFTING
FGIILNRST	FIRSTLING
FGIILNRZZ	FRIZZLING
FGIILNTTY	FITTINGLY
FGIIMNNOR	INFORMING
FGIINNOPR	PINING FOR
FGIINNOPS	NIPS OF GIN
FGIINNOTT	FITTING ON
FGIINNOTY	NOTIFYING
FGIINNTTU	UNFITTING
FGIINOPRT	PROFITING
FGIINOSSY	OSSIFYING
FGIINPRUY	PURIFYING
FGIINPTTU	FITTING UP
FGIINPTYY	TYPIFYING
FGIINRSST	FIRST SIGN
FGIINRSSU	FISSURING
FGIJKLMOU	JUG OF MILK
FGIKLLNOS	GOLF LINKS
FGIKNNOPU	POKING FUN
FGIKNORSU	FOUR KINGS
FGILLNOOW	FOLLOWING
FGILLNSUW	FULL SWING
FGILNNOOO	NO FOOLING
FGILNNRUU	UNFURLING
FGILNOPUU	FOULING UP
FGILNOSTU	FLINGS OUT
FGILNPRUU	FURLING UP
FGILNRRUY	FLURRYING
FGIMNNORS	FORM RINGS
FGIMRSTUU	FRUIT GUMS
FGINNOORT	GO IN FRONT
FGINOORTV	VOTING FOR
FGINORRUW	FURROWING
FGINORSST	FROSTINGS
FGINORSTW	FROWSTING
FGINRRSTU	FIRST RUNG
FGIOORSTT	FIRST TO GO
FGIORRTUW	GROW FRUIT
FGKLNOOSS	FOLK SONGS
FGKLNOOUY	YOUNG FOLK
FGLLNORUW	FULL GROWN
FGLOOOSST	FOOTSLOGS
FGNOOORTW	WRONG FOOT
	WRONG-FOOT
FGOORRSSU	FOUR GROSS
FHHIKOOSS	FISHHOOKS
FHHIOPSSS	FISH SHOPS
FHHIORTTW	FORTHWITH
FHIIIKLLS	KILLIFISH
FHIILOPST	PILOT FISH
FHIILRTTW	FLIRT WITH
FHIILRTTY	THRIFTILY
FHIIORSTX	HIT FOR SIX
FHIKORSTW	SHIFT WORK
FHILLOOST	FOOTHILLS
FHILLOOSY	FOOLISHLY
FHILLORST	HILLFORTS
FHILLOSWY	WOLFISHLY
FHILLSUWY	WISHFULLY
FHILMOSSW	FILM SHOWS
FHILOPPSY	FOPPISHLY
FHILOPSST	SHOPLIFTS

FHIMORSTX	SIXTH FORM	FLNOOPSSU	SPOONFULS
FHIORRSTT	THIRST FOR		SPOONSFUL
FHIORSSTY	FISH STORY	FLOORRSUW	SORROWFUL
FHLLRTUUY	HURTFULLY	FLOPRSSUU	PLUS FOURS
FHLMOSTUU	MOUTHFULS	FLORSSUUU	SULFUROUS
FHLOOOPRS	SHOP FLOOR	FMNNOOORW	FROM NOW ON
	SHOPFLOOR	FMNOOOORRT	FRONT ROOM
FHLOOORSW	FLOOR SHOW	FMNOORRSU	MOURNS FOR
FHLOORTUW	FOUL THROW	FMOORSTTU	TOTS OF RUM
FHMOOOPRT	MOTHPROOF	FNNOOPRUW	FROWN UPON
FHNOOOORTW	OF NO WORTH	FNOOOTTUW	OUT OF TOWN
FHNOOPRST	SHOP FRONT	FNOORTTUU	OUT OF TURN
	SHOPFRONT	FNORSSTTU	TURNS SOFT
FHOOPRRTU	POUR FORTH	FOOPRRSTU	RUSTPROOF
FHOORRSUU	FOUR HOURS	FOOPSSTUY	PUSSYFOOT
FHOORRTTW	FORT WORTH	GGGHHIINO	GOING HIGH
FHOORRTUW	FOURTH ROW	GGGHINRSU	SHRUGGING
FIIILNOPS	FILIPINOS	GGGIILNRW	WRIGGLING
FIIILSSTY	FISSILITY	GGGIINPRS	SPRIGGING
FIIIMNRTY	INFIRMITY	GGGIINPRU	RIGGING UP
FIIKLNNST	SKINFLINT	GGGILMNSU	SMUGGLING
FIIILLPTUY	PITIFULLY	GGGILNNSU	SNUGGLING
FIIILMPRST	FILM STRIP	GGGIMNPUU	MUGGING UP
	FILMSTRIP	GGHHHIILT	HIGHLIGHT
FIIILORTVY	FRIVOLITY	GGHHIINSS	SINGS HIGH
FIIILPRSST	FIRST SLIP	GGHHOORTU	GO THROUGH
FIIMMNORS	MISINFORM	GGHIIILRW	WHIRLIGIG
FIIMNNORU	IN UNIFORM	GGHIIKNNT	KNIGHTING
FIIMORRTU	TRIFORIUM	GGHIILNNS	SHINGLING
FIINNOSSU	INFUSIONS	GGHIILNNT	LIGHTNING
FIINORSST	IRON FISTS	GGHIILNPT	PLIGHTING
FIINORSTU	FRUITIONS	GGHIILNST	SLIGHTING
FIKLLLSUY	SKILFULLY	GGHIILPSY	PIGGISHLY
FIKLLRSTU	FULL SKIRT	GGHIINNNU	UNHINGING
FIKLOORSU	FOUR KILOS	GGHIINRTW	RIGHT WING
FILLLMORU	FLOUR MILL		RIGHT-WING
FILLLOOSY	SILLY FOOL	GGHIIPRTT	TIGHT GRIP
FILLSTUWY	WISTFULLY	GGHILNNOT	LONG NIGHT
FILMMORTU	MULTIFORM	GGHILNOPU	PLOUGHING
FILMNORUY	UNIFORMLY	GGHILNOST	LONG SIGHT
FILMNSTTU	FILM STUNT	GGHILNOSU	SLOUGHING
FILOOOPRT	PORTFOLIO	GGHILOOPR	LOGOGRIPH
FILOORSSU	FLUOROSIS	GGHINNORT	THRONGING
FILOORSUV	FRIVOLOUS	GGHINNOTW	NIGHTGOWN
FILOOSTUW	SOUL OF WIT	GGHINOPTU	GOING PHUT
FILOPSTUU	FOULS IT UP	GGHOSTUUY	TOUGH GUYS
FILORSUUY	FURIOUSLY	GGIIIMNNP	IMPINGING
FILOSSTUU	FISTULOUS	GGIIIMNSV	MISGIVING
FIMNOOPRT	IN TOP FORM	GGIIINNNR	RINGING IN
FIMNORSSY	FOR MY SINS	GGIILMNPS	GLIMPSING
FIMOORTTU	OUT OF TRIM	GGIILNNRY	RINGINGLY
FINOOPRSU	PROFUSION	GGIILNNSS	GIN SLINGS
FINOOPRTT	FOOTPRINT	GGIILNRZZ	GRIZZLING
FINOOPSTU	TIN OF SOUP	GGIIMNNPU	IMPUGNING
FINORRSTU	RUNS FOR IT	GGIIMNOSS	GO MISSING
FIOOPTTUY	OUT OF PITY	GGIIMPSSY	MISS PIGGY
FIOORSSTT	TOSS FOR IT	GGIINNNOS	SIGNING ON
FIOORSTTW	WORST OF IT	GGIINNORW	INGROWING
FIPRSSTTU	PUTS FIRST	GGIINNPRU	RINGING UP
FKLNOOSTW	TOWNSFOLK	GGIINNPSU	SIGNING UP
FKLOOOPRS	POOR FOLKS	GGIINNRSY	SYRINGING
FKLOORSTY	FOLK STORY	GGIINNSWW	SWING-WING
FKOOORTUW	OUT OF WORK	GGIINOPSS	GOSSIPING
FKOORRSTW	FROSTWORK	GGIINOTUV	GIVING OUT
FLLLOSUUY	SOULFULLY	GGILLNNOY	LONGINGLY
FLLNOOOSW	FLOWN SOLO	GGILLNOOP	GOLLOPING
	FOLLOWS ON	GGILLNOWY	GLOWINGLY
FLLNOORRY	FORLORNLY	GGILLOOSW	GOLLIWOGS
FLLOOPSUW	FOLLOWS UP	GGILNNOUY	YOUNGLING
FLLOPSSTU	FULL STOPS	GGILNOOSW	GOING SLOW
FLLORSTUY	FULL STORY	GGILNORUY	YOUNG GIRL

GGILNORWY	GROWINGLY	GHILMNOOT	MOONLIGHT
GGILNPRSU	SPLURGING	GHILNOOPT	POTHOLING
GGIMNOOTV	GOT MOVING	GHILNOOTU	HOLING OUT
GGINNOORW	GROWING ON	GHILNOPSS	LONGSHIPS
GGINNOSSS	SING SONGS		SPLOSHING
	SINGSONGS	GHILNOPYY	PHILOGYNY
GGINOOSTU	OUTGOINGS	GHILNOSST	SLINGSHOT
GGINOPRSU	GROUPINGS	GHILNOSTW	NIGHT OWLS
GGINOPRUW	GROWING UP	GHILNSTTU	SHUTTLING
GHHIIJKNS	HIGH JINKS	GHILNSTUY	UNSIGHTLY
GHHIILPST	LIGHTSHIP	GHILOOPRT	POOR LIGHT
GHHIIPSTT	TIGHT SHIP	GHILOOSTY	HISTOLOGY
GHHIJMPSU	HIGH JUMPS	GHILOPRSS	SHOP GIRLS
GHHIKOORT	RIGHT HOOK	GHILOPSTT	SPOTLIGHT
GHHILRSTU	RUSHLIGHT		STOP LIGHT
GHHINOOSW	WHOOSHING	GHILORSSW	SHOW GIRLS
GHHINOSTT	HOT NIGHTS		SHOWGIRLS
GHHINPSUU	HUSHING UP	GHILORSUY	ROGUISHLY
GHHIOPSST	HIGH SPOTS	GHILOSSTT	LOST SIGHT
	HIGHSPOTS	GHILOSTTU	LIGHTS OUT
GHHIOSTTU	TOUGH SHIT!		LIGHTS-OUT
GHHISTTTU	SHUT TIGHT	GHILPRSTY	SPRIGHTLY
GHHLOOSTY	HOLY GHOST	GHILPRTUY	UPRIGHTLY
GHHNOOTTU	THOUGHT ON	GHIMMNRTU	THRUMMING
GHHNOTTUU	UNTHOUGHT	GHIMMNTUY	THINGUMMY
GHHOPTTUU	THOUGHT UP	GHIMNOOST	SMOOTHING
GHIIIJRSS	IRISH JIGS	GHIMNORTY	ON MY RIGHT
GHIIIKLNS	LIGHT SKIN	GHIMNORUU	HUMOURING
GHIIKNOOT	HOOKING IT	GHIMNSSTU	GUNSMITHS
GHIIKNSTT	SKINTIGHT	GHIMOPSTY	GIPSY MOTH
GHIILLNOT	GILLIONTH	GHIMRRTTU	GRIM TRUTH
GHIILLNRS	SHRILLING	GHINNNOOT	NOTHING ON
GHIILLNRT	THRILLING	GHINNOORU	HONOURING
GHIILLNSS	SHILLINGS	GHINNOPPU	PHONING UP
GHIILMSTT	LIGHT MIST	GHINNOPSU	PUSHING ON
GHIILNNWY	WHININGLY	GHINNOPSY	SYPHONING
GHIILNOPS	POLISHING	GHINNORST	NORTHINGS
GHIILNSTW	WHISTLING	GHINNORSU	UNHORSING
GHIILNTTW	WHITTLING	GHINOOPRT	POOR THING
GHIILSTTU	LIGHT SUIT	GHINOOSST	SHOOTINGS
GHIIMMNSY	SHIMMYING	GHINOOSSW	SWOOSHING
GHIIMNPRS	SHRIMPING	GHINOPRSU	SHORING UP
GHIIMRSST	MISS RIGHT	GHINOPSTT	NIGHT SPOT
GHIINNNOP	PHONING IN	GHINOPSUW	SHOWING UP
GHIINNNWY	WHINNYING	GHINORSST	STRONGISH
GHIINNOPP	HOPPING IN	GHINORSTW	INGROWTHS
GHIINNOPS	SIPHONING	GHINORTUW	IN-WROUGHT
GHIINNOSW	SHOWING IN	GHINOSSSW	SHOW SIGNS
GHIINNPSU	PUNISHING	GHINPPSUU	PUSHING UP
GHIINNRSU	RUSHING IN	GHINPRSUU	RUSHING UP
GHIINOPPT	HOPPING IT	GHINPSSSU	SHIPS GUNS
	PIPING HOT	GHINRRTTU	RIGHT TURN
GHIINORTU	HIRING OUT		TURN RIGHT
GHIINOSSU	SQUISHING	GHIOOPRST	POOR SIGHT
GHIINRRRW	WHIRRRING	GHIOOTTUW	GO WITHOUT
GHIINRSTT	THIRSTING	GHIOPSTTT	TIGHT SPOT
GHIIOSSTV	VISIGOTHS	GHIOSTTUW	WITH GUSTO
GHIIOTTTW	GOT WITH IT	GHIPRSTTU	PUTS RIGHT
GHIIRSSTT	RIGHTISTS	GHKOORRUW	ROUGH WORK
GHIISSTTT	SITS TIGHT	GHLMOOTYY	MYTHOLOGY
GHIJRSTTU	JUST RIGHT	GHLNNOORS	LONGHORNS
GHIKLOORT	LOOK RIGHT	GHLNOOOPY	PHONOLOGY
GHIKLORTW	LIGHT WORK	GHLNOORSU	LONG HOURS
GHIKLSSTY	SKYLIGHTS	GHNNOOPRR	PRONGHORN
GHIKNNOOU	UNHOOKING	GHNNORTUY	NOT HUNGRY
GHIKNOOPU	HOOKING UP	GHNOOSTTW	GHOST TOWN
GHIKNORTW	NIGHT WORK	GHNOSSTUW	SHOWN GUTS
GHILLNOOW	HOLLOWING	GHNOSTTUU	TOUGH NUTS
GHILLOOPY	PHILOLOGY	GHOOORSTT	OSTROGOTH
GHILLOOTY	LITHOLOGY	GHOOPSTTU	TOUGH SPOT
GHILLPTTU	PULL TIGHT	GHOORSTUU	ROUGHS OUT

GHOORTTUW	OUTGROWTH	GIIMNORRR	MIRRORING
GHOOSTTUU	SOUGHT OUT	GIIMNORST	MORTISING
GHOSSSTUW	SHOWS GUTS	GIIMNOTTW	TWO-TIMING
GIIIJNNNO	JOINING IN	GIIMNQRSU	SQUIRMING
GIIIKNNNS	SINKING IN	GIIMNRSSU	SURMISING
GIIILNNOS	LIONISING	GIINNNNPU	UNPINNING
GIIILNNOZ	LIONIZING	GIINNNNRU	RUNNING IN
GIIILNNTY	LYING IN IT	GIINNNOWW	WINNOWING
GIIILNSTU	UTILISING	GIINNNPPU	PINNING UP
GIIILNTUZ	UTILIZING	GIINNNRTU	TURNING IN
GIIILOSTU	LITIGIOUS	GIINNOOPS	POISONING
GIIIMMNST	MISTIMING	GIINNOOPT	OPTIONING
GIIINNNOP	PINIONING	GIINNOPPP	POPPING IN
GIIINNPRS	INSPIRING	GIINNOSTT	SITTING ON
GIIINNQRU	INQUIRING	GIINNOTUW	WINING OUT
GIIINNRTW	IN WRITING	GIINNPPUZ	UNZIPPING
	WRITING IN	GIINNPRST	PRINTINGS
GIIINNSST	INSISTING		SPRINTING
GIIINNSTT	SITTING IN	GIINNPTTU	INPUTTING
GIIINNSTU	UNITISING		PUTTING IN
GIIINNTTU	INTUITING	GIINNQSTU	SQUINTING
GIIINNTUZ	UNITIZING	GIINNRSSU	RISING SUN
GIIINPRST	SPIRITING	GIINNTTUW	UNWITTING
GIIINRTVY	VIRGINITY	GIINOPTUW	WIPING OUT
GIIJMNNPU	JUMPING IN	GIINORTTU	TIRING OUT
GIIKLLLNY	KILLINGLY	GIINPPPTU	TIPPING UP
GIIKLNNOO	LOOKING IN	GIINPPRST	STRIPPING
GIIKLNNPU	LINKING UP	GIINPRRTU	IRRUPTING
GIIKLNNRW	WRINKLING	GIINPRSSU	UPRISINGS
GIIKLNNTW	TWINKLING	GIINPRTUW	WRITING UP
GIIKNNORW	WORKING IN	GIINPSTTU	SITTING UP
GIIKNNSTT	KNITTINGS	GIINQRSTU	SQUIRTING
GIIKNSVVY	SKIVVYING	GIINRSUVV	SURVIVING
GIIILLLNTY	LILTINGLY	GIJMNNOPU	JUMPING ON
GIIILLLNWY	WILLINGLY	GIJMNPPUU	JUMPING UP
GIIILLMNSY	SMILINGLY	GIJNNNORU	NONJURING
GIIILLNNOR	ROLLING IN	GIKKNOORS	KINGS ROOK
GIIILNNPU	PILING IN	GIKLLNORST	KING STORK
GIIILNNUW	UNWILLING	GIKLMOORS	LOOKS GRIM
GIIILNOPW	PILLOWING	GIKLNNNSY	KINGS LYNN
GIIILNORS	GRILLIONS	GIKLNNOOO	LOOKING ON
GIIILMNOPR	IMPLORING		ONLOOKING
GIIILMNPTU	LUMPING IT	GIKLNNOWY	KNOWINGLY
GIIILMNRSU	MISRULING	GIKLNOOOT	LOOKING TO
GIIILNNNWY	WINNINGLY	GIKLNOOPU	LOOKING UP
GIIILNNOTU	OUTLINING	GIKLNORST	LONG SKIRT
GIIILNNOVV	INVOLVING	GIKLNOSSW	SILK GOWNS
GIIILNNPST	SPLINTING	GIKMNNOOS	NO SMOKING
GIIILNNSTU	INSULTING	GIKNNNOOW	NO KNOWING
GIIILNOQRU	LIQUORING	GIKNNNOUW	UNKNOWING
GIIILNOSTV	LONG VISIT	GIKNNOORW	WORKING ON
GIIILNOTUV	LIVING OUT	GIKNOOPRV	PROVOKING
	OUTLIVING	GIKNOOSTW	TOOK WINGS
GIIILNPPRU	PIN-UP GIRL	GIKNOOTWW	KOWTOWING
GIIILNPPST	STIPPLING	GIKNOPRUW	WORKING UP
GIIILNPRST	STRIPLING	GIKNOPSST	KING POSTS
GIIILNPRSY	SPRINGILY	GILLLNOOP	LOLLOPING
GIIILNPSTT	SPLITTING	GILLMNOOY	LIMNOLOGY
GIIILNPTYY	PITYINGLY	GILLMOORR	GRILL ROOM
GIIILNQSSU	QUISLINGS	GILLMOSSY	SYLLOGISM
GIIILNRSTW	TWIN GIRLS	GILLNNOOR	ROLLING ON
GIIILNSSTU	LINGUISTS	GILLNNOPU	PULLING ON
GIIILNSSTY	STYLISING	GILLNNORU	UNROLLING
GIIILNSTYZ	STYLIZING	GILLNOPRU	ROLLING UP
GIIILRSTTU	LITURGIST	GILLNOPTU	POLLUTING
GIIIMMNRST	TRIMMINGS	GILLNORST	STROLLING
GIIMMNNOOT	MOTIONING	GILLNOSST	LONG LISTS
GIIMMNNSSU	MINUS SIGN	GILLNPPUU	PULLING UP
GIIMNOPRS	PROMISING	GILLNPRSU	RING PULLS
GIIMNOPRT	IMPORTING		RING-PULLS
GIIMNOPRV	IMPROVING	GILLOOOPY	OLIGOPOLY

GILLOOPSW	POLLIWOGS	GINRSTTTU	STRUTTING
GILMMNOOS	MONGOLISM	GKLLOOSUY	UGLY LOOKS
GILNNOOSU	UNLOOSING	GKNOOOTTW	GOT TO KNOW
GILNNORSU	LOSING RUN	GKNORTUUY	YOUNG TURK
GILNNRSSU	NURSLINGS	GLLOOPSTY	POLYGLOTS
GILNOOSTU	LOSING OUT	GLMOORSWW	GLOW WORMS
GILNOPPSU	SLOPING UP		GLOWWORMS
GILNOPRUY	POURINGLY	GLNNOOOPS	LONG SPOON
GILNOPSUW	SLOWING UP	GLNOOPSST	LONG STOPS
GILNORTUU	RULING OUT	GLNOORSTY	LONG STORY
GILNOSSTU	SLINGS OUT	GLOOOPRTY	TROPOLOGY
GILNOSSWW	SWINGS LOW	GMMNOSTUY	TOMMY GUNS
GILNOSTUU	GLUTINOUS	GNNORRTUW	WRONG TURN
GILNOTTUY	NOT GUILTY	GNOOORSTT	TOO STRONG
GILNPPSUY	SUPPLYING	GNOORSTWW	TWO WRONGS
GILNPSSSU	PLUS SIGNS	GNOPRSTUU	SPRUNG OUT
GILOOOSTZ	ZOOLOGIST	GNORSTTUU	STRUNG OUT
GILOOPRRS	POOR GIRLS	GOOPPPRSU	POP GROUPS
GILOORSTU	UROLOGIST	HHIJMNOST	JOHN SMITH
GIMMNNOSU	SUMMONING	HHIMNOSTT	THIS MONTH
GIMMNPSUU	SUMMING UP	HHINOORSU	HIS HONOUR
	SUMMING-UP	HHMNOOOPY	HOMOPHONY
GIMMNRRUU	MURMURING	HHNOORRST	SHORTHORN
GIMMNRSTU	STRUMMING	HHOOOOPPS	POOH-POOHS
GIMNNOORS	MONSIGNOR	HHOOPPRSS	PHOSPHORS
GIMNNORSU	MOURNINGS	HHOOPRSSU	SHOP HOURS
GIMNOOPRT	PROMOTING	HHPPPSUUY	HUSH PUPPY
GIMNOOTUV	MOVING OUT	HIIJLLMMY	JIMMY HILL
GIMNOPPPU	MOPPING UP	HIIKLLSTW	WITH SKILL
GIMNOPPRT	PROMPTING	HIIKNNOTT	THINK ON IT
GIMNORRUU	RUMOURING	HIILLMNOT	MILLIONTH
GIMOPRUUY	UROPYGIUM	HIILLOOOP	HOI POLLOI
GINNNNORU	RUNNING ON	HIILOSTTY	HOSTILITY
GINNNORTU	NO TURNING	HIILRSTTY	THIRSTILY
	RUNNING TO	HIIMNOSST	SHINTOISM
	TURNING ON	HIIMNPRTU	IN TRIUMPH
GINNNPRUU	RUNNING UP	HIIMNSSTT	TINSMITHS
GINNOOPRT	ORPINGTON	HIIMORSST	HIT OR MISS
GINNOOSTU	NOSING OUT		HIT-OR-MISS
GINNOPTTU	PUTTING ON	HIIMRSSTU	HIRSUTISM
GINNORSST	NO STRINGS	HIIMSSSTU	HUSSITISM
GINNORSTU	TONSURING	HIINOSSTT	SHINTOIST
GINNPRTUU	TURNING UP	HIIOPPRRS	PRIORSHIP
	UPTURNING	HIIOTTTUW	OUT WITH IT
GINNRRTUU	NURTURING	HIJKNSTTU	JUST THINK
GINNRSSTU	UNSTRINGS	HIJLLMNOS	JOHN MILLS
GINOOPPRS	PROPOSING	HIKNNORST	STINKHORN
GINOOPRSS	PROGNOSIS	HIKNOSTTU	THINKS OUT
GINOOPRTU	UPROOTING	HILLMORUU	ILL HUMOUR
GINOOPWWW	POWWOWING	HILLMPSUY	LUMPISHLY
GINOORRSW	SORROWING	HILLOOPRW	WHIRLPOOL
GINOOTTUV	OUTVOTING	HILLSSTYY	STYLISHLY
GINOPPPTU	TOPPING UP	HILMNOOST	MONOLITHS
GINOPPRST	STROPPING	HILMOOTTY	LITHOTOMY
GINOPPRSU	PURPOSING	HILOOPTXY	TOXOPHILY
GINOPPSSU	SUPPOSING	HILOOSSTW	SOLO WHIST
GINOPRSTU	POSTURING	HILORSSTT	SHORT LIST
	SPRING OUT		SHORT-LIST
	SPROUTING	HILRSTTUY	RUTTISHLY
GINOPSSST	SIGNPOSTS	HIMNOPSTY	HYPNOTISM
GINOPSSTU	TOSSING UP	HIMNOSSTX	SIX MONTHS
GINOPTTTU	TOTTING-UP	HIMORSSTU	HUMORISTS
GINORRTTU	TORTURING	HIMPSSSYY	SYMPHYSIS
GINORSTTU	STRING OUT	HINNOOPTT	THIN ON TOP
GINORSTUW	WRINGS OUT	HINNOSTTW	TWO NINTHS
GINORTTUY	TRYING OUT	HINOPPRRY	PORPHYRIN
GINOSSTUW	OUTSWINGS	HINOPPRST	PRINT SHOP
GINPPRSSU	SPRINGS UP	HINOPPSTW	TOWNSHIPS
GINPPTTUU	PUTTING UP	HINOPSTTY	HYPNOTIST
GINPRRTUU	RUPTURING	HINOPSTWY	SHOWN PITY
GINPRSSTU	STRINGS UP	HINORSTTY	THIN STORY

HIOOPPRST	TROOP SHIP	IILMNOPSU	IMPULSION
HIOOPPTUW	WHOOP IT UP	IILMOPSSS	SOLIPSISM
HIOOSTTTU	SHOT IT OUT	IILMOPSUY	IMPIOUSLY
HIOPRSSTY	SOPHISTRY	IILMPRSTW	LIMP WRIST
HIOPRSTTU	TUTORSHIP	IILNOOPST	POSTILION
HIOPRTTTY	TOP THIRTY	IILNOOSTV	VOLITIONS
HIOPSSTWY	SHOWS PITY	IILNOPSST	SLIPS INTO
HIOQSSUWZ	QUIZ SHOWS	IILNPPSST	SPLIT PINS
HIORRSTTY	THYRISTOR	IILOPRTXY	PROLIXITY
HIPPTTUUW	PUT UP WITH	IILOPSSST	SOLIPSIST
HJKNOPSSU	JUNK SHOPS	IILOSTVVZ	SLIVOVITZ
HJORSSTTU	JUST SHORT	IIMNNOOPY	MY OPINION
HKKNNOOTY	HONKY-TONK	IIMNNOSTU	MUNITIONS
HKLOORSTU	LOOKS HURT	IIMNOOSSS	OMISSIONS
HKMMNORRU	KRUMMHORN	IIMNOPRSS	IMPRISONS
HKMOOORSW	HOOKWORMS	IIMNORSTT	INTROMITS
HKOOPRSSW	WORKSHOPS	IIMNPRSST	MISPRINTS
HKOORRSTW	SHORT WORK	IIMOPRTXY	PROXIMITY
HLLNOPSUY	SULPHONYL	IIMOPSSTT	OPTIMISTS
HLLOOOTUW	HOLLOW OUT	IIMRRSTUV	TRIUMVIRS
HLMORSUUY	SLY HUMOUR	IIMSSSTUW	SWIM SUITS
HLNOOPPYY	POLYPHONY		SWIMSUITS
HLNOORUWY	UNHOLY ROW	IINNOPPST	PINPOINTS
HLOOOOPST	SHOOT POOL	IINNORSTU	INTRUSION
HLOOOPSSW	WOOL SHOPS	IINNORTTU	NUTRITION
HMMOORSSU	MUSHROOMS	IINNOSSTU	UNIONISTS
HMNOOSTTW	TWO MONTHS	IINNRSTTU	TURNS IT IN
HMOOORSSW	SHOWROOMS	IINOOPRSV	PROVISION
HMOOORSTW	MOTOR SHOW	IINOOPSST	POSITIONS
HMOOOSTTU	SMOOTH OUT	IINOOPSVY	POISON IVY
HNOOOOTTT	NOT TOO HOT	IINOPRSST	NO SPIRITS
HNOOOSTTU	SUTTON HOO	IINOPSSTX	SIX POINTS
HNOOPSTUW	PUT ON SHOW	IINOPSSTY	SPINOSITY
HNOORTTUW	THROWN OUT	IINOSSTUY	SINUOSITY
HNORRSSTU	RUNS SHORT	IINOSSTVY	SYNOVITIS
HOOOPRSST	POOR SHOTS	IINPRSTUU	IN PURSUIT
HOOORTTTW	TOOTHWORT	IIOOPSSTV	OVIPOSITS
HOOOSSTTU	SHOOT-OUTS	IIOPRSSTU	SPIRITOUS
	SHOOTS OUT	IIOPSTTTU	SPIT IT OUT
HOOPRSSTT	STOP SHORT	IIOSSTTTU	SITS IT OUT
HOORSTTUW	THROWS OUT	IIPRSSTTU	STIRS IT UP
HOOSSTTUU	SHOUTS OUT	IJMNOPSTU	JUMPS INTO
HORRSSTTU	THRUSTORS	IJMOPSTTU	JUMPS TO IT
HPRSSTTUU	UPTHRUSTS	IJMPSSTUU	JUMPSUITS
IIIKLLNPS	SPILLIKIN	IKKOORSST	TOOK RISKS
IIIKMNRST	MINI SKIRT	IKLLLOOSY	LOOK SILLY
IIILLMNPS	MINIPILLS	IKLLLOSST	LOST SKILL
IIILNOPPS	PILIPINOS	IKLLOOPST	TOOK PILLS
IIILNOSTV	VIOLINIST	IKLMORSSW	SILKWORMS
IIILNTTUY	INUTILITY	IKLMOSTTU	MILK STOUT
IIIMPRSST	SPIRITISM	IKLNOOOOT	TOOK ON OIL
IIIMRRTUV	TRIUMVIRI	IKLNOOOST	LOOKS INTO
IIINNNRTT	RIN TIN TIN	IKLNOOPPY	LOOK NIPPY
IIINNOTTU	INTUITION	IKLNOPSST	SLIP KNOTS
IIINPRSST	INSPIRITS		SLIPKNOTS
IIINSSSTU	SINUSITIS	IKLOOPSTU	LOOKS IT UP
IIIPRSSTT	SPIRITIST	IKLOPSSTY	SKY PILOTS
IIJLLNOTW	JOINT WILL	IKNOORRSW	IRON WORKS
IIJNORSUU	INJURIOUS		IRONWORKS
IIKLLLMPS	SPILL MILK	IKOOOTTTU	TOOK IT OUT
IIKLLMPST	SPILT MILK	IKOORTTUW	WORK IT OUT
IIKLRSSTT	SLIT SKIRT	IKORSSTTU	OUTSKIRTS
IIKNNNOOS	ONION SKIN	ILLLLORST	TILL ROLLS
IIKNNSSTU	SINK UNITS	ILLLMOPSS	PLIMSOLLS
IILLMNOPU	POLLINIUM	ILLLOOPPS	LOLLIPOPS
IILLMPRSU	SPIRILLUM	ILLLOSUVY	VILLOUSLY
IILLNORST	TRILLIONS	ILLMOORST	STILL ROOM
IILLNOSSU	ILLUSIONS	ILLNOOPTU	POLLUTION
IILLNOTWW	WILL TO WIN	ILLNOPVYY	POLYVINYL
IILLSSSTT	SITS STILL	ILLOOQSUY	SOLILOQUY
IILMNOOPS	IMPLOSION	ILLORSSSW	SWISS ROLL

ILMNOOSUY	OMINOUSLY	LMOORSSWW	SLOWWORMS
ILMNOPTUU	PLUTONIUM	LNNOOTTUW	LUTON TOWN
ILNOOPSSW	POOLS WINS	LNOOOPRST	POLTROONS
ILNOOSSTU	SOLUTIONS	LNOOSSWWY	SNOWY OWLS
ILNOOSUXY	NOXIOUSLY	LOOOPRSSU	POOR SOULS
ILNOPRXYY	PYROXYLIN	LOOOSSTTW	TWO STOOLS
ILNORSUUY	RUINOUSLY	LORSTUUUV	VULTUROUS
ILNOSSUUY	SINUOUSLY	MMNOPSSUU	SUMMONS UP
ILOOPPUVX	VOX POPULI	MMORRSUUU	MURMUROUS
ILOORSTUY	RIOTOUSLY	MNOORSSTU	MONSTROUS
ILOPPSSTU	POPULISTS	MNOORSSTW	SNOW STORM
ILOPRSSYY	PYROLYSIS		SNOWSTORM
ILORSUUUX	LUXURIOUS	MNORSSTUU	SURMOUNTS
IMMMNOORS	MORMONISM	MOOORRTTU	MOTOR TOUR
IMMOPPRTU	IMPROMPTU	MOPSSTUUU	SUMPTUOUS
IMMOPSSUY	SYMPOSIUM	NNOOOPSST	SPONTOONS
IMNNOOPTW	TOPMINNOW	NNOPRSTUU	TURNS UPON
IMNOOOPRT	PROMOTION	NOOOOPRTZ	PROTOZOON
IMNOOOPTT	MOOT POINT	NOOOPPSSU	SOUP SPOON
IMNORSTTU	STRONTIUM	NORRSSTUU	TURNS SOUR
IMOOPPSTY	POMPOSITY	OOOOPPRRST	POOR SPORT
IMOOPRRSS	PROMISORS	OOOOPRSTTU	TROOPS OUT
IMOOPRSST	IMPOSTORS	OOPRSSTUU	STUPOROUS
IMOOQSSTU	MOSQUITOS	OOPRSTTTY	TRY TO STOP
IMOORSSTT	MOTORISTS	OOPRTTTUU	PUT TO ROUT
IMPRSTTUU	TRUMP SUIT		
IMRSSSTTU	MISTRUSTS		
INNNORSTU	TRUNNIONS		
INNOOOPSU	ONION SOUP		
INNOORTTW	TORN IN TWO		
INNORSTTU	TURNS INTO		
	TURNS IT ON		
INNOSTTWW	TWIN TOWNS		
INOOOPSSU	POISONOUS		
INOOORSTU	NOTORIOUS		
INOOPRSST	POSITRONS		
INOOPSSTT	SPITTOONS		
INOOPSTTU	OUTPOINTS		
	POINTS OUT		
INOOPSTTW	TWO POINTS		
INOOPTTTU	NOT UP TO IT		
INOPPRSTU	IN SUPPORT		
INOPRSTTU	PRINTOUTS		
INPRSSTTU	TURNSPITS		
INPRSTTUU	TURNS IT UP		
INRSTTTUU	UNIT TRUST		
IOOORRRST	ORRISROOT		
IOOPPRRTU	POT POURRI		
	POTPOURRI		
IOOPPRSST	PROPTOSIS		
IOOPRRSVY	PROVISORY		
IOORSSTUV	VIRTUOSOS		
IOORSTTTU	SORT IT OUT		
IOORTTTTU	TROT IT OUT		
IOOSSTTUZ	ZOOT SUITS		
IOPRSSTTU	OUTSTRIPS		
IORRSSUVV	SURVIVORS		
IOSSSTTUU	SUSS IT OUT		
JNNOORRSU	NONJURORS		
KLLMNSSUU	NUMSKULLS		
KLNOOOPSU	LOOKS UPON		
KLNORSSTY	KLYSTRONS		
KLOOOPSTU	LOOKS UP TO		
KLOOPRSSY	LOOKS SPRY		
KMOOORRSW	WORKROOMS		
KNOORSTTU	TOOK TURNS		
KOOPRSSTW	STOPS WORK		
KOOPRTTUW	PUT TO WORK		
LLOOSSSTU	LOST SOULS		
LMOOOORST	TOOLROOMS		
LMOOPPSUY	POMPOUSLY		

AAAABBDDIS	ADDIS ABABA	AAABDELLNR	ARABLE LAND
AAAABCHNST	ATHABASCAN	AAABDGMMRR	BAD GRAMMAR
AAAABCLLSV	BALACLAVAS	AAABDGNNOY	GAY ABANDON
AAAABEINRS	ARABIAN SEA	AAABDKLNRW	DRAW A BLANK
AAAABIKLLS	BALALAIKAS	AAABDMNRRU	BARRAMUNDA
AAAACDGMRS	MADAGASCAR	AAABDMORSS	AMBASSADOR
AAAACDJNRS	JACARANDAS	AAABDORRST	ASTARBOARD
AAAACDMMRT	TARMACADAM	AAABEEGLMN	MANAGEABLE
AAAACGMNRT	MAGNA CARTA	AAABEEKKMR	MAKE A BREAK
AAAACINNRU	ARAUCANIAN	AAABEELLPP	APPEALABLE
AAAACIRRSU	ARAUCARIAS	AAABEELMNS	ABLE SEAMAN
AAAACMNRST	CATAMARANS	AAABEELPPS	APPEASABLE
AAAADFNRWY	FAR AND AWAY	AAABEFKLLR	BREAK A FALL
AAAADNRSTW	ANWAR SADAT	AAABEFKLOS	BAKES A LOAF
AAAAEGLMMT	AMAI GAMATE	AAABEFLMRR	ARABLE FARM
AAAAGHRSTY	SATYAGRAHA	AAABEGGINN	BEGAN AGAIN
AAAAGKLRSY	GAY AS A LARK	AAABEGGMNR	GARBAGE MAN
AAAAHHJMRS	MAHARAJAHS	AAABEGLMWY	GAMBLE AWAY
AAAAHINNST	ATHANASIAN	AAABEHHMST	THE BAHAMAS
AAAAHKNPST	ATHAPASKAN	AAABEHKNTT	TAKEN A BATH
AAAAILRTTV	LA TRAVIATA	AAABEHKSTT	TAKES A BATH
AAAAIMNRST	SANTA MARIA	AAABEHLPTZ	BLAZE A PATH
AAABBCILST	SABBATICAL	AAABEHPSTT	BEATS A PATH
AAABBDGINR	BAD BARGAIN	AAABEILLSS	ASSAILABLE
AAABBDHSTY	SABBATH DAY	AAABEILNTT	ATTAINABLE
AAABBDLLNT	BAT AND BALL	AAABEKMNRR	BREAK AN ARM
AAABBEMRST	BABE AT ARMS	AAABEKPRRT	BREAK APART
AAABBEPRRY	BARBARY APE	AAABEKRSWY	BREAKAWAYS
AAABBINRRS	BARBARIANS		BREAKS AWAY
AAABCCCHRT	CATCH A CRAB	AAABELLNSY	ANALYSABLE
AAABCCDELL	CALLED A CAB	AAABENRRST	RAN ABREAST
AAABCCEIRR	ARABIC RACE	AAABERSSTT	ARAB STATES
AAABCCHLLT	CATCH A BALL	AAABIKNNNS	BANANA SKIN
AAABCCHLNS	BACCHANALS	AAABIMNPST	ANABAPTISM
AAABCCHNRS	CHARABANCS	AAABINPSTT	ANABAPTIST
AAABCCKNSV	CANVASBACK	AAACCDEHHN	HAD A CHANCE
AAABCDEEKK	BAKED A CAKE	AAACCDELSV	CAVALCADES
AAABCDEHIL	HAILED A CAB	AAACCEGHTV	GAVE A CATCH
AAABCDEIRS	SCARABAEID	AAACCEHHNS	HAS A CHANCE
AAABCDEKWY	BACKED AWAY	AAACCEHKRV	HAVE A CRACK
AAABCDELNR	CANDELABRA	AAACCEHKTT	TAKE A CATCH
AAABCDRRSU	BARRACUDAS	AAACCFLTTU	ACTUAL FACT
AAABCEEKKS	BAKES A CAKE	AAACCINSSU	CAUCASIANS
AAABCEGGNR	GARBAGE CAN	AAACCIPRTT	PARATACTIC
AAABCEHHMO	OMAHA BEACH	AAACCIRSTT	ATARACTICS
AAABCEHLMR	BEACH-LA-MAR	AAACDDEEHR	RACED AHEAD
AAABCEHLSS	CALABASHES	AAACDDEELN	LEAD A DANCE
AAABCEHLTT	ATTACHABLE	AAACDDELRS	DEALS A CARD
AAABCEKKNT	TAKEN ABACK	AAACDDELRT	DEALT A CARD
AAABCEKKST	TAKES ABACK	AAACDDEMNR	CARED A DAMN
AAABCELRTU	ACETABULAR	AAACDDENRR	CARED A DARN
AAABCEMRST	CARBAMATES	AAACDEEHRS	RACES AHEAD
AAABCERSSU	SCARABAEUS	AAACDEELNS	LEADS AN ACE
AAABCGIKNT	TAKING A CAB	AAACDEHLLN	EACH AND ALL
AAABCHINRT	BATRACHIAN	AAACDEHLNV	AVALANCHED
AAABCIKLMR	BLACK MARIA	AAACDEHSWY	CHASED AWAY
AAABCORRTU	BARRACOUTA	AAACDEILMM	MADE A CLAIM
AAABCORSTV	COSTA BRAVA	AAACDEIMMS	MACADAMISE
AAABDDEINT	AID AND ABET	AAACDEKNPY	PANCAKE DAY
AAABDEEKMR	MADE A BREAK	AAACDEKNRT	TAKEN A CARD
AAABDEEKRT	BREAK A DATE	AAACDEKRST	TAKES A CARD
AAABDEFKLO	BAKED A LOAF	AAACDELMNR	CALAMANDER
AAABDEKRTY	AT DAYBREAK	AAACDELMRS	SALAD CREAM

AAACDELNTV	NAVAL CADET	AAACILLRTU	URAL-ALTAIC
AAACDELRSY	CLEAR AS DAY	AAACILLSTX	CALLS A TAXI
AAACDEMNRS	CARES A DAMN	AAACILMMNO	AMMONIACAL
AAACDENNRV	CARAVANNED	AAACILMNOT	ANATOMICAL
AAACDENNRW	DRAWN AN ACE	AAACILNRSS	CARNASSIAL
AAACDENRRS	CARES A DARN	AAACILNRST	SCARLATINA
AAACDENRSW	DRAWS AN ACE	AAACIMNPTY	PANAMA CITY
AAACDEPRTT	ACTED A PART	AAACINRRTT	TRACTARIAN
AAACDERTWY	CARTED AWAY	AAACLNSSTU	SANTA CLAUS
AAACDGLNNR	GRAND CANAL	AAACNRTTTT	ATTRACTANT
AAACDILLTY	CALL IT A DAY	AAACPRSTWW	WARSAW PACT
AAACDILMRT	DRAMATICAL	AAADDEEMNV	ADAM AND EVE
AAACDILNRS	CALANDRIAS	AAADDEHSWY	DASHED AWAY
AAACDLPRSY	PLAYS A CARD	AAADDEIMTY	MADE IT A DAY
AAACDLRSUW	CASUAL WARD	AAADDELNNS	LAND AND SEA
AAACEEFKMS	MAKES A FACE	AAADDEMNST	MADE A STAND
AAACEEGRSV	SAVAGE RACE	AAADDENVWW	WAVED A WAND
AAACEEKKMS	MAKES A CAKE	AAADDHHIOR	HAD A HAIR-DO
AAACEENPPR	APPEARANCE	AAADDHMRSY	HAMADRYADS
AAACEENRSS	CAESAREANS	AAADEEFTWY	AWAY DEFEAT
AAACEESSTT	STATE A CASE	AAADEEGLRT	A GREAT DEAL
AAACEFHLNR	HALF AN ACRE	AAADEEHINV	HAVE AN IDEA
AAACEFILTU	CAFE AU LAIT	AAADEEHLPS	LEAPS AHEAD
AAACEFIRST	EAST AFRICA	AAADEEHLPT	LEAPT AHEAD
AAACEFLQTU	CATAFALQUE	AAADEEHMRV	HAVE A DREAM
AAACEGNSTT	ACT AS AGENT	AAADEEKLMS	MAKES A DEAL
AAACEHHIRV	HAVE A CHAIR	AAADEEKLWY	LEAKED AWAY
AAACEHIKRT	TAKE A CHAIR	AAADEEKMST	MAKES A DATE
AAACEHIMNN	MANICHAEAN	AAADEEKRST	TAKE AS READ
AAACEHKNSV	HAVE A SNACK	AAADEFIOST	ASAFOETIDA
AAACEHLNSV	AVALANCHES	AAADEFNNRR	FAR AND NEAR
AAACEHSSWY	CHASES AWAY		NEAR AND FAR
AAACEIKLMM	MAKE A CLAIM	AAADEGGHNR	GARAGE HAND
AAACEINPSS	CASPIAN SEA	AAADEGGRTV	AGGRAVATED
AAACEINPST	ANAPAESTIC	AAADEGILRW	LAID A WAGER
	SEA CAPTAIN	AAADEGINRV	DEVANAGARI
AAACEINRSS	CAESARIANS	AAADEGKRWW	AWKWARD AGE
AAACEINRTV	AT VARIANCE	AAADEGLMNR	ARM AND A LEG
AAACEJKNPS	JACKANAPES	AAADEGMPSY	PAY DAMAGES
AAACEKLLMS	MAKES A CALL	AAADEGNRRS	AS ARRANGED
AAACEKLLNT	TAKEN A CALL	AAADEGNRTV	AVANT GARDE
AAACEKLLST	TAKES A CALL		AVANT-GARDE
AAACEKLSST	TAKE A CLASS	AAADEGNSTV	ADVANTAGES
AAACELLPSY	PLAY A SCALE	AAADEGNWWY	GNAWED AWAY
AAACELMPRT	METACARPAL	AAADEHHRTT	HAD AT HEART
AAACELNPSY	PLAYS AN ACE	AAADEHINRS	RAISE A HAND
AAACELNSWY	CLEANS AWAY	AAADEHKNNT	TAKEN A HAND
AAACELRSWY	CLEARS AWAY	AAADEHKNST	TAKES A HAND
AAACENNRRV	CARAVANNER	AAADEHLLVY	HAVE ALL DAY
AAACFHLRST	FATAL CRASH	AAADEHLMNV	VEAL AND HAM
AAACFLNRTV	NAVAL CRAFT	AAADEHLNPP	HAD AN APPLE
AAACGGILNO	ANAGOGICAL	AAADEHLNPS	PLANS AHEAD
AAACGHNRTT	TRAGACANTH	AAADEHLNTT	HAD A TALENT
AAACGILLMY	AGAMICALLY	AAADEHLUWY	HAULED AWAY
AAACGILLNO	ANALOGICAL	AAADEHNNRT	NEAR AT HAND
AAACGILLNS	CALLS AGAIN	AAADEHSSTY	STAYS AHEAD
AAACGIMSWY	MAGICS AWAY	AAADEHSSWY	DASHES AWAY
AAACGKSSTT	GAS ATTACKS	AAADEHSWWY	WASHED AWAY
AAACGLLNTT	GALLANT ACT	AAADEIKMTY	MAKE IT A DAY
AAACHILMNR	ALARM CHAIN	AAADEILSWY	SAILED AWAY
AAACHILSTY	SAIL A YACHT	AAADEILTWY	TAILED AWAY
AAACHLLLST	CALLS A HALT	AAADEIMNNT	ADAMANTINE
AAACHLNOTU	ANACOLUTHA	AAADEKLWWY	WALKED AWAY
AAACHLNRST	CHARLATANS	AAADEKMNST	MAKE A STAND
AAACHNPRTY	PYRACANTHA	AAADEKNSTT	TAKE A STAND
AAACHNSTWY	SNATCH AWAY	AAADELMMRS	MARMALADES
AAACIJMMRU	JAMAICA RUM	AAADELMNRS	SALAMANDER
AAACIKLMNP	PACK ANIMAL	AAADELMPPS	ADAMS APPLE
AAACIKLMNR	LAMARCKIAN	AAADELNPQU	AQUAPLANED
AAACIKLRTU	AUTARKICAL	AAADELPRTY	LEAD A PARTY
AAACILLMNU	ANIMALCULA	AAADELPSSW	PASSED A LAW

AAADELPWYY	PLAYED AWAY	AAAEGINTWY	EATING AWAY
AAADELRSTY	LEAD ASTRAY	AAAEGLMPSY	PLAYS A GAME
AAADELSTWY	SALTED AWAY	AAAEGLRSWY	LAYS A WAGER
AAADELSVWY	SLAVED AWAY	AAAEGMNRTY	A GREAT MANY
AAADEMRSTT	MADE A START	AAAEGNNTTT	AT A TANGENT
AAADENNWWX	WAX AND WANE	AAAEGPRTVY	GAVE A PARTY
AAADENRWWY	WANDER AWAY	AAAEGPSSWY	PASSAGEWAY
AAADEPRRWY	PAY A REWARD	AAAEHHKMSS	MAKES A HASH
AAADEPSSWY	PASSED AWAY	AAAEHHMSTW	WHAT A SHAME!
AAADESTWWY	WASTED AWAY	AAAEHHRSTT	HAS AT HEART
AAADESTWYY	STAYED AWAY	AAAEHILLNP	ALL IN A HEAP
AAADFGINWY	FADING AWAY	AAAEHINSTU	EUTHANASIA
AAADFMNNSY	FANNY ADAMS	AAAEHITVWY	HAVE IT AWAY
AAADGHILRS	SIR GALAHAD	AAAEHKNOTT	TAKE AN OATH
AAADGILLNR	GRANADILLA	AAAEHLNPPS	HAS AN APPLE
AAADGINNPT	GIANT PANDA	AAAEHLNSTT	HAS A TALENT
AAADGMNORR	MANDRAGORA	AAAEHLORSW	WEARS A HALO
AAADGNOPPR	PROPAGANDA	AAAEHMMOST	HAEMATOMAS
AAADHHIORS	HAS A HAIR-DO	AAAEHMMRWY	HAMMER AWAY
AAADHLLNTT	AND ALL THAT	AAAEHPPRRS	PARAPHRASE
AAADHLNNOY	LAY A HAND ON	AAAEHPRTVY	HAVE A PARTY
AAADHMMMNU	MUHAMMADAN	AAAEIILNTT	ITALIANATE
AAADHMNSSU	UMS AND AAHS	AAAEIKNRTT	TAKE A TRAIN
AAADIKLLLO	ALKALOIDAL	AAAEIKNTTX	TAKEN A TAXI
AAADIKLPST	DAS KAPITAL	AAAEIKSTTX	TAKES A TAXI
AAADILMNST	DALMATIANS	AAAEIKTTWY	TAKE IT AWAY
AAADINOPTT	ADAPTATION	AAAEILLLPS	PALALALISE
AAADINRSWY	DRAINS AWAY	AAAEILLPTZ	PALATALIZE
AAADLNNSSY	ANALYSANDS	AAAEILMMNT	TAME ANIMAL
AAADLNQRTU	QUADRANTAL	AAAEILMPST	METAPLASIA
AAADMNNQRUU	QUADRUMANA	AAAEILMRTU	TULARAEMIA
AAADNOTUWY	OUT AND AWAY	AAAEILNORS	RAISE A LOAN
AAADNPRRTW	DRAWN APART	AAAEILNPRT	PLANETARIA
AAADNPRSTT	STAND APART	AAAEILNPTT	PALATINATE
AAADNSSTWY	STANDS AWAY	AAAEIMNPRS	PARAMNESIA
AAADORSTTU	AUTOSTRADA	AAAEIMNQRU	AQUAMARINE
AAADPRRSTW	DRAWS APART	AAAEINNPST	NEAT AS A PIN
AAAEEELMNT	EATEN A MEAL	AAAEKKLNTW	TAKEN A WALK
AAAEEGGLRS	GARAGE SALE	AAAEKKLSTW	TAKES A WALK
AAAEEGLNNN	ANNA NEAGLE	AAAEKKMMRS	MAKES A MARK
AAAEEGLPSV	LEAVES A GAP	AAAEKLMPSY	MAKES A PLAY
AAAEEGMNRV	AVERAGE MAN	AAAEKMPSSS	MAKES A PASS
AAAEEGNRSW	EARNS A WAGE	AAAEKMRSSW	WEARS A MASK
AAAEEGRRTT	TARGET AREA	AAAEKMRSTT	MAKE A START
AAAEEHHRTV	HAVE A HEART	AAAEKNPRTT	TAKEN A PART
AAAEEHKRST	TAKE A SHARE		TAKEN APART
AAAEEKLMMS	MAKES A MEAL	AAAEKNSSWY	SNEAKS AWAY
AAAEEKLMRV	LEAVE A MARK	AAAEKPRSTT	TAKES A PART
AAAEEKLMSS	MAKES A SALE		TAKES APART
AAAEEKMMNS	MAKES A NAME	AAAEKSSTWY	STAYS AWAKE
AAAEEKNSTT	TAKEN A SEAT	AAAELLNRTT	TARANTELLA
AAAEEKSSTT	TAKES A SEAT	AAAELMMNOT	MELANOMATA
AAAEEMNNRS	EARNS A NAME	AAAELMPPSS	MASS APPEAL
AAAEFFILST	FIT AS A FLEA	AAAELMRSTT	METATARSAL
AAAEFFIMRT	TAME AFFAIR	AAAELNOPRY	REPAY A LOAN
AAAEFHHKLS	HALF A SHAKE	AAAELNPQRU	AQUAPLANER
AAAEFHLLOP	ALL OF A HEAP	AAAELNPQSU	AQUAPLANES
AAAEFHLRST	SHARE A FLAT	AAAELNRTTU	TARANTULAE
AAAEFIRRRW	AIR WARFARE	AAAELPSSSW	PASSES A LAW
AAAEFKLLNT	TAKEN A FALL	AAAELRSWWY	SAW A LAWYER
AAAEFKLLST	TAKES A FALL	AAAELSSTWY	STEALS AWAY
AAAEFLLMRS	FALSE ALARM	AAAELSSVWY	SLAVES AWAY
AAAEFLLNWY	FALLEN AWAY	AAAEPRRSTT	TEARS APART
AAAEFLSSTT	SAFE AT LAST	AAAEPRRSYY	SAY A PRAYER
AAAEGGIMNT	GAMETANGIA	AAAEPSSSWY	PASSES AWAY
AAAEGGRSTV	AGGRAVATES	AAAESSTWWY	WASTES AWAY
AAAEGILMNR	MANAGERIAL	AAAFFIILNN	FIANNA FAIL
AAAEGILMSS	MALAGASIES	AAAFFKKNRZ	FRANZ KAFKA
AAAEGILNST	EAST ANGLIA	AAAFGGHINV	HAVING A FAG
AAAEGILPPR	PARAPLEGIA	AAAFGHLLSS	HALF A GLASS
AAAEGINPRS	ASPARAGINE	AAAFHKNSST	SANK A SHAFT

AAAFHLMSTT	AT HALF-MAST
AAAFIINRWY	IN A FAIR WAY
AAAFIKPRRS	SAFARI PARK
AAAFILMMNR	ANIMAL FARM
	FARM ANIMAL
AAAFKORSUV	ASK A FAVOUR
AAAFLLPRST	FALLS APART
AAAFLORSST	SOLFATARAS
AAAFNORTWY	NOT FAR AWAY
AAAGGILLNO	ALGOLAGNIA
AAAGGNNRTU	GARGANTUAN
AAAGGNOORT	ANGORA GOAT
AAAGHINNPV	HAVING A NAP
AAAGHLSUWY	LAUGHS AWAY
AAAGHNPSTU	AGAPANTHUS
AAAGHPPRRS	PARAGRAPHS
AAAGIILMNR	MARGINALIA
AAAGIKLMNW	MAKING A LAW
AAAGIKNNPT	TAKING A NAP
AAAGIKNTWY	TAKING AWAY
AAAGILMRRV	MARGRAVIAL
AAAGIMMNRR	GRAMMARIAN
AAAGIMNORT	MAORITANGA
AAAGIMNSTT	ANASTIGMAT
AAAGINNRST	RAN AGAINST
AAAGINRSTT	START AGAIN
AAAGLNNSTW	NASAL TWANG
AAAGLNRSTU	NATURAL GAS
AAAGLRSSTU	ASTRAGALUS
AAAGNPRSWY	SPRANG AWAY
AAAHIILSTX	HAILS A TAXI
AAAHILMRRS	AIR MARSHAL
AAAHIMNSTY	MAHAYANIST
AAAHKNRSST	ASTRAKHANS
AAAHKNRSWY	SHRANK AWAY
AAAHLLOSTY	AYATOLLAHS
AAAHLMNPST	PHANTASMAL
AAAHMNNSTT	MANHATTANS
AAAIILRTTW	AWAIT TRIAL
AAAIIMNRTU	MAURITANIA
AAAILLLPTY	PALATIALLY
AAAILLMNNZ	MANZANILLA
AAAILLMRTW	MARTIAL LAW
AAAILLNOTV	LAVATIONAL
AAAILLORTV	LAVATORIAL
AAAILMNORZ	MARIO LANZA
AAAILMNRWY	RAILWAYMAN
AAAILMRRTT	MARTIAL ART
AAAILNNPRS	PLANARIANS
AAAILNORTT	NATATORIAL
AAAILNRSTU	AUSTRALIAN
	SATURNALIA
AAAILNSSST	ASSAILANTS
AAAILPPRSS	APPRAISALS
AAAIMNORST	INAMORATAS
AAAIMNRSST	SAMARITANS
AAAINNSSSS	SASSANIANS
AAAINPRRTT	RAT IN A TRAP
AAAKLNPPRY	PLAY A PRANK
AAALLNRTUW	NATURAL LAW
AAALLPTWYZ	PLAY A WALTZ
AAALMNOPRR	PARANORMAL
AAALNRSTTU	TARANTULAS
AAALPPRSTY	PLAYS A PART
AAAMMMNNOST	AS MAN TO MAN
AAAMNOPRSY	PAY A RANSOM
AAAMRTZZZZ	RAZZMATAZZ
AAAPRSSTTY	STAYS APART
AAARRSSTTW	STARTS A WAR
AABBBELORS	ABSORBABLE

AABBCCKKOT	BACK TO BACK
	BACK-TO-BACK
AABBCDEEGR	RED CABBAGE
AABBCDEKLR	BLACK BEARD
AABBCDKLOR	BLACKBOARD
AABBCDKORS	BACKBOARDS
AABBCEEHLL	BLEACHABLE
AABBCEEKNT	BEATEN BACK
AABBCEILRS	ASCRIBABLE
AABBCEKKRS	BREAKS BACK
AABBCEKLST	BLACK BEAST
AABBCERRSU	BARBACUERS
AABBCFKOSU	BACK OF A BUS
AABBCIJKRT	JACK RABBIT
AABBCILLPT	LIB-LAB PACT
AABBCKLLLS	BLACKBALLS
AABBDDEEKR	BAKED BREAD
AABBDDEENN	BADEN BADEN
AABBDDEORR	BREAD BOARD
AABBDEEKNS	BAKED BEANS
AABBDEEKRR	BREAK BREAD
AABBDEEKRS	BAKES BREAD
AABBDEGINR	BIG BAND ERA
AABBDEGMMO	BOMB DAMAGE
AABBDEGORR	BARGEBOARD
AABBDEHLSY	SHABBY DEAL
AABBDEIRRS	BARBARISED
AABBDEIRRZ	BARBARIZED
AABBDELORS	ADSORBABLE
AABBDENORS	BROAD BEANS
AABBDEOORV	ABOVE BOARD
	ABOVEBOARD
AABBDEORSS	BASEBOARDS
AABBDGNRSY	BABY GRANDS
AABBDORSSU	BOARDS A BUS
AABBEEIRTV	ABBREVIATE
AABBEEKNOR	BREAK A BONE
AABBEELLLL	LABELLABLE
AABBEELNRU	UNBEARABLE
AABBEELNTU	UNBEATABLE
AABBEESSUY	BUSY AS A BEE
AABBEGINWY	EBBING AWAY
AABBEGORRX	BOX BARRAGE
AABBEHHSTT	THE SABBATH
AABBEILMNO	ABOMINABLE
AABBEILNOT	OBTAINABLE
AABBEIMNRS	BABE IN ARMS
AABBEINRST	RABBINATES
AABBEIRRSS	BARBARISES
AABBEIRRSZ	BARBARIZES
AABBEKLLST	BASKETBALL
AABBEKLOOT	BOOK A TABLE
AABBEKMMOS	MAKES A BOMB
AABBELNRUY	UNBEARABLY
AABBELNTUY	UNBEATABLY
AABBEMMNORS	EARNS A BOMB
AABBIKORUY	ABOUKIR BAY
AABBILMNOY	ABOMINABLY
AABBIORSSU	BABIROUSSA
AABBIRSSSU	BABIRUSSAS
AABBMMNPYY	NAMBY-PAMBY
AABCCDEHKR	ARCHED BACK
AABCCDEKKP	BACKPACKED
AABCCDEKLL	CALLED BACK
AABCCDEKPS	BACKSPACED
AABCCDISTT	BAD TACTICS
AABCCDNOTU	BAD ACCOUNT
AABCCEEHNR	BARE CHANCE
AABCCEELPT	ACCEPTABLE
AABCCEGKLN	GLANCE BACK
AABCCEHKNY	HACKNEY CAB

AABCCEHNST	BACCHANTES	AABCDKLRWY	BACKWARDLY
AABCCEKKPR	BACKPACKER	AABCDKNSST	STANDS BACK
AABCCEKLMS	CAMELBACKS	AABCDLLNPU	CUP AND BALL
AABCCEKPSS	BACKSPACES	AABCDMNOPY	BAD COMPANY
AABCCELLLU	CALCULABLE	AABCDNNORT	CONTRABAND
AABCCELPTY	ACCEPTABLY	AABCDNOORS	CARBONADOS
AABCCGIKLM	BLACK MAGIC	AABCDORSST	BROADCASTS
AABCCHHKST	HATCHBACKS	AABCEEEFFL	EFFACEABLE
AABCCHKLPT	BLACK PATCH	AABCEEEMNS	BECAME SANE
AABCCIILST	CABALISTIC	AABCEEERTX	EXACERBATE
AABCCIKLLL	CILLA BLACK	AABCEEGHLN	CHANGEABLE
AABCCIKRRS	CRACKS A RIB	AABCEEGHLR	CHARGEABLE
AABCCIORST	ACROBATICS	AABCEEHILV	ACHIEVABLE
AABCCJKKLS	BLACKJACKS	AABCEEHLMP	PEACH MELBA
AABCCKKRST	BACKTRACKS	AABCEEHLRS	SEARCHABLE
AABCCKMNOT	BANTAM COCK	AABCEEHRST	SABRETACHE
AABCCLLLUY	CALCULABLY	AABCEEHTWY	EACH-WAY BET
AABCDDEEHK	HEADED BACK	AABCEEILMR	AMERCIABLE
AABCDDEHKN	BACKHANDED		BEAR MALICE
	HANDED BACK	AABCEEINNY	IN ABEYANCE
AABCDDEIRR	BARRICADED	AABCEEINRR	CARABINEER
AABCDDEKLS	SADDLEBACK	AABCEEKLNR	CLEAN BREAK
AABCDEEHHS	BEACHHEADS	AABCEELLLR	RECALLABLE
AABCDEEHHY	BEACHY HEAD	AABCEELMRT	TABLE CREAM
AABCDEEHLT	DETACHABLE	AABCEELNRT	TABERNACLE
AABCDEEILH	ERADICABLE	AABCEELNST	SENT A CABLE
AABCDEELLR	DECLARABLE	AABCEELPPR	RECAPPABLE
AABCDEELNS	ASCENDABLE	AABCEELPST	PLACES A BET
	SEND A CABLE	AABCEELRTU	TRABECULAE
AABCDEELNU	BALANCE DUE	AABCEFFLNO	OFF BALANCE
AABCDEELPT	PLACED A BET	AABCEFIILP	PACIFIABLE
AABCDEERSU	BREAD SAUCE	AABCEFIRST	FABRICATES
AABCDEFFIRT	FABRICATED	AABCEFKLLN	FALLEN BACK
AABCDEFOTU	ABOUT-FACED	AABCEFLORT	FACTORABLE
AABCDEGKNR	BACK GARDEN	AABCEFOSTU	ABOUT-FACES
AABCDEHIRT	BRACHIATED	AABCEGHLNY	CHANGEABLY
AABCDEHKLS	BLACKHEADS	AABCEGHMRS	GAS CHAMBER
AABCDEHKLT	BLACK DEATH	AABCEGINRS	BRING A CASE
AABCDEHKNR	BACKHANDER	AABCEGIRRR	CARRIER BAG
AABCDEHLTY	DETACHABLY	AABCEGKLLR	CLARK GABLE
AABCDEHNSY	SANDY BEACH	AABCEGLLOU	COAGULABLE
AABCDEHPST	BAD PATCHES	AABCEGLMNN	BLANCMANGE
AABCDEIIRS	ARABICISED	AABCEGLMRS	CABLEGRAMS
AABCDEIIRZ	ARABICIZED	AABCEGPRST	CARPETBAGS
AABCDEILRT	CALIBRATED	AABCEHIIMM	MIAMI BEACH
AABCDEIRRS	BARRICADES	AABCEHILMN	MACHINABLE
AABCDEKKLT	TALKED BACK	AABCEHILRT	CHARITABLE
AABCDEKKLW	WALKED BACK	AABCEHINRT	BRANCHIATE
AABCDEKLPS	BACKPEDALS	AABCEHIRST	BRACHIATES
AABCDEKLPY	PLAYED BACK	AABCEHKLRS	BACKLASHER
AABCDEKPSS	PASSED BACK	AABCEHKLRT	BLACK HEART
AABCDEKSWY	SWAYBACKED	AABCEHKLSS	BACKLASHES
AABCDELNNU	UNBALANCED	AABCEHKLSW	WHALEBACKS
AABCDELNPU	BALANCED UP	AABCEHKORS	BACK A HORSE
AABCDEMSSU	AMBUSCADES	AABCEHKSSW	BACKWASHES
AABCDENNOR	CARBONNADE	AABCEHLMRR	MARBLE ARCH
AABCDENNSU	ABUNDANCES	AABCEIINTU	BEAUTICIAN
AABCDENORT	CARBONATED	AABCEIIRSS	ARABICISES
AABCDERSST	BAD ACTRESS	AABCEIIRSZ	ARABICIZES
AABCDERSTT	ABSTRACTED	AABCEIKKTT	TAKE IT BACK
AABCDGIINT	ABDICATING	AABCEILLMP	IMPLACABLE
AABCDGIKNT	BACKDATING	AABCEILLPP	APPLICABLE
AABCDGKLRU	BLACKGUARD	AABCEILMNS	IMBALANCES
AABCDGKORW	GO BACKWARD	AABCEILNOT	ACTIONABLE
AABCDHIPSY	PAID BY CASH	AABCEILOSS	ASSOCIABLE
AABCDHMORT	MATCHBOARD	AABCEILOST	CATABOLISE
AABCDHOPRT	PATCHBOARD	AABCEILOTT	CATABOLITE
AABCDIILLO	DIABOLICAL	AABCEILOTZ	CATABOLIZE
AABCDIINOT	ABDICATION	AABCEILQRU	ACQUIRABLE
AABCDIMNOS	CAMBODIANS	AABCEILRST	CALIBRATES
AABCDIORST	ABDICATORS	AABCEINORT	ABREACTION

417

AABCEINRRS	CARABINERS	AABCILMOST	CATABOLISM
AABCEIORST	AEROBATICS	AABCILNNUU	INCUNABULA
AABCEJKLST	BLACK AS JET	AABCILNOTY	ACTIONABLY
AABCEKKMRR	BACK MARKER	AABCILNSUV	SUBCLAVIAN
AABCEKLLPR	BLACK PEARL	AABCILORRT	CALIBRATOR
AABCEKLLSY	BACK ALLEYS	AABCINNORS	CARBANIONS
AABCEKLNPS	BLANK SPACE	AABCIQSTUU	SUBAQUATIC
AABCEKLORS	BACK A LOSER	AABCKLLMPS	LAMPBLACKS
AABCEKLRSW	WEARS BLACK	AABCKLMOOR	BLACKAMOOR
AABCEKLRTW	BLACKWATER	AABCKLMPST	BLACK STAMP
AABCEKMPRS	BREAKS CAMP	AABCKRSSST	BRASS TACKS
AABCEKNRSW	ANSWER BACK	AABCLLNNNO	CANNON BALL
AABCEKPPRS	PAPERBACKS		CANNONBALL
AABCEKPSSS	PASSES BACK	AABCLMOPRU	LABOUR CAMP
AABCEKRRRS	BARRACKERS	AABCLMOPRY	COMPARABLY
AABCEKRSTW	BACK WATERS	AABCLORTUW	CRAWL ABOUT
	BACKWATERS	AABCLORUVY	VOCABULARY
AABCELLMNY	CALL BY NAME	AABCLRSTTY	ABSTRACTLY
AABCELLORR	BARCAROLLE	AABCMNOSTT	COMBATANTS
AABCELLORS	CABALLEROS	AABCNORSST	CONTRABASS
AABCELMNSU	AMBULANCES	AABCORRSTT	ABSTRACTOR
AABCELMOPR	COMPARABLE	AABCORRTUY	CARRY ABOUT
AABCELMTUU	ACETABULUM	AABCOSSTTU	CASTS ABOUT
AABCELNNSU	UNBALANCES	AABDDDGNOO	GOOD AND BAD
AABCELNOTU	BALANCE OUT	AABDDEEEHR	BAREHEADED
	OUTBALANCE	AABDDEEGLR	DEGRADABLE
AABCELNPSU	BALANCES UP	AABDDEEHNR	BARE-HANDED
AABCELOOSS	CALABOOSES	AABDDEELMN	DEMANDABLE
AABCELORRS	BARCAROLES	AABDDEELNR	BAND LEADER
AABCELPPRS	CRAB APPLES		BANDLEADER
AABCELRRTU	TRABECULAR	AABDDEGGNS	SANDBAGGED
AABCELRSTU	TRABECULAS	AABDDEGLSS	SADDLEBAGS
AABCEMORSX	BOX CAMERAS	AABDDEHLMO	HEBDOMADAL
AABCENORST	CARBONATES	AABDDEHLRS	BALDERDASH
AABCEORRSS	BEAR A CROSS	AABDDEHMNY	MADE BY HAND
AABCERRSTT	ABSTRACTER	AABDDEHORS	HEADBOARDS
AABCERRTTY	CAR BATTERY	AABDDEILRY	DAILY BREAD
AABCERRTUU	BUREAUCRAT	AABDDEJLNO	LANDED A JOB
AABCFHKLSS	FLASHBACKS	AABDDELOPT	PADDLE BOAT
AABCFIORRT	FABRICATOR	AABDDEMRTU	ADUMBRATED
AABCFKLLNO	FALL BACK ON	AABDDHORSS	DASHBOARDS
AABCGHIINR	HIRING A CAB	AABDDIMNOO	IN A BAD MOOD
AABCGHINPT	BATHING CAP	AABDDMNNOR	DON BRADMAN
AABCGHSTUU	CAUGHT A BUS	AABDDNNSST	BANDSTANDS
AABCGIINRR	BRACING AIR	AABDDNORRR	DR.BARNARDO
AABCGIKKNT	TAKING BACK	AABDDNORTU	DO A BAD TURN
AABCGIKNPY	PAYING BACK	AABDDORRST	DARTBOARDS
AABCGIKNRR	BARRACKING		DARTS BOARD
AABCGILPST	PLASTIC BAG	AABDDRRYYY	YARD BY YARD
AABCGKMMNO	BACKGAMMON	AABDEEELMS	SEALED-BEAM
AABCGKNPRS	SPRANG BACK	AABDEEFINR	BEEN AFRAID
AABCGLRRTU	CAT BURGLAR	AABDEEFLRS	FALSE BEARD
AABCHHIRST	BATH CHAIRS	AABDEEFLRY	DEFRAYABLE
AABCHILRTY	CHARITABLY	AABDEEGLLS	BALD EAGLES
AABCHINOTT	COHABITANT	AABDEEGNRR	BEAR GARDEN
AABCHIOOPR	ACROPHOBIA	AABDEEGRRW	GREW A BEARD
AABCHKKNRS	SHRANK BACK	AABDEEHLLN	HANDLEABLE
AABCHKLPSS	SPLASHBACK	AABDEEHRRT	THREADBARE
AABCHPSSYY	PAYS BY CASH	AABDEEHRTW	BAD WEATHER
AABCIIKLST	KABALISTIC	AABDEEKLPP	BAKED APPLE
AABCIILPTY	CAPABILITY	AABDEEKLPR	BRAKE PEDAL
AABCIILTTY	ACTABILITY	AABDEEKORT	BROKE A DATE
AABCIIOPRT	PARABIOTIC	AABDEELMPX	BAD EXAMPLE
AABCIKKLNS	BLACK AS INK	AABDEELNOR	BREAD ALONE
AABCIKLLMS	BLACKMAILS	AABDEELNPX	EXPANDABLE
AABCIKLNPT	BLACK PAINT	AABDEELNRR	BAD LEARNER
AABCIKLNRS	LACK BRAINS	AABDEELORT	ELABORATED
AABCIKRSST	BACK STAIRS	AABDEELPRS	SPREADABLE
	BACKSTAIRS	AABDEELRRW	REWARDABLE
AABCILLMPY	IMPLACABLY	AABDEELRST	STALE BREAD
AABCILMORU	COLUMBARIA	AABDEFFLOR	AFFORDABLE

AABDEFIIRS	BAD FAIRIES	AABDFHLNOT	NOT HALF BAD
AABDEFKORY	BREAK OF DAY	AABDFHLORS	HALF-BOARDS
AABDEGGINR	BRIGANDAGE	AABDFINOPT	DAB OF PAINT
AABDEGGIPR	BRIDGE A GAP	AABDFMOORR	FROM ABROAD
AABDEGHLNS	BANGLADESH	AABDFNOORV	BARD OF AVON
AABDEGINRS	GABARDINES	AABDGIIKMN	MAKING A BID
AABDEGLNOY	DONEGAL BAY	AABDGIILNW	LAW-ABIDING
AABDEGLNRY	BY AND LARGE	AABDGIILRS	GARIBALDIS
AABDEGLSSS	GLASS BEADS	AABDGIINST	BID AGAINST
AABDEGNOOR	GONE ABOARD	AABDGILNOY	LOADING BAY
	GONE ABROAD	AABDGLORST	OLD RATBAGS
AABDEGOORS	GOES ABOARD	AABDGNNOSW	BANDWAGONS
	GOES ABROAD	AABDHIILTY	DAILY HABIT
AABDEGORRW	GROW A BEARD	AABDHIIMTW	WHAT AM I BID?
AABDEHILSU	HAILED A BUS	AABDHIOPRS	ABOARD SHIP
AABDEHINPS	IN BAD SHAPE	AABDHLORRU	HARD LABOUR
AABDEHINRT	BRAIN DEATH	AABDHLOSTY	HOLDS AT BAY
AABDEHINWY	WIN BY A HEAD	AABDHNORRW	HANDBARROW
AABDEHITTU	HABITUATED	AABDHORSSW	WASHBOARDS
AABDEHLNRS	HANDLEBARS	AABDIILNST	TIDAL BASIN
AABDEHNOWY	WON BY A HEAD	AABDIINNRR	BRAIN DRAIN
AABDEHORRT	HARD TO BEAR	AABDIJOORU	OUIJA BOARD
AABDEHORTU	HEARD ABOUT	AABDILMMNU	DUMB ANIMAL
AABDEHRRTW	DRAW BREATH	AABDILMNOR	LOMBARDIAN
AABDFIILRS	RAISED BAIL	AABDILMNRU	MANDIBULAR
AABDEIITTW	WAITED A BIT	AABDILNSST	STANDS BAIL
AABDEIKKOR	KODIAK BEAR	AABDILOOPR	PARABOLOID
AABDEIKLNS	BALKANISED	AABDILORSS	BAD SAILORS
AABDEIKLNZ	BALKANIZED	AABDILORST	TAILBOARDS
AABDEIKMST	BAD MISTAKE	AABDILQTUY	BAD QUALITY
AABDEIKNRR	BANK RAIDER	AABDIMNRRU	BARRAMUNDI
AABDEILLNR	BANDERILLA	AABDINSSTW	WAISTBANDS
AABDEILLSY	DIALYSABLE	AABDIOPRRT	TRIP ABROAD
AABDEILMOW	AIMED A BLOW	AABDKLORSW	BOARDWALKS
AABDEILOWY	BOILED AWAY	AABDKMNORW	BAD WORKMAN
AABDEIMNOT	ABOMINATED	AABDLLNOSW	LANDS A BLOW
AABDEINNOT	ONE AND A BIT	AABDLLORSW	WALLBOARDS
AABDEINSTT	IN BAD TASTE	AABDLNNTUY	ABUNDANTLY
AABDEIOPPR	PIPE ABOARD	AABDLNOPRY	PARDONABLY
AABDEIRRTT	ARBITRATED	AABDLNSSST	SANDBLASTS
AABDEIRSST	BASTARDISE	AABDLNSTWY	WANTS BADLY
AABDEIRSTZ	BASTARDIZE	AABDLORRTY	BARDOLATRY
AABDEJLSTU	ADJUSTABLE	AABDLORSTY	ASTRAL BODY
AABDEKLLMS	MASKED BALL	AABDNNPRSY	BRANDY SNAP
AABDEKLNRW	DREW A BLANK	AABDNOORWY	ON BROADWAY
AABDEKOORS	READS A BOOK	AABDNOPTUU	UP AND ABOUT
AABDEKORST	SKATEBOARD	AABDNOSTTU	STAND ABOUT
AABDELLLPY	PLAYED BALL	AABDOORRRW	BROAD ARROW
AABDELLNNO	BELLADONNA	AABDORRSST	STARBOARDS
AABDELLOSW	DEALS A BLOW	AABDORRSTW	STRAWBOARD
AABDELLOTW	DEALT A BLOW	AABEEELLPR	REPEALABLE
AABDELNNRR	BARREN LAND	AABEEELLRV	REVEALABLE
AABDELNOPR	PARDONABLE	AABEEELPRT	REPEATABLE
AABDELOOPT	PEDALO BOAT	AABEEELRRT	TALEBEARER
AABDELORRT	BARDOLATER	AABEEESVWW	WEAVES A WEB
AABDELORRZ	RAZOR BLADE	AABEEFHORT	FEATHER BOA
AABDELPRSY	BAD PLAYERS	AABEEFNSST	BEANFEASTS
AABDELRSTU	BALUSTRADE	AABEEGKLRS	BREAKS A LEG
AABDELRTTY	TREAT BADLY	AABEEGLLST	BAGATELLES
AABDEMNNNO	ONE-MAN BAND	AABEEGLMSS	ASSEMBLAGE
AABDEMNNRS	BAD MANNERS	AABEEGLTTV	GAVE BATTLE
AABDEMNRST	BAND MASTER	AABEEGNORT	BARONETAGE
	BANDMASTER	AABEEHIRTT	BEAT THE AIR
AABDEMORST	DREAMBOATS	AABEEHKRRT	HEARTBREAK
AABDEMRSTU	ADUMBRATES	AABEEHLORT	ABLE TO HEAR
AABDENORSY	DRY AS A BONE	AABEEHLQTU	BEQUEATHAL
AABDENRSTV	BAD SERVANT	AABEEHPSSU	HEAPS ABUSE
AABDENSSTW	SWEATBANDS	AABEEHRRTT	THEATRE BAR
AABDEOPRST	PASTEBOARD	AABEEHRSTT	HEARTBEATS
AABDEORRTW	WATER BOARD	AABEEIKNTT	TAKEN A BITE
AABDFHIINT	IN BAD FAITH	AABEEIKSTT	TAKES A BITE

AABEEILLRS	REALISABLE
AABEEILLRZ	REALIZABLE
AABEEILMNX	EXAMINABLE
AABEEILNRT	RETAINABLE
AABEEJKRRW	JAWBREAKER
AABEEKLMRR	REMARKABLE
AABEEKLMRT	MARKETABLE
AABEEKLOSV	BAKE LOAVES
AABEEKLRRU	BREAK A RULE
AABEEKLRRW	LAWBREAKER
AABEEKMRRT	BEAR MARKET
AABEEKNOPT	KEEP A TAB ON
AABEEKPSTY	KEEPS AT BAY
AABEEKRRTW	BREAKWATER
AABEELLMNT	LAMENTABLE
AABEELLPRR	PALLBEARER
AABEELMRSU	MEASURABLE
AABEELMSST	BASE METALS
AABEELMSTT	METASTABLE
	STABLE MATE
AABEELNNTT	TENANTABLE
AABEELNORS	REASONABLE
AABEELNOSS	SEASONABLE
AABEELNPTT	PATENTABLE
AABEELNNRSW	ANSWERABLE
AABEELORST	ELABORATES
AABEELRRST	ARBALESTER
	ARRESTABLE
AABEELRTTW	TABLE WATER
	WATER TABLE
AABEELSSSS	ASSESSABLE
AABEELSSTT	SEA BATTLES
AABEELSTTX	BATTLE-AXES
AABEEORTVW	ABOVE WATER
AABEEQRSSU	ARABESQUES
AABEERRSTT	STREET ARAB
AABEERSTTX	TAX REBATES
AABEFFILMR	AFFIRMABLE
AABEFGORUV	BEG A FAVOUR
AABEFHIKRT	BREAK FAITH
AABEFHLMOT	FATHOMABLE
AABEFHLOSY	BALES OF HAY
AABEFIIKLS	FAKE ALIBIS
AABEFIILLS	FALSE ALIBI
AABEFILLNT	INFLATABLE
AABEFIMORS	FRAMBOESIA
AABEFKLLOR	BROKE A FALL
AABEFKRSST	BREAKFASTS
AABEFLLTUW	ALL BUT A FEW
AABEFLORUV	FAVOURABLE
AABEFLOTTU	TALE OF A TUB
AABEGGIINN	BEGIN AGAIN
AABEGGINNU	BEGUN AGAIN
AABEGGORRT	GRETA GARBO
AABEGHINST	SEA BATHING
AABEGHINTV	HAVING A BET
AABEGHOOPR	AGORAPHOBE
AABEGHORRU	HARBOURAGE
AABEGIILMN	IMAGINABLE
AABEGIKMNT	MAKING A BET
AABEGIKNTT	TAKING A BET
AABEGILNOZ	ZABAGLIONE
AABEGILNRY	LAYING BARE
AABEGILNSS	ASSIGNABLE
AABEGILNTY	LAYING A BET
AABEGILRST	ALGEBRAIST
AABEGINNOT	ABNEGATION
AABEGINRRS	BARGAINERS
AABEGLLMNO	AMBLE ALONG
AABEGLOPPR	PROPAGABLE
AABEGLOSVW	SAVAGE BLOW

AABEGMNRST	BAR MAGNETS
AABEHHISTW	WAHHABITES
AABEHISTTU	HABITUATES
AABEHKLNSU	UNSHAKABLE
AABEHLLLRT	ALBERT HALL
AABEHLOSTW	WHALEBOATS
AABEHLRSTT	LAST BREATH
AABEHORRSS	ARAB HORSES
AABEHORSTU	HEARS ABOUT
AABEHRSTWY	BARS THE WAY
AABEIILNRV	INVARIABLE
AABEIILRSS	RAISES BAIL
AABEIILRSV	BRAAIVLEIS
AABEIIMNRS	BAIN-MARIES
AABEIJKLRS	BREAKS JAIL
	JAILBREAKS
AABEIJLOSU	BEAUJOLAIS
AABEIKLNSS	BALKANISES
AABEIKLNSZ	BALKANIZES
AABEIKNRRS	KARABINERS
AABEILLMPP	IMPALPABLE
AABEILLNRS	BALLERINAS
AABEILLNUV	INVALUABLE
AABEILLOST	ISOLATABLE
AABEILLOTV	ABOVE IT ALL
AABEILMNRS	LAMEBRAINS
AABEILMNTV	AMBIVALENT
AABEILMPRT	IMPARTABLE
AABEILRSTT	AIR BATTLES
AABEILRSVY	ABRASIVELY
AABEILRTTT	TITRATABLE
AABEIMNOPS	IMPOSE A BAN
AABEIMNORU	MARIA BUENO
AABEIMNOST	ABOMINATES
AABEIMPRTV	VAMPIRE BAT
AABEINORRT	ABERRATION
AABEINRSST	ABSTAINERS
AABEIORRTV	ARBORVITAE
AABEIPRRTV	PRIVATE BAR
AABEIRRSTT	ARBITRATES
AABEJKNOOT	TAKE ON A JOB
AABEJLMMOS	JAMES BOLAM
AABEKKMOOS	MAKES A BOOK
AABEKKNRRS	BREAK RANKS
AABEKLMRRY	REMARKABLY
AABEKLNRST	BLANK STARE
AABEKMNORR	BROKE AN ARM
AABEKNOPTT	KEPT A TAB ON
AABEKNORWY	BROKEN AWAY
AABEKNOSTU	SNEAK ABOUT
AABEKNRSTU	BREAKS A NUT
AABEKOOSST	BOOKS A SEAT
AABEKOPRRT	BROKE APART
AABELLMNSY	BY ALL MEANS
AABELLMNTY	LAMENTABLY
AABELLNPUY	UNPLAYABLE
AABELLORRY	ARBOREALLY
AABELMOSTT	MELBA TOAST
AABELMRSUY	MEASURABLY
AABELMSTTY	METASTABLY
AABELNORSY	REASONABLY
AABELNORTU	LEARN ABOUT
AABELNOSSY	SEASONABLY
AABELNRRTY	ABERRANTLY
AABELOPSTU	LEAPS ABOUT
AABELOPTTU	LEAPT ABOUT
AABELORSST	ASTROLABES
AABELORSUV	SAVE LABOUR
AABELPRSST	BRASS PLATE
AABELPRSYY	PLAYS BY EAR
AABELRRRST	TAR BARRELS

AABEMNNSYY	BY ANY MEANS	AABIMNOORT	ABOMINATOR
AABEMOSSTT	STEAMBOATS	AABINORSTT	BOAT TRAINS
AABEMRSTTU	MASTURBATE	AABINOSSTW	BOATSWAINS
AABENRRSTU	RUN ABREAST	AABIORRRTT	ARBITRATOR
AABEOORSSV	SOARS ABOVE	AABIOSTTUW	SAW ABOUT IT
AABEORSTTU	TEARS ABOUT	AABKKOORRU	KOOKABURRA
AABFFIILTY	AFFABILITY	AABKLNSTUV	BANK VAULTS
AABFGILNOS	BAG OF NAILS	AABKLORSTU	LARKS ABOUT
AABFLLOSTU	FALLS ABOUT	AABKLOSTTU	TALKS ABOUT
AABFLMNOTY	FLAMBOYANT	AABKLOSTUW	WALKABOUTS
AABFLOOTTU	FLOAT ABOUT		WALKS ABOUT
AABFLORUVY	FAVOURABLY	AABLLMNORY	ABNORMALLY
AABFOOPRSS	BARS OF SOAP	AABLLMOSTU	SALBUTAMOL
AABGGIINNR	BARGAINING	AABLMMPSTU	STAMP ALBUM
AABGGINORT	ABROGATING	AABLMORTUY	AMBULATORY
AABGGINOST	SABOTAGING	AABLOORRTY	LABORATORY
AABGHIJNOV	HAVING A JOB	AABLOPSTUY	PLAYS ABOUT
AABGHLOTUU	LAUGH ABOUT	AABLORSTTU	TABULATORS
AABGHNOSTU	HANGS ABOUT	AABLSTTTUY	STATUTABLY
AABGHOPRRS	BAROGRAPHS	AABMNORRTY	MARY BARTON
AABGIILMNY	IMAGINABLY	AACCCDEIIT	ACETIC ACID
AABGIILNOR	ABORIGINAL	AACCCDEKOR	CRACK A CODE
AABGIINNST	ABSTAINING	AACCCDENOR	ACCORDANCE
AABGIJKNOT	TAKING A JOB	AACCCDERSS	ACCESS CARD
AABGIKMNNOW	MAKING A BOW	AACCCDHLOT	CATCH A COLD
AABGIKNOTW	TAKING A BOW	AACCCEENPT	ACCEPTANCE
AABGIKNPRY	PARKING BAY	AACCCEILTT	CATALECTIC
AABGIKNRTY	BAKING TRAY	AACCCINRUY	INACCURACY
AABGIKNSTU	TAKING A BUS	AACCDDFHKN	CACK-HANDED
AABGILLNST	BALLASTING	AACCDDELST	SCALDED CAT
AABGILMNST	LAMBASTING	AACCDEEMRS	MADE SCARCE
AABGILNOWY	WIN BY A GOAL	AACCDEENNS	ASCENDANCE
AABGILNRSU	BULGARIANS	AACCDEEPST	SPACE CADET
AABGILNTTU	TABULATING	AACCDEFFST	FACED FACTS
AABGINOORT	ABROGATION	AACCDEGHRR	CHARGE CARD
AABGINRSTU	RUB AGAINST	AACCDEHHIO	HAD A CHOICE
AABGINRSWY	BRINGS AWAY	AACCDEHIRS	SACCHARIDE
AABGLNOOWY	WON BY A GOAL	AACCDEHNOR	ARCHDEACON
AABHIILLRZ	BILHARZIAL	AACCDEILMT	ACCLIMATED
AABHIIMNPS	AMPHIBIANS	AACCDEILNT	ACCIDENTAL
AABHIINNTT	INHABITANT	AACCDEINTV	VACCINATED
AABHIINOTT	HABITATION	AACCDEIOSV	ADVOCACIES
AABHIKKLNU	KUBLAI KHAN	AACCDELLTU	CALCULATED
AABHILLTUY	HABITUALLY	AACCDELRST	CATS CRADLE
AABHIMMNRS	BRAHMANISM	AACCDENNSY	ASCENDANCY
AABHINRRUU	AUBURN HAIR	AACCDENRRW	CANCER WARD
AABHINSSSW	WASHBASINS	AACCDEORSS	ACCESS ROAD
AABHINSTTY	NASTY HABIT	AACCDGINRR	RACING CARD
AABHLLLOOU	HULLABALOO	AACCDHIINP	HAD A PICNIC
AABHLPSSYY	HYPABYSSAL	AACCDHOPRT	DROP A CATCH
AABHOPRTUV	VAPOUR BATH	AACCDHPRST	SCRATCH PAD
AABIIILMTY	AMIABILITY	AACCEEELRT	ACCELERATE
AABIILLSTY	SALABILITY	AACCEEFFOT	FACE TO FACE
AABIILNRRS	LIBRARIANS	AACCEEGPRS	SCAPEGRACE
AABIILNRVY	INVARIABLY	AACCEEHNRR	RARE CHANCE
AABIILNSTY	INSATIABLY	AACCEEIMNR	CINE CAMERA
AABIINPRST	BIPARTISAN		CINECAMERA
AABIIOPRSS	PARABIOSIS	AACCEEKMRS	MAKE SCARCE
AABIIPSTTT	A BIT PAST IT	AACCEELNRS	CLEARANCES
AABIJNORTU	ABJURATION	AACCEELPRS	CLEAR SPACE
AABIKMMORS	ARMS AKIMBO	AACCEENTTU	ACCENTUATE
AABILLLOSW	ALLOWS BAIL	AACCEEORTV	COACERVATE
AABILLMPPY	IMPALPABLY	AACCEEPRSU	CAPER SAUCE
AABILLMSUX	SUBMAXILLA	AACCEESSSY	EASY ACCESS
AABILLNNUY	BIANNUALLY	AACCEFFSST	FACES FACTS
AABILLNPRU	RAN UP A BILL	AACCEFGORT	ACT OF GRACE
AABILLNRUY	BINAURALLY	AACCEFHINR	FAIR CHANCE
AABILLNUVY	INVALUABLY	AACCEFINNT	FINANCE ACT
AABILMPSSY	IMPASSABLY	AACCEFPRST	SPACECRAFT
AABILNOSTT	BATTALIONS	AACCEGHITV	GIVE A CATCH
AABILNOTTU	TABULATION	AACCEGHOST	STAGECOACH

421

AACCEGINSS	GAIN ACCESS	AACCILMPST	PLASTIC MAC
AACCEGKRST	GETS A CRACK	AACCILNNOS	CANONICALS
AACCEHILLM	ALCHEMICAL	AACCILNOOS	OCCASIONAL
AACCEHILMN	MECHANICAL	AACCILORST	ACROSTICAL
AACCEHIMNN	MAIN CHANCE	AACCILPRST	PRACTICALS
AACCEHINNT	CACHINNATE	AACCILRTUY	ARTICULACY
AACCEHINRS	CANE CHAIRS	AACCIMNORS	CARCINOMAS
	SACCHARINE	AACCINORTV	VACCINATOR
AACCEHJKPS	CHEAP-JACKS	AACCINOSTU	ACCUSATION
AACCEHLNOT	COELACANTH	AACCIOPRST	CAPACITORS
AACCEHLNST	LAST CHANCE	AACCIORTTU	AUTOCRATIC
AACCEHLSST	TEACH CLASS	AACCKKQQUU	QUACK,QUACK
AACCEHNNOT	NOT A CHANCE	AACCKLLMOR	ALARM CLOCK
AACCEHORSS	SACCHAROSE	AACCKNRSTU	CRACKS A NUT
AACCEHOSTT	STATE COACH	AACCLLORTU	CALCULATOR
AACCEHRRSS	CAR CRASHES	AACCLMSSTY	CATACLYSMS
AACCEHRRST	CHARACTERS	AACCLNRRUU	CARUNCULAR
AACCEHSSTW	WATCH-CASES	AACCLOSTTU	CAST A CLOUT
AACCEIIPST	CAPACITIES	AACCMNORTY	CARTOMANCY
AACCEIIPTV	CAPACITIVE	AACCNNOTTU	ACCOUNTANT
AACCEILMST	ACCLIMATES	AACCNORSST	SACROSANCT
AACCEILPTT	CATALEPTIC	AACCORSTUY	ACCUSATORY
AACCEINNRS	CANCERIANS	AACDDEEEFT	DEFAECATED
AACCEINORV	COVARIANCE	AACDDEEFHT	FACED DEATH
AACCEINPRT	PANCREATIC		HAD A DEFECT
AACCEINRTU	INACCURATE	AACDDEEFLT	DEFALCATED
AACCEINSTV	VACCINATES	AACDDEEIMP	AIDE-DE-CAMP
AACCEIRRTU	CARICATURE	AACDDEEIRT	ERADICATED
AACCEISTUV	ACCUSATIVE	AACDDEEIST	TEA CADDIES
AACCEJKKOR	CRACK A JOKE	AACDDEELNR	CALENDARED
AACCEKNRSS	CRANKCASES	AACDDEEMNS	DAMASCENED
AACCELLLOR	COAL CELLAR	AACDDEEMRT	DEMARCATED
AACCELLRTU	CALL A TRUCE	AACDDEGIJN	DANCED A JIG
AACCELLSTU	CALCULATES	AACDDEIJTU	ADJUDICATE
AACCELMTUU	ACCUMULATE	AACDDEILMY	DECIMAL DAY
AACCELORSU	CALCAREOUS	AACDDEILTU	ACIDULATED
AACCELRTUY	ACCURATELY	AACDDEINOR	ENDOCARDIA
AACCEMORSS	CAME ACROSS	AACDDEINST	CANDIDATES
AACCENRSTU	CRUSTACEAN	AACDDEKLPS	PACKSADDLE
AACCEORSST	ASCOT RACES	AACDDENNNO	CANNONADED
AACCEPRSTU	CUTS A CAPER	AACDDHOSTU	ADDS A TOUCH
AACCFHHIST	CATCH A FISH	AACDDILLYY	DYADICALLY
AACCFILLRY	FARCICALLY	AACDDIOTTU	AUTODIDACT
AACCFILRSU	FASCICULAR	AACDEEEFFT	FACE DEFEAT
AACCFINNRS	FRANCISCAN	AACDEEEFNS	DEFEASANCE
AACCFKLOOS	SACK OF COAL	AACDEEEFST	DEFAECATES
AACCFORTTY	FACTORY ACT	AACDEEEMNS	MADE A SCENE
AACCGHLOSS	GLASS COACH	AACDEEFGNR	FACE DANGER
AACCGHOPRY	CACOGRAPHY	AACDEEFHMS	SHAMEFACED
AACCGIILMN	ACCLAIMING	AACDEEFHNR	FACE-HARDEN
AACCHHINTW	WATCH CHAIN	AACDEEFHST	FACES DEATH
AACCHIIMST	CHIASMATIC	AACDEEFLST	DEFALCATES
AACCHIIRST	ARCHAISTIC	AACDEEGIVV	GAVE ADVICE
AACCHILNPY	CHAPLAINCY	AACDEEHHST	HAD THE ACES
AACCHIMORT	ACHROMATIC	AACDEEHHTT	CHEAT DEATH
AACCHIMSST	MISS A CATCH	AACDEEHRRT	RACE HATRED
AACCHINNOR	ANACHRONIC	AACDEEHRST	HAD A SECRET
AACCHKNPPU	PACK A PUNCH	AACDEEIKTV	TAKE ADVICE
AACCHKOOTT	TOOK A CATCH	AACDEEILLP	IDEAL PLACE
AACCHLNORY	ACRONYCHAL	AACDEEIPTT	DECAPITATE
AACCHMNRST	SCRATCH MAN	AACDEEIRST	ERADICATES
AACCHMORSU	SCARAMOUCH	AACDEEISTV	DATIVE CASE
AACCHNORST	CAST ANCHOR	AACDEEITTV	DEACTIVATE
AACCHNOTYY	CHATOYANCY	AACDEEJLTU	EJACULATED
AACCHOPRTY	COACH PARTY	AACDEELLOS	CLOSE A DEAL
AACCIINRSS	CIRCASSIAN	AACDEELRRW	DECLARE WAR
AACCIINSTT	TACTICIANS	AACDEEMNSS	DAMASCENES
AACCILLLOS	SOCIAL CALL	AACDEEMRST	DEMARCATES
AACCILLRUV	CLAVICULAR	AACDEEMRTU	MADE A TRUCE
AACCILLTTY	TACTICALLY	AACDEENNTT	ATTENDANCE
AACCILMMUY	IMMACULACY	AACDEEORRW	ROWED A RACE

AACDEEPSSV	SAVED SPACE	AACDEIMNTT	ADMITTANCE
AACDEEPSTY	STEADY PACE	AACDEIMRRY	DAIRY CREAM
AACDEFFLTT	FATTED CALF	AACDEIMSTT	MASTICATED
AACDEFFNST	STAFF DANCE	AACDEINNOR	DANCE ON AIR
AACDEFGILT	CADGE A LIFT	AACDEINNRT	INCARNATED
AACDEFGORY	DAY OF GRACE	AACDEINOST	DIACONATES
AACDEFHLSS	CHEF'S SALAD	AACDEINOTV	VACATIONED
AACDEFILNP	FIND A PLACE	AACDEINPSU	CAUSED PAIN
AACDEFIMRT	CAME ADRIFT	AACDEINQTU	ACQUAINTED
AACDEFINRR	AFRICANDER	AACDEINQUY	INADEQUACY
AACDEFINRU	FRICANDEAU	AACDEINRRV	DRIVEN A CAR
AACDEFINST	FANTACISED	AACDEINRTX	TAXI DANCER
	FASCINATED	AACDEIOPRS	PAID A SCORE
AACDEFLORT	DEFALCATOR	AACDEIORRT	ERADICATOR
AACDEFNNRS	FAN DANCERS	AACDEIOSST	ASSOCIATED
AACDEFORRW	FORCE A DRAW	AACDEIPTTV	CAPTIVATED
AACDEGHHNR	CHARGE HAND	AACDEIRRSV	DRIVES A CAR
	CHARGEHAND	AACDEIRSTY	CARYATIDES
AACDEGHINT	ACTING HEAD	AACDEISSST	CASTS ASIDE
AACDEGIJNS	DANCES A JIG	AACDEJLNTY	ADJACENTLY
AACDEGIMNP	CAMPAIGNED	AACDEKLMNO	ALMOND CAKE
AACDEGISTT	CASTIGATED	AACDEKLOWY	LOCKED AWAY
AACDEGISTU	ACT AS GUIDE	AACDEKMRST	MADE TRACKS
AACDEGKNPU	PACKED A GUN	AACDEKNSST	CAKE STANDS
AACDEGLNRS	GRAND SCALE	AACDEKTUWY	TUCKED AWAY
AACDEGLOTU	CATALOGUED	AACDELLNOW	ALLOWANCED
	COAGULATED	AACDELMOPR	CAMELOPARD
AACDEGNOOT	GO TO A DANCE	AACDELMRSU	CLEAR AS MUD
AACDEHHTTW	DEATHWATCH	AACDELMSTY	STAYED CALM
AACDEHILRS	CHARLADIES	AACDELNOPR	ENDOCARPAL
AACDEHIMNT	MACHINATED	AACDELNPRS	LANDSCAPER
AACDEHIMPT	MADE A PITCH	AACDELNPSS	LANDSCAPES
AACDEHINRS	SEDAN CHAIR	AACDELNRST	DECLARANTS
AACDEHKLRT	HARD TACKLE		STAND CLEAR
AACDEHKPRT	PACKTHREAD	AACDELNSST	SAND CASTLE
AACDEHLLSS	CALLS HEADS		SANDCASTLE
AACDEHLNNS	CLEAN HANDS	AACDELNSWX	WAX CANDLES
AACDEHLORT	OCTAHEDRAL	AACDELORST	SACERDOTAL
AACDEHLRST	CATHEDRALS	AACDELOTUV	AUTOCLAVED
AACDEHMNOT	CAME TO HAND	AACDELPRRY	CARD PLAYER
AACDEHMPRY	MY DEAR CHAP	AACDELPTTU	CATAPULTED
AACDEHNTTU	UNATTACHED	AACDEMRSTY	ARMY CADETS
AACDEHOORT	CARED A HOOT	AACDENNNOS	CANNONADES
AACDEHOPPR	APPROACHED	AACDENNSST	ASCENDANTS
AACDEHORTY	CATHODE RAY	AACDENORRS	CARRONADES
	CATHODE-RAY	AACDENPRST	TAP DANCERS
AACDEHPRTU	PARACHUTED	AACDENRSTT	TRANSACTED
AACDEIILPR	EPICARDIAL	AACDEORSUV	CADAVEROUS
AACDEIILRS	RADICALISE	AACDFGILRS	FISCAL DRAG
AACDEIILRZ	RADICALIZE	AACDFHINRT	HANDICRAFT
AACDEIINRR	IRRADIANCE	AACDFHNRST	HANDCRAFTS
AACDEIINRS	RAISED CAIN	AACDFIINOO	AFICIONADO
AACDEIIPRR	PERICARDIA	AACDFLLOOO	LOAD OF COAL
AACDEIIPRT	PAEDIATRIC	AACDGHMNRR	GRAND MARCH
AACDEIIRTV	DIVARICATE	AACDGIKOSS	SICK AS A DOG
AACDEIJLTV	ADJECTIVAL	AACDGILNPR	PLACARDING
AACDEIKLLT	KILLED A CAT	AACDGINNPT	TAP DANCING
AACDEIKPRS	SICK PARADE	AACDGINOTV	ADVOCATING
AACDEIKSSV	ASKS ADVICE	AACDGNNOPW	CAP AND GOWN
AACDEILLNS	DALLIANCES	AACDGNRSUY	SUGAR CANDY
AACDEILLTV	VACILLATED	AACDGORSTU	COASTGUARD
AACDEILMMN	MEDICAL MAN	AACDHHINNS	CASH IN HAND
AACDEILMNR	ALDERMANIC	AACDHIINPS	PAID IN CASH
AACDEILNNO	CALEDONIAN	AACDHIINSY	DAISY CHAIN
AACDEILNOS	LAODICEANS	AACDHINORS	ARACHNOIDS
AACDEILNPS	SNAIL-PACED	AACDHJMMNO	JOHN MCADAM
AACDEILNSS	SCANDALISE	AACDHKNORT	ON HARD TACK
AACDEILNSZ	SCANDALIZE	AACDHLNPSS	CLAPS HANDS
AACDEILOTT	TAILCOATED		CLASP HANDS
AACDEILPSY	SPECIAL DAY	AACDHLNRSS	CRASH-LANDS
AACDEILSTU	ACIDULATES	AACDHLOPRY	PLAY A CHORD

AACDHMNOPY	HAD COMPANY	AACEEILMRZ	CARAMELIZE
AACDHMNRTW	DRAWN MATCH	AACEEILPRT	ALTARPIECE
AACDHMRSTT	DARTS MATCH	AACEEIMNPT	EMANCIPATE
AACDHPRRSS	CARDSHARPS	AACEEIMSST	SIAMESE CAT
AACDIILMRS	RADICALISM	AACEEIPPRT	APPRECIATE
AACDIILMRT	MATRICIDAL	AACEEIRTTV	REACTIVATE
AACDIILPRR	PARRICIDAL	AACEEIRTWY	TWICE A YEAR
AACDIILPRT	PATRICIDAL	AACEEITUVV	EVACUATIVE
AACDILLMTU	TALMUDICAL	AACEEJLSTU	EJACULATES
AACDILLNOP	PAID ON CALL	AACEEKKLRW	CAKEWALKER
AACDILLNOY	ANODICALLY	AACEEKLLTT	LATE TACKLE
AACDILLNRY	CARDINALLY	AACEEKLMRS	MAKES CLEAR
AACDILLOOR	LOCAL RADIO	AACEEKLNPT	TAKEN PLACE
AACDILMORY	MYOCARDIAL	AACEEKLPST	TAKES PLACE
AACDILMRRY	LYRIC DRAMA	AACEEKMPRS	PACEMAKERS
AACDIMMNOR	AIR COMMAND	AACEEKMRTU	MAKE A TRUCE
AACDINORRT	RATION CARD	AACEEKRRST	CARETAKERS
AACDIQRSTU	QUADRATICS	AACEELLNOT	LANCEOLATE
AACDLLOPST	OLD PALS ACT	AACEELLNST	CLEAN SLATE
AACDLMORRU	ARMOUR-CLAD	AACEELLPRT	CARPELLATE
AACDLNOSSU	SCANDALOUS	AACEELMNPS	PLACE-NAMES
AACDLPRSSY	PLAYS CARDS	AACEELMNST	MENTAL CASE
AACDMMNNOT	COMMANDANT	AACEELMOOT	ACOELOMATE
AACDOORSTW	SAW A DOCTOR	AACEELMRVW	MARCEL WAVE
AACDOORTVY	ADVOCATORY	AACEELMSTU	EMASCULATE
AACDORSSTW	COASTWARDS	AACEELNRTW	CLEAN WATER
AACDPRRSSY	SCRAPYARDS	AACEELOPTT	TOTAL PEACE
AACEEEKMNS	MAKE A SCENE	AACEELPPSU	APPLE SAUCE
AACEEEKMPS	MAKES PEACE	AACEELPRST	PARACLETES
AACEEELMNP	ELECAMPANE	AACEELRRTW	CLEAR WATER
AACEEELNOP	PALAEOCENE	AACEEMNNOPW	PEACE WOMAN
AACEEEMNRR	CAME NEARER	AACEEMRRST	MASTER RACE
AACEEENRSV	SERVE AN ACE	AACEENORSU	ARENACEOUS
AACEEFFOSS	SEA OF FACES	AACEENRRTV	VETERAN CAR
AACEEFIRST	CAFETERIAS	AACEENSSTY	CASTS AN EYE
AACEEFKMSS	MAKES FACES	AACEEPRTTZ	TRAPEZE ACT
AACEEFKORT	TAKE CARE OF	AACEEPSSSV	SAVES SPACE
AACEEFLPST	FACEPLATES	AACEFFFIOR	FAIR OF FACE
	LEFT A SPACE	AACEFFIMNR	AFFIRMANCE
AACEEFMNOP	MAN OF PEACE	AACEFFIRST	AFFRICATES
AACEEFRSSV	FACE-SAVERS	AACEFGHNOR	FOR A CHANGE
AACEEGGHNR	CHANGE GEAR	AACEFGINST	FACING EAST
AACEEGGHNV	GAVE CHANGE	AACEFGINSV	FACE-SAVING
AACEEGHIMN	MACHINE AGE		SAVING FACE
AACEEGHKRT	TAKE CHARGE	AACEFGLMOU	CAMOUFLAGE
AACEEGHRUV	CHE GUEVARA	AACEFGLNOR	CAN OF LAGER
AACEEGILLN	ALLEGIANCE	AACEFGNRRS	FRAGRANCES
AACEEGILMR	CLEAR IMAGE	AACEFGRSTT	STAGECRAFT
AACEEGKPPR	PREPACKAGE	AACEFHLLNP	CHAPFALLEN
AACEEGKPTW	WAGE PACKET	AACEFHLSST	HALF-CASTES
AACEEGLLRS	LARGE SCALE	AACEFIILLM	FILE A CLAIM
	LARGE-SCALE	AACEFIILTT	FACILITATE
AACEEGLNTU	ACUTE ANGLE	AACEFIIMPR	PRIMA FACIE
AACEEGNOST	ACT ONES AGE	AACEFIINRS	AFRICANISE
AACEEHHRST	HEARTACHES	AACEFIINRZ	AFRICANIZE
AACEEHHSST	HAS THE ACES	AACEFIINST	FANATICISE
AACEEHILNT	CHATELAINE	AACEFIINTZ	FANATICIZE
AACEEHIPRT	APHAERETIC	AACEFIKLRT	FAIR TACKLE
AACEEHKPST	CHEAP SKATE	AACEFILRSY	FISCAL YEAR
	CHEAPSKATE	AACEFINSST	FANTACIES
AACEEHLLST	ALL THE ACES		FASCINATES
AACEEHLLSW	LECH WALESA	AACEFIOPRS	PAIR OF ACES
AACEEHLMNR	MENARCHEAL	AACEFIRSTW	WEST AFRICA
AACEEHLNPT	ANTECHAPEL	AACEFKLRST	FLARESTACK
AACEEHLSTW	TEACHES LAW	AACEFKOOPS	CAKE OF SOAP
AACEEHMORS	CAME ASHORE	AACEFLLMSS	SMALL FACES
AACEEHNNRT	ANTHRACENE	AACEFLLPSU	PULLS A FACE
AACEEHPPRS	PAPER CHASE	AACEFLMORT	MALEFACTOR
AACEEHRRTT	THE RAT RACE	AACEFLMRTT	CATTLE FARM
AACEEHRSTT	TEACHES ART	AACEFLNPSU	FUN PALACES
AACEEIJNNR	JEAN RACINE	AACEFOPRRT	FORCE APART

AACEFRRTTW	WATERCRAFT	AACEHKOPRT	KARATE CHOP
AACEFRSTTT	STATECRAFT	AACEHKORVW	WREAK HAVOC
AACEGGHHNT	HATCH AN EGG	AACEHKRSSV	HAVERSACKS
AACEGHINNV	GAVE AN INCH	AACEHLLOTT	AT THE LOCAL
AACEGHINOR	ARCHEGONIA	AACEHLMOST	LOSE A MATCH
AACEGHLNRS	ARCHANGELS	AACEHLNPRS	PLANE CRASH
AACEGHMNPS	CHAMPAGNES	AACEHLOPSU	ACEPHALOUS
AACEGHMOPR	MACROPHAGE	AACEHLPRTY	ARCHETYPAL
AACEGHMRRT	GREAT MARCH	AACEHLRRSY	RAY CHARLES
AACEGHNORT	COAT HANGER	AACEHMMORT	CAME TO HARM
AACEGHOTTT	ACT THE GOAT	AACEHMNPRY	PARENCHYMA
AACEGHRRST	GREAT CRASH	AACEHMNTTT	ATTACHMENT
AACEGHRSTX	TAX CHARGES	AACEHMOPRT	CAMPHORATE
AACEGIIMNT	EMACIATING	AACEHMRSSS	CAR SMASHES
AACEGIKMNP	PACEMAKING	AACEHNSSSS	SASSENACHS
AACEGIKNRT	TAKING CARE	AACEHNSSTU	ACANTHUSES
AACEGILLLM	LEGAL CLAIM	AACEHOORST	CARES A HOOT
AACEGILLLT	ILLEGAL ACT	AACEHOPPRS	APPROACHES
AACEGILNRT	LACERATING	AACEHOPRTY	APOTHECARY
AACEGIINST	ESCALATING	AACEHPRSTU	PARACHUTES
AACEGILPPR	PARAPLEGIC	AACEHPRTTT	ACT THE PART
AACEGILRST	CARTILAGES	AACEHRSTTT	AT A STRETCH
AACEGILRTT	TRAGIC TALE	AACEIILLNN	IN ALLIANCE
AACEGIMNPR	CAMPAIGNER	AACEIILLNV	VANILLA ICE
AACEGIMNRT	MACERATING	AACEIILMST	CALAMITIES
AACEGINNRT	GIANT CRANE	AACEIILPST	CAPITALISE
AACEGINNTT	CATENATING	AACEIILPTZ	CAPITALIZE
AACEGINRTV	VINTAGE CAR	AACEIIMNOT	EMACIATION
AACEGINTUV	EVACUATING	AACEIIMNRT	MARTI CAINE
AACEGINTVX	EXCAVATING	AACEIINNRV	INVARIANCE
AACEGISSTT	CASTIGATES	AACEIINPRR	PERICRANIA
AACEGLMORY	ACROMEGALY	AACEIINPTT	ANTICIPATE
AACEGLOORS	SCORE A GOAL	AACEIINRSS	RAISES CAIN
AACEGLORTU	CATALOGUER	AACEIINRST	INSECTARIA
AACEGLOSTU	CATALOGUES	AACEIINTTV	INACTIVATE
	COAGULATES		VATICINATE
AACEGOPSST	SCAPEGOATS	AACEIIPRTT	PATRICIATE
AACEGORSTT	GREATCOATS	AACEIKKRTT	TAKE A TRICK
AACEHHKOSV	HAVE A SHOCK	AACEIKLMPT	MAIL PACKET
AACEHHMNTT	HATCHET MAN	AACEIKLNSV	CANVASLIKE
AACEHHMSTT	TEACH MATHS	AACEIKMPST	PICKS A TEAM
AACEHHRSTW	WASH THE CAR	AACEIKNOTT	TAKE ACTION
AACEHIKLMR	LIKE A CHARM	AACEIKPRSS	ASKS A PRICE
AACEHIKMPT	MAKE A PITCH	AACEILLMNU	ANIMALCULE
AACEHIKNSZ	ASHKENAZIC	AACEILLMNY	ANEMICALLY
AACEHILMMS	MICHAELMAS	AACEILLOSU	ALLIACEOUS
AACEHILMPR	ALPHAMERIC	AACEILLPRU	LUPERCALIA
AACEHILNPT	CHINA PLATE	AACEILLRRS	CAR RALLIES
AACEHILNSS	SELACHIANS	AACEILLRVY	CAVALIERLY
AACEHILPTT	THE CAPITAL	AACEILLSTV	VACILLATES
AACEHILRSV	LAVISH CARE	AACEILLSTY	SALICYLATE
AACEHILRTT	THEATRICAL	AACEILLTTV	CAVALETTI
AACEHIMNST	MACHINATES	AACEILMMNR	REMAIN CALM
AACEHIMPRS	PHARMACIES	AACEILMMTU	IMMACULATE
AACEHINRST	CHARENTAIS	AACEILMNPS	CAMPANILES
AACEHINRTT	ANTHRACITE	AACEILMNRT	CAMEL TRAIN
AACEHINSTT	ACT IN HASTE	AACEILMNRU	UNICAMERAL
	IN THAT CASE	AACEILMNST	CAME IN LAST
AACEHINSTU	EUSTACHIAN	AACEILMNSU	MAIN CLAUSE
	EUTHANASIC	AACEILMNTU	CALUMNIATE
AACEHINTTV	THE VATICAN	AACEILMRSU	MUSICAL EAR
AACEHIPSTT	CHAPATTIES	AACEILMRTU	TULARAEMIC
AACEHIRRTV	ARCHITRAVE	AACEILMSTV	CALMATIVES
AACEHIRSSY	EASY CHAIRS	AACEILNORT	LACERATION
AACEHJKMMR	JACKHAMMER	AACEILNOST	ESCALATION
AACEHKLMRS	RAMSHACKLE	AACEILNOSV	NASAL VOICE
AACEHKMMRT	MATCHMAKER	AACEILNPPS	APPLIANCES
AACEHKMNPU	KAMPUCHEAN	AACEILNPSS	SNAILS PACE
AACEHKMORS	HACKAMORES	AACEILNPTU	PANICULATE
AACEHKMRTW	WATCHMAKER	AACEILOOPZ	PALAEOZOIC
AACEHKNPTU	TAKE A PUNCH	AACEILPTTU	CAPITULATE

AACEILRSUV	RIVAL CAUSE	AACELNRRUW	NUCLEAR WAR
AACEILRTTU	ARTICULATE	AACELNRTTU	TENTACULAR
AACEILSSTU	CASUALTIES	AACELNSSSU	CASUALNESS
AACEILSTTT	STALACTITE	AACELOPPSY	APOCALYPSE
AACEIMMPRU	PARAMECIUM	AACELORSST	ESCALATORS
AACEIMNNRU	UN-AMERICAN	AACELORSTY	ESCALATORY
AACEIMNNST	ANAMNESTIC	AACELOSTUV	AUTOCLAVES
AACEIMNORS	MACARONIES	AACELRSSST	ART CLASSES
AACEIMNORT	MACERATION	AACELRSTUW	CATERWAULS
AACEIMNORU	OCEANARIUM	AACELSTTUU	AUSCULTATE
AACEIMNRRW	CRIMEAN WAR	AACEMNRSST	SACRAMENTS
AACEIMOPST	APOSEMATIC	AACEMOPRST	COMES APART
AACEIMORRT	CREMATORIA	AACEMOPSST	CAME TO PASS
AACEIMPRRT	PARAMETRIC	AACEMOSTTY	CAME TO STAY
AACEIMSSTT	MASTICATES	AACEMPRSTU	METACARPUS
AACEIMSTTT	METASTATIC	AACENNNOSY	ANNOYANCES
AACEINNNTU	ANNUNCIATE	AACENNSSTV	VACANTNESS
AACEINNOTT	CATENATION	AACENRSSSU	ASSURANCES
AACEINNPRT	PANCREATIN	AACENRSSSV	CANVASSERS
AACEINNRST	INCARNATES	AACEOPRSSY	PAYS A SCORE
AACEINORTV	VACATIONER	AACEORRTTT	TERRA COTTA
AACEINOTUV	EVACUATION		TERRACOTTA
AACEINOTVX	EXCAVATION	AACEOSSTTV	CASTS A VOTE
AACEINPRST	PERSIAN CAT	AACEPPPRRS	SCRAP PAPER
AACEINPRTY	AT ANY PRICE	AACFFGIINN	AFFIANCING
AACEINPSSU	CAUSES PAIN	AACFFHIOTT	ACT OF FAITH
AACEINRSST	ASCERTAINS	AACFFIINPR	PARAFFINIC
	SECTARIANS	AACFFIIRRT	AIR TRAFFIC
AACEINSSST	ASSISTANCE	AACFFIJMRT	TRAFFIC JAM
AACEINSTVY	VANITY CASE	AACFGIIMNT	MAGNIFICAT
AACEIORSTU	CAUSE A RIOT	AACFGILNRT	FLAT RACING
AACEIOSSST	ASSOCIATES		FLAT-RACING
AACEIOSTVV	VASOACTIVE	AACFHHILNN	HALF AN INCH
AACEIPRRTV	PRIVATE CAR	AACFHHLMSU	HALF AS MUCH
AACEIPRTTV	ACTIVE PART	AACFHIKLST	LACKS FAITH
AACEIPSTTV	CAPTIVATES	AACFHKLRST	HALF-TRACKS
AACEIRSSST	STAIRCASES	AACFHKNRST	CRANKSHAFT
AACEIRSSTU	CAUSE A STIR	AACFHLNORW	HALF A CROWN
AACEIRTTTV	ATTRACTIVE		HALF-A-CROWN
AACEIRTTVY	VARIETY ACT	AACFIIILRT	ARTIFICIAL
AACEJKNRRW	JACK WARNER	AACFIILSTT	FATALISTIC
AACEJKNRTT	NATTERJACK	AACFIIMNRS	AFRICANISM
AACEJLMORS	MAJOR SCALE	AACFIIMNNT	FANATICISM
AACEKKKNOT	TAKE A KNOCK	AACFIINOST	FASCIATION
AACEKKMRST	MAKE TRACKS	AACFIINRST	AFRICANIST
AACEKLMOOS	COOKS A MEAL	AACFIKMNOR	MARK OF CAIN
AACEKLMRST	SMART ALECK	AACFILLOSU	FALLACIOUS
AACEKNOPTY	TAKEN A COPY	AACFILMOOT	COAT OF MAIL
AACEKNOTTU	TAKE A COUNT	AACFILMSST	CASTS A FILM
AACEKOPSTY	TAKES A COPY	AACFILNORT	FRACTIONAL
AACEKPPSTY	PAY-PACKETS	AACFILNPST	PLAIN FACTS
AACELLLMSS	SMALL SCALE	AACFILOSTT	FAILS TO ACT
	SMALL-SCALE	AACFILRSTY	ACTS FAIRLY
AACELLLORT	COLLATERAL	AACFILTTUY	FACTUALITY
AACELLLRST	SALT CELLAR	AACFINORST	FASCINATOR
	SALTCELLAR	AACFLLLMOR	FORMAL CALL
AACELLNOSW	ALLOWANCES	AACFLLMRST	SMALL CRAFT
AACELLNSST	CASTELLANS	AACFMOORST	COAT OF ARMS
AACELLOPPR	LOCAL PAPER	AACFNRSTTU	SURFACTANT
AACELLORST	LOCAL RATES	AACFRRTTYY	ARTY-CRAFTY
AACELLOTTV	CAVALLETTO	AACGGIILNT	GLACIATING
AACELLPRRY	CARPELLARY	AACGGILLNO	ALGOLAGNIC
AACELLPSST	CAST A SPELL	AACGHHINPR	CHINAGRAPH
AACELLRSWY	SAW CLEARLY	AACGHHOPRT	TACHOGRAPH
AACELMOPSU	PALMACEOUS	AACGHIINRR	HIRING A CAR
AACELMORRT	RECLAMATOR	AACGHILNPY	ANAGLYPHIC
AACELMPRST	SCRAP METAL	AACGHINPSY	PAYING CASH
AACELMSSST	CLASSMATES	AACGHIOPRS	SARCOPHAGI
AACELNOPTU	CANTALOUPE	AACGHIPRRT	GRAPHIC ART
AACELNOPTY	ONE-ACT PLAY	AACGHLSSTW	WATCHGLASS
AACELNRRUV	VERNACULAR	AACGIILNNS	CANALISING

AACGIILNNZ	CANALIZING	AACHMNOPSY	HAS COMPANY
AACGIILNOT	GLACIATION	AACHMORRTW	MARCH TO WAR
AACGIIMSTT	ASTIGMATIC	AACHOOPSTT	CAPS A TOOTH
AACGIINNPT	CAPTAINING	AACHOSSSTT	ACTS AS HOST
AACGIINTTV	ACTIVATING	AACHOSSSTW	CASTS A SHOW
	CAVITATING	AACIILLMRV	RIVAL CLAIM
AACGIJNORT	CARING A JOT	AACIILLNNT	ANTICLINAL
AACGIKNNRS	RANSACKING	AACIILMNOS	SIMONIACAL
AACGIKNPRR	CAR PARKING	AACIILMNST	TALISMANIC
AACGIKNTTU	TAKING A CUT	AACIILMNTX	ANTICLIMAX
AACGILLMNT	MATING CALL	AACIILMPST	CAPITALISM
AACGILLNOT	ALLOCATING	AACIILNNST	ANNALISTIC
AACGILLRST	GARLIC SALT	AACIILNOST	ANTISOCIAL
AACGILLRTY	TRAGICALLY	AACIILNOTT	CITATIONAL
AACGILMNNY	MALIGNANCY	AACIILNSST	CASTILIANS
AACGILNORS	COR ANGLAIS	AACIILPSTT	CAPITALIST
AACGILNORT	CARING A LOT	AACIILRRTU	URTICARIAL
AACGILNPTY	PLAY ACTING	AACIILRSST	RACIALISTS
	PLAYACTING	AACIIMSSTT	ASTATICISM
AACGILNSTY	CATALYSING	AACIINNOPS	POINCIANAS
AACGILPRTY	TRAGIC PLAY	AACIINOPTT	CAPITATION
AACGIMNNORT	MORGANATIC	AACIINORTV	VICTORIANA
AACGIMNRSS	MASSACRING	AACIINOTTV	ACTIVATION
AACGIMRSTY	MAGISTRACY		CAVITATION
AACGINNSSV	CANVASSING	AACIINPRST	PATRICIANS
AACGINPRST	PAST CARING	AACIIORSUV	AVARICIOUS
AACGINRSTT	CASTRATING	AACIJMNORS	CANIS MAJOR
AACGINRTTT	ATTRACTING	AACIJMOPRT	APRICOT JAM
AACGIORSTT	CASTIGATOR	AACIKLMMRS	LAMARCKISM
AACGLLMOOY	MALACOLOGY	AACIKLNORS	SOCIAL RANK
AACGLLSSWY	SCALLYWAGS	AACIKLPRTY	PLAY A TRICK
AACGLNOORV	VOCAL ORGAN	AACIKNSSTY	KANSAS CITY
AACGLNOSTU	COAGULANTS	AACILLLSST	CALLS TAILS
AACGMNOPSY	GAS COMPANY	AACILLMOTY	ATOMICALLY
AACGMNOPYY	GAY COMPANY		LAY CLAIM TO
AACGMORRST	CARTOGRAMS	AACILLNOOT	ALLOCATION
AACHHHISUU	CHIHUAHUAS		LOCATIONAL
AACHHIMNNU	HUMAN CHAIN	AACILLNORT	LOCAL TRAIN
AACHHLOPTT	HATCH A PLOT	AACILLNTUY	NAUTICALLY
AACHILLOPT	ALLOPATHIC	AACILLOPTT	TO CAP IT ALL
AACHILLPTY	PHATICALLY	AACILLORTV	VACILLATOR
AACHILMNOR	MONARCHIAL	AACILLPTYY	ATYPICALLY
AACHILMRTT	TRIAL MATCH	AACILLSTTY	STATICALLY
AACHILNNPT	PLAINCHANT	AACILMNOTU	MACULATION
AACHILNPSS	SHIP CANALS	AACILMOSTU	CALAMITOUS
AACHILOPST	CHIPOLATAS	AACILMPSTU	CAPITAL SUM
AACHIMMNRS	RACHMANISM	AACILNNOOT	CONATIONAL
AACHIMNOPR	ANAMORPHIC	AACILNNRTY	TYRANNICAL
AACHIMNORS	HARMONICAS	AACILNOOTV	VOCATIONAL
	MARASCHINO	AACILNOPTY	NYCTALOPIA
AACHIMNORT	MACHINATOR	AACILNORTT	TRACTIONAL
AACHIMNPST	PHANTASMIC	AACILNOSTT	LACTATIONS
AACHIMNSTW	WINS A MATCH	AACILNPPST	APPLICANTS
AACHIMPRST	PHARMACIST	AACILOPPRT	APPLICATOR
AACHIMRRST	MATRIARCHS	AACILORRTU	CURATORIAL
AACHIMRRTY	MATRIARCHY	AACILPRRSU	SPIRACULAR
AACHINORST	TOCHARIANS	AACILPRRTU	PARTICULAR
AACHINPSSY	PAYS IN CASH	AACILPRSTY	PARALYTICS
AACHINRRST	TRAIN CRASH	AACILQSTTU	ACQUITTALS
AACHINRSST	ANARCHISTS	AACIMMNNOO	MONOMANIAC
AACHINRSTU	CARTHUSIAN	AACIMMOSST	ATOMIC MASS
AACHIPRRST	PATRIARCHS	AACIMNNNSU	MANCUNIANS
AACHIPRRTY	PATRIARCHY	AACIMNOPRY	PYROMANIAC
AACHKKNPPY	HAPPY KNACK	AACIMORSTT	MASTICATOR
AACHLLORTT	ALTAR CLOTH	AACIMOSTTU	AUTOMATICS
AACHLMOSTT	LOST A MATCH	AACINNOOTV	ON VACATION
AACHLNNNOT	NONCHALANT	AACINNOOTZ	ACTINOZOAN
AACHLOPPRY	APOCRYPHAL	AACINNORST	CARNATIONS
AACHLOPSVY	PLAYS HAVOC	AACINNORSW	WIN AN OSCAR
AACHLORTYY	ROYAL YACHT	AACINOOSTV	AVOCATIONS
AACHMNNORR	NORMAN ARCH		NOVA SCOTIA

AACINOPRSS	CAPARISONS	AADDEGIMMR	DIAGRAMMED
AACINORSTT	CASTRATION	AADDEGIPRS	DISPARAGED
AACINORTTT	ATTRACTION	AADDEGIRRT	TARDIGRADE
AACINORTTU	ART AUCTION	AADDEGMNOR	ARMAGEDDON
AACINORTUY	CAUTIONARY	AADDEGMRRU	ARMED GUARD
AACINOSSTU	CAUSATIONS	AADDEGNNOR	DRAGONNADE
AACINOSTTU	ACTUATIONS	AADDEHIMNN	HANDMAIDEN
AACINPPRST	CAPRI PANTS	AADDEHINWY	HIDDEN AWAY
AACINRSSST	SACRISTANS	AADDEHIPTT	HAD IT TAPED
AACIORRSTT	ARISTOCRAT	AADDEHLMNN	MANHANDLED
AACIOSSTTW	WAISTCOATS	AADDEHLMOT	THE OLD ADAM
AACJKPRSTT	JACK SPRATT	AADDEHLNNP	PANHANDLED
AACJLMRSUU	MAJUSCULAR	AADDEHLNNS	LENDS A HAND
AACJLNORSU	JUAN CARLOS	AADDEHLPRY	PLAYED HARD
AACKLNOOTV	VACANT LOOK	AADDEHNOSY	HAD ONE'S DAY
AACKLOOSST	CASTS A LOOK	AADDEHNSTY	STEADY HAND
	TOOK A CLASS	AADDEIILMS	LADIES MAID
AACKLORSSW	WALK ACROSS	AADDEIIRRT	IRRADIATED
AACKNSSTTY	TASTY SNACK	AADDEILLNS	LANDLADIES
AACLLMNPRU	PULLMAN CAR	AADDEILMMY	MIDDAY MEAL
AACLLMORST	CALL TO ARMS	AADDEILMRR	REAL MADRID
AACLLNOPSY	PAYS ON CALL		RED ADMIRAL
AACLLOORST	ALLOCATORS	AADDEILNSV	VANDALISED
AACLLORRUY	ORACULARLY	AADDEILNVZ	VANDALIZED
AACLLOSSTT	AT ALL COSTS	AADDEILORR	RAILROADED
AACLMMOPSY	MYCOPLASMA	AADDEILPRY	PAID DEARLY
AACLMNOPWY	COMPANY LAW	AADDEIMRST	DRAMATISED
AACLMOPRSS	SARCOPLASM	AADDEIMRTZ	DRAMATIZED
AACLNOPSTU	CANTALOUPS	AADDEINRWY	RIDDEN AWAY
AACLOORRTU	COLORATURA	AADDEINSST	STAND ASIDE
AACLOORSTY	ROYAL ASCOT	AADDEIRRSY	DISARRAYED
AACLOPPRTU	PAPAL COURT	AADDELMNST	LAST DEMAND
AACLOPTTWY	TWO-ACT PLAY	AADDELORSU	READS ALOUD
AACLORTUUY	YOUR ACTUAL	AADDEMNNST	DEMANDANTS
AACMNNORTY	MARC ANTONY	AADDEMNOSU	MADE A SOUND
AACMNOPTXY	COMPANY TAX	AADDEMNSTX	TAX DEMANDS
AACMNOSTTU	CATAMOUNTS	AADDEMSTUY	MADE A STUDY
AACMOOPRRT	COMPARATOR	AADDENRSTY	STAND READY
AACMORSSSW	SWAM ACROSS	AADDEOSTTY	TODAYS DATE
AACNNNOSTT	CONSTANTAN	AADDFHOOSS	DASH OF SODA
AACNNOORSW	WON AN OSCAR	AADDFIORUV	DID A FAVOUR
AACNNOPTTU	PUT ON AN ACT	AADDFQRSUU	FRAUD SQUAD
AACNORRSTT	TRANSACTOR	AADDGIIINT	DID IT AGAIN
AACNORRSTW	RAN TWO CARS	AADDGILOVY	LADY GODIVA
AACORRRSTW	RAW CARROTS	AADDGNNRST	GRANDSTAND
AACORRSTTT	ATTRACTORS	AADDGNOPWY	PADDY WAGON
AADDDDEEEH	DEADHEADED	AADDGNRSTU	STAND GUARD
AADDDEEHHR	HARDHEADED	AADDHHINNN	HAND IN HAND
AADDDEEHIT	DIED A DEATH	AADDHHNNOT	HAND TO HAND
AADDDEELUV	VALUE-ADDED		HAND-TO-HAND
AADDDEERTW	ADDED WATER	AADDHIMOTT	HAD TO ADMIT
AADDDEGOOS	GOOD AS DEAD	AADDHNNSST	HANDSTANDS
AADDDEIKSS	DID AS ASKED	AADDHNRSWY	WASH AND DRY
AADDDGRSUY	SUGAR DADDY	AADDIILNOT	ADDITIONAL
AADDEEEHST	THE DEAD SEA	AADDIINRSV	DRAVIDIANS
AADDEEELSV	DEAD LEAVES	AADDINORRT	RITARDANDO
AADDEEERRR	DEAR READER	AADDKKNORV	DRANK VODKA
AADDEEFITX	FIXED A DATE	AADDLNNOSW	DONALD SWAN
AADDEEHHST	DEATH'S-HEAD	AADDLNOOSW	SANDALWOOD
	DEATHS HEAD	AADDNNRRUU	DURAN DURAN
AADDEEHIMN	MAIDENHEAD	AADDORRSWW	DRAW A SWORD
AADDEEHIST	DIES A DEATH	AADEEEGGNV	GAVE AN EDGE
AADDEEIRST	DESIDERATA	AADEEEGHNV	HAVE AN EDGE
AADDEELRRW	EDWARD LEAR	AADEEEGLPR	LEADER PAGE
AADDEEMMNS	MADE AMENDS	AADEEEHKPS	KEEPS AHEAD
AADDEEMRTT	DEAD MATTER	AADEEEHMTT	MADE THE TEA
AADDEESTTV	DEVASTATED	AADEEEKPST	KEEPS A DATE
AADDEFINRW	FAR AND WIDE	AADEEELRSY	DAY RELEASE
AADDEGGIKR	KRAGDADIGE	AADEEEMSTY	MADE EYES AT
AADDEGILNO	DOING A DEAL	AADEEERVWY	VEERED AWAY
AADDEGILWY	GLIDED AWAY	AADEEESTVX	EVADE TAXES

428

AADEEFGHOR	FORGE AHEAD	AADEEIMPRS	SPARE A DIME
AADEEFGLRT	DEFLAGRATE	AADEEIMSTY	MADE IT EASY
AADEEFHRTT	AFTER DEATH	AADEEINQTU	INADEQUATE
AADEEFISTX	FIXES A DATE	AADEEINSTW	WAIT AND SEE
AADEEFKLMN	NAKED FLAME	AADEEIPTTX	EXPATIATED
AADEEFKRST	ASKED AFTER	AADEEISTTV	AESTIVATED
AADEEFLLRW	FEDERAL LAW	AADEEKMMNS	MAKE AMENDS
AADEEFLPSY	PLAYED SAFE	AADEEKMNST	MAKES A DENT
AADEEFPRRS	SPREAD FEAR	AADEEKMRSY	MAKES READY
AADEEFRRST	FAST READER	AADEELLLPR	PARALLELED
AADEEGGGRT	AGGREGATED	AADEELLPPR	APPARELLED
AADEEGGNRT	GARDEN GATE	AADEELMNNR	LEARNED MAN
AADEEGHRSU	SURGE AHEAD	AADEELMORR	ORDER A MEAL
AADEEGILNV	GIVEN A LEAD	AADEELMRRS	ARMS DEALER
AADEEGILSV	GIVES A LEAD	AADEELMRTT	MALTREATED
AADEEGINST	GETS AN IDEA	AADEELMSTT	STALEMATED
AADEEGIRTV	VARIEGATED	AADEELMTWY	MELTED AWAY
AADEEGKMRR	GREEK DRAMA	AADEELNNRS	LENDS AN EAR
AADEEGLNRR	REAL DANGER	AADEELNNWZ	NEW ZEALAND
AADEEGLNRS	GREEN SALAD	AADEELNPSS	ESPLANADES
AADEEGLNSS	AGENDALESS	AADEELNPST	PLANT A SEED
AADEEGMNRW	GAME WARDEN	AADEELNRSX	ALEXANDERS
AADEEGMNST	GAME AND SET	AADEELNRTT	ALTERNATED
AADEEGMNTV	MEAT AND VEG	AADEELQRSU	SQUARE DEAL
AADEEGMSSU	MADE A GUESS	AADEELQTUY	ADEQUATELY
AADEEGNPPS	APPENDAGES	AADEELRRST	ART DEALERS
AADEEGNPRS	GARDEN PEAS	AADEELRHSW	WAR LEADERS
AADEEGNRST	GARDEN SEAT	AADEELRSTV	SLAVE TRADE
	TEA GARDENS	AADEELRTTU	ADULTERATE
AADEEGNRTU	GUARANTEED	AADEEMMNNS	NAMED NAMES
AADEEGPSSU	USED AS A PEG	AADEEMPSSS	MADE PASSES
AADEEGRTTT	TARGET DATE	AADEEMORSU	MASQUERADE
AADEEHHMMR	HAMMERHEAD	AADEEMQSTU	DESQUAMATE
AADEEHIMTV	HAVE IT MADE	AADEENRSTY	STAYED NEAR
AADEEHINOV	HAVE NO IDEA	AADEENSTVZ	ZEND-AVESTA
AADEEHIRTW	HEAD WAITER	AADEENTTTU	ATTENUATED
	HEADWAITER	AADEEOPRTV	EVAPORATED
AADEEHKNSS	SNAKE'S-HEAD	AADEEPPRRT	TRADE PAPER
AADEEHLMTW	MADE THE LAW	AADEEPPRWX	WAXED PAPER
AADEEHLNTV	LEAD THE VAN	AADEERRTTW	TREAD WATER
AADEEHLTWY	LEAD THE WAY	AADEESSTTV	DEVASTATES
AADEEHMNTY	NAME THE DAY	AADEFFIILT	AFFILIATED
AADEEHMRST	HEADMASTER	AADEFFNORT	FORE AND AFT
AADEEHNNOY	HAD AN EYE ON		FORE-AND-AFT
AADEEHNRVW	HEAVENWARD	AADEFGILLP	FILLED A GAP
AADEEHPRSS	PRESS AHEAD	AADEFGKMOS	SMOKED A FAG
	SPEARHEADS	AADEFGLNRT	GARDEN FLAT
AADEEHQRSU	SQUAREHEAD	AADEFGRSSU	SAFEGUARDS
AADEEHRRTT	TETRAHEDRA	AADEFHHIOR	HEAD OF HAIR
AADEEHRRST	SHEDS A TEAR	AADEFHLNOZ	HALF A DOZEN
AADEEHRSTW	HEADWATERS	AADEFHLNRT	FATHERLAND
AADEEHRTTY	AT THE READY	AADEFHNOPS	HEAP OF SAND
AADEEHRTVY	HEAVY TREAD	AADEFHRSTY	FATHERS DAY
AADEEHSTVY	SAVE THE DAY	AADEFIIKLL	ALKALIFIED
AADEEIILLN	NAILED A LIE	AADEFIILRS	FAIR LADIES
AADEEIKLMR	LIKE A DREAM	AADEFILLNT	FLAT DENIAL
AADEEIKLNS	NEIL SEDAKA	AADEFILPRY	PLAYED FAIR
AADEEIKNST	TAKEN ASIDE	AADEFIMNNW	MAN AND WIFE
AADEEIKNTV	TAKEN A DIVE	AADEFIMNOS	MAN OF IDEAS
AADEEIKPRT	TAKE A PRIDE	AADEFIMNOT	DEFAMATION
AADEEIKPRY	KEEP A DIARY	AADEFINSTZ	FANTASIZED
AADEEIKSST	TAKES ASIDE	AADEFINTTU	INFATUATED
AADEEIKSTV	TAKES A DIVE	AADEFKLSTT	FAST-TALKED
AADEEILLTV	ALLEVIATED	AADEFLNORS	FARANDOLES
AADEEILNST	DESALINATE	AADEFMOORT	ROAD TO FAME
AADEEILPPW	WIDE APPEAL	AADEFMORTY	DEFAMATORY
AADEEILPSS	SAID PLEASE	AADEFMRSST	FARMSTEADS
AADEEILRTT	RETALIATED	AADEFORSTY	ROAD SAFETY
AADEEIMMNN	MAIDEN NAME	AADEFORTTY	AFTER TODAY
AADEEIMNOS	MADE A NOISE	AADEFRRSTW	AFTERWARDS
AADEEIMNTX	MADE AN EXIT	AADEGGHINO	GOING AHEAD

AADEGGHHMNS	HAM AND EGGS	AADEHINPST	PHANTASIED
AADEGGINRS	AGGRANDISE	AADEHINSSW	SANDIE SHAW
	SANG A DIRGE	AADEHIPSTT	HAS IT TAPED
AADEGGINRZ	AGGRANDIZE	AADEHJMPSU	JUMPS AHEAD
AADEGGIRSV	DIGS A GRAVE	AADEHKLLMR	HALLMARKED
AADEGGOSSU	SAUSAGE DOG	AADEHKLOOS	LOOKS AHEAD
AADEGHHINS	SHANGHAIED	AADEHKMNTY	TAKE MY HAND
AADEGHHIRT	RIGHT AHEAD	AADEHKORST	HAD A STROKE
AADEGHIINR	HEARING AID	AADEHKORTT	HARD TO TAKE
AADEGHIMOP	PAID HOMAGE	AADEHLLMRS	MARSHALLED
AADEGHINNV	GIVEN A HAND	AADEHLLOSS	HOLDS A SALE
AADEGHINSV	GIVES A HAND	AADEHLLPSU	PULLS AHEAD
AADEGHINTY	GAIN THE DAY	AADEHLLSST	HEADSTALLS
AADEGHLRTU	DRAUGHT ALE	AADEHLMNNS	MANHANDLES
AADEGHNPRT	GARDEN PATH	AADEHLMPSS	LAMPSHADES
AADEGHNRSY	HYDRANGEAS	AADEHLNNPR	PANHANDLER
AADEGHNSST	STAGEHANDS	AADEHLNNPS	PANHANDLES
AADEGIILNV	LIVED AGAIN	AADEHLNRST	HEARTLANDS
AADEGIINRT	TRIED AGAIN	AADEHLPRTY	HELD A PARTY
AADEGILMNN	LEADING MAN	AADEHMMMNO	MOHAMMEDAN
AADEGILNOS	ANALOGISED	AADEHMNOSY	MOSHE DAYAN
AADEGILNOZ	ANALOGIZED	AADEHMORTW	DRAW AT HOME
AADEGILNSV	GALVANISED	AADEHMRRST	HARD MASTER
AADEGILNVZ	GALVANIZED	AADEHNOOSZ	HAD A SNOOZE
AADEGILSWY	GLIDES AWAY	AADEHNORTY	ANOTHER DAY
AADEGILTTY	AGITATEDLY	AADEHNOSSY	HAD ONE'S SAY
AADEGIMMNS	MISMANAGED		HAS ONE'S DAY
AADEGIMNNV	GIVEN A DAMN	AADEHNOSWY	HAD ONE'S WAY
AADEGIMNPR	MAP READING	AADEHNRRST	HARD ASTERN
AADEGIMNST	DIAMAGNETS	AADEHOOSWY	SHOOED AWAY
AADEGIMNSV	GIVES A DAMN	AADEHORRSW	ARROWHEADS
AADEGINNRV	GIVEN A DARN	AADEHPSUWY	PUSHED AWAY
AADEGINNTT	ANTEDATING	AADEHRRSTW	EARTHWARDS
AADEGINRRS	DISARRANGE	AADEHRSUWY	RUSHED AWAY
AADEGINRST	TRAGEDIANS	AADEIIKLNR	LIKE A DRAIN
AADEGINRSV	GIVES A DARN	AADEIILMMN	IN A DILEMMA
AADEGINSWY	SIGNED AWAY	AADEIILMNN	INDIAN MEAL
AADEGINTVX	EVADING TAX	AADEIILMNS	ANIMALISED
AADEGIPRSS	DISPARAGES	AADEIILMNZ	ANIMALIZED
AADEGIRTTV	GRAVITATED	AADEIILNOT	IDEATIONAL
AADEGKLORV	LARGE VODKA	AADEIILNTV	INVALIDATE
AADEGKNRTU	TAKEN A DRUG	AADEIILPRS	LAPIDARIES
AADEGKRSTU	TAKES A DRUG	AADEIIMNNR	AMERINDIAN
AADEGLLNRW	GARDEN WALL	AADEIIMNNT	MAINTAINED
AADEGLNQRU	QUADRANGLE	AADEIIMNST	MEDIASTINA
AADEGLNRTU	GRANULATED	AADEIINNST	EAST INDIAN
AADEGMNOOS	GOOD SEAMAN	AADEIINPPR	INDIA PAPER
AADEGMOOSV	SAVAGE MOOD	AADEIINPRS	IN PARADISE
AADEGNOPRR	GRAND OPERA	AADEIINQTU	QUAINT IDEA
AADEGOPPRT	PROPAGATED	AADEIIRRST	IRRADIATES
AADEGRRSVY	GRAVEYARDS	AADEIJMNOT	MADE A JOINT
AADEHHIKNT	THINK AHEAD	AADEIJNSTU	JUST AN IDEA
AADEHHINNV	HAVE IN HAND	AADEIJORTY	RADIATE JOY
AADEHHKNSS	HANDSHAKES	AADEIKLMNR	RAN LIKE MAD
	SHAKE HANDS	AADEIKPRTY	KEPT A DIARY
AADEHHNORT	HAD ANOTHER	AADEILLMMT	MAMILLATED
AADEHHOOST	SHOOT AHEAD	AADEILLNNO	ALAIN DELON
AADEHHORSW	HAD A SHOWER	AADEILMNNR	MAINLANDER
AADEHHORTY	HAD A THEORY	AADEILMNTY	ANIMATEDLY
AADEHHRTWY	THE HARD WAY	AADEILMORT	TAILOR-MADE
AADEHIIMNR	MAIDENHAIR	AADEILNNRW	DRAWN A LINE
AADEHIINRT	ANTHERIDIA	AADEILNNSW	WALDENSIAN
AADEHIKNNT	TAKE IN HAND	AADEILNNTV	NATIVE LAND
AADEHIKNRV	HAVE A DRINK	AADEILNRSW	DRAWS A LINE
AADEHIKRTT	TAKE IT HARD	AADEILNRVW	DRAWN A VEIL
AADEHILNNT	LANTHANIDE	AADEILNSSV	VANDALISES
AADEHILNOS	ADHESIONAL	AADEILNSTT	TANTALISED
AADEHILORR	DIARRHOEAL	AADEILNSVZ	VANDALIZES
AADEHILOTT	HEAD TO TAIL	AADEILNTTZ	TANTALIZED
AADEHILRSW	HAWSER-LAID	AADEILORRR	RAILROADER
AADEHIMRTT	MATTED HAIR	AADEILORST	ASTEROIDAL

AADEILPPRY	DAILY PAPER	AADELNNPTT	LAND PATENT
AADEILPPTT	PALPITATED	AADELNNRUY	DANNY LA RUE
AADEILPRTV	LIVED APART	AADELNOPRS	PERSONAL AD
AADEILPTVY	ADAPTIVELY	AADELNORVW	LOVE AND WAR
AADEILRRTY	RADIAL TYRE	AADELNOTTW	WANTED A LOT
AADEILRSVW	DRAWS A VEIL	AADELNPPSY	PLAYED SNAP
AADEILSSWY	SLIDES AWAY	AADELNRSTT	TRANSLATED
AADEIMMNOT	AMMONIATED	AADELNRTTU	ADULTERANT
AADEIMMNRR	MARRIED MAN	AADELPRSTW	DRAWPLATES
AADEIMMRTW	MADE IT WARM	AADELPRSYY	PAYS DEARLY
AADEIMNNRT	DEAN MARTIN	AADEMMNSSU	MANDAMUSES
	TRAINED MAN	AADEMNPRSS	AMPERSANDS
AADEIMNNTU	MAIDEN AUNT	AADEMNQRUU	QUADRUMANE
AADEIMNOPT	MADE A POINT	AADEMPSSTT	DATE STAMPS
AADEIMNOST	ANATOMISED		DATESTAMPS
AADEIMNOTZ	ANATOMIZED	AADEMRRSTY	YARDMASTER
AADEIMNRTV	ANIMADVERT	AADENNNORR	ON AN ERRAND
AADEIMORST	AROMATISED	AADENNPPST	APPENDANTS
	STEAM RADIO	AADENNRRRS	RAN ERRANDS
AADEIMORTZ	AROMATIZED	AADENNRTTU	DENATURANT
AADEIMRSST	DRAMATISES	AADENNSTTT	ATTENDANTS
AADEIMRSTZ	DRAMATIZES	AADENORRRY	RAY REARDON
AADEINNOPT	ANTIPODEAN	AADENPPRSS	SANDPAPERS
AADEINNQRU	QUADRENNIA	AADENPPRSY	SANDPAPERY
AADEINNSTW	STAND IN AWE	AADENPRSTY	PARENTS DAY
AADEINOPPS	PEAS IN A POD	AADENRRTWW	DRAWN WATER
AADEINORRT	TREAD ON AIR	AADENRSTTT	STAND TREAT
AADEINPUSU	PASQUINADE	AADENRTUWY	TURNED AWAY
AADEINQRSU	QUANDARIES	AADENSSSTY	STANDS EASY
AADEINQTTU	ANTIQUATED	AADEORRSTY	READ A STORY
AADEINRSST	STERADIANS	AADEORSTTU	AUTOSTRADE
AADEINRSTT	ANTITRADES	AADEORSTTV	DEVASTATOR
AADEINRSTY	STEADY RAIN	AADEORSTWY	STORED AWAY
AADEINRVWY	DRIVEN AWAY	AADEOSSTWY	TOSSED AWAY
AADEIOPQRU	RADIOPAQUE	AADEOSTWWY	STOWED AWAY
AADEIORSVW	RADIO WAVES	AADEQRRSUY	SQUARE YARD
AADEIPPRSS	DISAPPEARS	AADEQRRTUU	QUADRATURE
AADEIPRRWZ	DRAW A PRIZE	AADEQRRTUY	QUARTER DAY
AADEIPSSTV	PASSIVATED	AADERRSTWW	DRAWS WATER
AADEIRRSTW	AIR STEWARD	AADFFFLNOR	FAR-OFF LAND
AADEIRSVWY	DRIVES AWAY	AADFFIISTV	AFFIDAVITS
AADEJMRSTU	JUST A DREAM	AADFFILLRU	DULL AFFAIR
AADEKKNRST	STARK NAKED	AADFFILNST	FINDS A FLAT
AADEKLLLTW	WALKED TALL	AADFFLNOTU	FOUND A FLAT
AADEKLLMNS	DAN MASKELL	AADFGHHIRT	HAD A FRIGHT
AADEKLLOTT	TALKED A LOT	AADFGHLOOS	HALF AS GOOD
AADEKLMORW	MEADOW LARK	AADFGINPSS	PASSING FAD
AADEKLOOWY	LOOKED AWAY	AADFHILNST	LIFTS A HAND
AADEKLOPSU	SPEAK ALOUD	AADFHLLLOR	HALF DOLLAR
AADEKLPSTW	WALKED PAST	AADFHLNOPU	HALF A POUND
AADEKMNNOW	NAKED WOMAN	AADFHOOPRT	DROP OF A HAT
AADEKMNOSU	MAKE A SOUND	AADFIILNTU	FINAL AUDIT
AADEKMORSS	DAMASK ROSE		LATIFUNDIA
AADEKMRRST	TRADEMARKS	AADFILMNOO	ANIMAL FOOD
AADEKMSTUY	MAKE A STUDY	AADFILMRYY	MY FAIR LADY
AADEKNOPRT	TAKEN A DROP	AADFILRSTU	FRUIT SALAD
AADEKNRRTW	DRANK WATER	AADFILRSTY	LAST FRIDAY
AADEKOORST	TOOK AS READ	AADFIPRRTT	DRIFT APART
AADEKOPRST	TAKES A DROP	AADFIRSTWY	DRIFTS AWAY
AADELLNPRS	LAPLANDERS	AADFLLLNOW	FALLOW LAND
AADELLNPTT	PLATTELAND	AADFLNOOST	STAND ALOOF
AADELLNSTU	LANDAULETS	AADFLNOTUW	FATAL WOUND
AADELLORSV	EL SALVADOR	AADFNSSSTT	STANDS FAST
AADELLRRRY	LARRY ADLER	AADGGIINTV	DIVAGATING
AADELMMORS	MELODRAMAS	AADGGILNNR	GARLANDING
AADELMNRTW	MENTAL WARD	AADGGINRTU	GRADUATING
AADELMNSSS	LANDMASSES	AADGHIINWY	HIDING AWAY
AADELMOSTT	MADE TO LAST	AADGHIKNRT	TAKING HARD
AADELMPRTU	LEAD A TRUMP	AADGHILNNS	HAND SIGNAL
AADELNNOOR	LONDON AREA	AADGHIMPRS	DIAPHRAGMS
AADELNNOST	STAND ALONE	AADGHINSWY	WASHING DAY

431

AADGHIOPRR	RADIOGRAPH	AADILNOPTT	TOP AND TAIL
AADGHNNORU	HANG AROUND	AADILNRSTT	STAND TRIAL
AADGIILNPS	PALISADING	AADILORSTU	AUSTRALOID
AADGIILNTV	VALIDATING	AADILOSSVW	DISAVOWALS
AADGIIMNNR	MARINADING	AADIMMORRS	SIR OR MADAM
AADGIINNRT	GRANT-IN-AID	AADIMMSSVY	SAMMY DAVIS
AADGIINOTV	DIVAGATION	AADIMNNOPR	PRIMA DONNA
AADGIINRWY	RIDING AWAY	AADIMNOPRS	PAID RANSOM
AADGIJNRUU	JAGUARUNDI	AADIMRSSTT	DRAMATISTS
AADGILLNOY	DIAGONALLY	AADINORTUW	WAIT AROUND
AADGILMNSU	SALMAGUNDI	AADJMNNPRU	PANJANDRUM
AADGILNPPU	APPLAUDING	AADJMNOOSY	JOY ADAMSON
AADGILORST	GLADIATORS	AADJORRTUY	ADJURATORY
AADGILRRSU	GUARDRAILS	AADKLNORUW	WALK AROUND
AADGIMORRS	RADIOGRAMS	AADKNOOSTT	TOOK A STAND
AADGINNOPR	GRAND PIANO	AADLLMNOOR	NORMAL LOAD
AADGINOOWY	IN A GOOD WAY	AADLLNSSTT	STANDS TALL
AADGINORRY	DORIAN GRAY	AADLLORSTW	WORLD ATLAS
AADGINORST	GRADATIONS	AADLMNNNOS	NO MANS LAND
AADGINORTU	GRADUATION		NO-MAN'S-LAND
AADGINPRWY	DRAWING PAY	AADLMNORTU	LAUNDROMAT
AADGLLLNOY	ALL DAY LONG	AADLMNORTY	LAY DORMANT
AADGLNORTT	GRAND TOTAL	AADLMNOSTY	LAST MONDAY
AADGLNRSSS	GRASSLANDS	AADLMNPSUY	PALM SUNDAY
AADGLOORSY	GOOD SALARY	AADLNOPRTW	DAWN PATROL
AADGLORRUY	ROYAL GUARD	AADLNOPRUY	PLAY AROUND
AADGMOPRRU	DRAMA GROUP	AADLNSSTUY	LAST SUNDAY
AADGMRRTUY	DRAMATURGY	AADLOPRSUY	PRAYS ALOUD
AADGMRSSTU	MUSTARD GAS	AADLPRSSTY	PLAYS DARTS
AADGNNOPRS	SNAPDRAGON	AADMNOORSU	ANADROMOUS
AADGNNORRU	RAN AGROUND	AADNOOPPSW	SAPPANWOOD
AADGNNORSU	SANG A ROUND	AADNOORRRW	NARROW ROAD
AADGNNRSTU	GRANDAUNTS	AADNOPRRUW	WRAPAROUND
AADHHIRSTT	HAD A THIRST	AADNORSTUY	ON SATURDAY
AADHHLORWW	LORD HAW-HAW	AADOOPRSTT	STOOD APART
AADHIKNNST	TASK IN HAND	AADOPPRSST	STRAPPADOS
AADHILOPYY	HOLIDAY PAY	AAEEEEFLST	FEEL AT EASE
AADHILRTWW	WITHDRAWAL	AAEEEFLSTT	FELT AT EASE
AADHIMOSTT	HAS TO ADMIT	AAEEEGGLMU	LEAGUE GAME
AADHINOPSU	DIAPHANOUS	AAEEEGGRTX	EXAGGERATE
AADHINORRS	HARD AS IRON	AAEEEGKLNV	LAKE GENEVA
AADHINQSTU	HAD A SQUINT	AAEEEGLRSX	AXLE GREASE
AADHIOTWWY	DO AWAY WITH	AAEEEHKMTT	MAKE THE TEA
AADHKORRTW	HARD AT WORK	AAEEEHNRST	NEAR THE SEA
AADHLLNNOS	ON ALL HANDS	AAEEEHPRSS	APHAERESES
AADHLLNSST	HALLSTANDS	AAEEEHRSST	HEARTS EASE
AADHLNNOSY	LAY HANDS ON		HEARTSEASE
AADHLNORWY	ANDY WARHOL	AAEEEINRVY	AIREY NEAVE
AADHLOPRTY	HOLD A PARTY	AAEEEKLNTV	TAKEN LEAVE
AADHNOSTTW	SHOT AT DAWN	AAEEEKLSTV	TAKES LEAVE
AADHNSSSTW	WASHSTANDS	AAEEEKMSTY	MAKE EYES AT
AADIIIPSTV	PAID A VISIT	AAEEEKNPPT	TAKEN A PEEP
AADIIJLLNN	LAND IN JAIL	AAEEEKPPST	TAKES A PEEP
AADIILLMNW	WILD ANIMAL	AAEEELLNOV	LEAVE ALONE
AADIILLPST	PLASTIDIAL	AAEEELLRVY	LEAVE EARLY
AADIILMMOT	OMMATIDIAL	AAEEELMNRW	ENAMELWARE
AADIILNOTT	DILATATION	AAEEELMRSV	SERVE A MEAL
AADIILNOTV	VALIDATION	AAEEELNOTV	LEAVE A NOTE
AADIIMMNOR	MAID MARION	AAEEELNPRS	PARASELENE
AADIIMNOPS	DIPSOMANIA	AAEEELRSTT	REAL ESTATE
AADIIMNORT	ADMIRATION	AAEEELRSWY	SEE A LAWYER
AADIINNRSS	SARDINIANS	AAEEEMNNOS	SEA ANEMONE
AADIINNRSW	DARWINIANS	AAEEENOSST	AT ONES EASE
AADIINORST	RADIATIONS	AAEEEPRSTX	EXASPERATE
AADIINORTX	X-RADIATION	AAEEERSSTV	ASSEVERATE
AADIINRRSY	IN DISARRAY	AAEEESSSTT	SETS AT EASE
AADIIORRRT	IRRADIATOR	AAEEFGILMS	FALSE IMAGE
AADIIPRSST	ASPIDISTRA	AAEEFGIMRT	AFTERIMAGE
AADIIPTTVY	ADAPTIVITY	AAEEFGINPY	PAYING A FEE
AADIJNORTU	ADJURATION	AAEEFGLLLT	FLAGELLATE
AADILLMORS	ARMADILLOS	AAEEFGMRSW	SEWAGE FARM

AAEEFGRSST	FARE STAGES	AAEEHKLMOS	MAKES A HOLE
AAEEFHIKTT	TAKE A THIEF	AAEEHKLMTW	MAKE THE LAW
AAEEFHLLPS	HALF ASLEEP	AAEEHKMOSV	HAVE A SMOKE
AAEEFHLMRT	HALF A METRE	AAEEHKMSST	MAKES HASTE
AAEEFHMOST	SAFE AT HOME	AAEEHKNPST	TAKEN SHAPE
AAEEFHNORV	HAVE NO FEAR	AAEEHKNRTT	TAKEN HEART
AAEEFHNRST	FAN HEATERS	AAEEHKPRTT	TAKE THE RAP
AAEEFHRSTT	THE FAR EAST	AAEEHKPSST	TAKES SHAPE
AAEEFHRSTV	AFTER-SHAVE	AAEEHKQRTU	EARTHQUAKE
AAEEFIKMRS	MAKES A FIRE	AAEEHKRSTT	TAKES HEART
AAEEFIKNTW	TAKEN A WIFE	AAEEHLLMST	ALL THE SAME
AAEEFIKSTW	TAKES A WIFE	AAEEHLLRTY	ALL THE YEAR
AAEEFIMRTT	AFTER A TIME	AAEEHLMRTY	HEARTY MEAL
AAEEFKKQSU	KAFKAESQUE	AAEEHLMTVY	HEAVY METAL
AAEEFKLOPT	KEEP AFLOAT	AAEEHLNRST	THE ARSENAL
AAEEFKNRTT	TAKEN AFTER	AAEEHLNTTT	LATENT HEAT
AAEEFKRSTT	TAKES AFTER	AAEEHLQRSU	EQUAL SHARE
AAEEFLLLPS	FALL ASLEEP	AAEEHLRRSS	REHEARSALS
AAEEFLPSST	FAST ASLEEP	AAEEHLRRTT	RATHER LATE
AAEEFLRSSV	I ASSA FEVER	AAEEHLSTTT	AT THE LEAST
AAEEFMNNOT	NO MEAN FEAT	AAEEHMNRTW	WEATHERMAN
AAEEFRSSTU	SURE AS FATE	AAEEHMNTTY	EATEN MY HAT
AAEEFRSTTT	AFTERTASTE	AAEEHMOSTT	EATS AT HOME
AAEEGGGRST	AGGREGATES	AAEEHMPRTW	WEATHER MAP
AAEEGGLPUV	GAVE A LEG UP	AAEEHMOSTT	AT THE SEAMS
AAEEGHHISV	HEAVE A SIGH	AAEEHNNOSY	HAS AN EYE ON
AAEEGHKLNS	SHAKEN A LEG	AAEEHNOSTT	ATE ONE'S HAT
AAEEGHKLSS	SHAKES A LEG		EAT ONE'S HAT
AAEEGHLLRT	ALL THE RAGE	AAEEHNRTVW	WHAT A NERVE!
AAEEGHLNOT	HALOGENATE	AAEEHOPRTT	AT THE OPERA
AAEEGHRRTT	GREAT HEART	AAEEHPTVWY	PAVE THE WAY
AAEEGHRSST	GAS HEATERS	AAEEHRRSTW	SHEARWATER
AAEEGHSSUV	HAVE A GUESS	AAEEHRSTWY	THERE'S A WAY
AAEEGILMNN	EMALANGENI	AAEEHRTVWY	HEAVY WATER
AAEEGILNRZ	GENERAL ZIA	AAEEHSTVXY	HEAVY TAXES
AAEEGIMSSX	SEXAGESIMA	AAEEIILRVW	AERIAL VIEW
AAEEGINNRV	NEVER AGAIN	AAEEIKLMNS	SEAMANLIKE
AAEEGINRTV	VEGETARIAN	AAEEIKLMNT	TAKEN A MILE
AAEEGIPRSV	GAVE PRAISE	AAEEIKLMPS	MAKES A PILE
AAEEGIRSTV	VARIEGATES	AAEEIKLMST	TAKES A MILE
AAEEGKLRST	GREAT LAKES	AAEEIKMNOS	MAKE A NOISE
AAEEGKMSSU	MAKE A GUESS	AAEEIKMNTX	MAKE AN EXIT
AAEEGKNOPT	KEEP A TAG ON	AAEEIKMSTY	MAKE IT EASY
AAEEGKSSTU	TAKE A GUESS	AAEEIKNRST	TAKEN A RISE
AAEEGLMOSS	LOSES A GAME	AAEEIKNTVW	TAKEN A VIEW
AAEEGLRRVY	EARLY GRAVE	AAEEIKSTTY	TAKE IT EASY
AAEEGLRSTT	SET AT LARGE	AAEEIKSTVW	TAKES A VIEW
AAEEGLRSTY	EARLY STAGE	AAEEILLLVW	LEAVE A WILL
AAEEGLRTUV	GREAT VALUE	AAEEILLRTT	ALLITERATE
AAEEGMMNNT	MANAGEMENT	AAEEILLSTV	ALLEVIATES
AAEEGMNRTV	RAVAGEMENT	AAEEILMNNS	MELANESIAN
AAEEGNPRRR	PREARRANGE	AAEEILMORT	AMELIORATE
AAEEGNRSTU	GUARANTEES	AAEEILMRSS	LAMASERIES
AAEEGNSSSV	SAVAGENESS	AAEEILNPRT	PENETRALIA
AAEEGORTUV	AVERAGE OUT	AAEEILNPVW	PLAIN-WEAVE
AAEEGOSSVY	SEA VOYAGES	AAEEILPSTV	LEAVES A TIP
AAEEGPSSSU	USES AS A PEG	AAEEILRRTV	ARRIVE LATE
AAEEGQRRTU	QUARTERAGE	AAEEILRSTT	RETALIATES
AAEEGRSSTT	GREAT ASSET	AAEEILTUVV	EVALUATIVE
AAEEGRSTTY	EASY TARGET	AAEEIMNOTT	ONE AT A TIME
AAEEGRSUVW	WEAVES A RUG	AAEEIPRRTT	REPATRIATE
AAEEGSSSTY	EASY STAGES	AAEEIPRRTV	REPARATIVE
AAEEHHRTVY	HEAVY HEART	AAEEIPRSTT	TEA PARTIES
AAEEHIKLRS	SHARE ALIKE	AAEEIPRSTV	SEPARATIVE
AAEEHIKNST	TAKE A SHINE	AAEEIPRTTX	EXPATRIATE
AAEEHIKRTT	TAKE THE AIR	AAEEIPSTTX	EXPATIATES
AAEEHILRTX	EXHILARATE	AAEEIRSSTX	RAISE TAXES
AAEEHIMPRY	HYPERAEMIA	AAEEISSSTT	EAST IS EAST
AAEEHINSST	ANESTHESIA	AAEEISSTTV	AESTIVATES
AAEEHIPRSS	APHAERESIS	AAEEJKKMOS	MAKES A JOKE
AAEEHIRSTW	WASHETERIA	AAEEJNNSTU	JANE AUSTEN

AAEEJPRRSW	JASPER WARE
AAEEKKWWYY	WAKEY WAKEY!
AAEEKLMRSU	MAKES A RULE
AAEEKLPTUW	WAKE UP LATE
AAEEKLRSWY	WAKES EARLY
AAEEKMMOSV	MAKES A MOVE
AAEEKMMRTT	MEAT MARKET
AAEEKMMSSS	MAKES A MESS
AAEEKMNOST	MAKES A NOTE
AAEEKMNRST	MEAN STREAK
AAEEKMPRUW	WEAR MAKE-UP
AAEEKMPSSS	MAKE PASSES
AAEEKMRSTW	MAKES WATER
AAEEKMRSTY	EASY MARKET
AAEEKMSSVW	MAKES WAVES
AAEEKNNOTT	TAKEN A NOTE
AAEEKNOSTT	TAKES A NOTE
AAEEKNOTTV	TAKEN A VOTE
AAEEKNRSTT	TAKEN A REST
AAEEKNSTTT	TAKEN A TEST
AAEEKOSTTV	TAKES A VOTE
AAEEKPPRST	KEEPS APART
AAEEKPRRST	PARRAKEETS
AAEEKRSSTT	TAKES A REST
AAEEKSSTTT	TAKES A TEST
AAEELLLSTT	TELLS A TALE
AAEELLMNRY	REALLY MEAN
AAEELLMPTT	METAL PLATE
AAEELLNNSW	ANNA SEWELL
AAEELLPRTY	PLATELAYER
AAEELLQRSU	AQUARELLES
AAEELLQUUV	EQUAL VALUE
AAEELMMNPS	AMPLE MEANS
AAEELMNPST	NAMEPLATES
AAEELMOSTV	MEAT LOAVES
AAEELMQRSU	SQUARE MEAL
AAEELMSSTT	STALEMATES
AAEELNNOST	EATS NO LEAN
AAEELNOPRS	AEROPLANES
AAEELNORSS	LOSES AN EAR
AAEELNPRRT	PARENTERAL
AAEELNPRST	PLEASANTER
AAEELNPRTT	PLANT A TREE
	TEA PLANTER
AAEELNRRTT	RARE TALENT
AAEELNRSTT	ALTERNATES
AAEELPRSTY	SEPARATELY
AAEELPSSSY	SAYS PLEASE
AAEELSSTTV	SLAVE STATE
AAEEMMNNSS	NAMES NAMES
AAEEMMNRRT	REARMAMENT
AAEEMMNNRSY	EASY MANNER
AAEEMNNSSU	AMANUENSES
AAEEMNOSTT	EATS NO MEAT
AAEEMPRRST	PARAMETERS
AAEEMSSSTT	METASTASES
AAEENRRSTW	WARRANTEES
AAEENSTTTU	ATTENUATES
AAEEOPRSTV	EVAPORATES
AAEEORRTYY	YEAR TO YEAR
AAEEPPRSTW	WASTE PAPER
	WASTEPAPER
AAEEPRRSTY	RATEPAYERS
AAEEPSSTTU	PUTS AT EASE
AAEEPSSWWY	SWEEPS AWAY
AAEERSSTTT	TEA TASTERS
AAEFFGLRST	LARGE STAFF
AAEFFHLLMO	HALL OF FAME
AAEFFIILST	AFFILIATES
AAEFFILNRW	WIN A RAFFLE
AAEFFILORV	LOVE AFFAIR

AAEFFLLLNT	FALLEN FLAT
AAEFFLNORW	WON A RAFFLE
AAEFFLSSST	SALES STAFF
AAEFGGLMNR	GERMAN FLAG
AAEFGHHITV	HAVE A FIGHT
AAEFGHILNV	HAVE A FLING
AAEFGHINVW	HAVING A FEW
AAEFGIKMNS	MAKING SAFE
AAEFGIKMST	MAKES A GIFT
AAEFGILNST	FINAL STAGE
AAEFGILPRT	PIRATE FLAG
AAEFGINNPR	FRANGIPANE
AAEFGKMOSS	SMOKES A FAG
AAEFGLLLNT	FLAGELLANT
AAEFGLLMRU	FRUGAL MEAL
AAEFGLLOSS	GLASS OF ALE
AAEFGLNRTT	ALF GARNETT
AAEFHHLMNT	HALF THE MAN
AAEFHHLMRT	HEALTH FARM
AAEFHHLRSS	HALF SHARES
AAEFHIKLLS	LIKE A FLASH
AAEFHILNRT	TEAR IN HALF
AAEFHILNRX	FLAXEN HAIR
AAEFHINRTT	FAINT HEART
AAEFHIRRSS	FAIR SHARES
AAEFHLLRTT	LATTER HALF
AAEFHLLRYY	HALF YEARLY
AAEFHLMTWY	MET HALFWAY
AAEFHLRRTT	RATHER FLAT
AAEFHMRSTT	AFTERMATHS
AAEFIIKLLS	ALKALIFIES
AAEFIILLMN	ANIMAL LIFE
AAEFIILRSS	FILARIASES
AAEFIILSTT	FATALITIES
AAEFIKLNRW	WALK IN FEAR
AAEFIKNRRS	AFRIKANERS
AAEFILLNRX	FRAXINELLA
AAEFILLRTT	LEFT A TRAIL
AAEFILMMNY	FAMILY NAME
AAEFILMPRS	FAIR SAMPLE
AAEFILMRRS	FIRE ALARMS
AAEFILMSTY	FAMILY SEAT
AAEFILORST	RAISE ALOFT
AAEFILORSV	FIRE A SALVO
AAEFILPSTY	PLAY IT SAFE
AAEFIMRRRT	TERRA FIRMA
AAEFINSSTZ	FANTASIZES
AAEFINSTTU	INFATUATES
AAEFIRRSTT	START A FIRE
AAEFKLLSST	LEAFSTALKS
AAEFKLOPSS	SOAP FLAKES
AAEFKLOPTT	KEPT AFLOAT
AAEFKMSSSU	MAKES A FUSS
AAEFKOORTT	TAKE TOO FAR
AAEFLLLOST	LEAST OF ALL
AAEFLLMMRS	SMALL FRAME
AAEFLLPSSY	PLAYS FALSE
AAEFLLRSTW	FATS WALLER
	WATERFALLS
AAEFLLRUWY	FULLY AWARE
AAEFLLSTTW	FAT WALLETS
AAEFLMORRT	MORTAL FEAR
AAEFLMPSTY	SAFETY LAMP
AAEFLNOSST	FLAT SEASON
AAEFLNOTWZ	WANT OF ZEAL
AAEFLNRSST	LEARNS FAST
AAEFLNRSTT	LEARNT FAST
	RENTS A FLAT
AAEFLOPSTT	SOFT PALATE
AAEFLORRRT	FATAL ERROR
AAEFLRSSTT	FALSE START

AAEFMMNNOS	MAN OF MEANS	AAEGIPRTVY	GIVE A PARTY
AAEFMMNOSU	FAMOUS NAME	AAEGIRSTTV	GRAVITATES
AAEFMNOSTT	MAN OF TASTE	AAEGIRTTVY	GAVE IT A TRY
AAEFNOORSS	FOR A SEASON	AAEGJORRST	STORAGE JAR
AAEFORRSTT	AFTER A SORT	AAEGKMMNRR	GERMAN MARK
AAEFORSTTW	STATE OF WAR	AAEGKNOPTT	KEPT A TAG ON
AAEGGGLNUV	LUGGAGE VAN	AAEGKNRSSS	GRASS SNAKE
AAEGGIKMMN	MAKING GAME	AAEGLLPSST	PLATE GLASS
AAEGGILNSW	GLASWEGIAN	AAEGLLRRTY	ART GALLERY
AAEGGILOSU	SIALAGOGUE	AAEGLMPRSU	MAPLE SUGAR
AAEGGIMNSV	SAVING GAME	AAEGLMPSSY	PLAYS GAMES
AAEGHHNSVY	HANGS HEAVY	AAEGLMSTTU	GLUTAMATES
AAEGHILNRT	HEALING ART	AAEGLNNOPT	PENTAGONAL
AAEGHINNNS	SHENANIGAN	AAEGLNORST	TEARS ALONG
AAEGHKNSTV	GAVE THANKS	AAEGLNORTT	TETRAGONAL
AAEGHILNOPT	HEPTAGONAL	AAEGLNRSTU	GRANULATES
AAEGHLNPRY	PHARYNGEAL	AAEGLOPRSS	OPERA GLASS
AAEGHLPRTV	GRAVEL PATH	AAEGLPPRSS	GLASSPAPER
AAEGHMNOPR	ANEMOGRAPH	AAFGLPRRRT	LARGER PART
	PHANEROGAM	AAEGLPRRYY	GARY PLAYER
AAEGHMOPSY	PAYS HOMAGE	AAEGLRSTTU	GASTRULATE
AAEGHNOPRS	ORPHANAGES	AAEGMNNRST	STRANGE MAN
AAEGHORRTW	GROWTH AREA	AAEGMNORTW	GREAT WOMAN
AAEGHOSTUV	GAVE A SHOUT	AAEGMNPRST	PENTAGRAMS
AAEGIILNNT	ALIENATING	AAEGMNRSTT	TERMAGANTS
AAEGIILNSV	LIVES AGAIN	AAEGMRSSTT	STRATAGEMS
AAEGIILPRS	PLAGIARISE	AAEGNOPRSS	PARSONAGES
AAEGIILPRZ	PLAGIARIZE	AAEGNOPRST	APRON STAGE
AAEGIINNTV	INVAGINATE	AAEGNORSTY	GONE ASTRAY
AAEGIINRST	TRIES AGAIN	AAEGNOTTUV	VANTAGE OUT
AAEGIINRTT	INGRATIATE	AAEGNPRTTY	PARTY AGENT
AAEGIKLMNR	MAKING REAL	AAEGNRSTTT	STATE GRANT
AAEGIKLNTV	GIVEN A TALK	AAEGNRSTTU	GREAT-AUNTS
AAEGIKLNWY	LYING AWAKE	AAEGOPPRST	PROPAGATES
AAEGIKLSTV	GIVES A TALK	AAEGORSSTY	GOES ASTRAY
AAEGIKMNRR	EARMARKING	AAEGRRSSTZ	STARGAZERS
AAEGIKMNSS	MAKES A SIGN	AAEGRSSTTT	GETS A START
AAEGIKMNSY	MAKING EASY	AAEHHJLLLU	HALLELUJAH
AAEGIKNPRT	TAKEN A GRIP	AAEHHLPRTY	HYPAETHRAL
AAEGIKNPTW	TAKING A PEW	AAEHHNORST	HAS ANOTHER
AAEGIKPRST	TAKES A GRIP	AAEHHPSSTT	PASS THE HAT
AAEGILLNOT	ALLEGATION	AAEHHRRSTU	ARTHUR ASHE
AAEGILMNNOT	OIL MAGNATE	AAEHIILNNT	ANNIHILATE
AAEGILMNRT	MARTINGALE	AAEHIILTWW	WAIT AWHILE
AAEGILMSTT	STALAGMITE	AAEHIIRRRS	HAIR-RAISER
AAEGILNNOT	NEGATIONAL	AAEHIKMNSZ	ASHKENAZIM
AAEGILNNST	GALANTINES	AAEHIKMSSW	MAKES A WISH
AAEGILNNTT	TANGENTIAL	AAEHIKNNTT	TAKEN A HINT
AAEGILNOSS	ANALOGISES	AAEHIKNSTT	TAKES A HINT
AAEGILNOSZ	ANALOGIZES	AAEHIKRTTT	EARTHA KITT
AAEGILNPRS	RINGS A PEAL	AAEHILMNST	THE ANIMALS
AAEGILNPSS	PELASGIANS	AAEHILNOPR	EOLIAN HARP
AAEGILNRSV	GALVANISER	AAEHILNOTX	EXHALATION
AAEGILNRVZ	GALVANIZER	AAEHILNSTV	LEVIATHANS
AAEGILNSSV	GALVANISES	AAEHILSTWY	STAY AWHILE
AAEGILNSVZ	GALVANIZES	AAEHIMNPSS	SEAMANSHIP
AAEGILNSWX	SEALING WAX	AAEHIMNSTT	AT THE MAINS
AAEGILNTUV	EVALUATING	AAEHIMNSTY	MYASTHENIA
AAEGIMMNSS	MISMANAGES	AAEHIMRSTU	AMATEURISH
AAEGIMNNSY	SAYING AMEN	AAEHINNORV	HANOVERIAN
AAEGIMNRRV	MARGRAVINE	AAEHINPSST	PHANTASIES
AAEGIMNRVY	MARVIN GAYE	AAEHIPSTXY	ASPHYXIATE
AAEGIMRSTT	MAGISTRATE	AAEHIRTWWY	WITHER AWAY
AAEGINNOST	ANTAGONISE	AAEHJLNORW	JEAN HARLOW
AAEGINNOTZ	ANTAGONIZE	AAEHKLLMRT	MARKET HALL
AAEGINNSTU	NAUSEATING	AAEHKMOSSW	MAKES A SHOW
AAEGINPRST	SEPARATING	AAEHKMRTUZ	THE MAZURKA
AAEGINRSTU	GUARANTIES	AAEHKNOSTT	TAKEN A SHOT
AAEGINRTUU	INAUGURATE	AAEHKOOPTT	TAKE A PHOTO
AAEGINSSTT	SET AGAINST	AAEHKOORST	TOOK A SHARE
AAEGIORRTV	VARIEGATOR	AAEHKOSSTT	TAKES A SHOT

AAEHKSSTWY	ASKS THE WAY	AAEILLPSSS	PAILLASSES
AAEHLLMPTY	PLAY HAMLET		PALLIASSES
AAEHLLPSTT	THE LAST LAP	AAEILLRRTT	TRILATERAL
AAEHLMNTWY	WEALTHY MAN	AAEILLRRTY	ARTERIALLY
AAEHLMOPTY	PLAY AT HOME	AAEILMNNPT	MENTAL PAIN
AAEHLMQSUV	HAVE QUALMS	AAEILMNNSS	ANIMALNESS
AAEHLOPPRS	PHALAROPES	AAEILMNNSU	SEMIANNUAL
AAEHLORTTT	TO THE ALTAR	AAEILMNPRT	PARLIAMENT
AAEHMMNNOR	MEAN NO HARM	AAEILMNPTU	MANIPULATE
AAEHMNORTW	WOMAN HATER	AAEILMNRTY	ALIMENTARY
AAEHMNRSST	HARASSMENT	AAEILMNRWY	RAILWAYMEN
AAEHMNRSTV	HARVESTMAN	AAEILMNSTU	ALUMINATES
AAEHMORTTX	METATHORAX	AAEILMORRT	MARIOLATER
AAEHMOSTTY	STAY AT HOME	AAEILMPRST	MILES APART
	STAY-AT-HOME		SPERMATIAL
AAEHMRRRTW	RATHER WARM	AAEILNNOPT	NEAPOLITAN
AAEHMRSSTU	SHAMATEURS	AAEILNNOTV	VENATIONAL
AAEHNORRTT	RAN TO EARTH	AAEILNOORT	AREOLATION
AAEHNORTWY	ANOTHER WAY	AAEILNOQTU	EQUATIONAL
AAEHNOSSSY	HAS ONE'S SAY	AAEILNORST	ALIENATORS
AAEHNOSSWY	HAS ONE'S WAY		RATIONALES
AAEHPRSSTT	SHARP TASTE		SENATORIAL
AAEHPSSUWY	PUSHES AWAY	AAEILNORTT	ALTERATION
AAEHRSSUWY	RUSHES AWAY	AAEILNORTX	RELAXATION
AAEHRSTTTT	AT THE START	AAEILNOTTX	EXALTATION
AAEIIJNRSZ	JANIZARIES	AAEILNOTUV	EVALUATION
AAEIIKLLMN	ANIMALLIKE	AAEILNPPPR	PLAIN PAPER
AAEIIILLPTV	PALLIATIVE	AAEILNPSTT	PLAIN TASTE
AAEIILMMRT	IMMATERIAL	AAEILNRRTY	EARLY TRAIN
AAEIILMNSS	ANIMALISES	AAEILNRRVW	NEW ARRIVAL
AAEIILMNSZ	ANIMALIZES	AAEILNRSTT	TANTALISER
AAEIILMSST	ASSIMILATE	AAEILNRSTU	NATURALISE
AAEIILNNOT	ALIENATION	AAEILNRTTZ	TANTALIZER
AAEIILNNST	SALIENTIAN	AAEILNRTUZ	NATURALIZE
AAEIILNSTT	NATALITIES	AAEILNSSTT	TANTALISES
AAEIIMNNRS	SEMINARIAN	AAEILNSTTY	LAY IN STATE
AAEIIMNNRT	MAINTAINER	AAEILNSTTZ	TANTALIZES
AAEIIMPPRR	PRIMIPARAE	AAEILOPRRT	PRAETORIAL
AAEIIMRRTT	TERMITARIA	AAEILOQRTU	EQUATORIAL
AAEIIPRSST	PARASITISE	AAEILORRRT	ARTERIOLAR
AAEIIPRSTZ	PARASITIZE	AAEILORSTV	LAVATORIES
AAEIJKMNOT	MAKE A JOINT		ROAST ALIVE
AAEIJMNSST	SAINT JAMES	AAEILPPSTT	PALPITATES
AAEIKKLLMS	MAKES A KILL	AAEILPRSTV	LIVES APART
AAEIKKNRST	TAKEN A RISK	AAEILPRTVW	PRIVATE LAW
AAEIKKRSST	TAKES A RISK	AAEILPRTWY	WRITE A PLAY
AAEIKLLMSW	MAKES A WILL	AAEILQRSSU	SQUARE SAIL
AAEIKLLNPT	TAKEN A PILL	AAEILRSSSW	WASSAILERS
AAEIKLLPST	TAKES A PILL	AAEILRSTTT	STATE TRIAL
AAEIKLMNPS	MAKES PLAIN	AAEILSSTUV	ASSAULTIVE
AAEIKLMPSS	MAKES A SLIP	AAEILSSTVY	STAYS ALIVE
AAEIKLMSST	MAKES A LIST	AAEIMMNOST	AMMONIATES
AAEIKLSSST	STEAL A KISS	AAEIMMNRST	MAIN STREAM
AAEIKMMNST	MAKES A MINT		MAINSTREAM
AAEIKMMRTW	MAKE IT WARM	AAEIMMPRTU	AT A PREMIUM
AAEIKMNOPT	MAKE A POINT	AAEIMMRSTU	AMATEURISM
AAEIKMNSST	TAKEN AMISS	AAEIMNNOPR	POMERANIAN
AAEIKMPSTY	MAKES IT PAY	AAEIMNNORS	MAIN REASON
AAEIKMSSST	TAKES AMISS	AAEIMNNOST	EMANATIONS
AAEIKNNPST	TAKEN PAINS	AAEIMNNOSY	MAYONNAISE
AAEIKNPRTT	TAKEN A TRIP	AAEIMNNRST	EARNS A MINT
AAEIKNPSST	TAKES PAINS	AAEIMNNSSU	AMANUENSIS
AAEIKPRSTT	TAKES A TRIP	AAEIMNNTTT	ATTAINMENT
AAEILLLNPR	IN PARALLEL	AAEIMNOORT	EROTOMANIA
AAEILLMRTY	MATERIALLY	AAEIMNORTT	MEAT RATION
AAEILLMSTT	AT ALL TIMES	AAEIMNOSST	ANATOMISES
AAEILLNORT	RELATIONAL	AAEIMNOSTY	I MEAN TO SAY
AAEILLNPRS	SAILPLANER	AAEIMNOSTZ	ANATOMIZES
AAEILLNPSS	SAILPLANES	AAEIMNPRST	PERSIAN MAT
AAEILLNPST	TAILPLANES	AAEIMNPRTZ	NITRAZEPAM
AAEILLNRTU	UNILATERAL	AAEIMNRRTY	MAIN ARTERY

AAEIMNRSTT	STEAM TRAIN	AAELLNPRTY	PARENTALLY
AAEIMNRTTT	ANTIMATTER		PATERNALLY
AAEIMNRTVW	VIETNAM WAR		PRENATALLY
AAEIMORSST	AROMATISES	AAELLNPSTY	PLEASANTLY
AAEIMORSTZ	AROMATIZES	AAELLNRSTU	STAN LAUREL
AAEIMOTTTW	TWO AT A TIME	AAELLPPRSW	WALLPAPERS
AAEIMPRSST	SEPARATISM	AAELMMNORV	REMOVAL MAN
AAEIMQRSTU	MARQUISATE	AAELMNNORT	ORNAMENTAL
AAEIMSSSTT	METASTASIS	AAELMNNPUW	PAUL NEWMAN
AAEINNNOTX	ANNEXATION	AAELMNOPSU	MENOPAUSAL
AAEINNOTTV	ANNOTATIVE	AAELMNORSS	LOSES AN ARM
AAEINNQRTU	QUARANTINE	AAELMNORVV	REMOVAL VAN
AAEINNRSST	STANNARIES	AAELMNOSSW	SALESWOMAN
AAEINOPRRT	PRAETORIAN	AAELMNPRST	MASTER PLAN
	REPARATION	AAELMNRRTW	TRAWLERMAN
AAEINOPRST	SEPARATION	AAELMNRSUY	ANEURYSMAL
AAEINOPSST	PASSIONATE	AAELMNTTUU	LATE AUTUMN
AAEINOSTVX	TAX EVASION	AAELMRRTUX	EXTRAMURAL
AAEINPPRST	APPERTAINS	AAELNNNPRU	PENANNULAR
AAEINRRSTV	NARRATIVES	AAELNNPSTU	UNPLEASANT
AAEINRRSTW	WARRANTIES	AAELNOPRVW	NAVAL POWER
AAEINRSSTU	RUSSIAN TEA	AAELNORRTT	ALTERNATOR
AAEIOPSSTT	APOSTATISE	AAELNOSSST	LAST SEASON
AAEIOPSTTZ	APOSTATIZE	AAELNOSTWY	STOLEN AWAY
AAEIPPRRSS	APPRAISERS	AAELNPPRTY	APPARENTLY
AAEIPRRTVW	PRIVATE WAR	AAELNPRRSU	SUPRARENAL
AAEIPRRSTT	SEPARATIST	AAELNPRSTT	TRANSEPTAL
AAEIPSSSTV	PASSIVATES	AAELNPRSTY	PLEASANTRY
AAEJKLOPRY	PLAY A JOKER	AAELNPSTUY	PLAYS A TUNE
AAEJKLOPSY	PLAYS A JOKE	AAELNRSSTT	TRANSLATES
AAEJLNNRTW	LANTERN JAW	AAELOPPRST	POLES APART
AAEJMMNOSS	JAMES MASON	AAELOPRSST	PASTORALES
AAEJMORSST	MAJOR ASSET	AAELOPRSTT	POSTAL RATE
AAEKKLNOOT	TAKEN A LOOK	AAELOPRTWY	WROTE A PLAY
AAEKKLOOST	TAKES A LOOK	AAELORSTTZ	LAZARETTOS
AAEKKOSTTT	TAKE TO TASK	AAELORSTUV	EVALUATORS
AAEKLMNPSS	MAKES PLANS	AAELPQRSTU	EQUAL PARTS
AAEKLMOSSS	MAKES A LOSS	AAELPRRSTY	STAR PLAYER
AAEKLMPRST	PLATE-MARKS	AAELPRSSUU	AS PER USUAL
AAEKLNRTUY	NATURAL KEY	AAELPSSSTT	STEALS PAST
AAEKLOORTT	LOOK A TREAT	AAELPSTTUY	STAY UP LATE
AAEKLOPSST	STOPS A LEAK	AAELRRSTTY	EARLY START
AAEKMMRSST	MASS MARKET	AAELRSSSTU	ASSAULTERS
AAEKMNOORT	TAKEN A ROOM	AAELSTTTUW	STATUTE LAW
AAEKMOORST	TAKES A ROOM	AAEMNNORTT	TRAMONTANE
AAEKMORSTT	TAKE TO ARMS	AAEMNNRSTV	MANSERVANT
AAEKMPRSTU	TAKE UP ARMS	AAEMNOOSST	ANASTOMOSE
AAEKMRRSTW	WATERMARKS	AAEMNORSSW	WARM SEASON
AAEKMRSSTT	TASKMASTER	AAEMNOSSTY	MEANS TO SAY
AAEKNNRTTU	TAKEN A TURN	AAEMNOSTTY	MEANT TO SAY
AAEKNOPRTT	TAKE NO PART	AAEMNPRSTT	APARTMENTS
AAEKNPRRSY	RAYNES PARK	AAEMPRSSTT	PAST MASTER
AAEKNPSSST	SNEAKS PAST	AAEMPRSSTY	PAYMASTERS
AAEKNRSTTU	TAKES A TURN	AAEMRRSSTT	ART MASTERS
AAEKPRSSTT	STREAK PAST	AAEMRSSTTU	METATARSUS
AAEKRRSTUU	SAUERKRAUT	AAENOPRTTW	WATER ON TAP
AAELLLLSWW	ALL WAS WELL	AAENOPSWYY	PAY ONES WAY
AAELLLMNOS	SALMONELLA	AAENORTTTU	ATTENUATOR
AAELLLORST	SALTARELLO	AAENORTUUV	ART NOUVEAU
AAELLMMNSS	SMALL MEANS	AAENOSSSYY	SAY ONE'S SAY
AAELLMNRTY	MATERNALLY	AAENOSSWWY	SAW ONE'S WAY
AAELLMNSTT	TALLEST MAN	AAENOQRRTUY	QUATERNARY
AAELLMOPRS	MORAL LAPSE	AAENRRRSTW	WARRANTERS
AAELLMORZZ	MOZZARELLA	AAENRRSTTU	RESTAURANT
AAELLMPPSU	SLAP-UP MEAL	AAENRSSTTW	STARTS ANEW
AAELLMRRST	SMELLS A RAT	AAENSSTTTY	NASTY TASTE
AAELLNNTUY	ANNULATELY	AAEOOPRRTV	EVAPORATOR
AAELLNOSSY	SEASONALLY	AAEOPRRSST	SEPARATORS
AAELLNPPST	APPELLANTS	AAEOPRSTWY	SOAPY WATER
		AAEORSSTWY	STORES AWAY
		AAEOSSSTWY	TOSSES AWAY

AAEOSTUWYY	EASY WAY OUT	AAGHIIKNNT	THINK AGAIN
AAEPPRRSST	SPARE PARTS	AAGHIIKNPV	HAVING A KIP
AAESSTTTWY	TESSA WYATT	AAGHIILRST	LIGHT AS AIR
AAFFGIMNRU	RAGAMUFFIN	AAGHILOPPY	POLYPHAGIA
AAFFIINOTX	AFFIXATION	AAGHINNRSU	HUNGARIANS
AAFGGILNPV	PAVING FLAG	AAGHINORVW	HAVING A ROW
AAFGGILNVW	FLAG-WAVING	AAGHINRSTW	GRANT A WISH
AAFGHIINTV	HAVING A FIT	AAGHINRTVY	HAVING A TRY
AAFGHILNOS	GO IN A FLASH	AAGHNOPPRT	PANTOGRAPH
AAFGIILNWY	FILING AWAY	AAGHOPRSTU	AUTOGRAPHS
AAFGIINNPR	FRANGIPANI	AAGHOPRTUY	AUTOGRAPHY
AAFGIINRWY	FIRING AWAY	AAGIIKNPTT	TAKING A TIP
AAFGIJNNOU	JUAN FANGIO	AAGIILLNPT	PALLIATING
AAFGIKMNST	MAKING FAST	AAGIILMNNT	LAMINATING
AAFGILLLSS	FILL A GLASS	AAGIILMPRS	PLAGIARISM
AAFGILNSST	FALANGISTS	AAGIILNNSS	NASALISING
AAFGILNSWY	FLINGS AWAY	AAGIILNNSZ	NASALIZING
AAFGILNWYY	FLYING AWAY	AAGIILNNUV	UNAVAILING
AAFGINORUV	GAIN FAVOUR	AAGIILNRTV	TRAVAILING
AAFGKLOORW	GO FOR A WALK	AAGIILNSTV	SALIVATING
AAFGLLLOOW	ALL OF A GLOW	AAGIILPRRU	AU PAIR GIRL
AAFGLLNRTY	FLAGRANTLY	AAGIILPRST	PLAGIARIST
AAFGLLORST	ALLOGRAFTS	AAGIIMNNRT	MARINATING
AAFGLNRRTY	FRAGRANTLY	AAGIINNOPT	PAGINATION
AAFGORSTTU	AUTOGRAFTS	AAGIINNOTV	NAVIGATION
AAFHHINORS	SHAH OF IRAN	AAGIINOSTT	AGITATIONS
AAFHHLNORU	HALF AN HOUR	AAGIINPPRS	APPRAISING
AAFHIINNOS	IN A FASHION	AAGIINPRST	ASPIRATING
AAFHIKNSST	SINK A SHAFT	AAGIINPWWY	WIPING AWAY
AAFHKNSSTU	SUNK A SHAFT	AAGIJKLNWY	JAYWALKING
AAFHLLORTT	FOR ALL THAT	AAGIKLLNTY	ALKYLATING
AAFIIILRSS	FILARIASIS	AAGIKLMNPY	MAKING PLAY
AAFIILLMRY	FAMILIARLY	AAGIKLMNSW	MAKING LAWS
AAFIILMNRU	UNFAMILIAR	AAGIKLNNOS	ALGONKIANS
AAFIINNRRTU	FRUITARIAN	AAGIKMNNPU	MAKING A PUN
AAFIINRTVY	VANITY FAIR	AAGIKMNOVW	MAKING A VOW
AAFILMOPTY	MAP OF ITALY	AAGIKNOTVW	TAKING A VOW
AAFILMRRWY	FAIRLY WARM	AAGIKNPRTT	TAKING PART
AAFILNOORT	FLOAT ON AIR	AAGIKNSTWY	TAKING WAYS
AAFILNOOTT	FLOATATION	AAGILLMNPS	SIGNAL LAMP
AAFILNOSTX	AFLATOXINS	AAGILLMNRY	ALARMINGLY
AAFILOPSST	FAIL TO PASS		MARGINALLY
AAFILOPSTY	FAILS TO PAY	AAGILLNOSS	SAILS ALONG
AAFIMNORTU	FAIR AMOUNT	AAGILLNSTV	GALLIVANTS
AAFINOOPRR	ROAR OF PAIN	AAGILLORST	ALLIGATORS
AAFINRSSTT	FAST TRAINS	AAGILLSTTY	SAGITTALLY
AAFIOOQRSTU	AQUA FORTIS	AAGILMNNSU	SIGN MANUAL
AAFMNOORTY	FAR TOO MANY	AAGILMNORS	ORGANISMAL
AAFMNOPRST	MAN OF PARTS	AAGILNNOQU	ALGONQUIAN
AAFMNORSTW	MAN OF STRAW	AAGILNOPRS	SPORANGIAL
AAFNNOOSVW	SWAN OF AVON	AAGILNORTY	GYRATIONAL
AAFNORRSTY	ROTARY FANS	AAGILNOSST	ANALOGISTS
AAGGHILNTU	LAUGHING AT	AAGILNPPUY	PAYING PAUL
AAGGHINNRU	HARANGUING	AAGILNRRTU	TRIANGULAR
AAGGIILLNN	ILANG-ILANG	AAGILNRSUV	VULGARIANS
AAGGIILNTT	TAILGATING	AAGILNRTUY	ANGULARITY
AAGGIINNPT	PAGINATING	AAGILNSSTU	ASSAULTING
AAGGIINNRR	ARRAIGNING	AAGILOSUVY	YUGOSLAVIA
AAGGIINNRS	RINGS AGAIN	AAGIMMPRST	PRAGMATISM
AAGGIINNTV	NAVIGATING	AAGIMNNOST	ANTAGONISM
AAGGIINVWY	GIVING AWAY	AAGIMNNPRW	WARMING PAN
AAGGINNSTT	STAGNATING	AAGIMNOTTU	AUTOMATING
AAGGINORRT	ARROGATING	AAGIMNOVWY	MOVING AWAY
AAGGINRSTZ	STARGAZING	AAGIMNPTTU	AMPUTATING
AAGGKLNNPS	GANGPLANKS	AAGIMPRSTT	PRAGMATIST
AAGGLLNNYY	YLANG-YLANG	AAGINNNOTT	ANNOTATING
AAGGLNOOWY	GO A LONG WAY	AAGINNORTW	WAGON TRAIN
AAGHHILLMR	GRAHAM HILL	AAGINNOSTT	ANTAGONIST
AAGHHILRSY	HIGH SALARY		STAGNATION
AAGHHIMNWY	HIGHWAYMAN	AAGINNPPST	SNAPPING AT
AAGHIIKMNT	MAKING A HIT	AAGINNRRTW	WARRANTING

AAGINNNRSTU	RUN AGAINST	AAIIKLLNTY	ALKALINITY
	TURNS AGAIN	AAIIKMNNST	KANTIANISM
AAGINNRSUY	SANGUINARY	AAIIKNNRSU	UKRAINIANS
AAGINOORRT	ARROGATION	AAIIKNPSST	PAKISTANIS
AAGINPRSWY	SPRING AWAY	AAIILLNOPT	PALLIATION
AAGINRRTVY	GRAVY TRAIN	AAIILLNUXY	UNIAXIALLY
AAGINRSTTU	SATURATING	AAIILMMSTX	MAXIMALIST
AAGKLLNOSW	WALKS ALONG	AAIILMNNOT	ANTIMONIAL
AAGLLNOPSY	PLAYS ALONG		LAMINATION
AAGLLNOPTT	TOPGALLANT	AAIILMNSST	ANIMALISTS
AAGLLNOSTT	AT LONG LAST	AAIILNORRT	IRRATIONAL
AAGLLNRRUY	GRANULARLY	AAIILNOSTV	SALIVATION
AAGLNNOOSX	ANGLO-SAXON	AAIILPRTTY	PARTIALITY
AAGLNNSTTY	STAGNANTLY		PATRIALITY
AAGLNOOORW	ANGORA WOOL	AAIILPSTTY	SPATIALITY
AAGLNORRTU	GRANULATOR	AAIIMNNNOT	ANTINOMIAN
AAGLNORRTY	ARROGANTLY	AAIIMNNOST	ANIMATIONS
AAGLSSTTUU	LAST AUGUST	AAIIMPPRRS	PRIMIPARAS
AAGMOOSTUU	AUTOGAMOUS	AAIIMPRSST	PARASITISM
AAGNNORSTU	ORANGUTANS	AAIINNOPSS	IN A PASSION
AAGNOPRRTW	GROWN APART	AAIINNOSTT	SANITATION
AAGNORRSTU	GUARANTORS	AAIINNRRTU	RURITANIAN
AAGNPRSUWY	SPRUNG AWAY	AAIINNRSTU	UNITARIANS
AAGOOPPRRT	PROPAGATOR	AAIINNRSTY	INSANITARY
AAGOOPSUYY	PAY AS YOU GO	AAIINOPPRT	APPARITION
AAGOPRRSTW	GROWS APART	AAIINOPRST	ASPIRATION
AAHHIIMRSS	MAHARISHIS	AAIINORSTV	VARIATIONS
AAHHILMOPT	OPHTHALMIA	AAIIPRSTWY	SPIRIT AWAY
AAHHIMRRTY	ARRHYTHMIA	AAIIPSSTVY	PAYS A VISIT
AAHHISTTWW	WHAT IS WHAT	AAIIRSSSTY	SATYRIASIS
AAHIILNNOT	INHALATION	AAIJRSSSTW	SWARAJISTS
AAHIILNNTU	LITHUANIAN	AAIKLLNOTY	ALKYLATION
AAHIILPSSS	SAILS A SHIP	AAIKLNORSW	WALKS ON AIR
AAHIIMPRSS	PHARISAISM	AAIKLNSSWY	SLINKS AWAY
AAHIINNSTY	HINAYANIST	AAIKLPRSTV	VITAL SPARK
AAHIKMNNRV	HANK MARVIN	AAIKNOORTT	TOOK A TRAIN
AAHIIKNRSWY	SHRINK AWAY	AAIKOOTTWY	TOOK IT AWAY
AAHIKRSSTY	KSHATRIYAS	AAILLMNORV	ROMAN VILLA
AAHILLOPRT	PROTHALLIA	AAILLMOPPS	PAPILLOMAS
AAHILMNPSU	ALPHA MINUS	AAILLMORRY	ARMORIALLY
AAHILMNSTU	MALTHUSIAN	AAILLMSSTW	SMALL WAIST
AAHILMTTUZ	ALTAZIMUTH	AAILLNNOTY	NATIONALLY
AAHILNNOPT	ANTIPHONAL	AAILLNOPST	SPALLATION
AAHILOPPSY	HYPOPLASIA	AAILLNORTY	NOTARIALLY
AAHIMNRSTW	MARTIN SHAW		RATIONALLY
AAHIMNSSST	SHAMANISTS	AAILLNOSTV	ASTON VILLA
AAHINORRSV	HARROVIANS	AAILLRSTUY	SALUTARILY
AAHINRRSTU	TURNS A HAIR	AAILMNNSUY	IN AN ASYLUM
AAHKKKNNPYY	HANKY-PANKY	AAILMNOTTU	MUTATIONAL
AAHKLNOSTT	THANKS A LOT	AAILMNRRTU	INTRAMURAL
AAHKMNNSTY	MANY THANKS	AAILMNRSTU	NATURALISM
AAHKNOOOTT	TOOK AN OATH	AAILMORRTY	MARIOLATRY
AAHKNRSUWY	SHRUNK AWAY	AAILMPRSSU	MARSUPIALS
AAHKOPTUUW	POHUTUKAWA	AAILNNOOTT	NOTATIONAL
AAHLLLLOSW	ALL HALLOWS	AAILNNOPTT	PLANTATION
AAHLLMOPSY	HYALOPLASM	AAILNNOSSV	SLAVONIANS
AAHLLMMOPTY	LYMPHOMATA	AAILNNOTTU	NUTATIONAL
AAHLORSTWY	SHAW TAYLOR	AAILNNPQSU	PALANQUINS
AAHLPQSSUY	PLAY SQUASH	AAILNNRTUY	ANNULARITY
AAHMMMNNOST	THOMAS MANN	AAILNOORTT	ROTATIONAL
AAHMNNOPPWY	HAPPY WOMAN	AAILNORRTY	ROYAL TRAIN
AAHMOOSTWY	SMOOTH AWAY	AAILNOSSTV	SALVATIONS
AAHNNOOSTZ	ANTHOZOANS	AAILNOSTTU	SALUTATION
AAHNOPRRTW	NARROW PATH	AAILNOSTUV	VALUATIONS
AAHNORTWWY	THROWN AWAY	AAILNPRSTU	TARPAULINS
AAHOPRRRSZ	RAZOR SHARP	AAILNPSSTU	SAINT PAUL'S
AAHORSTWWY	THROWAWAYS	AAILNPSSTV	VAST PLAINS
	THROWS AWAY	AAILNRSTTU	NATURALIST
AAHOSSTTTY	THATS TO SAY	AAILNRTTUW	NATURAL WIT
AAIIILMMNT	MILITIAMAN	AAILOPPRRU	POPULAR AIR
AAIIJLNORT	JANITORIAL	AAILORSTTT	ALTOSTRATI

AAIMMMNSTY	TAMMANYISM	AAORRSSTTW	STARTS A ROW
AAIMMOSTTU	AUTOMATISM	ABBBBEHLTU	BUBBLE BATH
AAIMMRSTTU	TRAUMATISM	ABBBCIKRTU	BUCK RABBIT
AAIMNNORSU	ROUMANIANS	ABBBCLMOOT	COBALT BOMB
AAIMNNRTTU	IN A TANTRUM	ABBBDEHIOR	BOBBED HAIR
AAIMNNSWYY	IN MANY WAYS	ABBBDENRRU	RUBBER BAND
AAIMNOOTTU	AUTOMATION	ABBBDHIRSU	BAD RUBBISH
AAIMNOPTTU	AMPUTATION	ABBBDINORY	BOBBY DARIN
AAIMNORSTU	SANATORIUM	ABBBEELMNT	BABBLEMENT
AAIMNORTTU	MATURATION	ABBBEGILNR	BLABBERING
AAIMNOSSTT	ANATOMISTS	ABBBEHMNOT	BAN THE BOMB
AAIMNPRSST	SPARTANISM	ABBBEIRRRT	BRER RABBIT
AAIMOSTTTU	AUTOMATIST	ABBBEKNORR	BANK ROBBER
AAINNNOOST	SAN ANTONIO	ABBBELLRRU	RUBBER BALL
AAINNNOOTT	ANNOTATION	ABBBELOPSU	SOAP BUBBLE
AAINNNSTTU	ANNUITANTS	ABBCCDEKMO	BACKCOMBED
AAINNOPRRU	IN AN UPROAR	ABBCCEKNOU	BOUNCE BACK
AAINNORRST	NARRATIONS	ABBCCKKLSU	BLACKBUCKS
AAINNPRSSY	SPINS A YARN	ABBCDEKLOU	DOUBLE BACK
AAINOORRST	ORATORIANS	ABBCDEMRRU	BREADCRUMB
AAINOPSSTT	ANTIPASTOS	ABBCDIKLRS	BLACKBIRDS
AAINOPSTTY	PAY STATION	ABBCDKLOOR	BLOCKBOARD
AAINORSTTU	SATURATION	ABBCDKMOUY	BOMBAY DUCK
AAINORSTTV	STARVATION	ABBCDKORSU	BUCKBOARDS
AAINORSTTY	STATIONARY	ABBCDMMORU	DUMB CRAMBO
AAINRSTTUY	STAY IN A RUT	ABBCEEILOS	BE SOCIABLE
AAINSSSSTT	ASSISTANTS	ABBCEEKLRT	BLACK BERET
AAIOPRRSST	ASPIRATORS	ABBCEGINRU	BARBECUING
AAIORRSTTT	START A RIOT	ABBCEIKNTT	BACKBITTEN
	TRATTORIAS	ABBCEIKRST	BACKBITERS
AAKLMNORUW	MANUAL WORK	ABBCEILLSS	BIBLE CLASS
AAKLNOPRTW	WALK-ON PART	ABBCEILMNO	COMBINABLE
AAKMMNORSW	MARKSWOMAN	ABBCEILRSU	SUBCALIBRE
AALLLLNNUU	NULLA-NULLA	ABBCEJLLOT	OBJECT BALL
AALLLLOTWW	WALL TO WALL	ABBCEKKNOR	BROKEN BACK
	WALL-TO-WALL	ABBCEKLRRY	BLACKBERRY
AALLLOSSTW	ALL WAS LOST	ABBCEKMNRU	BACK NUMBER
AALLMMNOSW	SMALL WOMAN	ABBCEKNNOO	NO BACKBONE
AALLMNTUUY	AUTUMNALLY	ABBCELLOTU	COBALT BLUE
AALLNNOPSY	POLLYANNAS	ABBCELRRSS	SCRABBLERS
AALLOPRSTY	PASTORALLY	ABBCENORSY	ABSORBENCY
AALLOPRTXY	PAYROLL TAX	ABBCFGINNO	CONFABBING
AALLPPRSTU	PULLS APART	ABBCGHKOTU	BOUGHT BACK
AALLRSTTWY	STALWARTLY	ABBCGIKNRS	BRINGS BACK
AALMNOSTTU	LAST MAN OUT	ABBCGIKNUY	BUYING BACK
AALMNPRSUY	SUN-RAY LAMP	ABBCGILNRS	SCRABBLING
AALMNSTTUU	LAST AUTUMN	ABBCHHOOTY	BOOBY HATCH
AALMOOPRTY	LAPAROTOMY	ABBCIILLLY	BIBLICALLY
AALMOOPSTX	TOXOPLASMA	ABBCIIRRTU	BARBITURIC
AALMOPRSXY	PAROXYSMAL	ABBCIMMOOT	ATOMIC BOMB
AALNNOOPST	PANTALOONS	ABBCKKLOOS	BLACK BOOKS
AALNNOSTUV	ANOVULANTS	ABBCLLORUU	LABOUR CLUB
AALNNPRSTT	TRANSPLANT	ABBCMOOSST	COSTS A BOMB
AALNOOPPRV	ON APPROVAL	ABBCNOORST	BOSTON CRAB
AALNOOPUZZ	POZZUOLANA	ABBDDEEILO	ABLE-BODIED
AALNORRSTT	TRANSLATOR	ABBDEEGILR	BRIDGEABLE
AALNORSSTU	RUN AT A LOSS	ABBDEEHLPS	PEBBLEDASH
AALNPRTTUY	PLAY TRUANT	ABBDEEIRRW	BARBED WIRE
AALOPRRSTY	PORTRAYALS	ABBDEEKORR	BROKE BREAD
AALORSTTUY	SALUTATORY	ABBDEELNUU	BLUE DANUBE
AAMMNORSTW	SMART WOMAN	ABBDEELORU	BELABOURED
AAMMNOTTTU	TANTAMOUNT	ABBDEENRSS	BARBEDNESS
AAMNOOSTTU	AUTOMATONS	ABBDEFIORR	FIBREBOARD
AAMNOPRSSY	PAYS RANSOM	ABBDEFLNOW	EBB AND FLOW
AAMOPRSTTU	AMPUTATORS	ABBDEHIINS	BISHAN BEDI
AAMRRSTTUY	MARY STUART	ABBDEHINRS	BEHIND BARS
AANNOORSTT	ANNOTATORS	ABBDEHORTY	BY THE BOARD
AANORRRSTW	WARRANTORS	ABBDEILLNN	BILL AND BEN
AANORSSTTU	ASTRONAUTS	ABBDEILRST	BIRD TABLES
AAOOPPRRST	PARATROOPS	ABBDEIMNRY	BABY-MINDER
AAORRSSTTU	SATURATORS	ABBDEIMORR	BOMBARDIER

ABBDELLNRU	LANDLUBBER	ABCCEELLRY	RECYCLABLE
ABBDELMOOZ	BAMBOOZLED	ABCCEENRSU	BUCCANEERS
ABBDELOSSU	DOUBLE BASS	ABCCEFLOSU	ACE OF CLUBS
ABBDEMNOPS	SPEND A BOMB	ABCCEHKKOS	CHOKES BACK
ABBDENORRW	BROWN BREAD	ABCCEIKRTT	CRICKET BAT
ABBDFGILOW	BIG BAD WOLF	ABCCEILMPY	IMPECCABLY
ABBDGIMNOR	BOMBARDING	ABCCEILSSY	ACCESSIBLY
ABBDHLOOST	BLOODBATHS	ABCCEJNSUY	SUBJACENCY
ABBDIINRRS	BIRD BRAINS	ABCCELNRSU	CARBUNCLES
	BIRDBRAINS	ABCCELNRUV	CAVERN CLUB
ABBDILLORS	BILLBOARDS	ABCCGIKMNO	COMING BACK
ABBDMOOPRS	DROPS A BOMB	ABCCHHKNSU	HUNCHBACKS
ABBEEEILLV	BELIEVABLE	ABCCHIKLPT	PITCH BLACK
ABBEEELRRR	BEER BARREL		PITCH-BLACK
ABBEEEENNST	BEEN ABSENT	ABCCHIKSTT	BACKSTITCH
ABBEEILLRR	BEARER BILL	ABCCHIKSTW	SWITCHBACK
ABBEEIRRRS	BARBERRIES	ABCCHILOTU	COACHBUILT
ABBEEKNOOR	BROKE A BONE	ABCCHKLOST	BACKCLOTHS
ABBEELMNRU	NUMBERABLE	ABCCIKLMSU	BLACK MUSIC
ABBEELORSV	OBSERVABLE	ABCCILLOSU	SOCIAL CLUB
ABBEELRTTU	REBUTTABLE	ABCCILNORY	CARBONYLIC
ABBEENORST	BREASTBONE	ABCCILORXY	CARBOXYLIC
ABBEENORTW	SNOWBEATEN	ABCCIKKKNOO	KNOCKS BACK
ABBEENRTTU	BUTTER BEAN	ABCCKKLOSS	BLACK SOCKS
ABBEFGNOOS	BAG OF BONES	ABCCKKRSTU	STRUCK BACK
ABBEFILNSS	FLABBINESS	ABCCMOPSTU	SUBCOMPACT
ABBEFMORRU	FOAM RUBBER	ABCCNOOPRY	CARBON COPY
ABBEFGNOOTY	GOES BY BOAT	ABCCOOONTW	TODAOOO NOW
ABBEGOOSTY	GOES BY BOAT	ABCDDEFKLO	FOLDED BACK
ABBEHINSSS	SHABBINESS	ABCDDEKNOW	BACKED DOWN
ABBEHOPRRS	BARBERSHOP	ABCDDKORSU	DUCKBOARDS
ABBEHORSWY	BABY SHOWER	ABCDEEEHSU	DEBAUCHEES
ABBEILMOPR	IMPROBABLE	ABCDEEEILV	DECEIVABLE
ABBEILMORR	MAIL ROBBER	ABCDEEELLT	DELECTABLE
ABBEILOPSY	BOB PAISLEY	ABCDEEELRT	CELEBRATED
ABBEINRRUW	WIN A RUBBER	ABCDEEELTT	DETECTABLE
ABBEIRSTTY	BABY SITTER	ABCDEEENNR	CANNED BEER
	BABY-SITTER	ABCDEEEOST	CEASED TO BE
ABBELLOWYY	YELLOW BABY	ABCDEEERRT	CEREBRATED
ABBELLRTTU	BUTTERBALL	ABCDEEHLLY	BELLYACHED
ABBELMOOSZ	BAMBOOZLES	ABCDEEHRSU	DEBAUCHERS
ABBELORSVY	OBSERVABLY	ABCDEEHRUY	DEBAUCHERY
ABBELQRSSU	SQUABBLERS	ABCDEEILLN	DECLINABLE
ABBEMNOPST	SPENT A BOMB	ABCDEEILNS	ASCENDIBLE
ABBEMNRRTU	BURNT AMBER	ABCDEEILPR	PREDICABLE
ABBENORRUW	WON A RUBBER	ABCDEEILPS	DESPICABLE
ABBENORSST	ABSORBENTS	ABCDEEILRT	CREDITABLE
ABBEORRRTY	ART ROBBERY	ABCDEELLTY	DELECTABLY
ABBFHLLSSU	FLASHBULBS	ABCDEELLUX	EXCLUDABLE
ABBFILORST	FIBROBLAST	ABCDEELORR	RECORDABLE
ABBGGIMNOO	GOING A BOMB	ABCDEENRTY	CYBERNATED
ABBGILLNOS	BILLABONGS	ABCDEFIILO	CODIFIABLE
ABBGILOOST	OBBLIGATOS	ABCDEFINOR	FRIED BACON
ABBGINORTU	BRING ABOUT	ABCDEFIRTU	BIFURCATED
ABBHIINORR	HAIR RIBBON	ABCDEFOSTU	OBFUSCATED
ABBILORSTU	SUBORBITAL	ABCDEGHINU	DEBAUCHING
ABBKNORSSS	BRASS KNOBS	ABCDEHIILR	HERBICIDAL
ABBLOORSTY	BORSTAL BOY	ABCDEHKLOS	BLOCKHEADS
ABBOOPRSTY	BOOBY-TRAPS	ABCDEHKMPU	HUMPBACKED
ABCCCEFIOS	BECCAFICOS	ABCDEHKPSU	PUSHED BACK
ABCCCKKLOS	BLACKCOCKS	ABCDEHORSS	CHESSBOARD
ABCCDDNOTU	BAD CONDUCT	ABCDEIILNT	INDICTABLE
ABCCDEHKKO	CHOKED BACK	ABCDEIILNV	VINDICABLE
ABCCDEIKKK	KICKED BACK	ABCDEIIMRT	IMBRICATED
ABCCDEINTY	BY ACCIDENT	ABCDEIKLRS	BACKSLIDER
ABCCDELNRU	CARBUNCLED	ABCDEIKLSS	BACKSLIDES
ABCCDKLLOU	BLACK CLOUD		SLIDES BACK
ABCCEEHNST	BEST CHANCE	ABCDEIKNRT	BANK CREDIT
ABCCEEIKLP	BLACK PIECE	ABCDEIKRSS	DISC BRAKES
ABCCEEILMP	IMPECCABLE	ABCDEIKRSU	RUDBECKIAS
ABCCEEILSS	ACCESSIBLE	ABCDEILLNU	INCLUDABLE

441

ABCDEILMPU	MADE PUBLIC	ABCEEHKLPS	BLACK SHEEP
ABCDEILPSY	DESPICABLY	ABCEEHLLRY	BELLYACHER
ABCDEILRTU	LUBRICATED	ABCEEHLLSY	BELLYACHES
ABCDEILRTY	CREDITABLY	ABCEEHLLTT	BELL THE CAT
ABCDEINORS	CARBONISED	ABCEEHLNQU	QUENCHABLE
ABCDEINORZ	CARBONIZED	ABCEEHLNSU	CHELSEA BUN
ABCDEIPRRS	CRISPBREAD	ABCEEHNORR	ABHORRENCE
ABCDEIRRSV	CAB DRIVERS	ABCEEHORSU	HERBACEOUS
ABCDEIRRTU	RUBRICATED	ABCEEILLPR	PRICE LABEL
ABCDEJKMPU	JUMPED BACK		REPLICABLE
ABCDEJKOOT	JACKBOOTED	ABCEEILLPX	EXPLICABLE
ABCDEKKLOO	LOOKED BACK	ABCEEILMMT	EMBLEMATIC
ABCDEKLLOR	ROLLED BACK	ABCEEILMOR	BORE MALICE
ABCDEKLLPU	PULLED BACK	ABCEEILMRT	CLIMB A TREE
ABCDEKLORS	BLOCKADERS	ABCEEILNNU	ENUNCIABLE
ABCDEKLOTU	BLACKED OUT	ABCEEILNOT	NOTICEABLE
ABCDEKLPRU	PARBUCKLED	ABCEEILRTX	EXTRICABLE
ABCDEKLRSS	BLACK DRESS	ABCEEINNST	ABSTINENCE
ABCDEKNRTU	TURNED BACK	ABCEEINOSS	OBEISANCES
ABCDEKOORS	SACRED BOOK	ABCEEIOPRV	ABOVE PRICE
ABCDELNNOO	CONDONABLE	ABCEEIRTVV	ACTIVE VERB
ABCDENORSS	ABSCONDERS	ABCEEJNSST	ABJECTNESS
ABCDENOSSU	SUBDEACONS	ABCEEKLNQU	BLACK QUEEN
ABCDEOORRS	SCOREBOARD	ABCEEKORRV	BREAK COVER
ABCDERSTTU	SUBTRACTED	ABCEEKORST	ROCKET BASE
ABCDGIKLNO	BLOCKADING	ABCEEKRSTT	BACK STREET
ABCDGINNOS	ABSCONDING		BACKSTREET
ABCDGKNORU	BACKGROUND	ABCEEKSTTU	BUCKET SEAT
ABCDHIILNR	BRAIN CHILD	ABCEELLORT	BROCATELLE
	BRAINCHILD	ABCEELLRRY	CEREBRALLY
ABCDHINNRU	NUDIBRANCH	ABCEELMRRS	CLAMBERERS
ABCDHIOOPR	BRACHIOPOD	ABCEELNRST	CELEBRANTS
ABCDHLOORT	BROADCLOTH	ABCEELNRSU	CENSURABLE
ABCDIILNNU	INDIAN CLUB	ABCEELOOPT	ABLE TO COPE
ABCDIKLOWW	BLACK WIDOW	ABCEELOPRU	RECOUPABLE
ABCDIKNORT	DICK BARTON	ABCEELORRT	CELEBRATOR
ABCDIKOPRR	DROP A BRICK	ABCEELORST	BRACTEOLES
ABCDIKRRSY	BRICKYARDS	ABCEELPTXY	EXPECTABLY
ABCDILLNOO	BILL AND COO	ABCEENORSV	OBSERVANCE
ABCDILOPRS	CLIPBOARDS	ABCEEOPPRS	SPACE PROBE
ABCDILOPRU	PUBLIC ROAD	ABCEEOSSUX	SAUCEBOXES
ABCDINOOST	BANDICOOTS	ABCEFHLSSU	FLASHCUBES
ABCDINOSTU	ABDUCTIONS	ABCEFHOSTW	FOB WATCHES
ABCDKLOORS	ROADBLOCKS	ABCEFIKLLS	BLACKFLIES
ABCDKORSSW	BACKSWORDS	ABCEFIRSTU	BIFURCATES
ABCDLMNOUY	MONDAY CLUB	ABCEFKLLNO	FELL BACK ON
ABCDOSSTTU	CASTS DOUBT	ABCEFOSSTU	OBFUSCATES
ABCEEEFFNO	COFFEE BEAN	ABCEGHIMNR	CHAMBERING
ABCEEEFLTT	BEEF CATTLE		CHAMBREING
ABCEEEIKRR	ICEBREAKER	ABCEGHIMST	BIG MATCHES
ABCEEEILRV	RECEIVABLE	ABCEGIKLNN	BLACKENING
ABCEEEELLRR	BEER CELLAR	ABCEGIKNNO	GONE BACK IN
	CEREBELLAR	ABCEGIKNOS	GOES BACK IN
ABCEEELMSS	BECAME LESS	ABCEGIKNRT	BRACKETING
ABCEEELNRS	SCREENABLE	ABCEGILMNR	CLAMBERING
ABCEEELPTX	EXPECTABLE	ABCEGILNOS	COGNISABLE
ABCEEELRST	CELEBRATES	ABCEGILNOZ	COGNIZABLE
	RESECTABLE	ABCEGINNNY	BENIGNANCY
ABCEEELTUX	EXECUTABLE	ABCEGINTTT	BETTING ACT
ABCEEEMNOS	BECOME SANE	ABCEGIORSX	CIGAR BOXES
ABCEEENRUX	EXUBERANCE	ABCEGNOORR	ROGER BACON
ABCEEEOSST	CEASES TO BE	ABCEHHORTY	TYCHO BRAHE
ABCEEERRST	CEREBRATES	ABCEHIKLNT	IN THE BLACK
ABCEEFHNNR	FRENCH BEAN	ABCEHILNNR	BRANCH LINE
ABCEEFIILN	BENEFICIAL	ABCEHILSTW	SWITCHABLE
ABCEEFIRSS	BRIEFCASES	ABCEHIMNRS	IN CHAMBERS
ABCEEFNORS	CANS OF BEER	ABCEHIMNSU	SUBMACHINE
ABCEEFNORT	BENEFACTOR	ABCEHIMRRT	HERMIT CRAB
ABCEEGKNRS	GREENBACKS	ABCEHINOST	AITCHBONES
ABCEEHHNOT	ON THE BEACH	ABCEHIPRRY	HYPERBARIC
ABCEEHINTT	THE CABINET	ABCEHKLLOY	HOCKEY BALL

ABCEHKLNRU	LUNCH BREAK	ABCEKRSTUW	WATERBUCKS
ABCEHKLORS	BLACK HORSE	ABCELLLORU	BLUE COLLAR
ABCEHKLOSS	BLACK SHOES		BLUE-COLLAR
ABCEHKMNRS	BENCHMARKS	ABCELLMTTU	LAMB CUTLET
ABCEHKPSSU	PUSHES BACK	ABCELLNOOR	COLLARBONE
ABCEHKSTUW	BUCKWHEATS	ABCELLNOOS	CONSOLABLE
ABCEHLLOTT	TABLECLOTH	ABCELLOORU	COLOURABLE
ABCEHLNRSS	BRANCHLESS	ABCELLOOST	BLASTOCOEL
ABCEHLPUYY	BUY CHEAPLY	ABCELLORSU	SCORE A BULL
ABCEHMMNRU	MACH NUMBER	ABCELLRSSW	SCREWBALLS
ABCEHMOPRT	CHAMBER POT	ABCELMMOTU	COMMUTABLE
ABCEHOQRSU	QUEBRACHOS	ABCELMNOSU	CONSUMABLE
ABCEHORTTX	CHATTERBOX	ABCELMNRSU	UNSCRAMBLE
ABCEIILLMT	BIMETALLIC	ABCELMOPTU	COMPUTABLE
ABCEIILLNR	BRILLIANCE	ABCELNORRY	BARLEYCORN
ABCEIILMTU	UMBILICATE	ABCELNORSS	CARBONLESS
ABCEIILPST	EPIBLASTIC	ABCELNORUY	BLUE CRAYON
ABCEIIMRST	IMBRICATES	ABCELNOSST	CONSTABLES
ABCEIINTUV	INCUBATIVE	ABCELOPRRU	PROCURABLE
ABCEIJNOST	ABJECTIONS	ABCELOSSTT	ECTOBLASTS
ABCEIKKRST	STRIKE BACK	ABCELPSSUY	BUSY PLACES
ABCEIKLMPU	MAKE PUBLIC	ABCELRRTUU	TUBERCULAR
ABCEIKLRRY	BRICKLAYER	ABCELSSSSU	SUBCLASSES
ABCEIKNNTW	WENT BACK IN	ABCEMOOSTU	COMES ABOUT
ABCEIKNNWY	WIN BY A NECK	ABCEMPRRSU	BUMPER CARS
ABCEIKNRST	IN BRACKETS	ABCENOOPTU	PONCE ABOUT
ABCEIKRSTW	WRITES BACK	ABCENSSSTU	SUBSTANCES
ABCEILLLOP	POLICE BALL	ABCEOORRSS	BORE A CROSS
ABCEILLNNO	ABE LINCOLN	ABCEORRRRT	ROBERT CARR
ABCEILLNPU	INCULPABLE	ABCERRSTTU	SUBTRACTER
ABCEILLNRS	CRANESBILL	ABCFFGIKNO	BACKING OFF
ABCEILLPSU	PUBLIC SALE	ABCFGHIKST	FIGHTS BACK
ABCEILLPXY	EXPLICABLY	ABCFGHKOTU	FOUGHT BACK
ABCEILMOPT	COMPATIBLE	ABCFGIIKNR	BACKFIRING
ABCEILNNSU	INCUNABLES	ABCFIIKLRS	SILK FABRIC
ABCEILNORS	BRIAN CLOSE	ABCFKOOSTU	BACKS OUT OF
ABCEILNOSU	UNSOCIABLE	ABCGGIIKNV	GIVING BACK
ABCEILNOTY	NOTICEABLY	ABCGGIKPSY	PIGGYBACKS
ABCEILNPRU	REPUBLICAN	ABCGGINORY	GOING BY CAR
ABCEILNRRU	INCURRABLE	ABCGHIINOT	COHABITING
ABCEILORST	CABRIOLETS	ABCGHIIOPR	BIOGRAPHIC
ABCEILORTU	ORBICULATE	ABCGHIKRST	RIGHT-BACKS
ABCEILPSSU	SPECIAL BUS	ABCGHKLOPU	PLOUGH BACK
ABCEILRSTU	LUBRICATES	ABCGHMRTUY	RUGBY MATCH
ABCEIMMRRW	MR.MICAWBER	ABCGIILLOO	BIOLOGICAL
ABCEIMORRT	BAROMETRIC	ABCGIINNTU	INCUBATING
ABCEIMOSTT	CAME TO BITS	ABCGIKLNPU	BLACKING UP
ABCEINORSS	CARBONISES	ABCGIKLNSS	SLINGBACKS
ABCEINORSZ	CARBONIZES	ABCGIKMNOV	MOVING BACK
ABCEINOSTU	COUNT BASIE	ABCGIKNOTU	BACKING OUT
ABCEINRRST	TRANSCRIBE	ABCGIKNPRS	SPRING BACK
ABCEIOSSSV	BASS VOICES	ABCGIKNSSW	BACKSWINGS
ABCEIRRSTU	RUBRICATES		SWINGS BACK
ABCEJKKOOT	BOOK JACKET	ABCGILMNRS	SCRAMBLING
ABCEJKLMRU	LUMBERJACK	ABCGILNOSY	COGNISABLY
ABCEJRSTTU	ART SUBJECT	ABCGILNOYZ	COGNIZABLY
ABCEKKLNRS	BANK CLERKS	ABCGIMNOTT	COMBATTING
ABCEKKLRUY	LUCKY BREAK	ABCGKNPRSU	SPRUNG BACK
ABCEKKORRS	BREAK ROCKS	ABCHHIOPRS	ARCHBISHOP
ABCEKKORST	BACK STROKE	ABCHHJNNOU	JOHN BUCHAN
	BACKSTROKE	ABCHHKSSUW	BUSHWHACKS
ABCEKLNNPY	PENNY BLACK	ABCHIILLLM	CLIMB A HILL
ABCEKLNORU	COAL BUNKER	ABCHIILLNS	CHILBLAINS
ABCEKLOPRW	BLACK POWER	ABCHIILOPS	BASOPHILIC
ABCEKLPRSU	PARBUCKLES	ABCHIKKNRS	SHRINK BACK
ABCEKLSSTU	CLUB STEAKS	ABCHIKKNST	THINKS BACK
ABCEKMNOPR	BROKEN CAMP	ABCHIKLMST	BLACKSMITH
ABCEKMOOOT	CAME TO BOOK	ABCHIKLRST	BLACK SHIRT
ABCEKNNOOS	ON ONES BACK		BLACKSHIRT
ABCEKNNOWY	WON BY A NECK	ABCHILPPTU	PUBLIC PATH
ABCEKOPRRT	REPORT BACK	ABCHIRSTTU	BASIC TRUTH

ABCHKKNRSU	SHRUNK BACK	ABDDEELMRU	DEAD LUMBER
ABCHKLNORT	BLACKTHORN	ABDDEELNPY	DEPENDABLY
ABCHKMSTTU	THUMB TACKS	ABDDEELOTU	DOUBLE DATE
	THUMBTACKS	ABDDEEPRSS	BEDSPREADS
ABCHKNORTW	THROWN BACK	ABDDEGHINR	BRIDGE HAND
ABCHKORSTW	THROWBACKS	ABDDEGILOR	OLD BRIGADE
	THROWS BACK	ABDDEGINRU	UNABRIDGED
ABCIIIKLSW	BAILIWICKS	ABDDEGINSS	BAD DESIGNS
ABCIIINOTT	ANTIBIOTIC	ABDDEGIORR	ROAD BRIDGE
ABCIIJMNOS	JACOBINISM	ABDDEGIRRW	DRAWBRIDGE
ABCIIJMOST	JACOBITISM	ABDDEHHINN	BEHINDHAND
ABCIILLNOY	BIONICALLY	ABDDEHILOR	HARD-BOILED
ABCIILLNRY	BRILLIANCY	ABDDEHINRS	BRANDISHED
ABCIILLSST	BALLISTICS	ABDDEHNNOY	DONE BY HAND
ABCIILMNOO	BIONOMICAL	ABDDEHNNSY	SEND BY HAND
ABCIILRTUY	CURABILITY	ABDDEHNORY	HARD DONE-BY
ABCIIMRSST	STRABISMIC	ABDDEHNOSY	DOES BY HAND
ABCIINNOTU	INCUBATION	ABDDEIILOS	DIABOLISED
ABCIINOSSS	ABSCISSION	ABDDEIILOZ	DIABOLIZED
ABCIKKOOTT	TOOK IT BACK	ABDDEIIMRS	BRIDESMAID
ABCIKLLSST	BLACKLISTS	ABDDEIIOVW	DAVID BOWIE
ABCIKLORVY	IVORY BLACK	ABDDEILOPU	PAID DOUBLE
ABCIKLPPRU	PUBLIC PARK	ABDDEIORSS	BROADSIDES
ABCILLRTUU	BICULTURAL		SIDEBOARDS
ABCILMOPTY	COMPATIBLY	ABDDEIRRSV	BAD DRIVERS
ABCILMOSUX	MUSICAL BOX	ABDDELLOWY	DEADLY BLOW
ABCILMSSTY	CYMBALISTS	ABDDELMOOS	MADE SO BOLD
ABCILNORSU	BINOCULARS	ABDDENOOST	AND SO TO BED
ABCILNOSUY	UNSOCIABLY	ABDDGIINNS	DISBANDING
ABCILNRSTU	LUBRICANTS	ABDDGIINRW	WADING BIRD
ABCILOPRTT	BALTIC PORT	ABDDGILNOW	OLD WINDBAG
ABCILORRTU	LUBRICATOR	ABDDGILNOY	DOING BADLY
ABCINNOSTY	OBSTINANCY	ABDDGJOOOO	DO A GOOD JOB
ABCINORSTU	INCUBATORS	ABDDGORSUY	BODYGUARDS
ABCINORTUY	INCUBATORY	ABDDHIINNR	BIRD IN HAND
ABCIORRRTU	RUBRICATOR	ABDDHNOOTU	HAD NO DOUBT
ABCKKLLOOS	LOOKS BLACK	ABDDINOORU	IN BAD ODOUR
ABCKKNOOTU	KNOCK ABOUT	ABDDLMOORU	MOULDBOARD
	KNOCKABOUT	ABDDLNOORW	DRAWN BLOOD
ABCKKOORTW	BACK TO WORK	ABDDLOORSW	DRAWS BLOOD
ABCKLNRSTU	TURNS BLACK	ABDDNOORSU	SOUNDBOARD
ABCKMOSTUU	MUCKS ABOUT	ABDDNORSWY	BANDY WORDS
ABCKNPRTUY	BANKRUPTCY	ABDDOORRSW	BROADSWORD
ABCKOOPRSS	SCRAPBOOKS	ABDEEEELMR	REDEEMABLE
ABCLLOORUY	COLOURABLY	ABDEEEFHRT	FEATHER BED
ABCLMOSSUU	SUBMUCOSAL		FEATHERBED
ABCLMPRUYZ	PLUMB CRAZY	ABDEEEFILS	DEFEASIBLE
ABCLORRTUY	ROTARY CLUB	ABDEEEFLRR	DEFERRABLE
ABCLORSSUY	SCABROUSLY	ABDEEEFLST	SALTED BEEF
ABCLOSSTTY	BLASTOCYST	ABDEEEFRST	BREAST-FEED
ABCNNRRTUU	CURRANT BUN	ABDEEEGNRR	BEER GARDEN
ABCNOORRST	BORN ACTORS	ABDEEEHKMT	MAKE THE BED
ABCNORSTTY	BY CONTRAST	ABDEEEHPRT	DEEP BREATH
ABDDDEEIOS	DEAD BODIES	ABDEEEHQTU	BEQUEATHED
ABDDDEEJNO	DEAD-END JOB	ABDEEEILMR	REMEDIABLE
ABDDDEMOYY	MY DEAD BODY	ABDEEEILRT	DELIBERATE
ABDDEEEFLN	DEFENDABLE	ABDEEEIRTT	BETTER IDEA
ABDDEEEHMT	MADE THE BED	ABDEEEILRT	BELTED EARL
ABDDEEEHNO	BONEHEADED	ABDEEELNPX	EXPENDABLE
ABDDEEELNP	DEPENDABLE	ABDEEELNTX	EXTENDABLE
ABDDEEERTT	BETTER DEAD	ABDEEELSTT	DETESTABLE
ABDDEEFIOX	FIXED ABODE	ABDEEEMNST	DEBASEMENT
ABDDEEFIRR	FRIED BREAD	ABDEEEMRTT	MADE BETTER
ABDDEEGGLR	BEDRAGGLED	ABDEEENNRW	BEEN WARNED
ABDDEEGHIR	BRIDGEHEAD	ABDEEEPPRR	BE PREPARED
ABDDEEGIOR	BIODEGRADE	ABDEEERSTW	SWEETBREAD
ABDDEEGIRR	RED BRIGADE	ABDEEFFHLU	BUFFLEHEAD
ABDDEEHLLU	BULLHEADED	ABDEEFGILN	FEELING BAD
ABDDEEINRS	READS IN BED	ABDEEFHILR	HELD A BRIEF
ABDDEEKORY	KEYBOARDED	ABDEEFHLRS	HALF-BREEDS
ABDDEELLMS	SMELLED BAD	ABDEEFHNOR	BEFOREHAND

ABDEEFHRRS	FRESH BREAD	ABDEERRSST	REDBREASTS
ABDEEFIITU	BEAUTIFIED	ABDEERSTTY	BETTER DAYS
ABDEEFIKNR	BREAD KNIFE	ABDEFHILLN	FALL BEHIND
ABDEEFLNRU	REFUNDABLE	ABDEFHILOR	HOLD A BRIEF
ABDEEFNORW	BEFORE DAWN	ABDEFHNOOP	BAND OF HOPE
ABDEEFRSST	FRED BASSET	ABDEFIILMO	MODIFIABLE
ABDEEGGILR	IDLE BEGGAR	ABDEFILMOR	FORMIDABLE
ABDEEGGLRS	BEDRAGGLES	ABDEFILNOS	BED OF NAILS
ABDEEGHHLT	HELD THE BAG	ABDEFIMORR	MORBID FEAR
ABDEEGHIRT	BIGHEARTED	ABDEFINRRS	FIREBRANDS
ABDEEGHNRR	HERB GARDEN	ABDEFIRRTU	BREAD FRUIT
ABDEEGINRS	GABERDINES		BREADFRUIT
ABDEEGLNTW	TANGLED WEB		FRUIT BREAD
ABDEEGLORT	GOLDBEATER	ABDEFNORTU	BAD FORTUNE
ABDEEGORRS	GARDEROBES	ABDEFOOSTX	BOX OF DATES
ABDEEGRRSY	GREYBEARDS	ABDEGGGIOS	DOGGIE BAGS
ABDEEHILLS	DESHABILLE	ABDEGGIRRU	BUDGERIGAR
ABDEEHILRR	HALBERDIER	ABDEGGKNOR	DOGGER BANK
ABDEEHIMSV	MISBEHAVED	ABDEGGNOOT	TOBOGGANED
ABDEEHINRT	BREATHED IN	ABDEGHHLOT	HOLD THE BAG
	HIBERNATED	ABDEGHIIRT	BRIGHT IDEA
ABDEEHIRST	AIR THE BEDS	ABDEGHILNS	LAGS BEHIND
ABDEEHIRTW	WHITE BEARD	ABDEGHINSU	SUBHEADING
	WHITE BREAD	ABDEGHOOTT	GO TO THE BAD
	WHITEBEARD	ABDEGHIORTU	BOUGHT DEAR
ABDEEHLMPS	BLASPHEMED	ABDEGIINNR	BRIGANDINE
ABDEEIILOOR	BORED A HOLE	ABDEGIIRRS	BRIGADIERS
ABDEEHLOTT	TABLE DHOTE	ABDEGIKNRR	RINGBARKED
ABDEEHORST	BROADSHEET	ABDEGILLOS	GLOBALISED
ABDEEHPPRY	HAPPY BREED	ABDEGILLOZ	GLOBALIZED
ABDEEHRRTW	DREW BREATH	ABDEGILLRU	LARGE BUILD
ABDEEHRSSW	SHEWBREADS	ABDEGILPRY	PLAY BRIDGE
ABDEEIIKRS	RIDES A BIKE	ABDEGIMNRT	ABRIDGMENT
ABDEEIILTT	DEBILITATE	ABDEGINNOR	BROADENING
ABDEEIINRT	INEBRIATED	ABDEGINORT	BARGED INTO
ABDEEIKNNY	KIDNEY BEAN	ABDEGINOTW	OWING A DEBT
ABDEEILMTT	TIMETABLED	ABDEGINRUY	BUYING DEAR
ABDEEILNNU	UNDENIABLE	ABDEGJSTUU	SUBJUGATED
ABDEEILNRS	BREADLINES	ABDEGKOSST	DOG BASKETS
ABDEEILRSV	VERBALISED	ABDEGLNNOY	GONE BY LAND
ABDEEILRVZ	VERBALIZED	ABDEGLNORS	OLD BANGERS
ABDEEIPRTT	BETTER PAID	ABDEGLNOSY	GOES BY LAND
ABDEEIRSVW	BAD REVIEWS	ABDEGNOORY	GONE BY ROAD
ABDEEISTTV	BETTE DAVIS	ABDEGNOPRS	BEGS PARDON
ABDEEKLOOS	SEALED BOOK	ABDEGNOSYY	BYGONE DAYS
ABDEEKLOTU	DOUBLE TAKE		DAYS GONE BY
ABDEEKORRY	KEYBOARDER	ABDEGOORSY	GOES BY ROAD
ABDEELLOPR	DEPLORABLE	ABDEGOOSYY	SAY GOODBYE
ABDEELLOPY	DEPLOYABLE	ABDEGORTUV	GRAVE DOUBT
ABDEELLOTT	BOTTLED ALE	ABDEGSTTUU	BUSTED A GUT
ABDEELLPSS	SPEEDBALLS	ABDEHIILLS	DISHABILLE
ABDEELMNOZ	EMBLAZONED	ABDEHIKLNW	WALK BEHIND
ABDEELMRRU	DEMURRABLE	ABDEHILNOR	BLONDE HAIR
ABDEELMSTW	STEWED LAMB	ABDEHILNSU	DANISH BLUE
ABDEELNORR	BORN LEADER	ABDEHILPRT	BRIDLE PATH
ABDEELNORS	BANDEROLES	ABDEHILUVY	HEAVY BUILD
	ENDORSABLE	ABDEHIMRTU	THUMB A RIDE
ABDEELNOTT	DONE BATTLE	ABDEHINRSS	BRANDISHES
ABDEELORTY	EARLY TO BED	ABDEHINRTT	HARD-BITTEN
ABDEELOSTT	DOES BATTLE	ABDEHINSTY	STAY BEHIND
ABDEELRTUX	EXTRUDABLE	ABDEHIRSSU	BRUSH ASIDE
ABDEELSTTY	DETESTABLY	ABDEHLNOSS	ASH BLONDES
ABDEEMRSTY	STREAMED BY	ABDEHLORTU	HAD TROUBLE
ABDEENNOTW	BEATEN DOWN	ABDEHLOSTW	DEATHBLOWS
ABDEENOPSU	SUBPOENAED	ABDEHNNSTY	SENT BY HAND
ABDEENPRRY	PREBENDARY	ABDEHNOORT	ON THE BOARD
ABDEENRRST	BARTENDERS	ABDEHNORTU	EARTHBOUND
ABDEENRSTT	STREET BAND	ABDEHNOSTT	AT BOTH ENDS
ABDEENSTTU	DEBUTANTES	ABDEHNRSTU	SUBTRAHEND
ABDEEOPRRT	REPROBATED	ABDEHORRST	SHORTBREAD
ABDEEORRUX	BORDEREAUX	ABDEHORSSW	SHOWBREADS

ABDEHOSTUV	HAVE DOUBTS	ABDEOPRRST	BAD REPORTS
ABDEIILLRV	BRIDAL VEIL	ABDEORRSWY	WORRY BEADS
ABDEIILMSS	ADMISSIBLE	ABDERRTTYY	DRY BATTERY
ABDEIILOSS	DIABOLISES	ABDFGOORSX	OXFORD BAGS
ABDEIILOSX	OXIDISABLE	ABDFHIILNT	BLIND FAITH
ABDEIILOSZ	DIABOLIZES	ABDFILMORY	FORMIDABLY
ABDEIILOXZ	OXIDIZABLE	ABDFILNORU	FLORIBUNDA
ABDEIILSST	STABILISED	ABDFINSSTU	IFS AND BUTS
ABDEIILSTZ	STABILIZED	ABDFOOORST	FOOTBOARDS
ABDEIILTYY	DYEABILITY	ABDFORRSSU	SURFBOARDS
ABDEIIMMNNR	BEAR IN MIND	ABDGGIKNOR	BARKING DOG
ABDEIINOST	ANTIBODIES	ABDGGILNOY	GOING BADLY
ABDEIINOTW	TIED IN A BOW	ABDGHHOTTU	BAD THOUGHT
ABDEIJLMPU	JUMPED BAIL	ABDGHILTYY	BY DAYLIGHT
ABDEIKMRSS	DISEMBARKS	ABDGHINNSU	HUSBANDING
ABDEIKNNOT	BANKED ON IT	ABDGHIOOST	GOOD HABITS
ABDEIKNRSW	BREAKS WIND	ABDGIIMNRS	BRIGANDISM
	WINDBREAKS	ABDGIINPRU	UPBRAIDING
ABDEIKRRST	BRISK TRADE	ABDGIINRRS	DISBARRING
ABDEIILLNY	BLIND ALLEY	ABDGIINRTW	BAD WRITING
ABDEILMNSY	SEND BY MAIL	ABDGIINSSU	DISABUSING
ABDEILMORS	BROMELIADS	ABDGIKLMNO	MAKING BOLD
ABDEILMSTU	SUBLIMATED	ABDGIKNNOU	DOING A BUNK
ABDEILNNUY	UNDENIABLY	ABDGILNORW	BRIDAL GOWN
ABDEILNORS	BANDOLIERS	ABDGILNORY	BOY AND GIRL
ABDEILNORY	DEBONAIRLY	ABDGINNRST	STRING BAND
ABDEILNRSW	SWEAR BLIND	ABDGINNSTY	STANDING BY
ABDEILOPSS	DISPOSABLE	ABDGINOPRU	BOARDING UP
ABDEILPSTU	DISPUTABLE	ABDGINORSS	SIGNBOARDS
ABDEILRSTU	BRUTALISED	ABDGINORTU	GROUND BAIT
ABDEILRTUZ	BRUTALIZED		GROUNDBAIT
ABDEIMNRST	DISBARMENT	ABDHIINNRS	HINDBRAINS
ABDEIMNSTU	SUBMEDIANT	ABDHIIRTTY	DIRTY HABIT
ABDEIMRTUW	DUMB WAITER	ABDHILMORY	BODILY HARM
ABDEINORSU	BOUNDARIES	ABDHIMRSTY	DITHYRAMBS
ABDEINRSUV	DRIVEN A BUS	ABDHNOOSTU	HAS NO DOUBT
ABDEINSSTY	STAYS IN BED	ABDIIILSTY	DISABILITY
ABDEIPRRSU	UPBRAIDERS	ABDIIILTUY	AUDIBILITY
ABDEIRSSUV	DRIVES A BUS	ABDIIKNNRY	BRADYKININ
ABDEIRTTTU	ATTRIBUTED	ABDIILLNPU	UNPAID BILL
ABDEKLLOTU	DOUBLE-TALK	ABDIILNOPY	BODILY PAIN
ABDEKLMOOS	MAKE SO BOLD	ABDIILOSST	DIABOLISTS
ABDEKLOPRU	DOUBLE-PARK	ABDIILRTUY	DURABILITY
ABDEKNORSW	BREAKDOWNS	ABDIIRSSUY	SUBSIDIARY
	BREAKS DOWN	ABDIKNRSUY	BUYS A DRINK
ABDEKNPRTU	BANKRUPTED	ABDILLLLOR	DOLLAR BILL
ABDELLLNSY	BELLY-LANDS	ABDILLLMSU	SMALL BUILD
ABDELLNOOR	RED BALLOON	ABDILNOOST	BLOODSTAIN
ABDELLNOSW	SNOWBALLED	ABDILNRUZZ	BUZZ ALDRIN
ABDELLNSUY	BUY AND SELL	ABDILOORWZ	BRAZILWOOD
ABDELLOPRY	DEPLORABLY	ABDILPSTUY	DISPUTABLY
ABDELLORST	LORDS TABLE	ABDIMPQSSU	DAMP SQUIBS
ABDELMNOUY	BLUE MONDAY	ABDINOSWWY	BAY WINDOWS
ABDELNORTU	ROUND TABLE	ABDINRSSTW	WRISTBANDS
	ROUND-TABLE	ABDIORSXXY	SIX-YARD BOX
ABDELOORST	STABLE DOOR	ABDKLLNOSY	LLOYDS BANK
ABDELOOSTT	TASTE BLOOD	ABDLLOOORY	BLOOD ROYAL
ABDELOOSTW	SWEAT BLOOD		ROYAL BLOOD
ABDELOPSUY	PAYS DOUBLE	ABDLMNPRUY	PLUM BRANDY
ABDELORSTU	DOUBLE STAR	ABDLMOORYY	BLOODY MARY
ABDELORSUV	BOULEVARDS	ABDLNNOTTU	NUT AND BOLT
ABDELORTUY	OBDURATELY	ABDMNORSUU	BUMS AROUND
ABDEMNORST	ON BAD TERMS	ABDMOOORRS	BOARDROOMS
ABDEMOOTUV	MOVED ABOUT	ABDNOOPRTU	PUT ON BOARD
ABDEMORSYY	MY DEAR BOYS	ABDNOORTUU	ROUND ABOUT
ABDENNOORW	BEAR DOWN ON		ROUNDABOUT
ABDENNOTTW	BATTEN DOWN	ABDNORSUUY	BUYS A ROUND
ABDENRSSSU	ABSURDNESS	ABDOOOSTTU	STOOD ABOUT
ABDENRSSTY	BYSTANDERS	ABDOOPRSTU	PROUD BOAST
ABDENSSTUY	SUNDAY BEST	ABDOORRTUU	TROUBADOUR
ABDEOORRTT	OTTERBOARD	ABEEEEFRST	BEEFEATERS

ABEEEERSSZ	SEA BREEZES	**ABEEGNNOST**	GONE ABSENT
ABEEEEFIRTW	WIFE BEATER	**ABEEGNOSST**	GOES ABSENT
ABEEEEFLPRR	PREFERABLE	**ABEEHILLRS**	RELISHABLE
ABEEEEFNRTW	FAR BETWEEN	**ABEEHILPRS**	PERISHABLE
ABEEEEGGRST	EGG BEATERS	**ABEEHIMNTT**	BENTHAMITE
ABEEEEGINRZ	GREEN BAIZE	**ABEEHIMRTW**	BEAR WITH ME
ABEEEEGLRSU	BELEAGUERS	**ABEEHIMSSV**	MISBEHAVES
ABEEEEGLSTT	STAG BEETLE	**ABEEHINRST**	BREATHES IN
ABEEEEGLSTV	VEGETABLES		HIBERNATES
ABEEEEGNNRS	GREEN BEANS	**ABEEHIRSTT**	BREATHIEST
ABEEEEGNOTY	TEENAGE BOY	**ABEEHKLNST**	BLANK SHEET
ABEEEEHLLVW	BEHAVE WELL	**ABEEHKLOSU**	BLEAK HOUSE
ABEEEEHLSTT	THE BEATLES	**ABEEHKOSSU**	BAKEHOUSES
ABEEEEHNNOT	BENEATH ONE	**ABEEHLLOST**	BALLET SHOE
ABEEEEHRRST	THREE BEARS	**ABEEHLLRST**	THREE BALLS
ABEEEEHRSTT	HARTEBEEST	**ABEEHLLSTT**	ALL THE BEST
ABEEEEIKLNR	BERKELEIAN	**ABEEHLLSUW**	BLUE WHALES
ABEEEEILLRV	RELIEVABLE	**ABEEHLMPRS**	BLASPHEMER
ABEEEEIMNTT	BEATEN TIME	**ABEEHLMPSS**	BLASPHEMES
ABEEEEKMRTT	MAKE BETTER	**ABEEHLNOSW**	WHALEBONES
ABEEEEKNRSV	BREAKS EVEN	**ABEEHLNOTT**	ON THE TABLE
ABEEEEKPRRS	BARKEEPERS	**ABEEHLOORS**	BORES A HOLE
ABEEEELLLPX	EXPELLABLE	**ABEEHLOPRY**	HYPERBOLAE
ABEEEELLNTW	WELL BEATEN	**ABEEHLRSST**	BREATHLESS
ABEEEELMNRU	ENUMERABLE	**ABEEHMNSTT**	THE BEST MAN
ABEEEELMPRT	TEMPERABLE	**ABEEHMORTT**	BATHOMETER
ABEEEELNPRT	PENETRABLE	**ABEEHNORSS**	HORSEBEANS
ABEEEELQQUZ	SQUEEZABLE	**ABEEHNRTTT**	BETTER THAN
ABEEEELRSTT	RESETTABLE	**ABEEHNRTTY**	BATTERY HEN
ABEEEEMRSTY	MERSEY BEAT	**ABEEHOORRS**	SEBORRHOEA
ABEEEENRSTT	BEEN AT REST	**ABEEHORRTV**	OVER THE BAR
ABEEEEORSTT	STEREOBATE	**ABEEHORRTW**	THE BOER WAR
ABEEEERRTTV	VERTEBRATE	**ABEEHORSTU**	HEREABOUTS
ABEEEFFHMOT	OFF THE BEAM	**ABEEHORTTU**	BREATHE OUT
ABEEEFFLMNT	BAFFLEMENT	**ABEEHORTTX**	THEATRE BOX
ABEEEFFLMTU	BUFFET MEAL	**ABEEHRSTTT**	BREATH TEST
ABEEEFFLRSU	SUFFERABLE	**ABEEIILLRS**	LIBERALISE
ABEEEFGGINO	BEING OF AGE	**ABEEIIILLRZ**	LIBERALIZE
ABEEEFGLRTU	BE GRATEFUL	**ABEEIILNTV**	INEVITABLE
ABEEEFHLMRU	HUMBLE FARE	**ABEEIILSST**	BESTIALISE
ABEEEFHLRTT	BETTER HALF	**ABEEIILSTZ**	BESTIALIZE
ABEEEFIILRV	VERIFIABLE	**ABEEIINRST**	INEBRIATES
ABEEEFIIRTU	BEAUTIFIER	**ABEEIIRRSV**	BREVIARIES
ABEEEFIISTU	BEAUTIFIES	**ABEEIIRSST**	BESTIARIES
ABEEEFIKLNT	TABLE KNIFE	**ABEEIJLLRW**	LIBERAL JEW
ABEEEFIKRRS	FIREBREAKS	**ABEEIKKLST**	BASKETLIKE
ABEEEFILLLR	REFILLABLE	**ABEEIKLLSZ**	LIKE BLAZES
ABEEEFILLRT	FILTERABLE	**ABEEIKLOTY**	KATIE BOYLE
ABEEEFILNTT	FLEA-BITTEN	**ABEEIKMNST**	BE MISTAKEN
ABEEEFILPST	PAST BELIEF	**ABEEIKRSTW**	WIRE BASKET
ABEEEFILRSS	BAS-RELIEFS	**ABEEILLNNT**	TABLE LINEN
ABEEEFILRST	LETS BE FAIR	**ABEEILLNPY**	PLEBEIANLY
ABEEEFILRSU	REFUSE BAIL	**ABEEILLNRU**	UNRELIABLE
ABEEEFINRRV	BRAIN FEVER	**ABEEILLRTT**	LITTLE BEAR
ABEEEFIORZZ	FOZZIE BEAR	**ABEEILMNRT**	TERMINABLE
ABEEEFLMORR	REFORMABLE	**ABEEILMOST**	METABOLISE
ABEEEFLORSW	SAFEBLOWER	**ABEEILMOTT**	METABOLITE
ABEEEFLPRRY	PREFERABLY	**ABEEILMOTZ**	METABOLIZE
ABEEEFLSSSU	SELF-ABUSES	**ABEEILMRTT**	REMITTABLE
ABEEEFLSTTY	SAFETY BELT	**ABEEILMSSS**	ASSEMBLIES
ABEEEGHHTUV	HAVE THE BUG	**ABEEILMSTT**	TIMETABLES
ABEEEGHLSUU	BUSH LEAGUE	**ABEEILNNUV**	UNENVIABLE
ABEEEGHNORS	HABERGEONS	**ABEEILNOPR**	INOPERABLE
ABEEEGILNNO	BEEN IN GOAL	**ABEEILNORX**	INEXORABLE
ABEEEGILNOT	NEGOTIABLE	**ABEEILNPSX**	EXPANSIBLE
ABEEEGILNRT	INTEGRABLE	**ABEEILNRSS**	BLEARINESS
ABEEEGILTTV	GIVE BATTLE	**ABEEILNRST**	EAST BERLIN
ABEEEGKLNOR	BROKEN A LEG	**ABEEILNRWY**	BARLEY WINE
ABEEEGLNORV	GOVERNABLE	**ABEEILNSTV**	INVESTABLE
ABEEEGLNOSS	NOBLE GASES	**ABEEILORTT**	OBLITERATE
ABEEEGLOPRS	PORBEAGLES	**ABEEILPRRS**	RESPIRABLE

ABEEILRRSV	VERBALISER	ABEEPRRRTU	RUPERT BEAR
ABEEILRRVZ	VERBALIZER	ABEEPRSSTT	BESPATTERS
ABEEILRSSV	VERBALISES	ABEFFGINOT	BEATING OFF
ABEEILRSVZ	VERBALIZES	ABEFFHLLOT	OFF THE BALL
ABEEILSSTT	BEASTLIEST	ABEFFHLNOO	ON BEHALF OF
ABEEIMOSTV	BASE MOTIVE	ABEFFIKORT	BREAK IT OFF
ABEEINORSV	RISEN ABOVE	ABEFFILLOR	BALL OF FIRE
ABEEINRTUX	EXURBANITE		BILL OF FARE
ABEEIORSSV	RISES ABOVE	ABEFFLRSUY	SUFFERABLY
ABEEIOSTTU	SEE ABOUT IT	ABEFGIINTY	BEATIFYING
ABEEIRRSSS	BRASSERIES	ABEFGILORV	FORGIVABLE
	BRASSIERES	ABEFGILRSS	FIBREGLASS
ABEEJKMRSU	JAMES BURKE	ABEFGIMOST	BAGS OF TIME
ABEEJLLMSU	JUMBLE SALE	ABEFGLLMOS	LEGS OF LAMB
ABEEJMMNNT	ENJAMBMENT	ABEFHIKORT	BROKE FAITH
ABEEKLNRSV	BLANK VERSE	ABEFHIRRTT	AFTERBIRTH
ABEEKLNTTW	WET BLANKET	ABEFHLLOTT	HALF BOTTLE
ABEEKLOORS	BREAK LOOSE	ABEFHLSSTU	FLASHTUBES
ABEEKLORRU	BROKE A RULE	ABEFIILLLN	INFALLIBLE
ABEEKLRRSU	BREAK RULES	ABEFIILLRT	FIBRILLATE
ABEEKLRSTU	BLUE STREAK	ABEFIILNOT	NOTIFIABLE
ABEEKMMNNT	EMBANKMENT	ABEFIJKOOT	BIT OF A JOKE
ABEEKMMNRT	EMBARKMENT	ABEFILLLOS	BILL OF SALE
ABEEKNOORW	RENEW A BOOK	ABEFILMORR	MORAL FIBRE
ABEEKNOPRS	BREAKS OPEN	ABEFILOPRT	PROFITABLE
ABEEKNOPST	KEEP TABS ON	ABEFILOSTU	FLIES ABOUT
ABEEKNOSTT	T-BONE STEAK	ABEFIMOSST	BIT OF A MESS
ABEEKORRST	ROBERT ASKE	ABEFINNOST	TIN OF BEANS
ABEEILLMPY	AMPLE BELLY	ABEFINRRUY	IN FEBRUARY
ABEELLMNTU	ANTEBELLUM	ABEFIOPPRT	BIT OF PAPER
ABEELLMOPY	EMPLOYABLE	ABEFIRRSTU	BEARS FRUIT
ABEELLNRUV	VULNERABLE	ABEFLLLMUY	BLAMEFULLY
ABEELLORSV	RESOLVABLE	ABEFLLOORT	FOOTBALLER
ABEELLORVV	REVOLVABLE	ABEFLOPSST	BEST OF PALS
ABEELMMMNT	EMBALMMENT	ABEFLORSTW	FAST BOWLER
ABEELMNOTY	TABLE MONEY	ABEFMORRSY	FARMERS BOY
ABEELMNRSU	LEBENSRAUM	ABEFMRRTTU	FARM BUTTER
	MENSURABLE	ABEFNOORSW	ROW OF BEANS
ABEELMNTTT	BATTLEMENT	ABEFNORRTV	BRAVE FRONT
ABEELMORST	BLASTOMERE	ABEFNRRRYY	BRYAN FERRY
ABEELMOSTX	METAL BOXES	ABEGGILNOS	BOILS AN EGG
ABEELMPRSU	PRESUMABLE	ABEGGINOOV	GOING ABOVE
ABEELMRSSS	ASSEMBLERS	ABEGGINOSY	GOING BY SEA
ABEELMRSTU	RUMBLE SEAT	ABEGGOOPRR	POOR BEGGAR
ABEELMWWYY	WEMBLEY WAY	ABEGHILMRT	AMBER LIGHT
ABEELNNNOY	ANNE BOLEYN	ABEGHIMNNU	HUMAN BEING
ABEELNOPRS	PERSONABLE	ABEGHINRRS	HARBINGERS
ABEELNOSST	OBLATENESS	ABEGHIOPRR	BIOGRAPHER
ABEELNQTTU	BLANQUETTE	ABEGHIRRST	BEARS RIGHT
ABEELNRRTU	RETURNABLE	ABEGHKORTU	TOUGH BREAK
ABEELNSSST	STABLENESS	ABEGHLLOPU	PLOUGHABLE
ABEELNSSSU	USABLENESS	ABEGHLNOOP	ANGLOPHOBE
ABEELOPRRT	REPORTABLE	ABEGHLORST	THE GORBALS
ABEELOPRTX	EXPORTABLE	ABEGHLOSTT	BAGS THE LOT
ABEELORRST	RESTORABLE	ABEGHMRRSU	HAMBURGERS
ABEEMMNSTY	EMBAYMENTS	ABEGHNRRSU	BUSHRANGER
ABEEMNRSUY	EASY NUMBER	ABEGHOORTT	GO TO THE BAR
ABEEMORRST	BAROMETERS	ABEGHOSUUU	USQUEBAUGH
ABEEMRRSSU	EMBRASURES	ABEGIIKMST	MAKES IT BIG
ABEENNNORT	ANNE BRONTE	ABEGIIKNNR	BREAKING IN
ABEENNNRRU	RUNNER BEAN	ABEGIILNNT	INTANGIBLE
ABEENNRRSS	BARRENNESS	ABEGIILNRT	LIBERATING
ABEENNRSSZ	BRAZENNESS	ABEGIILNRV	BRING ALIVE
ABEENORRTW	WATERBORNE	ABEGIINNRT	BRIGANTINE
ABEENORSSS	BARONESSES	ABEGIINORS	ABORIGINES
ABEENORSWY	WEARY BONES	ABEGIINOST	ABIOGENIST
ABEENOSSTT	AT ONES BEST	ABEGIKLNNT	BLANKETING
ABEENQRSTU	BANQUETERS	ABEGIKLRST	BIG TALKERS
ABEENQSTTU	BANQUETTES	ABEGIKNPRU	BREAKING UP
ABEEOPRRST	REPROBATES	ABEGIKNSTT	TAKING BETS
ABEEOSSSST	ASBESTOSES	ABEGILLNRR	BARRELLING

ABEGILLNRS	RINGS A BELL	ABEHKORRST	BREAK SHORT
ABEGILLOSS	GLOBALISES	ABEHKPRSSY	KHYBER PASS
ABEGILLOSZ	GLOBALIZES	ABEHLLOOTW	BEAT HOLLOW
ABEGILLOTY	OBLIGATELY	ABEHLMNTTY	BATTLE HYMN
ABEGILMNPU	IMPUGNABLE	ABEHLNOORU	HONOURABLE
ABEGILMNSS	ASSEMBLING	ABEHLNORSU	BURNS A HOLE
ABEGILMNTT	EMBATTLING	ABEHLOPRSY	HYPERBOLAS
ABEGILNORY	GONE BY RAIL	ABEHLORRTY	LAY BROTHER
ABEGILNSSU	SUBLEASING	ABEHLORSTT	BETROTHALS
ABEGILORSY	GOES BY RAIL	ABEHLORSTU	HAS TROUBLE
ABEGILRRSU	BURGLARIES	ABEHLOSTTW	BATH TOWELS
	BURGLARISE	ABEHLRSSUU	HURLS ABUSE
ABEGILRRUZ	BURGLARIZE	ABEHMMNSTU	AMBUSHMENT
ABEGIMNNTT	BETTING MAN	ABEHMNOOTY	BAY THE MOON
ABEGINNOPT	OPENING BAT	ABEHMRSSTU	BUSHMASTER
ABEGINNOTY	BAYONETING	ABEHOORTUV	HOVER ABOUT
ABEGINNQTU	BANQUETING	ABEHOOSSTU	BOATHOUSES
ABEGINNRST	STRING BEAN		HOUSEBOATS
ABEGINORST	BARGES INTO	ABEHOPSTUY	BEAUTY SHOP
ABEGINORTU	BEARING OUT	ABEHORTTUW	THREW ABOUT
ABEGINOTTU	BEATING OUT	ABEHOSSUUY	BUYS A HOUSE
ABEGINOTXY	GONE BY TAXI	ABEHRSSSUY	BUYS SHARES
ABEGINRSTU	GAS TURBINE	ABEIIILMNT	INIMITABLE
ABEGINRSWY	SWEARING BY	ABEIIILQRU	EQUILIBRIA
ABEGIOSTXY	GOES BY TAXI	ABEIIKLLRS	KAISER BILL
ABEGJSSTUU	SUBJUGATES	ABEIILLMRS	LIBERALISM
ABEGKRSSTU	GRUBSTAKES	ABEIILLNNY	BIENNIALLY
ABEGLLNOOU	BLUE LAGOON	ABEIILLNOV	INVIOLABLE
ABEGLNORRY	LOGANBERRY	ABEIILLRST	LIBERALIST
ABEGLNSTTU	GUN BATTLES	ABEIILLRTY	LIBERALITY
ABEGLOOSTZ	GO TO BLAZES!	ABEIILLSTU	UTILISABLE
ABEGMNOORS	BOOMERANGS	ABEIILLTUZ	UTILIZABLE
ABEGMNOOTY	MONTEGO BAY	ABEIILMNSS	LESBIANISM
ABEGMNORTY	GONE BY TRAM	ABEIILMPRT	IMPARTIBLE
ABEGMOORTT	BOTTOM GEAR	ABEIILMPSS	IMPASSIBLE
ABEGMORSTY	GOES BY TRAM	ABEIILNORT	LIBERATION
ABEGMORSUU	UMBRAGEOUS	ABEIILNTTU	INTUITABLE
ABEGNNORSW	GROWN BEANS	ABEIILNTTY	TENABILITY
ABEGNOORTU	BATON ROUGE	ABEIILNTVY	INEVITABLY
ABEGNORSSW	GROWS BEANS	ABEIILQTUY	EQUABILITY
ABEGNOSSTU	GETS ON A BUS	ABEIILRSST	STABILISER
ABEGOOOOST	BO TO A GOOSE	ABEIILRSTZ	STABILIZER
ABEGOOPRSTU	BEAT GROUPS	ABEIILSSST	STABILISES
ABEGORRSSY	GARY SOBERS	ABEIILSSTZ	STABILIZES
ABEHHIRSTT	HITS THE BAR	ABEIILSTTY	BESTIALITY
ABEHHORRTT	HEARTTHROB	ABEIINNRSS	BRAININESS
ABEHHORSTW	SHOWER BATH	ABEIINOSTW	TIES IN A BOW
ABEHHOSSTU	BATHHOUSES	ABEIINRRSV	RIVER BASIN
ABEHIILMNT	HABILIMENT	ABEIIORSTU	OBITUARIES
ABEHIKLNRS	SHRINKABLE	ABEIJKLNOR	BROKEN JAIL
ABEHIKRSWY	BY A WHISKER	ABEIJLNOTT	JOIN BATTLE
ABEHILLPTY	PAY THE BILL	ABEIKLNNSU	UNSINKABLE
ABEHILMOPS	AMPHIBOLES	ABEIKNORSW	WAKE-ROBINS
ABEHILNPSU	PUNISHABLE	ABEIKNORTW	BREAK IN TWO
ABEHILOPSS	BASOPHILES	ABEIKOORTW	WRITE A BOOK
ABEHILOPST	HOSPITABLE	ABEIKPRSTU	BREAKS IT UP
ABEHILORSS	ABOLISHERS	ABEILLLMTT	LITTLE LAMB
ABEHILORTV	BATH OLIVER	ABEILLLNRW	BERLIN WALL
ABEHILPSTT	BATTLESHIP	ABEILLMOSS	LOSES A LIMB
ABEHILRSST	HERBALISTS	ABEILLNNST	TENNIS BALL
ABEHIMMNST	BENTHAMISM	ABEILLNOSV	INSOLVABLE
ABEHIMNNST	BANISHMENT	ABEILLSUXY	BISEXUALLY
ABEHINNORT	ON THE BRAIN	ABEILMMOST	METABOLISM
ABEHINOOPX	XENOPHOBIA	ABEILMMOSV	IMMOVABLES
ABEHINOPRV	VIBRAPHONE	ABEILMNQRU	LAMBREQUIN
ABEHINORRT	HIBERNATOR	ABEILMNSTY	SENT BY MAIL
ABEHIORSUV	BEHAVIOURS	ABEILMOOTU	AUTOMOBILE
ABEHIRRSSU	AIRBRUSHES	ABEILMOPRT	IMPORTABLE
ABEHIRRSTT	BIRTHRATES	ABEILMOPRV	IMPROVABLE
ABEHKOOPRS	PHRASE BOOK	ABEILMSSTU	SUBLIMATES
ABEHKOPRSS	BAKERS SHOP	ABEILNORXY	INEXORABLY

ABEILNOSTY	OBEISANTLY	ABELLOSTTT	LOST BATTLE
ABEILNOTTT	INTO BATTLE	ABELLOSTUY	ABSOLUTELY
ABEILNRSUV	BURNS ALIVE	ABELLSSSUY	SYLLABUSES
ABEILNRTUV	BURNT ALIVE	ABELMNORYZ	EMBLAZONRY
ABEILNSTUU	UNSUITABLE	ABELMPRSUY	PRESUMABLY
ABEILOPRRV	PROVERBIAL	ABELMPSSTU	BLUE STAMPS
ABEILORRST	LIBERATORS	ABELNNORUV	VERBAL NOUN
ABEILORSTU	LABOURITES	ABELNOOPST	TABLESPOON
ABEILORSTW	BOILS WATER	ABELNOPTXY	PENALTY BOX
ABEILORTVY	ABORTIVELY	ABELNOSTTU	LAST BUT ONE
ABEILPRSTY	BIT PLAYERS	ABELNRSSTU	SUBALTERNS
ABEILRRTTU	TRITURABLE	ABELNRSTTU	TURNTABLES
ABEILRSSTU	BRUTALISES	ABELNSSTTU	UNSTABLEST
ABEILRSTUV	VESTIBULAR	ABELOORTUV	LABOUR VOTE
ABEILRSTUZ	BRUTALIZES		VOTE LABOUR
ABEILRSUVV	SURVIVABLE	ABELOOTTUW	OUT AT ELBOW
ABEIMMOQUZ	MOZAMBIQUE	ABELOPPSSU	SUPPOSABLE
ABEIMNNOTT	OBTAINMENT	ABELPPSSUY	SUPPLY BASE
ABEIMNOORR	BRIAN MOORE	ABELRSSTUY	ABSTRUSELY
ABEIMNORTT	MONTBRETIA	ABEMMNORSU	MEMBRANOUS
ABEIMNORTU	TAMBOURINE	ABEMNOORRW	MARROW BONE
ABEIMNRRSU	SUBMARINER		MARROWBONE
ABEIMNRSSU	SUBMARINES	ABEMOOPRRS	BROOMRAPES
ABEIMOSSTU	ABSTEMIOUS	ABEMOOSTUV	MOVES ABOUT
ABEINNOSTT	ABSTENTION	ABEMOPSTTY	EMPTY BOAST
ABEINNRSST	BANNISTERS	ABEMORRSTU	ARBORETUMS
ABEINNRSSW	BRAWNINESS	ABENNOPRSX	BOX SPANNER
ABEINOPPTT	BON APPETIT	ABENNSSTTU	SUBTENANTS
ABEINOPRRW	BRAINPOWER	ABENOPPRRW	BROWN PAPER
ABEINOPSTX	PAINT BOXES	ABENOPRRSS	PRESS BARON
ABEINORTTX	EXORBITANT	ABENOPSSUY	PAY ONES SUB
ABEINRSSSS	BRASSINESS	ABENORSTUZ	BRAZENS OUT
ABEIOPPRSY	PRESBYOPIA	ABENOSSSUY	BUSY SEASON
ABEIOPRSTV	ABSORPTIVE	ABENPRSSTU	ABRUPTNESS
ABEIORSTTT	TEAR TO BITS	ABEOORRSST	BARE TORSOS
ABEIORTTUW	WRITE ABOUT	ABEOORTTUW	WROTE ABOUT
ABEIOSSSST	ASBESTOSIS	ABEOPRRSTT	POTTERS BAR
ABEIPRRSST	STRIPS BARE	ABEOPSTTUY	BEAUTY SPOT
ABEIPRSTTY	BAPTISTERY	ABEOQSSUUU	SUBAQUEOUS
ABEIPRTTUX	ABRUPT EXIT	ABEORSSSTY	STAYS SOBER
ABEIPRTTUY	PAY TRIBUTE	ABERRRSTWY	STRAWBERRY
ABEIRRRSST	BARRISTERS	ABERRSTTUY	BURST A TYRE
ABEIRRTTTU	ATTRIBUTER	ABFFGILLNY	BAFFLINGLY
ABEIRSSTWY	SWEARS BY IT	ABFFGLOORU	BAG OF FLOUR
ABEIRSTTTU	ATTRIBUTES	ABFGHKNORU	FRANK BOUGH
ABEJNNORTW	JANET BROWN	ABFGILNOTY	FLYING BOAT
ABEKKMOORS	BOOKMAKERS	ABFGILORVY	FORGIVABLY
ABEKKNORRS	BROKE RANKS	ABFGOPRRSU	UP FOR GRABS
ABEKKORSTW	BASKETWORK	ABFHILMTTU	THUMB A LIFT
	WORKBASKET	ABFHINORTW	FAITH BROWN
ABEKLLMRTU	BULL MARKET	ABFIIILRTY	FRIABILITY
ABEKLNNOUW	UNKNOWABLE	ABFIILLLNY	INFALLIBLY
ABEKLNORUW	UNWORKABLE	ABFIILNORV	RIBOFLAVIN
ABEKLOOPST	BOOKPLATES	ABFILLOSTT	FALL TO BITS
ABEKLOOSWX	OX-BOW LAKES	ABFILOOPSY	SLIP OF A BOY
ABEKLOPRRR	PORK BARREL	ABFILOPRTY	PROFITABLY
ABEKLORSTW	WORKTABLES	ABFILOSTTU	FLITS ABOUT
ABEKMNNOTU	MOUNTEBANK	ABFIMNORRY	BINARY FORM
ABEKNNORTU	BROKEN A NUT	ABFJOORRTY	TRY FOR A JOB
ABEKNOOOPS	OPENS A BOOK	ABFKNNORRU	FRANK BRUNO
ABEKNOPRRW	PAWNBROKER	ABFLLLOOOW	BALL OF WOOL
ABEKNOPSTT	KEPT TABS ON	ABFLLOSTUY	BOASTFULLY
ABEKOOORTW	WROTE A BOOK	ABFLLOSUUY	FABULOUSLY
ABEKOOPRRY	PRAYER BOOK	ABFLNOOTUW	FLOWN ABOUT
ABEKOOSSST	BOOKS SEATS	ABFLNOSTTU	ALFS BUTTON
ABEKORRSTW	BREASTWORK	ABFLOOOSTU	FOOLS ABOUT
ABELLLLOVY	VOLLEY BALL	ABGGIIKLNT	TALKING BIG
	VOLLEYBALL	ABGGIILNOT	OBLIGATING
ABELLLOSUW	SAUL BELLOW	ABGGIIMNRS	BIG MARGINS
ABELLNRUVY	VULNERABLY	ABGGIINORY	GOING BY AIR
ABELLORRRU	BULL-ROARER	ABGGINOOTU	GOING ABOUT

ABGHIILNOS	ABOLISHING	ABIILOPTTY	POTABILITY
ABGHINNSTU	SUNBATHING	ABIIMRSSTY	SYBARITISM
ABGHINORRU	HARBOURING	ABIINNOTTU	INTUBATION
ABGHIORTTU	RIGHT ABOUT	ABIINORSTV	VIBRATIONS
ABGHIRSTTY	STRAIGHT BY	ABIJLLNTUY	JUBILANTLY
ABGHNOTUYY	NAUGHTY BOY	ABIKLNNOPT	POINT BLANK
ABGHOORRUY	YARBOROUGH		POINT-BLANK
ABGIILNNTY	INTANGIBLY	ABIKLNOSSW	BLOWN A KISS
ABGIILNOOT	OBLIGATION	ABIKLOSSSW	BLOWS A KISS
ABGIILNOPR	PARBOILING	ABIKNOOORT	RATION BOOK
ABGIILNOTU	BAILING OUT	ABILLNOOST	BALLOONIST
ABGIINNOST	BOTANISING	ABILLNOPST	BALL POINTS
ABGIINNOTZ	BOTANIZING		BALLPOINTS
ABGIINNRSU	URBANISING	ABILLNOSST	BALLONISTS
ABGIINNRUZ	URBANIZING	ABILLNOSVY	INSOLVABLY
ABGIINORRS	ARBORISING	ABILLNPRUU	RUN UP A BILL
ABGIINORRZ	ARBORIZING	ABILLORRSZ	RAZORBILLS
ABGIINRSTU	BRING A SUIT	ABILMNOOTU	OUT ON A LIMB
ABGIKKMNOU	BOOKMAKING	ABILMNNUSUU	ALBUMINOUS
ABGILLMNRY	RAMBLINGLY	ABILMOSSTU	ABSOLUTISM
ABGILLNNOO	BALLOONING	ABILNNOORU	LABOR UNION
ABGILMOSUY	BIGAMOUSLY	ABILNOOSTU	ABSOLUTION
ABGILNOPSY	PLAYS BINGO	ABILNRSSTU	RUBS SALT IN
ABGILNORWZ	BLAZING ROW	ABILNSTUUY	UNSUITABLY
ABGILNOTUW	BAWLING OUT	ABILOPRSTT	SPOILT BRAT
ABGILNOTUY	LYING ABOUT	ABILORSSUU	SALUBRIOUS
ABGILOORTY	OBLIGATORY	ABILOSSTTU	ABSOLUTIST
ABGILRRTUY	RUGBY TRIAL	ABILPPSTUU	PUTS UP BAIL
ABGIMNORTU	TAMBOURING	ABILRTTUUY	TUBULARITY
ABGINOORTW	ROWING BOAT	ABIMMNNRSUU	MANUBRIUMS
ABGINORTTU	OBTURATING	ABIMNORRST	BRAIN STORM
ABGIORSTUU	SUBJUGATOR		BRAINSTORM
ABGKLOORTU	OLGA KORBUT	ABIMRSSSTU	STRABISMUS
ABGKNOPRTU	GO BANKRUPT	ABINNOPRTW	BROWN PAINT
ABGLLNOOSW	BOWLS ALONG	ABINOOPRST	ABSORPTION
ABGLMNOOSS	BOOMSLANGS		PROBATIONS
ABGLPRSUYY	PLAYS RUGBY	ABINOORTTU	OBTURATION
ABGNORRSUW	BROWN SUGAR	ABINOOSSST	BASSOONIST
ABHHILOSTT	BATHOLITHS	ABINOPRRSS	PRISON BARS
ABHIIJRRST	BRITISH RAJ	ABINOSSTTU	BUS STATION
ABHIIMMNRS	BRAHMINISM		SUBSTATION
ABHIIMOPSU	AMPHIBIOUS	ABIOPTTTUU	PUT IT ABOUT
ABHIKLLSSW	HAWKSBILLS	ABJMOPSTUU	JUMPS ABOUT
ABHIKMNOST	MONKS HABIT	ABKLLOOSST	BOOKSTALLS
ABHIKMRRST	BIRTHMARKS	ABKMOOOORS	BOOKS A ROOM
ABHIKNOTTU	THINK ABOUT	ABLLMOORTW	MORTAL BLOW
ABHILNRSTY	LABYRINTHS	ABLLOPSSWY	PLAYS BOWLS
ABHILOPSTY	HOSPITABLY	ABLMMOOSSY	MAY BLOSSOM
ABHILORRTY	ROYAL BIRTH	ABLOOPRTTT	PORT TALBOT
ABHINPRSTU	PAINTBRUSH	ABLOOPRTUW	PROWL ABOUT
ABHIIOOTTUW	HOW ABOUT IT?	ABMNOOOSTU	MOONS ABOUT
ABHJNNNOUY	JOHN BUNYAN	ABMNORRSST	BARNSTORMS
ABHLLMSTTU	THUMBSTALL	ABMOOORSTT	MOTORBOATS
ABHLMNORSS	SHORN LAMBS	ABMRRRUUYY	RUBY MURRAY
ABHOORTTUW	THROW ABOUT	ABMRSSTTUU	SUBSTRATUM
ABIIIKLLTY	LIKABILITY	ABNORSTTTU	BURNT TOAST
ABIIILLPTY	PLIABILITY	ABNORSTTUU	ABOUT-TURNS
ABIIILMNTY	INIMITABLY		TURNS ABOUT
ABIIINOSST	ANTIBIOSIS	ABOOPRSSTT	BOOTSTRAPS
ABIIJLNOTU	JUBILATION	ABOORSTTUU	ROUSTABOUT
ABIIILLLORS	SAILOR BILL	ACCCDIIIRT	CITRIC ACID
ABIILLMNOY	BINOMIALLY	ACCCDILORT	ARCTIC COLD
ABIILLMNSU	SUBLIMINAL	ACCCEEEKLS	ECCLES CAKE
ABIILLNOVY	INVIOLABLY	ACCCEEILNR	CAR LICENCE
ABIILLNSTY	SIBILANTLY	ACCCEFHKOR	COCKCHAFER
ABIILMPRTY	IMPARTIBLY	ACCCEHORTW	COWCATCHER
ABIILMPSSY	IMPASSIBLY	ACCCEHORUU	ACCOUCHEUR
ABIILMTTUY	MUTABILITY	ACCCEIIRST	CICATRICES
ABIILNORST	LIBRATIONS	ACCCEIKORT	COCKATRICE
ABIILNOTTY	NOTABILITY	ACCCEIKPRT	CRICKET CAP
ABIILOPRTY	BIPOLARITY	ACCCEILLNY	ENCYCLICAL

ACCCEILMOP	ACCOMPLICE
ACCCFOOOPU	CUP OF COCOA
ACCCGLNOOO	GONOCOCCAL
ACCCHKOPST	SPATCHCOCK
ACCCHOOTUU	CAOUTCHOUC
ACCCILLLYY	CYCLICALLY
ACCCINOPPU	CAPPUCCINO
ACCDDEEIRT	ACCREDITED
ACCDDEEIST	DESICCATED
ACCDDEIRRT	CREDIT CARD
ACCDEEHIST	CATECHISED
ACCDEEHITZ	CATECHIZED
ACCDEEHKMT	CHECKMATED
ACCDEEHNOR	ENCROACHED
ACCDEEHQRU	CHEQUE CARD
ACCDEEHSTU	THE ACCUSED
ACCDEEIILS	DELICACIES
ACCDEEINNS	INCANDESCE
ACCDEEIQSU	ACQUIESCED
ACCDEEISST	DESICCATES
ACCDEELPST	SPECTACLED
ACCDEELPTY	ACCEPTEDLY
ACCDEELRTY	TRADE CYCLE
ACCDEEMNOS	CAME SECOND
ACCDEENNST	CANDESCENT
ACCDEENNTU	UNACCENTED
ACCDEENSSY	DENY ACCESS
ACCDEFHKLO	HALF-COCKED
ACCDEFIIRS	SACRIFICED
ACCDEGHNOO	GOOD CHANCE
ACCDEGHNOS	DOGS CHANCE
ACCDEGLNOR	CLOG DANCER
ACCDEGLNOS	CLOG DANCES
ACCDEHIKRS	DECK CHAIRS
ACCDEHIORV	CRIED HAVOC
ACCDEHLNOY	CHALCEDONY
ACCDEIILNY	INDELICACY
ACCDEIILST	DIALECTICS
ACCDEIIOPT	APODEICTIC
ACCDEIIRST	CICATRISED
ACCDEIIRTZ	CICATRIZED
ACCDEIKLNW	CANDLEWICK
ACCDEILLOP	PECCADILLO
ACCDEILNOT	OCCIDENTAL
ACCDEILNTU	INCULCATED
ACCDEILOPY	CYCLOPEDIA
ACCDEILRTU	CIRCULATED
ACCDEIMNNY	MENDICANCY
ACCDEIMNSU	DANCE MUSIC
ACCDEIMORT	DEMOCRATIC
ACCDEINNTU	INDUCTANCE
ACCDEINOOS	OCCASIONED
ACCDEINSST	DESICCANTS
ACCDEIORST	DESICCATOR
ACCDEKORSU	SCORE A DUCK
ACCDELLOOT	COLLOCATED
ACCDELRSUY	ACCURSEDLY
ACCDEMNOOS	CACODEMONS
ACCDEMOSTU	ACCUSTOMED
ACCDENOOST	SECOND COAT
ACCDENORTT	CONTRACTED
ACCDEOPRST	CADET CORPS
ACCDEORRTU	CUT A RECORD
ACCDEORSTU	CORUSCATED
ACCDFIILTY	FLACCIDITY
ACCDFIIMOR	FORMIC ACID
ACCDFKLOOO	LOAD OF COCK
ACCDGHLOTU	CAUGHT COLD
ACCDGIOOTT	GOOD TACTIC
ACCDHHRRUY	CHURCHYARD
ACCDHIINOR	DIACHRONIC
ACCDHILNOO	CONCHOIDAL
ACCDHILORV	CLAVICHORD
ACCDHORSTW	CATCHWORDS
ACCDIIINRT	NITRIC ACID
ACCDIIIRST	DIACRITICS
ACCDIILSST	CLADISTICS
ACCDIKRRST	CARD TRICKS
ACCDINOORS	ACCORDIONS
ACCDINORTT	CONTRADICT
ACCDKLNOSS	COLD SNACKS
ACCDKNORSW	CRACKDOWNS
ACCDLOORSV	VOCAL CORDS
ACCDNNOORT	CONCORDANT
ACCDNOORST	CONCORDATS
ACCDORRSTU	COURT CARDS
ACCEEEEHKS	CHEESECAKE
ACCEEEFFKO	COFFEE CAKE
ACCEEEFRSS	FREE ACCESS
ACCEEEHNNV	EVEN CHANCE
ACCEEEHRTY	EYE-CATCHER
ACCEEELPRT	RECEPTACLE
ACCEEENNRS	RENASCENCE
ACCEEENPTX	EXPECTANCE
ACCEEGLMSY	MEGACYCLES
ACCEEHHSVY	CHEVY CHASE
ACCEEHILNP	ENCEPHALIC
ACCEEHINRS	CHANCERIES
ACCEEHIRST	CATECHISER
ACCEEHIRTZ	CATECHIZER
ACCEEHISST	CATECHISES
ACCEEHISTZ	CATECHIZES
ACCEEHKMST	CHECKMATES
ACCEEHKTTU	CUT THE CAKE
ACCEEHLNSS	CHANCELESS
ACCEEHMNTU	CATECHUMEN
ACCEEHNORS	ENCROACHES
ACCEEHNPRU	PURE CHANCE
ACCEEIILLRT	ELECTRICAL
ACCEEIILMNU	ECUMENICAL
ACCEEIILNPS	PENCIL CASE
ACCEEIILNTY	ACETYLENIC
ACCEEIILORV	CLEAR VOICE
	VARICOCELE
ACCEEIORSU	ERICACEOUS
ACCEEIQSSU	ACQUIESCES
ACCEEIRTUX	EXCRUCIATE
ACCEELLNRS	CANCELLERS
ACCEELMNOS	COMES CLEAN
ACCEELMORS	CAME CLOSER
ACCEELNORS	CONCEALERS
ACCEELNOSV	CONVALESCE
ACCEELNRTU	RELUCTANCE
ACCEELNSST	ACCENTLESS
ACCEELNSTU	CAULESCENT
ACCEELPSST	SPECTACLES
ACCEEMNOOT	COME AT ONCE
ACCEEMNRTU	ACCRUEMENT
ACCEEMORST	SOCCER TEAM
ACCEEMOSTY	ASCOMYCETE
ACCEENNOVY	CONVEYANCE
ACCEENOPRR	COPARCENER
ACCEENORST	CONSECRATE
ACCEENPTXY	EXPECTANCY
ACCEENRSSS	SCARCENESS
ACCEEOPPRS	PEACE CORPS
ACCEEORRSU	RACECOURSE
ACCEEORSTU	CRETACEOUS
ACCEEPRSTT	SECRET PACT
ACCEFFIINY	INEFFICACY
ACCEFFIITY	EFFICACITY
ACCEFHIIPT	THE PACIFIC

ACCEFHILST	CATCHFLIES	ACCEIINRST	CISTERCIAN
ACCEFHLOST	FACECLOTHS	ACCEIIPRST	ACCIPITERS
ACCEFHLRTY	FLYCATCHER	ACCEIIRSST	CICATRISES
ACCEFIIRRS	SACRIFICER	ACCEIIRSTZ	CICATRIZES
ACCEFIIRSS	SACRIFICES	ACCEIKKLPS	PLACEKICKS
ACCEFILLOR	CALCIFEROL	ACCEIKLNPS	PICKS CLEAN
ACCEFILRSU	FLEA CIRCUS	ACCEIKRSSW	WISECRACKS
ACCEFILSSU	FASCICULES	ACCEILLLRY	CLERICALLY
ACCEFINOST	CONFISCATE	ACCEILLNSY	SCENICALLY
ACCEFINPRY	FANCY PRICE	ACCEILMMOR	COMMERCIAL
ACCEFIRSUY	ICY SURFACE	ACCEILMNOO	ECONOMICAL
ACCEFKKOOS	SACK OF COKE	ACCEILMNOP	COMPLIANCE
ACCEFLLOTU	FLOCCULATE	ACCEILMOPT	COMPLICATE
ACCEFMORTY	ACT OF MERCY	ACCEILMOST	CACOMISTLE
ACCEGILLNN	CANCELLING	ACCEILNNOV	IN CONCLAVE
ACCEGILLNO	COLLAGENIC	ACCEILNOSS	NEOCLASSIC
ACCEGILLOO	ECOLOGICAL	ACCEILOPPT	APOPLECTIC
ACCEGILNNO	CONCEALING	ACCEILOPRR	RECIPROCAL
ACCEGILNOS	COALESCING	ACCEILORTU	CIRCULATES
ACCEGINNOR	CARCINOGEN	ACCEIMOOPR	COMIC OPERA
ACCEGINNOS	COGNISANCE	ACCEINNNOV	CONNIVANCE
ACCEGINNOZ	COGNIZANCE	ACCEINNOPR	COPERNICAN
ACCEGKORRS	GO CRACKERS	ACCEINNORT	CONCERTINA
ACCEHHMSST	CHESS MATCH	ACCEINNSSY	INCESSANCY
ACCEHHOORS	COACH HORSE	ACCEINORST	ACCRETIONS
ACCEHHOOSU	COACH HOUSE	ACCEINOSSS	ACCESSIONS
ACCEHIILMR	CHIMERICAL	ACCEINRRTT	ARCTIC TERN
ACCEHIINNT	TECHNICIAN	ACCEIOPPSY	EPISCOPACY
ACCEHIKPRT	CHEAP TRICK	ACCEIORTUY	EUCARYOTIC
ACCEHILLMY	CHEMICALLY	ACCEJKOPSY	JOCKEYS CAP
ACCEHILLTY	HECTICALLY	ACCEKLNOSS	CLEAN SOCKS
ACCEHILMNS	SLIM CHANCE	ACCEKLORTW	WATER CLOCK
ACCEHILNOS	COCHINEALS	ACCEKNOPRS	CRACKS OPEN
ACCEHIMNSS	MISCHANCES	ACCEKNORRS	CORNCRAKES
ACCEHIMSST	CATECHISMS	ACCEKNRRTU	NUTCRACKER
ACCEHINNRY	IN CHANCERY	ACCELLNOSU	CANCELLOUS
ACCEHINNSS	CHANCINESS	ACCELLOOST	COLLOCATES
ACCEHIORSV	CRIES HAVOC	ACCELLORRT	ALL CORRECT
ACCEHIORTT	THEOCRATIC	ACCELLSSUU	CALCULUSES
ACCEHIPSTY	ICY PATCHES	ACCELMNOPT	COMPLACENT
ACCEHIRRST	SCRATCHIER	ACCELMOPRS	CAMEL CORPS
ACCEHIRRTT	TETRARCHIC	ACCELNOOPY	CAPE COLONY
ACCEHIRSTT	ARCHITECTS	ACCELNOPTU	CONCEPTUAL
ACCEHISSTT	CATECHISTS	ACCELNOSTU	CANCELS OUT
ACCEHKKSTU	CHUCK STEAK	ACCELOORSV	VOCAL SCORE
ACCEHKLOST	SCOTCH KALE	ACCELOPRSY	PLAY SOCCER
ACCEHKPTTU	CUT THE PACK	ACCEMMNNOY	NECROMANCY
ACCEHLLNOR	CHANCELLOR	ACCEMOORSS	COME ACROSS
ACCEHLMOST	CLOSE MATCH	ACCENNNOOS	CONSONANCE
ACCEHLNNOY	ONLY CHANCE	ACCENOPRRU	PROCURANCE
ACCEHLNOST	LOST CHANCE	ACCENORRTU	CUT A CORNER
ACCEHLOOST	CHOCOLATES	ACCENORTTU	COUNTERACT
ACCEHLOSTW	CLOSE WATCH	ACCENRSUVY	CYRUS VANCE
ACCEHMNSTT	CATCHMENTS	ACCEORRSSW	SCARECROWS
ACCEHMPSTU	CUP MATCHES	ACCEORSSTU	CORUSCATES
ACCEHNNPTY	CATCHPENNY	ACCEORSUUV	CURVACEOUS
ACCEHNNRTY	TRENCHANCY	ACCEPRSSTU	CUTS CAPERS
ACCEHNOOPR	POOR CHANCE	ACCFFFFHHI	CHIFFCHAFF
ACCEHNORTT	TECHNOCRAT	ACCFFHORST	SCRATCH OFF
	TRENCH COAT	ACCFFIOPRT	TRAFFIC COP
ACCEHNOSTT	NEAT SCOTCH	ACCFGIILNY	CALCIFYING
ACCEHNTTUY	CATCHY TUNE	ACCFGMOOOU	MUG OF COCOA
ACCEHORSTU	CARTOUCHES	ACCFHIMORY	COMFY CHAIR
ACCEHOSTTU	CATCHES OUT	ACCFHIRTTW	WITCHCRAFT
ACCEHRRSST	SCRATCHERS	ACCFILSSUU	FASCICULUS
ACCEIILNOT	CONCILIATE	ACCFINNOSU	CONFUCIANS
ACCEIILSSS	CLASSICISE	ACCFINOOUT	TIN OF COCOA
ACCEIILSSZ	CLASSICIZE	ACCFKNOORS	SACK OF CORN
ACCEIIMRST	CERAMICIST	ACCFLLNOOY	CONFOCALLY
ACCEIIMSST	ASCETICISM	ACCFLLNOTU	FLOCCULANT
ACCEIINPRT	IN PRACTICE	ACCGHHISTT	CATCH SIGHT

ACCGHIILOR	OLIGARCHIC	ACCILNORUW	WAR COUNCIL
ACCGHIINNT	CHANCING IT	ACCILORRTU	CIRCULATOR
ACCGHIINTT	CATCHING IT	ACCILRRRUU	CURRICULAR
ACCGHIMOTU	MAGIC TOUCH	ACCIMNOOPR	MONOCARPIC
ACCGHINNOT	CATCHING ON	ACCIMNOOPT	COMPACTION
ACCGHINPTU	CATCHING UP	ACCIMORSSY	COSMIC RAYS
ACCGHINRST	SCRATCHING	ACCINNOOOS	ON OCCASION
ACCGHIOPTY	PHAGOCYTIC	ACCINNORTT	CONTRACT IN
ACCGHORSSU	COUCH GRASS	ACCINOOPRU	CORNUCOPIA
ACCGIIKMRT	MAGIC TRICK	ACCINOOPTU	OCCUPATION
ACCGIIMORT	TRAGICOMIC	ACCINOPRRS	CAPRICORNS
ACCGIKNPRU	CRACKING UP	ACCINOPRSY	CONSPIRACY
ACCGILNSUY	ACCUSINGLY	ACCINSSTTY	SYNTACTICS
ACCGIMNOPT	COMPACTING	ACCKKNOOOS	COCK A SNOOK
ACCGINNOTT	CONTACTING	ACCKMPRSTU	STRUCK CAMP
ACCGINNOTU	ACCOUNTING	ACCKOORSTY	ROCKY COAST
ACCHHIILLN	CHINCHILLA	ACCKOPSSTU	SCOUT PACKS
ACCHHMRRUY	CHURCH ARMY	ACCLOPRTUY	PLUTOCRACY
ACCHHORSST	CROSSHATCH	ACCMOOPRST	COMPACTORS
ACCHIIILST	CHILIASTIC	ACCNOORRTT	CONTRACTOR
ACCHIIMSST	SCHISMATIC	ACCORSSSTU	CUTS ACROSS
ACCHIINORT	ANCHORITIC	ACDDDEEILO	LOADED DICE
ACCHIKMQRU	QUICK MARCH	ACDDDEELLP	PADDED CELL
ACCHIKMSTT	MATCHSTICK	ACDDDEIOPT	DOPE ADDICT
ACCHILLOOS	ALCOHOLICS	ACDDDEORWY	CROWDED DAY
ACCHILMOPS	ACCOMPLISH	ACDDDGIRTU	DRUG ADDICT
ACCHILNNPS	SPLANCHNIC	ACDDDKLNOU	DONALD DUCK
ACCHILNOOT	CATHOLICON	ACDDEEEKNU	DUNDEE CAKE
ACCHILOSST	SCHOLASTIC	ACDDEEENRT	DEAD CENTRE
ACCHIMNORY	CHIROMANCY	ACDDEEEPRT	DEPRECATED
ACCHIOPRSZ	SCHIZOCARP	ACDDEEERST	DESECRATED
ACCHIOPTTY	HYPOTACTIC	ACDDEEERTU	REEDUCATED
ACCHIOSSTT	STOCHASTIC	ACDDEEFNTU	FECUNDATED
ACCHKLMOST	MATCHLOCKS	ACDDEEGGIL	GILDED CAGE
ACCHKLMRUY	LUCKY CHARM	ACDDEEHLOO	COOLHEADED
ACCHKLPPUY	PLUCKY CHAP	ACDDEEHLRS	HELD SACRED
ACCHKLPTUY	LUCKY PATCH	ACDDEEHLTY	DETACHEDLY
ACCHNOPSYY	SYCOPHANCY	ACDDEEHPST	DESPATCHED
ACCHNORRST	CORNSTARCH	ACDDEEIITV	DEDICATIVE
ACCHOPRSST	CROSSPATCH	ACDDEEILPY	PLAYED DICE
ACCHORSTTU	SCRATCH OUT	ACDDEEILTU	ELUCIDATED
ACCIIILLLP	PICCALILLI	ACDDEEINNP	DID PENANCE
ACCIIILNNS	CLINICIANS	ACDDEEIPRT	PREDICATED
ACCIIISTTV	ACTIVISTIC	ACDDEELLSY	CLYDESDALE
ACCIIILLNY	CLINICALLY	ACDDEELNRY	DRY CLEANED
ACCIIILNOY	ICONICALLY		DRY-CLEANED
ACCIIILRTY	CRITICALLY	ACDDEELNTY	DECADENTLY
ACCIILMNOS	LACONICISM	ACDDEELTUY	EDUCATEDLY
ACCIILMSSS	CLASSICISM	ACDDEENNST	DESCENDANT
ACCIILNNOT	CALCITONIN	ACDDEENRTU	UNDERACTED
ACCIILNRTU	UNCRITICAL	ACDDEENTUU	UNEDUCATED
ACCIILSSST	CLASSICIST	ACDDEFFHNU	HANDCUFFED
ACCIIMNRSU	MUSCARINIC	ACDDEFFIRT	DIFFRACTED
ACCIIMORTT	TIMOCRATIC	ACDDEGHIRS	DISCHARGED
ACCIINNNPY	PICCANINNY	ACDDEGIINT	DEDICATING
ACCIINNOTY	CANONICITY	ACDDEGIOOV	GOOD ADVICE
ACCIIOPRSU	CAPRICIOUS	ACDDEGMORS	DODGEM CARS
ACCIIRRSTT	ART CRITICS	ACDDEGNOOS	DODECAGONS
ACCIISTTUW	CAUSTIC WIT	ACDDEHIKNP	HANDPICKED
ACCIISTTUY	CAUSTICITY	ACDDEHINSW	SANDWICHED
ACCIKKKKNN	KNICK-KNACK	ACDDEHIPST	DISPATCHED
ACCIKKLOPS	PICKS A LOCK	ACDDEHIRSV	CRASH-DIVED
ACCIKKNQSU	QUICK SNACK	ACDDEHLLRY	CHERYL LADD
ACCIKOQTTU	QUICK TO ACT	ACDDEHLORS	HOLD SACRED
ACCILLMOSY	COSMICALLY	ACDDEHNNOS	SECOND HAND
ACCILLORTY	CORTICALLY		SECONDHAND
ACCILLRRUY	CIRCULARLY	ACDDEIILMS	DISCLAIMED
ACCILMNOOS	ICONOCLASM	ACDDEIINOT	DEDICATION
ACCILMOSUV	VOCAL MUSIC	ACDDEIINTV	VINDICATED
ACCILNOOST	ICONOCLAST	ACDDEIINVW	CANDID VIEW
ACCILNORTU	INCULCATOR	ACDDEILMOU	DUODECIMAL

ACDDEILORU	CRIED ALOUD	ACDEEFGINT	DEFECATING
ACDDEILOST	DISLOCATED	ACDEEFIINN	IN DEFIANCE
ACDDEILPTU	DUPLICATED	ACDEEFINOT	DEFECATION
ACDDEINNSS	CANDIDNESS	ACDEEFINPS	FINDS PEACE
ACDDEINSTY	SYNDICATED	ACDEEFINRT	INTERFACED
ACDDEIORST	DEDICATORS	ACDEEFKOPR	POKER-FACED
ACDDEIORTY	DEDICATORY	ACDEEFLNOR	CONFEDERAL
ACDDEIRSTT	DISTRACTED	ACDEEFLORS	FORCED SALE
ACDDEKLLNO	LANDLOCKED	ACDEEFMORR	ARMED FORCE
ACDDEKLORS	DREADLOCKS	ACDEEFNOPU	FOUND PEACE
ACDDELLTUY	DUTY CALLED	ACDEEFNSTU	FECUNDATES
ACDDELMNOW	CALMED DOWN	ACDEEFOPRW	FACE POWDER
ACDDELNNOO	COLONNADED	ACDEEFORST	FORECASTED
ACDDELNOOW	CANDLEWOOD	ACDEEGGHOP	POACHED EGG
ACDDELNOSW	SCALED DOWN	ACDEEGHIRS	DISCHARGEE
ACDDENNORU	ROUND DANCE	ACDEEGHLLN	CHALLENGED
ACDDENNRUY	REDUNDANCY	ACDEEGHNNS	CHANGE ENDS
ACDDENORSW	SWORD DANCE	ACDEEGIIVV	GIVE ADVICE
ACDDEOOPSU	DECAPODOUS	ACDEEGINNR	GRANDNIECE
ACDDFHIORU	CHAUDFROID	ACDEEGINRR	ADRENERGIC
ACDDFIILMT	FILM ADDICT	ACDEEGINRS	DECREASING
ACDDGHILNR	GRANDCHILD	ACDEEGINRT	CENTIGRADE
ACDDGHNRUY	GRAND DUCHY	ACDEEGIRTV	GAVE CREDIT
ACDDGIINRS	DISCARDING	ACDEEGNOPS	SECOND PAGE
ACDDHHNSSU	DACHSHUNDS	ACDEEGNORS	SECOND GEAR
ACDDHLNOOT	HOT AND COLD	ACDEEGNORU	ENCOURAGED
ACDDIINOST	ADDICTIONS	ACDEEGOPSU	DECOUPAGES
ACDDINORST	DISCORDANT	ACDEEGORRT	RECORD GATE
ACDDINOSTU	ADDUCTIONS	AODCCIIILNR	CHANDELIER
ACDDKLORSU	DARK CLOUDS	ACDEEHIMNS	MECHANISED
ACDDLOORSU	ADDS COLOUR	ACDEEHIMNZ	MECHANIZED
ACDDLOORTY	LADY DOCTOR	ACDEEHIMRS	CHILD SHAME
ACDEEEEHHS	CHEESEHEAD	ACDEEHINOS	ON EACH SIDE
	HEADCHEESE	ACDEEHIORS	ICOSEHEDRA
ACDEEEEHMS	EDAM CHEESE	ACDEEHKLLS	SHELLACKED
AODCCEELNT	DECELERATE	ACDEEHLNRW	D H LAWRENCE
ACDEEEEPRS	PREDECEASE	ACDEEHLORT	CLOTH-EARED
ACDEEEFHNT	FACE THE END	ACDEEHLRRU	HURDLE RACE
ACDEEEFHTT	FEED THE CAT	ACDEEHLSTT	CATTLE SHED
ACDEEEFINR	AIR DEFENCE	ACDEEHMMSS	MAD SCHEMES
ACDEEEFIRS	CEASED FIRE	ACDEEHMNTT	DETACHMENT
ACDEEEFIRV	FREE ADVICE	ACDEEHNOPR	CHAPERONED
ACDEEEFLNR	FER-DE-LANCE	ACDEEHNOST	SECOND HEAT
	FREELANCED	ACDEEHNRRI	HARD CENTRE
ACDEEEFLRS	FALSE CREED	ACDEEHOPRR	REPROACHED
ACDEEEFMNT	DEFACEMENT	ACDEEHORTU	OUTREACHED
ACDEEEGNRY	DEGENERACY		REACHED OUT
ACDEEEHHRS	HARD CHEESE	ACDEEHPSST	DESPATCHES
ACDEEEHIPS	HEADPIECES	ACDEEHRRST	THREE CARDS
ACDEEEHLTT	DECATHLETE	ACDEEIILMP	EPIDEMICAL
ACDEEEHNST	DEATH SCENE	ACDEEIILMS	DECIMALISE
ACDEEEHRRS	RESEARCHED	ACDEEIILMZ	DECIMALIZE
ACDEEEIKSV	SEEK ADVICE	ACDEEIILNN	IN A DECLINE
ACDEEEILRV	CLEVER IDEA	ACDEEIILNT	INDELICATE
ACDEEEIPRT	DEPRECIATE	ACDEEIIMNS	CAME INSIDE
ACDEEEKNPP	KNEECAPPED	ACDEEIJSTV	ADJECTIVES
ACDEEELNTU	ENUCLEATED	ACDEEIKRTT	TAKE CREDIT
ACDEEELSTT	TELECASTED	ACDEEILLMT	CALLED TIME
ACDEEEMNOS	COME AND SEE	ACDEEILLNP	LEAD PENCIL
ACDEEENNTT	ANTECEDENT	ACDEEILLNR	CINDERELLA
ACDEEENRRT	TENDER CARE	ACDEEILLPR	CALLIPERED
ACDEEENRTT	RECENT DATE	ACDEEILLRS	ESCADRILLE
ACDEEEPRST	DEPRECATES	ACDEEILLTY	DELICATELY
ACDEEERSST	DESECRATES	ACDEEILMRS	DECLAIMERS
ACDEEERSTU	REEDUCATES	ACDEEILMRV	DECEMVIRAL
ACDEEFFHIO	HEAD OFFICE	ACDEEILNNS	CELANDINES
ACDEEFFHRT	FARFETCHED	ACDEEILNOR	COIN DEALER
ACDEEFFLOR	CLEARED OFF	ACDEEILNPW	WIPED CLEAN
ACDEEFFLTY	AFFECTEDLY	ACDEEILNRS	ICELANDERS
ACDEEFFNTU	UNAFFECTED	ACDEEILNRT	CREDENTIAL
ACDEEFGIMO	GAME OF DICE		INTERLACED

ACDEEILPPR	CIDER APPLE
ACDEEILPPY	PIPE-CLAYED
ACDEEILPRT	REPLICATED
ACDEEILPTX	EXPLICATED
ACDEEILRST	DECALITRES
ACDEEILSTU	ELUCIDATES
ACDEEIMMNN	MICE AND MEN
ACDEEIMMNT	MEDICAMENT
	MINCED MEAT
ACDEEIMNOS	MACEDOINES
ACDEEIMNPS	IMPEDANCES
ACDEEIMPRT	IMPRECATED
ACDEEIMRST	MISCREATED
ACDEEIMRTT	METRICATED
ACDEEINNTU	ENUNCIATED
ACDEEINOTV	ADVICE NOTE
ACDEEINPPS	APPENDICES
ACDEEINRTT	INTERACTED
ACDEEINSST	DESISTANCE
ACDEEIORTV	DECORATIVE
ACDEEIORTX	EXCORIATED
ACDEEIOTTX	DETOXICATE
ACDEEIPRRT	TRADE PRICE
ACDEEIPRST	PEDERASTIC
	PREDICATES
ACDEEIPRTT	CREPITATED
ACDEEIRRST	SACRED RITE
ACDEEIRSTU	CAUTERISED
ACDEEIRTTV	DETRACTIVE
ACDEEIRTTX	EXTRICATED
ACDEEIRTUZ	CAUTERIZED
ACDEEITTUX	EXACTITUDE
ACDEEKLOSV	DOCK LEAVES
ACDEEKMOOT	COOKED MEAT
ACDEEKMRSY	ASKED MERCY
ACDEEKRRST	DARK SECRET
ACDEELLLPW	WELL PLACED
ACDEELLMOS	SCALE MODEL
ACDEELLORV	CALLED OVER
	OVERCALLED
ACDEELLOSV	LEAVES COLD
ACDEELMORT	ECTODERMAL
ACDEELMRTU	CRUDE METAL
ACDEELNOST	ADOLESCENT
ACDEELNOTU	CLEANED OUT
ACDEELNRRY	DRY CLEANER
ACDEELOPRT	PERCOLATED
ACDEELORRS	RECORD SALE
ACDEELORRT	CORRELATED
ACDEELORSS	CASSEROLED
ACDEELORTU	CLEARED OUT
ACDEELPRSY	CLEPSYDRAE
ACDEELPSTU	SPECULATED
ACDEELPTUX	EXCULPATED
ACDEELRRSW	ARC WELDERS
ACDEELRRTT	LETTER CARD
ACDEEMMNOR	COMMANDEER
ACDEEMMNPT	DECAMPMENT
ACDEEMNNOS	SECOND NAME
ACDEEMNNOU	CAME UNDONE
ACDEEMNORV	DEVON CREAM
ACDEEMNOST	SECOND MATE
	SECOND TEAM
ACDEEMNRRY	MERRY DANCE
ACDEEMRRSU	MURDER CASE
ACDEEMRRTU	ARMED TRUCE
ACDEENNOST	CONDENSATE
ACDEENNOTV	COVENANTED
ACDEENNRSU	ENDURANCES
ACDEENOPRR	ROPEDANCER

ACDEENORST	DOESN'T CARE
	SECOND RATE
	SECOND-RATE
ACDEENORSY	SECOND YEAR
ACDEENRSSS	SACREDNESS
ACDEENRSSV	SEVEN CARDS
ACDEENRSTT	STAND ERECT
	TRANSECTED
ACDEEOOPRT	COOPERATED
ACDEEOORST	SEE A DOCTOR
ACDEEOPRRT	PROCREATED
	TAPE-RECORD
ACDEEOPRRY	COPYREADER
ACDEEORRST	DESECRATOR
	SET A RECORD
ACDEEORVWY	COVERED WAY
ACDEEPRRTU	RECAPTURED
ACDEFFGLNO	GLANCED OFF
ACDEFFHMOR	MARCHED OFF
ACDEFFIIOT	OFFICIATED
ACDEFFIKRT	TRAFFICKED
ACDEFFIORR	CARRIED OFF
ACDEFFISST	DISAFFECTS
ACDEFFKLOS	SLACKED OFF
ACDEFFLOTU	DUFFEL COAT
ACDEFFOPRS	SCRAPED OFF
ACDEFFOSTU	SUFFOCATED
ACDEFGHIRT	FACED RIGHT
ACDEFGLLNO	GOLDEN CALF
ACDEFHHILN	HALF-INCHED
ACDEFHINRS	FRANCHISED
ACDEFHLNOS	SECOND HALF
ACDEFHNORT	FACED NORTH
ACDEFHOSTU	FACED SOUTH
ACDEFHOSUV	VOUCHSAFED
ACDEFIIIRS	ACIDIFIERS
ACDEFIILSS	CLASSIFIED
ACDEFIIMRV	FIRM ADVICE
ACDEFIINST	SANCTIFIED
ACDEFIIRRT	FRATRICIDE
ACDEFIJKKN	JACKKNIFED
ACDEFILLOS	COAL FIELDS
	COALFIELDS
	SLICED LOAF
ACDEFILSSY	DECLASSIFY
ACDEFIMORT	COME ADRIFT
ACDEFINORT	FORNICATED
ACDEFIORST	FACTORISED
ACDEFIORTZ	FACTORIZED
ACDEFKLNOR	FOLK DANCER
ACDEFKLNOS	FOLK DANCES
ACDEFLMORS	COLD FRAMES
ACDEFLNORS	FORCE-LANDS
	LAND FORCES
ACDEFLOOPS	DOSE OF CLAP
ACDEFLOOSY	CLOSE OF DAY
ACDEFLOOTT	CATTLE FOOD
ACDEFLORTU	CUT FOR DEAL
ACDEFLTTUU	FLUCTUATED
ACDEFNRSSY	FANCY DRESS
ACDEFORTUY	DUTY OF CARE
ACDEGGIOPS	PEDAGOGICS
ACDEGGOORS	GOOD GRACES
ACDEGGRSTU	EGG CUSTARD
ACDEGHILLN	ANGEL CHILD
ACDEGHINRT	DIG A TRENCH
ACDEGHIRRS	DISCHARGER
ACDEGHIRSS	DISCHARGES
ACDEGHLLOR	GRALLOCHED
ACDEGHNNOW	CHANGE DOWN
ACDEGHNRTU	DUG A TRENCH

ACDEGHOSTW	DOGWATCHES	ACDEHNORST	ON THE CARDS
ACDEGHRRSU	SURCHARGED	ACDEHNORSZ	SCHERZANDO
ACDEGIILLS	GALLICISED	ACDEHNOSTU	COUNT HEADS
ACDEGIILLZ	GALLICIZED	ACDEHNPSTU	SNATCHED UP
ACDEGIILMN	DECLAIMING	ACDEHOPTTW	WATCHED POT
ACDEGIILMR	GERMICIDAL	ACDEHORRTT	TETRACHORD
ACDEGIILNS	ANGLICISED	ACDEHORSSS	CROSSHEADS
ACDEGIILNZ	ANGLICIZED	ACDEHORSTT	DO A STRETCH
ACDEGIIMNT	DECIMATING	ACDEHOTTUW	WATCHED OUT
	MEDICATING	ACDEHRTTTU	DUTCH TREAT
ACDEGIIMOR	IDEOGRAMIC	ACDEIIILST	IDEALISTIC
ACDEGIINOR	RADIOGENIC		ITALICISED
ACDEGIINRS	IN DISGRACE	ACDEIIILTZ	ITALICIZED
ACDEGILNRW	ARC-WELDING	ACDEIIINST	DIETICIANS
ACDEGILRTT	CATTLE GRID	ACDEIIINTV	INDICATIVE
ACDEGIMMRS	SCRIMMAGED	ACDEIIJKNT	JACKED IT IN
ACDEGINNOR	ANDROGENIC	ACDEIIKNNS	DICKENSIAN
ACDEGINNST	DESCANTING	ACDEIIKNPT	PACKED IT IN
ACDEGINORR	CORRIGENDA	ACDEIILLOT	IDIOLEOTAL
ACDEGINORT	DECORATING	ACDEIILMMT	DILEMMATIC
ACDEGINOTU	ACID TONGUE	ACDEIILMPT	IMPLICATED
ACDEGINRTT	DETRACTING	ACDEIILMRS	DISCLAIMER
ACDEGINRTY	GARDEN CITY	ACDEIILNNT	INCIDENTAL
ACDEGINRWY	WENDY CRAIG	ACDEIILNOS	DECISIONAL
ACDEGINSUY	DYING CAUSE	ACDEIILOPR	PERIODICAL
ACDEGIORSU	DISCOURAGE		POLICE RAID
ACDEGIRRST	CARTRIDGES	ACDEIILOSS	SOCIALISED
ACDEGJNOTU	CONJUGATED	ACDEIILOSZ	SOCIALIZED
ACDEGKLOOT	GOOD TACKLE	ACDEIILRSV	LARVICIDES
ACDEGKNORR	ROCK GARDEN	ACDEIILTWY	TWICE DAILY
ACDEGKORRT	TRACKER DOG	ACDEIIMNOT	DECIMATION
ACDEGLNNRU	GRANDUNCLE		MEDICATION
ACDEGLNORS	CRADLE SONG	ACDEIIMNRT	CRIMINATED
ACDEGLNORU	CLANGOURED	ACDEIIMNTV	ACTIVE MIND
ACDEGLORRW	LARGE CROWD	ACDEIIMPRU	EPICARDIUM
ACDEGMMRSU	SCRUMMAGED	ACDEIIMRRS	MISCARRIED
ACDEGORRTU	CORRUGATED	ACDEIIMRST	MATRICIDES
ACDEHHIKST	THICKHEADS	ACDEIIMRTX	TAXIDERMIC
ACDEHIIINR	ENCHIRIDIA	ACDEIINNRY	INCENDIARY
ACDEHIIMRT	DIATHERMIC	ACDEIINSTV	VINDICATES
ACDEHIIORR	DIARRHOEIC	ACDEIIORSU	IRIDACEOUS
ACDEHILMOT	METHODICAL	ACDEIIOSST	DISSOCIATE
ACDEHILNPR	HARD PENCIL	ACDEIIPRRS	PARRICIDES
ACDEHILPRT	THIRD PLACE	ACDEIIPRST	PATRICIDES
ACDEHIMMST	MISMATCHED	ACDEIJNTUV	ADJUNCTIVE
ACDEHIMNOP	CHAMPIONED	ACDEIJRTUU	JUDICATURE
ACDEHIMORT	DICHROMATE	ACDEIKNORT	DONE A TRICK
ACDEHINNRS	HINDRANCES	ACDEIKOOTV	TOOK ADVICE
ACDEHINNST	DISENCHANT	ACDEIKORST	DOES A TRICK
ACDEHINOPT	DICTAPHONE	ACDEIKPPTU	PACKED IT UP
ACDEHINSSW	SANDWICHES	ACDEIKRSST	SIDETRACKS
ACDEHIOPRS	HARD COPIES	ACDEILLMOT	COLLIMATED
ACDEHIORRR	RICHARD ROE	ACDEILLORR	CORDILLERA
ACDEHIORST	SCORED A HIT	ACDEILLOST	OSCILLATED
ACDEHIPRST	DISPATCHER	ACDEILLTUV	VICTUALLED
ACDEHIPSST	DISPATCHES	ACDEILMNOP	COMPLAINED
ACDEHIRRRW	RICH REWARD	ACDEILMNTU	CULMINATED
ACDEHIRSSV	CRASH-DIVES	ACDEILMOPR	PROCLAIMED
ACDEHIRTTW	DITCH WATER	ACDEILMRTY	DRY CLIMATE
ACDEHKLNSU	UNSHACKLED	ACDEILNNRU	CUNARD LINE
ACDEHLNOST	DECATHLONS	ACDEILNORT	CENTROIDAL
ACDEHLOOPP	CEPHALOPOD	ACDEILNOTU	INOCULATED
ACDEHLORRT	RATHER COLD	ACDEILNPSS	PLACIDNESS
ACDEHLORST	COLD HEARTS	ACDEILNPTU	INCULPATED
ACDEHLORTW	THE COLD WAR	ACDEILNSUV	VULCANISED
ACDEHLOUVY	HEAVY CLOUD	ACDEILNUVZ	VULCANIZED
ACDEHMNOOT	COME TO HAND	ACDEILORRW	COWARDLIER
ACDEHMNORY	HAD NO MERCY	ACDEILORST	DO ARTICLES
ACDEHMOTTU	OUTMATCHED	ACDEILORSU	CRIES ALOUD
ACDEHMPRSY	PACHYDERMS	ACDEILORSW	OSCAR WILDE
ACDEHNOORT	OCTAHEDRON	ACDEILORTU	ELUCIDATOR

ACDEILORVW	DIVORCE LAW
ACDEILOSST	DISLOCATES
ACDEILOTTU	COLATITUDE
ACDEILPSSU	CAPSULISED
ACDEILPSTU	DUPLICATES
ACDEILPSUZ	CAPSULIZED
ACDEILRTTW	WILDCATTER
ACDEILTTUV	CULTIVATED
ACDEIMMORY	IMMODERACY
ACDEIMNNST	MENDICANTS
ACDEIMNORU	ANDROECIUM
ACDEIMNOSU	MENDACIOUS
ACDEIMNSSU	MUSCADINES
ACDEIMOPRR	MADREPORIC
ACDEIMPPTU	CAMPED IT UP
ACDEIMQRSU	CRIME SQUAD
ACDEIMRSSU	READS MUSIC
ACDEIMRTTU	MICTURATED
ACDEINNORS	ORDINANCES
ACDEINNOSS	DISSONANCE
ACDEINNOST	NO DISTANCE
	SANCTIONED
ACDEINNOSW	SNOW AND ICE
ACDEINNRSS	RANCIDNESS
ACDEINOORT	CAROTENOID
	COORDINATE
	DECORATION
ACDEINOOTT	DO IT AT ONCE
ACDEINORRW	CORDWAINER
ACDEINORST	DESCRATION
ACDEINORTT	DETRACTION
ACDEINOSTT	ANECDOTIST
ACDEINOSTU	EDUCATIONS
ACDEINOSTV	ADVECTIONS
ACDEINOSWX	COXSWAINED
ACDEINOTTX	DETOXICANT
ACDEINPRST	DISCREPANT
ACDEINSSTY	SYNDICATES
ACDEIOPRSU	PREDACIOUS
ACDEIORRTU	CARRIED OUT
ACDEIORSST	OSTRACISED
ACDEIORSTZ	OSTRACIZED
ACDEIPQRSU	QUADRICEPS
ACDEIPRSTU	CUSTARD PIE
ACDEIRRRSV	CAR DRIVERS
ACDEIRRSTW	SACRED WRIT
ACDEIRSSTU	CRASSITUDE
ACDEIRSTTU	RUSTICATED
ACDEITTUVY	ACTIVE DUTY
ACDEJKPRUY	PACKED JURY
ACDEJKSTTU	DUST JACKET
ACDEKKLNOY	LOCK AND KEY
ACDEKKMOPR	POCKMARKED
ACDEKMNOOR	CROOKED MAN
ACDEKMORST	DOCK MASTER
ACDEKNORRR	DARK CORNER
ACDEKNORRY	ROCK AND RYE
ACDELLNOPU	CALLED UPON
ACDELLOOPY	PLAYED COOL
ACDELLORWY	YELLOW CARD
ACDELNNOOS	COLONNADES
ACDELNNOOY	CONAN DOYLE
ACDELNOORS	COLD REASON
ACDELNOORW	NOEL COWARD
ACDELNOOSS	COLD SEASON
ACDELNOOSW	LANCEWOODS
ACDELNORRU	CLEAR ROUND
ACDELNOSSW	SCALES DOWN
ACDELNPRUU	PEDUNCULAR
ACDELOORST	STOOD CLEAR
ACDELOPPTU	CLAPPED OUT

ACDELOPRRU	PROCEDURAL
ACDELORTYY	DOYLY CARTE
ACDELOSSTU	OUTCLASSED
ACDELPRSSY	CLEPSYDRAS
ACDEMMNOOS	COMMANDOES
ACDEMMNORS	COMMANDERS
ACDEMMOSTU	CUSTOM-MADE
ACDEMNNOTW	CAMDEN TOWN
ACDEMOORST	MOTORCADES
ACDEMOOSTY	DAYS TO COME
ACDEMOPRSU	DAMP COURSE
ACDENNNOOR	ORDONNANCE
ACDENNRSST	TRANSCENDS
ACDENOPPSW	SNOWCAPPED
ACDENOPRST	SECOND PART
ACDENOPSTY	SYNCOPATED
ACDENORRSU	SCORED A RUN
ACDENORRSY	RED CRAYONS
ACDENORSTT	CONTRASTED
ACDENORSTU	UNDERCOATS
ACDENPTTUU	PUNCTUATED
ACDENRRRTU	RED CURRANT
	REDCURRANT
ACDENRRSTU	TRANSDUCER
ACDENRSTTU	REDUCTANTS
ACDEOORRST	DECORATORS
ACDEOORRVW	WOOD CARVER
ACDEOPRRRT	REPORT CARD
ACDEOPRRST	PAST RECORD
ACDEOPRRTT	PROTRACTED
ACDEOPRSUU	DRUPACEOUS
ACDEORRRSW	WAR RECORDS
ACDEORRSTT	DETRACTORS
ACDEORRSTY	SCORED A TRY
ACDFFKLOOO	LACK OF FOOD
ACDFGIIINY	ACIDIFYING
ACDFGIILNU	FUNGICIDAL
ACDFGNOOSY	FANCY GOODS
ACDFIILLUY	FIDUCIALLY
ACDFIKNNOR	CAN OF DRINK
ACDFILOSST	SOLID FACTS
ACDFINNOST	CONFIDANTS
ACDFIRSTTU	CUTS ADRIFT
ACDFLLOTUY	CALL OF DUTY
ACDFLNOSSY	CANDY FLOSS
ACDFNSTTUY	CANDYTUFTS
ACDFOORSTW	WOODCRAFTS
ACDGGIIINRS	DISGRACING
ACDGHHLOTU	CAUGHT HOLD
ACDGHNOOTU	TOUCH AND GO
ACDGIIINNT	INDICATING
ACDGIILNPS	DISPLACING
ACDGIINNST	DISTANCING
ACDGIINORT	RIDING COAT
ACDGIINOST	DIAGNOSTIC
ACDGIKNOST	STOCKADING
ACDGILNNOO	CANOODLING
ACDGIMMNNO	COMMANDING
ACDGIMORSW	MAGIC SWORD
	MAGIC WORDS
ACDGLLOORS	DOG COLLARS
ACDGLOTYYZ	ZYGODACTYL
ACDHHILPPY	HAPPY CHILD
ACDHIIIOPT	IDIOPATHIC
ACDHILLLMS	SMALL CHILD
ACDHILLPSY	CHILDS PLAY
ACDHILRSST	THIRD CLASS
	THIRD-CLASS
ACDHILRSSY	CHRYSALIDS
ACDHILRSUY	HYDRAULICS
ACDHIMNRSW	MARCH WINDS

ACDHIMORST	CHROMATIDS	ACDLLMORSW	SMALL CROWD
ACDHIMOSTU	MIDAS TOUCH	ACDLLNOSTU	DON'T CALL US
ACDHINNOSW	CHAINS DOWN	ACDLLOOPSW	CODSWALLOP
ACDHIRSTWY	SWITCHYARD	ACDLLOPTYY	POLYDACTYL
ACDHJMOORR	MAJOR CHORD	ACDLLORSSW	WORLD-CLASS
ACDHKKNORS	HARD KNOCKS	ACDLMMNNOO	COMMON LAND
ACDHKNORTU	HAD NO TRUCK	ACDLMNOPSW	CLAMPS DOWN
ACDHLOORRU	UROCHORDAL	ACDLNSTYYY	SYNDACTYLY
ACDHLOOSSY	DAY SCHOOLS	ACDMMNORSU	COMMUNARDS
	SCHOOL DAYS	ACDMOORRTY	ARMY DOCTOR
ACDHNNOSTU	COUNT HANDS	ACDOORRSSS	CROSSROADS
ACDHNOOPRR	DROP ANCHOR	ACDORRSTUY	COURTYARDS
ACDHNORSUW	DAWN CHORUS	ACEEEEKPSS	SEEKS PEACE
ACDHOOPPSS	SCAPHOPODS	ACEEEFFKTT	TAKE EFFECT
ACDHOPSTUW	WHATS UP DOC?	ACEEEFFLOR	REAL COFFEE
ACDHORSTWW	WATCHWORDS	ACEEEFFMNT	EFFACEMENT
ACDIIINNOT	INDICATION	ACEEEFFOPR	PEACE OFFER
ACDIIJLLUY	JUDICIALLY	ACEEEFFTTU	EFFECTUATE
ACDIILLSUY	JUICIALLY	AOEEEFIFRS	FIRE ESOAPE
ACDIILMOPT	DIPLOMATIC	ACEEEFIRSS	CEASE-FIRES
ACDIILNOSV	COLIN DAVIS		CEASES FIRE
ACDIILORST	CLOSTRIDIA	ACEEEFKNNS	SNAKE FENCE
ACDIILORTY	CORDIALITY	ACEEEFLNRS	FREELANCES
ACDIILPSSS	SLIPS A DISC	ACEEEFLRUY	CAREFUL EYE
ACDIIMNNOS	DOMINICANS	ACEEEFRSSX	EXCESS FARE
ACDIIMNORT	ANTIDROMIC	ACEEEGHPRS	REPECHAGES
ACDIIMNOSY	ISODYNAMIC	ACEEEGILNN	INELEGANCE
ACDIIMNOTU	COATIMUNDI	ACEEEGILPR	LARGE PIECE
ACDIIMNSTY	DYNAMISTIC	ACEEEGILTX	EXEGETICAL
ACDIINNNOR	INDIAN CORN	ACEEEGINRT	GREAT NIECE
ACDIINOORT	CAROTINOID		GREAT-NIECE
ACDIINOORV	ORDOVICIAN	ACEEEGNPRT	PERCENTAGE
ACDIINORST	INDICATORS	ACEEEGNRRY	REGENERACY
ACDIINORSU	DINOSAURIC	ACEEEHIKLL	LIKE A LEECH
ACDIINORTV	VINDICATOR	ACEEEHLMOO	HAEMOCOELE
ACDIINORTY	DICTIONARY	ACEEEHLMOT	CAME TO HEEL
	INDICATORY	ACEEEHLNST	CLEAN SHEET
ACDIINOSTT	DICTATIONS	ACEEEHPSTT	SET THE PACE
ACDIKKNSST	KICKSTANDS	ACEEEHPSTY	EYE PATCHES
ACDIKNNPTU	NIP AND TUCK	ACEEEHRRRS	RESEARCHER
ACDIKNQSSU	QUICKSANDS	ACEEEHRRSS	RESEARCHES
ACDIKRRSTT	DIRT TRACKS	ACEEEIILNP	LIE IN PEACE
ACDIKRSSTY	YARDSTICKS	ACEEEIKTWW	TWICE A WEEK
ACDILLMNOO	DON CAMILLO	ACEEEIMRRS	CREAMERIES
ACDILLMNOT	CALL TO MIND	ACEEEIPPRV	APPERCEIVE
ACDILMOORU	DICOUMAROL	ACEEEIRRST	SECRETAIRE
ACDILMPRUY	PLAID CYMRU	ACEEEIRSTV	EVISCERATE
ACDILNOPRS	SPINAL CORD		TEA SERVICE
ACDILOPRTU	DUPLICATOR	ACEEEIRTVX	EXECRATIVE
ACDILPSSTY	DYSPLASTIC	ACEEEKLPRS	KEEPS CLEAR
ACDIMMORUY	MYOCARDIUM	ACEEEKRRST	RACKETEERS
ACDIMNPSTU	NUDIST CAMP	ACEEEKSUWX	WEAK EXCUSE
ACDIMNSSTU	MUSIC STAND	ACEEELLRSY	SEE CLEARLY
ACDIMOORSU	MORDACIOUS	ACEEELMNNT	ENLACEMENT
ACDINOORSW	COINS A WORD	ACEEELMSUX	LAME EXCUSE
ACDINOPSTU	SUCTION PAD	ACEEELNPRV	PREVALENCE
ACDINORRTU	CURTAIN ROD	ACEEELNPSW	CLEAN SWEEP
ACDINORSTY	SYNDICATOR		SWEEP CLEAN
ACDINORSWW	CAR WINDOWS	ACEEELNRTW	T.E.LAWRENCE
ACDINOSSTU	CUSTODIANS	ACEEELNSTU	ENUCLEATES
ACDIOOPRSY	RADIOSCOPY	ACEEELORTT	ELECTORATE
ACDIORTVYY	VICTORY DAY	ACEEELRRST	STEER CLEAR
ACDJKLNNOO	JACK LONDON	ACEEELRSSS	CREASELESS
ACDJOORSTU	COADJUTORS	ACEEELRSTT	TELECASTER
ACDKLMOSSY	LADY'S-SMOCK	ACEEEMMNRT	AMERCEMENT
ACDKLMUYYY	MY LUCKY DAY	ACEEEMNNPR	PERMANENCE
ACDKLOORRU	DARK COLOUR	ACEEEMNNRS	REMANENCES
ACDKNORSTU	SOUND TRACK	ACEEEMNNST	ENCASEMENT
ACDKNORSTW	TRACKS DOWN	ACEEEMNOPW	PEACE WOMEN
ACDKORSSTY	STOCKYARDS	ACEEEMNORR	COME NEARER
ACDLLMNOOS	ALL MOD CONS	ACEEEMNPRT	TEMPERANCE

ACEEEMNPST	ESCAPEMENT	ACEEGHLLNS	CHALLENGES
ACEEEMNRTT	METACENTRE	ACEEGHLNSS	CHANGELESS
ACEEEMPRST	PEACE TERMS	ACEEGHNORV	CHANGE OVER
ACEEEMRSTU	RESCUE TEAM		CHANGE-OVER
ACEEENNPRT	REPENTANCE	ACEEGHNPST	CHANGE STEP
ACEEENNSTV	EVANESCENT	ACEEGHNSSU	GAUCHENESS
ACEEEPPPRR	CREPE PAPER	ACEEGHORRV	OVERCHARGE
ACEEEPRRTU	RECUPERATE	ACEEGIINRS	GRECIANISE
ACEEEPRSTT	PACESETTER	ACEEGIINRZ	GRECIANIZE
ACEEERSSUY	SAUCER EYES	ACEEGIJPRU	GRAPE JUICE
ACEEFFHRSU	RECHAUFFES	ACEEGIKTTW	WICKET GATE
ACEEFFIKOT	TAKE OFFICE	ACEEGILLNR	ALLERGENIC
ACEEFFIMNY	EFFEMINACY	ACEEGILLOT	COLLEGIATE
ACEEFFLOTY	FEET OF CLAY	ACEEGILNPV	GIVEN PLACE
ACEEFFMNST	EFFECTS MAN	ACEEGILPSV	GIVES PLACE
ACEEFFNRSU	SUFFERANCE	ACEEGILRRR	CAREER GIRL
ACEEFGHINT	ACHING FEET	ACEEGIMNOR	CINEMAGOER
ACEEFGMOOS	COMES OF AGE	ACEEGINOTV	GAVE NOTICE
ACEEFHHTTW	CHEW THE FAT	ACEEGINRRT	RECREATING
ACEEFHIOSW	CHOSE A WIFE	ACEEGINRSV	GRIEVANCES
ACEEFHIRTV	VIC FEATHER	ACEEGINRTX	EXECRATING
ACEEFHLNRT	CENTRE HALF	ACEEGIOPTT	COTTAGE PIE
	CENTRE-HALF	ACEEGIORST	CATEGORIES
ACEEFHLNTU	NEUFCHATEL		CATEGORISE
ACEEFHMRRS	FRESH CREAM	ACEEGIORTZ	CATEGORIZE
ACEEFHNOST	HONEST FACE	ACEEGIOTTX	EXCOGITATE
ACEEFHOSTT	CHEST OF TEA	ACEEGIRSTT	CIGARETTES
ACEEFIILTT	FELICITATE	ACEEGKLLRY	GRACE KELLY
ACEEFIILTV	ACTIVE LIFE	ACEEGKLRSW	WAGES CLERK
ACEEFIIRST	ACETIFIERS	ACEEGKNOPS	SPONGE CAKE
ACEEFIJKLT	LIFE JACKET	ACEEGLLOSU	COLLEAGUES
ACEEFILMNT	MALEFICENT	ACEEGLMNOR	CAMERLENGO
ACEEFILMOT	CAME TO LIFE	ACEEGLNOPS	GONE PLACES
ACEEFILNNS	FINAL SCENE	ACEEGLNORV	GLANCE OVER
ACEEFILNSS	FACILENESS	ACEEGLNRST	RECTANGLES
ACEEFILPRS	FIREPLACES	ACEEGLNRTU	GREAT UNCLE
ACEEFILRSU	LUCIFERASE		GREAT-UNCLE
ACEEFILSTT	LETS FACE IT	ACEEGLOPSS	GOES PLACES
ACEEFINRST	INTERFACES	ACEEGMMOSU	GEMMACEOUS
ACEEFIOPSS	PIECE OF ASS	ACEEGMNPTY	TEMP AGENCY
ACEEFIORTV	VOCIFERATE	ACEEGNNORV	GOVERNANCE
ACEEFIRRRS	CAR FERRIES	ACEEGNNPRU	REPUGNANCE
ACEEFIRRTV	REFRACTIVE	ACEEGNNRSY	ANGRY SCENE
ACEEFIRSSS	FRICASSEES	ACEEGNNSWY	NEWS AGENCY
ACEEFIRSUX	FAIR EXCUSE	ACEEGNORST	GRACE NOTES
ACEEFLLNTU	FLATULENCE	ACEEGNORSU	ENCOURAGES
ACEEFLLORV	CLOVER LEAF	ACEEGNRSSV	SCAVENGERS
	CLOVERLEAF	ACEEHHILNW	CHAINWHEEL
ACEEFLLPUY	PEACEFULLY	ACEEHHILRW	WHEELCHAIR
ACEEFLNSST	FALSE SCENT	ACEEHHILSS	CHEHALISES
ACEEFLNSTV	FLAVESCENT	ACEEHHIMRT	CAME HITHER
ACEEFLORSS	SALES FORCE	ACEEHHIRRS	HERESIARCH
ACEEFLORST	FORECASTLE	ACEEHHIRST	HATCHERIES
ACEEFLOSTW	FACE TOWELS	ACEEHHLNNT	THE CHANNEL
ACEEFNOOST	TO ONES FACE	ACEEHHNOPT	ON THE CHEAP
ACEEFNORSW	CAFÉ OWNERS	ACEEHHRRST	THE ARCHERS
ACEEFORRST	FORECASTER	ACEEHIIPRS	HAIRPIECES
ACEEFPRTTY	PRETTY FACE	ACEEHILNNS	CHANNELISE
ACEEGGHINV	GIVE CHANGE	ACEEHILNNZ	CHANNELIZE
ACEEGGIKNR	GINGER CAKE	ACEEHILNRT	IN THE CLEAR
ACEEGGNORT	CONGREGATE	ACEEHILPTT	TELEPATHIC
ACEEGGRSTU	CURATES EGG	ACEEHILRSV	CHEVALIERS
ACEEGHHRTW	CHEW THE RAG	ACEEHIMNPZ	CHIMPANZEE
ACEEGHINNP	CHEAPENING	ACEEHIMNSS	MECHANISES
ACEEGHINNX	IN EXCHANGE	ACEEHIMNSZ	MECHANIZES
ACEEGHINST	ESCHEATING	ACEEHIMPTT	EMPATHETIC
ACEEGHINSV	GIVEN CHASE	ACEEHIMRSS	CRIES SHAME
ACEEGHIRSU	GAUCHERIES	ACEEHIMSST	SCHEMATISE
ACEEGHISSV	GIVES CHASE	ACEEHIMTTT	METATHETIC
ACEEGHKSTT	GET THE SACK	ACEEHINNPT	PHENACETIN
ACEEGHLLNR	CHALLENGER	ACEEHINRRT	RATHER NICE

ACEEHINRTW	WIN THE RACE	ACEEIKOPST	TAKE COPIES
ACEEHINSTT	ANESTHETIC	ACEEIKPRTT	TICKER TAPE
ACEEHIORRT	CHARIOTEER	ACEEIKSTWY	EASY WICKET
ACEEHIORSV	HEAR VOICES	ACEEILLMTY	EMETICALLY
ACEEHISSTT	AESTHETICS	ACEEILLNNN	CLEAN LINEN
ACEEHISTUW	WHITE SAUCE	ACEEILLNRV	CLEAN LIVER
ACEEHJKRST	THREE JACKS	ACEEILLNRW	WINE CELLAR
ACEEHKLNRT	HALTER NECK	ACEEILLPSY	ESPECIALLY
ACEEHKMOTY	HOCKEY TEAM	ACEEILMNOR	CEREMONIAL
ACEEHKPSTW	KEEPS WATCH		REAL INCOME
ACEEHLLLOR	LA ROCHELLE	ACEEILMNRT	MERCANTILE
ACEEHLLNOP	CELLOPHANE	ACEEILMNST	CENTESIMAL
ACEEHLMNOS	CHAMELEONS	ACEEILMOSV	COMES ALIVE
ACEEHLMRSU	CRUEL SHAME	ACEEILMRST	CARMELITES
ACEEHLNNOP	ENCEPHALON	ACEEILMTTW	WET CLIMATE
ACEEHLNPRU	LEPRECHAUN	ACEEILNNNT	CENTENNIAL
ACEEHLNRST	THE LANCERS	ACEEILNNOR	OCEAN LINER
ACEEHLOPTY	POLYCHAETE	ACEEILNPRT	EPICENTRAL
ACEEHILOSSV	CLOSE SHAVE	ACEEILNPSW	WIPES CLEAN
ACEEHLRSTW	CARTWHEELS	ACEEILNRST	CENTRALISE
ACEEHLSSST	SCATHELESS		INTERLACES
ACEEHMMRSU	MEERSCHAUM		TRIAL SCENE
ACEEHMNNST	ENCASHMENT	ACEEILNRTV	CANTILEVER
ACEEHMOORS	COME ASHORE	ACEEILNRTZ	CENTRALIZE
ACEEHMOPRS	SCRAPE HOME	ACEEILPPRT	TEA CLIPPER
ACEEHMORTT	TACHOMETER	ACEEILPRST	REPLICATES
ACEEHMOSTY	HAEMOCYTES	ACEEILPSTX	EXPLICATES
ACEEHMRTTY	TACHYMETER	ACEEILQRTU	QUITE CLEAR
ACEEHNNOOT	ON THE OCEAN	ACEEILRRTT	RETRACTILE
ACEEHNNRST	ENCHANTER'S	ACEEILRSSU	SECULARISE
	ENCHANTERS	ACEEILRSUZ	SECULARIZE
ACEEHNOPRT	CHAPTER ONE	ACEEILRTTU	RETICULATE
ACEEHNORTW	WON THE RACE	ACEEILRTUV	ULCERATIVE
ACEEHNPRTT	CHAPTER TEN	ACEEILRTVY	CREATIVELY
ACEEHNPRTW	NEW CHAPTER		REACTIVELY
ACEEHNPTTU	PENTATEUCH	ACEEILSSWX	EXCISE LAWS
ACEEHNRSST	CHASTENERS	ACEEILSTUV	VESICULATE
ACEEHNRSTT	ENTRECHATS	ACEEIMNRSS	CREAMINESS
ACEEHNSSST	CHASTENESS	ACEEIMNRSV	SERVICEMAN
ACEEHNSSTU	CHANTEUSES	ACEEIMNRTT	REMITTANCE
ACEEHOPRRR	REPROACHER	ACEEIMPRST	IMPRECATES
ACEEHOPRRS	REPROACHES		SPERMACETI
ACEEHORSTU	OUTREACHES	ACEEIMPRSU	PRIME CAUSE
	REACHES OUT	ACEEIMRSST	MISCREATES
ACEEHPPRSY	HYPERSPACE	ACEEIMRSTT	METRICATES
ACEEHPRSTY	ARCHETYPES	ACEEINNOPT	NO PATIENCE
ACEEHPTTTU	CUT THE TAPE	ACEEINNPRS	INNER SPACE
ACEEHRRRST	CHARTERERS	ACEEINNRST	NECTARINES
ACEEHRRSTT	CHATTERERS		TRANSIENCE
ACEEHRRSTU	CHARTREUSE	ACEEINNSTU	ENUNCIATES
ACEEIILMRT	EREMITICAL	ACEEINOORT	RECREATION
ACEEIILMST	ELEATICISM	ACEEINORTU	AUCTIONEER
ACEEIILNTT	LICENTIATE	ACEEINORTV	RAVE NOTICE
ACEEIILPSS	SPECIALISE	ACEEINORTX	EXECRATION
ACEEIILPST	TAILPIECES	ACEEINPPRT	APPRENTICE
ACEEIILPSZ	SPECIALIZE	ACEEINPRST	INTERSPACE
ACEEIILSTZ	ELASTICIZE	ACEEINPRSU	EPICUREANS
ACEEIIMNPT	IMPATIENCE	ACEEINQSUU	UNIQUE CASE
ACEEIIMRRU	MARIE CURIE	ACEEINRSST	RESISTANCE
ACEEIINNRT	CREATININE	ACEEINRTVY	INVETERACY
	INCINERATE	ACEEINSSTV	ACTIVENESS
ACEEIIRRSV	AIR SERVICE	ACEEIOPPST	EPISCOPATE
ACEEIIRTTV	RECITATIVE	ACEEIOQTUV	EQUIVOCATE
ACEEIITTVX	EXCITATIVE	ACEEIORSTX	EXCORIATES
ACEEIJLMSV	CLIVE JAMES	ACEEIOSSSS	ECOSSAISES
ACEEIKLMNS	SIMNEL CAKE	ACEEIPPRTY	PARTY PIECE
ACEEIKLMTT	MEAL TICKET	ACEEIPQRSU	PICARESQUE
ACEEIKLNRT	TRANCELIKE	ACEEIPRSTT	CREPITATES
ACEEIKLRSS	CLEAR SKIES	ACEEIRRSST	CAREERISTS
ACEEIKLRSU	SAUCERLIKE	ACEEIRSSSU	SEA CRUISES
ACEEIKNOTT	TAKE NOTICE	ACEEIRSSTU	CAUTERISES

ACEEIRSSVW	SAW SERVICE	ACEENORSSS	COARSENESS
ACEEIRSTTX	EXTRICATES	ACEENPRRST	CARPENTERS
ACEEIRSTUZ	CAUTERIZES	ACEENPRSTT	RECENT PAST
ACEEIRTTVX	EXTRACTIVE	ACEENPRUVY	PURVEYANCE
ACEEJJMOSY	JAMES JOYCE	ACEENRSSTW	NEWSCASTER
ACEEJKMSST	MESS JACKET	ACEENRSTTU	UTTERANCES
ACEEJKNOTT	ETON JACKET	ACEENSSTTV	CAT STEVENS
ACEEJKOORS	COARSE JOKE	ACEENSTTUX	EXECUTANTS
ACEEJNOSSY	CASEY JONES	ACEEOOPRRS	OPERA SCORE
ACEEKKPRST	KEEPS TRACK	ACEEOOPRST	COOPERATES
ACEEKLLRSS	SALES CLERK	ACEEOPPRRR	PROPER CARE
	SALESCLERK	ACEEOPPRST	PROCREATES
ACEEKLNSSS	LACKS SENSE	ACEEOPRSTU	OUTER SPACE
ACEEKLRRTT	LETTER RACK	ACEEORRTVX	EXTRA COVER
ACEEKNORTV	TAKEN COVER	ACEEORSSTU	SET A COURSE
ACEEKNRRRT	RACK-RENTER	ACEEORSTTT	CATO STREET
ACEEKNRTTV	TRACK EVENT	ACEEORSTUY	EUCARYOTES
ACEEKORRSW	CASEWORKER	ACEEOSSTTU	TESTACEOUS
ACEEKORRSTV	TAKES COVER	ACEEPRRSTU	RECAPTURES
ACEELLNOTW	CLEAN TOWEL	ACEERRSSTT	SCATTERERS
ACEELLORWY	YELLOW RACE		STREETCARS
ACEELLRSSY	CARELESSLY	ACEERRSSTW	WATER CRESS
ACEELLRSTY	CELERY SALT		WATERCRESS
ACEELLSTTU	SCUTELLATE	ACEFFFILOT	FACT OF LIFE
ACEELLTTUV	VEAL CUTLET	ACEFFGHLNR	FRENCH FLAG
ACEELMNOPY	PLACE MONEY	ACEFFGILNT	FACING LEFT
ACEELMNOST	SOLACEMENT	ACEFFGLNOS	GLANCES OFF
ACEELMOOST	COELOMATES	ACEFFHLNOR	FRENCH LOAF
ACEELMOPPS	AMPLE SCOPE	ACEFFHMORS	MARCHES OFF
ACEELMORSY	COMES EARLY	ACEFFHRSUU	CHAUFFEURS
ACEELNOPST	OPALESCENT	ACEFFIIOST	OFFICIATES
ACEELNOPSY	CLAP EYES ON	ACEFFIKRRT	TRAFFICKER
ACEELNORST	TOLERANCES	ACEFFILORW	LAW OFFICER
ACEELNPRSY	SCREENPLAY	ACEFFINOST	AFFECTIONS
ACEELNPRTY	PLAY CENTRE	ACEFFIORRS	CARRIES OFF
ACEELNPSTW	SWEPT CLEAN	ACEFFIRSST	SCARE STIFF
ACEELNRRSU	RURAL SCENE	ACEFFKLNOS	SLACKEN OFF
ACEELNRSTW	LAW CENTRES	ACEFFLOORW	FORCE OF LAW
	ST.LAWRENCE	ACEFFLOOSS	LOSS OF FACE
ACEELOOPRT	COLEOPTERA	ACEFFMOPRS	SCAMPER OFF
ACEELOPRST	PERCOLATES	ACEFFOPRSS	SCRAPES OFF
ACEELOPRTU	OPERCULATE	ACEFFOSSTU	SUFFOCATES
ACEELORRST	CORRELATES	ACEFFOSTUU	TUFFACEOUS
ACEELORSSS	CASSEROLES	ACEFGHILNT	CLEAN FIGHT
ACEELPPRTU	PERCEPTUAL	ACEFGHIMNR	CHAMFERING
ACEELPSSTU	SPECULATES	ACEFGHIRRT	FREIGHT CAR
ACEELPSTUX	EXCULPATES	ACEFGHIRST	FACES RIGHT
ACEELQRRUU	CRAQUELURE	ACEFGHIRTU	CAUGHT FIRE
ACEELRRTUY	CREATURELY	ACEFGIINTY	ACETIFYING
ACEEMMNNPT	ENCAMPMENT	ACEFGILLOS	FALSE LOGIC
ACEEMMNOTT	COMMENTATE	ACEFGILMTU	MAGIC FLUTE
ACEEMMNNORR	AMEN CORNER	ACEFGILNOS	LOSING FACE
ACEEMMNPRY	PERMANENCY	ACEFGINRRT	REFRACTING
ACEEMNOPST	COMPENSATE	ACEFGINSTW	FACING WEST
ACEEMNPRST	ESCARPMENT	ACEFGIRTUU	CUT A FIGURE
ACEEMOPRSS	EPSOM RACES	ACEFGKOORS	ROCK OF AGES
ACEEMORSTT	CAME TO REST	ACEFGLLRUY	GRACEFULLY
	OCTAMETERS	ACEFGLNORR	CORNER FLAG
ACEEMORSTU	MEAT COURSE	ACEFGLNORS	GERFALCONS
ACEEMOSTUZ	ECZEMATOUS	ACEFGLNRUU	UNGRACEFUL
ACEEMPPSTY	EMPTY SPACE	ACEFHHILNS	HALF-INCHES
ACEENNNORT	NO ENTRANCE	ACEFHHINSW	HAWFINCHES
ACEENNOPRS	CAN OPENERS	ACEFHHIRRS	ARCHERFISH
ACEENNOPRV	PROVENANCE	ACEFHIINST	CHIEFTAINS
ACEENNORSS	RESONANCES	ACEFHINRSS	FRANCHISES
ACEENNORTV	CONTRAVENE	ACEFHIORSS	COARSE FISH
	COVENANTER	ACEFHIRTTY	CITY FATHER
ACEENNOSSS	CANONESSES	ACEFHKLOOT	HECK OF A LOT
ACEENNRSSV	CRAVENNESS	ACEFHKOORW	HECK OF A ROW
ACEENNSSTU	SUSTENANCE	ACEFHLLSTU	SATCHELFUL
ACEENORRST	CORNER SEAT	ACEFHLNPRS	FRENCH ALPS

ACEFHLNRTU	AFTER LUNCH	ACEGGIJKMR	MICK JAGGER
ACEFHLOOTT	ACT THE FOOL	ACEGGILLOO	GEOLOGICAL
ACEFHLOPRY	HYPERFOCAL	ACEGGILNNO	CONGEALING
ACEFHMOOST	SMOOTH FACE	ACEGGINNOO	OCEANGOING
ACEFHMORTU	CAME FOURTH	ACEGGINNOR	GONE RACING
ACEFHNORST	FACES NORTH	ACEGGINNSV	SCAVENGING
ACEFHOORTU	OUT OF REACH	ACEGGINORS	GOES RACING
ACEFHORRTV	HOVERCRAFT	ACEGGINRSS	CRAGGINESS
ACEFHORSTU	HOUSECRAFT	ACEGGIRSST	SCRAGGIEST
ACEFHOSSTU	FACES SOUTH	ACEGHHILPS	HIGH PLACES
ACEFHOSSUV	VOUCHSAFES	ACEGHHINOT	HIGH OCTANE
ACEFIIILST	FACILITIES		HIGH-OCTANE
ACEFIILLOS	SOCIAL LIFE	ACEGHIILMT	MEGALITHIC
ACEFIILMSS	FACSIMILES	ACEGHIIMNP	IMPEACHING
ACEFIILRRS	CLARIFIERS	ACEGHIIMTW	WHITE MAGIC
ACEFIILRSS	CLASSIFIER	ACEGHIINNV	GIVE AN INCH
ACEFIILSSS	CLASSIFIES	ACEGHIINRS	CASHIERING
ACEFIIMNOR	FAIR INCOME	ACEGHIIPPR	EPIGRAPHIC
ACEFIINNRS	FINANCIERS	ACEGHIILLCT	GETS A CHILL
ACEFIINSST	SANCTIFIES	ACEGHIILMPT	PHLEGMATIC
ACEFIIOPRS	FAIR COPIES	ACEGHILOTT	LATE GOTHIC
ACEFIIPRRS	FAIR PRICES	ACEGHILPRT	RIGHT PLACE
ACEFIIRRST	ARTIFICERS	ACEGHILRTU	THEURGICAL
ACEFIIRSTV	FRICATIVES	ACEGHIMNNU	MACHINE GUN
ACEFIJKKNS	JACKKNIFES		MACHINE-GUN
ACEFIKLLNS	FALLEN SICK	ACEGHIMNOP	MEGAPHONIC
ACEFIKLMOT	LACK OF TIME	ACEGHIMOPR	MICROPHAGE
ACEFIKLOPS	PACK OF LIES	ACEGHINNNT	ENCHANTING
ACEFIKNOSW	CASK OF WINE	ACEGHINNST	CHASTENING
ACEFIKSTTW	FAST WICKET	ACEGHINOPT	PATHOGENIC
ACEFILNORS	FALCONRIES	ACEGHINRRT	CHARTERING
	FINAL SCORE	ACEGHINRTT	CHATTERING
ACEFILOOSU	FOLIACEOUS	ACEGHIOOPS	HAGIOSCOPE
ACEFILOPSY	SAFE POLICY	ACEGHIRSTW	SWITCHGEAR
ACEFILORST	FORTALICES	ACEGHKOORT	TOOK CHARGE
ACEFILORTV	VITAL FORCE	ACEGHKORST	GREAT SHOCK
ACEFILPRST	FIRST PLACE	ACEGHKOSST	GETS A SHOCK
ACEFIMORTT	TIME FACTOR	ACEGHKOSTT	GOT THE SACK
ACEFINORRT	FOR CERTAIN	ACEGHLNOTV	THE LONG VAC
	REFRACTION	ACEGHOPSTY	PHAGOCYTES
ACEFINORST	FORNICATES	ACEGHRRSSU	SURCHARGES
ACEFINORTV	VOCIFERANT	ACEGIIKNST	ICE SKATING
ACEFINRSST	CRAFTINESS	ACEGIILLSS	GALLICISES
ACEFIOPTTU	FACE UP TO IT	ACEGIILLST	LEGALISTIC
ACEFIORSST	FACTORISES	ACEGIILLSZ	GALLICIZES
ACEFIORSTZ	FACTORIZES	ACEGIILMNR	RECLAIMING
ACEFIRRRTV	RIVER CRAFT	ACEGIILMNX	EXCLAIMING
ACEFIRRTTU	TRIFURCATE	ACEGIILMTY	LEGITIMACY
ACEFKLNORS	CORN FLAKES	ACEGIILNNO	LIGNOCAINE
	CORNFLAKES	ACEGIILNPR	CALIPERING
ACEFKOOORT	TOOK CARE OF	ACEGIILNSS	ANGLICISES
ACEFLLNOOR	ONCE FOR ALL	ACEGIILNSZ	ANGLICIZES
ACEFLLNTUY	FLATULENCY	ACEGIILOOT	AETIOLOGIC
ACEFLLPSSU	PULLS FACES	ACEGIILOST	EGOISTICAL
ACEFLOOPRS	FLOOR SPACE	ACEGIIMNNT	GENTAMICIN
ACEFLOOPTU	OUT OF PLACE	ACEGIIMNTT	MAGNETITIC
ACEFLSTTUU	FLUCTUATES	ACEGIIMPTT	PEGMATITIC
ACEFMOPTUY	MY CUP OF TEA	ACEGIINNRS	INCREASING
ACEFNOORRS	EARS OF CORN	ACEGIINORT	IATROGENIC
ACEFNOPRTT	PONTEFRACT	ACEGIINSTV	VESICATING
ACEFNOPRTV	PROVEN FACT	ACEGIIOTTV	COGITATIVE
ACEFOPRTUW	CUP OF WATER	ACEGIIPRST	EPIGASTRIC
ACEFORRRST	REFRACTORS	ACEGIIRRST	GERIATRICS
ACEFORRRTY	REFRACTORY	ACEGIKKNNR	KNACKERING
ACEGGHILNN	CHANGELING	ACEGIKLNNS	SLACKENING
ACEGGHINNX	EXCHANGING	ACEGIKLNOR	CAROLE KING
ACEGGHINOP	GOING CHEAP	ACEGIKMORS	CIGAR SMOKE
ACEGGHINRR	RECHARGING	ACEGIKNNTU	KING CANUTE
ACEGGHIOPR	GEOGRAPHIC	ACEGILLMPS	MAGIC SPELL
ACEGGIINRS	GRAECISING	ACEGILLNOO	NEOLOGICAL
ACEGGIINRZ	GRAECIZING	ACEGILLNOS	COLLEGIANS

ACEGILLNPR	PARCELLING
ACEGILLNTW	ACTING WELL
ACEGILLOOS	OLIGOCLASE
ACEGILMNNY	MENACINGLY
ACEGILNNOT	CONGENITAL
ACEGILNNPU	CLEANING UP
ACEGILNNTU	NUCLEATING
ACEGILNOPY	CLAY PIGEON
ACEGILNORV	LOVING CARE
ACEGILNPRU	CLEARING UP
ACEGILNPTU	PECULATING
ACEGILNQRU	LACQUERING
ACEGILNRTT	CLATTERING
ACEGILNRTU	ULCERATING
ACEGILNTXY	EXACTINGLY
ACEGILRSTU	CURTILAGES
	GRATICULES
ACEGIMMRSS	SCRIMMAGES
ACEGIMNNOR	COMING NEAR
ACEGIMNPRS	SCAMPERING
ACEGIMNRST	CENTIGRAMS
ACEGIMOPRW	MAGIC POWER
ACEGIMORSU	GRACIOUS ME!
ACEGIMRSTU	TRAGIC MUSE
ACEGINNNRT	ENTRANCING
ACEGINNORS	COARSENING
ACEGINNRRU	GRECIAN URN
ACEGINOPRS	SAPROGENIC
ACEGINORTV	OVERACTING
ACEGINORTW	EATING CROW
ACEGINPRRS	SCARPERING
ACEGINPRSY	PANEGYRICS
ACEGINPRSZ	CAP GRIS-NEZ
ACEGINPSTT	SPECTATING
ACEGINRRTT	RETRACTING
ACEGINRSTT	SCATTERING
ACEGINRSTW	TRAGIC NEWS
ACEGINRTTX	EXTRACTING
ACEGIOPRRS	PAREGORICS
ACEGIORRST	CIGAR STORE
ACEGJNOSTU	CONJUGATES
ACEGKLORST	LARGE STOCK
ACEGKOORSS	GAS COOKERS
ACEGKORSTU	GOATSUCKER
ACEGLLOSST	LEGAL COSTS
ACEGLMNOOS	COMES ALONG
ACEGLMOSUU	GLUMACEOUS
ACEGLNOPRW	WRONG PLACE
ACEGLOOPSY	ESCAPOLOGY
ACEGMMRSSU	SCRUMMAGES
ACEGMNOOPT	GONE TO CAMP
ACEGMOOPST	GOES TO CAMP
ACEGNNORTW	CROWN AGENT
ACEGNNOSTT	COTANGENTS
ACEGNOORSS	GONE ACROSS
ACEGNORSST	STRONG CASE
ACEGNPSTUU	UNCUT PAGES
ACEGNRSTTU	SCATTER-GUN
ACEGOOPRRY	GARY COOPER
ACEGOORSSS	GOES ACROSS
ACEGOORSUU	COURAGEOUS
ACEGOPRRSU	SUPERCARGO
ACEGORRSTU	CORRUGATES
ACEGORSSST	GETS ACROSS
ACEGORSTTT	GREAT SCOTT!
ACEHHIINRT	IN THE CHAIR
ACEHHIKLTW	WHITE CHALK
ACEHHIKRTT	HIT THE RACK
ACEHHIKSTT	HIT THE SACK
ACEHHILTWZ	WITCH HAZEL
ACEHHIORSV	HARSH VOICE

ACEHHLNOTT	ON THE LATCH
ACEHHMNORT	ON THE MARCH
ACEHHMNSTT	HATCHMENTS
ACEHHMRRTU	RATHER MUCH
ACEHHNORSU	RANCH HOUSE
ACEHHNPUVY	HEAVY PUNCH
ACEHHNSTTU	NUTHATCHES
ACEHHOOSTT	TOOTHACHES
ACEHHOSTTT	ACT THE HOST
ACEHHOTUVY	HEAVY TOUCH
ACEHIILLPT	PHILATELIC
ACEHIILSTT	THEISTICAL
ACEHIILTTY	ETHICALITY
ACEHIIMRTT	ARITHMETIC
ACEHIINNOP	PHOENICIAN
ACEHIINORT	ANTI-HEROIC
ACEHIINOTV	INCHOATIVE
ACEHIINTTT	IN THE ATTIC
	THE TITANIC
ACEHIKMNOS	CHAIN SMOKE
	CHAIN-SMOKE
ACEHIKORST	ARTICHOKES
ACEHIKRRTW	HACK WRITER
ACEHILLNOT	IN THE LOCAL
ACEHILLNTY	ETHNICALLY
ACEHILLORY	HEROICALLY
ACEHILLPRY	CAERPHILLY
ACEHILMMOS	CHAMOMILES
ACEHILMOTT	HOT CLIMATE
ACEHILMOTY	HAEMOLYTIC
ACEHILMSST	ALCHEMISTS
ACEHILNORT	CHLORINATE
ACEHILNOTY	INCHOATELY
ACEHILNRST	CLEAN SHIRT
ACEHILOPTT	THE CAPITOL
ACEHILORRT	RHETORICAL
ACEHILRSTY	HYSTERICAL
ACEHIMMNSS	MECHANISMS
ACEHIMMSST	MISMATCHES
ACEHIMNNOP	ONE-INCH MAP
ACEHIMNNOR	ENHARMONIC
ACEHIMNOPT	PHONEMATIC
ACEHIMNORS	MONARCHIES
ACEHIMNOUV	HUMAN VOICE
ACEHIMNRSV	REVANCHISM
ACEHIMNSTW	WIN MATCHES
ACEHIMNSTY	MYASTHENIC
ACEHIMOPRT	AMPHOTERIC
	METAPHORIC
ACEHIMOSTX	CHEMOTAXIS
ACEHIMPRTY	EMPTY CHAIR
ACEHIMPSTY	METAPHYSIC
ACEHIMRSTU	RHEUMATICS
ACEHIMSUVY	HEAVY MUSIC
ACEHINNOST	CHINA STONE
ACEHINNOTT	IN ON THE ACT
ACEHINORRT	CHITARRONE
ACEHINORST	ANCHORITES
	CHAIN STORE
ACEHINORTV	CHEVROTAIN
ACEHINPSST	PATCHINESS
ACEHINPTTT	PITCH A TENT
ACEHINQRSU	SQUARE CHIN
	SQUARE INCH
ACEHINRRSU	HURRICANES
ACEHINRSSU	SEA URCHINS
ACEHINRSTV	REVANCHIST
ACEHINSSTT	CHATTINESS
ACEHIOPRSV	SHARP VOICE
ACEHIORSST	SCORES A HIT
ACEHIORSTT	RHEOSTATIC

ACEHIORTTT	THE RIOT ACT
ACEHIPPSSS	SPACESHIPS
ACEHIPRSSU	HARUSPICES
ACEHIPRSSZ	CASH PRIZES
ACEHIPRTTU	PICTURE HAT
ACEHIRRTTU	HAIRCUTTER
ACEHIRSSST	CHASTISERS
ACEHIRSSTT	STARCHIEST
ACEHIRSSTU	EUCHARISTS
ACEHIRSTTV	TSAREVITCH
ACEHIRTVWY	VICHY WATER
ACEHJKNORR	JACK HORNER
ACEHJKOPTT	THE JACKPOT
ACEHJNNORV	JOHN CRAVEN
ACEHKLLLTU	ALL THE LUCK
ACEHKLMMOR	HAMMERLOCK
ACEHKLNNTU	TAKEN LUNCH
ACEHKLNSSU	UNSHACKLES
ACEHKLNSTU	TAKES LUNCH
ACEHKLOPYY	PLAY HOCKEY
ACEHKOPRSS	PACKHORSES
ACEHKORSST	SHORTCAKES
ACEHLLMNOY	MELANCHOLY
ACEHLLMOOS	SCHOOL MEAL
ACEHLLNRUY	EARLY LUNCH
ACEHLLOORS	REAL SCHOOL
ACEHLLOOSV	COAL SHOVEL
ACEHLLPRSU	SEPULCHRAL
ACEHLLTTWY	WATCH TELLY
ACEHLMOOST	SCHOOLMATE
ACEHLMORSU	MALE CHORUS
ACEHLMORSY	LACHRYMOSE
ACEHLNORSS	ANCHORLESS
ACEHLNORST	CHARLESTON
ACEHLNTTUW	CUT THE LAWN
ACEHLOORRT	RATHER COOL
ACEHLOORST	ORTHOCLASE
ACEHLOORSY	SCHOOL YEAR
ACEHLORRST	ORCHESTRAL
ACEHLORSSU	HOUSECARLS
ACEHLOSTTW	CATTLE SHOW
ACEHLPRTYY	PHYLACTERY
ACEHLPSSSY	PLAYS CHESS
ACEHMMOOQRT	COME TO HARM
ACEHMNNOOT	ONCE A MONTH
ACEHMNORSY	HAS NO MERCY
ACEHMNOTUV	AVOUCHMENT
ACEHMNPRST	PARCHMENTS
ACEHMOOTTT	COME TO THAT
ACEHMORRTU	ROUTE MARCH
ACEHMORSST	STOMACHERS
ACEHMOSSTU	MOUSTACHES
ACEHMOSTTU	OUTMATCHES
ACEHNNOORU	ONCE AN HOUR
ACEHNOOSTT	ON THE COAST
ACEHNOPTYY	CYANOPHYTE
ACEHNORRTT	TROCHANTER
ACEHNOSSTT	STONECHATS
ACEHNPSSTU	SNATCHES UP
ACEHNRRSTU	RUNS THE CAR
ACEHNRSSUZ	SCHNAUZERS
ACEHNSSTTU	STAUNCHEST
ACEHOOSSTU	HOUSECOATS
ACEHOPPRTU	TOUCH PAPER
	TOUCHPAPER
ACEHOPRSUY	CORYPHAEUS
ACEHOPRTTW	CHAPTER TWO
ACEHORRSST	ORCHESTRAS
ACEHORSTTU	UTTER CHAOS
ACEHORTTWW	WATCHTOWER
ACEHOSTTUW	WATCHES OUT

ACEHRRRTTY	CHERRY TART
ACEIIILSST	ITALICISES
ACEIIILSTZ	ITALICIZES
ACEIIIMNST	INTIMACIES
ACEIIISTTV	ACTIVITIES
ACEIIJLSTU	JESUITICAL
ACEIIKLQTU	QUITE A LICK
ACEIIKMNST	KINEMATICS
ACEIIKRSTT	RICKETTSIA
ACEIILLLPT	ELLIPTICAL
ACEIILLOST	LOCALITIES
ACEIILLOSU	LILIACEOUS
ACEIILLOSV	SOCIAL EVIL
ACEIILLRTY	ILLITERACY
ACEIILLTXY	LEXICALITY
ACEIILMMST	MELISMATIC
ACEIILMOPT	ATOMIC PILE
ACEIILMPSS	SPECIALISM
ACEIILMPST	IMPLICATES
ACEIILNNST	ANTICLINES
ACEIILNOSV	VIOLIN CASE
ACEIILNPST	IN ITS PLACE
	PLASTICINE
ACEIILNRST	IN ARTICLES
ACEIILNTVY	INACTIVELY
ACEIILORSS	SOCIALISER
ACEIILORSZ	SOCIALIZER
ACEIILOSSS	SOCIALISES
ACEIILOSST	SOCIALITES
ACEIILOSSZ	SOCIALIZES
ACEIILPPRT	PARTICIPLE
ACEIILPRTT	TRIPLICATE
ACEIILPSST	PLASTICISE
	SPECIALIST
ACEIILPSTY	SPECIALITY
ACEIILPSTZ	PLASTICIZE
ACEIILPTTY	ITALIC TYPE
ACEIILRSTT	RECITALIST
ACEIILRSTV	CLAVIERIST
ACEIILSTTV	ACTIVE LIST
ACEIILSTTY	ELASTICITY
ACEIIMNORS	ACRIMONIES
ACEIIMNRRU	CINERARIUM
ACEIIMNRST	CRIMINATES
ACEIIMRRSS	MISCARRIES
ACEIIMRRST	ERRATICISM
ACEIIMRSST	ARMISTICES
ACEIINNRTY	ITINERANCY
ACEIINNSST	INSTANCIES
ACEIINORTT	RECITATION
ACEIINOSTV	VESICATION
ACEIINOTTX	EXCITATION
	INTOXICATE
ACEIINPSTT	ANTISEPTIC
	PSITTACINE
ACEIIORRRT	CERTIORARI
ACEIIORSTT	ATROCITIES
ACEIIRRSSU	CUIRASSIER
ACEIIRSSST	SACRISTIES
ACEIIRTTVY	REACTIVITY
ACEIISSSTY	ESSAYISTIC
ACEIJKKNSV	JACKKNIVES
ACEIJNSSTU	JUST IN CASE
ACEIKLNSSY	ASKS NICELY
ACEIKLOPSS	LACKS POISE
ACEIKLORST	LOSE A TRICK
ACEIKLRSTV	TRAVEL SICK
ACEIKMMSSU	MAKES MUSIC
ACEIKMPRST	STRIKE CAMP
ACEIKMRRSY	ICY REMARKS
ACEIKNNRSS	CRANKINESS

ACEIKOPRST	AIR POCKETS	ACEILPSSSU	CAPSULISES
ACEIKORTUY	EUKARYOTIC	ACEILPSSUZ	CAPSULIZES
ACEILLLTUY	LUETICALLY	ACEILRRSTU	CURTAILERS
ACEILLMNSY	MISCELLANY	ACEILRSSTU	SECULARIST
ACEILLMOST	COLLIMATES	ACEILRSSTY	CRYSTALISE
ACEILLMOSV	SMALL VOICE	ACEILRSTTU	TESTICULAR
ACEILLMRTY	METRICALLY	ACEILRSTUY	SECULARITY
ACEILLNNNO	CANNELLONI	ACEILRSTYZ	CRYSTALIZE
ACEILLNOOT	OCELLATION	ACEILRTUVY	CURATIVELY
ACEILLNORS	CORALLINES	ACEILSSTWY	ACTS WISELY
ACEILLNORT	CITRONELLA	ACEILSSUWY	SLUICEWAYS
ACEILLNRTU	LENTICULAR	ACEILSTTUV	CULTIVATES
ACEILLOPSW	PILLOWCASE	ACEIMMNORT	MANOMETRIC
ACEILLOPTY	POETICALLY	ACEIMMRSTY	ASYMMETRIC
ACEILLORST	ALLOSTERIC	ACEIMNNRUY	INNUMERACY
	SCLEROTIAL	ACEIMNOPRT	IMPORTANCE
ACEILLORTV	VORTICELLA	ACEIMNORST	CREMATIONS
ACEILLORTY	EROTICALLY	ACEIMNORSU	MAIN COURSE
ACEILLOSST	OSCILLATES	ACEIMNOSST	ENCOMIASTS
ACEILLOSTY	SOCIETALLY	ACEIMNPSTU	PNEUMATICS
ACEILLOTXY	EXOTICALLY	ACEIMOORTV	MOVIE ACTOR
ACEILLPRUY	PECULIARLY	ACEIMOPRSU	OPERA MUSIC
ACEILLRSTY	STERICALLY	ACEIMORSVW	MICROWAVES
ACEILLRSVY	VISCERALLY	ACEIMORTTT	TETRATOMIC
ACEILLRTUV	VICTUALLER	ACEIMORTTU	TAUTOMERIC
ACEILLRTVY	VERTICALLY	ACEIMPPRSU	MUSIC PAPER
ACEILMMNSS	CLAMMINESS	ACEIMRSTTU	MICTURATES
ACEILMNOPR	COMPLAINER	ACEIMRSTUW	WATER MUSIC
ACEILMNORS	COAL MINERS	ACEIMSSTTY	SYSTEMATIC
	MINOR SCALE	ACEINNNSTU	UNCANNIEST
ACEILMNOST	COME IN LAST	ACEINNOPTT	PENTATONIC
ACEILMNRST	CENTRALISM	ACEINNORST	CONTAINERS
ACEILMNRSU	LEARN MUSIC	ACEINNORTU	ENUNCIATOR
ACEILMNRUW	LAWRENCIUM	ACEINNOSSS	ASCENSIONS
ACEILMNSSU	MASCULINES	ACEINNRSST	CANNISTERS
ACEILMNSTU	CULMINATES	ACEINNRSSU	INSURANCES
ACEILMOPRR	PROCLAIMER	ACEINNRSTY	TRANSIENCY
ACEILMRRUV	VERMICULAR	ACEINNRTUU	NUNCIATURE
ACEILMRSSU	SECULARISM	ACEINNSSST	SCANTINESS
ACEILMTUUV	CUMULATIVE	ACEINOOPRS	PIANO SCORE
ACEILNNOOP	NAPOLEONIC	ACEINOORRS	CORONARIES
ACEILNNOTU	NUCLEATION	ACEINOORTV	REVOCATION
ACEILNOPRT	PRATINCOLE	ACEINOPRTU	PRECAUTION
ACEILNOPRV	PLAIN COVER	ACEINOPSTT	CONSTIPATE
ACEILNOPST	NEOPLASTIC	ACEINORRSV	CARNIVORES
ACEILNOPTU	PECULATION	ACEINORRTT	RETRACTION
ACEILNORTU	ULCERATION	ACEINORTTU	ERUCTATION
ACEILNORTY	LECTIONARY	ACEINORTTW	TONIC WATER
ACEILNOSST	COASTLINES		WINTER COAT
ACEILNOSTU	INOCULATES	ACEINORTTX	EXTRACTION
	INOSCULATE	ACEINOSSST	CESSATIONS
ACEILNPPTU	PUT IN PLACE	ACEINQSTTU	QUITTANCES
ACEILNPRRT	CLEAR PRINT	ACEIOOPRTZ	AZEOTROPIC
ACEILNPSTU	INCULPATES	ACEIOOPTTV	CO-OPTATIVE
ACEILNRSTT	CENTRALIST	ACEIOORTTU	AUTOEROTIC
ACEILNRSTU	LACUSTRINE	ACEIOPRRSU	PRECARIOUS
ACEILNRTTY	CENTRALITY	ACEIOPSTTT	PETTICOATS
ACEILNRUUX	LUXURIANCE	ACEIORRSTU	CARRIES OUT
ACEILNSSSS	CLASSINESS	ACEIORSSST	OSTRACISES
ACEILNSSUV	VULCANISES	ACEIORSSTT	CASTROITES
ACEILNSUVZ	VULCANIZES	ACEIORSSTZ	OSTRACIZES
ACEILOOSUV	OLIVACEOUS	ACEIORTTXY	EXCITATORY
	VIOLACEOUS	ACEIPPRSST	SCRAPPIEST
ACEILOPPRT	POLICE TRAP	ACEIRRRTUW	RAW RECRUIT
ACEILOPRTX	EXPLICATOR	ACEIRSSTTU	RUSTIC SEAT
ACEILOPTUV	COPULATIVE		RUSTICATES
ACEILORSSV	VOCALISERS	ACEISSTTTY	CITY-STATES
ACEILORSVZ	VOCALIZERS	ACEJKKMOSS	SMOKEJACKS
ACEILOSTWY	LAW SOCIETY	ACEJKKRSSY	SKYJACKERS
ACEILPPSTU	SUPPLICATE	ACEJKLLOWY	YELLOW JACK
ACEILPRTUU	APICULTURE	ACEJLMPRSU	JUMPS CLEAR

ACEJLMSSUU	MAJUSCULES	**ACEMPPSSTU**	SETS UP CAMP
ACEJORRTTY	TRAJECTORY	**ACENNNORSU**	ANNOUNCERS
ACEKKLNOSS	ANKLE SOCKS	**ACENNORSTV**	CONVERSANT
ACEKKLOORW	LOOK A WRECK	**ACENNOSTTT**	CONTESTANT
ACEKKMOSST	SMOKESTACK	**ACENOORRSZ**	SCORZONERA
ACEKKNOSTT	TAKEN STOCK	**ACENOPRRST**	COPARTNERS
ACEKKOSSTT	TAKES STOCK	**ACENOPRRSU**	PAN SCOURER
ACEKLLLRTY	TALLY CLERK	**ACENOPRSTT**	PAR CONTEST
ACEKLLRSTU	LACKLUSTRE	**ACENOPRTTT**	PROTECTANT
ACEKLMNOSU	SUCK A LEMON	**ACENOPSSTW**	TOWNSCAPES
ACEKLMNOSY	LACKS MONEY	**ACENOPSSTY**	SYNCOPATES
ACEKLNOPST	ALPENSTOCK	**ACENORRSSU**	SCORES A RUN
ACEKLNORSS	CLOSE RANKS	**ACENORRSTU**	RACONTEURS
ACEKLORSST	LOSES TRACK	**ACENORSSTU**	COURTESANS
ACEKLORTTW	TOTAL WRECK	**ACENPSTTUU**	PUNCTUATES
ACEKMNOOTW	CAME TO KNOW	**ACEOOOPRRT**	COOPERATOR
ACEKPRRSSY	SKYSCRAPER	**ACEOOPPRRS**	CARPOSPORE
ACELLLLRUY	CELLULARLY	**ACEOOPPRRT**	PROCREATOR
ACELLLORSS	COLLARLESS	**ACEOOPRRTY**	PROCARYOTE
ACELLNOORT	ETON COLLAR	**ACEOOSTTVW**	TWO OCTAVES
ACELLNOSSW	CALLOWNESS	**ACEOPRSSTT**	SPECTATORS
ACELLNOTVY	COVALENTLY	**ACEOPRSTTY**	COPY TASTER
ACELLOPTUY	EUCALYPTOL		COPYTASTER
ACELLORSSW	LOWER CLASS	**ACEORRRSTT**	RETRACTORS
ACELLPRSTY	SPECTRALLY	**ACEORRSSTY**	SCORES A TRY
ACELLPRSUY	SPECULARLY	**ACEORRSUWY**	CAUSE WORRY
ACELLSSTTY	TACTLESSLY	**ACEORSTUXY**	EXCUSATORY
ACELMNNOTT	MALCONTENT	**ACEQRSSTUU**	SQUARE CUTS
ACELMNOORT	MONTE CARLO	**ACERRSTUUV**	CURVATURES
ACELMNOOSV	MOONCALVES	**ACFFGIILNT**	AFFLICTING
ACELMNSTUU	TENACULUMS	**ACFFGILLNO**	CALLING OFF
ACELMOOSTT	LAST TO COME	**ACFFGINOST**	CASTING OFF
ACELMOPSST	ECTOPLASMS	**ACFFIILLOY**	OFFICIALLY
ACELNNNORU	NONNUCLEAR	**ACFFIILNNO**	COFFIN NAIL
ACELNNOSSU	CONSENSUAL	**ACFFIILNOT**	AFFLICTION
ACELNNOTUV	CONVENTUAL	**ACFFIILNOU**	UNOFFICIAL
ACELNNTTUU	CUT A TUNNEL	**ACFFILLNUY**	FANCIFULLY
ACELNOPRSV	PROVENCALS	**ACFFILLOST**	CALLS IT OFF
ACELNOPRSY	NARCOLEPSY	**ACFFINOOTU**	AUCTION OFF
ACELNOSSTU	CONSULATES	**ACFFIORRTY**	CARRY IT OFF
ACELNOTTUX	CONTEXTUAL	**ACFGHHISTU**	CAUGHT FISH
ACELOOPRRT	PERCOLATOR	**ACFGHIIKPT**	PICK A FIGHT
ACELOORSTW	WATER-COOLS	**ACFGHILNNU**	FLAUNCHING
ACELOOSSST	CASTS LOOSE	**ACFGIILNOS**	FOCALISING
ACELOPPRST	PARCEL POST	**ACFGIILNOZ**	FOCALIZING
ACELOPRSTU	SPECULATOR	**ACFGIILNRY**	CLARIFYING
ACELOPRSWY	COW PARSLEY	**ACFGIINNRU**	FACING RUIN
ACELOPSTTT	CATTLESTOP	**ACFGIINRSY**	SCARIFYING
ACELORRSSU	CARROUSELS	**ACFGIKNOOT**	COOKING FAT
ACELORRSTU	EARLS COURT	**ACFGILLNOR**	CALLING FOR
ACELORSSTU	LAST COURSE	**ACFGILNNOT**	CONFLATING
ACELOSSSTU	OUTCLASSES	**ACFGILOPRY**	PROFLIGACY
ACELOSSSTY	STAYS CLOSE	**ACFGIMNORR**	RACING FORM
ACELPPRRSU	CURLPAPERS	**ACFGINOPTU**	FACING UP TO
ACELPPRSSU	UPPER CLASS	**ACFGINRRTU**	FRACTURING
	UPPER-CLASS	**ACFGLNORSY**	GYRFALCONS
ACELPSTUUY	EUCALYPTUS	**ACFHHIILTT**	HITCH A LIFT
ACELRSSTTY	CRYSTAL SET	**ACFHIIKLNS**	LACK FINISH
ACEMMMNNOO	COMMON NAME	**ACFHIKLOOR**	LOCK OF HAIR
ACEMMMPRSU	SUMMER CAMP	**ACFHILNOTU**	FINAL TOUCH
ACEMMNORTY	COMMENTARY	**ACFHILNSTU**	CUTS IN HALF
ACEMMNOSTU	CONSUMMATE	**ACFHIOPRST**	FACTORSHIP
ACEMMOSTTY	MASTECTOMY	**ACFHKOOTUW**	OUT OF WHACK
ACEMNNNOTT	CANTONMENT	**ACFHLLORST**	CALLS FORTH
ACEMNNORST	MONSTRANCE	**ACFHLLTUWY**	WATCHFULLY
ACEMNOOTYZ	MYCETOZOAN	**ACFHLMRSSU**	SCRUM-HALFS
ACEMNOSTTY	NEMATOCYST	**ACFHLORSTW**	FLOWCHARTS
ACEMOOPSST	COME TO PASS	**ACFHMOORTU**	FAR TOO MUCH
ACEMOORSSV	MOVE ACROSS	**ACFIILLLMY**	FILMICALLY
ACEMOOSTTY	COME TO STAY	**ACFIILLMTV**	FALL VICTIM
ACEMORSSTU	SCREAMS OUT	**ACFIILNOPS**	FLIPS A COIN

ACFIILNOPT	PONTIFICAL	ACGHIRRTTW	CARTWRIGHT
ACFIILNORT	FRICTIONAL	ACGHKORRTU	ROUGH TRACK
ACFIINNORS	INFRASONIC	ACGHMNOORR	CHRONOGRAM
ACFIINNORT	INFARCTION	ACGHOOPPRY	COPROPHAGY
	INFRACTION	ACGHORSSTU	ROUGHCASTS
ACFIIOSTTU	FACTITIOUS	ACGIIKKNST	TAKING SICK
ACFIKLLLTU	AT FULL LICK	ACGIIKKNST	STICKING AT
ACFIKSSSTT	STICKS FAST	ACGIILLMSS	GALLICISMS
ACFILLLORU	FOLLICULAR	ACGIILLNOS	LOCALISING
ACFILMORST	FILM ACTORS	ACGIILLNOZ	LOCALIZING
ACFILNNOOT	CONFLATION	ACGIILLORS	CIGARILLOS
ACFILNNORS	FRANCOLINS	ACGIILLOTY	LOGICALITY
ACFILNNOTU	FINAL COUNT	ACGIILLRTU	LITURGICAL
	FUNCTIONAL	ACGIILMNPS	MISPLACING
ACFILNOOPT	FOCAL POINT	ACGIILNNNP	PINNACLING
ACFILNOOST	OLFACTIONS	ACGIILNOOR	AIR-COOLING
ACFILOSTUY	FACTIOUSLY	ACGIILNOSV	VOCALISING
ACFILRSSST	FIRST CLASS	ACGIILNOVZ	VOCALIZING
	FIRST-CLASS	ACGIILNRTU	CURTAILING
ACFIMNPRSY	FRANCIS PYM	ACGIILNRTY	LARYNGITIC
ACFINNOOTU	ACT OF UNION	ACGIILNSST	ANGLICISTS
ACFINOORRT	FORNICATOR	ACGIIMNNRU	MANICURING
ACFINRSSSW	SWISS FRANC	ACGIIMNORS	ORGANISMIC
ACFIORSTTT	FIRST TO ACT	ACGIIMSSTT	STIGMATICS
ACFKOPRRTY	PARTY FROCK	ACGIINNNOS	CANONISING
ACFLLMOPUY	LUMP OF CLAY	ACGIINNNOT	CONTAINING
ACFLLOOPRT	PORT OF CALL	ACGIINNNOZ	CANONIZING
ACFLLORRSU	FUR COLLARS	ACGIINNNST	INSTANCING
ACFLNOOOST	TONS OF COAL	ACGIINNOPS	CAPONISING
ACFLNRRUUU	FURUNCULAR	ACGIINNOPZ	CAPONIZING
ACFLOORSTU	COLOURFAST	ACGIINNOTU	AUCTIONING
	FAST COLOUR		CAUTIONING
ACFLOORTUW	COURT OF LAW	ACGIINOOTT	COGITATION
ACFLORSTUY	CRUSTY LOAF	ACGIINPRST	PRACTISING
ACGGHINNNU	UNCHANGING	ACGIINOTTU	ACQUITTING
ACGGHINNPU	CHANGING UP	ACGIINRRSU	CURARISING
ACGGHINOPY	HYPNAGOGIC	ACGIINRRUZ	CURARIZING
ACGGIILNNO	GANGLIONIC	ACGIINRTTU	URTICATING
ACGGIINOTT	COGITATING	ACGIJKKNSY	SKYJACKING
ACGGIINRSU	ICING SUGAR	ACGIKKMMNO	MAKING MOCK
ACGGILLNNY	GLANCINGLY	ACGIKKMNRU	MUCKRAKING
ACGGILLOOY	GLACIOLOGY	ACGIKLLNNY	CLANKINGLY
ACGGILNNPU	GLANCING UP	ACGIKMNOPS	SMOKING CAP
ACGGINORYZ	GOING CRAZY	ACGIKMNSTU	MAKING CUTS
ACGHHILLOR	HIGH COLLAR	ACGIKNOPTU	PACKING OUT
ACGHHILNST	HATCHLINGS	ACGILLNOPS	COLLAPSING
ACGHHINTTW	NIGHT WATCH		SCALLOPING
ACGHIINNNU	UNCHAINING	ACGILLNORR	CORRALLING
ACGHIINSST	CHASTISING	ACGILLNOTU	CALLING OUT
ACGHIIPRRT	TRIGRAPHIC	ACGILLOOOZ	ZOOLOGICAL
ACGHIKLNPU	CHALKING UP	ACGILLOORU	UROLOGICAL
ACGHIKLNST	LIGHT SNACK	ACGILLOSST	COLLAGISTS
ACGHIKNPSU	SHACKING UP	ACGILLRSUY	SURGICALLY
ACGHIKRRTT	RIGHT TRACK	ACGILMNNOO	COGNOMINAL
ACGHILLOTY	GOTHICALLY	ACGILMNORU	CLAMOURING
ACGHILMNRY	CHARMINGLY	ACGILMNOST	COMING LAST
ACGHILNNTU	UNLATCHING	ACGILMNTUU	CUMULATING
ACGHILNRTU	NAUTCH GIRL	ACGILNNPRY	PRANCINGLY
ACGHILNSTY	SCATHINGLY	ACGILNNPSU	UNCLASPING
ACGHILOOPT	PATHOLOGIC	ACGILNOORY	CRANIOLOGY
ACGHIMNNOP	CHAMPIGNON	ACGILNOPTU	COPULATING
ACGHIMNOST	STOMACHING	ACGILNOSTU	OSCULATING
ACGHIMNPTU	MATCHING UP	ACGILORSUY	GLYCOSURIA
ACGHINNSTU	STAUNCHING		GRACIOUSLY
ACGHINOPRT	PROGNATHIC	ACGIMNOPSS	COMPASSING
ACGHINPPTU	PATCHING UP	ACGIMNOPTU	CAMPING OUT
ACGHINPRSU	PURCHASING	ACGIMNORRS	CAIRNGORMS
ACGHINTTVW	WATCHING T.V.	ACGIMNORSU	ORGAN MUSIC
ACGHIOOPRR	OROGRAPHIC	ACGIMNSSTY	GYMNASTICS
ACGHIOPPRT	PICTOGRAPH	ACGINNNNOU	ANNOUNCING
ACGHIOPRSS	SHIPS CARGO		

ACGINNORRY	CARRYING ON	ACHIMOSSST	MASOCHISTS
	CARRYING-ON	ACHIMOSSTU	MUSTACHIOS
ACGINNRRWY	WARNING CRY	ACHIMRSSSW	SCRIMSHAWS
ACGINNRTTU	TRUNCATING	ACHINNOSST	STANCHIONS
ACGINOOSTU	CONTAGIOUS	ACHINOSTTT	NOT A STITCH
ACGINOPSTU	SPACING OUT	ACHIOPRRSZ	RHIZOCARPS
ACGINOPSUU	PUGNACIOUS	ACHIOPRSTY	PHYSIOCRAT
ACGINORRTU	TOURING CAR	ACHIOPSTTY	HYPOSTATIC
ACGINORSUU	UNGRACIOUS	ACHIPRSTYY	PSYCHIATRY
ACGINORTUV	CARVING OUT	ACHIRSTTWW	WRIST WATCH
ACGINOSTTU	CASTING OUT		WRISTWATCH
ACGINPPRSU	SCRAPING UP	ACHKMOOOST	THOMAS COOK
ACGJLLNOUY	CONJUGALLY	ACHKMOOSTU	ASK TOO MUCH
ACGJNNOSTU	CONJUGANTS	ACHKMORSTU	TOUCHMARKS
ACGKNORRTW	WRONG TRACK	ACHKNOOPTU	TOOK A PUNCH
ACGLNOORSU	CLANGOROUS	ACHKNORSTU	HAS NO TRUCK
ACGLNORSSW	CROWN GLASS	ACHKNOSSTY	NASTY SHOCK
ACGLOORSUY	GAY COLOURS	ACHLLNOTUY	COUNTY HALL
ACGMOPRRTY	CRYPTOGRAM	ACHLLOOPST	PHOTOCALLS
ACGMOPRSTY	CRYPTOGAMS	ACHLLOOSSW	LAW SCHOOLS
ACGORRSSTU	GRASS COURT	ACHLMMOORS	SCHOOLMARM
ACHHILMOPT	OPHTHALMIC	ACHLOORSST	ART SCHOOLS
ACHHIMRRTY	ARRHYTHMIC	ACHLOOSSTU	HOLOCAUSTS
ACHHIOPPST	PHOSPHATIC	ACHNNORSYY	ASYNCHRONY
ACHHIPRSCU	PUSHCHAIRS	ACHNOORSTT	NORTH COAST
ACHHJNNOSY	JOHNNY CASH	ACHNOPSSTY	SYCOPHANTS
ACHHLOSSTW	WASH CLOTHS	ACHOOSSTTU	SOUTH COAST
	WASHCLOTHS	ACHOOSTTTU	CUTS A TOOTH
ACHHNOOTTU	AUTOCHTHON	ACHOPSSTUY	HYPOCAUSTS
ACHHOPPSTY	PSYCHOPATH	ACHORSTTTU	CUTTHROATS
ACHIIIMNST	HISTAMINIC	ACIIILLMNP	AMPICILLIN
ACHIIIRSST	TRICHIASIS	ACIIILLMNY	INIMICALLY
ACHIILLLTY	LITHICALLY	ACIIILNOPT	POLITICIAN
ACHIILORST	HISTORICAL	ACIIILSTTV	VITALISTIC
ACHIIMNSST	MACHINISTS	ACIIINNOTT	INCITATION
ACHIIMNSTU	HUMANISTIC	ACIIINNRST	INARTISTIC
ACHIIMNSUV	CHAUVINISM	ACIIINNTTV	INACTIVITY
ACHIIMOPPP	HIPPOCAMPI	ACIIJRSTUY	JUSTICIARY
ACHIINNORT	CORINTHIAN	ACIIKLPRST	LACK SPIRIT
ACHIINORSU	AIR CUSHION	ACIIKMRSST	MISS A TRICK
	AIR-CUSHION	ACIIKNNNPY	PICKANINNY
ACHIINPSSY	PHYSICIANS	ACIIKNRSTW	WINS A TRICK
ACHIINPSUY	PICAYUNISH	ACIIKSSTTT	STICKS AT IT
ACHIINRSST	CHRISTIANS	ACIILLMNRY	CRIMINALLY
ACHIINRSTT	ANTICHRIST	ACIILLNORY	IRONICALLY
ACHIINSTUV	CHAUVINIST	ACIILMNOST	MONISTICAL
ACHIIOPRST	APHORISTIC	ACIILMOPRR	PRIOR CLAIM
ACHIIOPSST	PISTACHIOS	ACIILMORST	MORALISTIC
ACHIIRSSTV	ARCHIVISTS	ACIILMQSTU	QUITCLAIMS
ACHIJLNNOV	JOHN CALVIN	ACIILMSTUY	MUSICALITY
ACHIKLLOPS	LACK POLISH	ACIILNOOST	COALITIONS
ACHIKLMSST	MAHLSTICKS	ACIILNOPRV	PROVINCIAL
ACHIKLPSTU	CHALKS IT UP	ACIILNOPST	PLICATIONS
ACHIKMNOST	MACKINTOSH	ACIILNORTT	TINCTORIAL
ACHIKMNRSS	SCRIMSHANK	ACIILNOSTT	SOLICITANT
ACHILLMOOS	ALCOHOLISM	ACIILNPPRS	PRINCIPALS
ACHILLMTYY	MYTHICALLY	ACIILNSSTV	CALVINISTS
ACHILLNNSY	CLANNISHLY	ACIILOPTTY	TOPICALITY
ACHILLNOOP	ALLOPHONIC	ACIILOSSST	SOCIALISTS
ACHILLNOPY	PHONICALLY	ACIILOSSUV	LASCIVIOUS
ACHILLOPTY	PHOTICALLY	ACIILPSTTY	PLASTICITY
ACHILLPSYY	PHYSICALLY	ACIILPTTYY	TYPICALITY
ACHILMOPTY	POLYMATHIC	ACIILRSTTU	ALTRUISTIC
ACHILNOORS	ISOCHRONAL		ULTRAISTIC
ACHILNOSST	ST.NICHOLAS	ACIILSSSTV	SLAVICISTS
ACHILORSUV	CHIVALROUS	ACIIMMNOPT	PANTOMIMIC
ACHILOSSST	SCHOLIASTS	ACIIMMNNSTU	NUMISMATIC
ACHIMMNNORS	MONARCHISM	ACIIMNNORS	CANIS MINOR
ACHIMNOPTT	MATCH POINT	ACIIMNOPST	IMPACTIONS
ACHIMNORST	MONARCHIST	ACIIMNOPSU	PIANO MUSIC
ACHIMORRYZ	MYCORRHIZA		

ACIIMNORST	MORTICIANS	ACILNOOSSS	COLOSSIANS
	ROMANISTIC	ACILNOOSTU	OSCULATION
ACIIMNPTTY	TYMPANITIC	ACILNORRTY	CONTRARILY
ACIIMNRSSS	NARCISSISM	ACILNORSSU	INCUR A LOSS
ACIIMNRSTU	MANICURIST	ACILNORSTU	ULTRASONIC
ACIINNOOTV	INVOCATION	ACILNPPSTU	SUPPLICANT
ACIINNOPSS	SPINS A COIN	ACILOOPRRT	PROCTORIAL
ACIINNOSTU	INSOUCIANT	ACILOOQSUU	LOQUACIOUS
ACIINNOTTX	INTOXICANT	ACILOOSSUX	SAXICOLOUS
ACIINOPRST	ASCRIPTION	ACILOPSSUY	SPACIOUSLY
ACIINORSTV	VICTORIANS	ACILOPSTUY	CAPTIOUSLY
ACIINORTTU	URTICATION	ACILORTTUV	CULTIVATOR
ACIINRSSST	NARCISSIST	ACILOSTUUY	CAUTIOUSLY
ACIIOPSSUU	AUSPICIOUS	ACILPRRSTU	SCRIPTURAL
ACIIOQRSTU	ACQUISITOR	ACIMMNORTY	MATRONYMIC
ACIIORSTVY	VARICOSITY	ACIMMORSSS	COMMISSARS
ACIIPSSTTY	SPASTICITY	ACIMMORSSY	COMMISSARY
ACIIQRTTUZ	QUARTZITIC	ACIMNNNOOR	MINOR CANON
ACIISSSTTT	STATISTICS	ACIMNNOOPS	COMPANIONS
ACIJLNNOTU	JUNCTIONAL	ACIMNNORTU	ROMAN TUNIC
ACIJLORTUY	JOCULARITY	ACIMNOOPRS	COMPARISON
ACIKKOORTT	TOOK A TRICK	ACIMNOOPSS	COMPASSION
ACIKKOPRUW	KICK UP A ROW	ACIMNOPPRS	PRISON CAMP
ACIKLMSSTU	MAULSTICKS	ACIMNOPRTY	PATRONYMIC
ACIKLNNOPT	PLANKTONIC	ACIMNPRSTU	MANUSCRIPT
ACIKLNOSTY	LAY IN STOCK	ACIMOOPRTT	COMPATRIOT
ACIKLOORSW	SOCIAL WORK	ACIMOPSTTY	ASYMPTOTIC
ACIKLORSTT	LOST A TRICK	ACIMORSSSW	SWIM ACROSS
ACIKLPRSTY	PLAY TRICKS	ACINNNOSTT	INCONSTANT
ACIKLPSSSS	SKIPS CLASS	ACINNNOTTU	CONTINUANT
ACIKLPSSST	SLAPSTICKS	ACINNOOORT	CORONATION
ACIKNOOOTT	TOOK ACTION	ACINNOPTTU	PUNCTUATION
ACIKNRSTTY	NASTY TRICK	ACINNORSST	CONSTRAINS
ACIKOPRTYY	KARYOTYPIC	ACINNORSTT	CONSTRAINT
ACIKPRRTTY	PARTY TRICK		IN CONTRAST
ACIKPRSSTW	PICK STRAWS	ACINNORTTU	TRUNCATION
ACILLLNOOY	COLONIALLY	ACINOOOPTT	CO-OPTATION
ACILLLOOQU	COLLOQUIAL	ACINOORSTT	CARTOONIST
ACILLMNNOO	MONOCLINAL	ACINOORTVY	INVOCATORY
ACILLMOORT	COLLIMATOR	ACINORSSST	CROISSANTS
	MORTAL COIL	ACINPRRSTT	TRANSCRIPT
ACILLMOPYY	MYOPICALLY	ACIOORSTVY	IVORY COAST
ACILLMOTUU	ALTOCUMULI	ACIORRSTTU	RUSTICATOR
ACILLMSTYY	MYSTICALLY	ACJKOPRSST	JOCKSTRAPS
ACILLNOOTU	ALLOCUTION	ACKKKNOOOT	TOOK A KNOCK
ACILLNORTW	CROWN IT ALL	ACKLMMNOOT	COMMON TALK
ACILLNORUU	UNILOCULAR	ACKLMNOORS	ROCK SALMON
ACILLNORUV	INVOLUCRAL	ACKLMOOORS	CLOAKROOMS
ACILLNOSUY	UNSOCIALLY	ACKLRSSTUY	LUCKY STARS
ACILLNOUVY	UNIVOCALLY	ACKMMNOOST	COMMON TASK
ACILLOOPRT	ALLOTROPIC	ACKNOOOTTU	TOOK A COUNT
ACILLOOPTY	PLAY IT COOL	ACKOOPRSTY	PASTRY COOK
ACILLOORST	OSCILLATOR	ACLLLOOSSY	COLOSSALLY
ACILLOPRTY	TROPICALLY	ACLLLRTUUY	CULTURALLY
ACILLRSTUY	RUSTICALLY	ACLLMMNOUY	COMMUNALLY
ACILMMOORS	MICROSOMAL	ACLLMPRSTU	CALL TRUMPS
ACILMMOSTT	COMMITTALS	ACLLMRSUUY	MUSCULARLY
ACILMMRSUU	SIMULACRUM	ACLLNPTUUY	PUNCTUALLY
ACILMNOOPY	OIL COMPANY	ACLLOOPRRY	CORPORALLY
ACILMNOORT	MICROTONAL	ACLLORRSSY	RALLYCROSS
ACILMNOPST	COMPLAINTS	ACLLPRSTUU	SCULPTURAL
ACILMNOSUU	CALUMNIOUS	ACLMMNOOST	COMMON SALT
ACILMNOTUU	CUMULATION	ACLMMNOOTY	COMMONALTY
ACILMOPRRY	MICROPYLAR	ACLMOORSSS	CLASSROOMS
ACILMORSUU	MIRACULOUS	ACLNNOSTTU	CONSULTANT
ACILMSTUWZ	WALTZ MUSIC	ACLNNOSTTY	CONSTANTLY
ACILNNOOOT	ON LOCATION	ACLNNOSTUV	CONVULSANT
ACILNOOORT	COLORATION	ACLNNRSUUU	RANUNCULUS
ACILNOOPTU	COPULATION	ACLNOORSTT	CONTRALTOS
ACILNOOPZZ	POZZOLANIC	ACLNOORSTU	COLOURANTS
ACILNOORTU	INOCULATOR	ACLNOPSTUY	POSTULANCY

ACLOOPRTUY	COPULATORY	ADDEEFINRR	DEAR FRIEND
ACLOORSSTY	ROYAL SCOTS	ADDEEFLORW	DEAD FLOWER
ACLRRSTTUU	STRUCTURAL	ADDEEFNNST	DEFENDANTS
ACMMNOSSTU	CUSTOMS MAN	ADDEEFRRSU	DEFRAUDERS
ACMMOORTTU	COMMUTATOR	ADDEEGGINS	DISENGAGED
ACMMPPUUUV	VACUUM PUMP	ADDEEGHITW	DEAD WEIGHT
ACMNNORTUY	COUNTRYMAN		DEADWEIGHT
ACMNOOPRTU	CONTOUR MAP	ADDEEGHLNO	LONGHEADED
ACMNOORRST	CORMORANTS	ADDEEGHNRS	GARDEN SHED
ACMNOOSSTU	COSMONAUTS	ADDEEGILMS	MIDDLE AGES
ACMNOOSSTW	SCOTSWOMAN	ADDEEGINRR	DEAD RINGER
ACMORSSSUW	SWUM ACROSS	ADDEEGINRT	DENIGRATED
ACNNNOOSST	CONSONANTS	ADDEEGINST	DESIGNATED
ACNOOPRSTY	SYNCOPATOR	ADDEEHHNOT	NOD THE HEAD
ACNOPRSSUY	SYNCARPOUS	ADDEEHIRSW	SHREWD IDEA
ACNOPRTTUU	PUNCTUATOR	ADDEEHLNRU	UNHERALDED
ACNORRSSSU	RUNS ACROSS	ADDEEHNNOP	OPENHANDED
ACNORRSTUW	RUN TWO CARS	ADDEEHNNSS	HANDEDNESS
ACNORSSUWY	RUSS CONWAY	ADDEEHNOOW	WOODENHEAD
ACNPRRRUWY	PRAWN CURRY	ADDEEHNORV	HANDED OVER
ACNPSTTUUY	CUT UP NASTY	ADDEEHRRTY	REHYDRATED
ACOOPRRRTT	PROTRACTOR	ADDEEHRSTY	DEHYDRATES
ACOOPRRRTU	PROCURATOR	ADDEEHRTUY	RUED THE DAY
ACOOPRSSTT	SPORTS COAT	ADDEEIKMNW	WEAK-MINDED
ACOPRSSSTU	PUTS ACROSS	ADDEEILLNT	ENDED IT ALL
ADDDDEEKLS	SKEDADDLED	ADDEEILMNS	DAMNED LIES
ADDDEEEELN	DEAD NEEDLE	ADDEEILMST	MIDDLE EAST
ADDDEEFPRT	DEPREDATED	ADDEEILNRY	DINED EARLY
ADDDEEFHIL	FIDDLEHEAD	ADDEEILNSS	DEADLINESS
ADDDEEGILM	MIDDLE-AGED	ADDEEILNTZ	DENTALIZED
ADDDEEGINO	DOING A DEED	ADDEEILOTV	DOVETAILED
ADDDEEHNRU	DUNDERHEAD	ADDEEILPSS	DISPLEASED
ADDDEEHRTY	DEHYDRATED	ADDEEILRSS	SADDLERIES
ADDDEEILSS	SIDESADDLE	ADDEEILRSV	DAREDEVILS
ADDDEEKLSS	SKEDADDLES	ADDEEILRWY	WIDELY READ
ADDDEENNOV	ODD AND EVEN	ADDEEILSTV	DAVID STEEL
ADDDEEPRSU	SUPERADDED	ADDEEIMNOR	MODERN IDEA
ADDDEFILPY	PADDY FIELD	ADDEEIMNOT	DEAD ON TIME
	PADDYFIELD	ADDEEINNRT	DINNER DATE
ADDDEGINWY	WEDDING DAY	ADDEEINSTU	UNSTEADIED
ADDDEGNORU	DEAD GROUND	ADDEEIOPTV	VIDEOTAPED
ADDDEGNORW	DOWNGRADED	ADDEEIORTY	READY TO DIE
ADDDEHIOTT	DID TO DEATH	ADDEEIPRSW	WIDESPREAD
ADDDEHNNOW	HANDED DOWN	ADDEEIPRTU	REPUDIATED
ADDDEILMOR	MIDDLE ROAD	ADDEEIRRST	ARID DESERT
ADDDELLLUY	DEADLY DULL	ADDEEIRSTV	ADVERTISED
ADDDEMNOOS	MADE NO ODDS	ADDEEIRTTX	EXTRADITED
ADDDEMNOPW	DAMPED DOWN	ADDEEISSVX	DAVID ESSEX
ADDEEEEPST	DEEP-SEATED	ADDEELLMTU	MEDULLATED
ADDEEEFGRY	FRAYED EDGE	ADDEELLSSS	SADDLELESS
ADDEEEFHNR	FREEHANDED	ADDEELMNOR	ENDODERMAL
ADDEEEFLOR	FREELOADED	ADDEELMNOY	ALMOND-EYED
ADDEEEGGGJ	JAGGED EDGE	ADDEELMOTU	DEMODULATE
ADDEEEGGGR	RAGGED EDGE	ADDEELNORV	OVERLANDED
ADDEEEGHHT	HAD THE EDGE	ADDEELOORV	OVERLOADED
ADDEEEGILR	EDDIE LARGE	ADDEELOPPR	DOPE PEDLAR
ADDEEEGNNR	ENDANGERED	ADDEELOPRR	ROPE LADDER
ADDEEEHNNV	EVENHANDED	ADDEELPRST	STEP LADDER
ADDEEEHORS	SOREHEADED		STEPLADDER
ADDEEEILNT	DELINEATED	ADDEELPRVY	DEPRAVEDLY
ADDEEELRST	SADDLETREE	ADDEEMNNRT	RENT DEMAND
ADDEEELRTT	DEAD LETTER	ADDEEMNOPR	PROMENADED
ADDEEEOORT	ORDERED TEA	ADDEEMNRRU	UNDERARMED
ADDEEEPRST	DEPREDATES	ADDEENNPST	DEPENDANTS
ADDEEERSSS	ADDRESSEES	ADDEENQRSU	SQUANDERED
ADDEEERTTU	DEUTERATED	ADDEENRRTU	UNDERRATED
ADDEEFFIOR	DIED OF FEAR	ADDEENRSSW	NEW ADDRESS
ADDEEFHLNT	LEFT-HANDED	ADDEENRTUV	ADVENTURED
ADDEEFHOST	SOFTHEADED	ADDEENSSWY	WEDNESDAYS
ADDEEFIINZ	DENAZIFIED	ADDEEOPRRT	DEPREDATOR
ADDEEFIISX	FIXED IDEAS	ADDEEOPRSS	DESPERADOS

471

ADDEFGIILN	DEFILADING	ADDEILMNST	DISMANTLED
ADDEFGINRU	DEFRAUDING	ADDEILMPRT	MIDDLE PART
ADDEFGLORR	GERALD FORD	ADDEILMTTY	ADMITTEDLY
ADDEFHINRS	HAD FRIENDS	ADDEILNNOR	ROD AND LINE
ADDEFHNORU	FOUR-HANDED	ADDEILNNOS	DANDELIONS
ADDEFHOTUY	FADED YOUTH	ADDEILNNOW	NAILED DOWN
ADDEFILLSU	FUSILLADED	ADDEILNOYZ	DAILY DOZEN
ADDEFILMNO	MANIFOLDED	ADDEILNQSU	LENDS A QUID
ADDEFILSTX	TAX FIDDLES	ADDEILNSST	STANDS IDLE
ADDEFLLOOP	FLAPDOODLE	ADDEILNSSW	WINDLASSED
ADDEFLLORU	FEUDAL LORD	ADDEILSTUW	STUDIED LAW
ADDEFLLRUY	DREADFULLY	ADDEIMNNOO	ONE DIAMOND
ADDEFLMORS	FOLDED ARMS	ADDEIMNORS	RANDOMISED
ADDEFLNOST	SOFT-LANDED	ADDEIMNORZ	RANDOMIZED
ADDEFMOOOW	MADE OF WOOD	ADDEIMNPRW	WARPED MIND
ADDEGGOOST	DOG EATS DOG	ADDEINNOTU	DENUDATION
ADDEGGORTU	DRAGGED OUT	ADDEINOORS	RADIOSONDE
ADDEGHHHIN	HIGH-HANDED	ADDEINSTWY	STEADY WIND
ADDEGHILST	DEADLIGHTS	ADDEIOOSST	STOOD ASIDE
ADDEGHINSS	HAD DESIGNS	ADDEIRSTTU	STUDIED ART
ADDEGHIRRT	THIRD GRADE	ADDEKLNOTW	TALKED DOWN
ADDEGHLORT	GOLD THREAD	ADDEKMNOOS	MAKE NO ODDS
ADDEGIKNRW	KING EDWARD	ADDEKMNORW	MARKED DOWN
ADDEGILLNW	WINDGALLED	ADDEKNORSW	NAKED SWORD
ADDEGILOOS	GOOD LADIES	ADDELLMNPU	DEMAND-PULL
ADDEGIMOTZ	DOGMATIZED	ADDELMORRW	DREAM WORLD
ADDEGINRSS	ADDRESSING	ADDELNNOPU	LEND A POUND
ADDEGIORVW	DAVID GOWER	ADDELNNORW	WONDERLAND
ADDEGIRRSS	DISREGARDS	ADDELNOORW	WOODLANDER
ADDEGLLNNO	OLD ENGLAND	ADDELNOPWY	PLAYED DOWN
ADDEGLLNOR	LONG LADDER	ADDELPQRUU	QUADRUPLED
ADDEGLNOSY	GOLDEN DAYS	ADDELRRSST	STRADDLERS
ADDEGNORRS	RED DRAGONS	ADDEMNNOUW	WOUNDED MAN
ADDEGNORSW	DOWNGRADES	ADDEMRTUWY	MUDDY WATER
ADDEGNRRSU	UNDERGRADS	ADDENNNOST	STAND ON END
ADDEHHPRSU	PUSHED HARD	ADDENNPRUU	UP AND UNDER
ADDEHIIMRS	DIE-HARDISM	ADDENNRSTU	UNDERSTAND
ADDEHIINNT	HANDED IT IN	ADDENOOPST	ADOPTED SON
ADDEHIKNRY	HEADY DRINK	ADDENOORST	DEODORANTS
ADDEHILMNS	MISHANDLED	ADDENOPSSW	PASSED DOWN
ADDEHIMNOO	MAIDENHOOD	ADDENORRTW	DROWNED RAT
ADDEHIMNOS	ADMONISHED	ADDENORSTW	STARED DOWN
ADDEHINRRV	DRIVEN HARD		TREADS DOWN
ADDEHINRSY	ANHYDRIDES	ADDENOSTWY	STAYED DOWN
ADDEHIRRSV	DRIVES HARD	ADDEOORSTY	STOOD READY
ADDEHKORRW	WORKED HARD	ADDEORRSWW	DREW A SWORD
ADDEHLLNOR	LANDHOLDER	ADDEOSSSTT	SETS AT ODDS
ADDEHLLPRU	PULLED HARD	ADDEPQRSUU	QUADRUPEDS
ADDEHLNOOR	DOOR HANDLE	ADDFGIINNY	DANDIFYING
ADDEHLOSTY	LAY THE ODDS	ADDFGIOORY	GOOD FRIDAY
ADDEHMNNOW	HAND-ME-DOWN	ADDFIILNSU	DISDAINFUL
ADDEHMNOOS	DO HANDSOME	ADDFIINNOO	INDIAN FOOD
ADDEHMNORY	HOME AND DRY	ADDFIORSTV	DAVID FROST
ADDEHNOORT	HORNED TOAD	ADDGGLOOOS	GOOD AS GOLD
ADDEHNORSU	ROUNDHEADS	ADDGHHINRY	HIGH AND DRY
ADDEHNOSWW	WASHED DOWN	ADDGHLOORS	HOARDS GOLD
ADDEHOORST	DEATHS DOOR	ADDGHNORRU	HARD GROUND
ADDEHOOSST	SHOOTS DEAD	ADDGIIINNS	DISDAINING
ADDEHORRTY	DEHYDRATOR	ADDGIILNRY	DAILY GRIND
ADDEIILLSV	ILL-ADVISED	ADDGIIMNRV	DRIVING MAD
ADDEIILMPY	EPIDIDYMAL	ADDGIINSST	SAD TIDINGS
ADDEIILQTU	LIQUIDATED	ADDGIINSSU	DISSUADING
ADDEIILTVY	ADDITIVELY	ADDGILNNSU	UNSADDLING
ADDEIINNRS	RED INDIANS	ADDGILNPSU	SADDLING UP
ADDEIINNVV	DAVID NIVEN	ADDGILNRST	STRADDLING
ADDEIINOTU	AUDITIONED	ADDGINNOPU	UP AND DOING
ADDEIINRST	DISTRAINED	ADDGOORSTU	STOOD GUARD
ADDEIIPRSS	DISPRAISED	ADDHHLNOSS	HOLDS HANDS
ADDEIIPSST	DISSIPATED	ADDHHLOORT	HARD TO HOLD
ADDEILLNSS	LANDSLIDES	ADDHIINSTY	DAINTY DISH
ADDEILLOSW	DISALLOWED	ADDHIKNRRS	HARD DRINKS

ADDHILNSYY	DANDYISHLY	ADEEELNNUV	UNLEAVENED
ADDHILORSU	SHROUD-LAID	ADEEELNOPT	OPENED LATE
ADDHHNNORSU	HANDS ROUND	ADEEELNSVY	ELEVEN DAYS
ADDIIIKNNP	PAID IN KIND	ADEEELPRTY	REPEATEDLY
ADDIIILNUV	INDIVIDUAL	ADEEEMNNOY	ONE-EYED MAN
ADDIIINNOT	IN ADDITION	ADEEEMNNRT	ENDEARMENT
ADDIIITTVY	ADDITIVITY	ADEEEMNORR	EARNED MORE
ADDIINNOVX	DAVID NIXON	ADEEEMNRTT	TENDER MEAT
ADDIKKNORV	DRINK VODKA	ADEEEMNRTU	ENUMERATED
ADDILLLLYY	DILLY DALLY	ADEEEMNRUV	MANEUVERED
	DILLYDALLY	ADEEEMSTTW	STEWED MEAT
ADDILLQRSU	SQUAD DRILL	ADEEENORTX	EXONERATED
ADDILNORUY	DAILY ROUND	ADEEENPRTT	PENETRATED
ADDKKNORUV	DRUNK VODKA	ADEEENRRSS	SERENADERS
ADDLMMOSUY	SOLD A DUMMY	ADEEENRRSW	NEW READERS
ADDLNOOOSS	OLD SO-AND-SO		NEWSREADER
ADDLNORWWY	DOWNWARDLY	ADEEENRSST	EAST ENDERS
ADDNNOOTUW	DOWN AND OUT	ADEEENSSST	SEDATENESS
	DOWN-AND-OUT	ADEEENTTUV	EVENTUATED
ADDNNOSSTW	STANDS DOWN	ADEEENTTUX	EXTENUATED
ADDNORRSWW	DRAWN SWORD	ADEEEPRSTW	DEEP WATERS
ADEEEEFLNS	FEELS A NEED	ADEEERRSSV	READS VERSE
ADEEEEFLNT	LEADEN FEET	ADEEERSTTU	DEUTERATES
ADEEEEGNRT	DEGENERATE	ADEEERSTWW	WATERWEEDS
ADEEEELMRS	SEEMED REAL	ADEEFFILRS	FIELDFARES
ADEEEERSST	SEEDEATERS	ADEEFFIORS	DIES OF FEAR
ADEEEFGNRT	GARDEN FETE	ADEEFFKNOS	SNEAKED OFF
ADEEFFHMOT	HOME DEFEAT	ADEEFFOPRT	TAPERED OFF
ADEEEFHNRR	FREEHANDER	ADEEFFORST	AFFORESTED
ADEEEFHRRZ	FREEZE HARD	ADEEFGHIRU	FIGUREHEAD
ADEEEFIMRS	SEEMED FAIR	ADEEFGHLRT	THE RED FLAG
ADEEEFIRTV	FEDERATIVE	ADEEFGILNS	FEELING SAD
ADEEEFKPRS	SPEED FREAK		SAD FEELING
ADEEEFLORR	FREELOADER	ADEEFGINRT	FEDERATING
ADEEEGGLGNT	GET ENGAGED	ADEEFGLNNW	NEWFANGLED
ADEEEGGINV	GIVE AN EDGE	ADEEFGLRRS	SELF-REGARD
ADEEEGGNST	GETS AN EDGE	ADEEFGMNRT	FRAGMENTED
ADEEEGGPSU	SPEED GAUGE	ADEEFHILOX	FIXED A HOLE
ADEEEGGRST	SEGREGATED	ADEEFHILTW	WHEAT FIELD
ADEEEGHHST	HAS THE EDGE	ADEEFHIRSS	FRESH IDEAS
ADEEEGHITT	GET THE IDEA	ADEEFHITTX	FIX THE DATE
ADEEEGHLTY	THE GLAD EYE	ADEEFHLNRT	LEFT-HANDER
ADEEEGHRRT	GRADE THREE	ADEEFHLRST	SELF-HATRED
ADEEEGIMRT	MEAGRE DIET	ADEEFHMOST	SAFE METHOD
ADEEEGPRST	GREAT SPEED	ADEEFHORSW	SHOWED FEAR
ADEEEGRSTW	WATERS EDGE	ADEEFHORSY	HAD EYES FOR
ADEEEHISST	THE SEASIDE	ADEEFIIMTX	FIXED A TIME
ADEEEHKLLU	KEELHAULED	ADEEFIINSZ	DENAZIFIES
ADEEEHLNOT	HEEL AND TOE	ADEEFIKRWY	FRIDAY WEEK
	HEEL-AND-TOE	ADEEFILLNS	FILLS A NEED
ADEEEHLPSY	SLEEPYHEAD		SELF-DENIAL
ADEEEHLRTT	LETTERHEAD	ADEEFILMRS	FEDERALISM
ADEEEHNNRT	NEAR THE END	ADEEFILNRR	REAL FRIEND
ADEEEHNQSU	QUEENS HEAD	ADEEFILOTX	EXFOLIATED
ADEEEHNRTT	THREATENED	ADEEFILPRS	FALSE PRIDE
ADEEEHNRTT	THE EAST END	ADEEFILRST	FEDERALIST
ADEEEHORTV	OVERHEATED	ADEEFILSTW	WASTED LIFE
ADEEEHRSTY	STAYED HERE	ADEEFIMNST	MANIFESTED
ADEEEILNST	DELINEATES	ADEEFINNOY	ONE FINE DAY
ADEEEILOTV	LEAVE TO DIE	ADEEFINNTV	FIVE AND TEN
ADEEEINRTY	TRAINED EYE	ADEEFINORT	FEDERATION
ADEEEINSSV	SEVEN A SIDE	ADEEFIPSSV	FIVE SPADES
ADEEEIPRRT	PIED-A-TERRE	ADEEFISSTT	DEFEATISTS
ADEEEIPSSW	SWEEP ASIDE	ADEEFKORTU	FREAKED OUT
ADEEEIRRTT	REITERATED	ADEEFLLLNN	FLANNELLED
ADEEEKLNST	NAKED STEEL	ADEEFLLNOX	FELLED AN OX
ADEEEKNPSS	PEAKEDNESS	ADEEFLLORW	FALLOW DEER
ADEEEKNSSW	SNAKEWEEDS	ADEEFLRSTU	DEFAULTERS
ADEEELLMNP	EMPANELLED	ADEEFMNSSU	MENDS A FUSE
ADEEELLRSS	LEADERLESS	ADEEFNNSTU	UNFASTENED
ADEEELNNSS	LEADENNESS	ADEEFNOPRR	FREE PARDON

ADEEFNORRW	FOREWARNED
ADEEFNORRY	YEARNED FOR
ADEEFNORVW	FAWNED OVER
ADEEFNPTTU	FATTENED UP
ADEEFOPRRT	PERFORATED
ADEEGGGNOT	GOT ENGAGED
ADEEGGHJRU	JUGGED HARE
ADEEGGHLOR	LOGGERHEAD
ADEEGGILNT	DELEGATING
ADEEGGILNW	NEW-LAID EGG
ADEEGGINSS	DISENGAGES
ADEEGGJNSS	JAGGEDNESS
ADEEGGLNOT	GOLDEN GATE
ADEEGGMOSU	DEMAGOGUES
ADEEGGNORS	GEORGE SAND
ADEEGGNRSS	RAGGEDNESS
ADEEGGOPSU	PEDAGOGUES
ADEEGHHNOT	HEATHEN GOD
ADEEGHIKNT	TAKING HEED
ADEEGHILTW	LEAD WEIGHT
ADEEGHINRT	GATHERED IN
ADEEGHIOTT	GOT THE IDEA
ADEEGHIRTW	AGREED WITH
ADEEGHLOSW	SHOWED A LEG
ADEEGHNORS	GARDEN HOSE
ADEEGHNOSV	GOD'S HEAVEN
ADEEGHPRTU	GATHERED UP
ADEEGHRRST	HAD REGRETS
ADEEGIIMNT	GAINED TIME
ADEEGIIRRT	RIDE A TIGER
ADEEGIJLNR	DARJEELING
ADEEGILLST	LEGISLATED
ADEEGILMNR	MALINGERED
ADEEGILNNR	DANGER LINE
ADEEGILNOT	DELEGATION
ADEEGILNRR	RINGLEADER
ADEEGILOPR	RIPE OLD AGE
ADEEGIMNNR	MEANDERING
ADEEGIMNNT	EMENDATING
ADEEGIMNRT	GERMINATED
ADEEGIMNST	MAGNETISED
ADEEGIMNTZ	MAGNETIZED
ADEEGIMRRT	GET MARRIED
ADEEGINNRS	GRENADINES
	SERENADING
ADEEGINOTT	NEGOTIATED
ADEEGINPSS	GAINS SPEED
ADEEGINRRS	GRENADIERS
ADEEGINRRT	INTERGRADE
	RETREADING
ADEEGINRRW	WEARING RED
ADEEGINRST	DENIGRATES
ADEEGINRTT	INTEGRATED
ADEEGINSST	DESIGNATES
ADEEGIORRT	RODE A TIGER
ADEEGIORTV	DEROGATIVE
ADEEGIPTTT	GET IT TAPED
ADEEGKNRSW	KEW GARDENS
ADEEGKPRSU	KEEPS GUARD
ADEEGLLNTY	DEAL GENTLY
ADEEGLMNNO	GOLDEN MEAN
ADEEGLNNNW	NEW ENGLAND
ADEEGLNTTU	GAUNTLETED
ADEEGLORRR	LARGE ORDER
ADEEGLRRSS	REGARDLESS
ADEEGLRTTT	GET RATTLED
ADEEGNORRS	ROSE GARDEN
ADEEGNOSTY	GONE STEADY
ADEEGNOTXY	OXYGENATED
ADEEGNPRST	GARDEN PEST
ADEEGNRRSW	GREENSWARD

ADEEGOPSTU	POSTAGE DUE
ADEEGORRRT	RETROGRADE
ADEEGORRSV	GAVE ORDERS
ADEEGOSSTY	GOES STEADY
ADEEGPRTUX	EXPURGATED
ADEEGRSTTT	GET STARTED
ADEEHHILMR	HEMIHEDRAL
ADEEHHINST	IN THE SHADE
ADEEHHISTW	WHITEHEADS
ADEEHHLRTU	RUDE HEALTH
ADEEHHMNOT	HEATHENDOM
ADEEHHNOPS	HEADPHONES
ADEEHHNORX	HEXAHEDRON
ADEEHHNPTY	HYPHENATED
ADEEHHNRTU	HEAD HUNTER
	HEADHUNTER
ADEEHHNSTU	UNSHEATHED
ADEEHHOTTT	TO THE DEATH
ADEEHHOTTV	HAD THE VOTE
ADEEHIIKRR	KEIR HARDIE
ADEEHIIPRS	HESPERIDIA
ADEEHIIRRW	WIREHAIRED
ADEEHIKLNT	AND THE LIKE
ADEEHIKLRT	THREADLIKE
ADEEHILLRS	RAISED HELL
ADEEHILNNR	IRENE HANDL
ADEEHILNTT	THE TAIL-END
ADEEHILOPP	PAEDOPHILE
ADEEHILPPR	HARELIPPED
ADEEHILPRS	LEADERSHIP
ADEEHILRRS	HERALDRIES
ADEEHILRTT	IDLE THREAT
ADEEHILSVY	ADHESIVELY
ADEEHILTVY	THE EVIL DAY
ADEEHIMMNR	HAMMERED IN
ADEEHIMNOT	DINE AT HOME
ADEEHIMNSU	DEHUMANISE
ADEEHIMNUZ	DEHUMANIZE
ADEEHIMPSS	EMPHASISED
ADEEHIMPSZ	EMPHASIZED
ADEEHIMSST	MEAT DISHES
ADEEHINNOS	IN ONES HEAD
ADEEHINNRV	HAVE DINNER
ADEEHINRRT	REND THE AIR
ADEEHINRST	DISHEARTEN
ADEEHINRSX	SHARE INDEX
ADEEHINRTT	IN THE TRADE
ADEEHINSTV	EDITH EVANS
ADEEHIORRT	RADIO THREE
ADEEHIOSSV	SHOVE ASIDE
ADEEHIPRRS	READERSHIP
ADEEHIRRSS	SHERARDISE
ADEEHIRRSZ	SHERARDIZE
ADEEHIRRTY	HEREDITARY
ADEEHKLLNT	DEATH KNELL
ADEEHKLRSS	SHELDRAKES
ADEEHKNOOY	HOOK AND EYE
ADEEHLLLPY	PLAYED HELL
ADEEHLLNRT	ENTHRALLED
ADEEHLLNSS	HANDLELESS
ADEEHLLOSS	LEASEHOLDS
ADEEHLLOST	LETHAL DOSE
ADEEHLLOSV	LEAVES HOLD
ADEEHLMTTY	METHYLATED
ADEEHLNOTW	DOWN AT HEEL
ADEEHLORUV	HAULED OVER
	OVERHAULED
ADEEHLOSTY	LOSE THE DAY
ADEEHLRRVY	HARDLY EVER
ADEEHLRSST	THREADLESS
ADEEHMMMOR	RAMMED HOME

ADEEHMMMNOR	REMAND HOME	ADEEILMNPT	PEDIMENTAL
ADEEHMNPRU	UNHAMPERED	ADEEILMNRT	DERAILMENT
ADEEHMOPRS	SEMAPHORED	ADEEILMNTY	MYELINATED
ADEEHMORSU	DREAM HOUSE	ADEEILMORS	DEMORALISE
ADEEHMORTW	DREW AT HOME	ADEEILMORT	MELIORATED
ADEEHMOSST	HOMESTEADS	ADEEILMORZ	DEMORALIZE
ADEEHMOSTY	STAYED HOME	ADEEILMPRR	PERIDERMAL
ADEEHMRRTY	THE RED ARMY	ADEEILNNRT	LATE DINNER
ADEEHNNORW	HERE AND NOW	ADEEILNORS	RIDES ALONE
ADEEHNNRTU	UNDERNEATH	ADEEILNORT	DELINEATOR
ADEEHNOSST	HEADSTONES	ADEEILNOSY	EASILY DONE
ADEEHNPPRS	APPREHENDS		LAID EYES ON
ADEEHNRSTT	AND THE REST	ADEEILNPPR	LINED PAPER
ADEEHNSTUU	UNDUE HASTE	ADEEILNRST	TAILENDERS
ADEEHNSTVY	SEVENTH DAY	ADEEILNRSV	VERNALISED
ADEEHOPRRT	HEAD PORTER	ADEEILNRSY	DINES EARLY
ADEEHORSUW	WAREHOUSED	ADEEILNRVZ	VERNALIZED
ADEEHORSVW	WASHED OVER	ADEEILNSSV	SEVEN DIALS
ADEEHORTTY	THE YEAR DOT	ADEEILNSTZ	DENTALIZES
ADEEHOSSWY	EYE SHADOWS	ADEEILNTTT	DILETTANTE
ADEEHRRSTT	THREE DARTS	ADEEILNTTV	VENTILATED
ADEEHRRSTY	REHYDRATES	ADEEILOPRS	DEPOLARISE
	THREE YARDS	ADEEILOPRZ	DEPOLARIZE
ADEEHRRTWY	DRY WEATHER	ADEEILOPTT	PETIOLATED
ADEEHRSSST	SHEDS TEARS	ADEEILPRRS	LIP READERS
ADEEHRSSTW	WATERSHEDS	ADEEILPRRV	PEARL DIVER
ADEEHRSTUY	RUES THE DAY	ADEEILPRST	SPEED TRIAL
ADEEHIILAT	THE ALIENS	ADEEILPSSS	DISPLEASES
ADEEIIJNRR	JARDINIERE	ADEEILPSTT	STAPLE DIET
ADEEIILMNT	ELIMINATED	ADEEILRSTU	ADULTERIES
ADEEIILMPS	SIMPLE IDEA	ADEEILRTTU	ELUTRIATED
ADEEIILMTT	DELIMITATE	ADEEILSSUX	SEXUALISED
ADEEIILNNS	INSIDE LANE	ADEEILSUXZ	SEXUALIZED
ADEEIILNNY	ANILINE DYE	ADEEIMMORT	IMMODERATE
ADEEIILNTV	EVIDENTIAL	ADEEIMMRRU	MEDIUM RARE
ADEEIILRSS	SERIALISED	ADEEIMMUVW	MEDIUM WAVE
ADEEIILRSZ	SERIALIZED	ADEEIMNNOT	DENOMINATE
ADEEIILSTV	DEVITALISE		EMENDATION
ADEEIILTVZ	DEVITALIZE		MATED IN ONE
ADEEIIMTTV	MEDITATIVE	ADEEIMNNTT	TINNED MEAT
ADEEIINRST	DISTRAINEE	ADEEIMNORT	ENDOMETRIA
ADEEIINRTT	ITINERATED	ADEEIMNORV	MAIDEN OVER
ADEEIINRVV	VIVANDIERE	ADEEIMNRRS	REMAINDERS
ADEEIINSST	EAST INDIES	ADEEIMNRRT	RETIRED MAN
ADEEIIRTTW	TIDEWAITER	ADEEIMNRSS	DREAMINESS
ADEEIIRTVV	DERIVATIVE	ADEEIMNRST	STREAMED IN
ADEEIJOPRS	JEOPARDISE	ADEEIMNRTT	TERMINATED
ADEEIJOPRZ	JEOPARDIZE	ADEEIMORRT	RADIOMETER
ADEEIKKPRT	KEEP IT DARK	ADEEIMORTU	AUDIOMETER
ADEEIKLMNN	KENNEL MAID	ADEEIMRSTT	MISTREATED
ADEEIKMMRT	MARKED TIME	ADEEIMSSST	DEMITASSES
ADEEIKNPRT	TAKEN PRIDE	ADEEIMSTTW	WASTED TIME
ADEEIKNRRT	TEA DRINKER	ADEEINNRST	EATS DINNER
ADEEIKNSST	TAKEN SIDES		END IN TEARS
ADEEIKPRST	TAKES PRIDE	ADEEINNRTV	INNERVATED
ADEEIKRSST	ASTERISKED	ADEEINORTT	ORIENTATED
ADEEIKSSST	TAKES SIDES		ROTTEN IDEA
ADEEIKSWXY	SIX-DAY WEEK	ADEEINOSST	AT ONES SIDE
ADEEILLMRY	REMEDIALLY	ADEEINOTTV	DENOTATIVE
ADEEILLMST	METALLISED		DETONATIVE
ADEEILLMTZ	METALLIZED	ADEEINPPSX	APPENDIXES
ADEEILLMVY	MEDIEVALLY	ADEEINPRST	PEDESTRIAN
ADEEILLNOV	LIVED ALONE	ADEEINRRSS	DREARINESS
ADEEILLPRS	ESPADRILLE	ADEEINRRST	RESTRAINED
ADEEILLPSS	SEALED LIPS	ADEEINRSSW	SENDS A WIRE
ADEEILLPST	PALLETISED	ADEEINRSTT	REINSTATED
ADEEILLPTZ	PALLETIZED		STRAITENED
ADEEILLRTT	ILL-TREATED	ADEEINRSTU	UNSTEADIER
ADEEILLSVV	SLIDE VALVE	ADEEINSSST	STEADINESS
ADEEILLSVW	ADVISE WELL	ADEEINSSTU	UNSTEADIES
ADEEILLUVV	VAUDEVILLE	ADEEIOPSTV	VIDEOTAPES

ADEEIOSSTY	EASY DOES IT	ADEELRSSTY	STEELYARDS
ADEEIOSXYY	OX-EYE DAISY	ADEELSTUVY	STUDY LEAVE
ADEEIPPRSU	PAUPERISED	ADEELSTVWY	TWELVE DAYS
ADEEIPPRUZ	PAUPERIZED	ADEEMMNNOY	MONEYED MAN
ADEEIPRRWZ	DREW A PRIZE	ADEEMMNNST	AMENDMENTS
ADEEIPRSTT	TAPESTRIED	ADEEMNNORT	ORNAMENTED
ADEEIPRSTU	REPUDIATES	ADEEMNNORV	OVERMANNED
ADEEIPRTTW	TEPID WATER	ADEEMNOPRR	PROMENADER
ADEEIPRTTX	EXTIRPATED	ADEEMNOPRS	PROMENADES
ADEEIPSSST	STEPS ASIDE	ADEEMNORTW	WANTED MORE
ADEEIPSSTW	SWEPT ASIDE	ADEEMNORTY	EMENDATORY
ADEEIQRRSU	AS REQUIRED	ADEEMNORUV	MANOEUVRED
ADEEIRRSTV	ADVERTISER	ADEEMNORYY	READY MONEY
ADEEIRRSTW	WATERSIDER	ADEEMNOSVY	SAVED MONEY
ADEEIRSSTV	ADVERTISES	ADEEMNPRTT	DEPARTMENT
ADEEIRSTTV	TRAVESTIED	ADEEMNRSTU	UNDER STEAM
ADEEIRSTTW	TIDEWATERS		UNSTREAMED
ADEEIRSTTX	EXTRADITES	ADEEMOORRS	AERODROMES
ADEEISSTVV	STEVE DAVIS	ADEEMOPTTT	POTTED MEAT
ADEEKLLMRW	MARKED WELL	ADEEMRRSTT	TRADE TERMS
ADEEKLLLOOP	LOOKED PALE	ADEEMRRSUY	DRY MEASURE
ADEEKLLPUY	ALL KEYED UP	ADEEMRRWXY	WAXED MERRY
ADEEKLOORT	OLD OAK TREE	ADEENNORSY	YEARS ON END
ADEEKLORTV	TALKED OVER	ADEENNRSUW	UNANSWERED
ADEEKLORTW	WORKED LATE	ADEENOOSTW	WOODEN SEAT
ADEEKLORVW	WALKED OVER	ADEENOPRRW	OPEN DRAWER
ADEEKMNOWY	MONDAY WEEK	ADEENOPRST	PERSONATED
ADEEKMRRRU	RUDE REMARK	ADEENOPSTY	STAYED OPEN
ADEEKMRRSS	DRESSMAKER	ADEENOQRSU	ONE SQUARED
ADEEKNNRTU	UNDERTAKEN	ADEENORRVW	EVER ONWARD
ADEEKNOSTU	SNEAKED OUT		WANDER OVER
ADEEKNRRTU	UNDERTAKER	ADEENORSUV	ENDEAVOURS
ADEEKNRSTU	UNDERTAKES	ADEENPPRRU	UNPREPARED
ADEEKNSUWY	SUNDAY WEEK	ADEENPPRSS	DAPPERNESS
ADEEKORRST	TAKE ORDERS	ADEENPRRTT	TENDER TRAP
ADEEKORSTV	SKATED OVER	ADEENPRRTU	ENRAPTURED
ADEELLLPWY	PLAYED WELL	ADEENPRSST	DEPRESSANT
	WELL PLAYED	ADEENPRSTY	PRESENT DAY
ADEELLMMRT	TRAMMELLED		PRESENT-DAY
ADEELLMNOP	MODEL PLANE	ADEENQRRSU	SQUANDERER
ADEELLNQUU	UNEQUALLED	ADEENQRSTU	TEN SQUARED
ADEELLNRUV	UNRAVELLED	ADEENRRSTU	UNDERRATES
ADEELLNRVW	DRAWN LEVEL	ADEENRRSUW	RUDE ANSWER
ADEELLOPST	SELLOTAPED	ADEENRRTUV	ADVENTURER
ADEELLORSS	LOSS LEADER	ADEENRRTUW	UNDER WATER
ADEELLORTT	LORD ATTLEE		UNDERWATER
ADEELLORVY	LOVE DEARLY	ADEENRSTTU	UNDERSTATE
ADEELLOSTY	DESOLATELY	ADEENRSTUV	ADVENTURES
ADEELLQRRU	QUARRELLED	ADEEOPRSSV	EAVESDROPS
ADEELLRSVW	DRAWS LEVEL		PASSED OVER
ADEELMMORS	MESODERMAL	ADEEORRTTU	TRADE ROUTE
ADEELMNORT	ALMOND TREE	ADEEORSTTV	OVERSTATED
ADEELMOORT	LEAD TO ROME	ADEEORSTVY	OVERSTAYED
ADEELMORRV	DREAM LOVER	ADEEPRRSST	TRADE PRESS
ADEELMORTY	MODERATELY	ADEEPRRSTU	DEPARTURES
ADEELMRSUY	MEASUREDLY	ADEEPRSSST	TRESPASSED
ADEELNNRTU	LAND TENURE	ADEERRSSTT	DESERT RATS
ADEELNORRV	OVERLANDER	ADEERRSTYY	STARRY-EYED
ADEELNPRTU	TURNED PALE	ADEERSSSTW	STEWARDESS
ADEELNRRSS	SLANDERERS	ADEERSSTYY	YESTERDAYS
ADEELNRUUV	UNDERVALUE	ADEESTTTUY	ESTATE DUTY
ADEELOPPRV	OVERLAPPED	ADEFFGHINO	HEADING OFF
ADEELOPPTU	DEPOPULATE	ADEFFGHLOU	LAUGHED OFF
ADEELOPRVY	OVERPLAYED	ADEFFGILNO	LEADING OFF
ADEELORRST	SOLE TRADER	ADEFFGINOR	READING OFF
ADEELORRTY	TORY LEADER	ADEFFGLNOU	GULF OF ADEN
ADEELORSVW	LEAVES WORD	ADEFFHLNOT	OFF THE LAND
ADEELPRRYY	READY REPLY	ADEFFIINSW	FINDS A WIFE
ADEELPRSTT	SPLATTERED	ADEFFILMUY	FAMILY FEUD
ADEELRRSSW	REWARDLESS	ADEFFILNOW	DAWN OF LIFE
ADEELRRSTU	ADULTERERS	ADEFFILNRU	FEARFUL DIN

ADEFFILORT	TRAILED OFF	**ADEFILOORT**	DEFOLIATOR
ADEFFIMORR	MARRIED OFF	**ADEFILOORW**	WORD OF A LIE
ADEFFINOUW	FOUND A WIFE	**ADEFILORTU**	FLUORIDATE
ADEFFKOPRS	SPARKED OFF	**ADEFIMNOOR**	MADE OF IRON
ADEFFLOOTT	FLAT-FOOTED	**ADEFIMNOTW**	DAWN OF TIME
ADEFFLORTT	RATTLED OFF	**ADEFIMNRRW**	WARM FRIEND
ADEFFNORSW	WANDERS OFF	**ADEFINNOTU**	FOUNTAINED
ADEFFOQRSU	SQUARED OFF	**ADEFINOORR**	FOREORDAIN
ADEFFORSTT	STARTED OFF	**ADEFINRSTX**	TRANSFIXED
ADEFGGINOR	GOD-FEARING	**ADEFINRTXY**	NEXT FRIDAY
ADEFGHILTU	FIGHT A DUEL	**ADEFIORRTY**	READY FOR IT
ADEFGHINOR	HEADING FOR	**ADEFIRSSTX**	FIXED STARS
ADEFGHOORT	GATHER FOOD	**ADEFKLNOTU**	OUTFLANKED
ADEFGHORST	GODFATHERS	**ADEFKNOPTU**	POKED FUN AT
ADEFGIILNN	ENFILADING	**ADEFLLMRUY**	DREAMFULLY
ADEFGIILNS	FLING ASIDE		FULLY ARMED
ADEFGIKLNR	KING ALFRED	**ADEFLLNNOW**	DOWNFALLEN
ADEFGILLNU	FALLING DUE		FALLEN DOWN
ADEFGILNSU	FLUNG ASIDE	**ADEFLLNRSU**	FALLS UNDER
ADEFGILNTU	DEFAULTING	**ADEFLMNORR**	LAND REFORM
ADEFGILRSU	LIFEGUARDS	**ADEFLMORTU**	FORMULATED
ADEFGIOORR	GO FOR A RIDE	**ADEFLNOOST**	TONS OF LEAD
ADEFGIRRST	FIRST GRADE	**ADEFLNORST**	FOREST LAND
ADEFGIRRSU	FIREGUARDS		SOFT-LANDER
ADEFGKNORR	GARDEN FORK	**ADEFLNRTUU**	FRAUDULENT
ADEFGLLOPY	PLAYED GOLF	**ADEFLOORTW**	FLOOD WATER
ADEFGLOOOS	SALE OF GOOD	**ADEFLOPSST**	SOFT-PEDALS
ADEFGLOOST	FLOOD GATES	**ADEFLOSTWY**	STEADY FLOW
	FLOODGATES	**ADEFMNNSTU**	FUNDAMENTS
ADEFGMOOST	TEAM OF DOGS	**ADEFMOORRS**	DOOR-FRAMES
ADEFGNOORR	ROOF GARDEN	**ADEFNNOPRT**	FOND PARENT
ADEFGNORSU	SAFE GROUND	**ADEFNOOPRS**	ROPE OF SAND
ADEFHHLOOT	HEALTH FOOD	**ADEFNOOSTW**	WAD OF NOTES
ADEFHHOORT	FATHERHOOD	**ADEFNRSSTU**	TRANSFUSED
ADEFHILTTW	HALF-WITTED	**ADEFOOPRRS**	PROOFREADS
ADEFHIMNOS	FINDS A HOME	**ADEFOOPSST**	SOFT-SOAPED
ADEFHIMNOT	HAND OF TIME	**ADEFOORSYY**	DAYS OF YORE
ADEFHINPRT	PATHFINDER	**ADEFOPRSSU**	FOUR SPADES
ADEFHINRSS	HAS FRIENDS	**ADEFORRSTV**	OVERDRAFTS
ADEFHINTWY	FIND THE WAY	**ADEFORRSTW**	FORWARDEST
ADEFHIORST	FIRED A SHOT	**ADEFORSSTT**	SET OF DARTS
ADEFHIRRSY	DAIRY FRESH	**ADEFRRRSTU**	FUR TRADERS
ADEFHIRIWW	WHITE DWARF	**ADEFRRSTTU**	FRUSTRATED
ADEFHLOOSS	FALSEHOODS	**ADEGGHHIRR**	HIGH REGARD
ADEFHLTTWY	TWELFTH DAY	**ADEGGHIINV**	GIVING HEAD
ADEFHMNOOU	FOUND A HOME	**ADEGGHILNR**	HANG GLIDER
ADEFHNNOOT	NOTE OF HAND		HANG-GLIDER
ADEFHNNORY	HENRY FONDA	**ADEGGIINRS**	SING A DIRGE
ADEFHNORRZ	FROZEN HARD	**ADEGGIMNTT**	GETTING MAD
ADEFHOOOTT	HEAD TO FOOT	**ADEGGINORT**	DEROGATING
ADEFHOORSW	FORESHADOW	**ADEGGINRSU**	SUNG A DIRGE
ADEFIIILNN	INDIAN FILE	**ADEGGINSSU**	DEGAUSSING
ADEFIILMNR	FIRM DENIAL	**ADEGGNOPTU**	GET UP AND GO
ADEFIILMST	MAILED FIST	**ADEGGNORUV**	GAVE GROUND
ADEFIILSTU	FILED A SUIT	**ADEGHHIILS**	HIGH IDEALS
ADEFIINOPS	SAPONIFIED	**ADEGHHIILT**	HIGHTAILED
ADEFIINQTU	QUANTIFIED	**ADEGHHIKNR**	RANKED HIGH
ADEFIINRTU	INFURIATED	**ADEGHHILNR**	HIGHLANDER
ADEFIINRTW	DRAW IT FINE	**ADEGHHILPY**	PLAYED HIGH
ADEFIIRRST	FIRST-AIDER	**ADEGHHILST**	HEADLIGHTS
ADEFIIRSTT	STRATIFIED	**ADEGHHINST**	NIGHTSHADE
ADEFIKORST	ASKED FOR IT	**ADEGHHLOOT**	GOOD HEALTH
ADEFILLLNO	FALLEN IDOL	**ADEGHIKLNT**	NAKED LIGHT
ADEFILLNTW	FIT AND WELL	**ADEGHILLMR**	GRILLED HAM
ADEFILLSSU	FUSILLADES	**ADEGHILNOR**	GOLDEN HAIR
ADEFILMNTU	FULMINATED		LONG-HAIRED
ADEFILMORS	FORMALISED	**ADEGHILNSU**	LANGUISHED
ADEFILMORZ	FORMALIZED	**ADEGHILRTT**	LIGHT TREAD
ADEFILNOST	DEFLATIONS	**ADEGHINNOV**	HAVING DONE
	DEFOLIANTS	**ADEGHINNRS**	HARDENINGS
ADEFILNSTU	LEFT UNSAID	**ADEGHINOSU**	ENOUGH SAID

ADEGHINPRS	HEADSPRING	ADEGIMNNOS	IN GOD'S NAME
ADEGHINSSS	HAS DESIGNS		MADE NO SIGN
ADEGHIOPRS	IDEOGRAPHS	ADEGIMNNRU	MAUNDERING
ADEGHIOPRY	IDEOGRAPHY	ADEGIMNORS	GORMANDISE
ADEGHIRRTU	DRAUGHTIER	ADEGIMNORT	MODERATING
ADEGHIRSST	SIGHT-READS	ADEGIMNORZ	GORMANDIZE
ADEGHIRSTW	EIGHT DRAWS	ADEGIMNPST	STAMPEDING
ADEGHISTYY	EIGHTY DAYS	ADEGIMNRST	GREAT MINDS
ADEGHKLOTW	WALK THE DOG	ADEGIMNSTU	MAGNITUDES
ADEGHLNORT	GRAND HOTEL	ADEGIMORRT	GOT MARRIED
ADEGHLNOST	ANGLED SHOT	ADEGIMORTZ	DOGMATIZER
ADEGHLORSS	GASHOLDERS	ADEGIMOSTZ	DOGMATIZES
	GOLD SHARES	ADEGINNOPY	OPENING DAY
ADEGHLRRUV	VULGAR HERD	ADEGINNORT	TREADING ON
ADEGHLRTUY	DAUGHTERLY	ADEGINNOTT	DETONATING
ADEGHMOPRY	DEMOGRAPHY	ADEGINNRSS	DARINGNESS
ADEGHNOOTT	DO THE TANGO	ADEGINNRST	INTEGRANDS
ADEGHNORST	HEADSTRONG	ADEGINNRSW	WANDERINGS
	STRONG HEAD	ADEGINNRTU	DENATURING
ADEGHOOOORT	GOOD TO HEAR	ADEGINNRYY	YARN-DYEING
ADEGHOOORRT	RATHER GOOD	ADEGINOORT	DEROGATION
ADEGHORSUU	GUARDHOUSE	ADEGINORRS	GARRISONED
ADEGIIILNS	IDEALISING	ADEGINORRT	DENIGRATOR
ADEGIIILNZ	IDEALIZING		DOG TRAINER
ADEGIIILST	DIGITALISE	ADEGINORST	DESIGNATOR
ADEGIIILTZ	DIGITALIZE	ADEGINORTW	GET A WORD IN
ADEGIILLSU	SEGUIDILLA	ADEGINORTX	AXE TO GRIND
ADEGIILMNN	GIN AND LIME	ADEGINPRSU	PERSUADING
ADEGIILMNP	IMPLEADING	ADEGINRSTW	STEWARDING
ADEGIILMNS	MISALIGNED	ADEGIOOPRR	GOOD REPAIR
	MISDEALING	ADEGIOPTTT	GOT IT TAPED
ADEGIILNNT	DINING LATE	ADEGIPRRST	PARTRIDGES
ADEGIILNOT	GADOLINITE	ADEGJLMNTU	JUDGMENTAL
ADEGIILNPP	LEAD PIPING	ADEGKLLOOZ	GLAZED LOOK
ADEGIILNPR	LIPREADING	ADEGKNRRRU	KRUGERRAND
ADEGIILNPT	DEPILATING	ADEGKNRSTU	TAKEN DRUGS
ADEGIILNRT	RING-TAILED	ADEGKRSSTU	TAKES DRUGS
ADEGIILNSS	SIGNALISED	ADEGLLMOSY	GLADSOMELY
ADEGIILNSZ	SIGNALIZED	ADEGLLNOST	LASTED LONG
ADEGIILTTY	DIGITATELY	ADEGLMNOOV	MOVED ALONG
ADEGIIMMRT	IMMIGRATED	ADEGLNORST	STRONG LEAD
ADEGIIMNRW	WIDE MARGIN	ADEGLNOSTY	LONGEST DAY
ADEGIIMNTT	MEDITATING	ADEGLNRSTY	GRAND STYLE
ADEGIINNRT	DETRAINING	ADEGLOOPRY	GOOD PLAYER
ADEGIINORT	ORIGINATED	ADEGLORSST	OLD STAGERS
ADEGIINPRS	DESPAIRING	ADEGLORSTT	GOLD STATER
ADEGIINRST	EAST RIDING	ADEGLORTTT	GOT RATTLED
	RIDING SEAT	ADEGMMOPRR	PROGRAMMED
ADEGIINRTT	EATING DIRT	ADEGMNOOSU	ENDOGAMOUS
ADEGIINSTT	INSTIGATED	ADEGMNORTU	GROUND MEAT
ADEGIIOPRR	PRAIRIE DOG	ADEGMOORST	GOOD MASTER
ADEGILLNPY	PLEADINGLY	ADEGNNOORU	GONE AROUND
ADEGILMORS	GLAMORISED	ADEGNOOORS	GOOD REASON
ADEGILMORZ	GLAMORIZED	ADEGNOOORW	ORANGEWOOD
ADEGILMOTY	GAY OLD TIME	ADEGNOORSS	GOOSANDERS
ADEGILMRRY	MY DEAR GIRL	ADEGNOORSU	GOES AROUND
ADEGILNNNO	NONALIGNED	ADEGNOORTU	GOOD NATURE
ADEGILNNOS	ENDS IN GAOL	ADEGNOPRST	GODPARENTS
ADEGILNNRS	SANDERLING	ADEGNORSTU	GETS AROUND
	SLANDERING	ADEGOOPRST	GASTEROPOD
ADEGILNNRU	LAUNDERING	ADEGOORRTY	DEROGATORY
ADEGILNORS	GIRANDOLES	ADEGOORSTY	GOOD STAYER
ADEGILNOST	DESOLATING	ADEGORRSVW	GRAVE WORDS
ADEGILNOTU	LEADING OUT	ADEGORSTTT	GOT STARTED
ADEGILNRST	DANGER LIST	ADEGPRSTTU	TRUDGE PAST
ADEGILNRUV	GERUNDIVAL	ADEHHIIORR	HIDE OR HAIR
ADEGILNSTW	DELTA WINGS	ADEHHIIPRT	DIPHTHERIA
ADEGILOOPS	APOLOGISED	ADEHHINRSS	HIS AND HERS
ADEGILOOPZ	APOLOGIZED	ADEHHIORTT	HIT THE ROAD
ADEGILRSUV	VULGARISED	ADEHHIRSSW	DISHWASHER
ADEGILRUVZ	VULGARIZED	ADEHHLLOOR	HOLOHEDRAL

ADEHHLLOST	DO THE HALLS	ADEHLLOORT	ROAD TO HELL
ADEHHMPRRU	HARRUMPHED	ADEHLLOPRY	POLYHEDRAL
ADEHHNOPRY	HYDROPHANE	ADEHLMNNORT	MOTHERLAND
ADEHHOSSTW	THE SHADOWS	ADEHLMNOSY	HANDSOMELY
ADEHHPRSSU	PUSHES HARD	ADEHLNNNOS	DEL SHANNON
ADEHIILMST	DELIA SMITH	ADEHLNOPRY	HYDROPLANE
ADEHIILMTU	HUMILIATED	ADEHLNORSS	HARD LESSON
ADEHIILOPU	AUDIOPHILE	ADEHLOPSTY	PLAYED HOST
ADEHIILRSS	HAIR-SLIDES	ADEHLORSSS	SOLD SHARES
ADEHIIMNNP	INDIAN HEMP	ADEHLORSTW	HOLDS WATER
ADEHIIMNNV	HAVE IN MIND	ADEHLOSTTY	LOST THE DAY
ADEHIIMNSS	MAIN DISHES	ADEHLOTTWZ	DO THE WALTZ
ADEHIIMRTT	MITHRIDATE	ADEHLSTTUY	LAY THE DUST
ADEHIINNOT	HAD IT IN ONE	ADEHMNNOOR	DONE NO HARM
ADEHIJNRUY	HEAD INJURY		NO HARM DONE
ADEHIKNPSS	HANDSPIKES	ADEHMNOORS	DOES NO HARM
ADEHIKNSTT	HAD KITTENS	ADEHMNOSST	HANDSOMEST
ADEHILLNNW	WELL IN HAND	ADEHMORRTW	THREADWORM
ADEHILLORU	LOUD HAILER	ADEHMORSTY	MOTHERS DAY
	LOUD-HAILER	ADEHNNNOTW	NOW AND THEN
ADEHILMNSS	MISHANDLES	ADEHNNOSTT	ON THE STAND
ADEHILNNRT	HINTERLAND	ADEHNOOPRT	PARENTHOOD
ADEHILNOPS	SPHENOIDAL	ADEHNOPPRS	SANDHOPPER
ADEHILNPRS	PHILANDERS	ADEHNORRRT	TRADER HORN
ADEHILOPRS	SPHEROIDAL	ADEHOORSSU	ROADHOUSES
ADEHILOSVW	HOLDS A VIEW	ADEHOORSVW	OVERSHADOW
ADEHILPTWY	PLAYED WITH	ADEHOORUWY	HOW DARE YOU!
ADEHIMMPTU	HAMMED IT UP	ADEHOPRRTU	PROUD HEART
ADEHIMNNTU	MINUTE HAND	ADEHOPTTTU	PUT TO DEATH
ADEHIMNORS	ADMONISHER	ADEHORRSSW	SHOREWARDS
	HARMONISED	ADEHORRSSY	DRAY HORSES
ADEHIMNORZ	HARMONIZED		DRAYHORSES
ADEHIMNOSS	ADMONISHES	ADEHORSTWW	WESTWARD HO!
ADEHIMORTU	RHEUMATOID	ADEHORSTWY	SAY THE WORD
ADEHIMOSSU	HOUSEMAIDS	ADEHPPSSTU	PUSHED PAST
ADEHIMRTTU	MADE IT HURT	ADEIIILLNT	INITIALLED
ADEHINNORS	SON AND HEIR	ADEIIILTVX	LIXIVIATED
ADEHINNPSU	DUENNASHIP	ADEIIIMNTT	INTIMIDATE
ADEHINNSTT	IN THE STAND	ADEIIINSTT	DIETITIANS
ADEHINOORS	DO ONES HAIR	ADEIIJLNNS	ENDS IN JAIL
ADEHINOORT	ON THE RADIO	ADEIILLSTT	DISTILLATE
ADEHINORST	HAD IN STORE		SAID LITTLE
ADEHINORTV	HAND IT OVER	ADEIILLTTT	TITILLATED
ADEHINOSST	ASTONISHED	ADEIILMMTU	MULTIMEDIA
ADEHINPRSW	WARDENSHIP	ADEIILMNOR	MERIDIONAL
ADEHINQSUV	VANQUISHED	ADEIILMNSU	ALUMINISED
ADEHINRRTW	HARD WINTER	ADEIILMNUZ	ALUMINIZED
ADEHINSTWY	WINS THE DAY	ADEIILMOST	MODALITIES
ADEHIOPRSS	RHAPSODIES	ADEIILMPPS	MISAPPLIED
	RHAPSODISE	ADEIILNOPT	DEPILATION
ADEHIOPRSZ	RHAPSODIZE	ADEIILNOPV	PAVILIONED
ADEHIOPSSS	SOAP DISHES	ADEIILNORV	LIVED ON AIR
ADEHIORSTU	AUTHORISED	ADEIILNPST	PLATINISED
ADEHIORTUZ	AUTHORIZED	ADEIILNPTZ	PLATINIZED
ADEHIOSSTW	SHADOWIEST	ADEIILNRTT	INTERTIDAL
ADEHIOSTTT	THAT DOES IT!	ADEIILNSST	DISENTAILS
ADEHIOTUVY	YOUVE HAD IT	ADEIILNTTT	DILETTANTI
ADEHIPRRSW	WARDERSHIP	ADEIILORST	EDITORIALS
ADEHIPRTTW	PARTED WITH	ADEIILQSTU	LIQUIDATES
ADEHIRRRTT	THIRD-RATER	ADEIILRRRV	RAIL DRIVER
ADEHKLOOPT	DO THE POLKA	ADEIILRSTU	RITUALISED
ADEHKLOPST	TALKED SHOP	ADEIILRTUZ	RITUALIZED
ADEHKNNOSW	SHAKEN DOWN	ADEIILSSUV	VISUALISED
ADEHKNORRW	HANDWORKER	ADEIILSUVZ	VISUALIZED
	WORK-HARDEN	ADEIIMNNOR	IRON MAIDEN
ADEHKNOSSW	SHAKEDOWNS	ADEIIMNOTT	MEDITATION
	SHAKES DOWN	ADEIIMNOTV	DOMINATIVE
ADEHKNRTTU	NAKED TRUTH	ADEIIMNPRU	UNIMPAIRED
ADEHKORRRW	HARD WORKER	ADEIIMNRST	ADMINISTER
ADEHKORRSS	DARK HORSES	ADEIIMORST	RADIO TIMES
ADEHLLNOSW	SHALLOW END	ADEIIMOSTT	DIATOMITES

479

ADEIIMPRSU	PRAESIDIUM
ADEIIMRSTT	DERMATITIS
ADEIINNNOS	INDONESIAN
ADEIINNORT	INORDINATE
ADEIINNOTX	INDEXATION
ADEIINNRST	SARDINE TIN
ADEIINNSST	DAINTINESS
ADEIINNSTU	INSINUATED
ADEIINNSTW	WEST INDIAN
ADEIINNSWY	WAYSIDE INN
ADEIINORRS	ORDINARIES
ADEIINORTV	DERIVATION
ADEIINOSTV	DEVIATIONS
ADEIINPPRS	DRAINPIPES
ADEIINPTTU	INAPTITUDE
ADEIINRRST	DISTRAINER
ADEIINRTUV	INDURATIVE
ADEIINSSTY	STAY INSIDE
ADEIIPRSSS	DISPRAISES
ADEIIPRSST	DISSIPATER
ADEIIPSSST	DISSIPATES
ADEIIRRTVX	TAXI DRIVER
ADEIISSSUV	DISSUASIVE
ADEIITTTTV	TITTIVATED
ADEIJLNOPT	LAP-JOINTED
ADEIJLNORU	JUNIOR LEAD
ADEIJMMNRW	WINDJAMMER
ADEIJMPTTU	JUMPED AT IT
ADEIJNOPRY	IN JEOPARDY
ADEIKKLNTY	TAKE KINDLY
ADEIKKPRTT	KEPT IT DARK
ADEIKLLLRY	LADY-KILLER
ADEIKLLLSY	LIKELY LADS
ADEIKLLMMT	MALTED MILK
ADEIKLLMNS	SKILLED MAN
ADEIKLMNRU	RUN LIKE MAD
ADEIKLNOOP	PAINED LOOK
ADEIKLNOTW	WALKED INTO
ADEIKNNRSS	IN DARKNESS
ADEIKNNRTU	KIND NATURE
ADEIKNPRSS	SPIKENARDS
ADEIKNRRTW	DRINK WATER
ADEIKOOPRT	TOOK A PRIDE
ADEIKOPSWW	WIDOWS PEAK
ADEILLMNOS	MEDALLIONS
ADEILLMORY	MARIE LLOYD
ADEILLMOST	METALLOIDS
ADEILLMPUX	ALL MIXED UP
ADEILLMRST	TREADMILLS
ADEILLNOOS	SOLENOIDAL
ADEILLNOPT	POLLINATED
ADEILLNORR	ALL IN ORDER
ADEILLNOSS	ON ALL SIDES
ADEILLNOSU	DELUSIONAL
ADEILLNPSS	PALLIDNESS
ADEILLNRTU	ILL-NATURED
ADEILLNRUV	UNRIVALLED
ADEILLPSSU	PULLS ASIDE
ADEILLQRSU	QUADRILLES
ADEILLRSUY	RESIDUALLY
ADEILMNOPR	PALINDROME
ADEILMNORS	NORMALISED
ADEILMNORT	LIE DORMANT
	MODEL TRAIN
ADEILMNORZ	NORMALIZED
ADEILMNOTY	ANY OLD TIME
ADEILMNRTU	RUDIMENTAL
ADEILMNSSS	DISMALNESS
ADEILMNSST	DISMANTLES
ADEILMOORS	LADIES' ROOM
ADEILMOPST	DIPLOMATES

ADEILMOPSY	POLYAMIDES
ADEILMPSTU	AMPLITUDES
ADEILMRTWY	MARTY WILDE
ADEILMSTTU	STIMULATED
ADEILNNOOT	OLD ETONIAN
ADEILNNORT	INTERNODAL
ADEILNNPTU	PINNULATED
ADEILNOOST	DESOLATION
ADEILNOOTV	DEVOTIONAL
ADEILNOPRS	DROPS A LINE
ADEILNOPST	PLANETOIDS
ADEILNORSU	LIES AROUND
ADEILNPRTU	PRUDENTIAL
ADEILNRRST	INTERLARDS
ADEILNRRTU	UNDER TRIAL
ADEILNRSTU	UITLANDERS
ADEILNRTTU	TURNED TAIL
ADEILNSSSW	WINDLASSES
ADEILNSTTT	LET IT STAND
ADEILNSTUY	UNSTEADILY
ADEILNSTWY	WALT DISNEY
ADEILOORST	OESTRADIOL
ADEILOPRSU	LOUD PRAISE
ADEILOPRTT	TETRAPLOID
ADEILOPRTY	DEPILATORY
ADEILOPSTW	LOWEST-PAID
ADEILOPTVY	ADOPTIVELY
	DEVIL TO PAY
ADEILOQSSU	ODALISQUES
ADEILORSTT	LAID TO REST
ADEILOSSTT	SOLID-STATE
ADEILPPRSU	RAPID PULSE
ADEILPRSSY	DAILY PRESS
ADEILPRUZZ	PUZZLED AIR
ADEILPSTTU	PLATITUDES
	STIPULATED
ADEILRSTTU	STRIDULATE
ADEILRTTXY	DEXTRALITY
ADEILRTUUX	LUXURIATED
ADEILSSTUW	STUDIES LAW
ADEIMMNRST	MASTERMIND
ADEIMMNRTU	MATURE MIND
ADEIMMNTTU	MANUMITTED
ADEIMMRSSU	SUMMARISED
ADEIMMRSUZ	SUMMARIZED
ADEIMNNORT	ORDAINMENT
ADEIMNOORT	MODERATION
ADEIMNORRS	RANDOMISER
ADEIMNORRW	WORRIED MAN
ADEIMNORRZ	RANDOMIZER
ADEIMNORSS	RANDOMISES
ADEIMNORSZ	RANDOMIZES
ADEIMNOTTW	MATED IN TWO
ADEIMNPRRS	REPRIMANDS
ADEIMNRSSU	NURSEMAIDS
ADEIMNSSTV	ADVENTISMS
ADEIMOPRSS	AS PROMISED
ADEIMORRTY	RADIOMETRY
ADEIMORTUY	AUDIOMETRY
ADEIMPRTXY	MIXED PARTY
ADEIMRRRTV	TRAM DRIVER
ADEIMRRSSY	MY DEAR SIRS
ADEIMRSTUX	ADMIXTURES
ADEINNNSTT	INTENDANTS
ADEINNOORS	IN ONE'S ROAD
ADEINNOOTT	DENOTATION
	DETONATION
ADEINNOPWW	WINDOW PANE
ADEINNORTU	TRADE UNION
ADEINNRSSW	INWARDNESS
ADEINNRSTY	TYRANNISED

ADEINNRTYZ	TYRANNIZED	ADELNOOOST	STOOD ALONE
ADEINOOSTW	STOOD IN AWE	ADELNOOPRS	DOOR PANELS
ADEINOPRRS	PREORDAINS	ADELNOPTTU	PLANTED OUT
ADEINOPRST	PATRONISED	ADELNORSSU	SLANDEROUS
ADEINOPRTZ	PATRONIZED	ADELNORSUY	ROUNDELAYS
ADEINOPSST	PASSED IT ON	ADELNPPSTU	SUPPLANTED
ADEINOPTTU	DEPUTATION	ADELNPRSUY	UNDERPLAYS
	PAINTED OUT	ADELNRSTUW	WANDERLUST
ADEINOPTUW	WAITED UPON	ADELNSTTUW	LAW STUDENT
ADEINORRWW	REAR WINDOW	ADELOORSST	DESOLATORS
ADEINORSST	ADROITNESS	ADELOPPTUY	PLAYED UP TO
ADEINOSTVY	VIDEO NASTY	ADELOPQRUU	QUADRUPOLE
ADEINPPRSS	SANDPIPERS	ADELOPSTTU	POSTULATED
ADEINPPSST	STANDPIPES	ADELORRSST	LAST ORDERS
ADEINPRRST	TRANSPIRED	ADELORRTUY	EARLY TUDOR
ADEINPRSST	DISPERSANT	ADELORRWWY	WORLD-WEARY
ADEINPRSSY	DISPENSARY	ADELORSTTW	LATEST WORD
ADEINPRSTV	DRIVEN PAST	ADELORSTUU	ADULTEROUS
ADEINRRSVV	VAN DRIVERS	ADELPORSUU	QUADRUPLES
ADEINRSSST	SATIN DRESS	ADELPQRTUU	QUADRUPLET
ADEINRSSTU	TURNS ASIDE	ADEMMMMNORU	MEMORANDUM
ADEINRSSTW	TAWDRINESS	ADEMMRRSSU	MASS MURDER
ADEINSSSTU	UNASSISTED	ADEMNNORSS	RANDOMNESS
ADEINSSTTV	ADVENTISTS	ADEMNNORST	ADORNMENTS
	VEDANTISTS	ADEMNNORWY	DRAWN MONEY
ADEIOPPRSV	DISAPPROVE	ADEMNNOTXY	NEXT MONDAY
ADEIOPRSTV	ADSORPTIVE	ADEMNORSTW	DOWNSTREAM
ADEIOPRSTY	DEPOSITARY	ADEMNORSWY	DRAWS MONEY
ADEIOPRSTZ	TRAPEZOIDS	ADEMNRSTTU	TRANSMUTED
ADEIORSTTY	TRIED TO SAY	ADEMOORRST	MODERATORS
ADEIPPRRTY	DAY TRIPPER	ADEMOPSTTU	STAMPED OUT
ADEIPRSSTV	DRIVES PAST	ADEMORRRSS	ORDERS ARMS
ADEIQRSSUX	SIX SQUARED	ADEMORSTTU	OUTSMARTED
ADEIRRSSTW	WARD SISTER	ADENNOPTTU	PUT AN END TO
ADEIRRTTTU	TRITURATED	ADENNORRRU	ROADRUNNER
ADEIRRTTWY	DIRTY WATER	ADENNORTUW	WENT AROUND
ADEIRSSTTU	STUDIES ART	ADENNOSSST	NODS ASSENT
ADEJMNSTTU	ADJUSTMENT	ADENNPRSTU	UNDERPANTS
ADEJOPSTUX	JUXTAPOSED	ADENNRRRSU	RUN ERRANDS
ADEJRRSTUW	JUST REWARD	ADENNSSSTW	NEWSSTANDS
ADEKLLNPRU	PULLED RANK	ADENNSTUXY	NEXT SUNDAY
ADEKLMOORY	DREAMY LOOK	ADENOOOPRS	OPENS A DOOR
ADEKLOOPSU	SPOKE ALOUD	ADENOOORST	AT ONES DOOR
ADEKMNNNRU	DRUNKEN MAN	ADENOOPPRT	PTEROPODAN
ADEKMNORTW	DOWN MARKET	ADENOOPRST	DO ONE'S PART
	DOWN-MARKET	ADENOORSTT	DETONATORS
ADEKMOPRST	POSTMARKED	ADENOORTUV	OVER AND OUT
ADEKMORTWY	TAKE MY WORD	ADENOPPRRU	PAPER ROUND
ADEKNRRTUW	DRUNK WATER	ADENOPRSST	TRANSPOSED
ADELLLPTUU	PULLULATED	ADENOPRSTV	DAVENPORTS
ADELLMMSUY	SELL A DUMMY	ADENOPSSSW	PASSES DOWN
ADELLMORRS	SMALL ORDER	ADENORSSTV	STANDS OVER
ADELLNOOWY	WOODY ALLEN	ADENORSSTW	STARES DOWN
ADELLNORRU	ALL-ROUNDER	ADENORSTUW	WANDERS OUT
ADELLNORST	TEN DOLLARS	ADENOSSUVW	SOUND WAVES
ADELLNORSW	LOWLANDERS	ADENPRRSTU	UNDERPARTS
ADELLOOPPY	PLAYED POLO	ADENPRSTUU	PUT ASUNDER
	PLAYED POOL	ADENRRSSTW	STERNWARDS
ADELLOORRU	EURODOLLAR	ADENRRSTUY	DAY-RETURNS
ADELLOORST	ROLLED OATS	ADENRRSUYY	DAY NURSERY
ADELLOORSW	LOW-LOADERS	ADENRSTTTU	ART STUDENT
ADELMNOPRT	TRAMPLED ON	ADENSTTWYY	TWENTY DAYS
ADELMOPRSS	SLOPED ARMS	ADEOOPPRSW	SOAP POWDER
ADELMOPSTU	DEUTOPLASM	ADEOOORSTT	STOOD TREAT
ADELMORSST	OLD MASTERS	ADEOPRRSSS	PASS ORDERS
ADELMPRSTU	LEAD TRUMPS	ADEOPRRSTT	PROSTRATED
ADELMPTTUY	PUTTY MEDAL	ADEOPRSSTU	SPREADS OUT
ADELNNNOOY	ONE AND ONLY	ADEOQRRSUW	WORD SQUARE
ADELNNOOOR	LORNA DOONE	ADEOQRRSTUW	TWO SQUARED
ADELNNOOST	EAST LONDON	ADEORRSTTW	ROD STEWART
ADELNNOPTU	LENT A POUND	ADEORRTTUW	UTTER A WORD

ADEORSSTWW	WASTE WORDS
ADEORSTTTU	STARTED OUT
ADEORSTTUV	STARVED OUT
ADEPRRSSTY	PARTY DRESS
ADFFGHINNO	HANDING OFF
ADFFGHINOS	DASHING OFF
ADFFGILNOO	OFF-LOADING
ADFFGINORT	TRADING OFF
ADFFGINORW	DRAWING OFF
	WARDING OFF
ADFFHILLMO	HALF OF MILD
ADFFIIMRSS	DISAFFIRMS
ADFFILNSTU	FIND FAULTS
	FINDS FAULT
ADFFINORUV	FIND FAVOUR
ADFFIRRSTT	FIRST DRAFT
ADFFLNOOSU	LOADS OF FUN
ADFFLNOTUU	FOUND FAULT
ADFGGLOOST	OLD FAGGOTS
ADFGHORRTU	ROUGH DRAFT
ADFGIILRRY	GIRL FRIDAY
ADFGIIMNNY	DAMNIFYING
ADFGIKNOOT	TAKING FOOD
ADFGILMOOY	GOOD FAMILY
ADFGILNORT	DRIFT ALONG
ADFGILOORY	FAIRLY GOOD
ADFGILORSU	DOUGLAS FIR
ADFGINORRU	FAIRGROUND
ADFGINORRW	FORWARDING
ADFGLNORTU	FLAT GROUND
ADFHIIRSTY	THIS FRIDAY
ADFHIMORTY	THIRD OF MAY
ADFHINNORU	FOUR IN HAND
	FOUR-IN-HAND
ADFHLLOOST	HOLDS ALOFT
ADFHNOORST	AND SO FORTH
ADFHNORRTW	DRAWN FORTH
ADFHORRSTW	DRAWS FORTH
ADFIILLNPU	PAID IN FULL
ADFIILLTUY	FILIAL DUTY
ADFIILMRSU	DISULFIRAM
ADFIIOSSTU	FASTIDIOUS
ADFIISSSTY	DISSATISFY
ADFIKNOOTW	TWO OF A KIND
ADFILLMNOY	MANIFOLDLY
ADFILLNOOP	FLOODPLAIN
ADFILNNORU	FINAL ROUND
ADFILOSTTU	STUDIO FLAT
ADFIMNOOST	FATS DOMINO
ADFIMNRSST	FIRM STANDS
	STANDS FIRM
ADFINNOOTU	FOUNDATION
ADFINNOSTU	FAINT SOUND
ADFINOOPRR	DROP OF RAIN
ADFINORSTT	STAND FOR IT
ADFINORSUX	FOUR AND SIX
ADFIOORWZZ	WIZARD OF OZ
ADFIORSSUV	DISFAVOURS
ADFJKLNOOU	LOAD OF JUNK
ADFLLNOOPT	PLOT OF LAND
ADFLLNOPRU	FULL PARDON
ADFLLOOSST	FALDSTOOLS
ADFLMNTUUU	MUTUAL FUND
ADFLNOOORU	FOOL AROUND
ADFLNOOSTW	FLOATS DOWN
ADFLOOOOST	STOOD ALOOF
ADFMMNOOOS	MAN OF MOODS
ADFNOORSSZ	SFORZANDOS
ADFNOPRSTU	STAND UP FOR
ADFNPRSTUY	PARTY FUNDS
ADFOORRSWW	WAR OF WORDS
ADFOPRRTUW	PUT FORWARD
ADGGGGILNRY	DRAGGINGLY
ADGGGINPRU	DRAGGING UP
ADGGHINOOT	A GOOD THING
ADGGIILNSS	GLISSADING
ADGGIINNOS	DIAGNOSING
ADGGIKMNOO	MAKING GOOD
ADGGILLNNY	DANGLINGLY
ADGGILNORW	GROWING LAD
ADGGINNOOR	DRAGOONING
	GADROONING
ADGGINNORU	GAIN GROUND
ADGGINNOWW	WIG AND GOWN
ADGGLLRSUY	SLUGGARDLY
ADGGNOORSY	GAY GORDONS
ADGHHIILPY	HIGHLY PAID
ADGHHILNOW	HIGH AND LOW
ADGHIILLNN	DINING HALL
ADGHIILNOY	HOLIDAYING
ADGHIILNTY	IN DAYLIGHT
ADGHIKLNOR	KING HAROLD
ADGHIKLNOT	TAKING HOLD
ADGHILNNNO	IN LONGHAND
ADGHILNNOS	LOSING HAND
ADGHILNSST	SIGHTS LAND
ADGHIMNOPP	HOPPING MAD
ADGHINNOTU	HANDING OUT
ADGHINNPRS	HANDSPRING
ADGHINOSTU	DASHING OUT
ADGHINPPYY	DYING HAPPY
ADGHINRRTY	TRYING HARD
ADGHINRSTU	INDRAUGHTS
ADGHINRTTW	DRAWN TIGHT
ADGHIRRSTW	RIGHTWARDS
ADGHIRSTTU	DISTRAUGHT
ADGHIRSTTW	DRAWS TIGHT
ADGHLNOOSW	LONG SHADOW
ADGHNNORST	STRONG HAND
ADGHNNORUU	HUNG AROUND
ADGHPRSTUU	UPDRAUGHTS
ADGIIILNNV	INVALIDING
ADGIIINOTT	DIGITATION
ADGIIKNNPP	KIDNAPPING
ADGIILLNOT	DOING IT ALL
ADGIILMNOU	GADOLINIUM
ADGIILMNRY	ADMIRINGLY
ADGIILNNRV	VIRGIN LAND
ADGIILNPSY	DISPLAYING
ADGIILOSST	DIALOGISTS
ADGIIMMNOT	DOMINATING
ADGIIMNNTY	DYNAMITING
ADGIIMNPRS	RISING DAMP
ADGIIMNSST	DISMASTING
ADGIINNNST	STANDING IN
ADGIINNNTU	INUNDATING
ADGIINNPRW	DRAWING PIN
ADGIINNRTU	INDURATING
ADGIINOSVW	DISAVOWING
ADGIINRSST	DISTRINGAS
ADGIJNNORU	ADJOURNING
ADGIKMNORW	WORD MAKING
ADGIKNNOTW	TAKING DOWN
ADGIKNORWY	WORKING DAY
ADGILLNNOS	LONG ISLAND
ADGILLNOPR	POLLARDING
ADGILLNOPY	POLLING DAY
ADGILLNRWY	DRAWLINGLY
ADGILLNYZZ	DAZZLINGLY
ADGILLOPRY	PRODIGALLY
ADGILMNOTU	MODULATING

ADGILNNTUU	UNDULATING	ADHINOOPRT	ANTHROPOID
ADGILNNTUY	DAUNTINGLY	ADHINOOPRZ	RHIZOPODAN
ADGILNOSSS	GLISSANDOS	ADHINOPRST	DROPS A HINT
ADGILNOSSY	OLD SAYINGS	ADHINOSSWW	WINDOW SASH
ADGILOOORS	GOOD SAILOR	ADHINOSTTU	HANDS IT OUT
ADGIMMOSST	DOGMATISMS	ADHINSSTTW	WITHSTANDS
ADGINNNORU	GRAND UNION	ADHINSSTUY	THIS SUNDAY
ADGINNOOSU	IGUANODONS	ADHINSTUWY	WHIT SUNDAY
ADGINNOOTU	GO IN AND OUT		WHITSUNDAY
ADGINNORSU	SING A ROUND	ADHIOPRSST	RHAPSODIST
ADGINNOSTT	STANDING TO	ADHIPRRTTY	THIRD PARTY
ADGINNOSTU	ASTOUNDING		THIRD-PARTY
ADGINNPSTU	STANDING UP	ADHIRSTTYY	THIRTY DAYS
	UPSTANDING	ADHJLNNOOT	JOHN DALTON
ADGINNRSTU	TRANSUDING	ADHKNNOORW	WORK ON HAND
ADGINOOPRT	IN GOOD PART	ADHLNOPSSW	SPLASHDOWN
ADGINOORST	GOODS TRAIN	ADHMNOORST	RANDOM SHOT
ADGINOORTW	GOT A WORD IN	ADHMOOPRSY	DRY SHAMPOO
ADGINOPSTT	POSTDATING	ADHMSSTTUY	STUDY MATHS
ADGINORTTU	DARTING OUT	ADHNOOPSSY	SODA SYPHON
ADGINORTUW	DRAWING OUT	ADHNOPRSUU	PUSH AROUND
ADGINOTUWY	OWING A DUTY	ADHNORRSTW	NORTHWARDS
ADGINRRSTW	DRAWSTRING	ADHNORSTUY	ON THURSDAY
ADGIORSSWW	GRASS WIDOW	ADHOOPRRST	ARTHROPODS
ADGJNORRRU	GRAND JUROR	ADHOORRTWY	ROADWORTHY
ADGLLMOOSS	SMALLGOODS	ADHOPRRSSW	SHARP WORDS
ADGLLNOOPS	PLODS ALONG	ADHORSSTUW	SOUTHWARDS
ADGLMNOSWY	SAM GOLDWYN	ADIIILMRSS	DISSIMILAR
ADGLNNOPRU	GROUND PLAN	ADIIILNOSV	DIVISIONAL
ADGLNOPRUY	PLAYGROUND	ADIIILNTVY	INVALIDITY
ADGLOOPSVV	PAVLOVS DOG	ADIIINNOOT	IODINATION
ADGMNNORSU	GROUNDSMAN	ADIIINNOTV	DIVINATION
ADGMNORTUU	MOUNT GUARD	ADIIKLLMMS	MILD AS MILK
ADGMOORRSU	GUARDROOMS	ADIIKNNPSY	PAYS IN KIND
ADGNNORRUU	RUN AGROUND	ADIILLORTY	DILATORILY
ADGNNORSUU	SUNG A ROUND	ADIILMOPRR	PRIMORDIAL
ADGNNORSUY	GYNANDROUS	ADIILNOPTV	VALID POINT
ADGOOPRSST	GASTROPODS	ADIILNORRY	ORDINARILY
ADHHIKNNRST	THINKS HARD	ADIILNOTUV	INVALID OUT
ADHHKNOOSS	SHOOK HANDS	ADIILNRSTU	INDUSTRIAL
ADHHMOOOST	THOMAS HOOD	ADILLOQRTU	LIQUIDATOR
ADHHNOOOPR	ORPHANHOOD	ADIILORSTY	SOLIDARITY
ADHHNORSSU	HARSH SOUND	ADIIMMMOTU	OMMATIDIUM
ADHHNOSTTU	THOUSANDTH	ADIIMNNNOO	ANNO DOMINI
ADHHOPRTYY	HYDROPATHY	ADIIMNNOOT	ADMONITION
ADHHORRSSW	HARSH WORDS		DOMINATION
ADHIIKKNNT	KITH AND KIN	ADIIMNOSSS	ADMISSIONS
ADHIIMMNPS	MIDSHIPMAN	ADIIMNNRTY	DRY MARTINI
ADHIIMNSST	HIT AND MISS	ADIIMORTUU	AUDITORIUM
	HIT-AND-MISS	ADIIMQRUUV	QUADRIVIUM
ADHIINNSTU	HINDUSTANI	ADIINNNOTU	INUNDATION
ADHIJLNNOS	JOHN LANDIS	ADIINNOORT	ORDINATION
ADHIJMORRT	MAJOR THIRD	ADIINNORTU	INDURATION
ADHIJMOTWY	MAD WITH JOY	ADIINOPPST	DISAPPOINT
ADHIJNNOSS	JOINS HANDS	ADIINORSTT	TRADITIONS
ADHIKLNOTU	THINK ALOUD	ADIINORTVY	DIVINATORY
ADHIKNNOOT	TOOK IN HAND	ADIINOSSSU	DISSUASION
ADHIKNNORW	WORK IN HAND	ADIINRSSTT	DISTRAINTS
ADHIKOORTT	TOOK IT HARD	ADIINRSSTW	DARWINISTS
ADHILLNOSY	HOLY ISLAND	ADIIOPRSTT	PODIATRIST
ADHILNNOOT	HAND LOTION	ADIJNNORUY	DO AN INJURY
ADHILNOSTU	OUTLANDISH	ADILLLOSYY	DISLOYALLY
ADHILOOPRS	DROSOPHILA	ADILLNSSTT	STAND STILL
ADHILOOPRZ	RHIZOPODAL		STANDSTILL
ADHILOQRRU	HARD LIQUOR	ADILLOORTY	TOROIDALLY
ADHIMNORSY	DISHARMONY	ADILLORSSX	SIX DOLLARS
ADHIIMNOSTY	THIS MONDAY	ADILLOSTYY	DISLOYALTY
ADHIMNOTWY	WHIT MONDAY	ADILMMOPSU	PLASMODIUM
	WHITMONDAY		SODIUM LAMP
ADHINNOOOT	NATIONHOOD	ADILMNNOTY	DOMINANTLY
ADHINNPSTU	PUTS IN HAND	ADILMNOOTU	MODULATION

ADILMORTUY	MODULARITY	AEEEEHRRTW	THERE WE ARE
ADILMSSTTU	TALMUDISTS	AEEEEHRTWY	WEATHER EYE
ADILNNOORY	ANY OLD IRON	AEEEEKRSTW	EASTER WEEK
ADILNNOOTU	NODULATION	AEEEELPRRS	PRE-RELEASE
ADILNNOPRT	INLAND PORT	AEEEEFFILOS	LIFE OF EASE
ADILNNOTUU	UNDULATION	AEEEEFFIMNT	EFFEMINATE
ADILNOPRSW	PLAIN WORDS	AEEEEFFSTWY	SWEET EFFAY
	SPIRAL DOWN	AEEEFGKRTU	TAKE REFUGE
ADILNORSSU	SAILS ROUND	AEEEEFGLLRT	LARGE FLEET
ADILOORRRW	OLD WARRIOR	AEEEEFGLRST	FEELS GREAT
ADILOORSTT	STOOD TRIAL	AEEEEFGLRVY	GAVE FREELY
ADILOORSTU	IDOLATROUS	AEEEEFGNRST	FREE AGENTS
ADILORRTWY	TROD WARILY	AEEEEFGRSTV	STAGE FEVER
ADIMNNORRW	NARROW MIND	AEEEEFHLMOT	FEEL AT HOME
ADIMNNTUUW	AUTUMN WIND	AEEEEFHLMSS	FEELS SHAME
ADIMNOORTY	ADMONITORY	AEEEEFHLSTT	FALSE TEETH
ADIMNORTTW	MORDANT WIT	AEEEEFHRRTT	THEREAFTER
ADIMNOSTWW	WANT WISDOM	AEEEEFINRTZ	ANTIFREEZE
ADINNOPSTT	STANDPOINT	AEEEEFIRRST	FIRE EATERS
ADINNORSTW	DOWN TRAINS		FIRE-EATERS
ADINNOSSTU	INS AND OUTS	AEEEEFKMRRT	FREE MARKET
ADINNOSTTW	STAND TO WIN	AEEEEFKRSST	SEEKS AFTER
ADINOOPRST	ADSORPTION	AEEEEFLLLPS	FELL ASLEEP
	POISON DART	AEEEEFLMNSS	FEMALENESS
ADINOOORRTU	ROAD TO RUIN	AEEEEFLMPRS	FREE SAMPLE
ADINOPRRSY	PRISON YARD	AEEEEFLNRTT	FETTER LANE
ADINOPRTUW	PUT IN A WORD	AEEEEFNOSTT	AT ONES FEET
ADINORSSTU	SITS AROUND	AEEEEFNRRST	TRANSFEREE
ADINORSSTW	DOWNSTAIRS	AEEEEFNRSTV	EVEN FASTER
ADIOPPSTTU	PUTS PAID TO	AEEEEGGGNRS	GREENGAGES
ADIORSSSTU	DISASTROUS	AEEEEGGMNNT	ENGAGEMENT
ADIORSSTTU	ART STUDIOS	AEEEEGGRSST	SEGREGATES
ADJLOPRTUU	PLAT DU JOUR	AEEEEGHILTV	GAVE THE LIE
ADJMMOOORS	MAJORDOMOS	AEEEEGHNRRT	GREENHEART
ADKLNOOORU	LOOK AROUND	AEEEEGHPRST	THREE PAGES
ADKLNORSTU	TALKS ROUND	AEEEEGHRSTT	STAGE THREE
ADLLLMORSW	SMALL WORLD	AEEEEGILNRS	GENERALISE
ADLLLNNOOW	LONDON WALL	AEEEEGILNRZ	GENERALIZE
ADLLMORSSW	SMALLSWORD	AEEEEGILNSV	EVANGELISE
ADLLNORRUV	RALLY ROUND	AEEEEGILNUV	EIGENVALUE
ADLLOORSTW	TWO DOLLARS	AEEEEGILNVZ	EVANGELIZE
ADLMMNOOWY	MY OLD WOMAN	AEEEEGIMNRS	MENAGERIES
ADLMOOORSU	MALODOROUS	AEEEEGINRTV	GENERATIVE
ADLMOORTUY	MODULATORY	AEEEEGITTVV	VEGETATIVE
ADLNORSTUU	ULTRASOUND	AEEEEGKLOPR	GOALKEEPER
ADLNORTUUY	UNDULATORY	AEEEEGKLWWY	WEEKLY WAGE
ADLNORTUWY	UNTOWARDLY	AEEEEGLNOPR	ORANGE PEEL
ADLOOOSSTT	TOADSTOOLS	AEEEEGLNPPR	APPLE GREEN
ADLOORSTTY	TOLD A STORY	AEEEEGLNSST	EAGLES NEST
ADLOPRSSWY	SWORDPLAYS	AEEEEGLRSSS	GREASELESS
ADLOPRTTUY	PATROL DUTY	AEEEEGLSSSY	EYEGLASSES
ADMNNNOOSU	SUN AND MOON	AEEEEGMNNTY	ENEMY AGENT
ADMNNOORSU	MONANDROUS	AEEEEGMNRSS	MEAGRENESS
ADMNOPSSTW	STAMPS DOWN	AEEEEGMNRST	AGREEMENTS
ADMNORSSST	SANDSTORMS	AEEEEGNORRT	ORANGE TREE
ADMOPRSTTU	MUSTARD POT	AEEEEGNPPRR	GREEN PAPER
ADMPRSSTUW	DRAW STUMPS	AEEEEGRSTTZ	GAZETTEERS
ADNNNOOSUY	NOONDAY SUN	AEEEHHINST	HEATHENISE
ADNNOORRWW	NARROW DOWN	AEEEHHINTZ	HEATHENIZE
ADNNORRSUU	RUNS AROUND	AEEEHHLTTW	AT THE WHEEL
ADNNORRTUU	TURN AROUND	AEEEHHPRST	PHASE THREE
ADNOORUWWY	DOWN OUR WAY		THREE-PHASE
ADNOOSTUYY	YOU DON'T SAY	AEEEHHRTTT	THE THEATRE
ADNOPRRSUW	WRAPS ROUND	AEEEHHRTTW	THE WEATHER
ADNOPRSSTW	STRAPS DOWN	AEEEHKPRST	THE SPEAKER
ADNOPSSTTU	STANDS UP TO	AEEEHLLRTY	ETHEREALLY
AEEEEFGRWZ	WAGE FREEZE	AEEEHLMOSV	LEAVES HOME
AEEEEGKMPR	GAMEKEEPER	AEEEHLMSTT	SHEET METAL
AEEEEGKPRT	GATEKEEPER	AEEEHLORSV	SHORE LEAVE
AEEEEGLLNR	GENERAL LEE	AEEEHLPRSW	SPARE WHEEL
AEEEEGNRRT	REGENERATE	AEEEHLPSVY	HEAVY SLEEP

AEEEHLRTWW	WATERWHEEL	AEEENRRVVW	NEVER WAVER
AEEEHMNRTW	WEATHERMEN	AEEENRSSSV	AVERSENESS
AEEEHMPRTT	HEPTAMETER	AEEENRSSVY	SEVEN YEARS
AEEEHMSSTT	METATHESES	AEEENSTTUV	EVENTUATES
AEEEHNNSTV	HEAVEN-SENT	AEEENSTTUX	EXTENUATES
AEEEHNORTY	THE YEAR ONE	AEEEPPRRTT	PERPETRATE
AEEEHNRRTT	THREATENER	AEEEPPRRTTU	PERPETUATE
AEEEHNRTWY	THE NEW YEAR	AEEERRRSTYY	YESTERYEAR
AEEEHORRUY	HERE YOU ARE	AEEERSSTTY	EASY STREET
AEEEHORSTV	OVER THE SEA	AEEFFHINRT	FAN THE FIRE
AEEEHRRSTY	THREE YEARS	AEEFFHORRT	FOREFATHER
AEEEHRSTTW	SWEETHEART	AEEFFILLNT	FIFTEEN ALL
AEEEHRTTWW	WET WEATHER	AEEFFILNST	FEELS FAINT
AEEEIIKLSV	LIKE A SIEVE	AEEFFLLOOS	FEELS A FOOL
AEEEIIPPRT	PERIPETEIA	AEEFFLLORR	FREE FOR ALL
AEEEIKLPSV	KEEPS ALIVE		FREE-FOR-ALL
AEEEILLPSS	LIES ASLEEP	AEEFFLLSUW	FEELS AWFUL
AEEEILMPST	TIME,PLEASE	AEEFFLNRTY	AFFERENTLY
AEEEILNRST	ETERNALISE	AEEFFORRST	REAFFOREST
AEEEILNRTV	INTERLEAVE	AEEFFSSTUY	SAFETY FUSE
AEEEILNRTZ	ETERNALIZE	AEEFGHINRT	FEATHERING
AEEEILNSVV	VINE LEAVES	AEEFGHLNRS	GREEN FLASH
AEEEILRSST	EASTERLIES	AEEFGHORRT	FOREGATHER
AEEEIMNSTV	VIETNAMESE	AEEFGIINRT	FIRE-EATING
AEEEIMRSTT	EASTER TIME	AEEFGIKMNR	MAKING FREE
AEEEINNSTT	SENTENTIAE	AEEFGILMSS	SELF IMAGES
AEEEINPRSV	SEVERE PAIN	AEEFGILNRR	RIFLE RANGE
AEEEINRSTT	ENTREATIES	AEEFGILNRS	SINGLE FARE
AEEEINRTTV	INVETERATE	AEEFGILPRS	PERSIFLAGE
AEEEINRTVW	INTERWEAVE	AEEFGINNOR	GONE IN FEAR
AEEEIPRTVY	PRIVATE EYE	AEEFGINORS	GOES IN FEAR
AEEEIRRSTT	REITERATES	AEEFGINRTU	NEAT FIGURE
AEEEIRRVVW	RAVE REVIEW	AEEFGLLOST	FLAGEOLETS
AEEEJJMSSS	JESSE JAMES	AEEFGLNOSS	GAS ONESELF
AEEEJKRRRT	TEARJERKER	AEEFGLNRSY	FEELS ANGRY
AEEEJNRTUV	REJUVENATE	AEEFGLPRSU	PRESAGEFUL
AEEEKLSTTT	TEA KETTLES	AEEFGLRSTU	LAST REFUGE
AEEEKMNSSS	MAKES SENSE	AEEFGRSTTT	GETS FATTER
AEEEKNSSSW	WEAKNESSES	AEEFHHINRT	FAHRENHEIT
AEEEKPSSTW	SWEEPSTAKE	AEEFHHRRST	FRESH HEART
AEEELLRTVW	WATER LEVEL	AEEFHIKLRT	LIKE FATHER
AEEELLSSTT	TESSELLATE	AEEFHIKNST	SNEAK THIEF
AEEELMNRTV	REVEALMENT	AEEFHIKPST	KEEPS FAITH
AEEELMNRTY	ELEMENTARY	AEEFHILOSX	FIXES A HOLE
AEEELNOPSV	LEAVES OPEN	AEEFHIMRTT	FATHER TIME
AEEELNOSSY	LOSES AN EYE	AEEFHINRRT	RATHER FINE
AEEELNOSTT	TELEOSTEAN	AEEFHIORSU	HOUSE AFIRE
AEEELNPRTT	TERNEPLATE	AEEFHIRSTV	FIVE HEARTS
AEEELNPSTX	NEXT PLEASE	AEEFHIRSTX	THE FAIR SEX
AEEELORSVV	LEAVES OVER	AEEFHISSTT	SETS A THIEF
AEEELPRRUV	PAUL REVERE	AEEFHKNOPR	PHONE FREAK
AEEELPSTTU	EPAULETTES	AEEFHLLSTV	LEFT HALVES
AEEELRRTTT	LETTER RATE	AEEFHLMOTT	FELT AT HOME
AEEEMMNORT	ANEMOMETER	AEEFHLOPPR	LEAFHOPPER
AEEEMNOPSS	OPEN SESAME	AEEFHLPPSY	FEELS HAPPY
AEEEMNPRTT	PENTAMETER	AEEFHLRSST	FATHERLESS
AEEEMNRRTU	REMUNERATE	AEEFHMORSU	FRAME HOUSE
AEEEMNRSTU	ENUMERATES	AEEFHMORTT	FATHOMETER
AEEEMPPRRY	EMERY PAPER	AEEFHORSSY	HAS EYES FOR
AEEEMRRSTT	EASTER TERM	AEEFHPRSTT	STEPFATHER
AEEEMRRTTT	TETRAMETER	AEEFHRRSTW	FRESH WATER
AEEEMRSTUW	WET MEASURE		FRESHWATER
AEEEMSSTTW	SWEETMEATS	AEEFIIKLST	FLIES A KITE
AEEENNORSS	SEEN REASON	AEEFIILLNR	IN REAL LIFE
AEEENORSSS	SEES REASON	AEEFIILLNT	LATE IN LIFE
AEEENORSTX	EXONERATES	AEEFIILMNR	MARINE LIFE
AEEENOSSWY	SEE ONES WAY	AEEFIILNRV	LIVE IN FEAR
AEEENPRSST	SEA SERPENT	AEEFIIMSTX	FIXES A TIME
AEEENPRSTT	PENETRATES	AEEFIIRRRS	FIRE-RAISER
AEEENQRSUW	QUEENS WARE	AEEFIJORRZ	JOE FRAZIER
AEEENRRSST	EASTERNERS	AEEFILMNNO	NOMINAL FEE

AEEFILMOTT	FAIL TO MEET	AEEGHINRSS	GARNISHEES
AEEFILMPRS	SIMPLE FARE	AEEGHINRTV	IN THE GRAVE
AEEFILMRTY	FAMILY TREE	AEEGHINRTW	WEATHERING
AEEFILNNTT	LIFE TENANT	AEEGHIPPRR	EPIGRAPHER
AEEFILNNTV	FINAL EVENT	AEEGHIPPTV	GAVE THE PIP
AEEFILNOPS	OPENS A FILE	AEEGHIRSTW	AGREES WITH
AEEFILOSST	FAILS TO SEE	AEEGHIRSTY	EIGHT YEARS
AEEFILOSTX	EXFOLIATES	AEEGHKNNRS	GREENSHANK
AEEFILRSSV	LIFESAVERS	AEEGHKOTTY	GET THE OKAY
AEEFIMNRRT	FREEMARTIN	AEEGHLMORT	GEOTHERMAL
AEEFIMNRST	MANIFESTER	AEEGHLNOSV	GONE HALVES
AEEFIMORTT	TIME FOR TEA	AEEGHLNOWW	WAGON WHEEL
AEEFIMORTY	TIME OF YEAR	AEEGHLNTVW	WAVELENGTH
AEEFINPSSS	FINE PASSES	AEEGHLORSU	LARGE HOUSE
AEEFINQRUY	FAIRY QUEEN	AEEGHLORTT	ALTOGETHER
AEEFINRRRU	FUNERARIER	AEEGHLOSSV	GOES HALVES
AEEFINRRST	FRATERNISE	AEEGHLPRST	TELEGRAPHS
AEEFINRRTZ	FRATERNIZE	AEEGHLPRTY	TELEGRAPHY
AEEFJLMOSW	JAMES WOLFE	AEEGHLSSST	SHEET GLASS
AEEFKLNORZ	FROZEN LAKE	AEEGHMNOOT	HOMOGENATE
AEEFKLNOTU	TAKE ON FUEL	AEEGHMNOPS	MEGAPHONES
AEEFLLLMSS	FEELS SMALL	AEEGHMNOTW	WON THE GAME
AEEFLLNNOT	FONTANELLE	AEEGHMNRST	THE GERMANS
AEEFLLNORV	FALLEN OVER	AEEGHMORTY	GAME THEORY
AEEFLLNPRY	FALLEN PREY		HETEROGAMY
AEEFLLNRUY	FUNEREALLY	AEEGHMPSTU	THE GAMES UP
AEEFLLRSSY	FEARLESSLY	AEEGHNNORU	NEAR ENOUGH
AEEFLMNOST	MAN OF STEEL	AEEGHNOORS	GONE ASHORE
AEEFLMOPRX	FOR EXAMPLE	AEEGHNOOTV	GO TO HEAVEN
AEEFLMORSY	FEARSOMELY	AEEGHNORSY	SHEER AGONY
AEEFMNORSS	FREEMASONS	AEEGHNOSST	SEEN A GHOST
AEEFMNORTZ	FROZEN MEAT	AEEGHNOSTT	ON THE STAGE
AEEFMOQRUU	FORM A QUEUE	AEEGHNOSTU	HOUSE AGENT
AEEFMPSTTT	TEMPTS FATE	AEEGHOORSS	GOES ASHORE
AEEFNOPRSZ	FROZEN PEAS	AEEGHOPPUV	GAVE UP HOPE
AEEFNRRRTU	RETURN FARE	AEEGHOPRST	GREAT HOPES
AEEFNRRTUU	NEAR FUTURE	AEEGHOPSTT	THE GESTAPO
AEEFNSSSST	FASTNESSES	AEEGHORSTT	GETS TO HEAR
AEEFOPRRST	PERFORATES	AEEGHORTTV	TO THE GRAVE
AEEFORSSTT	FORETASTES	AEEGHOSSST	SEES A GHOST
AEEGGHHNTT	GET THE HANG	AEEGHOSSTU	GATEHOUSES
AEEGGHILRT	LIGHTERAGE	AEEGHRRSST	HAS REGRETS
AEEGGHOPRR	GEOGRAPHER	AEEGIILLNV	VILLEINAGE
AEEGGILNRT	RELEGATING	AEEGIILLST	LEGALITIES
AEEGGILPUV	GIVE A LEG UP	AEEGIILMTT	LEGITIMATE
AEEGGINNRT	GENERATING	AEEGIILNST	GELATINISE
AEEGGINNSS	GAS ENGINES	AEEGIILNTZ	GELATINIZE
AEEGGINTTV	VEGETATING	AEEGIIMNRZ	NAZI REGIME
AEEGGIRSSV	AGGRESSIVE	AEEGIIPRSV	GIVE PRAISE
AEEGGLRRRW	GREW LARGER	AEEGIKLNSX	SEX-LINKAGE
AEEGGLRSYY	GRAYS ELEGY	AEEGIKMNSY	MAKING EYES
AEEGGMORST	MORTGAGEES	AEEGIKORTV	GIVE OR TAKE
AEEGGNOTUV	GAVE TONGUE	AEEGIKPPRS	KEEPS A GRIP
AEEGGNRRSS	GREEN GRASS	AEEGIILLLTT	LEGAL TITLE
AEEGGRRSST	STAGGERERS	AEEGILLMNN	ENAMELLING
AEEGGRRSSV	GRASS VERGE	AEEGILLNST	TEASELLING
AEEGGRRSSW	SWAGGERERS	AEEGILLORS	ALLEGORIES
AEEGGRSSSU	SURE AS EGGS		ALLEGORISE
AEEGHHHINV	HIGH HEAVEN	AEEGILLORZ	ALLEGORIZE
AEEGHHHIST	THE HIGH SEA	AEEGILLSST	LEGISLATES
AEEGHHNOUV	HAVE ENOUGH	AEEGILLSSU	LEGAL ISSUE
AEEGHIILMP	HEMIPLEGIA	AEEGILMNRR	MALINGERER
AEEGHIKMTW	MAKEWEIGHT	AEEGILMNRT	REGIMENTAL
AEEGHIKNNR	HEARKENING	AEEGILMNSV	EVANGELISM
AEEGHILNRT	LEATHERING	AEEGILMNTY	GEMINATELY
AEEGHILNSS	SINGHALESE	AEEGILNNOT	GET A LINE ON
AEEGHILPST	LEGATESHIP	AEEGILNNSS	GENIALNESS
AEEGHIMNTW	WIN THE GAME	AEEGILNNST	EGLANTINES
AEEGHIMRST	HERMITAGES	AEEGILNORT	REGELATION
AEEGHINNRT	HEARTENING		RELEGATION
AEEGHINRRS	REHEARSING	AEEGILNRST	GENERALIST

AEEGILNRTY	GENERALITY	AEEGMORSST	GASOMETERS
AEEGILNSTV	EVANGELIST	AEEGMPRTUU	UP A GUM TREE
AEEGILNTVY	NEGATIVELY	AEEGMPSTTU	GET UP STEAM
AEEGILOSTY	LAY SIEGE TO	AEEGMRRTTY	GREY MATTER
AEEGILRRSU	REGULARISE	AEEGNNORSS	SENSE ORGAN
AEEGILRRUZ	REGULARIZE	AEEGNNORST	GONE ASTERN
AEEGILRSTU	GAULEITERS	AEEGNNRRRU	REAR GUNNER
AEEGILRTUV	REGULATIVE	AEEGNNSSTW	NEWSAGENTS
AEEGIMNNRW	GERMAN WINE	AEEGNOOPRS	GO ON A SPREE
AEEGIMNORT	ERGOTAMINE	AEEGNOPRSS	PERSONAGES
AEEGIMNPRT	IMPREGNATE	AEEGNORRRV	RANGE ROVER
	PERMEATING	AEEGNORRST	GENERATORS
AEEGIMNRST	GERMINATES	AEEGNORSST	GOES ASTERN
	MAGNETISER	AEEGNORSTU	ENTOURAGES
AEEGIMNRTZ	MAGNETIZER	AEEGNORSTV	GRAVESTONE
AEEGIMNSST	GET IN A MESS	AEEGNOSTTW	WAGONETTES
	MAGNETISES	AEEGNOSTWY	GET ONE'S WAY
AEEGIMNSTZ	MAGNETIZES	AEEGNOSTXY	OXYGENATES
AEEGIMRRTT	GREAT MERIT	AEEGNOTTVW	GAVE VENT TO
AEEGIMRRTV	GRAVIMETER	AEEGNPRSSS	PASSENGERS
AEEGINNORT	GENERATION	AEEGNPRSST	PRESS AGENT
AEEGINNPRT	GREEN PAINT	AEEGOORSSV	GO OVERSEAS
AEEGINNRRT	INTERREGNA	AEEGOPRRST	PORTERAGES
AEEGINNRST	TANGERINES	AEEGPRSTUX	EXPURGATES
AEEGINNRTT	ENTREATING	AEEHHHINST	HEATHENISH
AEEGINNRTV	ENERVATING	AEEHHILSTT	HEALTHIEST
	VENERATING	AEEHHIMNST	HEATHENISM
AEEGINORRS	ORANGERIES	AEEHHIMSST	THE MESSIAH
AEEGINORTV	GIVEN EAR TO	AEEHHINRST	EARTHSHINE
AEEGINOSTT	NEGOTIATES	AEEHHISTTW	WITH THE SEA
AEEGINOTTV	VEGETATION	AEEHHKNPSS	SHEEPSHANK
AEEGINPRRS	PARIS GREEN	AEEHHLMSTU	METHUSELAH
AEEGINPRSV	GRAPEVINES	AEEHHMMMOR	HAMMER HOME
AEEGINPSUV	GIVEN PAUSE	AEEHHNOOPV	HAVE NO HOPE
AEEGINRRTT	RETREATING	AEEHHNOPRT	OPEN HEARTH
AEEGINRRTV	VAIN REGRET		OPEN-HEARTH
AEEGINRSSS	GREASINESS	AEEHHNPSTY	HYPHENATES
AEEGINRSST	INERT GASES	AEEHHNSSTU	UNSHEATHES
AEEGINRSTT	INTEGRATES	AEEHHORTTW	HOT WEATHER
AEEGINSTTW	GET IN A STEW	AEEHHOSTTT	THE HOT SEAT
AEEGIORSTV	GAVE RISE TO	AEEHHOSTTV	HAS THE VOTE
	GIVES EAR TO	AEEHIILLPT	EPITHELIAL
AEEGIPPRRT	PAPER TIGER	AEEHIINPRS	HEPARINISE
AEEGIPSSUV	GIVES PAUSE	AEEHIINPRZ	HEPARINIZE
AEEGIRSSTT	STRATEGIES	AEEHIINVVW	HAVE IN VIEW
AEEGKRRSTY	GREY STREAK	AEEHIIRRTV	THE RIVIERA
AEEGLLNORS	ORGANELLES	AEEHIISTTV	HESITATIVE
AEEGLLNORW	LEGAL OWNER	AEEHIKMSSW	MAKE WISHES
AEEGLLNOSS	LOS ANGELES	AEEHILLMTT	ALL THE TIME
AEEGLLORTT	ALLEGRETTO	AEEHILLRSS	RAISES HELL
AEEGLLRRTW	GREW TALLER	AEEHILMNSW	MEANWHILES
AEEGLMMOSY	GAMESOMELY	AEEHILMSSW	LIMEWASHES
AEEGLMNTTU	TEGUMENTAL	AEEHILNNOP	ANOPHELINE
AEEGLMRRSW	LEG-WARMERS	AEEHILNORV	HEAR NO EVIL
AEEGLNNORR	LONE RANGER	AEEHILNPTT	TAP THE LINE
AEEGLNNPST	PENTANGLES	AEEHILNSTT	IN THE LEAST
AEEGLNOPSW	SWEEP ALONG	AEEHILORST	OIL HEATERS
AEEGLNORTU	OUTGENERAL	AEEHILOSTT	TO THE AISLE
AEEGLOPRSY	GREASY POLE	AEEHILPPRR	PERIPHERAL
AEEGLORSWW	LOWER WAGES	AEEHILPPSY	EPIPHYSEAL
AEEGLORTUV	TRAVELOGUE	AEEHILPRST	SPHALERITE
AEEGLPPRSW	GREW APPLES	AEEHILPSST	SHAPELIEST
AEEGLPRTUY	GET UP EARLY	AEEHILRSTT	STEALTHIER
AEEGLPSTTU	GETS UP LATE	AEEHILRSTW	REST AWHILE
AEEGMNNOST	MANGOSTEEN		THE WAILERS
AEEGMNOOTV	GET A MOVE ON	AEEHILSTVW	WHITE SLAVE
AEEGMNOPSW	WOMENS PAGE	AEEHIIMNOTV	HAVE NO TIME
AEEGMNRRSS	MERGANSERS	AEEHIMNRST	THE MARINES
AEEGMNRRTU	RETURN GAME	AEEHIMPSSS	EMPHASISES
AEEGMNRSTU	AUGMENTERS	AEEHIMPSSZ	EMPHASIZES
AEEGMNRSTY	SEGMENTARY	AEEHIMRSTY	MY HEARTIES

AEEHIMSSTT	METATHESIS	AEEHNPRRSS	SHARPENERS
AEEHINNNRS	HENNA RINSE	AEEHNPRTTY	PAY THE RENT
AEEHINPPRT	IN THE PAPER	AEEHNPSTTU	UPS THE ANTE
AEEHINPRST	HEN PARTIES	AEEHOOPRRS	HORSE OPERA
	INTERPHASE	AEEHOOPRST	PEASHOOTER
AEEHINRRTT	RENT THE AIR	AEEHOOPRSU	OPERA HOUSE
AEEHINRSST	EARTHINESS	AEEHOOPSST	APOTHEOSES
	HEARTINESS	AEEHOPRSST	STEP ASHORE
AEEHINRSTV	HITS A NERVE	AEEHOPRTTU	POUR THE TEA
AEEHINRTTW	IN THE WATER	AEEHORRSUW	WAREHOUSER
AEEHINSSTT	ANTITHESES	AEEHORSSUW	WAREHOUSES
AEEHIPPRTW	WHITE PAPER	AEEHORSTVW	WHATSOEVER
AEEHIPRRST	THREE PAIRS	AEEHORTVWY	OVER THE WAY
AEEHIRSTTW	THERE IT WAS	AEEHOSSTTU	STATEHOUSE
	WHERE IT'S AT	AEEHPRRSTT	THREE PARTS
AEEHIRSTWW	WEARS WHITE	AEEHPRSSST	SET PHRASES
AEEHISTUVX	EXHAUSTIVE	AEEHPRSSTU	SUPERHEATS
AEEHJKOSTW	SAW THE JOKE	AEEHRRSSTT	THREE STARS
AEEHJMNRSY	HENRY JAMES	AEEIIJKLNP	KEEP IN JAIL
AEEHJMRSTY	HER MAJESTY	AEEIIKNRST	KERATINISE
AEEHKKNRUZ	HAKENKREUZ	AEEIIKNRTZ	KERATINIZE
AEEHKLMOSW	MAKES WHOLE	AEEIILLRTT	ILLITERATE
AEEHKLPSSW	SPEAK WELSH	AEEIILMNRS	MINERALISE
AEEHKMMORT	HOME MARKET	AEEIILMNRZ	MINERALIZE
AEEHKMORSS	SHOEMAKERS	AEEIILMNST	ELIMINATES
AEEHKOPSSV	SPOKESHAVE	AEEIILNNSU	ELEUSINIAN
AEEHKORSTT	HEAT STROKE	AEEIILNSTT	LIE IN STATE
	HEATSTROKE	AEEIILQSTU	EQUALITIES
AEEHKOSSTU	STEAK HOUSE	AEEIILRSSS	SERIALISES
AEEHKQRSTU	THE QUAKERS	AEEIILRSST	ISRAELITES
AEEHLLMORT	ALL THE MORE	AEEIILRSSZ	SERIALIZES
AEEHLLORSW	WHOLESALER	AEEIILRSTV	REVITALISE
AEEHLLOSSW	WHOLESALES	AEEIILRTVZ	REVITALIZE
AEEHLLPSSS	SHELLS PEAS	AEEIIMNNST	INSEMINATE
AEEHLLRSSS	SELL SHARES	AEEIIMNRSS	SEMINARIES
AEEHLLRSSU	SURE AS HELL	AEEIIMNSTT	ANTI-SEMITE
AEEHLLRSTT	ALL THE REST	AEEIIMPRTV	IMPERATIVE
AEEHLLSVWY	HEAVY SWELL	AEEIIMRSSS	EMISSARIES
AEEHLMMNOT	MENTAL HOME	AEEIIMSTTV	ESTIMATIVE
AEEHLMNNOP	PHENOMENAL	AEEIINRSTT	ITINERATES
AEEHLMPRSW	SPERM WHALE	AEEIINRTWW	WINE WAITER
AEEHLMSTTY	METHYLATES	AEEIIPPTTV	APPETITIVE
AEEHLNORTT	ON THE ALERT	AEEIIPRSST	PATISSERIE
AEEHLNOSTT	ON THE SLATE	AEEIJKLLLY	LIKE A JELLY
AEEHLNPSTT	THE PLANETS	AEEIJNNORR	JEAN RENOIR
AEEHLOQRSU	SQUARE HOLE	AEEIJOPRTV	PEJORATIVE
AEEHLORSST	LOSES HEART	AEEIKKMSST	KISS ME KATE
	SHORT LEASE	AEEIKLLLTY	LIKELY TALE
AEEHLORTWY	THE ROYAL WE	AEEIKLNNOV	LIKE AN OVEN
AEEHLOSTWY	LOSE THE WAY	AEEIKLNPPY	KEEP IN PLAY
AEEHLPRRSY	PALE SHERRY	AEEIKLNSSW	WEAKLINESS
AEEHMMORST	HAMMER TOES	AEEIKMOPPS	SMOKE A PIPE
	HAMMERTOES	AEEIKNNOSW	IN ONE'S WAKE
AEEHMMRSTU	SUMMER HEAT	AEEIKNRRSS	INK ERASERS
AEEHMNNTTX	THE NEXT MAN	AEEIKNSSTU	TAKEN ISSUE
AEEHMNOORR	MENORRHOEA	AEEIKRRSTW	WATER-SKIER
AEEHMNOPRT	PROMETHEAN	AEEIKSSSTU	TAKES ISSUE
AEEHMNOSTT	NOT THE SAME	AEEIILLLNV	VILLANELLE
AEEHMNRSTV	HARVESTMEN	AEEIILLMRSV	SILVER LAME
AEEHMOPRRU	AMPERE-HOUR	AEEIILLMSST	METALLISES
AEEHMOPRSS	SEMAPHORES	AEEIILLMSTZ	METALLIZES
AEEHMOPRST	ATMOSPHERE	AEEIILLNNOT	LINOLENATE
AEEHMORSTW	HOME WATERS	AEEIILLNOSV	LIVES ALONE
AEEHMRRRTY	MERRY HEART	AEEIILLPRST	PALLETISER
AEEHNNOORT	ONE ANOTHER	AEEIILLPRTZ	PALLETIZER
AEEHNOPRTT	NEAR THE TOP	AEEIILLPSST	PALLETISES
AEEHNORSSS	HOARSENESS	AEEIILLPSTT	PAILLETTES
AEEHNORSTU	RENT A HOUSE	AEEIILLPSTZ	PALLETIZES
AEEHNORTTW	ON THE WATER	AEEIILLRTTY	LITERATELY
AEEHNOSSST	THE SEASONS	AEEIILLRTVY	RELATIVELY
AEEHNPPTVY	HAPPY EVENT	AEEIILLSSTT	SATELLITES

AEEILLSTUV	TELEVISUAL	AEEIMPSSST	PASSES TIME
AEEILMMNPT	IMPALEMENT	AEEIMQRSUV	SEMIQUAVER
AEEILMNNST	LINEAMENTS	AEEIMRSTTX	TAXIMETERS
AEEILMNNTT	ENTAILMENT	AEEIMSSTTW	WASTES TIME
AEEILMNPRT	PLANIMETER	AEEIMSSTVW	EMITS WAVES
AEEILMNRST	STREAMLINE	AEEINNNPWY	PENNINE WAY
AEEILMNRSY	MINELAYERS	AEEINNNSST	INNATENESS
AEEILMORST	MELIORATES	AEEINNNTVY	IN ANY EVENT
AEEILMQRSU	SQUARE MILE	AEEINNORTV	ENERVATION
AEEILMRSTT	ALTIMETERS		VENERATION
AEEILNNPPS	PENEPLAINS	AEEINNRSTT	ENTERTAINS
AEEILNNPST	SEPTENNIAL	AEEINNRSTV	INNERVATES
AEEILNNRST	REAL TENNIS	AEEINNRSWY	EASY WINNER
AEEILNNSSV	VENIALNESS	AEEINNRTUV	AVENTURINE
AEEILNNSTT	SENTENTIAL	AEEINNSSSU	UNEASINESS
AEEILNNSTV	VALENTINES	AEEINNSSTV	NATIVENESS
AEEILNNTTU	LIEUTENANT	AEEINOPPST	APPOINTEES
AEEILNOPRT	PERITONEAL	AEEINOPPTT	NO APPETITE
AEEILNOPST	PLAIN TO SEE	AEEINOPRST	PROTEINASE
AEEILNORTV	REVELATION	AEEINOPTTT	POTENTIATE
AEEILNOSTV	ELEVATIONS	AEEINORSTT	ORIENTATES
AEEILNPPPS	PINEAPPLES	AEEINORTTW	WRITE A NOTE
AEEILNQSTU	SEQUENTIAL	AEEINPPRSS	PAPERINESS
AEEILNQTUV	EQUIVALENT	AEEINPRSTT	SAINT PETER
AEEILNRRSY	RISEN EARLY	AEEINPRSTU	RESUPINATE
AEEILNRRTV	IRRELEVANT	AEEINQRSTU	EQUESTRIAN
AEEILNRSSV	VERNALISES	AEEINQSSSU	QUEASINESS
AEEILNRSTU	NEUTRALISE	AEEINRRRST	RESTRAINER
AEEILNRSTV	LATIN VERSE	AEEINRRTTV	TRAVERTINE
AEEILNRSTW	WINTER SALE	AEEINRRTVY	VETERINARY
AEEILNRSVZ	VERNALIZES	AEEINRSSTT	REINSTATES
AEEILNSSST	ESSENTIALS	AEEINRSSTW	EAR WITNESS
AEEILNSSSU	SENSUALISE		WATERINESS
AEEILNSSSZ	SLEAZINESS	AEEINRSTTT	INTERSTATE
AEEILNSSUZ	SENSUALIZE	AEEINRSTTW	WINE TASTER
AEEILNSTTV	VENTILATES	AEEINRVWYY	IN EVERY WAY
AEEILOPRST	PERIOSTEAL	AEEINSSSTW	SWEATINESS
AEEILORTTV	TOLERATIVE	AEEINSSSTY	YEASTINESS
AEEILPRRTV	RIVER PLATE	AEEIOPRSTV	OPERATIVES
AEEILPRSST	PSALTERIES	AEEIPPRSST	APPETISERS
AEEILPRSSY	ERYSIPELAS	AEEIPPRSSU	PAUPERISES
AEEILRRRSY	EARLY RISER	AEEIPPRSTZ	APPETIZERS
AEEILRRSSY	RISES EARLY	AEEIPPRSUZ	PAUPERIZES
AEEILRRSTT	AIR LETTERS	AEEIPRRSTV	PRIVATEERS
AEEILRRSTV	RETRIEVALS	AEEIPRSSTT	STRIP TEASE
AEEILRRSVW	SILVERWARE		STRIPTEASE
AEEILRRTTU	LITERATURE		TAPESTRIES
AEEILRSSTT	LIES AT REST	AEEIPRSSTU	PASTEURISE
AEEILRSTTU	ELUTRIATES	AEEIPRSSUV	PERSUASIVE
AEEILSSSUX	SEXUALISES	AEEIPRSSYZ	PRIZE ESSAY
AEEILSSTTT	STATELIEST	AEEIPRSTTX	EXTIRPATES
AEEILSSUXZ	SEXUALIZES	AEEIPRSTUZ	PASTEURIZE
AEEIMMMRST	METAMERISM	AEEIPRTTUV	VITUPERATE
AEEIMNNORT	ENANTIOMER	AEEIRRSSTU	TREASURIES
AEEIMNNOST	MATES IN ONE	AEEIRRSTVW	SERVE A WRIT
AEEIMNNPRT	PINE MARTEN	AEEIRSSTTV	TRAVESTIES
AEEIMNNRTU	INNUMERATE	AEEIRSTUVY	EASY VIRTUE
AEEIMNOPRT	PERMEATION	AEEJLNORSU	JOURNALESE
AEEIMNORSY	RAISE MONEY	AEEJNOSSTW	SET ONE'S JAW
AEEIMNORTT	MARIONETTE	AEEKLLLSTY	SKELETALLY
AEEIMNOSTT	MAISONETTE	AEEKLLPSSW	SPEAKS WELL
AEEIMNPRRU	PRAEMUNIRE	AEEKLMOSSS	MAKE LOSSES
AEEIMNRSSS	NEAR MISSES	AEEKLMSSUY	SEEK ASYLUM
AEEIMNRSTT	MAIN STREET	AEEKLNORWY	WOKEN EARLY
	MARTENSITE	AEEKLNSSST	TALKS SENSE
	TERMINATES	AEEKLOPRRW	ROPEWALKER
AEEIMNSSST	STEAMINESS	AEEKLOPTUW	WOKE UP LATE
AEEIMNSSTT	ESTAMINETS	AEEKLORSVW	LEAVES WORK
AEEIMOPRTU	OPIUM EATER	AEEKLSSTTW	SWEET-TALKS
AEEIMOPRTW	WRITE A POEM	AEEKMMNORY	MONEY-MAKER
AEEIMPRRSS	SPERMARIES	AEEKMMNOSY	MAKES MONEY

AEEKMMRRRY	MERRYMAKER
AEEKMMRRSY	MAKES MERRY
AEEKMMRSST	MAKES TERMS
AEEKMNOPRT	OPEN MARKET
AEEKMNOSTY	STAKE MONEY
AEEKMOPRUW	WORE MAKE-UP
AEEKMORSSW	MAKES WORSE
AEEKMPRRTV	VERKRAMPTE
AEEKNNOSTT	TAKEN NOTES
AEEKNOSSTT	TAKES NOTES
AEEKNPSSTT	TAKEN STEPS
AEEKORSSTV	SKATES OVER
AEEKORSTUY	EUKARYOTES
AEEKPSSSTT	TAKES STEPS
AEELLLOPWY	PALE YELLOW
AEELLLPRUW	PAUL WELLER
AEELLLSSTT	TELLS TALES
AEELLMNOTV	MALEVOLENT
AEELLMNRTU	ALLUREMENT
AEELLMNSSY	NAMELESSLY
AEELLNORSV	LOVERS LANE
AEELLNPRST	ALL PRESENT
AEELLNRTVY	RELEVANTLY
AEELLNRTXY	EXTERNALLY
AEELLNSSTT	TALENTLESS
AEELLNTUVY	EVENTUALLY
AEELLOPRSV	LOVERS LEAP
AEELLOPSST	SELLOTAPES
	SOLEPLATES
AEELLOPSVW	WOVE A SPELL
AEELLORTTY	TEA TROLLEY
AEELLQRRRU	QUARRELLER
AEELLRRSTV	TRAVELLERS
AEELLRSTTW	TREATS WELL
	WALL STREET
AEELMMNORY	MEMORY LANE
AEELMMRSSU	SUMMER SALE
AEELMMRSTU	LATE SUMMER
AEELMNOPRT	TREPONEMAL
AEELMNORSS	MORAL SENSE
AEELMNORTV	OVERMANTEL
AEELMNORTW	WATER MELON
	WATERMELON
AEELMNOSSW	SALESWOMEN
AEELMNRRTW	TRAWLERMEN
AEELMNSTTT	MENTAL TEST
AEELMNSTTV	VESTMENTAL
AEELMOORSV	LEAVES ROOM
AEELMOPSTT	PALMETTOES
AEELMORSST	ELASTOMERS
AEELMORTTV	VOLTAMETER
AEELMPRSTT	STREET LAMP
AEELMPRSTU	TRUE SAMPLE
AEELMQRSTU	EQUAL TERMS
AEELNNORSW	NEW ORLEANS
AEELNNSSTT	TENANTLESS
AEELNOPRRS	REAL PERSON
AEELNORRVY	NEARLY OVER
AEELNOSSSY	EASY LESSON
AEELNOSSYY	LAYS EYES ON
AEELNPRTTW	WENTLETRAP
AEELNRRTYY	YEARLY RENT
AEELNRRVYY	VERY NEARLY
AEELNRTTUW	WALNUT TREE
AEELNSSTTW	LATEST NEWS
AEELOOPPTT	POTATO PEEL
AEELOORTTV	LEAVE TO ROT
AEELOPPRRT	POPLAR TREE
AEELORRTVY	REVELATORY
AEELORSTTU	LOTUS EATER
	LOTUS-EATER

AEELPRSTTY	PLAY STREET
AEELRRSTUW	LUSTREWARE
AEEMMNORST	MANOMETERS
AEEMMNORTT	ANTEMORTEM
AEEMMNORTY	ANEMOMETRY
AEEMMNSSTU	AMUSEMENTS
AEEMMRRSST	STAMMERERS
AEEMNNORSY	EARNS MONEY
AEEMNNORUV	MAVOURNEEN
AEEMNNOSTT	ATONEMENTS
AEEMNNPRST	PERMANENTS
AEEMNNPRTT	ENTRAPMENT
AEEMNNTTTU	ATTUNEMENT
AEEMNOPPRR	PROPER NAME
AEEMNOPPRY	PAPER MONEY
AEEMNOPSST	STEAMS OPEN
AEEMNOQRSU	ROMANESQUE
AEEMNORRTU	ENUMERATOR
AEEMNORRUV	MANOEUVRER
AEEMNORSST	SEA MONSTER
AEEMNORSUV	MANOEUVRES
AEEMNORSVY	EVER SO MANY
AEEMNORTXY	EXTRA MONEY
AEEMNORVWY	EVERY WOMAN
AEEMNOSSVY	SAVES MONEY
AEEMNOSTWY	WASTE MONEY
AEEMNPPRTY	PREPAYMENT
AEEMNRRSTT	ARRESTMENT
AEEMNRSSTU	MATURENESS
AEEMNRSTTU	MENSTRUATE
AEEMNSSSST	ASSESSMENT
AEEMNSSTTT	STATEMENTS
	TESTAMENTS
AEEMOOPRTW	WROTE A POEM
AEEMOPRSTW	STEAM POWER
AEEMORRSTV	OVERMASTER
AEEMORSSSY	MAYORESSES
AEEMORSTUU	MEASURE OUT
AEEMPRRSTY	MARY PETERS
AEEMPRRTTU	EAR TRUMPET
AEEMQRSSSU	MARQUESSES
AEEMRRSWXY	WAXES MERRY
AEEMRSSSST	SEAMSTRESS
AEEMRSSSTT	MATTRESSES
AEENNOOPSS	OPEN SEASON
AEENNOPSTT	TEN PAST ONE
AEENNORSST	ORNATENESS
AEENNOSSTX	NEXT SEASON
AEENNOTTTX	TO AN EXTENT
AEENNPQSUW	QUEENS PAWN
AEENNPSTTT	TEN PAST TEN
AEENNRRSTT	REENTRANTS
AEENOORTTW	WROTE A NOTE
AEENOPQSSU	OPAQUENESS
AEENOPRSST	ESPERANTOS
	PERSONATES
AEENOPSTTT	POTENTATES
AEENOQRRTU	ONE QUARTER
AEENORRSTV	VENERATORS
AEENORSTUX	EXTRANEOUS
AEENORTTUX	EXTENUATOR
AEENPPRSSW	NEWSPAPERS
AEENPPRSTT	STEPPARENT
AEENPRRSTU	ENRAPTURES
AEENPRSSSS	SPARSENESS
AEENQRSSUZ	SQUARENESS
AEENRRSSTU	SAUNTERERS
AEENRRSSTV	TRANSVERSE
AEENSSSTTU	ASTUTENESS
AEENSTTTVX	VAST EXTENT
AEEOOPRSTZ	AZEOTROPES

AEEOPPRRSV	PAPERS OVER	**AEFGHIILNV**	HAVING LIFE
AEEOPPRRSSU	PEA-SOUPERS	**AEFGHIILRT**	LIGHT A FIRE
AEEOPRRTWW	WATER POWER	**AEFGHIIRRT**	AIR FREIGHT
	WATERPOWER	**AEFGHIKLTT**	TAKE FLIGHT
AEEOPRRTWX	EXTRA POWER	**AEFGHIKRTT**	TAKE FRIGHT
AEEOPRSSSV	OVERPASSES	**AEFGHILLPT**	FILL THE GAP
	PASSES OVER	**AEFGHILNST**	SELF-HATING
AEEOPRSSTT	POETASTERS	**AEFGHILOST**	LOSE A FIGHT
AEEORRTTWW	WATER TOWER	**AEFGHINORU**	FAIR ENOUGH
AEEORSSTTV	OVERSTATES	**AEFGHINRRW**	WHARFINGER
AEEOSSTTTW	EAST TO WEST	**AEFGHIRSST**	GEARSHIFTS
AEEPPSSSTW	SWEEPS PAST		SHIFTS GEAR
AEEPRRSSST	TRESPASSER	**AEFGHLRTUW**	THE GULF WAR
AEEPRSSSST	TRESPASSES	**AEFGHORRST**	FORGATHERS
AEEPRSSWXY	EXPRESSWAY	**AEFGHORRTU**	FOURTH GEAR
AEEQRSSSTU	SET SQUARES	**AEFGHORTTW**	GET WHAT FOR
AEEQSSTTUU	STATUESQUE	**AEFGIIKLNT**	TAKING LIFE
AEERRRSSTU	TREASURERS	**AEFGIILLOR**	FLORILEGIA
AEERRRSSTV	TRAVERSERS	**AEFGIILMNN**	IAN FLEMING
AEERRSTTVX	EXTRAVERTS	**AEFGIILNNR**	FINGERNAIL
AEERSSSTTT	SETS AT REST	**AEFGIILNSV**	LIFESAVING
AEESSSSTUX	EAST SUSSEX	**AEFGIILNTV**	GIVEN A LIFT
AEESSTTTTU	STATUETTES	**AEFGIILSTV**	GIVES A LIFT
AEFFFILNOR	FINAL OFFER	**AEFGIINNRR**	REFRAINING
AEFFGGORST	STAGGER OFF	**AEFGIIRTUV**	FIGURATIVE
AEFFGHLLTY	FLY THE FLAG	**AEFGIKMNRR**	FINGERMARK
AEFFGILNOS	SEALING OFF	**AEFGILMNNU**	MEANINGFUL
AEFFGILNUV	LEAVING OFF	**AEFGILMNOS**	FLAMINGOES
AEFFGINORT	FIT OF ANGER	**AEFGILNNTT**	FLATTENING
	TEARING OFF	**AEFGILNOUW**	GUINEA FOWL
AEFFGINORW	WEARING OFF	**AEFGILNRSS**	RINGS FALSE
AEFFGIORST	FITS OF RAGE	**AEFGILNRTT**	FLATTERING
AEFFHIKOST	SHAKE IT OFF	**AEFGILNSTY**	FLYING EAST
AEFFHKMORT	OFF THE MARK	**AEFGILOPRT**	PROFLIGATE
AEFFHLLOTU	FULL OF HATE	**AEFGIMNORR**	FOREARMING
AEFFHLLOTW	OFF THE WALL	**AEFGINNSST**	FASTENINGS
AEFFHILOSTT	HOTEL STAFF	**AEFGINOSSW**	WAGES OF SIN
AEFFHSTUVY	HEAVY STUFF	**AEFGIORSSS**	OSSIFRAGES
AEFFIIINST	AFFINITIES	**AEFGIPRRTU**	GRAPEFRUIT
AEFFIILLMY	FAMILY LIFE	**AEFGIRSSTT**	FIRST STAGE
AEFFIKLLOW	WALK OF LIFE		GAS FITTERS
AEFFIKPSST	PIKESTAFFS		GETS A FIRST
AEFFILLORW	WALL OF FIRE	**AEFGIRSUWX**	WAX FIGURES
AEFFILNOPS	SPAN OF LIFE	**AEFGLLLMSU**	FLAGELLUMS
AEFFILNORW	WAFFLE IRON	**AEFGLLORSW**	WELLS FARGO
AEFFILNSTU	INSUFFLATE	**AEFGLLRTUY**	GRATEFULLY
AEFFIMNSTX	AFFIXMENTS	**AEFGLMRSTU**	GULF STREAM
AEFFIMORRS	MARRIES OFF	**AEFGLNRTUU**	UNGRATEFUL
AEFFINORTV	VAIN EFFORT	**AEFGLORSTW**	AFTERGLOWS
AEFFIRSTUX	AFFIXTURES	**AEFGNOOORT**	GONE TOO FAR
AEFFIRSTYY	FIFTY YEARS		TOO FAR GONE
AEFFKMNOSU	MAKES FUN OF	**AEFGNOORTU**	OUT OF RANGE
AEFFKNNSTU	TAKEN SNUFF	**AEFGOOORST**	GOES TOO FAR
AEFFKNSSTU	TAKES SNUFF	**AEFHHLORTY**	HOLY FATHER
AEFFLLLNOU	FALLEN FOUL	**AEFHIILLRT**	FILL THE AIR
AEFFLLLOTW	LEFT FALLOW	**AEFHIILNNT**	IN THE FINAL
AEFFLLLOUZ	FULL OF ZEAL	**AEFHIIRRTW**	WHITE FRIAR
AEFFLLNTUY	AFFLUENTLY	**AEFHIKLRSY**	FREAKISHLY
AEFFLMOOPR	FLAMEPROOF	**AEFHIKMRST**	FISH MARKET
AEFFLNORST	FALSE FRONT	**AEFHIKMSST**	MAKES SHIFT
AEFFLORSTT	RATTLES OFF	**AEFHIKNPRS**	SHARP KNIFE
AEFFMOORTU	TEAM OF FOUR	**AEFHIKSSST**	FISH STEAKS
AEFFNOOSSS	OFF-SEASONS	**AEFHILNORT**	TORE IN HALF
AEFFNRSSTU	STAFF NURSE	**AEFHILNSSS**	FLASHINESS
AEFFOOPRTY	OFFER TO PAY	**AEFHILOSST**	LOSES FAITH
AEFFOQRSSU	SQUARES OFF	**AEFHILPSST**	FISHPLATES
AEFFRSSTUX	SUFFERS TAX	**AEFHILRSST**	HALF SISTER
AEFGGHIRTT	GET A FRIGHT	**AEFHINNOSW**	NEW FASHION
AEFGGINORT	GOING AFTER	**AEFHINOSSS**	OAFISHNESS
AEFGHHLLNT	HALF LENGTH	**AEFHINOTTU**	UNIT OF HEAT
	HALF-LENGTH	**AEFHINPRST**	FRESH PAINT

AEFHIORSST	FIRES A SHOT	AEFIMORSTV	FORMATIVES
AEFHJNOORY	JAR OF HONEY	AEFIMORSTW	TIMES OF WAR
AEFHKLOPRS	ASK FOR HELP	AEFINNRSSU	UNFAIRNESS
AEFHLLLOOT	HELL OF A LOT	AEFINOOPRT	PIANOFORTE
AEFHLLLOVY	HALF VOLLEY	AEFINOPPPS	PIPES OF PAN
	HALF-VOLLEY	AEFINOPRRS	PORIFERANS
AEFHLLMSUY	SHAMEFULLY		PRISON FARE
AEFHLLNNOS	HALF NELSON	AEFINOPRST	PAIR OF TENS
AEFHLLOORW	HELL OF A ROW	AEFINORRST	RAIN FOREST
AEFHLMNTTW	TWELFTH MAN	AEFINORTTU	REFUTATION
AEFHLMOSST	FATHOMLESS	AEFINOSTTT	NO FIT STATE
AEFHLNOPRR	RAN FOR HELP	AEFINRRRTY	TRAIN FERRY
AEFHMNOORR	RAN FOR HOME	AEFINRRTTY	FRATERNITY
AEFHMNOSTT	TEN FATHOMS	AEFINRSSTX	TRANSFIXES
AEFHMNOTTY	TENTH OF MAY	AEFIOQRSUU	AQUIFEROUS
AEFHMORRSS	FARM HORSES	AEFIORRSUU	AURIFEROUS
AEFHMORSSU	FARMHOUSES	AEFIORSTUV	FAVOURITES
AEFHNNOOTT	NONE OF THAT	AEFIPRRTTY	PRETTY FAIR
AEFHNORSST	FATHER'S SON	AEFIRRRSTT	FIRST-RATER
AEFHNORTTT	AT THE FRONT	AEFIRRSTTW	FIRST WATER
AEFHOOPSTU	OUT OF SHAPE	AEFJLOOPRY	LEAP FOR JOY
AEFHORRSTU	AFTER HOURS	AEFKLNOSSW	SNOWFLAKES
	AFTER-HOURS	AEFKLOORST	LOOKS AFTER
	FOUR HEARTS	AEFKLOORSW	SALE OF WORK
AEFHRRSSTT	FRESH START	AEFKLORSSW	FALSEWORKS
AEFIIILNST	FINALITIES	AEFKMOORRS	ASK FOR MORE
AEFIILLLNN	FALL IN LINE	AEFKMORRRW	FARM WORKER
AEFIILLTUV	FLUVIATILE	AEFKMORRSW	FRAMEWORKS
AEFIILMNSS	SEMIFINALS	AEFKNOPSTU	POKES FUN AT
AEFIILMPRS	AMPLIFIERS	AEFKNORSUV	FOUR KNAVES
AEFIILMSTY	FAMILY TIES	AEFKORRSTW	FAST WORKER
AEFIILMSYZ	FAMILY SIZE	AEFLLLOPWY	PLAYFELLOW
AEFIILNRTT	INFILTRATE	AEFLLLORWW	WALLFLOWER
AEFIILORTT	TRIFOLIATE	AEFLLLSSWY	FLAWLESSLY
AEFIILQRSU	QUALIFIERS	AEFLLMRRSY	SMALLER FRY
AEFIILSSTU	FILES A SUIT	AEFLLNORTY	LEARN TO FLY
AEFIIMMNOR	AMMONIFIER	AEFLLNOSSW	FALLOWNESS
AEFIINOPRS	SAPONIFIER	AEFLLNSSUW	LAWFULNESS
AEFIINOPSS	SAPONIFIES	AEFLLORSST	FORESTALLS
AEFIINQRTU	QUANTIFIER	AEFLLPRTTU	PLATTERFUL
AEFIINQSTU	QUANTIFIES	AEFLLSTTUY	TASTEFULLY
AEFIINRSTU	INFURIATES	AEFLLSTUWY	WASTEFULLY
AEFIIRSSTT	STRATIFIES	AEFLMNOORU	FORMULA ONE
AEFIKLNOTW	FLOWN A KITE	AEFLMORSTU	FORMULATES
AEFIKLORSS	ISLE OF SARK		SET FORMULA
AEFIKNOPRS	FAIR-SPOKEN	AEFLMORSTW	FLEW TO ARMS
AEFILLLNOV	FALL IN LOVE	AEFLNNRRUU	FUNERAL URN
AEFILLLNST	FALL SILENT	AEFLNOORST	NOT FOR SALE
AEFILLLOSW	LIES FALLOW	AEFLNOOTVW	WANT OF LOVE
AEFILLLRWY	FAIRLY WELL	AEFLNOTTTU	FLATTEN OUT
AEFILLMNOR	NORMAL LIFE	AEFLNRSSTU	ARTFULNESS
AEFILLMORT	FOR ALL TIME	AEFLOOPSTT	FOOTPLATES
AEFILLNNRY	INFERNALLY	AEFLOORSUV	LOSE FAVOUR
AEFILLPRXY	PREFIXALLY	AEFLORRSUW	RULES OF WAR
AEFILMMORS	SEMIFORMAL	AEFLORSTWW	WATERFOWLS
AEFILMNORS	FORMS A LINE	AEFLRSTTWY	FLYSWATTER
	LIFE ON MARS	AEFMMORRST	FORM MASTER
AEFILMNSTU	FULMINATES	AEFMNOSSSU	FAMOUSNESS
AEFILMNSTY	MANIFESTLY	AEFMOPRRST	PERMAFROST
AEFILMOOTV	FAIL TO MOVE	AEFNNOORST	AFTERNOONS
AEFILMORSS	FORMALISES	AEFNNOOSTT	OFTEN AS NOT
AEFILMORSZ	FORMALIZES	AEFNNRRSTU	FAST RUNNER
AEFILMORTW	WOLFRAMITE	AEFNORRRST	TRANSFEROR
AEFILMRSTX	FILM EXTRAS	AEFNORRTTW	WATERFRONT
AEFILNORST	REFLATIONS	AEFNORSSTU	FAR-OUTNESS
AEFILNORTU	FLUORINATE	AEFNORSSTW	SOFT ANSWER
AEFILNRTTU	IN A FLUTTER	AEFNRSSSTU	TRANSFUSES
AEFILNSSTU	FAULTINESS	AEFOOPRRRT	PERFORATOR
AEFILOQRTU	QUATREFOIL	AEFOOPRRTW	WATERPROOF
AEFILQTUUW	QUITE AWFUL	AEFOOPRSST	SOFT-SOAPER
AEFIMNOSST	MANIFESTOS	AEFOOQRSTU	SQUARE FOOT

AEFOORRSTT	TORTFEASOR	AEGGORRSSS	AGGRESSORS
AEFOORTTUW	OUT OF WATER	AEGHHIIPRS	HIGH PRAISE
AEFOQRRSUU	FOURSQUARE	AEGHHIKNRR	HIGHER RANK
AEFORRSTYY	FORTY YEARS	AEGHHIKSST	HIGH STAKES
AEFRRSSTTU	FRUSTRATES	AEGHHILLLS	SHILLELAGH
AEGGGIINRV	AGGRIEVING	AEGHHILMOR	HIGH MORALE
AEGGGILNNY	ENGAGINGLY	AEGHHILOPR	HELIOGRAPH
AEGGGINNNR	GANGRENING	AEGHHILRTT	EARTHLIGHT
AEGGGINRST	STAGGERING		LIGHT HEART
AEGGGINRSW	SWAGGERING	AEGHHIMNWY	HIGHWAYMEN
AEGGHHIINT	GAIN HEIGHT	AEGHHIMRTY	EIGHTH ARMY
AEGGHHIMNR	HIGH GERMAN	AEGHHINOSS	HIGH SEASON
AEGGHHLNOU	LOUGH NEAGH	AEGHHIPRTT	EIGHTH PART
AEGGHHNOTT	GOT THE HANG	AEGHHISTTU	HAUGHTIEST
AEGGHIILRS	GEISHA GIRL	AEGHHLORSU	HORSE LAUGH
AEGGHIINTW	GAIN WEIGHT		HORSELAUGH
AEGGHILLRT	LEGAL RIGHT	AEGHHMOPPT	APOPHTHEGM
AEGGHILNRT	RIGHT ANGLE	AEGHHNRTTU	GARETH HUNT
	RIGHT-ANGLE	AEGHIILMST	ALMIGHTIES
AEGGHILRST	GAS LIGHTER	AEGHIILPPT	LIGHT A PIPE
AEGGHINOVY	HEAVY GOING	AEGHIINNTV	GIVEN A HINT
AFGGHINRST	GATHERINGS	AEGHIINRSV	VINEGARISH
AEGGHINRTT	GREAT THING	AEGHIINSTT	HESITATING
AEGGHMOOPS	EGG SHAMPOO	AEGHIINSTV	GIVES A HINT
AEGGIILMPR	PILGRIMAGE	AEGHIIPRST	GRAPHITISE
AEGGIILNNR	REALIGNING	AEGHIIPRTZ	GRAPHITIZE
AEGGIILNTV	LEVIGATING	AEGHIKLMST	MAKES LIGHT
AEGGIILNVW	LIVING WAGE	AEGHIKMSTT	MAKES TIGHT
AEGGIILNZZ	ZIG-ZAG LINE	AEGHIKNSTV	GIVE THANKS
	ZIGZAG LINE	AEGHIKRRST	TIGER SHARK
AEGGIIMNNT	GEMINATING	AEGHILLNOP	ANGLOPHILE
AEGGIIMNRT	EMIGRATING	AEGHILLNSW	ENGLISH LAW
AEGGIINNNR	ENGRAINING	AEGHILLRTT	GET A THRILL
AEGGIINNRV	GIVEN A RING	AEGHILLRTY	EARLY LIGHT
AEGGIINNSV	ENVISAGING	AEGHILMNNS	ENGLISHMAN
	GIVEN A SIGN	AEGHILMNTT	ALIGHTMENT
AEGGIINNTV	NEGATIVING	AEGHILNNSU	UNLEASHING
AEGGIINOTV	GIVEN IT A GO	AEGHILNOOT	THEOLOGIAN
AEGGIINRSV	GIVES A RING	AEGHILNOST	GENIAL HOST
AEGGIINSSV	GIVES A SIGN	AEGHILNRST	EARTHLINGS
AEGGIIOSTV	GIVES IT A GO	AEGHILNRTY	EARLY NIGHT
AEGGILLNOS	LOSING A LEG	AEGHILNSSU	LANGUISHES
AEGGILLNRV	GRAVELLING	AEGHILNSVW	WING HALVES
AEGGILMNOS	LOSING GAME	AEGHILOPRT	LIGHT OPERA
AEGGILNNNT	ENTANGLING	AEGHILRRST	REAR LIGHTS
AEGGILNNOT	ELONGATING	AEGHILRSTY	LIGHT-YEARS
AEGGILNRTU	REGULATING	AEGHILSSTT	SETS ALIGHT
AEGGIMNNTU	AUGMENTING	AEGHIMMNRS	HAMMERINGS
AEGGINNORS	GONE IN RAGS	AEGHIMNRST	NIGHTMARES
AEGGINNPRS	GINGER SNAP	AEGHIMPRST	TEPHIGRAMS
AEGGINNRST	ESTRANGING	AEGHINNPPS	HAPPENINGS
AFGGINNRSV	ENGRAVINGS	AEGHINNPRS	SHARPENING
AEGGINOOST	GOING TO SEA	AEGHINNRSS	HARNESSING
AEGGINOPRS	GOING SPARE	AEGHINNRTU	UNEARTHING
AEGGINORSS	AGGRESSION	AEGHINNSWY	SAYING WHEN
	GOES IN RAGS	AEGHINOOTV	GIVEN A HOOT
AEGGINRSST	STAGGERS IN	AEGHINORSS	GARISHNESS
AEGGIORRSU	GREGARIOUS	AEGHINRSTT	SHATTERING
AEGGIRRSTW	GAG WRITERS		STRAIGHTEN
AEGGJNRTUU	JUGGERNAUT	AEGHINRSTV	HARVESTING
AEGGLNOOOT	GONE TO GAOL	AEGHINSSTY	EASY THINGS
AEGGLNOOVY	LONG VOYAGE	AEGHINSTTU	NAUGHTIEST
AEGGLOOOST	GOES TO GAOL	AEGHINSTUX	EXHAUSTING
AEGGLORRRW	GROW LARGER	AEGHIOOSTV	GIVES A HOOT
AEGGLPRRUY	PLAY RUGGER	AEGHIOSTUV	GIVE A SHOUT
AEGGLRRSST	STRAGGLERS	AEGHIPRRSS	SERIGRAPHS
AEGGLRRUUY	REGULAR GUY	AEGHIPRRSY	SERIGRAPHY
AEGGNNORSU	GANGRENOUS	AEGHIRRSTT	STRAIGHTER
AEGGNOOSTT	EGG ON TOAST	AEGHIRSTUW	WHITE SUGAR
AEGGNOSSUY	SYNAGOGUES	AEGHIRTTTW	WATERTIGHT
AEGGNPRSSS	PRESS-GANGS	AEGHKOOTTY	GOT THE OKAY

AEGHLLMOOP	GALLOP HOME	AEGIIMSTTZ	STIGMATIZE
AEGHLLNOPS	HELPS ALONG	AEGIINNNRT	ENTRAINING
AEGHLLOSTW	THE GALLOWS	AEGIINNOTT	EATING INTO
AEGHLMNRST	ARMS LENGTH	AEGIINNPRT	PERTAINING
AEGHLMOOOT	HOMOLOGATE	AEGIINNRSS	GRAININESS
AEGHLNNOOP	ANGLOPHONE	AEGIINNRSW	SWEARING IN
AEGHLNOOSS	HANGS LOOSE	AEGIINNSTT	TETANISING
AEGHLNOOSU	HALOGENOUS	AEGIINNTTZ	TETANIZING
AEGHLNSTWY	LENGTHWAYS	AEGIINORST	ORIGINATES
AEGHLOOORR	LOGORRHOEA	AEGIINORTV	INVIGORATE
AEGHLOOPRS	OLEOGRAPHS	AEGIINPPST	APPETISING
AEGHLOOPRY	OLEOGRAPHY	AEGIINPPTZ	APPETIZING
AEGHLOORTW	WOOLGATHER	AEGIINSSTT	INSTIGATES
AEGHLORSTT	LARGHETTOS	AEGIINTTVY	NEGATIVITY
AEGHLORSUV	LAUGHS OVER	AEGIINTUVX	EXUVIATING
AEGHLOSSSU	GLASS HOUSE	AEGIIRSTTU	GRATUITIES
	GLASSHOUSE	AEGIIRTTVY	GIVE IT A TRY
AEGHLRSSTU	SLAUGHTERS	AEGIJLNOOT	GONE TO JAIL
AEGHLRTTUY	UGLY THREAT	AEGIJLOOST	GOES TO JAIL
AEGHMMORRT	THERMOGRAM	AEGIKKMNRS	KINGMAKERS
AEGHMNNSTU	MAN THE GUNS	AEGIKLMNOV	LOVEMAKING
AEGHMNOOPR	GRAMOPHONE		MAKING LOVE
AEGHNNOOTW	ON THE WAGON	AEGIKLNNSY	SNEAKINGLY
AEGHNOOORR	GONORRHOEA	AEGIKLNOOT	GET A LOOK IN
AEGHNOORST	NO SHORTAGE	AEGIKLNOTU	LEAKING OUT
AEGHNOORSU	HOUSE ORGAN	AEGIKLNPRY	PEARLY KING
AEGHNOOSTW	WHAT GOES ON?	AEGIKMNNOS	MAKE NO SIGN
AEGHNORRST	SHORT RANGE	AEGIKMNNSW	MAKING NEWS
	SHORT-RANGE	AEGIKMNORV	MAKING OVER
AEGHOOPSSU	OESOPHAGUS	AEGIKMNRSU	MAKING SURE
AEGHOPPSTT	STOP THE GAP	AEGIKNNOTT	TAKING NOTE
AEGHOPRRXY	XEROGRAPHY	AEGIKNNPSU	SNEAKING UP
AEGHORRTUW	ROUGH WATER	AEGIKNNSTW	TAKEN WINGS
AEGIIILLNV	LIVING A LIE	AEGIKNORRV	RAKING OVER
AEGIIILNTV	INVIGILATE	AEGIKNORTV	OVERTAKING
AEGIIKMMNT	MAKING TIME		TAKING OVER
AEGIIKMNTT	TAKING TIME	AEGIKNOSTW	SOAKING WET
AEGIIKNNNS	SNEAKING IN	AEGIKNPPSU	SPEAKING UP
AEGIIKNOPP	PIG IN A POKE	AEGIKNSSTW	TAKES WINGS
AEGIILLLMT	LEGAL LIMIT	AEGILLLLNT	TELLING ALL
AEGIILLLTY	ILLEGALITY	AEGILLLNSU	GALLINULES
AEGIILLPRS	ASPERGILLI	AEGILLLRVY	GRAVELLY ILL
AEGIILMNNP	IMPANELING	AEGILLMNRV	MARVELLING
AEGIILMNNS	MELANISING	AEGILLMNRY	GERMINALLY
AEGIILMNNZ	MELANIZING	AEGILLNORU	NEUROGLIAL
AEGIILMNRT	TRIGEMINAL	AEGILLNORY	REGIONALLY
AEGIILMNST	TIME SIGNAL	AEGILLNPSY	PLEASINGLY
AEGIILNNPS	PENALISING	AEGILLNRSS	SIGNALLERS
AEGIILNNPX	EXPLAINING	AEGILLNRTV	TRAVELLING
AEGIILNNPZ	PENALIZING	AEGILLNRTY	INTEGRALLY
AEGIILNNRU	UNGAINLIER	AEGILLNSST	TASSELLING
AEGIILNOTT	ETIOLATING	AEGILLOPTT	EPIGLOTTAL
AEGIILNOTV	LEVIGATION	AEGILLORST	ALLEGORIST
AEGIILNPRV	PREVAILING		LEGISLATOR
AEGIILNQSU	EQUALISING	AEGILLRRSU	GUERRILLAS
AEGIILNQUZ	EQUALIZING	AEGILLRSSS	SALESGIRLS
AEGIILNRST	RISING LATE	AEGILMNORY	MINERALOGY
AEGIILNSSS	SIGNALISES	AEGILMNOST	LOSING TEAM
AEGIILNSSZ	SIGNALIZES	AEGILMOPSY	POLYGAMISE
AEGIILNSTV	VIGILANTES	AEGILMOPYZ	POLYGAMIZE
AEGIILNSVY	EASY LIVING	AEGILMORSS	GLAMORISES
AEGIILNTTV	LEVITATING	AEGILMORSZ	GLAMORIZES
AEGIIMMRST	IMMIGRATES	AEGILMRSSV	ALMSGIVERS
AEGIIMMNOT	GEMINATION	AEGILMSTTU	MULTISTAGE
AEGIIMMNST	STEAMING IN	AEGILNNNRU	UNLEARNING
AEGIIMNORT	EMIGRATION	AEGILNNOOT	ELONGATION
AEGIIMNSSV	GIVEN A MISS		GOT A LINE ON
AEGIIMNSTT	ESTIMATING	AEGILNNPRT	REPLANTING
AEGIIMNSTV	SAVING TIME	AEGILNNPTX	EXPLANTING
AEGIIMSSSV	GIVES A MISS	AEGILNNRYY	YEARNINGLY
AEGIIMSSTT	STIGMATISE	AEGILNOOSU	OLEAGINOUS

AEGILNORTT	TOLERATING
AEGILNORTU	REGULATION
	UROGENITAL
AEGILNOSTU	GELATINOUS
AEGILNOTUV	LEAVING OUT
AEGILNPRRT	LARGE PRINT
AEGILNPRST	LATE SPRING
	PLASTERING
AEGILNPRSU	PLEASURING
AEGILNPSSY	PAYING LESS
AEGILNPSTU	STEALING UP
AEGILNQSSU	EQUALS SIGN
AEGILNRSTV	STARVELING
AEGILNRVWY	WAVERINGLY
AEGILNSSSS	GLASSINESS
AEGILOOPSS	APOLOGISES
AEGILOOPSZ	APOLOGIZES
AEGILOORST	AEROLOGIST
AEGILOPRTT	GRAPTOLITE
AEGILORSSS	GLOSSARIES
AEGILRRRSU	IRREGULARS
AEGILRRSUV	VULGARISER
AEGILRRTUY	REGULARITY
AEGILRRUVZ	VULGARIZER
AEGILRSSUV	VULGARISES
AEGILRSUVZ	VULGARIZES
AEGIMMNRST	STAMMERING
AEGIMMORSS	SEISMOGRAM
AEGIMMNORT	MORNING TEA
AEGIMNNORU	ENAMOURING
AEGIMNNRST	SMARTENING
AEGIMNNRSV	SERVING MAN
AEGIMNNSST	ASSIGNMENT
AEGIMNOPRS	ANGIOSPERM
AEGIMNOPRY	PAYING MORE
AEGIMNORSU	GRAMINEOUS
AEGIMNOSST	GOT IN A MESS
AEGIMNPRTY	PIGMENTARY
AEGIMNPTTT	ATTEMPTING
AEGIMNRRST	RINGMASTER
AEGIMNRSST	GERMANISTS
AEGIMNRSTT	SMATTERING
AEGIMORRSU	ARMIGEROUS
AEGINNNPRT	TREPANNING
AEGINNNSTU	SANG IN TUNE
AEGINNORST	RESONATING
AEGINNORSW	NORWEGIANS
AEGINNORTV	RENOVATING
AEGINNPPRT	ENTRAPPING
AEGINNPRRT	PARTNERING
AEGINNPRTT	PATTERNING
AEGINNPRTY	PAYING RENT
AEGINNRSTT	ASTRINGENT
AEGINNRTUV	GIVEN A TURN
AEGINNRUVW	UNWAVERING
AEGINOORTT	NEGOTIATOR
AEGINOPRST	PRISON GATE
AEGINOPRSW	GAINS POWER
	SPIRO AGNEW
AEGINOPRVY	OVERPAYING
AEGINORRSS	ORGANISERS
AEGINORRSZ	ORGANIZERS
AEGINORRTT	INTEGRATOR
AEGINORRTV	OVERRATING
AEGINORSTW	WRITE A SONG
AEGINORTUW	WEARING OUT
AEGINORTVX	OVERTAXING
AEGINOSSTT	GESTATIONS
AEGINOSTTW	GOT IN A STEW
AEGINPQRTU	PARQUETING
AEGINPRRSU	PERSIAN RUG

AEGINPRSTT	SPATTERING
AEGINPRSTU	PUTS IN GEAR
	SUPERGIANT
AEGINPRSTY	PANEGYRIST
AEGINPSTTU	SEPTUAGINT
AEGINQRRTU	QUARTERING
AEGINRRSSU	REASSURING
AEGINRRSTU	GARNITURES
	TREASURING
AEGINRRSTV	TRAVERSING
AEGINRSSTU	SIGNATURES
AEGINRSTUV	GIVES A TURN
AEGINRSTWW	WATER WINGS
AEGIORTTUU	ARGUE IT OUT
AEGIPRSTUV	PURGATIVES
AEGIRRRSST	REGISTRARS
AEGIRSSTTT	STRATEGIST
AEGJKLORUV	VULGAR JOKE
AEGJMNOPSS	JAM SPONGES
AEGKLLMRSS	MRS.GASKELL
AEGKLPRRUU	PAUL KRUGER
AEGKMNOSXY	OXYGEN MASK
AEGKMNPSUY	MAGNUS PYKE
AEGKOOSSTU	TOOK A GUESS
AEGKOPRUVW	GAVE UP WORK
AEGLLMOORS	LOOMS LARGE
AEGLLMORRU	GLOMERULAR
AEGLLMRTUY	METALLURGY
AEGLLNNOST	TEN GALLONS
AEGLLNNPTY	PLANGENTLY
AEGLLNOOTU	GONE ALL OUT
AEGLLNOPRY	LONG PLAYER
AEGLLNOSST	GALLSTONES
AEGLLOOSTT	ALL SET TO GO
AEGLLOOSTU	GOES ALL OUT
AEGLLOPRSU	PELLAGROUS
AEGLLORRTW	GROW TALLER
AEGLLRSUUW	AUGURS WELL
AEGLMNOOSV	MOVES ALONG
AEGLMNORSS	LEMONGRASS
AEGLMOPRTU	PROMULGATE
AEGLMPSSTY	EMPTY GLASS
AEGLNNPRTY	PREGNANTLY
AEGLNOPRSY	GYROPLANES
AEGLNOPSTW	SWEPT ALONG
AEGLNORSTW	GROWN STALE
AEGLNOSTWY	LONGEST WAY
AEGLNRRSST	STRANGLERS
AEGLNSSSSU	SUNGLASSES
AEGLOORRST	ASTROLOGER
AEGLOORSTV	GLOATS OVER
AEGLOORTTY	TERATOLOGY
AEGLOPPRSW	GROW APPLES
AEGLOPPSTU	PLAGUE SPOT
AEGLOPRTUY	GOT UP EARLY
AEGLORRTUY	REGULATORY
AEGLORSSTW	GROWS STALE
AEGLORSSUV	GROSS VALUE
AEGLPSSSSY	SPYGLASSES
AEGMMOPRRR	PROGRAMMER
AEGMMOPRRS	PROGRAMMES
AEGMMNNORST	MAGNETRONS
AEGMNOOOTV	GOT A MOVE ON
AEGMNOORST	GASTRONOME
	GO ON STREAM
AEGMNOOSST	GONE TO MASS
AEGMNORRSW	WARMONGERS
AEGMNORSTT	STRONG MEAT
AEGMNORSTU	AUGMENTORS
AEGMNOSTTU	MAO TSE TUNG
AEGMOOSSST	GOES TO MASS

AEGMOPSTTU	GOT UP STEAM	AEHILLMPTT	LIT THE LAMP
AEGNNOPPRS	SPRANG OPEN	AEHILLSTTY	STEALTHILY
AEGNNORRST	NO STRANGER	AEHILMNNUY	INHUMANELY
AEGNOORSTW	WROTE A SONG	AEHILMNOPY	ANEMOPHILY
AEGNOORTXY	OXYGENATOR	AEHILMORST	ISOTHERMAL
AEGNOOSTUU	AUTOGENOUS	AEHILMOSSY	HAEMOLYSIS
AEGNOOSTWY	GOT ONE'S WAY	AEHILMRRTY	HILARY TERM
AEGNOPRRSV	SPRANG OVER	AEHILNNOST	ANTHELIONS
AEGNORRTWY	TERRY WOGAN	AEHILNOOST	SHOOT A LINE
AEGNORRWWY	GROWN WEARY	AEHILNOPTT	THIOPENTAL
AEGNRRSSST	TRANSGRESS	AEHILNORSS	LIONS SHARE
AEGNSSSTUU	AUGUSTNESS	AEHILNORST	ON THE RAILS
AEGNSTTUUX	NEXT AUGUST	AEHILNORTT	ON THE TRAIL
AEGOORSTUU	OUTRAGEOUS	AEHILNOSST	HAILSTONES
AEGOPPRSST	SPORTS PAGE	AEHILNQRSU	HARLEQUINS
AEGOPRRSSU	SOUR GRAPES	AEHILNSSSV	LAVISHNESS
AEGOPRRTUX	EXPURGATOR	AEHILNSTTY	HESITANTLY
AEGORRSSTU	SURROGATES	AEHILOPRST	RETAIL SHOP
AEGORRSWWY	GROWS WEARY	AEHILOSSTT	HELIOSTATS
AEGORSSSTU	STEGOSAURS	AEHILRSSTY	HAIRSTYLES
AEHHHISTTY	HITS THE HAY	AEHILRSTVY	SHRIEVALTY
AEHHIIRSTW	WHITE HAIRS	AEHIMMPRRT	TRIP-HAMMER
AEHHIKMRTT	HIT THE MARK	AEHIMMRSTU	RHEUMATISM
AEHHIKRSTW	WHITE SHARK	AEHIMNNPPS	PENMANSHIP
AEHHILPSSW	WHIPLASHES	AEHIMNORRS	HARMONISER
AEHHIMNNTT	THE THIN MAN	AEHIMNORRZ	HARMONIZER
AEHHIMNPST	MAN THE SHIP	AEHIMNORSS	HARMONISES
AEHHINOPRT	HIEROPHANT	AEHIMNORSZ	HARMONIZES
AEHHIRSTTW	WHITE TRASH	AEHIMNOTUX	EXHUMATION
AEHHKOOSSV	SHAVEHOOKS	AEHIMNRSSS	MARSHINESS
AEHHLMMOPY	HAEMOLYMPH	AEHIMNRSTV	RAVISHMENT
AEHHLOOPRT	POOR HEALTH	AEHIMNSSTU	ENTHUSIASM
AEHHMOOOPT	HOMOEOPATH	AEHIMPRSST	MASTERSHIP
AEHHNOORTW	HOW ON EARTH	AEHIMPSSST	STEAMSHIPS
AEHHNORSTW	RAN THE SHOW	AEHIMPSSTY	SYMPATHIES
AEHHOPPSST	PHOSPHATES		SYMPATHISE
AEHHOSSSUW	WASHHOUSES	AEHIMPSTYZ	SYMPATHIZE
AEHHOSTWWY	SHOW THE WAY	AEHINNORTT	ON THE TRAIN
AEHIIILRST	HILARITIES	AEHINOPPTX	PAT PHOENIX
AEHIIKKLNT	THINK ALIKE	AEHINOPSTT	TIP ONE'S HAT
AEHIIKLNRS	SILKEN HAIR	AEHINORRTV	HOVERTRAIN
AEHIILMSTU	HUMILIATES	AEHINORSST	HAS IN STORE
AEHIILMSTW	WITH A SMILE	AEHINORSTU	HOUSETRAIN
AEHIILOSTX	HELIOTAXIS	AEHINORTTW	IN HOT WATER
AEHIILRRSV	SILVER HAIR	AEHINOSSST	ASTONISHES
AEHIIMMPSX	AMPHIMIXES		THIS SEASON
AEHIIMNSTU	HUMANITIES	AEHINOSTUX	EXHAUSTION
AEHIINNOST	HAS IT IN ONE	AEHINPPRST	PARENT SHIP
AEHIINOPST	ETHIOPIANS	AEHINPPSTU	UNHAPPIEST
AEHIINOSTT	HESITATION	AEHINQRSUV	VANQUISHER
AEHIINPPRS	SAPPHIRINE	AEHINQSSUV	VANQUISHES
AEHIINPRSW	IN A WHISPER	AEHINRRSSV	VARNISHERS
AEHIINPRTU	UP IN THE AIR	AEHINRRTTU	RITA HUNTER
AEHIINPTTW	WHITE PAINT	AEHINRSSST	TRASHINESS
AEHIINSSTT	ANTITHESIS	AEHINRSTWW	WINS THE WAR
AEHIIPPRST	PIRATE SHIP	AEHINSSTTU	ENTHUSIAST
AEHIJLSTUW	JUST A WHILE	AEHIOOPSST	APOTHEOSIS
AEHIJMSSTY	HIS MAJESTY	AEHIOPPRRS	REPAIR SHOP
AEHIJNNOPR	JOHN NAPIER	AEHIORRSTU	AUTHORISER
AEHIJNNORY	JOHNNIE RAY	AEHIORRTUZ	AUTHORIZER
AEHIKMNNST	KENTISHMAN	AEHIORSSST	AIR HOSTESS
AEHIKMOSTT	MAKES IT HOT	AEHIORSSTU	AUTHORISES
AEHIKMRTTU	MAKE IT HURT	AEHIORSTTT	THROATIEST
AEHIKNOOST	TOOK A SHINE	AEHIORSTUZ	AUTHORIZES
AEHIKNRRST	RAN THE RISK	AEHIPPQTUY	QUITE HAPPY
AEHIKNRSSS	RAKISHNESS	AEHIPRSSTT	THERAPISTS
AEHIKNSSTT	HAS KITTENS	AEHIRSSTTW	SWARTHIEST
AEHIKNSTWY	NEAT WHISKY		SWEAT SHIRT
AEHIKOORTT	TOOK THE AIR	AEHJKLNORW	JOHN WALKER
AEHIKOPPRT	PORK-PIE HAT	AEHJKNNOOS	JOHN NOAKES
AEHIKRSSTW	THREW A KISS	AEHJMNSTTU	JUST THE MAN

AEHKLLLSTW	WHELK STALL	AEHNOOSSUW	OWNS A HOUSE
AEHKLOOPYY	PLAY HOOKEY	AEHNOPRTUY	NEUROPATHY
AEHKLOPRSW	SHOPWALKER	AEHNOPTUWY	ON THE WAY UP
AEHKNOORRT	NORTH KOREA	AEHNORRSSU	RUNS ASHORE
AEHKNORRST	OTHER RANKS	AEHNORRTTU	RUN TO EARTH
AEHKNORSTT	TAKEN SHORT	AEHNORSTTY	STONY HEART
AEHKOOPRTT	TOOK THE RAP	AEHOOPPRST	APOSTROPHE
AEHKOORSTU	SOUTH KOREA	AEHOOPRRTT	ORTHOPTERA
AEHKORRSTW	EARTHWORKS	AEHOOPSTTT	TOOTHPASTE
AEHLLMOSSU	SMALL HOUSE	AEHOOPSTTY	OSTEOPATHY
AEHLLMRSSY	HARMLESSLY	AEHOORRSTT	SORE THROAT
AEHLLMSTUU	HAUSTELLUM	AEHOORSSTY	SOOTHSAYER
AEHLLNOOPS	ALLOPHONES	AEHOPPRSTY	SAPROPHYTE
AEHLLOORWW	HOLLOWWARE	AEHOPRSTUY	HOUSE PARTY
AEHLLOPRRT	HALL PORTER	AEHOPSSSTW	SWEATSHOPS
AEHLLOPRXY	PHYLLOXERA	AEHORSTTTU	STOUT HEART
AEHLLORRSZ	RAZOR SHELL	AEHORSTTTW	AT THE WORST
	RAZOR-SHELL	AEHPPSSSTU	PUSHES PAST
AEHLLOSSTW	SHALLOWEST	AEHPRSSTTY	STRATHSPEY
AEHLMNOOPR	PHEROMONAL	AEIIIINTTV	INITIATIVE
AEHLMNOOST	SOLEMN OATH	AEIIILMMNS	MINIMALISE
AEHLMNOTWW	MOW THE LAWN	AEIIILMMNT	MILITIAMEN
AEHLMOOSUX	HOMOSEXUAL	AEIIILMMNZ	MINIMALIZE
AEHLMORRYY	RHYME ROYAL	AEIIILMRST	MILITARISE
AEHLMORTTY	METHYLATOR	AEIIILMRTZ	MILITARIZE
AEHLMOSSSU	ALMS HOUSES	AEIIILMTTV	LIMITATIVE
	ALMSHOUSES	AEIIILNNTW	WAIT IN LINE
AEHLMPSSYY	SYMPHYSEAL	AEIIILNSTW	LIES IN WAIT
AEHLNNOPRS	ALPENHORNS	AEIIILRSTV	TRIVIALISE
AEHLNNOPTT	PENTATHLON	AEIIILRTVZ	TRIVIALIZE
AEHLNNOSTT	ON THE SLANT	AEIIILSTVX	LIXIVIATES
AEHLNOPSTU	HOUSEPLANT	AEIIIMNSTV	VITAMINISE
	SULPHONATE	AEIIIMNTVZ	VITAMINIZE
AEHLNORSTW	NORTH WALES	AEIIINSTTV	NATIVITIES
AEHLNOSTTW	SHOW TALENT	AEIIIRRTTV	IRRITATIVE
	TALENT SHOW	AEIIJKLNPT	KEPT IN JAIL
AEHLOORSUY	ROYAL HOUSE	AEIIJMORST	MAJORITIES
AEHLOOSTVY	SAVOY HOTEL	AEIIKKSTTW	KITTIWAKES
AEHLOPSSUY	PLAYHOUSES	AEIIKLLNPR	PAINKILLER
AEHLORRSTW	RATHER SLOW	AEIIKLRRST	RAIL STRIKE
AEHLORRSUY	EARLY HOURS	AEIILLLMMS	MILLESIMAL
AEHLORRTUW	ARTHUR LOWE	AEIILLLMNN	MILLENNIAL
AEHLOSSTUW	SOUTH WALES	AEIILLLTVY	ILLATIVELY
AEHLOSTTWY	LOST THE WAY	AEIILLMNOR	MINERAL OIL
AEHLPRSTUU	SULPHURATE	AEIILLMNTU	ILLUMINATE
AEHLRTTUUV	TRUTH-VALUE	AEIILLMPRY	IMPERIALLY
AEHMMOORST	THOMAS MORE	AEIILLMRST	LITERALISM
AEHMMORSTU	HAMMERS OUT	AEIILLNRTY	INERTIALLY
AEHMNNOOSW	ONE-MAN SHOW	AEIILLOSTV	VOLATILISE
AEHMNNOWWY	NEW-MOWN HAY	AEIILLOTVZ	VOLATILIZE
AEHMNOOPRT	HOMOPTERAN	AEIILLPSTT	PISTILLATE
AEHMNOOPTY	PAY THE MOON	AEIILLRRTT	TRILITERAL
AEHMNOORSU	MANOR HOUSE	AEIILLRRTY	LITERARILY
	ROMAN HOUSE	AEIILLRSTT	LITERALIST
AEHMNOORSW	HORSEWOMAN	AEIILLRTTY	LITERALITY
AEHMNOOSUY	SHAME ON YOU!	AEIILLRTWW	WRITE A WILL
AEHMNORRRU	HUMAN ERROR	AEIILLSTTT	TITILLATES
AEHMNPRSUU	SUPERHUMAN	AEIILMMMOR	IMMEMORIAL
AEHMNPRTWY	WATER NYMPH	AEIILMNORT	ELIMINATOR
AEHMOOPSTT	STOP AT HOME	AEIILMNRSU	LUMINARIES
AEHMOOPSTW	WET SHAMPOO	AEIILMNSSU	ALUMINISES
AEHMOPPRST	TOP-HAMPERS	AEIILMNSUZ	ALUMINIZES
AEHMOPRSTT	AT THE PROMS	AEIILMNTTY	INTIMATELY
AEHMOPRWYY	WHY PAY MORE?	AEIILMOSSS	ISOSEISMAL
AEHMOPSTTU	PUT TO SHAME	AEIILMPPSS	MISAPPLIES
AEHMORRSTW	EARTHWORMS	AEIILMRSTV	RELATIVISM
AEHMORSTTT	THERMOSTAT	AEIILMRSVV	REVIVALISM
AEHMORSTVY	HEAVY STORM	AEIILNNORS	ROSANILINE
AEHNOOPPSS	OPENS A SHOP	AEIILNNOST	LINEATIONS
AEHNOOPSSU	SOUSAPHONE	AEIILNNOVV	LOVE IN VAIN
AEHNOOPSSX	SAXOPHONES	AEIILNNSTT	INTESTINAL

AEIILNNTVW	LIVE IN WANT	AEIKLNOOST	TAKES ON OIL
AEIILNOOTT	ETIOLATION	AEIKLNORST	OIL TANKERS
AEIILNOPRT	OIL PAINTER	AEIKLNPPTY	KEPT IN PLAY
AEIILNORSV	LIVES ON AIR	AEIKLNPSTW	WALK IN STEP
AEIILNORTT	LITERATION	AEIKLORTTV	TALK IT OVER
AEIILNOTTV	LEVITATION	AEIKLOSSST	STOLE A KISS
AEIILNPRZZ	LIPIZZANER	AEIKLPRSTT	TALKS TRIPE
AEIILNPSST	PLATINISES	AEIKMNOSST	NO MISTAKES
AEIILNQTUY	INEQUALITY	AEIKNNOPTT	POINT TAKEN
AEIILNSSTW	WAISTLINES	AEIKNNOTTU	UNTIE A KNOT
AEIILNSSWY	WINS EASILY	AEIKNNPRSS	SPINNAKERS
AEIILRSSST	SERIALISTS	AEIKNOOPST	TAKE POISON
AEIILRSSTU	RITUALISES	AEIKNOPTTY	TAKE PITY ON
AEIILRSTTV	RELATIVIST	AEIKNORSTU	KERATINOUS
AEIILRSTUZ	RITUALIZES	AEIKNOTTTU	TAKEN IT OUT
AEIILRSTVV	REVIVALIST	AEIKOOSTTY	TOOK IT EASY
AEIILRTTVY	RELATIVITY	AEIKOSTTTU	TAKES IT OUT
AEIILSSSUV	VISUALISES	AEIKOSTTTW	IT TAKES TWO
AEIILSSUVZ	VISUALIZES	AEIKPPQSSU	PIP-SQUEAKS
AEIIMMMNOR	IN MEMORIAM	AEILLLMOTW	ALL-TIME LOW
AEIIMMNPRT	IMPAIRMENT	AEILLLMSTT	LITTLE SLAM
AEIIMMNSSS	MESSIANISM	AEILLLSUVY	ALLUSIVELY
AEIIMNNNOT	INNOMINATE	AEILLMMORY	MEMORIALLY
AEIIMNNOTT	ANTIMONITE	AEILLMMRST	SMALL-TIMER
AEIIMNNOTV	NOMINATIVE	AEILLMNNOS	MEANS NO ILL
AEIIMNOSTT	ESTIMATION	AEILLMNNOT	MEANT NO ILL
AEIIMNQTUY	EQUANIMITY	AEILLMNNRS	ILL MANNERS
AEIIMNRRSS	RISE IN ARMS	AEILLMPRVY	PRIMEVALLY
AEIIMNRSST	SEMINARIST	AEILLMTTUY	ULTIMATELY
AEIIMNRSTU	MINIATURES	AEILLNNRTY	INTERNALLY
AEIIMNRTUV	RUMINATIVE	AEILLNOPST	POLLINATES
AEIIMOPRRS	IMPRESARIO	AEILLNOPTT	POTENTILLA
AEIIMPRSTT	TEAM SPIRIT	AEILLNPSTT	PANELLISTS
AEIIMPTTUV	IMPUTATIVE	AEILLNPSSY	PAINLESSLY
AEIINNOTVV	INNOVATIVE	AEILLOPRVW	PROVE A WILL
AEIINNPRTW	TIP A WINNER	AEILLORTUV	TROUVAILLE
AEIINNPSTT	INPATIENTS	AEILLORTWW	WROTE A WILL
AEIINNRSTW	ITS A WINNER	AEILLPSSTT	PASTELLIST
AEIINNSSTU	INSINUATES	AEILLRSSTW	STAIRWELLS
AEIINOPPST	INAPPOSITE	AEILLRSTTT	LITTLE STAR
AEIINOPPTV	APPOINTIVE	AEILLRSTTU	ILLUSTRATE
AEIINOPRTX	EXPIRATION	AEILLRSTTW	STILL WATER
AEIINOPSTT	POINSETTIA	AEILLSSSSY	SILLY ASSES
AEIINOQTTU	EQUITATION	AEILLSSTTY	SAYS LITTLE
AEIINOSTTV	NOVITIATES	AEILMMMNNTY	IMMANENTLY
AEIINOTUVX	EXUVIATION	AEILMMNPRS	MINERS LAMP
AEIINPRSWZ	WINS A PRIZE	AEILMMRTUY	IMMATURELY
AEIINPSSST	ANTISEPSIS	AEILMNNNOY	IN NAME ONLY
	INSPISSATE	AEILMNNSTT	INSTALMENT
AEIINQSTTU	QUANTITIES	AEILMNOPRS	IMPERSONAL
AEIINRSTTV	TRANSITIVE	AEILMNOPRT	TRAMPOLINE
AEIIOPPRTT	PROPITIATE	AEILMNOPTU	OUTLINE MAP
AEIIORRSSU	SERIOUS AIR	AEILMNORRV	OL MAN RIVER
AEIIPRRTTT	TRIPARTITE	AEILMNORSS	NORMALISES
AEIIRSSTUW	ISSUE A WRIT	AEILMNORSZ	NORMALIZES
AEIISSTTTV	STATE VISIT	AEILMNORTU	TOURMALINE
AEIISTTTTV	TITTIVATES	AEILMNORTY	MONETARILY
AEIJLNORSU	JOURNALISE	AEILMNPRST	PLAIN TERMS
AEIJLNORUZ	JOURNALIZE	AEILMNRSTU	NEUTRALISM
AEIJMNOSSS	JAM SESSION	AEILMNSSSU	SENSUALISM
AEIJMORSSU	MAJOR ISSUE	AEILMNSTTU	LAST MINUTE
AEIJNNSSTU	JAUNTINESS	AEILMOPSTT	PTOLEMAIST
AEIKKLLOOS	LOOK-ALIKES	AEILMORSSU	MORAL ISSUE
	LOOKS ALIKE	AEILMPPSST	PALIMPSEST
AEIKKNRSST	TAKEN RISKS	AEILMPPRST	SLIPSTREAM
AEIKKRSSST	TAKES RISKS	AEILMPRSYY	MISERLY PAY
AEIKLLNPST	TAKEN PILLS	AEILMPRTUU	PARI MUTUEL
AEIKLLNSSW	SINKS A WELL		PARI-MUTUEL
AEIKLLPSST	TAKES PILLS	AEILMRRSSU	SURREALISM
AEIKLMNSTY	MISTAKENLY	AEILMRRSTT	TRIMESTRAL
AEIKLNNOOT	TAKEN ON OIL	AEILMSSTTU	STIMULATES

AEILNNNPPY	PENNY PLAIN	AEIMNOPRSZ	MAZE PRISON
AEILNNNSTW	LAWN TENNIS	AEIMNOPRTT	PORTAMENTI
AEILNNOPRS	NONPAREILS	AEIMNOPTTT	TEMPTATION
AEILNNOPSY	POLYNESIAN	AEIMNORRSS	ROSE IN ARMS
AEILNNOPVW	PLAIN-WOVEN	AEIMNORRTT	TERMINATOR
AEILNNORTT	INTOLERANT	AEIMNORSSW	WOMANISERS
AEILNNPRSU	PENINSULAR	AEIMNORSTT	MONETARIST
AEILNNPSST	PLIANTNESS	AEIMNORSTU	MOUSTERIAN
AEILNNPSSU	PENINSULAS	AEIMNORSWZ	WOMANIZERS
AEILNNPSTY	PLAY TENNIS	AEIMNOSSWY	IN SOME WAYS
AEILNNPTUY	PLAY IN TUNE	AEIMNOSTTW	MATES IN TWO
AEILNOOPSS	POLONAISES	AEIMNPPRST	PENTAPRISM
AEILNOORTT	TOLERATION	AEIMNPRSST	SPEARMINTS
AEILNOOSTT	NOSE TO TAIL	AEIMNPRTTY	TRYPTAMINE
AEILNOPRST	LATIN PROSE	AEIMNPSSSW	SWAMPINESS
AEILNOPSTT	POTENTIALS	AEIMNPSTTY	TYMPANITES
AEILNOPSTY	TOY SPANIEL	AEIMNRRRTY	INTERMARRY
AEILNORRTT	TORRENTIAL	AEIMNRSSTU	ANTISERUMS
AEILNORRTY	ANTERIORLY	AEIMNRSSTX	AXMINSTERS
AEILNORTTV	VENTILATOR	AEIMOOPRTT	RIPE TOMATO
AEILNORTWW	IN LOW WATER	AEIMOOTTUV	AUTOMOTIVE
AEILNOTTUX	EXULTATION	AEIMOPRRST	IMPERATORS
AEILNPRSST	PALTRINESS	AEIMORRSTU	MORTUARIES
AEILNPRSTY	INTERPLAYS	AEIMPRSTUZ	TRAPEZIUMS
AEILNRSSUV	UNIVERSALS	AEIMPSSTUV	ASSUMPTIVE
AEILNRSTTU	NEUTRALIST	AEIMQRSTUZ	QUIZ MASTER
AEILNRSTTW	LAST WINTER	AEIMRRRSTU	TERRARIUMS
AEILNRTTUY	NEUTRALITY	AEINNNOQSU	SINE QUA NON
AEILNRTTWW	WRITTEN LAW	AEINNOORTV	RENOVATION
AEILNSSSTU	SENSUALIST	AEINNOPRSV	VAIN PERSON
AEILNSSTUU	NAUTILUSES	AEINNOPRTU	PIANO TUNER
AEILNSSTUY	SENSUALITY	AEINNOPSSX	EXPANSIONS
AEILOOPSTT	TOILET SOAP	AEINNOORTU	QUATERNION
AEILOPPRSU	POPULARISE	AEINNORSTT	STENTORIAN
AEILOPPRUZ	POPULARIZE	AEINNOSSST	SENSATIONS
AEILOPPSTY	APPOSITELY	AEINNOSTTT	ATTENTIONS
AEILOPRSSU	PLESIOSAUR	AEINNPPSSS	SNAPPINESS
AEILOPRSTY	EPISTOLARY	AEINNQSSTU	QUAINTNESS
AEILOPRTVW	VITAL POWER	AEINNRSSTT	TENNIS STAR
AEILORRRTV	VITAL ERROR	AEINNRSSTY	TYRANNISES
AEILORRTTU	ELUTRIATOR	AEINNRSTYZ	TYRANNIZES
AEILORSSTT	TOTALISERS	AEINOOPPRT	PROPIONATE
AEILORSTTZ	TOTALIZERS	AEINOOPRRT	PERORATION
AEILORSTUY	ROYAL SUITE	AEINOOPRST	OPERATIONS
AEILPRSTWY	WRITE PLAYS	AEINOOPSTY	EASY OPTION
AEILPSSTTU	STIPULATES	AEINOPRSSS	ASPERSIONS
AEILPTTUVY	PUTATIVELY	AEINOPRSST	PATRONISES
AEILRRSSTU	SURREALIST	AEINOPRSSU	PERSUASION
AEILRRSSTV	SILVER STAR	AEINOPRSTV	PAINTS OVER
AEILRRSTUV	ULTRA VIRES	AEINOPRSTZ	PATRONIZES
AEILRRSTVY	SILVER TRAY	AEINOPRTTU	REPUTATION
AEILRSTUUX	LUXURIATES	AEINOPSSST	PASSES IT ON
AEIMMNNRSS	MANNERISMS	AEINOPTTTU	OUTPATIENT
AEIMMNOPST	PANTOMIMES	AEINORRSST	SERRATIONS
AEIMMNORST	MONETARISM	AEINORRSTV	OVERTRAINS
	ROMAN TIMES	AEINORRVWW	NARROW VIEW
AEIMMNOTUU	AUTOIMMUNE	AEINORSSST	ASSERTIONS
AEIMMNPRTT	IMPARTMENT	AEINORSSTT	STATIONERS
AEIMMNSTZZ	MIZZENMAST	AEINORSTTW	TEARS IN TWO
AEIMMORRSW	WAR MEMOIRS	AEINORSTTY	STATIONERY
AEIMMPRSTU	SPERMATIUM	AEINPRRSST	TRANSPIRES
AEIMMRRSSU	SUMMARISER	AEINPRRTTU	PARTURIENT
AEIMMRRSUZ	SUMMARIZER	AEINPSSTTX	TEN PAST SIX
AEIMMRSSSU	SUMMARISES	AEINQRTTUY	QUATERNITY
AEIMMRSSUZ	SUMMARIZES	AEINRRSSTT	RESTRAINTS
AEIMNNNOTT	ANOINTMENT	AEINRSSSTT	STRAITNESS
AEIMNNNQSU	MANNEQUINS	AEINRSSSTU	SUSTAINERS
AEIMNNORTU	NUMERATION	AEINRSTUYZ	SUZERAINTY
AEIMNNOSSS	SESSION MAN	AEIOPRRRST	RESPIRATOR
AEIMNNRTUU	RUN A MINUTE	AEIOPRRSSV	VAPORISERS
AEIMNOOSTZ	ZOO INMATES	AEIOPRRSVZ	VAPORIZERS

AEIOPRRTTX	EXTIRPATOR	AELMMRSSTU	LAST SUMMER
AEIOPRRTXY	EXPIRATORY	AELMNNNRUY	UNMANNERLY
AEIORSSTTY	TRIES TO SAY	AELMNNOOPS	MONOPLANES
AEIOSSTTTU	TITUS OATES	AELMNNOOTV	MONOVALENT
AEIOSTTTUW	SWEAT IT OUT	AELMNOOOSW	LOOSE WOMAN
AEIQRSTTTU	QUIET START	AELMNOOPRY	LAMPOONERY
AEIRRSTTTU	TRITURATES	AELMNOPRST	TRAMPLES ON
AEIRSSTXYY	SIXTY YEARS	AELMOORSTV	ALMOST OVER
AEJLLSSTUW	JUST AS WELL	AELMOPRSSS	SLOPES ARMS
AEJMNNORUY	JOURNEYMAN	AELMOPRTTU	PETROLATUM
AEJMOOPRRW	MAJOR POWER	AELMOPSSST	EPSOM SALTS
AEJOPSSTUX	JUXTAPOSES	AELMORRSSU	ARMOURLESS
AEKKLRRSSY	SKYLARKERS	AELMORRSSW	MARROWLESS
AEKKLRTTUY	TALK TURKEY	AELMORSSTU	SOMERSAULT
AEKLLMRUWY	LUKEWARMLY	AELMPPRSUY	MAPLE SYRUP
AEKLMNOSTY	MONEY TALKS	AELNNOOWYY	ONE WAY ONLY
	TALKS MONEY	AELNNOPRYY	PENNYROYAL
AEKLMOORST	TOOLMAKERS	AELNNORSTY	RESONANTLY
AEKLMOOSSS	LOOKS A MESS	AELNOPPRTW	POWER PLANT
AEKLNOPRTT	PETROL TANK	AELNOPRSST	LAST PERSON
AEKLOORSWY	LOOKS WEARY	AELNOPRSTY	PERSONALTY
AEKLNPPRSY	PLAYS POKER	AELNOPRSYZ	LAZY PERSON
AEKLOPRSTY	STROKE PLAY	AELNOPSTT	STOLEN PAST
AEKLORRSWY	EARLY WORKS	AELNOPSSTU	PUTS ON SALE
AEKMMNORSW	MARKSWOMEN		STEALS UP ON
AEKMMOOPRU	MAKE-UP ROOM	AELNORSSST	ART LESSONS
AEKMNNOTUY	MOUNT KENYA	AELNORSUVY	RAVENOUSLY
AEKMNOOQSU	MOONQUAKES	AELNOSSUUY	NAUSEOUSLY
AEKMNOPRUW	WORN MAKE-UP	AELNOSTUVV	VOL-AU-VENTS
AEKMNORTTW	MARKET TOWN	AELNPPRSTU	SUPPLANTER
AEKMNPRRRY	MERRY PRANK	AELNRSSTTU	RESULTANTS
AEKMOPRSST	MAKES SPORT	AELOOOPRTY	AEOLOTROPY
AEKMPRRSSS	PRESSMARKS	AELOOOPRSW	SOLAR POWER
AEKNNOPSSU	SNEAKS UP ON	AELOORRSTT	TOLERATORS
AEKNNRSTTU	TAKEN TURNS	AELOPPRRRU	POURPARLER
AEKNOORSTT	NOT A STROKE	AELOPPRTUV	UPPER VOLTA
AEKNOOQRSTU	SQUARE KNOT	AELOPRRSTW	LAW REPORTS
AEKNPRRSST	PRANKSTERS	AELOPRSSTY	POSTS EARLY
AEKNRSSTTU	TAKES TURNS	AELOPRSTWY	WROTE PLAYS
AEKOOPRRTY	PROKARYOTE	AELOPSSTTU	POSTULATES
AEKORRSTWW	WATERWORKS	AELORRSSTT	LAST RESORT
AEKORRSSTTU	STREAKS OUT	AELORRSSTY	LAYS TO REST
AELLLLOOTW	ALL TOO WELL	AELORSTTUW	LOW STATURE
AELLLNPSSY	PLANLESSLY	AELORSTUVV	VAULTS OVER
AELLLPSTUU	PULLULATES	AELPPRSSTU	LAST SUPPER
AELLMNORST	STAN MELLOR	AELPPSSTUY	PLATYPUSES
AELLMNOSTT	ALLOTMENTS	AEMMNNOORSU	MAN OR MOUSE?
AELLMOPRTY	TEMPORALLY	AEMMNRSTYY	MYSTERY MAN
AELLMOPSSY	PLASMOLYSE	AEMMRSSTUU	ART MUSEUMS
AELLMOPSYZ	PLASMOLYZE	AEMNNNOOSW	ONE'S OWN MAN
AELLMOTUUV	MUTUAL LOVE	AEMNNOOOTY	ONE TOO MANY
AELLNOOSWW	ONE SWALLOW	AEMNNOORTTU	TOURNAMENT
AELLNOPPRT	PROPELLANT	AEMNNPPSTY	PENNY STAMP
AELLNOPRSY	PERSONALLY	AEMNNRRSUY	NURSERYMAN
AELLNOPTVY	POLYVALENT	AEMNNTTUUX	NEXT AUTUMN
AELLNORTTY	TOLERANTLY	AEMNNOOPRTT	PORTAMENTO
AELLNOSSSW	SALLOWNESS	AEMNOORRST	ASTRONOMER
AELLNOSSTW	STONE WALLS	AEMNOOPRRSY	PERRY MASON
	STONEWALLS	AEMNORRSTT	MONTSERRAT
AELLNPTTUY	PETULANTLY	AEMNORRSTU	NUMERATORS
AELLNRSTTY	SLATTERNLY	AEMNORRTUY	URANOMETRY
AELLNTTUXY	EXULTANTLY	AEMNORSSTT	ASSORTMENT
AELLOOPPRY	POLO PLAYER	AEMNPRSSTU	SMARTENS UP
AELLOOPRST	ALLOTROPES	AEMNRSSTTU	TRANSMUTES
AELLOPPRSU	ALL-PURPOSE	AEMOOPSTTY	SOMATOTYPE
AELLORSSWW	SWALLOWERS	AEMOORSSTT	STATEROOMS
AELLORSTTY	TELL A STORY	AEMOPRSSTT	POSTMASTER
AELLRSSTTW	STARTS WELL	AEMOPRSSTU	MOUSETRAPS
AELMMNNOTU	MONUMENTAL	AEMOPSSTTY	ASYMPTOTES
AELMMNOSTT	LAST MOMENT	AEMORRSSVW	SWARMS OVER
AELMMOSSUU	MAUSOLEUMS	AEMORRSTTW	STORMWATER

AEMORSSTTU	STREAMS OUT
AEMPRSSSTU	PASS MUSTER
AENNNOSSTW	WANTONNESS
AENNOOSWWY	ONES OWN WAY
AENNORRSSW	NARROWNESS
AENNORRSTT	NONSTARTER
AENOOPRRST	PERSONATOR
AENOOPSSTT	AT ONES POST
AENOORRSST	RESONATORS
AENOORSSTU	TREASONOUS
AENOPPPRTU	PUT ON PAPER
AENOPPSSTU	PUTS ON TAPE
AENOPRSSST	TRANSPOSES
AENOPRSSUV	SUPERNOVAS
AENOPRSTTT	PROTESTANT
AENOPSTTTW	TEN PAST TWO
AENOQRSTUW	TOWN SQUARE
AENORRSTUU	SOUR NATURE
AENORSSTTY	STONY STARE
AENPSTTTWY	TWENTY PAST
AENRRSTTUX	TAX RETURNS
AEOOPPRSTU	TROPOPAUSE
AEOOQRRSTU	SQUARE ROOT
AEOORSTTUU	AUTOROUTES
AEOPPRRRTU	RAPPORTEUR
AEOPRRSSTT	PROSTRATES
AEOPRRSSTU	PTEROSAURS
AEOPRRTTTY	TREATY PORT
AEOPRSTTUW	WATERSPOUT
AEORRSSTTY	SORRY STATE
AEORSSSTUU	TROUSSEAUS
AEORSSTTUV	STARVES OUT
AEORSSTUUX	TROUSSEAUX
AEPPRSSTTY	PRETTY PASS
AEPPRSSTUU	SUPPURATES
AFFFCILLNO	FALLING OFF
AFFFHIIORW	WHIFF OF AIR
AFFFHIMOTY	FIFTH OF MAY
AFFFLLLOOU	FALL FOUL OF
AFFGHIIRST	FAIR FIGHTS
	FIGHTS FAIR
AFFGHIKNOS	SHAKING OFF
AFFGHILOTU	LAUGH IT OFF
AFFGHIORTU	FOUGHT FAIR
AFFGIILLNN	FINAL FLING
AFFGIILNOT	TAILING OFF
AFFGIILNSY	FALSIFYING
AFFGIINOPR	PAIRING OFF
AFFGIKLNOW	WALKING OFF
AFFGIKMNOR	MARKING OFF
AFFGILLNOR	FALLING FOR
AFFGILNOPY	PLAYING OFF
AFFGINNORT	AFFRONTING
AFFGINNORW	WARNING OFF
AFFGINOPSS	PASSING OFF
AFFGINOSTV	STAVING OFF
AFFGIRSSTU	SUFFRAGIST
AFFGLLOOPS	GALLOPS OFF
AFFGNOOORST	STROGANOFF
AFFHILLTUY	FAITHFULLY
AFFHILNTUU	UNFAITHFUL
AFFHIORTTU	TUFT OF HAIR
AFFHIORTTY	FIRTH OF TAY
AFFIILMMRY	FAMILY FIRM
AFFIILNPST	PLAINTIFFS
AFFIIMNRSU	RUFFIANISM
AFFILLORST	FALLS FOR IT
	FIRST OF ALL
AFFIMORSTY	FIRST OF MAY
AFFINOORUV	IN FAVOUR OF
AFFIOPRSTT	FAT PROFITS

AFFLLNOOSW	FALL OF SNOW
AFFLLOORTY	FALL OF TROY
AFFLLORUUV	FLAVOURFUL
AFFLOORSTU	LAST OF FOUR
AFFLOOSTTU	FOOT FAULTS
AFFPPRSTUY	PUFF PASTRY
AFGGGIIINV	GIVING A FIG
AFGGGILNNU	UNFLAGGING
AFGGHIORTT	GOT A FRIGHT
AFGGIIMNNY	MAGNIFYING
AFGGIIMNTU	FUMIGATING
AFGGIINRTY	GRATIFYING
AFGGINNORW	FOG WARNING
AFGGNOOORS	GO FOR A SONG
AFGHHILLST	FLASHLIGHT
	HALF-LIGHTS
AFGHHILPTT	FLIGHT PATH
AFGHHIORUV	HIGH FAVOUR
AFGHIILNTT	FAINT LIGHT
AFGHIINNOS	FASHIONING
AFGHIINSTW	WINS A FIGHT
AFGHIKLNRT	RIGHT FLANK
AFGHILORTY	RAY OF LIGHT
AFGHILOSTT	LOST A FIGHT
AFGHILSTUW	AWFUL SIGHT
AFGHIORTWY	RIGHT OF WAY
AFGHMOORST	HOMOGRAFTS
AFGHOORTTW	GOT WHAT FOR
AFGIIILNNS	FINALISING
AFGIIILNNZ	FINALIZING
AFGIIKMMNR	MAKING FIRM
AFGIIKMNOS	KING OF SIAM
AFGIILLLLN	FALLING ILL
AFGIILMNPY	AMPLIFYING
AFGIILNPST	FILING PAST
AFGIILNQUY	QUALIFYING
AFGIILNRTT	FILTRATING
AFGIILNSTV	FAST LIVING
AFGIIMNOTU	FUMIGATION
AFGIINORTU	FIGURATION
AFGIINORTW	WAITING FOR
AFGIINSSTY	SATISFYING
AFGIKKNORU	KING FAROUK
AFGIKLNOTU	FLAKING OUT
AFGIKMNORS	KING OF ARMS
AFGILLNOTU	FALLING OUT
AFGILLNSST	FLINT GLASS
AFGILMNORW	FLAMING ROW
AFGILNORUV	FLAVOURING
AFGIMNORRS	FORMS A RING
AFGIMNORTU	FARMING OUT
AFGIMNOSTV	MOVING FAST
AFGIMOORSW	GO FOR A SWIM
AFGINOOPRS	GO FOR A SPIN
AFGINOORTW	WAR FOOTING
AFGINOPRSS	PASSING FOR
AFGIOOPRRT	GO FOR A TRIP
AFGJNOORSY	SANG FOR JOY
AFGLLLLOPU	FULL GALLOP
AFGLLNNOUY	GO ALL FUNNY
AFHHLLORUY	HALF-HOURLY
AFHHLRSTTU	HALF-TRUTHS
AFHIILLNTW	FALL IN WITH
AFHIILNSST	FINISH LAST
AFHIIMNSTT	MATT FINISH
AFHIKNOORT	KNOT OF HAIR
AFHIKNSSTT	THINKS FAST
AFHILNNORT	TORN IN HALF
AFHILNPSSY	SPANISH FLY
AFHILORRRS	ROLF HARRIS
AFHIMNNOTY	NINTH OF MAY

AFHIMORRTY	MORAY FIRTH	AGGGILNRST	STRAGGLING
AFHIMOSTXY	SIXTH OF MAY	AGGGIMNORT	MORTGAGING
AFHINORTTW	THROWN A FIT	AGGHHIIIMN	AIMING HIGH
AFHKLLNTUY	THANKFULLY	AGGHIINNRS	GARNISHING
AFHLLORSST	FALLS SHORT	AGGHILLNUY	LAUGHINGLY
	SHORTFALLS	AGGHILMNPU	GALUMPHING
AFHLLORSTY	SALLY FORTH	AGGHINNOTU	HANGING OUT
AFHLLORSUY	ROYAL FLUSH	AGGHIORSTT	GO STRAIGHT
AFHLLORSWY	SHALLOW FRY	AGGHIPRSTT	TIGHT GRASP
AFHMOOSTTW	TWO FATHOMS	AGGHLOOPRS	LOGOGRAPHS
AFHOOPRSTU	PUSH TOO FAR	AGGHLOOPRY	GRAPHOLOGY
AFHOORRSST	HOARFROSTS	AGGIIILNTT	LITIGATING
AFHOORSUVW	SHOW FAVOUR	AGGIIIMNTT	MITIGATING
AFHOPRRSST	SHARP FROST	AGGIIINNNR	INGRAINING
AFHORSSTUY	TRUSS OF HAY	AGGIIINPTV	GIVING A TIP
AFIIILNOST	FILIATIONS	AGGIIINRRT	IRRIGATING
AFIIKLLMOP	PAIL OF MILK	AGGIIJNOTV	GIVING A JOT
AFIILLRRTY	FRITILLARY	AGGIIKNNTW	TAKING WING
AFIILNNOPT	FINAL POINT	AGGIILLNNS	SIGNALLING
AFIILNNOST	INFLATIONS	AGGIILMNSV	ALMSGIVING
AFIILNOORT	FLORIATION	AGGIILNNTU	AGGLUTININ
AFIILNORSU	INFUSORIAL	AGGIILNNTW	WANGLING IT
AFIILNORTT	FILTRATION	AGGIINNORS	ORGANISING
	FLIRTATION	AGGIINNORZ	ORGANIZING
AFIILNOSTW	FAILS TO WIN	AGGILLNOTY	GLOATINGLY
AFIIMNNRST	FIRST MAN IN	AGGILNNNTU	UNTANGLING
AFIINNOPTT	TIN OF PAINT	AGGILNNOSW	SWING ALONG
AFIINNORSU	INFUSORIAN	AGGILNNRST	STRANGLING
AFIKLOSSST	SOFT AS SILK	AGGILNPRSY	GRASPINGLY
AFILLLNOPY	PLAIN FOLLY	AGGINNOSSS	SINGS A SONG
AFILLLTTTU	AT FULL TILT	AGGINNOTTU	TOTING A GUN
AFILLMNORY	INFORMALLY	AGGINOORRT	RARING TO GO
AFILLNPPTY	FLIPPANTLY	AGGINOORTW	GOING TO WAR
AFILLNPSUY	PAYS IN FULL	AGGINORRSS	GROSGRAINS
AFILLOPSST	FILLS A POST	AGGINORRTT	GARROTTING
AFILMNORTU	FULMINATOR	AGGLNNOOOT	NOT LONG AGO
AFILMNOSUY	INFAMOUSLY	AGGLNNOSUW	SWUNG ALONG
AFILNOOPTW	POINT OF LAW	AGGLNOOORZ	GORGONZOLA
AFILNOOSTT	FLOTATIONS	AGGMOORRST	MORTGAGORS
AFILNRSTZZ	FRANZ LISZT	AGGNNORRWY	GROWN ANGRY
AFIMNOORST	FORMATIONS	AGGNORRSWY	GROWS ANGRY
AFIMNORSTW	FIRST WOMAN	AGHHIIMOOT	AIM TOO HIGH
AFINNORTWY	WAY IN FRONT	AGHHIKNSTW	NIGHTHAWKS
AFINOOPPTT	POT OF PAINT	AGHHILOPRT	LITHOGRAPH
AFINOOPRRS	RAINPROOFS	AGHHIMNRTU	HUMAN RIGHT
AFINORSUVW	WINS FAVOUR	AGHHISSTTU	HIGH STATUS
AFIOOPRSTW	PAIR OF TWOS	AGHHLOOPRS	HOLOGRAPHS
AFIOPRSTTX	PROFITS TAX	AGHHLOOPRY	HOLOGRAPHY
AFIORRSTYY	FAIRY STORY	AGHHMOOPRS	HOMOGRAPHS
AFIPRRSTTY	FIRST PARTY	AGHHNOOPPR	PHONOGRAPH
AFKLLOOOOS	LOOKS A FOOL	AGHHNORRTU	RAN THROUGH
AFKMOORSUW	FAMOUS WORK	AGHHOOPPRT	PHOTOGRAPH
AFKOOOORTT	TOOK TOO FAR	AGHHOPPTYY	PHYTOPHAGY
AFLLLMOSTU	ALMOST FULL	AGHHORSTUW	SAW THROUGH
AFLLLNOORR	ALL FORLORN	AGHIILNNPS	PLANISHING
AFLLLNUUWY	UNLAWFULLY	AGHIILNORS	ANGLO-IRISH
AFLLMOOPRS	FLOOR LAMPS	AGHIILRRTT	RIGHT TRAIL
AFLLNOORSU	ON ALL FOURS	AGHIIMMNNSU	HUMANISING
AFLLOORSTW	WORST OF ALL	AGHIIMMNNUZ	HUMANIZING
AFLLRTUUXY	LUXURY FLAT	AGHIINNRST	TARNISHING
AFLMOORRTU	FORMULATOR	AGHIINNRSV	VARNISHING
AFLOORSTUV	LOST FAVOUR	AGHIINNRTT	NIGHT TRAIN
AFMMNOORRU	ROMAN FORUM	AGHIINNRTU	THURINGIAN
AFMNORRSST	TRANSFORMS	AGHIINOPRS	APHORISING
AFOQRRSTUU	FOUR QUARTS	AGHIINOPRZ	APHORIZING
AGGGGIINWW	WIGWAGGING	AGHIINPRRS	HAIRSPRING
AGGGGIINZZ	ZIGZAGGING	AGHIINPTVY	HAVING PITY
AGGGIINTUV	GIVING A TUG	AGHIINRSTT	STRAIGHT IN
AGGGILNNOO	GOING ALONG	AGHIINRTWW	WAINWRIGHT
AGGGILNNTU	GATLING GUN	AGHIKNOSTU	SHAKING OUT
		AGHIKNRRTU	KING ARTHUR

AGHILLMNST	SMALL THING	AGIIIMMNXZ	MAXIMIZING
AGHILLNOPY	ANGLOPHILY	AGIIIMNNTT	INTIMATING
AGHILLNOSW	SHALLOWING	AGIIIMNOTT	MITIGATION
AGHILLNPTU	UP ALL NIGHT	AGIIINNNRT	IN TRAINING
AGHILLNSSY	SLASHINGLY	AGIIINNSST	SANITISING
AGHILLORTT	GOT A THRILL	AGIIINNSTZ	SANITIZING
AGHILMNSSY	SMASHINGLY	AGIIINORRT	IRRIGATION
AGHILMORRT	MORAL RIGHT	AGIIINRRTT	IRRITATING
AGHILMORST	ALGORITHMS	AGIIINRSST	SATIRISING
	LOGARITHMS	AGIIINRSTZ	SATIRIZING
AGHILNNTUY	HAUNTINGLY	AGIIINTTTV	TITIVATING
AGHILNOPRR	ORPHAN GIRL	AGIIKKLNST	TAKING SILK
AGHILNORST	GRANOLITHS	AGIIKKMNNR	MARKING INK
AGHILNOSTU	LASHING OUT	AGIIKMNPTU	MAKING IT UP
AGHILNPSTY	PLAYTHINGS	AGIIKNNNPR	NAPKIN RING
AGHILNRSTT	STRINGHALT	AGIIKNPTTU	TAKING IT UP
AGHILNSTUU	USUAL THING	AGIIKNPTTY	TAKING PITY
AGHILOPPSY	GYPSOPHILA	AGIILLMMRS	MILLIGRAMS
AGHILORRTY	RIGHT ROYAL	AGIILLNNST	INSTALLING
AGHILPRTWY	PLAYWRIGHT	AGIILLNORY	ORIGINALLY
AGHIMNOOPS	SHAMPOOING	AGIILLNPRS	SPIRALLING
AGHIMNORTW	RIGHT WOMAN	AGIILLNRTU	TRILINGUAL
AGHIMNPRTU	UPRIGHT MAN	AGIILLNRVY	VIRGINALLY
AGHIMNPSSU	SMASHING UP	AGIILLNTVY	VIGILANTLY
AGHIMNRSST	HAMSTRINGS	AGIILMMNOT	IMMOLATING
AGHIMORSST	HISTOGRAMS	AGIILMNNRS	MORALISING
AGHINNOSSW	SHOWN A SIGN	AGIILMNORZ	MORALIZING
AGHINNOSTW	SAW NOTHING	AGIILMNSTU	SIMULATING
AGHINNOSTY	SAY NOTHING	AGIILMNTTU	MUTILATING
AGHINOOSTT	SHOOTING AT	AGIILNNORU	UNORIGINAL
AGHINOPRTY	ATROPHYING	AGIILNNOTY	LAYING IT ON
AGHINOPSTU	PHASING OUT	AGIILNNSTU	INSULATING
AGHINOPSTY	PAY ON SIGHT	AGIILNOPRS	POLARISING
AGHINORSTT	GHOST TRAIN	AGIILNOPRZ	POLARIZING
	STRAIGHT ON	AGIILNOPST	SPOLIATING
AGHINORSTU	SHARING OUT	AGIILNORSS	SOLARISING
AGHINOSSSW	SHOWS A SIGN	AGIILNORSV	VALORISING
AGHINOSTUW	WASHING OUT	AGIILNORSZ	SOLARIZING
AGHINPPSUV	HAVING PUPS	AGIILNORVZ	VALORIZING
AGHINPRTTY	PARTY NIGHT	AGIILNOSTT	TOTALISING
AGHIOPPRRS	SPIROGRAPH	AGIILNOTTU	TAILING OUT
AGHIOSTTTU	OUTTA SIGHT!	AGIILNOTTZ	TOTALIZING
AGHIPRSTTU	SAT UPRIGHT	AGIILNPRST	SPRINGTAIL
	STRAIGHT UP	AGIILNRSTY	LARYNGITIS
AGHIPRTUWY	RIGHT WAY UP	AGIIMMNNRST	IMMIGRANTS
AGHLMOOPRS	LAGOMORPHS	AGIIMMOSST	MISOGAMIST
AGHLMOOSTU	GOALMOUTHS	AGIIMMNNNOT	NOMINATING
AGHLNOOORT	ORTHOGONAL	AGIIMNNORS	ROMANISING
AGHLNORRUY	HURRY ALONG	AGIIMNNORZ	ROMANIZING
AGHLOPPRSY	POLYGRAPHS	AGIIMNNOSW	WOMANISING
AGHLOPRSTY	STYLOGRAPH	AGIIMNNOWZ	WOMANIZING
AGHLOPRSUY	PLAYS ROUGH	AGIIMNNPRS	MAINSPRING
AGHLOPRXYY	XYLOGRAPHY	AGIIMNNRTU	RUMINATING
AGHMNOOPRS	MONOGRAPHS	AGIIMNORST	AMORTISING
	PHONOGRAMS	AGIIMNORSU	MIGRAINOUS
AGHMNOOPRY	NOMOGRAPHY	AGIIMNORTZ	AMORTIZING
AGHMNOORTU	MOUTH ORGAN	AGIIMNOTTV	MOTIVATING
AGHMOOPRTY	TOMOGRAPHY	AGIIMNRRVY	VIRGIN MARY
AGHNNOOPRU	HARPOON GUN	AGIIMNSSTT	MISSTATING
AGHOOPPRTY	TOPOGRAPHY	AGIIMNSSUV	VAGINISMUS
AGHOPPRTYY	TYPOGRAPHY	AGIIMORTTY	MITIGATORY
AGIIIINNTT	INITIATING	AGIINNNOTT	INTONATING
AGIIIKNNTT	TAKING IT IN	AGIINNNOTV	INNOVATING
AGIIILMNNN	MAINLINING	AGIINNOPPT	APPOINTING
AGIIILMNTT	MILITATING	AGIINNORSS	SIGNORINAS
AGIIILNNST	LATINISING	AGIINNORST	NOTARISING
AGIIILNNTZ	LATINIZING	AGIINNORTZ	NOTARIZING
AGIIILNOTT	LITIGATION	AGIINNOSTT	STATIONING
AGIIILNSTV	VITALISING	AGIINNPSTU	SUPINATING
AGIIILNTVZ	VITALIZING	AGIINNQSTU	QUANTISING
AGIIIMMNSX	MAXIMISING	AGIINNQTUZ	QUANTIZING

AGIINNSSTU	SUSTAINING	AGINNPPSUW	SWAN UPPING
AGIINNSTUY	SANGUINITY		SWAN-UPPING
AGIINOORRT	ORIGINATOR	AGINOPRRTY	PORTRAYING
AGIINOPRRR	RIP-ROARING	AGINOPRSTU	PURGATIONS
AGIINOPRSV	VAPORISING	AGINOPSSTU	PASSING OUT
AGIINOPRVZ	VAPORIZING	AGINORRRST	RINGO STARR
AGIINORSTT	INSTIGATOR	AGINORSTTU	OUTSTARING
AGIINORSUV	VIRAGINOUS	AGINOSTTUY	OUTSTAYING
AGIINPRTUV	RAVING IT UP	AGINPPPRUW	WRAPPING UP
AGIKKLNRSY	SKYLARKING	AGINPQRSUU	SQUARING UP
AGIKLLNOTT	TAKING TOLL	AGINPRSSSU	SURPASSING
AGIKLMNOOT	TOOLMAKING	AGINPRSTTU	STARTING UP
AGIKLNNOSY	ANKYLOSING	AGINPSTTUY	STAYING PUT
AGIKLNNPSY	SPANKINGLY	AGIOPRSSTU	GO UPSTAIRS
AGIKLNOOOT	GOT A LOOK IN	AGIORSTTUU	GRATUITOUS
AGIKLNOPRT	PARKING LOT	AGJKNORRSU	KURRAJONGS
AGIKLNOTTU	TALKING OUT	AGKLLOOSSY	GLASSY LOOK
AGIKLNOTUW	WALKING OUT	AGKLORSSSW	GLASSWORKS
AGIKMMNOOR	MAKING ROOM	AGKLPPRSSU	SPARK PLUGS
AGIKMNNORW	WORKING MAN	AGKNNNORTY	GRANNY KNOT
	WORKINGMAN	AGLLLLOPPU	GALLUP POLL
AGIKMNNRSU	MAKING RUNS	AGLLLNOORS	ROLLS ALONG
AGIKMNOPTU	MAKING UP TO	AGLLLOOPRY	PYROGALLOL
AGIKMNORTU	MARKING OUT	AGLLNOOPYY	PALYNOLOGY
AGIKNNORTU	OUTRANKING	AGLLNOOSTW	TWO GALLONS
AGIKNNOTTY	TYING A KNOT	AGLLOOOPTT	GO ALL TO POT
AGIKNOORTT	TAKING ROOT	AGLLRTTUUY	GUTTURALLY
AGIKNOSTTU	STAKING OUT	AGLMOOPSUY	POLYGAMOUS
AGIKNOSTVW	TAKING VOWS	AGLMOORSUU	GLAMOUROUS
AGIKRRSSST	GRASS SKIRT	AGLMPRSSUU	SUGARPLUMS
AGILLNNSTY	SLANTINGLY	AGLNOORSUU	LANGUOROUS
AGILLNOPRT	PATROLLING	AGLNOOTUWY	LONG WAY OUT
AGILLNORTY	TRIGONALLY	AGLOOOSTUU	AUTOLOGOUS
AGILLNOSSX	SIX GALLONS	AGLOPPRSUY	PLAYGROUPS
AGILLNOSWW	SWALLOWING	AGLORRSTUV	VULGAR SORT
AGILLNRSUY	SINGULARLY	AGMMNOOOSU	MONOGAMOUS
AGILLNRTTY	RATTLINGLY	AGMMNOPSUU	MAGNUM OPUS
AGILLOOSSS	ISOGLOSSAL	AGMNNOORWW	GROWN WOMAN
AGILMNNOOP	LAMPOONING		WRONG WOMAN
AGILMNNOOS	MONGOLIANS	AGMNNOOUWY	YOUNG WOMAN
AGILMOPSTY	POLYGAMIST	AGMNOORSTY	GASTRONOMY
AGILNNNOYY	ANNOYINGLY	AGMNORRUYY	MARRY YOUNG
AGILNNOPSS	PLAINSONGS	AGNOPRUWWY	WRONG WAY UP
AGILNNOPTY	POIGNANTLY	AGNORSTTUY	START YOUNG
AGILNNOQSU	ALGONQUINS	AGNOSSTUYY	STAYS YOUNG
AGILNNORTY	IGNORANTLY	AGOORRSSST	GRASS ROOTS
AGILNNTTUY	TAUNTINGLY		GRASS-ROOTS
AGILNNTUVY	VAUNTINGLY	AGOORSSTTT	STARTS TO GO
AGILNOPPTU	POPULATING	AHHIMNOSTY	MISHNAYOTH
AGILNOPSST	GLOSS PAINT	AHHIOPRSTU	AUTHORSHIP
AGILNOPTUY	OUTPLAYING	AHHIORRSST	SHORT HAIRS
	PLAYING OUT	AHHIORSTTT	THIS OR THAT
AGILNOSSTW	WAGONS-LITS	AHHISSWWYY	WISHY-WASHY
AGILNOSTTU	OUTLASTING	AHHLMNNOTU	HOLMAN HUNT
AGILNPRSST	LAST SPRING	AHHORRRTWY	HARRY WORTH
AGILNRSTTU	LUSTRATING	AHIIMMPSX	AMPHIMIXIS
AGILOOPSST	APOLOGISTS	AHIIINNSVW	WISH IN VAIN
AGILOORSTU	GUITAR SOLO	AHIILLMMNP	HILLMAN IMP
AGIMMNOOST	MONOGAMIST	AHIILLNOPS	NAIL POLISH
AGIMMNNSSUY	GYMNASIUMS	AHIILMNOPY	HYPOLIMNIA
AGIMNNNOOW	WANING MOON	AHIILNOORT	HAIR LOTION
AGIMNNOOWX	WAXING MOON	AHIILOSSST	HOISTS SAIL
AGIMNNSSUU	UNASSUMING	AHIILPRSST	SPLIT HAIRS
AGIMNOORST	AGRONOMIST	AHIIMNNOTU	INHUMATION
AGIMNOPPTU	MAPPING OUT	AHIIMNNTUY	INHUMANITY
AGIMNOPRSU	SPORANGIUM	AHIIMNORSW	IRISHWOMAN
AGIMNPRRSW	WARM SPRING	AHIIMORSTU	MOHAIR SUIT
AGINNOPTTU	AT GUNPOINT	AHIINORSST	HISTORIANS
AGINNOTTUW	WANTING OUT	AHIJNNNOOS	JOHNSONIAN
AGINNPPRUW	UNWRAPPING	AHIKLLLPUW	UPHILL WALK
		AHIKLLMNSU	HUMAN SKILL

AHIKLLPSTU	UPHILL TASK	AIIINNOOST	IONISATION
AHIKLMSTWY	MALT WHISKY	AIIINNOOTZ	IONIZATION
AHIKNPRRSW	SHRINK-WRAP	AIIINNOTTV	INVITATION
AHIKORSSTW	THROW A KISS	AIIINORRTT	IRRITATION
AHILLOPSSV	SLAVOPHILS	AIIINORTTY	INITIATORY
AHILMNOPYY	POLYHYMNIA	AIIINOSTTV	VISITATION
AHILMNOSWY	WOMANISHLY	AIIINOTTTV	TITIVATION
AHILMPSSYY	SYMPHYSIAL	AIIIPRSSTY	PITYRIASIS
AHILNOORRY	HONORARILY	AIIIPRTVVY	VIVIPARITY
AHILNPPSSY	SNAPPISHLY	AIIJLNPSTU	PUTS IN JAIL
AHILNPRTTU	PLAIN TRUTH	AIIKLLMOST	AIMS TO KILL
AHILPSSTWY	PLAYS WHIST	AIILLLNOSU	ILLUSIONAL
AHIMMNORSU	HARMONIUMS	AIILLMNTTY	MILITANTLY
AHIMNOORRU	HONORARIUM	AIILLNOOTV	VOLITIONAL
AHIMNOORSU	HARMONIOUS	AIILLNOSUV	VILLAINOUS
AHIMNORSST	HARMONISTS	AIILLNOSVY	VISIONALLY
AHIMNPRTTU	TRIUMPHANT	AIILLORSTY	SOLITARILY
AHIMNPSTYY	IN SYMPATHY	AIILLOSSTT	SOLSTITIAL
AHIMNSTTUU	THIS AUTUMN	AIILLOTTVY	VOLATILITY
AHIMOOPSST	SHAMPOOIST	AIILMMNNOS	NOMINALISM
AHIMPPPRSU	PARISH PUMP	AIILMMNOOT	IMMOLATION
AHINOPPRST	SHARP POINT	AIILMMORTY	IMMORALITY
AHINOSTTWW	IT WONT WASH	AIILMNNOST	NOMINALIST
AHINPRSSST	TRANSSHIPS	AIILMNOORT	MONITORIAL
AHIOPPRSST	PASTORSHIP	AIILMNORTU	IN A TURMOIL
AHIOPSSSTY	HYPOSTASIS	AIILMNOSTU	SIMULATION
AHIOSTTUWY	THIS WAY OUT	AIILMNOTTU	MUTILATION
AHIPRSSTTW	SHARP TWIST	AIILMNRSSU	INSULARISM
AHIRSSTTTW	STARTS WITH	AIILMPPRST	SPIRIT LAMP
AHJLNOORTT	JOHN ARLOTT	AIILMRRTUV	TRIUMVIRAL
AHJMNNOOSY	AMY JOHNSON	AIILMSSSVY	SYLVIA SIMS
AHKLOOPPSY	LOOKS HAPPY	AIILNNOOST	INSOLATION
AHKLOOPRSS	LOOKS SHARP	AIILNNORTV	NONTRIVIAL
AHKNNOOTUY	NO THANK YOU	AIILNNOSTU	INSULATION
AHKNNOPSSY	SHANKS PONY	AIILNNRSUY	LAY IN RUINS
AHKOOOOPTT	TOOK A PHOTO	AIILNOOPST	POSITIONAL
AHLLMNOORY	HORMONALLY		SPOLIATION
AHLLMOOPRS	ALLOMORPHS	AIILNOPTTV	VITAL POINT
AHLLMORSSU	SMALL HOURS	AIILNRSUYY	URINALYSIS
AHLLOPRSTU	PROTHALLUS	AIILNRSTUY	INSULARITY
AHLLOPTXYY	PHYLLOTAXY	AIILNSSSTT	STALINISTS
AHLMNNORTU	LUNAR MONTH	AIILORSSTU	SAILOR SUIT
AHLMNOORST	SOLAR MONTH	AIILORSTVY	ROYAL VISIT
AHLNOPSTUY	POLYANTHUS	AIILPRSSST	SPRITSAILS
AHLOORSUVW	SHOW VALOUR	AIILPRSSTU	SPIRITUALS
AHMNOORSUW	WOMANS HOUR	AIIMMNNOTU	AMMUNITION
AHNNOSTTWY	SHANTY TOWN	AIIMMPRRTU	IMPRIMATUR
	SHANTYTOWN	AIIMMRTTUY	IMMATURITY
AHNOOPSTTU	PUTS ON OATH	AIIMNNNOOT	NOMINATION
AHNOOPSTUW	PUT ON A SHOW	AIIMNNORTU	RUMINATION
AHNOPPRTTY	TRYPTOPHAN	AIIMNNOSTU	MOUNT SINAI
AHNOPRSSTT	SHORT PANTS	AIIMNNRSTT	MINISTRANT
AHOOPSSTTT	PHOTOSTATS	AIIMNOOTTV	MOTIVATION
AHOPRRRTTU	PORT ARTHUR	AIIMNOPRTV	PROVITAMIN
AHORSSTUWY	WHATS YOURS?	AIIMNOPSSS	IMPASSIONS
AHPRSSTTTU	THRUST PAST	AIIMNOPSTU	UTOPIANISM
AIIIINNOTT	INITIATION	AIIMNOPTTU	IMPUTATION
AIIILLMNTU	ILLUMINATI	AIIMNORSSY	MISSIONARY
AIIILLMRTY	MILITARILY	AIIMNPRSTU	PURITANISM
AIIILMMNST	MINIMALIST	AIIMNPSSTT	TIMPANISTS
AIIILMMRST	MILITARISM	AIIMOPRSTT	PATRIOTISM
AIIILMNOSS	MONILIASIS	AIIMOSSTTT	STOMATITIS
AIIILMNOTT	LIMITATION	AIIINNNOOTT	INTONATION
AIIILMRSTT	MILITARIST	AIIINNNOOTV	INNOVATION
AIIILMRSTY	SIMILARITY	AIIINNOORRT	IRON RATION
AIIILNOPTX	PIXILATION	AIIINNOORTT	IN ROTATION
AIIILNQTUY	AQUILINITY	AIIINNOPSTT	SNAP INTO IT
AIIILRTTVY	TRIVIALITY	AIIINNOPSTU	SUPINATION
AIIIMNNOTT	INTIMATION	AIIINNOPSTW	WINS A POINT
AIIIMNOPSS	PIANISSIMO	AIIINNORSTT	TRANSITION
AIIIMNOSTT	IMITATIONS	AIIINNORSTU	INSINUATOR

AIINNOSTTX	ANTITOXINS	AINNOORTVY	INNOVATORY
AIINOOPPST	APPOSITION	AINOOPPRST	APPORTIONS
AIINOOQRSU	IROQUOIANS	AINOOPPTTU	UP TO A POINT
AIINOPRRST	INSPIRATOR	AINOOPRSTY	ANISOTROPY
AIINOPRSTT	PARTITIONS	AINOOQSTTU	QUOTATIONS
AIINOPRSTV	PRIVATIONS	AINOORSTTU	RATIONS OUT
AIINORSTTT	ATTRITIONS	AINOOSTTTU	OUTSTATION
AIINORTTVY	INVITATORY	AINOPRSSTU	PUTS ON AIRS
AIINOSSSVW	SAW VISIONS	AINOPRSTTT	START POINT
AIINOSSTTU	SITUATIONS	AINOPRSTUU	USURPATION
AIIOPRSUVV	VIVIPAROUS	AINORRSSTT	TRANSISTOR
AIJLMNORSU	JOURNALISM	AINORRSTTY	TRANSITORY
AIJLNORSTU	JOURNALIST	AINPRSSSUY	RUSSIAN SPY
AIKLLLOPTW	PILLOW TALK	AINPRSTUUV	PURSUIVANT
AIKLLNNOTW	KNOWN IT ALL	AIOOPRRSUU	UPROARIOUS
AIKLLNOSTW	KNOW-IT-ALLS	AIOORRSTTU	TRAITOROUS
	KNOWS IT ALL	AIOOSSTTTT	TATTOOISTS
AIKLMNNOPS	SALMON PINK	AIOPPPRSUU	PUPIPAROUS
AIKLOSTTTU	TALKS IT OUT	AIOPPRSSTT	POP ARTISTS
AIKLRSSTTY	STARLIT SKY	AIORRRTTTU	TRITURATOR
AIKNOPRSTW	PAINTWORKS	AIORSSTTTW	AT ITS WORST
AIKNPSSTTU	SINKS A PUTT	AKKKLLNUUX	KU KLUX KLAN
AILLMMORTY	IMMORTALLY	AKKOOOSTTT	TOOK TO TASK
AILLMNOOPY	POLYNOMIAL	AKLLLOSWWY	WALK SLOWLY
AILLMNPRST	SMALL PRINT	AKLMNOOOTU	LOOK-OUT MAN
AILLMOPRXY	PROXIMALLY	AKLMOORSST	LOOKS SMART
AILLMOQRTU	MALT LIQUOR	AKLNNNOOWW	KNOWN NO LAW
AILLNNOOTY	NOTIONALLY	AKLNNOOSWW	KNOWS NO LAW
AILLNOOPRT	POLLINATOR	AKLNOOSTUW	WALKS OUT ON
AILLNOOPTY	OPTIONALLY	AKMNNNOOTW	KNOWN TO MAN
AILLNPSSTY	NASTY SPILL	AKMNOORSWW	WOMANS WORK
AILLNQRTUY	TRANQUILLY	AKMOOORSTT	TOOK TO ARMS
AILLOOPTTT	TO TOP IT ALL	AKMOOPRSTU	TOOK UP ARMS
AILLOPSTTW	STOP AT WILL	AKNOOOPRTT	TOOK NO PART
AILLOQRSUW	LIQUOR LAWS	AKORRSSTTW	STARTS WORK
AILLOQTUWY	LOW QUALITY	ALLMOORRTY	MOTOR RALLY
AILLORTTUY	TUTORIALLY	ALLNOOOOST	ALL TOO SOON
AILLSSSTTY	STAYS STILL	ALLOORSUVY	VALOROUSLY
AILMMNNOSU	NOMINAL SUM	ALLOPSSUWW	SWALLOWS UP
AILMMSTTUU	ULTIMATUMS	ALLOPSTUUY	PATULOUSLY
AILMNNOOPR	PRONOMINAL	ALLRRRTUUY	TRULY RURAL
AILMNOOPST	LAMPOONIST	ALMMNSSSUU	MUSSULMANS
AILMNSSTTU	STIMULANTS	ALMMPRSUYY	PLAYS RUMMY
AILMOOPRST	PROSTOMIAL	ALMOOPPRST	PROTOPLASM
AILMORSSTU	SIMULATORS	ALMOPPSSUY	PLAY POSSUM
AILMORSTTU	STIMULATOR	ALMPPRSTUY	PLAY TRUMPS
AILMPSTTUY	STUMPY TAIL	ALNOPRRSUU	SUN PARLOUR
AILNOOOPST	PIANO STOOL	ALNOPSSTTU	POSTULANTS
AILNOOPPTU	POPULATION	ALOOPPRSTT	PROTOPLAST
AILNOOPRSS	SPONSORIAL	ALOOPPRTTY	PROTOTYPAL
AILNOOSTTW	LOW STATION	ALOOPRSUVY	VAPOROUSLY
AILNOPRTTU	PUT ON TRIAL	ALOORRSTUY	ROYAL TOURS
AILNOPSSTU	PULSATIONS	ALOPRTUUVY	VOLUPTUARY
AILNOPSTWY	PLAYS TO WIN	AMMOOSTUXY	MYXOMATOUS
AILNORSSTU	INSULATORS	AMNNOOSTUY	ANTONYMOUS
AILNORSTTU	LUSTRATION	AMNOOOSTUU	AUTONOMOUS
AILOOPRSST	SPOLIATORS	AMNOOPRSUY	PARONYMOUS
AILOOPSTUX	OXTAIL SOUP	AMNOOSTTUW	STOUT WOMAN
AILOPPRTUY	POPULARITY	AMOOOPSTTU	TOMATO SOUP
AILOPQTTUY	TOP QUALITY	AMOOOSTTUU	AUTOTOMOUS
AILOPRSTTU	STIPULATOR	AMOOPPSSSU	POMPOUS ASS
AIMMNOSSTU	SUMMATIONS	AMOPPRSTTU	POSTPARTUM
AIMMOORRTU	MORATORIUM	ANNRSSTTUY	TURNS NASTY
AIMMRRSTWY	TWIST MY ARM	ANOOOPRSSZ	SPOROZOANS
AIMNNORRSU	ROMAN RUINS	ANOOOPRSTZ	PROTOZOANS
AIMNOOSTTU	AUTONOMIST	ANOOPPRTTU	NOT UP TO PAR
AIMNOOSTTX	TAXONOMIST	ANOPRRSSTT	TRANSPORTS
AIMNOPSSTU	ASSUMPTION	AOOOPPSTTU	POTATO SOUP
AIMNORRSTU	RUM RATIONS	AOOORRSTTV	ROTOVATORS
AIMNRSTTUU	NASTURTIUM	AOOPPSTTTU	PUT A STOP TO
AINNOOPRSS	SOPRANINOS	AOOPRRRSTZ	RAZOR STROP

AOOPRSSTTU	AUTOSPORTS	BBEELORRSU	RUBBER SOLE
AOORRSSTYY	SORRY TO SAY	BBEERRRTUY	RUBBER TYRE
BBBEEELMSU	BUMBLEBEES	BBEGHILOSS	BOBSLEIGHS
BBBEEIINRW	WINE BIBBER	BBEGHILRTU	BRIGHT BLUE
BBBEELORUV	BUBBLE OVER	BBEGHIORRT	BIG BROTHER
BBBEERRTUU	RUBBER TUBE	BBEGIILLSU	BIG BULLIES
BBBEGILNRU	BLUBBERING	BBEGILNORS	SLOBBERING
BBBEIKORSS	SKIBOBBERS	BBEGILORTU	BIG TROUBLE
BBBEILNORU	BLUE RIBBON	BBEGINRSSU	GRUBBINESS
BBBEJNOOSY	BOBBY JONES	BBEHHILOST	SHIBBOLETH
BBBEMOOORY	BOBBY MOORE	BBEHHOORSY	HOBBY HORSE
BBBEOORSXY	BOBBY-SOXER		HOBBYHORSE
BBBGGIORSY	BOBBY RIGGS	BBEHILNORT	NOBLE BIRTH
BBBGHINNOO	HOBNOBBING	BBEHLLMOSS	BOMBSHELLS
BBBGIIKNOS	SKIBOBBING	BBEHRSSTUU	THE SUBURBS
BBBGILNPUU	BUBBLING UP	BBEIIKLNOR	RIBBONLIKE
BBBHRSSUUY	SUBSHRUBBY	BBEILNOSSW	WOBBLINESS
BBBLLOOWWY	BLOW BY BLOW	BBEILNOSUY	BOYS IN BLUE
	BLOW-BY-BLOW	BBEILORTTW	BITTER BLOW
BBCDEGILRU	BRIDGE CLUB	BBEIOOPRYZ	BOOBY PRIZE
BBCDEIRSSU	SUBSCRIBED	BBELLMOOTT	BELL-BOTTOM
BBCDEKRRUU	RUBBER DUCK	BBEMNORSUX	BOX NUMBERS
BBCDHLSTUU	DUTCH BULBS	BBEOOORTVV	BOVVER BOOT
BBCEEKNRRU	RUBBERNECK	BBEOORSVVY	BOVVER BOYS
BBCEELMMRU	CLUB MEMBER	BBERRSTTUU	BUTTERBURS
BBCEGILNOR	CLOBBERING	BBFFFGINOO	FOBBING OFF
BBCEHINSSU	CHUBBINESS	BBFGILMNOY	FLYING BOMB
BBCEILRRSS	SCRIBBLERS	BBFHIINORS	RIBBONFISH
BBCEIRRSSU	SUBSCRIBER	BBGGILNOPU	GOBBLING UP
BBCEIRSSSU	SUBSCRIBES	BBGGINOSUY	GOING BY BUS
BBCGIILNRS	SCRIBBLING	BBGHIINRSU	RUBBISHING
BBCGINORSY	BING CROSBY	BBGHILNOOS	HOBGOBLINS
BBCIIOSTUX	BISCUIT BOX	BBGHIMOSST	BOMBSIGHTS
BBCIKMOSTY	STICKY BOMB	BBGIKLNUUY	BULK BUYING
BBDDDDIIYY	BIDDY-BIDDY	BBGILLMNUY	BUMBLINGLY
BBDDEEIMOV	DIVE-BOMBED	BBGINORTUU	RUBBING OUT
BBDDEELNOU	BEND DOUBLE	BBHIIPRSTU	RUBBISH TIP
	DOUBLE BEND	BBHIIRSTUY	BUY BRITISH
BBDDELMNOU	DUMB BLONDE	BBHILNOSSY	SNOBBISHLY
BBDDENORUW	RUBBED DOWN	BBIIKKNTUZ	KIBBUTZNIK
BBDEEEEFTW	WEBBED FEET	BBIKLNSUUY	BUYS IN BULK
BBDEEEFILO	BOILED BEEF	BBIKMNOSST	STINK-BOMBS
BBDEEEINNT	BEEN IN DEBT	BBILLOSUUY	BIBULOUSLY
BBDEEIMORV	DIVE BOMBER	BBIMNOORSU	BOURBONISM
	DIVE-BOMBER	BBJMMMOOUU	MUMBO JUMBO
BBDEEIRRSU	RUBBERISED	BBLNORSTUY	STUBBORNLY
BBDEEIRRUZ	RUBBERIZED	BBNOOORSTW	BROWN BOOTS
BBDEELLOUU	DOUBLE BLUE	BCCDEHKOSY	BODY CHECKS
BBDEELNOTU	BENT DOUBLE	BCCEEENPSU	PUBESCENCE
BBDEIINRTU	RUBBED IT IN	BCCEEGIINS	BIG SCIENCE
BBDEIKNOOR	BOOKBINDER	BCCEEINRTY	CYBERNETIC
BBDEILLNOU	I'LL BE BOUND	BCCEELLSTU	SELECT CLUB
BBDEINORRS	RED RIBBONS	BCCEEMNRUY	RECUMBENCY
BBDEIOSSUY	BUSYBODIES	BCCEFIKLOO	BLOCK OF ICE
BBDELLNOOO	NOBLE BLOOD	BCCEGISSSU	BIG SUCCESS
BBEEEEHLMSU	HUMBLE-BEES	BCCEHHLLRU	CHURCH BELL
BBEEEILNSS	BE SENSIBLE	BCCEHKLOTY	BY THE CLOCK
BBEEEIRRTT	BITTER BEER	BCCEHKLOUY	HOCKEY CLUB
BBEEEELORTT	BEER BOTTLE	BCCEHKRRUY	CHUCK BERRY
BBEEFFIORS	RIBS OF BEEF	BCCEIINOOT	COENOBITIC
BBEEGNOTUY	GONE BY TUBE	BCCEIMNNUY	INCUMBENCY
BBEEGOSTUY	GOES BY TUBE	BCCEINNOSU	CONCUBINES
BBEEHILNOT	ON THE BIBLE	BCCEJKLOUY	JOCKEY CLUB
BBEEHORRSU	RUBBER HOSE	BCCEKRSTUY	CRY BUCKETS
BBEEIILRRS	BILBERRIES	BCCGIMNSUU	SUCCUMBING
BBEEIRRSSU	RUBBERISES	BCCHHIINNY	INCH BY INCH
BBEEIRRSUZ	RUBBERIZES	BCCHIINORT	BRONCHITIC
BBEEIRSTTT	BEST BITTER	BCCIIKOORT	BOOK CRITIC
BBEEKNNOOR	BROKEN BONE	BCCIILSSTY	BICYCLISTS
BBEELLOTTU	BLUEBOTTLE	BCCMORRSUY	CURRYCOMBS
BBEELMORTT	LETTER BOMB	BCDDEEILTU	DEDUCTIBLE

BCDDEIIKRY	DICKEYBIRD
BCDDEIKLLU	DUCKBILLED
BCDEEEEHMR	BECHE-DE-MER
BCDEEEFNOR	CORNED BEEF
BCDEEEIINT	BENEDICITE
BCDEEEIMNR	IN DECEMBER
BCDEEEMNRU	ENCUMBERED
BCDEEEMOSU	BECOMES DUE
BCDEEHIIRS	HERBICIDES
BCDEEHIMRS	BESMIRCHED
BCDEEHLOST	BEDCLOTHES
BCDEEIILNR	INCREDIBLE
BCDEEIILOR	BOILED RICE
BCDEEINSSU	SUBSIDENCE
BCDEEINSTU	BENEDICTUS
BCDEEIPRRS	PRESCRIBED
BCDEEKLLNU	BULLNECKED
BCDEELOORS	EL CORDOBES
BCDEEMOOST	COMES TO BED
BCDEENOSST	SECOND BEST
	SECOND-BEST
BCDEEORRSS	CROSSBREED
BCDEFFLOTU	COLD BUFFET
BCDEFIIKLR	BRICKFIELD
BCDEFLOOTU	CLUBFOOTED
BCDEGHINOU	DEBOUCHING
BCDEGIINRS	DESCRIBING
BCDEHILNOU	DOUBLE CHIN
BCDEHIMNUX	MIXED BUNCH
BCDEIILLNU	INCLUDIBLE
BCDEIILNRY	INCREDIBLY
BCDEIILPSU	PUBLICISED
BCDEIILPUZ	PUBLICIZED
BCDEIKLOOT	BOOTLICKED
BCDEILNRSU	DINERS CLUB
BCDEILOORR	CORRODIBLE
BCDEILOPRU	PRODUCIBLE
BCDEIOPRRS	PROSCRIBED
BCDEKLLOOU	DOUBLE LOCK
BCDEKLNOUW	BUCKLE DOWN
BCDEKLOOOS	CLOSED BOOK
BCDEKLOOTU	BLOCKED OUT
BCDELNOORU	CORDON BLEU
BCDELNOOUW	WOODEN CLUB
BCDELORRUY	CLOUDBERRY
BCDEMMNRUU	CUMMERBUND
BCDENORRWY	CROWN DERBY
BCDEORSTTU	OBSTRUCTED
BCDGIILNOS	CLOSING BID
BCDGIIOSTU	DOG BISCUIT
BCDGIKLORS	GOLDBRICKS
BCDGILOOPU	PUBLIC GOOD
BCDHHIILRT	CHILDBIRTH
BCDHIKLOOT	THICK BLOOD
BCDILMNOSW	CLIMBS DOWN
BCDIMOORSS	SCOMBROIDS
BCDKLOOOST	BLOODSTOCK
BCDKLOOOSW	WOODBLOCKS
BCDKMRSTUU	DUMBSTRUCK
	STRUCK DUMB
BCDLLNNOOU	LONDON CLUB
BCDLNOOOTU	BLOOD COUNT
BCDLORSTUU	CLOUDBURST
BCDNORSSUW	SCRUBS DOWN
BCDOPRSTUY	BY-PRODUCTS
BCEEEEHLSU	BLUE CHEESE
BCEEEEFINNT	BENEFICENT
BCEEEFLLRT	TREBLE CLEF
BCEEEEHKNOS	CHEEKBONES
BCEEEEIILLNU	EBULLIENCE
BCEEEELLMRU	CEREBELLUM

BCEEELMOSS	BECOME LESS
BCEEELOORZ	COOL BREEZE
BCEEEMNOOS	BECOMES ONE
BCEEFIKRTU	FIRE BUCKET
BCEEFILMRU	BE MERCIFUL
BCEEFIOPRS	FIBRESCOPE
BCEEFORRTU	BRUTE FORCE
BCEEGIINOT	BIOGENETIC
BCEEGLLOOY	COLLEGE BOY
BCEEHHNNOT	ON THE BENCH
BCEEHIMRSS	BESMIRCHES
BCEEHINOSX	CHINESE BOX
BCEEHIRSTU	BUTCHERIES
BCEEHKOOQU	CHEQUE BOOK
	CHEQUEBOOK
BCEEHKORRY	CHOKEBERRY
BCEEHLRSTU	THREE CLUBS
BCEEHMORUU	EMBOUCHURE
BCEEHMRTTU	MUCH BETTER
BCEEHNORRX	BRONX CHEER
BCEEHORSTT	BROCHETTES
BCEEHORSTY	BY THE SCORE
BCEEIILLSX	EXCISE BILL
BCEEIILMNT	BELEMNITIC
BCEEIILPST	PLEBISCITE
BCEEIJOSTV	OBJECTIVES
BCEEIJSTUV	SUBJECTIVE
BCEEIKOOPR	RECIPE BOOK
BCEEILLNPU	BLUE PENCIL
	BLUE-PENCIL
BCEEILLOOS	CELLOBIOSE
BCEEILMOST	COMESTIBLE
BCEEILMPST	STEEP CLIMB
BCEEILNOTY	BY-ELECTION
BCEEILOPRW	BELOW PRICE
BCEEINNOTT	ONCE BITTEN
BCEEIPRRRS	PRESCRIBER
BCEEIPRRSS	PRESCRIBES
BCEEIPSSSU	SUBSPECIES
BCEEJLOSST	OBJECTLESS
BCEEJNORST	JOB CENTRES
BCEEKKNNOR	BROKEN NECK
BCEEKLLNNU	KENNEL CLUB
BCEEKLNOTT	BOTTLENECK
BCEEKOORRV	BROKE COVER
BCEELNOTTU	CUTTLEBONE
BCEELNRTUU	TURBULENCE
BCEELNSSUV	SEVEN CLUBS
BCEEMMORSU	CUMBERSOME
BCEEOOOORRR	CORROBOREE
BCEFHNNORT	FRONT BENCH
BCEFIIKRRS	FIREBRICKS
BCEFIIOPRT	FIBRE-OPTIC
BCEFILOORW	BOWL OF RICE
BCEFKLOSTU	BEST OF LUCK
BCEFKLSTUU	BUCKETFULS
	BUCKETSFUL
BCEFLMORRU	REFORM CLUB
BCEFLNOSTU	TEN OF CLUBS
BCEFLOSSTU	SET OF CLUBS
BCEGHIINTW	BEWITCHING
BCEGHIKNNS	KINGS BENCH
BCEGHINPSU	BIG PUNCHES
BCEGHINRTU	BUTCHERING
BCEGIIJNST	SUBJECTING
BCEGILLNOR	CORBELLING
BCEGILMNOY	BECOMINGLY
BCEGILNOPU	GONE PUBLIC
BCEGILOPSU	GOES PUBLIC
BCEGIMNNOU	UNBECOMING
BCEGRRSSUW	GRUB-SCREWS

BCEHIIMOST	BIOCHEMIST	BCGIKLLNOO	BOLLOCKING
BCEHIINSST	BITCHINESS	BCGIKLNNUU	UNBUCKLING
BCEHIKNOTY	KITCHEN BOY	BCGIKLNPUU	BUCKLING UP
BCEHILNOOR	BRONCHIOLE	BCGILNORUW	ROWING CLUB
BCEHILOPRY	HYPERBOLIC	BCGIMNOSTU	COMBUSTING
BCEHIMORSS	CHEMISORBS	BCGINNOPUU	BOUNCING UP
BCEHINOOPX	XENOPHOBIC	BCGINOOTTY	BOYCOTTING
BCEHKKOOST	SKETCH BOOK	BCGMRRSUUY	RUGBY SCRUM
	SKETCHBOOK	BCHIINORST	BRONCHITIS
BCEHKLOOSU	BLOCKHOUSE	BCHIIOPRSS	BISHOPRICS
BCEHKOPSTU	BUCKET SHOP	BCHIIOPSSY	BIOPHYSICS
BCEHLLLOOS	SCHOOL BELL	BCHIMOORTT	THROMBOTIC
BCEHMNOOSY	HONEYCOMBS	BCHIOPRTYY	BRYOPHYTIC
BCEHMOORSS	CHEMOSORBS	BCHKLOOOOS	SCHOOL BOOK
BCEHMRSTUW	THUMBSCREW	BCHKNORSTU	BUCKTHORNS
BCEIIILMMS	IMMISCIBLE	BCHLOOOSSY	BOYS SCHOOL
BCEIIILMTY	IMBECILITY		SCHOOLBOYS
BCEIIILNNV	INVINCIBLE	BCHMOOOSTT	TOOTHCOMBS
BCEIILMMOS	EMBOLISMIC	BCIIILMMSY	IMMISCIBLY
BCEIILPSSU	PUBLICISES	BCIIILNNVY	INVINCIBLY
BCEIILPSUZ	PUBLICIZES	BCIIINSTTU	BISCUIT TIN
BCEIIMORST	BIOMETRICS	BCIILNOPSY	PSILOCYBIN
BCEIINNOTT	BENTONITIC	BCIILORSUU	LUBRICIOUS
BCEIJNOOST	OBJECTIONS	BCIILPSSTU	PUBLICISTS
BCEIJNOSTU	SUBJECTION	BCIIMMNORS	BORN MIMICS
BCEIKLOORT	BOOTLICKER	BCIIMNOSTY	SYMBIONTIC
BCEIKNOOPT	BONE TO PICK	BCIINNSTTY	BY INSTINCT
BCEIKRSSTU	BUS TICKETS	BCIKLNOPRT	BLOCK PRINT
BCEIILMOORT	BOLOMETRIC	BCIKMOORST	BROOMSTICK
BCEILMORSV	CLIMBS OVER	BCIKNOSTUY	BUYS ON TICK
BCEILNNSTU	TENNIS CLUB	BCILLORSSS	CROSSBILLS
BCEILNOOST	BOLECTIONS	BCILMOOPRU	PUBLIC ROOM
BCEILNRTUU	TUBERCULIN	BCILOOSTUU	TUBICOLOUS
BCEILOOSTV	SOVIET BLOC	BCIMNOOSTU	COMBUSTION
BCEILOPSTY	BEST POLICY	BCIOPRSSTU	SUBTROPICS
BCEIMNNSTU	INCUMBENTS	BCIPRSSSTU	SUBSCRIPTS
BCEIMOOSTT	COME TO BITS	BCKMOOORTT	ROCK BOTTOM
BCEIMOSSUX	MUSIC BOXES		ROCK-BOTTOM
BCEIMOSTUV	COMBUSTIVE	BCLMORSUUY	CUMBROUSLY
BCEINNOORZ	BRONZE COIN	BCLOPRSSTU	SPORTS CLUB
BCEINORTTU	CONTRIBUTE	BCNOPRTUUY	COUNTRY PUB
BCEINOSSTU	SUBSECTION	BCOORRSTTU	OBSTRUCTOR
BCEIOPPRSY	PRESBYOPIC	BDDDDEENOW	BEDDED DOWN
BCEIOPRRRS	PROSCRIBER	BDDDEEFNTU	FUNDED DEBT
BCEIOPRRSS	PROSCRIBES	BDDDEELOOR	RED-BLOODED
BCEIORSSTT	OBSTETRICS	BDDDEIISUV	SUBDIVIDED
BCEKKOOOPT	POCKET BOOK	BDDDGIINSU	DISBUDDING
	POCKETBOOK	BDDEEEEKNN	BENDED KNEE
BCEKKOORRS	BROKE ROCKS	BDDEEEEFINR	BEFRIENDED
BCEKLNRTUU	TURNBUCKLE	BDDEEEGORR	DOG BREEDER
BCEKLOORTW	TOWER BLOCK	BDDEEEILLV	BEDEVILLED
BCEKMOOOOT	COME TO BOOK	BDDEEEILRW	BEWILDERED
BCELORSSTW	SCREW-BOLTS	BDDEEEINPT	DEEP IN DEBT
BCELRSTUUU	SUBCULTURE	BDDEEELMNO	EMBOLDENED
BCEMNOPRTU	PROCUMBENT	BDDEEGLNOU	BLUDGEONED
BCEMOPPRRU	BUMPER CROP	BDDEEIISSY	SIDE BY SIDE
BCENOORSSS	CROSSBONES		SIDE-BY-SIDE
BCENORRSST	BRENT CROSS	BDDEEILMSS	DISSEMBLED
BCEOORSTTY	BOYCOTTERS	BDDEEIMNNR	MINDBENDER
BCEPRSTTUU	BUTTERCUPS	BDDEEINRST	BESTRIDDEN
BCFFIILMST	STIFF CLIMB	BDDEEIORSS	SOBERSIDED
BCFGIKNORU	BUCKING FOR	BDDEENNRUU	UNBURDENED
BCFHILRTTU	THRIFT CLUB	BDDEENORTU	DONT BE RUDE
BCFIIMORRR	CRIBRIFORM	BDDEFGILNU	BEFUDDLING
BCFILOSSUX	SIX OF CLUBS	BDDEFILLOU	FULL-BODIED
BCFLOOSTUW	TWO OF CLUBS	BDDEFORSUY	BODYSURFED
BCGHIIINPTU	RITCHING UP	BDDEGGIINW	BIG WEDDING
BCGHILNSTU	NIGHTCLUBS	BDDEGGNOOW	BOGGED DOWN
BCGHIPRTUY	RUGBY PITCH	BDDEGIILOS	DISOBLIGED
BCGHORTUUY	TOUCH RUGBY	BDDEGIINNY	DYING IN BED
BCGIIINNRS	INSCRIBING	BDDEGILNOS	BOLD DESIGN

BDDEGINOTU	BEDDING OUT	BDEEFILOUV	DOUBLE FIVE
BDDEGIOOSS	DOGSBODIES	BDEEFIMORT	TIME FOR BED
BDDEGLOOSU	DOODLEBUGS	BDEEFINRST	BEST FRIEND
BDDEHINOPR	DROP BEHIND	BDEEFKORSU	BEFORE DUSK
BDDEHLNOOR	BONDHOLDER	BDEEFLLOSW	BEDFELLOWS
BDDEHLOOOT	HOT-BLOODED	BDEEFOORSS	BED OF ROSES
BDDEHLOOSS	SHEDS BLOOD	BDEEGGIIOR	BIG GEORDIE
BDDEIINOST	DID ONE'S BIT	BDEEGGLOOT	BOOTLEGGED
BDDEIISSSU	SUBSIDISED	BDEEGGRRSU	BEGRUDGERS
BDDEIISSUV	SUBDIVIDES	BDEEGHINRT	BRIGHTENED
BDDEIISSUZ	SUBSIDIZED	BDEEGHINST	GETS BEHIND
BDDEILMORW	MIDDLEBROW	BDEEGHIRTT	GET THE BIRD
BDDEILNOOW	BOILED DOWN	BDEEGIILST	DIGESTIBLE
BDDEINNRUW	WINDBURNED	BDEEGIINNR	INBREEDING
BDDEINRSSU	DISBURDENS	BDEEGIMOSU	DISEMBOGUE
BDDELNOSUW	SUDDEN BLOW	BDEEGINTTW	BED-WETTING
BDDEMNORSU	ODD NUMBERS	BDEEGIORST	GOBI DESERT
BDDFGIINOR	FORBIDDING	BDEEGLMOSS	GOD BLESS ME!
BDDFILLNOS	BLINDFOLDS	BDEEGNNOOY	GONE BEYOND
BDDFMNOSUU	DUMBFOUNDS	BDEEGNOOSY	GOES BEYOND
BDDGIIINRV	DIVING BIRD	BDEEHIIMNT	BEHIND TIME
BDDHLLOUYY	BUDDY HOLLY	BDEEHILLNW	WELL BEHIND
BDDHLNOOOU	BLOODHOUND	BDEEHIMOOS	HOMEBODIES
BDDIILLOSU	SOLID BUILD	BDEEHIMRSX	MIXED HERBS
BDDIILNSTU	DUSTBIN LID	BDEEHINOTW	BE DONE WITH
BDDIKLNNRU	BLIND DRUNK	BDEEHLNNOR	HORNBLENDE
BDDLNOOOOR	BLOOD DONOR	BDEEHNOOPY	BEYOND HOPE
BDDLNOOOTY	TOLD NOBODY	BDEEHNOTYZ	BY THE DOZEN
BDDMOOSTUY	MUDDY BOOTS	BDEEHORRSY	DERBY HORSE
BDDOOOORSUY	BODY ODOURS	BDEEIILMOS	DEMOBILISE
BDDOOOPPRRY	DROP BY DROP	BDEEIILMOZ	DEMOBILIZE
BDEEEEFSTW	STEWED BEEF	BDEEIKLMRU	MILD REBUKE
BDEEEELRSV	BELVEDERES	BDEEIKNNNU	BEEN UNKIND
BDEEEEMMRR	REMEMBERED	BDEEIKNRRS	DRINKS BEER
BDEEEESSTT	BEDSETTEES	BDEEILLNNR	DINNER BELL
BDEEEFFIOS	SIDE OF BEEF	BDEEILLOPT	POTBELLIED
BDEEEFFLOT	BEETLED OFF	BDEEILMNRU	UNLIMBERED
BDEEEFILMN	FEEBLE MIND	BDEEILMOSW	DISEMBOWEL
BDEEEFILNS	DEFENSIBLE	BDEEILMOTU	DOUBLE TIME
BDEEEFINTT	BENEFITTED	BDEEILMPRU	LIMBERED UP
BDEEEFLOTT	BOTTLE-FEED	BDEEILMRSS	DISSEMBLER
BDEEEHILTW	BLEED WHITE	BDEEILMSSS	DISSEMBLES
BDEEEHLNOR	BEHOLDENER	BDEEILNNOU	DOUBLE NINE
BDEEEIILSV	DISBELIEVE	BDEEILNORR	BORDERLINE
BDEEEILNSS	EDIBLENESS	BDEEILNOTY	OBEDIENTLY
BDEEEILNTX	EXTENDIBLE	BDEEILOORV	BOILED OVER
BDEEEILSTW	WILDEBEEST	BDEEILORSW	BOWDLERISE
BDEEEIMRTT	EMBITTERED	BDEEILORWZ	BOWDLERIZE
BDEEEINNRZ	BENZEDRINE	BDEEILSTUV	VESTIBULED
BDEEEINRRT	INTERBREED	BDEEIMMNNOT	EMBODIMENT
BDEEEIRRSW	DEWBERRIES	BDEEIMMRSS	DISMEMBERS
BDEEEKNORR	BROKEN REED	BDEEIMOOSS	SOMEBODIES
BDEEELMTUW	TUMBLEWEED	BDEEIMORRS	EMBROIDERS
BDEEELNOSS	NOSEBLEEDS	BDEEIMORRY	EMBROIDERY
BDEEELNOSU	SEEN DOUBLE	BDEEIMRRSU	REIMBURSED
BDEEELOSSU	SEES DOUBLE	BDEEINRTTY	DEBIT ENTRY
BDEEELRRRY	ELDERBERRY	BDEEIORSSS	SOBERSIDES
BDEEEMNRRU	RENUMBERED	BDEEIPRSSW	SPIDERS WEB
BDEEENORTT	DONE BETTER		SPIDERWEBS
BDEEENRSTU	DEBENTURES	BDEEIRSSTT	BED-SITTERS
BDEEEORSTT	DOES BETTER	BDEEKOOORV	OVERBOOKED
BDEEEPRSWY	DERBY SWEEP	BDEELLNRUY	UNDERBELLY
BDEEFFILNO	FOND BELIEF	BDEELMRRUU	BLUE MURDER
BDEEFGIINR	DEBRIEFING	BDEELNOOSY	NOBODY ELSE
BDEEFHILLN	FELL BEHIND	BDEELNOSSU	DOUBLENESS
BDEEFHILNT	LEFT BEHIND	BDEELNRTUU	TURNED BLUE
BDEEFILLOR	BOLD RELIEF	BDEELOORVW	BOWLED OVER
BDEEFILLOU	DOUBLE LIFE	BDEELOPRUW	POWDER BLUE
BDEEFILNNO	LOBE-FINNED	BDEELQRSUU	BURLESQUED
BDEEFILNRS	SELF-BINDER	BDEEMNNRUU	UNNUMBERED
BDEEFILNSY	DEFENSIBLY	BDEEMNORSU	BURDENSOME

BDEENOOSST	DO ONES BEST
BDEENORRUV	OVERBURDEN
BDEENORSTT	BOND STREET
BDEENORSUV	UNOBSERVED
BDEEOORRSY	OBEY ORDERS
BDEEORSVWY	BODY SWERVE
BDEEPRTTUU	BUTTERED UP
BDEERSSTTU	BUTTRESSED
BDEFFHORSU	BRUSHED OFF
BDEFFIILSU	DIFFUSIBLE
BDEFFILLOU	BULLIED OFF
BDEFFIORST	BORED STIFF
BDEFFLMOTU	TUMBLED OFF
BDEFFLORSU	OLD BUFFERS
BDEFFNOORW	BROWNED OFF
	BROWNED-OFF
BDEFGGLORS	FRED BLOGGS
BDEFGILRUY	RUGBY FIELD
BDEFGINOOR	FOREBODING
BDEFGIOORT	FOOTBRIDGE
BDEFGSSTUU	FUSSBUDGET
BDEFHIILOS	BOILED FISH
BDEFIIMNOR	FROM BEHIND
BDEFILOOST	SOFT-BOILED
BDEFINORSY	BOY FRIENDS
	BOYFRIENDS
BDEFIOPRRY	BIRD OF PREY
BDEFLOORUU	DOUBLE FOUR
BDEFLOORUX	OXFORD BLUE
BDEFORRSUY	BODYSURFER
BDEGGGINRU	BEGRUDGING
BDEGGIINNO	GOING IN BED
BDEGHHIORW	HIGHBROWED
BDEGHIIRST	BRIGHT SIDE
BDEGHILSSU	SHIELDBUGS
BDEGHIMOTU	BIGMOUTHED
BDEGHIORTT	GOT THE BIRD
BDEGIIILRS	DIRIGIBLES
BDEGIILLNV	DIVING BELL
BDEGIILNNY	LYING IN BED
BDEGIILNOV	BODING EVIL
BDEGIILNSW	BIG SWINDLE
BDEGIILOSS	DISOBLIGES
BDEGIINNOP	OPENING BID
BDEGIINOSY	DISOBEYING
BDEGIINSTU	SUBEDITING
BDEGIIPPRS	BIG DIPPERS
BDEGIKOOSU	GUIDEBOOKS
BDEGIKORRW	BRIDGEWORK
BDEGILLNOW	BODING WELL
BDEGILLORR	BRIDGE ROLL
BDEGILLORT	TOLL BRIDGE
BDEGILNNOW	BENDING LOW
BDEGILNNRU	BLUNDERING
BDEGILNOOV	GIVEN BLOOD
BDEGILNORU	REDOUBLING
BDEGILNSSU	BLIND GUESS
BDEGILOOSV	GIVES BLOOD
BDEGILORSW	LOW BRIDGES
BDEGIMOORR	BRIDEGROOM
BDEGINNORU	REBOUNDING
BDEGINNSTU	SUBTENDING
BDEGINPRSS	BEDSPRINGS
BDEGINRSUU	BURGUNDIES
BDEGIORRSX	BOX GIRDERS
	BOX-GIRDERS
BDEGMNOORU	GOOD NUMBER
BDEHIIOPRT	PROHIBITED
BDEHIKORRT	KID BROTHER
BDEHILNOOT	IN THE BLOOD
BDEHILNORS	BLIND HORSE
BDEHIMNTUX	THUMB INDEX
	THUMB-INDEX
BDEHIRSTTU	BUTTER DISH
BDEHISTTTU	BIT THE DUST
BDEHLOOORS	BLOOD HORSE
BDEHNOOSUU	HOUSEBOUND
BDEHNRRSUU	UNDERBRUSH
	UNDERSHRUB
BDEIIKRRST	BIRDSTRIKE
BDEIILLRTT	LITTLE BIRD
BDEIILMORS	DISEMBROIL
BDEIILRRSV	LIVER BIRDS
BDEIIMNNOR	BORE IN MIND
BDEIINRTTW	BITTER WIND
BDEIIRSSSU	SUBSIDISER
BDEIIRSSUZ	SUBSIDIZER
BDEIIRSTTU	DISTRIBUTE
BDEIISSSSU	SUBSIDISES
BDEIISSSUZ	SUBSIDIZES
BDEIJLRRUY	JERRY-BUILD
BDEIKMRSTU	STRIKE DUMB
BDEIKNNORW	BROKEN WIND
	WIND-BROKEN
BDEILLOSSU	DISSOLUBLE
BDEILLOTUX	BILLET-DOUX
BDEILMNORW	MINDBLOWER
BDEILMOSSY	SYMBOLISED
BDEILMOSYZ	SYMBOLIZED
BDEILNNOST	STONE BLIND
BDEILNOOSS	BLOODINESS
BDEILNORSW	SWORD BLIND
BDEILOORRV	BLOOD RIVER
BDEILORRSW	BLOW-DRIERS
BDEILORSUV	OVERBUILDS
BDEIMNOPTU	BUMPED INTO
BDEIMNORSS	MORBIDNESS
BDEINOORSS	BROODINESS
BDEINOPSST	STOPS IN BED
BDEINOSSSU	DO BUSINESS
BDEINRSSTU	TURBIDNESS
BDEIORSSTU	SUBEDITORS
BDEIRRSSSU	DISBURSERS
BDEIRRSSUV	BUS DRIVERS
BDEKLOORST	BOLD STROKE
BDEKNNOORW	BROKEN DOWN
	BROKEN-DOWN
BDEKNOORRW	BROKEN WORD
BDELLNOOTY	TELL NOBODY
BDELLNOPSU	SPELLBOUND
BDELLOOSTT	OLD BOTTLES
BDELLORSTY	STROLLED BY
BDELLORSUZ	BULLDOZERS
BDELMMNOUY	MOLYBDENUM
BDELMNOOOY	BLOOD MONEY
BDELMNOOWW	BLOW ME DOWN
BDELMNOTUW	TUMBLE DOWN
	TUMBLEDOWN
BDELMOOORU	DOUBLE ROOM
BDELMOTTUU	TUMBLED OUT
BDELNOOOST	BLOODSTONE
BDELNOOOSY	BLOODY NOSE
BDELNORTUU	UNTROUBLED
BDELOOTTTU	BLOTTED OUT
BDELORSUUY	DOUBLY SURE
BDELORTTUU	BLURTED OUT
BDEMMORRUY	DRUMMER BOY
BDENNOOORW	BORE DOWN ON
BDENNOTTUU	UNBUTTONED
BDENOPSSTY	SEND BY POST
BDENOPTTUU	BUTTONED UP
BDFILOORST	FIRST BLOOD

BDFLLOTUUY	DOUBTFULLY	BEEEGRRTTW	GREW BETTER
BDGHIILNNT	NIGHT-BLIND	BEEEGRSTTT	GETS BETTER
BDGIIINNTW	BITING WIND	BEEEHKNOTW	BOW THE KNEE
BDGIILLNNY	BLINDINGLY	BEEEHLLRTW	BELLWETHER
BDGIILNNRU	UNBRIDLING	BEEEHMRTTY	BY THE METRE
BDGIILNPUU	BUILDING UP	BEEEHRSSTW	SWEET HERBS
BDGIINRSSU	DISBURSING	BEEEIIKLSW	BIWEEKLIES
BDGIINRSTU	DISTURBING	BEEEIINNRV	ERNIE BEVIN
BDGILLNOUZ	BULLDOZING	BEEEILMNST	BELEMNITES
BDGILNOORY	BROODINGLY	BEEEILNNOV	BEEN IN LOVE
BDGILNOPUU	DOUBLING UP	BEEEILNOPT	BEEN POLITE
BDGILNORUY	RULING BODY	BEEEILNRUV	UNBELIEVER
BDGILNORWY	BLOW-DRYING	BEEEILNSTX	EXTENSIBLE
BDGILNOTUY	DOUBTINGLY	BEEEILRRSV	REVERSIBLE
BDGINNOORW	DOING BROWN	BEEEILRRTV	REVERTIBLE
BDGINNOOWW	BOWING DOWN	BEEEIMRSSV	SEMIBREVES
BDGINNORRU	BRING ROUND	BEEEINRSSZ	BREEZINESS
BDGINNORSW	BRINGS DOWN	BEEEIRRSTW	SWEETBRIER
BDGINOPPRY	DROPPING BY	BEEEKKOOPR	BOOKKEEPER
BDGINORRSW	BRINGS WORD	BEEEKNNORV	BROKEN EVEN
BDGLNOOOUY	YOUNG BLOOD	BEEEKNRTTW	KNEW BETTER
BDGLOOOPRU	BLOOD GROUP	BEEEKOPRSS	KEEPS SOBER
BDHHIOOOPS	BISHOPHOOD	BEEELLRSST	BEST SELLER
BDHIILRRWY	WHIRLYBIRD		BEST-SELLER
BDHILNOOOT	IN HOT BLOOD	BEEELMMNST	EMBLEMENTS
BDHIMNOORY	MONOHYBRID	BEEELNNOTV	BENEVOLENT
BDHMNOSTUW	THUMBS DOWN	BEEELOPRRT	ROBERT PEEL
	THUMBS-DOWN	BEEELORSVW	SEVERE BLOW
BDIIILNOSU	LIBIDINOUS	BEEEMMNNRSW	NEW MEMBERS
BDIIIMNOTU	BITUMINOID	BEEEMMNSTU	BEMUSEMENT
BDIILOPRST	BOLD SPIRIT	BEEEMNNOOR	BEEN NO MORE
BDIKLLNOSU	SOLD IN BULK	BEEEMNNRUV	EVEN NUMBER
BDIKOORSTY	DIRTY BOOKS	BEEEMNRTTT	BETTERMENT
BDILLLOOPS	SPILL BLOOD	BEEEMPRSST	SEPTEMBERS
BDILLOOPST	SPILT BLOOD	BEEENORRSV	SEVERN BORE
BDILMNORSW	BLINDWORMS	BEEENORSTT	BONESETTER
BDILNNORSW	SWORN BLIND	BEEEOQSUXZ	SQUEEZE BOX
BDILNOOOTW	BOIL DOWN TO		SQUEEZE-BOX
BDINNOORRU	ROUND ROBIN	BEEFFGIRSU	FEBRIFUGES
BDINOOSWWW	BOW WINDOWS	BEEFFIILMR	FIRM BELIEF
BDIOPSSTUY	STUPID BOYS	BEEFFIOSTV	BEST OF FIVE
BDLMOOORSW	BLOODWORMS	BEEFGIKNOO	BOOKING FEE
BDLOOOPRST	BLOOD SPORT	BEEFGLNOOR	BEFORE LONG
BDMNOORSTU	STORMBOUND	BEEFGMOORR	BEG FOR MORE
BDNNOOTTUW	BUTTON-DOWN	BEEFGRSTUU	SUBTERFUGE
BDNORSTUWY	BROWN STUDY	BEEFHORSTT	FOR THE BEST
BEEEEEGHST	THE BEE GEES	BEEFIIKNOW	BOWIE KNIFE
BEEEEFJKLO	FEEBLE JOKE	BEEFIILLNX	INFLEXIBLE
BEEEEFLNSS	FEEBLENESS	BEEFIINORR	BE INFERIOR
BEEEEFLRTT	FEEL BETTER	BEEFIINRTV	FINITE VERB
BEEEEGNRRT	GREEN BERET	BEEFILLMRU	UMBELLIFER
BEEEEKKWWY	WEEK BY WEEK	BEEFIMNRUV	NUMBER FIVE
BEEEEKMMNR	KEEN MEMBER	BEEFINOPRT	PINT OF BEER
BEEEELORRT	ROBERT E.LEE	BEEFJORSTU	JUST BEFORE
BEEEELRSSZ	BREEZELESS	BEEFLLLORW	BELLFLOWER
BEEEENRTTV	EVEN BETTER	BEEFLLORUW	BLUE FLOWER
BEEEFFLOST	BEETLES OFF	BEEFLORSUY	BE YOURSELF
BEEEFGILNN	ENFEEBLING	BEEFNNOOOR	BEFORE NOON
BEEEFGNOOR	GONE BEFORE	BEEGGGIRRW	GREW BIGGER
BEEEFGOORS	GOES BEFORE	BEEGGHORSU	GEORGE BUSH
BEEEFILMMR	LIFE MEMBER	BEEGGHOTTY	GET THE GO-BY
BEEEFILRTU	TRUE BELIEF	BEEGGHSTTU	GETS THE BUG
BEEEFIMORT	BEFORE TIME	BEEGGIILLN	NEGLIGIBLE
BEEEFLOSUY	EYES OF BLUE	BEEGGLOORT	BOOTLEGGER
BEEEFLRSTT	BETTER SELF	BEEGHIILLN	GHIBELLINE
BEEEFLRTTT	FELT BETTER	BEEGHIIMTT	THE BIG TIME
BEEEFOORRT	FREEBOOTER	BEEGHILNRT	BLETHERING
BEEEGGINRR	GINGER BEER	BEEGHINRRT	BRIGHTENER
BEEEGGORST	GEORGE BEST	BEEGHIRSTY	BRIGHT EYES
BEEEGNOSTW	GO-BETWEENS	BEEGHOOTTT	GET THE BOOT
		BEEGIIILLN	INELIGIBLE

BEEGIILNST	INGESTIBLE	BEEIMNNNRU	NUMBER NINE
BEEGIINNRZ	BREEZING IN	BEEIMNNORV	IN NOVEMBER
BEEGIINOSS	BIOGENESIS	BEEIMRRSSU	REIMBURSES
BEEGIKNNOT	BETOKENING	BEEINNNPSU	BUN PENNIES
BEEGILLNSW	BEGINS WELL	BEEINRSSTT	BITTERNESS
BEEGILMNRS	RESEMBLING	BEEINSSSSU	BUSINESSES
BEEGILMNZZ	EMBEZZLING	BEEIOPRRSU	BE SUPERIOR
BEEGILNNSU	BLUE ENSIGN	BEEIPRSUVW	SUPERB VIEW
BEEGINRTTV	BREVETTING	BEEIQRRSUU	BRUSQUERIE
BEEGOOORSY	GOOSEBERRY	BEEIQRSTTU	BRIQUETTES
BEEGORRTTW	GROW BETTER	BEEIRSSUVV	SUBVERSIVE
BEEHIIITVX	EXHIBITIVE	BEEKKOOPSS	KEEPS BOOKS
BEEHILMMOO	MOBILE HOME	BEEKLLOORS	BOOKSELLER
BEEHILOSSV	BOLSHEVISE	BEEKLOOORS	BROKE LOOSE
BEEHILOSVZ	BOLSHEVIZE	BEEKLORRSU	BROKE RULES
BEEHIMMPRS	MEMBERSHIP	BEEKNNOOPR	BROKEN OPEN
BEEHIORRSV	HERBIVORES	BEEKNNOORS	BROKEN NOSE
BEEHIRRTVY	BY THE RIVER	BEEKNNORSS	BROKENNESS
BEEHISSSTW	BEST WISHES	BEEKNOORST	STONE-BROKE
BEEHKMNOOR	BROKEN HOME	BEEKNORSST	KERBSTONES
BEEHLLLLSS	HELLS BELLS	BEEKNORTTW	KNOW BETTER
BEEHLLLOTU	BULLET HOLE	BEELLLOTWY	YELLOW BELT
BEEHLLOTTW	BLEW THE LOT	BEELMNRSSU	NUMBERLESS
BEEHLMNSSU	HUMBLENESS	BEELMOORST	BOLOMETERS
BEEHLMOSTW	THE WOMBLES	BEELMORTUV	TUMBLE OVER
BEEHLOPTTU	POT THE BLUE	BEELMRRSSU	SLUMBERERS
BEEHLORRTW	LOWER BERTH	BEELNOORST	BOSTON REEL
BEEHLRSSTU	BUS SHELTER	BEELNSSSTU	SUBTLENESS
	BUS-SHELTER	BEELOOOSSX	LOOSE BOXES
BEEHMOORST	BOTHERSOME	BEELORRSST	BOLSTERERS
BEEHNOOOTZ	ON THE BOOZE	BEELQRSSUU	BURLESQUES
BEEHNOOPSX	PHONE BOXES	BEELRRSSTU	BLUSTERERS
	XENOPHOBES	BEELRSSTTU	BUTTERLESS
BEEHNOOPTX	OPEN THE BOX	BEEMMNNOTT	ENTOMBMENT
BEEHNORSTT	THE BRONTES	BEEMMNOSST	EMBOSSMENT
BEEHOORSSX	HORSEBOXES	BEEMOPSTXY	EMPTY BOXES
BEEHORSSSU	ROSE BUSHES	BEEMRRSSSU	BRESSUMERS
	ROSEBUSHES	BEENNOTTUX	NEXT BUT ONE
BEEHORTTWY	THREE BY TWO	BEENOORRTW	ROBERT OWEN
	TWO BY THREE	BEENOSSSTU	OBTUSENESS
BEEHPPRRTU	UPPER BERTH	BEENPRSSSU	SUPERBNESS
BEEIIJORTU	BIJOUTERIE	BEENQSSTUU	SUBSEQUENT
BEEIIKLMOZ	ZOMBIELIKE	BEEORSSTTU	SOUBRETTES
BEEIILMMRS	IMMERSIBLE	BEEORSSTTY	SET STORE BY
BEEIILMNRT	TIMBER LINE	BEEPPSSTTY	STEP BY STEP
	TIMBERLINE		STEP-BY-STEP
BEEIILNNSS	INSENSIBLE	BEEPRRSSTY	PRESBYTERS
BEEIILNRST	LIBERTINES	BEEPRRSTYY	PRESBYTERY
BEEIILNRTV	INVERTIBLE	BEERRSSTUV	SUBVERTERS
BEEIILRSST	RESISTIBLE	BEERSSSTTU	BUTTRESSES
BEEIKKNORR	KNOBKERRIE	BEERSSTTUY	BUSY STREET
BEEIKLNPRS	BESPRINKLE	BEFFGIORST	BIG EFFORTS
BEEIKOORVW	BOOK REVIEW	BEFFHIJNNO	JOHN BIFFEN
BEEILLLSSY	SELSEY BILL	BEFFHILOOT	OFF THE BOIL
BEEILLNORS	REBELLIONS	BEFFHORSSU	BRUSHES OFF
BEEILLOPST	POTBELLIES	BEFFIKOORT	BROKE IT OFF
BEEILLORSU	REBELLIOUS	BEFFILLOSU	BULLIES OFF
BEEILLRSTT	BELITTLERS	BEFFIORSST	BORES STIFF
	BELLETRIST	BEFFNOORUY	BUFFOONERY
BEEILMNNSS	NIMBLENESS	BEFFNOSSUX	SNUFF BOXES
BEEILMNRSS	LIMBERNESS		SNUFFBOXES
BEEILMRRSU	MULBERRIES	BEFGHIORTU	THE BIG FOUR
BEEILNOPRZ	NOBEL PRIZE	BEFGIINNOR	FIBRINOGEN
BEEILNOSST	OSTENSIBLE	BEFGILNORW	FINGER BOWL
BEEILNOTTW	WINE BOTTLE		FINGERBOWL
BEEILNRSTW	WEST BERLIN	BEFGNOOOTY	GONE BY FOOT
BEEILOSTTU	OUBLIETTES	BEFGOOOSTY	GOES BY FOOT
BEEILRRSTT	TERRIBLEST	BEFHIILLTT	FIT THE BILL
BEEILRRSVY	REVERSIBLY	BEFHILLMTU	THIMBLEFUL
BEEILSSTTU	SUBTLETIES	BEFHIRSTTU	BUTTERFISH
BEEILSSTUV	VESTIBULES	BEFIIIRSTV	BRIEF VISIT

BEFIILLNXY	INFLEXIBLY	BEGLLORUVY	LOVELY GRUB
BEFIILLORS	FIBRILLOSE	BEGLMOORYY	EMBRYOLOGY
BEFIILOPSS	IF POSSIBLE	BEGLNRSTUY	RUBS GENTLY
BEFIILRSTU	FILIBUSTER	BEGNORRSTW	STRONG BREW
BEFILLMORR	REFORM BILL	BEGOOPPRST	GOBSTOPPER
BEFILLOSTT	FELL TO BITS	BEHHIIRSTT	THE BRITISH
BEFINOPSTT	PINT OF BEST	BEHHILTTU	HIT THE BULL
BEFLLLOTTU	FULL BOTTLE	BEHHNORSTY	BY THE HORNS
BEFLLMRTUU	TUMBLERFUL	BEHIIIINTV	INHIBITIVE
BEFLLOSTTU	BOTTLEFULS	BEHIIINOTX	EXHIBITION
BEFMNORRUU	NUMBER FOUR	BEHIIKLOSV	BOLSHEVIKI
BEFMNORSTU	SOFT NUMBER	BEHIIORTXY	EXHIBITORY
BEFMOPRRSU	SUPERB FORM	BEHIIRRSST	BRITISHERS
BEGGGIORRW	GROW BIGGER	BEHIKLNNRU	BUNKER HILL
BEGGHMRUUY	HUMBUGGERY	BEHIKLNNOT	ON THE BLINK
BEGGHOOTTY	GOT THE GO-BY	BEHIKLOSSV	BOLSHEVIKS
BEGGIILLNY	NEGLIGIBLY	BEHILLOPTT	TOP THE BILL
BEGGIINNNS	BEGINNINGS	BEHILLORTT	ROB THE TILL
BEGGIINSTV	GIVING BEST	BEHILLORWW	WILLOWHERB
BEGGIKNOOR	GOING BROKE	BEHILMOSSV	BOLSHEVISM
BEGGILNNOS	BELONGINGS	BEHILNOSSS	BOLSHINESS
BEGGILNOOW	GOING BELOW	BEHILNSSSU	BLUISHNESS
BEGGILNOTU	GLIB TONGUE	BEHILNSTTU	SUBTLE HINT
BEGGIMNRSU	SUBMERGING	BEHILOSSTV	BOLSHEVIST
BEGGINNORU	BURGEONING	BEHILPRSSU	PUBLISHERS
BEGHHIMNRU	HIGH NUMBER	BEHILRSSTU	BLUE SHIRTS
BEGHHINOST	THIGHBONES	BEHIMSSSTU	MISS THE BUS
BEGHIIINTX	EXHIBITING	BEHINOSSSY	BOYISHNESS
BEGHIILMNS	BLEMISHING	BEHJJOSTTU	JUST THE JOB
BEGHIILMRT	THIMBLERIG	BEHKOORRST	BROKE SHORT
BEGHIILNRT	BLITHERING	BEHLLOOTTW	BLOW THE LOT
BEGHIINRTV	GIVEN BIRTH	BEHLLORRYY	HOLLY BERRY
BEGHIIRSTT	BIG HITTERS	BEHLMOOPTY	PHLEBOTOMY
BEGHIIRSTV	GIVES BIRTH	BEHLNOOTTU	BUTTONHOLE
BEGHILLSTU	LIGHT BLUES	BEHMNORSTU	HOT NUMBERS
BEGHILORTW	RIGHT ELBOW	BEHMOOOORST	SMOOTHBORE
BEGHIMNORS	BRINGS HOME	BEHMOORSST	THROMBOSES
BEGHINOPSY	GONE BY SHIP	BEHMOORSTY	MOTHERS BOY
BEGHINORSU	NEIGHBOURS	BEHMPRTTUU	TUB-THUMPER
BEGHINORTT	BETROTHING	BEHNOORSSW	BROWN SHOES
BEGHINPRTU	BRIGHTEN UP	BEHOPRSTYY	BRYOPHYTES
BEGHINRSST	BRIGHTNESS	BEHOPSSTTU	STOP THE BUS
BEGHINSSTT	BEST THINGS	BEHORRSTTU	SOBER TRUTH
BEGHIOPSSY	GOES BY SHIP	BEIIILMMOS	IMMOBILISE
BEGHOOOTTT	GOT THE BOOT	BEIIILMMOZ	IMMOBILIZE
BEGIIILLTY	LEGIBILITY	BEIIILNSSV	INVISIBLES
BEGIIKLRTZ	BLITZKRIEG	BEIIIMNSTU	BITUMINISE
BEGIILLNTT	BELITTLING	BEIIIMNTUZ	BITUMINIZE
BEGIILMNOR	EMBROILING	BEIILLNNOO	ONE BILLION
BEGIILNRST	BLISTERING	BEIILLNOTU	EBULLITION
BEGIILNRTT	BITTERLING	BEIILLOSSU	SOLUBILISE
BEGIINNNTW	WINNING BET	BEIILLOSUZ	SOLUBILIZE
BEGIINRRST	BESTIRRING	BEIILLPRTT	BITTER PILL
BEGIIORSST	BIG STORIES	BEIILMOPSS	IMPOSSIBLE
BEGIJRSTTU	JITTERBUGS	BEIILNNSSY	INSENSIBLY
BEGIKNORSW	BEGINS WORK	BEIILNOPST	BIT ONE'S LIP
BEGILLNOSW	SINGLE BLOW	BEIILORSTT	TRILOBITES
BEGILMNOTV	MOVING BELT	BEIILORSTU	BOILER SUIT
BEGILMNRSU	SLUMBERING	BEIILRSTTT	LIBRETTIST
BEGILMORTY	BOY MET GIRL	BEIILSUYZZ	BUSY LIZZIE
BEGILNORST	BOLSTERING	BEIIMSSSUV	SUBMISSIVE
BEGILNRSTU	BLUSTERING	BEIINNOTTT	BITTEN INTO
BEGILOOOXY	EXOBIOLOGY	BEIINNSSSU	IN BUSINESS
BEGILPSTTU	SPITTLEBUG	BEIINORSTY	INSOBRIETY
BEGILRSTTU	LITTERBUGS	BEIJLRRTUY	JERRY BUILT
BEGINORRSV	BRINGS OVER		JERRY-BUILT
BEGINORSSU	SUBREGIONS	BEIKLLLNSU	SELL IN BULK
BEGINPRRTU	PERTURBING	BEIKLLLORW	KILLER BLOW
BEGINRSSUV	SUBSERVING	BEIKLLMOTT	MILK BOTTLE
BEGINRSTUV	SUBVERTING	BEIKLMRTTU	BUTTERMILK
BEGJKLNOOU	JUNGLE BOOK	BEIKLNOSTT	INK BOTTLES

BEIKLOOSTT	BOOK TITLES	BEMNOOOTTT	BOTTOM NOTE
BEIKLOSSSW	BLOW KISSES	BEMNOOSSTT	TOMBSTONES
BEIKMNOOTU	MINUTE BOOK	BEMNORSTUU	OUTNUMBERS
BEIKMOORST	MOTOR BIKES	BEMPPPRSUU	BUMP SUPPER
BEIKNOORTW	BROKE IN TWO	BENNNOSSTU	SUN BONNETS
BEIKNOPRTU	BROKEN IT UP		SUNBONNETS
BEIKOORSTW	WRITE BOOKS	BENOPRSSTU	BURSTS OPEN
BEILLNSUUU	LUIS BUNUEL	BENOPSSTTY	SENT BY POST
BEILLOPRST	BILLPOSTER	BENORSSSTU	ROBUSTNESS
BEILMNOOSW	SNOWMOBILE	BENRSTTTUU	BUTTERNUTS
BEILMNOOTT	BOTTOM LINE	BEORRTTTUW	BUTTERWORT
BEILMOOORR	BOILER ROOM	BFFFFILOTU	BIT OF FLUFF
BEILMOOOST	LOBOTOMISE	BFFFIOSTTU	BIT OF STUFF
BEILMOOOTZ	LOBOTOMIZE	BFFGHOORTU	BROUGHT OFF
BEILMOSSSY	SYMBOLISES	BFFGIINORT	BRING IT OFF
BEILMOSSYZ	SYMBOLIZES	BFFGIKNNOU	BUNKING OFF
BEILMPSUUY	IMPULSE BUY	BFFGILNOOW	BLOWING OFF
BEILNOORST	ORIONS BELT	BFFGIMNOPU	BUMPING OFF
BEILNOPRSW	SPIN BOWLER	BFFOORRUUY	FOUR BY FOUR
BEILNOPTTT	PINT BOTTLE	BFGHIINRSU	FURBISHING
BEILNOSSTY	OSTENSIBLY	BFGHILLSTU	BULL FIGHTS
BEILNOSTUY	NEBULOSITY		BULLFIGHTS
BEILNPRSTU	BLUEPRINTS	BFGHILNTYY	FLY BY NIGHT
BEILNRRSSU	BLURRINESS		FLY-BY-NIGHT
BEILOOPRST	POT BOILERS	BFGHINORRT	BRING FORTH
	POTBOILERS	BFGIIOPRST	BIG PROFITS
BEIMNORSSU	SUBMERSION	BFGILLMNUY	FUMBLINGLY
BEINNOSSSU	UN BUSINESS	BFHORRSTTU	BURST FORTH
BEINNOSTUV	SUBVENTION	BFIIILSTUY	FUSIBILITY
BEINOOSSSS	OBSESSIONS	BFIIIORSST	FIBROSITIS
BEINORSSUV	SUBVERSION	BFIIKORSTT	BIT OF SKIRT
BEINORSTUU	SUBROUTINE	BFILLLSSUY	BLISSFULLY
BEINOSSSSY	BYSSINOSES	BFILLOOPSX	BOX OF PILLS
BEINOSSSUU	BONUS ISSUE	BFIORSTTTU	FIT TO BURST
BEINOSSTWX	WITNESS BOX	BFLOOOPSUW	BOWL OF SOUP
	WITNESS-BOX	BGGGHIMNUU	HUMBUGGING
BEIN333TTU	SUBSISTENT	BGGHHIOTTU	THOUGHT BIG
BEIOOQSSUU	OBSEQUIOUS	BGGHIIILLN	BIGGIN HILL
BEIOORSSST	SOB STORIES	BGGIIINNNR	BRINGING IN
BEIOORSSTU	BOISTEROUS	BGGIILLNOY	OBLIGINGLY
BEIOORSTTT	TORE TO BITS	BGGIILNORS	GIBSON GIRL
BEIOQRSSTU	SOBRIQUETS	BGGIINNNOR	BRINGING ON
BEIOQRSTUU	SOUBRIQUET	BGGIINNORT	BRINGING TO
BEIORSSSST	SOB SISTERS	BGGIINNORX	BOXING RING
BEIPRRSSUY	BY SURPRISE	BGGIINNPRU	BRINGING UP
BEISSTTTUU	SUBSTITUTE		UPBRINGING
BEJNORRRWY	JERRY BROWN	BGGINOORWY	GROWING BOY
BEKKNOOOST	BOOK TOKENS	BGHHIIRRTT	BIRTHRIGHT
BEKLOOORSV	BOOK LOVERS	BGHHIJNORT	JOHN BRIGHT
BEKNOORSTY	STONY BROKE	BGHIIIINNT	INHIBITING
	STONY-BROKE	BGHIILLRST	BIG THRILLS
BEKNOSTTUY	KEYBUTTONS	BGHIILNOOT	BOILING HOT
BEKOOORSTW	WROTE BOOKS	BGHIILNPSU	PUBLISHING
BEKORRSUWY	BUSY WORKER	BGHIINNRSU	BURNISHING
BELLNOSUUY	NEBULOUSLY	BGHIKOORST	BOOK RIGHTS
BELLOORSWW	SLOW BOWLER	BGHIKORRTW	BRIGHTWORK
BELLOOSSTY	BOOTLESSLY	BGHILLNSUY	BLUSHINGLY
BELLORSTUY	TROLLEY BUS	BGHILNNSUU	UNBLUSHING
	TROLLEYBUS	BGHILNOOTW	BLOWING HOT
BELMMOORRU	LUMBER ROOM	BGHILNORTW	LIGHT BROWN
BELMNOOPRS	NO PROBLEMS	BGHINNOTTU	NOTHING BUT
BELMNORSUW	LOW NUMBERS	BGHINPRSUU	BRUSHING UP
BELMOOSSTT	BOTTOMLESS	BGHIOPRSTT	BRIGHT SPOT
BELMOSSSXY	SEX SYMBOLS	BGHLOORTUW	BROUGHT LOW
BELNNRRUYY	YUL BRYNNER	BGHOORTTUU	BROUGHT OUT
BELNOORRTU	BORN TO RULE	BGIIILLNOO	BOILING OIL
BELNOSSTTU	BUTTONLESS	BGIIILMNOS	MOBILISING
BELOOPRSTT	LOBSTER POT	BGIIILMNOZ	MOBILIZING
BELOPRSSTU	BOLSTERS UP	BGIIILNOTY	IGNOBILITY
BELORSSTUU	BLUSTEROUS	BGIIINNOTT	BITING INTO
BEMMNOORRU	ROOM NUMBER	BGIIJNNOSU	SUBJOINING

BGIIKLNNNU	UNBLINKING	CCCCGINOOO	GONOCOCCIC
BGIIILLNOPT	TOP BILLING	CCCDEILOPY	CYCLOPEDIC
BGIILMNOWX	MIXING BOWL	CCCDIILOOP	DIPLOCOCCI
BGIILMOORS	IMBROGLIOS	CCCEEINNOS	CONSCIENCE
BGIILNNORU	BURNING OIL	CCCEEINRST	ECCENTRICS
BGIILNRSST	BRISTLINGS	CCCEELNSUU	SUCCULENCE
BGIILOOSST	BIOLOGISTS	CCCEENORRU	OCCURRENCE
BGIIMNSTTU	SUBMITTING	CCCEHHIMRU	CHURCH MICE
BGIINNRSTU	BURSTING IN	CCCEHIILNO	COLCHICINE
BGIINORSUU	RUBIGINOUS	CCCEHKORSS	CROSS-CHECK
BGIINPRSTU	BRINGS IT UP	CCCEIILPRY	PERICYCLIC
BGIINSSSTU	SUBSISTING	CCCEIIMRSU	CIRCUMCISE
BGIKNOPRSS	SPRINGBOKS	CCCEIINNORT	CONCENTRIC
BGILLNRRUY	BLURRINGLY	CCCEINOOTV	CONCOCTIVE
BGILLNSTUY	BUSTLINGLY	CCCEINOOTY	COENOCYTIC
BGILMNOOSS	BLOSSOMING	CCCENOORST	CONCOCTERS
BGILMNOOTW	TOM BOWLING	CCCGINNOOT	CONCOCTING
BGILNOOTUW	BLOWING OUT	CCCGNOOOSU	GONOCOCCUS
	BOWLING OUT	CCCIKKLLNU	CLUNK CLICK
BGILNOPTTU	BOTTLING UP	CCCILNSTUY	SUCCINCTLY
BGILORSUUU	LUGUBRIOUS	CCCINNOOOT	CONCOCTION
BGIMNNOOSU	UNBOSOMING	CCCLOORSSY	CYCLO-CROSS
BGINNORSTU	BINTURONGS	CCDDEENNOS	CONDESCEND
BGINNORTUU	BURNING OUT	CCDEEEENPR	PRECEDENCE
BGINNORUUY	RUGBY UNION	CCDEEEEFFIO	ICED COFFEE
BGMNOORTTU	BOTTOM RUNG	CCDEEEHINS	DEHISCENCE
BHHIMORSTY	BIORHYTHMS	CCDEEEENRST	DECRESCENT
BHHOORRUUY	HOUR BY HOUR	CCDEEEORST	SECRET CODE
BHHOORSTTU	TOOTHBRUSH	CCDEEERRSU	RECRUDESCE
BHIIIINNOT	INHIBITION	CCDEEERRSSU	SUCCEEDERS
BHIIINORST	INHIBITORS	CCDEEFIINY	DEFICIENCY
BHIIINORTY	INHIBITORY	CCDEEFINNO	CONFIDENCE
BHIILLMPSY	BLIMPISHLY	CCDEEGILNO	DOG LICENCE
BHIILLRSTT	STILLBIRTH	CCDEEGINSU	SUCCEEDING
BHIIPRSSTY	BRITISH SPY	CCDEEHHTUW	CHEW THE CUD
BHILOOOPST	BOOT POLISH	CCDEEHIIOW	WIDE CHOICE
BHIMNPRTTU	THUMBPRINT	CCDEEHIORT	RICOCHETED
BHIMOORSST	THROMBOSIS	CCDEEHKOTU	CHECKED OUT
BHINORRSTW	BROWN SHIRT	CCDEEHNOSY	SYNECDOCHE
	BROWNSHIRT	CCDEEIILRT	DIELECTRIC
BHKNOOOTTU	BUTTONHOOK	CCDEEIILRW	WIDE CIRCLE
BHLLOOOSTT	TOLLBOOTHS	CCDEEIINNS	INCIDENCES
BHLLRRUUYY	HURLY-BURLY	CCDEEIKLRV	CLEVER DICK
BHNOPSTTUU	PUSH-BUTTON		CLEVER-DICK
BHORRSSTTU	SHORT BURST	CCDEEILNOR	RECONCILED
BIIIILRSTY	RISIBILITY	CCDEEIMORT	ECTODERMIC
BIIILMMOTY	IMMOBILITY	CCDEEKLOYY	COCKEYEDLY
BIILLLLSYY	SILLY BILLY	CCDEELNNOO	CONDOLENCE
	SILLY-BILLY	CCDEEMNOOS	COME SECOND
BIILLOSTUY	SOLUBILITY	CCDEENORSS	CRESCENDOS
BIILLOTUVY	VOLUBILITY	CCDEENORSW	CROWD SCENE
BIILMOPSSY	IMPOSSIBLY	CCDEFILNOT	CONFLICTED
BIIMNOSSSU	SUBMISSION	CCDEGHIOOO	GOOD CHOICE
BIIMNOSTUU	BITUMINOUS	CCDEGIILRY	GLYCERIDIC
BIINOSSSSY	BYSSINOSIS	CCDEHKOTUU	CHUCKED OUT
BIIOOSTUUU	UBIQUITOUS	CCDEHLNTUU	DUTCH UNCLE
BIKKNOOSTY	KINKY BOOTS	CCDEIIILOT	IDIOLECTIC
BIKLLORSST	STORKSBILL	CCDEIIPRV	CIVIC PRIDE
BILLNOOPSS	SPOONBILLS	CCDEIIIRST	CRITICISED
BILMOSSSTY	SYMBOLISTS	CCDEIIIRTZ	CRITICIZED
BIMNOORSTT	TROMBONIST	CCDEIILOPY	EPICYCLOID
BIMOOPPRRU	OPPROBRIUM	CCDEIINNOT	COINCIDENT
BINOOOORRSY	ROY ORBISON	CCDEIJKOSY	DISC JOCKEY
BINOORSTTT	TORN TO BITS	CCDEIKOPTU	COCKED IT UP
BKLLMNSSUU	NUMBSKULLS	CCDEILOORS	CROCODILES
BKMOOOPPRT	PROMPT BOOK	CCDEIMOOOT	OCTODECIMO
BMMOOOSTTT	BOTTOMMOST	CCDEINNOST	DISCONNECT
BMOOOSTTTU	BOTTOMS OUT	CCDEINOOPS	ENDOSCOPIC
BNNORRSTUW	TURNS BROWN	CCDEINOPUU	UNOCCUPIED
BNOORRTTUW	BROWN TROUT	CCDEINORST	DISCONCERT
BOOPPRRSTU	TURBOPROPS	CCDEINOTUV	CONDUCTIVE

CCDEKLOOTU	CLOCKED OUT	CCEEINNNOT	CONTINENCE
CCDEKLORSU	CUCKOLDERS	CCEEINNOTV	CONNECTIVE
CCDENOOPRS	SECOND CROP	CCEEINNRRU	INCURRENCE
CCDGIIINNO	COINCIDING	CCEEINOPRW	CROWN PIECE
CCDGIILOSU	GLUCOSIDIC	CCEEINOPTV	CONCEPTIVE
CCDGIILOSY	GLYCOSIDIC	CCEEINORST	CONCRETISE
CCDGIKLNOU	CUCKOLDING		ICE CORNETS
CCDGILNNOU	CONCLUDING	CCEEINORSV	CONCEIVERS
CCDGINNOTU	CONDUCTING	CCEEINORTZ	CONCRETIZE
CCDHIINORT	CHONDRITIC	CCEEINOSSV	CONCESSIVE
CCDHIKLOTU	THICK CLOUD	CCEEINOTVV	CONVECTIVE
CCDHKOOSUW	WOODCHUCKS	CCEEINRRSU	CURRENCIES
CCDHNOORUW	CROUCH DOWN	CCEEINRTTY	CITY CENTRE
CCDIIOORST	CORTICOIDS	CCEEIOPRSS	CROSSPIECE
CCDIMNNOSTU	MISCONDUCT	CCEEIORRTV	CORRECTIVE
CCDINNOOTU	CONDUCTION	CCEEISSSUV	SUCCESSIVE
CCDKKLNOOS	KNOCKS COLD	CCEEJNORTU	CONJECTURE
CCDLMMNOOO	COMMON COLD	CCEELLORST	RECOLLECTS
CCDNOORSTU	CONDUCTORS	CCEELMOORS	COME CLOSER
CCEEEELLNX	EXCELLENCE	CCEELMOOSS	COMES CLOSE
CCEEEENNSS	SENESCENCE	CCEELMORTY	CYCLOMETER
CCEEEFHIOR	FREE CHOICE	CCEELNOPRU	CORPULENCE
CCEEEFFNNOR	CONFERENCE	CCEELNORTY	CONCRETELY
CCEEEHIPSS	CHESS PIECE	CCEELNRTUU	TRUCULENCE
CCEEEHIRRSS	SCREECHERS	CCEELOSTTU	COS LETTUCE
CCEEEINPRS	PRESCIENCE	CCEELOSTUY	LEUCOCYTES
CCEEEINQSU	QUIESCENCE	CCEENNORST	CONNECTERS
CCEEEINRSV	VIRESCENCE	CCEENOPRRT	PRECONCERT
CCEEEIOPSS	ECOSPECIES	CCEEORRSTT	CORRECTEST
CCEEEIRSTV	SECRET VICE	CCEFFIIOTY	CITY OFFICE
CCEEEMNOPT	COMPETENCE	CCEFHIIMOR	MICROFICHE
CCEEEMNSTU	TUMESCENCE	CCEFHIMMOS	COMMIS CHEF
CCEEENRRRU	RECURRENCE	CCEFHIOSTU	CHIEF SCOUT
CCEEENRSTX	EXCRESCENT	CCEFIIINST	SCIENTIFIC
CCEEFFIINY	EFFICIENCY	CCEFIIRSUX	CRUCIFIXES
CCEEFFILNO	OFF LICENCE	CCEFIKLOOV	FIVE O CLOCK
	OFF LICENCE	CCEFIKLSTT	CLEFT STICK
CCEEFHHRRU	FREE CHURCH	CCEFILLLRU	FULL CIRCLE
CCEEFHIKLR	CHIEF CLERK	CCEFILMRUX	CIRCUMFLEX
CCEEFINTTU	FETTUCCINE	CCEFINNOOT	CONFECTION
CCEEFLNNOU	CONFLUENCE	CCEFLLNOTU	FLOCCULENT
CCEEGHIKNR	CHECKERING	CCEFLSSSUU	SUCCESSFUL
CCEEGHINRS	SCREECHING	CCEGHIIKNN	CHECKING IN
CCEEGILNNU	GUN LICENCE	CCEGHINORT	CROCHETING
CCEEGINNOR	CONGENERIC	CCEGIILNNR	ENCIRCLING
CCEEGINORS	CONCIERGES	CCEGIINNOV	CONCEIVING
CCEEGINORT	EGOCENTRIC	CCEGILLNOT	COLLECTING
	GEOCENTRIC	CCEGIMMNNO	COMMENCING
CCEEGNNORU	CONGRUENCE	CCEGINNNOR	CONCERNING
CCEEHIIMTT	HECTIC TIME	CCEGINNNOS	ENSCONCING
CCEEHIIOSW	WISE CHOICE	CCEGINNNOT	CONNECTING
CCEEHINOSS	CHOICENESS	CCEGINNORT	CONCRETING
CCEEHKORSV	CHECKS OVER	CCEGINORRT	CORRECTING
CCEEHLORST	CERECLOTHS	CCEGINORSY	CRYOGENICS
CCEEHLORSW	SCREECH OWL	CCEHHILOTV	CLOVE HITCH
CCEEHNOSTU	ESCUTCHEON	CCEHIILNNS	IN CLINCHES
CCEEHORRST	CROCHETERS	CCEHIINNNO	CINCHONINE
CCEEHOSTTU	COUCHETTES	CCEHIIRSTT	THE CRITICS
CCEEIIINNP	INCIPIENCE	CCEHIKLSST	CHECKLISTS
CCEEIIILLNR	CIRCLE LINE	CCEHIKNNRU	CHICKEN RUN
CCEEIIILMRS	SEMICIRCLE	CCEHIKNOPT	CHECK POINT
CCEEIIPPRS	PRECIPICES		CHECKPOINT
CCEEIKLLLS	SICKLE-CELL	CCEHIKNOSY	COCKNEYISH
CCEEIKRRST	CRICKETERS	CCEHIKNOTU	CHICKEN OUT
CCEEILLOTV	COLLECTIVE	CCEHILNOOY	ONLY CHOICE
CCEEILMNNY	INCLEMENCY	CCEHILNORR	CHRONICLER
CCEEILNORR	RECONCILER	CCEHILNORS	CHRONICLES
CCEEILNORS	RECONCILES	CCEHILOOPR	PLEOCHROIC
CCEEILNORT	ELECTRONIC	CCEHINOPST	SCOTCH PINE
CCEEILOPST	TELESCOPIC	CCEHINORST	CHRONICEST
CCEEIMORSV	COMIC VERSE	CCEHINRSTU	CRUNCHIEST

CCEHIOOOPR	POOR CHOICE	CCFIILNNOT	IN CONFLICT
CCEHIOORUY	YOUR CHOICE	CCFKLOOORU	FOUR O CLOCK
CCEHIORRSU	RICH SOURCE	CCGHHHHIRU	HIGH CHURCH
CCEHKMOORS	CHECKROOMS	CCGHHOORTU	GO TO CHURCH
CCEHKOPSST	SPOT-CHECKS	CCGHIIKNNU	CHUCKING IN
CCEHKORTUU	CHUCKER-OUT	CCGHIIKNTU	CHUCKING IT
CCEHMOORTY	CYTOCHROME	CCGHIINPPU	HICCUPPING
CCEHNORSTU	ON CRUTCHES	CCGHIKNPUU	CHUCKING UP
CCEHOSTTTU	CUT THE COST	CCGHINNRSU	SCRUNCHING
CCEHOSTTUZ	ZUCCHETTOS	CCGHLNOOOY	CONCHOLOGY
CCEIIINNPY	INCIPIENCY	CCGIIKNNP	PICNICKING
CCEIIIRSST	CRITICISES	CCGIIKLNNO	CLOCKING IN
CCEIIIRSTZ	CRITICIZES	CCGIILNRTY	TRICYCLING
CCEIILOPTY	CITY POLICE	CCGIINNNOV	CONVINCING
CCEIILOSST	SOLECISTIC	CCGIINNOTV	CONVICTING
CCEIILSSTT	CELTICISTS	CCGIKLNNOO	CLOCKING ON
CCEIIMOORS	SERIOCOMIC	CCGILLOTYY	GLYCOLYTIC
CCEIIMOTXY	MEXICO CITY	CCGILMOOOS	COSMOLOGIC
CCEIIMPSST	SCEPTICISM	CCGILORSUY	GLYCOSURIC
CCEIINPRTU	CUT IN PRICE	CCGIMNOOOS	COSMOGONIC
CCEIINRTTY	CENTRICITY	CCGINNORRU	CONCURRING
CCEIIOPPRS	PERISCOPIC	CCGINNOSSU	CONCUSSING
CCEIKKNORR	CORNER KICK	CCGINORSUU	SUCCOURING
CCEIKKNOTW	KNOCK TWICE	CCGIOOPRSY	GYROSCOPIC
CCEIKKOPPT	PICKPOCKET	CCHHHOOPTT	HOTCHPOTCH
CCEIKLLOSY	KILOCYCLES	CCHIIKNSTU	CHUCKS IT IN
CCEIKLNNOO	NINE O CLOCK	CCHIINORTY	CHRONICITY
CCEIKMNOSY	COCKNEYISM	CCHIKLNQUU	QUICK LUNCH
CCEIKNORTT	NOT CRICKET	CCHIKLOSTT	LOCKSTITCH
CCEILLNOOT	COLLECTION	CCHIKOPSST	CHOPSTICKS
CCEILNOSUV	CONCLUSIVE	CCHIKOTTUU	CHUCK IT OUT
CCEILOSTTU	CUT IT CLOSE	CCHIMOSSTT	SCOTCH MIST
CCEIMNNOOU	UNECONOMIC	CCHINNORSY	SYNCHRONIC
CCEIMNRTUV	CIRCUMVENT	CCHIORSTTY	TRICHOCYST
CCEIMOOPRS	MICROSCOPE	CCHKLNOSUU	NO SUCH LUCK
CCEINNNOOT	CONNECTION	CCHMMNOOPU	NOT MUCH COP
CCEINNOOPT	CONCEPTION	CCHNOOSTUY	COCONUT SHY
CCEINNOORT	CONCERTINO	CCHOOPSSUU	HOCUS POCUS
	CONCRETION		HOCUS-POCUS
CCEINNOOSS	CONCESSION	CCIIIMRSST	CRITICISMS
CCEINNOOTV	CONVECTION	CCIILMNNOO	MONOCLINIC
CCEINOOPPR	COPPER COIN	CCIILMOPTY	COMPLICITY
CCEINOORRT	CORRECTION	CCIILNSTUY	UNICYCLIST
CCEINOSSSU	SUCCESSION	CCIILOOPRT	COPROLITIC
CCEINOSSUV	CONCUSSIVE	CCIILOOPST	PICCOLOIST
CCEIOOPRSU	PRECOCIOUS	CCIILORTUV	CIVIL COURT
CCEIOOTTXY	EXOCYTOTIC	CCIILRSTTY	TRICYCLIST
CCEKKNNOOS	KNOCKS ONCE	CCIIMOPRST	COMIC STRIP
CCEKKORTUY	TURKEY COCK	CCIIMOSSTT	SCOTTICISM
CCEKLOORTW	CLOCK TOWER	CCIINNNOTY	CONCINNITY
CCEKLORSUY	COCKSURELY	CCIINNOOTV	CONVICTION
CCEKORRSSW	CORKSCREWS	CCIIORSTUU	CIRCUITOUS
CCELLOORST	COLLECTORS	CCIKNOOPTU	CUCKOO PINT
CCELLOSTYY	CYCLOSTYLE		CUCKOOPINT
CCELMOORTY	MOTOR CYCLE	CCILLNOORU	COUNCILLOR
	MOTORCYCLE	CCILMRRUUU	CURRICULUM
CCELMOOSTY	CYCLOSTOME	CCILNNOOSU	CONCLUSION
CCELNRTUUY	TRUCULENCY	CCILNOOOTU	COCONUT OIL
CCELOPRSSU	CORPUSCLES	CCILNOORSU	COUNCILORS
CCENNOORST	CONNECTORS	CCILNOOSSU	OCCLUSIONS
CCENNORRTU	CONCURRENT	CCIMOOPRSY	MICROSCOPY
CCENOOPPRT	POP CONCERT	CCINNOOSSU	CONCUSSION
CCENOORSSU	CONCOURSES	CCINOPRSST	CONSCRIPTS
CCENOORSTV	CONVECTORS	CCINORSSTT	CONSTRICTS
CCENOPSSTU	CONSPECTUS	CCINOSTUVY	VISCOUNTCY
CCENORRSTU	CUT CORNERS	CCIORRSSSS	CRISSCROSS
CCEOORRRST	CORRECTORS	CCKNOORTUY	COUNTY CORK
CCEORSSSSU	SUCCESSORS	CCLNOORSTY	CYCLOTRONS
CCFGIINRUY	CRUCIFYING	CCNOORRTUW	CROWN COURT
CCFIIILMRT	FILM CRITIC	CCNORSSTTU	CONSTRUCTS
		CCOORRSSTU	CROSSCOURT

CDDDEEGGGLO	CODDLED EGG	CDDNOORRUW	CROWD ROUND
CDDDEEIKLM	MIDDLE DECK	CDEEEEFNRR	REFERENCED
CDDEEEHIOR	HEROIC DEED	CDEEEEGLTT	GET ELECTED
CDDEEEHIPR	DECIPHERED	CDEEEEHRSS	RED CHEESES
CDDEEEINRT	INTERCEDED	CDEEEEENRRT	DETERRENCE
CDDEEEINUV	UNDECEIVED	CDEEEEENRRV	REVERENCED
CDDEEEIRRT	REDIRECTED	CDEEEFFHOS	CHEESED OFF
CDDEEEJLTY	DEJECTEDLY	CDEEEFFINR	DIFFERENCE
CDDEEEELNOR	NEEDLECORD	CDEEEFFIST	SIDE EFFECT
CDDEEEENNPY	DEPENDENCY	CDEEEFFORS	FORCE FEEDS
CDDEEENRSU	DESCENDEUR		FORCE-FEEDS
CDDEEENTTU	UNDETECTED	CDEEEFILTV	DEFLECTIVE
CDDEEFFIIN	DIFFIDENCE	CDEEEFISTV	DEFECTIVES
CDDEEFOSSU	DEFOCUSSED	CDEEEGIIPR	RIDGEPIECE
CDDEEGINNS	DESCENDING	CDEEEGINRV	DIVERGENCE
CDDEEHOSUU	DUD CHEQUES	CDEEEGITTX	GET EXCITED
CDDEEIINSS	DISSIDENCE	CDEEEGLOTT	GOT ELECTED
CDDEEIJPRU	PREJUDICED	CDEEEHHISS	CHEESE DISH
CDDEEILNRY	CYLINDERED	CDEEEHINPR	ENCIPHERED
CDDEEINORS	CONSIDERED	CDEEEHIPRR	DECIPHERER
CDDEEINORT	DONE CREDIT	CDEEEHIRRT	ERIC THE RED
CDDEEINPRS	PRESCINDED	CDEEEHNNRT	ENTRENCHED
CDDEEIORSV	DISCOVERED	CDEEEHNRRT	RETRENCHED
CDDEEKMRXY	EDDY MERCKX	CDEEEHORVW	CHEWED OVER
CDDEELLSUY	SECLUDEDLY	CDEEEINNNV	IN EVIDENCE
CDDEELMOSU	CUDDLESOME	CDEEEIINRS	DECREE NISI
CDDEEMNOTU	DOCUMENTED	CDEEEILOPV	VELOCIPEDE
CDDEEMOOPS	DECOMPOSED	CDEEEILQSU	DELIQUESCE
CDDEENORSW	DENSE CROWD	CDEEEIMRRS	MERCERISED
CDDEEOPRRU	REPRODUCED	CDEEEIMRRZ	MERCERIZED
CDDEERSTTU	DESTRUCTED	CDEEEIMRST	DECIMETRES
CDDEFIKORS	DISFROCKED	CDEEEINNST	TENDENCIES
CDDEFNNOOU	CONFOUNDED	CDEEEINPST	CENTIPEDES
CDDEGILNOS	GOLDEN DISC	CDEEEINPXY	EXPEDIENCY
CDDEGIOORT	GOOD CREDIT	CDEEEINRSS	RESIDENCES
CDDEGLOORR	GOLD RECORD	CDEEEINRST	INTERCEDES
CDDEGLOORS	OLD CODGERS	CDEEEINRSW	WIDE SCREEN
CDDEGNOOOS	GOOD SECOND		WIDE-SCREEN
CDDEGNOORR	CORN DODGER	CDEEEINSUV	UNDECEIVES
CDDEGOOORR	GOOD RECORD	CDEEEIOPSV	DEEP VOICES
CDDEHIILOR	DICHLORIDE	CDEEEISTTV	DETECTIVES
CDDEHILOSS	COLD DISHES	CDEEEKNOSW	SECOND WEEK
CDDEHKNOOW	CHOKED DOWN	CDEEELOPST	TELESCOPED
CDDEHLOOPP	COPPED HOLD	CDEEELORST	ELECTRODES
CDDEIIJSTU	DID JUSTICE	CDEEELOSSY	CLOSED EYES
CDDEIIOSSV	VIDEODISCS	CDEEELPTXY	EXPECTEDLY
CDDEIIRSST	DISCREDITS	CDEEENPRST	PRECEDENTS
CDDEILMNOS	CLOSED MIND	CDEEENPTUX	UNEXPECTED
CDDEIMMNOO	INCOMMODED	CDEEEPRSTU	DUE RESPECT
CDDEIMOOSU	DUODECIMOS		PERSECUTED
CDDEINNOSW	SECOND WIND	CDEEFFHILO	HELD OFFICE
CDDEINOOPW	COPIED DOWN	CDEEFFIKOS	OFFICE DESK
CDDEINORTU	INTRODUCED	CDEEFGILNT	DEFLECTING
CDDEINOSTU	DEDUCTIONS	CDEEFIINRT	DENTIFRICE
	DISCOUNTED	CDEEFIIPRX	FIXED PRICE
CDDEIORSSU	DISCOURSED	CDEEFILNNU	INFLUENCED
CDDEKLLOOO	LOOKED COLD	CDEEFILNOT	DEFLECTION
CDDEKLOOOR	LOCKED DOOR	CDEEFINORR	REINFORCED
CDDELNOOOW	COOLED DOWN	CDEEFINOST	DEFECTIONS
CDDELNOOSW	CLOSED DOWN	CDEEFINOSW	SECOND WIFE
CDDELNORTU	TURNED COLD	CDEEFKLPSY	FLYSPECKED
CDDELOOORS	CLOSED DOOR	CDEEFLNORT	CENTREFOLD
CDDELOORRS	OLD RECORDS	CDEEFLOORS	FORECLOSED
CDDEMNOOPU	COMPOUNDED	CDEEFLORST	DEFLECTORS
CDDENOPRTU	END PRODUCT	CDEEFNNORU	FENCE ROUND
CDDEOORTUW	CROWDED OUT	CDEEFNOOPR	FORCED OPEN
CDDGILNPUU	CUDDLING UP	CDEEFOORST	DOCTORS FEE
CDDHHIILRT	THIRD CHILD	CDEEGGKSSU	SUCKED EGGS
CDDHHILOOS	CHILDHOODS	CDEEGHHITT	GET HITCHED
CDDIKLNORS	COLD DRINKS	CDEEGHOOPS	GOOD SPEECH
CDDILOOPSU	DIPLODOCUS	CDEEGIIMRS	GERMICIDES

519

CDEEGIINNV	EVIDENCING	CDEEIILPRTY	DECREPITLY
CDEEGIINPY	PIECE-DYING	CDEEIILRRTU	DIRECT RULE
CDEEGIIRTV	GIVE CREDIT	CDEEIILRRVY	RIVER CLYDE
CDEEGIKNNR	RING-NECKED	CDEEIILRSTY	DISCREETLY
CDEEGILNNU	INDULGENCE		DISCRETELY
CDEEGILNUV	DIVULGENCE	CDEEIMMORS	MESODERMIC
CDEEGINNOR	ENDERGONIC	CDEEIMMNNSU	DECENNIUMS
CDEEGINOPR	PROCEEDING	CDEEIMMNNTU	INDUCEMENT
CDEEGINORS	RECOGNISED	CDEEIMNOOS	ECONOMISED
CDEEGINORT	GONE DIRECT	CDEEIMNOOZ	ECONOMIZED
CDEEGINORZ	RECOGNIZED	CDEEIMNOST	SECOND TIME
CDEEGIOOPS	PIECE GOODS	CDEEIMNPRU	IMPRUDENCE
CDEEGIORST	GOES DIRECT	CDEEIMNSTU	INTUMESCED
CDEEGIOTTX	GOT EXCITED	CDEEIMORRT	RECORD TIME
CDEEGOOSUX	GOOD EXCUSE	CDEEINNRSW	WINDSCREEN
CDEEHHIKTT	HIT THE DECK	CDEEINOPRT	OPEN CREDIT
CDEEHIMNOR	ECHINODERM	CDEEINOPRV	PROVIDENCE
CDEEHINNRT	INTRENCHED	CDEEINOPST	DECEPTIONS
CDEEHINRST	CHRISTENED	CDEEINORRS	RECONSIDER
CDEEHKOSSU	DECKHOUSES	CDEEINORTT	CREDIT NOTE
CDEEHKRSTU	HUCKSTERED	CDEEINOSSV	VOICEDNESS
CDEEHLNOSU	ON SCHEDULE	CDEEINPRRU	UNDERPRICE
CDEEHLORSU	LOUD CHEERS	CDEEINPRSY	PRESIDENCY
CDEEHLRSSU	SCHEDULERS	CDEEINRRSS	DISCERNERS
CDEEHLRTWY	WRETCHEDLY	CDEEINRSST	DIRECTNESS
CDEEHMNOOS	SECOND HOME	CDEEINRSTY	DYSENTERIC
CDEEHMNOPR	COMPREHEND	CDEEIORRSV	DISCOVERER
CDEEHNOSST	THE SECONDS	CDEEIORRVV	COVER DRIVE
CDEEIIINSV	INDECISIVE	CDEEIPRSST	DISRESPECT
CDEEIILNRT	DIRECT LINE	CDEEIRRSTT	DERESTRICT
CDEEIILRST	DECILITRES		RESTRICTED
CDEEIILSVY	DECISIVELY	CDEEISTUXY	EXCISE DUTY
CDEEIIMNOS	COME INSIDE	CDEEKKKNNO	KNOCK-KNEED
CDEEIIMNRS	REMINISCED	CDEEKKLRSS	DESK CLERKS
CDEEIIMNTY	ENDEMICITY	CDEEKNNOOR	RECKONED ON
CDEEIIMPRR	PERIDERMIC	CDEEKNOPRU	RECKONED UP
CDEEIIMPRS	SPERMICIDE	CDEEKOOPRW	WOODPECKER
CDEEIINPRX	PRICE INDEX	CDEELLNRSU	CULLENDERS
CDEEIINRST	INDISCREET	CDEEMMNORS	RECOMMENDS
	INDISCRETE	CDEEMNNOOU	COME UNDONE
	IRIDESCENT	CDEEMNNOST	SECONDMENT
CDEEIIOPST	POETICISED	CDEEMNORST	SECOND TERM
CDEEIIOPTZ	POETICIZED	CDEEMNORSU	COMES UNDER
CDEEIIPRRS	CIRRIPEDES	CDEEMOOPRS	DECOMPOSER
CDEEIIPRTV	PREDICTIVE	CDEEMOOPSS	DECOMPOSES
CDEEIIPSST	PESTICIDES	CDEEMOPRSS	COMPRESSED
CDEEIIRSSV	DISSERVICE		DECOMPRESS
CDEEIIRSTV	DIRECTIVES	CDEENNORSS	CONDENSERS
CDEEIISTVV	VIVISECTED	CDEENNORST	CONTENDERS
CDEEIJPRSU	PREJUDICES	CDEENNORSU	DENOUNCERS
CDEEIKKORV	KICKED OVER	CDEENNOSST	TEN SECONDS
CDEEIKNNST	DECK TENNIS	CDEENNOTTU	COUNTED TEN
CDEEIKNSSW	WICKEDNESS	CDEENOOPSS	ENDOSCOPES
CDEEIKOPST	SIDE POCKET	CDEENOORSU	UNDERSCORE
CDEEIKORTV	TICKED OVER	CDEENORRSW	NEW RECORDS
CDEEILMNSU	LUMINESCED	CDEENORRUV	UNDER COVER
CDEEILNNOS	DECLENSION		UNDERCOVER
	SECOND LINE	CDEENOSSTT	SECOND TEST
CDEEILNNOY	DONE NICELY	CDEENRSSSU	CURSEDNESS
CDEEILNNSU	UNLICENSED	CDEENSSSSU	CUSSEDNESS
CDEEILNNTY	INDECENTLY	CDEEOOORRST	SECRET DOOR
CDEEILNOOS	DECOLONISE	CDEEOOORRVW	CROWED OVER
CDEEILNOOZ	DECOLONIZE	CDEEOOORSTT	STOOD ERECT
CDEEILNORS	SCREEN IDOL	CDEEOOORSTY	EYE DOCTORS
CDEEILNOSU	NUCLEOSIDE	CDEEOPPRST	PROSPECTED
CDEEILNOSY	DOES NICELY	CDEEOPPRRS	PRERECORDS
CDEEILNOTU	NUCLEOTIDE	CDEEOPRRRU	REPRODUCER
CDEEILNPRS	RED PENCILS	CDEEOPRRSU	PROCEDURES
CDEEILOORS	DECOLORISE		REPRODUCES
CDEEILOORZ	DECOLORIZE	CDEEOPRSSU	DUE PROCESS
CDEEILORST	CLOISTERED	CDEEOPRSTU	PROSECUTED

CDEERSSSTU	SEDUCTRESS	CDEHINOSTW	SWITCHED ON
CDEFFHILOO	HOLD OFFICE		SWITCHED-ON
CDEFFHOOTU	TOUCHED OFF	CDEHIPSTTU	STITCHED UP
CDEFFIIRTU	FRUCTIFIED	CDEHIPSTUW	SWITCHED UP
CDEFFKKNOO	KNOCKED OFF	CDEHKNOOSW	CHOKES DOWN
CDEFFOORSS	CROSSED OFF	CDEHLLOOSS	HOLDS CLOSE
CDEFGHIKLT	FLIGHT DECK	CDEHLLOOST	OLD CLOTHES
CDEFGIINSU	FUNGICIDES	CDEHLNOOSU	UNSCHOOLED
CDEFGIKNOR	DEFROCKING	CDEHLNORRU	ORDER LUNCH
CDEFGINOOR	FORGED COIN	CDEHLNORSU	CHONDRULES
CDEFGINOSU	DEFOCUSING	CDEHLOOPPR	CLODHOPPER
CDEFHIKOOS	DIE OF SHOCK	CDEHLOOPRY	COPYHOLDER
CDEFHOORSW	HERD OF COWS	CDEHLOOPSS	CLOSED SHOP
CDEFHOORUV	VOUCHED FOR	CDEHLOORSW	COLD SHOWER
CDEFIIILS	SILICIFIED	CDEHMMNOOR	COMMON HERD
CDEFIIINSST	DISINFECTS	CDEHNORTUU	CHURNED OUT
CDEFILLOST	COD FILLETS	CDEHOOPRRS	RECORD SHOP
CDEFILNOUU	FLUID OUNCE	CDEHOPSTUY	PSYCHED OUT
CDEFIINNNOU	UNCONFINED	CDEHOPTTUY	TOUCH-TYPED
CDEFINNOTU	FUNCTIONED	CDEIIILNPS	DISCIPLINE
CDEFLNOSUY	CONFUSEDLY	CDEIIIMRSV	RECIDIVISM
CDEFMNOORS	SECOND FORM	CDEIIIMSTV	VICTIMISED
CDEFNNOORT	CONFRONTED	CDEIIIMTVZ	VICTIMIZED
CDEFNNOORU	CONFOUNDER	CDEIIINNOS	INDECISION
CDEFNORRTU	UNDERCROFT	CDEIIINNOT	COINED IT IN
CDEGGILLNU	CUDGELLING	CDEIIINTVV	VINDICTIVE
CDEGHHIMOY	HIGH COMEDY	CDEIIIRSTV	RECIDIVIST
CDEGHHIOTT	GOT HITCHED	CDEIIKLLLP	DILL PICKLE
CDEGHILNSU	SCHEDULING	CDEIIKPPTU	PICKED IT UP
CDEGHINNRU	CHUNDERING	CDEIILNPPR	PRINCIPLED
CDEGHJOTUU	TOUCH JUDGE	CDEIILNRTY	INDIRECTLY
CDEGIIINNRS	DISCERNING	CDEIILOSTU	SOLICITUDE
	RESCINDING	CDEIILRSSV	SILVER DISC
CDEGIIINPRT	PREDICTING	CDEIIMNNTT	INDICTMENT
CDEGIIINSST	DISSECTING	CDEIIMNOTY	TIDY INCOME
CDEGIKNOST	STOCKINGED	CDEIIMORRS	MISERICORD
CDEGIKOOTW	GOOD WICKET	CDEIIMORST	DOSIMETRIC
CDEGILMMNO	COMMINGLED	CDEIIMORTY	MEDIOCRITY
CDEGILNOOR	COLD REGION	CDEIIMPPSU	PIPED MUSIC
CDEGILNOPU	DECOUPLING	CDEIIMRSST	MISDIRECTS
CDEGILNPRU	PRECLUDING	CDEIINOPRT	PREDICTION
CDEGIMMNNO	COMMENDING	CDEIINOPST	DEPICTIONS
CDEGIMMNNO	CONDEMNING	CDEIINORST	DIRECTIONS
CDEGINNNOS	CONDENSING		DISCRETION
CDEGINNNOT	CONTENDING	CDEIINOSST	DISSECTION
CDEGINNNOU	DENOUNCING	CDEIINRSTT	INTERDICTS
CDEGINOOOT	GOOD NOTICE	CDEIIORTTY	CITY EDITOR
CDEGINOPSY	SIGNED COPY	CDEIIRSSUV	DISCURSIVE
CDEGINORRS	RECORDINGS	CDEIIRSTTT	STRICT DIET
CDEGINORRU	GROUND RICE	CDEIKLLSUV	DEVILS LUCK
CDEGLNOOTU	COLD TONGUE	CDEIKLLUVY	LUCKY DEVIL
CDEGLORSST	GOLDCRESTS	CDEIKLOPST	STOCKPILED
CDEGMNORUU	CURMUDGEON	CDEIKOORTT	TOOK CREDIT
CDEGNOOORR	GO ON RECORD	CDEIKOQSTU	DECK QUOITS
CDEGNORRUW	GROUND CREW	CDEILLLOSU	CELLULOIDS
CDEHHHIIKT	HITCH HIKED	CDEILLLOVY	CLIVE LLOYD
	HITCHHIKED	CDEILLLPUY	PELLUCIDLY
CDEHHIIRRT	THIRD REICH	CDEILNOORS	OLD CRONIES
CDEHHIJNOR	JOHN EDRICH	CDEILNOPSS	SECOND SLIP
CDEHIIMSTY	MYTHICISED	CDEILNORTW	COLD WINTER
CDEHIIMTYZ	MYTHICIZED	CDEILNOSSU	CLOUDINESS
CDEHIINOST	HEDONISTIC	CDEILOPSUU	PEDICULOUS
CDEHIKORTT	DO THE TRICK	CDEILORSSS	DISCLOSERS
CDEHILOPTW	LOW-PITCHED	CDEILORSSU	DISCLOSURE
CDEHILOSTW	OLD WITCHES	CDEIMMNOOS	INCOMMODES
CDEHILOTUW	WHITE CLOUD	CDEIMMNOPU	COMPENDIUM
CDEHILRRWY	WILD CHERRY	CDEIMMNOSU	COMMUNISED
CDEHIMOPRY	HYPODERMIC	CDEIMMNOTU	COMMINUTED
CDEHIMORST	COMES THIRD	CDEIMMNOUZ	COMMUNIZED
CDEHINOPTY	ENDOPHYTIC	CDEIMNNOST	CONDIMENTS
		CDEIMNOOST	ENDOSMOTIC

CDEIMNOOSY	DISECONOMY	CDFHLOOOPS	COPS HOLD OF
CDEIMNORSW	MINCE WORDS	CDFHNOOTUU	FOUND TOUCH
CDEIMNOSTU	MISCOUNTED	CDFIIMOSST	DISCOMFITS
CDEIMOOPSS	DISCOMPOSE	CDFIMOORST	DISCOMFORT
CDEIMOOSTY	DICTYOSOME	CDGGHINOTU	GOING DUTCH
CDEIMOSSTU	CUSTOMISED	CDGHILLOST	SLIGHT COLD
CDEIMOSTUZ	CUSTOMIZED	CDGHILNOST	COLD NIGHTS
CDEINNOSTT	DISCONTENT	CDGHILNOUY	YOUNG CHILD
CDEINOOPRS	ENDOSPORIC	CDGHILOORY	HYDROLOGIC
CDEINOOPSW	COPIES DOWN	CDGHLOOOOS	GOOD SCHOOL
CDEINOORSU	INDECOROUS	CDGIIILMNO	DOMICILING
CDEINORSTU	INTRODUCES	CDGIIILNRU	RIDICULING
	REDUCTIONS	CDGIIKNNOO	IN GOOD NICK
CDEINORTUW	TWICE ROUND	CDGIILNOSS	DISCLOSING
CDEINOSSTU	SEDUCTIONS	CDGIINOPRR	RIDING CROP
CDEINRSTTU	INSTRUCTED	CDGIINSSSU	DISCUSSING
CDEIOORRTY	ROY DOTRICE	CDGILNOOSU	SOUND LOGIC
CDEIOPRTUV	PRODUCTIVE	CDGIMNNOOW	COMING DOWN
CDEIORRSST	RECORDISTS	CDGINNORWY	CRYING DOWN
CDEIORRSSU	DISCOURSER	CDGKLORSTU	STRUCK GOLD
CDEIORSSSU	DISCOURSES	CDGMMNOOOO	COMMON GOOD
CDEJNOPRUU	CONJURED UP	CDGNNOORRU	GROUND CORN
CDEKKNOOTU	KNOCKED OUT	CDHHIILLSY	CHILDISHLY
CDEKLLOOOO	LOOKED COOL	CDHHILOSST	DISH CLOTHS
CDEKLORTUY	COLD TURKEY	CDHHIMNOOR	CHIRONOMID
CDELLLOPSS	COLD SPELLS	CDHIIOSSTU	DISTICHOUS
CDELLNOORT	CONTROLLED	CDHIKLOORY	OLD HICKORY
CDELLOOPSU	OLD COUPLES	CDHIKLOOSS	SCHOOLKIDS
CDELMOOPSY	COMPOSEDLY	CDHILLORSY	CHRIS LLOYD
CDELMPPRUU	CRUMPLED UP	CDHILOORSV	DICHLORVOS
CDELNOOSSW	CLOSEDOWNS	CDHILORTYY	HYDROLYTIC
	CLOSES DOWN	CDHILORXYY	HYDROXYLIC
CDELNOOTUV	CONVOLUTED	CDHILPTTUU	DUTCH TULIP
CDELNORSSU	SCOUNDRELS	CDHIMNOORR	MINOR CHORD
CDELOOORUV	DOVE-COLOUR	CDHIMNOORY	MONOHYDRIC
CDELOORSUV	CLOUDS OVER	CDHINOOOSU	COUSINHOOD
	OVERCLOUDS	CDHINOOPRY	HYDROPONIC
CDELOORSUY	DECOROUSLY	CDHIOOPRST	DOCTORSHIP
CDELPRSTUU	SCULPTURED	CDHKNNPRUU	PUNCH DRUNK
CDEMMOOORS	COMMODORES		PUNCH-DRUNK
	COSMODROME	CDHKNOORSU	ROCK HUDSON
CDEMNOOPRU	COMPOUNDER	CDHLLMNOOO	LOCH LOMOND
CDEMNOORSU	COMES ROUND	CDHLOORSTU	HOLDS COURT
CDENNOOORS	DES O'CONNOR	CDHMNOOORS	MONOCHORDS
CDENNOOOTT	COTTONED ON	CDHNOOOTTU	DO NOT TOUCH
CDENNOOPRU	PRONOUNCED	CDHNOOSTUW	TOUCHDOWNS
CDENOOOPRS	POOR SECOND	CDIIINNSTT	INDISTINCT
CDENOOPRRS	CORRESPOND	CDIIIOSSUV	SID VICIOUS
CDENOOPRSS	DROP SCONES	CDIIKNPRTU	DICK TURPIN
CDENOOSSTU	SECONDS OUT	CDIIKRRTTY	DIRTY TRICK
CDENOOSSTW	TWO SECONDS	CDIILNSTTY	DISTINCTLY
CDENOOTTUU	COUNTED OUT	CDIILORSUU	RIDICULOUS
CDENORSSWW	SCREWS DOWN	CDIINNOOST	CONDITIONS
CDEOOOPSTU	SCOOPED OUT	CDIINNOSTU	INDUCTIONS
CDEOOPPRRS	POP RECORDS	CDIINOSSSU	DISCUSSION
CDEOOPPRTU	OUTCROPPED	CDIKLNOORS	COOL DRINKS
CDEOORRRTU	COURT ORDER	CDIKMRSTU	DRUMSTICKS
CDEOORRSVW	OVERCROWDS	CDIKORSSTW	SWORDSTICK
CDEOORSSTU	CROSSED OUT	CDILMOOORX	LOXODROMIC
CDEOORTTUW	WOODCUTTER	CDILMOOPUY	LYCOPODIUM
CDEOOSTTUU	SCOUTED OUT	CDILMORSUW	MUSIC WORLD
CDEORRSSTU	COURT DRESS	CDILOORSSU	DISCOLOURS
CDEORRSTTU	DESTRUCTOR	CDIMMOOOSU	COMMODIOUS
CDEORSSTUV	DUST COVERS	CDIMSSTUUY	STUDY MUSIC
	DUSTCOVERS	CDINOOPRTU	PRODUCTION
CDERRSTTUU	STRUCTURED	CDINORSSSW	CROSS WINDS
CDFFIILTUY	DIFFICULTY		CROSSWINDS
CDFFNOOORS	CORDONS OFF	CDKKNNOOSW	KNOCKDOWNS
CDFHIILRST	FIRST CHILD		KNOCKS DOWN
CDFHILOOPR	CHILDPROOF	CDKNORSTUW	STRUCK DOWN
CDFHINOSTU	FINDS TOUCH	CDLLLOORUU	DULL COLOUR

CDLLOOORUU	LOUD COLOUR
CDLMOORSTU	STORM CLOUD
CDLMOOSSTU	OLD CUSTOMS
CDLNOORTUY	OLD COUNTRY
CDLOORRTUW	WORLD COURT
CDLOORTUUY	CRY OUT LOUD
CDMNNORSUU	CONUNDRUMS
CDNNOOSTUW	COUNTDOWNS
	COUNTS DOWN
CDNNOOTUWY	COUNTY DOWN
CDNOOOTTWW	COTTONWOOD
CDNOORSTUU	SCOUT ROUND
CDOOOOPSTU	OCTOPODOUS
CDOORRSSSW	CROSS WORDS
CEEEEFFRSV	EFFERVESCE
CEEEEFHPRS	FREE SPEECH
CEEEEFLRSU	FEEL SECURE
CEEEEFNPRR	PREFERENCE
CEEEEFNRRS	REFERENCES
CEEEEGMNRS	EMERGENCES
CEEEEHNPRT	THREE PENCE
CEEEEHNRST	SCENE THREE
CEEEEIMRST	CEMETERIES
CEEEEINPRX	EXPERIENCE
CEEEEIRSSV	SEE SERVICE
CEEEEKPRST	KEEP SECRET
CEEEENNPSV	SEVEN PENCE
CEEEENRRRV	REVERENCER
CEEEENRRSV	REVERENCES
CEEEFFGLNU	EFFULGENCE
CEEEFFHIRR	ERIC HEFFER
CEEEFFHNRR	FREE FRENCH
CEEEFFIKOS	SEEK OFFICE
CEEEFFISTV	EFFECTIVES
CEEEFFLNSU	EFFLUENCES
CEEEFFLORS	EFFLORESCE
CEEEFGLNRU	REFULGENCE
CEEEFHIOST	SHEET OF ICE
CEEEFHNNOT	ON THE FENCE
CEEEFHORRS	SHEER FORCE
CEEEFIKRTT	FREE TICKET
CEEEFILRST	SECRET FILE
	SECRET LIFE
CEEEFILRTV	REFLECTIVE
CEEEFINNRS	INFERENCES
CEEEFINRRS	FIRE SCREEN
CEEEFINRSS	FIERCENESS
CEEEFIOPRS	FREE COPIES
CEEEFIPRTV	PERFECTIVE
CEEEFLRSTU	FELT SECURE
CEEEFPRRTU	PREFECTURE
CEEEGGILNN	NEGLIGENCE
CEEEGGLOOR	GEORGE COLE
CEEEGHINPT	EIGHT PENCE
CEEEGIINPT	EPIGENETIC
CEEEGIINSX	EXIGENCIES
CEEEGINRST	ENERGETICS
CEEEGLLNOW	NEW COLLEGE
CEEEGNRRSU	RESURGENCE
CEEEHHKORT	OTHER CHEEK
CEEEHIIPTW	WHITE PIECE
CEEEHIKNSS	CHEEKINESS
CEEEHIKRSV	KERCHIEVES
CEEEHILMTT	MELT THE ICE
CEEEHINRSS	CHEERINESS
CEEEHINSSS	CHEESINESS
CEEEHIRTTW	TWICE THREE
CEEEHJLNOS	JOHN CLEESE
CEEEHKPRTU	UP THE CREEK
CEEEHLLORS	CHEESE ROLL
CEEEHLLSSY	SEYCHELLES
CEEEHLMOOT	COME TO HEEL
CEEEHLPSSS	SPEECHLESS
CEEEHNNRST	ENTRENCHES
CEEEHNOPQU	OPEN CHEQUE
CEEEHNORSS	CHERSONESE
CEEEHNRRST	RETRENCHES
CEEEHORRST	THREE SCORE
	THREESCORE
CEEEHQRSUX	EXCHEQUERS
CEEEHRRRTY	CHERRY TREE
CEEEIILNRS	RESILIENCE
CEEEIIMPST	TIMEPIECES
CEEEIINNOP	IN ONE PIECE
CEEEIKKPTW	KEEP WICKET
CEEEIKNOPS	KEEPS ON ICE
CEEEIILPRV	PRICE LEVEL
CEEEIILTVY	ELECTIVELY
CEEEILMNNT	CLEMENTINE
CEEEILMRTT	TELEMETRIC
CEEEILNOPP	NICE PEOPLE
CEEEILNPRT	PERCENTILE
CEEEILNPST	PESTILENCE
CEEEIMNNTT	ENTICEMENT
CEEEIMNORS	CEREMONIES
CEEEIMNRST	MESENTERIC
CEEEIMNRSV	SERVICEMEN
CEEEIMNRTT	CENTIMETRE
CEEEIMNTTX	EXCITEMENT
CEEEIMRRSS	MERCERISES
CEEEIMRRSZ	MERCERIZES
CEEEINNPRT	PERTINENCE
CEEEINNQSU	IN SEQUENCE
CEEEINOPSS	NOSEPIECES
CEEEINPRST	EPICENTRES
CEEEINSSTX	EXISTENCES
CEEEINSTVW	TWICE SEVEN
CEEEINTTWY	WINCEYETTE
CEEEIORRST	CORSETIERE
CEEEIORRSV	RECOVERIES
CEEEIPPRST	STEEP PRICE
CEEEIPPRTV	PERCEPTIVE
	PRECEPTIVE
CEEEIPRSSV	EPIC VERSES
CEEEIPRSTV	RESPECTIVE
CEEEIRTTXY	EXETER CITY
CEEEISTUVX	EXECUTIVES
CEEEKKLOPR	LOCKKEEPER
CEEEKLOPSS	KEEPS CLOSE
CEEEKOPRSS	KEEPS SCORE
CEEEKPRSTT	KEPT SECRET
CEEEKRRSSU	SEERSUCKER
CEEELLORSV	LEVEL SCORE
CEEELMORVV	CLEVER MOVE
CEEELNRSSV	CLEVERNESS
CEEELNSSST	SELECTNESS
CEEELOPRSS	CREPE SOLES
CEEELOPSST	TELESCOPES
CEEELORSTT	CORSELETTE
CEEEMNOPRS	RECOMPENSE
CEEEMNORRT	CENTROMERE
CEEEMNRSTU	SECUREMENT
CEEENNOPRT	ONE PER CENT
CEEENNPRTT	TEN PER CENT
CEEENNRSST	RECENTNESS
CEEENOPRST	OPEN SECRET
CEEENORSSV	EVEN SCORES
CEEENORSTT	ENTRECOTES
CEEENQRSSU	SEQUENCERS
CEEENRSSSU	SECURENESS
CEEENRSSTT	SCREEN TEST
CEEEORRSTT	ERECTOR SET

CEEEORSTTV	SECRET VOTE	CEEGIINPRT	RECEIPTING
CEEEPRSSTU	PERSECUTES	CEEGIINPRV	PERCEIVING
CEEFFHIMOO	HOME OFFICE	CEEGIINRSX	EXERCISING
CEEFFHITTW	WITH EFFECT	CEEGIINSTT	GENETICIST
CEEFFINPTY	FIFTY PENCE	CEEGIINSTU	EUGENICIST
CEEFFIOSSU	COIFFEUSES	CEEGIKNRST	GREENSTICK
CEEFFIPRTT	PERFECT FIT	CEEGIMMNSU	E.E.CUMMINGS
CEEFFKOOTT	TOOK EFFECT	CEEGIMORRT	ERGOMETRIC
CEEFFOORST	FREE OF COST	CEEGINNNST	SENTENCING
CEEFGHINNR	GREENFINCH	CEEGINNOSS	CONSIGNEES
CEEFGILNRT	REFLECTING	CEEGINNQSU	SEQUENCING
CEEFGINPRT	PERFECTING	CEEGINNRSS	SCREENINGS
CEEFGINRRY	REFRIGENCY	CEEGINNRSU	INSURGENCE
CEEFGINRTU	CENTRIFUGE	CEEGINOORT	EROTOGENIC
CEEFGLLNTU	NEGLECTFUL	CEEGINORRV	RECOVERING
CEEFGLNSTU	GENUFLECTS	CEEGINORSS	RECOGNISES
CEEFGOORST	GO SCOT-FREE	CEEGINORSZ	RECOGNIZES
CEEFHHNORT	HENCEFORTH	CEEGINOSTV	CONGESTIVE
CEEFHINNRW	FRENCH WINE	CEEGINPPRU	CREEPING UP
CEEFHINPRT	PETER FINCH	CEEGINPRSS	PRECESSING
CEEFHIPRTV	FEVER PITCH	CEEGINPRST	RESPECTING
CEEFHLLRUY	CHEERFULLY	CEEGINPRTX	EXCERPTING
CEEFHLOORS	FREE SCHOOL	CEEGINRSST	SECRET SIGN
CEEFHLOOSS	SCHOOL FEES	CEEGIOOPST	GO TO PIECES
CEEFHMOORS	HOME FORCES	CEEGKNOOSS	GOOSENECKS
CEEFHNNRSS	FRENCHNESS	CEEGKORRSS	GREEK CROSS
CEEFIIILST	FELICITIES	CEEGLRSTTU	LEG CUTTERS
CEEFIILNTV	INFLECTIVE	CEEGNNORRW	CROWN GREEN
CEEFIIORST	FEROCITIES	CEEGNNORTV	CONVERGENT
CEEFIIPRSS	SPECIFIERS	CEEGNOOSTU	ECTOGENOUS
CEEFIIRRST	CERTIFIERS	CEEGNORSSS	CONGRESSES
	RECTIFIERS	CEEGNRSTTU	TURGESCENT
CEEFIKLNSS	FICKLENESS	CEEGORSTTU	COURGETTES
CEEFILMOOT	COME TO LIFE	CEEHHIMORT	COME HITHER
CEEFILNNSU	INFLUENCES		COME-HITHER
CEEFILNORT	REFLECTION	CEEHIIMRST	ERETHISMIC
CEEFINOPRT	PERFECTION	CEEHIKLRRY	CHERRYLIKE
CEEFINORRR	REINFORCER	CEEHIKORST	THE ROCKIES
CEEFINORRS	REINFORCES	CEEHIKPPRS	SCHIPPERKE
CEEFINORST	REFECTIONS	CEEHIKSSTT	SKETCHIEST
CEEFINOSUV	FIVE OUNCES	CEEHILLRSS	CHISELLERS
CEEFIRRSST	FIRECRESTS	CEEHILNNST	LINEN CHEST
CEEFKLLSSY	FECKLESSLY	CEEHILNOPR	NECROPHILE
CEEFLNORST	FLORESCENT	CEEHILNOPT	TELEPHONIC
CEEFLOORSS	FORECLOSES	CEEHILOPPR	RICH PEOPLE
CEEFLORRST	REFLECTORS	CEEHILOPRT	HELICOPTER
CEEFLORRSU	FLUORESCER	CEEHILOSVY	COHESIVELY
CEEFLPPRTU	PLUPERFECT	CEEHIMMSTU	THEME MUSIC
CEEFLPRSTU	RESPECTFUL	CEEHIMNNRT	ENRICHMENT
CEEFNOOPRS	FORCES OPEN	CEEHIMNTTU	TECHNETIUM
CEEFNOPRST	SPENT FORCE	CEEHIMOPTU	MOUTHPIECE
CEEFNOPRTY	FORTY PENCE	CEEHIMORTX	EXOTHERMIC
CEEFNORRRS	CONFERRERS	CEEHIMSSTU	SHEET MUSIC
CEEFNORRTY	FORCE ENTRY	CEEHINNORT	INCOHERENT
CEEFNORSTT	SOFT CENTRE	CEEHINNRST	INTRENCHES
CEEFNRSTTU	FRUTESCENT	CEEHINQSTU	TECHNIQUES
CEEFOORRSS	CROSS-REFER	CEEHINSSTT	TETCHINESS
CEEFORRSST	C.S.FORESTER	CEEHINSTUX	THIN EXCUSE
CEEGGILNNT	NEGLECTING	CEEHIOPPRS	PROPHECIES
CEEGHHOPTT	GET THE CHOP	CEEHIOPRST	SPIROCHETE
CEEGHIILMP	HEMIPLEGIC	CEEHIOPRSX	EXOSPHERIC
CEEGHIITTW	TWICE EIGHT	CEEHIOPSSW	SHOWPIECES
CEEGHIMNOR	COMING HERE	CEEHIORTVW	CHEW IT OVER
CEEGHINPRU	CHEERING UP	CEEHIRRSTV	CHRIS EVERT
CEEGHINQRU	CHEQUERING	CEEHIRSTTY	HYSTERETIC
CEEGHLNOPS	LONG SPEECH	CEEHKKOOYY	HOKEY COKEY
CEEGHLNORT	GREEN CLOTH	CEEHKNPRUY	KEYPUNCHER
CEEGHLOPST	CLOTHES PEG	CEEHKNPSUY	KEY PUNCHES
CEEGIINNPR	CREEPING IN		KEYPUNCHES
CEEGIINOTV	GIVE NOTICE	CEEHKORRST	THE ROCKERS
CEEGIINOVV	GIVEN VOICE	CEEHKORSSY	ROSY CHEEKS

CEEHLMORTY	EMERY CLOTH
CEEHLMOSZZ	SCHEMOZZLE
CEEHLNORTY	COHERENTLY
CEEHLNOSTW	NEW CLOTHES
CEEHLNQSSU	QUENCHLESS
CEEHLNSSTU	SET LUNCHES
CEEHLOSTTW	WET CLOTHES
CEEHLPRSSU	SEPULCHERS
	SEPULCHRES
CEEHMMOORR	CHROMOMERE
CEEHMORSUV	EVER SO MUCH
CEEHNNOSTT	ON THE SCENT
CEEHNOOPRT	CTENOPHORE
CEEHNOPRRS	PERCHERONS
CEEHNOPSTU	COUNT SHEEP
CEEHNORSTT	ON THE CREST
CEEHRRSSTT	STRETCHERS
CEEIIJLMRU	LIME-JUICER
CEEIIKLNPR	PINCERLIKE
CEEIIKLNPT	PICKET LINE
CEEIILLLOS	ICE LOLLIES
CEEIILLMRV	VERMICELLI
CEEIILLORS	COLLIERIES
CEEIILMOPS	POLEMICISE
CEEIILMOPZ	POLEMICIZE
CEEIILNOSU	ISOLEUCINE
CEEIILNRTT	CENTILITRE
CEEIILOSTV	VELOCITIES
CEEIILPPST	EPILEPTICS
CEEIILPRSV	LIP SERVICE
CEEIILRTTY	ERECTILITY
CEEIIMNNTT	INCITEMENT
CEEIIMNRSS	REMINISCES
CEEIIMORTT	METEORITIC
CEEIINNSST	INSISTENCE
CEEIINNSTV	INCENTIVES
CEEIINOPTV	POETIC VEIN
CEEIINPPRT	PERCIPIENT
CEEIINPRST	RECIPIENTS
CEEIINPSTV	INSPECTIVE
CEEIINRSTT	INTERSTICE
CEEIINSTVV	INVECTIVES
CEEIINTTVX	EXTINCTIVE
CEEIIOPSST	POETICISES
CEEIIOPSTZ	POETICIZES
CEEIIRSSTU	SECURITIES
CEEIJLMNOU	LEMON JUICE
CEEIJLOPRT	PROJECTILE
CEEIJNRSTT	INTERJECTS
CEEIJOPRTV	PROJECTIVE
CEEIJRSTYY	JERSEY CITY
CEEIKKPTTW	KEPT WICKET
CEEIKLNOST	SKELETONIC
CEEIKLNRSS	SILK SCREEN
	SILK-SCREEN
CEEIKNPRTY	PERNICKETY
CEEIKNRRSS	SNICKERERS
CEEIKNSSSS	SICKNESSES
CEEIKNSTTW	TEN WICKETS
CEEIKOPSTZ	POCKET-SIZE
CEEIKORSTT	ROCKET SITE
CEEIKOTTTV	TICKET VOTE
CEEIKSTTTW	TEST WICKET
CEEILLMPSU	SIMPLE CLUE
CEEILLNRST	STENCILLER
CEEILLNSTT	INTELLECTS
CEEILLOOPT	COLEOPTILE
CEEILLRSSU	SCULLERIES
CEEILMNOPT	INCOMPLETE
CEEILMNORT	CLINOMETER
CEEILMNOSS	COMELINESS

CEEILMNSSU	LUMINESCES
CEEILMOPTV	COMPLETIVE
CEEILNOORW	WINE COOLER
CEEILNOSST	SELECTIONS
CEEILNQSTU	LIQUESCENT
CEEILNRSTV	VENTRICLES
CEEILNRSUY	INSECURELY
CEEILNRTTY	RETICENTLY
CEEILOQSTU	QUITE CLOSE
CEEILPRSUV	PRECLUSIVE
CEEILRRSVY	LYRIC VERSE
CEEILSSUVX	EXCLUSIVES
CEEIMMOOTT	TIME TO COME
CEEIMMORRT	MICROMETER
CEEIMMOSTT	COMMITTEES
CEEIMNNOPR	PROMINENCE
CEEIMNNRST	INCREMENTS
CEEIMNOORS	ECONOMISER
CEEIMNOORZ	ECONOMIZER
CEEIMNOOSS	ECONOMISES
CEEIMNOOSZ	ECONOMIZES
CEEIMNOPPR	COPPER MINE
CEEIMNOSST	CENTESIMOS
CEEIMNSSSU	MENISCUSES
CEEIMNSSTU	INTUMESCES
CEEIMORSTV	VISCOMETER
CEEIMPRTTY	PETTY CRIME
CEEIMSSTUW	SWEET MUSIC
CEEINNNOSU	NINE OUNCES
CEEINNNOTV	CONVENIENT
CEEINNOPRS	NICE PERSON
CEEINNORSS	RECENSIONS
CEEINNPRTY	PERTINENCY
CEEINOORTV	TENOR VOICE
CEEINOPPRT	PERCEPTION
CEEINOPRSS	PRECESSION
CEEINOPRST	RECEPTIONS
CEEINOPRTV	OPTIC NERVE
CEEINOPRTX	EXCERPTION
CEEINOPSTX	EXCEPTIONS
CEEINORRST	CORNER SITE
CEEINORRSW	CORNERWISE
CEEINORSSS	RECESSIONS
CEEINORSST	SECRETIONS
CEEINOSSSS	SECESSIONS
CEEINOSSTX	EXOTICNESS
CEEINOSTTX	COEXISTENT
CEEINOSTUX	EXECUTIONS
CEEINPRSSS	PRINCESSES
CEEINPRSTT	INTERCEPTS
CEEINPRSTX	SIX PER CENT
CEEINPSTXY	SIXTY PENCE
CEEINRRSSV	SCRIVENERS
CEEINRRSTU	SCRUTINEER
CEEINRRTUW	NEW RECRUIT
CEEINRSSSW	SCREWINESS
CEEINRSSTT	INTERSECTS
CEEIOORSVV	VOICE-OVERS
CEEIOPPRRW	COPPER WIRE
CEEIOPPRSS	PERISCOPES
CEEIOPPRTY	EPIC POETRY
CEEIOPRTTV	PROTECTIVE
CEEIORSSTU	COURTESIES
CEEIPPRSTU	UPSET PRICE
CEEIPRSSUV	PERCUSSIVE
CEEIPSSTUV	SUSCEPTIVE
CEEIRSTTTY	CITY STREET
CEEJNOOSSS	JOCOSENESS
CEEKKKNNOS	KNOCK-KNEES
CEEKKOPSST	KEEPS STOCK
CEEKLLRSSY	RECKLESSLY

CEEKLNRTTU	TURTLE NECK	CEFFIIKKLN	FLICK KNIFE
	TURTLENECK		FLICK-KNIFE
CEEKLOORRV	OVERLOCKER	CEFFIINSTU	SUFFICIENT
CEEKLORRST	STORE CLERK	CEFFIIPRST	STIFF PRICE
CEEKLORRWW	CREWELWORK	CEFFIIRSTU	FRUCTIFIES
CEEKNNNOOS	ON ONE'S NECK	CEFFIKOOOT	TOOK OFFICE
CEEKNOPSTU	KEEPS COUNT	CEFFIKOORW	OFFICE WORK
CEEKOOPTTV	POCKET VETO	CEFFIOOPST	POST OFFICE
CEEKOPSTTV	VEST POCKET	CEFFIRSSTU	SCRUFFIEST
	VEST-POCKET	CEFFLLORUY	FORCEFULLY
CEEKORRSUW	RESCUE WORK	CEFFLOSTTU	SCUTTLE OFF
CEELLMOPTY	COMPLETELY	CEFFOORSSS	CROSSES OFF
CEELMMNOPT	COMPLEMENT	CEFFORSTTU	OFF CUTTERS
CEELMNNOOS	SOMNOLENCE	CEFGHILNTY	FETCHINGLY
CEELMNRSUU	UNCLE REMUS	CEFGHINPTU	FETCHING UP
CEELMOOOSS	COMES LOOSE	CEFGIIKLNR	FLICKERING
CEELMOPSTT	COMPLETEST	CEFGIILNNT	INFLECTING
CEELNOOPRS	NECROPOLES	CEFGIILNPSY	SPECIFYING
CEELNOORTT	COTTON REEL	CEFGIINRTY	CERTIFYING
CEELNORSSU	ENCLOSURES		RECTIFYING
CEELNORSVY	CONVERSELY	CEFGINNORR	CONFERRING
CEELOOORSV	LOOSE COVER	CEFGINNOSS	CONFESSING
CEELOOPRRT	COLE PORTER	CEFGINORSU	USING FORCE
CEELOORSSW	SCREW LOOSE	CEFGLOORSU	GOLF COURSE
CEELORRSTY	CLERESTORY	CEFHHNNORR	FRENCH HORN
CEELORSSSU	SOURCELESS	CEFHHOOPRT	FOR THE CHOP
CEEMMOOOORT	MORE TO COME	CEFHIILSSU	SUCH IS LIFE
CEEMNNORST	CONTEMNERS	CEFHIINNOU	UNION CHIEF
CEEMNNSTTY	ENCYSTMENT	CEFHIKKORT	FOR THE KICK
CEEMNOOORV	COME ON OVER	CEFHIKNRSS	FRENCH-KISS
CEEMNOORST	CENTROSOME	CEFHILNOST	FINE CLOTHS
CEEMNOOTTX	NEXT TO COME	CEFHILSTTU	CUTTLE FISH
CEEMOORSTT	COME TO REST		CUTTLEFISH
CEEMOPRSSS	COMPRESSES	CEFHIORSSU	FISH COURSE
CEENNOQSTU	CONSEQUENT	CEFHLLNORR	FRENCH ROLL
CEENNORSST	CONSENTERS	CEFHLLOOST	LEFT SCHOOL
CEENNORSTU	ENCOUNTERS	CEFHLNOOOV	CLOVEN HOOF
CEENNORTTW	TOWN CENTRE	CEFHLOPRRY	CRY FOR HELP
CEENNORTVW	NEW CONVERT	CEFHMOORTU	COME FOURTH
CEENOOPSST	COPESTONES	CEFHOORSUV	VOUCHES FOR
CEENOPPPRR	PEPPERCORN	CEFIIIILSS	SILICIFIES
CEENOPPRTY	PREPOTENCY	CEFIIILNTY	INFELICITY
CEENOPRRST	PRECENTORS	CEFIIIMNST	FEMINISTIC
CEENOPRTTW	TWO PER CENT	CEFIIJRTUU	FRUIT JUICE
CEENORRSSV	CONSERVERS	CEFIIKMNNY	MICKEY FINN
CEENORRSTV	CONVERTERS	CEFIIKMNOT	NICK OF TIME
CEENORRTUV	REV COUNTER	CEFIIKRSTV	FIVE TRICKS
CEENORSSTT	CONTESTERS	CEFIILLMTV	FELL VICTIM
CEENORSSTV	COVERTNESS	CEFIILLOPY	LIFE POLICY
CEENOSSSTU	COUNTESSES	CEFIILNNOT	INFLECTION
CEENPRSSSU	SPRUCENESS	CEFIILNOQU	CINQUEFOIL
CEENPRSTTU	PUTRESCENT	CEFIILOSTU	FELICITOUS
CEEOOPRSUX	POOR EXCUSE	CEFIILRSSU	FUEL CRISIS
CEEOORRTUV	OUTER COVER	CEFIIMNNTU	MUNIFICENT
CEEOPPRRST	PRECEPTORS	CEFIIMPRRS	FIRM PRICES
CEEOPRRSTT	RETROSPECT	CEFIINNOST	INFECTIONS
CEEOPRRSTU	PERSECUTOR	CEFIINOPRT	PROFICIENT
CEEOPRSSTU	PROSECUTES	CEFIINOPST	PONTIFICES
CEEOPRSTTT	PETER SCOTT	CEFIINOSTU	INFECTIOUS
CEEOQRSTTU	CROQUETTES	CEFIINSTTU	CUTS IT FINE
CEEORRSSST	CROSSTREES	CEFIJNOORS	JOIN FORCES
CEEORSSSTU	SETS COURSE	CEFIJOORSY	CRIES OF JOY
CEERRRSSTU	RESURRECTS	CEFIKOQRUZ	QUICK-FROZE
CEFFFFHOTU	OFF THE CUFF	CEFIKOSTTW	SOFT WICKET
	OFF-THE-CUFF	CEFIKRRSTU	FIRE TRUCKS
CEFFGHHIIO	HIGH OFFICE	CEFILLMRUY	MERCIFULLY
CEFFGIILOR	OFFICE GIRL	CEFILMNORS	FILM CENSOR
CEFFGIINOR	OFFICERING	CEFILMOORS	FROLICSOME
CEFFGIORUV	GRUFF VOICE	CEFILMORSU	FOUL CRIMES
CEFFHIINOR	CHIFFONIER	CEFILNOPST	SOFT PENCIL
CEFFHOOSTU	TOUCHES OFF	CEFIMNORSU	CUNEIFORMS

CEFIMORSST	COMES FIRST
CEFINNOOSS	CONFESSION
CEFINOORSU	CONIFEROUS
CEFINOORTU	OUT IN FORCE
CEFIOORSUV	VOCIFEROUS
CEFIORRSSY	FIERY CROSS
CEFIORSTUV	FIVES COURT
CEFKNOOOST	TONS OF COKE
CEFKOORRSW	WORKFORCES
CEFLNNOSTU	CONFLUENTS
CEFLNOOOTV	CLOVEN FOOT
CEFLNOORRW	CORNFLOWER
CEFLORSTUW	CUT FLOWERS
CEFMNNOORRS	CONFORMERS
CEFMOORRST	COMFORTERS
CEFNNOORRT	CONFRONTER
CEFNOORRTV	FRONT COVER
CEFNOORSSS	CONFESSORS
CEFNOORSUU	FOUR OUNCES
CEFOORRSTU	FORECOURTS
CEGGHIMNUW	CHEWING GUM
CEGGIINOTW	GOING TWICE
CEGGINNORV	CONVERGING
CEGGINNOST	CONGESTING
CEGHHIIMNO	HIGH INCOME
CEGHHIINRS	CHERISHING
CEGHIIIOOPTT	GOT THE CHOP
CEGHIILLNS	CHISELLING
CEGHIINNST	NICE THINGS
CEGHIINNUY	UNHYGIENIC
CEGHILNOOT	ETHNOLOGIC
CEGHILNOPY	PHYLOGENIC
CEGHILNOST	CLOSE THING
CEGHILNQSU	SQUELCHING
CEGHILORSW	WELSH CORGI
CEGHIMMNOO	COMING HOME
	HOMECOMING
CEGHIMOOPR	GEOMORPHIC
CEGHIMORST	COMES RIGHT
CEGHINNRTU	CHUNTERING
CEGHINOOPT	PHOTOGENIC
CEGHINORRU	CHIRURGEON
CEGHINORTU	RETOUCHING
	RIGHT ON CUE
CEGHINOTUW	CHEWING OUT
CEGHINRSTT	STRETCHING
CEGHIOPSSY	GEOPHYSICS
CEGHKNORSU	ROUGHNECKS
CEGHLNOOTY	TECHNOLOGY
CEGHOOPRSY	HYGROSCOPE
CEGIIIMNNT	MENINGITIC
CEGIIKNNQU	QUICKENING
CEGIIKNNRS	SNICKERING
CEGIIKNSTV	GIVEN STICK
CEGIIKSSTV	GIVES STICK
CEGIILLNNP	PENCILLING
CEGIILLNOW	LOW CEILING
CEGIILMOOR	OLIGOMERIC
CEGIILNNPR	PRINCELING
CEGIILNPRY	PIERCINGLY
CEGIILNTXY	EXCITINGLY
CEGIILOPTT	EPIGLOTTIC
CEGIILOSTU	EULOGISTIC
CEGIINNOST	SECTIONING
CEGIINNPRS	CRISPENING
CEGIINNPST	INSPECTING
CEGIINOPRR	PRINCE IGOR
CEGIINORSX	EXORCISING
CEGIINOSTX	COEXISTING
CEGIINPRRS	PRICE-RINGS
CEGIINRRTU	RECRUITING

CEGIINRSTT	TRISECTING
CEGIJNOPRT	PROJECTING
CEGIKNNORS	RECKONINGS
CEGIKNSTTU	GET STUCK IN
CEGILLMNOP	COMPELLING
CEGILLOOXY	LEXICOLOGY
CEGILMMNOS	COMMINGLES
CEGILMNOPT	COMPLETING
CEGILNNOST	CLINGSTONE
CEGILNNOSU	COUNSELING
CEGILNOORU	NEUROLOGIC
CEGILNORSU	LONG CRUISE
CEGILNRSTU	CLUSTERING
CEGILNRTTU	CLUTTERING
CEGILOOPRT	PETROLOGIC
CEGIMMMNNOT	COMMENTING
CEGIMNNNOT	CONTEMNING
CEGIMNNOTX	COMING NEXT
CEGIMNOORS	ERGONOMICS
CEGIMNOORV	COMING OVER
CEGIMNORTU	COMING TRUE
CEGINNNORU	RENOUNCING
CEGINNNOST	CONSENTING
CEGINNNOTT	CONTENTING
	CONTINGENT
CEGINNOOST	CONGESTION
CEGINNOQRU	CONQUERING
CEGINNORSV	CONSERVING
	CONVERSING
CEGINNORTU	COUNTERING
	RECOUNTING
CEGINNORTV	CONVERTING
CEGINNORUV	UNCOVERING
CEGINNOSTT	CONTESTING
CEGINNRSTU	ENCRUSTING
CEGINNRSTY	STRINGENCY
CEGINNRSUW	UNSCREWING
CEGINNRSUY	INSURGENCY
CEGINOORST	CREOSOTING
CEGINOPRSS	PROCESSING
CEGINOPRTT	PROTECTING
CEGINOPRUV	COVERING UP
CEGINPPRSU	SCUPPERING
CEGINPRSSU	PERCUSSING
CEGINPRSUW	SCREWING UP
CEGINPSSTU	SUSPECTING
CEGINRSTTU	SCUTTERING
CEGKLSSUUY	LUCKY GUESS
CEGLNOOSYY	SYNECOLOGY
CEGNNORSSU	SCROUNGERS
CEGOOPRSSY	GYROSCOPES
CEHHHIIKRT	HITCHHIKER
CEHHHIIKST	HITCH HIKES
	HITCHHIKES
CEHHIILMNT	HELMINTHIC
CEHHILNRTU	IN THE LURCH
CEHHIMRTUY	EURHYTHMIC
CEHHJNNOOT	JOHN CONTEH
CEHHKLLOSS	SHELL-SHOCK
CEHHLNOSTU	HOT LUNCHES
CEHHOOPSSU	CHOPHOUSES
CEHIIKLRST	CHRISTLIKE
CEHIIKNTTW	THINK TWICE
CEHIILLNSS	CHILLINESS
CEHIILMOST	HOMILETICS
	MESOLITHIC
CEHIILNOTX	XENOLITHIC
CEHIILOPST	ISOPLETHIC
CEHIIMNORT	THERMIONIC
CEHIIMRSTY	MYTHICISER
CEHIIMRTYZ	MYTHICIZER

CEHIIMSSTY	MYTHICISES	CEHMMNOOOR	MONOCHROME
CEHIIMSTTW	TIME SWITCH	CEHMMNOOST	THE COMMONS
CEHIIMSTYZ	MYTHICIZES	CEHMMOOORS	CHROMOSOME
CEHIINPPRS	PRINCESHIP	CEHMNOOTUY	HOME COUNTY
CEHIINPRSS	CHIRPINESS	CEHMNORSWY	SHOWN MERCY
CEHIINSSTT	IN STITCHES	CEHMOOPRST	ECTOMORPHS
CEHIIOSTTY	HISTIOCYTE	CEHMOORSST	COMES SHORT
CEHIIPRSTY	SPHERICITY	CEHMORSSWY	SHOWS MERCY
CEHIIPSTUU	EUPHUISTIC	CEHMOSSTTU	THE CUSTOMS
CEHIIRSSTU	HEURISTICS	CEHMPRTTUY	PRETTY MUCH
CEHIKLOPSS	PICKS HOLES	CEHNNORSTU	TRUNCHEONS
CEHIKNNSSU	CHUNKINESS	CEHNOOPRRS	CORNER SHOP
CEHIKOPPRS	HOP PICKERS	CEHNOOPRTT	TOPNOTCHER
CEHIKOQTTU	TO THE QUICK	CEHNOORSST	ON THE CROSS
CEHIKOSSTW	WHITE SOCKS	CEHNOOSTTU	TOUCHSTONE
CEHIKOSUVY	HUSKY VOICE	CEHNOPRSSU	SUN PORCHES
CEHIKPRSSW	SHIPWRECKS	CEHNOPRSTY	PHENOCRYST
CEHIKPSTTU	UP THE STICK	CEHOOOPRSS	HOROSCOPES
CEHILNOPST	CLOTHES PIN	CEHOOPRRSS	POOR WRETCH
	CLOTHESPIN	CEHOORSTUU	COURT HOUSE
CEHILNOSTU	TOUCHLINES		COURTHOUSE
CEHILNSSTZ	SCHNITZELS	CEHOPSSTUY	PSYCHES OUT
CEHILORSTY	CHRYSOLITE	CEHOPSTTUY	TOUCH-TYPES
	CHRYSOTILE	CEHORRSTUU	COURT USHER
CEHILPRRSY	CHERRY LIPS	CEHORSSSTT	CROSS THE T'S
CEHIMMNSSU	CHUMMINESS	CEHORSTTTU	OUTSTRETCH
CEHIMMOPRS	MORPHEMICS		STRETCH OUT
CEHIMNNOSU	ICHNEUMONS	CEIIIINSTV	VICINITIES
CEHIMNOOPR	MICROPHONE	CEIIILLNNP	PENICILLIN
CEHIMNOPTY	CHIMNEY POT	CEIIILNSVY	INCISIVELY
	CHIMNEY TOP	CEIIILOPST	POLITICISE
CEHIMOPSTY	MESOPHYTIC	CEIIILOPTZ	POLITICIZE
CEHIMRSTUY	EURYTHMICS	CEIIILRSSV	CIVILISERS
CEHINNRSTY	STRYCHNINE	CEIIILRSVZ	CIVILIZERS
CEHINOOIRRS	RHINOCEROS	CEIIIMMPRS	EMPIRICISM
CEHINOPPTY	PHENOTYPIC	CEIIIMPRST	EMPIRICIST
CEHINOPRRS	RICH PERSON	CEIIIMRSTV	VICTIMISER
CEHINOPRSS	CENSORSHIP	CEIIIMRTVZ	VICTIMIZER
CEHINOPRSY	HYPERSONIC	CEIIIMSSTV	VICTIMISES
CEHINOPRTY	HYPERTONIC	CEIIIMSSTY	SEISMICITY
CEHINOSSTU	TOUCHINESS	CEIIIMSTVZ	VICTIMIZES
CEHINOSSTW	SWITCHES ON	CEIIJNNOST	INJECTIONS
CEHINPSTUW	WINS THE CUP	CEIIJNNTUV	INJUNCTIVE
CEHINRRTTU	CURRENT HIT	CEIIJNSSTU	INJUSTICES
CEHIOPRRST	RECTORSHIP	CEIIKLNSSS	SICKLINESS
	SHORT PRICE	CEIIKLPRST	PRICKLIEST
CEHIOPRSTT	PROSTHETIC	CEIIKMPSST	SKEPTICISM
	THE TROPICS	CEIIKNNRST	NINE TRICKS
CEHIOPRSTY	HYPOCRITES	CEIIKNRSST	TRICKINESS
CEHIOPRTXY	XEROPHYTIC	CEIIKNSSST	STICKINESS
CEHIOQSTTU	COQUETTISH	CEIIKRSSTT	TRICKSIEST
CEHIORRSST	CHORISTERS	CEIIKSSTWX	SIX WICKETS
CEHIORRSTU	HOT CURRIES	CEIILLLSTU	CELLULITIS
CEHIORSTVW	SWITCH OVER	CEIILLPTXY	EXPLICITLY
	SWITCHOVER	CEIILMOPST	POLEMICIST
CEHIPSSTTU	STITCHES UP	CEIILMORTT	TREMOLITIC
CEHIPSSTUW	SWITCHES UP	CEIILNNORS	CRINOLINES
CEHKKNNOOT	ON THE KNOCK	CEIILNORSV	SILVER COIN
CEHKLNORSS	SCHNORKELS	CEIILNOSTU	LICENTIOUS
CEHKMORSTU	STRUCK HOME	CEIILNOSTV	NOVELISTIC
CEHKNOORST	ON THE ROCKS	CEIILNPPRS	PRINCIPLES
CEHKOOOSSU	COOKHOUSES	CEIILOOPST	POLITICOES
CEHLLOOPST	PHOTOCELLS	CEIILORSST	CLITORISES
CEHLMOOPRY	POLYCHROME	CEIIMNNOST	OMNISCIENT
CEHLMOORST	SCHOOL TERM	CEIIMNOSYZ	ISOENZYMIC
CEHLMOPTYY	LYMPHOCYTE	CEIIMNRTTU	METRIC UNIT
CEHLNOOSSU	NO SLOUCHES	CEIIMNTTVX	NEXT VICTIM
CEHLNOOSSW	NEW SCHOOLS	CEIIMORSST	ISOMETRICS
CEHLOOOPRT	TOCOPHEROL	CEIIMRSTUW	WRITE MUSIC
CEHLOOPPRS	PREP SCHOOL	CEIINNOPST	INCEPTIONS
CEHLOOSSTU	LOSES TOUCH		INSPECTION

CEIINNOTTX	EXTINCTION	CEILOPRSUY	PRECIOUSLY
CEIINOPRSS	PRECISIONS	CEILOPSSUY	SPECIOUSLY
CEIINOPRST	ISENTROPIC	CEIMMMNOTT	COMMITMENT
CEIINOPRSU	PERNICIOUS	CEIMMNOORT	METRONOMIC
CEIINOPRTV	VOICEPRINT	CEIMMNOQUU	COMMUNIQUE
CEIINORRST	CRITERIONS	CEIMMNORTY	METRONYMIC
CEIINORSSS	RESCISSION	CEIMMNOSSU	COMMUNISES
CEIINORSTT	TRISECTION	CEIMMNOSTU	COMMINUTES
CEIINPRSSS	CRISPINESS	CEIMMNOSUZ	COMMUNIZES
CEIINRSTUY	INSECURITY	CEIMMOOPRS	COMPROMISE
CEIINRSTUZ	SCRUTINIZE	CEIMMOORSS	MICROSOMES
CEIINSSSTT	SCIENTISTS	CEIMMOORST	MICROTOMES
CEIIOOPSTZ	EPIZOOTICS		OSMOMETRIC
CEIIOPRSTY	PRECIOSITY	CEIMMORSSU	COMMISSURE
CEIIOPSSTY	SPECIOSITY	CEIMNNOOSY	COINS MONEY
CEIIORSTVV	VIVISECTOR	CEIMNOOOSU	MONOECIOUS
CEIIPRSSSU	SCRIP ISSUE	CEIMNOORST	MICROTONES
CEIJNOOPRT	PROJECTION	CEIMNOORTT	TONOMETRIC
CEIJNORSTT	INTROJECTS	CEIMNOOSST	ECONOMISTS
CEIKKORRWW	WICKERWORK	CEIMNOPRSU	PROSCENIUM
CEIKLLORRU	KILL OR CURE	CEIMNORSUU	CERUMINOUS
CEIKLLORTT	LITTLE ROCK	CEIMNRSSTY	SYNCRETISM
CEIKLNNORS	RICK NELSON	CEIMOOPRTT	COMPETITOR
CEIKLNORST	INTERLOCKS		OPTOMETRIC
CEIKLNPSSU	PLUCKINESS	CEIMOOPSST	COMPOSITES
CEIKLNSTUU	UNLUCKIEST	CEIMOORSTY	SOCIOMETRY
CEIKLOPSST	STOCKPILES	CEIMOPRRTY	PYROMETRIC
CEIKLOSTWW	SLOW WICKET	CEIMORRSTY	CRIME STORY
CEIKMOOSTT	SOCK IT TO ME!	CEIMORSSTU	COSTUMIERS
CEIKMOPOTU	QUICK TEMPO	CEIMORSTUW	WROTE MUSIC
CEIKMSSSTY	STICKY MESS	CEIMORSTVY	VISCOMETRY
CEIKNNOOTW	NICE TO KNOW	CEIMOSSSTU	CUSTOMISES
CEIKNOOOTT	TOOK NOTICE	CEIMOSSTTU	SET TO MUSIC
CEIKNOPRSS	SICK PERSON	CEIMOSSTUV	MUSCOVITES
CEIKNOSSST	STOCKINESS	CEIMOSSTUZ	CUSTOMIZES
CEIKOPRRST	REPORT SICK	CEINNNOOTT	CONTENTION
CEIKORRSTV	OVERTRICKS	CEINNNOOTV	CONVENTION
CEIKORRTWY	CITY WORKER	CEINNNOSTT	CONTINENTS
CEIKOSTTWW	TWO WICKETS	CEINNOORSV	CONVERSION
CEIKOTTTTU	TICKET TOUT	CEINNOPSSU	IN ONE'S CUPS
CEIKPQSSTU	QUICKSTEPS	CEINNOPTUX	EXPUNCTION
CEIKRRSSTT	TRICKSTERS	CEINNORSTU	CENTURIONS
CEILLNOPRS	PRISON CELL		CONTINUERS
CEILMMNOPT	COMPLIMENT	CEINNOSSTT	CONSISTENT
CEILMNNOOS	MONOCLINES	CEINNPRSUW	CUP WINNERS
CEILMNOOPT	COMPLETION	CEINNQSUUX	QUINCUNXES
CEILMNOOPX	COMPLEXION	CEINOOPRSS	PROCESSION
CEILMNOOSS	SEMICOLONS	CEINOOPRTT	PROTECTION
CEILMNORTY	CLINOMETRY	CEINOOPRTV	COVER POINT
CEILMNOSTU	MONTICULES		COVER-POINT
CEILMNSSSU	CLUMSINESS	CEINOOPSTY	PINOCYTOSE
CEILMOOOTV	LOCOMOTIVE	CEINOORSSU	CENSORIOUS
CEILMOPSUV	COMPULSIVE	CEINOORTTV	CONTORTIVE
CEILMOPTXY	COMPLEXITY	CEINOPPRST	IN PROSPECT
CEILMORSTU	SCLEROTIUM	CEINOPPRSU	PORCUPINES
CEILMORSUV	MUSIC LOVER	CEINOPQRTU	CINQUE PORT
CEILMORTUV	VOLUMETRIC	CEINOPRSST	INSPECTORS
CEILMOSTUU	METICULOUS		INTERCROPS
CEILNNNOTY	INNOCENTLY	CEINOPRSSU	PERCUSSION
CEILNNOSVY	INSOLVENCY		SUPERSONIC
CEILNOOPRS	NECROPOLIS	CEINOPRSTT	INTROSPECT
CEILNOORSS	COLONISERS	CEINOPRSTU	SUPERTONIC
CEILNOORSZ	COLONIZERS	CEINORRSST	INTERCROSS
CEILNOOSTU	ELOCUTIONS	CEINORRSSU	RECURSIONS
CEILNOPRSU	PRECLUSION	CEINORRSTV	CONTRIVERS
CEILNOPSTU	PLEUSTONIC	CEINORSSTT	CORNETISTS
CEILNORSUV	INVOLUCRES	CEINORSSUX	EXCURSIONS
CEILNORTTY	CONTRITELY	CEINORSTTT	CORNETTIST
CEILNOSSST	COSTLINESS	CEINORSTTU	TURNS TO ICE
CEILNOSUVV	CONVULSIVE	CEINORSTUV	NERVOUS TIC
CEILOOPRST	COPROLITES	CEINOSSTUU	INCESTUOUS

CEINOSTTTU	CONSTITUTE	CEOPRRRSSU	PRECURSORS
CEINRSSSTT	STRICTNESS	CEOPRRRSTU	CORRUPTERS
CEINRSSSTU	CRUSTINESS	CEOPRRSTTU	CORRUPTEST
CEINRSSSUV	SCURVINESS	CEORRSTTTY	TERRY SCOTT
CEINRSSTTY	SYNCRETIST	CEPPRRSTUU	UPPER CRUST
CEIOOPRRTU	PUERTO RICO	CERRSSTTUU	STRUCTURES
CEIOOSSTXY	EXOCYTOSIS	CFFFIISSTU	FISTICUFFS
CEIOPRRTUV	CORRUPTIVE	CFFGHIKNOO	CHOKING OFF
CEIOPRRTUZ	PRIZE COURT	CFFGIIKKNO	KICKING OFF
CEIOPRRTWY	COPYWRITER	CFFGIIKNOP	PICKING OFF
CEIORRSSTT	TRISECTORS	CFFGIIKNOT	TICKING OFF
CEIORRSTUU	COUTURIERS	CFFGILNOOO	COOLING OFF
CEIPPRRSST	PRESCRIPTS		COOLING-OFF
CEIPPRSTTY	TYPESCRIPT	CFFGINOORS	SCORING OFF
CEIPRRSSTU	SCRIPTURES	CFFGINOTTU	CUTTING OFF
CEIRRSSTTU	STRICTURES	CFFIKKNOOT	KNOCK IT OFF
CEJNOPRSUU	CONJURES UP	CFFIMMNNORU	CORN MUFFIN
CEJOOPRRST	PROJECTORS	CFFIOORSST	CROSS IT OFF
CEKKNOORSV	KNOCKS OVER	CFFOOOSTUU	OUT OF FOCUS
CEKKORSSTY	SKYROCKETS	CFGIIILNNT	INFLICTING
CEKLMORTTU	MOCK TURTLE	CFGIIKKLNY	FLYING KICK
CEKLNNPUYY	LUCKY PENNY	CFGIIKLNOR	FROLICKING
CEKLNORTTU	ROTTEN LUCK	CFGIIKNOSS	FOSSICKING
CEKLOPRSTY	STOCK REPLY	CFGIIMMNOR	CONFIRMING
CEKMNOOOTW	COME TO KNOW	CFGIIINNORU	FINNO-UGRIC
CELLNOORRT	CONTROLLER	CFGIKNNORU	UNFROCKING
CELLNOORSU	COUNSELLOR	CFGILNORWY	CRYING WOLF
CELLOOORSU	LOSE COLOUR	CFGILNOSTY	FLYING SCOT
CELLOORRSY	ROLLS ROYCE	CFGIMMNOOR	COMING FROM
CELLOORSSU	COLOURLESS	CFGIMMNOOR	CONFORMING
CELMOPRSUU	OPERCULUMS	CFGIMNOORT	COMFORTING
CELMPPRSUU	CRUMPLES UP	CFGINOOPTU	GIFT COUPON
CELNOORSSU	COUNSELORS	CFGINOORTU	FORCING OUT
CELNOOSSTU	LOSES COUNT	CFHIKOPRST	PITCHFORKS
CELNOOSTUV	CONVOLUTES	CFHIOORTUV	VOUCH FOR IT
CELNOPRSUU	UNCOUPLERS	CFHKOOOPRS	SHOCKPROOF
CELNORSSTU	CONSULTERS	CFHLLOOORT	FLOOR CLOTH
CELOOPRRTU	COLPORTEUR	CFHLLORSUU	FULL CHORUS
CELOOPRRUU	PURE COLOUR	CFHLMOOORR	CHLOROFORM
CELOOPRSSU	SUPERCOOLS	CFHOOOTTUU	OUT OF TOUCH
CELOOSSSSU	COLOSSUSES	CFIIILNNOT	INFLICTION
CELOOSTUVY	COVETOUSLY	CFIIINOSTT	FICTIONIST
CELPRSSTUU	SCULPTURES	CFIIIOSTTU	FICTITIOUS
CEMMNNOORU	UNCOMMONER	CFIIKPRSTU	PICKS FRUIT
CEMMNNOOSS	COMMONNESS	CFIILMMORS	MICROFILMS
CEMMNOOPTY	COMMON TYPE	CFIIRSTTUU	FUTURISTIC
CEMMNOOPST	COMPONENTS	CFIKKOORSW	SICK OF WORK
CEMNNOORST	CONTEMNORS	CFIKLLNOST	FLINTLOCKS
CEMNNORTUY	COUNTRYMEN	CFIKLMOPSU	CUPS OF MILK
CEMNOOSSTW	SCOTSWOMEN	CFIKOPRSTU	STICK UP FOR
CEMNOOTTUU	COUNT ME OUT	CFIKORRSTU	FOUR TRICKS
CEMOOPRRSS	COMPRESSOR	CFILLMOORU	COLOUR FILM
CEMOOPRSST	COMPOSTERS	CFIMMNOORS	CONFORMISM
CENNOOPPUU	POUNCE UPON	CFIMNOORST	CONFORMIST
CENNOOPRRU	PRONOUNCER	CFIMNOORTY	CONFORMITY
CENNOOPRSU	PRONOUNCES	CFINNOOSSU	CONFUSIONS
CENNORRTUU	RUN COUNTER	CFKOOOSTTU	OUT OF STOCK
CENNOSTTUU	UNCUT STONE	CFKOOSTTUU	OUT OF STUCK
CENOOOSSTT	TO ONE'S COST	CFKOPRSTUU	STUCK UP FOR
CENOOPRSST	STONECROPS	CFLLLOORUU	FULL COLOUR
CENOOQRRSU	CONQUERORS	CFLOOORSTU	SOFT COLOUR
CENOOORRTTV	CONTROVERT	CFLOOOSSTT	COLTSFOOTS
CEOOPPRRST	PROSPECTOR	CFLOORSSUU	SCROFULOUS
CEOOPRRSSS	PROCESSORS	CFMMMNOOOR	COMMON FORM
CEOOPRRSTT	PROTECTORS	CFOOORTTUU	OUT OF COURT
CEOOPRRSTU	PROSECUTOR	CGGHINOPUU	COUGHING UP
CEOOPRRTTY	PROTECTORY	CGGIIKNPSU	SUCKING PIG
CEOOPRSSUU	SOUP COURSE	CGGIILNNNO	CLINGING ON
CEOORSSSTU	CROSSES OUT	CGGIIINNNOS	CONSIGNING
CEOORSSTUW	TWO COURSES	CGGINNORSU	SCROUNGING
CEOPPRRSTU	PROSPECTUS	CGHHHILOOS	HIGH SCHOOL

CGHHILLNTU	LIGHT LUNCH	CGIINORSST	RISING COST
CGHHILOORU	HIGH COLOUR	CGIINOTTUY	CONTIGUITY
CGHHILOTTU	LIGHT TOUCH	CGIKKNNNOO	KNOCKING ON
CGHHORTTUU	CUT THROUGH	CGIKKNNOPU	KNOCKING UP
CGHIIINNPT	PITCHING IN	CGIKLNOOTU	LOCKING OUT
CGHIIIOSTV	VISIGOTHIC	CGIKLNOTUU	LUCKING OUT
CGHIIKNPSY	PHYSICKING	CGIKNOOOPT	COOKING POT
CGHIIKNSTT	NIGHT STICK	CGIKNOPSTU	STOCKING UP
CGHIIKSTTT	STICK TIGHT	CGIKNORSSS	KINGS CROSS
CGHIILLLNY	CHILLINGLY	CGIKNOSTTU	GOT STUCK IN
CGHIILLNSS	SCHILLINGS	CGILLOSSYY	GLYCOLYSIS
CGHIILLOOT	LITHOLOGIC	CGILMOOSTY	MYCOLOGIST
CGHIILMSTU	LIGHT MUSIC	CGILMOOSUY	MUSICOLOGY
CGHIILOOST	HISTOLOGIC	CGILNNNOUW	LOW CUNNING
CGHIILOPST	PHLOGISTIC	CGILNNOPUU	UNCOUPLING
CGHIILSTTY	CITY LIGHTS	CGILNNOSTU	CONSULTING
CGHIIMNSTU	MUSIC NIGHT	CGILNNOSUV	CONVULSING
CGHIINNOSU	CUSHIONING	CGILNOOOST	ONCOLOGIST
CGHIINOPTW	COPING WITH	CGILOOOPRT	TROPOLOGIC
CGHIINPRRU	CHIRRUPING	CGILOOOTXY	TOXICOLOGY
CGHIKLNOSY	SHOCKINGLY	CGILOOSTTY	CYTOLOGIST
CGHIKSTTTU	STUCK TIGHT	CGILORSSTU	GIRL SCOUTS
CGHILLOORS	SCHOOLGIRL	CGIMNNOOOS	COMING SOON
CGHILNNOTU	UNCLOTHING	CGIMNNOOPU	COMING UPON
CGHILNOOOP	PHONOLOGIC	CGIMNOOPRT	COMPORTING
CGHILNOPST	SPLOTCHING	CGIMNOOPST	COMPOSTING
CGHILNOTUY	TOUCHINGLY	CGIMNOOPTU	COMING UP TO
CGHILOORTY	TRICHOLOGY	CGINNNOOPU	POUNCING ON
CGHILORRSU	CHORUS GIRL	CGINNNOOTU	COUNTING ON
CGIIINNOOTU	TOUCHING ON	CGINNOORSS	CONSIGNORS
CGIHINOPTUU	TOUCHING UP	CGINNOORST	CONSORTING
CGHIOORTUV	VICTOR HUGO	CGINNOORTT	CONTORTING
CGHIOPRSTY	COPYRIGHTS	CGINNOORTU	CONTOURING
CGHLNOOOORY	CHRONOLOGY	CGINNOPTUU	COUNTING UP
CGHLNOOOSS	SCHOOL SONG	CGINNORSTU	CONSTRUING
CGHLOOOOST	GO TO SCHOOL	CGINNPRTUU	PUNCTURING
CGHLOOPSYY	PSYCHOLOGY	CGINOOPRST	PROGNOSTIC
CGHOPRTUUU	CUT UP ROUGH	CGINOOPTUY	COPYING OUT
CGIIILNSV	CIVILISING	CGINOORSTU	OUTSCORING
CGIIIILNVZ	CIVILIZING	CGINOOSTUU	CONTIGUOUS
CGIIIJNOST	JINGOISTIC	CGINOPRRTU	CORRUPTING
CGIIIKNNPT	NIT PICKING	CGINOPRSTY	STOP CRYING
	NIT-PICKING	CGINOTTTUU	CUTTING OUT
CGIIILNOST	SOLICITING	CGINPPRSUU	SPRUCING UP
CGIIILNSTU	LINGUISTIC	CGKOOPRRSU	ROCK GROUPS
CGIIILPSTU	PUGILISTIC	CGLOOOPRTY	PROCTOLOGY
CGIIJNNNOO	CONJOINING	CHHIIPSTTW	WHIPSTITCH
CGIIKKNOTU	KICKING OUT	CHHILLRSUY	CHURLISHLY
CGIIKLLNOR	ROLLICKING	CHHILOOPTY	HOLOPHYTIC
CGIIKLNRST	STRICKLING	CHHIMNOOOP	HOMOPHONIC
CGIIKNNOPY	COPYING INK	CHHIMNOOST	SMOOTH CHIN
CGIIKNOPTU	PICKING OUT	CHHINSTTUW	WITCH-HUNTS
CGIIKNOSTT	STICKING TO	CHHIOOPPRS	PHOSPHORIC
CGIIKNPSTU	STICKING UP	CHHKLLOOSY	HOLLYHOCKS
CGIILNNOOS	COLONISING	CHIIILLNST	NIHILISTIC
CGIILNNOOZ	COLONIZING	CHIIILLOPP	LIPOPHILIC
CGIILNOPTU	POULTICING	CHIIILPSTY	SYPHILITIC
CGIILNORVW	CIVIL WRONG	CHIIINORST	HISTRIONIC
CGIIMMNOTT	COMMITTING	CHIIKLLSTY	TICKLISHLY
CGIIMNNORS	CRIMSONING	CHIILLQSUY	CLIQUISHLY
CGIIMNOPRS	COMPRISING	CHIILMNOOT	MONOLITHIC
CGIIMNOSST	GNOSTICISM	CHIILMORST	MICROLITHS
CGIIMNSSUW	SWING MUSIC	CHIILMRSTY	CYRIL SMITH
CGIINNNOTU	CONTINUING	CHIILPSSTT	SLIPSTITCH
	COUNTING IN	CHIIMOOPRS	ISOMORPHIC
CGIINNOPRS	CONSPIRING	CHIIMOPRRT	TRIMORPHIC
CGIINNORTV	CONTRIVING	CHIIMORSTU	HUMORISTIC
CGIINNOSST	CONSISTING	CHIINNOPSU	PIN CUSHION
CGIINNRSTU	INCRUSTING		PINCUSHION
CGIINNRTTU	TINCTURING	CHIINOPSSU	COUSINSHIP
CGIINORSSS	SCISSORING	CHIINORSTU	TRICHINOUS

531

CHIIPSSSTY	PHYSICISTS	CIJLNNOOTY	CONJOINTLY
CHIJORTWYY	CRY WITH JOY	CIKKLLOOSY	LOOK SICKLY
CHIKKLLSTU	THICK SKULL	CIKLLOSSTT	STOCK STILL
CHIKLMOSST	LOCKSMITHS		STOCK-STILL
CHIKMORSUU	SICK HUMOUR	CIKLNOORSU	SKIN COLOUR
CHIKNOQRTU	QUICKTHORN	CIKLNORSSS	CROSS-LINKS
CHIKOOPSTT	TOOTHPICKS	CIKOOOPRRY	POOR YORICK
CHIKOPSSTW	WHIPSTOCKS	CIKOORRTTW	TRICK OR TWO
CHIKORSSTW	HOW'S TRICKS?	CIKOSTTTUU	STUCK IT OUT
CHILLNOOST	LOINCLOTHS	CILLMNOOST	TOM COLLINS
CHILLNOSWY	CLOWNISHLY	CILLMNOOTT	COTTON MILL
CHILLOOPTT	PILOT-CLOTH	CILLMOOQUU	COLLOQUIUM
CHILNOOPPY	POLYPHONIC	CILLMORSUY	COLLYRIUMS
CHILNOPSSU	CONSULSHIP	CILLNOOSSU	COLLUSIONS
CHILOOPTTY	PHOTOLYTIC	CILLNOOUVV	CONVOLVULI
CHIMNNOOOP	MONOPHONIC	CILLOOORSU	OIL COLOURS
CHIMOOOPRS	SOPHOMORIC	CILLOOSTVY	SOLVOLYTIC
CHIMOOOPRZ	ZOOMORPHIC	CILLOPRSTU	PORTCULLIS
CHIMOOPRSY	HYPOCORISM	CILLOSSUUY	LUSCIOUSLY
CHIMOORTTY	TRICHOTOMY	CILMNOOOOT	LOCOMOTION
CHIOOPPRRY	PYROPHORIC	CILMNOOPSU	COMPULSION
CHIOOPTTXY	PHYTOTOXIC	CILMNOSSTU	COLUMNISTS
CHIOPRSSTU	COURTSHIPS	CILMOOSSTU	MUSIC STOOL
CHIORSTTTU	CUT IT SHORT	CILNNOOSUV	CONVULSION
CHIORSTTTW	STITCHWORT	CILNOOOSTY	OIL TYCOONS
CHKLNOORSS	LOCKS HORNS	CILNOOQRRU	CORN LIQUOR
CHKLOOORSW	SCHOOLWORK	CILOOPRTYY	TORY POLICY
CHKLOOPPSU	LOCK-UP SHOP	CILOORRSTU	TRICOLOURS
CHKOORSSST	SHORT SOCKS	CILOORSSTU	COLOURISTS
CHLMNOSUUU	HOMUNCULUS	CILORRSSUU	SCURRILOUS
CHLMOOOORS	SCHOOLROOM	CIMMNNOOSU	COMMUNIONS
CHLMOOPRYY	POLYCHROMY	CIMMNOOOST	COMMOTIONS
CHMNOOPTTU	MUTTON CHOP	CIMMNOSSTU	COMMUNISTS
CHORRSSTTU	SHORTCRUST	CIMMNOOOPP	NINCOMPOOP
CIIIILNOTV	OLIVINITIC	CIMNNOOSTU	CONTINUUMS
CIIIILNTVY	INCIVILITY	CIMNOORSTU	CONSORTIUM
CIIILLMPTY	IMPLICITLY	CIMNOOSTXY	MYCOTOXINS
CIIILMNRTU	TRICLINIUM	CIMOOOPRST	COMPOSITOR
CIIILMPSST	SIMPLISTIC	CIMOPSTTUU	PUT TO MUSIC
CIIILMPSTY	SIMPLICITY	CINNNORTUY	COUNTRY INN
CIIILMSTTY	CITY LIMITS	CINNOOORTT	CONTORTION
CIIILNOPST	IN POLITICS	CINNOOSSTU	CONTUSIONS
CIIILPRTTY	TRIPLICITY	CINNOOSTTU	COUNTS ON IT
CIIIMOPSTT	OPTIMISTIC	CINNOOSTUU	CONTINUOUS
CIIIMSSTTW	WITTICISMS	CINOOPRRTU	CORRUPTION
CIIJLNOPST	CLIP JOINTS	CINOORSSTY	CONSISTORY
CIIJNNNOTU	INJUNCTION	CINORRSTTU	INSTRUCTOR
CIIKNOSSTT	STICKS IT ON	CINORSTTUY	TONY CURTIS
CIIKOSSTTT	STICKS TO IT	CIOOPRSTTU	PROSCIUTTO
CIIKOSTTTU	STICK IT OUT	CIOORSSTTU	CROSS IT OUT
CIIILLNOOSS	COLLISIONS	CIOPPRSSTT	POSTSCRIPT
CIILNNOSSU	INCLUSIONS	CIOPPSTTYY	COPY TYPIST
CIILNOPSTU	PUNCTILIOS	CIOPRSSTYY	SPICY STORY
CIILOORSST	SOLICITORS	CIPPRRSTUU	STIRRUP CUP
CIILOOSSTU	SOLICITOUS	CJKLMSTUUY	JUST MY LUCK
CIILOPPSTU	POPULISTIC	CKMNOORSTU	MOONSTRUCK
CIILOPRTVY	PROCLIVITY	CKOPRSSTTU	TRUCK STOPS
CIILRRSTUY	SCURRILITY	CLLMNNOOOY	MO CONNOLLY
CIILSSSTTY	STYLISTICS	CLLOOORSTU	LOST COLOUR
CIIMMNOOSS	COMMISSION	CLMMNNOOUY	UNCOMMONLY
CIINNNOOPT	CONNIPTION	CLMOOPRSUY	COMPULSORY
CIINNOORTT	CONTRITION	CLNOOOOTTW	COTTON WOOL
CIINNORSSU	INCURSIONS	CLNOOPRSSU	PROCONSULS
CIINNOTTUY	CONTINUITY	CLNOSTUUUY	UNCTUOUSLY
CIINOPSSSU	SUSPICIONS	CLOOORSTUW	TWO COLOURS
CIIOORSTUV	VICTORIOUS	CLOPRSSUUU	SCRUPULOUS
CIIOPRSTTU	PROSCIUTTI	CMMMNOOOOR	COMMON ROOM
CIIOPSSSUU	SUSPICIOUS	CMMNNNOOOU	COMMON NOUN
CIIORSSTTV	VORTICISTS	CMMNOOORST	COMMON SORT
CIJKNOOSTT	JOINT STOCK	CNNOOPSTUU	COUNTS UPON
	JOINT-STOCK	CNNOOTTUWY	COUNTY TOWN

COOPRRRSTU	CORRUPTORS	DDEEHIMOST	METHODISED
COOPRSSSTY	SPOROCYSTS	DDEEHIMOTZ	METHODIZED
DDDDDFUUYY	FUDDY-DUDDY	DDEEHIOOPT	HOPED TO DIE
DDDDEEEHIT	DID THE DEED	DDEEHLNOPW	HELPED DOWN
DDDEEEFIWW	WEDDED WIFE	DDEEHLORSU	SHOULDERED
DDDEEEHOST	DO THE DEEDS	DDEEHNNORU	ONE HUNDRED
DDDEEELOPP	PEDDLE DOPE	DDEEHNORSU	DEERHOUNDS
DDDEEFIOST	EISTEDDFOD		ENSHROUDED
DDDEEIINVX	EX DIVIDEND	DDEEHOORTU	OUT-HERODED
DDDEEINOSW	DISENDOWED	DDEEIIKLMN	LIKE-MINDED
DDDEEIOORS	DEODORISED	DDEEIIMOPR	EPIDERMOID
DDDEEIOORZ	DEODORIZED	DDEEIINRSW	SIDEWINDER
DDDEEIORRS	DISORDERED	DDEEIIOPSX	EPOXIDISED
DDDEFFLOOT	TODDLED OFF	DDEEIIOPXZ	EPOXIDIZED
DDDEFLNOOW	FOLDED DOWN	DDEEIIOSST	SIDE TO SIDE
DDDEGIIOOR	DIDGERIDOO	DDEEIIPPST	DIPEPTIDES
DDDEINORSW	DID WONDERS	DDEEIIQSTU	DISQUIETED
DDDENOSTUW	DUSTED DOWN	DDEEILLNRT	TENDRILLED
DDDEOOQSTU	QUOTED ODDS	DDEEILMMRT	MIDDLE TERM
DDEEEEELTW	TWEEDLEDEE	DDEEILNNRU	UNDERLINED
DDEEEEGNNR	ENGENDERED	DDEEILNOSY	ONE-SIDEDLY
DDEEEEHNPT	THE DEEP END	DDEEILNOTT	DOTTED LINE
DDEEEEPSTY	DEEPEST DYE	DDEEIMMNOS	DEMIMONDES
DDEEEFGHOT	FEED THE DOG	DDEEIMNNOP	OPEN-MINDED
DDEEEFHORR	HERD OF DEER	DDEEIMNNRU	UNDERMINED
DDEEEFLORW	DEFLOWERED	DDEEIMNNSS	MINDEDNESS
DDEEEFNRSU	UNDERFEEDS	DDEEIMNORS	MODERNISED
DDEEEGIINS	INSIDE EDGE	DDEEIMNORZ	MODERNIZED
DDEEEGILLM	MILLED EDGE	DDEEINNRTU	INDENTURED
DDEEEGRSST	GET DRESSED	DDEEINORRV	OVERRIDDEN
DDEEEHHPRS	SHEPHERDED		RIDDEN OVER
DDEEEIINNR	IN DIRE NEED	DDEEINRRSS	DRESS IN RED
DDEEEIILSTT	TITLE DEEDS	DDEEINRSUZ	UNDERSIZED
DDEEEIMNOR	DOMINEERED	DDEEIOORRS	DEODORISER
DDEEEIMNRT	DETERMINED	DDEEIOORRZ	DEODORIZER
DDEEEINOPW	OPENED WIDE	DDEEIOORSS	DEODORISES
DDEEEINRGT	TENDERISED	DDEEIOORSZ	DEODORIZES
DDEEEINRTZ	TENDERIZED	DDEEIORUVY	DID YOU EVER?
DDEEEIRSSV	DISSEVERED	DDEEIPRRSS	RED SPIDERS
DDEEELLMOR	REMODELLED	DDEEIRSSST	DISTRESSED
DDEEELMMOS	MEDDLESOME	DDEEKMOOPS	SMOKED DOPE
DDEEELMNTY	DEMENTEDLY	DDEELLOORW	OLDE-WORLDE
DDEEELMTUW	TWEEDLEDUM	DDEELMNOTW	MELTED DOWN
DDEEELNTXY	EXTENDEDLY	DDEELMORSU	SMOULDERED
DDEEELOPRY	REDEPLOYED	DDEELNNOSY	NELSON EDDY
DDEEELRSVY	DESERVEDLY	DDEELNOPUX	UNEXPLODED
DDEEENRRTU	UNDETERRED	DDEELORSSS	OLD DRESSES
DDEEENRSUV	UNDESERVED	DDEELRRSSU	RUDDERLESS
DDEEENRSUX	UNDERSEXED	DDEENNOOPR	PONDERED ON
DDEEEOOPRT	DEEP-ROOTED	DDEENNOPST	DESPONDENT
DDEEEOORRS	RED RED ROSE	DDEENNOSSS	SODDENNESS
DDEEEORSTV	STEVEDORED	DDEENNSSSU	SUDDENNESS
DDEEEPRSSU	SUPERSEDED	DDEENOOTTT	DOTTED NOTE
DDEEFFGIOT	DEED OF GIFT	DDEENOPPST	END-STOPPED
DDEEFFOORR	ORDERED OFF	DDEENRRSSU	UNDERDRESS
DDEEFGILSY	FEELS GIDDY	DDEEOOORRTU	ORDERED OUT
DDEEFGJORU	FOREJUDGED	DDEEOPRSST	TOP-DRESSED
DDEEFIIINT	IDENTIFIED	DDEFFLOOST	TODDLES OFF
DDEEFIILMS	MISFIELDED	DDEFFNOORU	ROUNDED OFF
DDEEFIIOTX	DETOXIFIED	DDEFFNOOSU	SOUNDED OFF
DDEEFINOPS	DOPE FIENDS	DDEFFOOPPR	DROPPED OFF
DDEEFLNORU	FLOUNDERED	DDEFGIIRSU	DISFIGURED
DDEEFLOORV	FOLDED OVER	DDEFGINOOR	GOOD FRIEND
DDEEGGHOOP	HODGEPODGE	DDEFGINRSU	DRUG FIENDS
DDEEGGNOSS	DOGGEDNESS	DDEFGOOPRR	DROP-FORGED
DDEEGILNSY	DESIGNEDLY	DDEFHIIIMU	HUMIDIFIED
DDEEGORSST	GOT DRESSED	DDEFHIIMUY	DEHUMIDIFY
DDEEHIILNS	LIES HIDDEN	DDEFIIKNNR	KIND FRIEND
DDEEHIISSS	SIDE DISHES	DDEFIIRRTU	DRIED FRUIT
DDEEHILLWY	WIDELY HELD	DDEFILNORS	OLD FRIENDS
DDEEHILMOS	DEMOLISHED	DDEFINNOOT	TINNED FOOD

DDEFLMOORT	MODEL T FORD	DDEJMNOPUW	JUMPED DOWN
DDEFLOOOTU	FLOODED OUT	DDEKLNOOOW	LOOKED DOWN
DDEGHHIIMN	HIGH-MINDED	DDELLNOPUW	PULLED DOWN
DDEGHHIINR	RIDDEN HIGH	DDELNOOPSW	SLOPED DOWN
DDEGHILNNO	GOLDEN HIND	DDELNOOSWW	SLOWED DOWN
DDEGHINRSU	SHUDDERING	DDELNORRUW	UNDERWORLD
DDEGHIORRU	ROUGH-DRIED	DDEMMNOOST	ODD MOMENTS
DDEGHOOOPT	HOPED TO GOD	DDEMMORTUU	DRUMMED OUT
DDEGIINNST	DISTENDING	DDEMNOORUV	MOVED ROUND
DDEGILLNUY	DELUDINGLY	DDENNOOOST	STOOD ON END
DDEGILNNOW	LONG-WINDED	DDENNOORUZ	ROUND DOZEN
DDEGINNOOR	GOOD DINNER	DDENNORTUW	TURNED DOWN
DDEGINNORS	DOGS DINNER	DDENOOOPRU	DO ONE PROUD
DDEGINNORU	REDOUNDING	DDENOOPPRU	PROPOUNDED
DDEGIOORRV	GOOD DRIVER	DDENOORSTU	UNDERSTOOD
DDEGKLOOOO	LOOKED GOOD	DDENOORTUW	DROWNED OUT
DDEGLLLOOR	ROLLED GOLD	DDENOOSTUU	SOUNDED OUT
DDEGLNOPUW	GULPED DOWN	DDENOOSTUY	DO ONES DUTY
DDEGMOOOOS	DO SOME GOOD	DDENOPSSTU	SUDDEN STOP
DDEGNNOOOO	DONE NO GOOD	DDENORRSUU	SURROUNDED
DDEGNOOOOS	DOES NO GOOD	DDENRSTUUY	UNDERSTUDY
DDEGNORRUW	WONDER DRUG	DDEOOOPRTU	DROPPED OUT
DDEGOOPSTT	SPOTTED DOG	DDEOOOPPSU	PSEUDOPODS
DDEHHNNORTU	HOT HUNDRED	DDEOOOQSSTU	QUOTES ODDS
DDEHIIIMNS	DIMINISHED	DDFFGINNOO	NODDING OFF
DDEHIILNSW	WINDSHIELD	DDFGGILOOR	DIG FOR GOLD
DDEHIILPSU	DISULPHIDE	DDFGGLOORU	DUG FOR GOLD
DDEHIKNOOW	HOODWINKED	DDFGOOOSTY	STODGY FOOD
DDEHINOSSS	SHODDINESS	DDFIILOOQU	LIQUID FOOD
DDEHINOTTW	DID THE TOWN	DDFINNOOWW	DOWN WIND OF
DDEHINRSUX	SIX HUNDRED	DDFINORSSW	FINDS WORDS
DDEHIOOSTT	HOT TODDIES	DDFNOORSUW	FOUND WORDS
DDEHIORSXY	HYDROXIDES	DDGGHIINOO	GOOD HIDING
DDEHIORTTY	DO THE DIRTY	DDGGIILNOS	DISLODGING
DDEHJNNORY	JOHN DRYDEN	DDGGIINOSV	GIVING ODDS
DDEHLMOOST	OLD METHODS	DDGGNOOORU	GOOD GROUND
DDEHLNOOWW	HOWLED DOWN	DDGGOOOOYY	GOODY-GOODY
DDEHLORSYY	HYDROLYSED	DDGHIINNOT	DID NOTHING
DDEHLORYYZ	HYDROLYZED	DDGHIINOOR	RIDING HOOD
DDEHMOSSUY	MUDDY SHOES	DDGHRRUUYY	HURDY-GURDY
DDEHNNOTUW	HUNTED DOWN	DDGIIILMTY	GIDDY LIMIT
DDEHNOPRTU	TOP HUNDRED	DDGIIKNOOS	SKIDDOOING
DDEHNOPSUW	PUSHED DOWN	DDGIILLMNY	MIDDLINGLY
DDEHNORTUW	TWO HUNDRED	DDGIINPRRY	DRIP-DRYING
DDEIIILQSU	LIQUIDISED	DDGILLNOPY	PLODDINGLY
DDEIIILQTU	LIQUID DIET	DDGILNOPTU	TODDLING UP
DDEIIILQUZ	LIQUIDIZED	DDGINNORSW	GRINDS DOWN
DDEIIIMPSY	EPIDIDYMIS	DDGINOOPRU	DOING PROUD
DDEIIIPRST	DISPIRITED	DDGINORSWY	DYING WORDS
DDEIIIQSTU	QUIDDITIES	DDGNNOORUW	GROUND DOWN
DDEIIJNOST	DISJOINTED	DDGOOOORSU	GOOD ODOURS
DDEIIKMNRX	MIXED DRINK	DDHIIOTTUW	DID WITHOUT
DDEIIKMPUX	MIXED-UP KID	DDHIJKNNOY	JOHNNY KIDD
DDEIILLMNW	WINDMILLED	DDHILORRTW	THIRD WORLD
DDEIIMNNOU	DIMINUENDO	DDHINORRTU	THIRD ROUND
DDEIINOPSS	INDISPOSED	DDHNNOOSUW	HOUNDS DOWN
DDEIINSSST	DISSIDENTS	DDHOOOOUWY	HOW DO YOU DO?
DDEIKNNRUW	WUNDERKIND		HOW-DO-YOU-DO
DDEILLNPSY	SPLENDIDLY	DDIIIKKNSW	KIDDIWINKS
DDEILLOORS	OLD SOLDIER	DDIIMNNTUY	UNTIDY MIND
DDEILLOPSY	LOPSIDEDLY	DDIKNNORUW	UNKIND WORD
DDEILLORTT	DR.DOLITTLE	DDOOOOORRT	DOOR TO DOOR
DDEILNOSSW	SLIDES DOWN		DOOR-TO-DOOR
DDEILORRSY	DISORDERLY	DDOSSTTTUU	DUST TO DUST
DDEIMNOSTU	DISMOUNTED	DEEEEEFPRZ	DEEP FREEZE
DDEINNNOPW	PINNED DOWN		DEEP-FREEZE
DDEINNOSTU	DID ONE'S NUT		
DDEINOPSUW	UPSIDE DOWN	DEEEEELNSY	NEEDLES EYE
	UPSIDE-DOWN	DEEEEFFLRS	SELF-FEEDER
DDEINORSSS	SORDIDNESS	DEEEEFILLN	LEE-ENFIELD
DDEIRSSTTU	DISTRUSTED	DEEEEFLLPY	FEEL DEEPLY
		DEEEEFLRTV	VEERED LEFT

534

DEEEEFNRTT	ENFETTERED	DEEEHNORTY	HETERODYNE
	TENDERFEET	DEEEHNORTZ	THREE DOZEN
DEEEEGGHTT	GET THE EDGE	DEEEHNPRRS	REPREHENDS
DEEEEGINNR	ENGINEERED	DEEEHNRRTU	THEREUNDER
DEEEEGNRST	TEN DEGREES	DEEEHNSTTW	THE WEST END
DEEEEGPRRT	DEEP REGRET	DEEEHOSSSU	SUEDE SHOES
DEEEEHLLLW	WELL-HEELED	DEEEHOSSTW	SOW THE SEED
DEEEEHLNST	THE NEEDLES	DEEEHRSTYY	DRY THE EYES
DEEEEHLORV	HEELED OVER	DEEEIILRSV	DELIVERIES
DEEEEIKLLN	NEEDLELIKE	DEEEIKLLRW	WEED KILLER
DEEEEILNNP	PINE NEEDLE	DEEEILLMOS	DEMOISELLE
DEEEEKLORV	KEELED OVER	DEEEILLMPS	MILLEPEDES
DEEEEKNRSW	WEEKENDERS	DEEEILLRVY	RELIEVEDLY
DEEEEKNTWW	WET WEEKEND	DEEEILNQUV	ELEVEN QUID
DEEEEPRRSV	PERSEVERED	DEEEILNRUV	UNRELIEVED
DEEEFFGHOT	OFF THE EDGE	DEEEILNSVW	WIND-SLEEVE
DEEEFFHORS	SHEERED OFF	DEEEILPRTT	DEEP LITTER
DEEEFGILNR	GREEN FIELD	DEEEILRRSV	DELIVERERS
DEEEFHLNTU	THE NEEDFUL	DEEEILRSSW	WIRELESSED
DEEEFHLORR	FREEHOLDER	DEEEILRSVW	SILVERWEED
DEEEFIIRST	ESTERIFIED	DEEEIMMRSS	MESMERISED
DEEEFILLSU	DIESEL FUEL	DEEEIMMRSZ	MESMERIZED
DEEEFILMNT	DEFILEMENT	DEEEIMNORS	NO REMEDIES
DEEEFILNTV	FIELD EVENT	DEEEIMNOST	DEMONETISE
DEEEFILRST	FEELS TIRED	DEEEIMNOTZ	DEMONETIZE
DEEEFINOPR	OPENED FIRE	DEEEIMNRRT	DETERMINER
DEEEFINRRT	INTERFERED	DEEEIMNRST	DETERMINES
DEEEFINOTY	FIERY STEED	DEEEIMPRTV	REDEMPTIVE
DEEEFLLNOV	ELEVENFOLD	DEEEIMRSTV	SERVED TIME
DEEEFLLPTY	DEEPLY FELT	DEEEINNRTV	INTERVENED
	FELT DEEPLY		REINVENTED
DEEEFLORRW	DEFLOWERER	DEEEINPRST	PREDESTINE
DEEEFMNRRU	REFERENDUM	DEEEINPSSS	SPEEDINESS
DEEEFNOPRZ	DEEP-FROZEN	DEEEINPSTX	EXPEDIENTS
DEEEFNQRTU	FREQUENTED	DEEEINQSUZ	SQUEEZED IN
DEEEFNRTTU	UNFETTERED	DEEEINRRST	TENDERISER
DEEEFORRRT	REFERRED TO	DEEEINRRTZ	TENDERIZER
DEEEFORRST	DEER FOREST	DEEEINRSST	TENDERISES
DEEEGGGLOY	GOGGLE-EYED	DEEEINRSTT	INTERESTED
DEEEGGHHIR	HIGH DEGREE	DEEEINRSTV	REINVESTED
DEEEGGHOTT	GOT THE EDGE	DEEEINRSTZ	TENDERIZES
DEEEGGLORV	LEGGED OVER	DEEEINSSTW	TWEEDINESS
DEEEGHHINT	HEIGHTENED	DEEEIPRSSV	DEPRESSIVE
DEEEGHLNNT	LENGTHENED	DEEEIRSSTT	SIDE STREET
DEEEGIIMRV	DEMI-VIERGE	DEEEKLNORW	NEEDLEWORK
DEEEGIKNNW	WEEKENDING	DEEEKNPRSU	KEEPS UNDER
DEEEGILNRW	GENE WILDER	DEEEKOOPRR	DOORKEEPER
DEEEGIMNRT	REGIMENTED	DEEEKOPPST	KEEP POSTED
DEEEGINRSS	GREEDINESS	DEEEKOPRRS	KEEPS ORDER
DEEEGINRSU	UNDER SIEGE	DEEELLNORW	NE'ER-DO-WELL
DEEEGIRRST	REGISTERED	DEEELLNSSY	NEEDLESSLY
DEEEGLNOSY	GOLDENEYES	DEEELLPSSW	SPEEDWELLS
DEEEGNNRTU	URGENT NEED	DEEELLRSVW	SERVED WELL
DEEEGNOOST	GONE TO SEED		WELL VERSED
DEEEGNOSST	SETS ON EDGE		WELL-VERSED
DEEEGNRRSS	GREEN DRESS	DEEELNORSS	ONES ELDERS
DEEEGNRSTT	DETERGENTS	DEEELNORTV	TENDER LOVE
DEEEGOOSST	GOES TO SEED	DEEELNRTTU	UNLETTERED
DEEEGORSTW	TWO DEGREES	DEEELOPRSV	DEVELOPERS
DEEEHHKLTY	HELD THE KEY		REDEVELOPS
DEEEHIMNRT	METHEDRINE	DEEELOPRTT	TELEPORTED
DEEEHIMPSU	EUPHEMISED	DEEELPPPRU	DEEP PURPLE
DEEEHIMPUZ	EUPHEMIZED	DEEELRRSTT	RED LETTERS
DEEEHINOTY	DO IN THE EYE	DEEELRRSVY	RESERVEDLY
DEEEHIRSST	THREE SIDES	DEEEMNNOST	MET ONE'S END
DEEEHLLSSY	HEEDLESSLY	DEEEMNNOTU	DENOUEMENT
DEEEHLNOPT	TELEPHONED	DEEEMNRSSU	DEMURENESS
DEEEHLNORS	LEDERHOSEN	DEEEMOPRST	PEDOMETERS
DEEEHLNORW	LED NOWHERE	DEEENNRSST	TENDERNESS
DEEEHLOTUW	WHEELED OUT	DEEENORTVX	OVEREXTEND
DEEEHLPRTU	THE PRELUDE	DEEENPRRST	PRETENDERS

535

DEEENPRSUV	SUPERVENED
DEEENRRSTT	DETERRENTS
DEEENRRSTU	UNDERSTEER
DEEENRRSUV	UNRESERVED
DEEENRSSSS	DRESS SENSE
DEEENRSSSW	NEW DRESSES
DEEEOPRTTU	PETERED OUT
DEEEORSSTV	STEVEDORES
DEEEPPPRRS	RED PEPPERS
DEEEPPRRSSU	SUPERSEDER
DEEEPRSSST	SPEEDSTERS
DEEEPRSSSU	SUPERSEDES
DEEEQRSUYZ	SQUEEZE DRY
DEEERRSSTT	RED SETTERS
DEEFFGINRU	FIND REFUGE
DEEFFGSTTU	GET STUFFED!
DEEFFHLRSU	RESHUFFLED
DEEFFIILNR	FIND RELIEF
DEEFFIILOS	SIDE OF LIFE
DEEFFILNRU	RELIEF FUND
DEEFFORTUY	FREE OF DUTY
DEEFGHINRT	FRIGHTENED
DEEFGILLNO	FEELING OLD
DEEFGINPRY	DEEP-FRYING
DEEFGINSST	GIFTEDNESS
DEEFGIPRRU	PREFIGURED
DEEFGJORSU	FOREJUDGES
DEEFGLOOTT	GOOD FETTLE
DEEFGNOORT	FORGED NOTE
DEEFHIORSV	OVERFISHED
DEEFHLOPSS	SHEEPFOLDS
DEEFHNOORU	HOUR OF NEED
DEEFIIILST	FIDELITIES
DEEFIIINNT	INDEFINITE
DEEFIIINRT	IDENTIFIER
DEEFIIINST	IDENTIFIES
DEEFIIINTV	DEFINITIVE
DEEFIIIRVV	REVIVIFIED
DEEFIILMSU	EMULSIFIED
DEEFIILMSX	FIXED SMILE
DEEFIILNOR	REFINED OIL
DEEFIILNRR	FRIENDLIER
DEEFIILNRS	FRIENDLIES
DEEFIILNRT	FILTERED IN
	INTERFILED
DEEFIILNST	INSIDE LEFT
	INSIDE-LEFT
DEEFIILNTY	DEFINITELY
DEEFIILRST	FERTILISED
DEEFIILRTZ	FERTILIZED
DEEFIIMSTT	SEMIFITTED
DEEFIINRVW	VIEWFINDER
DEEFIIOSTX	DETOXIFIES
DEEFIIPRTT	PRETTIFIED
DEEFIKLNOS	KID ONESELF
DEEFIKNRRS	FREE DRINKS
DEEFILLLSW	SELF-WILLED
DEEFILLRSU	FLEUR-DE-LIS
DEEFILLTTW	FITTED WELL
DEEFILNRSS	FRIENDLESS
DEEFILNRYZ	FRENZIEDLY
DEEFILOORV	DIE FOR LOVE
DEEFILORTU	OUTFIELDER
DEEFIMNORW	WIN FREEDOM
DEEFINNPRS	PEN FRIENDS
	PEN-FRIENDS
DEEFINNRSW	NEW FRIENDS
DEEFINOPRW	FINE POWDER
DEEFINORRX	FERREDOXIN
DEEFINRRTU	TRUE FRIEND
DEEFINRSSV	FERVIDNESS

DEEFINRSTU	INTERFUSED
DEEFKKNOTU	DUKE OF KENT
DEEFKLNRSU	FEELS DRUNK
DEEFLLLOOV	FLOOD LEVEL
DEEFLLOTVW	TWELVEFOLD
DEEFLLRSUY	FLEUR-DE-LYS
DEEFLLSSTY	SELF-STYLED
DEEFLNNOTU	LEFT UNDONE
DEEFLNNORY	DRY ONESELF
DEEFLNRTTU	TURNED LEFT
DEEFLOORVW	FLOWED OVER
	OVERFLOWED
DEEFLORRSW	RED FLOWERS
DEEFMNOORW	WON FREEDOM
DEEFMPRSUU	REFUSE DUMP
DEEFNOOPSS	SPOON FEEDS
	SPOON-FEEDS
DEEFNOORTT	TENDERFOOT
DEEFNOPSTU	SOFTENED UP
DEEFOORSTU	SUREFOOTED
DEEGGGLNOS	GOLDEN EGGS
DEEGGIIPRW	PERIWIGGED
DEEGGINPRU	GINGERED UP
DEEGGNRSSU	RUGGEDNESS
DEEGGRSTUY	GREEDY-GUTS
DEEGHIILRS	SLEIGH RIDE
DEEGHILNTW	LEND WEIGHT
DEEGHILPSY	SIGH DEEPLY
DEEGHILRST	DELIGHTERS
DEEGHINOPS	DIPHOSGENE
DEEGHINORR	RED HERRING
DEEGHIOOST	THE GIDEONS
DEEGHIOOST	THE GOODIES
DEEGHIOTUW	OUTWEIGHED
DEEGIIINNS	INDIGENISE
DEEGIIINNZ	INDIGENIZE
DEEGIILNRV	DELIVERING
DEEGIILNSU	GUIDELINES
DEEGIILOOS	IDEOLOGIES
DEEGIILPRV	PRIVILEGED
DEEGIINNOS	GONE INSIDE
DEEGIINNRT	INGREDIENT
DEEGIINOSS	GOES INSIDE
DEEGIINPTX	EXPEDITING
DEEGIINSTY	TIE-DYEINGS
DEEGIIRSSV	DIGRESSIVE
DEEGIISSTV	DIGESTIVES
DEEGIKLLST	GETS KILLED
DEEGILLMNO	GOLDEN MILE
DEEGILNNOR	LINGERED ON
DEEGILNOPV	DEVELOPING
DEEGILNRSY	RESIGNEDLY
DEEGILOOSU	IDEOLOGUES
DEEGILOPRS	RIDGEPOLES
DEEGIMORST	GEOMETRIDS
DEEGINNNOT	NEEDING NOT
DEEGINNPRT	PRETENDING
DEEGINNRRS	RENDERINGS
DEEGINOOPT	PIGEON-TOED
DEEGINORRR	REORDERING
DEEGINORST	REDINGOTES
DEEGINOTTU	TONGUE-TIED
DEEGINOTUW	WEEDING OUT
DEEGINPPSU	SPEEDING UP
DEEGINPRSS	DEPRESSING
DEEGINRRRS	DERRINGERS
DEEGINRRSS	REDRESSING
DEEGIOORVW	GOOD REVIEW
DEEGIORRSV	GIVE ORDERS
DEEGIORRTW	GET WORRIED
DEEGIPRSST	PREDIGESTS

DEEGJNOSUY	JUDY GEESON	DEEIILLSTT	LET IT SLIDE
DEEGKLNNOS	DOG KENNELS	DEEIILMPST	SIMPLE DIET
DEEGKNOTTT	GET KNOTTED!		SPEED LIMIT
DEEGLLNORU	GOLDEN RULE	DEEIILNNRT	INTERLINED
DEEGLNNOSS	GOLDENNESS	DEEIILNNST	LISTENED IN
DEEGLOOOPP	GOOD PEOPLE	DEEIILNRUW	UNWIELDIER
DEEGMNOOSS	GOODNESS ME!	DEEIILNSTU	LUTEINISED
DEEGMOOPRT	GOOD TEMPER	DEEIILNTUZ	LUTEINIZED
DEEGMRSSSY	GYM DRESSES	DEEIILPRRV	PILE DRIVER
DEEGNNOOSU	ENDOGENOUS	DEEIILRSST	STERILISED
DEEGNNOPRU	GREEN POUND	DEEIILRSSV	SILVERSIDE
DEEGNOOSSS	GOODNESSES	DEEIILRSTV	DEVILTRIES
DEEGNORSST	DESERT SONG	DEEIILRSTZ	STERILIZED
DEEGNRRTUY	TURNED GREY	DEEIILRSVY	DERISIVELY
DEEGOOPRTU	GOOD REPUTE	DEEIIMMNPT	IMPEDIMENT
DEEGOPRRSS	PROGRESSED	DEEIIMMSUZ	MEDIUM SIZE
DEEHHILOSY	HIDEY-HOLES	DEEIIMNNRT	DINNER TIME
DEEHHKLOTY	HOLD THE KEY	DEEIIMNRST	MINISTERED
DEEHHMOPRT	DROP THE HEM	DEEIIMOPST	EPITOMISED
DEEHHNNOORS	SHOE-HORNED	DEEIIMOPTZ	EPITOMIZED
DEEHIIOOSTU	DO THE HOUSE	DEEIINNOSV	ENVISIONED
DEEHILLRSV	SHRIVELLED	DEEIINNOTW	NEW EDITION
DEEHILMORS	DEMOLISHER	DEEIINNRTT	TRIDENTINE
DEEHILMOSS	DEMOLISHES	DEEIINNSSV	DIVINENESS
DEEHILNOST	ON THE SLIDE	DEEIINOPTT	PETITIONED
DEEHILOOTT	THEODOLITE	DEEIINOPTX	EXPEDITION
DEEHIMNORV	DRIVEN HOME	DEEIINPSST	STEP INSIDE
DEEHIMNPST	THE MENDIPS	DEEIINPTTU	INEPTITUDE
DEEHIMORSV	DRIVES HOME	DEEIINQTUU	INQUIETUDE
DEEHIMOSST	METHODISES	DEEIINRSTW	WINTERISED
DEEHIMOSTZ	METHODIZES	DEEIINRTWZ	WINTERIZED
DEEHINNRRS	NED SHERRIN	DEEIINSSST	SENSITISED
DEEHINORST	DINOTHERES	DEEIINSSTW	WEST INDIES
DEEHINRSSW	SWINEHERDS	DEEIINSSTZ	SENSITIZED
DEEHIOOPST	HOPES TO DIE	DEEIIOPSSX	EPOXIDISES
DEEHIOPPRS	PROPHESIED	DEEIIOPSXZ	EPOXIDIZES
DEEHIORSTV	SHROVETIDE	DEEIIPRSSV	DISPERSIVE
DEEHIRRSTV	THIRD VERSE	DEEIIPSSSW	SIDESWIPES
DEEHKNOOOS	HOOKED NOSE	DEEIJMNOSW	JIMSONWEED
DEEHLLMOPR	PHELLODERM	DEEIJNORRS	REJOINDERS
DEEHLLOSTU	SHELLED OUT	DEEIJNOSTT	JETTISONED
DEEHLNOPRS	PENHOLDERS	DEEIJNOSTY	SEEDY JOINT
DEEHLPRTUY	DEEPLY HURT	DEEIKKLLOO	LOOKED LIKE
DEEHMMOOPR	ROMPED HOME	DEEIKLLOPW	KEWPIE DOLL
DEEHMNOOST	SMOOTHENED	DEEIKLLORV	OVERKILLED
DEEHMNOSTW	NEW METHODS	DEEIKMMNOR	DEREK NIMMO
DEEHMOOSUV	MOVED HOUSE	DEEIKMNNOS	END IN SMOKE
DEEHMORRTY	HYDROMETER	DEEIKNSSTW	STINKWEEDS
DEEHMORSVW	SHREWD MOVE	DEEIKORSST	SIDESTROKE
DEEHNOOOSW	WOODEN SHOE	DEEILLMNUW	MULLED WINE
DEEHNOOPPS	OPENED SHOP	DEEILLMPSS	MISSPELLED
DEEHNOPSTY	ENDOPHYTES	DEEILLNOTW	DONE IT WELL
DEEHNORRTU	ROUND THREE	DEEILLORRS	DROLLERIES
DEEHNRRSTU	THUNDERERS	DEEILLOSTW	DOES IT WELL
DEEHNRSSSW	SHREWDNESS	DEEILLSTTU	LITTLE USED
DEEHOORSVW	SHOWED OVER	DEEILLSUVY	DELUSIVELY
DEEHOORTXY	HETERODOXY	DEEILMMNOT	IDLE MOMENT
DEEHOPRSTT	POTS THE RED	DEEILMNOSS	SOLEMNISED
DEEHOPRSUV	PUSHED OVER	DEEILMNOST	OLDEN TIMES
DEEHORRSTW	THREE WORDS	DEEILMNOSV	DIME NOVELS
DEEHORSTUU	USHERED OUT	DEEILMNOSZ	SOLEMNIZED
DEEHSSSTTU	DUSTSHEETS	DEEILNNORT	TENDERLOIN
DEEIIINPPR	PIPERIDINE	DEEILNNOTV	VIOLENT END
DEEIIINSTT	IDENTITIES	DEEILNNQTU	DELINQUENT
DEEIIKLLMT	KILLED TIME	DEEILNNRSU	UNDERLINES
DEEIIKLOSW	DO LIKEWISE	DEEILNOPRU	RELIED UPON
DEEIIKMNNP	KEEP IN MIND	DEEILNORVY	ON DELIVERY
DEEIILLMPR	IMPERILLED	DEEILNOSSS	SOLID SENSE
DEEIILLMPS	MILLIPEDES	DEEILNOSTT	LISTENED TO
DEEIILLNOS	LINSEED OIL	DEEILNPRST	SPLINTERED
DEEIILLOPT	LEPIDOLITE	DEEILNPSTU	PLENITUDES

DEEILNRSSW	WILDERNESS	DEEKLNORSY	LORD KEYNES
DEEILNRSTU	INTERLUDES	DEEKLOOORV	LOOKED OVER
DEEILNSSTU	DILUTENESS		OVERLOOKED
DEEILOPRSS	DESPOILERS	DEEKMOOPSS	SMOKES DOPE
DEEILOPRWW	WIELD POWER	DEEKNOOPRW	OPEN-WORKED
DEEILPRSUV	PULVERISED	DEEKOORRVW	OVERWORKED
DEEILPRUVZ	PULVERIZED		WORKED OVER
DEEILQTUVW	TWELVE QUID	DEEKOPPSTT	KEPT POSTED
DEEILRRSSV	DRIVERLESS	DEELLNORTY	REDOLENTLY
DEEIMMNNOSU	EUDEMONISM	DEELLNRSSU	UNDERSELLS
DEEIMMNSUW	NEWS MEDIUM	DEELLNRTUW	WELL-TURNED
DEEIMNNNTT	INTENDMENT	DEELLOORRV	ROLLED OVER
DEEIMNNRSU	UNDERMINES	DEELLOPRUV	PULLED OVER
DEEIMNOOPS	EMPOISONED	DEELLOPSTU	SPELLED OUT
DEEIMNOPRT	REDEMPTION	DEELLORVWY	DO VERY WELL
DEEIMNORSS	MODERNISES	DEELLOSTUW	SWELLED OUT
	SERMONISED	DEELMMNOPU	NOM DE PLUME
DEEIMNORSZ	MODERNIZES	DEELMNNOSY	LENDS MONEY
	SERMONIZED	DEELMNOPTY	DEPLOYMENT
DEEIMNOSTU	EUDEMONIST	DEELMNOPUY	UNEMPLOYED
DEEIMNPSST	SPENDS TIME	DEELMOOORV	LOOMED OVER
DEEIMNSTTV	DIVESTMENT	DEELMORSVY	VERY SELDOM
DEEIMOORST	METEOROIDS	DEELNNOOSU	UNLOOSENED
DEEIMOORTV	DO OVERTIME	DEELNNOOTW	LET ONE DOWN
DEEIMOPRST	TEMPORISED	DEELNNOSTW	NESTLE DOWN
DEEIMOPRTZ	TEMPORIZED	DEELNOOPSU	LOOSENED UP
DEEIMORSST	DIME STORES	DEELNOOSST	LODESTONES
	DOSIMETERS	DEELNOPRUX	UNEXPLORED
DEEIMPRSST	DISTEMPERS	DEELNOPSSU	SOUND SLEEP
DEEIMPSSTU	MESSED IT UP	DEELNOSTTW	SETTLE DOWN
DEEIMSSSTY	SYSTEMISED	DEELNOSTUU	EDENTULOUS
DEEIMSSTYZ	SYSTEMIZED	DEELOPRRTY	REPORTEDLY
DEEINNNOSU	INNUENDOES	DEELOPRSTY	PROSELYTED
DEEINNOPRS	PREDNISONE	DEELORTTUV	TURTLE DOVE
DEEINNORST	INTERNODES		TURTLEDOVE
DEEINNOSTT	DETENTIONS	DEELPRSTTU	SPLUTTERED
DEEINNRSTU	INDENTURES	DEEMNNOPSY	SPEND MONEY
DEEINOPRSS	DEPRESSION	DEEMNNORSS	MODERNNESS
DEEINOPRST	INTERPOSED	DEEMNNORTW	WONDERMENT
DEEINOPSUZ	SEIZED UPON	DEEMNNOSTW	ENDOWMENTS
DEEINOQSTU	QUESTIONED	DEEMNOORRY	MONEY ORDER
DEEINORRST	SET IN ORDER	DEEMNOPRTT	DEPORTMENT
DEEINORSST	DESERTIONS	DEEMNORSTU	TREMENDOUS
DEEINORSTW	NEWS EDITOR	DEEMNOOSSW	WOODENNESS
DEEINPRRST	RINDERPEST	DEENNOPRST	RESPONDENT
DEEINPRSSS	DISPENSERS	DEENNORSTU	UNDERTONES
DEEINPRSST	PRESIDENTS	DEENNORSUV	ROUND SEVEN
DEEINQRTUU	UNREQUITED	DEENNORSVW	NEWSVENDOR
DEEINRRTUW	UNDERWRITE	DEENNOSSSU	SOUND SENSE
DEEINRSSSS	DRESSINESS	DEENNOSSTW	WONTEDNESS
DEEINRSSST	DISSENTERS	DEENOOPRSS	ENDOSPORES
DEEINRSTTV	TEST-DRIVEN	DEENOORSST	ROOTEDNESS
DEEIOORSTV	OVERDOES IT	DEENOPPRUY	PREYED UPON
DEEIOPPRRT	PROPERTIED	DEENOPPSTU	PUT ON SPEED
DEEIOPPRSS	PREDISPOSE	DEENOPRRSU	RUDE PERSON
DEEIOPPRST	REST PERIOD	DEENOPRSSV	OVERSPENDS
DEEIOPRSUX	OEDIPUS REX	DEENOPRSTT	TENDER SPOT
DEEIORRRST	TERRORISED	DEENOPSSWW	SWEEPS DOWN
DEEIORRRSV	OVER-RIDERS	DEENOQRTUU	UNDERQUOTE
DEEIORRRTZ	TERRORIZED	DEENOORSUV	VEERS ROUND
DEEIPPSSTU	SPEEDS IT UP	DEENORRTUV	OVERTURNED
DEEIPRSSUV	SUPERVISED		TURNED OVER
DEEIRSSSST	DISTRESSES	DEENORRTUW	UNDERWROTE
DEEIRSSTTV	TEST-DRIVES	DEENORSSTU	RUNS TO SEED
DEEJMOPRUV	JUMPED OVER	DEENORSUVZ	RENDEZVOUS
DEEJOPRTUX	JUDO EXPERT	DEENOSSTUV	DEVOUTNESS
DEEKLLLOOW	LOOKED WELL	DEENOSSTUW	SWEET SOUND
DEEKLLORWW	WORKED WELL	DEENPRSSSU	SUSPENDERS
DEEKLMRTTU	KETTLE DRUM	DEENRRRSSU	SURRENDERS
	KETTLEDRUM	DEENRSSSTU	UNSTRESSED
DEEKLNNOSW	KNEELS DOWN	DEEOOPPRTV	OVERTOPPED

DEEEOOPRRSW	DEEP SORROW	DEFHLOSTUU	FLUSHED OUT
DEEEOORRSTT	STREET DOOR	DEFHNORSST	SENDS FORTH
DEEEOORSTUW	SWEET ODOUR	DEFIIILMPS	SIMPLIFIED
DEEEOPPRSSU	SUPERPOSED	DEFIIILNTY	INFIDELITY
DEEEOPPSTTU	STEPPED OUT	DEFIIILORS	SOLIDIFIER
DEEEOPRRSSS	DEPRESSORS	DEFIIINNOT	DEFINITION
DEEEOPRRTUV	PROVED TRUE	DEFIIINNTU	INFINITUDE
DEEEOPRSSST	TOP-DRESSES	DEFIILLNSU	FULL INSIDE
DEEEORRSSTY	DESTROYERS	DEFIILLQUU	LIQUID FUEL
DEEORSSTWW	SWEET WORDS	DEFIILLRRS	FIRE DRILLS
DEEPPRSSSU	SUPPRESSED	DEFIILMORT	FILM EDITOR
DEFFFLOTUU	FLUFFED OUT	DEFIILORSS	SOLDIFIERS
DEFFGINNOR	FORFENDING	DEFIILOSSS	FOSSILISED
DEFFGINNOS	SENDING OFF	DEFIILOSSZ	FOSSILIZED
DEFFGNOOPS	SPONGED OFF	DEFIILRTUY	YIELD FRUIT
DEFFGOOORT	GOOD EFFORT	DEFIILSTTU	STULTIFIED
DEFFHIKOSW	WHISKED OFF	DEFIIMRTUX	MIXED FRUIT
DEFFHIMORS	SHERIFFDOM	DEFIINOPTX	FIXED POINT
DEFFHIORRU	HURRIED OFF		FIXED-POINT
DEFFIIMNRR	FIRM FRIEND	DEFIINSSST	DISINFESTS
DEFFIKOPPS	SKIPPED OFF	DEFIIOPRSU	PERFIDIOUS
DEFFILNOSU	FOUL FIENDS	DEFIIORRTT	TRIED FOR IT
DEFFNOOORZ	FROZEN FOOD	DEFIKLORSW	FIELDWORKS
DEFFOOOPRT	TROOPED OFF	DEFIKNNOUW	KNIFE WOUND
DEFFOOPPST	STOPPED OFF	DEFILLORWW	WILD FLOWER
DEFFOORTTT	TROTTED OFF		WILDFOWLER
DEFFOPPRUW	POWDER PUFF	DEFILNNOOS	DEN OF LIONS
DEFFRRTUYY	TEDDY DUFFY	DEFILNNOTY	NINETYFOLD
DEFGGILLNS	FLEDGLINGS	DEFILNNRUY	UNFRIENDLY
DEFGGIOORU	GOOD FIGURE	DEFILNORSS	FLORIDNESS
DEFGHILLTU	DELIGHTFUL	DEFILNORWW	WINDFLOWER
DEFGHILNOR	FINGERHOLD	DEFILNOTUY	LINE OF DUTY
DEFGHILOTY	EIGHTYFOLD	DEFILOPRST	FIELD SPORT
DEFGHIOPRS	HERD OF PIGS	DEFILOPTUU	FOULED IT UP
DEFGHLORUU	FURLOUGHED	DEFILOTUZZ	FIZZLED OUT
DEFGHOOOSU	HOUSE OF GOD	DEFIMOORSX	FOOD MIXERS
DEFGIILNRR	GIRL FRIEND	DEFIMRSTTU	FRED TITMUS
	GIRLFRIEND	DEFINOPSUV	FIVE POUNDS
DEFGIINNUY	UNEDIFYING	DEFINORSUV	FIVE ROUNDS
DEFGIINORT	FRIGID TONE	DEFIOOPRRV	PROVIDE FOR
DEFGIINORZ	FRIGID ZONE	DEFIORRRST	FIRST ORDER
DEFGIINOTW	DOTING WIFE	DEFKKOORUY	DUKE OF YORK
DEFGIINRSS	FRIGIDNESS	DEFLLLOOSW	OLD FELLOWS
DEFGIIRSSU	DISFIGURES	DEFLLNOOOW	FOLLOWED ON
DEFGILNNSY	SEND FLYING		FOLLOWED-ON
DEFGILOOSS	ISLE OF DOGS	DEFLLOOPUW	FOLLOWED UP
DEFGINNORS	SENDING FOR	DEFLNOTTWY	TWENTYFOLD
DEFGINNORU	FOUNDERING	DEFLOPPRRU	DROPPERFUL
DEFGINOOTW	WING-FOOTED	DEFMNOORRU	MOURNED FOR
DEFGINORST	DEFROSTING	DEFNNOOPRZ	FROZEN POND
DEFGINOSTW	GETS WIND OF	DEFNOOPRRU	UNDERPROOF
DEFGLLOOOW	GOOD FELLOW	DEFNORSTTU	TURNED SOFT
DEFGNOOOOR	GOOD FOR ONE	DEFOOORRTU	OUT OF ORDER
DEFGNOORRU	FOREGROUND	DEFOOOORSST	FOOD STORES
DEFGNOORTT	DONT FORGET	DEFOSSSTTU	SET OF STUDS
DEFGOOPRRS	DROP-FORGES	DEGGGLNOTU	GOLD NUGGET
DEFHIIIMRU	HUMIDIFIER	DEGGHIILNT	DELIGHTING
DEFHIIIMSU	HUMIDIFIES	DEGGHIIPRS	SHIP-RIGGED
DEFHIILNSY	FIENDISHLY	DEGGHIORUU	ROUGH GUIDE
DEFHIINNRS	FISH DINNER	DEGGHLNOOT	GOOD LENGTH
DEFHIINNST	TINNED FISH	DEGGHNOOOU	GOOD ENOUGH
DEFHIINNSU	UNFINISHED	DEGGIINRSS	DIGRESSING
DEFHIINPRS	FRIENDSHIP	DEGGIINRTT	GETTING RID
DEFHIINPSU	FINISHED UP	DEGGIJNPRU	PREJUDGING
DEFHIKMOSS	SMOKED FISH	DEGGILLNOR	GOLDEN GIRL
DEFHILMORT	THE OLD FIRM	DEGGILMNSU	SMUGGLED IN
DEFHILOPST	SHOPLIFTED	DEGGILNNOR	GOLDEN RING
DEFHILORSU	FLOURISHED	DEGGILNOTT	GETTING OLD
DEFHLNOSUW	FLESH WOUND	DEGGINNNOR	DINNER GONG
DEFHLOOOSW	WHOLEFOODS	DEGGINNORU	GOING UNDER
DEFHLORSSU	RUDOLF HESS		UNDERGOING

539

DEGGINORUV	GIVE GROUND	DEGIKLMOOR	LOOKED GRIM
DEGGLNPSUU	SNUGGLED UP	DEGIKLORST	GOLD STRIKE
DEGHHILSST	SHEDS LIGHT		STRIKE GOLD
DEGHHINOTU	IN THE DOUGH	DEGILLNNOW	DWELLING ON
DEGHIILSST	SIDELIGHTS	DEGILLOOTT	LITTLE GOOD
DEGHIINNST	END IN SIGHT	DEGILLORST	OLDEST GIRL
DEGHILLTUY	HELD GUILTY	DEGILLOSSY	SYLLOGISED
DEGHILNOTW	WIN THE GOLD	DEGILLOSYZ	SYLLOGIZED
DEGHILORUV	LIVED ROUGH	DEGILMNORR	MODERN GIRL
DEGHINNORT	DETHRONING	DEGILMNORS	SMOLDERING
DEGHINNRTU	THUNDERING	DEGILMNORU	MOULDERING
DEGHINORTU	ROUND EIGHT		REMOULDING
DEGHINOSWW	WEIGHS DOWN	DEGILNNPRU	PLUNDERING
DEGHINRSST	NIGHTDRESS	DEGILNNRSU	UNDERLINGS
DEGHIOOSSW	GOOD WISHES	DEGILNNRUY	UNDERLYING
DEGHIORRSU	RIDES ROUGH	DEGILNNSSW	LENDS WINGS
	ROUGH RIDES	DEGILNOOPR	LONG PERIOD
	ROUGH-DRIES	DEGILNOORS	GONDOLIERS
DEGHIOSTTU	DOUGHTIEST	DEGILNOSTU	LONGITUDES
DEGHIRSSTT	TIGHT DRESS		SINGLED OUT
DEGHLNNOOR	LONG-HORNED	DEGILNRSTU	DELUSTRING
DEGHLNOORU	GOLDEN HOUR	DEGILOOOSX	DOXOLOGIES
DEGHLNOOTW	WON THE GOLD	DEGILOOPST	PEDOLOGIST
DEGHMNOORU	HOME GROUND	DEGIMNNORW	MORNING DEW
DEGHMOORST	GODMOTHERS	DEGIMNNOTU	DEMOUNTING
DEGHNOOOTU	ENOUGH TO DO	DEGIMNSSSU	SMUDGINESS
DEGHNORSUY	GREYHOUNDS	DEGIMOOOTV	GOOD MOTIVE
DEGHOOOPST	HOPES TO GOD	DEGIMRSSTY	GRID SYSTEM
DEGHOORTUU	ROUGHED OUT	DEGINNOOTT	GOOD INTENT
DEGHOSSTUW	SHOWED GUTS	DEGINNOPRS	RESPONDING
DEGHPRRSUU	DRUG PUSHER	DEGINNOPRT	PORTENDING
DEGIIILMNT	DELIMITING	DEGINNOPUX	EXPOUNDING
DEGIIILNSV	LIVE IN DIGS	DEGINNORST	GRINDSTONE
DEGIIIMNRS	DIMERISING	DEGINNORSU	RESOUNDING
DEGIIIMNRZ	DIMERIZING	DEGINNOSTU	SENDING OUT
DEGIIINNOS	DEIONISING	DEGINNPSSU	SUSPENDING
DEGIIINNOZ	DEIONIZING	DEGINNRRTU	TURNING RED
DEGIIINRST	RISING TIDE	DEGINNRSSU	UNDRESSING
DEGIIINSSS	DISSEISING	DEGINOOOPW	WOOD PIGEON
DEGIIINSSU	IN DISGUISE		WOODPIGEON
DEGIIIRSST	DIGITISERS	DEGINOOPRT	TORPEDOING
DEGIIIRSTZ	DIGITIZERS	DEGINOORSV	OVERDOSING
DEGIILLMRX	MIXED GRILL	DEGINOORSW	DOING WORSE
DEGIILLNNW	INDWELLING	DEGINOPSST	SIGNPOSTED
DEGIILLNPS	DISPELLING	DEGINORRTW	GROWN TIRED
DEGIILLNRV	DRIVELLING	DEGINORRUW	GROUND WIRE
DEGIILLNTY	DILIGENTLY	DEGINORSST	STRONG SIDE
DEGIILNNUY	UNYIELDING	DEGINORSTY	DESTROYING
DEGIILNOPS	DESPOILING	DEGINOSSST	STODGINESS
DEGIILNORS	SOLDIERING	DEGINOSTTW	GETS IT DOWN
DEGIILNOSS	LOSING SIDE	DEGINPRSSU	DRESSING UP
DEGIILOOST	IDEOLOGIST	DEGINRSSTU	TURGIDNESS
DEGIILOPSS	IDLE GOSSIP	DEGIOORRTW	GOT WORRIED
DEGIIMNNOS	DEMONISING	DEGIOPSSTU	GUIDEPOSTS
DEGIIMNNOZ	DEMONIZING	DEGIORRSTW	GROWS TIRED
DEGIIMNOOT	IN GOOD TIME	DEGKLOOOOR	GOOD LOOKER
DEGIIMNRSY	SEMIDRYING		GOOD-LOOKER
DEGIINNOSU	INDIGENOUS	DEGLLNOOWW	GO DOWN WELL
DEGIINNPSS	DISPENSING	DEGLMNOOOY	DEMONOLOGY
DEGIINNSST	DISSENTING	DEGLNNRSUU	UNDERSLUNG
DEGIINOPRX	PEROXIDING	DEGLNOOOTY	DEONTOLOGY
DEGIINOPST	DEPOSITING	DEGLNOORRW	GROWN OLDER
DEGIINORRV	OVERRIDING	DEGLNOORSU	LOSE GROUND
	RIDING OVER	DEGLNORSSU	GROUNDLESS
DEGIINORSS	DIGRESSION	DEGLOORRSW	GROWS OLDER
DEGIINORTV	TIDING OVER	DEGLOORSTU	GOOD RESULT
DEGIINPRSS	DISPERSING	DEGLOORTTY	TROGLODYTE
DEGIINPRST	SPRING TIDE	DEGMMOOORY	GOOD MEMORY
DEGIINPSTU	DEPUTISING	DEGMNNORSU	GROUNDSMEN
DEGIINPTUZ	DEPUTIZING	DEGMNOOSSY	MY GOODNESS!
DEGIINRSTW	WEST RIDING	DEGMOSSSTY	STODGY MESS

DEGNNOOPSW	SPONGE DOWN	DEHIOORSST	SISTERHOOD
DEGNNOOTUY	GONE ON DUTY	DEHIOPPRSW	WORSHIPPED
DEGNNORRTU	GROUND RENT	DEHIOPSTWY	SHOWED PITY
DEGNOOOOPRS	GOOD PERSON	DEHIORRSTV	SHORT DRIVE
DEGNOORRSW	WRONGDOERS	DEHIORRTUU	HURRIED OUT
DEGNOORRUV	OVERGROUND	DEHIOSTTTW	DO THE TWIST
DEGNOOSTUY	GOES ON DUTY	DEHIPPRRTU	UPPER THIRD
DEGNORRSUU	SURE GROUND	DEHIRRSSST	DRESS SHIRT
DEGOOOOPRRT	GOOD REPORT	DEHKLOORTU	LOOKED HURT
DEGOOPRTTY	PRETTY GOOD	DEHKLOOSST	STOKEHOLDS
DEGORRSSTU	DRUG STORES	DEHKNNORUW	HUNKER DOWN
	DRUGSTORES	DEHLLLLOOY	HELLO DOLLY
DEHHIIOOPP	HIPPIEHOOD	DEHLLOOORT	TOOLHOLDER
DEHHILORTW	WITHHOLDER	DEHLLOORWW	WHOLE WORLD
DEHHIOPPSS	PHOSPHIDES	DEHLLOOSSU	DOLLS HOUSE
DEHHLLNOSU	HELLHOUNDS	DEHLNOOPRY	POLYHEDRON
DEHHLOOSSU	HOUSEHOLDS	DEHLNOOSTY	HOLYSTONED
DEHHLORSST	THRESHOLDS	DEHLNOOTWW	THE LOW-DOWN
DEHHMOOORT	MOTHERHOOD	DEHLOORRSY	HOLY ORDERS
DEHHNOOPRY	HYDROPHONE	DEHLOORRTW	OTHER WORLD
DEHHOOOOPP	POOH-POOHED	DEHLORSSYY	HYDROLYSES
DEHHOPRTYY	HYDROPHYTE	DEHLORSYYZ	HYDROLYZES
DEHIIIMNSS	DIMINISHES	DEHMMOORSU	MUSHROOMED
DEHIIIMSTU	HUMIDITIES	DEHMNOOPRS	ENDOMORPHS
DEHIIINRST	DISINHERIT	DEHMNOOPRY	ENDOMORPHY
DEHIIKLLOO	LIKELIHOOD	DEHMNOOSST	THE OSMONDS
DEHIIKMRSS	SKIRMISHED	DEHMORRTYY	HYDROMETRY
DEHIIKNNRT	IN THE DRINK	DEHNNOOPST	SPHENODONT
DEHIILLOOV	LIVELIHOOD	DEHNNOORSU	HOURS ON END
DEHIILLSVY	DEVILISHLY	DEHNNORTTU	TENTH ROUND
DEHIILMNPU	DELPHINIUM	DEHNOORRSU	HORRENDOUS
DEHIILNSTW	IN THE WILDS	DEHNOORSTU	UNDERSHOOT
DEHIIMMNPS	MIDSHIPMEN	DEHNOORSUU	ROUNDHOUSE
DEHIINOSST	ON THIS SIDE	DEHNOPSSUW	PUSHES DOWN
DEHIIOPRST	EDITORSHIP	DEHNOORRTUU	HENRY TUDOR
DEHIIPRRTZ	THIRD PRIZE	DEHNORSTUU	THUNDEROUS
DEHIIPSSTU	THIS SIDE UP	DEHNORSWWY	WONDERS WHY
DEHIIRSTVW	WHIST DRIVE	DEHOOPRSUU	HOUSE-PROUD
DEHIKNOORW	HOODWINKER	DEHOOORRRST	SHORT ORDER
DEHIKORSST	KISS THE ROD	DEHOORSTUU	TUDOR HOUSE
DEHILNORTW	IN THE WORLD	DEHOOSSSSU	DOSS HOUSES
DEHILOOPSS	SHOPSOILED		DOSSHOUSES
DEHILOPPSU	POLISHED UP	DEHOOSTTUU	SHOUTED OUT
DEHILORRTW	LOWER THIRD	DEHORRSSST	SHORT DRESS
DEHILORSSW	WILD HORSES	DEIIIINSTV	DIVINITIES
DEHILORSTV	SHORT-LIVED	DEIIIKNSST	SINK-TIDIES
DEHILOSSTW	DISH TOWELS	DEIIILMQSU	SEMILIQUID
DEHIMMNORR	HORN-RIMMED	DEIIILMSTU	SIMILITUDE
DEHIMNOSSS	MODISHNESS	DEIIILNNSV	LIVED IN SIN
DEHIMNPSTU	IN THE DUMPS	DEIIILQRSU	LIQUIDISER
DEHIMOOPPR	HIPPODROME	DEIIILQRUZ	LIQUIDIZER
DEHIMOSSTT	METHODISTS	DEIIILQSSU	LIQUIDISES
DEHINNORRU	DINNER HOUR	DEIIILQSUZ	LIQUIDIZES
DEHINNORST	HOT DINNERS	DEIIILSVVY	DIVISIVELY
DEHINNORTU	IN THE ROUND	DEIIIMNPRY	PYRIMIDINE
DEHINNOTTU	THINNED OUT	DEIIIMNTUV	DIMINUTIVE
DEHINOOSTW	IN THE WOODS	DEIIIMSSSV	DISMISSIVE
DEHINOPSTY	HYPNOTISED	DEIIINPRST	INSPIRITED
DEHINOPTTW	DOWN THE PIT	DEIIINSSTU	DISUNITIES
DEHINOPTYZ	HYPNOTIZED	DEIIIOPRTZ	PRIZE IDIOT
DEHINORRSS	HORRIDNESS	DEIIKKLNRS	KILDERKINS
DEHINORSTT	THRENODIST	DEIIKLMNNT	TINNED MILK
DEHINORSTU	RUSHED INTO	DEIIKLNNSS	KINDLINESS
DEHINORSVW	WINDHOVERS	DEIIKLNOOS	LOOK INSIDE
DEHINOSSSV	DOVISHNESS	DEIIKMNNPT	KEPT IN MIND
DEHINOSSTY	DISHONESTY	DEIIKNNRSW	DRINKS WINE
DEHINOSTTW	TO THE WINDS	DEIIKRSSST	KID SISTERS
DEHINOSTWW	SOW THE WIND	DEIIKRSSTY	DIRTY SKIES
DEHINOTTUW	WITHOUT END	DEIILLLSVY	SILLY DEVIL
DEHINSTTUY	IN THE STUDY	DEIILLMNVY	LIVELY MIND
DEHIOOPRST	PRIESTHOOD	DEIILLMPTU	MULTIPLIED

DEIILLNUWY	UNWIELDILY	DEILLOPRRW	POWER DRILL
DEIILLOPSS	ELLIPSOIDS	DEILLOPRTT	LITTLE DROP
DEIILLRSST	DISTILLERS	DEILLORSTW	WORLDLIEST
DEIILLRSTY	DISTILLERY	DEILLORTTW	WORLD TITLE
DEIILMMNPS	SIMPLE MIND	DEILLPSYZZ	DIZZY SPELL
DEIILMNOOT	DEMOLITION	DEILLRSTUY	LURID STYLE
DEIILMNPSS	LIMPIDNESS	DEILMMOSTY	IMMODESTLY
DEIILMNRTW	MILD WINTER	DEILMNPTUY	IMPUDENTLY
DEIILNNRTY	DIRTY LINEN	DEILMORRUU	IDLE RUMOUR
DEIILNORST	TIN SOLDIER	DEILMORTWY	TIMELY WORD
DEIILNOTUV	VIOLIN DUET	DEILMSTTUU	MULTITUDES
DEIILNOTVW	LIVE IT DOWN	DEILNNNTUW	WIND TUNNEL
DEIILNPRTY	INTREPIDLY	DEILNOORSS	SOLDIERS ON
DEIILNPSST	SPINDLIEST	DEILNOORTU	OLD ROUTINE
DEIILNQSSU	LIQUIDNESS	DEILNOOTUV	DEVOLUTION
DEIILPRSTY	SPIRITEDLY	DEILNOSSWW	WINDOWLESS
DEIIMNNNOS	IN ONES MIND	DEILNOSTWY	LOW DENSITY
DEIIMNNOSS	DIMENSIONS	DEILNPQTUU	QUINTUPLED
DEIIMNOPRS	IMPRISONED	DEILNRSTTY	STRIDENTLY
DEIIMNOSSS	DEMISSIONS	DEILOORRTV	LORD IT OVER
DEIIMNPRST	MISPRINTED	DEILOORSST	OLD STORIES
DEIIMOPRSV	IMPROVISED	DEILOORSTY	TOY SOLDIER
DEIIMOSTWW	WIDOWS MITE	DEILOPPSTU	SLIPPED OUT
DEIIMPRSSU	PRESIDIUMS	DEILOSTTWW	SLOW-WITTED
DEIINNNOST	INDENTIONS	DEIMMNNORSS	MODERN MISS
DEIINNOPPT	PINPOINTED	DEIMMNORSW	SIMMER DOWN
DEIINNORST	RENDITIONS	DEIMMPSTUU	SUMMED IT UP
DEIINNOSSS	DISSENSION	DEIMNNNOOS	ON ONES MIND
DEIINNOSST	DISTENSION	DEIMNOOSSS	ENDOSMOSIS
DEIINNRSTU	DINNER SUIT	DEIMNOPRTU	IMPORTUNED
DEIINNRTTU	TURNED IT IN	DEIMNOPRUV	UNIMPROVED
DEIINNSSTU	UNTIDINESS	DEIMNORTYY	DIRTY MONEY
DEIINOOPST	DEPOSITION	DEIMORRWWY	MERRY WIDOW
	POSITIONED	DEIMRSSTTU	MISTRUSTED
DEIINOPRSS	DISPERSION	DEINNNOOSW	DOWNS IN ONE
DEIINOPRST	PRISON DIET	DEINNNOPSU	NINE POUNDS
DEIINOPRXY	PYRIDOXINE	DEINNOOPWW	OPEN WINDOW
DEIINOPSSS	INDISPOSES	DEINNOPSTU	TINNED SOUP
DEIINORSST	DISORIENTS	DEINNORSVW	DRIVEN SNOW
DEIINORSSV	DIVERSIONS	DEINNORTTU	TURNED INTO
DEIINPPRST	PIN-STRIPED		TURNED IT ON
DEIINPRRSS	SPIN-DRIERS	DEINOOPRST	DESORPTION
DEIINRSSST	IN DISTRESS	DEINOOPRXY	PYROXENOID
DEIINRSSTU	INDUSTRIES	DEINOOPTTU	OUTPOINTED
DEIINSTTTU	INSTITUTED		POINTED OUT
DEIIOOPSTV	OVIPOSITED	DEINOOQTUX	DON QUIXOTE
DEIIORSTTU	RIDES IT OUT	DEINOORRTZ	TORRID ZONE
DEIIORTTTU	TRIED IT OUT	DEINOOSSST	DOTS ONE'S I'S
DEIIPRSTUV	DISRUPTIVE	DEINOOSSSU	ODIOUSNESS
DEIJKLORSW	JOKERS WILD	DEINOPRRTU	PUT IN ORDER
DEIJMNOPTU	JUMPED INTO	DEINOPRSST	DRIPSTONES
DEIJMOPTTU	JUMPED TO IT	DEINORRSST	TORRIDNESS
DEIJNNNOOR	NONJOINDER	DEINORSSSW	DROWSINESS
DEIKLMNNOR	LEMON DRINK	DEINORSTWW	WRITE-DOWNS
DEIKLNOOOT	LOOKED INTO		WRITES DOWN
DEIKLNOTUW	WINKLED OUT	DEINPRRSST	PRINT DRESS
DEIKLOOPTU	LOOKED IT UP	DEINPRSSTU	PUTRIDNESS
DEIKLOORST	LOOKS TIRED	DEINPRTTUU	TURNED IT UP
DEIKNNNSSU	UNKINDNESS	DEINPSSSTU	STUPIDNESS
DEIKNNOPRS	KIND PERSON	DEINOTTUWY	TWENTY QUID
DEIKNORSTW	STRIKE DOWN	DEINRSSSTU	STURDINESS
DEIKOORRTW	RIDE TO WORK	DEIOOPRSST	DEPOSITORS
DEIKOPPSTU	SKIPPED OUT	DEIOOPRSTY	DEPOSITORY
DEILLMNSSY	MINDLESSLY	DEIOPRRSTW	SPIDERWORT
DEILLNNOTY	INDOLENTLY	DEIOPSSSSS	DISPOSSESS
DEILLNOOST	TOLD NO LIES	DEIORSSTTU	STRIDES OUT
DEILLNOPTT	LITTLE POND	DEJLLLMOUY	JELLY MOULD
DEILLNORSS	LORDLINESS	DEKKNOORWY	DONKEY WORK
DEILLNOVVY	INVOLVEDLY		DONKEYWORK
DEILLNSSWY	WINDLESSLY	DEKLNOOOPU	LOOKED UPON
DEILLOOSWW	WISE OLD OWL	DEKLOOOPTU	LOOKED UP TO

DEKLOOPRSY	LOOKED SPRY
DEKNNOOSTW	DOESN'T KNOW
DEKNOOPRSW	SPOKEN WORD
DEKNOOPRUV	UNPROVOKED
DEKNOORSTW	DOWNSTROKE
DEKOOORRST	TOOK ORDERS
DEKOOORRTW	RODE TO WORK
DEKOOORRWW	WOODWORKER
DELLMMNOTU	DULL MOMENT
DELLNNOORS	LORD NELSON
DELLNOPSUW	DWELLS UPON
DELLOSSUUY	SEDULOUSLY
DELMOOOORSX	LOXODROMES
DELNNOOSTW	WEST LONDON
DELNNOPSSU	NONPLUSSED
DELNNOTUWY	UNWONTEDLY
DELNOOPSSW	SLOPES DOWN
DELNOOPTTY	PLENTY TO DO
DELNOOSUVW	VOWEL SOUND
DELNOPRSSU	SPLENDOURS
DELNOPRSSU	SPLENDROUS
DELOOOPSTY	TOY POODLES
DELOOPRRTU	LOUD REPORT
DELOOPRRWW	WORLD POWER
DELOPPSSUY	SUPPOSEDLY
DELORSTTUY	TUDOR STYLE
DEMMNOPSUU	SUMMONED UP
DEMNOOPSSW	EPSOM DOWNS
DEMNOORSUV	MOVES ROUND
DEMNOPSSUY	PSEUDONYMS
DEMNORSTUU	SURMOUNTED
DEMOOOOPRRW	POWDER ROOM
DEMOPRSTWY	EMPTY WORDS
DEMPRSSTUW	DREW STUMPS
DENNOPRTUU	TURNED UPON
DENNORSSTU	ROTUNDNESS
DENOOORTTW	ROTTEN WOOD
DENOOPPRRU	PROPOUNDER
DENOORRTUW	ROUND TOWER
DENOPSSTUU	STUPENDOUS
DENORRSSTW	STERN WORDS
DENORRSTUU	TURNED SOUR
DENRSTTUYY	SENTRY DUTY
DEOOOPRTTU	TROOPED OUT
DEOOPPSTTU	STOPPED OUT
DEOORTTTTU	TROTTED OUT
DEORRSTTUY	DUTY ROSTER
DEPRSSSSTU	PRESS-STUDS
DFFFINOPUW	PUFF OF WIND
DFFFOOSSTU	FOODSTUFFS
DFFGHILNOO	HOLDING OFF
DFFGIINORV	DRIVING OFF
DFFHINORTU	FIFTH ROUND
DFFIIKNRST	STIFF DRINK
DFFIMMNOOT	DOM MINTOFF
DFFNOOSTUU	OUT OF FUNDS
DFGGIIINNY	DIGNIFYING
DFGHIINORS	FISHING ROD
DFGHILLOOT	FLOODLIGHT
DFGHIORSTW	SWORD FIGHT
DFGIIILNSU	FLUIDISING
DFGIIILNUZ	FLUIDIZING
DFGIILNNOW	FILING DOWN
DFGIILNTUY	FIND GUILTY
DFGIINNOTU	FINDING OUT
DFGILLMOOS	MILLS OF GOD
DFGILNNOSU	FOUNDLINGS
DFGILNNOSW	FLINGS DOWN
DFGIMNOOOR	IN GOOD FORM
DFGIMNORRU	FIRM GROUND
DFGINOSTUW	GUST OF WIND

DFGLNOOOST	TONS OF GOLD
DFGLOOOOSW	LOGS OF WOOD
DFGNOORSTU	SOFT GROUND
DFGOOOORUY	GOOD FOR YOU
DFHHIIRSTT	THIRD SHIFT
DFHHLOORST	HOLDS FORTH
DFHILMOOTY	FILTHY MOOD
DFHILOORRT	THIRD FLOOR
DFHILOORSY	HYDROFOILS
DFHILORTTY	THIRTYFOLD
DFHLNOOSUW	WOLFHOUNDS
DFHLNSSSUU	SLUSH FUNDS
DFHLOOOOPT	PHOTOFLOOD
DFHMOOOORU	HOUR OF DOOM
DFIIKNRRTU	FRUIT DRINK
DFIILMNOPT	PINT OF MILD
DFIILMOSTU	FILM STUDIO
DFIKLOPPSY	FLOPPY DISK
DFILOOPSTU	STUPID FOOL
DFINOPRTUY	PROFUNDITY
DFINORRSTU	FIRST ROUND
DFINORSSTW	SNOWDRIFTS
DFIOOORSTT	STOOD FOR IT
DFKLNNOOOW	KNOWN OF OLD
DFKLNOOOSW	KNOWS OF OLD
DFLNOOPRUY	PROFOUNDLY
DFLOOPPSUY	FOOD SUPPLY
DFLOOORTTY	TROLL VOTLEY
DFNOOOPRSU	SOUNDPROOF
DFNOOPRSUU	FOUR POUNDS
DFNORTTUUY	TURN OF DUTY
DFOOOOORSTU	OUT OF DOORS
DFOOOPRSTU	STOOD UP FOR
DFOORTTUUY	TOUR OF DUTY
DGGGIINORS	DISGORGING
DGGGILNOOY	LYING DOGGO
DGGGILNRUY	GRUDGINGLY
DGGGINNRUU	UNGRUDGING
DGGHHIIINR	RIDING HIGH
DGGHHIIINV	HIGH DIVING
DGGHHINORU	HIGH GROUND
DGGHIINORT	DOING RIGHT
DGGHINNOTU	HUNTING DOG
DGGHINOOST	GOOD THINGS
DGGIIIINST	DIGITISING
DGGIIIINTZ	DIGITIZING
DGGIIIMNSU	MISGUIDING
DGGIIINSSU	DISGUISING
DGGIIJMNSU	MISJUDGING
DGGIILLNOW	GOD WILLING
DGGIILLNNRY	GRINDINGLY
DGGIILNOOV	GOOD LIVING
DGGIIMNOOT	GOOD TIMING
DGGIINSSTU	DISGUSTING
DGGILNNORU	GROUNDLING
DGGILNOOOV	GOOD LOVING
DGGILNOORW	GROWING OLD
DGGINNOORU	GOING ROUND
DGGINNOORW	DOING WRONG
	WRONGDOING
DGGINNOUYY	DYING YOUNG
DGGNOOORTU	GO TO GROUND
DGHHIKNOOT	KNIGHTHOOD
DGHHILOSTT	HOLDS TIGHT
DGHHINOPST	DIPHTHONGS
DGHIIINPRW	RIDING WHIP
DGHIIINSTW	SIDING WITH
DGHIIIORTT	RIGHT IDIOT
DGHIILMNTY	MIDNIGHTLY
DGHIINOSTU	DISHING OUT
DGHILLNOOW	GO DOWNHILL

DGHILLOTUY	HOLD GUILTY	DHIIQRTTUY	THIRTY QUID
DGHILMOSST	GOLDSMITHS	DHIKNORRST	SHORT DRINK
DGHILNOOTU	HOLDING OUT	DHILLLOSST	HOLDS STILL
DGHINNOOSW	HOSING DOWN	DHILNORRUW	WHIRL ROUND
DGHINORRTU	RIGHT ROUND	DHILORSSYY	HYDROLYSIS
DGHLNOORST	STRONGHOLD	DHIMMSTUWY	DUMMY WHIST
DGHLNOORUY	HOLY GROUND	DHIMOOPRSU	DIMORPHOUS
DGHMOOORUU	GOOD HUMOUR	DHINNNORTU	NINTH ROUND
DGIIIJNNOS	DISJOINING	DHINOOPSWW	SHOP WINDOW
DGIIIKNNNR	DRINKING IN		SHOPWINDOW
DGIIIKNNSV	SKIN DIVING		WINDOW-SHOP
DGIIILLNST	DISTILLING	DHINOORSSU	DISHONOURS
DGIIIMNSSS	DISMISSING	DHINOPRSUW	WHIP-ROUNDS
DGIIINNSTU	DISUNITING	DHINORSTUX	SIXTH ROUND
DGIIINSTUV	DIVING SUIT	DHLLOOPPSY	PHYLLOPODS
DGIIKNNPRU	DRINKING UP	DHLLPRSUYY	SULPHYDRYL
DGIILMNTUY	GUILTY MIND	DHLMOOSTUU	LOUDMOUTHS
DGIILNNOVW	LIVING DOWN	DHLOOORTXY	ORTHODOXLY
DGIILNOSSV	DISSOLVING	DHMNOOOSTW	SMOOTH DOWN
DGIILNYYZZ	DIZZYINGLY	DHNNOORSTW	NORTH DOWNS
DGIILPRSTU	STUPID GIRL	DHNNOORSUW	SHOWN ROUND
DGIIMNNOOR	DINING ROOM	DHNNOORTWW	THROWN DOWN
DGIIMNNOPU	IMPOUNDING	DHNOOORTUX	UNORTHODOX
DGIIMNOORT	IN GOOD TRIM	DHNOOOSSTW	SHOOTS DOWN
DGIINNOPPR	DROPPING IN	DHNOORSSUW	SHOWS ROUND
DGIINNOPPW	PIPING DOWN	DHNOORSTWW	THROWS DOWN
DGIINNPRSY	SPIN-DRYING	DHNOOSSTUW	SHOUTS DOWN
DGIINOPPRT	DROPPING IT		SOUTH DOWNS
DGIINOPRST	DISPORTING	DHOOPRRSST	DROPS SHORT
DGIINOPRSV	DISPROVING	DIIIINPSTY	INSIPIDITY
DGIINORSTT	DISTORTING	DIIILLOSTY	SILLY IDIOT
DGIINORTUV	DRIVING OUT	DIIIMMORSU	OSMIRIDIUM
DGIINPRSTU	DISRUPTING	DIIIMMNOTU	DIMINUTION
DGIIOOPRSU	PRODIGIOUS	DIIILLMNOSY	SILLY MID-ON
DGILLNORSW	WORLDLINGS	DIIMMOPRRU	PRIMORDIUM
DGILNNOSUY	SOUNDINGLY	DIIMNNOSTW	IN TWO MINDS
DGILNOOPRY	DROOPINGLY	DIIMNNPSTU	PUTS IN MIND
DGILOOPRTT	PROGLOTTID	DIINOORSTT	DISTORTION
DGIMNOOOWW	MOWING DOWN	DIINOPRSTU	DISRUPTION
DGIMNNORST	STRONG MIND	DIJNOOSTTW	JOTS IT DOWN
DGIMNRSSUY	GRUNDYISMS	DIKKLNOOTY	TOOK KINDLY
DGINNNOORU	ROUNDING ON	DIKNORRSTU	SKIRT ROUND
DGINNNOOTW	NOTING DOWN	DILLLOSSTY	LLOYDS LIST
	TONING DOWN	DILLMNOOWY	WOOLLY MIND
DGINNNORUU	UNROUNDING	DILLOOPPYY	POLYPLOIDY
DGINNOOPPR	DROPPING ON	DILLOOSSTT	STOOD STILL
DGINNOOTVW	VOTING DOWN	DILNORRTUW	TWIRL ROUND
DGINNOPRUU	ROUNDING UP	DILOSSTUUY	STUDIOUSLY
DGINNORRSU	RINGS ROUND	DIMOPRSSUY	DYSPROSIUM
DGINNORSTW	STRONG WIND	DIMOPRTTUY	IMPORT DUTY
DGINNORSUW	SWING ROUND	DINNNOSTUY	TINNY SOUND
DGINOORSSW	SWING DOORS	DINNOPRSSU	SPINS ROUND
DGINOPRRTU	PROTRUDING	DINNORTTUW	TURN IT DOWN
DGKNOOOOTW	GOOD TO KNOW	DINOOOSTTW	STOOD TO WIN
DGKNOORRUW	GROUNDWORK	DINOORTTUY	OROTUNDITY
DGLNOOOOTY	ODONTOLOGY	DINOPRSTUW	PUT IN WORDS
DGLNOOOPRU	POLO GROUND	DINOPSTTUW	PUTS IT DOWN
DGLNOORSTU	LOST GROUND	DIOOPPQRUU	QUID PRO QUO
DGLNOORTTU	TURN TO GOLD	DIORRSTTYY	DIRTY STORY
DGLOOPPSUY	GOOD SUPPLY	DKLNNOOOOW	LOOK DOWN ON
DGMOOOORRW	GOOD MORROW	DKLNOOORSU	LOOKS ROUND
DGNNORSTUU	GROUNDNUTS	DLLNOORTTY	LORD LYTTON
DGNNORSUUW	SWUNG ROUND	DLLOOORSUY	DOLOROUSLY
DGNOOOOPTU	UP TO NO GOOD	DLNNNOOOTW	LONDON TOWN
DGOOOORSTU	GO OUTDOORS	DLNOORSUWY	WONDROUSLY
DHHILMOOSU	HOODLUMISH	DMNOOPRUWY	UPON MY WORD
DHHIMNORTT	THIRD MONTH	DMNOORRSUW	ROUNDWORMS
DHIIKNNOTT	I DON'T THINK	DMOOORRSST	STORM DOORS
DHIILNRSWW	WHIRLWINDS	DMORSSSTTU	DUST STORMS
DHIIMMOPRS	DIMORPHISM	DNNORRSTUU	TURNS ROUND
DHIIMNORRT	MINOR THIRD	DNOOOPSSTW	STOOPS DOWN

DNOOOPSSWW	SWOOPS DOWN	EEEFIIRSST	ESTERIFIES
DNOOSSTTUY	NOT SO DUSTY	EEEFILLRTT	LETTER FILE
DNORSTTTUU	TURN TO DUST	EEEFILRSVX	REFLEXIVES
EEEEEFHRRT	THE REFEREE	EEEFIMNNRT	REFINEMENT
EEEEEFLNTV	ELEVEN FEET	EEEFIMRSTV	FIVE METRES
EEEEEHMTTY	MEET THE EYE	EEEFINRRST	INTERFERES
EEEEFFILLR	FEEL RELIEF	EEEFINSSSU	USE FINESSE
EEEEFFNSST	EFFETENESS	EEEFINSSSV	FIVE SENSES
EEEEFGHLTT	GET THE FEEL	EEEFKNOPRS	FREE-SPOKEN
EEEEFGINRR	REFEREEING	EEEFLLORRT	FORETELLER
EEEEFGKRSU	SEEK REFUGE	EEEFLLPSTY	FELT SLEEPY
EEEEFHLRSW	FREEWHEELS	EEEFMNPRRT	PREFERMENT
EEEEFKLRSS	SELF-SEEKER	EEEFNNOOST	ON ONES FEET
EEEEFLLPSY	FEEL SLEEPY	EEEFNNORSU	UNFORESEEN
EEEEFLMNTY	ENEMY FLEET	EEEFNORSST	FREESTONES
EEEEFLMSST	SELF-ESTEEM	EEEFNQRRTU	FREQUENTER
EEEEFLTTVW	TWELVE FEET	EEEFNTTTWY	TWENTY FEET
EEEEFORRVZ	FREEZE OVER	EEEFORSTUZ	FREEZES OUT
EEEEGKRRSV	GREEK VERSE	EEEGGILNRS	GLEE SINGER
EEEEGLLNSV	LEGS ELEVEN	EEEGGNOORS	GOOSE GREEN
EEEEGNRRSV	EVERGREENS	EEEGHHIMST	HIGH ESTEEM
EEEEHHRRTT	THERE,THERE	EEEGHHINRV	EVEN HIGHER
EEEEHILTVY	THE EVIL EYE	EEEGHIIINTT	EIGHTEENTH
EEEEHIMRSU	EUHEMERISE	EEEGHIILTV	GIVE THE LIE
EEEEHIMRUZ	EUHEMERIZE	EEEGHIKSTW	EIGHT WEEKS
EEEEHJKOST	SEE THE JOKE	EEEGHIMNOT	EIGHTEENMO
EEEEHKRSST	THE SEEKERS	EEEGHLRSTT	THE SLEDGER
EEEEHKRSTW	THREE WEEKS	EEEGHINNORT	ON THE GREEN
EEEEHNSTWY	THE SWEENEY	EEEGHNORSU	GREENHOUSE
EEEEHPSSSY	SHEEPS EYES	EEEGHNORTV	ON THE VERGE
EEEEHRRVWY	EVERYWHERE	EEEGHNORTW	GET NOWHERE
EEEEIKMPRT	TIMEKEEPER	EEEGIINPSS	EPIGENESIS
EEEEILNPRS	PERISELENE	EEEGIJNNST	JET ENGINES
EEEEILNSVZ	SIZE ELEVEN	EEEGILMNST	GENTEELISM
EEEEKMRRSY	KERSEYMERE	EEEGILNNSS	ENGINELESS
EEEEKNSSVW	SEVEN WEEKS	EEEGILNORV	OLIVE GREEN
EEEELLORRT	REEL-TO-REEL	EEEGINNOPY	EYE-OPENING
EEEELLSSSV	SLEEVELESS	EEEGINNPST	STEEPENING
EEEELMRSTT	TELEMETERS	EEEGINNPTY	GENE PITNEY
EEEEMNPRTV	EVEN TEMPER	EEEGINNSTW	SWEETENING
EEEENNRRVV	NEVER NEVER	EEEGINOPRY	EPEIROGENY
	NEVER-NEVER	EEEGINORSV	SEEING OVER
EEEENNRSSS	SERENENESS	EEEGINPRRS	PEREGRINES
EEEENNSTVV	EVEN STEVEN	EEEGINRRRV	GREEN RIVER
EEEENNTWYY	TEENY WEENY	EEEGIRRSSV	REGRESSIVE
EEEENOPRSY	EYE-OPENERS	EEEGIRSSTY	TIGER'S-EYES
EEEENRSSTW	SWEETENERS	EEEGKOPRRS	GREEK PROSE
EEEEPRRSSV	PERSEVERES	EEEGLNNSST	GENTLENESS
EEEERSSTTV	SEVERE TEST	EEEGMNRSSS	MESSENGERS
EEEFFHLORT	OFF THE REEL	EEEGMORRST	ERGOMETERS
EEEFFILLRT	FELT RELIEF	EEEGNNNTUY	GENE TUNNEY
EEEFFILNTT	FINE FETTLE	EEEGNNORST	GREENSTONE
EEEFFILORT	TREE OF LIFE	EEEHHIMPRS	HEMISPHERE
EEEFFIMNNT	FIFTEEN MEN	EEEHHINTTT	IN THE TEETH
EEEFFLNRTY	EFFERENTLY	EEEHHISTTW	WHITE SHEET
EEEFGHLOTT	GOT THE FEEL	EEEHHLORSW	WHEELHORSE
EEEFGIILNS	SEEING LIFE	EEEHHLOSUW	WHEELHOUSE
EEEFGIINNR	FIRE ENGINE	EEEHHRRSTT	THE THREE RS
EEEFGILNRS	GREENFLIES	EEEHIKLLMT	HELMETLIKE
EEEFGILRVY	GIVE FREELY	EEEHIKLPSS	SPIKE HEELS
EEEFGINORS	FORESEEING	EEEHILMRST	THREE MILES
EEEFHIJLTW	JEWEL THIEF	EEEHILNOTT	TOE THE LINE
EEEFHIRSTV	THREE FIVES	EEEHILNOTV	THE EVIL ONE
EEEFHKLRSU	SHEER FLUKE	EEEHILNPRS	PREHENSILE
EEEFHKPRSS	KEEPS FRESH	EEEHIMMRSU	EUHEMERISM
EEEFHOORRT	HERETOFORE	EEEHIMPRSU	EUPHEMISER
EEEFHORRSW	WHEREFORES	EEEHIMPRUZ	EUPHEMIZER
EEEFHORSST	FORESHEETS	EEEHIMPSSU	EUPHEMISES
EEEFHOSTTT	SET OF TEETH	EEEHIMPSUZ	EUPHEMIZES
EEEFHRRRSS	REFRESHERS	EEEHIMRSTT	THREE TIMES
EEEFIINRRS	REFINERIES	EEEHIMRSTU	EUHEMERIST

EEEHINNNTT	NINETEENTH
EEEHINNORT	ONE IN THREE
	THREE IN ONE
EEEHINNRST	THREE NINES
EEEHINNTTV	IN THE EVENT
EEEHINQTUU	IN THE QUEUE
EEEHINQTUW	WHITE QUEEN
EEEHINSSWZ	WHEEZINESS
EEEHINSTTV	SEVENTIETH
EEEHIRSSTX	THREE SIXES
EEEHJNOSST	THE JONESES
EEEHKOPPRS	SHOPKEEPER
EEEHKOPSSU	KEEPS HOUSE
EEEHLLNOTV	ON THE LEVEL
EEEHLMNTVY	VEHEMENTLY
EEEHLMSSTV	THEMSELVES
EEEHLNOPRT	TELEPHONER
EEEHLNOPST	TELEPHONES
EEEHMMNNST	ENMESHMENT
EEEHMNOPRS	EPHEMERONS
EEEHMOPRSS	MESOSPHERE
EEEHMORSSW	SOMEWHERES
EEEHMPSTTT	THE TEMPEST
EEEHNNOSTV	ONE SEVENTH
EEEHNOORTT	THREE TO ONE
EEEHNORSSS	HORSE SENSE
EEEHNORSVW	WHENSOEVER
EEEHNORTTT	TEN TO THREE
EEEHNORTVY	THE VERY ONE
EEEHNPRSTT	THE PRESENT
EEEHOPRRST	PETER SHORE
EEEHORRTVY	EVERY OTHER
EEEIIKNPVW	KEEP IN VIEW
EEEIINRRSV	RIVER SEINE
EEEIINRSTT	ENTIRETIES
EEEIIPRTTV	REPETITIVE
EEEIKLMSWY	SEMIWEEKLY
EEEIKLNPST	KEEP SILENT
EEEIKLNSSS	LIKENESSES
EEEIKNNPRS	INNKEEPERS
EEEIKNNPTU	KEEP IN TUNE
EEEIKNPPST	KEEP IN STEP
EEEIKPQSTU	KEEPS QUIET
EEEILLNRVW	WELL I NEVER!
EEEILLRRVV	RIVER LEVEL
EEEILLRSSV	LESSER EVIL
EEEILMNNSY	ENEMY LINES
EEEILMNRSU	UNSEEMLIER
EEEILMNRTV	REVILEMENT
EEEILMNSSS	SEEMLINESS
EEEILMNSSV	SEVEN MILES
EEEILMPRTV	EVIL TEMPER
EEEILMRSTT	LIME STREET
EEEILMSSTW	SWEET SMILE
EEEILNORTV	LEE TREVINO
EEEILNPRRT	TERREPLEIN
EEEILNPSSS	SLEEPINESS
EEEILNSSST	STEELINESS
EEEILNSSVV	SEVEN VEILS
EEEILPRTUV	EVIL REPUTE
EEEILPSTVX	EXPLETIVES
EEEILRRSTW	WESTERLIER
EEEILRSSSW	WIRELESSES
EEEILRSSTW	WESTERLIES
EEEILSTVWZ	SIZE TWELVE
EEEIMMRRSS	MESMERISER
EEEIMMRRSZ	MESMERIZER
EEEIMMRSSS	MESMERISES
EEEIMMRSSZ	MESMERIZES
EEEIMNNPRT	PREEMINENT
EEEIMNNRST	NINE METRES

EEEIMNORST	REMONETISE
EEEIMNORTZ	REMONETIZE
EEEIMNPRTX	EXPERIMENT
EEEIMNPSSY	ENEMY SPIES
EEEIMNRRTT	RETIREMENT
EEEIMNRSTT	TENSIMETER
EEEIMNSSTV	SEVEN TIMES
EEEIMOPRTZ	PIEZOMETER
EEEIMORSTT	METEORITES
EEEIMPPRTV	PREEMPTIVE
EEEIMPRRST	PERIMETERS
EEEIMRRSTV	TIMESERVER
EEEIMRSSTV	SERVES TIME
EEEINNNOSS	IN ONE SENSE
EEEINNNOSV	ONE IN SEVEN
EEEINNPRST	SERPENTINE
EEEINNPRTV	PREVENIENT
EEEINNRSST	ENTIRENESS
EEEINNRSTV	INTERVENES
EEEINPRRST	ENTERPRISE
EEEINPRSTV	VESPERTINE
EEEINPRTVV	PREVENTIVE
EEEINQSSUZ	SQUEEZES IN
EEEINRRRTV	IRREVERENT
EEEINRSSTW	WESTERNISE
EEEINRSTWZ	WESTERNIZE
EEEINRSVWW	NEWS REVIEW
EEEINSSTWY	EYE WITNESS
	EYEWITNESS
EEEINSSVVW	SEVEN WIVES
EEEIOPRRRT	REPERTOIRE
EEEIOPRSWZ	SEIZE POWER
EEEIPPPRRT	PETER PIPER
EEEIPRRSSV	REPRESSIVE
EEEIPRRSVV	PERVERSIVE
EEEIPRRTTU	REPETITEUR
EEEIPRSSVX	EXPRESSIVE
EEEIRRRSTV	RETRIEVERS
EEEIRRSTVW	WRITE VERSE
EEEIRSSTTV	SERVIETTES
EEEJJNNSSU	JEJUNENESS
EEEJKMNORR	JEROME KERN
EEEJLNRSUV	JULES VERNE
EEEJNOPRTW	JON PERTWEE
EEEJNOSSSW	JESSE OWENS
EEEKLNRTWY	WEEKLY RENT
EEEKLOORSV	SEVERE LOOK
EEEKMRSSTU	MUSKETEERS
EEELLLORVW	LOWER LEVEL
EEELLLPSSW	SLEEPS WELL
EEELLMSSTW	SWEET SMELL
EEELLNPRST	REPELLENTS
EEELLNPSUV	ELEVEN PLUS
	ELEVEN-PLUS
EEELLNRRTY	ELLEN TERRY
EEELLNRSST	RELENTLESS
EEELLOPSSS	LOSES SLEEP
EEELLORTTV	LOVE LETTER
EEELLPRSSY	PEERLESSLY
EEELLRSSVW	SERVES WELL
EEELMMOSTT	METTLESOME
EEELMNOTVV	EVOLVEMENT
EEELMNSTTT	SETTLEMENT
EEELNOPRTT	OPEN LETTER
EEELNORSVV	NEW RESOLVE
EEELNOSTTV	NOVELETTES
EEELNOTTVW	TWELVE-NOTE
	TWELVE-TONE
EEELNRRTVY	REVERENTLY
EEELNRSTTW	NEWS LETTER
	NEWSLETTER

EEELNSSSTV	SVELTENESS	EEFGHLOOSS	GOOSEFLESH
EEEELOPRRRT	PETER LORRE	EEFGIIKLNR	FINGERLIKE
EEEELOPRSSV	OVERSLEEPS	EEFGIIKNPT	KEEPING FIT
EEELORSSSV	SEVERE LOSS	EEFGIILLLN	FEELING ILL
EEEELORSVWW	WEREWOLVES		ILL FEELING
EEEELPRRSVY	PERVERSELY	EEFGIILLNS	SINGLE FILE
EEEMNNNOOW	NEW ONE ON ME	EEFGIILNRV	FREE-LIVING
EEEMNNRSTT	RESENTMENT	EEFGIINNRU	FIGURE NINE
EEEMNOOPRW	WEEP NO MORE	EEFGILLNRU	REFUELLING
EEEMNORSST	REMOTENESS	EEFGILLNTY	FLEETINGLY
EEEMNRSTTV	REVETMENTS	EEFGILLTUY	FEEL GUILTY
EEENNNSSUV	UNEVENNESS	EEFGILNOTU	FEELING OUT
EEENNOOSTV	SEVEN TO ONE	EEFGILNRTW	LEFT WINGER
EEENNORSST	SONNETEERS		LEFT-WINGER
EEENNOSTTV	TEN TO SEVEN	EEFGILNRYZ	FREEZINGLY
EEENORSTWZ	SNEEZEWORT	EEFGIMNNRT	FERMENTING
EEENOSSSTY	SETS EYES ON	EEFGIMNOOR	MOORING FEE
EEENPRRSST	PRESENTERS	EEFGINNRRT	REFRINGENT
	REPRESENTS	EEFGINNRUZ	UNFREEZING
EEENPRSSTX	EXPERTNESS	EEFGINORRS	FOREIGNERS
EEENPRSSUV	SUPERVENES	EEFGINPRRR	PREFERRING
EEENPSSTUW	SWEETENS UP	EEFGINPRUZ	FREEZING UP
EEENRRSSTW	WESTERNERS	EEFGIPRRSU	PREFIGURES
EEEOPRSTTY	STEREOTYPE	EEFGKLLNOT	GENTLEFOLK
EEEOQSTUUZ	SQUEEZE OUT	EEFGKOORTU	TOOK REFUGE
EEEORRSSTV	OVERSTEERS	EEFGLLMNOR	FELLMONGER
EEEORRSTVW	WROTE VERSE	EEFGLLNUVY	VENGEFULLY
EEEOSTTTVV	STEVE OVETT	EEFGLMNNTU	ENGULFMENT
EEEPRSTTTY	TYPESETTER	EEFGOORSTU	REFUSE TO GO
EEEQRSSSTU	SEQUESTERS	EEFHHILNST	IN THE FLESH
EEFFFGINNO	ENFEOFFING	EEFHHIORST	HORSE THIEF
EEFFFKLRSU	KERFUFFLES	EEFHHLNOST	ON THE SHELF
EEFFFMNOST	FEOFFMENTS	EEFHIILSTW	WHITEFLIES
EEFFGIINRU	FINE FIGURE	EEFHIKLSTT	FISH KETTLE
EEFFGIIRUV	FIGURE FIVE	EEFHILNSSS	FLESHINESS
EEFFGIKNOP	KEEPING OFF	EEFHILORSS	HORSEFLIES
EEFFGILNOP	PEELING OFF	EEFHILORSV	HOVERFLIES
EEFFGILNOR	REELING OFF	EEFHILOSSU	HOUSE FLIES
EEFFGINORR	FOREFINGER		HOUSEFLIES
	REOFFERING	EEFHILRSVY	FEVERISHLY
EEFFGNRSTU	GREEN STUFF	EEFHINORSW	FINE SHOWER
	GREENSTUFF	EEFHINSTTV	FIVE TENTHS
EEFFHIISSV	FIVE FISHES	EEFHIORSSV	OVERFISHES
EEFFHII3TT	THE FIFTIES	EEFHIORSTT	THE FORTIES
EEFFHLRSSU	RESHUFFLES	EEFHIPTTTY	PETTY THIEF
EEFFIILMOT	TIME OF LIFE	EEFHIRTTTY	THIRTY FEET
EEFFIILNOR	LINE OF FIRE	EEFHKLOORS	FOLK HEROES
EEFFIIOTVV	FIVE TO FIVE	EEFHLLORSY	SHEER FOLLY
EEFFILLNOW	FINE FELLOW	EEFHLNORTW	FRONT WHEEL
EEFFILOPST	SLEEP IT OFF	EEFHLNOTTW	ONE TWELFTH
EEFFILSUVY	EFFUSIVELY	EEFHLORSUW	FOUR WHEELS
EEFFINOSSV	OFFENSIVES	EEFHNORTTT	FRONT TEETH
EEFFINRSST	STIFFENERS	EEFHNORTTU	FOURTEENTH
EEFFIORRST	FOREST FIRE	EEFHNPRSSU	FRESHENS UP
EEFFIORRTU	FORFEITURE	EEFHOOPRST	FOSTER HOPE
EEFFIRTUUW	FUTURE WIFE	EEFHORRSTU	FOUR THREES
EEFFLNNSUY	FEELS FUNNY		THREE FOURS
EEFFLORSST	EFFORTLESS	EEFHPTTTTY	PETTY THEFT
	LESS EFFORT	EEFIIIRSVV	REVIVIFIES
EEFFNORRTY	EFFRONTERY	EEFIILLLNN	FELL IN LINE
EEFGGGLORY	FEEL GROGGY	EEFIILLMPS	SIMPLE LIFE
EEFGGHIOTW	WHITE OF EGG	EEFIILMNNY	FEMININELY
EEFGGILNTU	GUT FEELING	EEFIILMRSU	EMULSIFIER
EEFGHHIILR	HIGH RELIEF	EEFIILMRVW	FILM REVIEW
EEFGHILNOT	FEELING HOT	EEFIILMSSU	EMULSIFIES
EEFGHILRST	FEELS RIGHT	EEFIILNRST	INTERFILES
EEFGHINNRS	FRESHENING	EEFIILNSSW	WIFELINESS
EEFGHINRRS	REFRESHING	EEFIILRRST	FERTILISER
EEFGHIOSTT	SET OF EIGHT	EEFIILRRTZ	FERTILIZER
EEFGHIRRST	FREIGHTERS	EEFIILRSST	FERTILISES
EEFGHLNRUY	FEEL HUNGRY	EEFIILRSTV	FIVE LITRES

EEFIILRSTZ	FERTILIZES
EEFIINNOTV	FIVE TO NINE
	NINE TO FIVE
EEFIINNSST	FINITENESS
EEFIIPPRRS	FRIPPERIES
EEFIIPRSTT	PRETTIFIES
EEFIIRRSSV	VERSIFIERS
EEFIIRSSTT	TESTIFIERS
EEFIJLNOSY	ENJOYS LIFE
EEFIKLOSSY	ISLE OF SKYE
EEFILLLNOV	FELL IN LOVE
EEFILLLNST	FELL SILENT
EEFILLLSSY	FEELS SILLY
	LIFELESSLY
EEFILLSSTY	LIFE-STYLES
EEFILMMRSU	FLUMMERIES
EEFILMRSTT	FILMSETTER
EEFILNOPTY	FEEL NO PITY
EEFILNSSTU	FUTILENESS
EEFILOOPRR	POOR RELIEF
EEFILOPTTU	FEEL UP TO IT
EEFILORTTU	TRUE TO LIFE
EEFILRSSST	STRIFELESS
EEFIMOSTTT	TEST OF TIME
EEFINNORRT	INTERFERON
EEFINOPRST	PINE FOREST
EEFINORSST	SETS ON FIRE
EEFINPRTTY	PRETTY FINE
EEFINRRRTU	RETURN FIRE
EEFINRSSTU	INTERFUSES
EEFIOPRRST	PROFITEERS
EEFIORRRTX	FOX TERRIER
EEFIORSSTT	SETS FIRE TO
EEFIRRRSTU	FRUITERERS
EEFIRRSSTU	SURFEITERS
EEFIRRSSTV	FIRST VERSE
EEFJMORRSW	REFORM JEWS
EEFJOOPRWY	WEEP FOR JOY
EEFKNOORST	FORETOKENS
EEFLLLSSSY	SELFLESSLY
EEFLLNTUVY	EVENTFULLY
EEFLLORSSW	FLOWERLESS
EEFLMOPRTU	FOUL TEMPER
EEFLMORRSU	REMORSEFUL
EEFLNNTUUV	UNEVENTFUL
EEFLNOSSUW	WOEFULNESS
EEFLNQRTUY	FREQUENTLY
EEFLNRSSUU	RUEFULNESS
EEFLNSSSUU	USEFULNESS
EEFLORRSSY	FEELS SORRY
EEFLORRTTU	FOUR-LETTER
EEFLORSSTU	SET OF RULES
EEFLORSUVY	FEVEROUSLY
EEFLRSSTUU	FUTURELESS
EEFMOPRRRS	PERFORMERS
EEFMORRSTU	FOUR METRES
EEFNNORRRU	FORERUNNER
EEFNNORSSZ	FROZENNESS
EEFNOORRVZ	FROZEN OVER
EEFNOOTTWW	OWN TWO FEET
EEFNOORSUU	FOUR QUEENS
EEFNORSSUV	FOUR SEVENS
EEFOORRSTW	ROW OF TREES
EEFORRSSST	FORTRESSES
EEFORRSTTU	FERRETS OUT
EEGGGGISSS	EGGS IS EGGS
EEGGGIKNOR	KING GEORGE
EEGGGINNOR	GOING GREEN
EEGGHHINRY	HIGH-ENERGY
EEGGHILNRT	GREEN LIGHT
	LIGHT GREEN
EEGGHHOORTT	GO TOGETHER
EEGGIINNRS	ENERGISING
EEGGIINNRW	GINGER WINE
EEGGIINNRZ	ENERGIZING
EEGGIKNOPS	KEEPS GOING
EEGGIMNNST	SEGMENTING
EEGGINOOST	GOING TO SEE
EEGGINOTUV	GIVE TONGUE
EEGGINRRSS	SNIGGERERS
EEGGINRRTT	REGRETTING
EEGGINRSSU	SNUGGERIES
EEGGINSTTT	GETTING SET
EEGGISSTUV	SUGGESTIVE
EEGGNOORTW	GEORGE TOWN
EEGGRSSSTU	SUGGESTERS
EEGHHIIRRS	RISE HIGHER
EEGHHILNST	THE ENGLISH
EEGHHILOST	LOSE HEIGHT
EEGHHINSSS	HIGHNESSES
EEGHHIORRS	ROSE HIGHER
EEGHHIPRTU	HIGH REPUTE
EEGHHIRSTT	HIGH STREET
EEGHHMPTTU	GET THE HUMP
EEGHHORSTU	SEE THROUGH
	SEE-THROUGH
EEGHHPSTTU	GET THE PUSH
EEGHIILMST	EIGHT MILES
EEGHIIMSTT	EIGHT TIMES
EEGHIINNOT	ONE IN EIGHT
EEGHIINRST	ETHERISING
EEGHIINRTZ	ETHERIZING
EEGHIIPPTV	GIVE THE PIP
EEGHIISTTW	WEIGHTIEST
EEGHIKLRSU	KIESELGUHR
EEGHIKNOTV	GIVEN THE O.K.
EEGHIKNRST	THREE KINGS
EEGHIKNSTW	WEEKNIGHTS
EEGHIKOSTV	GIVES THE O.K.
EEGHIKPSST	KEEPS SIGHT
EEGHILLPST	LIGHT SLEEP
EEGHILMNNS	ENGLISHMEN
EEGHILMRTT	LIGHT METER
EEGHILNNST	ENLIGHTENS
EEGHILNOOP	PIGEONHOLE
EEGHILNRST	SHELTERING
EEGHILNTTW	LENT WEIGHT
EEGHILOSTW	LOSE WEIGHT
EEGHILPSTT	GET THE SLIP
	SLEEP TIGHT
EEGHILRSTV	LIGHT VERSE
EEGHILSSTW	WEIGHTLESS
EEGHIMNOOS	HOMOGENISE
EEGHIMNOOZ	HOMOGENIZE
EEGHIMNOTU	ENOUGH TIME
	TIME ENOUGH
EEGHINNOST	SEE NOTHING
EEGHINNSST	SEEN THINGS
EEGHINOOTT	EIGHT TO ONE
EEGHINOTTT	TEN TO EIGHT
EEGHINOTUV	IN THE VOGUE
EEGHINRSTT	TIGHTENERS
EEGHINRTVY	EVERY NIGHT
	EVERYTHING
EEGHINSSST	SEES THINGS
EEGHIOPPUV	GIVE UP HOPE
EEGHIORTVW	OVERWEIGHT
EEGHIPPSTT	GETS THE PIP
EEGHIRRSTV	SERVE RIGHT
	VEERS RIGHT
EEGHIRRTTW	WITH REGRET
EEGHKMORRU	KHMER ROUGE

EEGHLLNOOT	GONE TO HELL	EEGINORRWW	WINEGROWER
EEGHLLNOUW	WELL ENOUGH	EEGINORSSV	SOVEREIGNS
EEGHLLOOST	GOES TO HELL	EEGINORSTY	GENEROSITY
EEGHLNPSTU	GENTLE PUSH	EEGINOSTTU	TONGUE-TIES
EEGHLOPRSU	SLEEP ROUGH	EEGINOTTVV	GIVE VENT TO
EEGHMORRTY	HYGROMETER	EEGINPPSUW	SWEEPING UP
EEGHNNORRS	GREENHORNS	EEGINPQUUU	QUEUEING UP
EEGHNNRSTT	STRENGTHEN	EEGINPRRSS	REPRESSING
EEGHNNRSTU	THE GUNNERS	EEGINPRRSV	PRESERVING
EEGHNOOPRU	ENOUGH ROPE	EEGINPRRTV	PERVERTING
EEGHNOORTW	GOT NOWHERE	EEGINPRSSX	EXPRESSING
EEGHNOORTY	HETEROGONY	EEGINQRSTU	REQUESTING
EEGHNORSUU	SURE ENOUGH	EEGIOPPRRT	EGO-TRIPPER
EEGHORRSST	THREE GROSS	EEGIRRSSSU	REGISSEURS
EEGHOSSTUU	GUEST HOUSE	EEGJLMOORY	JOE GORMLEY
	GUESTHOUSE	EEGKOOPSST	STOKE POGES
	HOUSEGUEST	EEGLLMORSU	GLOMERULES
EEGIIKLPSV	KEEPS VIGIL	EEGLLMRTUY	GREY MULLET
EEGIILNNNV	ENLIVENING	EEGLLNNNWY	NELL GWYNNE
EEGIILNNPS	SLEEPING IN	EEGLLNOOSY	SELENOLOGY
EEGIILNNST	GETS IN LINE	EEGLLNOOWY	GONE YELLOW
EEGIILNSTV	TELEVISING	EEGLLNORTT	LONG LETTER
EEGIILNSUV	EVIL GENIUS	EEGLLNOSTW	GETS ON WELL
EEGIILPRSV	PRIVILEGES	EEGLLOOPSY	SPELEOLOGY
EEGIINNOPR	PIONEERING	EEGLLOOSWY	GOES YELLOW
EEGIINNQTU	QUEENING IT	EEGLMORSUY	GRUESOMELY
	QUIETENING	EEGLNNOOSS	ON ONES LEGS
EEGIINNRTT	ENTERING IT	EEGLNOOSVV	OVEN GLOVES
EEGIINOSTT	SEEING TO IT	EEGLNORSTT	LORGNETTES
EEGIINPRRV	REPRIEVING	EEGLNORSUY	GENEROUSLY
EEGIINPRVW	PREVIEWING	EEGLNOSSTU	TONGUELESS
EEGIINRRRV	RIVER NIGER	EEGLOORRST	ERGOSTEROL
EEGIINRRTV	RETRIEVING	EEGLOSTTUW	GUEST TOWEL
EEGIIORSTV	GIVE RISE TO	EEGMNNORSW	NEWSMONGER
EEGIIRRSST	REGISTRIES	EEGMNNORTV	GOVERNMENT
EEGIKLLNNN	KENNELLING	EEGMNNOORRS	GREENROOMS
EEGIKLNOTU	TONGUELIKE	EEGMOOORRR	ROGER MOORE
EEGIKMMNPU	KEEPING MUM	EEGNNORRVW	NEVER WRONG
EEGIKMNOPV	KEEP MOVING	EEGNNORSUU	UNGENEROUS
EEGIKNOPTU	KEEPING OUT	EEGNNOTTXY	OXYGEN TENT
EEGIKNOSTU	SEEKING OUT	EEGNNRRSTU	TURNS GREEN
EEGIKNPRTY	KEEP TRYING	EEGNOORSST	OESTROGENS
EEGILLNORS	NEGRILLOES	EEGNOPSSTW	WET SPONGES
EEGILLNPRS	RESPELLING	EEGNPQSUYY	GYPSY QUEEN
EEGILMNORS	MONGRELISE	EEGOPRRSSS	PROGRESSES
EEGILMNORZ	MONGRELIZE	EEGOPRSTUU	PORTUGUESE
EEGILMOOSY	SEMEIOLOGY	EEGORRRSST	RETROGRESS
EEGILNNOPS	SLEEPING ON	EEHHHLLOTW	HOW THE HELL
EEGILNNOPV	ENVELOPING		WHO THE HELL
EEGILNNSSS	SINGLENESS	EEHHHLLTWY	WHY THE HELL
EEGILNOSTV	SINGLE VOTE	EEHHIKNRTT	THE THINKER
EEGILNPPRX	PERPLEXING	EEHHILLNOP	HOPE IN HELL
EEGILNPSWY	SWEEPINGLY	EEHHILLOST	THE HOLLIES
EEGILNRSTW	SWELTERING	EEHHILMPTT	PITH HELMET
EEGILOORVV	OLIVE GROVE	EEHHILNOTT	THE HOT LINE
EEGIMNNNOV	ENVENOMING	EEHHILPSSY	SHEEPISHLY
EEGIMNNOOR	ENGINE ROOM	EEHHINOSTU	IN THE HOUSE
EEGIMNNOTT	MIGNONETTE	EEHHINRTTT	THIRTEENTH
EEGIMNNTTU	INTEGUMENT	EEHHIORRSS	SHIRE HORSE
EEGIMNOORT	GONIOMETER	EEHHIORSTW	WHITE HORSE
EEGIMNOPPT	PEEPING TOM	EEHHIOSTUW	WHITE HOUSE
EEGIMNOPRW	EMPOWERING	EEHHIRSSTV	THE SHIVERS
EEGIMNPPRT	PREEMPTING	EEHHLNOOTW	ON THE WHOLE
EEGIMNRSTV	GIVEN TERMS	EEHHNNOOPT	ON THE PHONE
EEGIMRSSTV	GIVES TERMS	EEHHNOOSTU	ON THE HOUSE
EEGINNOPRT	PORT ENGINE	EEHHOORRSS	HORSESHOER
EEGINNPRST	PRESENTING	EEHHOORSSS	HORSESHOES
EEGINNPRTV	PREVENTING	EEHHOORSUW	WHOREHOUSE
EEGINOPSTU	SEEPING OUT	EEHHOPSSTY	HYPOTHESES
EEGINORRSS	REGRESSION	EEHHORRSTU	THREE HOURS
EEGINORRVW	VINE GROWER	EEHIILLSTW	THE WILLIES

EEHIILMPTU	EPITHELIUM	EEHJLNOSWY	JOHN WESLEY
EEHIILNOPR	PERIHELION	EEHJNNOOSS	JOHNSONESE
EEHIILNOPV	LIVE IN HOPE	EEHKLNOOTW	THE NEW LOOK
EEHIIMNNOT	METHIONINE	EEHKLNORRV	HERRENVOLK
EEHIIMRSST	SMITHERIES	EEHKLOOSST	STOKEHOLES
EEHIINRRRV	RIVER RHINE	EEHKLOPSSW	SPOKE WELSH
EEHIINRRTV	IN THE RIVER	EEHKMOORRW	HOMEWORKER
EEHIINSTTU	THE UNITIES	EEHKNOORTT	TENTERHOOK
EEHIIPRSSW	IRISH SWEEP	EEHKNORSTY	THE ORKNEYS
EEHIISSTTX	THE SIXTIES	EEHKNRTTUY	TURN THE KEY
EEHIKLMNRT	THE KREMLIN	EEHKORRSTW	THE WORKERS
EEHIKLORST	THREE KILOS	EEHLLLPSSY	HELPLESSLY
EEHIKMNNST	KENTISHMEN	EEHLLMNOOP	MELLOPHONE
EEHIKMNSSV	MENSHEVIKS	EEHLLMOPTY	HOLY TEMPLE
EEHIKMORST	STRIKE HOME	EEHLLMPSTY	EMPTY BELLY
EEHIKNOTTT	TIE THE KNOT	EEHLLNOTTY	ON THE TELLY
EEHIKNPSSS	SHEEPSKINS	EEHLLOPSSY	HOPELESSLY
EEHIKPPTUW	KEEP UP WITH	EEHLLORSSV	SHOVELLERS
EEHILLLNSW	HELEN WILLS	EEHLLORSTU	OUTER SHELL
EEHILLNOOT	LEO THE LION	EEHLMNSSTU	SUN HELMETS
EEHILLNSST	HELLENISTS	EEHLMOORTV	MOTHER LOVE
EEHILLOPTT	LITTLE HOPE	EEHLMORSST	MOTHERLESS
EEHILLRSTT	STILL THERE	EEHLMORSVW	OVERWHELMS
EEHILLRSWW	WELL-WISHER	EEHLMOSSZZ	SHEMOZZLES
EEHILMNOSS	HOMELINESS	EEHLMPRSTU	THREE LUMPS
EEHILMNSTT	TIN HELMETS	EEHLNOOOST	ON THE LOOSE
EEHILMOPRT	THERMOPILE	EEHLNOPSTU	ON THE PULSE
EEHILNNRTY	INHERENTLY	EEHLOORSUW	LOWER HOUSE
EEHILNOOPS	OENOPHILES	EEHLOOSTTU	HOUSE TO LET
EEHILNOSTT	ON THE TILES	EEHLORSSUU	HOUSE RULES
EEHILNOTTV	LIT THE OVEN	EEHMNNNOOP	PHENOMENON
EEHILNSTUV	NEVIL SHUTE	EEHMNOOPRS	PHEROMONES
EEHILOOPRT	HELIOTROPE	EEHMNOORRY	HENRY MOORE
EEHILOPRST	PRIEST HOLE	EEHMNOORSW	HORSEWOMEN
EEHILOPRSX	XEROPHILES	EEHMNOORTY	HETERONOMY
EEHILORSST	HOSTELRIES	EEHMNORRTU	RETURN HOME
EEHILOSTTU	HOTEL SUITE	EEHMNORSTT	NETHERMOST
	SILHOUETTE	EEHMNORSTY	HETERONYMS
EEHILPRSTU	SPHERULITE	EEHMNORTVY	EVERY MONTH
EEHIMMNSSV	MENSHEVISM	EEHMNOSTUY	SOUTH YEMEN
EEHIMMOOSV	HOME MOVIES	EEHMOOPRTT	PHOTOMETER
EEHIMMPSSU	EUPHEMISMS	EEHMOORSVW	WHOMSOEVER
EEHIMNNORW	WHEN IN ROME	EEHMOOSSUV	MOVES HOUSE
EEHIMNNOTY	IN THE MONEY	EEHMOPRSTT	STEPMOTHER
EEHIMNSSTV	MENSHEVIST	EEHMOPSSTU	SETS UP HOME
EEHIMORSTW	WRITES HOME	EEHMOPSTUY	EMPTY HOUSE
EEHINNNSTT	NINE TENTHS	EEHMOQRSUU	HUMORESQUE
EEHINNOPRS	PREHENSION	EEHMORSSUW	SHREWMOUSE
EEHINNORST	RHINESTONE	EEHMPSSTTU	SETS THEM UP
EEHINNORSU	INNER HOUSE	EEHMRRSSTY	RHYMESTERS
EEHINOOPRS	IONOSPHERE	EEHNNOPTTY	TO THE PENNY
EEHINOPSVW	VIEWPHONES	EEHNNORRRT	NORTHERNER
EEHINOQTTU	ON THE QUIET	EEHNNOSSTV	SEVENTH SON
EEHINORTTW	IN THE TOWER	EEHNOOPRST	ON THE ROPES
EEHINPRSST	IN THE PRESS	EEHNOPPSTY	PHENOTYPES
EEHINPRSTT	THREE PINTS	EEHNOPSSTU	PENTHOUSES
EEHINSSSTX	SIXTH SENSE	EEHNOPSTUY	HYPOTENUSE
EEHINSSSTY	SYNTHESISE	EEHNOPTTTY	NOT THE TYPE
EEHINSSTYZ	SYNTHESIZE	EEHNORRSTU	SOUTHERNER
EEHIOPPRRS	PROPHESIER	EEHNORSSUV	SEVEN HOURS
EEHIOPPRSS	PROPHESIES	EEHOOPRRSW	HORSE POWER
EEHIORRSST	THEORISERS		HORSEPOWER
EEHIORRSTZ	THEORIZERS	EEHOOPRSUW	POWER HOUSE
EEHIORSSTW	WHITE ROSES		POWERHOUSE
EEHIORTTWW	WHITE TOWER	EEHOOPRTTV	OVER THE TOP
EEHIOSSUVW	HOUSEWIVES	EEHOOPSTTY	OSTEOPHYTE
EEHIPRRSSW	WHISPERERS	EEHOORRTTW	TWO OR THREE
EEHIPRRTUV	UP THE RIVER	EEHOORSSTU	STOREHOUSE
EEHIPRTTTU	PUT IT THERE!	EEHOORSTUU	OUTER HOUSE
EEHIRRRTTU	RETIRE HURT	EEHOOSTTTW	SWEET TOOTH
EEHIRSSSTY	HYSTERESIS	EEHOPPPRST	HOT PEPPERS

EEHOPPRSUU	UPPER HOUSE
EEHOPRSSST	PROSTHESES
EEHOPRSSUV	PUSHES OVER
EEHOPRSTTX	EXPERT SHOT
EEHOPRSTXY	XEROPHYTES
EEHOPSSTUU	SET UP HOUSE
EEIIINQSTUV	INEQUITIES
EEIIKLLNRU	UNLIKELIER
EEIIKLMORT	MORE LIKE IT
EEIIKLNPRW	PERIWINKLE
EEIIKLNRTW	WINTERLIKE
EEIIKNPTVW	KEPT IN VIEW
EEIIILLMMRT	MILLIMETRE
EEIIILLMTTT	LITTLE TIME
EEIIILLNSSV	LIVELINESS
EEIIILMNOSW	SIMONE WEIL
EEIIILMNRSV	SILVER MINE
EEIIILMNSST	TIMELINESS
EEIIILMPRTT	TRIPLE TIME
EEIIILMTTXY	TIMELY EXIT
EEIIILNNNOS	IN ONE'S LINE
EEIIILNNNTX	NEXT IN LINE
EEIIILNNNRST	INTERLINES
	LISTENER-IN
	NINE LITRES
EEIIILNOSTV	TELEVISION
EEIIILNSSTU	LUTEINISES
EEIIILNSTUZ	LUTEINIZES
EEIIILOPTVX	EXPLOITIVE
EEIIILORSTT	TOILETRIES
EEIIILRRSST	STERILISER
EEIIILRRSTZ	STERILIZER
EEIIILRSSST	STERILISES
EEIIILRSSTZ	STERILIZES
EEIIMMOTTT	TIME TO TIME
EEIIMMNOST	IN ONE'S TIME
EEIIMNORST	ENORMITIES
EEIIMNRSTX	IN EXTREMIS
EEIIMNRTTW	WINTER TIME
EEIIMNRTZZ	INTERMEZZI
EEIIMOPSST	EPITOMISES
EEIIMOPSTZ	EPITOMIZES
EEIIMPRSSV	IMPRESSIVE
	PERMISSIVE
EEIIMPRTTX	EXIT PERMIT
EEIINNNSTT	INSENTIENT
EEIINNRTTW	INTERTWINE
EEIINNSSTT	INTESTINES
EEIINOPRTT	PETITIONER
	REPETITION
EEIINOSSSV	SEE VISIONS
EEIINRSSST	SENSITISER
EEIINRSSTW	WINTERISES
EEIINRSSTZ	SENSITIZER
EEIINRSTVW	INTERVIEWS
EEIINRSTWZ	WINTERIZES
EEIINSSSST	SENSITISES
EEIINSSSTZ	SENSITIZES
EEIIOPSTVX	EXPOSITIVE
EEIIORRSST	ROTISSERIE
EEIIPQRSTU	PERQUISITE
EEIJLLNUVY	JUVENILELY
EEIJLRRSWY	JERRY LEWIS
EEIJOSSTVW	SOVIET JEWS
EEIKLLPSST	KEEPS STILL
EEIKLLRVYY	VERY LIKELY
EEIKLMORST	KILOMETRES
EEIKLNNSSU	UNLIKENESS
EEIKLNOSSV	SEVEN KILOS
EEIKLNPSTT	KEPT SILENT
EEIKMRSSTU	MUSKETRIES

EEIKNNPTTU	KEPT IN TUNE
EEIKNPPSTT	KEPT IN STEP
EEIKNSSTTX	SEX KITTENS
EEIKNSSTWY	KEY WITNESS
EEIKOPSTTU	KEEPS IT OUT
EEILLLLNTT	LITTLE NELL
EEILLLNOST	TELL NO LIES
	TELLS NO LIE
EEILLLPSTV	SPLIT LEVEL
	SPLIT-LEVEL
EEILLMMORT	IMMORTELLE
EEILLMNOST	EMOLLIENTS
EEILLMORTT	LITTLE MORE
EEILLMOTVY	LOVELY TIME
EEILLMPPPR	PEPPER MILL
EEILLMSSTY	TIMELESSLY
EEILLNNOSS	LONELINESS
EEILLNOSSV	LOVELINESS
EEILLNRSSV	SNIVELLERS
EEILLNSSTT	LITTLENESS
EEILLORTWW	WILLOW TREE
EEILLPSTVY	STEP LIVELY
EEILLRSSTY	TIRELESSLY
EEILLRSTWW	WRITES WELL
EEILLRTTVY	VERY LITTLE
EEILLSSVWY	VIEWLESSLY
EEILMMNPST	IMPLEMENTS
EEILMMORST	MILOMETERS
EEILMNNSTT	ENLISTMENT
EEILMNOOST	LOSE NO TIME
EEILMNOSSS	SOLEMNISES
EEILMNOSST	MILESTONES
EEILMNOSSU	MOUSSELINE
EEILMNOSSZ	SOLEMNIZES
EEILMNPSSS	SIMPLENESS
EEILMOOSTT	TIME TO LOSE
EEILMOPRSY	POLYMERISE
EEILMOPRYZ	POLYMERIZE
EEILMORSTY	TIRESOMELY
EEILMOSSTV	MOTIVELESS
EEILMOSSVW	SEMIVOWELS
EEILMPRSTU	PULSIMETER
EEILNNPTTY	PENITENTLY
EEILNNSSST	SILENTNESS
EEILNNSTTY	SENTIENTLY
EEILNOPRRT	INTERLOPER
EEILNOPRSU	RELIES UPON
EEILNOPSST	POLITENESS
	SLEEPS ON IT
EEILNORSVW	WOLVERINES
EEILNPRTXY	INEXPERTLY
EEILNPSTTY	SILENT TYPE
EEILNRSSTW	WINTERLESS
EEILNRSTUY	ESURIENTLY
EEILOOPRTV	OVER POLITE
EEILOPRSST	PISTOLEERS
EEILOPSSVX	EXPLOSIVES
EEILORRSTU	IRRESOLUTE
EEILORRTXY	EXTERIORLY
EEILOSSTTT	STILETTOES
EEILPPRTXY	PERPLEXITY
EEILPPSTUV	SUPPLETIVE
EEILPRRSUV	PULVERISER
	PURE SILVER
EEILPRRUVZ	PULVERIZER
EEILPRSSST	STRIPELESS
EEILPRSSTY	PERISTYLES
EEILPRSSUV	PULVERISES
EEILPRSUVZ	PULVERIZES
EEILPRTUVY	ERUPTIVELY
EEILRSSSST	RESISTLESS

EEILRSSTUV	VIRTUELESS
EEIMMMNRTU	IMMUREMENT
EEIMMMRSTU	SUMMER TIME
	SUMMERTIME
EEIMMOPRRV	PRIME MOVER
EEIMMRSSTU	SUMMERIEST
EEIMMRSSTW	SWIMMERETS
EEIMMRSTYZ	SYMMETRIZE
EEIMNNNRTT	INTERNMENT
EEIMNNOPTT	PENTIMENTO
EEIMNNORST	MINESTRONE
EEIMNNRSTT	INTERMENTS
EEIMNNSSTT	SENTIMENTS
EEIMNNSSTU	MINUTENESS
EEIMNNSTTU	TEN MINUTES
EEIMNNSTTV	INVESTMENT
EEIMNOPPRT	PREEMPTION
EEIMNOPRST	SIMON PETER
EEIMNOPRTU	PERITONEUM
EEIMNOPRYZ	MONEY PRIZE
	PRIZE MONEY
EEIMNORRSS	SERMONISER
EEIMNORRSZ	SERMONIZER
EEIMNORSSS	SERMONISES
EEIMNORSSZ	SERMONIZES
EEIMNORTZZ	INTERMEZZO
EEIMNOSSYZ	ISOENZYMES
EEIMNPPPRT	PEPPERMINT
EEIMNPQSTU	EQUIPMENTS
EEIMNRRSUV	MR.UNIVERSE
EEIMNRSSSS	REMISSNESS
EEIMOPPRRT	PROPER TIME
EEIMOPRRST	SPIROMETER
	TEMPORISER
EEIMOPRRTZ	TEMPORIZER
EEIMOPRSST	TEMPORISES
EEIMOPRSTU	PERIOSTEUM
EEIMOPRSTZ	TEMPORIZES
EEIMOPRTYZ	PIEZOMETRY
EEIMPSSSTU	MESSES IT UP
EEIMRRSVWY	MERRY WIVES
EEIMRSSSST	MISTRESSES
EEIMRSSTTU	SESTERTIUM
EEIMSSSSTY	SYSTEMISES
EEIMSSSTYZ	SYSTEMIZES
EEINNNSSTT	INTENTNESS
EEINNOPRSS	IN RESPONSE
	PENSIONERS
EEINNOPRST	PRETENSION
	TIN OPENERS
EEINNOPRTV	PREVENTION
EEINNORRSS	ORNERINESS
EEINNORRTV	INTERVENOR
EEINNORSST	TENSIONERS
EEINNORSTT	ENTERS INTO
	NO INTEREST
	RETENTIONS
EEINNORSVW	NEW VERSION
EEINNORTVW	INTERWOVEN
EEINNOSSTX	EXTENSIONS
EEINNPRSST	SPINNERETS
EEINNPRTTU	TURPENTINE
EEINNPSSSU	IN SUSPENSE
	SUPINENESS
EEINNPSSTV	SEVEN PINTS
EEINNQSSUU	UNIQUENESS
EEINNRSSTV	INVENTRESS
EEINNRTTWX	NEXT WINTER
EEINOOPTVW	OPEN TO VIEW
EEINOOSSST	OTIOSENESS
EEINOPRRSS	REPRESSION
EEINOPRRST	INTERPOSER
EEINOPRRSV	PERVERSION
EEINOPRSST	INTERPOSES
EEINOPRSSV	RESPONSIVE
EEINOPRSSX	EXPRESSION
EEINOPRTXY	PYROXENITE
EEINOPSSUZ	SEIZES UPON
EEINOQRSTU	QUESTIONER
EEINORRSSV	REVERSIONS
EEINORRTVW	OVERWINTER
EEINORSSVX	SIX OR SEVEN
EEINOSSTVV	VOTIVENESS
EEINPRRSTT	INTERPRETS
EEINPRSSTT	PERSISTENT
	PRETTINESS
EEINPRSTUV	PUT IN VERSE
EEINPSSSUV	SUSPENSIVE
EEINRRRTTV	RIVER TRENT
EEIOPPRRST	PROPERTIES
EEIOPPRSSV	OPPRESSIVE
EEIOPPSSTV	STOVEPIPES
EEIOPRRSSS	PRIORESSES
EEIOPRRSTV	RESORPTIVE
EEIOPRSTTT	OPERETTIST
EEIOPRSTTU	PIROUETTES
EEIOPSSSSV	POSSESSIVE
EEIOQQSUUV	EQUIVOQUES
EEIORRRSST	TERRORISES
EEIORRRSSV	RESERVOIRS
EEIORRRSTZ	TERRORIZES
EEIORRRTTY	TOY TERRIER
EEIORRSTVW	OVERWRITES
EEIPPRTTUY	PERPETUITY
EEIPRRSSSU	PRESSURISE
EEIPRRSSUZ	PRESSURIZE
EEIPRRSTVY	PERVERSITY
EEIPRRTTTU	UTTER TRIPE
EEIPRRTTWY	TYPEWRITER
EEIPRSSSTT	STEPSISTER
EEIPRSSSUV	SUPERVISES
EEIPRSTTWY	TYPEWRITES
EEIRRSSSTV	RESERVISTS
EEIRRSSTTU	SESTERTIUS
EEISSSTTWW	WEST IS WEST
EEJMNNORUY	JOURNEYMEN
EEJMPQSUUU	QUEUE-JUMPS
EEJNORRSTY	TERRY JONES
EEKKORRSWY	KEY WORKERS
EEKLLNOPSW	SPOKEN WELL
	WELL SPOKEN
	WELL-SPOKEN
EEKLLNRSSU	KEN RUSSELL
EEKLNORRSS	SNORKELERS
EEKLNPRSSU	SPELUNKERS
EEKLOOPPRW	WORKPEOPLE
EEKLORSSTW	STEEL WORKS
	STEELWORKS
EEKMMNOSTY	KEY MOMENTS
EEKMNNOOTY	TOKEN MONEY
EEKNOOQRSU	QUEENS ROOK
EEKNORRSWY	NEW YORKERS
EELLLOSSVY	LOVELESSLY
EELLMNOOSY	LONESOMELY
EELLMNOSSW	MELLOWNESS
EELLNNOOST	TELLS NO ONE
EELLNNSSSU	SULLENNESS
EELLNOPPRT	PROPELLENT
EELLNOQTUY	ELOQUENTLY
EELLNOSSTY	TONELESSLY
EELLNSSTUY	TUNELESSLY
EELLOORSWY	YELLOW ROSE

EELLOPPRRS	PROPELLERS	EENOPPRRSS	PROPERNESS
EELLORSTUY	RESOLUTELY	EENOPRRSTW	NEWS REPORT
EELLPRTTWY	PRETTY WELL	EENOPRRTUV	PROVEN TRUE
EELLRSSSTU	LUSTRELESS	EENOPSSSTT	STONE STEPS
EELLRSSSTY	RESTLESSLY	EENORRRVWY	NEVER WORRY
EELMMNOPTY	EMPLOYMENT	EENORTTUUV	VENTURE OUT
EELMMNOSTU	EMOLUMENTS	EENPRTTTUY	PRETTY TUNE
EELMNNOSSS	SOLEMNNESS	EEOOPRRSVW	OVERPOWERS
EELMNOOSSY	LOSES MONEY	EEOPPRRSSU	PRESUPPOSE
EELMNOPRTY	PLENTY MORE	EEOPPRRSSW	POWER PRESS
EELMNPPSTU	SUPPLEMENT	EEOPPRRSUW	SUPERPOWER
EELMNPTUZZ	PUZZLEMENT	EEOPPRSSSS	PREPOSSESS
EELMOOPPST	MOST PEOPLE	EEOPPRSSSU	SUPERPOSES
EELMOORRSS	MORE OR LESS	EEOPPRSSTU	SET PURPOSE
EELMORSTTV	VOLTMETERS	EEOPRRRTTU	TRUE REPORT
EELMSSSSTY	SYSTEMLESS	EEOPRRSSTU	SUPERSTORE
EELNNOOTVW	TWELVE NOON	EEOPRRSTUV	PROVES TRUE
EELNOOPRTV	OPEN REVOLT	EEOPRTTTUY	TRUE TO TYPE
EELNOPRSTW	SPLEENWORT	EEORRSTTVX	EXTROVERTS
EELNORSSTV	RESOLVENTS	EEORSSSTUW	SOU'WESTERS
EELNORSTUV	VOLUNTEERS	EEPPRSSSSU	SUPPRESSES
EELNPPSSSU	SUPPLENESS	EEPRRSSTTU	SPUTTERERS
EELNRSSTTU	NET RESULTS	EEPRRSTTUY	PRETTY SURE
EELOOOOPPPR	POOR PEOPLE	EERRSSTTTU	STUTTERERS
EELOOPPRTV	TOPPLE OVER	EESSSSTUWX	WEST SUSSEX
EELOORSSTU	SURE TO LOSE	EFFFFHLOSU	SHUFFLE OFF
EELOPPSTTU	PUT TO SLEEP	EFFFGIILLOT	GIFT OF LIFE
EELOPRRSTU	POULTERERS	EFFFILLLOU	FULL OF LIFE
EELOPRSSTY	POLYESTERS	EFFFILNSSU	FLUFFINESS
	PROSELYTES	EFFFIMORRS	FIRM OFFERS
EELOPRSTTT	LETTER POST	EFFFLLLOOU	FELL FOUL OF
EELOPRUVZZ	PUZZLE OVER	EFFFOOPRRU	UP FOR OFFER
EELORRRSTY	RETRORSELY	EFFGGINOTT	GETTING OFF
EELORSSUVY	YOURSELVES	EFFGGIORRT	TRIGGER OFF
EELPSSTTUX	SEXTUPLETS	EFFGHIINRS	FISH FINGER
EELRSSSSST	STRESSLESS	EFFGHIIRST	FIGHTS FIRE
EEMMMRRSTU	SUMMER TERM		FIREFIGHTS
EEMMNOORST	METRONOMES	EFFGHIORTU	FOUGHT FIRE
	MONOTREMES	EFFGIILNOS	SIGN OF LIFE
EEMMNRSTUX	NEXT SUMMER	EFFGIINNST	STIFFENING
EEMMOORSST	OSMOMETERS	EFFGIINORT	FORFEITING
EEMMORSTTY	MEMORY TEST	EFFGILLNOS	SELLING OFF
EEMMRSSTUW	WET SUMMERS	EFFGILLNOT	TELLING OFF
EEMNNOPSTT	PENTSTEMON		TELLING-OFF
EEMNNOPSTY	SPENT MONEY	EFFGILNOTT	LETTING OFF
EEMNNORSWY	SWORN ENEMY	EFFGILNSSU	SNIFFS GLUE
EEMNNORTYY	ENTRY MONEY	EFFGINOPRR	PROFFERING
EEMNNRRSUY	NURSERYMEN	EFFGINOPRU	OFFERING UP
EEMNOORRSY	ROY EMERSON	EFFGINOSTT	SETTING OFF
EEMNOORSSS	MOROSENESS	EFFGINRSSU	SUFFERINGS
EEMNOORSTT	TONOMETERS	EFFGIORRUU	FIGURE FOUR
EEMNORRSTT	TORMENTERS	EFFGLOSUUZ	GULF OF SUEZ
EEMOPPRRTY	PEREMPTORY	EFFGNOOPSS	SPONGES OFF
EEMOPPRRSTY	PYROMETERS	EFFHHKOOOT	OFF THE HOOK
EEMOQRSTTU	QUOTE TERMS	EFFHIINOTW	IN OFF WHITE
EEMORSSTTU	METOESTRUS	EFFHIKLORS	FISHERFOLK
EEMPPRSTUY	EMPTY PURSE	EFFHINORSZ	FROZEN FISH
EEMPRRSTTU	TRUMPETERS	EFFHINOSSS	OFFISHNESS
EEMPRSSSST	SEMPSTRESS	EFFHIORRSU	HURRIES OFF
EEMPRSSTTY	PRETTY MESS	EFFHIRRSTU	FRESH FRUIT
EENNNNOOSS	NO NONSENSE	EFFHLLOOPU	FULL OF HOPE
	NO-NONSENSE	EFFIIKLOSS	KISS OF LIFE
EENNOOOSST	ON ONES TOES	EFFIILMSTY	FIFTY MILES
EENNOOPRSS	NO RESPONSE	EFFIIMNNOR	IN FINE FORM
EENNOORRVW	NOW OR NEVER	EFFIINNOTY	ONE IN FIFTY
EENNOPRSTT	NOT PRESENT	EFFIINNSSS	SNIFFINESS
EENNOPRSTX	NEXT PERSON	EFFIIORTTW	WRITE IT OFF
EENNORSSTT	ROTTENNESS	EFFIIQSSTU	SQUIFFIEST
EENOOOSSUY	SEE YOU SOON	EFFIKORSST	STRIKES OFF
EENOOPRTTY	TONE POETRY	EFFILLMNTU	FULFILMENT
EENOOPRTUV	PUT ONE OVER	EFFILLOOSS	LOSS OF LIFE

EFFILLOSSU	FOSSIL FUEL	EFGILLNNNU	FUNNELLING
EFFILMSUUV	EFFLUVIUMS	EFGILLNOSV	SELF-LOVING
EFFILNSSTU	FITFULNESS	EFGILLNTTY	LETTING FLY
EFFILOPSTT	SLEPT IT OFF	EFGILLORRW	FLOWER GIRL
EFFILORSTV	LOVERS TIFF	EFGILLTTUY	FELT GUILTY
EFFIMMSSTU	MISS MUFFET	EFGILNNSTY	SENT FLYING
EFFINNOOPS	PENSION OFF	EFGILNORST	FOSTERLING
EFFINOOTTY	FIFTY TO ONE	EFGILNORVY	FLYING OVER
EFFINORSTT	FIRST OF TEN	EFGILNOSSW	SELF-SOWING
EFFINORTTW	WRITTEN OFF	EFGILNRSTU	FLUSTERING
EFFINSSSTU	STUFFINESS	EFGILNRTTU	FLUTTERING
EFFIOORRUV	FOUR OR FIVE	EFGILNSTWY	FLYING WEST
EFFIOORTTW	WROTE IT OFF	EFGILRSTUU	FULGURITES
EFFIOORTUV	FIVE TO FOUR	EFGIMNOPRR	PERFORMING
EFFLLOOUUV	FULL OF LOVE		PREFORMING
EFFLOOORST	SOLO EFFORT	EFGINNOOST	FESTOONING
EFFLORSSSU	SUFFER LOSS	EFGINOPRSS	PROFESSING
EFFMMNOOST	OFF MOMENTS	EFGINOPRST	FINGERPOST
EFFNNOOSTU	OFF ONES NUT	EFGINORSTW	TWO FINGERS
EFFORSSTUV	OVERSTUFFS	EFGINPRTUY	PUTREFYING
EFGGGLORTY	FELT GROGGY	EFGINPSTUY	STUPEFYING
EFGGHIINRT	FREIGHTING	EFGIOOPRRU	POOR FIGURE
EFGGIIILNV	LIFE-GIVING	EFGIRSSSTU	FIRST GUESS
EFGGIILNSV	SELF-GIVING	EFGKLOOPRS	LEGS OF PORK
EFGGIINNRR	RING FINGER	EFGLNNOORU	ONE FURLONG
EFGGINORTT	FORGETTING	EFGLNOOOSV	SONG OF LOVE
EFGHHIILRS	HIGH-FLIERS	EFGNNOOOOT	GONE ON FOOT
EFGHHIIKNRS	KINGFISHER	EFGNOOOOST	GOES ON FOOT
EFGHIILSTT	FLIGHTIEST	EFGNOOOPRTU	GROUP OF TEN
EFGHIILTTT	TITLE FIGHT	EFHHINORST	SHINE FORTH
EFGHIIMNTY	MIGHTY FINE	EFHHIOORTT	HIT THE ROOF
EFGHIIINNST	FISHING NET	EFHHLOSSTU	HOT FLUSHES
EFGHIIPRTZ	PRIZE FIGHT	EFHHNOORST	SHONE FORTH
	PRIZEFIGHT	EFHIIKNSSV	FISH KNIVES
EFGHILLSST	FLIGHTLESS	EFHIILLNTW	FELL IN WITH
EFGHILMNOY	FLYING HOME	EFHIILLSTT	LITTLE FISH
EFGHILORTV	OVERFLIGHT	EFHIILNSST	FILTHINESS
EFGHILSTTT	TEST FLIGHT	EFHIILRSSV	SILVERFISH
EFGHILSTWY	FLYWEIGHTS	EFHIILRTTW	TRIFLE WITH
EFGHIMNORS	FISHMONGER	EFHIINNSTV	FIVE NINTHS
EFGHINORTV	GIVEN FORTH	EFHIINPSSU	FINISHES UP
EFGHINRRTU	FURTHERING	EFHIINSSST	SHIFTINESS
EFGHIOPRTU	HUGE PROFIT	EFHIISSTVX	FIVE SIXTHS
EFGHIORSTU	FOUR EIGHTS	EFHILLOPSW	FELLOWSHIP
EFGHIORSTV	GIVES FORTH	EFHILNORST	FLIES NORTH
EFGHLLLNTU	FULL LENGTH	EFHILNSTUU	USEFUL HINT
	FULL-LENGTH	EFHILOPRST	SHOPLIFTER
EFGHLLNORU	FLUGELHORN	EFHILORSSU	FLOURISHES
EFGHLNRTUY	FELT HUNGRY	EFHILORSTW	WHISTLE FOR
EFGHOOPPRR	FROGHOPPER	EFHILOSSTU	FLIES SOUTH
EFGIIILNNR	FIRING LINE	EFHILRSSTT	THRIFTLESS
EFGIIIMNNS	FEMINISING	EFHIMNOSTV	FIVE MONTHS
EFGIIIMNNZ	FEMINIZING	EFHIMORTTU	FOURTH TIME
EFGIIINRSS	SIGNIFIERS	EFHINNORTT	IN THE FRONT
EFGIILMRSU	SLIM FIGURE	EFHINORSST	FROTHINESS
EFGIILNOVW	LOVING WIFE	EFHINORSTU	FINEST HOUR
EFGIILNQUY	LIQUEFYING	EFHIORRRTV	RIVER FORTH
EFGIILNRTT	FLITTERING	EFHIORSSTU	FIRST HOUSE
EFGIILTUVY	FUGITIVELY		ISSUE FORTH
EFGIIMNORS	FOREIGNISM	EFHIORSTTW	WHITE FROST
EFGIIMRRTU	TRIM FIGURE	EFHIPPRSSU	FISH SUPPER
EFGIINPRST	FINGERTIPS	EFHKLOORSS	LOOKS FRESH
EFGIINPRTY	PETRIFYING	EFHLLOOPRS	SHELLPROOF
EFGIINRRTY	TERRIFYING	EFHLLOSSUV	SHOVELFULS
EFGIINRSTT	GET IN FIRST		SHOVELSFUL
EFGIINRSTU	SURFEITING	EFHLNOOORT	ON THE FLOOR
EFGIINRSVY	VERSIFYING	EFHLNOORTT	TENTH FLOOR
EFGIINSTTY	TESTIFYING	EFHLNOPRRU	RUN FOR HELP
EFGIIRSSUX	SIX FIGURES	EFHLOORSWW	FLOWER SHOW
EFGIKLNORS	FOLK SINGER	EFHLOSSTUU	FLUSHES OUT
EFGILLLUUY	GUILEFULLY	EFHMMOORRT	THERMOFORM

EFHMNOORRU	RUN FOR HOME
EFHMOOPRTT	FROM THE TOP
EFHNOOOPTY	POT OF HONEY
EFHNORSTTU	FOUR TENTHS
EFHNORSTUX	FOXHUNTERS
EFHORSTTTU	FOURTH TEST
EFIIIINNTV	INFINITIVE
EFIIILLMNT	FILL IN TIME
EFIIILMPRS	SIMPLIFIER
EFIIILMPSS	SIMPLIFIES
EFIIILNNTY	INFINITELY
EFIIIMNNTY	FEMININITY
EFIIKNRSSS	FRISKINESS
EFIILLMNST	SILENT FILM
EFIILLNUVW	IN FULL VIEW
EFIILLORSV	SILVER FOIL
EFIILMNSSS	FLIMSINESS
EFIILNORRY	INFERIORLY
EFIILOOOOO	FOOOILIOEO
EFIILOSSSZ	FOSSILIZES
EFIILSSTTU	STULTIFIES
EFIIMNOTTU	UNIT OF TIME
EFIIMORRSU	FOURIERISM
EFIINNOPST	FINE POINTS
EFIINOPSTV	FIVE POINTS
EFIINRSSTU	FRUITINESS
EFIINRSSZZ	FRIZZINESS
EFIIORRSTT	TRIES FOR IT
EFIIORRSTU	FOURIERIST
EFIIPRRSTZ	FIRST PRIZE
EFIIRSSSTU	FIRST ISSUE
EFIJLLRTUY	FRUIT JELLY
EFIKLLLOTT	LITTLE FOLK
EFIKLNOSSS	FOLKSINESS
EFILLLMOSU	ISLE OF MULL
EFILLMORST	STELLIFORM
EFILLNORTU	ILL FORTUNE
EFILLNSSUW	WILFULNESS
EFILLOOPRW	LOW PROFILE
EFILLPSTUY	SPITEFULLY
EFILMOOSST	LOSS OF TIME
EFILMOOSTT	LOTS OF TIME
EFILMORSTY	FORTY MILES
EFILNNSSSU	SINFULNESS
EFILNOPPSS	FLOPPINESS
EFILNOPTTY	FELT NO PITY
EFILNORSTV	FIRST NOVEL
EFILNORTWW	TWINFLOWER
EFILOPRSST	PROFITLESS
EFILOPTTTU	FELT UP TO IT
EFILORRSTU	FOUR LITRES
EFILOSTUZZ	FIZZLES OUT
EFIMNORSTU	MISFORTUNE
EFIMOOPRSU	POMIFEROUS
EFINNORRTY	FORTY-NINER
EFINOOPRSS	PROFESSION
EFINOPRSTT	NET PROFITS
EFINORSSST	FROSTINESS
EFINORSSTT	FIRST STONE
EFIOOPSTTU	OUT OF SPITE
EFIOPRSTTU	PETIT FOURS
EFIORRSTYZ	TRY FOR SIZE
EFIORSTTTU	OUTFITTERS
EFIPRSSSTT	FIRST STEPS
EFJLNOSSUY	JOYFULNESS
EFJOOPRTWY	WEPT FOR JOY
EFKLNOOOTU	TOOK ON FUEL
EFKLOORSTU	FOUL STROKE
EFKNOOPSST	SOFT-SPOKEN
EFKOORRSTU	FOUR-STROKE
EFLLLMOSSU	FOUL SMELLS

EFLLLMOUUV	FULL VOLUME
EFLLLNNOSU	FULL NELSON
EFLLLOOSWW	LOW FELLOWS
EFLLMORSSY	FORMLESSLY
EFLLMORSUW	RUM FELLOWS
EFLLNNORRY	ERROL FLYNN
EFLLOOOPRW	POOR FELLOW
EFLLOPRRTU	FULL REPORT
EFLLOPRUWY	POWERFULLY
EFLLOSUUXY	FLEXUOUSLY
EFLMOOORTY	TOMFOOLERY
EFLMOORUUV	VOLUME FOUR
EFLNNORTTU	NO LEFT TURN
EFLNORSSUW	SUNFLOWERS
EFLOOOSSTT	SET OF TOOLS
EFLOOPRSTW	FLOWERPOTS
EFLOOSTTUY	OUT OF STYLE
EFLOPPRSUU	PURPOSEFUL
EFMMMOORRY	FROM MEMORY
EFMMNOORYY	FOR MY MONEY
EFMMNOOSUY	SUM OF MONEY
EFMNOOOTUY	OUT OF MONEY
EFMOORRTTU	TRUE TO FORM
EFNNOORRSU	NONFERROUS
EFNNOORSWZ	FROZEN SNOW
EFNOOORTTY	FORTY TO ONE
EFNOOOOSTT	GETS ON FOOT
EFNOORRSTT	STOREFRONT
EFOOPRRSSS	PROFESSORS
EFOOPRRSTU	FOUR-POSTER
EFOORRSTVY	FORTY OVERS
EGGGIINNRS	SNIGGERING
EGGGIINRRT	TRIGGERING
EGGGINOPTU	PEGGING OUT
EGGGINORSS	GROGGINESS
EGGGINSSTU	SUGGESTING
EGGHHORTTU	GET THROUGH
EGGHIIINNV	INVEIGHING
EGGHIIINNW	WEIGHING IN
EGGHIILLNV	GIVING HELL
EGGHIILNNT	LIGHTENING
EGGHIILNRT	LIGHTERING
EGGHIINNTT	TIGHTENING
EGGHIINOTW	GOING WHITE
EGGHIINPUW	WEIGHING UP
EGGHIIRTTT	GET IT RIGHT
EGGHINNORU	ROUGHENING
EGGHINNOTU	TOUGHENING
EGGHINSTTU	GUEST NIGHT
EGGHIPTTTU	GET UPTIGHT
EGGHIRRSTU	GUESS RIGHT
EGGIINNORUY	GONE HUNGRY
EGGHNORSUY	GOES HUNGRY
EGGHORSSUU	ROUGH GUESS
EGGIIILNNV	INVEIGLING
EGGIIINRSV	GIVING RISE
EGGIIILLNRS	SINGLE GIRL
EGGIILMMNR	GLIMMERING
EGGIILMNNST	GLISTENING
EGGIILNOSU	EULOGISING
EGGIILNOUZ	EULOGIZING
EGGIILNRST	GLISTERING
EGGIILNRTT	GLITTERING
EGGIIMNNPT	PIGMENTING
EGGIINNRST	SIGNET RING
EGGIINNTVV	GIVING VENT
EGGIINORVV	GIVING OVER
EGGIILLNORV	GROVELLING
EGGILMNSSU	SMUGGLES IN
EGGILNNRSU	GUNSLINGER
EGGILOOSST	GEOLOGISTS

EGGILORTUW	WRIGGLE OUT	EGHILOOSTT	ETHOLOGIST
EGGIMNOSTV	GETS MOVING	EGHILOPSTT	GOT THE SLIP
EGGINNORSS	ENGROSSING	EGHILORSST	SOLE RIGHTS
EGGINORTTW	GET IT WRONG	EGHILORSUV	LIVES ROUGH
EGGINOSSTU	SUGGESTION	EGHILOSSST	LOSES SIGHT
EGGINOTTTU	GETTING OUT	EGHILOSTTW	LOST WEIGHT
EGGIOPRSTT	GET TO GRIPS	EGHILPSTTT	SLEPT TIGHT
EGGIORRSTU	OUTRIGGERS	EGHIMNOORS	SIGH NO MORE
EGGLLOOOPX	GOOGOLPLEX	EGHIMNORST	SMOTHERING
EGGLMOSTUU	SMUGGLE OUT	EGHIMORTVY	OVERMIGHTY
EGGLNORSTU	STRUGGLE ON	EGHINNNORT	ENTHRONING
EGGLNPSSUU	SNUGGLES UP	EGHINNNOTW	NOTHING NEW
EGGLOOPTYY	EGYPTOLOGY	EGHINNORST	SHORTENING
EGGLOORSUY	GORGEOUSLY	EGHINNORTW	IN THE WRONG
EGGLRRSSTU	STRUGGLERS	EGHINNPPSU	PEN PUSHING
EGGMNOPTUY	PEGGY MOUNT	EGHINNRSSU	HUNGRINESS
EGGNNOORST	GONE STRONG	EGHINNRSTT	IN STRENGTH
EGGNOORSST	GOES STRONG	EGHINNRSTU	NIGHT NURSE
EGGNORSSUW	GUESS WRONG	EGHINORRST	SHORT REIGN
EGHHIILTTW	WHITE LIGHT	EGHINORSST	SHOE STRING
EGHHIINNTT	IN THE NIGHT		SHOESTRING
EGHHIINORS	SENIOR HIGH	EGHINPSTTU	TIGHTENS UP
EGHHIINRTT	IN THE RIGHT	EGHINRSTTU	SHUTTERING
EGHHIIPRST	HIGH PRIEST	EGHIOPRSTT	TIGHTROPES
EGHHILOPRY	HIEROGLYPH	EGHIORSSTV	OVERSIGHTS
EGHHILOSTT	LOST HEIGHT	EGHIORSTTW	GHOSTWRITE
EGHHILOSTU	LIGHTHOUSE	EGHIORTTWY	TROY WEIGHT
EGHHINORTT	ON THE RIGHT	EGHIRSSTTU	THEURGISTS
EGHHINORTU	IN THE ROUGH	EGHJMNPTUU	JUMP THE GUN
EGHHIORSTU	EIGHT HOURS	EGHJNOSTUU	JUST ENOUGH
EGHHIORTTT	TO THE RIGHT	EGHLMOOOSU	HOMOLOGUES
EGHHLOOSTT	HOGS THE LOT	EGHLNOOPRY	PHRENOLOGY
EGHHMOPTTU	GOT THE HUMP	EGHLNOSTTW	TWO LENGTHS
EGHHOORSUU	ROUGH HOUSE	EGHLOOPPSY	PSEPHOLOGY
	ROUGHHOUSE	EGHLOPRSTU	SLEPT ROUGH
EGHHOPSTTU	GOT THE PUSH	EGHMNOOORU	ENOUGH ROOM
EGHHORTTUW	WET THROUGH	EGHMNOOOSU	HOMOGENOUS
EGHIIINNRT	INHERITING	EGHMOOOTYZ	HOMOZYGOTE
EGHIIKLOST	EIGHT KILOS	EGHMORRTYY	HYGROMETRY
EGHIIKNSST	NIGHT SKIES	EGHNNOOOSU	SOON ENOUGH
EGHIIKNSTV	THE VIKINGS	EGHNOORRSW	WRONG HORSE
EGHIILLMST	LIMELIGHTS	EGHNOORSTU	ROUGH STONE
EGHIILMOTT	GO THE LIMIT	EGHNOPSTUU	TOUGHENS UP
EGHIILNNRT	INNER LIGHT	EGHNRRUVYY	VERY HUNGRY
EGHIILNRST	RIGHT LINES	EGHOOOOTTZ	GO TO THE ZOO
	SLITHERING	EGHOORRTVW	OVERGROWTH
EGHIILRSTY	TIGERISHLY	EGHOORSSTU	SHOT GROUSE
EGHIIMMNRS	SHIMMERING	EGHOORSTTW	GHOSTWROTE
EGHIIMNPRW	WHIMPERING	EGIIILMMST	LEGITIMISM
EGHIIMNSST	MIGHTINESS	EGIIILMSTT	LEGITIMIST
EGHIINNNRS	ENSHRINING	EGIIILNORR	IRRELIGION
EGHIINNPRT	TREPHINING	EGIIIMNNST	MENINGITIS
EGHIINNRSU	USHERING IN	EGIIKNPPRS	SKIPPERING
EGHIINNSTW	IN THE SWING	EGIIKNRSTT	SKITTERING
	IN THE WINGS	EGIILLLNVW	LIVING WELL
EGHIINORST	THEORISING	EGIILLLRTT	LITTLE GIRL
EGHIINORTZ	THEORIZING	EGIILLNNSV	SNIVELLING
EGHIINPRSW	WHISPERING	EGIILLNOTU	GUILLOTINE
EGHIINPSTT	EIGHT PINTS	EGIILLNRST	TRELLISING
EGHIINSTUX	EXTINGUISH	EGIILMNOPS	POLEMISING
EGHIIQRTTU	QUITE RIGHT	EGIILMNOPZ	POLEMIZING
EGHIISTTTW	GETS WITH IT	EGIILMNOST	LOSING TIME
EGHILLMORY	HOMELY GIRL	EGIILNNPUV	LIVENING UP
EGHILLNOPU	GONE UPHILL	EGIILNNRST	IN STERLING
EGHILLNOSV	SHOVELLING	EGIILNNSSV	LIVINGNESS
EGHILLOPSU	GOES UPHILL	EGIILNNSTT	SETTLING IN
EGHILMOOOZ	HOMOLOGIZE	EGIILNOPTX	EXPLOITING
EGHILNOOPS	LOSING HOPE	EGIILNORRS	SENIOR GIRL
EGHILNOPTU	HELPING OUT	EGIILNPRTT	LETTING RIP
EGHILNSSST	SLIGHTNESS	EGIILNRRSV	SILVER RING
EGHILOORST	RHEOLOGIST	EGIILNRRTY	RETIRINGLY

EGIILNRSSS	GRISLINESS
EGIILNSSTU	GUILTINESS
EGIILOPSTT	EPIGLOTTIS
EGIIMMNNORS	MEMORISING
EGIIMMNNORZ	MEMORIZING
EGIIMMNNNOT	MENTIONING
EGIIMNPRSS	IMPRESSING
EGIIMNPRST	SPRINGTIME
EGIIMNPRTT	PERMITTING
EGIIMNRTTY	TRYING TIME
EGIINNNOPS	PENSIONING
EGIINNNORV	ENVIRONING
EGIINNNOST	TENSIONING
EGIINNNSTU	SING IN TUNE
EGIINNPPST	STEPPING IN
EGIINNRRSU	REINSURING
EGIINNSSST	STINGINESS
EGIINNSSTW	WITNESSING
EGIINORRST	ROISTERING
EGIINPPRRS	PERSPIRING
EGIINPRSST	PERSISTING
	SPRINGIEST
EGIINRSSTT	GRITTINESS
	STRINGIEST
EGIINRTTTW	TWITTERING
EGIINSTTTV	VIGNETTIST
EGIKILOSSV	SILK GLOVES
EGIKLNNOOS	INGLENOOKS
EGIKLNNORS	SNORKELING
EGIKLNNOSV	LONG KNIVES
EGIKLNNPSU	SPELUNKING
EGIKMNNORW	WORKINGMEN
EGIKMNOPTV	KEPT MOVING
EGIKNNOORS	SNOOKERING
EGIKNNORTW	NETWORKING
EGIKNOORST	GO ON STRIKE
EGIKNPRTTY	KEPT TRYING
EGIKOPRUVW	GIVE UP WORK
EGILLMMNOP	POMMELLING
EGILLMMNPU	PUMMELLING
EGILLMOSTU	GUILLEMOTS
EGILLNNNTU	TUNNELLING
EGILLNNOTW	NOTING WELL
	WELLINGTON
EGILLNOPPR	PROPELLING
EGILLNORTW	TROWELLING
EGILLNOSTU	SELLING OUT
EGILLNPRSW	WELLSPRING
EGILLNPSUW	SWELLING UP
EGILLNTUXY	EXULTINGLY
EGILLOOSSY	SILLY GOOSE
EGILLOSSSY	SYLLOGISES
EGILLOSSYZ	SYLLOGIZES
EGILMMNPTU	PLUMMETING
EGILMNOORS	SINGLE ROOM
EGILMNOOSS	GLOOMINESS
EGILMNOPTT	MELTING POT
EGILMNOSUU	LEGUMINOUS
EGILMNPTTY	TEMPTINGLY
EGILMOOSSY	SEISMOLOGY
EGILNNORST	STRONG LINE
EGILNNORTW	LONG WINTER
EGILNNOSST	SINGLETONS
EGILNNOSTT	SETTLING ON
EGILNNRRUY	UNERRINGLY
EGILNNSTTU	UNSETTLING
EGILNOOPST	PENOLOGIST
EGILNORRUV	OVERRULING
EGILNORTUV	REVOLUTING
EGILNORTWY	TOWERINGLY
EGILNOSSSS	GLOSSINESS

EGILNOSSTU	SINGLES OUT
EGILNOSTUU	LOUNGE SUIT
EGILNOTTTU	LETTING OUT
EGILNPRSSY	PRESSINGLY
EGILNPSTTU	SETTLING UP
EGILNPSTUX	SEXTUPLING
EGILNRSSST	STRINGLESS
EGILOORSST	SEROLOGIST
EGILORSUVY	GRIEVOUSLY
EGILOSUUXY	EXIGUOUSLY
EGILPRRTTY	PRETTY GIRL
EGILRSSTUY	UGLY SISTER
EGIMNNOORR	IRONMONGER
EGIMNNOOWY	OWING MONEY
EGIMMNNORTT	TORMENTING
EGIMNNORTU	REMOUNTING
EGIMNOORST	ERGONOMIST
EGIMNOORTY	GONIOMETRY
EGIMNOORVV	MOVING OVER
EGIMNORSSV	MISGOVERNS
EGIMNPRRST	SPRING TERM
EGIMNPRSSU	GRUMPINESS
EGIMNPRTTU	TRUMPETING
EGIMOOPRST	GEOTROPISM
EGINNNNSTUU	SUNG IN TUNE
EGINNOOPTU	OPENING OUT
EGINNOPPRS	SPRING OPEN
EGINNOPRSS	PRESSING ON
EGINNOPSSS	SPONGINESS
EGINNORTTU	RENTING OUT
EGINNORTUY	TOURNEYING
EGINNPRSTX	NEXT SPRING
EGINNRSSTU	INSURGENTS
EGINNRSTTU	ENTRUSTING
EGINNRSTUW	WET NURSING
	WET-NURSING
EGINNRSUVW	UNSWERVING
EGINNSSTTU	SETTING SUN
EGINOOOPTT	GO ON TIPTOE
EGINOOPPST	PIGEON POST
EGINOOPRRT	PROGENITOR
EGINOOPRRV	PORING OVER
EGINOPPRRS	PROSPERING
EGINOPPRSS	OPPRESSING
	POP SINGERS
EGINOPPRST	STOPPERING
EGINOPPSTW	SOPPING WET
EGINOPRRRS	PORRINGERS
EGINOPRRSS	IN PROGRESS
EGINOPRRST	SPORTINGER
EGINOPRRSV	SPRING OVER
EGINOPRSTT	PROTESTING
EGINOPRSUY	PERIGYNOUS
EGINOPRTUW	POURING WET
EGINOPSSSS	POSSESSING
EGINOQRTUW	QUITE WRONG
EGINORRSTW	SONG WRITER
	SONGWRITER
EGINORSTUV	SERVING OUT
EGINORSTUW	OUTSWINGER
EGINOSTTTU	SETTING OUT
EGINPPPSTU	STEPPING UP
EGINPPRSSU	PRESSING UP
EGINPRRSSU	PRESSURING
EGINPRSTTU	SPUTTERING
EGINRSSSTY	SYNERGISTS
EGINRSSTTV	STRING VEST
EGINRSTTTU	STUTTERING
EGJLLOORRY	JOLLY ROGER
EGKNOOORTW	GONE TO WORK
EGKNOOSTTW	GETS TO KNOW

EGKOOOORSTW	GOES TO WORK
EGLLMORSUU	GLOMERULUS
EGLLNNNOTU	LONG TUNNEL
EGLMMNOORY	LONG MEMORY
EGLMMNNORSU	LONG SUMMER
EGLMNOOOSU	MONOLOGUES
EGLMNOOOTY	ENTOMOLOGY
EGLMNOORUY	NUMEROLOGY
EGLMNOOYYZ	ENZYMOLOGY
EGLNNOSSUU	SUN LOUNGES
	SUNLOUNGES
EGMMNOPRSY	GYMNOSPERM
EGMOOOORRSU	GROUSE MOOR
EGNNNRRSUU	GUN RUNNERS
	GUNRUNNERS
EGNNOOOTTW	GONE TO TOWN
EGNNOORSUY	YOUNGER SON
EGNNOPPRSU	SPRUNG OPEN
EGNNORSTTW	WENT STRONG
EGNOOOSTTW	GOES TO TOWN
EGNOPRRSUV	SPRUNG OVER
EGNORRSTUV	OVERSTRUNG
EGNORSSTUY	YOUNGSTERS
EGNRRSTTUU	GUN TURRETS
EGOOPRSSYZ	ZYGOSPORES
EGOPPRSTTU	GET SUPPORT
EHHIIMSTTW	WHITESMITH
EHHIIRSTTW	WHITE SHIRT
EHHILLLSSW	WELSH HILLS
EHHILOOPSS	SHOE POLISH
EHHILOPTTY	LITHOPHYTE
EHHILORTWW	WORTHWHILE
EHHILRSSWY	SHREWISHLY
EHHIMNOTTU	IN THE MOUTH
EHHIMOPRST	MOTHER SHIP
EHHINNORTT	IN THE NORTH
EHHINOSTTU	IN THE SOUTH
EHHINOTTTW	HIT THE TOWN
EHHIOPRSSW	HORSEWHIPS
EHHIOPSSTY	HYPOTHESIS
EHHIOPSTTT	HIT THE POST
EHHLOOOOPPR	LOPHOPHORE
EHHLORTTUW	WHOLE TRUTH
EHHMNOOOPS	HOMOPHONES
EHHMORSTTU	HOME TRUTHS
EHHNOORTTT	TO THE NORTH
EHHNORSTUW	RUN THE SHOW
EHHOOOOPPRT	PHOTOPHORE
EHHOORRRST	THE HORRORS
EHHOORSSTW	HOT SHOWERS
EHHOOSTTTU	TO THE SOUTH
EHHOPPSSYY	HYPOPHYSES
EHHOPSTTTU	PUT THE SHOT
EHIIILNNRS	IRISH LINEN
EHIIILNPST	PHILISTINE
EHIIINRRTX	INHERITRIX
EHIIIPRSVZ	VIZIERSHIP
EHIIJMMTWY	JIMMY WHITE
EHIIKMRRSS	SKIRMISHER
EHIIKMRSSS	SKIRMISHES
EHIIKNPTTW	TIP THE WINK
EHIIKNRTTW	TINKER WITH
EHIIKNTTTY	IN THE KITTY
EHIILLOPSY	LYOPHILISE
EHIILLOPYZ	LYOPHILIZE
EHIILNOOPS	EOSINOPHIL
EHIILNPSST	IN THE SLIPS
EHIILNQRSU	RELINQUISH
EHIILNSTTW	TIN WHISTLE
EHIILNSVXY	VIXENISHLY
EHIIMNORSW	IRISHWOMEN

EHIIMNPSSS	IMPISHNESS
EHIIMNSTTU	THIS MINUTE
EHIIMOPRSV	IMPOVERISH
EHIINNPRST	INTERNSHIP
EHIINPPRSW	WHIPPERS-IN
EHIINPRSSW	IN WHISPERS
EHIINRSTTW	THIS WINTER
EHIIPRSSST	SISTER SHIP
EHIIQSSSTU	SQUISHIEST
EHIIRRSTTU	URETHRITIS
EHIIRSSTTT	THIRSTIEST
EHIIRSSTTZ	ZITHERISTS
EHIJKLNOSW	JOHN WILKES
EHIJLLNOTT	LITTLE JOHN
EHIKNOPPTT	POT THE PINK
EHIKNORSTV	THINKS OVER
EHIKNORSTW	IN THE WORKS
EHIKNPSTUY	UP IN THE SKY
EHIKNRRSTU	RUN THE RISK
EHIKORSSTU	SHRIEKS OUT
EHIKPPTTUW	KEPT UP WITH
EHILLNORST	ROTS IN HELL
	SHRILL NOTE
	SHRILL TONE
EHILLNRSSS	SHRILLNESS
EHILMNSSSU	MULISHNESS
EHILMOPSTY	POLYTHEISM
EHILNNOSSU	UNHOLINESS
EHILNOOSTT	HONEST TOIL
EHILNOPRTU	NEUTROPHIL
EHILNPSSSU	PLUSHINESS
EHILOPPSSU	POLISHES UP
EHILOPSTTY	POLYTHEIST
EHILORSTWX	LOWER SIXTH
EHILORTTVY	LOVE THIRTY
	THIRTY LOVE
EHILPRSSUU	SULPHURISE
EHILPRSSUV	SHRIVELS UP
EHILPRSUUZ	SULPHURIZE
EHIMMNOOST	MONOTHEISM
EHIMMNOSTT	THIS MOMENT
EHIMMOPRTU	PROMETHIUM
EHIMMRSSTU	THIS SUMMER
EHIMNNNOST	NINE MONTHS
EHIMNNOORS	MOONSHINER
EHIMNNOOSS	MOONSHINES
EHIMNNPSTU	PUNISHMENT
EHIMNOOSTT	MONOTHEIST
EHIMNOPSSY	SYMPHONIES
EHIMNOPSUU	EUPHONIUMS
EHIMORRSTT	THERMISTOR
EHIMORRTUV	RIVER MOUTH
EHINNOOPTT	ON THE POINT
EHINNORSST	THORNINESS
EHINOOPSUU	EUPHONIOUS
EHINOOPTTT	TO THE POINT
EHINOPRSSW	SHIPOWNERS
EHINOPSSTY	HYPNOTISES
EHINOPSTYZ	HYPNOTIZES
EHINORRTUW	UNWORTHIER
EHINORSSTU	RUSHES INTO
EHINORSSTW	WORTHINESS
EHINORSTUU	RUTHENIOUS
EHINOSSTTW	WIN THE TOSS
EHINOSTWWY	SNOWY WHITE
EHINPPSSSU	UPPISHNESS
EHINRSTTUW	TURNS WHITE
EHINSSSTTY	SYNTHESIST
EHIOOPRSTT	ORTHOEPIST
EHIOORSSTX	SIX-SHOOTER
EHIOPPRRSW	WORSHIPPER

EHIOPRRSTY	PREHISTORY
EHIOPRSSST	PROSTHESIS
EHIOPRSTTT	STIR THE POT
EHIORRSTUU	HURRIES OUT
EHIPPRSTUX	UPPER SIXTH
EHIPRSSTUY	SURETYSHIP
EHJLLORTTU	JETHRO TULL
EHJLNNNNOO	JOHN LENNON
EHJMOPRSUW	SHOW JUMPER
	SHOWJUMPER
EHKLNOOOST	HONEST LOOK
EHKNNNOTUW	THE UNKNOWN
EHKNOOOSSU	USE NO HOOKS
EHKNOORSTW	HONEST WORK
EHKOORSSTU	HOUSE STORK
EHKOORSSUW	WORKHOUSES
EHLLNOOSSW	HOLLOWNESS
EHLLOOSSTU	TOLLHOUSES
EHLLOPRSST	SHORT SPELL
EHLLORSSST	SELLS SHORT
EHLLRSSTUY	RUTHLESSLY
EHLMNOPPTY	NYMPHOLEPT
EHLMORSSUU	HUMOURLESS
EHLNOOOPST	ON THE POOLS
EHLNOOPRTW	ON THE PROWL
EHLNOOPSXY	XYLOPHONES
EHLNOOSSTY	HOLYSTONES
EHLNOSSTWY	SHOWN STYLE
EHLOOOOSTT	LOOSE TOOTH
EHLOOORRTY	HOLY TERROR
EHLOPRSSTU	UPHOLSTERS
EHLOPRSTUY	UPHOLSTERY
EHLORRSTTT	THROTTLERS
EHLOSSSTWY	SLOWS STYLE
EHMMNORRTY	MERRY MONTH
EHMMOOPRSY	MESOMORPHY
EHMNNOOOST	THE MONSOON
EHMNNOOOSY	HONEYMOONS
EHMNOOORRT	THRONE ROOM
EHMNOORSST	MOTHER'S SON
EHMNOOSSST	SMOOTHNESS
EHMOOOPRSS	SOPHOMORES
EHMOOORSTV	SMOOTH OVER
EHMOOPRRRT	OH,MR.PORTER!
EHMOOPRTTY	PHOTOMETRY
EHMPRRSTUY	PYRETHRUMS
EHMRRSTTUU	TRUTH SERUM
EHNNOOPRTW	THROWN OPEN
EHNNOPRTWY	PENNYWORTH
EHNOOPRSTW	THROWS OPEN
EHNOORRTVW	OVERTHROWN
	THROWN OVER
EHNOORTTWY	NOTEWORTHY
EHNOOSSTTW	WON THE TOSS
EHNOPRSTTU	POTHUNTERS
	THRUST OPEN
EHNOQSTTUU	QUONSET HUT
EHNORSTWWY	NEWSWORTHY
EHOOOPRSSU	POORHOUSES
EHOOORSSTV	OVERSHOOTS
EHOOPPRSTY	SPOROPHYTE
EHOOPRRSTV	HOVERPORTS
EHOOPRSSST	POST-HORSES
EHOOPRSTTT	STOP THE ROT
EHOORRSTVW	OVERTHROWS
	THROWS OVER
EHOPPPSTUW	PUPPET SHOW
EHOPPSSSTU	SETS UP SHOP
EHOPPSTTUU	UP THE SPOUT
EHOPRSTTTU	SHOT-PUTTER
EHORRSSTTW	THROWSTERS
EHORSSTTUU	TRUST HOUSE
EIIIINQSTU	INIQUITIES
EIIIKNNRTW	WRITE IN INK
EIIILMNNOP	EPILIMNION
EIIILNNQSU	INQUILINES
EIIILNNRSU	LIE IN RUINS
EIIILNNSSV	LIVES IN SIN
EIIILNSTZZ	TIN LIZZIES
EIIILPRSTV	EVIL SPIRIT
EIIIMNORST	MINORITIES
EIIIMNPSTU	IMPUNITIES
EIIIMNRSST	MINISTRIES
EIIIMPRSTV	PRIMITIVES
EIIIMSSTVY	EMISSIVITY
EIIIOPRRST	PRIORITIES
EIIJLNTUVY	JUVENILITY
EIIJMNRTUY	INJURY TIME
	INJURY-TIME
EIIJMNOTTU	JUST IN TIME
EIIJNOSSSU	JOINS ISSUE
EIIKLLLOWW	WILLOWLIKE
EIIKLLMOTT	TIME TO KILL
EIIKLMORRR	MIRRORLIKE
EIIKLNNSSS	SLINKINESS
EIIKLNORST	TRISKELION
EIIKLORSST	STRIKES OIL
EIIKMNPSSS	SKIMPINESS
EIIKNNNSSS	SKINNINESS
EIIKNNORTW	WROTE IN INK
EIIKNNOSTT	TIE IN KNOTS
EIILLLOTVW	WILL TO LIVE
EIILLMMNNU	MILLENNIUM
EIILLMMNSU	MILLENIUMS
EIILLMNNOO	ONE MILLION
EIILLMNNOT	TEN MILLION
EIILLMOPTY	IMPOLITELY
EIILLMORTW	LOWER LIMIT
EIILLMPRTU	MULTIPLIER
EIILLMPSTU	MULTIPLIES
EIILLNORRT	RITORNELLI
EIILLOSTWW	WILLOWIEST
EIILLPSSTY	PITILESSLY
EIILLQSTTU	QUITE STILL
EIILMMNNIY	IMMINENTLY
EIILMNOSSU	LIMOUSINES
EIILMOSTTV	LEITMOTIVS
EIILMPPRTU	UPPER LIMIT
EIILMSSTXY	SIXTY MILES
EIILNORRTY	INTERIORLY
EIILNOSSSV	VISIONLESS
EIILNPRSTY	PRISTINELY
EIILNRSSTY	SINISTERLY
EIILOPSTVY	POSITIVELY
EIILOPTTUV	LIVE UP TO IT
EIILPRSSST	SPIRITLESS
EIIMMNORSS	IMMERSIONS
EIIMMNNORTW	WIN ON MERIT
EIIMNNRSTU	TRIENNIUMS
EIIMNOPRSS	IMPRESSION
	PERMISSION
EIIMNOPSTT	STOP IN TIME
EIIMNORSSS	MISSIONERS
	REMISSIONS
EIIMNSSTUX	SIX MINUTES
EIIMOPRRSV	IMPROVISER
EIIMOPRSSV	IMPROVISES
EIIMOPRSUV	IMPERVIOUS
EIIMORSSTU	MOISTURISE
EIIMORSTUZ	MOISTURIZE
EIIMPSSSST	PESSIMISTS
EIINNNOPST	NINE POINTS

EIINNNOSTT	INTENTIONS	EILNOOOPPS	POLO PONIES
EIINNNOSTV	INVENTIONS	EILNOOOPTV	LOVE POTION
EIINNOQSTU	IN QUESTION	EILNOOPSSX	EXPLOSIONS
EIINNORSST	INSERTIONS	EILNOORSTU	RESOLUTION
EIINNORSSV	INVERSIONS	EILNOORTUV	REVOLUTION
EIINNRSSTW	WINTRINESS	EILNOOSTUV	EVOLUTIONS
EIINOOPSTX	EXPOSITION	EILNOPPRTW	NIPPLEWORT
EIINOORSUV	EUROVISION	EILNOPPSSS	SLOPPINESS
EIINOPRSSV	PREVISIONS	EILNOPPSST	SPLITS OPEN
EIINOPSTVW	VIEWPOINTS	EILNOPPSTU	SUPPLETION
EIINORTTWZ	ZWITTERION	EILNOPRSST	PORTLINESS
EIINPPRSST	PINSTRIPES	EILNOPRSSU	REPULSIONS
EIINPRSSSS	PRISSINESS	EILNOPSSUX	EXPULSIONS
EIINRSSTTW	TWIN SISTER	EILNOSTUUV	VELUTINOUS
EIINRSTUVY	UNIVERSITY	EILNPQSTUU	QUINTUPLES
EIINSSTTTU	INSTITUTES	EILNPQTTUU	QUINTUPLET
EIIOOPRRST	POSTERIORI	EILNRSSSTU	SULTRINESS
EIIOORRSST	SORORITIES	EILNRSSTTU	TURNSTILES
EIIOPPSSTT	PETITS POIS	EILOOPPSTY	OPPOSITELY
EIIORSTTTU	TRIES IT OUT	EILOOSTTVW	LOST TO VIEW
EIJKNNORSY	ROY JENKINS	EILOPPRSUV	PROPULSIVE
EIJLMPPRTU	TRIPLE JUMP	EILOPRRSUY	SUPERIORLY
EIKLLLOOVY	LOOK LIVELY	EILOPRSTVY	SPORTIVELY
EIKLLMOORY	ILKLEY MOOR	EILOPRSUVY	PREVIOUSLY
EIKLLMOSTY	MOST LIKELY		VIPEROUSLY
EIKLLOPSTY	LIKELY SPOT	EILOPSSSTX	SEX PISTOLS
EIKLNOSTUW	WINKLES OUT	EILOPSTTTU	SPELT IT OUT
EIKLNPRRSS	SPRINKLERS	EILORRSTVW	LIVERWORTS
EIKLOSTTTU	SKITTLE OUT	EILORSTUVY	VITREOUSLY
EIKMOPRRTW	WORK PERMIT	EIMMNOPRSS	PERSIMMONS
EIKNNOSSTT	KNOTTINESS	EIMNNOOORS	IN ONES ROOM
EIKNORRSSW	OWNERS RISK	EIMNNOOPTT	OMNIPOTENT
EIKOPPRRST	STRIP POKER	EIMNNOORTW	WON ON MERIT
EIKOPRRSTW	PIT WORKERS	EIMNNRSTTU	INSTRUMENT
EIKORSSTTU	STRIKES OUT	EIMNOOPRSS	SPOONERISM
EIKORSTTTY	TROTSKYITE	EIMNOPRRTU	IMPORTUNER
EILLLOORTT	TOILET ROLL	EIMNOPRSTU	IMPORTUNES
EILLLSSSTY	LISTLESSLY		RESUMPTION
EILLMMOSUV	SLIM VOLUME	EIMNORSSST	STORMINESS
EILLMNOSST	MILLSTONES	EIMNORSSSU	SENSORIUMS
EILLMOORTT	LITTLE ROOM	EIMNOSTTUW	TWO MINUTES
EILLMOPSSU	SIMPLE SOUL	EIMNOSTTZZ	MEZZOTINTS
EILLNNOSTY	INSOLENTLY	EIMNSSSTTU	SMUTTINESS
EILLNOORRT	RITORNELLO	EIMOOQSSTU	MOSQUITOES
EILLNOOSSW	WOOLLINESS	EIMOOQSTUY	MOSQUITOEY
EILLNOPSTU	LENTIL SOUP	EIMOPRRSST	MISREPORTS
EILLNOTUVY	INVOLUTELY	EIMOPRRSTU	ROMPER SUIT
EILLNRTUVY	VIRULENTLY	EIMOPRRSTY	SPIROMETRY
EILLOOPRSY	ROLY-POLIES	EIMOPRSSTU	IMPOSTURES
EILLOPRRST	ILL REPORTS	EIMORSSTUY	MYSTERIOUS
EILLOPRSSV	SPILLS OVER	EINNNOOPSS	ON ONES PINS
EILLOPRSUY	PERILOUSLY	EINNNORSWW	WINS RENOWN
EILLOPSTTU	SPELL IT OUT	EINNOOPPRS	OPEN PRISON
EILLORRTUY	ULTERIORLY	EINNOOPRRS	POOR SINNER
EILLORTTTU	LITTER LOUT	EINNOOPRST	PRENOTIONS
	LITTERLOUT	EINNOOQSTU	NO QUESTION
EILLPRSSUW	PULLS WIRES	EINNOORSTW	TWO RONNIES
EILMNNSSUY	SUNNY SMILE	EINNOOSSST	SNOOTINESS
EILMNOOOPS	MONOPOLIES	EINNOPSSSU	SUSPENSION
	MONOPOLISE	EINOOOPRTZ	ZERO OPTION
EILMNOOOPZ	MONOPOLIZE	EINOOPPRSS	OPPRESSION
EILMNOOSST	MOTIONLESS	EINOOPPRTW	POWER POINT
EILMNOOSTT	LOST NO TIME	EINOOPRRST	RESORPTION
EILMNOPSST	SIMPLETONS	EINOOPSSSS	POSSESSION
EILMNOPTTY	IMPOTENTLY	EINOORSTTX	EXTORTIONS
EILMNRSSTY	MINSTRELSY	EINOOSTTXY	SIXTY TO ONE
EILMOOPRST	METROPOLIS	EINOPPRSTY	PROPENSITY
EILMOPPRRY	IMPROPERLY	EINOPPRTUW	PUT IN POWER
EILNNNOOTV	NONVIOLENT	EINOPRRSTV	OVERPRINTS
EILNNOOSTW	LOW-TENSION	EINOPRSSST	SPORTINESS
EILNNRSSUU	UNRULINESS	EINOPSSSTT	SPOTTINESS

EINOQRTTUU	TOURNIQUET	EMMNRSSTUU	MENSTRUUMS
EINORRSSTTV	INTROVERTS	EMMOOOORTV	ROOM TO MOVE
EINORTTTUW	WRITTEN OUT	EMMOOPRSTT	POST MORTEM
EINOSSSTUY	SENSUOSITY		POSTMORTEM
EINPPSSTUY	UPPITYNESS	EMNNOOOSST	MOONSTONES
EINPRRRTTU	RETURN TRIP	EMNNOOPRTU	ONE NO-TRUMP
EINPRRSTTU	INTERRUPTS	EMNNRRRSUU	RUM RUNNERS
EINRSSSTTU	TRUSTINESS	EMNOORRSTT	TORMENTORS
EIOOOPRSTZ	SPOROZOITE	EMNOPPRSST	PROMPTNESS
EIOOPRRRRT	PROPRIETOR	EMNORSSTUU	MENSTRUOUS
EIOOPRRSST	POSTERIORS	EMOOORRSST	STOREROOMS
EIOOPRRSTY	REPOSITORY	EMOOORRSTV	SERVOMOTOR
EIOOPRSTXY	EXPOSITORY	EMOPRRSTUV	OVERTRUMPS
EIOORRTVWY	IVORY TOWER	ENNNORRTUV	TREVOR NUNN
EIOPPRRSTY	PROSPERITY	ENNOOOOTTW	TWO TO ONE ON
EIOPPRSSTT	STROPPIEST	ENNOOPPRRU	PROPER NOUN
EIOPPRSTUV	SUPPORTIVE	ENNOOPPRST	PROPONENTS
EIOPPRSSUV	SUPERVISOR	ENNOOTTTWW	WENT TO TOWN
EIOPRRSTUV	PROTRUSIVE	ENOOOPPRRC	POON PENCON
EIOPRSSTTW	TWO STRIPES	ENOOPRRRTU	POOR RETURN
EIOPRSTTTU	PROSTITUTE	ENOOPRRSSY	RESPONSORY
EIOPRSTTUV	PUTS IT OVER	ENOOPRSSSU	POROUSNESS
EIORRRSSTT	TERRORISTS	ENOOPRSTTU	PORTENTOUS
EIORRRTTUV	RIVER TROUT	ENOORSSTTW	STONEWORTS
EIORSSTVXY	SIXTY OVERS	ENOPRSSSTT	STERNPOSTS
EIPPRRSUVY	PRIVY PURSE	ENOPRSSSUY	SUSPENSORY
EIPRRRSSSU	SURPRISERS	EOOPPRRSSS	OPPRESSORS
EIPRSSTTTY	SITS PRETTY	EOOPPRRSSU	PROSPEROUS
EJMRSSTUYY	JURY SYSTEM	EOOPPRSTTY	PROTOTYPES
EJNNSSSTUU	UNJUSTNESS	EOOPRRSSTU	PRO-OESTRUS
EJNOORRSSU	SOJOURNERS	EOOPRSSSSS	POSSESSORS
EJNOOSSSUY	JOYOUSNESS	EOOPRSSSSY	POSSESSORY
EJNOSTTTUY	NOT JUST YET	EOORRSSTTU	STERTOROUS
EKLLMNOOOS	SOLEMN LOOK	EOORRSTTVY	TORY VOTERS
EKLMMNOSSU	MUSKMELONS	EOPPRRSSSU	SUPPRESSOR
EKLNOORSTV	LOVERS KNOT	EOPPRRSSTU	SUPPORTERS
EKLOOORSSW	WORKS LOOSE	EOPRSSSSUU	SOURPUSSES
EKLOORRSWW	SLOW WORKER	FFFFIITTYY	FIFTY-FIFTY
EKLOORRTUW	WORK TO RULE	FFFGGINOOO	GOOFING OFF
	WORK-TO-RULE	FFFGIILNOT	LIFTING OFF
EKMNNOSTUY	MONKEY NUTS	FFFHILOORT	FIFTH FLOOR
EKNOORSSTW	STONEWORKS	FFFHIORSTU	FOUR FIFTHS
EKNORSSSTT	STORKS NEST	FFGGIINNOR	RINGING OFF
EKOORSSTTW	SETS TO WORK	FFGGIINNOS	SIGNING OFF
EKORRTTTUY	TURKEY TROT	FFGHHIOSTY	FIGHT SHY OF
ELLLOOOTVY	LOVELY LOOT	FFGHIILNSY	FLY FISHING
ELLLOSSSUY	SOULLESSLY		FLY-FISHING
ELLMNOORST	MELLOTRONS		FLYING FISH
ELLMOOSVWY	MOVE SLOWLY	FFGHIIORTT	FIGHT FOR IT
ELLMORSSTU	ROSTELLUMS	FFGHINOOPP	HOPPING OFF
ELLNNPSSUY	SUNNY SPELL	FFGHINOOSV	SHOVING OFF
ELLNOQOSTV	NO LOVE LOST	FFGHINOOSW	SHOWING OFF
ELLNOOSTUW	SWOLLEN OUT	FFGHINOPSU	PUSHING OFF
ELLNORTUWY	TURN YELLOW	FFGHORSTUU	ROUGH STUFF
ELLOOOSTTY	LEO TOLSTOY	FFGIIKLLNO	KILLING OFF
ELLOPPRTTY	PRETTY POLL	FFGIILLLNU	FULFILLING
ELLOPSSSTY	SPOTLESSLY	FFGIINNSTU	SNUFFING IT
ELMNOORSUY	ENORMOUSLY	FFGIINOPPR	RIPPING OFF
ELMNOOSUVY	VENOMOUSLY	FFGIINOPPT	TIPPING OFF
ELMNORSUUY	NUMEROUSLY	FFGIINORTW	WRITING OFF
ELMOOPSSUY	POLYSEMOUS	FFGIINORTY	FORTIFYING
ELMOPPPRTU	PETROL PUMP	FFGIJMNOPU	JUMPING-OFF
ELNNOOPSTU	STOLEN UP ON	FFGIKNOORW	WORKING OFF
ELNOOORSTU	TURNS LOOSE	FFGILLNOPU	PULLING OFF
ELNOSSSUUY	SENSUOUSLY	FFGILMNPUU	MUFFLING UP
ELNPPRRTUU	TURN PURPLE	FFGILNOOPS	SLOPING OFF
ELNRRTTTUU	TURN TURTLE	FFGINNNORU	RUNNING OFF
ELOOPPRRTU	POOR RESULT	FFGINNORTU	TURNING OFF
ELOORSSVVW	LOVERS VOWS	FFGINOOPPP	POPPING OFF
ELOPPRSTUY	SUPPLETORY	FFGINOPTTU	OFF-PUTTING
ELOPRSTTUU	TURTLE SOUP		PUTTING OFF

FFHIIRSSTT	FIRST SHIFT	FGHLLORTUW	FULL GROWTH
FFHIKOOOST	SHOOK IT OFF	FGIIINNRTY	NITRIFYING
FFHILOORSW	FISH OR FOWL	FGIIINRTVY	VITRIFYING
FFHILRSSTU	FIRST FLUSH	FGIIJNSTUY	JUSTIFYING
FFHIOORRTU	HIT FOR FOUR	FGIILLMNOY	MOLLIFYING
FFHIOOTUWY	OFF WITH YOU	FGIILLNNUY	NULLIFYING
FFHMOORRTU	FOURTH FORM	FGIILLNOTU	FILLING OUT
FFIIKLOSTY	FIFTY KILOS	FGIILLNSTY	STIFLINGLY
FFIINORTTU	TIN OF FRUIT	FGIILNOSUU	FULIGINOUS
FFIIORSSTX	FIRST OF SIX	FGIILNRSST	FIRSTLINGS
FFIKOORRTW	FIT FOR WORK	FGIIMMMNUY	MUMMIFYING
FFILLOPSTU	PULLS IT OFF	FGIIMNNORU	UNIFORMING
FFILLRTUUY	FRUITFULLY	FGIIMNORTY	MORTIFYING
FFILOORRST	FIRST FLOOR	FGIIMNSTYY	MYSTIFYING
FFINORSTTU	TURNS IT OFF	FGIINNOPRU	FIRING UPON
FFIOORSTTW	FIRST OF TWO	FGIINOOPRR	GRIP OF IRON
FFIORRSTWY	WORRY STIFF	FGIINORSTT	GOT IN FIRST
FFJNORSTUU	JUST FOR FUN	FGIINORSTW	SWING FOR IT
FFLLLOOSUU	FULL OF SOUL	FGIINOTTTU	FITTING OUT
FFMOORSTUY	STUFFY ROOM		OUTFITTING
FGGGHINOTY	FOGGY NIGHT	FGIINRRSTY	STIR-FRYING
FGGHHIILNY	FLYING HIGH	FGIJKLMOSU	JUGS OF MILK
	HIGH FLYING	FGIJLMNPUY	FLYING JUMP
	HIGH-FLYING	FGIJNOORSY	SING FOR JOY
FGGHHIOTTU	TOUGH FIGHT	FGIKNNORTU	TUNING FORK
FGGHIIINNT	INFIGHTING	FGIKNOORRW	WORKING FOR
FGGHIIINTT	FIGHTING IT	FGIKNOORTU	FORKING OUT
FGGHIINNOT	FIGHTING ON	FGILLNOOSY	FLYING SOLO
FGGHIINOORT	GOING FORTH	FGILMMNOUX	FLUMMOXING
FGGIIILNNY	LIGNIFYING	FGILMNOORS	LOSING FORM
FGGIIINNNR	INFRINGING	FGILNNORWY	FROWNINGLY
FGGIIINNSY	SIGNIFYING	FGILNOPSTY	FLYPOSTING
FGGIILNORY	GLORIFYING	FGINORRTUW	GROWN FRUIT
FGGIINNOOR	GOING IN FOR	FGINORSTUW	SWUNG FOR IT
FGGIINOORT	GOING FOR IT	FGINORTTUU	TURFING OUT
FGGIINORST	GOING FIRST	FGIORRSTUW	GROWS FRUIT
FGGINOOPRR	GROPING FOR	FGJNOORSUY	SUNG FOR JOY
FGHHIINSTT	NIGHT SHIFT	FGLLNORUWY	FULLY GROWN
FGHHIISTTW	FIGHTS WITH		WRONGFULLY
FGHHINOSTW	SHOWN FIGHT	FGLOORTUUY	FUTUROLOGY
FGHHIORRTT	FORTHRIGHT	FGNOOORSTW	WRONG-FOOTS
FGHHIOSSTW	SHOWS FIGHT	FHHIOPRSTT	THRIFT SHOP
FGHHIOTTUW	FOUGHT WITH	FHIILRSTTW	FLIRTS WITH
FGHHLOTTUU	THOUGHTFUL	FHIIMNORTW	FROM WITHIN
FGHIIKNNOT	THINKING OF	FHIIORSSTX	HITS FOR SIX
FGHIILMRST	FILM RIGHTS	FHILLMRTUY	MIRTHFULLY
FGHIILNSTU	INSIGHTFUL	FHILMOORRR	HORROR FILM
FGHIILRSTT	FIRST LIGHT	FHILOPRSTU	FOURTH SLIP
FGHIINNRSU	FURNISHING	FHILOPRSUW	WORSHIPFUL
FGHIINORRY	HORRIFYING	FHIMNORSTT	FIRST MONTH
FGHIINOSTU	FISHING OUT	FHINNORSTU	FOUR NINTHS
FGHIINRSTT	FIRST NIGHT	FHINOOORTT	HOT TIN ROOF
	FIRST THING	FHIORRSSTT	THIRSTS FOR
FGHIINSSTW	SWING SHIFT	FHIORSSTYY	FISHY STORY
FGHIIOTTTU	FIGHT IT OUT	FHKOOORSWW	SHOW OF WORK
FGHIIRSSTT	FIRST SIGHT	FHLLLOSTUY	SLOTHFULLY
FGHIKLOOTT	TOOK FLIGHT	FHLLOTUUYY	YOUTHFULLY
FGHIKOORTT	TOOK FRIGHT	FHLLRTTUUY	TRUTHFULLY
FGHILLOOST	SOLO FLIGHT	FHLNNOORTW	FLOWN NORTH
FGHILLRTUY	RIGHTFULLY	FHLNOOSTUW	FLOWN SOUTH
FGHILNOSTY	FLYING SHOT	FHLNRTTUUU	UNTRUTHFUL
FGHILOOPRT	LIGHTPROOF	FHLOOOPRSS	SHOPFLOORS
FGHILOOSTT	FOOTLIGHTS	FHMNOORSTU	FOUR MONTHS
FGHINNNTUY	FUNNY THING	FHMOOOPRST	MOTHPROOFS
FGHINNOORT	FOR NOTHING	FHNOOPRSST	SHOPFRONTS
FGHINNOTUX	FOX HUNTING	FHOOORSTUU	OUT OF HOURS
	FOXHUNTING	FHOOPRRSTU	POURS FORTH
FGHINOOOTT	HOTFOOTING	FIIJLLMTX	JIMLL FIX IT
FGHINOPRSU	PUSHING FOR	FIIKLMNOPT	PINT OF MILK
FGHINORSTT	FORTNIGHTS	FIIKLNNSST	SKINFLINTS
FGHIOOSTTU	OUT OF SIGHT	FIILLNOORW	WILL OF IRON

FIILMMNOOR	MONILIFORM	GGIIINPTUV	GIVING IT UP
FIILMOORRS	LORISIFORM	GGIILLNNTY	TINGLINGLY
FIILMPRSST	FILM STRIPS	GGIILNNNPU	PLUNGING IN
	FILMSTRIPS	GGIILNNNSU	UNSLINGING
FIIMMNORSS	MISINFORMS	GGIILNNOSW	SINGING LOW
FIIMNORTUY	UNIFORMITY	GGIILNNSTY	STINGINGLY
FIIMOORSST	FORTISSIMO	GGIILNPPRY	GRIPPINGLY
FIJNOOOTTU	OUT OF JOINT	GGIIMMNOSW	GO SWIMMING
FIKLLOORST	FOLKLORIST	GGIINNORTU	RINGING OUT
FIKLOORSTY	FORTY KILOS	GGIINNOSTU	SINGING OUT
FIKNOORTUW	UNIT OF WORK	GGILLLNOOR	LOGROLLING
FIKNORSTWY	FORTY WINKS	GGILNNOOPR	PROLONGING
FILLOOSTUW	FOLLOW SUIT	GGILNNOSUY	YOUNGLINGS
FILMNSSTTU	FILM STUNTS	GGINNNNRUU	GUNRUNNING
FILOOOPRST	PORTFOLIOS	GGINNOPRSS	SPRING SONG
FIMNOOOPRT	OF NO IMPORT	GGINOOOPTT	GOING TO POT
FINNOORTTU	OUT IN FRONT	GGINOOPRRU	PROROGUING
FINNOPRTTU	PUT IN FRONT	GGINOORTTW	GOT IT WRONG
FINOOOPSTT	SOFT OPTION	GGINOORTUW	GROWING OUT
FINOOPRSTT	FOOTPRINTS	GGINOPRRST	STRONG GRIP
FINOOPRSTU	FOUR POINTS	GGIOOPRSTT	GOT TO GRIPS
FINOOPRSTW	FOR TWO PINS	GHHIIJNORU	JUNIOR HIGH
FINOOPRTTU	OUT OF PRINT	GHHIILPSST	LIGHTSHIPS
FINOOPSSTU	TINS OF SOUP	GHHIINRSTT	NIGHTSHIRT
FIOORSTTUU	FORTUITOUS	GHHIIPRSTW	SHIPWRIGHT
FJJMOOPRUY	JUMP FOR JOY	GHHILLOSUY	GHOULISHLY
FLLMNORUUY	MOURNFULLY	GHHILRSSTU	RUSHLIGHTS
FLLRSTTUUY	TRUSTFULLY	GHHINOPRTT	TRIPHTHONG
FLMOOOORST	LOTS OF ROOM	GHHINORTUW	WIN THROUGH
FMOOOORRTW	ROOM FOR TWO	GHHIORSSTT	SHORT SIGHT
FNNOOPRSUW	FROWNS UPON	GHHISSTTTU	SHUTS TIGHT
FNNORSTUYY	FUNNY STORY	GHHLOORTUY	THOROUGHLY
FOOORSSTTU	OUT OF SORTS	GHHNOORTUW	WON THROUGH
FOOPSSSTUY	PUSSYFOOTS	GHHNORRTUU	RUN THROUGH
FUUWYYZZZZ	FUZZY-WUZZY		RUN-THROUGH
GGGGIILLNY	GIGGLINGLY	GHHNORSSTU	SONG THRUSH
GGGHIINORT	GOING RIGHT	GHHOORTTUU	THROUGHOUT
GGGHINOORU	ROUGH GOING	GHHOOTTTUU	THOUGHT OUT
GGGIILLNNY	NIGGLINGLY	GHHOPRTTUU	PUT THROUGH
GGGIILNNPU	PLUGGING IN		THROUGHPUT
GGGIILNQSU	SQUIGGLING	GHIIINNNTW	WINNING HIT
GGGIINORTU	RIGGING OUT	GHIIKNNNOT	THINKING ON
GGGILNNPUU	UNPLUGGING	GHIIKNNNTU	UNTHINKING
GGGILNRSTU	STRUGGLING	GHIIKNNPTU	THINKING UP
GGGINNOORW	GOING WRONG	GHIIKRSTTT	TIGHT SKIRT
GGHHHIILST	HIGHLIGHTS	GHIILLMRTW	MILLWRIGHT
GGHHIIILNV	HIGH LIVING	GHIILLNORT	GRILLIONTH
GGHHIILNTT	NIGHT-LIGHT	GHIILLOPTT	PILOT LIGHT
GGHHIINRTT	RIGHT THING	GHIILNSSWY	SWISHINGLY
GGHHINORTU	ROUGH NIGHT	GHIILPRSTT	STRIP LIGHT
GGHHINRSTU	HIGH-STRUNG	GHIIMNPRTU	TRIUMPHING
GGHHOORTTU	GOT THROUGH	GHIINNORSU	NOURISHING
GGHIIILRSW	WHIRLIGIGS	GHIINNORTW	THROWING IN
GGHIILNPTU	LIGHTING UP	GHIINNPPSU	UNSHIPPING
GGHIILPRSY	PRIGGISHLY	GHIINPRSST	THIS SPRING
GGHIINNSTU	UNSIGHTING	GHIIPRSTTU	SIT UPRIGHT
GGHIINORTU	ROUGHING IT	GHIKLOORST	LOOKS RIGHT
GGHIIORTTT	GOT IT RIGHT	GHIKNNOOWW	KNOWING HOW
GGHILLSSUY	SLUGGISHLY	GHILLNOOOP	LOOPHOLING
GGHILOOPRS	LOGOGRIPHS	GHILLPSTTU	PULLS TIGHT
GGHINNOORT	GOING NORTH	GHILMNOOST	MOONLIGHTS
GGHINNOSTW	NIGHTGOWNS	GHILNOOPST	PHLOGISTON
GGHINOOOST	GO SHOOTING	GHILNOOSTY	SOOTHINGLY
GGHINOOOPS	GO SHOPPING	GHILNORTTT	THROTTLING
GGHINOORST	GOING SHORT	GHILNPRSUU	SULPHURING
GGHINOOSTU	GOING SOUTH	GHILOOOORST	HOROLOGIST
GGHINOPRUU	ROUGHING UP	GHILOOPSYY	PHYSIOLOGY
GGIIIMNSSV	MISGIVINGS	GHILOPSSTT	SPOTLIGHTS
GGIIINNOTV	GIVING IN TO	GHIMMNOPTU	HUMMING TOP
GGIIINNRTU	INTRIGUING	GHINNOOSSW	SHOW NO SIGN
GGIIINNSTW	SWINGING IT		

GHINNOPTTU	POT HUNTING
	POTHUNTING
GHINNOSSSW	SHOWN SIGNS
GHINOOPRTT	RIGHT ON TOP
GHINOOPSTU	SHOOTING UP
GHINOORTTW	THING OR TWO
GHINOOSTUW	SHOWING OUT
GHINOPRSST	HOT SPRINGS
GHINOPRTUW	THROWING UP
GHINOPSTUU	PUSHING OUT
GHINOSSSSW	SHOWS SIGNS
GHINPRRUUY	HURRYING UP
GHINRRSTTU	TURNS RIGHT
GHIORRSSTY	SORRY SIGHT
GHKLNOORUY	HUNGRY LOOK
GHKOORSTUW	SOUGHT WORK
GHLMOOOOSU	HOMOLOGOUS
GHLMOOOPRY	MORPHOLOGY
GHLNOOPSUW	SNOWPLOUGH
GHLOORSTWW	SLOW GROWTH
GHMOOOSUYZ	HOMOZYGOUS
GHMOOPRYYZ	ZYGOMORPHY
GHNNOOPRRS	PRONGHORNS
GHNOOPSUYY	HYPOGYNOUS
GHOOORSSTT	OSTROGOTHS
GHOORSSTTY	GHOST STORY
GHOORSTTUW	OUTGROWTHS
GIIIIMMNNS	MINIMISING
GIIIIMMNNZ	MINIMIZING
GIIILLMNNU	ILLUMINING
GIIILLNNST	INSTILLING
GIIILNNOPT	PILING IT ON
GIIILNNTTU	INTITULING
GIIILNNTVY	INVITINGLY
GIIILNORSV	VIRGIN SOIL
GIIILNPTUV	LIVING IT UP
GIIIMNNPRT	IMPRINTING
GIIINNNOSU	UNIONISING
GIIINNNOUZ	UNIONIZING
GIIKLMNNRSY	SMIRKINGLY
GIIKLNNPRS	SPRINKLING
GIIKLNRSTY	STRIKINGLY
GIIKNPRSTU	STRIKING UP
GIIKNRSTWY	SKYWRITING
GIIILLLNSTY	LYING STILL
GIIILLNNOPR	ROLLING PIN
GIIILLNOPRY	PILLORYING
GIIILLNOSTW	STILL OWING
GIIILLNOSUV	LIVING SOUL
GIIILLNRSWY	SWIRLINGLY
GIIILMMNSWY	SWIMMINGLY
GIIILMNOORV	LIVING ROOM
GIIILMNOPSY	IMPOSINGLY
GIIILNNOPPS	SLIPPING ON
GIIILNNOPRU	PURLOINING
GIIILNNOTUV	INVOLUTING
GIIILNOOPRU	POURING OIL
GIIILNOORSU	INGLORIOUS
GIIILNOPTUV	LIVING UP TO
GIIILNPPPSU	SLIPPING UP
GIIILNPPRSU	PIN-UP GIRLS
GIIILNPPRTY	TRIPPINGLY
GIIILNPRSST	STRIPLINGS
GIIILOORSTV	VIROLOGIST
GIIILRSSTTU	LITURGISTS
GIIMNNNORU	IN MOURNING
GIIMNNOORS	MONSIGNORI
GIIMNNOORT	MONITORING
GIIMNOORST	MOTORISING
GIIMNOORTZ	MOTORIZING
GIIMNNOQSTU	MISQUOTING
GIIMNORRRW	WING MIRROR
GIIMNOSSTU	MISSING OUT
GIIMNOSSTY	MISOGYNIST
GIINNNNRUW	WINNING RUN
GIINNNRTWY	WINNING TRY
GIINNNSTTU	UNSTINTING
GIINNOOPRT	PORTIONING
GIINNOORTU	IRONING OUT
GIINNORSTU	RINSING OUT
GIINNORTTY	TRYING IT ON
GIINNRSTTU	INTRUSTING
	TRUSTING IN
GIINOPPSTT	STOPPING IT
GIINORRSTT	STRING TRIO
GIINORTTUW	WRITING OUT
GIINOSTTTU	SITTING OUT
GIINOTTTUW	OUTWITTING
GIINPPPRTU	TRIPPING UP
GIINPRRSSU	SURPRISING
GIINPRRSTU	STIRRING UP
GIJMNOPTUU	JUMPING OUT
GIJNNOORSU	SOJOURNING
GIKLLOOTUY	GUILTY LOOK
GIKMNOOSTU	SMOKING OUT
GIKNNOORTW	NOT WORKING
GIKNOORTUW	WORKING OUT
GILLNOORTU	ROLLING OUT
GILLNOPTUU	PULLING OUT
GILLNORSTW	STRONG WILL
GILLOORSUY	GLORIOUSLY
GILMMNOOUY	IMMUNOLOGY
GILMNOOOST	MONOLOGIST
GILMOOOPST	POMOLOGIST
GILNNNSTUY	STUNNINGLY
GILNNOOSWY	SWOONINGLY
GILNOOOSTT	ONTOLOGIST
GILNOOPPTY	TYPING POOL
GILNOPRSTY	SPORTINGLY
GILNOPRSYY	PYROLYSING
GILNRSTTUY	TRUSTINGLY
GILOOOPSTT	TOPOLOGIST
GILOOOSSTZ	ZOOLOGISTS
GILOOPRSTT	PROGLOTTIS
GILOOPSTTY	TYPOLOGIST
GILOORRSUY	RIGOROUSLY
GILOORSSTU	UROLOGISTS
GILOORSUVY	VIGOROUSLY
GIMMNNOSSU	SUMMONSING
GIMMNPSSUU	SUMMING-UPS
GIMNNNORSU	MORNING SUN
GIMNNOORSS	MONSIGNORS
GIMNNOPTUU	MOUNTING UP
GIMNOOSSUY	MISOGYNOUS
GIMNOPPTUU	PUMPING OUT
GINNNORTUU	RUNNING OUT
GINNOOPPST	POSTPONING
GINNOOPRSS	SPONSORING
GINNOOPTUW	OWNING UP TO
GINNOPPSTU	UNSTOPPING
GINNORTTUU	TURNING OUT
GINOOOPRST	GO TO PRISON
GINOOORTTU	ROOTING OUT
GINOOPPPTU	POPPING OUT
GINOOPRTUU	OUTPOURING
	POURING OUT
GINOORSTTU	SORTING OUT
GINOORTTVY	VOTING TORY
GINOPPPPRU	PROPPING UP
GINOPPPSTU	STOPPING UP
GINOPPRRTU	PURPORTING
GINOPPRSTU	SUPPORTING

GINOPRSSTU	SPRINGS OUT
GINOPTTTUU	PUTTING OUT
GINORSSTTU	STRINGS OUT
	STRONG SUIT
GINOSSSTUU	SUSSING OUT
GINPRSSTUU	TRUSSING UP
GKNORSTUUY	YOUNG TURKS
GLMORRUUUY	UGLY RUMOUR
GLNOOPSUYY	POLYGYNOUS
GLNOOSTTUU	GLUTTONOUS
GMNNOOOSUY	MONOGYNOUS
GMNOOORRST	STRONG ROOM
GOOPPRSTTU	GOT SUPPORT
HHIIOPRSSW	HIS WORSHIP
HHILOOPPSY	PHILOSOPHY
HHIOPPSSYY	HYPOPHYSIS
HHJNNOOSTU	JOHN HUSTON
HHLMOPRTYY	POLYRHYTHM
HHMMOOOPRY	HOMOMORPHY
HHOOPPRSSU	PHOSPHORUS
HHOORRSSTU	SHORT HOURS
HHOPPSSTUU	SHUT UP SHOP
HIIKLSSTTY	SKITTISHLY
HIIKNNOSTT	THINKS ON IT
HIIKNOTTTU	THINK IT OUT
HIILLNORTT	TRILLIONTH
HIILOPRSTY	HOLY SPIRIT
HIIMMNOPRS	MORPHINISM
HIINOSSSTT	SHINTOISTS
HIIOOTTTYY	HOITY-TOITY
HIIOPRSSTW	SHOW SPIRIT
HIIORSSTTV	SHORT VISIT
HIJKNNORSU	JOHN RUSKIN
HIJLMNNOOT	JOHN MILTON
HIKLLOOSTT	SHOT TO KILL
HIKLLOPRUW	UPHILL WORK
HIKMNOOSST	SMOOTH SKIN
HIKNNORSST	STINKHORNS
HIKORRSSTT	SHORT SKIRT
HILLOOPRSW	WHIRLPOOLS
HILLSSTTUY	SLUTTISHLY
HILMNOOSTU	LIONS MOUTH
HILNORTUWY	UNWORTHILY
HILOOOPSUZ	ZOOPHILOUS
HILOOPSSTT	PISTOL SHOT
HILOOPSSTY	PHOTOLYSIS
HILORSSSTT	SHORT-LISTS
HILPPPSSUY	SUPPLY SHIP
HIMNOPSSTY	SYMPHONIST
HINNOORSUW	WIN HONOURS
HINOOPSTWY	SHOW NO PITY
HINOORTTTW	NOT WORTH IT
HINOPRSSUW	SUN WORSHIP
HIOOOSTTTU	SHOOT IT OUT
HIOOPPSTUW	WHOOPS IT UP
HIOOPRTTXY	THIXOTROPY
HIOPRSTTUU	HOT PURSUIT
HIORSSTTUU	STRUTHIOUS
HIPPSTTUUW	PUTS UP WITH
HJMNNOOOST	JOHN MOTSON
HKKNNOOSTY	HONKY-TONKS
HKMMNORRSU	KRUMMHORNS
HKNOOOUWWY	YOU-KNOW-WHO
HLLOOOSTUW	HOLLOWS OUT
HLMOORSUUY	HUMOROUSLY
HLOOOOPSST	SHOOTS POOL
HLOPRSSUUU	SULPHUROUS
HMMNOOOSUY	HOMONYMOUS
HMNNOOORUY	ON MY HONOUR
HMOOPSSTUU	POSTHUMOUS
HNNOOOORSUW	WON HONOURS

HNOOOPRSTU	TOP HONOURS
HNOOORRUUY	YOUR HONOUR
HNOOPSSTUW	PUTS ON SHOW
HOOOPPRRTT	PROTOTROPH
HOOPRSSSTT	STOPS SHORT
HOORRSSTTY	SHORT STORY
IIILNOSSTV	VIOLINISTS
IIIMNOOPST	IMPOSITION
IIIMNOPRSS	MISPRISION
IIIMOPSSTV	POSITIVISM
IIINNOOPST	IN POSITION
IIINNOSTTU	INTUITIONS
IIINOQRSTU	INQUISITOR
IIINOQSTUU	INIQUITOUS
IIIOPSSTTV	POSITIVIST
IIIPRSSSTT	SPIRITISTS
IIKLLLMPSS	SPILLS MILK
IIKLNOOOTT	LOOK INTO IT
IIKLOSSTXY	SIXTY KILOG
IIKMNORSSW	SINK OR SWIM
IILLLLNWYY	WILLY NILLY
IILLLLWWYY	WILLY-WILLY
IILLLORSUY	ILLUSORILY
IILLMNOOTW	TWO MILLION
IILLNOOOSV	VIOLIN SOLO
IILLNOOPSS	POLLINOSIS
IILLNOPSTY	SILLY POINT
IILMNOOPSS	IMPLOSIONS
IILMNOPSSU	IMPULSIONS
IILMNOSTUY	LUMINOSITY
IILNNOOOPW	LOW OPINION
IILNNOOTUV	INVOLUTION
IILNOOPSST	POSTILIONS
IILNOPSTTW	SPLIT IN TWO
IILOPRSSTW	LOW SPIRITS
IILOPSSSST	SOLIPSISTS
IIMNNOOPRT	MINOR POINT
IINNOPRSTU	PUT IN IRONS
IINNORSSTU	INTRUSIONS
IINOOOPPST	OPPOSITION
IINOOPRSSV	PROVISIONS
IINOPRRSTU	IRRUPTIONS
IINORSTTUU	NUTRITIOUS
IIOOPPRSTU	PROPITIOUS
IIOPRSSTUU	SPIRITUOUS
IIOPSSTTTU	SPITS IT OUT
IIORSTTUVY	VIRTUOSITY
IKLLLOOSSY	LOOKS SILLY
IKLLOOPPSY	LOOK SLIPPY
IKLNOOPPSY	LOOKS NIPPY
IKMORSSTTY	TROTSKYISM
IKNOOOOPST	TOOK POISON
IKNOOOPTTY	TOOK PITY ON
IKOORSTTUW	WORKS IT OUT
IKORSSTTTY	TROTSKYIST
ILLMNOSUUY	LUMINOUSLY
ILLOOQSSUY	SOLILOQUYS
ILLOOSSSVY	SOLVOLYSIS
ILMNOOOPST	MONOPOLIST
ILMNOOOSTW	SLOW MOTION
	SLOW-MOTION
ILMNOOSUUV	VOLUMINOUS
ILMNOSTUUY	MUTINOUSLY
ILMOORSTUY	TIMOROUSLY
ILNOOPPRSU	PROPULSION
ILOOPPRSST	SPOILSPORT
ILOORSTTUY	TORTIOUSLY
ILOORSUUXY	UXORIOUSLY
ILOPRSSUUY	SPURIOUSLY
ILORSSUUUY	USURIOUSLY
ILORSTUUVY	VIRTUOUSLY

IMMNOPRSSS	MRS. SIMPSON
IMMOOPRSTU	PROSTOMIUM
IMMOPPRSTU	IMPROMPTUS
IMMOPSSSUY	SYMPOSIUMS
IMNNOSTYYY	SYNONYMITY
IMNOOOPRST	PROMOTIONS
IMNOOORSUV	OMNIVOROUS
IMOOPPPPUY	OPIUM POPPY
IMOOPRRSSY	PROMISSORY
INOOOPPRRT	PROPORTION
INOOOPRTTU	PORTION OUT
INOOPRRSTU	PROTRUSION
INOOPRTTTW	TRIP TO TOWN
IOOPPRRSTU	POTPOURRIS
IOORSSTTTU	SORTS IT OUT
IOORSTTTTU	TROTS IT OUT
IOORSTTTUY	TORTUOSITY
JNNOOSTTUW	NOT JUST NOW
KOOPRSTTUW	PUTS TO WORK
LLOOPPSUUY	POPULOUSLY
LLORSSTUUY	LUSTROUSLY
LMNOOPSUUY	UPON MY SOUL
LMOSTTUUUU	TUMULTUOUS
LNOOORSSUY	SONOROUSLY
LNOORTTUUW	LOW TURNOUT
LNOPRRTUUY	POULTRY RUN
LOOPPPRSUY	POOR SUPPLY
LOOPSTUUUV	VOLUPTUOUS
LOORSTTUUY	TORTUOUSLY
LORRSTUUYY	YOURS TRULY
MMOOPRRSUU	RUMPUS ROOM
MNNOOOOSTU	MONOTONOUS
MNNOOSSUYY	SYNONYMOUS
MNOOOOPRRTY	PROMONTORY
MNOOOORRTTU	ROOM TO TURN
MNOORSSSTW	SNOWSTORMS
NOOOOPRRUWW	ROW UPON ROW
NOOOORRTTWY	NOT TO WORRY
OOPRSTTTUU	PUTS TO ROUT
OPRSTTUVYY	TOPSY-TURVY

AAAAAABBCDRR	ABRACADABRA
AAAAACLMNNP	PANAMA CANAL
AAAAABBBCHRR	BARBARA BACH
AAAAABBINRST	SABBATARIAN
AAAAABCCHILN	BACCHANALIA
AAAABCEKRST	ACT AS A BRAKE
AAAAABCESSSY	AS EASY AS A B C
AAAAABCHNSST	ATHABASCANS
AAAABDIIRSU	SAUDI ARABIA
AAAACCDHNVY	HAD A VACANCY
AAAACCHNSVY	HAS A VACANCY
AAAACDFMNOP	MAP OF CANADA
AAAACDGMOSV	VASCO DA GAMA
AAAACGILPSS	PASSACAGLIA
AAAACILLMHS	MARIA CALLAS
AAAACINNRSU	ARAUCANIANS
AAAADDENRYY	YEAR AND A DAY
AAAADDLMOSS	AS OLD AS ADAM
AAAADEGLMMT	AMALGAMATED
AAAADELMRSS	DAR ES SALAAM
AAAADELNPPY	AN APPLE A DAY
AAAADEMPSST	MADE A PASS AT
AAAADLRRSWY	DRAW A SALARY
AAAAEGLMMST	AMALGAMATES
AAAAEKMPSST	MAKE A PASS AT
AAAAFGIPSST	AS FAT AS A PIG
AAAAFGMNORT	FATA MORGANA
AAAAFINRRST	RASTAFARIAN
AAAAHKNPSST	ATHAPASKANS
AAAALNNOPVV	ANNA PAVLOVA
AAAABBBELLST	BASEBALL BAT
AAABBCEEFGL	CABBAGE LEAF
AAABBCEKLNN	BANK BALANCE
AAAABBCILSST	SABBATICALS
AAABBDILNST	BLIND AS A BAT
AAABBEHIKRT	BREAK A HABIT
AAABCCGHRTU	CAUGHT A CRAB
AAABCCGILLN	CALLING A CAB
AAABCCKLLOS	BLACK AS COAL
AAABCCKNSSV	CANVASBACKS
AAABCCLLOWY	CAB CALLOWAY
AAABCDDIRRY	BRADYCARDIA
AAABCDEILNN	CAIN AND ABEL
AAABCDELNRS	CANDELABRAS
AAABCDGINRY	CARDIGAN BAY
AAABCDHKNNS	CASH AND BANK
AAABCDKLNNT	BLACK AND TAN
AAABCDLOOST	BALD AS A COOT
AAABCEEEMRW	BECAME AWARE
AAABCEEIMRT	BACTERAEMIA
AAABCEEKLNR	BREAK A LANCE
AAABCEGIKKN	BAKING A CAKE
AAABCEGIMNR	CAMBRIAN AGE
AAABCEGKPSS	BACK PASSAGE
AAABCEHNNRS	ANABRANCHES
AAABCELLLOT	ALLOCATABLE
AAABCELRTTT	ATTRACTABLE
AAABCERRSTT	CABARET STAR
AAABCGHIILN	HAILING A CAB
AAABCGHLLTU	CAUGHT A BALL
AAABCGIKKNT	TAKING ABACK
AAABCGIKNWY	BACKING AWAY

AAABCHINRST	BATRACHIANS
AAABCLLOPSS	PABLO CASALS
AAABCRRSTTT	ABSTRACT ART
AAABDDEHIMT	HAD A BAD TIME
AAABDDEJMNR	BREAD AND JAM
AAABDEEGMNT	GET A BAD NAME
AAABDEEKRST	BREAKS A DATE
AAABDEGGLNU	BAD LANGUAGE
AAABDEGGNOV	VAGABONDAGE
AAABDEGIMNR	BRAIN DAMAGE
AAABDEGLMWY	GAMBLED AWAY
AAABDEGMNOT	GOT A BAD NAME
AAABDEHIMST	HAS A BAD TIME
AAABDEHLPTZ	BLAZED A PATH
AAABDEINSTT	IN A BAD STATE
AAABDELLPPU	APPLAUDABLE
AAABDEMNNST	MAN AND BEAST
AAABDENORRS	AARONS BEARD
AAABDFGLNNU	BUD FLANAGAN
AAABDGHINRR	HARD BARGAIN
AAABDKLNNRW	DRAWN A BLANK
AAABDKLNRSW	DRAWS A BLANK
AAABDMNRRSU	BARRAMUNDAS
AAABDMORSSS	AMBASSADORS
AAABEEGLLSV	SALVAGEABLE
AAABEEGSSTV	SAVAGE BEAST
AAABEEHNPTT	BEATEN A PATH
AAABEEKKMRS	MAKES A BREAK
AAABEEKLMMS	MEEK AS A LAMB
AAABEFKLLRS	BREAKS A FALL
AAABEGGILPR	GARBAGE PAIL
AAABEGILNRS	BARGAIN SALE
AAABEGKMNNR	BANK MANAGER
AAABEGLLTTU	BULL AT A GATE
AAABEGLMSWY	GAMBLES AWAY
AAABEHIMNPS	AMPHISBAENA
AAABEHLPSTZ	BLAZES A PATH
AAABEIILNRS	RABELAISIAN
AAABEILLNUV	UNAVAILABLE
AAABEILLRTZ	BLAZE A TRAIL
AAABEILNRST	ALABASTRINE
AAABEILRSTU	BURIAL AT SEA
AAABEILTTTW	WAIT AT TABLE
AAABEKMNRRS	BREAKS AN ARM
AAABEKPRRST	BREAKS APART
AAABELLNPTU	UNPALATABLE
AAABELLNTTV	NAVAL BATTLE
AAABELMOTTU	AUTOMATABLE
AAABELNRRTW	WARRANTABLE
AAABELRRTTY	BATTLE ARRAY
AAABENNPRYZ	PENNY BAZAAR
AAABEOOTTTT	BEAT A TATTOO
AAABFGIKLNO	BAKING A LOAF
AAABGHHINSV	HAVING A BASH
AAABGHHINTV	HAVING A BATH
AAABGHIKNTT	TAKING A BATH
AAABGHILLNV	HAVING A BALL
AAABGHINSTV	HAVING A STAB
AAABGHIOOPR	AGORAPHOBIA
AAABGORSSZZ	ZSA ZSA GABOR
AAABILNNPST	BANANA SPLIT
AAABINPSSTT	ANABAPTISTS
AAACCCEILTT	ACATALECTIC

AAAACCCEINPT	CAPACITANCE	AAACDELNTWZ	DANCE A WALTZ
AAAACCDEHNSV	CASH ADVANCE	AAACDEOOPRV	AVOCADO PEAR
AAAACCDEIIMN	ACADEMICIAN	AAACDFIINOS	AFICIONADAS
AAAACCDEILMS	ACADEMICALS	AAACDGIKNRT	TAKING A CARD
AAAACCDHIRTY	TACHYCARDIA	AAACDGIMNNR	CARING A DAMN
AAAACCEEGHNV	GAVE A CHANCE	AAACDGINNRR	CARING A DARN
AAAACCEEHHNV	HAVE A CHANCE	AAACDHHIRTU	HAD A HAIRCUT
AAAACCEEHKNT	TAKE A CHANCE	AAACDHOSSTW	CAST A SHADOW
AAAACCEEHSTT	ATTACHE CASE	AAACDILLSTY	CALLS IT A DAY
AAAACCEEKNPR	PANCAKE RACE	AAACDILOPRX	PARADOXICAL
AAAACCEFHHLN	HALF A CHANCE	AAACDIMRRTT	DRAMATIC ART
AAAACCEGLNST	CAST A GLANCE	AAACDLOORST	COASTAL ROAD
AAAACCEHHLTW	CATCH A WHALE	AAACEEEELPSV	LEAVE A SPACE
AAAACCEHINPU	IPECACUANHA	AAACEEFGMSS	FACE MASSAGE
AAAACCEHKNTT	TAKEN A CATCH	AAACEEFLMNS	MALFEASANCE
AAAACCEHKSTT	TAKES A CATCH	AAACEEFRRSU	SURFACE AREA
AAAACCEHLNPT	CATCH A PLANE	AAACEEGHKMN	MAKE A CHANGE
AAAACCEIIRST	ASIATIC RACE	AAACEEGNNRR	CARRAGEENAN
AAAACCEILLOR	CALCEOLARIA	AAACEEGRRST	GREAT CAESAR
AAAACCEILPRT	PALAEARCTIC	AAACEEGRSTV	VAST ACREAGE
AAAACCEKTTTU	ACUTE ATTACK	AAACEEKKMPT	MAKE A PACKET
AAAACCELNNST	NASAL ACCENT	AAACEEKPSTU	TAKE UP A CASE
AAAACCGNRTVY	VAGRANCY ACT	AAACEENPPRS	APPEARANCES
AAAACCHILLRY	ARCHAICALLY	AAACEESSSTT	STATES A CASE
AAAACCHINRTT	CATCH A TRAIN	AAACEFGIKMN	MAKING A FACE
AAAACCILLPRT	PARALLACTIC	AAACEFLQSTU	CATAFALQUES
AAAACCILMNOT	ACCLAMATION	AAACEFLRTTU	ARTEFACTUAL
AAAACCILRRTU	CARICATURAL	AAACEGHINRV	HAVING A CARE
AAAACCILRTTW	TACTICAL WAR	AAACEGHINSV	HAVING A CASE
AAAACCIMNORT	CARCINOMATA	AAACEGIKKMN	MAKING A CAKE
AAAACCLLMSTY	CATACLYSMAL	AAACEGIRRWY	CARRIAGEWAY
AAAACCOTTUWY	CUT-AWAY COAT	AAACEGNSSTT	ACTS AS AGENT
AAAACDDEEGNV	ADVANCED AGE	AAACEHIMNNS	MANICHAEANS
AAAACDDEELNS	LEADS A DANCE	AAACEHKRTTT	HEART ATTACK
AAAACDDEIMMS	MACADAMISED	AAACEHLMOTT	CAME TO A HALT
AAAACDDEIMMZ	MACADAMIZED	AAACEHLMRST	STEAL A MARCH
AAAACDDELPRY	PLAYED A CARD	AAACEHMRSWY	MARCHES AWAY
AAAACDDENORW	DO A WAR-DANCE	AAACEHMSTWY	AWAY MATCHES
AAAACDEEGHMN	MADE A CHANGE	AAACEIIKLMN	LIKE A MANIAC
AAAACDEEGKLP	PACKAGE DEAL	AAACEIKLMMS	MAKES A CLAIM
AAAACDEEGMSU	CAUSE DAMAGE	AAACEIKLMPT	MAKE CAPITAL
AAAACDEEHMOT	CAME TO A HEAD	AAACEIKLMST	STAKE A CLAIM
AAAACDEEIKMR	MADEIRA CAKE	AAACEILLMNR	ALL-AMERICAN
AAAACDEEIMRR	CAMARADERIE	AAACEILLMNY	ANAEMICALLY
AAAACDEEKLNS	CAKES AND ALE	AAACEILMNRW	AMERICAN LAW
AAAACDEEKMPT	MADE A PACKET	AAACEILNNPS	CLEAN AS A PIN
AAAACDEEKNST	TEA AND CAKES	AAACEILNPSU	AESCULAPIAN
AAAACDEELNPY	PLAYED AN ACE	AAACEILNRST	CENTRAL ASIA
AAAACDEELNWY	CLEANED AWAY	AAACEIMNPTT	TEAM CAPTAIN
AAAACDEELRWY	CLEARED AWAY	AAACEIMNRRW	AMERICAN WAR
AAAACDEENPRW	WAR AND PEACE	AAACEINRSTV	CARAVAN SITE
AAAACDEESSTT	STATED A CASE	AAACEIRRSWY	CARRIES AWAY
AAAACDEGHINR	RACING AHEAD	AAACEKLNSST	TAKEN A CLASS
AAAACDEGILLN	CALLED AGAIN	AAACEKLSSST	TAKES A CLASS
AAAACDEGILMN	CAGED ANIMAL	AAACELLOPRY	ROYAL PALACE
AAAACDEGLPRU	PALACE GUARD	AAACELLPSSY	PLAYS A SCALE
AAAACDEGNNOT	DANCE A TANGO	AAACELMNPTU	CAMPANULATE
AAAACDEHLLLT	CALLED A HALT	AAACELMNRSS	CAR SALESMAN
AAAACDEHMRWY	MARCHED AWAY	AAACELMNRST	SACRAMENTAL
AAAACDEIILPT	CAPITAL IDEA	AAACELMOPRT	PARACETAMOL
AAAACDEIIRST	ADRIATIC SEA	AAACELMPRST	METACARPALS
AAAACDEILLTX	CALLED A TAXI	AAACENNRRSV	CARAVANNERS
AAAACDEILMPR	PARAMEDICAL	AAACENRSTTV	VACANT STARE
AAAACDEILMPT	MADE CAPITAL	AAACEPPRSSS	SCRAPE A PASS
AAAACDEILNRT	CARDINALATE	AAACFGILNPT	FLAG CAPTAIN
AAAACDEILPSS	PAS DE CALAIS	AAACFIIORST	AFRO-ASIATIC
AAAACDEIMMSS	MACADAMISES	AAACFILLNTY	FANATICALLY
AAAACDEIMMSZ	MACADAMIZES	AAACFILNSTT	FANTASTICAL
AAAACDEINSTT	AT A DISTANCE	AAACFILRTTU	ARTIFACTUAL
AAAACDEIRRWY	CARRIED AWAY	AAACFIMNRRT	AIRCRAFTMAN
AAAACDEKNRTY	TAKE ANY CARD	AAACFKKLNTT	FLANK ATTACK

AAACGHHINTV	HAVING A CHAT	AAADEEIKMNS	MAKE AN ASIDE
AAACGHILNNV	AVALANCHING	AAADEEKMMRR	MADE A REMARK
AAACGHIMNSU	AS MUCH AGAIN	AAADEEKNRST	TAKEN AS READ
AAACGHINSWY	CHASING AWAY	AAADEEKNSWY	SNEAKED AWAY
AAACGHIPPRR	PARAGRAPHIC	AAADEEKRSST	TAKES AS READ
AAACGIILNPT	CAPITAL GAIN	AAADEEKSTWY	STAYED AWAKE
AAACGIINNRU	AURIGNACIAN	AAADEEELNRRT	LEARN A TRADE
AAACGIKLLMN	MAKING A CALL	AAADEENRRTW	WEAR AND TEAR
AAACGIKLLNT	TAKING A CALL	AAADEENSSTT	STAND AT EASE
AAACGILLNPY	PAYING A CALL	AAADEEPRRRW	REAP A REWARD
AAACGILMMRT	GRAMMATICAL	AAADEFFKOTY	TAKE A DAY OFF
AAACGINNNRV	CARAVANNING	AAADEFFNNOR	FANFARONADE
AAACGINPRTT	ACTING A PART	AAADEFHLNNO	ONE AND A HALF
AAACGINRTWY	CARTING AWAY	AAADEFHLNNT	TEN AND A HALF
AAACGINSTWY	CASTING AWAY	AAADEFHLRST	SHARED A FLAT
AAACHHIRSTU	HAS A HAIRCUT	AAADEFOPSST	DEAF AS A POST
AAACHIKNSTY	IN A HAYSTACK	AAADEGHINTV	HAVING A DATE
AAACHIKPPRT	APPARATCHIK	AAADEGHLORU	ROAD HAULAGE
AAACHILMRRT	MATRIARCHAL	AAADEGHLUWY	LAUGHED AWAY
AAACHILPRRT	PATRIARCHAL	AAADEGHOORS	HAS A GOOD EAR
AAACHILSSTY	SAILS A YACHT	AAADEGIKLMN	MAKING A DEAL
AAACHKPRSTT	SHARP ATTACK	AAADEGIKMNT	MAKING A DATE
AAACHLLLOTT	CALL TO A HALT	AAADEGILMNN	MAGDALENIAN
AAACHLNORTY	LAY AT ANCHOR	AAADEGILMNS	MADE A SIGNAL
AAACHLNRRTY	CHARLATANRY	AAADEGMPSSY	PAYS DAMAGES
AAACHNNOPSZ	SANCHO PANZA	AAADEHHIORV	HAVE A HAIR-DO
AAACHNPRSTY	PYRACANTHAS	AAADEHIILTX	HAILED A TAXI
AAACIILPRST	PARADITICAL	AAADEHINRSS	RAISES A HAND
AAACIIMOSSV	ISAAC ASIMOV	AAADEHIINRTT	RADIANT HEAT
AAACILLMNRU	ANIMALCULAR	AAADEHLMPSS	MADE A SPLASH
AAACILLNOTT	LACTATIONAL	AAADEHMNOWY	HOME AND AWAY
AAACILLNRST	SCARLATINAL	AAADEHPPRRS	PARAPHRASED
AAACILLNSTY	SATANICALLY	AAADEIJMNNP	MADE IN JAPAN
AAACILLQTUY	AQUATICALLY	AAADEIKMSTY	MAKES IT A DAY
AAACILLRTUY	ACTUARIALLY	AAADEILMRRR	REAR ADMIRAL
AAACILLSTTY	ASTATICALLY	AAADEILNNRX	ALEXANDRIAN
AAACILMMNOS	SAL AMMONIAC	AAADEILNOPR	REPAID A LOAN
AAACILMORSS	MACASSAR OIL	AAADEILNORS	RAISED A LOAN
AAACILNNRST	LANCASTRIAN	AAADEIPRRSY	SAID A PRAYER
AAACILNOOTV	AVOCATIONAL	AAADEKMNSST	MAKES A STAND
AAACJMPSSTY	CAT'S PYJAMAS	AAADEKNNSTT	TAKEN A STAND
AAACLLRSSTT	ALL-STAR CAST	AAADEKNSSTT	TAKES A STAND
AAACNRSTTTT	ATTRACTANTS	AAADELMNRSS	SALAMANDERS
AAADDDDEOOS	DEAD AS A DODO	AAADELNPSTY	PLEASANT DAY
AAADDDNSSYY	DAYS AND DAYS	AAADELPPRTY	PLAYED A PART
AAADDEEHMWY	MADE HEADWAY	AAADELPRSTY	LEADS A PARTY
AAADDEEHSTY	STAYED AHEAD	AAADELRRSWY	DREW A SALARY
AAADDEEIMNS	MADE AN ASIDE	AAADELRSSTY	LEADS ASTRAY
AAADDEENNRR	NEAR AND DEAR	AAADENNNRRR	RAN AN ERRAND
AAADDEENRVY	EVER AND A DAY	AAADENNRRTV	RANT AND RAVE
AAADDEFRTYY	DAY AFTER DAY	AAADENOSTTT	TEA AND TOAST
AAADDEGHOOR	HAD A GOOD EAR	AAADENRSWWY	WANDERS AWAY
AAADDEGIMPS	PAID DAMAGES	AAADEPRRSWY	PAYS A REWARD
AAADDEGINST	DEAD AGAINST	AAADEPRSTTY	STAYED APART
AAADDEHILNT	HEAD AND TAIL	AAADERRSTTW	STARTED A WAR
AAADDEHINRS	RAISED A HAND	AAADFFHHLLN	HALF AND HALF
AAADDEINRWY	DRAINED AWAY		HALF-AND-HALF
AAADDEIPRRW	PAID A REWARD	AAADFHILNSX	SIX AND A HALF
AAADDEKNNRT	ATE AND DRANK	AAADFHLLLOR	HALF A DOLLAR
AAADDEMMMRY	MY DEAR MADAM	AAADFHLNOTW	TWO AND A HALF
AAADDFHNRST	HARD AND FAST	AAADGHIKNNT	TAKING A HAND
	HARD-AND-FAST	AAADGHINSWY	DASHING AWAY
AAADDHILNNO	LAID A HAND ON	AAADGHNSSTT	STAND AGHAST
AAADEEEGNRW	EARNED A WAGE	AAADGIILMNR	MADRIGALIAN
AAADEEEMNNR	EARNED A NAME	AAADGILLNRS	GRANADILLAS
AAADEEGGNSS	AGES AND AGES	AAADGILNORT	GRADATIONAL
AAADEEGLMPY	PLAYED A GAME	AAADGINNNOW	NOW AND AGAIN
AAADEEHKMWY	MAKE HEADWAY	AAADGINNVWW	WAVING A WAND
AAADEEHLPRS	HAD A RELAPSE	AAADGINRWWY	DRAWING AWAY
AAADEEHLPST	PALE AS DEATH	AAADGNOPPRS	PROPAGANDAS
AAADEEHLSVY	HEAVY AS LEAD	AAADHHITWWY	HAD A WAY WITH

AAADHHLPRYZ	HAPHAZARDLY	AAAEGILRSSS	RAISE A GLASS
AAADHILMMMU	MUHAMMAD ALI	AAAEGINRWWY	WEARING AWAY
AAADHILNRSS	HARD AS NAILS	AAAEGJLMSWY	JAMES GALWAY
AAADHLNNOSY	LAYS A HAND ON	AAAEGKLNPRS	SPRANG A LEAK
AAADHLNNRUY	HARDY ANNUAL	AAAEGLLRRSY	LARGE SALARY
AAADIILNORR	RADIOLARIAN	AAAEGNNRRST	NARRAGANSET
AAADIILNORT	RADIATIONAL	AAAEGNRTTVX	EXTRAVAGANT
AAADIMNOPRS	PAID A RANSOM	AAAEGPSSSWY	PASSAGEWAYS
AAADINNQRUY	IN A QUANDARY	AAAEHHJLMTT	THE TAJ MAHAL
AAADINOPSTT	ADAPTATIONS	AAAEHIILMPT	EPITHALAMIA
AAADKNORSTT	DRANK A TOAST	AAAEHIKNRST	THIN AS A RAKE
AAADLLNRSTW	WARTS AND ALL	AAAEHILNOPR	AEOLIAN HARP
AAADLMNQRUU	QUADRUMANAL	AAAEHIMNNRT	AMARANTHINE
AAADLNORSSV	SAN SALVADOR	AAAEHKLMPSS	MAKE A SPLASH
AAADLNPPRUW	DRAW UP A PLAN	AAAEHKNNOTT	TAKEN AN OATH
AAADLOOPSTT	POTATO SALAD	AAAEHKNOSTT	TAKES AN OATH
AAADMMNNNOW	MAN AND WOMAN	AAAEHLLMRRS	EARL MARSHAL
AAADNPRSSTT	STANDS APART	AAAEHLNPSXY	ANAPHYLAXES
AAADORSSTTU	AUTOSTRADAS	AAAEHMMRSWY	HAMMERS AWAY
AAAEEEGGRVW	AVERAGE WAGE	AAAEHNORSTW	SWEAR AN OATH
AAAEEELNPRS	PARASELENAE	AAAEHPPRRRS	PARAPHRASER
AAAEEFGHLLU	HALF A LEAGUE	AAAEHPPRRSS	PARAPHRASES
AAAEEFGPSSS	SAFE PASSAGE	AAAEIKNNRTT	TAKEN A TRAIN
AAAEEFIRRSS	AS FREE AS AIR	AAAEIKNRSTT	TAKES A TRAIN
AAAEEGGMNST	STAGE-MANAGE	AAAEIKNTTWY	TAKEN IT AWAY
AAAEEGILMNT	EATING A MEAL	AAAEIKSTTWY	TAKES IT AWAY
AAAEEGMSSTU	SAUSAGE MEAT	AAAEILLRRTV	LATE ARRIVAL
AAAEEGNORSV	GAVE A REASON	AAAEILMNNOT	EMANATIONAL
AAAEEHHRRTV	HAVE AT HEART	AAAEILMRRTW	RAW MATERIAL
AAAEEHINSST	ANAESTHESIA	AAAEILNORSS	RAISES A LOAN
AAAEEHKNRST	TAKEN A SHARE	AAAEILNPSTT	PALATINATES
AAAEEHKRSST	TAKES A SHARE	AAAEILNPWXY	EXPLAIN AWAY
AAAEEHLNPPV	HAVE AN APPLE	AAAEIMNQRSU	AQUAMARINES
AAAEEHLNTTV	HAVE A TALENT	AAAEINSSSST	ASSASSINATE
AAAEEHLPRSS	HAS A RELAPSE	AAAEKMORSTW	WORK AS A TEAM
AAAEEHMNTTX	EXANTHEMATA	AAAEKMPRRSS	PASS A REMARK
AAAEEHNPPST	HAPPEN AT SEA	AAAEKMRSSTT	MAKES A START
AAAEEILLRTV	LEAVE A TRAIL	AAAELLLLPRY	LAY PARALLEL
AAAEEIPSSSY	AS EASY AS PIE	AAAELLLNPRR	RAN PARALLEL
AAAEEKKMMRR	MAKE A REMARK	AAAELLMMMPS	PLASMALEMMA
AAAEEKLMRSV	LEAVES A MARK	AAAELLNPRST	ASTRAL PLANE
AAAEELLNNUV	ANNUAL LEAVE	AAAELMNPRTT	APARTMENTAL
AAAEELNPRTY	PENALTY AREA	AAAELMRSSTT	METATARSALS
AAAEEMMRRTU	AMATEUR TEAM	AAAELMSSTTY	MALAY STATES
AAAEERSTTVX	EXTRAVASATE	AAAELNOPRSY	REPAYS A LOAN
AAAEFFGIRRV	GRAVE AFFAIR	AAAELNPPTYY	PAY A PENALTY
AAAEFFGJNOR	JAFFA ORANGE	AAAEPPRSSTU	APPARATUSES
AAAEFGGNRRW	GANG WARFARE	AAAEPRRSSYY	SAYS A PRAYER
AAAEFGMMNRR	FARM MANAGER	AAAFGHILLNV	HAVING A FALL
AAAEFHKLLOS	ALL OF A SHAKE	AAAFGHINNST	AFGHANISTAN
AAAEFHLRSST	SHARES A FLAT	AAAFGHLLLNO	HALF A GALLON
AAAEFKNRRTW	TANK WARFARE	AAAFGIKLLNT	TAKING A FALL
AAAEFLLNPRT	FALLEN APART	AAAFGILLNWY	FALLING AWAY
AAAEFLLOSTW	ALL OF A SWEAT	AAAFGIMMNNOT	GIANT OF A MAN
AAAEFNPRRST	SPARTAN FARE	AAAFIKPRRSS	SAFARI PARKS
AAAEGGILNPV	LEAVING A GAP	AAAFILLNUVY	AVIFAUNALLY
AAAEGGILNSV	GAVE A SIGNAL	AAAFKLNOORS	ASK FOR A LOAN
AAAEGHILMNV	HAVING A MEAL	AAAFKLOORWY	FAR-AWAY LOOK
AAAEGHILNSV	HAVING A SALE	AAAFKORSSUV	ASKS A FAVOUR
AAAEGHILRSU	RAISE A LAUGH	AAAFLLPUWYY	FLY AWAY PAUL
AAAEGHINNRV	HAVING AN EAR	AAAGGGINRTV	AGGRAVATING
AAAEGIILNRT	EGALITARIAN	AAAGGINNWWY	GNAWING AWAY
AAAEGIILNRZ	NAZI REGALIA	AAAGGINORTV	AGGRAVATION
AAAEGIKLMMN	MAKING A MEAL	AAAGHHIKMNS	MAKING A HASH
AAAEGIKLMNS	MAKE A SIGNAL	AAAGHIKLNRV	HAVING A LARK
	MAKING A SALE	AAAGHILNNPV	HAVING A PLAN
AAAEGIKLNWY	LEAKING AWAY	AAAGHILNUWY	HAULING AWAY
AAAEGIKMMNN	MAKING A NAME	AAAGHLMNNRY	LARRY HAGMAN
AAAEGIKNSTT	TAKING A SEAT	AAAGIIKNTTX	TAKING A TAXI
AAAEGILMMNO	MEGALOMANIA	AAAGIILNOTT	AGITATIONAL
AAAEGILNNST	LEAN AGAINST	AAAGIILNPTY	PLAY IT AGAIN

AAAGIILNSWY	SAILING AWAY	AABBCEINORT	BICARBONATE
AAAGIILNTWY	TAILING AWAY	AABBCEINPTW	CAPTAIN WEBB
AAAGIIMNRRS	AGRARIANISM	AABBCEKLTUY	BLACK BEAUTY
AAAGIINRSTT	SAGITTARIAN	AABBCEKNRUY	BANBURY CAKE
AAAGIKKLNTW	TAKING A WALK	AABBCFIOSYY	BAY OF BISCAY
AAAGIKKMMNR	MAKING A MARK	AABBDDDENOR	BED AND BOARD
AAAGIKLMNPY	MAKING A PLAY	AABBDDEORSU	BOARDED A BUS
AAAGIKLNWWY	WALKING AWAY	AABBDEEHLVY	BEHAVE BADLY
AAAGIKMNPSS	MAKING A PASS	AABBDEEHNTT	BEAT THE BAND
AAAGIKNPRTT	TAKING A PART	AABBDEEHRTT	BATED BREATH
	TAKING APART	AABBDEEIRTV	ABBREVIATED
AAAGILLMNRS	ALARM SIGNAL	AABBDEEKRRS	BREAKS BREAD
AAAGILNNPQU	AQUAPLANING	AABBDEEKRST	BREAD BASKET
AAAGILNNRTV	NAVAL RATING		BREADBASKET
AAAGILNPRTY	LAYING A TRAP	AABBDEEMNOR	EARNED A BOMB
AAAGILNPSSW	PASSING A LAW	AABBDEEORRV	BEAVERBOARD
AAAGILNPSTY	PLAY AGAINST	AABBDEGIKNR	BAKING BREAD
AAAGILNPWYY	PLAYING AWAY	AABBDEGORRS	BARGEBOARDS
AAAGILNSTWY	SALTING AWAY	AABBDFORRRW	BARRED ARROW
AAAGILNSVWY	SLAVING AWAY	AABBDLORSSS	BOLD AS BRASS
AAAGINPSSWY	PASSING AWAY	AABBEEIRRTV	REBARBATIVE
AAAGINRSSTT	STARTS AGAIN	AABBEEIRSTV	ABBREVIATES
AAAGINSTWWY	WASTING AWAY	AABBEEIRSTW	WATER BABIES
AAAGINSTWYY	STAYING AWAY	AABBEEKLNRU	UNBREAKABLE
AAAGMPPRSSS	PAMPAS GRASS	AABBEFGLNOY	BAY OF BENGAL
AAAGNPPRRST	SPRANG A TRAP	AABBEFGLRST	FLABBERGAST
	SPRANG APART	AABBEGIINRT	BEAR BAITING
AAAHHIKNNOR	NOHAN KANHAI		BEARBAITING
AAAHHILNSTT	THIN AS A LATH	AABBEGILLNR	BALL BEARING
AAAHHISTWWY	HAS A WAY WITH	AABBEHIILNT	INHABITABLE
AAAHIKNRRSV	RAVI SHANKAR	AABBEHIKORT	BROKE A HABIT
AAAHILMOPRT	PROTHALAMIA	AABBEHILLOS	ABOLISHABLE
AAAHILNPSXY	ANAPHYLAXIS	AABBEIIRRST	BARBARITIES
AAAHJLLTTZZ	ALL THAT JAZZ	AABBEIORRTV	ABBREVIATOR
AAAHKMMUHYY	OMAR KHAYYAM	AABBEIRRTTU	BARBITURATE
AAAHLLMMNTY	TAMMANY HALL	AABBEKLLSST	BASKETBALLS
AAAIILLNPST	ITALIAN ALPS	AABBEKLOOST	BOOKS A TABLE
AAAIILNORTV	VARIATIONAL	AABBGHIMNOT	THINGAMABOB
AAAIILRSTTW	AWAITS TRIAL	AABBGIINRRS	BARBARISING
AAAIINNQRTU	ANTIQUARIAN	AABBGIINRRZ	BARBARIZING
AAAIKLNOTWZ	IZAAK WALTON	AABBGIKMMNO	MAKING A BOMB
AAAILLMNSWY	IN A SMALL WAY	AABBHRRRTTU	RHUBARB TART
AAAILLMOPPT	PAPILLOMATA	AABBILNNOSY	BABYLONIANS
AAAILLNOSTV	SALVATIONAL	AABBIORSSSU	BABI OUSSAS
AAAILLNOTUV	VALUATIONAL	AABBLORRSUY	BARBAROUSLY
AAAILMRRSTT	MARTIAL ARTS	AABCCDEGKLN	GLANCED BACK
AAAILNNORRT	NARRATIONAL	AABCCDEIKRR	CRACKED A RIB
AAAILNNRSTU	SATURNALIAN	AABCCDEJKKL	BLACKJACKED
AAAILNRSSTU	AUSTRALIANS	AABCCDEKKRT	BACKTRACKED
	SATURNALIAS	AABCCDEKLLN	BECK AND CALL
AAAIMNNOOST	ANTONOMASIA	AABCCDENORT	BROAD ACCENT
AAAIMNOOPRS	PARONOMASIA	AABCCDOOORT	TOBACCO ROAD
AAAJLNRSTUY	LAST JANUARY	AABCCEELLLN	CANCELLABLE
AAAJMPPRTYY	PYJAMA PARTY	AABCCEELLNO	CONCEALABLE
AAAKLNPPRSY	PLAYS A PRANK	AABCCEGKLNS	GLANCES BACK
AAALLPSTWYZ	PLAYS A WALTZ	AABCCEILLRY	ACERBICALLY
AAALNOPRTTU	RAN UP A TOTAL	AABCCEILPRT	PRACTICABLE
AAAMNOPRSSY	PAYS A RANSOM	AABCCEKKPRS	BACKPACKERS
AAAMNORRTTU	MOUNT ARARAT	AABCCEKLLST	BLACK CASTLE
AAAMORSSTTW	WARM AS TOAST	AABCCELNOTU	ACCOUNTABLE
AABBBDEKNOR	ROBBED A BANK	AABCCERRUUY	BUREAUCRACY
AABBCCKKOST	BACK-TO-BACKS	AABCCGIKKNP	BACKPACKING
AABBCDEINRT	BRACE AND BIT	AABCCGIKLLN	CALLING BACK
AABBCDEKLLL	BLACKBALLED	AABCCGIKNPS	BACKSPACING
AABBCDKLORS	BLACKBOARDS	AABCCHLLNOR	LOCAL BRANCH
AABBCDKORWY	BACKWARD BOY	AABCCIKLORT	COCKTAIL BAR
AABBCEFGORS	CABBAGE ROSE	AABCCILPRTY	PRACTICABLY
AABBCEEPTXY	EXPECT A BABY	AABCCKNNOTU	BANK ACCOUNT
AABBCEGHMOT	CABBAGE MOTH	AABCCLNOTUY	ACCOUNTABLY
AABBCEGIKNT	BEATING BACK	AABCCLNRRUU	CARBUNCULAR
AABBCEHINRT	THE BARBICAN	AABCDDEHMRU	DUMB CHARADE

AABCDDEKLNR	RED AND BLACK	AABCEEINRRS	CARABINEERS
AABCDDEKLSS	SADDLEBACKS	AABCEEKNRTT	BEATEN TRACK
AABCDDELLPY	BADLY PLACED	AABCEELNORV	OVERBALANCE
AABCDDEORST	BROADCASTED	AABCEELNPSS	CAPABLENESS
AABCDDIKMNO	DIAMONDBACK	AABCEELNRST	CLEAN BREAST
AABCDEEERTX	EXACERBATED		TABERNACLES
AABCDEEFLRY	BAREFACEDLY	AABCEELNRTU	UNTRACEABLE
AABCDEEFNRZ	BRAZEN-FACED	AABCEELORTT	BRACTEOLATE
AABCDEELNSS	SENDS A CABLE	AABCEELRRTT	RETRACTABLE
AABCDEEORRT	BEAT A RECORD	AABCEELRTTU	TRABECULATE
AABCDEFNORS	SEND FOR A CAB	AABCEELRTTX	EXTRACTABLE
AABCDEFNOST	BASED ON FACT	AABCEFLMNOY	FLAMBOYANCE
AABCDEGGNNO	BACON AND EGG	AABCEFLNOTU	CONFABULATE
	EGG AND BACON	AABCEFNORST	SENT FOR A CAB
AABCDEGHIKN	HEADING BACK	AABCEGHKNRS	BANK CHARGES
AABCDEGIMRT	AT CAMBRIDGE	AABCEGHLORY	GAY BACHELOR
AABCDEGINNR	DANCING BEAR	AABCEGHNRST	BAG SNATCHER
AABCDEHIMMR	CHAMBERMAID	AABCEGIKLNN	LEANING BACK
AABCDEHKNRS	BACKHANDERS	AABCEGILNNT	ENABLING ACT
AABCDEHLMTY	LADY MACBETH	AABCEGILNPT	PLACING A BET
AABCDEHLOPR	BACHELOR PAD	AABCEGINRSS	BRINGS A CASE
AABCDEHNPRY	PEACH BRANDY	AABCEGLMNNS	BLANCMANGES
AABCDEIKLLM	BLACKMAILED	AABCEHHPSTY	BATHYSCAPHE
AABCDEILNST	ELASTIC BAND	AABCEHIKLVY	BACK HEAVILY
AABCDEILOST	CATABOLISED	AABCEHIKNRS	BANK CASHIER
AABCDEILOTZ	CATABOLIZED	AABCEHIKRST	BASKET CHAIR
AABCDEINNSU	ABUNDANCIES	AABCEHILLRY	HEBRAICALLY
AABCDEINOOR	RADIO BEACON	AABCEHILMNR	CHAMBERLAIN
AABCDEKLPPS	BACKSLAPPED	AABCEHINORT	HARICOT BEAN
AABCDEKORRZ	RAZOR-BACKED	AABCEHKLRSS	BACKLASHERS
AABCDELLNPS	CAP AND BELLS	AABCEHKNWWY	WAY BACK WHEN
AABCDELMMNO	COMMANDABLE	AABCEHKORSS	BACKS A HORSE
AABCDELMMRS	MAD SCRAMBLE	AABCEHKORTT	BACK TO EARTH
AABCDELNOTU	BALANCED OUT	AABCEHLLMRS	CHARLES LAMB
	OUTBALANCED	AABCEHLMPTY	PLAY MACBETH
AABCDEMMORT	ARMED COMBAT	AABCEHLOPRU	CHEAP LABOUR
AABCDEORRST	BROADCASTER	AABCEHLPRSU	PURCHASABLE
AABCDFIKLRY	BLACK FRIDAY	AABCEHMRRST	STAR CHAMBER
AABCDGGIOOR	BRAGGADOCIO	AABCEHNRRTW	BRANCH WATER
AABCDGHIKNN	BACKHANDING	AABCEIIINRR	CARABINIERI
	HANDING BACK	AABCEIILNNS	CANNIBALISE
AABCDGIINRR	BARRICADING	AABCEIILNNZ	CANNIBALIZE
AABCDGIKNRW	DRAWING BACK	AABCEIINSTU	BEAUTICIANS
AABCDGILNOR	LANGOBARDIC	AABCEIKKNTT	TAKEN IT BACK
AABCDGKLRSU	BLACKGUARDS	AABCEIKKSTT	TAKES IT BACK
AABCDGKORSW	GO BACKWARDS	AABCEIKLLMR	BLACKMAILER
AABCDHINNOS	DANISH BACON	AABCEIKNNRW	BACK A WINNER
AABCDHINRSW	SANDWICH BAR	AABCEILLPRU	BURIAL PLACE
AABCDHMORST	MATCHBOARDS	AABCEILLRTY	BACTERIALLY
AABCDHOPRST	PATCHBOARDS	AABCEILNNOT	CONTAINABLE
AABCDIINOST	ABDICATIONS	AABCEILNPSY	INESCAPABLY
AABCDINOORR	RADIOCARBON	AABCEILNRTT	INTRACTABLE
AABCDKLMNOY	BLACK MONDAY	AABCEILOSST	CATABOLISES
AABCEEEHLST	ESCHEATABLE	AABCEILOSTZ	CATABOLIZES
AABCEEELLPR	REPLACEABLE	AABCEILPPRY	APPRECIABLY
AABCEEELRRT	RECREATABLE	AABCEIMNPRR	PRECAMBRIAN
AABCEEEMORW	BECOME AWARE	AABCEINORST	ABREACTIONS
AABCEEERSTX	EXACERBATES	AABCEIRSTTV	ABSTRACTIVE
AABCEEFNORR	FORBEARANCE	AABCEKKLMRT	BLACK MARKET
AABCEEGLLNO	CONGEALABLE	AABCEKLORSS	BACKS A LOSER
AABCEEHILMN	MACHINEABLE	AABCEKLPPRS	BACKSLAPPER
AABCEEHILMP	IMPEACHABLE	AABCEKLQRSU	BLACK SQUARE
AABCEEHMNRT	ANTECHAMBER	AABCEKMNPTY	BACK PAYMENT
AABCEEHORTT	THE BOAT RACE	AABCEKNRSSW	ANSWERS BACK
AABCEEHRSST	SABRETACHES	AABCELLMNSY	CALLS BY NAME
AABCEEILLMR	RECLAIMABLE	AABCELLOORT	COLLABORATE
AABCEEILMNV	AMBIVALENCE	AABCELLORRS	BARCAROLLES
AABCEEILMRS	BEARS MALICE	AABCELMOPSS	COMPASSABLE
AABCEEILNPS	INESCAPABLE	AABCELMRSTU	ALBERT CAMUS
AABCEEILNRS	INCREASABLE	AABCELMRUWY	CRUMBLE AWAY
AABCEEILPPR	APPRECIABLE	AABCELMSTUU	ACETABULUMS

AABCELNOSTU	BALANCES OUT
	OUTBALANCES
AABCELNOSTY	BALCONY SEAT
AABCELORSXY	CARBOXYLASE
AABCELORTXY	CARBOXYLATE
AABCENOPPRR	CARBON PAPER
AABCENOPRTU	PRANCE ABOUT
AABCEOORTTZ	AZOTOBACTER
AABCEORRSSS	BEARS A CROSS
AABCERRSTUU	BUREAUCRATS
AABCFGIINRT	FABRICATING
AABCFGIKLLN	FALLING BACK
AABCFGINOTU	ABOUT-FACING
AABCFIINORT	FABRICATION
AABCFIORRST	FABRICATORS
AABCFIORRVY	VICAR OF BRAY
AABCFKLLNOS	FALLS BACK ON
AABCFLMNOYY	FLAMBOYANCY
AABCGGHIKNN	HANGING BACK
AABCGHIINRT	BRACHIATING
AABCGHIOOPR	AGORAPHOBIC
AABCGHIOPRR	BAROGRAPHIC
AABCGIIINRS	ARABICISING
AABCGIIINRZ	ARABICIZING
AABCGIILNRT	CALIBRATING
AABCGIKKLNT	TALKING BACK
AABCGIKKLNW	WALKING BACK
AABCGIKLNPY	PLAYING BACK
AABCGIKNPSS	PASSING BACK
AABCGILNNNU	UNBALANCING
AABCGILNNPU	BALANCING UP
AABCGINNORT	CARBONATING
AABCGINRSTT	ABSTRACTING
AABCHIILMNR	BRAHMINICAL
AABCHIINNTY	INHABITANCY
AABCHIINORT	BRACHIATION
AABCHIJMORR	ARMCHAIR JOB
AABCHKLPSSS	SPLASHBACKS
AABCIIILMTY	AMICABILITY
AABCIIKLPTY	PACKABILITY
AABCIILLOTY	ABIOTICALLY
AABCIILMNNS	CANNIBALISM
AABCIILNORT	CALIBRATION
AABCIKLNRSS	LACKS BRAINS
AABCILLNOTY	BOTANICALLY
AABCILNRTTY	INTRACTABLY
AABCILORRST	CALIBRATORS
AABCINNOORT	CARBONATION
AABCINORRTU	CARBURATION
AABCINORSTT	ABSTRACTION
AABCKLLOPTY	BLACK TO PLAY
AABCKLMOORS	BLACKAMOORS
AABCKLOOSST	BLACK AS SOOT
AABCKMOORRR	BARRACK ROOM
AABCLLLRSTY	CRYSTAL BALL
AABCLLNNNOS	CANNONBALLS
AABCLORSTUW	CRAWLS ABOUT
AABDDDEELRY	BEARDED LADY
AABDDDEFMNU	DEAF AND DUMB
AABDDDEGOTU	GADDED ABOUT
AABDDDINRTU	DID A BAD TURN
AABDDEEFTUY	FADED BEAUTY
AABDDEELNRS	BANDLEADERS
AABDDEELORV	BROAD-LEAVED
AABDDEELRSS	ADDRESSABLE
AABDDEFORRT	BAD FOR TRADE
AABDDEGGIPR	BRIDGED A GAP
AABDDEIMNRT	ARMED BANDIT
AABDDEIOPPR	PIPED ABOARD
AABDDEIRSST	BASTARDISED
AABDDEIRSTZ	BASTARDIZED
AABDDELLNOW	LANDED A BLOW
AABDDELNSST	SANDBLASTED
AABDDELNTWY	WANTED BADLY
AABDDEMNSSS	MASSED BANDS
AABDDEOORST	STARBOARDED
AABDDIKLMNN	MIDLAND BANK
AABDDNRSSTU	SUBSTANDARD
AABDEEEGRTT	GREAT DEBATE
AABDEEEHPSU	HEAPED ABUSE
AABDEEEMMMR	MADE A MEMBER
AABDEEENTTY	BATTED AN EYE
AABDEEFIRRS	FREE AS A BIRD
AABDEEFKRST	BREAKFASTED
AABDEEGGRRU	BEAR A GRUDGE
AABDEEHHRRS	HABERDASHER
AABDEEHHRRT	BREATHE HARD
AABDEEHINRR	HAREBRAINED
AABDEEILLNS	ANISEED BALL
AABDEEILLRR	READ BRAILLE
AABDEEILMNR	LAMEBRAINED
AABDEEILNTY	BAT AN EYELID
AABDEEIMRRT	ADMIT BEARER
AABDEEIRSTU	BURIED AT SEA
AABDEEKLPRS	BRAKE PEDALS
AABDEEKNORT	BROKEN A DATE
AABDEEKNRRT	BEER TANKARD
AABDEEKOOST	BOOKED A SEAT
AABDEELNOPP	ONE BAD APPLE
AABDEELNOTT	DETONATABLE
AABDEELPRSU	PERSUADABLE
AABDEELPRYY	PLAYED BY EAR
AABDEEMRRSS	EMBARRASSED
AABDEENSSUU	USE AND ABUSE
AABDEEOORSV	SOARED ABOVE
AABDEFFLOOR	LOAF OF BREAD
AABDEFGIINR	BEING AFRAID
AABDEGGHRSY	SHAGGY BEARD
AABDEGGIPRS	BRIDGES A GAP
AABDEGHILNS	BANGLADESHI
AABDEGILNOS	DIAGNOSABLE
AABDEGIMNRT	RAGTIME BAND
AABDEGLLMNO	AMBLED ALONG
AABDEGLNRRY	LARGE BRANDY
AABDEGNORRW	GROWN A BEARD
AABDEGORRSW	GROWS A BEARD
AABDEHHIRRT	HAIRBREADTH
AABDEHINSWY	WINS BY A HEAD
AABDEHKLNSY	BADLY SHAKEN
AABDEHLNSTU	LATE HUSBAND
AABDEHNNOOP	ABANDON HOPE
AABDEHNNRSW	BERNARD SHAW
AABDEHNRRTW	DRAWN BREATH
AABDEHOSTTT	STAB TO DEATH
AABDEHRRSTW	DRAWS BREATH
AABDEHRSTWY	BREADTHWAYS
AABDEHRSUWY	BRUSHED AWAY
AABDEIILNSV	INADVISABLE
AABDEIILRTY	READABILITY
AABDEIINNRV	INDIAN BRAVE
AABDEIINRRS	RAISIN BREAD
AABDEILLLOW	ALLOWED BAIL
AABDEILLNRS	BANDERILLAS
AABDEILLRVY	ADVERBIALLY
AABDEILMNRU	DIAL A NUMBER
AABDEILMNTU	MANDIBULATE
AABDEILNNRW	BRIAN WALDEN
AABDEILNOUV	UNAVOIDABLE
AABDEILORRT	LABRADORITE
AABDEIMNOPS	IMPOSED A BAN
AABDEIMRTUV	ADUMBRATIVE
AABDEINORRT	BREAD RATION

AABDEINOSST	BASTINADOES	AABEEGIRSTV	SAVAGE TRIBE
AABDEIOPPRS	PIPES ABOARD	AABEEGKMRTU	TAKE UMBRAGE
AABDEIRRSVY	BARRY DAVIES	AABEEGLLLTT	LEGAL BATTLE
AABDEIRSSST	BASTARDISES	AABEEGLMNTU	AUGMENTABLE
AABDEIRSSTZ	BASTARDIZES	AABEEGLMSSS	ASSEMBLAGES
AABDEKLORTU	LARKED ABOUT	AABEEGLNOSV	NOBLE SAVAGE
AABDEKLOTTU	TALKED ABOUT	AABEEGRTTUY	GREAT BEAUTY
AABDEKLOTUW	WALKED ABOUT	AABEEHHLPTT	THE ALPHABET
AABDEKNOORT	TAKE ON BOARD	AABEEHHNNRRT	BARREN HEATH
AABDEKOOPTT	BAKED POTATO	AABEEHIKTTT	TAKE THE BAIT
AABDEKORSST	SKATEBOARDS	AABEEHILNTZ	ELIZABETHAN
AABDELLLNOO	LEAD BALLOON	AABEEHILPST	ALPHABETISE
AABDELLNNOS	BELLADONNAS	AABEEHILPTZ	ALPHABETIZE
AABDELNRSST	SANDBLASTER	AABEEHIRRRT	HEAT BARRIER
AABDELOPTUY	PLAYED ABOUT	AABEEHIRSTT	BEATS THE AIR
AABDELORRUY	DAY LABOURER	AABEEHKLRRT	HALTERBREAK
AABDELORSUV	SAVED LABOUR	AABEEHKLRTW	BREAK THE LAW
AABDELRSSTU	BALUSTRADES	AABEEHKRRST	HEARTBREAKS
AABDELRSTTY	TREATS BADLY	AABEEHLLTTY	LAY THE TABLE
AABDEMNRSST	BANDMASTERS	AABEEHLMPRT	BEAR THE PALM
AABDENORTUW	WANDER ABOUT	AABEEHLOTVW	ABOVE THE LAW
AABDGGGINNS	SANDBAGGING	AABEEHLPRTY	PLAY THE BEAR
AABDGGINOOR	GOING ABOARD	AABEEHLRSTV	HARVESTABLE
	GOING ABROAD	AABEEHLRSTY	BREATHALYSE
	GOOD BARGAIN	AABEEHLRTYZ	BREATHALYZE
AABDGHIILNT	IN A BAD LIGHT	AABEEHNOPSU	HEAP ABUSE ON
AABDGHINOSV	VAGABONDISH	AABEEIILLNN	INALIENABLE
AABDGIILRTY	GRADABILITY	AABEEIJMRRS	JAMES BARRIE
AABDGIINSST	BIDS AGAINST	AABEEILLNNU	UNALIENABLE
AABDGIJLNNO	LANDING A JOB	AABEEILLNPX	EXPLAINABLE
AABDGIMNOSV	VAGABONDISM	AABEEILMNSS	AMIABLENESS
AABDGIMNRTU	ADUMBRATING	AABEEILNPRS	INSEPARABLE
AABDGINORWW	DRAWING A BOW	AABEEILORTV	ELABORATIVE
AABDGLNRSSY	BRANDY GLASS	AABEEILPRRR	IRREPARABLE
AABDHIKLNOY	BANK HOLIDAY	AABEEINNNST	ANNIE BESANT
AABDHINNOPS	ABANDON SHIP	AABEEINRRRT	TRAINBEARER
AABDHINNOTW	WITH ABANDON	AABEEINRRST	BRAINTEASER
AABDHIOSTTV	BODHISATTVA	AABEEIRSSTU	BURIES AT SEA
AABDHNORRSW	HANDBARROWS	AABEEJKRRSW	JAWBREAKERS
AABDHOOSTTT	THAT'S TOO BAD	AABEEKKMORR	MAKE OR BREAK
AABDIILLTUY	LAUDABILITY	AABEEKLMTTU	TAKE A TUMBLE
AABDIILMQRU	LIQUIDAMBAR	AABEEKLNPSU	UNSPEAKABLE
AABDIILNRRT	BRIDAL TRAIN	AABEEKLOPST	ABLE TO SPEAK
AABDIILNTUY	BUILT IN A DAY	AABEEKLRRSU	BREAKS A RULE
AABDIILORTY	ADORABILITY	AABEEKLRRSW	LAWBREAKERS
AABDILLMNOY	ABDOMINALLY	AABEEKMNRTU	TAKE A NUMBER
AABDILLMNRY	BILL MAYNARD	AABEEKNOPST	KEEPS A TAB ON
AABDILLNOOS	BOLD AS A LION	AABEEKPRSTT	KEPT ABREAST
AABDILNOUVY	UNAVOIDABLY	AABEEKRRSTW	BREAKWATERS
AABDIMNNORTU	ADUMBRATION	AABEEKSSTTW	WASTEBASKET
AABDIMNRRSU	BARRAMUNDIS	AABEELLMNOT	BALLETOMANE
AABDMOORRRT	MORTARBOARD	AABEELLMNTT	NETBALL TEAM
AABDNOOPRSX	PANDORAS BOX	AABEELLNRTU	UNALTERABLE
AABDNOORRWW	BOW AND ARROW	AABEELLORTY	ELABORATELY
AABDNOOTTUU	OUT AND ABOUT	AABEELLPRRS	PALLBEARERS
AABDNOSSTTU	STANDS ABOUT	AABEELLPRSU	PLEASURABLE
AABEEEEGRRV	EAGER BEAVER	AABEELMPRTU	PERAMBULATE
AABEEEFGSSU	BEEF SAUSAGE	AABEELMPTTU	ATTEMPTABLE
AABEEEFKRRS	SAFEBREAKER	AABEELNNNTT	ALAN BENNETT
AABEEEGLLTU	LEAGUE TABLE	AABEELNORST	TREASONABLE
AABEEEHMNRT	BEAR THE NAME	AABEELNRTTU	ENTABLATURE
AABEEEKPRST	KEEP ABREAST	AABEELORRRV	OVER A BARREL
AABEEELRRST	TALEBEARERS	AABEELPRSTT	BREASTPLATE
AABEEERRRTW	WATER BEARER	AABEELRRSTV	TRAVERSABLE
AABEEFFLLOR	BEFORE A FALL	AABEELRRTWY	BARLEY WATER
AABEEFGIRTV	FIVE-BAR GATE	AABEELRSTVY	TRAVEL BY SEA
AABEEFKORRT	BREAK FOR TEA	AABEEMRRSSS	EMBARRASSES
AABEEFKRRST	BREAKFASTER	AABEENNRRSTW	BARREN WASTE
AABEEGGIIRR	ARGIE-BARGIE	AABEFGORSUV	BEGS A FAVOUR
AABEEGILNRT	TALEBEARING	AABEFHIKRST	BREAKS FAITH
AABEEGINVWW	WEAVING A WEB	AABEFHILNOS	FASHIONABLE

AABEFHILOSU	HAIL OF ABUSE	AABEILRRTVY	TRAVEL BY AIR
AABEFHIORRT	BREATH OF AIR	AABEIMNOPSS	IMPOSES A BAN
AABEFHLLOTT	HALF A BOTTLE	AABEIMNRRTT	ARBITRAMENT
AABEFIILLQU	QUALIFIABLE	AABEINORRST	ABERRATIONS
AABEFIILSST	SATISFIABLE	AABEIORSSTV	ABOVE STAIRS
AABEFILLMMN	INFLAMMABLE	AABEJKLOORU	LABOUR A JOKE
AABEFILLNST	INFLATABLES	AABEJKNNOOT	TAKEN ON A JOB
AABEFILLNTT	FINAL BATTLE	AABEJKNOOST	TAKES ON A JOB
AABEFIMNRSY	BY FAIR MEANS	AABEKKNRRSS	BREAKS RANKS
AABEFKLLNOR	BROKEN A FALL	AABEKLNPSUY	UNSPEAKABLY
AABEFLLNOTU	FALLEN ABOUT	AABEKMNNORR	BROKEN AN ARM
AABEFLLNPPU	UNFLAPPABLE	AABEKNNSTTW	NATWEST BANK
AABEFLNOPSY	BAY OF NAPLES	AABEKNOPRRT	BROKEN APART
AABEFLORSTW	BALE OF STRAW	AABEKNOPRTU	PUT A BRAKE ON
AABEGGIINNS	BEGINS AGAIN	AABEKNOSSTU	SNEAKS ABOUT
AABEGGILMNT	GAMING TABLE	AABELLLOSWW	SWALLOWABLE
AABEGHIIINTV	HAVING A BITE	AABELLMPRSY	PLAY MARBLES
AABEGHOOPRS	AGORAPHOBES	AABELLOPPRT	BALLOT PAPER
AABEGHORRSU	HARBOURAGES	AABELLORSUV	SLAVE LABOUR
AABEGIIKNTT	TAKING A BITE	AABELLORTTY	BATTLE ROYAL
AABEGIKLNRW	LAWBREAKING	AABELLPRSUY	PLEASURABLY
AABEGILNORT	ELABORATING	AABELMNOORV	ABOVE NORMAL
AABEGILRSST	ALGEBRAISTS	AABELNNRTTU	NATURAL BENT
AABEGIMNRRS	BEARING ARMS	AABELNOOTUY	LAY ABOUT ONE
AABEGINNOST	ABNEGATIONS	AABELNOPTUY	UNABLE TO PAY
AABEGLLMNOS	AMBLES ALONG	AABELNORSTU	LEARNS ABOUT
AABEGLLNOPT	BEGAN TO PALL	AABELNORSTY	TREASONABLY
AABEGLNORRR	BARREL ORGAN	AABELNORTTU	LEARNT ABOUT
AABEGLRRSUY	BARLEY SUGAR	AABELNOSTUY	BEAUTY SALON
AABEGMRSVXY	MAX BYGRAVES	AABELORSSST	ALBATROSSES
AABEHILNRST	TARNISHABLE	AABELORSSUV	SAVES LABOUR
AABEHILORUV	BEHAVIOURAL	AABELORTTUV	TRAVEL ABOUT
AABEHIMNSST	THAMES BASIN	AABELPRSSSU	SURPASSABLE
AABEHINRRSW	BRAINWASHER	AABEMNOOSSY	SOON AS MAYBE
AABEHIPHITT	BAIT THE TRAP	AABENRRSSTU	RUNS ABREAST
AABEHKLLMTW	LAMBETH WALK	AABFFILNOOT	FOOTBALL FAN
AABEHKNOSTT	SANK THE BOAT	AABFGHLOTTU	BOUGHT A FLAT
AABEHLLLPTY	PLAY THE BALL	AABFGILNTUY	BUYING A FLAT
AABEHLLPSST	PASS THE BALL	AABFHILNOSY	FASHIONABLY
AABEHLOPRRR	PEARL HARBOR	AABFILLMMUY	FAMILY ALBUM
AABEHMNRSTU	HUMAN BREAST	AABFLLLSTTU	AT FULL BLAST
AABEHMOTTUW	WHAT ABOUT ME?	AABFLOOSTTU	FLOATS ABOUT
AABEHRSSUWY	BRUSHES AWAY	AABGGILMMNN	GAMBLING MAN
AABEIILLMSS	ASSIMILABLE	AABGHIIINSU	HAILING A BUS
AABEIILLNNY	INALIENABLY	AABGHIINTTU	HABITUATING
AABEIILMMOR	MEMORABILIA	AABGHILLMRY	BILLY GRAHAM
AABEIILMNTY	AMENABILITY	AABGHILNOOP	ANGLOPHOBIA
AABEIILNRRT	LIBERTARIAN	AABGHIRSTTT	STRAIGHT BAT
AABEIILRSTY	ERASABILITY	AABGHLOSTUU	LAUGHS ABOUT
AABEIIRRTTV	ARBITRATIVE	AABGHORTUWY	BROUGHT AWAY
AABEIJLMNRU	JULIAN BREAM	AABGIIILNRS	RAISING BAIL
AABEIKLNNPT	TABLE NAPKIN	AABGIIINTTW	WAITING A BIT
AABEIKMNORT	EMBARKATION	AABGIIKLNNS	BALKANISING
AABEILLLRTY	BILATERALLY	AABGIIKLNNZ	BALKANIZING
AABEILLMNPT	IMPLANTABLE	AABGIILLNPY	PAYING A BILL
AABEILLMSUX	SUBMAXILLAE	AABGIILMNOW	AIMING A BLOW
AABEILLOPRS	POLARISABLE	AABGIILNORS	ABORIGINALS
AABEILLOPRZ	POLARIZABLE	AABGIILNOST	SAILING BOAT
AABEILLRRST	LIBERAL ARTS	AABGIILNOWY	BOILING AWAY
AABEILLRRTZ	TRAILBLAZER	AABGIIMNNOT	ABOMINATING
AABEILMNPRS	PERSIAN LAMB	AABGIINRRTT	ARBITRATING
AABEILMORST	AMORTISABLE	AABGIKKMNOO	MAKING A BOOK
AABEILMORTZ	AMORTIZABLE	AABGIKNNSSV	SAVINGS BANK
AABEILNOORT	ELABORATION	AABGIKNRSTY	BAKING TRAYS
AABEILNPRSY	INSEPARABLY	AABGILLLNPY	PLAYING BALL
AABEILNSSTU	SUSTAINABLE	AABGILNOSWY	WINS BY A GOAL
AABEILOPRSV	VAPORISABLE	AABGILNOTUY	LAYING ABOUT
AABEILOPRVZ	VAPORIZABLE	AABGILNOWWY	BLOWING AWAY
AABEILPRRRY	IRREPARABLY	AABGINOORST	ABROGATIONS
AABEILPRTUU	BUILT-UP AREA	AABGINRSSTU	RUBS AGAINST
AABEILPRTYY	PLAY IT BY EAR	AABHHORSTTU	THRASH ABOUT

AABHIILSTWY	WASHABILITY	AACCDEIRRTU	CARICATURED
AABHIINOSTT	HABITATIONS	AACCDEKNRTU	CRACKED A NUT
AABHIINOTTU	HABITATION	AACCDEKORRS	SODA CRACKER
AABHILMNSUY	LAY IN AMBUSH	AACCDELMTUU	ACCUMULATED
AABHIMNOPST	BOATMANSHIP	AACCDEMMOOT	ACCOMMODATE
AABHIMNPSST	BATSMANSHIP	AACCDEMNOTT	MADE CONTACT
AABHIOTTTUW	WHAT ABOUT IT?	AACCDENOPVY	ADVANCE COPY
AABHOPRRSUY	HARBOUR A SPY	AACCDFKNORW	CRACK OF DAWN
AABIIILRTVY	VARIABILITY	AACCDFKOPRS	PACK OF CARDS
AABIIILLNORT	LIBRATIONAL	AACCDGHLOTU	CAUGHT A COLD
AABIILLPPTY	PALPABILITY	AACCDGILLNR	CALLING CARD
AABIILLPTYY	PLAYABILITY	AACCDHHORTT	HARD TO CATCH
AABIILMNRUU	ALBUMINURIA	AACCDHILNOR	CHANCROIDAL
AABIILNORTV	VIBRATIONAL	AACCDHOPRST	DROPS A CATCH
AABIILRRRTY	ARBITRARILY	AACCDHPRSST	SCRATCH PADS
AABIIMNNOOT	ABOMINATION	AACCDIIILRT	DIACRITICAL
AABIINORRTT	ARBITRATION	AACCDIIMRRT	DRAMA CRITIC
AABIJNORSTU	ABJURATIONS	AACCDINOPTU	ACCOUNT PAID
AABILLMPSTY	BAPTISMALLY	AACCDIOSSTU	CAUSTIC SODA
AABILLMSSUX	SUBMAXILLAS	AACCDLLMNOO	COOL AND CALM
AABILMNORTY	ABNORMALITY	AACCDLLOORT	CALL A DOCTOR
AABILNOOPRT	PROBATIONAL	AACCDLNORTY	ACCORDANTLY
AABILNORTUY	ABLUTIONARY	AACCEEELLNV	CANCEL LEAVE
AABILNOSSTT	LAST BASTION	AACCEEELRST	ACCELERATES
AABILNSSTTU	SUBSTANTIAL	AACCEEENSSU	CAUSE A SCENE
AABIMNOORST	ABOMINATORS	AACCEEFKRRS	SAFECRACKER
AABIMNOPRST	BONAPARTISM	AACCEEGHINV	GIVE A CHANCE
AABINOOPPRT	APPROBATION	AACCEEGHNRT	GREAT CHANCE
AABINOPRSTT	BONAPARTIST	AACCEEGNRTV	GRAVE ACCENT
AABINORRSST	A STAR IS BORN	AACCEEGPRSS	SCAPEGRACES
AABIORRRSTT	ARBITRATORS	AACCEEHHIOV	HAVE A CHOICE
AABKKOORRSU	KOOKABURRAS	AACCEEHHPST	ESCAPE HATCH
AABLOPRRTUY	LABOUR PARTY	AACCEEHHQSU	CASH A CHEQUE
AABMNNORRRY	BARRY NORMAN	AACCEEHIKMO	MAKE A CHOICE
AABOOPPRRTY	APPROBATORY	AACCEEHKNST	TAKE CHANCES
AACCCDEKORS	CRACKS A CODE	AACCEEHLNOS	LOSE A CHANCE
AACCCDENORS	ACCORDANCES	AACCEEHLNQU	EQUAL CHANCE
AACCCEENPST	ACCEPTANCES	AACCEEHORTV	CREATE HAVOC
AACCCEENTTU	ACUTE ACCENT	AACCEEHRSST	CATACHRESES
AACCCEILRSS	CLASSIC RACE	AACCEEHSSTY	EASY CATCHES
AACCCEINORT	ARCTIC OCEAN	AACCEEILPRS	SPECIAL CARE
AACCCEJKKRR	CRACKERJACK	AACCEEILPSS	SPECIAL CASE
AACCCHHILLT	CATCH A CHILL	AACCEEIMMNR	ICE-CREAM MAN
AACCCHNOSTU	CASH ACCOUNT	AACCEEIMNRS	CINECAMERAS
AACCCIIILRT	CICATRICIAL	AACCEEINRRT	INCARCERATE
AACCCILMSTY	CATACLYSMIC	AACCEEIRSSS	ACCESSARIES
AACCCLPTTUU	CALCUTTA CUP	AACCEEJNOTU	JEAN COCTEAU
AACCCNNOTUY	ACCOUNTANCY	AACCEELORRT	ACCELERATOR
AACCDDDIILO	ADD A CODICIL	AACCEENNOTT	CONCATENATE
AACCDEEELRT	ACCELERATED	AACCEENSTTU	ACCENTUATES
AACCDEEHIMO	MADE A CHOICE	AACCEFHHITT	CATCH A THIEF
AACCDEEIIMZ	ACADEMICIZE	AACCEFHSTTY	SAFETY CATCH
AACCDEEILMR	MEDICAL CARE	AACCEFILSTU	FASCICULATE
AACCDEEILMS	MEDICAL CASE	AACCEFINPRT	FRANTIC PACE
AACCDEELNOR	ACCELERANDO	AACCEFLORTY	CALEFACTORY
AACCDEENTTU	ACCENTUATED	AACCEFPRSST	SPACECRAFTS
AACCDEEPSST	SPACE CADETS	AACCEGHILNR	ARCHANGELIC
AACCDEERSSY	READY ACCESS	AACCEGHINTV	GIVEN A CATCH
AACCDEHILLN	CLINCH A DEAL	AACCEGHISTV	GIVES A CATCH
AACCDEHINNT	CACHINNATED	AACCEGILMOR	ACROMEGALIC
AACCDEHNORS	ARCHDEACONS	AACCEGILORT	CATEGORICAL
AACCDEIILLT	DIALECTICAL	AACCEGIMPRT	MAGIC CARPET
AACCDEIIMMS	ACADEMICISM	AACCEGINSSS	GAINS ACCESS
AACCDEILNOT	ANECDOTICAL	AACCEGKLORU	LACK COURAGE
AACCDEILNST	ACCIDENTALS	AACCEGNRSST	GRANT ACCESS
AACCDEILOPY	CYCLOPAEDIA	AACCEHHMOST	STOMACH ACHE
AACCDEILRRU	RADICAL CURE	AACCEHHNPPY	HAPPY CHANCE
AACCDEILRRW	DRAW A CIRCLE	AACCEHHPRST	CATCH PHRASE
AACCDEIMNOP	ACCOMPANIED		CATCHPHRASE
AACCDEIMNOR	NOMADIC RACE	AACCEHIIMNN	MECHANICIAN
AACCDEINOTV	ACT ON ADVICE	AACCEHIINPV	HAVE A PICNIC

AACCEHILMOT	MACHICOLATE
AACCEHILMST	CATECHISMAL
AACCEHIMNSS	MISS A CHANCE
AACCEHINNST	CACHINNATES
AACCEHINRRT	IN CHARACTER
AACCEHIOORZ	ARCHAEOZOIC
AACCEHIORRT	CHARIOT RACE
AACCEHIRSST	CATACHRESIS
AACCEHJNSTU	JUST A CHANCE
AACCEHKNOOT	TOOK A CHANCE
AACCEHLLMNS	SMALL CHANCE
AACCEHLNNNO	NONCHALANCE
AACCEHLNOST	COELACANTHS
	LOST A CHANCE
AACCEHLNRTT	CATTLE RANCH
AACCEHMORSU	SCARAMOUCHE
AACCEHMRSTT	SCRATCH TEAM
AACCEHNRRTY	CARRY THE CAN
AACCEIILMST	ACCLIMATISE
AACCEIILMTZ	ACCLIMATIZE
AACCEILLOSS	SOCIAL SCALE
AACCEILLSTY	ASCETICALLY
AACCEILLTUV	CALCULATIVE
AACCEILMPRT	MALPRACTICE
AACCEILNOSS	ACCESSIONAL
AACCEILPSTY	TYPICAL CASE
AACCEIMNOPS	ACCOMPANIES
AACCEINNOSV	NO VACANCIES
AACCEINOPTT	ACCEPTATION
AACCEINORSV	COVARIANCES
AACCEINQTTU	ACQUITTANCE
AACCEIORSTU	AUTOCRACIES
AACCEIRRSTU	CARICATURES
AACCEISSTUV	ACCUSATIVES
AACCEJKKORS	CRACKS A JOKE
AACCEJKKORU	JACK KEROUAC
AACCEKKTYYY	YACKETY-YACK
AACCEKMNOTT	MAKE CONTACT
AACCEKNOTTU	TAKE ACCOUNT
AACCEKOPSTT	COST A PACKET
AACCELLLNOR	CLEAN COLLAR
AACCELLMNOW	EWAN MACCOLL
AACCELLNTUY	ACCENTUALLY
AACCELLRSTU	CALLS A TRUCE
AACCELMNUUV	VACUUM-CLEAN
AACCELMSTUU	ACCUMULATES
AACCELNRTUU	CARUNCULATE
AACCELPRSTU	SPECTACULAR
AACCELRTTUU	ACCULTURATE
AACCENRSSTU	CRUSTACEANS
AACCFFGINST	FACING FACTS
AACCFIIILRS	SACRIFICIAL
AACCFIILLPY	PACIFICALLY
AACCFIILRTY	FARCICALITY
AACCFINNRSS	FRANCISCANS
AACCFORSTTY	FACTORY ACTS
AACCGHIMOPR	MACROPHAGIC
AACCGHINPTY	YACHTING CAP
AACCGHINRTY	RACING YACHT
	YACHT RACING
AACCGIILMNT	ACCLIMATING
AACCGIINNTV	VACCINATING
AACCGILLNTU	CALCULATING
AACCHIIMRST	CHARISMATIC
AACCHIINRST	ANARCHISTIC
AACCHIINRTT	ANTHRACITIC
AACCHILLOTY	CHAOTICALLY
AACCHILMNOR	MONARCHICAL
AACCHILNOSV	VOLCANIC ASH
AACCHILNOTU	ANACOLUTHIC
AACCHKNPPSU	PACKS A PUNCH

AACCHNORSST	CASTS ANCHOR
AACCHORRRTY	CARRY A TORCH
AACCIIILRST	RACIALISTIC
AACCIILMNOT	ACCLIMATION
AACCIILMPRT	IMPRACTICAL
AACCIILNNOT	CALCINATION
AACCIILPTTY	CAPITAL CITY
AACCIILSSTU	CASUISTICAL
AACCIILSTTT	STALACTITIC
AACCIINNOTV	VACCINATION
AACCIINOSTU	ACOUSTICIAN
AACCIINTTVY	VATICAN CITY
AACCIKNOOPT	CAPTAIN COOK
AACCILLLNOR	CLARION CALL
AACCILLLNOY	LACONICALLY
AACCILLLORY	CALORICALLY
AACCILLLOVY	VOCALICALLY
AACCILLLSSY	CLASSICALLY
AACCILLNNOY	CANONICALLY
AACCILLNOTU	CALCULATION
AACCILLNRTU	CURTAIN CALL
AACCILLOSSS	SOCIAL CLASS
AACCILLPRTY	PRACTICALLY
AACCILLSTUY	CAUSTICALLY
AACCILNOSTU	SACCULATION
AACCILOPPTY	APOCALYPTIC
AACCILOPSUY	CAPACIOUSLY
AACCILRRSUW	CIRCULAR SAW
AACCILSSSUY	CASSIUS CLAY
AACCIMNOPST	ACCOMPANIST
AACCINOORTT	COARCTATION
AACCINORSTV	VACCINATORS
AACCINOSSTU	ACCUSATIONS
AACCIORRSTY	ARISTOCRACY
AACCLLORSTU	CALCULATORS
AACCLMORTUU	ACCUMULATOR
AACCLNOPRTY	PLANTOCRACY
AACCLNORTTU	CONTRACTUAL
AACCLNORTTW	CONTRACT LAW
AACCLOSSTTU	CASTS A CLOUT
AACCNNOSTTU	ACCOUNTANTS
AACCORRRSSY	CARRY ACROSS
AACCORRSTTY	STRATOCRACY
AACDDDEEHOR	DODECAHEDRA
AACDDDEHHRR	HARD CHEDDAR
AACDDDEHOTU	ADDED A TOUCH
AACDDDEIJTU	ADJUDICATED
AACDDEEEFFT	FACED DEFEAT
AACDDEEEHLR	CLEARHEADED
AACDDEEFGNR	FACED DANGER
AACDDEEHLLN	HELD A CANDLE
AACDDEEHLLS	CALLED HEADS
AACDDEEHLNR	REACHED LAND
AACDDEEIKSV	ASKED ADVICE
AACDDEEIMPS	AIDES-DE-CAMP
AACDDEEINRT	DEAD CERTAIN
AACDDEEIPTT	DECAPITATED
AACDDEEITTV	DEACTIVATED
AACDDEELLOS	CLOSED A DEAL
AACDDEELRRW	DECLARED WAR
AACDDEEMNTU	EDUCATED MAN
AACDDEEMORR	MADE A RECORD
AACDDEFGILT	CADGED A LIFT
AACDDEFHNRT	HANDCRAFTED
AACDDEFORRW	FORCED A DRAW
AACDDEGLNOO	DODECAGONAL
AACDDEHINPP	HANDICAPPED
AACDDEHLLNO	HOLD A CANDLE
AACDDEHLNRS	CRASH-LANDED
AACDDEHLOST	COLD AS DEATH
AACDDEHMMOU	MADE MUCH ADO

AACDDEIIRTV	DIVARICATED	AACDEELPRRS	SCRAP DEALER
AACDDEIJSTU	ADJUDICATES	AACDEELRRSW	DECLARES WAR
AACDDEILNOR	ENDOCARDIAL	AACDEELRTUW	CATERWAULED
AACDDEILNRR	CARDINAL RED	AACDEEMNNOT	CAME TO AN END
AACDDEILNSS	SCANDALISED	AACDEEMNNTV	ADVANCEMENT
AACDDEILNSZ	SCANDALIZED	AACDEEMNNTW	CAME AND WENT
AACDDEINNOR	DANCED ON AIR	AACDEENNSTT	ATTENDANCES
AACDDEINRTU	CANDIDATURE	AACDEENQRSU	SQUARE DANCE
AACDDEKLPSS	PACKSADDLES	AACDEENRRRS	RADAR SCREEN
AACDDEKMRRS	MARKED CARDS	AACDEFGHINT	FACING DEATH
AACDDELPRSY	PLAYED CARDS	AACDEFGILNT	DEFALCATING
AACDDEMMORY	COMEDY DRAMA	AACDEFGILST	CADGES A LIFT
AACDDGNOSST	CATS AND DOGS	AACDEFGLMOU	CAMOUFLAGED
AACDDHILOPT	ADOPT A CHILD	AACDEFGMORS	GAME OF CARDS
AACDDIIINSS	CANDIDIASIS	AACDEFGORSY	DAYS OF GRACE
AACDDIIKNPT	CAPTAIN KIDD	AACDEFHIKLT	LACKED FAITH
AACDDIJORTU	ADJUDICATOR	AACDEFHKLRT	HALF-TRACKED
AACDDIOSTTU	AUTODIDACTS	AACDEFHLNOS	HALF A SECOND
AACDEEEENRT	CREATE A NEED	AACDEFHRRSU	HARD SURFACE
AACDEEEEFFST	FACES DEFEAT	AACDEFIILLM	FILED A CLAIM
AACDEEEFHTV	HAVE A DEFECT	AACDEFIILTT	FACILITATED
AACDEEEHHRT	HEAD TEACHER	AACDEFIINRS	AFRICANISED
AACDEEEHLSS	CHEESE SALAD	AACDEFIINRZ	AFRICANIZED
AACDEEEHMPS	MADE A SPEECH	AACDEFILNOT	DEFALCATION
AACDEEEHMPT	MADE THE PACE	AACDEFILNPS	FINDS A PLACE
AACDEEEHPRS	READ A SPEECH	AACDEFILOTT	FAILED TO ACT
AACDEEEHPST	ESCAPE DEATH	AACDEFILRTY	ACTED FAIRLY
AACDEEENRSV	SERVED AN ACE	AACDEFINRRS	AFRICANDERS
AACDEEFGINT	DEFAECATING	AACDEFINRST	FAR DISTANCE
AACDEEFGNRS	FACES DANGER	AACDEFINRUX	FRICANDEAUX
AACDEEFINOT	DEFAECATION	AACDEFLLNOR	FLORAL DANCE
AACDEEFINPT	PAINTED FACE	AACDEFLNOPU	FOUND A PLACE
AACDEEFLLPU	PULLED A FACE	AACDEFLORST	DEFALCATORS
AACDEEFOPSS	ACE OF SPADES	AACDEFMORRW	CAME FORWARD
AACDEEGGHNR	CHANGED GEAR	AACDEFOPRRT	FORCED APART
AACDEEGHMNS	MADE CHANGES	AACDEFORRSU	ROAD SURFACE
AACDEEGILLV	LEGAL ADVICE	AACDEFORRSW	FORCES A DRAW
AACDEEGKPPR	PREPACKAGED	AACDEGGILMO	DEMAGOGICAL
AACDEEHHSTT	CHEATS DEATH	AACDEGGILOP	PEDAGOGICAL
AACDEEHILMX	HEXADECIMAL	AACDEGHHNNS	CHANGE HANDS
AACDEEHIMMN	MACHINE MADE	AACDEGHHNRS	CHARGEHANDS
AACDEEHKLPT	DEAL THE PACK	AACDEGHIINT	TEACHING AID
AACDEEHKNOS	HAD ONE'S CAKE	AACDEGHINPR	RAPID CHANGE
AACDEEHLNRS	REACHES LAND	AACDEGHINRR	GARDEN CHAIR
AACDEEHLNSW	WASHED CLEAN	AACDEGHIRTT	TRAGIC DEATH
AACDEEHMOOT	COME TO A HEAD	AACDEGIIMNT	DIAMAGNETIC
AACDEEHORTT	TEACH TO READ	AACDEGIINRT	ERADICATING
AACDEEHRRST	SACRED HEART	AACDEGILNNR	CALENDARING
AACDEEIILNT	ACETANILIDE	AACDEGILNPR	RAPID GLANCE
AACDEEIIRTV	ERADICATIVE	AACDEGIMNNS	DAMASCENING
AACDEEIKMPT	PICKED A TEAM	AACDEGIMNRT	DEMARCATING
AACDEEIKNTV	TAKEN ADVICE	AACDEGINPST	SIGNED A PACT
AACDEEIKPRS	ASKED A PRICE	AACDEGINRRU	CARRIED A GUN
AACDEEIKSTV	TAKES ADVICE	AACDEGINRVW	CAVE DRAWING
AACDEEILMRT	MADE IT CLEAR	AACDEGISSTU	ACTS AS GUIDE
AACDEEILRTV	DECLARATIVE	AACDEGLOORS	SCORED A GOAL
AACDEEILSTT	ELASTICATED	AACDEGORSTU	SUGAR-COATED
AACDEEIMNPT	EMANCIPATED	AACDEHHIMMN	MACHINE HAND
AACDEEIMNRT	MADE CERTAIN	AACDEHILLPY	EDAPHICALLY
AACDEEINNSY	NICE AND EASY	AACDEHILORS	ICOSAHEDRAL
AACDEEINRST	ASCERTAINED	AACDEHIMNNY	CAME IN HANDY
AACDEEIPPRT	APPRECIATED	AACDEHINPPR	HANDICAPPER
AACDEEIPSTT	DECAPITATES	AACDEHINRST	CANTHARIDES
AACDEEIRTTV	REACTIVATED	AACDEHIPRST	CHEAP AS DIRT
AACDEEISTTV	DEACTIVATES	AACDEHKMMOU	MAKE MUCH ADO
AACDEEKLMOO	COOKED A MEAL	AACDEHKLMPRY	PACHYDERMAL
AACDEEKMORR	MAKE A RECORD	AACDEHLNOST	CLOSE AT HAND
AACDEELLOSS	CLOSES A DEAL	AACDEHLOPVY	PLAYED HAVOC
AACDEELLSTT	CASTELLATED	AACDEHLRSST	CLASS HATRED
AACDEELMSTU	EMASCULATED	AACDEHMNSTT	SET AND MATCH
AACDEELNPRS	SEND A PARCEL	AACDEHMOPRT	CAMPHORATED

AACDEHMPPST	DAMP PATCHES	AACDENNRSUV	UNDER CANVAS
AACDEHMPRST	MARCHED PAST	AACDENOSSWY	SECONDS AWAY
AACDEHNRSSW	ANDREW SACHS	AACDFFIORRT	ROAD TRAFFIC
AACDEHORSTY	CATHODE RAYS	AACDFHINRST	HANDICRAFTS
AACDEHOSSTT	ACTED AS HOST	AACDFHNORTY	FACTORY HAND
AACDEHRRTYY	CARRY THE DAY	AACDFIILRRT	FRATRICIDAL
AACDEIILPRR	PERICARDIAL	AACDFIINOOS	AFICIONADOS
AACDEIILPST	CAPITALISED	AACDGGIIJNN	DANCING A JIG
AACDEIILPTZ	CAPITALIZED	AACDGHILNOV	HAVING A COLD
AACDEIILRVW	RADICAL VIEW	AACDGHINTUU	DUTCH GUIANA
AACDEIINNNO	INDIAN OCEAN	AACDGIILNTU	ACIDULATING
AACDEIINNNR	INCARNADINE	AACDGIINRRV	DRIVING A CAR
AACDEIINORT	ERADICATION	AACDGILNNPS	LANDSCAPING
AACDEIINPTT	ANTICIPATED	AACDGILNPRY	PLAYING CARD
AACDEIINTTV	VATICINATED	AACDGIMRRTU	DRAMATURGIC
AACDEIIORTV	RADIOACTIVE	AACDGINNNNO	CANNONADING
AACDEIIPRST	PAEDIATRICS	AACDGKNOPPU	PACK UP AND GO
AACDEIIRSTV	DIVARICATES	AACDGNNNORY	GRAND CANYON
AACDEILLLST	CALLED TAILS	AACDGORRSSTU	COASTGUARDS
AACDEILLLTY	DIALECTALLY	AACDHHIIMNSW	HAM SANDWICH
AACDEILLOTV	LA DOLCE VITA	AACDHHNORSU	HAD A CRUSH ON
AACDEILLPPT	CAPPED IT ALL	AACDHIINPSU	UPANISHADIC
AACDEILMNOT	DECLAMATION	AACDHIIOPRS	APHRODISIAC
AACDEILMNTU	CALUMNIATED	AACDHIJMNSW	JAM SANDWICH
AACDEILNORT	DECLARATION	AACDHILMOPY	HOLIDAY CAMP
AACDEILNOTU	EDUCATIONAL	AACDHILOPRS	RHAPSODICAL
AACDEILNPSU	SAUCEPAN LID	AACDHIMMNTU	IM A DUTCHMAN
AACDEILNRSS	RADICALNESS	AACDHLMOORS	DRAMA SCHOOL
	SCANDALISER	AACDHLNOSYY	HALCYON DAYS
AACDEILNRSZ	SCANDALIZER	AACDHLNPSSS	CLASPS HANDS
AACDEILNRTU	RITUAL DANCE	AACDHLOPRSY	PLAYS A CHORD
AACDEILNSSS	SCANDALISES	AACDHNOPSWY	PAY CASH DOWN
AACDEILNSSZ	SCANDALIZES	AACDIILLMOT	LAID CLAIM TO
AACDEILPRTY	DIRECT A PLAY	AACDIILMNTT	MID-ATLANTIC
AACDEILPTTU	CAPITULATED	AACDIILNNRS	CARDINAL SIN
AACDEILRSTT	STRAITLACED	AACDIILNOTU	ACIDULATION
AACDEILRTTU	ARTICULATED	AACDIILNSTV	VANDALISTIC
AACDEILRTTY	DAIRY CATTLE	AACDIILORTT	DICTATORIAL
AACDEIMNNRW	NICE AND WARM	AACDIIMNOPS	DIPSOMANIAC
AACDEIMNORT	DEMARCATION	AACDIJJKLLN	JACK AND JILL
AACDEIMNORY	AERODYNAMIC	AACDIKNNRRU	RACK AND RUIN
AACDEIMNSTT	ADMITTANCES	AACDIKRSSTY	DRY AS A STICK
AACDEIMRRRS	CARRIED ARMS	AACDILLLOOR	CORALLOIDAL
AACDEINNNTU	ANNUNCIATED	AACDILLMNYY	DYNAMICALLY
AACDEINNORS	DANCES ON AIR	AACDILLNORS	CORAL ISLAND
AACDEINNOTT	DECANTATION	AACDILLRSTY	DRASTICALLY
AACDEINOSTW	WAIT A SECOND	AACDILMOPSS	SPASMODICAL
AACDEIOPRTT	DECAPITATOR	AACDILNNOOV	VAL DOONICAN
AACDEIORSTU	CAUSED A RIOT	AACDILOSUUY	AUDACIOUSLY
AACDEIORTTV	DEACTIVATOR	AACDINOSTTU	AT A DISCOUNT
AACDEIOSTTW	WAISTCOATED	AACDMMNNOST	COMMANDANTS
AACDEIRSSTU	CAUSED A STIR	AACDMOORSTU	CATADROMOUS
AACDEKMMNOT	TAKE COMMAND	AACDMRRRSUY	MADRAS CURRY
AACDEKNRTTU	UNDER ATTACK	AACDRRSTTU	CUSTARD TART
AACDELLNNOO	ALL ONE CAN DO	AACEEEGHNTV	GAVE THE CANE
	DO ALL ONE CAN	AACEEEHHSTV	HAVE THE ACES
AACDELLNOTY	ANECDOTALLY	AACEEEHIRRS	RAISE A CHEER
AACDELLRSTY	SCARLET LADY	AACEEEHKKTT	TAKE THE CAKE
AACDELMNNOR	ROMAN CANDLE	AACEEEHKMPS	MAKE A SPEECH
AACDELMOPRS	CAMELOPARDS	AACEEEHKMPT	MAKE THE PACE
AACDELMORTY	DECLAMATORY	AACEEEHRSTV	HAVE A SECRET
AACDELNNSTY	ASCENDANTLY	AACEEEKMNSS	MAKES A SCENE
AACDELNRSST	STANDS CLEAR	AACEEELMRTV	MEAT CLEAVER
AACDELNSSST	SANDCASTLES	AACEEENPSUY	UNEASY PEACE
AACDELOPRRY	PLAY A RECORD	AACEEENRSSV	SERVES AN ACE
AACDELORRTY	DECLARATORY	AACEEEPRTTY	PEACE TREATY
AACDELORSTW	DRAW TO SCALE	AACEEFGHLRS	FALSE CHARGE
AACDEMNNOPR	ORDNANCE MAP	AACEEFGORRY	YEAR OF GRACE
AACDEMNOSTU	CAT AND MOUSE	AACEEFHORST	ACE OF HEARTS
	CAT-AND-MOUSE	AACEEFHRSTY	REACH SAFETY
AACDEMORRRU	ARMOURED CAR	AACEEFILLOP	ALL OF A PIECE

AACEEFILRTY	FACE REALITY	AACEEIPPRST	APPRECIATES
AACEEFIMNSS	MISFEASANCE	AACEEIPRRTV	PREVARICATE
AACEEFIRRTV	RAREFACTIVE	AACEEIRRSTT	CREATE A STIR
AACEEFIRSSW	CAESARS WIFE		SECRETARIAT
AACEEFKNORT	TAKEN CARE OF	AACEEIRSTTV	REACTIVATES
AACEEFKORST	TAKES CARE OF	AACEEKLMPRT	MARKET PLACE
AACEEFLLPTT	CLEFT PALATE		MARKETPLACE
AACEEFNNNOS	NONFEASANCE	AACEEKLOPST	LOSE A PACKET
AACEEGGHNRS	CHANGES GEAR	AACEEKLPRSW	SPACEWALKER
AACEEGHKMNS	MAKE CHANGES	AACEEKMRSTU	MAKES A TRUCE
AACEEGHKNRT	TAKEN CHARGE	AACEEKNORRT	TAKE A CORNER
AACEEGHKRST	TAKES CHARGE	AACEEKNSSTU	TAKE A CENSUS
AACEEGHKSTV	GAVE THE SACK	AACEEKORSTU	TAKE A COURSE
AACEEGHLMTU	LEAGUE MATCH	AACEELMPRRU	CAME A PURLER
AACEEGHMNRT	TEACH GERMAN	AACEELMSSTU	EMASCULATES
AACEEGHNOPR	CHAPERONAGE	AACEELNNPUZ	PAUL CEZANNE
AACEEGHRRST	GATE-CRASHER	AACEELNPRST	SENT A PARCEL
AACEEGHRRTX	EXTRA CHARGE	AACEELNPSTU	ENCAPSULATE
AACEEGIKMNP	MAKING PEACE	AACEELPRSTV	SPACE TRAVEL
AACEEGILLLY	ELEGIACALLY	AACEELRRTTT	TREACLE TART
AACEEGILLNS	ALLEGIANCES	AACEELRSTTZ	LATEST CRAZE
AACEEGILLNV	EVANGELICAL	AACEEMNNORRW	CAREER WOMAN
AACEEGJMNSY	JAMES CAGNEY	AACEEMNOSWY	CAME ONE'S WAY
AACEEGKORTU	TAKE COURAGE	AACEEMRTTTX	MEAT EXTRACT
AACEEGKPPRS	PREPACKAGES	AACEFFHINRS	AFFRANCHISE
AACEEGMMNRV	GEMMA CRAVEN	AACEFFIIRTV	AFFRICATIVE
AACEEGNOSST	ACTS ONE'S AGE	AACEFFILNOT	AFFECTIONAL
AACEEHHLLRT	HEAR THE CALL	AACEFFILNRT	TRAFFIC LANE
AACEEHILRRT	CLEAR THE AIR	AACEFFILNOTT	AFFECTATION
AACEEHIMNPT	TAPE MACHINE	AACEFFLRSTU	FLAT SURFACE
AACEEHIMNTT	AT THE CINEMA	AACEFFMNOPR	MAP OF FRANCE
AACEEHIMPPR	PAPIER MACHE	AACEFGHINOR	CHANGE OF AIR
	PAPIER-MACHE	AACEFGHINRR	FAR-REACHING
AACEEHINSTT	ANAESTHETIC	AACEFGIKMNS	MAKING FACES
AACEEHKMPRR	CHEAP REMARK	AACEFGILNSV	FINGALS CAVE
AACEEHKNOSS	HAS ONE'S CAKE	AACEFGLMOSU	CAMOUFLAGES
AACEEHKPSST	CHEAPSKATES	AACEFGLOOTT	COTTAGE LOAF
AACEEHLLLRT	THE ALL CLEAR	AACEFGORTTY	FACTORY GATE
AACEEHLMNNS	SAME CHANNEL	AACEFHKOSTW	SACK OF WHEAT
AACEEHLMRTW	CALM WEATHER	AACEFHLNNOU	HALF AN OUNCE
AACEEHLNNSV	CLEAN-SHAVEN	AACEFHMSTTY	SAFETY MATCH
AACEEHLNPST	ANTECHAPELS	AACEFIILLMS	FILES A CLAIM
AACEEHLNSSW	WASHES CLEAN	AACEFIILNOT	INTERFACIAL
AACEEHLORTT	LEATHER COAT	AACEFIILNRV	ACRIFLAVINE
AACEEHLPRRY	LAY PREACHER	AACEFIILQTU	AQUATIC LIFE
AACEEHLRTWY	CLEAR THE WAY	AACEFIILSTT	FACILITATES
AACEEHMORTT	CAME TO EARTH	AACEFIINRSS	AFRICANISES
AACEEHMPRST	SPERMATHECA	AACEFIINRSZ	AFRICANIZES
AACEEHPSTTY	STAY THE PACE	AACEFIJRRTT	JET AIRCRAFT
AACEEIIMNRS	AMERICANISE	AACEFILLLNP	FALL IN PLACE
AACEEIIMNRZ	AMERICANIZE	AACEFILLORR	FOR ALL I CARE
AACEEIIMPST	SEPTICAEMIA	AACEFILMMOT	CLAIM TO FAME
AACEEIKKTTW	TAKE A WICKET	AACEFILMNOT	MALEFACTION
AACEEIKLMRT	MAKE IT CLEAR	AACEFILMRSU	SURFACE MAIL
AACEEIKMNRT	MAKE CERTAIN	AACEFILTTUV	FACULTATIVE
AACEEIKPTTV	TAKE CAPTIVE	AACEFIMNRRT	AIRCRAFTMEN
AACEEIKRSTU	TAKE A CRUISE	AACEFINNRSS	AFRICANNESS
AACEEILLMNS	MESALLIANCE	AACEFINORRT	RAREFACTION
	MISCELLANEA	AACEFINORSU	FARINACEOUS
AACEEILNPRS	PARASELENIC	AACEFINORTT	FRACTIONATE
AACEEILNRTT	INTERCALATE	AACEFINORWY	FORCE A WAY IN
AACEEILPRST	ALTARPIECES	AACEFISSTTW	TWICE AS FAST
AACEEILRRST	SECRETARIAL	AACEFKLOSTT	LACK OF TASTE
AACEEIMNNNT	MAINTENANCE	AACEFKLRSST	FLARESTACKS
AACEEIMNPST	EMANCIPATES	AACEFLMORST	MALEFACTORS
AACEEINNNRT	CENTENARIAN	AACEFLNSSTU	FACTUALNESS
AACEEINNRRT	REINCARNATE	AACEFMNRTUU	MANUFACTURE
AACEEINNRSS	RENAISSANCE	AACEFMRSTTU	MATT SURFACE
AACEEINPRSY	PAY INCREASE	AACEFOPRRST	FORCES APART
AACEEINRSTT	TEA CANISTER	AACEGGGKLRU	LUGGAGE RACK
AACEEINRSTX	TAX INCREASE	AACEGGINPSS	ESCAPING GAS

AACEGGINRSV	SAVING GRACE
AACEGGINRSY	SAYING GRACE
AACEGHHINRT	ACHING HEART
AACEGHHNOTT	CHAETOGNATH
AACEGHILNOR	ARCHEGONIAL
AACEGHILNTW	TEACHING LAW
AACEGHILNUV	HAVING A CLUE
AACEGHIMNNR	MAN IN CHARGE
AACEGHINRTT	TEACHING ART
AACEGHLLMNS	SMALL CHANGE
AACEGHLLMRS	SMALL CHARGE
AACEGHLLSSV	CHEVAL GLASS
AACEGHLOORY	ARCHAEOLOGY
AACEGHMOPRS	MACROPHAGES
AACEGHNOPRU	UP ON A CHARGE
AACEGHOSTTT	ACTS THE GOAT
AACEGHPRTTU	GUTTA-PERCHA
AACEGIIMRRS	MISCARRIAGE
AACEGIINNRT	CERTAIN GAIN
AACEGIJLNTU	EJACULATING
AACEGIKLMNR	MAKING CLEAR
AACEGIKLNPT	TAKING PLACE
AACEGIKLNPW	WALKING PACE
AACEGIKLNRW	WALKING RACE
AACEGIKMORS	SMOKE A CIGAR
AACEGILLLNY	ANGELICALLY
AACEGILLLOR	ALLEGORICAL
AACEGILLMNN	NAME-CALLING
AACEGILLMTY	GAMETICALLY
AACEGILLNOT	LEGAL ACTION
AACEGILLOOR	AEROLOGICAL
AACEGILLOPS	PLAGIOCLASE
AACEGILLMNRR	OLEAN MARGIN
AACEGILNPRY	PANEGYRICAL
AACEGIMNPRS	CAMPAIGNERS
AACEGIMQRSU	MAGIC SQUARE
AACEGINNRTW	WATERING CAN
AACEGINNSTT	CASTING A NET
AACEGINORRS	COARSE GRAIN
AACEGINORRW	ROWING A RACE
AACEGINPPRT	RATE CAPPING
AACEGINPSSV	SAVING SPACE
AACEGINRRSU	CARRIES A GUN
AACEGKOPRTU	PACKAGE TOUR
AACEGLNRRTU	RECTANGULAR
AACEGLOORSS	SCORES A GOAL
AACEGLORSTU	CATALOGUERS
AACEGMNOORR	GRAECO-ROMAN
AACEGNRRTTU	GRANT A TRUCE
AACEGORRSSS	COARSE GRASS
AACEGRRSSTU	CASTER SUGAR
AACEHIILSTT	ATHEISTICAL
AACEHIIMMNS	MANICHAEISM
AACEHIINNTW	WITHIN AN ACE
AACEHIKLNRW	ALAN WHICKER
AACEHIKMPST	MAKES A PITCH
AACEHIKRSTT	SICK AT HEART
AACEHILLMNO	MELANCHOLIA
AACEHILLNTU	HALLUCINATE
AACEHILMRSV	VICE-MARSHAL
AACEHILNORT	LIE AT ANCHOR
AACEHILNTTT	THE ATLANTIC
AACEHILRSTT	THEATRICALS
AACEHIMMSTT	MATHEMATICS
AACEHIMNNOY	HAEMOCYANIN
AACEHIMNRXY	X-RAY MACHINE
AACEHIMORTT	HAEMATOCRIT
AACEHIMORTZ	ACHROMATIZE
AACEHIMOSTT	HAEMOSTATIC
AACEHINOPRS	COIN A PHRASE
AACEHJKMMRS	JACKHAMMERS

AACEHKMMRST	MATCHMAKERS
AACEHKMNPSU	KAMPUCHEANS
AACEHKMOSTW	WEAK STOMACH
AACEHKMRSTW	WATCHMAKERS
AACEHKNNPTU	TAKEN A PUNCH
AACEHKNOTTT	ON THE ATTACK
AACEHKNPSTU	TAKES A PUNCH
AACEHKORSVW	WREAKS HAVOC
AACEHLLLNRT	CENTRAL HALL
AACEHLLOPRY	CHAPEL ROYAL
AACEHLMNRTW	LAW MERCHANT
	LAWMERCHANT
AACEHLMNSTU	STEAM LAUNCH
AACEHLMOOTT	COME TO A HALT
AACEHLMORST	STOLE A MARCH
AACEHLMOSST	LOSES A MATCH
AACEHLPRSTT	LAST CHAPTER
AACEHMMNNRT	MERCHANTMAN
AACEHMMOTWY	COME WHAT MAY
AACEHMNOPVY	HAVE COMPANY
AACEHMNPSTY	CASH PAYMENT
AACEHMNSTTT	ATTACHMENTS
AACEHMOPRST	CAMPHORATES
AACEHMPRSST	MARCHES PAST
AACEHMSSSTU	MASSACHUSET
AACEHNOPPRW	NEW APPROACH
AACEHNOSSSV	CANVAS SHOES
AACEHOPRSTT	CATASTROPHE
AACEHPRRSTY	SEARCH PARTY
AACEHPRSTTT	ACTS THE PART
AACEHPRSTUX	PURCHASE TAX
AACEHQSSSTU	SASQUATCHES
AACEIIKLMNT	KINEMATICAL
AACEIILLMNS	MISALLIANCE
AACEIILLNRS	ANCILLARIES
AACEIILLPRS	CAPILLARIES
AACEIILNPRR	PERICRANIAL
AACEIILPPTV	APPLICATIVE
AACEIILPSST	CAPITALISES
AACEIILPSTZ	CAPITALIZES
AACEIILSSTU	CAUSALITIES
AACEIILSTTU	ACTUALITIES
AACEIIMMNNS	AMERICANISM
AACEIIMNRTV	CARMINATIVE
AACEIINORTT	RATIOCINATE
AACEIINPSTT	ANTICIPATES
AACEIINSTTV	VATICINATES
AACEIIOSSTV	ASSOCIATIVE
AACEIIPPRTT	PARTICIPATE
AACEIIPRSTT	PATRICIATES
AACEIJLNOTU	EJACULATION
AACEIJQSTTU	JACQUES TATI
AACEIKKNRTT	TAKEN A TRICK
AACEIKKRSTT	TAKES A TRICK
AACEIKNNOTT	TAKEN ACTION
AACEIKNOSTT	TAKES ACTION
AACEILLLSTY	ELASTICALLY
AACEILLMNSU	ANIMALCULES
AACEILLMPRY	MIRACLE PLAY
AACEILLNPRU	LUPERCALIAN
AACEILLNTTY	TETANICALLY
AACEILLPRRT	CATERPILLAR
AACEILLPSTY	ASEPTICALLY
AACEILLRRTY	ERRATICALLY
AACEILLSSTY	SALICYLATES
AACEILLTUXY	AUXETICALLY
AACEILMMNRS	REMAINS CALM
AACEILMMRTW	WARM CLIMATE
AACEILMNORT	RECLAMATION
AACEILMNOTX	EXCLAMATION
AACEILMNSTU	CALUMNIATES

581

AACEILMPRSS	PRESS A CLAIM	AACEMNOTTUX	EXACT AMOUNT
AACEILMPSTT	METAPLASTIC	AACEMOOPSTT	CAME TO A STOP
AACEILMRTTU	MATRICULATE	AACEMOOSTTU	TOMATO SAUCE
AACEILNORST	LACERATIONS	AACENOOPSSU	SAPONACEOUS
AACEILNORTT	ALTERCATION	AACENOPRRSU	RAN UP A SCORE
AACEILNOSTU	AUCTION SALE	AACFFHIKLOT	LACK OF FAITH
AACEILNRRTY	INTERCALARY	AACFFIINORT	AFFRICATION
AACEILOPRST	TROPICAL SEA	AACFFIKLLOR	LACK OF FLAIR
AACEILOPSST	CASTILE SOAP	AACFFIMRRST	ARMS TRAFFIC
AACEILPRSTW	PRACTISE LAW	AACFFIORRTT	TRAFFICATOR
AACEILPRTTU	PARTICULATE	AACFGHHISTU	CAUGHT A FISH
AACEILPSTTU	CAPITULATES	AACFGIINNST	FANTACISING
AACEILRSSUV	VASCULARISE		FASCINATING
AACEILRSTTU	ARTICULATES	AACFHINORRT	NORTH AFRICA
AACEILRSUVZ	VASCULARIZE	AACFHIORSTU	SOUTH AFRICA
AACEILSSTTT	STALACTITES	AACFHKNRSST	CRANKSHAFTS
AACEILSTUVY	CAUSATIVELY	AACFHLNORSW	HALF-A-CROWNS
AACEIMMPRSU	PARAMECIUMS	AACFIILLNNY	FINANCIALLY
AACEIMNNOPT	CAPTAIN NEMO	AACFIILORTT	FACILITATOR
AACEIMNNOTT	CONTAMINATE	AACFIIMNRSS	AFRICANISMS
AACEIMNOORT	EROTOMANIAC	AACFIINNOST	FASCINATION
AACEIMNOPRT	EMANCIPATOR	AACFIINRSST	AFRICANISTS
AACEIMNORSU	OCEANARIUMS	AACFIIOPRST	ITS A FAIR COP
AACEIMNPRSY	AMERICAN SPY	AACFIJKOPRS	PAIR OF JACKS
AACEIMOPRTV	COMPARATIVE	AACFIKMORRS	FIRM AS A ROCK
AACEIMRRRSS	CARRIES ARMS	AACFILLNOTY	FACTIONALLY
AACEINNNSTU	ANNUNCIATES	AACFILLNRTY	FRANTICALLY
AACEINNORTT	RECANTATION	AACFIMNNOOT	MAN OF ACTION
AACEINNOSTW	ISAAC NEWTON	AACFINOOPTT	COAT OF PAINT
AACEINNRTTT	INTERACTANT	AACFJNOORST	ST JOAN OF ARC
AACEINORRTY	REACTIONARY	AACFKLMSUUV	VACUUM FLASK
AACEINORSTU	AERONAUTICS	AACFLLNTUUW	UNLAWFUL ACT
AACEINORSTV	VACATIONERS	AACFLNORRTU	CURRANT LOAF
AACEINRSSTU	SANCTUARIES	AACFMNORTUY	MANUFACTORY
AACEINSSTWY	SWANSEA CITY	AACFNRSSTTU	SURFACTANTS
AACEIOPPRRT	APPRECIATOR	AACFOORRRTY	CARRY TOO FAR
AACEIORSSSW	CASSOWARIES	AACGGHHMOOR	GRAHAM GOOCH
AACEIORSSTU	CAUSES A RIOT	AACGGIIMNNP	CAMPAIGNING
AACEIPRRSST	STAIR CARPET	AACGGIINSTT	CASTIGATING
AACEIRSSSTU	CAUSES A STIR	AACGGIKNNPU	PACKING A GUN
AACEJKNRSTT	NATTERJACKS	AACGGILNOTU	CATALOGUING
AACEJLORTUY	EJACULATORY		COAGULATING
AACEJNOORTT	NOT CARE A JOT	AACGHHILMTT	LIGHT A MATCH
AACEKKKNNOT	TAKEN A KNOCK	AACGHHOPRST	TACHOGRAPHS
AACEKKKNOST	TAKES A KNOCK	AACGHHPRTYY	TACHYGRAPHY
AACEKKLLPRS	LACK SPARKLE	AACGHIIMNNT	MACHINATING
AACEKKLNOOS	LOOK ASKANCE	AACGHIKMMNT	MATCHMAKING
AACEKKMRSST	MAKES TRACKS	AACGHIKMNTW	WATCHMAKING
AACEKLLPRTU	PETULA CLARK	AACGHILLPRY	CALLIGRAPHY
AACEKLMNNRS	LACK MANNERS		GRAPHICALLY
AACEKLMRSTY	SMART-ALECKY	AACGHINOORT	CARING A HOOT
AACEKLNOSSS	SLACK SEASON	AACGHINOPPR	APPROACHING
AACEKLNPRRT	CENTRAL PARK	AACGHINPRTU	PARACHUTING
AACEKLOPSTT	LOST A PACKET	AACGHIPRRST	GRAPHIC ARTS
AACEKMRRTTY	CATTY REMARK	AACGHLMOORU	CHAULMOOGRA
AACEKNNOTTU	TAKEN A COUNT	AACGHLSSTTU	TAUGHT CLASS
AACEKNOSTTU	TAKES A COUNT	AACGHOPRRTY	CARTOGRAPHY
AACEKOOPSTU	TOOK UP A CASE	AACGHOPRSSU	SARCOPHAGUS
AACELLLMPRS	SMALL PARCEL	AACGIIINNRS	RAISING CAIN
AACELLLNOTT	LOCAL TALENT	AACGIIKKNST	KICK AGAINST
AACELLLRSST	SALTCELLARS	AACGIIKLLNT	KILLING A CAT
AACELLNOTTV	VOCAL TALENT	AACGIILLMNY	LAYING CLAIM
AACELLNRRTU	RETURN A CALL	AACGIILLNTV	VACILLATING
AACELLNRSTY	ANCESTRALLY	AACGIILLOOX	AXIOLOGICAL
AACELLPSSST	CASTS A SPELL	AACGIILMNNS	ANGLICANISM
AACELMORSTU	EMASCULATOR	AACGIILMSTT	STALAGMITIC
AACELMORTXY	EXCLAMATORY	AACGIILNNOR	CAROLINGIAN
AACELMPPRSY	SCRAPPY MEAL	AACGIIMNSTT	MASTICATING
AACELNOPSTU	CANTALOUPES	AACGIINNNRT	INCARNATING
AACELOPPRTU	APPEAL COURT	AACGIINNOTV	VACATIONING
AACELPRSSTT	PLASTER CAST	AACGIINNPSU	CAUSING PAIN

AACGIINNQTU	ACQUAINTING
AACGIINOSST	ASSOCIATING
AACGIINOSTT	CASTIGATION
AACGIINPTTV	CAPTIVATING
AACGIJNNRTU	JAUNTING CAR
AACGIKLNOWY	LOCKING AWAY
AACGIKLNRTY	TRACKLAYING
AACGIKNOPTY	TAKING A COPY
AACGIKNTUWY	TUCKING AWAY
AACGILLNNOW	ALLOWANCING
AACGILLNORY	ORGANICALLY
AACGILMNSTY	STAYING CALM
AACGILNOOTU	COAGULATION
AACGILNOPST	CAPTAINS LOG
AACGILNOTUV	AUTOCLAVING
AACGILNPTTU	CATAPULTING
AACGILOPRRU	RACIAL GROUP
AACGILOSSUY	SAGACIOUSLY
AACGIMNOPRT	COMING APART
AACGINNNRRU	RUNNING A CAR
AACGINNRSTT	TRANSACTING
AACGINPRVYZ	CRAZY PAVING
AACGINTTUWY	CUTTING AWAY
AACGIORSSTT	CASTIGATORS
AACGLLNOOTY	OCTAGONALLY
AACGLMNOOPY	CAMPANOLOGY
AACGLNORSUY	YOUNG RASCAL
AACGORRSSTU	CASTOR SUGAR
AACHHNORSSU	HAS A CRUSH ON
AACHIIINRST	CHRISTIANIA
AACHIILLNRV	ARCH VILLAIN
AACHIIMNNOT	MACHINATION
AACHIINPPST	CAPTAINSHIP
AACHIJKKNSW	JACK HAWKINS
AACHIKNOOPT	CAPTAIN HOOK
AACHILLLLPY	PHALLICALLY
AACHILLMNOS	MASONIC HALL
AACHILLOPRY	PAROCHIALLY
AACHILMOPPP	HIPPOCAMPAL
AACHILNNPST	PLAINCHANTS
AACHIMMORST	ACHROMATISM
AACHIMNNORS	ANACHRONISM
AACHIMNORSS	MARASCHINOS
AACHIMPRSST	PHARMACISTS
AACHINNNOTY	ANTHOCYANIN
AACHINRSSTU	CARTHUSIANS
AACHIPRSTTU	PARACHUTIST
AACHLMORRTY	LACHRYMATOR
AACHLNNOOTU	ANACOLUTHON
AACHLNORTTT	TARTAN CLOTH
AACHMMRRSUU	HARUM-SCARUM
AACHMNOSTWY	YACHTSWOMAN
AACHNNOORSU	ANACHRONOUS
AACHQRTTUWZ	QUARTZ WATCH
AACIIILMNST	ANIMALISTIC
AACIIILNNOT	LACINIATION
AACIIILNOST	LAICISATION
AACIIILNOTZ	LAICIZATION
AACIIILPPRT	PARTICIPIAL
AACIIJNOTTT	JACTITATION
AACIIKKNPRT	CAPTAIN KIRK
AACIILLMNRW	CRIMINAL LAW
AACIILLMRTU	MULTIRACIAL
AACIILLNNOY	ANIONICALLY
AACIILLNOTV	VACILLATION
AACIILLNTTY	TITANICALLY
AACIILLNUXY	AUXINICALLY
AACIILLPRTY	CAPILLARITY
	PIRATICALLY
AACIILMNORT	LACRIMATION
AACIILMNOST	ANOMALISTIC

AACIILMNPTU	PUT IN A CLAIM
AACIILMNRRW	WAR CRIMINAL
AACIILNOSTT	ATONALISTIC
AACIILNPRTU	PURITANICAL
AACIILNRRTU	CURTAIN RAIL
AACIILNTTYY	ANALYTICITY
AACIILPSSTT	CAPITALISTS
AACIILPTTYY	ATYPICALITY
AACIILSSTTT	STATISTICAL
AACIIMNOSTT	MASTICATION
AACIIMORTTY	AROMATICITY
AACIINNNORT	INCARNATION
AACIINNNOTT	INCANTATION
AACIINOOSST	ASSOCIATION
AACIINOPRTT	ANTICIPATOR
AACIINOPTTV	CAPTIVATION
AACIINORTTV	VATICINATOR
AACIINPPRTT	PARTICIPANT
AACIKLNOSTY	LAY IN A STOCK
AACIKLPRSTY	PLAYS A TRICK
AACILLLPSTY	PLASTICALLY
AACILLMMNUU	ANIMALCULUM
AACILLMOSTY	LAYS CLAIM TO
	SOMATICALLY
AACILLNOORW	COLONIAL WAR
AACILLNOOST	ALLOCATIONS
AACILLNOPRS	RAPSCALLION
AACILLOPRSY	PROSAICALLY
AACILLORSTV	VACILLATORS
AACILLOSSUY	SALACIOUSLY
AACILLPRTUU	APICULTURAL
AACILLPSSTY	SPASTICALLY
AACILMMOPRT	MORAL IMPACT
AACILMNNOPT	COMPLAINANT
AACILMNOPST	COMPLAISANT
AACILMNORTU	CALUMNIATOR
AACILNNNOTU	CANNULATION
AACILNNOPSY	CALYPSONIAN
AACILNOOTUV	VACUOLATION
AACILNOPRTY	COPLANARITY
AACILNORTVY	CLAIRVOYANT
AACILNRRTUY	CULINARY ART
AACILNRSTUY	CUT IN SALARY
AACILNRTUVY	CAVALRY UNIT
AACILOPPRST	APPLICATORS
AACILOPPRTY	APPLICATORY
AACILOPRSUY	RAPACIOUSLY
AACILORRTTU	ARTICULATOR
AACILPRRSTU	PARTICULARS
AACILRSTUVY	VASCULARITY
AACIMNNNOTT	CONTAMINANT
AACIMNOOSTT	ANASTOMOTIC
AACIMNORRTT	ROMANTIC ART
AACIMORSTTY	MASTICATORY
AACINNNORTU	ANNUNCIATOR
AACINNOOSTZ	ACTINOZOANS
AACINNORSSW	WINS AN OSCAR
AACINNORSTT	TRANSACTION
AACINNORTTY	INCANTATORY
AACINNRRSTU	TRANSURANIC
AACINORSTTT	ATTRACTIONS
AACINORSTTU	ASTRONAUTIC
AACIOORSSTY	ASSOCIATORY
AACIORRSSTT	ARISTOCRATS
AACLLMMOPSY	MYCOPLASMAL
AACLLMORSST	CALLS TO ARMS
AACLMMOPSSY	MYCOPLASMAS
AACLNNNOOST	CONSONANTAL
AACMNOPPRTY	PART COMPANY
AACMOOPRRST	COMPARATORS
AACMOORSSTU	SARCOMATOUS

AACNNOPSTTU	PUTS ON AN ACT	AADDEHHLNOV	HAVE AND HOLD
AACNORRSSTT	TRANSACTORS	AADDEHILLLN	HILL AND DALE
AADDDEEGHIN	DEADHEADING	AADDEHIMNNS	HANDMAIDENS
AADDDEEGNNO	DEAD AND GONE	AADDEHNORTY	READY TO HAND
AADDDEEMMNS	MADE DEMANDS	AADDEIILNTV	INVALIDATED
AADDDEIILPT	DILAPIDATED	AADDEIJORTY	RADIATED JOY
AADDDEINNOS	SAID AND DONE	AADDEIKNNRT	EAT AND DRINK
AADDDGILORS	LISA GODDARD	AADDEILLNOY	ADENOIDALLY
AADDDISSTVY	ST.DAVIDS DAY	AADDEILNPTY	PAINTED LADY
AADDDLLNORY	LORD AND LADY	AADDEILNWWY	DWINDLE AWAY
AADDEEEGLMP	MADE A PLEDGE	AADDEIMNORS	MADE INROADS
AADDEEEHKTW	WAKE THE DEAD	AADDEINNTTY	NEAT AND TIDY
AADDEEEHPRS	SPEARHEADED	AADDEINRSST	STANDARDISE
AADDEEENRST	DEAD EARNEST	AADDEINRSTZ	STANDARDIZE
AADDEEFGHOR	FORGED AHEAD	AADDEINSSST	STANDS ASIDE
AADDEEFGIMR	FIRE DAMAGED	AADDEJLMSTU	MALADJUSTED
AADDEEFGLRT	DEFLAGRATED	AADDEKLLTTW	TALK TWADDLE
AADDEEFGRSU	SAFEGUARDED	AADDELLLNOR	LEND A DOLLAR
AADDEEFHLTY	FATHEADEDLY	AADDELNORRW	LAW AND ORDER
AADDEEFIMTT	ADMIT DEFEAT	AADDELOPRUY	PRAYED ALOUD
AADDEEFIOTV	AVOID DEFEAT	AADDELPQRUU	QUADRUPEDAL
AADDEEGHNNR	HAND GRENADE	AADDELPRSTY	PLAYED DARTS
AADDEEGHRSU	SURGED AHEAD	AADDEMNNOPY	PAY ON DEMAND
AADDEEGLRRW	EDWARD ELGAR	AADDENNORTW	DRAW TO AN END
AADDEEGNPRS	GARDEN SPADE	AADDENRSSTT	SET STANDARD
AADDEEHHNVY	HEAVY-HANDED	AADDENRSSTY	STANDS READY
AADDEEHHRRT	HARDHEARTED	AADDFFMNOOR	FOND OF A DRAM
AADDEEHHRTW	EDWARD HEATH	AADDFHNNOOT	HAND AND FOOT
AADDEEHHSST	DEATH'S-HEADS	AADDFIORSTV	STAR OF DAVID
AADDEEHIMNS	MAIDENHEADS	AADDFNORTUX	ROAD FUND TAX
AADDEEHJMPU	JUMPED AHEAD	AADDFORRRTW	DART FORWARD
AADDEEHKLOO	LOOKED AHEAD	AADDGHINNTY	DAY AND NIGHT
AADDEEHLLPU	PULLED AHEAD		NIGHT AND DAY
AADDEEHLPRY	PARALDEHYDE	AADDGINOSST	AGAINST ODDS
AADDEEHMNTY	NAMED THE DAY		ODDS AGAINST
AADDEEHSTVY	SAVED THE DAY	AADDGINPRRS	GRAND RAPIDS
AADDEEILNST	DESALINATED	AADDGJLNRUY	JUDY GARLAND
AADDEEILORV	ALIVE OR DEAD	AADDGLMNNOR	GRAND OLD MAN
	DEAD OR ALIVE	AADDGNNRSST	GRANDSTANDS
AADDEEILPRT	PLIED A TRADE	AADDGNOPSWY	PADDY WAGONS
AADDEEIMNRT	RIDE A TANDEM	AADDGNRSSTU	STANDS GUARD
AADDEEINRTW	IN DEAD WATER	AADDHIILOPY	PAID HOLIDAY
AADDEEIPPRS	DISAPPEARED	AADDHIITWWY	DID AWAY WITH
AADDEEKMMNN	MAKE AND MEND	AADDHILNNOS	LAID HANDS ON
AADDEEKMMNS	MAKE DEMANDS	AADDIKLMNOS	SODA AND MILK
AADDEEKNOSS	DONE AS ASKED	AADDIKNNRST	STAND A DRINK
AADDEEKOSSS	DOES AS ASKED	AADDILMNRUY	LAUNDRY MAID
AADDEELMPPR	DAMPER PEDAL	AADDINNNORU	IN AND AROUND
AADDEELRTTU	ADULTERATED	AADDINORRST	RITARDANDOS
AADDEEMMRRS	DREAM DREAMS	AADDINOTUYY	DAY IN,DAY OUT
AADDEEMNORT	RODE A TANDEM	AADDLNORSTW	LOW STANDARD
AADDEEMNOSY	MADE ONE'S DAY	AADDNNNORST	NONSTANDARD
AADDEEMORTU	MADE A DETOUR	AADDNNORSTU	STAND A ROUND
AADDEEMQRSU	MASQUERADED		STAND AROUND
AADDEEMQSTU	DESQUAMATED	AADDNORRSWW	DRAWN A SWORD
AADDEENPPRS	SANDPAPERED	AADDORRSSWW	DRAWS A SWORD
AADDEENPSST	ADAPTEDNESS	AADDRSSSTUY	AS DRY AS DUST
AADDEFGLMOO	FLOOD DAMAGE	AADEEEEGKRT	TAKE A DEGREE
AADDEFHHNOT	HAND OF DEATH	AADEEEELRST	RELEASE DATE
AADDEFHILNT	LIFTED A HAND	AADEEEFHHRT	FEATHERHEAD
AADDEFILMNN	FINAL DEMAND	AADEEEFHLMS	FEEL ASHAMED
AADDEFIRTWY	DRIFTED AWAY	AADEEEFNRSY	FREE AND EASY
AADDEGGINRS	AGGRANDISED	AADEEEGGRTX	EXAGGERATED
AADDEGGINRZ	AGGRANDIZED	AADEEEGHINS	SEEING AHEAD
AADDEGGNRST	STANDARD EGG	AADEEEGILNR	GENERAL IDEA
AADDEGHINTY	DYING A DEATH	AADEEEGKLMP	MAKE A PLEDGE
AADDEGILLNY	LEADING LADY	AADEEEGLPRS	SPREAD-EAGLE
AADDEGINORT	DEGRADATION	AADEEEHKLTT	TAKE THE LEAD
AADDEGINRRS	DISARRANGED	AADEEEHLTVW	EVADE THE LAW
AADDEGINRTW	ADDING WATER	AADEEELMRSV	SERVED A MEAL
AADDEGNNORS	DRAGONNADES	AADEEEPRSTX	EXASPERATED

AADEEEERSSTV	ASSEVERATED	AADEEHNOSVY	HAVE ONES DAY
AADEEFFHORT	FEAR OF DEATH	AADEEHNRSVW	HEAVENWARDS
AADEEFFILNT	FINAL DEFEAT	AADEEHPTVWY	PAVED THE WAY
AADEEFFMNOR	MADE AN OFFER	AADEEHQRSSU	SQUAREHEADS
AADEEFGHILN	HAD A FEELING	AADEEHSTVYY	SAVEY THE DAY
AADEEFGHORS	FORGES AHEAD	AADEEIIMNRW	MADEIRA WINE
AADEEFGILLY	LED A GAY LIFE	AADEEIKNNOT	DIANE KEATON
AADEEFGLLLT	FLAGELLATED	AADEEIKNPRT	TAKEN A PRIDE
AADEEFGLRST	DEFLAGRATES	AADEEIKPRST	TAKES A PRIDE
AADEEFHHLRT	HALFHEARTED	AADEEIKPRSY	KEEPS A DIARY
AADEEFHIMOT	AHEAD OF TIME	AADEEILLRTT	ALLITERATED
AADEEFHLMST	FELT ASHAMED	AADEEILLSSS	SALESLADIES
AADEEFHOSTT	HEAD OF STATE	AADEEILMORT	AMELIORATED
AADEEFHRTTY	THE DAY AFTER	AADEEILNNRX	ALEXANDRINE
AADEEFIRRST	FRED ASTAIRE	AADEEILNRTX	ALEXANDRITE
AADEEFJLNRS	FLARED JEANS	AADEEILNSST	DESALINATES
AADEEFLLNSW	SAFE AND WELL	AADEEILNSUV	LEAVE UNSAID
AADEEFLLPSY	PLAYED FALSE	AADEEILPRST	PLIES A TRADE
AADEEFLLRSW	SAD FAREWELL	AADEEILRRTT	RETAIL TRADE
AADEEFLMMNS	SELF-MADE MAN	AADEEILRRTV	ARRIVED LATE
AADEEFLMSTY	STEADY FLAME	AADEEILSTVY	STAYED ALIVE
AADEEFLNRST	LEARNED FAST	AADEEIMMNRR	MARRIED NAME
AADEEFLNRTT	RENIED A FLAT	AADEEIMMNRT	EARNED A MINT
AADEEFLOTTT	TOTAL DEFEAT	AADEEIMRSTU	AMATEUR SIDE
AADEEFNRSSU	SAFE AND SURE	AADEEINPPRT	APPERTAINED
AADEEFORRTT	FEAR TO TREAD	AADEEINSTVX	VEXED A SAINT
AADEEFPRRSS	SPREADS FEAR	AADEEIPRRTT	REPATRIATED
AADEEGGHINP	PAGE HEADING	AADEEIPRTTX	EXPATRIATED
AADEEGGHHNRRT	GREAT DANGER	AADEEIRRSSV	ADVERSARIES
AADEEGHHHNT	HANG THE HEAD	AADEEIRSSTX	RAISED TAXES
AADEEGHHISV	HEAVED A SIGH	AADEEIRSTVV	ADVERSATIVE
AADEEGHKRST	THE DARK AGES	AADEEJKLOPY	PLAYED A JOKE
AADEEGHLLNR	HERALD ANGEL	AADEEKMMNSS	MAKES AMENDS
AADEEGHNNOO	GONE AHEAD ON	AADEEKMNOSY	MAKE ONES DAY
AADEEGHNNOT	ON THE AGENDA	AADEEKMORTU	MAKE A DETOUR
AADEEGHNOOS	GOES AHEAD ON	AADEEKMRRTW	WATERMARKED
AADEEGHRSSU	SURGES AHEAD	AADEEKNPSST	SNEAKED PAST
AADEEGIKNTV	GIVE AND TAKE	AADEEKOPRTW	TAKE A POWDER
	GIVE-AND-TAKE	AADEELLMNRW	WELL-READ MAN
AADEEGILRTT	GREAT DETAIL	AADEELLMRST	SMELLED A RAT
AADEEGILSTV	GAVE DETAILS	AADEELLPPRW	WALLPAPERED
AADEEGINPSU	SPADE GUINEA	AADEELMNRSU	LAND MEASURE
AADEEGJLPPU	APPEAL JUDGE	AADEELMORRS	ORDERS A MEAL
AADEEGLMMOS	SAME OLD GAME	AADEELMPRST	STAMP DEALER
AADEEGLMPSY	PLAYED GAMES	AADEELNOOST	AT A LOOSE END
AADEEGNORRV	GAVE AN ORDER	AADEELNOPST	ON A PEDESTAL
AADEEGNPRRR	PREARRANGED	AADEELNORRT	LEARN TO READ
AADEEGNRRTW	WATER GARDEN	AADEELNORSS	READ A LESSON
AADEEGOPRST	GAS-OPERATED	AADEELNPSST	PLANTS A SEED
AADEEGORTUV	AVERAGED OUT	AADEELNPTUY	PLAYED A TUNE
AADEEHHMMRS	HAMMERHEADS	AADEELNRRYY	NEARLY READY
AADEEHILRTX	EXHILARATED	AADEELORSTT	SAD TO RELATE
AADEEHIPTTV	HAVE IT TAPED	AADEELORSTV	VOLSTEAD ERA
AADEEHIRRST	REAR ITS HEAD	AADEELPRRTY	PARTY LEADER
AADEEHIRSTW	HEADWAITERS	AADEELRRSTV	SLAVE TRADER
AADEEHJMMMO	HOME-MADE JAM	AADEELRSTTU	ADULTERATES
AADEEHLLPTY	DEATHLY PALE	AADEEMMNNSSU	ASSUMED NAME
	PLAY THE LEAD	AADEEMMNNRTY	MADE AN ENTRY
AADEEHLNNRT	NEANDERTHAL	AADEEMNNORRR	MADE AN ERROR
AADEEHLNOTV	LOVE AND HATE	AADEEMNOSWY	MADE ONE'S WAY
AADEEHLNRTT	THEATRE LAND	AADEEMQRRSU	MASQUERADER
AADEEHLNSTV	LEADS THE VAN	AADEEMQRSSU	MASQUERADES
AADEEHLPSST	PASTEL SHADE	AADEEMQSSTU	DESQUAMATES
AADEEHLRRTT	TETRAHEDRAL	AADEEMRRSUY	YARD MEASURE
AADEEHLRSST	HARD AS STEEL	AADEENNNORV	EVER AND ANON
AADEEHLRTTT	DEATH RATTLE	AADEENNOSSY	AYES AND NOES
AADEEHLSTWY	LEADS THE WAY	AADEENNPPPR	PEN AND PAPER
AADEEHMMNSTY	NAMES THE DAY	AADEENNRTWY	TYNE AND WEAR
AADEEHMRRTW	WARMHEARTED	AADEENQRSUW	QUEENS AWARD
AADEEHMRSST	HEADMASTERS	AADEENRRSTU	TEAR ASUNDER
AADEEHNNOTW	WENT AHEAD ON	AADEENRRSWY	READY ANSWER

AADEENRSTTW	STARTED ANEW	AADEGIILNOS	DIAGONALISE
AADEENRSTVY	VETERANS' DAY	AADEGIILNOZ	DIAGONALIZE
AADEENRSWYY	NEW YEARS DAY	AADEGIILNSY	LAYING ASIDE
AADEENSSTTW	EAST AND WEST	AADEGIILPRS	PLAGIARISED
AADEEOOSSTT	STOOD AT EASE	AADEGIILPRZ	PLAGIARIZED
AADEEORRTWY	READY TO WEAR	AADEGIINNOT	DONE IT AGAIN
	READY-TO-WEAR	AADEGIINNTV	INVAGINATED
AADEEORRUYY	ARE YOU READY?	AADEGIINOST	DOES IT AGAIN
AADEEPPRSTW	WASTED PAPER	AADEGIINRTT	INGRATIATED
AADEEPRSSTW	PASSED WATER	AADEGIINSST	SIDE AGAINST
AADEERRSTTW	TREADS WATER	AADEGIKMNNT	MAKING A DENT
AADEFFLMOOO	MADE A FOOL OF	AADEGIKMNRY	MAKING READY
AADEFFMOSSU	MADE A FUSS OF	AADEGILLNOS	SAILED ALONG
AADEFGHNRRT	GRANDFATHER	AADEGILLNTV	GALLIVANTED
AADEFGIINTX	FIXING A DATE	AADEGILMNPR	READING LAMP
AADEFGILNNR	GRAND FINALE	AADEGILMOOS	GOOD AS A MILE
AADEFGILNNS	SAFE LANDING	AADEGILNNSS	SEND A SIGNAL
AADEFGIMOOT	MADE A GO OF IT	AADEGILNPRT	LEADING PART
AADEFGMNNSU	FUN AND GAMES		PLANTIGRADE
AADEFGORRRW	FORWARD GEAR	AADEGINNOST	ANTAGONISED
AADEFHINNSS	IN SAFE HANDS	AADEGINNOTZ	ANTAGONIZED
AADEFHINNTT	INFANT DEATH	AADEGINNRRW	DRAWING NEAR
AADEFHINOPT	PAIN OF DEATH	AADEGINNRTU	TURNED AGAIN
AADEFHJOSTW	JAWS OF DEATH	AADEGINNSWY	SENDING AWAY
AADEFHLLOTW	WALL OF DEATH	AADEGINRRSS	DISARRANGES
AADEFHLRTTU	HAD A FLUTTER	AADEGINRTUU	INAUGURATED
AADEFIINNRR	FIRE AND RAIN	AADEGINSTTV	DEVASTATING
AADEFIKLNNR	RANK AND FILE	AADEGIOPPST	POSTAGE PAID
AADEFILLNRS	RISE AND FALL	AADEGKLLNOW	WALKED ALONG
AADEFILOPTY	FAILED TO PAY	AADEGKLRSSS	DARK GLASSES
AADEFILORST	RAISED ALOFT	AADEGLLNOPY	PLAYED ALONG
AADEFILORSV	FIRED A SALVO	AADEGLMNRSS	ARMS AND LEGS
AADEFILRSXY	FIXED SALARY	AADEGLMNRST	STRANGE LAND
AADEFIMOPRT	MADE A PROFIT	AADEGLNOPSS	PASSED ALONG
AADEFINRRRY	INFRARED RAY	AADEGLNQRSU	QUADRANGLES
AADEFINRRTU	TRUE AND FAIR	AADEGLNRSSU	GRADUALNESS
AADEFKLMRRS	ALFRED MARKS	AADEGLRSTTU	GASTRULATED
AADEFLLLOOW	FOLLOW A LEAD	AADEGMNNNRR	GRAND MANNER
AADEFLLNOTU	UNFOLD A TALE	AADEGMNRRST	GRAND MASTER
AADEFLMNNTU	FUNDAMENTAL	AADEGNNPRRT	GRANDPARENT
AADEFLNORRW	LEAN FORWARD	AADEGNOOSSW	AS GOOD AS NEW
AADEFLSSTTY	STEADFASTLY	AADEGNPRRTY	GARDEN PARTY
AADEFMMNNNR	MANFRED MANN	AADEGOPPPST	STOPPED A GAP
AADEFMOORUV	DO ME A FAVOUR	AADEHHIKNST	THINKS AHEAD
AADEFMORSTW	MADE OF STRAW	AADEHHKNNSS	SHAKEN HANDS
AADEFNOORUV	DONE A FAVOUR	AADEHHOOSST	SHOOTS AHEAD
AADEFOORSUV	DOES A FAVOUR	AADEHIILNNT	ANNIHILATED
AADEFOORTTW	TWO OF A TRADE	AADEHIILNRT	ANTHERIDIAL
AADEFOPRRYY	DAY OF PRAYER	AADEHIILOPP	PAEDOPHILIA
AADEGGGLNOT	TAGGED ALONG	AADEHIILPSS	SAILED A SHIP
AADEGGGHNRSS	HAGGARDNESS	AADEHIKNNNT	TAKEN IN HAND
AADEGGIILNV	GIVING A LEAD	AADEHIKNNST	TAKES IN HAND
AADEGGILNNR	LANDING GEAR	AADEHIKNRTT	TAKEN IT HARD
AADEGGILNOR	READING GAOL	AADEHIKRSTT	TAKES IT HARD
AADEGGINRRT	GREAT DARING	AADEHILLNOS	HOLLANDAISE
AADEGGINRSS	AGGRANDISES	AADEHILMMMU	MUHAMMED ALI
AADEGGINRSZ	AGGRANDIZES	AADEHILMNNO	NOMINAL HEAD
AADEGGLOSWY	SLOGGED AWAY	AADEHILMPPT	APPLIED MATH
AADEGGLPUWY	PLUGGED AWAY	AADEHILNNST	LANTHANIDES
AADEGGMNOOR	GOOD MANAGER	AADEHIMOTTV	HAVE TO ADMIT
AADEGGOSSSU	SAUSAGE DOGS	AADEHIMSSTU	SHEA STADIUM
AADEGHILNUV	HAVING A DUEL	AADEHINRRTU	TURNED A HAIR
AADEGHIMRTW	MAD WITH RAGE	AADEHIRRUWY	HURRIED AWAY
AADEGHINRRW	HARDWEARING	AADEHLLPSUW	ALL WASHED UP
AADEGHINRTU	THE GUARDIAN	AADEHLMNSUY	UNASHAMEDLY
AADEGHINSTY	GAINS THE DAY	AADEHLRRRUY	HARRY LAUDER
AADEGHOORTT	GOOD AT HEART	AADEHMMNNOS	HANDSOME MAN
AADEGHOPRTU	AUTOGRAPHED	AADEHMNORTW	DRAWN AT HOME
AADEGIIKNST	TAKING ASIDE	AADEHMNPTTU	UP AND AT THEM
AADEGIIKNTV	TAKING A DIVE	AADEHMORSTW	DRAWS AT HOME
AADEGIILMNV	MADE A LIVING	AADEHNOPPRY	HOPE AND PRAY

AADEHNORTTW	DOWN AT HEART
AADEHRSTTTY	START THE DAY
AADEIIIRRTV	IRRADIATIVE
AADEIILMNPT	MADE IT PLAIN
AADEIILMNST	MEDIASTINAL
AADEIILMNTY	MADE IN ITALY
AADEIILMRST	ADMIRALTIES
AADEIILMSST	ASSIMILATED
AADEIILNSTV	INVALIDATES
AADEIIMNNRS	AMERINDIANS
AADEIINRRTV	DRIVE A TRAIN
AADEIINRSTT	TRIED A SAINT
AADEIIOPRRT	PIRATE RADIO
AADEIJORSTY	RADIATES JOY
AADEIKLNORW	WALKED ON AIR
AADEIKMMRST	MADE ITS MARK
AADEIKMNORS	MAKE INROADS
AADEIKMRTWW	AWKWARD TIME
AADEILLLLRV	ALVAR LIDELL
AADEILLNNRT	RALLENTANDI
AADEILLNOPT	PLANETOIDAL
AADEILLNOST	ALLANTOIDES
AADEILLNPSU	PAUL DANIELS
AADEILMMORY	MEMORIAL DAY
AADEILMNPTU	MANIPULATED
AADEILNNQRU	QUADRENNIAL
AADEILNOOTW	NATALIE WOOD
AADEILNORST	DESALINATOR
AADEILNORSV	VALID REASON
AADEILNOTUV	DEVALUATION
AADEILNPPRR	PREPRANDIAL
AADEILNRSTU	NATURALISED
AADEILNRTUZ	NATURALIZED
AADEILOPRTZ	TRAPEZOIDAL
AADEILPPSWY	SLIPPED AWAY
AADEILPRSTY	DISPARATELY
AADEILRRTWY	TREAD WARILY
AADEILRSTTW	TIDAL WATERS
AADEIMMNRST	DISARMAMENT
AADEIMNNRTT	NEAT AND TRIM
AADEIMNOPRR	MADREPORIAN
AADEIMNORST	MANDATORIES
AADEIMNRSTV	ANIMADVERTS
	MAIDSERVANT
AADEIINNOPST	ANTIPODEANS
AADEIINNQRTU	QUARANTINED
AADEIINNRSTW	SAINT ANDREW
AADEINNSSTW	STANDS IN AWE
AADEINOPRTV	DEPRAVATION
AADEINOPSWY	PAID ONE'S WAY
AADEINOORST	TREADS ON AIR
AADEINORRTT	RETARDATION
AADEINORRTV	DROVE A TRAIN
AADEINOSSSY	SAID ONE'S SAY
AADEINOSTTV	DEVASTATION
AADEINPQSSU	PASQUINADES
AADEINPRRWZ	DRAWN A PRIZE
AADEINPRSTV	PAID SERVANT
AADEINSSTTW	SAW A DENTIST
AADEIOPRRRS	ROAD REPAIRS
AADEIOPRRTV	PRIVATE ROAD
AADEIOPSSTT	APOSTATISED
AADEIOPSTTZ	APOSTATIZED
AADEIPRRTVW	PRIVATE WARD
AADEIPSSTWW	WASP-WAISTED
AADEKLNNRRT	DARK LANTERN
AADEKLOPSSU	SPEAKS ALOUD
AADEKMNOSSU	MAKES A SOUND
AADEKMNRSSS	MASSED RANKS
AADEKMOPRRR	DROP A REMARK
AADEKMSSTUY	MAKES A STUDY

AADEKNRSSWW	AWKWARDNESS
AADELLLNORT	LENT A DOLLAR
AADELLMNORY	LADY ALMONER
AADELLMRRST	SMALL TRADER
AADELLNNORT	RALLENTANDO
AADELLPPRTU	PULLED APART
AADELMMOPSS	PLASMODESMA
AADELMNOPST	ALMOND PASTE
AADELMPRSTU	LEADS A TRUMP
AADELNNOSST	STANDS ALONE
AADELNORSTW	LEAN TOWARDS
AADELNPPRUW	DREW UP A PLAN
AADELNRSTTU	ADULTERANTS
AADELORRTTU	ADULTERATOR
AADELPRRSTY	DARTS PLAYER
AADELSSTTUY	LAST TUESDAY
AADEMNOOSST	ANASTOMOSED
AADEMNOOSTU	ADENOMATOUS
AADEMRRSSTY	YARDMASTERS
AADENNNRRRU	RUN AN ERRAND
AADENNRRTUW	UNWARRANTED
AADENPPRSUY	SUNDAY PAPER
AADENRSSTTT	STANDS TREAT
AADENRSSWWY	WAYWARDNESS
AADENRSTTUU	UNSATURATED
AADEOPPRSST	STRAPPADOES
AADEOQRRTUW	EQUATORWARD
AADEORRSSTY	READS A STORY
AADEORRSTTW	STARTED A ROW
AADEORSSTTV	DEVASTATORS
AADEORRSTUU	QUADRATURES
AADFFIILNORU	FAIR AND FOUL
AADFFKOOOTY	TOOK A DAY OFF
AADFGHHNNOU	AFGHAN HOUND
AADFGIINNWY	FINDING A WAY
AADFGIKNORY	KING FOR A DAY
AADFGINNORS	GRAIN OF SAND
AADFHHILLOY	HALF HOLIDAY
	HALF-HOLIDAY
AADFHINOPRS	PAIR OF HANDS
AADFHINRSTT	AT FIRST HAND
AADFHLNOWWY	HALF WAY DOWN
AADFHNORSTT	SHORT AND FAT
AADFIINORST	STAR OF INDIA
AADFILNORST	TRAIL OF SAND
AADFINOTUWY	FIND A WAY OUT
AADFIPRRSTT	DRIFTS APART
AADFLLLLNOW	ALL FALL DOWN
AADFLLLOOSY	ALL FOOLS DAY
AADFLLNORST	STAND OR FALL
AADFLNOOSST	STANDS ALOOF
AADFLOPRRWY	FORWARD PLAY
AADFMNOORRS	MANSARD ROOF
AADFOORSUUV	DO US A FAVOUR
AADFOPRRSSW	FORWARD PASS
AADGGGGMNOO	GOG AND MAGOG
AADGGHIINNV	GIVING A HAND
AADGGHKLOOR	HAGGARD LOOK
AADGGIILNWY	GLIDING AWAY
AADGGIIMMNR	DIAGRAMMING
AADGGIIMNNV	GIVING A DAMN
AADGGIINNRV	GIVING A DARN
AADGGIINPRS	DISPARAGING
AADGGIKNRTU	TAKING A DRUG
AADGGINNRUW	DRAWING A GUN
AADGGMMOORR	GOOD GRAMMAR
AADGHILMNNN	MANHANDLING
AADGHILNNNP	PANHANDLING
AADGHILNPRY	PLAYING HARD
AADGHILSTWY	SAW DAYLIGHT
AADGHINORVW	HAVING A WORD

AADGHINOSSW	WASHING SODA
AADGHIOPRRS	RADIOGRAPHS
AADGHMNRSTU	DRAUGHTSMAN
AADGHNNORSU	HANGS AROUND
AADGHOOSSTT	STOOD AGHAST
AADGHOPRRST	HARD TO GRASP
AADGIIINRRT	IRRADIATING
AADGIILNNNO	ANGLO-INDIAN
AADGIILNNSV	VANDALISING
AADGIILNNVZ	VANDALIZING
AADGIILNORR	RAILROADING
AADGIILNORS	RADIO SIGNAL
AADGIILNSWY	SLIDING AWAY
AADGIIMNRST	DRAMATISING
AADGIIMNRTZ	DRAMATIZING
AADGIINNPRT	DARTING PAIN
AADGIINNRST	GRANTS-IN-AID
AADGIINRRSY	DISARRAYING
AADGIINRVWY	DRIVING AWAY
AADGIJNRSUU	JAGUARUNDIS
AADGIKNOOSW	GOOD AS A WINK
AADGIKNOPRT	TAKING A DROP
AADGINNOSTT	STAND TO GAIN
AADGINNPSTT	STANDING PAT
AADGLLLNRUY	GLANDULARLY
AADGLORRSUY	ROYAL GUARDS
AADGNOOPRST	GASTROPODAN
AADHHINSTTT	THIS AND THAT
AADHHMMNSSUW	HUMS AND HAWS
AADHHMORSTY	THOMAS HARDY
AADHIKLOSTY	HOLIDAY TASK
AADHILLNNTT	TALL AND THIN
AADHILLOYYZ	LAZY HOLIDAY
AADHILNOPSY	HOLIDAY SNAP
AADHILRSTWW	WITHDRAWALS
AADHIOPPRTY	PARATYPHOID
AADHIOPRRTY	PARATHYROID
AADHJMMNNOO	JOAN HAMMOND
AADHKNOORTT	NORTH DAKOTA
AADHKOOSTTU	SOUTH DAKOTA
AADHLMNOSTY	DYLAN THOMAS
AADHLNNOSSY	LAYS HANDS ON
AADHLOPRSTY	HOLDS A PARTY
AADHLORSUYZ	HAZARDOUSLY
AADHMMNNOUY	HUMAN DYNAMO
AADHNOOSTTW	SHOOT AT DAWN
AADHNOPQRUY	QUADRAPHONY
AADIIILMRTY	MILITARY AID
AADIIIINNNOR	INDO-IRANIAN
AADIIIINORRT	IRRADIATION
AADIIJLLNNS	LANDS IN JAIL
AADIIKNNPRT	DRINK A PINTA
AADIILLNTTU	ALTITUDINAL
	LATITUDINAL
AADIILNORTT	TRADITIONAL
AADIILNPTTU	APTITUDINAL
AADIILNTTTU	ATTITUDINAL
AADIILOSUUV	AUDIOVISUAL
AADIINNOOST	ANODISATION
AADIINNOOTZ	ANODIZATION
AADIINNORSU	DINOSAURIAN
AADIINNOTTX	ANTIOXIDANT
AADIINNQSUW	INDIAN SQUAW
AADIIPRSSST	ASPIDISTRAS
AADIKNNPRTT	PINT TANKARD
AADIKNORSTT	DRINK A TOAST
AADILLLMNST	TALL AND SLIM
AADILLMNNOY	MADONNA LILY
AADILLMNOOT	AMONTILLADO
AADILLMNORW	ANIMAL WORLD
AADILMOPRRU	PARLOUR MAID
AADILNRSSTT	STANDS TRIAL
AADILOORSTV	VASODILATOR
AADILOPPRSV	DISAPPROVAL
AADIMNNORRY	ORDINARY MAN
AADINORSTUW	WAITS AROUND
AADINPSSTTT	DISTANT PAST
AADJMNNPRSU	PANJANDRUMS
AADKLNOPRWY	WORK AND PLAY
AADKLORSTWW	WALK TOWARDS
AADKNNOPRSW	SANDOWN PARK
AADKNORSTTU	DRUNK A TOAST
AADLLLOSSUY	ALL SOULS DAY
AADLLOOSSST	SOLD AT A LOSS
AADLMNORSTU	LAUNDROMATS
AADLNOOPRRY	ROYAL PARDON
AADLNOPRSUY	PLAYS AROUND
AADLNPPRSUW	DRAW UP PLANS
AADLOPQRRUU	QUADRUPOLAR
AADLOPRRSTW	WORLDS APART
AADNNOPPRTY	PONY AND TRAP
AADNNOPPSST	POTS AND PANS
AADNOPRRSUW	WRAPAROUNDS
AAEEEEFLSST	FEELS AT EASE
AAEEEELNRSW	RENEW A LEASE
AAEEEFFLMMT	FEMME FATALE
AAEEEFGPRSS	FREE PASSAGE
AAEEEFLPRSS	FARES PLEASE
AAEEEGGRSTX	EXAGGERATES
AAEEEGHLRRT	GREAT HEALER
AAEEEGKRTTW	REGATTA WEEK
AAEEEGLLSTT	LEGAL ESTATE
AAEEEGLNRRT	GENERAL RATE
AAEEEGNRSSV	AVERAGENESS
AAEEEGNSTTT	ESTATE AGENT
AAEEEGPRTVY	AVERAGE TYPE
AAEEEGRSTWY	STEERAGE-WAY
AAEEEHINPST	EASE THE PAIN
AAEEEHKMSTT	MAKES THE TEA
AAEEEHLNPST	SEA ELEPHANT
AAEEEHMNNSV	HEAVEN'S NAME
AAEEEHMNOTT	EATEN AT HOME
AAEEEHNNOVY	HAVE AN EYE ON
AAEEEHNPRST	ENTER A PHASE
AAEEEHNRRTW	EARTHENWARE
AAEEEHRRTTW	WATER HEATER
AAEEEHRRTTY	HEARTY EATER
AAEEEHRSTTT	THEATRE SEAT
AAEEEIKPSSS	SPEAKEASIES
AAEEEILLSXY	ALEXEI SAYLE
AAEEEKLORTV	TAKE OR LEAVE
AAEEEKLRTTT	TAKE A LETTER
AAEEEKMSSTY	MAKES EYES AT
AAEEELLNOSV	LEAVES ALONE
AAEEELLPSVW	WEAVE A SPELL
AAEEELLRSVY	LEAVES EARLY
AAEEELMPRRX	RARE EXAMPLE
AAEEELNNNOT	EATEN NO LEAN
AAEEELNOSTV	LEAVES A NOTE
AAEEELNRSWY	SEEN A LAWYER
AAEEELRSSWY	SEES A LAWYER
AAEEEMNNOTT	EATEN NO MEAT
AAEEEMNPPST	APPEASEMENT
AAEEEMPRSTU	TAPE MEASURE
AAEEEPRSSTX	EXASPERATES
AAEEERSSSTV	ASSEVERATES
AAEEFFHLMNT	FAN THE FLAME
AAEEFFKMNOR	MAKE AN OFFER
AAEEFFKNORT	TAKE AN OFFER
AAEEFFKOPRT	OFF-PEAK RATE
AAEEFGHILNS	HAS A FEELING
AAEEFGHIMRT	FATHER IMAGE

AAEEFGILLRS	LARGE AS LIFE
AAEEFGILORT	FAIL TO AGREE
AAEEFGIMRST	AFTERIMAGES
AAEEFGLLLNN	FALLEN ANGEL
AAEEFGLLLST	FLAGELLATES
AAEEFGMRRRW	GERM WARFARE
AAEEFGORRST	TEARS OF RAGE
AAEEFHHILRT	FAITH HEALER
AAEEFHILRTW	AFTER A WHILE
	WHAT A RELIEF!
AAEEFHIRRTW	FAIR WEATHER
	FAIR-WEATHER
AAEEFHKNRRT	HANKER AFTER
AAEEFHLMRSU	HALF MEASURE
AAEEFHLMTWY	MEET HALFWAY
AAEEFHLOSTW	LAW OF THE SEA
AAEEFHMORST	ARM OF THE SEA
AAEEFHRRTTW	AFTER THE WAR
AAEEFIMNRTU	MAIN FEATURE
AAEEFKLOPST	KEEPS AFLOAT
AAEEFLLLOVW	LEAVE FALLOW
AAEEFLLLPSS	FALLS ASLEEP
AAEEFLLSSUV	FALSE VALUES
AAEEFLRRSST	FALSE ARREST
AAEEFLRSTUV	SERVE A FAULT
AAEEFLSTVVY	SAFETY VALVE
AAEEFMOPPRR	REAM OF PAPER
AAEEFNOPRRW	OPEN WARFARE
AAEEFNRRSST	TRANSFERASE
AAEEFRSSTTT	AFTERTASTES
AAEEGGGIRTV	AGGREGATIVE
AAEEGGGLRTY	AGGREGATELY
AAEEGGHINRT	IN THE GARAGE
AAEEGGILNNV	GALA EVENING
AAEEGGIMNRV	GRAVEN IMAGE
AAEEGGLMORT	AGGLOMERATE
AAEEGGLPRTU	GREAT PLAGUE
AAEEGGORRTX	EXAGGERATOR
AAEEGGHHISSV	HEAVES A SIGH
AAEEGHHMORR	HAEMORRHAGE
AAEEGHIMRTT	THE GREAT I AM
AAEEGHKOSTT	TAKE HOSTAGE
AAEEGHKOTVY	GAVE THE OKAY
AAEEGHKRSST	GREAT SHAKES
AAEEGHLMPTV	GAVE THE PALM
AAEEGHLMPTY	PLAY THE GAME
AAEEGHLNRTW	WALTER HAGEN
AAEEGHLOOPS	OESOPHAGEAL
AAEEGHLPSTT	THE LAST PAGE
AAEEGHLRTTW	GREAT WEALTH
AAEEGHNPPRR	PAPERHANGER
AAEEGHRRTTW	THE GREAT WAR
AAEEGIIKLPT	ATE LIKE A PIG
	EAT LIKE A PIG
AAEEGIKLNSV	ASKING LEAVE
AAEEGIKLNTV	LEAVE-TAKING
	TAKING LEAVE
AAEEGIKNPPT	TAKING A PEEP
AAEEGIKNPWY	KEEPING AWAY
AAEEGILLLTT	TAGLIATELLE
AAEEGILLTTV	GAVE A LITTLE
AAEEGILMMNT	MENTAL IMAGE
AAEEGILMNNR	REAL MEANING
AAEEGILMSSX	SEXAGESIMAL
AAEEGILNPPT	EATING APPLE
AAEEGIMSSSX	SEXAGESIMAS
AAEEGINORSV	GIVE A REASON
AAEEGINPRST	GREASE PAINT
	GREASEPAINT
AAEEGINRRTW	GRANITEWARE
AAEEGINRSTV	VEGETARIANS
AAEEGINRTVY	VINTAGE YEAR
AAEEGINRVWY	VEERING AWAY
AAEEGIRSTTV	GAVE IT A REST
AAEEGJMNNRS	JAMES GARNER
AAEEGKLRRTT	GREAT TALKER
AAEEGKMNPRS	SPEAK GERMAN
AAEEGKMPSTU	STAGE MAKE-UP
AAEEGKMSSSU	MAKES A GUESS
AAEEGKNOPST	KEEPS A TAG ON
AAEEGKNRRST	GARTER SNAKE
AAEEGKNSSTU	TAKEN A GUESS
AAEEGKSSSTU	TAKES A GUESS
AAEEGLLLSVY	GALLEY SLAVE
AAEEGLLMRTT	LEGAL MATTER
AAEEGLLNOSV	GAVE ONE'S ALL
AAEEGLLRTTY	TATE GALLERY
AAEEGLMMRSU	RUMMAGE SALE
AAEEGLNNORV	NAVEL ORANGE
AAEEGLNNPTT	PLANTAGENET
AAEEGLNOSSV	GAVE A LESSON
AAEEGLNRTTV	TRAVEL AGENT
AAEEGLPRSTY	PEARLY GATES
	STAGE PLAYER
AAEEGLRSSTT	SETS AT LARGE
AAEEGLRSSTY	EARLY STAGES
AAEEGMMMNNST	MANAGEMENTS
AAEEGMMRSST	GAMES MASTER
AAEEGMNNRRT	ARRANGEMENT
AAEEGMNOPRT	POMEGRANATE
AAEEGMNRSTY	EAST GERMANY
AAEEGMNSSTU	ASSUAGEMENT
AAEEGMRRTTV	GRAVE MATTER
AAEEGNNPTTT	PATENT AGENT
AAEEGNPRRRS	PREARRANGES
AAEEGORSTUV	AVERAGES OUT
AAEEGPRRRTT	GREATER PART
AAEEGLPRRTU	QUARTERAGES
AAEEGQRRTUV	GAVE QUARTER
AAEEGRRTVWY	WATERY GRAVE
AAEEHHINTTV	NATIVE HEATH
AAEEHHKNNTV	THANK HEAVEN!
AAEEHHKOTTT	TAKE THE OATH
AAEEHHLNNPT	NAPHTHALENE
AAEEHHLRSTW	WASH LEATHER
	WASH-LEATHER
AAEEHHNORTV	HAVE ANOTHER
AAEEHHORSVW	HAVE A SHOWER
AAEEHHORTVY	HAVE A THEORY
AAEEHHPRTTY	HEAT THERAPY
	PAY THE EARTH
AAEEHIKNNST	TAKEN A SHINE
AAEEHIKNRTT	TAKEN THE AIR
AAEEHIKNSST	TAKES A SHINE
AAEEHIKRSTT	TAKES THE AIR
AAEEHILNNST	SAINT HELENA
AAEEHILRSTX	EXHILARATES
AAEEHIMMNPT	AMPHETAMINE
AAEEHINSSST	ANESTHESIAS
	SEA SHANTIES
AAEEHIRSSTW	WASHETERIAS
AAEEHKLMSTW	MAKES THE LAW
AAEEHKMNRRT	NEAR THE MARK
AAEEHKMOPTY	TAKE-HOME PAY
AAEEHKMRSTV	SAVE THE MARK
AAEEHKNPRTT	TAKEN THE RAP
AAEEHKORSTV	HAVE A STROKE
AAEEHKORTTT	TAKE TO HEART
AAEEHKPRSTT	TAKES THE RAP
AAEEHKQRSTU	EARTHQUAKES
AAEEHLLSTTU	HAUSTELLATE

AAEEHLMNNPT	ELEPHANT MAN	AAEEELLPRSTY	PLATELAYERS
AAEEHLMRSTT	SET THE ALARM	AAEEELMNSTTT	MENTAL STATE
AAEEHLNORTT	LEARN TO HATE	AAEEELMORSSU	ASSUME A ROLE
AAEEHLNPRSS	ENA SHARPLES	AAEEELNNNTUV	ANNUAL EVENT
AAEEHLNPRTT	PLANET EARTH	AAEEELNOSSTT	ATE ONE'S SALT
AAEEHLQRSSU	EQUAL SHARES		EAT ONE'S SALT
AAEEHMNOORR	AMENORRHOEA	AAEEELNPRSTT	PLANTS A TREE
AAEEHMRRTWW	WARM WEATHER	AAEEELNPSSTT	PLEASANTEST
AAEEHNOOSVZ	HAVE A SNOOZE	AAEEELNRRSTT	RETRANSLATE
AAEEHNOSSVY	HAVE ONES SAY	AAEEELNRTTTV	TETRAVALENT
AAEEHNOSVWY	HAVE ONES WAY	AAEEELOPRTTX	EXTRAPOLATE
AAEEHPSTVWY	PAVES THE WAY	AAEEELRRSTTT	LATE STARTER
AAEEIIILLTVV	ALLEVIATIVE	AAEEMMMNNNOS	NAME NO NAMES
AAEEIILMRST	MATERIALISE	AAEEMMMNNOST	ONE MANS MEAT
AAEEIILMRTZ	MATERIALIZE	AAEEMMNNRSUV	SUAVE MANNER
AAEEIILNSST	ILIE NASTASE	AAEEMNOPRTT	TREPONEMATA
AAEEIILRRST	ARTERIALISE	AAEEMNPRSTT	SAME PATTERN
AAEEIILRRTZ	ARTERIALIZE	AAEEMQRSSTU	MARQUESSATE
AAEEIILRTTV	RETALIATIVE	AAEEMRRSTUY	MATURE YEARS
AAEEIIKKLRST	LIKE A STREAK	AAEENNPPRSY	SPARE A PENNY
AAEEIKLNNOY	ANNIE OAKLEY	AAEENNRSSUW	UNAWARENESS
AAEEIKLNSSV	SNAKES ALIVE!	AAEENPSSTVX	VAST EXPANSE
AAEEIKMNOSS	MAKES A NOISE	AAEEPPRSSTW	WASTES PAPER
AAEEIKMNSTX	MAKES AN EXIT	AAEEPRSSSTW	PASSES WATER
AAEEIKMSSTY	MAKES IT EASY	AAEFFHIMORS	HOME AFFAIRS
AAEEIKNSTTY	TAKEN IT EASY	AAEFFIIMRTV	AFFIRMATIVE
AAEEIKSSTTY	TAKES IT EASY	AAEFFILNRSW	WINS A RAFFLE
AAEEIILLLLPR	LIE PARALLEL	AAEFFIOPRTY	PAY A FORFEIT
AAEEIILLLSVW	LEAVES A WILL	AAEFFKLMOOO	MAKE A FOOL OF
AAEEIILLMNNT	LINEAMENTAL	AAEFFKMOSSU	MAKE A FUSS OF
AAEEIILLNOTV	ELEVATIONAL	AAEFFLLLMOW	WALL OF FLAME
AAEEIILLPPTV	APPELLATIVE	AAEFFLLORST	FLAT FOR SALE
AAEEIILLQRTU	EQUILATERAL	AAEFFLLRSTU	FLAT REFUSAL
AAEEIILLRSTT	ALLITERATES	AAEFGHHIRTV	HAVE A FRIGHT
AAEEIILMNNSS	MELANESIANS	AAEFGHHLLNT	HALF A LENGTH
AAEEIILMOPST	AIM TO PLEASE	AAEFGHIINRR	FAIR HEARING
AAEEIILMORRS	RAISE MORALE	AAEFGHILNRT	FARTHINGALE
AAEEIILMORST	AMELIORATES	AAEFGHLNOWY	GONE HALF-WAY
AAEEIILNPTVX	EXPLANATIVE	AAEFGHLOSWY	GOES HALF-WAY
AAEEIILNRTTV	ALTERNATIVE	AAEFGIIKMNR	MAKING A FIRE
	TEA INTERVAL	AAEFGIIKNTW	TAKING A WIFE
AAEEIILPRSTV	PRIVATE SALE	AAEFGIILNRY	LAYING A FIRE
AAEEIILRRRVY	ARRIVE EARLY	AAEFGIINNPY	PAYING A FINE
AAEEIILRRSTV	ARRIVES LATE	AAEFGIKMOOT	MAKE A GO OF IT
AAEEIMNNSST	ANIMATENESS	AAEFGIKNRST	ASKING AFTER
AAEEIMSSSTT	METASTASISE	AAEFGIKNRTT	TAKING AFTER
AAEEIMSSTTZ	METASTASIZE	AAEFGILLLRU	FULL REGALIA
AAEEINRRSTT	TEA STRAINER	AAEFGILLMRY	LARGE FAMILY
AAEEINSSTVX	VEXES A SAINT	AAEFGILNPSY	PLAYING SAFE
AAEEIOPRTVV	EVAPORATIVE	AAEFGIMMNOR	FORM AN IMAGE
AAEEIPPRRTV	PREPARATIVE	AAEFGINNOTT	EATING NO FAT
AAEEIPRRSTT	REPATRIATES	AAEFGINNPRS	FRANGIPANES
AAEEIPRSTTX	EXPATRIATES	AAEFGLLLNST	FLAGELLANTS
AAEEIRSSSTX	RAISES TAXES	AAEFGLNOPSS	PANE OF GLASS
AAEEKLMRSTV	SLAVE MARKET	AAEFGMNNRRTY	FRAGMENTARY
AAEEKLMRTUV	MARKET VALUE	AAEFGMORTWY	GET AWAY FROM
AAEEKLNRSTT	RATTLESNAKE	AAEFGORRTUV	GREAT FAVOUR
AAEEKLPRUWY	WAKE UP EARLY	AAEFGORSSTY	FORSYTE SAGA
AAEEKLPSTUW	WAKES UP LATE	AAEFHILLMSS	FLASH A SMILE
AAEEKMNNRTY	MAKE AN ENTRY	AAEFHILLNWY	HALFWAY LINE
AAEEKMNORRR	MAKE AN ERROR	AAEFHILMNTU	HALF A MINUTE
AAEEKMNOSWY	MAKE ONES WAY	AAEFHILNRST	TEARS IN HALF
AAEEKMNRRST	MARKET RASEN	AAEFHILNRTW	FATHER-IN-LAW
AAEEKMPRSUW	WEARS MAKE-UP	AAEFHKLSTTU	HATEFUL TASK
AAEEKMPSSSS	MAKES PASSES	AAEFHLLORTT	FALL TO EARTH
AAEEKOSTUWY	SEEK A WAY OUT	AAEFHLLOTWY	ALL OF THE WAY
AAEELLLMNOS	SALMONELLAE	AAEFHLMMNOT	HALF A MOMENT
AAEELLMNPST	MENTAL LAPSE	AAEFHLMNOTW	MAN OF WEALTH
AAEELLNRTTY	ALTERNATELY	AAEFHLMORTW	ARM OF THE LAW
AAEELLNSTTV	AT ALL EVENTS	AAEFHLNTWWY	WENT HALF-WAY
AAEELLOSTTV	LAST TO LEAVE	AAEFHLRSTTU	HAS A FLUTTER

AAEFHORRTTW	THREAT OF WAR	AAEGHIMNTTY	EATING MY HAT
AAEFHRRSSTT	START AFRESH	AAEGHINNNSS	SHENANIGANS
AAEFIIILMRS	FAMILIARISE	AAEGHINRSTV	HAVING A REST
AAEFIIILMRZ	FAMILIARIZE	AAEGHINSTTV	HAVING TASTE
AAEFIINPRST	FAINT PRAISE	AAEGHLLNOXY	HEXAGONALLY
AAEFIIORRSV	SAVOIR FAIRE	AAEGHLLOTWY	GO ALL THE WAY
AAEFIKLNRSW	WALKS IN FEAR	AAEGHLMOOTY	HAEMATOLOGY
AAEFIKMOPRT	MAKE A PROFIT	AAEGHLMRSSW	GRESHAMS LAW
AAEFIKORRSS	ASK FOR A RISE	AAEGHLPSSTT	THE LAST GASP
AAEFILLLNUV	FALL IN VALUE	AAEGHMNOPRS	ANEMOGRAPHS
AAEFILLNRTU	NATURAL LIFE		PHANEROGAMS
AAEFILMMNNRT	FIRMAMENTAL	AAEGHMOPRRS	PHRASEOGRAM
AAEFILMNOOR	REMAIN ALOOF	AAEGHNOPRTY	PYTHAGOREAN
AAEFILMNRTY	FILAMENTARY	AAEGHNORSST	NORTH SEA GAS
AAEFILNNRSW	FINAL ANSWER	AAEGHNPRRST	STRAPHANGER
AAEFILNORRS	ISLE OF ARRAN	AAEGHNSTTTU	SET AT NAUGHT
AAEFILNSTVY	FALSE VANITY	AAEGHORRTTU	GREAT AUTHOR
AAEFILNSTWY	STIFLE A YAWN	AAEGIIILLNN	NAILING A LIE
AAEFILOPRTW	PAIL OF WATER	AAEGIIIMNTV	IMAGINATIVE
AAEFILORSST	RAISES ALOFT	AAEGIIKLMNP	MAKING A PILE
AAEFILORSSV	FIRES A SALVO	AAEGIIKLMNT	TAKING A MILE
AAEFILPSSTY	PLAYS IT SAFE	AAEGIIKLMNV	MAKE A LIVING
AAEFIMNNRSU	UNFAIR MEANS	AAEGIIKNRST	TAKING A RISE
AAEFIMORTTU	FOUR AT A TIME	AAEGIIKNTVW	TAKING A VIEW
AAEFIOPPRRT	REAP A PROFIT	AAEGIILLNTV	ALLEVIATING
AAEFIRRSSTT	STARTS A FIRE	AAEGIILMNPS	PELAGIANISM
AAEFIRRTTWY	FRITTER AWAY	AAEGIILMRST	MAGISTERIAL
AAEFKNOORTT	TAKEN TOO FAR	AAEGIILNNRV	EARN A LIVING
AAEFLLMMRRS	SMALL FARMER	AAEGIILNNUV	GAIN IN VALUE
AAEFLLNRRTY	FRATERNALLY	AAEGIILNPTV	LEAVING A TIP
AAEFLNORTUW	LAW OF NATURE	AAEGIILNRTT	RETALIATING
AAEFLNRRRST	TRANSFERRAL	AAEGIILPRRS	PLAGIARISER
AAEFLOPSTTY	STATE OF PLAY	AAEGIILPRRZ	PLAGIARIZER
AAEFLPPSSTU	SLAP-UP FEAST	AAEGIILPRSS	PLAGIARISES
AAEFMNOPRRY	MAN OF PRAYER	AAEGIILPRSZ	PLAGIARIZES
AAEFORRSTYZ	SAFETY RAZOR	AAEGIIMNSTT	AGAINST TIME
AAEGGGGINRT	AGGREGATING	AAEGIIMSSTV	GAVE IT A MISS
AAEGGGILNNY	LAYING AN EGG	AAEGIINNOTV	EVAGINATION
AAEGGGINORT	AGGREGATION	AAEGIINNSTV	INVAGINATES
AAEGGHIKLNS	SHAKING A LEG	AAEGIINORTV	VARIEGATION
AAEGGIILNSV	GIVE A SIGNAL	AAEGIINPTTX	EXPATIATING
AAEGGIIMNTW	WAITING GAME	AAEGIINRSST	RISE AGAINST
AAEGGIINRTV	VARIEGATING	AAEGIINRSTT	INGRATIATES
AAEGGILMNOS	LOSING A GAME	AAEGIINSTTV	AESTIVATING
AAEGGILNNRW	GALE WARNING	AAEGIIRTTVV	GRAVITATIVE
AAEGGILNRUV	GAVE A RULING	AAEGIJKKMNO	MAKING A JOKE
AAEGGILNSSW	GLASWEGIANS	AAEGIKLMNRU	MAKING A RULE
AAEGGILNTTU	AGGLUTINATE	AAEGIKLNPRS	SPRING A LEAK
AAEGGIMMNTU	GAMETANGIUM	AAEGIKLNRWY	WAKING EARLY
AAEGGINNRVW	GAVE WARNING	AAEGIKMMNOV	MAKING A MOVE
AAEGGINNTTT	GETTING A TAN	AAEGIKMMNSS	MAKING A MESS
AAEGGINOSST	GOES AGAINST	AAEGIKMNNOT	MAKING A NOTE
AAEGGINPSSU	USING AS A PEG	AAEGIKMNRTW	MAKING WATER
AAEGGINPSWY	PAYING WAGES	AAEGIKMNSVW	MAKING WAVES
AAEGGINRUVW	WEAVING A RUG	AAEGIKNNOTT	TAKING A NOTE
AAEGGINTTWY	GETTING AWAY	AAEGIKNNRTW	TAKE WARNING
AAEGGJLLNOR	LEGAL JARGON	AAEGIKNOTTV	TAKING A VOTE
AAEGGLMMORU	GRAMMALOGUE	AAEGIKNRSTT	TAKING A REST
AAEGGNORRUW	NARROW GAUGE	AAEGIKNSTTT	TAKING A TEST
AAEGHHINOPV	HAVING A HOPE	AAEGILLLNPR	PARALLELING
AAEGHHLORSU	HOARSE LAUGH	AAEGILLNOST	ALLEGATIONS
AAEGHHLRTUY	HEARTY LAUGH	AAEGILLNPPR	APPARELLING
AAEGHIKLMNO	MAKING A HOLE	AAEGILLNPPY	APPEALINGLY
AAEGHIKMNST	MAKING HASTE	AAEGILLNRST	GALLANTRIES
AAEGHIKNPST	TAKING SHAPE	AAEGILLRRUW	GUERILLA WAR
AAEGHIKNRTT	TAKING HEART	AAEGILMMNOS	MAGLEMOSIAN
AAEGHILLLLV	VILLAGE HALL	AAEGILMNRST	MARTINGALES
AAEGHILNTTT	LATE AT NIGHT	AAEGILMNRTT	MALTREATING
AAEGHIMNNORR	MENORRHAGIA	AAEGILMNRTV	MALT VINEGAR
AAEGHIMNPRS	MANAGERSHIP	AAEGILMNRTY	LIGAMENTARY
AAEGHIMNPRV	HAVING A PERM	AAEGILMNSTT	STALEMATING

AAEGILMNTWY	MELTING AWAY
AAEGILMSSTT	STALAGMITES
AAEGILNNORS	LOSING AN EAR
AAEGILNNPPU	UNAPPEALING
AAEGILNNRTT	ALTERNATING
AAEGILNNSST	SENT A SIGNAL
AAEGILNOSTT	GESTATIONAL
AAEGILNQRUU	EQUIANGULAR
AAEGILNRTTU	TRIANGULATE
AAEGILNRTUV	GRANULATIVE
AAEGILNSTWY	LAYING WASTE
AAEGIMMNNNS	NAMING NAMES
AAEGIMNNRRT	ARRAIGNMENT
AAEGIMNNRYZ	NAZI GERMANY
AAEGIMNRRSV	MARGRAVINES
AAEGIMNRSTY	GAIN MASTERY
AAEGIMRSSTT	MAGISTRATES
AAEGINNOSST	ANTAGONISES
AAEGINNOSTZ	ANTAGONIZES
AAEGINNRSTY	STAYING NEAR
AAEGINNSTTW	WENT AGAINST
AAEGINNTTTU	ATTENUATING
AAEGINOPRTV	EVAPORATING
AAEGINORSST	ROSE AGAINST
AAEGINOSTTV	VOTE AGAINST
AAEGINPRTVY	GIVEN A PARTY
AAEGINPRTXY	PAYING EXTRA
AAEGINRRSTT	GREAT STRAIN
AAEGINRSTUU	INAUGURATES
AAEGIOPPRTV	PROPAGATIVE
AAEGIOPSTTY	STEATOPYGIA
AAEGIORRSTV	VARIEGATORS
AAEGIPRSTVY	GIVES A PARTY
AAEGIRRSTTT	GREAT ARTIST
AAEGKLNPRSU	SPRUNG A LEAK
AAEGKMMNOST	GAMMON STEAK
AAEGKOPRSSU	PORK SAUSAGE
AAEGLLNOPTY	PENALTY GOAL
AAEGLLNORTV	TRAVEL ALONG
AAEGLLORSSU	SAUSAGE ROLL
AAEGLMNORTU	LARGE AMOUNT
AAEGLMNPRST	MENTAL GRASP
AAEGLMOPRRU	PARLOUR GAME
AAEGLMRRRUY	REGULAR ARMY
AAEGLNOPSSS	PASSES ALONG
AAEGLNRSTTU	STRANGULATE
AAEGLPRRSTT	LARGEST PART
AAEGLRSSTTU	GASTRULATES
AAEGLRSTTUV	VULGAR TASTE
AAEGMNORTTU	GREAT AMOUNT
AAEGMRRSSTT	ST.MARGARETS
AAEGOPRSSTY	EASY TO GRASP
AAEHHIRSTTV	HAVE A THIRST
AAEHHJLLLSU	HALLELUJAHS
AAEHHMNORTT	THE MARATHON
AAEHHOTUVWY	WHAT HAVE YOU
AAEHHSTTTWY	THATS THE WAY
AAEHIILNNST	ANNIHILATES
AAEHIILNSTT	THE ITALIANS
AAEHIILSTWW	WAITS AWHILE
AAEHIINPSTT	ANTIPATHIES
AAEHIIRRRSS	HAIR-RAISERS
AAEHIJLNNOU	JEAN ANOUILH
AAEHILLMTTY	I'LL EAT MY HAT
AAEHILMNOST	THE MONA LISA
AAEHILNNOTT	THE NATIONAL
AAEHILNOSTT	EAST LOTHIAN
AAEHILNOSTX	EXHALATIONS
AAEHILPPRSY	HYPERPLASIA
AAEHILRRTWY	TARRY AWHILE
AAEHILSSTWY	STAYS AWHILE

AAEHIMOSSST	HAEMOSTASIS
AAEHINPRSTT	THESPIAN ART
AAEHINQSTUV	HAVE A SQUINT
AAEHIRRSUWY	HURRIES AWAY
AAEHIRSTWWY	WITHERS AWAY
AAEHKMNRSSS	SHANKSS MARE
AAEHKNOOPTT	TAKEN A PHOTO
AAEHKOOPSTT	TAKES A PHOTO
AAEHKRRSTUY	ARTHUR ASKEY
AAEHLLLPPST	PAST ALL HELP
AAEHLLMNSTW	MAN THE WALLS
AAEHLLMPSTY	PLAYS HAMLET
AAEHLLNOOPT	NO HOPE AT ALL
AAEHLLPPVYY	HAPPY VALLEY
AAEHLMOPSTY	PLAYS AT HOME
AAEHLNPRSTY	PHALANSTERY
AAEHLPPRTTY	PLAY THE PART
AAEHLPSSSTT	PASS THE SALT
AAEHMMMNNORS	MEANS NO HARM
AAEHMMMNNORT	MEANT NO HARM
AAEHMMMRSSTT	MATHS MASTER
AAEHMMNRTUU	HUMAN NATURE
AAEHMNORSTT	TAM-O'-SHANTER
AAEHMNORSWW	WASHERWOMAN
AAEHMOSSTTY	STAY-AT-HOMES
	STAYS AT HOME
AAEHNOORSTW	SWEAR ON OATH
	SWORE AN OATH
AAEHNORRSVW	NARROW SHAVE
AAEHNPRRSSW	SHARP ANSWER
AAEHOPRTTTW	HOT-WATER TAP
AAEHPRRTTWY	THREW A PARTY
AAEHPRRTXYY	X-RAY THERAPY
AAEHRRSSTTU	ARTHURS SEAT
AAEIIILMNST	ANIMALITIES
AAEIIILNNTW	ITALIAN WINE
AAEIILRSUX	AUXILIARIES
AAEIIJNRSSS	JANISSARIES
AAEIIKLMNPT	MAKE IT PLAIN
AAEIIKNRSST	RAISE A STINK
AAEIILLMNNR	MILLENARIAN
AAEIILLMNRT	MATRILINEAL
AAEIILLNOTV	ALLEVIATION
AAEIILLNPRT	PATRILINEAL
AAEIILLNRWY	RAILWAY LINE
AAEIILLPRST	IPSILATERAL
AAEIILLPTXY	EPITAXIALLY
AAEIILMMRST	MATERIALISM
AAEIILMMRTW	MARITIME LAW
AAEIILMNNTY	INANIMATELY
AAEIILMNRRT	AIR TERMINAL
AAEIILMRSTT	MATERIALIST
AAEIILMRTTY	MATERIALITY
AAEIILMSSST	ASSIMILATES
AAEIILNNOST	ALIENATIONS
	NATIONALISE
AAEIILNNOTZ	NATIONALIZE
AAEIILNORST	RATIONALISE
	REALISATION
AAEIILNORTT	RETALIATION
AAEIILNORTZ	RATIONALIZE
	REALIZATION
AAEIILNSSTV	SAINTS ALIVE
AAEIILQTTUV	QUALITATIVE
AAEIIMMNNOTX	EXAMINATION
AAEIIMNNRSS	SEMINARIANS
AAEIIMNRSST	ERASTIANISM
AAEIIMNRSTT	MENAI STRAIT
AAEIIMNTTUW	WAIT A MINUTE
AAEIINNSTTT	INSTANTIATE
AAEIINOPTTX	EXPATIATION

AAEIINOSTTV	AESTIVATION	AAEIMMPPRUY	PAY A PREMIUM
AAEIINQRSTU	ANTIQUARIES	AAEIMNNOPRS	POMERANIANS
AAEIINRSSTT	TRIES A SAINT	AAEIMNNRRST	TRANSMARINE
AAEIJKLNORT	LIKE A TROJAN	AAEIMNNSTTT	ATTAINMENTS
AAEIJKMNOST	MAKES A JOINT	AAEIMNORRVZ	RIVER AMAZON
AAEIJLNOPPT	JOINT APPEAL	AAEIMNPTTTV	VAIN ATTEMPT
AAEIKKMMRST	MAKE ITS MARK	AAEIMOPPRTX	APPROXIMATE
AAEIKLLTTVY	TALKATIVELY	AAEINNORSSY	RAINY SEASON
AAEIKLMNOPT	KLEPTOMANIA	AAEINNOTTTT	AT ATTENTION
AAEIKLNORRW	LIKE AN ARROW	AAEINNOTTTU	ATTENUATION
AAEIKLNOSST	AS LIKE AS NOT	AAEINNQRSTU	QUARANTINES
AAEIKLOPRRT	LIKE A PARROT	AAEINNRRSVY	ANNIVERSARY
AAEIKLSSSST	STEALS A KISS	AAEINOOPRTV	EVAPORATION
AAEIKMMRSTW	MAKES IT WARM	AAEINOPPRRT	PREPARATION
AAEIKMNOPST	MAKES A POINT	AAEINOPRRST	REPARATIONS
AAEILLLMNOT	LAMELLATION	AAEINOPRSST	SEPARATIONS
AAEILLLMPRS	PARALLELISM	AAEINOSTTTT	ATTESTATION
AAEILLLOSTV	SAL VOLATILE	AAEIOPPPRRT	APPROPRIATE
AAEILLMNORV	ANIMAL LOVER	AAEIOPRSSTT	APOSTATISED
AAEILLMNOTT	NO TIME AT ALL	AAEIOPSSTTZ	APOSTATIZES
AAEILLMNRST	MINERAL SALT	AAEIORSSTTV	ASSORTATIVE
AAEILLMRSSY	AMARYLLISES	AAEIPRSSSTT	SEPARATISTS
AAEILLNNPTY	TIN PAN ALLEY	AAEJKLOPRSY	PLAYS A JOKER
AAEILLNOPPT	APPELLATION	AAEJLMNOPRT	MAJOR PLANET
AAEILLNPRSS	SAILPLANERS	AAEJNNRTUXY	NEXT JANUARY
AAEILLORSSW	LOW SALARIES	AAEKKNOSTTT	TAKEN TO TASK
AAEILLORTTU	RATATOUILLE	AAEKKOSSTTT	TAKES TO TASK
AAEILLORTVY	ALLEVIATORY	AAEKLLNORTT	LEARN TO TALK
AAEILLQRSTU	AQUARELLIST	AAEKLLNORTW	LEARN TO WALK
AAEILMMORRW	WAR MEMORIAL	AAEKLLORSTT	TAKE A STROLL
AAEILMNNORT	NOMINAL RATE	AAEKLMNOSST	SALMON STEAK
AAEILMNNOTT	LAMENTATION	AAEKLMRRSTT	SMART TALKER
AAEILMNPRST	PARLIAMENTS	AAEKLNORTWW	WALK ON WATER
	PATERNALISM	AAEKLOORSTT	LOOKS A TREAT
AAEILMNPRTU	PLANETARIUM	AAEKMNORSTT	TAKEN TO ARMS
AAEILMNPSTU	MANIPULATES	AAEKMNPRSTU	TAKEN UP ARMS
AAEILMNRRSS	SILAS MARNER	AAEKMORSSTT	TAKES TO ARMS
AAEILMNRRTU	ULTRAMARINE	AAEKMPRSSTU	TAKES UP ARMS
AAEILMNRRTY	LITERARY MAN	AAEKMRSSSTT	TASKMASTERS
AAEILMNRSTT	LATIN MASTER	AAEKNNOPRTT	TAKEN NO PART
AAEILNNOPST	NEAPOLITANS	AAEKNOPRSTT	TAKES NO PART
AAEILNNOPSX	EXPANSIONAL	AAEKPRSSSTT	STREAKS PAST
AAEILNNOPTX	EXPLANATION	AAELLLLMNOSS	SALMONELLAS
AAEILNNORTT	ALTERNATION	AAELLLNPRRU	RUN PARALLEL
AAEILNNOSST	SENSATIONAL	AAELLLOSSST	SELL AT A LOSS
AAEILNNOTTT	ATTENTIONAL	AAELLMMRSTT	SMALL MATTER
AAEILNNPRST	TRANSALPINE	AAELLOPSSTT	ELASTOPLAST
AAEILNNPRSW	PLAIN ANSWER	AAELLORSTUY	ROYAL SALUTE
AAEILNNSSTV	VALIANTNESS	AAELLQRRSTU	ALL QUARTERS
AAEILNOOPRT	OPERATIONAL	AAELMNNSUUU	UNUSUAL NAME
AAEILNOPPRY	PIANO PLAYER	AAELMNOPPRU	POPULAR NAME
	PLAYER PIANO	AAELMNORSTT	NORMAL STATE
AAEILNOPRRT	PROLETARIAN	AAELMNRTUUY	EARLY AUTUMN
AAEILNORRTT	ORIENTAL ART	AAELMNSSTTY	STATESMANLY
AAEILNORSTT	ALTERATIONS	AAELMOPRRTU	ARMOUR PLATE
AAEILNOSSWW	WISE AS AN OWL		PLATE ARMOUR
AAEILNOSTTX	EXALTATIONS	AAELNNRRSSTU	NATURALNESS
AAEILNPRSTT	PATERNALIST	AAELNOPRTXY	EXPLANATORY
AAEILNRRTVY	NARRATIVELY	AAELNORRSTT	ALTERNATORS
AAEILNRSSTT	TANTALISERS	AAELNORSSTY	ROYAL ASSENT
AAEILNRSSTU	NATURALISES	AAELNRRSTSV	TRANSVERSAL
AAEILNRSTTV	AT INTERVALS	AAELNRRSSTW	WARRANTLESS
AAEILNRSTTZ	TANTALIZERS	AAELNRSSTUX	TRANSSEXUAL
AAEILNRSTUZ	NATURALIZES	AAELNRSTTUY	STAY NEUTRAL
AAEILOPRRTT	PROLETARIAT	AAELOOORRTVY	LAEVOROTARY
AAEILORRTTY	RETALIATORY	AAELORRTVVY	ROTARY VALVE
AAEILORSSTV	ROASTS ALIVE	AAELPSSTTUY	STAYS UP LATE
AAEILPRSTWY	WRITES A PLAY	AAELQRRSTTU	LAST QUARTER
AAEILQRRTUY	RARE QUALITY	AAEMNNRSSTV	MANSERVANTS
AAEILRRTUVY	RARITY VALUE	AAEMNOOSSST	ANASTOMOSES
AAEIMMNOTTW	WAIT A MOMENT	AAEMNOPRTTU	PORTMANTEAU

AAEMNOSSTTW	STATESWOMAN	AAFLLLNOOPW	FOLLOW A PLAN
AAEMNPPRTTY	PART PAYMENT	AAFLLMOORST	FAR TOO SMALL
AAEMOOPRSTZ	SPERMATOZOA	AAFMMMNNORRS	MAN FROM MARS
AAEMOORSTTW	RAW TOMATOES	AAFMMNOOSUW	FAMOUS WOMAN
AAEMORSSTTT	TOASTMASTER	AAFMNOORRRY	RAN FOR MAYOR
AAENNPPRRTTU	APPURTENANT	AAFMNORSSTW	SWARM OF ANTS
AAENNPRRSTT	TRANSPARENT	AAFNOOPRRTT	PATRON OF ART
AAENNPRSTTU	SUPERNATANT	AAGGGHILNSU	LAUGHING GAS
AAENOPRRSST	SPORTS ARENA	AAGGGIINNNP	NAGGING PAIN
AAENOPSSSWY	PASS ONE'S WAY	AAGGHHIINNS	SHANGHAIING
AAENOPSSWYY	PAYS ONE'S WAY	AAGGHHIOPRY	HAGIOGRAPHY
AAENORSTTTU	ATTENUATORS	AAGGHIIJMNT	THINGAMAJIG
AAENOSSSSYY	SAYS ONE'S SAY	AAGGHIILNTT	HALTING GAIT
AAENRRSSTTU	RESTAURANTS	AAGGIIILNNV	LIVING AGAIN
AAEOOPPRRRT	PARATROOPER	AAGGIIKLNTV	GIVING A TALK
AAEOOPPQRRTU	QUARTO PAPER	AAGGIIKMNNS	MAKING A SIGN
AAEOPPPRRRTY	PREPARATORY	AAGGIIKNPRT	TAKING A GRIP
AAEOPRRTUVW	WATER VAPOUR	AAGGIILNNOS	ANALOGISING
AAEPQRRSTTU	QUARTER PAST	AAGGIILNNOZ	ANALOGIZING
AAFFFINNRUY	FUNNY AFFAIR	AAGGIILNNSV	GALVANISING
AAFFGIIILNT	AFFILIATING	AAGGIILNNVZ	GALVANIZING
AAFFGILLLNT	FALLING FLAT	AAGGIIMMNNS	MISMANAGING
AAFFGIMNRSU	RAGAMUFFINS	AAGGIINNNPW	GNAWING PAIN
AAFFIIILNOT	AFFILIATION	AAGGIINNRTY	TRYING AGAIN
AAFFIIMNORT	AFFIRMATION	AAGGIINNSWY	SIGNING AWAY
AAFFIKLNNRY	FRANK FINLAY	AAGGIINRRUY	YURI GAGARIN
AAFGGIIKMNT	MAKING A GIFT	AAGGIINRTTV	GRAVITATING
AAFGGIILLNP	FILLING A GAP	AAGGIILNOST	ALGOLAGNIST
AAFGGIKMNOS	SMOKING A FAG	AAGGILNNRTU	GRANULATING
AAFGHHIINTV	HAVING FAITH	AAGGILNPUUU	PAUL GAUGUIN
AAFGHIRSTTT	START A FIGHT	AAGGINOPPRT	PROPAGATING
AAFGIIKLLNY	ALKALIFYING	AAGGINORSTY	GOING ASTRAY
AAFGIILNPRY	PLAYING FAIR	AAGGLLNNSYY	YLANG-YLANGS
AAFGIINNRRW	FAIR WARNING	AAGHHINOSTV	HAVING A SHOT
AAFGIINNSTZ	FANTASIZING	AAGHHLOPPRY	HAPLOGRAPHY
AAFGIINNTTU	INFATUATING	AAGHHMSTTTU	TAUGHT MATHS
AAFGIKLNSTT	FAST-TALKING	AAGHIIINRRS	HAIR-RAISING
AAFGIKMNSSU	MAKING A FUSS	AAGHIIKMNSW	MAKING A WISH
AAFGILLLSSS	FILLS A GLASS	AAGHIIKNNST	THINKS AGAIN
AAFGILLMRUY	GALLIMAUFRY	AAGHIIKNNTT	TAKING A HINT
AAFGILLNRST	FALLING STAR	AAGHIILLNOP	ANGLOPHILIA
AAFGILNORST	GRAIN OF SALT	AAGHIINRRST	RIGHT AS RAIN
AAFGILNOSTT	STAGFLATION	AAGHIKLLMNR	HALLMARKING
AAFGILNRTTU	NATURAL GIFT	AAGHIKLNOOV	HAVING A LOOK
AAFGINORSUV	GAINS FAVOUR	AAGHIKMNOSW	MAKING A SHOW
AAFGMOORTWY	GOT AWAY FROM	AAGHIKNOSTT	TAKING A SHOT
AAFGNOORSTU	RAN OUT OF GAS	AAGHILLMNRS	MARSHALLING
AAFHHIINPRS	PIRANHA FISH	AAGHILLRSTT	ALL STRAIGHT
AAFHIKNSSST	SINKS A SHAFT	AAGHILOORTY	GAY LOTHARIO
AAFHILMPPYY	HAPPY FAMILY	AAGHIMNRSTT	STRAIGHT MAN
AAFHILNOTWX	HALIFAX TOWN	AAGHINNPSTY	PHANTASYING
AAFIIILMRTY	FAMILIARITY	AAGHINOOSWY	SHOOING AWAY
AAFIILMTTW	WILLIAM TAFT	AAGHINOPSSV	SHAVING SOAP
AAFIILMOORT	TOO FAMILIAR	AAGHINOPSSW	WASHING SOAP
AAFIILNNPST	IN A FLAT SPIN	AAGHINPSUWY	PUSHING AWAY
AAFIINNOTTU	INFATUATION	AAGHINRRSTT	RAN STRAIGHT
AAFIINRRSTU	FRUITARIANS	AAGHINRSSTW	GRANTS A WISH
AAFIJLNRTUY	FATAL INJURY	AAGHINRSUWY	RUSHING AWAY
AAFILLLMMSY	SMALL FAMILY	AAGHIRSSTTW	SAW STRAIGHT
AAFILLLNORW	LOW RAINFALL	AAGHIRSTTWY	STRAIGHTWAY
AAFILLMORYY	ROYAL FAMILY	AAGHLNOPPRY	PLANOGRAPHY
AAFILLNORUV	ALL IN FAVOUR	AAGHMRRTTUUY	THAUMATURGY
AAFILMNOORT	FORMATIONAL	AAGHNOPPRST	PANTOGRAPHS
AAFILNOORST	FLOATS ON AIR	AAGHNOPRRUY	URANOGRAPHY
AAFILNOOSTT	FLOATATIONS	AAGIIILMNNS	ANIMALISING
AAFILOPSSST	FAILS TO PASS	AAGIIILMNNZ	ANIMALIZING
AAFIMNNNRTY	INFANTRYMAN	AAGIIILMNRY	IMAGINARILY
AAFINNOOPRT	PROFANATION	AAGIIIMNNNT	MAINTAINING
AAFINOPRRRY	PRAY FOR RAIN	AAGIIIMNNOT	IMAGINATION
AAFIOPPRSST	PAIR OF SPATS	AAGIIKKLLMN	MAKING A KILL
AAFKLPRSTYY	FLAKY PASTRY	AAGIIKKNRST	TAKING A RISK

AAGIIKLLMNW	MAKING A WILL
AAGIIKLLNPT	TAKING A PILL
AAGIIKLMNNP	MAKING PLAIN
AAGIIKLMNPS	MAKING A SLIP
AAGIIKLMNST	MAKING A LIST
AAGIIKMMNNT	MAKING A MINT
AAGIIKMNPTY	MAKING IT PAY
AAGIIKMNSST	TAKING AMISS
AAGIIKNNPST	PAINSTAKING
AAGIIKNPRTT	TAKING A TRIP
AAGIILLLNWW	WAILING WALL
AAGIILMNNRS	ARM IN A SLING
AAGIILMNORT	MIGRATIONAL
AAGIILMNRTY	MARGINALITY
AAGIILMPRSS	PLAGIARISMS
AAGIILNNSTT	TANTALISING
AAGIILNNTTZ	TANTALIZING
AAGIILNPPTT	PALPITATING
AAGIILNPRTV	LIVING APART
AAGIIMMNNOT	AMMONIATING
AAGIIMMNNTY	MAGNANIMITY
AAGIIMMSSTT	ASTIGMATISM
AAGIIMMNNOST	ANATOMISING
AAGIIMMNNOTZ	ANATOMIZING
AAGIINNOGGT	ASSIGNATION
AAGIINNOSTV	NAVIGATIONS
AAGIINNSTUU	AUGUSTINIAN
AAGIINNORTTV	GRAVITATION
AAGIINPSSTV	PASSIVATING
AAGIINPSTTU	UP AGAINST IT
AAGIINRTTVY	ANTIGRAVITY
AAGIIRSSTTU	SAGITTARIUS
AAGIJKNOPRT	JOKING APART
AAGIKKKLNOOT	LOOK AT A KING
	TAKING A LOOK
AAGIKLLLNTW	WALKING TALL
AAGIKLLNOTT	TALKING A LOT
AAGIKLMNNPS	MAKING PLANS
AAGIKLMNOSS	MAKING A LOSS
AAGIKLNOOWY	LOOKING AWAY
AAGIKLNPSTW	WALKING PAST
AAGIKMNOORT	TAKING A ROOM
AAGIKNNNTTU	ANTI-TANK GUN
AAGIKNNRTTU	TAKING A TURN
AAGIKNORSTW	WORK AGAINST
AAGILLLLNPPY	APPALLINGLY
AAGILLLOOSS	GLOSSOLALIA
AAGILLMNNTY	MALIGNANTLY
AAGILLMRSTY	MAGISTRALLY
AAGILMNNORS	LOSING AN ARM
AAGILNNOQSU	ALGONQUIANS
AAGILNNORTU	GRANULATION
AAGILNNOTTW	WANTING A LOT
AAGILNNPPSY	PLAYING SNAP
AAGILNNRSTT	TRANSLATING
AAGILNRRTUY	GRANULARITY
AAGILNSSSUY	AS UGLY AS SIN
AAGILOPRRTU	PURGATORIAL
AAGIMMMNNOSU	MAGNANIMOUS
AAGIMMMNNRRY	MARRYING MAN
AAGIMNNNORT	IGNORANT MAN
AAGIMNRSSTY	SMART SAYING
AAGINNNRUWY	RUNNING AWAY
AAGINNNOSSTT	ANTAGONISTS
AAGINNRSSTU	RUNS AGAINST
AAGINNRSTTU	TURN AGAINST
AAGINNRTUWY	TURNING AWAY
AAGINOOPPRT	PROPAGATION
AAGINORRTUU	INAUGURATOR
AAGINORSTWY	STORING AWAY
AAGINOSTWWY	STOWING AWAY

AAGINPPRRST	SPRING A TRAP
	SPRING APART
AAGINPRSSWY	SPRINGS AWAY
AAGINPTTUWY	PUTTING AWAY
AAGINRRTTYY	TRY,TRY AGAIN
AAGINRSSTTV	START SAVING
AAGLLMMMOOY	MAMMALOLOGY
AAGLLNOOSUY	ANALOGOUSLY
AAGLMNNNOOR	ANGLO-NORMAN
AAGLMNOORTY	MORTAL AGONY
AAGLMNRSTUY	GRANT ASYLUM
AAGLNNOOSSX	ANGLO-SAXONS
AAGLNOOTUWY	A LONG WAY OUT
AAGNPPRRSTU	SPRUNG A TRAP
	SPRUNG APART
AAHHILMPRSS	MARSHALSHIP
AAHIILNNORT	ANNIHILATOR
AAHIILNNOST	INHALATIONS
AAHIILNNRSV	NAIL VARNISH
AAHIILNNSTU	LITHUANIANS
AAHIIMNNPSS	SPANISH MAIN
AAHIKLSTWWY	WALK THIS WAY
AAHIKNRSSWY	SHRINKS AWAY
AAHILLLOPRT	PROTHALLIAL
AAHILLMTUYZ	AZIMUTHALLY
AAHILMORSTT	MARSHAL TITO
AAHIMMNNOPY	NYMPHOMANIA
AAHIMNNOSTU	MOUNTAIN ASH
AAHIMNOPRSS	OARSMANSHIP
AAHINNOPRTY	ANTIPHONARY
AAHIOPRSTXY	ASPHYXIATOR
AAHIOSSTTTY	THAT IS TO SAY
AAHIOTUWWYY	AWAY WITH YOU!
AAHIPSSSTWY	PASS THIS WAY
AAHJKNRRRTU	J.ARTHUR RANK
AAHKOPSTUUW	POHUTUKAWAS
AAHLLMMORSW	MARSHMALLOW
AAHLPQSSSUY	PLAYS SQUASH
AAHMNNRRTUY	HARRY TRUMAN
AAHMOOSSTWY	SMOOTHS AWAY
AAHNNOORSTW	SWORN AN OATH
AAHNOPRTTUY	NATUROPATHY
AAHOPRRTTWY	THROW A PARTY
AAIIILMNOTT	IMITATIONAL
AAIIILMRSST	ALISTAIR SIM
AAIIILNRTTU	UTILITARIAN
AAIIILRTTXY	TRIAXIALITY
AAIIINNRRTT	TRINITARIAN
AAIIJNPSTZZ	JAZZ PIANIST
AAIIILLLPSUZ	LAPIS LAZULI
AAIIILLMPRTY	IMPARTIALLY
AAIIILLMRTWY	MILITARY LAW
AAIIILMMNORS	MANORIALISM
AAIIILMMNORT	MATRIMONIAL
AAIIILMMNRTY	MILITARY MAN
AAIIILMMSSTX	MAXIMALISTS
AAIIILMNNOST	LAMINATIONS
	NATIONALISM
AAIIILMNOPRT	PATRIMONIAL
AAIIILMNORST	RATIONALISM
AAIIILMORSST	ASSIMILATOR
AAIIILNNOSTT	NATIONALIST
AAIIILNNOTTY	NATIONALITY
AAIIILNOPPTT	PALPITATION
AAIIILNORRST	IRRATIONALS
AAIIILNORSTT	RATIONALIST
AAIIILNORTTT	ATTRITIONAL
AAIIILNORTTY	RATIONALITY
AAIIILNOSTTU	SITUATIONAL
AAIIIMMNNOOT	AMMONIATION
AAIIIMNNNOST	ANTINOMIANS

AAIIMNOOSTT	ATOMISATION	ABBBENNORWY	NEW-BORN BABY
AAIIMNOOTTZ	ATOMIZATION	ABBBENORUWY	WOBURN ABBEY
AAIIMNOPRTT	IMPARTATION	ABBBGINNTUY	BABY BUNTING
AAIINNNNSTT	IN AN INSTANT	ABBBINNRTUY	BUNNY RABBIT
AAIINOPPRST	APPARITIONS	ABBCCDEKNOU	BOUNCED BACK
AAIINOPRSST	ASPIRATIONS	ABBCCEEHKNR	BACK BENCHER
AAIINOPSSTV	PASSIVATION		BACK-BENCHER
AAIINQSTTTU	AQUATINTIST	ABBCCEEHKNS	BACK BENCHES
AAIIPRSSTWY	SPIRITS AWAY	ABBCCEEHMOR	BEACHCOMBER
AAIJMNNOTTW	WANT JAM ON IT	ABBCCEKNOSU	BOUNCES BACK
AAIKNRRSTTT	TARTAN SKIRT	ABBCCGIKMNO	BACKCOMBING
AAILLLOSTWW	SWALLOWTAIL	ABBCCHIORTT	BOB CRATCHIT
AAILLORRSTY	SARTORIALLY	ABBCDDEKLOU	DOUBLED BACK
AAILMMNOSTU	SUMMATIONAL	ABBCDEEFIKO	BIOFEEDBACK
AAILMMOPPRS	MALAPROPISM	ABBCDEEILRS	DESCRIBABLE
AAILMNNOPRT	LION RAMPANT	ABBCDEENRSS	CRABBEDNESS
AAILMNOOPRT	POINT A MORAL	ABBCDEGIKNN	BENDING BACK
AAILMNOPRTU	MANIPULATOR	ABBCDEKLOSU	DOUBLES BACK
AAILMNORSTY	SOLITARY MAN	ABBCDEMRRSU	BREADCRUMBS
AAILMNRSTTT	TRANSMITTAL	ABBCDKLOORS	BLOCKBOARDS
AAILMOPRSST	PASTORALISM	ABBCEEEKLLT	BLACK BEETLE
AAILNNOPSST	LION PASSANT	ABBCEEKLORT	BETA-BLOCKER
AAILNNOPSTT	PLANTATIONS	ABBCEHIILOT	BIBLIOTHECA
AAILNNORSTT	TRANSLATION	ABBCELMNORU	NUCLEAR BOMB
AAILNOPPSSY	PASSION PLAY	ABBCGHKORTU	BROUGHT BACK
AAILNOSSTTU	SALUTATIONS	ABBCHHIRTTU	RABBIT HUTCH
AAILNRSSTTU	NATURALISTS	ABBCHIKLOPS	BLACK BISHOP
AAILOORSTTT	TOTALISATOR	ABBCHIKRSTY	SHABBY TRICK
AAILOORTTTZ	TOTALIZATOR	ABBCHILPSTU	PUBLIC BATHS
AAILOPRRTUV	VAPOUR TRAIL	ABBCHIMNOOP	BOB CHAMPION
AAILOPRSSTT	PASTORALIST	ABBCHINPRTU	RABBIT PUNCH
AAILPPRSTTY	PLAY ITS PART	ABBCKMOOORY	BACK-ROOM BOY
AAILQRSTTUY	STAR QUALITY		BACKROOM BOY
AAIMMNOSSUY	IMMUNOASSAY	ABBDDEERRUY	READY RUBBED
AAIMNNORSTT	ASTON MARTIN	ABBDDEIINRR	BIRDBRAINED
AAIMNOOSSST	ANASTOMOSIS	ABBDDELNOYY	BADLY DONE BY
AAIMNOPSTTU	AMPUTATIONS	ABBDDENNORR	BORN AND BRED
AAIMNORSSTU	SANATORIUMS	ABBDDEORRSW	BARBED WORDS
AAIMOSSTTTU	AUTOMATISTS	ABBDDIIILTY	BIDDABILITY
AAINNNOOSTT	ANNOTATIONS	ABBDEEEFIRS	BRAISED BEEF
AAINNOPRSTT	PATRON SAINT	ABBDEEGILRT	BRIDGE TABLE
AAINOOORRSTZ	ZOROASTRIAN	ABBDEEHHLTY	HELD THE BABY
AAINRSSTTUY	STAYS IN A RUT	ABBDEEINORU	BURIED A BONE
AAIORRSSTTT	STARTS A RIOT	ABBDEEKNORR	BROKEN BREAD
AAKLLMPRUUU	KUALA LUMPUR	ABBDEELORTU	REDOUBTABLE
AAKNNORSSUY	SUSANNA YORK	ABBDEEMORRR	ARMED ROBBER
AALLLLNNSUU	NULLA-NULLAS	ABBDEGGILNR	BLIND BEGGAR
AALLMMNOSTU	SMALL AMOUNT	ABBDEGIORSY	BOYS BRIGADE
AALLMNOOSUY	ANOMALOUSLY	ABBDEHHLOTY	HOLD THE BABY
AALLMOOSTUY	AUTOSOMALLY	ABBDEHIMNTY	MIND THE BABY
AALLNNRTUUY	UNNATURALLY	ABBDEHNOSTU	HUSBAND TO BE
AALLNOPSTTY	POSTNATALLY	ABBDEIILNTU	INDUBITABLE
AALMMOOPSST	SOMATOPLASM	ABBDEIINRRU	INDIA RUBBER
AALMMOPPRRS	MRS.MALAPROP	ABBDEILMNOR	MEDAL RIBBON
AALMNOOTTTU	TOTAL AMOUNT	ABBDEIMNRSY	BABY-MINDERS
AALNNPRSSTT	TRANSPLANTS	ABBDEIMORRS	BOMBARDIERS
AALNOORTUVY	ANOVULATORY	ABBDEKLLNOU	DOUBLE BLANK
AALNOPRTTUU	RUN UP A TOTAL	ABBDELLNRSU	LANDLUBBERS
AALNORRSSTT	TRANSLATORS	ABBDELORTUY	REDOUBTABLY
AALNORSSSTU	RUNS AT A LOSS	ABBDEMMNORT	BOMBARDMENT
AALNPRSTTUY	PLAYS TRUANT	ABBDEMNOPSS	SPENDS A BOMB
AALORSSTTTU	ALTOSTRATUS	ABBDGIIMNNY	BABY-MINDING
AALORSSUWYY	YOURS ALWAYS	ABBDGIMRSSU	BIG BASS DRUM
AAMNPRSSTTY	SMARTY-PANTS	ABBDGINNRUY	BRING AND BUY
AANNORRSTUY	TYRANNOSAUR	ABBDGMNOOOW	GO DOWN A BOMB
AAOOOPRSTTT	ROAST POTATO	ABBDHLLNSUU	BULL AND BUSH
ABBBCEEEHLP	PEBBLE BEACH	ABBDIILNTUY	INDUBITABLY
ABBBDINOSST	BITS AND BOBS	ABBEEEHSTTT	BEAT THE BEST
ABBBEENNORW	NEW-BORN BABE	ABBEEEILRRS	BLAEBERRIES
ABBBEKNORRY	BANK ROBBERY	ABBEEFFNOOR	BARON OF BEEF
ABBBELOPSSU	SOAP BUBBLES	ABBEEFRRTTY	BETTER BY FAR

ABBEEGINNST	BEING ABSENT
ABBEEGLRTTY	BETTY GRABLE
ABBEEGORRRV	GRAVE ROBBER
ABBEEHMMORX	MAX BEERBOHM
ABBEEHMORVY	HEAVY BOMBER
ABBEEINORSU	BURIES A BONE
ABBEEKNNOOR	BROKEN A BONE
ABBEELOPRRS	BARBERS POLE
ABBEELPRRTU	PERTURBABLE
ABBEEMNSSTU	SUBBASEMENT
ABBEENRSTTU	BUTTER BEANS
ABBEFIILLMY	FAMILY BIBLE
ABBEFLOORUY	BLUE FOR A BOY
ABBEGIKLMOO	GO LIKE A BOMB
ABBEGILNORU	BELABOURING
ABBEGINORRT	BRING TO BEAR
ABBEGINORTW	BROWBEATING
ABBEHHIPRSU	RUBBISH HEAP
ABBEHIIRTTW	WHITE RABBIT
ABBEHILRSTW	WELSH RABBIT
ABBEHOPRRSS	BARBERS SHOP
	BARBERSHOPS
ABBEINORRRT	TRAIN ROBBER
ABBEINRRSUW	WINS A RUBBER
ABBEINRSSUU	SUBURBANISE
ABBEINRSTUU	SUBURBANITE
ABBEINRSUUZ	SUBURBANIZE
ABBEIRSSTTY	BABY-SITTERS
ABBELLRSTTU	BUTTERBALLS
ABBELMOOORS	AEROSOL BOMB
ABBELMSSSUY	SUBASSEMBLY
ABBELNPRRTU	RUBBER PLANT
ABBEMPRRSTU	RUBBER STAMP
	RUBBER-STAMP
ABBENNOOSST	BOSTON BEANS
ABBENNOOTTW	NEWTON ABBOT
ABBFFILLLOU	BUFFALO BILL
ABBFHOOORTY	BROTH OF A BOY
ABBFILORSST	FIBROBLASTS
ABBFIOORSTT	RABBITS FOOT
ABBGGINOOTY	GOING BY BOAT
ABBGIILLNTU	BULL BAITING
ABBGILMNNOOZ	BAMBOOZLING
ABBGILNORSY	ABSORBINGLY
ABBGINORSTU	BRINGS ABOUT
ABBHIKLRSTU	TALK RUBBISH
ABBIILOPRTY	PROBABILITY
ABBIILORSTY	SORBABILITY
ABBIKLOORRY	LIBRARY BOOK
ABBKOOOORRW	BORROW A BOOK
ABBMMNNORSTU	STUBBORN MAN
ABBNNOORRSY	BRYAN ROBSON
ABCCCEEFIOS	BECCAFICOES
ABCCCEEILRY	BICYCLE RACE
ABCCCHKKLOO	CHOCK-A-BLOCK
ABCCDEEIIRT	BACTERICIDE
ABCCDEHHKNU	HUNCHBACKED
ABCCDEHILNN	BLIND CHANCE
ABCCDEKKKNO	KNOCKED BACK
ABCCDEKLMOY	BLACK COMEDY
ABCCDKLLNOU	COCK AND BULL
	COCK-AND-BULL
ABCCDKLLOSU	BLACK CLOUDS
ABCCEEFFKLO	BLACK COFFEE
ABCCEEHHMOR	ECHO CHAMBER
ABCCEEILNOT	CECIL BEATON
ABCCEEILNOV	CONCEIVABLE
ABCCEEKLMOW	WELCOME BACK
ABCCEEKLOPU	PEACOCK BLUE
ABCCEELLLOT	COLLECTABLE
ABCCEELNNOT	CONNECTABLE

ABCCEELORRT	CORRECTABLE
ABCCEEMNNRU	ENCUMBRANCE
ABCCEFILNOS	CONFISCABLE
ABCCEGHNOOY	GONE BY COACH
ABCCEGHOOSY	GOES BY COACH
ABCCEGINNOU	CONCUBINAGE
ABCCEHHSTTU	CATCH THE BUS
ABCCEHIILMO	BIOCHEMICAL
ABCCEHILSTT	CABLE STITCH
ABCCEHNOTWY	WENT BY COACH
ABCCEIILNOT	CENOBITICAL
ABCCEIKKLST	STICKLEBACK
ABCCEIKLLRT	CRICKET BALL
ABCCEIKLNPR	BLACK PRINCE
ABCCEILMOPT	COMPACTIBLE
ABCCEILNORS	BACON SLICER
ABCCEILNOVY	CONCEIVABLY
ABCCEILOSTT	ECTOBLASTIC
ABCCEIOOPFT	PIPE TOBACCO
ABCCELMOOST	CLOSE COMBAT
ABCCFJKLOSU	JACK OF CLUBS
ABCCGHIKKNO	CHOKING BACK
ABCCGIIKKKN	KICKING BACK
ABCCGIKNTTU	CUTTING BACK
ABCCHIKSSTW	SWITCHBACKS
ABCCIILLNSU	SUBCLINICAL
ABCCIILRSTU	SUBCRITICAL
ABCCIIMOORT	MACROBIOTIC
ABCCIINOTVY	BICONCAVITY
ABCCIKKKNOT	KNOCK IT BACK
ABCCILLLOUY	BUCOLICALLY
ABCCINOOSTT	TOBACCONIST
ABCCKNOOOTU	ACCOUNT BOOK
ABCCLLNORTU	CARLTON CLUB
ABCCNORSTTU	SUBCONTRACT
ABCDDEEFLOU	DOUBLE-FACED
ABCDDEEILRS	SLICED BREAD
ABCDDEERRSS	DRESSED CRAB
ABCDDEKOPPR	DROPPED BACK
ABCDDEMOORY	BROAD COMEDY
ABCDEEEERRT	DECEREBRATE
ABCDEEEHORS	CHEESE BOARD
ABCDEEEILPR	DEPRECIABLE
ABCDEEFHNRR	FRENCH BREAD
ABCDEEFLORT	CLEAR OF DEBT
ABCDEEFMNOR	FOND EMBRACE
ABCDEEIILMM	IMMEDICABLE
ABCDEEILNRS	DISCERNABLE
ABCDEEILOTY	DELICATE BOY
ABCDEEILPRT	PREDICTABLE
ABCDEEINORS	DECARBONISE
ABCDEEINORZ	DECARBONIZE
ABCDEEKPPST	STEPPED BACK
ABCDEELLNOW	CLEAN BOWLED
ABCDEELLNRY	BELLY DANCER
ABCDEELMMNO	COMMENDABLE
ABCDEELMNNO	CONDEMNABLE
ABCDEELMORU	DOUBLE CREAM
ABCDEELNNOS	CONDENSABLE
ABCDEENORRT	CENTREBOARD
ABCDEERRTTU	CARBURETTED
ABCDEFFHNOR	BRANCHED OFF
ABCDEFIINRR	BIRD FANCIER
ABCDEFINOOS	SIDE OF BACON
ABCDEFKOOTU	BACKED OUT OF
ABCDEGHILOOS	SCHOOL BADGE
ABCDEGIKNNS	SENDING BACK
ABCDEHHKSUW	BUSHWHACKED
ABCDEHIKRRU	HURRIED BACK
ABCDEHILSTW	SWITCHBLADE

ABCDEHIRRTW	BIRD WATCHER
	BIRD-WATCHER
ABCDEHLMOOR	BACHELORDOM
ABCDEHLMORU	DOUBLE MARCH
ABCDEHLOTTU	CLUB TO DEATH
ABCDEHNORTU	BRANCHED OUT
ABCDEHORSSS	CHESSBOARDS
ABCDEIILLRU	BILLIARD CUE
ABCDEIILMMY	IMMEDICABLY
ABCDEIIORTT	OBITER DICTA
ABCDEIJKNRU	INJURED BACK
ABCDEIKLPPS	SLIPPED BACK
ABCDEIKLRSS	BACKSLIDERS
ABCDEILPRTY	PREDICTABLY
ABCDEILSSSU	DISCUSSABLE
ABCDEINOORT	NOTICE BOARD
	NOTICE-BOARD
ABCDEINRRST	TRANSCRIBED
ABCDEINRSTU	DISTURBANCE
ABCDEIPRRSS	CRISPBREADS
ABCDEKKLLOO	LOOKED BLACK
ABCDEKLNRTU	TURNED BLACK
ABCDEKLORTU	DOUBLE TRACK
ABCDEKMOTUU	MUCKED ABOUT
ABCDELLORSU	SCORED A BULL
ABCDELMMNOY	COMMENDABLY
ABCDELMNRSU	UNSCRAMBLED
ABCDELMORRU	RECORD ALBUM
ABCDENOOPTU	PONCED ABOUT
ABCDEOORRSS	SCOREBOARDS
ABCDFGIKLNO	FOLDING BACK
ABCDGHIKLNO	HOLDING BACK
ABCDGIIKLNS	SLIDING BACK
ABCDGIKNNOW	BACKING DOWN
ABCDGKNORSU	BACKGROUNDS
ABCDHHINRSU	RICH HUSBAND
ABCDHIILNRS	BRAINCHILDS
ABCDHIIMRTY	DITHYRAMBIC
ABCDHILLORU	CHILD LABOUR
ABCDHINOOPR	BRANCHIOPOD
ABCDHIOOPRS	BRACHIOPODS
ABCDHIOPSTX	DISPATCH BOX
ABCDHIORSTW	SWITCHBOARD
ABCDHLOOORS	BOARD SCHOOL
	SCHOOL BOARD
ABCDHNOORRY	HYDROCARBON
ABCDIILNNSU	INDIAN CLUBS
ABCDIINNOWW	CABIN WINDOW
ABCDIKOPRRS	DROPS A BRICK
ABCDMNORRUU	CARBORUNDUM
ABCEEEEMNTW	CAME BETWEEN
ABCEEEEFFKOR	COFFEE BREAK
ABCEEEEFFLOT	COFFEE TABLE
	COFFEE-TABLE
ABCEEEEFFNOS	COFFEE BEANS
ABCEEEFIINT	BENEFICIATE
ABCEEEEFLNOR	ENFORCEABLE
ABCEEEEFLNRU	BEEN CAREFUL
ABCEEEEFRTTX	BEEF EXTRACT
ABCEEEEHIKRT	BREAK THE ICE
ABCEEEIKRRS	ICEBREAKERS
ABCEEEEILPRV	PERCEIVABLE
ABCEEEEILRSV	SERVICEABLE
ABCEEEEILRSX	EXERCISABLE
ABCEEEINNRT	BEEN CERTAIN
ABCEEEELMNRS	RESEMBLANCE
ABCEEEELORRV	RECOVERABLE
ABCEEEELPRST	RESPECTABLE
ABCEEEEMMNRR	REMEMBRANCE
ABCEEEEMNOSS	BECOMES SANE
ABCEEEFFLOST	FLEET OF CABS
ABCEEFFMOST	CAME OFF BEST
ABCEEFHNNRS	FRENCH BEANS
ABCEEFIILPS	SPECIFIABLE
ABCEEFIILRT	CERTIFIABLE
	RECTIFIABLE
ABCEEFIINRY	BENEFICIARY
ABCEEFINNOT	BENEFACTION
ABCEEFINRTU	RUBEFACIENT
ABCEEFKORTY	TAKE BY FORCE
ABCEEFLNORR	CONFERRABLE
ABCEEFLNOSS	CONFESSABLE
ABCEEFNORST	BENEFACTORS
ABCEEGHNSSU	CHANGE BUSES
ABCEEGIINOT	ABIOGENETIC
ABCEEGIKKNP	KEEPING BACK
ABCEEGILNRT	CELEBRATING
ABCEEGINOST	CEASING TO BE
ABCEEGINRRT	CEREBRATING
ABCEEHHILRS	CHERISHABLE
ABCEEHJOTVY	HEAVY OBJECT
ABCEEHKLNQU	BLANK CHEQUE
ABCEEHLLRSY	BELLYACHERS
ABCEEHLLSTT	BELLS THE CAT
ABCEEHLRSTT	STRETCHABLE
ABCEEHLRTTU	THEATRE CLUB
ABCEEHORRRT	TORCHBEARER
ABCEEHORSTT	BEAR THE COST
ABCEEHPQUYY	PAY BY CHEQUE
ABCEEIILRST	BE REALISTIC
ABCEEIILLNTU	INELUCTABLE
ABCEEIILMRST	CLIMBS A TREE
ABCEEIILNORT	CELEBRATION
ABCEEIILNPSS	BASIL SPENCE
ABCEEIILNSUX	INEXCUSABLE
ABCEEIILORRV	IRREVOCABLE
ABCEEIILPRVY	PERCEIVABLY
ABCEEIILRSVY	SERVICEABLY
ABCEEIILRTTX	EXTRACTIBLE
ABCEEINNRTY	BICENTENARY
ABCEEEINORRT	CEREBRATION
ABCEEINORTX	EXORBITANCE
ABCEEINRRRS	CRANBERRIES
ABCEEJLOPRT	PROJECTABLE
ABCEEKLLRTT	BLACK LETTER
ABCEEKLLTVV	BLACK VELVET
ABCEEKLNOSY	LOSE BY A NECK
ABCEEKLPPPR	BLACK PEPPER
ABCEEKORRSV	BREAKS COVER
ABCEELLLMOP	COMPELLABLE
ABCEELMOPRR	RACE PROBLEM
ABCEELNORRT	CORNER TABLE
ABCEELNORST	EASTERN BLOC
ABCEELNOSTT	CONTESTABLE
ABCEELNRSSU	CURABLENESS
ABCEELOPRSS	PROCESSABLE
ABCEELORRST	CELEBRATORS
ABCEELORRTY	CELEBRATORY
ABCEELPRSTY	RESPECTABLY
ABCEELRTTUU	TUBERCULATE
ABCEEMOSTTU	CAME OUT BEST
ABCEENNORRST	ARBORESCENT
ABCEENORSSV	OBSERVANCES
ABCEFFHNORS	BRANCHES OFF
ABCEFIILLNN	FINANCE BILL
ABCEFIILRTY	CERTIFIABLY
ABCEFILMNOR	CONFIRMABLE
ABCEFIMNORY	BY MAIN FORCE
ABCEFINORVW	WOVEN FABRIC
ABCEFKLLLOW	BLACKFELLOW
ABCEFKLORST	BLACK FOREST
ABCEFLMNOOR	CONFORMABLE

ABCEFLMOORT	COMFORTABLE
ABCEFLOORRU	LABOUR FORCE
ABCEGGIKNTT	GETTING BACK
ABCEGGKLRUY	LUCKY BEGGAR
ABCEGHHIMTT	THE BIG MATCH
ABCEGHHOPTU	BOUGHT CHEAP
ABCEGHILLNY	BELLYACHING
ABCEGHINPUY	BUYING CHEAP
ABCEGHORRTU	TURBOCHARGE
ABCEGIILMPU	PUBLIC IMAGE
ABCEGIKNSTT	SETTING BACK
ABCEGILMNRY	EMBRACINGLY
ABCEGILNNOS	CONSIGNABLE
ABCEGIMMNRU	MAGIC NUMBER
ABCEGKLRTUY	RUGBY TACKLE
ABCEGKNOOTU	GONE BACK OUT
ABCEGKOOSTU	GOES BACK OUT
ABCEHHKRSUW	BUSHWHACKER
ABCEHIKMRST	THE BISMARCK
ABCEHIKRRSU	HURRIES BACK
ABCEHILNORV	OLIVE BRANCH
ABCEHKLOPTT	POT THE BLACK
ABCEHKLOTWY	BLOCK THE WAY
ABCEHKNOORS	ON HORSEBACK
ABCEHKOORTT	ROCK THE BOAT
ABCEHKPSSTU	PASS THE BUCK
ABCEHLLOSTT	TABLECLOTHS
ABCEHLNOTUU	UNTOUCHABLE
ABCEHLPSUYY	BUYS CHEAPLY
ABCEHMOPRST	CHAMBER POTS
ABCEHNORSTU	BRANCHES OUT
ABCEIIILLSV	CIVILISABLE
ABCEIIILLVZ	CIVILIZABLE
ABCEIIJLSTU	JUSTICIABLE
ABCEIILLNOT	LIBEL ACTION
ABCEIILMORT	BIOMETRICAL
ABCEIILMRTY	IMBRICATELY
ABCEIILNOSV	CABLEVISION
ABCEIILRTUV	LUBRICATIVE
ABCEIIMNOTV	COMBINATIVE
ABCEIKKRSST	STRIKES BACK
ABCEIKLLSTY	STICKY LABEL
ABCEIKLMPSU	MAKES PUBLIC
ABCEIKLRRSY	BRICKLAYERS
ABCEIKNNSWY	WINS BY A NECK
ABCEIKNOOPT	A BONE TO PICK
ABCEIKNORTW	CABINETWORK
ABCEIKNRTTW	WRITTEN BACK
ABCEILLLMNR	BILL MCLAREN
ABCEILLLOPS	COLLAPSIBLE
ABCEILLMORU	BIMOLECULAR
ABCEILLNRSS	CRANESBILLS
ABCEILLNTUY	INELUCTABLY
ABCEILLRTUV	CARVEL-BUILT
ABCEILMMOTT	COMMITTABLE
ABCEILMOPRT	PROBLEMATIC
ABCEILMORST	BLASTOMERIC
ABCEILMOSST	MESOBLASTIC
ABCEILMOTVY	COMBATIVELY
ABCEILNPRSU	REPUBLICANS
ABCEILNRSTU	INSCRUTABLE
ABCEILNSUXY	INEXCUSABLY
ABCEILOOPRR	POOR CALIBRE
ABCEILORRVY	IRREVOCABLY
ABCEILPSTTU	PLASTIC TUBE
	PUBLIC TASTE
ABCEIMNNORT	RECOMBINANT
ABCEIMNOORT	EMBROCATION
ABCEINNORTY	CYBERNATION
ABCEINOPSTT	CABINET POST
ABCEINORRTU	CARBURETION
ABCEINRRRST	TRANSCRIBER
ABCEINRRSST	TRANSCRIBES
ABCEIRSTTUV	SUBTRACTIVE
ABCEJKLMRSU	LUMBERJACKS
ABCEJMNORSU	JAMES COBURN
ABCEJRSSTTU	ARTS SUBJECT
ABCEKKKORRSS	BREAKS ROCKS
ABCEKKORRST	BACKSTROKER
ABCEKLMOOTV	BLACK TO MOVE
ABCEKLNOSTY	LOST BY A NECK
ABCEKNOTTUW	WENT BACK OUT
ABCEKOPRRST	REPORTS BACK
ABCELLLRSUU	SUBCELLULAR
ABCELLMOSTU	COSTUME BALL
ABCELLNOORS	COLLARBONES
ABCELLOQRTU	CROQUET BALL
ABCELLORSSU	SCORES A BULL
ABCELMNORUV	VOCAL NUMBER
ABCELMNOSSU	CONSUMABLES
ABCELMNNRSU	UNSCRAMBLER
ABCELMNNRSSU	UNSCRAMBLES
ABCELMOOSTW	CAME TO BLOWS
ABCELNORSTU	CONSTRUABLE
ABCELOORSTT	LAST OCTOBER
ABCENOOPSTU	PONCES ABOUT
ABCENORRSST	BORN ACTRESS
ABCEOOOORRRT	CORROBORATE
ABCEORRRTTU	CARBURETTOR
ABCEORSTUUY	BUTYRACEOUS
ABCERRSSTTU	SUBTRACTERS
ABCFGIINRTU	BIFURCATING
ABCFGIKORST	BAG OF TRICKS
ABCFGINOSTU	OBFUSCATING
ABCFGIOORSX	BOX OF CIGARS
ABCFGIOPRSS	BAG OF CRISPS
ABCFIINORTU	BIFURCATION
ABCFINOOSTU	OBFUSCATION
ABCFKNOORTT	BACK TO FRONT
ABCFLMNOORY	CONFORMABLY
ABCFLMOORTY	COMFORTABLY
ABCFOORSTUY	OBFUSCATORY
ABCGGIIKNNO	GOING BACK IN
ABCGGIIKNNR	RINGING BACK
ABCGGILLNNU	ANGLING CLUB
ABCGHHKOTTU	THOUGHT BACK
ABCGHIIKNTT	HITTING BACK
ABCGHIIRSST	BASIC RIGHTS
ABCGHIKKLNT	BLACK KNIGHT
ABCGHIKNPSU	PUSHING BACK
ABCGHILNOOP	ANGLOPHOBIC
ABCGHILNORU	BRIAN CLOUGH
ABCGHIMNOTX	BOXING MATCH
ABCGHKLOPSU	PLOUGHS BACK
ABCGIIIMNRT	IMBRICATING
ABCGIIKLNRY	BRICKLAYING
ABCGIIKNNNW	WINNING BACK
ABCGIIKNRTW	WRITING BACK
ABCGIIKNSTT	SITTING BACK
ABCGIILLNSU	SAILING CLUB
ABCGIILNRTU	LUBRICATING
ABCGIINNORS	CARBONISING
ABCGIINNORZ	CARBONIZING
ABCGIINRRTU	RUBRICATING
ABCGIJKMNPU	JUMPING BACK
ABCGIKKLNOO	LOOKING BACK
ABCGIKLLNOR	ROLLING BACK
ABCGIKLLNPU	PULLING BACK
ABCGIKLNOTU	BLACKING OUT
ABCGIKLNPRU	PARBUCKLING
ABCGIKNNNRU	RUNNING BACK
ABCGIKNNRTU	TURNING BACK

ABCGIKNPRSS	SPRINGS BACK	ABDDEGIRRSW	DRAWBRIDGES
ABCGIMNOOTU	COMING ABOUT	ABDDEGJMNTU	BAD JUDGMENT
ABCGINRSTTU	SUBTRACTING	ABDDEHLLNOO	LO AND BEHOLD
ABCHHIILOTT	BATHOLITHIC	ABDDEHNNSSY	SENDS BY HAND
ABCHHIOPRSS	ARCHBISHOPS	ABDDEHOOSWX	SHADOW-BOXED
ABCHIILLLMS	CLIMBS A HILL	ABDDEIIMRSS	BRIDESMAIDS
ABCHIILOPSY	BIOPHYSICAL	ABDDEIMMNNST	DISBANDMENT
ABCHIIMPRST	BRITISH CAMP	ABDDEIMOORV	DAVID BROOME
ABCHIKKNRSS	SHRINKS BACK	ABDDEKLOOUV	DOUBLE VODKA
ABCHIKLMSST	BLACKSMITHS	ABDDEKOORSS	ADDRESS BOOK
ABCHIKLRSST	BLACKSHIRTS	ABDDELMOORW	WARM-BLOODED
ABCHILLNORY	BRONCHIALLY	ABDDELNOOTY	BADLY DONE TO
ABCHILNOORR	BRONCHIOLAR	ABDDELOOSTT	TASTED BLOOD
ABCHILOPSTY	HYPOBLASTIC	ABDDELORRTW	BLADDERWORT
ABCHOSTTUWY	CUT BOTH WAYS	ABDDFGIIINR	BIDDING FAIR
ABCIIILLOTY	COILABILITY	ABDDGHINNOY	DOING BY HAND
ABCIIILOSTY	SOCIABILITY	ABDDGHNOOSU	GOOD HUSBAND
ABCIIIMNORT	IMBRICATION	ABDDGIINORV	DIVING BOARD
ABCIIINOSTT	ANTIBIOTICS	ABDDGLNOOWY	GO DOWN BADLY
ABCIILLPTUY	CULPABILITY	ABDDIILMNNW	WIND AND LIMB
ABCIIILLRSTY	TRISYLLABIC	ABDDILNNOSU	BUILD ON SAND
ABCIILMNRUU	ALBUMINURIC	ABDDLMOORSU	MOULDBOARDS
ABCIILNOPTU	PUBLICATION	ABDDLNOOSUY	BODY AND SOUL
ABCIILNORTU	LUBRICATION	ABDDNOORSSU	SOUNDBOARDS
ABCIIMNNOOT	COMBINATION	ABDDOORRSSW	BROADSWORDS
ABCIINORRTU	RUBRICATION	ABDEEEEGGLV	BEGGED LEAVE
ABCIINOSSSS	ABSCISSIONS	ABDEEEEGLRU	BELEAGUERED
ABCILLNNOUY	CONNUBIALLY	ABDEEEEILMV	MADE BELIEVE
ABCILLNORUY	BINOCULARLY	ABDEEEEELLRR	REBEL LEADER
ABCILLNORYY	BYRONICALLY	ABDEEEEELPSU	DEEP BLUE SEA
ABCILLORRUY	ORBICULARLY	ABDEEEFHRST	FEATHERBEDS
ABCILMMORUU	COLUMBARIUM	ABDEEEFRSST	BREAST-FEEDS
ABCILMNNUUU	INCUNABULUM	ABDEEEGINST	BEING SEATED
ABCILNORTUU	LUCUBRATION	ABDEEEGLLOU	DOUBLE EAGLE
ABCILNRSTUY	INSCRUTABLY	ABDEEEGNNNO	BEEN AND GONE
ABCILOPRSTU	SUBTROPICAL	ABDEEEGNOTY	TEENAGED BOY
ABCINNOORTU	CONURBATION	ABDEEEHILNV	LEAVE BEHIND
ABCINOORSTU	OBSCURATION	ABDEEEHKMST	MAKES THE BED
ABCINORSTTU	SUBTRACTION	ABDEEEHLLVW	BEHAVED WELL
ABCKKNOOSTU	KNOCKS ABOUT		WELL-BEHAVED
ABCKLORSTUW	STRUCK A BLOW	ABDEEEILLRV	DELIVERABLE
ABCLLRSTUUU	SUBCULTURAL	ABDEEEILPPP	APPLE-PIE BED
ABCLOOPSWYY	PLAY COWBOYS	ABDEEEILRST	DELIBERATES
ABCLOSSSTTY	BLASTOCYSTS	ABDEEEKMNOS	MAKE ONES BED
ABCMNOORSSW	CROSSBOWMAN	ABDEEELLOPV	DEVELOPABLE
ABCNOOOORRT	CORROBORANT	ABDEEELMNRU	DENUMERABLE
ABDDDEGINNW	WEDDING BAND	ABDEEELNSST	BELATEDNESS
ABDDDEIMNOR	BROAD-MINDED	ABDEEEPRSTT	BESPATTERED
ABDDDGIJOOO	DID A GOOD JOB	ABDEEERSSTW	SWEETBREADS
ABDDDIMNNOY	MIND AND BODY	ABDEEFFHLSU	BUFFLEHEADS
ABDDEEEILRT	DELIBERATED	ABDEEFFILOR	BREAD OF LIFE
ABDDEEEINSV	BEEN ADVISED	ABDEEFGIIRR	FIRE BRIGADE
ABDDEEELORV	DEAR BELOVED	ABDEEFGILNS	BAD FEELINGS
ABDDEEEMNOS	MADE ONE'S BED	ABDEEFHIRTY	DEATH BY FIRE
ABDDEEENRSS	BEARDEDNESS	ABDEEFIILNN	INDEFINABLE
ABDDEEFORRY	READY FOR BED	ABDEEFILLRW	BID FAREWELL
ABDDEEGHIRS	BRIDGEHEADS	ABDEEFILRSU	REFUSED BAIL
ABDDEEIIKNR	RIDDEN A BIKE	ABDEEFLLNOR	ALFRED NOBEL
ABDDEEIILTT	DEBILITATED	ABDEEFNOORR	FREE ON BOARD
ABDDEEIKMRS	DISEMBARKED	ABDEEGGILNO	BOILED AN EGG
ABDDEEILLMN	ILL BE DAMNED!	ABDEEGGINRR	GINGERBREAD
ABDDEEILLNR	I'LL BE DARNED!	ABDEEGGORRU	BORE A GRUDGE
ABDDEEILMPS	BEDSIDE LAMP	ABDEEGHILLN	ILL BE HANGED!
ABDDEEINSTY	STAYED IN BED	ABDEEGHIRTV	GAVE THE BIRD
ABDDEEKNRSU	SUDDEN BREAK	ABDEEGHISTY	BAD EYESIGHT
ABDDEELLLNY	BELLY-LANDED	ABDEEGHRRTU	DRAUGHT BEER
ABDDEFHLLOO	HALF-BLOODED	ABDEEGINNRW	BEING WARNED
ABDDEFILOTU	FIDDLE ABOUT	ABDEEGINRRW	DEBRA WINGER
ABDDEFNORRW	BEND FORWARD	ABDEEGLLMMU	GUMMED LABEL
ABDDEGIKORR	DIRK BOGARDE	ABDEEGLLOUZ	DOUBLE-GLAZE
ABDDEGIOOSY	SAID GOODBYE	ABDEEGLNNOU	GONE A BUNDLE

ABDEEGLNOSU	GOES A BUNDLE	ABDEFGINORR	FINGER BOARD
ABDEEGLNOTU	DOUBLE AGENT		FINGERBOARD
ABDEEGLOOTT	GO TO BED LATE	ABDEFGLOTUY	GO BY DEFAULT
ABDEEGLORST	GOLDBEATERS	ABDEFHILLNS	FALLS BEHIND
ABDEEGNNOOR	GO ON A BENDER	ABDEFHILORS	HOLDS A BRIEF
ABDEEGNRRTU	GREAT BURDEN	ABDEFHIORTT	DATE OF BIRTH
ABDEEGOOVWY	WAVE GOODBYE	ABDEFHLNOUY	BUNDLE OF HAY
ABDEEGRRSST	BEST REGARDS	ABDEFIILLMN	LIFE AND LIMB
ABDEEHHLSTU	HAD THE BLUES	ABDEFIILLSY	SYLLABIFIED
ABDEEHIIMTW	ABIDE WITH ME	ABDEFIILNNY	INDEFINABLY
ABDEEHIIRST	RAISE THE BID	ABDEFLLOTUU	DOUBLE FAULT
ABDEEHILSST	ESTABLISHED		DOUBLE-FAULT
ABDEEHILTTW	WIELD THE BAT	ABDEFLOOOTU	FOOLED ABOUT
ABDEEHIRSTW	WHITEBEARDS	ABDEFNORRTW	BENT FORWARD
ABDEEHKORRR	DEBORAH KERR	ABDEFORRRSU	SURFBOARDER
ABDEEHLNORU	BURNED A HOLE	ABDEGGILMNN	GAMBLING DEN
ABDEEHLORSU	DOUBLE SHARE	ABDEGGILNOT	GOLDBEATING
ABDEEHLOTTU	AT THE DOUBLE	ABDEGGINOOT	GOOD BEATING
ABDEEHLRSUU	HURLED ABUSE	ABDEGGINORR	RAGGED ROBIN
ABDEEHMRTTU	BEAT THE DRUM	ABDEGGIRRSU	BUDGERIGARS
ABDEEHNOOSW	BOW ONES HEAD	ABDEGGLOTUU	LUGGED ABOUT
ABDEEHNRUVY	HEAVY BURDEN	ABDEGHHLOST	HOLDS THE BAG
ABDEEHOORTT	BORE TO DEATH	ABDEGHINRTY	DYING BREATH
ABDEEHORSST	BROADSHEETS	ABDEGHLORSU	SHOULDER BAG
ABDEEHORTTU	BREATHED OUT	ABDEGIIMNNTU	BANG THE DRUM
ABDEEIILLRS	LIBERALISED	ABDEGIIIKNR	RIDING A BIKE
ABDEEIILLRZ	LIBERALIZED	ABDEGIILNNT	DINING TABLE
ABDEEIILNTT	DIE IN BATTLE	ABDEGIINSTT	BATTING SIDE
ABDEEIILRUV	BURIED ALIVE	ABDEGIKNORY	KEYBOARDING
ABDEEIILSST	BESTIALISED	ABDEGILLMNS	SMELLING BAD
ABDEEIILSTT	DEBILITATES	ABDEGILLNRV	GRAVEL-BLIND
ABDEEIILSTZ	BESTIALIZED	ABDEGILNOPY	PLAYED BINGO
ABDEEIKNNSY	KIDNEY BEANS	ABDEGILNOTT	DOING BATTLE
ABDEEIKORTV	TAKEOVER BID	ABDEGILPRSY	PLAYS BRIDGE
ABDEEILMNST	DISABLEMENT	ABDEGILRRSU	BURGLARISED
ABDEEILMSSS	DISASSEMBLE	ABDEGILRRUZ	BURGLARIZED
ABDEEILNNOO	DANIEL BOONE	ABDEGIMNOST	DOG BITES MAN
ABDEEILNNRT	DINNER TABLE		MAN BITES DOG
ABDEEILNPSS	DISPENSABLE	ABDEGIMNRST	ABRIDGMENTS
ABDEEILNRSU	UNDESIRABLE	ABDEGINNORW	BEARING DOWN
ABDEEILNRUV	BURNED ALIVE	ABDEGINNOTW	BEATING DOWN
ABDEEILORTT	OBLITERATED	ABDEGIPRRTY	BRIDGE PARTY
ABDEEILORTW	BOILED WATER	ABDEGKNORRU	BREAK GROUND
ABDEEIMRRTT	TIMBER TRADE	ABDEGLLNOOW	BOWLED ALONG
ABDEEINNNST	TINNED BEANS	ABDEGLPRUYY	PLAYED RUGBY
ABDEEINNRRW	BREAD WINNER	ABDEGNNOOOR	GONE ON BOARD
	BREADWINNER	ABDEGNOOORS	GOES ON BOARD
ABDEEINRRUV	RIVER DANUBE	ABDEGNOORUV	ABOVE GROUND
ABDEEJKNOOY	BEYOND A JOKE		ABOVEGROUND
ABDEEKLOPSU	DOUBLESPEAK	ABDEGOOORRV	GO OVERBOARD
ABDEEKNOOOP	OPENED A BOOK	ABDEGOOSSYY	SAYS GOODBYE
ABDEEKNORSZ	BAKERS DOZEN	ABDEGORSTUV	GRAVE DOUBTS
ABDEEKOOSST	BOOKED SEATS	ABDEHHLOTYY	HEALTHY BODY
ABDEEKRSSTY	DERBY STAKES	ABDEHHMOORR	RHOMBOHEDRA
ABDEELLNOPW	BADEN POWELL	ABDEHIILLPT	PAID THE BILL
ABDEELMNORZ	BRONZE MEDAL	ABDEHIILNRT	TRAIL BEHIND
ABDEELMNNOTU	DEMOUNTABLE	ABDEHIIMRST	BRITISH MADE
ABDEELMNRUY	DENUMERABLY	ABDEHIINNPR	HAIRPIN BEND
ABDEELMORTU	MADE TROUBLE	ABDEHIINNTU	UNINHABITED
ABDEELNNRUU	UNENDURABLE	ABDEHILOPST	HOSPITAL BED
ABDEELNNTUW	WENT A BUNDLE	ABDEHILOSUU	BUILD A HOUSE
ABDEELNRSSU	DURABLENESS	ABDEHIMRSTU	THUMBS A RIDE
ABDEELORRTT	BATTLE ORDER	ABDEHINSSTY	STAYS BEHIND
ABDEELRSSTT	BATTLEDRESS	ABDEHMNOOSY	HANDSOME BOY
ABDEEMNNOOS	MADE NO BONES	ABDEHNOORST	ON THE BOARDS
ABDEEMOSSTU	MESSED ABOUT	ABDEHNOOTUV	HAVE NO DOUBT
ABDEENORTUZ	BRAZENED OUT	ABDEHNOSSTU	BASSET HOUND
ABDEEORRSTT	BROAD STREET	ABDEHOOSSWX	SHADOW-BOXES
ABDEEORSSTY	STAYED SOBER	ABDEHORRSST	SHORTBREADS
ABDEERRRSWY	BREWERS DRAY	ABDEHORSTUU	RUSHED ABOUT
ABDEFFIIMRR	BARE MIDRIFF	ABDEHPRSSTU	BRUSHED PAST

ABDEIIINNRT	INDIAN TRIBE
ABDEIILLTWY	WELDABILITY
ABDEIILMNOT	INDOMITABLE
ABDEIILRSTU	BRIDAL SUITE
ABDEIIMNNRS	BEARS IN MIND
ABDEIIPRTTU	PAID TRIBUTE
ABDEIKLNNRU	UNDRINKABLE
ABDEIKLNRTT	BRITT EKLAND
ABDEIKNNNOS	SKIN AND BONE
ABDEIKNOPST	BANK DEPOSIT
ABDEILLOSSV	DISSOLVABLE
ABDEILMNSSY	SENDS BY MAIL
ABDEILMSSSY	DISASSEMBLY
ABDEILNOORV	LIVE ON BOARD
ABDEILNRSSW	SWEARS BLIND
ABDEILNRSUY	UNDESIRABLY
ABDEILOPRSV	DISPROVABLE
ABDEILOPSSS	DISPOSABLES
ABDEINNORSW	RAINBOWS END
ABDEINNORTT	RAN INTO DEBT
ABDEINOOPPR	PIPE ON BOARD
ABDEINOPSSU	PAID ONE'S SUB
ABDEINORSTU	SUBORDINATE
ABDEIRRTTUY	DAIRY BUTTER
ABDEJMOPTUU	JUMPED ABOUT
ABDEKLLOSTU	DOUBLE-TALKS
ABDEKLMOOSS	MAKES SO BOLD
ABDEKLOPRSU	DOUBLE-PARKS
ABDEKMOOOOR	BOOKED A ROOM
ABDELLMOOPS	BLOOD SAMPLE
ABDELLOPSWY	PLAYED BOWLS
ABDELLOSTTU	SUBTOTALLED
ABDELMOORST	BLOOD STREAM
	BLOODSTREAM
ABDELMOPTTT	BOLD ATTEMPT
ABDELOORTUV	VOTED LABOUR
ABDELOOSSTT	TASTES BLOOD
ABDELOOSSTW	SWEATS BLOOD
ABDEMNOOOTU	MOONED ABOUT
ABDEMNORRST	BARNSTORMED
ABDENNOORSW	BEARS DOWN ON
ABDENNOORTW	WENT ON BOARD
ABDENNOSTTW	BATTENS DOWN
ABDENOORTUW	WONDER ABOUT
ABDENORRSTY	ANDY ROBERTS
ABDENORTTUU	TURNED ABOUT
ABDEOOOPRTT	TORPEDO BOAT
ABDEOOORRSTT	OTTERBOARDS
ABDEOOSSTTU	TOSSED ABOUT
ABDEOPRTTUY	PROBATE DUTY
ABDFFLNOPUW	PUFF AND BLOW
ABDFGIIJNNO	FINDING A JOB
ABDFIILNNUU	INFUNDIBULA
ABDFIIORSTX	FIRST-AID BOX
ABDFILNORSU	FLORIBUNDAS
ABDFINNOPRY	NIP OF BRANDY
ABDFINOPRSY	SIP OF BRANDY
ABDGGIIKNORS	BARKING DOGS
ABDGGILNNOY	GOING BY LAND
ABDGGILNORS	RONALD BIGGS
ABDGGINOORY	GOING BY ROAD
ABDGHIIINRT	RIDING HABIT
ABDGHIILNOR	HARD-BOILING
ABDGHIINNRS	BRANDISHING
ABDGHILNORW	BLOWING HARD
ABDGHINPSSU	SPUD-BASHING
ABDGIIILNOS	DIABOLISING
ABDGIIILNOZ	DIABOLIZING
ABDGIIKLNRT	TALKING BIRD
ABDGIIINRSUV	DRIVING A BUS
ABDGINNOSSV	SAVINGS BOND

ABDGINOPRRS	SPRINGBOARD
ABDGJOOOOOT	A GOOD JOB TOO
ABDGKNNOORS	GORDON BANKS
ABDGMOORRSS	SMORGASBORD
ABDHHIIOOPRY	HYDROPHOBIA
ABDHIIRSTTY	DIRTY HABITS
ABDHINOOPRS	ON BOARD SHIP
ABDHNOSSTUW	TWO HUSBANDS
ABDIILLNRTW	WILLI BRANDT
ABDIILMNOTY	INDOMITABLY
ABDIINORTTY	BY TRADITION
ABDIINOSTUU	SUBAUDITION
ABDILNNOSTU	BUILT ON SAND
ABDILNOOSST	BLOODSTAINS
ABDILNOPRSU	SPIRAL-BOUND
ABDIMNNOSTU	SUBDOMINANT
ABDIOOOQRRUW	BORROW A QUID
ABDKNOOOORT	TOOK ON BOARD
ABDLMNNORTU	BURNT ALMOND
ABDLNNORRYY	BARRY LYNDON
ABDMNORRRUY	RAYMOND BURR
ABDNOOPRSTU	PUTS ON BOARD
ABDNOORSTUU	ROUNDABOUTS
ABDOOORRSTUU	TROUBADOURS
ABEEEEFLORS	FORESEEABLE
ABEEEEGLNRR	REGENERABLE
ABEEEEIKLMV	MAKE BELIEVE
	MAKE-BELIEVE
ABEEEEMNRTV	BEREAVEMENT
ABEEEEERRRTV	REVERBERATE
ABEEEFFLMOR	FREE OF BLAME
ABEEEFGLPRS	FEEBLE GRASP
ABEEEFHIRRT	BREATHE FIRE
ABEEEFIRRRR	BARRIER REEF
ABEEEFLMNRT	FERMENTABLE
ABEEEGLORSW	ELBOW GREASE
ABEEEGLRRTT	REGRETTABLE
ABEEEGLRSSS	BEER GLASSES
ABEEEGNOSTY	TEENAGE BOYS
ABEEEGRSTTW	BETTER WAGES
ABEEEHHIINPR	HEBEPHRENIA
ABEEEHLLRTT	LEATHER BELT
ABEEEHLLSVW	BEHAVES WELL
ABEEEHLSTTT	SET THE TABLE
ABEEEHMNORT	BORE THE NAME
ABEEEHNNORT	NEAR THE BONE
ABEEEIJLRUY	JUBILEE YEAR
ABEEEILMMPR	IMPERMEABLE
ABEEEILMMST	EMBLEMATISE
ABEEEILMMTZ	EMBLEMATIZE
ABEEEILRRTV	RETRIEVABLE
ABEEEIMNSST	ABSENTEEISM
ABEEEKMRSTT	MAKES BETTER
ABEEEKNRRSV	RESERVE BANK
ABEEEKRRSTT	BAKER STREET
ABEEELMNNTT	ENTABLEMENT
ABEEELNPRST	PRESENTABLE
ABEEELNPRTV	PREVENTABLE
ABEEELPRRSV	PRESERVABLE
ABEEELPRSTT	PRESETTABLE
ABEEELPSTUY	BEAUTY SLEEP
ABEEELRTTUV	BETTER VALUE
ABEEENQTUUY	BEAUTY QUEEN
ABEEENRNRTV	REVERBERANT
ABEEERRSTTV	VERTEBRATES
ABEEFFGHLTW	BLEW THE GAFF
ABEEFFILORT	FORFEITABLE
ABEEFFLORRU	FEARFUL BORE
ABEEFFOOPRU	OPERA BOUFFE
ABEEFFORRTV	BRAVE EFFORT
ABEEFFRSTTU	BUFFER STATE

ABEEFGILNRR	REFRANGIBLE	ABEEHINRSST	BREATHINESS
ABEEFGILNRT	BEARING LEFT	ABEEHKLORRT	HALTERBROKE
ABEEFGLORSS	GLASS OF BEER	ABEEHKLORTW	BROKE THE LAW
ABEEFGLORTT	FORGETTABLE	ABEEHKNORRT	BROKEN HEART
ABEEFGNORSV	BAG OF NERVES		HEARTBROKEN
ABEEFGOSSTW	BAG OF SWEETS	ABEEHKNRTWY	KNEW BY HEART
ABEEFIILLQU	LIQUEFIABLE	ABEEHLMPRSS	BLASPHEMERS
ABEEFIIRSTU	BEAUTIFIERS	ABEEHLORRSU	BARRELHOUSE
ABEEFILNRSS	FRIABLENESS	ABEEHLORRWW	WHEELBARROW
ABEEFILRRTU	IRREFUTABLE	ABEEHLORTUV	HAVE TROUBLE
ABEEFILRSSU	REFUSES BAIL	ABEEHMOOPRS	BEER SHAMPOO
ABEEFKLNORS	BARK ONESELF	ABEEHMORSTT	BATHOMETERS
ABEEFKOORRT	BROKE FOR TEA	ABEEHNOPRRY	HYPERBOREAN
ABEEFLLLOPS	PEAL OF BELLS	ABEEHORSTTU	BREATHES OUT
ABEEFLLNSSU	BALEFULNESS		THEREABOUTS
ABEEFLMOPRR	PERFORMABLE	ABEEHORSTUW	WHEREABOUTS
ABEEFLORSSW	SAFEBLOWERS	ABEEHPRSTTT	THE BEST PART
ABEEFMORSSW	SWARM OF BEES	ABEEHQRSSUU	HARQUEBUSES
ABEEFMORSTU	TERM OF ABUSE	ABEEIILLRSS	LIBERALISES
ABEEFNNORSZ	FROZEN BEANS	ABEEIILLRSZ	LIBERALIZES
ABEEFNRRRTU	AFTERBURNER	ABEEIILLRVW	LIBERAL VIEW
ABEEFOORSTT	ROBE OF STATE	ABEEIILMNPS	PLEBEIANISM
ABEEFOPRSTY	BEAST OF PREY	ABEEIILMNST	INESTIMABLE
ABEEFOSSTTT	BEST OF TASTE	ABEEIILNQTU	INEQUITABLE
ABEEGGHOTVY	GAVE THE GO-BY	ABEEIILQRTU	EQUILIBRATE
ABEEGGILNPS	SLEEPING BAG	ABEEIILRSUV	BURIES ALIVE
ABEEGGLRUUY	RUGBY LEAGUE	ABEEIILSSST	BESTIALISES
ABEEGHILPPT	THE BIG APPLE	ABEEIILSSTZ	BESTIALIZES
ABEEGHINQTU	BEQUEATHING	ABEEIINRRTV	NATIVE TRIBE
ABEEGHILLNRT	HANG THE BELL	ABEEIJLLRSW	LIBERAL JEWS
ABEEGHMPTTY	EMPTY THE BAG	ABEEIKLLNSS	LIKABLENESS
ABEEGHOOTTV	GAVE THE BOOT	ABEEIKLNNST	LINEN BASKET
ABEEGIILNRT	LIBERTINAGE	ABEEILLNORT	INTOLERABLE
ABEEGIIMNTT	BEATING TIME	ABEEILLNPSS	PLIABLENESS
ABEEGIINOSS	ABIOGENESIS	ABEEILLNRSS	LIBERALNESS
ABEEGIKLPRS	GLIB SPEAKER	ABEEILLNSSV	LIVABLENESS
ABEEGIKNPST	KEEPING TABS	ABEEILLOPTX	EXPLOITABLE
ABEEGILMNPR	IMPREGNABLE	ABEEILLORTV	LIBERAL VOTE
ABEEGILNRUW	WEARING BLUE		VOTE LIBERAL
ABEEGILNTTV	GIVEN BATTLE	ABEEILMMORS	MEMORISABLE
ABEEGILRRST	REGISTRABLE	ABEEILMMORZ	MEMORIZABLE
ABEEGILSTTV	GIVES BATTLE	ABEEILMMPRY	IMPERMEABLY
ABEEGINORRV	OVERBEARING	ABEEILMNNOT	MENTIONABLE
ABEEGINOSTU	SEEING ABOUT	ABEEILMNNRU	INNUMERABLE
ABEEGINRSTT	BEING AT REST	ABEEILMNNSS	SENSIBLE MAN
ABEEGLMNNRRU	LARGE NUMBER	ABEEILNNOPS	PENSIONABLE
ABEEGLMORTY	TELEGRAM BOY	ABEEILNNSTT	TABLE TENNIS
ABEEGLNNOPY	GONE BY PLANE	ABEEILNPRSU	INSUPERABLE
ABEEGLNOPSY	GOES BY PLANE	ABEEILNSSST	BEASTLINESS
ABEEGLNOSTU	OBTUSE ANGLE	ABEEILNSSSZ	SIZABLENESS
ABEEGLORTUV	GAVE TROUBLE	ABEEILORSTT	OBLITERATES
ABEEGLRRRUV	REGULAR VERB	ABEEILPRSSU	PERSUASIBLE
ABEEGLRRTTY	REGRETTABLY	ABEEILRRSSV	VERBALISERS
ABEEGMNRRTU	GREAT NUMBER	ABEEILRRSVZ	VERBALIZERS
ABEEGNORSYY	YEARS GONE BY	ABEEILRRTVY	RETRIEVABLY
ABEEGNORTWY	GONE BY WATER	ABEEIMNORTV	OVERTIME BAN
ABEEGORSTWY	GOES BY WATER	ABEEINNORTU	BARQUENTINE
ABEEHHLSSTU	HAS THE BLUES	ABEEINORSSU	BUENOS AIRES
ABEEHHPRSTY	BATHYSPHERE	ABEEINOSTTU	SEEN ABOUT IT
ABEEHIILNRT	INHERITABLE	ABEEINRRSSZ	BIZARRENESS
ABEEHILLRST	THE LIBERALS	ABEEINRSSTW	BEAR WITNESS
ABEEHILLSTT	THE BASTILLE	ABEEINSSSUV	ABUSIVENESS
ABEEHILLSTW	WHISTLEABLE	ABEEIOPRRSS	SOAPBERRIES
ABEEHILMPSS	BLASPHEMIES	ABEEIOPRRTV	REPROBATIVE
ABEEHILPRSS	PERISHABLES	ABEEIOSSTTU	SEES ABOUT IT
ABEEHILRSST	ESTABLISHER	ABEEIPRRRSS	RASPBERRIES
ABEEHILSSST	ESTABLISHES	ABEEIPRSSVV	PASSIVE VERB
ABEEHILSTUX	EXHAUSTIBLE	ABEEIQRRSUU	ARQUEBUSIER
ABEEHIMNSTT	BENTHAMITES	ABEEIRRSTTT	BITTER TEARS
ABEEHINNORT	IN ONE BREATH	ABEEIRSTTTT	BITTER TASTE
ABEEHINRSSS	BEARISHNESS	ABEEKKLNNOR	BROKEN ANKLE

ABEEKLMORTU	MAKE TROUBLE	ABEFILLTUUY	BEAUTIFULLY
ABEEKLNORRU	BROKEN A RULE	ABEFILRRTUY	IRREFUTABLY
ABEEKLNOSTX	SEXTON BLAKE	ABEFINOSTXY	FIX BAYONETS
ABEEKLOORSS	BREAKS LOOSE	ABEFLLLMSYY	ALL BY MYSELF
ABEEKLRRSSU	BREAKS RULES	ABEFLLOORST	FOOTBALLERS
ABEEKMMMNNST	EMBANKMENTS	ABEFLMOOSTT	FALSE BOTTOM
ABEEKMNNOOS	MAKE NO BONES	ABEFLNOOSST	SLAB OF STONE
ABEEKNOORSW	RENEWS A BOOK	ABEFLOORTTW	TABLE FOR TWO
ABEEKNOPSST	KEEPS TABS ON	ABEFOPRTTTU	PAT OF BUTTER
ABEELLLMSSY	BLAMELESSLY	ABEFORRRSTY	BARRY FOSTER
ABEELLLNOSY	ONE SYLLABLE	ABEGGHIMNTU	HUNT BIG GAME
ABEELLMNORY	LEMON BARLEY	ABEGGIILNNO	BEING IN GOAL
ABEELLNOSSV	LOVABLENESS	ABEGGIJNOTT	GETTING A JOB
ABEELMNPRTU	NUMBER PLATE	ABEGGINNOST	GOING ABSENT
	NUMBERPLATE	ABEGGLMNRVY	MELVYN BRAGG
ABEELMNSSTU	MUTABLENESS	ABEGHIIMNSV	MISBEHAVING
ABEELMNSTTT	BATTLEMENTS	ABEGHIINNRT	BREATHING IN
ABEELMOPRST	SET A PROBLEM		HIBERNATING
ABEELMOPTVY	MOVABLE TYPE	ABEGHIINRTW	BEARING WITH
ABEELMORRRS	RAMBLER ROSE	ABEGHIINSTT	ITS IN THE BAG
ABEELMORSST	BLASTOMERES	ABEGHIIOPRS	BIOGRAPHIES
ABEELNNOORR	ELEANOR BRON	ABEGHILMNOO	HAEMOGLOBIN
ABEELNNORTU	BORE A TUNNEL	ABEGHILMNPS	BLASPHEMING
ABEELNNOSST	NOTABLENESS	ABEGHILNOOR	BORING A HOLE
ABEELNNPTWY	WENT BY PLANE	ABEGHIOPRRS	BIOGRAPHERS
ABEELNOOPTT	OPEN A BOTTLE	ABEGHLLOOTT	GO TO THE BALL
ABEELNOOSTW	AT ONES ELBOW	ABEGHLNOOPS	ANGLOPHOBES
ABEELNOPSST	POTABLENESS	ABEGHNRRSSU	BUSHRANGERS
ABEELNPRSTY	PRESENTABLY	ABEGIILMMT	IMMITIGABLE
ABEELNRTTUU	UNUTTERABLE	ABEGIIIMSTU	AMBIGUITIES
ABEELNRTUXY	EXUBERANTLY	ABEGIIINNRT	INEBRIATING
ABEELORUVYY	BY YOUR LEAVE	ABEGIILMNTT	TIMETABLING
	BY-YOUR-LEAVE	ABEGIILNNST	INTANGIBLES
ABEELOSTUUY	BEAUTEOUSLY	ABEGIILNRSV	BRINGS ALIVE
ABEELPPRSTU	SUPPER TABLE		VERBALISING
ABEELPPRTTU	APPLE BUTTER	ABEGIILNRVZ	VERBALIZING
ABEEMMPRRTY	PARTY MEMBER	ABEGIINNRST	BRIGANTINES
ABEEMOSSSTU	MESSES ABOUT	ABEGIINORSV	RISING ABOVE
ABEENNNNRSU	RUNNER BEANS	ABEGIINOSST	ABIOGENISTS
ABEENOPRRSV	BRAVE PERSON	ABEGIJMNNPU	JUMPING BEAN
ABEENRTTWWY	WENT BY WATER	ABEGIKNORTU	BREAKING OUT
ABEEOOORRSTT	BORE TO TEARS	ABEGIKNRRSU	BEARSKIN RUG
ABEFFGHLOTW	BLOW THE GAFF	ABEGILLNOPT	BEGIN TO PALL
ABEFFGIKNOR	BREAKING OFF	ABEGILMNNOZ	EMBLAZONING
ABEFFHPRRSU	SHARP REBUFF	ABEGILMNOSW	SEAM BOWLING
ABEFFIKORST	BREAKS IT OFF	ABEGILMNPRY	IMPREGNABLY
ABEFFLLNOSU	FULL OF BEANS	ABEGILNNNTY	BENIGNANTLY
ABEFFLORSUW	SUFFER A BLOW	ABEGILNNRTY	BANTERINGLY
ABEFGHILMOT	BEAM OF LIGHT	ABEGILNORSU	SUBREGIONAL
ABEFGHOOTTU	OUT OF THE BAG	ABEGILNOSSX	SIGNALBOXES
ABEFGIIILNS	SIGNIFIABLE	ABEGILRRSSU	BURGLARISES
ABEFGIILLNT	TELLING A FIB	ABEGILRRSUZ	BURGLARIZES
ABEFGIILNNR	INFRANGIBLE	ABEGILRRYZZ	GRIZZLY BEAR
ABEFGIILNRZ	BLAZING FIRE	ABEGIMNRSTY	STREAMING BY
ABEFGIINTUY	BEAUTIFYING	ABEGINNOPSU	SUBPOENAING
ABEFGILNOSW	SAFEBLOWING	ABEGINNORRT	INTERROBANG
ABEFGLMOOSW	GAME OF BOWLS	ABEGINNORTY	GONE BY TRAIN
ABEFGMNOOSY	BAGS OF MONEY	ABEGINNRSST	STRING BEANS
ABEFHHLORRT	HALF BROTHER	ABEGINOPRRT	REPROBATING
ABEFHIKNORT	BROKEN FAITH	ABEGINORSTY	GOES BY TRAIN
ABEFHIRRSTT	AFTERBIRTHS	ABEGKLNORSS	BROKEN GLASS
ABEFHLNSSSU	BASHFULNESS	ABEGKMOORTU	TOOK UMBRAGE
ABEFHOORTTU	OUT OF BREATH	ABEGLLNOPTU	BEGUN TO PALL
ABEFIIILRTV	VITRIFIABLE	ABEGLLORSSW	GLASS BLOWER
ABEFIIILSTY	FEASIBILITY		GLASSBLOWER
ABEFIIJLSTU	JUSTIFIABLE	ABEGLNOOTUU	LOUNGE ABOUT
ABEFIILLSSY	SYLLABIFIES	ABEGLPRRUUY	RUGBY PLAYER
ABEFIILNORT	LIT A BONFIRE	ABEGMORRSTU	BURGOMASTER
ABEFIILNOSS	FISSIONABLE	ABEHHHRRSTU	HEARTH BRUSH
ABEFIKLNNUU	IN A BLUE FUNK	ABEHHILNNOS	HANS HOLBEIN
ABEFILLMNOY	NOBLE FAMILY	ABEHHIRRSSU	HAIRBRUSHES

ABEHHORRSTT	HEARTTHROBS
ABEHIILMNST	HABILIMENTS
ABEHIILMNSU	LIE IN AMBUSH
ABEHIINNORT	HIBERNATION
ABEHIKLNNTU	UNTHINKABLE
ABEHIKNOSTT	SINK THE BOAT
ABEHIKOOTTT	TOOK THE BAIT
ABEHILLLRTY	LIBERTY HALL
ABEHILLPSTY	PAYS THE BILL
ABEHILMNOST	ABOLISHMENT
ABEHILOSTUU	BUILT A HOUSE
ABEHILPSSTT	BATTLESHIPS
ABEHIMOSSTT	MISS THE BOAT
ABEHINOORTT	BOTHERATION
ABEHINOPRSV	VIBRAPHONES
ABEHJMNNOOT	MAN ON THE JOB
ABEHKNORTWY	KNOW BY HEART
ABEHKNOSTTU	SUNK THE BOAT
ABEHKORRSST	BREAKS SHORT
ABEHLLOOSTW	BEATS HOLLOW
ABEHLLOPSTT	SPOT THE BALL
ABEHLMOPSSU	BLASPHEMOUS
ABEHLMORTWY	BLAMEWORTHY
ABEHLMOSSTU	LAST BUS HOME
ABEHLNORRTY	ABHORRENTLY
ABEHMNOOSTY	BAYS THE MOON
ABEHMOOTTTT	AT THE BOTTOM
ABEHMRSSSTU	BUSHMASTERS
ABEHNORSSTU	BURN TO ASHES
ABEHNORSTTY	EAST BY NORTH
	NORTH BY EAST
ABEHOORSTUV	HOVERS ABOUT
ABEHOPRSSTT	THE TOP BRASS
ABEHORSSTUU	RUSHES ABOUT
ABEHOSSTTUY	EAST BY SOUTH
	SOUTH BY EAST
ABEHPRSSSTU	BRUSHES PAST
ABEIIIILLST	LIABILITIES
ABEIIILLNST	INABILITIES
ABEIIILLNOR	BILLIONAIRE
ABEIIILLRTY	RELIABILITY
ABEIIINNORT	INEBRIATION
ABEIILLLLRW	BEAR ILL-WILL
ABEIILLLLRY	ILLIBERALLY
ABEIILLLMNU	ILLUMINABLE
ABEIILLMNRY	BIMILLENARY
ABEIILLMPSU	IMPLAUSIBLE
ABEIILLPRTV	PRIVATE BILL
ABEIILLRSTT	BRISTLETAIL
ABEIILMMSSY	MISS BY A MILE
ABEIILMNSTY	INESTIMABLY
ABEIILNOPRT	PRELIBATION
ABEIILNOPTY	OPENABILITY
ABEIILNORST	LIBERATIONS
ABEIILNQTUY	INEQUITABLY
ABEIILNRTTY	RENTABILITY
ABEIILOPPRT	PROPITIABLE
ABEIILOPRTY	OPERABILITY
ABEIILPRTTY	BIPARTITELY
ABEIILRSSST	STABILISERS
ABEIILRSSTZ	STABILIZERS
ABEIILSTUXY	BISEXUALITY
ABEIILTTTWY	WETTABILITY
ABEIIMMMNRU	BARE MINIMUM
ABEIIMNORSV	AMBIVERSION
ABEIINNOSTT	SINO-TIBETAN
ABEIINRRSST	BAR SINISTER
ABEIIRRSTTU	TRIBUTARIES
ABEIIRTTTUV	ATTRIBUTIVE
ABEIJLNOSTT	JOINS BATTLE
ABEIJMOPRTT	PART-TIME JOB

ABEIKLORSTW	STRIKE A BLOW
ABEIKNORSTW	BREAKS IN TWO
ABEIKOORSTW	WRITES A BOOK
ABEILLLRSTY	TRISYLLABLE
ABEILLNORTY	INTOLERABLY
ABEILLNRSSY	BRAINLESSLY
ABEILLOPRSX	PILLAR-BOXES
ABEILMMNOPR	MAIN PROBLEM
ABEILMMOSST	METABOLISMS
ABEILMNNRUY	INNUMERABLY
ABEILMNQRSU	LAMBREQUINS
ABEILMNRSTU	SUBTERMINAL
ABEILMOOSTU	AUTOMOBILES
ABEILNNORTT	LEON BRITTAN
ABEILNNPRTU	UNPRINTABLE
ABEILNNSTTY	ABSTINENTLY
ABEILNOOSSS	OBSESSIONAL
ABEILNORSSU	BELORUSSIAN
ABEILNOSTTY	OBSTINATELY
ABEILNPRSUY	INSUPERABLY
ABEILOORRTT	OBLITERATOR
ABEILORSSTW	BELOW STAIRS
ABEILQSTTUY	BEST QUALITY
ABEIMNNSSSU	BUSINESSMAN
ABEIMMNORSTT	MONTBRETIAS
ABEIMNORSTU	TAMBOURINES
ABEIMNRRSSU	SUBMARINERS
ABEINNNOORS	ON ONE'S BRAIN
ABEINNNRSTU	BURNT SIENNA
ABEINNORSTV	INOBSERVANT
ABEINNOSSTT	ABSTENTIONS
ABEINNRTTWY	WENT BY TRAIN
ABEINOOPRRT	PROBATIONER
	REPROBATION
ABEINOORSTV	OBSERVATION
ABEINOOSTTT	OBTESTATION
ABEINORTTUZ	BRAZEN IT OUT
ABEINOSSTTU	ABSTENTIOUS
ABEINOSTTTU	TUBE STATION
ABEINSSTTUV	SUBSTANTIVE
ABEIORSSTTT	TEARS TO BITS
ABEIORSTTUW	WRITES ABOUT
ABEIPRSTTUY	PAYS TRIBUTE
ABEIRRSTTTU	ATTRIBUTERS
ABEKKNNORRS	BROKEN RANKS
ABEKKORSSTW	WORKBASKETS
ABEKLMNRRTU	BLUNT REMARK
ABEKLMOOTTU	TOOK A TUMBLE
ABEKLOORRWY	BOWL A YORKER
ABEKMNNOSTU	MOUNTEBANKS
ABEKMNOORTU	TOOK A NUMBER
ABEKMNOOTUY	MONKEY ABOUT
ABEKMNORSSY	BRASS MONKEY
ABEKMORSTTY	TAKE BY STORM
ABEKNOPRRSW	PAWNBROKERS
ABEKOOSTTTU	STATUTE BOOK
ABEKORRSSTW	BREASTWORKS
ABELLMMNRSU	SMALL NUMBER
ABELLMOPPRY	PROBLEM PLAY
ABELLOPSTTU	STOP A BULLET
ABELLORRRSU	BULL-ROARERS
ABELLRSTTUY	STRAY BULLET
ABELMNORTTU	TOTAL NUMBER
ABELNOOPPST	POSTPONEABLE
ABELNOOPRSU	PAUL ROBESON
ABELNOOPSST	TABLESPOONS
ABELNOPPSTU	UNSTOPPABLE
ABELNORRTUW	RETURN A BLOW
ABELNORSTVY	OBSERVANTLY
ABELNRTTUUY	UNUTTERABLY
ABELOORRTUV	LABOUR VOTER

ABELOORSTUV	VOTES LABOUR
ABELOOSTTUW	OUT AT ELBOWS
ABELOPPRSTU	SUPPORTABLE
ABELOPRTTTY	BOTTLE PARTY
ABELOQRTTTU	QUART BOTTLE
ABEMNORRRST	BARNSTORMER
ABENOPRRTTU	PROTUBERANT
ABENOPSSSUY	PAYS ONE'S SUB
ABEOOPRRRTY	REPROBATORY
ABEOOPRTTTU	POTTER ABOUT
ABEOORRSTVY	OBSERVATORY
ABEOORTTTTU	TOTTER ABOUT
ABEOOSSSTTU	TOSSES ABOUT
ABERRSSTTUY	BURSTS A TYRE
ABFFHIIILPS	BAILIFFSHIP
ABFFIIMRRTU	FIRM BUT FAIR
ABFFILLMSTU	BULL MASTIFF
ABFGHIILRST	BRITISH FLAG
ABFGHIINOST	FISHING BOAT
ABFGHIKLOOT	BOOK A FLIGHT
ABFGIILNNRY	INFRANGIBLY
ABFGIILNORT	FLOATING RIB
ABFGILNOSTW	FAST BOWLING
ABFGILNOTUY	FLYING ABOUT
ABFHILLOOSW	HAIL OF BLOWS
ABFHILMSTTU	THUMBS A LIFT
ABFIIILLLTY	FALLIBILITY
ABFIIIMNORT	FIMBRIATION
ABFIIJLSTUY	JUSTIFIABLY
ABFIINOOTTT	NOT A BIT OF IT
ABFIJLMNOOT	JOINT OF LAMB
ABFILLLNSTU	IN FULL BLAST
ABFILLOSSTT	FALLS TO BITS
ABFILMNSTUU	FUNAMBULIST
ABFIMOORSTU	FIBROMATOUS
ABFINOOPSTX	BOX OF PAINTS
ABFIOOOPRST	PAIR OF BOOTS
ABFJKLOOOOR	LOOK FOR A JOB
ABFLNOOORRS	FLORA ROBSON
ABGGGINNOOT	TOBOGGANING
ABGGHINOPPS	SHOPPING BAG
ABGGIIIKMNT	MAKING IT BIG
ABGGIIKNNRR	RINGBARKING
ABGGIILLNOS	GLOBALISING
ABGGIILLNOZ	GLOBALIZING
ABGGIILNORY	GOING BY RAIL
ABGGIINNORT	BARGING INTO
ABGGIINOTXY	GOING BY TAXI
ABGGIJNSTUU	SUBJUGATING
ABGGILNNSUZ	GUNS BLAZING
ABGGIMNORTY	GOING BY TRAM
ABGGINNOOST	BOATING SONG
ABGGINOOSTT	TOBOGGANIST
ABGGINSTTUU	BUSTING A GUT
ABGGLLOOOWY	BOWL A GOOGLY
ABGGNNOORTU	TOBOGGAN RUN
ABGHIINSTTU	BATHING SUIT
ABGHIKLLNOO	BOOKING HALL
ABGHIKPRRST	BRIGHT SPARK
ABGHILNOOPT	BATHING POOL
ABGHINNTTUY	ANYTHING BUT
ABGHOORRSUY	YARBOROUGHS
ABGIIILMMTY	IMMITIGABLY
ABGIIILNSST	STABILISING
ABGIIILNSTZ	STABILIZING
ABGIIILNTTY	TANGIBILITY
ABGIIJLMNPU	JUMPING BAIL
ABGIIKNNNOT	BANKING ON IT
ABGIILLLNUY	BILINGUALLY
ABGIILLMNOS	LOSING A LIMB
ABGIILLNRST	STAR BILLING
ABGIILMNSTU	SUBLIMATING
ABGIILNOOST	OBLIGATIONS
ABGIILNRSTU	BRUTALISING
ABGIILNRTUZ	BRUTALIZING
ABGIINNOTWY	TYING IN A BOW
ABGIINRSSTU	BRINGS A SUIT
ABGIINRTTTU	ATTRIBUTING
ABGIJNOSTUU	SUBJUGATION
ABGIKNNOPRW	PAWNBROKING
ABGIKNNPRTU	BANKRUPTING
ABGIKNRRSTY	STRINGYBARK
ABGILLNNOOS	BALLOONINGS
ABGILLNNOSW	SNOWBALLING
ABGILMOSUUY	AMBIGUOUSLY
ABGIMNOOTUV	MOVING ABOUT
ABGIMNOSUUU	UNAMBIGUOUS
ABGJORSSTUU	SUBJUGATORS
ABHHIKRSTTU	TURKISH BATH
ABHHIOOOPPT	PHOTOPHOBIA
ABHIIILRRST	BRITISH RAIL
ABHIILOSTWY	SHOW ABILITY
ABHIIMRRSTY	BRITISH ARMY
ABHIINRSTVY	BRITISH NAVY
ABHIKLLLNSY	BILL SHANKLY
ABHIKLNNTUY	UNTHINKABLY
ABHIKNOSTTU	THINKS ABOUT
ABHILRRSSTU	ARTHUR BLISS
ABHIMNPRRUY	BRIAN MURPHY
ABHINOPPSSW	BISHOPS PAWN
ABHIORTTUYY	BY AUTHORITY
ABHLLOOOSTW	HOLLOW BOAST
ABHLOOPRSTT	TROPHOBLAST
ABHNOORTTUW	THROWN ABOUT
ABHOORSTTUW	THROWS ABOUT
ABIIILNSTTY	INSTABILITY
ABIIILRTTVY	VIBRATILITY
ABIIILSTTUY	SUITABILITY
ABIIINOPRTT	BIPARTITION
ABIIJNNRRUY	BRAIN INJURY
ABIIKLORTWY	WORKABILITY
ABIILLLNRTY	BRILLIANTLY
ABIILLMPSUY	IMPLAUSIBLY
ABIILLOSTVY	SOLVABILITY
ABIILMNOSTU	SUBLIMATION
ABIILMOSTUY	AMBITIOUSLY
ABIILNORTTU	TRIBULATION
ABIILNRSTUY	INSALUBRITY
ABIILOPRTTY	PORTABILITY
ABIINNOSTTU	INTUBATIONS
ABIINOORSTT	ABORTIONIST
ABIINORTTTU	ATTRIBUTION
ABIJLRRTUYY	TRIAL BY JURY
ABILLNPRSUU	RUNS UP A BILL
ABILLOORSUY	LABORIOUSLY
ABILLORSTTU	SUBLITTORAL
ABILLOSTTTU	BUILT TO LAST
ABILNOOSSTU	ABSOLUTIONS
ABIMNORRSST	BRAINSTORMS
ABIMNORRTUU	BRAIN TUMOUR
ABINNOOOPRT	ON PROBATION
ABINOOSSSST	BASSOONISTS
ABINOSSSTTU	SUBSTATIONS
ABINRRSSTTU	BRAINS TRUST
ABIOPSTTTUU	PUTS IT ABOUT
ABKMMOORSTT	BOTTOM MARKS
ABLLMNORSUY	SUBNORMALLY
ABLNOPPSTUY	UNSTOPPABLY
ABLOOPRSTUW	PROWLS ABOUT
ABLOPPRSTUY	SUPPORTABLY
ABOORSSTTUU	ROUSTABOUTS
ACCCDEEENNS	CANDESCENCE

ACCCDEHILNO	CHALCEDONIC
ACCCDEHLOST	CATCHES COLD
ACCCDEIMNOO	CACODEMONIC
ACCCDENNOOR	CONCORDANCE
ACCCDENNOTU	CONDUCTANCE
ACCCDILLOOP	DIPLOCOCCAL
ACCCEEELNOS	COALESCENCE
ACCCEFHKORS	COCKCHAFERS
ACCCEGIILMR	MAGIC CIRCLE
ACCCEGILNRY	CYCLE RACING
ACCCEHIKNTT	THICK ACCENT
ACCCEHIMOTT	CHEMOTACTIC
ACCCEHKLNUY	LUCKY CHANCE
ACCCEHKOORS	COCKROACHES
ACCCEHMORST	SOCCER MATCH
ACCCEIINORTY	TECHNOCRACY
ACCCEHORSTW	COWCATCHERS
ACCCEHORSUU	ACCOUCHEURS
ACCCEFHRRSTW	SCRATCH CREW
ACCCEIILMRT	CLIMACTERIC
ACCCEIKORST	COCKATRICES
ACCCEILLNSY	ENCYCLICALS
ACCCEILMOPS	ACCOMPLICES
ACCCEINOPSU	OCCUPANCIES
ACCCELLLLOT	CALL COLLECT
ACCCELMNOPY	COMPLACENCY
ACCCENORSTT	CATS CONCERT
ACCCENOSSTT	SCOTS ACCENT
ACCCHKOPSST	SPATCHCOCKS
ACCCIKLMOOT	ATOMIC CLOCK
ACCCIMMOORS	MACROCOSMIC
ACCCIMOOPRS	MACROSCOPIC
ACCDDEEFIIL	DECALCIFIED
ACCDDEFKORS	DECK OF CARDS
ACCDDEINORS	DISCORDANCE
ACCDDEKORSU	SCORED A DUCK
ACCDDHINOPS	COD AND CHIPS
ACCDDIIIMST	DIDACTICISM
ACCDDINORSY	DISCORDANCY
ACCDEEEIMRR	CREAMED RICE
ACCDEEELNOS	ADOLESCENCE
ACCDEEFIILS	DECALCIFIES
ACCDEEFNORY	CONFEDERACY
ACCDEEGOPRU	COUP DE GRACE
ACCDEEHHKLU	CHUCKLEHEAD
ACCDEEHIORS	ARCHDIOCESE
ACCDEEHISTT	CAST THE DICE
ACCDEEIISTV	DESICCATIVE
ACCDEEIKKLP	PLACEKICKED
ACCDEEIKLNP	PICKED CLEAN
ACCDEEIKRSW	WISECRACKED
ACCDEEILOPT	POLICE CADET
ACCDEEILRRW	DREW A CIRCLE
ACCDEEIMORS	DEMOCRACIES
ACCDEEINOSS	ACCESSIONED
ACCDEEIORSV	DIVORCE CASE
ACCDEEIORTT	DECORTICATE
ACCDEEKKNNN	NECK AND NECK
ACCDEEKNOPR	CRACKED OPEN
ACCDEELNNOU	UNCONCEALED
ACCDEELNOPS	SECOND PLACE
ACCDEELNORR	CLEAN RECORD
ACCDEELNOSV	CONVALESCED
ACCDEENORST	CONSECRATED
ACCDEFHMORR	FORCED MARCH
ACCDEFINOST	CONFISCATED
ACCDEFLLOTU	FLOCCULATED
ACCDEFNOSTU	SAFE CONDUCT
	SAFE-CONDUCT
ACCDEGIINRT	ACCREDITING

ACCDEGIINST	CASTING DICE
	DESICCATING
ACCDEGIMNNO	COME DANCING
ACCDEHHITTT	CHITCHATTED
ACCDEHHLOST	CATCHES HOLD
ACCDEHHRSSU	ARCHDUCHESS
ACCDEHIMPPT	PITCHED CAMP
ACCDEHIRSST	SCRATCH SIDE
ACCDEHKLNPU	PACKED LUNCH
ACCDEHLMORW	CLAM CHOWDER
ACCDEHNPRSU	CARD PUNCHES
ACCDEHRSTTU	CUT THE CARDS
ACCDEIILNOT	CONCILIATED
ACCDEIILSSS	CLASSICISED
ACCDEIILSSZ	CLASSICIZED
ACCDEIIMNOO	ECONOMIC AID
ACCDEIINOST	DESICCATION
ACCDEIIPSTU	SUICIDE PACT
ACCDEIKKLOP	PICKED A LOCK
ACCDEIKLNST	CANDLESTICK
ACCDEIKLNSW	CANDLEWICKS
ACCDEIKNRRT	CINDER TRACK
ACCDEIKPRST	CRICKET PADS
ACCDEILLMOT	COLD CLIMATE
ACCDEILLOPS	PECCADILLOS
ACCDEILMOPT	COMPLICATED
ACCDEILNNOO	NICE AND COOL
ACCDEILNOST	OCCIDENTALS
ACCDEILOPSY	CYCLOPEDIAS
ACCDEIMNNSU	CANNED MUSIC
ACCDEIMRSSU	SACRED MUSIC
ACCDEINNSTU	INDUCTANCES
ACCDEINOOTU	COEDUCATION
ACCDEINPRSY	DISCREPANCY
ACCDEIORSST	DESICCATORS
ACCDEKNNOPR	NECK AND CROP
ACCDEKORRRT	TRACK RECORD
ACCDEKORSSU	SCORES A DUCK
ACCDELNOSSS	SECOND CLASS
	SECOND-CLASS
ACCDEMOORTY	COMEDY ACTOR
ACCDENNOTUU	UNACCOUNTED
ACCDEORRSTU	CUTS A RECORD
ACCDFFIIRTY	CARDIFF CITY
ACCDFIIKNRS	DICK FRANCIS
ACCDFKMOOOR	CRACK OF DOOM
ACCDGHIINTV	DIVING CATCH
ACCDGILNORY	ACCORDINGLY
ACCDGIOOSTT	GOOD TACTICS
ACCDGNOOOTU	GOOD ACCOUNT
ACCDHHNSSUU	SUCH AND SUCH
ACCDHHRRSUY	CHURCHYARDS
ACCDHIIILOP	ACIDOPHILIC
ACCDHIIMORT	DICHROMATIC
ACCDHILORSV	CLAVICHORDS
ACCDHINORYY	HYDROCYANIC
ACCDHKNORST	DRANK SCOTCH
ACCDIILLNRY	CYLINDRICAL
ACCDIILNOOR	CROCODILIAN
ACCDIILPSST	PLASTIC DISC
ACCDIIOOPRS	RADIOSCOPIC
ACCDIIPRSSU	PRUSSIC ACID
ACCDINORSTT	CONTRADICTS
ACCDKOOOQRTU	QUACK DOCTOR
ACCDNNOOTTY	COTTON CANDY
ACCEEEEHKSS	CHEESECAKES
ACCEEEEHMRS	CREAM CHEESE
ACCEEEENNSV	EVANESCENCE
ACCEEEFFKOS	COFFEE CAKES
ACCEEEFFMOR	COFFEE CREAM
ACCEEEFIKOP	PIECE OF CAKE

ACCEEEFILMN	MALEFICENCE	ACCEFIIIMPT	PACIFIC TIME
ACCEEEFPRST	PERFECT CASE	ACCEFIILRRY	FAIRY CIRCLE
ACCEEEGHNNS	SCENE CHANGE	ACCEFILORSU	CALCIFEROUS
ACCEEEGILMN	GAME LICENCE	ACCEFINOSST	CONFISCATES
ACCEEEIKKLO	COCK-A-LEEKIE	ACCEFKLOOPS	LACK OF SCOPE
ACCEEELMNRY	RAY CLEMENCE	ACCEFLLOSTU	FLOCCULATES
ACCEEELNOPS	OPALESCENCE	ACCEGGIKNRT	GET CRACKING
ACCEEELPRST	RECEPTACLES	ACCEGHIINTZ	CATECHIZING
	SECRET PLACE	ACCEGHIKMNT	CHECKMATING
ACCEEFHHNRT	TEACH FRENCH	ACCEGHINNOR	ENCROACHING
ACCEEFHIRST	CATCHES FIRE	ACCEGHLORST	LARGE SCOTCH
ACCEEFIIRTT	CERTIFICATE	ACCEGIINQSU	ACQUIESCING
ACCEEFIKLOS	SLICE OF CAKE	ACCEGIKLNQU	QUICK GLANCE
ACCEEFILNRT	ELECTRIC FAN	ACCEGIKMRRY	GIMCRACKERY
ACCEEGHINTY	EYE-CATCHING	ACCEGILMNNO	COMING CLEAN
ACCEEGHORRV	COVER CHARGE	ACCEGINNORS	CARCINOGENS
ACCEEGILRRT	GREAT CIRCLE	ACCEHHIINSW	IN WHICH CASE
ACCEEGINRST	TRAGIC SCENE	ACCEHHKMOTY	HOCKEY MATCH
ACCEEHHIRST	CHESHIRE CAT	ACCEHHLRRUY	EARLY CHURCH
ACCEEHIKPTT	CHEAP TICKET	ACCEHHNSTTU	CATCH THE SUN
ACCEEHILMNO	CHAMELEONIC	ACCEHIIKRRW	WICKER CHAIR
ACCEEHILNRT	CHANTICLEER	ACCEHIILNST	CALISTHENIC
ACCEEHIORST	THEOCRACIES	ACCEHIILOTZ	CATHOLICIZE
ACCEEHIRSST	CATECHISERS	ACCEHIIMNST	MECHANISTIC
ACCEEHIRSTZ	CATECHIZERS	ACCEHIINNST	TECHNICIANS
ACCEEHKORTW	WEATHERCOCK	ACCEHIIRSTU	EUCHARISTIC
ACCEEHKSTTU	CUTS THE CAKE	ACCEHILLMNO	MELANCHOLIC
ACCEEHLLNRY	CHANCELLERY	ACCEHILLNTY	TECHNICALLY
ACCEEHLNOXY	CYCLOHEXANE	ACCEHILSSST	THE CLASSICS
ACCEEHLNSTW	WELSH ACCENT	ACCEHIMNNOR	CHROMINANCE
ACCEEIILNRT	ELECTRICIAN	ACCEHIMNORR	CHIROMANCER
ACCEEIIOTVV	ACTIVE VOICE	ACCEHIMORTU	EUCHROMATIC
ACCEEIKKLPR	PLACEKICKER	ACCEHIMPPST	PITCHES CAMP
ACCEEIKMRTT	CRICKET TEAM	ACCEHIMSTUW	TWICE AS MUCH
ACCEEIKRRSW	WISECRACKER	ACCEHINNNRY	CHANCERY INN
ACCEEILMNOU	OECUMENICAL	ACCEHINOOPS	CACOPHONIES
ACCEEILOOPR	ALICE COOPER	ACCEHIRSSTT	SCRATCHIEST
ACCEEILRRTY	ELECTRIC RAY	ACCEHIRSTTU	AT THE CIRCUS
ACCEEIMNOPS	CINEMASCOPE	ACCEHKNOOST	TOOK CHANCES
ACCEEIMNRTT	METACENTRIC	ACCEHKOPTTW	WATCH POCKET
ACCEEINPRTT	NET PRACTICE	ACCEHKPSTTU	CUTS THE PACK
ACCEEINQSTU	ACQUIESCENT	ACCEHLLMNOY	COLLENCHYMA
ACCEEINRRTU	CERTAIN CURE	ACCEHLLNORS	CHANCELLORS
ACCEEIOORSV	COARSE VOICE	ACCEHLLNORT	CONCERT HALL
ACCEEIOPRRT	RECIPROCATE	ACCEHLOORST	COARSE CLOTH
ACCEEIORSSS	ACCESSORIES	ACCEHLOOSSW	SLOW COACHES
ACCEEKLPSUY	LUCKY ESCAPE		SLOWCOACHES
ACCEEKOPRST	SPACE ROCKET	ACCEHLSTTUW	CUT THE CLAWS
ACCEELMNNOT	CONCEALMENT	ACCEHORRSSU	CRASH COURSE
ACCEELNOSSV	CONVALESCES	ACCEIIILSTV	ACCLIVITIES
ACCEEMNNORR	NECROMANCER	ACCEIIINPRT	ACCIPITRINE
ACCEEMNOPPU	COME-UPPANCE	ACCEIIKKMNR	CAMIKNICKER
ACCEENNNOTU	COUNTENANCE	ACCEIILLMRS	CLERICALISM
ACCEENNORTT	CONCENTRATE	ACCEIILLNPR	PRECLINICAL
ACCEENNORVY	CONVEYANCER	ACCEIILLRST	CLERICALIST
ACCEENNOSVY	CONVEYANCES	ACCEIILMRTU	CRUCIAL TIME
ACCEENOPRRS	COPARCENERS	ACCEIILNOST	CONCILIATES
ACCEENORRRT	CATERCORNER	ACCEIILNRTY	CIRCINATELY
ACCEENORSST	CONSECRATES	ACCEIILRRSU	CIRCULARISE
ACCEEORRSSU	RACECOURSES	ACCEIILRRUZ	CIRCULARIZE
ACCEFFHHINS	CHAFFINCHES	ACCEIILRTUV	CIRCULATIVE
ACCEFFHNNRR	FRENCH FRANC	ACCEIILSSSS	CLASSICISES
ACCEFFIIOSU	EFFICACIOUS	ACCEIILSSSZ	CLASSICIZES
ACCEFHHISST	CATCHES FISH	ACCEIIMNOST	COSMETICIAN
ACCEFHHKLNR	FRENCH CHALK		ENCOMIASTIC
ACCEFHIILNO	FINAL CHOICE	ACCEIIMRSST	CERAMICISTS
ACCEFHIINTY	CHIEFTAINCY	ACCEIINNOSU	INSOUCIANCE
ACCEFHIKMNR	CHICKEN FARM	ACCEIINNTTY	ANCIENT CITY
ACCEFHINRVY	VICHY FRANCE	ACCEIINRSST	CISTERCIANS
ACCEFHLRSTY	FLYCATCHERS	ACCEIKKOPPT	PICK A POCKET
ACCEFHNORST	FRENCH COAST	ACCEIKKOTTT	TICKTACKTOE

ACCEIKLPRTY	PLAY CRICKET	ACCGIIINRTZ	CICATRIZING
ACCEIKNRSSS	CARSICKNESS	ACCGIILNNTU	INCULCATING
ACCEILLNRTY	CENTRICALLY	ACCGIILNRTU	CIRCULATING
ACCEILLOPRR	POLAR CIRCLE	ACCGIINNOOP	GO ON A PICNIC
ACCEILLOPTY	ECTOPICALLY	ACCGIINNOOS	OCCASIONING
ACCEILLORRY	ROYAL CIRCLE	ACCGILLMOOY	MYCOLOGICAL
ACCEILMMORS	COMMERCIALS	ACCGILLNOOO	ONCOLOGICAL
ACCEILMNOOW	ECONOMIC LAW	ACCGILLNOOT	COLLOCATING
ACCEILMOPST	COMPLICATES	ACCGILLOOTY	CYTOLOGICAL
	ECTOPLASMIC	ACCGIMNOSTU	ACCUSTOMING
ACCEILMOSST	CACOMISTLES	ACCGIMOPRTY	CRYPTOGAMIC
ACCEILNNOTY	ANTICYCLONE	ACCGINNORTT	CONTRACTING
ACCEILNOPRT	ERIC CLAPTON	ACCGINNOSTU	ACCOUNTINGS
	NARCOLEPTIC	ACCGINORSTU	CORUSCATING
ACCEILNORTT	CONTRACTILE	ACCGLNNOOTU	LONG ACCOUNT
ACCEILOPRRS	RECIPROCALS	ACCHHIILLNS	CHINCHILLAS
ACCEILOPRST	CEROPLASTIC	ACCHHIINSTT	CHAIN STITCH
ACCEILRSTTU	CRUCIAL TEST	ACCHHJKNNOO	JOHN HANCOCK
ACCEIMMNOTU	COMMUNICATE	ACCHIIILMOOR3	CHARM SCHOOL
ACCEIMNNORT	NECROMANTIC	ACCHHMNORRU	ROMAN CHURCH
ACCEIMNNOTT	CONTACT MINE	ACCHHMNORUW	CHURCHWOMAN
ACCEIMNOTYZ	COENZYMATIC	ACCHIIIMMPT	AMPHIMICTIC
ACCEIMORRTY	MERITOCRACY	ACCHIILMOST	CATHOLICISM
ACCEINNNOSV	CONNIVANCES	ACCHIILOSST	SCHOLIASTIC
ACCEINNNOTU	CONTINUANCE	ACCHIILOTTY	CATHOLICITY
ACCEINNOPRS	COPERNICANS	ACCHIIMNORT	CHROMATINIC
ACCEINNORST	CONCERTINAS	ACCHIIMOSST	MASOCHISTIC
ACCEINNORTV	CONTRIVANCE	ACCHIIOPPRT	HIPPOCRATIC
ACCEINORTTV	CONTRACTIVE	ACCHIIOPRRZ	RHIZOCARPIC
ACCEINPRRTU	PRACTICE RUN	ACCHIIPRSTY	PSYCHIATRIC
ACCEIOORSSU	SCORIACEOUS	ACCHIKMSSTT	MATCHSTICKS
ACCEIOPRRST	PRE-SOCRATIC	ACCHIKPSTTY	STICKY PATCH
ACCEJLNORTU	CONJECTURAL	ACCHILLNORY	CHRONICALLY
ACCEKLRTTTU	CATTLE TRUCK	ACCHILLPSYY	PSYCHICALLY
ACCEKMNSTUU	CAME UNSTUCK	ACCHILMOTYY	CYCLOTHYMIA
ACCEKNRRSTU	NUTCRACKERS	ACCHIMRSTTY	MCCARTHYIST
ACCELLOSTTU	COAL SCUTTLE	ACCHINOPSTY	SYCOPHANTIC
ACCELMMNOOP	COMMONPLACE	ACCHIOOPRRT	PROTHORACIC
ACCELNNOSTT	CONTACT LENS	ACCHIOORRSU	CHIAROSCURO
ACCELNORSUY	CANCEROUSLY	ACCHKNNOOTY	TONY HANCOCK
ACCELNORTUY	COUNTY CLARE	ACCHLOORRTU	COLOUR CHART
ACCELOPRSSY	PLAYS SOCCER	ACCHMNOTTUY	COUNTY MATCH
ACCELPRRSUU	CREPUSCULAR	ACCHNOOOPSU	CACOPHONOUS
ACCEMMNOOSU	COMMON CAUSE	ACCHOPRSTTU	UP TO SCRATCH
ACCEMNOPSST	COMPACTNESS	ACCIIIKKNPW	PICKWICKIAN
ACCEMOORSSS	COMES ACROSS	ACCIIILNOTV	CIVIL ACTION
ACCENNOOPTU	OPEN ACCOUNT	ACCIIILNSTV	CALVINISTIC
ACCENNORSVY	CONSERVANCY	ACCIIILOSST	SOCIALISTIC
ACCENOORRST	CONSECRATOR	ACCIIILRTTY	CRITICALITY
ACCENOOSTTU	CUT ONE'S COAT	ACCIILLNORY	CONCILIARLY
ACCENORRSTU	CUTS A CORNER	ACCIILLOPTY	OCCIPITALLY
ACCENORRTTU	CONTRACTURE	ACCIILMSSSS	CLASSICISMS
ACCENORSTTU	COUNTERACTS	ACCIILNNOTU	INCULCATION
ACCENORTTUU	TRUE ACCOUNT	ACCIILNNQUU	QUINCUNCIAL
ACCENPRTUUU	ACUPUNCTURE	ACCIILNOORT	CONCILIATOR
ACCEORRSTUY	COURTESY CAR	ACCIILNORTU	CIRCULATION
ACCEORSSTUU	CRUSTACEOUS	ACCIILNOSTY	CYCLISATION
ACCFGIIINRS	SACRIFICING	ACCIILNOTVY	VOLCANICITY
ACCFHMORRST	FROM SCRATCH	ACCIILNOTYZ	CYCLIZATION
ACCFIILOPRY	PROLIFICACY	ACCIILRRTUY	CIRCULARITY
ACCFILLNOTU	COUNCIL FLAT	ACCIILSSSST	CLASSICISTS
ACCFINOORST	CONFISCATOR	ACCIINORRSU	ROSICRUCIAN
ACCFLLNOTUU	FULL ACCOUNT	ACCIINPPRTY	PICNIC PARTY
ACCFNNOOOTU	OF NO ACCOUNT	ACCIIOPSTTT	PSITTACOTIC
ACCGGHKNOUW	CHUCK WAGGON	ACCIJNNOTUV	CONJUNCTIVA
ACCGGIILLOO	GLACIOLOGIC	ACCIKKKKNNS	KNICK-KNACKS
ACCGGIKNORT	GOT CRACKING	ACCIKNORSTW	WATSON-CRICK
ACCGHHNORRU	CHURCH ORGAN	ACCILLNOOOT	COLLOCATION
ACCGHINORVY	CRYING HAVOC	ACCILLPRTYY	CRYPTICALLY
ACCGHINOTTU	CATCHING OUT	ACCILMNRRUU	CIRCUMLUNAR
ACCGIIINRST	CICATRISING	ACCILMOPRRU	CIRCUMPOLAR

ACCILMOPSTY	CYTOPLASMIC	ACDDEEMNNOR	MODERN DANCE
ACCILNOOSST	ICONOCLASTS	ACDDEEMNRUV	DEMAND CURVE
ACCILNOOTTU	OCCULTATION	ACDDEENNRST	TRANSCENDED
ACCILNORSTU	ARTS COUNCIL	ACDDEENNSST	DESCENDANTS
ACCILOPRSTY	PYROCLASTIC	ACDDEGHNNOW	CHANGED DOWN
ACCILOPRTTU	PLUTOCRATIC	ACDDEGINTTU	CUTTING DEAD
ACCILORRSTU	CIRCULATORS	ACDDEGIORSU	DISCOURAGED
ACCILORRTUY	CIRCULATORY	ACDDEGNNOOS	CANNED GOODS
ACCIMMNNOTU	COMMUNICANT	ACDDEHINNOW	CHAINED DOWN
ACCIMNNOOTT	CONCOMITANT	ACDDEHIRSTT	DID A STRETCH
ACCINNNOSTY	INCONSTANCY	ACDDEHKMORU	ARCHDUKEDOM
ACCINNOOOSS	ON OCCASIONS	ACDDEHLLOST	SADDLECLOTH
ACCINNOOOTV	CONVOCATION	ACDDEHLORSS	HOLDS SACRED
ACCINNOOPRU	CORNUCOPIAN	ACDDEHNOOPY	DODECAPHONY
ACCINNOORTT	CONTRACTION	ACDDEHNORSW	CRASHED DOWN
ACCINNORSTT	CONTRACTS IN	ACDDEHNPPSU	CUPPED HANDS
ACCINOOPRSU	CORNUCOPIAS	ACDDEIILNRT	DENDRITICAL
ACCINOOPSTU	OCCUPATIONS	ACDDEIILRST	DID ARTICLES
ACCINOORRRW	CARRION CROW	ACDDEIINOST	DEDICATIONS
ACCIOOPPRRS	CARPOSPORIC	ACDDEIIOSST	DISSOCIATED
ACCIOOPRRTY	PROCARYOTIC	ACDDEIKKNVY	DICK VAN DYKE
ACCKKNOOOSS	COCKS A SNOOK	ACDDEIKNNNR	CANNED DRINK
ACCKLMOSTUY	LUCKY MASCOT	ACDDEILLMSS	MIDDLE CLASS
ACCKLOQRTUZ	QUARTZ CLOCK		MIDDLE-CLASS
ACCKNOOOTTU	TOOK ACCOUNT	ACDDEILORRY	DAILY RECORD
ACCKOOPRRST	CRACK TROOPS	ACDDEIMMNORU	ENDOCARDIUM
ACCKOOPRRSW	COCK SPARROW	ACDDEINOORT	COORDINATED
ACCLLLOOORU	LOCAL COLOUR	ACDDEINOORW	COINED A WORD
ACCLLMOOSTU	LOCAL CUSTOM	ACDDEINOSUV	SOUND ADVICE
ACCLMNOOPTU	COCONUT PALM	ACDDEKNORTW	TRACKED DOWN
ACCLNNOSTUY	CONSULTANCY	ACDDELMNOPW	CLAMPED DOWN
ACCLOPRRSUU	CORPUSCULAR	ACDDELNORUU	UNDER A CLOUD
ACCNNNOOOTU	ON NO ACCOUNT	ACDDIIMOPTU	OPIUM ADDICT
ACCNOOOPRTU	POOR ACCOUNT	ACDEEEEHLRR	CHEER LEADER
ACCNOORRSTT	CONTRACTORS		CHEERLEADER
ACCNOORTTTU	CONTRACT OUT	ACDEEEELRST	DECELERATES
ACCOORTTUUY	CUT YOUR COAT	ACDEEEEPRSS	PREDECEASES
ACDDDEEILTY	DEDICATEDLY	ACDEEEFFTTU	EFFECTUATED
ACDDDEGINRW	WEDDING CARD	ACDEEEFGNNR	GARDEN FENCE
ACDDDEEINRTU	CUT AND DRIED	ACDEEEFHNST	FACES THE END
	CUT-AND-DRIED	ACDEEEFHSTT	FEEDS THE CAT
ACDDDELOORU	ADDED COLOUR	ACDEEEFLNPU	PEACEFUL END
ACDDEEEELRT	DECELERATED	ACDEEEFNORT	CONFEDERATE
ACDDEEEEPRS	PREDECEASED	ACDEEEFOOPV	DOVE OF PEACE
ACDDEEEFHNT	FACED THE END	ACDEEEGHOSU	GOUDA CHEESE
ACDDEEEFRRU	REDUCED FARE	ACDEEEGLLOT	DECOLLETAGE
ACDDEEEILNP	CANDIED PEEL	ACDEEEHHLST	HELD THE ACES
ACDDEEEILNS	DEAD SILENCE	ACDEEEHHMOR	REACHED HOME
ACDDEEEIPRT	DEPRECIATED	ACDEEEHHNRT	REACH THE END
ACDDEEERRTU	REDUCED RATE	ACDEEEHLMNT	NEEDLE MATCH
ACDDEEFFIST	DISAFFECTED	ACDEEEHLRTW	CARTWHEELED
ACDDEEFHOST	FACE THE ODDS	ACDEEEHLSTT	DECATHLETES
ACDDEEFLNOR	FORCE-LANDED	ACDEEEHORRV	OVERREACHED
ACDDEEGHNNS	CHANGED ENDS	ACDEEEIKSSV	SEEKS ADVICE
ACDDEEGIKLR	GRIDDLE CAKE	ACDEEEILLPT	PEDICELLATE
ACDDEEGIKNW	WEDDING CAKE	ACDEEEILNRV	DELIVERANCE
ACDDEEGNORS	SECOND GRADE	ACDEEEILNSY	SENILE DECAY
ACDDEEHHIKT	THICK-HEADED	ACDEEEIMRTV	DECEMVIRATE
ACDDEEHHKOS	SHOCK-HEADED	ACDEEEINNNV	NICE AND EVEN
ACDDEEHILOT	LOAD THE DICE	ACDEEEIPRRS	PIERCED EARS
ACDDEEHNORW	CROWNED HEAD	ACDEEEIPRST	DEPRECIATES
	REACHED DOWN	ACDEEEIPRTT	DECREPITATE
ACDDEEIILMS	DECIMALISED	ACDEEEIRSTV	EVISCERATED
ACDDEEIILMZ	DECIMALIZED	ACDEEEIRTUV	REEDUCATIVE
ACDDEEIKRST	SIDETRACKED	ACDEEEJKSTU	SUEDE JACKET
ACDDEEILMRY	DEADLY CRIME	ACDEEEJKTTW	TWEED JACKET
ACDDEEINNNR	DINNER DANCE	ACDEEEKLNSS	LACKED SENSE
ACDDEEINRSX	CARD INDEXES	ACDEEEKNNPY	CAPE KENNEDY
ACDDEEIOTTX	DETOXICATED	ACDEEELLNRT	CRENELLATED
ACDDEELLSSY	CLYDESDALES	ACDEEELLRVW	CAVE DWELLER
		ACDEEELMMOW	MADE WELCOME

ACDEEELMNST	MALE DESCENT	ACDEEHLLMTW	WELL MATCHED
ACDEEELORRT	DECELERATOR	ACDEEHLLOSU	CLOSE-HAULED
ACDEEEMSSUX	MADE EXCUSES	ACDEEHLLSSS	HELD CLASSES
ACDEEENNNOP	DONE PENANCE	ACDEEHLORTW	COLD WEATHER
ACDEEENNOPS	DOES PENANCE	ACDEEHLPSSY	PLAYED CHESS
ACDEEENNSTT	ANTECEDENTS	ACDEEHMNORW	REACH-ME-DOWN
ACDEEENOSSS	DEACONESSES	ACDEEHMNRTW	WRETCHED MAN
ACDEEENPRRT	CARPENTERED	ACDEEHMNSTT	DETACHMENTS
ACDEEEOORRTV	OVERREACTED	ACDEEHMOPRS	SCRAPED HOME
ACDEEEPRRTU	RECUPERATED	ACDEEHNORSW	REACHES DOWN
ACDEEERRSTT	TRADE SECRET	ACDEEHOPRST	DROP THE CASE
ACDEEFFHRUU	CHAUFFEURED	ACDEEHORSTU	SEARCHED OUT
ACDEEFFIORV	OFFER ADVICE	ACDEEHORTVW	WATCHED OVER
ACDEEFGHIRX	FIXED CHARGE	ACDEEHRSSTU	THE CRUSADES
ACDEEFHILMR	CHARMED LIFE	ACDEEIILLTY	EIDETICALLY
ACDEEFHORRS	SEARCHED FOR	ACDEEIILMSS	DECIMALISES
ACDEEFIILTT	FELICITATED	ACDEEIILMSZ	DECIMALIZES
ACDEEFIIPRX	FIXED A PRICE	ACDEEIILPSS	SPECIALISED
ACDEEFILNOP	PIECE OF LAND	ACDEEIILPST	SPECIAL DIET
ACDEEFIMNOP	PEACE OF MIND	ACDEEIILPSZ	SPECIALIZED
ACDEEFIORTV	VOCIFERATED	ACDEEIILTUV	ELUCIDATIVE
ACDEEFLLPSU	PULLED FACES	ACDEEIIMMNN	MEDICINE MAN
ACDEEFLMORT	MORAL DEFECT	ACDEEIINNRT	INCINERATED
ACDEEFLNRUU	FRAUDULENCE	ACDEEIIOPPS	EPIDIASCOPE
ACDEEFLPRTY	PERFECT LADY	ACDEEIIORSV	RAISED VOICE
ACDEEFMORRS	ARMED FORCES	ACDEEIIPRTV	PREDICATIVE
ACDEEFRSSUY	DREYFUS CASE	ACDEEIKLNSY	ASKED NICELY
ACDEEGGNORT	CONGREGATED	ACDEEIKLOPS	LACKED POISE
ACDEEGHHPRT	DEPTH CHARGE	ACDEEIKMRTT	DREAM TICKET
ACDEEGHINSS	CHANGE SIDES	ACDEEIKNRTT	TAKEN CREDIT
ACDEEGHIRRR	RICHARD GERE	ACDEEIKNRTV	DICK TAVERNE
ACDEEGHIRSS	DISCHARGEES	ACDEEIKRSTT	TAKES CREDIT
ACDEEGHNNSS	CHANGES ENDS	ACDEEILLMNY	ENDEMICALLY
ACDEEGHNORV	CHANGED OVER	ACDEEILLNNY	DECENNIALLY
ACDEEGHNPST	CHANGED STEP	ACDEEILLRSS	ESCADRILLES
ACDEEGHNRRU	UNDERCHARGE	ACDEEILMSTT	MEDICAL TEST
ACDEEGHORRV	OVERCHARGED	ACDEEILNNST	CLANDESTINE
ACDEEGIINRV	DIVINE GRACE	ACDEEILNOPT	DECEPTIONAL
ACDEEGIINVV	GIVEN ADVICE	ACDEEILNOTT	DELECTATION
ACDEEGIISVV	GIVES ADVICE	ACDEEILNOTY	ELECTION DAY
ACDEEGIMMRY	MAGIC REMEDY	ACDEEILNRST	CREDENTIALS
ACDEEGINNRS	GRANDNIECES	ACDEEILNRTZ	CENTRALIZED
ACDEEGINPRT	DEPRECATING	ACDEEILPRTU	REDUPLICATE
ACDEEGINRST	DESECRATING	ACDEEILRSSU	SECULARISED
ACDEEGINRTU	REEDUCATING	ACDEEILRSUZ	SECULARIZED
ACDEEGIORST	CATEGORISED	ACDEEILSTWY	ACTED WISELY
ACDEEGIORTV	GET A DIVORCE	ACDEEIMMNST	MEDICAMENTS
ACDEEGIORTZ	CATEGORIZED	ACDEEIMNPRT	PREDICAMENT
ACDEEGIOTTT	TIED COTTAGE	ACDEEIMNRTY	DETERMINACY
ACDEEGIOTTX	EXCOGITATED	ACDEEIMORST	DEMOCRATISE
ACDEEGKLNOW	ACKNOWLEDGE	ACDEEIMORTZ	DEMOCRATIZE
ACDEEGLNORU	GRAND COULEE	ACDEEIMOSTT	DOMESTICATE
ACDEEGLNORV	GLANCED OVER	ACDEEIMOSTU	CAME OUTSIDE
ACDEEGNOSST	SECOND STAGE	ACDEEINOPRT	DEPRECATION
ACDEEHHLOST	HOLD THE ACES	ACDEEINORSS	SECONDARIES
ACDEEHILLTV	EDITH CAVELL	ACDEEINORST	CONSIDERATE
ACDEEHILNNS	CHANNELISED	ACDEEINORTU	REEDUCATION
ACDEEHILNNZ	CHANNELIZED	ACDEEINPPRT	APPRENTICED
ACDEEHILNPP	CHIPPENDALE	ACDEEINPRST	INTERSPACED
ACDEEHILNRS	CHANDELIERS	ACDEEINRRRV	CRANE DRIVER
ACDEEHILNRT	IN THE CRADLE	ACDEEIOPRRT	DEPRECIATOR
ACDEEHILPTV	HELD CAPTIVE	ACDEEIOPTTT	PETTICOATED
ACDEEHIMNRS	MERCHANDISE	ACDEEIOQTUV	EQUIVOCATED
ACDEEHIMSST	SCHEMATISED	ACDEEIORRRV	CARRIED OVER
ACDEEHIMSTZ	SCHEMATIZED	ACDEEIORRSV	SERVICE ROAD
ACDEEHINOTT	DEATH NOTICE	ACDEEIORRTT	DIRECTORATE
ACDEEHIINRTW	WINDCHEATER	ACDEEIORRTV	DIVORCE RATE
ACDEEHIORSV	HEARD VOICES	ACDEEIOSTTX	DETOXICATES
ACDEEHIORTT	TEACH TO RIDE	ACDEEJKKNNY	JACK KENNEDY
ACDEEHISTTT	THE ACID TEST	ACDEEJKMPSY	JACK DEMPSEY
ACDEEHKOPSU	PACKED HOUSE	ACDEEJLMPRU	JUMPED CLEAR

ACDEEKLLSTW	WELL-STACKED
ACDEEKLMNOY	LACKED MONEY
ACDEEKMQRUY	QUACK REMEDY
ACDEEKQRRTU	QUARTER DECK
	QUARTERDECK
ACDEELLSTTU	SCUTELLATED
ACDEELMNOTU	CLAUDE MONET
ACDEELNOPRW	CANDLEPOWER
ACDEELNORSU	SECURED LOAN
ACDEELNOSST	ADOLESCENTS
	SECONDS LATE
ACDEELNPTUU	PEDUNCULATE
ACDEELNRRSY	DRY CLEANERS
ACDEELOORTW	WATER-COOLED
ACDEELOPRTU	OPERCULATED
ACDEELORSTV	DOVER CASTLE
ACDEELORSTW	DREW TO SCALE
ACDEELOSSTY	STAYED CLOSE
ACDEELSSTUY	DECUSSATELY
ACDEEMMNORS	COMMANDEERS
ACDEEMMNOTT	COMMENTATED
ACDEEMNNOOT	COME TO AN END
ACDEEMNOPSS	ENCOMPASSED
ACDEEMNOPST	COMPENSATED
ACDEEMNRRRY	MERRY DANCER
ACDEEMNRTTU	TRADUCEMENT
ACDEEMORRST	ARMED ESCORT
ACDEEMORSTU	SCREAMED OUT
ACDEENNORTV	CONTRAVENED
ACDEENNOSST	CONDENSATES
ACDEENOORST	SEEN A DOCTOR
ACDEENOPRRS	ROPEDANCERS
ACDEENOPRTU	DANCE TROUPE
ACDEENOPSST	SCENTED SOAP
ACDEENORRST	SECOND-RATER
ACDEENRRSUU	UNDER A CURSE
ACDEENRRTTU	CURRENT DATE
ACDEENRSSTT	STANDS ERECT
ACDEEOORSST	SEES A DOCTOR
ACDEEOPRRST	TAPE-RECORDS
ACDEEOPRRSY	COPYREADERS
ACDEEOPRRTY	DEPRECATORY
ACDEEORRSST	DESECRATORS
	SETS A RECORD
ACDEFFILLOT	CALLED IT OFF
ACDEFFIRSST	SCARED STIFF
ACDEFFNOOPS	DOFF ONES CAP
ACDEFGHLORU	FORCED LAUGH
ACDEFGHMORR	FROGMARCHED
ACDEFGILRSU	DISGRACEFUL
ACDEFGINNTU	FECUNDATING
ACDEFHIIMOS	DO A MISCHIEF
ACDEFHILPST	FELDSPATHIC
ACDEFHIMORS	IDES OF MARCH
ACDEFHLLORT	CALLED FORTH
ACDEFIIINNT	INFANTICIDE
ACDEFIIINOT	DEIFICATION
	EDIFICATION
ACDEFIIKRWY	WICKED FAIRY
ACDEFIILSTU	FEUDALISTIC
ACDEFIIORTY	EDIFICATORY
ACDEFIIRRST	FRATRICIDES
ACDEFILNRTY	FRIENDLY ACT
ACDEFILORST	FIDEL CASTRO
ACDEFIMORST	COMES ADRIFT
ACDEFINNOTU	FECUNDATION
ACDEFINNRTU	CANNED FRUIT
ACDEFIOPTTU	FACED UP TO IT
ACDEFJNOORY	DANCE FOR JOY
ACDEFLLNORU	UNCALLED FOR
	UNCALLED-FOR

ACDEFLMMNOS	SELF-COMMAND
ACDEFLORSTU	CUTS FOR DEAL
ACDEFMNOOSY	SECOND OF MAY
ACDEFMOORRW	COME FORWARD
ACDEFMOPRRU	FARM PRODUCE
ACDEFOSSTUY	SAFE CUSTODY
ACDEGGHINPS	EGG AND CHIPS
ACDEGGHINSW	EGG SANDWICH
ACDEGGILNOO	GOLD COINAGE
ACDEGGINNNO	GONE DANCING
ACDEGGINNOS	GOES DANCING
ACDEGHHIOWY	HIGHWAY CODE
ACDEGHIILNP	HIDING PLACE
ACDEGHIIOPR	IDEOGRAPHIC
ACDEGHIMOPR	DEMOGRAPHIC
ACDEGHINPST	DESPATCHING
ACDEGHINRST	DIGS A TRENCH
ACDEGHIRRSS	DISCHARGERS
ACDEGHLOORS	GRADE SCHOOL
ACDEGHNNORU	CHANGE ROUND
ACDEGHNNOSW	CHANGES DOWN
ACDEGIILLOO	IDEOLOGICAL
ACDEGIILMRU	DEMIURGICAL
ACDEGIILNPY	PLAYING DICE
ACDEGIILNTU	ELUCIDATING
ACDEGIIMMOR	IDEOGRAMMIC
ACDEGIIMNSU	MISGUIDANCE
ACDEGIINPRT	PREDICATING
ACDEGIKNNPS	SEND PACKING
ACDEGILLNOV	LEAVING COLD
ACDEGILLOOP	PEDOLOGICAL
ACDEGILMNOR	RACING MODEL
ACDEGILMRRU	MIRACLE DRUG
ACDEGILNNRY	DRY CLEANING
	DRY-CLEANING
ACDEGILNOST	CLOSING DATE
ACDEGIMORTY	TRAGICOMEDY
ACDEGINNNTW	WENT DANCING
ACDEGINNOPR	ROPEDANCING
ACDEGINNRTU	UNDERACTING
ACDEGINRRTT	DIRECT GRANT
ACDEGIOORTV	GOT A DIVORCE
ACDEGIOOSTW	TWICE AS GOOD
ACDEGIORSSU	DISCOURAGES
ACDEGLNNRSU	GRANDUNCLES
ACDEGLOORST	COLD STORAGE
ACDEGOORSST	GOOD ACTRESS
ACDEHHIKNNT	KITCHEN HAND
ACDEHHILSTW	CLASHED WITH
ACDEHIIKMNT	KITCHEN MAID
ACDEHIIMNRT	CAME IN THIRD
ACDEHIIOPRT	DIAPHORETIC
ACDEHIIORRT	DIARRHOETIC
ACDEHIKLPTU	CHALKED IT UP
ACDEHIKLSTY	DAILY SKETCH
ACDEHIKMNOS	CHAIN SMOKED
	CHAIN-SMOKED
ACDEHIKOSTT	SICK TO DEATH
ACDEHILLLPY	DELPHICALLY
ACDEHILLNOY	HEDONICALLY
ACDEHILNORT	CHLORINATED
ACDEHILOPTV	HOLD CAPTIVE
ACDEHILRSSY	CHRYSALIDES
ACDEHIMNNOY	COME IN HANDY
ACDEHIMOPRS	COMRADESHIP
ACDEHIMORST	DICHROMATES
ACDEHIMOSTU	MUSTACHIOED
ACDEHINNOST	STANCHIONED
ACDEHINNSST	DISENCHANTS
ACDEHINOORS	ICOSAHEDRON
ACDEHINOORW	WOODEN CHAIR

ACDEHINOPST	DICTAPHONES	ACDEILRSTTW	WILDCATTERS
ACDEHIOOPRT	ORTHOPAEDIC	ACDEILRSTYZ	CRYSTALIZED
ACDEHIOPPRR	CROPPED HAIR	ACDEIMNORRS	MORRIS DANCE
ACDEHIPPTTU	PATCHED IT UP	ACDEIMNOTTU	MADE IT COUNT
ACDEHKLORST	DARK CLOTHES	ACDEINNORST	CONSTRAINED
ACDEHKOOPRT	CROOKED PATH	ACDEINNOSSS	DISSONANCES
ACDEHLLOSSS	HOLD CLASSES	ACDEINOORST	CAROTENOIDS
ACDEHLNPRTU	THUNDERCLAP		COORDINATES
ACDEHLOOPPS	CEPHALOPODS		DECORATIONS
ACDEHLOORST	RED-HOT COALS	ACDEINOOSST	TOSSED A COIN
ACDEHLOSUVY	HEAVY CLOUDS	ACDEINOPSTT	CONSTIPATED
ACDEHMNOOST	COMES TO HAND	ACDEINORRSW	CORDWAINERS
ACDEHMOORTT	METHOD ACTOR	ACDEINORRWY	CORDWAINERY
ACDEHNOORST	OCTAHEDRONS	ACDEINOSSTT	ANECDOTISTS
ACDEHNORSSW	CRASHES DOWN	ACDEINOSSTU	DECUSSATION
ACDEHNORSSZ	SCHERZANDOS	ACDEINOSTTU	OUTDISTANCE
ACDEHNORSTT	HARD CONTEST	ACDEINOSTTX	DETOXICANTS
ACDEHNOSSTU	COUNTS HEADS	ACDEINPRSTY	CANDY STRIPE
ACDEIIJLPRU	PREJUDICIAL	ACDEIOPRSSY	CARYOPSIDES
ACDEIIKMQTU	MADE IT QUICK	ACDEIORRRTT	ART DIRECTOR
ACDEIIKMSTT	MADE IT STICK	ACDEJNOSSTU	JUST A SECOND
ACDEIIKNRST	INSIDE TRACK	ACDEKLNORSS	CLOSED RANKS
ACDEIILLMMT	MILD CLIMATE	ACDEKOSTTUY	TAKE CUSTODY
ACDEIILLMNY	MEDICINALLY	ACDELLNOOTY	COTYLEDONAL
ACDEIILLMOR	LIME CORDIAL	ACDELLOORRT	CALL TO ORDER
ACDEIILLRVY	VERIDICALLY	ACDELLOOSST	COSTA DEL SOL
ACDEIILLSTY	DEISTICALLY	ACDELMNOORU	COLOURED MAN
ACDEIILMNOT	MALEDICTION	ACDELNOOPRT	PANEL DOCTOR
ACDEIILMPRS	SPERMICIDAL	ACDEMMMNNOT	COMMANDMENT
ACDEIILMRSS	DISCLAIMERS	ACDEMMNOSTU	CONSUMMATED
ACDEIILNNOT	DECLINATION	ACDEMNNORTU	COUNTERMAND
ACDEIILNNST	INCIDENTALS	ACDEMNORTUY	DOCUMENTARY
ACDEIILNORT	DIRECTIONAL	ACDEMOORSSV	MOVED ACROSS
ACDEIILNOTU	ELUCIDATION	ACDEMOPRSSU	MASS PRODUCE
ACDEIILNOTV	VALEDICTION	ACDENNNNOUU	UNANNOUNCED
ACDEIILNPTU	IN DUPLICATE	ACDENNNOORS	ORDONNANCES
ACDEIILOPRS	PERIODICALS	ACDENOORRSW	NO-SCORE DRAW
ACDEIILORRT	DIRECTORIAL	ACDENOPRSTY	SECOND PARTY
ACDEIILPRTT	TRIPLICATED	ACDENRRRSTU	REDCURRANTS
ACDEIILPTUV	DUPLICATIVE	ACDENRRSSTU	TRANSDUCERS
ACDEIILRTUV	DIVERTICULA	ACDEOOPRSTU	DEAR OCTOPUS
ACDEIIMORTU	AUDIOMETRIC	ACDEORRSSST	STAR-CROSSED
ACDEIIMPRRU	PERICARDIUM	ACDEORRSUWY	CAUSED WORRY
ACDEIIMSSSU	MASS SUICIDE	ACDFFGHINNU	HANDCUFFING
ACDEIINNRTY	TYRANNICIDE	ACDFFGIINRT	DIFFRACTING
ACDEIINOPRT	PREDICATION	ACDFFGILNOS	SCAFFOLDING
ACDEIINORRT	DOCTRINAIRE	ACDFFGIRRTU	DRUG TRAFFIC
ACDEIINOTTX	INTOXICATED	ACDFFIILMOO	OFFICIALDOM
ACDEIINRTTX	INDIRECT TAX	ACDFFIINORT	DIFFRACTION
ACDEIIOSSST	DISSOCIATES	ACDFFIRTTUY	TRAFFIC DUTY
ACDEIIRSTTV	DISTRACTIVE	ACDFGHHIINS	CHAFING DISH
ACDEIKNSSSY	CANDY KISSES	ACDFGIKLNNO	FOLK DANCING
ACDEILLLMOY	MELODICALLY	ACDFIORSSTU	SUIT OF CARDS
ACDEILLMNOY	DEMONICALLY	ACDFKLOORRW	LOCK FORWARD
ACDEILLNORR	CORDILLERAN	ACDFKOORTUU	OUT FOR A DUCK
ACDEILLORTW	ALLOW CREDIT	ACDFLOOORTW	DOCTOR OF LAW
ACDEILMNOOW	LOW COMEDIAN	ACDFOORRTUW	WARD OF COURT
ACDEILMNOPS	ENDOPLASMIC	ACDGGHIINRS	DISCHARGING
ACDEILMORTY	MALEDICTORY	ACDGGIILNNR	DANCING GIRL
ACDEILNNOSY	CONEY ISLAND	ACDGHHIMMNO	HIGH COMMAND
ACDEILNOOST	CONSOLIDATE	ACDGHIIKNNP	HANDPICKING
ACDEILNORSS	CORDIALNESS	ACDGHIIKNRR	KING RICHARD
ACDEILNORSY	SECONDARILY	ACDGHIIMNOT	HAD IT COMING
ACDEILNOSTU	INOSCULATED	ACDGHIINNSW	SANDWICHING
ACDEILNRRSU	LAND CRUISER	ACDGHIINPST	DISPATCHING
ACDEILORSTW	COWARDLIEST	ACDGHIINRSV	CRASH-DIVING
ACDEILORTVY	VALEDICTORY	ACDGHIOPRSY	DISCOGRAPHY
ACDEILOSTYY	SOCIETY LADY	ACDGHLOOORS	GOOD SCHOLAR
ACDEILPPSTU	SUPPLICATED	ACDGIIILMNS	DISCLAIMING
ACDEILPSTUY	SPECIAL DUTY	ACDGIIILOST	DIALOGISTIC
ACDEILRSSTY	CRYSTALISED	ACDGIIINNTV	VINDICATING

ACDGIIKNORT	DOING A TRICK
ACDGIILLMNO	LOGICAL MIND
ACDGIILNOST	DISLOCATING
ACDGIILNTTW	WILDCATTING
ACDGIINNNOT	GIN AND TONIC
ACDGIINNNRW	WINNING CARD
ACDGIINNSTY	SYNDICATING
ACDGIINOSST	DIAGNOSTICS
ACDGIINRSTT	DISTRACTING
ACDGILLNTUY	DUTY CALLING
ACDGILMNNOW	CALMING DOWN
ACDGILNNOSW	SCALING DOWN
ACDGILNORRW	RACING WORLD
ACDGILNORUY	CRYING ALOUD
ACDGIMNNOPU	UP AND COMING
	UP-AND-COMING
ACDGINOORVW	WOOD CARVING
ACDGINOPRSU	SCOURING PAD
ACDGLLOOTYY	DACTYLOLOGY
ACDGMNOOOPY	GOOD COMPANY
ACDGORSSSTU	SCOTS GUARDS
ACDHHILNOPR	ORPHAN CHILD
ACDHHIOPRRS	HARPSICHORD
ACDHHIOPRTY	HYDROPATHIC
ACDHIINOOPR	RADIOPHONIC
ACDHIIOPRST	DIASTROPHIC
ACDHIIRRSVV	VIV RICHARDS
ACDHIKNNOST	STOCK IN HAND
ACDHIMNOORT	TRICHOMONAD
ACDHINOOPRR	RICH AND POOR
ACDHIOPRSTT	DROP A STITCH
ACDHIORSTTY	HYDROSTATIC
ACDHLLOOOOW	WOOD ALCOHOL
ACDHLNNSUUY	SUNDAY LUNCH
ACDHLNOOORT	NOTOCHORDAL
ACDHLOOOPPR	POOR OLD CHAP
ACDHNNOSSTU	COUNTS HANDS
ACDHNOOPRRS	DROPS ANCHOR
ACDIIILLNPS	DISCIPLINAL
ACDIIILLOTY	IDIOTICALLY
ACDIIILLRVY	VIRICIDALLY
ACDIIILMORY	DOMICILIARY
ACDIIINNOST	INDICATIONS
ACDIIINNOTV	VINDICATION
ACDIIINRSTW	DARWINISTIC
ACDIIJLLRUY	JURIDICALLY
ACDIIKLNOST	LAID IN STOCK
ACDIILLLLYY	IDYLLICALLY
ACDIILLMOWY	WILLIAM CODY
ACDIILLNOTY	DICTIONALLY
ACDIILLORST	CLOSTRIDIAL
ACDIILMNOPR	PALINDROMIC
ACDIILMNSSY	SYNDICALISM
ACDIILNNOOT	CONDITIONAL
ACDIILNOOST	DISLOCATION
ACDIILNOPTU	DUPLICATION
ACDIILNSSTY	SYNDICALIST
ACDIILOSTUY	ACIDULOSITY
ACDIIMORSTY	MYOCARDITIS
ACDIINNOSTY	SYNDICATION
ACDIINOORST	CAROTINOIDS
ACDIINORSTT	DISTRACTION
ACDIINORSTV	VINDICATORS
ACDIINORTVY	VINDICATORY
ACDIIOORRRR	AIR CORRIDOR
ACDIKKPSTUU	KICK UP A DUST
ACDIKLLNOPR	NO PACK DRILL
ACDIKLNOOSS	COOK ISLANDS
ACDILLLLOOY	COLLOIDALLY
ACDILLMNOOY	MONODICALLY
ACDILLMNOST	CALLS TO MIND

ACDILLNORTY	DOCTRINALLY
ACDILLORSTY	CRYSTALLOID
ACDILNOORSU	SOCIAL ROUND
ACDILOPRSTU	DUPLICATORS
ACDIMNOOSTT	MASTODONTIC
ACDINNNOOOT	CONDONATION
ACDINOOORRT	COORDINATOR
ACDINORSSTY	SYNDICATORS
ACDINRRSTUY	CAR INDUSTRY
ACDIOPRRSUW	CUPIDS ARROW
ACDKKNNOORU	KNOCK AROUND
ACDKLLNOORR	ROCK AND ROLL
ACDKMMNOOOT	TOOK COMMAND
ACDLLNOORTU	DUAL CONTROL
ACDLLOPTYYY	POLYDACTYLY
ACDLNOOORTY	CONDOLATORY
ACDNNOOPRSS	PROS AND CONS
ACDNOORSTUU	SCOUT AROUND
ACDOPRRSTUY	DROP A CURTSY
ACEEEEFNNRT	ENTRANCE FEE
ACEEEEKPRST	KEEP A SECRET
ACEEEEMRSTX	EXTREME CASE
ACEEEFFFRTT	AFTEREFFECT
ACEEEFFGNOV	GAVE OFFENCE
ACEEEFFGSTT	STAGE EFFECT
ACEEEFFKNOT	TAKE OFFENCE
ACEEEFFKNTT	TAKEN EFFECT
ACEEEFFKSTT	TAKES EFFECT
ACEEEFFOORT	TEA OR COFFEE
ACEEEFFSTTU	EFFECTUATES
ACEEEFGILRR	FIERCE GLARE
ACEEEFGMPRU	REFUGEE CAMP
ACEEEFHLNRV	FRENCH LEAVE
ACEEEFILMOV	FEMALE VOICE
ACEEEFILNRT	FEEL CERTAIN
ACEEEFIOPPR	PIPE OF PEACE
ACEEEFNPRRT	NEAR PERFECT
ACEEEFOPRSU	SUE FOR PEACE
ACEEEGHHRST	CHARGE SHEET
ACEEEGHPRSV	GRAVE SPEECH
ACEEEGHRRST	THREE GRACES
ACEEEGIKNPP	KEEPING PACE
ACEEEGIMNNR	GENERIC NAME
ACEEEGIMNRT	RACE MEETING
ACEEEGIMNTT	METAGENETIC
ACEEEGINNSU	GENUINE CASE
ACEEEGINRST	GREAT-NIECES
ACEEEGLNRRS	LARGE SCREEN
ACEEEGNNORT	GET AN ENCORE
ACEEEGNPRST	PERCENTAGES
ACEEEGNRSTT	SECRET AGENT
ACEEEHHMORS	REACHES HOME
ACEEEHHRRTY	HEARTY CHEER
ACEEEHILMNS	CHINESE MEAL
ACEEEHIMNRS	ARCH ENEMIES
ACEEEHIMNTV	ACHIEVEMENT
ACEEEHINNTT	CANINE TEETH
ACEEEHINRTW	NICE WEATHER
ACEEEHIRSTT	CATHETERISE
ACEEEHIRTTZ	CATHETERIZE
ACEEEHKLNRT	LEATHERNECK
ACEEEHLLNRT	CHANTERELLE
ACEEEHLORST	LOSE THE RACE
ACEEEHLRSTU	THE CRUEL SEA
ACEEEHMNNNT	ENHANCEMENT
ACEEEHNOPST	OPEN THE CASE
ACEEEHORRSV	OVERREACHES
ACEEEHPRSTT	TEACHERS PET
ACEEEHPSSTT	SETS THE PACE
ACEEEHRRSSS	RESEARCHERS
ACEEEIILNPV	LIVE IN PEACE

ACEEEILMNPT	MANTELPIECE
ACEEEILNPPR	PIPE CLEANER
ACEEEILNQUV	EQUIVALENCE
ACEEEILNRRV	IRRELEVANCE
ACEEEILOSTV	CEASE TO LIVE
ACEEEIMNQUU	CINEMA QUEUE
ACEEEIMNRRS	MERCENARIES
ACEEEIMPRST	MASTERPIECE
ACEEEINNRST	CENTENARIES
ACEEEINPRST	REST IN PEACE
ACEEEINSSTT	NECESSITATE
ACEEEIRRSST	SECRETAIRES
	SECRETARIES
ACEEEIRSSTV	EVISCERATES
ACEEEJKLPST	STEEPLEJACK
ACEEEJORSTT	EJECTOR SEAT
ACEEEKLLNRU	LAKE LUCERNE
ACEEEKLMMOW	MAKE WELCOME
ACEEEKMSSUX	MAKE EXCUSES
ACEEEKNOSTU	TAKE ONES CUE
ACEEEKPRSTT	KEPT A SECRET
ACEEELLMNOV	MALEVOLENCE
ACEEELLNRSY	CLEARLY SEEN
	SEEN CLEARLY
ACEEELLRSSY	SEES CLEARLY
ACEEELLSSSY	CEASELESSLY
ACEEELMMNPT	EMPLACEMENT
ACEEELMNPRT	REPLACEMENT
ACEEELMNRTX	EXCREMENTAL
ACEEELNPRST	SECRET PANEL
ACEEELNPSSW	SWEEPS CLEAN
ACEEELORSTT	ELECTORATES
ACEEELRRSST	STEERS CLEAR
ACEEELRSSTT	TELECASTERS
ACEEEMNORRS	COMES NEARER
ACEEEMNPSST	ESCAPEMENTS
ACEEENRRSTY	RECENT YEARS
ACEEEOPRSTU	ESCAPE ROUTE
ACEEEOPRTTX	EXPECTORATE
ACEEEPRRSTU	RECUPERATES
ACEEEPRSSTT	PACESETTERS
ACEEERRSTTY	CAREY STREET
ACEEERSSTTT	STATE SECRET
ACEEFFIILOS	OFFICIALESE
ACEEFFIKNOT	TAKEN OFFICE
ACEEFFIKOST	TAKES OFFICE
ACEEFFILNTU	INEFFECTUAL
ACEEFFILTVY	AFFECTIVELY
ACEEFFIMOPR	PRICE OF FAME
ACEEFFIOPRR	OFFER A PRICE
ACEEFFLLMOW	CAME OFF WELL
ACEEFFLLTUY	EFFECTUALLY
ACEEFFLORST	FLEET OF CARS
ACEEFGHMOSS	GAME OF CHESS
ACEEFGHSTTT	GET THE FACTS
ACEEFGIINRS	CEASING FIRE
ACEEFGILNNR	FREELANCING
ACEEFGIMORT	CAME TO GRIEF
ACEEFHHSTTW	CHEWS THE FAT
ACEEFHIINTV	NATIVE CHIEF
ACEEFHILTTT	CATTLE THIEF
ACEEFHILTTX	FELIX THE CAT
ACEEFHINNRS	ENFRANCHISE
ACEEFHINOSW	CHOSEN A WIFE
ACEEFHIOOSW	CHOOSE A WIFE
ACEEFHIORRT	THE AIR FORCE
ACEEFHIPRTV	CHAPTER FIVE
ACEEFHIRRTW	FIRE-WATCHER
ACEEFHKLOST	LOCK THE SAFE
ACEEFHKNPRS	SPEAK FRENCH
ACEEFHLTUWY	WATCHFUL EYE
ACEEFHNRRTU	FURTHERANCE
ACEEFHORRSS	SEARCHES FOR
ACEEFHRTTVY	THE VERY FACT
ACEEFIILSTT	FELICITATES
ACEEFIIMNPR	FAMINE PRICE
ACEEFIIPRSX	FIXES A PRICE
ACEEFIKLLPS	SCAFELL PIKE
ACEEFILLLNP	FELL IN PLACE
ACEEFILMOST	SLICE OF MEAT
ACEEFILNRTT	FELT CERTAIN
ACEEFILRSTV	SERVICE FLAT
ACEEFIMOPST	SPACE OF TIME
ACEEFIORSTV	VOCIFERATES
ACEEFKLLOPS	LACK OF SLEEP
ACEEFKLNOSS	LACK OF SENSE
ACEEFKNOPTT	PACKET OF TEN
ACEEFLLNRST	CRESTFALLEN
ACEEFLLORSV	CLOVERLEAFS
ACEEFLNORTT	LEFT NO TRACE
ACEEFLNRSSU	CAREFULNESS
ACEEFLOPRST	PLACE OF REST
ACEEFLORSST	FORECASTLES
ACEEFLPRRTU	PREFECTURAL
ACEEFMNOPRR	PERFORMANCE
ACEEFORSTTU	REFUSE TO ACT
ACEEGGHINNV	GIVEN CHANGE
ACEEGGHINSV	GIVES CHANGE
ACEEGGHNNOT	GET NO CHANGE
ACEEGGIMNOT	GEOMAGNETIC
ACEEGGLLNOT	GLANCE TO LEG
ACEEGGLORSU	GEORGE LUCAS
ACEEGGNORST	CONGREGATES
ACEEGHHOPTV	GAVE THE CHOP
ACEEGHHRSTW	CHEWS THE RAG
ACEEGHIKSTV	GIVE THE SACK
ACEEGHILOOT	OLIGOCHAETE
ACEEGHILPRT	TELEGRAPHIC
ACEEGHIMNST	TIMES CHANGE
ACEEGHIINNRT	INTERCHANGE
ACEEGHINRRS	RESEARCHING
ACEEGHKSSTT	GETS THE SACK
ACEEGHLLNRS	CHALLENGERS
ACEEGHLNOOS	LOOSE CHANGE
ACEEGHLNRST	THE CLANGERS
ACEEGHLOPST	CLOSE THE GAP
ACEEGHNORSV	CHANGE-OVERS
	CHANGES OVER
ACEEGHNPSST	CHANGES STEP
ACEEGHOPSTU	SOUGHT PEACE
ACEEGHORRSV	OVERCHARGES
ACEEGHORTTT	ACT TOGETHER
ACEEGHPRRSU	SUPERCHARGE
ACEEGIINPRR	EARPIERCING
ACEEGIJNORU	ORANGE JUICE
ACEEGIKLMNP	KEEPING CALM
ACEEGIKNNPP	KNEECAPPING
ACEEGIKNTTT	TICKET AGENT
ACEEGILLNRY	GENERICALLY
ACEEGILLNTY	GENETICALLY
	LEGAL NICETY
ACEEGILLNUY	EUGENICALLY
ACEEGILLRVY	VICEREGALLY
ACEEGILMNOR	LARGE INCOME
ACEEGILMNRS	SINGLE CREAM
ACEEGILNNTU	ENUCLEATING
ACEEGILNPRS	SLEEPING CAR
ACEEGILNPSS	SINGLE-SPACE
ACEEGILNRSS	GRACILENESS
ACEEGILNSTT	TELECASTING
ACEEGILSSTU	SLUICE GATES
ACEEGILSTTU	GESTICULATE

ACEEGIMNORS	CINEMAGOERS	ACEEHLLNTTU	CALL THE TUNE
ACEEGIMRRRR	GERM CARRIER	ACEEHLLOOSV	LEAVE SCHOOL
ACEEGINNORS	GRECIAN NOSE	ACEEHLLQRUW	RAQUEL WELCH
ACEEGINNPRS	PREGNANCIES	ACEEHLNOPTW	COW ELEPHANT
ACEEGINORTT	TERATOGENIC	ACEEHLNPRSU	LEPRECHAUNS
ACEEGINRTTV	TRAGIC EVENT	ACEEHLNRSUY	SHEER LUNACY
ACEEGIOPSTY	SOCIETY PAGE	ACEEHLOORRU	LEUCORRHOEA
ACEEGIORSST	CATEGORISES	ACEEHLOPSTY	POLYCHAETES
ACEEGIORSTZ	CATEGORIZES	ACEEHLORSTT	LOST THE RACE
ACEEGIOSTTX	EXCOGITATES	ACEEHLPRSSY	CHESS PLAYER
ACEEGKNORRT	ROCKET RANGE	ACEEHMMNNRT	MERCHANTMEN
ACEEGLLRSSY	GRACELESSLY	ACEEHMMRRSSU	MEERSCHAUMS
ACEEGLMNNOT	CONGEALMENT	ACEEHMNNNTT	ENCHANTMENT
ACEEGLMNORS	CAMERLENGOS	ACEEHMNNRRT	TRENCHERMAN
ACEEGLNORSV	GLANCES OVER	ACEEHMNORVY	HAVE NO MERCY
ACEEGLNRSTU	GREAT-UNCLES	ACEEHMOORSS	COMES ASHORE
ACEEGLORSSV	CARGO VESSEL	ACEEHMOORTT	COME TO EARTH
ACEEGMNORRS	SCAREMONGER	ACEEHMOPRSS	SCRAPES HOME
ACEEGMOSTTW	MEWS COTTAGE	ACEEHMORSTT	TACHOMETERS
ACEEGNNOORT	GOT AN ENCORE	ACEEHMRSTTY	TACHYMETERS
ACEEGNNORSV	GOVERNANCES	ACEEHNNRSST	ENCHANTRESS
ACEEGNNOSST	COGNATENESS	ACEEHNOPRTT	ON THE CARPET
ACEEGPRRSSU	SECURE GRASP	ACEEHNORTUV	TOUCH A NERVE
ACEEHHHKTTW	WHAT THE HECK	ACEEHNPRRTU	CHEAP RETURN
ACEEHHIIRRS	HIERARCHIES	ACEEHNPRTTX	NEXT CHAPTER
ACEEHHIKLST	HEAL THE SICK	ACEEHNRSTTU	SECRET HAUNT
ACEEHHILNSW	CHAINWHEELS	ACEEHORRSTT	ORCHESTRATE
ACEEHHILRSW	WHEELCHAIRS	ACEEHORRSTU	TREACHEROUS
ACEEHHLMRST	CRASH HELMET	ACEEHORSSST	CROSS THE SEA
ACEEHHMMSTU	MUCH THE SAME	ACEEHORSSTT	THE COASTERS
ACEEHHNOPTT	THE CENOTAPH	ACEEHORSTVW	WATCHES OVER
ACEEHHNORST	SHEET ANCHOR	ACEEHPSTTTU	CUTS THE TAPE
ACEEHHOPRTT	REACH THE TOP	ACEEIIKNNTZ	CITIZEN KANE
ACEEHIILPTT	EPITHETICAL	ACEEIIKRSTT	RICKETTSIAE
ACEEHIIMMNT	TIME MACHINE	ACEEIILLNPS	ALL IN PIECES
ACEEHIIMMNNT	IN THE CINEMA	ACEEIILLNPT	PENICILLATE
ACEEHIINNRT	INHERITANCE	ACEEIILNRRT	RECTILINEAR
ACEEHIKMPTT	PICK THE TEAM	ACEEIILNSTT	LICENTIATES
ACEEHIKPRST	ASK THE PRICE	ACEEIILPRRT	RETAIL PRICE
ACEEHIKTTTW	AT THE WICKET	ACEEIILPRTV	REPLICATIVE
ACEEHILLNRT	IN THE CELLAR	ACEEIILPSSS	SPECIALISES
ACEEHILLRTY	HERETICALLY	ACEEIILPSST	SPECIALTIES
ACEEHILNNSS	CHANNELISES	ACEEIILPSSZ	SPECIALIZES
ACEEHILNNSZ	CHANNELIZES	ACEEIILPTVX	EXPLICATIVE
ACEEHILNPPS	PLAIN SPEECH	ACEEIIMNRRT	RECRIMINATE
ACEEHILNRTT	CHAIN LETTER	ACEEIINNRST	INCINERATES
ACEEHILNSST	ETHICALNESS	ACEEIINNRST	INSECTARIES
ACEEHILORTT	THEORETICAL	ACEEIINRSTT	CERTAINTIES
ACEEHILPSTT	TIP THE SCALE	ACEEIINRTTV	INTERACTIVE
ACEEHILRSTV	STAR VEHICLE	ACEEIIPPRTT	PERIPATETIC
ACEEHILSTTW	WHITE CASTLE		PRECIPITATE
ACEEHIMMNPT	IMPEACHMENT	ACEEIIPRRSS	RAISE PRICES
ACEEHIMNOST	THE SAME COIN	ACEEIIRSSTT	CASSITERITE
ACEEHIMNPSZ	CHIMPANZEES	ACEEIIRSTTV	RECITATIVES
ACEEHIMNRSU	CINEMA USHER	ACEEIKMPRRT	MARKET PRICE
ACEEHIMNTTW	TWICE THE MAN	ACEEIKMRTUX	CAKE MIXTURE
ACEEHIMORTT	THEOREMATIC	ACEEIKNNOTT	TAKEN NOTICE
ACEEHIMRRTT	HERMETIC ART	ACEEIKNOSTT	TAKES NOTICE
ACEEHIMSSST	SCHEMATISES	ACEEIKNSSSS	SEASICKNESS
ACEEHIMSSTZ	SCHEMATIZES	ACEEILLLSTY	CELESTIALLY
ACEEHINORTT	THE CREATION	ACEEILLNNRT	CENTRAL LINE
ACEEHINPRTT	PARENTHETIC	ACEEILLNNSS	CLEANLINESS
ACEEHINRSTW	WINS THE RACE	ACEEILLNPST	SLATE PENCIL
ACEEHIOORSV	HOARSE VOICE	ACEEILLOPTV	PLACE TO LIVE
ACEEHIOPRST	SPIROCHAETE	ACEEILLORTV	VORTICELLAE
ACEEHIORRST	CHARIOTEERS	ACEEILMNNRT	INCREMENTAL
ACEEHIORSSV	HEARS VOICES	ACEEILMNORS	CEREMONIALS
ACEEHIPPRTY	PAY THE PRICE	ACEEILMNRRY	MERCENARILY
ACEEHIPRTTU	THERAPEUTIC	ACEEILMNRST	MISTER CLEAN
ACEEHKKOOTT	TOOK THE CAKE	ACEEILMORRT	CALORIMETER
ACEEHLLLRTU	LECTURE HALL	ACEEILMORST	ELASTOMERIC

ACEEILMQTUY	CAME QUIETLY
ACEEILMRTUV	VERMICULATE
ACEEILNNNST	CENTENNIALS
ACEEILNNORT	INTOLERANCE
ACEEILNNOTU	ENUCLEATION
ACEEILNNTUU	UNINUCLEATE
ACEEILNNTUY	LIEUTENANCY
ACEEILNOPST	SPECIAL NOTE
ACEEILNOPTX	EXCEPTIONAL
ACEEILNORSS	RECESSIONAL
ACEEILNPRTT	CENTRIPETAL
ACEEILNPSSS	SPECIALNESS
ACEEILNPSST	PLICATENESS
ACEEILNQUVY	EQUIVALENCY
ACEEILNRRST	CENTRALISER
ACEEILNRRTZ	CENTRALIZER
ACEEILNRRVY	IRRELEVANCY
ACEEILNRSST	CENTRALISES
ACEEILNRSSY	NECESSARILY
ACEEILNRSTV	CANTILEVERS
ACEEILNRSTZ	CENTRALIZES
ACEEILNRTTY	ETERNAL CITY
ACEEILOPSTT	POLICE STATE
ACEEILORRTV	CORRELATIVE
ACEEILORTUX	EXECUTORIAL
ACEEILOTVVY	EVOCATIVELY
ACEEILPRSVY	VERY SPECIAL
ACEEILPRTTZ	PRIZE CATTLE
ACEEILPSTUV	SPECULATIVE
ACEEILRRSSU	SECULARISER
ACEEILRRSUZ	SECULARIZER
ACEEILRSSSU	SECULARISES
ACEEILRSSUZ	SECULARIZES
ACEEILRTWYY	TWICE YEARLY
ACEEIMMNORT	ANEMOMETRIC
ACEEIMNNNRS	NICE MANNERS
ACEEIMNNORT	ANCIENT ROME
ACEEIMNNOTT	CEMENTATION
ACEEIMNNOTY	ENEMY ACTION
ACEEIMNORTT	ACTINOMETER
ACEEIMNQRTU	ACQUIREMENT
ACEEIMNRSTT	REMITTANCES
ACEEIMNRSTU	MANICURE SET
ACEEIMOSSTV	VASECTOMIES
	VASECTOMISE
ACEEIMOSTVZ	VASECTOMIZE
ACEEINNRRSU	REINSURANCE
ACEEINNSSTX	INEXACTNESS
ACEEINOPTTX	EXPECTATION
ACEEINORRST	RECREATIONS
ACEEINORSTU	AUCTIONEERS
ACEEINPPRST	APPRENTICES
ACEEINPRSST	INTERSPACES
ACEEINRRSTV	TRANSCEIVER
ACEEINRSSST	RESISTANCES
ACEEIOOPRTV	COOPERATIVE
ACEEIOPPSST	EPISCOPATES
ACEEIOPRRTV	PROCREATIVE
ACEEIOQSTUV	EQUIVOCATES
ACEEIORRRSV	CARRIES OVER
ACEEIORRTTV	RETROACTIVE
ACEEIRSSTTU	RESUSCITATE
ACEEJMNNORS	CARMEN JONES
ACEEJNPRSTU	SUPERJACENT
ACEEKKLMRSY	MACKEREL SKY
ACEEKKPRRRY	KERRY PACKER
ACEEKLLRSSS	SALES CLERKS
	SALESCLERKS
ACEEKLNOSTU	TAKE COUNSEL
ACEEKMNNSTT	MACK SENNETT
ACEEKMNOPPY	KEEP COMPANY

ACEEKORRSSW	CASEWORKERS
ACEELLLOPRY	CELLO PLAYER
ACEELLMNRSS	SMALL SCREEN
ACEELLMOTUW	CAME OUT WELL
ACEELLNOPVY	POLYVALENCE
ACEELMMORWW	WARM WELCOME
ACEELMMOSUV	MOVE A MUSCLE
ACEELMNOPTT	CONTEMPLATE
ACEELMOPRRU	COME A PURLER
ACEELMOPSST	COMPLETE ASS
ACEELNNNSSU	UNCLEANNESS
ACEELNOOPRT	COLEOPTERAN
ACEELNOOSSS	CLOSE SEASON
ACEELNOPSSY	CLAPS EYES ON
ACEELNOPSTT	PENTECOSTAL
ACEELNPRSSY	SCREENPLAYS
ACEELNPTTXY	EXPECTANTLY
ACEELNRRTUU	CRUEL NATURE
ACEFFLNRSTTW	WEST CENTRAL
ACEELOORRTW	WATER COOLER
ACEELOPPPRR	PROPER PLACE
ACEELOPPPRT	COPPERPLATE
ACEELORRSTU	ALTER COURSE
ACEELORSSTT	LATEST SCORE
ACEELORSTTU	TRUE TO SCALE
ACEELORSTTW	WATER CLOSET
ACEELOSSTUY	SETACEOUSLY
ACEEMMMOORT	COMMEMORATE
ACEEMMNNPST	ENCAMPMENTS
ACEEMMNOSTT	COMMENTATES
ACEEMMORSTT	CAME TO TERMS
ACEEMNOOSWY	COME ONE'S WAY
ACEEMNOPSSS	ENCOMPASSES
ACEEMNOPSST	COMPENSATES
ACEEMNORSTY	AT ONE'S MERCY
ACEEMNPRSST	ESCARPMENTS
ACEEMOOPRTW	CAME TO POWER
ACEEMOORSTY	YEARS TO COME
ACEEMOPRSSU	CAME UP ROSES
ACEENNNORSY	SEAN CONNERY
ACEENNOPRSV	PROVENANCES
ACEENNOPRTU	COUNTERPANE
ACEENNORRTV	CONTRAVENER
ACEENNORETV	CONTRAVENES
	COVENANTERS
ACEENNRSSUY	UNNECESSARY
ACEENOORSTT	COTONEASTER
ACEENOPPRRU	EUROPEAN CUP
ACEENOPRTTX	EXPECTORANT
ACEENOPSSTU	PUT ONES CASE
ACEENORSTTW	CROWN ESTATE
ACEENPRRTTY	CENTRE PARTY
ACEENRRTUYY	CURRENT YEAR
ACEENRSTUUY	UNEASY TRUCE
ACEEOQRRSUV	SQUARE COVER
ACEEORRSTUW	WATERCOURSE
ACEEORSSSTU	SETS A COURSE
ACEEPRRSTUY	RESCUE PARTY
ACEFFFFIOST	OFFICE STAFF
ACEFFFGILOR	FLAG OFFICER
ACEFFFILOST	FACTS OF LIFE
ACEFFGHILNR	CLIFF HANGER
	CLIFF-HANGER
ACEFFGILNOR	CLEARING OFF
ACEFFGILNTY	AFFECTINGLY
ACEFFGLLORU	FULL OF GRACE
ACEFFGLORTU	FLAG OF TRUCE
ACEFFHKORTT	OFF THE TRACK
ACEFFHNOORS	SHEAF OF CORN
ACEFFHOOSTT	OFF THE COAST
ACEFFIILPST	SPIFFLICATE

ACEFFIITTVY	AFFECTIVITY
ACEFFIKRRST	TRAFFICKERS
ACEFFIMORRY	ARMY OFFICER
ACEFFIOPRTY	OFFICE PARTY
ACEFFIOSTUV	SUFFOCATIVE
ACEFFIRSSST	SCARES STIFF
ACEFFKLNOSS	SLACKENS OFF
ACEFFLOORTV	VOCAL EFFORT
ACEFFMOORRS	FORCE OF ARMS
ACEFFMOPRSS	SCAMPERS OFF
ACEFGGIMNOO	COMING OF AGE
ACEFGHHIINN	HIGH FINANCE
ACEFGHILPST	SPACE FLIGHT
	SPACEFLIGHT
ACEFGHIRRST	FREIGHT CARS
ACEFGHLLNUY	CHANGEFULLY
ACEFGHLNNOR	ANGLO-FRENCH
ACEFGHMORRS	FROGMARCHES
ACEFGHOSTTT	GOT THE FACTS
ACEFGIILNOR	ORGANIC LIFE
ACEFGIILPST	SPECIAL GIFT
ACEFGIIMNNT	MAGNIFICENT
ACEFGIINNRT	INTERFACING
ACEFGILNRST	FIRST GLANCE
ACEFGILNRTU	CENTRIFUGAL
ACEFGILNSTW	SWIFT GLANCE
ACEFGIRSTUU	CUTS A FIGURE
ACEFGLNOORT	CLEAN FORGOT
ACEFGLORTUY	GLUE FACTORY
ACEFHILMOOT	MICHAEL FOOT
ACEFHIMMORT	MARCH OF TIME
ACEFHIORSST	SET OF CHAIRS
ACEFHIRSTTY	CITY FATHERS
ACEFHLLSSTU	SATCHELFULS
ACEFHLNNORU	CHANNEL FOUR
ACEFHLOORST	AFTER SCHOOL
ACEFHLOOSTT	ACTS THE FOOL
ACEFHLOPRRU	REPROACHFUL
ACEFHMNNORW	FRENCHWOMAN
ACEFHNNOOPR	FRANCOPHONE
ACEFHNORSTT	FRENCH TOAST
ACEFHOPRRTU	CHAPTER FOUR
ACEFIIINORT	REIFICATION
ACEFIILLNPR	FALL IN PRICE
ACEFIILNNOT	FINAL NOTICE
ACEFIILNNSS	FINICALNESS
ACEFIILORTT	FELICITATOR
ACEFIILPRSU	SUPERFICIAL
ACEFIILRSSS	CLASSIFIERS
ACEFIILTTVY	FACTITIVELY
ACEFIIMNRST	CAME IN FIRST
ACEFIIMORRS	FORMICARIES
ACEFIINOPTT	PONTIFICATE
ACEFIINRRTU	FIRE CURTAIN
ACEFIJKNOSV	JACKSON FIVE
ACEFIKLOPRW	PICK A FLOWER
ACEFILLLOTU	FOLLICULATE
ACEFILLORSY	FAIRLY CLOSE
ACEFILLORUW	CAULIFLOWER
ACEFILMRSST	FILM ACTRESS
ACEFILOORST	FAIL TO SCORE
ACEFILOPRRT	CLEAR PROFIT
ACEFILOPRRU	CROP FAILURE
ACEFILORSTU	LACTIFEROUS
ACEFILOSTUY	FACETIOUSLY
ACEFIMMNORT	FAIR COMMENT
ACEFIMNOTTU	TUMEFACTION
ACEFIMOPRRT	PRIME FACTOR
ACEFIMORRSU	EAR FOR MUSIC
ACEFINNORST	FOR INSTANCE
ACEFINNRSST	FRANTICNESS

ACEFIOORRTV	VOCIFERATOR
ACEFIOPRSUU	FURIOUS PACE
ACEFIOPSTTU	FACES UP TO IT
ACEFKLLOORU	CAREFUL LOOK
ACEFKLMNOOY	LACK OF MONEY
ACEFKMOORTT	TAKE COMFORT
ACEFKMORRSY	ASK FOR MERCY
ACEFLLOOPSY	CLOSE OF PLAY
ACEFLLOORSU	FALSE COLOUR
ACEFLNOOPRT	CAN OF PETROL
ACEFLNSSTTU	TACTFULNESS
ACEFMOPRSTU	ACE OF TRUMPS
ACEFNOORRRV	RAN FOR COVER
ACEGGHIINSV	GIVING CHASE
ACEGGHILLNN	CHALLENGING
ACEGGHILNNS	CHANGELINGS
ACEGGHMRRTU	RUGGER MATCH
ACEGGHNNOOT	GOT NO CHANGE
ACEGGHNNORW	WRONG CHANGE
ACEGGIILNPV	GIVING PLACE
ACEGGIIMNNO	CINEMAGOING
ACEGGILNOPS	GOING PLACES
ACEGGINNORU	ENCOURAGING
ACEGGKLLOPT	KELLOGG PACT
ACEGGLNOOYY	GYNAECOLOGY
ACEGHHIIRTW	HIGH-WIRE ACT
ACEGHHILRSS	HIGHER CLASS
ACEGHHILRST	SEARCHLIGHT
ACEGHHINORW	WEIGH ANCHOR
ACEGHHMNRRU	HUNGER MARCH
ACEGHHMORTU	CAME THROUGH
ACEGHHNORST	SHORT CHANGE
	SHORTCHANGE
ACEGHHOOPRR	CHOREOGRAPH
ACEGHIIKLNW	WHACKING LIE
ACEGHIIMNNS	MECHANISING
ACEGHIIMNNZ	MECHANIZING
ACEGHIINNNV	GIVEN AN INCH
ACEGHIINNSV	GIVES AN INCH
ACEGHIKLLNS	SHELLACKING
ACEGHIKLNRS	KING CHARLES
ACEGHIKMNOP	EPOCH-MAKING
ACEGHILLNNN	CHANNELLING
ACEGHILLOOR	RHEOLOGICAL
ACEGHILLOOT	ETHOLOGICAL
	THEOLOGICAL
ACEGHILMOTT	CAME TO LIGHT
ACEGHILNNTU	EATING LUNCH
ACEGHILNOST	ANGELIC HOST
ACEGHILNPRY	PREACHINGLY
ACEGHILNRSY	SEARCHINGLY
ACEGHILOOPR	OLEOGRAPHIC
ACEGHILOPSY	GEOPHYSICAL
ACEGHILORTY	EARLY GOTHIC
ACEGHIMNORR	MENORRHAGIC
ACEGHIMNORU	ARCHEGONIUM
ACEGHIMNNRSY	CRYING SHAME
ACEGHIMNRVY	HAVING MERCY
ACEGHIMNSTT	MATCHING SET
ACEGHINNOPR	CHAPERONING
ACEGHINNOPRR	REPROACHING
ACEGHINORRS	HORSE RACING
ACEGHINORTU	OUTREACHING
	REACHING OUT
ACEGHINPRSS	GRAPHICNESS
ACEGHINPRTU	PUT IN CHARGE
ACEGHIOOPSS	HAGIOSCOPES
ACEGHIOPRRX	XEROGRAPHIC
ACEGHIOPSTY	PHAGOCYTISE
ACEGHIOPTYZ	PHAGOCYTIZE
ACEGHIRRTWY	CARRY WEIGHT

ACEGHLOOSST	STAGE SCHOOL
ACEGHLOOSTY	ESCHATOLOGY
ACEGHOOPSTY	PHAGOCYTOSE
ACEGHOORSUW	SHOW COURAGE
ACEGHRSSTTU	CUT THE GRASS
ACEGIIKLLNP	KILLING PACE
ACEGIIKNPRS	ASKING PRICE
ACEGIILLMNT	CALLING TIME
ACEGIILLNPR	CALLIPERING
ACEGIILLOOT	ETIOLOGICAL
ACEGIILLOTV	COLLIGATIVE
ACEGIILMNOV	COMING ALIVE
ACEGIILNNPW	WIPING CLEAN
ACEGIILNNRT	INTERLACING
ACEGIILNPPY	PIPE-CLAYING
ACEGIILNPRT	REPLICATING
ACEGIILNPSV	LIVING SPACE
ACEGIILNPTX	EXPLICATING
ACEGIILOSTT	EGOTISTICAL
ACEGIIMNPRT	IMPRECATING
ACEGIIMNPST	CAMPING SITE
ACEGIIMNRST	MISCREATING
ACEGIIMNRTT	METRICATING
ACEGIIMRRTV	GRAVIMETRIC
ACEGIINNNTU	ENUNCIATING
ACEGIINNRTT	INTERACTING
ACEGIINORTX	EXCORIATING
ACEGIINPRTT	CREPITATING
ACEGIINRSTU	CAUTERISING
ACEGIINRTTX	EXTRICATING
ACEGIINRTUZ	CAUTERIZING
ACEGIIRRSSV	GRAVE CRISIS
ACEGIJMMNYY	JIMMY CAGNEY
ACEGIJNOTUV	CONJUGATIVE
ACEGIKLNNOT	NAT KING COLE
ACEGIKLNRST	SINGLE TRACK
ACEGIKMNRSY	ASKING MERCY
ACEGIKNNPST	SENT PACKING
ACEGIKNORST	ORANGE-STICK
ACEGIKNORTV	TAKING COVER
ACEGILLLLOY	COLLEGIALLY
ACEGILLNOOP	PENOLOGICAL
ACEGILLNORV	CALLING OVER
	OVERCALLING
ACEGILLNOSS	LOGICALNESS
ACEGILLOORS	SEROLOGICAL
ACEGILLOPST	LOGICAL STEP
ACEGILMNORY	COMING EARLY
ACEGILMNRSY	SCREAMINGLY
ACEGILNNNOU	UNCONGENIAL
ACEGILNNOOT	CONGELATION
ACEGILNNOTU	CLEANING OUT
ACEGILNNPRS	SPRING CLEAN
	SPRING-CLEAN
ACEGILNOPRT	PERCOLATING
ACEGILNOPTY	GENOTYPICAL
ACEGILNORRS	CAROL SINGER
ACEGILNORRT	CORRELATING
ACEGILNORSS	CASSEROLING
ACEGILNORST	SONG RECITAL
ACEGILNORTU	CLEARING OUT
ACEGILNPSTU	SPECULATING
ACEGILNPTUX	EXCULPATING
ACEGILNRSSY	CARESSINGLY
ACEGILNSSSW	SEWING CLASS
ACEGILOOPST	APOLOGETICS
ACEGILRRTUU	AGRICULTURE
ACEGIMMMNOT	MAGIC MOMENT
ACEGIMOPRST	CAME TO GRIPS
ACEGINNNOTV	COVENANTING
ACEGINNRSTT	TRANSECTING
ACEGINNRSTY	ASTRINGENCY
ACEGINNSSTW	NEWSCASTING
ACEGINOOPRT	COOPERATING
ACEGINOORSU	GO ON A CRUISE
ACEGINOPRRT	PROCREATING
ACEGINORSTV	OVERCASTING
ACEGINORTTU	GUT REACTION
ACEGINOSTTV	CASTING VOTE
ACEGINPRRTU	RECAPTURING
ACEGINPSTTY	TYPECASTING
ACEGIOPSTTY	STEATOPYGIC
ACEGIORRSST	CIGAR STORES
ACEGJLNOTUY	CONJUGATELY
ACEGKOOORTU	TOOK COURAGE
ACEGKORSSTU	GOATSUCKERS
ACEGKRSSTTU	STAGE STRUCK
	STAGESTRUCK
ACEGLLNOOSU	COLLAGENOUS
ACEGLNORTUY	GRANULOCYTE
ACEGMMNOOSU	COMMON USAGE
ACEGMNNORSS	CONGRESSMAN
ACEGMOPRRST	SPECTROGRAM
ACEGNOORRTT	GERONTOCRAT
ACEGNRSSTTU	SCATTER-GUNS
ACEHHIILMOP	HAEMOPHILIC
ACEHHIINNTY	HYACINTHINE
ACEHHIINRTW	WITHIN REACH
ACEHHIKRSTT	HITS THE RACK
ACEHHIKSSTT	HITS THE SACK
ACEHHILLPRT	CHEAP THRILL
ACEHHILSSTW	CLASHES WITH
ACEHHIMNOPS	MACHINE SHOP
ACEHHIMNOPT	THE CHAMPION
ACEHHIMNTTW	WIN THE MATCH
ACEHHINRSTT	IN THE CHARTS
ACEHHIRRSTV	RICH HARVEST
ACEHHMNOTTW	WON THE MATCH
ACEHHMRRSTT	MRS. THATCHER
ACEHHNPRTUW	THREW A PUNCH
ACEHHOSSTTT	ACTS THE HOST
ACEHIIINPSS	HISPANICISE
ACEHIIINPSZ	HISPANICIZE
ACEHIILMSTT	ATHLETICISM
ACEHIILNOPR	NECROPHILIA
ACEHIILRSVW	SWIVEL CHAIR
ACEHIIMSSST	SCHISMATISE
ACEHIIMSSTZ	SCHISMATIZE
ACEHIINNOPS	PHOENICIANS
ACEHIINNOPT	PHONETICIAN
ACEHIINORRT	RHETORICIAN
ACEHIINPSTT	PANTHEISTIC
ACEHIKLMORY	MICHAEL YORK
ACEHIKLPRRS	PARISH CLERK
ACEHIKLPRTY	PRICKLY HEAT
ACEHIKMNORS	CHAIN SMOKER
ACEHIKMNOSS	CHAIN SMOKES
	CHAIN-SMOKES
ACEHIKMRTUY	RHEUMATICKY
ACEHIKRSSTW	CATS WHISKER
ACEHILLOPTT	COAT THE PILL
ACEHILLORTW	WHITE COLLAR
	WHITE-COLLAR
ACEHILLPRSY	SPHERICALLY
ACEHILMNNSW	CHANNEL SWIM
ACEHILMNOOT	MACHINE TOOL
ACEHILMNOST	SLOT MACHINE
ACEHILNNOOT	HONITON LACE
ACEHILNORST	CHLORINATES
ACEHILNPRST	SPHINCTERAL
ACEHILOSSTT	SHEILA SCOTT
ACEHILRSSSY	CHRYSALISES

ACEHILSSSTW	SWISS CHALET
ACEHIMMOPRT	METAMORPHIC
ACEHIMMNNSTT	TENNIS MATCH
ACEHIMNORSS	MARCHIONESS
ACEHIMNORTU	EUCHROMATIN
ACEHIMNOSYY	HYOSCYAMINE
ACEHIMNOTTW	TWICE A MONTH
ACEHIMNPRST	MARCH IN STEP
ACEHIMNRSST	CHRIST'S NAME
ACEHIMOPRST	ATMOSPHERIC
ACEHIMORRST	CHOIR MASTER
ACEHIMORRYZ	MYCORRHIZAE
ACEHIMOSTTW	TEACH TO SWIM
ACEHIMPSSTY	METAPHYSICS
ACEHIMPSTTY	SYMPATHETIC
ACEHIMRSSST	CHRISTMASES
ACEHINNOOTT	CANINE TOOTH
ACEHINNOPTT	PANTOTHENIC
ACEHINNRSSU	RAUNCHINESS
ACEHINOPRRS	CHAIRPERSON
ACEHINOPRRT	CHIROPTERAN
ACEHINOPRTU	NEUROPATHIC
ACEHINORSTU	CUT ONES HAIR
ACEHINRSSST	STARCHINESS
ACEHIOOPSTT	OSTEOPATHIC
ACEHIORSSTY	CASE HISTORY
ACEHIPPSTTU	PATCHES IT UP
ACEHIQRRSUY	SQUIREARCHY
ACEHJKNOSST	THE JACKSONS
ACEHJKORSTT	SHORT JACKET
ACEHJOOOTYY	YOOTHA JOYCE
ACEHKLMMORS	HAMMERLOCKS
ACEHKLMNOST	MENTAL SHOCK
ACEHKLOOSTW	THE WOOLSACK
ACEHKLOPSYY	PLAYS HOCKEY
ACEHKMOOTTU	TAKE TOO MUCH
ACEHKNORTUV	HAVE NO TRUCK
ACEHKOPRSST	STOCK PHRASE
ACEHLLLLORT	CALL THE ROLL
ACEHLLMOOSS	SCHOOL MEALS
ACEHLLMSSTY	MATCHLESSLY
ACEHLLOOPRU	PURE ALCOHOL
ACEHLMOOSST	SCHOOLMATES
ACEHLMORSTW	WARM CLOTHES
ACEHLNNRTTY	TRENCHANTLY
ACEHLNOPRTY	LYCANTHROPE
ACEHLNORSST	CHARLESTONS
ACEHLNSTTUW	CUTS THE LAWN
ACEHLOOSSTT	STATE SCHOOL
ACEHLOPPPUY	HAPPY COUPLE
ACEHLPPPRTU	PURPLE PATCH
ACEHMMOORST	COMES TO HARM
ACEHMNOSTWY	YACHTSWOMEN
ACEHMNRRTTU	RETURN MATCH
ACEHMOOPPST	COMPOST HEAP
ACEHMOPRSTU	CHAMPERTOUS
ACEHNNOOPRT	CTENOPHORAN
ACEHNNSSSTU	STAUNCHNESS
ACEHNOPRRRS	SHARP CORNER
ACEHNORRSTT	TROCHANTERS
ACEHOPSSTTW	STOPWATCHES
ACEHOPSSTTY	PAY THE COSTS
ACEHORSTTWW	WATCHTOWERS
ACEHORSTUWY	WORTHY CAUSE
ACEHRRSSTTU	EARTHS CRUST
ACEIIIILNVZ	CIVILIANIZE
ACEIIILMPTV	IMPLICATIVE
ACEIIILNOTT	ELICITATION
ACEIIILPSTT	PIETISTICAL
ACEIIIMNNRT	INCRIMINATE
ACEIIIMNSTT	ANTI-SEMITIC
ACEIIIQSTUV	ACQUISITIVE
ACEIIKKMQTU	MAKE IT QUICK
ACEIIKKMSTT	MAKE IT STICK
ACEIIKLLOOR	KILOCALORIE
ACEIIKLRSTT	RICKETTSIAL
ACEIIKNNPRW	PICK A WINNER
ACEIIKNRSSS	AIRSICKNESS
ACEIIKNRTTT	TRAIN TICKET
ACEIIKRSSTT	RICKETTSIAS
ACEIILLMMTY	MIMETICALLY
ACEIILLMOTY	MEIOTICALLY
ACEIILLMPRY	EMPIRICALLY
ACEIILLNOOS	COLONIALISE
ACEIILLNOOZ	COLONIALIZE
ACEIILLNSTT	SCINTILLATE
ACEIILLOSST	CALLOSITIES
ACEIILLRSTY	ERISTICALLY
ACEIILMNPRT	PLANIMETRIC
ACEIILMNSSU	MASCULINISE
ACEIILMNSUZ	MASCULINIZE
ACEIILMPSST	SEMIPLASTIC
ACEIILNOOVV	IN A LOW VOICE
ACEIILNOPRT	REPLICATION
ACEIILNOPTX	EXPLICATION
ACEIILNOQTU	EQUINOCTIAL
ACEIILNOTUV	INOCULATIVE
ACEIILNPRUY	PECUNIARILY
ACEIILNRRUV	CURVILINEAR
ACEIILNRSTT	CLARINETIST
ACEIILNRSTU	UNREALISTIC
ACEIILNRTTY	INTRICATELY
ACEIILORSSS	SOCIALISERS
ACEIILORSSZ	SOCIALIZERS
ACEIILPPRST	PARTICIPLES
ACEIILPRRTU	PICTURE RAIL
ACEIILPRSST	PLASTICISER
ACEIILPRSTT	PERISTALTIC
	TRIPLICATES
ACEIILPRSTZ	PLASTICIZER
ACEIILPRTUY	PECULIARITY
ACEIILPSSST	SPECIALISTS
ACEIILRRSTV	CIVIL ARREST
ACEIILRRTWY	WRITE A LYRIC
ACEIILRSSTV	CLAVIERISTS
ACEIILRTTVY	VERTICALITY
ACEIIMNNORS	MICRONESIAN
ACEIIMNNRST	MANNERISTIC
ACEIIMNOPRT	IMPRECATION
ACEIIMNORST	ROMANTICISE
ACEIIMNORTT	INTERATOMIC
	METRICATION
ACEIIMNORTZ	ROMANTICIZE
ACEIIMNPRRU	PERICRANIUM
ACEIIMNRSTT	MARTENSITIC
ACEIIMNRSTU	INSECTARIUM
ACEIIMNSSTT	SEMANTICIST
ACEIINNNOTU	ENUNCIATION
ACEIINNNRTU	ANCIENT RUIN
ACEIINNOPST	CASE IN POINT
ACEIINNOPTT	PECTINATION
ACEIINNORRT	INCINERATOR
ACEIINNORTT	INTERACTION
ACEIINOORTX	EXCORIATION
ACEIINOPRTT	CREPITATION
ACEIINORSTT	CREATIONIST
	RECITATIONS
ACEIINORTTX	EXTRICATION
ACEIINOSTTX	INTOXICATES
ACEIINPPRTT	PRECIPITANT
ACEIINPRTTY	PERTINACITY
ACEIINPSSTT	ANTISEPTICS

ACEIIOOPPST	APOSIOPETIC
ACEIIRRSSSU	CUIRASSIERS
ACEIJMMRRTY	JIMMY CARTER
ACEIJMOOTTU	TOMATO JUICE
ACEIKKLLNNTY	KILKENNY CAT
ACEIKKLNPTY	PENALTY KICK
ACEIKKLQRTU	QUICK TALKER
ACEIKKOOTTW	TOOK A WICKET
ACEIKKRRSTT	KICK-STARTER
ACEIKLLPSTY	SKEPTICALLY
ACEIKLMOPRY	POLICY MAKER
ACEIKLORSST	LOSES A TRICK
ACEIKLORTTW	LATTICE WORK
	LATTICEWORK
ACEIKLPPRRY	PRICKLY PEAR
ACEIKMNOTTU	MAKE IT COUNT
ACEIKMPRSST	STRIKES CAMP
ACEIKNQRSUW	QUICK ANSWER
ACEIKOOPTTV	TOOK CAPTIVE
ACEIKOORSTU	TOOK A CRUISE
ACEIKPPRSTY	STICKY PAPER
ACEIKPSSSSY	SISSY SPACER
ACEIKQSTUWY	QUICKEST WAY
ACEILLLMNOR	LAMELLICORN
ACEILLLNRUU	UNICELLULAR
ACEILLLRTUY	CELLULARITY
ACEILLMMNOS	SMALL INCOME
ACEILLMMNNOT	NONMETALLIC
ACEILLMNRUY	NUMERICALLY
ACEILLMNSUY	MASCULINELY
ACEILLMNYYZ	ENZYMICALLY
ACEILLMRRUY	MERCURIALLY
ACEILLNNOOO	NEOCOLONIAL
ACEILLNOPTU	CUPELLATION
ACEILLNORST	CITRONELLAS
	SIR LANCELOT
ACEILLNOSTY	SECTIONALLY
ACEILLNOTTY	TONETICALLY
ACEILLNRSTY	CRYSTALLINE
ACEILLOORRS	COROLLARIES
ACEILLOPPSY	EPISCOPALLY
ACEILLOPSSW	PILLOWCASES
ACEILLOQUVY	EQUIVOCALLY
ACEILLORSTV	VORTICELLAS
ACEILLRSSTY	CRYSTALLISE
ACEILLRSTTY	CRYSTALLITE
ACEILLRSTUV	VICTUALLERS
ACEILLRSTYZ	CRYSTALLIZE
ACEILLRTUVY	LUCRATIVELY
ACEILMMNNOSU	COMMUNALISE
ACEILMMNOUZ	COMMUNALIZE
ACEILMMOPTY	OLYMPIC TEAM
ACEILMMRSTY	SYMMETRICAL
ACEILMNOOPS	SCOPOLAMINE
ACEILMNOPRS	COMPLAINERS
ACEILMNOSST	COMES IN LAST
ACEILMNOSTU	MUSICAL NOTE
ACEILMNRSSU	LEARNS MUSIC
ACEILMNRSTU	LEARNT MUSIC
ACEILMNRTTU	CURTAILMENT
ACEILMORRTY	CALORIMETRY
ACEILMORTTV	VOLTAMETRIC
ACEILMRRTUU	MARICULTURE
ACEILNNNOSS	NONSENSICAL
ACEILNNNOTT	CONTINENTAL
ACEILNNRTUY	UNCERTAINLY
ACEILNNSSTY	INCESSANTLY
ACEILNOOPRR	INCORPOREAL
ACEILNOOPRT	NEOTROPICAL
	PERCOLATION
ACEILNOORRT	CORRELATION
ACEILNOPRST	PRATINCOLES
ACEILNOPSST	CAPTIONLESS
ACEILNOPSTU	SPECULATION
ACEILNOPTUX	EXCULPATION
ACEILNOQUUV	UNEQUIVOCAL
ACEILNORSTT	INTERCOSTAL
ACEILNORSTU	ULCERATIONS
ACEILNORTUV	COUNTERVAIL
ACEILNOSSTT	SELINA SCOTT
ACEILNOSSTU	INOSCULATES
ACEILNOSTUY	TENACIOUSLY
ACEILNPPSTU	PUTS IN PLACE
ACEILNPSSTY	TYPICALNESS
ACEILNRRTUV	VENTRICULAR
ACEILNRSSTT	CENTRALISTS
ACEILOOOOPRT	AEOLOTROPIC
ACEILOOPPRS	POLARISCOPE
ACEILOPRRTT	PROTRACTILE
ACEILOPRTXY	EXPLICATORY
ACEILOPSTUV	COPULATIVES
ACEILORRTWY	WROTE A LYRIC
ACEILORSUVY	VERACIOUSLY
ACEILORTVYY	VICEROYALTY
ACEILPPSSTU	SUPPLICATES
ACEILPRSTTY	SPECTRALITY
ACEILPRSTUY	SPECULARITY
ACEILRRSSTY	CRYSTALISER
ACEILRRSTYZ	CRYSTALIZER
ACEILRSSSTU	SECULARISTS
ACEILRSSSTY	CRYSTALISES
ACEILRSSTYZ	CRYSTALIZES
ACEIMMORRTU	CREMATORIUM
ACEIMMOTTUV	COMMUTATIVE
ACEIMMRSSTU	MUSIC MASTER
ACEIMNNNNOT	INNOCENT MAN
ACEIMNNNOTT	CONTAINMENT
ACEIMNOPRRS	MARINE CORPS
ACEIMNORTTY	ACTINOMETRY
ACEIMOOPRTW	ATOMIC POWER
ACEIMOORTVY	OVARIECTOMY
ACEIMOPRRTY	IMPRECATORY
ACEIMPRSSTU	SUPREMACIST
ACEIMSSSTTY	SYSTEMATICS
ACEINNNNSSU	UNCANNINESS
ACEINNOOTTV	CONNOTATIVE
ACEINNOPSTW	NEWS CAPTION
ACEINNORSTT	TRANSECTION
ACEINNORSTTY	ENCYSTATION
ACEINNRSSSW	SCRAWNINESS
ACEINNRSTTU	INSTANT CURE
ACEINNRTTUY	UNCERTAINTY
ACEINOOOPRT	COOPERATION
ACEINOOPRRT	INCORPORATE
	PROCREATION
ACEINOOPRST	SCORE A POINT
ACEINOORRTT	RETROACTION
ACEINOOSSST	ICONOSTASES
	TOSSES A COIN
ACEINOPRSTU	PRECAUTIONS
ACEINOPSSTT	CONSTIPATES
ACEINOPSTVY	SYNCOPATIVE
ACEINORRSTT	RETRACTIONS
ACEINORRTTY	CONTRARIETY
ACEINORSTTU	ERUCTATIONS
ACEINORSTTV	CONTRASTIVE
ACEINORSTTX	EXTRACTIONS
ACEINPPRSTY	PRESYNAPTIC
ACEINRSSSSU	NARCISSUSES
ACEIOOPRTVV	PROVOCATIVE
ACEIOOQRTUV	EQUIVOCATOR

ACEIOPRRSTT	TRICERATOPS	ACEMOOPSSST	COMES TO PASS
ACEIOPRRTTV	PROTRACTIVE	ACEMOORSSSV	MOVES ACROSS
ACEIORSSTUZ	ASSIZE COURT	ACEMOOSSTTY	COMES TO STAY
ACEIORSTVYY	EASY VICTORY	ACEMORSSTTU	SCOUT MASTER
ACEKKLOORSW	LOOKS A WRECK		SCOUTMASTER
ACEKKLOPTTU	TAKE POT LUCK	ACENNOSSTTT	CONTESTANTS
ACEKKLRSTUY	LUCKY STREAK	ACENNOSSTTU	CONSTANT USE
ACEKKMORSTT	STOCK MARKET	ACENOORRSTV	CONSERVATOR
ACEKKMOSSST	SMOKESTACKS	ACENOPRRSTU	PROCRUSTEAN
ACEKLLLRSTY	TALLY CLERKS	ACENOPRRSUU	RUN UP A SCORE
ACEKLMNOSSU	SUCKS A LEMON	ACENOPRRTTU	COUNTERPART
ACEKLNOORTT	TAKE CONTROL	ACENORRTTVY	CONVERT A TRY
ACEKLNOPSST	ALPENSTOCKS	ACENORSSSUU	RAUCOUSNESS
ACEKLNORSSS	CLOSES RANKS	ACENORSTTUY	COUNTRY SEAT
ACEKMNOPPTY	KEPT COMPANY	ACENOSSSUUV	VACUOUSNESS
ACEKNOOORRT	TOOK A CORNER	ACEOOOPRRST	COOPERATORS
ACEKNOOSSTU	TOOK A CENSUS	ACEOPRSSTTY	COPYTASTERS
ACEKNOPPRRS	COPPERS NARK	ACEORRSSUWY	CAUSES WORRY
ACEKNORSTTU	STRUCK A NOTE	ACFFGGILNNO	GLANCING OFF
ACEKOOORSTU	TOOK A COURSE	ACFFGHIMNOR	MARCHING OFF
ACEKOORTTTU	TAKE TO COURT	ACFFGIIINOT	OFFICIATING
ACEKOPRSSTU	STRUCK A POSE	ACFFGIIKNRT	TRAFFICKING
ACEKORSSTVY	OVERCAST SKY	ACFFGIKLNOS	SLACKING OFF
ACEKPRRSSSY	SKYSCRAPERS	ACFFGINOPRS	SCRAPING OFF
ACELLLLOUWY	WE'LL CALL YOU	ACFFGINORRY	CARRYING OFF
ACELLLMORUY	MOLECULARLY	ACFFGINOSTU	SUFFOCATING
ACELLLMPSUU	PULL A MUSCLE	ACFFIIILMOS	OFFICIALISM
ACELLMMNOSY	COMMENSALLY	ACFFIIINOOT	OFFICIATION
ACELLMORRST	STORM CELLAR	ACFFIILLNOY	OFFICINALLY
ACELLMPRTTU	TRUMPET CALL	ACFFIILNOST	AFFLICTIONS
ACELLNNOOPY	PENAL COLONY	ACFFILLORST	STIFF COLLAR
ACELLNOSSSU	CALLOUSNESS	ACFFINOOPTT	POINT OF FACT
ACELLNRTTUY	RELUCTANTLY	ACFFINOOSTU	AUCTIONS OFF
ACELLOOPRRY	CORPOREALLY		SUFFOCATION
ACELLOOPRTU	COLOUR PLATE	ACFFKLOOOPS	PACK OF FOOLS
ACELMMNOOPS	COMMON PLEAS	ACFFKLOORSU	SACK OF FLOUR
ACELMMNOSTT	MALCONTENTS	ACFGGHIINRT	FACING RIGHT
ACELMOORSTU	TEAM COLOURS	ACFGHHIILNN	HALF-INCHING
ACELMOPSTUY	COSTUME PLAY	ACFGHIIKPST	PICKS A FIGHT
ACELMRSTUUU	MUSCULATURE	ACFGHIILORT	CHIT OF A GIRL
ACELNNOOPVX	PLANO-CONVEX	ACFGHIINNRS	FRANCHISING
ACELNNORTUY	COUNTRY LANE	ACFGHINNORT	FACING NORTH
ACELNNRSTTU	TRANSLUCENT	ACFGHINOSTU	FACING SOUTH
ACELNNSTTUU	CUTS A TUNNEL	ACFGHINOSUV	VOUCHSAFING
ACELNOPRRST	CORN PLASTER	ACFGIIINNST	SIGNIFICANT
ACELNOQRTUW	CROQUET LAWN	ACFGIIJKKNN	JACKKNIFING
ACELNORSUVY	CAVERNOUSLY	ACFGIIKLLNS	FALLING SICK
ACELNOSSTTU	SANSCULOTTE	ACFGIILNSSY	CLASSIFYING
ACELNOSTTTU	TALENT SCOUT	ACFGIINNORT	FORNICATING
ACELNOSTUUY	CUTANEOUSLY	ACFGIINNSTY	SANCTIFYING
ACELNRRTTUY	CRUEL TYRANT	ACFGIINORST	FACTORISING
ACELNRSTTUY	LAST CENTURY	ACFGIINORTZ	FACTORIZING
ACELOOPRRST	PERCOLATORS	ACFGILNTTUU	FLUCTUATING
ACELOOPRRTY	CORPORATELY	ACFGILOOPRS	PAIR OF CLOGS
ACELOOPRSTU	PLOT A COURSE	ACFHHIKOORS	SHOCK OF HAIR
ACELOORRTUW	WATER COLOUR	ACFHHOORSST	SHORT OF CASH
	WATERCOLOUR	ACFHIIKLNSS	LACKS FINISH
ACELOPRSSTU	SPECULATORS	ACFHILNOPST	PINCH OF SALT
ACELOPRSTTY	POTTERS CLAY	ACFHLOOORST	SCHOOL OF ART
ACELOPRTUXY	EXCULPATORY	ACFIIINNOTU	UNIFICATION
ACELOPSSTTT	CATTLESTOPS	ACFIIKLNOPT	LICK OF PAINT
ACELORSTTTW	WALTER SCOTT	ACFIILLMSTV	FALLS VICTIM
ACELRRSSTTU	STAR CLUSTER	ACFIILLNOTY	FICTIONALLY
ACEMMNOORTT	COMMENTATOR	ACFIILMNORU	CALIFORNIUM
ACEMMNOPRTT	COMPARTMENT	ACFIILMORST	FORMALISTIC
ACEMMNOPSST	PASS COMMENT	ACFIINNOORT	FORNICATION
ACEMMNOSSTU	CONSUMMATES	ACFIINNORST	INFRACTIONS
ACEMNNNOSTT	CANTONMENTS	ACFIIOPRRTU	PURIFICATOR
ACEMNNORSST	MONSTRANCES	ACFIKKPSSUU	KICK UP A FUSS
ACEMNOOPRST	COMPENSATOR	ACFIKOOPRSS	PAIR OF SOCKS
ACEMOOOPSTT	COME TO A STOP	ACFILMMNOPY	FILM COMPANY

ACFILMNNOTU	MALFUNCTION	ACGHMOORRUX	GROUCHO MARX
ACFILNOTTUU	FLUCTUATION	ACGIIIILNST	ITALICISING
ACFILORSTUY	FRACTIOUSLY	ACGIIIILNTZ	ITALICIZING
ACFINNOOTTU	CONFUTATION	ACGIIIJKNNT	JACKING IT IN
ACFINNORTUY	FUNCTIONARY	ACGIIIKNNPT	PACKING IT IN
ACFINOOOSST	TOSS OF A COIN	ACGIIILMNPT	IMPLICATING
ACFINOOOTTU	OUT OF ACTION	ACGIIILNOSS	SOCIALISING
ACFINOORRST	FORNICATORS	ACGIIILNOSZ	SOCIALIZING
ACFKKOORSTW	STACK OF WORK	ACGIIIMNNRT	CRIMINATING
ACFLMMNOOTU	COMMON FAULT	ACGIIJNORST	JARGONISTIC
ACFLOORSSTU	FAST COLOURS	ACGIIKMMNSU	MAKING MUSIC
ACFORRRUUVY	CURRY FAVOUR	ACGIIKNPPTU	PACKING IT UP
ACGGGIINNOR	GOING RACING	ACGIILLLLOY	ILLOGICALLY
ACGGGIJLNTU	JUGGLING ACT	ACGIILLMNOT	COLLIMATING
ACGGHHIILLN	HIGH CALLING	ACGIILLNOOS	SINOLOGICAL
ACGGHHISTTU	CAUGHT SIGHT	ACGIILLNOST	OSCILLATING
ACGGHINRRSU	SURCHARGING	ACGIILLNTUV	VICTUALLING
ACGGIIILLNS	GALLICISING	ACGIILLOORV	VIROLOGICAL
ACGGIIILNNS	ANGLICISING	ACGIII MNNOP	COMPLAINING
ACGGIIILNNZ	ANGLICIZING	ACGIILMNNTU	CULMINATING
ACGGIIMMNRS	SCRIMMAGING	ACGIILMNOPR	PROCLAIMING
ACGGIINNSST	SCAT SINGING	ACGIILMNOOT	COGNITIONAL
ACGGIJNNOTU	CONJUGATING	ACGIILNNOTU	INOCULATING
ACGGILMNNOO	COMING ALONG	ACGIILNNPTU	INCULPATING
ACGGILNNORU	CLANGOURING	ACGIILNNSUV	VULCANISING
ACGGIMMNRSU	SCRUMMAGING	ACGIILNNUVZ	VULCANIZING
ACGGIMNOOPT	GOING TO CAMP	ACGIILNPSSU	CAPSULISING
ACGGIMNOORV	GOING ACROSS	ACGIILNPSUZ	CAPSULIZING
ACGGINORRTU	CORRUGATING	ACGIILNTTUV	CULTIVATING
ACGHHILNNUV	HAVING LUNCH	ACGIIMNOOPT	MAGIC POTION
ACGHHILOOPR	HOLOGRAPHIC	ACGIIMNOSST	AGNOSTICISM
ACGHHIMOOPR	HOMOGRAPHIC	ACGIIMNPPTU	CAMPING IT UP
ACGHHINOOTT	ACHING TOOTH	ACGIIMNRRSY	MISCARRYING
ACGHHIOPRRY	CHIROGRAPHY	ACGIIMNRTTU	MICTURATING
ACGHHNOOPRR	CHRONOGRAPH	ACGIINNNOST	SANCTIONING
ACGHHORSTTU	CAUGHT SHORT	ACGIINNNOTZ	INCOGNIZANT
ACGHIIKNNPT	THINKING CAP	ACGIINNOSTW	WAINSCOTING
ACGHIILLNOP	ANGLOPHILIC	ACGIINNOSWX	COXSWAINING
ACGHIILMNPT	ITCHING PALM	ACGIINOOSTT	COGITATIONS
ACGHIILMORT	ALGORITHMIC	ACGIINORRTY	TRAGIC IRONY
	LOGARITHMIC	ACGIINORSST	OSTRACISING
ACGHIILNORT	GRANOLITHIC	ACGIINORSTZ	OSTRACIZING
ACGHIIMMNST	MISMATCHING	ACGIINRSTTU	RUSTICATING
ACGHIIMNNOP	CHAMPIONING	ACGIJJKMNPU	JUMPING JACK
ACGHIIMNOST	HAS IT COMING	ACGIJLNOTUY	CONJUGALITY
ACGHIINORST	SCORING A HIT	ACGIJNNOOTU	CONJUGATION
ACGHIINRTTU	HAIRCUTTING	ACGIKKNOSTT	TAKING STOCK
ACGHIKLNNSU	UNSHACKLING	ACGIKKNOSTT	TAKING STOCK
ACGHIKLNNTU	TAKING LUNCH	ACGIKLNORST	LOSING TRACK
ACGHILLOOOR	HOROLOGICAL	ACGILLLOOOY	OOLOGICALLY
ACGHILMOOPR	LAGOMORPHIC	ACGILLMNNOR	MORNING CALL
ACGHILNOSTT	CAST LIGHT ON	ACGILLMOOOP	POMOLOGICAL
ACGHILOPPRY	POLYGRAPHIC	ACGILLMOOTY	CLIMATOLOGY
ACGHILOPRXY	XYLOGRAPHIC	ACGILLNNOPU	CALLING UPON
ACGHIMNNOPS	CHAMPIGNONS	ACGILLNNPRU	RING-PULL CAN
ACGHIMNOOPR	MONOGRAPHIC	ACGILLNOOOS	NOSOLOGICAL
	NOMOGRAPHIC	ACGILLNOOOT	ONTOLOGICAL
	PHONOGRAMIC	ACGILLNOOPY	PALYNOLOGIC
ACGHIMNOTTU	OUTMATCHING		PLAYING COOL
ACGHIMNPTUW	WIGHTMAN CUP	ACGILLNRRYY	RALLYING CRY
ACGHIMORRST	CHRISTOGRAM	ACGILLNRSSU	RULING CLASS
ACGHINNPSTU	SNATCHING UP	ACGILLOOOPT	TOPOLOGICAL
ACGHINOOPRY	ICONOGRAPHY	ACGILLOOPSS	LOCAL GOSSIP
ACGHINOTTUW	WATCHING OUT	ACGILLOOPTY	TYPOLOGICAL
ACGHIOPPRST	PICTOGRAPHS	ACGILNNOORT	GAIN CONTROL
ACGHIOPPRTY	PICTOGRAPHY	ACGILNOPRSS	SIGNAL CORPS
	TYPOGRAPHIC	ACGILNOSSTT	CASTING LOTS
ACGHIRRSTTW	CARTWRIGHTS	ACGILNOSSTU	OUTCLASSING
ACGHLLNOOSU	SLOUCH ALONG	ACGILOOPRSU	SOCIAL GROUP
ACGHMNOORRS	CHRONOGRAMS	ACGIMNNOORT	MORNING COAT
ACGHMOOPRSY	COSMOGRAPHY	ACGIMNOORRT	MOTOR RACING

ACGIMNOORST	GASTRONOMIC	ACHKMOOSSTU	ASKS TOO MUCH
ACGINNOPSTY	SYNCOPATING	ACHLLOOPRST	CHLOROPLAST
ACGINNORRSU	SCORING A RUN	ACHLLOOTUWY	CALLOW YOUTH
ACGINNORRSY	CARRYINGS-ON	ACHLMMOOORS	CHROMOSOMAL
ACGINNORSTT	CONTRASTING	ACHLMMOORSS	SCHOOLMARMS
ACGINNPTTUU	PUNCTUATING	ACHLMNOORTU	MOTOR LAUNCH
ACGINOORRTU	CORRUGATION	ACHLMOOPRST	CHROMOPLAST
ACGINOPRRTT	PROTRACTING	ACHLMOOSSTTU	TOO MUCH SALT
ACGINOPSSTY	PAYING COSTS	ACHLNOPRTYY	LYCANTHROPY
ACGINORRSTY	SCORING A TRY	ACHLNOSTTUY	STAY TO LUNCH
ACGINORRTUY	CARRYING OUT	ACHLPRSSSUU	SURPLUS CASH
ACGLLNOOOVY	VOLCANOLOGY	ACHMNNOPSUY	SHUN COMPANY
ACGLLNOOUVY	VULCANOLOGY	ACHNOOORTTW	CROWN A TOOTH
ACGLMNNOOUY	AGONY COLUMN	ACHOQRSSTUU	SQUASH COURT
ACGMOOPRRTU	COMPURGATOR	ACIILMNOPT	IMPLICATION
ACGMOOPRSSY	GYROCOMPASS	ACIIILMNRTY	CRIMINALITY
ACGMOOPRRSTY	CRYPTOGRAMS	ACIIILNNNOT	INCLINATION
ACHHIILLPTY	ITHYPHALLIC	ACIIILNOPST	POLITICIANS
ACHHIKNRSTT	THANK CHRIST!	ACIIILRSTTU	RITUALISTIC
ACHHILOPRSS	SCHOLARSHIP	ACIIIMNNORT	CRIMINATION
ACHHIORSTUY	ICHTHYOSAUR	ACIIINOQSTU	ACQUISITION
ACHHNOOSTTU	AUTOCHTHONS	ACIIINPTTVY	IN CAPTIVITY
ACHHNOOTTUY	AUTOCHTHONY	ACIIJMORRSS	MAJOR CRISIS
ACHHNOPRTUW	THROW A PUNCH	ACIIKLPRSST	LACKS SPIRIT
ACHHOPPSSTY	PSYCHOPATHS	ACIIKNRSTTU	STICK IN A RUT
ACHHOPPSTYY	PSYCHOPATHY	ACIILLLNOOS	COLLISIONAL
ACHIIIMNPSS	HISPANICISM	ACIILLLOPTY	POLITICALLY
ACHIIINPSST	HISPANICIST	ACIILLMNOOS	COLONIALISM
ACHIILLLOPT	CAPITOL HILL	ACIILLMNOOT	COLLIMATION
ACHIILLMSWY	WHIMSICALLY	ACIILLMNPUY	MUNICIPALLY
ACHIILLORSW	SOCIAL WHIRL	ACIILLMOSUY	MALICIOUSLY
ACHIILMPSTU	MULTIPHASIC	ACIILLNNSTT	SCINTILLANT
ACHIILNRSTY	CHRISTIANLY	ACIILLNOOST	COLONIALIST
ACHIILOOPPR	COPROPHILIA		OSCILLATION
ACHIILOPSST	SOPHISTICAL	ACIILLNOPTU	UNPOLITICAL
ACHIILPSTYY	PHYSICALITY	ACIILLNOVVY	CONVIVIALLY
ACHIIMNORST	HARMONISTIC	ACIILLNPPRY	PRINCIPALLY
ACHIIMNSSTW	MAINS SWITCH	ACIILLOPRTY	PICTORIALLY
ACHIINNORST	CORINTHIANS	ACIILLPRSTU	PLURALISTIC
ACHIINNRSTU	UNCHRISTIAN	ACIILLQSTTU	CALL IT QUITS
ACHIINORSSU	AIR CUSHIONS	ACIILLQUYZZ	QUIZZICALLY
	AIR-CUSHIONS	ACIILMNNOTU	CULMINATION
ACHIINPRTWY	CRY WITH PAIN	ACIILMNOOPT	COMPILATION
ACHIINSSTTT	SATIN STITCH	ACIILMNSTUY	MASCULINITY
ACHIINSSTUV	CHAUVINISTS	ACIILMSTTUU	MUTUALISTIC
ACHIKLLOPSS	LACKS POLISH	ACIILNNOOTU	INOCULATION
ACHIKMNOPTW	HAMPTON WICK	ACIILNNOPRS	CLAP IN IRONS
ACHIKMNRSSS	SCRIMSHANKS	ACIILNNOPTU	INCULPATION
ACHIKNOORTU	CURTAIN HOOK	ACIILNNSTTU	INSTINCTUAL
ACHILLMOOPR	ALLOMORPHIC	ACIILNOPRSV	PROVINCIALS
ACHILLOPRTY	TROPHICALLY	ACIILNOPSTT	PLATONISTIC
ACHILMNOORT	TRICHOMONAL	ACIILNOTTUV	CULTIVATION
ACHILMORRYZ	MYCORRHIZAL	ACIILORSUVY	VICARIOUSLY
ACHILMOSSUW	MUSICAL SHOW	ACIILOSUVVY	VIVACIOUSLY
ACHILNOOORT	CHLORINATOR	ACIIMMNORST	ROMANTICISM
ACHILNORSUV	ANVIL CHORUS	ACIIMMNOSST	MONASTICISM
ACHILOPPSTY	HYPOPLASTIC	ACIIMMNSSTU	NUMISMATICS
ACHILOSSTTW	SCOTTISH LAW	ACIIMNOORSU	ACRIMONIOUS
ACHIMNORSST	MONARCHISTS	ACIINNNOSTU	ACT IN UNISON
ACHIMOPPPSU	HIPPOCAMPUS	ACIINNOOSTV	INVOCATIONS
ACHIMORRSYZ	MYCORRHIZAS	ACIINNORRTU	IRON CURTAIN
ACHIMRSSSTY	CHRISTMASSY	ACIINOOPRST	ANISOTROPIC
ACHIOOPPRST	APOSTROPHIC	ACIINOOSSST	ICONOSTASIS
ACHIOOPPSTT	POTATO CHIPS	ACIINOPRSST	ASCRIPTIONS
ACHIOOPRTTU	AUTOTROPHIC	ACIINOPRRTU	UNPATRIOTIC
ACHIOOPRTUX	AUXOTROPHIC	ACIINORSTTU	RUSTICATION
ACHIOOPSTTT	PHOTOSTATIC	ACIINRTTTUY	TACITURNITY
ACHIOPPRSTY	SAPROPHYTIC	ACIIOPSSSTT	PSITTACOSIS
ACHIOPRRSTU	CURATORSHIP	ACIIOQRSSTU	ACQUISITORS
ACHIOPRSSTY	PHYSIOCRATS	ACIJKLNNOTY	TONY JACKLIN
ACHKLMOOTTU	TALK TOO MUCH	ACIJLLNNOOS	JOAN COLLINS

ACIJNNOORTU	CONJURATION
ACIKKLLQUWY	WALK QUICKLY
ACIKKOPRSUW	KICKS UP A ROW
ACIKLMORSUW	MUSICAL WORK
ACIKLNOSSTY	LAYS IN STOCK
ACIKLPRSSTY	PLAYS TRICKS
ACIKNNNOPST	NON-STICK PAN
ACIKNRSTTUU	STUCK IN A RUT
ACIKOOPRRTY	PROKARYOTIC
ACIKPRSSSTW	PICKS STRAWS
ACILLMNOPTY	COMPLIANTLY
ACILLMOORST	COLLIMATORS
ACILLMOPSTY	PLASMOLYTIC
ACILLMOTYYZ	ZYMOTICALLY
ACILLNNOTUY	CONTINUALLY
ACILLNOOSTU	ALLOCUTIONS
ACILLNORSTW	CROWNS IT ALL
ACILLOOPSTY	PLAYS IT COOL
ACILLOORSST	OSCILLATORS
ACILLOORSTY	OSCILLATORY
ACILMMMNOSU	COMMUNALISM
ACILMMNOOTY	COMMONALITY
ACILMMNOOTU	COMMUNALIST
ACILMMNOTUY	COMMUNALITY
ACILMMORSSU	COMMISSURAL
ACILMMRSSUU	SIMULACRUMS
ACILMNNOSYY	SYNONYMICAL
ACILMNOOPTY	TOPONYMICAL
ACILMOOPSTX	TOXOPLASMIC
ACILMORSTUY	CUSTOMARILY
ACILMRSTUUY	MUSCULARITY
ACILNNOOOST	CONSOLATION
ACILNOOORTU	COLOURATION
ACILNOPRSTU	TROPICAL SUN
ACILNOPRTUY	INCULPATORY
ACILNORSSSU	INCURS A LOSS
ACILNORSSTU	ULTRASONICS
ACILNPTTUUY	PUNCTUALITY
ACILOOPRRTY	CORPORALITY
ACILOORSTUY	ATROCIOUSLY
ACILOORSUVY	VORACIOUSLY
ACILORSTTUV	CULTIVATORS
ACIMMNNOOTTU	COMMUTATION
ACIMMOPSTTY	SYMPTOMATIC
ACIMNOOORTU	AUCTION ROOM
ACIMNOOPRSS	COMPARISONS
ACIMNOOPSSU	POISON SUMAC
ACIMNOOPTTU	COMPUTATION
ACIMNPRSSTU	MANUSCRIPTS
ACIMOOPRRST	CORPORATISM
ACIMOOPRSTT	COMPATRIOTS
ACIMOOPSTTY	SOMATOTYPIC
ACIMORSSSSW	SWIMS ACROSS
ACINNNNOOST	INCONSONANT
ACINNNOOOTT	CONNOTATION
ACINNNOSTTU	CONTINUANTS
ACINNOOORST	CORONATIONS
ACINNOOPRTT	CONTRAPTION
ACINNOOPSTY	SYNCOPATION
ACINNOORTYZ	CRAZY NOTION
ACINNOPTTUU	PUNCTUATION
ACINNORSSTT	CONSTRAINTS
ACINOOOPRRT	CORPORATION
ACINOOOPRTV	PROVOCATION
ACINOOPRRST	CONSPIRATOR
ACINOOPRRTT	PROTRACTION
ACINOOPRRTU	PROCURATION
ACINOORRSUV	CARNIVOROUS
ACINOORSSTT	CARTOONISTS
ACINPRRSSTT	TRANSCRIPTS
ACIOOPPRSTT	POTATO CRISP
ACIOOPRRSTT	CORPORATIST
ACIOPRSSTTU	PUT IT ACROSS
ACKLNORTUWY	COUNTRY WALK
ACKLNRSTUUY	UNLUCKY STAR
ACKNNORTTUW	WANT NO TRUCK
ACKNOOORTTU	COOK TO A TURN
ACLLMNOORUY	MONOCULARLY
ACLLMOORSUY	CLAMOROUSLY
ACLLMOSTUUU	ALTOCUMULUS
ACLLMPRSSTU	CALLS TRUMPS
ACLLNNORTUY	NOCTURNALLY
ACLMOSSTUUU	USUAL CUSTOM
ACLNNNOOSTY	CONSONANTLY
ACLNNOOPTTT	COTTON PLANT
ACLNNOSSTTU	CONSULTANTS
ACLNOOORSTY	CONSOLATORY
ACLNOOPRRSU	PROCONSULAR
ACMMNOORSTU	CONSUMMATOR
ACMMOORSTTU	COMMUTATORS
ACMNOOPSTWY	TWOS COMPANY
ACMNORRTUWY	WARM COUNTRY
ACMOOOSSTTU	SCOTOMATOUS
ACNOOPRSSTY	SYNCOPATORS
ACNORRSSTUW	RUNS TWO CARS
ACNPSSTTUUY	CUTS UP NASTY
ACOOPRRRSTT	PROTRACTORS
ACOOPRRRSTU	PROCURATORS
ADDDDEEOPPR	DROPPED DEAD
ADDDDENNOSS	ODDS AND ENDS
ADDDDNOOSSS	ODDS AND SODS
ADDDEEFHILS	FIDDLEHEADS
ADDDEEGIRRS	DISREGARDED
ADDDEEHILRS	ADDED RELISH
ADDDEEHNORU	ROUNDHEADED
ADDDEEHNRSU	DUNDERHEADS
ADDDEEHNSTU	SUDDEN DEATH
ADDDEELMOTU	DEMODULATED
ADDDEEOPPST	STOPPED DEAD
ADDDEFGORRT	DRAFT DODGER
ADDDEFILPSY	PADDYFIELDS
ADDDEGGNORW	DRAGGED DOWN
ADDDEGHLOOR	HOARDED GOLD
ADDDEGIKLNS	SKEDADDLING
ADDDEGOORSS	GOOD ADDRESS
ADDDEHILOST	LAID THE ODDS
ADDDEHIMNOS	DID HANDSOME
ADDDEHIRSTU	STUDIED HARD
ADDDEHNNORU	HANDED ROUND
ADDDEHNRSUY	HUNDRED DAYS
ADDDEILNORT	OLD AND SHOT
	OLD AND TIRED
ADDDERSSTTU	STAR STUDDED
	STAR-STUDDED
ADDDGLOOOSY	GOOD OLD DAYS
ADDDNNOOSST	DO'S AND DON'TS
ADDEEEEGNRT	DEGENERATED
ADDEEEEHLLV	LEVELHEADED
ADDEEEFILLN	FILLED A NEED
ADDEEEFILNO	DANIEL DEFOE
ADDEEEFMNSU	MENDED A FUSE
ADDEEEFPRRY	DEFERRED PAY
ADDEEEFRRTX	DEFERRED TAX
ADDEEEGGGRS	RAGGED EDGES
ADDEEEGGILN	LEADING EDGE
ADDEEEGINPS	GAINED SPEED
ADDEEEHHITT	DIE THE DEATH
ADDEEEHHILLT	HELD THE LEAD
ADDEEEHHNRT	THREE-HANDED
ADDEEEHIKNS	HIDE AND SEEK
	HIDE-AND-SEEK
ADDEEEHKOTW	WOKE THE DEAD

ADDEEEHMPTY	EMPTY-HEADED
ADDEEEHNPPR	APPREHENDED
ADDEEEHRSSS	HEADDRESSES
ADDEEEIMNRR	REMAINDERED
ADDEEEILMNYY	DEADLY ENEMY
ADDEEENORUV	ENDEAVOURED
ADDEEEOPRSS	DESPERADOES
ADDEEFFNORW	WANDERED OFF
ADDEEFGILOO	DIE OF OLD AGE
ADDEEFHNOTY	END OF THE DAY
ADDEEFIMNRS	MADE FRIENDS
ADDEEFIMNRY	FIND A REMEDY
ADDEEFINRRS	DEAR FRIENDS
ADDEEGGHLRU	HELD A GRUDGE
ADDEEGHHILT	LIGHT-HEADED
ADDEEGHISTW	DEADWEIGHTS
ADDEEGHNORW	WRONGHEADED
ADDEEGHOORT	GOOD-HEARTED
ADDEEGIIKLO	DIE LIKE A DOG
ADDEEGIINRW	EDDIE WARING
	WIDE READING
ADDEEGIIRTV	GREAT DIVIDE
ADDEEGIKNRS	READING DESK
ADDEEGILNNO	ENDED IN GOAL
ADDEEGILNNY	DEADENINGLY
ADDEEGILNTW	DELTA-WINGED
ADDEEGINPRT	DEPREDATING
ADDEEGINRRT	INTERGRADED
ADDEEGNRSSU	GUARDEDNESS
ADDEEGORRRT	RETROGRADED
ADDEEHHLLOT	HOLD THE LEAD
ADDEEHHLORT	HELD THE ROAD
ADDEEHHLOTY	HOTHEADEDLY
ADDEEHHNOST	NODS THE HEAD
ADDEEHHNRTU	THUNDERHEAD
ADDEEHHOPSS	DASHED HOPES
ADDEEHIKNRT	KINDHEARTED
ADDEEHILNNP	HIDDEN PANEL
ADDEEHILNPR	PHILANDERED
ADDEEHILNST	IN THE SADDLE
ADDEEHIMNOT	DINED AT HOME
ADDEEHIMNSU	DEHUMANISED
ADDEEHIMNUZ	DEHUMANIZED
ADDEEHINRTW	RED AND WHITE
ADDEEHIOSSV	SHOVED ASIDE
ADDEEHIPSSU	PUSHED ASIDE
ADDEEHIRRRT	TRIED HARDER
ADDEEHIRRSS	SHERARDISED
ADDEEHIRRSZ	SHERARDIZED
ADDEEHISTTU	DEATH DUTIES
ADDEEHMNPTY	EMPTY-HANDED
ADDEEHNNOOS	NOD ONES HEAD
ADDEEHNOOSW	WOODENHEADS
ADDEEHNOOTT	DONE TO DEATH
ADDEEHNORTW	DOWNHEARTED
ADDEEHOOSTT	DOES TO DEATH
ADDEEHORSTW	HEATED WORDS
ADDEEHPRRSS	HARD PRESSED
	PRESSED HARD
ADDEEIIJLNN	ENDED IN JAIL
ADDEEIILMTT	DELIMITATED
ADDEEIILNRV	LIVE IN DREAD
ADDEEIILNST	DISENTAILED
ADDEEIILSTV	DEVITALISED
ADDEEIILTVZ	DEVITALIZED
ADDEEIIMNTT	TIME AND TIDE
ADDEEIINNNW	WINE AND DINE
ADDEEIJOPRS	JEOPARDISED
ADDEEIJOPRZ	JEOPARDIZED
ADDEEIKLMMN	MEEK AND MILD
ADDEEIILLPRY	DEADLY PERIL
ADDEEIILLPSU	PULLED ASIDE
ADDEEIILLSVW	ADVISED WELL
	WELL-ADVISED
ADDEEIILMORS	DEMORALISED
ADDEEIILMORZ	DEMORALIZED
ADDEEIILNNOR	RIDDEN ALONE
ADDEEIILNRRT	INTERLARDED
ADDEEIILNSST	DILATEDNESS
ADDEEIILOPRS	DEPOLARISED
ADDEEIILOPRZ	DEPOLARIZED
ADDEEIILRRVY	DAREDEVILRY
ADDEEIMNNOT	DENOMINATED
ADDEEIMNORV	DRIVE ONE MAD
ADDEEIMNPRR	REPRIMANDED
ADDEEIMORRS	DROMEDARIES
ADDEEIMRSST	MADE STRIDES
ADDEEIMRSTU	DESIDERATUM
ADDEEINNNST	STAND IN NEED
ADDEEINOPRR	PREORDAINED
ADDEEINOPRT	DEPREDATION
ADDEEINRRSU	DUNDREARIES
ADDEEINRSTU	TURNED ASIDE
ADDEEIOSSST	TOSSED ASIDE
ADDEELLORVY	LOVED DEARLY
ADDEELMOSTU	DEMODULATES
ADDEELNPRUY	UNDERPLAYED
ADDEELNRUUV	UNDERVALUED
ADDEELOPPTU	DEPOPULATED
ADDEELPRSST	STEPLADDERS
ADDEEMNNNRU	UNDERMANNED
ADDEEMNOORV	DROVE ONE MAD
ADDEEMOORRT	MADE TO ORDER
ADDEEMRSSTU	MUSTARD SEED
ADDEENNORRS	SEND AN ORDER
ADDEENNORTW	DREW TO AN END
ADDEENNOSSY	END ONES DAYS
ADDEENNOSWY	ON WEDNESDAY
ADDEENOOOPR	OPENED A DOOR
ADDEENORTUW	WANDERED OUT
ADDEENORTWW	WATERED-DOWN
ADDEENRSSST	DESERT SANDS
ADDEENRSTTU	UNDERSTATED
ADDEENRSTTY	STEADY TREND
ADDEEOPRRST	DEPREDATORS
ADDEEOPRRTY	DEPREDATORY
ADDEFFHLNOY	OFFHANDEDLY
ADDEFFIIMRS	DISAFFIRMED
ADDEFFIISST	DISTAFF SIDE
ADDEFGGLNOW	FLAGGED DOWN
ADDEFGHINOT	DEAD OF NIGHT
ADDEFGLORTU	ARTFUL DODGE
ADDEFGNORRS	FOND REGARDS
ADDEFHILNTY	FIND THE LADY
ADDEFHINSSS	FADDISHNESS
ADDEFIIKNSW	WIFE AND KIDS
ADDEFILORTU	FLUORIDATED
ADDEFIORSUV	DISFAVOURED
ADDEFLLRSSU	FULL ADDRESS
ADDEFLNOOTW	FLOATED DOWN
ADDEGGHLORU	HOLD A GRUDGE
ADDEGGHORTU	GODDAUGHTER
ADDEGGIIIRT	DIGITIGRADE
ADDEGGILNRY	DEGRADINGLY
ADDEGGINOOR	GOOD READING
ADDEGHHINRT	RIGHT-HANDED
ADDEGHILNOR	HOLDING DEAR
ADDEGHILNST	SIGHTED LAND
ADDEGHINOTT	DID THE TANGO
ADDEGHINRST	DARNED SIGHT
ADDEGHINRTY	DEHYDRATING
ADDEGHIPPRR	GRIPPED HARD

ADDEGHLORTU	THE OLD GUARD	ADDEKLOOPTT	POLKA-DOTTED
ADDEGHNORTU	DREADNOUGHT	ADDEKMNOOSS	MAKES NO ODDS
ADDEGIIILST	DIGITALISED	ADDELLNORVY	DOLLY VARDEN
ADDEGIIILTZ	DIGITALIZED	ADDELMOORTU	DEMODULATOR
ADDEGIKNRRS	KIND REGARDS	ADDELNNOPSU	LENDS A POUND
ADDEGILLNRU	DULL READING	ADDELNNORSW	WONDERLANDS
ADDEGILMNNY	DEMANDINGLY	ADDELNNRTUY	REDUNDANTLY
ADDEGILNOOV	GOOD AND EVIL	ADDELNNTUUY	UNDAUNTEDLY
ADDEGIMNNNU	UNDEMANDING	ADDELNOORSW	WOODLANDERS
ADDEGIMNORS	GORMANDISED	ADDELNOPPSW	SLAPPED DOWN
ADDEGIMNORZ	GORMANDIZED	ADDEMNNOOSU	MADE NO SOUND
ADDEGINOOST	IN GOOD STEAD	ADDEMNOOORT	RODOMONTADE
ADDEGINPRSU	SUPERADDING	ADDEMNOPSTW	STAMPED DOWN
ADDEGJMNTUY	JUDGMENT DAY	ADDEMRSTUWY	MUDDY WATERS
ADDEGLLNOOW	WELL AND GOOD	ADDENNNOSST	STANDS ON END
ADDEGLNNOSS	GOLDEN SANDS	ADDENNRSSTU	UNDERSTANDS
ADDEGLNRUUY	UNGUARDEDLY	ADDENOORRUV	DROVE AROUND
ADDEGLOOPPR	DROPPED GOAL	ADDENOPRSSU	PASSED ROUND
ADDEGNOORTU	GOOD-NATURED	ADDENOOTTUY	STUDENT DAYS
ADDEGPRSTTU	TRUDGED PAST	ADDEOOPRRTY	READY TO DROP
ADDEHHILLST	DID THE HALLS	ADDFFLOORRT	OLD TRAFFORD
ADDEHHINOTW	HAD DONE WITH	ADDFILNOOSY	IN DAYS OF OLD
ADDEHHLOORT	HOLD THE ROAD	ADDGGHIINNU	GUIDING HAND
ADDEHHNORST	SHORTHANDED	ADDGGIILNST	GLAD TIDINGS
ADDEHIILMOT	THALIDOMIDE	ADDGGINNORW	DOWNGRADING
ADDEHIINORS	DID ONE'S HAIR	ADDGGINOPSU	SAGO PUDDING
ADDEHIJNNOS	JOINED HANDS	ADDGHHILNOR	HOLDING HARD
ADDEHIKLOPT	DID THE POLKA	ADDGHIINRRV	DRIVING HARD
ADDEHIKNRRR	HARD DRINKER		HARD DRIVING
ADDEHILLLRT	LIDDELL HART	ADDGHILLNNO	LANDHOLDING
ADDEHILMNST	THE MIDLANDS	ADDGHILNOOR	ROADHOLDING
ADDEHILNOPR	PHILODENDRA	ADDGHINNNOW	HANDING DOWN
ADDEHILNORS	RHODE ISLAND	ADDGHINNOOS	IN GOOD HANDS
ADDEHILOPSU	DIADELPHOUS	ADDGHNOOSTT	HOT DOG STAND
ADDEHILSTTU	LAID THE DUST	ADDGHNORTUW	DOWNDRAUGHT
ADDEHILTTWZ	DID THE WALTZ	ADDGIIMNNOR	DIAMOND RING
ADDEHINORTY	DEHYDRATION	ADDGIINNORW	WINDING ROAD
ADDEHINOTTU	HANDED IT OUT	ADDGIMNNOPW	DAMPING DOWN
ADDEHIOPRSS	RHAPSODISED	ADDGIMNOOOO	IN A GOOD MOOD
ADDEHIOPRSZ	RHAPSODIZED	ADDGLNNOOUY	OLD AND YOUNG
ADDEHIORSTW	SAID THE WORD		YOUNG AND OLD
ADDEHIRSSTU	STUDIES HARD	ADDGNOOORTU	DO A GOOD TURN
ADDEHLLNORS	LANDHOLDERS	ADDHILMOOOY	HOLIDAY MOOD
ADDEHLOOSWY	LADY WHO DOES	ADDHINNORSW	SWORD IN HAND
ADDEHLOSSTY	LAYS THE ODDS	ADDHLLLOORY	HAROLD LLOYD
ADDEHMNNOSW	HAND-ME-DOWNS	ADDIIILNSUV	INDIVIDUALS
ADDEHNOORTW	DOWN THE ROAD	ADDIIJMNOSV	JIM DAVIDSON
ADDEIIILTVV	VIVID DETAIL	ADDIIJNNRUY	DID AN INJURY
ADDEIIIMNTT	INTIMIDATED	ADDIIMNOSSX	SIX DIAMONDS
ADDEIIINTUV	INDIVIDUATE	ADDIKKNORSV	DRINKS VODKA
ADDEIIKMNRX	MIXED A DRINK	ADDIKNOORST	STOOD A DRINK
ADDEIILLRTU	LURID DETAIL	ADDILLNNOUV	NULL AND VOID
ADDEIIMMNNO	DIAMOND MINE	ADDILLNNSUY	LUNDY ISLAND
ADDEIINNORS	ROADSIDE INN	ADDILMNORTY	DIRTY OLD MAN
ADDEIJNOPRY	PRIDE AND JOY	ADDILNNOOOR	RADIO LONDON
ADDEIKNORRR	ORDER A DRINK	ADDIMNOOSTW	TWO DIAMONDS
ADDEILLMMNS	SMALL-MINDED	ADDNNOOSTUW	DOWN-AND-OUTS
ADDEILLNNSU	DISANNULLED	ADDNNOPSSUW	UPS AND DOWNS
ADDEILMSSSY	SADLY MISSED	ADDNOOORSTU	STOOD A ROUND
ADDEILNORSU	SAILED ROUND		STOOD AROUND
ADDEILNSUVY	UNADVISEDLY	ADEEEEFGHRT	FEATHEREDGE
ADDEILRSTTU	STRIDULATED	ADEEEEGGHTV	GAVE THE EDGE
ADDEINOORSS	RADIOSONDES	ADEEEEGGRST	DESEGREGATE
ADDEINOPRST	DID ONE'S PART	ADEEEEGHHTV	HAVE THE EDGE
ADDEINOPRTW	PARTIED DOWN	ADEEEEGHNRT	NEAR THE EDGE
ADDEINORRUV	DRIVE AROUND	ADEEEEGNRRT	REGENERATED
ADDEIOOPPSU	PSEUDOPODIA	ADEEEEGNRST	DEGENERATES
ADDEIOPPRSV	DISAPPROVED	ADEEEEHKNTY	THE NAKED EYE
ADDEKLNOORT	OLD KENT ROAD	ADEEEEILNSV	ELEVEN A SIDE
ADDEKLNOORW	LOOKED DRAWN	ADEEEEIMMNS	MADE ENEMIES
ADDEKLNORTU	TALKED ROUND	ADEEEELPRRS	PRE-RELEASED

ADEEEEENRRVV	EVER AND EVER	ADEEEINNRTT	ENTERTAINED
ADEEEFGNOSX	FOX AND GEESE	ADEEEINNRTV	VENETIAN RED
ADEEEFHNRST	FREEHANDEST	ADEEEINPRTW	IN DEEP WATER
ADEEEFHRRSZ	FREEZES HARD	ADEEEINRSVY	NEVER SAY DIE
ADEEEFIKVWY	FIVE-DAY WEEK	ADEEEINRTVW	INTERWEAVED
ADEEEFILNOP	OPENED A FILE	ADEEEINRTVW	INTERWEAVED
ADEEEFILNRT	DEFERENTIAL	ADEEEINSSTT	SEE A DENTIST
ADEEEFILOST	FAILED TO SEE	ADEEEIORRTT	DETERIORATE
ADEEEFLMOST	MADE OF STEEL	ADEEEIPRRST	PIEDS-A-TERRE
ADEEEFMPTTT	TEMPTED FATE	ADEEEIPSSSW	SWEEPS ASIDE
ADEEEFNRSTT	FENESTRATED	ADEEEJNRTUV	REJUVENATED
ADEEEFRTTTU	UTTER DEFEAT	ADEEEKLNSST	TALKED SENSE
ADEEEGGGNST	GETS ENGAGED	ADEEEKLRRST	DEERSTALKER
ADEEEGGINNV	GIVEN AN EDGE	ADEEEKLSTTW	SWEET-TALKED
ADEEEGGINSV	GIVES AN EDGE	ADEEEKNRSTT	TENDER STEAK
ADEEEGGLLNO	GOLDEN EAGLE	ADEEEKSTUWY	TUESDAY WEEK
ADEEEGGLMOR	GEORGE MEDAL	ADEEELLNSWY	WENSLEYDALE
ADEEEGGLNOR	GREEN OLD AGE	ADEEELLRTTW	TREATED WELL
ADEEEGGNNOT	ENGAGED TONE	ADEEELLSSTT	TESSELLATED
ADEEEGHHLPT	HELP THE AGED	ADEEELMNNOW	NEEDLEWOMAN
ADEEEGHISTT	GETS THE IDEA	ADEEELNNOUV	LEAVE UNDONE
ADEEEGHLPRT	TELEGRAPHED	ADEEELNNRSS	LEARNEDNESS
ADEEEGHPRST	GATHER SPEED	ADEEELNRSST	RELATEDNESS
ADEEEGILMNR	LEGERDEMAIN	ADEEELNRSTT	SEND A LETTER
ADEEEGILNRS	GENERALISED	ADEEELNRTTU	LAUNDERETTE
ADEEEGILNRZ	GENERALIZED	ADEEELPRSTY	DESPERATELY
ADEEEGILNSV	EVANGELISED	ADEEELPRSVY	VERY PLEASED
ADEEEGILNVZ	EVANGELIZED	ADEEEMNNORY	EARNED MONEY
ADEEEGIMNRR	GENDARMERIE	ADEEEMNNRST	ENDEARMENTS
ADEEEGIMNST	DEMAGNETISE	ADEEEMNOPST	STEAMED OPEN
ADEEEGIMNTZ	DEMAGNETIZE	ADEEEMNRRTU	REMUNERATED
ADEEEGKOORT	TOOK A DEGREE	ADEEEMOSTWW	MEADOWSWEET
ADEEEGLLMRY	LEGAL REMEDY	ADEEEMRSSTW	SWEET DREAMS
ADEEEGLLNRT	LEGAL TENDER	ADEEENNNORS	NEAR ONES END
ADEEEGLLRSS	SALES LEDGER	ADEEENPSSSV	SEVEN SPADES
ADEEEGMNNRT	DERANGEMENT	ADEEENRRSSW	NEWSREADERS
ADEEEGNOSWY	EDGE ONES WAY	ADEEENRRSTY	TENDER YEARS
ADEEEGNOTXY	DEOXYGENATE	ADEEENRSSSV	ADVERSENESS
ADEEEGRRVYY	RED-EYE GRAVY	ADEEEOPPRRV	PAPERED OVER
ADEEEHILNSY	DENIS HEALEY	ADEEEOPPRSW	ROAD SWEEPER
ADEEEHIRSTW	WEATHER SIDE	ADEEEORRRSS	ROSES ARE RED
ADEEEHIRTVY	THE VERY IDEA!	ADEEEPPRRTT	PERPETRATED
ADEEEHLLORS	LEASEHOLDER	ADEEEPPRTTU	PERPETUATED
ADEEEHLLPSS	SHELLED PEAS	ADEEEQRSSTU	AS REQUESTED
ADEEEHLNORW	LEAD NOWHERE	ADEEERSSTTW	DESERT WASTE
ADEEEHLNTVY	ELEVENTH DAY	ADEEFFGINRU	FIND A REFUGE
ADEEEHLORRS	HORSE DEALER	ADEEFFHNOOS	OFF ONES HEAD
ADEEEHLPSSY	SLEEPYHEADS	ADEEFFIINRT	DIFFERENTIA
ADEEEHLRSTT	LETTERHEADS	ADEEFFILNRS	FALSE FRIEND
ADEEEHMNNSTW	MADE THE NEWS	ADEEFFILORR	FOR DEAR LIFE
ADEEEHMOOPW	MADE WHOOPEE	ADEEFFRSTUX	SUFFERED TAX
ADEEEHMORST	HOMESTEADER	ADEEFGGLOPR	LEAPFROGGED
ADEEEHNOPRT	OPENHEARTED	ADEEFGHIRST	SHIFTED GEAR
ADEEEHNOSSU	USE ONES HEAD	ADEEFGHIRSU	FIGUREHEADS
ADEEEHNRRTT	TENDER HEART	ADEEFGHOOST	GOD OF THE SEA
ADEEEHNRSTU	UNDER THE SEA	ADEEFGHORRT	FORGATHERED
ADEEEHPRSST	THREE SPADES	ADEEFGILNNY	DEAFENINGLY
ADEEEHPRSTU	SUPERHEATED	ADEEFGILNOR	FREELOADING
ADEEEIILNTV	DELINEATIVE	ADEEFGINRRT	GREAT FRIEND
ADEEEIIMMOR	AIDE MEMOIRE	ADEEFGLRRSS	SELF-REGARDS
	AIDE-MEMOIRE	ADEEFHHMOOR	HEAD FOR HOME
ADEEEILLMRS	EMERALD ISLE	ADEEFHILORT	LIFE OR DEATH
ADEEEILMNTY	DEMYELINATE	ADEEFHIMOTT	TIME OF DEATH
ADEEEILNRTV	INTERLEAVED	ADEEFHIMSST	STEAMED FISH
ADEEEILOSTV	LEAVES TO DIE	ADEEFHINRSV	HAVE FRIENDS
ADEEEILRTVY	EVERY DETAIL	ADEEFHLNRST	LEFT-HANDERS
ADEEEILSSUX	DESEXUALISE	ADEEFHLOORW	LOW FOREHEAD
ADEEEILSUXZ	DESEXUALIZE	ADEEFHNORTW	END OF THE WAR
ADEEEIMNRTT	DETERMINATE	ADEEFHOOTVY	HEAVY-FOOTED
ADEEEIMPRTT	PREMEDITATE	ADEEFHORSTT	SOFTHEARTED
ADEEEINNNRT	EATEN DINNER	ADEEFIILMRR	MARRIED LIFE
		ADEEFIILNRV	LIVED IN FEAR

ADEEFIKMNRS	MAKE FRIENDS	ADEEGILNOST	DELEGATIONS
ADEEFILLMSS	DAMSELFLIES	ADEEGILNRRS	RINGLEADERS
ADEEFILLNRT	FERTILE LAND	ADEEGIMNPRT	IMPREGNATED
ADEEFILMNOR	FORMED A LINE	ADEEGIMRRST	GETS MARRIED
ADEEFILRSST	FEDERALISTS	ADEEGINNNOS	GAIN ONES END
ADEEFINNRRT	AFTER DINNER	ADEEGINNOOT	GONE ON A DIET
ADEEFINORST	FEDERATIONS	ADEEGINOOST	GOES ON A DIET
ADEEFINRRST	FRATERNISED	ADEEGINOPRW	GAINED POWER
ADEEFINRRTW	WATER-FINDER	ADEEGINORRT	ORDERING TEA
ADEEFINRRTZ	FRATERNIZED	ADEEGINORRV	GIVE AN ORDER
ADEEFIOPSST	SAFE DEPOSIT	ADEEGINPPRT	PRINTED PAGE
ADEEFIQRSUV	FIVE SQUARED	ADEEGINRRST	INTERGRADES
ADEEFIRRVYY	EVERY FRIDAY	ADEEGINRRTU	TRUE READING
ADEEFISSSTX	FIXED ASSETS	ADEEGINRTTU	DEUTERATING
ADEEFKLOORT	LOOKED AFTER	ADEEGIPSTTT	GETS IT TAPED
ADEEFKORUWY	FOUR-DAY WEEK	ADEEGKOOPRS	GOOD SPEAKER
ADEEFLLNNRU	FALLEN UNDER	ADEEGLLMNRS	SMELL DANGER
ADEEFLLORST	FORESTALLED	ADEEGLLMOOR	LOOMED LARGE
ADEEFLLORSV	SEVERALFOLD	ADEEGLLNOPP	GOLDEN APPLE
ADEEFLLPSTU	AT FULL SPEED	ADEEGLLNPRS	SPELL DANGER
ADEEFMMNOOY	MADE OF MONEY	ADEEGLLNSTY	DEALS GENTLY
ADEEFMNOORW	WOODEN FRAME	ADEEGLLNTTY	DEALT GENTLY
ADEEFMNORTU	DAME FORTUNE	ADEEGLLRUUW	AUGURED WELL
ADEEFMNRRTU	FRED TRUEMAN	ADEEGLMNRST	SMELT DANGER
ADEEFNOPSST	TEN OF SPADES	ADEEGLMOOPX	GOOD EXAMPLE
ADEEFNRRRST	TRANSFERRED	ADEEGLMORRY	OLD GREY MARE
ADEEFNRSSVW	SEVEN DWARFS	ADEEGLNOORR	GOOD LEARNER
ADEEFOOPRRR	PROOF READER	ADEEGLNPRST	SPELT DANGER
	PROOFREADER	ADEEGLOORTV	GLOATED OVER
ADEEGGHLORS	LOGGERHEADS	ADEEGLRSTTT	GETS RATTLED
ADEEGGIINRS	DISAGREEING	ADEEGMNNORY	DANGER MONEY
ADEEGGIKNOP	KEEPING A DOG	ADEEGMNRRRY	GERRYMANDER
ADEEGGILRVY	AGGRIEVEDLY	ADEEGMOORSU	GOOD MEASURE
ADEEGGINNNR	ENDANGERING	ADEEGNRTUWY	GET UNDER WAY
ADEEGGINRST	STAGGERED IN	ADEEGORRRST	RETROGRADES
ADEEGGLORTW	WATERLOGGED	ADEEGRSSTTT	GETS STARTED
ADEEGGMORUY	DEMAGOGUERY	ADEEHHILSTT	HEAD THE LIST
ADEEGHHHNTU	HUNG THE HEAD	ADEEHHISSTW	DEATH-WISHES
ADEEGHHLOST	HELD HOSTAGE	ADEEHHISTWW	WHITEWASHED
ADEEGHILSTY	SEE DAYLIGHT	ADEEHHLLMPT	HELD THE PALM
ADEEGHINNRT	IN THE GARDEN	ADEEHHLORRS	SHAREHOLDER
ADEEGHINPTW	WIDEN THE GAP	ADEEHHLPSST	HELD THE PASS
ADEEGHINRST	NEARSIGHTED	ADEEHHNORSX	HEXAHEDRONS
ADEEGHINSSV	HAVE DESIGNS	ADEEHHORSTT	DEATH THROES
ADEEGHLLNOP	HELPED ALONG	ADEEHHORTTY	THE OTHER DAY
ADEEGHLORUV	LAUGHED OVER	ADEEHIIPSTT	HEPATITIDES
ADEEGHLRSTU	SLAUGHTERED	ADEEHILLNOT	ENDOTHELIAL
ADEEGHMOPRR	DEMOGRAPHER	ADEEHILMRRU	HURRIED MEAL
ADEEGHNNPRW	GRANDNEPHEW	ADEEHILMRTW	MILD WEATHER
ADEEGHNNOOSV	GOOD HEAVENS	ADEEHILNORT	LIONHEARTED
ADEEGHNORTY	HYDROGENATE	ADEEHILNORV	HEARD NO EVIL
ADEEGHNORUY	READY ENOUGH	ADEEHILNPRR	PHILANDERER
ADEEGHOORTW	GOOD WEATHER	ADEEHILNRTW	DRAW THE LINE
ADEEGHORTVW	GAVE THE WORD	ADEEHILPTVY	PAY THE DEVIL
ADEEGIILMTT	LEGITIMATED	ADEEHIMNOST	DINES AT HOME
ADEEGIILNNT	DELINEATING	ADEEHIMNSSU	DEHUMANISES
ADEEGIILOST	LAID SIEGE TO	ADEEHIMNSUZ	DEHUMANIZES
ADEEGIILSTV	GIVE DETAILS	ADEEHINNOST	TAN ONE'S HIDE
ADEEGIIRRST	RIDES A TIGER	ADEEHINNRTW	NEAR THE WIND
ADEEGIKKNPR	KEEPING DARK	ADEEHINORSY	DYE ONES HAIR
ADEEGILLNOR	LEADING ROLE	ADEEHINPRTT	PAID THE RENT
ADEEGILLNRS	SELLING DEAR	ADEEHINRRST	RENDS THE AIR
ADEEGILLNRW	READING WELL	ADEEHINRSST	DISHEARTENS
ADEEGILLORS	ALLEGORISED	ADEEHINRSTX	THREE AND SIX
ADEEGILLORZ	ALLEGORIZED	ADEEHIOSSSV	SHOVES ASIDE
ADEEGILMNRR	EMERALD RING	ADEEHIPSSSU	PUSHES ASIDE
ADEEGILNNOT	LEADING NOTE	ADEEHIRRRSS	HAIRDRESSER
ADEEGILNNRT	LENDING RATE	ADEEHIRRRST	TRIES HARDER
ADEEGILNNRW	LEADING WREN	ADEEHIRRSSS	SHERARDISES
ADEEGILNNRY	ENDEARINGLY	ADEEHIRRSSZ	SHERARDIZES
ADEEGILNNST	DISENTANGLE	ADEEHIRRSTW	HARRIS TWEED

ADEEHKLOOTT	TOOK THE LEAD	ADEEILMNRTT	DETRIMENTAL
ADEEHKMNORT	MOTHER-NAKED	ADEEILMNRVY	DELIVERY MAN
ADEEHLLNOSW	SWOLLEN HEAD		DELIVERYMAN
ADEEHLLOTTT	TOLD THE TALE	ADEEILMNTTU	ULTIMATE END
ADEEHLLRTUW	DULL WEATHER	ADEEILMOORT	METEOROIDAL
ADEEHLLSSTY	DEATHLESSLY	ADEEILMORSS	DEMORALISES
ADEEHLMNOTT	MENTHOLATED	ADEEILMORSZ	DEMORALIZES
ADEEHLOORST	LOOSE THREAD	ADEEILMOSVY	EASILY MOVED
ADEEHLORTUY	YOUTH LEADER	ADEEILNNORU	UNION LEADER
ADEEHLOSSTY	LOSES THE DAY	ADEEILNNPRR	LINEN DRAPER
ADEEHMMNNTUU	HUMMED A TUNE	ADEEILNNPRT	DINNER PLATE
ADEEHMMORTU	HAMMERED OUT	ADEEILNNPUX	UNEXPLAINED
ADEEHMNRTTU	UNDER THE MAT	ADEEILNNRRY	EARLY DINNER
ADEEHMOPRST	ATMOSPHERED	ADEEILNOPWY	LAY WIDE OPEN
ADEEHNNNNOTY	ANTHONY EDEN	ADEEILNORRT	LEARN TO RIDE
ADEEHNOOPPS	OPENED A SHOP	ADEEILNORST	DELINEATORS
ADEEHNOOPRT	THE OPEN ROAD	ADEEILNOSTU	OUTSIDE LANE
ADEEHNOOSUW	OWNED A HOUSE	ADEEILNRSTU	NEUTRALISED
ADEEHNORRTT	TETRAHEDRON	ADEEILNRTUZ	NEUTRALIZED
ADEEHOORRTV	OVER THE ROAD	ADEEILNSSSU	SENSUALISED
ADEEHOPRRST	SPARE THE ROD	ADEEILNSSUZ	SENSUALIZED
ADEEHORRRST	HORSE TRADER	ADEEILLSTTT	DILETTANTES
ADEEHORRSST	ARTHRODESES	ADEEILOPPRT	LEPIDOPTERA
ADEEHPRRSSS	PRESSES HARD	ADEEILOPRRS	DEPOLARISER
ADEEIIJNRRS	JARDINIERES	ADEEILOPRRZ	DEPOLARIZER
ADEEIIKNSSS	SKIN DISEASE	ADEEILOPRSS	DEPOLARISES
ADEEIILMMSV	MEDIEVALISM	ADEEILOPRSZ	DEPOLARIZES
ADEEIILMMTY	IMMEDIATELY	ADEEILPRSSU	DISPLEASURE
ADEEIILMNOT	MATINEE IDOL	ADEEILRRSVV	SLAVE DRIVER
ADEEIILMNRS	MINERALISED	ADEEIMNNOOS	MADE NO NOISE
ADEEIILMNRZ	MINERALIZED	ADEEIMNNOST	DENOMINATES
ADEEIILMSTT	DELIMITATES		EMENDATIONS
ADEEIILMSTV	MEDIEVALIST	ADEEIMNNRTT	DETERMINANT
ADEEIILNNOT	DELINEATION		DETRAINMENT
ADEEIILNOTT	LATE EDITION	ADEEIMNOPRT	PREDOMINATE
ADEEIILNRST	DIESEL TRAIN	ADEEIMNORSY	RAISED MONEY
	RESIDENTIAL	ADEEIMNRSTY	SEDIMENTARY
ADEEIILNSST	DESTALINISE	ADEEIMORRST	RADIOMETERS
ADEEIILNSTZ	DESTALINIZE	ADEEIMORSTU	AUDIOMETERS
ADEEIILRSTV	REVITALISED	ADEEIMORSTW	MADE IT WORSE
ADEEIILRTVZ	REVITALIZED	ADEEIMRRVWY	RIVER MEDWAY
ADEEIILSSTV	DEVITALISES	ADEEINNORSV	DROVE INSANE
ADEEIILSTVZ	DEVITALIZES	ADEEINNOTTW	WENT ON A DIET
ADEEIIMMNPT	IMPEDIMENTA	ADEEINNPRRV	ANDRE PREVIN
ADEEIIMNNST	INSEMINATED	ADEEINNPRST	TINNED PEARS
ADEEIIMNSST	DISSEMINATE	ADEEINNQRSU	NINE SQUARED
ADEEIINNRSS	IN READINESS	ADEEINNRSST	ENDS IN TEARS
ADEEIINNRSV	DRIVE INSANE	ADEEINNRTTV	INADVERTENT
ADEEIINRTVY	EVIDENTIARY	ADEEINNSSVX	SEVEN AND SIX
ADEEIIRSSTV	ADVERSITIES	ADEEINOPRST	DESPERATION
ADEEIIRSTTW	TIDEWAITERS	ADEEINOPRTV	PAINTED OVER
ADEEIIRSTVV	DERIVATIVES	ADEEINOPTTT	POTENTIATED
ADEEIIRTVWY	WIDE VARIETY	ADEEINORRST	RAISON DETRE
ADEEIJOPRSS	JEOPARDISES	ADEEINORRTV	OVERTRAINED
ADEEIJOPRSZ	JEOPARDIZES	ADEEINORTTU	DEUTERATION
ADEEIKKLLOO	LOOKED ALIKE	ADEEINOSSTW	SEASIDE TOWN
ADEEIKKPRST	KEEPS IT DARK	ADEEINOSTTT	DETESTATION
ADEEIKLPRTT	TALKED TRIPE	ADEEINPRSST	PEDESTRIANS
ADEEIKLRSTW	WATERED SILK	ADEEINRSSTV	NATIVE DRESS
ADEEIKMMSTU	MEDIUM STEAK	ADEEINSSTTU	UNSTEADIEST
ADEEIKMOPPS	SMOKED A PIPE	ADEEIORSTTV	TRIED TO SAVE
ADEEIKMRSST	MAKE STRIDES	ADEEIOSSSST	TOSSES ASIDE
ADEEILLMNNR	ILL-MANNERED	ADEEIPRTTUV	VITUPERATED
ADEEILLMRRW	MARRIED WELL	ADEEIRRSSTV	ADVERTISERS
ADEEILLMRSV	SILVER MEDAL	ADEEIRRSSTW	WATERSIDERS
ADEEILLPRSS	ESPADRILLES	ADEEIRRSTVW	SERVED A WRIT
ADEEILLSSVW	ADVISES WELL	ADEEKLLOOPS	LOOK PLEASED
ADEEILMNNST	ENLISTED MAN	ADEEKLMMORY	MELODY MAKER
ADEEILMNOPR	DROP ME A LINE	ADEEKLMNOTY	TALKED MONEY
ADEEILMNORT	ENDOMETRIAL	ADEEKLMOOSS	LOOKED A MESS
ADEEILMNRST	STREAMLINED	ADEEKLOORWY	LOOKED WEARY

ADEEKLOPPRY	PLAYED POKER	ADEFFILLOSU	FULL OF IDEAS
ADEEKLOPRSU	LOUD SPEAKER	ADEFFILNRTU	FAULTFINDER
	LOUDSPEAKER	ADEFFILNSTU	INSUFFLATED
ADEEKMNRRTT	MARKET TREND	ADEFFIMMNOR	FRAME OF MIND
ADEEKMOORRT	MAKE TO ORDER	ADEFFINRRUY	FIRE AND FURY
ADEEKMRRSSS	DRESSMAKERS	ADEFFINRSST	FAST FRIENDS
ADEEKNNOPSU	SNEAKED UP ON	ADEFGHILMOT	MADE LIGHT OF
ADEEKNNORRST	TAKEN ORDERS	ADEFGHILSTU	FIGHTS A DUEL
ADEEKNRRSTU	UNDERTAKERS	ADEFGHINOPS	FADING HOPES
ADEEKORRSST	TAKES ORDERS	ADEFGHLOORT	HEART OF GOLD
ADEEKORSTTU	STREAKED OUT	ADEFGHLOOTT	FLOG TO DEATH
ADEELLLNNPW	PLANNED WELL	ADEFGHLOTUU	FOUGHT A DUEL
ADEELLMOSTT	LATEST MODEL	ADEFGHOORST	GATHERS FOOD
ADEELLMRSSY	DREAMLESSLY		HERD OF GOATS
ADEELLNOSTW	STONEWALLED	ADEFGIILNSS	FLINGS ASIDE
ADEELLNPRSU	UNDER A SPELL	ADEFGIINNYZ	DENAZIFYING
ADEELLNSSSS	LESS AND LESS	ADEFGILLNOS	SELF-LOADING
ADEELLORSVY	LOVES DEARLY	ADEFGILNNOR	FOREIGN LAND
ADEELLRSTTW	STARTED WELL	ADEFGILNORS	DRAGONFLIES
ADEELMPRRTY	EMPTY LARDER	ADEFGIMNORR	FORMED A RING
ADEELNOORST	ALDOSTERONE	ADEFGIMNOTW	GIFTED WOMAN
ADEELNOPSSU	SOUND ASLEEP	ADEFGIMOOSW	AGE OF WISDOM
ADEELNRSUUV	UNDERVALUES	ADEFGINOOPR	GONE FOR A DIP
ADEELOPPSTU	DEPOPULATES	ADEFGIOOPRS	GOES FOR A DIP
ADEELOPRSTY	POSTED EARLY	ADEFGITTUUY	FATIGUE DUTY
ADEELORTUVV	VAULTED OVER	ADEFGKNOORS	GODFORSAKEN
ADEELPSSTUY	STEADY PULSE	ADEFGKOORSS	FOR GOD'S SAKE!
ADEEMMNNNOW	MEN AND WOMEN	ADEFGLLNORW	GRAND FELLOW
ADEEMMNNOORR	MORE AND MORE	ADEFGNNORRT	FRONT GARDEN
ADEEMMNNORTY	DYNAMOMETER	ADEFGNOORRW	GONE FORWARD
ADEEMMNNOSST	MODEST MEANS	ADEFGNOORTU	OUT OF DANGER
ADEEMMNNNSSU	MUNDANENESS	ADEFGNORTWW	GWEN WATFORD
ADEEMNOPPRR	NAME DROPPER	ADEFGOORRSW	GOES FORWARD
	NAME-DROPPER	ADEFHIILOOS	FOOLISH IDEA
ADEEMNOPRRS	PROMENADERS	ADEFHIKOSST	KISS OF DEATH
ADEEMNORSTT	DEMONSTRATE	ADEFHILLORT	ADOLF HITLER
ADEEMNORVYY	EVERY MONDAY	ADEFHINNOOT	HAD NONE OF IT
ADEEMNOSTWY	WASTED MONEY	ADEFHINPRST	PATHFINDERS
ADEEMNPRSTT	DEPARTMENTS	ADEFHINRRTY	FIRE HYDRANT
ADEEMNPRSTU	SMARTENED UP	ADEFHNOTUWY	FOUND THE WAY
ADEEMNRRRWY	MERRY ANDREW	ADEFHOORSSW	FORESHADOWS
ADEEMORRSVW	SWARMED OVER	ADEFHOPRRTU	PROUD FATHER
ADEEMORSSTTU	STREAMED OUT	ADEFHOPRTUY	UP FOR THE DAY
ADEEMORSTUU	MEASURED OUT	ADEFIIKLNTU	FLUID INTAKE
ADEENNNPPSY	SPEND A PENNY	ADEFIILLMOS	OLD FAMILIES
ADEENNNRTTU	UNDERTENANT	ADEFIILMPRY	FAMILY PRIDE
ADEENNORRST	SENT AN ORDER	ADEFIILNOOT	DEFOLIATION
ADEENNOSWWY	WEND ONES WAY	ADEFIILNOTW	FAILED TO WIN
ADEENNRRSTU	RENT ASUNDER	ADEFIILNQUU	UNQUALIFIED
ADEENOORRVV	OVER AND OVER	ADEFIILNRTT	INFILTRATED
ADEENORRSTU	TORE ASUNDER	ADEFIILRSST	LADIES FIRST
ADEENORRSVW	WANDERS OVER	ADEFILLLSTU	FULL DETAILS
ADEENPPSSWW	SWAPPED NEWS	ADEFILLNORR	FILL AN ORDER
ADEENPRSSST	DEPRESSANTS	ADEFILLNOSU	LIFE AND SOUL
ADEENPRSSSU	UNDERPASSES	ADEFILLOPST	FILLED A POST
ADEENQRRSSU	SQUANDERERS	ADEFILLORSV	FIVE DOLLARS
ADEENRRRSTU	UNDER ARREST	ADEFILLORUV	ILL-FAVOURED
ADEENRRSTUV	ADVENTURERS	ADEFILMORSW	WORDS FAIL ME
ADEENRSSSSU	ASSUREDNESS	ADEFILNOORT	DEFLORATION
ADEENRSSTTU	UNDERSTATES	ADEFILNORRW	FORWARD LINE
ADEENRSUVYY	EVERY SUNDAY	ADEFILNORTU	FLUORINATED
ADEENSTTUXY	NEXT TUESDAY	ADEFILOOPRT	LOAD OF TRIPE
ADEEOPPRSVW	SWAPPED OVER	ADEFILORSTU	FLUORIDATES
ADEEOPRRTTX	EXPORT TRADE	ADEFILSSTTU	DISTASTEFUL
ADEERRSSSTU	REST ASSURED	ADEFIMNOORT	DEFORMATION
ADEFFGINORY	DYING OF FEAR	ADEFIMNORWW	WINDOW FRAME
	FEAR OF DYING	ADEFIMNOSST	SANDS OF TIME
ADEFFGLLOOP	GALLOPED OFF	ADEFIMNOSTT	STATE OF MIND
ADEFFHNOOST	DOFF ONES HAT	ADEFIMNOTUX	FIXED AMOUNT
ADEFFIIKLNR	FRANK IFIELD	ADEFIMOORTT	FRIED TOMATO
ADEFFILLOPY	FIELD OF PLAY	ADEFIMOPRTU	MADE UP FOR IT

ADEFINNOSWY	FIND ONES WAY
ADEFINOOPRR	RAINPROOFED
ADEFINOORRS	FOREORDAINS
ADEFINOPRTW	WENT FOR A DIP
ADEFINORSWW	IN A FEW WORDS
ADEFINPRRST	PART FRIENDS
ADEFIOPSSSX	SIX OF SPADES
ADEFKLLOOOO	LOOKED A FOOL
ADEFLMORRSS	FORMAL DRESS
ADEFLNOORRS	FOOLS ERRAND
ADEFLOOPSTY	SPLAYFOOTED
ADEFLOORTUV	VAULTED ROOF
ADEFLOOSSST	DOSE OF SALTS
ADEFLORSTTY	TREAD SOFTLY
ADEFMNORRST	TRANSFORMED
ADEFMOOPRST	MADE SPORT OF
ADEFMOORRVW	MOVE FORWARD
ADEFMRRSTUY	STURDY FRAME
ADEFNNOPRST	FOND PARENTS
ADEFNORRSSW	FORWARDNESS
	FROWARDNESS
ADEFNORRTWW	WENT FORWARD
ADEFOOPRRTW	DROP OF WATER
ADEFOOPSSTW	TWO OF SPADES
ADEFOPRRSTW	STEP FORWARD
ADEFOQRRSUU	FOUR SQUARED
ADEGGGIINNS	DISENGAGING
ADEGGHIILNU	DIE LAUGHING
ADEGGHILNRS	HANG-GLIDERS
ADEGGHILNRT	RIGHT-ANGLED
ADEGGHINOOR	GOOD HEARING
ADEGGHNOORS	GORGONS HEAD
ADEGGIIMNOS	IN GODS IMAGE
ADEGGIINNRT	DENIGRATING
ADEGGIINNST	DESIGNATING
ADEGGIINRSS	SINGS A DIRGE
ADEGGIKNRTT	GETTING DARK
ADEGGINOPTY	EGYPTIAN GOD
ADEGGINOSTY	GOING STEADY
ADEGGKLOORS	LOOK DAGGERS
ADEGGNNOOPS	EGG AND SPOON
ADEGGNNOORU	GONE AGROUND
ADEGGNOORSU	GOES AGROUND
ADEGHHILNNP	HELPING HAND
ADEGHHINNTU	HEAD-HUNTING
ADEGHHINRRT	RIGHT-HANDER
ADEGHHLOOST	HOLD HOSTAGE
ADEGHHORRTU	READ THROUGH
ADEGHHORTUW	WADE THROUGH
ADEGHIIKNNT	THE KING AND I
ADEGHIILNTV	LIVING DEATH
ADEGHIILNTW	DEALING WITH
ADEGHIIMRTT	MADE IT RIGHT
ADEGHILLNOV	LEAVING HOLD
ADEGHILNNOV	HAND IN GLOVE
ADEGHILNNST	THIS ENGLAND
ADEGHINNORV	HANDING OVER
ADEGHINNPPY	HAPPY ENDING
ADEGHINOOPS	IN GOOD SHAPE
ADEGHINOORT	IN GOOD HEART
ADEGHINORTW	WHITE DRAGON
ADEGHINOSSW	SHOWED A SIGN
ADEGHINPRSS	HEADSPRINGS
ADEGHINRRTY	REHYDRATING
ADEGHINRTUY	RUING THE DAY
ADEGHIRSTTU	DRAUGHTIEST
ADEGHKLOSTW	WALKS THE DOG
ADEGHLMOOOT	HOMOLOGATED
ADEGHLNOOPP	HOPPED ALONG
ADEGHLOPRUY	PLAYED ROUGH
ADEGHMNORRT	GRANDMOTHER

ADEGHMNRSTU	DRAUGHTSMEN
ADEGHNOORST	ON GODS EARTH
ADEGHNORRTU	GATHER ROUND
ADEGHOORSTV	GOOD HARVEST
ADEGHORRSSU	HORSE GUARDS
ADEGHORSSUU	GUARDHOUSES
ADEGIIILNTV	INVIGILATED
ADEGIIILSST	DIGITALISES
ADEGIIILSTZ	DIGITALIZES
ADEGIIINNRV	INDIAN GIVER
ADEGIIINRST	DIGNITARIES
ADEGIIKNPRT	TAKING PRIDE
ADEGIIKNSST	TAKING SIDES
ADEGIILLNNT	ENDING IT ALL
ADEGIILNNNW	WINNING LEAD
ADEGIILNNOR	RIDING ALONE
ADEGIILNNRW	LINE DRAWING
ADEGIILNNRY	DINING EARLY
	INGRAINEDLY
ADEGIILNNTZ	DENTALIZING
ADEGIILNOTV	DOVETAILING
ADEGIILNPSS	DISPLEASING
ADEGIILNRST	READING LIST
ADEGIILNSST	SLIDING SEAT
ADEGIIMNTTU	UNMITIGATED
ADEGIIMSSTT	STIGMATISED
ADEGIIMSTTZ	STIGMATIZED
ADEGIINNORT	DENIGRATION
ADEGIINNOST	DESIGNATION
ADEGIINNRRW	DRAWING REIN
ADEGIINOPTV	VIDEOTAPING
ADEGIINORSS	DISORGANISE
ADEGIINORSZ	DISORGANIZE
ADEGIINORTV	INVIGORATED
ADEGIINPRTU	REPUDIATING
ADEGIINRRVZ	GRAND VIZIER
ADEGIINRSTT	GIANT STRIDE
ADEGIINRSTV	ADVERTISING
ADEGIINRTTU	IN GRATITUDE
	INGRATITUDE
ADEGIINRTTX	EXTRADITING
ADEGIKMNRSS	DRESSMAKING
ADEGIKNNORR	ORANGE DRINK
ADEGIKNNRTU	UNDERTAKING
ADEGILLNOPV	VILLAGE POND
ADEGILLNOVY	LIVELONG DAY
ADEGILLPTUY	PLEAD GUILTY
ADEGILMMNRY	ME AND MY GIRL
ADEGILMNNNO	GIN AND LEMON
ADEGILMNNNS	MISS ENGLAND
ADEGILNNORV	OVERLANDING
ADEGILNNRSS	SANDERLINGS
ADEGILNNSSU	LANGUIDNESS
ADEGILNOPTU	LEADING UP TO
ADEGILNORSY	GRANDIOSELY
ADEGILNORVW	LEAVING WORD
ADEGILNOSTW	LONG-WAISTED
ADEGILNPRTY	PANTY GIRDLE
ADEGILNSTTY	SETTLING DAY
ADEGIMNNOPR	PROMENADING
ADEGIMNNRRU	UNDERARMING
ADEGIMNOORR	READING ROOM
ADEGIMNOORS	INDOOR GAMES
ADEGIMNORRS	GORMANDISER
ADEGIMNORRZ	GORMANDIZER
ADEGIMNORSS	GORMANDISES
ADEGIMNORSZ	GORMANDIZES
ADEGINNOPRU	READING UP ON
ADEGINNORTU	GET A ROUND IN
ADEGINNORTW	TEARING DOWN
ADEGINNORWW	WEARING DOWN

ADEGINNPRTU	PUT IN DANGER	ADEHILLNPTU	DULL THE PAIN
ADEGINNQRSU	SQUANDERING	ADEHILLORSU	LOUD HAILERS
ADEGINNRRTU	UNDERRATING		LOUD-HAILERS
ADEGINNRRUW	UNREWARDING	ADEHILORSTU	TOUSLED HAIR
ADEGINNRTUV	ADVENTURING	ADEHILPSTWY	PLAYED WHIST
ADEGINNSTUY	UNSTEADYING	ADEHILRSWWZ	WELSH WIZARD
ADEGINOOSTT	IN GOOD TASTE	ADEHIMMPPUY	HAPPY MEDIUM
ADEGINORRST	DENIGRATORS	ADEHIMNOOPT	PAID THE MOON
ADEGINORRTY	DENIGRATORY	ADEHIMNOPST	HANDSOME TIP
ADEGINORSST	DESIGNATORS	ADEHIMNORSS	ADMONISHERS
ADEGINORSTW	GETS A WORD IN	ADEHIMORSTY	MADE HISTORY
ADEGINORSTY	DESIGNATORY	ADEHIMPRSTY	THE PYRAMIDS
ADEGINRRSSS	DRESS IN RAGS	ADEHIMPSSTY	SYMPATHISED
ADEGIOPRSST	TRADE GOSSIP	ADEHIMPSTYZ	SYMPATHIZED
ADEGIORTTUU	ARGUED IT OUT	ADEHINNRSTU	UNTARNISHED
ADEGKLMOSSS	SMOKED GLASS	ADEHINNRSUV	UNVARNISHED
ADEGKNRRRSU	KRUGERRANDS	ADEHINOOSUW	WODEHOUSIAN
ADEGLLLNOOR	ROLLED ALONG	ADEHINORRTY	REHYDRATION
ADEGLMOOPRS	SPREAD GLOOM	ADEHINORSTV	HANDS IT OVER
ADEGLMOOPRT	GOOD TEMPLAR	ADEHINOSSSW	SHADOWINESS
ADEGLMOORTY	DERMATOLOGY	ADEHINOSTTT	THATS DONE IT
ADEGLMOPRTU	PROMULGATED	ADEHINQRRTU	HINDQUARTER
ADEGLNNOOST	LONDON STAGE	ADEHIOPRSSS	RHAPSODISES
ADEGLNOORRW	GOLDEN ARROW	ADEHIOPRSSZ	RHAPSODIZES
ADEGLNOORST	GARDEN TOOLS	ADEHIORRSST	ARTHRODESIS
ADEGLNORSUY	DANGEROUSLY	ADEHIPRSSTW	STEWARDSHIP
ADEGMNNOORS	GOOD MANNERS	ADEHIRRRSTT	THIRD-RATERS
ADEGMNNQTUY	STUDY GERMAN	ADEHIRSTTTU	TITHOT ASIDE
ADEGMOOORTU	OUTDOOR GAME	ADEHIRSTTTW	STARTED WITH
ADEGNNNNOOO	GONE ON AND ON	ADEHIRSTVYY	THIS VERY DAY
ADEGNNNOOOS	GOES ON AND ON	ADEHISSTTUY	THIS TUESDAY
ADEGNNOORSU	ON ONES GUARD	ADEHKLOOPPY	LOOKED HAPPY
ADEGNNORTUW	WENT AGROUND	ADEHKLOOPRS	LOOKED SHARP
ADEGNOORSTV	GOOD SERVANT	ADEHKNORRSW	WORK-HARDENS
ADEGNOORSTW	GONE TOWARDS	ADEHKNRRRSY	DRANK SHERRY
ADEGNORSTUW	WASTE GROUND	ADEHKOORTTW	WORK TO DEATH
ADEGNORSTWX	WAXED STRONG	ADEHKORRSTU	DARKEST HOUR
ADEGNORTUWY	GOT UNDER WAY	ADEHLLLMORS	SMALLHOLDER
ADEGNOSTUYY	STAYED YOUNG	ADEHLLLORST	STALLHOLDER
ADEGNRSSTTU	STUDENTS RAG	ADEHLLLORTW	ALL THE WORLD
ADEGOOPRSST	GASTEROPODS	ADEHLLNOSTW	THE LOWLANDS
ADEGOORSSTW	GOES TOWARDS	ADEHLMNOOTW	THE OLD WOMAN
ADEGOORSTTT	STARTED TO GO	ADEHLMOORST	SLAM THE DOOR
ADEGPRRSUWW	GREW UPWARDS	ADEHLNOPRSY	HYDROPLANES
ADEGPRSSTTU	TRUDGES PAST	ADEHLOORRSW	OLD WARHORSE
ADEHHHINPTW	THE WHIP-HAND	ADEHLOPSSST	SOLD THE PASS
ADEHHHLSTUY	DEATHLY HUSH	ADEHLORSTTW	THE LAST WORD
ADEHHIILPRT	DIPHTHERIAL	ADEHLORSTWW	SAW THE WORLD
ADEHHIINORR	HIDE NOR HAIR	ADEHLORTXYY	HYDROXYLATE
ADEHHIINPRT	DIPHTHERIAN	ADEHLPRSTUU	SULPHURATED
ADEHHILMNTY	HEALTHY MIND	ADEHLSSTTUY	LAYS THE DUST
ADEHHILMOOY	HOLIDAY HOME	ADEHMMNOSSU	HANDSOME SUM
ADEHHILPRSY	HER LADYSHIP	ADEHMORRSTW	THREADWORMS
ADEHHIMNRTT	THE THIRD MAN	ADEHNNNOOSS	ON ONES HANDS
ADEHHIMOORR	HAEMORRHOID	ADEHNNOOSTU	ONE THOUSAND
ADEHHIMRTTY	MAY THE THIRD	ADEHNNOPSTU	OPEN AND SHUT
ADEHHINOSTW	HAS DONE WITH		OPEN-AND-SHUT
ADEHHIORRSS	HORSERADISH	ADEHNNORSTY	TRY ONES HAND
ADEHHIORSTT	HITS THE ROAD	ADEHNNOSTTU	TEN THOUSAND
ADEHHIRSSSW	DISHWASHERS	ADEHNOOPTTY	PAY ON THE DOT
ADEHHLLMOPT	HOLD THE PALM	ADEHNOORRSU	HORSE AROUND
ADEHHLLNOTY	THE HOLY LAND	ADEHNOORTTW	DOWN TO EARTH
ADEHHLOPSST	HOLD THE PASS		DOWN-TO-EARTH
ADEHHORSTTU	THRASHED OUT	ADEHNOPPRSS	SANDHOPPERS
ADEHIILMOTY	HOLIDAY TIME	ADEHOOPSTTT	PHOTOSTATED
ADEHIILOPSU	AUDIOPHILES	ADEHOORSSVW	OVERSHADOWS
ADEHIILOSST	HOISTED SAIL	ADEHOPRSSTW	SHOP STEWARD
ADEHIIMNRTU	ANTHERIDIUM	ADEHOPSTTTU	PUTS TO DEATH
ADEHIINPPST	PAINTED SHIP	ADEHORSSTTY	SHORTEST DAY
ADEHIIRRSTT	ARTHRITIDES	ADEHORSSTWY	SAYS THE WORD
ADEHIKMRSSY	KISS ME,HARDY	ADEIIIKLNOT	LIKE AN IDIOT

ADEIIILMRST	MILITARISED	ADEIKNNOTTU	UNTIED A KNOT
ADEIIILMRTZ	MILITARIZED	ADEIKNPRTTW	WARP-KNITTED
ADEIIILRSTV	TRIVIALISED	ADEIKNRRSTW	DRINKS WATER
ADEIIILRTVZ	TRIVIALIZED	ADEILLNNORS	NINE DOLLARS
ADEIIIMNSTT	INTIMIDATES	ADEILLOPPTT	TOPPED IT ALL
ADEIIIMNSTV	VITAMINISED	ADEILLOPRVW	PROVED A WILL
ADEIIIMNTVZ	VITAMINIZED	ADEILLORTUV	ALL-OUT DRIVE
ADEIIINNRTV	TRIED IN VAIN	ADEILLOSVWW	SWALLOW DIVE
ADEIIINNTTU	UNINITIATED	ADEILLOTTUW	LOW ALTITUDE
ADEIIIOPSTV	DIAPOSITIVE	ADEILLRSTTU	ILLUSTRATED
ADEIIIPRSST	DISPARITIES	ADEILLSSTTY	STAYED STILL
ADEIIIPSSTV	DISSIPATIVE	ADEILMNOPRS	PALINDROMES
ADEIIKLLMOT	AIMED TO KILL	ADEILMNORRV	OLD MAN RIVER
ADEIIKMNRSX	MIXES A DRINK	ADEILMNORST	LIES DORMANT
ADEIIKNPPTW	TIPPED A WINK	ADEILMORSTT	SOLID MATTER
ADEIIILLLOPS	ELLIPSOIDAL	ADEILMRRRTU	MURDER TRIAL
ADEIIILLMNTU	ILLUMINATED	ADEILNOOPRT	PERIODONTAL
ADEIIILLORTY	EDITORIALLY	ADEILNOPTWY	PLAYED TO WIN
ADEIIILLOSTV	VOLATILISED	ADEILNORSUY	DELUSIONARY
ADEIIILLOTVZ	VOLATILIZED	ADEILNQSSSU	SQUALIDNESS
ADEIIILLSSTT	DISTILLATES	ADEILNRSTWW	WINDLESTRAW
ADEIIILMNNOS	DIMENSIONAL	ADEILNRSTWZ	SWITZERLAND
ADEIIILMNORT	MINOR DETAIL	ADEILNSSTTT	LETS IT STAND
ADEIIILMNRSU	SEMIDIURNAL	ADEILOPPRSU	POPULARISED
ADEIIILMSSTU	DISSIMULATE	ADEILOPPRUZ	POPULARIZED
ADEIIILNNNST	STAND IN LINE	ADEILOPRRTY	DAILY REPORT
ADEIIILNNOVV	LOVED IN VAIN		PREDATORILY
ADEIIILNNTVW	LIVED IN WANT	ADEILOPRSSY	SOLDIERS PAY
ADEIIILNOPTY	YIELD A POINT	ADEILOPRTTY	TETRAPLOIDY
ADEIIILOPRRT	TRIAL PERIOD	ADEILPPPSST	SLIPPED PAST
ADEIIILRRRSV	RAIL DRIVERS	ADEILRSSTTU	STRIDULATES
ADEIIMMNNSTU	MEDIASTINUM	ADEIMMNNOPU	PANDEMONIUM
ADEIIMNOPSS	IMPASSIONED	ADEIMMNRSST	MASTERMINDS
ADEIIMNRSST	ADMINISTERS	ADEIMMOORTY	AID TO MEMORY
ADEIIMPRSSU	PRAESIDIUMS	ADEIMMNOORT	DENOMINATOR
ADEIIMRSTTX	TAXIDERMIST	ADEIMNNOPRT	PREDOMINANT
ADEIIINNNOSS	INDONESIANS	ADEIMNNOTUW	MOUNTAIN DEW
ADEIIINNNOTT	INDENTATION	ADEIMNNQRUU	QUADRENNIUM
ADEIIINNOOPT	OPINIONATED	ADEIMNOORST	MODERATIONS
ADEIIINNOSTT	DESTINATION	ADEIMNORRVW	WOMAN DRIVER
ADEIIINOPRTT	PARTITIONED	ADEIMNRRSUY	NURSERY MAID
	TREPIDATION	ADEIMNRRTUY	RUDIMENTARY
ADEIIINOPRTU	REPUDIATION	ADEIMNRSTTT	TRANSMITTED
ADEIIINOPRTV	DEPRIVATION	ADEIMNRSTUV	ADVENTURISM
ADEIIINOPSST	PASSIONTIDE	ADEIMNSSTUY	SUNDAY TIMES
ADEIIINORSTV	DERIVATIONS	ADEIMOPSTUY	IMPOSE A DUTY
ADEIIINORSTY	SEDITIONARY	ADEINNOOSTT	DETONATIONS
ADEIIINORTTX	EXTRADITION	ADEINNOPRSW	OPEN INWARDS
ADEIINPRSTY	STIPENDIARY	ADEINNOSWWY	WIND ONES WAY
ADEIINPSSST	INSPISSATED	ADEINNPRRTY	DINNER PARTY
ADEIINPSTTU	INAPTITUDES	ADEINNRRSTU	UNDER STRAIN
ADEIINQSTTU	EQUIDISTANT	ADEINNSSSTT	DISTANTNESS
ADEIINSSSTY	STAYS INSIDE	ADEINOOPPRT	APPORTIONED
ADEIIOPPRTT	PROPITIATED	ADEINOOPRTT	DEPORTATION
ADEIIRRSSTT	DIRE STRAITS	ADEINOORTTU	RATIONED OUT
ADEIIRSSTUW	ISSUED A WRIT	ADEINOPRRTW	WORD PAINTER
ADEIJLNORSU	JOURNALISED	ADEINOPRSTW	PARTIES DOWN
ADEIJLNORUZ	JOURNALIZED	ADEINOPSTTU	DEPUTATIONS
ADEIJMMNRSW	WINDJAMMERS	ADEINPRSSST	DISPERSANTS
ADEIJMRRSTU	JUST MARRIED	ADEINRSTTUV	ADVENTURIST
ADEIJNORRRV	RIVER JORDAN	ADEIOPPRRSV	DISAPPROVER
ADEIKKLNNTY	TAKEN KINDLY	ADEIOPPRSSV	DISAPPROVES
ADEIKKLNSTY	TAKES KINDLY	ADEIOPPRRSTT	DROP A SITTER
ADEIKKNORTT	TAKE TO DRINK	ADEIOSSTTUY	STAY OUTSIDE
ADEIKLLLRSY	LADY-KILLERS	ADEIPPPRTUW	WRAPPED IT UP
ADEIKLLMPSY	SPEAK MILDLY	ADEJMNNORTU	ADJOURNMENT
ADEIKLMNRSU	RUNS LIKE MAD	ADEJMNNORRTY	TOM AND JERRY
ADEIKLOTTTU	TALKED IT OUT	ADEJMNSSTTU	ADJUSTMENTS
ADEIKMNNOTW	MADE IT KNOWN	ADEJNORSUYY	DAYS JOURNEY
ADEIKMNNOTY	DOMINANT KEY	ADEKLMOORST	LOOKED SMART
ADEIKMOORWY	MIKE YARWOOD	ADEKLNOOPSU	SPOKEN ALOUD

ADEKLNOOTUW	WALKED OUT ON	ADFGIINNNTW	FIND WANTING
ADEKMNNOOSU	MAKE NO SOUND	ADFGIINQRSU	FIRING SQUAD
ADEKORRSTTW	STARTED WORK	ADFGILLNNOW	FALLING DOWN
ADELLMMSSUY	SELLS A DUMMY	ADFGILNNOST	SOFT LANDING
ADELLMNORSW	SMALL WONDER		SOFT-LANDING
ADELLNORRSU	ALL-ROUNDERS	ADFGILNORST	DRIFTS ALONG
ADELLNSSTUY	DAUNTLESSLY	ADFGILNQSUY	FLYING SQUAD
ADELLOOPRRT	PETRODOLLAR	ADFGINNORST	STANDING FOR
ADELLOORRSU	EURODOLLARS	ADFGINORRSU	FAIRGROUNDS
ADELLOPSUWW	SWALLOWED UP	ADFGINORRWW	WING FORWARD
ADELMMPRUYY	PLAYED RUMMY	ADFGOOOORSS	SO FAR SO GOOD
ADELMMNOPRTW	TRAMPLE DOWN	ADFHHNOOSSW	SHOW OF HANDS
ADELMPRSSTU	LEADS TRUMPS	ADFHILLOORY	FOOLHARDILY
ADELNOOOPRSW	SNOW LEOPARD	ADFHIMNOOOR	MAID OF HONOR
ADELNOORRWW	WORLD WAR ONE	ADFHINNORSU	FOUR-IN-HANDS
ADELNOOSSTT	STAND TO LOSE	ADFHOPRRSUW	PUSH FORWARD
ADELNOPPTTT	POTTED PLANT	ADFHORRRSUW	RUSH FORWARD
ADELNOPRSUY	SOUND PLAYER	ADFIIIMNNTU	AD INFINITUM
ADELNORSSUW	SLOW AND SURE	ADFIILMNTUU	LATIFUNDIUM
ADELNPPRSUW	DREW UP PLANS	ADFIJKOSSSU	KISS OF JUDAS
ADELOOPPRTU	DEPOPULATOR	ADFILLNOOPS	FLOODPLAINS
ADELOOPRRST	POSTAL ORDER	ADFILLPPUUY	FULLY PAID-UP
ADELOPPPSTY	STOPPED PLAY	ADFILNOPRST	STRIP OF LAND
ADELOPPRSUU	DUAL PURPOSE	ADFILORSTTU	TRAIL OF DUST
	DUAL-PURPOSE	ADFINNOOPRU	IN FOR A POUND
ADELOPRRRSY	LORDS PRAYER	ADFINNOOSTU	FOUNDATIONS
ADELOPRRSWY	SWORDPLAYER	ADFINORSSTT	STANDS FOR IT
ADELOORRSUW	SQUARE WORLD	ADFKLOOOORW	LOOK FORWARD
ADELPQRSTUU	QUADRUPLETS	ADFLLOORRSU	FOUR DOLLARS
ADEMMMMNORSU	MEMORANDUMS	ADFLMNNOOOP	MAP OF LONDON
ADEMMNNORSU	DONNA SUMMER	ADFLNOOORSU	FOOLS AROUND
ADEMMNNOUYY	MAUNDY MONEY	ADFLOORSTWW	FLOW TOWARDS
ADEMMNORTYY	DYNAMOMETRY	ADFNOPRSSTU	STANDS UP FOR
ADEMNNOORWW	WONDER WOMAN	ADFOOORSUVY	SAVOURY FOOD
ADEMNNOPTWY	DOWN PAYMENT	ADFOOPPRRRW	PROP FORWARD
ADEMMNOSTVY	YVES MONTAND	ADFOPRRSTUW	PUTS FORWARD
ADEMOORSTVW	MOVE TOWARDS	ADGGGHIILNN	HANG GLIDING
ADENNNNOOTW	WENT ON AND ON	ADGGGINORTU	DRAGGING OUT
ADENNOORSSU	SOUND REASON	ADGGHIINNRW	DRAWING NIGH
ADENNOORTTU	DONE TO A TURN	ADGGHILMOTY	ALMIGHTY GOD
ADENNOPOSSS	ONE'S P'S AND Q'S	ADGGHINNNOW	HANGING DOWN
ADENNOPSTTU	PUTS AN END TO	ADGGHKLNOOO	HANG-DOG LOOK
ADENNORRSU	ROADRUNNERS	ADGGIIMNNOTZ	DOGMATIZING
ADENNORRSTU	TORN ASUNDER	ADGGIINNNSS	SINGING SAND
ADENNRRRSSU	RUNS ERRANDS	ADGGIINRSTU	GUIDING STAR
ADENNRSTTUY	TURNED NASTY	ADGGIKNORRW	GROWING DARK
ADENOORTTUU	OUT-AND-OUTER	ADGGIKNRSTU	TAKING DRUGS
ADENOPRRSSW	PRESS ONWARD	ADGGINNOORU	GOING AROUND
ADENOPRRSTT	TRANSPORTED	ADGGINNORSU	GAINS GROUND
ADENOPRSSSU	PASSES ROUND	ADGHHHIINPT	HIP AND THIGH
ADENORSSSUU	ARDUOUSNESS	ADGHHHORSTU	DASH THROUGH
ADENORSTTWW	WENT TOWARDS	ADGHHHORTTU	THOUGHT HARD
ADENORSTUUV	ADVENTUROUS	ADGHHIINRTT	HARD-HITTING
ADENPRSSTUU	PUTS ASUNDER		HITTING HARD
ADENRSTTUUY	NATURE STUDY	ADGHHILNOPT	DIPHTHONGAL
ADEORSSSTWW	WASTES WORDS	ADGHHINPRSU	PUSHING HARD
ADFFFFHNPUU	HUFF AND PUFF	ADGHHNNORTUW	HANDWROUGHT
ADFFGINNOST	STANDING OFF	ADGHHOORRTU	THROUGH ROAD
ADFFGNORSTU	GROUNDSTAFF	ADGHHOPRRYY	HYDROGRAPHY
ADFFHILLOTU	OLD FAITHFUL	ADGHIIINNNT	HANDING IT IN
ADFFHINOSST	STANDOFFISH	ADGHIILLNNW	WILLING HAND
ADFFIILNOSU	DIFFUSIONAL	ADGHIILMNNS	MISHANDLING
ADFFINORSUV	FINDS FAVOUR	ADGHIIMNNOS	ADMONISHING
ADFFNOORUUV	FOUND FAVOUR	ADGHIINNNNW	WINNING HAND
ADFGGHIILNT	FADING LIGHT	ADGHIINNOST	SAID NOTHING
ADFGHIINNPT	PATHFINDING	ADGHIINNRTW	HANDWRITING
ADFGHIINOOT	IN GOOD FAITH	ADGHIINRTWW	WITHDRAWING
ADFGHIINRTY	FRIDAY NIGHT	ADGHIIRRSSU	IRISH GUARDS
ADFGHILNOST	HOLDING FAST	ADGHIKNNOSW	SHAKING DOWN
ADFGIILLNSU	FUSILLADING	ADGHIKNORRW	WORKING HARD
ADFGIILMNNO	MANIFOLDING	ADGHILLNOOY	LONG HOLIDAY

ADGHILLNPRU	PULLING HARD
ADGHILNOOOY	GO ON HOLIDAY
ADGHILNOPSS	SPANISH GOLD
ADGHILNOSWY	HOLDING SWAY
ADGHIMNNOOR	DOING NO HARM
ADGHIMNNOTY	MONDAY NIGHT
ADGHINNNRRU	RUNNING HARD
ADGHINNPRSS	HANDSPRINGS
ADGHINNSTUY	SUNDAY NIGHT
ADGHINORSVW	HAVING WORDS
ADGHIOPRRTW	RAPID GROWTH
ADGHIOPRTTY	DITTOGRAPHY
ADGHNOPRTUY	HANG UP TO DRY
ADGHNORTUWY	NAUGHTY WORD
ADGIIILNQTU	LIQUIDATING
ADGIIINNNOT	INDIGNATION
ADGIIINNOTU	AUDITIONING
ADGIIINNRRV	DRIVING RAIN
ADGIIINNRST	DISTRAINING
ADGIIINPRSS	DISPRAISING
ADGIIINPSST	DISSIPATING
ADGIIINSTVY	VISITING DAY
ADGIILLMOSY	SIGMOIDALLY
ADGIILLNOSW	DISALLOWING
ADGIILMNNST	DISMANTLING
ADGIILMNRSY	DISARMINGLY
ADGIILMNSYY	DISMAYINGLY
ADGIILNNNOW	NAILING DOWN
ADGIILNNNTY	INDIGNANTLY
ADGIILNNSSW	WINDLASSING
ADGIILNTWZZ	DAZZLING WIT
ADGIILOORST	RADIOLOGIST
ADGIILOOSTU	AUDIOLOGIST
ADGIILOPRTY	PRODIGALITY
ADGIIMNNORS	RANDOMISING
ADGIIMNNORZ	RANDOMIZING
ADGIINORSTY	GRANDIOSITY
ADGIINPPTTU	PUTTING PAID
ADGIINPRSTV	DRIVING PAST
ADGIKKLORSU	KIRK DOUGLAS
ADGIKLLLNOT	TALKING DOLL
ADGIKLNNOTW	TALKING DOWN
ADGIKMNNORW	MARKING DOWN
ADGIKNNOORT	GORDIAN KNOT
ADGIKNNOPRS	KINGS PARDON
ADGILMNNNOO	MOON LANDING
ADGILNNOPWY	PLAYING DOWN
ADGILNNORUY	LYING AROUND
ADGILNOOPRS	PRODIGAL SON
ADGILNORSTW	DRAWING LOTS
ADGILNPQRUU	QUADRUPLING
ADGILNSTUWY	STUDYING LAW
ADGILOOQTUY	GOOD QUALITY
ADGILOORSUY	GLORIOUS DAY
ADGIMMNORSU	GOURMANDISM
ADGIMNNNORW	DROWNING MAN
ADGIMNNSTYY	MING DYNASTY
ADGIMNOORRW	DRAWING ROOM
ADGINNOORTU	GOT A ROUND IN
ADGINNOPSSW	PASSING DOWN
ADGINNORSSU	SINGS A ROUND
ADGINNORSTW	STARING DOWN
ADGINNOSTTU	OUTSTANDING
	STANDING OUT
ADGINNOSTWY	STAYING DOWN
ADGINOOOSTT	STOOD TO GAIN
ADGINOOPRST	GOOD IN PARTS
ADGINOPRRSU	PRISON GUARD
ADGINOPRSTT	TRADING POST
ADGINORSTUW	OUTWARD SIGN
ADGINRRSSTW	DRAWSTRINGS
ADGINRSTTUY	STUDYING ART
ADGIRSSSSUW	SWISS GUARDS
ADGKMNOOORW	GOOD WORKMAN
ADGLNOPRSUY	PLAYGROUNDS
ADGMNORSTUU	MOUNTS GUARD
ADGNNNOOTWW	TOWN AND GOWN
ADGNNOORRTU	RAN TO GROUND
ADGNNOORSUY	ANDROGYNOUS
ADGNNORRSUU	RUNS AGROUND
ADGNOOOPSST	DO NOT PASS GO
ADGOPRRSUWW	GROW UPWARDS
ADHHILLOSSW	SHALLOW DISH
ADHHIINNOPSS	HANDS ON HIPS
ADHHINNNORST	IN SHORTHAND
ADHHMNOOTTU	HAND TO MOUTH
ADHHOORRTXY	HYDROTHORAX
ADHIKKNRSWY	DRANK WHISKY
ADHIKLNOSTU	THINKS ALOUD
ADHILLLNORW	ROWLAND HILL
ADHILNNORST	NORTH ISLAND
ADHILNOSSTU	SOUTH ISLAND
ADHIMORRTUU	RUMOUR HAD IT
ADHINOOORTT	ORTHODONTIA
ADHINOSSTUX	SIX THOUSAND
ADHIOPRTTTU	HARD PUT TO IT
ADHJKNNOOOY	JOHN AND YOKO
ADHLLNOOPPY	PHYLLOPODAN
ADHLLNPPSUU	PUSH AND PULL
ADHLNOPSSSW	SPLASHDOWNS
ADHNOOSTTUW	TWO THOUSAND
ADHOORSTUWW	OUTWARD SHOW
ADIIILNOOST	IDOLISATION
ADIIILNOOTZ	IDOLIZATION
ADIIILNOQTU	LIQUIDATION
ADIIIMNORTT	INTIMIDATOR
ADIIIMOSSTT	MASTOIDITIS
ADIIINNOSTV	DIVINATIONS
ADIIINOPSST	DISSIPATION
ADIILLMNOOT	TOIL AND MOIL
ADIILLNOQRU	QUADRILLION
ADIILLNSTTW	IT WILL STAND
ADIILMOOSSY	AMYLOIDOSIS
ADIILMOPSTT	DIPLOMATIST
ADIILMORRRY	DAILY MIRROR
ADIILNOPRTZ	LIZARD POINT
ADIILNPPSTU	PLAIN STUPID
ADIILNPSTUY	DISPLAY UNIT
ADIILOQRSTU	LIQUIDATORS
ADIIMNNOOSS	NO ADMISSION
ADIIMNNOOST	ADMONITIONS
ADIIMNOOPRT	RAPID MOTION
ADIIMORSTUU	AUDITORIUMS
ADIINNOORST	ORDINATIONS
ADIINOPPSST	DISAPPOINTS
ADIINOPSTTU	DISPUTATION
ADIINOSSSSU	DISSUASIONS
ADIIOOPRSUV	AVOIRDUPOIS
ADIIOPSTTUY	AUDIO TYPIST
ADIJNNOSTUY	SUNDAY JOINT
ADILLMNOUWW	WALLOW IN MUD
ADILLNSSSTT	STANDS STILL
	STANDSTILLS
ADILMNNOPTW	PILTDOWN MAN
ADILNNORTWY	TINY ROWLAND
ADILNNOSSTY	DISSONANTLY
ADILNNOSTUU	UNDULATIONS
ADILOOSSTWW	SOW WILD OATS
ADILOSSSUUY	ASSIDUOUSLY
ADIMNOPSTUW	STUPID WOMAN
ADIMNOSSTWW	WANTS WISDOM
ADINNOPSSTT	STANDPOINTS

ADINNOSSTTW	STANDS TO WIN	AEEEFHNOPST	OPEN THE SAFE
ADINOOPRSST	ADSORPTIONS	AEEEFHORSVY	HAVE EYES FOR
	POISON DARTS	AEEEFILLNRT	ETERNAL LIFE
ADINOORSSTY	STAY INDOORS	AEEEFILNRRT	REFERENTIAL
ADINOPRSTUW	PUTS IN A WORD	AEEEFKLPRSY	SPEAK FREELY
ADKLNOOORSU	LOOKS AROUND	AEEEFKOPRST	FREE TO SPEAK
ADKMMORRSWY	MARK MY WORDS	AEEEFLLNNTT	FLANNELETTE
ADLLMORSSSW	SMALLSWORDS	AEEEFLNOSST	SEAT ONESELF
ADLLNOOPRTY	DOLLY PARTON	AEEEFLNOSSV	SAVE ONESELF
ADLLNOOSSTT	LOTS AND LOTS	AEEEFLNOSWY	FEEL ONES WAY
ADLMNOORTUW	MORTAL WOUND	AEEEFLRSSTU	FEATURELESS
ADLNOOPRSUY	POLYANDROUS	AEEEFNOPSTT	TAP ONES FEET
ADLNOOPRSWY	PLAY ON WORDS	AEEEFNRRSST	TRANSFEREES
ADLOORRTWWW	WORLD WAR TWO	AEEEGGILNOS	GENEALOGIES
ADMNNNOORUY	DAMON RUNYON	AEEEGGILNRT	TEENAGE GIRL
ADMNPRSSTUW	DRAWN STUMPS	AEEEGGIRSTV	SEGREGATIVE
ADMOOPPRSTT	TOM STOPPARD	AEEEGGMNNST	ENGAGEMENTS
ADMPRSSSTUW	DRAWS STUMPS	AEEEGGNNRRT	GRETNA GREEN
ADNNNOOSSTT	TONS AND TONS	AEEEGGRRRTT	GREAT REGRET
ADNNORRSTUU	TURNS AROUND	AEEEGHIKNNR	KEEN HEARING
ADNNORSSTTU	TOSS AND TURN	AEEEGHLMOST	LOSE THE GAME
ADNOORRSSWW	ROWS AND ROWS	AEEEGHLPRRT	TELEGRAPHER
ADNOOORSUUYY	YOU AND YOUNG	AEEEGHNOPTT	OPEN THE GATE
AEEEEFGILPR	LIFE PEERAGE	AEEEGHNPRTW	GREAT NEPHEW
AEEEEFGLNOS	FEEL ONE'S AGE		GREAT-NEPHEW
AEEEEFHHLTT	FEEL THE HEAT	AEEEGHNRSTV	THE AVENGERS
AEEEEFNORYY	EYE FOR AN EYE	AEEEGHRRSTV	HAVE REGRETS
AEEEEGKMPRS	GAMEKEEPERS	AEEEGHRSTTT	THE GREATEST
AEEEEGKPRST	GATEKEEPERS	AEEEGHSSTTT	SET THE STAGE
AEEEEGMRRSV	GAME RESERVE	AEEEGHSTTTT	GET THE TASTE
AEEEEGNRRST	REGENERATES	AEEEGIKKNNV	KEVIN KEEGAN
AEEEEGRRRSV	REVERSE GEAR	AEEEGILMMRR	LAMMERGEIER
AEEEEHILRST	ETHEREALISE	AEEEGILMNNV	EVENING MEAL
AEEEEHILRTZ	ETHEREALIZE	AEEEGILMNRS	SEEMING REAL
AEEEEHILRTTT	LEATHERETTE	AEEEGILNNTV	LATE EVENING
AEEEEIKMMNS	MAKE ENEMIES	AEEEGILNRRS	GENERALISER
AEEEEJLMSST	LESE MAJESTE	AEEEGILNRRZ	GENERALIZER
AEEEEKNNOPY	KEEP AN EYE ON	AEEEGILNRSS	GENERALISES
AEEEELNRSVY	ELEVEN YEARS	AEEEGILNRSZ	GENERALIZES
AEEEELPRRSS	PRE-RELEASES	AEEEGILNRVW	GENERAL VIEW
AEEEEMRRSTV	RESERVE TEAM	AEEEGILNSSV	EVANGELISES
AEEEENRSVWY	NEW YEARS EVE	AEEEGILNSUV	EIGENVALUES
AEEEEOSTWYY	SAW EYE TO EYE	AEEEGILNSVZ	EVANGELIZES
AEEEEPRRSTV	PERSEVERATE	AEEEGIMNNRT	IN AGREEMENT
AEEEFFGILNS	FEELING SAFE	AEEEGIMNNST	STEAM ENGINE
AEEEFFHINRT	FINE FEATHER	AEEEGIMNSST	METAGENESIS
AEEEFFILLOS	LEASE OF LIFE	AEEEGINPRRT	PEREGRINATE
AEEEFFLOPPT	TOFFEE APPLE	AEEEGKLOPRS	GOALKEEPERS
	TOFFEE-APPLE	AEEEGKRSTTU	GREEK STATUE
AEEEFFNRRST	TRANSFER FEE	AEEEGLLNRRU	GENERAL RULE
AEEEFGGIMOR	GEORGIE FAME	AEEEGLMNNRT	ENLARGEMENT
AEEEFGIKNPS	KEEPING SAFE	AEEEGLNSSSS	AGELESSNESS
	SAFE KEEPING	AEEEGLPRSTT	LETTERS PAGE
	SAFEKEEPING	AEEEGNORRRT	REGENERATOR
AEEEFGILLTV	VILLAGE FETE	AEEEHHLORST	SHOE LEATHER
AEEEFGILNVW	GAVE NEW LIFE	AEEEHHOTTVV	HAVE THE VOTE
AEEEFGILRRT	GREAT RELIEF	AEEEHHRRSTT	THREE HEARTS
AEEEFGIRRRT	REFRIGERATE	AEEEHIKLTTV	TAKE THE VEIL
AEEEFGKNRTU	TAKEN REFUGE	AEEEHIKRSTT	TAKE THE RISE
AEEEFGKRSTU	TAKES REFUGE	AEEEHIKTTVW	TAKE THE VIEW
AEEEFGLLNRX	REFLEX ANGLE	AEEEHILNNPT	ELEPHANTINE
AEEEFGLNOST	FELT ONE'S AGE	AEEEHILRTTV	LIVE THEATRE
AEEEFGLNRST	FEEL STRANGE	AEEEHILRTTY	ETHEREALITY
AEEEFGOPRST	POSTAGE FREE	AEEEHIMNRTT	MATE IN THREE
AEEEFHHLTTT	FELT THE HEAT	AEEEHINNSTT	INTENSE HEAT
AEEEFHILNPT	FEEL THE PAIN	AEEEHINSTTZ	ANESTHETIZE
AEEEFHINRRT	HEREINAFTER	AEEEHIOSSST	TESSIE O'SHEA
AEEEFHINRTW	FINE WEATHER	AEEEHIRSTWW	WEATHER-WISE
AEEEFHLMNOS	FEEL NO SHAME	AEEEHKLRSTT	TAKE SHELTER
AEEEFHLMOST	FEELS AT HOME	AEEEHKMNSTW	MAKE THE NEWS
AEEEFHMPRRS	SHEEP FARMER	AEEEHKMOOPW	MAKE WHOOPEE

AEEEHKNRSTV	THREE KNAVES	AEEELNPRSTT	TERNEPLATES
AEEEHKSTTTT	TAKE THE TEST	AEEELNRRSTT	ETERNAL REST
AEEEHLLLTTT	TELL THE TALE	AEEELNRSTTT	SENT A LETTER
AEEEHLLMPRY	EPHEMERALLY	AEEELPQRSTU	PLATERESQUE
AEEEHLLORST	LEATHER SOLE	AEEELPRTTTY	TYPE A LETTER
AEEEHLMMOTT	HAM OMELETTE	AEEELRSTVWY	TWELVE YEARS
AEEEHLMNOOV	HOME ON LEAVE	AEEEMMNORST	ANEMOMETERS
AEEEHLMPPRT	PAMPHLETEER	AEEEMMNPRTT	TEMPERAMENT
AEEEHLNOSST	AT ONES HEELS	AEEEMMNRSTU	MEASUREMENT
AEEEHLNPTTT	PENTATHLETE	AEEEMMNRTTT	ENTREATMENT
AEEEHLNRRTY	NEARLY THERE	AEEEMNOSSSW	AWESOMENESS
AEEEHLRSTWW	WATERWHEELS	AEEEMNPRSTT	PENTAMETERS
AEEEHMRSTVY	THE VERY SAME	AEEEMNRRSTU	REMUNERATES
AEEEHNNORRW	NOWHERE NEAR	AEEEMNRSTTT	RESTATEMENT
AEEEHNNPRTY	THREE A PENNY	AEEEMPRRTTU	TEMPERATURE
AEEEHNOSSTU	SENATE HOUSE	AEEEMQRRSTU	SQUARE METRE
AEEEHNPRSST	PARENTHESES	AEEEMRRRSVY	ARMY RESERVE
AEEEHNRRSTT	THREATENERS	AEEEMRRSTTT	TETRAMETERS
AEEEHNRSSTV	SEVEN HEARTS	AEEENNOSSWY	SEEN ONE'S WAY
AEEEHORRTUY	THERE YOU ARE	AEEENNRSSST	EARNESTNESS
AEEEHPRRSTU	SUPERHEATER	AEEENORSSSU	USE ONES EARS
AEEEHRSSTTW	SWEETHEARTS	AEEENOSSSWY	SEES ONE'S WAY
AEEEIILNRRT	INERTIA REEL	AEEENPSSTVX	VAST EXPENSE
AEEEIIRRTTV	REITERATIVE	AEEENRSSSTU	AUSTERENESS
AEEEILLMPSS	SMILE PLEASE	AEEEPPRRSTT	PERPETRATES
AEEEILMMNNT	MAIN ELEMENT	AEEEPPRSTTU	PERPETUATES
AEEEILMOTTV	LEAVE IT TO ME	AEEEQRSSTTU	SEQUESTRATE
	TIME TO LEAVE	AEEFFGHLLTW	FLEW THE FLAG
AEEEILNNRST	ELSIE TANNER	AEEFFGHOSTT	OFF THE STAGE
AEEEILNORRS	SIERRA LEONE	AEEFFGIISWX	WAX EFFIGIES
AEEEILNRRTT	INTERRELATE	AEEFFGIRSTU	REFUSE A GIFT
AEEEILNRRTV	REVERENTIAL	AEEFFGORRTT	GREAT EFFORT
AEEEILNRSTV	INTERLEAVES	AEEFFGRSTTU	SUFFRAGETTE
AEEEILNRSTX	EXTERNALISE	AEEFFHHLOST	OFF THE LEASH
AEEEILNRTXZ	EXTERNALIZE	AEEFFHINRST	FANS THE FIRE
AEEEILPQSTU	QUIET PLEASE	AEEFFHINTUV	FIFTH AVENUE
AEEEILPRRTT	PRELITERATE	AEEFFHLLRTU	FULL FEATHER
AEEEIMMRSTU	MEASURE TIME	AEEFFHMORRR	FAR FROM HERE
AEEEIMNNNNT	NEMERTINEAN	AEEFFHORRST	FOREFATHERS
AEEEIMNPRTT	INTEMPERATE	AEEFFIKMOTT	TAKE TIME OFF
AEEEIMNPRTX	EXTREME PAIN	AEEFFILMRTU	FEATURE FILM
AEEEIMNRSTT	EASTERN TIME	AEEFFILORTW	WATER OF LIFE
AEEEIMNRTTX	EXTERMINATE	AEEFFIMRRSW	FARMERS WIFE
AEEEIMNRTUV	ENUMERATIVE	AEEFFLMOSTT	LET OFF STEAM
AEEEIMPRSTT	EMPIRE STATE	AEEFFLNOSTV	FLEET OF VANS
AEEEINNRRTT	ENTERTAINER	AEEFFLNRSSU	FEARFULNESS
AEEEINOPRSU	EUROPEANISE	AEEFFLNSSTU	FATEFULNESS
AEEEINOPRUZ	EUROPEANIZE	AEEFFORRSST	REAFFORESTS
AEEEINORTVX	EXONERATIVE	AEEFGGGLLTU	LEFT LUGGAGE
AEEEINPRTTV	PENETRATIVE		LEFT-LUGGAGE
AEEEINRRSVW	SWANEE RIVER	AEEFGHHHIRT	HIGH FEATHER
AEEEINRSTVW	INTERWEAVES	AEEFGHLMOOP	GLEAM OF HOPE
AEEEISNSSVVO	EVASIVENESS	AEEFGHLNNOS	HANG ONESELF
AEEEJKRRRST	TEARJERKERS	AEEFGHORRST	FOREGATHERS
AEEEJNRSTUV	REJUVENATES	AEEFGHORRTT	HETEROGRAFT
AEEEKLLOSTX	EXOSKELETAL	AEEFGIILLLV	VILLAGE LIFE
AEEEKLLPRSW	SLEEPWALKER	AEEFGIILLNP	FEELING PAIN
AEEEKLNNORT	KEEN TO LEARN	AEEFGIIMNRS	SEEMING FAIR
AEEEKLPPRWY	WEEKLY PAPER	AEEFGIKNPRR	FREE PARKING
AEEEKLPRRTW	PETER WALKER	AEEFGILLNSS	SELF-SEALING
AEEEKNNOPTY	KEPT AN EYE ON	AEEFGILLNYZ	FEELING LAZY
AEEEKPSSSTW	SWEEPSTAKES	AEEFGILMNRW	FEELING WARM
AEEELLLMNTY	ELEMENTALLY	AEEFGILMRRS	FARMER GILES
AEEELLORTTT	TEETOTALLER	AEEFGILNPRT	FINGERPLATE
AEEELLSSSTT	TESSELLATES	AEEFGIMNRRT	FERRIMAGNET
AEEELMNNSTV	ENSLAVEMENT	AEEFGINRRRT	REFRIGERANT
AEEELMPRTTY	TEMPERATELY	AEEFGLLLNRU	FULL GENERAL
AEEELMRSSSU	MEASURELESS	AEEFGLLMORR	LEGAL REFORM
AEEELNNRSST	ETERNALNESS	AEEFGLNRSTT	FELT STRANGE
AEEELNOPRTT	OPEN A LETTER	AEEFGOOPRRS	GREASEPROOF
AEEELNPQRUY	PEARLY QUEEN	AEEFHHILMTT	HALF THE TIME

AEEFHHLLSTY	HEAL THYSELF	AEEFLLOORST	FOR ALL TO SEE
AEEFHHORSTU	HOUSEFATHER	AEEFLLORRST	FORESTALLER
AEEFHIKLSSW	FLESH IS WEAK	AEEFLLOTTTW	TWO-FEET TALL
AEEFHIKLTTT	TAKE THE LIFT	AEEFLLRRTTU	FULL RETREAT
AEEFHIKNOTW	IN THE WAKE OF	AEEFLMNOPRR	PENAL REFORM
AEEFHILLMOT	HELL OF A TIME	AEEFLMNORUV	ROMAN-FLEUVE
AEEFHILNNPS	HALFPENNIES	AEEFLMRSSTY	SELF-MASTERY
AEEFHILNORT	LIFE ON EARTH	AEEFLNOOSSU	USE ONES LOAF
AEEFHILNPTT	FELT THE PAIN	AEEFLNOSTWY	FELT ONE'S WAY
AEEFHILOPRS	PAIR OF HEELS	AEEFLNPRRUY	FUNERAL PYRE
AEEFHILSTTT	FAIL THE TEST	AEEFLNRSSTU	TEARFULNESS
AEEFHIMNNOT	IN THE NAME OF	AEEFLOPRRST	FALSE REPORT
AEEFHINRSTT	THE FINE ARTS	AEEFLOPRRSU	FOR PLEASURE
AEEFHKNOPRS	PHONE FREAKS	AEEFLORRSTV	LAST FOR EVER
AEEFHLLMNST	MANTELSHELF	AEEFLRRSSTT	SELF STARTER
AEEFHLLMOSS	HELL OF A MESS	AEEFMNOPRTU	MAN OF REPUTE
AEEFHLLORTT	FELL TO EARTH	AEEFMNORRSY	FREEMASONRY
AEEFHLMNOST	FELT NO SHAME	AEEFMOOPPRU	MAP OF EUROPE
AEEFHLNSSTU	HATEFULNESS	AEEFMOQRSUU	FORMS A QUEUE
AEEFHLOPPRS	LEAFHOPPERS	AEEFMORRSTY	TERM OF YEARS
AEEFHLORSTT	LAST OF THREE	AEEFNNOPRSS	PROFANENESS
AEEFHLORTUW	FOUL WEATHER	AEEFNOPSSTW	SPATE OF NEWS
AEEFHMORSTT	FATHOMETERS	AEEFNORRSVW	WAR OF NERVES
	FROM THE EAST	AEEFNORRTWZ	FROZEN WATER
AEEFHNORSTT	TEN OF HEARTS	AEEFNRRRRST	TRANSFERRER
AEEFHNORSTV	HAVEN OF REST	AEEFNRSSTTU	AFTER SUNSET
AEEFIIIPRRR	PRAIRIE FIRE	AEEFOPRSTUY	REFUSE TO PAY
AEEFIILLNRY	EARLY IN LIFE	AEEFOQRRRTU	FOREQUARTER
AEEFIILNNRT	INFERENTIAL	AEEFPPRRSTU	AFTER SUPPER
AEEFIILNOPR	OPEN-AIR LIFE	AEEGGGINRST	SEGREGATING
AEEFIILNRSV	LIVES IN FEAR	AEEGGHHIRSW	HIGHER WAGES
AEEFIILOTVX	EXFOLIATIVE	AEEGGHHIRTT	GREAT HEIGHT
AEEFIILPRTV	PRIVATE LIFE	AEEGGHHNSTT	GETS THE HANG
AEEFIJLOSUW	JEALOUS WIFE	AEEGGHINSTV	GAVE THE SIGN
AEEFIKLLSTT	FILLET STEAK	AEEGGHIRTTW	GREAT WEIGHT
AEEFILLLNUV	FELL IN VALUE	AEEGGHOPRRS	GEOGRAPHERS
AEEFILLNOST	ATE ONE'S FILL	AEEGGIILNSY	LAYING SIEGE
	EAT ONES FILL	AEEGGIINORS	SEIGNIORAGE
AEEFILLNOTT	LEFT IT ALONE	AEEGGIINRRT	RETIRING AGE
AEEFILLNPRU	FUNERAL PILE	AEEGGIKLNOP	GOALKEEPING
AEEFILLNRST	SELF-RELIANT		KEEPING GOAL
AEEFILLNRVY	ALL VERY FINE	AEEGGILNOST	GENEALOGIST
AEEFILLORVY	FIRE A VOLLEY	AEEGGILNPUV	GIVEN A LEG UP
AEEFILLSTTX	SIX FEET TALL	AEEGGILNRRS	GLENGARRIES
AEEFILMOPST	LAPSE OF TIME	AEEGGILPSUV	GIVES A LEG UP
AEEFILMOSTT	FAILS TO MEET	AEEGGINORST	SAINT GEORGE
AEEFILOPRRT	PROLIFERATE		SEGREGATION
AEEFILOPSUY	IF YOU PLEASE	AEEGGINORTT	GET INTO GEAR
AEEFILPPRRT	FILTER PAPER	AEEGGINRRST	GREAT SINGER
AEEFIMNOSST	MANIFESTOES	AEEGGIRRTTU	REGURGITATE
AEEFIMNRRST	FREEMARTINS	AEEGGLLNOSS	ALL ONE'S EGGS
AEEFIMOPRRT	IMPERFORATE	AEEGGLOPRTU	PETROL GAUGE
AEEFIMORRTV	REFORMATIVE	AEEGGNOOSTT	GET ONES GOAT
AEEFIMOSTTW	WASTE OF TIME	AEEGGNORRRS	GREER GARSON
AEEFINNOPSS	SENSE OF PAIN	AEEGGNORSSU	SUSAN GEORGE
AEEFINOPSTV	FIVE PAST ONE	AEEGHHHISST	THE HIGH SEAS
AEEFINPRSTZ	ZIP FASTENER	AEEGHHILQTU	EQUAL HEIGHT
AEEFINPSTTV	FIVE PAST TEN	AEEGHHITVWY	HEAVY WEIGHT
	TEN PAST FIVE		HEAVYWEIGHT
AEEFINRRSST	FRATERNISES	AEEGHHMPTUV	GAVE THE HUMP
AEEFINRRSTU	FUNERARIEST	AEEGHHPSTUV	GAVE THE PUSH
AEEFINRRSTZ	FRATERNIZES	AEEGHHSTTTU	SHUT THE GATE
AEEFJNORSUY	SAFE JOURNEY	AEEGHIILMNS	HEGELIANISM
AEEFJOORRVY	A JOY FOREVER	AEEGHIIPPRS	EPIGRAPHIES
AEEFJORSSTW	JAR OF SWEETS	AEEGHIKLLNU	KEELHAULING
AEEFKLNNOTU	TAKEN ON FUEL	AEEGHIKMSTW	MAKEWEIGHTS
AEEFKLNOSTU	TAKES ON FUEL	AEEGHIKOTVY	GIVE THE OKAY
AEEFKLNSSUW	WAKEFULNESS	AEEGHILLNRT	HEARING TELL
AEEFKLORRWW	WELFARE WORK	AEEGHILMNOV	LEAVING HOME
AEEFLLMRSUU	FULL MEASURE	AEEGHILMPTV	GIVE THE PALM
AEEFLLNNOST	FONTANELLES	AEEGHILNPRS	GENERALSHIP

AEEGHILNPSS	SINGLE-PHASE
AEEGHILPSTV	GAVE THE SLIP
AEEGHIMMORT	MOTHER IMAGE
AEEGHIMNSTW	WINS THE GAME
AEEGHIMPSTU	THE GAME IS UP
AEEGHINNRTT	THREATENING
AEEGHINNSSV	HAVING SENSE
AEEGHINORTV	OVERHEATING
AEEGHINORWY	GONE HAYWIRE
AEEGHINOSSW	SEEING A SHOW
AEEGHINOSTU	EATING HOUSE
AEEGHINRSTY	STAYING HERE
AEEGHINTTWY	GET IN THE WAY
AEEGHIORSWY	GOES HAYWIRE
AEEGHIPPRTW	PAPERWEIGHT
AEEGHIRSSTT	SEE STRAIGHT
AEEGHIRSTYY	EIGHTY YEARS
AEEGHKNNRSS	GREENSHANKS
AEEGHKOSTTY	GETS THE OKAY
AEEGHLLLNSS	HELLS ANGELS
AEEGHLLNOOP	ALL HOPE GONE
AEEGHLLORTT	ALL TOGETHER
AEEGHLLOTUV	ALL THE VOGUE
AEEGHLMOSTT	LOST THE GAME
AEEGHLNNPTU	ELEPHANT GUN
AEEGHLNOSWW	WAGON WHEELS
AEEGHLNSTVW	WAVELENGTHS
AEEGHLNUVWY	EVELYN WAUGH
AEEGHLORRRU	REGULAR HERO
AEEGHLRRRSY	LARGE SHERRY
AEEGHLRRSTU	SLAUGHTERER
AEEGHLRTUWY	UGLY WEATHER
AEEGHMNOOST	HOMOGENATES
AEEGHMOPTTY	GAMETOPHYTE
AEEGHNNOPTT	THE PENTAGON
AEEGHNOORTT	GONE TO EARTH
AEEGHNOOSSW	SHOW ONES AGE
AEEGHNPRTTU	TURN THE PAGE
AEEGHOORSTT	GOES TO EARTH
AEEGHORRSST	GATHER ROSES
AEEGHOSTTTT	GOT THE TASTE
AEEGIIKLNRT	GRANITELIKE
AEEGIIKNPTT	KEEPING AT IT
AEEGIIKNPTW	KEEP WAITING
AEEGIILLLNT	TELLING A LIE
AEEGIILLNST	SEEING IT ALL
AEEGIILLSTV	LEGISLATIVE
AEEGIILLTTU	AIGUILLETTE
AEEGIILLTTV	GIVE A LITTLE
AEEGIILMSTT	LEGITIMATES
AEEGIILNNOR	LEGIONAIRE
AEEGIILNORS	LEGIONARIES
	REGIONALISE
AEEGIILNORZ	REGIONALIZE
AEEGIILOOST	AETIOLOGIES
AEEGIIMNNRT	TEEMING RAIN
AEEGIIMNRTV	GERMINATIVE
AEEGIINNRVW	WINE VINEGAR
AEEGIINNSTY	GAY NINETIES
AEEGIINNTVW	VINTAGE WINE
AEEGIINPRSV	GIVEN PRAISE
AEEGIINRRTT	REITERATING
AEEGIINRTTV	INTEGRATIVE
	VINAIGRETTE
AEEGIINSTTV	INVESTIGATE
AEEGIIPRSSV	GIVES PRAISE
AEEGIIRSTTV	GIVE IT A REST
AEEGIJKNRRT	TEAR-JERKING
AEEGIKMNNSS	MAKING SENSE
AEEGIKMNPRW	KEEPING WARM
AEEGILLLLNT	LITTLE ANGEL

AEEGILLMNNP	EMPANELLING
AEEGILLMNNW	MEANING WELL
	WELL-MEANING
AEEGILLNNTY	INELEGANTLY
AEEGILLNOSV	GIVE ONES ALL
AEEGILLNPSY	LYING ASLEEP
AEEGILLNTTY	LEGAL ENTITY
AEEGILLORRS	ALLEGORISER
AEEGILLORRZ	ALLEGORIZER
AEEGILLORSS	ALLEGORISES
AEEGILLORSZ	ALLEGORIZES
AEEGILLRSTU	LEGISLATURE
AEEGILMNNRT	REALIGNMENT
AEEGILMNNSS	MEANINGLESS
AEEGILMNRST	REGIMENTALS
AEEGILNNOOT	GONE IT ALONE
AEEGILNNOPT	OPENING LATE
AEEGILNNOPV	LEAVING OPEN
AEEGILNNORV	LEANING OVER
AEEGILNNOST	GETS A LINE ON
AEEGILNNOSY	LOSING AN EYE
AEEGILNOOST	GOES IT ALONE
AEEGILNOPRV	LEAPING OVER
AEEGILNORTV	VIOLENT RAGE
AEEGILNORVV	LEAVING OVER
AEEGILNOSSV	GIVE A LESSON
AEEGILNRSST	GENERALISTS
AEEGILNRSTV	EVERLASTING
AEEGILNRTVY	VITAL ENERGY
AEEGILNSSSW	WINEGLASSES
AEEGILNSSTT	SINGLE STATE
AEEGILNSSTV	EVANGELISTS
AEEGILOSSTY	LAYS SEIGE TO
AEEGILSSTTV	LAST VESTIGE
AEEGIMMNSST	MASS MEETING
AEEGIMMOOST	SOME TIME AGO
AEEGIMNNOTT	GET A MENTION
AEEGIMNNRTU	ENUMERATING
	TRUE MEANING
AEEGIMNNRUV	MANEUVERING
AEEGIMNOTTW	WITENAGEMOT
AEEGIMNPRST	IMPREGNATES
AEEGIMNSSST	GETS IN A MESS
AEEGIMNSSTU	MUTAGENESIS
AEEGIMRRSTU	MARGUERITES
AEEGIMRRSTV	GRAVIMETERS
AEEGIMSSTTU	GUESSTIMATE
AEEGINNOPRT	TEARING OPEN
AEEGINNORST	GENERATIONS
AEEGINNORTX	EXONERATING
AEEGINNPRTT	PENETRATING
AEEGINNRSTV	EVENING STAR
AEEGINNTTUV	EVENTUATING
AEEGINNTTUX	EXTENUATING
AEEGINOPRRS	OPERA SINGER
AEEGINORRTT	INTERROGATE
AEEGINRSSST	SEEING STARS
AEEGINSSTTW	GETS IN A STEW
AEEGIOPRRTV	PREROGATIVE
AEEGIORRTUV	GIVE QUARTER
AEEGKLLLNOW	ALL WEEK LONG
AEEGKLNOOOS	LOOK ONES AGE
AEEGKMNOPRS	SPOKE GERMAN
AEEGKNPRRST	REGENTS PARK
AEEGKORSSWW	SEWAGE WORKS
AEEGLLLLOSW	ALL GOES WELL
AEEGLLMNNTY	GENTLEMANLY
AEEGLLMORUV	LARGE VOLUME
AEEGLLMRRSW	GREW SMALLER
AEEGLLOPSWY	YELLOW PAGES
AEEGLMNNNOT	NO GENTLEMAN

AEEGLMNNOTW	GENTLEWOMAN
AEEGLMNOOPR	PROLEGOMENA
AEEGLMNNORSU	LONG MEASURE
AEEGLNNOPRU	ENLARGE UPON
AEEGLNOOORSS	LOSE ONE'S RAG
AEEGLNOPRST	GENERAL POST
AEEGLNOPSSW	SWEEPS ALONG
AEEGLNORRSY	SOLAR ENERGY
AEEGLNORSTU	OUTGENERALS
AEEGLNOSSSV	GAVE LESSONS
AEEGLORSTUV	TRAVELOGUES
AEEGLPRSTUY	GETS UP EARLY
AEEGMNNOOSW	ONE'S OWN GAME
AEEGMNOORTV	MOVE TO ANGER
AEEGMNOOSTV	GETS A MOVE ON
AEEGMNRSTWY	WEST GERMANY
AEEGMNRTTUY	TEGUMENTARY
AEEGMPSSTTU	GETS UP STEAM
AEEGNNOOSWY	GONE ONE'S WAY
AEEGNNRSSST	STRANGENESS
AEEGNOOORRTV	GOVERNORATE
AEEGNOOSSTT	GET ONE'S OATS
AEEGNOOSSWY	GOES ONE'S WAY
AEEGNOOSTTW	GONE TO WASTE
AEEGNOPRSTT	POSTERN GATE
	TOP SERGEANT
AEEGNORRRSV	RANGE ROVERS
AEEGNORSSTV	GRAVESTONES
AEEGNOSSSSU	GASEOUSNESS
AEEGNRRSTVY	VERY STRANGE
AEEGOOSSTTW	GOES TO WASTE
AEEGOPRRSTT	REPORT STAGE
AEEHHHLLTTW	WHAT THE HELL
AEEHHIKNTTT	TAKE THE HINT
AEEHHILLLTW	ALL THE WHILE
AEEHHILNSST	HEALTHINESS
AEEHHILRTWW	WHEREWITHAL
AEEHHINSSTW	WIN THE ASHES
AEEHHINTTTZ	AT THE ZENITH
AEEHHIRSTWW	WHITEWASHER
AEEHHISSTWW	WHITEWASHES
AEEHHLLNORT	HELL ON EARTH
AEEHHLOPRTY	PLAY THE HERO
AEEHHMMMORS	HAMMERS HOME
AEEHHMNORTT	THE OTHER MAN
AEEHHMNOSTT	ON THE THAMES
AEEHHMNTTTY	MAY THE TENTH
AEEHHMORRTT	MOTHER EARTH
AEEHHMORSTV	HARVEST HOME
AEEHHMPSTTU	UP THE THAMES
AEEHHNNOPTT	THE PANTHEON
AEEHHNOPPTT	TAP THE PHONE
AEEHHNORSTT	HEARTHSTONE
AEEHHNOSSTW	WON THE ASHES
AEEHHNOSTTV	THE HAVE-NOTS
AEEHHORSTTW	THEATRE SHOW
AEEHHPRRSSU	SHARE-PUSHER
AEEHIIKNSST	KINESTHESIA
AEEHIILNRTT	LET IN THE AIR
AEEHIINNOTV	HAVE IT IN ONE
AEEHIKKLSTT	TAKE THE SILK
AEEHIKLLLRW	KILLER WHALE
AEEHIKLLPTT	TAKE THE PILL
AEEHIKLMRRS	SHAREMILKER
AEEHIKMNRTT	IN THE MARKET
AEEHIKNSTTV	HAVE KITTENS
AEEHIKPPRSS	SPEAKERSHIP
AEEHIKPSSTT	TAKE THE PISS
AEEHILLMNNS	IN HELL'S NAME
AEEHILLNTVY	IN THE VALLEY
AEEHILLPRTV	PRIVATE HELL

AEEHILLRTTT	AT THE TILLER
AEEHILMPRST	SIMPLE HEART
AEEHILNPPRS	PLANISPHERE
AEEHILNPSSS	SHAPELINESS
AEEHILNPSTT	TAPS THE LINE
AEEHILNRSST	EARTHLINESS
AEEHILNSSTW	WEALTHINESS
AEEHILPSTTT	TELEPATHIST
AEEHILRSSTW	RESTS AWHILE
AEEHILSSTTT	STEALTHIEST
AEEHIMNNNRT	THE INNER MAN
AEEHIMNORTT	ANOTHER TIME
AEEHIMNSTTY	AMETHYSTINE
AEEHIMOQTTU	QUITE AT HOME
AEEHIMPSSTT	PASS THE TIME
AEEHIMRRSTV	RIVER THAMES
AEEHIMRSTTV	HARVEST TIME
AEEHINNORST	IN ONES HEART
AEEHINNOSST	IN THE OCEAON
AEEHINORSTV	HAVE IN STORE
AEEHINPPRST	IN THE PAPERS
AEEHINPRRTU	PURE IN HEART
AEEHINPRSST	INTERPHASES
	PARENTHESIS
AEEHINRTWWY	WENT HAYWIRE
AEEHINSSTTT	ANESTHETIST
	IN THE STATES
AEEHIOOPSST	APOTHEOSISE
AEEHIOOPSTZ	APOTHEOSIZE
AEEHIORTTVX	EXHORTATIVE
AEEHIPPPRTY	PAY THE PIPER
AEEHIPPRRSS	PERIPHRASES
AEEHIPPSTUX	EXHAUST PIPE
AEEHIQRSTUW	WHITE SQUARE
AEEHIRSSSSU	ISSUE SHARES
AEEHJMSSTTU	JUST THE SAME
AEEHKLPSSSW	SPEAKS WELSH
AEEHKMNORTT	ON THE MARKET
AEEHKMORRTV	OVER THE MARK
AEEHKMORSVY	HEAVY SMOKER
AEEHKMPRRTY	HYPERMARKET
AEEHKNNOSVW	HEAVEN KNOWS
AEEHKOPSSSV	SPOKESHAVES
AEEHKORSTTT	AT THE STROKE
AEEHLLMSSSY	SHAMELESSLY
AEEHLLNORTT	NOT ALL THERE
AEEHLLORSSW	WHOLESALERS
AEEHLLORTVW	OVER THE WALL
AEEHLLPSSST	SELL THE PASS
AEEHLLPSSSY	SHAPELESSLY
AEEHLLRSSSS	SELLS SHARES
AEEHLLRSSTY	HEARTLESSLY
AEEHLMNNRTT	ENTHRALMENT
AEEHLMNOOPR	MELANOPHORE
AEEHLMORSTT	ALMOST THERE
AEEHLMOSTTY	STATELY HOME
AEEHLNORTZZ	ON THE RAZZLE
AEEHLNPSSSS	HAPLESSNESS
AEEHLOSSTWY	LOSES THE WAY
AEEHLPPRRTU	PURPLE HEART
AEEHLRTVWYY	VERY WEALTHY
AEEHMMNOTTT	AT THE MOMENT
AEEHMMNOORT	MORE THAN ONE
AEEHMNOOSST	TO ONES SHAME
AEEHMNORSWW	WASHERWOMEN
AEEHMOPRRSU	AMPERE-HOURS
AEEHMOPRSST	ATMOSPHERES
AEEHMORRRTT	EARTH TREMOR
AEEHMORRSTW	WHOREMASTER
AEEHMORRSTY	THE MARY ROSE

AEEHMORSSTU	HOUSE MASTER
	HOUSEMASTER
AEEHMPPRRST	SHARP TEMPER
AEEHMPRSTTY	HASTY TEMPER
AEEHMPRTTTY	EMPTY THREAT
AEEHNNORTTU	ANOTHER TUNE
AEEHNOPRSTU	HOUSEPARENT
AEEHNOQRSTU	ON THE SQUARE
AEEHNORRSST	ENARTHROSES
AEEHNORRTWW	WEATHERWORN
AEEHNORSSTU	RENTS A HOUSE
AEEHNORSSTTW	THREW A STONE
AEEHNORTTTW	WENT TO EARTH
AEEHNOSSTTW	HONEST SWEAT
AEEHNPRSTTY	PAYS THE RENT
AEEHOOPRSST	PEASHOOTERS
AEEHOPPPRST	HOT AS PEPPER
AEEHOPRSSST	STEPS ASHORE
AEEHOPRSTTU	POURS THE TEA
	UP TO THE EARS
AEEHORRSSTU	HOUSE ARREST
AEEHORRSSUW	WAREHOUSERS
AEEHOSSSTTU	STATEHOUSES
AEEHOSTTTTU	AT THE OUTSET
AEEHPSSSTTT	PASS THE TEST
AEEHQRRSTTU	THREE QUARTS
AEEHRRSTTUY	THE TREASURY
AEEHRSSSTUU	THESAURUSES
AEEIIILMNTV	ELIMINATIVE
AEEIIINNNST	EINSTEINIAN
AEEIIINRRST	ITINERARIES
AEEIIJKLNPS	KEEPS IN JAIL
AEEIIILLMNRS	MILLENARIES
AEEIIILMMNTU	MILE A MINUTE
AEEIIILMMORS	MEMORIALISE
AEEIIILMMORZ	MEMORIALIZE
AEEIILMNNRV	MINERAL VEIN
AEEIILMNRSS	MINERALISES
AEEIILMNRSZ	MINERALIZES
AEEIILMNSTT	MENTALITIES
AEEIILMORTV	MELIORATIVE
AEEIILMRRST	SEMITRAILER
AEEIILNNPTT	PENITENTIAL
AEEIILNNRRT	INTERLINEAR
AEEIILNNRST	INTERNALISE
AEEIILNNRTZ	INTERNALIZE
AEEIILNNSST	INESSENTIAL
AEEIILNSSTT	LIES IN STATE
AEEIILNSTTX	EXISTENTIAL
AEEIILNTTVV	VENTILATIVE
AEEIILQRRSU	RELIQUARIES
AEEIILRSSTV	REVITALISES
AEEIILRSTVZ	REVITALIZES
AEEIILRTTVY	ITERATIVELY
AEEIIMNNSST	INSEMINATES
AEEIIMPRSTV	IMPERATIVES
AEEIINNTTTV	INATTENTIVE
AEEIINOPRTV	INOPERATIVE
AEEIINORRTT	REITERATION
AEEIIPRSSST	PATISSERIES
AEEIIPRTTVX	EXTIRPATIVE
AEEIIRSSTTU	AUSTERITIES
AEEIJKNPSST	SPEAK IN JEST
AEEIKKLNSTW	WEAKEST LINK
AEEIKLLNTTW	KNEW A LITTLE
AEEIKLNOPSV	SPEAK NO EVIL
AEEIKLNPPSY	KEEPS IN PLAY
AEEIKMNNOOS	MAKE NO NOISE
AEEIKMNSTTU	MINUTE STEAK
AEEIKMOPPSS	SMOKES A PIPE
AEEIKMORSTW	MAKE IT WORSE

AEEIKMOTTTU	TAKE TIME OUT
AEEIKMRRRTT	TRITE REMARK
AEEIKNOPSSW	PASSION WEEK
AEEIKNORSTT	STRIKE A NOTE
AEEIKNRSSST	STREAKINESS
AEEIKOPRSST	RISE TO SPEAK
	STRIKE A POSE
AEEIKRRSSTW	WATER-SKIERS
AEEILLMPRXY	EXEMPLARILY
AEEILLMRRSW	MARRIES WELL
AEEILLNNPRY	PERENNIALLY
AEEILLNNPTY	PENALTY LINE
AEEILLNOPPP	PLAIN PEOPLE
AEEILLNRSST	LITERALNESS
AEEILLNSSTY	ESSENTIALLY
AEEILLPRSST	PETER ALLISS
AEEILLPRSTV	SILVER PLATE
AEEILLRSTVY	VERSATILELY
AEEILLRTTTX	LITTLE EXTRA
AEEILMNNSTT	SENTIMENTAL
AEEILMNORRV	OLE MAN RIVER
AEEILMNPRST	PLANIMETERS
	SEMPITERNAL
AEEILMNPRSU	URINE SAMPLE
AEEILMNPTTU	PENULTIMATE
AEEILMNRSST	STREAMLINES
AEEILMNRSTT	MELT IN TEARS
AEEILMNSSSS	AIMLESSNESS
AEEILMNSSWY	WESLEYANISM
AEEILMNSTTU	MINUTES LATE
AEEILMOPRRT	POLARIMETER
AEEILMORSWY	WEARISOMELY
AEEILMOSTTT	TEETOTALISM
AEEILMPRTXY	EXEMPLARITY
AEEILMPSSTT	SIMPLE TASTE
AEEILMQRRTU	QUARTER MILE
AEEILMSTTTU	STATUTE MILE
AEEILNNOPST	ON PENALTIES
AEEILNNOPTX	EXPONENTIAL
AEEILNNOTTW	WENT IT ALONE
AEEILNNSSTY	INSENSATELY
AEEILNNSTTU	LIEUTENANTS
AEEILNNSTTV	ST.VALENTINE
AEEILNOPRSS	PERSONALISE
AEEILNOPRST	AT ONES PERIL
AEEILNOPRSZ	PERSONALIZE
AEEILNOPRTT	INTERPOLATE
AEEILNORSTV	REVELATIONS
AEEILNORTVW	WRITE A NOVEL
AEEILNOSSTT	TESSELATION
AEEILNPSVXY	EXPANSIVELY
AEEILNRSSSS	AIRLESSNESS
AEEILNRSSTU	NEUTRALISES
AEEILNRSTTW	WINTERS TALE
AEEILNRSTUX	INTERSEXUAL
AEEILNRSTUZ	NEUTRALIZES
AEEILNRTTXY	EXTERNALITY
AEEILNSSSSU	SENSUALISES
AEEILNSSSTT	STATELINESS
AEEILNSSSUZ	SENSUALIZES
AEEILNTTTVY	ATTENTIVELY
	TENTATIVELY
AEEILNTTUVY	EVENTUALITY
AEEILOPPRTT	TOILET PAPER
AEEILOPRSSV	PASSIVE ROLE
AEEILOPRTVX	EXPLORATIVE
AEEILOPRTVY	OPERATIVELY
AEEILORRSTY	EARLY TO RISE
AEEILORTTTW	TOILET WATER
AEEILPPRRSV	SILVER PAPER
AEEILPRSTUV	SUPERLATIVE

AEEILPRSVVY	PERVASIVELY	AEEKLOPRRSW	ROPEWALKERS
AEEILPSTTUX	EXSTIPULATE	AEEKLOPRUWY	WOKE UP EARLY
AEEILQRRSTU	QUARTERLIES	AEEKMMNORSY	MONEY-MAKERS
AEEILRRRSTT	TERRESTRIAL	AEEKMMNORTY	MONEY MARKET
AEEILRRTTTU	LITTERATEUR	AEEKMMRRRSY	MERRYMAKERS
AEEILRSSTVY	ASSERTIVELY	AEEKMORRTTV	MARKET OVERT
AEEILSSSTTU	LATEST ISSUE	AEEKMPRRSTU	SUPERMARKET
AEEIMMNNNPRT	IMPERMANENT	AEEKNNOSWWY	KNEW ONE'S WAY
AEEIMMNOPRR	ROMAN EMPIRE	AEEKNOORSTT	AT ONE STROKE
AEEIMMQRSSU	REQUIEM MASS	AEEKNOPRRSY	NOSEY PARKER
AEEIMNNNRTT	ENTRAINMENT	AEEKNPRRSTU	SUPERTANKER
AEEIMNNORTU	ENUMERATION	AEEKOOPRSST	ROSE TO SPEAK
	MOUNTAINEER	AEELLLLRVWY	ALL VERY WELL
AEEIMNOPRST	IMPERSONATE	AEELLLNOOSS	LOSE ONES ALL
AEEIMNOPRSU	EUROPEANISM	AEELLLNOSTT	TELL NO TALES
AEEIMNORSST	MONASTERIES	AEELLLORSST	SALTERELLOS
AEEIMNORSSY	RAISES MONEY	AEELLMMNOTT	MOLTEN METAL
AEEIMNORSTT	MARIONETTES	AEELLMORRST	STEAMROLLER
AEEIMNOSSTT	MAISONETTES	AEELLNOQORTV	LEARN TO LOVE
AEEIMNPRRSU	PRAEMUNIRES	AEELLNOPSVW	WOVEN A SPELL
AEEIMNPRSTU	PINT MEASURE	AEELLNORSTW	STONEWALLER
AEEIMNSSSSV	MASSIVENESS	AEELLNPRTVY	PREVALENTLY
AEEIMOPRSST	MARIE STOPES	AEELLNSSSSW	LAWLESSNESS
AEEIMOPRSTT	TIME TO SPARE	AEELLOPRTUV	POLE VAULTER
AEEIMOPRSTW	WRITES A POEM		POLE-VAULTER
AEEIMOPRTVY	OVERTIME PAY	AEELLORSTTY	TEA TROLLEYS
	PAY OVERTIME	AEELLPPRTUY	PERPETUALLY
AEEIMOSTTTW	TIME TO WASTE	AEELLSSSTTY	TASTELESSLY
AEEIMQRSSUV	SEMIQUAVERS	AEELLSSTTTY	LATEST STYLE
AEEIMSSSTTY	SYSTEMATISE	AEELMMNORTY	MORTAL ENEMY
AEEIMSSTTYZ	SYSTEMATIZE	AEELMMORSSU	SAMUEL MORSE
AEEINNNPSTT	TEN PAST NINE	AEELMMRRSUY	EARLY SUMMER
AEEINNOORTX	EXONERATION	AEELMNNPRTY	PERMANENTLY
AEEINNOPRTT	PENETRATION	AEELMNOPRTW	MENTAL POWER
AEEINNOTTUX	EXTENUATION	AEELMNOPRTY	ENEMY PATROL
AEEINNRSTYY	NINETY YEARS	AEELMNORSTV	OVERMANTELS
AEEINOPRSTV	PERSONATIVE	AEELMNORSTW	WATERMELONS
	PET AVERSION	AEELMNPSSTY	PENAL SYSTEM
AEEINOPSTTT	POTENTIATES	AEELMOPPRST	SMART PEOPLE
AEEINORRSTV	RESERVATION	AEELMOQRRSU	QUARRELSOME
AEEINORSSTT	STIR ONES TEA	AEELMORSTTV	VOLTAMETERS
AEEINORSTTW	WRITES A NOTE	AEELMPPSSUY	SAMUEL PEPYS
AEEINPRRSUV	NURSE A VIPER	AEELMPRRTUY	PREMATURELY
AEEINPRSSTT	ESPERANTIST	AEELNNOOPST	ON ONES PLATE
AEEINPRSSTV	PRIVATENESS	AEELNNORTUZ	NEUTRAL ZONE
AEEINPRSTTY	PAY INTEREST	AEELNOORTVW	WROTE A NOVEL
AEEINPSSSSV	PASSIVENESS	AEELNOOSSWY	LOSE ONES WAY
AEEINQRSSTU	EQUESTRIANS	AEELNOPPRTT	ROTTEN APPLE
AEEIOOPPSSS	APOSIOPESES	AEELNOPPSTY	NASTY PEOPLE
AEEIOPPRRTX	EXPROPRIATE	AEELNOPRSSS	SALESPERSON
AEEIORRSTTV	RESTORATIVE	AEELNOPTTTY	PLENTY TO EAT
AEEIORSSTTV	TRIES TO SAVE	AEELNORRTUV	NATURE LOVER
AEEIPPRSSTU	TISSUE PAPER	AEELNOSSSUZ	ZEALOUSNESS
AEEIPRRSSTT	STRIPTEASER	AEELNPSSSSS	SAPLESSNESS
AEEIPRRSTTW	WATER SPRITE	AEELNRRSTUY	NURSERY TALE
AEEIPRSSSTT	STRIPTEASES	AEELNRSSSST	ARTLESSNESS
AEEIPRSTTUV	VITUPERATES	AEELOORSTTV	LEAVES TO ROT
AEEIRRSSTVW	SERVES A WRIT	AEELOPPRSUY	PAY UP OR ELSE!
AEEJLNOSSSU	JEALOUSNESS	AEELOPRSTTT	POST A LETTER
AEEJMNORSUY	JANE SEYMOUR	AEELOPRSTTY	TRY TO PLEASE
AEEJNORRTUV	REJUVENATOR	AEELOPSTTUX	EXPOSTULATE
AEEJNOSSSTW	SETS ONE'S JAW	AEELORSSTTU	LOTUS EATERS
AEEKLLNORSW	KEN ROSEWALL		LOTUS-EATERS
AEEKLLORRST	ROLLER-SKATE	AEELQRSSTTU	LAST REQUEST
AEEKLMORRTW	METALWORKER	AEEMMNNORTTY	MONEY MATTER
AEEKLMSSSUY	SEEKS ASYLUM	AEEMNOPRSTU	PENTAMEROUS
AEEKLNOPPSY	SPEAK OPENLY	AEEMNORRRTU	REMUNERATOR
AEEKLNOPTUW	WOKEN UP LATE	AEEMNORRSTT	REMONSTRATE
AEEKLNOSSST	TAKE LESSONS	AEEMNORSSTT	EASTERNMOST
AEEKLOORTTT	TOOK A LETTER	AEEMNORSSTY	ON EASY TERMS
AEEKLOPPRRY	POKER PLAYER	AEEMNOSSTTW	STATESWOMEN

AEEMNPRRSST	PRESENT ARMS	AEFGHHILTTW	FIGHT THE LAW
AEEMNPRSTTY	NASTY TEMPER	AEFGHHIMOTY	EIGHTH OF MAY
AEEMNSSSSST	ASSESSMENTS	AEFGHHLOSTW	SHOW THE FLAG
AEEMOORSSTTV	MOVE TO TEARS	AEFGHIILNOX	FIXING A HOLE
AEEMOPRRTXY	EXTEMPORARY	AEFGHIILRST	LIGHTS A FIRE
AEEMORRSSTV	OVERMASTERS	AEFGHIKLMOT	MAKE LIGHT OF
AEEMORRSTTU	TETRAMEROUS	AEFGHIKLNTT	TAKEN FLIGHT
AEEMORSSTUU	MEASURES OUT	AEFGHIKLSTT	TAKES FLIGHT
AEENNNNOOTT	NO,NO,NANETTE	AEFGHIKNRTT	TAKEN FRIGHT
AEENNNPPSTY	SPENT A PENNY	AEFGHIKRSTT	TAKES FRIGHT
AEENNOPRRTU	NEUROPTERAN	AEFGHILLPST	FILLS THE GAP
AEENNOSTWWY	WENT ONE'S WAY	AEFGHILOSST	LOSES A FIGHT
AEENOOPSTTW	NEW POTATOES	AEFGHIMOSTW	GAME OF WHIST
AEENOPRRSTT	PATER NOSTER	AEFGHINNORT	ONE FARTHING
	PATERNOSTER	AEFGHINORSW	SHOWING FEAR
AEENORTTUXY	EXTENUATORY	AEFGHINRRSW	WHARFINGERS
AEENOSTTTWW	WENT TO WASTE	AEFGHIOORTT	GO TO THE FAIR
AEENPRSSTUW	PASTURES NEW	AEFGHLOPRXY	FLEXOGRAPHY
AEENRRTTUVY	AT EVERY TURN	AEFGHORSTTU	SOUGHT AFTER
AEENRSTTWYY	TWENTY YEARS		SOUGHT-AFTER
AEEOOPSTTTW	SWEET POTATO	AEFGHORSTTW	GETS WHAT FOR
AEEOPPRRRTT	PERPETRATOR	AEFGIIIMNTX	FIXING A TIME
	PRET-A-PORTER	AEFGIIINRRS	FIRE-RAISING
AEEOPPRRTTU	PERPETUATOR	AEFGIIKLNTY	FLYING A KITE
AEEOPRRRRTW	WAR REPORTER	AEFGIIKNNPR	PARKING FINE
AEEPRRSTTTY	STREET PARTY	AEFGIILNNRS	FINGERNAILS
AEEPRSSSWXY	EXPRESSWAYS	AEFGIILNOTX	EXFOLIATING
AEEPRSTTTTY	PRETTY STATE	AEFGIILNPRU	PLAIN FIGURE
AEFFFFILOST	STAFF OF LIFE	AEFGIILNRSS	SELF-RAISING
AEFFFHILTUW	FAITHFUL FEW	AEFGIILNSSV	LIFE SAVINGS
AEFFFLMOORR	FORMAL OFFER	AEFGIIMNNNW	WINNING FAME
AEFFGGORSST	STAGGERS OFF	AEFGIIMNNST	MANIFESTING
AEFFGIILNRT	LIFT A FINGER	AEFGIINORRR	ROARING FIRE
AEFFGIKNNOS	SNEAKING OFF	AEFGIINOTTX	GET INTO A FIX
AEFFGINOPRT	TAPERING OFF	AEFGIINRRST	STIR A FINGER
AEFFGINORST	AFFORESTING	AEFGIJLMNNU	FLAMING JUNE
AEFFHHILOTT	THE HALF OF IT	AEFGIKLLMOS	GAME OF SKILL
AEFFHHILTTU	THE FAITHFUL	AEFGIKMNRRS	FINGERMARKS
AEFFHHIMTTY	MAY THE FIFTH	AEFGIKNOPRS	SPEAKING FOR
AEFFHIKNOST	SHAKEN IT OFF	AEFGIKNORTU	FREAKING OUT
AEFFHIKOSST	SHAKES IT OFF	AEFGILLLNNN	FLANNELLING
AEFFHILORST	OFF THE RAILS	AEFGILLLNTT	LETTING FALL
AEFFHIMOSTV	FIVE FATHOMS	AEFGILLNNOX	FELLING AN OX
AEFFHINRSSS	RAFFISHNESS	AEFGILLNORV	FALLING OVER
AEFFHMMOORR	FAR FROM HOME	AEFGILLNOSV	FIVE GALLONS
AEFFHMNORTU	HUMAN EFFORT	AEFGILLNPRY	FALLING PREY
AEFFIIMNORR	FORAMINIFER	AEFGILLNRST	FINGERSTALL
AEFFIIOPRSV	PAIR OF FIVES	AEFGILLNRTY	FALTERINGLY
AEFFIKLNOSW	FLASK OF WINE	AEFGILMNRUY	MANLY FIGURE
AEFFILLMMMR	FLIMFLAMMER	AEFGILNNRTU	UNFALTERING
AEFFILLNORT	FALLEN FOR IT	AEFGILNOSSW	GLASS OF WINE
AEFFILNSSTU	INSUFFLATES	AEFGILNPRSU	PERSIAN GULF
AEFFIOSTTTW	TWIST OF FATE	AEFGILOPRRT	LARGE PROFIT
AEFFIRSSTTY	SAFETY FIRST	AEFGILOPRST	PROFLIGATES
AEFFKNOOORT	TOOK AN OFFER	AEFGIMNNOSU	MAN OF GENIUS
AEFFKNRRRTU	FRANKFURTER	AEFGIMNOOST	SAME FOOTING
AEFFLLOORTW	FOLLOW AFTER	AEFGIMNORRT	IN GREAT FORM
AEFFLORSSSU	SUFFER A LOSS	AEFGINNNSTU	UNFASTENING
AEFFLOSTTUX	STATE OF FLUX	AEFGINNORRW	FOREWARNING
AEFFNOOOSST	OFF ONE'S OATS	AEFGINNORRY	YEARNING FOR
AEFFOOPRSTY	OFFERS TO PAY	AEFGINNORVW	FAWNING OVER
AEFGGGIINNW	NAGGING WIFE	AEFGINNPTTU	FATTENING UP
AEFGGHIINNR	HANGING FIRE	AEFGINOPRRT	PERFORATING
AEFGGHIRSTT	GETS A FRIGHT	AEFGINORSSW	SIGNS OF WEAR
	STAGE FRIGHT	AEFGINRRSTU	TRANSFIGURE
AEFGGIINNOR	GOING IN FEAR	AEFGJNOORTW	WENT FOR A JOG
AEFGGIMNNRT	FRAGMENTING	AEFGLLOOPRY	GALLEY PROOF
AEFGGJNOOOR	GONE FOR A JOG	AEFGLNNORSU	FUNERAL SONG
AEFGGJOOORS	GOES FOR A JOG	AEFGLNOORTW	WENT FOR GOAL
AEFGGLNOOOR	GONE FOR GOAL	AEFGLNOOTTU	GONE FLAT OUT
AEFGGLOOORS	GOES FOR GOAL	AEFGLOOSTTU	GOES FLAT OUT

AEFGMMMORUY	GAME OF RUMMY	AEFILNOOPST	POINT OF SALE
AEFGNNOORRU	GONE FOR A RUN		POINT-OF-SALE
AEFGNOORRSU	GOES FOR A RUN	AEFILNOPRRT	FINAL REPORT
AEFHHIINSTT	AT THE FINISH	AEFILNORSTU	FLUORINATES
AEFHIILLRST	FILLS THE AIR	AEFILNORSUY	NEFARIOUSLY
AEFHIILMNTY	IN THE FAMILY	AEFILOPPPRS	SLIP OF PAPER
AEFHIILNRSY	FINISH EARLY	AEFILOPPSTV	POP FESTIVAL
AEFHIINNNPS	PHINEAS FINN	AEFILOPRRTY	PREFATORILY
AEFHILLMOTY	FAMILY HOTEL	AEFIMNNNRTY	INFANTRYMEN
AEFHILLSSTY	FAITHLESSLY	AEFIMNNOOTT	FOMENTATION
AEFHIMNOPRS	H.M.S.PINAFORE	AEFIMNOORRT	REFORMATION
AEFHIMRSTTY	MAY THE FIRST	AEFINNNOPRY	IN FOR A PENNY
AEFHINNOOST	HAS NONE OF IT	AEFINNNOPTU	FOUNTAIN PEN
AEFHINOPTVY	PINT OF HEAVY	AEFINNORTUW	WIN A FORTUNE
AEFHIOOPRSS	PAIR OF SHOES	AEFINOOPRRT	PERFORATION
AEFHIOPSSTT	SHIP OF STATE	AEFINOOPRST	PIANOFORTES
AEFHIORSSTX	SIX OF HEARTS	AEFINOORSTT	FORESTATION
AEFHIRRSTTT	THIRST AFTER	AEFINORSSWW	SINEWS OF WAR
AEFHKLOPRSS	ASKS FOR HELP	AEFIOOPRSTW	TOWER OF PISA
AEFIIKOORTTU	OUT OF THE ARK	AEFIOPPPRRT	PAPER PROFIT
AEFHLLLOSVY	HALF-VOLLEYS	AEFIOPRSTTY	TEARS OF PITY
AEFHLLNORST	FALLEN SHORT	AEFIOPSTTVW	FIVE PAST TWO
AEFHLLOOPTY	PLAY THE FOOL	AEFISSTTTUY	FATTY TISSUE
AEFHLMNNRUY	FUNERAL HYMN	AEFJLOOPRSY	LEAPS FOR JOY
AEFHLMNORSS	FRESH SALMON	AEFJLOOPRTY	LEAPT FOR JOY
AEFHLMNRSSU	HARMFULNESS	AEFJMMNOORY	MONEY FOR JAM
AEFHMOOPRRS	SHAPE OR FORM	AEFKLLOORRW	FLOORWALKER
AEFHMORRSTT	FARTHERMOST	AEFKLOORRTW	LATE FOR WORK
	STREAM FORTH	AEFKLOPSSTY	SPEAK SOFTLY
AEFHOORSTTW	TWO OF HEARTS	AEFKMNOORSY	ASK FOR MONEY
AEFHOOTTUWY	OUT OF THE WAY	AEFKMOOPRST	MAKE SPORT OF
	OUT-OF-THE-WAY	AEFKMOORRSS	ASKS FOR MORE
AEFIIIMNRRS	INFIRMARIES	AEFKNOORSTT	RATE OF KNOTS
AEFIILLLNNS	FALLS IN LINE	AEFLLLNTTUY	FLATULENTLY
AEFIILLNNTU	INFLUENTIAL	AEFLLLOPRUW	ALL-POWERFUL
AEFIILMORST	FORMALITIES	AEFLLLOPSWY	PLAYFELLOWS
AEFIILNOOTX	EXFOLIATION	AEFLLLORSWW	WALLFLOWERS
AEFIILNRSTT	INFILTRATES	AEFLLLSSTUY	FAULTLESSLY
AEFIILOPRRW	PRAIRIE WOLF	AEFLLMMOPTU	LUMP OF METAL
AEFIIMMMMNUX	MAXIMUM FINE	AEFLLMRSTUY	MASTERFULLY
AEFIIMNORTV	INFORMATIVE	AEFLLNOOOTT	ONE FOOT TALL
AEFIINNOPRS	PAIR OF NINES	AEFLLNORSTY	LEARNS TO FLY
AEFIINNOSTT	INFESTATION	AEFLLNORTTY	LEARNT TO FLY
	SINFONIETTA	AEFLLNPSSUY	PLAYFULNESS
AEFIINNRSTT	TRANSFINITE	AEFLLOOPPRR	ROLL OF PAPER
AEFIINOPRSS	SAPONIFIERS	AEFLLORSSUV	FLAVOURLESS
AEFIINOPRST	PROFANITIES	AEFLMOORSUV	FLAVOURSOME
AEFIINORSTT	FIRE STATION	AEFLNOOPSTU	TEASPOONFUL
AEFIIOPRSSX	PAIR OF SIXES	AEFLNORTTUY	FORTUNATELY
AEFIIPSSTVX	FIVE PAST SIX	AEFLNOSTTTU	FLATTENS OUT
AEFIJMNOOTT	JOINT OF MEAT	AEFLNOTTTUW	WENT FLAT OUT
AEFIKLMRSTT	LEFT ITS MARK	AEFLNPRSTUU	FUTURE PLANS
AEFIKMOPRTU	MAKE UP FOR IT	AEFLNRRTTUY	RUNFLAT TYRE
AEFIKMRRTTU	FRUIT MARKET	AEFLOORSSUV	LOSES FAVOUR
AEFILLLNOSV	FALLS IN LOVE	AEFLPRTTUWY	PRETTY AWFUL
AEFILLLNSST	FALLS SILENT	AEFLRSSTTWY	FLYSWATTERS
AEFILLMORUV	LIME FLAVOUR	AEFMMNOOSUW	FAMOUS WOMEN
AEFILLNRSTU	FINAL RESULT	AEFMNNNOORW	MAN OF RENOWN
AEFILLOPRTY	FAIL TO REPLY	AEFMNORRRST	TRANSFORMER
AEFILMNOSST	LIST OF NAMES	AEFMOOPPRRT	TAMPERPROOF
AEFILMNOSTU	FILAMENTOUS	AEFMOORRRTY	REFORMATORY
AEFILMOOSTV	FAILS TO MOVE	AEFMOPSSSTT	SET OF STAMPS
AEFILMOPRTY	PLAY FOR TIME	AEFNNOORTUW	WON A FORTUNE
AEFILMORRSU	FORMULARIES	AEFNNORRTUW	WENT FOR A RUN
	FORMULARISE	AEFNNORTTUU	UNFORTUNATE
AEFILMORRUZ	FORMULARIZE	AEFNOOOPSTT	TAP ONE'S FOOT
AEFILMORSST	FLIES TO ARMS	AEFNOOOSSTU	OUT OF SEASON
AEFILMORTVY	FORMATIVELY	AEFNOOPRRST	FOR ONE'S PART
AEFILMPPRSY	FLIMSY PAPER	AEFNOORSSSU	FOUR SEASONS
AEFILNNPSSU	PAINFULNESS	AEFNOPRSTTU	TEN PAST FOUR
		AEFNORRRSST	TRANSFERORS

AEFNOSSSTUU	FATUOUSNESS	AEGHHILNOST	SHONE A LIGHT
AEFOOPPRRSU	FOR A PURPOSE	AEGHHILNRSS	HASH SLINGER
AEFOOPRRSTW	WATERPROOFS	AEGHHILOPRS	HELIOGRAPHS
AEFOOPRSSST	SOFT-SOAPERS	AEGHHILOPRY	HELIOGRAPHY
AEFOORRSSTT	TORTFEASORS	AEGHHILRSTV	RIGHT-HALVES
AEFORRRSSTT	FOR STARTERS	AEGHHILSTTW	SAW THE LIGHT
AEGGGNORSTU	GO GREAT GUNS	AEGHHILTTWY	LIGHT THE WAY
AEGGHHIINST	GAINS HEIGHT	AEGHHINNORT	HEAR NOTHING
AEGGHHIKNNS	GENGHIS KHAN	AEGHHINNPTY	HYPHENATING
AEGGHHILOTV	HIGH VOLTAGE	AEGHHINNSTU	UNSHEATHING
AEGGHHILSTT	LIGHT THE GAS	AEGHHINORST	HIGH TREASON
AEGGHIILNNT	NIGHTINGALE	AEGHHINSSTU	HAUGHTINESS
AEGGHIILNSX	ALEX HIGGINS	AEGHHLOPRSU	PLOUGHSHARE
AEGGHIIMMST	MAGGIE SMITH	AEGHHLORSSU	HORSELAUGHS
AEGGHIINNRT	GATHERING IN	AEGHHLOSTTY	LAY THE GHOST
AEGGHIINSTW	GAINS WEIGHT	AEGHHMOPRRT	THERMOGRAPH
AEGGHIIRRRT	HAIR-TRIGGER	AEGHHNOPRTY	ETHNOGRAPHY
AEGGHILNOSV	GOING HALVES	AEGHIIKMNNT	IN THE MAKING
AEGGHILNOSW	SHOWING A LEG	AEGHIIKMRTT	MAKE IT RIGHT
AEGGHILNRST	RIGHT ANGLES	AEGHIILLNRS	RAISING HELL
AEGGHIMNOSU	GAMING HOUSE	AEGHIILNNSW	WASHING LINE
AEGGHINNORV	HANGING OVER	AEGHIILPPST	LIGHTS A PIPE
AEGGHINOORS	GOING ASHORE	AEGHIIMMNNR	HAMMERING IN
AEGGHINPRTU	GATHERING UP	AEGHIIMNNTW	WITH MEANING
AEGGHINRSTT	GREAT THINGS	AEGHIIMNPSS	EMPHASISING
AEGGHINSSSW	WAGGISHNESS	AEGHIIMNPSZ	EMPHASIZING
AEGGHIRSTTT	GET STRAIGHT	AEGHIIMNRST	TIME-SHARING
AEGGIIILMNV	LIVING IMAGE	AEGHIIMNRTW	WITHIN RANGE
AEGGIIIMNNT	GAINING TIME	AEGHIINSVVW	HAVING VIEWS
AEGGIIKNSST	KISSING GATE	AEGHIIPPRST	EPIGRAPHIST
AEGGIILLNST	LEGISLATING	AEGHIKLLTTY	TAKE LIGHTLY
AEGGIILMNNR	MALINGERING	AEGHIKLMNOW	MAKING WHOLE
AEGGIILMPRS	PILGRIMAGES	AEGHIKLRSWY	LARGE WHISKY
AEGGIILNNOS	GONE SAILING	AEGHIKNNSTV	GIVEN THANKS
AEGGIILNOSS	GOES SAILING	AEGHIKNSSSW	GAWKISHNESS
AEGGIILNRUV	GIVE A RULING	AEGHIKNSSTV	GIVES THANKS
AEGGIIMNNNW	WINNING GAME	AEGHILLLNPY	PLAYING HELL
AEGGIIMNNRT	GERMINATING	AEGHILLMPRT	LAMPLIGHTER
AEGGIIMNNST	MAGNETISING	AEGHILLMSTW	MIGHT AS WELL
AEGGIIMNNTZ	MAGNETIZING	AEGHILLNNRT	ENTHRALLING
AEGGIINNOTT	NEGOTIATING	AEGHILLNOPS	ANGLOPHILES
AEGGIINNRTT	INTEGRATING	AEGHILLNSST	ALL THE SIGNS
AEGGIINNRVW	GIVE WARNING	AEGHILLOPSV	VILLAGE SHOP
AEGGIINORTV	GIVING EAR TO	AEGHILLRSTT	GETS A THRILL
AEGGIINPSUV	GIVING PAUSE	AEGHILLRTTV	TRAVEL LIGHT
AEGGIINRTTU	INGURGITATE	AEGHILMNTTY	METHYLATING
AEGGIKNNOST	GONE SKATING	AEGHILNOOST	ANTHOLOGIES
AEGGIKNORWW	GROWING WEAK		ANTHOLOGISE
AEGGIKNOSST	GOES SKATING		THEOLOGIANS
AEGGILMNOOT	LONG TIME AGO	AEGHILNOOTZ	ANTHOLOGIZE
AEGGILNNRSS	GLARINGNESS	AEGHILNORST	LOSING HEART
AEGGILNOPRW	GROWING PALE	AEGHILNORUV	HAULING OVER
AEGGILRRTTY	GARY GLITTER		OVERHAULING
AEGGIMNRSST	GANGSTERISM	AEGHILNOTTU	GLUTATHIONE
AEGGIMNRTTW	GETTING WARM	AEGHILNSSST	GHASTLINESS
AEGGINNORST	GOING ASTERN	AEGHILNSTTT	LATEST THING
AEGGINNOTXY	OXYGENATING	AEGHILNSTVY	HAVING STYLE
AEGGINOORTT	GOT INTO GEAR	AEGHILOORST	OIL SHORTAGE
AEGGINPRTUX	EXPURGATING	AEGHILPSSTU	SLIGHT PAUSE
AEGGINPSTUY	PAYING GUEST	AEGHILQRSTU	EQUAL RIGHTS
AEGGJNRSTUU	JUGGERNAUTS	AEGHIMMMNOR	RAMMING HOME
AEGGLNORRRW	GROWN LARGER	AEGHIMNNNOT	MEAN NOTHING
AEGGLORRRSW	GROWS LARGER	AEGHIMNNRST	GARNISHMENT
AEGGLPRRSUY	PLAYS RUGGER	AEGHIMNOPRS	SEMAPHORING
AEGGNOOOSTT	GOT ONE'S GOAT	AEGHIMNOSTT	STEAMING HOT
AEGGOSSTTUU	AUTOSUGGEST	AEGHIMNOSTY	STAYING HOME
AEGHHIILLMT	ALL-TIME HIGH	AEGHIMOPRSS	SEISMOGRAPH
AEGHHIILNST	SHINE A LIGHT	AEGHINNOSTV	SAVE NOTHING
AEGHHIIINORS	RAISE ON HIGH	AEGHINNSSTU	NAUGHTINESS
AEGHHILLLSS	SHILLELAGHS	AEGHINORSUW	WAREHOUSING
AEGHHILMTTY	THE ALMIGHTY	AEGHINOSTUV	GIVEN A SHOUT

AEGHINOTTWY	GOT IN THE WAY
AEGHINRRSTW	RIGHT ANSWER
AEGHINRSSTT	STRAIGHTENS
AEGHIORRTUY	RIGHT YOU ARE
AEGHIOSSTUV	GIVES A SHOUT
AEGHIRSSTTT	SET STRAIGHT
	STRAIGHT SET
	STRAIGHTEST
AEGHKOOOSTT	TOOK HOSTAGE
AEGHLLMOOPS	GALLOPS HOME
AEGHLLOOTTW	GO TO THE WALL
AEGHLLOPTUW	GO UP THE WALL
AEGHLMOOOST	HOMOLOGATES
AEGHLMSSSTY	GHASTLY MESS
AEGHLNNOOPS	ANGLOPHONES
AEGHLNOOORR	GONORRHOEAL
AEGHLOOPRSY	PHRASEOLOGY
AEGHLOPRRXY	XYLOGRAPHER
AEGHLORSSSU	HOURGLASSES
AEGHLOSSSSU	GLASS HOUSES
	GLASSHOUSES
AEGHLRRSSSY	SHERRY GLASS
AEGHMMORRST	THERMOGRAMS
AEGHMNNORRU	ROUGH MANNER
AEGHMNNORRY	HENRY MORGAN
AEGHMNNSSTU	MANS THE GUNS
AEGHMNOOPRS	GRAMOPHONES
AEGHNOOOSTW	GONE TO A SHOW
AEGHNOORRTU	GREAT HONOUR
AEGHNOPRSTU	SHARP TONGUE
AEGHNOPRSTY	STENOGRAPHY
AEGHNORSTTU	HART'S-TONGUE
AEGHNORSUVY	YOUNG SHAVER
AEGHNRRSTUU	ARTHUR NEGUS
AEGHOOOSSTW	GOES TO A SHOW
AEGHOOPPRRT	TOPOGRAPHER
AEGHOORSTTW	GO TO THE WARS
AEGHOPPRRRY	REPROGRAPHY
AEGHOPPRRSS	GRASSHOPPER
AEGHOPPRRTY	PETROGRAPHY
	TYPOGRAPHER
AEGHOPPSSTT	STOPS THE GAP
AEGIIILMNNT	ELIMINATING
AEGIIILMNST	SAILING TIME
AEGIIILNRSS	SERIALISING
AEGIIILNRSZ	SERIALIZING
AEGIIILNSTV	INVIGILATES
AEGIIIMSSTV	GIVE IT A MISS
AEGIIINNRTT	ITINERATING
AEGIIJMNSTU	JUST IMAGINE
AEGIIKLLNRT	GIANT KILLER
AEGIIKMMNRT	MARKING TIME
AEGIIKNPTTW	KEPT WAITING
AEGIIKNRSST	ASTERISKING
AEGIIKNRSTW	WATER SKIING
	WATER-SKIING
AEGIIKNSSTU	TAKING ISSUE
AEGIILLMNST	METALLISING
AEGIILLMNTZ	METALLIZING
AEGIILLNNOV	LIVING ALONE
AEGIILLNOST	LEGISLATION
AEGIILLNPST	PALLETISING
AEGIILLNPTZ	PALLETIZING
AEGIILLNRTT	ILL-TREATING
AEGIILLNTVY	GENITIVALLY
AEGIILLRSTX	LEGISLATRIX
AEGIILLSTVY	VESTIGIALLY
AEGIILMNNOT	MAGINOT LINE
AEGIILMNORS	REGIONALISM
AEGIILMNORT	MELIORATING
AEGIILNNPRT	PELTING RAIN
AEGIILNNRSV	VERNALISING
AEGIILNNRVZ	VERNALIZING
AEGIILNNSTU	UNGAINLIEST
AEGIILNNSTW	WENT SAILING
AEGIILNNTTV	VENTILATING
AEGIILNORST	REGIONALIST
AEGIILNRRSY	RISING EARLY
AEGIILNRSSU	SINGULARISE
AEGIILNRSUZ	SINGULARIZE
AEGIILNRTTU	ELUTRIATING
AEGIILNRTTY	INTEGRALITY
AEGIILNRTVW	LIVING WATER
AEGIILNSSTT	SETTING SAIL
AEGIILNSSUX	SEXUALISING
AEGIILNSUXZ	SEXUALIZING
AEGIIMMMNUW	MINIMUM WAGE
AEGIIMMORRR	MIRROR IMAGE
AEGIIMMNNOT	MATING IN ONE
AEGIIMNNNTW	WINNING TEAM
AEGIIMNNORT	GERMINATION
AEGIIMNNORV	MEROVINGIAN
AEGIIMNNRST	STREAMING IN
AEGIIMNNRTT	TERMINATING
AEGIIMNPSST	PASSING TIME
AEGIIMNNRST	MISTREATING
AEGIIMNSTTW	WASTING TIME
AEGIIMSSSTT	STIGMATISES
AEGIIMSSTTZ	STIGMATIZES
AEGIINNNOST	ANGIOTENSIN
AEGIINNNRTV	INNERVATING
AEGIINNOOTT	NEGOTIATION
AEGIINNORST	RESIGNATION
AEGIINNORTT	INTEGRATION
	ORIENTATING
AEGIINNRRST	RESTRAINING
AEGIINNRSTT	REINSTATING
	STRAITENING
AEGIINNSTTW	WINE TASTING
AEGIINORSST	SIGNATORIES
AEGIINORSTV	INVIGORATES
AEGIINPPRSU	PAUPERISING
AEGIINPPRTW	WIRETAPPING
AEGIINPPRUZ	PAUPERIZING
AEGIINPRTTU	TEARING IT UP
AEGIINPRTTX	EXTIRPATING
AEGIINRTTVY	GIVEN IT A TRY
AEGIIRSTTVY	GIVES IT A TRY
AEGIJLNRUUV	JUGULAR VEIN
AEGIJNOOTTV	NOT GIVE A JOT
AEGIKLLMNRW	MARKING WELL
AEGIKLLNOOP	LOOKING PALE
AEGIKLMNOSS	SMOKE SIGNAL
AEGIKLNOOST	GETS A LOOK IN
AEGIKLNORTV	TALKING OVER
AEGIKLNORTW	WORKING LATE
AEGIKLNORVW	LEAVING WORK
	WALKING OVER
AEGIKMMNNOY	MAKING MONEY
	MONEYMAKING
AEGIKMMNRRY	MAKING MERRY
	MERRYMAKING
AEGIKMMNRST	MAKING TERMS
AEGIKMNNOSS	MAKES NO SIGN
AEGIKMNORSW	MAKING WORSE
AEGIKNNOPST	NOT SPEAKING
AEGIKNNOSTT	TAKING NOTES
AEGIKNNOSTU	SNEAKING OUT
AEGIKNNSTTW	WENT SKATING
AEGIKNOPSTU	SPEAKING OUT
AEGIKNORRWY	WORKING YEAR
AEGIKNORSTV	SKATING OVER

AEGIKNPSSTT	TAKING STEPS
AEGILLLNPWY	PLAYING WELL
AEGILLMMNRT	TRAMMELLING
AEGILLMOOPS	MEGALOPOLIS
AEGILLMPPUV	VILLAGE PUMP
AEGILLNNNOS	NINE GALLONS
AEGILLNNOSW	NIGEL LAWSON
AEGILLNNRUV	UNRAVELLING
AEGILLNOPST	SELLOTAPING
AEGILLNQRRU	QUARRELLING
AEGILLORSST	ALLEGORISTS
	LEGISLATORS
AEGILLPRSSU	ASPERGILLUS
AEGILLRRRUY	IRREGULARLY
AEGILMMNOTU	GEMMULATION
AEGILMNNOPS	PLASMINOGEN
AEGILMNNORT	LATE MORNING
AEGILMNNOSW	SINGLE WOMAN
AEGILMNOORV	LEAVING ROOM
AEGILMNOPRU	PELARGONIUM
AEGILMNORSS	MORSE SIGNAL
AEGILMNOSTU	LIGAMENTOUS
AEGILNNOOST	ELONGATIONS
AEGILNNPRTU	TURNING PALE
AEGILNNSSST	LASTINGNESS
AEGILNOOPRR	POLAR REGION
AEGILNOPPRV	OVERLAPPING
AEGILNOPRVY	OVERPLAYING
AEGILNORSTU	REGULATIONS
AEGILNPRRSY	EARLY SPRING
AEGILNPRSTT	SPLATTERING
AEGILNPSTTT	LETTING PAST
AEGILNQRUVY	QUAVERINGLY
AEGILNRRSTV	SERVANT GIRL
AEGILNRRSTY	ARRESTINGLY
AEGILNRSSTV	STARVELINGS
AEGILNRSTTY	LYING AT REST
AEGILOORSST	AEROLOGISTS
AEGILOOSTTU	TAUTOLOGIES
AEGILOPRSTT	GRAPTOLITES
AEGILRRSSUV	VULGARISERS
AEGILRRSUVZ	VULGARIZERS
AEGILRSTTUU	GUTTURALISE
AEGILRTTUUZ	GUTTURALIZE
AEGIMMORSSS	SEISMOGRAMS
AEGIMNNNORT	ORNAMENTING
AEGIMNNNORV	OVERMANNING
AEGIMNNOOTT	GOT A MENTION
AEGIMNNORTW	WANTING MORE
AEGIMNNORUV	MANOEUVRING
AEGIMNNORVW	WARMING OVEN
AEGIMNNOSVY	SAVING MONEY
AEGIMNNSSST	ASSIGNMENTS
AEGIMNNSSSU	AMUSINGNESS
AEGIMNOPRRT	IMPREGNATOR
AEGIMNOPRSS	ANGIOSPERMS
AEGIMNORSSU	IGNORAMUSES
AEGIMNRRSST	RINGMASTERS
AEGIMNRRWXY	WAXING MERRY
AEGIMNRSSTT	SMATTERINGS
AEGIMOPRRTT	GREAT IMPORT
AEGINNNORSU	UNREASONING
AEGINNNORTW	WARNING NOTE
AEGINNOOTXY	OXYGENATION
AEGINNOPRSS	IN ONES GRASP
AEGINNOPRST	PERSONATING
AEGINNOPSTV	PAVING STONE
AEGINNOPSTY	STAYING OPEN
AEGINNOSSUU	SANGUINEOUS
AEGINNOSWWY	WING ONES WAY
AEGINNPRRTU	ENRAPTURING

AEGINNRSSTT	ASTRINGENTS
AEGINOORSTT	NEGOTIATORS
AEGINOORTTW	GET INTO A ROW
AEGINOORTTY	NEGOTIATORY
AEGINOPPRTV	VOTING PAPER
AEGINOPRSST	PRISON GATES
AEGINOPRSSV	PASSING OVER
AEGINOPRTTV	VINTAGE PORT
AEGINOPRTUX	EXPURGATION
AEGINORRSTT	INTEGRATORS
AEGINORSSTW	WRITES A SONG
AEGINORSTTV	OVERSTATING
AEGINORSTVY	OVERSTAYING
AEGINORTTTU	GET INTO A RUT
AEGINPRRSTW	SPRING WATER
AEGINPRSSST	TRESPASSING
AEGINPRSSTU	SUPERGIANTS
AEGINRSTTVY	TRAVESTYING
AEGIORRTVYZ	ZERO GRAVITY
AEGIORSTTUU	ARGUES IT OUT
AEGIRSSSTTT	STRATEGISTS
AEGIRSSTTTU	GUEST ARTIST
AEGLLMORRSW	GROW SMALLER
AEGLLNORRTW	GROWN TALLER
AEGLLORRSTW	GROWS TALLER
AEGLMOPRSTU	PROMULGATES
AEGLNNPRTUY	REPUGNANTLY
AEGLNOORSST	LOST ONE'S RAG
	NO GREAT LOSS
AEGLNOORSTW	SLOW TO ANGER
AEGLNOPPRSW	GROWN APPLES
AEGLOORRSST	ASTROLOGERS
AEGLOPPRSSW	GROWS APPLES
AEGLORSSSSY	ROSY GLASSES
AEGMMOPRRRS	PROGRAMMERS
AEGMNOORSST	GASTRONOMES
AEGNNORRSWW	WRONG ANSWER
AEGNOOOSSTT	GOT ONE'S OATS
AEGNOOPRSSY	GREASY SPOON
AEGNORRSTTX	EXTRA STRONG
AEGNORSSTTT	STRONG TASTE
AEGNORSSTWX	WAXES STRONG
AEGNRRSSTTU	STARTERS GUN
AEGOORRRSTW	GREAT SORROW
AEGOPPRSTUV	GAVE SUPPORT
AEGOPRRTUXY	EXPURGATORY
AEGORSSSTUU	STEGOSAURUS
AEHHIILRTTT	HIT THE TRAIL
AEHHIIMPSSS	MESSIAHSHIP
AEHHIKLRTTW	WITH THE LARK
AEHHIKMRSTT	HITS THE MARK
AEHHIKNOTTT	HATE TO THINK
AEHHIKNSSSW	HAWKISHNESS
AEHHILLNTUY	UNHEALTHILY
AEHHILNOTTT	AT THE HILTON
AEHHIMNNTTY	MAY THE NINTH
AEHHIMNPSST	MANS THE SHIP
AEHHIMOPRTY	HYPOTHERMIA
AEHHIMRSTVY	HARVEY SMITH
AEHHIMSTTXY	MAY THE SIXTH
AEHHINNOPTY	HYPHENATION
AEHHINOPRST	HIEROPHANTS
AEHHINORSTW	NOW HEAR THIS
AEHHIORTTTW	WHITETHROAT
AEHHKOOOTTT	TOOK THE OATH
AEHHLLOPTTY	THALLOPHYTE
AEHHLOPPSYY	HYPOPHYSEAL
AEHHLOPSTTY	PLAY THE HOST
AEHHMMORRTW	HAMMER THROW
AEHHMOOOPST	HOMEOPATHS
AEHHMOOOPTY	HOMEOPATHY

AEHHNOSTWWY	SHOWN THE WAY	AEHINNPPSSU	UNHAPPINESS
AEHHORSSTTU	THRASHES OUT	AEHINOOPPRS	IN POOR SHAPE
AEHHOSSTWWY	SHOWS THE WAY	AEHINOORTTX	EXHORTATION
AEHIIINNPRT	NIP IN THE AIR	AEHINOPQSTU	ANTIQUE SHOP
AEHIIKKLNST	THINKS ALIKE	AEHINOPRSST	SENATORSHIP
AEHIIKLLNTT	IN AT THE KILL	AEHINOPRSTT	ANTISTROPHE
AEHIILLPSTT	PHILATELIST	AEHINOPSSTT	STEPHANOTIS
AEHIILOPSST	HOSPITALISE		TIPS ONE'S HAT
AEHIILOPSTZ	HOSPITALIZE	AEHINOPSTTW	SAW THE POINT
AEHIIMPPRST	PRIMATESHIP	AEHINOPTTWY	POINT THE WAY
AEHIINNORRS	RAIN OR SHINE	AEHINORRRSX	REX HARRISON
AEHIINNPSSW	SPANISH WINE	AEHINORRSST	ENARTHROSIS
AEHIINOPRRS	PARISHIONER	AEHINORRSTV	HOVERTRAINS
AEHIINPRSTX	XIPHISTERNA	AEHINORSSTT	ON THE STAIRS
AEHIIORSTTU	AUTHORITIES		THROATINESS
AEHIIPPRRSS	PERIPHRASIS	AEHINORSSTU	HOUSETRAINS
AEHIIRSSTUW	WHITE RUSSIA	AEHINOSSTWW	WHITE AS SNOW
AEHIJMNORTY	JOIN THE ARMY	AEHINPPRRST	PARTNERSHIP
AEHIJMORTTY	THE MAJORITY	AEHINPSSSSW	WASPISHNESS
AEHIJNNOTVY	JOIN THE NAVY	AEHINPTTUWY	PUT IN THE WAY
AEHIJNOPSST	SAINT JOSEPH	AEHINQRSSUV	VANQUISHERS
AEHIKLMNOPT	PHANTOMLIKE	AEHINQSSSSU	SQUASHINESS
AEHIKMMRSST	MISS THE MARK	AEHINRSSSTW	SWARTHINESS
AEHIKMNSSSW	MAWKISHNESS	AEHINSSSTTU	ENTHUSIASTS
AEHIKMORSTY	MAKE HISTORY	AEHIOPPRRST	PRAETORSHIP
AEHIKMPRRTY	PITHY REMARK	AEHIOPSSTTY	HYPOSTATISE
AEHIKMRSTTU	MAKES IT HURT	AEHIOPSTTYZ	HYPOSTATIZE
AEHIKNNPPRT	PINK PANTHER	AEHIORRRSTV	RAITH ROVERS
AEHIKNOPPRX	PHOENIX PARK	AEHIORRSSTU	AUTHORISERS
AEHIKNOSSTW	IN TWO SHAKES	AEHIORRSTUZ	AUTHORIZERS
AEHILLLSTTT	TILL THE LAST	AEHIORSTVWY	VARIETY SHOW
AEHILLMOPST	METAL POLISH	AEHIPRSSTTU	UP THE STAIRS
AEHILLNNSTU	IN A NUTSHELL	AEHIPSSTTWY	STEP THIS WAY
AEHILLNPRTU	IN THE PLURAL	AEHIRRSTTYY	THIRTY YEARS
AEHILLNSSTT	IN THE STALLS	AEHJNOORRST	TROJAN HORSE
AEHILLOPPPS	APPLE-POLISH	AEHKLLNSSTY	THANKLESSLY
AEHILLOPRST	HOSPITALLER	AEHKLOOPRTT	LOOK THE PART
AEHILMMPRTT	TRIM THE LAMP	AEHKLOOPSYY	PLAYS HOOKEY
AEHILMNORTW	MOTHER-IN-LAW	AEHKLOPRSSW	SHOPWALKERS
AEHILMNOTTY	METHYLATION	AEHKMOPRSTT	MARK THE SPOT
AEHILMNPSSY	MISSHAPENLY	AEHKMOPRTTU	UP TO THE MARK
AEHILMNRSTU	LUTHERANISM	AEHKOOORTTT	TOOK TO HEART
AEHILMNRTTU	THERMAL UNIT	AEHKOPRSTTU	TAKE UP SHORT
AEHILMNSTWY	WHATS MY LINE?	AEHKORSTWWX	THE WAXWORKS
AEHILMQSSUY	SQUEAMISHLY	AEHLLLMOOPR	ALLELOMORPH
AEHILNOOPRS	SOPHIA LOREN	AEHLLMOOSTY	LOATHSOMELY
AEHILNOORST	NORTH SEA OIL	AEHLLMORRSY	LARRY HOLMES
AEHILNOOSST	SHOOTS A LINE	AEHLLMRRSSY	SMALL SHERRY
AEHILNOSTTW	WEST LOTHIAN	AEHLLNOPRXY	PHYLLOXERAN
AEHILNSSSSV	SLAVISHNESS	AEHLLNOSSSW	SHALLOWNESS
AEHILOPPSST	APOSTLESHIP	AEHLLORRSSZ	RAZOR-SHELLS
AEHILOPRRSW	APRIL SHOWER	AEHLLOTTUWY	TELL YOU WHAT
AEHILOPTTWY	WHITE TO PLAY	AEHLMNMNOTWW	MOWN THE LAWN
AEHILORTTVY	HORTATIVELY	AEHLMNOQSSU	LEMON SQUASH
AEHIMMPRRST	TRIP-HAMMERS	AEHLMNOSSST	MATHS LESSON
AEHIMMSTTTU	AT THE SUMMIT	AEHLMNOSTWW	MOWS THE LAWN
AEHIMNNNSSS	MANNISHNESS	AEHLMOOSSUX	HOMOSEXUALS
AEHIMNNTTUU	IN THE AUTUMN	AEHLNNOPSTT	PENTATHLONS
AEHIMNOOPSS	HOMO SAPIENS	AEHLNNOSTTW	SHOWN TALENT
AEHIMNOPRST	MISANTHROPE	AEHLNOPRSSS	SHARP LESSON
AEHIMNORSTU	HOUSE MARTIN	AEHLNOPSSTU	HOUSEPLANTS
AEHIMNSSSTU	ENTHUSIASMS	AEHLNOSSTTW	SHOWS TALENT
AEHIMOPRRSS	RASH PROMISE	AEHLOOPPRRU	POPULAR HERO
AEHIMOPSSUX	AMPHIOXUSES	AEHLOPPRSXY	PROPHYLAXES
AEHIMORSTTX	THERMOTAXIS	AEHLOPSSTTT	THE LAST POST
AEHIMPRSSST	SHIPS MASTER	AEHLPRSSTUU	SULPHURATES
AEHIMPRSSTY	SYMPATHISER	AEHMMMNPPSTU	MAN THE PUMPS
AEHIMPRSTYZ	SYMPATHIZER	AEHMMOOORST	THOMAS MOORE
AEHIMPSSSTY	SYMPATHISES	AEHMMOPPRYY	HAPPY MEMORY
AEHIMPSSTYZ	SYMPATHIZES	AEHMNNNORTU	MAN ON THE RUN
AEHIMRSTTTW	TWIST THE ARM	AEHMNNOOSTW	HONEST WOMAN

AEHMNOOPSTY	PAYS THE MOON	AEIILLMNNPW	WILLIAM PENN
AEHMNOORSTU	MOUNT A HORSE	AEIILLMNSTU	ILLUMINATES
AEHMNOORSTV	HARVEST MOON	AEIILLNNRTY	TRIENNIALLY
AEHMNOORTTW	NO MATTER HOW	AEIILLNOPST	PILLION SEAT
	NO MATTER WHO	AEIILLNOTVY	INVIOLATELY
AEHMNOPPTTU	PUT ON THE MAP	AEIILLNPTVY	PLAINTIVELY
AEHMNORTTWY	NO MATTER WHY	AEIILLOSSTV	VOLATILISES
AEHMOOPSSTT	STOPS AT HOME	AEIILLOSTVZ	VOLATILIZES
AEHMOPSSTTU	PUTS TO SHAME	AEIILLOTTVW	VOLATILE WIT
AEHMORRSTTY	TERRY THOMAS	AEIILLRSTWW	WRITES A WILL
AEHMORRTWWY	WHAT – ME WORRY?	AEIILMMORST	IMMORTALISE
AEHMORSSTTT	THERMOSTATS	AEIILMMORTZ	IMMORTALIZE
AEHNOOOORSTW	SWORE ON OATH	AEIILMNOORT	MELIORATION
AEHNOOPRRTT	ORTHOPTERAN	AEIILMNOSTT	TESTIMONIAL
AEHNOOPSSSU	SOUSAPHONES	AEIILMNOSTV	LOVE-IN-A-MIST
AEHNOORSTTU	AUTHORS NOTE	AEIILMNPRRT	LATIN PRIMER
AEHNOORSTTW	THROW A STONE	AEIILMNPRRY	PRELIMINARY
AEHNOOSTTWW	WENT TO A SHOW	AEIILMNPTTY	IMPATIENTLY
AEHNOOTTUWY	ON THE WAY OUT	AEIILMPSSVY	IMPASSIVELY
AEHNORRSSTW	SHORT ANSWER	AEIILMRRSTT	TRIMESTRIAL
AEHNORRSTTU	RUNS TO EARTH	AEIILMSTTUV	STIMULATIVE
AEHNORSSTTU	TURN TO ASHES	AEIILNNNOST	INTENSIONAL
AEHOOOOPSTTT	HOT POTATOES	AEIILNNNOTT	INTENTIONAL
AEHOOOPPRSST	APOSTROPHES	AEIILNNORST	INSERTIONAL
AEHOOPRRSTT	TRAPSHOOTER	AEIILNNOSVV	LOVES IN VAIN
AEHOOPRRSTV	POOR HARVEST	AEIILNNOTTV	VENTILATION
AEHOOPRRSTX	PROTHORAXES	AEIILNNRTTY	INTERNALITY
AEHOOPSSTTT	TOOTHPASTES	AEIILNNSSST	SAINTLINESS
AEHOORRTTXY	EXHORTATORY	AEIILNNSTVW	LIVES IN WANT
AEHOORSSSTY	SOOTHSAYERS	AEIILNOPRSV	PREVISIONAL
AEHOPPSSTTT	PAST THE POST	AEIILNORSTT	ORIENTALIST
AEHORSSTTWY	SHORTEST WAY	AEIILNRSSTV	TRIVIALNESS
AEHPRRRSTYY	SHERRY PARTY	AEIILNRSSTW	SISTER-IN-LAW
AEIIIINSTTV	INITIATIVES	AEIILORRRTT	TERRITORIAL
AEIIILLMNOR	MILLIONAIRE	AEIILPRSSST	PERISTALSIS
AEIIILLMNST	SILLIMANITE	AEIILPRTTVY	PARTITIVELY
AEIIILLTTTV	TITILLATIVE	AEIILRSSTVV	REVIVALISTS
AEIIILMMPRS	IMPERIALISM	AEIILRSTTVY	VERSATILITY
AEIIILMNNOT	ELIMINATION	AEIIMMNNOPT	IN PANTOMIME
AEIIILMNOTV	INITIAL MOVE	AEIIMMRRTTU	TERMITARIUM
AEIIILMNRST	MINISTERIAL	AEIIMNNORST	INSEMINATOR
AEIIILMNSST	LAMINITISES		NITROSAMINE
AEIIILMPRST	IMPERIALIST	AEIIMNNORTT	TERMINATION
AEIIILMRSST	MILITARISES	AEIIMNNRRSS	RISEN IN ARMS
AEIIILMRSTZ	MILITARIZES	AEIIMNOSSTT	ESTIMATIONS
AEIIILMTTVY	IMITATIVELY	AEIIMNOSTUX	ANXIOUS TIME
AEIIILNNSTW	WAITS IN LINE	AEIIMNRRSSS	RISES IN ARMS
AEIIILNPRST	PLEINAIRIST	AEIIMNRRSTU	AIR TERMINUS
AEIIILRSSTV	TRIVIALISES	AEIIMNRRSTW	WAR MINISTER
AEIIILRSTVZ	TRIVIALIZES	AEIIMNRSSST	SEMINARISTS
AEIIIMNNRTU	IN MINIATURE	AEIIMOPRRSS	IMPRESARIOS
AEIIIMNOSST	ANIMOSITIES	AEIIMRRTTUV	TRIUMVIRATE
AEIIIMNOSTT	ITEMISATION	AEIIMRSSSTT	MISS A SITTER
AEIIIMNOTTZ	ITEMIZATION	AEIINNNORTV	INNERVATION
AEIIIMNRRST	AIR MINISTER	AEIINNNOTTT	INATTENTION
AEIIIMNRSTU	MINIATURISE	AEIINNNQQUU	QUINQUENNIA
AEIIIMNRTUZ	MINIATURIZE	AEIINNOOPRT	IN OPERATION
AEIIIMNSSTV	VITAMINISES	AEIINNOORTT	ORIENTATION
AEIIIMNSTVZ	VITAMINIZES	AEIINNPRSTW	TIPS A WINNER
AEIIINNORTT	ITINERATION	AEIINOPRRST	RESPIRATION
AEIIINNRSTV	TRIES IN VAIN	AEIINOPRSTX	EXPIRATIONS
AEIIINNSTUV	INSINUATIVE	AEIINOPRTTX	EXTIRPATION
AEIIINORSSV	VISIONARIES	AEIINOPRTTY	PETITIONARY
AEIIINQSTTU	ANTIQUITIES	AEIINOPSSTT	POINSETTIAS
AEIIJLMMSVY	JIMMY SAVILE	AEIINORRSVY	REVISIONARY
AEIIKLLNPRS	PAINKILLERS	AEIINPRSSSU	PRUSSIANISE
AEIIKLLOPRT	REALPOLITIK	AEIINPRSSUZ	PRUSSIANIZE
AEIIKLOSTUY	AS YOU LIKE IT	AEIINPSSSST	INSPISSATES
AEIILLLLMTW	WILLIAM TELL	AEIINPSTVXY	EXPANSIVITY
AEIILLLMMSS	MILLESIMALS	AEIINSSTTUV	ANTITUSSIVE
AEIILLLOOTV	VOLATILE OIL	AEIIOOPPSSS	APOSIOPESIS

AEIIOPPRSTT	PROPITIATES	AEILNNOOPSS	PIANO LESSON
AEIIOPRRRSU	SUPERIOR AIR	AEILNNOPSSY	POLYNESIANS
AEIIRSSSTUW	ISSUES A WRIT	AEILNNORSTY	ROYAL TENNIS
AEIJLLSTTTU	JUST A LITTLE	AEILNNPSSTY	PLAYS TENNIS
AEIJLNORRUZ	JOURNALIZER	AEILNNPSTUY	PLAYS IN TUNE
AEIJLNORSSU	JOURNALISES	AEILNNRSTTY	TRANSIENTLY
AEIJLNORSUZ	JOURNALIZES	AEILNNRSTUY	SATURNINELY
AEIJMMNNOSS	JEAN SIMMONS	AEILNOOPRTX	EXPLORATION
AEIJMNSTTUU	JUST A MINUTE	AEILNOPRSTY	PERSONALITY
AEIJNNNOTTT	JOINT TENANT	AEILNORSTTV	VENTILATORS
AEIJNOSSSZZ	JAZZ SESSION	AEILNORSTUV	VOLUNTARIES
AEIKKLMNORW	WORKMANLIKE	AEILNSSSSTU	SENSUALISTS
AEIKKMMNNOTW	MAKE IT KNOWN	AEILOORRTTV	IL TROVATORE
AEIKKNORSST	TAKE NO RISKS	AEILOPPRRSU	POPULARISER
AEIKLLMRRSY	SILLY REMARK	AEILOPPRRUZ	POPULARIZER
AEIKLLNOSTY	LIKELY AS NOT	AEILOPPRSSU	POPULARISES
AEIKLLNOTTW	KNOW A LITTLE	AEILOPPRSUZ	POPULARIZES
AEIKLLOSTTT	TAKE ITS TOLL	AEILOPRRRTV	RIVER PATROL
AEIKLLOSUWY	WELL, I ASK YOU	AEILOPRRTUY	AT YOUR PERIL
AEIKLLOTTUV	TALK QUIETLY	AEILOPRSSSU	PLESIOSAURS
AEIKLNNOPPS	PLAINSPOKEN	AEILOPRSTTW	WATER PISTOL
AEIKLNOSSST	STOLEN A KISS	AEILOPRSTUV	SPORULATIVE
AEIKLNPSSTW	WALKS IN STEP	AEILORRSSTY	SERIAL STORY
AEIKLORSSTU	SERIOUS TALK	AEILOSTUVXY	VEXATIOUSLY
AEIKLORSTTV	TALKS IT OVER	AEILPRSSTWY	WRITES PLAYS
AEIKMRRTTWY	WITTY REMARK	AEILRRSSSTU	SURREALISTS
AEIKNNOOPSS	SNAKE POISON	AFIMMNOOSST	MASS EMOTION
AEIKNNOOPST	TAKEN POISON	AEIMMMNORRTT	MINOR MATTER
AEIKNNOPTTY	TAKEN PITY ON	AEIMMORSTTU	TAUTOMERISM
AEIKNNOSTTU	UNTIES A KNOT	AEIMMRRSSSU	SUMMARISERS
AEIKNOOPSST	TAKES POISON	AEIMMRRSSUZ	SUMMARIZERS
AEIKNOPSTTY	TAKES PITY ON	AEIMNNOPPTT	APPOINTMENT
AEILLLLMNTY	MENTALLY ILL	AEIMNNORSTU	MENSURATION
AEILLMNOOPS	OIL ONE'S PALM	AEIMNOPPRRY	OPEN PRIMARY
AEILLMNOOTY	EMOTIONALLY	AEIMNOPPRSU	MAIN PURPOSE
AEILLMOPRRT	MORTAL PERIL	AEIMNOPRTTU	IMPORTUNATE
AEILLNOORSY	EROSIONALLY		PERMUTATION
AEILLNOPTTY	POTENTIALLY	AEIMNOPSTTT	TEMPTATIONS
AEILLNOPTWY	YELLOW PAINT	AEIMNORRSTT	TERMINATORS
AEILLNOSSSY	SILLY SEASON	AEIMNORRSTT	MONETARISTS
AEILLNRSSWY	SILLY ANSWER	AEIMNPPRSST	PENTAPRISMS
AEILLNRSTUV	SURVEILLANT	AEIMNRRSTTT	TRANSMITTER
AEILLNRSUVY	UNIVERSALLY	AEIMOOPRRTV	PRIVATE ROOM
AEILLNSSSTY	STAINLESSLY	AEIMOORSTTU	AUTOEROTISM
AEILLNSUUXY	UNISEXUALLY	AEIMPRRTTUY	PREMATURITY
AEILLOOPRST	ALLOTROPIES	AEIMSSSTTTY	SYSTEMATIST
AEILLOPRSVW	PROVES A WILL	AEINNNOORTW	ON TO A WINNER
AEILLORTTUV	ULTRA VIOLET	AEINNOOPRST	PERSONATION
	ULTRAVIOLET	AEINNOOSTTT	OSTENTATION
AEILLPRTVYY	LIVELY PARTY	AEINNOPSTTY	SPONTANEITY
AEILLRSSTTU	ILLUSTRATES	AEINNOQRSTU	QUATERNIONS
AEILLRSSTTW	STILL WATERS	AEINNORSTUV	INTRAVENOUS
AEILMMNORTY	MOMENTARILY	AEINNOSSSUX	ANXIOUSNESS
AEILMNNNORT	NOMINAL RENT	AEINNPQSSTU	PIQUANTNESS
AEILMNNNSSU	UNMANLINESS	AEINOOPPRTV	PROVE A POINT
AEILMNNOPRT	MINOR PLANET	AEINOOPRRST	PERORATIONS
AEILMNNOSSW	WOMANLINESS	AEINOOPRSTT	IN POOR TASTE
AEILMNNSSTT	INSTALMENTS	AEINOOPRTTT	POTENTIATOR
AEILMNOOSTT	MOLESTATION	AEINOOPRTTX	EXPORTATION
AEILMNOPRRT	TRAMPOLINER	AEINOORRSTT	RESTORATION
AEILMNOPRST	TRAMPOLINES	AEINOORSUVX	OVER ANXIOUS
AEILMNORTVY	NORMATIVELY	AEINOPPRRTT	PEN PORTRAIT
AEILMNTTUWZ	MINUTE WALTZ	AEINOPRSSSU	PERSUASIONS
AEILMOPRRTY	POLARIMETRY	AEINOPRSSSV	VASOPRESSIN
	TEMPORARILY	AEINOPRSSTT	STATE PRISON
AEILMOPRTTY	TEMPORALITY	AEINOPRSSTU	REPUTATIONS
AEILMOPRTXY	PROXIMATELY	AEINOPSTTTU	OUTPATIENTS
AEILMPPRSTU	LITMUS PAPER	AEINORSSSUV	VARIOUSNESS
AEILMPPSSST	PALIMPSESTS	AEIOPPRRRTY	PROPRIETARY
AEILMPRSSST	SLIPSTREAMS	AEIOPRRRSST	RESPIRATORS
AEILMRTTTWY	WALTER MITTY	AEIOPRRRSTY	RESPIRATORY

AEIOPRRRTTU	PORTRAITURE
AEIOPRRTTUV	VITUPERATOR
AEIORRSTTWY	WRITE A STORY
AEIOSSTTTUW	SWEATS IT OUT
AEIPPRSTUUV	SUPPURATIVE
AEJLNORSTUY	LAST JOURNEY
AEJMMNOSTTU	JUST A MOMENT
AEJMORSTUYY	YOUR MAJESTY
AEKKLRSTTUY	TALKS TURKEY
AEKKMNOPPRT	KEMPTON PARK
AEKLLMORUWY	MARK YOU WELL
AEKLLOPSSWY	SPEAK SLOWLY
AEKLNOOPRSY	PLAY SNOOKER
AEKLOPRRSTW	PLASTERWORK
AEKMNOOPSSW	SPOKESWOMAN
AEKNNOOSWWY	KNOW ONES WAY
AEKNOORSSTU	ONEROUS TASK
AEKNOORSWWY	WORK ONES WAY
AEKNORSTTTU	TAKE ON TRUST
AEKOOPRRSTY	PROKARYOTES
AEKORRSTTUY	ROAST TURKEY
AELLLMMNOOY	MOLLY MALONE
AELLLNOOSST	LOST ONE'S ALL
AELLMNOORSS	MORAL LESSON
AELLMOOORSS	LOOSE MORALS
AELLNOORSTW	SLOW TO LEARN
AELLNOPPRST	PROPELLANTS
AELLNRSTTUY	RESULTANTLY
AELLOPRSSUX	SOLAR PLEXUS
AELLORSSTTY	TELLS A STORY
AELMMOOSTUY	MYELOMATOUS
AELMNNORSTY	NORMAN STYLE
AELMNOOTUYY	LAY OUT MONEY
AELMNOPRRSU	SUPERNORMAL
AELMOPSSTUY	SYMPETALOUS
AELMORSSSTU	SOMERSAULTS
AELMORSSSTY	SOLAR SYSTEM
AELMORSSTTY	TASTY MORSEL
AELMPRSTYYY	MYSTERY PLAY
AELNNNOPRTW	TOWN PLANNER
AELNNSSSUUU	UNUSUALNESS
AELNOOOPRTU	OUT ON PAROLE
AELNOOPPRTU	PUT ON PAROLE
AELNOOSSTWY	LOST ONE'S WAY
AELNOPPRTUU	POPULAR TUNE
AELNOPPSTTY	PENALTY SPOT
AELNOPRSTTY	PORT STANLEY
AELNPRRSUUY	SUPERLUNARY
AELOOPRRTXY	EXPLORATORY
AELOPPRRRSU	POURPARLERS
AELORRSSTTW	SLOW STARTER
AELPPRSTUWY	WATER SUPPLY
AEMMNNOORSY	RANSOM MONEY
AEMMNRSSUWY	NEWS SUMMARY
AEMNNORSTTU	TOURNAMENTS
AEMNNORTVYY	NOT VERY MANY
AEMNOOPPRSS	MAN PROPOSES
AEMNOOPRSTY	TRYPANOSOME
AEMNOORRSST	ASTRONOMERS
AEMNOORSSSU	AMOROUSNESS
AEMNOORSWWY	WORM ONES WAY
AEMNOPPSTTY	STOP PAYMENT
AEMNOPRRSST	SMART PERSON
AEMNORSSSTT	ASSORTMENTS
AEMOOOPRRST	ROOM TO SPARE
AEMOPPRSTTU	TEAM SUPPORT
AEMOPRSSSTT	POSTMASTERS
AEMORRRSTTT	SMART RETORT
AEMORRSTTTU	TROUT STREAM
AEMPRRSTTTY	PRETTY SMART
AEMPRSSTTYY	PARTY SYSTEM

AENNOOPRSSS	PARSONS NOSE
AENNOOPSSTU	SPONTANEOUS
AENNOPRSSTY	NASTY PERSON
AENNORRSSTT	NONSTARTERS
AENOOOSSSTW	SOW ONE'S OATS
AENOPPPRSTU	PUTS ON PAPER
AENOPRRRSTT	TRANSPORTER
AENOPRSSTTT	PROTESTANTS
AENOQRRSTUY	STONE QUARRY
AENORRSTTTU	STERNUTATOR
AENPRTTTTYY	PETTY TYRANT
AEOOPRRRTWY	ROTARY POWER
AEOOPRRSSSV	VASOPRESSOR
AEOOPSTTTUU	PUT OUT TO SEA
AEOORRSTTWY	WROTE A STORY
AEOPPRRRSTU	RAPPORTEURS
AEOPPRRTTXY	PROPERTY TAX
AEOPRRRSSTY	ROTARY PRESS
AEOPRRSSTTW	WATER SPORTS
AEPPPRRSTUY	SUPPER PARTY
AFFFLLLOOSU	FALLS FOUL OF
AFFGGHILNOU	LAUGHING OFF
AFFGHIINOTV	HAVING IT OFF
AFFGHIIORRT	FIGHT FOR AIR
AFFGHILOSTU	LAUGHS IT OFF
AFFGHIORSTT	STRAIGHT OFF
AFFGIIINNTT	FAINTING FIT
AFFGIIKNORT	FIT FOR A KING
AFFGIILNORT	TRAILING OFF
AFFGIKMNNOU	MAKING FUN OF
AFFGIKNNSTU	TAKING SNUFF
AFFGIKNOPRS	SPARKING OFF
AFFGILLLNOU	FALLING FOUL
AFFGILNORTT	RATTLING OFF
AFFGIMNORRY	MARRYING OFF
AFFGINOQRSU	SQUARING OFF
AFFGINORSTT	STARTING OFF
AFFGIRSSSTU	SUFFRAGISTS
AFFGORSSTTU	TUFT OF GRASS
AFFHHILOOSS	SHOAL OF FISH
AFFHIKLOTWW	WALK OFF WITH
AFFHILOOSST	LOSS OF FAITH
AFFHMOORSTU	FOUR FATHOMS
AFFHMOORTUY	FOURTH OF MAY
AFFHOORSTWY	SHORT WAY OFF
AFFIILLMNOR	FILL IN A FORM
AFFIINOSTUX	SUFFIXATION
AFFILNORSTU	INSUFFLATOR
AFFIMNORSTY	FIRST OF MANY
AFFIOOPRRSU	PAIR OF FOURS
AFFLLLNORTU	FULL FRONTAL
AFFLLLORUUV	FULL FLAVOUR
AFFOOORTUUV	OUT OF FAVOUR
AFGGHIIMNNT	FIGHTING MAN
AFGGIIILNTV	GIVING A LIFT
AFGGIILNNST	SINGING FLAT
AFGGIILNTUY	FATIGUINGLY
AFGGIINPRTT	PARTING GIFT
AFGGILLNOPY	PLAYING GOLF
AFGGINOOORT	GOING TOO FAR
AFGHHHIINOS	HIGH FASHION
AFGHHIILNTU	HIGHFALUTIN
AFGHHLLORTU	FALL THROUGH
AFGHHOSTTTU	THOUGHT FAST
AFGHIIKMNST	MAKING SHIFT
AFGHIILNORW	FLOWING HAIR
AFGHIILNOST	LOSING FAITH
AFGHIILRSTY	FAIRY LIGHTS
AFGHIINORST	FIRING A SHOT
AFGHIKLOORT	LOOK A FRIGHT
AFGHILMOPRY	FILMOGRAPHY

AFGHILNNTTU	FLAT HUNTING
AFGHINNORTY	FOR ANYTHING
AFGHINORSTT	STRONG FAITH
AFGHIPPTTUU	PUT UP A FIGHT
AFGHJNNOOTU	JOHN OF GAUNT
AFGIIILNSTU	FILING A SUIT
AFGIIINNRTU	INFURIATING
AFGIIKNNOPS	KING OF SPAIN
AFGIIKNOPRS	PAIR OF KINGS
AFGIIKNORST	ASKING FOR IT
AFGIILLNNUY	UNFAILINGLY
AFGIILLOPRS	SLIP OF A GIRL
AFGIILMNNTU	FULMINATING
AFGIILMNORS	FORMALISING
AFGIILMNORZ	FORMALIZING
AFGIINNNNORU	FINNO-UGRIAN
AFGIINNNOTU	FOUNTAINING
AFGIINNOPSY	SAPONIFYING
AFGIINNQTUY	QUANTIFYING
AFGIINNRSTX	TRANSFIXING
AFGIINOOTTX	GOT INTO A FIX
AFGIINOPRTY	PAYING FOR IT
AFGIINORSTU	FIGURATIONS
AFGIINPRRTY	FIRING PARTY
AFGIINRSTTY	STRATIFYING
AFGIKLLMOSS	GLASS OF MILK
AFGIKLNNOTU	OUTFLANKING
AFGIKNNOPTU	POKING FUN AT
AFGILLLNOOO	GALLON OF OIL
AFGILLLNOWY	LYING FALLOW
AFGILLNNTUY	FLAUNTINGLY
AFGILMNORTU	FORMULATING
AFGILNRSTTY	FLYING START
AFGINNRSSTU	TRANSFUSING
AFGINOOPRST	PAIR OF TONGS
AFGINOOPSST	SOFT-SOAPING
AFGINRRSTTU	FRUSTRATING
AFGLLLOOPUY	FULL APOLOGY
AFGLLNOORSU	FOUR GALLONS
AFGLMOPRSUU	LUMP OF SUGAR
AFGLOOPRSST	GLASS OF PORT
AFGNNOORRTW	NOT FAR WRONG
AFGNOORSTUU	RUN OUT OF GAS
AFHHINOOSSW	FASHION SHOW
AFHIIINNSST	SATIN FINISH
AFHIILLNSTW	FALLS IN WITH
AFHIILOTTUW	WITHOUT FAIL
AFHIKLLOOST	FOOLISH TALK
AFHILORSTWY	SOLWAY FIRTH
AFHINOOPRRS	PAIR OF HORNS
AFHIOOPRSTW	SHOW A PROFIT
AFHLNOOOPRU	LAP OF HONOUR
AFHMNNOOORU	MAN OF HONOUR
AFHNOORSUVW	SHOWN FAVOUR
AFHOORSSUVW	SHOWS FAVOUR
AFIIIILNNTV	INFINITIVAL
AFIIILMNNST	INFANTILISM
AFIILLMORTW	FORT WILLIAM
AFIILLNNRSU	FALL IN RUINS
AFIILMNNOTU	FULMINATION
AFIILMNORTY	INFORMALITY
AFIILMORSTV	FORMAL VISIT
AFIILNORRTT	INFILTRATOR
AFIILNORSTT	FILTRATIONS
	FLIRTATIONS
AFIILORSTTU	FLIRTATIOUS
AFIIMNNOORT	IN FORMATION
	INFORMATION
AFIIMNOPRST	MAN OF SPIRIT
AFIIMORSTUV	FAVOURITISM
AFIINNORSTX	TRANSFIXION
AFIIOPRSSSU	FISSIPAROUS
AFIKLLNOORW	FOR ALL I KNOW
AFIKLNNORTW	WALK IN FRONT
AFILLMOOPRT	OIL PLATFORM
AFILLMOPRST	SMALL PROFIT
AFILLMPSUWY	SIMPLY AWFUL
AFILMMOOTTY	FAMILY MOTTO
AFILMNNOOST	TIN OF SALMON
AFILMNOORTU	FORMULATION
AFILMNORTUV	MINT FLAVOUR
AFILNOOORTU	RAN OUT OF OIL
AFILOOPRSSW	SPOILS OF WAR
AFILORSSTTT	FIRST TO LAST
AFIMNNOORRT	RAN INTO FORM
AFIMOPPPRSU	PAIR OF PUMPS
AFINNORSSTU	TRANSFUSION
AFINOOPPRST	PORT OF SPAIN
AFINOOPSTTU	SNAP OUT OF IT
AFINORRSTTU	FRUSTRATION
AFKKLMPRTUU	KULTURKAMPF
AFKMOOOORRRZ	MARK OF ZORRO
AFLLOPRUUXY	LAP OF LUXURY
AFLMNOORSTW	FLOWN TO ARMS
AFLMOPRRTUY	POULTRY FARM
AFMNOORRRUY	RUN FOR MAYOR
AGGGIIINNRV	GIVING A RING
AGGGIIINNSV	GIVING A SIGN
AGGGIIINOTV	GIVING IT A GO
AGGGIINNORS	GOING IN RAGS
AGGGILNOOOT	GOING TO GAOL
AGGGLLNNOOO	LONG LONG AGO
AGGHHIIILNT	HIGHTAILING
AGGHHIIKNNR	RANKING HIGH
AGGHHIILNPY	PLAYING HIGH
AGGHIIINNTV	GIVING A HINT
AGGHIIJMNTU	THINGUMAJIG
AGGHIIKLMNT	MAKING LIGHT
AGGHIIKMNTT	MAKING TIGHT
AGGHIIILLNST	SIGNAL LIGHT
AGGHIILNNSU	LANGUISHING
AGGHIILNNTW	WANING LIGHT
AGGHIINOOTV	GIVING A HOOT
AGGHILNRTUY	NAUGHTY GIRL
AGGHINNNOOT	HANGING ON TO
AGGHINNORRTW	RIGHT A WRONG
AGGHIORSTTT	GOT STRAIGHT
AGGIIILNNSS	SIGNALISING
AGGIIILNNSZ	SIGNALIZING
AGGIIIMMNRT	IMMIGRATING
AGGIIIMNSSV	GIVING A MISS
AGGIIINNORT	ORIGINATING
AGGIIINNSTT	INSTIGATING
AGGIIJLNOOT	GOING TO JAIL
AGGIIKNNSTW	TAKING WINGS
AGGIILLNORT	ROLLING GAIT
AGGIILMNORS	GLAMORISING
AGGIILMNORZ	GLAMORIZING
AGGIILNNNOW	WINNING GOAL
AGGIILNNOSY	AGONISINGLY
AGGIILNNOYZ	AGONIZINGLY
AGGIILNNSTU	AGGLUTININS
AGGIILNOOPS	APOLOGISING
AGGIILNOOPZ	APOLOGIZING
AGGIILNRSUV	VULGARISING
AGGIILNRUVZ	VULGARIZING
AGGIINNOPRW	GROWING PAIN
AGGIINNORRS	GARRISONING
AGGIINNRTUV	GIVING A TURN
AGGILLMORRU	GLAMOUR GIRL
AGGILLNNOPY	LONG PLAYING
AGGILLNNOST	LASTING LONG

AGGILLNOOTU	GOING ALL OUT
AGGILMNNOOV	MOVING ALONG
AGGILNNORST	STRING ALONG
AGGILNNOSSW	SWINGS ALONG
AGGILNOORTV	GRAVING TOOL
AGGIMMNNOPRR	PROGRAMMING
AGGIMNOOSST	GOING TO MASS
AGGIMNORRWW	GROWING WARM
AGGINNRSTTU	STARTING GUN
AGGLNNORSTU	STRUNG ALONG
AGGLOOPRSTW	PORT GLASGOW
AGHHIILQTUY	HIGH QUALITY
AGHHIIMNRST	NIGHTMARISH
AGHHIIMOOST	AIMS TOO HIGH
AGHHIINOSTT	HIGH STATION
AGHHIIRSSTT	STRAIGHTISH
AGHHIIRSTTT	STRAIGHT HIT
AGHHILOPRST	LITHOGRAPHS
AGHHILOPRTY	LITHOGRAPHY
AGHHIMNPRRU	HARRUMPHING
AGHHIMNRSTU	HUMAN RIGHTS
AGHHKLORTUW	WALK-THROUGH
AGHHLLLOOUW	HOLLOW LAUGH
AGHHNOOPPRS	PHONOGRAPHS
AGHHNOOPPRY	PHONOGRAPHY
AGHHOOPPRST	PHOTOGRAPHS
AGHHOOPPRTY	PHOTOGRAPHY
AGHHOOPPRRTY	ORTHOGRAPHY
AGHHOPPRSYY	HYPSOGRAPHY
AGHHOPPRTYY	PHYTOGRAPHY
AGHHOPRSSTU	PASS THROUGH
AGHIIILMNTU	HUMILIATING
AGHIIILNPSS	SAILING SHIP
AGHIIINSTTX	HITTING A SIX
AGHIIKMNOTT	MAKING IT HOT
AGHIILLRSTT	IT'S ALL RIGHT
AGHIILMNOOS	HOOLIGANISM
AGHIILNPTWY	PLAYING WITH
AGHIILNRSTY	HAIRSTYLING
AGHIILNRSVY	RAVISHINGLY
AGHIIMMNPTU	HAMMING IT UP
AGHIIMNNORS	HARMONISING
AGHIIMNNORZ	HARMONIZING
AGHIIMNPSSW	PASSING WHIM
AGHIINNOSST	ASTONISHING
AGHIINNQSUV	VANQUISHING
AGHIINNRSTU	THURINGIANS
AGHIINNSTVW	HAVING TWINS
AGHIINORSTU	AUTHORISING
AGHIINORTUZ	AUTHORIZING
AGHIINOTTUV	HAVING IT OUT
AGHIINPRRSS	HAIRSPRINGS
AGHIINPRSTY	PHARYNGITIS
AGHIINPRTTW	PARTING WITH
AGHIINRSTTW	STRAIGHT WIN
AGHIINRSTWW	WAINWRIGHTS
AGHIINSSTTY	STAY IN SIGHT
AGHIIPRSTTT	STRAIGHT TIP
AGHIJNOSTWY	SANG WITH JOY
AGHIKLNOPST	TALKING SHOP
AGHIKNNPSTW	KNIGHTS PAWN
AGHIKNORSUW	WAKING HOURS
AGHILLOPRST	POLAR LIGHTS
AGHILNOPSTY	PLAYING HOST
AGHILOOPSTT	PATHOLOGIST
AGHILPRSTWY	PLAYWRIGHTS
AGHIMNNRSTY	GRANNY SMITH
AGHINNORSTW	WARNING SHOT
AGHINNOSSTY	SAYS NOTHING
AGHINOORSTT	ROASTING HOT
AGHINOORSTW	SHOOTING WAR
AGHINOORTTW	A THING OR TWO
AGHINOOSSTY	SOOTHSAYING
AGHINOPRSTT	PARTING SHOT
AGHINOPSSSW	PASSING SHOW
AGHINPPSSTU	PUSHING PAST
AGHINRRSTTU	RUN STRAIGHT
	STRAIGHT RUN
AGHINRRSTTY	STARRY NIGHT
AGHIOPPRRSS	SPIROGRAPHS
AGHIOPPRRSY	SPIROGRAPHY
AGHIORSTTTU	STRAIGHT OUT
	STRAIGHT-OUT
AGHIPRSTTTU	PUT STRAIGHT
AGHJNOOORST	JOHN OGROATS
AGHKLLOOSTY	LOOK GHASTLY
AGHLLOOPSSY	HYPOGLOSSAL
AGHLOOPPSUY	POLYPHAGOUS
AGHLOPRSSTY	STYLOGRAPHS
AGHLOSSTTUV	GUSTAV HOLST
AGHNOOPPRRY	PORNOGRAPHY
AGHNOOPRSTU	PROGNATHOUS
AGIIIILLNNT	INITIALLING
AGIIIILNTVX	LIXIVIATING
AGIIIKLLMNW	KING WILLIAM
AGIIIKLLNNP	PAINKILLING
AGIIILLMNST	MAILING LIST
AGIIILLNTTT	TITILLATING
AGIIILMNNSU	ALUMINISING
AGIIILMNNUZ	ALUMINIZING
AGIIILNNOPT	OIL PAINTING
AGIIILNNOPV	PAVILIONING
AGIIILNNORS	ORIGINAL SIN
AGIIILNNORV	LIVING ON AIR
AGIIILNNPST	PLATINISING
AGIIILNNPTZ	PLATINIZING
AGIIILNNTWY	LYING IN WAIT
AGIIILNORTV	INVIGILATOR
AGIIILNORTY	ORIGINALITY
AGIIILNRSTU	RITUALISING
AGIIILNRTUZ	RITUALIZING
AGIIILNSSUV	VISUALISING
AGIIILNSTTW	WAITING LIST
AGIIILNSUVZ	VISUALIZING
AGIIIMMNORT	IMMIGRATION
AGIIINNNSTU	INSINUATING
AGIIINNOORT	ORIGINATION
AGIIINNOSTT	INSTIGATION
AGIIINTTTTV	TITTIVATING
AGIIJMNPTTU	JUMPING AT IT
AGIIKKNNRST	SKATING RINK
AGIIKKNRSST	TAKING RISKS
AGIIKLLNPST	TAKING PILLS
AGIIKLNNOOT	TAKING ON OIL
AGIIKLNNOTW	WALKING INTO
AGIIKNOTTTU	TAKING IT OUT
AGIIILLNNOPT	POLLINATING
AGIIILMNNORS	NORMALISING
AGIIILMNNORZ	NORMALIZING
AGIIILMNPPSY	MISAPPLYING
AGIIILMNSTTU	STIMULATING
AGIIILNNRTTU	TURNING TAIL
AGIIILNPRSST	SPRINGTAILS
AGIIILNPSTTU	STIPULATING
AGIIILNRSTUY	SINGULARITY
AGIIILNRTUUX	LUXURIATING
AGIIIMMNNTTU	MANUMITTING
AGIIIMMNRSSU	SUMMARISING
AGIIIMMNRSUZ	SUMMARIZING
AGIIIMMOSSST	MISOGAMISTS
AGIIIMNNOTTW	MATING IN TWO
AGIIIMNOORTW	WAITING ROOM

AGIINNNRSTY	TYRANNISING	AGLMOORRTYY	MARTYROLOGY
AGIINNNRTYZ	TYRANNIZING	AGLNOOOSTTY	STAY TOO LONG
AGIINNNSWWY	WINNING WAYS	AGLNOOPPRSU	POPULAR SONG
AGIINNOPRRU	POURING RAIN	AGLOOOPTTUY	GO OUT TO PLAY
AGIINNOPRST	PATRONISING	AGLOOOSTTUU	TAUTOLOGOUS
AGIINNOPRTZ	PATRONIZING	AGNORSSTTUY	STARTS YOUNG
AGIINNOPSST	PASSING IT ON	AHHIIMOSTWW	HIM WHO WAITS
AGIINNOPTTU	PAINTING OUT	AHHIKKORSST	KHAKI SHORTS
AGIINNOPTUW	WAITING UPON	AHHILNOORTU	HOLOTHURIAN
AGIINNPPRRY	RIPPING YARN	AHHILOPPSYY	HYPOPHYSIAL
AGIINNPRRST	TRANSPIRING	AHHIMNOPPST	PHANTOM SHIP
AGIINOORRST	ORIGINATORS	AHHIMNOPSSW	SHOWMANSHIP
AGIINOORRTV	INVIGORATOR	AHHIORSTTTU	THRASH IT OUT
AGIINRRTTTU	TRITURATING	AHHLLNOPTXY	XANTHOPHYLL
AGIJNOPSTUX	JUXTAPOSING	AHIIILMNOTU	HUMILIATION
AGIKKMNNNOW	MAKING KNOWN	AHIIILNPPPS	PHILIPPIANS
AGIKLLNNPRU	PULLING RANK	AHIIINNORTT	INTO THIN AIR
AGIKLNNOORW	WARNING LOOK	AHIILLNRTTY	TRINITY HALL
AGIKLNOPSTT	STOP TALKING	AHIILLORSUY	HILARIOUSLY
AGIKLNORTUW	WALKING TOUR	AHIILMMNSTW	SLIM WHITMAN
AGIKMNNNORU	RUNNING AMOK	AHIILOPSTTY	HOSPITALITY
AGIKMNNORSS	KINGS RANSOM	AHIILPRSSST	SPLITS HAIRS
AGIKMNOPRST	MAKING SPORT	AHIILRSSTTY	HAIR STYLIST
	POSTMARKING		HAIRSTYLIST
AGIKNNOORTW	TOOK WARNING	AHIIMNNRRTU	ANTIRRHINUM
AGIKNNRSTTU	TAKING TURNS	AHIIMOOPPPT	HIPPOPOTAMI
AGILLLNPTUU	PULLULATING	AHIINNPRSTU	HUNT IN PAIRS
AGILLMNNOOU	MONOLINGUAL	AHIINNSSTTT	THIS INSTANT
AGILLNOOPPY	PLAYING POLO	AHIINOPSTTT	AT THIS POINT
	PLAYING POOL	AHIINORTTUY	IN AUTHORITY
AGILLNPRTTY	PRATTLINGLY	AHIKKOORRSW	KWASHIORKOR
AGILLNRSTTY	STARTLINGLY	AHIKMNOPRSW	WORKMANSHIP
AGILMNNOPRT	TRAMPLING ON	AHIKNORSSTW	THROWN A KISS
AGILMNORSST	STORM SIGNAL	AHIKNPRRSSW	SHRINK-WRAPS
AGILMNPPRSS	PALM SPRINGS	AHIKORSSSTW	THROWS A KISS
AGILMOOPRTY	PRIMATOLOGY	AHILLMOPRTU	PROTHALLIUM
AGILNNOPTTU	PLANTING OUT	AHILLNNOPSY	POLLYANNISH
AGILNNPPSTU	SUPPLANTING	AHILLOTUWWY	WHAT YOU WILL
AGILNNPRSUY	UNSPARINGLY	AHILOPPRSXY	PROPHYLAXIS
AGILNOPPRVY	APPROVINGLY	AHIIMNOORRSU	HONORARIUMS
AGILNOPPTUY	PLAYING UP TO	AHIMNOPRSTY	MISANTHROPY
AGILNOPSSTY	GLOSSY PAINT	AHIMOOPSSST	SHAMPOOISTS
AGILNOPSTTU	POSTULATING	AHIMOORSTUZ	RHIZOMATOUS
AGILNPRRTUY	RULING PARTY	AHIMORRSTUU	RUMOUR HAS IT
AGILOORSSYY	ASSYRIOLOGY	AHINOOPSSTX	SAXOPHONIST
AGILORSTTUY	GUSTATORILY	AHINOORTTUY	NO AUTHORITY
AGILPRTTUYY	GUILTY PARTY		ON AUTHORITY
AGIMNNOPRST	SPORTING MAN	AHINORSTTTT	THATS TORN IT
AGIMNNORRST	MORNING STAR	AHIOPRSSTTY	PAST HISTORY
AGIMNNRSTTU	TRANSMUTING	AHJKMNOOOSU	JOSHUA NKOMO
AGIMNOORSST	AGRONOMISTS	AHKNNOPSSSY	SHANKSS PONY
AGIMNOPRSTV	MOVING PARTS	AHLMNOORSTY	RAN SMOOTHLY
AGIMNOPSTTU	STAMPING OUT	AHLMOOPRSUY	AMORPHOUSLY
AGIMNORSTTU	OUTSMARTING	AHLNOORSUVW	SHOWN VALOUR
AGINNNPRSTU	RUNNING PAST	AHLOORSSUVW	SHOWS VALOUR
AGINNOPRSST	TRANSPOSING	AHLOPRRSTUU	SULPHURATOR
AGINOOOPRRT	PROROGATION	AHNNOOOORSTW	SWORN ON OATH
AGINOOORTTW	GOT INTO A ROW	AHNNOSSTTWY	SHANTYTOWNS
AGINOOPRSTT	PROTAGONIST	AHNOOPSSTUW	PUTS ON A SHOW
AGINOORTTTU	GOT INTO A RUT	AHOPRRSSTTY	SHORT PASTRY
AGINOPRRSTT	PROSTRATING	AHPRSSSTTTU	THRUSTS PAST
AGINORSTTTU	STARTING OUT	AIIILNOTVX	LIXIVIATION
AGINORSTTUV	STARVING OUT	AIIIINNOSTT	INITIATIONS
AGINORSTTYY	TRYING TO SAY	AIIILLLNPTU	LILLIPUTIAN
AGINPPRSTUU	SUPPURATING	AIIILLMNPTV	VITAMIN PILL
AGLILLNOOPYY	POLYGONALLY	AIIILLMPTTW	WILLIAM PITT
AGLLLOOPTTY	POLYGLOTTAL	AIIILLNOTTT	TITILLATION
AGLLMOORSUY	GLAMOROUSLY	AIIILMMNSST	MINIMALISTS
AGLLORRSUUY	GARRULOUSLY	AIIILMNOSTT	LIMITATIONS
AGLMOOOSTTY	STOMATOLOGY	AIIILNNOOST	LIONISATION
AGLMOOPRRTU	PROMULGATOR	AIIILNNOOTZ	LIONIZATION

AIIILNNOPST	PAINT IN OILS	AILMNORSTUV	VOLUNTARISM
AIIILNNOTTU	INTUITIONAL	AILMOOPRSTUU	MULTIPAROUS
AIIILNOSTTU	UTILISATION	AILMORSSTTU	STIMULATORS
AIIILNOTTUZ	UTILIZATION	AILNNORTUVY	INVOLUNTARY
AIIIMNNORTY	IN A MINORITY	AILNOOPPSTU	POPULATIONS
AIIIMNRRSTY	AIR MINISTRY	AILNOOPRSTU	SPORULATION
AIIIMNRSTTU	MINIATURIST	AILNOOPSTTU	POSTULATION
AIIIMPPRRTY	PRIMIPARITY	AILNOPPSTTU	POSTNUPTIAL
AIIIMPSSTVY	IMPASSIVITY	AILNOPRSTTU	PUTS ON TRIAL
AIIINNNOSTU	INSINUATION	AILNOPSTTUU	PUSTULATION
AIIINNOPRST	INSPIRATION	AILNORSTTUV	VOLUNTARIST
AIIINNOSTTV	INVITATIONS	AILOOPQRTUY	POOR QUALITY
AIIINOSSTTV	VISITATIONS	AILOOPRSUVY	OVIPAROUSLY
AIIJLLMSTUW	JUST WILLIAM	AILOPRSSTTU	STIPULATORS
AIIILLMNORTU	ILLUMINATOR	AILOPRSTTUY	STIPULATORY
AIIILLNNOOPT	POLLINATION	AILORSTTTUY	STATUTORILY
AIIILLNRSSTY	SINISTRALLY	AIMMNORRTUU	MURMURATION
AIIILLPRSTUY	SPIRITUALLY	AIMMNSSTTUU	AUTUMN MISTS
AIIILMMORTTY	IMMORTALITY	AIMMOORRSTU	MORATORIUMS
AIIILMNOOSTZ	SOLMIZATION	AIMMOOSSTXY	MYXOMATOSIS
AIIILMNOSTTU	STIMULATION	AIMMRSSTTWY	TWISTS MY ARM
AIIILMNPRSTY	MANLY SPIRIT	AIMNNOOPTTU	MOUNTAIN TOP
AIIILNNOOTTY	NOTIONALITY	AIMNNOOSTUU	MOUNTAINOUS
AIIILNNORTTU	NUTRITIONAL	AIMNNOPRTTU	UNIMPORTANT
AIIILNOOPRSV	PROVISIONAL	AIMNOOSSTTU	AUTONOMISTS
AIIILNOPRTUY	UNIPOLARITY	AIMNOOSSTTX	TAXONOMISTS
AIIILNOPSTTU	STIPULATION	AIMNOPPPRSY	MARY POPPINS
AIIILNOSSTTY	STYLISATION	AIMNOPSSSTU	ASSUMPTIONS
AIIILNOSTTYZ	STYLIZATION	AIMNRSSTTUU	NASTURTIUMS
AIIMMNNOSSU	MANUMISSION	AINOOPRRSTT	PROSTRATION
AIIMMNSSTTU	NUMISMATIST	AINOOSSTTTU	OUTSTATIONS
AIIMMPRRSTU	IMPRIMATURS	AINOPPRSTUU	SUPPURATION
AIIMNNOOSTU	ANTIMONIOUS	AINORRRTTTU	TURN TRAITOR
AIIMNOOPRTT	IMPORTATION	AINORRSSSTT	TRANSISTORS
AIIMNOPRSTV	PROVITAMINS	AINORRSSTUU	SUSURRATION
AIIMOPPRRSU	PRIMIPAROUS	AINPRSSTUUV	PURSUIVANTS
AIINNNOOSTT	INTONATIONS	AIORRRSTTTU	TRITURATORS
AIINNOORRST	IRON RATIONS	AJMMOOORRTW	JAM TOMORROW
AIINNOPSSTT	SNAPS INTO IT	AKLLOOORSTT	TOOK A STROLL
AIINNORSSTT	TRANSITIONS	AKLNNOOOPTZ	ZOOPLANKTON
AIINNOSTWWY	IN ITS OWN WAY	AKMNOORRSUY	ON YOUR MARKS
AIINOPRRSST	INSPIRATORS	ALLLNOOPTYY	POLYTONALLY
AIINOPRRSTY	INSPIRATORY	ALLNOOOPPRR	PROPRANOLOL
AIINOPRRTTU	PARTURITION	ALLOORSTWWW	SWALLOWWORT
AIINORRTTTU	TRITURATION	ALLOOSSTWWW	TWO SWALLOWS
AIIOOPPRRTT	PROPITIATOR	ALMNNOOSUYY	ANONYMOUSLY
AIIOPRRSTTT	PORTRAITIST	ALMNOORSTTU	SALMON TROUT
AIIPPRRSTTY	PARTY SPIRIT	ALMOPPSSSUY	PLAYS POSSUM
AIJLNORSSTU	JOURNALISTS	ALMPPRSSTUY	PLAYS TRUMPS
AIKLMMSSTTU	SUMMIT TALKS	ALMPRRSSUUY	ARMY SURPLUS
AIKLNOORSST	SAILORS KNOT	ALNNOOOPPTY	PLAY PONTOON
AIKMMNOSSTY	TOMMY ATKINS	ALOOPPRSSTT	PROTOPLASTS
AILLLLMORTY	MORTALLY ILL	ALOOPTTTTUU	TOTAL OUTPUT
AILLLLMNOOPP	LOLLIPOP MAN	ALOPRRSTUUY	RAPTUROUSLY
AILLLNOOPRU	ALLOPURINOL	AMMNOOORRST	MARSTON MOOR
AILLLNOPTUU	PULLULATION	AMNOOPRSSTW	SPORTSWOMAN
AILLMNOOPSY	POLYNOMIALS	AMNOORSTTTU	ROAST MUTTON
AILLMOPSSSY	PLASMOLYSIS	AMOOPRRSTTU	STUMP ORATOR
AILLNNOOPST	ON ALL POINTS	ANOOOPRRTTY	PROTONOTARY
AILLNOPPRRU	PURL OR PLAIN	ANOPPRSTTUU	PUT ON A SPURT
AILLNOPRSSW	PRISON WALLS	AOOPPSSTTTU	PUTS A STOP TO
AILLNOPRSUU	NULLIPAROUS	BBBBEELLSUW	BLEW BUBBLES
AILLNORTUVY	VOLUNTARILY	BBBBELLOSUW	BLOW BUBBLES
AILLNPPSTUY	SUPPLIANTLY	BBBBNOOORSY	BOBBY ROBSON
AILLNRTUUXY	LUXURIANTLY	BBBDDEILNOR	ROBBED BLIND
AILLOPSSTTW	STOPS AT WILL	BBBDEELORUV	BUBBLED OVER
AILLORRSTTU	ILLUSTRATOR	BBBEELORSUV	BUBBLES OVER
AILMNNOSUUY	UNANIMOUSLY	BBBEINORRSU	ROBBIE BURNS
AILMNOOOPRT	PROMOTIONAL	BBBEMNOORRW	BROWN BOMBER
AILMNOPPSSS	SIMPLON PASS	BBBEOORSSXY	BOBBY-SOXERS
AILMNOPRTTY	IMPORTANTLY	BBCCEEHKLOR	BREECHBLOCK

BBCCEEILLLY	BICYCLE BELL
BBCDEHIRRTU	BUTCHER-BIRD
BBCDEORSTUU	SCRUBBED OUT
BBCEEEKLORZ	BREEZE BLOCK
	BREEZE-BLOCK
BBCEEHNNOOU	BONNE BOUCHE
BBCEEKNRRSU	RUBBERNECKS
BBCEELNOOST	COBBLESTONE
BBCEHILLOOS	BIBLE SCHOOL
BBCEILMOSTU	COMBUSTIBLE
BBCEIRRSSSU	SUBSCRIBERS
BBCEJKOORST	STOCKJOBBER
BBCEKLORSTU	BLOCKBUSTER
BBCGIINRRSU	SUBSCRIBING
BBCILMOSTUY	COMBUSTIBLY
BBDDEFLLOOU	BLUE-BLOODED
BBDDEELNOSU	BENDS DOUBLE
BBDDEILLNOU	DOUBLE-BLIND
BBDDENOOTUY	BEYOND DOUBT
BBDEEELORTT	BOTTLED BEER
BBDEEELOUYY	BLUE-EYED BOY
BBDEEEOPRRT	ROBBED PETER
BBDEEGIILNO	GIDEON BIBLE
BBDEEGIINNT	BEING IN DEBT
BBDEEHHLOOY	HOBBLEDEHOY
DDDCEIILORTU	DOUBLE BERTH
BBDEEILLLOW	ILL BE BLOWED!
BBDEENORSSU	RUBBED NOSES
DDDCGIIMNOV	DIVE-BOMBING
BBDEIKNOORS	BOOKBINDERS
BBDEIKNOORY	BOOKBINDERY
BBDELNRSSUU	BLUNDERBUSS
BBDGIIKNNOO	BOOKBINDING
BBDGINNORUW	RUBBING DOWN
BBDHIMPRSUU	RUBBISH DUMP
BBDHLOOORTY	LORD BOOTHBY
BBEEEILRRSU	BLUEBERRIES
BBEEGIILLNR	GIBBERELLIN
BBEEHIIRTTT	THE BITER BIT
BBEEHIRRSSU	SHRUBBERIES
BBEEHLMORST	BOMB SHELTER
BBEEILMRSSU	SUBMERSIBLE
BBEEILNOSSY	SENSIBLE BOY
BBEEKNNOORS	BROKEN BONES
BBEELLOSTTU	BLUEBOTTLES
BBEELOORRTY	ROBERT BOYLE
BBEELORRSSU	RUBBER SOLES
BBEENORRSYY	BOYSENBERRY
BBEGGGILNOW	BEGGING BOWL
BBEGHILMORT	LIGHT BOMBER
BBEGHKOOOTY	GO BY THE BOOK
BBEGIINRRSU	RUBBERISING
BBEGIINRRUZ	RUBBERIZING
BBEGIINSSSU	BIG BUSINESS
BBEGINOSSSU	GIBBOUSNESS
BBEHHILMRTU	HUMBLE BIRTH
BBEHHOORSSY	HOBBYHORSES
BBEHIIILLOP	BIBLIOPHILE
BBEHIKLORST	HOBBLE SKIRT
BBEILLNRTUY	BILLY BUNTER
BBEILMOOPRT	BOMBER PILOT
BBEILORSTTY	SOB BITTERLY
BBELLMOOSTT	BELL-BOTTOMS
BBEMNNOORTU	NEUTRON BOMB
BBEMNOSTTUU	BUT ME NO BUTS
BBENORRRSTU	ROBERT BURNS
BBEOOOORSTVV	BOVVER BOOTS
BBFLLOOORWW	BLOW FOR BLOW
BBGHINNRSUU	BURNING BUSH
BBGHINOOOTX	BOXING BOOTH
BBGIIINNRTU	RUBBING IT IN
BBGIKNOOORT	BRING TO BOOK
BBHIIILLOPY	BIBLIOPHILY
BBHIIRSSTUY	BUYS BRITISH
BBIIKKNSTUZ	KIBBUTZNIKS
BCCCEIKLRTU	CRICKET CLUB
BCCCGILLNUY	CYCLING CLUB
BCCDEEHKLOU	DOUBLE CHECK
BCCDEILNOTU	CONDUCTIBLE
BCCEEEEFINN	BENEFICENCE
BCCEEEHOPPR	COPPER BEECH
BCCEEHILRTU	THE CRUCIBLE
BCCEEILLLOT	COLLECTIBLE
BCCEEILNNOT	CONNECTIBLE
BCCEEILRSST	BEST CIRCLES
BCCEEINRSTY	CYBERNETICS
BCCEFFIKLOO	OFFICE BLOCK
BCCEFIIPSSU	SUBSPECIFIC
BCCEHHLLRSU	CHURCH BELLS
BCCEHKKLOST	SKETCHBLOCK
BCCEIILNORU	RIBONUCLEIC
BCCEILMPPUY	BICYCLE PUMP
BCCEINOOPPR	CORNCOB PIPE
BCCELLRTUUU	CULTURE CLUB
BCCHHOORSTT	SCOTCH BROTH
BCCLLOORSUU	CLUB COLOURS
BCCLNORTUUY	COUNTRY CLUB
BCDDDELLOOO	COLD BLOODED
BCDDEHLOTUU	DOUBLE DUTCH
BCDDEIIKRSY	DICKEYBIRDS
BCDDEILMNOW	CLIMBED DOWN
BCDDEKLNOUW	BUCKLED DOWN
BCDDGILNPUU	PUDDING CLUB
BCDDILLNOOO	IN COLD BLOOD
BCDEEEFHIPP	CHIPPED BEEF
BCDEEEEFIOTW	WEB OF DECEIT
BCDEEEIINNT	BENEDICTINE
BCDEEEIINST	BENEDICITES
BCDEEELORVX	BOXED CLEVER
BCDEEFIIJOT	OBJECTIFIED
BCDEEGIMNOU	BECOMING DUE
BCDEEGIPRTU	BUDGET PRICE
BCDEEHILNOS	CLOSE BEHIND
BCDEEHILNPT	PITCHBLENDE
BCDEEHIMORS	CHEMISORBED
BCDEEHMNOOY	HONEYCOMBED
BCDEEHMNOTU	DEBOUCHMENT
BCDEEHMOORS	CHEMOSORBED
BCDEEHNNOOW	WOODEN BENCH
BCDEEIILNRS	DISCERNIBLE
BCDEEIILRRU	IRREDUCIBLE
BCDEEIINNOT	BENEDICTION
BCDEEIKLNTY	DICK BENTLEY
BCDEEILMORV	CLIMBED OVER
BCDEEIMNRSU	DISENCUMBER
BCDEEIMRSST	DECEMBRISTS
BCDEEINOPRY	BEYOND PRICE
BCDEEORRSSS	CROSSBREEDS
BCDEFIIKLRS	BRICKFIELDS
BCDEGHILMOU	MUCH OBLIGED
BCDEGHNRRSU	BERGSCHRUND
BCDEGIMNOOT	COMING TO BED
BCDEHILNNOR	HORNBLENDIC
BCDEHKOOTTU	BUCK-TOOTHED
BCDEIIILRTY	CREDIBILITY
BCDEIILNRSY	DISCERNIBLY
BCDEIILRRUY	IRREDUCIBLY
BCDEIILSSSU	DISCUSSIBLE
BCDEIKLOQUU	DOUBLE-QUICK
BCDEILNNORR	BLIND CORNER
BCDEILORTUU	TUBERCULOID
BCDEINORTTU	CONTRIBUTED

BCDEINORTUY	BUY ON CREDIT
BCDEIOOPRSS	PROBOSCIDES
BCDEJNOORTU	ROUND OBJECT
BCDEKLNOSUW	BUCKLES DOWN
BCDEKLOORSU	BLOODSUCKER
BCDELMNOSUU	MUSCLE-BOUND
BCDELNOOTUU	COUNT DOUBLE
BCDELOORSSU	DOUBLE CROSS
	DOUBLE-CROSS
BCDEMMNRSUU	CUMMERBUNDS
BCDENORTUYY	DERBY COUNTY
BCDFILNPSUU	PUBLIC FUNDS
BCDFKLOOOOW	BLOCK OF WOOD
BCDGHHIILRT	BRIGHT CHILD
BCDGIIKMNOR	MOCKING BIRD
	MOCKINGBIRD
BCDGILLNOOW	BLOWING COLD
BCDHHIILRST	CHILDBIRTHS
BCDHHIOOPRY	HYDROPHOBIC
BCDHILNNORU	UNBORN CHILD
BCDHIMOORRY	HYDROBROMIC
BCDIILOOPTY	BODY POLITIC
BCDIINRTUUY	RUBICUNDITY
BCDIKLNRSTU	STRUCK BLIND
BCDILLNOORU	COLOUR BLIND
	COLOUR-BLIND
BCDLORSSTUU	CLOUDBURSTS
BCEEEEFILOV	FEEBLE VOICE
BCEEEELNNOV	BENEVOLENCE
BCEEEEMNOTW	COME BETWEEN
BCEEEFILPRT	PERFECTIBLE
BCEEEFIORSV	BE OF SERVICE
BCEEEGMNRSU	SUBMERGENCE
BCEEEHHINPR	HEBEPHRENIC
BCEEEHIKORT	BROKE THE ICE
BCEEEHHNNQSU	QUEENS BENCH
BCEEEIILRST	CELEBRITIES
BCEEEILPPRT	PERCEPTIBLE
BCEEEELLMRSU	CEREBELLUMS
BCEEEELMOSSS	BECOMES LESS
BCEEEELORSVX	BOXES CLEVER
BCEEFFMOOST	COME OFF BEST
BCEEFGMORRY	BEG FOR MERCY
BCEEFHIKRST	BRIEF SKETCH
BCEEFHLNORU	BEFORE LUNCH
BCEEFIIJOST	OBJECTIFIES
BCEEGHINRTY	BY THE CRINGE
BCEEGILLMNT	GENTLE CLIMB
BCEEGIMNNOO	BECOMING ONE
BCEEGIMNNRU	ENCUMBERING
BCEEHIKPSTT	PICK THE BEST
BCEEHIMNTTW	BEWITCHMENT
BCEEHIPSSSU	SPICEBUSHES
BCEEHIRSTWW	WITCHES BREW
BCEEHJKLOWY	CHEEK BY JOWL
BCEEHKLRRUY	HUCKLEBERRY
BCEEHKNORSW	WORKBENCHES
BCEEHKOOQSU	CHEQUEBOOKS
BCEEHLOSSTT	BEST CLOTHES
BCEEHMNOSSU	BONUS SCHEME
BCEEHMORSUU	EMBOUCHURES
BCEEHOORSTT	BORE THE COST
BCEEIILPSST	PLEBISCITES
BCEEIINOSST	OBSCENITIES
BCEEIJLOTVY	OBJECTIVELY
BCEEIKOOPRT	RECEIPT BOOK
BCEEILLLOSY	BELLICOSELY
BCEEILLNPSU	BLUE-PENCILS
BCEEILMNOOV	MOB VIOLENCE
BCEEILMNPUY	PUBLIC ENEMY
BCEEILMOSST	COMESTIBLE
BCEEILNOSTY	BY-ELECTIONS
BCEEILNOSTY	BY-ELECTIONS
BCEEILOPRSS	PROCESSIBLE
BCEEILORRSU	LE CORBUSIER
BCEEILORRTV	ROBERT CLIVE
BCEEILPPRTY	PERCEPTIBLY
BCEEINSSSTU	SUBSISTENCE
BCEEIORRRSW	CROWBERRIES
BCEEIPRRSSU	SUPERSCRIBE
BCEEJLSSSTU	SUBJECTLESS
BCEEKKLNNOU	KNUCKLEBONE
BCEEKLNOSTT	BOTTLENECKS
BCEEKNOORRV	BROKEN COVER
BCEELMMOOTY	EMBOLECTOMY
BCEELMNRTUY	RECUMBENTLY
BCEELNOOSST	OBSOLESCENT
BCEELNOSTTT	SCENT BOTTLE
BCEELNOSTTU	CUTTLEBONES
BCEEMOOSTTU	COME OUT BEST
BCEENOORTTX	NEXT OCTOBER
BCEENORSSSU	OBSCURENESS
BCEEOOOORRRS	CORROBOREES
BCEEOPRRRTU	CUB REPORTER
BCEFFILOSUV	FIVE OF CLUBS
BCEFHILLNSU	BULLFINCHES
BCEFHKNOSUY	BUNCH OF KEYS
BCEFIIOPRST	FIBRE OPTICS
BCEFILNNOSU	NINE OF CLUBS
BCEFKOOORTY	TOOK BY FORCE
BCEGHHIMOWY	HIGH WYCOMBE
BCEGHIIMNRS	BESMIRCHING
BCEGIIINOTY	BIOGENICITY
BCEGIINPRRS	PRESCRIBING
BCEGIINPRYU	BUYING PRICE
BCEGILMOORY	EMBRYOLOGIC
BCEHIILRRSV	SILVER BIRCH
BCEHIIMOSST	BIOCHEMISTS
BCEHIJLNOTU	JOIN THE CLUB
BCEHILOPSUU	PUBLIC HOUSE
BCEHKKOOSST	SKETCHBOOKS
BCEHKLOOSSU	BLOCKHOUSES
BCEHKOPRRTU	PORK BUTCHER
BCEHLMORTUU	MUCH TROUBLE
BCEHLOORSTW	BLOWTORCHES
BCEHLORRSYY	CHRYSOBERYL
BCEHMNRSUUY	CUSHY NUMBER
BCEHMOORTTY	THROMBOCYTE
BCEHMRSSTUW	THUMBSCREWS
BCEIIJMOSTV	OBJECTIVISM
BCEIIJOSTTV	OBJECTIVIST
BCEIIJOTTVY	OBJECTIVITY
BCEIIKLLRST	BILLSTICKER
BCEIILLOSTY	BELLICOSITY
BCEIILMSSUU	UMBILICUSES
BCEIINOTVXY	BICONVEXITY
BCEIIORRSTW	ERIC BRISTOW
BCEIIORRSSTU	OBSCURITIES
BCEIJNNOOOT	NO OBJECTION
BCEIJNSTUUV	SUBJUNCTIVE
BCEIKLOORST	BOOTLICKERS
BCEIKOOPRTU	PICTURE BOOK
BCEILLORSSU	BRUCELLOSIS
BCEILMNOPUY	PUBLIC MONEY
BCEILMORTUU	MICROTUBULE
BCEILNORTVY	CONVERTIBLY
BCEILOPRRTU	CORRUPTIBLE
BCEILPPRSUU	PUBLIC PURSE
BCEILPSSTUY	SUSCEPTIBLY
BCEIMOOSSTT	COMES TO BITS
BCEINORSTTU	CONTRIBUTES
BCEINOSSSTU	SUBSECTIONS

BCEIORSTTUV	OBSTRUCTIVE
BCEKKNOORRS	BROKEN ROCKS
BCEKKOOOORY	COOKERY BOOK
BCEKKOOOPST	POCKET BOOKS
	POCKETBOOKS
BCEKKOORRST	STOCKBROKER
BCEKLMNRUUY	LUCKY NUMBER
BCEKLNRSTUU	TURNBUCKLES
BCEKLOORSTW	TOWER BLOCKS
BCEKMOOOOST	COMES TO BOOK
BCELMOOOSTW	COME TO BLOWS
BCELMOORSYY	CORYMBOSELY
BCELOOORRSU	SOBER COLOUR
BCELORSTUUU	TUBERCULOUS
BCELRSSTUUU	SUBCULTURES
BCELSTTTTUU	SCUTTLEBUTT
BCEMNOORSSW	CROSSBOWMEN
BCEOOOPRSST	STROBOSCOPE
BCFFLOORSUU	FOUR OF CLUBS
BCFGIKLNOSU	KING OF CLUBS
BCFHLNOOPUW	BOWL OF PUNCH
BCFIKNOORST	TON OF BRICKS
BCFIKOORSTX	BOX OF TRICKS
BCFILLOOSSI	BILL OF COSTS
BCFJMOOORST	JOBS COMFORT
BCGGIILNOPU	GOING PUBLIC
BCGHOORSTTU	BROUGH SCOTT
BCGIIILNPSU	PUBLICISING
BCGIIILNPUZ	PUBLICIZING
BCGIIKLNOOT	BOOTLICKING
BCGIINOPRRS	PROSCRIBING
BCGIKLLNOOS	BOLLOCKINGS
BCGIKLNOOTU	BLOCKING OUT
BCGILNORTUU	TOURING CLUB
BCGINORSTTU	OBSTRUCTING
BCHHIIMORTY	BIORHYTHMIC
BCHHIOOOPPT	PHOTOPHOBIC
BCHIILLMPU	UPHILL CLIMB
BCHMOOOTTTU	TOUCH BOTTOM
BCHNOORSSTU	HOT CROSS BUN
BCIIIILMSTY	MISCIBILITY
BCIIIILNTVY	VINCIBILITY
BCIILMOSSTY	SYMBOLISTIC
BCIILORSTTY	BRISTOL CITY
BCIJNNOOTUX	BOX JUNCTION
BCIKLOPRSUW	PUBLIC WORKS
BCIKMOORSST	BROOMSTICKS
BCILMOSTTUU	CUSTOM-BUILT
BCILOPRRTUY	CORRUPTIBLY
BCINOORRTTU	CONTRIBUTOR
BCINOORSTTU	OBSTRUCTION
BCOOORRSSTTU	OBSTRUCTORS
BDDDEEEGLOU	DOUBLE-EDGED
BDDDEEEELNOU	DOUBLE-ENDED
BDDDEEIIMOS	DISEMBODIED
BDDDEEILSSW	WEDDED BLISS
BDDDEEINRRU	UNDERBIDDER
BDDDEEINRSU	DISBURDENED
BDDDEFILLNO	BLINDFOLDED
BDDDEFMNOUU	DUMBFOUNDED
BDDDEGINNOW	BEDDING DOWN
BDDEEEEKNNS	BENDED KNEES
BDDEEEIILSV	DISBELIEVED
BDDEEEIMMRS	DISMEMBERED
BDDEEEIMNRT	DEBRIDEMENT
BDDEEEIMORR	EMBROIDERED
BDDEEFGIINR	BRIDGE FIEND
BDDEEGHILST	DEBS DELIGHT
BDDEEGIIRRV	BRIDGE DRIVE
BDDEEGIMOSU	DISEMBOGUED
BDDEEHIMNNT	BEND THE MIND

BDDEEIILMOS	DEMOBILISED
BDDEEIILMOZ	DEMOBILIZED
BDDEEIIMOSS	DISEMBODIES
BDDEEIINOST	DISOBEDIENT
BDDEEIINTVY	DIVIDE BY TEN
BDDEEILMRTU	TUMBLE-DRIED
BDDEEILORSW	BOWDLERISED
BDDEEILORWZ	BOWDLERIZED
BDDEEINORRR	RED RED ROBIN
BDDEEINORSU	UNDERBODIES
BDDEEINOSST	DID ONE'S BEST
BDDEEKMNRUU	EDMUND BURKE
BDDEELNOOSS	BLOODEDNESS
BDDEFFIRSTU	STUFFED BIRD
BDDEFIMNRSU	DUMB FRIENDS
BDDEFLLLOOU	FULL-BLOODED
BDDEGIIMNNN	MINDBENDING
BDDEGINNNOW	BENDING DOWN
BDDEGINOPTU	BUDDING POET
BDDEGINRUWY	RUBY WEDDING
BDDEHINOPRS	DROPS BEHIND
BDDEHLNOORS	BONDHOLDERS
BDDEHNORSUW	BRUSHED DOWN
BDDEIISVXY	DIVIDE BY SIX
BDDEIILMMUU	MEDIUM BUILD
BDDEIILORSW	WISE OLD BIRD
BDDEIINSSSU	DID BUSINESS
BDDEIIOTVWY	DIVIDE BY TWO
BDDEIIRSTTU	DISTRIBUTED
BDDEILNNOSW	SNOW-BLINDED
BDDEINRSTUU	UNDISTURBED
BDDELMNOTUW	TUMBLED DOWN
BDDELNOTUUY	UNDOUBTEDLY
BDDELOOORSU	DOUBLE DOORS
BDDENOSTTUY	STUDENT BODY
BDDFLOOOOPR	DROP OF BLOOD
BDDGIINSUV	SUBDIVIDING
BDDGILNOPUW	PUDDING BOWL
BDDHLNOOOSU	BLOODHOUNDS
BDDIILNNOWW	WINDOW BLIND
BDDILRSTUUY	STURDY BUILD
BDEEEEFPRSS	PRESSED BEEF
BDEEEEHKNNT	BEND THE KNEE
BDEEEEIIMRR	BIEDERMEIER
BDEEEELRRSS	LESSER BREED
BDEEEFFINRT	BE DIFFERENT
BDEEEFINNRS	BEEN FRIENDS
BDEEEFLOSTT	BOTTLE-FEEDS
BDEEEFORRVW	FEVERED BROW
BDEEEGHNSTT	GET THE BENDS
BDEEEHHIRST	THE HEBRIDES
BDEEEHILLMS	EMBELLISHED
BDEEEHILSTW	BLEEDS WHITE
BDEEEHINRSW	NEW HEBRIDES
BDEEEHLORTU	DOUBLE THREE
BDEEEIILRSV	DISBELIEVER
BDEEEIILSSV	DISBELIEVES
BDEEEILMNTV	BEDEVILMENT
BDEEEILOSTW	BOILED SWEET
BDEEEILSSTW	WILDEBEESTS
BDEEEIMMRRS	DISREMEMBER
BDEEEIMORRR	EMBROIDERER
BDEEEINNRSZ	BENZEDRINES
BDEEEINRRST	INTERBREEDS
BDEEEINRSSV	SEVEN BRIDES
BDEEEIORRTT	RETIRE TO BED
BDEEEKNORRS	BROKEN REEDS
BDEEELLNSST	ENDLESS BELT
BDEEELMSTUW	TUMBLEWEEDS
BDEEELNOSUV	DOUBLE SEVEN
BDEEELNOTUV	DOUBLE EVENT

BDEEEELNSSSS	BLESSEDNESS	BDEEMNORTUU	OUTNUMBERED
BDEEELOPPRY	PROBE DEEPLY	BDEENORRSUV	OVERBURDENS
BDEEEENNPRTU	BEEN PRUDENT	BDEENPRRTUU	UNPERTURBED
BDEEFFGIORT	BEG TO DIFFER	BDEEOORRSSY	OBEYS ORDERS
BDEEFGIILNU	EDIBLE FUNGI	BDEFFLNNOUU	BUNDLE OF FUN
BDEEFGIINNR	BEFRIENDING	BDEFGHIORRT	FORTH BRIDGE
BDEEFGOOOTTU	GET OUT OF BED	BDEFGINOORS	FOREBODINGS
BDEEFHIRRSU	REFURBISHED	BDEFGINOORY	FOREIGN BODY
BDEEGGHIIRW	WEIGHBRIDGE	BDEFGIOORST	FOOTBRIDGES
BDEEGHIIRTV	GIVE THE BIRD	BDEFGOOOTTU	GOT OUT OF BED
BDEEGHILNTY	BENIGHTEDLY	BDEFGSSSTUU	FUSSBUDGETS
BDEEGHILOTU	DOUBLE EIGHT	BDEFGSSTUUY	FUSSBUDGETY
BDEEGHINORU	NEIGHBOURED	BDEFHIORRST	FOR THE BIRDS
BDEEGHIRSTT	GETS THE BIRD	BDEFHNOORST	BED OF THORNS
BDEEGHNOSTT	GOT THE BENDS	BDEFILOOOST	TIES OF BLOOD
BDEEGIIINNV	DIVINE BEING	BDEFILORSTU	DOUBLE FIRST
BDEEGIILLNV	BEDEVILLING	BDEFIMNOORS	BOSOM FRIEND
BDEEGIILNRW	BEWILDERING	BDEFKLLOOUY	FULLY BOOKED
BDEEGIINNRS	INBREEDINGS	BDEFLNOOTTU	LEFT NO DOUBT
BDEEGILMNNO	EMBOLDENING	BDEFORRSSUY	BODYSURFERS
BDEEGIMNRSY	DYING EMBERS	BDEGGHITTTU	TIGHT BUDGET
BDEEGIMOSSU	DISEMBOGUES	BDEGGHLNOOU	GOLDEN BOUGH
BDEEGINNORV	BENDING OVER	BDEGGILNNOU	BLUDGEONING
BDEEGINNRTU	REED BUNTING	BDEGGINNOOW	GONE DOWN BIG
BDEEGINORTT	DOING BETTER	BDEGGINNOOY	GOING BEYOND
BDEEGINORTU	OUTBREEDING	BDEGGINOOSW	GOES DOWN BIG
BDEEGINOTTT	GET INTO DEBT	BDEGHIRRSST	BRIGHT DRESS
BDEEGINRRTT	TRENT BRIDGE	BDEGHKOOOOT	THE GOOD BOOK
BDEEGIORRTW	TOWER BRIDGE	BDEGIIKNNNU	BEING UNKIND
BDEEHHOPRSY	SHEPHERD BOY	BDEGIILLNNS	SINGLE-BLIND
BDEEHILMNSU	UNBLEMISHED	BDEGIILMNSS	DISSEMBLING
BDEEHILOSSV	BOLSHEVISED	BDEGIINNORV	BINDING OVER
BDEEHILOSVZ	BOLSHEVIZED	BDEGILLORRS	BILL RODGERS
BDEEHIMNNTT	BENT THE MIND	BDEGIMOORRS	BRIDEGROOMS
BDEEHINRTWY	WIN THE DERBY	BDEGINNNRUU	UNBURDENING
BDEEHISTTTU	BITE THE DUST	BDEGINNOTWW	WENT DOWN BIG
BDEEHLNOOTU	ON THE DOUBLE	BDEGINOOTTT	GOT INTO DEBT
BDEEHLORRSW	WELSH BORDER	BDEGKNOORRU	BROKE GROUND
BDEEHNORTWY	WON THE DERBY	BDEGLMOPRRU	DRUG PROBLEM
BDEEHORRSUV	BRUSHED OVER	BDEGLNNOORW	GOLDEN BROWN
BDEEIILMOSS	DEMOBILISES	BDEGLNOORUW	BELOW GROUND
BDEEIILMOSZ	DEMOBILIZES	BDEGLOOSSUY	GOD BLESS YOU
BDEEIILNSST	DISTENSIBLE	BDEHHOOOORT	BROTHERHOOD
BDEEIILPRSS	DISPERSIBLE	BDEHIIINNTU	UNINHIBITED
BDEEIIKLNPRS	BESPRINKLED	BDEHIIKLLTY	BILLY THE KID
BDEEIILLMOOS	LOOSE-LIMBED	BDEHIILORST	BOILED SHIRT
BDEEIILLNPRS	SPELLBINDER	BDEHIILPRSU	SHIPBUILDER
BDEEIILLOSVW	DEVILS ELBOW	BDEHIINNPTU	NIP IN THE BUD
BDEEIILMNOTY	MOLYBDENITE	BDEHIKLNOTU	DOUBLETHINK
BDEEIILMOSSW	DISEMBOWELS	BDEHILOOPRY	HYPERBOLOID
BDEEIILMRRTU	TUMBLE-DRIER	BDEHJLOOOTY	JOY TO BEHOLD
BDEEIILMRSTU	TUMBLE-DRIES	BDEHLNOOTTU	BUTTONHOLED
BDEEIILNORRS	BORDERLINES	BDEHLNORTTU	THUNDERBOLT
BDEEIILNRSSU	DRESS IN BLUE	BDEHLOOOORTT	BOLT THE DOOR
BDEEIILORRSW	BOWDLERISER	BDEHNORSSUW	BRUSHES DOWN
BDEEIILORRTU	DIRE TROUBLE	BDEHNRRSSUU	UNDERSHRUBS
BDEEIILORRWZ	BOWDLERIZER	BDEIIIILNSV	INDIVISIBLE
BDEEIILORSSW	BOWDLERISES	BDEIIILMMOS	IMMOBILISED
BDEEIILORSWZ	BOWDLERIZES	BDEIIILMMOZ	IMMOBILIZED
BDEEIIMMORRV	BRIMMED OVER	BDEIIILMSSS	DISMISSIBLE
BDEEIINNOOST	DONE ONE'S BIT	BDEIIIMNSTU	BITUMINISED
BDEEINNRRWY	DERBY WINNER	BDEIIIMNTUZ	BITUMINIZED
BDEEINOOSST	DOES ONE'S BIT	BDEIIKLNRST	STRIKE BLIND
BDEEINORSTX	TINDERBOXES	BDEIIKRRSST	BIRDSTRIKES
BDEEIOORSXY	DEOXYRIBOSE	BDEIILLLRWY	BILLY WILDER
BDEELLOOSSV	BLOOD VESSEL	BDEIILLNSSV	LOVE IS BLIND
BDEELMNOORW	DEMON BOWLER	BDEIILLOSSU	SOLUBILISED
BDEELMORTUV	TUMBLED OVER	BDEIILLOSUZ	SOLUBILIZED
BDEELNOOSTT	BOTTLE-NOSED	BDEIILMORSS	DISEMBROILS
BDEELNORTUY	DOUBLE ENTRY	BDEIIRSSSSU	SUBSIDISERS
BDEELOPRSTU	BOLSTERED UP	BDEIIRSSSUZ	SUBSIDIZERS

BDEIIRSSTTU	DISTRIBUTES	BEEEEGNNOTW	GONE BETWEEN
BDEIJRRTUYY	TRIED BY JURY	BEEEEGNOSTW	GOES BETWEEN
BDEIKMRSSTU	STRIKES DUMB	BEEEEHKNNTT	BENT THE KNEE
BDEIKNNORSZ	BRONZED SKIN	BEEEEENNPRST	BEEN PRESENT
BDEIKNORSTU	STRIKEBOUND	BEEEEENNTTWW	WENT BETWEEN
BDEIKNORTTW	KNITTED BROW	BEEEFFIRSTZ	STIFF BREEZE
BDEILLNOOTU	BOLD OUTLINE	BEEEFGILLNU	FEELING BLUE
BDEILLOSTUX	BILLETS-DOUX	BEEEFHORSTT	BEST OF THREE
BDEILNNNOOS	NONE SO BLIND	BEEEFINOSTT	FIT TO BE SEEN
BDEILNNOOOS	IN ONE'S BLOOD	BEEEFLORRTU	TROUBLE FREE
BDEIMMNOPRU	PREMIUM BOND	BEEEFOORRST	FREEBOOTERS
BDEINNORTTU	RUN INTO DEBT	BEEEGHILPST	THE BIG SLEEP
BDEINOSSSUU	DUBIOUSNESS	BEEEGHILRTZ	LIGHT BREEZE
BDEISSTTTUU	SUBSTITUTED	BEEEGHLOTTW	GET THE ELBOW
BDELLLOOSSY	BLOODLESSLY	BEEEGILLNPS	SPELLING BEE
BDELLNOOSTY	TELLS NOBODY	BEEEGILLNRT	BELLIGERENT
BDELLNOSSUY	BOUNDLESSLY	BEEEGILMNTU	BEGUILEMENT
BDELLNOTUUW	BULLET WOUND	BEEEGIMMNRR	REMEMBERING
BDELMNOSTUW	TUMBLES DOWN	BEEEGINOSUY	BE SEEING YOU
BDELOOORTWY	BLOODY TOWER	BEEEGKNORRS	GONE BERSERK
BDEMNNORRUU	ROUND NUMBER	BEEEGKORRSS	GOES BERSERK
BDEMOOORSTW	TWO BEDROOMS	BEEEGLNORTT	BOTTLE GREEN
BDEMOOOTTTU	BOTTOMED OUT		GREEN BOTTLE
BDENNORRTUW	TURNED BROWN	BEEEGMNRSSY	BY MESSENGER
BDENOOOPTTU	OPEN TO DOUBT	BEEEGNOORTT	GO ONE BETTER
BDENOOOORTXY	BOY NEXT DOOR	BEEEHILLMRS	EMBELLISHER
BDENOPSSSTY	SENDS BY POST	BEEEHILLMSS	EMBELLISHES
BDFGHIIINRS	FISHING BIRD	BEEEHILLNOR	HELLEBORINE
BDFGHIKNORE	KING OF BIRDS	BEEEHKNOSTW	BOWS THE KNEE
BDFGIILLNNY	BLIND FLYING	BEEEHLLRSTW	BELLWETHERS
BDFGINORSUY	BODYSURFING	BEEEHMNNRRTU	NUMBER THREE
BDFILNOOOPT	PINT OF BLOOD	BEEEHORRSTV	THE OBSERVER
BDFLLOOOOSS	LOSS OF BLOOD	BEEEHRSTTVY	THE VERY BEST
BDFLNOOOOSY	NOBODYS FOOL	BEEEIIJLLNU	JUBILEE LINE
BDFLOOOORTU	OUT FOR BLOOD	BEEEILNPRTV	PREVENTIBLE
BDFNOOOSTUU	OUT OF BOUNDS	BEEEILNRSUV	UNBELIEVERS
	OUT-OF-BOUNDS	BEEEILPRRSS	REPRESSIBLE
BDGGGINNOOW	BOGGING DOWN	BEEEILPRSSX	EXPRESSIBLE
BDGGIIILNOS	DISOBLIGING	BEEEILRRSSV	REVERSIBLES
BDGGIIINNRS	SINGING BIRD	BEEEIMNPRST	IN SEPTEMBER
BDGGIILNOOV	GIVING BLOOD	BEEEIMNRTTY	BITTER ENEMY
BDGHIIMMNRU	HUMMING BIRD	BEEEIMRSTTT	BETTER TIMES
	HUMMINGBIRD	BEEEINNRSTV	ERNEST BEVIN
BDGHILOSTTU	SLIGHT DOUBT	BEEEINORSSU	BEEN SERIOUS
BDGHNOORTUW	BROUGHT DOWN	BEEEIRSTTTW	BITTER SWEET
BDGHOORRTUW	BROUGHT WORD		BITTERSWEET
BDGIIINSSSU	SUBSIDISING	BEEEKNRRSTU	STERN REBUKE
BDGIIINSSUZ	SUBSIDIZING	BEEEKNRRSTW	WENT BERSERK
BDGIILMNNOW	MIND-BLOWING	BEEELLRSSST	BEST-SELLERS
BDGIILNNOOW	BOILING DOWN	BEEELMNNNOT	ENNOBLEMENT
BDGIILNOTUU	OUTBUILDING	BEEEMNNRSUV	EVEN NUMBERS
BDGIIMNNORT	BRING TO MIND		NUMBER SEVEN
BDGIINOORST	RIDING BOOTS	BEEENOPPRTY	TEENY BOPPER
BDGIINORSTT	GRIND TO BITS		TEENYBOPPER
BDGILLLNOOU	GOLD BULLION	BEEENOPPRWY	WEENY BOPPER
BDGILNNOOWW	BLOWING DOWN		WEENYBOPPER
BDGINNNORUW	BURNING DOWN	BEEENORSSSV	VERBOSENESS
BDGINNORRSU	BRINGS ROUND	BEEENORSSTT	BONESETTERS
BDHIILRRSWY	WHIRLYBIRDS		ONES BETTERS
BDHIMNOORSY	MONOHYBRIDS	BEEFFGILNOT	BEETLING OFF
BDHNNOOORUU	HONOUR BOUND	BEEFFHOOOTZ	OFF THE BOOZE
BDIIINOSSUV	SUBDIVISION	BEEFFIJNOOT	JOINT OF BEEF
BDIIMNORTUY	MORIBUNDITY	BEEFFLNOORT	NOBLE EFFORT
BDIIORRSTTU	DISTRIBUTOR	BEEFGGINOOR	GOING BEFORE
BDILLLOOPSS	SPILLS BLOOD	BEEFGIINNTT	BENEFITTING
BDILNOOOSTW	BOILS DOWN TO	BEEFGIIRRTT	BITTER GRIEF
BDLOOOPRSST	BLOOD SPORTS	BEEFGILNORU	NOBLE FIGURE
BEEEEFHRRSZ	FRESH BREEZE	BEEFGLLOORW	GLOBEFLOWER
BEEEEFLNNOS	BEEN ONESELF	BEEFGMOORRS	BEGS FOR MORE
BEEEEFLRSTT	FEELS BETTER	BEEFHIOSTTT	THE BEST OF IT
BEEEEFNORRV	NEVER BEFORE	BEEFHIRRSSU	REFURBISHES

BEEFHRRSTTU	FRESH BUTTER
BEEFIINNRSW	NEWS IN BRIEF
BEEFIKNRTTU	BUTTER KNIFE
BEEFILLMRSU	UMBELLIFERS
BEEFILLORSU	SUE FOR LIBEL
BEEFILORTUY	BET YOUR LIFE
BEEFILRSTTU	BUTTERFLIES
BEEFIMMNORT	BRIEF MOMENT
BEEFIMOSSTT	BEST OF TIMES
BEEFKOOORSV	BOOK OF VERSE
BEEFLLLORSW	BELLFLOWERS
BEEFLNORSUY	BURY ONESELF
BEEGGGGINNO	GONE BEGGING
BEEGGGGINOS	GOES BEGGING
BEEGGGINNTW	WENT BEGGING
BEEGGGLOOSX	GOGGLE BOXES
BEEGGHINRRT	BRIGHT GREEN
BEEGGHIOTVY	GIVE THE GO-BY
BEEGGHOSTTY	GETS THE GO-BY
BEEGGIKLRUY	LIKE BUGGERY
BEEGGILNSUY	BULGING EYES
BEEGGILSSTU	SUGGESTIBLE
BEEGGINOORV	GONE OVER BIG
BEEGGIOORSV	GOES OVER BIG
BEEGGLOORST	BOOTLEGGERS
BEEGGNOORRW	GEORGE BROWN
BEEGGNORRSU	GEORGE BURNS
BEEGHIILLNS	GHIBELLINES
BEEGHILLLSS	SLEIGH BELLS
BEEGHILLNRT	RING THE BELL
BEEGHILNORT	BRING TO HEEL
BEEGHILNRST	SINGLE BERTH
BEEGHIMNOST	SEETHING MOB
BEEGHIMNRTU	NUMBER EIGHT
BEEGHINNORR	HERRINGBONE
BEEGHIOOTTV	GIVE THE BOOT
BEEGHLLNRTU	RUNG THE BELL
BEEGHLOOTTW	GOT THE ELBOW
BEEGHMNRSTU	GREEN THUMBS
BEEGHOORSSU	BROGUE SHOES
BEEGHOOSTTT	GETS THE BOOT
BEEGHORRTTU	RUB TOGETHER
BEEGIILNNOV	BEING IN LOVE
BEEGIILNNUV	UNBELIEVING
BEEGIILNOPT	BEING POLITE
BEEGIILNTTT	LETTING IT BE
BEEGIIMNRTT	EMBITTERING
BEEGIIOORSU	BOURGEOISIE
BEEGIJLLLNS	JINGLE BELLS
BEEGIKKNOOP	BOOKKEEPING
BEEGIKLNNSY	BEN KINGSLEY
BEEGIKNPSUY	KEEPING BUSY
BEEGILLNSST	BEST-SELLING
BEEGILNNOSS	IGNOBLENESS
BEEGILNRSSU	BLUES SINGER
BEEGILORTUV	GIVE TROUBLE
BEEGIMNNOOR	BEING NO MORE
BEEGIMNNRRU	RENUMBERING
BEEGIMNOSTT	MISBEGOTTEN
BEEGIMNOSTY	BYGONE TIMES
BEEGINORTVW	WENT OVER BIG
BEEGINPRSUY	BUYING SPREE
BEEGNORRTTW	GROWN BETTER
BEEGORRSTTW	GROWS BETTER
BEEHHINSSTU	IN THE BUSHES
BEEHHISTTTW	WITH THE BEST
BEEHHLLPSTU	PUSH THE BELL
BEEHIIKNNRS	HENRIK IBSEN
BEEHIIMSSST	BESSIE SMITH
BEEHILNOTTU	INTO THE BLUE
BEEHILOPRYZ	HYPERBOLIZE
BEEHILOPTTW	TIP THE ELBOW
BEEHILOSSSV	BOLSHEVISES
BEEHILOSSVZ	BOLSHEVIZES
BEEHIMNOORT	THEOBROMINE
BEEHINORSTW	THE BROWNIES
BEEHJNOOTTW	NEW TO THE JOB
BEEHKNOORSU	HOUSEBROKEN
BEEHLLLLOTT	TOLL THE BELL
BEEHLLLOSTU	BULLET HOLES
BEEHLNOOTTT	ON THE BOTTLE
BEEHLNOSTTY	ONLY THE BEST
BEEHLOORRTV	BROTHER LOVE
BEEHLOPSTTU	POTS THE BLUE
BEEHLRRTTTU	RHETT BUTLER
BEEHLRSSSTU	BUS-SHELTERS
BEEHMNNOPRU	PHONE NUMBER
BEEHMNORSUU	HOUSE NUMBER
BEEHMOOTTTT	BOTTOM TEETH
BEEHMOPRTYY	EMBRYOPHYTE
BEEHNNOORST	THE SORBONNE
BEEHNOOPSTX	OPENS THE BOX
BEEHOPRRSTT	STEPBROTHER
BEEHORRSSUV	BRUSHES OVER
BEEIILLNNOR	IN REBELLION
BEEIILMNRST	TIMBERLINES
BEEIILMPRSS	IMPRESSIBLE
	PERMISSIBLE
BEEIILNOPST	BITE ONES LIP
BEEIILNSSSV	VISIBLENESS
BEEIIRRTTUV	RETRIBUTIVE
BEEIJLPRSTY	J.B.PRIESTLEY
BEEIKKNORRS	KNOBKERRIES
BEEIKLNPRSS	BESPRINKLES
BEEILLLNTUY	EBULLIENTLY
BEEILLOSTTX	LITTLE BOXES
BEEILLRRRTU	BULL TERRIER
BEEILMMNORT	EMBROILMENT
BEEILMNORTT	BITTER LEMON
BEEILMNORTY	EMILY BRONTE
BEEILNNOSTW	TENNIS ELBOW
BEEILNOPRSS	RESPONSIBLE
BEEILNOQSSU	OBLIQUENESS
BEEILNRSSTT	BRITTLENESS
BEEILOSSSVY	OBSESSIVELY
BEEIMMNPRRU	PRIME NUMBER
BEEIMNNSSSU	BUSINESSMEN
BEEINORRSSW	SNOWBERRIES
BEEINORRSTW	BORE WITNESS
BEEINRSSTUV	SUBSERVIENT
BEEJKNNOOSW	KNEW ONE'S JOB
BEEKLLOORSS	BOOKSELLERS
BEEKLNOOORS	BROKEN LOOSE
BEEKLNORRSU	BROKEN RULES
BEEKNNORTTW	KNOWN BETTER
BEEKNORSTTW	KNOWS BETTER
BEELLNOSSSU	SOLUBLENESS
BEELLNOSSUV	VOLUBLENESS
BEELLORSSTU	LESS TROUBLE
BEELMMNNORSY	MEMBERS ONLY
BEELMOORSTU	TROUBLESOME
BEELMOPTTTY	EMPTY BOTTLE
BEELMORSTUV	STUMBLE OVER
	TUMBLES OVER
BEELNOOPSTW	BLEW ONE'S TOP
BEENNNOOOSW	BE ON ONES OWN
BEENOOPRRSS	SOBER PERSON
BEENOOSSTTU	STUB ONES TOE
BEENORSSTTY	TRY ONES BEST
BEENORSSSUU	BRUSQUENESS
BEEORSSSTTY	SETS STORE BY
BEFFGINRTUY	BURNT EFFIGY

BEFFIKNOORT	BROKEN IT OFF	BEHIIILLLLS	HILLBILLIES
BEFFIORRSTU	BURST OF FIRE	BEHIIINOSTX	EXHIBITIONS
BEFGHILLRTU	BULLFIGHTER	BEHIIIOPRTV	PROHIBITIVE
BEFGIILLNST	TELLING FIBS	BEHIILRRSTU	BRITISH RULE
BEFGIILNORT	BRING TO LIFE	BEHIINORSTZ	BRITISH ZONE
BEFGIILNTTY	BEFITTINGLY	BEHIINPRSTU	TRIBUNESHIP
BEFGILNOOTT	BOTTLE OF GIN	BEHIINRSSST	BRITISHNESS
BEFHIIILLLLT	FILL THE BILL	BEHIKNOOSSS	BOOKISHNESS
BEFHIILLSTT	FITS THE BILL	BEHILLNSSSU	BULLISHNESS
BEFHILLMSTU	THIMBLEFULS	BEHILLOPSTT	TOPS THE BILL
BEFHILLOOTT	FOOT THE BILL	BEHILLORSTT	ROBS THE TILL
BEFHLMORTUU	RULE OF THUMB	BEHILLORSWW	WILLOWHERBS
BEFIIILLTXY	FLEXIBILITY	BEHILNOOTWW	WITH ONE BLOW
BEFIILRSSTU	FILIBUSTERS	BEHILOPRSTY	HYPERBOLIST
BEFIJLLMOTU	FULL-TIME JOB	BEHILOSSSTV	BOLSHEVISTS
BEFIKLNOOTT	BOTTLE OF INK	BEHINORRTTW	TWIN BROTHER
BEFIKLOOOPS	PILE OF BOOKS	BEHIOOORRSUV	HERBIVOROUS
BEFINORSSSU	FIBROUSNESS	BEHJNNOOORS	JOHN OSBORNE
BEFINORSTTT	FROSTBITTEN	BEHKNOORRST	BROKEN SHORT
BEFINORSTTU	FIRST BUT ONE	BEHLLNOOTTW	DLOWN THE LOT
BEFLLOOPRTU	BULLETPROOF	BEHLLOOSTTW	BLOWS THE LOT
BEFLMOORTTU	BOTTLE OF RUM	BEHLNOORTTU	BUTTONHOLER
BEFOOORRRSTT	ROBERT FROST	BEHLNOOSTTU	BUTTONHOLES
BEGGGILNOOT	BOOTLEGGING	BEHLOORRSTU	SOUL BROTHER
BEGGGINORRW	GROWN BIGGER	BEHMOOORSST	SMOOTHBORES
BEGGGIORRSW	GROWS BIGGER	BEHMOOOTTTT	TO THE BOTTOM
BEGGHIINNRT	BRIGHTENING	BEHMPRSTTUU	TUB-THUMPERS
BEGGIILLNUY	BEGUILINGLY	BEHNNOOOORRT	NORTH BORNEO
BEGGILLRSUY	SILLY BUGGER	BEHNNOOTTTU	ON THE BUTTON
BEGGILNOOVX	BOXING GLOVE	BEHNNOOTTUY	ON THE BOUNTY
BEGGINOORRS	BOGNOR REGIS	BEHNOOPRTTW	POT THE BROWN
BEGHHIKLSWY	BLEW SKY-HIGH	BEHNORSTTWY	NORTH BY WEST
BEGHHMOORTU	BROUGHT HOME		WEST BY NORTH
BEGHIILMRST	BRIGHT SMILE	BEHOORRSSTX	BOXER SHORTS
	THIMBLERIGS	BEHOPSSSTTU	STOPS THE BUS
BEGHIIORRSU	IRISH BROGUE	BEHOSSTTUWY	SOUTH BY WEST
BEGHIKNSTWY	KNEW BY SIGHT		WEST BY SOUTH
BEGHILNORUY	NEIGHBOURLY	BEIIILMMORS	IMMOBILISER
BEGHIMNRRTU	RIGHT NUMBER	BEIIILMMORZ	IMMOBILIZER
BEGHINNORTW	NEW BRIGHTON	BEIIILMMOSS	IMMOBILISES
BEGHINOPSTT	BETTING SHOP	BEIIILMMOSZ	IMMOBILIZES
BEGHINPRSTU	BRIGHTENS UP	BEIIILMNRST	LIBERTINISM
BEGHOOORRTUV	BROUGHT OVER	BEIIILMQRUU	EQUILIBRIUM
BEGIIIILLTY	ELIGIBILITY	BEIIILNSSTY	SENSIBILITY
BEGIILMNNRU	UNLIMBERING	BEIIIMNSSTU	BITUMINISES
BEGIILMNPRU	LIMBERING UP	BEIIIMNSSTUZ	BITUMINIZES
BEGIILNOORV	BOILING OVER	BEIIJLSSTUV	JUST VISIBLE
BEGIILNPSTT	BETTING SLIP	BEIILLLORW	BORE ILL-WILL
BEGIILNRSTT	BITTERLINGS	BEIIILLOSSSU	SOLUBILISES
BEGIIMNRRSU	REIMBURSING	BEIILLOSSUZ	SOLUBILIZES
BEGIKNNOSTW	KNOWING BEST	BEIILMPRSSY	PERMISSIBLY
BEGIKNOOORV	OVERBOOKING	BEIILNOSSSU	BILIOUSNESS
BEGILNNOOPW	BLOWING OPEN	BEIILRRSSTV	VERS LIBRIST
BEGILNNRTUU	TURNING BLUE	BEIINNPSTXY	SIXPENNY BIT
BEGILNOORVW	BLOWING OVER	BEIINORRTTU	RETRIBUTION
	BOWLING OVER	BEIINORRTTY	BITTER IRONY
BEGILNQRSUU	BURLESQUING	BEIJRRSTUYY	TRIES BY JURY
BEGILPSSTTU	SPITTLEBUGS	BEIKLLLNSSU	SELLS IN BULK
BEGINORRSTT	BRING TO REST	BEIKLNOSTTT	INK-BLOT TEST
BEGINPRTTUU	BUTTERING UP	BEIKNNOORTW	BROKEN IN TWO
BEGJLNNNUUY	JUNGLE BUNNY	BEIKOORSSTW	WRITES BOOKS
BEGMNNORRUW	WRONG NUMBER	BEILLMPSTUU	SUBMULTIPLE
BEGNNRSTTUU	GET SUNBURNT	BEILLNOOTVW	VIOLENT BLOW
BEGNOORSSTX	STRONG BOXES	BEILLNOSSSU	BULL SESSION
	STRONGBOXES	BEILLOPRSST	BILL POSTERS
BEGNOOSTUYY	YOUNGEST BOY		BILLPOSTERS
BEGOOPPRSST	GOBSTOPPERS	BEILMNOOOTT	MILTON OBOTE
BEHHIIOPSTW	WHITE BISHOP	BEILMNOOSSW	SNOWMOBILES
BEHHILLSTTU	HITS THE BULL	BEILMNORSTY	MINSTREL BOY
BEHHIORSTTW	BE SHORT WITH	BEILNOOPSST	NOT POSSIBLE
BEHHMRSSTUU	THE BUM'S RUSH	BEILNOPRSSY	RESPONSIBLY

BEILORSTUVY	OBTRUSIVELY	BGIILMNOSSY	SYMBOLISING
BEIMNRSSTUU	BUS TERMINUS	BGIILMNOSYZ	SYMBOLIZING
BEINNOSSTUV	SUBVENTIONS	BGIILOORSTT	TRIBOLOGIST
BEINOOSSSUV	OBVIOUSNESS	BGIIMNNOPTU	BUMPING INTO
BEINORSSTUU	SUBROUTINES	BGIINOOORTT	GO INTO ORBIT
BEINORSTUUV	UNOBTRUSIVE	BGIKNNOSTUY	KINGS BOUNTY
BEINSSTTTUU	SUBSTITUENT	BGILLMNSTUY	STUMBLINGLY
BEIOQRSSTUU	SOUBRIQUETS	BGILLNOOSWW	SLOW BOWLING
BEIORRRTTUY	RETRIBUTORY	BGILLNORSTY	STROLLING BY
BEISSSTTTUU	SUBSTITUTES	BGILMNOTTUU	TUMBLING OUT
BEJJKORUUXY	JUKE-BOX JURY	BGILNOOTTTU	BLOTTING OUT
BEJKNNOOOSW	KNOW ONES JOB	BGILNORTTUU	BLURTING OUT
BEKNNNORRUU	UNBROKEN RUN	BGIMNORSTWY	GRIMSBY TOWN
BELLMOSSSUY	BLESS MY SOUL!	BGINNNOTTUU	UNBUTTONING
BELLNRTTUUY	TURBULENTLY	BGINNOPTTUU	BUTTONING UP
BELMNOPSTUU	STUMBLE UPON	BGINORSTTUU	BURSTING OUT
BELNOOOPSTW	BLOW ONES TOP	BGLLOOORTWY	BLOW TO GLORY
BELNOOSTUUY	BOUNTEOUSLY	BGNNORSTTUU	GOT SUNBURNT
BELOOPRSTTU	TROUBLE SPOT	BHHHHJOSSUU	HUSH-HUSH JOB
BELORSSTUUW	SLOW BUT SURE	BHIIIINNOST	INHIBITIONS
BEMNNOORTUY	MONEY TO BURN	BHIIILNORST	BRITISH LION
BEMNOOOOPRSW	MOP ONES BROW	BHIIINOOPRT	PROHIBITION
BEMNOOORRWY	BORROW MONEY	BHIIIOPRSTU	TRIPHIBIOUS
BEOOPRTVXYY	VOTE BY PROXY	BHIILLRSSTT	STILLBIRTHS
BEORRSTTTUW	BUTTERWORTS	BHIKNNOOSTW	WITH KNOBS ON
BFFGGIINNOR	BRINGING OFF	BHIKOOORSTY	HISTORY BOOK
BFFGHINORSU	BRUSHING OFF	BHILMOOSTYY	TOMBOYISHLY
BFFGIINORST	BORING STIFF	BHIMNOOPRRT	PROTHROMBIN
	BRINGS IT OFF	BHIMNPRSTTU	THUMBPRINTS
BFFGILLNOUY	BULLYING OFF	BHINORRSSTW	BROWNSHIRTS
BFFGILMNOTU	TUMBLING OFF	BHKNOOOSTTU	BUTTONHOOKS
BFFILOORTUW	BOWL OF FRUIT	BIIILOPSSTY	POSSIBILITY
BFGGINOOOTY	GOING BY FOOT	BIIKLLMORST	BRISTOL MILK
BFGGMOOOTTY	FOGGY BOTTOM	BIILLOOSUVY	OBLIVIOUSLY
BFGHILNSTYY	FLY-BY-NIGHTS	BIIMNOSSSSU	SUBMISSIONS
BFGHINORRST	BRINGS FORTH	BILMOPSTUUY	BUMPTIOUSLY
BFGIIILNTUY	FUNGIBILITY	BILNOOOSUXY	OBNOXIOUSLY
BFGIILNOOST	SOFT-BOILING	BIMNOORSSTT	TROMBONISTS
BFGIIOOPSST	BIT OF GOSSIP	BIMNOPSSTUU	SUBSUMPTION
BFHIIILMRST	BRITISH FILM	BIMORSSTUUU	RUMBUSTIOUS
BFHILLORSTY	BILL FORSYTH	BINOOPSSSTU	PUSS IN BOOTS
BFHORRSSTTU	BURSTS FORTH	BIOOOPPRRSU	OPPROBRIOUS
BFILLLMNOOU	IN FULL BLOOM	BKMOOOORSTTY	TOOK BY STORM
BFILLNOTUUY	BOUNTIFULLY	BMOOOOPTTTT	TOP TO BOTTOM
BFLLOORUUYY	BULLY FOR YOU	CCCCDIILOOP	DIPLOCOCCIC
BGGHHIILRTT	BRIGHT LIGHT	CCCCKKLOOOU	CUCKOO CLOCK
BGGHIIIKNNT	THINKING BIG	CCCDEEIINNO	COINCIDENCE
BGGHIIINRTV	GIVING BIRTH	CCCDEHIKLNO	COLD CHICKEN
BGGHIINOPSY	GOING BY SHIP	CCCDEIIMRSU	CIRCUMCISED
BGGIILNNORW	BRINGING LOW	CCCDEIIOOSS	COCCIDIOSES
BGGIILNORSS	GIBSON GIRLS	CCCDIIIOOSS	COCCIDIOSIS
BGGIINNORTU	BRINGING OUT	CCCDILOOPSU	DIPLOCOCCUS
BGGILLMNRUY	GRUMBLINGLY	CCCEEEEENRSX	EXCRESCENCE
BGHHHILNOOR	HIGH HOLBORN	CCCEEFIIOPS	ECOSPECIFIC
BGHHIIMORSW	HIGHBROWISM	CCCEEFLLNOU	FLOCCULENCE
BGHHIKLOSWY	BLOW SKY-HIGH	CCCEEIILMST	ECLECTICISM
BGHIIIINOPRT	PROHIBITING	CCCEEINNOSS	CONSCIENCES
BGHIIIINRRTV	VIRGIN BIRTH	CCCEENNORRU	CONCURRENCE
BGHIIKNOPSS	KINGS BISHOP	CCCEENNORST	CONCRESCENT
BGHIILPPRTU	BRIGHT PUPIL	CCCEENORRSU	OCCURRENCES
BGHIINOPPWY	WHIPPING BOY	CCCEHIKNOOP	CHICKEN COOP
BGHIKNOSTWY	KNOW BY SIGHT	CCCEHIOPRST	SOCCER PITCH
BGHILMNOOTY	BY MOONLIGHT	CCCEHKORSSS	CROSS-CHECKS
BGHILOPRTTU	BOLT UPRIGHT	CCCEIIMRRSU	CIRCUMCISER
BGHIMNPTTUU	TUB-THUMPING	CCCEIIMRSSU	CIRCUMCISES
BGHINOOOSTX	SHOOTING BOX	CCCEILORSST	CELTIC CROSS
BGHIOPRTTUU	BROUGHT IT UP	CCCEILPRTUY	CRYPTIC CLUE
BGHIORRTTUUY	BUY OUTRIGHT	CCCEIMNOOPU	PNEUMOCOCCI
BGIIILLLTUY	GULLIBILITY	CCCEIMPRSTU	CIRCUMSPECT
BGIIILLNOPST	BILLPOSTING	CCCEKNOORRT	ROCK CONCERT
BGIILLNSTTU	SITTING BULL	CCCHHHIORRU	CHURCH CHOIR

CCCHHIMRSUU	CHURCH MUSIC
CCCHILMOTYY	CYCLOTHYMIC
CCCIIIMRSTU	MUSIC CRITIC
CCCIILNOTUY	CITY COUNCIL
CCCIIMMOORS	MICROCOSMIC
CCCIIMOOPRS	MICROSCOPIC
CCDDEEEENORS	DECRESCENDO
CCDDEEEERRSU	RECRUDESCED
CCDDEENNOSS	CONDESCENDS
CCDDEHILNOS	SECOND CHILD
CCDDEKKLNOO	KNOCKED COLD
CCDDEOORRRW	RECORD CROWD
CCDDGNOOOTU	GOOD CONDUCT
CCDEEEFHIKN	CHICKEN FEED
CCDEEEHHSTU	DUTCH CHEESE
CCDEEEHKORV	CHECKED OVER
CCDEEEIINRS	IRIDESCENCE
CCDEEEELLORT	RECOLLECTED
CCDEEEENNOPR	DEEP CONCERN
CCDEEEENONCS	CRESCENDOES
CCDEEERRSSU	RECRUDESCES
CCDEEFINNOS	CONFIDENCES
CCDEEHHIKLN	HELD IN CHECK
CCDEEHHSTUW	CHEWS THE CUD
CCDEEHILORS	CECIL RHODES
CCDEEHILPSY	PSYCHEDELIC
CCDEEHIORTT	RICOCHETTED
CCDEEHKOPST	SPOT-CHECKED
CCDEEIIINST	INSECTICIDE
CCDEEIIRRST	DIRECTRICES
CCDEEIKLNUW	WICKED UNCLE
CCDEEIKLRSV	CLEVER-DICKS
CCDEEILNOTY	CONCEITEDLY
CCDEEILRRSS	DRESS CIRCLE
CCDEEINONST	CONCRETISED
CCDEEINORTZ	CONCRETIZED
CCDEEIOPPRU	PREOCCUPIED
CCDEEJNORTU	CONJECTURED
CCDEEKKNNOO	KNOCKED ONCE
CCDEEKORRSW	CORKSCREWED
CCDEELLLOTY	COLLECTEDLY
CCDEELLMOOW	COLD WELCOME
CCDEELNNOOS	CONDOLENCES
CCDEELNNOTY	CONNECTEDLY
CCDEELNOOSS	CLOSE SECOND
CCDEELNORTY	CONCERTEDLY
CCDEEMNOOSS	COMES SECOND
CCDEENNNORU	UNCONCERNED
CCDEEOOORRS	RECORD SCORE
CCDEHHIIORT	THIRD CHOICE
CCDEHHIKLNO	HOLD IN CHECK
CCDEHIIKNTU	CHUCKED IT IN
CCDEHIIKTWW	WICKED WITCH
CCDEHLOORUW	CROUCHED LOW
CCDEIILOORT	CROCIDOLITE
CCDEIIRRRSU	CIRCUS RIDER
CCDEILLOPPP	CLIP-CLOPPED
CCDEILNOTUV	EVIL CONDUCT
CCDEINNOSST	DISCONNECTS
CCDEINOOTTY	ENDOCYTOTIC
CCDEINOPRST	CONSCRIPTED
CCDEINORSST	DISCONCERTS
CCDEINORSTT	CONSTRICTED
CCDELLOSTTU	COLLECT DUST
CCDELLOSTYY	CYCLOSTYLED
CCDENOORTUY	COUNTRY CODE
CCDENORSSTU	CONDUCTRESS
CCDENORSTTU	CONSTRUCTED
CCDFGKLOOOR	CROCK OF GOLD
CCDFLMOOORT	COLD COMFORT

CCDHHILLOOS	SCHOOL CHILD
	SCHOOLCHILD
CCDHIKNORST	DRINK SCOTCH
CCDHILOOPYY	HYPOCYCLOID
CCDHIOORTTW	WITCH DOCTOR
CCDHIOOSTUU	STUDIO COUCH
CCDHKNORSTU	DRUNK SCOTCH
CCDHMMNOOOR	COMMON CHORD
CCDIMNOSSTU	MISCONDUCTS
CCDINNOOSTU	CONDUCTIONS
CCDKOOOOPRST	DOCTOR SPOCK
CCEEEEILLRT	ELECTRIC EEL
CCEEEEILRTY	ELECTRIC EYE
CCEEEEINPRT	CENTREPIECE
CCEEEEELLNSX	EXCELLENCES
CCEEEEFHIKNR	NECKERCHIEF
CCEEEFIKNPT	PICKET FENCE
CCEEEEFLNORS	FLORESCENCE
CCEEEFNNORS	CONFERENCES
CCEEEGNNORV	CONVERGENCE
CCEEEGNRSTU	TURGESCENCE
CCEEEHHLOST	CHEESECLOTH
CCEEEHIKKNP	KEEP IN CHECK
CCEEEHINNOR	INCOHERENCE
CCEEEHLORTY	HETEROCYCLE
CCEEEIINPPR	PERCIPIENCE
CCEEEINNNOV	CONVENIENCE
CCEEEINOPRV	PRECONCEIVE
CCEEEINOPSS	CENOSPECIES
CCEEEINOSTX	COEXISTENCE
CCEEEINPRSU	PURE SCIENCE
CCEEEIRSTUX	EXECUTRICES
CCEEELORSST	CLOSE SECRET
CCEEELORTTU	ELECTROCUTE
CCEEENNOOSU	QUONODUENCE
CCEEENPRSTU	PUTRESCENCE
CCEEFFFOOPU	CUP OF COFFEE
CCEEFFIINOT	COEFFICIENT
CCEEFFIKLOR	OFFICE CLERK
CCEEFFILNOS	OFF-LICENCES
CCEEFIILMOR	COMIC RELIEF
CCEEFIIMNNU	MUNIFICENCE
CCEEFIKLOPU	PIECE OF LUCK
CCEEFILOOPR	POLICE FORCE
CCEEFLNOPST	SELF-CONCEPT
CCEEGHHKRRU	GREEK CHURCH
CCEEGHSSSUU	HUGE SUCCESS
CCEEGKLNOOS	COCK ONES LEG
CCEEGNNOOST	COGNOSCENTE
CCEEHIIKNRW	CHICKEN WIRE
CCEEHIKKNPT	KEPT IN CHECK
CCEEHINNORY	INCOHERENCY
CCEEHKLLLOS	COCKLESHELL
CCEEHKLMOSU	CHUCKLESOME
CCEEHKLOORT	THREE O CLOCK
CCEEHLMNOWY	COMELY WENCH
CCEEHNOSSTU	ESCUTCHEONS
CCEEIIKPRTT	PRICE TICKET
CCEEIILMRSS	SEMICIRCLES
CCEEIILNNRR	INNER CIRCLE
CCEEIILORST	ISOELECTRIC
CCEEIILRTTY	ELECTRICITY
CCEEIIMNNOS	OMNISCIENCE
CCEEIIMNOSV	MISCONCEIVE
CCEEIKLRRTV	CLEVER TRICK
CCEEIKRSTTT	TEST CRICKET
CCEEILLOSTV	COLLECTIVES
CCEEILNNOTV	CONVENTICLE
CCEEILNORST	ELECTRONICS
CCEEILORRTU	OUTER CIRCLE
CCEEILPPRRU	UPPER CIRCLE

CCEEIMNOORT	ECONOMETRIC
CCEEIMNORRT	CENTROMERIC
CCEEIMNRSTU	MUSIC CENTRE
CCEEIMORRTT	CORRECT TIME
CCEEINNOQTU	CINQUECENTO
CCEEINNOSSS	CONCISENESS
CCEEINOORTW	ONCE OR TWICE
CCEEINORSST	CONCRETISES
CCEEINORSTZ	CONCRETIZES
CCEEINOSTUV	CONSECUTIVE
CCEEIOPPRSU	PREOCCUPIES
CCEEIOPRSSS	CROSSPIECES
CCEEIOPSTTU	CUT TO PIECES
CCEEJNORRTU	CONJECTURER
CCEEJNORSTU	CONJECTURES
CCEEKLNOOSV	SEVEN O CLOCK
CCEEKOSSTUX	STOCK EXCUSE
CCEELMOORSS	COMES CLOSER
CCEELMORSTY	CYCLOMETERS
CCEENOPRRST	PRECONCERTS
CCEENORRSST	CORRECTNESS
CCEENORRTTU	CENTRE COURT
CCEFFGHIKNO	CHECKING OFF
CCEFFIINSUY	SUFFICIENCY
CCEFGHNNOOR	FRENCH CONGO
CCEFGIKLNOS	SELF-COCKING
CCEFHHILSTU	HECTIC FLUSH
CCEFHIIMORS	MICROFICHES
CCEFHIIORST	FIRST CHOICE
CCEFHIOOOTW	CHOICE OF TWO
CCEFIIIPSTY	SPECIFICITY
CCEFIINOPRY	PROFICIENCY
CCEFIKLLOSU	SLICE OF LUCK
CCEFINNOOST	CONFECTIONS
CCEFIORRSUU	CRUCIFEROUS
CCEGHHIILRS	HIGH CIRCLES
CCEGHIILNOR	CHOLINERGIC
CCEGHIINORT	RICOCHETING
CCEGHIKLOOT	EIGHT O CLOCK
CCEGHIKNOTU	CHECKING OUT
CCEGHINOPSY	PSYCHOGENIC
CCEGIILNNOR	RECONCILING
CCEGILMNOOS	COMING CLOSE
CCEGINNNOTY	CONTINGENCY
CCEGINNOOST	COGNOSCENTI
CCEGINOPRTY	CRYPTOGENIC
CCEHHIOSSTT	SCHOTTISCHE
CCEHHIPRRSU	CHURCH SPIRE
CCEHHMNORUW	CHURCHWOMEN
CCEHHMORSUU	CHURCH MOUSE
CCEHIILNOPR	NECROPHILIC
CCEHIKKLOPT	PICK THE LOCK
CCEHIKKOSTY	HOCKEY STICK
CCEHIKNOPST	CHECKPOINTS
CCEHIKNOPSU	CHICKEN SOUP
CCEHILNOORT	TECHNICOLOR
CCEHILNOPTY	POLYTECHNIC
CCEHILNORRS	CHRONICLERS
CCEHILOSTTY	CHOLECYSTIT
CCEHIMMOORR	CHROMOMERIC
CCEHIMOOPRT	CHEMOTROPIC
	ECTOMORPHIC
CCEHINNRSSU	CRUNCHINESS
CCEHINOPRTY	PYROTECHNIC
CCEHKLOSTTU	SHUTTLECOCK
CCEHKNPRSUU	SUCKER PUNCH
CCEHKORSTUU	CHUCKERS-OUT
CCEHLOORSUW	CROUCHES LOW
CCEHMOORSTY	CYTOCHROMES
CCEHOSSTTTU	CUTS THE COST
CCEIIKNOTTY	CYTOKINETIC

CCEIIKNSSTT	STICK INSECT
CCEIILMNORT	CLINOMETRIC
CCEIIMOOPRS	MICROCOPIES
CCEIIMOORST	SOCIOMETRIC
CCEIIMORSTV	VISCOMETRIC
CCEIINOPRTU	OPEN CIRCUIT
	OPEN-CIRCUIT
CCEIINPRSTU	CUTS IN PRICE
CCEIIOPRRTY	RECIPROCITY
CCEIJNNOTUV	CONJUNCTIVE
CCEIKKNOSTW	KNOCKS TWICE
CCEIKKOPPST	PICK POCKETS
	PICKPOCKETS
CCEIKLMOORT	MORTICE LOCK
CCEIKLNOPRU	CUPRO-NICKEL
CCEILLNOOST	COLLECTIONS
CCEILNORRTY	INCORRECTLY
CCEILOOPRTU	POLICE COURT
CCEILOSSTTU	CUTS IT CLOSE
CCEIMNOORST	CENTROSOMIC
CCEIMNRSTUV	CIRCUMVENTS
CCEIMOOPRSS	MICROSCOPES
CCEINNNOOST	CONNECTIONS
CCEINNOOPST	CONCEPTIONS
CCEINNOORST	CONCERTINOS
CCEINNOOSSS	CONCESSIONS
CCEINNOPRRW	CROWN PRINCE
CCEINNOSSTY	CONSISTENCY
CCEINOORRST	CORRECTIONS
CCEJNNORTUU	CONJUNCTURE
CCEKLOORTWY	CYCLE TO WORK
CCEKMNOSTUU	COME UNSTUCK
CCELLNSTUUY	SUCCULENTLY
CCELLOSSTYY	CYCLOSTYLES
CCELMOORSTY	MOTORCYCLES
CCELMOOSSTY	CYCLOSTOMES
CCEMNOOPRRT	PROM CONCERT
CCENORRSSTU	CUTS CORNERS
CCENORRSTTU	RECONSTRUCT
CCFGIILNNOT	CONFLICTING
CCFIIINORUX	CRUCIFIXION
CCFIILNNOOT	CONFLICTION
CCFIKKOORST	STICK OF ROCK
CCFIKOORSTU	FIRST CUCKOO
CCFILMORRUY	CRUCIFORMLY
CCFKNOOORTT	COTTON FROCK
CCGHIILLNNY	CLINCHINGLY
CCGHIILNNOR	CHRONICLING
CCGHIKLLNUY	CHUCKLINGLY
CCGHIKNOTUU	CHUCKING OUT
CCGHILNORSY	SCORCHINGLY
CCGHIOOPRSY	HYGROSCOPIC
CCGIIINNRST	CRITICISING
CCGIIINNRTZ	CRITICIZING
CCGIIKNOPTU	COCKING IT UP
CCGIKLNOOTU	CLOCKING OUT
CCGILOOOPRT	PROCTOLOGIC
CCHHLLNOOSU	SCHOOL LUNCH
CCHIIIOSTTY	HISTIOCYTIC
CCHIIMNOOPR	MICROPHONIC
CCHIIMORSTW	MICROSWITCH
CCHIINORTWY	NORWICH CITY
CCHIKOSTTUU	CHUCKS IT OUT
CCHILMNOORY	CHYLOMICRON
CCHILMOOSSU	MUSIC SCHOOL
CCHILMOPTYY	LYMPHOCYTIC
CCHIMMNOOOR	MONOCHROMIC
CCHIMOOOORRR	HORROR COMIC
CCHIOOOPRST	ORTHOSCOPIC
CCHIORSSSTT	CROSS-STITCH
CCHMMNOOOTU	COMMON TOUCH

CCIILLNNOTY	LINCOLN CITY
CCIILNSSTUY	UNICYCLISTS
CCIILRSSTTY	TRICYCLISTS
CCIIMMNOSTU	COMMUNISTIC
CCIINNOOSTV	CONVICTIONS
CCIINOOPTTY	PINOCYTOTIC
CCIINOPRTTY	NYCTITROPIC
CCIJNNNOOTU	CONJUNCTION
CCIKKPPRTUU	PICK-UP TRUCK
CCIKNOOPSTU	CUCKOOPINTS
CCILLNOORSU	COUNCILLORS
CCILMRRSUUU	CURRICULUMS
CCILNNOOSSU	CONCLUSIONS
CCILNNOOTUW	TOWN COUNCIL
CCILNOOSSUY	CONSCIOUSLY
CCIMNNOOPTU	COMPUNCTION
CCINNOOSSUU	UNCONSCIOUS
CCINOOPSSUU	CONSPICUOUS
CCINOORRSTT	CONSTRICTOR
CCIOOPRSCTY	PROROCYSTIC
CCKKLRSTUUY	STRUCK LUCKY
CCKMMNOOOST	COMMON STOCK
CCKNOOOSSTT	COTTON SOCKS
CCKNOORRTUY	COUNTRY ROCK
CCLNNOOORWY	CROWN COLONY
CCNOORRSTTU	CONSTRUCTOR
CCNOORTTUUY	COUNTY COURT
CDDDEEEEGKL	DECKLE-EDGED
CDDDEEEEINSS	DECIDEDNESS
CDDDEEENNSU	UNDESCENDED
CDDDECIIRST	DISCREDITED
CDDDEEILNUY	UNDECIDEDLY
CDDEEEEPRSU	REDUCE SPEED
CDDEEEFGNOO	GOOD DEFENCE
CDDEFFGLORV	CLEVER DODGE
CDDEEEILQSU	DELIQUESCED
CDDEEEIPRTU	DECREPITUDE
CDDEEEMMNOR	RECOMMENDED
CDDEEENRSSU	DESCENDEURS
CDDEEEOPRRR	PRERECORDED
CDDEEEOPRRS	SPEED RECORD
CDDEEFIINST	DISINFECTED
CDDEEFILNSU	SELF-INDUCED
CDDEEFNNORU	FENCED ROUND
CDDEEHNNRSU	SUNDRENCHED
CDDEEIIMRST	MISDIRECTED
CDDEEIINORT	RODENTICIDE
CDDEEIINRTT	INTERDICTED
CDDEEILNOOS	DECOLONISED
CDDEEILNOOZ	DECOLONIZED
CDDEEILOORS	DECOLORISED
CDDEEILOORZ	DECOLORIZED
CDDEEILTUVY	DEDUCTIVELY
CDDEEINPRRU	UNDERPRICED
CDDEELOORUV	CLOUDED OVER
	OVERCLOUDED
CDDEENNOPSY	DESPONDENCY
CDDEENORRSU	UNDERSCORED
CDDEENORSWW	SCREWED DOWN
CDDEEOORRVW	OVERCROWDED
CDDEFFNOOOR	CORDONED OFF
CDDEFHIKOOS	DIED OF SHOCK
CDDEFIIMOST	DISCOMFITED
CDDEGHILNOR	GODCHILDREN
CDDEGIINORT	DOING CREDIT
CDDEGIINPRU	RICE PUDDING
CDDEGNOORRS	CORN DODGERS
CDDEHIIKRTT	DID THE TRICK
CDDEHIILMNR	CHILDMINDER
CDDEHKNOSSU	SUDDEN SHOCK
CDDEHNOOPPW	CHOPPED DOWN

CDDEHNOOTUW	TOUCHED DOWN
CDDEHOOOTUW	TOUCHED WOOD
CDDEHOORRUW	CROWDED HOUR
CDDEIIILNNS	DISINCLINED
CDDEIIILNPS	DISCIPLINED
CDDEIILPPSS	SLIPPED DISC
CDDEIINNOOT	CONDITIONED
CDDEIKKOPPR	DROPPED KICK
CDDEIKLLMRU	CURDLED MILK
CDDEIKOPSTT	SPOTTED DICK
CDDEILNOOTY	DICOTYLEDON
CDDEILNOSSU	UNDISCLOSED
CDDEILOORSU	DISCOLOURED
CDDEILOSUUY	DECIDUOUSLY
CDDEIMNORSW	MINCED WORDS
CDDEIMOOPSS	DISCOMPOSED
CDDEKKNNOOW	KNOCKED DOWN
CDDEKLOOORS	LOCKED DOORS
CDDELLLMOOY	MOLLYCODDLE
CDDELOOORSS	CLOSED DOORS
CDDELOORRRW	WORLD RECORD
CDDEMOOORRW	CROWDED ROOM
CDDENNOORSU	SECOND ROUND
CDDENNOOTUW	COUNTED DOWN
CDDFLOOSTUU	CLOUD OF DUST
CDDGIINOOOT	GOOD DICTION
CDDKLNNOOOS	LONDON DOCKS
CDDNOORRSUW	CROWDS ROUND
CDEEEEFFLNS	SELF DEFENCE
	SELF-DEFENCE
CDEEEEFFRSV	EFFERVESCED
CDEEEEFLNSS	DEFENCELESS
CDEEEEGLSTT	GETS ELECTED
CDEEEEHKRRT	THREE-DECKER
CDEEEEINNVW	NEW EVIDENCE
CDEEEEINPRX	EXPERIENCED
CDEEEFFINRS	DIFFERENCES
CDEEEFFLORS	EFFLORESCED
CDEEEFGLNTU	GENUFLECTED
CDEEEFGLOTT	GET COLD FEET
CDEEEFHIIPS	SPEECHIFIED
CDEEEFHIMNR	CHEMIN DE FER
CDEEEFHLLOT	FEEL THE COLD
CDEEEFIILRT	ELECTRIFIED
CDEEEFILTVY	DEFECTIVELY
CDEEEFKNORW	DEFENCE WORK
CDEEEFLNRST	SELF-CENTRED
CDEEEGIIPRS	RIDGEPIECES
CDEEEGILNXY	EXCEEDINGLY
CDEEEGINRSV	DIVERGENCES
CDEEEGISTTX	GETS EXCITED
CDEEEGKLLRR	LEDGER CLERK
CDEEEGKMORY	GREEK COMEDY
CDEEEGKNOOS	GOOSENECKED
CDEEEHIPRRS	DECIPHERERS
CDEEEIINNRS	IN RESIDENCE
CDEEEIIOPPR	PERIOD PIECE
CDEEEIJNRTT	INTERJECTED
CDEEEILOPSV	VELOCIPEDES
CDEEEILORTT	LIE DETECTOR
CDEEEILPTVY	DECEPTIVELY
CDEEEILQSSU	DELIQUESCES
CDEEEINPRTT	INTERCEPTED
CDEEEINRSTT	INTERSECTED
CDEEEINSTTU	SENECTITUDE
CDEEEMNOORV	ONCE REMOVED
CDEEEMNOPRS	RECOMPENSED
CDEEEMNRRTY	TENDER MERCY
CDEEEMNSTTU	DETUMESCENT
CDEEENNORTU	ENCOUNTERED
CDEEENOPSSW	SWEEP-SECOND

CDEEENORSSV	SECOND VERSE	CDEEIILNORT	DERELICTION
CDEEEOPRRSS	PREDECESSOR	CDEEIILRTTT	CREDIT TITLE
CDEEERRRSTU	RESURRECTED	CDEEIIMNOSS	COMES INSIDE
CDEEFFHINRR	FRENCH FRIED	CDEEIIMPSSX	MIXED SPICES
CDEEFFIKNST	STIFF-NECKED	CDEEIINORRT	REDIRECTION
CDEEFFNOSTU	SOUND EFFECT	CDEEIINOSTU	SUICIDE NOTE
CDEEFGILLNO	FEELING COLD	CDEEIINRSTV	VIRIDESCENT
CDEEFGINRTU	CENTRIFUGED	CDEEIINRTTU	INCERTITUDE
CDEEFGLOOTT	GOT COLD FEET	CDEEIIORRST	DIRECTORIES
CDEEFHIKLOY	FIELD HOCKEY	CDEEIIORSSV	DISCOVERIES
CDEEFHINOOS	CHINESE FOOD	CDEEIIPRSTV	DESCRIPTIVE
CDEEFHLLOTT	FELT THE COLD	CDEEIIRRSTX	DIRECTRIXES
CDEEFIILNTY	DEFICIENTLY	CDEEIIRSSSV	DISSERVICES
CDEEFIIMNOX	FIXED INCOME	CDEEIJNORTT	INTROJECTED
CDEEFIINPSU	UNSPECIFIED	CDEEIJNOSTU	DONE JUSTICE
CDEEFIIOPRT	PIECE OF DIRT	CDEEIJOSSTU	DOES JUSTICE
CDEEFILLTUY	DECEITFULLY	CDEEIKLMOOR	CROOKED MILE
CDEEFILMORS	FORCED SMILE	CDEEIKLNNOO	NICKELODEON
CDEEFILNORS	CLOSE FRIEND	CDEEIKLNORT	INTERLOCKED
CDEEFILNOST	DEFLECTIONS	CDEEIKPPPSU	PICK UP SPEED
CDEEFILORSU	FIELD COURSE	CDEEILLNOSW	SLOW DECLINE
CDEEFILOSST	CLOSEFISTED	CDEEILNNOSS	DECLENSIONS
CDEEFINOSSV	FIVE SECONDS	CDEEILNNOST	INTENSE COLD
CDEEFLLNOOT	LEFT ONE COLD	CDEEILNNQUY	DELINQUENCY
CDEEFLNORST	CENTREFOLDS	CDEEILNOOSS	DECOLONISES
CDEEFLNOSSY	CONFESSEDLY	CDEEILNOOSZ	DECOLONIZES
CDEEFNNORSU	FENCES ROUND	CDEEILNORTY	RECONDITELY
CDEEFNORRTY	FORCED ENTRY	CDEEILOORRS	DECOLORISER
CDEEFOORRRR	FORCED ERROR	CDEEILOORRZ	DECOLORIZER
CDEEFOORRTU	TOUR DE FORCE	CDEEILOORSS	DECOLORISES
CDEEFOPRRTW	WORD PERFECT	CDEEILOORSU	DECOLOURISE
	WORD-PERFECT	CDEEILOORSZ	DECOLORIZES
CDEEGGINTTU	CUTTING EDGE	CDEEILOORUZ	DECOLOURIZE
CDEEGGLORSS	CROSS-LEGGED	CDEEILRSTTY	DIRECT STYLE
CDEEGHHISTT	GETS HITCHED	CDEEILSTUVY	SEDUCTIVELY
CDEEGHIINPR	DECIPHERING	CDEEIMNNOOY	COINED MONEY
CDEEGIILNVY	DECEIVINGLY	CDEEIMNNRST	DISCERNMENT
CDEEGIINNRT	INTERCEDING		RESCINDMENT
CDEEGIINNUV	UNDECEIVING	CDEEIMNNSTU	INDUCEMENTS
CDEEGIINRRT	REDIRECTING	CDEEIMNOORR	CRIED NO MORE
CDEEGIINRTV	GIVEN CREDIT	CDEEIMNOPRS	ENDOSPERMIC
CDEEGIIRSTV	GIVES CREDIT	CDEEIMOOSTU	COME OUTSIDE
CDEEGIKOPTU	POCKET GUIDE	CDEEIMOPSTT	DOMESTIC PET
CDEEGILNNSU	INDULGENCES	CDEEIMRRSTT	CREDIT TERMS
CDEEGILNSUV	DIVULGENCES	CDEEINNORTU	UNDER NOTICE
CDEEGINOPRS	PROCEEDINGS	CDEEINNRSSW	WINDSCREENS
CDEEGIOORSV	GOOD SERVICE	CDEEINOORTT	CONDOTTIERE
CDEEGNOSSSU	SECOND GUESS	CDEEINOPRSZ	SECOND PRIZE
CDEEHHIKSTT	HITS THE DECK	CDEEINOPRTV	OPEN VERDICT
CDEEHHIMSTT	HEMSTITCHED	CDEEINORRSS	RECONSIDERS
CDEEHHIOSUV	HUSHED VOICE	CDEEINORSUU	IN DUE COURSE
CDEEHIINNOS	INDO-CHINESE	CDEEINORTTU	TURNED TO ICE
CDEEHIINNST	INDEHISCENT	CDEEINPRRSU	UNDERPRICES
CDEEHIKLOPS	PICKED HOLES	CDEEINRRTTY	CREDIT ENTRY
CDEEHIKNSTT	TEND THE SICK	CDEEIOPQRTU	QUOTED PRICE
CDEEHIKPRSW	SHIPWRECKED	CDEEIORRSSV	DISCOVERERS
CDEEHIMNORS	ECHINODERMS	CDEEIORRTTU	DIRECT ROUTE
CDEEHIMNORT	ENDOTHERMIC	CDEEIORRTXY	EX-DIRECTORY
CDEEHIOPRTV	OVERPITCHED	CDEEIPRSSST	DISRESPECTS
CDEEHIOQSTU	DISCOTHEQUE	CDEEIRRRSVW	SCREWDRIVER
CDEEHMNOPRS	COMPREHENDS	CDEEIRRSSTT	DERESTRICTS
CDEEHMORSWY	SHOWED MERCY	CDEEIRSTTUV	DESTRUCTIVE
CDEEHNOORRT	ON THE RECORD	CDEEKKNOORV	KNOCKED OVER
CDEEHNOOSSU	SECOND HOUSE	CDEEKNOORRT	RECORD TOKEN
CDEEHNOOSTT	TO THE SECOND	CDEEKNOORSS	CROOKEDNESS
CDEEHPRSTTU	STRETCHED UP	CDEEKOOPRSW	WOODPECKERS
CDEEIIMPTY	EPIDEMICITY	CDEELNNOTTY	CONTENTEDLY
CDEEIIKLNSS	SLICKENSIDE	CDEELNOSTTU	DULCET TONES
CDEEIILLNNP	PENCILLED IN	CDEELOOPRSU	SUPERCOOLED
CDEEIILMOPS	POLEMICISED	CDEEMNNOOSU	COMES UNDONE
CDEEIILMOPZ	POLEMICIZED	CDEEMOOPRSS	DECOMPOSERS

CDEENNOQRUU	UNCONQUERED	CDEHIIMNORT	COME IN THIRD
CDEENOPRTTU	UNPROTECTED	CDEHIIMOOST	DICHOTOMIES
CDEENORRSSU	UNDERSCORES	CDEHIIMOSTT	METHODISTIC
CDEEOOPRRUV	OVERPRODUCE	CDEHIINOPTT	PITCHED INTO
CDEEOORRSSV	CROSSED OVER	CDEHIKLSTTU	LICK THE DUST
CDEFFGIOOOS	GOOD OFFICES	CDEHILNOSTU	IN THE CLOUDS
CDEFFHILOOS	HOLDS OFFICE	CDEHILPRTUU	PULCHRITUDE
CDEFFHIOSTW	SWITCHED OFF	CDEHIMNOOPR	ENDOMORPHIC
CDEFFIORTUY	DUTY OFFICER	CDEHIMNORST	CHRISTENDOM
CDEFFLOSTTU	SCUTTLED OFF	CDEHIMOPRSY	HYPODERMICS
CDEFGHILNOS	GOLDFINCHES	CDEHIMORRTY	HYDROMETRIC
CDEFGILOOPR	PRICE OF GOLD	CDEHIOOOPPT	PHOTOCOPIED
CDEFGINOSSU	DEFOCUSSING	CDEHIORRSTU	THIRD COURSE
CDEFHIKOOSS	DIES OF SHOCK	CDEHKLLOOWY	HOLY WEDLOCK
CDEFHIKOPRT	PITCHFORKED	CDEHKLNOORS	LOCKED HORNS
CDEFHILORST	FOSTER CHILD	CDEHKLOOORT	LOCK THE DOOR
CDEFHINOSST	SECOND SHIFT	CDEHLNORRSU	ORDERS LUNCH
CDEFHNRSTUY	STUDY FRENCH	CDEHLOOPPRS	CLODHOPPERS
CDEFIIKPRTU	PICKED FRUIT	CDEHLOOPRSY	COPYHOLDERS
CDEFIINORTU	COUNTRIFIED	CDEHLOPRTUW	THE WORLD CUP
CDEFIJOORRY	CRIED FOR JOY	CDEHMNNOOST	SECOND MONTH
CDEFILMNORY	CONFIRMEDLY	CDEHNOOPTUU	TOUCHED UPON
CDEFILNNOTY	CONFIDENTLY	CDEHNOOSTUW	TOUCHES DOWN
CDEFILNOOTT	COTTON FIELD	CDEHOOOORST	HORSE DOCTOR
CDEFIMOOOOV	VOICE OF DOOM	CDEHOOOSTUW	TOUCHES WOOD
CDEFIORRRST	FIRST RECORD	CDEIIILNPRS	DISCIPLINER
CDEFKOPSSTU	SPECK OF DUST	CDEIIILNPSS	DISCIPLINES
CDEFLNOOORS	SECOND FLOOR	CDEIIILNSUV	UNCIVILISED
CDEFNNOORST	SECOND FRONT	CDEIIILNUVZ	UNCIVILIZED
CDEFNNOORSU	CONFOUNDERS	CDEIIILOPST	POLITICISED
CDEFNOOORTU	FOOD COUNTER	CDEIIILOPTZ	POLITICIZED
CDEFNOORSSU	FOUR SECONDS	CDEIIINNOSS	INDECISIONS
CDEFNORRSTU	UNDERCROFTS	CDEIIINSTTV	DISTINCTIVE
CDEGGIINORT	GOING DIRECT	CDEIIIOPRTY	PERIODICITY
CDEGGILNOTT	GETTING COLD	CDEIIIRSSTV	RECIDIVISTS
CDEGHHHIIPT	HIGH-PITCHED	CDEIIISSTUV	VICISSITUDE
CDEGHIILNSU	CHILD GENIUS	CDEIIJNSTUV	DISJUNCTIVE
CDEGHILLOPR	GRILLED CHOP	CDEIIKKLNPT	TICKLED PINK
CDEGHILMOTY	LIGHT COMEDY	CDEIIKNOPSW	DIP ONE'S WICK
CDEGHINOSST	SECOND SIGHT	CDEIIKORRSW	WORRIED SICK
CDEGHIOPRTY	COPYRIGHTED	CDEIIKQTTUW	QUICK-WITTED
CDEGHLNOOTU	GOLDEN TOUCH	CDEIILLOORV	COD-LIVER OIL
CDEGIIJNPRU	PREJUDICING	CDEIILLOSUY	DELICIOUSLY
CDEGIILNNOY	DOING NICELY	CDEIILLPTUY	PELLUCIDITY
CDEGIINNORS	CONSIDERING	CDEIILNOSTU	UNSOLICITED
CDEGIINNPRS	PRESCINDING	CDEIILNRTUY	INCREDULITY
CDEGIINOOOV	IN GOOD VOICE	CDEIILNTUVY	INDUCTIVELY
CDEGIINOOTZ	GOOD CITIZEN	CDEIILOOSUY	DIOECIOUSLY
CDEGIINOPTY	COPY-EDITING	CDEIILOPSSU	PEDICULOSIS
CDEGIINORSV	DISCOVERING	CDEIILOSTUV	DECLIVITOUS
CDEGIKLLNOO	OLD KING COLE	CDEIIMMOOST	COMMODITIES
CDEGIKMMNOO	KINGDOM COME	CDEIIMNNSTT	INDICTMENTS
CDEGIMNNORU	COMING UNDER	CDEIIMNORST	MODERNISTIC
CDEGIMNNOTU	DOCUMENTING	CDEIIMORRSS	MISERICORDS
CDEGIMNOOPS	DECOMPOSING	CDEIIMOSTTY	DOMESTICITY
CDEGIMNORRU	CORRIGENDUM	CDEIIMPPRUY	CYPRIPEDIUM
CDEGINOPRRU	REPRODUCING	CDEIINNOORT	CONDITIONER
CDEGINOPRSU	GROUND SPICE		RECONDITION
CDEGINRSTTU	DESTRUCTING	CDEIINNOPRW	DOWN IN PRICE
CDEGIOOOSTY	GOOD SOCIETY	CDEIINNOSTU	DISCONTINUE
CDEGLLNORSU	GOLDEN CURLS	CDEIINOORTT	CONDOTTIERI
CDEGMNORSUU	CURMUDGEONS	CDEIINOPPRR	DROP IN PRICE
CDEGNOORRUV	COVER GROUND	CDEIINOPRST	DESCRIPTION
CDEHIIIINNOR	ENCHIRIDION		PREDICTIONS
CDEHIIINRST	TRICHINISED	CDEIINORSST	DISCRETIONS
CDEHIIINRTZ	TRICHINIZED	CDEIINOSSST	DISSECTIONS
CDEHIIKRTTW	THIRD WICKET	CDEIINRSTUZ	SCRUTINIZED
CDEHIIKTTTW	THICK-WITTED	CDEIIORSTUV	DIVORCE SUIT
CDEHIILLLTT	LITTLE CHILD	CDEIJLORSTU	LORD JUSTICE
CDEHIILOOTT	THEODOLITIC	CDEIKLOSSTT	SOLD TICKETS
CDEHIILORRT	TRICHLORIDE	CDEIKRRRTUV	TRUCK DRIVER

CDEILMMNOTU	LUCID MOMENT	CDGINNOOPWY	COPYING DOWN
CDEILNNNOOU	ON CLOUD NINE	CDGINNOTTUW	CUTTING DOWN
CDEILNNOORS	LONDON CRIES	CDGINOORTUW	CROWDING OUT
CDEILNOPSST	SPLIT SECOND	CDGINOOTTUW	WOODCUTTING
	SPLIT-SECOND	CDHHIILOPRY	HYDROPHILIC
CDEILNORSUU	INCREDULOUS	CDHHIOPRTYY	HYDROPHYTIC
CDEILORRSUW	WORLD CRUISE	CDHIILLNQUU	LIQUID LUNCH
CDEILORSSSU	DISCLOSURES	CDHIILLOPST	SPOILT CHILD
CDEIMMNOPSU	COMPENDIUMS	CDHIIMORRSU	IRIS MURDOCH
CDEIMMNNORSU	MODERN MUSIC	CDHIIOOPRST	CHIROPODIST
CDEIMMNOTTU	UNCOMMITTED	CDHILPSTTUU	DUTCH TULIPS
CDEIMMOOPRS	COMPROMISED	CDHIMOOOSTU	DICHOTOMOUS
CDEIMNOOPSU	COMPENDIOUS	CDHINOOORTT	ORTHODONTIC
CDEIMNORSSW	MINCES WORDS	CDHINOOPRSY	HYDROPONICS
CDEIMOOPSSS	DISCOMPOSES	CDHIOOPRRTY	HYDROTROPIC
CDEINNOOTTU	COUNTED ON IT	CDHIOOPRSST	SHIPS DOCTOR
CDEINNOPRST	NONDESCRIPT	CDIIJNOSUU	INJUDICIOUS
CDEINNOSSTT	DISCONTENTS	CDIIINNNOOT	IN CONDITION
CDEINOOSSTY	ENDOCYTOSIS	CDIIINNOSTT	DISTINCTION
CDEINORSTTU	DESTRUCTION	CDIIJLOSUUY	JUDICIOUSLY
CDEINOSTTTU	CONSTITUTED	CDIIJNNOSTU	DISJUNCTION
CDEIOPRRTUW	WORD PICTURE	CDIILMORSTU	CLOSTRIDIUM
CDEIORRRSTT	STRICT ORDER	CDIILOORUVV	VIVID COLOUR
CDEIORRSSSU	DISCOURSERS	CDIILOPSTUU	DUPLICITOUS
CDEIORSSTUY	DISCOURTESY	CDIIMMNNOOU	CONDOMINIUM
CDEKKLNNOUW	KNUCKLE DOWN	CDIINOOOPRT	POOR DICTION
CDELLNORSUY	SCOUNDRELLY	CDIINOSSSSU	DISCUSSIONS
CDELLORSUUY	CREDULOUSLY	CDIKLNOPSSU	SPONDULICKS
CDELMOORSTU	OLD CUSTOMER	CDIKORSSSTW	SWORDSTICKS
CDELMOORTWY	MOTLEY CROWD	CDILLORSUUY	LUDICROUSLY
CDEMMOOORSS	COSMODROMES	CDILNOOPSUY	SOUND POLICY
CDEMNOOPRSU	COMPOUNDERS	CDILNORTUWY	WILD COUNTRY
CDENNOOPPUU	POUNCED UPON	CDILOOORUUU	DOUROUCOULI
CDENNOOPTUU	COUNTED UPON	CDINOOPRSTU	PRODUCTIONS
CDENOOPRRSS	CORRESPONDS	CDKKNNOOOOW	KNOCK ON WOOD
CDENOOPRRTU	PUT ON RECORD	CDKOOOSTTUY	TOOK CUSTODY
CDENOORSSTT	COTTON DRESS	CDLMOORSSTU	STORM CLOUDS
CDENOORSSTY	SECOND-STORY	CDMOSSTTUUY	CUSTOMS DUTY
CDEOORSTTUW	WOODCUTTERS	CDNOORSSTUU	SCOUTS ROUND
CDEOPRRRUWY	CURRY POWDER	CDOORRSSSSW	CROSS SWORDS
CDEORRSSTTU	DESTRUCTORS	CEEEEEGHNRS	GREEN CHEESE
CDFFIILLTUY	DIFFICULTLY	CEEEEELLNPV	ELEVEN PENCE
CDFFIMNOORT	FIND COMFORT	CEEEEEPRRRT	TREECREEPER
CDFGHLLOOOT	CLOTH OF GOLD	CEEEEFFRSSV	EFFERVESCES
CDFGIIKNORS	DISFROCKING	CEEEEFIPRRZ	PRICE FREEZE
CDFGINNNOOU	CONFOUNDING	CEEEEFIRRSV	FREE SERVICE
CDFIINNOSTU	DISFUNCTION	CEEEEFLRSSU	FEELS SECURE
CDFIMOORSST	DISCOMFORTS	CEEEEFNPRRS	PREFERENCES
CDFINNOSTUY	DYSFUNCTION	CEEEEGIMNRS	EMERGENCIES
CDGGILNOORW	GROWING COLD	CEEEEHHRRST	THREE CHEERS
CDGHIIMNORT	COMING THIRD	CEEEEHIRRTV	THE RECEIVER
CDGHIKNNOOW	CHOKING DOWN	CEEEEHNSSTT	SET THE SCENE
CDGHILNOOPP	CLODHOPPING	CEEEEHPRSST	TERSE SPEECH
	COPPING HOLD	CEEEEILNORT	ELECTIONEER
CDGHMNOOOTU	NOT MUCH GOOD	CEEEEILNTVW	TWICE ELEVEN
CDGHNOORTUU	TOUCH GROUND	CEEEEIMNNPR	PREEMINENCE
CDGIIIKNRRT	TRICK RIDING	CEEEEIMNNSS	MISE-EN-SCENE
CDGIIKNSTTU	SITTING DUCK	CEEEEINPRSX	EXPERIENCES
CDGIIMMNNOO	INCOMMODING	CEEEEINRRRV	IRREVERENCE
CDGIINNORTU	INTRODUCING	CEEEEINRSSV	SEEN SERVICE
CDGIINNOSTU	DISCOUNTING	CEEEEIRSSSV	SEES SERVICE
CDGIINORSSU	DISCOURSING	CEEEEJNRSUV	REJUVENESCE
CDGIKLLNOOO	LOOKING COLD	CEEEEKPRSST	KEEPS SECRET
CDGILNNNORU	RUNNING COLD	CEEEELNOORT	ENTEROCOELE
CDGILNNOOOW	COOLING DOWN	CEEEELNPTVW	TWELVE PENCE
CDGILNNOOSW	CLOSING DOWN	CEEEEMNRSTY	SECRET ENEMY
CDGILNNORTU	TURNING COLD	CEEEENNNPTW	TEN NEW PENCE
CDGILOORTTY	TROGLODYTIC	CEEEENNNSTW	NEW SENTENCE
CDGIMNNOOPU	COMPOUNDING	CEEEENNRRTV	NERVE CENTRE
CDGIMNNOORU	COMING ROUND	CEEEENRSSTT	STREET SCENE
		CEEEFFGINOV	GIVE OFFENCE

CEEEFFGLNSU	EFFULGENCES	CEEEIIRRSVW	WIRE SERVICE
CEEEFFHIOTW	WHITE COFFEE	CEEEIKKPSTW	KEEPS WICKET
CEEEFFHOOSU	COFFEE HOUSE	CEEEIKLPSTW	SWEET PICKLE
	COFFEEHOUSE	CEEEIKLTWWY	TWICE WEEKLY
CEEEFFIINTV	INEFFECTIVE	CEEEIKNNRSS	SNICKERSNEE
CEEEFFIKOSS	SEEKS OFFICE	CEEEIKNOSTW	WEEKS NOTICE
CEEEFFILNOS	OFF-LICENSEE	CEEEIKOPRRW	PIECEWORKER
CEEEFFILTVY	EFFECTIVELY	CEEEILLMOPT	COMPLETE LIE
CEEEFFIPRTW	PERFECT WIFE	CEEEILLSTVY	SELECTIVELY
CEEEFFLNOSS	OFFENCELESS	CEEEILMNNST	CLEMENTINES
CEEEFFLORSS	EFFLORESCES	CEEEILNOPST	PLEISTOCENE
CEEEFGINNRR	REFERENCING	CEEEILNOSUV	USE VIOLENCE
	REFRINGENCE	CEEEILNPRST	PERCENTILES
CEEEFGIRRTU	ERECT FIGURE	CEEEILNPSST	PESTILENCES
CEEEFHIIPSS	SPEECHIFIES	CEEEILPRTVY	RECEPTIVELY
CEEEFHIKLPS	FEEL PECKISH	CEEEILRSSVY	RECESSIVELY
CEEEFHIPRSY	FIERY SPEECH	CEEEILRSTVY	SECRETIVELY
CEEEFHLORSY	CHOSE FREELY	CEEEILSSVXY	EXCESSIVELY
CEEEFHNRRTV	TRENCH FEVER	CEEEILTTVWW	TWICE TWELVE
CEEEFIILHST	ELECTRIFIES	CEEEIMMNRTX	CEMENT MIXER
CEEEFIIRRSV	FIRE SERVICE	CEEEIMMPSUU	MUSEUM PIECE
CEEEFIKQRUZ	QUICK FREEZE	CEEEIMNRSTT	CENTIMETRES
	QUICK-FREEZE	CEEEINNNPRT	NINE PER CENT
CEEEFILRSSV	SELF-SERVICE	CEEEINNNPTY	NINETY PENCE
CEEEFINPRTV	FIVE PER CENT	CEEEINNOSTV	VENESECTION
CEEEFINQRSU	FREQUENCIES	CEEEINNRSSS	SINCERENESS
CEEEFIORRST	REFECTORIES	CEEEINORSTV	SERVE NOTICE
CEEEFLORRSY	SCORE FREELY	CEEEINORTUX	EXECUTIONER
CEEEFLPRSST	SELF-RESPECT	CEEEINOSTVX	COEXTENSIVE
CEEEFMNNORT	ENFORCEMENT	CEEEINPRSSS	PRECISENESS
CEEEFMNOORY	FREE ECONOMY	CEEEINPRSST	PERSISTENCE
CEEEFNPRSST	PERFECTNESS	CEEEINPRSTT	NET RECEIPTS
CEEEFPPRRSTU	PREFECTURES	CEEEINROOTU	RECENT ISSUE
CEEEGGHINNS	GEGENSCHEIN	CEEEIORRSST	CORSETIERES
CEEEGGNORRR	GREENGROCER	CEEEIPPRSTV	PERSPECTIVE
CEEEGHINPTY	EIGHTY PENCE	CEEEIRRSSTT	STREET CRIES
CEEEGIILNPS	SINGLE PIECE	CEEEKKLOPRS	LOCKKEEPERS
CEEEGIINOPR	EPEIROGENIC	CEEEKLNOPSU	KEEP COUNSEL
CEEEGILNOTV	GENTLE VOICE	CEEEKMNORSS	SMOKE SCREEN
CEEEGINNRRV	REVERENCING	CEEEKNNOSTT	KEEN CONTEST
CEEEGINORTV	EIGENVECTOR	CEEELLLNTXY	EXCELLENTLY
CEEEGLLNOOT	ETON COLLEGE	CEEELLORSTY	ELECTROLYSE
CEEEGNRRSSU	RESURGENCES	CEEELLORTTY	ELECTROLYTE
CEEEHHMOPRS	CHEMOSPHERE	CEEELMNOSSW	WELCOMENESS
CEEEHIIMNNS	HIS EMINENCE	CEEELMNOSWW	WELCOME NEWS
CEEEHIKNTTT	KITCHENETTE	CEEELMOPSTT	COMPLETE SET
CEEEHIKOOST	COOKIE SHEET	CEEELMORVWY	VERY WELCOME
CEEEHILMSTT	MELTS THE ICE	CEEELOPRRST	PRESELECTOR
CEEEHILORTT	HETEROCLITE	CEEELOPRTTY	ELECTROTYPE
CEEEHIMNRTU	HERMENEUTIC	CEEELORSSTT	CORSELETTES
CEEEHIMORSV	HOME SERVICE	CEEEMNOPRSS	RECOMPENSES
CEEEHINNRTT	IN THE CENTRE	CEEENNOPTWW	TWO NEW PENCE
CEEEHIORRSV	HEROIC VERSE	CEEENNOSSUV	SEVEN OUNCES
CEEEHIRSSTV	THE SERVICES	CEEENNPTTWY	TWENTY PENCE
CEEEHISSSSW	SWISS CHEESE	CEEEOOPRSST	STEREOSCOPE
CEEEHKORSSV	SEVERE SHOCK	CEEEORRSSTT	ERECTOR SETS
CEEEHLLRSSY	CHEERLESSLY	CEEEFFFOOOPT	POT OF COFFEE
CEEEHLMMOOW	WELCOME HOME	CEEEFFHIIORS	IRISH COFFEE
CEEEHLMOOST	COMES TO HEEL	CEEEFFHNOSTT	OFF THE SCENT
CEEEHMNNRRT	TRENCHERMEN	CEEEFFIIINNT	INEFFICIENT
CEEEHNNORST	ON THE SCREEN	CEEEFFIILMOR	LIFE OF CRIME
CEEEHNOORTV	THE ONCE-OVER	CEEEFFIILNTY	EFFICIENTLY
CEEEHNORSTU	THREE OUNCES	CEEEFFIILOPS	SPICE OF LIFE
CEEEHORSTTU	TO THE RESCUE	CEEEFFILOOTT	OFFICE TO LET
CEEEIIKLNTT	TELEKINETIC	CEEEFFIOPRSS	PRESS OFFICE
CEEEIILNRSV	SERVICE LINE	CEEEFFKNOOOT	TOOK OFFENCE
CEEEIIMPRST	PRECISE TIME	CEEEFFLIMOOW	COME OFF WELL
CEEEIINNNRT	INTERNECINE	CEEEFFLOOPRT	PERFECT FOOL
CEEEIINNNST	INSENTIENCE	CEEEFFLOORRU	RULE OF FORCE
CEEEIINNSTX	IN EXISTENCE	CEEEFFLRSTUV	CLEVER STUFF
CEEEIINSSST	NECESSITIES	CEEEFGIIKLNS	FEELING SICK

CEEFGIMOORT	COME TO GRIEF
CEEFGINRSTU	CENTRIFUGES
CEEFGLNORTU	GENUFLECTOR
CEEFHHNORTT	THENCEFORTH
CEEFHIIKNRT	KITCHEN FIRE
CEEFHIIPRTX	FIX THE PRICE
CEEFHIKLPST	FELT PECKISH
CEEFHIKORST	CHIEF STOKER
CEEFHINOSTU	FINE TOUCHES
CEEFHKNOPRS	SPOKE FRENCH
CEEFHMNNORW	FRENCHWOMEN
CEEFHNNOORT	FOR THE NONCE
CEEFHOPRSTT	PERFECT HOST
CEEFIIINNOV	IN FINE VOICE
CEEFIIKSTVW	FIVE WICKETS
CEEFIILLNPR	FELL IN PRICE
CEEFIILNORS	LEIF ERICSON
CEEFIILRSTV	SERVICE LIFT
CEEFIIPRSSU	SUPERFICIES
CEEFIKKLNOS	KICK ONESELF
CEEFIKKNOPT	POCKETKNIFE
CEEFIKOOPRW	PIECE OF WORK
CEEFIKORRST	STRIKE FORCE
CEEFILLRSUV	FULL SERVICE
CEEFILMOOST	COMES TO LIFE
CEEFILMPRTY	IMPERFECTLY
CEEFILNORST	REFLECTIONS
CEEFIMNNNOT	CONFINEMENT
CEEFIMOORTV	MOTIVE FORCE
CEEFINNQRUY	INFREQUENCY
CEEFINOOOTV	TONE OF VOICE
CEEFINORTTU	COUNTERFEIT
CEEFLMOORRT	ELECTROFORM
CEEFLNNOSTT	SELF-CONTENT
CEEFLNORSTU	FLUORESCENT
CEEFLOORRSU	FORECLOSURE
CEEFLORRSUU	RESOURCEFUL
CEEFNOPRRTU	FOUR PER CENT
CEEFNORRSTY	FORCES ENTRY
CEEFNORRTUY	FREE COUNTRY
CEEFORRRSSS	CROSS-REFERS
CEEGGILLLOR	COLLEGE GIRL
CEEGGKOORRU	GEORGE CUKOR
CEEGGKOPRRY	GREGORY PECK
CEEGGOORRSS	GEORGE CROSS
CEEGHHIOPTV	GIVE THE CHOP
CEEGHHOPSTT	GETS THE CHOP
CEEGHIINNPR	ENCIPHERING
CEEGHILLNOV	LONG VEHICLE
CEEGHINNNRT	ENTRENCHING
CEEGHINNRRT	RETRENCHING
CEEGHINORVW	CHEWING OVER
CEEGHINOSTU	EIGHT OUNCES
CEEGHINRSST	SIGHT SCREEN
CEEGHKORRSU	GREEK CHORUS
CEEGHLNOTTU	GENTLE TOUCH
CEEGIILNOSV	SINGLE VOICE
CEEGIIMNRRS	MERCERISING
CEEGIIMNRRZ	MERCERIZING
CEEGIINNOTV	GIVEN NOTICE
CEEGIINOSTV	GIVES NOTICE
CEEGIINPRST	STRINGPIECE
CEEGIJJLNUU	JUNGLE JUICE
CEEGIKLNOOP	KEEPING COOL
CEEGILLPTTU	GILLETTE CUP
CEEGILMNOSW	WELCOME SIGN
CEEGILNOPST	TELESCOPING
CEEGILNOPTY	POLYGENETIC
CEEGILNORSV	LONG SERVICE
CEEGIMNNOOT	MONOGENETIC
CEEGIMNNOSV	MOVING SCENE
CEEGIMNORST	EGOCENTRISM
CEEGINNOOSS	ONCOGENESIS
CEEGINNOOTT	ONTOGENETIC
CEEGINOORST	OESTROGENIC
CEEGINOPRTU	CREEPING OUT
CEEGINPRSTU	PERSECUTING
CEEGMNNORSS	CONGRESSMEN
CEEGNNOORSU	CONGENEROUS
CEEHHIIMPRS	HEMISPHERIC
CEEHHIIMSST	HEMISTICHES
CEEHHIMORST	COMES HITHER
CEEHHIMSSTT	HEMSTITCHES
CEEHHIORSVW	WHICHSOEVER
CEEHHIOSTTV	THE CHEVIOTS
CEEHHMORSTT	HOME STRETCH
	HOMESTRETCH
CEEHHOPRSST	SHORT SPEECH
CEEHIIINORS	CHINOISERIE
CEEHIIKNSTT	KINESTHETIC
CEEHIILLNST	HELLENISTIC
CEEHIIMMRST	HERMETICISM
CEEHIIMPSTU	EUPHEMISTIC
CEEHIIMRSTT	HERMETICIST
CEEHIJKNNSU	CHINESE JUNK
CEEHIKNOPTU	KEEP IN TOUCH
CEEHIKNSSST	SKETCHINESS
CEEHIKNTTTW	TENTH WICKET
CEEHIKRRSTT	THREE TRICKS
CEEHILLNOPU	NUCLEOPHILE
CEEHILLNOST	CLOTHES LINE
	CLOTHESLINE
CEEHILMNORT	THERMOCLINE
CEEHILMOPST	PILOT SCHEME
CEEHILNOOST	THE COLONIES
CEEHILOPRST	HELICOPTERS
CEEHILPRRSV	SILVER PERCH
CEEHIMOPRSS	MESOSPHERIC
CEEHIMOPSTU	MOUTHPIECES
CEEHINNNOTT	THE INNOCENT
CEEHINNORRT	IN THE CORNER
CEEHINPRTTY	THIRTY PENCE
CEEHIOPRSST	SPIROCHETES
CEEHIOPRSTV	OVERPITCHES
CEEHIORSTVW	CHEWS IT OVER
CEEHIPRSTTW	WITH RESPECT
CEEHIPSTTWY	WITTY SPEECH
CEEHJMNNOOR	JOHN MCENROE
CEEHKLNOSUY	HONEYSUCKLE
CEEHKNOPTTU	UP TO THE NECK
CEEHLLNOOPW	ENOCH POWELL
CEEHLLOORST	CHOLESTEROL
CEEHLLOORWY	YELLOW OCHRE
CEEHLLORSUY	LECHEROUSLY
CEEHLMOOOST	CLOSE TO HOME
CEEHLMRSTWZ	WELTSCHMERZ
CEEHLOORRTU	THREE-COLOUR
CEEHMMOORRS	CHROMOMERES
CEEHMNOORRT	CHRONOMETER
CEEHNNOORRT	ON THE CORNER
CEEHNOOPRRY	HENRY COOPER
CEEHNOOPRST	CTENOPHORES
CEEHNOORRSU	CORNER HOUSE
CEEHNOPSSTU	COUNTS SHEEP
CEEHNORTTUY	YOUTH CENTRE
CEEHOOPSSTT	STETHOSCOPE
CEEHOPRSSTW	SHOW RESPECT
CEEHORRTTYY	ERYTHROCYTE
CEEHPRSSTTU	STRETCHES UP
CEEIIINPRRS	RISE IN PRICE
CEEIIJLMRSU	LIME-JUICERS
CEEIIKNNSTW	NINE WICKETS

CEEIILMOPSS	POLEMICISES	CEEINOPRSTU	PERSECUTION
CEEIILMOPSZ	POLEMICIZES	CEEINORRSST	INTERCESSOR
CEEIILMRTUV	VERMICULITE	CEEINORRSTU	INTERCOURSE
CEEIILNNRSY	INSINCERELY	CEEINOSSSTU	NECESSITOUS
CEEIILNPTVY	INCEPTIVELY	CEEINOSSSTV	COSTIVENESS
CEEIILNRSTT	CENTILITRES	CEEINOSSTWY	SOCIETY NEWS
CEEIILNTVVY	INVECTIVELY	CEEINPRSSTY	PERSISTENCY
CEEIILOPRRV	RIVER POLICE	CEEINRSSSUV	CURSIVENESS
CEEIILSTTVY	SELECTIVITY	CEEIOPPRSTV	PROSPECTIVE
CEEIIMMNOTT	IN COMMITTEE	CEEIOPRSTTY	STEREOTYPIC
CEEIIMNNRST	REMINISCENT	CEEIPQRSTUU	PICTURESQUE
CEEIIMOPRTZ	PIEZOMETRIC	CEEIPRRTTUU	TRUE PICTURE
CEEIIMOPTTV	COMPETITIVE	CEEIRSTTVVY	CIVVY STREET
CEEIIMORSST	ESOTERICISM	CEEJLNORSWW	CROWN JEWELS
CEEIINNOSTV	VENISECTION	CEEJORRSTTU	COURT JESTER
CEEIINOPRRS	ROSE IN PRICE	CEEKLNOPSTU	KEPT COUNSEL
CEEIINORSTV	INSECTIVORE	CEEKLNRSTTU	TURTLENECKS
CEEIINRSSTT	INTERSTICES	CEEKLOOPRST	ROCK TO SLEEP
CEEIIORRSST	ESCRITOIRES	CEEKLORRSST	STORE CLERKS
CEEIIPRTTVY	RECEPTIVITY	CEEKMNOOPTY	POCKET MONEY
CEEIIRRSTTV	RESTRICTIVE	CEEKMOPPTTY	EMPTY POCKET
CEEIJLOPRST	PROJECTILES	CEEKOORRRTT	RETRO-ROCKET
CEEIJNORRTT	INTERJECTOR	CEEKOPSSTTV	VEST POCKETS
CEEIJRRSUVY	JURY SERVICE	CEELLMOOTUW	COME OUT WELL
CEEIKKNOPST	KEEP IN STOCK	CEELLNNOTTW	WELL CONTENT
CEEIKLLSSTT	SELL TICKETS	CEELMMNOPST	COMPLEMENTS
CEEIKMMOSUY	MICKEY MOUSE	CEELMNNOSTU	LOCUM TENENS
CEEIKMPQRTU	QUICK TEMPER	CEELMNOPSTY	SPLENECTOMY
CEEIKNPRSTY	PERSNICKETY	CEELMNOPTTY	COMPETENTLY
CEEIKNRSSTV	SEVEN TRICKS	CEELNRRRTUY	RECURRENTLY
CEEIKSSTTWY	STICKY SWEET	CEELORRTTUU	LECTURE TOUR
CEEILLMNNTY	INCLEMENTLY	CEEMMMNNOOY	COMMON ENEMY
CEEILLMRSSY	MERCILESSLY	CEEMMNNOOSS	COMMON SENSE
CEEILLNRSST	STENCILLERS		COMMONSENSE
CEEILLOSSVY	VOICELESSLY	CEEMMOOPRTT	COMPTOMETER
CEEILLSSUVY	SECLUSIVELY	CEEMMOORSTT	COME TO TERMS
CEEILLSUVXY	EXCLUSIVELY	CEEMNNNOTTT	CONTENTMENT
CEEILMNNSTU	LUMINESCENT	CEEMNOORTUV	COUNTERMOVE
CEEILMNORST	CLINOMETERS	CEEMNOPRRTU	PROCUREMENT
CEEILMOORRT	COLORIMETER	CEEMNOPRSTT	CONTRETEMPS
CEEILMOQTUY	COME QUIETLY	CEEMNORRSTT	STORM CENTRE
CEEILNNNOOV	NONVIOLENCE	CEEMOOOPRTW	COME TO POWER
CEEILNOOPRS	NECROPOLEIS	CEEMOOORSTW	WORSE TO COME
CEEILNOPRTU	NEUROLEPTIC	CEEMOOPRSSU	COME UP ROSES
CEEILNPRSTY	PRESCIENTLY	CEEMOORSSTT	COMES TO REST
CEEILNQSTUY	QUIESCENTLY	CEENNNOSTTW	NEWS CONTENT
CEEILOPSTTY	POETIC STYLE	CEENNOORRST	CORNERSTONE
CEEILRRSTUU	SERICULTURE		NONSECRETOR
CEEILRRSUVY	RECURSIVELY	CEENNRRSSTU	CURRENTNESS
CEEILRSUVXY	EXCURSIVELY	CEENNRRSTUW	CURRENT NEWS
CEEIMMORRST	MICROMETERS	CEENNRTTUXY	NEXT CENTURY
CEEIMNNOOPT	OMNIPOTENCE	CEENOOPRRST	POETS CORNER
CEEIMNNOPRS	PROMINENCES	CEENOOPRRTY	CYPROTERONE
CEEIMNNOPTT	INCOMPETENT	CEENOPPPRRS	PEPPERCORNS
CEEIMNNORTU	COUNTERMINE	CEEOOPRRRSS	COREPRESSOR
CEEIMNNSTTU	INTUMESCENT	CEEOOPRRSUW	POWER SOURCE
CEEIMNOORRS	CRIES NO MORE	CEEOOPRSSTY	STEREOSCOPY
CEEIMNOORSU	CEREMONIOUS	CEEOORRSSSV	CROSSES OVER
CEEIMNOOSYZ	ECONOMY SIZE	CEEOPRRSSTU	PERSECUTORS
CEEIMNOPSTU	PUMICE STONE	CEEOPRRSTUY	PERSECUTORY
CEEIMNRRTTU	RECRUITMENT	CEEORRSSUXY	SORRY EXCUSE
CEEIMOORRSV	ROOM SERVICE	CEERRRSTTUU	RESTRUCTURE
CEEIMOPRSTU	COMPUTERISE	CEFFFIOOOTU	OUT OF OFFICE
CEEIMOPRTUZ	COMPUTERIZE	CEFFHIIKTTW	FIFTH WICKET
CEEIMORSSTV	VISCOMETERS	CEFFHIILSTW	WHITE CLIFFS
CEEINNOOPTX	NO EXCEPTION	CEFFHIOORSU	OFFICE HOURS
CEEINNOORRT	RECONNOITRE	CEFFHIOSSTW	SWITCHES OFF
CEEINNOPRST	IN NO RESPECT	CEFFHIRSSTT	FESTSCHRIFT
CEEINOPPRST	PERCEPTIONS	CEFFHKOORST	OFF THE ROCKS
CEEINOPRRTT	INTERCEPTOR	CEFFHOOORSW	SHOW OF FORCE
CEEINOPRSST	PRESS NOTICE	CEFFINRSSSU	SCRUFFINESS

CEFFLOSSTTU	SCUTTLES OFF
CEFGHINRTUW	NIGHT CURFEW
CEFGHIORTUV	GIFT VOUCHER
CEFGIIKLLNR	FILING CLERK
CEFGIILNNNU	INFLUENCING
CEFGIINNOOR	FOREIGN COIN
CEFGIINNORR	REINFORCING
CEFGILNOORS	FORECLOSING
CEFGIMNOORV	MOVING FORCE
CEFGINNOOPR	FORCING OPEN
CEFHIIISSTT	FETISHISTIC
CEFHIILNOSS	CLOSE FINISH
CEFHILLRTUY	FILTHY LUCRE
CEFHIMMNOOT	COMMON THIEF
CEFHLLOORSU	FLESH COLOUR
CEFHLLRSTTU	FULL STRETCH
CEFHMOORSTU	COMES FOURTH
CEFHOOPTTUU	OUT OF THE CUP
CEFHOPPRTUU	UP FOR THE CUP
CEFIIIKNNSS	FINICKINESS
CEFIIKKLNSV	FLICK KNIVES
	FLICKKNIVES
CEFIIKPRRTU	FRUIT PICKER
CEFIIKRSTTW	FIRST WICKET
CEFIILNNOST	INFLECTIONS
CEFIIMNORST	COME IN FIRST
CEFIINOPRTU	PURE FICTION
CEFIIORTUVY	FRUITY VOICE
CEFIJNOORSS	JOINS FORCES
CEFIJOORRSY	CRIES FOR JOY
CEFIKLOPRSW	PICK FLOWERS
CEFIKNOQRUZ	QUICK-FROZEN
CEFIKORSTUW	FOUR WICKETS
CEFILMNORSS	FILM CENSORS
CEFILNOORTU	COUNTERFOIL
CEFILNORTUY	COUNTRY LIFE
CEFILOOOSSV	LOSS OF VOICE
CEFILOORSUY	FEROCIOUSLY
CEFIMOORSTT	FIRST TO COME
CEFINNOOSSS	CONFESSIONS
CEFIORRSSTU	FIRST COURSE
CEFJNOORSTU	JUST FOR ONCE
CEFKLLLOUWY	LUCKY FELLOW
CEFKLMOORSU	CURL OF SMOKE
CEFKOOOPTTU	OUT OF POCKET
	OUT-OF-POCKET
CEFLLNNOSTU	FULL CONSENT
CEFLLNOORST	SELF CONTROL
	SELF-CONTROL
CEFLMOORSST	COMFORTLESS
CEFLNOORRSW	CORNFLOWERS
CEFLOOOPRSU	FLUOROSCOPE
CEFMNOOOSTY	COST OF MONEY
CEFNNOORRST	CONFRONTERS
CEFNOORRRSU	FOUR CORNERS
CEFNOORRRUV	RUN FOR COVER
CEFNOPRRTUY	PERFUNCTORY
CEFOORRSSUU	FOUR COURSES
CEGGGIKNSSU	SUCKING EGGS
CEGGHHIIILN	HIGH CEILING
CEGGHIINRTT	GETTING RICH
CEGGIIINOVV	GIVING VOICE
CEGGIIKNSTT	GETTING SICK
CEGGIINNORS	RECOGNISING
CEGGIINNORZ	RECOGNIZING
CEGGIINOORT	GOITROGENIC
CEGGMRRRSUU	RUGGER SCRUM
CEGHHIIOSTY	HIGH SOCIETY
CEGHHIIORRTU	HIGHER COURT
CEGHHKORSTU	ROUGH SKETCH
CEGHHMOORTU	COME THROUGH

CEGHIIKRSTT	EIGHT TRICKS
CEGHIILNRTT	CHITTERLING
CEGHIINNNRT	INTRENCHING
CEGHIINNRST	CHRISTENING
CEGHIKMNOOO	HOME COOKING
CEGHIKNRSTU	HUCKSTERING
CEGHILLMTUY	GUY MITCHELL
CEGHILMOOTT	COME TO LIGHT
CEGHILNORTY	HECTORINGLY
CEGHILOSTTY	GOTHIC STYLE
CEGHIMMNOOS	HOMECOMINGS
CEGHIMNORUZ	ZURICH GNOME
CEGHIMORRTY	HYGROMETRIC
CEGHINORRST	TORCH SINGER
CEGHINORRSU	CHIRURGEONS
CEGHINORRTT	TIGHT CORNER
CEGHIOOPRST	GEOSTROPHIC
CEGHLNNOOTU	GONE TO LUNCH
CEGHLNOOORR	CHRONOLOGER
CEGHLNOOSTU	GOES TO LUNCH
CEGHLNORSTT	LONG STRETCH
CEGHOOPRSSY	HYGROSCOPES
CEGIIIMNNRS	REMINISCING
CEGIIINOPST	POETICISING
CEGIIINOPTZ	POETICIZING
CEGIIINSTVV	VIVISECTING
CEGIIJLNORY	REJOICINGLY
CEGIIKKNORV	KICKING OVER
CEGIIKLNNSY	SICKENINGLY
CEGIIKLNSST	SINGLESTICK
CEGIIKNORTV	TICKING OVER
CEGIILLNNST	STENCILLING
CEGIILMNNSU	LUMINESCING
CEGIILMNOST	CLOSING TIME
CEGIILNNPRS	PRINCELINGS
CEGIILNOOST	NEOLOGISTIC
CEGIILNOTUV	CIVIL TONGUE
CEGIILNPRRU	RULING PRICE
CEGIILOOPST	GEOPOLITICS
CEGIIMNNOOS	ECONOMISING
CEGIIMNNOOZ	ECONOMIZING
CEGIIMNNSTU	INTUMESCING
CEGIIMNOORT	GONIOMETRIC
CEGIINNOORT	RECOGNITION
CEGIINNRRST	RESTRICTING
CEGIINRSSTY	SYNERGISTIC
CEGIKLNOORV	OVERLOCKING
CEGIKNNNOOR	RECKONING ON
CEGIKNNOPRU	RECKONING UP
CEGIKNOORSU	IGNEOUS ROCK
CEGIKNOQTUU	QUICK TONGUE
CEGIKNSSTTU	GETS STUCK IN
CEGILLNNOSU	COUNSELLING
CEGILMNOOOS	COMING LOOSE
CEGILMOPSSU	GOSPEL MUSIC
CEGILNNOSST	CLINGSTONES
CEGILNOORST	NECROLOGIST
CEGILNOOSTY	SCIENTOLOGY
CEGIMNNNOST	CONSIGNMENT
CEGIMNNOORS	GROSS INCOME
CEGIMNOPRSS	COMPRESSING
CEGIMOOPRST	COME TO GRIPS
CEGINNNNSSU	CUNNINGNESS
CEGINNNOSTT	CONTINGENTS
CEGINNNOTTU	COUNTING TEN
CEGINNOOPST	COPINGSTONE
CEGINNOPRTY	CORN IN EGYPT
CEGINNOPTTU	CUTTING OPEN
CEGINNORSTU	COUNTERSIGN
CEGINOORRVW	CROWING OVER
CEGINOPPRST	PROSPECTING

CEGINOPRSTU	PROSECUTING	CEHIOOPSTTY	OSTEOPHYTIC
CEGLMOOOSTY	COSMETOLOGY	CEHIOPRSSTT	PROSTHETICS
CEGLNNORTUY	CONGRUENTLY	CEHIOPRSTUW	PICTURE SHOW
CEGNNOOSSTT	SONG CONTEST	CEHKMNOOTUW	KNEW TOO MUCH
CEGNOORRSUW	WRONG COURSE	CEHKNOOSSTT	ON THE STOCKS
CEGNOORRSUY	CRYOSURGEON	CEHLLOOORSW	LOWER SCHOOL
CEGORRRSUYY	CRYOSURGERY	CEHLLOORTUW	HOLLOW TRUCE
CEHHIINPRTT	PINCH HITTER	CEHLMOPSTYY	LYMPHOCYTES
CEHHILOTTYY	THE HOLY CITY	CEHLNNOTTUW	WENT TO LUNCH
CEHHIMOPRTY	HYPOTHERMIC	CEHLOOPPRSU	UPPER SCHOOL
CEHHIMRSTUY	EURHYTHMICS	CEHMMOOORSS	CHROMOSOMES
CEHHINRTTUW	WITCH-HUNTER	CEHMNOORRTY	CHRONOMETRY
CEHHIOSSTTT	THE SCOTTISH	CEHMNOORSWY	SHOW NO MERCY
CEHHLOOOSSU	SCHOOL HOUSE	CEHMNOORTUY	HOME COUNTRY
	SCHOOLHOUSE	CEHMNORTUVY	NOT VERY MUCH
CEHHMNORSSY	SYNCHROMESH	CEHMOOSSTUU	CUSTOM HOUSE
CEHHMOOOPRR	CHROMOPHORE	CEHMOPRSSTU	CHOSE TRUMPS
CEHHNOSTTTU	HOT CHESTNUT	CEHMOPRSTYY	PSYCHOMETRY
CEHHOOOPRRT	TROCHOPHORE	CEHNNOSSTUU	UNCOUTHNESS
CEHIIINPSTZ	CITIZENSHIP	CEHNOOPRSTT	TOPNOTCHERS
CEHIIKKNNST	KITCHEN SINK	CEHNOOPRSTU	SHOP COUNTER
	KITCHEN-SINK	CEHNOOPSTUU	TOUCHES UPON
CEHIIKLNOPS	PICK HOLES IN	CEHNOOSSTTU	TOUCHSTONES
CEHIIKMRTTW	TRIM THE WICK	CEHNOPRSSTY	PHENOCRYSTS
CEHIIKNNOPS	PHONE IN SICK	CEHOOOPQRTU	CROQUET HOOP
CEHIIKNNTTU	KITCHEN UNIT	CEHOOPSSTTY	STETHOSCOPY
CEHIIKNNTTW	NINTH WICKET	CEHOORSSTUU	COURTHOUSES
CEHIIKNRTTW	WIN THE TRICK	CEIIILLLOTV	ILLICIT LOVE
CEHIIKNSTTW	THINKS TWICE	CEIIILLPTTY	ELLIPTICITY
CEHIIKSTTWX	SIXTH WICKET	CEIIILNNPPR	IN PRINCIPLE
CEHIILLORSV	SHRILL VOICE	CEIIILNNPTY	INCIPIENTLY
CEHIILOOPRT	HELIOTROPIC	CEIIILOPSST	POLITICISES
CEHIILPRSTU	SPHERULITIC	CEIIILOPSTZ	POLITICIZES
CEHIIMOSSUV	MISCHIEVOUS	CEIIIMPRSST	EMPIRICISTS
CEHIINOOPRS	IONOSPHERIC	CEIIIMPSSST	PESSIMISTIC
CEHIINOPSTT	PITCHES INTO	CEIIIMRSSTV	VICTIMISERS
CEHIINRSSTY	IN HYSTERICS	CEIIIMRSTVZ	VICTIMIZERS
CEHIIOPRRST	PREHISTORIC	CEIIINNRSTY	INSINCERITY
CEHIIOPRSVY	VICEROYSHIP	CEIIINNSTTV	INSTINCTIVE
CEHIIOSSSVY	VICHYSSOISE	CEIIINOSTVV	VIVISECTION
CEHIJRSSSTU	JESUS CHRIST	CEIIINPRSTV	INSCRIPTIVE
CEHIKMPSTTU	STICK THEM UP!	CEIIIORSSTU	CURIOSITIES
CEHIKNOPSTU	SOUP KITCHEN	CEIIKKLNNNO	NEIL KINNOCK
CEHIKNOPTTU	KEPT IN TOUCH	CEIIKLLMSSY	SICKLY SMILE
CEHIKNORTTW	WON THE TRICK	CEIIKLNPRSS	PRICKLINESS
CEHIKNOSSTT	IN THE STOCKS	CEIIKLNPRST	PENCIL SKIRT
CEHILLMOPSY	MESOPHYLLIC	CEIIKLQRSUV	QUICKSILVER
CEHILLNNOPU	PUNCHINELLO	CEIIKNOSSTY	CYTOKINESIS
CEHILLPSSTW	WITCHS SPELL	CEIIKNRSSST	TRICKSINESS
CEHILMOOPPR	PLEOMORPHIC	CEIIKORRSSW	WORRIES SICK
CEHILMOOPRS	PLEOCHROISM	CEIIILLSSSY	SCILLY ISLES
CEHILMOPSTY	THE OLYMPICS	CEIIILNSUVY	INCLUSIVELY
CEIILNOOQRU	CHLOROQUINE	CEIILNNOPPR	ON PRINCIPLE
CEHILNOPSST	CLOTHES PINS	CEIILNNOSSU	IN SECLUSION
	CLOTHESPINS	CEIILNOPSWW	COWSLIP WINE
CEHILNOSSST	COLTISHNESS	CEIILNRTUUV	VINICULTURE
CEHILNOSSSU	CUSHIONLESS	CEIILRTTUUV	VITICULTURE
CEHILORSSTY	CHRYSOLITES	CEIILSTUVXY	EXCLUSIVITY
CEHIMMOOPRS	MESOMORPHIC	CEIIMMNOSTU	COMMUNITIES
CEHIMNOOPRS	MICROPHONES	CEIIMNOOPTT	COMPETITION
CEHIMNOPSTY	CHIMNEY TOPS	CEIIMNOPSUU	IMPECUNIOUS
CEHIMOOPRTT	PHOTOMETRIC	CEIIMNORSTU	NEUROTICISM
CEHIMOOSSST	SCHISTOSOME	CEIIMOPRRST	SPIROMETRIC
CEHIMOPPRST	COPPERSMITH	CEIIMRSSTTY	MYSTIC RITES
CEHINNORSSY	SYNCHRONISE	CEIIMRSSTUW	WRITES MUSIC
CEHINNORSYZ	SYNCHRONIZE	CEIINNNNOTT	INCONTINENT
CEHINOORSTT	SHORT NOTICE	CEIINNOSTTX	EXTINCTIONS
CEHINOOTTTW	WHITE COTTON	CEIINOPRSTV	VOICEPRINTS
CEHINRSTTUY	THIS CENTURY	CEIINOPRTXY	PYROXENITIC
CEHIOOOPPRT	PHOTOCOPIER	CEIINORRSTT	RESTRICTION
CEHIOOOPPST	PHOTOCOPIES	CEIINOSSSUV	VICIOUSNESS

CEIINRRSTUZ	SCRUTINIZER
CEIINRSSTUZ	SCRUTINIZES
CEIINRSTTUV	INSTRUCTIVE
CEIIOPPRSTU	PRECIPITOUS
CEIIORRRSTT	TERRORISTIC
CEIIORSSTVV	VIVISECTORS
CEIIORSTUVY	VOYEURISTIC
CEIIPPRSTUY	PERSPICUITY
CEIJNOOPRST	PROJECTIONS
CEIKKLRSTUY	LUCKY STRIKE
	STRIKE LUCKY
CEIKKNOPSTT	KEPT IN STOCK
CEIKKOQRRUW	QUICK WORKER
CEIKKORRSWW	WICKERWORKS
CEIKLMOQUVY	MOVE QUICKLY
CEIKLNNRUWY	LUCKY WINNER
CEIKLNNSSUU	UNLUCKINESS
CEIKLORTTTU	TICKLE TROUT
CEIKNNORSTU	COUNTERSINK
CEIKNORRTTY	KITTY CORNER
CEIKNORTWYY	NEW YORK CITY
CEIKNORRTUU	QUICK RETURN
CEIKNRSSSTU	TINKERS CUSS
CEIKOPRRSST	REPORTS SICK
CEIKOSTTTTU	TICKET TOUTS
CEILLLNOOOV	VIOLONCELLO
CEILLLOSUVY	COLLUSIVELY
CEILLMOOSTT	STILL TO COME
CEILLNOPRSU	CURL ONES LIP
CEILMMNOPST	COMPLIMENTS
CEILMMNOSSU	SOLEMN MUSIC
CEILMNOOPSX	COMPLEXIONS
CEILMNOSSSU	MUSIC LESSON
CEILMOOOPST	COSMOPOLITE
CEILMOOOSST	COLOSTOMIES
CEILMOOOSTV	LOCOMOTIVES
CEILMOOPSTY	COMPOSITELY
CEILMOORRTY	COLORIMETRY
CEILNNNOTTY	CONTINENTLY
CEILNNOORTU	CONTOUR LINE
CEILNOPRRTW	TRIPLE CROWN
CEILNORRSVW	SILVER CROWN
CEILNORSSTU	COURTLINESS
CEILOOPRTTY	PROTEOLYTIC
CEILOORRSTU	TERRICOLOUS
CEILOORRSUV	VERSICOLOUR
CEILOORRSVY	CORROSIVELY
CEILOPRRTYY	LYRIC POETRY
CEIMMMNOSTT	COMMITMENTS
CEIMMNOQSUU	COMMUNIQUES
CEIMMNORSSU	CONSUMERISM
CEIMMOOPRRS	COMPROMISER
CEIMMOOPRSS	COMPROMISES
CEIMMORSSSU	COMMISSURES
CEIMNOOPRSS	COMPRESSION
CEIMNOORSTU	COTERMINOUS
CEIMNOPRSSU	PROSCENIUMS
CEIMNOPSTUV	CONSUMPTIVE
CEIMNORSSTU	CONSUMERIST
	MISCONSTRUE
CEIMOOPRSTT	COMPETITORS
CEIMOPRSTTT	STRICT TEMPO
CEIMOSSSTTU	SETS TO MUSIC
CEINNNOOOSW	ONE'S OWN COIN
CEINNNOOSTT	CONTENTIONS
CEINNNOOSTV	CONVENTIONS
CEINNOORSSV	CONVERSIONS
CEINNOOSTTU	CONTENTIOUS
CEINNORSTTU	TENNIS COURT
CEINNOSTTTU	CONSTITUENT
CEINOOPRSSS	PROCESSIONS

CEINOOPRSTU	PROSECUTION
CEINOPQRSTU	CINQUE PORTS
CEINOPRSSSU	PERCUSSIONS
CEINOPRSSTT	INTROSPECTS
CEINORRSSSU	CURSORINESS
CEINORSSSUU	CURIOUSNESS
CEINORSSTTT	CORNETTISTS
CEINOSSSSUV	VISCOUSNESS
CEINOSSSTUV	VISCOUNTESS
CEINOSSTTTU	CONSTITUTES
CEINRSSSTTY	SYNCRETISTS
CEIOOOPRRTZ	PROTEROZOIC
CEIOPPRSSUU	PERSPICUOUS
CEIOPPRSTTU	PICTURE POST
CEIOPRRSTUY	ROSY PICTURE
CEIOPRRSTWY	COPYWRITERS
CEIPPRRSSTU	SUPERSCRIPT
CEIPPRSSTTY	TYPESCRIPTS
CEKLNOOOSTU	TOOK COUNSEL
CEKLNORSTUY	TRY ONES LUCK
CEKMMORSSTU	SUMMER STOCK
CEKMMORTTUY	TOMMY TUCKER
CEKMNOOOSTW	COMES TO KNOW
CEKNNORSTUU	COUNTERSUNK
CELLMOOPRRT	COMPTROLLER
CELLNOOORST	LOSE CONTROL
CELLNOORRST	CONTROLLERS
CELLNOORSSU	COUNSELLORS
CELLNRTTUUY	TRUCULENTLY
CELLOOORSSU	LOSES COLOUR
CELLOORSSWY	SCORE SLOWLY
CELMNOORTUU	MONOCULTURE
CELNNOORRTT	RENT CONTROL
CELOOPRRSTU	COLPORTEURS
CELOOPRSSSW	SLOW PROCESS
CELOORRSTUU	TRUE COLOURS
CELOORSTUUY	COURTEOUSLY
CEMMNNOOSTU	UNCOMMONEST
CEMMOOOPRTY	TOMMY COOPER
CEMOOPRRSSS	COMPRESSORS
CENNOOPPSUU	POUNCES UPON
CENNOOPRTUY	OPEN COUNTRY
CENOORRSTTV	CONTROVERTS
CENOORRSTVY	CONTROVERSY
CENOORSSSST	CROSS ONE'S T'S
CENOPRRSSTU	CORRUPTNESS
CENORSTTUWY	WEST COUNTRY
CEOOPRRSSTU	PROSECUTORS
CFFGHIOOTU	TOUCHING OFF
CFFGIINRTUY	FRUCTIFYING
CFFGIKKNNOO	KNOCKING OFF
CFFGINOORSS	CROSSING OFF
CFFGINOORSU	OFFSCOURING
CFFHIIOSTTW	SWITCH IT OFF
CFFHILMNOTU	FIFTH COLUMN
CFFHINOOSTW	ON-OFF SWITCH
CFFIILOOSUY	OFFICIOUSLY
CFFIKKNOOST	KNOCKS IT OFF
CFFIKSSTTUY	STICKY STUFF
CFFIMNNORSU	CORN MUFFINS
CFGHIILLNNY	FLINCHINGLY
CFGHIILNNNU	UNFLINCHING
CFGHIMNOORT	COMING FORTH
	FORTHCOMING
CFGHINOORUV	VOUCHING FOR
CFGIIIILNSY	SILICIFYING
CFGIIMNORST	COMING FIRST
CFGIINNNOTU	FUNCTIONING
CFGIKKLNNOY	KNOCK FLYING
CFGILNNOSUY	CONFUSINGLY
CFGILNOPRSY	FLYING CORPS

CFGINNNOORT	CONFRONTING
CFHHIKMNOTU	THINK MUCH OF
CFHLMOOORRS	CHLOROFORMS
CFHLOOOOSTU	OUT OF SCHOOL
CFHLOOOOSSTU	LOSS OF TOUCH
CFIIILOPRTY	PROLIFICITY
CFIIKOPQRTU	QUICK PROFIT
CFIILNOPPTU	PULP FICTION
CFIINNNOOSU	IN CONFUSION
CFIINORSSTU	FIRST COUSIN
CFIIRRSTTUU	CITRUS FRUIT
CFIKKNOORSX	KNOCK FOR SIX
CFIKKOORSTU	OUT FOR KICKS
CFIKOPRSSTU	STICKS UP FOR
CFILMNOORRT	FIRM CONTROL
CFIMNOORSST	CONFORMISTS
CFINNOORSTU	INNS OF COURT
CFINOOOPPSU	CUP OF POISON
CFIOOORRTVVY	V FOR VICTORY
CFIOOATTTUU	CUT OUT FOR IT
CFKMOOOOORTT	TOOK COMFORT
CFLLLOORUUY	COLOURFULLY
CFLNORSUUUU	FURUNCULOUS
CFLOOOOPRSUY	FLUOROSCOPY
CFLOOOORRSUU	FOUR COLOURS
CFMMNNOOOORT	COMMON FRONT
CFOOOPRRSUW	CUP OF SORROW
CCGHIIIMNNORT	COMING RIGHT
CGGHIINORRW	GROWING RICH
CGGIIIKNPST	PIGSTICKING
CGGIIIKNSTV	GIVING STICK
CGGIILMMNNO	COMMINGLING
CGHHHIIIKNT	HITCH HIKING
	HITCHHIKING
CGHHIILSTTW	LIGHT SWITCH
CGHHILNOOST	NIGHT SCHOOL
CGHHIMNNOTU	NOTHING MUCH
CGHHORSTTUU	CUTS THROUGH
CGHIIILRSTV	CIVIL RIGHTS
CGHIIIMNSTY	MYTHICISING
CGHIIIMNTYZ	MYTHICIZING
CGHIIKNSSTT	NIGHTSTICKS
CGHIIKSSTTT	STICKS TIGHT
CGHIINNOSTW	SWITCHING ON
CGHIINPSTTU	STITCHING UP
CGHIINPSTUW	SWITCHING UP
CGHILLOORSS	GIRLS SCHOOL
	SCHOOLGIRLS
CGHILLOORTU	LIGHT COLOUR
CGHILNOOSTU	LOSING TOUCH
CGHILORRSSU	CHORUS GIRLS
CGHIMNOORST	COMING SHORT
	SHORTCOMING
CGHIMOOPRYZ	ZYGOMORPHIC
CGHINNORTUU	CHURNING OUT
CGHINOPSTUY	PSYCHING OUT
CGHINOPTTUY	TOUCH TYPING
	TOUCH-TYPING
CGHIOOORSTT	OSTROGOTHIC
CGHOPRSTUUU	CUTS UP ROUGH
CGIIIIMNSTV	VICTIMISING
CGIIIIMNTVZ	VICTIMIZING
CGIIIINNNOT	COINING IT IN
CGIIKNPPTU	PICKING IT UP
CGIIILNSSTU	LINGUISTICS
CGIIKKMNSSU	KINGS MUSICK
CGIIKLNOPST	STOCKPILING
CGIIKNOSTTU	STICKING OUT
CGIILLOSSTY	SYLLOGISTIC
CGIILMMNOOU	IMMUNOLOGIC
CGIILMNOORY	CRIMINOLOGY

CGIILLNNORRU	CURLING IRON
CGIILOOOSST	SOCIOLOGIST
CGIIMMNNNOSU	COMMUNISING
CGIIMMNNOTU	COMMINUTING
CGIIMMNNOUZ	COMMUNIZING
CGIIMNNOSTU	MISCOUNTING
CGIIMNOSSTU	CUSTOMISING
CGIIMNOSTUZ	CUSTOMIZING
CGIIMNRSSTU	STRING MUSIC
CGIINNORTUY	INCONGRUITY
CGIINNRSTTU	INSTRUCTING
CGIINORSSST	RISING COSTS
CGIINORSTVY	VICTORY SIGN
CGIJNNOPRUU	CONJURING UP
CGIKKNNOOTU	KNOCKING OUT
CGIKLLNOOOO	LOOKING COOL
CGILLNNOORT	CONTROLLING
CGILLNNOOSY	CONSOLINGLY
CGILMNNOSUY	CONSUMINGLY
CGILMOOOSST	COSMOLOGIST
CGILNNOOSTU	LOSING COUNT
CGILNNOOTUV	CONVOLUTING
CGILNPRSTUU	SCULPTURING
CGILOOSSTTY	CYTOLOGISTS
CGIMNOOOSST	COSMOGONIST
CGIMNOOOTYZ	MONOZYGOTIC
CGINNNOOOTT	COTTONING ON
CGINNNOOPRU	PRONOUNCING
CGINNNORSTU	RUNNING COST
CGINNOORSUU	INCONGRUOUS
CGINNOOTTUU	COUNTING OUT
CGINOOOPSTU	SCOOPING OUT
CGINOOPPRTU	OUTCROPPING
CGINOORSSTU	CROSSING OUT
CGINOOSTTUU	SCOUTING OUT
CGINOPRSSTY	STOPS CRYING
CGINRRSTTUU	STRUCTURING
CGLNOORSUUY	CONGRUOUSLY
CHHIILOPTTY	LITHOPHYTIC
CHHIIMRTTYY	RHYTHMICITY
CHHIMMOOOPR	HOMOMORPHIC
CHHKOOOORRS	SHOCK HORROR
CHHLLLOOPRY	CHLOROPHYLL
CHHLOOORSSU	SCHOOL HOURS
CHIIIMORSST	HISTORICISM
CHIIINORSST	HISTRIONICS
	TRICHINOSIS
CHIIINOSSTT	SHINTOISTIC
CHIIIORSSTT	HISTORICIST
CHIIIORSTTY	HISTORICITY
CHIIMNOORSS	ISOCHRONISM
CHIINNOPSSU	PINCUSHIONS
CHIINOPSTWW	IPSWICH TOWN
CHIIOOPRTTX	THIXOTROPIC
CHIIOPPRRTY	PORPHYRITIC
CHIKNORSSTW	CHRIST KNOWS
CHILLNORTUY	HILL COUNTRY
CHILMOOPPRY	POLYMORPHIC
CHILNNOOTUY	HOLY UNCTION
CHILOORSTUU	ULOTRICHOUS
CHIMNNORSSY	SYNCHRONISM
CHIMNOOPPPY	HYPNOPOMPIC
CHIOOOPPRTT	PHOTOTROPIC
CHIOOPPRRST	PROCTORSHIP
CHIOOPPRSTY	SPOROPHYTIC
CHIOPSTTTUY	TOUCH TYPIST
CHIORSSTTTU	CUTS IT SHORT
CHIRRSTTTTU	STRICT TRUTH
CHKMNOOOTUW	KNOW TOO MUCH
CHKMOOOOTTU	TOOK TOO MUCH
CHKOOOPRSST	SHOCK TROOPS

CHLMOOOORSS	SCHOOLROOMS
CHLOOOOPRTU	COLOUR PHOTO
CHMMOOOORTU	TOO MUCH ROOM
CHMNOOPSTTU	MUTTONCHOPS
CHMNOOPTTUU	NOT UP TO MUCH
CHMOOOOPRSTY	PSYCHOMOTOR
CHNNOORRSTY	SYNCHROTRON
CHNNOORSSUY	SYNCHRONOUS
CIIIPRSSTT	SPIRITISTIC
CIIILLMOPTY	IMPOLITICLY
CIIILLNNOOS	IN COLLISION
CIIILOPSSST	SOLIPSISTIC
CIIIMNORTTU	MICTURITION
CIIINNOPRST	INSCRIPTION
CIIINOOSTTY	ISOTONICITY
CIIINORSTUY	INCURIOSITY
CIIJNNNOSTU	INJUNCTIONS
CIIKOSSTTTU	STICKS IT OUT
CIILLLMNOOO	COOL MILLION
CIILLNNNNOS	LINCOLNS INN
CIILLNNOOSU	IN COLLUSION
CIILLOORSTT	TORTICOLLIS
CIILNOPSTUU	PUNCTILIOUS
CIILNORSUUY	INCURIOUSLY
CIIMMNNOOTU	COMMINUTION
CIIMMNOOSSS	COMMISSIONS
CIIMNOOOPST	COMPOSITION
CIIMOPRSTUY	PROMISCUITY
CIINNORSTTU	INSTRUCTION
CIINOOPSSTY	PINOCYTOSIS
CIJLNOOPSTT	SCOTT JOPLIN
CIKKLLOOSSY	LOOKS SICKLY
CILLMOOOSUU	COLLOQUIUMS
CILLOORRTVY	VICTORY ROLL
CILMNOOOOST	LOCOMOTIONS
CILMNOOPSSU	COMPULSIONS
CILNNOOOTUV	CONVOLUTION
CILNNOORTTU	CONTROL UNIT
CILNNOOSSUV	CONVULSIONS
CILNNOOSUUY	INNOCUOUSLY
CILNOOPRRTU	COLOUR PRINT
CIMNNOOOOPPS	NINCOMPOOPS
CIMNNOOPSTU	CONSUMPTION
CIMNNORRSTU	TURN CRIMSON
CIMNOORSSTU	CONSORTIUMS
CIMOOOPRSST	COMPOSITORS
CIMOOPRSSUU	PROMISCUOUS
CIMOPRSSTUU	SCRUMPTIOUS
CIMOPSSTTUU	PUTS TO MUSIC
CINNOOOORSTT	CONTORTIONS
CINOOPRRSTU	CORRUPTIONS
CINORRSSTTU	INSTRUCTORS
CIOOPRSSTTU	PROSCIUTTOS
CIOORRTTVYY	TORY VICTORY
CIOPPRSSSTT	POSTSCRIPTS
CKKLOOOPTTU	TOOK POT LUCK
CKLNOOOORTT	TOOK CONTROL
CKLORSTTTUU	TRUST TO LUCK
CKOOOORTTTU	TOOK TO COURT
CLLNOOORSTT	LOST CONTROL
CLLNOOSUUVV	CONVOLVULUS
CLNOOOOPPSU	POOLS COUPON
CNNOORTTUWY	COUNTRY TOWN
CNNOOSTTTUY	NOTTS COUNTY
DDDEEEEHNOT	DONE THE DEED
DDDEEEEHOST	DOES THE DEED
DDDEEEELOPPR	DOPE PEDDLER
DDDEEEELOPPS	PEDDLES DOPE
DDDEEFIOSST	EISTEDDFODS
DDDEEGLPRRU	DRUG PEDDLER
DDDEEIILORV	LIVED OR DIED

DDDEEIMOOOT	DOOMED TO DIE
DDDEENORSSW	DRESSED DOWN
DDDEGIIOORS	DIDGERIDOOS
DDDEGIMOOOS	DID SOME GOOD
DDDEHIIRTTY	DID THE DIRTY
DDDEHINQRUU	HUNDRED QUID
DDDEHNNOOUW	HOUNDED DOWN
DDDEINOOPRU	DID ONE PROUD
DDDEINOSTUY	DID ONE'S DUTY
DDDENNOORTW	DOWNTRODDEN
	TRODDEN DOWN
DDDENOOPPRW	DROPPED DOWN
DDDGHOOOSSY	SHODDY GOODS
DDEEEEFIRRZ	FREEZE DRIED
	FREEZE-DRIED
DDEEEEHNPRR	REPREHENDED
DDEEEELOPRV	REDEVELOPED
DDEEEEPRRSS	DEREPRESSED
DDEEEFGHOST	FEEDS THE DOG
DDEEEFHIIRS	EDDIE FISHER
DDEEEFHNRTU	HUNDRED FEET
DDEEEFIOTVW	DEVOTED WIFE
DDEEEGHHOPP	HEDGEHOPPED
DDEEEGHIRRT	THIRD DEGREE
	THIRD-DEGREE
DDEEEGHISTW	DIG THE WEEDS
DDEEEGHSTUW	DUG THE WEEDS
DDEEEGIPRST	PREDIGESTED
DDEEEGRSSST	GETS DRESSED
DDEEEHHKLTY	HELD THE DYKE
DDEEEHIINTY	DID IN THE EYE
DDEEEHILLSV	DISHEVELLED
DDEEEILNSTU	LEEDS UNITED
DDEEEIMNOST	DEMONETISED
DDEEEIMNOTZ	DEMONETIZED
DDEEEIMPRST	DISTEMPERED
DDEEEINNNPT	INDEPENDENT
DDEEEINNPRT	INTERDEPEND
DDEEEINPRST	PREDESTINED
DDEEEIPPSST	SIDESTEPPED
DDEEELLMOUX	DE-LUXE MODEL
DDEEELLRSSW	DRESSED WELL
DDEEELMOPVY	DEEPLY MOVED
DDEEELNNPTY	DEPENDENTLY
DDEEELNOPUV	UNDEVELOPED
DDEEELNPRTY	PRETENDEDLY
DDEEENORRUV	VEERED ROUND
DDEEENOSTWY	SWEENEY TODD
DDEEENRRRSU	SURRENDERED
DDEEEORRSSV	OVERDRESSED
DDEEEQRSUYZ	SQUEEZED DRY
DDEEFFGLLLU	FULL-FLEDGED
DDEEFFLNOOR	OLD OFFENDER
DDEEFHILNOT	ON THE FIDDLE
DDEEFHINRUV	FIVE HUNDRED
DDEEFIIIMNN	INDEMNIFIED
DDEEFIIINRT	DENITRIFIED
DDEEFIIIRSV	DIVERSIFIED
DDEEFIIMSTY	DEMYSTIFIED
DDEEFIINSST	DISINFESTED
DDEEFILOORV	DIED FOR LOVE
DDEEFLLNOUW	WELL-FOUNDED
DDEEGGGIINP	DIGGING DEEP
DDEEGHILLTY	DELIGHTEDLY
DDEEGHLLNNO	GLENN HODDLE
DDEEGILNOWW	WINDOW LEDGE
DDEEGINNRSU	UNDERSIGNED
DDEEGNOPRSU	GROUND SPEED
DDEEHHIOSTU	DID THE HOUSE
DDEEHHKLOTY	HOLD THE DYKE
DDEEHIILMNT	IN THE MIDDLE

DDEEHIIMNRT	HIDDEN MERIT	DDEGHLOOOORT	THE GOOD LORD
DDEEHILNOOT	ENDOTHELOID	DDEGIIILNSV	LIVED IN DIGS
DDEEHIMPRUY	EDDIE MURPHY	DDEGIILMSUY	MISGUIDEDLY
DDEEHINNNRU	NINE HUNDRED	DDEGIILSSUY	DISGUISEDLY
DDEEHINRSSS	REDDISHNESS	DDEGIINNOSW	DISENDOWING
DDEEHIOSTTT	DOTTED THE I'S	DDEGIINOORS	DEODORISING
DDEEHNORSTU	UNDER THE SOD	DDEGIINOORZ	DEODORIZING
DDEEHNORWWY	WONDERED WHY	DDEGIINORRS	DISORDERING
DDEEHOORSTV	OVER THE ODDS	DDEGIINORST	OTIS REDDING
DDEEIIIKLSW	DID LIKEWISE	DDEGIINSSUU	UNDISGUISED
DDEEIIKLNNX	INDEX-LINKED	DDEGILNNNOR	LORD DENNING
DDEEIILPPSS	SIDESLIPPED	DDEGILNRSTU	DISGRUNTLED
DDEEIIMNNOS	DIMENSIONED	DDEGILOOORS	GOOD SOLDIER
DDEEIIMORTV	DID OVERTIME	DDEGILOOOSS	SOILED GOODS
DDEEIINORST	DISORIENTED	DDEGILSSTUY	DISGUSTEDLY
DDEEIINRRST	DISINTERRED	DDEGINNNOSW	SENDING DOWN
DDEEIINRSSW	SIDEWINDERS	DDEGINNOOST	TINNED GOODS
DDEEIIQSTUU	DISQUIETUDE	DDEGINNORSW	SENDING WORD
DDEEIKLOORT	LOOKED TIRED	DDEGINOSVWW	WEDDING VOWS
DDEEILLRVWY	DID VERY WELL	DDEGINPSTUU	SUET PUDDING
DDEEILNOORS	SOLDIERED ON	DDEGIOOPSSS	GOD DISPOSES
DDEEILPRSSY	DISPERSEDLY	DDEGMNOOOSS	MOON GODDESS
DDEEINNNOOW	DOWNED IN ONE	DDEGNNOOPSW	SPONGED DOWN
DDEEINNNORS	DENIS NORDEN	DDEGNNORRUU	UNDER GROUND
DDEEINNNPRU	UNDERPINNED		UNDERGROUND
DDEEINNOOST	STOOD IN NEED		
DDEEINNORRR	ORDER DINNER	DDEHHIIOPRT	DIPHTHEROID
DDEEINNRRSS	DINNER DRESS	DDEHIILNSSW	WINDSHIELDS
DDEEIOPPRSS	PREDISPOSED	DDEHIILPSSU	DISULPHIDES
DDEEIOPRRSS	PERIOD DRESS	DDEHIINRSSW	WIDDERSHINS
DDEEIOSSWWW	WIDOWS WEEDS	DDEHIISTTTW	DID THE TWIST
DDEELLNOPUW	DWELLED UPON	DDEHINOORSU	DISHONOURED
DDEELLNORUW	WELL ROUNDED	DDEHINORRUW	HURRIED DOWN
DDEELMNNOOS	NOEL EDMONDS	DDEHINORSTW	SHORT-WINDED
DDEELMOORUY	DUDLEY MOORE	DDEHLLOORTW	THE OLD WORLD
DDEELNNOSTW	NESTLED DOWN	DDEHLMOOTUU	LOUDMOUTHED
DDEELNOSTTW	SETTLED DOWN	DDEHNOORSTU	DO THE ROUNDS
DDEEMNNORRT	MODERN TREND	DDEHNOORSUW	SHOWED ROUND
DDEEMNORRSS	MODERN DRESS	DDEHNOOSTUW	SHOUTED DOWN
DDEENNNOOOW	DONE ONE DOWN	DDEIILMTTWY	DIM-WITTEDLY
DDEENNOOOSW	DOES ONE DOWN	DDEIILNOTVW	LIVED IT DOWN
DDEENNOORSW	DONE WONDERS	DDEIIMMNOOR	MODERN IDIOM
DDEENNORSSU	ROUNDEDNESS	DDEIIMNNOSU	DIMINUENDOS
DDEENNORSUW	SNOWED UNDER	DDEIINORTTU	RIDDEN IT OUT
DDEENOORSSW	DOES WONDERS	DDEIKLNORSU	KINDRED SOUL
DDEENOPPSTW	STEPPED DOWN	DDEILMMPSTU	MIDDLE STUMP
DDEENOPRSSW	PRESSED DOWN	DDEILMNORTY	DIRTY OLD MEN
DDEENOQRTUU	UNDERQUOTED	DDEILNNOOPR	LONDON PRIDE
DDEENORRRSU	UNDER ORDERS	DDEINOPRRTW	PRINTED WORD
DDEENORSSSW	DRESSES DOWN	DDEINORSSWW	WINDOW-DRESS
DDEENRRSSUU	UNDER DURESS	DDEIOOPRRTU	TUDOR PERIOD
DDEEOOPPRRV	DROPPED OVER	DDEKLNOOORU	LOOKED ROUND
DDEFFGNOOOS	GOOD SEND OFF	DDELORRTUYY	ORDERLY DUTY
DDEFFIILNTY	DIFFIDENTLY	DDENNORRTUU	TURNED ROUND
DDEFFIILRST	FIRST FIDDLE	DDENOOOPSTW	STOOPED DOWN
DDEFGGIINTW	WEDDING GIFT	DDENOOOPSWW	SWOOPED DOWN
DDEFGIIINNU	UNDIGNIFIED	DDFFGILNOOT	TODDLING OFF
DDEFGINOORS	GOOD FRIENDS	DDFGGILOORS	DIGS FOR GOLD
DDEFHNORRUU	FOUR HUNDRED	DDFGILNNOOW	FOLDING DOWN
DDEFIMORSTU	STUDIED FORM	DDFGLOOOORW	WORLD OF GOOD
DDEFINOPRSU	DE PROFUNDIS	DDFOOORRWW	WORD FOR WORD
DDEFIOOPRRV	PROVIDED FOR		WORD-FOR-WORD
DDEGGHHINOU	HIGH DUDGEON		
DDEGGIINNRW	WEDDING RING	DDGGHILNOOO	HOLDING GOOD
DDEGHIILLTW	WILD DELIGHT	DDGGIINOOST	GOOD TIDINGS
DDEGHIILNNY	LYING HIDDEN	DDGGINNOOOO	DOING NO GOOD
DDEGHIIMNRT	RIGHT-MINDED	DDGHILNNOOW	HOLDING DOWN
DDEGHILOTUY	GILDED YOUTH	DDGIINNORV	DIVINING ROD
DDEGHIMNOTU	TOUGH-MINDED	DDGIIKLMNPU	MILK PUDDING
DDEGHINORRU	RIDDEN ROUGH	DDGIILNNOSW	SLIDING DOWN
DDEGHLNOOUY	ODDLY ENOUGH	DDGIILNOORS	SLIDING DOOR
		DDGIINNNOWW	WINDING DOWN
		DDGILMNPPUU	PLUM PUDDING

DDGILNOORSU	SOLID GROUND	DEEEFORRTTU	FERRETED OUT
DDGINNOSTUW	DUSTING DOWN	DEEEGGINNNR	ENGENDERING
DDGINOOOORU	IN GOOD ODOUR	DEEEGHHOPPR	HEDGEHOPPER
DDGINOOQSTU	QUOTING ODDS	DEEEGHILNNT	ENLIGHTENED
DDGINORSTTU	GRIND TO DUST	DEEEGHIPRTV	PRIVET HEDGE
DDGNNOORRUU	GROUND ROUND	DEEEGHIRRTV	VEERED RIGHT
DDIIKLNSTWY	TIDDLYWINKS	DEEEGIIMRSV	DEMI-VIERGES
DDIIMNNNOSU	SOUND IN MIND	DEEEGILRRST	STEEL GIRDER
DDIKNOOPRRT	DROP TO DRINK	DEEEGINNNRV	NEVER ENDING
DDILOOOPPSU	DIPLOPODOUS	DEEEGJLNNSU	DENSE JUNGLE
DDIMNNNOSUU	UNSOUND MIND	DEEEGKLNNOW	LONG WEEK-END
DDLLOOORSTY	OLD OLD STORY		LONG WEEKEND
DDLNNOOORSW	LORD SNOWDON	DEEEGMNORRU	NOM DE GUERRE
DDMNNNOOOSY	DONNY OSMOND	DEEEGNNRRTU	TURNED GREEN
DEEEEEFHLNT	FEEL THE NEED	DEEEGRRSTUU	RUDE GESTURE
DEEEEEFHLRW	FREEWHEELED	DEEEHHILLNT	HELD THE LINE
DEEEEEFPRSZ	DEEP-FREEZES	DEEEHIKNPRT	DEEP THINKER
DEEEEFGILNP	DEEP FEELING	DEEEHILNOTT	TOED THE LINE
	DEEP FINE LEG	DEEEHILNPRS	REPLENISHED
DEEEEFGIRSV	FIVE DEGREES	DEEEHILNRTW	DREW THE LINE
DEEEEFHLNTT	FELT THE NEED	DEEEHIMNSTY	THE MINDS EYE
DEEEEFILLNS	LEE-ENFIELDS	DEEEHIMSTTT	STEM THE TIDE
DEEEEFIRRSZ	FREEZE-DRIES	DEEEHINRSTT	IN THE DESERT
DEEEEFLLPSY	FEELS DEEPLY	DEEEHLMORVW	OVERWHELMED
DEEEEGGHITV	GIVE THE EDGE	DEEEHLNNORT	HELDENTENOR
DEEEEGGHLRT	THREE-LEGGED	DEEEHLNOPRS	SLENDER HOPE
DEEEEGGHSTT	GETS THE EDGE	DEEEHLORSTW	SEE THE WORLD
DEEEEGGKLNR	GREEK LEGEND	DEEEHMOPRSS	PRESSED HOME
DEEEEGHNOTT	TEETH ON EDGE	DEEEHMRRRSU	SHEER MURDER
DEEEEGHORTV	OVER THE EDGE	DEEEHNRSTTT	SET THE TREND
DEEEEHHPRRS	SHEEPHERDER	DEEEHOSSSTW	SOWS THE SEED
DEEEEHIMPRS	EPHEMERIDES	DEEEIIJORVV	JOIE DE VIVRE
DEEEEHNOPRW	RENEWED HOPE	DEEEIINNPTX	INEXPEDIENT
DEEEEHNRRTV	THE REVEREND	DEEEIINSSST	DESENSITISE
DEEEEIJLLLS	JELLIED EELS	DEEEIINSSTZ	DESENSITIZE
DEEEEILNNPS	PINE NEEDLES	DEEEILLMOSS	DEMOISELLES
DEEEELLRRTW	TREE DWELLER	DEEEILLMPRT	ILL-TEMPERED
DEEEELMNNOW	NEEDLEWOMEN	DEEEILLNPPZ	LED ZEPPELIN
DEEEELOPRRV	REDEVELOPER	DEEEILLNRSS	ELDERLINESS
DEEEEMNNOST	MEET ONES END	DEEEILMMNPT	IMPLEMENTED
DEEEEMOPRRS	DEEP REMORSE	DEEEILMMNUV	MENDELEVIUM
DEEEEMOPRST	SPEEDOMETER	DEEEILMNRVY	DELIVERYMEN
DEEEENPRRST	REPRESENTED	DEEEILMNSST	ENDLESS TIME
DEEEENPSTUW	SWEETENED UP	DEEEILNNOPT	NEEDLE POINT
DEEEEPRRSSS	DEREPRESSES		NEEDLEPOINT
DEEEEQRSSTU	SEQUESTERED	DEEEILNPTXY	EXPEDIENTLY
DEEEFFLLLOV	LEVELLED OFF	DEEEILNSSVW	WIND-SLEEVES
DEEEFFNOOST	TOFFEE-NOSED	DEEEILORSTU	DELETERIOUS
DEEEFGIIMNT	FEEDING TIME	DEEEILRRSST	ELDER SISTER
DEEEFGILLNW	FEEDING WELL	DEEEILRSSVW	SILVERWEEDS
DEEEFGILNRS	GREEN FIELDS	DEEEIMNNOSY	MIND ONE'S EYE
DEEEFGIRRST	FIRST DEGREE	DEEEIMNORST	REMONETISED
	FIRST-DEGREE	DEEEIMNORTZ	REMONETIZED
DEEEFGORRSU	FOUR DEGREES	DEEEIMNOSTZ	DEMONETIZES
DEEEFHILNTW	FEEL THE WIND	DEEEIMNRRST	DETERMINERS
DEEEFHLNSSU	HEEDFULNESS	DEEEINNORTT	ENTERED INTO
DEEEFHLORRS	FREEHOLDERS	DEEEINNRRSV	SERVE DINNER
DEEEFHNPRSU	FRESHENED UP	DEEEINOORTV	TIDE ONE OVER
DEEEFIILMPX	EXEMPLIFIED	DEEEINORSVY	ON EVERY SIDE
DEEEFIJLNOY	ENJOYED LIFE	DEEEINPRRTT	INTERPRETED
DEEEFILNNOS	END ONES LIFE	DEEEINPRSST	PREDESTINES
DEEEFILNSTV	FIELD EVENTS	DEEEINPRTUX	EXPENDITURE
	SELF-EVIDENT	DEEEINRRSST	TENDERISERS
DEEEFILNSVY	DEFENSIVELY	DEEEINRRSSV	VINEDRESSER
DEEEFIMOSST	SEEDS OF TIME	DEEEINRRSTZ	TENDERIZERS
DEEEFINSSSU	USED FINESSE	DEEEINRRUVW	UNDER REVIEW
DEEEFKNOORT	FORETOKENED	DEEEINRSSSV	DIVERSENESS
DEEEFLNNSSU	NEEDFULNESS	DEEEINRSSTW	WESTERNISED
DEEEFLORRSW	DEFLOWERERS	DEEEINRSTWZ	WESTERNIZED
DEEEFMNRRSU	REFERENDUMS	DEEEIOPRSWZ	SEIZED POWER
DEEEFNORSST	DENSE FOREST	DEEEIPRSSSV	DEPRESSIVES

DEEEJMPQUUU	QUEUE-JUMPED	DEEFHHLORTT	HELD THE FORT
DEEEKNNSTTU	KEEN STUDENT	DEEFHIILNST	IN THE FIELDS
DEEEKOOPRRS	DOORKEEPERS	DEEFHIIMNTT	FIND THE TIME
DEEEKOPPSST	KEEPS POSTED	DEEFHILNRST	FIND SHELTER
DEEEELLLOTUV	LEVELLED OUT	DEEFHILNTTW	FELT THE WIND
DEEEELLNORSW	NE'ER-DO-WELLS	DEEFHINORSW	HERD OF SWINE
DEEEELLPPRXY	PERPLEXEDLY	DEEFHIRRSTT	THE DRIFTERS
DEEEELLRSSSW	DRESSES WELL	DEEFHKLOORS	LOOKED FRESH
DEEEELMNNORY	MONEY LENDER	DEEFHLNOPRS	SEND FOR HELP
	MONEYLENDER	DEEFHOOORWW	HEWER OF WOOD
DEEEELMNOPTV	DEVELOPMENT	DEEFHOORTTU	OUT OF THE RED
DEEEELNNPRST	RESPLENDENT	DEEFIIIMNNS	INDEMNIFIES
DEEEELNNRSSS	SLENDERNESS	DEEFIIIMRSW	MIDWIFERIES
DEEEELNNSSSS	ENDLESSNESS	DEEFIIINNST	INTENSIFIED
DEEEELNOPSST	SEND TO SLEEP	DEEFIIINRST	DENITRIFIES
DEEEELNORTUV	VOLUNTEERED	DEEFIIIRRSV	DIVERSIFIER
DEEEELNOTVWZ	TWELVE DOZEN	DEEFIIIRSSV	DIVERSIFIES
DEEEELNRRTTY	DETERRENTLY	DEEFIILMNRT	FERTILE MIND
DEEEELPRRTVY	PERVERTEDLY	DEEFIILNORS	FINE SOLDIER
DEEEELRRSSUV	VERDURELESS	DEEFIILNRST	FRIENDLIEST
DEEEEMNNORST	ENDORSEMENT	DEEFIILNSST	INSIDE LEFTS
DEEEEMNNOSTU	DENOUEMENTS	DEEFIIMORST	DEFORMITIES
DEEEEMPRSTYY	DEEP MYSTERY	DEEFIIMSSTY	DEMYSTIFIES
DEEEENOPRRSV	OVERSPENDER	DEEFIINOPRS	PERSONIFIED
DEEEENOPRSUX	UNDEREXPOSE	DEEFIINRSVW	VIEWFINDERS
DEEEENORSSYY	DRY ONES EYES	DEEFIJOORST	JODIE FOSTER
DEEEENORSTVX	OVEREXTENDS	DEEFIKLNOSS	KIDS ONESELF
DEEEENORSSTU	UNDERNOTEENG	DEEFIKLOHRW	FIELD-WORKER
DEEEENRRSTTT	TREND SETTER	DEEFIKNTTTW	WEFT KNITTED
	TRENDSETTER	DEEFILLRSSU	FLEURS-DE-LIS
DEEEOOPRRVW	OVERPOWERED	DEEFILNORSS	LOSE FRIENDS
DEEEOPPRSTV	OVERSTEPPED	DEEFILOORSV	DIES FOR LOVE
	STEPPED OVER	DEEFILORSTU	OUTFIELDERS
DEEEOPRRSSS	SORE PRESSED	DEEFILOSTTU	LEFT OUTSIDE
DEEEOPRSSSS	REPOSSESSED		OUTSIDE LEFT
DEEEOPRSTTY	STEREOTYPED		OUTSIDE-LEFT
DEEEOQSTUUZ	SQUEEZED OUT	DEEFIMNOR3W	WINS FREEDOM
DEEEOORRSSSV	OVERDRESSES	DEEFIMOOSTV	FESTIVE MOOD
DEEEORRTTVX	EXTROVERTED	DEEFINOOSSV	VOID OF SENSE
DEEEPRRSSST	PRESTRESSED	DEEFIORRTTT	RETROFITTED
DEEEPRRSSSU	SUPERSEDERS	DEEFIRRSSTV	FIRST SERVED
DEEEPRRSSUU	SUPERSEDURE	DEEFIRSTTUW	STEWED FRUIT
DEEEORSSUYZ	SQUEEZES DRY	DEEFKORRSST	DESSERT FORK
DEEFFGILNSU	SNIFFED GLUE	DEEFLLNOOSS	ONE'S OLD SELF
DEEFFGINRSU	FINDS REFUGE	DEEFLLNOSSU	DOLEFULNESS
DEEFFGNORUU	FOUND REFUGE	DEEFLLRSSUY	FLEURS-DE-LYS
DEEFFHILRSS	FRESH FIELDS	DEEFLNOOSTV	FONDEST LOVE
DEEFFIILNRS	FINDS RELIEF	DEEFLOORSTV	F.D.ROOSEVELT
DEEFFIILORT	TIRED OF LIFE	DEEFLOPRSSY	PROFESSEDLY
DEEFFILNNOS	FIND ONESELF	DEEFNOORSTT	TENDERFOOTS
DEEFFILNORU	FOUND RELIEF	DEEFNOPRSTU	TURN OF SPEED
DEEFFILNRTY	DIFFERENTLY	DEEFNOPRTUY	TYPEFOUNDER
DEEFFILORSU	OFF-SIDE RULE	DEEFNOSSTUY	SENSE OF DUTY
DEEFFINOORR	FRIEND OR FOE	DEEGGILNOPS	SLEEPING DOG
DEEFFINSSSU	DIFFUSENESS		SLOPING EDGE
DEEFFORSTUV	OVERSTUFFED	DEEGGINNOOV	GOOD EVENING
DEEFGGILNOO	FEELING GOOD	DEEGGINOOST	GOING TO SEED
	GOOD FEELING	DEEGGLLOORY	LLOYD GEORGE
DEEFGGIOPTT	PETTIFOGGED	DEEGGLNOOOS	GOLDEN GOOSE
DEEFGHIINRT	IN THE FRIDGE	DEEGHHILRTT	THE RED LIGHT
DEEFGHILOOT	THE GOOD LIFE	DEEGHHINPRS	SHEPHERDING
DEEFGHINORU	DIE OF HUNGER	DEEGHHIOPRW	HIGH-POWERED
DEEFGHIORST	FORESIGHTED	DEEGHHOPTTU	DEEP THOUGHT
DEEFGIINNRX	INDEX FINGER	DEEGHIILRST	LIGHTER SIDE
DEEFGILNNSY	SELF-DENYING	DEEGHIINPST	DEEP INSIGHT
DEEFGILNORW	DEFLOWERING	DEEGHILNNOT	LEN DEIGHTON
DEEFGILNPSY	FLYING SPEED	DEEGHILNNPS	SENDING HELP
DEEFGINORST	DEFORESTING	DEEGHILNOOP	PIGEONHOLED
DEEFGLLMOOU	GLEEFUL MOOD	DEEGHILNSTW	LENDS WEIGHT
DEEFGOORSTU	REFUSED TO GO	DEEGHILPSSY	SIGHS DEEPLY
DEEFHHIPTWY	DEFY THE WHIP	DEEGHIMNNOS	SENDING HOME

DEEGHIMNOOS	HOMOGENISED	DEEHILLNRWY	WENDY HILLER
DEEGHIMNOOZ	HOMOGENIZED	DEEHILLORTT	TITLE HOLDER
DEEGHINORSW	WINGED HORSE	DEEHILMNOTU	ENDOTHELIUM
DEEGHINPTTU	TIGHTENED UP	DEEHILMORSS	DEMOLISHERS
DEEGHINRTUW	UNDERWEIGHT	DEEHILMOTTT	TOLD THE TIME
DEEGHIORTVW	GIVE THE WORD	DEEHILNNOTW	DOWN THE LINE
DEEGHIRRSTV	SERVED RIGHT	DEEHILOOSTT	THEODOLITES
DEEGHLMOOPS	SO HELP ME GOD	DEEHILOPRTT	TRIED TO HELP
DEEGHLNOOOT	GO ON THE DOLE	DEEHILOSTTU	SILHOUETTED
DEEGHNOPTUU	TOUGHENED UP	DEEHILRRTTT	THIRD LETTER
DEEGHNORSTU	GROUNDSHEET	DEEHIMNNNOTW	DOWN THE MINE
DEEGHOOPSUW	P.G.WODEHOUSE	DEEHIMNPSTT	MIND THE STEP
DEEGHRSSSUW	SHREWD GUESS	DEEHINNOPST	OPEN THIS END
DEEGIILSTVY	DIGESTIVELY	DEEHINOPRRV	HORNED VIPER
DEEGIIMNNOR	DOMINEERING	DEEHINORSUU	RUINED HOUSE
DEEGIIMNNRT	DETERMINING	DEEHINOSSSU	HIDEOUSNESS
DEEGIINNOPW	OPENING WIDE	DEEHINRTTTU	TURN THE TIDE
DEEGIINNRST	INGREDIENTS	DEEHINRTTUW	TURNED WHITE
	TENDERISING	DEEHINSSSTY	SYNTHESISED
DEEGIINNRTZ	TENDERIZING	DEEHINSSTYZ	SYNTHESIZED
DEEGIINRSSV	DISSEVERING	DEEHIOOPRSU	PERIOD HOUSE
DEEGIKNNOPW	KEEPING DOWN	DEEHIOPRSTU	OTHER SIDE UP
DEEGIKNRSTU	KIND GESTURE	DEEHIOPRTWW	WHITE POWDER
DEEGILLLORS	GRILLED SOLE	DEEHIRRRTTU	RETIRED HURT
DEEGILLMNOR	REMODELLING	DEEHJKNNNOY	JOHN KENNEDY
DEEGILNOPRY	REDEPLOYING	DEEHKOOPRRT	RED-HOT POKER
DEEGILNOTVV	GET INVOLVED	DEEHLLNRRTU	RUTH RENDELL
DEEGILNRTVY	DIVERGENTLY	DEEHLLOOTTW	THE WELL-TO-DO
DEEGILNRUVY	GERUNDIVELY	DEEHLNNOOSW	HELD ONE'S OWN
DEEGIMNORSV	MISGOVERNED	DEEHLNORRTW	NETHER WORLD
DEEGIMORSUU	DEMIURGEOUS		NETHERWORLD
DEEGINNNPRU	RUNNING DEEP	DEEHLNORTWW	THE NEW WORLD
DEEGINNORSU	SEEING ROUND	DEEHLOPRSTU	UPHOLSTERED
DEEGINNRSUV	UNDESERVING	DEEHLOPSUUX	DUPLEX HOUSE
DEEGINOOSTU	GONE OUTSIDE	DEEHLOSSTWY	SHOWED STYLE
DEEGINORRSV	GIVEN ORDERS	DEEHMNNORSY	HENRY ESMOND
DEEGINORSTV	STEVEDORING	DEEHMNOOPTU	OPENMOUTHED
DEEGINPPSTY	TYPING SPEED	DEEHMNOORSU	MODERN HOUSE
DEEGINPRSSU	SUPERSEDING	DEEHMOOPPST	STOPPED HOME
DEEGIOOSSTU	GOES OUTSIDE	DEEHMOOPSST	MODEST HOPES
DEEGIORRSSV	GIVES ORDERS	DEEHMORRSTY	HYDROMETERS
DEEGIORRSTW	GETS WORRIED	DEEHNNOOTTW	DONE THE TOWN
DEEGJLRSSUU	JUDGE'S RULES	DEEHNNRSTUU	UNDER THE SUN
DEEGJMNPRTU	PREJUDGMENT	DEEHNOOOPRT	OPEN THE DOOR
DEEGLLMOORW	WELL GROOMED	DEEHNOOORSW	WOODEN HORSE
	WELL-GROOMED	DEEHNOOSTTW	DOES THE TOWN
DEEGLLNORUV	GROUND LEVEL	DEEHNOPRSTU	THREE POUNDS
DEEGLNNOOOR	NOELE GORDON	DEEHNORRSTU	THREE ROUNDS
DEEGLNOORUV	LONG OVERDUE	DEEHOORRSUV	HORS DOEUVRE
DEEGLNOSSSS	GODLESSNESS	DEEIIILMMTT	LIMITED TIME
DEEGLOORSSV	GLOSSED OVER	DEEIIIMNNST	INDEMNITIES
DEEGMOOPRTT	GET PROMOTED	DEEIIIRSSTV	DIVERSITIES
DEEHHIITTTW	WITH THE TIDE	DEEIIJNOSSU	JOINED ISSUE
DEEHHILLNOT	HOLD THE LINE	DEEIIKLLMSS	SEMISKILLED
DEEHHIMORRU	HURRIED HOME	DEEIIKMNNPS	KEEPS IN MIND
DEEHHINPSTT	IN THE DEPTHS	DEEIIILLLRVY	LILY-LIVERED
DEEHHKLOSTY	HOLDS THE KEY	DEEIIILLTTV	LITTLE DEVIL
DEEHHLOOPTU	HELD OUT HOPE	DEEIIILLNNOS	SOILED LINEN
DEEHHLOORSU	HOUSEHOLDER	DEEIIILLSSTT	LETS IT SLIDE
DEEHHMOPRST	DROPS THE HEM	DEEIIILMNSST	LIMITEDNESS
DEEHHNOSSTU	HUSHED TONES	DEEIIILNSTUW	UNWIELDIEST
DEEHHOPRRSY	HYDROSPHERE	DEEIIILORSSV	LIVES OR DIES
DEEHIIILOPT	EPITHELIOID	DEEIIILPRRSV	PILE DRIVERS
DEEHIIKLLRR	HIRED KILLER	DEEIIMMNPST	IMPEDIMENTS
DEEHIIKLNTW	LIKE THE WIND	DEEIIMMNRST	DETERMINISM
DEEHIILNNRT	THIN RED LINE	DEEIIMNRRST	IRREDENTISM
DEEHIILNOPV	LIVED IN HOPE	DEEIIMNRSTT	DETERMINIST
DEEHIIMPRSU	HESPERIDIUM	DEEIIMNRTTT	INTERMITTED
DEEHIINNOST	ON THE INSIDE	DEEIINNORTV	INVENTORIED
DEEHIINPRST	NEPHRITIDES	DEEIINNRTTW	INTERTWINED
DEEHIKORSTU	SHRIEKED OUT	DEEIINNSSTT	DISSENTIENT

DEEIINOPSTX	EXPEDITIONS
DEEIINPRSTY	SERENDIPITY
DEEIINPSSST	STEPS INSIDE
DEEIINRRSTT	IRREDENTIST
DEEIINRSSTT	DISINTEREST
DEEIIOPSTUX	EXPEDITIOUS
DEEIIRSTTUV	DIVESTITURE
DEEIJNNOSST	JOINTEDNESS
DEEIKLLOPSW	KEWPIE DOLLS
DEEIKLNPRRS	SPRINKLERED
DEEIKMMORSV	SKIMMED OVER
DEEIKMNNOSS	ENDS IN SMOKE
DEEIKOPPRSV	SKIPPED OVER
DEEILLMPTUX	MULTIPLEXED
DEEILLOPRSV	SPILLED OVER
DEEILLPRSUW	PULLED WIRES
DEEILMMOORS	OLD MEMORIES
DEEILMNNTUY	UNTIMELY END
DEEILMNOPST	DESPOILMENT
DEEILMNOSUV	VENUS DE MILO
DEEILNNQSTU	DELINQUENTS
DEEILNORRSS	ORDERLINESS
DEEILNSSSTT	STILTEDNESS
DEEILOPPPTY	POLYPEPTIDE
DEEILOPRSWW	WIELDS POWER
DEEILORRSST	OLDER SISTER
DEEILORRSSW	WORLD SERIES
DEEILORRSTY	SORELY TRIED
DEEILQRRRSU	RED SQUIRREL
DEEIMMMRSTU	MEDIUM TERMS
DEEIMMNORST	MODERN TIMES
DEEIMMNORTU	ENDOMETRIUM
DEEIMNNNSTT	INTENDMENTS
DEEIMNOOPSV	PENSIVE MOOD
DEEIMNOPRSY	MONEY SPIDER
DEEIMNOPRVW	NEW IMPROVED
DEEIMNORUYY	MIND YOUR EYE!
DEEIMNPRSSU	UNIMPRESSED
DEEIMNSSTTV	DIVESTMENTS
DEEIMOPRRST	MISREPORTED
DEEINNNORST	NONRESIDENT
DEEINNOPSST	POINTEDNESS
DEEINNOQTUW	QUIETEN DOWN
DEEINNOSTTU	TENDENTIOUS
DEEINNPRSTU	SUPERINTEND
DEEINNPRTTU	TURPENTINED
DEEINNRSSST	TENNIS DRESS
DEEINOPPSTT	STEPPED INTO
	STEPPED ON IT
DEEINOPRSSS	DEPRESSIONS
DEEINORRRVW	OWNER DRIVER
DEEINORRSST	SETS IN ORDER
DEEINORRTTV	INTROVERTED
DEEINOSSSTU	TEDIOUSNESS
DEEINOSSSUV	DEVIOUSNESS
DEEINOSTTUW	WENT OUTSIDE
DEEINRRRTUW	UNDERWRITER
DEEINRRSTUW	UNDERWRITES
DEEIOPPRRTV	TRIPPED OVER
DEEIOPPRSSS	PREDISPOSES
DEEIOPRRTVX	EXPORT DRIVE
DEEIOPSSTTU	STEP OUTSIDE
DEEIORRRVWY	VERY WORRIED
DEEIOSTTTUU	TOUT DE SUITE
DEEIPRRSSSU	PRESSURISED
DEEIPRRSSUZ	PRESSURIZED
DEEJNNORSUY	JOURNEYS END
DEEJRSSSTTU	JUST DESERTS
DEEKLMRSTTU	KETTLEDRUMS
DEEKLOOORSW	WORKED LOOSE
DEEKNNNRSSU	DRUNKENNESS
DEELLLMRSUW	SLUM DWELLER
DEELLNORTWW	TOWN DWELLER
DEELMNNOORV	MODERN NOVEL
DEELMNORSTY	MODERN STYLE
DEELNNOOSTW	LETS ONE DOWN
DEELNNOSSTW	NESTLES DOWN
DEELNOOORTV	NEVER TOO OLD
DEELNOORSTU	TURNED LOOSE
DEELNORSTVW	WORLD EVENTS
DEELNOSSTTW	SETTLES DOWN
DEELOOPPRSV	SLOPPED OVER
DEELOOPPRTV	TOPPLED OVER
DEELOPRUVZZ	PUZZLED OVER
DEELOPSSSSY	POSSESSEDLY
DEELORRSTXY	DEXTRORSELY
DEELORSTTUV	TURTLEDOVES
DEELORSTUXY	DEXTEROUSLY
DEEMMRRSSSU	SUMMER DRESS
DEEMNNOPSSY	SPENDS MONEY
DEEMNOORTUY	DEUTERONOMY
DEEMNORSSUY	MERSEY SOUND
DEEMOPRRTUV	OVERTRUMPED
DEEMOPSSTTU	UTMOST SPEED
DEEMOQRSTTU	QUOTED TERMS
DEENNNOOSTU	DONE ONE'S NUT
DEENNOOSSTU	DOES ONE'S NUT
DEENNOPRSST	RESPONDENTS
DEENNOPSSUV	SEVEN POUNDS
DEENNORSSVW	NEWSVENDORS
DEENNSSSTTU	STUNTEDNESS
DEENOPPSSTU	PUTS ON SPEED
DEENOPPSSWW	SWOPPED NEWS
DEENOPRSSSW	PRESSES DOWN
DEENOQRSTUU	UNDERQUOTES
DEENORTTUUV	VENTURED OUT
DEENRRSSSTU	UNDER STRESS
DEEOOPPRSTV	STOPPED OVER
DEEOOPPRSVW	SWOPPED OVER
DEEOOPRRRTX	EXPORT ORDER
DEEOOPPRSSU	PRESUPPOSED
DEERSSTTTUY	TRUSTY STEED
DEFFFFHLOSU	SHUFFLED OFF
DEFFFHIINOS	FINISHED OFF
DEFFFNOOOOS	OFF ONES FOOD
DEFFGGHORSU	SHRUGGED OFF
DEFFGGINOOR	FINGER OF GOD
DEFFGHIIORT	DIE OF FRIGHT
DEFFGINOORR	ORDERING OFF
DEFFGNOOTUY	GONE OFF DUTY
DEFFGOOSTUY	GOES OFF DUTY
DEFFHILOOPS	POLISHED OFF
DEFFIIMNRRS	FIRM FRIENDS
DEFFILLLNUU	UNFULFILLED
DEFFILLOPRU	FULL OF PRIDE
DEFFILLOPTU	PULLED IT OFF
DEFFILLRSUY	SILLY DUFFER
DEFFINOORRU	ROUND OF FIRE
DEFFINORTTU	TURNED IT OFF
DEFFIOPPRST	STRIPPED OFF
DEFFMOORRSU	FORMED FOURS
DEFFNOOSSTU	DO ONE'S STUFF
DEFFNOTTUWY	WENT OFF DUTY
DEFGGHIIINT	DIE FIGHTING
DEFGGIJNORU	FOREJUDGING
DEFGGLOOOST	FOOTSLOGGED
DEFGGNOOOOR	GONE FOR GOOD
DEFGGOOOORS	GOES FOR GOOD
DEFGHHIOSTW	SHOWED FIGHT
DEFGHIILLRS	GRILLED FISH
DEFGHIINRRT	THIRD FINGER
DEFGHIISTTT	TIGHTFISTED

DEFGHILOOTT	LIGHT-FOOTED
DEFGHMOOOOR	HOME FOR GOOD
DEFGHNORRSU	FRESH GROUND
DEFGIIILMNS	MISFIELDING
DEFGIIIMMNT	FINDING TIME
DEFGIIIINNTY	IDENTIFYING
DEFGIILNNSW	SELF-WINDING
DEFGIILNRRS	GIRLFRIENDS
DEFGIILORSU	SOLID FIGURE
DEFGIIINOTXY	DETOXIFYING
DEFGILNNORU	FLOUNDERING
DEFGILNNSSY	SENDS FLYING
DEFGILNOORV	FOLDING OVER
DEFGINORRUU	ROUND FIGURE
DEFGNOOORTU	GOOD FORTUNE
DEFGNOOOORTW	WENT FOR GOOD
	WRONG-FOOTED
DEFGNOORRSU	FOREGROUNDS
DEFGOOOOPRW	POWER OF GOOD
DEFHHLOORTT	HOLD THE FORT
DEFHIIIMRSU	HUMIDIFIERS
DEFHIILRTTW	FLIRTED WITH
	TRIFLED WITH
DEFHIINPRSS	FRIENDSHIPS
DEFHIIORSTT	DIE OF THIRST
DEFHIJNORTU	THIRD OF JUNE
DEFHILORSTW	WHISTLED FOR
DEFHINNRSUU	UNFURNISHED
DEFHINPRSTT	SPENDTHRIFT
DEFHIORRSTT	THIRSTED FOR
DEFHIORSSTU	ISSUED FORTH
DEFHKLLOOST	THE OLD FOLKS
DEFHLLMOTUU	FULLMOUTHED
DEFHLMOOTUU	FOULMOUTHED
DEFHLOORRTW	FOR THE WORLD
DEFHMOOOPRT	MOTHPROOFED
DEFHMOOOORTW	FROM THE WOOD
DEFHNORRTUW	FURTHER DOWN
DEFHOOORSSX	OXFORD SHOES
DEFHOOPRRTU	POURED FORTH
DEFIIINNOST	DEFINITIONS
DEFIILNPRTY	FRIENDLY TIP
DEFIILRSTUY	YIELDS FRUIT
DEFIIMMNORS	MISINFORMED
DEFIINNOORS	FRIED ONIONS
DEFIINNRTTU	TINNED FRUIT
DEFIKOORRTW	TIRED OF WORK
DEFIKORRRST	RORKE'S DRIFT
DEFILLORSTY	FLORID STYLE
DEFILLORSWW	WILD FLOWERS
	WILDFOWLERS
DEFILMNNSSU	MINDFULNESS
DEFILMOOPRR	MILD REPROOF
DEFILMOORST	FOR OLD TIMES
DEFILNOORSZ	FROZEN SOLID
DEFILNORSST	LOST FRIENDS
DEFILNORSWW	WINDFLOWERS
DEFILNSSTUU	DUTIFULNESS
DEFILOOORST	FOOT SOLDIER
DEFILOOORTU	OUTDOOR LIFE
DEFILOOPRSS	LOSS OF PRIDE
DEFILOPRSST	FIELD SPORTS
DEFILRSSSTU	DISTRESSFUL
DEFIMOORSTW	DIET OF WORMS
DEFIMORSSTU	STUDIES FORM
DEFINNNOPSU	PENSION FUND
DEFINNORTTU	UNITED FRONT
DEFIOOORRSU	ODORIFEROUS
DEFIOOPRRSV	PROVIDES FOR
DEFIOORSSTT	TOSSED FOR IT
DEFKLLLOOOU	DOLEFUL LOOK
DEFKLNOOORU	UNLOOKED-FOR
DEFLLNORUWY	WONDERFULLY
DEFLLOOORST	STOOD OR FELL
DEFLLOPSTUY	SPELL OF DUTY
DEFLNORTTUW	FLUTTER DOWN
DEFNNOOPRUW	FROWNED UPON
DEFNOPRTUYY	TYPEFOUNDRY
DEFOOPSSTUY	PUSSYFOOTED
DEGGHHHIILT	HIGHLIGHTED
DEGGHIJLNOU	JOHN GIELGUD
DEGGHILNOST	LONGSIGHTED
DEGGHILNOTT	GETTING HOLD
DEGGHOOOSTT	GO TO THE DOGS
DEGGIIINNOS	GOING INSIDE
DEGGIIINNTTW	GETTING WIND
DEGGILORTUW	WRIGGLED OUT
DEGGINNOOOP	GOOD OPENING
DEGGINNORUV	GIVEN GROUND
DEGGINNOTTW	GETTING DOWN
DEGGINORSUV	GIVES GROUND
DEGGKLRSUUY	SKULDUGGERY
DEGGLMOSTUU	SMUGGLED OUT
DEGGLNORSTU	STRUGGLED ON
DEGHHIILMOT	HIGH OLD TIME
DEGHHIINSTY	HIGH DENSITY
DEGHHIITYZZ	DIZZY HEIGHT
DEGHHILNOST	SHED LIGHT ON
DEGHHILNOTT	HELD ON TIGHT
DEGHHILOTTU	IDLE THOUGHT
DEGHHINORTU	EIGHTH ROUND
DEGHHIOSSTT	DO THE SIGHTS
DEGHHLORSTU	THE GOLD RUSH
DEGHIIINRST	INSIDE RIGHT
	INSIDE-RIGHT
	RIGHT INSIDE
DEGHIIINRTV	DIVINE RIGHT
DEGHIIILLLPT	GILD THE PILL
DEGHIIILLLTY	GILD THE LILY
DEGHIILMNOS	DEMOLISHING
DEGHIILPPTT	TIGHT-LIPPED
DEGHIILSTTU	LIGHT DUTIES
DEGHIIMNORV	DRIVING HOME
DEGHIIMNOST	METHODISING
DEGHIIMNOTZ	METHODIZING
DEGHIINOOPT	HOPING TO DIE
DEGHIINORTT	NIGHT EDITOR
DEGHIIPRSTU	RIGHT SIDE UP
DEGHIKLOORT	LOOKED RIGHT
DEGHILLPTTU	PULLED TIGHT
DEGHILMNOOT	MOONLIGHTED
DEGHILNNOPW	HELPING DOWN
DEGHILNOORV	HOLDING OVER
DEGHILNORSU	SHOULDERING
DEGHILNORTU	HOLDING TRUE
DEGHILNOSTW	WINS THE GOLD
DEGHILOPSTT	SPOTLIGHTED
DEGHINNNOOT	DONE NOTHING
DEGHINNOOST	DO ONE'S THING
	DOES NOTHING
DEGHINNORSU	ENSHROUDING
DEGHINNORTU	IN THE GROUND
DEGHINNRSTU	UNDERTHINGS
DEGHINOORTU	OUT-HERODING
DEGHINOPSTT	POTTING SHED
DEGHINOPSTU	EIGHT POUNDS
DEGHINORSTU	EIGHT ROUNDS
DEGHINOSSSW	SHOWED SIGNS
DEGHINOSSTU	DOUGHTINESS
DEGHINRRTTU	TURNED RIGHT
DEGHLMOOOTY	METHODOLOGY
DEGHNNOORTU	ON THE GROUND

DEGHNOOOSTT	HONEST TO GOD	DEHHILLNOTW	DOWN THE HILL
DEGHNOORSTU	GO THE ROUNDS	DEHHILORSTW	WITHHOLDERS
DEGHNOORSUY	HYDROGENOUS	DEHHLNOSTUU	SLEUTHHOUND
DEGHNORRTUW	UNDERGROWTH	DEHHLOOOPTU	HOLD OUT HOPE
DEGIIIINNST	INDIGNITIES	DEHHOOORSTW	SHOW THE DOOR
DEGIIILNSSV	LIVES IN DIGS	DEHHOORSTTU	SHUT THE DOOR
DEGIIINNNSW	WINNING SIDE	DEHIIIJMNRX	JIMI HENDRIX
DEGIIINNOST	INDIGESTION	DEHIIINRSST	DISINHERITS
DEGIIINNRST	DISINTERING	DEHIIKLLOOS	LIKELIHOODS
DEGIIINOPSX	EPOXIDISING	DEHIIKNNNST	THIN-SKINNED
DEGIIINOPXZ	EPOXIDIZING	DEHIILLMNPS	MENDIP HILLS
DEGIIINQSTU	DISQUIETING	DEHIILLMNTW	THE WINDMILL
DEGIIKLNORS	SOLDIER KING	DEHIILLOPSY	LYOPHILISED
DEGIIKNRSTW	WRITING DESK	DEHIILLOPYZ	LYOPHILIZED
DEGIILLNOTW	DOING IT WELL	DEHIILMNPSU	DELPHINIUMS
DEGIILLNRSU	SLIDING RULE	DEHIILOPRSS	SOLDIERSHIP
DEGIILLOPRT	GLIDER PILOT	DEHIINNOTTW	INTO THE WIND
DEGIILNNNRU	UNDERLINING	DEHIINNOTWW	IN THE WINDOW
DEGIILNOTTU	DEGLUTITION	DEHIINSTTUW	WHITSUNTIDE
DEGIIMNNNRU	UNDERMINING	DEHIKNNOSTW	DOWN THE SINK
DEGIIMNNORS	MODERNISING	DEHIKNRRRSY	DRINK SHERRY
DEGIIMNNORZ	MODERNIZING	DEHIKSSSTTU	KISS THE DUST
DEGIINNNRTU	INDENTURING	DEHILMORTUV	THIRD VOLUME
DEGIINNRSTU	SIDE TURNING	DEHILNOPTTU	PUT THE LID ON
DEGIINOORTV	OVERDOING IT	DEHILNORSST	THIRD LESSON
DEGIINORSSS	DIGRESSIONS	DEHILNOSSST	DOLTISHNESS
DEGIINPPRTW	DRIPPING WET	DEHILNOSSTY	DISHONESTLY
DEGIINRSSST	DISTRESSING	DEHILNOSTTW	THISTLEDOWN
DEGIINRSTTV	DRIVING TEST	DEHILNOTTWW	WHITTLE DOWN
	TEST-DRIVING	DEHILNRRUUY	UNHURRIEDLY
DEGIJMMNSTU	MISJUDGMENT	DEHILNRSTTU	HELD IN TRUST
DEGIKLLOPRR	GRILLED PORK	DEHILOPSSTT	DO THE SPLITS
DEGIKLORSST	STRIKES GOLD	DEHILORSSTT	SHORT-LISTED
DEGIKMNOOPS	SMOKING DOPE	DEHILPRSSUU	SULPHURISED
DEGILLNNTUY	INDULGENTLY	DEHILPRSUUZ	SULPHURIZED
DEGILLNOPRY	DEPLORINGLY	DEHIMOOPPRS	HIPPODROMES
DEGILMNNOTW	MELTING DOWN	DEHINNNOSSS	DONNISHNESS
DEGILMNORSU	SMOULDERING	DEHINOOTTUW	DONE WITHOUT
DEGILNNOSSU	UNGODLINESS	DEHINOPRRST	THIRD PERSON
DEGILNNOTTW	LETTING DOWN	DEHINORRSUW	HURRIES DOWN
DEGILNNOUVY	UNDYING LOVE	DEHINORSSTT	THRENODISTS
DEGILNOOTVV	GOT INVOLVED	DEHINPRSSSU	PRUDISHNESS
DEGILNOPRTT	LETTING DROP	DEHINPSSTTU	STUDENTSHIP
DEGILNORSST	LONG STRIDES	DEHIOOOPPRT	PHOTOPERIOD
DEGILOOPRTY	PTERIDOLOGY	DEHIOOPPTUW	WHOOPED IT UP
DEGIMMOORSW	GOOD SWIMMER	DEHIOOPRRST	SHORT PERIOD
DEGINNNOOPR	PONDERING ON	DEHIOOSTTUW	DOES WITHOUT
DEGINNNOOOS	GONE INDOORS	DEHIORRSTTY	THIRD STOREY
DEGINNORSST	GRINDSTONES	DEHJOOORTWX	ORTHODOX JEW
DEGINNOSTTW	SETTING DOWN	DEHJORSTTUW	JUST THE WORD
DEGINOOOPSW	WOODPIGEONS	DEHKMPRSTUY	MURKY DEPTHS
DEGINOOORSS	GOES INDOORS	DEHKNNORSUW	HUNKERS DOWN
DEGINOORRTU	ORDERING OUT	DEHKNRRRSUY	DRUNK SHERRY
DEGINOOTTTW	GET DOWN TO IT	DEHLLNNOOSW	LONDON WELSH
DEGINOPRSST	TOP-DRESSING	DEHLLOOORST	TOOLHOLDERS
	TOPDRESSING	DEHLLOOOTUW	HOLLOWED OUT
DEGIOOPRTUW	GOOD WRITE-UP	DEHLNNOOOSW	HOLD ONES OWN
DEGKNNORRUY	DRUNKEN ORGY	DEHLNOOPRSY	POLYHEDRONS
DEGLLNORSUW	GROUND SWELL	DEHMMORSTUW	MUMS THE WORD
DEGLNOOOSST	STOLEN GOODS	DEHMNOORTUY	MODERN YOUTH
DEGLNOORSSU	LOSES GROUND	DEHMOOOSTTU	SMOOTHED OUT
DEGLNOPRSUY	GOLDEN SYRUP	DEHMOOPPRSU	PSEUDOMORPH
DEGLNORRSUU	GROUND RULES	DEHNOORSSTU	UNDERSHOOTS
DEGLOORSTTY	TROGLODYTES	DEHNOORSSUU	ROUNDHOUSES
DEGLOORSTUY	SURELY TO GOD	DEHOOOPRTTW	TOOTH POWDER
DEGMNOOORST	ON GOOD TERMS	DEIIILLNOPR	PILLION RIDE
DEGMOOOPRTT	GOT PROMOTED	DEIIILQRSSU	LIQUIDISERS
DEGNNOOORTU	ONE GOOD TURN	DEIIILQRSUZ	LIQUIDIZERS
DEGNNOOPSSW	SPONGES DOWN	DEIIIMNSTUV	DIMINUTIVES
DEGNNOORSTU	STONE-GROUND	DEIIINNOOSV	DIVISION ONE
DEHHIINTTWW	WITH THE WIND	DEIIINPRTTY	INTREPIDITY

DEIIKKLMMMS	SKIMMED MILK
DEIIKLNOOSS	LOOKS INSIDE
DEIIKLORSST	SOLDIERS KIT
DEIIKNNOSTT	TIED IN KNOTS
DEIILLMNSTT	LITTLE MINDS
DEIILLMNTUY	UNLIMITEDLY
DEIILLORSSV	SOLID SILVER
DEIILLORSUY	DELIRIOUSLY
DEIILMNOOST	DEMOLITIONS
DEIILNNOOST	STOOD IN LINE
DEIILNOORWW	ORIEL WINDOW
DEIILNOPPST	SLIPPED INTO
DEIILNORSST	TIN SOLDIERS
DEIILNOSTTY	DO IT IN STYLE
DEIILNOSTVW	LIVES IT DOWN
DEIILOPRSTW	LOW-SPIRITED
DEIILOPTTUV	LIVED UP TO IT
DEIILOSSTUY	SEDITIOUSLY
DEIIMNOPRTV	IMPROVIDENT
DEIIMNORSSU	SERIOUS MIND
DEIIMNORTTT	INTROMITTED
DEIIMOORRST	DORMITORIES
DEIIMORSSTU	MOISTURISED
DEIIMORSTUZ	MOISTURIZED
DEIINNOSSSS	DISSENSIONS
DEIINOOPRSV	PROVISIONED
DEIINOOPSST	DEPOSITIONS
DEIINOPPTTW	TIPPED TO WIN
DEIINOPRSSS	DISPERSIONS
DEIINORSSTY	INSIDE STORY
DEIINORTTWW	WRITE IT DOWN
DEIINOSTTTU	DESTITUTION
DEIIPRRSTTU	STIRRED IT UP
DEIJKLNOORU	INJURED LOOK
DEIKKLLORSW	SKILLED WORK
DEIKLLLOOSY	LOOKED SILLY
DEIKLLMOPSY	SPOKE MILDLY
DEIKLLORSST	DRESS TO KILL
DEIKLNOOPPY	LOOKED NIPPY
DEIKLNRSSSY	SLINKY DRESS
DEIKLOOORRW	LOOK WORRIED
	WORRIED LOOK
DEIKLOOOSTU	LOOK OUTSIDE
DEIKLOSTTTU	SKITTLED OUT
DEIKNORSSTW	STRIKES DOWN
DEIKNRSTUYY	KEY INDUSTRY
DEIKOORRSTW	RIDES TO WORK
DEIKOORRTVW	DRIVE TO WORK
DEIKOORSTUW	OUTSIDE WORK
	TEDIOUS WORK
DEIKOORTTUW	WORKED IT OUT
DEILLLOPSWY	DILYS POWELL
DEILLMOOSUY	MELODIOUSLY
DEILLMRSTUY	DUSTY MILLER
DEILLNORSSW	WORLDLINESS
DEILLNORTUU	DULL ROUTINE
DEILLORSTUY	DESULTORILY
DEILLORSVWY	DRIVE SLOWLY
DEILLORSWWY	WORLDLY WISE
	WORLDLY-WISE
DEILLOSSTUY	DISSOLUTELY
DEILMNOOOPS	MONOPOLISED
DEILMNOOOPZ	MONOPOLIZED
DEILMNPRTUY	IMPRUDENTLY
DEILNOOSTUV	DEVOLUTIONS
DEILNOPRTVY	PROVIDENTLY
DEILOOORRSTV	LORDS IT OVER
DEILORRRRVY	LORRY DRIVER
DEIMMNNOPTU	IMPOUNDMENT
DEIMMNORSSW	SIMMERS DOWN
DEIMMRSSTYY	DISSYMMETRY

DEIMOOORSSU	SERIOUS MOOD
DEIMOPPRTTU	PROMPTITUDE
DEINNOORSTW	WENT INDOORS
DEINNOPRSUY	SUNNY PERIOD
DEINNORTTWW	WRITTEN DOWN
DEINNPSSUUY	SUNNY SIDE UP
DEINOORTTWW	WROTE IT DOWN
DEINOPRRSTU	PUTS IN ORDER
DEINORRTTWW	WRITTEN WORD
DEIOOPRSTTT	TRIED TO STOP
DEIOOPSSTTU	STOP OUTSIDE
DEIOORSTTTU	SORTED IT OUT
DEIOPPRSTTU	OUTSTRIPPED
DEIOPRSTTTU	PROSTITUTED
DEIOSSSTTUU	SUSSED IT OUT
DEKLLOOPRST	ROLL-TOP DESK
DEKMOORSTTU	SMOKED TROUT
DEKNOORRSWW	WORK WONDERS
DEKNOORSSTW	DOWNSTROKES
DEKOOORRSWW	WOODWORKERS
DEKOOORRTVW	DROVE TO WORK
DEKOOPPRSTW	STOPPED WORK
DELLLORRSSU	LORD RUSSELL
DELLMOOSVWY	MOVED SLOWLY
DELLNOPSUUY	PENDULOUSLY
DELLNOSSSUY	SOUNDLESSLY
DELLOORSVWY	DROVE SLOWLY
DELMOOOORRRY	ORDERLY ROOM
DELMOOPRSST	SPORTS MODEL
DELMORRSUUY	MURDEROUSLY
DELNOOPRSSU	SPLENDOROUS
DELNOPPRSTU	LEND SUPPORT
DELOOOOSSTT	STOOD TO LOSE
DELOOPRSTTU	LOUD PROTEST
DELOPPPSTUY	SUPPLY DEPOT
DELOPPRRSSU	LORDS SUPPER
DEMNNNOOOWY	NO MONEY DOWN
DENNNOSSSUU	UNSOUNDNESS
DENNOOOOPSW	WOODEN SPOON
DENNOOSSTUY	NONE SO DUSTY
DENNORRSSUU	SENSURROUND
DENOOOPRSSU	ENDOSPOROUS
DENOOORSSTW	DO ONES WORST
DENOPPRSTUU	UNSUPPORTED
DFFGINNOORU	ROUNDING OFF
DFFGINNOOSU	SOUNDING OFF
DFFGINOOPPR	DROPPING OFF
DFFGLNOOORU	ROUND OF GOLF
DFFHOOOORST	SHORT OF FOOD
DFFIILLMOSY	SILLY MID-OFF
DFFIILLNOOU	IN FULL FLOOD
DFFINOPSTUY	FIFTY POUNDS
DFFLOOORSWW	FLOW OF WORDS
DFGGIIINRSU	DISFIGURING
DFGGIILLLNO	GOLD FILLING
DFGGIILMNNU	FLINGING MUD
DFGGINOOPRR	DROP-FORGING
DFGHIIIMNUY	HUMIDIFYING
DFGHILLOOST	FLOODLIGHTS
DFGIIKNNNSU	SINKING FUND
DFGIILLNOWW	WILDFOWLING
DFGIILNOORS	SLIDING ROOF
DFGIILNSTUY	FINDS GUILTY
DFGIIMNNOOR	FINDING ROOM
DFGIINNRSUW	WIND-SURFING
DFGILNOOOTU	FLOODING OUT
DFGILNOTUUY	FOUND GUILTY
DFGLNOOORRU	GROUND FLOOR
DFGNOORRSTU	GROUND FROST
DFHHIIINRST	FINISH THIRD
DFHIJLORTUY	THIRD OF JULY

DFHLOORRTUW	FOURTH WORLD
DFHMOOORTUW	WORD OF MOUTH
DFHNOORRTUU	FOURTH ROUND
DFIKLOPPSSY	FLOPPY DISKS
DFILRSSTTUU	DISTRUSTFUL
DFIMOOORSUU	FURIOUS MOOD
DFINNOOORUX	OXFORD UNION
DFINNOORRUY	IRON FOUNDRY
DFINNOORTWW	FRONT WINDOW
DFLNOOOSSSU	LOSS OF SOUND
DFNOOPRSTUY	FORTY POUNDS
DGGHIINORRU	RIDING ROUGH
DGGHINNOOTU	GOOD HUNTING
DGGHINOOOPT	HOPING TO GOD
DGGHINORRUY	ROUGH-DRYING
DGGHNOORRUU	ROUGH GROUND
DGGIILMNNSU	SLINGING MUD
DGGIILNORWW	GROWING WILD
DGGIINNNOOS	GOOD INNINGS
DGGIINNNORW	RINGING DOWN
DGGIINNRRWY	WRINGING DRY
DGGIKLNOOOO	GOOD-LOOKING
	LOOKING GOOD
DGGILNNOPUW	GULPING DOWN
DGGILNNORSU	GROUNDLINGS
DGGIMNNOOOR	GOOD MORNING
DGGINNOOTUY	GOING ON DUTY
DGGINOOPRST	SPORTING DOG
DGHHIILNOTW	HOLDING WITH
DGHHIKNOTTU	KIND THOUGHT
DGHHILNOOTT	HOLD ON TIGHT
DGHIIIIMNNS	DIMINISHING
DGHIIILMNOT	MIDNIGHT OIL
DGHIIINSSTU	DISTINGUISH
DGHIIKNNOOW	HOODWINKING
DGHIILNNOWW	HOWLING WIND
DGHIIMNNSTU	MIDNIGHT SUN
DGHIINNORRT	NORTH RIDING
DGHIINORSTU	SOUTH RIDING
DGHILLORTTY	TROD LIGHTLY
DGHILLOSTUY	HOLDS GUILTY
DGHILNNOOOT	HOLDING ON TO
DGHILNNOOWW	HOWLING DOWN
DGHILNORSYY	HYDROLYSING
DGHILNORTWY	DOWNRIGHTLY
DGHILNORYYZ	HYDROLYZING
DGHILOORSTY	HYDROLOGIST
DGHIMNORTUW	THROWING MUD
DGHINNNOTUW	HUNTING DOWN
DGHINNOOOTT	NOTHING TO DO
DGHINNOPSUW	PUSHING DOWN
DGHLNOORSST	STRONGHOLDS
DGHNOPRTUUY	HUNG UP TO DRY
DGIIIILNQSU	LIQUIDISING
DGIIIILNQUZ	LIQUIDIZING
DGIIIINPRST	DISPIRITING
DGIIIJNNOST	DISJOINTING
DGIIILLMNNW	WINDMILLING
DGIIINNOPSS	INDISPOSING
DGIIINNORRV	DRIVING IRON
DGIIINNORTY	NONRIGIDITY
DGIIINORTTU	RIDING IT OUT
DGIIKNNNOSW	SINKING DOWN
DGIILNNNRUW	RUNNING WILD
DGIILPRSSTU	STUPID GIRLS
DGIIMNNOSTU	DISMOUNTING
DGIINNNNOPW	PINNING DOWN
DGIINNOOOOP	GOOD OPINION
DGIINNOORTW	WRITING DOWN
DGIINNOSTTW	SITTING DOWN
DGIINORSTTU	STRIDING OUT

DGIINRSSTTU	DISTRUSTING
DGIIOOPRSST	GOOD SPIRITS
DGIJMNNOPUW	JUMPING DOWN
DGIKLNNOOOW	LOOKING DOWN
DGIKNNORRST	STRONG DRINK
DGIKNOOORWW	WOODWORKING
DGILLNNOPUW	PULLING DOWN
DGILMOORSUU	GLORIOUS MUD
DGILNNOOPSW	SLOPING DOWN
DGILNNOOSWW	SLOWING DOWN
DGILOOPRSTT	PROGLOTTIDS
DGIMMNORTUU	DRUMMING OUT
DGIMNNOORUV	MOVING ROUND
DGIMNOORSVW	MOVING WORDS
DGINNNNORUW	RUNNING DOWN
DGINNNORTUW	TURNING DOWN
DGINNOOPPRU	PROPOUNDING
DGINNOORTUW	DROWNING OUT
DGINNOOSTUU	SOUNDING OUT
DGINNOPTTUW	PUTTING DOWN
DGINNORRSUU	SURROUNDING
DGINNORSSUW	SWINGS ROUND
DGINOOORRST	GORDON RIOTS
DGINOOOTTTW	GOT DOWN TO IT
DGINOOPPRTU	DROPPING OUT
DGLNOORSTTU	TURNS TO GOLD
DGLOORSUUXY	LUXURY GOODS
DGNNOOPRSTU	STRONG POUND
DGNNOORRTUU	RUN TO GROUND
DGNNOORSTUY	STONY GROUND
DGNOORRSSTW	STRONG WORDS
DHHIILOPRSS	HIS LORDSHIP
DHHIOOPRTYY	HYPOTHYROID
DHHNOOOSTTU	HOUNDSTOOTH
DHIIKKNRSWY	DRINK WHISKY
DHIILNNOORS	LONDON IRISH
DHIKKNRSUWY	DRUNK WHISKY
DHILLNOOPPY	PODOPHYLLIN
DHILLNORSSU	SHRILL SOUND
DHILNORRSUW	WHIRLS ROUND
DHILNORSTTU	HOLD IN TRUST
DHIMOOOSTTW	WISDOM TOOTH
DHINOOPSSWW	SHOPWINDOWS
	WINDOW-SHOPS
DHIOOOPRSUZ	RHIZOPODOUS
DHJNOOOSSTW	ST.JOHNS WOOD
DHLLNOOOSUW	HOLLOW SOUND
DHLMNOOORST	LORD THOMSON
DHLNNNOOORT	NORTH LONDON
DHLNNOOOSTU	SOUTH LONDON
DHMNOOOSSTW	SMOOTHS DOWN
DHNOOOORTUXY	UNORTHODOXY
DHNOOPRSSTU	POUND'S WORTH
DHORRSSTTUW	SWORD THRUST
DIIILLNOSSU	DISILLUSION
DIIILNOSSUY	INSIDIOUSLY
DIIILNOSUVY	INVIDIOUSLY
DIIIMNNOSTU	DIMINUTIONS
DIIIMNOSSUV	DIVISION SUM
DIIINOOPSST	DISPOSITION
DIIINOOSTVW	DIVISION TWO
DIILLMPTTUY	PUT IT MILDLY
DIILNOOSSTU	DISSOLUTION
DIILNOPSSTY	SPONDYLITIS
DIINOPRSSTU	DISRUPTIONS
DIINORSSTUU	INDUSTRIOUS
DIKKNOOORTT	TOOK TO DRINK
DIKNORRSSTU	SKIRTS ROUND
DILNORRSTUW	TWIRLS ROUND
DINNNOOSTWW	SWINDON TOWN
DINNORSTTUW	TURNS IT DOWN

DINOPRSSTUW	PUTS IN WORDS
DINOPSSTUXY	SIXTY POUNDS
DKLNNOOOOSW	LOOKS DOWN ON
DLLOOOOPRSU	POOR OLD SOUL
DLOOOPRRSTV	LORD PROVOST
DNORSSTTTUU	TURNS TO DUST
DOOORRSTUWY	DO YOUR WORST
DORRSSTTUWY	TRUSTY SWORD
EEEEEEOSTYY	SEE EYE TO EYE
EEEEEFHLRRW	FREEWHEELER
EEEEEHMSTTY	MEETS THE EYE
EEEEEKNSTWX	SEE NEXT WEEK
EEEEEFGILNR	FEELING FREE
EEEEEFFILLRS	FEELS RELIEF
EEEEEFFLLNOS	FEEL ONESELF
EEEEEFFLNORS	FREE ONESELF
EEEEEFGHLRTU	FEEL THE URGE
EEEEEFGHLSTT	GETS THE FEEL
EEEEEFGKRSSU	SEEKS REFUGE
EEEEEFKLRSSS	SELF-SEEKERS
EEEEEFLLPSSY	FEELS SLEEPY
EEEEEFLMORRS	FEEL REMORSE
EEEEEFLRSTTT	FLEET STREET
EEEEEFORRSVZ	FREEZES OVER
EEEEEGHNPSUX	HUGE EXPENSE
EEEEEGLNNSST	GENTEELNESS
EEEEEGNPPPRR	GREEN PEPPER
EEEEEHHLRSTW	THREE WHEELS
EEEEEHHRRSTT	THREE THREES
EEEEEHINNNOTY	ONE IN THE EYE
EEEEEHIPSTWY	WIPE THE EYES
EEEEEHJKNOST	SEEN THE JOKE
EEEEEHJKOSST	SEES THE JOKE
EEEEEHKLOPRT	HOTEL KEEPER
EEEEEHKOPRSU	HOUSEKEEPER
EEEEEHLLMSTT	STEEL HELMET
EEEEEHLMNSTT	THE ELEMENTS
EEEEEHMRRSTT	THREE METRES
EEEEEHNNPSTV	EVEN STEPHEN
EEEEEHNNSTTV	SEVENTEENTH
EEEEEHNOPSTY	OPEN THE EYES
EEEEEHNPRSTY	THE PYRENEES
EEEEEHNQRSTU	THREE QUEENS
EEEEEHNRSSTV	THREE SEVENS
EEEEEHRRSSTV	THREE VERSES
EEEEEIINRTVW	INTERVIEWEE
EEEEEIKMPRST	TIMEKEEPERS
EEEEEILLMNSV	ELEVEN MILES
EEEEEILMNSTV	ELEVEN TIMES
EEEEEIMNPRSW	MINESWEEPER
EEEEEINNNNTT	NINETEEN TEN
EEEEKOPRRST	STOREKEEPER
EEEEELLRSTTV	STREET LEVEL
EEEEELMNOOSS	SOMEONE ELSE
EEEEELNNORTV	TEN OR ELEVEN
EEEEELNNOTTV	TEN TO ELEVEN
EEEEELNPRSST	REPLETENESS
EEEEELRRSTTT	TRESTLETREE
EEEEEMNRSSTV	SEVEN METRES
EEEEEMNRSSTX	EXTREMENESS
EEEEEMPRSTTW	SWEET TEMPER
EEEEENOSSSUY	USE ONES EYES
EEEEENPRRRST	REPRESENTER
EEEEEQRRSTTU	QUEER STREET
EEEEFFFMNNOT	ENFEOFFMENT
EEEEFFFNOOST	OFF ONE'S FEET
EEEEFFGIILNN	FEELING FINE
EEEEFFHILRTW	WHIFFLETREE
EEEEFFHNOOTW	ONE OF THE FEW
EEEEFFILLRST	SELF-FERTILE

EEEEFFILNOTV	FIFTEEN LOVE
	LOVE FIFTEEN
EEEEFFILORTW	EIFFEL TOWER
EEEEFFLLNOST	FELT ONESELF
EEEEFFLOTTTW	TWO LEFT FEET
EEEFGHIRRTU	FIGURE THREE
EEEFGHLRTTU	FELT THE URGE
EEEEFGIIKLLN	FEELING LIKE
EEEFGIIKNNP	KEEPING FINE
EEEFGIILNVW	GIVE NEW LIFE
EEEEFGIKLNSS	SELF-SEEKING
EEEEFGILLLNW	FEELING WELL
EEEFGILNORS	FEELING SORE
EEEFGILNRSU	FEELING SURE
EEEEFGILNRTV	VEERING LEFT
EEEEFGILNRVY	GIVEN FREELY
EEEFGILRSVY	GIVES FREELY
EEEFGINNRTT	ENFETTERING
EEEFGINRSTT	SETTING FREE
EEEFGINRSUV	FIGURE SEVEN
EEEFGJLNRUV	JUNGLE FEVER
EEEFGLLNSSU	GLEEFULNESS
EEEFGLLNSUW	GLEEFUL NEWS
EEEFGNOORRV	GONE FOR EVER
EEEFGNORRTV	NEVER FORGET
EEEFGOORRSV	GOES FOR EVER
EEEFHIKNRRT	FREE THINKER
	FREETHINKER
EEEFHIKOPRT	POKE THE FIRE
EEEFHILRRSW	FERRIS WHEEL
EEEFHIORTTV	FIVE TO THREE
EEEFHLLNOPS	HELP ONESELF
EEEFHLNSTTT	LEFT THE NEST
EEEFHLORRTU	RULE OF THREE
EEEFHMNNRRST	REFRESHMENT
EEEFHNOPRTV	FERVENT HOPE
EEEFHOORRTT	THERETOFORE
EEEFIILMPSX	EXEMPLIFIES
EEEFILLRSST	SELF-STERILE
EEEFILLRVXY	REFLEXIVELY
EEEFILMNOOT	FEEL EMOTION
EEEFILNRSST	FERTILENESS
EEEFILNRSTV	FIRST ELEVEN
EEEFILORRVV	LIVE FOR EVER
EEEFIMNNRST	REFINEMENTS
EEEFIMPRRSU	PERFUMERIES
EEEFIMPRRTY	FIERY TEMPER
EEEFINOSTVV	FIVE TO SEVEN
EEEFINSSSSU	USES FINESSE
EEEFINSSSTV	FESTIVENESS
EEEFKLOPRSY	SPOKE FREELY
EEEFLLNNRSS	FRESNEL LENS
EEEFLLNOOSS	LOSE ONESELF
EEEFLLORVWY	YELLOW FEVER
EEEFLMORRST	FELT REMORSE
EEEFMNPRRST	PREFERMENTS
EEEFNORRTVW	WENT FOR EVER
EEEFNRSTTUU	FUTURE TENSE
EEEFORRSSTV	SEVERE FROST
EEEGGGINNRR	GREEN GINGER
EEEGGHHINRU	HUGHIE GREEN
EEEGGHORTTT	GET TOGETHER
	GET-TOGETHER
EEEGGIINNNR	ENGINEERING
EEEGGIILNRSS	GLEE SINGERS
EEEGGILOORT	GEORGE ELIOT
EEEGGINNTTV	GETTING EVEN
EEEGGLLMORY	GEORGE MELLY
EEEGGMNNORT	ENGORGEMENT
EEEGHHIISTT	THE EIGHTIES
EEEGHHILLRV	HIGHER LEVEL

EEEGHHILSTT	SEE THE LIGHT
EEEGHHIRSTT	THREE EIGHTS
EEEGHIILNTV	GIVEN THE LIE
EEEGHIILSTV	GIVES THE LIE
EEEGHILNORV	HEELING OVER
EEEGHILOPTU	THE EPILOGUE
EEEGHIMNNOST	EIGHTEENMOS
EEEGHIMRSTT	EIGHT METRES
EEEGHINNOSU	ENGINE HOUSE
EEEGHINTTVW	GET EVEN WITH
EEEGHNOPRTT	POT THE GREEN
EEEGHNORSSU	GREENHOUSES
EEEGHNORSTW	GETS NOWHERE
EEEGHOORSSV	OVER SHE GOES
EEEGIIKMNPT	KEEPING TIME
	TIMEKEEPING
EEEGIKLLNPW	KEEPING WELL
EEEGIKLNORV	KEELING OVER
EEEGIKNNOPP	KEEPING OPEN
EEEGILMNORS	SIMON LEGREE
EEEGILNRSTW	SWINGLETREE
EEEGIMNNOPT	OPEN MEETING
EEEGINNNSSU	GENUINENESS
EEEGINNNSVW	EVENING NEWS
EEEGINNOPRW	ENGINE POWER
EEEGINNORVW	OVERWEENING
EEEGINNRRTW	WINTERGREEN
EEEGINPRRSV	PERSEVERING
EEEGKMNNORY	GREEN MONKEY
EEEGLLNOPST	GENTLE SLOPE
EEEGLLOTVVV	VELVET GLOVE
EEEGLMNNOTW	GENTLEWOMEN
EEEGLNOOPST	GONE TO SLEEP
EEEGLNOORVY	VENEREOLOGY
EEEGLOOPSST	GOES TO SLEEP
EEEGNORRSTU	TREE SURGEON
EEEGNORRSTW	GREW ON TREES
EEEGNORSSSV	GOVERNESSES
EEEGRRRSTUY	TREE SURGERY
EEEHHHLLNTW	WHEN THE HELL
EEEHHILPPTW	HEPPLEWHITE
EEEHHIMPRSS	HEMISPHERES
EEEHHIRSSTW	THREE WISHES
EEEHHLORSSW	WHEELHORSES
EEEHHLOSSUW	WHEELHOUSES
EEEHHNOORTT	THE OTHER ONE
EEEHHNOPSTU	USE THE PHONE
EEEHHNPRSTY	HYPERSTHENE
EEEHHNRSTTT	THREE TENTHS
EEEHHORSTUW	THE WEE HOURS
EEEHIINNPPR	EPINEPHRINE
EEEHIINNSTT	THE NINETIES
EEEHIIPPRRS	PERIPHERIES
EEEHILLMTTT	TELL THE TIME
EEEHILMNNRR	HELEN MIRREN
EEEHILNORTV	OVER THE LINE
EEEHILNOSTT	TOES THE LINE
EEEHILNPRSS	REPLENISHES
EEEHILNRSTT	THE LISTENER
EEEHILPPRTW	WHIPPLETREE
EEEHILRRSTT	THREE LITRES
EEEHILRSSTV	SHIRT-SLEEVE
EEEHIMNRSST	SMITHEREENS
EEEHINNNPST	THE PENNINES
EEEHINOPSTT	SEE THE POINT
EEEHINORSTW	NEW THEORIES
EEEHINPSSSV	PEEVISHNESS
EEEHINRSTTT	IN THE STREET
EEEHINRSTUV	THE UNIVERSE
EEEHINSTTTW	THE TWENTIES
EEEHIPPPRTW	WHITE PEPPER

EEEHKMNNORT	KENNETH MORE
EEEHKOPPRSS	SHOPKEEPERS
EEEHLMORTUV	VOLUME THREE
EEEHLNNOSST	NONE THE LESS
	NONETHELESS
EEEHLNOPRST	TELEPHONERS
EEEHLNORSUV	ELEVEN HOURS
EEEHLOOPPRT	OTHER PEOPLE
EEEHLOOSTTV	LOSE THE VOTE
EEEHLORTTTT	TO THE LETTER
EEEHMMORRTT	THERMOMETER
EEEHMNOQRTU	QUEEN MOTHER
EEEHMOPRRST	SPHEROMETER
EEEHMOPRSSS	PRESSES HOME
EEEHMPRSSTU	THE SUPREMES
EEEHNNSSTTV	SEVEN TENTHS
EEEHNORSTTT	ON THE STREET
EEEHOORSSVW	WHOSESOEVER
EEEHOPSTTUY	UP TO THE EYES
EEEHPRSTTTU	UP THE STREET
EEEHRRSSTWY	SWEET SHERRY
EEEIIKKLLMT	LIKE MET LIKE
EEEIIKLNSST	TELEKINESIS
EEEIIKNPSVW	KEEPS IN VIEW
EEEIILMRSTU	LEISURE TIME
EEEIIMRSTTX	EXTREMITIES
EEEIINNPSVX	INEXPENSIVE
EEEIINRRTVW	INTERVIEWER
EEEIIORRSTX	EXTERIORISE
EEEIIORRTXZ	EXTERIORIZE
EEEIJNPRRTU	JUNIPER TREE
EEEIKLNOSST	SKELETONISE
EEEIKLNOSTZ	SKELETONIZE
EEEIKLNPSST	KEEPS SILENT
EEEIKNNPSTU	KEEPS IN TUNE
EEEIKNPPSST	KEEPS IN STEP
EEEIKRRRSTY	SKYE TERRIER
EEEILLMNOSW	MOSELLE WINE
EEEILLMSTVW	TWELVE MILES
EEEILLPPRSY	SLIPPERY EEL
EEEILLRSSSU	LEISURELESS
EEEILMNNNTV	ENLIVENMENT
EEEILMNNPRT	INNER TEMPLE
EEEILMNNTTT	ENTITLEMENT
EEEILMNSSTU	UNSEEMLIEST
EEEILMSTTVW	TWELVE TIMES
EEEILNNOPSS	IN ONES SLEEP
EEEILNNOTVW	ONE IN TWELVE
EEEILNPRRTT	TELEPRINTER
EEEILNPRSTW	WINTER SLEEP
EEEILNPRTTV	TRIPLE EVENT
EEEILNPSVXY	EXPENSIVELY
EEEILNRSSTV	SEVEN LITRES
EEEILNRTTVY	RETENTIVELY
EEEILNSSSUV	ELUSIVENESS
EEEILNSTVXY	EXTENSIVELY
EEEILRSSSTW	WIRELESS SET
EEEILRSSTTW	WESTERLIEST
EEEIMMNNSSS	IMMENSENESS
EEEIMMNOORT	ONE MORE TIME
EEEIMNORSST	REMONETISES
EEEIMNORSTZ	REMONETIZES
EEEIMNPRSTT	PRESENT TIME
EEEIMNPRSTX	EXPERIMENTS
EEEIMNQRRTU	REQUIREMENT
EEEIMNRTUVY	EVERY MINUTE
EEEIMOPRSTX	EXTEMPORISE
EEEIMOPRTXZ	EXTEMPORIZE
EEEIMPRRSTZ	TEMPERIZERS
EEEIMRRRSVY	RIVER MERSEY
EEEINNNOSST	IN ONES TEENS

EEEINNNSSST	INTENSENESS
EEEINNPRSTT	PRESENTIENT
EEEINNPSSSV	PENSIVENESS
EEEINORRRSV	REVERSIONER
EEEINPRRRST	ENTERPRISER
EEEINPRRRTT	INTERPRETER
EEEINPRRSST	ENTERPRISES
	INTERSPERSE
EEEINPRSTTX	PREEXISTENT
EEEINPRSTVV	PREVENTIVES
EEEINRRRSVV	RIVER SEVERN
EEEINRSSSTV	RESTIVENESS
EEEINRSSSTW	WESTERNISES
EEEINRSSTWZ	WESTERNIZES
EEEIOPRRRST	REPERTOIRES
	REPERTORIES
EEEIOPRSSWZ	SEIZES POWER
EEEIPRRSTTU	REPETITEURS
EEEIPRSSSST	PRIESTESSES
EEEIRRSSTVW	WRITES VERSE
EEEJMPQRUUU	QUEUE JUMPER
	QUEUE-JUMPER
EEEKKLNOSTY	SKELETON KEY
EEEKLNOOSTX	EXOSKELETON
EEEKLORRSTW	STEELWORKER
EEEKNNNOOSS	ON ONES KNEES
EEEKNSTTWWY	TWENTY WEEKS
EEELLLNPRTY	REPELLENTLY
EEELLLPSSSY	SLEEPLESSLY
EEELLNRSSVY	NERVELESSLY
EEELLNSSSSY	SENSELESSLY
EEELLORSTTV	LOVE LETTERS
EEELMMOSTTY	TOMMY STEELE
EEELMNNOPTV	ENVELOPMENT
EEELMNSSTTT	SETTLEMENTS
EEELMOORRVW	LOWER REMOVE
EEELMORRSSS	REMORSELESS
EEELNOPSSTT	SENT TO SLEEP
EEELNOPSTTW	WENT TO SLEEP
EEELNOTTTVW	TEN TO TWELVE
EEELNRSSTTW	NEWSLETTERS
EEELNSSSSSU	USELESSNESS
EEELOOOPRTT	PETER OTOOLE
EEELPRRSSTT	LETTERPRESS
EEEMMMNNOSTT	TENSE MOMENT
EEEMMNOPRTW	EMPOWERMENT
EEEMNNOSTUX	EXEUNT OMNES
EEEMNNPRSTT	PRESENTMENT
EEEMNORSTUV	VENTURESOME
EEEMOPPRRUV	UPPER REMOVE
EEEMORSTTWX	TWO EXTREMES
EEEMPRSSSTT	TEMPTRESSES
EEENNNNOPWY	ONE NEW PENNY
EEENNPRSSST	PRESENTNESS
EEENOPPRRSS	PROPER SENSE
EEENOPQRRSU	QUEER PERSON
EEENOPSSTUY	SET EYES UPON
EEENORSSTWZ	SNEEZEWORTS
EEEOPRRSTTY	STEREOTYPER
EEEOPRSSSSS	REPOSSESSES
EEEOPRSSTTY	STEREOTYPES
EEEOQSSTUUZ	SQUEEZES OUT
EEEPRRSSSST	PRESTRESSES
EEEPRSSTTTY	TYPESETTERS
EEFFFLOOOTT	FLEET OF FOOT
EEFFGHINORS	SHEERING OFF
EEFFGIIRSUV	FIVE FIGURES
EEFFGILNOPS	SLEEPING OFF
EEFFGILNRSU	GLUE-SNIFFER
EEFFGILORTU	FREE OF GUILT
EEFFGINORRS	FOREFINGERS

EEFFGLNOOSS	OFF ONE'S LEGS
EEFFHHIRSTT	THREE FIFTHS
EEFFHIIMOTT	THIEF OF TIME
EEFFHNOOOPR	OFFER NO HOPE
EEFFIILLORY	LIFE OF RILEY
EEFFIILMOPR	PRIME OF LIFE
EEFFIINNOSV	INOFFENSIVE
EEFFILNOORS	FOR ONE'S LIFE
EEFFILNOSVY	OFFENSIVELY
EEFFIMOPRTT	FIT OF TEMPER
EEFFIMRSTTY	FIFTY METRES
EEFFINORSTV	FIT OF NERVES
EEFFIOORRST	OFFERTORIES
EEFFLLORVWY	VERY WELL OFF
EEFFLNRSSTU	FRETFULNESS
EEFFNOOOPRT	OPEN TO OFFER
EEFGGGLORSY	FEELS GROGGY
EEFGGHIIRTU	FIGURE EIGHT
EEFGGIOPRTT	PETTIFOGGER
EEFGHHHIILT	THE HIGH LIFE
EEFGHHIISTV	FIVE EIGHTHS
EEFGHHORTTU	FREE THOUGHT
EEFGHIILLRT	LIGHT RELIEF
EEFGHIIOTTV	FIVE TO EIGHT
EEFGHIKOPST	KEEP SIGHT OF
EEFGHILLRTU	LIGHTER FUEL
EEFGHILNNOT	FEEL NOTHING
EEFGHILNOSW	SHOW FEELING
EEFGHINNORT	ON THE FRINGE
EEFGHLNOOPR	GONE FOR HELP
EEFGHLNRSUY	FEELS HUNGRY
EEFGHLOOPRS	GOES FOR HELP
EEFGHNORRTU	GONE FURTHER
EEFGHORRSTU	GOES FURTHER
EEFGIINNOPR	OPENING FIRE
EEFGIINNRRT	INTERFERING
EEFGIINRSTT	SETTING FIRE
EEFGIINRSTY	ESTERIFYING
EEFGILLNNUY	UNFEELINGLY
EEFGILLSTUY	FEELS GUILTY
EEFGILNNOUX	GENUFLEXION
EEFGILNOPTU	FEELING UP TO
EEFGILNORRU	FOREIGN RULE
EEFGILNRSSV	SELF-SERVING
EEFGILPRSTU	PRESTIGEFUL
EEFGINNNRRU	RUNNING FREE
EEFGINNORSS	FOREIGNNESS
EEFGINNORSW	FOREIGN NEWS
EEFGINNQRTU	FREQUENTING
EEFGINNRTTU	UNFETTERING
EEFGINORRRT	REFERRING TO
EEFGINORSSV	FORGIVENESS
EEFGINORTUZ	FREEZING OUT
EEFGINPRRSV	SPRING FEVER
EEFGIOORSTY	SIEGE OF TROY
EEFGLLMNORS	FELLMONGERS
EEFGLLMNORY	FELLMONGERY
EEFGLLNRTUY	REFULGENTLY
EEFGLLRRTUY	REGRETFULLY
EEFGMNOORTT	FORGET ME NOT
	FORGET-ME-NOT
EEFGNOOORRV	GO ON FOR EVER
EEFGOORSSTU	REFUSES TO GO
EEFHIIINNTT	THE INFINITE
EEFHIILLTTV	LIFT THE VEIL
EEFHIINORTT	INTO THE FIRE
EEFHIIOSTTZ	THE SIZE OF IT
EEFHILNSSSS	SELFISHNESS
EEFHILOSUWY	HOUSEWIFELY
EEFHIMRSTTX	FIX THE TERMS
EEFHINOORSU	HOUSE ON FIRE

EEFHINORSTT	IN THE FOREST
EEFHINRTTUU	IN THE FUTURE
EEFHIORSUWY	HOUSEWIFERY
EEFHJNNOTTU	TENTH OF JUNE
EEFHKOOSSUY	HOUSE OF KEYS
EEFHLLNPSSU	HELPFULNESS
EEFHLMOORTT	LEFT THE ROOM
EEFHLNOORTY	HELEN OF TROY
EEFHLNOOSST	SHOT ONESELF
EEFHLNOOSSW	SHOW ONESELF
EEFHLNOPRST	SENT FOR HELP
EEFHLNOPRTW	WENT FOR HELP
EEFHLNOPSSU	HOPEFULNESS
EEFHMORRRTU	FURTHERMORE
EEFHMORSTTW	FROM THE WEST
EEFHNOORRST	FORESHORTEN
EEFHNOOTTTU	TO THE TUNE OF
EEFHNRRTTUW	WENT FURTHER
EEFHOOPRSST	FOSTERS HOPE
EEFHOORRRTU	THREE OR FOUR
EEFHOORRSTW	FOR THE WORSE
EEFIIINNRST	INTENSIFIER
EEFIIINNSST	INTENSIFIES
EEFIIISSTTV	FESTIVITIES
EEFIILLNORW	IN LOW RELIEF
EEFIILLORST	FERTILE SOIL
EEFIILLNNSTY	IN FINE STYLE
EEFIILNORRY	OIL REFINERY
EEFIILRRSST	FERTILISERS
EEFIILRRSTZ	FERTILIZERS
EEFIIMNSTUV	FIVE MINUTES
EEFIINOPRRS	PERSONIFIER
EEFIINOPRSS	PERSONIFIES
EEFIINOSTTU	TUITION FEES
EEFIIRRSSST	FIRST SERIES
EEFIKLLLNOS	KILL ONESELF
EEFIKLNOPSW	WINK OF SLEEP
EEFIKOOPTTU	KEEP OUT OF IT
EEFILLMORSU	MELLIFEROUS
EEFILLNORWW	OWN FREE WILL
EEFILLOPRTU	OF ILL REPUTE
EEFILMNOOPY	PILE OF MONEY
EEFILMNOOTT	FELT EMOTION
EEFILMORRSV	FIRM RESOLVE
EEFILMORRTU	FLUORIMETER
EEFILNNORSU	RUIN ONESELF
EEFILNOPSTY	FEELS NO PITY
EEFILNORSSW	FLOWERINESS
EEFILNOSSTU	SUIT ONESELF
EEFILOOPRRT	PROFITEROLE
EEFILOORSST	LOOSESTRIFE
EEFILOPSTTU	FEELS UP TO IT
EEFILPRSSTX	EXPRESS LIFT
EEFILRRSTTT	FIRST LETTER
EEFIMMOORST	FOR SOME TIME
EEFIMMORRST	FORMER TIMES
EEFINRRRSTU	RETURNS FIRE
EEFINRSSTUV	FURTIVENESS
EEFIOPRSSTU	PESTIFEROUS
EEFJOOPRSWY	WEEPS FOR JOY
EEFKLNOOOTV	TOKEN OF LOVE
EEFLLNOOSST	LOST ONESELF
EEFLLNRSTUY	RESENTFULLY
EEFLMNOOOVY	LOVE OF MONEY
EEFLMNOSSSU	FULSOMENESS
EEFLMOPRSTU	PETROL FUMES
EEFLNNSSTUU	TUNEFULNESS
EEFLNOOSSSS	SENSE OF LOSS
EEFLNPSSSUU	SUSPENSEFUL
EEFLNRSSSTU	RESTFULNESS
EEFLOOOPRVW	POWER OF LOVE

EEFMORRSTTY	FORTY METRES
EEFNNOORSSW	NOSE FOR NEWS
EEFNNOOTTTU	TEN OUT OF TEN
EEFNNORRRSU	FORERUNNERS
EEFNOPRSSSU	PROFUSENESS
EEFOOOPRTVW	POWER OF VETO
EEGGGILNORV	LEGGING OVER
EEGGHHIINNT	HEIGHTENING
EEGGHIINRST	SEEING RIGHT
EEGGHIINSST	SIGHTSEEING
EEGGHIINSTV	GIVE THE SIGN
EEGGHILNNNT	LENGTHENING
EEGGHILNPTT	GETTING HELP
EEGGHIMNNOT	GETTING HOME
EEGGHOORTTT	GOT TOGETHER
EEGGIIKNOPT	KEEP IT GOING
EEGGIIMNNRT	REGIMENTING
EEGGIINRRST	REGISTERING
EEGGILLNNTY	NEGLIGENTLY
EEGGILLNTTW	GETTING WELL
EEGGILORSUY	EGREGIOUSLY
EEGGINNNOVW	EVENING GOWN
EEGGINNOTUV	GIVEN TONGUE
EEGGINORTTV	GETTING OVER
EEGGINOSTUV	GIVES TONGUE
EEGGNOOPRST	PROGESTOGEN
EEGGNORRUWY	GREW YOUNGER
EEGGOOPPRRY	POPE GREGORY
EEGHIIIINRSS	HER HIGHNESS
EEGHHHLOOTW	THE WHOLE HOG
EEGHHHORSTU	HUG THE SHORE
EEGHHIINRRS	RISEN HIGHER
EEGHHIIRRSS	RISES HIGHER
EEGHHILOSST	LOSES HEIGHT
EEGHHILRTWW	WHEELWRIGHT
EEGHHIMPTUV	GIVE THE HUMP
EEGHHINSTTT	EIGHT TENTHS
EEGHHIOPRRW	HIGHER POWER
EEGHHIPPRST	HIGH-STEPPER
EEGHHIPSTUV	GIVE THE PUSH
EEGHHLLNOTW	WHOLE-LENGTH
EEGHHLMNSUY	EMLYN HUGHES
EEGHHMORTTU	MERE THOUGHT
EEGHHMPSTTU	GETS THE HUMP
EEGHHNORSTU	SEEN THROUGH
EEGHHNRSSUY	NERYS HUGHES
EEGHHORSSTU	SEES THROUGH
EEGHHPSSTTU	GETS THE PUSH
EEGHIIILNVV	VIVIEN LEIGH
EEGHIIKNPST	KEEP IN SIGHT
EEGHIILMSTY	EIGHTY MILES
EEGHIILNRTV	LIGHTER VEIN
EEGHIILPSTV	GIVE THE SLIP
EEGHIILRSTT	EIGHT LITRES
EEGHIIMNPSU	EUPHEMISING
EEGHIIMNPUZ	EUPHEMIZING
EEGHIINNORT	EIGHT OR NINE
EEGHIINNSTW	WHITE ENSIGN
EEGHIINPPTV	GIVEN THE PIP
EEGHIINSSTW	WEIGHTINESS
EEGHIIPPSTV	GIVES THE PIP
EEGHIJLNNTU	IN THE JUNGLE
EEGHIKNOPPS	KEEPING SHOP
EEGHIKNOPRT	KEEP RIGHT ON
EEGHILNNOPT	TELEPHONING
EEGHILNNOST	NOTHING ELSE
EEGHILNNSSS	ENGLISHNESS
EEGHILNNSST	LENGTHINESS
EEGHILNOOPS	PIGEONHOLES
EEGHILNORSS	ENGLISH ROSE
EEGHILNOTUW	WHEELING OUT

EEGHILNRTTT	NIGHT LETTER
EEGHILOSSTW	LOSES WEIGHT
EEGHILOSTVW	WHITE GLOVES
EEGHILPSSTT	GETS THE SLIP
	SLEEPS TIGHT
EEGHILRSTTT	STREET LIGHT
EEGHIMNNORT	MERE NOTHING
EEGHIMNOORS	HOMOGENISER
EEGHIMNOORZ	HOMOGENIZER
EEGHIMNOOSS	HOMOGENISES
EEGHIMNOOSZ	HOMOGENIZES
EEGHIMNOOTY	HOMOGENEITY
EEGHINNNOST	SEEN NOTHING
EEGHINNOSST	SEES NOTHING
EEGHINNPTWY	PENNYWEIGHT
EEGHINOORTV	IN THE GROOVE
EEGHINOPPUV	GIVEN UP HOPE
EEGHINOPTTT	GET THE POINT
EEGHINOQTUU	QUITE ENOUGH
EEGHINORSTW	WORTH SEEING
EEGHINOSSTW	GET ONES WISH
EEGHINOTTVW	GOT EVEN WITH
EEGHINRTTTU	IN THE GUTTER
EEGHINSSTTW	SWEET THINGS
EEGHIOPPSUV	GIVES UP HOPE
EEGHIRRSSTV	SERVES RIGHT
EEGHKORSTTW	GET THE WORKS
EEGHLLNOOTU	HOTEL LOUNGE
EEGHLOOPRTU	THE PROLOGUE
EEGHLOOPRTY	HERPETOLOGY
EEGHLOPRSSU	SLEEPS ROUGH
EEGHMNOOOSU	HOMOGENEOUS
EEGHMNOORRW	WHOREMONGER
EEGHMORRSTY	HYGROMETERS
EEGHNNNRSTT	STRENGTHENS
EEGHNOOORTW	NOWHERE TO GO
EEGHOOPTTTT	GET TO THE TOP
EEGHOPRTTTU	PUT TOGETHER
EEGHOSSSTUU	GUESTHOUSES
	HOUSEGUESTS
EEGIIIKNNPT	KEEPING IT IN
EEGIIILNSTT	GENTILITIES
EEGIIINNSTU	INGENUITIES
EEGIIKLMNPS	KEEP SMILING
EEGIIKNPPTU	KEEPING IT UP
EEGIILLLNST	TELLING LIES
EEGIILLNNTT	INTELLIGENT
EEGIILMNNRT	INTERMINGLE
EEGIILNOOTX	GO INTO EXILE
EEGIILNOPSS	LIPOGENESIS
EEGIILNRSSW	WIRELESSING
EEGIIMMNNPT	IMPINGEMENT
EEGIIMMNRSS	MESMERISING
EEGIIMMNRSZ	MESMERIZING
EEGIIMMNNNRS	MINNESINGER
EEGIIMNNOPT	OPENING TIME
EEGIIMNNRSTV	SERVING TIME
EEGIIMNSTTT	TESTING TIME
EEGIIINNNRTV	INTERVENING
	REINVENTING
EEGIINNQRUV	VIRGIN QUEEN
EEGIINNQSUZ	SQUEEZING IN
EEGIINNRSTT	INTERESTING
EEGIINNRSTV	REINVESTING
EEGIINORSTV	GIVEN RISE TO
EEGIINOSTTU	SEEING IT OUT
EEGIIORSSTV	GIVES RISE TO
EEGIIOSTTTW	GET WISE TO IT
EEGIKKNORSW	SEEKING WORK
EEGIKKNORWW	WORKING WEEK
EEGIKMNOPSV	KEEPS MOVING
EEGIKNPRSTY	KEEPS TRYING
EEGILLLLNSW	SELLING WELL
EEGILLLMNNR	GLENN MILLER
EEGILLLSSUY	GUILELESSLY
EEGILLNOPSS	LOSING SLEEP
EEGILLNRSVW	SERVING WELL
EEGILLOOSTT	TELEOLOGIST
EEGILMOOSTY	ETYMOLOGISE
EEGILMOOTYZ	ETYMOLOGIZE
EEGILNNNRTU	UNRELENTING
EEGILNNRSTY	SINGLE ENTRY
EEGILNOPRTT	TELEPORTING
EEGILNOPSSY	POLYGENESIS
EEGILNOPSTU	SLEEPING OUT
EEGILNOQTUY	GONE QUIETLY
EEGILNORSVY	SOVEREIGNLY
EEGILNOSSSV	GIVE LESSONS
EEGILOPRSTT	POLTERGEIST
EEGILOQSTUY	GOES QUIETLY
EEGIMNNOOPV	OPENING MOVE
EEGIMNNOOSS	MONOGENESIS
EEGIMNNOSTT	MIGNONETTES
EEGIMNNOTTW	TOWN MEETING
EEGIMNNRRTU	INTERREGNUM
EEGIMNNSTTU	INTEGUMENTS
EEGIMNOORST	GONIOMETERS
EEGIMNORSTW	SWINGOMETER
EEGIMNPSTTU	SETTING 'EM UP
EEGIMOPRTTU	TIME TO GET UP
EEGINNOOSST	ONTOGENESIS
EEGINNOTTVV	GIVEN VENT TO
EEGINNPRSUV	SUPERVENING
EEGINOORRTU	ROUGE ET NOIR
EEGINOPRTTU	PETERING OUT
EEGINOPSTTT	GET INTO STEP
EEGINOPSTUW	SWEEPING OUT
EEGINOQTTUU	QUIET TONGUE
EEGINORRSSS	REGRESSIONS
EEGINORRSTU	TERRIGENOUS
EEGINORRSWW	WINEGROWERS
EEGINORSTVY	SOVEREIGNTY
EEGINOSTTVV	GIVES VENT TO
EEGINPRSTTU	GUTTERSNIPE
EEGINPSTTTY	TYPESETTING
EEGIOPRRSSV	PROGRESSIVE
EEGLLLNOPSU	PULL ONES LEG
EEGLLNOOSTW	GET WELL SOON
EEGLMNOOSUY	MYELOGENOUS
EEGLMOOORTY	METEOROLOGY
EEGLNOOPPUY	YOUNG PEOPLE
EEGLNOOSUXY	EXOGENOUSLY
EEGLNSSSSTU	GUTLESSNESS
EEGLOORSSSV	GLOSSES OVER
EEGLOPPPTUV	GLOVE PUPPET
EEGLOQRSTUY	GROTESQUELY
EEGLORSSTVW	TWELVE GROSS
EEGMNNORSST	ENGROSSMENT
EEGMNNORSSW	NEWSMONGERS
EEGMNNORSTV	GOVERNMENTS
EEGNOOPRSST	GONE TO PRESS
EEGNOORRSTW	GROW ON TREES
EEGOOPRSSST	GOES TO PRESS
EEGPRRSSTTU	GUTTER PRESS
EEHHIINNRSW	RHENISH WINE
EEHHIIRSTTT	THE THIRTIES
EEHHIJKOPST	KEITH JOSEPH
EEHHILLNSSS	HELLISHNESS
EEHHILLORTV	OVER THE HILL
EEHHILMOPRT	THERMOPHILE
EEHHILOPRST	LITHOSPHERE
EEHHILORTUV	THE EVIL HOUR

EEHHIMORRSU	HURRIES HOME
EEHHINORSTT	IN THE THROES
EEHHIOPSSTY	HYPOTHESISE
EEHHIOPSTYZ	HYPOTHESIZE
EEHHIORSSTW	WHITE HORSES
EEHHLLOOTTW	THE WHOLE LOT
EEHHLMOPRST	MOTHERS HELP
EEHHMNORSTT	THREE MONTHS
EEHHMOORSTU	HOUSE MOTHER
	HOUSEMOTHER
EEHHMOPRTUV	OVER THE HUMP
EEHHNNOORTT	ON THE THRONE
EEHHNORSTUU	HOUSE HUNTER
EEHHOOPPRST	PHOTOSPHERE
EEHHOOPRRTT	HETEROTROPH
EEHHOORSSUW	WHOREHOUSES
EEHIIKLNOPX	PHOENIXLIKE
EEHIIKNPSTY	PIE IN THE SKY
EEHIIKNSSST	KINESTHESIS
EEHIILLLTTW	LITTLE WHILE
EEHIILNOPSV	LIVES IN HOPE
EEHIILNTTTW	WIN THE TITLE
EEHIIMPPRRS	PREMIERSHIP
EEHIINNRTTW	IN THE WINTER
EEHIINORRTT	THE INTERIOR
EEHIINPRTWZ	WIN THE PRIZE
EEHIINRRSST	INHERITRESS
EEHIIRRSSTT	IRISH SETTER
EEHIJLNNNOT	JOHN TENNIEL
EEHIKLOOTTV	TOOK THE VEIL
EEHIKMORSST	STRIKES HOME
EEHIKNSTUWW	WHITSUN WEEK
EEHIKOORSTT	TOOK THE RISE
EEHIKOOTTVW	TOOK THE VIEW
EEHIKPPSTUW	KEEPS UP WITH
EEHILLNNOSS	IN ONE'S SHELL
EEHILLRSSWW	WELL-WISHERS
EEHILMOPRST	THERMOPILES
EEHILNNSTTU	LET IN THE SUN
EEHILNOPSTT	TELEPHONIST
EEHILNORRST	NORTHERLIES
EEHILNOSTTV	NOVELETTISH
EEHILNOTTTW	WON THE TITLE
EEHILOPRSST	PRIESTS HOLE
EEHILOPRSTT	TRIES TO HELP
EEHILORSSTU	SOUTHERLIES
EEHILOSSTTU	SILHOUETTES
EEHILOSTTTV	LIT THE STOVE
EEHILPRSSTU	SPHERULITES
EEHILRSTTWW	WRESTLE WITH
EEHIMMNRSTU	IN THE SUMMER
EEHIMNORTTW	WRITTEN HOME
EEHIMNOSTTU	THE MOUNTIES
EEHIMNOTTTU	TO THE MINUTE
EEHIMOOTTVW	WHITE TO MOVE
EEHIMOPPRRS	EMPERORSHIP
EEHINNNSSTV	SEVEN NINTHS
EEHINNOOPTT	THIOPENTONE
EEHINNOOSSS	IN ONE'S SHOES
EEHINNOPRSS	PREHENSIONS
EEHINNORSST	RHINESTONES
EEHINNOSSST	TENNIS SHOES
EEHINNOSSSU	HEINOUSNESS
EEHINOPRRST	THE PRISONER
EEHINOPRSTT	THREE POINTS
EEHINOPRTWZ	WON THE PRIZE
EEHINOPSTVY	HYPOTENSIVE
EEHINORSTTT	THE ROT SET IN
EEHINRSSSTU	HIRSUTENESS
EEHINRSSSTY	SYNTHESISER
EEHINRSSTYZ	SYNTHESIZER

EEHINSSSSTY	SYNTHESISES
EEHINSSSTVX	SIX SEVENTHS
EEHINSSSTYZ	SYNTHESIZES
EEHIOPRTTUW	WITHOUT PEER
EEHIPRSSTTU	TRUSTEESHIP
EEHIRRRSTTU	RETIRES HURT
EEHJNOPRRST	PRESTER JOHN
EEHKLNOOORW	NOW LOOK HERE
EEHKLNOPSSW	SPOKEN WELSH
EEHKLOORSTT	TOOK SHELTER
EEHKNOORSTT	ON THE STROKE
	TENTERHOOKS
EEHKNRSTTUY	TURNS THE KEY
EEHKOOSTTTT	TOOK THE TEST
EEHLLMNOOPS	MELLOPHONES
EEHLMNOTTVW	TWELVEMONTH
EEHLNOOSTWW	ON TWO WHEELS
EEHLOOPRRTT	HOTEL PORTER
EEHLOOSSSTT	LOSE THE TOSS
EEHLOOSSUVY	SHE LOVES YOU
EEHLOOSTTTV	LOST THE VOTE
EEHLOPRRSTU	UPHOLSTERER
EEHLORRSTTT	SHORT LETTER
EEHLORSTUVW	TWELVE HOURS
EEHLRSSSTTU	SHUTTERLESS
EEHMMNNOTTU	THE MONUMENT
EEHMMORRTTY	THERMOMETRY
EEHMMORSSUU	SUMMER HOUSE
	SUMMERHOUSE
EEHMNNNOOPS	PHENOMENONS
EEHMNNOOORY	HONEYMOONER
EEHMNNOSSTV	SEVEN MONTHS
EEHMNOOORTV	OVER THE MOON
EEHMNORRSTU	RETURNS HOME
EEHMOOPRSTT	PHOTOMETERS
EEHMOPRRSTT	SHORT TEMPER
EEHMOQRSSUU	HUMORESQUES
EEHNNNOPSTY	HONEST PENNY
EEHNNOORSUV	HONOURS EVEN
EEHNNORRRST	NORTHERNERS
EEHNNORSSTT	HORNETS NEST
EEHNOOPRSTY	STEREOPHONY
EEHNOPSSSTY	PYTHONESSES
EEHNORRSSTU	SOUTHERNERS
EEHNORSSTTW	THREW STONES
EEHNORSTTTY	TENTH STOREY
EEHNOSSTTVW	TWO SEVENTHS
EEHOOPPRRST	TROPOSPHERE
EEHOOPRRSTU	PORTERHOUSE
EEHOOPRSSUW	POWERHOUSES
EEHOOPRSTTT	PHOTOSETTER
EEHOORSSSTU	STOREHOUSES
EEHOPRSTTVY	THE VERY SPOT
EEHOPSSSTUU	SETS UP HOUSE
EEHORSSTTUW	SOUTHWESTER
EEIIIMNNSTU	EINSTEINIUM
EEIIINNSSTV	INSENSITIVE
EEIIINORRTZ	INTERIORIZE
EEIIKLLNSTU	UNLIKELIEST
EEIIKLLQTUY	QUITE LIKELY
EEIIKLNPRSW	PERIWINKLES
EEIIKMRSSTT	IT STRIKES ME
EEIILLLOORS	LE ROI SOLEIL
EEIILLMMRST	MILLIMETRES
EEIILLNRSTY	RESILIENTLY
EEIILLNSTVY	LIVE IN STYLE
EEIILLOPRST	PELLITORIES
EEIILLPPRST	PIPISTRELLE
EEIILLPRSTV	SPIRIT LEVEL
EEIILMMNPRT	IMPERILMENT
EEIILMNNSTY	NINETY MILES

EEIILMNRSSS	MISERLINESS	EEILMNSTTWY	TWENTY MILES
EEIILNNSTVY	INTENSIVELY	EEILMPRSSTU	PULSIMETERS
EEIILNNTVVY	INVENTIVELY	EEILNNOPSSS	PENSIONLESS
EEIILNOSSTV	TELEVISIONS	EEILNNOSSST	TENSIONLESS
EEIILNRSSSV	SILVERINESS	EEILNNPRSVY	SILVER PENNY
EEIILNSSTVY	SENSITIVELY	EEILNNPRTTY	PERTINENTLY
EEIILQSTUXY	EXQUISITELY	EEILNNSSSSS	SINLESSNESS
EEIILRRSSST	STERILISERS	EEILNOPRRST	INTERLOPERS
EEIILRRSSTZ	STERILIZERS	EEILNOPRTVY	POVERTY LINE
EEIILRSSTVY	RESISTIVELY	EEILNOPSSTW	WET ONES LIPS
EEIIMMNNOSU	MINNIE MOUSE	EEILNOSSTVY	OSTENSIVELY
EEIIMMNOSTY	TIME IS MONEY	EEILNQTTUWY	WENT QUIETLY
EEIIMMNNNSTU	NINE MINUTES	EEILOPPRRTT	PROPER TITLE
EEIIMNNOPRS	IN ONES PRIME	EEILOPRSSTY	PROSELYTISE
EEIIMNNPRTT	IMPERTINENT	EEILOPRSTYZ	PROSELYTIZE
EEIIMNRSSTY	YES, MINISTER	EEIMMMRSSTU	SUMMERTIMES
EEIINNNORTV	REINVENTION	EEIMMNOPRTV	IMPROVEMENT
EEIINNNOSTT	NONENTITIES	EEIMMNPRSST	IMPRESSMENT
EEIINNORSTV	INVENTORIES	EEIMMORSSTY	SEISMOMETRY
EEIINNOSSSV	SEEN VISIONS	EEIMNNNORTV	ENVIRONMENT
EEIINNRSTTW	INTERTWINES	EEIMNNOOSSS	NOISOMENESS
EEIINOPRSTT	PETITIONERS	EEIMNNOPRST	OMNIPRESENT
	REPETITIONS	EEIMNNOSSSW	WINSOMENESS
EEIINORSSUV	SERIOUS VEIN	EEIMNNSSTTV	INVESTMENTS
EEIINOSSSSV	SEES VISIONS	EEIMNOPRSTU	PERITONEUMS
EEIINRSTTUV	INVESTITURE	EEIMNORRSSS	SERMONISERS
EEIIOPPRSTV	PREPOSITIVE	EEIMNORRSSZ	SERMONIZERS
EEIIOPRSTTU	REPETITIOUS	EEIMNORSTZZ	INTERMEZZOS
EEIIORRRSTT	TERRITORIES	EEIMNPPPRST	PEPPERMINTS
EEIIORRSSST	ROTISSERIES	EEIMNPPPRTY	PEPPERMINTY
EEIIORRTTXY	EXTERIORITY	EEIMNPRRTTY	ENTRY PERMIT
EEIIORSSUVW	SERIOUS VIEW	EEIMNRSSTTW	WESTMINSTER
EEIIPQRSSTU	PERQUISITES	EEIMOOPRTVW	MOTIVE POWER
EEIIJJLLMMWY	JIMMY JEWELL	EEIMOPPRRSU	IMPROPER USE
EEIJKNOPSST	SPOKE IN JEST	EEIMOPPRSSU	SUPERIMPOSE
EEIJMNORRSY	JEREMY IRONS	EEIMOPRRSST	SPIROMETERS
EEIKKLLNOOW	LOOK LIKE NEW		TEMPORISERS
EEIKKNORSTT	TOKEN STRIKE	EEIMPPRSTUV	PRESUMPTIVE
EEIKLMPRTTU	TRUMPETLIKE	EEIMRRSTTUY	UTTER MISERY
EEIKLNOOPSV	SPOKE NO EVIL	EEIMRSSTTXY	SIXTY METRES
EEIKMNORSSS	IRKSOMENESS	EEINNNOTTWY	ONE IN TWENTY
EEIKNNOORST	IN ONE STROKE	EEINNOOPRSW	IN ONES POWER
EEIKNOQSTUY	KEY QUESTION	EEINNOPPRSST	PRETENSIONS
EEIILLLNOSST	TELLS NO LIES	EEINNOPSSTV	SEVEN POINTS
EEIILLLOPRWY	YELLOW PERIL	EEINNOSSSUV	ENVIOUSNESS
EEIILLMMORST	IMMORTELLES	EEINNOSSTTU	SENTENTIOUS
EEIILLMMSTUV	SUMMIT LEVEL	EEINNPRSTTU	TURPENTINES
EEIILLMNOTTW	LITTLE WOMEN	EEINNQSSTUU	UNQUIETNESS
EEIILLMOPRSW	PROMISE WELL	EEINOORRTTX	EXTORTIONER
EEIILLMPRTUX	MULTIPLEXER	EEINOPRRSSS	REPRESSIONS
EEIILLMPSSTY	SIMPLE STYLE	EEINOPRRSSV	PERVERSIONS
EEIILLMPSTUX	MULTIPLEXES	EEINOPRRTVY	IN EVERY PORT
EEIILLNNOORS	ONION SELLER	EEINOPRSSSX	EXPRESSIONS
EEIILLNOPQTU	EQUIPOLLENT	EEINOPRSTTU	PRETENTIOUS
EEIILLNOSSSY	NOISELESSLY	EEINOPSSSTU	PITEOUSNESS
EEIILLNPSSSY	SPINELESSLY	EEINOQRSSTU	QUESTIONERS
EEIILLNPSTTY	PESTILENTLY	EEINORRSTVW	OVERWINTERS
EEIILLNRTTWW	WELL WRITTEN	EEINORRTTVW	OVERWRITTEN
	WRITTEN WELL	EEINORSSSSU	SERIOUSNESS
EEIILLOPSVXY	EXPLOSIVELY	EEINOSSSTUW	USE ONES WITS
EEIILLORRVWY	YELLOW RIVER	EEINPRRRTTU	INTERRUPTER
EEIILLPRSUVY	PRELUSIVELY	EEINPRSSTUV	PUTS IN VERSE
	REPULSIVELY	EEINPRTTTWY	TYPEWRITTEN
EEIILLPSSTVY	STEPS LIVELY	EEIOOPPSSTX	OPPOSITE SEX
EEIILMNNOOVW	WOMEN IN LOVE	EEIOOPRRSTW	RISE TO POWER
EEIILMNNOTVV	INVOLVEMENT	EEIOPRRTTWY	WRITE POETRY
EEIILMNOOSST	EMOTIONLESS	EEIOPRSSSTU	SERIOUS STEP
	LOSES NO TIME	EEIOPSSSSSV	POSSESSIVES
EEIILMNORSVY	SILVER MONEY	EEIPPRSSSUV	SUPPRESSIVE
EEIILMNOSSSU	MOUSSELINES	EEIPRRRSSSU	PRESSURISER
EEIILMNRTTTY	REMITTENTLY	EEIPRRRSSUZ	PRESSURIZER

EEIPRRSSSSU	PRESSURISES
EEIPRRSSSUZ	PRESSURIZES
EEIPRRSTTWY	TYPEWRITERS
EEIPRSSSSTT	STEPSISTERS
EEJLNOSSSSY	JOYLESSNESS
EEKKOORRRTV	VOORTREKKER
EEKLNOOPPSY	SPOKE OPENLY
EEKMNOOPSSW	SPOKESWOMEN
EEKNOORRSTW	STONEWORKER
EELLLMNOOWY	LEMON YELLOW
EELLLOORRTW	ROLLER TOWEL
EELLMNOOVYY	LOVELY MONEY
EELLNOORSSW	ORSON WELLES
EELLNOPSTUY	PLENTEOUSLY
EELLNORRSTW	WESTERN ROLL
EELLNORTVWY	NOT VERY WELL
EELLNPRTUUV	PULVERULENT
EELLOPRSSWY	POWERLESSLY
	YELLOW PRESS
EELLORRSTTY	STORY TELLER
	STORYTELLER
EELMMNOPSTY	EMPLOYMENTS
EELMNOOORVY	LOVE OR MONEY
EELMNPPSSTU	SUPPLEMENTS
EELNOOPPSTW	TOWNSPEOPLE
EELNOOPRUWW	PURE NEW WOOL
EELNOORRSUY	ERRONEOUSLY
EELNOPPRTTY	PREPOTENTLY
EELNOPRSSTW	SPLEENWORTS
EELNOPRSTYY	POLYSTYRENE
EELOOPPRSTV	TOPPLES OVER
EELOPPRSSSU	PURPOSELESS
EELOPPSSTTU	PUTS TO SLEEP
EELOPRRSSUW	LOW PRESSURE
EELOPRSUVEZ	PUZZLES OVER
EEMNNRSTTTU	ENTRUSTMENT
EEMNOOPRSTY	ENEMY TROOPS
EEMNORSSTTT	STEM TO STERN
EEMNORSSTTW	WESTERNMOST
EEMOPSSTTUU	TEMPESTUOUS
EEMOQRSSTTU	QUOTES TERMS
EENNNNOOPTY	NOT ONE PENNY
EENNOOPSTTY	NOT ONES TYPE
EENNOORSSSU	ONEROUSNESS
EENNOORSTTT	ROTTENSTONE
EENNOORSVWY	ONES VERY OWN
EENNOOTTTWY	TWENTY TO ONE
EENNORSSSUV	NERVOUSNESS
EENNOSSSTUU	TENUOUSNESS
EENNPPRTTYY	PRETTY PENNY
EENOOOOPRRRT	OPEN TO ERROR
EENOOPRSTUV	PUTS ONE OVER
EENOPPRSSXY	PONY EXPRESS
EENOPRSSTTW	WENT TO PRESS
EENORSTTUUV	VENTURES OUT
EEOOOPPRRSTW	ROSE TO POWER
EEOOPPRRSTY	PROSE POETRY
EEOOPRRTTWY	WROTE POETRY
EEOOPRSTTTV	PROTEST VOTE
EEOPPPRSSSU	PRESUPPOSES
EEOPPRRSSUW	SUPERPOWERS
EEOPPRRSTTT	PORT ST.PETER
EEOPPRRSTUY	UPPER STOREY
EEOPPRSSSTX	EXPRESS POST
EEOPQRSSTTU	REQUEST STOP
EEOPRRSSSTU	SUPERSTORES
EFFFFHLOSSU	SHUFFLES OFF
EFFFGHINORT	FRIGHTEN OFF
EFFFGINORUU	FIGURE OF FUN
EFFFHIINOSS	FINISHES OFF
EFFFHIJNOTU	FIFTH OF JUNE

EFFFIIORSTV	FIRST OF FIVE
EFFFINORSTZ	FROZEN STIFF
EFFFKMOOPSU	PUFF OF SMOKE
EFFFLOORSSU	SUFFER FOOLS
EFFGGIORRST	TRIGGERS OFF
EFFGHHHIIRS	HIGH SHERIFF
EFFGHIINNOT	IN THE OFFING
EFFGHIINRSS	FISH FINGERS
EFFGHILNRSU	RESHUFFLING
EFFGHIOORRS	OFF-SHORE RIG
EFFGIINRRST	FIRST FINGER
EFFGIMNOOTY	GIFT OF MONEY
EFFGIOOPRUV	GROUP OF FIVE
EFFGIORRSUU	FOUR FIGURES
EFFGLLORTUY	FORGETFULLY
EFFHHLOOPSU	FLUSH OF HOPE
EFFHILOOPSS	POLISHES OFF
EFFHIORSTTY	FIFTH STOREY
EFFHJMNOOST	JEFF THOMSON
EFFHLORRSUU	FOUR FLUSHER
EFFHOOOOPSTT	PHOTO-OFFSET
EFFIILNORRU	RUIN FOR LIFE
EFFIIORSTTW	WRITES IT OFF
EFFIJNOORTT	JOINT EFFORT
EFFIJNORSTU	FIRST OF JUNE
EFFIKMOOOTT	TOOK TIME OFF
EFFILLORSTU	LUST FOR LIFE
EFFINNOOPSS	PENSIONS OFF
EFFINORSTUU	UNFIT FOR USE
EFFIOORRRTT	FIT OF TERROR
EFFIOORRSTT	FIRSTFOOTER
EFFKLOORRTW	LEFT FOR WORK
EFFLORSSSSU	SUFFERS LOSS
EFGGHIINNOS	GONE FISHING
EFGGHIINNRT	FRIGHTENING
EFGGHIINOSS	GOES FISHING
EFGGIINPRRU	PREFIGURING
EFGGLOOORST	FOOTSLOGGER
EFGHHINNTTW	WIN THE FIGHT
EFGHHILOTTY	LOFTY HEIGHT
EFGHHINOTTW	WON THE FIGHT
EFGHHLLORTU	FELL THROUGH
EFGHHOORTTU	FORETHOUGHT
EFGHIIILNNS	FISHING LINE
EFGHIIKNRSS	KINGFISHERS
EFGHIILNOST	LINE OF SIGHT
EFGHIILNSST	FLIGHTINESS
EFGHIILOSTW	ISLE OF WIGHT
EFGHIIMNNTT	TIME OF NIGHT
EFGHIINNSTW	WENT FISHING
EFGHIINORSV	OVERFISHING
EFGHIKOPSTT	KEPT SIGHT OF
EFGHILNNOTT	FELT NOTHING
	NOTHING LEFT
EFGHILNOPSU	HOPEFUL SIGN
EFGHILOOSST	LOSE SIGHT OF
EFGHILORSTV	OVERFLIGHTS
EFGHIMNORSS	FISHMONGERS
EFGHINNOORT	FOR ONE THING
EFGHINRRTTU	RETURN FIGHT
EFGHLLNORSU	FLUGELHORNS
EFGHOOPPRRS	FROGHOPPERS
EFGIIILNNRT	FILTERING IN
	INTERFILING
EFGIIILNRST	FERTILISING
EFGIIILNRTZ	FERTILIZING
EFGIIINNRTW	FINE WRITING
EFGIIINRVVY	REVIVIFYING
EFGIIKLNORW	WORKING LIFE
EFGIIKNORWW	WORKING WIFE
EFGIILLMORU	FLORILEGIUM

EFGIILLNTTW	FITTING WELL	EFHNOOSTTUU	OUT OF THE SUN
EFGIILMNSTT	FILMSETTING	EFHOOOPRRSW	SHOWERPROOF
EFGIILMNSUY	EMULSIFYING	EFHOOORSSUW	ROW OF HOUSES
EFGIILNOORS	FOREIGN SOIL	EFHOOPRRSST	FRESH TROOPS
EFGIILNPSTY	SELF-PITYING	EFHOOPRSTTU	THE FOUR TOPS
EFGIILNRSST	FIRST SINGLE	EFIIIIMNRST	INFIRMITIES
EFGIINNNRRU	RUNNING FIRE	EFIIILLMNOV	FIVE MILLION
EFGIINNPRRT	FINGERPRINT	EFIIILLMNST	FILLS IN TIME
EFGIINNRSTU	INTERFUSING	EFIIILMPRSS	SIMPLIFIERS
EFGIINNSSTT	FITTINGNESS	EFIIILNNRST	FIRST IN LINE
EFGIINPRTTY	PRETTIFYING	EFIIILNRTTY	INFERTILITY
EFGIINRSSTT	GETS IN FIRST	EFIIINORRTY	INFERIORITY
EFGIIORTTUU	FIGURE IT OUT	EFIIIPRRSTY	FIERY SPIRIT
EFGILLLORWY	GILLYFLOWER	EFIILLNNRSU	FELL IN RUINS
EFGILNNRTTU	TURNING LEFT	EFIILMOSSTT	LIST OF ITEMS
EFGILNOORVW	FLOWING OVER	EFIILNPSSTU	PITIFULNESS
	OVERFLOWING	EFIILRSTTUX	FIXTURE LIST
EFGILNORSST	FOSTERLINGS	EFIIMMOPRRS	FIRM PROMISE
EFGIMPSTTUU	TEMPUS FUGIT	EFIIMNOOPTT	POINT OF TIME
EFGINNNNOORT	GONE IN FRONT	EFIIMNORSUZ	UNIFORM SIZE
EFGINNOORST	GOES IN FRONT	EFIINNORSTU	INTERFUSION
EFGINNOPSTU	SOFTENING UP	EFIINOOPTVW	POINT OF VIEW
EFGINOOORSS	RING OF ROSES	EFIKLLOSSTT	TEST OF SKILL
EFGINOOORSTU	SURE FOOTING	EFIKLOORSST	FOLK STORIES
EFGINOORTTT	FORGOTTEN IT	EFIKMOOPSTW	TOM WEISKOPF
EFGINOOSTTT	SETTING FOOT	EFIKOOPTTTU	KEPT OUT OF IT
EFGINOPRSST	FINGERPOSTS	EFIKORRSSTT	FIRST STROKE
EFGINORRSUU	FERRUGINOUS	EFILLLMOSUU	MELLIFLUOUS
EFGIOOPRRSU	POOR FIGURES	EFILLLNPTUY	PLENTIFULLY
EFGIOPRSSUY	GYPSIFEROUS	EFILLNNORTW	WELL IN FRONT
EFGIORRRSUY	SORRY FIGURE	EFILLNOOSUY	FELONIOUSLY
EFGLMNOOTTU	LEG OF MUTTON	EFILLOOTTUW	WELL OUT OF IT
	LEG-OF-MUTTON	EFILLRSSTUY	FRUITLESSLY
EFHHINORSST	SHINES FORTH	EFILMOPPRRU	FORMER PUPIL
EFHHIOORSTT	HITS THE ROOF	EFILMORRTUY	FLUORIMETRY
EFHHLORTTUW	TWELFTH HOUR	EFILMORSSTY	FROSTY SMILE
EFHIILORSTY	LIFE HISTORY	EFILMORSTUV	FIRST VOLUME
EFHIILRSTTW	TRIFLES WITH	EFILNORSSST	FIRST LESSON
EFHIINRSSTT	THRIFTINESS	EFILNORSTTU	STOLEN FRUIT
EFHIJNNNOTU	NINTH OF JUNE	EFILNSSSTUW	WISTFULNESS
EFHIJNOSTUX	SIXTH OF JUNE	EFILOOPRRSU	PROLIFEROUS
EFHIKLOOTTT	TOOK THE LIFT	EFILOPPRSTU	SUPPORT LIFE
EFHIKORRSTW	SHIFT WORKER	EFILPRSTUUY	SUPERFLUITY
EFHILLNSSUY	UNSELFISHLY	EFIMMNNOOTY	MINT OF MONEY
EFHILLOPSSW	FELLOWSHIPS	EFIMNNORSSU	UNIFORMNESS
EFHILLOSTWW	WOLF WHISTLE	EFIMNOORSSU	SOMNIFEROUS
	WOLF-WHISTLE	EFIMNORSTUU	FOUR MINUTES
EFHILLSSSTY	SHIFTLESSLY	EFINNNORTTW	WENT IN FRONT
EFHILNOOSSS	FOOLISHNESS	EFINNOORSSS	FOR ONE'S SINS
EFHILNOPSTU	SPOIL THE FUN	EFINOOORSUZ	OZONIFEROUS
EFHILNOSSSW	WOLFISHNESS	EFINOOPRSSS	PROFESSIONS
EFHILNSSSUW	WISHFULNESS	EFINOOSTTUX	SIX OUT OF TEN
EFHILOPRSST	SHOPLIFTERS	EFINOPRRSST	FIRST PERSON
EFHILORSSTW	WHISTLES FOR	EFIOOPRRSSU	SPORIFEROUS
EFHIMOORSTT	SHORT OF TIME	EFIOORSSSTT	TOSSES FOR IT
EFHIMORRSTX	SIXTH-FORMER	EFIORRSSTTY	FIRST STOREY
EFHINOPPSSS	FOPPISHNESS	EFKLOOPSSTY	SPOKE SOFTLY
EFHIORSSSTU	ISSUES FORTH	EFLLLMOOSSS	LOSS OF SMELL
EFHJLNOTTUY	TENTH OF JULY	EFLLNOSSSUU	SOULFULNESS
EFHKLNOSTWY	KNOW THYSELF	EFLLOORRSWY	SORRY FELLOW
EFHKOOORSUY	HOUSE OF YORK	EFLLOOSTTUW	STOUT FELLOW
EFHLMOOOPRT	MOP THE FLOOR	EFLLRSSSTUY	STRESSFULLY
EFHLNOOOOPRR	FORLORN HOPE	EFLMNOOOSSY	LOSS OF MONEY
EFHLNOPRRSU	RUNS FOR HELP	EFLMNOOOSTY	LOTS OF MONEY
EFHLNRSSTUU	HURTFULNESS	EFLNNOOOPSU	ONE SPOONFUL
EFHLOOPSTTW	STOP THE FLOW	EFLOOOOPRTTU	OUT OF PETROL
EFHLOORTTUV	LOVE OF TRUTH	EFLOOOORTTU	TWO-FOOT RULE
EFHMNOORRSU	RUNS FOR HOME	EFLOPRSSUUU	SUPERFLUOUS
EFHMOOPRSTT	FROM THE SPOT	EFMNNOOOSTY	TONS OF MONEY
EFHMORRSTTU	FURTHERMOST	EFMNOOOPSTY	POTS OF MONEY
EFHNNOORRTZ	FROZEN NORTH	EFMNOPRSTTU	TEN OF TRUMPS

EFNNNOPRSUY	FUNNY PERSON	EGHHINNOORS	SHOE-HORNING
EFNNNORRRTU	FRONT-RUNNER	EGHHINNOTTT	NOT THE THING
EFNOORRSSTT	STOREFRONTS	EGHHINSSTTU	THE HUSTINGS
EFNOORSSTTT	NOTTS FOREST	EGHHIORSTTW	SHORT WEIGHT
EFNOORSSTTU	STORE OF NUTS	EGHHLOSSTTU	THOUGHTLESS
EFOOPRRSSTU	FOUR-POSTERS	EGHHNOOOSTW	THE GOON SHOW
EGGGHHIINTT	GETTING HIGH	EGHHNORTTUW	WENT THROUGH
EGGGIINNPRU	GINGERING UP	EGHHOORTTUV	THOUGHT OVER
EGGGINOPRRU	GINGER GROUP	EGHIIIMSTTT	TIME IS TIGHT
EGGHHHIILRT	HIGHLIGHTER	EGHIIKLNNOT	NOTHING LIKE
EGGHHIILTTW	LIGHT WEIGHT	EGHIIKLOSTY	EIGHTY KILOS
	LIGHTWEIGHT	EGHIIKNNSSU	KING HUSSEIN
EGGHHNOORTU	GONE THROUGH	EGHIIKNPSTT	KEPT IN SIGHT
EGGHHOORSTU	GOES THROUGH	EGHIILLLNPW	WILLING HELP
EGGHHORSTTU	GETS THROUGH	EGHIILLNNOS	ONE SHILLING
EGGHIIKNOTV	GIVING THE O.K.	EGHIILLNRSV	SHRIVELLING
EGGHIINOTUW	OUTWEIGHING	EGHIILLNSWW	WELL-WISHING
EGGHIINPSSS	PIGGISHNESS		WISHING WELL
EGGHIINRRTW	RIGHT WINGER	EGHIILLNTTT	LITTLE THING
	RIGHTWINGER	EGHIILNNSTT	SILENT NIGHT
EGGHIIRSTTT	GETS IT RIGHT	EGHIILNOPPW	WHOPPING LIE
EGGHILLNOOT	GOING TO HELL	EGHIILNPRSY	PERISHINGLY
EGGHILLNRRU	HERRING GULL	EGHIILNRSSS	GIRLISHNESS
EGGHINOSTTT	GETTING SHOT	EGHIILNRTWY	WITHERINGLY
EGGHIPSTTTU	GETS UPTIGHT	EGHIILNSSST	SIGHTLINESS
EGGHLNOORSW	HORNSWOGGLE	EGHIIMMNSTU	THINGUMMIES
EGGHNOORTUU	ROUGH TONGUE	EGHIIMNORTT	RIGHT ON TIME
EGGIIILNPRV	PRIVILEGING	EGHIIMNORTW	WRITING HOME
EGGIIKNNNPU	KING PENGUIN	EGHIIMRRSTT	MISTER RIGHT
EGGIIKNOPTT	KEPT IT GOING	EGHIINNPRST	IN THE SPRING
EGGIILLNNRY	LINGERINGLY	EGHIINNRRVY	HENRY IRVING
EGGIILLNRSS	SINGLE GIRLS	EGHIINOPSTT	EIGHT POINTS
EGGIILMMNRS	GLIMMERINGS	EGHIINOTTTW	GET ON WITH IT
EGGIILNNNOR	LINGERING ON	EGHIINRSSTT	NIGHT SISTER
EGGIILNOTTT	LETTING IT GO	EGHIKNNNOTW	KNEW NOTHING
EGGIIMNNOSS	GONE MISSING	EGHIKNOPRTT	KEPT RIGHT ON
EGGIIMNOSSS	GOES MISSING	EGHIKNORRTW	NIGHT WORKER
EGGIIMNRSTV	GIVING TERMS	EGHILLMNOOR	ROLLING HOME
EGGIINNNORT	RINGING TONE	EGHILLNOSTU	SHELLING OUT
EGGIINNOTTT	GETTING INTO	EGHILLOSTVY	LOVELY SIGHT
	GETTING IT ON	EGHILMNOORT	MOONLIGHTER
EGGIINNRRTU	RINGING TRUE	EGHILMOOSTY	MYTHOLOGIES
EGGIINNRTWW	WRINGING WET		MYTHOLOGISE
EGGILLNOOWY	GOING YELLOW	EGHILMOOTYZ	MYTHOLOGIZE
EGGILNNRSSU	GUNSLINGERS	EGHILNOOSTT	ETHNOLOGIST
EGGILNOSTTT	GETTING LOST	EGHILNOSSST	GHOSTLINESS
EGGILORSTUW	WRIGGLES OUT	EGHILORSTUY	RIGHTEOUSLY
EGGINNNRRTUY	TURNING GREY	EGHIMMNOOPR	ROMPING HOME
EGGINOPRRSS	PROGRESSING	EGHIMMNORTT	RIGHT MOMENT
EGGINORSTTW	GETS IT WRONG	EGHIMNNOOST	SMOOTHENING
EGGINOSSSTU	SUGGESTIONS	EGHIMNNORSU	NURSING HOME
EGGIOPRSSTT	GETS TO GRIPS	EGHIMNOOSUV	MOVING HOUSE
EGGLMOSSTUU	SMUGGLES OUT	EGHINNNOSST	NOTHINGNESS
EGGLNOOORTY	GERONTOLOGY	EGHINNOOPPS	OPENING SHOP
EGGLNORSSTU	STRUGGLES ON	EGHINNOSSTW	ON THE SWINGS
EGGNOORRUWY	GROW YOUNGER	EGHINOOPTTT	GOT THE POINT
EGHHHIINSSS	HIS HIGHNESS	EGHINOORSVW	SHOWING OVER
EGHHHIOPSTT	THE HIGH SPOT	EGHINOOSSTW	GOT ONE'S WISH
EGHHIIKNTTW	WHITE KNIGHT	EGHINOOTTUW	GONE WITHOUT
EGHHIIMNOTT	HITTING HOME	EGHINOPPRSY	PROPHESYING
EGHHIIMOOTT	HIGH TIME TOO!	EGHINOPRRST	RIGHT PERSON
EGHHIIMOSTV	HIGH MOTIVES	EGHINOPRRTT	NIGHT PORTER
EGHHIINNOST	HIGH TENSION	EGHINOPRSUV	PUSHING OVER
EGHHIINNSTT	EIGHT NINTHS	EGHINOPTTUW	PUT ON WEIGHT
EGHHILNNORS	ENGLISH HORN	EGHINORRTTW	INTERGROWTH
EGHHILOPRSY	HIEROGLYPHS	EGHINORSSST	SHOESTRINGS
EGHHILORTUV	LIVE THROUGH	EGHINORSSSU	ROGUISHNESS
EGHHILOSSTU	HOUSELIGHTS	EGHINORSSTW	WORSE THINGS
	LIGHTHOUSES	EGHINORSTUU	USHERING OUT
EGHHILOTTUV	EVIL THOUGHT	EGHINPRSSTU	UPRIGHTNESS
EGHHIMNOSTT	EIGHT MONTHS	EGHINPSSTTU	UPTIGHTNESS

EGHIOORTTTV	RIGHT TO VOTE
EGHIOOSTTUW	GOES WITHOUT
EGHIORRSTTW	GHOST WRITER
	GHOST-WRITER
EGHIORSSTTT	SET TO RIGHTS
EGHIORSSTTW	GHOSTWRITES
EGHIPPRSTTU	STEP RIGHT UP
EGHIPRSTTTY	PRETTY SIGHT
EGHJMNPSTUU	JUMPS THE GUN
EGHKOORSTTW	GOT THE WORKS
EGHLOPRSTTU	GOSPEL TRUTH
EGHMNOOOOTT	GO TO THE MOON
EGHMNOORTTU	GUN THE MOTOR
EGHMOOOSTYZ	HOMOZYGOTES
EGHOOOPTTTT	GOT TO THE TOP
EGHOOORSSTU	SHOOT GROUSE
EGHOORRTUVW	OVERWROUGHT
EGIIIKLLMNT	KILLING TIME
EGIIIKNNOTY	IGNITION KEY
EGIIILLMNPR	IMPERILLING
EGIIILMNORS	RELIGIONISM
EGIIILNNNRT	INTERLINING
EGIIILNNNST	LISTENING IN
EGIIILNNSTU	LUTEINISING
EGIIILNNTUZ	LUTEINIZING
EGIIILNORST	RELIGIONIST
EGIIILNRSST	STERILISING
EGIIILNRSTZ	STERILIZING
EGIIILORRSU	IRRELIGIOUS
EGIIILORSTY	RELIGIOSITY
EGIIIMNNNTW	WINNING TIME
EGIIIMNNNRST	MINISTERING
EGIIIMNOPST	EPITOMISING
EGIIIMNOPTZ	EPITOMIZING
EGIIINNNOSV	ENVISIONING
EGIIINNOPRT	PREIGNITION
EGIIINNOPTT	PETITIONING
EGIIINNRSTW	WINTERISING
EGIIINNRTWZ	WINTERIZING
EGIIINNSSST	SENSITISING
EGIIINNSSTZ	SENSITIZING
EGIIINRSSVW	WISE VIRGINS
EGIIJNNOSTT	JETTISONING
EGIIKKLLNOO	LOOKING LIKE
EGIIKLLNORV	OVERKILLING
EGIIKLMNOPS	PIGEONS MILK
EGIIKLMNPST	KEPT SMILING
EGIIILLNNSSW	WILLINGNESS
EGIIILLNOOSV	LOOSE LIVING
EGIIILLNOSTU	GUILLOTINES
EGIIILLNPSTT	LETTING SLIP
EGIIILLNRTWW	WRITING WELL
EGIIILLORSUY	RELIGIOUSLY
EGIILMNNOSS	SOLEMNISING
EGIILMNNOSZ	SOLEMNIZING
EGIILNNOSTT	LISTENING TO
EGIILNNOSUY	INGENIOUSLY
EGIILNNPRST	SPLINTERING
EGIILNPRSUV	PULVERISING
EGIILNPRUVZ	PULVERIZING
EGIILNRSSST	GRISTLINESS
EGIIMNNNOVW	WINNING MOVE
EGIIMNNOOPS	EMPOISONING
EGIIMNNORSS	SERMONISING
EGIIMNNORSZ	SERMONIZING
EGIIMNNRTTU	UNREMITTING
EGIIMNNSSTW	WENT MISSING
EGIIMNOPRST	TEMPORISING
EGIIMNOPRTZ	TEMPORIZING
EGIIMNPSSTU	MESSING IT UP
EGIIMNRSTTY	TRYING TIMES

EGIIMNSSSTY	SYSTEMISING
EGIIMNSSTYZ	SYSTEMIZING
EGIINNNORVW	WINNING OVER
EGIINNNSSTU	SINGS IN TUNE
EGIINNOPRST	INTERPOSING
EGIINNOPSUZ	SEIZING UPON
EGIINNOQSTU	QUESTIONING
EGIINNPRSSS	SPRINGINESS
EGIINNRSSST	STRINGINESS
EGIINOPRSSU	SERPIGINOUS
EGIINORRRST	TERRORISING
EGIINORRRTZ	TERRORIZING
EGIINORSTUV	VERTIGINOUS
EGIINPRSSUV	SUPERVISING
EGIINSSTTTV	VIGNETTISTS
EGIIOOSTTTW	GOT WISE TO IT
EGIIOPRSSTU	PRESTIGIOUS
EGIJKNOORUY	YOURE JOKING!
EGIJMNOPPRU	JUMPING ROPE
EGIJMNOPRUV	JUMPING OVER
EGIKLLLNOOW	LOOKING WELL
EGIKLLNNOWW	KNOWING WELL
EGIKLLNORWW	WORKING WELL
EGIKLNOOORV	LOOKING OVER
	OVERLOOKING
EGIKMNOOPSU	GO UP IN SMOKE
EGIKNOORRVW	OVERWORKING
	WORKING OVER
EGIKNOPRUVW	GIVEN UP WORK
EGIKOPRSUVW	GIVES UP WORK
EGILLNNNRUW	RUNNING WELL
EGILLNOORRV	ROLLING OVER
EGILLNOPRUV	PULLING OVER
EGILLNOPSTU	SPELLING OUT
EGILLNOSTTU	STILL TONGUE
EGILLNOSTUW	SWELLING OUT
EGILLNPRSSW	WELLSPRINGS
EGILMNNOOSY	LOSING MONEY
EGILMNOOORV	LOOMING OVER
EGILMNOORTY	TERMINOLOGY
EGILMNOORUU	MOULIN ROUGE
EGILMNPRSUY	PRESUMINGLY
EGILMOOSTTY	ETYMOLOGIST
EGILNNNOOSU	UNLOOSENING
EGILNNNRUVY	UNNERVINGLY
EGILNNOOPSU	LOOSENING UP
EGILNNOORSV	LONG VERSION
EGILNNOPRUY	RELYING UPON
EGILNNOSUUY	INGENUOUSLY
EGILNNRSTTY	STRINGENTLY
EGILNOOOPST	STOOL PIGEON
EGILNOORSTU	NEUROLOGIST
EGILNOPRRUW	RULING POWER
EGILNOPRRVY	REPROVINGLY
EGILNOPRSTY	PROSELYTING
EGILNPRSTTU	SPLUTTERING
EGILOOORSTY	SOTERIOLOGY
EGILOOPRSTT	PETROLOGIST
EGILOORSSST	SEROLOGISTS
EGILOPRTUVY	PROVE GUILTY
EGILRSSSTUY	UGLY SISTERS
EGIMMNOORTY	MONOGERMITY
EGIMMNOORRS	IRONMONGERS
EGIMMNOORRY	IRONMONGERY
EGINNNORRSU	RUNNING SORE
EGINNNORRUV	RUNNING OVER
EGINNOORSTU	NITROGENOUS
EGINNOPPRSS	SPRINGS OPEN
EGINNOPPRUY	PREYING UPON
EGINNOPSTTU	SETTING UPON

EGINNORRTUV	OVERTURNING	EHIINQSSSSU	SQUISHINESS
	TURNING OVER	EHIINRSSSTT	THIRSTINESS
EGINOOPPRTV	OVERTOPPING	EHIIOPRSSST	SOPHISTRIES
EGINOOPRRSS	PROGRESSION	EHIJNNNOSTU	HONEST INJUN
EGINOOPRRST	PROGENITORS	EHIKKLOOSTT	TOOK THE SILK
EGINOOPSTTT	GOT INTO STEP	EHIKLLOOPTT	TOOK THE PILL
EGINOPPSTTU	STEPPING OUT	EHIKLMMORST	MOTHERS MILK
EGINOPRRRTY	TYPING ERROR	EHIKNNOSTTW	KENTISH TOWN
EGINOPRRSSV	SPRINGS OVER	EHIKNOPPSTT	POTS THE PINK
EGINOPRRTUV	PROVING TRUE	EHIKNOPSSTT	THE INKSPOTS
EGINOPRSSTT	SPORTINGEST	EHIKNRRSSTU	RUNS THE RISK
EGINOPRTTUV	PUTTING OVER	EHIKOPRSSST	SHIPS STOKER
EGINORRSSTW	SONGWRITERS	EHILLLLMSUW	MUSWELL HILL
EGINORSSTUW	OUTSWINGERS	EHILLORTTWW	WELL WORTH IT
EGINORSSTVW	STRONG VIEWS	EHILMMNOSTY	SEMIMONTHLY
EGINPPRSSSU	SUPPRESSING	EHILMNOOPTY	ENTOMOPHILY
EGIOPPRSTUV	GIVE SUPPORT	EHILMNPSSSU	LUMPISHNESS
EGJLNNOORUY	LONG JOURNEY	EHILMPRSTTU	SIMPLE TRUTH
EGLLMNORSST	STRONG SMELL	EHILNNOOSUY	UNHOLY NOISE
EGMMNNOORTW	WRONG MOMENT	EHILNOOPSTW	WIN THE POOLS
EGMMNOPRSYY	GYMNOSPERMY	EHILNSSSSTY	STYLISHNESS
EGNNOOPRRSW	WRONG PERSON	EHILOOPRSST	HORSE PISTOL
EGNNOOPRSUY	YOUNG PERSON	EHILOOPRSUX	XEROPHILOUS
EGNNOOSSTUY	YOUNGEST SON	EHILOPSSTTW	WHISTLE-STOP
EGNOOOPRSSU	SPOROGENOUS	EHILPRSSSUU	SULPHURISES
EGNORSSTTWY	TWENTY GROSS	EHILPRSSUUZ	SULPHURIZES
EGOPPRSSTTU	GETS SUPPORT	EHIMMNNOORSS	MOONSHINERS
EHHIINRSSTW	WITHERSHINS	EHIMMNORSTU	NOURISHMENT
EHHIKNOOTTT	TOOK THE HINT	EHIMMNPSSTU	PUNISHMENTS
EHHILLNOOTT	HILTON HOTEL	EHIMNOORSTT	ON SHORT TIME
EHHILOOPPRS	PHILOSOPHER	EHIMNORRSTU	MOTHERS RUIN
EHHILOPTTTU	UP TO THE HILT	EHIMOOPRSSW	SHOW PROMISE
EHHILORTTUY	HITLER YOUTH	EHIMOPRRTUV	TRIUMPH OVER
EHHIMMOOORT	HOMOIOTHERM	EHIMOPRSTXY	XEROPHYTISM
EHHIMNNORTT	R IN THE MONTH	EHIMORRSSTT	THERMISTORS
EHHINOSTTTW	HITS THE TOWN	EHIMOSTTTWY	TIMOTHY WEST
EHHIOOPPRST	PHOSPHORITE	EHIMPRSSTYY	MYSTERY SHIP
EHHIOOPRRSW	HERO WORSHIP	EHINNOOPSTY	HYPOTENSION
	HERO WORSHIP	EHINNOOPTTT	NOT THE POINT
EHHIOOPRSST	SHIP TO SHORE	EHINNOOPTTW	WON THE POINT
EHHIOOPSSTT	THEOSOPHIST	EHINOORTTTY	THIRTY TO ONE
EHHIOPSSTTT	HITS THE POST	EHINORSTTUW	UNWORTHIEST
EHHIPPPSSUU	HUSH PUPPIES	EHINOSSSTTW	WINS THE TOSS
EHHLOOSTTUY	YOUTH HOSTEL	EHINOTTTUWW	WENT WITHOUT
EHHMOORSSTU	HORSES MOUTH	EHINRSSSTTU	RUTTISHNESS
EHHNORSSTUW	RUNS THE SHOW	EHINSSSSTTY	SYNTHESISTS
EHHNORSTTTU	HONEST TRUTH	EHIOORSSSTX	SIX-SHOOTERS
EHHOOOPPRST	PHOTOPHORES	EHIOPPRRSSW	WORSHIPPERS
EHHOPPRRTYY	HYPERTROPHY	EHIOPRSSTTT	STIRS THE POT
EHHOPSTTTTU	PUTT THE SHOT	EHJNNOOSSTT	ST.JOHNSTONE
EHIIILNPPPS	PHILIPPINES	EHLLOOOOPPT	LOOP THE LOOP
EHIIILNPSST	PHILISTINES	EHLLORSSTWY	WORTHLESSLY
EHIIILOSSTT	HOSTILITIES	EHLLORTTTTU	TRUTH TO TELL
EHIIIPRSTTW	WHITE SPIRIT	EHLLORTUUXY	LUXURY HOTEL
EHIIKMNOTTT	TIME TO THINK	EHLMNNORTTY	MONTHLY RENT
EHIIKMRRSSS	SKIRMISHERS	EHLMNOPPSYY	NYMPHOLEPSY
EHIIKNORTTV	THINK IT OVER	EHLMNORSTTU	SOLEMN TRUTH
EHIIKNPSTTW	TIPS THE WINK	EHLMOOOSTTY	TOOTHSOMELY
EHIIKNRSTTW	TINKERS WITH	EHLNOOOPSTW	WON THE POOLS
EHIILLLOSTT	TILL THE SOIL	EHLNOORSSST	SHORT LESSON
EHIILLOPSSY	LYOPHILISES	EHLOOSSSTTT	LOST THE TOSS
EHIILLOPSYZ	LYOPHILIZES	EHLORSSSTUW	SHOW RESULTS
EHIILLPRSSV	PHIL SILVERS	EHMMOORRSTY	SHORT MEMORY
EHIILMRSSTV	SILVERSMITH	EHMMNNOORSTU	HUNTERS MOON
EHIILMRSTTY	THIRTY MILES	EHMNOOORRTW	ON THE MORROW
EHIILOOPTTX	TOXOPHILITE	EHMNOORSTWY	MONEYS WORTH
EHIIMNORRRT	IN THE MIRROR	EHMOOOPRSTU	HOMOPTEROUS
EHIIMNORTTY	THE MINORITY	EHMOOORSSTV	SMOOTHS OVER
EHIIMNRSTTY	THE MINISTRY	EHMOOSTTTTU	TO THE UTMOST
EHIINNOPTTW	WIN THE POINT	EHNNOPRSTWY	PENNYWORTHS
EHIINPRSSST	SPINSTERISH		

EHNOORSSTTW	STONES THROW
	THROW STONES
EHNOPRSSTTU	THRUSTS OPEN
EHNORSTTUWY	TWENTY HOURS
EHOOPPRRTTY	HOT PROPERTY
EHOOPPRSSTY	SPOROPHYTES
EHOOPRSSTTT	STOPS THE ROT
EHOPRSSTTTU	SHOT-PUTTERS
EIIIINQSTUV	INQUISITIVE
EIIIKNNRSTW	WRITES IN INK
EIIILLLMRST	MILLILITRES
EIIILMPRTVY	PRIMITIVELY
EIIILNNRSSU	LIES IN RUINS
EIIILNTTUVY	INTUITIVELY
EIIIMNNOPTT	POINT IN TIME
EIIIMNORSSV	REVISIONISM
EIIIMOPRSTX	PROXIMITIES
EIIINOPRSTT	PERITONITIS
EIIINOQRSTU	REQUISITION
EIIINORRTTY	INTERIORITY
EIIINORSSTV	REVISIONIST
EIIINSSTTVY	SENSITIVITY
EIIIOPRSSTT	PERIOSTITIS
EIIIRSSTTVY	RESISTIVITY
EIIKLNNOSTY	NINETY KILOS
EIIKLNOORTT	LIKE IT OR NOT
EIIKLNORSST	TRISKELIONS
EIIKNNOSSTT	TIES IN KNOTS
EIIKNNPRRST	PRINTERS INK
EIIKNOOPSTY	KEY POSITION
EIIILLLMSSTY	LIMITLESSLY
EIIILLMNNSTT	INSTILLMENT
EIIILLMPRSTU	MULTIPLIERS
EIIILLMPSUVY	IMPULSIVELY
EIIILLOOQSUZ	SOLILOQUIZE
EIIILMMNOPSS	SIMPLE SIMON
EIIILMOPRSUY	IMPERIOUSLY
EIIILNNSSTTY	INSISTENTLY
EIIILNOOORSS	SOIL EROSION
EIIILNOOPPRT	LIPOPROTEIN
EIIILNOPPRSU	SENIOR PUPIL
EIIILNRSTUVY	INTRUSIVELY
EIIILNRTTUVY	NUTRITIVELY
EIIILOPSTTUV	LIVES UP TO IT
EIIILORSTTVW	OLIVER TWIST
EIIILPRRTUVY	IRRUPTIVELY
EIIMNNOOPRT	PREMONITION
EIIMNNOOSTT	SET IN MOTION
EIIMNNORSTW	WINS ON MERIT
EIIMNOPRSSS	IMPRESSIONS
	PERMISSIONS
EIIMOORRSTU	MERITORIOUS
EIIMOPPRRTY	IMPROPRIETY
EIIMOPSTTUY	IMPETUOSITY
EIIMORRSSTU	MOISTURISER
EIIMORRSTUZ	MOISTURIZER
EIIMORSSSTU	MOISTURISES
EIIMORSSTUZ	MOISTURIZES
EIINNOOSTUV	SOVIET UNION
EIINOOPPRST	PREPOSITION
EIINOOPSSTX	EXPOSITIONS
EIINOPRRSTY	IRON PYRITES
EIINOPRSSUV	SUPERVISION
EIINOPSSTTW	PIT ONES WITS
EIINORRSSST	SINISTRORSE
EIINORRSSSY	YES SIR,NO SIR
EIINORSTTTU	RESTITUTION
EIINRRSTTUV	RETURN VISIT
EIINRSSSTTW	TWIN SISTERS
EIIOPPSSTUV	SUPPOSITIVE
EIIOPRRSTUY	SUPERIORITY

EIKLLNNOTTW	LITTLE KNOWN
EIKLLORRSTW	TRELLISWORK
EIKLLORSTYY	LIKELY STORY
EIKLNOSTTWY	TWENTY KILOS
EIKLOOORSSU	SERIOUS LOOK
EIKLOSSTTTU	SKITTLES OUT
EIKMMOOPRSU	OPIUM SMOKER
EIKMNNORRSTY	YORK MINSTER
EIKMOOOTTTU	TOOK TIME OUT
EIKNOORSTTU	OUT ON STRIKE
EILLMOPRTUX	MULTIPLEXOR
EILLNNOOORT	ROLL INTO ONE
EILLNOOORVV	IVOR NOVELLO
EILLNOORRST	RITORNELLOS
EILLNOPRSSY	SILLY PERSON
EILLNOPSSTY	POINTLESSLY
EILLOPSSTTU	SPELLS IT OUT
EILLORSTTTU	LITTERLOUTS
EILMNNOPRTY	PROMINENTLY
EILMNOOOPRS	MONOPOLISER
EILMNOOOPRZ	MONOPOLIZER
EILMNOOOPSS	MONOPOLISES
EILMNOOOPSZ	MONOPOLIZES
EILMNOORSVY	SILVERY MOON
EILMNORSUVY	VERMINOUSLY
EILMOORRSWY	WORRISOMELY
EILMOPRSSTY	PROSELYTISM
EILMOPSTUUY	IMPETUOUSLY
EILMORSTTUY	MULTI-STOREY
EILNOOPRSST	PORTIONLESS
EILNOOPRSSV	SILVER SPOON
EILNOOPRTTU	LUTEOTROPIN
EILNOORSSTU	RESOLUTIONS
EILNOORSTUV	REVOLUTIONS
EILNOPRSUUY	PENURIOUSLY
EILNPQSTTUU	QUINTUPLETS
EILOOPRRSTY	POSTERIORLY
EILOOPRSSTY	PROTEOLYSIS
EILOORSSSSU	SERIOUS LOSS
EILOPPRSUVY	PURPOSIVELY
EILOPTTUUZZ	PUZZLE IT OUT
EILRSTUUUXY	LUXURY SUITE
EIMMOOPRRSW	POOR SWIMMER
EIMMNOOSSSU	OMINOUSNESS
EIMMNNRSSTTU	INSTRUMENTS
EIMNOOPRRTY	PREMONITORY
EIMNOOPRSSS	SPOONERISMS
EIMNOOQSTTU	MOSQUITO NET
EIMNOPPRSTU	PRESUMPTION
EIMOOPRSTTT	OPTOMETRIST
EIMOPRSSTUV	PRIMUS STOVE
EIMPRRSTTYY	MYSTERY TRIP
EINNOOPPRTU	INOPPORTUNE
EINNOOQSSTU	NO QUESTIONS
EINNOOSSSUX	NOXIOUSNESS
EINNOPSSSSU	SUSPENSIONS
EINNORSSSUU	RUINOUSNESS
EINNOSSSSUU	SINUOUSNESS
EINOOPPRSSS	OPPRESSIONS
EINOOPRRSST	RESORPTIONS
EINOOPSSSSS	POSSESSIONS
EINOORSSSTU	RIOTOUSNESS
EINOPPRSSSU	SUPPRESSION
EINOPPRSTUW	PUTS IN POWER
EINOPSSTTTY	STENOTYPIST
EINOQRSTTUU	TOURNIQUETS
EINORSSTTUY	STRENUOSITY
EINPRSSSTTU	SUNSET STRIP
EIOOOPRSSTZ	SPOROZOITES
EIOOPPRRRST	PROPRIETORS
EIOOPRSSTTT	TRIES TO STOP

EIOPRRSSSUV	SUPERVISORS
EIOPRRSSUVY	SUPERVISORY
EIOPRSSTTTU	PROSTITUTES
EIORRRSTTWY	STORY WRITER
EIORRSSTTUU	TROUSER SUIT
EIORRTTTTWY	WITTY RETORT
EIOSSSSTTUU	SUSSES IT OUT
EKLLOOPSSWY	SPOKE SLOWLY
EKLNOOOSSST	TOOK LESSONS
EKLNOOPSTUY	OUTSPOKENLY
EKLNOORSTTY	LEON TROTSKY
EKLNOPRSTUY	TRULY SPOKEN
EKLOORRSTUW	WORKS TO RULE
	WORK-TO-RULES
ELLMNNOOSTY	SOMNOLENTLY
ELLMOOSSVWY	MOVES SLOWLY
ELLMORSTUUY	TREMULOUSLY
ELLNORSTUWY	TURNS YELLOW
ELLNORTTUUW	TURN OUT WELL
ELLOPPRTTYY	PRETTY POLLY
ELLOQRSUUUY	QUERULOUSLY
ELMMOPSSSTY	SYMPTOMLESS
ELMOPPPRRTY	PROMPT REPLY
ELNOOPPRTUY	OPPORTUNELY
ELNOPPRSTTU	LENT SUPPORT
ELNORSSTUUY	STRENUOUSLY
ELNORSTUUVY	VENTUROUSLY
ELNPPRRSTUU	TURNS PURPLE
ELNRRSTTTUU	TURNS TURTLE
ELOOPPRSSTU	SOLE SUPPORT
ELOPPPRSUWY	POWER SUPPLY
EMMOOPRSSTT	POSTMORTEMS
EMNOOORSSTU	MONOESTROUS
EMNOOPPSSSU	POMPOUSNESS
EMNOOPRSSTW	SPORTSWOMEN
EMOOOPRRSST	MOSS-TROOPER
EMOOORRSSTV	SERVOMOTORS
EMORRSTTUYY	MYSTERY TOUR
ENNNOOOOOST	NONE TOO SOON
ENNOORSTTTU	TURN TO STONE
ENOOOPPRSTU	TO NO PURPOSE
ENOORRUVWYY	YOUR VERY OWN
EOPPRRSSSSU	SUPPRESSORS
FFFGGHIINOT	FIGHTING OFF
FFFGGIILNNO	FLINGING OFF
FFFGHILLOTU	FULL OF FIGHT
FFFGILNOTUU	FLUFFING OUT
FFFHIJLOTUY	FIFTH OF JULY
FFFIOOOSTTW	SWIFT OF FOOT
FFFIOORRSTU	FIRST OF FOUR
FFGGHIIINTT	FIGHTING FIT
FFGGHIINORT	FIGHTING FOR
FFGGINNOOPS	SPONGING OFF
FFGHHIOSSTY	FIGHTS SHY OF
FFGHHOOSTUY	FOUGHT SHY OF
FFGHIIKNOSW	WHISKING OFF
FFGHIILRSTT	FIRST FLIGHT
FFGHIIORSTT	FIGHTS FOR IT
FFGHILLRTUY	FRIGHTFULLY
FFGHINOOOST	SHOOTING OFF
FFGHINOORTW	THROWING OFF
FFGHINORRUY	HURRYING OFF
FFGHINOSTTU	SHUTTING OFF
FFGHIOORTTU	FOUGHT FOR IT
FFGIIKNOPPS	SKIPPING OFF
FFGIIKNORST	STRIKING OFF
FFGIILNOPPS	SLIPPING OFF
FFGIINNNOPS	SPINNING OFF
FFGINNOSTUU	SNUFFING OUT
FFGINOOOPRT	TROOPING OFF
FFGINOOPPST	STOPPING OFF

FFGINOORTTT	TROTTING OFF
FFGIOPRSSUY	SYRUP OF FIGS
FFGNORSSTTU	STRONG STUFF
FFGOOOPRRUU	GROUP OF FOUR
FFHIIINRSST	FINISH FIRST
FFHILNOORSW	FISH NOR FOWL
FFHIOORRSTU	HITS FOR FOUR
FFHLOOORRTU	FOURTH FLOOR
FFIINOPSTTY	FIFTY POINTS
FFIIRRSSTTU	FIRST FRUITS
	FIRSTFRUITS
FFIJLORSTUY	FIRST OF JULY
FFNOOOOPRSU	ONUS OF PROOF
FGGHHIILNTT	NIGHT FLIGHT
FGGHHIINSTY	FIGHTING SHY
FGGHIIINNST	INFIGHTINGS
FGGHIILNNTY	NIGHT FLYING
FGGHIINORTV	GIVING FORTH
FGGIIKKNNOO	KING OF KINGS
FGGIILNNOTU	FLINGING OUT
FGGIILNORVY	FORGIVINGLY
FGGINNOOOOT	GOING ON FOOT
FGGNNOOOSSS	SONG OF SONGS
FGHHIILLPTU	UPHILL FIGHT
FGHHLOORTUW	FLOW THROUGH
FGHIIINNPSU	FINISHING UP
FGHIILLOPTW	PILLOW FIGHT
FGHIILNOPST	SHOPLIFTING
FGHIILNORSU	FLOURISHING
FGHIILNOSSS	GLOSS FINISH
FGHIINNRSSU	FURNISHINGS
FGHIIOSTTTU	FIGHTS IT OUT
FGHILNNORTY	FLYING NORTH
FGHILNORSTT	FRONT LIGHTS
FGHILNORTTY	FORTNIGHTLY
FGHILNOSTUU	FLUSHING OUT
FGHILNOSTUY	FLYING SOUTH
FGHILOOSSST	LOSS OF SIGHT
FGHILOOSSTT	LOST SIGHT OF
FGHILOPTTTU	PUT TO FLIGHT
FGHINOOSTTU	OUT OF THINGS
FGHINORRTTU	RING OF TRUTH
FGHINORSTTY	FORTY NIGHTS
FGHIOOTTTUU	FOUGHT IT OUT
FGIIILMNPSY	SIMPLIFYING
FGIIILNNORS	IRON FILINGS
FGIIILNOSSS	FOSSILISING
FGIIILNOSSZ	FOSSILIZING
FGIIILNSTVY	FLYING VISIT
FGIILLNNSUW	IN FULL SWING
FGIILNOOPRV	LIVING PROOF
FGIILNOPTUU	FOULING IT UP
FGIILNOTUZZ	FIZZLING OUT
FGIILNSTTUY	STULTIFYING
FGIIMNOORTT	FITTING ROOM
FGIINORRTTY	TRYING FOR IT
FGIINORSSTW	SWINGS FOR IT
FGIINRRSSTT	FIRST-STRING
FGIJNOORSSY	SINGS FOR JOY
FGILLNNOOOW	FOLLOWING ON
	FOLLOWING-ON
FGILLNOOPUW	FOLLOWING UP
FGILNNSTTUY	STUNT FLYING
FGILNOOOPRS	SLOPING ROOF
FGILNOORSUU	GLORIOUS FUN
FGIMNNOORRU	MOURNING FOR
FGINNORSTTU	TURNING SOFT
FGIOOPRRSST	GROSS PROFIT
FGIOORRSUUV	FRUGIVOROUS
FGLNOORSTUW	TWO FURLONGS
FHHIINOOPST	PHOTO FINISH

FHHIOPRSSTT	THRIFT SHOPS
FHHIORRSSTT	SHORT SHRIFT
FHIJLNNOTUY	NINTH OF JULY
FHIJLOSTUXY	SIXTH OF JULY
FHIKLLOOOOS	LOOK FOOLISH
FHIKOOSTTWY	TOT OF WHISKY
FHILLOOOPRS	FLOOR POLISH
FHILNOORSSU	FOOLS RUSH IN
FHIMOORTTUW	FROM WITHOUT
FHIORRTTTYY	FORTY THIRTY
	THIRTY FORTY
FHJOOORSTUY	SHOUT FOR JOY
FHKOOOORRSTW	SHORT OF WORK
FHKOOOORRSUW	HOURS OF WORK
FHMOOORTUUU	OUT OF HUMOUR
FIIILNORSTV	FIRST VIOLIN
FIIIMNNOOPR	FIRM OPINION
FIILLMNOORU	FOUR MILLION
FIIOOPPRRST	PROOF SPIRIT
FIIRTTTTTUU	TUTTI-FRUTTI
FIJKNOOOPRT	JOINT OF PORK
FIKLNOORSTU	NORFOLK SUIT
FILLOORSUVY	FRIVOLOUSLY
FILLOOSSTUW	FOLLOWS SUIT
FILMRSSTTUU	MISTRUSTFUL
FILNOOORTUU	RUN OUT OF OIL
FIMNNOORRTU	RUN INTO FORM
FIMOPRSSTUX	SIX OF TRUMPS
FINNOPRSTTU	PUTS IN FRONT
FINOOPSTTTU	PINT OF STOUT
FJJMOOPRSUY	JUMPS FOR JOY
FKKLOOOOORRW	LOOK FOR WORK
FLLOORRSUWY	SORROWFULLY
FLLOPPRSTUU	FULL SUPPORT
FLOOORSTTWX	SLOW FOXTROT
FMOOPRSTTUW	TWO OF TRUMPS
GGGHHIIINNS	SINGING HIGH
GGGHINNORUY	GOING HUNGRY
GGGIILMNNSU	SMUGGLING IN
GGGIILNORRW	GROWING GIRL
GGGIILNNPSUU	SNUGGLING UP
GGGINNOORST	GOING STRONG
GGHHIILNSTT	NIGHT-LIGHTS
GGHHIINNNRU	RUNNING HIGH
GGHHLOTTUUY	UGLY THOUGHT
GGHIIILNNTV	LIVING THING
GGHIIKKNNST	KINGS KNIGHT
GGHIILLNOPU	GOING UPHILL
GGHIILLNSTY	SLIGHTINGLY
GGHIILNORUV	LIVING ROUGH
GGHIILNOSST	LOSING SIGHT
GGHIIMNOSTV	MOVING SIGHT
GGHILNORSTT	STRONG LIGHT
GGHINOSSTUW	SHOWING GUTS
GGIIKLMNOOR	LOOKING GRIM
GGIIKLNORRW	WORKING GIRL
GGIILLNOSSY	SYLLOGISING
GGIILLNOSYZ	SYLLOGIZING
GGIILNNNNOS	LONG INNINGS
GGIILNNOSTU	SINGLING OUT
	SLINGING OUT
GGIILNNOSWW	SWINGING LOW
GGIINNNRSTU	UNSTRINGING
GGIINNOPSST	SIGNPOSTING
GGIINNORSTW	SONGWRITING
GGIINNORTUW	WRINGING OUT
GGIINNPPRSU	SPRINGING UP
GGIINNPRSTU	STRINGING UP
GGIKNOOORTW	GOING TO WORK
GGINNOOOTTW	GOING TO TOWN
GGINNOORSSU	ROUSING SONG
GGINNOPRSTU	SPORTING GUN
GHHHOORSTTU	SHOT THROUGH
GHHHOPRSTUU	PUSH THROUGH
GHHHORRSTUU	RUSH THROUGH
GHHIIINNOOP	HIGH OPINION
GHHIIINSTTW	WITHIN SIGHT
GHHIIIPRSST	HIGH SPIRITS
GHHIINNORSU	SHINING HOUR
GHHIINRSSTT	NIGHTSHIRTS
GHHIIPRSSTW	SHIPWRIGHTS
GHHIKMORSTU	SKIM THROUGH
GHHILOPRSTU	SLIP THROUGH
GHHINNNORTU	HUNTING HORN
GHHINOOOOPP	POOH-POOHING
GHHINOOTTTU	THOUGHT ON IT
GHHINORSTUW	WINS THROUGH
GHHINORTTUU	HIGH TURNOUT
GHHKLOOOORTU	LOOK THROUGH
GHHLLOPRTUU	PULL THROUGH
	PULLTHROUGH
GHHNORRSTUU	RUNS THROUGH
	RUN-THROUGHS
GHHOPRSTTUU	PUTS THROUGH
GHIIKMNRSS	SKIRMISHING
GHIIIKNNPSS	SINKING SHIP
GHIIINNNOTT	NOTHING IN IT
GHIIJNOSTWY	SING WITH JOY
GHIIKNNNPTU	HUNTING PINK
GHIIKNNOTTU	THINKING OUT
GHIILLLNRTY	THRILLINGLY
GHIILLMRSTW	MILLWRIGHTS
GHIILLNOPST	STILL HOPING
GHIILLNOSWW	SHOW WILLING
GHIILLOOPST	PHILOLOGIST
GHIILLPRTTY	TRIP LIGHTLY
GHIILNOPPSU	POLISHING UP
GHIILOOSSTT	HISTOLOGIST
GHIIMNNORST	THIS MORNING
GHIIMNNOSST	MISS NOTHING
GHIIMNORSTY	HOMINY GRITS
GHIINNNOSTW	WINNING SHOT
GHIINNNOTTU	THINNING OUT
GHIINNOOTTT	NOTHING TO IT
GHIINNOPSTY	HYPNOTISING
GHIINNOPTYZ	HYPNOTIZING
GHIINNORSTU	RUSHING INTO
GHIINOOTTTW	GOT ON WITH IT
GHIINOPPRSW	WORSHIPPING
GHIINOPSTWY	SHOWING PITY
GHIINORTTUW	OUTRIGHT WIN
	WIN OUTRIGHT
GHIIPRSSTTU	SITS UPRIGHT
GHIJLNNOSSY	GLYNIS JOHNS
GHIJMNOPSUW	SHOW JUMPING
	SHOWJUMPING
GHIJNOSTUWY	SUNG WITH JOY
GHIKLLOOTTY	TOOK LIGHTLY
GHIKLNOORTU	LOOKING HURT
GHIKNNNOOTW	KNOW NOTHING
GHIKOORRTTW	RIGHT TO WORK
GHILMOOSTTY	MYTHOLOGIST
GHILNNOOSTY	HOLYSTONING
GHILNOOOPST	PHONOLOGIST
GHILNOOORTY	ORNITHOLOGY
GHILOOSSTTT	LOST TO SIGHT
GHILOPRRSTY	SORRY PLIGHT
GHIMMNOORSU	MUSHROOMING
GHIMNOOPSYY	PHYSIOGNOMY
GHIMNORSTTY	STORMY NIGHT
GHIMOOOSSYZ	HOMOZYGOSIS
GHINNNOOSSW	SHOWN NO SIGN

GHINNOOSSSW	SHOWS NO SIGN
GHINNORRTTU	NO RIGHT TURN
GHINOOOSTTU	SHOOTING OUT
GHINOORRTUW	WROUGHT IRON
GHINOORSTUW	TOURING SHOW
GHINOORTTUW	THROWING OUT
	WON OUTRIGHT
GHINOOSTTUU	SHOUTING OUT
GHINOPSTTTU	SHOT-PUTTING
GHINORRTUUY	HURRYING OUT
GHINOSTTTUU	SHUTTING OUT
GHIOPRSTTTU	PUT TO RIGHTS
GHJLLNORUYY	JOLLY HUNGRY
GHLNOOPSSUW	SNOWPLOUGHS
GIIIILNNNSV	LIVING IN SIN
GIIIINNPRST	INSPIRITING
GIIIKLMNNSS	MISSING LINK
GIIIKLNORST	STRIKING OIL
GIIIKNNNPRT	PRINTING INK
GIIILLNNORT	ROLLING IN IT
GIIILLOSTUY	LITIGIOUSLY
GIIILNNQRUY	INQUIRINGLY
GIIIMNNOOSU	IGNOMINIOUS
GIIIMNNOPRS	IMPRISONING
GIIIMNNPRST	IMPRINTINGS
	MISPRINTING
GIIIMNOPRSV	IMPROVISING
GIIINNNNOPPT	PINPOINTING
GIIINNNPRSU	UNINSPIRING
GIIINNNRTTU	TURNING IT IN
GIIINNOOPST	POSITIONING
GIIINNSTTTU	INSTITUTING
GIIINOOPSTV	OVIPOSITING
GIIJMNNOPTU	JUMPING INTO
GIIJMNOPTTU	JUMPING TO IT
GIIKLNNOOOT	LOOKING INTO
GIIKLNNOTUW	WINKLING OUT
GIIKLNNPRSS	SPRINKLINGS
GIIKLNOOPTU	LOOKING IT UP
GIIKNOPPSTU	SKIPPING OUT
GIIKNORSTTU	STRIKING OUT
GIIILLLNNUWY	UNWILLINGLY
GIILLMNOOST	LIMNOLOGIST
GIILLMNPTUY	MULTIPLYING
GIILLNNSTUY	INSULTINGLY
GIILLOOOPST	OLIGOPOLIST
GIILMNOPRSY	PROMISINGLY
GIILNNPQTUU	QUINTUPLING
GIILNNQSTUY	SQUINTINGLY
GIILNNTTUWY	UNWITTINGLY
GIILNOOSSST	SINOLOGISTS
GIILNOPPSTU	SLIPPING OUT
GIILNPPSTTU	SPLITTING UP
GIILOORSSTV	VIROLOGISTS
GIIMNNOPRSU	UNPROMISING
GIIMNNOPRTU	IMPORTUNING
GIIMNNORSTU	MORNING SUIT
GIIMNOORSTT	SITTING ROOM
GIIMNOSSSTY	MISOGYNISTS
GIIMNRSSTTU	MISTRUSTING
GIIMOORRRST	RIGOR MORTIS
GIINNNNORTU	RUNNING INTO
GIINNNOOPRS	SPRING ONION
GIINNNOPPST	SPINNING TOP
GIINNNOPSTU	SPINNING OUT
GIINNNOPSTW	WINNING POST
GIINNNORRTU	RUNNING RIOT
GIINNNORTTU	TURNING INTO
	TURNING IT ON
GIINNOOPTTU	OUTPOINTING
	POINTING OUT

GIINNPRTTUU	TURNING IT UP
GIINOPRRSUU	PRURIGINOUS
GIINOPSTTTU	SPITTING OUT
GIINORTTTUY	TRYING IT OUT
GIINRTTTTYY	NITTY GRITTY
	NITTY-GRITTY
GIJMNNNPRUU	RUNNING JUMP
GIKKLNNOOOW	KNOWING LOOK
GIKLMNNOOOS	KING SOLOMON
GIKLMOOORTU	GRIM OUTLOOK
GIKLNNNOUWY	UNKNOWINGLY
GIKLNNOOOPU	LOOKING UPON
GIKLNOOOPTU	LOOKING UP TO
GIKLNOOPRSY	LOOKING SPRY
GIKLNOOPRVY	PROVOKINGLY
GIKMMNOOORS	SMOKING ROOM
GIKMNOOPSST	STOP SMOKING
GIKNNNNORTU	RUNNING KNOT
GIKNOOPRSTW	STOP WORKING
GIKNOORSTUW	WORKS OUTING
GILLNOSTUUY	GLUTINOUSLY
GILLNPRSSTU	PULL STRINGS
GILMNOOOSTU	MONOLOGUIST
GILNNNOPSSU	NONPLUSSING
GILOOOPSSTT	TOPOLOGISTS
GILOOPSSTTY	TYPOLOGISTS
GIMMNNOOORR	MORNING ROOM
GIMMNNOPSUU	SUMMONING UP
GIMNNNORSTUU	SURMOUNTING
GIMNOORSTVY	MOVING STORY
GINNNOPRTUU	TURNING UPON
GINNOOPRSTT	STRONG POINT
	STRONGPOINT
GINNORRSTUU	TURNING SOUR
GINOOOPRTTU	TROOPING OUT
GINOOPPSTTU	STOPPING OUT
GINOOPRSTUU	OUTPOURINGS
GINOORTTTTU	TROTTING OUT
GKOOOORTTUW	GO OUT TO WORK
HHIIIKRSSWY	IRISH WHISKY
HHIJNNORSTU	SIR JOHN HUNT
HHINOORSTUW	WITH HONOURS
HHLLOORTTUW	HOLLOW TRUTH
HHLMOPRSTYY	POLYRHYTHMS
HHMNOOOOPSU	HOMOPHONOUS
HHOOOPPRSSU	PHOSPHOROUS
HHOPPSSSTUU	SHUTS UP SHOP
HIIKLORSTTY	THIRTY KILOS
HIIKNOSTTTU	THINKS IT OUT
HIILMNNOOPY	HYPOLIMNION
HIILNORTTYY	HOLY TRINITY
HIILOPPSSTW	PISTOL WHIPS
HIIMMOOPRSS	ISOMORPHISM
HIIMMOPRRST	TRIMORPHISM
HIIMNOOPRST	MONITORSHIP
HIINOPRSSTW	SHOWN SPIRIT
HIIOPRSSSTW	SHOWS SPIRIT
HIIOPTTTUWY	WITHOUT PITY
HIJJMOPTUWY	JUMP WITH JOY
HIKLLOOOSTT	SHOOT TO KILL
HIKNOOPSTTT	STOP TO THINK
HIKORRSTTWY	THIRSTY WORK
HILNOOORSTZ	LOST HORIZON
HILNOOPSTXY	XYLOPHONIST
HILNOORSTSU	HONOURS LIST
HILOOSSTTUW	WITHOUT LOSS
HIMNOPSSSTY	SYMPHONISTS
HIMOOOPRSSU	ISOMORPHOUS
HINNOOPSTWY	SHOWN NO PITY
HINNOORSSUW	WINS HONOURS
HINOOPPRSSS	SPONSORSHIP

HINOOPSSTWY	SHOWS NO PITY
HIOOOSSTTTU	SHOOTS IT OUT
HIOOPRRSUWY	YOUR WORSHIP
HIOPRRSSSTT	SPORTS SHIRT
HKOOOPRSTTU	TOOK UP SHORT
HLLOPPRSTUU	PULL UP SHORT
HLMNOORSTUY	RUN SMOOTHLY
HLOPPRSSTUY	SHORT SUPPLY
HMNNOOPTTYY	MONTY PYTHON
HNNOOOPSSTW	NON-STOP SHOW
HOOOPPRRTTY	PROTOTROPHY
HORRSTTTUWY	TRUSTWORTHY
IIIILMNNQSU	INQUILINISM
IIIIMMPRSTV	PRIMITIVISM
IIIIMPRSTTV	PRIMITIVIST
IIIIMPRTTVY	PRIMITIVITY
IIIINNOQSTU	INQUISITION
IIILLMNOPST	POINTILLISM
IIILLNOPSTT	POINTILLIST
IIILLNOSSTT	TONSILLITIS
IIILLNOSSTU	ILLUSIONIST
IIILNNOQSUU	INQUILINOUS
IIIMNNNOOPY	IN MY OPINION
IIIMNOOPSST	IMPOSITIONS
IIINNOSTTTU	INSTITUTION
IIINOOOOPSTV	OVIPOSITION
IIINOQRSSTU	INQUISITORS
IIJLNORSUUY	INJURIOUSLY
IIJMNNORRUY	MINOR INJURY
IIKLNOOOSTT	LOOKS INTO IT
IILLNNOOOPP	OPINION POLL
IILLNNOOSSU	NO ILLUSIONS
IILLOOQSSTU	SOLILOQUIST
IILLORSSTUU	ILLUSTRIOUS
IILNNOOSTUV	INVOLUTIONS
IILNOOOPSTW	LOW POSITION
IILNOPSSTTW	SPLITS IN TWO
IIMNOOPRSTU	POSITRONIUM
IIMNOPRTTUY	IMPORTUNITY
IINNNOOPSTW	WIN ON POINTS
IINNOOOOOPPR	POOR OPINION
IINNOOOPRUY	YOUR OPINION
IINNOPPRSTU	PUT IN PRISON
IINNOPRSSTU	PUTS IN IRONS
IINOOOOPPRST	PROPOSITION
IINOOOOPPSST	OPPOSITIONS
IINOOOPPSSTU	SUPPOSITION
IINOPPQRTUY	PROPINQUITY
IIOOOPRSSTV	OVIPOSITORS
IKKNOOOORSST	TOOK NO RISKS
IKLLOOOSTTT	TOOK ITS TOLL
IKLLOOPPSSY	LOOKS SLIPPY
IKORSSSTTTY	TROTSKYISTS
ILLORSUUUXY	LUXURIOUSLY
ILMNOOOPSST	MONOPOLISTS
ILMNOPRSSUU	PLUS OR MINUS
ILNNNOOSSTY	SONNY LISTON
ILNOOOPSSUY	POISONOUSLY
ILNOOOORSTUY	NOTORIOUSLY
ILNOOPPRSSU	PROPULSIONS
ILOOPPRSSST	SPOILSPORTS
IMNOOPPRSTU	OPPORTUNISM
IMNOORSSTTY	MONSTROSITY
IMNOPRSSTUX	SIX NO-TRUMPS
IMPPPRRSTUU	STIRRUP PUMP
INNNOOOPSTW	WON ON POINTS
INOOOOPPRRST	PROPORTIONS
INOOOOPRSTTU	PORTIONS OUT
INOOPPRSTTU	OPPORTUNIST
INOOPPRTTUY	OPPORTUNITY
IOOPPRSSTUY	SUPPOSITORY

KLOOOOOOPRTU	POOR OUTLOOK
KNOOOORSTTTU	TOOK ON TRUST
LMMORRSUUUY	MURMUROUSLY
LMNOORSSTUY	MONSTROUSLY
LMOPSSTUUUY	SUMPTUOUSLY
MNOOPRSTTUW	TWO NO-TRUMPS
MOOOPRRSSTT	STORM TROOPS

AAAAAALMRSTT	TARAMASALATA	AAAAGILMMNOT	AMALGAMATION
AAAAABBNRRST	SANTA BARBARA	AAAAGLNOWWYY	A LONG WAY AWAY
AAAAACDKLLNS	ALAS AND ALACK	AAAAHHIKLMRS	RAS AL-KHAIMAH
AAAAAGKLRSSY	AS GAY AS A LARK	AAAAHKLPPRSY	HAPPY AS A LARK
AAAABBINRSST	SABBATARIANS	AAAAILLPRRSS	SARSAPARILLA
AAAABBJMORRR	MAJOR BARBARA	AAAAILNRSSTU	AUSTRALASIAN
AAAABCCHILNN	BACCHANALIAN	AAAALLNNRSUY	ANNUAL SALARY
AAAABCEILRTU	ACETABULARIA	AAABBCCEGHPT	CABBAGE PATCH
AAAABCEKRSST	ACTS AS A BRAKE	AAABBCEEINRS	CARIBBEAN SEA
AAAABDEGIMNR	MADE A BARGAIN	AAABBCEGIRRY	BABY CARRIAGE
AAAABEGIKMNR	MAKE A BARGAIN	AAABBCILLRRY	DABDARICALLY
AAAABEGILNRS	SEAL A BARGAIN	AAABBCKLNRSY	BARCLAYS BANK
AAAACCCCIRTU	ACCIACCATURA	AAABBCORRSTY	BARBARY COAST
AAAACCEHNVVY	HAVE A VACANCY	AAABBEELLMST	BASEBALL TEAM
AAAACCHRRTTT	CATCH A TARTAR	AAABBEESSSUY	AS BUSY AS A BEE
AAAACDDEMRWY	ACADEMY AWARD	AAABBEGHINNT	THE BIG BANANA
AAAACDELMMRT	MARMALADE CAT	AAABBEHIKRST	BREAKS A HABIT
AAAACDELMNVY	NAVAL ACADEMY	AAABBIIMNRRS	BARBARIANISM
AAAACDELRSSY	AS CLEAR AS DAY	AAABCCCEHRST	CATCHES A CRAB
AAAAODIILPRO	PARADISAICAL	AAABCCDEHRRT	BAD CHARACTER
AAAACEFRSTWY	CAST AWAY FEAR	AAABCCEHLLST	CATCHES A BALL
AAAACEGKSTTV	SAVAGE ATTACK	AAABCCGILNNT	BALANCING ACT
AAAACEGLNSTW	SAW AT A GLANCE	AAABCCHHRRUZ	CHURCH BAZAAR
AAAACEHLNTTV	NAVAL ATTACHE	AAABCDEHLNPS	CAPABLE HANDS
AAAACEINRRSV	CARAVANSERAI	AAABCDEHNOTY	DAYTONA BEACH
AAAACENNRRTV	RENT A CARAVAN	AAABCDEIRSTT	ABSTRACT IDEA
AAAACGILPSSS	PASSACAGLIAS	AAABCDHHIPTT	HIT A BAD PATCH
AAAACGIMMNRT	ANAGRAMMATIC	AAABCDHILLNN	BALL AND CHAIN
AAAACHKPRSST	SHARP AS A TACK	AAABCDKLNNST	BLACK AND TANS
AAAACIMNRSST	ANTIMACASSAR	AAABCEEILSTV	ABLATIVE CASE
AAAADDEGMRSW	AWARD DAMAGES	AAABCEELLLRS	CLEAR AS A BELL
AAAADDFHLNRY	YARD AND A HALF	AAABCEGKPSSS	BACK PASSAGES
AAAADEEGMTWY	MADE A GETAWAY	AAABCEHILLPT	ALPHABETICAL
AAAADEEGNRRT	ARRANGE A DATE	AAABCEHKSTTT	SAT AT THE BACK
AAAADEELRTTT	AT A LATER DATE	AAABCEHLOPPR	APPROACHABLE
AAAADEFHLNRY	YEAR AND A HALF	AAABCEILLNRT	TRIAL BALANCE
AAAADEFMPSUX	MADE A FAUX PAS	AAABCEILLPSS	BLAISE PASCAL
AAAADEGLMNNR	AN ARM AND A LEG	AAABCEILLRWY	CABLE RAILWAY
AAAADEHMRSTT	MAD AS A HATTER	AAABCEKLRTTV	VERBAL ATTACK
AAAADHLLRSTZ	AT ALL HAZARDS	AAABCELLLNRU	LAUREN BACALL
AAAADILNOPTT	ADAPTATIONAL	AAABCELMMNNU	AMBULANCE MAN
AAAADLNRRSWY	DRAWN A SALARY	AAABCELNRRTU	TABERNACULAR
AAAADLRRSSWY	DRAWS A SALARY	AAABCGIINNRT	CANTABRIGIAN
AAAAEEGKMTWY	MAKE A GETAWAY	AAABCIKKLNSS	AS BLACK AS INK
AAAAEEKLMNPP	MAKE AN APPEAL	AAABCLLORSUU	CASUAL LABOUR
AAAAEEFFILSST	AS FIT AS A FLEA	AAABDDDEGLMY	BADLY DAMAGED
AAAAEFGIPRWY	PAY A FAIR WAGE	AAABDDEINSST	AIDS AND ABETS
AAAAEFKMPSUX	MAKE A FAUX PAS	AAABDDGHHINT	HAD A BAD NIGHT
AAAAEFLNRRVW	NAVAL WARFARE	AAABDDJNNORY	DARBY AND JOAN
AAAAEGNRTVXZ	EXTRAVAGANZA	AAABDDLMNNST	DAMN AND BLAST!
AAAAEHHNNTWY	ANNE HATHAWAY	AAABDEEGMNST	GETS A BAD NAME
AAAAEHILMSST	THALASSAEMIA	AAABDEEHHRRT	HAD A BREATHER
AAAAEIKNNNNR	ANNA KARENINA	AAABDEEHIMTV	HAVE A BAD TIME
AAAAEIMMNRRT	ARMAMENTARIA	AAABDEFHKRST	HAD BREAKFAST
AAAAEINNPSST	AS NEAT AS A PIN	AAABDEFILLMN	FABLED ANIMAL
AAAAEKMPSSST	MAKES A PASS AT	AAABDEHKNSTU	TAKE A HUSBAND
AAAAENORSTWY	RAN AWAY TO SEA	AAABDEILLRTZ	BLAZED A TRAIL
AAAAFGILLNRS	NIAGARA FALLS	AAABDEILMRST	DRAMATISABLE
AAAAFINRRSST	RASTAFARIANS	AAABDEILMRTZ	DRAMATIZABLE
AAAAFIRRSSTY	YASSIR ARAFAT	AAABDEILORRTV	TRAVEL ABROAD
AAAAGGILMMNT	AMALGAMATING	AAABDEMMORVY	MADAME BOVARY
AAAAGHHNRSUV	SARAH VAUGHAN	AAABDEMRSSSS	AMBASSADRESS
AAAAGHINSTTY	SAY THAT AGAIN	AAABDENORSSY	AS DRY AS A BONE

AAABDFHRSSTU	DAFT AS A BRUSH
AAABDGHHINST	HAS A BAD NIGHT
AAABDGHMNRSS	SMASH AND GRAB
	SMASH-AND-GRAB
AAABDIILPTTY	ADAPTABILITY
AAABDILLOOPR	PARABOLOIDAL
AAABDNRRSSST	STARS AND BARS
AAABEEEGORVV	ABOVE AVERAGE
AAABEEEERRTTT	BEAT A RETREAT
AAABEEGHINRT	BREATHE AGAIN
AAABEEGIKNTT	TAKE A BEATING
AAABEEGILMRR	MARRIAGEABLE
AAABEEGILRRV	VARIABLE GEAR
AAABEEGLMNNU	UNMANAGEABLE
AAABEEGORTUV	ABOUT AVERAGE
AAABEEHHRRST	HAS A BREATHER
AAABEEILRRTV	VARIABLE RATE
AAABEEIMRRST	ARAB EMIRATES
AAABEELLRTUV	RATABLE VALUE
AAABEELOPRTV	EVAPORATABLE
AAABEFHKRSST	HAS BREAKFAST
AAABEGHINPTT	BEATING A PATH
AAABEGIKKMNR	MAKING A BREAK
AAABEGIKNRWY	BREAKING AWAY
AAABEGKOOPSS	BOOK A PASSAGE
AAABEHIKPPPT	PHI BETA KAPPA
AAABEHNNOPTT	THE TOP BANANA
AAABEIILMNNT	MAINTAINABLE
AAABEILLMNOT	BALLETOMANIA
AAABEILLNOTV	NOT AVAILABLE
AAABEILLNSSU	UNASSAILABLE
AAABEILLRSTZ	BLAZES A TRAIL
AAABEILNNTTU	UNATTAINABLE
AAABEILNORRT	ABERRATIONAL
AAABEILNORSV	BRAVE AS A LION
AAABEILSTTTW	WAITS AT TABLE
AAABEINNSSST	SAN SEBASTIAN
AAABEKLNRRTU	NATURAL BREAK
AAABEKLNRTUW	BREAK A WALNUT
AAABELLLPRRS	PARALLEL BARS
AAABELLNRSTT	TRANSLATABLE
AAABELNOOPTY	PALAEOBOTANY
AAABEOOSTTTT	BEATS A TATTOO
AAABFILMRRSS	FRIARS BALSAM
AAABGGILMNWY	GAMBLING AWAY
AAABGHILNPTZ	BLAZING A PATH
AAABGLLMRRRU	BURGLAR ALARM
AAABHIILLRTU	HABITUAL LIAR
AAABIILLTVY	AVAILABILITY
AAABIILLPTTY	PALATABILITY
AAABIKLNNNOT	NATIONAL BANK
AAABILLNSSUY	UNASSAILABLY
AAABILMRRUWY	BURMA RAILWAY
AAABLLMNORUU	MANUAL LABOUR
AAACCDDEIMNR	CANDID CAMERA
AAACCDEHINPR	HANDICAP RACE
AAACCDEHNNST	STAND A CHANCE
AAACCDEHRSTT	CHEAT AT CARDS
AAACCDEIIMNS	ACADEMICIANS
AAACCDEILLMY	ACADEMICALLY
AAACCDFFNNTY	FACT AND FANCY
AAACCDHINOPR	COACH AND PAIR
AAACCDHNRRSY	CASH AND CARRY
	CASH-AND-CARRY
AAACCEEHKNNT	TAKEN A CHANCE
AAACCEEHKNST	TAKES A CHANCE
AAACCEGLLNSU	CASUAL GLANCE
AAACCEGLNSST	CASTS A GLANCE
AAACCEIINPTT	INCAPACITATE
AAACCEINNQTU	ACQUAINTANCE
AAACCFILLNVY	FILL A VACANCY
AAACCGHIKNRV	HAVING A CRACK
AAACCGHIKNTT	TAKING A CATCH
AAACCGILNOOS	GALA OCCASION
AAACCHILLNRY	ANARCHICALLY
AAACCHILNPTY	ANAPHYLACTIC
AAACCILLRSST	CLASSICAL ART
AAACCILMNOST	ACCLAMATIONS
AAACCILORSTU	ACCUSATORIAL
AAACCKLNRTUW	CRACK A WALNUT
AAACDDDEEINV	ADVANCED IDEA
AAACDDDEINRW	DID A WAR-DANCE
AAACDDEEGMSU	CAUSED DAMAGE
AAACDDEEMNSV	MADE ADVANCES
AAACDDEGILNR	DEALING A CARD
AAACDDEGNNOT	DANCED A TANGO
AAACDDEGNRUV	ADVANCE GUARD
AAACDDEILLTY	CALLED IT A DAY
AAACDDEILNSV	ALADDINS CAVE
AAACDDELNTWZ	DANCED A WALTZ
AAACDDHNRTWW	WATCH AND WARD
AAACDEEFHPRY	CHEAP-DAY FARE
AAACDEEGILNN	LEADING AN ACE
AAACDEEGLLRW	EDGAR WALLACE
AAACDEEGMSSU	CAUSES DAMAGE
AAACDEEGNSTT	ACTED AS AGENT
AAACDEEKMNSV	MAKE ADVANCES
AAACDEELLPSY	PLAYED A SCALE
AAACDEELNRRY	CALENDAR YEAR
AAACDEERSSWY	CARAWAY SEEDS
AAACDEGHMMNT	GAME AND MATCH
AAACDEGIIPRR	CARRIAGE PAID
AAACDEGIKMWY	MAGICKED AWAY
AAACDEGILMMS	CLAIM DAMAGES
AAACDEGILMRS	SCALE DIAGRAM
AAACDEGINNRW	DRAWING AN ACE
AAACDEGNNOST	DANCES A TANGO
AAACDEHILRRT	RACIAL HATRED
AAACDEHILSTY	SAILED A YACHT
AAACDEHNSTWY	SNATCHED AWAY
AAACDEIKLMST	STAKED A CLAIM
AAACDEILMRRW	CLAIM A REWARD
AAACDEINNPVY	PAY IN ADVANCE
AAACDEINOTVX	TAX AVOIDANCE
AAACDEINRSTT	TRADESCANTIA
AAACDELLRUWY	AWAY DULL CARE!
AAACDELMORYY	ROYAL ACADEMY
AAACDELMRSSU	AS CLEAR AS MUD
AAACDELNSTWZ	DANCES A WALTZ
AAACDENPRTVY	ADVANCE PARTY
AAACDEPPRSSS	SCRAPED A PASS
AAACDFIIILNN	FINANCIAL AID
AAACDGIIMMNS	MACADAMISING
AAACDGIIMMNZ	MACADAMIZING
AAACDGIIMMRT	DIAGRAMMATIC
AAACDGIIMPRT	PARADIGMATIC
AAACDGIKOSSS	AS SICK AS A DOG
AAACDGILNPRY	PLAYING A CARD
AAACDHILNRST	CARDINALS HAT
AAACDHNPRTWY	WATCH AND PRAY
AAACDHOOPPRR	APPROACH ROAD
AAACDHOSSSTW	CASTS A SHADOW
AAACDIILOPRT	CAPITAL RADIO
AAACDIINNNSV	SCANDINAVIAN
AAACDILLMRTY	DRAMATICALLY
AAACDILMPRTY	DRAMATIC PLAY
AAACDLMMNNOV	NAVAL COMMAND
AAACDLRSTUWY	CASUALTY WARD
AAACEEEGLLVY	LEAVE A LEGACY
AAACEEEGLNST	SEE AT A GLANCE
AAACEEEKMNPS	MAKE AN ESCAPE
AAACEEELPSSV	LEAVES A SPACE

AAACEEEPPRRS	PREPARE A CASE	AAACGINRRWYY	CARRYING AWAY
AAACEEFLMNSS	MALFEASANCES	AAACHIIKPPRT	APPARATCHIKI
AAACEEGHKMNS	MAKES A CHANGE	AAACHIIMNSTY	MAHAYANISTIC
AAACEEGLNTWY	GET CLEAN AWAY	AAACHIKPPRST	APPARATCHIKS
AAACEEGLPRSS	CLEAR PASSAGE	AAACHILMNPRY	ARMY CHAPLAIN
AAACEEGLRTWY	GET CLEAR AWAY	AAACHILMNRST	CHARLATANISM
AAACEEGNRTVX	EXTRAVAGANCE	AAACHIPPRRST	PARAPHRASTIC
AAACEEINNPPR	IN APPEARANCE	AAACHLLLOSTT	CALLS TO A HALT
AAACEEKKKMPST	MAKES A PACKET	AAACHLMNRRTU	NATURAL CHARM
AAACEEKMOSTU	MAKE OUT A CASE	AAACIILNNOST	CANALISATION
AAACEEKNPSTU	TAKEN UP A CASE	AAACIILNNOTZ	CANALIZATION
AAACEEKPSSTU	TAKES UP A CASE	AAACIILNNRRT	INTRACRANIAL
AAACEERRSTTU	SAUCE TARTARE	AAACILLLNTYY	ANALYTICALLY
	TARTARE SAUCE	AAACILLMNOTY	ANATOMICALLY
AAACEFFIILMR	FAMILIAR FACE	AAACILLMORTY	AROMATICALLY
AAACEFGILMNR	AMERICAN FLAG	AAACILMNOPRY	PYROMANIACAL
AAACEFIMMOPR	MAP OF AMERICA	AAACILNNRSST	LANCASTRIANS
AAACEFLRRSSW	CLASS WARFARE	AAACILNPQTTU	AQUATIC PLANT
AAACEGHHLTUW	CAUGHT A WHALE	AAACIMNNOTTU	CAT-A-MOUNTAIN
AAACEGHLNPTU	CAUGHT A PLANE	AAACINNNRSTY	NANCY SINATRA
AAACEGIKMNRZ	MAGAZINE RACK	AAACLMMOPSTY	MYCOPLASMATA
AAACEGILMMNO	MEGALOMANIAC	AAADDDEFFMST	MADE A DEAD SET
AAACEGILNNPY	PLAYING AN ACE	AAADDDEFHILY	HAD A FIELD DAY
AAACEGILNNWY	CLEANING AWAY	AAADDDEGOOSS	AS GOOD AS DEAD
AAACEGILNRWY	CLEARING AWAY	AAADDDHHNNOST	DO A HANDSTAND
AAACEGIMNPRT	PARAMAGNETIC	AAADDEEEHKTW	AWAKE THE DEAD
AAACEGINRSTT	REACT AGAINST	AAADDEEEKMST	MAKE A DEAD SET
AAACEGINSSTT	STATING A CASE	AAADDEEGGLNU	DEAD LANGUAGE
AAACEGIRRSWY	CARRIAGEWAYS	AAADDEEGINRW	EDWARDIAN AGE
AAACEGLMNOWY	CAME A LONG WAY	AAADDEEHLNNP	PLANNED AHEAD
AAACEGLNOTWY	GOT CLEAN AWAY	AAADDEEINRRW	EDWARDIAN ERA
AAACEGLORTWY	GOT CLEAR AWAY	AAADDEENRWWY	WANDERED AWAY
AAACEGMNORRT	ACTOR MANAGER	AAADDEFHILSY	HAS A FIELD DAY
AAACEHHIRTUV	HAVE A HAIRCUT	AAADDEFIMOTY	MADE A DAY OF IT
AAACEHIILNTT	TEACH ITALIAN	AAADDEGINSTV	DISADVANTAGE
AAACEHILMMTT	MATHEMATICAL	AAADDENRRSTT	STANDARD RATE
AAACEHILPRST	SHARE CAPITAL	AAADDENRSSTT	SET A STANDARD
AAACEHIPRRTT	PATRIARCHATE	AAADDFHHILMN	HAD HALF A MIND
AAACEHLMRSST	STEALS A MARCH	AAADDFHLLOOO	ALL OF A DOODAH
AAACEHMNORRT	MARATHON RACE	AAADDFLLORSW	WALDORF SALAD
AAACEHNSSTWY	SNATCHES AWAY	AAADDHHIKLMNS	MILK AND A DASH
AAACEIILMNRT	LATIN AMERICA	AAADDIIMNORT	DIAMOND TIARA
AAACEIIOPRRT	OPERATIC ARIA	AAADDILLMNPS	ALADDINS LAMP
AAACEIJLMNTY	CALAMITY JANE	AAADDILLORSV	SALVADOR DALI
AAACEIKLMPST	MAKES CAPITAL	AAADDKQRSUWW	AWKWARD SQUAD
AAACEIKLMSST	STAKES A CLAIM	AAADDLMNPRST	STANDARD LAMP
AAACEILMNNPR	AMERICAN PLAN	AAADEEEPPRRST	EASTER PARADE
AAACEILMOOST	OSTEOMALACIA	AAADEEERRTTW	AERATED WATER
AAACEILMPRRT	PARAMETRICAL	AAADEEFGILLY	LEAD A GAY LIFE
AAACEILNORTU	AERONAUTICAL	AAADEEFILSST	FATAL DISEASE
AAACEINNRTTW	WIN AT A CANTER	AAADEEFNRRTU	TURN A DEAF EAR
AAACEINOPSTT	CAPTAIN OATES	AAADEEGGMNST	STAGE-MANAGED
AAACEKLMRRSU	CASUAL REMARK	AAADEEGHILNP	LEAPING AHEAD
AAACEKNOPSST	TOSS A PANCAKE	AAADEEGHOORV	HAVE A GOOD EAR
AAACEMORRTTU	AMATEUR ACTOR	AAADEEGIKNRT	TAKE A READING
AAACEPPRSSSS	SCRAPES A PASS	AAADEEHKMSWY	MAKES HEADWAY
AAACFFILLORS	LOCAL AFFAIRS	AAADEEHMMRWY	HAMMERED AWAY
AAACFKLNOPTT	PLAN OF ATTACK	AAADEEHRRSST	SAHARA DESERT
AAACGGIILLNN	CALLING AGAIN	AAADEEIKMMST	MADE A MISTAKE
AAACGGILLNOY	ANAGOGICALLY	AAADEEIKMNSS	MAKES AN ASIDE
AAACGHIKNNSV	HAVING A SNACK	AAADEEIKRSTT	TAKE IT AS READ
AAACGHILLLNT	CALLING A HALT	AAADEEIRRSST	DISASTER AREA
AAACGHIMNRWY	MARCHING AWAY	AAADEELNRRST	LEARNS A TRADE
AAACGHINRTTU	CAUGHT A TRAIN	AAADEELNRRTT	LEARNT A TRADE
AAACGIIKLMMN	MAKING A CLAIM	AAADEENSSSTT	STANDS AT EASE
AAACGIILLNTX	CALLING A TAXI	AAADEEPRRRSW	REAPS A REWARD
AAACGIILNPST	CAPITAL GAINS	AAADEERSTTVX	EXTRAVASATED
AAACGIIMNSTT	ANASTIGMATIC	AAADEFFHILNV	FIVE AND A HALF
AAACGIKLNSST	TAKING A CLASS	AAADEFFHLLOR	HEAD FOR A FALL
AAACGILLLNOY	ANALOGICALLY	AAADEFFKNOTY	TAKEN A DAY OFF
AAACGILLLNVY	GALVANICALLY	AAADEFFKOSTY	TAKES A DAY OFF

AAADEFFNNORS	FANFARONADES
AAADEFGOOSST	GOOD AS A FEAST
AAADEFHILMNT	TIME AND A HALF
AAADEFHILNNN	NINE AND A HALF
AAADEFIKMOTY	MAKE A DAY OF IT
AAADEFKLNORT	TANKARD OF ALE
AAADEFKORSUV	ASKED A FAVOUR
AAADEGHIINNV	HAVING AN IDEA
AAADEGHILRSU	RAISED A LAUGH
AAADEGHIMNRV	HAVING A DREAM
AAADEGHINSTY	STAYING AHEAD
AAADEGHRSSUZ	HAZARD A GUESS
AAADEGIIMNNR	MAIN DRAINAGE
AAADEGIIMNNT	TIME AND AGAIN
AAADEGIKNRST	TAKING AS READ
AAADEGILRSSS	RAISED A GLASS
AAADEGIMQRSU	QUADRAGESIMA
AAADEGINRSTT	STARTED AGAIN
AAADEGLNNORR	RONALD REAGAN
AAADEGNOSTUV	ADVANTAGEOUS
AAADEHIKLOTY	TAKE A HOLIDAY
AAADEHLNRTTU	NATURAL DEATH
AAADEHNORRTT	EAR AND THROAT
AAADEHNRRTTW	DEATH WARRANT
AAADEIILRTTW	AWAITED TRIAL
AAADEILMNNRS	SALAMANDRINE
AAADEILNPPTY	PAID A PENALTY
AAADEILORRRT	ARTERIAL ROAD
AAADEINSSSST	ASSASSINATED
AAADEKLNPPRY	PLAYED A PRANK
AAADEKNPSTTU	TAKE UP A STAND
AAADELLPTWYZ	PLAYED A WALTZ
AAADELMNRRUX	ANDRE MALRAUX
AAADEMNNSSWY	WAYS AND MEANS
AAADENOPRSTW	SOAP AND WATER
AAADFFHHLLNS	HALF-AND-HALFS
AAADFFHLNORU	FOUR AND A HALF
AAADFHHILMNS	HAS HALF A MIND
AAADFHLNSTTT	AND THATS FLAT!
AAADFINORRYY	FOR A RAINY DAY
AAADFLOPRRWY	PLAY FOR A DRAW
AAADGGINRSTU	GUARD AGAINST
AAADGHIINNRS	RAISING A HAND
AAADGHILLNVY	HAVING ALL DAY
AAADGHNSSSTT	STANDS AGHAST
AAADGIIKMNTY	MAKING IT A DAY
AAADGIILLORT	GLADIATORIAL
AAADGIINNRWY	DRAINING AWAY
AAADGIKMNNST	MAKING A STAND
AAADGIKNNSTT	TAKING A STAND
AAADGILLMNNR	MARGINAL LAND
AAADGIMNRSTV	AVANT-GARDISM
AAADGINNSSTT	STAND AGAINST
AAADGINNSTWY	STANDING AWAY
AAADGINPRRTW	DRAWING APART
AAADGINRSTTV	AVANT-GARDIST
AAADGLMNNOYY	MANY A LONG DAY
AAADGLNQRRUU	QUADRANGULAR
AAADHILLNRSW	HADRIANS WALL
AAADIILLMNPS	PALLADIANISM
AAADIILLNOTT	DILATATIONAL
AAADIILNORRS	RADIOLARIANS
AAADILLNSSTY	ALL SAINTS DAY
AAADILNRSSSU	RUSSIAN SALAD
AAADINORRSTT	RADAR STATION
AAADLNNPPRUW	DRAWN UP A PLAN
AAADLNPPRSUW	DRAWS UP A PLAN
AAADLRSSTTUY	LAST SATURDAY
AAAEEEHLPRSV	HAVE A RELAPSE
AAAEEEELMPPRR	PREPARE A MEAL
AAAEEFRSSSTU	AS SURE AS FATE
AAAEEGGINNRW	EARNING A WAGE
AAAEEGGLMNTU	METALANGUAGE
AAAEEGGMNRST	STAGE MANAGER
AAAEEGGMNSST	STAGE-MANAGES
AAAEEGHIKSTV	GAVE IT A SHAKE
AAAEEGIMNNNR	EARNING A NAME
AAAEEGIMRRRT	MARRIAGE RATE
AAAEEGINNRSX	SEXAGENARIAN
AAAEEGLMNRSS	SALES MANAGER
AAAEEGMNNPRT	PERMANGANATE
AAAEEGMRSTTU	AMATEUR STAGE
AAAEEHHRTTVY	HEAVY AT HEART
AAAEEHIKLNRR	RAN LIKE A HARE
AAAEEHIMNSTT	ANATHEMATISE
AAAEEHIMNTTZ	ANATHEMATIZE
AAAEEHIMRRST	MARIA THERESA
AAAEEHIPRSST	PARAESTHESIA
AAAEEIKKMMST	MAKE A MISTAKE
AAAEEILLRSTV	LEAVES A TRAIL
AAAEEKKMMRRS	MAKES A REMARK
AAAEEKLNPTTY	TAKE A PENALTY
AAAEEKMNRRST	MAKE AN ARREST
AAAEEKNORRSZ	KEEN AS A RAZOR
AAAEEKNRSTUW	TAKE UNAWARES
AAAEEPRSSTWY	SEPARATE WAYS
AAAEERSSTTVX	EXTRAVASATES
AAAEFGIMNNRS	SEAFARING MAN
AAAEFIILMRSY	RAISE A FAMILY
AAAEFIKLMSTT	FATAL MISTAKE
AAAEFIKNRSSW	AS FAR AS I KNEW
AAAEFILOPPRT	FAIL TO APPEAR
AAAEFKKLORTW	TAKE FOR A WALK
AAAEGGHIINNR	GAIN A HEARING
AAAEGGILMNPY	PLAYING A GAME
AAAEGGILNRWY	LAYING A WAGER
AAAEGHIKNRST	TAKING A SHARE
AAAEGHILNORW	WEARING A HALO
AAAEGHILRSSU	RAISES A LAUGH
AAAEGHLMOOPT	ALPHA TO OMEGA
AAAEGHLOPPRY	PALAEOGRAPHY
AAAEGHLOPSST	PALE AS A GHOST
AAAEGHNPPRRW	NEW PARAGRAPH
AAAEGIILMNRT	MATERIAL GAIN
AAAEGIKLMNRV	LEAVING A MARK
AAAEGIKLMNSS	MAKES A SIGNAL
AAAEGIKMNRSW	WEARING A MASK
AAAEGIKNNSWY	SNEAKING AWAY
AAAEGIKNSTWY	STAYING AWAKE
AAAEGILLNORV	ALL OVER AGAIN
AAAEGILMNNOT	NATIONAL GAME
AAAEGILMNRST	MARGINAL SEAT
AAAEGILNNSST	LEANS AGAINST
AAAEGILNNSTT	LEANT AGAINST
AAAEGILNSTWY	STEALING AWAY
AAAEGILRSSSS	RAISES A GLASS
AAAEGINNNNOR	NONAGENARIAN
AAAEGINPRRTT	TEARING APART
AAAEGMMRSUVY	GAVE A SUMMARY
AAAEGMNORSYY	MANY YEARS AGO
AAAEGNOPRRST	PERSONA GRATA
AAAEHHILMSTY	THE HIMALAYAS
AAAEHHITVWWY	HAVE A WAY WITH
AAAEHILNRTTV	VALIANT HEART
AAAEHIMNNSTW	WHAT'S IN A NAME
AAAEHKLMPSSS	MAKES A SPLASH
AAAEHNORSSTW	SWEARS AN OATH
AAAEIIKKNRTW	KIRI TE KANAWA
AAAEIILKNPST	SPEAK ITALIAN
AAAEIILMMNNR	MARINE ANIMAL
AAAEIILNQRTU	EQUALITARIAN
AAAEIKLLLMST	ALKALI METALS

AAAEILLMNPPR	MANILLA PAPER	AAAKLMMMNNOTT	MAN-TO-MAN TALK
AAAEILLNPSST	PALATIALNESS	AAALLMNOPRRY	PARANORMALLY
AAAEILMRRSTT	STAR MATERIAL	AAALNORRRTWY	ROYAL WARRANT
AAAEILMRRSTW	RAW MATERIALS	AABBBGIKNNOR	ROBBING A BANK
AAAEILMRRTTX	EXTRAMARITAL	AABBCDDEKNRW	BEND BACKWARD
AAAEILNNNOTX	ANNEXATIONAL	AABBCDDOORRX	CARDBOARD BOX
AAAEILNPSWXY	EXPLAINS AWAY	AABBCDEEIKRR	RIDE BARE-BACK
AAAEIMNPTTWY	AWAIT PAYMENT	AABBCDEEILNT	DEBIT BALANCE
AAAEINSSSSST	ASSASSINATES	AABBCDEKLLNU	BLACK AND BLUE
AAAEJLNRSSUY	JANUARY SALES		BLACK-AND-BLUE
AAAEKKLMRTTU	KEMAL ATATURK	AABBCDEOPRRU	BARE CUPBOARD
AAAEKMORSSTW	WORKS AS A TEAM	AABBCEEGHITW	CABBAGE WHITE
AAAELLNORRSY	ROYAL ARSENAL	AABBCEEHKKRT	BREAK THE BACK
AAAELLOSTTTY	TOTALLY AT SEA	AABBCEEMMORY	MORECAMBE BAY
AAAELMOPPRST	APPEAL TO ARMS	AABBCEEPSTXY	EXPECTS A BABY
AAAELNPPSTYY	PAYS A PENALTY	AABBCEGHHINT	BATHING BEACH
AAAELNRSTTTU	NATURAL STATE	AABBCEGIKKNR	BACKBREAKING
AAAEMMRRSSTT	MASTER-AT-ARMS		BREAKING BACK
AAAENOPRSUYY	PAY AS YOU EARN	AABBCEHHRRKS	BARBERS CHAIR
	PAY-AS-YOU-EARN	AABBCEHNRSTY	BABY SNATCHER
AAAENORSTUWY	RUN AWAY TO SEA	AABBCEIKLRYY	CRY LIKE A BABY
AAAFFFIILMRY	FAMILY AFFAIR	AABBCEINORST	BICARBONATES
AAAFFGLNNOPU	GULF OF PANAMA	AABBCGIKLLLN	BLACKBALLING
AAAFFILMNPPR	PARAFFIN LAMP	AABBCIILLNRY	RABBINICALLY
AAAFGHILNNGT	SHARING A FLAT	AABBDDEEHLVY	BADLY BEHAVED
AAAFGILLNNOT	NATIONAL FLAG		BEHAVED BADLY
AAAFGILLNPRT	FALLING APART	AABBDEEHLSVY	BEHAVES BADLY
AAAFIKNNNNGT	FRANK SINATRA	AABBDEEHNSTT	BEATS THE BAND
AAAFIKNORSSW	AS FAR AS I KNOW	AABBDEEKLOOT	BOOKED A TABLE
AAAFKLNOORSS	ASKS FOR A LOAN	AABBDEEKRSST	BREADBASKETS
AAAGGHILNUWY	LAUGHING AWAY	AABBDEELNORY	BY BREAD ALONE
AAAGGINORSTV	AGGRAVATIONS	AABBDEGNRRUY	BARNABY RUDGE
AAAGGIOPPHIU	APPOGGIATURA	AABBDEHIORUV	BAD BEHAVIOUR
AAAGHIIILNTX	HAILING A TAXI	AABBDGIILNNR	BLIND BARGAIN
AAAGHIILRSST	AS LIGHT AS AIR	AABBDGINORSU	BOARDING A BUS
AAAGHIIMNOSS	NAGISA OSHIMA	AABBDIILLLLR	BILLIARD BALL
AAAGHIINTVWY	HAVING IT AWAY	AABBDIILLRRS	BAR BILLIARDS
AAAGHIKNNOTT	TAKING AN OATH	AABBEEEEHLMRT	BEAR THE BLAME
AAAGHINPPRRS	PARAPHRASING	AABBEEHKKNRT	BREAK THE BANK
AAAGHINPRTVY	HAVING A PARTY	AABBEEHPRRSY	BARBARY SHEEP
AAAGHIRSTTWY	STRAIGHT AWAY	AABBEEKLORTT	BREAK A BOTTLE
	STRAIGHTAWAY	AABBEENRRSSS	BENARES BRASS
AAAGHLMORRTY	GRAHAM TAYLOR	AABBEFGLRSST	FLABBERGASTS
AAAGIIKNNRTT	TAKING A TRAIN	AABBEGIINRTV	ABBREVIATING
AAAGIIKNTTWY	TAKING IT AWAY	AABBEGILLNRS	BALL BEARINGS
AAAGIILLNNORS	RAISING A LOAN	AABBEGIMNNOR	EARNING A BOMB
AAAGIILNNOTV	NAVIGATIONAL	AABBEHIKNORT	BROKEN A HABIT
AAAGIILNPSTY	PLAYS IT AGAIN	AABBEIINORTV	ABBREVIATION
AAAGIIMNRRSS	AGRARIANISMS	AABBEILNNOTU	UNOBTAINABLE
AAAGIKMNRSTT	MAKING A START	AABBEILRTTTU	ATTRIBUTABLE
AAAGILMMNRRT	LATIN GRAMMAR	AABBEINNRRTW	RABBIT WARREN
AAAGILNPPRTY	PLAYING A PART	AABBEIORRSTV	ABBREVIATORS
AAAGILNPSSTY	PLAYS AGAINST	AABBEIRRSTTU	BARBITURATES
AAAGINPRSTTY	STAYING APART	AABBGHIMNOST	THINGAMABOBS
AAAGINRRSTTW	STARTING A WAR	AABBGIINNPST	STABBING PAIN
AAAHIIMNNRTU	HUMANITARIAN	AABBHIIILTTY	HABITABILITY
AAAHLLLMNPRS	MARSHALL PLAN	AABCCCDIILOR	CARBOLIC ACID
AAAHLPPRRSYY	HAPPY AS LARRY	AABCCDEEILRT	ACCREDITABLE
AAAIILMPRRTY	PARAMILITARY	AABCCDEIILRT	BACTERICIDAL
AAAIILNNOSST	NASALISATION	AABCCDEILLSY	DECASYLLABIC
AAAIILNNOSTZ	NASALIZATION	AABCCEEHLNRT	CARTE BLANCHE
AAAIILNOPPRT	APPARITIONAL	AABCCEEKNNRT	BACK ENTRANCE
AAAIILNORTTT	TOTALITARIAN	AABCCEELNPTU	UNACCEPTABLE
AAAIILNRRTWY	RAILWAY TRAIN	AABCCEELORST	OBSTACLE RACE
AAAIINNQRSTU	ANTIQUARIANS	AABCCEFIORRS	COARSE FABRIC
AAAIKLNNOPRT	NATIONAL PARK	AABCCEHHLLTT	CATCH THE BALL
AAAILLNOSTTU	SALUTATIONAL	AABCCEHIINNT	CHINA CABINET
AAAILMNORTTU	MATURATIONAL	AABCCEHKNORS	ARCH ONES BACK
AAAILNOPRSTY	PARALYSATION	AABCCEHLOORT	CHOCOLATE BAR
AAAINNRRTUWY	RUNAWAY TRAIN	AABCCEILLLNU	INCALCULABLE
AAAINORSSSST	ASSASSINATOR	AABCCEILLRTU	CIRCULATABLE

AABCCEIRRTUU	BUREAUCRATIC
AABCCEKLORTT	CRACK A BOTTLE
AABCCEKNORTT	BREAK CONTACT
AABCCENOORSU	CARBONACEOUS
AABCCFINNORS	FRANCIS BACON
AABCCGGIKLNN	GLANCING BACK
AABCCGHINSTU	CATCHING A BUS
AABCCGIIKNRR	CRACKING A RIB
AABCCGIJKKLN	BLACKJACKING
AABCCGIKKNRT	BACKTRACKING
AABCCHIKLPST	BLACK AS PITCH
AABCCIIKNNOT	BACK IN ACTION
AABCCIKLLOPT	BLOCK CAPITAL
AABCCILLLNUY	INCALCULABLY
AABCCILOOPRS	CARBOLIC SOAP
AABCCINOOSTT	TOBACCO STAIN
AABCCINRSTTU	SUBANTARCTIC
AABCCIOSSSTU	ACOUSTIC BASS
AABCCKLNRRTU	BLACKCURRANT
AABCCLNOOPTT	TOBACCO PLANT
AABCDDEEILNT	BALANCED DIET
AABCDDEEKLLP	BACKPEDALLED
AABCDDEEHKLNY	BACKHANDEDLY
AABCDDEIKNSS	BACK AND SIDES
AABCDDEILLMR	CLIMB A LADDER
AABCDDEILMNN	BALANCED MIND
AABCDDEJLORS	JACOBS LADDER
AABCDDHIRRTY	BIRTHDAY CARD
AABCDDIKLMNO	BLACK DIAMOND
AABCDDIKMNOS	DIAMONDBACKS
AABCDEEEFILR	BAREFACED LIE
AABCDEEEKLPY	BLACK-EYED PEA
AABCDEEHHMRT	DEATH CHAMBER
AABCDEEHKNRT	THERE AND BACK
AABCDEEHKORS	BACKED A HORSE
AABCDEEIILNR	INERADICABLE
AABCDEEILLPS	DISPLACEABLE
AABCDEEKLORS	BACKED A LOSER
AABCDEEKNRSW	ANSWERED BACK
AABCDEEKORRR	BREAK A RECORD
AABCDEELLLSY	DECASYLLABLE
AABCDEELLMNY	CALLED BY NAME
AABCDEELLNRT	BALLET DANCER
AABCDEELLNRY	DRY-CLEANABLE
AABCDEELNORV	OVERBALANCED
AABCDEEORRST	BEATS A RECORD
AABCDEFLNOTU	CONFABULATED
AABCDEFNORSS	SENDS FOR A CAB
AABCDEGGNNOS	BACON AND EGGS
	EGGS AND BACON
AABCDEGHIRTW	WITH BAD GRACE
AABCDEGIKLRW	BIRDCAGE WALK
AABCDEGKNORW	GONE BACKWARD
AABCDEGKORSW	GOES BACKWARD
AABCDEHHRSTU	HAD A BUTCHER'S
AABCDEHIKRRR	RICHARD BAKER
AABCDEHIKRTY	BIRTHDAY CAKE
AABCDEHIMMRS	CHAMBERMAIDS
AABCDEHORRTY	CARBOHYDRATE
AABCDEIILNNS	CANNIBALISED
AABCDEIILNNZ	CANNIBALIZED
AABCDEIILNRY	INERADICABLY
AABCDEIKLNRS	LACKED BRAINS
AABCDEIKLPRS	BLACK DESPAIR
AABCDEINOSTU	SUBDIACONATE
AABCDEINRSTW	CABIN STEWARD
AABCDEIORRTU	CARRIED ABOUT
AABCDEKNRSSW	BACKWARDNESS
AABCDEKNRTWW	WENT BACKWARD
AABCDEKPRSTW	BACKWARD STEP
	STEP BACKWARD
AABCDELLMORS	COLD AS MARBLE
AABCDELLOORT	COLLABORATED
AABCDELMNRSU	CANDELABRUMS
AABCDELMRUWY	CRUMBLED AWAY
AABCDELOPPRR	CLAPPER-BOARD
AABCDELORTUW	CRAWLED ABOUT
AABCDELORTXY	CARBOXYLATED
AABCDELRSTTY	ABSTRACTEDLY
AABCDEMNOPPR	COMB AND PAPER
AABCDENOPRSW	BOW AND SCRAPE
AABCDENOPRTU	PRANCED ABOUT
AABCDEOPRRRS	SCRAPERBOARD
AABCDEORRSST	BROADCASTERS
AABCDFHKNORT	BACK AND FORTH
AABCDFILNOST	BIT OF SCANDAL
AABCDFKNNORT	BACK AND FRONT
AABCDGIKLRRW	BACKWARD GIRL
AABCDGIKNNST	STANDING BACK
AABCDGINNORT	CARBON DATING
AABCDGINORST	BROADCASTING
AABCDGKLLRUY	BLACKGUARDLY
AABCDIILLLOY	DIABOLICALLY
AABCDKKLNOTT	DONT TALK BACK
AABCDKMNOOSW	BACKWOODSMAN
AABCEEEEFKLTT	FEEBLE ATTACK
AABCEEEGHLNX	EXCHANGEABLE
AABCEEEGHLRR	RECHARGEABLE
AABCEEEGINPT	BEING AT PEACE
AABCEEEHLLNW	BALANCE WHEEL
AABCEEEHLNST	BALANCE SHEET
AABCEEEHLRRS	RESEARCHABLE
AABCEEEMORSW	BECOMES AWARE
AABCEEEPRRTT	CARPET BEATER
AABCEEFIPRRT	PREFABRICATE
AABCEEFKRRSU	BREAK SURFACE
AABCEEFNORRS	FORBEARANCES
AABCEEGGPRRT	CARPET BAGGER
	CARPETBAGGER
AABCEEGHLNNU	UNCHANGEABLE
AABCEEGINRTX	EXACERBATING
AABCEEGLLNNR	BENGAL LANCER
AABCEEHILNNT	IN THE BALANCE
AABCEEHILSTT	THE BALTIC SEA
AABCEEHIPRTV	PRIVATE BEACH
AABCEEHLMNRT	MERCHANTABLE
AABCEEHLOPRR	REPROACHABLE
AABCEEHMNRST	ANTECHAMBERS
AABCEEIKMNRT	CABINET MAKER
	CABINETMAKER
AABCEEILMNSS	AMICABLENESS
AABCEEINORTX	EXACERBATION
AABCEEINOSST	SEBASTIAN COE
AABCEELLORRT	CORRELATABLE
AABCEELNORSV	OVERBALANCES
AABCEENORTUY	BUT ONCE A YEAR
AABCEFHLLORT	BACHELOR FLAT
AABCEFHOSTWY	FACE BOTH WAYS
AABCEFIILLSS	CLASSIFIABLE
AABCEFIILLTY	BEATIFICALLY
AABCEFIOPRRS	PAIR OF BRACES
AABCEFKLLNNO	FALLEN BACK ON
AABCEFKPRSTU	BREAKFAST CUP
AABCEFLNOOTU	OUT OF BALANCE
AABCEFLNOSTU	CONFABULATES
AABCEFLNRSTU	BLAST FURNACE
AABCEFNNNORT	ANNE BANCROFT
AABCEGGHINRR	BRING A CHARGE
AABCEGHORSTU	BROUGHT A CASE
AABCEGIINPRR	BARGAIN PRICE
AABCEGIKLNNR	CLEARING BANK
AABCEGIKLNRW	WEARING BLACK

710

Code	Phrase	Code	Phrase
AABCEGIKMNPR	BREAKING CAMP	AABCGILNNOTU	BALANCING OUT
AABCEGILLMNR	ALL-EMBRACING		OUTBALANCING
AABCEGILNRST	RACING STABLE	AABCGINOSTTU	CASTING ABOUT
AABCEGKNOPSS	PACK ONES BAGS	AABCHIIMORTT	MICROHABITAT
AABCEHHPSSTY	BATHYSCAPHES	AABCHIINOOTT	COHABITATION
AABCEHHRSSTU	HAS A BUTCHER'S	AABCHILLLNOS	NICHOLAS BALL
AABCEHIILTTY	TEACHABILITY	AABCHILNRTUY	UNCHARITABLY
AABCEHIKLSVY	BACKS HEAVILY	AABCIIILNPTY	INCAPABILITY
AABCEHIKNSTT	SAT IN THE BACK	AABCIILNORST	CALIBRATIONS
AABCEHIKSTTT	SIT AT THE BACK	AABCIILRTTTY	TRACTABILITY
AABCEHILLTTY	BATHETICALLY	AABCIINORSTU	CUBARISATION
AABCEHILMNRS	CHAMBERLAINS	AABCILLLLSYY	SYLLABICALLY
AABCEHILNRTU	UNCHARITABLE	AABCILOOPPSS	PABLO PICASSO
AABCEHINORST	HARICOT BEANS	AABCINORSSTT	ABSTRACTIONS
AABCEHIRRRRS	CRASH BARRIER	AABCKLMNOORT	BACK TO NORMAL
AABCEHKLLLST	THE ALL-BLACKS	AABCLLOOORRT	COLLABORATOR
AABCEHKMNNRT	MERCHANT BANK	AABCLNORSTUY	CONSTABULARY
AABCEHKNOPTT	PAT ON THE BACK	AABCMNNNOOTT	NONCOMBATANT
AABCEHLLNNST	CALL THE BANNS	AABCNNORSTTU	ABSTRACT NOUN
AABCEHLLORTT	CALL TO THE BAR	AABDDDEEHNNR	NAB RED-HANDED
AABCEHLMNORS	ELASMOBRANCH	AABDDDLNNOOS	BLOOD AND SAND
AABCEHLMNRSU	BURNHAM SCALE	AABDDEEHHRRT	BREATHED HARD
AABCEHLMPSTY	PLAYS MACBETH	AABDDEEHINRR	BRIAN REDHEAD
AABCEHOPRSSU	HABEAS CORPUS	AABDDEEILLLN	DEAD-BALL LINE
AABCEIIILPST	CAPABILITIES	AABDDEEINNRW	BREAD AND WINE
AABCEIILLNPP	INAPPLICABLE	AABDDEEIORRS	RESIDE ABROAD
AABCEIILMMRS	BICAMERALISM	AABDDEELRTTY	TREATED BADLY
AABCEIILNNSS	CANNIBALISES	AABDDEFOORRT	BOARD OF TRADE
AABCEIILNNSZ	CANNIBALIZES	AABDDEHHNRST	HANDS BREADTH
AABCEIKLLMRS	BLACKMAILERS	AABDDEHILNSU	IDEAL HUSBAND
AABCEIKNNRSW	BACKS A WINNER	AABDDEHLLMOY	HEBDOMADALLY
AABCEIKRTTTT	BITTER ATTACK	AABDDEIKLMNR	BREAD AND MILK
AABCEILLTTUV	CULTIVATABLE	AABDDEILLMVY	DAVID BELLAMY
AABCEILMNOPR	INCOMPARABLE	AABDDELMNORS	OLD MANS BEARD
AABCEILMORRT	BAROMETRICAL	AABDDENORSTU	DOES A BAD TURN
AABCEILNRSST	BASS CLARINET	AABDDFHINNSU	FIND A HUSBAND
AABCEILORSUV	VOCABULARIES	AABDDGGINOTU	GADDING ABOUT
AABCEILSSTTT	BALTIC STATES	AABDDGHORRTU	DRAUGHTBOARD
AABCEINRRSTT	SCATTERBRAIN	AABDDGINORRW	DRAWING BOARD
AABCEIORRSTU	CARRIES ABOUT	AABDDIJNRTTU	ADJUTANT BIRD
AABCEKLPPRSS	BACKSLAPPERS	AABDEEEEILMN	MADE A BEE-LINE
AABCEKNORSTY	STREAKY BACON	AABDEEEGILRS	DISAGREEABLE
AABCEKNORTTU	BACK TO NATURE	AABDEEEHNORS	BARE ONES HEAD
AABCELLOORST	COLLABORATES	AABDEEELLNRSS	READABLENESS
AABCELMRSUWY	CRUMBLES AWAY	AABDEEEMQSTU	MADE A BEQUEST
AABCELNORSTT	CONTRASTABLE	AABDEEFIMMNR	MAN-MADE FIBRE
AABCELORSTXY	CARBOXYLATES		MANMADE FIBRE
AABCEMRRSTTT	ABSTRACT TERM	AABDEEFIMNOR	MADE A BONFIRE
AABCENNORTWY	WON BY A CANTER	AABDEEGGRRSU	BEARS A GRUDGE
AABCENOPRSTU	PRANCES ABOUT	AABDEEGHIRVY	HEAVY BRIGADE
AABCENORRSTY	CARRY ONES BAT	AABDEEGHNNOS	BANG ONES HEAD
AABCENORSSST	CONTRABASSES	AABDEEGILNOS	DIAGNOSEABLE
AABCENRSSSTT	ABSTRACTNESS	AABDEEGILRSY	DISAGREEABLY
AABCEOORSTTZ	AZOTOBACTERS	AABDEEHHRRSS	HABERDASHERS
AABCFFIILPRU	PUBLIC AFFAIR	AABDEEHHRRST	BREATHES HARD
AABCFIINORST	FABRICATIONS	AABDEEHHRRSY	HABERDASHERY
AABCFIKLNORS	LACK OF BRAINS	AABDEEHILLTT	LAID THE TABLE
AABCFKLLNOPU	FALL BACK UPON	AABDEEHILPST	ALPHABETISED
AABCFKLOORRY	BACK OF A LORRY	AABDEEHILPTZ	ALPHABETIZED
AABCGHIILNPT	CAPTAIN BLIGH	AABDEEHLORTU	TROUBLE AHEAD
AABCGHIILOPR	BIOGRAPHICAL	AABDEEHLRSTY	BREATHALYSED
AABCGHIKLNST	BLACK AS NIGHT	AABDEEHLRTYZ	BREATHALYZED
AABCGHIKRSTT	BACK STRAIGHT	AABDEEHORRTW	WEATHERBOARD
	STRAIGHT BACK	AABDEEHRRTWY	BARRED THE WAY
AABCGHINPSYY	PAYING BY CASH	AABDEEIKRSST	BRAISED STEAK
AABCGHKLLNOY	BY A LONG CHALK	AABDEEILLRRS	READS BRAILLE
AABCGIIKKNTT	TAKING IT BACK	AABDEEILMPSS	BIASED SAMPLE
AABCGIIKLLMN	BLACKMAILING	AABDEEILNSTY	BATS AN EYELID
AABCGIILNOST	CATABOLISING	AABDEEILRTTX	EXTRADITABLE
AABCGIILNOTZ	CATABOLIZING	AABDEEKNOSTU	SNEAKED ABOUT
AABCGIKLNPPS	BACKSLAPPING	AABDEEKORRST	SKATEBOARDER

AABDEELLNSSU	LAUDABLENESS
AABDEELLORRU	LABOUR LEADER
AABDEELLOTTX	OLD BATTLE-AXE
AABDEELMNNSS	DAMNABLENESS
AABDEELMPRTU	PERAMBULATED
AABDEELNORSS	ADORABLENESS
AABDEEMNRTTT	BAD TREATMENT
AABDEENOORVV	OVER AND ABOVE
AABDEFGILLMO	BALM OF GILEAD
AABDEFGINTUY	FADING BEAUTY
AABDEFGLORSS	BLADE OF GRASS
AABDEFILTUUY	BEAUTIFUL DAY
AABDEFKNRRST	BANKERS DRAFT
AABDEFLLNRTU	FATAL BLUNDER
AABDEFLOOTTU	FLOATED ABOUT
AABDEGGLNOST	GLADSTONE BAG
AABDEGHINORT	BRING TO A HEAD
AABDEGHLOTUU	LAUGHED ABOUT
AABDEGIIMSTU	DISAMBIGUATE
AABDEGIJMORR	BRIGADE MAJOR
AABDEGIKNOOR	READING A BOOK
AABDEGILLNOW	DEALING A BLOW
AABDEGILLNRS	BALLAD SINGER
AABDEGLNNTUU	ANNUAL BUDGET
AABDEGNNORSS	RAGS AND BONES
AABDEGNOPTTU	BANG UP TO DATE
AABDEHHIRRST	HAIRS BREADTH
AABDEHHORSTY	BY A SHORT HEAD
AABDEHILRTWW	WITHDRAWABLE
AABDEHNNOOPS	ABANDONS HOPE
AABDEHOSSTTT	STABS TO DEATH
AABDEIILNRST	DISTRAINABLE
AABDEIILNRVW	VARIABLE WIND
AABDEIILPRTY	DRAPEABILITY
AABDEIILQSTU	BAD QUALITIES
AABDEILLMNOS	BLIND AS A MOLE
AABDEILLNPRY	PLAY A BLINDER
AABDEILLNPST	BEST LAID PLAN
AABDEILMNRSU	DIALS A NUMBER
AABDEILNNOTT	NATIONAL DEBT
AABDEILNOOTU	LAID ABOUT ONE
AABDEILOPPRR	AIR-DROPPABLE
AABDEIMRSTUV	ADUMBRATIVES
AABDEINNRRST	SAINT BERNARD
AABDEINORRTW	WINTER ABROAD
AABDEKNNOORT	TAKEN ON BOARD
AABDEKNNOPRS	PORK AND BEANS
AABDEKNOORST	TAKES ON BOARD
AABDELLNOSSU	SOUND AS A BELL
AABDELLNRTVY	TRAVEL BY LAND
AABDELNNOPRU	UNPARDONABLE
AABDELNRSSST	SANDBLASTERS
AABDELOPRRST	PLASTERBOARD
AABDEMNNRRSU	ABSURD MANNER
AABDEMNOORRV	MAN OVERBOARD
AABDENNORTUV	OVERABUNDANT
AABDENORSTUW	WANDERS ABOUT
AABDFFIILNNS	BAFFIN ISLAND
AABDFLNORRWY	BARNYARD FOWL
AABDGGGIINPR	BRIDGING A GAP
AABDGHILNOTY	HOLDING AT BAY
AABDGIILNNST	STANDING BAIL
AABDGIINOPPR	PIPING ABOARD
AABDGIINRSST	BASTARDISING
AABDGIINRSTZ	BASTARDIZING
AABDGILLNNOW	LANDING A BLOW
AABDGILNNSST	SANDBLASTING
AABDGILNNTWY	WANTING BADLY
AABDGINORRST	STARBOARDING
AABDHIILLLLR	BILLIARD HALL
AABDHIINSTTY	DAINTY HABITS

AABDHINNOPSS	ABANDONS SHIP
AABDHINORTUY	HIT A BOUNDARY
AABDHKNOOSTU	TOOK A HUSBAND
AABDIIILLTTY	DILATABILITY
AABDIIILMRTY	ADMIRABILITY
AABDIIILSTVY	ADVISABILITY
AABDIILMNRTY	MILITARY BAND
AABDIILOPTTY	ADOPTABILITY
AABDILNOPRUU	UNPAID LABOUR
AABDIMNORSTU	ADUMBRATIONS
AABDINOOTTUY	AUTOANTIBODY
AABDLLNOOTTU	NO DOUBT AT ALL
AABDLMNNOORR	MARLON BRANDO
AABDLNOPPRRU	POPULAR BRAND
AABDMOOORRRST	MORTARBOARDS
AABEEEEIKLMN	MAKE A BEE-LINE
AABEEEFGLTTV	VEGETABLE FAT
AABEEEFGSSSU	BEEF SAUSAGES
AABEEEFKRRSS	SAFEBREAKERS
AABEEEGGLLTT	GATE-LEG TABLE
AABEEEGLORVW	BELOW AVERAGE
AABEEEHINRTT	BEATEN THE AIR
AABEEEHKLMTT	TAKE THE BLAME
AABEEEHKLRST	BREAK THE SEAL
AABEEEHMNRST	BEARS THE NAME
AABEEEHNOSVV	HEAVENS ABOVE!
AABEEEHPRRTY	PAY THE BEARER
AABEEEKMQSTU	MAKE A BEQUEST
AABEEEKPRSST	KEEPS ABREAST
AABEEELMNRWY	WEMBLEY ARENA
AABEEELNPRTU	UNREPEATABLE
AABEEELRSTTV	SERVE AT TABLE
AABEEERRRSTW	WATER BEARERS
AABEEFGGINNO	BEING OF AN AGE
AABEEFGIKNRS	SAFEBREAKING
AABEEFHINRRT	FEATHERBRAIN
AABEEFHLLRTT	AFTER THE BALL
AABEEFHLOTTT	HEAT OF BATTLE
AABEEFIKMNOR	MAKE A BONFIRE
AABEEFKORRST	BREAKS FOR TEA
AABEEFKRRSST	BREAKFASTERS
AABEEFLMNSTT	BASEMENT FLAT
AABEEFLMOSTV	MOVABLE FEAST
AABEEFLNRRST	TRANSFERABLE
AABEEFLOPSSS	AESOPS FABLES
AABEEGGGLLLU	LUGGAGE LABEL
AABEEGGIKLNR	BREAKING A LEG
AABEEGGILNNN	BEING AN ANGEL
AABEEGGOPRRS	BEGGARS OPERA
AABEEGHINPSU	HEAPING ABUSE
AABEEGIKNPTY	KEEPING AT BAY
AABEEGIKNRST	TAKE BEARINGS
AABEEGILMNST	MAGNETISABLE
AABEEGILMNTZ	MAGNETIZABLE
AABEEGILMNUZ	BLUE MAGAZINE
AABEEGINNTTY	BATTING AN EYE
AABEEGIRRSTT	GASTARBEITER
AABEEGKMNRTU	TAKEN UMBRAGE
AABEEGKMRSTU	TAKES UMBRAGE
AABEEGRRRTVY	GREAT BRAVERY
AABEEGSSSTYY	BY EASY STAGES
AABEEHIILRTT	REHABILITATE
AABEEHIKNTTT	TAKEN THE BAIT
AABEEHIKSTTT	TAKES THE BAIT
AABEEHILLRRS	LIBERAL SHARE
AABEEHILPRST	ALPHABETISER
AABEEHILPRTZ	ALPHABETIZER
AABEEHILPSST	ALPHABETISES
AABEEHILPSTZ	ALPHABETIZES
AABEEHKLRSTW	BREAKS THE LAW
AABEEHLLSTTY	LAYS THE TABLE

AABEEHLNRRTY	LEARN BY HEART	AABEGIINRRTT	GREAT BRITAIN
AABEEHLOSTTV	ABOVE THE SALT	AABEGIINSSUU	GUINEA BISSAU
AABEEHLPRSTY	PLAYS THE BEAR		GUINEA-BISSAU
AABEEHLRRSTY	BREATHALYSER	AABEGIKNNRTU	BREAKING A NUT
AABEEHLRRTYZ	BREATHALYZER	AABEGIKNOOST	BOOKING A SEAT
AABEEHLRSSTY	BREATHALYSES	AABEGIKNOOTT	TOOK A BEATING
AABEEHLRSTYZ	BREATHALYZES	AABEGILNOPTU	LEAPING ABOUT
AABEEHNOPSSU	HEAPS ABUSE ON	AABEGILNPRYY	PLAYING BY EAR
AABEEIKLRTTY	TAKE A LIBERTY	AABEGILNSSTU	SALUTING BASE
AABEEILMMRSU	IMMEASURABLE	AABEGIMNRRSS	EMBARRASSING
AABEEILNRRST	RESTRAINABLE	AABEGIMNRRTT	BATTERING RAM
AABEEILNRSSV	VARIABLENESS	AABEGINOORSV	SOARING ABOVE
AABEEILORRSW	SAILOR BEWARE	AABEGINORTTU	TEARING ABOUT
AABEEINNNRUV	ANEURIN BEVAN	AABEGINRSTUY	BURYING AT SEA
AABEEINRRRST	TRAINBEARERS	AABEGLMMOPRR	PROGRAMMABLE
AABEEINRRSST	BRAINTEASERS	AABEHIILRSSZ	BILHARZIASES
AABEEINRSSSV	ABRASIVENESS	AABEHILNQSUV	VANQUISHABLE
AABEEJKLLNOW	JOAN BAKEWELL	AABEHILNSSTU	HABITUALNESS
AABEEKLLRTTW	BAKEWELL TART	AABEHILRTTWY	WHAT A LIBERTY!
AABEEKLMNTTU	TAKEN A TUMBLE	AABEHINOTTUW	WITHOUT A BEAN
AABEEKLMOSTU	MAKE ABSOLUTE	AABEHINRRSSW	BRAINWASHERS
AABEEKLMSTTU	TAKES A TUMBLE	AABEHIPRSTTT	BAITS THE TRAP
AABEEKMNNRTU	TAKEN A NUMBER	AABEHLLLMSSY	ASSEMBLY HALL
AABEEKMNORRS	BREAK ONES ARM	AABEHLLLPSTY	PLAYS THE BALL
AABEEKMNRSTU	TAKES A NUMBER	AABEHLOPRRRU	PEARL HARBOUR
AABEEKSSSTTW	WASTEBASKETS	AABEHMNOOTTY	BAY AT THE MOON
AABEELLMNOST	BALLETOMANES	AABEIIILLNTY	ALIENABILITY
AABEELLMRSTT	BALLET MASTER	AABEIIKLLLMW	WILLIAM BLAKE
AABEELLNSSUV	VALUABLENESS	AABEIILLLMTY	MALLEABILITY
AABEELMNNRST	TABLE MANNERS	AABEIILLMRST	BILATERALISM
AABEELMNORUV	MANOEUVRABLE	AABEIILLRTTY	ALTERABILITY
AABEELMORUWZ	ABEL MUZOREWA	AABEIILMRSTY	MILITARY BASE
AABEELMPRSTU	PERAMBULATES	AABEIILNRRST	LIBERTARIANS
AABEELNNORSU	UNREASONABLE	AABEIILPRSTY	SEPARABILITY
AABEELNNOSSU	UNSEASONABLE	AABEIKLMNSTU	UNMISTAKABLE
AABEELNNRRUW	URBAN RENEWAL	AABEILLMNORS	NORMALISABLE
AABEELNNRSUW	UNANSWERABLE	AABEILLMNORZ	NORMALIZABLE
AABEELNRSTTU	ENTABLATURES	AABEILLMNTVY	AMBIVALENTLY
AABEELOPRSTU	PLEASURE BOAT	AABEILLNRSTU	TURBELLARIAN
AABEELPRSSTT	BREASTPLATES	AABEILLPRRTY	LIBERAL PARTY
AABEELRRTUUV	TRAVEL BUREAU	AABEILLRRSTZ	TRAILBLAZERS
AABEELRSSTVY	TRAVELS BY SEA	AABEILMMRSUY	IMMEASURABLY
AABEEMORRTUX	AMATEUR BOXER	AABEILMNOOTT	TABLE A MOTION
AABEEMPRTTTV	BRAVE ATTEMPT	AABEILMORSTU	AMBULATORIES
AABEENNRRSTU	SUBTERRANEAN	AABEILOORRST	LABORATORIES
AABEENRRTTWY	WARREN BEATTY	AABEILOPPPRR	APPROPRIABLE
AABEFFLORTUW	WATER BUFFALO	AABEILPRSTYY	PLAYS IT BY EAR
AABEFGIKNRST	BREAKFASTING	AABEILRRSTVY	TRAVELS BY AIR
AABEFGILNTTU	BEING AT FAULT	AABEINSSTTTU	SUBSTANTIATE
AABEFHIKORSY	SHEIK OF ARABY	AABEIORRRRVW	BRAVE WARRIOR
AABEFHLLTWYY	FALL BY THE WAY	AABEJKLOORSU	LABOURS A JOKE
AABEFIILNOPS	SAPONIFIABLE	AABEJMPRRRSY	RASPBERRY JAM
AABEFIILNQTU	QUANTIFIABLE	AABEKKMNPRTU	MAKE BANKRUPT
AABEFILNRRTU	NATURAL FIBRE	AABEKLMORRTU	LABOUR MARKET
AABEFJKOOWYY	BY WAY OF A JOKE	AABEKLNORTUW	BROKE A WALNUT
AABEFLLMMNNO	NONFLAMMABLE	AABEKNOPRSTU	PUTS A BRAKE ON
AABEFLLMOOTT	FOOTBALL TEAM	AABELLMPRSSY	PLAYS MARBLES
AABEFLMORRRU	FARM LABOURER	AABELMMNOSTU	SOMNAMBULATE
AABEFLNORUUV	UNFAVOURABLE	AABELMNRSTTU	TRANSMUTABLE
AABEFLNRSSTU	TRANSFUSABLE	AABELMOPRRTU	PERAMBULATOR
AABEFLOOPSTT	TABLET OF SOAP	AABELNNORSUY	UNREASONABLY
AABEFLRRSTUY	LAST FEBRUARY	AABELNNOSSUY	UNSEASONABLY
AABEGGGILMMN	GAMBLING GAME	AABELNNRSUWY	UNANSWERABLY
AABEGGIILNRS	SAILING BARGE	AABELNOOSTUY	LAYS ABOUT ONE
AABEGGNNORTT	BANG ON TARGET	AABELNOPRSST	TRANSPOSABLE
AABEGHIKNRTT	BREATHTAKING	AABELORRSTTY	SOLAR BATTERY
AABEGHILRRTU	REGULAR HABIT	AABELORSTTUV	TRAVELS ABOUT
AABEGHIMNTTW	BANTAMWEIGHT	AABEMNNPRRTU	ABRUPT MANNER
AABEGHINORTU	HEARING ABOUT	AABENNOOSSTT	BEANS ON TOAST
AABEGHKMRSTU	HAMBURG STEAK	AABFGIIILTTY	FATIGABILITY
AABEGIIJKLNR	BREAKING JAIL	AABFGILLNOTU	FALLING ABOUT

AABFIILLMMTY	FLAMMABILITY
AABFIIMNOPRT	MAP OF BRITAIN
AABFILLOPPRY	APPLY FOR BAIL
AABFJLOOPPRY	APPLY FOR A JOB
AABFLLLOOPTY	PLAY FOOTBALL
AABFLLMNOTYY	FLAMBOYANTLY
AABFLNORUUVY	UNFAVOURABLY
AABGGHINNOTU	HANGING ABOUT
AABGGIINNRWY	BRINGING AWAY
AABGGILLMNNO	AMBLING ALONG
AABGHIINNRSW	BRAINWASHING
AABGHINRSSTU	BRUSH AGAINST
AABGHINRSUWY	BRUSHING AWAY
AABGIIILNTVY	NAVIGABILITY
AABGIILLLNOW	ALLOWING BAIL
AABGIILLNORY	ABORIGINALLY
AABGIILLNRTZ	TRAILBLAZING
AABGIIMNNOPS	IMPOSING A BAN
AABGIJKNNOOT	TAKING ON A JOB
AABGIKLNORTU	LARKING ABOUT
AABGIKLNOTTU	TALKING ABOUT
AABGIKLNOTUW	WALKING ABOUT
AABGILNOPTUY	PLAYING ABOUT
AABGILNORSUV	LABOURSAVING
	SAVING LABOUR
AABGINNSSWYY	YAWNING ABYSS
AABHHMOOPRST	PHARAOHS TOMB
AABHHOOTTTUW	HOW ABOUT THAT
AABHIIILRSSZ	BILHARZIASIS
AABHIIINNOTT	INHABITATION
AABHIINOSTTU	HABITUATIONS
AABHIMNOPSST	BOATSMANSHIP
AABHOPRRSSUY	HARBOURS A SPY
AABIILMSSTUY	ASSUMABILITY
AABIILNNORUV	LABOUR IN VAIN
AABIILNOORTY	ABOLITIONARY
AABIIMNNOOST	ABOMINATIONS
AABIINNORSTU	URBANISATION
AABIINNORTUZ	URBANIZATION
AABIINOORRST	ARBORISATION
AABIINOORRTZ	ARBORIZATION
AABIINORRSTT	ARBITRATIONS
AABIKLMNSTUY	UNMISTAKABLY
AABILLMRSUXY	SUBMAXILLARY
AABILLNOSTTU	BLASTULATION
AABILMNORRWY	BARRY MANILOW
AABILNSSTTUV	SUBSTANTIVAL
AABILOPRRSTU	SUPRAORBITAL
AABIMNORSTTU	MASTURBATION
AABINOOPRRTY	PROBATIONARY
AABLMMNNOSTU	SOMNAMBULANT
AABMNNOOTTUW	MAN ABOUT TOWN
	MAN-ABOUT-TOWN
AABMORRSSTTUY	MASTURBATORY
AACCCDDEEKOR	CRACKED A CODE
AACCCDEEIPTV	ACCEPT ADVICE
AACCCDEHLOST	CATCHES A COLD
AACCCEEKMRRR	CREAM CRACKER
AACCCEFIINOP	PACIFIC OCEAN
AACCCEGIKNPR	CRACKING PACE
AACCCEHIRSTT	CATACHRESTIC
AACCCEIINRSU	INACCURACIES
AACCCEJKKRRS	CRACKERJACKS
AACCCENOTTUX	EXACT ACCOUNT
AACCDDDIILOS	ADDS A CODICIL
AACCDDEHIIRS	DISACCHARIDE
AACCDDEINORT	ROAD ACCIDENT
AACCDDEMMOOT	ACCOMMODATED
AACCDDENSSTU	STAND ACCUSED
AACCDDIILLTY	DIDACTICALLY
AACCDDIIOTTU	AUTODIDACTIC

AACCDEEEFPTT	ACCEPT DEFEAT
AACCDEEENSSU	CAUSED A SCENE
AACCDEEFGIRS	FACE DISGRACE
AACCDEEGINSS	GAINED ACCESS
AACCDEEHORTV	CREATED HAVOC
AACCDEEHPSST	DESPATCH CASE
AACCDEEIMORS	ICE-CREAM SODA
AACCDEEINNSS	ASCENDANCIES
AACCDEEINRRT	INCARCERATED
AACCDEEJKKOR	CRACKED A JOKE
AACCDEELLRTU	CALLED A TRUCE
AACCDEENNOTT	CONCATENATED
AACCDEHHPRRU	CHURCH PARADE
AACCDEHIKNSW	SANDWICH CAKE
AACCDEHIMSST	MISSED A CATCH
AACCDEHINORS	ARCHDIOCESAN
AACCDEHIPSST	DISPATCH CASE
AACCDEHKNPPU	PACKED A PUNCH
AACCDEIIILNT	DIALECTICIAN
AACCDEIILMST	ACCLIMATISED
AACCDEIILMTZ	ACCLIMATIZED
AACCDEIINNNT	IN AN ACCIDENT
AACCDEIKOPRT	CRACK-POT IDEA
	CRACKPOT IDEA
AACCDEILLLOT	LOCAL DIALECT
AACCDEILLNTY	ACCIDENTALLY
AACCDEILNRRW	DRAWN A CIRCLE
AACCDEILOPSY	CYCLOPAEDIAS
AACCDEILRRSW	DRAWS A CIRCLE
AACCDEINOSTV	ACTS ON ADVICE
AACCDEKMPUUV	VACUUM-PACKED
AACCDELLLTUY	CALCULATEDLY
AACCDELNRTUU	CARUNCULATED
AACCDEMMOOST	ACCOMMODATES
AACCDEMNORSS	RANDOM-ACCESS
AACCDENPRSUU	CUP AND SAUCER
AACCDFHNOORU	COACH AND FOUR
AACCDGINRRRY	CARD-CARRYING
AACCDIILNOTU	CLAUDICATION
AACCDILLNSTY	SCANTILY CLAD
AACCDKLRSTUY	LUCKY AT CARDS
AACCDLLOORST	CALLS A DOCTOR
AACCDLNORTUU	COUNT DRACULA
AACCEEEENRST	CREATE A SCENE
AACCEEEFIKOP	A PIECE OF CAKE
AACCEEEILRTV	ACCELERATIVE
AACCEEEKLPRT	CEREAL PACKET
AACCEEELLNSV	CANCELS LEAVE
AACCEEELPSSU	ESCAPE CLAUSE
AACCEEENSSSU	CAUSES A SCENE
AACCEEFFGHNO	CHANGE OF FACE
AACCEEFFHSTT	FACE THE FACTS
AACCEEFGHMNO	GAME OF CHANCE
AACCEEFIKRTT	FIERCE ATTACK
AACCEEFKRRSS	SAFECRACKERS
AACCEEGHINNV	GIVEN A CHANCE
AACCEEGHINSV	GIVES A CHANCE
AACCEEGHLNPS	CHANGE PLACES
AACCEEGHOSST	STAGECOACHES
AACCEEGILNRT	ACCELERATING
AACCEEGIMPRT	PRACTICE GAME
AACCEEGMNNRT	GERMAN ACCENT
AACCEEGNORTV	GAVE A CONCERT
AACCEEHIKMOS	MAKES A CHOICE
AACCEEHIRRST	CHARACTERISE
AACCEEHIRRTZ	CHARACTERIZE
AACCEEHKMNRR	CHANCE REMARK
AACCEEHKNNST	TAKEN CHANCES
AACCEEHKNSST	TAKES CHANCES
AACCEEHLNOSS	LOSES A CHANCE
AACCEEHLSSST	TEACHES CLASS

AACCEEHORSTV	CREATES HAVOC
AACCEEIILLPR	CAPERCAILLIE
AACCEEILNORT	ACCELERATION
AACCEEINRRST	INCARCERATES
AACCEEIOSTVV	VOCATIVE CASE
AACCEEKNOPSS	PACK ONES CASE
AACCEELMOOST	CAME TO A CLOSE
AACCEELORRST	ACCELERATORS
AACCEELPPSSU	SPACE CAPSULE
AACCEEMOPPRR	CAME A CROPPER
AACCEENNOSTT	CONCATENATES
AACCEENOPTUY	ACCOUNT PAYEE
AACCEENRSSTU	ACCURATENESS
AACCEFFINOTV	VACANT OFFICE
AACCEFGIKNRS	SAFECRACKING
AACCEFGOORTU	ACT OF COURAGE
AACCEFHHISST	CATCHES A FISH
AACCEFLNOSTU	FALSE ACCOUNT
AACCEGHIILPR	ARCHIPELAGIC
AACCEGHMNPPU	CHAMPAGNE CUP
AACCEGIKMNRS	MAKING SCARCE
AACCEGINNTTU	ACCENTUATING
AACCEGKLORSU	LACKS COURAGE
AACCEGNORTTU	GREAT ACCOUNT
AACCEGNRSSST	GRANTS ACCESS
AACCEHHIILRR	HIERARCHICAL
AACCEHHIILPTW	AT WHICH PLACE
AACCEHHPRSST	CATCHPHRASES
AACCEHIIMNNS	MECHANICIANS
AACCEHILLLPY	CEPHALICALLY
AACCEHILLMNO	MELANCHOLIAC
AACCEHILLMNY	MECHANICALLY
AACCEHILORTT	THEOCRATICAL
AACCEHILPRTY	ARCHETYPICAL
AACCEHIMORTT	METATHORACIC
AACCEHIMSSST	MISSES A CATCH
AACCEHINNTTW	WITH AN ACCENT
AACCEHINRTTT	THE ANTARCTIC
AACCEHKNOSST	SCOTCH A SNAKE
AACCEHLMNORT	COAL MERCHANT
AACCEHLMOPRY	MACROCEPHALY
AACCEIIINPST	INCAPACITIES
AACCEIILLNRT	ANTICLERICAL
AACCEIIIMNRS	CRIMINAL CASE
AACCEIILMPRT	CAPITAL CRIME
AACCEIILMRST	ACCLIMATISER
AACCEIILMRTZ	ACCLIMATIZER
AACCEIILMSST	ACCLIMATISES
AACCEIILMSTZ	ACCLIMATIZES
AACCEIILPTVY	CAPACITIVELY
AACCEIKLOPST	PEACOCKS TAIL
AACCEILLMSSU	MUSICAL SCALE
AACCEILLMSTU	MISCALCULATE
AACCEILLNNOT	CANCELLATION
AACCEILLSTTY	ECSTATICALLY
AACCEILMMORT	MACROCLIMATE
AACCEILMNOPS	COMPLAISANCE
AACCEILMPRST	MALPRACTICES
AACCEILMTUUV	ACCUMULATIVE
AACCEILNORVY	CLAIRVOYANCE
AACCEILNRRTT	RECALCITRANT
AACCEILNRTUY	INACCURATELY
AACCEILORSST	COAST IS CLEAR
AACCEIMNOPST	COMPANIES ACT
AACCEINNOTTU	ACCENTUATION
AACCEINOORRS	RARE OCCASION
AACCEINOORTV	COACERVATION
AACCEINOPSTT	ACCEPTATIONS
AACCEINORRTY	ACCRETIONARY
AACCEINORSST	CAST-IRON CASE
AACCEINQSTTU	ACQUITTANCES

AACCEKKSTYYY	YACKETY-YACKS
AACCEKMNOSTT	MAKES CONTACT
AACCEKNNOTTU	TAKEN ACCOUNT
AACCEKNOSTTU	TAKES ACCOUNT
AACCEKOPSSTT	COSTS A PACKET
AACCELLORSUY	CALCAREOUSLY
AACCELLRRSTY	CRYSTAL CLEAR
AACCELNNOOPV	PLANO-CONCAVE
AACCELPRSSTU	SPECTACULARS
AACCFIIINOPT	PACIFICATION
AACCFIILMOPT	FAIT ACCOMPLI
AACCFIIOPRTY	PACIFICATORY
AACCFILLPTUY	FULL CAPACITY
AACCFILNNOTU	FINAL ACCOUNT
AACCFINNORSS	SAN FRANCISCO
AACCGGHIINTV	GIVING A CATCH
AACCGGHHILLTU	CAUGHT A CHILL
AACCGHHIPRTY	TACHYGRAPHIC
AACCGHIILLNO	LOGICAL CHAIN
AACCGHIILLOR	OLIGARCHICAL
AACCGHIILLPR	CALLIGRAPHIC
AACCGHIINNNT	CACHINNATING
AACCGHINNPPT	CATCH NAPPING
AACCGHIOPRRT	CARTOGRAPHIC
AACCGIILMORT	TRAGICOMICAL
AACCGIINRRTU	CARICATURING
AACCGIKNNRTU	CRACKING A NUT
AACCGILLOOST	SCATOLOGICAL
AACCGILMNTUU	ACCUMULATING
AACCGIMNNOPY	ACCOMPANYING
AACCHHIMRTTY	CHARITY MATCH
AACCHIILPRTT	CRITICAL PATH
AACCHIINNNOT	CACHINNATION
AACCHIINRSTY	SACCHARINITY
AACCHILLMSTU	MUSIC-HALL ACT
AACCHIMMRSTY	MACCARTHYISM
AACCHIMNOPRT	PANCHROMATIC
AACCHIMOOPRT	APOCHROMATIC
AACCHINOOSTT	COACH STATION
AACCHIOPRSTT	CATASTROPHIC
AACCHJKLNORT	JACK CHARLTON
AACCHKMRSTTU	STRUCK A MATCH
AACCIIILLMTY	CLIMATICALLY
AACCIIILLSST	CLASSICALIST
AACCIILLSSTY	CLASSICALITY
AACCIILMORTT	TIMOCRATICAL
AACCIILMRSST	CRITICAL MASS
AACCIILNTTTY	ATLANTIC CITY
AACCIILPRTTY	PRACTICALITY
AACCIINNOPRR	CAPRICORNIAN
AACCIINOSSTU	ACOUSTICIANS
AACCIIORRSTT	ARISTOCRATIC
AACCIIRRSTTU	CARICATURIST
AACCIJKKLNSU	JACK NICKLAUS
AACCILLLNOVY	VOLCANICALLY
AACCILLNOOSY	OCCASIONALLY
AACCILLNORTY	NARCOTICALLY
AACCILLNOSTU	CALCULATIONS
AACCILLORSTY	ACROSTICALLY
	SOCRATICALLY
AACCILLOSTUY	ACOUSTICALLY
AACCILMNOTUU	ACCUMULATION
AACCILMOPRSS	SARCOPLASMIC
AACCILNOOPTU	OCCUPATIONAL
AACCIMNOPSST	ACCOMPANISTS
AACCINOPSTTT	CAPTAIN SCOTT
AACCLMORSTUU	ACCUMULATORS
AACCOOOSSTTT	COAST TO COAST
AACDDDEEHLOR	DODECAHEDRAL
AACDDDEFILNT	CAT AND FIDDLE
AACDDDIISSVY	DAVID CASSIDY

AACDDEEEHHTT	CHEATED DEATH	AACDEEHKLPST	DEALS THE PACK
AACDDEEEHLTY	ACETALDEHYDE	AACDEEHKLPTT	DEALT THE PACK
AACDDEEEHNRS	CASE-HARDENED	AACDEEHKORVW	WREAKED HAVOC
AACDDEEEHPST	ESCAPED DEATH	AACDEEHLLNSW	SHALL WE DANCE?
AACDDEEEELNNO	LED ONE A DANCE	AACDEEHLORRT	CLEAR THE ROAD
AACDDEEFHNOT	DANCE OF DEATH	AACDEEHMOOST	COMES TO A HEAD
AACDDEEFIORS	ROADSIDE CAFE	AACDEEHNPSTT	STAND THE PACE
AACDDEEGISTU	ACTED AS GUIDE	AACDEEHPRTTT	ACTED THE PART
AACDDEEHLRST	DEAL THE CARDS	AACDEEIIMNRS	AMERICANISED
AACDDEEHRRST	READ THE CARDS	AACDEEIIMNRZ	AMERICANIZED
AACDDEEIRSTT	ITS A DEAD CERT	AACDEEIJKNTT	JACKET AND TIE
AACDDEEKLNRS	DESK CALENDAR	AACDEEIKMTVY	TAKE MY ADVICE
AACDDEELLNVW	WELL ADVANCED	AACDEEILMMNR	REMAINED CALM
AACDDEFIILSS	CLASSIFIED AD	AACDEEILMNPT	TIME AND PLACE
AACDDEGHHNNS	CHANGED HANDS	AACDEEILMRVY	DEVIL MAY CARE
AACDDEGNNNOS	SONG AND DANCE		DEVIL-MAY-CARE
AACDDEHINNNY	NICE AND HANDY	AACDEEILNNOW	NEW CALEDONIA
AACDDEHLLNOS	HOLDS A CANDLE	AACDEEILNRTT	INTERCALATED
AACDDEHLNPPS	CLAPPED HANDS	AACDEEILOSST	ISOLATED CASE
AACDDEHLNPSS	CLASPED HANDS	AACDEEILSTTX	EXACT DETAILS
AACDDEHLOPRY	PLAYED A CHORD	AACDEEIMNPST	TIME AND SPACE
AACDDEHMNNOS	CASH ON DEMAND	AACDEEINNNTT	IN ATTENDANCE
AACDDEHNNOST	AT SECOND HAND	AACDEEINNOPT	PAINTED OCEAN
AACDDEIIJTUV	ADJUDICATIVE	AACDEEINNRRT	REINCARNATED
AACDDEIINNNR	INCARNADINED	AACDEEINNRST	NEAR DISTANCE
AACDDEILMNOV	DAVID COLEMAN	AACDEEINPRSY	INCREASED PAY
AACDDEINRSTU	CANDIDATURES	AACDEEIPRRTV	PREVARICATED
AACDDEKNSTTU	SUDDEN ATTACK	AACDEEIRRSTT	CREATED A STIR
AACDDELLNORU	LOUD AND CLEAR	AACDEEKMORRS	MAKES A RECORD
AACDDELOORTV	LORD ADVOCATE	AACDEEKNPPST	SPEND A PACKET
AACDDGHINOTU	ADDING A TOUCH	AACDEELMNOPY	MAYPOLE DANCE
AACDDGIIJNTU	ADJUDICATING	AACDEELNOPRR	PLACE AN ORDER
AACDDGIIKRRV	DAVID GARRICK	AACDEELNPRSS	SENDS A PARCEL
AACDDHILOPST	ADOPTS A CHILD	AACDEELNPSTU	ENCAPSULATED
AACDDHILRWWY	WAYWARD CHILD	AACDEEMMNNSTV	ADVANCEMENTS
AACDDHINOPSW	PAID CASH DOWN	AACDEEMMNRTUY	MADE A CENTURY
AACDDIIJNOTU	ADJUDICATION	AACDEEMRSTUY	MADE A CURTSEY
AACDDIIJORSTU	ADJUDICATORS	AACDEENNOTTW	WENT TO A DANCE
AACDDIIJORTUY	ADJUDICATORY	AACDEFFILMST	MEDICAL STAFF
AACDDIKMNNRU	MANDARIN DUCK	AACDEFGGINNR	FACING DANGER
AACDDILMNOPS	DIAMOND CLASP	AACDEFHIMTVY	FIVE-DAY MATCH
AACDDIMMNOOR	COMMANDO RAID	AACDEFHINRRT	HANDICRAFTER
AACDDLNORSTY	SCOTLAND YARD	AACDEFHORRRW	REACH FORWARD
AACDDORSTUWY	AWARD CUSTODY	AACDEFIILPTX	FIXED CAPITAL
AACDEEEENRST	CREATES A NEED	AACDEFIKNRRS	FRANCIS DRAKE
AACDEEEGLNRS	CANDLE GREASE	AACDEFIKORSV	ASK FOR ADVICE
AACDEEEGNOST	ACTED ONE'S AGE	AACDEFINORTT	FRACTIONATED
AACDEEEHIRRS	RAISED A CHEER	AACDEFINORWY	FORCED A WAY IN
AACDEEEHKMMO	HOME-MADE CAKE	AACDEFJKOPSS	JACK OF SPADES
AACDEEEHNRVY	EACH AND EVERY	AACDEFMNRTUU	MANUFACTURED
AACDEEEHPRSS	READS A SPEECH	AACDEFMRRRTU	FRACTURED ARM
AACDEEEHPSST	ESCAPES DEATH	AACDEGGILNRR	GRACE DARLING
AACDEEELLRTT	CATTLE DEALER	AACDEGHHNNSS	CHANGES HANDS
AACDEEFFGINT	FACING DEFEAT	AACDEGHILLNS	CALLING HEADS
AACDEEFHLMSY	SHAMEFACEDLY	AACDEGHILLNT	LIGHT A CANDLE
AACDEEFHLOTT	HEAD OF CATTLE	AACDEGHILNNR	REACHING LAND
AACDEEFILRTY	FACED REALITY	AACDEGHNNORU	CHANGE AROUND
AACDEEFIMNNR	MADE IN FRANCE	AACDEGIIKNSV	ASKING ADVICE
AACDEEFINSST	SAFE DISTANCE	AACDEGIIKNTV	TAKING ADVICE
AACDEEGGHHNT	HATCHED AN EGG	AACDEGIINPTT	DECAPITATING
AACDEEGHILRV	AVERAGE CHILD	AACDEGIINSST	CASTING ASIDE
AACDEEGHOTTT	ACTED THE GOAT	AACDEGIINTTV	DEACTIVATING
AACDEEGKOORT	TAKE GOOD CARE	AACDEGIKMORS	SMOKED A CIGAR
AACDEEGNNOOT	GONE TO A DANCE	AACDEGILLNNP	LANDING PLACE
AACDEEGNOOST	GOES TO A DANCE	AACDEGILLNOS	CLOSING A DEAL
AACDEEHHLLRT	HEARD THE CALL	AACDEGILNORT	LEADING ACTOR
AACDEEHHRSTW	WASHED THE CAR	AACDEGILNRRW	DECLARING WAR
AACDEEHILLNU	AUDIENCE HALL	AACDEGILNRSW	SCALE DRAWING
AACDEEHILRSV	LAVISHED CARE	AACDEGLNNRRT	GRAND CENTRAL
AACDEEHINRTT	CERTAIN DEATH	AACDEGLNNRRY	GRAND LARCENY
AACDEEHINSTT	ACTED IN HASTE	AACDEGLNOPRR	DROP A CLANGER

AACDEHHLOPTT	HATCHED A PLOT	AACDELPPRSTU	CUSTARD APPLE
AACDEHHOSSSW	CHASE SHADOWS	AACDFGGIILNT	CADGING A LIFT
AACDEHIKNOQU	HAD A QUICK ONE	AACDFGHINNRT	HANDCRAFTING
AACDEHILLLRY	HERALDICALLY	AACDFGILNNRT	LANDING CRAFT
AACDEHILLNTU	HALLUCINATED	AACDFGINORRW	FORCING A DRAW
AACDEHILMNRU	CARDINAL HUME	AACDFHIKNSTT	THICK AND FAST
AACDEHIMNSTW	MEAT SANDWICH	AACDFHMORRRW	FORWARD MARCH
AACDEHINORRT	RIDE AT ANCHOR	AACDFIMMORRT	DRAMATIC FORM
AACDEHINPPRS	HANDICAPPERS	AACDFORRRRWY	CARRY FORWARD
AACDEHKMMOSU	MAKES MUCH ADO	AACDGHIILTTW	DIGITAL WATCH
AACDEHKMRRST	MARK THE CARDS	AACDGHIINNPP	HANDICAPPING
AACDEHLLORTY	OCTAHEDRALLY	AACDGHIIOPRR	RADIOGRAPHIC
AACDEHLNOOPP	CEPHALOPODAN	AACDGHILNNPU	LAUNCHING PAD
AACDEHLNORSS	LEONARD SACHS	AACDGHILNNRS	CRASH LANDING
AACDEHLOPPRR	APPLE ORCHARD		CRASH-LANDING
AACDEHMORRTW	MARCHED TO WAR	AACDGHINSTTU	CUTTING A DASH
AACDEHNORRST	HORSE AND CART	AACDGIIINRTV	DIVARICATING
AACDEHOOPPTT	CAPPED A TOOTH	AACDGIILLLOY	DIALOGICALLY
AACDEIILRSVW	RADICAL VIEWS	AACDGIILLOOR	RADIOLOGICAL
AACDEIIMNORT	ROMANTIC IDEA	AACDGIILLOOU	AUDIOLOGICAL
AACDEIIMRSTY	ARMISTICE DAY	AACDGIILNNSS	SCANDALISING
AACDEIINNNRS	INCARNADINES	AACDGIILNNSZ	SCANDALIZING
AACDEIINOPTT	DECAPITATION	AACDGIINNNOR	DANCING ON AIR
AACDEIINORTT	RATIOCINATED	AACDGILLMOTY	DOGMATICALLY
AACDEIINOTTV	DEACTIVATION	AACDGILNPRSY	PLAYING CARDS
AACDEIIOSSST	DISASSOCIATE	AACDGILOOPST	CAPITAL GOODS
AACDEIIPPRTT	PARTICIPATED	AACDGILORSUY	GRACIOUS LADY
AACDEIJLLTVY	ADJECTIVALLY	AACDGILRRSUW	SURGICAL WARD
AACDEIKLPRTY	PLAYED A TRICK	AACDHIIILNRV	INVALID CHAIR
AACDEILLMNOY	DEMONIACALLY	AACDHIIINRST	CHRISTIAN AID
AACDEILLNORT	COLLAR AND TIE	AACDHIIJLOTU	JUDICIAL OATH
AACDEILLNOSW	DISALLOWANCE	AACDHIILNPRS	CARDINALSHIP
AACDEILMMORT	MELODRAMATIC	AACDHIIOPRSS	APHRODISIACS
AACDEILMNNOT	CAME IN TO LAND	AACDHILLNRTU	NATURAL CHILD
AACDEILMNRTY	CITY ALDERMAN	AACDHILMRRUY	HYDRAULIC RAM
AACDEILMRTTU	MATRICULATED	AACDHIMRSSTY	CHRISTMAS DAY
AACDEILNNSVY	CANVEY ISLAND	AACDHINOPQRU	QUADRAPHONIC
AACDEILNORST	DECLARATIONS	AACDHLNOOTTW	TOOTH AND CLAW
AACDEILNOSTT	ANECDOTALIST	AACDHNOPSSWY	PAYS CASH DOWN
AACDEILNOSTW	IN A COLD SWEAT	AACDIIINORTV	DIVARICATION
AACDEILNRSSS	SCANDALISERS	AACDIIKLNOST	LAID IN A STOCK
AACDEILNRSSZ	SCANDALIZERS	AACDIILLNOTY	DIATONICALLY
AACDEILPRSTW	PRACTISED LAW	AACDIILLSSTY	SADISTICALLY
AACDEILPRSTY	DIRECTS A PLAY	AACDIKNNPPSS	SPICK AND SPAN
AACDEILRSSUV	VASCULARISED		SPICK-AND-SPAN
AACDEILRSUVZ	VASCULARIZED	AACDILLNORSY	SARDONICALLY
AACDEIMMOPRT	DRAMATIC POEM	AACDILLNSTYY	DYNASTICALLY
AACDEIMNNOTT	CONTAMINATED	AACDILLOPRSY	SPORADICALLY
	NO ADMITTANCE	AACDILMNOORT	ANIMAL DOCTOR
AACDEIMNORSY	AERODYNAMICS	AACDINOPRSSW	PASS IN A CROWD
AACDEIMOOSTU	DIATOMACEOUS	AACDLMMNOORY	ROYAL COMMAND
AACDEIMOPRTT	DRAMATIC POET	AACEEEFHNOPV	HAVEN OF PEACE
AACDEINNOSSY	ASCENSION DAY	AACEEEFNOSSV	SAVE ONES FACE
AACDEINNRSSU	RUSSIAN DANCE	AACEEEFOPSTT	STATE OF PEACE
AACDEIOPRSTT	DECAPITATORS	AACEEEGHNRTX	EXCHANGE RATE
AACDEIORSTTV	DEACTIVATORS	AACEEEGHRSTU	ARGUE THE CASE
AACDEIPRRTUW	DRAW A PICTURE	AACEEEGINRSW	WAGE INCREASE
AACDEKKNRRSY	KNACKERS YARD	AACEEEGLRTUV	GAVE A LECTURE
AACDEKLLRSUY	ALL-DAY SUCKER	AACEEEHINPTV	HAVE PATIENCE
AACDEKLORSSW	WALKED ACROSS	AACEEEHIRRSS	RAISES A CHEER
AACDEKMMNNOT	TAKEN COMMAND	AACEEEHKKNTT	TAKEN THE CAKE
AACDEKMMNOST	TAKES COMMAND	AACEEEHKKSTT	TAKES THE CAKE
AACDELLLNOTW	TALLOW CANDLE	AACEEEHKMPSS	MAKES A SPEECH
AACDELLMORST	CALLED TO ARMS	AACEEEHKMPST	MAKES THE PACE
AACDELLORSTY	SACERDOTALLY	AACEEEHKNOSV	HAVE ONE'S CAKE
AACDELNORSTW	DRAWN TO SCALE	AACEEEHMRRST	RESEARCH TEAM
AACDELOORSTW	DRAW TO A CLOSE	AACEEEIINOPRT	PEACE ON EARTH
AACDELOPRRSY	PLAYS A RECORD	AACEEEIRRSSU	AIR-SEA RESCUE
AACDELOPRTTW	COLD-WATER TAP	AACEEEKRSTTV	SEVERE ATTACK
AACDELORSSTW	DRAWS TO SCALE	AACEEELNORTV	LEAVE NO TRACE
AACDELORSUVY	CADAVEROUSLY	AACEEENNRRRT	REAR ENTRANCE

AACEEEENPRSVY	SEVERANCE PAY	AACEEHLNOTUV	NOT HAVE A CLUE
AACEEEPSSTTT	CASSETTE TAPE	AACEEHLNPRRT	CHARTER PLANE
AACEEFFHRTTT	AFTER THE FACT	AACEEHLNPTTU	PENTATEUCHAL
AACEEFFINORW	CARAFE OF WINE	AACEEHLPPRTT	THE APPLE-CART
AACEEFFINOTT	AFFECTIONATE	AACEEHLPRTTY	THREE-ACT PLAY
AACEEFGHINRX	FAIR EXCHANGE	AACEEHLRSTWY	CLEARS THE WAY
AACEEFGHNORT	RATE OF CHANGE	AACEEHNNPPST	HAPPENSTANCE
AACEEFHHNORV	ARCH OF HEAVEN	AACEEHNORSTT	NEAR THE COAST
AACEEFHLLNRS	FALLEN ARCHES	AACEEHORSSST	ACROSS THE SEA
AACEEFHLLOST	CALL OF THE SEA	AACEEHPSSSTU	PASS THE SAUCE
AACEEFHNOSSW	WASH ONES FACE	AACEEHPSSTTY	STAYS THE PACE
AACEEFILRSTY	FACES REALITY	AACEEIIMNRSS	AMERICANISES
AACEEFIMNNOR	A FINE ROMANCE	AACEEIIMNRSZ	AMERICANIZES
AACEEFINNQRU	AFRICAN QUEEN	AACEEIINRSST	SECTARIANISE
AACEEFLMRRTT	CATTLE FARMER	AACEEIINRSTZ	SECTARIANIZE
AACEEFLNRTTV	RELEVANT FACT	AACEEIIPPRTV	APPRECIATIVE
AACEEFNNNOSS	NONFEASANCES	AACEEIKKNTTW	TAKEN A WICKET
AACEEFOPPRRY	PRAY FOR PEACE	AACEEIKKSTTW	TAKES A WICKET
AACEEFORSTVW	CREST OF A WAVE	AACEEIKLMOTV	MOVE LIKE A CAT
AACEEGGHHNST	HATCHES AN EGG	AACEEIKLMRST	MAKES IT CLEAR
AACEEGGIKNRT	CREAKING GATE	AACEEIKLNORV	VERONICA LAKE
AACEEGGILLNO	GENEALOGICAL	AACEEIKLNRVW	CARNIVAL WEEK
AACEEGHILLNR	CARNEGIE HALL	AACEEIKMNRST	MAKES CERTAIN
AACEEGHINORT	ARCHEGONIATE	AACEEIKNPTTV	TAKEN CAPTIVE
AACEEGHIRSTT	CIGARETTE ASH	AACEEIKNRSTT	CREATE A STINK
AACEEGHKMNSS	MAKES CHANGES	AACEEIKNRSTU	TAKEN A CRUISE
AACEEGHLNNPS	CHANGE PLANES	AACEEIKPSTTV	TAKES CAPTIVE
AACEEGHNPRTX	PART EXCHANGE	AACEEIKRSSTU	TAKES A CRUISE
	PART-EXCHANGE	AACEEILLMNSS	MESALLIANCES
AACEEGHRRSST	GATE-CRASHERS	AACEEILMPPRS	PRE-ECLAMPSIA
AACEEGIKMNNS	MAKING A SCENE	AACEEILNORRT	RECREATIONAL
AACEEGILLMNT	CALL A MEETING	AACEEILNRRRY	CLAIRE RAYNER
AACEEGILNPST	LASTING PEACE	AACEEILNRSTT	INTERCALATES
	SPECIAL AGENT	AACEEILNRSVV	NAVAL SERVICE
AACEEGILNRRV	VICAR-GENERAL	AACEEILPRSTX	EXTRA SPECIAL
AACEEGIMNNTX	EXACT MEANING	AACEEILPRTTU	RECAPITULATE
AACEEGIMNPTT	MAGNETIC TAPE	AACEEIMNNNRT	MAIN ENTRANCE
AACEEGINNRSV	SERVING AN ACE	AACEEINNNRST	CENTENARIANS
AACEEGINNSTY	CASTING AN EYE	AACEEINNRRST	REINCARNATES
AACEEGKNORTU	TAKEN COURAGE	AACEEIOPRSTT	ECTOPARASITE
AACEEGKORSTU	TAKES COURAGE	AACEEIPRRSTV	PREVARICATES
AACEEGLLLNOV	NAVAL COLLEGE	AACEEIRRSSTT	CREATES A STIR
AACEEGLNNRST	REGENT'S CANAL	AACEEJKMNRVY	EVERY MAN JACK
AACEEGLNPRST	STRANGE PLACE	AACEEKLLPRSY	SPEAK CLEARLY
AACEEGLNRTVY	TRAVEL AGENCY	AACEEKLLRSST	CARELESS TALK
AACEEGNORTTT	RENT A COTTAGE	AACEEKLMPRST	MARKETPLACES
AACEEGOPRSST	STORAGE SPACE	AACEEKLMRTTT	CATTLE MARKET
AACEEHHHMRRT	THE MARCH HARE	AACEEKLOPSST	LOSES A PACKET
AACEEHHIRSST	RAISE THE CASH	AACEEKLPRSSW	SPACEWALKERS
AACEEHHKKNTV	HAVE THE KNACK	AACEEKMNRTUY	MAKE A CENTURY
AACEEHHLLRST	HEARS THE CALL	AACEEKMRSTUY	MAKE A CURTSEY
AACEEHHLPRTT	CLEAR THE PATH	AACEEKNNORRT	TAKEN A CORNER
AACEEHHMSSTT	TEACHES MATHS	AACEEKNNSSTU	TAKEN A CENSUS
AACEEHHRRTTW	WEATHER CHART	AACEEKNORRST	TAKES A CORNER
AACEEHHRSSTW	WASHES THE CAR	AACEEKNORSTU	TAKEN A COURSE
AACEEHIINSTT	AESTHETICIAN	AACEEKNPPSTT	SPENT A PACKET
AACEEHILLMPS	MICHAEL ASPEL	AACEEKNSSSTU	TAKES A CENSUS
AACEEHILMTTT	METATHETICAL	AACEEKORSSTU	TAKES A COURSE
AACEEHILRRST	CLEARS THE AIR	AACEELNPSSTU	ENCAPSULATES
AACEEHILRSSV	LAVISHES CARE	AACEEMMNORST	CAME ON STREAM
AACEEHILRSTV	THE CAVALIERS	AACEEMMNNORRS	COARSE MANNER
AACEEHIMNRST	THE AMERICANS	AACEEMOPRTTV	CAVEAT EMPTOR
AACEEHINSSTT	ANAESTHETICS	AACEENNPPRTU	APPURTENANCE
AACEEHINTTTU	AUTHENTICATE	AACEENNPRRST	TRANSPARENCE
AACEEHIOPRST	APOTHECARIES	AACEENOPRRSW	NARROW ESCAPE
AACEEHISTVWY	TWICE AS HEAVY	AACEENORSSTW	CASE TO ANSWER
AACEEHKMNRRS	SNAKE CHARMER	AACEEOPPPRRS	SPARE A COPPER
AACEEHLLNNRT	ENTRANCE HALL	AACEFFHINRSS	AFFRANCHISES
AACEEHLMPRST	SPERMATHECAL	AACEFFILNORV	NAVAL OFFICER
AACEEHLNOPRT	ANOTHER PLACE	AACEFFILRSTV	SLAVE TRAFFIC
AACEEHLNOSST	TEACH A LESSON	AACEFFINOSTT	AFFECTATIONS

AACEFFMORTTT	MATTER OF FACT	AACEGILMNNRT	MAGIC LANTERN
	MATTER-OF-FACT	AACEGILMNSTU	EMASCULATING
AACEFFOOPRSY	PAY OFF A SCORE	AACEGILMORSV	LIAM COSGRAVE
AACEFFORSTTY	SAFETY FACTOR	AACEGILNNRRW	CLEAR WARNING
AACEFGHHITTU	CAUGHT A THIEF	AACEGILNORRT	ORGAN RECITAL
AACEFGHINNRU	FRENCH GUIANA	AACEGILNPPSS	PASSING PLACE
AACEFGHIRSTT	STRAIGHT FACE	AACEGILNRTUW	CATERWAULING
AACEFGHLNNOP	CHANGE OF PLAN	AACEGILNSSUV	SAVING CLAUSE
AACEFGIKNORT	TAKING CARE OF	AACEGINNNRRU	RUNNING A RACE
AACEFGILLNPU	PULLING A FACE	AACEGINNOORT	OCTOGENARIAN
AACEFGINORST	RACE OF GIANTS	AACEGINNORSS	RACING SEASON
AACEFHINRSTT	FRANTIC HASTE	AACEGINOOPTT	COTTAGE PIANO
AACEFHJKORST	JACK OF HEARTS	AACEGINOPRSY	PAYING A SCORE
AACEFHLMNNRRU	FUNERAL MARCH	AACEGINOSTTV	CASTING A VOTE
AACEFHOPRTTT	PART OF THE ACT	AACEGINPPRRT	TRACING PAPER
AACEFIIILTTV	FACILITATIVE	AACEGINRRTTW	WATERING CART
AACEFIILLNTU	NAUTICAL LIFE	AACEGKNNORSU	SUCK AN ORANGE
AACEFIILMMNR	AMERICAN FILM	AACEGLMNOOWY	COME A LONG WAY
AACEFIKLLOOT	ACT LIKE A FOOL	AACEGLMOORRU	MORAL COURAGE
AACEFILLLNPS	FALLS IN PLACE	AACEGLNORTTU	CONGRATULATE
AACEFILOPRSS	PAIR OF SCALES	AACEGLNORTUY	AGRANULOCYTE
AACEFIMOPRRU	CAME UP FOR AIR	AACEGNRRSTTU	GRANTS A TRUCE
AACEFINORSTT	FRACTIONATES	AACEHHIILMOP	HAEMOPHILIAC
AACEFINORSWY	FORCES A WAY IN	AACEHHILNNPT	NAPHTHALENIC
AACEFINOSSST	OF ASSISTANCE	AACEHHIINPSST	TEACH SPANISH
AACEFMNRRTUU	MANUFACTURER	AACEHHLOPSTT	HATCHES A PLOT
AACEFMNRSTUU	MANUFACTURES	AACEHHNORSUV	HAVE A CRUSH ON
AACEFNOORSTT	ACT OF TREASON	AACEHIILLMNP	MICHAEL PALIN
AACEFNORRTTX	EXTRACTOR FAN	AACEHIILLOPT	PALAEOLITHIC
AACEFOPPPRRS	SCRAP OF PAPER	AACEHIILLRTY	HIERATICALLY
AACEGGGHINNR	CHANGING GEAR	AACEHIILMRTT	ARITHMETICAL
AACEGGHIKNRT	TAKING CHARGE	AACEHIILNTTT	ANTITHETICAL
AACEGGHILOPR	GEOGRAPHICAL	AACEHIIMMRRST	MATRIARCHIES
AACEGGIKNPPR	PREPACKAGING	AACEHIINNRSV	SEARCH IN VAIN
AACEGGCKLOPRU	LOCK-UP GARAGE	AACEHIINPTTT	ANTIPATHETIC
AACEGHHIMORR	HAEMORRHAGIC	AACEHIINRRST	CHRISTIAN ERA
AACEGHIIKLMN	LAKE MICHIGAN	AACEHIKLRRTY	LITERARY HACK
AACEGHILLPRR	CALLIGRAPHER	AACEHIKMRSTT	STRIKE A MATCH
AACEGHILMOOT	HAEMATOLOGIC	AACEHIKNOQSU	HAS A QUICK ONE
AACEGHILNNSW	WASHING CLEAN	AACEHILLLNOY	HOLY ALLIANCE
AACEGHILOPRS	ARCHIPELAGOS	AACEHILLLTTY	ATHLETICALLY
AACEGHIMNOPR	ANEMOGRAPHIC	AACEHILLMPTY	EMPHATICALLY
	PHANEROGAMIC	AACEHILLMTTY	THEMATICALLY
AACEGHINNNRST	CHANGE TRAINS	AACEHILLNSTU	HALLUCINATES
AACEGHLNOOST	SHOOT A GLANCE	AACEHILLPTTY	PATHETICALLY
AACEGHLOORST	COAL SHORTAGE	AACEHILLRTTY	THEATRICALLY
AACEGHLSSSTW	WATCHGLASSES	AACEHILMNPRU	ALPHANUMERIC
AACEGHNOOPRY	OCEANOGRAPHY	AACEHILMOPRT	METAPHORICAL
AACEGHOPRRRT	CARTOGRAPHER	AACEHILMPSTY	METAPHYSICAL
AACEGIIINRRT	GERIATRICIAN	AACEHILNORST	LIES AT ANCHOR
AACEGIIKMNPT	PICKING A TEAM	AACEHILNRSSW	CHARLESS WAIN
AACEGIIKNPRS	ASKING A PRICE	AACEHILOPRST	SPIROCHAETAL
AACEGIILLOOT	AETIOLOGICAL	AACEHILOPRTT	TROPICAL HEAT
AACEGIIMMPRT	EPIGRAMMATIC	AACEHILOPSST	HOSPITAL CASE
AACEGIIMNNPT	EMANCIPATING	AACEHIMNORRT	NORTH AMERICA
AACEGIIMRRSS	MISCARRIAGES	AACEHIMNPRTY	PARTY MACHINE
AACEGIINNNRW	WINNING A RACE	AACEHIMORSTT	HAEMATOCRITS
AACEGIINNPTV	CAVE PAINTING	AACEHIMORSTU	SOUTH AMERICA
AACEGIINNRST	ASCERTAINING	AACEHINOPRSS	COINS A PHRASE
AACEGIINORTV	VICTORIAN AGE	AACEHINRSSTU	TEACH RUSSIAN
AACEGIINPPRT	APPRECIATING	AACEHIORTTUW	WITHOUT A CARE
AACEGIINRRTTV	REACTIVATING	AACEHKOPRTTW	WORTH A PACKET
AACEGIKLMNOO	COOKING A MEAL	AACEHLLPRTYY	ARCHETYPALLY
AACEGIKLNPPR	PARKING PLACE	AACEHLMMNORST	STOLEN A MARCH
AACEGIKLNPSW	SPACEWALKING	AACEHLMOOSTT	COMES TO A HALT
AACEGIKMNRTU	MAKING A TRUCE	AACEHLNRSTUY	CHARLEYS AUNT
AACEGIKMORSS	SMOKES A CIGAR	AACEHLORRRTY	ROYAL CHARTER
AACEGIKNPPRS	PARKING SPACE	AACEHLPRRSTY	REACT SHARPLY
AACEGILLMNTY	MAGNETICALLY	AACEHMMNOORT	CAME TO NO HARM
AACEGILLNOSU	GALLINACEOUS	AACEHMNNRSTU	TRANSHUMANCE
AACEGILLORSU	ARGILLACEOUS	AACEHMNNRTVY	MERCHANT NAVY

AACEHMORRSTW	MARCHES TO WAR
AACEHMSSSSTU	MASSACHUSETS
AACEHNOOORTT	NOT CARE A HOOT
AACEHOPRSSTT	CATASTROPHES
AACEHORSSTWY	ACROSS THE WAY
AACEHPRRRTTY	CHARTER PARTY
	CHARTERPARTY
AACEIIINPTTV	ANTICIPATIVE
AACEIIKLORTV	LAKE VICTORIA
AACEIIKLQTTU	AT QUITE A LICK
AACEIILLMNTU	NAUTICAL MILE
AACEIILMNRTY	RAINY CLIMATE
AACEIILMNSTX	ANTICLIMAXES
AACEIILNOPPS	EPISCOPALIAN
AACEIILNOPRT	PIANO RECITAL
AACEIILNPRST	SPECIAL TRAIN
AACEIILNPRTT	ANTIPARTICLE
AACEIILNRTTU	INARTICULATE
AACEIILRTTUV	ARTICULATIVE
AACEIIMMNRSS	AMERICANISMS
AACEIIMNNOPT	EMANCIPATION
AACEIIMNNORST	RACEMISATION
AACEIIMNNORTZ	RACEMIZATION
AACEIIMNRSST	CARTESIANISM
	SECTARIANISM
AACEIINOPPRT	APPRECIATION
AACEIINORRTV	VICTORIAN ERA
AACEIINORSTT	RATIOCINATES
AACEIINORTTV	REACTIVATION
AACEIIPPRSTT	PARTICIPATES
AACEIJKRSTTT	STRAIT JACKET
	STRAITJACKET
AACEIJLLMSTY	MAJESTICALLY
AACEIJLRSSUU	JULIUS CAESAR
AACEIKLLSTTY	SALT LAKE CITY
AACEIKLMNOPT	KLEPTOMANIAC
AACEIKLMORRW	WORK A MIRACLE
AACEIKLNOSST	SEALSKIN COAT
AACEIKLPQRRU	PICK A QUARREL
AACEILLLLMTY	METALLICALLY
AACEILLMMTUY	IMMACULATELY
AACEILLMNNTW	CAN'T WIN 'EM ALL
AACEILLMNRUY	UNICAMERALLY
AACEILLMNSTY	SEMANTICALLY
AACEILLOPRTY	OPERATICALLY
AACEILLPRRST	CATERPILLARS
AACEILLRTTUY	ARTICULATELY
AACEILMMNORT	MANOMETRICAL
AACEILMNNNOU	ANNUAL INCOME
AACEILMNOSTU	EMASCULATION
AACEILMNOSTX	EXCLAMATIONS
AACEILMRSTTU	MATRICULATES
AACEILNNOPTT	PLACENTATION
AACEILNORSTT	ALTERCATIONS
AACEILPRSSTW	PRACTISES LAW
AACEILPRSTTU	PARTICULATES
AACEILRSSSUV	VASCULARISES
AACEILRSSUVZ	VASCULARIZES
AACEILRSTTTU	STRATICULATE
AACEILRTTTVY	ATTRACTIVELY
AACEIMNNNORT	ANCIENT ROMAN
AACEIMNNOOPT	COMPANIONATE
AACEIMNNOSTT	CONTAMINATES
AACEIMNOOPTT	CAME TO A POINT
AACEIMOPRSTV	COMPARATIVES
AACEIMOPSSTT	IT CAME TO PASS
AACEINNNORST	NONSECTARIAN
AACEINOPSSTT	SPACE STATION
AACEINRTTTUV	UNATTRACTIVE
AACEIOPPRRST	APPRECIATORS
AACEIOPPRRTY	APPRECIATORY

AACEIOPRRRTV	PREVARICATOR
AACEJKLNNORT	JACK-O'-LANTERN
AACEJKOOPTTT	JACKET POTATO
AACEKKLLPRSS	LACKS SPARKLE
AACEKKLNOOSS	LOOKS ASKANCE
AACEKLMNNRSS	LACKS MANNERS
AACEKLORRSUW	CASUAL WORKER
AACEKNNORSTU	CANTANKEROUS
AACEKNOOPTTT	OPEN TO ATTACK
AACELLLLORTY	COLLATERALLY
AACELLLMPRSS	SMALL PARCELS
AACELLLNOPRS	PERSONAL CALL
AACELLMNRTUY	TRACEY ULLMAN
AACELLNORWYY	CANARY YELLOW
AACELLNRRSTU	RETURNS A CALL
AACELLNRRUVY	VERNACULARLY
AACELLOPRRTY	CALL TO PRAYER
AACELLOQTTUZ	QUETZALCOATL
AACELMNORSTW	SCARLET WOMAN
AACEMNOPRTTU	TRUMAN CAPOTE
AACENNPRRSTY	TRANSPARENCY
AACFFIORRSTT	TRAFFICATORS
AACFFKNOORTW	KNOW FOR A FACT
AACFGGILMNOU	CAMOUFLAGING
AACFGHIIKLNT	LACKING FAITH
AACFGIIILLMN	FILING A CLAIM
AACFGIIILNTT	FACILITATING
AACFGIIINNRS	AFRICANISING
AACFGIIINNRZ	AFRICANIZING
AACFGIIINOST	GASIFICATION
AACFGIILMNST	CASTING A FILM
AACFGIILNOTT	FAILING TO ACT
AACFGIILNRTY	ACTING FAIRLY
AACFGILMMORU	MAGIC FORMULA
AACFGINNPSSY	PASSING FANCY
AACFGINOPRRT	FORCING APART
AACFGLORSSTY	GLASS FACTORY
AACFHILLOTTW	ALL OF A TWITCH
AACFHINORSTU	SOUTH AFRICAN
AACFIIILLRTY	ARTIFICIALLY
AACFIIILNOTT	FACILITATION
AACFIIIMNORT	RAMIFICATION
AACFIIINNOTZ	NAZIFICATION
AACFIIINORTT	RATIFICATION
AACFIIINSTUV	AVIFAUNISTIC
AACFIILMNOST	FACTIONALISM
AACFIILNNRTU	FINAL CURTAIN
AACFIILNOOST	FOCALISATION
AACFIILNOOTZ	FOCALIZATION
AACFIILNORTV	RIVAL FACTION
AACFIINNRSST	SAINT FRANCIS
AACFIINOSSTT	SATISFACTION
AACFIKLOPRSS	PAIR OF SLACKS
AACFILLLOSUY	FALLACIOUSLY
AACFILMORTWY	TWO-CAR FAMILY
AACFILNNOOPT	PLAN OF ACTION
AACFINOORRTT	FRACTIONATOR
AACFIORRSSUZ	CZAR OF RUSSIA
AACFIORSSTTY	SATISFACTORY
AACFIPRSSTTY	FASCIST PARTY
AACFRRSSTTYY	ARTSY-CRAFTSY
AACGGHHIIOPR	HAGIOGRAPHIC
AACGGIILLNTY	GIGANTICALLY
AACGGIINNPST	SIGNING A PACT
AACGGILNOORS	SCORING A GOAL
AACGGINNRRUY	CARRYING A GUN
AACGGINORSTU	SUGAR COATING
AACGHHIKNOSV	HAVING A SHOCK
AACGHHILMSTT	LIGHTS A MATCH
AACGHHIRSSTT	STRAIGHT CASH
AACGHIIKMNPT	MAKING A PITCH

AACGHIILLNTT	CALL IT A NIGHT
AACGHIIMNPRT	MATCHING PAIR
AACGHIINNPSY	PAYING IN CASH
AACGHIKNNPTU	TAKING A PUNCH
AACGHILLOOPT	PATHOLOGICAL
AACGHILLRTVY	LIGHT CAVALRY
AACGHILMNOST	LOSING A MATCH
AACGHILNOPPR	PLANOGRAPHIC
AACGHILNOPVY	PLAYING HAVOC
AACGHILOOPRR	OROGRAPHICAL
AACGHIMNOPRT	CAMPHORATING
AACGHIMNPRST	MARCHING PAST
AACGHIMRTTUU	THAUMATURGIC
AACGHINOPPRT	PANTOGRAPHIC
AACGHINOPRRU	URANOGRAPHIC
AACGHINOSSTT	ACTING AS HOST
AACGHINOSSTW	CASTING A SHOW
AACGHLMOOPRY	PHARMACOLOGY
AACGHMMOORRT	CHROMATOGRAM
AACGIIILNPST	CAPITALISING
AACGIIILNPTZ	CAPITALIZING
AACGIIILPRST	PLAGIARISTIC
AACGIIINNPTT	ANTICIPATING
AACGIIINNTTV	VATICINATING
AACGIIKKNRTT	TAKING A TRICK
AACGIIKKNSST	KICKS AGAINST
AACGIIKNNOTT	TAKING ACTION
AAOGGIILLLNQT	CALLING TAILS
AACGIIILLNPPT	CAPPING IT ALL
AACGIILMNNTU	CALUMNIATING
AACGIILNNORS	CAROLINGIANS
AACGIILNPTTU	CAPITULATING
AACGIILNRTTU	ARTICULATING
AACGIIMPRSTT	PRAGMATISTIC
AACGIINNNNTU	ANNUNCIATING
AACGIINNOSTT	ANTAGONISTIC
AACGIINORSTU	CAUSING A RIOT
AACGIINORTVY	GAIN A VICTORY
AACGIINRSSTU	CAUSING A STIR
AACGIKKKNNOT	TAKING A KNOCK
AACGIKKMNRST	MAKING TRACKS
AACGIKKNNOST	KNOCK AGAINST
AACGIKLNOOST	CASTING A LOOK
AACGIKNNOTTU	TAKING A COUNT
AACGIKNPRSTT	START PACKING
AACGILLMOOST	MALACOLOGIST
AACGILLNNOPY	PAYING ON CALL
AACGILLOORST	ASTROLOGICAL
AACGILLOOTTU	TAUTOLOGICAL
AACGILLOPSST	OPTICAL GLASS
AACGILLRRTUU	AGRICULTURAL
AACGILMNORST	MARGINAL COST
AACGILNNNNPT	CANNING PLANT
AACGILNNOOTV	LONG VACATION
AACGILOPRRSU	RACIAL GROUPS
AACGIMMMOPRRT	PROGRAMMATIC
AACGIMNRRRSY	CARRYING ARMS
AACGINOPPRTU	GROUP CAPTAIN
AACGLLRSSSTY	CRYSTAL GLASS
AACHHIILNPPS	CHAPLAINSHIP
AACHHIIMNPRS	CHAIRMANSHIP
AACHHILMOPTY	HYPOTHALAMIC
AACHHILMRRTY	ARRHYTHMICAL
AACHHOOPPRST	APPROACH SHOT
AACHIIINNSTY	HINAYANISTIC
AACHIIKNSSTT	THIN AS A STICK
AACHIILMOPRS	PAROCHIALISM
AACHIILNPPSY	PHYSICAL PAIN
AACHIIMNNOST	MACHINATIONS
AACHIINPPSST	SHIPS CAPTAIN
AACHIKLMOOTY	OKLAHOMA CITY

AACHILLMNORY	HARMONICALLY
AACHILLNORST	LATIN SCHOLAR
AACHILMNORTY	LACHRYMATION
AACHILOPSTTY	HYPOSTATICAL
AACHIMMMNNOPY	NYMPHOMANIAC
AACHIMNNORSS	ANACHRONISMS
AACHIMRSTTVY	VARSITY MATCH
AACHINOPRTTU	NATUROPATHIC
AACHLLNNNOTY	NONCHALANTLY
AACHLLOPPRYY	APOCRYPHALLY
AACHLMORRSTY	LACHRYMATORS
AACHLMORRTYY	LACHRYMATORY
AACHLNNOOSTU	ANACOLUTHONS
AACHMOORSTTU	TRACHOMATOUS
AACIIIMNOTTV	AVITAMINOTIC
AACIIINNOPTT	ANTICIPATION
AACIIINNOTTV	VATICINATION
AACIIINSSTTT	STATISTICIAN
AACIIJMNSUZZ	JAZZ MUSICIAN
AACIIKNPRSTT	SAINT PATRICK
AACIILLMNPUW	MUNICIPAL LAW
AACIILLMOPPT	POLITICAL MAP
AACIILLNOOST	LOCALISATION
AACIILLNOOTZ	LOCALIZATION
AACIILLORSTY	AORISTICALLY
AACIILLRSTTY	ARTISTICALLY
AACIILMMPRTY	MILITARY CAMP
AACIILMMNOTU	MARTIAL MUSIC
AACIILMNNOTU	CALUMNIATION
AACIILMNORST	LACRIMATIONS
AACIILMNPSTU	PUTS IN A CLAIM
AACIILNNOOTV	INVOCATIONAL
AACIILNOOSTV	VOCALISATION
AACIILNOOTVZ	VOCALIZATION
AACIILNOPPST	APPLICATIONS
AACIILNOPRRT	TROPICAL RAIN
AACIILNOPTTU	CAPITULATION
AACIILNORTTU	ARTICULATION
AACIILNPRRTU	IN PARTICULAR
AACIILNRSTTU	NATURALISTIC
AACIILOPRRTT	PICTORIAL ART
AACIILORSUVY	AVARICIOUSLY
AACIIMMORSST	COMMISSARIAT
AACIIMOTTTUY	AUTOMATICITY
AACIINNNNOTU	ANNUNCIATION
AACIINNNOOST	CANONISATION
AACIINNNOOTZ	CANONIZATION
AACIINNNOSTT	INCANTATIONS
AACIINOORRTT	RATIOCINATOR
AACIINOOSSST	ASSOCIATIONS
AACIINOPRSTT	ANTICIPATORS
AACIINOPRTTY	ANTICIPATORY
AACIINORRTUZ	CURARIZATION
AACIINORSTTV	VATICINATORS
AACIIOPRRTT	PARTICIPATOR
AACIIOSTTVVY	VASOACTIVITY
AACIKLNOSSTY	LAYS IN A STOCK
AACILLLNOOTY	LOCATIONALLY
AACILLLNOPTY	CALL INTO PLAY
	PLATONICALLY
AACILLLRTVWY	CAVALRY TWILL
AACILLMNORTY	ROMANTICALLY
AACILLMNOSTY	MONASTICALLY
AACILLMOSTUY	CALAMITOUSLY
AACILLNNRTYY	TYRANNICALLY
AACILLNOOTVY	VOCATIONALLY
AACILLNOPRSS	RAPSCALLIONS
AACILLPRRTUY	PARTICULARLY
AACILLSSTTUY	CASUALTY LIST
AACILMNNOPST	COMPLAINANTS
AACILMNOOPRT	PROCLAMATION

AACILMNOORST	ASTRONOMICAL
AACILMNORSTU	CALUMNIATORS
AACILMORRTTU	COURT MARTIAL
	COURT-MARTIAL
AACILNORSTVY	CLAIRVOYANTS
AACILNOSTTUU	AUSCULTATION
AACILORRSTTU	ARTICULATORS
AACILORRTTUY	ARTICULATORY
AACILOSSSTTU	SOCIAL STATUS
AACIMMOPSTTY	ASYMPTOMATIC
AACIMNNNOSTT	CONTAMINANTS
AACIMNNOOPWY	COMPANIONWAY
AACIMNNOORTT	CONTAMINATOR
AACIMNOOPRST	PARONOMASTIC
AACIMNOPSTTU	STAMP AUCTION
AACINNNORSTU	ANNUNCIATORS
AACINNNORTUY	ANNUNCIATORY
AACINNORSSTT	TRANSACTIONS
AACINOORRTTY	ROTARY ACTION
AACINORSSTTU	ASTRONAUTICS
AACIOPQRSTTU	AQUATIC SPORT
AACKNRRTUUWY	RUNAWAY TRUCK
AACLNNOPRTTU	CONTRAPUNTAL
AACMNNOPPRSTY	PARTS COMPANY
AACMOPPRRSYY	ARMY PAY CORPS
AADDDEEEPRRT	DEAR DEPARTED
AADDDEEGLNRY	DEADLY DANGER
AADDDEEHHLRY	HARDHEADEDLY
AADDDEEHMNRU	MADE A HUNDRED
AADDDEELNRRU	UNDER A LADDER
AADDDEEMNSTY	STEADY DEMAND
AADDDEFINNNY	FINE AND DANDY
AADDDEFORSWW	ADD A FEW WORDS
AADDDEGGMOOS	DAMAGED GOODS
AADDDEGNOORY	GOOD AND READY
AADDDEIINPVY	PAY A DIVIDEND
AADDDEILNWWY	DWINDLED AWAY
AADDDEIMNNOP	PAID ON DEMAND
AADDDEINRSST	STANDARDISED
AADDDEINRSTZ	STANDARDIZED
AADDDGHIMNOO	HAD A GOOD MIND
AADDDGLNORST	GOLD STANDARD
AADDEEEFLORV	LEAVE FOR DEAD
AADDEEEFNRTW	FEED AND WATER
AADDEEEGHNRR	HEAD GARDENER
AADDEEEGLPRS	SPREAD-EAGLED
AADDEEEHIRST	RAISE THE DEAD
AADDEEEHKOTW	AWOKE THE DEAD
AADDEEEHKSTW	WAKES THE DEAD
AADDEEEHLLNW	WHEEL AND DEAL
AADDEEEHLTVW	EVADED THE LAW
AADDEEEHPRSS	PRESSED AHEAD
AADDEEEILMNT	MET A DEADLINE
AADDEEELMORR	ORDERED A MEAL
AADDEEELNPST	PLANTED A SEED
AADDEEENPRST	DESPERATE DEAD
AADDEEFGLRTU	GRATEFUL DEAD
AADDEEFHILNT	LIFE AND DEATH
	LIFE-AND-DEATH
AADDEEFHNNST	HANDS AND FEET
AADDEEFIMSTT	ADMITS DEFEAT
AADDEEFIOSTV	AVOIDS DEFEAT
AADDEEFIRSTU	DEAD SEA FRUIT
AADDEEFLRSSS	FALSE ADDRESS
AADDEEGHINTY	GAINED THE DAY
AADDEEGLLNRW	WALLED GARDEN
AADDEEHKMNRU	MAKE A HUNDRED
AADDEEHNSSWY	ASH WEDNESDAY
AADDEEILLNPT	DETAILED PLAN
AADDEEILOPRT	PORT ADELAIDE
AADDEEIMNRST	RIDES A TANDEM
AADDEEIMNRTV	ANIMADVERTED
AADDEEIMQSSU	MAQUIS DE SADE
AADDEEINRRTW	READ AND WRITE
AADDEEKLLNRR	DEREK RANDALL
AADDEEKMMNSS	MAKES DEMANDS
AADDEELNOPWY	DEADLY WEAPON
AADDEEMMRRSS	DREAMS DREAMS
AADDEEMMRRST	DREAMT DREAMS
AADDEFFIILST	FIT AS A FIDDLE
AADDEFGILLNU	LEGAL AID FUND
AADDEFHIINNN	FINNAN HADDIE
AADDEFINORTU	DEFRAUDATION
AADDEFIPRRTT	DRIFTED APART
AADDEFKNOPRS	SPADE AND FORK
AADDEFLLNOSU	ALL OF A SUDDEN
AADDEFNNOSSU	SAFE AND SOUND
AADDEGGHIRRR	RIDER HAGGARD
AADDEGGNRRSW	DAGGERS DRAWN
AADDEGHILNNN	LENDING A HAND
AADDEGHIMOOT	HAD A GOOD TIME
AADDEGHIRSTT	DEAD STRAIGHT
AADDEGIILNOS	DIAGONALISED
AADDEGIILNOZ	DIAGONALIZED
AADDEGIINSST	SIDED AGAINST
AADDEGIKNOSS	DOING AS ASKED
AADDEGILNORU	READING ALOUD
AADDEGLMNOTU	UNTOLD DAMAGE
AADDEGNOPRRU	PARADE GROUND
AADDEHHLNORT	HARD TO HANDLE
AADDEHHNNORU	HARE AND HOUND
AADDEHHNNORV	HAND OVER HAND
AADDEHOORSTT	AT DEATHS DOOR
AADDEIIJLLNN	LANDED IN JAIL
AADDEIKMNNRT	MEAT AND DRINK
AADDEIMNNRSTT	STANDARD TIME
AADDEINORTUW	WAITED AROUND
AADDEINRSSST	STANDARDISES
AADDEINRSSTZ	STANDARD SIZE
	STANDARDIZES
AADDEJRSTTUW	JUST ADD WATER
AADDEKLLSTTW	TALKS TWADDLE
AADDEKLNORUW	WALKED AROUND
AADDELLLNORS	LENDS A DOLLAR
AADDELMNORTU	MOUNT A LADDER
AADDELNOPRUY	PLAYED AROUND
AADDEMNNOPSY	PAYS ON DEMAND
AADDEMNOSTTU	DEAD AS MUTTON
AADDENNNORTW	DRAWN TO AN END
AADDENNORSTW	DRAWS TO AN END
AADDENRSSTWY	ST.ANDREWS DAY
AADDFHHILMOR	HAD A FIRM HOLD
AADDFMOORTYY	FROM DAY TO DAY
AADDFORRRSTW	DARTS FORWARD
AADDGGLOOOSS	AS GOOD AS GOLD
AADDGHHINNNO	GO HAND IN HAND
AADDGHINNRST	HIGH STANDARD
AADDGHIIINNR	INDIRA GANDHI
AADDGHIILRTY	DAYLIGHT RAID
AADDGHIKLNRT	LIGHT AND DARK
AADDGHINNRST	HARDSTANDING
AADDGOOORSWY	SAY A GOOD WORD
AADDHHIORTWW	HAD A WORD WITH
AADDHHLNOOTU	HOLD OUT A HAND
AADDHHNNORSTU	DO A HANDS TURN
AADDHHNOPRTWW	DOWNWARD PATH
AADDHNPRSUWY	WASH AND DRY UP
AADDIIILNOPT	DILAPIDATION
AADDIILLNOTY	ADDITIONALLY
AADDIKNNRSST	STANDS A DRINK
AADDKLNORRSU	DRUNK AS A LORD
AADDKNORRSTW	STANDARD WORK

AADDLLNNRSUY	ALL AND SUNDRY	AADEEGHHNNOS	HANG ONES HEAD
AADDNNORSSTU	STANDS A ROUND	AADEEGHINPRS	SPEARHEADING
	STANDS AROUND	AADEEGHINRVY	HEAVY READING
AADDNOPRSTTU	UP TO STANDARD	AADEEGHLLNRS	HERALD ANGELS
AADEEEEGKNRT	TAKEN A DEGREE	AADEEGILLMNR	LAGER AND LIME
AADEEEEGKRST	TAKES A DEGREE	AADEEGILLRSV	LEGAL ADVISER
AADEEEEGMNRT	TEENAGE DREAM	AADEEGILNNNR	LENDING AN EAR
AADEEEEGPRSV	AVERAGE SPEED	AADEEGILNNPR	ALPINE GARDEN
AADEEEFGLNRT	FEDERAL AGENT	AADEEGIMNOST	ADMIT ONES AGE
AADEEEFHHRST	FEATHERHEADS	AADEEGIMNOVY	MAIDEN VOYAGE
AADEEEFHLMSS	FEELS ASHAMED	AADEEGIMORSS	RADIO MESSAGE
AADEEEGHIKNP	KEEPING AHEAD	AADEEGINSTTT	SETTING A DATE
AADEEEGHKMRT	MAKE THE GRADE	AADEEGJLNRYY	LADY JANE GREY
AADEEEGHRRTT	GREATHEARTED	AADEEGKMNRRT	MARKET GARDEN
AADEEEGIKNPT	KEEPING A DATE	AADEEGKNOPTW	TAKE DOWN A PEG
AADEEEGKLMPS	MAKES A PLEDGE	AADEEGOORSSV	AS GOOD AS EVER
AADEEEGLPRSS	SPREAD-EAGLES	AADEEHHIINRT	HEAD IN THE AIR
AADEEEGMNSSS	SEND A MESSAGE	AADEEHHINTTT	IN AT THE DEATH
AADEEEGMRSTU	MADE A GESTURE	AADEEHHIPRTT	PAID THE EARTH
AADEEEHHHKST	SHAKE THE HEAD	AADEEHIIILORST	SHARE THE LOAD
AADEEEHHRTVY	HEAVYHEARTED	AADEEHHMRTTT	THE MAD HATTER
AADEEEHILSTT	THE LEAST IDEA	AADEEHHNOPTT	PAT ON THE HEAD
AADEEEHINPST	EASED THE PAIN		TAP ON THE HEAD
AADEEEHIPSTV	ADHESIVE TAPE	AADEEHHNRSTW	HAD THE ANSWER
AADEEEHIRSST	HEART DISEASE	AADEEHHNSTTT	STAND THE HEAT
AADEEEHISSTT	AT THE SEASIDE	AADEEHHPSSTT	PASSED THE HAT
AADEEEHKLNTT	TAKEN THE LEAD	AADEEHIILTWW	WAITED AWHILE
AADEEEHKLSTT	TAKES THE LEAD	AADEEHILNQRU	HARLEQUINADE
AADEEEHLSTVW	EVADES THE LAW	AADEEHILNTTY	LATE IN THE DAY
AADEEEHMNOOV	ONE MOVE AHEAD	AADEEHILSTWY	STAYED AWHILE
AADEEEHNNOPY	HAD AN EYE OPEN	AADEEHIRRSST	REARS ITS HEAD
AADEEEHNOPST	ONE STEP AHEAD	AADEEHIRTWWY	WITHERED AWAY
AADEEEHNORRS	REAR ONES HEAD	AADEEHJMNOPU	ONE JUMP AHEAD
AADEEEHORRSV	HEAD OVER EARS	AADEEHKNNRSY	SARAH KENNEDY
AADEEEHPRSSS	PRESSES AHEAD	AADEEHKNSTTT	TAKE THE STAND
AADEEEHRRSTT	DEAREST HEART	AADEEHLLMPTY	PLAYED HAMLET
AADEEEHRSSTT	STREETS AHEAD	AADEEHLLPSTY	PLAYS THE LEAD
AADEEEIMNRST	REMAIN SEATED	AADEEHLMOPTY	PLAYED AT HOME
AADEEELLMNTT	LATE LAMENTED	AADEEHLNPTTY	DEATH PENALTY
AADEEELNNRWZ	NEW ZEALANDER	AADEEHLNSTTW	THE WASTE LAND
AADEEELNPRTT	PLANTED A TREE	AADEEHLOPRST	HARD TO PLEASE
AADEEELORTVY	READY TO LEAVE	AADEEHMMRSSY	DAME MYRA HESS
AADEEEMNPRST	DESPERATE MAN	AADEEHMNRTTT	HAD TREATMENT
AADEEEMORSTU	MADE A REQUEST	AADEEHMOSTTY	STAYED AT HOME
AADEEENQSSTU	ADEQUATENESS	AADEEHOOSTTU	HEAD OUT TO SEA
AADEEFFGMRSU	SUFFER DAMAGE	AADEEHORRTTT	READ THE TAROT
AADEEFFORRRW	OFFER A REWARD	AADEEHQRRSTU	HEADQUARTERS
AADEEFGHLNOT	ANGEL OF DEATH	AADEEHRRSSTT	READ THE STARS
AADEEFGILNNR	FINE AND LARGE	AADEEHRRSTTY	SHADY RETREAT
AADEEFGILNRS	FALSE READING	AADEEIIKMNST	MISTAKEN IDEA
AADEEFGILNST	SIGNAL DEFEAT	AADEEIIKMTVW	TAKE A DIM VIEW
AADEEFGIMNOR	GERM OF AN IDEA	AADEEIILMNRV	LIVE IN A DREAM
AADEEFHHOTTY	HEAT OF THE DAY	AADEEIILMRST	MATERIALISED
AADEEFHINRTT	FAINTHEARTED	AADEEIILMRTZ	MATERIALIZED
AADEEFIINSTT	FAINTEST IDEA	AADEEIILRRST	ARTERIALISED
AADEEFIKLNRW	WALKED IN FEAR	AADEEIILRRTZ	ARTERIALIZED
AADEEFIKORRT	TAKE FOR A RIDE	AADEEIIMNNRT	ANTE MERIDIAN
AADEEFILPSTY	PLAYED IT SAFE	AADEEIKMNSST	MAIDEN STAKES
AADEEFINRRTW	FIRE AND WATER	AADEEILLNNRV	LIVE AND LEARN
AADEEFIRRSTT	STARTED A FIRE	AADEEILMORRS	RAISED MORALE
AADEEFLMNRRS	FLANDERS MARE	AADEEILNNRSX	ALEXANDRINES
AADEEFLRSTUV	SERVED A FAULT	AADEEILNPRRY	LEAD IN PRAYER
AADEEFMNORTU	MADE A FORTUNE	AADEEILNQTUY	INADEQUATELY
AADEEFNOORST	DEAF TO REASON	AADEEILNRSST	EASTER ISLAND
AADEEFNORRTW	NARROW DEFEAT	AADEEILNSSUV	LEAVES UNSAID
AADEEFORRSTT	FEARS TO TREAD	AADEEILORSTV	ROASTED ALIVE
AADEEGGHINNV	HAVING AN EDGE	AADEEILRRRTT	RETAIL TRADER
AADEEGGHINTT	GETTING AHEAD	AADEEILRRRVY	ARRIVED EARLY
AADEEGGLMORT	AGGLOMERATED	AADEEIMMOPRS	MADE A PROMISE
AADEEGGRRTTY	GREAT TRAGEDY	AADEEINOPRST	ENDOPARASITE
AADEEGHHHNST	HANGS THE HEAD	AADEEINPSSTV	ADAPTIVENESS

AADEEJKLOPRY	PLAYED A JOKER
AADEEJMRSTYY	JAM YESTERDAY
AADEEKLOORTT	LOOKED A TREAT
AADEEKLOPPST	STOPPED A LEAK
AADEEKMNOSSY	MAKES ONE'S DAY
AADEEKMORSTU	MAKES A DETOUR
AADEEKPRSSTT	STREAKED PAST
AADEEKRSTUWY	SATURDAY WEEK
AADEELLLNPRU	UNPARALLELED
AADEELLMPSTU	ALL STEAMED UP
AADEELLOPRRT	PATROL LEADER
AADEELLRZZZZ	RAZZLE-DAZZLE
AADEELMNOPRS	READ ONES PALM
AADEELMNOPSY	MADE ONE'S PLAY
AADEELMNPRTT	DEPARTMENTAL
AADEELMORSSU	ASSUMED A ROLE
AADEELNORRST	LEARNS TO READ
AADEELNORRTT	LEARNT TO READ
AADEELNORSSS	READS A LESSON
AADEELNORSTY	LED ONE ASTRAY
AADEELNRRSTT	RETRANSLATED
AADEELOPRTTX	EXTRAPOLATED
AADEELPSTTUY	STAYED UP LATE
AADEEMMNNNOS	NAMED NO NAMES
AADEEMMNORTT	MADE NO MATTER
AADEEMMNRSTW	NEW AMSTERDAM
AADEEMNNNOST	MEANS TO AN END
AADEEMNNNRTUX	EXTRAMUNDANE
AADEEMNORSTY	EASTER MONDAY
AADEEMOPRSTT	MADE A PROTEST
AADEEMORRSTU	TROD A MEASURE
AADEENNOSVWW	WAVE ONE'S WAND
AADEENNPPRSY	SPARED A PENNY
AADEENPRRTUW	WARPED NATURE
AADEENRRSSTU	TEARS ASUNDER
AADEENRSSTUY	EASTER SUNDAY
AADEFFHLNOTT	FAT OF THE LAND
AADEFFIIILST	DISAFFILIATE
AADEFFIIOPRT	PAID A FORFEIT
AADEFFILLORR	RIDE FOR A FALL
AADEFGGHINOR	FORGING AHEAD
AADEFGGILNRT	DEFLAGRATING
AADEFGGINRSU	SAFEGUARDING
AADEFGHLLLNO	FALL HEADLONG
AADEFGHNRRST	GRANDFATHERS
AADEFGILLLSS	FILLED A GLASS
AADEFGILLMUW	WILFUL DAMAGE
AADEFGILNORT	DEFLAGRATION
AADEFGINORUV	GAINED FAVOUR
AADEFGLMNNOP	MAP OF ENGLAND
AADEFGLMNORR	FORMAL GARDEN
AADEFHILLMRS	FIELD MARSHAL
AADEFHILLORT	ALL OF A DITHER
AADEFHILNPTU	PAINFUL DEATH
AADEFHINNOTU	FOUNTAINHEAD
AADEFHINNSTT	INFANT DEATHS
AADEFHKLLNST	THE FALKLANDS
AADEFHLLNOTW	LAW OF THE LAND
AADEFHLLNOTY	LAY OF THE LAND
AADEFHNNORST	FATHER AND SON
AADEFIIILMRS	FAMILIARISED
AADEFIIILMRZ	FAMILIARIZED
AADEFIKMNORR	AFRIKANERDOM
AADEFILMNOPR	MAP OF IRELAND
AADEFILMNPRR	INFRARED LAMP
AADEFILNNRSS	FARNE ISLANDS
AADEFILNOORT	FLOATED ON AIR
AADEFILNORSS	FAROE ISLANDS
AADEFILNORTY	DEFLATIONARY
AADEFILNSTWY	STIFLED A YAWN
AADEFILOPSST	FAILED TO PASS

AADEFILOSTTW	TWO FAT LADIES
AADEFIMNORRT	FIRE AT RANDOM
AADEFINRRRSY	INFRARED RAYS
AADEFKMMNORW	KNEW FROM ADAM
AADEFLLLOOSW	FOLLOWS A LEAD
AADEFLLNOSTU	UNFOLDS A TALE
AADEFLLOOPPR	LORD OF APPEAL
AADEFLMMNRTY	MARTY FELDMAN
AADEFLMNNSTU	FUNDAMENTALS
AADEFLNNRRST	LAND TRANSFER
AADEFLNOOSST	FAST AND LOOSE
AADEFLNORRRS	RONALD FRASER
AADEFLNORRSW	LEANS FORWARD
AADEFLNORRTW	LEANT FORWARD
AADEFNOOORUV	DO ONE A FAVOUR
AADEFORSSWWY	SAY A FEW WORDS
AADEGGHILMST	SLIGHT DAMAGE
AADEGGHINNOO	GOING AHEAD ON
AADEGGHINRSU	SURGING AHEAD
AADEGGILNNOT	GANGLIONATED
AADEGGILNNRS	DANGER SIGNAL
AADEGGILNRSS	READING GLASS
AADEGGILNTTU	AGGLUTINATED
AADEGGIMNNOR	DOG IN A MANGER
AADEGGINNNOR	GIN AND ORANGE
AADEGHHHOTTU	THOUGHT AHEAD
AADEGHIIMNTV	HAVING IT MADE
AADEGHIINNOV	HAVING NO IDEA
AADEGHIJMNPU	JUMPING AHEAD
AADEGHIKLNOO	LOOKING AHEAD
AADEGHILLNOS	HOLDING A SALE
AADEGHILLNPU	PULLING AHEAD
AADEGHILRSTT	STRAIGHT DEAL
AADEGHIMNNTY	NAMING THE DAY
AADEGHIMOOST	HAS A GOOD TIME
AADEGHINNNRU	RUNNING AHEAD
AADEGHINRSTW	GRANTED A WISH
AADEGHINSTVY	SAVING THE DAY
AADEGHIOPRRR	RADIOGRAPHER
AADEGHLNOORT	ALONG THE ROAD
AADEGHMNNOTU	HAM AND TONGUE
AADEGHORTTTU	TAUGHT TO READ
AADEGIIILNOR	ORIGINAL IDEA
AADEGIIINRVW	VIRGINIA WADE
AADEGIIKLLMN	MADE A KILLING
AADEGIIKNPRT	TAKING A PRIDE
AADEGIILLNNO	DIAGONAL LINE
AADEGIILLNNP	PLAIN DEALING
AADEGIILNNRW	DRAWING A LINE
AADEGIILNNST	DESALINATING
AADEGIILNOSS	DIAGONALISES
AADEGIILNOSZ	DIAGONALIZES
AADEGIILNRVW	DRAWING A VEIL
AADEGIILPQRU	QUADRIPLEGIA
AADEGIILRUWY	RAILWAY GUIDE
AADEGIIMMNST	DIAMAGNETISM
AADEGIINPPRS	DISAPPEARING
AADEGIINSSST	SIDES AGAINST
AADEGIKMMNNS	MAKING AMENDS
AADEGIKNOORT	TOOK A READING
AADEGILNNSSS	SENDS A SIGNAL
AADEGILNPRTY	PLYING A TRADE
AADEGILNPRYY	PAYING DEARLY
AADEGILNRTTU	ADULTERATING
	TRIANGULATED
AADEGILNSSST	STAINED GLASS
AADEGIMNQRSU	MASQUERADING
AADEGIMNQSTU	DESQUAMATING
AADEGINNNOOS	SAGE AND ONION
AADEGINNORTX	AN AXE TO GRIND
AADEGINNPPRS	SANDPAPERING

AADEGINNSSTY	STANDING EASY	AADEIKOORSTT	TOOK IT AS READ
AADEGINOPPRS	PROPAGANDISE	AADEILLMORWY	MODEL RAILWAY
AADEGINOPPRZ	PROPAGANDIZE	AADEILLPPSUW	WILD APPLAUSE
AADEGINORRRT	ROARING TRADE	AADEILNNNNRU	ANNUAL DINNER
AADEGINOSTTV	VOTED AGAINST	AADEILNNNORR	NORADRENALIN
AADEGINPPRRW	DRAWING PAPER	AADEILNNORVW	IN LOVE AND WAR
AADEGINRRTWW	DRAWING WATER	AADEILNNSSTT	STATEN ISLAND
AADEGKNRRRST	DARK STRANGER	AADEILNORSST	DESALINATORS
AADEGLLNNSUY	AULD LANG SYNE	AADEILNORTTU	ADULTERATION
AADEGLLORSSW	GOAL-LESS DRAW	AADEILNOSTUV	DEVALUATIONS
AADEGLMNNORRT	MORTAL DANGER	AADEILNPRRTU	NATURAL PRIDE
AADEGLMRRTUU	MUTUAL REGARD	AADEILNRTUVY	VALETUDINARY
AADEGLNPRSST	STAR-SPANGLED	AADEILOPRSST	PARADISE LOST
AADEGLNRSTTU	STRANGULATED	AADEILRRSTWY	TREADS WARILY
AADEGMNNORSU	DANGEROUS MAN	AADEIMMNNRRU	UNMARRIED MAN
AADEGNNNOORR	GO ON AN ERRAND	AADEIMMNORRW	MARRIED WOMAN
AADEGNNPRRST	GRANDPARENTS	AADEIMNNORRSU	DESQUAMATION
AADEGOPRSTTU	POSTGRADUATE	AADEIMNNORRSU	ANDRE MAUROIS
AADEHHIIMNTT	HAD A THIN TIME	AADEIMNRSSTV	MAIDSERVANTS
AADEHIKLMORY	HOLIDAYMAKER	AADEIMOPPRTX	APPROXIMATED
AADEHIKLNRVY	DRANK HEAVILY	AADEINNOPRSW	DRAW A PENSION
AADEHIKNRSTW	SAW IN THE DARK	AADEINNORTTU	DENATURATION
AADEHILLMPTU	THE PALLADIUM	AADEINNRRSTU	UNDER A STRAIN
AADEHILLNSSW	WHEN ALL'S SAID	AADEINRSTTUY	STAYED IN A RUT
AADEHIILMPPST	APPLIED MATHS	AADEIOPPPRRT	APPROPRIATED
AADEHILORSST	HEADS OR TAILS	AADEIORRSTTT	STARTED A RIOT
AADEHILPRSSV	LAVISH SPREAD	AADEJLMNSTTU	ADJUSTMENTAL
AADEHINOPRRR	HEAD A PIN DROP	AADEJLNORRTU	TRADE JOURNAL
AADEHINOSTWY	HAD IT ONE'S WAY	AADEKLLOSTTT	ALLOTTED TASK
AADEIIINOTWWY	DONE AWAY WITH	AADEKMOPRRRS	DROPS A REMARK
AADEHIOPRRTY	RADIOTHERAPY	AADELLMNOPRR	ARNOLD PALMER
AADEHIOSTWWY	DOES AWAY WITH	AADELLNNORST	RALLENTANDOS
AADEHJJNNNOT	JANET AND JOHN	AADELLOPPSUU	LOUD APPLAUSE
AADEHLLOSTUW	ALL WASHED OUT	AADELMMNOPRS	RANDOM SAMPLE
AADEHLMRTTUU	MUTUAL HATRED	AADELMMOPSSS	PLASMODESMAS
AADEHLNORSTU	HEART AND SOUL	AADELNNPRSTT	TRANSPLANTED
AADEHLPQSSUY	PLAYED SQUASH	AADELNOR33TW	LEANS TOWARDS
AADEHMOOSTWY	SMOOTHED AWAY	AADELNORSTTW	LEANT TOWARDS
AADEHMRRRSSTT	HARD MATTRESS	AADELNPRTTUY	PLAYED TRUANT
AADEHNNNORSS	HANS ANDERSON	AADELORRSTTU	ADULTERATORS
AADEHNNOSSTY	STAY ONE'S HAND	AADEMNOPPRTU	PUT A DAMPER ON
AADEHNOPRRST	HORSE AND TRAP	AADEMNORSTWY	MY DEAR WATSON
AADEHNRRTTWY	WATER AND TRAP	AADENNNRRRSU	RUNS AN ERRAND
AADEHOOPRTTT	TAP AT THE DOOR	AADENORR&TWW	WAR TO END WARS
AADEHRSSTTTY	STARTS THE DAY	AADENRSTTUXY	NEXT SATURDAY
AADEIIIILNOST	IDEALISATION	AADEOQRRSTUW	EQUATORWARDS
AADEIIILNOTZ	IDEALIZATION	AADEORRSTTTY	READY TO START
AADEIIKNRSST	RAISED A STINK	AADFFGIILNNT	FINDING A FLAT
AADEIIILLMMNO	MADE A MILLION	AADFFGINOSTY	DAY OF FASTING
AADEIILMNRST	RADIANT SMILE	AADFFGLNOOSS	FOND OF A GLASS
AADEIILNNOST	DESALINATION	AADFFILMNORU	FIND A FORMULA
	NATIONALISED	AADFGHIILNNT	LIFTING A HAND
AADEIILNNOTZ	NATIONALIZED	AADFGHIILLOOT	ALL GOOD FAITH
AADEIILNNTUV	ANTEDILUVIAN	AADFGIIMNRRY	DAIRY FARMING
AADEIILNOORR	INDOOR AERIAL	AADFGIINRTWY	DRIFTING AWAY
AADEIILNORST	RATIONALISED	AADFGINNSSTT	STANDING FAST
AADEIILNORTV	DERIVATIONAL	AADFGINOORUV	DOING A FAVOUR
AADEIILNORTZ	RATIONALIZED	AADFHHILLOSY	HALF-HOLIDAYS
AADEIIMMPPRU	PAID A PREMIUM	AADFHHILMORS	HAS A FIRM HOLD
AADEIIMNNRST	ADMINISTRATE	AADFHHINORRST	STRAND OF HAIR
AADEIINNRRTV	DRIVEN A TRAIN	AADFHLOOPSSS	SPLASH OF SODA
AADEIINNSTTT	INSTANTIATED	AADFHOOPSSTT	HAD A SOFT SPOT
AADEIINRRSTV	DRIVES A TRAIN	AADFIKORRSWY	FAIR DAYS WORK
AADEIIPRSTWY	SPIRITED AWAY	AADFILNNOOTU	FOUNDATIONAL
AADEIJMMNOSS	JAMES MADISON	AADFILNRSSTT	FIRST AND LAST
AADEIKLMNRTW	MILK AND WATER	AADFINNOOSTU	SODA FOUNTAIN
	MILK-AND-WATER	AADFINOSTUWY	FINDS A WAY OUT
AADEIKLPPRSY	SPEAK RAPIDLY	AADFKMMNOORW	KNOW FROM ADAM
AADEIKLSSWWY	WALK SIDEWAYS	AADFLOOPRTYY	PLAY FOR TODAY
AADEIKMNNOST	AND NO MISTAKE	AADFNOORSTWY	SWAY TO AND FRO
AADEIKMNORSS	MAKES INROADS	AADFNOOTUUWY	FOUND A WAY OUT

AADGGGIINNRS	AGGRANDISING	AADILNNOSTTU	NATIONAL STUD
AADGGGIINNRZ	AGGRANDIZING	AADILNOPPRST	POSTPRANDIAL
AADGGIIINNOT	DOING IT AGAIN	AADILOORSSTV	VASODILATORS
AADGGIINNRRS	DISARRANGING	AADIMNNOORTU	MOUNTAIN ROAD
AADGGILMMNOR	MID GLAMORGAN	AADINNORSTTU	TRANSUDATION
AADGHHIINNNV	HAVING IN HAND	AADKLORSSTWW	WALKS TOWARDS
AADGHHIKNNSS	SHAKING HANDS	AADKNOOPSTTU	TOOK UP A STAND
AADGHHIMNNRT	RIGHT-HAND MAN	AADLLNOOSTTW	ALLOW TO STAND
AADGHHNNNOOR	HANNAH GORDON	AADLNPPRSSUW	DRAWS UP PLANS
AADGHIIKNNNT	TAKING IN HAND	AADMNNOORSST	MOON AND STARS
AADGHIIKNNRV	HAVING A DRINK	AADMNOQRSUUU	QUADRUMANOUS
AADGHIIKNRTT	TAKING IT HARD	AADNOPRSSTTT	STOP AND START
AADGHIIMMNNT	MIGHT AND MAIN	AAEEEEGNRSTY	TEENAGE YEARS
AADGHIINNRRT	HARD TRAINING	AAEEEEKNOSST	TAKE ONES EASE
AADGHIINPRSU	GUARDIANSHIP	AAEEEELNRSSW	RENEWS A LEASE
AADGHILNNPPY	HAPPY LANDING	AAEEEENOSSTT	SET ONE AT EASE
AADGHILNORSZ	LOSING HAZARD	AAEEEFFKKOTW	TAKE A WEEK OFF
AADGHILNORTT	GRIND TO A HALT	AAEEEFGHILNV	HAVE A FEELING
AADGHIORRSTT	STRAIGHT ROAD	AAEEEFGILLOS	SEA OF GALILEE
AADGHLPRSTUY	PLAY DRAUGHTS	AAEEEFGIRRSW	SIEGE WARFARE
AADGIIILNNTV	INVALIDATING	AAEEEFGLMSST	LEFT A MESSAGE
AADGIIJNORTY	RADIATING JOY	AAEEEFHIRRST	FREE AS THE AIR
AADGIILNNNOS	ANGLO-INDIANS	AAEEEFLLLNSV	FALLEN LEAVES
AADGIILNNORT	NATIONAL GRID	AAEEEFLNOSST	SEAL ONE'S FATE
AADGIKLMNRSU	MILK AND SUGAR	AAEEEFLRSTTW	WELFARE STATE
AADGIKMNNOSU	MAKING A SOUND	AAEEEGGHMNRR	GRAHAM GREENE
AADGIKMNSTUY	MAKING A STUDY	AAEEEGGHRTUW	WEATHER GAUGE
AADGILLNNSTT	STANDING TALL	AAEEEGGIRTVX	EXAGGERATIVE
AADGILNNPRTY	LANDING PARTY	AAEEEGGLNRSU	GENERAL USAGE
AADGILNOORST	IT'S A LONG ROAD	AAEEEGHKMOTW	TAKE-HOME WAGE
AADGILNOPRUY	PRAYING ALOUD	AAEEEGHKSTTT	TAKE THE STAGE
AADGILNPPRST	STRAPPING LAD	AAEEEGKMRSTU	MAKE A GESTURE
AADGILNPRSTY	PLAYING DARTS	AAEEEGLLNRRT	GENERAL ALERT
AADGIMNNRSTY	STANDING ARMY	AAEEEGLLNRSV	RAGLAN SLEEVE
AADGIMNNOPPRS	PROPAGANDISM	AAEEEGLLRSTY	EASTERLY GALE
AADGIMNPRSTT	TRADING STAMP	AAEEEGLNPRSX	LARGE EXPANSE
AADGINNNOSSTT	STANDS TO GAIN	AAEEEGMNSSST	SENT A MESSAGE
AADGINOORSTY	ROGATION DAYS	AAEEEGNPRSTV	GAVE A PRESENT
AADGINOOSSTT	STOOD AGAINST	AAEEEGNRRSTT	GREAT EASTERN
AADGINOPPRST	PROPAGANDIST	AAEEEHHMNSTV	HAVE THE MEANS
AADGLNOOPTUY	GO OUT AND PLAY	AAEEEHHRTTTT	AT THE THEATRE
AADHHIIKNNST	HAD A THIN SKIN	AAEEEHHRTVWY	HEAVY WEATHER
AADHHILNOTUY	HOLIDAY HAUNT	AAEEEHILSSTT	TELAESTHESIA
AADHHILOPPYY	HAPPY HOLIDAY	AAEEEHIMRTTT	THREE AT A TIME
AADHHIORSTWW	HAS A WORD WITH	AAEEEHINPSST	EASES THE PAIN
AADHHOOOTTTU	HAD A TOOTH OUT	AAEEEHINRSTT	RAISE THE ANTE
AADHIKLOOOTY	TOOK A HOLIDAY	AAEEEHINSSTT	ANAESTHETISE
AADHILLMNOTY	LADY HAMILTON	AAEEEHINSTTZ	ANAESTHETIZE
AADHILNNOOTT	TOOTH AND NAIL	AAEEEHLMNRST	ETERNAL SHAME
AADHILNOORRV	OLD HARROVIAN	AAEEEHLPPRSY	HAPPY RELEASE
AADHILNOPSUY	DIAPHANOUSLY	AAEEEHNNOPSY	HAS AN EYE OPEN
AADHILOPRSTW	HOSPITAL WARD	AAEEEHNNOSST	SHEENA EASTON
AADHINPRSSTY	DANISH PASTRY	AAEEEHNNOSTT	EATEN ONE'S HAT
AADHIRSSTTUY	THIS SATURDAY	AAEEEHNPRSST	ENTERS A PHASE
AADHLMNOORST	THOMAS ARNOLD	AAEEEILLNOTV	LEAVE IT ALONE
AADHLRSSTTUY	LAST THURSDAY	AAEEEIMPRRST	PARAMETERISE
AADHNOOSSTTW	SHOOTS AT DAWN	AAEEEIRSSTVV	ASSEVERATIVE
AADHOOSTUWYY	WHAT DO YOU SAY?	AAEEEKKLOOST	TAKE A LOOK-SEE
AADIIILNNOTV	INVALIDATION	AAEEEKLMPUWY	MAKE UP LEEWAY
AADIILLMNSWY	ANDY WILLIAMS	AAEEEKLNRTTT	TAKEN A LETTER
AADIILNOOSTV	VASODILATION	AAEEEKLPRSTU	TAKE PLEASURE
AADIILNSTTUY	STUDY ITALIAN	AAEEEKLQRRSU	SEEK A QUARREL
AADIIMNNRSTT	ADMINISTRANT	AAEEEKLRSTTT	TAKES A LETTER
AADIINNOSTTX	ANTIOXIDANTS	AAEEEKMNNOST	TAKE ONES NAME
AADIINOORSTT	RADIO STATION	AAEEEKMQRSTU	MAKE A REQUEST
AADIINPRRSTT	RAPID TRANSIT	AAEEEKMRSSTU	TAKE MEASURES
AADIJMMRSSVY	SAMMY DAVIS JR.	AAEEEKPRRTTX	KARATE EXPERT
AADIKNORSSTT	DRINKS A TOAST	AAEEELLPSSVW	WEAVES A SPELL
AADILLMNOOST	AMONTILLADOS	AAEEELMNPSTX	SET AN EXAMPLE
AADILLNNPPRU	PLAIN AND PURL	AAEEELMPRSUV	SERVE UP A MEAL
	PURL AND PLAIN	AAEEELNRRSVV	NAVAL RESERVE

AAEEELOPRTTU	POET LAUREATE
AAEEELOPSSTY	EASY TO PLEASE
AAEEEMRRSTUW	WATER MEASURE
AAEEEENNORRVY	RAN AN EYE OVER
AAEEEENPRSSST	SEPARATENESS
AAEEFFGLNRST	GENERAL STAFF
AAEEFFHHOSTW	SHEAF OF WHEAT
AAEEFFHHLMNST	FAN THE FLAMES
	FANS THE FLAME
AAEEFFKMNORS	MAKES AN OFFER
AAEEFFKMNORT	MAKE AN EFFORT
AAEEFFKNNORT	TAKEN AN OFFER
AAEEFFKNORST	TAKES AN OFFER
AAEEFGHILRST	RAISE THE FLAG
AAEEFGILMTTU	METAL FATIGUE
AAEEFGILORST	FAILS TO AGREE
AAEEFHHMRSTT	FATHER THAMES
AAEEFHILMOTW	WHALE OF A TIME
AAEEFHILRRTU	HEART FAILURE
AAEEFHKNRRST	HANKERS AFTER
AAEEFHLMRSSU	HALF MEASURES
AAEEFHLMSTWY	MEETS HALFWAY
AAEEFHLORSSV	HALF SEAS OVER
AAEEFHLRTTUV	HAVE A FLUTTER
AAEEFHMORSST	TEARS OF SHAME
AAEEFHMORSTU	FARMHOUSE TEA
AAEEFHORRTTW	THEATRE OF WAR
AAEEFHOSSSSU	SAFE AS HOUSES
AAEEFIIKLNNR	FRANKIE LAINE
AAEEFIILRSSZ	LAISSEZ FAIRE
	LAISSEZ-FAIRE
AAEEFILNPRVY	FIVE-YEAR PLAN
AAEEFILOSSSY	ESSAYS OF ELIA
AAEEFIMNNORS	ONES FAIR NAME
AAEEFKMNORTU	MAKE A FORTUNE
AAEEFLLLOSVW	LEAVES FALLOW
AAEEFLLNOPSY	PLAY ONE FALSE
AAEEFLMOPSTT	PLATES OF MEAT
AAEEFLNNRTUW	TURN A NEW LEAF
AAEEFLNRSTTU	STATE FUNERAL
AAEEFLPRTWYY	FLY AWAY PETER
AAEEFLRSSTUV	SERVES A FAULT
AAEEFMNNRRTT	TENANT FARMER
AAEEFMNNORSY	ANY MORE FARES
AAEEFMOORRRT	FROM EAR TO EAR
AAEEFNNOORTT	AFTERNOON TEA
AAEEGGGGLLRT	RAGGLE-TAGGLE
AAEEGGGINRTX	EXAGGERATING
AAEEGGGMORTT	GET A MORTGAGE
AAEEGGIMNRTV	GRAM-NEGATIVE
AAEEGGINNRTU	GUARANTEEING
AAEEGGINORTT	GET INTO A RAGE
AAEEGGINORTX	EXAGGERATION
AAEEGGGLMORST	AGGLOMERATES
AAEEGGLNNRRT	GENERAL GRANT
AAEEGGMORRTT	MORTGAGE RATE
AAEEGGNRRSSS	GREEN AS GRASS
AAEEGGORRTXY	EXAGGERATORY
AAEEGGRSSSSU	AS SURE AS EGGS
AAEEGHHMORRS	HAEMORRHAGES
AAEEGHHMSTTW	WHAT'S THE GAME?
AAEEGHIIKSTV	GIVE IT A SHAKE
AAEEGHIKMNTT	MAKING THE TEA
AAEEGHILLMNT	ALL IN THE GAME
AAEEGHILMRTV	GIVE THE ALARM
AAEEGHKNOSTT	TAKEN HOSTAGE
AAEEGHKOSSTT	TAKE HOSTAGE
	TAKES HOSTAGE
AAEEGHLMNORT	HOTEL MANAGER
AAEEGHLMPSTY	PLAYS THE GAME

AAEEGHLRSSTW	WEATHER GLASS
	WEATHERGLASS
AAEEGHMNOPRT	ON THE RAMPAGE
AAEEGHMOSTWY	GO THE SAME WAY
AAEEGHNPPRRS	PAPERHANGERS
AAEEGHPRRSTV	GRAPE HARVEST
AAEEGIIKLPST	EATS LIKE A PIG
AAEEGIKLNSTV	LEAVE-TAKINGS
AAEEGIKMNSTY	MAKING EYES AT
AAEEGIKMRSTV	GRAVE MISTAKE
AAEEGIKNPPRT	KEEPING APART
AAEEGIKRSSTT	STAGE A STRIKE
AAEEGILLLNTT	TELLING A TALE
AAEEGILLNNOV	LEAVING ALONE
AAEEGILLNNST	SALIENT ANGLE
AAEEGILLNRVY	LEAVING EARLY
AAEEGILMNRSV	SERVING A MEAL
AAEEGILNNNOT	EATING NO LEAN
AAEEGILNNORT	GENERATIONAL
AAEEGILNNOTV	LEAVING A NOTE
AAEEGILNOTTV	VEGETATIONAL
AAEEGILNPSSY	SAYING PLEASE
AAEEGILNRRST	STEALING AREA
AAEEGILRRTVY	LARGE VARIETY
AAEEGILRSSUV	LIVER SAUSAGE
AAEEGIMNNOTT	EATING NO MEAT
AAEEGIMNORST	MENAGE A TROIS
AAEEGIMNNTTUV	AUGMENTATIVE
AAEEGIMPSSTU	SEPTUAGESIMA
AAEEGINNORSV	GIVEN A REASON
AAEEGINNSTUX	EXSANGUINATE
AAEEGINORSSV	GIVES A REASON
AAEEGINPRRSS	AIR PASSENGER
AAEEGINPRRTT	GREAT PAINTER
AAEEGINPRSST	GREASEPAINTS
AAEEGINPRSTX	EXASPERATING
AAEEGINPSWWY	SWEEPING AWAY
AAEEGINRRSTV	ASSEVERATING
AAEEGINSSSTY	IN EASY STAGES
AAEEGIRRTTVY	GREAT VARIETY
AAEEGIRSTTVY	VARIETY STAGE
AAEEGJLMNORR	MAJOR GENERAL
AAEEGKLOPSST	TAKE AS GOSPEL
AAEEGKMNPRSS	SPEAKS GERMAN
AAEEGKMNRTUW	WEAK ARGUMENT
AAEEGLLMNOTW	ETON WALL-GAME
AAEEGLLMRRSU	REGULAR MEALS
AAEEGLMNORTV	GALVANOMETER
AAEEGLMNRRTV	GREAT MALVERN
AAEEGLNRSTTV	TRAVEL AGENTS
AAEEGLOPRSSS	OPERA GLASSES
AAEEGMMNRRST	GERMAN MASTER
AAEEGMNNRRST	ARRANGEMENTS
AAEEGMNOPRST	POMEGRANATES
AAEEGMNOPSTU	MAGNETOPAUSE
AAEEGNNORTUV	GAVE ONE A TURN
AAEEGRRSTTTU	GREAT STATURE
AAEEGRSSSTUW	SWEET AS SUGAR
AAEEHHIMPRTT	AMPHITHEATRE
AAEEHHKMRTTY	THE HAYMARKET
AAEEHHKNNSTV	THANK HEAVENS!
	THANKS HEAVEN
AAEEHHKNOTTT	TAKEN THE OATH
AAEEHHKOSTTT	TAKES THE OATH
AAEEHHLLMNTT	MENTAL HEALTH
AAEEHHLNNPST	NAPHTHALENES
AAEEHHLRSSTW	WASH-LEATHERS
AAEEHHMRRTTW	WARM THE HEART
AAEEHHNNRSSTW	HAS THE ANSWER
AAEEHHORRTTT	HEART TO HEART
	HEART-TO-HEART

AAEEHHOSSSST	ASHES TO ASHES	AAEEILMORRSS	RAISES MORALE
AAEEHHPRSTTY	PAYS THE EARTH	AAEEILNNORRT	NEAR RELATION
AAEEHHPSSSTT	PASSES THE HAT	AAEEILNPRSST	PLEASANTRIES
AAEEHIIKNSST	KINAESTHESIA	AAEEILNPRSTW	WATER SPANIEL
AAEEHIILNPRT	LEAP IN THE AIR	AAEEILNRSTTV	ALTERNATIVES
AAEEHIILRTVX	EXHILARATIVE	AAEEILNSSTVX	LAXATIVENESS
AAEEHIKLNRRU	RUN LIKE A HARE	AAEEILPRSSTU	ITS A PLEASURE
AAEEHIKNRTTT	TAKE THE TRAIN	AAEEILRRRSVY	ARRIVES EARLY
AAEEHIKORTTT	TAKE TO THE AIR	AAEEIMNPPRST	APPRAISEMENT
AAEEHILPRSTU	LAUREATESHIP	AAEEIMNPRSTV	PRIVATE MEANS
AAEEHIMMNORT	REMAIN AT HOME	AAEEIMPRRSTU	TRIP A MEASURE
AAEEHIMMNPST	AMPHETAMINES	AAEEINOPRSTX	EXASPERATION
AAEEHIMORRRS	MOIRA SHEARER	AAEEINORSSTV	ASSEVERATION
AAEEHINNRSTU	NEURASTHENIA	AAEEINORRSTU	QUATERNARIES
AAEEHINORRST	TEAR ONES HAIR	AAEEINRSSTWY	WRITE AN ESSAY
AAEEHINORSST	RAISE ONES HAT	AAEEIPPRRSTV	PREPARATIVES
AAEEHINPPRRT	HEIR APPARENT	AAEEJMRSSTTW	JAMES STEWART
AAEEHINRRTVW	HIT A RAW NERVE	AAEEKKMMNORS	MAKE ONES MARK
AAEEHINRRTWY	RAINY WEATHER	AAEEKLMNOPSY	MAKE ONE'S PLAY
AAEEHINSSSTY	SYNAESTHESIA	AAEEKLNRSSTT	RATTLESNAKES
AAEEHINSSTTT	ANAESTHETIST	AAEEKLPRSUWY	WAKES UP EARLY
AAEEHIRSSTTU	ISSUE A THREAT	AAEEKMMNORTT	MAKE NO MATTER
AAEEHKMNORST	ASK ME ANOTHER	AAEEKMNNRSTY	MAKES AN ENTRY
AAEEHKNORTTT	TAKEN TO HEART	AAEEKMNORRRS	MAKES AN ERROR
AAEEHKORSTTT	TAKES TO HEART	AAEEKMNOSSWY	MAKES ONE'S WAY
AAEEHLLMSTVY	THAMES VALLEY	AAEEKMNPRRTT	PATTERN MAKER
AAEEHLLNOPTW	LETHAL WEAPON	AAEEKMOPRSTT	MAKE A PROTEST
AAEEHLLPPRTW	PAPER THE WALL	AAEEKMQRRSTU	MARKET SQUARE
AAEEHLLRRTUW	LAUREL WREATH	AAEEKNOPRSTT	TAKE ONE'S PART
AAEEHLLRSSSU	AS SURE AS HELL	AAEEKOSSTUWY	SEEKS A WAY OUT
AAEEHLMRSSTT	SETS THE ALARM	AAEELLMMRSSU	SMALL MEASURE
AAEEHLNORSTT	LEARNS TO HATE	AAEELLMNORTV	MATERNAL LOVE
AAEEHLNORTTT	LEARNT TO HATE	AAEELLNNORSS	LEARN A LESSON
AAEEHLNPTVYY	HEAVY PENALTY	AAEELLNNTTTT	LATENT TALENT
AAEEHLORRTTY	THEATRE ROYAL	AAEELLNOPRTV	PATERNAL LOVE
AAEEHMNNTTTU	NAME THAT TUNE	AAEELLNPRRTY	PARENTERALLY
AAEEHMNORSUW	WAREHOUSEMAN	AAEELMMNRTTT	MALTREATMENT
AAEEHMNRSTTT	HAS TREATMENT	AAEELMNNRTUY	NATURAL ENEMY
AAEEHNOPRSSY	PAY ONES SHARE	AAEELMNSTUUV	AUTUMN LEAVES
AAEEHNORRSTW	THERES A WAR ON	AAEELMORSSSU	ASSUMES A ROLE
AAEEHNPPRWYY	HAPPY NEW YEAR	AAEELNNOPPRU	EUROPEAN PLAN
AAEEHNPRRSSW	SAW SHARPENER	AAEELNNPSSST	PLEASANTNESS
AAEEHNPRSTTW	WEAR THE PANTS	AAEELNOPSTTY	STAY OPEN LATE
AAEEHNRSSTTY	HEARTY ASSENT	AAEELNOQRSSU	SLOANE SQUARE
AAEEHRRSTTTY	HASTY RETREAT	AAEELNORSSTV	NEVER AT A LOSS
AAEEHRRTTTTU	UTTER A THREAT	AAEELNOSSSTT	EATS ONE'S SALT
AAEEIIKKLLTW	WALKIE-TALKIE	AAEELNRRSSTT	RETRANSLATES
AAEEIILLRTTV	ALLITERATIVE	AAEELNRSTTTU	NEUTRAL STATE
AAEEIILMMNTU	A MILE A MINUTE	AAEELOPRSTTX	EXTRAPOLATES
AAEEIILMNTTV	ALIMENTATIVE	AAEEMMNNNOSS	NAMES NO NAMES
AAEEIILMORTV	AMELIORATIVE	AAEEMMPRRSTT	TRAMP STEAMER
AAEEIILMRSST	MATERIALISES	AAEEMNNPPRSW	NEWSPAPERMAN
AAEEIILMRSTZ	MATERIALIZES	AAEEMNNSSTTW	NEW STATESMAN
AAEEIILRRSST	ARTERIALISES	AAEEMNORSSTW	WESTERN SAMOA
AAEEIILRRSTZ	ARTERIALIZES	AAEEMNPSSTYY	EASY PAYMENTS
AAEEIINNRRTV	VETERINARIAN	AAEEMNNRSTTY	TESTAMENTARY
AAEEIJLNNQUU	QUEEN JULIANA	AAEENNPPRSSY	SPARES A PENNY
AAEEIKLMRSTV	LEAVE ITS MARK	AAEENNPRSTUU	SUPERANNUATE
AAEEIKLNPPRS	PLAIN SPEAKER	AAEENORSSTWY	WROTE AN ESSAY
AAEEIKMMOPRS	MAKE A PROMISE	AAEERRRSSTTU	ART TREASURES
AAEEIKNRSTTW	KNIT A SWEATER	AAEERRRSTTUU	RESTAURATEUR
AAEEIILLLLPRS	LIES PARALLEL	AAEFFHLLMNOT	THE FALL OF MAN
AAEEIILLLRSSZ	LAISSEZ-ALLER	AAEFFIIMNORR	FORAMINIFERA
AAEEIILLMNPST	PLANETESIMAL	AAEFFIIMRSTV	AFFIRMATIVES
AAEEIILLNPRUV	PAUL VERLAINE	AAEFFIOPRSTY	PAYS A FORFEIT
AAEEIILLNRSTW	ARTESIAN WELL	AAEFFKLMOOOS	MAKES A FOOL OF
AAEEIILLRRRTV	AIR TRAVELLER	AAEFFKLOOORT	TAKE FOR A FOOL
AAEEIILLRTTTX	A LITTLE EXTRA	AAEFFNORRSTY	RAN FOR SAFETY
AAEEIILMNPSTT	PLEASANT TIME	AAEFFOORRRUV	FEAR OR FAVOUR
AAEEIILMNRRTW	MINERAL WATER	AAEFFQRRSTTU	QUARTERSTAFF
AAEEILMOPSST	AIMS TO PLEASE	AAEFGGILLLNT	FLAGELLATING

AAEFGGLLNOUU	FOUL LANGUAGE	AAEFNNOOSSTT	AS OFTEN AS NOT
AAEFGHHIILNT	FAITH HEALING	AAEGGGILNNSU	SIGN LANGUAGE
AAEFGHILNNOS	GONE IN A FLASH	AAEGGGILNOTT	GETTING A GOAL
AAEFGHILNOSS	GOES IN A FLASH	AAEGGGINORST	AGGREGATIONS
AAEFGHILNRST	FARTHINGALES	AAEGGGMOORTT	GOT A MORTGAGE
AAEFGHINNORV	HAVING NO FEAR	AAEGGHHIINSV	HEAVING A SIGH
AAEFGHINRTWY	FRIGHTEN AWAY	AAEGGHHINNVY	HANGING HEAVY
AAEFGHLNPRTU	RAN UP THE FLAG	AAEGGHHIOPRR	HAGIOGRAPHER
AAEFGIILMMNZ	FILM MAGAZINE	AAEGGHIMNOPY	PAYING HOMAGE
AAEFGIKMOOST	MAKES A GO OF IT	AAEGGHINNPPR	PAPERHANGING
AAEFGIILLNOT	FLAGELLATION	AAEGGHINSSUV	HAVING A GUESS
AAEFGILLLNSS	FALLING SALES	AAEGGHMNRTTU	TAUGHT GERMAN
AAEFGILLNPSY	PLAYING FALSE	AAEGGHOPRSSU	ROUGH PASSAGE
AAEFGILNNORY	LAY A FINGER ON	AAEGGIILNNPR	RINGING A PEAL
AAEFGILNNRST	LEARNING FAST	AAEGGIILNNSV	GIVEN A SIGNAL
AAEFGILNNRTT	RENTING A FLAT	AAEGGIILNSSV	GIVES A SIGNAL
AAEFGILNORTY	FLY INTO A RAGE	AAEGGIIMNNNW	WINNING A GAME
AAEFGIMMNORS	FORMS AN IMAGE	AAEGGIKMNSSU	MAKING A GUESS
AAEFGIMNRSTY	SAFETY MARGIN	AAEGGIKNSSTU	TAKING A GUESS
AAEFGIRRTTUY	FATIGUE PARTY	AAEGGILMNOOT	A LONG TIME AGO
AAEFGKLNOORW	GONE FOR A WALK	AAEGGILMNPSY	PLAYING GAMES
AAEFGKLOORSW	GOES FOR A WALK	AAEGGILNNORT	TEARING ALONG
AAEFGLLOPPRY	PLAY LEAP FROG	AAEGGILNSTTU	AGGLUTINATES
AAEFGLNOORTU	GO TO A FUNERAL	AAEGGINNPRRR	PREARRANGING
AAEFGLORSSTW	GLASS OF WATER	AAEGGINOORTT	GOT INTO A RAGE
AAEFGMMNOPRY	MAP OF GERMANY	AAEGGINORTUV	AVERAGING OUT
AAEFGMORSTWY	GETS AWAY FROM	AAEGGLMMORSU	GRAMMALOGUES
AAEFHHIOPRSS	SHAH OF PERSIA	AAEGGLNNOOWY	GONE A LONG WAY
AAEFHHLOSUWY	HALFWAY HOUSE	AAEFGGLNOOSWY	GOES A LONG WAY
AAEFHILLLMTY	ALL THE FAMILY	AAEGHHIKNRST	EARTHSHAKING
AAEFHILLLSTV	FESTIVAL HALL	AAEGHHILRTTT	LIGHT AT HEART
AAEFHILMTWYY	THE FAMILY WAY	AAEGHHIORTWY	HOARY WITH AGE
AAEFHILNNSTW	WENT IN A FLASH	AAEGHHLLSTTU	THE LAST LAUGH
AAEFHILNOPST	FASHION PLATE	AAEGHHOPPRRS	PHRASEOGRAPH
AAEFHILNRSTW	FATHERS-IN-LAW	AAEGHIIKNNST	TAKING A SHINE
AAEFHINPRSST	FRESH AS PAINT	AAEGHIIKNRTT	TAKING THE AIR
AAEFHLLORSTT	FALLS TO EARTH	AAEGHIILNRTX	EXHILARATING
AAEFHMMOORWY	AWAY FROM HOME	AAEGHIILRTVW	GAVE IT A WHIRL
AAEFHOPRTTWY	PART OF THE WAY	AAEGHIKLMNTW	MAKING THE LAW
AAEFHRRSSCTT	STARTS AFRESH	AAEGHIKMNOSV	HAVING A SMOKE
AAEFIIILMRSS	FAMILIARISES	AAEGHIKNPRTT	TAKING THE RAP
AAEFIIILMRSZ	FAMILIARIZES	AAEGHIKNSTWY	ASKING THE WAY
AAEFIILLSTUW	FILE A LAWSUIT	AAEGHILMNRRV	MARVIN HAGLER
AAEFIILMNRSS	FAMILIARNESS	AAEGHILNNOOT	HALOGENATION
AALFIILORRTV	FAIL TO ARRIVE	AAEGHILOORRT	HORATIO ALGER
AAEFIJLSTVZZ	JAZZ FESTIVAL	AAEGHIMMNPSS	GAMESMANSHIP
AAEFIKMOPRST	MAKES A PROFIT	AAEGHIMNPRST	THE GRAMPIANS
AAEFIKOPRSST	PAIR OF SKATES	AAEGHIMNRRTW	HEARTWARMING
AAEFIKORRSSS	ASKS FOR A RISE	AAEGHIMORRRT	METRORRHAGIA
AAEFILLLNSUV	FALLS IN VALUE	AAEGHINOSSTT	THOSE AGAINST
AAEFILLMRWYY	FAMILY LAWYER	AAEGHINPPSSS	PASSING PHASE
AAEFILLOQRUV	ALL OF A QUIVER	AAEGHINPTVWY	PAVING THE WAY
AAEFILMMMORT	IMMORTAL FAME	AAEGHINRRSTV	GRAIN HARVEST
AAEFILMMRTTY	FAMILY MATTER	AAEGHIORRRTW	ROAR WITH RAGE
AAEFILMNNPTY	FINAL PAYMENT	AAEGHKLLNTTT	TALK AT LENGTH
AAEFILMNOORS	REMAINS ALOOF	AAEGHLLNNOTT	TEN-GALLON HAT
AAEFILMNPTTT	FINAL ATTEMPT	AAEGHLMNRSTT	AT ARMS LENGTH
AAEFILMNRRST	FRATERNALISM	AAEGHLMNRSTU	MANSLAUGHTER
AAEFILNORRTY	REFLATIONARY	AAEGHLMRSTUV	GUSTAV MAHLER
AAEFILNQRRTU	QUARTER FINAL	AAEGHLNOPRTY	PLAY THE ORGAN
	QUARTERFINAL	AAEGHMNNOPRS	HANGMANS ROPE
AAEFILNSSTWY	STIFLES A YAWN	AAEGHMOPRRSS	PHRASEOGRAMS
AAEFIMNOOPTT	POTATO FAMINE	AAEGHNOPRRTW	NARROW THE GAP
AAEFIMNPTTTT	FAINT ATTEMPT	AAEGHNOQRSSU	ORANGE SQUASH
AAEFIOPPRRST	REAPS A PROFIT	AAEGHNORTTUY	YOUNG AT HEART
AAEFIRRSTTWY	FRITTERS AWAY	AAEGHNPRRSST	STRAPHANGERS
AAEFKLNORTWW	WENT FOR A WALK	AAEGHNSSTTTU	SETS AT NAUGHT
AAEFLLNOPSTU	PULL A FAST ONE	AAEGHOPRSSST	SHORT PASSAGE
AAEFMMORSSTT	FOAM MATTRESS	AAEGIIKKLLMN	MAKE A KILLING
AAEFMORRSSTT	MASTER OF ARTS	AAEGIIKLMNSV	MAKES A LIVING
AAEFNNNOOPRT	AFTERNOON NAP	AAEGIIKMNNOS	MAKING A NOISE

729

AAEGIIKMNNTX	MAKING AN EXIT
AAEGIIKMNSTY	MAKING IT EASY
AAEGIIKNSTTY	TAKING IT EASY
AAEGIILLLNVW	LEAVING A WILL
AAEGIILLNOST	LEGALISATION
AAEGIILLNOTZ	LEGALIZATION
AAEGIILLNRTT	ALLITERATING
AAEGIILMNORT	AMELIORATING
AAEGIILNNRSV	EARNS A LIVING
AAEGIILNNSUV	GAINS IN VALUE
AAEGIILNRRTV	ARRIVING LATE
AAEGIILNSTVY	STAYING ALIVE
AAEGIIMNNNNW	WINNING A NAME
AAEGIIMNNNRT	EARNING A MINT
AAEGIINNOSTV	EVAGINATIONS
AAEGIINNPPRT	APPERTAINING
AAEGIINNRSST	RISEN AGAINST
AAEGIINNSTVX	VEXING A SAINT
AAEGIINPRRTT	REPATRIATING
AAEGIINPRTTX	EXPATRIATING
AAEGIINRSSST	RISES AGAINST
AAEGIINRSSTX	RAISING TAXES
AAEGIISTTTVW	GAVE IT A TWIST
AAEGIJKLNOPY	PLAYING A JOKE
AAEGIKLNPRSS	SPRINGS A LEAK
AAEGIKLNPTUW	WAKING UP LATE
AAEGIKMNORRT	MARRIAGE KNOT
AAEGIKMNPSSS	MAKING PASSES
AAEGIKMNRRTW	WATERMARKING
AAEGIKNNNRTW	TAKEN WARNING
AAEGIKNNPSST	SNEAKING PAST
AAEGIKNNRSTW	TAKES WARNING
AAEGIKNPPRST	SPEAKING PART
AAEGIKNSSTTT	SETTING A TASK
AAEGILLMMNRST	SMELLING A RAT
AAEGILLNNOST	IT'S A LONG LANE
AAEGILLNNTTY	TANGENTIALLY
AAEGILLNPPRW	WALLPAPERING
AAEGILLRRRUW	GUERRILLA WAR
AAEGILMNOPPV	MOVING APPEAL
AAEGILNNOPPR	ANGELA RIPPON
AAEGILNNOPRS	PERSONAL GAIN
AAEGILNNPTUY	PLAYING A TUNE
AAEGILNNRRWY	EARLY WARNING
AAEGILNNSTUY	NAUSEATINGLY
AAEGILNPRRTT	INTEGRAL PART
AAEGILNPSSTT	STEALING PAST
AAEGILNRSTTU	TRIANGULATES
AAEGILPRTUY	GUITAR PLAYER
AAEGIMMRSUVY	GIVE A SUMMARY
AAEGIMNNOSST	MATING SEASON
AAEGIMNNOSTY	MEANING TO SAY
AAEGIMNNOTTU	AUGMENTATION
AAEGIMNNRRST	ARRAIGNMENTS
AAEGIMNRRSTT	TRANSMIGRATE
AAEGIMNRRSSTY	GAINS MASTERY
AAEGIMORRSVW	MARRIAGE VOWS
AAEGINNOPTTV	VANTAGE POINT
AAEGINNRSTTW	STARTING ANEW
AAEGINOSSTTV	VOTES AGAINST
AAEGINPPRSTW	WASTING PAPER
AAEGINPRSSTW	PASSING WATER
AAEGINPRSTTT	SETTING A TRAP
	SETTING APART
AAEGIORRSTTT	TRAITORS GATE
AAEGKMNORRSW	WORKS MANAGER
AAEGKOPRSSSU	PORK SAUSAGES
AAEGLLNNOPTY	PENTAGONALLY
AAEGLLNORSTV	TRAVELS ALONG
AAEGLLNORTTY	TETRAGONALLY
AAEGLMOOPSSU	GAMOSEPALOUS

AAEGLMOOPSTU	GAMOPETALOUS
AAEGLNNOTWWY	WENT A LONG WAY
AAEGLNOOPUUY	A PLAGUE ON YOU!
AAEGLNOPSSST	ONE'S LAST GASP
AAEGLNRSSTTU	STRANGULATES
AAEGMNNORSTW	STRANGE WOMAN
AAEGMOPPSSTT	POSTAGE STAMP
AAEGNORSSTTY	STRANGE TO SAY
AAEGOPRRSSST	ESPARTO GRASS
AAEHHIIMNSTT	HAS A THIN TIME
AAEHHILLSTTW	WITH ALL HASTE
AAEHHILNTTTU	ATTILA THE HUN
AAEHHINORSSW	WASH ONES HAIR
AAEHHLLLPSTY	PLAY THE HALLS
AAEHHNOPRTTW	ON THE WARPATH
AAEHHOPPRTWW	WHAT A WHOPPER!
AAEHIILLNNTV	ANNIHILATIVE
AAEHIILMMPTU	EPITHALAMIUM
AAEHIILMNRTT	THIN MATERIAL
AAEHIILNORTX	EXHILARATION
AAEHIILPRSSV	LAVISH PRAISE
AAEHIKNOSTTV	STAKHANOVITE
AAEHIKNPPSSS	SPEAK SPANISH
AAEHIILLMMOR	MEMORIAL HALL
AAEHILLNPTTW	PAINT THE WALL
AAEHILLORTWY	RAILWAY HOTEL
AAEHILLPSSWY	PAISLEY SHAWL
AAEHILMNPSSS	SALESMANSHIP
AAEHILMRSTUY	AMATEURISHLY
AAEHILNNOORT	NATIONAL HERO
AAEHILNNPOTY	PAY ON THE NAIL
AAEHILNNPSSY	NEPHANALYSIS
AAEHILNOPPTY	PLAY THE PIANO
AAEHILNRSTTT	THE LAST TRAIN
AAEHIMMNNRSU	HUMAN REMAINS
AAEHIMMNOOTT	AIM AT THE MOON
AAEHIMMRSSTU	SHAMATEURISM
AAEHIMNRRSTY	MARRY IN HASTE
AAEHIMNSTTTW	SAINT MATTHEW
AAEHIMRSSSTY	MASS HYSTERIA
AAEHINOPRRST	PART ONES HAIR
AAEHINOSSTWY	HAS IT ONE'S WAY
AAEHINOSTTTT	AT THE STATION
AAEHKKLLNPTW	WALK THE PLANK
AAEHKOOPSTTT	TAKE A POT-SHOT
AAEHLLMNSSTW	MANS THE WALLS
AAEHLLNRSSTV	SERVANTS HALL
AAEHLLORSTWW	SHALLOW WATER
AAEHLLSTTTWZ	THE LAST WALTZ
AAEHLMNOSTTT	TO THE LAST MAN
AAEHLNORTVYY	THE ROYAL NAVY
AAEHLPPRSTTY	PLAYS THE PART
AAEHLRSSTTTW	THE LAST STRAW
AAEHMNORSSTT	TAM-O'-SHANTERS
AAEHMNORTTTW	NO MATTER WHAT
AAEHMOORSTTU	ATHEROMATOUS
AAEHNOORSSTW	SWEARS ON OATH
AAEHNOORSTTT	AT ONE'S THROAT
AAEHNORRSUWY	RUNAWAY HORSE
AAEIIILMSSTV	ASSIMILATIVE
AAEIIILPRSTT	PARTIALITIES
AAEIIKLLMMNO	MAKE A MILLION
AAEIIKLMNPST	MAKES IT PLAIN
AAEIIKLNOPST	SPOKE ITALIAN
AAEIIKNRSSST	RAISES A STINK
AAEIIILMMRTY	IMMATERIALLY
AAEIIILLNORTT	ALLITERATION
AAEIIILLNOTTV	LEVITATIONAL
AAEIILMNNOST	MELANISATION
AAEIILMNNOTT	ALIMENTATION
AAEIILMNNOTZ	MELANIZATION

AAEIILMNNPRT	IN PARLIAMENT	AAEIMMNNORRS	ROMAN REMAINS
AAEIILMNOORT	AMELIORATION	AAEIMMNOSTTW	WAITS A MOMENT
AAEIILMNPTUV	MANIPULATIVE	AAEIMMPPRSUY	PAYS A PREMIUM
AAEIILMOPRRT	IMPERATORIAL	AAEIMNOOOOPT	ONOMATOPOEIA
AAEIILNNOPST	PENALISATION	AAEIMOPPRSTX	APPROXIMATES
AAEIILNNOPTZ	PENALIZATION	AAEINNOPPRSS	SPARE NO PAINS
AAEIILNNORST	NATIONALISER	AAEINNOPRSXY	EXPANSIONARY
AAEIILNNORTZ	NATIONALIZER	AAEINNOPTTTY	PAY ATTENTION
AAEIILNNOSST	NATIONALISES	AAEINNORSSTU	AUSTRONESIAN
AAEIILNNOSTZ	NATIONALIZES	AAEINNOSSTTT	NATION-STATES
AAEIILNOQSTU	EQUALISATION	AAEINOPPRRST	PREPARATIONS
AAEIILNOQTUZ	EQUALIZATION	AAEINOSSTTTT	ATTESTATIONS
AAEIILNORRST	RATIONALISER	AAEIOPPPRRST	APPROPRIATES
AAEIILNORRTZ	RATIONALIZER	AAEIPPRRTTVY	PRIVATE PARTY
AAEIILNORSST	RATIONALISES	AAEJKMNOOTTY	JOMO KENYATTA
AAEIILNORSTT	ARISTOTELIAN	AAEJKMPRSSST	ST.JAMESS PARK
AAEIILNORSTZ	RATIONALIZES	AAEJLLMNNOUY	JOANNA LUMLEY
AAEIIMNNOSTX	EXAMINATIONS	AAEKLLNORSTT	LEARNS TO TALK
AAEIIMNOSSTV	AVITAMINOSES		TAKEN A STROLL
AAEIIMNRSSTT	MENAI STRAITS	AAEKLLNORSTW	LEARNS TO WALK
AAEIIMNSTTUW	WAITS A MINUTE	AAEKLLNORTTT	LEARNT TO TALK
AAEIINNNQRTU	IN QUARANTINE	AAEKLLNORTTW	LEARNT TO WALK
AAEIINNSSTTT	INSTANTIATES	AACKLLOR33TT	TAKES A STROLL
AAEIINOPRRTT	REPATRIATION	AAEKLMNORRUW	MANUAL WORKER
AAEIINOPRTTX	EXPATRIATION	AAEKLNOOPTTY	TOOK A PENALTY
AAEIINOSSTTV	AESTIVATIONS	AAEKLNORSTWW	WALKS ON WATER
AAEIINOTTTUV	QUANTITATIVE	AAEKNOORSTUW	TOOK UNAWARES
AAEIKKMMRSST	MAKES ITS MARK	AAEKNOQPRSTU	ASK NO QUARTER
AAEIKLLNPPSY	SPEAK PLAINLY	AAEKNOQRRSUW	NARROW SQUEAK
AAEIKLMMNNTU	IMMANUEL KANT	AAELLLNPRRSU	RUNS PARALLEL
AAEIKLMNNOTU	MOUNTAIN LAKE	AAELLLOSSSST	SELLS AT A LOSS
AAEIKLRRSTTY	STARK REALITY	AAELLMMNSTUY	MENTAL ASYLUM
AAEIKMNNOPTU	MOUNTAIN PEAK	AAELLMNNORTY	ORNAMENTALLY
AAEIKMNPPSTY	MAKE IT SNAPPY	AAELLMRRTUXY	EXTRAMURALLY
AAEIKMPRSTTU	MAKE-UP ARTIST	AAELLNNOOPRS	PERSONAL LOAN
AAEIKNOQSSTU	ASK A QUESTION	AAELLNNPSTUY	UNPLEASANTLY
AAEIKNPRSSSU	SPEAK RUSSIAN	AAELMMNNORRU	ROMAN NUMERAL
AAEIILLLMRTTU	MULTILATERAL	AAELMNNORTTU	ULTRAMONTANE
AAEIILLLNRTUY	UNILATERALLY	AAELMOOPPRST	PASTORAL POEM
AAEIILLLRRTTY	TRILATERALLY	AAELMOOPRSTZ	SPERMATOZOAL
AAEIILLMNNOUV	NOMINAL VALUE	AAELNNNRRTUU	ANNUAL RETURN
AAEIILLMNNSUY	SEMIANNUALLY	AAELNNOPRRTU	ANNUAL REPORT
AAEIILLNOPPST	APPELLATIONS	AAELNNPRRSTT	TRANSPLANTER
AAEIILLNOQTUY	EQUATIONALLY	AAELNOPPRSTY	PLAY ONES PART
AAEIILLQRSSTU	QUASI-STELLAR	AAELNPRRSTUU	SUPERNATURAL
AAEIILMMMNORT	IMMORTAL NAME	AAELNRRSSSTV	TRANSVERSALS
AAEIILMMNNORR	NORMAN MAILER	AAELNRSSSTTW	STALWARTNESS
AAEIILMNNOSTT	LAMENTATIONS	AAELNRSSSTUX	TRANSSEXUALS
AAEIILMNNNRSTT	MENTAL STRAIN	AAELNRSSTTUY	STAYS NEUTRAL
AAEIILMNNSSUY	INSANE ASYLUM	AAELOOPRRTTX	EXTRAPOLATOR
AAEIILMNORRSY	ROYAL MARINES	AAELOORSTTTT	START TOO LATE
AAEIILMNORSTV	MALVERSATION	AAELOPRRSTTY	LAY PROSTRATE
AAEIILMNPRSTU	PLANETARIUMS	AAELOPRSSTTU	PARLOUS STATE
AAEIILMOOPRST	LAPAROTOMIES	AAEMNOPRSTTU	PORTMANTEAUS
AAEIILMORRSTT	MASTER TAILOR	AAEMNOPRTTUX	PORTMANTEAUX
AAEIILNNNOSTW	NATIONAL NEWS	AAEMOORSTTTU	TERATOMATOUS
AAEIILNNOORTT	NOTIONAL RATE	AAEMORSSSTTT	TOASTMASTERS
AAEIILNNOPSTX	EXPLANATIONS	AAEMQRRRSTUY	ARMY QUARTERS
AAEIILNNOPTTX	EXPLANTATION	AAENNPRSSTTU	SUPERNATANTS
AAEIILNNORSST	RATIONALNESS	AAEOOPPRRRST	PARATROOPERS
AAEIILNNORSTT	ALTERNATIONS	AAEOPPRSSTTU	PASSE-PARTOUT
AAEIILNOOPRRT	PERORATIONAL	AAFFGHHILNRT	HALF FARTHING
AAEIILNOPRRST	PROLETARIANS	AAFFIIILNOST	AFFILIATIONS
AAEIILNOPSSTY	PASSIONATELY	AAFFIIMNNORST	AFFIRMATIONS
AAEIILNPPPRRW	PLAIN WRAPPER	AAFGGHHIINTV	HAVING A FIGHT
AAEIILNPPRSTT	PLEASANT TRIP	AAFGGHIILNNV	HAVING A FLING
AAEIILNPRSSTT	PLASTER SAINT	AAFGGHIINSTT	FIGHT AGAINST
AAEIILNPRTTWY	WRITTEN A PLAY	AAFGGHILNOWY	GOING HALF-WAY
AAEIILNQRRTTU	LATIN QUARTER	AAFGGIILNNWY	FLINGING AWAY
AAEIILNRSSSTU	SALUTARINESS	AAFGHHIILLNR	HIGH RAINFALL
AAEIILORRSTTV	LAST TO ARRIVE	AAFGHIILMNNU	HUMAN FAILING

AAFGHIRSSTTT	STARTS A FIGHT	AAGHILPRSTTY	STRAIGHT PLAY
AAFGIIILMNRR	FAMILIAR RING	AAGHINORTWWY	THROWING AWAY
AAFGIILNNNRW	FINAL WARNING	AAGHINRRUWYY	HURRYING AWAY
AAFGIILNOPTY	FAILING TO PAY	AAGHIPRRSTTT	STRAIGHT PART
AAFGIILNORST	RAISING ALOFT	AAGHIPRRSTTY	STRATIGRAPHY
AAFGIILNORSV	FIRING A SALVO	AAGHIPRSSTTT	STRAIGHT PAST
AAFGIKNOORTT	TAKING TOO FAR	AAGHOOPPRSSU	SAPROPHAGOUS
AAFGILORTVWY	LAW OF GRAVITY	AAGIIILLNNPS	PLAIN SAILING
AAFGLLNORRTY	FOR GALLANTRY	AAGIIILMNSST	ASSIMILATING
AAFHILMNRTUY	HUMAN FRAILTY	AAGIIIMNNOST	IMAGINATIONS
AAFHOOPSSSTT	HAS A SOFT SPOT	AAGIIINNNOTV	INVAGINATION
AAFIIILNNOST	FINALISATION	AAGIIINNORTT	INGRATIATION
AAFIIILNNOTZ	FINALIZATION	AAGIIINPSTVY	PAYING A VISIT
AAFIILLMNRUY	UNFAMILIARLY	AAGIIJKMNNOT	MAKING A JOINT
AAFIILMMNNOT	INFLAMMATION	AAGIIKLNNORW	WALKING ON AIR
AAFIILNNORTY	INFLATIONARY	AAGIIKLNNSWY	SLINKING AWAY
AAFILLLOPRST	PILLAR OF SALT	AAGIIKMMNRTW	MAKING IT WARM
AAFILMMNOORT	MALFORMATION	AAGIIKMNNOPT	MAKING A POINT
AAFILMMNORTY	INFLAMMATORY	AAGIILLNNOPR	ORIGINAL PLAN
AAFILMNNORUV	NAVAL UNIFORM	AAGIILLNNPTW	WALL PAINTING
AAFIMMNNOORTW	WAIT FOR NO MAN	AAGIILLNNUVY	UNAVAILINGLY
AAFINNOOPRST	PROFANATIONS	AAGIILMNNPTU	MANIPULATING
AAFINOPRRRSY	PRAYS FOR RAIN	AAGIILNNRSTU	NATURALISING
AAFIORRSSSTU	TSAR OF RUSSIA	AAGIILNNRSUY	SANGUINARILY
AAFJKLORRSTU	JUST FOR A LARK	AAGIILNNRTUZ	NATURALIZING
AAFKNOORSSUV	ASK NO FAVOURS	AAGIILNPPRSY	APPRAISINGLY
AAFLLLNOOPSW	FOLLOWS A PLAN	AAGIILNPPSWY	SLIPPING AWAY
AAFLLLOOPRTY	ALL TO PLAY FOR	AAGIILNPRTWY	WRITING A PLAY
AAGGGGILNNOT	TAGGING ALONG	AAGIIMNNOTWW	WAITING WOMAN
AAGGGIIINNNR	RINGING AGAIN	AAGIINNNQRTU	QUARANTINING
AAGGGIINNOST	GOING AGAINST	AAGIINNOORST	ORGANISATION
AAGGGILNOSWY	SLOGGING AWAY	AAGIINNOORTZ	ORGANIZATION
AAGGGILNPUWY	PLUGGING AWAY	AAGIINNORTUU	INAUGURATION
AAGGHHINOTTU	THOUGHT AGAIN	AAGIINNOSSST	ASSIGNATIONS
AAGGHIIJMNST	THINGAMAJIGS	AAGIINNRSTTY	TRYING A SAINT
AAGGHIINNSTT	HITTING A SNAG	AAGIINNSSTUU	AUGUSTINIANS
AAGGHINNPRST	STRAPHANGING	AAGIINOPSSTT	APOSTASISING
AAGGHINOPRTU	AUTOGRAPHING	AAGIINOPSTTZ	APOSTATIZING
AAGGIIILNPRS	PLAGIARISING	AAGIINORRTTY	INGRATIATORY
AAGGIIILNPRZ	PLAGIARIZING	AAGIKKNOSTTT	TAKING TO TASK
AAGGIIINNNTV	INVAGINATING	AAGIKLNRSTTT	START TALKING
AAGGIIINNRTT	INGRATIATING	AAGIKMNORSTT	TAKING TO ARMS
AAGGIILLNNOS	SAILING ALONG	AAGIKMNPRSTU	TAKING UP ARMS
AAGGIILLNNTV	GALLIVANTING	AAGIKNNOPRTT	TAKING NO PART
AAGGIILMMNSW	SWIMMING GALA	AAGIKNORSSTW	WORKS AGAINST
AAGGIINNNOST	ANTAGONISING	AAGILLMNTUWY	MULLIGATAWNY
AAGGIINNNOTZ	ANTAGONIZING	AAGILLNPPRTU	PULLING APART
AAGGIINNNRTU	TURNING AGAIN	AAGILLNRRTUY	TRIANGULARLY
AAGGIINNRTUU	INAUGURATING	AAGILNNNOTUU	ANNUAL OUTING
AAGGIINPRTVY	GIVING A PARTY	AAGILNORSTTU	GASTRULATION
AAGGIKLLNNOW	WALKING ALONG	AAGILOOPRSTY	PARASITOLOGY
AAGGILLNNOPY	PLAYING ALONG	AAGIMNNOOSST	ANASTOMOSING
AAGGILLNOSST	ALGOLAGNISTS	AAGIMNNOOTTU	MOUNTAIN GOAT
AAGGILNNOPSS	PASSING ALONG	AAGIMNNOPRSY	PAYING RANSOM
AAGGILNRSTTU	GASTRULATING	AAGIMNNORRRW	NARROW MARGIN
AAGGINOPPPST	STOPPING A GAP	AAGIMNPSSSTV	SAVINGS STAMP
AAGGINOPRRTW	GROWING APART	AAGINNOOSTTW	STATION WAGON
AAGHHIIRRSTT	STRAIGHT HAIR	AAGINNRSSTTU	TURNS AGAINST
AAGHHIPRSTTT	STRAIGHT PATH	AAGINOOPPRST	PROPAGATIONS
AAGHHLORTTUY	THROATY LAUGH	AAGINORRSTTW	STARTING A ROW
AAGHIIILNNNT	ANNIHILATING	AAGINPPRRSST	SPRINGS A TRAP
AAGHIIILNPSS	SAILING A SHIP		SPRINGS APART
AAGHIINNRRTU	TURNING A HAIR	AAGINRSSSTTV	STARTS SAVING
AAGHIJKNNNOT	JONATHAN KING	AAGLMNNRSTUY	GRANTS ASYLUM
AAGHIKLRSTTT	STRAIGHT TALK	AAGLNORRRSYY	LARRY GRAYSON
	TALK STRAIGHT	AAGMMNNORRST	STRONG-ARM MAN
AAGHIKLRSTTW	WALK STRAIGHT	AAGNNOORSSTX	STRONG AS AN OX
AAGHIKNOOPTT	TAKING A PHOTO	AAGOPRRRSSSW	SPARROWGRASS
AAGHILLNNOTT	NOTHING AT ALL	AAHHIIKNNSST	HAS A THIN SKIN
AAGHILMNQSUV	HAVING QUALMS	AAHHINOPRSTT	PARTHIAN SHOT
AAGHILNOSSTU	TOUGH AS NAILS	AAHHLLLOSTTY	ALL THAT'S HOLY

AAHHLMOPSTUY	HYPOTHALAMUS
AAHHNORRRTWY	HARRY WHARTON
AAHHOOOSTTTU	HAS A TOOTH OUT
AAHIIILNNNOT	ANNIHILATION
AAHIIKLLMNSW	HANK WILLIAMS
AAHIILNNORST	ANNIHILATORS
AAHIILNNORTY	ANNIHILATORY
AAHIIMNNOSTU	HUMANISATION
AAHIIMNNOTUZ	HUMANIZATION
AAHIINOPRRTW	ROAR WITH PAIN
AAHIINOPSTXY	ASPHYXIATION
AAHIINPPRSST	PARTISANSHIP
AAHIKMMNPRSS	MARKSMANSHIP
AAHIKMNOSSTV	STAKHANOVISM
AAHILLNNOPSY	POLLYANNAISH
AAHILMNOOPRT	PROTHALAMION
AAHILNNNOTTU	NATIONAL HUNT
AAHILPRRTTTU	PARTIAL TRUTH
AAHIOPRSSTXY	ASPHYXIATORS
AAHJLNOORTTV	JOHN TRAVOLTA
AAHKNNORSSUY	SUSANNAH YORK
AAHLLMMORSSW	MARSHMALLOWS
AAHLLMMORSWY	MARSHMALLOWY
AAHMNRRRSTUY	HARRY S.TRUMAN
AAHNOPRRTTWY	THROWN A PARTY
AAHOPRRSTTWY	THROWS A PARTY
AAIIIKLMMNRR	MIRIAM KARLIN
AAIIIILMNOTT	LIMITATIONAL
AAIIILMNOSST	ASSIMILATION
	ISLAMISATION
AAIIILMNOSTZ	ISLAMIZATION
AAIIILMPRTTY	IMPARTIALITY
AAIIILNNOSTT	LATINISATION
AAIIILNNOTTV	INVITATIONAL
AAIIILNNOTTZ	LATINIZATION
AAIIILNOSTTV	VISITATIONAL
	VITALISATION
AAIIILNOTTVZ	VITALIZATION
AAIIILNRSTTU	UTILITARIANS
AAIIILORSTTV	VISITATORIAL
AAIIIMMNOSTX	MAXIMISATION
AAIIIMMNOTXZ	MAXIMIZATION
AAIIIMNNRSTU	UNITARIANISM
AAIIIMNOSSTV	AVITAMINOSIS
AAIIINNOSSTT	SANITISATION
AAIIINNOSTTZ	SANITIZATION
AAIIINNRRSTT	TRINITARIANS
AAIIKLMNRRTY	MILITARY RANK
AAIIKNNNOPRS	PARKINSONIAN
AAIILLNNOSTT	INSTALLATION
AAIILLNORRTY	IRRATIONALLY
AAIILMNNOPTT	IMPLANTATION
AAIILMNNOPTU	MANIPULATION
AAIILMNOORST	MORALISATION
AAIILMNOORTZ	MORALIZATION
AAIILMNOSSTV	SALVATIONISM
AAIILMORSSST	ASSIMILATORS
AAIILMORSSTY	ASSIMILATORY
AAIILNNORSTT	TRANSITIONAL
AAIILNNOSSTT	NATIONALISTS
AAIILNOOPPST	APPOSITIONAL
AAIILNOOPRST	POLARISATION
AAIILNOOPRTZ	POLARIZATION
AAIILNOORSST	SOLARISATION
AAIILNOORSTV	VALORISATION
AAIILNOORSTZ	SOLARIZATION
AAIILNOORTVZ	VALORIZATION
AAIILNOSSTTV	SALVATIONIST
AAIILNPTTVYY	NATIVITY PLAY
AAIIMNNOORST	ROMANISATION
AAIIMNNOORTZ	ROMANIZATION

AAIIMNNOORSTT	AMORTISATION
AAIIMNOORTTZ	AMORTIZATION
AAIINNOPRSTT	STRAIN A POINT
AAIINNOOQSTTU	QUANTISATION
AAIINNOOQTTUZ	QUANTIZATION
AAIINNORSTTU	INSTAURATION
AAIINOOPRSTV	VAPORISATION
AAIINOOPRTVZ	VAPORIZATION
AAIINQSSTTTU	AQUATINTISTS
AAIJMNNOSTTW	WANTS JAM ON IT
AAILLLOSSTWW	SWALLOWTAILS
AAILLMNOPRTT	ALL-IMPORTANT
AAILLMNOTTUY	MUTATIONALLY
AAILLMNRRTUY	INTRAMURALLY
AAILLMOPRTYY	MORALITY PLAY
AAILLNOOTUVW	LOW VALUATION
AAILMMOPPRSS	MALAPROPISMS
AAILMNOPRTUY	MANIPULATORY
AAILNNORSSTT	TRANSLATIONS
AAILNOSSSSTU	SUSTAIN A LOSS
AAILOORSSTTT	TOTALISATORS
AAILOORSTTTZ	TOTALIZATORS
AAILOPRSSSTT	PASTORALISTS
AAILPPRSSTTY	PLAYS ITS PART
AAIMMMNOSSUY	IMMUNOASSAYS
AAIMNNNORTTU	MOUNTAIN TARN
AAIMNNOPSSTU	MOUNTAIN PASS
AAINOOPQTTTU	APT QUOTATION
AAINOPRRRSTT	AIR TRANSPORT
AAINQSTTTUVY	VAST QUANTITY
AAIOOPPPRRRT	APPROPRIATOR
AAJOSSSTUUYY	JUST AS YOU SAY
AALNOPRSTTUU	RUNS UP A TOTAL
AALNORRRUWYY	RUNAWAY LORRY
AAMMMNNOOOTWW	WOMAN TO WOMAN
AAMORRRSTTUU	START A RUMOUR
AANNORRSSTUY	TYRANNOSAURS
ABBBCGINNOUY	BOUNCING BABY
ABBBEESTTTUY	TEST-TUBE BABY
ABBBEHLMORTU	BLABBERMOUTH
ABBBGINRRSSU	BRASS RUBBING
ABBCCEEHKNRS	BACK BENCHERS
	BACK-BENCHERS
ABBCCEEHMORS	BEACHCOMBERS
ABBCCEEILMPU	BECAME PUBLIC
ABBCCGIKNNOU	BOUNCING BACK
ABBCDDEEMRRU	BREADCRUMBED
ABBCDEFIORRS	BRACE OF BIRDS
ABBCDEFKNOOY	BACK OF BEYOND
ABBCDEIKNRTU	BIB AND TUCKER
ABBCDGIKLNOU	DOUBLING BACK
ABBCDHMNORSU	BRUSH AND COMB
ABBCEEEILNOS	BEEN SOCIABLE
ABBCEEHHOSTY	THE BEACH BOYS
ABBCEEHIILOT	BIBLIOTHECAE
ABBCEEHKKORT	BROKE THE BACK
ABBCEEIKLRRS	BLACKBERRIES
ABBCEEKLORST	BETA-BLOCKERS
ABBCEHIILLOT	BIBLIOTHECAL
ABBCEHIILOST	BIBLIOTHECAS
ABBCEIKKLLNU	BLUE-BLACK INK
ABBCFIILORST	FIBROBLASTIC
ABBCFLLLOOTU	FOOTBALL CLUB
ABBCGGIIKNNR	BRINGING BACK
ABBCGIMNOOST	COSTING A BOMB
ABBCKMOOORSY	BACK-ROOM BOYS
	BACKROOM BOYS
ABBCNORRSSUY	BANBURY CROSS
ABBDDEEEILST	BEDSIDE TABLE
ABBDDEGIILRU	BUILD A BRIDGE
ABBDDEGINORW	EDWARD GIBBON

ABBDDEHLLOOU	HAD BLUE BLOOD	ABCCDEEIIRST	BACTERICIDES
ABBDDELNORUY	DOUBLE BRANDY	ABCCDEEILORY	RODE A BICYCLE
ABBDDEMOOPPR	DROPPED A BOMB	ABCCDEEKLMOW	WELCOMED BACK
ABBDDENOOTUY	BEYOND A DOUBT	ABCCDEHILORU	COACHBUILDER
ABBDDNNOOPUW	BOB UP AND DOWN	ABCCDEHLMORU	CLOUD CHAMBER
ABBDEEFLORSS	SELF-ABSORBED	ABCCDEILLSYY	LADYS BICYCLE
ABBDEEGIILRY	BAILEY BRIDGE	ABCCDHILNSUW	CLUB SANDWICH
ABBDEEGILRRT	ALBERT BRIDGE	ABCCEEEELRSU	CAUSE CELEBRE
ABBDEEHHINRT	BEHIND THE BAR	ABCCEEEEHLNRT	TREBLE CHANCE
ABBDEELLORRU	DOUBLE BARREL	ABCCEEENORRS	ARBORESCENCE
ABBDEEMORRRY	ARMED ROBBERY	ABCCEEHHTTTU	CATCH THE TUBE
ABBDEFLNOSSW	EBBS AND FLOWS	ABCCEEHKLOTT	BEAT THE CLOCK
ABBDEGGIINNN	BAD BEGINNING	ABCCEEHKMMOO	COME BACK HOME
ABBDEGGILMNT	GAMBLING DEBT	ABCCEEIILNSS	INACCESSIBLE
ABBDEGGILNRS	BLIND BEGGARS	ABCCEEIILLNOR	RECONCILABLE
ABBDEGHOORTY	GO BY THE BOARD	ABCCEEIMRSUU	CUBIC MEASURE
ABBDEGNRRSUU	GARDEN SUBURB	ABCCEEKLMOSW	WELCOMES BACK
ABBDEHHLOSTY	HOLDS THE BABY	ABCCEEKNNORT	BROKEN ACCENT
ABBDEHIILRSY	HYBRIDISABLE	ABCCEELNNOSY	BALCONY SCENE
ABBDEHIILRYZ	HYBRIDIZABLE	ABCCEEMNNRSU	ENCUMBRANCES
ABBDEHLLOOSU	HAS BLUE BLOOD	ABCCEFFHINOR	BRANCH OFFICE
ABBDEILLMRRU	UMBRELLA BIRD	ABCCEHIKSSTT	BACKSTITCHES
ABBDEILNRSTU	RUBBED SALT IN	ABCCEHIMMRSU	CHAMBER MUSIC
ABBDEINRSSUU	SUBURBANISED	ABCCEHKLLOST	BLACK CLOTHES
ABBDEINRSUUZ	SUBURBANIZED	ABCCEHLOOOTX	CHOCOLATE BOX
ABBDELLLNRUY	LANDLUBBERLY		CHOCOLATE-BOX
ABBDELNORTTY	BRANDY BOTTLE	ABCCEIIKNPST	PICNIC BASKET
ABBDENRRTTUY	BRANDY BUTTER	ABCCEIINRRSU	CABIN CRUISER
ABBDILMOOPSS	BOMB DISPOSAL	ABCCEIKKLSST	STICKLEBACKS
ABBEEEFLORRR	BARREL OF BEER	ABCCEILLOOST	BLASTOCOELIC
ABBEEEEHNORST	THE BARE BONES	ABCCEILMMNOU	COMMUNICABLE
ABBEEEHSSTTT	BEATS THE BEST	ABCCEILNORTT	CONTRACTIBLE
ABBEEEEILLNUV	UNBELIEVABLE	ABCCEKMNOOOS	COME BACK SOON
ABBEEFHRSTTY	BY FAR THE BEST	ABCCEKMOOOST	TOBACCO SMOKE
ABBEEFLOORTW	TOWER OF BABEL	ABCCEKNOORTT	BROKE CONTACT
ABBEEGIKNORS	ONES BIG BREAK	ABCCGGHINOOY	GOING BY COACH
ABBEEGILNNOR	NOBLE BEARING	ABCCGHILNTUY	YACHTING CLUB
ABBEEGMORRTU	ROBERT MUGABE	ABCCGIKKKNNO	KNOCKING BACK
ABBEEHINRRTU	BRUIN THE BEAR	ABCCHIKLLOTY	BILLYCOCK HAT
ABBEEHKKNORT	BROKE THE BANK	ABCCHKLOOOST	BACK TO SCHOOL
ABBEEHNRRTTU	BEAR THE BRUNT	ABCCIKKKNOST	KNOCKS IT BACK
ABBEEILLNUVY	UNBELIEVABLY	ABCCILLOOSTY	OCTOSYLLABIC
ABBEEILMRRSU	REIMBURSABLE	ABCCILMMNOUY	COMMUNICABLY
ABBEEILOPQRU	EQUIPROBABLE	ABCCINOOSSTT	TOBACCONISTS
ABBEEINNRTTY	TINTERN ABBEY	ABCCKLNORTUY	BLACK COUNTRY
ABBEEJLLLMRY	BRAMBLE JELLY	ABCCNORSSTTU	SUBCONTRACTS
ABBEEKLOORTT	BROKE A BOTTLE	ABCDDEEEERRT	DECEREBRATED
ABBEELLMMRUU	BEAU BRUMMELL	ABCDDEEINORS	DECARBONISED
ABBEELLOSTWZ	BLEW TO BLAZES	ABCDDEEINORZ	DECARBONIZED
ABBEELORRRSU	RABBLE-ROUSER	ABCDDEIILLTY	DECIDABILITY
ABBEEMNSSSTU	SUBBASEMENTS	ABCDDEILMNPU	PUBLIC DEMAND
ABBEGINNORUY	BURYING A BONE	ABCDDFIORRTY	BRADFORD CITY
ABBEGINORRST	BRINGS TO BEAR	ABCDDGIKLNPU	BLACK PUDDING
ABBEILLMNOTU	BILL BEAUMONT	ABCDDGINORTU	BUDDING ACTOR
ABBEINORRRTY	TRAIN ROBBERY	ABCDEEEERRST	DECEREBRATES
ABBEINRSSSUU	SUBURBANISES	ABCDEEEFIINT	BENEFICIATED
ABBEINRSSTUU	SUBURBANITES	ABCDEEEFIOPR	PIECE OF BREAD
ABBEINRSSUUZ	SUBURBANIZES	ABCDEEEHILPR	DECIPHERABLE
ABBELLOOSTWZ	BLOW TO BLAZES	ABCDEEEHLLTT	BELLED THE CAT
ABBEMPRRSSTU	RUBBER-STAMPS	ABCDEEEHLNPT	CANT BE HELPED
ABBGHIILOPRY	BIBLIOGRAPHY	ABCDEEEHLORR	BREECHLOADER
ABBGHOORTTUU	BROUGHT ABOUT	ABCDEEEILMRT	CLIMBED A TREE
ABBHIKLRSSTU	TALKS RUBBISH	ABCDEEELMRST	LAST DECEMBER
ABBHMOOOOSST	BAMBOO SHOOTS	ABCDEEELNTTU	UNDETECTABLE
ABBKOOOORRSW	BORROWS A BOOK	ABCDEEFHINSW	BEEF SANDWICH
ABCCCEHIILNY	BICYCLE CHAIN	ABCDEEFILNNU	BAD INFLUENCE
ABCCCHOOOPTU	TOBACCO POUCH	ABCDEEFILORS	SLICE OF BREAD
ABCCDDNOORTU	BAD CONDUCTOR	ABCDEEGGLMRS	SCRAMBLED EGG
ABCCDEEEELPST	BESPECTACLED	ABCDEEGHNSSU	CHANGED BUSES
ABCCDEEHNNOS	DEACON'S BENCH	ABCDEEGLLORT	GOLD BRACELET
ABCCDEEIILRY	RIDE A BICYCLE	ABCDEEHIINRU	RICHIE BENAUD

ABCDEEHIKLST	THE BLACK SIDE	ABCEEEIMMRTV	ACTIVE MEMBER
ABCDEEHIPQUY	PAID BY CHEQUE	ABCEEEKLMORW	WELCOME BREAK
ABCDEEIILLMN	MEDICINE BALL	ABCEEEMMNRRR	REMEMBRANCER
ABCDEEIILLNN	INDECLINABLE	ABCEEEMMNRRS	REMEMBRANCES
ABCDEEILNORS	CONSIDERABLE	ABCEEEOPRRTT	BETA-RECEPTOR
ABCDEEILORSV	DISCOVERABLE	ABCEEFGILNRU	BEING CAREFUL
ABCDEEINORRS	DECARBONISER	ABCEEFHIMNTT	BENEFIT MATCH
ABCDEEINORRZ	DECARBONIZER	ABCEEFIILLNY	BENEFICIALLY
ABCDEEINORSS	DECARBONISES	ABCEEFILORRU	AIR-FORCE BLUE
ABCDEEINORSZ	DECARBONIZES	ABCEEFINNOST	BENEFACTIONS
ABCDEEKOPRRT	REPORTED BACK	ABCEEFKNORTY	TAKEN BY FORCE
ABCDEEKORRRS	BREAK RECORDS	ABCEEFKORRSU	BROKE SURFACE
ABCDEELLNORY	BEYOND RECALL	ABCEEFKORSTY	TAKES BY FORCE
ABCDEELMOOPS	DECOMPOSABLE	ABCEEGHLLNST	CABLES LENGTH
ABCDEELRTTUU	TUBERCULATED	ABCEEGHNSSSU	CHANGES BUSES
ABCDEEMRRTUU	DUMB CREATURE	ABCEEGIIMNRT	BEING CERTAIN
ABCDEENNOOST	BEST ONE CAN DO	ABCEEGILNORS	RECOGNISABLE
ABCDEENORRST	CENTREBOARDS	ABCEEGILNORZ	RECOGNIZABLE
ABCDEENORSST	ONE'S BEST CARD	ABCEEGIMNNOS	BECOMING SANE
ABCDEFIRRRTU	FRACTURED RIB	ABCEEHHLORST	THE BACHELORS
ABCDEFLOORRU	FORCED LABOUR	ABCEEHIINNTT	IN THE CABINET
ABCDEFMOPRUU	FUME CUPBOARD	ABCEEHIKLNTT	KITCHEN TABLE
ABCDEFORRSTU	CRUST OF BREAD	ABCEEHILLLST	SLICE THE BALL
ABCDEGHHINTU	CAUGHT BEHIND	ABCEEHKLORST	BACK THE LOSER
ABCDEGHKLOPU	PLOUGHED BACK	ABCEEHKMOSTT	THOMAS BECKET
ABCDEGILLNOR	GRILLED BACON	ABCEEHKNRSTU	BURN THE CAKES
ABCDEGILNOTU	DOUBLE ACTING	ABCEEHLMORRW	LOWER CHAMBER
ABCDEHIILOOON	BACHELORHOOD	ABCEEHLORRSY	CHARLES BOYER
ABCDEHIILLLM	CLIMBED A HILL	ABCEEHMMNNRT	EMBRANCHMENT
ABCDEHILNORR	RICHARD NODLE	ABCEEHMMORRSY	HARRY SECOMBE
ABCDEHILSSTW	SWITCHBLADES	ABCEEHMPPRRU	UPPER CHAMBER
ABCDEHKNORTU	ROUND THE BACK	ABCEEHNOTTTU	BEAT THE COUNT
ABCDEHLMOSTU	DOUBLES MATCH	ABCEEHORRRST	TORCHBEARERS
ABCDEHLOSTTU	CLUBS TO DEATH	ABCEEHORSSTT	BEARS THE COST
ABCDEHMOORST	HORS DE COMBAT		TOSS THE CABER
ABCDEHMOORTY	HARD TO COME BY	ABCEEHORSTTX	CHATTERBOXES
ABCDEHNOORRV	CHEVRON BOARD	ABCEEHPOSUYY	PAYS BY CHEQUE
ABCDEHNORSTY	BODY SNATCHER	ABCEEHPRRTUY	REACH PUBERTY
ABCDEHNRRRYY	CHERRY BRANDY	ABCEEIILLNPX	INEXPLICABLE
ABCDEIILRSTT	DISTRACTIBLE	ABCEEIILNNNT	BICENTENNIAL
ABCDEIINNSTZ	CITIZENS' BAND	ABCEEIILNRTX	INEXTRICABLE
ABCDEIKLNRSS	DRESS IN BLACK	ABCEEIILPPRT	PRECIPITABLE
ABCDEILNORSY	CONSIDERABLY	ABCEEIJNOPST	JACOB EPSTEIN
ABCDEILNOSTU	DISCOUNTABLE	ABCEEIKKRSTW	WICKER BASKET
ABCDEINOOPRS	PROBOSCIDEAN	ABCEEIKMMOST	SOME TIME BACK
ABCDEINOORST	NOTICE-BOARDS	ABCEEILNORST	CELEBRATIONS
ABCDEINRSSTU	DISTURBANCES	ABCEEILNOSSS	SOCIABLENESS
ABCDEKKNOOTU	KNOCKED ABOUT	ABCEEILNPRRT	PRINCE ALBERT
ABCDEKMNOOSW	BACKWOODSMEN	ABCEEINNORSV	INOBSERVANCE
ABCDELLOOSTU	ABSOLUTE COLD	ABCEEINOPRSU	PRECIOUS BANE
ABCDELMNOOPU	COMPOUNDABLE	ABCEEJKLMRTU	LUMBER JACKET
ABCDELOOPRUV	CUPBOARD LOVE	ABCEEKLNOSSY	LOSES BY A NECK
ABCDEOOOORRRT	CORROBORATED	ABCEEKLORRTW	LOWER BRACKET
ABCDFKLNORUU	RUN OF BAD LUCK	ABCEEKOPRSTT	BREAST POCKET
ABCDGHIINRTW	BIRD WATCHING	ABCEELLMPPRU	APPLE CRUMBLE
	BIRD-WATCHING	ABCEELLNOOST	CONSOLE TABLE
ABCDGIKNOPPR	DROPPING BACK	ABCEELLNPSSU	CULPABLENESS
ABCDGINOSTTU	CASTING DOUBT	ABCEELLOOSST	BLASTOCOELES
ABCDHINOOPRS	BRANCHIOPODS	ABCEELLORSTT	SECRET BALLOT
ABCDHIORSSTW	SWITCHBOARDS	ABCEELLRRTTU	TRACER BULLET
ABCDHNOORRSY	HYDROCARBONS	ABCEELNOOPTU	UNABLE TO COPE
ABCDIILOPRRT	TROPICAL BIRD	ABCEELOPRRSV	PROCES-VERBAL
ABCDILLNOOSS	BILLS AND COOS	ABCEELORSTUU	CAUSE TROUBLE
ABCDINORTUYY	CITY BOUNDARY	ABCEENOPRRTU	PROTUBERANCE
ABCEEEEHQRRU	BEARER CHEQUE	ABCEFFHIOORT	FORCE OF HABIT
ABCEEEFIINST	BENEFICIATES	ABCEFHILOPRT	PLACE OF BIRTH
ABCEEEFLNORS	BRACE ONESELF	ABCEFHMOOSTX	BOX OF MATCHES
ABCEEEHHKTTT	THE BACK TEETH	ABCEFIIORRTY	BOY ARTIFICER
ABCEEEHIKRST	BREAKS THE ICE	ABCEFKLLLOSW	BLACKFELLOWS
ABCEEEHLMRWY	REACH WEMBLEY	ABCEFKLNOSUV	KNAVE OF CLUBS
ABCEEEILMNST	BECAME SILENT	ABCEFLNOOTUU	FLOUNCE ABOUT

ABCEGGHINRRS	BRING CHARGES
ABCEGGILNNOO	BELGIAN CONGO
ABCEGHHSTTUU	CAUGHT THE BUS
ABCEGHIILNSS	BASIC ENGLISH
ABCEGHILLORR	BACHELOR GIRL
ABCEGHINORRS	CRASHING BORE
ABCEGHORRRTU	TURBOCHARGER
ABCEGIKNPPST	STEPPING BACK
ABCEGILMNOST	SINGLE COMBAT
ABCEGILNORSY	RECOGNISABLY
ABCEGILNORYZ	RECOGNIZABLY
ABCEGILOORTY	BACTERIOLOGY
ABCEGINRRTTU	CARBURETTING
ABCEHHIIKKTT	KICK THE HABIT
ABCEHHILLPTU	PUBLIC HEALTH
ABCEHIIKNSTT	SIT IN THE BACK
ABCEHIILLTTW	HIT BALL TWICE
ABCEHIJKNOTX	JACK-IN-THE-BOX
ABCEHIKLORTW	BLACK OR WHITE
ABCEHIKMRRTY	BITCHY REMARK
ABCEHIKNRSSS	BRACKISHNESS
ABCEHIKPPTTU	PICK UP THE TAB
ABCEHILNNOTY	IN THE BALCONY
ABCEHILSTTTY	CHASTITY BELT
ABCEHIMNNRUY	BAYERN MUNICH
ABCEHIMNOORS	COMB ONES HAIR
ABCEHIRRRRSU	CRUSH BARRIER
ABCEHKLOPSTT	POTS THE BLACK
ABCEHKLOSTWY	BLOCKS THE WAY
ABCEHKLRSSUW	SWASHBUCKLER
ABCEHKMOORTT	BACK TO MOTHER
ABCEHKOORSTT	ROCKS THE BOAT
ABCEHLLLOOST	BALLET SCHOOL
ABCEHLLOORSZ	SCHOOL BLAZER
ABCEHLMOOPSS	PEACH BLOSSOM
ABCEHLNNOOTY	ON THE BALCONY
ABCEHLNOSTUU	UNTOUCHABLES
ABCEHNNORRTT	ROTTEN BRANCH
ABCEHORRRTTY	HARRY CORBETT
ABCEIIILLRST	LIBERALISTIC
ABCEIIILTTXY	EXCITABILITY
ABCEIIJPRSTT	ABJECT SPIRIT
ABCEIILLNPXY	INEXPLICABLY
ABCEIILMNOPT	INCOMPATIBLE
ABCEIILNRTXY	INEXTRICABLY
ABCEIILPRSTY	PLEBISCITARY
ABCEIINORRRS	SONIC BARRIER
ABCEIINORSTT	OBSTETRICIAN
ABCEIIRSTTUW	WATER BISCUIT
ABCEIKMNORST	MINOR SET-BACK
ABCEIKNPRSTU	BANKRUPTCIES
ABCEILLNNOOS	INCONSOLABLE
ABCEILMMNOTU	INCOMMUTABLE
ABCEILMORRST	BRISTOL CREAM
ABCEILNOOPRR	INCORPORABLE
ABCEIMMNORTU	ATOMIC NUMBER
ABCEIMNOORST	EMBROCATIONS
ABCEINORRTUU	TUBOCURARINE
ABCEINORSSST	BRASS SECTION
ABCEINRRRSST	TRANSCRIBERS
ABCEJLLOSTUY	LOYAL SUBJECT
ABCEKKORRSST	BACKSTROKERS
ABCEKNNORSTU	TURN ONES BACK
ABCELLLNOORT	CONTROLLABLE
ABCELLLOOSTY	OCTOSYLLABLE
ABCELLRRTUUY	TUBERCULARLY
ABCELMNRRSSU	UNSCRAMBLERS
ABCELMOTTUUV	VACUUM BOTTLE
ABCELNORSTTU	COUNTERBLAST
ABCENORSSSSU	SCABROUSNESS
ABCENOSSTUUU	SUBCUTANEOUS

ABCEOOOORRRST	CORROBORATES
ABCEOOPRRTTU	PROBATE COURT
ABCEORRRSTTU	CARBURETTORS
ABCFFGHINNOR	BRANCHING OFF
ABCFFKLLOOST	BLOCK OF FLATS
ABCFGGHIIKNT	FIGHTING BACK
ABCFGIKNOOTU	BACKING OUT OF
ABCFLNOOORRU	FLUOROCARBON
ABCGGIIKNNSW	SWINGING BACK
ABCGGIKNOOTU	GOING BACK OUT
ABCGGILLNNOW	GLANCING BLOW
ABCGHHIKNSUW	BUSHWHACKING
ABCGHIIKKNNT	THINKING BACK
ABCGHIKLPSTU	BACK-UP LIGHTS
ABCGHIKNORTW	THROWING BACK
ABCGHIKNRRUY	HURRYING BACK
ABCGHINNORTU	BRANCHING OUT
ABCGIIKKNRST	STRIKING BACK
ABCGIIKLMNPU	MAKING PUBLIC
ABCGIIKLNPPS	SLIPPING BACK
ABCGIILLLOOY	BIOLOGICALLY
ABCGIILLOORT	TRIBOLOGICAL
ABCGIINNRRST	TRANSCRIBING
ABCGIKKLLNOO	LOOKING BLACK
ABCGIKLNNRTU	TURNING BLACK
ABCGIKMNOTUU	MUCKING ABOUT
ABCGILLNORSU	SCORING A BULL
ABCGILMNNRSU	UNSCRAMBLING
ABCGINNOOPTU	PONCING ABOUT
ABCGKKOOOORTW	GO BACK TO WORK
ABCHIIILMOPT	AMPHIBOLITIC
ABCHIMORSSTX	CHRISTMAS BOX
ABCHOSSTTUWY	CUTS BOTH WAYS
ABCIIIILRSTY	IRASCIBILITY
ABCIIILMNOTU	UMBILICATION
ABCIILLMNOOY	BIONOMICALLY
ABCIILLMNOPTY	INCOMPATIBLY
ABCIILLNNOTUY	CONNUBIALITY
ABCIILNOPPRY	PRINCIPAL BOY
ABCIILNOPSTU	PUBLICATIONS
ABCIILORRTUY	ORBICULARITY
ABCIILOSSTTU	ABSOLUTISTIC
ABCIIMNNOOST	COMBINATIONS
ABCIJKMMRTUY	JIMMY TARBUCK
ABCIJKNNOORS	JACK ROBINSON
ABCILLLMOSYY	SYMBOLICALLY
ABCILLLOPSYY	POLYSYLLABIC
ABCILLMNOOSY	MONOSYLLABIC
ABCILLNNOOSY	INCONSOLABLY
ABCILLNOSSUY	SUBSONICALLY
ABCILLOOPRUY	LABOUR POLICY
ABCILMMNOTUY	INCOMMUTABLY
ABCILMMNNOOSU	NO-CLAIM BONUS
ABCILMORRTUU	MICROTUBULAR
ABCILMORSTTU	TRIBAL CUSTOM
ABCILNOPRTUY	NOTARY PUBLIC
ABCILOOPRRTU	PUBLIC ORATOR
ABCIMNOOPRSY	BY COMPARISON
ABCIMNORSSTU	OBSCURANTISM
ABCIMNORSTUU	RAMBUNCTIOUS
ABCINNOORSTU	CONURBATIONS
ABCINORSSTTU	OBSCURANTIST
	SUBTRACTIONS
ABCLOOPSSWYY	PLAYS COWBOYS
ABCMOOOPRSTT	COMBAT TROOPS
ABCOOOOORRRT	CORROBORATOR
ABDDDEEEEILV	BELIEVED DEAD
ABDDDEFILOTU	FIDDLED ABOUT
ABDDDEGINPRU	BREAD PUDDING
ABDDDEINORSW	BANDIED WORDS
ABDDDELNOUWY	BADLY WOUNDED

ABDDEEEEHLLTU	BULLETHEADED	ABDEEEIILMRR	IRREMEDIABLE
ABDDEEEEHLNYZ	BENZALDEHYDE	ABDEEEIILRTV	DELIBERATIVE
ABDDEEEEHLORU	DOUBLEHEADER	ABDEEEILLRTY	DELIBERATELY
ABDDEEEIPRST	DESPERATE BID	ABDEEEILLTVY	LIVELY DEBATE
ABDDEEEELLORU	DOUBLE DEALER	ABDEEEILMMST	EMBLEMATISED
ABDDEEFHLNNT	LEFT-HAND BEND	ABDEEEILMMTZ	EMBLEMATIZED
ABDDEEFINOOX	NO FIXED ABODE	ABDEEEILMNRT	DETERMINABLE
ABDDEEFLORRU	DREADFUL BORE	ABDEEEILMRRY	IRREDEEMABLY
ABDDEEGGHILN	LAGGED BEHIND	ABDEEEINPRRS	PREBENDARIES
ABDDEEGGNOPR	BEGGED PARDON	ABDEEEKMNOSS	MAKES ONE'S BED
ABDDEEGIINNR	READING IN BED	ABDEEEKNOORW	RENEWED A BOOK
ABDDEEGIINSV	BEING ADVISED	ABDEEELLNRUV	LAVENDER BLUE
ABDDEEGILPRY	PLAYED BRIDGE	ABDEEELMNTTT	BATTLEMENTED
ABDDEEGIOPRS	GOD BE PRAISED	ABDEEENNSTTW	STAND BETWEEN
ABDDEEGOOVWY	WAVED GOODBYE	ABDEEFNRRRST	BARREN DESERT
ABDDEEHHLNTY	LED BY THE HAND	ABDEEFGGIMOR	GAME OF BRIDGE
ABDDEEHIIRST	RAISED THE BID	ABDEEFGIMORT	BADGE OF MERIT
ABDDEEHIKLNW	WALKED BEHIND	ABDEEFHHOSTT	HAD THE BEST OF
ABDDEEHIMRTU	THUMBED A RIDE	ABDEEFHILMRT	HALF-TIMBERED
ABDDEEHINSTY	STAYED BEHIND	ABDEEFHINORV	HEAVEN FORBID!
ABDDEEHIRSSU	BRUSHED ASIDE	ABDEEFHNOORS	BAND OF HEROES
ABDDEEHLLLUY	BULLHEADEDLY	ABDEEFIIILNT	IDENTIFIABLE
ABDDEEHOORTT	BORED TO DEATH	ABDEEFIIILRT	DEFIBRILLATE
ABDDEEIILNTT	DIED IN BATTLE	ABDEEFIILNSY	INDEFEASIBLY
ABDDEEILMNRU	IN DEAD LUMBER	ADDEEFILLR3W	BID3 FAREWELL
ABDDEEILMSSS	DISASSEMBLED	ABDEEFILORRY	ORDEAL BY FIRE
ABDDEEIMNNST	ABSENTMINDED	ABDEEFINNNOU	BEEF AND ONION
ABDDEEKLOPRU	DOUBLE PARKED	ABDEEFIOORTV	FESTIVE BOARD
ABDDEELMNOOS	MADE OLD BONES	ABDEEFLLRSUY	BLUE-ARSED FLY
ABDDEELOOSTW	SWEATED BLOOD	ABDEEFNORTTU	DEBT OF NATURE
ABDDEENNOTTW	BATTENED DOWN	ABDEEGGHIPRT	BRIDGE THE GAP
ABDDEFILOSTU	FIDDLES ABOUT	ABDEEGGHLOTT	BAGGED THE LOT
ABDDEFNORRSW	BENDS FORWARD	ABDEEGHIKMNT	MAKING THE BED
ABDDEGJNOOOO	DONE A GOOD JOB	ABDEEGHILRTY	BIGHEARTEDLY
ABDDEGJOOOOS	DOES A GOOD JOB	ABDEEGHNOOTT	GONE TO THE BAD
ABDDEGLOORSU	DURABLE GOODS	ABDEEGHNORTT	BAND TOGETHER
ABDDEHILNRTW	DRAW THE BLIND	ABDEEGHOOSTT	GOES TO THE BAD
ABDDEHLMNOSU	MODEL HUSBAND	ABDEEGIILNRT	DELIBERATING
ABDDEILNOORV	LIVED ON BOARD	ABDEEGILPRRY	BRIDGE PLAYER
ABDDEILNOOST	BLOODSTAINED	ABDEEGIMNORT	BOARD MEETING
ABDDEINOOPPR	PIPED ON BOARD	ABDEEGLOORTY	GO TO BED EARLY
ABDDEINORSSW	BANDIES WORDS	ABDEEGOOSVWY	WAVES GOODBYE
ABDDEINORSTU	SUBORDINATED	ABDEEHIIRSST	RAISES THE BID
ABDDEKMOOOSY	DOMESDAY BOOK	ABDEEHILLOTY	THE OLD BAILEY
ABDDELORRSTW	BLADDERWORTS	ABDEEHILNORT	BEARD THE LION
ABDDEMMNORUU	BUMMED AROUND	ABDEEHILSTTW	WIELDS THE BAT
ABDDEMNNOOSY	DOMBEY AND SON	ABDEEHIRSSSU	BRUSHES ASIDE
ABDDFNOOPRRY	DROP OF BRANDY	ABDEEHISTWYY	BY THE WAYSIDE
ABDDGIILLNNU	BUILDING LAND	ABDEEHKLRSTU	THE DARK BLUES
ABDDGIINNPSU	PUDDING BASIN	ABDEEHLNOTWY	BEYOND THE LAW
ABDDGILNOORW	DRAWING BLOOD	ABDEEHLNOVYY	HEAVENLY BODY
ABDDGLNOOORS	DRAGONS BLOOD	ABDEEHLNRSUU	UNDER A BUSHEL
ABDDHJLNOOOW	HOLD DOWN A JOB	ABDEEHMNOOTY	BAYED THE MOON
ABDDILNNOOOR	BLOOD AND IRON	ABDEEHMRSTTU	BEATS THE DRUM
ABDDILNNOSSU	BUILDS ON SAND	ABDEEHNOOSSW	BOWS ONE'S HEAD
ABDDKMOOOOSY	DOOMSDAY BOOK	ABDEEHNOPTTU	POUND THE BEAT
ABDDLNOOSUYY	BLOODY SUNDAY	ABDEEHNORSUY	BURY ONES HEAD
ABDDNOORTUUW	OUTWARD BOUND	ABDEEHNORTUW	WEATHER-BOUND
	OUTWARD-BOUND	ABDEEHNOTTTW	WENT TO THE BAD
ABDEEEEHISST	BESIDE THE SEA	ABDEEHOORSTT	BORES TO DEATH
ABDEEEEILMRR	IRREDEEMABLE		SABRE-TOOTHED
ABDEEEENPPRR	BEEN PREPARED	ABDEEHOORTUV	HOVERED ABOUT
ABDEEEERRRTV	REVERBERATED	ABDEEIIKLRST	EAST KILBRIDE
ABDEEEFHIRRT	BREATHED FIRE	ABDEEIILMRRY	IRREMEDIABLY
ABDEEEFHORTY	THE DAY BEFORE	ABDEEIILNORT	DELIBERATION
ABDEEEFIILNS	INDEFEASIBLE	ABDEEIILNSTT	DIES IN BATTLE
ABDEEEGNOSTY	TEENAGED BOYS	ABDEEIILQRTU	EQUILIBRATED
ABDEEEHILNRT	THE BREADLINE	ABDEEIIJLNOTT	JOINED BATTLE
ABDEEEHILNSV	LEAVES BEHIND	ABDEEIILLNORR	BANDERILLERO
ABDEEEHISSTY	BY THE SEASIDE	ABDEEIILLORTV	VOTED LIBERAL
ABDEEEHLMRRY	HERBAL REMEDY	ABDEEILMNOPR	IMPONDERABLE

ABDEEILMNRRS	BERNARD MILES
ABDEEILMNRTY	DETERMINABLY
ABDEEILMRSTU	BUILDERS MATE
ABDEEILMSSSS	DISASSEMBLES
ABDEEILNRSSU	UNDESIRABLES
ABDEEILNSSSU	BUSINESS DEAL
ABDEEILPRSTU	DISREPUTABLE
ABDEEIMMPPRU	PAID-UP MEMBER
ABDEEINNORSS	DEBONAIRNESS
ABDEEINNRRSW	BREADWINNERS
ABDEEINNSSSU	UNBIASEDNESS
ABDEEINOPRRY	BEYOND REPAIR
ABDEEIPPRRST	STRIPPED BARE
ABDEEJNORSTY	SEDENTARY JOB
ABDEEKLLORTU	DOUBLE-TALKER
ABDEEKLMNOOS	MAKE OLD BONES
ABDEEKNORRRS	BANKERS ORDER
ABDEELLLNOST	LONSDALE BELT
ABDEELMNORST	DEMONSTRABLE
ABDEELNNORTU	BORED A TUNNEL
ABDEELNOOTUV	LEAVE NO DOUBT
ABDEELORTTTW	BOTTLED WATER
ABDEELRSTTTU	SALTED BUTTER
ABDEEMOOPRRS	SPARE BEDROOM
ABDEEMORSTTY	STORMY DEBATE
ABDEEENORSSTU	OBDURATENESS
ABDEEOOORRSTT	BORED TO TEARS
ABDEFFHLORSU	SHUFFLEBOARD
ABDEFGILNOTT	FLOATING DEBT
ABDEFGINORRS	FINGERBOARDS
ABDEFHIILORY	BRIEF HOLIDAY
ABDEFHILMTTU	THUMBED A LIFT
ABDEFIIILNTY	IDENTIFIABLY
ABDEFIIKLLRY	FLY LIKE A BIRD
ABDEFIJOORRT	TRIED FOR A JOB
ABDEFILOTTTU	FLITTED ABOUT
ABDEFLLOSTUU	DOUBLE-FAULTS
ABDEFORRRSSU	SURFBOARDERS
ABDEGGHIILRT	LIGHT BRIGADE
ABDEGGILNNOU	GOING A BUNDLE
ABDEGGINNORU	BEING ON GUARD
ABDEGGINNRRY	GINGER BRANDY
ABDEGHIIMNTX	MIXED BATHING
ABDEGHINRSST	BATHING DRESS
ABDEGHIRRSTT	STRAIGHTBRED
ABDEGHMNRSTU	BANGS THE DRUM
ABDEGIIILNTT	DEBILITATING
ABDEGIIKMNRS	DISEMBARKING
ABDEGIIKNNRW	BREAKING WIND
ABDEGIILLNTT	BIG AND LITTLE
ABDEGIILNRST	RIDING STABLE
ABDEGIINNNRW	BREADWINNING
ABDEGIINNSTY	STAYING IN BED
ABDEGIKNNORW	BREAKING DOWN
ABDEGIKNOPRW	BAKING POWDER
ABDEGILLLNNY	BELLY-LANDING
ABDEGILNNRSY	SINGLE BRANDY
ABDEGILNOPUY	PAYING DOUBLE
ABDEGILNORRU	ORGAN BUILDER
ABDEGINNNORT	BRING TO AN END
ABDEGINORRTT	BATTING ORDER
ABDEGJNOORSU	DANGEROUS JOB
ABDEGKNORRSU	BREAKS GROUND
ABDEGLLLNOUY	LEGALLY BOUND
ABDEGLNOOTUU	LOUNGED ABOUT
ABDEGMNNNOOY	BENNY GOODMAN
ABDEGNOPRSSY	PORGY AND BESS
ABDEHHIJNNOT	THE JOB IN HAND
ABDEHHLMOORR	RHOMBOHEDRAL
ABDEHIIILMNS	DIMINISHABLE
ABDEHIILNRST	TRAILS BEHIND

ABDEHIILSSST	DISESTABLISH
ABDEHILMNNST	BLANDISHMENT
ABDEHILOSTVY	DO IT BY HALVES
ABDEHINRSTTY	BITTER SHANDY
ABDEHLLORSYY	HYDROLYSABLE
ABDEHLLORYYZ	HYDROLYZABLE
ABDEHLNOORTU	HAD NO TROUBLE
ABDEHNNORSSU	RUB ONES HANDS
ABDEHNOOSTUV	HAVE NO DOUBTS
ABDEIIILSST	DISABILITIES
ABDEIIILMNSS	INADMISSIBLE
ABDEIIILNOTT	DEBILITATION
ABDEIIILRSTY	DESIRABILITY
ABDEIIIRSSSU	SUBSIDIARIES
ABDEIILMRRSS	MARRIED BLISS
ABDEIILNPSTU	INDISPUTABLE
ABDEIIILORSTU	SUBEDITORIAL
ABDEIIOOPRSS	BASIDIOSPORE
ABDEIKNNNOSS	SKIN AND BONES
ABDEILLOPRRX	PILLAR-BOX RED
ABDEILMNOPRY	IMPONDERABLY
ABDEILMNORTT	BITTER ALMOND
ABDEILNNORUY	BOUNDARY LINE
ABDEILNOORSV	LIVES ON BOARD
ABDEILNOORTU	BROAD OUTLINE
ABDEILPRSTUY	DISREPUTABLY
ABDEIMORSTUX	AMBIDEXTROUS
ABDEINOOPPRS	PIPES ON BOARD
ABDEINORRRSU	SOUND BARRIER
ABDEINORSSTU	SUBORDINATES
ABDEISSSTTUY	STATE SUBSIDY
ABDEKLNNRRUW	DRUNKEN BRAWL
ABDELLORRTUV	ROBERT DUVALL
ABDELMNORSTY	DEMONSTRABLY
ABDELMOORSST	BLOODSTREAMS
ABDELMRRRTUU	BRUTAL MURDER
ABDELOOPRTUW	PROWLED ABOUT
ABDEMOORRTTW	BOTTOM DRAWER
ABDENNOOPRUW	BEAR DOWN UPON
ABDENNOORSSY	ONES BORN DAYS
ABDENOOORSTUW	WONDERS ABOUT
ABDENOQRRTUU	QUARTER-BOUND
ABDENORRSTUY	TREASURY BOND
ABDENORSTTUY	TRUST AND OBEY
ABDEORRSTTUY	READY TO BURST
ABDFGHIIRTTY	BIRTHDAY GIFT
ABDFGIIILLNO	BILL OF LADING
ABDFGIILMNRU	FARM BUILDING
ABDFGINORRRW	BRING FORWARD
ABDFIILNNRUU	INFUNDIBULAR
ABDFLNOOSTUY	NOBODYS FAULT
ABDGGGINNOTU	NAGGING DOUBT
ABDGGIILNNOR	BRIDGING LOAN
ABDGGINNOOOR	GOING ON BOARD
ABDGHIKNORTU	BOUGHT A DRINK
ABDGHINOOSWX	SHADOW BOXING
	SHADOW-BOXING
ABDGHINOSTUV	HAVING DOUBTS
ABDGHNOORTUU	BOUGHT A ROUND
ABDGIIKNNRUV	BUYING A DRINK
ABDGIINNNORR	BRANDING IRON
ABDGIINNOORR	IRONING BOARD
ABDGIKLMNOOS	MAKING SO BOLD
ABDGILNOOSTT	TASTING BLOOD
ABDGILNORRUU	BURIAL GROUND
ABDGILNORSSY	BOYS AND GIRLS
	GIRLS AND BOYS
ABDGINNNORRU	RUNNING BOARD
ABDGINNORUUY	BUYING A ROUND
ABDGINOPRRSS	SPRINGBOARDS
ABDHIIRSTTUY	BIRTHDAY SUIT

ABDIILLMOORR	BILLIARD ROOM
ABDIILMORTYY	MILITARY BODY
ABDIILNPSTUY	INDISPUTABLY
ABDIINOSSTUU	SUBAUDITIONS
ABDIIRRSTTUY	DISTRIBUTARY
ABDILLLNOPRT	PORTLAND BILL
ABDIOOOQRRSUW	BORROWS A QUID
ABDKLNOOOTTY	TALK TO NOBODY
ABDKLOOOORTU	BROAD OUTLOOK
ABDLLMOOOORTT	BOTTOM DOLLAR
ABDLMNNORSTU	BURNT ALMONDS
ABDLNNOSSTTU	NUTS AND BOLTS
ABDNOOOPRRUW	BORROW A POUND
ABEEEEFILMRT	MERE FLEA-BITE
ABEEEEIKLMSV	MAKES BELIEVE
ABEEEEELMNSTW	BETWEEN MEALS
ABEEEEEMNRSTV	BEREAVEMENTS
ABEEEEERRRSTV	REVERBERATES
ABEEEFGLNRTU	BEEN GRATEFUL
ABEEEEFHIRRST	BREATHES FIRE
ABEEEFHMNRST	FAN THE EMBERS
ABEEEFHNOQSU	QUEEN OF SHEBA
ABEEEFHORRTW	BEFORE THE WAR
ABEEEFILNSSS	FEASIBLENESS
ABEEEEFINORST	SEEN TO BE FAIR
ABEEEFLNOOSV	ABOVE ONESELF
ABEEEFLNOSSU	ABUSE ONESELF
ADCEEFORTUYY	EYE FOR BEAUTY
ABEEEGGGILNV	DEGGING LEAVE
ABEEEGGILNRU	BELEAGUERING
ABEEEGGINNOS	BEING ONE'S AGE
ABEEEGHLLNTU	THE BLUE ANGEL
ABEEEGHLNNRT	BETHNAL GREEN
ABEEEGHLORTT	GLOBE THEATRE
ABEEEGHLOTVW	GAVE THE ELBOW
ABEEEGIKNNRV	BREAKING EVEN
ABEEEGILLOTV	VEGETABLE OIL
ABEEEGKLNORS	BREAK ONES LEG
ABEEEHHLSTUV	HAVE THE BLUES
ABEEEHILMPTU	ATE HUMBLE PIE
	EAT HUMBLE PIE
ABEEEHILNOTV	ABOVE THE LINE
ABEEEHKLORST	BROKE THE SEAL
ABEEEHKLRRTU	BREAK THE RULE
ABEEEHKNRSTW	BREAK THE NEWS
ABEEEHKORRRS	HORSEBREAKER
ABEEEHKORRSU	HOUSEBREAKER
ABEEEHLLRTTT	ALL THE BETTER
ABEEEHLMNUVY	MY BLUE HEAVEN
ABEEEHLSSTTT	SETS THE TABLE
ABEEEIKMNNST	BEEN MISTAKEN
ABEEEILLNRSS	RELIABLENESS
ABEEEILMMSST	EMBLEMATISES
ABEEEILMMSTZ	EMBLEMATIZES
ABEEEILMNPRT	IMPENETRABLE
ABEEEILNNSSV	ENVIABLENESS
ABEEEINRRTTV	INVERTEBRATE
ABEEEKLOOPRS	BOOK A SLEEPER
ABEEELLRSTTT	TRESTLE TABLE
ABEEELMNNSTT	ENTABLEMENTS
ABEEELMNPRSU	NUMBER,PLEASE
ABEEELMNSSST	BASEMENTLESS
ABEEEMNNRRYZ	BREEZY MANNER
ABEEENNORSTT	EASTER BONNET
ABEEEORRRRTV	REVERBERATOR
ABEEEPRRSTTY	PRESBYTERATE
ABEEFFFGOOST	BAG OF TOFFEES
ABEEFFHILORT	BREATH OF LIFE
ABEEFFILNRSU	INSUFFERABLE
ABEEFHHLOSTT	BEST OF HEALTH
ABEEFHHOSSTT	HAS THE BEST OF
ABEEFHILRTYZ	ELIZABETH FRY
ABEEFHLLTWYY	FELL BY THE WAY
ABEEFIILLMSU	EMULSIFIABLE
ABEEFIILLRST	FERTILISABLE
ABEEFIILLRTZ	FERTILIZABLE
ABEEFIILNRRT	FERTILE BRAIN
ABEEFILLNOTT	LINE OF BATTLE
ABEEFILNNRTY	ALBERT FINNEY
ABEEFKLNORSS	BARKS ONESELF
ABEEFKNOORRT	BROKEN FOR TEA
ABEEFLLLNOSY	ALL BY ONESELF
ABEEFLNOSSTT	NEST OF TABLES
ABEEFNRRTUXY	NEXT FEBRUARY
ABEEGGILNRSS	BEGGARLINESS
ABEEGGILNSSV	GAVE BLESSING
ABEEGHHIRSTT	BEAR THE SIGHT
ABEEGHILLNVW	BEHAVING WELL
ABEEGHLNOPTY	POLYTHENE BAG
ABEEGHLOPRTY	TELEGRAPH BOY
ABEEGHNOORTT	GONE TO THE BAR
ABEEGIILMMNS	BEAMING SMILE
ABEEGIKMNRTT	MAKING BETTER
ABEEGIKNNOPR	BREAKING OPEN
ABEEGILLLLNW	ALL BEING WELL
ABEEGILLMNRS	ELGIN MARBLES
ABEEGILLNOQU	OBLIQUE ANGLE
ABEEGILNNSST	TANGIBLENESS
ABEEGILNORRS	LOGANBERRIES
ABEEGIMNNNNR	BENIGN MANNER
ABEEGIMOSSTY	AS TIME GOES BY
ABEEGINORRTT	BITTER ORANGE
ABEEGINPRSTT	BESPATTERING
ABEEGLNNORUV	UNGOVERNABLE
ABEEHHPRSSTY	BATHYSPHERES
ABEEHIILMPRS	IMPERISHABLE
ABEEHILLMORT	THERMOLABILE
ABEEHILLSTWW	BLEW A WHISTLE
ABEEHILNTTTW	WIN THE BATTLE
ABEEHILRRSTW	WELSH RAREBIT
ABEEHJJMNNOT	JOHN BETJEMAN
ABEEHJMRRSTU	JAMES THURBER
ABEEHKLMORTW	BELOW THE MARK
ABEEHKLNORRT	HALTERBROKEN
ABEEHKLNORST	HORSE BLANKET
ABEEHKLNORTW	BROKEN THE LAW
ABEEHKLSSTUY	BLUE AS THE SKY
ABEEHLLLNPTU	BULL ELEPHANT
ABEEHLLNOOTW	BEATEN HOLLOW
ABEEHLLOSTTW	BELOW THE SALT
ABEEHLLRSSTY	BREATHLESSLY
ABEEHLMORSTT	THERMOSTABLE
ABEEHLNOTTTW	WON THE BATTLE
ABEEHLORRSSU	BARRELHOUSES
ABEEHLORRTTU	HEART TROUBLE
ABEEHNOORSTX	BOX ON THE EARS
ABEEHNORTTTW	WENT TO THE BAR
ABEEHOPRSTTW	POWERS THAT BE
ABEEIIILSSTT	BESTIALITIES
ABEEIIKLRRTW	WARLIKE TRIBE
ABEEIILLRSST	STERILISABLE
ABEEIILLRSTZ	STERILIZABLE
ABEEIILLRSVW	LIBERAL VIEWS
ABEEIILMNNRT	INTERMINABLE
ABEEIILMNSSV	VISIBLE MEANS
ABEEIILMPRTY	PERMEABILITY
ABEEIILNPSST	PITIABLENESS
ABEEIILNRTVY	VENERABILITY
ABEEIILNRTWY	RENEWABILITY
ABEEIILORTTV	OBLITERATIVE
ABEEIILQRSTU	EQUILIBRATES
ABEEIIMRRVZZ	ZAMBEZI RIVER

ABEEIJLNOSTT	JETTISONABLE	ABEENRSSSSTU	ABSTRUSENESS
ABEEIJMOPRST	SPARE-TIME JOB	ABEEOORRSSTT	BORES TO TEARS
ABEEIKLLNOOR	BAKERLOO LINE	ABEFFGGHIOTT	GIFT OF THE GAB
ABEEIKLNRRSW	WEAR BLINKERS	ABEFFGHLNOTW	BLOWN THE GAFF
ABEEIKLRSTTT	LITTER BASKET	ABEFFGHLOSTW	BLOWS THE GAFF
ABEEIKNNORRR	RONNIE BARKER	ABEFFHILORTT	HALF OF BITTER
ABEEIKNNRSTT	BANK INTEREST	ABEFFILNRSUY	INSUFFERABLY
ABEEILLMNSSY	ASSEMBLY LINE	ABEFFLMOOSTW	BLOW OFF STEAM
ABEEILLNNRUV	INVULNERABLE	ABEFFLMOPRST	STAFF PROBLEM
ABEEILLORRTV	LIBERAL VOTER	ABEFFLORSSUW	SUFFERS A BLOW
ABEEILLORSTV	LIBERAL VOTES	ABEFGHILLOTZ	BLAZE OF LIGHT
	VOTES LIBERAL	ABEFGIILNRSU	REFUSING BAIL
ABEEILLPRSUV	PULVERISABLE	ABEFGIINRRTU	BEARING FRUIT
ABEEILLPRUVZ	PULVERIZABLE	ABEFGIKNOSST	KING OF BEASTS
ABEEILMMOSSV	IMMOVABLESES	ABEFGILNORUV	UNFORGIVABLE
ABEEILMNPRTY	IMPENETRABLY	ABEFGLLOORYZ	BLAZE OF GLORY
ABEEILMNRRSU	SERIAL NUMBER	ABEFGNORRSTU	BURST OF ANGER
ABEEILMPSTUY	SIMPLE BEAUTY	ABEFHHILLLOT	BILL OF HEALTH
ABEEILNOQSTU	QUESTIONABLE	ABEFHILLMOTW	LIMB OF THE LAW
ABEEILNSSSTU	SUITABLENESS	ABEFHJMNOORT	MAN FOR THE JOB
ABEEILPRRSTY	PRESBYTERIAL	ABEFHLLOOTTU	BAT OUT OF HELL
ABEEILRSTTTY	SET AT LIBERTY	ABEFIJOORRST	TRIES FOR A JOB
ABEEIMNNSSSU	MEAN BUSINESS	ABEFILLNOSTT	FALLEN TO BITS
ABEEIMNRSTTU	STEAM TURBINE	ABEFILNOPRTU	UNPROFITABLE
ABEEINNOPRSS	NAPIERS BONES	ABEFILNRSSTU	TRANSFUSIBLE
ABEEINNORSSU	USE ONES BRAIN	ABEFILOSSSTT	STATE OF BLISS
ABEEINNQRSTU	BARQUENTINES	ABEFILOSTTTW	BATTLE OF WITS
ABEEINORSSTV	ABORTIVENESS	ABEFIMMRRSUY	BRIEF SUMMARY
ABEEINPRRSTY	PRESBYTERIAN	ABEFINOPSTTU	BIT OF AN UPSET
ABEEINRSSSTW	BEARS WITNESS	ABEFIOORRRVW	BORROW A FIVER
ABEEIRRRSSTW	STRAWBERRIES	ABEFLLOOORUV	LABOUR OF LOVE
ABEEJLLMOSSW	JAMES BOSWELL	ABEFLLOOOSTU	ABSOLUTE FOOL
ABEEJMNNOPRT	PERMANENT JOB	ABEFLNOSSSTU	BOASTFULNESS
ABEEKLMORRTU	TROUBLEMAKER	ABEFLNOSSSUU	FABULOUSNESS
ABEEKLMORSTU	MAKES TROUBLE	ABEFORSSTTTU	SOFT AS BUTTER
ABEEKLNORSSW	WORKABLENESS	ABEGGGIILNNO	BOILING AN EGG
ABEEKMNNOOSS	MAKES NO BONES	ABEGGHHINTUV	HAVING THE BUG
ABEEKMNOORRS	BROKE ONE'S ARM	ABEGGHIINRRT	BEARING RIGHT
ABEEKMRRSTUY	BUYERS MARKET	ABEGGHIMNSTU	HUNTS BIG GAME
ABEEKNORSTTU	BUSTER KEATON	ABEGGHINORTV	OVERNIGHT BAG
ABEEKORRSSTT	BREAST STROKE	ABEGGIILLNNR	RINGING A BELL
	BREASTSTROKE	ABEGGIILNTTV	GIVING BATTLE
ABEELLMNNOPUY	UNEMPLOYABLE	ABEGGILNNOPY	GOING BY PLANE
ABEELLMNOTTT	BALLOTTEMENT	ABEGGINNORSW	GROWING BEANS
ABEELLMRSTUU	SAMUEL BUTLER	ABEGGINORTWY	GOING BY WATER
ABEELLORSTUU	ABSOLUTE RULE	ABEGGINOTTTU	GETTING ABOUT
ABEELMMNNOTZ	EMBLAZONMENT	ABEGHHKORRTU	BREAK THROUGH
ABEELMMPRSTU	PLUMBERS MATE		BREAKTHROUGH
ABEELMNOOTUV	UNABLE TO MOVE	ABEGHHOOSTUU	BOUGHT A HOUSE
ABEELMNORSTV	LAST NOVEMBER	ABEGHHORSSTU	BOUGHT SHARES
ABEELMNPRSTU	NUMBERPLATES	ABEGHIILNSST	ESTABLISHING
ABEELMOOPPRS	POSE A PROBLEM	ABEGHILNNORU	BURNING A HOLE
ABEELMOPRSST	SETS A PROBLEM	ABEGHILNNTWY	WIN BY A LENGTH
ABEELNNORSTU	BORES A TUNNEL	ABEGHILNRSUU	HURLING ABUSE
ABEELNNORSTY	BLARNEY STONE	ABEGHILORTUV	BROUGHT ALIVE
ABEELNNOSSWY	BONNY WEE LASS	ABEGHIMNNRSU	BURNING SHAME
ABEELNNSSSTU	UNSTABLENESS	ABEGHINORRTT	BRING TO EARTH
ABEELNOOPSTT	OPENS A BOTTLE	ABEGHINORTTU	BREATHING OUT
ABEELNOORSSU	BARE ONE'S SOUL	ABEGHINOSUUY	BUYING A HOUSE
ABEELNOOSWWY	ELBOW ONES WAY	ABEGHINRSSUY	BUYING SHARES
ABEELNOSSSTU	ABSOLUTENESS	ABEGHLNNOTWY	WON BY A LENGTH
ABEELOORSTUZ	ABSOLUTE ZERO	ABEGIIILLNRS	LIBERALISING
ABEELOOSTTUV	ABSOLUTE VETO	ABEGIIILLNRZ	LIBERALIZING
ABEELOPPRSSU	SUPERPOSABLE	ABEGIIKNPRTU	BREAKING IT UP
ABEELOQRSTUY	BAROQUE STYLE	ABEGIILNNRUV	BURNING ALIVE
ABEEMLORRSWW	WHEELBARROWS	ABEGIILNORTT	OBLITERATING
ABEEMMRRSSTU	BREASTSUMMER	ABEGIILNORTW	BOILING WATER
ABEEMMNQRRSUU	SQUARE NUMBER	ABEGIILNRTTW	WRITING TABLE
ABEENOPSSSTT	PAST ONES BEST	ABEGIILNRUVY	BURYING ALIVE
ABEENORRSTTU	RETURN TO BASE	ABEGIINNNPSW	SPINNING A WEB
ABEENPRTTTUU	PEANUT BUTTER	ABEGIINRRSTT	BERING STRAIT

ABEGIINRSTWY	SWEARING BY IT
ABEGIKLNNOOR	BOOK LEARNING
ABEGIKNNOOOP	OPENING A BOOK
ABEGIKNOOSST	BOOKING SEATS
ABEGILLLNOST	ALL BEING LOST
ABEGILLLNOWY	BOWLING ALLEY
ABEGILLNOPST	BEGINS TO PALL
ABEGILLNOSTT	LOSING BATTLE
ABEGILMNORRS	RAMBLING ROSE
ABEGILNOOTTT	GO INTO BATTLE
ABEGIMNOORTT	IN BOTTOM GEAR
ABEGIMNOSSTU	MESSING ABOUT
ABEGINNORRSU	BRAIN SURGEON
ABEGINNORTUZ	BRAZENING OUT
ABEGINOQRTUU	BOUQUET GARNI
ABEGINORSSTY	STAYING SOBER
ABEGINOSTTTU	SETTING ABOUT
ABEGINRRRSUY	BRAIN SURGERY
ABEGKNNOPRTU	GONE BANKRUPT
ABEGKNOOSSTY	SKYE BOAT SONG
ABEGKNOPRSTU	GOES BANKRUPT
ABEGLLMRSSTU	GLASS TUMBLER
ABEGLLNORSSU	GLOBULARNESS
ABEGLMORSUUY	UMBRAGEOUSLY
ABEGLNOOSTUU	LOUNGES ABOUT
ABEGLNORSSSU	GLABROUSNESS
ABEGMORRSSTU	BURGOMASTERS
ABEHHLORSTTU	ROBUST HEALTH
ABEHHOPRTUYY	PAY BY THE HOUR
ABEHIIILRTTY	HERITABILITY
ABEHIILMNSSU	LIES IN AMBUSH
ABEHIILMPRSY	IMPERISHABLY
ABEHIILNNRTY	LABYRINTHINE
ABEHIILNOPST	INHOSPITABLE
ABEHIIMORSUV	BEHAVIOURISM
	MISBEHAVIOUR
ABEHIKNNSSTU	BASK IN THE SUN
ABEHIKNOSSTT	SINKS THE BOAT
ABEHILLLPTTU	UPHILL BATTLE
ABEHILLOSTWW	BLOW A WHISTLE
ABEHILNOPSTY	HYPNOTISABLE
ABEHILNOPTYZ	HYPNOTIZABLE
ABEHILNORRTW	BROTHER-IN-LAW
ABEHILORRTTW	LOW BIRTH-RATE
ABEHINPRSSTU	PAINTBRUSHES
ABEHKNNNORTU	RUN ON THE BANK
ABEHKNNORTWY	KNOWN BY HEART
ABEHKNORSTWY	KNOWS BY HEART
ABEHLNOORSTU	HAS NO TROUBLE
	HONEST LABOUR
ABEHLORRSTTY	ERYTHROBLAST
ABEHMORRRSTX	MARX BROTHERS
ABEHNORSSSTU	BURNS TO ASHES
ABEHNORSSTTU	BURNT TO ASHES
ABEHNORSTTTU	BURN THE TOAST
ABEHOPPPRRTU	PROP UP THE BAR
ABEIIILLLMRS	ILLIBERALISM
ABEIIILLLRTY	ILLIBERALITY
ABEIIILLNNRT	BRILLIANTINE
ABEIIILLNORS	BILLIONAIRES
ABEIIILMNNSV	INVISIBLE MAN
ABEIIILNOSTT	NOTABILITIES
ABEIIILQTTUY	EQUITABILITY
ABEIIILLLLRSW	BEARS ILL-WILL
ABEIIILLMPTU	MULTIPLIABLE
ABEIIILLORSU	LOUIS BRAILLE
ABEIIILLORTTY	TOLERABILITY
ABEIIILLRSSTT	BRISTLETAILS
ABEIILMMORTY	MEMORABILITY
ABEIILMNNRTY	INTERMINABLY
ABEIILMNOSST	AMBITIONLESS

ABEIILMORTVY	REMOVABILITY
ABEIILNNOSST	BIT ONE'S NAILS
ABEIILNNTTUY	UNTENABILITY
ABEIILNOORTT	OBLITERATION
ABEIILNOPRST	PRELIBATIONS
ABEIILOQRRTU	EQUILIBRATOR
ABEIILPRTTUY	REPUTABILITY
ABEIINORSSTU	SUBERISATION
ABEIINORSTUZ	SUBERIZATION
ABEIKLNSSSTU	TALK BUSINESS
ABEIKLOORTTY	TOOK A LIBERTY
ABEIKLORSSTW	STRIKES A BLOW
ABEIKNOORTTW	WRITTEN A BOOK
ABEILLLRSSTY	TRISYLLABLES
ABEILLMMRRST	BERTRAM MILLS
ABEILLNNOPPT	BALL-POINT PEN
ABEILLNNRUVY	INVULNERABLY
ABEILLOPRRVY	PROVERBIALLY
ABFIILRRSTUY	TREASURY BILL
ADEILMO3STUY	ABSTEMIOUSLY
ABEILMRSSTTY	TRIBAL SYSTEM
ABEILNNRRTTU	RENT TRIBUNAL
ABEILNOQSTUY	QUESTIONABLY
ABEILNORSSSU	BELORUSSIANS
ABEILNORSSUY	BYELORUSSIAN
ABEILNORTTXY	EXORBITANTLY
ABEILNPRSSUU	PRUSSIAN BLUE
ABEIMOOOTTTU	ABOUT TIME TOO
ABEINOOPRRST	PROBATIONERS
ABEINOORSSTV	OBSERVATIONS
ABEINOPRRTTU	PERTURBATION
ABEINORSTTUZ	BRAZENS IT OUT
ABEINORTTTUW	WRITTEN ABOUT
ABEINSSSTTUV	SUBSTANTIVES
ABEIOSSSSTTU	ASBESTOS SUIT
ABEJLMMOOPRR	MAJOR PROBLEM
ABEJMOOPRRTY	TEMPORARY JOB
ABEKKLLOOOTU	BLEAK OUTLOOK
ABEKLOORRSWY	BOWLS A YORKER
ABEKMNOOSTUY	MONKEYS ABOUT
ABEKMNORSTTY	TAKEN BY STORM
ABEKNNPRTTUW	WENT BANKRUPT
ABELLLLOPSYY	POLYSYLLABLE
ABELLLMNOOSY	MONOSYLLABLE
ABELLLOSSTWY	TWO SYLLABLES
ABELLMOOPPSS	APPLE BLOSSOM
ABELLOPSSTTU	STOPS A BULLET
ABELMMOORSSY	ASSEMBLY ROOM
ABELMNORSTUU	SURMOUNTABLE
ABELMOPRSTUW	BLEW UP A STORM
ABELMPRSTTTU	TRUMPET BLAST
ABELNORRSTUW	RETURNS A BLOW
ABELOORRSTUV	LABOUR VOTERS
ABELOPRSTTTY	LOBSTER PATTY
ABEMMNNORRSU	ROMAN NUMBERS
ABEMNNOOTTUW	MEN-ABOUT-TOWN
ABEMNORRRSST	BARNSTORMERS
ABENNOOSTTUW	SEW ON A BUTTON
ABEOOPRSTTTU	POTTERS ABOUT
ABEOORSTTTTU	TOTTERS ABOUT
ABFFGHIKLLNU	BLUFF KING HAL
ABFFIKLOORRS	BORIS KARLOFF
ABFGHIIMNORT	HABIT FORMING
	HABIT-FORMING
ABFGHIKLOOST	BOOKS A FLIGHT
ABFGIIILLNSYY	SYLLABIFYING
ABFGILLNORST	BALL OF STRING
ABFGILNOOOTU	FOOLING ABOUT
ABFGNOOORRTU	GO FOR A BURTON
ABFIIILLNORT	FIBRILLATION
ABFIIILLMORRY	MYOFIBRILLAR

ABFIKNPRRSUY	FINSBURY PARK
ABFILLORSTTU	OUT FIRST BALL
ABFILMMNSSUU	FUNAMBULISMS
ABFJKLOOOORS	LOOKS FOR A JOB
ABFKLMOOOPSS	BOOK OF PSALMS
ABFKMOOOPSST	BOOK OF STAMPS
ABFLLOOOOPRU	POOL OF LABOUR
ABGGGILNOTUU	LUGGING ABOUT
ABGGHINORSTT	BANG TO RIGHTS
ABGGIILNNOPY	PLAYING BINGO
ABGGIILNRRSU	BURGLARISING
ABGGIILNRRUZ	BURGLARIZING
ABGGIINNORTY	GOING BY TRAIN
ABGGILLNNOOW	BOWLING ALONG
ABGGILLNNOPP	PING-PONG BALL
ABGGILLNOSSW	GLASSBLOWING
ABGGILNNRSSU	BURNING GLASS
ABGGILNPRUYY	PLAYING RUGBY
ABGGINOOSSTT	TOBOGGANISTS
ABGGLLOOOSWY	BOWLS A GOOGLY
ABGHHILORRTU	HARBOUR LIGHT
ABGHHINRSSUV	SHAVING BRUSH
ABGHHOORSSTU	THOROUGHBASS
ABGHHOOTTTUU	THOUGHT ABOUT
ABGHIIMMNSTW	SWIMMING BATH
ABGHIKNNORSU	BANKING HOURS
ABGHINORSTUU	RUSHING ABOUT
ABGHINPRSSTU	BRUSHING PAST
ABGHIORSTTUU	BROUGHT A SUIT
ABGIIIILLMNSU	BILINGUALISM
ABGIIKLNOSSW	BLOWING A KISS
ABGIIKNNOOPT	PAINTING BOOK
ABGIIKNNOOPY	PAYING-IN BOOK
ABGIIKNOORTW	WRITING A BOOK
ABGIILLOORTY	OBLIGATORILY
ABGIILNNOOOT	NO OBLIGATION
ABGIILNORRTT	BRING TO TRIAL
ABGIINORTTUW	WRITING ABOUT
ABGIINOSTTTU	SITTING ABOUT
ABGIJMNOPTUU	JUMPING ABOUT
ABGIKMNOOOOR	BOOKING A ROOM
ABGILLNOPSWY	PLAYING BOWLS
ABGILLNOSTTU	SUBTOTALLING
ABGILMNOPSUU	PLUMBAGINOUS
ABGILNOORTUV	VOTING LABOUR
ABGIMNNOOOTU	MOONING ABOUT
ABGIMNNORRST	BARNSTORMING
ABGINNNORTUU	RUNNING ABOUT
ABGINNORTTUU	TURNING ABOUT
ABGINOOSSTTU	TOSSING ABOUT
ABGINOPTTTUU	PUTTING ABOUT
ABHIIKMNNPRS	BRINKMANSHIP
ABHIIKNOTTTU	THINK ABOUT IT
ABHIILLMOOTW	WILLIAM BOOTH
ABHIILMOPSUY	AMPHIBIOUSLY
ABHIILNOPSTY	INHOSPITABLY
ABHIILNOSTWY	SHOWN ABILITY
ABHIILOSSTWY	SHOWS ABILITY
ABHIINOPRSTV	VIBRAPHONIST
ABHIMNNORRTU	NORTHUMBRIAN
ABHINOOPPRSS	BISHOPS APRON
ABHKLOOOSTWY	LOOK BOTH WAYS
ABHLNNOOSUVW	HANS VON BULOW
ABIIIILRRTTY	IRRITABILITY
ABIIIILNRTTW	BRILLIANT WIT
ABIIIILPSTUY	PLAUSIBILITY
ABIIILMMOTVY	IMMOVABILITY
ABIIILMMTTUY	IMMUTABILITY
ABIIILMNOOST	ABOLITIONISM
	MOBILISATION
ABIIILMNOOTZ	MOBILIZATION
ABIIILMOTTXY	ABILITY TO MIX
ABIIILNOOSTT	ABOLITIONIST
ABIIILNPRTTY	PRINTABILITY
ABIILLLMNSUY	SUBLIMINALLY
ABIILMNOORSV	SIMON BOLIVAR
ABIILMOOSTTU	AUTOMOBILIST
ABIILNOORSTT	STROBILATION
ABIILNORSSUU	INSALUBRIOUS
ABIILNORSTTU	TRIBULATIONS
ABIINOORSSTT	ABORTIONISTS
ABIJLNOOPPSU	SLIP UP ON A JOB
ABIKOPRSSSSY	BORIS SPASSKY
ABILLORSSUUY	SALUBRIOUSLY
ABILMMMNOSSU	SOMNAMBULISM
ABILMMNOSSTU	SOMNAMBULIST
ABILMNORSTUY	SUBNORMALITY
ABIMNORSSTTU	NIMBOSTRATUS
ABINOORRTTUW	RAINBOW TROUT
ABLMOOPRSTUW	BLOW UP A STORM
ABLMOSSSTTUY	STATUS SYMBOL
ABMNOOORSTTW	BOOMTOWN RATS
ABNOORRSSTUU	BRONTOSAURUS
ACCCCEIILRRT	ARCTIC CIRCLE
ACCCDEEHIKLM	MEDICAL CHECK
ACCCDEEHKORT	CRACK THE CODE
ACCCDEEHNNOS	SECOND CHANCE
ACCCDENNOORS	CONCORDANCES
ACCCDGHILNOT	CATCHING COLD
ACCCEEEHINST	TEACH SCIENCE
ACCCEEEILLNN	CLEAN LICENCE
ACCCEEEIMNOR	ICE-CREAM CONE
ACCCEEEINOSU	ACQUIESCENCE
ACCCEEEINSTX	EXACT SCIENCE
ACCCEEFFIOPT	ACCEPT OFFICE
ACCCEEFHNNRT	FRENCH ACCENT
ACCCEEHKLTTU	CUT THE CACKLE
ACCCEEIILSST	ECCLESIASTIC
ACCCEEILLLTY	ECLECTICALLY
ACCCEFHOOSST	CASE OF SCOTCH
ACCCEGIINNOR	CARCINOGENIC
ACCCEHIKMRTT	CRICKET MATCH
ACCCEHIKNOPR	INCHCAPE ROCK
ACCCEHINORTT	TECHNOCRATIC
ACCCEHKLORTW	CLOCK WATCHER
	CLOCK-WATCHER
ACCCEIILLORS	SOCIAL CIRCLE
ACCCEIMNNOOT	CONCOMITANCE
ACCCEIMNRSTU	CIRCUMSTANCE
ACCCEINNORTT	ACT IN CONCERT
ACCCELMNOOPU	PNEUMOCOCCAL
ACCCELNOORRT	CAROL CONCERT
ACCCELNOOSTT	CLOSE CONTACT
ACCCEMMNNOOT	COMMON ACCENT
ACCCHIIOPRRT	CHIROPRACTIC
ACCCHIKOSSTT	SHOCK TACTICS
ACCCIIILSSST	CLASSICISTIC
ACCCIILNNOTY	ANTICYCLONIC
ACCCIILNOOST	ICONOCLASTIC
ACCCIKLNOORV	VOLCANIC ROCK
ACCCNOOSSTTU	COST ACCOUNTS
ACCDDEEEINSS	DENIED ACCESS
ACCDDEEHINOR	EDDIE COCHRAN
ACCDDEEIORTT	DECORTICATED
ACCDDEHINOOP	DODECAPHONIC
ACCDDEHNNOOS	ODDS-ON CHANCE
ACCDDEHOPPRT	DROPPED CATCH
ACCDDEINORTT	CONTRADICTED
ACCDDEOOSSTU	STOOD ACCUSED
ACCDEEEEHKLRT	CLEAR THE DECK
ACCDEEEEINSSS	DENIES ACCESS
ACCDEEEKSSTT	CASSETTE DECK

ACCDEEFFIORT	OFFICER CADET	ACCDHINOTTUU	DUTCH AUCTION
ACCDEEFIIRTT	CERTIFICATED	ACCDHKORRSTU	STRUCK A CHORD
ACCDEEGLNNOS	SECOND GLANCE	ACCDIILNOORS	CROCODILIANS
ACCDEEHHHIOT	HAD THE CHOICE	ACCDIINOORST	ACCORDIONIST
ACCDEEHHKLSU	CHUCKLEHEADS	ACCDILNOORTU	CONDUCTORIAL
ACCDEEHIMNSS	MISSED CHANCE	ACCDINOORRTT	CONTRADICTOR
ACCDEEHISSTT	CASTS THE DICE	ACCDINOSSTTU	SOUND TACTICS
ACCDEEIILNOT	INDOLEACETIC	ACCDLMNOORTU	MORAL CONDUCT
ACCDEEIILNPY	NICELY PLACED	ACCDLNNOORTY	CONCORDANTLY
ACCDEEIILLOPS	PECCADILLOES	ACCEEEEFPPRT	PERFECT PEACE
ACCDEEILNOPY	ENCYCLOPEDIA	ACCEEEFFNOSU	CAUSE OFFENCE
ACCDEEINNNST	INCANDESCENT	ACCEEEFHOPRT	FORCE THE PACE
ACCDEEINNORT	CONCERTINAED	ACCEEEGLLLOR	CLARE COLLEGE
ACCDEEINPRTU	PURE ACCIDENT	ACCEEEHILRRT	ELECTRIC HARE
ACCDEEIOPRRT	RECIPROCATED	ACCEEEHMNORT	REMOTE CHANCE
ACCDEEIORSTT	DECORTICATES	ACCEEEHNNNUV	UNEVEN CHANCE
ACCDEELLNOTU	CANCELLED OUT	ACCEEEHNORRS	CHOSEN CAREER
ACCDEELMORTT	CLOTTED CREAM	ACCEEEHNOSTY	CATCH ONE'S EYE
ACCDEELOPRSY	PLAYED SOCCER	ACCEEFILSSST	ECCLESIASTES
ACCDEFNNNOTU	COUNTENANCED	ACCEEEIMNNRS	CINEMA SCREEN
ACCDEEHNNORTT	CONCENTRATED	ACCEEEINOPST	ESCAPE NOTICE
ACCDEENORTTU	COUNTERACTED	ACCEEFFHIOOR	OFFER A CHOICE
ACCDEENNR333U	ACCURSEDNESS	ACCEEFGIIMNN	MAGNIFICENCE
ACCDEFFHORST	SCRATCHED OFF	ACCEEFGIIMOP	PIECE OF MAGIC
ACCDEFGIILNY	DECALCIFYING	ACCEEFGLLORS	COLLEGE SCARF
ACCDEFIMNORY	DYNAMIC FORCE	ACCEEFGMOORS	GAME OF SOCCER
ACCDEFNOSSTU	SAFE-CONDUCTS	ACCEEFHHIIRS	CHIEF CASHIER
ACCDEGHORTUU	DUTCH COURAGE	ACCEEFHIIPST	SPECIFIC HEAT
ACCDEGIOOPRT	GOOD PRACTICE	ACCEEFHIKLOP	PIECE OF CHALK
ACCDEGNNORRT	CONCERT GRAND	ACCEEFHIMSTU	FACE THE MUSIC
ACCDEHHNOTTU	UNDO THE CATCH	ACCEEFHKOTTU	CUT OF THE CAKE
ACCDEHHNRRUW	CHURCH WARDEN	ACCEEFHLNOTT	LEFT TO CHANCE
	CHURCHWARDEN	ACCEEFHMPRTT	PERFECT MATCH
ACCDEHHNRTTU	ATTEND CHURCH	ACCEEFIIPRRT	FIRE PRACTICE
ACCDEHHORSST	CROSSHATCHED	ACCEEFIIRSTT	CERTIFICATES
ACCDEHIILOTZ	CATHOLICIZED	ACCEEFIIRTTU	U CERTIFICATE
ACCDEHILMOPS	ACCOMPLISHED	ACCEEFIIRTTX	X CERTIFICATE
ACCDEHNNRRUY	HARD CURRENCY	ACCEEFIMNNOS	MAN OF SCIENCE
ACCDEHORSTTU	SCRATCHED OUT	ACCEEGGHLOOT	CHOCOLATE EGG
ACCDEHRSSTTU	CUTS THE CARDS	ACCEEGHLLNPU	CHALLENGE CUP
ACCDEIIILNST	INSECTICIDAL	ACCEEGHNNORX	CORN EXCHANGE
ACCDEIILMNOR	CRIMINAL CODE	ACCEEGHNORSU	CHANGE COURSE
ACCDEIILNNOT	COINCIDENTAL	ACCEEGINNORS	RECOGNISANCE
ACCDEIILORST	SOCIAL CREDIT	ACCEEGINNORZ	RECOGNIZANCE
ACCDEIILRRSU	CIRCULARISED	ACCEEGINORTV	GIVE A CONCERT
ACCDEIILRRUZ	CIRCULARIZED	ACCEEGKNORRS	GONE CRACKERS
ACCDEIINORTT	DIRECT ACTION	ACCEEGKORRSS	GOES CRACKERS
ACCDEIKLNSST	CANDLESTICKS	ACCEEGNORSTY	ESCORT AGENCY
ACCDEIKLORRS	CRACK SOLDIER	ACCEEGRSSSTU	GREAT SUCCESS
ACCDEILLNOTY	OCCIDENTALLY	ACCEEHHHIOST	HAS THE CHOICE
ACCDEIMMNNOTU	COMMUNICATED	ACCEEHHILLNN	CHANCE IN HELL
ACCDEIMNNOTV	CONVICTED MAN	ACCEEHHINOOV	HAVE NO CHOICE
ACCDEIMNORTU	UNDEMOCRATIC	ACCEEHIILNPT	ENCEPHALITIC
ACCDEINNORTT	CONTRACTED IN	ACCEEHIKOPST	HACK TO PIECES
ACCDEINOPSTT	ACCIDENT SPOT	ACCEEHILLNTT	LITTLE CHANCE
ACCDEIOORRTT	DECORTICATOR	ACCEEHILMSTT	CHEMICAL TEST
ACCDEKKNOOOS	COCKED A SNOOK	ACCEEHIMRSTU	MUSIC TEACHER
ACCDEKORRRST	TRACK RECORDS	ACCEEHINNPST	CATCHPENNIES
ACCDEMNOSTUU	UNACCUSTOMED	ACCEEHIRRTTU	ARCHITECTURE
ACCDENNORTUY	COUNTRY DANCE	ACCEEHKORSTW	WEATHERCOCKS
ACCDFFHIILRR	CLIFF RICHARD	ACCEEHLMNRSY	SCLERENCHYMA
ACCDFIIINOOT	CODIFICATION	ACCEEHLMORTY	THE REAL MCCOY
ACCDGHHILNOT	CATCHING HOLD	ACCEEHMMNOPT	CHEAP COMMENT
ACCDGHIIOPRS	DISCOGRAPHIC	ACCEEHMNNORT	ENCROACHMENT
ACCDGIIKLLOT	DIGITAL CLOCK	ACCEEHNNOOPT	OPEN TO CHANCE
ACCDGIINSTTU	CUTTING A DISC	ACCEEHNOPRTT	CONCRETE PATH
ACCDGIKNORSU	SCORING A DUCK	ACCEEIILMPSU	MUSICAL PIECE
ACCDGLOOPSTU	ASCOT GOLD CUP	ACCEEIILNRST	ELECTRICIANS
ACCDHHINOPPS	CHOP AND CHIPS	ACCEEIILPPRS	SPECIAL PRICE
ACCDHILLNOOY	CONCHOIDALLY	ACCEEIINPPRT	PRECIPITANCE
ACCDHILOOOSU	I SHOULD COCOA!	ACCEEIIOPPSS	EPISCOPACIES

ACCEEIKRRSSW	WISECRACKERS
ACCEEILLLRTY	ELECTRICALLY
ACCEEILLMNUY	ECUMENICALLY
ACCEEILLMPRT	ELECTRIC LAMP
ACCEEILNRTTY	TETRACYCLINE
ACCEEIOPRRST	RECIPROCATES
ACCEEJOPQSUU	COUPE JACQUES
ACCEEKNOPSTU	KEEP ACCOUNTS
ACCEEKNRRSTW	WENT CRACKERS
ACCEELLOSTTX	COLLECT TAXES
ACCEELMOOOST	COME TO A CLOSE
ACCEELNNOSTV	CONVALESCENT
ACCEELNNRSTU	TRANSLUCENCE
ACCEELOPRRSY	SOCCER PLAYER
ACCEELORSTUY	CRETACEOUSLY
ACCEELPRRWYY	CREEPY-CRAWLY
ACCEEMNORTTU	ACCOUTREMENT
ACCEEMOOPPRR	COME A CROPPER
ACCEENNNOSTU	COUNTENANCES
ACCEENNORSTT	CONCENTRATES
ACCEENPRRSTY	SPENCER TRACY
ACCEENRRRTUZ	CURRENT CRAZE
ACCEFFHORSST	SCRATCHES OFF
ACCEFFIIJKNO	JACK IN OFFICE
	JACK-IN-OFFICE
ACCEFGHIINRT	CATCHING FIRE
ACCEFGHKLNOU	CHANGE OF LUCK
ACCEFGIIINNS	SIGNIFICANCE
ACCEFHIINORU	UNFAIR CHOICE
ACCEFHILMRTU	LUCIFER MATCH
ACCEFIILLMRY	FAMILY CIRCLE
ACCEFIILLPSY	SPECIFICALLY
ACCEFIILLRST	SELF-CRITICAL
ACCEFIINOPST	SPACE FICTION
ACCEGGILNOOY	GYNAECOLOGIC
ACCEGHHILNST	SLIGHT CHANCE
ACCEGHHISSTT	CATCHES SIGHT
ACCEGHINORRY	GROCERY CHAIN
ACCEGHLNOORU	CHANGE COLOUR
ACCEGIIKKLNP	PLACEKICKING
ACCEGIIKLNNP	PICKING CLEAN
ACCEGIIKNRSW	WISECRACKING
ACCEGIINNNOZ	INCOGNIZANCE
ACCEGIINNOSS	ACCESSIONING
ACCEGIINORRT	ARCTIC REGION
ACCEGIINRTUX	EXCRUCIATING
ACCEGIKNNOPR	CRACKING OPEN
ACCEGILLLOOY	ECOLOGICALLY
ACCEGILLNNOY	CONCEALINGLY
ACCEGILLNOOR	NECROLOGICAL
ACCEGILNNOSV	CONVALESCING
ACCEGINNNOVY	CONVEYANCING
ACCEGINNORST	CONSECRATING
ACCEGLMOORTY	CROMOGLYCATE
ACCEGNOORRTY	GERONTOCRACY
ACCEHHIKPRTW	CRACK THE WHIP
ACCEHHLOOOTT	HOT CHOCOLATE
ACCEHHOPSTTT	CATCH THE POST
ACCEHHORSSST	CROSSHATCHES
ACCEHIILLMRY	CHIMERICALLY
ACCEHIILLNST	CALLISTHENIC
ACCEHIILNOPR	NECROPHILIAC
ACCEHIILNSST	CALISTHENICS
ACCEHIILNTTY	TECHNICALITY
ACCEHIILOSTZ	CATHOLICIZES
ACCEHIIMNPPR	PICNIC HAMPER
ACCEHIKMNSTY	CHIMNEY STACK
ACCEHIKNORST	ROAST CHICKEN
ACCEHILMOPRS	ACCOMPLISHER
ACCEHILMOPRY	MICROCEPHALY
ACCEHILMOPSS	ACCOMPLISHES

ACCEHILNOOOT	ECHOLOCATION
ACCEHILOPRTY	CHALCOPYRITE
ACCEHIMNORRS	CORNISH CREAM
ACCEHIMORTTT	THERMOTACTIC
ACCEHINNNOPT	PANTECHNICON
ACCEHINORRTT	TROCHANTERIC
ACCEHINRSSST	SCRATCHINESS
ACCEHIOPSTVY	PSYCHOACTIVE
ACCEHLLOSTWY	WATCH CLOSELY
ACCEHLOOPRTY	PYROCATECHOL
ACCEHLOORSSU	SCHORLACEOUS
ACCEHLSSTTUW	CUTS THE CLAWS
ACCEHMNORRTU	COUNTERMARCH
ACCEHMMORSSTU	CASH CUSTOMER
ACCEHNOOPSTU	TOUCH ONES CAP
ACCEHOPRSSST	CROSSPATCHES
ACCEHORSSTTU	SCRATCHES OUT
ACCEIIILMRTT	CRITICAL TIME
ACCEIIILNOTV	CONCILIATIVE
ACCEIIILPSST	SPECIALISTIC
ACCEIIINNNPS	PICCANINNIES
ACCEIIKKMNRS	CAMIKNICKERS
ACCEIIKQSTUW	TWICE AS QUICK
ACCEIIILLLNTY	ENCLITICALLY
ACCEIIILLMNSY	CYNICAL SMILE
ACCEIIILLRSST	CLERICALISTS
ACCEIILMMORT	MICROCLIMATE
ACCEIILMORRT	CALORIMETRIC
ACCEIILMRRSU	SEMICIRCULAR
ACCEIILNRSTT	CENTRALISTIC
ACCEIILRRSSU	CIRCULARISES
ACCEIILRRSUZ	CIRCULARIZES
ACCEIILRSSTU	SECULARISTIC
ACCEIIMMMORT	COMMIT A CRIME
ACCEIIMNORTT	ACTINOMETRIC
ACCEIIMNNOSST	COSMETICIANS
ACCEIIMORRTT	MERITOCRATIC
ACCEIINOPRSS	CONSPIRACIES
ACCEIINPPRTY	PRECIPITANCY
ACCEIINRRTTW	ARCTIC WINTER
ACCEIIPPRSTY	PERSPICACITY
ACCEIJNNOTUV	CONJUNCTIVAE
ACCEIKKOPPST	PICKS A POCKET
ACCEIKLLORRW	CLERICAL WORK
ACCEILLMMORY	COMMERCIALLY
ACCEILLMNOOY	ECONOMICALLY
ACCEILLMOSTY	COSMETICALLY
ACCEILLNOTTY	TECTONICALLY
ACCEILLOPRRY	RECIPROCALLY
ACCEILLOPTYY	ECOTYPICALLY
ACCEILLSSSTY	CLASSIC STYLE
ACCEILMMNORU	UNCOMMERCIAL
ACCEILMNORTU	COUNTERCLAIM
ACCEILMORSSU	MUSICAL SCORE
ACCEILNNNOOT	CONNECTIONAL
ACCEILNNOOPT	CONCEPTIONAL
ACCEILNNOOSS	CONCESSIONAL
ACCEILNNOOTV	CONVECTIONAL
ACCEILNNORTV	VITAL CONCERN
ACCEILNNOSTY	ANTICYCLONES
ACCEILNOORRT	CORRECTIONAL
ACCEILNOSSSU	SUCCESSIONAL
ACCEILNRRSSU	CIRCULARNESS
ACCEILOPRSTU	PLUTOCRACIES
ACCEIMMNOSTU	COMMUNICATES
ACCEINNNOOOS	INCONSONANCE
ACCEINNOORST	CONSECRATION
ACCEINNORSTV	CONTRIVANCES
ACCEINOORRSU	ENRICO CARUSO
ACCEIOOPRRRT	RECIPROCATOR
ACCEKLOORSSY	COOKERY CLASS

ACCEKLRSTTTU	CATTLE TRUCKS	ACCIIILNNOOT	CONCILIATION
ACCELLMNOPTY	COMPLACENTLY	ACCIIILPRSTT	ITALIC SCRIPT
ACCELLNOPTUY	CONCEPTUALLY	ACCIIINRSSST	NARCISSISTIC
ACCELLOORTTX	TAX COLLECTOR	ACCIILLNRTUY	UNCRITICALLY
ACCELMMNOOPS	COMMONPLACES	ACCIILLRSTTY	CRYSTALLITIC
ACCELNNRSTUY	TRANSLUCENCY	ACCIILMNOOPT	COMPLICATION
ACCELNOOPSTU	SOLE OCCUPANT	ACCIILNNOSTU	SAT IN COUNCIL
ACCEMOOSSTUY	ASCOMYCETOUS	ACCIILNOORST	CONCILIATORS
ACCENNOORRTT	CONCENTRATOR	ACCIILNOORTY	CONCILIATORY
ACCENOORRSST	CONSECRATORS	ACCIILOOPPRS	POLARISCOPIC
ACCENOORRSTY	CONSECRATORY	ACCIILOPRSUY	CAPRICIOUSLY
ACCENOOSSTTU	CUTS ONE'S COAT	ACCIIMOOPRTT	COMPATRIOTIC
ACCENOPRRSTU	COUNTERSCARP	ACCIINNOOOST	CONSOCIATION
ACCENOPRRTTY	CONCERT PARTY	ACCIINORRSSU	ROSICRUCIANS
ACCEOORSTTUU	COURTEOUS ACT	ACCIJLNNOTUV	CONJUNCTIVAL
ACCFGHHIINST	CATCHING FISH	ACCIJNNOOTTU	JOINT ACCOUNT
ACCFGHHIOSTT	CATCH SIGHT OF	ACCIJNNOSTUV	CONJUNCTIVAS
ACCFGIINNOST	CONFISCATING	ACCILMORRSTY	MICROCRYSTAL
ACCFGILLNOTU	FLOCCULATING	ACCILNOOQTTU	OCCULTATIONS
ACCFHIIOPSTU	SOUTH PACIFIC	ACCILNOSSTTU	SANSCULOTTIC
ACCFHIKKLOST	STICK OF CHALK	ACCILORRRTUU	CIRCULAR TOUR
ACCFHLOOSSTU	TOUCH OF CLASS	ACCIMMNNOSTU	COMMUNICANTS
ACCFILLOPSY	FISCAL POLICY	ACCIMMNOORTU	COMMUNICATOR
ACCFIIMNNOSU	CONFUCIANISM	ACCIMNNOOSTT	CONCOMITANTS
ACCFIINNOOST	CONFISCATION	ACCIMNOOSTUU	CONTUMACIOUS
ACCFILLNOOTU	FLOCCULATION	ACCINNOOOSTV	CONVOCATIONS
ACCFILNOORUW	COUNCIL OF WAR	ACCINNOORSTT	CONTRACTIONS
ACCFINOORSST	CONFISCATORS	ACCKMNOOPSTY	STOCK COMPANY
ACCFINOORSTY	CONFISCATORY	ACCMNORSTUUU	AUTUMN CROCUS
ACCFMMNOOORT	COMMON FACTOR	ACCNOOPRSTTT	CONTACT SPORT
ACCGGHHIKNOU	HACKING COUGH	ACCNOOPTTTUU	PUT TO ACCOUNT
ACCGGHKNOSUW	CHUCK WAGGONS	ACCNOORSTTTU	CONTRACTS OUT
ACCGHHIINTTT	CHITCHATTING	ACDDDEEFHOST	FACED THE ODDS
ACCGHHIIOPRR	CHIROGRAPHIC	ACDDDEEHIMNT	DETACHED MIND
ACCGHIIKNORR	ROCKING CHAIR	ACDDDEEHNOOR	DODECAHEDRON
ACCGHIIMNPPT	PITCHING CAMP	ACDDDEGINOOR	GOOD RIDDANCE
ACCGHIINOOPR	ICONOGRAPHIC	ACDDDEHILOPT	ADOPTED CHILD
ACCGHIIOPPRT	PICTOGRAPHIC	ACDDDEHILOTW	DEAD WITH COLD
ACCGHIMOOPRS	COSMOGRAPHIC	ACDDDGIMNORW	MADDING CROWD
ACCGHINORRSS	CHARING CROSS	ACDDEEEEFLMN	DEFENCE MEDAL
ACCGHIOOPTTY	PHAGOCYTOTIC	ACDDEEEFNORT	CONFEDERATED
ACCGIIILNNOT	CONCILIATING	ACDDEEEFRRSU	REDUCED FARES
ACCGIIILNSSS	CLASSICISING	ACDDEEEGLPRS	SACRED PLEDGE
ACCGIIILNSSZ	CLASSICIZING	ACDDEEEGMOSS	CODED MESSAGE
ACCGIIKKLNOP	PICKING A LOCK	ACDDEEEHIMST	SEMIDETACHED
ACCGIILLNOOO	ICONOLOGICAL	ACDDEEEHINRV	HARD EVIDENCE
ACCGIILLOOOS	SOCIOLOGICAL	ACDDEEEHITVW	DETACHED VIEW
ACCGIILMNOPT	COMPLICATING	ACDDEEEIJNUY	JAUNDICED EYE
ACCGILLMOOOS	COSMOLOGICAL	ACDDEEEIPRTT	DECREPITATED
ACCGILMNOOOS	COSMOGONICAL	ACDDEEELLTUW	WELL EDUCATED
ACCGILNORTUY	GRANULOCYTIC	ACDDEEELRSTY	DEADLY SECRET
ACCGILORRSUY	CRYOSURGICAL	ACDDEEEMMNOR	COMMANDEERED
ACCGIMNOORSS	COMING ACROSS	ACDDEEEMNSSX	EXCESS DEMAND
ACCHHHIPRRSU	PARISH CHURCH	ACDDEEENSSTU	EDUCATEDNESS
ACCHHIOPPSTY	PSYCHOPATHIC	ACDDEEEOPRRT	TAPE-RECORDED
ACCHIIINSTUV	CHAUVINISTIC	ACDDEEFHOSST	FACES THE ODDS
ACCHIILOOPPR	COPROPHILIAC	ACDDEEFIILSS	DECLASSIFIED
ACCHIILOPRTY	HYPOCRITICAL	ACDDEEFIIRTT	TRADE DEFICIT
ACCHIIMMORST	CHROMATICISM	ACDDEEGGHORR	CHEDDAR GORGE
ACCHIIMNORST	MONARCHISTIC	ACDDEEGHINSS	CHANGED SIDES
ACCHIIMORRTT	TRICHROMATIC	ACDDEEGHNNSU	SUDDEN CHANGE
ACCHIIMORTTY	CHROMATICITY	ACDDEEGHNRRU	UNDERCHARGED
ACCHIIOPRSTY	PHYSIOCRATIC	ACDDEEGKLNOW	ACKNOWLEDGED
ACCHILLOPTTY	PHYLLOTACTIC	ACDDEEHILNRY	CYLINDER HEAD
ACCHILNOPRTY	LYCANTHROPIC	ACDDEEHILOST	LOADS THE DICE
ACCHILOOPSSY	PSYCHOSOCIAL	ACDDEEHIMNRS	MERCHANDISED
ACCHILOPPRTY	PROPHYLACTIC	ACDDEEHINNRS	DRESDEN CHINA
ACCHIOOPRRRT	CHIROPRACTOR	ACDDEEHINNST	DISENCHANTED
ACCHIOORRSSU	CHIAROSCUROS	ACDDEEHKNOSU	DUCK ONES HEAD
ACCHNOORSTTU	SHORT ACCOUNT	ACDDEEHNORSW	CROWNED HEADS
ACCIIILLRSTT	CRITICAL LIST	ACDDEEHNOSTU	COUNTED HEADS

ACDDEEIIIKSV	DICKIE DAVIES	ACDEEEHIMNPS	MAIDEN SPEECH
ACDDEEIILNPR	RAPID DECLINE	ACDEEEHIRSTT	CATHETERISED
ACDDEEILMNOT	OLD-TIME DANCE	ACDEEEHIRTTZ	CATHETERIZED
ACDDEEILPSWY	WIDELY SPACED	ACDEEEHMNOTT	CAME TO THE END
ACDDEEIMORST	DEMOCRATISED	ACDEEEHMNRST	SEED MERCHANT
ACDDEEIMORTZ	DEMOCRATIZED	ACDEEEHPRRTT	THE RED CARPET
ACDDEEIMOSTT	DOMESTICATED	ACDEEEIILNPV	LIVED IN PEACE
ACDDEEINNRSU	REDUNDANCIES	ACDEEEIILNUV	LIVE AUDIENCE
ACDDEEINORRV	COVERED DRAIN	ACDEEEIIPRTV	DEPRECIATIVE
ACDDEEINPRRW	PRINCE EDWARD	ACDEEEILNORT	DECELERATION
ACDDEELNPTUU	PEDUNCULATED	ACDEEEILNOTT	ELECTION DATE
ACDDEEMMMNNNO	CONDEMNED MAN	ACDEEEILNRST	DECENTRALISE
ACDDEFHIIIMS	DID A MISCHIEF	ACDEEEILNRSU	DENUCLEARISE
ACDDEFIOORVW	WORD OF ADVICE	ACDEEEILNRTZ	DECENTRALIZE
ACDDEFJNOORY	DANCED FOR JOY	ACDEEEILNRUZ	DENUCLEARIZE
ACDDEFNNNOOR	CANNON FODDER	ACDEEEILNSST	DELICATENESS
ACDDEGHIMNRW	WEDDING MARCH	ACDEEEILOSTV	CEASED TO LIVE
ACDDEGHIRRTU	DRAUGHT CIDER	ACDEEEIMNNOR	EARNED INCOME
ACDDEGHNNORU	CHANGED ROUND	ACDEEEINNRST	SIDE ENTRANCE
ACDDEGHNRSSU	GRAND DUCHESS	ACDEEEINNRTV	INADVERTENCE
ACDDEGIILLNO	DIALLING CODE	ACDEEEINRSSV	DISSEVERANCE
ACDDEHHLORST	HOLD THE CARDS	ACDEEEINSSTT	NECESSITATED
ACDDEHIKMTUW	CAKED WITH MUD	ACDEEEIPRSTT	DECREPITATES
ACDDEHIMMNNU	MUCH IN DEMAND	ACDEEEIPRTVX	EXPERT ADVICE
ACDDEHNNOSTU	COUNTED HANDS	ACDEEEIRRSXY	EXERCISE YARD
ACDDEHNRSUWY	CURDS AND WHEY	ACDEEEKLNPSS	SLACKEN SPEED
ACDDEIIKNRST	SICK AND TIRED	ACDEEELLNOOV	LEAVE ONE COLD
ACDDEIILPPSS	SLIPPED A DISC	ACDEEELNNTTY	ANTECEDENTLY
ACDDEIINORST	ENDOCARDITIS	ACDEEELORRST	DECELERATORS
ACDDEIINRTTY	IDENTITY CARD	ACDEEENPPRST	SCENTED PAPER
ACDDEILLMNOT	CALLED TO MIND	ACDEEENRRRST	SECRET ERRAND
ACDDEILNOOST	CONSOLIDATED	ACDEEEOPRRRT	TAPE RECORDER
ACDDEILNPRUU	CURL UP AND DIE	ACDEEEOPRTTX	EXPECTORATED
ACDDEILRSTTY	DISTRACTEDLY	ACDEEFFILNRY	FRIENDLY FACE
ACDDEINOSTTU	OUTDISTANCED	ACDEEFFIORSV	OFFERS ADVICE
ACDDEIOPRRUY	DAIRY PRODUCE	ACDEEFFKLNOS	SLACKENED OFF
ACDDEMOPRSSU	MASS-PRODUCED	ACDEEFFLNTUY	UNAFFECTEDLY
ACDDFHIILRSY	FRIDAYS CHILD	ACDEEFFMOPRS	SCAMPERED OFF
ACDDFIOORSSV	CROSS OF DAVID	ACDEEFGHINNT	FACING THE END
ACDDGGHOOOTW	GOOD WATCH-DOG	ACDEEFGIILRS	GRACIE FIELDS
ACDDGHLNOOOT	GO HOT AND COLD	ACDEEFGIINNP	FINDING PEACE
ACDDGILNOORU	ADDING COLOUR	ACDEEFGIORTY	FORCED GAIETY
ACDDHILMNOSY	MONDAYS CHILD	ACDEEFGLRRTU	FRACTURED LEG
ACDDHILNSSUY	SUNDAYS CHILD	ACDEEFHHIKNR	HANDKERCHIEF
ACDDHIMNORYY	HYDRODYNAMIC	ACDEEFHIIRST	FIRESIDE CHAT
ACDDHJNNPUUY	PUNCH AND JUDY	ACDEEFHILLRW	CHILD WELFARE
ACDDILNORSTY	DISCORDANTLY	ACDEEFHILNRU	HURL DEFIANCE
ACDDIMNNOTUU	UNCUT DIAMOND	ACDEEFHINNRS	ENFRANCHISED
ACDEEEEGHRST	GRATED CHEESE	ACDEEFHIRSTW	CHIEF STEWARD
ACDEEEEHLRRS	CHEERLEADERS	ACDEEFHLOOTT	ACTED THE FOOL
ACDEEEELRRST	STEERED CLEAR	ACDEEFHLORTT	HERD OF CATTLE
ACDEEEFFNSST	AFFECTEDNESS	ACDEEFHNOPRT	END OF CHAPTER
ACDEEEFHHTTW	CHEWED THE FAT	ACDEEFHNORRW	HENCEFORWARD
ACDEEEFHINOS	HIDE ONES FACE	ACDEEFIILSSS	DECLASSIFIES
ACDEEEFHINRT	RED IN THE FACE	ACDEEFILLORS	ALLIED FORCES
ACDEEEFHIRRT	FIERCE HATRED	ACDEEFILOPPR	PRIDE OF PLACE
ACDEEEFHLOTV	HAVE COLD FEET	ACDEEFILRSTV	FALSE VERDICT
ACDEEEFINNOS	IN CASE OF NEED	ACDEEFIMMNNNO	OF MICE AND MEN
ACDEEEFISTVY	SAFETY DEVICE	ACDEEFIPRTTT	FITTED CARPET
ACDEEEFLMNTT	MENTAL DEFECT	ACDEEFLMOOTW	FLEETWOOD MAC
ACDEEEFNORST	CONFEDERATES	ACDEEFLNORST	LEFT ONE'S CARD
ACDEEEFOPRSU	SUED FOR PEACE	ACDEEFLORRTU	FEDERAL COURT
ACDEEEGHHRTW	CHEWED THE RAG	ACDEEFMNNOST	DESCENT OF MAN
ACDEEEGIKNSU	SEEK GUIDANCE	ACDEEFMORRSU	CASE OF MURDER
ACDEEEGILNRT	DECELERATING	ACDEEFNORRTU	TOUR DE FRANCE
ACDEEEGINPRS	PREDECEASING	ACDEEFNOSSTW	TWO-FACEDNESS
ACDEEEGINRTT	CIGARETTE END	ACDEEFNRRSUU	UNDERSURFACE
ACDEEEGLNOOU	EAU DE COLOGNE	ACDEEFORSTTU	REFUSED TO ACT
ACDEEEGLNOSU	SECOND LEAGUE	ACDEEGHILRST	CLEAR-SIGHTED
ACDEEEGLORSU	SECURE OLD-AGE	ACDEEGHINNRT	INTERCHANGED
ACDEEEHHTTUW	WHAT THE DEUCE?	ACDEEGHINSSS	CHANGES SIDES

ACDEEGHLLNNU	UNCHALLENGED	ACDEEIKLOOPS	KALEIDOSCOPE
ACDEEGHLOPST	CLOSED THE GAP	ACDEEIKLPTUY	DUPLICATE KEY
ACDEEGHMRRRU	MURDER CHARGE	ACDEEILLMNRY	ENDERMICALLY
ACDEEGHNRRSU	UNDERCHARGES	ACDEEILLMTTW	WELL-TIMED ACT
ACDEEGHPRRSU	SUPERCHARGED	ACDEEILLNNOS	DECLENSIONAL
ACDEEGIINPRT	DEPRECIATING	ACDEEILMNPST	DISPLACEMENT
ACDEEGILLOTY	GEODETICALLY	ACDEEILMNRSU	LEARNED MUSIC
ACDEEGILMNOY	EALING COMEDY	ACDEEILMNNOU	NON-EUCLIDEAN
ACDEEGILNPSS	SINGLE-SPACED	ACDEEILNNNPP	PEN AND PENCIL
ACDEEGILNRSY	DECREASINGLY	ACDEEILNOPRR	PLACE IN ORDER
ACDEEGILSTTU	GESTICULATED	ACDEEILNORST	DONE ARTICLES
ACDEEGIMNOTT	COME AND GET IT	ACDEEILNRSTU	RUINED CASTLE
ACDEEGINNNOP	DOING PENANCE	ACDEEILOPRRS	SPECIAL ORDER
ACDEEGINRSSS	DRESSING CASE	ACDEEILORSST	DOES ARTICLES
ACDEEGIORSTV	GETS A DIVORCE	ACDEEILORTVY	DECORATIVELY
ACDEEGKLNOSW	ACKNOWLEDGES	ACDEEIMMORST	COMMISERATED
ACDEEGMNOOPW	COME DOWN A PEG	ACDEEIMNNOPR	PREDOMINANCE
ACDEEGMNOOSS	COMES AND GOES	ACDEEIMNOSTY	STEADY INCOME
ACDEEGNNORTV	COVENT GARDEN	ACDEEIMNPRST	PREDICAMENTS
ACDEEGNNOSTT	DECONGESTANT	ACDEEIMOORTV	CREATIVE MOOD
ACDEEGNNORSST	GET ONES CARDS	ACDEEIMORRST	DEMOCRATISER
ACDEEHHIMORT	HEMICHORDATE	ACDEEIMORRTZ	DEMOCRATIZER
ACDEEHHLOSST	HOLDS THE ACES	ACDEEIMORSST	DEMOCRATISES
ACDEEHHOSTTT	ACTED THE HOST	ACDEEIMORSTZ	DEMOCRATIZES
ACDEEHIILNTT	DELICATE HINT	ACDEEIMOSSTT	DOMESTICATES
ACDEEHIISSTT	THE DIE IS CAST	ACDEEIMOSSTV	VASECTOMISED
ACDEEHIJNNOT	JOIN THE DANCE	ACDEEIMOSTVZ	VASECTOMIZED
ACDEEHIINNSS	ENDLESS CHAIN	ACDEEIMRSTTT	DICTATE TERMS
ACDEEHIMNRRS	MERCHANDISER	ACDEEINNOSSS	DANCE SESSION
ACDEEHIMNRSS	MERCHANDISES	ACDEEINNPRRW	PRINCE ANDREW
ACDEEHIMPPRW	WHIPPED CREAM	ACDEEIOPRRST	DEPRECIATORS
ACDEEHINNRST	DISENCHANTER	ACDEEIOPRRTY	DEPRECIATORY
ACDEEHINPTTT	PITCHED A TENT	ACDEEIPRRTUW	DREW A PICTURE
ACDEEHINRSTW	WINDCHEATERS	ACDEEIRSSTTU	RESUSCITATED
ACDEEHIOPSST	DASH TO PIECES	ACDEEJKKNOTY	DONKEY JACKET
ACDEEHKLOPYY	PLAYED HOCKEY	ACDEEKKLOORW	LOOKED A WRECK
ACDEEHLLORT	CALLED THE ROLL	ACDEEKLMNOSU	SUCKED A LEMON
ACDEEHLLTTWY	WATCHED TELLY	ACDEELMMOSUV	MOVED A MUSCLE
ACDEEHLNNOOR	LEONARD COHEN	ACDEELMNOPTT	CONTEMPLATED
ACDEEHLNORST	CHARLESTONED	ACDEELNNOOOP	CODE NAPOLEON
ACDEEHLOOSTT	CLOSE TO DEATH	ACDEELNORSTY	ROYAL DESCENT
ACDEEHMNORSW	REACH-ME-DOWNS	ACDEELOORSTW	DREW TO A CLOSE
ACDEEHMNOSTY	MAY THE SECOND	ACDEELOPRRRY	RECORD PLAYER
ACDEEHNOPSTT	DESPATCH NOTE	ACDEEMMMOORT	COMMEMORATED
ACDEEHNORSST	HAD NO SECRETS	ACDEEMNNOOST	COMES TO AN END
ACDEEHNORSTT	DONE A STRETCH	ACDEEMNOPPTY	APPENDECTOMY
ACDEEHNOSSST	DANCE HOSTESS	ACDEEMNRRRSY	MERRY DANCERS
ACDEEHOOPSTT	STOOD THE PACE	ACDEENNNRSTT	TRANSCENDENT
ACDEEHOPRSST	DROPS THE CASE	ACDEENNORSTU	SECOND NATURE
ACDEEHORRSTT	ORCHESTRATED	ACDEFFGIINST	DISAFFECTING
ACDEEHORRSTW	THREES A CROWD	ACDEFFIILPST	SPIFFLICATED
ACDEEHORSSTT	DOES A STRETCH	ACDEFFIINOST	DISAFFECTION
ACDEEIINNHS	INCENDIARIES	ACDEFFIIORRT	CARRIED IT OFF
ACDEEIILLMPY	EPIDEMICALLY	ACDEFFINOOTU	AUCTIONED OFF
ACDEEIILLNTY	INDELICATELY	ACDEFFNOOPSS	DOFFS ONES CAP
ACDEEIILLTTY	DIETETICALLY	ACDEFGHIIKPT	PICKED A FIGHT
ACDEEIILMPST	LIMITED SPACE	ACDEFGHIMNNO	CHANGE OF MIND
ACDEEIILMTVY	TIMELY ADVICE	ACDEFGHINNOW	WIND OF CHANGE
ACDEEIILRSVY	DAILY SERVICE	ACDEFGILNNOR	FORCE-LANDING
ACDEEIIMNRRT	RECRIMINATED	ACDEFGLNNOOU	GOOD CLEAN FUN
ACDEEIIMNRTV	CREATIVE MIND	ACDEFHHIILTT	HITCHED A LIFT
ACDEEIIMNRTY	INTERMEDIACY	ACDEFHHOORTT	THATCHED ROOF
ACDEEIINOPRT	DEPRECIATION	ACDEFHIIKLNS	LACKED FINISH
ACDEEIINORTV	TRAINED VOICE	ACDEFHIINRSS	DISFRANCHISE
ACDEEIINQSTU	EQUIDISTANCE	ACDEFHILNRTY	FRIENDLY CHAT
ACDEEIINTTUX	INEXACTITUDE	ACDEFHOORSSU	HOUSE OF CARDS
ACDEEIIOPPSS	EPIDIASCOPES	ACDEFIIILNOV	CLIVE OF INDIA
ACDEEIIORSSV	RAISED VOICES	ACDEFIIINNST	INFANTICIDES
ACDEEIIPPRTT	PRECIPITATED	ACDEFIIINORS	FAIR DECISION
ACDEEIIPRRSS	RAISED PRICES	ACDEFIILNNOT	CONFIDENTIAL
ACDEEIJKNNRT	DINNER JACKET	ACDEFIILNOPP	FLIPPED A COIN

ACDEFIILNSSU	UNCLASSIFIED	ACDEHKMOOSTU	ASKED TOO MUCH
ACDEFIINNSTT	DISINFECTANT	ACDEHLLOSSSS	HOLDS CLASSES
ACDEFIINOPTT	PONTIFICATED	ACDEHLNPRSTU	THUNDERCLAPS
ACDEFIKORRST	ASK FOR CREDIT	ACDEHLPSTTTU	PLATTDEUTSCH
ACDEFILLLOTU	FOLLICULATED	ACDEHMMNOORT	COMMON HATRED
ACDEFILLOOVW	FOLLOW ADVICE	ACDEHNNNORSY	SONNY AND CHER
ACDEFILNORTU	FUR-LINED COAT	ACDEHNNOPSSU	CUP ONE'S HANDS
ACDEFIOPRRSY	CRY OF DESPAIR	ACDEHNOORSSW	SHOW ONES CARD
ACDEFJNOORSY	DANCES FOR JOY	ACDEHNOORTTT	COTTON THREAD
ACDEFLMOOSTU	CLOUD OF STEAM	ACDEHNOSTTUY	COUNT THE DAYS
ACDEFLRSTUUY	CAREFUL STUDY	ACDEHOORRSST	CROSS THE ROAD
ACDEFMOORRSW	COMES FORWARD	ACDEIIILNVZ	CIVILIANIZED
ACDEGGHINNNS	CHANGING ENDS	ACDEIIILNTVY	INDICATIVELY
ACDEGGIIINVV	GIVING ADVICE	ACDEIIILRTVY	VERIDICALITY
ACDEGGIINNRT	TRAGIC ENDING	ACDEIIIMMORT	RADIOMIMETIC
ACDEGHHNORST	SHORTCHANGED	ACDEIIIMNNOT	NICOTINAMIDE
ACDEGHIMNOTT	METHOD ACTING	ACDEIIIMNNRS	INCENDIARISM
ACDEGHINNORW	REACHING DOWN	ACDEIIIMNNRT	INCRIMINATED
ACDEGHIOPRRS	DISCOGRAPHER	ACDEIIIMNRST	DISCRIMINATE
ACDEGHIOSTUV	SOUGHT ADVICE	ACDEIIINORST	DICTIONARIES
ACDEGHNNORSU	CHANGES ROUND	ACDEIIINPPST	APPENDICITIS
ACDEGIIILMNS	DECIMALISING	ACDEIIIOPRTY	APERIODICITY
ACDEGIIILMNZ	DECIMALIZING	ACDEIIIOSSTV	DISSOCIATIVE
ACDEGIIKNRST	SIDETRACKING	ACDEIIIPRRST	PERICARDITIS
ACDEGIIKNRTT	TAKING CREDIT	ACDEIIKLPRST	LACKED SPIRIT
ACDEGIILLMRY	GERMICIDALLY	ACDEIIKLRSTT	LAKE DISTRICT
ACDEGIILLNSS	SLIDING SCALE	ACDEIIKMRSST	MISSED A TRICK
ACDEGIILPQRU	QUADRIPLEGIC	ACDEIIKPRSTT	PEAK DISTRICT
ACDEGIIMNNOR	INDO-GERMANIC	ACDEIIILLNNTY	INCIDENTALLY
ACDEGIIMNRSU	READING MUSIC	ACDEIIILLNOOS	COLONIALISED
ACDEGIINOTTX	DETOXICATING	ACDEIIILLNOOZ	COLONIALIZED
ACDEGIINRRRV	RACING DRIVER	ACDEIIILLNSTT	SCINTILLATED
ACDEGIINRRTT	CREDIT RATING	ACDEIIILLOPRY	PERIODICALLY
ACDEGIKNNPSS	SENDS PACKING	ACDEIIILLOPSY	EPISODICALLY
ACDEGILLOORR	LOGICAL ORDER	ACDEIIILLRTUY	DIURETICALLY
ACDEGILLOOTY	DIALECTOLOGY	ACDEIIILMNOPT	DECIMAL POINT
ACDEGILMNOOS	MASONIC LODGE	ACDEIIILMNOST	MALEDICTIONS
ACDEGILMOORT	DERMATOLOGIC	ACDEIIILNNOST	DECLINATIONS
ACDEGILNNOST	LONG DISTANCE	ACDEIIMNORST	ROMANTICISED
	LONG-DISTANCE	ACDEIIMNORTZ	ROMANTICIZED
ACDEGINNNRST	TRANSCENDING	ACDEIIMNNOSTU	CINEMA STUDIO
ACDEGINORRSS	CROSS-GRAINED	ACDEIINNNOTU	DENUNCIATION
ACDEGLLOSTUY	LEGAL CUSTODY	ACDEIINNOPSS	SNAP DECISION
ACDEGMNOOOOT	CAME TO NO GOOD	ACDEIINNORTT	INDOCTRINATE
ACDEGNOORSST	GOT ONE'S CARDS	ACDEIINNOTTU	UNITED ACTION
ACDEHHHNOTTW	DOWN THE HATCH	ACDEIINOORTV	COORDINATIVE
ACDEHHILNNRT	THIRD CHANNEL	ACDEIINOOTTX	DETOXICATION
ACDEHHINOPSS	HAD ONE'S CHIPS	ACDEIINOPRST	PREDICATIONS
ACDEHHINORSW	HERO SANDWICH	ACDEIINORRST	DOCTRINAIRES
ACDEHHIPRRTT	THIRD CHAPTER	ACDEIINOSTTU	EDUCATIONIST
ACDEHHIRSSTY	HAD HYSTERICS	ACDEIJLNTUVY	ADJUNCTIVELY
ACDEHIIMNNOT	INDOMETHACIN	ACDEIKKOPRUW	KICKED UP A ROW
ACDEHIIMORST	RADIOCHEMIST	ACDEIKLPPSSS	SKIPPED CLASS
ACDEHIIMSSST	SCHISMATISED	ACDEIKLPRSTY	PLAYED TRICKS
ACDEHIIMSSTZ	SCHISMATIZED	ACDEIKMNNORT	ONE-TRACK MIND
ACDEHIINOPRR	PERICHONDRIA	ACDEIKNORSTT	STOCK IN TRADE
ACDEHIIJNOTWY	DANCE WITH JOY		STOCK-IN-TRADE
ACDEHIKLLOPS	LACKED POLISH	ACDEIKNOSTTU	TAKE DISCOUNT
ACDEHIKMNNOT	MAN IN THE DOCK	ACDEIKORSTTU	OUTSIDE TRACK
ACDEHIKMNRSS	SCRIMSHANKED	ACDEIKPRSSTW	PICKED STRAWS
ACDEHIKORRST	STRIKE A CHORD	ACDEILLMMOPY	OLYMPIC MEDAL
ACDEHILLMOTY	METHODICALLY	ACDEILLMNORT	RECALL TO MIND
ACDEHILOPSTV	HOLDS CAPTIVE	ACDEILLMOSTY	DOMESTICALLY
ACDEHIMNNOSY	COMES IN HANDY	ACDEILLMRSUY	SCULLERY MAID
ACDEHIMORSSS	MASSED CHOIRS	ACDEILLNORTW	CROWNED IT ALL
ACDEHINNOPSW	OPEN SANDWICH	ACDEILLOOPTY	PLAYED IT COOL
ACDEHINOORSS	ICOSAHEDRONS	ACDEILLOPSTY	DESPOTICALLY
ACDEHINOSSTT	DISHONEST ACT	ACDEILLORSTW	ALLOWS CREDIT
ACDEHIOOPRST	ORTHOPAEDICS	ACDEILLRSSTY	CRYSTALLISED
ACDEHIOPSSTT	PAID THE COSTS	ACDEILLRSTYZ	CRYSTALLIZED
ACDEHJNOOPRS	JOSEPH CONRAD	ACDEILMMNOSU	COMMUNALISED

ACDEILMMNOUZ	COMMUNALIZED	ACDGIINNOORT	COORDINATING
ACDEILMNNOOT	COME IN TO LAND	ACDGIINNOORW	COINING A WORD
ACDEILMNOSUY	MENDACIOUSLY	ACDGIINNORRS	SARDONIC GRIN
ACDEILMOPSTU	DEUTOPLASMIC	ACDGIKNNORTW	TRACKING DOWN
ACDEILMORTVY	VICTORY MEDAL	ACDGILMMNNOY	COMMANDINGLY
ACDEILNNORTW	ANCIENT WORLD	ACDGILMNNOPW	CLAMPING DOWN
ACDEILNOORTY	COORDINATELY	ACDHHIIKNNTT	THICK AND THIN
ACDEILNOOSST	CONSOLIDATES	ACDHHIILNTWY	WILD HYACINTH
	DISCONSOLATE	ACDHHIILSSWY	CHILDISH WAYS
ACDEILNORSSW	COWARDLINESS	ACDHHINOOPRY	HYPOCHONDRIA
ACDEILNPRSTY	DISCREPANTLY	ACDHHIOPRRSS	HARPSICHORDS
ACDEILNRRSSU	LAND CRUISERS	ACDHIIMMORST	DICHROMATISM
ACDEILNTTUUV	UNCULTIVATED	ACDHIIMNOORT	MITOCHONDRIA
ACDEILOORRUV	VARICOLOURED	ACDHIINNORRX	RICHARD NIXON
ACDEIMMNNOOT	COMMENDATION	ACDHIINORRSW	WINDSOR CHAIR
ACDEIMMNOPXY	MIXED COMPANY	ACDHIIOPRSTT	DICTATORSHIP
ACDEIMMNORTY	DYNAMOMETRIC	ACDHIKMNOPRR	RICHMOND PARK
ACDEIMMOOORR	AIR COMMODORE	ACDHIKNOPRSW	PORK SANDWICH
ACDEIMNNNOOT	CONDEMNATION	ACDHIIMNOORST	TRICHOMONADS
ACDEIMNORRRS	MORRIS DANCER	ACDHINOPSSTT	PITCH AND TOSS
ACDEINNNOOST	CONDENSATION	ACDHINPPTTTU	PITCH AND PUTT
ACDEINOOPRRT	INCORPORATED	ACDHIOPRRRRY	RICHARD PRYOR
ACDEINOOPRST	SCORED A POINT	ACDHIOPRSSTT	DROPS A STITCH
ACDEINOSSTTU	OUTDISTANCES	ACDHIORSSTTY	HYDROSTATICS
ACDEKNOSTTUY	TAKEN CUSTODY	ACDHLNOOOSTU	COOL THOUSAND
ACDEKOSSTTUY	TAKES CUSTODY	ACDHLNOOSSUY	SUNDAY SCHOOL
ACDELLMPRSTU	CALLED TRUMPS	ACDHNOPPRSUU	PROUD AS PUNCH
ACDELLOORRST	CALLS TO ORDER	ACDHNRSTTTUU	CUT AND THRUST
ACDELLOPRRUY	PROCEDURALLY	ACDIIIIMOTTY	IDIOMATICITY
ACDELLORRSWY	WORLDLY CARES	ACDIIILNPRSY	DISCIPLINARY
ACDELMOPRTUW	TALCUM POWDER	ACDIIIMNNRST	DISCRIMINANT
ACDELNOORTYY	COTYLEDONARY	ACDIIINNOORT	AIR-CONDITION
ACDELOPRSTTY	PTERODACTYLS	ACDIIINOOSST	DISSOCIATION
ACDEMMMNNOST	COMMANDMENTS	ACDIILLMNPTU	MULTIPLICAND
ACDEMMNOORTY	COMMENDATORY	ACDIILNOOSST	DISLOCATIONS
ACDEMNNOORTY	CONDEMNATORY	ACDIILNOPRTW	TROPICAL WIND
ACDEMNNORSTU	COUNTERMANDS	ACDIILNOPSTU	DUPLICATIONS
ACDEMOPRSSSU	MASS-PRODUCES	ACDIILNSSSTY	SYNDICALISTS
ACDENNNOOSWY	ANY SECOND NOW	ACDIINNOOORT	COORDINATION
ACDENNOORRSW	ROSE AND CROWN	ACDIINORRSST	DISTRACTIONS
ACDEOPRRSTUY	DROP A CURTSEY	ACDIINORSSYY	IDIOSYNCRASY
ACDEOPRSTTUW	WASTE PRODUCT	ACDIJNNOORTU	ROAD JUNCTION
ACDFFIILOTUY	OFFICIAL DUTY	ACDIKKPSSTUU	KICKS UP A DUST
ACDFGHIILNOR	FOLDING CHAIR	ACDILLORSSTY	CRYSTALLOIDS
ACDFGIILLNUY	FUNGICIDALLY	ACDILMNOSSUU	MUSICAL SOUND
ACDFGIIMNORT	COMING ADRIFT	ACDILNOOORST	CONSOLIDATOR
ACDFGIKLNOOT	FLOATING DOCK	ACDILNOOPRTU	PRODUCTIONAL
ACDFHHIINPSS	FISH AND CHIPS	ACDILNORSTUY	COAL INDUSTRY
ACDFHHIMORRT	THIRD OF MARCH	ACDIMMNNOOTU	COMMANDO UNIT
ACDFHKNOOPSU	PACK OF HOUNDS	ACDIMMNOORST	COMMON AS DIRT
ACDFIIINNNOT	NIDIFICATION	ACDINOOORRST	COORDINATORS
ACDFIIIMNOOT	MODIFICATION	ACDINOOQRSTU	CONQUISTADOR
ACDFIKLMOOSW	LACK OF WISDOM	ACDKKNNOORSU	KNOCKS AROUND
ACDFIKMOPRRY	MARY PICKFORD	ACDNOOORSTTW	DOCTOR WATSON
ACDFILMOORTY	FAMILY DOCTOR	ACDNOORSSTUU	SCOUTS AROUND
ACDGGGIINNNO	GOING DANCING	ACDOPRRSSTUY	DROPS A CURTSY
ACDGGHINNNOW	CHANGING DOWN	ACEEEEEHKPPT	KEEP THE PEACE
ACDGGIILNNRS	DANCING GIRLS	ACEEEEFHMNTY	FACE THE ENEMY
ACDGGIINORSU	DISCOURAGING	ACEEEEFJKRRT	REEFER JACKET
ACDGGIOOORSU	GOOD GRACIOUS	ACEEEEFNNRRT	ENTRANCE FREE
ACDGHHILNTUY	NAUGHTY CHILD	ACEEEEGIKNPS	SEEKING PEACE
ACDGHHIOPRRY	HYDROGRAPHIC	ACEEEEHLPSST	STEEPLECHASE
ACDGHIINNNOW	CHAINING DOWN	ACEEEEILMRST	MARIE CELESTE
ACDGHIIOPRTT	DITTOGRAPHIC	ACEEEEKPRSST	KEEPS A SECRET
ACDGHILLOORY	HYDROLOGICAL	ACEEEELNORTT	COELENTERATE
ACDGHIMNNOOT	COMING TO HAND	ACEEEELNRSST	SCENE STEALER
ACDGHINNORSW	CRASHING DOWN	ACEEEENPRRSV	PERSEVERANCE
ACDGHINNPPSU	CUPPING HANDS	ACEEEEOPRRST	RESTORE PEACE
ACDGIIINOSST	DISSOCIATING	ACEEEFFFRSTT	AFTEREFFECTS
ACDGIIINRSTV	VISITING CARD	ACEEEFFGHORR	FREE OF CHARGE
ACDGIIKLOSST	DIGITAL SOCKS	ACEEEFFGNORV	GRAVE OFFENCE

ACEEEFFGSSTT	STAGE EFFECTS
ACEEEFFKNNOT	TAKEN OFFENCE
ACEEEFFKNOST	TAKES OFFENCE
ACEEEFFMORRR	FREE FROM CARE
ACEEEFGHOQRU	FORGE A CHEQUE
ACEEEFGIMPRT	PERFECT IMAGE
ACEEEFHISSTU	FACE THE ISSUE
ACEEEFILLNRS	SELF-RELIANCE
ACEEEFILNRST	FEELS CERTAIN
ACEEEFIOPPPR	PIECE OF PAPER
ACEEEFLLNORS	CLEAR ONESELF
ACEEEFLNNOSV	ANNE OF CLEVES
ACEEEFLNPSSU	PEACEFULNESS
ACEEEFLNSSSS	FACELESSNESS
ACEEEFLORRST	STEER CLEAR OF
ACEEEFLRRSTV	SCARLET FEVER
ACEEEFNNRRST	TRANSFERENCE
ACEEEFOPRSSU	SUES FOR PEACE
ACEEEGHINNTV	GIVEN THE CANE
ACEEEGHINPRS	CHEESEPARING
ACEEEGHINSTV	GIVES THE CANE
ACEEEGHLOSTT	CLOSE THE GATE
ACEEEGIIMNNR	ANCIEN REGIME
ACEEEGIINSTV	GENITIVE CASE
ACEEEGIKLNPR	KEEPING CLEAR
ACEEEGILMNPT	MEETING PLACE
ACEEEGILRTUV	GIVE A LECTURE
ACEEEGINNORV	GIVE AN ENCORE
ACEEEGLNNOST	GAOL SENTENCE
ACEEEGLRRSTU	CEST LA GUERRE
ACEEEGNNORST	GETS AN ENCORE
ACEEEGPRRSTT	GREAT RESPECT
ACEEEHHILLLS	ACHILLES HEEL
ACEEEHHILNOT	ACE IN THE HOLE
ACEEEHHILVVY	HEAVY VEHICLE
ACEEEHHIRRSS	HERESIARCHES
ACEEEHHLNRTT	HEALTH CENTRE
ACEEEHHLRTTW	RATCHET WHEEL
ACEEEHHPRRTT	CHAPTER THREE
ACEEEHHRRSST	THE SEARCHERS
ACEEEHIKPPTW	KEEP PACE WITH
ACEEEHIMNSTV	ACHIEVEMENTS
ACEEEHINSTTY	CAST IN THE EYE
ACEEEHIQRTUW	WRITE A CHEQUE
ACEEEHIRSSTT	CATHETERISES
ACEEEHIRSTTZ	CATHETERIZES
ACEEEHKLNRST	LEATHERNECKS
ACEEEHLOPSSS	HOPELESS CASE
ACEEEHLORSST	LOSES THE RACE
ACEEEHLPRTVY	THE VERY PLACE
ACEEEHMNNRRY	CHEERY MANNER
ACEEEHNOORTV	OVER THE OCEAN
ACEEEHNOPSST	OPENS THE CASE
ACEEEHNSTTUV	STEVE CAUTHEN
ACEEEHORSTTV	THREE OCTAVES
ACEEEHRSSSTW	CHEESE STRAWS
ACEEEIILNPSV	LIVES IN PEACE
ACEEEIINPRST	TEAR IN PIECES
ACEEEIJLNNST	JAIL SENTENCE
ACEEEIKOPSTT	TAKE TO PIECES
ACEEEIILLNPST	LICENSE PLATE
ACEEEIILMNPST	MANTELPIECES
ACEEEIILNOPST	LOSE PATIENCE
ACEEEIILNORTY	ELECTION YEAR
ACEEEIILOSSTV	CEASES TO LIVE
ACEEEIMMNNNPR	IMPERMANENCE
ACEEEIMMNNQSU	MAIN SEQUENCE
	MAIN-SEQUENCE
ACEEEIMNPRTT	MERE PITTANCE
ACEEEIMNRSVX	EX-SERVICE MAN
ACEEEIMORSTT	TEA-TIME SCORE

ACEEEIMPRSST	MASTERPIECES
ACEEEIMRRSXY	ARMY EXERCISE
ACEEEINOPSSY	SAY ONES PIECE
ACEEEINPRSST	RESTS IN PEACE
ACEEEINRSSTV	CREATIVENESS
	REACTIVENESS
ACEEEINSSSTT	NECESSITATES
ACEEEIOPRSTT	TEAR TO PIECES
ACEEEIOSSTTX	CEASE TO EXIST
ACEEEIPPPRTV	APPERCEPTIVE
ACEEEIPRRTUV	RECUPERATIVE
ACEEEJKLPSST	STEEPLEJACKS
ACEEEKLMMOSW	MAKES WELCOME
ACEEEKMSSSUX	MAKES EXCUSES
ACEEEKNNOSSV	SAVE ONES NECK
ACEEEKNNOSTU	TAKEN ONE'S CUE
ACEEEKNOSSTU	TAKES ONE'S CUE
ACEEELLOPRTT	ELECTROPLATE
ACEEELLORSVV	CLOVERLEAVES
ACEEELMMNPST	EMPLACEMENTS
ACEEELMNNRRV	CLEVER MANNER
ACEEELMNPRST	REPLACEMENTS
ACEEELNNOVWY	EVONNE CAWLEY
ACEEELNOTXYY	OXYACETYLENE
ACEEELNRSSSS	CARELESSNESS
ACEEELORSSTT	SETTLE A SCORE
ACEEEMNNNRTT	ENTRANCEMENT
ACEEEMORRSTY	SYCAMORE TREE
ACEEENNPSSST	PASS SENTENCE
ACEEENNRRTTY	TERCENTENARY
ACEEENOPRSTW	SECRET WEAPON
ACEEENORSSST	REST ONES CASE
ACEEENRRRSTU	RETURN CREASE
ACEEEOPRSTTX	EXPECTORATES
ACEEFFFGILNS	SELF-EFFACING
ACEEFFGHILNO	CHANGE OF LIFE
ACEEFFGIKNTT	TAKING EFFECT
ACEEFFGINTTU	EFFECTUATING
ACEEFFGLLOST	STAFF COLLEGE
ACEEFFHILNTY	FLY IN THE FACE
ACEEFFHNORTT	FACE THE FRONT
ACEEFFIILRTY	FREE FACILITY
ACEEFFIKLRTT	RAFFLE TICKET
ACEEFFIKOPTU	TAKE UP OFFICE
ACEEFFILOPRS	SPECIAL OFFER
ACEEFFILTTUY	EFFECTUALITY
ACEEFFINOPTT	PATENT OFFICE
ACEEFFINOTTU	EFFECTUATION
ACEEFFIOPRRS	OFFERS A PRICE
ACEEFFLNNOSY	FANCY ONESELF
ACEEFGHIMNST	GEMEINSCHAFT
ACEEFGHISTTV	GIVE THE FACTS
ACEEFGHLLSST	GESELLSCHAFT
ACEEFGHSSTTT	GETS THE FACTS
ACEEFGILNRST	SELF-CATERING
ACEEFGILRTUX	GRACEFUL EXIT
ACEEFGKLNORY	LACK OF ENERGY
ACEEFGLLNNOT	FALCON-GENTLE
ACEEFGLMNORY	ANGEL OF MERCY
ACEEFGLNRSSU	GRACEFULNESS
ACEEFGNNOOST	AGE OF CONSENT
ACEEFHHLMNOR	MEN OF HARLECH
ACEEFHHPRRST	FRESH CHAPTER
ACEEFHHRTTTU	FACE THE TRUTH
ACEEFHIIMMNS	MEAN MISCHIEF
ACEEFHIIRRRS	CARRIE FISHER
ACEEFHINNRSS	ENFRANCHISES
ACEEFHIOOSSW	CHOOSES A WIFE
ACEEFHIRRSTW	FIRE-WATCHERS
ACEEFHKLOSST	LOCKS THE SAFE
ACEEFHKNPRSS	SPEAKS FRENCH

ACEEFHLLOSST	CLASH OF STEEL	ACEEGILNNSSV	EVENING CLASS
ACEEFHLMNRTU	FUEL MERCHANT	ACEEGILNPRST	RESTING PLACE
ACEEFHLMOPRS	FORMAL SPEECH	ACEEGILNPSSS	SINGLE-SPACES
ACEEFHLNNRRY	CHANNEL FERRY	ACEEGILPSSTU	SPECIAL GUEST
ACEEFHLOPRRS	SELF-REPROACH	ACEEGILSSTTU	GESTICULATES
ACEEFHMNRRST	FRENCH MASTER	ACEEGIMNNORR	COMING NEARER
ACEEFHNOOSSW	SHOW ONES FACE	ACEEGIMNORTY	ATOMIC ENERGY
ACEEFHNORSTU	ON THE SURFACE	ACEEGINNPRRT	CARPENTERING
ACEEFHOORTTU	OUT OF THE RACE	ACEEGINNSSTX	EXACTINGNESS
ACEEFHOPPRST	PART OF SPEECH	ACEEGINORRTV	OVERREACTING
ACEEFILNQTU	LIQUEFACIENT	ACEEGINPRRTU	RECUPERATING
ACEEFIKLPSST	KEEP-FIT CLASS	ACEEGLLMMORU	GRAM MOLECULE
ACEEFIKNNNRS	FRANKINCENSE	ACEEGLLOPRSS	LEGAL PROCESS
ACEEFILLLORT	RECALL TO LIFE	ACEEGLMNOORT	CONGLOMERATE
ACEEFILLNORT	REFLECTIONAL	ACEEGMNORRSS	SCAREMONGERS
ACEEFILLNRTY	FRENETICALLY	ACEEGNPRTTUU	GET A PUNCTURE
ACEEFILLOPST	FALL TO PIECES	ACEEHHIKLSST	HEALS THE SICK
ACEEFILNNORT	CONFERENTIAL	ACEEHHILMSTT	THE ALCHEMIST
ACEEFILNORTX	REFLEX ACTION	ACEEHHILORRS	QUARRELLE HOUSE
ACEEFIMPRRTU	PICTURE FRAME	ACEEHHIPRRSU	HIRE PURCHASE
ACEEFIORRRST	REFRACTORIES	ACEEHHLMOSTT	LOSE THE MATCH
ACEEFIPRTTUV	PUTREFACTIVE	ACEEHHLNORSU	CHARNEL HOUSE
ACEEFKOOPRRW	WORK FOR PEACE	ACEEHHLORTTW	WEAR THE CLOTH
ACEEFLMNOOSY	FALSE ECONOMY	ACEEHHMOPRTY	CHEMOTHERAPY
ACEEFLMOPRRY	PLEA FOR MERCY	ACEEHHOPRSTU	CHAPTER HOUSE
ACEEFMNOPRRS	PERFORMANCES	ACEEHHORRSTU	CHARTERHOUSE
ACEEFNNORRTY	FORCE AN ENTRY	ACEEHHORSTTT	COST THE EARTH
ACEEFNOORSWY	FORCE ONE WAY	ACEEHIIKNSTT	KINAESTHETIC
ACEEFORSSTTU	REFUSES TO ACT	ACEEHIILNNOW	ONCE IN A WHILE
ACEEGGHLLPPR	GREG CHAPPELL	ACEEHIILNPST	ENCEPHALITIS
ACEEGGHHNNOST	GETS NO CHANGE	ACEEHIILRRTV	RICH RELATIVE
ACEEGGGILNRTT	GETTING CLEAR	ACEEHIIMOQPT	HAEMOPOIETIC
ACEEGHHILNST	TEACH ENGLISH	ACEEHIIMSSTT	AESTHETICISM
ACEEGHHIMNOR	REACHING HOME	ACEEHIINNRST	INHERITANCES
ACEEGHHNORSS	CHANGE HORSES	ACEEHIINORTT	THEORETICIAN
ACEEGHIKNNRT	KITCHEN RANGE	ACEEHIJNOSTT	CASE THE JOINT
ACEEGHIKNPTW	KEEPING WATCH	ACEEHIKKLOST	LIKE HOT CAKES
ACEEGHIKNSTV	GIVEN THE SACK	ACEEHIKKMTTY	TAKE THE MICKY
ACEEGHIKSSTV	GIVES THE SACK	ACEEHIKLLPTT	LICK THE PLATE
ACEEGHILNOSU	CHAISE LONGUE	ACEEHIKMPSTT	PICKS THE TEAM
ACEEGHILNRTW	CARTWHEELING	ACEEHIKPRSST	ASKS THE PRICE
ACEEGHINNORX	ION-EXCHANGER	ACEEHILLMRTY	HERMETICALLY
ACEEGHINNRST	INTERCHANGES	ACEEHILLNRST	INCHES TALLER
ACEEGHINOPTT	PATHOGENETIC	ACEEHILLSTTT	TILT THE SCALE
ACEEGHINORRV	OVERREACHING	ACEEHILPPRTU	PUPIL TEACHER
ACEEGHIRRSST	CASH REGISTER	ACEEHILPRSTY	PHYLACTERIES
ACEEGHKLORRS	GREEK SCHOLAR	ACEEHILPSSTT	TIP THE SCALE
ACEEGHLLNSSY	CHANGELESSLY		TIPS THE SCALE
ACEEGHLOPSST	CLOSES THE GAP	ACEEHIMNNRTW	WINE MERCHANT
ACEEGHMNNORY	MONEY CHANGER	ACEEHIMNPSSU	HUMAN SPECIES
ACEEGHNOPSTX	POST EXCHANGE	ACEEHIMNSSTT	CHASTISEMENT
ACEEGHOORSTT	GO TO THE RACES	ACEEHIMRSSTV	CHRISTMAS EVE
ACEEGHORSTTT	ACTS TOGETHER	ACEEHINNOSST	INCHOATENESS
ACEEGHPRRRSU	SUPERCHARGER	ACEEHINNOSTU	ANCIENT HOUSE
ACEEGHPRRSSU	SUPERCHARGES	ACEEHINNRSTU	NEURASTHENIC
ACEEGIILLMNS	ANGELIC SMILE	ACEEHINORRST	HIRE AN ESCORT
ACEEGIILNNPT	PALINGENETIC	ACEEHINORUUV	NOUVEAU RICHE
ACEEGIILNSTV	EVANGELISTIC	ACEEHINPSTTT	PITCHES A TENT
ACEEGIIMMNNT	MAGNETIC MINE	ACEEHINRTTVY	IN THE VERY ACT
ACEEGIINNORX	ANOREXIGENIC	ACEEHINSSTTY	SYNAESTHETIC
ACEEGIINRSTV	EVISCERATING	ACEEHIOPRSST	SPIROCHAETES
ACEEGIIOTTVX	EXCOGITATIVE	ACEEHIORSTTW	SWEET CHARIOT
ACEEGIKKNPRT	KEEPING TRACK	ACEEHIPPRSTY	PAYS THE PRICE
ACEEGIKLNNSS	LACKING SENSE	ACEEHIPRSTTU	THERAPEUTICS
ACEEGIKMNRTT	TRACK MEETING	ACEEHIPRSTTW	CHEAP TWISTER
ACEEGIKNNRRV	NERVE-RACKING	ACEEHIRSSTTV	TSAREVITCHES
ACEEGILLLOOT	TELEOLOGICAL	ACEEHKKLNNRT	KENNETH CLARK
ACEEGILLLOTY	COLLEGIATELY	ACEEHKLLMORY	HOLY MACKEREL
ACEEGILMNOPT	MAGNETIC POLE	ACEEHKLLOSSW	SALLOW CHEEKS
ACEEGILNNRSY	ANGRY SILENCE	ACEEHKLOPRYY	HOCKEY PLAYER
ACEEGILNNSSU	ALEC GUINNESS	ACEEHKNOTTTU	TAKE THE COUNT

ACEEHKORRRSW	RESEARCH WORK
ACEEHKORSTTT	STROKE THE CAT
ACEEHLLMOSTY	HALLEYS COMET
ACEEHLLNSTTU	CALLS THE TUNE
ACEEHLLOORSV	SCHOOL-LEAVER
ACEEHLLOOSSV	LEAVES SCHOOL
ACEEHLLSTTWY	WATCHES TELLY
ACEEHLMNNOTU	LUNCHEON MEAT
ACEEHLNRSTTU	TURN THE SCALE
ACEEHLOORSTV	OVER THE COALS
ACEEHLOTTTTU	LET THE CAT OUT
ACEEHLPRSSUV	HAVE SCRUPLES
ACEEHMMNOSTT	MET ONE'S MATCH
ACEEHMNNOORT	MORE THAN ONCE
ACEEHMOORSTT	COMES TO EARTH
ACEEHNORRSTT	ON A STRETCHER
ACEEHNORRTWW	WEAR THE CROWN
ACEEHNORSSST	HAS NO SECRETS
ACEEHOPPRRRS	SHARECROPPER
ACEEHOPRSTTT	THE SPECTATOR
ACEEHORRSSTT	ORCHESTRATES
ACEEHORTTUUU	HAUTE COUTURE
ACEEIIILPSST	SPECIALITIES
ACEEIILLMMST	SEMIMETALLIC
ACEEIILLNRTV	VERTICAL LINE
ACEEIILLRTTV	VERTICILLATE
ACEEIILMORTT	METEORITICAL
ACEEIILNOSTZ	SECTIONALIZE
ACEEIILPSSSU	SPECIAL ISSUE
ACEEIIMMRSTT	MERISTEMATIC
ACEEIIMMNNORT	ENANTIOMERIC
ACEEIIMNNSTT	ANCIENT TIMES
ACEEIIMNPRSU	EPICUREANISM
ACEEIIMNNRRST	RECRIMINATES
ACEEIINNORST	CONTAINERISE
ACEEIINNORTZ	CONTAINERIZE
ACEEIINNRTUV	RENUNCIATIVE
ACEEIINORSTV	EVISCERATION
ACEEIINORSVV	VARICOSE VEIN
ACEEIINQRTTU	QUITE CERTAIN
ACEEIINRRRRT	CAIRN TERRIER
ACEEIINRRSTV	TRAIN SERVICE
ACEEIIOPSSVV	PASSIVE VOICE
ACEEIIPPRSTT	PERIPATETICS
	PRECIPITATES
ACEEIIPRRSSS	RAISES PRICES
ACEEIJORRSTT	TRAJECTORIES
ACEEIKKNOPST	TAKE ONES PICK
ACEEIKLNRSTT	LACK INTEREST
ACEEIKNNOOTT	TAKE NO NOTICE
ACEEIKNNRSTT	TENNIS RACKET
ACEEIKNOSSTT	SEASON TICKET
ACEEIKORRTVW	CREATIVE WORK
ACEEILLLNTTU	INTELLECTUAL
ACEEILLMMRSS	SMALL MERCIES
ACEEILLMNORY	CEREMONIALLY
ACEEILLMORTY	METEORICALLY
ACEEILLNNNTY	CENTENNIALLY
ACEEILLNNORT	CRENELLATION
ACEEILLNRSUV	SURVEILLANCE
ACEEILLOPRSS	SOLAR ECLIPSE
ACEEILLOPSTT	TOTAL ECLIPSE
ACEEILLORSTY	ESOTERICALLY
ACEEILLORTXY	EXOTERICALLY
ACEEILLRTTUY	RETICULATELY
ACEEILMMNPST	MISPLACEMENT
ACEEILMORRST	CALORIMETERS
ACEEILMPRSST	SPECIAL TERMS
ACEEILNNRRTU	INTERNUCLEAR
ACEEILNOPPRT	PERCEPTIONAL
ACEEILNOPRRT	PRECENTORIAL

ACEEILNOPRSS	PRECESSIONAL
ACEEILNORSSS	RECESSIONALS
ACEEILNRRSST	CENTRALISERS
ACEEILNRRSTZ	CENTRALIZERS
ACEEILNRSSTV	VERTICALNESS
ACEEILOPPRRT	PRECEPTORIAL
ACEEILOPPRSU	PILE UP A SCORE
ACEEILRRSSSU	SECULARISERS
ACEEILRRSSUZ	SECULARIZERS
ACEEILRTTVXY	EXTRACTIVELY
ACEEIMMMNNOTT	COMMITTEEMAN
ACEEIMMNNPRY	IMPERMANENCY
ACEEIMMNORST	COMMENTARIES
ACEEIMMNRSTT	MINCE MATTERS
ACEEIMMORSST	COMMISERATES
ACEEIMMOSSTT	MASTECTOMIES
ACEEIMNNNOTU	CEMENT A UNION
ACEEIMNNOPST	OPEN-CAST MINE
ACEEIMNOPSTV	COMPENSATIVE
ACEEIMNORSSX	CROSS-EXAMINE
ACEEIMNORSTT	ACTINOMETERS
ACEEIMOOPQRU	OPERA COMIQUE
ACEEIMOSSSTV	VASECTOMISES
ACEEIMOSSTVZ	VASECTOMIZES
ACEEINNNPRSS	PRINCESS ANNE
ACEEINNPRSTY	IN ANY RESPECT
ACEEINOORRTV	OVERREACTION
ACEEINOPPPRT	APPERCEPTION
ACEEINOPRRTU	RECUPERATION
ACEEINOPRSTT	INSPECTORATE
ACEEINOPSTTX	EXPECTATIONS
ACEEINOQRSTU	RACE QUESTION
ACEEINORRSSY	RECESSIONARY
ACEEINORRSTY	SECRETIONARY
ACEEINORSTVV	CONSERVATIVE
ACEEINRRSSTV	TRANSCEIVERS
ACEEIOOPRSTV	COOPERATIVES
ACEEIOPRSSUV	PRECIOUS VASE
ACEEIRSSSTTU	RESUSCITATES
ACEEJJKNOSSS	JESSE JACKSON
ACEEJKKMNOTY	MONKEY JACKET
ACEEKLLOPRSY	SPOKE CLEARLY
ACEEKLNNOSTU	TAKEN COUNSEL
ACEEKLNOSSTU	TAKES COUNSEL
ACEEKMNOPPSY	KEEPS COMPANY
ACEEKNNORSTW	WORKS CANTEEN
ACEELLMMNOPT	COMPLEMENTAL
ACEELLMOORWY	ROYAL WELCOME
ACEELLORSSSW	LOWER CLASSES
ACEELMMOSSUV	MOVES A MUSCLE
ACEELMNNORTU	NOMENCLATURE
ACEELMNOPSTT	CONTEMPLATES
ACEELMOPRRSU	COMES A PURLER
ACEELMORSSST	MALTESE CROSS
ACEELNOOPRST	COLEOPTERANS
ACEELNOOPRSU	PORCELANEOUS
ACEELNOPRRUW	NUCLEAR POWER
ACEELNOQSTTU	EQUAL CONTEST
ACEELNPRTTYY	PETTY LARCENY
ACEELNSSSSTT	TACTLESSNESS
ACEELORRSSTU	ALTERS COURSE
ACEELPPRSSSU	UPPER CLASSES
ACEELPSSTUUY	EUCALYPTUSES
ACEEMMMOORST	COMMEMORATES
ACEEMMNNOORST	COME ON STREAM
ACEEMMNNORSTU	COMMENSURATE
ACEEMNNNNOTU	ANNOUNCEMENT
ACEEMNNORRST	REMONSTRANCE
ACEEMNOOPRST	COMPARE NOTES
ACEEMNOOSSWY	COMES ONE'S WAY
ACEEMNPRSSTY	MANY RESPECTS

ACEEMOPRSTTY	SPERMATOCYTE	ACEFIILLRRTY	TERRIFICALLY
ACEEMORRRSTY	STORMY CAREER	ACEFIILNNOOT	LINE OF ACTION
ACEENNNORSTT	CANNON STREET	ACEFIILNOQTU	LIQUEFACTION
ACEENNOPRSTU	COUNTERPANES	ACEFIILORSTU	LATICIFEROUS
ACEENNORRSTV	CONTRAVENERS	ACEFIINOORTV	VOCIFERATION
ACEENOOSSTTV	CAST ONES VOTE	ACEFIINOPRTT	PETRIFACTION
ACEENOPRSTTX	EXPECTORANTS	ACEFIINOPSTT	PONTIFICATES
ACEENOPRSTUU	PERCUTANEOUS	ACEFIIRRTTVY	REFRACTIVITY
ACEENOPSSSTU	PUTS ONE'S CASE	ACEFIKLOPRSW	PICKS A FLOWER
ACEENORRSSWY	CRY ONES WARES	ACEFIKLOQRSU	FOR QUICK SALE
ACEENORSSTTW	CROWN ESTATES	ACEFIKLORSTV	ROCK FESTIVAL
ACEEOOPRRRTU	POOR CREATURE	ACEFILLNORSY	FORENSICALLY
ACEEOOPRRTTT	PROTECTORATE	ACEFILLORSUW	CAULIFLOWERS
ACEEORRSSTUW	WATERCOURSES	ACEFILMNOOTU	FINAL OUTCOME
ACEFFFFHIOST	CHIEF OF STAFF	ACEFILNNOOSS	CONFESSIONAL
ACEFFFFIORST	STAFF OFFICER	ACEFILOORSST	FAILS TO SCORE
ACEFFFINOORR	RAN FOR OFFICE	ACEFILOOSSTT	SLICE OF TOAST
ACEFFGHILNRS	CLIFF-HANGERS	ACEFIMOOPRRU	COME UP FOR AIR
ACEFFGHINRUU	CHAUFFEURING	ACEFINOPRTTU	PUTREFACTION
ACEFFGHOSTTU	CUT OFF THE GAS	ACEFINOPSTTU	STUPEFACTION
ACEFFGIIKNOT	TAKING OFFICE	ACEFINORRRTU	CURRENT OF AIR
ACEFFGIKNNOR	KING OF FRANCE	ACEFINOSSSTU	FACTIOUSNESS
ACEFFHIIPSTT	IF THE CAP FITS	ACEFIOORRSTV	VOCIFERATORS
ACEFFIIILLNO	OFFICIAL LINE	ACEFIOPPRRST	FAIR PROSPECT
ACEFFIIILMOS	SEMIOFFICIAL	ACEFKKLORSTU	STREAK OF LUCK
ACEFFIIILOVW	OFFICIAL VIEW	ACEFKLOOPSVW	PACK OF WOLVES
ACEFFIILPSST	SPIFFLICATES	ACEFKMNOORTT	TAKEN COMFORT
ACEFFIIORRST	CARRIES IT OFF	ACEFKMOORSTT	TAKES COMFORT
ACEFFIIRRRTV	RIVER TRAFFIC	ACEFKMORRSSY	ASKS FOR MERCY
ACEFFIKLLOTW	FALL OF WICKET	ACEFLLMOOPRW	CAMP FOLLOWER
ACEFFILNNSSU	FANCIFULNESS	ACEFLLOORSSU	FALSE COLOURS
ACEFGHHIKLOT	LACK OF HEIGHT	ACEFMOPRRRYY	PRAY FOR MERCY
ACEFGHHNRTTU	TAUGHT FRENCH	ACEGGGHIINNV	GIVING CHANGE
ACEFGHIINRTW	FIRE-WATCHING	ACEGGGINNORT	CONGREGATING
ACEFGHILOPRX	FLEXOGRAPHIC	ACEGGHHILNST	SLIGHT CHANGE
ACEFGHILPSST	SPACEFLIGHTS	ACEGGHINNORV	CHANGING OVER
ACEFGHINORRS	SEARCHING FOR	ACEGGHINNPST	CHANGING STEP
ACEFGHORRSUU	ROUGH SURFACE	ACEGGHINORRV	OVERCHARGING
ACEFGIIILNTT	FELICITATING	ACEGGIINNOPR	RACING PIGEON
ACEFGIIINPRX	FIXING A PRICE	ACEGGIINORST	CATEGORISING
ACEFGIIKNNRV	CARVING KNIFE	ACEGGIINORTV	GRATING VOICE
ACEFGIILLNOT	LEGAL FICTION	ACEGGIINORTZ	CATEGORIZING
ACEFGIINORTV	VOCIFERATING	ACEGGIINOTTX	EXCOGITATING
ACEFGIKLLNTY	FLYING TACKLE	ACEGGILLLOOY	GEOLOGICALLY
ACEFGILLNPSU	PULLING FACES	ACEGGILNNOOT	COOLING AGENT
ACEFGILNPRTY	FLYING CARPET	ACEGGILNNORV	GLANCING OVER
ACEFGILNRSUY	FLYING SAUCER	ACEGGIMNNORY	GYROMAGNETIC
ACEFGINORSSS	SAFE CROSSING	ACEGGINNOORT	CONGREGATION
ACEFHHIILSTT	HITCHES A LIFT	ACEGGIORSUZZ	ZIGZAG COURSE
ACEFHHMNORTT	TENTH OF MARCH	ACEGHHIILNPS	IN HIGH PLACES
ACEFHIIMNRTU	FRUIT MACHINE	ACEGHHIILOPR	HELIOGRAPHIC
ACEFHIKOSSWY	CASE OF WHISKY	ACEGHHIILRRT	RIGHT CHARLIE
ACEFHILOSSVW	CLASH OF VIEWS	ACEGHHILNOTU	HEALING TOUCH
ACEFHIPRRSTT	FIRST CHAPTER	ACEGHHILRSST	SEARCHLIGHTS
ACEFHJMNNOOR	JOHN FRANCOME	ACEGHHINOPRT	ETHNOGRAPHIC
ACEFHKNOSTTW	KNOW THE FACTS	ACEGHHINORSW	WEIGHS ANCHOR
ACEFHKOOSSTT	STATE OF SHOCK	ACEGHHINRSTV	SERVING HATCH
ACEFHLNOPSTY	PLENTY OF CASH	ACEGHHIOPRRR	CHIROGRAPHER
ACEFHLNSSTUW	WATCHFULNESS	ACEGHHLORTTU	CLEAR THOUGHT
ACEFHNORSTTU	COUNTERSHAFT	ACEGHHNORSST	SHORTCHANGES
ACEFHNPRRSTY	FRENCH PASTRY	ACEGHHNSTTUU	CAUGHT THE SUN
ACEFHOOPRSST	SHORT OF SPACE	ACEGHHOOPRRS	CHOREOGRAPHS
ACEFIIIILLNV	CIVILIAN LIFE	ACEGHHOOPRRY	CHOREOGRAPHY
ACEFIIILNOST	FICTIONALISE	ACEGHIILLNYY	HYGIENICALLY
ACEFIIILNOTT	FELICITATION	ACEGHIILNNNS	CHANNELISING
ACEFIIILNOTZ	FICTIONALIZE	ACEGHIILNNNZ	CHANNELIZING
ACEFIIINORTV	VERIFICATION	ACEGHIIMNOTV	HAVE IT COMING
ACEFIILLMNTV	FALLEN VICTIM	ACEGHIIMNSST	SCHEMATISING
ACEFIILLNNOT	INFLECTIONAL	ACEGHIIMNSTZ	SCHEMATIZING
ACEFIILLNPRS	FALL IN PRICES	ACEGHIIMOTTW	ATOMIC WEIGHT
	FALLS IN PRICE	ACEGHIKNPRTT	CARPET KNIGHT

ACEGHILLNNOU	HALLUCINOGEN	ACEGILLNRTTY	CLATTERINGLY
ACEGHILLNOOT	ETHNOLOGICAL	ACEGILLOOPRT	PETROLOGICAL
ACEGHILMNSST	SINGLES MATCH	ACEGILLOORRR	LOGICAL ERROR
ACEGHILNNNTY	ENCHANTINGLY	ACEGILMMOPSY	OLYMPIC GAMES
ACEGHILNPSSY	PLAYING CHESS	ACEGILNNPRSS	SPRING-CLEANS
ACEGHILNRRTW	NIGHT CRAWLER	ACEGILNOOPRT	ORGANOLEPTIC
ACEGHILNSSST	NIGHT CLASSES	ACEGILNOORTW	WATER-COOLING
ACEGHILOPRXY	LEXICOGRAPHY	ACEGILNOOSST	CASTING LOOSE
ACEGHILRTTXY	EXACTLY RIGHT	ACEGILNORRSS	CAROL SINGERS
ACEGHIMNOORS	COMING ASHORE	ACEGILNOSSTY	STAYING CLOSE
ACEGHIMNOPRS	SCRAPING HOME	ACEGILNRSTTY	SCATTERINGLY
ACEGHIMOPTTY	GAMETOPHYTIC	ACEGILOOPSST	ESCAPOLOGIST
ACEGHIMORRRT	METRORRHAGIC	ACEGILORSTTU	GESTICULATOR
ACEGHINOOPRR	ICONOGRAPHER	ACEGIMMNNOTT	COMMENTATING
ACEGHINOPRST	STENOGRAPHIC	ACEGIMNNOPSS	ENCOMPASSING
ACEGHINORSTU	SEARCHING OUT	ACEGIMNNOPST	COMPENSATING
ACEGHINORTVW	WATCHING OVER	ACEGIMNNORSU	COUSIN GERMAN
ACEGHINPRSTU	PUTS IN CHARGE	ACEGIMNNORSTU	SCREAMING OUT
ACEGHIOPPRRR	REPROGRAPHIC	ACEGINNNORTV	CONTRAVENING
ACEGHIOPPRRT	PETROGRAPHIC	ACEGINOORTTU	OUTER COATING
ACEGHIORRSST	RAGS TO RICHES	ACEGINORRRVY	CARRYING OVER
ACEGHMNOOTTU	COME TO NAUGHT	ACEGINORSSSU	GRACIOUSNESS
ACEGHMOOPRRS	COSMOGRAPHER	ACEGINORSTTU	GUT REACTIONS
ACEGHNOOPRSU	NECROPHAGOUS	ACEGIORRTTVY	GREAT VICTORY
ACEGHNOORSUW	SHOWN COURAGE	ACEGIOSSSTTW	SWISS COTTAGE
ACEGHOORSSUW	SHOWS COURAGE	ACEGLMNNOOOW	COME ALONG NOW
ACEGHOPPRRST	SPECTROGRAPH	ACEGLMNORTYY	LARYNGECTOMY
ACEGHRSSSTTU	CUTS THE GRASS	ACEGLMOOPSTY	GLOOMY ASPECT
ACEGIILLMTY	ILLEGITIMACY	ACEGLNNORSTY	LONG ANCESTRY
ACEGIIILNPSS	SPECIALISING	ACEGLNORSTUY	GRANULOCYTES
ACEGIIILNPSZ	SPECIALIZING	ACEGLNOSSSUU	GLAUCOUSNESS
ACEGIIINNNRT	INCINERATING	ACEGLOORSUUY	COURAGEOUSLY
ACEGIIINNTTY	ANTIGENICITY	ACEGMMNORSTU	GERMAN CUSTOM
ACEGIIKLMMSS	SALES GIMMICK	ACEGMOPRRSST	SPECTROGRAMS
ACEGIIKLNNSY	ASKING NICELY	ACEGNNORSTTU	SUGAR CONTENT
ACEGIIKLNOPS	LACKING POISE	ACEGNOPRTTUU	GOT A PUNCTURE
ACEGIIKNNOTT	TAKING NOTICE	ACEHHIINOPRT	HIEROPHANTIC
ACEGIILLLOTY	COLLEGIALITY	ACEHHILLPRST	CHEAP THRILLS
ACEGIILLMOOS	SEMIOLOGICAL	ACEHHILMOPTX	EXOPHTHALMIC
ACEGIILLNNSW	LICENSING LAW	ACEHHILOOPST	THEOSOPHICAL
ACEGIILLOOPT	GEOPOLITICAL	ACEHHILOPTTY	HYPOTHETICAL
ACEGIILLOSTY	EGOISTICALLY	ACEHHIMNPRST	MERCHANT SHIP
ACEGIILNNOST	SINGLE-ACTION	ACEHHIMNSTTW	WINS THE MATCH
ACEGIILNNOTY	CONGENIALITY	ACEHHIMOOOPT	HOMOEOPATHIC
ACEGIILNNRST	CENTRALISING	ACEHHINOPSSS	HAS ONE'S CHIPS
ACEGIILNNRSY	INCREASINGLY	ACEHHIRSSSTY	HAS HYSTERICS
ACEGIILNNRTZ	CENTRALIZING	ACEHHKNNOOTV	ANTON CHEKHOV
ACEGIILNPRSS	ALICE SPRINGS	ACEHHKOPRSTY	SHOCK THERAPY
ACEGIILNPTXY	EXCITING PLAY	ACEHHLLOSSTT	CALL THE SHOTS
ACEGIILNRSSU	SECULARISING	ACEHHLOOPRTY	ORTHOCEPHALY
ACEGIILNRSUZ	SECULARIZING	ACEHHNOOSTTU	AUTOCHTHONES
ACEGIILNSTWY	ACTING WISELY	ACEHIIINRSTZ	CHRISTIANIZE
ACEGIILORSSU	SACRILEGIOUS	ACEHIILMNNTT	ANTHELMINTIC
ACEGIIMNNTTUY	MUTAGENICITY	ACEHIILNORRT	RICH RELATION
ACEGIINNPPRT	APPRENTICING	ACEHIILNOTVY	INCHOATIVELY
ACEGIINNPRST	INTERSPACING	ACEHIILNPPRS	PLANISPHERIC
ACEGIINOOTTX	EXCOGITATION	ACEHIIMSSSST	SCHISMATISES
ACEGIINOPRSV	RASPING VOICE	ACEHIIMSSSTZ	SCHISMATIZES
ACEGIINOQTUV	EQUIVOCATING	ACEHIINORRST	RHETORICIANS
ACEGIJLMNPRU	JUMPING CLEAR	ACEHIINPRRST	PRE-CHRISTIAN
ACEGIKLLNSSS	CLINK GLASSES	ACEHIINSSTTU	ENTHUSIASTIC
ACEGIKLMNNOY	LACKING MONEY	ACEHIINTTTUY	AUTHENTICITY
ACEGIKLNOOPP	COOKING APPLE	ACEHIIOPSSTT	SOPHISTICATE
ACEGIKLNORSS	CROSS-LINKAGE	ACEHIIPPRRST	PERIPHRASTIC
ACEGIKNOQRTU	QUICK TO ANGER	ACEHIKMMNSTU	MUCH MISTAKEN
ACEGIKNORSST	ORANGE-STICKS	ACEHIKMNOSST	MACKINTOSHES
ACEGILLMOOTY	ETYMOLOGICAL	ACEHIKMNRRSS	SCRIMSHANKER
ACEGILLNNOTY	CONGENITALLY	ACEHIKRSSSTW	CATS WHISKERS
ACEGILLNOORU	NEUROLOGICAL	ACEHILLMNOPY	PHONEMICALLY
ACEGILLNORSY	EARLY CLOSING	ACEHILLNOPST	PLAIN CLOTHES
ACEGILLNRSYY	SYNERGICALLY	ACEHILLNOPTY	PHONETICALLY

ACEHILLNOPUY	EUPHONICALLY	ACEIIKNNPRSW	PICKS A WINNER
ACEHILLOPRUY	EUPHORICALLY	ACEIIKNORSTT	STRIKE ACTION
ACEHILLOPSTT	COATS THE PILL	ACEIILLLLPTY	ELLIPTICALLY
ACEHILLORRTY	RHETORICALLY	ACEIILLLNSUV	ALL-INCLUSIVE
ACEHILLRSTYY	HYSTERICALLY	ACEIILLMNSST	MISCELLANIST
ACEHILMNOOST	MACHINE TOOLS	ACEIILLNOOSS	COLONIALISES
ACEHILNNNSSS	CLANNISHNESS	ACEIILLNOOSZ	COLONIALIZES
ACEHILNOPPTY	PHENOTYPICAL	ACEIILLNORSW	WILLIE CARSON
ACEHILOOPRST	THE ACROPOLIS	ACEIILLNORTY	COLLINEARITY
ACEHILPPRSTY	HYPERPLASTIC	ACEIILLNPPRS	NAIL CLIPPERS
ACEHIMNNOOPP	OPEN CHAMPION	ACEIILLNSSTT	SCINTILLATES
ACEHIMOOOSTT	HOMOEOSTATIC	ACEIILMMNRST	MERCANTILISM
ACEHIMOORTTY	ATOMIC THEORY	ACEIILMNNOPR	NOMINAL PRICE
ACEHIMOPRSST	ATMOSPHERICS	ACEIILMNOSST	SECTIONALISM
ACEHIMORSTTT	THERMOSTATIC	ACEIILMNPRTY	CRIMINAL TYPE
ACEHINNRTTTW	TRENCHANT WIT	ACEIILMNRSTT	MERCANTILIST
ACEHINOPRRSS	CHAIRPERSONS	ACEIILMNRTTU	METRICAL UNIT
ACEHINOPRRTT	TRICHOPTERAN	ACEIILMOPRRT	POLARIMETRIC
ACEHINORSSTU	CUTS ONE'S HAIR	ACEIILMOPRST	SEMITROPICAL
ACEHINOTTTUW	WITHOUT A CENT	ACEIILNNNRTU	INTERNUNCIAL
ACEHIOPRRSTT	ORCHESTRA PIT	ACEIILNNORRS	CORN IN ISRAEL
ACEHIOSTTUUW	WITHOUT CAUSE	ACEIILNNORSS	IRONICALNESS
ACEHIRSSTTWW	WRISTWATCHES	ACEIILNOPRST	REPLICATIONS
ACEHKMNOOTTU	TAKEN TOO MUCH	ACEIILNORTTU	RETICULATION
ACEIIKMOOSTTU	TAKES TOO MUCH	ACEIILNPRTVY	PLAINTIVE CRY
ACEHKMRRSSTT	STRETCH MARKS	ACEIILNRSSTT	CLARINETISTS
ACEHKNOPRTTU	PUT ON THE RACK	ACEIILNRSTTT	CLARINETTIST
ACEIILLLLORST	CALLS THE ROLL	ACEIILNRSTTU	NEUTRALISTIC
ACEHLLLPRSUY	SEPULCHRALLY	ACEIILNRSTVV	CIVIL SERVANT
ACEHLLMORSYY	LACHRYMOSELY	ACEIILOQTUVY	EQUIVOCALITY
ACEHLLNOPTWY	PLAY THE CLOWN	ACEIILPRSSST	PLASTICISERS
ACEHLLORRSTY	ORCHESTRALLY	ACEIILPRSSTZ	PLASTICIZERS
ACEHLMMNOOTW	COMMONWEALTH	ACEIILRRSSTU	SURREALISTIC
ACEHLMNOORSY	CLOSE HARMONY	ACEIILRRSTWY	WRITES A LYRIC
ACEHLMOORSST	SCHOOLMASTER	ACEIILRRTTTY	RETRACTILITY
ACEHLMORSSTT	SMART CLOTHES	ACEIILRSTUVY	VESICULARITY
ACEHLNOPRSTY	LYCANTHROPES	ACEIIMMMPRUX	MAXIMUM PRICE
ACEHLNOSSSTT	LESS THAN COST	ACEIIMMORSTW	COMMIS WAITER
ACEHLOOPSTUY	POLYCHAETOUS	ACEIIMNNORSS	MICRONESIANS
ACEHLOPSSUXY	PSYCHOSEXUAL	ACEIIMNORSST	ROMANTICISES
ACEHMMNOOOORT	COME TO NO HARM	ACEIIMNORSTZ	ROMANTICIZES
ACEHMMNORRRY	MERRY MONARCH	ACEIIMNOSTYZ	ISOENZYMATIC
ACEHMMOPSTTY	EMPTY STOMACH	ACEIIMNPTTUY	PNEUMATICITY
ACEHMNOORRST	SHORT ROMANCE	ACEIIMNRSSTU	INSECTARIUMS
ACEHMNORRRTT	TRENCH MORTAR	ACEIIMNSSSTT	SEMANTICISTS
ACEHMOOPPTUY	HAPPY OUTCOME	ACEIINNNORTU	RENUNCIATION
ACEHMOPRRSTT	PROTEST MARCH	ACEIINNNRSTU	ANCIENT RUINS
ACEHOOORSTTW	CARE TWO HOOTS	ACEIINNORRST	INCINERATORS
ACEHOORRRSTT	ORCHESTRATOR	ACEIINOOQTUV	EQUIVOCATION
ACEHOPSSSTTY	PAYS THE COSTS	ACEIINOPRRTT	PRACTITIONER
ACEHOPTTTTUU	PUT OUT THE CAT	ACEIINOPRSTT	CREPITATIONS
	PUT THE CAT OUT	ACEIINOPRSTU	PERTINACIOUS
ACEHORRSTTTX	SHORT EXTRACT	ACEIINORRSTW	CONTRARIWISE
ACEIIILNSVZ	CIVILIANIZES	ACEIINORSSTT	CREATIONISTS
ACEIIIKNNNPS	PICKANINNIES	ACEIINORTTUX	EXCRUTIATION
ACEIIILLRSTT	LITERALISTIC	ACEIINPRSTTY	ANTIPYRETICS
ACEIIILMNPSU	MUNICIPALISE	ACEIIOPPRRTT	PRECIPITATOR
ACEIIILMNPUZ	MUNICIPALIZE	ACEIJLNOOPRT	PROJECTIONAL
ACEIIILNORTV	VICTORIA LINE	ACEIJNNNOTTY	JOINT TENANCY
ACEIIILNPRTT	IN TRIPLICATE	ACEIKKLNNSTY	KILKENNY CATS
ACEIIILNSTTY	INELASTICITY	ACEIKKOPRTUY	TAKE YOUR PICK
ACEIIILRSTTV	RELATIVISTIC	ACEIKKRRSSTT	KICK-STARTERS
ACEIIILRSTVV	REVIVALISTIC	ACEIKLLMNSTY	MENTALLY SICK
ACEIIIMNNRST	INCRIMINATES	ACEIKLMORRSW	WORK MIRACLES
ACEIIINNNORT	INCINERATION	ACEIKLOORRSW	SOCIAL WORKER
ACEIIJLLSTUY	JESUITICALLY	ACEIKMNOSTTU	MAKES IT COUNT
ACEIIKKMQSTU	MAKES IT QUICK	ACEIKMOOPRRT	PATRICK MOORE
ACEIIKKMSSTT	MAKES IT STICK	ACEIKMOPRRTW	PATRICK MOWER
ACEIIKKNORTY	KARYOKINETIC	ACEIKNNORSST	IN ONE'S TRACKS
ACEIIKLLOORS	KILOCALORIES	ACEIKNOPTTUU	PICK OUT A TUNE
ACEIIKMRSSST	MISSES A TRICK	ACEIKOOPRRTW	OPERATIC WORK

ACEIKORRRTTT	TRICK OR TREAT
ACEILLLORRSW	LEWIS CARROLL
ACEILLLRSTTW	WILL SCARLETT
ACEILLMMNNOY	MNEMONICALLY
ACEILLMNOOPX	COMPLEXIONAL
ACEILLMORTUY	MOLECULARITY
ACEILLMSSTYY	SYSTEMICALLY
ACEILLMTUUVY	CUMULATIVELY
ACEILLNNOOSS	COLONIALNESS
ACEILLNOOPTV	PLATONIC LOVE
ACEILLNORTUY	NEUROTICALLY
ACEILLOOPPRT	POLICE PATROL
ACEILLOOSUVY	VIOLACEOUSLY
ACEILLOPTUVY	COPULATIVELY
ACEILLRRSSTY	CRYSTALLISER
ACEILLRRSTUU	SERICULTURAL
ACEILLRRSTYZ	CRYSTALLIZER
ACEILLRSSSTY	CRYSTALLISES
ACEILLRSSTTY	CRYSTALLITES
ACEILMMMNOSS	COMMENSALISM
ACEILMMNOSSU	COMMUNALISES
ACEILMMNOSUZ	COMMUNALIZES
ACEILMNNOOPT	COMPONENTIAL
ACEILMNOOPTY	COME INTO PLAY
ACEILMNOPSTU	ACT ON IMPULSE
ACEILNNNOOTV	CONVENTIONAL
ACEILNNNOSTT	CONTINENTALS
ACEILNNOORSV	CONVERSIONAL
ACEILNNORTTY	CERTAINLY NOT
ACEILNNOSSTU	CUT ONES NAILS
ACEILNOOPRSS	PROCESSIONAL
ACEILNOOPRTZ	TROPICAL ZONE
ACEILNOORSTV	VIOLET CARSON
ACEILNOORTUY	ELOCUTIONARY
ACEILNORSSTU	SOCIAL UNREST
ACEILNORSTUV	COUNTERVAILS
ACEILNORSUXY	EXCLUSIONARY
ACEILNOSSSWX	COXSWAINLESS
ACEILNOSTTUV	CONSULTATIVE
ACEILOOPPRSS	POLARISCOPES
ACEILOOPRRTY	CORPOREALITY
ACEILOPRRSUY	PRECARIOUSLY
ACEILORSSUVY	SOCIAL SURVEY
ACEILRRSSSTY	CRYSTALISERS
ACEILRRSSTYZ	CRYSTALIZERS
ACEIMMNOSTUV	CONSUMMATIVE
ACEIMMORRSTU	CREMATORIUMS
ACEIMNNNRSTU	INNER SANCTUM
ACEIMNNOOPRT	NO IMPORTANCE
ACEIMNNOOPST	COMPENSATION
ACEIMNNOOTUY	CAUTION MONEY
ACEIMNOOOOPT	ONOMATOPOEIC
ACEIMNOOOPTT	COME TO A POINT
ACEIMNOOSTWY	SOCIETY WOMAN
ACEIMNORSSTV	CONSERVATISM
ACEIMNOSTTUV	NATIVE CUSTOM
ACEIMNSSTTUY	UNSYSTEMATIC
ACEIMOOPPPST	OPPOSITE CAMP
ACEIMOOSTUUV	CAUTIOUS MOVE
ACEIMOPRSSTU	COME UPSTAIRS
ACEIMORRTTUV	VICTOR MATURE
ACEIMPRRRSTW	WRITERS CRAMP
ACEIMPRSSSTU	SUPREMACISTS
ACEINNOORSTV	CONSERVATION
	CONVERSATION
ACEINNORRSST	CONTRARINESS
ACEINNORRTUY	RENUNCIATORY
ACEINNORSTTU	ENCRUSTATION
ACEINOOOOPRSV	SOPRANO VOICE
ACEINOOPRRST	INCORPORATES
ACEINOOPRSST	SCORES A POINT

ACEINOPPRRTU	PORT AU' PRINCE
ACEINOPRSTTX	TAX INSPECTOR
ACEINOPSSSSU	SPACIOUSNESS
ACEINOPSSSTU	CAPTIOUSNESS
ACEINORRSSTU	RAN ITS COURSE
ACEINOSSSTUU	CAUTIOUSNESS
ACEIOOPRRRRT	TROOP CARRIER
ACEIOPSTTUUY	CAUTIOUS TYPE
ACEIORRSSTTU	RESUSCITATOR
ACEJKOPRSSTT	SPORTS JACKET
ACEKKLNOPTTU	TAKEN POT LUCK
ACEKKLOPSTTU	TAKES POT LUCK
ACEKLNNOORTT	TAKEN CONTROL
ACEKLNOORSTT	TAKES CONTROL
ACEKMMMNOORT	COMMON MARKET
ACEKNOORTTTU	TAKEN TO COURT
ACEKOORSTTTU	TAKES TO COURT
ACELLLMPSSUU	PULLS A MUSCLE
ACELLNNOOPRT	CONTROL PANEL
ACELLNNOSSUY	CONSENSUALLY
ACELLNNOTUVY	CONVENTUALLY
ACELLNOTTUXY	CONTEXTUALLY
ACELLOOPRSTU	PASTEL COLOUR
ACELMMNOORWY	COMMON LAWYER
ACELMMNOSTUY	CONSUMMATELY
ACELMNOOPRTT	CONTEMPLATOR
ACELMOPRRSTU	MARCEL PROUST
ACELNNOORSTY	ROYAL CONSENT
ACELNNORSTVY	CONVERSANTLY
ACELNNRSSUUU	RANUNCULUSES
ACELNOOPRSTU	PROCONSULATE
ACELNOORSTTT	STATE CONTROL
ACELNOSSSTTU	SANSCULOTTES
ACELNRRSSSUY	NURSERY CLASS
ACELOOPRSSTU	PLOTS A COURSE
ACELOORRSTUW	WATER COLOURS
	WATERCOLOURS
ACELOPRRSTTU	COURT PLASTER
ACEMMNOOPRRY	COMMON PRAYER
ACEMMNOORSTT	COMMENTATORS
ACEMMNOPRSTT	COMPARTMENTS
ACEMNOOPRRTY	CONTEMPORARY
ACEMNOOPRSST	COMPENSATORS
ACEMNOOPRSTY	COMPENSATORY
ACEMNOORTTUY	TOM COURTENAY
ACEMOOOPSSTT	COMES TO A STOP
ACEMORSSSTTU	SCOUTMASTERS
ACENNOORRTTU	RAN COUNTER TO
ACENNOORRTYY	TORREY CANYON
ACENNOORSTTU	TURN ONE'S COAT
ACENOOQRTTTU	QUATTROCENTO
ACENOORRSSTV	CONSERVATORS
ACENOORRSTVY	CONSERVATORY
ACENOPRRSSUU	RUNS UP A SCORE
ACENOPRRSTTU	COUNTERPARTS
ACENORRSTTVY	CONVERTS A TRY
ACFFFHHIMORT	FIFTH OF MARCH
ACFFFIILMOOR	OFFICIAL FORM
ACFFGHHIIILO	HIGH OFFICIAL
ACFFGHIILRTT	TRAFFIC LIGHT
ACFFGIILLNOT	CALLING IT OFF
ACFFGIINRSST	SCARING STIFF
ACFFHIIKLNOS	LACK OF FINISH
ACFFHIMORRST	FIRST OF MARCH
ACFFIIILLOST	OFFICIAL LIST
ACFFIIMOPRTU	OPIUM TRAFFIC
ACFFMOOORRTY	RAY OF COMFORT
ACFGGHIMNORR	FROGMARCHING
ACFGHIIKMNSS	FISHING SMACK
ACFGHILLNORT	CALLING FORTH
ACFGHILMNOOP	GOLF CHAMPION

ACFGIIKNSSTT	STICKING FAST
ACFGIINOPTTU	FACING UP TO IT
ACFGIKLLNORS	FALLING ROCKS
ACFHHIMNNORT	NINTH OF MARCH
ACFHHIMORSTX	SIXTH OF MARCH
ACFHIIIMNOTU	HUMIFICATION
ACFHIILLORRY	HORRIFICALLY
ACFHIILOPRST	TROPICAL FISH
ACFHIINOORSU	CUSHION OF AIR
ACFHIKLLOOPS	LACK OF POLISH
ACFHILLOOSTY	ACT FOOLISHLY
ACFHILNNOOST	INFANT SCHOOL
ACFHILSTTUWY	FAULTY SWITCH
ACFHIOOPRSTW	ACT OF WORSHIP
ACFIIIINNOTV	VINIFICATION
ACFIIIINOTVV	VIVIFICATION
ACFIIILMOSST	SOCIAL MISFIT
ACFIIILNOTTY	FICTIONALITY
ACFIIINNNSTY	IN ITS INFANCY
ACFIIINNOOTT	NOTIFICATION
ACFIIINOOSST	OSSIFICATION
ACFIIINOPRTU	PURIFICATION
ACFIIINOPTTY	TYPIFICATION
ACFIIKLOPRST	LACK OF SPIRIT
ACFIILLLOPRY	PROLIFICALLY
ACFIILLNOPTY	PONTIFICALLY
ACFIILNORTVY	FINAL VICTORY
ACFIILNPSSTU	CUP FINALISTS
ACFIILOSTTUY	FACTITIOUSLY
ACFIIMNNOORT	CONFIRMATION
ACFIIMNOOSTU	ATOMIC FUSION
ACFIINNOORST	FORNICATIONS
ACFIINOOPRTT	PONTIFICATOR
ACFIINORRTTU	TRIFURCATION
ACFIIOPRRTUY	PURIFICATORY
ACFIKKPSSSUU	KICKS UP A FUSS
ACFILLNNOTUY	FUNCTIONALLY
ACFILMNNOSTU	MALFUNCTIONS
ACFILMNOOORT	ROMANTIC FOOL
ACFILMNOTUYY	COUNTY FAMILY
ACFILNOSTTUU	FLUCTUATIONS
ACFIMNNOOORT	CONFORMATION
ACFIMNOORRTY	CONFIRMATORY
ACFINOOPRTUU	UP FOR AUCTION
ACFJKMOPRSTU	JACK OF TRUMPS
ACFLLMMOORST	SMALL COMFORT
ACFLNNOOOSTY	COLONY OF ANTS
ACGGHIIINNNV	GIVING AN INCH
ACGGHIMNNOOR	CHANGING ROOM
ACGGHIMNNORS	MARCHING SONG
ACGGIILLOOST	GLACIOLOGIST
ACGGINRSSTTU	CUTTING GRASS
ACGHHIILNSTW	CLASHING WITH
ACGHHIILOPRT	LITHOGRAPHIC
ACGHHINOOPPR	PHONOGRAPHIC
ACGHHIOOPPRT	PHOTOGRAPHIC
ACGHHIOOPRRT	ORTHOGRAPHIC
ACGHHNOOPRRY	CHRONOGRAPHY
ACGHHOORTTUY	THROATY COUGH
ACGHHORRRTUY	CARRY THROUGH
ACGHIIKLNPTU	CHALKING IT UP
ACGHIIKMNNOS	CHAIN SMOKING
	CHAIN-SMOKING
ACGHIIKNSSTV	SHAVING STICK
ACGHIILLLOOP	PHILOLOGICAL
ACGHIILLLOOT	LITHOLOGICAL
ACGHIILLOOST	HISTOLOGICAL
ACGHIILMNPST	ITCHING PALMS
ACGHIILNNORT	CHLORINATING
ACGHIINNNOST	STANCHIONING
ACGHIINPPTTU	PATCHING IT UP
ACGHIINPRSTY	SCINTIGRAPHY
ACGHIIOPPRRS	SPIROGRAPHIC
ACGHIKLRSTTU	STRUCK A LIGHT
ACGHIKNOOSTW	WHATS COOKING?
ACGHILLMOOTY	MYTHOLOGICAL
ACGHILLNOOOP	PHONOLOGICAL
ACGHILLOOPRS	OSCILLOGRAPH
ACGHILNOSSTT	CASTS LIGHT ON
ACGHIMMNOOPR	PHONOGRAMMIC
ACGHIMMNOORT	COMING TO HARM
ACGHINOOPPRR	PORNOGRAPHIC
ACGHIOOPSSTY	PHAGOCYTOSIS
ACGHKLOPPUYY	HAPPY-GO-LUCKY
ACGHLNOORSTU	LAUGH TO SCORN
ACGHOOOPPRSU	COPROPHAGOUS
ACGHOPPRRTYY	CRYPTOGRAPHY
ACGIIIILLNST	ILLICIT GAINS
ACGIIIKNSTTT	STICKING AT IT
ACGIIILLLOTY	ILLOGICALITY
ACGIIILNPRTT	TRIPLICATING
ACGIIINNOTTX	INTOXICATING
ACGIIKLNNOOP	PLAIN COOKING
ACGIIKLNORST	LOSING A TRICK
ACGIIKMNPRST	STRIKING CAMP
ACGIILLLMNOO	LIMNOLOGICAL
ACGIILLLOSTY	LOGISTICALLY
ACGIILLLRTUY	LITURGICALLY
ACGIILMNNOST	COMING IN LAST
ACGIILMNOSUU	MUCILAGINOUS
ACGIILNNOSTU	INOSCULATING
ACGIILNOOPRY	ORIGINAL COPY
ACGIILNOORST	ORIGINAL COST
ACGIILNPPRTX	CRIPPLING TAX
ACGIILNPPSTU	SUPPLICATING
ACGIILNRSSTY	CRYSTALISING
ACGIILNRSTYZ	CRYSTALIZING
ACGIINNNORST	CONSTRAINING
ACGIINNOOOTT	GO INTO ACTION
ACGIINNOOSST	TOSSING A COIN
ACGIINNOPSTT	CONSTIPATING
ACGIJNNOOSTU	CONJUGATIONS
ACGIKLNNORSS	CLOSING RANKS
ACGIKLNORSSW	WORKING CLASS
	WORKING-CLASS
ACGIKMNNNRUU	RUNNING AMUCK
ACGIKNNNRRTU	RUNNING TRACK
ACGILLLOOOYZ	ZOOLOGICALLY
ACGILLOOOPRT	TROPOLOGICAL
ACGILNNOORST	GAINS CONTROL
ACGILNOOSTUY	CONTAGIOUSLY
ACGIMMNNOOSY	COMMON SAYING
ACGIMMNNOSTU	CONSUMMATING
ACGIMNOOPRTU	COMPURGATION
ACGIMNOOPSST	COMING TO PASS
ACGIMNOORSSV	MOVING ACROSS
ACGIMNOOSTTY	COMING TO STAY
ACGIMOORSSTU	MOST GRACIOUS
ACGINOORRSTU	CORRUGATIONS
ACGINORRSUWY	CAUSING WORRY
ACGLLNOORSUY	CLANGOROUSLY
ACGMNOOPRRTU	COMPURGATORS
ACGMOOPRSTUY	CRYPTOGAMOUS
ACHHIIINNNTW	WITHIN AN INCH
ACHHIILMNOPR	PHILHARMONIC
ACHHIIMNOPPS	CHAMPIONSHIP
ACHHIIMOSTYZ	SCHIZOTHYMIA
ACHHIINOPTTW	AT WHICH POINT
ACHHILLMRTYY	RHYTHMICALLY
ACHHILLOPTTY	THALLOPHYTIC
ACHHILOOPRSS	PARISH SCHOOL
ACHHILOOPRST	HOLOPHRASTIC

ACHHILOPRSSS	SCHOLARSHIPS
ACHHIORSSTUY	ICHTHYOSAURS
ACHHIORSTTWW	THROW A SWITCH
ACHHLOOOORRSW	HARROW SCHOOL
ACHHNNOPRTUW	THROWN A PUNCH
ACHHNOPRSTUW	THROWS A PUNCH
ACHIIILMSTWY	WHIMSICALITY
ACHIIIMNPSSU	MUSICIANSHIP
ACHIIINRSTTY	CHRISTIANITY
ACHIIKLNOTTY	LAY IT ON THICK
ACHIILLORSTY	HISTORICALLY
ACHIILNNOORT	CHLORINATION
ACHIIMNOPRST	MISANTHROPIC
ACHIINOPRSTT	ANTISTROPHIC
ACHIIOPRSSTT	PAST HISTORIC
ACHIIPRSSTTY	PSYCHIATRIST
ACHILLNOORSY	ISOCHRONALLY
ACHILLNOPTYY	HYPNOTICALLY
ACHILLORSUVY	CHIVALROUSLY
ACHILMOOSSST	SCHISTOSOMAL
ACHILNOORRST	CHLORINATORS
ACHILNO⊦SUUV	UNCHIVALROUS
ACHILOOOPTTV	PHOTOVOLTAIC
ACHIMNOOPRTY	ACTINOMORPHY
ACHIMOPPSSSS	SHIPS COMPASS
ACHINNORSTTU	TURN INTO CASH
ACHINOPRSSTY	CORNISH PASTY
ACHIOOPRRSUZ	RHIZOCARPOUS
ACHIOPRSSSTY	ASTROPHYSICS
ACHKLMOOSTTU	TALKS TOO MUCH
ACHLLMNOOORS	NORMAL SCHOOL
ACHLMOOPRSST	CHROMOPLASTS
ACHLNOSSTTUY	STAYS TO LUNCH
ACHMNNOPSSUY	SHUNS COMPANY
ACHMNOOPRTTU	HAMPTON COURT
ACHNNOORSSUY	ASYNCHRONOUS
ACHNOOORSTTW	CROWNS A TOOTH
ACIIIILMRSTT	MILITARISTIC
ACIIIILNOSTV	CIVILISATION
ACIIIILNOTVZ	CIVILIZATION
ACIIILMNNOST	NOMINALISTIC
ACIIILMNOPST	IMPLICATIONS
ACIIILMNPTUY	MUNICIPALITY
ACIIILMNRSTU	CRIMINAL SUIT
ACIIILNNNOST	INCLINATIONS
ACIIILNOOSTT	COALITIONIST
	SOLICITATION
ACIIILNOPRTT	TRIPLICATION
ACIIILNOTVVY	CONVIVIALITY
ACIIILNPPRTY	PRINCIPALITY
ACIIILQTUYZZ	QUIZZICALITY
ACIIINNOOTTX	INTOXICATION
ACIIINOPSSUU	INAUSPICIOUS
ACIIINOQSSTU	ACQUISITIONS
ACIIJLLRSTUY	JURISTICALLY
ACIIJLNORSTU	JOURNALISTIC
ACIIKKKNPSTU	KICK UP A STINK
ACIIKLLOPSTT	TALK POLITICS
ACIIKNOPSTTU	PUT A SOCK IN IT
ACIIKNRSSTTU	STICKS IN A RUT
ACIIKORRSTTW	ARTISTIC WORK
ACIIILNOOSST	COLONIALISTS
	OSCILLATIONS
ACIIILNORTTY	TINCTORIALLY
ACIILLOOPSTY	ISOTOPICALLY
ACIILLOQTUXY	QUIXOTICALLY
ACIILLOSSUVY	LASCIVIOUSLY
ACIILLQSSTTU	CALLS IT QUITS
ACIILLRTTUUV	VITICULTURAL
ACIILMNOOPST	COMPILATIONS
ACIILMOPRTUV	VICTORIA PLUM
ACIILMOPRTUY	MILITARY COUP
ACIILNNOOOST	COLONISATION
ACIILNNOOOTZ	COLONIZATION
ACIILNNOOSTU	INOSCULATION
ACIILNNOPRSS	CLAPS IN IRONS
ACIILNNOSTUY	INSOUCIANTLY
ACIILNOORSST	CONSISTORIAL
ACIILNOPPSTU	SUPPLICATION
ACIILNORSSSS	NAIL SCISSORS
ACIILOOPSTTY	APOSTOLICITY
ACIILOPSSUUY	AUSPICIOUSLY
ACIILPRSTTUU	APICULTURIST
ACIIMNOPRTTU	PROTACTINIUM
ACIINNNOOTTU	CONTINUATION
ACIINNNOSSTU	ACTS IN UNISON
ACIINNOOPSTT	CONSTIPATION
ACIINNORSTTU	INCRUSTATION
ACIKKLLQSUWY	WALKS QUICKLY
ACIKLLNPPRTY	PRICKLY PLANT
ACILLLLOOQUY	COLLOQUIALLY
ACILLMNNOPSU	SPINAL COLUMN
ACILLMNNOORTY	MICROTONALLY
ACILLMNOSUUY	CALUMNIOUSLY
ACILLMORSUUY	MIRACULOUSLY
ACILLNOORTTW	TO CROWN IT ALL
ACILLNOPSTYY	SYNOPTICALLY
ACILLNPPSTUY	SUPPLICANTLY
ACILLOOQSUUY	LOQUACIOUSLY
ACILLPRRSTUY	SCRIPTURALLY
ACILMMNNOOTT	NONCOMMITTAL
ACILMMNOSSTU	COMMUNALISTS
ACILMNOOOPST	COSMOPOLITAN
ACILMOOPPRST	PROTOPLASMIC
ACILMOORRTVY	MORAL VICTORY
ACILMOPPRSUU	POPULAR MUSIC
ACILNNNNOSTY	INCONSTANTLY
ACILNNOOOSST	CONSOLATIONS
ACILNNOOSTTU	CONSULTATION
ACILOOPPRSTT	PROTOPLASTIC
ACILOPPRSTUY	SUPPLICATORY
ACILORSSSTTU	TOURIST CLASS
ACIMMNNOOSTU	CONSUMMATION
ACIMMNOOSTTU	COMMUTATIONS
ACIMNNOOOPRS	NO COMPARISON
ACIMNNORTTUY	COUNTY ANTRIM
ACIMNOOORSTU	AUCTION ROOMS
ACIMNOOPPRTT	PROMPT ACTION
ACIMNOOPPSST	COMPASS POINT
ACIMNOOPSTTU	COMPUTATIONS
ACIMNOOSSTVW	MONASTIC VOWS
ACINNNOOOSTT	CONNOTATIONS
ACINNOOPRSTT	CONTRAPTIONS
ACINNOOPSSTY	SYNCOPATIONS
ACINOOOPRRRT	INCORPORATOR
ACINOOOPRRST	CORPORATIONS
ACINOOOPRRTT	CROP ROTATION
ACINOOOPRSTV	PROVOCATIONS
ACINOOPRRSST	CONSPIRATORS
ACINOOPRRSTT	CARTOON STRIP
	STRIP CARTOON
ACINOOPRRSTU	PROCURATIONS
ACINOPPSSTTY	POSTSYNAPTIC
ACIOOPPRSSTT	POTATO CRISPS
ACIOOPRRSSTT	CORPORATISTS
ACIOPRSSSTTU	PUTS IT ACROSS
ACIORRRSSTTU	CIRROSTRATUS
ACKMNOOOOSTY	TOO MANY COOKS
ACKNNORSTTUW	WANTS NO TRUCK
ACKNOOORSTTU	COOKS TO A TURN
ACKOOOPRSTUY	COOK UP A STORY
ACLLLPRSTUUY	SCULPTURALLY

ACLLMNOORTUU	MONOCULTURAL
ACLLOOORRSUY	ROYAL COLOURS
ACLLRRSTTUUY	STRUCTURALLY
ACMMNOORSSTU	CONSUMMATORS
ACMNOPRSTTUY	TRUST COMPANY
ADDDDEEEHLMU	MUDDLEHEADED
ADDDDEEEHNRU	DUNDERHEADED
ADDDDEEFFILL	FIDDLE-FADDLE
ADDDEEEHHITT	DIED THE DEATH
ADDDEEEHNOOW	WOODENHEADED
ADDDEEFGILOO	DIED OF OLD AGE
ADDDEEFIOSTU	EISTEDDFODAU
ADDDEEGHINNR	HIDDEN DANGER
ADDDEEGIIKLO	DIED LIKE A DOG
ADDDEEGILLMN	MIDDLE AND LEG
ADDDEEHHINOT	ODD IN THE HEAD
ADDDEEIILNRV	LIVED IN DREAD
ADDDEEILORSS	DEAD SOLDIERS
ADDDEENNOSST	NODDED ASSENT
ADDDEENNOSSV	ODDS AND EVENS
ADDDEFGORRST	DRAFT DODGERS
ADDDEGINOPPR	DROPPING DEAD
ADDDEGLLNOOP	PLODDED ALONG
ADDDEHNRRSUY	HUNDRED YARDS
ADDDEIIINTUV	INDIVIDUATED
ADDDEIILLLLY	DILLY DALLIED
	DILLYDALLIED
ADDDEIINPSVY	PAY DIVIDENDS
ADDDEILNNNOS	DONALD SINDEN
ADDDFIKNNOOR	FOOD AND DRINK
ADDDGINOORTU	DID A GOOD TURN
ADDEEEEGGRST	DESEGREGATED
ADDEEEEHNPTT	AT THE DEEP END
ADDEEEEIPRSV	DEEP-SEA DIVER
ADDEEEELPRSY	SEEDED PLAYER
ADDEEEFGNNOR	GARDEN OF EDEN
ADDEEEFHILLT	LEAD THE FIELD
ADDEEEFHITTX	FIXED THE DATE
ADDEEEFHLNRY	FREEHANDEDLY
ADDEEEGIMNST	DEMAGNETISED
ADDEEEGIMNTZ	DEMAGNETIZED
ADDEEEGJLNRU	LEARNED JUDGE
ADDEEEGNOSWY	EDGED ONE'S WAY
ADDEEEGNOTXY	DEOXYGENATED
ADDEEEHHINOS	HIDE ONES HEAD
ADDEEEHHISTT	DIES THE DEATH
ADDEEEHINRST	DISHEARTENED
ADDEEEHKNOTW	WOKEN THE DEAD
ADDEEEHLNNVY	EVENHANDEDLY
ADDEEEHNOSSU	USED ONE'S HEAD
ADDEEEIKMRST	STRIKE ME DEAD!
ADDEEEILMNTY	DEMYELINATED
ADDEEEEILRTVY	DELIVERY DATE
ADDEEEILSSUX	DESEXUALISED
ADDEEEILSUXZ	DESEXUALIZED
ADDEEEIMPRTT	PREMEDITATED
ADDEEEINNRST	ENDED IN TEARS
ADDEEEIORRTT	DETERIORATED
ADDEEEIPPSST	STEPPED ASIDE
ADDEEEJNNRRW	EDWARD JENNER
ADDEEEKLNOOY	YANKEE DOODLE
ADDEEELNPTXY	EXTENDED PLAY
ADDEEELORRSS	SEALED ORDERS
ADDEEELPRSST	PLEATED DRESS
ADDEEELPRTUY	DEPUTY LEADER
ADDEEELRRTTY	RED-LETTER DAY
ADDEEEOPPRSV	EAVESDROPPED
ADDEEFFIOORV	DEVOID OF FEAR
ADDEEFFNRSTU	UNDERSTAFFED
ADDEEFGHOORT	GATHERED FOOD
ADDEEFGILLOS	LED A DOG'S LIFE
ADDEEFGILOOS	DIES OF OLD AGE
ADDEEFGINSTW	WEDDING FEAST
ADDEEFGNORRR	RED FOR DANGER
ADDEEFHHNOOT	NOD OF THE HEAD
ADDEEFHILNST	LEFT-HAND SIDE
ADDEEFHLLNTY	LEFT-HANDEDLY
ADDEEFHLMORY	FORMALDEHYDE
ADDEEFHLOSTY	SOFTHEADEDLY
ADDEEFHNOORT	END OF THE ROAD
ADDEEFHOORSW	FORESHADOWED
ADDEEFILNRUV	VALUED FRIEND
ADDEEFIMNRSY	FINDS A REMEDY
ADDEEFINOORR	FOREORDAINED
ADDEEFINORTW	DEAD OF WINTER
ADDEEFIRRRST	FREDDIE STARR
ADDEEFLLOPST	SOFT-PEDALLED
ADDEEFLNRSSU	DREADFULNESS
ADDEEFMNORUY	FOUND A REMEDY
ADDEEFGGHINRT	DIG THE GARDEN
ADDEEGGIINRTU	DUG THE GARDEN
ADDEEGHILNNS	SINGLE-HANDED
ADDEEGHKLOTW	WALKED THE DOG
ADDEEGHNORTY	HYDROGENATED
ADDEEGIIKLOS	DIES LIKE A DOG
ADDEEGIINRRT	RIDDEN A TIGER
ADDEEGILNNST	DISENTANGLED
ADDEEGILNPRW	PEARL WEDDING
ADDEEGINPPSU	PEASE PUDDING
ADDEEGLNNRTY	LANDED GENTRY
ADDEEGLPRRUY	GUARDED REPLY
ADDEEGMNNRTU	URGENT DEMAND
ADDEEGNORSTU	ADDER'S-TONGUE
ADDEEHHILNTW	HIDDEN WEALTH
ADDEEHHLLOST	HOLDS THE LEAD
ADDEEHHLNNOS	HELD ONE'S HAND
ADDEEHHNRSTU	THUNDERHEADS
ADDEEHIILPTV	PAID THE DEVIL
ADDEEHILNNTT	HIDDEN TALENT
ADDEEHIMNPRT	DEEP THIRD MAN
ADDEEHINORSY	DYED ONE'S HAIR
ADDEEHINORTV	HANDED IT OVER
ADDEEHIORTTT	TIRED TO DEATH
ADDEEHKNORRW	WORK-HARDENED
ADDEEHLNNOPY	OPENHANDEDLY
ADDEEHLNOOSS	SHED ONES LOAD
ADDEEHNNOOSS	NODS ONE'S HEAD
ADDEEHNRRSUY	HUNDRED YEARS
ADDEEHOORSVW	OVERSHADOWED
ADDEEHOPRRST	SPARED THE ROD
ADDEEIILNOPW	LAID WIDE OPEN
ADDEEIILNRSV	LIVES IN DREAD
ADDEEIILNSST	DESTALINISED
ADDEEIILNSTZ	DESTALINIZED
ADDEEIIMMNNO	DEMIMONDAINE
ADDEEIIMNRST	ADMINISTERED
ADDEEIIMNSST	DISSEMINATED
ADDEEIINSSTY	STAYED INSIDE
ADDEEIILLMNTT	LITTLE DEMAND
ADDEEIILLNPST	IT ALL DEPENDS
ADDEEIILLOPPT	DEEP-LAID PLOT
ADDEEIILNNPST	PADDLE TENNIS
ADDEEIILNOPPR	DROPPED A LINE
ADDEEIILNRSST	DESERT ISLAND
ADDEEIIMMNRST	MASTERMINDED
ADDEEIIMNNORV	DRIVEN ONE MAD
ADDEEIIMNOPRT	PREDOMINATED
ADDEEIIMNORSV	DRIVES ONE MAD
ADDEEIINNNSST	STANDS IN NEED
ADDEEILLMNORY	ENDODERMALLY
ADDEEILLPRSSU	ALL DRESSED UP
ADDEEMNORSTT	DEMONSTRATED

ADDEEMOOORSS	DO AS ROME DOES
ADDEENNORRSS	SENDS AN ORDER
ADDEENNORRUV	OVER AND UNDER
	UNDER AND OVER
ADDEENNOSSSY	ENDS ONE'S DAYS
ADDEENORRTTW	TRODDEN WATER
ADDEEOPRRSSS	PASSED ORDERS
ADDEEOQRTTUV	DOTTED QUAVER
ADDEFFGNNORS	GRAND SEND-OFF
ADDEFGILNORT	DRIFTED ALONG
ADDEFGILRRSU	DISREGARDFUL
ADDEFGLORRTU	ARTFUL DODGER
ADDEFHILNOOS	OLD FASHIONED
	OLD-FASHIONED
ADDEFHLNNOOT	THE LAND OF NOD
ADDEFHLOORTY	DAY OF THE LORD
ADDEFIIILQSU	DISQUALIFIED
ADDEFIIISSST	DISSATISFIED
ADDEFIIMNOSV	FIVE DIAMONDS
ADDEFILNPRSY	SPIDER AND FLY
ADDEFINORRSW	FIRE AND SWORD
ADDEFIORRRVW	DRIVE FORWARD
ADDEFLNNNOUW	NEWFOUNDLAND
ADDEFLNOOORU	FOOLED AROUND
ADDEFMOORRVW	MOVED FORWARD
ADDEFOORRRVW	DROVE FORWARD
ADDEGGGINOOT	DOG EATING DOG
ADDEGGHIILNU	DIED LAUGHING
ADDEGGHIOTTY	THE GIDDY GOAT
ADDEGGHLORSU	HOLDS A GRUDGE
ADDEGGHORSTU	GODDAUGHTERS
ADDEGGIINRRS	DISREGARDING
ADDEGGINNORU	GAINED GROUND
ADDEGGINOOTW	GO TO A WEDDING
ADDEGHHHILNY	HIGH-HANDEDLY
ADDEGHHORTUW	WADED THROUGH
ADDEGHIINRRT	THIRD READING
ADDEGHILNORT	DEAR OLD THING
ADDEGHINNOSS	HAD DESIGNS ON
ADDEGHINOOST	SHOOTING DEAD
ADDEGHINOOTT	DOING TO DEATH
ADDEGHINRTUY	DURING THE DAY
ADDEGHIORSTT	DEAD TO RIGHTS
ADDEGHLLNOPU	PLOUGHED LAND
ADDEGHNORSTU	DREADNOUGHTS
ADDEGIILNNQU	LENDING A QUID
ADDEGIILNNST	STANDING IDLE
ADDEGIINORSS	DISORGANISED
ADDEGIINORSZ	DISORGANIZED
ADDEGIKMORRT	MARGOT KIDDER
ADDEGIKNPSTU	STEAK PUDDING
ADDEGILMNOTU	DEMODULATING
ADDEGILNOPRS	SPRING-LOADED
ADDEGILNORWY	ROYAL WEDDING
ADDEGINNORTW	TREADING DOWN
ADDEGINOOSTT	TAINTED GOODS
ADDEGINOPPST	STOPPING DEAD
ADDEGIOPRSST	TRADED GOSSIP
ADDEGJJNRUUY	JUDGE AND JURY
ADDEGMMNNORST	STRONG DEMAND
ADDEGMNORTUU	MOUNTED GUARD
ADDEGNORRSSW	WRONG ADDRESS
ADDEHHLNNOOS	HOLD ONE'S HAND
ADDEHHLOORST	HOLDS THE ROAD
ADDEHHLORRSU	HARD SHOULDER
ADDEHHNOOTTU	HOUND TO DEATH
ADDEHHOSSTTW	WHATS THE ODDS?
ADDEHILNOSSU	HAD DELUSIONS
ADDEHILNOSTY	IN THE OLD DAYS
ADDEHILOSTTT	ADD TO THE LIST
ADDEHIMNORUY	MIND YOUR HEAD

ADDEHIMSSTTU	STUDIED MATHS
ADDEHINNORTW	DOWN THE DRAIN
ADDEHINOOPTT	PAID ON THE DOT
ADDEHINOPPRT	DROPPED A HINT
ADDEHNOORRSU	HORSED AROUND
ADDEHNOPRSUU	PUSHED AROUND
ADDEHOOORSST	DO AS OTHERS DO
ADDEIIINSTUV	INDIVIDUATES
ADDEIILLLLSY	DILLY DALLIES
	DILLYDALLIES
ADDEIILLLSVY	ILL-ADVISEDLY
ADDEIILLNPSS	SLIP AND SLIDE
ADDEIILLNSSV	DEVILS ISLAND
ADDEIILMSSTU	DISSIMULATED
ADDEIILNOTUV	INVALIDED OUT
ADDEIILPSSTY	DISSIPATEDLY
ADDEIINOPPST	DISAPPOINTED
ADDEIIPRRSST	RAPID STRIDES
ADDEIJMMRSWY	JIMMY EDWARDS
ADDEIKNORRRS	ORDERS A DRINK
ADDEILLNORRU	RALLIED ROUND
ADDEILMNOOTU	DEMODULATION
ADDEILMNOPRS	PROMISED LAND
ADDEILMNSSTW	WEST MIDLANDS
ADDEILNOOPSY	DEADLY POISON
ADDEIMMMRSUY	MIDSUMMER DAY
ADDEIMNNORRW	NARROW-MINDED
ADDEIMNOSTWW	WANTED WISDOM
ADDEIMOPSTUY	IMPOSED A DUTY
ADDEINNNRSUY	SUNDAY DINNER
ADDEINNOORRT	TRODDEN ON AIR
ADDEINNOOSST	ODD SENSATION
ADDEINNORRUV	DRIVEN AROUND
ADDEINOOPRST	POISONED DART
ADDEINORRSUV	DRIVES AROUND
ADDEINRRSUVY	SUNDAY DRIVER
ADDEKLNOOORU	LOOKED AROUND
ADDELMNOPRTW	TRAMPLED DOWN
ADDELMOORSTU	DEMODULATORS
ADDELNOOOSST	DO AS ONES TOLD
ADDEMNOOORST	RODOMONTADES
ADDEMOORSTVW	MOVED TOWARDS
ADDENNORRTUU	TURNED AROUND
ADDENNORSSWW	DOWNWARDNESS
ADDENOORSSTU	AS UNDERSTOOD
ADDENOPPRRUW	WRAPPED ROUND
ADDENOPPRSTW	STRAPPED DOWN
ADDFFIKOOSSV	DAVID KOSSOFF
ADDFHNNOOSUX	FOX AND HOUNDS
ADDFIILLNSUY	DISDAINFULLY
ADDFILLNOOTW	DONALD WOLFIT
ADDFIMNOORSU	FOUR DIAMONDS
ADDFLNNOOSTU	LOST AND FOUND
ADDFNNORSUUY	SOUND AND FURY
ADDGGGINNORW	DRAGGING DOWN
ADDGGHILNOOR	HOARDING GOLD
ADDGGHNOORUY	GROUNDHOG DAY
ADDGHHILNNOS	HOLDING HANDS
ADDGHIIKNNRR	HARD DRINKING
ADDGHILNORTY	THYROID GLAND
ADDGHIMNOORU	ROUGH DIAMOND
ADDGHINNNORU	HANDING ROUND
ADDGHINNOOTT	NOTHING TO ADD
ADDGHINPSTUY	HASTY PUDDING
ADDGHINRSTUY	STUDYING HARD
ADDGHNORSTUW	DOWNDRAUGHTS
ADDGIIILLNVW	DIVIDING WALL
ADDGIIINNOST	ADDITION SIGN
ADDGIKMNNOOS	MAKING NO ODDS
ADDGILLNOOPP	PADDLING POOL
ADDGKOOOOPRW	GOODWOOD PARK

ADDGKOOORSWY	GOOD DAYS WORK
ADDHHIORSTWW	HAD WORDS WITH
ADDHINNNOSWW	WIN HANDS DOWN
ADDHNNNOOSWW	WON HANDS DOWN
ADDIIILLNUVY	INDIVIDUALLY
ADDIIMNOSTWW	WIT AND WISDOM
ADDILLMOOSTY	TILL DOOMSDAY
ADEEEEEFLNOY	EYE OF A NEEDLE
ADEEEEEKLNVW	WEEK-END LEAVE
ADEEEEFGILNN	FEELING A NEED
ADEEEEGGLRTT	GET REGELATED
ADEEEEGGRSST	DESEGREGATES
ADEEEEGINRTV	DEGENERATIVE
ADEEEEGLMNRR	EMERALD GREEN
ADEEEEGLNRRT	GENTLE READER
ADEEEEGLNRTY	DEGENERATELY
ADEEEEHHNRRT	HERE AND THERE
ADEEEEHKNOPS	KEEP ONES HEAD
ADEEEEHKRTWY	THREE-DAY WEEK
ADEEEEKMMNST	MAKE ENDS MEET
ADEEEEERRSSTV	RESERVED SEAT
ADEEEFFFRSTU	SUFFER DEFEAT
ADEEEFFIINRT	DIFFERENTIAE
ADEEEFFORRST	REAFFORESTED
ADEEEFGHORRT	FOREGATHERED
ADEEEFGIKNNO	ON A KNIFE EDGE
ADEEEFGIRRRT	REFRIGERATED
ADEEEFGNORST	DRAG ONES FEET
ADEEEFHIKLTT	TAKE THE FIELD
ADEEEFHISTTX	FIXES THE DATE
ADEEEFHKOTWY	DAY OF THE WEEK
ADEEEFHMPRUY	HEADY PERFUME
ADEEEFHNORTY	END OF THE YEAR
ADEEEFILMOTT	FAILED TO MEET
ADEEEFINRSTT	REFINED TASTE
ADEEEFLNOSSV	SAVED ONESELF
ADEEEFMNPRTY	DEFER PAYMENT
ADEEEFMOQRUU	FORMED A QUEUE
ADEEEGGILNRT	TEENAGED GIRL
ADEEEGGINNRT	DEGENERATING
ADEEEGGKRRTY	GREEK TRAGEDY
ADEEEGGLMNNO	ONE-LEGGED MAN
ADEEEGGLORTT	GOT RELEGATED
ADEEEGHILMNT	HELD A MEETING
ADEEEGHLMMRS	SLEDGE-HAMMER
	SLEDGEHAMMER
ADEEEGHPRSST	GATHERS SPEED
ADEEEGIMNRST	DEMAGNETISER
	DISAGREEMENT
ADEEEGIMNRTZ	DEMAGNETIZER
ADEEEGIMNSST	DEMAGNETISES
ADEEEGIMNSTZ	DEMAGNETIZES
ADEEEGINNORT	DEGENERATION
ADEEEGINRRSV	READING VERSE
ADEEEGLNNRRT	GENERAL TREND
ADEEEGLNRSST	ELEGANT DRESS
ADEEEGLPRSTT	GET PLASTERED
ADEEEGMNNNRT	ENDANGERMENT
ADEEEGMPSTTU	GET STEAMED UP
ADEEEGNOSSWY	EDGES ONE'S WAY
ADEEEGNOSTXY	DEOXYGENATES
ADEEEGNSSTTW	WEST-END STAGE
ADEEEHHLORTW	WHOLEHEARTED
ADEEEHHMMMOR	HAMMERED HOME
ADEEEHHNNRTT	THEN AND THERE
	THERE AND THEN
ADEEEHHNNRWW	WHEN AND WHERE
	WHERE AND WHEN
ADEEEHIKNRST	SEE IN THE DARK
ADEEEHILNNSW	HEADLINE NEWS
	NEWS HEADLINE

ADEEEHILRSTW	RESTED AWHILE
ADEEEHILRTTV	VEILED THREAT
ADEEEHIMNRTT	HEREDITAMENT
	MATED IN THREE
ADEEEHINSSSV	ADHESIVENESS
ADEEEHINSTTZ	ANESTHETIZED
ADEEEHIRRSST	HEARTS DESIRE
ADEEEHLNOOSS	LOSE ONES HEAD
ADEEEHLNORSW	LEADS NOWHERE
ADEEEHLNSSSS	HEADLESSNESS
ADEEEHNNOOSY	HAD ONE'S EYE ON
ADEEEHNOORSV	OVER ONES HEAD
ADEEEHNORSTU	RENTED A HOUSE
ADEEEHNOSSSU	USES ONE'S HEAD
ADEEEHNPPTTU	UPPED THE ANTE
ADEEEHOPRTTU	POURED THE TEA
ADEEEHQRRSTU	THREE SQUARED
ADEEEIILMNRS	DEMINERALISE
ADEEEIILMNRZ	DEMINERALIZE
ADEEEIIMMORS	AIDES-MEMOIRE
ADEEEIIMMRST	SEMIDIAMETER
ADEEEIIMNRTT	INTERMEDIATE
ADEEEIINSTTT	DIE INTESTATE
ADEEEIJLLNUV	JUVENILE LEAD
ADEEEIKLMRVY	MAKE DELIVERY
ADEEEIKLRTVY	TAKE DELIVERY
ADEEEIKNOSST	TAKE ONE'S SIDE
ADEEEIILLMMOS	MADEMOISELLE
ADEEEILMMRSU	MEASURED MILE
ADEEEILMNORT	RADIOELEMENT
ADEEEILMNSTY	DEMYELINATES
ADEEEILNPRRT	INTERPLEADER
ADEEEILNRRTT	INTERRELATED
ADEEEILNRSTX	EXTERNALISED
ADEEEILNRTXZ	EXTERNALIZED
ADEEEILOSTUV	LEAVE OUTSIDE
ADEEEILRRRTW	LEADER WRITER
ADEEEILSSSUX	DESEXUALISES
ADEEEILSSUXZ	DESEXUALIZES
ADEEEIMMRSTU	MEASURED TIME
ADEEEIMNNOSS	EASE ONES MIND
ADEEEIMNRTTX	EXTERMINATED
ADEEEIMPRSTT	PREMEDITATES
ADEEEIMSTTVW	EMITTED WAVES
ADEEEINNSSTT	SEEN A DENTIST
ADEEEINPRRSV	NEVER DESPAIR
ADEEEINPRSTT	PREDESTINATE
ADEEEINPRSTW	IN DEEP WATERS
ADEEEINSSSTT	SEES A DENTIST
ADEEEIORRSTT	DETERIORATES
ADEEEKLLNOST	ENDOSKELETAL
ADEEEKLRRSST	DEERSTALKERS
ADEEEKOPPTTU	KEEP UP-TO-DATE
ADEEELMNNNOS	LEND ONE'S NAME
ADEEELMNNRSS	SLENDER MEANS
ADEEELNNOSUV	LEAVES UNDONE
ADEEELNOSSST	DESOLATENESS
ADEEELNRSSTT	SENDS A LETTER
ADEEELNRSTTU	LAUNDERETTES
ADEEELPPSSTW	STEWED APPLES
ADEEELPRTTTY	TYPED A LETTER
ADEEEMNORSST	MODERATENESS
ADEEEMORRSTV	OVERMASTERED
ADEEENNNORSS	NEARS ONE'S END
ADEEENOPPRRT	PREPONDERATE
ADEEENORSSSU	USED ONE'S EARS
ADEEENPPRRSS	PREPAREDNESS
ADEEENPRRTUV	PERADVENTURE
ADEEENPRRTUW	NEW DEPARTURE
ADEEENPRSSWY	SPEEDY ANSWER
ADEEENQRSSUV	SEVEN SQUARED

ADEEENRSSVYY	EVERYDAYNESS	ADEEFLLORUVW	WELL-FAVOURED
ADEEEOPPRRSV	EAVESDROPPER	ADEEFLMNRSSU	DREAMFULNESS
ADEEEPPRRTTX	PREPARED TEXT	ADEEFLMOSSTY	FALSE MODESTY
ADEEEQRSSTTU	SEQUESTRATED	ADEEFLMSSTUY	FEUDAL SYSTEM
ADEEERRRSTTT	STREET TRADER	ADEEFLNOOSSU	USED ONE'S LOAF
ADEEERSSSSTW	STEWARDESSES	ADEEFLNOTTTU	FLATTENED OUT
ADEEERSTUVYY	EVERY TUESDAY	ADEEFMORRSTT	TERMS OF TRADE
ADEEFFFINRRT	FAR DIFFERENT	ADEEFNNOOPRT	END OF PART ONE
ADEEFFGGORST	STAGGERED OFF	ADEEFNORSTUY	FOURTEEN DAYS
ADEEFFGINRSU	FINDS A REFUGE	ADEEFOOPRRTW	WATERPROOFED
ADEEFFGIRSTU	REFUSED A GIFT	ADEEFOPRSTUY	REFUSED TO PAY
ADEEFFGNORUU	FOUND A REFUGE	ADEEGGGIINNV	GIVING AN EDGE
ADEEFFHILOTW	FIELD OF WHEAT	ADEEGGHHIINT	GAINED HEIGHT
ADEEFFHINRTT	FIRE AND THEFT	ADEEGGHIRSTT	STRAIGHTEDGE
ADEEFFIILNRT	DIFFERENTIAL	ADEEGGIINNPS	GAINING SPEED
ADEEFFIOPSSV	FIVE OF SPADES	ADEEGGIINSTT	GETTING IDEAS
ADEEFFNOORST	FOREST OF DEAN	ADEEGGIKNPRU	KEEPING GUARD
ADEEFFOOPRTY	OFFERED TO PAY	ADEEGGILNNOU	GOLDEN GUINEA
ADEEFFORSTTW	WASTED EFFORT	ADEEGGINORSV	DIG ONES GRAVE
ADEEFGGIIOST	FOGGIEST IDEA	ADEEGGINRTTY	GETTING READY
ADEEFGGLLNUY	FULLY ENGAGED	ADEEGGIQRRSU	SQUARE-RIGGED
ADEEFGHHHIOR	HIGH FOREHEAD	ADEEGGIRRTTU	REGURGITATED
ADEEFGHILLPT	FILLED THE GAP	ADEEGGLNOPPR	DOPPELGANGER
ADEEFGHILNRS	HARD FEELINGS	ADEEGGLPRRUY	PLAYED RUGGER
ADEEFGHINRRZ	FREEZING HARD	ADEEGGNORSUV	DUG ONE'S GRAVE
ADEEFGHLNRTU	UNDER THE FLAG	ADEEGGORSSTY	ST.GEORGES DAY
ADEEFGIILLNN	FILLING A NEED	ADEEGHHILLNR	HIGHLAND REEL
ADEEFGILLSSS	FIELD GLASSES	ADEEGHHILRTT	LIGHTHEARTED
ADEEFGIMNNRU	ENDURING FAME	ADEEGHHLOSTT	HOLD THE STAGE
ADEEFGIMNNSU	MENDING A FUSE	ADEEGHIIRSTW	DISAGREE WITH
ADEEFGINNORW	DEAFENING ROW	ADEEGHILMNOT	HOLD A MEETING
ADEEFGINNRST	FREESTANDING	ADEEGHILNSTW	SWING THE LEAD
ADEEFGINOORR	GONE FOR A RIDE	ADEEGHILNSTY	SEEN DAYLIGHT
ADEEFGINORRT	FOREIGN TRADE	ADEEGHILSSTY	SEES DAYLIGHT
ADEEFGINRRST	GREAT FRIENDS	ADEEGHINNOSV	IN GOD'S HEAVEN
ADEEFGINRRSU	REFINED SUGAR	ADEEGHINNPPR	APPREHENDING
ADEEFGIOORRS	GOES FOR A RIDE	ADEEGHINNRRT	HEARTRENDING
ADEEFGLNORRW	FLOWER GARDEN	ADEEGHINOTUY	THE YOUNG IDEA
ADEEFGOORSTU	GOOD FEATURES	ADEEGHINPSTW	WIDENS THE GAP
ADEEFHHMOORS	HEADS FOR HOME	ADEEGHINRSST	READ THE SIGNS
ADEEFHIILLRT	FILLED THE AIR	ADEEGHINRSTT	STRAIGHTENED
ADEEFHIIRSTT	THE FIRST IDEA	ADEEGHINRTUY	RUEING THE DAY
ADEEFHILLNOT	LIE OF THE LAND	ADEEGHIQRSTU	EIGHT SQUARED
ADEEFHILLPTY	PLAY THE FIELD	ADEEGHLLMOOP	GALLOPED HOME
ADEEFHINORST	ON THE FAR SIDE	ADEEGHLLNNTY	HANDLE GENTLY
ADEEFHKLOPRS	ASKED FOR HELP	ADEEGHLNSTUW	SWUNG THE LEAD
ADEEFHLNOOST	ONE OF THE LADS	ADEEGHLOORST	LEATHER GOODS
ADEEFHLRRTUY	FURTHER DELAY	ADEEGHLORTVW	GAVE THE WORLD
ADEEFHMOORST	HEADFOREMOST	ADEEGHLRSSTU	DAUGHTERLESS
ADEEFHOORRSW	FORESHADOWER	ADEEGHMOPPRS	DEMOGRAPHERS
ADEEFHOORTTZ	FROZE TO DEATH	ADEEGHNNOOTT	DONE THE TANGO
ADEEFIILMOTV	DEVIL OF A TIME	ADEEGHNNPRSW	GRANDNEPHEWS
ADEEFIILNNRU	END IN FAILURE	ADEEGHNOOOST	GO TO ONES HEAD
ADEEFIILNOPS	FINAL EPISODE	ADEEGHNOOSTT	DOES THE TANGO
ADEEFIKMNRSS	MAKES FRIENDS	ADEEGHNOPRTU	ON THE UP GRADE
ADEEFILLORVY	FIRED A VOLLEY		ON THE UPGRADE
ADEEFILMOOTV	FAILED TO MOVE	ADEEGHNORRST	HAD NO REGRETS
ADEEFILMOSSV	DEVIL OF A MESS	ADEEGHNORSTY	HYDROGENATES
ADEEFILMRSUU	FLUID MEASURE	ADEEGHOPRRSW	HEDGE SPARROW
ADEEFILNNORU	FEDERAL UNION	ADEEGHORRTTW	DRAW TOGETHER
ADEEFILNPRSU	FIND PLEASURE	ADEEGHPRSTTU	STEPDAUGHTER
ADEEFILOPRRT	PROLIFERATED	ADEEGIILNORS	REGIONALISED
ADEEFILORSUY	DAY OF LEISURE	ADEEGIILNORZ	REGIONALIZED
ADEEFIMNPTXY	FIXED PAYMENT	ADEEGIILNTUV	LEAVING TO DIE
ADEEFIMNRSST	MET AS FRIENDS	ADEEGIILNSTV	GIVEN DETAILS
ADEEFINNOPSS	NINE OF SPADES	ADEEGIILSSTV	GIVES DETAILS
ADEEFINORRTW	WENT FOR A RIDE	ADEEGIIMNNRR	REMAINDERING
ADEEFINRRSTW	WATER-FINDERS	ADEEGIINNNRT	EATING DINNER
ADEEFKMOORRS	ASKED FOR MORE	ADEEGIINNRSW	SENDING A WIRE
ADEEFLLMORWY	MY DEAR FELLOW	ADEEGIINRSST	RINGSIDE SEAT
ADEEFLLNORTY	LEARNED TO FLY	ADEEGIINRSTT	DISINTEGRATE

ADEEGIINSSTT	SETTING ASIDE
ADEEGIINSTTV	INVESTIGATED
ADEEGIJNNRWW	WANDERING JEW
ADEEGIKLLRST	GRILLED STEAK
ADEEGIKLNRSS	GREEK ISLANDS
ADEEGIKMMOOT	MAKE GOOD TIME
ADEEGIKNNNQU	KING AND QUEEN
ADEEGIKNNRRT	KINDERGARTEN
ADEEGILLNRVW	DRAWING LEVEL
ADEEGILNNOOS	IN ONES OLD AGE
ADEEGILNNSST	DISENTANGLES
ADEEGILORRST	GREAT SOLDIER
ADEEGINNNOSS	GAIN ONES ENDS
	GAINS ONE'S END
ADEEGINNORRV	GIVEN AN ORDER
ADEEGINNORSX	GRIND ONES AXE
ADEEGINNORUV	ENDEAVOURING
ADEEGINNRRTW	WINTER GARDEN
ADEEGINORRSV	GIVES AN ORDER
ADEEGINORRTT	INTERROGATED
ADEEGIOOPPTT	GOOD APPETITE
ADEEGIOPRRTV	PREROGATIVED
ADEEGIRRSSTT	GREAT STRIDES
ADEEGJMNSTTU	JUDGMENT SEAT
ADEEGKNNNRSU	SUNKEN GARDEN
ADEEGLLMNNOT	OLD GENTLEMAN
ADEEGLLMNRSS	SMELLS DANGER
ADEEGLLNORRR	GARDEN ROLLER
ADEEGLLNPRSS	SPELLS DANGER
ADEEGLLRRSSY	REGARDLESSLY
ADEEGLMNNRRY	MERRY ENGLAND
ADEEGLMNOSSS	GLADSOMENESS
ADEEGLNNOPRU	ENLARGED UPON
ADEEGLNORRTW	GARDEN TROWEL
ADEEGLOPRSTT	GOT PLASTERED
ADEEGLORRRTY	RETROGRADELY
	ROGER DALTREY
ADEEGMNNOOOS	ONE'S GOOD NAME
ADEEGMNNRRTU	UNDERGARMENT
ADEEGMNOORTV	MOVED TO ANGER
ADEEGMNRRRSY	GERRYMANDERS
ADEEGMOPSTTU	GOT STEAMED UP
ADEEGNPRTUUX	UNEXPURGATED
ADEEGNRRSSST	TRANSGRESSED
ADEEGNRSTUWY	GETS UNDER WAY
ADEEHHHINOTT	HIT ON THE HEAD
ADEEHHHKOOST	SHOOK THE HEAD
ADEEHHIKNRRS	HEAD SHRINKER
	HEADSHRINKER
ADEEHHILSSTT	HEADS THE LIST
ADEEHHILTTVW	WHAT THE DEVIL
ADEEHHILTTWY	DEATHLY WHITE
ADEEHHINOTVW	HAVE DONE WITH
ADEEHHLLNOST	DONE THE HALLS
ADEEHHLLOSST	DOES THE HALLS
ADEEHHLNSSTT	THE SHETLANDS
ADEEHHLORRSS	SHAREHOLDERS
ADEEHHMNOOSU	HOUSE AND HOME
ADEEHHNNNOOT	ON THE ONE HAND
ADEEHHNOOPSU	HAD OPEN HOUSE
ADEEHHNOSTUU	HAUNTED HOUSE
ADEEHHNPPRTU	THE UPPER HAND
ADEEHHOOSTTT	STOOD THE HEAT
ADEEHHOSTWWY	SHOWED THE WAY
ADEEHIILRRTY	HEREDITARILY
ADEEHIIMNTTY	IN THE DAYTIME
ADEEHIINNRSS	RISE AND SHINE
ADEEHIINRSTW	RAISE THE WIND
ADEEHIIPPPRT	PAID THE PIPER
ADEEHIKNRRVY	HEAVY DRINKER
ADEEHILLMPTY	YIELD THE PALM
ADEEHILLPSTW	WITH ALL SPEED
ADEEHILMORTT	MAITRE DHOTEL
ADEEHILNNRTW	DRAWN THE LINE
ADEEHILNOSTW	DOWN THE AISLE
ADEEHILNOTTV	VIOLENT DEATH
ADEEHILNRSTW	DRAWS THE LINE
ADEEHILPSTVY	PAYS THE DEVIL
ADEEHIMNPPRS	MISAPPREHEND
ADEEHIMRTUXY	HEADY MIXTURE
ADEEHINNOORS	DONE ONE'S HAIR
ADEEHINNOSST	TANS ONE'S HIDE
	TIE ONES HANDS
ADEEHINNOSYY	IN ONES HEYDAY
ADEEHINOORSS	DOES ONE'S HAIR
ADEEHINOPSTT	THE ANTIPODES
ADEEHINORSTU	HOUSE TRAINED
	HOUSETRAINED
ADEEHINRRSST	TEAR IN SHREDS
ADEEHINRRSTV	HIRED SERVANT
ADEEHINRTWWY	WINDY WEATHER
ADEEHIOSTTTU	AT THE OUTSIDE
ADEEHIRRRSSS	HAIRDRESSERS
ADEEHIRRTTWY	DIRTY WEATHER
ADEEHIRSSSSU	ISSUED SHARES
ADEEHIRSSTTU	RAISE THE DUST
ADEEHKLNOOPT	DONE THE POLKA
ADEEHKLOOPST	DOES THE POLKA
ADEEHKLOOPYY	PLAYED HOOKEY
ADEEHKNNRRST	RENDER THANKS
ADEEHKOPRSTW	SPEAK THE WORD
ADEEHKRSTUWY	THURSDAY WEEK
ADEEHLLORRST	THREE DOLLARS
ADEEHLMMOTUY	MEALY-MOUTHED
ADEEHLMNORTW	MEAN THE WORLD
ADEEHLMNOTWW	MOWED THE LAWN
ADEEHLNOSTTW	SHOWED TALENT
ADEEHLNOTTWZ	DONE THE WALTZ
ADEEHLOSTTWZ	DOES THE WALTZ
ADEEHLPPRSSU	PEDAL PUSHERS
ADEEHMMOOPSU	HOME-MADE SOUP
ADEEHMNNOSSS	HANDSOMENESS
ADEEHNNORSTU	TURN ONES HEAD
	UNDER ONES HAT
ADEEHNNOSSSU	USE ONES HANDS
ADEEHNOOSSST	TOSS ONES HEAD
ADEEHNOOSTTT	STONE TO DEATH
ADEEHNORRSTT	TETRAHEDRONS
ADEEHNORSTTY	STONYHEARTED
ADEEHNOSTTTY	STAY TO THE END
ADEEHNSSTTTT	STAND THE TEST
ADEEHOPRRTTW	THE TOP DRAWER
ADEEHORRSSTT	TEAR TO SHREDS
ADEEHORSTTTU	STOUTHEARTED
ADEEIIILMRST	DEMILITARISE
ADEEIIILMRTZ	DEMILITARIZE
ADEEIIILMTTV	DELIMITATIVE
ADEEIIILNNTW	WAITED IN LINE
ADEEIIILORST	EDITORIALISE
ADEEIIILORTZ	EDITORIALIZE
ADEEIIIMNNPR	INDIAN EMPIRE
ADEEIIJNOORR	RIO DE JANEIRO
ADEEIIKLNRSS	LIKE SARDINES
ADEEIIILNTVY	EVIDENTIALLY
ADEEIIILMMNST	LIMITED MEANS
ADEEIIILMNNSS	MAIDENLINESS
ADEEIIILMTTVY	MEDITATIVELY
ADEEIIILNNRST	INTERNALISED
ADEEIIILNNRTZ	INTERNALIZED
ADEEIIILNORTY	EARLY EDITION
ADEEIIILNPRST	PRESIDENTIAL
ADEEIIILNSSST	DESTALINISES

ADEEIILNSSTZ	DESTALINIZES
ADEEIILRTVVY	DERIVATIVELY
ADEEIIMNNOTV	DENOMINATIVE
ADEEIIMNRRRT	INTERMARRIED
ADEEIIMNSSST	DISSEMINATES
ADEEIIMOPRTV	PAID OVERTIME
ADEEIINNNRSV	DRIVEN INSANE
ADEEIINNRSSV	DRIVES INSANE
ADEEIINNRTUV	DIVINE NATURE
ADEEIINORSTT	DISORIENTATE
ADEEIINORTTX	EXTRA EDITION
ADEEIINOSSTV	VIDEO NASTIES
ADEEIINPRSSS	DISPENSARIES
ADEEIINPRSTT	PAID INTEREST
ADEEIINRRTVW	WATER DIVINER
	WATER-DIVINER
ADEEIIOPRSST	DEPOSITARIES
ADEEIJLNRSUW	JULIE ANDREWS
ADEEIKLMOSST	OLD TIMES' SAKE
ADEEIKLNPSTW	WALKED IN STEP
ADEEIKLORTTV	TALKED IT OVER
ADEEIKLPRSTT	PLEATED SKIRT
ADEEIKMNRSSS	SEMIDARKNESS
ADEEIKMRSSST	MAKES STRIDES
ADEEIKNORSTY	ONE-DAY STRIKE
ADEEIKNRRRSS	SERRIED RANKS
ADEEILLMRTUY	MULTILAYERED
ADEEILLMSTUW	WELL-MADE SUIT
ADEEILLNNOOS	ALL ON ONE SIDE
ADEEILLNNRST	LANTERN SLIDE
ADEEILLOSTVW	OLD WIVES TALE
ADEEILLRSTVY	LAST DELIVERY
ADEEILMMORTY	IMMODERATELY
ADEEILMNOPTT	MODEL PATIENT
ADEEILMNRRWY	NEWLY MARRIED
ADEEILMNTTTU	MULTIDENTATE
ADEEILMPRSST	SLIPSTREAMED
ADEEILMSSTTU	ASSUMED TITLE
ADEEILNNORST	IRON AND STEEL
ADEEILNNPSTY	PLAYED TENNIS
ADEEILNNPTUY	PLAYED IN TUNE
ADEEILNOPPRT	LEPIDOPTERAN
ADEEILNOPRSS	PERSONALISED
ADEEILNOPRSZ	PERSONALIZED
ADEEILNOPRTT	INTERPOLATED
ADEEILNOPSWY	LAYS WIDE OPEN
ADEEILNORRST	LEARNS TO RIDE
ADEEILNORRTT	LEARNT TO RIDE
ADEEILNORRTV	LEARN TO DRIVE
ADEEILNRRSTY	RESTRAINEDLY
ADEEILNRSSTW	SLENDER WAIST
ADEEILNRSTWY	EASTERLY WIND
ADEEILOPRRSS	DEPOLARISERS
ADEEILOPRRSZ	DEPOLARIZERS
ADEEILPRSSXY	DAILY EXPRESS
ADEEILPSTTTY	PETTY DETAILS
ADEEIMMMPSUX	MAXIMUM SPEED
ADEEIMMNNOTY	TIME AND MONEY
ADEEIMMNORSU	MISDEMEANOUR
ADEEIMNNNOWW	WINE AND WOMEN
ADEEIMNNRSTT	DETERMINANTS
ADEEIMNOPRST	IMPERSONATED
	PREDOMINATES
ADEEIMNOSSUV	DEVIOUS MEANS
ADEEIMNRSTUV	MISADVENTURE
ADEEIMOPRRTT	PREMEDITATOR
ADEEIMOSSVWY	MOVE SIDEWAYS
ADEEIMSSSTTY	SYSTEMATISED
ADEEIMSSTTYZ	SYSTEMATIZED
ADEEINNOOPRU	INDO-EUROPEAN
ADEEINNOPRSW	DREW A PENSION

ADEEINNRRSTU	TRAINED NURSE
	UNRESTRAINED
ADEEINNSSSTU	UNSTEADINESS
ADEEINPRRSUV	NURSED A VIPER
ADEEINSSTTTU	UNITED STATES
ADEEIOPPRRTX	EXPROPRIATED
ADEEIOSTTTUW	SWEATED IT OUT
ADEEIPSTTTTU	APTITUDE TEST
ADEEKKLRTTUY	TALKED TURKEY
ADEEKLLOOPSS	LOOKS PLEASED
ADEEKLNORRSW	ARNOLD WESKER
ADEEKLOPRSSU	LOUDSPEAKERS
ADEEKNNRSTTU	DRUNKEN STATE
ADEEKNOORSTW	TAKE ONES WORD
ADEEKNORSSYY	DONKEYS YEARS
ADEEKOPPTTTU	KEPT UP-TO-DATE
ADEELLLRSSSW	SADLERS WELLS
ADEELLMORUZZ	MUZZLE-LOADER
ADEELLNORSSV	SEVEN DOLLARS
ADEELLPPRSTU	APPLE STRUDEL
ADEELMNOSTTT	OLD TESTAMENT
ADEELNOPPSUY	SUNDAY PEOPLE
ADEELNOPRSSU	POLES ASUNDER
ADEELNOPRSTY	PLY ONES TRADE
ADEELNORRSTW	EASTERN WORLD
ADEELOPPRRTY	PROPERTY DEAL
ADEELOPPRTVY	PLEAD POVERTY
ADEELOPSTTUX	EXPOSTULATED
ADEEMMNORSTY	DYNAMOMETERS
ADEEMMRRRSSU	MASS MURDERER
ADEEMNNOSSWY	MEND ONES WAYS
ADEEMNOPRRUW	MURDER WEAPON
ADEEMNORRSTT	REMONSTRATED
ADEEMNORSSTT	DEMONSTRATES
ADEEMOORSTTV	MOVED TO TEARS
ADEEMPRSSSTU	PASSED MUSTER
ADEENNNPPSSY	SPENDS A PENNY
ADEENNNRSTTU	UNDERTENANTS
ADEENNOOPRST	DONE ONE'S PART
ADEENNOPPRRT	PREPONDERANT
ADEENNOPRSTW	WANTED PERSON
ADEENNOSSWWY	WENDS ONE'S WAY
ADEENNRRSSTU	RENTS ASUNDER
ADEENOOPRSST	DOES ONE'S PART
ADEENOORSSTW	ATE ONE'S WORDS
	EAT ONES WORDS
ADEENOPSSTTU	UP-TO-DATENESS
ADEENORSSTUW	SWEET AND SOUR
	SWEET-AND-SOUR
ADEEOPRRSSSS	PASSES ORDERS
ADEERRSSSSTU	RESTS ASSURED
ADEFFGHILOTU	LAUGHED IT OFF
ADEFFGIIINNW	FINDING A WIFE
ADEFFGINNORW	WANDERING OFF
ADEFFGNOORSU	OFF ONES GUARD
ADEFFHHRSTTU	THE HARD STUFF
ADEFFHLMNNOU	HANDFUL OF MEN
ADEFFHNNOOSS	OFF ONES HANDS
ADEFFHNOOSST	DOFFS ONE'S HAT
ADEFFIILMNRY	FAMILY FRIEND
ADEFFIIKKNNOR	KNIFE AND FORK
ADEFFIILNRSTU	FAULTFINDERS
ADEFFIIMNOSST	FIT OF MADNESS
ADEFFLLOOTTY	FLAT-FOOTEDLY
ADEFFLOOORST	FLOOD OF TEARS
ADEFFOOPRSSU	FOUR OF SPADES
ADEFGGINNORS	SIGN OF DANGER
ADEFGHHIIOORT	HAIR OF THE DOG
ADEFGHIILMNT	MAIDEN FLIGHT
ADEFGHILNNOS	HAD ONE'S FLING

ADEFGHILNRTT	LEFT AND RIGHT
	RIGHT AND LEFT
ADEFGHILRSTY	FARSIGHTEDLY
ADEFGHLOOPST	LAP OF THE GODS
ADEFGHLOOSTT	FLOGS TO DEATH
ADEFGHNOORRU	HOUR OF DANGER
ADEFGHNOOTTU	GET OUT OF HAND
ADEFGHOOORST	FOOD SHORTAGE
ADEFGIIIRSTV	GIVE FIRST AID
ADEFGIILLNPY	PLAYING FIELD
ADEFGIINRRST	FIRST READING
ADEFGIKNOPSS	KING OF SPADES
ADEFGILLNNRU	FALLING UNDER
ADEFGILNNSTT	LEFT STANDING
ADEFGIMNNORS	AMONG FRIENDS
ADEFGINOOPRR	PROOFREADING
ADEFGINRRSTU	TRANSFIGURED
ADEFGLORSSST	FROSTED GLASS
ADEFGNNOORSU	ON SAFE GROUND
ADEFGORRRSUW	SURGE FORWARD
ADEFHHOORTUY	HOUR OF THE DAY
ADEFHIILNSST	FINISHED LAST
ADEFHIILLOR3T	SALLIED FORTH
ADEFHILMNOOS	FASHION MODEL
ADEFHILMNORV	MILFORD HAVEN
ADEFHILNNOST	LIFT ONES HAND
ADEFHILNORTW	THE FINAL WORD
ADEFHILRSTTY	THE FIRST LADY
ADEFHINORSTV	HAND OVER FIST
ADEFHINOSTUV	FIVE THOUSAND
ADEFHINRSSSW	DWARFISHNESS
ADEFHLMNOOOR	MEDAL OF HONOR
ADEFHLNNRTTU	LEFT-HAND TURN
ADEFHMOORTUY	DREAM OF YOUTH
ADEFHOOORTTU	OUT OF THE ROAD
ADEFHOOPRSTU	PUSHED TOO FAR
ADEFHOOPSTUY	SOUP OF THE DAY
ADEFHOORSUVW	SHOWED FAVOUR
ADEFIIILNNOT	DEFINITIONAL
	FINAL EDITION
ADEFIIILQSSU	DISQUALIFIES
ADEFIIISSSST	DISSATISFIES
ADEFIILNPRSU	FREUDIAN SLIP
ADEFIIMMORTU	FAIR TO MEDIUM
ADEFIKNORRTW	DRINK OF WATER
ADEFILLMORSS	FROM ALL SIDES
ADEFILLNORRS	FILLS AN ORDER
ADEFILMNNOSS	MANIFOLDNESS
ADEFILMNRTUU	MUTUAL FRIEND
ADEFILMORRSU	FORMULARISED
ADEFILMORRUZ	FORMULARIZED
ADEFILOORTUV	OLD FAVOURITE
ADEFILOORTVY	LIVE FOR TODAY
ADEFILORRSST	FIRST SEA-LORD
ADEFIMNNOSTY	MAN OF DESTINY
ADEFINNOSSWY	FINDS ONE'S WAY
ADEFINOORSYY	IN DAYS OF YORE
ADEFINOPPRRT	FIT AND PROPER
ADEFLLLMNORS	MOLL FLANDERS
ADEFLLNNOPTY	LAND OF PLENTY
ADEFLLNRTUUY	FRAUDULENTLY
ADEFLMNOORSS	FOLD ONES ARMS
ADEFLMOOOPPS	APPLE OF SODOM
ADEFLNOSTTUW	STUDENT OF LAW
ADEFLORSSTTY	TREADS SOFTLY
ADEFMOORRSVW	MOVES FORWARD
ADEFNNOOSUWY	FOUND ONE'S WAY
ADEFNOOPRTTW	END OF PART TWO
ADEFOPRRRSSW	PRESS FORWARD
ADEFOPRRSSTW	STEPS FORWARD
ADEFORSSTUYY	YEARS OF STUDY

ADEGGGHIILNO	DIGGING A HOLE
ADEGGGHIJNNU	HANGING JUDGE
ADEGGHIILLNT	LEADING LIGHT
ADEGGHIILNRT	LIGHT READING
ADEGGHIILNSU	DIES LAUGHING
ADEGGHIINRST	SIGHT-READING
ADEGGHLRRSTU	STRUGGLE HARD
ADEGGHNORRTU	GATHER GROUND
ADEGGIIINRRT	RIDING A TIGER
ADEGGIILNNNO	ENDING IN GAOL
ADEGGIINNOOT	GOING ON A DIET
ADEGGIINNRRT	INTERGRADING
ADEGGIINRTTU	INGURGITATED
ADEGGINNNOPR	GRAND OPENING
ADEGGINNORRR	ORGAN GRINDER
	ORGAN-GRINDER
ADEGGINORRRT	RETROGRADING
ADEGGKLOORSS	LOOKS DAGGERS
ADEGGLNNNOUY	YOUNG ENGLAND
ADEGHHHILNST	THE HIGHLANDS
ADEGHHIILTTU	HIGH ALTITUDE
ADEGHHIIMOOT	AIMED TOO HIGH
ADEGHHIINORS	RAISED ON HIGH
ADEGHHILLUVY	HIGHLY VALUED
ADEGHHILMSUY	HIGHLY AMUSED
ADEGHHILNOOT	IN GOOD HEALTH
ADEGHHILOPRT	LITHOGRAPHED
ADEGHHILOSTT	LAID THE GHOST
ADEGHHINNORT	HEARD NOTHING
ADEGHHINOSTW	DO THE WASHING
ADEGHHINRRST	RIGHT-HANDERS
ADEGHHLNORSU	RUSH HEADLONG
ADEGHHLOOSST	HOLDS HOSTAGE
ADEGHHOPRRRY	HYDROGRAPHER
ADEGHHORRSTU	DRAUGHT HORSE
	READS THROUGH
ADEGHHORSTUW	WADES THROUGH
ADEGHIILNNPR	PHILANDERING
ADEGHIILNOVW	HOLDING A VIEW
ADEGHIIMNNOT	DINING AT HOME
ADEGHIIMNNSU	DEHUMANISING
ADEGHIIMNNUZ	DEHUMANIZING
ADEGHIINNNRV	HAVING DINNER
ADEGHIINOSSV	SHOVING ASIDE
ADEGHIINPSSU	PUSHING ASIDE
ADEGHIINRRSS	HAIRDRESSING
	SHERARDISING
ADEGHIINRRSZ	SHERARDIZING
ADEGHILLORST	EIGHT DOLLARS
ADEGHILLRTTY	TREAD LIGHTLY
ADEGHILLRTUW	WILD LAUGHTER
ADEGHILMNOST	SAME OLD THING
ADEGHILNOOST	ANTHOLOGISED
ADEGHILNOOTZ	ANTHOLOGIZED
ADEGHILNORRU	HURRIED ALONG
ADEGHILNORTW	HOLDING WATER
ADEGHILNOSTY	LOSING THE DAY
ADEGHILNRSTT	STRINGHALTED
ADEGHINNOSSS	HAS DESIGNS ON
ADEGHINNOSTV	SAVED NOTHING
ADEGHINORRST	HORSE TRADING
	HORSE-TRADING
ADEGHINPRRSS	PRESSING HARD
ADEGHINRRRTY	TRYING HARDER
ADEGHINRRTUW	DURING THE WAR
ADEGHINSTTUY	TUESDAY NIGHT
ADEGHIORTTTU	TAUGHT TO RIDE
ADEGHIPPSTTU	DIG UP THE PAST
ADEGHLLNORST	STRANGLEHOLD
ADEGHLLOOOTT	ALL TO THE GOOD
ADEGHLNORTUY	ONLY DAUGHTER

ADEGHLOORRTY	DEATH OR GLORY
ADEGHMNOORTY	HYDROGEN ATOM
ADEGHMNORRST	GRANDMOTHERS
ADEGHNOPRSTU	SHARP-TONGUED
ADEGHNOPRTUW	PAW THE GROUND
ADEGHNORRSTU	GATHERS ROUND
ADEGHPPSTTUU	DUG UP THE PAST
ADEGIIIJLNNN	ENDING IN JAIL
ADEGIIILLOTV	VILLAGE IDIOT
ADEGIIILMNTT	DELIMITATING
ADEGIIILNNST	DISENTAILING
ADEGIIILNSTV	DEVITALISING
ADEGIIILNTVZ	DEVITALIZING
ADEGIIJNOPRS	JEOPARDISING
ADEGIIJNOPRZ	JEOPARDIZING
ADEGIILLMNSY	MISLEADINGLY
ADEGIILLNNOT	DIALLING TONE
ADEGIILLNNPS	SLIDING PANEL
ADEGIILLNPSU	PULLING ASIDE
ADEGIILLNSVW	ADVISING WELL
ADEGIILMNORS	DEMORALISING
ADEGIILMNORZ	DEMORALIZING
ADEGIILNNRRT	INTERLARDING
ADEGIILNOOTT	GO INTO DETAIL
ADEGIILNOPRS	DEPOLARISING
ADEGIILNOPRZ	DEPOLARIZING
ADEGIILNORSS	DIGRESSIONAL
ADEGIILNPRSY	DESPAIRINGLY
ADEGIILNRSSU	SINGULARISED
ADEGIILNRSUZ	SINGULARIZED
ADEGIIMNNNOT	DENOMINATING
ADEGIIMNNPRR	REPRIMANDING
ADEGIIMNORTU	MINIATURE DOG
ADEGIIMNRRST	RIDING MASTER
ADEGIINNOPRR	PREORDAINING
ADEGIINNRSTU	TURNING ASIDE
ADEGIINOOPRR	IN GOOD REPAIR
ADEGIINORSSS	DISORGANISES
ADEGIINORSSZ	DISORGANIZES
ADEGIINOSSST	TOSSING ASIDE
ADEGIINPSTTU	PUTTING ASIDE
ADEGIJKNNOST	STANDING JOKE
ADEGIKKLOORW	WORK LIKE A DOG
ADEGIKNNRSTU	UNDERTAKINGS
ADEGIKNORRST	TAKING ORDERS
ADEGILLNORUZ	LOUNGE LIZARD
ADEGILLNORVY	LOVING DEARLY
ADEGILLPSTUY	PLEADS GUILTY
ADEGILNNORST	STRONG DENIAL
ADEGILNNPRUY	UNDERPLAYING
ADEGILNNRUUV	UNDERVALUING
ADEGILNOPPTU	DEPOPULATING
ADEGILOORRTY	DEROGATORILY
ADEGIMNNOPPR	NAME-DROPPING
ADEGIMNNORWY	DRAWING MONEY
ADEGIMNORRRS	ORDERING ARMS
ADEGIMNORRUY	MARRIED YOUNG
ADEGINNNOOTU	GONE IN AND OUT
ADEGINNOOOPR	OPENING A DOOR
ADEGINNORSTU	GETS A ROUND IN
ADEGINNORSTV	STANDING OVER
ADEGINNORTUW	WANDERING OUT
ADEGINNPRSTU	PUTS IN DANGER
ADEGINNRSTTU	UNDERSTATING
ADEGINOPRSTU	SPREADING OUT
ADEGIOPRSSST	TRADES GOSSIP
ADEGJLMNSTTU	LAST JUDGMENT
ADEGJMNNPSTU	SNAP JUDGMENT
ADEGJMNPSSTU	PASS JUDGMENT
ADEGLLNNORTU	TRUNDLE ALONG
ADEGLMNORSTY	STRONGLY MADE
ADEGLMOOPRSS	SPREADS GLOOM
ADEGLNNOOSTT	LEG TO STAND ON
ADEGLORSSTUV	SLAVE TO DRUGS
ADEGMOOORSTU	OUTDOOR GAMES
ADEGNNOPTTUW	GOT UP AND WENT
ADEGNNORSSTU	STRANGE SOUND
ADEGNOOOORRST	TOREADOR SONG
ADEGNORSTTUY	STARTED YOUNG
ADEHHHNOORTU	HAD THE HONOUR
ADEHHILLPPSU	PHILADELPHUS
ADEHHIMOORRS	HAEMORRHOIDS
ADEHHINOOPTT	HAD THE OPTION
ADEHHINOSSTW	IN THE SHADOWS
ADEHHKLNORTT	THANK THE LORD
ADEHHLLMOPST	HOLDS THE PALM
ADEHHLMORRTY	HYDROTHERMAL
ADEHHLOPSSST	HOLDS THE PASS
ADEHHMPRUVYY	HUMPHREY DAVY
ADEHHNNOOSSW	SHOW ONES HAND
ADEHHOOOORRTW	HARD ROW TO HOE
ADEHHOPRRTYY	HYDROTHERAPY
ADEHIIINNSVW	WISHED IN VAIN
ADEHIIKLNRVY	DRINK HEAVILY
ADEHIILLMNNT	ALL IN THE MIND
ADEHIILNSTTT	DILETTANTISH
ADEHIILOPSST	HOSPITALISED
ADEHIILOPSTZ	HOSPITALIZED
ADEHIIMNORSS	DISHARMONIES
ADEHIINNNOST	HONEST INDIAN
ADEHIKLMNNOY	MILK AND HONEY
ADEHIKLNRUVY	DRUNK HEAVILY
ADEHILLNPSTU	DULLS THE PAIN
ADEHILLOPRSY	SPHEROIDALLY
ADEHILMNOOYY	HOLIDAY MONEY
ADEHILMNOPSU	SULPHONAMIDE
ADEHILNOPRRT	HAROLD PINTER
ADEHILNOSSSU	HAS DELUSIONS
ADEHILNPRSTY	SPREAD THINLY
	THINLY SPREAD
ADEHILORSSVW	SILVER SHADOW
ADEHILOTTUWY	WITHOUT DELAY
ADEHILOTWWWY	WEALTHY WIDOW
ADEHIMMNNOST	ADMONISHMENT
ADEHIMNOOSST	THOMAS EDISON
ADEHIMNOSTTT	THAMES DITTON
ADEHIMSSSTTU	STUDIES MATHS
ADEHINNNOSTU	NINE THOUSAND
ADEHINOOPSWZ	WHIPSNADE ZOO
ADEHINOQRSTU	HARD QUESTION
ADEHINORSTUU	UNAUTHORISED
ADEHINORTUUZ	UNAUTHORIZED
ADEHINQRRSTU	HINDQUARTERS
ADEHIOOPRSTT	ORTHOPAEDIST
ADEHIOPSSTTY	HYPOSTATISED
ADEHIOPSTTYZ	HYPOSTATIZED
ADEHIORSSTTW	SHORT-WAISTED
ADEHIPRSSSTW	SHIPS STEWARD
ADEHIQRRRTTU	THIRD QUARTER
ADEHIRSSSTTU	THRUSTS ASIDE
ADEHJLNNOORT	JOHN ALDERTON
ADEHKOORSTTW	WORKS TO DEATH
ADEHLLLORSST	STALLHOLDERS
ADEHLLNOTTUW	UNTOLD WEALTH
ADEHLLOSUUXY	ALDOUS HUXLEY
ADEHLMMNOTYY	TOMMY HANDLEY
ADEHLMNOOPSU	MONADELPHOUS
ADEHLMOORSST	SLAMS THE DOOR
ADEHLMORRSSU	SHOULDER ARMS
ADEHLNNOPSTY	SHETLAND PONY
ADEHLNOORRTW	ANOTHER WORLD
ADEHLOOPPRTW	TOLD A WHOPPER

ADEHLOORSUVW	SHOWED VALOUR
ADEHMNNOORST	MOTHER AND SON
ADEHMORRRTTU	MORTE DARTHUR
ADEHNNOOTWWY	ON THE WAY DOWN
ADEHNNOPPTUU	ON THE UP-AND-UP
ADEHNOOPSTTY	PAYS ON THE DOT
ADEHNOORRSSU	HORSES AROUND
ADEHNOPRSSTU	PRESS HAND-OUT
ADEHNOPRSSUU	PUSHES AROUND
ADEHNRSTTUXY	NEXT THURSDAY
ADEHOORRRTVW	TREVOR HOWARD
ADEHOORRTTWY	WORRY TO DEATH
ADEIIILMNOTT	DELIMITATION
ADEIIIMNORST	DIMERISATION
ADEIIIMNORTZ	DIMERIZATION
ADEIIIMNOSTV	DEVIATIONISM
ADEIIIMNRSTU	MINIATURISED
ADEIIIMNRTUZ	MINIATURIZED
ADEIIINNOOST	DEIONISATION
ADEIIINNOOTZ	DEIONIZATION
ADEIIINNORRV	VIN ORDINAIRE
ADEIIINOSTTV	DEVIATIONIST
ADEIIINSTTTU	ATTITUDINISE
ADEIIINTTTUZ	ATTITUDINIZE
ADEIIKMOOTVW	TOOK A DIM VIEW
ADEIILLMMNOS	MADE MILLIONS
ADEIILLMNORY	MERIDIONALLY
ADEIILLNPRUV	LIVERPUDLIAN
ADEIILLNRTTY	INTERTIDALLY
ADEIILMNSTTT	DILETTANTISM
ADEIILMSSSTU	DISSIMULATES
ADEIILNNNSST	STANDS IN LINE
ADEIILNNORTY	INORDINATELY
ADEIILNOOPST	DEPOSITIONAL
	DESPOLIATION
ADEIILNOPRTV	PROVIDENTIAL
ADEIILNOPSTY	YIELDS A POINT
ADEIILNORSST	DILATORINESS
ADEIILNORTUY	DAILY ROUTINE
ADEIILORSTTU	TAILORED SUIT
ADEIILQSSSTU	LIQUID ASSETS
ADEIILSSSUVY	DISSUASIVELY
ADEIIMMNNRSU	INDIAN SUMMER
ADEIIMMNOORT	IMMODERATION
ADEIIMNNNOOT	DENOMINATION
ADEIIMNNOORT	IN MODERATION
ADEIIMNNOOST	DEMONISATION
ADEIIMNNOOTZ	DEMONIZATION
ADEIIMNNRSSY	SIN AND MISERY
ADEIIMNNRSTT	DISTRAINMENT
ADEIIMNOPRST	POST MERIDIAN
ADEIIMNORSST	DISSEMINATOR
ADEIIMNSSTTT	DISTANT TIMES
ADEIIMOSSTTT	STOMATITIDES
ADEIIMRSSTTX	TAXIDERMISTS
ADEIINNNOSTT	INDENTATIONS
ADEIINNOPSST	DISPENSATION
ADEIINNORRSS	ORDINARINESS
ADEIINNOSSTT	DESTINATIONS
ADEIINOOPRTX	PEROXIDATION
ADEIINOPRSTV	DEPRIVATIONS
ADEIINORRSVY	DIVERSIONARY
ADEIINORSSTT	DISSERTATION
ADEIINORSTTX	EXTRADITIONS
ADEIINOSTTUV	ADVENTITIOUS
ADEIINPRRSTT	ARDENT SPIRIT
ADEIINPRSSSU	PRUSSIANISED
ADEIINPRSSUZ	PRUSSIANIZED
ADEIIOOOPRST	RADIOISOTOPE
ADEIJMMNRTUY	JIMMY DURANTE
ADEIJNNNORUY	DONE AN INJURY
ADEIJNNORSUY	DOES AN INJURY
ADEIJNPRRTUY	INJURED PARTY
ADEIKKNNORTT	TAKEN TO DRINK
ADEIKKNORSTT	TAKES TO DRINK
ADEIKLLMPSSY	SPEAKS MILDLY
ADEIKLNORSTV	SLAVE TO DRINK
ADEIKLOOSSWY	LOOK SIDEWAYS
ADEIKLOPPRSY	SPOKE RAPIDLY
ADEIKNOORRTW	RADIO NETWORK
ADEIKNOPRRUW	UNPAID WORKER
ADEIKNORRSTU	RANK OUTSIDER
ADEIKNOTWWWY	WIDOW TWANKEY
ADEILLLNRTUY	ILL-NATUREDLY
ADEILLLORRSV	SILVER DOLLAR
ADEILLNOOTVY	DEVOTIONALLY
ADEILLNORRSU	RALLIES ROUND
ADEILLNPRTUY	PRUDENTIALLY
ADEILLOOPRST	ALLIED TROOPS
ADEILMNNNOST	TINNED SALMON
ADEILMNOOPSY	PLAY DOMINOES
ADEILMNOORRS	ROMAN SOLDIER
ADEILMNOOTUY	I AID OUT MONEY
ADEILMNOPRTT	PERMIT TO LAND
ADEILMORSSTT	ARTISTS MODEL
ADEILMRRRTUU	RITUAL MURDER
ADEILNOOPPTU	DEPOPULATION
ADEILOOSTTTV	DEVIL'S TATTOO
ADEILOPPRSTV	APPROVED LIST
ADEILOPRRSUY	LADY SUPERIOR
ADEIMMOPRSUY	PRASEODYMIUM
ADEIMMRSTTWY	TWISTED MY ARM
ADEIMNNOORST	DENOMINATORS
ADEIMNNQRSUU	QUADRENNIUMS
ADEIMOOPRSTZ	SPERMATOZOID
ADEIMOPSSTUY	IMPOSES A DUTY
ADEINNNOTTUW	WENT IN AND OUT
ADEINNOORSSW	WORD IN SEASON
ADEINNOPRSSW	OPENS INWARDS
ADEINNOPTTTU	PUT AN END TO IT
ADEINNORRSTT	STAY TO DINNER
ADEINNOSSWWY	WINDS ONE'S WAY
ADEINOOPPRTV	PROVED A POINT
ADEINOPRRRSW	PRISON WARDER
ADEINPRSSTUW	STUPID ANSWER
ADEINRSSTTUV	ADVENTURISTS
ADEIOPPRRSSV	DISAPPROVERS
ADEIOPPRRSSTT	DROPS A SITTER
ADEIORRSTTTU	TOURIST TRADE
ADEIOSSSTTUY	STAYS OUTSIDE
ADEJLORSSSTU	LOSS ADJUSTER
ADEJMNNORSTU	ADJOURNMENTS
ADEKLLLOSWWY	WALKED SLOWLY
ADEKLMMNOOSS	SMOKED SALMON
ADEKMNNOOSSU	MAKES NO SOUND
ADEKOPRRSTUW	UPWARD STROKE
ADELLLNRTUWY	WELL AND TRULY
ADELLMOOSSWY	OSWALD MOSLEY
ADELLNORSSUY	SLANDEROUSLY
ADELLOOPRRST	PETRODOLLARS
ADELLORSTUUY	ADULTEROUSLY
ADELMNOPRSTW	TRAMPLES DOWN
ADELMOORSSTY	SAME OLD STORY
ADELMOPPSSUY	PLAYED POSSUM
ADELMPPRSTUY	PLAYED TRUMPS
ADELNOORSSTW	ONES LAST WORD
ADELNOOSSSTT	STANDS TO LOSE
ADELNORRSUVY	LAND SURVEYOR
ADELOOPPRSTU	DEPOPULATORS
ADELOPRRSSWY	SWORDPLAYERS
ADELPRRSSTUU	TRADE SURPLUS
ADEMNNNOPTWY	TWOPENNY DAMN

ADEMNOOOPRTX	ROOM TO EXPAND	ADGGIIIILNST	DIGITALISING
ADEMNOORRSTT	DEMONSTRATOR	ADGGIIIILNTZ	DIGITALIZING
ADEMOORSSTVW	MOVES TOWARDS	ADGGIIMNNORS	GORMANDISING
ADENNOOSUWWY	WOUND ONE'S WAY	ADGGIIMNNORZ	GORMANDIZING
ADENNORSSTUW	UNTOWARDNESS	ADGGIKNNOOPS	GOOD SPANKING
ADENOOPRSTUW	OPEN OUTWARDS	ADGGILNNNOST	LONG STANDING
ADENOPRRSSSW	PRESS ONWARDS		LONG-STANDING
ADEOORRRTTXY	DEXTROROTARY	ADGGINNNNOOO	GOING ON AND ON
ADFFGIIIMNRS	DISAFFIRMING	ADGGINOORSTW	GOING TOWARDS
ADFFGIILNNTU	FAULTFINDING	ADGGINPRSTTU	TRUDGING PAST
	FINDING FAULT	ADGHHIIKNNRT	HARD THINKING
ADFFGILNNOTU	FLOATING FUND		THINKING HARD
ADFFGLOOOOTT	FAT LOT OF GOOD	ADGHHINNNOOT	HAD NOTHING ON
ADFFIILNNPSU	PUFFIN ISLAND	ADGHHKORSTTU	DARK THOUGHTS
ADFFILLORSTY	FIFTY DOLLARS	ADGHHLOOTTUU	THOUGHT ALOUD
ADFGGGGILNNOW	FLAGGING DOWN	ADGHIIMNNNV	HAVING IN MIND
ADFGGIINOOPR	GOING FOR A DIP	ADGHIIJNNNOS	JOINING HANDS
ADFGGINOORRW	GOING FORWARD	ADGHIILLNNSW	WILLING HANDS
ADFGHILLLTUY	FULL DAYLIGHT	ADGHIIMMNSST	MIDNIGHT MASS
ADFGHILLNOOT	HOLDING ALOFT	ADGHIIMNNOTT	ADMIT NOTHING
ADFGHILNNOST	SOFT HANDLING	ADGHIIMNPSTT	PAST MIDNIGHT
ADFGHINORRTW	DRAWING FORTH	ADGHIINNOTTU	HANDING IT OUT
ADFGHINPSTTU	STAND-UP FIGHT	ADGHIINNRSTW	HANDWRITINGS
ADFGHIORRRTW	RIGHT FORWARD	ADGHIINNSTTW	WITHSTANDING
ADFGHNOOOTTU	GOT OUT OF HAND	ADGHINOPRSS	RHAPSODISING
ADFGIIILNRYZ	FLYING LIZARD	ADGHIINOPRSZ	RHAPSODIZING
ADFGIIILNORTU	FLUORIDATING	ADGHIKLNORSW	WORLD-SHAKING
ADFGIIMNNRST	STANDING FIRM	ADGHILLLMNOS	SMALLHOLDING
ADFGIINNNSTW	FINDS WANTING	ADGHILLMORTY	LORD ALMIGHTY
ADFGIINORSUV	DISFAVOURING	ADGHILMNOOOT	DO A MOONLIGHT
ADFGILNNOOTW	FLOATING DOWN	ADGHILRSTTUY	DISTRAUGHTLY
ADFGINNNOTUW	FOUND WANTING	ADGHINOOSSVW	WOOD SHAVINGS
ADFGLNNOOORS	FOR AN OLD SONG	ADGHINOPPSSY	SHOPPING DAYS
ADFGNOOPRSUU	POUND OF SUGAR	ADGHINORSTTW	STRAIGHT DOWN
ADFHHMNOOOTU	HOOF AND MOUTH	ADGHINPRSTTU	STAND UPRIGHT
ADFHIILOPRRT	THIRD OF APRIL	ADGHKLLNOOOR	LONG HARD LOOK
ADFHIMNOOORU	MAID OF HONOUR	ADGHLLOOTUUU	LAUGH OUT LOUD
ADFHIMNOORSW	MAN OF HIS WORD	ADGHLMNOOPUY	PLOUGH MONDAY
ADFHINOORRRS	HARRISON FORD	ADGHMMNOOORU	GOOD HUMOR MAN
ADFHIOOPRSWY	DAY OF WORSHIP	ADGHNNOORSTT	HOT AND STRONG
ADFHMNOOOTTU	FOOT AND MOUTH	ADGHNOPRSTUY	HANGS UP TO DRY
	FOOT-AND-MOUTH	ADGIIIIMNNTT	INTIMIDATING
ADFHNOORSTUU	FOUR THOUSAND	ADGIIIINOSTT	DIGITISATION
ADFHOOOTTUYY	YOUTH OF TODAY	ADGIIIINOTTZ	DIGITIZATION
ADFIIILNNOST	DISINFLATION	ADGIIIKMNNRX	MIXING A DRINK
ADFIIILNOSTU	FLUIDISATION	ADGIIIKNNNPY	PAYING IN KIND
ADFIIILNOTUZ	FLUIDIZATION	ADGIIILNNRTW	WINDING TRAIL
ADFIILNOORTU	FLUORIDATION	ADGIIKKLNNTY	TAKING KINDLY
ADFIILOSSTUY	FASTIDIOUSLY	ADGIILLNNNSU	DISANNULLING
ADFIIOPRSSTT	FIRST-AID POST	ADGIIILLNNOTU	LONGITUDINAL
ADFIKLNOORRY	ORDINARY FOLK	ADGIILNNNOOS	DINING SALOON
ADFIKNNORRSW	FRANK WINDSOR	ADGIILNNORSU	SAILING ROUND
ADFINNNORSTT	STAND IN FRONT	ADGIILNNPRST	LANDING STRIP
ADFKLOOORRSW	LOOKS FORWARD	ADGIILNRSTTU	STRIDULATING
ADFKNNOOOPRS	SPOON AND FORK	ADGIILOORSST	RADIOLOGISTS
ADFLLOORRSTY	FORTY DOLLARS	ADGIILOOSSTU	AUDIOLOGISTS
ADFLOORSSTWW	FLOWS TOWARDS	ADGIIMNNORUVV	VIM AND VIGOUR
ADFNOOORSTTU	ROUND OF TOAST	ADGIINNOPRTW	WORD PAINTING
ADGGGGILNNORU	GRAND GUIGNOL	ADGIINOPPRSV	DISAPPROVING
ADGGGINNOORU	GOING AGROUND	ADGIKLNNOORW	LOOKING DRAWN
ADGGHHIINNST	HIGH STANDING	ADGIKLNNORTU	TALKING ROUND
ADGGHHORRTUU	ROUGH DRAUGHT	ADGIKNOOOPRS	GOODISON PARK
ADGGHIILNNST	SIGHTING LAND	ADGILMNNORTY	LYING DORMANT
ADGGHIILNOOT	IN A GOOD LIGHT	ADGILNNNOSTY	STANDING ONLY
ADGGHIINPPRR	GRIPPING HARD	ADGILNNOPPSW	SLAPPING DOWN
ADGGHIINRTTW	DRAWING TIGHT	ADGILNNOSTUY	ASTOUNDINGLY
ADGGHIKLNSTY	GLADYS KNIGHT	ADGILOOQSTUY	QUALITY GOODS
ADGGHILNOORT	LIGHT DRAGOON	ADGIMNNOOOST	SANTO DOMINGO
ADGGHINOOSTY	SAY GOODNIGHT	ADGIMNNOORST	STANDING ROOM
ADGGHINORRUW	ROUGH DRAWING	ADGIMNNOPRST	SPRANG TO MIND
ADGGHINPRRTU	UPRIGHT GRAND	ADGIMNNOPSTW	STAMPING DOWN

ADGINNNORSUW	WARNING SOUND	AEEEEGINRRTV	REGENERATIVE
ADGINNOPRSSU	PASSING ROUND	AEEEEGMPRRSV	GAME PRESERVE
ADGINNOPRTWY	PARTYING DOWN	AEEEEGNPRSTX	GREAT EXPENSE
ADGINNOPSTTU	STANDING UP TO	AEEEEHHKLTTW	TAKE THE WHEEL
ADGINOORSSTW	GO DOWNSTAIRS	AEEEEHHPRRSS	SHEEPSHEARER
ADGINOPRRSTW	PARTING WORDS	AEEEEHKRSTWX	THE WEAKER SEX
ADGINORSSTWW	WASTING WORDS	AEEEEHLNRSST	ETHEREALNESS
ADGLNNOORTUW	LONG DRAWN-OUT	AEEEEHLNSTTV	LEAVE THE NEST
	LONG-DRAWN-OUT	AEEEEHLPRSVY	HEAVY SLEEPER
ADGLNNOORUWY	LONG WAY ROUND	AEEEEHMNRSTV	NEVER THE SAME
ADGMNNNOOORW	DO NO MAN WRONG	AEEEEHNOSTYY	EASY ON THE EYE
ADGNOPRRSUWW	GROWN UPWARDS	AEEEEHNSSSTV	THE SEVEN SEAS
ADHHIINORRUY	HARRY HOUDINI	AEEEEHQRTTUU	THEATRE QUEUE
ADHHIORSSTWW	HAS WORDS WITH	AEEEEIKMMNSS	MAKES ENEMIES
ADHHIRSSTTUY	THIS THURSDAY	AEEEEIKNPPTT	KEEN APPETITE
ADHHOORSTTTU	SHUT THAT DOOR!	AEEEEKLNNNOV	ON AN EVEN KEEL
ADHIIMOPRSST	DIASTROPHISM	AEEEEKNNOPRS	EARN ONES KEEP
ADHILLNOORSW	HAROLD WILSON	AEEEEKNNOPSY	KEEPS AN EYE ON
ADHILLNOSTUY	OUTLANDISHLY	AEEEEKNOPSST	KEEP ONES SEAT
ADHILMMOOPTY	LYMPHOMATOID	AEEEELPRRSSS	PRESS RELEASE
ADHILOORSSTY	OLD AS HISTORY	AEEEENNRRSTU	SERENE NATURE
ADHINPSSSTUY	STUDY SPANISH	AEEEFFFMORRR	FREE FROM FEAR
ADHIOORTTUWW	WITHOUT A WORD	AEEEFFHILRTT	THE AFTERLIFE
ADHKNOOOTTWW	KNOW WHAT TO DO	AEEEFFHINRST	FINE FEATHERS
ADHLMNOOORST	HOLD TO RANSOM	AEEEFFHLMOST	SHEET OF FLAME
ADIIIIMNNOTT	INTIMIDATION	AEEEFFIILMNR	FAMINE RELIEF
ADIIIILLMRSSY	DISSIMILARLY	AEEEFFILLTTV	FIVE FEET TALL
ADIIILLNNSTW	ITS AN ILL WIND	AEEEFFINRSTU	FINE FEATURES
ADIIILLNOSTT	DISTILLATION	AEEEFFINRSTY	FIFTEEN YEARS
ADIIILMNNOTU	DIMINUTIONAL	AEEEFFLOPPST	TOFFEE-APPLES
ADIIIMNNNTUY	INDIAN MUTINY	AEEEFFNORRST	NEAREST OFFER
ADIIIMNORTTY	INTIMIDATORY	AEEEFFNRRRST	FREE TRANSFER
ADIIINOPSSST	DISSIPATIONS	AEEEFGGILNRT	FEELING GREAT
ADIIILLMOPRRY	PRIMORDIALLY	AEEEFGHILMNS	FEELING SHAME
ADIIILLNOQRSU	QUADRILLIONS	AEEEFGHILNSV	HAVE FEELINGS
ADIILLNRSTUY	INDUSTRIALLY	AEEEFGHIRRTT	THE GREAT FIRE
ADIILMNOORTY	ADMONITORILY	AEEEFGIINNRT	RETAINING FEE
ADIILMOPSSTT	DIPLOMATISTS	AEEEFGIKNRST	SEEKING AFTER
ADIILMORSSTU	DISSIMULATOR	AEEEFGIOSSTT	STATE OF SIEGE
ADIILMRTTUYY	MILITARY DUTY	AEEEFGIRRRST	REFRIGERATES
ADIILNOORSTT	DISTORTIONAL	AEEEFGLLNORW	GENERAL WOLFE
ADIILNORSTTU	STRIDULATION	AEEEFGLNRSST	FEELS STRANGE
ADIINOPSSTTU	DISPUTATIONS	AEEEFHHIRTTW	WHITE FEATHER
ADIIOPSSTTUU	DISPUTATIOUS	AEEEFHILNPST	FEELS THE PAIN
ADILLMNOSUWW	WALLOWS IN MUD	AEEEFHLMNOSS	FEELS NO SHAME
ADILLOORSTUY	IDOLATROUSLY	AEEEFHLOSTWY	EYES OF THE LAW
ADILLORSSTXY	SIXTY DOLLARS	AEEEFHMNOSSS	SENSE OF SHAME
ADILMMORSTUY	TAILORS DUMMY	AEEEFHNOPSST	OPENS THE SAFE
ADILMNNPSSUU	PLUS AND MINUS	AEEEFHOPPRST	SHEET OF PAPER
ADILOOSSSTWW	SOWS WILD OATS	AEEEFIKLNOST	TAKE ONES LIFE
ADILORRSTTUY	STRIDULATORY	AEEEFIKLNPTT	PALETTE KNIFE
ADILORSSSTUY	DISASTROUSLY	AEEEFILNOSSV	SAVE ONES LIFE
ADIMMNNOORSW	NORMAN WISDOM	AEEEFILNPRRT	PREFERENTIAL
ADIMNORRSUY	SUNDAY MIRROR	AEEEFIMNRTTV	FERMENTATIVE
ADIMOOPRSUUV	SODIUM-VAPOUR	AEEEFINQRRTU	ENQUIRE AFTER
ADIMOORSTTUY	AMOROUS DITTY	AEEEFKLPRSSY	SPEAKS FREELY
ADINNRSTTTUW	TWIST AND TURN	AEEEFKOPRSST	FOR PETE'S SAKE
ADINOORSSSTY	STAYS INDOORS	AEEEFLLNNSTT	FLANNELETTES
ADINRSSSTUUY	STUDY RUSSIAN	AEEEFLMNOSSU	AMUSE ONESELF
ADLOOPRRSTWW	POST-WAR WORLD	AEEEFLNOSSST	SEATS ONESELF
ADNOOOSSTUYY	YOU DON'T SAY SO	AEEEFLNOSSSV	SAVES ONESELF
AEEEEFGINRRV	GAVE FREE REIN	AEEEFLNOSSWY	FEELS ONE'S WAY
AEEEEFGLNOSS	FEELS ONE'S AGE	AEEEFLNRSSSS	FEARLESSNESS
AEEEEFHHLSTT	FEELS THE HEAT	AEEEFMNORSSS	FEARSOMENESS
AEEEEFHHRRTT	THE HEREAFTER	AEEEFNOPSSTT	TAPS ONE'S FEET
AEEEEFHLLRTW	FARE THEE WELL	AEEEFNOSSSTT	SENSE OF TASTE
AEEEEFLMNOTV	TEAM OF ELEVEN	AEEEFQRRRSTU	FREE QUARTERS
AEEEEFMNOSTT	MEET ONES FATE	AEEEGGILLNRV	VILLAGE GREEN
AEEEEGHKRRTT	GREEK THEATRE	AEEEGGILNRST	TEENAGE GIRLS
AEEEEGHLPRST	TELEGRAPHESE	AEEEGGINNRRT	REGENERATING
AEEEEGHMORTT	HETEROGAMETE	AEEEGGINRRST	STEERING GEAR

AEEEGHHIRTTV	GIVE THE EARTH
AEEEGHIMRTVY	THE VERY IMAGE
AEEEGHINNRTT	THE ARGENTINE
AEEEGHKORRTT	RAKE TOGETHER
AEEEGHLMOSST	LOSES THE GAME
AEEEGHLPRRST	TELEGRAPHERS
AEEEGHNNOOTV	GONE TO HEAVEN
AEEEGHNOOSTV	GOES TO HEAVEN
AEEEGHNOPSTT	OPENS THE GATE
AEEEGHNPRSTW	GREAT-NEPHEWS
AEEEGHSSTTTT	GETS THE TASTE
AEEEGIIKLNPV	KEEPING ALIVE
AEEEGIILNRST	GENERALITIES
AEEEGIIMNNNR	MARINE ENGINE
AEEEGILLNNST	ELEGANT LINES
AEEEGILNPRRS	PRE-RELEASING
AEEEGILNRSSU	GENERAL ISSUE
AEEEGILPRSUV	GIVE PLEASURE
AEEEGILTTVVY	VEGETATIVELY
AEEEGINNORRT	REGENERATION
AEEEGINNORSS	SEEING REASON
AEEEGINNPPRV	EVENING PAPER
AEEEGINNSSTV	NEGATIVENESS
AEEEGINOTTVV	NEGATIVE VOTE
AEEEGINPRSTV	GIVE A PRESENT
AEEEGIRRSTTV	TERGIVERSATE
AEEEGKLLMORT	ALL GREEK TO ME
AEEEGKMNORSY	GREASE MONKEY
AEEEGKPRSSTU	GUEST SPEAKER
AEEEGLLRSTWY	WESTERLY GALE
AEEEGLMNNNTT	ENTANGLEMENT
AEEEGLMNNRST	ENLARGEMENTS
AEEEGLMNNRTY	MENTAL ENERGY
AEEEGLMNNRST	GENERAL TERMS
AEEEGLNNOPRR	GENERAL PERON
AEEEGLNNRTTU	GENTLE NATURE
AEEEGLNNRTTY	LATENT ENERGY
AEEEGLNORRST	GENERAL STORE
AEEEGMMNORTT	MAGNETOMETER
AEEEGMMNOSSS	GAMESOMENESS
AEEEGMNNRSTT	ESTRANGEMENT
AEEEGMORRSTT	AGREE TO TERMS
AEEEGNNOOPRS	GONE ON A SPREE
AEEEGNOOPRSS	GOES ON A SPREE
AEEEGNOORSSV	GONE OVERSEAS
AEEEGNRRSTTW	GREAT WESTERN
AEEEGOORSSSV	GOES OVERSEAS
AEEEHHHIRTTW	WHITE HEATHER
AEEEHHLMRTTT	MELT THE HEART
AEEEHHLNPSUV	HEAVEN HELP US!
AEEEHHLOSSST	LOSE THE ASHES
AEEEHHMMNNRSS	HERMANN HESSE
AEEEHHMNOTVY	HAVE THE MONEY
AEEEHHNOOPTV	HOPE TO HEAVEN
AEEEHHRRSTTU	THEATRE USHER
AEEEHIKLNTTV	TAKEN THE VEIL
AEEEHIKLSTTV	TAKES THE VEIL
AEEEHIKNRSTT	TAKE THE REINS
	TAKEN THE RISE
AEEEHIKNTTVW	TAKEN THE VIEW
AEEEHIKRSSTT	TAKES THE RISE
AEEEHIKSTTVW	TAKES THE VIEW
AEEEHILMPRTY	EPHEMERALITY
AEEEHILNNSSV	HEAVENLINESS
AEEEHIMNNNOPP	EPIPHENOMENA
AEEEHIMNRSTT	MATES IN THREE
AEEEHIMNRTTT	MEET THE TRAIN
AEEEHIMORTTV	MOVIE THEATER
AEEEHINPPRSV	APPREHENSIVE
AEEEHINPRSST	PARENTHESISE
AEEEHINPRSTZ	PARENTHESIZE

AEEEHINSSTTZ	ANESTHETIZES
AEEEHIOPRRRS	SHOE REPAIRER
AEEEHKLMRSTU	MAKE THE RULES
AEEEHKLNRSTT	TAKEN SHELTER
AEEEHKLRSSTT	TAKES SHELTER
AEEEHKMNOTTY	TAKE THE MONEY
AEEEHKMNSSTW	MAKES THE NEWS
AEEEHKMOOPSW	MAKES WHOOPEE
AEEEHKNSTTTT	TAKEN THE TEST
AEEEHKSSTTTT	TAKES THE TEST
AEEEHLLLSTTT	TELLS THE TALE
AEEEHLLORSST	LEATHER SOLES
AEEEHLMMNNTU	HUMAN ELEMENT
AEEEHLMOORTV	LEAVE THE ROOM
AEEEHLMPPRST	PAMPHLETEERS
AEEEHLNOSSTT	SET THE SEAL ON
AEEEHLNPSTTT	PENTATHLETES
AEEEHLORSTUX	HETEROSEXUAL
AEEEHLRRSTTY	HARLEY STREET
AEEEHMNORRTV	MORE THAN EVER
AEEEHMNORSUW	WAREHOUSEMEN
AEEEHMORTTTX	METHOTREXATE
AEEEHNNOOSSY	HAS ONE'S EYE ON
AEEEHNNOTTVW	WENT TO HEAVEN
AEEEHNORRTTT	ON THE RETREAT
AEEEHNOSSTWY	SWEET AS HONEY
AEEEHNPRSTTT	TEN PAST THREE
AEEEHNRTTVWX	WHATEVER NEXT?
AEEEHORRSTVY	OVER THE YEARS
AEEEHORRTTVW	OVER THE WATER
AEEEHPRRSSTU	SUPERHEATERS
AEEEHQRRRTTU	THREE-QUARTER
AEEEIILNPRTX	EXPERIENTIAL
AEEEIINRRSTV	VETERINARIES
AEEEIINRSSTV	SENSITIVE EAR
AEEEIKLMNOPS	MAKE ONES PILE
AEEEIKMNOSTT	TAKE ONES TIME
AEEEIKMNOSTX	MAKE ONES EXIT
AEEEIKMOPPRS	KEEP A PROMISE
AEEEIKNNORST	ENTEROKINASE
AEEEIKNPRSVW	SNEAK PREVIEW
AEEEILLMNRTY	ELEMENTARILY
AEEEILLNPRTT	INTERPELLATE
AEEEILMNPRTX	EXPERIMENTAL
AEEEILMRSSTV	SEVERAL TIMES
AEEEILNRRSTT	INTERRELATES
AEEEILNRSSTT	LITERATENESS
AEEEILNRSSTV	RELATIVENESS
AEEEILNRSSTX	EXTERNALISES
AEEEILNRSTXZ	EXTERNALIZES
AEEEILNRTTVY	INVETERATELY
AEEEILRRTTTW	WRITE A LETTER
AEEEIMMRSSTU	MEASURES TIME
AEEEIMNRRTUV	REMUNERATIVE
AEEEIMNRSTTX	EXTERMINATES
AEEEIMORSTTV	OVERESTIMATE
AEEEINNRRSTT	EARN INTEREST
AEEEINPRSTTV	PRESENTATIVE
AEEEINRRSSTV	SEVERE STRAIN
AEEEINRRSTTT	INTEREST RATE
AEEEINRSSTXY	SIXTEEN YEARS
AEEEIOPPRRTV	PREOPERATIVE
AEEEIPRRSTVV	PRESERVATIVE
AEEEIPRSSVWX	EXPRESS A VIEW
AEEEJLMNRSUW	NEW JERUSALEM
AEEEKLLPRSSW	SLEEPWALKERS
AEEEKLRRSTTW	STREETWALKER
AEEEKMMMNORST	MET ONE'S MAKER
AEEEKMRRSTTT	STREET MARKET
AEEELLLLNOTW	LET WELL ALONE
AEEELLLNOOPV	APOLLO ELEVEN

AEEELLORSTTT	TEETOTALLERS	AEEFGILNPPRZ	GRAF ZEPPELIN
AEEELMNNNOST	LENT ONE'S NAME	AEEFGILNPRST	FINGERPLATES
AEEELMNNSSSS	NAMELESSNESS	AEEFGILRSSSU	SALES FIGURES
AEEELMNORSYY	ELEEMOSYNARY	AEEFGIMNNOST	GAME OF TENNIS
AEEELNOORTTV	NEVER TOO LATE	AEEFGIMNPTTT	TEMPTING FATE
AEEELNOOSSST	LOSE ONES SEAT	AEEFGINNORSS	GRAIN OF SENSE
AEEELNOPRSTT	OPENS A LETTER	AEEFGINRRRSU	SUGAR REFINER
AEEELOPRSSTU	SURE TO PLEASE	AEEFGIORRRRT	REFRIGERATOR
AEEELPRSTTTY	TYPES A LETTER	AEEFGLMNNRTU	FLUENT GERMAN
AEEEMMNRSSTU	MEASUREMENTS	AEEFGLNRSSTU	GRATEFULNESS
AEEEMNNPPRSW	NEWSPAPERMEN	AEEFHHIINSST	FISH IN THE SEA
AEEEMNNSTTTW	NEW TESTAMENT	AEEFHHLOORTV	HAVE THE FLOOR
AEEEMPRRSTTU	TEMPERATURES	AEEFHHMORSST	FROM THE ASHES
AEEEMRSSSSST	SEAMSTRESSES	AEEFHHMORSTT	THREE FATHOMS
AEEENNOPRSTW	WENT ON A SPREE	AEEFHHNOSTTU	HEAT OF THE SUN
AEEENNORRUVY	RUN AN EYE OVER	AEEFHHORSSTU	HOUSEFATHERS
AEEENNPSSTTV	TEN PAST SEVEN	AEEFHIILNRTT	LEFT IN THE AIR
AEEENORSSSSU	USES ONE'S EARS	AEEFHIKLNTTT	TAKEN THE LIFT
AEEENORSSTVW	WENT OVERSEAS	AEEFHIKLSTTT	TAKES THE LIFT
AEEENORSTTWY	ONE WAY STREET	AEEFHIKNRSSS	FREAKISHNESS
AEEENRSSTVYY	SEVENTY YEARS	AEEFHILLMOTT	ALL OF THE TIME
AEEEQRSSSTTU	SEQUESTRATES	AEEFHILLNOOS	HELL OF A NOISE
AEEFFFLOORRS	OFFER FOR SALE	AEEFHILLNOSV	HAVE ONES FILL
AEEFFGHHIMOT	HEIGHT OF FAME	AEEFHILLNOVW	WILL OF HEAVEN
AEEFFGHILLST	FLIES THE FLAG	AEEFHILPRRSS	PEARL FISHERS
AEEFFGHIRRTU	FATHER FIGURE	AEEFHILSSTTT	FAILS THE TEST
AEEFFGIILNNT	FEELING FAINT	AEEFHINNOOTV	HAVE NONE OF IT
AEEFFGIILLNOO	FEELING A FOOL	AEEFHINNORST	NINE OF HEARTS
AEEFFGILLNUW	FEELING AWFUL	AEEFHIOORRST	RAISE THE ROOF
AEEFFGILNORT	FREE-FLOATING	AEEFHIOPRRST	PAIR OF THREES
AEEFFGIORRST	TEARS OF GRIEF	AEEFHKLOORTT	TAKE THE FLOOR
AEEFFGIRSSTU	REFUSES A GIFT	AEEFHLLRRSTU	FULLERS EARTH
AEEFFGRSSTTU	SUFFRAGETTES	AEEFHLMNSSSU	SHAMEFULNESS
AEEFFHIORSTV	FIVE OF HEARTS	AEEFHLMORRTW	FLAMETHROWER
AEEFFHORRSTT	FOSTER FATHER	AEEFHLMORTWY	THE MAYFLOWER
AEEFFIILMORT	FOR A LIFETIME	AEEFHLMPSTYY	FEEL SYMPATHY
AEEFFIIPSTVV	FIVE PAST FIVE	AEEFHLOORSSU	HOUSE FOR SALE
AEEFFIKMNOTT	TAKEN TIME OFF	AEEFHLOOSTTT	ATHLETES FOOT
AEEFFIKMOSTT	TAKES TIME OFF	AEEFHLOPPRST	FALSE PROPHET
AEEFFILOSTTX	FLEET OF TAXIS	AEEFHMNNOOPSY	HEAPS OF MONEY
AEEFFIMNOPRR	FREE FROM PAIN	AEEFHMNOSTVY	SEVENTH OF MAY
AEEFFKKOOOTW	TOOK A WEEK OFF	AEEFHMOORSST	TEAM OF HORSES
AEEFFKOORSTT	STROKE OF FATE	AEEFHNOORSTT	HEART OF STONE
AEEFFLLORTTU	FOUR FEET TALL	AEEFHINOOSTTY	TASTE OF HONEY
AEEFFLMNORTT	MENTAL EFFORT	AEEFHOOPRRTW	WEATHERPROOF
AEEFFLMOSSTT	LETS OFF STEAM	AEEFHORRSTTW	FEAR THE WORST
AEEFFLNORTTU	LEFT A FORTUNE	AEEFHORSTTTU	FOURTH ESTATE
AEEFFMNORRTW	FREE FROM WANT	AEEFIILLLNNN	FALLEN IN LINE
AEEFGGHINOTW	WHITE OF AN EGG	AEEFIILMPPRR	PREAMPLIFIER
AEEFGGHINRTW	WAG THE FINGER	AEEFIIMOSTTY	EASY TIME OF IT
AEEFGGHNNOOT	ONE OF THE GANG	AEEFIINNPSTV	FIVE PAST NINE
AEEFGGHORTWY	FOGGY WEATHER	AEEFIINRRSTT	FRATERNITIES
AEEFGGIKNRTU	TAKING REFUGE	AEEFIKMMORTT	TAKE IT FROM ME
AEEFGGILNNRY	FEELING ANGRY	AEEFIKNNNRST	FRANKENSTEIN
AEEFGGINNORT	FOREIGN AGENT	AEEFILLLNNOV	FALLEN IN LOVE
AEEFGHILNPPY	FEELING HAPPY	AEEFILLNOPRW	ALPINE FLOWER
AEEFGHILNPRT	FIGHTER PLANE	AEEFILLNOSST	EATS ONE'S FILL
AEEFGHILNSSY	FLASHING EYES	AEEFILLORSVY	FIRES A VOLLEY
AEEFGHIMRTUW	FUME WITH RAGE	AEEFILMNORSU	MAN OF LEISURE
AEEFGHLLORTW	LOWER THE FLAG	AEEFILNRRSTU	FUNERAL RITES
AEEFGHLNNOSS	HANGS ONESELF	AEEFILNSSSTW	FALSE WITNESS
AEEFGHLOSSST	SHEET OF GLASS	AEEFILOPRRST	PROLIFERATES
AEEFGIILNNOP	OPENING A FILE	AEEFILORSTTV	FIRST TO LEAVE
AEEFGIILNOST	FAILING TO SEE	AEEFILPPRRTT	APPLE FRITTER
AEEFGIILNOTV	GIVE ONE A LIFT	AEEFILRRTTUU	UTTER FAILURE
AEEFGIIOPRSS	SIEGE OF PARIS	AEEFIMMRRSSU	FIRM MEASURES
AEEFGIKRRSTU	FIGURE SKATER	AEEFIMNNORTT	FERMENTATION
AEEFGILLLMNS	FEELING SMALL	AEEFINNORSTT	FENESTRATION
AEEFGILLNNOS	ALIGN ONESELF	AEEFINOPQRSU	PAIR OF QUEENS
AEEFGILLNRUV	GAVE FULL REIN	AEEFINOPRSSV	PAIR OF SEVENS
AEEFGILMNRSW	WARM FEELINGS	AEEFINRRSSTU	AFTER SUNRISE

AEEFKLMNORST	LEFT ONE'S MARK	AEEGHIILNTUW	IN LEAGUE WITH
AEEFKLOORRVW	LEAVE FOR WORK	AEEGHIINRTWW	WEARING WHITE
AEEFKLOPPRSY	PLAY FOR KEEPS	AEEGHIKLNPSS	SPEAK ENGLISH
AEEFKNOPSSXY	EXPANSE OF SKY	AEEGHIKMRRTT	RIG THE MARKET
AEEFLLNOPPSY	APPLY ONESELF	AEEGHIKNOTVY	GIVEN THE OKAY
AEEFLLNSSSSW	FLAWLESSNESS	AEEGHIKNRRTT	GREAT THINKER
AEEFLMNORSTT	MAN OF LETTERS	AEEGHIKOSTVY	GIVES THE OKAY
AEEFLNOORTUV	LOVE OF NATURE	AEEGHILLNPSS	SHELLING PEAS
AEEFLNOOSSSU	USES ONE'S LOAF	AEEGHILLNRSY	EARLY ENGLISH
AEEFLNSSSTTU	TASTEFULNESS	AEEGHILMNPTV	GIVEN THE PALM
AEEFLNSSSTUW	WASTEFULNESS	AEEGHILMPSTV	GIVES THE PALM
AEEFLOPQRSUW	PASQUEFLOWER	AEEGHILNNRTY	HEARTENINGLY
AEEFLOPRSTUY	REFUSE TO PLAY	AEEGHILNOPRW	HEALING POWER
AEEFLRRSSSTT	SELF-STARTERS	AEEGHILPRSTT	TELEGRAPHIST
AEEFMNNOORST	MASTER OF NONE	AEEGHIMNSSST	SEETHING MASS
AEEFMNOOSTWY	WASTE OF MONEY	AEEGHINNNRTW	RANG IN THE NEW
AEEFMNORSSSV	MASS OF NERVES	AEEGHINOPSST	PATHOGENESIS
AEEFMOORRTTY	TREATY OF ROME	AEEGHINPRSTU	SUPERHEATING
AEEFNNNOPRTY	TEN FOR A PENNY	AEEGHINPSTTT	TEN PAST EIGHT
AEEFNNORRSTT	EASTERN FRONT	AEEGHINPTTVY	HEAVY PETTING
AEEFNOPRRSTT	FOSTER PARENT	AEEGHINRRSTT	STRAIGHTENER
AEEFNORSSSTZ	FROZEN ASSETS	AEEGHINRSSTT	SEEN STRAIGHT
AEEFNRRRRSST	TRANSFERRERS	AEEGHINSTTWY	GETS IN THE WAY
AEEFOOPRRRTW	WATERPROOFER	AEEGHIPPRSTW	PAPERWEIGHTS
AEEFOOPRRSST	PROFESSORATE	AEEGHIPRRRSS	SERIGRAPHERS
AEEFOORRRSWW	WORSE FOR WEAR	AEEGHIPRSSTW	STAGE WHISPER
AEEFOPRSSTUY	REFUSES TO PAY	AEEGHIQSTTTU	QUIT THE STAGE
AEEFORRSTTUY	FEATURE STORY	AEEGHIRSSSTT	SEES STRAIGHT
AEEGGGILNOTW	GET A WIGGLE ON	AEEGHKLORTTW	WALK TOGETHER
AEEGGGIMNSSU	GUESSING GAME	AEEGHKOOSTTT	GO TO THE STAKE
AEEGGHHNORTT	HANG TOGETHER	AEEGHLLMORTY	GEOTHERMALLY
AEEGGHIINNRS	GARNISHEEING	AEEGHLLNORST	THREE GALLONS
AEEGGHIINRTW	AGREEING WITH	AEEGHLMNOSTT	AT SOME LENGTH
AEEGGHILLNPR	LARGE HELPING	AEEGHLNOPRSY	SELENOGRAPHY
AEEGGHILNPRT	TELEGRAPHING	AEEGHLOORRTW	WOOLGATHERER
AEEGGHINOSST	SEEING A GHOST	AEEGHLOSSTTU	TOUGH AS STEEL
AEEGGHINTTUV	GAVE IT THE GUN	AEEGHLRRSSTU	SLAUGHTERERS
AEEGGHMOORST	GEORGE THOMAS	AEEGHMOORSTU	HETEROGAMOUS
AEEGGHMRTUWY	MUGGY WEATHER	AEEGHMOPSTTY	GAMETOPHYTES
AEEGGHNOOSTT	GO ON THE STAGE	AEEGHNNOOSSW	SHOWN ONE'S AGE
AEEGGIIKNPPR	KEEPING A GRIP	AEEGHNOOPRTV	PHOTOENGRAVE
AEEGGIILNNRS	GENERALISING	AEEGHNOOSSSW	SHOWS ONE'S AGE
AEEGGIILNNRZ	GENERALIZING	AEEGHNOOPRRST	STENOGRAPHER
AEEGGIILNNSV	EVANGELISING	AEEGHNOPSSTT	STEP ON THE GAS
AEEGGIILNNVZ	EVANGELIZING	AEEGHNORRSST	HAS NO REGRETS
AEEGGIINNSTV	NEGATIVE SIGN	AEEGHNORSSTU	ANOTHER GUESS
AEEGGIINRSTT	GETTING A RISE	AEEGHNPRSTTU	TURN THE PAGES
AEEGGILNSTTT	GETTING STALE	AEEGHOOOPRTT	GO TO THE OPERA
AEEGGILRSSVY	AGGRESSIVELY	AEEGHOPPRRRT	PETROGRAPHER
AEEGGIMMNOST	GEOMAGNETISM	AEEGHOPRRSTY	STEREOGRAPHY
AEEGGIMNOSTT	GEOMAGNETIST	AEEGHORRSSST	GATHERS ROSES
AEEGGIMNPRRT	RAGING TEMPER	AEEGHORRSSTU	ARGUE THE TOSS
AEEGGINORRTW	TOWERING RAGE	AEEGHRRRSTUY	HEART SURGERY
AEEGGINSSTTT	STAGE SETTING	AEEGIIILLMTT	ILLEGITIMATE
AEEGGIQRRRSU	SQUARE-RIGGER	AEEGIIILNRRV	VIRGINIA REEL
AEEGGIRRSTTU	REGURGITATES	AEEGIIKNPSTW	KEEPS WAITING
AEEGGLNNOORW	GENERAL GOWON	AEEGIILLMTTY	LEGITIMATELY
AEEGGLPRRRUY	RUGGER PLAYER	AEEGIILLNTTV	GIVEN A LITTLE
AEEGGMNRRTTU	NUTMEG GRATER	AEEGIILLSTTV	GIVES A LITTLE
AEEGGNOOSSTT	GETS ONE'S GOAT	AEEGIILMNNRS	REMAIN SINGLE
AEEGGNOPRSTU	GET ONE'S RAG UP	AEEGIILNNORS	LEGIONNAIRES
AEEGHHHIMTTY	MAY THE EIGHTH	AEEGIILNNRTV	INTERLEAVING
AEEGHHIILVWY	WEIGH HEAVILY	AEEGIILNORSS	REGIONALISES
AEEGHHIIMSTT	HIGH ESTIMATE	AEEGIILNORSZ	REGIONALIZES
AEEGHHIILNRTT	THE REAL THING	AEEGIINNNRTT	ENTERTAINING
AEEGHHIIMNSTT	THE SAME THING	AEEGIINNRRSST	EASTER RISING
AEEGHHIRTTTT	HIT THE TARGET	AEEGIINNRSTT	GIVEN IT A REST
AEEGHHISTVWY	HEAVYWEIGHTS	AEEGIINSSTTV	INVESTIGATES
AEEGHHNOPRRT	ETHNOGRAPHER	AEEGIIRSSTTV	GIVES IT A REST
AEEGHHORRTUW	ROUGH WEATHER	AEEGIJLMMNNT	GENTLEMAN JIM
AEEGHHSSTTTU	SHUTS THE GATE		

AEEGIJMMRSVY	JIMMY GREAVES	AEEGNNOSSSUY	ANYONE'S GUESS
AEEGIJNNRTUV	REJUVENATING	AEEGNOOPRSWY	GROPE ONES WAY
AEEGIKLLNPSW	SPEAKING WELL	AEEGNOORSSSU	GROUSE SEASON
AEEGIKLNNSST	TALKING SENSE	AEEGNOOSSSTT	GETS ONE'S OATS
AEEGIKLNSTTW	SWEET-TALKING	AEEGNORRTUVY	RETURN VOYAGE
AEEGIKMNPRRT	PARKING METER	AEEGNRRSSSST	TRANSGRESSES
AEEGIKNOORTW	ROGATION WEEK	AEEHHIKNNTTT	TAKEN THE HINT
AEEGIKNRSTUY	KEY SIGNATURE	AEEHHIKNSTTT	TAKES THE HINT
AEEGILLLNRTY	ILLEGAL ENTRY	AEEHHILNOPRS	HELEN SHAPIRO
AEEGILLLNSTT	TELL-TALE SIGN	AEEHHILNORTT	THE LION HEART
	TELLING TALES	AEEHHIMNPRSW	NEW HAMPSHIRE
AEEGILLMNRTY	REGIMENTALLY	AEEHHIMPRRTY	HYPERTHERMIA
AEEGILLNNOSV	GIVEN ONE'S ALL	AEEHHINOSTTT	IN THE HOT SEAT
AEEGILLNNOTT	LETTING ALONE	AEEHHINSSSTW	WINS THE ASHES
AEEGILLNOSSV	GIVES ONE'S ALL	AEEHHIRSSTWW	WHITEWASHERS
AEEGILLNRTTW	TREATING WELL	AEEHHKORRSTW	SHARE THE WORK
AEEGILLNSSTT	TESSELLATING	AEEHHLLORSTT	ALL THE OTHERS
AEEGILLRSSST	LEGISLATRESS	AEEHHLNOSTVY	HEAVENLY HOST
AEEGILMNNTTU	INTEGUMENTAL	AEEHIILLOOPRTT	BILLARE THE LOOT
AEEGILNNORSW	REGIONAL NEWS	AEEHHLOPRSTY	PLAYS THE HERO
AEEGILNNORTW	LEANING TOWER	AEEHHLORRSTT	HEALTH RESORT
AEEGILNNOSSV	GIVEN A LESSON	AEEHHLOSSTTW	STEAL THE SHOW
AEEGILNNOSYY	LAYING EYES ON	AEEHHMNORTTW	WORTH THE NAME
AEEGILNNRTTY	ENTREATINGLY	AEEHHNNOPRTT	THE PARTHENON
AEEGILNOSSSV	GIVES A LESSON	AEEHHNNOPSVY	SHOVE HAPENNY
AEEGIMNNNORY	EARNING MONEY	AEEHHNNOOPSSU	HAS OPEN HOUSE
AEEGIMNNNOSS	SIGN ONES NAME	AEEHHNOPPSTT	TAPS THE PHONE
AEEGIMNNOPST	STEAMING OPEN	AEEHHNOPTTTU	PUT THE HEAT ON
AEEGIMNNOSTT	SEGMENTATION	AEEHHNORSSTT	HEARTHSTONES
AEEGIMNNRRTU	REMUNERATING	AEEHHNNORSTT	THE NORTH-EAST
AEEGIMNNOORTV	MOVE INTO GEAR	AEEHHNNRRTTTU	NEAR THE TRUTH
AEEGIMNOSSTT	GET INTO A MESS	AEEHHOSSTTTU	THE SOUTH-EAST
AEEGIMSSSTTU	GUESSTIMATES	AEEHHPRRSSSU	SHARE-PUSHERS
AEEGINNORRTY	ROTARY ENGINE	AEEHIIKNSSST	KINAESTHESIS
AEEGINNORTUV	GIVE ONE A TURN	AEEHIILNRSTT	LETS IN THE AIR
AEEGINNOTTUV	NATIVE TONGUE	AEEHIIMNRTTW	TEEM WITH RAIN
AEEGINNQRTUY	ENQUIRY AGENT	AEEHIIMOOPSS	HAEMOPOIESIS
AEEGINOPPRRV	PAPERING OVER	AEEHIINNOPRT	IN THE OPEN AIR
AEEGINORRSTT	INTERROGATES	AEEHIINNORST	NOSE IN THE AIR
AEEGINOSTTTW	GET INTO A STEW	AEEHIINNORST	ETHERISATION
AEEGINPPRRTT	PERPETRATING	AEEHIINORTTZ	ETHERIZATION
AEEGINPPRTTU	PERPETUATING	AEEHIJMNPSTU	JUMP IN THE SEA
AEEGINPPSSTW	SWEEPING PAST	AEEHIJMORRST	JAMES HERRIOT
AEEGINQRRTUV	GIVEN QUARTER	AEEHIKKLNSTT	TAKEN THE SILK
AEEGINRRSTVY	YANGTSE RIVER	AEEHIKKLSSTT	TAKES THE SILK
AEEGIOPRRSTV	PREROGATIVES	AEEHIKLLMNRU	HUMANE KILLER
AEEGIQRRSTUV	GIVES QUARTER	AEEHIKLLNPTT	TAKEN THE PILL
AEEGIRSSSTUW	SUGAR IS SWEET	AEEHIKLLPSTT	TAKES THE PILL
AEEGJNNRTTUY	JENNY AGUTTER	AEEHIKLMRRSS	SHAREMILKERS
AEEGKLNOOOSS	LOOKS ONE'S AGE	AEEHIKLNNPPT	PINK ELEPHANT
AEEGKMNNOPRS	GERMAN SPOKEN	AEEHIKMNOPTT	MAKE THE POINT
	SPOKEN GERMAN	AEEHIKNOPTTT	TAKE THE POINT
AEEGKMOPRRSS	MAKE PROGRESS	AEEHIKNPSSTT	TAKEN THE PISS
AEEGLLMNOPSY	SPLENOMEGALY	AEEHIKPSSSTT	TAKES THE PISS
AEEGLLMNRUWZ	MANGEL-WURZEL	AEEHILLNNOTY	LAY ON THE LINE
AEEGLLNNOSSV	SEVEN GALLONS	AEEHILLNOSVW	HAVE ONES WILL
AEEGLLPRRSSY	PRESS GALLERY	AEEHILLNOTVW	ON A LEVEL WITH
AEEGLMNNORSS	GERMAN LESSON	AEEHILLPPRRY	PERIPHERALLY
AEEGLMNNORTV	GOVERNMENTAL	AEEHILMMNRST	IN THE SLAMMER
AEEGLMNOORST	LOOSE GARMENT	AEEHILMMOOST	MESOTHELIOMA
AEEGLNNOPRSU	ENLARGES UPON	AEEHILMNPSST	MISS THE PLANE
AEEGLNOORSSS	LOSES ONE'S RAG	AEEHILMSSTTW	STEAM WHISTLE
AEEGMMNORTTY	MAGNETOMETRY	AEEHILNOORSS	LOSE ONES HAIR
AEEGMMOPRRST	SET PROGRAMME	AEEHILNRSSSS	HAIRLESSNESS
AEEGMNNOORST	GONE ON STREAM	AEEHILNSSSTT	STEALTHINESS
AEEGMNNRRSTU	MASTER GUNNER	AEEHILOPPRST	POLITE PHRASE
AEEGMNOORSST	GOES ON STREAM	AEEHILOPRTTV	PRIVATE HOTEL
AEEGMNOORSTV	MOVES TO ANGER	AEEHILOTTUVW	WITHOUT LEAVE
AEEGMNORRTTU	OUTER GARMENT	AEEHILPRSTUW	WITH PLEASURE
AEEGMNRRTTTU	URGENT MATTER	AEEHILPSSTTT	TELEPATHISTS
AEEGMRRSTTYY	GREAT MYSTERY	AEEHIMMNSTTY	MANYS THE TIME

AEEHIMNORRSS	HORSE MARINES
AEEHINNOPPRS	APPREHENSION
AEEHINNOPSTW	TWO HA'PENNIES
AEEHINNORSTW	WIN ONE'S HEART
AEEHINNPSSTT	SAINT STEPHEN
AEEHINOPRSTU	HOUSE PAINTER
AEEHINORRRST	HORSE TRAINER
AEEHINSSSTTT	ANESTHETISTS
AEEHIOPPRTTW	HOT-WATER PIPE
AEEHIOPPSTTV	STOVEPIPE HAT
AEEHIOPRSTUV	PRIVATE HOUSE
AEEHIORRRRST	HAIR RESTORER
AEEHIPPPRSTY	PAYS THE PIPER
AEEHIPRRSTTW	WEATHER-STRIP
AEEHIRSSSSSU	ISSUES SHARES
AEEHKLOPSSST	HOPELESS TASK
AEEHKMPRRSTY	HYPERMARKETS
AEEHKNNNNTTY	KENNETH TYNAN
AEEHLLMMORWY	YELLOW HAMMER
	YELLOWHAMMER
AEEHLLMNNOPY	PHENOMENALLY
AEEHLLNOTWWY	WELL ON THE WAY
AEEHLLOPPRTW	TELL A WHOPPER
AEEHLLPSSSST	SELLS THE PASS
AEEHLMNOOPRS	MELANOPHORES
AEEHLMNORSTT	SOLEMN THREAT
AEEHLMNRSSSS	HARMLESSNESS
AEEHLNNRSTYY	HENRY STANLEY
AEEHLNOPRTUY	POLYURETHANE
AEEHLNOPSTTU	PUT THE SEAL ON
AEEHLNORSTUY	NO EARTHLY USE
AEEHLNORTTUY	ETERNAL YOUTH
AEEHMMOOPRST	METAMORPHOSE
AEEHMNNOPRTY	HYMENOPTERAN
AEEHMNNORTTW	NO MATTER WHEN
AEEHMNORRTTU	MOTHER NATURE
AEEHMOOPPRRT	PAPER THE ROOM
AEEHMOPRSTTU	THE MOUSETRAP
AEEHMORRSSTU	SHORT MEASURE
AEEHMORRSSTW	WHOREMASTERS
AEEHMORSSSTU	HOUSEMASTERS
AEEHMORSSTUV	HARVEST MOUSE
AEEHMORSTTUY	ERYTHEMATOUS
AEEHNNOORSTW	WON ONE'S HEART
AEEHNNORRSTT	NORTHEASTERN
AEEHNNRSTUWY	SUNNY WEATHER
AEEHNOPRSSTU	HOUSEPARENTS
AEEHNOPRSTTW	WORE THE PANTS
AEEHNORSSTTU	SOUTHEASTERN
AEEHNRRSTTUU	TREASURE HUNT
AEEHOPRRSSTT	STRATOSPHERE
AEEHRRSTTTTU	UTTER THREATS
AEEIIILNQSTU	INEQUALITIES
AEEIIIMNQSTU	EQUANIMITIES
AEEIIJNOQSSU	JE NE SAIS QUOI
AEEIIKLMNNNR	IN LIKE MANNER
AEEIIKLMNPRS	MARLINESPIKE
AEEIIKMNNSSY	KEYNESIANISM
AEEIIILLRTTY	ILLITERATELY
AEEIIILLMPRRU	IMPERIAL RULE
AEEIIILLMRSTU	MITRAILLEUSE
AEEIIILLMSTWW	SWEET WILLIAM
AEEIIILLNOSST	ESSENTIAL OIL
AEEIIILLNPSTT	PESTILENTIAL
AEEIILMNNRST	REMAIN SILENT
AEEIILMNOOST	EMOTIONALISE
AEEIILMNOOTZ	EMOTIONALIZE
AEEIILMNSSST	ESSENTIALISM
AEEIILMPRTVY	IMPERATIVELY
AEEIILMRRSST	SEMITRAILERS
AEEIILNNOQSU	AQUILINE NOSE
AEEIILNNRSST	INTERNALISES
AEEIILNNRSTZ	INTERNALIZES
AEEIILNNSSST	INESSENTIALS
AEEIILNNSSTW	EINSTEINS LAW
AEEIILNOPRTT	REPETITIONAL
AEEIILNPRSTV	VESPERTILIAN
AEEIILNRRSST	LITERARINESS
AEEIILNRSSUV	UNIVERSALISE
AEEIILNRSUVZ	UNIVERSALIZE
AEEIILNSSSTT	ESSENTIALIST
AEEIILNSSTTY	ESSENTIALITY
AEEIILOPTTVX	EXPLOITATIVE
AEEIILPRSTVV	PRIVATE LIVES
AEEIIMNORRTV	ARRIVE ON TIME
AEEIIMNRRRST	INTERMARRIES
AEEIIMNRSTTW	SWEET MARTINI
AEEIIMNSSSTW	SIAMESE TWINS
AEEIINNPRTTY	PENITENTIARY
AEEIINNRRSTV	IT NEVER RAINS
AEEIINNRRTTU	INTRAUTERINE
AEEIINORSSVW	AIR ONES VIEWS
AEEIINNQRSTTU	QUATERNITIES
AEEIIPRTTUVV	VITUPERATIVE
AEEIJKNPSSST	SPEAKS IN JEST
AEEIJLOPRTVY	PEJORATIVELY
AEEIKKNORSSY	KARYOKINESES
AEEIKLLLSTTY	SKITTLE ALLEY
AEEIKLLMNOSW	MAKE ONES WILL
AEEIKLNOPSSV	SPEAKS NO EVIL
AEEIKLOOPRRT	LIKE A TROOPER
AEEIKLOPRRSU	LAKE SUPERIOR
AEEIKMNNOOSS	MAKES NO NOISE
AEEIKMNOTTTU	TAKEN TIME OUT
AEEIKMOPPRST	KEPT A PROMISE
AEEIKMORSSTW	MAKES IT WORSE
AEEIKMOSTTTU	TAKES TIME OUT
AEEIKNNOSSSV	SAVE ONES SKIN
AEEIKNOPRRST	TAKE PRISONER
AEEIKNOPRSST	RISEN TO SPEAK
AEEIKNOPRSTW	STRIKE WEAPON
AEEIKNOPSTTW	WEAKEST POINT
AEEIKNORSSTT	STRIKES A NOTE
AEEIKOPRSSST	RISES TO SPEAK
	STRIKES A POSE
AEEIILLMNRTTT	ILL-TREATMENT
AEEIILLNNPSTY	SEPTENNIALLY
AEEIILLNOPRTY	PERITONEALLY
AEEIILLNQSTUY	SEQUENTIALLY
AEEIILLNQTUVY	EQUIVALENTLY
AEEIILLNRRSTT	INTERSTELLAR
AEEIILLNRRTVY	IRRELEVANTLY
AEEIILLNSSSUV	ALLUSIVENESS
AEEIILLORRTWX	EXTERIOR WALL
AEEIILLRRSSVW	SILVER SALVER
AEEIILLTTTTTT	TITTLE TATTLE
	TITTLE-TATTLE
AEEIILMMPRSTT	SIMPLE MATTER
AEEIILMNNNRSS	MANNERLINESS
AEEIILMNPRSSW	SIMPLE ANSWER
AEEIILMNRSSST	MASTERLINESS
AEEIILMNRRSTT	MELTS IN TEARS
AEEIILMNSSTTU	ULTIMATENESS
AEEIILMOPRRST	POLARIMETERS
AEEIILMOPRRSY	EARLY PROMISE
AEEIILNNPRSTY	TENNIS PLAYER
AEEIILNNPRSUV	RIEN NE VA PLUS
AEEIILNNPSSSS	PAINLESSNESS
AEEIILNNOPRSS	PERSONALISES
AEEIILNOPRSSX	EXPRESSIONAL
AEEIILNOPRSSZ	PERSONALIZES
AEEIILNOPRSTT	INTERPOLATES

AEEILNORRTTW	LEARN TO WRITE
AEEILNORSTVW	WRITES A NOVEL
AEEILNPRRSTY	SILENT PRAYER
AEEILNRRSTTY	STERN REALITY
AEEILOOPRRTV	POOR RELATIVE
AEEILOPRRSTT	LIE PROSTRATE
AEEILOPRSTTV	SILVER TEAPOT
AEEILPPRRSTU	PLEASURE TRIP
AEEILPRSSTUV	SUPERLATIVES
AEEILPRSSUVY	PERSUASIVELY
AEEILRRSTTTU	LITTERATEURS
AEEIMMNRSSTU	IMMATURENESS
AEEIMMNRSTTT	MISTREATMENT
AEEIMMNSSTTT	MISSTATEMENT
AEEIMNNORRTU	REMUNERATION
AEEIMNOPRSST	IMPERSONATES
AEEIMNOPRTTW	WRITTEN A POEM
AEEIMNOPTTXX	TAX EXEMPTION
AEEIMNORRSST	SENIOR MASTER
AEEIMOPRSTVY	PAYS OVERTIME
AEEIMRSSSTTY	SYSTEMATISER
AEEIMRSSTTYZ	SYSTEMATIZER
AEEIMSSSSTTY	SYSTEMATISES
AEEIMSSSTTYZ	SYSTEMATIZES
AEEINNOPRSTT	NEAREST POINT
	PRESENTATION
AEEINNOPSSTT	STATE PENSION
AEEINNORSSTW	WINTER SEASON
AEEINNORTTTW	WRITTEN A NOTE
AEEINOORTTTX	EXTORTIONATE
AEEINOPPRRTT	PERPETRATION
AEEINOPPRTTU	PERPETUATION
AEEINOPPSSST	APPOSITENESS
AEEINOPRRSTV	PRESERVATION
AEEINORRRSVY	REVERSIONARY
AEEINORRSSTV	RESERVATIONS
AEEINORRSTTT	TREAT IN STORE
AEEINORSSSTT	STIRS ONE'S TEA
AEEINPRRSSTX	EXPRESS TRAIN
AEEINPRRSSUV	NURSES A VIPER
AEEINPRRSTUV	PRIVATE NURSE
AEEINPRSSTTY	PAYS INTEREST
AEEINRSSTTTV	TRANSVESTITE
AEEINSSTTTUV	SUSTENTATIVE
AEEIOPPRRSTX	EXPROPRIATES
AEEIOPRRRTTW	WRITE A REPORT
AEEIORRSSTTV	RESTORATIVES
AEEIPPRRTTTT	PITTER-PATTER
AEEIPRRSSSTT	STRIPTEASERS
AEEIRRSSTTTT	STREET ARTIST
AEEKKLOOOOST	TOOK A LOOK-SEE
AEEKKLOOOPTU	KEEP A LOOK-OUT
AEEKLLORRRST	ROLLER-SKATER
AEEKLLORRSST	ROLLER SKATES
	ROLLER-SKATES
AEEKLLORSTWY	YELLOW STREAK
AEEKLMNRSSUW	LUKEWARMNESS
AEEKLMOPSSUV	SPEAK VOLUMES
AEEKLMORRSTW	METALWORKERS
AEEKLNNNOSST	TALK NONSENSE
AEEKLNNOSSST	TAKEN LESSONS
AEEKLNOPPSSY	SPEAKS OPENLY
AEEKLNOPRUWY	WOKEN UP EARLY
AEEKLNOSSSST	TAKES LESSONS
AEEKMMOPRTUV	MOVE UP-MARKET
AEEKMNNOPTTY	TOKEN PAYMENT
AEEKMOPRRTTX	EXPORT MARKET
AEEKMORRSSTT	MASTER STROKE
	MASTERSTROKE
AEEKMPRRSSTU	SUPERMARKETS
AEEKNNORSTTU	TAKE ONES TURN

AEEKNORSTTWY	NEW YORK STATE
AEEKNPRRSSTU	SUPERTANKERS
AEELLLMNOTVY	MALEVOLENTLY
AEELLLMRSSTT	SMALL LETTERS
AEELLLNOOSSS	LOSES ONE'S ALL
AEELLLNOSSTT	TELLS NO TALES
AEELLMNPPSTU	SUPPLEMENTAL
AEELLMORRSST	STEAMROLLERS
AEELLMORSTTY	TELL ME A STORY
AEELLNOOPRSY	PLAY ONES ROLE
AEELLNOORSTV	LEARNS TO LOVE
AEELLNOORTTV	LEARNT TO LOVE
AEELLNORSSTW	STONEWALLERS
AEELLOPRTTUY	PLAY ROULETTE
AEELMNOOQRSTU	ON EQUAL TERMS
AEELMNPRRSTU	PREMENSTRUAL
AEELNNOOPRST	PERSONAL NOTE
AEELNOOSSSWY	LOSES ONE'S WAY
AEELNOPPRSTT	PLANE OF OTTER
AEELNOPRSSSS	SALESPERSONS
AEELNORRRSTU	SALE OR RETURN
AEELNORSTUXY	EXTRANEOUSLY
AEELNRRSSTVY	TRANSVERSELY
AEELOPPRRRTY	REAL PROPERTY
AEELOPRRSTTT	LATEST REPORT
AEELOPRSSTTT	POSTS A LETTER
AEELOPSSTTUX	EXPOSTULATES
AEELORSTTTY	STATE LOTTERY
AEELQSSTTUUY	STATUESQUELY
AEEMMMNOSSTV	MASS MOVEMENT
AEEMMNOOPRRR	ROMAN EMPEROR
AEEMMNORSSSU	SUMMER SEASON
AEEMMNORSTTY	MONEY MATTERS
AEEMMNNOOSSTW	ONE'S OWN STEAM
AEEMMNNORSTTW	WENT ON STREAM
AEEMMNOOPRSTY	MONEY TO SPARE
AEEMMNOORTUUV	OUTMANOEUVRE
AEEMMNORRSSTT	REMONSTRATES
AEEMMNPRRSSST	PRESENTS ARMS
AEEMOOORSSTTV	MOVES TO TEARS
AEEMPRSSSSTU	PASSES MUSTER
AEENNOOORSTU	OUT ON ONE'S EAR
AEENNOOPPRST	OPEN ONE'S TRAP
AEENNOSSSSUU	NAUSEOUSNESS
AEENOOPRSSST	STOP ONE'S EARS
AEENOOPRSSTU	UP TO ONE'S EARS
AEENOOQRRTTU	QUARTER TO ONE
AEENOORSTTTT	ROSETTA STONE
AEENOPRRSSTT	PATERNOSTERS
AEENOQRRTTTU	QUARTER TO TEN
AEENORRRSTTW	NARROW STREET
AEENORRSSTXY	EXTRASENSORY
AEENORRSTTUY	TREASURY NOTE
AEENORRTTTUU	TRUE TO NATURE
AEENORSSTTUV	NERVOUS STATE
AEENORSTTUVY	VENTURE TO SAY
AEEOOPRRSTTT	STATE TROOPER
AEEOPPRRRSTT	PERPETRATORS
AEEORRRTTTUW	WATER TORTURE
AEEORSTTTWWY	TWO-WAY STREET
AEEPRRSSSSST	TRESSPASSERS
AEFFFHINORTU	FUN OF THE FAIR
AEFFFLLLNOOU	FALLEN FOUL OF
AEFFGHILRSTU	FEARFUL SIGHT
AEFFGHLLNOTW	FLOWN THE FLAG
AEFFGIILNRST	LIFTS A FINGER
AEFFGILNNOOW	FLAGON OF WINE
AEFFGINRSTUX	SUFFERING TAX
AEFFHIKLOOST	OFF LIKE A SHOT
AEFFHILNSSTU	FAITHFULNESS
AEFFHLMOTTWY	TWELFTH OF MAY

AEFFHOORRSTU	FOUR OF HEARTS
AEFFIILLMSTV	FILM FESTIVAL
AEFFIILMNRST	FIREMANS LIFT
AEFFIIMNORRS	FORAMINIFERS
AEFFILMORSSW	SWARM OF FLIES
AEFFILNPSTTY	STIFF PENALTY
AEFFILRRSSTU	FIRST REFUSAL
AEFFIOPRSTUV	FIVE PAST FOUR
AEFFKMOORSTW	WORK OFF STEAM
AEFFKNRRRSTU	FRANKFURTERS
AEFFLLOORSTW	FOLLOWS AFTER
AEFFLLOOSTUU	FALL OUT OF USE
AEFFLORSSSSU	SUFFERS A LOSS
AEFFMNNOORTU	MAN OF FORTUNE
AEFFNNOPRRSU	SPURN AN OFFER
AEFFNORRSTUY	RUN FOR SAFETY
AEFGGGGILNOPR	LEAPFROGGING
AEFGGHIINRST	SHIFTING GEAR
AEFGGHILLMOT	GLEAM OF LIGHT
AEFGGHINORRT	FORGATHERING
AEFGGIILNNRS	RINGING FALSE
AEFGGIILNTTT	GETTING A LIFT
AEFGGLOOOTTU	GET OUT OF GAOL
AEFGGNNOOORS	GONE FOR A SONG
AEFGGNOOORSS	GOES FOR A SONG
AEFGHHILOSTT	HOIST THE FLAG
AEFGHHILSTTW	FIGHTS THE LAW
AEFGHHLOSSTW	SHOWS THE FLAG
AEFGHHLOTTUW	FOUGHT THE LAW
AEFGHHOORRTU	THOROUGHFARE
AEFGHHOORTTU	AFORETHOUGHT
AEFGHHORTTTU	AFTERTHOUGHT
AEFGHIILNPRS	PEARL FISHING
AEFGHIINRRTT	FREIGHT TRAIN
AEFGHIIOPRST	PAIR OF EIGHTS
AEFGHIIPRTTV	PRIVATE FIGHT
AEFGHIKLMOST	MAKES LIGHT OF
AEFGHIKLOTTT	TAKE TO FLIGHT
AEFGHIKNORST	FOR THE ASKING
	KING OF HEARTS
AEFGHIKNORTT	FOR THE TAKING
AEFGHILLNORS	RANGE OF HILLS
AEFGHILNNOSS	HAS ONE'S FLING
AEFGHILRSTTT	STRAIGHT LEFT
AEFGHINOSTWY	FIGHT ONES WAY
AEFGHLLLNTTU	AT FULL LENGTH
AEFGHLNPRTUU	RUN UP THE FLAG
AEFGHOORRTTW	RATE OF GROWTH
AEFGIIILNNRV	LIVING IN FEAR
AEFGIILMNNOR	FORMING A LINE
AEFGIILMNNOT	FLOATING MINE
AEFGIILRTUVY	FIGURATIVELY
AEFGIINNOPRT	POINT A FINGER
AEFGIINNOPTW	TWINGE OF PAIN
AEFGIINNRRST	FRATERNISING
AEFGIINNRRTZ	FRATERNIZING
AEFGIINPPSWW	WIFE-SWAPPING
AEFGIINRRSST	STIRS A FINGER
AEFGIJLOOTTU	GET OUT OF JAIL
AEFGIKLNNOTU	TAKING ON FUEL
AEFGIKLNOORT	LOOKING AFTER
AEFGIKMNORSU	MARK OF GENIUS
AEFGILLMNNUY	MEANINGFULLY
AEFGILLNORST	FORESTALLING
AEFGILLNRSST	FINGERSTALLS
AEFGILLNRTTY	FLATTERINGLY
AEFGILLOPRTY	PROFLIGATELY
AEFGILLOPTUY	PLEA OF GUILTY
AEFGILMNOPSU	GO UP IN FLAMES
AEFGILNNRTTU	UNFLATTERING
AEFGILNOOTTV	FLOATING VOTE
AEFGILNORTWW	FLOWING WATER
AEFGILNRSSTT	SELF-STARTING
AEFGILOOPRSV	PAIR OF GLOVES
AEFGIMNNORRT	MORNING AFTER
AEFGIMNOORSW	GONE FOR A SWIM
AEFGIMNOPRST	FOREIGN STAMP
AEFGIMOORSSW	GOES FOR A SWIM
AEFGINNNRRTU	RUNNING AFTER
AEFGINNOOPRS	GONE FOR A SPIN
AEFGINNRRRST	TRANSFERRING
AEFGINOOPRRT	GONE FOR A TRIP
AEFGINOOPRSS	GOES FOR A SPIN
	SONG OF PRAISE
AEFGINOPRRST	FOREIGN PARTS
AEFGINORRSTW	SWIFT TO ANGER
AEFGINRRSSTU	TRANSFIGURES
AEFGIOOPRRST	GOES FOR A TRIP
AEFGLLNNNOUY	GONE ALL FUNNY
AEFGLLNNOSUY	GOES ALL FUNNY
AEFGLLNNOTTW	LONG-FELT WANT
AEFGLLNOORSS	SELL FOR A SONG
AEFGLLNRTUUY	UNGRATEFULLY
AEFGNNOORSTW	WENT FOR A SONG
AEFHHINOOSSU	FASHION HOUSE
AEFHHLLOOSST	LOSS OF HEALTH
AEFHHMNOORTU	MAN OF THE HOUR
AEFHHMORTTUY	MAY THE FOURTH
AEFHIILLNNTW	FALLEN IN WITH
AEFHIILLNSTW	FINAL WHISTLE
AEFHIILNSSST	FINISHES LAST
AEFHIILPRTWY	PLAY WITH FIRE
AEFHIINNOPST	PIN ONES FAITH
AEFHIKLNRTTW	FRANK WHITTLE
AEFHILLOPSTT	LEFT HOSPITAL
AEFHILLORSST	SALLIES FORTH
AEFHILNOORSZ	FALSE HORIZON
AEFHILNOPRTT	TENTH OF APRIL
AEFHIMNOPRSY	HYMN OF PRAISE
AEFHINOORRSW	SHOWER OF RAIN
AEFHINOORTTU	OUT OF THE RAIN
AEFHIOORTTUV	HOT FAVOURITE
AEFHIRRSSTTT	THIRSTS AFTER
AEFHKLMORSST	THERMOS FLASK
AEFHKLNNSSTU	THANKFULNESS
AEFHKNOOSTTV	VOTE OF THANKS
AEFHLLLNOTWY	FLY ON THE WALL
AEFHLLMOSSTY	FATHOMLESSLY
AEFHLLOOPSTY	PLAYS THE FOOL
AEFHLORRSTTY	SHORTLY AFTER
AEFHMORRSSTT	STREAMS FORTH
AEFHMORRSTTT	FROM THE START
AEFHNOORSSTU	OUT OF HARNESS
AEFHNOPRRSTU	TURN OF PHRASE
AEFHOOORSTTU	OUT OF EARSHOT
AEFHOOPRSSTU	PUSHES TOO FAR
AEFHOORSTTTU	STOUT OF HEART
AEFHORRSSTTU	THAT'S FOR SURE
AEFIIILLRSTT	FRITILLARIES
AEFIIILMNSST	SEMIFINALIST
AEFIIILNRTTV	INFILTRATIVE
AEFIIIMNNOST	FEMINISATION
AEFIIIMNNOTZ	FEMINIZATION
AEFIILLLNNOT	FALL INTO LINE
AEFIILOPPRRS	PAIR OF PLIERS
AEFIINOQRSTU	FAIR QUESTION
AEFIIOPRRTTU	REPAIR OUTFIT
AEFIKLLOOPPS	KILO OF APPLES
AEFIKMNOOPRT	MAKE NO PROFIT
AEFIKMOPRSTU	MAKES UP FOR IT
AEFIKOPRSSTY	FOR PITYS SAKE
AEFILLMORSTT	STALL FOR TIME

AEFILLOPRSTY	FAILS TO REPLY
AEFILMMNNOOT	MONOFILAMENT
AEFILMNORSWY	FLOWERS IN MAY
AEFILMOPRSTY	PLAYS FOR TIME
AEFILMORRSSU	FORMULARISES
AEFILMORRSUZ	FORMULARIZES
AEFILNOOPRSS	PROFESSIONAL
AEFILNOOPRTV	FLAVOPROTEIN
AEFILNORRSTT	LAST FRONTIER
AEFILOOPRRSS	PROFESSORIAL
AEFILOPPSSTV	POP FESTIVALS
AEFILOPRRSTT	SELF-PORTRAIT
AEFIMNNOOSTT	FOMENTATIONS
AEFIMNNORRST	FRONTIERSMAN
AEFIMNOOPRRT	PREFORMATION
AEFIMNOORRST	REFORMATIONS
AEFIMNORSTWW	WENT FOR A SWIM
AEFIMNPRSTTY	FIRST PAYMENT
AEFIMORRSTYY	AIR OF MYSTERY
AEFIMPRSTTTT	FIRST ATTEMPT
AEFINNOORSUV	IN ONES FAVOUR
AEFINNOPRSTW	WENT FOR A SPIN
AEFINNORSTUW	WINS A FORTUNE
AEFINNRRTUUV	FURNITURE VAN
AEFINOOPRRST	PERFORATIONS
AEFINOORSTUV	FAVOURITE SON
AEFINOPRRTTW	WENT FOR A TRIP
AEFIOPPPRRST	STRIP OF PAPER
AEFIOPPRSTUW	SUPPORT A WIFE
AEFIQRRRSTTU	FIRST QUARTER
AEFKLLNORRRW	FRANK WORRELL
AEFKLLOORRSW	FLOORWALKERS
AEFKLOPSSSTY	SPEAKS SOFTLY
AEFKMNOORSSY	ASKS FOR MONEY
AEFKMOOPRSST	MAKES SPORT OF
AEFLLMNOORUV	LEMON FLAVOUR
AEFLLMNORSTU	SMALL FORTUNE
AEFLLMOOORSS	LOSS OF MORALE
AEFLLNNNTUWY	WENT ALL FUNNY
AEFLLNNSSUUW	UNLAWFULNESS
AEFLMNOOPRYY	PLAY FOR MONEY
AEFLNNOOSTUW	ONES OWN FAULT
AEFLNOOPSSTU	TEASPOONFULS
	TEASPOONSFUL
AEFLNPRSTUVY	VENUS FLY-TRAP
	VENUS'-FLYTRAP
AEFLOOPQRRTU	PARQUET FLOOR
AEFLOPPRSTUU	PUT UP FOR SALE
AEFMMNORSTYY	MAN OF MYSTERY
AEFMNORRRSST	TRANSFORMERS
AEFMORSSSTTT	SOFT MATTRESS
AEFNNOOPRTWY	TWO FOR A PENNY
AEFNNORSTTUU	UNFORTUNATES
AEFNOOOSTUWY	OUT OF ONES WAY
AEGGGIILNPUV	GIVING A LEG UP
AEGGGIINNRST	STAGGERING IN
AEGGGIINPRTT	GETTING A GRIP
AEGGGILNNOTT	GETTING ALONG
AEGGGILNORTW	WATERLOGGING
AEGGGILNRSTY	STAGGERINGLY
AEGGGILNRSWY	SWAGGERINGLY
AEGGGINNRTTY	GETTING ANGRY
AEGGHHILNOST	GOLAN HEIGHTS
AEGGHHILSSTT	LIGHTS THE GAS
AEGGHHINNOUV	HAVING ENOUGH
AEGGHIILNNST	NIGHTINGALES
AEGGHIINORWY	GOING HAYWIRE
AEGGHILLNNOP	HELPING ALONG
AEGGHILLNOST	EIGHT GALLONS
AEGGHILMRRTU	GRIM LAUGHTER
AEGGHILNNOOS	HANGING LOOSE

AEGGHILNORUV	LAUGHING OVER
AEGGHILNRSTU	SLAUGHTERING
AEGGHINNOSTY	ANYTHING GOES
AEGGHINNRSTT	GAIN STRENGTH
	STRANGE THING
AEGGHINOORTT	GOING TO EARTH
AEGGHINORSTT	GONE STRAIGHT
AEGGHINRSSTT	STRANGE SIGHT
AEGGHIOORSTU	SOUTH GEORGIA
AEGGHIORSSTT	GOES STRAIGHT
AEGGHIPPRRTY	TRIGGER HAPPY
	TRIGGER-HAPPY
AEGGHIRSSTTT	GETS STRAIGHT
AEGGHLNOOTWY	GO THE LONG WAY
AEGGHOOOPRYZ	ZOOGEOGRAPHY
AEGGIIILMNTT	LEGITIMATING
AEGGIIINPRSV	GIVING PRAISE
AEGGIILLNORS	ALLEGORISING
AEGGIILLNORZ	ALLEGORIZING
AEGGIILNNOOT	GOING IT ALONE
AEGGIILNNRUV	GIVEN A RULING
AEGGIILNPPRT	GRIPPING TALE
AEGGIILNRRTW	LARGE WRITING
AEGGIILNRSUV	GIVES A RULING
AEGGIIMNNPRT	IMPREGNATING
AEGGIINNNRVW	GIVEN WARNING
AEGGIINNOPRW	GAINING POWER
AEGGIINNRSVW	GIVES WARNING
AEGGIINRSTTU	INGURGITATES
AEGGILLMNOOR	LOOMING LARGE
AEGGILLNRUUW	AUGURING WELL
AEGGILNOORTV	GLOATING OVER
AEGGILNORRRR	GLARING ERROR
AEGGILNORSTW	GROWING STALE
AEGGILORRSUY	GREGARIOUSLY
AEGGIMNNNRVW	WRONG MEANING
AEGGIMNNORRW	WARMONGERING
AEGGIMNORTTV	MOVING TARGET
AEGGINNOOSWY	GOING ONE'S WAY
AEGGINNPRSSS	GRASPINGNESS
AEGGINNRTTTU	GETTING A TURN
AEGGINOOSTTW	GOING TO WASTE
AEGGINORRWWY	GROWING WEARY
AEGGINPSSTUY	PAYING GUESTS
AEGGMNNOOORT	RONTGENOGRAM
AEGGNNOOPRRT	RONTGENOGRAP
AEGGNNOORSST	GROSS TONNAGE
AEGGNOOPRSTU	GOT ONE'S RAG UP
AEGHHHIIINRT	HIGH IN THE AIR
AEGHHHMOSSTU	THOMAS HUGHES
AEGHHIILNSST	SHINES A LIGHT
AEGHHIINORSS	RAISES ON HIGH
AEGHHIINSTWW	WHITEWASHING
AEGHHIKLOTTU	THOUGHT ALIKE
AEGHHILLMPTT	LIGHT THE LAMP
AEGHHILNSTTT	THE LAST THING
AEGHHILSTTWY	LIGHTS THE WAY
AEGHHIMORSTT	HOME STRAIGHT
AEGHHINNOOPV	HAVING NO HOPE
AEGHHINNORST	HEARS NOTHING
AEGHHINNORTT	ANOTHER THING
AEGHHINSTTTY	STAY THE NIGHT
AEGHHIPRSUWY	SUPERHIGHWAY
AEGHHISSSTTW	SAW THE SIGHTS
AEGHHLOPRSSU	PLOUGHSHARES
AEGHHLOSSTTY	LAYS THE GHOST
AEGHHMOPRRST	THERMOGRAPHS
AEGHHMOPRRTY	THERMOGRAPHY
AEGHHOOPPRRT	PHOTOGRAPHER
AEGHIIILRTVW	GIVE IT A WHIRL
AEGHIIIINNVVW	HAVING IN VIEW

AEGHIIKLMNRS	SHAREMILKING
AEGHIIKLNNTY	LIKE ANYTHING
AEGHIIKLRSTT	STRIKE A LIGHT
AEGHIIKMRSTT	MAKES IT RIGHT
AEGHIIILLNNPS	PLAIN ENGLISH
AEGHIILMNNST	NAME IN LIGHTS
AEGHIILMNSST	ALMIGHTINESS
AEGHIILNNPPS	SHIPPING LANE
AEGHIILNRSTT	STRAIGHT LINE
AEGHIILNSTTY	HESITATINGLY
AEGHIILRRSST	SERIAL RIGHTS
AEGHIIMNNOTV	HAVING NO TIME
AEGHIINOPRTU	GO UP IN THE AIR
AEGHIINPPRRS	SAPPHIRE RING
AEGHIINRSSTT	AIRTIGHTNESS
AEGHIKLLNTTY	TAKEN LIGHTLY
AEGHIKLLSTTY	TAKES LIGHTLY
AEGHIKLNOSSW	WALKING SHOES
AEGHIKNNRRTT	ERRANT KNIGHT
	KNIGHT ERRANT
	KNIGHT-ERRANT
AEGHILLLMNPS	SMALL HELPING
AEGHILLMPRST	LAMPLIGHTERS
AEGHILLNNOPT	OPEN ALL NIGHT
AEGHILLORSTY	LEGAL HISTORY
AEGHILLPRSTU	SUGAR THE PILL
AEGHILLRSTTV	TRAVELS LIGHT
AEGHILLRTTTY	TREAT LIGHTLY
AEGHILMNNSTU	LANGUISHMENT
AEGHILNOORST	ANTHOLOGISER
AEGHILNOORTZ	ANTHOLOGIZER
AEGHILNOOSST	ANTHOLOGISES
AEGHILNOOSTZ	ANTHOLOGIZES
AEGHILNORRSU	HURRIES ALONG
AEGHILNOSTWY	LOSING THE WAY
AEGHILNPRRSW	WRANGLERSHIP
AEGHILNRSTTY	SHATTERINGLY
AEGHIMMMNNTUU	HUMMING A TUNE
AEGHIMMNORTU	HAMMERING OUT
AEGHIMNNNOST	MEANS NOTHING
AEGHIMNNNOTT	MEANT NOTHING
AEGHIMNNRSST	GARNISHMENTS
AEGHIMNORSUW	HOUSEWARMING
AEGHIMNOSSTY	SAY SOMETHING
AEGHIMOORSTT	SHORT TIME AGO
AEGHIMOPRSSS	SEISMOGRAPHS
AEGHIMOPRSSY	SEISMOGRAPHY
AEGHIMPRRTTU	GREAT TRIUMPH
AEGHINNNTTWY	ANYTHING WENT
AEGHINNOOPPS	OPENING A SHOP
AEGHINNOOSUW	OWNING A HOUSE
AEGHINNOOTTT	NOTHING TO EAT
AEGHINNORTUY	YOUNG IN HEART
AEGHINNOSSTV	SAVES NOTHING
AEGHINNOSTTT	SET AT NOTHING
AEGHINNOSTTW	WASTE NOTHING
AEGHINNPRSTU	HUNTING SPEAR
AEGHINOOOTTV	NOT GIVE A HOOT
AEGHINORSSTT	STRAIGHT NOSE
AEGHINPRSTTT	PATENT RIGHTS
AEGHINPRSTTU	STRAIGHTEN UP
AEGHINQTTUUY	HUGE QUANTITY
AEGHINRRRTUY	TEARING HURRY
AEGHINRRSSTT	HEARTSTRINGS
AEGHINRSSSTT	STRAIGHTNESS
AEGHINRSTTTW	WENT STRAIGHT
AEGHIRSSSTTT	SETS STRAIGHT
	STRAIGHT SETS
AEGHKOOOSSTT	TOOK HOSTAGES
AEGHLMNNOORS	LONGSHOREMAN
AEGHLMOORTUY	RHEUMATOLOGY

AEGHLOPRRSXY	XYLOGRAPHERS
AEGHLORRRSUU	REGULAR HOURS
AEGHMMNNORRSU	ROUGH MANNERS
AEGHNNOOPRTY	ANTHROPOGENY
AEGHNNORSTTU	TURN ON THE GAS
	TURN THE GAS ON
AEGHNOOPPRRR	PORNOGRAPHER
AEGHOOOSTTVW	GAVE TWO HOOTS
AEGHOOPPRRST	TOPOGRAPHERS
AEGHOOPRRTUV	PHOTOGRAVURE
AEGHOPPRRSSS	GRASSHOPPERS
AEGHOPPRRSTY	TYPOGRAPHERS
AEGHOPPRRTUY	GROUP THERAPY
AEGIIILMNNRS	MINERALISING
AEGIIILMNNRZ	MINERALIZING
AEGIIILMNOTT	LEGITIMATION
AEGIIILNRSTV	REVITALISING
AEGIIILNRTVZ	REVITALIZING
AEGIIIMNNNST	INSEMINATING
AEGIIIMNSSTV	GIVEN IT A MISS
AEGIIIMNSTTV	VISITING TEAM
AEGIIIMSSSTV	GIVES IT A MISS
AEGIIINNPSSU	GENIUS IS PAIN
AEGIIINRSTVW	WEST VIRGINIA
AEGIIISTTTVW	GIVE IT A TWIST
AEGIIKKLLNOO	LOOKING ALIKE
AEGIIKLLNNSW	SINKING A WELL
AEGIIKLMNSSY	KINGSLEY AMIS
AEGIIKLNPRTT	TALKING TRIPE
AEGIIKMNOPPS	SMOKING A PIPE
AEGIILLLNSVW	WILLING SLAVE
AEGIILLMNNNO	MEANING NO ILL
AEGIILLMRRTY	TERRY GILLIAM
AEGIILLNNOOP	LEGAL OPINION
AEGIILLNNOTW	WELLINGTONIA
AEGIILLNPRVY	PREVAILINGLY
AEGIILLNSTTY	SAYING LITTLE
AEGIILMMNNST	MISALIGNMENT
AEGIILMNNNRU	RUNNING A MILE
AEGIILMNNRST	STREAMLINING
AEGIILMNORST	MINERALOGIST
AEGIILNNNSSU	UNGAINLINESS
AEGIILNNORTU	URINOGENITAL
AEGIILNNRSTU	NEUTRALISING
AEGIILNNRTUZ	NEUTRALIZING
AEGIILNNSSSU	SENSUALISING
AEGIILNNSSUZ	SENSUALIZING
AEGIILNNSTTY	LYING IN STATE
AEGIILNPPSTY	APPETISINGLY
AEGIILNPPTYZ	APPETIZINGLY
AEGIILNPRSTT	EARSPLITTING
AEGIILNRRSTT	STIRRING TALE
AEGIILNRSSSU	SINGULARISES
AEGIILNRSSUZ	SINGULARIZES
AEGIILNRSTVV	VESTAL VIRGIN
AEGIILORRSSW	RELIGIOUS WAR
AEGIILRRRTUY	IRREGULARITY
AEGIIMNNOPRT	IMPREGNATION
AEGIIMNNOPTT	PIGMENTATION
AEGIIMNNORSV	MEROVINGIANS
AEGIIMNNORSY	RAISING MONEY
AEGIIMNOPRTW	WRITING A POEM
AEGIIMOPRSTV	GRAM-POSITIVE
AEGIINNNRSTT	INTRANSIGENT
AEGIINNOOSTT	NEGOTIATIONS
AEGIINNOPPPR	ORANGE PIPPIN
AEGIINNOPRTV	PAINTING OVER
AEGIINNOPTTT	POTENTIATING
AEGIINNORRTV	OVERTRAINING
AEGIINNORSST	RESIGNATIONS
AEGIINNORSTT	INTEGRATIONS

AEGIINNORTTW	TEARING IN TWO
	WRITING A NOTE
AEGIINNPPSTU	UNAPPETISING
AEGIINNPPTUZ	UNAPPETIZING
AEGIINNQRTUY	INQUIRY AGENT
AEGIINOPRSUV	GRIEVOUS PAIN
AEGIINORRSTT	REGISTRATION
AEGIINORSTTV	INVESTIGATOR
AEGIINPPRRTW	WRITING PAPER
AEGIINPRTTUV	VITUPERATING
AEGIINRRSTVW	SERVING A WRIT
AEGIJKMNORTT	JOKING MATTER
AEGIJLPSUWZZ	JIG-SAW PUZZLE
AEGIKLMNNOTY	TALKING MONEY
AEGIKLMNOOSS	LOOKING A MESS
AEGIKLMNOSSS	SMOKE SIGNALS
AEGIKLNOORWY	LOOKING WEARY
AEGIKLNOPPRY	PLAYING POKER
AEGIKLNORSST	LOSING STREAK
AEGIKNNNOPSU	SNEAKING UP ON
AEGIKNORSTTU	STREAKING OUT
AEGILLLNNNPW	PLANNING WELL
AEGILLMNRRWY	MARRYING WELL
AEGILLMNSTUW	MULLIGAN STEW
AEGILLMRSTTU	METALLURGIST
AEGILLNNOSTW	STONEWALLING
AEGILLNOOSUY	OLEAGINOUSLY
AEGILLNOSTUY	GELATINOUSLY
AEGILLNRSTTW	STARTING WELL
AEGILLPPRSSS	GLASS SLIPPER
AEGILMNNNNOT	NONALIGNMENT
AEGILMNNOQTU	MAGNILOQUENT
AEGILMNNORRY	EARLY MORNING
AEGILMNOPRSU	PELARGONIUMS
AEGILNNOPSTU	STEALING UP ON
AEGILNNRSTTY	ASTRINGENTLY
AEGILNNRUVWY	UNWAVERINGLY
AEGILNOOPRRT	LARGE PORTION
AEGILNOORTTV	LEAVING TO ROT
AEGILNOPRSTY	POSTING EARLY
AEGILNORRRST	STARRING ROLE
AEGILNORSTTY	LAYING TO REST
AEGILNORTUVV	VAULTING OVER
AEGILNRRSSUY	REASSURINGLY
AEGILOORSTTT	TERATOLOGIST
AEGIMNNOPPRR	MORNING PAPER
AEGIMNNOSTWY	WASTING MONEY
AEGIMNNPRSTU	SMARTENING UP
AEGIMNOOPPST	OPPOSING TEAM
AEGIMNOOSSTT	GOT INTO A MESS
AEGIMNORRSUY	MARRIES YOUNG
AEGIMNORRSVW	SWARMING OVER
AEGIMNORSTTU	STREAMING OUT
AEGIMNORSTUU	MEASURING OUT
AEGINNNRRTUW	RUNNING WATER
AEGINNORSTTW	WRITTEN A SONG
AEGINNOSSWWY	WINGS ONE'S WAY
AEGINNPPSSWW	SWAPPING NEWS
AEGINOORRRTT	INTERROGATOR
AEGINOORSTTW	GETS INTO A ROW
AEGINOOSTTTW	GOT INTO A STEW
AEGINOPPRSVW	SWAPPING OVER
AEGINOPRSSTU	GONE UPSTAIRS
AEGINOPRSTWY	STAYING POWER
AEGINOPSTTTU	PUTTING TO SEA
AEGINORSTTTU	GETS INTO A RUT
AEGINORSTTVY	TRYING TO SAVE
AEGIOPRSSSTU	GOES UPSTAIRS
AEGJMORRSUY	MAJOR SURGERY
AEGKLOOOPSST	TOOK AS GOSPEL
AEGLLMNNOORT	LONG-TERM LOAN
AEGLLMNORRSW	GROWN SMALLER
AEGLLMOSSSTY	ALL SYSTEMS GO
AEGLLNOOOPTT	GONE ALL TO POT
AEGLLOOOPSTT	GOES ALL TO POT
AEGLNOOSTUUY	AUTOGENOUSLY
AEGLOORSTUUY	OUTRAGEOUSLY
AEGNNOOOSWWY	GO ONES OWN WAY
AEGNORRRSSST	TRANSGRESSOR
AEGOOOPRSTTW	GROW POTATOES
AEGOOPSSTTUY	STEATOPYGOUS
AEHHHNOORSTU	HAS THE HONOUR
AEHHIILNTTWW	WITHIN THE LAW
AEHHIILRSTTT	HITS THE TRAIL
AEHHIIMPSSTW	WITH EMPHASIS
AEHHILMMNPSS	HELMSMANSHIP
AEHIIILNOOPRT	IN POOR HEALTH
AEHHILOPSTTU	THIOSULPHATE
AEHHIMMNOPRSS	HORSEMANSHIP
AEHHIMNORSTT	SHOT IN THE ARM
AEHHINOOPSTT	HAS THE OPTION
AEHHIOOPTTUW	WITHOUT A HOPE
AEHHIOPPRSTT	TRIPHOSPHATE
AEHHIORSTTTW	WHITETHROATS
AEHHLLOORTTW	HOLLOW THREAT
AEHHLMOOOPSTX	EXOPHTHALMOS
AEHHLOPSSTTY	PLAYS THE HOST
AEHHMOOSTTWY	SMOOTH THE WAY
AEHHNOPPRTYY	HYPNOTHERAPY
AEHHOOPRRSST	SHARPSHOOTER
AEHIIMSTTTW	WHAT TIME IS IT?
AEHIIINNPRTW	WRITHE IN PAIN
AEHIIINNSSVW	WISHES IN VAIN
AEHIILLNPTTY	PAINT THE LILY
AEHIILLNPTWY	YELL WITH PAIN
AEHIILLPSSTT	PHILATELISTS
AEHIILMRSSTT	TRIM THE SAILS
AEHIILNOPRST	RELATIONSHIP
AEHIILNPRTTW	PELT WITH RAIN
AEHIILOPRSST	HOSPITALISES
AEHIILOPSSTZ	HOSPITALIZES
AEHIILOTUWWY	WHILE YOU WAIT
AEHIILPRRSTT	HAIRSPLITTER
AEHIIMNORSTT	IN A SHORT TIME
AEHIIMNRSSTT	MISS THE TRAIN
AEHIINNORSTW	WITHIN REASON
AEHIINOPRRSS	PARISHIONERS
AEHIINOPRRST	PREHISTORIAN
AEHIINRSSTUW	WHITE RUSSIAN
AEHIIPPRRSST	PARISH PRIEST
AEHIIRRSSTTW	SHIRTWAISTER
AEHIISTTUVXY	EXHAUSTIVITY
AEHIJKLSTTTU	JUST LIKE THAT
AEHIJLLNUUXY	JULIAN HUXLEY
AEHIJLNOPSST	JOSEPH STALIN
AEHIJMNORSTY	JOINS THE ARMY
AEHIJNNOSTVY	JOINS THE NAVY
AEHIKMNORRSY	YORKSHIREMAN
AEHIKMORSSTY	MAKES HISTORY
AEHIKNOPPSSS	SPOKE SPANISH
AEHIKOOORTTT	TOOK TO THE AIR
AEHILLLPSSTT	SPILL THE SALT
AEHILLMRRRTU	ARTHUR MILLER
AEHILLNNOSTY	IN ALL HONESTY
AEHILLOPRSST	HOSPITALLERS
AEHILLPSSTTT	SPILT THE SALT
AEHILLRRTTTU	LITERAL TRUTH
AEHILMMPRSTT	TRIMS THE LAMP
AEHILMNOOPSU	ANEMOPHILOUS
AEHILMNORSTW	MOTHERS-IN-LAW
AEHILMNRRTTU	MARTIN LUTHER
AEHILMOPSTTT	SPLIT THE ATOM

779

AEHILMORTTYY	TIMOTHY LEARY	AEHNOORRSTTY	ANOTHER STORY
AEHILNOOSTTT	STATION HOTEL	AEHNOORSSTTW	THROWS A STONE
AEHILNOPRRTU	IN THE PARLOUR	AEHNOPRSSTTU	SHUT ONE'S TRAP
AEHILOPRRSSW	APRIL SHOWERS	AEHNOPSTTUWY	PUTS ON THE WAY
AEHIMMNNNOOT	MAN IN THE MOON	AEHNORRSSSTY	SYNARTHROSES
AEHIMNNNOOPRT	ENANTIOMORPH	AEHNORSSSTTU	TURNS TO ASHES
AEHIMNNOOSSU	MANSION HOUSE	AEHNPPRRSTUY	HAPPY RETURNS
AEHIMNNOPPSU	ONE-UPMANSHIP	AEHOOPRRSSTT	TRAPSHOOTERS
AEHIMNNORTTV	NORTH VIETNAM	AEHOOPRRSSUW	HOUSE SPARROW
AEHIMNNOSSSW	WOMANISHNESS	AEHOQSSTTTUU	THE STATUS QUO
AEHIMNNOSSTT	ASTONISHMENT	AEIIILLMNORS	MILLIONAIRES
AEHIMNOOPRTT	PAINT THE ROOM	AEIIILLMNTUV	ILLUMINATIVE
AEHIMNOPRSST	MISANTHROPES	AEIIILMNPPRT	IMPERIAL PINT
AEHIMNOPRSTW	WITH OPEN ARMS	AEIIILNRSTTT	INTERSTITIAL
AEHIMNORRSTU	TO ERR IS HUMAN	AEIIILPRSSTU	SPIRITUALISE
AEHIMNOSTTUV	SOUTH VIETNAM	AEIIILPRSTUZ	SPIRITUALIZE
AEHIMNOTWWWY	WAY WITH WOMEN	AEIIIMMNPRTV	PRIMITIVE MAN
AEHIMOOOSSST	HOMOEOSTASIS	AEIIIMMNSSTT	ANTI-SEMITISM
AEHIMOPPRRST	PRIMROSE PATH	AEIIIMNNNOST	INSEMINATION
AEHIMPRSSSTY	SYMPATHISERS	AEIIIMNORSSS	MISSIONARIES
AEHIMPRSSTYZ	SYMPATHIZERS	AEIIIMNRSSTU	MINIATURISES
AEHINNNORRSV	RIVER SHANNON	AEIIIMNRSTUZ	MINIATURIZES
AEHINNOOOPTV	HAVE NO OPTION	AEIIIMPRRTTV	PRIMITIVE ART
AEHINNPPSSSS	SNAPPISHNESS	AEIIINNRSTTV	INTRANSITIVE
AEHINOORSTTX	EXHORTATIONS	AEIIINNRSTVV	STRIVE IN VAIN
AEHINOPPSTTU	PUT INTO SHAPE	AEIIIPRSTTVV	PRIVATE VISIT
AEHINOPRSTTY	ATTORNEYSHIP	AEIIKKNORSSY	KARYOKINESIS
AEHINOPSTTWY	POINTS THE WAY	AEIIKLLMMNOS	MAKE MILLIONS
AEHINORSSTUY	YOURS IN HASTE	AEIIKLNNPRVW	RIP VAN WINKLE
AEHINPPRRSST	PARTNERSHIPS	AEIIKLNOPPST	SPIN LIKE A TOP
AEHIOOPPRSST	APOSTROPHISE	AEIIKLNORSST	SIRLOIN STEAK
AEHIOOPPRSTZ	APOSTROPHIZE	AEIIKNNRTTTU	TAKE IT IN TURN
AEHIOPPPSTTT	PIP AT THE POST	AEIIKOPRRTTY	TAKE PRIORITY
AEHIOPPRSTUW	WITH A PURPOSE	AEIIILLLLMMSY	MILLESIMALLY
AEHIOPRRSTWY	PRAISEWORTHY	AEIIILLMMMORY	IMMEMORIALLY
AEHIOPSSSTTY	HYPOSTATISES	AEIIILLMNORSY	MILLION YEARS
AEHIOPSSTTYZ	HYPOSTATIZES	AEIIILLNNSTTY	INTESTINALLY
AEHIOPSTTTUW	UP TO THE WAIST	AEIIILLNOPRVY	VIOLIN PLAYER
AEHIPRRRSTTU	RAPIER THRUST	AEIIILLNORRTW	INTERIOR WALL
AEHJLNOOPPPU	POPE JOHN PAUL	AEIIILLNORRTY	LITERARY LION
AEHJMOOPPRRT	MAJOR PROPHET	AEIIILLNQRSTU	TRANQUILLISE
AEHKLMOORSTT	SMOOTH TALKER	AEIIILLNQRTUZ	TRANQUILLIZE
AEHKLOOPRSTT	LOOKS THE PART	AEIIILLNRTTWW	WRITTEN A WILL
AEHKMOPRSSTT	MARKS THE SPOT	AEIIILLRSTTUV	ILLUSTRATIVE
AEHKNOPRSTTU	TAKEN UP SHORT	AEIIILMMNNORT	MINOR AILMENT
AEHKOPRSSTTU	TAKES UP SHORT	AEIIILMMNOOST	EMOTIONALISM
AEHLLLOOSWWW	SWALLOW WHOLE	AEIIILMNNNOTU	MOUNTAIN LINE
AEHLLMOOSUXY	HOMOSEXUALLY	AEIIILMNNSSTT	MILITANTNESS
AEHLLNOOPRSU	OPEN ALL HOURS	AEIIILMNOOSTT	EMOTIONALIST
AEHLLNOOPRTY	ON THE PAYROLL	AEIIILMNOOTTY	EMOTIONALITY
AEHLLOOQRSUW	HOLLOW SQUARE	AEIIILMNOSSTT	TESTIMONIALS
AEHLLRRSSTUY	RUSSELL HARTY	AEIIILMNRRSTU	RAIL TERMINUS
AEHLMNPRSUUY	SUPERHUMANLY	AEIIILMNRSSUV	UNIVERSALISM
AEHLMOOSSTWY	THOMAS WOLSEY	AEIIILMNRTUVY	RUMINATIVELY
AEHLNOPSSTUY	POLYANTHUSES	AEIIILMNSTTUY	SIMULTANEITY
AEHLOOPRRRTY	RATHER POORLY	AEIIILMPRTTTU	MULTIPARTITE
AEHMMNNNOOOT	MAN ON THE MOON	AEIIILNNNOQUU	QUINQUENNIAL
AEHMMNNOORST	SMOOTH MANNER	AEIIILNNOPSTT	SALIENT POINT
AEHMMNPPSSTU	MANS THE PUMPS	AEIIILNOOPSTX	EXPOSITIONAL
AEHMNNOOPSTT	MAN ON THE SPOT	AEIIILNOOPTTX	EXPLOITATION
AEHMNOOPRTUX	PNEUMOTHORAX	AEIIILNOPTTTY	POTENTIALITY
AEHMNOOORSSTU	MOUNTS A HORSE	AEIIILNORSSST	SOLITARINESS
AEHMNOPPSTTU	PUTS ON THE MAP	AEIIILNORSSTT	ORIENTALISTS
AEHMOOOPRTTT	ROOM AT THE TOP	AEIIILNRSSSTW	SISTERS-IN-LAW
AEHNNOOPRSTT	RAN ON THE SPOT	AEIIILNRSSTUV	UNIVERSALIST
AEHNNOORSTTW	THROWN A STONE	AEIIILNRSTTVY	TRANSITIVELY
AEHNNOPRSTTW	WORN THE PANTS	AEIIILNRSTUVY	UNIVERSALITY
AEHNNOPRTTTU	TURN ON THE TAP	AEIIILNSTUUXY	UNISEXUALITY
	TURN THE TAP ON	AEIIILORRRSTT	TERRITORIALS
AEHNOOPRRSSU	SARRUSOPHONE	AEIIILORRSSUV	SERIOUS RIVAL
AEHNOOPRRSTT	ORTHOPTERANS	AEIIILPRRTTTY	TRIPARTITELY

AEIIMMNOORST	MEMORISATION
AEIIMMNOORTZ	MEMORIZATION
AEIIMNNOPSSX	EXPANSIONISM
AEIIMNNORSST	NESTORIANISM
AEIIMNPRRSSU	RISE UP IN ARMS
AEIIMNRSSSTV	TRANSMISSIVE
AEIIMOSSSTTT	STOMATITISES
AEIIMRRSTTUV	TRIUMVIRATES
AEIINNOOPTTT	POTENTIATION
AEIINNOPRSTU	RESUPINATION
AEIINNOPSSTX	EXPANSIONIST
AEIINNORSTVV	STROVE IN VAIN
AEIINOPPRRST	PERSPIRATION
AEIINOPRRSST	RESPIRATIONS
AEIINOPRRSVY	PREVISIONARY
AEIINOPRTTUV	VITUPERATION
AEIINOPSSTTU	POINT AT ISSUE
AEIINPRSSSSU	PRUSSIANISES
AEIINPRSSSUZ	PRUSSIANIZES
AEIINRROTTUV	RETURN A VISIT
AEIINRSTTUVY	AT UNIVERSITY
AEIIORSSSTUV	SOVIET RUSSIA
AEIJLLNORTVY	JAYNE TORVILL
AEIJLMORRTUY	MAJORITY RULE
AEIJMMRSTTWY	JIMMY STEWART
AEIJMOORTTVY	MAJORITY VOTE
AEIJNNORRTUY	TRAIN JOURNEY
AEIKKMNNOSTW	MAKES IT KNOWN
AEIKKNNORSST	TAKEN NO RISKS
AEIKKNORSSST	TAKES NO RISKS
AEIKLLNNOTTW	KNOWN A LITTLE
AEIKLLNOPPSY	SPOKE PLAINLY
AEIKLLNOSTTT	TAKEN ITS TOLL
AEIKLLNOSTTW	KNOWS A LITTLE
AEIKLLORSTTU	ALL OUT STRIKE
AEIKLLOSSTTT	TAKES ITS TOLL
AEIKLLPSSTTY	PLAY SKITTLES
AEIKLLQSTTUY	TALKS QUIETLY
AEIKLNOOPTTW	WALK ON TIPTOE
AEIKLNOOSTUW	WEAK SOLUTION
AEIKLORRRTWY	LITERARY WORK
AEIKMMOPRRRU	MAKE-UP MIRROR
AEIKMNOQRSTU	QUESTION MARK
AEIKMOPRRTTW	PART-TIME WORK
AEIKNOPRRRSU	SUPERIOR RANK
AEIKNOPRSSSU	SPOKE RUSSIAN
AEIKNOQSSSTU	ASK QUESTIONS
AEIILLMNNORRU	NOMINAL RULER
AEIILLMNOOPSS	OILS ON'S PALM
AEIILLMNOPRSY	IMPERSONALLY
AEIILLNNORTTY	INTOLERANTLY
AEIILLNNOSTTT	TO ALL INTENTS
AEIILLNORRTTY	TORRENTIALLY
AEIILLOOSSTUY	TAILS YOU LOSE
AEIILMNNRSTTU	INSTRUMENTAL
AEIILMNOOPRTT	METROPOLITAN
AEIILMNOPRRST	TRAMPOLINERS
AEIILMNOSSTUU	SIMULTANEOUS
AEIILNNORSSUV	RUSSIAN NOVEL
AEIILNNRTTUWW	UNWRITTEN LAW
AEIILNOOOPRRT	POOR RELATION
AEIILNOOPRRTT	INTERPOLATOR
	PETROL RATION
AEIILNOOPSSSS	POSSESSIONAL
AEIILNOORTUVY	EVOLUTIONARY
AEIILNOOSSTUY	EASY SOLUTION
AEIILNPPRSSTU	SUPPLIANTERS
AEIILNPPRSTUU	PURSUIT PLANE
AEIILNPRSTTWY	WRITTEN PLAYS
AEIILNSSSTUVW	SULTANS WIVES
AEIILOOPPPSTY	PLAY OPPOSITE

AEILOPRSSTUU	LOUIS PASTEUR
AEIMMPRSSTUW	SWIM UPSTREAM
AEIMNNNOTUWY	ANY MINUTE NOW
AEIMNNOORSST	MONTESSORIAN
AEIMNNOPPSTT	APPOINTMENTS
AEIMNNORSTTU	MENSTRUATION
AEIMNNORTTUY	MONETARY UNIT
AEIMNOOPRRST	IMPERSONATOR
AEIMNOPRRSSU	ROSE UP IN ARMS
AEIMNOPRSTTU	PERMUTATIONS
AEIMNORSSTTW	TWIST ONES ARM
AEIMNRRSSTTT	TRANSMITTERS
AEIMNRSSSTTV	TRANSVESTISM
AEIMOOPPRSTY	PROMISE TO PAY
AEIMSSSSTTTY	SYSTEMATISTS
AEINNNOOSWWY	IN ONE'S OWN WAY
AEINNNOPRSTT	TRANSPONTINE
AEINNOOPRSTU	PUT IN ONE'S OAR
	BUT ONES OAR IN
AEINNOORSSTV	ROAST VENISON
AEINNOQSSTUY	ANY QUESTIONS
AEINNORSTTTU	STERNUTATION
AEINNORSTTUW	WAIT ONES TURN
AEINNOSSTTTU	SUSTENTATION
AEINOOPPRSTV	PROVES A POINT
AEINOOPRSTTT	PROTESTATION
AEINOOPRSTTV	NATIVE TROOPS
AEINOOPRSTTW	POWER STATION
AEINOOPRSTTX	EXPORTATIONS
AEINOORRSSTT	RESTORATIONS
AEINOOSSTTTU	OSTENTATIOUS
AEINOPPRRTWY	PARTY IN POWER
AEINOPQSSTTU	PAST QUESTION
AEINOPQSTTUU	PUT A QUESTION
AEINOPRRSTTT	TRAIN SPOTTER
AEINPRSSTTUW	WENT UPSTAIRS
AEIOOOOPPPRS	PROSOPOPOEIA
AEIOOPPRRRTX	EXPROPRIATOR
AEIOPPRRRSTY	PERSPIRATORY
AEIOPRRRSTTU	PORTRAITURES
AEIOPRRSTTUV	VITUPERATORS
AEIOQRRSTTUX	QUARTER TO SIX
AEIORRSSTTWY	WRITES A STORY
AEKKLOOOPTTU	KEPT A LOOK-OUT
AEKLLNNOPRSU	PULL ONE'S RANK
AEKLLOPSSSWY	SPEAKS SLOWLY
AEKLLPPSSTUU	PULL UP STAKES
AEKLNOOPRSSY	PLAYS SNOOKER
AEKNNNOOSWWY	KNOWN ONE'S WAY
AEKNNOOSSWWY	KNOWS ONE'S WAY
AEKNNORSTTTU	TAKEN ON TRUST
AEKNOOOPRSTT	TOOK ONE'S PART
AEKNOORSSWWY	WORKS ONE'S WAY
AEKNORSSTTTU	TAKES ON TRUST
AELLLMORSUVY	MARVELLOUSLY
AELLMMNNOTUY	MONUMENTALLY
AELLMMOORSST	SMALLEST ROOM
AELLMNOOOSSS	SOLOMONS SEAL
AELLNNNOOOSW	ALL ON ONES OWN
AELLNOOPPRUV	POPULAR NOVEL
AELLNOOPTTTW	WENT ALL TO POT
AELMNOOSTUYY	LAYS OUT MONEY
AELMOORRRRTT	MORTAL TERROR
AELNOOOPPSST	APOSTLE SPOON
AELNOOPPRSTU	PUTS ON PAROLE
AELNOPSSSTUU	PATULOUSNESS
AELOORSSSUUV	SAVE OUR SOULS
AELOPPPRRSSU	POPULAR PRESS
AEMMNNNOOTWY	ANY MOMENT NOW
AEMNNOSSTTYY	TANNOY SYSTEM
AEMNOOOPRSTZ	SPERMATOZOON

AEMNOOOPRSZZ	MEZZO SOPRANO	AFGIILNSSTYY	SATISFYINGLY
	MEZZO-SOPRANO	AFGIIMNOPRRT	PROFIT MARGIN
AEMNOORRRSTT	REMONSTRATOR	AFGIINNOOPRR	RAINPROOFING
AEMNOORSSWWY	WORMS ONE'S WAY	AFGIINNSSTUY	UNSATISFYING
AEMNOPPRRSTW	PROMPT ANSWER	AFGIJLOOOTTU	GOT OUT OF JAIL
AEMNOPPSSTTY	STOPS PAYMENT	AFGIKLLLMNOO	GALLON OF MILK
AEMOORRRSSTT	RESORT TO ARMS	AFGIKLLNOOOO	LOOKING A FOOL
AEMOPRRSSSTT	SPORTS MASTER	AFGIKNOORSTT	TOASTING FORK
AEMPRRSSTTUU	SUPERSTRATUM	AFGILMNORSTY	FLYING TO ARMS
AENNOOOSSSTW	SOWN ONE'S OATS	AFGILNOORSUV	LOSING FAVOUR
AENNOOOSTUWY	ON ONE'S WAY OUT	AFGIMNNORRST	TRANSFORMING
AENOOPRSSSUV	VAPOROUSNESS	AFGIMNORRSTY	TRANSMOGRIFY
AENOPRRRSSTT	TRANSPORTERS	AFGINNNORTTU	RUNNING TO FAT
AENORRSSTTTU	STERNUTATORS	AFGINNORTTWY	WANT OF TRYING
AENORRSTTTUY	STERNUTATORY	AFGLLNOOORSU	GO ON ALL FOURS
AEOOPRRSSSSV	VASOPRESSORS	AFGLLOOORRST	GO FOR A STROLL
AEOOPSSTTTUU	PUTS OUT TO SEA	AFGNOORSSTUU	RUNS OUT OF GAS
AEOOQRRTTTUW	QUARTER TO TWO	AFHIIKKMNORU	KHAKI UNIFORM
AFFFGINNORSU	GRAIN OF SNUFF	AFHIILNNOPRT	NINTH OF APRIL
AFFFHIILOPRT	FIFTH OF APRIL	AFHIILOPRSTX	SIXTH OF APRIL
AFFFHOORSSTT	SHORT OF STAFF	AFHIIMOPRRTU	AIR OF TRIUMPH
AFFGGHIIINRT	FIGHTING FAIR	AFHIINOORTTU	OUT OF THIN AIR
AFFGGILLNOOP	GALLOPING OFF	AFHIINOPSTTU	PUT A FINISH TO
AFFGHHILOSTT	SHAFT OF LIGHT	AFHILOTTTUUW	WITHOUT FAULT
AFFGHIIKNOST	SHAKING IT OFF	AFHIOOPRRSST	PAIR OF SHORTS
AFFGHIIORRST	FIGHTS FOR AIR	AFHIOOPRSSTW	SHOWS A PROFIT
AFFGHIOORRTU	FOUGHT FOR AIR	AFHMNOOORTUY	OUT OF HARMONY
AFFGIILLNORT	FALLING FOR IT	AFIIILNNORTT	INFILTRATION
AFFGIILNNSTU	INSUFFLATING	AFIILLMRSUUW	WILLIAM RUFUS
AFFHIIILNOST	FAIL TO FINISH	AFIILLNNORTU	FALL INTO RUIN
AFFHILLNTUUY	UNFAITHFULLY	AFIILLNNRSSU	FALLS IN RUINS
AFFHINOOOSTU	OUT OF FASHION	AFIILMORSTUU	MULTIFARIOUS
AFFIILLMNORS	FILLS IN A FORM	AFIILNNOORTU	FLUORINATION
AFFIILNNOSTU	INSUFFLATION	AFIINNNRRTUY	INFANTRY UNIT
AFFIILOPRRST	FIRST OF APRIL	AFIINOPRSSTU	PASSION FRUIT
AFFILLMOORTU	FILL OUT A FORM		PASSIONFRUIT
AFGGGIJNOOOR	GOING FOR A JOG	AFIKLNNORSTW	WALKS IN FRONT
AFGGGILLNNUY	UNFLAGGINGLY	AFIKNOPRRSTU	PAIR OF TRUNKS
AFGGGILNOOOR	GOING FOR GOAL	AFILLMOOPRST	OIL PLATFORMS
AFGGHIIILLNT	FAILING LIGHT	AFILLNOOPPTW	PINT OF WALLOP
AFGGHIIILNST	FAILING SIGHT	AFILMNOOOSTW	LAWS OF MOTION
AFGGHIIKLNTT	FIGHTING TALK	AFILMOOPPRRS	FIRM PROPOSAL
	TAKING FLIGHT	AFILNNOOORUV	ONION FLAVOUR
AFGGHIIKNRTT	TAKING FRIGHT	AFIMOORRSTUU	SUIT OF ARMOUR
AFGGHIILNOST	LOSING A FIGHT	AFINOOPSSTTU	SNAPS OUT OF IT
AFGGIILNRTYY	GRATIFYINGLY	AFINORRSSTTU	FRUSTRATIONS
AFGGIIMNNORR	FORMING A RING	AFIOOPRRSSTT	ARTISTS PROOF
AFGGIINPPRTW	GIFT WRAPPING	AFLNOOPPRRTU	POPULAR FRONT
AFGGILNOOTTU	GOING FLAT OUT	AFLNOOPPRRTU	FRONT PARLOUR
AFGGINNOORRU	GOING FOR A RUN	AFMNOORRRSUY	RUNS FOR MAYOR
AFGGLOOOOTTU	GOT OUT OF GAOL	AFORRSSSTTUW	TRUSS OF STRAW
AFGHHLLORSTU	FALLS THROUGH	AGGGHIILNNRU	RINGING LAUGH
AFGHIIKNNSTT	FAST THINKING	AGGGIIILNNOS	GOING SAILING
	THINKING FAST	AGGGIINNNOSS	SINGING A SONG
AFGHIILNOPST	SLIP OF A THING	AGGGINNORRWY	GROWING ANGRY
AFGHIINORTTU	HITTING A FOUR	AGGHHIIKNSWY	KINGS HIGHWAY
AFGHIINORTTW	THROWING A FIT	AGGHHILMOTUW	GOUGH WHITLAM
AFGHIIOPRSTT	PAIR OF TIGHTS	AGGHIIJMNSTU	THINGUMAJIGS
AFGHIIRSSTTT	AT FIRST SIGHT	AGGHIIKNNSTV	GIVING THANKS
AFGHIKLOORST	LOOKS A FRIGHT		THANKSGIVING
AFGHILLNORST	FALLING SHORT	AGGHIILNNRTW	WARNING LIGHT
AFGHINOORSST	SONG OF A SHIRT	AGGHIINNOSSW	SHOWING A SIGN
AFGHINORRTTU	GRAIN OF TRUTH	AGGHIINOSTUV	GIVING A SHOUT
AFGHIPPSTTUU	PUTS UP A FIGHT	AGGHIINOSTWW	GO WITH A SWING
AFGIIILLNNOTW	FAILING TO WIN	AGGHILLLNNOT	ALL NIGHT LONG
AFGIIILLNNRTT	INFILTRATING	AGGHILMNNRSY	RHYMING SLANG
AFGIIKLNOPRR	PINK FOR A GIRL	AGGHILNNOOPP	HOPPING ALONG
AFGIIKNOPRTT	PROFIT TAKING	AGGHILNOPRUY	PLAYING ROUGH
AFGIILLNNPUY	PAYING IN FULL	AGGHILNOPSTU	STOP LAUGHING
AFGIILLNOPST	FILLING A POST	AGGHILOOPRST	GRAPHOLOGIST
AFGIILNNORTU	FLUORINATING	AGGHINNOOSTW	WHAT'S GOING ON?

AGGHINOOOSTW	GOING TO A SHOW	AGHLNOOOPRTY	ANTHROPOLOGY
AGGHINORRSTW	RIGHTS A WRONG	AGIIIILMNRST	MILITARISING
AGGIIIILNNTV	INVIGILATING	AGIIIILMNRTZ	MILITARIZING
AGGIIIMNSSTT	STIGMATISING	AGIIIILNNOTV	INVIGILATION
AGGIIIMNSTTZ	STIGMATIZING	AGIIIILNRSTV	TRIVIALISING
AGGIIINNORTV	INVIGORATING	AGIIIILNRTVZ	TRIVIALIZING
AGGIIINRTTVY	GIVING IT A TRY	AGIIIIMNNSTV	VITAMINISING
AGGIIKMNNNOS	MAKING NO SIGN	AGIIIIMNNTVZ	VITAMINIZING
AGGIIMNORRSU	MARIUS GORING	AGIIIKLLMNOT	AIMING TO KILL
AGGIINNOOPSS	GAS POISONING	AGIIIKNNPPTW	TIPPING A WINK
AGGIINNOPRSW	GROWING PAINS	AGIIILLMNNTU	ILLUMINATING
AGGIINNORSTW	WRITING A SONG	AGIIILLNOSTV	VOLATILISING
AGGIINORTTUU	ARGUING IT OUT	AGIIILLNOTVZ	VOLATILIZING
AGGIINRRSTTU	GUITAR STRING	AGIIILLNRTWW	WRITING A WILL
AGGIKLNPPRSU	SPARKING PLUG	AGIIILLNSTTW	STILL WAITING
AGGILLLNNOOR	ROLLING ALONG	AGIIILNNNOVV	LOVING IN VAIN
AGGILMNOPRTU	PROMULGATING	AGIIILNNNTVW	LIVING IN WANT
AGGILNNNNORU	RUNNING ALONG	AGIIILNNPPSY	PAYING-IN SLIP
AGGILNNORSST	STRINGS ALONG	AGIIILNORSTV	INVIGILATORS
AGGINNNORSTWX	WAXING STRONG	AGIIILNRRTTY	IRRITATINGLY
AGGINNOSTUYY	STAYING YOUNG	AGIIIMNNOPSS	IMPASSIONING
AGGINOORSTTT	STARTING TO GO	AGIIIMNNRRSS	RISING IN ARMS
AGHHHOPPTTUY	HAPPY THOUGHT	AGIIINNNRTVY	TRYING IN VAIN
AGHHIIMNNOTU	HIGH MOUNTAIN	AGIIINNOORTV	INVIGORATION
AGHHILNNOOTT	NOTHING LOATH	AGIIINNOPRTT	PARTITIONING
AGHHILNOPRTT	TRIPHTHONGAL	AGIIINNPSSST	INSPISSATING
AGHHINNNOOST	HAS NOTHING ON	AGIIINOPPRTT	PROPITIATING
AGHHINORRTTU	THROUGH TRAIN	AGIIINRSSTUW	ISSUING A WRIT
AGHHINORSTTU	THRASHING OUT	AGIIJLNNORSU	JOURNALISING
AGHHIOPPRSYY	PHYSIOGRAPHY	AGIIJLNNORUZ	JOURNALIZING
AGHHIORSSTTT	SHOT STRAIGHT	AGIIKLLNNOTW	KNOWING IT ALL
AGHHIORSTTUW	SAW IT THROUGH	AGIIKLNNOPTT	TALKING POINT
AGHHOOPPSTUY	PHYTOPHAGOUS	AGIIKLNOORRW	ORIGINAL WORK
AGHIIILNOSST	HOISTING SAIL	AGIIKLNOTTTU	TALKING IT OUT
AGHIIINNPRST	TRAINING SHIP	AGIIKLNPRSTW	SPARKLING WIT
AGHIIKMNRTTU	MAKING IT HURT	AGIIKNNNRRSU	RUNNING A RISK
AGHIILLMNOPS	ANGLOPHILISM	AGIIKNNOOPST	TAKING POISON
AGHIILNPSTWY	PLAYING WHIST	AGIIKNNOPTTY	TAKING PITY ON
AGHIILNRSTTT	STARLIT NIGHT	AGIIKNNPSTTU	SINKING A PUTT
AGHIIMNNOSST	NOTHING AMISS	AGIILLLMNTUU	MULTILINGUAL
AGHIIMNPSSTY	SYMPATHISING	AGIILLLNRTUY	TRILINGUALLY
AGHIIMNPSTYZ	SYMPATHIZING	AGIILLNOPPTT	TOPPING IT ALL
AGHIINNOOPST	SHOOTING PAIN	AGIILLNOPRVW	PROVING A WILL
AGHIINOPPRTU	UPRIGHT PIANO	AGIILLNPRTWY	WILLING PARTY
AGHIINOPSTTT	IN A TIGHT SPOT	AGIILLNRSTTU	ILLUSTRATING
AGHIINRSTTTW	STARTING WITH	AGIILLNSSTTY	STAYING STILL
AGHIINSSSTTY	STAYS IN SIGHT	AGIILMNNOORS	MONSIGNORIAL
AGHIJKNNNOOT	JONATHON KING	AGIILMNNOPRT	TRAMPOLINING
AGHIKLNOOPPY	LOOKING HAPPY	AGIILNNOPTWY	PLAYING TO WIN
AGHIKLNOOPRS	LOOKING SHARP	AGIILNOORSUV	VAINGLORIOUS
AGHILLNNOORT	ALL OR NOTHING	AGIILNOPPRSU	POPULARISING
AGHILLORRTYY	RIGHT ROYALLY	AGIILNOPPRUZ	POPULARIZING
AGHILMNOOOOT	HOMOLOGATION	AGIILNPPPSST	SLIPPING PAST
AGHILNOOSSTT	ANTHOLOGISTS	AGIILNPRSTWY	WRITING PLAYS
AGHILNPRSTUU	SULPHURATING	AGIIMMNNRSTTT	TRANSMITTING
AGHILOOPSSTT	PATHOLOGISTS	AGIINNOOPPRT	APPORTIONING
AGHILOPSSTUY	GUYS HOSPITAL	AGIINNOORTTU	RATIONING OUT
AGHIMOSTTTUW	TAUGHT TO SWIM	AGIINPPPRTUW	WRAPPING IT UP
AGHINNOOPTTY	NOTHING TO PAY	AGIKLMNOORST	LOOKING SMART
AGHINNOOSTTY	NOTHING TO SAY	AGIKLNNNOOWW	KNOWING NO LAW
AGHINNORSSST	HAS NO STRINGS	AGIKLNNOOTUW	WALKING OUT ON
AGHINOOPRSTT	TRAPSHOOTING	AGIKLNOPSSTT	STOPS TALKING
AGHINOOPSTTT	PHOTOSTATING	AGIKNNNOTTUY	UNTYING A KNOT
AGHINOORSSTT	SHOOTING STAR	AGIKNOPRRTWY	WORKING PARTY
AGHINRRSSTTU	RUNS STRAIGHT	AGIKNORRSTTW	STARTING WORK
AGHIORSTTUUW	WITHOUT SUGAR	AGILLNOOPSTY	PALYNOLOGIST
AGHIPRSSTTTU	PUTS STRAIGHT	AGILLNOPSUWW	SWALLOWING UP
AGHKLLOOSSTY	LOOKS GHASTLY	AGILMMNPRUYY	PLAYING RUMMY
AGHLLNOOORTY	ORTHOGONALLY	AGILMNOOPRTU	PROMULGATION
AGHLMOOOPRSU	LAGOMORPHOUS	AGILNNNNOPTW	TOWN PLANNING
AGHLMOSSTUUY	SOUGHT ASYLUM		

AGILNNOOOPRT	PROLONGATION
AGILNOPPPSTY	STOPPING PLAY
AGILNPRSSSUY	SURPASSINGLY
AGILORSTTUUY	GRATUITOUSLY
AGIMNNORRSTW	STORM WARNING
AGINNNRSTTUY	TURNING NASTY
AGINNOORRSTW	GARRISON TOWN
AGINNOPRRSST	APRON STRINGS
AGINNOPRRSTT	TRANSPORTING
AGINNRRSSSTU	SATURNS RINGS
AGINOOPRSSTT	PROTAGONISTS
AGINOPRSSTTT	STARTING POST
AGLLMOOPSUYY	POLYGAMOUSLY
AGLLMOORSUUY	GLAMOUROUSLY
AGLLNOORSUUY	LANGUOROUSLY
AGLMMNOOOSUY	MONOGAMOUSLY
AGLNOOOSSTTY	STAYS TOO LONG
AHHHIIOOPPRY	HIP HIP HOORAY!
AHHIILOPPSST	HOSPITAL SHIP
AHHIJMNNOSTY	JOHNNY MATHIS
AHHILLLLSSYY	SHILLY-SHALLY
AHHILNOORSTU	HOLOTHURIANS
AHHILNOPPRTY	PHILANTHROPY
AHHINNOPRSTT	STROPHANTHIN
AHIIJLLMNOSW	JOHN WILLIAMS
AHIIKLLMPPRS	MARK PHILLIPS
AHIIMNNOORSU	INHARMONIOUS
AHIIMNNRRSTU	ANTIRRHINUMS
AHIINNNOOPSS	SPANISH ONION
AHIINOPRRTUW	POUR WITH RAIN
AHIKLOORTTUW	KILOWATT-HOUR
AHILLLLORSTU	TILL ALL HOURS
AHILLMMOOPRS	ALLOMORPHISM
AHILLNOORTYZ	HORIZONTALLY
AHILMNOORSUY	HARMONIOUSLY
AHILMNPRTTUY	TRIUMPHANTLY
AHILNOPRSTUU	SULPHURATION
AHIMNOORRSTY	ROMAN HISTORY
AHIMOOPPPSTU	HIPPOPOTAMUS
AHINNNNOOQTUY	ANTHONY QUINN
AHINNOPRSSTT	IN SHORT PANTS
AHINNOPRSSTU	SINANTHROPUS
AHINOOPSSSTX	SAXOPHONISTS
AHINORRSSSTY	SYNARTHROSIS
AHKLOOOPRSTU	SHARP LOOK-OUT
AHKOOOOPSTTT	TOOK A POT-SHOT
AHLMMOOPSTUY	LYMPHOMATOUS
AHLOPRRSSTUU	SULPHURATORS
AHMMORRSSTUY	SHORT SUMMARY
AHOPRRSTTUUY	SHUT YOUR TRAP!
AIIIIMMNNOST	MINIMISATION
AIIIIMMNNOTZ	MINIMIZATION
AIIILLLNPSTU	LILLIPUTIANS
AIIILLMNNOTU	ILLUMINATION
AIIILLNNOSTT	INSTILLATION
AIIILMNOOSST	ISOLATIONISM
AIIILMNRTTUY	MILITARY UNIT
AIIILMPRSSTU	SPIRITUALISM
AIIILNNOPSST	PAINTS IN OILS
AIIILNOOSSTT	ISOLATIONIST
AIIILPRSSTTU	SPIRITUALIST
AIIILPRSTTUY	SPIRITUALITY
AIIIMMNNOSTU	IMMUNISATION
AIIIMMNNOTUZ	IMMUNIZATION
AIIIMNNORSTT	MINISTRATION
AIIINNNOOSTU	UNIONISATION
AIIINNNOOTUZ	UNIONIZATION
AIIINNNOSSTU	INSINUATIONS
AIIINNOPRSST	INSPIRATIONS
AIIINOPSSSST	INSPISSATION
AIIINOOPPRTT	PROPITIATION
AIIINOPRRTTT	TRIPARTITION
AIIINOPRRSTT	PARTITIONIST
AIIINRSTTTVY	TRANSITIVITY
AIIKMNNOPRSS	PARKINSONISM
AIILLLNOSUVY	VILLAINOUSLY
AIILLNNRSTTU	ILLUSTRATION
AIILLNQRTTUY	TRANQUILLITY
AIILMNNNOOTU	MOUNTAIN LION
AIILMNNORTTU	MALNUTRITION
AIILNOOOPPST	OPPOSITIONAL
AIILNOPSSTTU	STIPULATIONS
AIILNORRSTTY	TRANSITORILY
AIILOPRSUVVY	VIVIPAROUSLY
AIIMMNNOTTUUY	AUTOIMMUNITY
AIIMMNSSSTTU	NUMISMATISTS
AIIMNNORSSST	TRANSMISSION
AIIMNOOORSTT	MOTORISATION
AIIMNOOORTTZ	MOTORIZATION
AIIMNOOPRSST	ANISOTROPISM
AIIMNOOPRSSU	PARSIMONIOUS
AIIMNOOQSTTU	MISQUOTATION
AIINNOPSSTUU	ANTONIUS PIUS
AIIOOPPRRTTY	PROPITIATORY
AIJMOORRTTYY	TORY MAJORITY
AIKLLLMMOPRS	PLIMSOLL MARK
AIKLLNOSSTTW	WALK ON STILTS
AIKMNOPPRSTT	TRAPPIST MONK
AILLLNOOSSTT	ALL IS NOT LOST
AILLMMOORSTU	IMMORTAL SOUL
AILLMNNOOPRY	PRONOMINALLY
AILLMNOOPRST	SMALL PORTION
AILLNOOPTTYY	POLYTONALITY
AILLOOPPRSTT	PILLAR TO POST
AILMNORSTUVY	VOLUNTARYISM
AILNNNOOSTTU	SUN-TAN LOTION
	SUNTAN LOTION
AILNOOOPPRRT	PROPORTIONAL
AILNOOPRRTTU	LUTON AIRPORT
AILNOPPRTUUY	UNPOPULARITY
AILNOPSSTTUU	PUSTULATIONS
AILNORSSTTUV	VOLUNTARISTS
AILNORSTTUVY	VOLUNTARYIST
AILOOPRRSUUY	UPROARIOUSLY
AILOORRSTTUY	TRAITOROUSLY
AIMMNNORRSTU	MURMURATIONS
AIMNNOOPRSSU	PONS ASINORUM
AIMNOOOPRSTT	SOMATOTROPIN
AIMNOOPRRSTT	PORT IN A STORM
AIMOOPRRSSTU	UPSTAIRS ROOM
AINNNOOPRSTT	NON-STOP TRAIN
AINORRRSTTTU	TURNS TRAITOR
AINORRSSSTUU	SUSURRATIONS
AIOOPPSTTTTU	PUT A STOP TO IT
AKLLMNOORWWY	ALL MY OWN WORK
ALLOOPPRSTUY	LOYAL SUPPORT
ALMNOOOSTUUY	AUTONOMOUSLY
ALMOOPPRRSTU	MORAL SUPPORT
ALNNOOOOPPSTY	PLAYS PONTOON
ALOOPPPRRSTU	POPULAR SPORT
ANOOOORSSTTT	START TOO SOON
ANOPPRSSTTUU	PUTS ON A SPURT
BBBBBEEHLLUU	HUBBLE-BUBBLE
BBBBELLNOSUW	BLOWN BUBBLES
BBBBELLOSSUW	BLOWS BUBBLES
BBBCCIIKKRRY	BRICK BY BRICK
BBBCEFHIORSY	BOBBY FISCHER
BBBDGIILNNOR	ROBBING BLIND
BBBEGILNORUV	BUBBLING OVER
BBCCEEHKLORS	BREECHBLOCKS
BBCCEEILLRTU	ELECTRIC BULB
BBCCEEILMOPU	BECOME PUBLIC

BBCDDENORSUW	SCRUBBED DOWN
BBCDEEEKNRRU	RUBBERNECKED
BBCDEELNOOST	COBBLESTONED
BBCDEHIRRSTU	BUTCHER-BIRDS
BBCEEEEHQRRUU	RUBBER CHEQUE
BBCEEEKLORSZ	BREEZE-BLOCKS
BBCEEELSTTUW	WEBB'S LETTUCE
BBCEEHKOORRS	BECHERS BROOK
BBCEEILNPRRU	PENCIL RUBBER
BBCEELNOOSST	COBBLESTONES
BBCEHILORSTY	SIR TOBY BELCH
BBCEJKOORSST	STOCKJOBBERS
BBCEKLORSSTU	BLOCKBUSTERS
BBCELLLOOSWY	COLLYWOBBLES
BBCGIKKLNOOO	BLOCK-BOOKING
BBCGINORSTUU	SCRUBBING OUT
BBCHIIIILLOP	BIBLIOPHILIC
BBCINOORSTTU	CUT TO RIBBONS
BBDDDDEIIISY	BIDDY-BIDDIES
BDDDEEGLLORU	BULLDOG BREED
BBDDENNOOSUY	BEYOND BOUNDS
BBDDGIILNOUY	BODY BUILDING
BBDEEEFILNQY	BEYOND BELIEF
BBDEEEHLNOTW	BEND THE ELBOW
BBDEEGGLORRU	RUBE GOLDBERG
BBDEEGLNRTUY	RUBBED GENTLY
BBDEEHHLOOSY	HOBBLEDEHOYS
BBDEGGKLOOOY	GOBBLEDYGOOK
BBDEGHINRRUY	RUBBER DINGHY
BBDEGHMNOORY	HYDROGEN BOMB
BBDEHLOOORRT	BLOOD BROTHER
BBDELMOOOTTU	DOUBLE BOTTOM
BBDLNNOORSUU	LONDON SUBURB
BBEEEEILNNSS	BEEN SENSIBLE
BBEEEFLOORTT	BOTTLE OF BEER
BBEEEGHINSTT	BEING THE BEST
BBEFFFHILOTTW	BELOW THE BELT
BBEEGINOPRRT	ROBBING PETER
BBEEGLORRSUV	RUBBER GLOVES
BBEEHHHILLOTY	THE HOLY BIBLE
BBEEHILLTTTU	BIT THE BULLET
BBEEHILMPRTU	BIBLE THUMPER
BBEEILLMNRRY	BILLY BREMNER
BBEEILLNRSSU	LUBBERLINESS
BBEENNNRRSUU	BUNSEN BURNER
BBEFILOORTTU	BIT OF TROUBLE
BBEGINNORSSU	RUBBING NOSES
BBEHIIILLOPS	BIBLIOPHILES
BBEHINNOSSSS	SNOBBISHNESS
BBEHINRSSTUU	IN THE SUBURBS
BBEHIRRSTTUU	UTTER RUBBISH
BBEHKMNOOOSU	BOB MONKHOUSE
BBEHLMRRSUUY	MULBERRY BUSH
BBEILLNOORWY	YELLOW RIBBON
BBEILNOSSSUU	BIBULOUSNESS
BBEILORSSTTY	SOBS BITTERLY
BBEMNNOORSTU	NEUTRON BOMBS
BBENNORSSSTU	STUBBORNNESS
BBFIILLMMMOR	LIMB FROM LIMB
BBGHIKLNOTUU	BOUGHT IN BULK
BBGIIKLNNUUY	BUYING IN BULK
BBGIKNOOORST	BRINGS TO BOOK
BCCCEIILLPSY	BICYCLE CLIPS
BCCCEIIMRRSU	CIRCUMSCRIBE
BCCDEEIJORTT	DIRECT OBJECT
BCCDEEIKRSTU	CRIED BUCKETS
BCCDEHLOOSTU	DOUBLE SCOTCH
BCCDNOORSTUU	BUS CONDUCTOR
BCCEEEEIIPPY	PIECE BY PIECE
BCCEEEILLLRT	ELECTRIC BELL
BCCEEEILLRTU	ELECTRIC BLUE
BCCEEELNOOSS	OBSOLESCENCE
BCCEEFHIILTY	BICYCLE THIEF
BCCEEGILNSTY	GENTS BICYCLE
BCCEEHHMMRRU	CHURCH MEMBER
BCCEEHILPPSU	PUBLIC SPEECH
BCCEEHNORRSS	CROSSBENCHER
BCCEEIIMNNSU	INCUMBENCIES
BCCEEIKRSSTU	CRIES BUCKETS
BCCEEIILLLOST	COLLECTIBLES
BCCEFFIILOPU	PUBLIC OFFICE
BCCEHKKLOSST	SKETCHBLOCKS
BCCEHNNOOORT	CORN ON THE COB
BCCEHORSTTTU	BUTTERSCOTCH
BCCEIILNOPTU	PUBLIC NOTICE
BCCEILOPRSTU	PUBLIC SECTOR
BCCHILLOOPSU	PUBLIC SCHOOL
BCCHIMOORTTY	THROMBOCYTIC
BCCILOPRTUUY	PUBLIC OUTCRY
BCCINOOSSSUU	SUBCONSCIOUS
BCCIOOOPRSST	STROBOSCOPIC
BCCKOORSSTTU	CROSS-BUTTOCK
BCDDEEEFNNOS	DEFENCE BONDS
BCDDEECIINOS	DISOBEDIENCE
BCDDEEEKLORU	DOUBLE DECKER
	DOUBLE-DECKER
BCDDEEILORTT	BOTTLED CIDER
BCDDHILNOOSY	NOBODYS CHILD
BCDEEEEGRRST	CRESTED GREBE
BCDEEEEINOOW	OWL OBEDIENCE
BCDEEEEMNRSZ	MERCEDES BENZ
BCDEEEEMNRTX	NEXT DECEMBER
BCDEEEEOPTTX	TO BE EXPECTED
BCDEEEGHPSTU	BUDGET SPEECH
BCDEEEIIMNST	BEST MEDICINE
BCDEEEIINNST	BENEDICTINES
BCDEEEKORRST	STOCKBREEDER
BCDEEELNNOST	NOBLE DESCENT
BCDEEFHIOOTV	HOTBED OF VICE
BCDEEFINNOOT	CONFINE TO BED
BCDEEHMNOSTU	DEBOUCHMENTS
BCDEEIINNOST	BENEDICTIONS
BCDEEIIOPRRU	REPRODUCIBLE
BCDEEILORRSU	CLOUDBERRIES
BCDEEILRSTTU	DESTRUCTIBLE
BCDEEIMNRSSU	DISENCUMBERS
BCDEEIPRRSSU	SUPERSCRIBED
BCDEEKOORRRS	BROKE RECORDS
BCDEELOORSUW	COULD BE WORSE
BCDEHILLMOPR	PROBLEM CHILD
BCDEHILLOTUW	BLUE WITH COLD
BCDEIIMORTTU	OBITER DICTUM
BCDEILLORTTY	BITTERLY COLD
BCDEINORSTUY	BUYS ON CREDIT
BCDEIOORRSTX	DIRECTORS BOX
BCDEKLOORSSU	BLOODSUCKERS
BCDELNOOSTUU	COUNTS DOUBLE
BCDENORSTTUU	UNOBSTRUCTED
BCDFFIIJLOTU	DIFFICULT JOB
BCDFFIKLOORS	FLOCK OF BIRDS
BCDGIIKMNORS	MOCKINGBIRDS
BCDGIILMNNOW	CLIMBING DOWN
BCDGIKLNNOUW	BUCKLING DOWN
BCDGIKLNOOSU	BLOODSUCKING
BCDGIKNOOSTY	BODY STOCKING
BCDHILMNOTUW	NUMB WITH COLD
BCDINOORSTVY	VICTORY BONDS
BCEEFFFFLSUX	FEEBLE EXCUSE
BCEEEEEHKNRS	KNEE BREECHES
BCEEEEGHHIST	THE BIG CHEESE
BCEEEEGILLNR	BELLIGERENCE
BCEEEEGKLLLO	KEBLE COLLEGE

BCEEEEMNOSTW	COMES BETWEEN
BCEEEFILMNRU	BEEN MERCIFUL
BCEEEFILNNTY	BENEFICENTLY
BCEEEGHILNSY	BESEECHINGLY
BCEEEGIINORT	BIOENERGETIC
BCEEEHIKNORT	BROKEN THE ICE
BCEEEHIKORRS	CHOKEBERRIES
BCEEEHILPTUY	THE PUBLIC EYE
BCEEEIKOORSX	EXERCISE BOOK
BCEEEILMNOST	BECOME SILENT
BCEEEILMRSTV	CLIMB EVEREST
BCEEEILOPSTW	BLEW TO PIECES
BCEEEINRSSUV	SUBSERVIENCE
BCEEEIRRRSVY	SERVICEBERRY
BCEEFFMOOSST	COMES OFF BEST
BCEEFGMORRSY	BEGS FOR MERCY
BCEEFHIORRST	BEFORE CHRIST
BCEEFHLORSTU	THREE OF CLUBS
BCEEFILNORSS	FORCIBLENESS
BCEEFLNOQSUU	QUEEN OF CLUBS
BCEEFLNOSSUV	SEVEN OF CLUBS
BCEEGHLORTTU	CLUB TOGETHER
BCEEGILMNOSS	BECOMING LESS
BCEEGILNORVX	BOXING CLEVER
BCEEGLLNOOOY	COLONEL BOGEY
BCEEHIKPSSTT	PICKS THE BEST
BCEEHJMNNOOW	JOHN NEWCOMBE
BCEEHJNOSTTU	ON THE SUBJECT
BCEEHLMOPRSS	CHESS PROBLEM
BCEEHNOOTTTU	CUT TO THE BONE
BCEEIIILMST	IMBECILITIES
BCEEIIJSSTUV	SUBJECTIVISE
BCEEIIJSTUVZ	SUBJECTIVIZE
BCEEIIILNNSSV	VINCIBLENESS
BCEEIJLSTUVY	SUBJECTIVELY
BCEEIJMNOOTT	TIME NO OBJECT
BCEEILMNOPTT	CONTEMPTIBLE
BCEEILMOPRSS	COMPRESSIBLE
BCEEILNORSTV	CONVERTIBLES
BCEEILOOPSTW	BLOW TO PIECES
BCEEIMMOSTTU	SUBCOMMITTEE
BCEEIPRRSSSU	SUPERSCRIBES
BCEEJLNOOSST	OBJECT LESSON
BCEEKKLNNOSU	KNUCKLEBONES
BCEEKLLORSTT	BLOCK LETTERS
BCEELLNOOOSW	BLEW ONE'S COOL
BCEELMMORSUY	CUMBERSOMELY
BCEEMOOSSTTU	COMES OUT BEST
BCEFFGOOOTTY	GEOFF BOYCOTT
BCEFFHINOSUV	BUNCH OF FIVES
BCEFGHILOSTU	EIGHT OF CLUBS
BCEFGIIJNOTY	OBJECTIFYING
BCEFGIILPRUU	PUBLIC FIGURE
BCEFGIJLNOTY	FLYING OBJECT
BCEFHNOORSSU	BUNCH OF ROSES
BCEFHORRSTUY	BRUCE FORSYTH
BCEFIJNOOSTU	CUT OF ONES JIB
BCEFIJOOPTTY	OBJECT OF PITY
BCEFIMOPRTTU	BIT OF CRUMPET
BCEFKLNOOOST	BLOCK OF STONE
BCEGHIILNTWY	BEWITCHINGLY
BCEGHIIMNORS	CHEMISORBING
BCEGHIMNNOOY	HONEYCOMBING
BCEGHIMNOORS	CHEMOSORBING
BCEGIIILNORR	INCORRIGIBLE
BCEGIIKMOORT	BIG-TIME CROOK
BCEGIIKNOOTX	EXCITING BOOK
BCEGIILMNOPR	CLIMBING ROPE
BCEGIILMNORV	CLIMBING OVER
BCEGIKKLNOOR	BOOKING CLERK
BCEGIKLNOSTU	BLUE STOCKING
	BLUESTOCKING
BCEGILMNNOUY	UNBECOMINGLY
BCEHHIILLNOR	HEINRICH BOLL
BCEHHLORSSTU	CLOTHES BRUSH
BCEHHOPRSSTU	BUTCHERS SHOP
BCEHIIMORSTY	BIOCHEMISTRY
BCEHIJLNOSTU	JOINS THE CLUB
BCEHIMOORSTW	WITCHES'-BROOM
BCEHIMORSTWW	WEST BROMWICH
BCEHKKOOOOST	COOK THE BOOKS
BCEIIILLRTVY	CIVIL LIBERTY
BCEIIJMSSTUV	SUBJECTIVISM
BCEIIJSSTTUV	SUBJECTIVIST
BCEIIJSTTUVY	SUBJECTIVITY
BCEIIKLLNRTU	CLINKER-BUILT
BCEIIKLLRSST	BILLSTICKERS
BCEIINNOORRS	ERIC ROBINSON
BCEIINORTTUV	CONTRIBUTIVE
BCEIJNSSTUUV	SUBJUNCTIVES
BCEIKNNRSUWW	NEW BRUNSWICK
BCEILLLMNOOP	COLONEL BLIMP
BCEILLMMNOOU	MOBILE COLUMN
BCEILMNOPTTY	CONTEMPTIBLY
BCEILMOOPRTW	CLIMB TO POWER
BCEILMORSTUU	MICROTUBULES
BCEILORSSTUU	TUBERCULOSIS
BCEINNNOSTTU	SUBCONTINENT
BCEKKOORRSST	STOCKBROKERS
BCELLNOOOOSW	BLOW ONE'S COOL
BCELMOOOSSTW	COMES TO BLOWS
BCELSSTTTTUU	SCUTTLEBUTTS
BCEMNORSSSUU	CUMBROUSNESS
BCEOOOOPRSST	STROBOSCOPES
BCERRSSTTUUU	SUBSTRUCTURE
BCGHIKNOORRT	BRIGHTON ROCK
BCGHIKNOOTTU	BOUGHT ON TICK
BCGHILNORSUW	CRUSHING BLOW
BCGHILOORRTU	BRIGHT COLOUR
BCGIIIKLLNST	BILLSTICKING
BCGIIILNORRY	INCORRIGIBLY
BCGIIKNNOTUY	BUYING ON TICK
BCGIILMMNSUW	SWIMMING CLUB
BCGIILMOOORY	MICROBIOLOGY
BCGIILOOOOSY	SOCIOBIOLOGY
BCGIIMNNOOST	COMING TO BITS
BCGIINNORTTU	CONTRIBUTING
BCGIKKNOORST	STOCKBROKING
BCGIKMNOOOOT	COMING TO BOOK
BCHHIMOOORRT	ORTHORHOMBIC
BCHIIIOPSSTY	BIOPHYSICIST
BCHIIIPSSSTU	SHIPS BISCUIT
BCHILNOORRTT	BIRTH CONTROL
BCHNOORSSSTU	HOT CROSS-BUNS
BCIIILPPRSTU	PUBLIC SPIRIT
BCIIKLLNOSST	STICK NO BILLS
BCIILLORSUUY	LUBRICIOUSLY
BCIINNOORSSU	ROBIN COUSINS
BCIINNOORTTU	CONTRIBUTION
BCIINNOPRSSTU	SUBSCRIPTION
BCIJNNOOSTUX	BOX JUNCTIONS
BCILMMNOSUUU	CUMULONIMBUS
BCINOORRSTTU	CONTRIBUTORS
BCINOORRTTUY	CONTRIBUTORY
BCINOORSSTTU	OBSTRUCTIONS
BCKMOORSTTTU	STRUCK BOTTOM
BDDDEEEGILNS	SINGLE-BEDDED
BDDDEEIINTVY	DIVIDED BY TEN
BDDDEGIINNRU	UNDERBIDDING
BDDDEIIISVXY	DIVIDED BY SIX
BDDDEIIOTVWY	DIVIDED BY TWO

BDDDEILMNOOY	BLOODY-MINDED	BDEEELLOTUVW	DOUBLE TWELVE
BDDEEEEFILMN	FEEBLEMINDED	BDEEEELMRTTTU	MELTED BUTTER
BDDEEEEKNNNO	ON BENDED KNEE	BDEEELOPPRSY	PROBES DEEPLY
BDDEEEFGNOOY	EDGE OF BEYOND	BDEEENNOOSST	DONE ONE'S BEST
BDDEEEFHIRST	FEED THE BIRDS	BDEEENNOPRTV	DEPONENT VERB
BDDEEEFLMNTU	BEFUDDLEMENT	BDEEENOOSSST	DOES ONE'S BEST
BDDEEEIINNOS	DIE IN ONES BED	BDEEENOOSTTW	STOOD BETWEEN
BDDEEEINNSST	INDEBTEDNESS	BDEEFFGIORST	BEGS TO DIFFER
BDDEEEELOPPRY	PROBED DEEPLY	BDEEFFLLOTUU	FEEL DOUBTFUL
BDDEEEENORRUV	OVERBURDENED	BDEEFGIINNRS	BEING FRIENDS
BDDEEEOOORRSY	OBEYED ORDERS	BDEEFGILNSUU	EDIBLE FUNGUS
BDDEEFIIIVVY	DIVIDE BY FIVE	BDEEFGOOSTTU	GETS OUT OF BED
BDDEEFOOSSTU	SEEDS OF DOUBT	BDEEFHINORTY	THE BOY FRIEND
BDDEEGGINOOR	GOOD BREEDING	BDEEFIILNNSY	INDEFENSIBLY
BDDEEGHHIIRR	HIGHER BIDDER	BDEEFIILRSTU	FILIBUSTERED
BDDEEGHIILST	BEDSIDE LIGHT	BDEEFILLORSU	SUED FOR LIBEL
BDDEEGILLNSW	WEDDING BELLS	BDEEFIMOORRT	TIMBERED ROOF
BDDEEGLOOUWW	WEDGWOOD BLUE	BDEEFIMOORSV	FIVE BEDROOMS
BDDEEHIMNNST	BENDS THE MIND	BDEEFLOOOPPY	BODY OF PEOPLE
BDDEEHNNORTU	ROUND THE BEND	BDEEFLOORRRW	FLOWER BORDER
BDDEEIIINNVY	DIVIDE BY NINE	BDEEFNOOORSS	NO BED OF ROSES
BDDEEIILMORS	DISEMBROILED	BDEEFOPRSSTU	BURST OF SPEED
BDDEEIINSTVY	DIVIDES BY TEN	BDEEGGHIIRSW	WEIGHBRIDGES
BDDEEIKNNORW	BROKEN-WINDED	BDEEGHIINRTV	GIVEN THE BIRD
BDDEEILMOSUX	MIXED DOUBLES	BDEEGHIIRSTV	GIVES THE BIRD
BDDEELORRTUY	ROBERT DUDLEY	BDEEGHINNORR	HERRINGBONED
BDDEEFIIORUVY	DIVIDE BY FOUR	BDEEGHINORTT	BIND TOGETHER
BDDEGHILSTUU	SUBDUED LIGHT	BDEEGHINPRTU	BRIGHTENED UP
BDDEGIIMNOSY	DISEMBODYING	BDEEGIIILNST	INDIGESTIBLE
BDDEGIINNRSU	DISBURDENING	BDEEGIIILNSV	DISBELIEVING
BDDEGILNNOOR	LONDON BRIDGE	BDEEGIIKNNRR	DRINKING BEER
BDDEIIISSVXY	DIVIDES BY SIX	BDEEGIIMMNRS	DISMEMBERING
BDDEIINNOOTU	BOUND EDITION	BDEEGIIMNORR	EMBROIDERING
BDDEIIOSTVWY	DIVIDES BY TWO	BDEEGINNPRTU	BEING PRUDENT
BDDEIILLLOOPS	SPILLED BLOOD	BDEEGINOSTTT	GETS INTO DEBT
BDDEILMNORTU	TROUBLED MIND	BDEEGINPRTUY	PUTNEY BRIDGE
BDDEILNOOOTW	BOILED DOWN TO	BDEEGLMNNORU	GOLDEN NUMBER
BDDELLMMTUUU	DUM-DUM BULLET	BDEEGLNOOTUU	DOUBLE-TONGUE
BDDFGIILLNNO	BLINDFOLDING	BDEEHIINOSTT	BIT ON THE SIDE
BDDFGIILNORY	FORBIDDINGLY	BDEEHIINOTTW	BE DONE WITH IT
BDDFGIMNNOUU	DUMBFOUNDING	BDEEHIMNOORT	IN THE BEDROOM
BDDGHINOTUUY	BUDDING YOUTH	BDEEHIMSSSTU	MISSED THE BUS
BDDHIKMNOSTU	BUDDHIST MONK	BDEEHINRSTWY	WINS THE DERBY
BDDINOORSTTU	DO NOT DISTURB	BDEEHISSTTTU	BITES THE DUST
BDEEEEHKNNST	BENDS THE KNEE	BDEEHLOORRRT	OLDER BROTHER
BDEEEEHKNOTW	BOWED THE KNEE	BDEEHNNOORTU	ON THE REBOUND
BDEEEEILLOTV	LED TO BELIEVE	BDEEIIKLLNN	INDELIBLE INK
BDEEEEILRRRS	ELDERBERRIES	BDEEIIINNRSST	BEND SINISTER
BDEEEELLNOUV	DOUBLE ELEVEN	BDEEIJLRRUY	JERRY-BUILDER
BDEEEFFMORRT	FREE FROM DEBT	BDEEILLNPRSS	SPELLBINDERS
BDEEEFIILNNS	INDEFENSIBLE	BDEEILMNNOSW	BLEW ONE'S MIND
BDEEEFINNORR	BEFORE DINNER	BDEEILMOORVY	REMOVE BODILY
BDEEEFLNOSTT	BED OF NETTLES	BDEEILMRRSTU	TUMBLE-DRIERS
BDEEEGHMNRTU	GREEN-THUMBED	BDEEILNOOPWW	BLOW WIDE OPEN
BDEEEGHNSSTT	GETS THE BENDS	BDEEILORRSSW	BOWDLERISERS
BDEEEGIILNTV	DIVING BEETLE	BDEEILORRSWZ	BOWDLERIZERS
BDEEEGILNOSU	SEEING DOUBLE	BDEEIMNRSSTU	DISBURSEMENT
BDEEEGINRRSV	SEVERN BRIDGE	BDEEIMOORRTW	BORROWED TIME
BDEEEHINOSTT	BET ON THE SIDE	BDEEIMORSTTY	BED-TIME STORY
BDEEEHINRTTT	THE BITTER END		BEDTIME STORY
BDEEEHLNOSTY	LED BY THE NOSE	BDEEINNORSTV	INVERTED SNOB
BDEEEHLORRRT	ELDER BROTHER	BDEEINNOSSSU	DONE BUSINESS
BDEEEHNOOPTX	OPENED THE BOX	BDEEINOORRRT	ROBERT DE NIRO
BDEEEIILRSSV	DISBELIEVERS	BDEEINOSSSSU	DOES BUSINESS
BDEEEIIMNOST	BIDE ONES TIME	BDEELMORSTUV	STUMBLED OVER
BDEEEIIRSVWY	BIRDS-EYE VIEW	BDEELNOTTUWY	DOUBLE TWENTY
BDEEEILLNRSU	UNDERBELLIES	BDEEOOORTUVYY	EVERYBODY OUT
BDEEEEILMNRTW	BEWILDERMENT	BDEFGILNOSTU	SELF-DOUBTING
BDEEEILNOPWW	BLEW WIDE OPEN	BDEFILOOORRV	RIVER OF BLOOD
BDEEEILOSSTW	BOILED SWEETS	BDEFILORTTTU	BOTTLED FRUIT
BDEEEIMMRRSS	DISREMEMBERS	BDEFIMNOORSS	BOSOM FRIENDS

BDEFKOOOOSUX	BOOK OF EXODUS
BDEFLNOOOOST	BOLT ONES FOOD
BDEFLNOSSTUU	DOUBTFULNESS
BDEFMOOOORRSU	FOUR BEDROOMS
BDEGGGILNRUY	BEGRUDGINGLY
BDEGGIIMNOSU	DISEMBOGUING
BDEGGINPRSTU	SPRING BUDGET
BDEGHHOORRTU	THOROUGHBRED
BDEGHIIINRST	DIG IN THE RIBS
BDEGHIILMNTU	MIDNIGHT BLUE
BDEGHIINRSTU	DUG IN THE RIBS
BDEGHIIOPRRT	BRIGHT PERIOD
BDEGHIOOTUWY	GOD BE WITH YOU
BDEGIIILMNOS	DEMOBILISING
BDEGIIILMNOZ	DEMOBILIZING
BDEGIIILNSTU	BUILDING SITE
BDEGIILLNNPS	SPELLBINDING
BDEGIILNORSW	BOWDLERISING
BDEGIILNORWZ	BOWDLERIZING
BDEGIINNOOST	DOING ONE'S BIT
BDEGIINNRSST	BIRD'S-NESTING
BDEGILLNNRUY	BLUNDERINGLY
BDEGILLNOOTT	BLOODLETTING
	LETTING BLOOD
BDEGILMNRTUY	TUMBLE-DRYING
BDEGINOOSSSU	GOOD BUSINESS
BDEGINOPTTTU	PUTTING TO BED
BDEGKNNOOORRU	BROKEN GROUND
BDEHHMNOOORR	RHOMBOHEDRON
BDEHHOOOORRST	BROTHERHOODS
BDEHIILPRSSU	SHIPBUILDERS
BDEHIINNPSTU	NIPS IN THE BUD
BDEHIKLOSUWY	DOUBLE WHISKY
BDEHILOORSTT	STIR THE BLOOD
BDEHLNORSTTU	THUNDERBOLTS
BDEHLOOORSTT	BOLTS THE DOOR
BDEHLORRSSUU	RUB SHOULDERS
BDEIIIILLNTY	INDELIBILITY
BDEIIIILLNOSV	DIVISION BELL
BDEIIIRSTTUV	DISTRIBUTIVE
BDEIIKLNRSST	STRIKES BLIND
BDEIILLMNPSU	BLIND IMPULSE
BDEIILLNOSSU	INDISSOLUBLE
BDEIILNOOSUV	DOUBLE VISION
BDEIJLNOOSVW	DEVIL'S OWN JOB
BDEIKNNOORWW	BROKEN WINDOW
BDEILMNNOOSW	BLOW ONE'S MIND
BDEILNNPRSSU	PURBLINDNESS
BDEIMMNOPRSU	PREMIUM BONDS
BDEINNORSTTU	RUNS INTO DEBT
BDEKNOORRRSU	DRUNK OR SOBER
BDELMNOPSTUU	STUMBLED UPON
BDELNORRSTUY	BURT REYNOLDS
BDEMNNORRSUU	ROUND NUMBERS
BDEOOOPRTVXYY	VOTED BY PROXY
BDFGHILLOOSW	GOLDFISH BOWL
BDFIILMNNUUU	INFUNDIBULUM
BDFMOOOORRTU	ROOM FOR DOUBT
BDFOOOOOPRSTY	BODY OF TROOPS
BDGGGIILMNNO	MIND-BOGGLING
BDGGGIINNOOW	GOING DOWN BIG
BDGGHHIIILNU	HIGH BUILDING
BDGGIINNNORW	BRINGING DOWN
BDGGIINNORRW	BRINGING WORD
BDGHIIILNPSU	SHIPBUILDING
BDGHIIMMNRSU	HUMMINGBIRDS
BDGHILNOTUWY	BLIGHTY WOUND
BDGHINNORSUW	BRUSHING DOWN
BDGHNOORRTUU	BROUGHT ROUND
BDGIIINRSTTU	DISTRIBUTING
BDGIIKMNRSTU	STRIKING DUMB
BDGIIKNNORTU	DRINKING BOUT
BDGIILLNOPTU	BUILDING PLOT
BDGIILNOSTUU	OUTBUILDINGS
BDGIILNRSTUY	DISTURBINGLY
BDGIIMNNORST	BRINGS TO MIND
BDGIINORSSTT	GRINDS TO BITS
BDGILMNNOTUW	TUMBLING DOWN
BDGINOOOORSUV	BORIS GODUNOV
BDGINOORSTTU	GROUND TO BITS
BDHIINNOSTUW	WITHIN BOUNDS
BDHILOORSTTY	BLOODTHIRSTY
BDHIOOTTTUUW	WITHOUT DOUBT
BDIIIIILSTVY	DIVISIBILITY
BDIIIILLNOSUY	LIBIDINOUSLY
BDIIINORSTTU	DISTRIBUTION
BDIIINOSSSUV	SUBDIVISIONS
BDIIKLLORSTW	KILL TWO BIRDS
BDIILLNOSSUY	INDISSOLUBLY
BDIIORRSSTTU	DISTRIBUTORS
BDINNOORRSWW	BROWN WINDSOR
BDKNNNOOOSUW	KNOW NO BOUNDS
BEEEEEFLMNNT	ENFEEBLEMENT
BEEEEEGLNRTZ	GENTLE BREEZE
BEEEEEHKNSST	THE BEES KNEES
BEEEEEFFFLORT	FEEBLE EFFORT
BEEEEHHRRTTY	THREE BY THREE
BEEEEHKLNOTW	BELOW THE KNEE
BEEEEILRRTUV	TRUE BELIEVER
BEEEEIMNSTTW	BETWEEN TIMES
	BETWEENTIMES
BEEEEKLMNRRT	KNEE TREMBLER
BEEEELMMNTZZ	EMBEZZLEMENT
BEEEELMNNRUV	NUMBER ELEVEN
BEEEEMNNOTVY	EVEN-MONEY BET
BEEEEOOQSSUXZ	SQUEEZE-BOXES
BEEEFFFILORT	BEREFT OF LIFE
BEEEFFHOOPRT	BEREFT OF HOPE
BEEEFGHOSTTT	GET THE BEST OF
BEEEFGILNNOS	BEING ONESELF
BEEEFHNOOSTT	ONE OF THE BEST
BEEEFHORRTTT	FOR THE BETTER
BEEEFIINNORR	BEEN INFERIOR
BEEEFLLMMORW	FELLOW MEMBER
BEEEFLNORSUY	BEEN YOURSELF
BEEEFOPPRRSU	BEFORE SUPPER
BEEEGGINNOTW	GOING BETWEEN
BEEEGHIIMNTT	THE TIME BEING
BEEEGHILOTVW	GIVE THE ELBOW
BEEEGHLOSTTW	GETS THE ELBOW
BEEEGIKNOPRS	KEEPING SOBER
BEEEGILLNRST	BELLIGERENTS
BEEEGILNNRSU	GREEN-LINE BUS
BEEEGINNOSTW	BEING SWEET ON
BEEEGINNPRST	BEING PRESENT
BEEEGINOSSTV	GIVE ONES BEST
BEEEGIOORRSS	GOOSEBERRIES
BEEEGKLNOORS	BROKE ONE'S LEG
BEEEGLNORSTU	NOBLE GESTURE
BEEEGMNORSSY	MESSENGER BOY
BEEEHHRRSTTU	THERES THE RUB
BEEEHIINNRTT	TEREBINTHINE
BEEEHILLNORS	HELLEBORINES
BEEEHILLNOTW	BELOW THE LINE
BEEEHKKOOPST	KEEP THE BOOKS
BEEEHKLORRTU	BROKE THE RULE
BEEEHKNORSTW	BROKE THE NEWS
BEEEHLLPRSST	PRESS THE BELL
BEEEHLNNTTWY	HYWEL BENNETT
BEEEHLNOOPTX	TELEPHONE BOX
BEEEIILMRRTT	TERRIBLE TIME
BEEEIILRRRSV	IRREVERSIBLE

BEEEIKOORRVW	BOOK REVIEWER
BEEEILLMNTTT	BELITTLEMENT
BEEEILNNSSSS	SENSIBLENESS
BEEEILNRRSST	TERRIBLENESS
BEEEIMMNORRS	SENIOR MEMBER
BEEEIMMNRTTT	EMBITTERMENT
BEEEINNNORTZ	NITROBENZENE
BEEEINOPRRSU	BEEN SUPERIOR
BEEEIPRRSSTY	PRESBYTERIES
BEEEIRSSTTTW	BITTERSWEETS
BEEEELLNNOTVY	BENEVOLENTLY
BEEEELMNRTUVW	NUMBER TWELVE
BEEELNOOPRTT	BOTTLE OPENER
BEEELNOOSSST	OBSOLETENESS
BEEELNRTTTWY	TREBLE TWENTY
BEEELRSSTTUY	TUBELESS TYRE
BEEEMNNORTVX	NEXT NOVEMBER
BEEENOPPRSTY	TEENY BOPPERS
	TEENYBOPPERS
BEEENOPPRSWY	WEENY BOPPERS
	WEENYBOPPERS
BEEFFINOORST	BORE ONE STIFF
BEEFGGMOORRY	GEORGE FORMBY
BEEFGHOOSTTT	GOT THE BEST OF
BEEFGIINNRRT	BIREFRINGENT
BEEFGLLOORSW	GLOBEFLOWERS
BEEFHIOSSTTX	SIX OF THE BEST
BEEFHLOOSTTT	BEST OF THE LOT
BEEFHLOOTTUU	OUT OF THE BLUE
BEEFHNOOOSTY	ONE OF THE BOYS
BEEFIILNORTU	BRIEF OUTLINE
BEEFIILNSSSU	BUSINESS LIFE
BEEFIIRRSTTT	BITTER STRIFE
BEEFILLORSSU	SUES FOR LIBEL
BEEFILNOOTTW	BOTTLE OF WINE
BEEFLNRTTTUY	BUTTERFLY NET
BEEGGHINOTVY	GIVEN THE GO-BY
BEEGGIILNSSV	GIVE BLESSING
BEEGGIIOOOOW	BOOGIE-WOOGIE
BEEGGIKNORRS	GOING BERSERK
BEEGGILNNORW	BOWLING GREEN
BEEGGILNOTTW	GETTING BELOW
BEEGHIILLMNS	EMBELLISHING
BEEGHILLNRST	RINGS THE BELL
BEEGHILNORST	BRINGS TO HEEL
BEEGHINNSSTU	SING THE BLUES
BEEGHINNORRS	HERRINGBONES
BEEGHINOOTTV	GIVEN THE BOOT
BEEGHINRSTTT	BETTER THINGS
BEEGHIOOSTTV	GIVES THE BOOT
BEEGHORRSTTU	RUBS TOGETHER
BEEGIIILLLNT	INTELLIGIBLE
BEEGIINNSSTT	BESETTING SIN
BEEGIINORSSU	BEING SERIOUS
BEEGIKKNOOPS	KEEPING BOOKS
BEEGILMOORSY	EMBRYOLOGIES
BEEGILMORSTY	BOY MEETS GIRL
BEEGILNORTUV	GIVEN TROUBLE
BEEGILORSTUV	GIVES TROUBLE
BEEGLOORRTTT	GLOBE-TROTTER
BEEGPRRSSTTU	ST.PETERSBURG
BEEHHILOTTTT	HIT THE BOTTLE
BEEHHINOOSSY	SHOE-SHINE BOY
BEEHHORRSTUV	OVER THE BRUSH
BEEHIIINORTX	EXHIBITIONER
BEEHIILRSSTT	BRITISH STEEL
BEEHILLRSVY	BEVERLY HILLS
BEEHILMOOPST	PHLEBOTOMIES
	PHLEBOTOMISE
BEEHILMOOPTZ	PHLEBOTOMIZE
BEEHILNORRSS	HORRIBLENESS

BEEHILOPSTTW	TIPS THE ELBOW
BEEHIMSSSSTU	MISSES THE BUS
BEEHINNNOTUV	BUN IN THE OVEN
BEEHINNORTWZ	WIN THE BRONZE
BEEHINOPQSSU	QUEENS BISHOP
BEEHINOSSSTY	BIOSYNTHESES
BEEHLLLLOSTT	TOLLS THE BELL
BEEHLLORSSSU	BLESS HER SOUL
BEEHLORRRTWY	WHORTLEBERRY
BEEHMOPRSTYY	EMBRYOPHYTES
BEEHNNOORTWZ	WON THE BRONZE
BEEHOPRRSSTT	STEPBROTHERS
BEEIIILRRSST	IRRESISTIBLE
BEEIIKLNSSLU	BUSINESSLIKE
BEEIILNOPSST	BITE ONES LIPS
	BITES ONE'S LIP
BEEIILNOSSTU	NEBULOSITIES
BEEIILRRRSVY	IRREVERSIBLY
BEEIKLNNNORU	UNBROKEN I INF
BEEILLLORSUY	REBELLIOUSLY
BEEILLLRSTUV	SILVER BULLET
BEEILLNNSTUW	NEWS BULLETIN
BEEILNOOPSTW	TIP ONE'S ELBOW
BEEILPPRSSSU	SUPPRESSIBLE
BEEILRSSUVVY	SUBVERSIVELY
BEEINOSSSTWX	WITNESS-BOXES
BEEKLNOOOSST	LOOK ONES BEST
BEEKNNOORTTW	KNOW NO BETTER
BEEKOOPRRRTU	RUPERT BROOKE
BEELLORSSTUY	TROLLEYBUSES
BEELMNOORTUY	MONEY TROUBLE
BEELMOORRRTY	ROBERT MORLEY
BEELMORSSTUV	STUMBLES OVER
BEELNNOSSSUU	NEBULOUSNESS
BEELNOOSSSST	BOOTLESSNESS
BEELNQSSTUUY	SUBSEQUENTLY
BEEMNNRTTUWY	NUMBER TWENTY
BEENOOSSSTTU	STUBS ONE'S TOE
BEEOOPRRSSTU	OBSTREPEROUS
BEFFHIOOTUWY	BE OFF WITH YOU
BEFGGIINORRT	BRING TO GRIEF
BEFGHIINNORT	BONFIRE NIGHT
BEFGHIINRRSU	REFURBISHING
BEFGHILLRSTU	BULLFIGHTERS
BEFGHILMNRTU	FLIGHT NUMBER
BEFGHLLOORTU	GO FOR THE BULL
BEFGIILNORST	BRINGS TO LIFE
BEFGINNRRSTU	BURNT FINGERS
BEFHHIIJNOST	FINISH THE JOB
BEFHIILLLLST	FILLS THE BILL
BEFHIINPRSSU	SUPERB FINISH
BEFHILLOOPTT	TOP OF THE BILL
BEFHILLOOSTT	FOOTS THE BILL
BEFHINNOOORS	ONE FOR HIS NOB
BEFHOOOPRSTT	SPOT OF BOTHER
BEFIINOPRTTT	PINT OF BITTER
BEFIKLLMOOTT	BOTTLE OF MILK
BEFIKLOORTTU	KILO OF BUTTER
BEFILLNSSSSU	BLISSFULNESS
BEFILNOOSTTU	BUILT OF STONE
BEFLOOOPRTTT	BOTTLE OF PORT
BEFLOOORTTUU	OUT OF TROUBLE
BEGGGGGIINNO	GOING BEGGING
BEGGGIINOORV	GOING OVER BIG
BEGGHIIMNNOR	BRINGING HOME
BEGGHIINNORU	NEIGHBOURING
BEGGIILNNOSS	OBLIGINGNESS
BEGGIINNORRV	BRINGING OVER
BEGGILLRSSUY	SILLY BUGGERS
BEGGILNOOSVX	BOXING GLOVES
BEGHHKOORRTU	BROKE THROUGH

BEGHIILMNORU	HUMBLE ORIGIN
BEGHIILNOSSV	BOLSHEVISING
BEGHIILNOSVZ	BOLSHEVIZING
BEGHIINOPRRT	BRIGHTON PIER
BEGHILLORTWY	BRIGHT YELLOW
BEGHILPPRRTU	BRIGHT PURPLE
BEGHINORRSUV	BRUSHING OVER
BEGIIIILLLTY	ILLEGIBILITY
BEGIIILLLNTY	INTELLIGIBLY
BEGIILNNNRRV	IRVING BERLIN
BEGIIKLNNPRS	BESPRINKLING
BEGIILLNRSTY	BLISTERINGLY
BEGIILOOOSTX	EXOBIOLOGIST
BEGIIMMNORRV	BRIMMING OVER
BEGIINNRSSUU	BURNING ISSUE
BEGIKLLNOOPS	SPELLING BOOK
BEGILLNRSTUY	BLUSTERINGLY
BEGILMNORTUV	TUMBLING OVER
BEGILMOORSTY	EMBRYOLOGIST
BEGILNOPRSTU	BOLSTERING UP
BEGIMNNORTUU	OUTNUMBERING
BEGIMNORRSTW	STORM BREWING
BEGINNOPRSTU	BURSTING OPEN
BEGINOPRRTUU	TRIBUNE GROUP
BEGINORRSSTT	BRINGS TO REST
BEGNNRSSTTUU	GETS SUNBURNT
BEHHIJNOOTTW	ON WITH THE JOB
BEHHINOSTTUW	TWO IN THE BUSH
BEHHOOPRSSTU	THE BOSPHORUS
BEHHOORSSTTU	TOOTHBRUSHES
BEHIIILPRSTT	BLITHE SPIRIT
BEHIIILRSSST	BRITISH ISLES
BEHIILMNPSSS	BLIMPISHNESS
BEHIINOSSSTY	BIOSYNTHESIS
BEHIKLOSTTWY	WHISKY BOTTLE
BEHILLMMRSTU	MILLER'S-THUMB
BEHILLOSSSSU	BLESS HIS SOUL
BEHILMOOPSTT	PHLEBOTOMIST
BEHIMNRRTTUY	NUMBER THIRTY
BEHINOOPTTTU	PUT THE BOOT IN
BEHINORRSTTW	TWIN BROTHERS
BEHINOSSSSUW	SHOW BUSINESS
BEHLNNOOORSW	BLOW ONES HORN
BEHLNOOOSSTT	SHOT ONES BOLT
BEHLNOORSTTU	BUTTONHOLERS
BEHLOORRSSTU	SOUL BROTHERS
BEHNNORTTUUY	BOUNTY HUNTER
BEHNOOPRSTTW	POTS THE BROWN
BEIIIKLNNSV	INVISIBLE INK
BEIIILLLLSSY	SILLY-BILLIES
BEIIILMQRSUU	EQUILIBRIUMS
BEIIILRRSSTY	IRRESISTIBLY
BEIIKNOPRRST	BROKEN SPIRIT
BEIILLOORSTU	LOUIS BLERIOT
BEIILMSSSUVY	SUBMISSIVELY
BEIIMOOQSTTU	MOSQUITO BITE
BEIINORRSTTU	RETRIBUTIONS
BEIINPRSSSTU	BUSINESS TRIP
BEIISSTTTUUV	SUBSTITUTIVE
BEIKLMNNRSUY	SLINKY NUMBER
BEIKMOORSTTT	STRIKE BOTTOM
BEIKNNOORSTW	KNIT ONES BROW
BEIKNOOOSSTU	SUIT ONE'S BOOK
BEIKNOORSTTW	WRITTEN BOOKS
BEILLOORSSTT	STILBOESTROL
BEILOOQSSUUY	OBSEQUIOUSLY
BEILOORSSTUY	BOISTEROUSLY
BEILOPPRSTUU	PURPOSE BUILT
	PURPOSE-BUILT
BEINSSSTTTUU	SUBSTITUENTS
BEJKNNNOOOSW	KNOWN ONE'S JOB

BEJKNNNOOOSSW	KNOWS ONE'S JOB
BEKMMNNOSSTUW	MUM KNOWS BEST
BELLMOOSSTTY	BOTTOMLESSLY
BELMNOPSSTUU	STUMBLES UPON
BELNNOOOPSTW	BLOWN ONE'S TOP
BELNOOOPRSTW	BLOWS ONE'S TOP
BEMNOOOPRSSW	MOPS ONE'S BROW
BEOOPRSTVXYY	VOTES BY PROXY
BFFGHIOORTTU	BROUGHT IT OFF
BFFGIILLNPUY	PUFFING BILLY
BFFIIILLMORR	FIBRILLIFORM
BFGHHOORRTTU	BROUGHT FORTH
BFGHIILLORST	BILL OF RIGHTS
BFGHIILNOSST	NIGHT OF BLISS
BFHLMOOOOTUY	BLOOM OF YOUTH
BFIIIILNSTUY	INFUSIBILITY
BFIIILNNORSY	FIBRINOLYSIN
BFINNOORRSST	FIRST-BORN SON
BGGGHIILNNTU	LIGHTNING BUG
BGGHHIILRSTT	BRIGHT LIGHTS
BGGHHINORRTU	BRING THROUGH
BGGHIILNORTT	BRING TO LIGHT
BGGIIINNPRTU	BRINGING IT UP
BGGIILNNOSTW	STINGING BLOW
BGHHIKLNOSWY	BLOWN SKY-HIGH
BGHHIKLOSSWY	BLOWS SKY-HIGH
BGHHINOORRTU	HONOUR BRIGHT
BGHIILRRTUWW	WILBUR WRIGHT
BGHIKNNOSTWY	KNOWN BY SIGHT
BGHIKNOSSTWY	KNOWS BY SIGHT
BGHILLNNSUUY	UNBLUSHINGLY
BGHILLNOOOPT	POLLING BOOTH
BGHILNNOOTTU	BUTTONHOLING
BGHIMNPSSTUU	THUMBS-UP SIGN
BGHINOPRRSTU	BRING UP SHORT
BGHIORSTTUUY	BUYS OUTRIGHT
BGIIIILMMNOS	IMMOBILISING
BGIIIILMMNOZ	IMMOBILIZING
BGIIILLNOSSU	SOLUBILISING
BGIIILLNOSUZ	SOLUBILIZING
BGIIILNNOOPT	BOILING POINT
BGIIKLLNNNUY	UNBLINKINGLY
BGIIKNOORSTW	WRITING BOOKS
BGIILOORSSTT	TRIBOLOGISTS
BGIINSSTTTUU	SUBSTITUTING
BGIJNRRTUYYY	TRYING BY JURY
BGILLORSUUUY	LUGUBRIOUSLY
BGILNNNOSTUW	STUNNING BLOW
BGINNNORRTUW	TURNING BROWN
BHHMMNNOOTTY	MONTH BY MONTH
BHIIINOOPRST	PROHIBITIONS
BIIIILNSTVY	INVISIBILITY
BIIILLNOSTUY	INSOLUBILITY
BIIKOOORSSTV	VISITORS BOOK
BIILOQSTUUUY	UBIQUITOUSLY
BIIMNOOPRSTT	BORN OPTIMIST
BIINNOOPPTTY	POINT BY POINT
BIINOSSTTTUU	SUBSTITUTION
BILLNPTTTUUY	PUT IT BLUNTLY
BLLMOOOSSSTU	LOTUS BLOSSOM
CCCCEEENNORS	CONCRESCENCE
CCCCEIMNOOPU	PNEUMOCOCCIC
CCCDEEHINOOS	SECOND CHOICE
CCCDEEHKORSS	CROSS-CHECKED
CCCDEEIINNOS	COINCIDENCES
CCCDEEILLORS	CLOSED CIRCLE
CCCDEEILNOPY	ENCYCLOPEDIC
CCCEEEENRSSX	EXCRESCENCES
CCCEEHILORTY	HETEROCYCLIC
CCCEEIILMOVW	CIVIC WELCOME
CCCEEIINRTTY	ECCENTRICITY

Code	Phrase	Code	Phrase
CCCEEIKORRST	CRICKET SCORE	CCDEILNOORWY	COLIN COWDREY
CCCEENNORRSU	CONCURRENCES	CCDEINNOOSSU	SECOND COUSIN
CCCEHIIKPRTT	CRICKET PITCH	CCDEIOORRTUV	DIVORCE COURT
CCCEHIKNRRUY	CHICKEN CURRY	CCDEIORRSSSS	CRISSCROSSED
CCCEHINOPRTT	CONCERT PITCH	CCDEKLOORTWY	CYCLED TO WORK
CCCEHLNOOOTW	COCO THE CLOWN	CCDELLOSSTTU	COLLECTS DUST
CCCEIIMRRSSU	CIRCUMCISERS	CCDELMOOPRSS	COLD COMPRESS
CCCEIINNOOST	CONIC SECTION	CCDFHOOOPRST	DROP OF SCOTCH
CCCEIMNORSTU	CONCERT MUSIC	CCDFIOORRSUX	OXFORD CIRCUS
CCCEINNOPSTU	CONCUPISCENT	CCDGHIKLNOOS	SHOCKING COLD
CCCEINNSSSTU	SUCCINCTNESS	CCDGIKKLNNOO	KNOCKING COLD
CCCEIOOPRSTT	STREPTOCOCCI	CCDHHILOORRY	HYDROCHLORIC
CCCEMNOOPSUU	PNEUMOCOCCUS	CCDHIKNORSST	DRINKS SCOTCH
CCCGHIIKLMNO	CHIMING CLOCK	CCDIINOTTUVY	CONDUCTIVITY
CCCGIIIMNRSU	CIRCUMCISING	CCDLLMOSUUUU	CUMULUS CLOUD
CCCHHHLOORSU	CHURCH SCHOOL	CCDNNNOOORTU	NONCONDUCTOR
CCCIIIMNORSU	CIRCUMCISION	CCEEEEHHKKOT	CHEEK TO CHEEK
CCCIIIMORRTU	MICROCIRCUIT	CCEEEEHLPRSV	CLEVER SPEECH
CCCIIKLRSTTY	TRICK CYCLIST	CCEEEEINPRST	CENTREPIECES
CCCIIORRTTUU	CIRCUIT COURT	CCEEEFFIIINS	EFFICIENCIES
CCDDDEEENNOS	CONDESCENDED	CCEEEFHHRRSU	FREE CHURCHES
CCDDEEEHHTUW	CHEWED THE CUD	CCEEEFHIKNRS	NECKERCHIEFS
CCDDEEEIPRRU	REDUCED PRICE	CCEEEFIILNCC	LIFE COINCIDE
CCDDEEENORSS	DECRESCENDOS	CCEEEFIILRRT	ELECTRIC FIRE
CCDDEEFINNOST	DISCONNECTED	CCEEEFINNNOR	IN CONFERENCE
CCDDEEINORST	DISCONCERTED	CCEEEFLNORSU	FLUORESCENCE
CCDDEHNOORUW	CROUCHED DOWN	CCEEEGNNORSV	CONVERGENCES
CCDEEEEFHPST	SPEECH DEFECT	CCEEEHIIMNPY	CHIMNEYPIECE
CCDEEEEGINRV	GIVE CREDENCE	CCEEEHIKKNPS	KEEPS IN CHECK
CCDEEEEHINPR	CREPE DE CHINE	CCEEEIILLRST	ELITE CIRCLES
CCDEEEEMNSTU	DETUMESCENCE	CCEEEIILRRTW	ELECTRIC WIRE
CCDEEEFIIINS	DEFICIENCIES	CCEEEIIMNNRS	REMINISCENCE
CCDEEEFIILNV	CIVIL DEFENCE	CCEEEIIRRSTV	SEVERE CRITIC
CCDEEEHIINNS	INDEHISCENCE	CCEEEILLORTV	RECOLLECTIVE
CCDEEEHIPRST	DIRECT SPEECH	CCEEEILMNNRT	ENCIRCLEMENT
CCDEEEIINRSS	IRIDESCENCES	CCEEEILMNNSU	LUMINESCENCE
CCDEEEILNNRU	UNDER LICENCE	CCEEEILNOORT	ENTEROCOELIC
CCDEEEINOPRV	PRECONCEIVED	CCEEEILNORTV	ELECTRIC OVEN
CCDEEEKNOSSY	COCKEYEDNESS	CCEEEILOPRST	SECRET POLICE
CCDEEELORTTU	ELECTROCUTED	CCEEEIMNNOPT	INCOMPETENCE
CCDEEENOPRRT	PRECONCERTED	CCEEEIMNNSTU	INTUMESCENCE
CCDEEENRRSTU	RECRUDESCENT	CCEEEIMOOPST	COME TO PIECES
CCDEEFFIOORR	RECORD OFFICE	CCEEEIMOPSTU	COSTUME PIECE
CCDEEFHILNST	CLENCHED FIST	CCEEEINNNOSV	CONVENIENCES
CCDEEFIINNNO	IN CONFIDENCE	CCEEEINOPRSV	PRECONCEIVES
CCDEEGINRRSU	RECRUDESCING	CCEEEKLLNOOV	ELEVEN O CLOCK
CCDEEIINSST	INSECTICIDES	CCEEEKNOPRTT	CENTRE POCKET
CCDEEIIMNOSV	MISCONCEIVED	CCEEELOOPRST	ELECTROSCOPE
CCDEEIKKNOTW	KNOCKED TWICE	CCEEELORSTTU	ELECTROCUTES
CCDEEIKNOSTW	SECOND WICKET	CCEEEMMMNNOT	COMMENCEMENT
CCDEEILOOPRR	POLICE RECORD	CCEEENNOQSSU	CONSEQUENCES
CCDEIMNNOOS	COME IN SECOND	CCEEENNORSST	CONCRETENESS
CCDEEIMNRTUV	CIRCUMVENTED	CCEEESSSSTUW	SWEET SUCCESS
CCDEEIORRSTU	DIRECT COURSE	CCEEFFFHIIOR	CHIEF OFFICER
CCDEELOOPPRS	CLOSE-CROPPED	CCEEFFIIINNY	INEFFICIENCY
CCDEELOPRRSU	RED CORPUSCLE	CCEEFFIIKOTT	TICKET OFFICE
CCDEENOORSSU	SECOND COURSE	CCEEFFIILNOV	CIVIL OFFENCE
CCDEEOORRRSU	COURSE RECORD	CCEEFFIINOST	COEFFICIENTS
CCDEEOORRTUV	COVERED COURT	CCEEFGIILNRT	CELTIC FRINGE
CCDEEORRRSST	CORRECT DRESS	CCEEFHIIJSTU	CHIEF JUSTICE
CCDEGIIJRTUU	CIRCUIT JUDGE	CCEEFHILNOOT	LEFT NO CHOICE
CCDEGIMNNOOS	COMING SECOND	CCEEFHIPSSTU	CHIEF SUSPECT
	SECOND COMING	CCEEFIIMOPSU	PIECE OF MUSIC
CCDEHHIKLNOS	HOLDS IN CHECK	CCEEFINNOORT	CONFECTIONER
CCDEHIKLNOTW	WIND THE CLOCK	CCEEGGILNOTY	GLYCOGENETIC
CCDEHIKOTTUU	CHUCKED IT OUT	CCEEGHIKNORV	CHECKING OVER
CCDEHIMOORTY	ORCHIDECTOMY	CCEEGILLNORT	RECOLLECTING
CCDEHNOORSUW	CROUCHES DOWN	CCEEGILLOOSY	ECCLESIOLOGY
CCDEIIIIRSTV	RECIDIVISTIC	CCEEGILLPRTU	ELECTRIC PLUG
CCDEIILNNOTY	COINCIDENTLY	CCEEGKLNOOSS	COCKS ONE'S LEG
CCDEILNOOOPR	POLICE CORDON	CCEEHHIKLLTT	CHECK THE TILL

CCEEHIILNORT	HELIOCENTRIC
CCEEHIKLNPST	PENCIL SKETCH
CCEEHIKNORTU	ROUTINE CHECK
CCEEHILMOORS	CHOICE MORSEL
CCEEHIMOSTYZ	SCHIZOMYCETE
CCEEHINNORTT	ETHNOCENTRIC
CCEEHINOOOPT	OPEN TO CHOICE
CCEEHINOSTVW	WITCHES COVEN
CCEEHKLLLOSS	COCKLESHELLS
CCEEHKLOORST	ELECTROSHOCK
CCEEHLMOORSU	COLOUR SCHEME
CCEEHMMNOOPS	COMMON SPEECH
CCEEHNORRTTU	CUT THE CORNER
CCEEHOORSTTV	COVER THE COST
CCEEIIILRSVV	CIVIL SERVICE
CCEEIIKLNORV	INVOICE CLERK
CCEEIIKOPPST	PICK TO PIECES
CCEEIILLOSTV	COLLECTIVISE
CCEEIILLOTVZ	COLLECTIVIZE
CCEEIILNORRT	ELECTRIC IRON
CCEEIIMNOSSV	MISCONCEIVES
CCEEIINNNNOT	INCONTINENCE
CCEEIINNPRTV	VINCENT PRICE
CCEEIINOPRTY	ICY RECEPTION
CCEEIKKOPTTT	TICKET POCKET
CCEEIILLLOTVY	COLLECTIVELY
CCEEIILLNOORT	RECOLLECTION
CCEEIILLORTTY	ELECTROLYTIC
CCEEIILMNOORT	MOTOR LICENCE
CCEEIILNNORTV	CONVENTICLER
CCEEIILNNOSTV	CONVENTICLES
CCEEIILNNOTVY	CONNECTIVELY
CCEEIILNOSSVY	CONCESSIVELY
CCEEIILOOPRST	POLICE ESCORT
CCEEIILORRTVY	CORRECTIVELY
CCEEIILORTTUY	RETICULOCYTE
CCEEIILSSSUVY	SUCCESSIVELY
CCEEIMNNOPTY	INCOMPETENCY
CCEEIMNOORST	ECONOMETRICS
CCEEIMNOPPSY	SPECIMEN COPY
CCEEIMNRSSTU	MUSIC CENTRES
CCEEINNNORTT	INTERCONNECT
CCEEINPRRRTU	CURRENT PRICE
CCEEIOOPRSST	STEREOSCOPIC
CCEEIOPSSTTU	CUTS TO PIECES
CCEEIOQRRTTU	QUITE CORRECT
CCEEJNORRSTU	CONJECTURERS
CCEEKLLOOTVW	TWELVE O CLOCK
CCEEKNOOPRRT	CORNER POCKET
CCEEKNORSSSU	COCKSURENESS
CCEELNOOSSTT	CLOSE CONTEST
CCEELORRSTTY	CORRECT STYLE
CCEEMNNOORST	CRESCENT MOON
CCEENNORRTUY	CURRENCY NOTE
CCEENOOPRSTT	CONCRETE POST
CCEENOPSSSTU	CONSPECTUSES
CCEEOOPPRSST	SPECTROSCOPE
CCEFFIIOORRTU	COURT OFFICER
CCEFGGHLOSTU	CLUTCH OF EGGS
CCEFHHMOORRU	CHURCH OF ROME
CCEFHMNORSTU	FRENCH CUSTOM
CCEFIIINNSTU	UNSCIENTIFIC
CCEFILNNOOPT	OPEN CONFLICT
CCEFKLOOORUW	CUCKOOFLOWER
CCEFLLSSSUUY	SUCCESSFULLY
CCEFLNSSSUUU	UNSUCCESSFUL
CCEFNORRSTUY	SOFT CURRENCY
CCEGGINNNOOR	GOING CONCERN
CCEGHHNOORTU	GONE TO CHURCH
CCEGHHOORSTU	GOES TO CHURCH
CCEGHIIKQRTU	GET RICH QUICK

CCEGHIINORTT	RICOCHETTING
CCEGHIKNOPST	SPOT-CHECKING
CCEGHILNOSST	SINGLE SCOTCH
CCEGIILNOPRS	CLOSING PRICE
CCEGIINNOOTY	ONCOGENICITY
CCEGIINNORST	CONCRETISING
CCEGIINNORTZ	CONCRETIZING
CCEGIINNOTTU	CUTTING NO ICE
CCEGIJNNORTU	CONJECTURING
CCEGIKKNNNOO	KNOCKING ONCE
CCEGIKNORRSW	CORKSCREWING
CCEGILMNOORS	COMING CLOSER
CCEGINOOPPRUY	PREOCCUPYING
CCEEHHNORTTUW	WENT TO CHURCH
CCEHIILLNOPU	NUCLEOPHILIC
CCEEHIKKLOPST	PICKS THE LOCK
CCEEHILNOORTU	TECHNICOLOUR
CCEEHILNOOSUU	COUNCIL HOUSE
CCEEHILNOPSTY	POLYTECHNICS
CCEEHIMNOORRT	CHRONOMETRIC
CCEEHIMOPRSTY	PSYCHOMETRIC
CCEEHINOORSUV	CUSHION COVER
CCEEHINOPRSTY	PHENOCRYSTIC
	PYROTECHNICS
CCEEHIOOPSSTT	STETHOSCOPIC
CCEEHIORRTTYY	ERYTHROCYTIC
CCEEHKLOOPSTT	STOP THE CLOCK
CCEEHKLOSSTTU	SHUTTLECOCKS
CCEEHNOOSTTTU	COUNT THE COST
CCEEIIILMOPST	COMPLICITIES
CCEEIIKKSSTTWY	STICKY WICKET
CCEEIILLMOSTV	COLLECTIVISM
CCEEIILLOSTTV	COLLECTIVIST
CCEEIILMOORRT	COLORIMETRIC
CCEEIILNNOSUV	INCONCLUSIVE
CCEEIINNOSSSU	IN SUCCESSION
CCEEIINNOTTVY	CONNECTIVITY
CCEEIINNORSTTV	CONSTRICTIVE
CCEEIINRSSTTY	SYNCRETISTIC
CCEEIJNNNOORT	JOINT CONCERN
CCEEIKKOPPSST	PICKS POCKETS
CCEEIKMPRSTTU	CRICKET STUMP
CCEEILLNOSUVY	CONCLUSIVELY
CCEEILLOOOPSS	OSCILLOSCOPE
CCEEILNOOPRRT	PRICE CONTROL
CCEEILNOPRSSU	PRESS COUNCIL
CCEEILNOSSUVY	CONCUSSIVELY
CCEEILOOPRSUY	PRECOCIOUSLY
CCEEIMMOOPSSU	COMPOSE MUSIC
CCEEINNOSTTUY	CONSTITUENCY
CCEEINNRRTUUY	CURRENCY UNIT
CCEEINOOPRSSU	PRECONSCIOUS
CCEEINOORSSST	CROSS SECTION
	CROSS-SECTION
CCEEINORSTTUV	CONSTRUCTIVE
CCEEINORTTVYY	COVENTRY CITY
CCEEIORRSSSSS	CRISSCROSSES
CCEEKLOORSTWY	CYCLES TO WORK
CCEEKMNOSSTUU	COMES UNSTUCK
CCEELMOOORSTU	COOL CUSTOMER
CCEELNNORRTUY	CONCURRENTLY
CCEEMNOOPRRST	PROM CONCERTS
CCEENORRRSSTU	CROSSCURRENT
CCEENORRSSTTU	RECONSTRUCTS
CCEEOOPPRSSTY	SPECTROSCOPY
CCEEORRSSSTUY	SUCCESS STORY
CCFGGHIIKNOT	COCKFIGHTING
	FIGHTING COCK
CCFGIILNRSUY	FLYING CIRCUS
CCFIIINORSUX	CRUCIFIXIONS
CCFILOOOPRSU	FLUOROSCOPIC

CCGHHIILNRUV	CHURCH LIVING	CDDEEIILNOTU	DINUCLEOTIDE
CCGHHINOORST	SCORCHING HOT	CDDEEIJNPRUU	UNPREJUDICED
CCGHIIIKNPRS	RICH PICKINGS	CDDEEIKLMOPT	MIDDLE POCKET
CCGHIIKOQRTU	GOT RICH QUICK	CDDEEILMORSU	MIDDLE COURSE
CCGHIIOPRSTT	GOTHIC SCRIPT	CDDEEILOORSU	DECOLOURISED
CCGHILNOOOST	CONCHOLOGIST	CDDEEILOORUZ	DECOLOURIZED
CCGHILNOORUW	CROUCHING LOW	CDDEEINNORSU	UNCONSIDERED
CCGIILLNOPPP	CLIP-CLOPPING	CDDEEINNOSTT	DISCONTENTED
CCGIILNNNOVY	CONVINCINGLY	CDDEELOOORUV	DOVE-COLOURED
CCGIINNNNOUV	UNCONVINCING	CDDEELOPSSTU	SECLUDED SPOT
CCGIINNOPRST	CONSCRIPTING	CDDEENOOPRRS	CORRESPONDED
CCGIINNORSTT	CONSTRICTING	CDDEEOOPRRUV	OVERPRODUCED
CCGILLNOSTYY	CYCLOSTYLING	CDDEEORSTTUU	REDUCE TO DUST
CCGINNORSTTU	CONSTRUCTING	CDDEFHLOOOPP	COPPED HOLD OF
CCHHHHIIISWW	WHICH IS WHICH?	CDDEFIIKLSST	FIDDLESTICKS
CCHHIIMOSTYZ	SCHIZOTHYMIC	CDDEFIMNNOSU	CONFUSED MIND
CCHHIKOSSTWY	SCOTCH WHISKY	CDDEFIMOORST	DISCOMFORTED
CCHHIMOOOPRR	CHROMOPHORIC	CDDEFLNNOOUY	CONFOUNDEDLY
CCHHIMOOOPRT	PHOTOCHROMIC	CDDEGIIINRST	DISCREDITING
CCHIIKRRSTTU	STRUCK IT RICH	CDDEHIILLOPS	SPOILED CHILD
CCHIIOOPRSTY	HYPOCORISTIC	CDDEHIILMNRS	CHILDMINDERS
CCHIIORRSTTU	SHORT CIRCUIT	CDDEHILLMOOS	MIDDLE SCHOOL
	SHORT-CIRCUIT	CDDEHILNOSSS	CLODDISHNESS
CCHILMOOPRTY	OLYMPIC TORCH	CDDEHINSTTUW	SUDDEN TWITCH
CCHIOOPPRSTY	PSYCHOTROPIC	CDDEHLLOORSU	COLD SHOULDER
CCHLNOOOSTUY	COUNTY SCHOOL		COLD-SHOULDER
CCIIILNNOSTU	SIT IN COUNCIL	CDDEHLNORTUU	THUNDERCLOUD
CCIILNNNOOSU	IN CONCLUSION	ODDEIIINSTTY	IDENTITY DISC
CCIILNOPRUVY	PRIVY COUNCIL	CDDEIIMSSTUU	STUDIED MUSIC
CCIILORSTUUY	CIRCUITOUSLY	CDDEIINNOSTU	DISCONTINUED
CCIIMOOPRSST	MICROSCOPIST	CDDEILNOOSTY	DICOTYLEDONS
CCIINNOOPRST	CONSCRIPTION	CDDEILOORTUU	CRIED OUT LOUD
CCIINNOORSTT	CONSTRICTION	CDDEKKLNNOUW	KNUCKLED DOWN
CCIIOOTTTXYY	CYTOTOXICITY	CDDELLLMOOSY	MOLLYCODDLES
CCIJNNNOOSTU	CONJUNCTIONS	CDDENOORSTUU	SCOUTED ROUND
CCIKKPPRSTUU	PICK-UP TRUCKS	CDDGHIIILMNN	CHILDMINDING
CCIKLNOORSUW	WORKS COUNCIL	CDDOOOOOOORTV	VOODOO DOCTOR
CCILMOORSTTY	MOTORCYCLIST	CDEEEEEHLMST	MELTED CHEESE
CCILMORRSUUU	CIRROCUMULUS	CDEEEEFGLLNO	GOLDEN FLEECE
CCIMNOOPSTUU	COMPUNCTIOUS	CDEEEEFHNNOT	ON THE DEFENCE
CCIMNORSTUUY	COUNTRY MUSIC	CDEEEEFILNSV	SELF-EVIDENCE
CCINNOORSTTU	CONSTRUCTION	CDEEEEGIINVV	GIVE EVIDENCE
CCINOORRSSTT	CONSTRICTORS	CDEEEEHIKLTU	LIKE THE DEUCE
CCKKLOOORTWY	CLOCKWORK TOY	CDEEEEHILMTT	MELTED THE ICE
CCNOORRSSTTU	CONSTRUCTORS	CDEEEEHKPSTW	SWEEP THE DECK
CCNOORRSSTUY	CROSS-COUNTRY	CDEEEEHKRRST	THREE-DECKERS
CDDDEEEEPRSU	REDUCED SPEED	CDEEEEILRRST	RED LEICESTER
CDDDEEELOPUW	WEDDED COUPLE	CDEEEELNNOSV	SECOND ELEVEN
CDDDEEFIIOST	EISTEDDFODIC	CDEEEELNNPRS	RESPLENDENCE
CDDDEEFILNOS	SECOND FIDDLE	CDEEEENPSSTX	EXPECTEDNESS
CDDDENOORRUW	CROWDED ROUND	CDEEEFFGINOR	FORCE FEEDING
CDDEEEEEFNRU	DUE DEFERENCE		FORCE-FEEDING
CDDEEFFGNORS	SECOND DEGREE	CDEEEFFIINNR	INDIFFERENCE
	SECOND-DEGREE	CDEEEFFINNOR	NO DIFFERENCE
CDDEEEEINNNP	INDEPENDENCE	CDEEEFGLOSTT	GETS COLD FEET
CDDEEEEINNPS	DEPENDENCIES	CDEEEFHILRST	CHESTERFIELD
CDDEEEEJNSST	DEJECTEDNESS	CDEEEFHLLOST	FEELS THE COLD
CDDEEEEPRSSU	REDUCES SPEED	CDEEEFILLORS	CLOSE FIELDER
CDDEEEGHILPP	CLIPPED HEDGE	CDEEEFIRRSTU	REFUSE CREDIT
CDDEEEHMNOPR	COMPREHENDED	CDEEEFLORRSY	SCORED FREELY
CDDEEEHNNPRU	HUNDRED PENCE	CDEEEGHIRTTT	GET THE CREDIT
CDDEEEINORRS	RECONSIDERED	CDEEEGIINNRV	RECEIVING END
CDDEEEINRTTX	EXTEND CREDIT	CDEEEGINNRST	DESIGN CENTRE
CDDEEEIRRSTT	DERESTRICTED	CDEEEHILNNOT	ON THE DECLINE
CDDEEELNSSSU	SECLUDEDNESS	CDEEEHIMNPRT	DECIPHERMENT
CDDEEEMOPRSS	DECOMPRESSED	CDEEEHIORTVW	CHEWED IT OVER
CDDEEGIINOTV	DECIDING VOTE	CDEEEHKPSTTW	SWEPT THE DECK
CDDEEHLNORRU	ORDERED LUNCH	CDEEEHLMMOOW	WELCOMED HOME
CDDEEHLOORRR	RECORD HOLDER	CDEEEHMNOOTT	COME TO THE END
CDDEEHMORSTU	CRUDE METHODS	CDEEEHNOPSTU	COUNTED SHEEP
CDDEEIIKLMTW	MIDDLE WICKET	CDEEEHNORSST	THREE SECONDS

CDEEEHNRSSTW	WRETCHEDNESS	CDEEHLOOORST	CLOSE THE DOOR
CDEEEIILMPSV	SIMPLE DEVICE	CDEEHLORSSST	DRESS CLOTHES
CDEEEIINSSSV	DECISIVENESS	CDEEHORSSSTT	CROSSED THE T'S
CDEEEILMNORT	DECLINOMETER	CDEEHORSTTTU	OUTSTRETCHED
CDEEEILNOSUV	USED VIOLENCE		STRETCHED OUT
CDEEEILNQSTU	DELIQUESCENT	CDEEIIILNSVY	INDECISIVELY
CDEEEILPRSST	SCEPTRED ISLE	CDEEIIILOPST	DEPOLITICISE
CDEEEIMNORTT	MINE DETECTOR	CDEEIIILOPTZ	DEPOLITICIZE
CDEEEIMORTVW	TWICE REMOVED	CDEEIIINNSTV	DISINCENTIVE
CDEEEINNNORS	NONRESIDENCE	CDEEIIINOSSW	WISE DECISION
CDEEEINORSSS	SECOND SERIES	CDEEIILNNNOS	SECOND IN LINE
CDEEEINORSTV	SERVED NOTICE	CDEEIILNOPRT	PREDILECTION
CDEEEINRSSST	DISCREETNESS	CDEEIILNOPSY	NICELY POISED
	DISCRETENESS	CDEEIILNRSTY	INDISCREETLY
CDEEEIOPRSTV	SERVICE DEPOT		IRIDESCENTLY
CDEEEIORSTUZ	REDUCE TO SIZE	CDEEIILPRTVY	PREDICTIVELY
CDEEEIRRSSSV	SERVICE DRESS	CDEEIILRSTTT	CREDIT TITLES
CDEEELMMNOPT	COMPLEMENTED	CDEEIIMNOOSS	DISECONOMIES
CDEEELNORSTT	SECOND LETTER	CDEEIIMNOPRV	IMPROVIDENCE
CDEEELNPTUXY	UNEXPECTEDLY	CDEEIIMNORRT	IN RECORD TIME
CDEEELOPRTTY	ELECTROTYPED	CDEEIIMNOSTU	EUDEMONISTIC
CDEEEMNNNOTU	DENOUNCEMENT	CDEEIINNRSST	INDIRECTNESS
CDEEEMOPRSSS	DECOMPRESSES	CDEEIINRSTTU	INCERTITUDES
CDEEEOPRRSSS	PREDECESSORS	CDEEIKLNNOOS	NICKELODEONS
CDEEERSSSSTU	SEDUCTRESSES	CDEEIKOPRRST	REPORTED SICK
CDEEFFFIILOR	FIELD OFFICER	CDEEIKPPPSSU	PICKS UP SPEED
CDEEFFGNOORU	GROUND COFFEE	CDEEILLNORST	SELL ON CREDIT
CDEEFFGNORTU	GROUND-EFFECT	CDEEILMMNOPT	COMPLIMENTED
CDEEFFHOORRT	OFF THE RECORD	CDEEILMNOOPX	COMPLEXIONED
	OFF-THE-RECORD	CDEEILNORSSS	CROSSED LINES
CDEEFFILMOUV	MUFFLED VOICE	CDEEILNORSTU	CENTURIES OLD
CDEEFFIMNOOT	DOMINO EFFECT	CDEEILOORRSS	DECOLORISERS
CDEEFFNOSSTU	SOUND EFFECTS	CDEEILOORRSU	DECOLOURISER
CDEEFGILNORZ	FREEZING COLD	CDEEILOORRSZ	DECOLORIZERS
CDEEFGINNORS	SECOND FINGER	CDEEILOORRUZ	DECOLOURIZER
CDEEFHIIKLNT	FIELD KITCHEN	CDEEILOORSSU	DECOLOURISES
CDEEFHILOPRR	CRIED FOR HELP	CDEEILOORSUZ	DECOLOURIZES
CDEEFHILORSV	FEVERISH COLD	CDEEILRRSTTY	RESTRICTEDLY
CDEEFHLMOORU	CHEERFUL MOOD	CDEEIMMNOOST	MODEST INCOME
CDEEFHLNOOOV	CLOVEN-HOOFED	CDEEIMMNOOXY	MIXED ECONOMY
CDEEFHLNOOPR	FRENCH POODLE	CDEEIMNNORTU	COUNTERMINED
CDEEFHOORRRT	FOR THE RECORD	CDEEIMNOORVY	ECONOMY DRIVE
CDEEFIJNOORS	JOINED FORCES	CDEEIMOOSSTU	COMES OUTSIDE
CDEEFIOORRVV	DIVE FOR COVER	CDEEIMOPRSTU	COMPUTERISED
CDEEFJNNOOSU	SECOND OF JUNE	CDEEIMOPRTUZ	COMPUTERIZED
CDEEFLLOORSU	SELF-COLOURED	CDEEINNNORSY	NONRESIDENCY
CDEEFLLRSUUY	FULLY SECURED	CDEEINNOORRT	RECONNOITRED
CDEEFLMOOPSS	SELF-COMPOSED	CDEEINOORSTT	TO ONES CREDIT
CDEEFLNOOOTV	CLOVEN-FOOTED	CDEEINOPPRRT	INTERCROPPED
CDEEFLRSSTTU	SELF-DESTRUCT	CDEEINOPRSTT	INTROSPECTED
CDEEGHIORTTT	GOT THE CREDIT	CDEEINRRSTTU	UNRESTRICTED
CDEEGIILNNTV	DECENT LIVING	CDEEIOPRRTUV	REPRODUCTIVE
CDEEGIILNQSU	DELIQUESCING	CDEEIOPSSSUY	PSEUDOCYESIS
CDEEGIINNSTW	WINGED INSECT	CDEEIORRSSSW	CROSSED WIRES
CDEEGIKNOPRR	PECKING ORDER	CDEEIRRRSSVW	SCREWDRIVERS
CDEEGILOPPTY	GLYCOPEPTIDE	CDEEKKLLNNRUU	KNUCKLE UNDER
CDEEGIMMNNOR	RECOMMENDING	CDEEKNNNOOSW	DOWN ONE'S NECK
CDEEGIMNOOPS	GOOD SPECIMEN	CDEELMNOOSUV	SECOND VOLUME
CDEEGINOPRRR	PRERECORDING	CDEELMNOOSUW	WELCOME SOUND
CDEEGNNOOORR	GONE ON RECORD	CDEELMOPRSSY	COMPRESSEDLY
CDEEGNOOOORRS	GOES ON RECORD	CDEELNNOOSSS	SECOND LESSON
CDEEHIIMORSU	HIDEOUS CRIME	CDEELOOOORRSU	ROSE-COLOURED
CDEEHIKLORTT	TICKET HOLDER	CDEELOPPRTUU	REDUCE TO PULP
CDEEHIKNORTT	DONE THE TRICK	CDEEMNOOPSSS	COMPOSEDNESS
CDEEHIKNSSTT	TENDS THE SICK	CDEENNNOOOST	SECOND TO NONE
CDEEHIKORSTT	DOES THE TRICK	CDEENNNOOPRSS	SECOND PERSON
CDEEHILMOPST	DOMESTIC HELP	CDEENNOOPRST	CO-RESPONDENT
CDEEHILNPRST	STEPCHILDREN	CDEENNOORRTW	WENT ON RECORD
CDEEHIOQSSTU	DISCOTHEQUES	CDEENNRRRTTU	CURRENT TREND
CDEEHIORSTVW	SWITCHED OVER	CDEENNRRRTUU	UNDERCURRENT
CDEEHLNORSTU	UNDERCLOTHES	CDEENOORRTTV	CONTROVERTED

CDEENOORSSSU	DECOROUSNESS
CDEENOORSSTY	SECOND STOREY
CDEEOOPRRSUV	OVERPRODUCES
CDEEOORRRSSSS	CROSS-DRESSER
CDEERRRSTTUU	RESTRUCTURED
CDEFFHIIORRT	THIRD OFFICER
CDEFFHILORTY	FIRTH OF CLYDE
CDEFFIIILSTU	DIFFICULTIES
CDEFFIKKNOOT	KNOCKED IT OFF
CDEFFIOORSST	CROSSED IT OFF
CDEFGIIINNST	DISINFECTING
CDEFGIINORRV	DRIVING FORCE
CDEFGINNNORU	FENCING ROUND
CDEFHIINNOSS	FINISH SECOND
CDEFHILNOORS	SCHOOL FRIEND
CDEFHINNORWW	FRENCH WINDOW
CDEFHIOORTUV	VOUCHED FOR IT
CDEFHLMOOORR	CHLOROFORMED
CDEFHNOOOORU	CODE OF HONOUR
CDEFIIIMNORS	FIRM DECISION
CDEFIIINNOST	DISINFECTION
CDEFIILMORRT	FILM DIRECTOR
CDEFIIMORSTU	DISCOMFITURE
CDEFILMOPRRU	FILM PRODUCER
CDEFIMMNNOOR	COMMON FRIEND
CDEFJLNOOSUY	SECOND OF JULY
CDEFKLMOOOSU	CLOUD OF SMOKE
CDEFKLOOOTUW	OUT OF WEDLOCK
CDEFLLMNOTUU	FLUTED COLUMN
CDEFOOOORRSTT	DOCTOR FOSTER
CDEFOORSTUUY	COURSE OF DUTY
CDEGGIIINRTV	GIVING CREDIT
CDEGHHILOORU	HIGH-COLOURED
CDEGHILLNOOS	HOLDING CLOSE
CDEGIIIMNNOS	COMING INSIDE
CDEGIIIMNNOT	INCOMING TIDE
CDEGIIIMNRST	MISDIRECTING
CDEGIIINNRTT	INTERDICTING
CDEGIIJNOSTU	DOING JUSTICE
CDEGIILNNOOS	DECOLONISING
CDEGIILNNOOZ	DECOLONIZING
CDEGIILNNRSY	DISCERNINGLY
CDEGIILNOORS	DECOLORISING
CDEGIILNOORZ	DECOLORIZING
CDEGIILNOPRS	COILED SPRING
CDEGIINNPRRU	UNDERPRICING
CDEGILNOORUV	CLOUDING OVER
	OVERCLOUDING
CDEGIMNNNOOU	COMING UNDONE
CDEGINNORRSU	UNDERSCORING
CDEGINNORSST	SECOND STRING
	SECOND-STRING
CDEGINNORSWW	SCREWING DOWN
CDEGINNRTTUU	UNDERCUTTING
CDEGINOORRVW	OVERCROWDING
CDEGJLMNOOTU	COOL JUDGMENT
CDEGLMNORUUY	CURMUDGEONLY
CDEGMNOOOOOT	COME TO NO GOOD
CDEGNOORRSUV	COVERS GROUND
CDEHHIIIPRTT	DIPHTHERITIC
CDEHHIILNSSS	CHILDISHNESS
CDEHHIOPRRSY	HYDROSPHERIC
CDEHHLLOOOST	THE OLD SCHOOL
CDEHHLOORSTT	THE LOST CHORD
CDEHIIILPPSS	DISCIPLESHIP
CDEHIIJORTWY	CRIED WITH JOY
CDEHIIKKNNST	THICK-SKINNED
CDEHIIKNNOPS	PHONED IN SICK
CDEHIIMNORST	COMES IN THIRD
CDEHIINNRSTT	HERD INSTINCT
CDEHIINOOOPR	CONIDIOPHORE
CDEHIINTTWYY	THE WINDY CITY
CDEHIIOPRRST	DIRECTORSHIP
CDEHIKLSSTTU	LICKS THE DUST
CDEHILLOOOST	OLD SCHOOL TIE
CDEHILLOOPRY	POLICYHOLDER
CDEHILNNOORS	SCHOOL DINNER
CDEHILNOOTTU	OUT IN THE COLD
CDEHILOORSTW	HOSTILE CROWD
CDEHIMMOPRUV	MUCH IMPROVED
CDEHINNORSSY	SYNCHRONISED
CDEHINNORSYZ	SYNCHRONIZED
CDEHINORSTTY	THIRTY-SECOND
CDEHINRRTTUY	THIRD CENTURY
CDEHIORRTTWY	CREDIT-WORTHY
CDEHKLOOOORST	LOCKS THE DOOR
CDEHLMNOOORS	MODERN SCHOOL
CDEHLOOSSTTW	THE COTSWOLDS
CDEIIIIINVVV	VENI VIDI VICI
CDEIIIILNNPS	INDISCIPLINE
CDEIIILNOSTZ	SOLID CITIZEN
CDEIIILNPRSS	DISCIPLINERS
CDEIIILNRSTT	DISTRICT LINE
CDEIIILNTVVY	VINDICTIVELY
CDEIIIMNORST	MISDIRECTION
CDEIIINNORST	INDISCRETION
CDEIIINNORTT	INTERDICTION
CDEIIIPRTUVV	VIVID PICTURE
CDEIIISSSTUV	VICISSITUDES
CDEIIJNSSTUV	DISJUNCTIVES
CDEIIKLNNOOP	PICKLED ONION
CDEIIILMRTUUV	DIVERTICULUM
CDEIIILNNOOSV	SECOND VIOLIN
CDEIIILNNPPRU	UNPRINCIPLED
CDEIILOPPPTY	POLYPEPTIDIC
CDEIILRSSUVY	DISCURSIVELY
CDEIIMMNNOOSS	COMMISSIONED
CDEIIMMRRTUV	MURDER VICTIM
CDEIIMMRSSTY	DISSYMMETRIC
CDEIIMNORSTU	REDUCTIONISM
CDEIIMSSSTUU	STUDIES MUSIC
CDEIINNNOOOT	ONE CONDITION
CDEIINNNOTUV	NONINDUCTIVE
CDEIINNOOPRT	PRECONDITION
CDEIINNOOQRST	CONDITIONERS
	RECONDITIONS
CDEIINNOSSTU	DISCONTINUES
CDEIINNSSSTT	DISTINCTNESS
CDEIINOOPRST	PERIODONTICS
CDEIINOPPRRS	DROPS IN PRICE
CDEIINOPRSST	DESCRIPTIONS
CDEIINORRTTY	INTERDICTORY
CDEIINORSTTU	REDUCTIONIST
CDEIKLMOQUVY	MOVED QUICKLY
CDEIKLORTTTU	TICKLED TROUT
CDEIKNNSTTUU	UNKINDEST CUT
CDEIKOOPPRST	PICKED TROOPS
CDEILOORSTUU	CRIES OUT LOUD
CDEILOPRTUVY	PRODUCTIVELY
CDEILPRTTUUY	PUT IT CRUDELY
CDEIMMMORRTU	COMMIT MURDER
CDEIMMNOOPTU	COMPOUND TIME
CDEIMMNNOOPST	DENIS COMPTON
CDEIMNORSSTU	MISCONSTRUED
CDEIMOOPRSSU	DISCOMPOSURE
CDEINOOPRRRS	PRISON RECORD
CDEINOOPRRTU	REPRODUCTION
CDEINOORRRTII	ORDER IN COURT
CDEINOSSSTXY	SIXTY SECONDS
CDEIOORSSTTU	CROSSED IT OUT
CDEIOORSSTUU	DISCOURTEOUS
CDEIOORRRSSTT	STRICT ORDERS

CDEJKLLOORTY	DOCTOR JEKYLL
CDEKKLNNOSUW	KNUCKLES DOWN
CDEKLLOSSSUY	CLOUDLESS SKY
CDEKNORRSTUW	WONDERSTRUCK
CDELLMNOOORU	CULLODEN MOOR
CDELLOORSSWY	SCORED SLOWLY
CDELLOPRRSUW	CROWDPULLERS
CDELLOSSTUYY	STUDY CLOSELY
CDELNNOOPRUY	PRONOUNCEDLY
CDELNNOORRTU	UNDER CONTROL
CDELNOOOSTUY	COTYLEDONOUS
CDEMMNOOSTUW	MUST COME DOWN
CDENOOPRRSTU	PUTS ON RECORD
CDFFGINNOOOR	CORDONING OFF
CDFFIIILNTUY	IN DIFFICULTY
CDFFIILMSTUU	DIFFICULT SUM
CDFFIMNOORST	FINDS COMFORT
CDFFMNOOORTU	FOUND COMFORT
CDFGHIINNOTU	FINDING TOUCH
CDFGHIKNOOSY	DYING OF SHOCK
CDFGIIIMNOST	DISCOMFITING
CDFGILNOORTY	FLYING DOCTOR
CDFHILMNOTUW	DUNMOW FLITCH
CDFHILOORRUY	HYDROFLUORIC
CDFIINNOSSTU	DISFUNCTIONS
CDFILNNOOOTY	CITY OF LONDON
CDFIMNOOSSUU	SOUND OF MUSIC
CDFINNOSSTUY	DYSFUNCTIONS
CDGGHIILNORW	GROWING CHILD
CDGGIKLLNUUY	UGLY DUCKLING
CDGHIILNOORS	RIDING SCHOOL
CDGHIKMNOOOS	SHOCKING MOOD
CDGHILNOORTU	HOLDING COURT
CDGHINNOOPPW	CHOPPING DOWN
CDGHINNOOTUW	TOUCHING DOWN
CDGHINOOOTUW	TOUCHING WOOD
CDGIIIILNNPS	DISCIPLINING
CDGIIINNNOOT	CONDITIONING
CDGIILNOORSU	DISCOLOURING
CDGIIMNNORSW	MINCING WORDS
CDGIIMNOOPSS	DISCOMPOSING
CDGIKKNNNOOW	KNOCKING DOWN
CDGIKLNOOSTU	DUCKING STOOL
CDGILMNNOORU	MORNING CLOUD
CDGINNNOOTUW	COUNTING DOWN
CDGINOOSTTUW	WOODCUTTINGS
CDGINORSTTUW	CUTTING WORDS
CDGMMNNOOORU	COMMON GROUND
CDHHILNOORRY	CHLOROHYDRIN
CDHIILOSSTUY	DISTICHOUSLY
CDHIIOOPRSST	CHIROPODISTS
CDHILMMNNOOO	HOLD IN COMMON
CDHINOOORSTT	ORTHODONTICS
CDIIIJNORSTU	JURISDICTION
CDIIILNNSTTY	INDISTINCTLY
CDIIINNOSSTT	DISTINCTIONS
CDIIJNNOSSTU	DISJUNCTIONS
CDIILLORSUUY	RIDICULOUSLY
CDIIMMNOOOSU	INCOMMODIOUS
CDIINNOORTTU	INTRODUCTION
CDIIOPRTTUVY	PRODUCTIVITY
CDIKLNOORTWW	LOW-DOWN TRICK
CDILMMOOOSUY	COMMODIOUSLY
CDILNNOOSTUY	NUDIST COLONY
CDINOORRTTUY	INTRODUCTORY
CDINOORSSUUU	CURIOUS SOUND
CDKKNNOOOOSW	KNOCKS ON WOOD
CEEEEEHLRVWZ	CLEVER WHEEZE
CEEEEEFFINNPT	FIFTEEN PENCE
CEEEEFFNRSTV	EFFERVESCENT
CEEEEFILNNST	LIFE SENTENCE
CEEEEFIMPRRT	FIERCE TEMPER
CEEEEFINNPVW	FIVE NEW PENCE
CEEEEFINNRRT	INTERFERENCE
CEEEEFLLNOSX	EXCEL ONESELF
CEEEEFNNOPRR	NO PREFERENCE
CEEEEFNPRSTT	PERFECT TENSE
CEEEEGHPRSTT	GET THE CREEPS
CEEEEGIMNNRY	GREY EMINENCE
CEEEEHIKORTV	RECEIVE THE O.K.
CEEEEHINRRSV	HIS REVERENCE
CEEEEHKOPRST	KEEP THE SCORE
CEEEEHMOORRV	COME OVER HERE
CEEEEHNORSVW	WHENCESOEVER
CEEEEHNPQSSU	QUEENS SPEECH
CEEEEHNPRRTT	THREE PER CENT
CEEEEHNSSSTT	SETS THE SCENE
CEEEEIINNPRX	INEXPERIENCE
CEEEEIKKPRTW	WICKET KEEPER
	WICKETKEEPER
CEEEEIKPRSTT	KEEP IT SECRET
CEEEEILNORST	ELECTIONEERS
CEEEEILNSSTV	ELECTIVENESS
CEEEEIMNRSTT	MEET IN SECRET
CEEEEINNPSTX	SIXTEEN PENCE
CEEEEINPRSTX	PREEXISTENCE
CEEEEIPRRRSV	RESERVE PRICE
CEEEELMNOTVW	WELCOME EVENT
CEEEELMORRTT	ELECTROMETER
CEEEELNNOSUV	ELEVEN OUNCES
CEEEELNORSVW	WE NEVER CLOSE
CEEEEMNQSTUV	STEVE MCQUEEN
CEEEENNPRSTV	SEVEN PER CENT
CEEEENNPSTVY	SEVENTY PENCE
CEEEENNRSTTV	RECENT EVENTS
CEEEEPRSTTUZ	CREPE SUZETTE
CEEEFFGINNOV	GIVEN OFFENCE
CEEEFFGINOSV	GIVES OFFENCE
CEEEFFGINRSV	EFFERVESCING
CEEEFFGKLOOS	FLOCK OF GEESE
CEEEFFHNORST	OFF THE SCREEN
CEEEFFHOOSSU	COFFEEHOUSES
CEEEFFIMNORRV	FREE FROM VICE
CEEEFFLNORST	EFFLORESCENT
CEEEFFLNORTT	LEFT OF CENTRE
CEEEFFNOPTTY	PETTY OFFENCE
CEEEFFOOPPRR	PROPER COFFEE
CEEEFGHIIOPT	PIECE OF EIGHT
CEEEFGHINNRS	GREENFINCHES
CEEEFGNOORST	GONE SCOT-FREE
CEEEFGOORSST	GOES SCOT-FREE
CEEEFHHILNPT	FEEL THE PINCH
CEEEFHHKNOSU	HUNK OF CHEESE
CEEEFHIKLMOS	FEEL HOMESICK
CEEEFHIKLPSS	FEELS PECKISH
CEEEFHILLOST	CLOSE THE FILE
CEEEFHINRSST	SCENE SHIFTER
	SCENESHIFTER
CEEEFHLNORSY	CHOSEN FREELY
CEEEFHLNRSSU	CHEERFULNESS
CEEEFHLOORSY	CHOOSE FREELY
CEEEFHOOORST	FREE TO CHOOSE
CEEEFIILRRSV	SERVICE RIFLE
CEEEFIIMNNPS	FINE SPECIMEN
CEEEFIIMPRTV	IMPERFECTIVE
CEEEFIKQRSUZ	QUICK-FREEZES
CEEEFILLLLMNU	MELLIFLUENCE
CEEEFILLRTVY	REFLECTIVELY
CEEEFILPRTVY	PERFECTIVELY
CEEEFKLNSSSS	FECKLESSNESS
CEEEFLORRSSY	SCORES FREELY
CEEEFNNOOSSU	OUNCE OF SENSE

CEEEFNNOPRUW	FOUR NEW PENCE	CEEEINORSSTV	SERVES NOTICE
CEEEFNORSTTW	WENT SCOT-FREE	CEEEINORSTUX	EXECUTIONERS
CEEEGGNORRRS	GREENGROCERS	CEEEINRRRSTW	SCREENWRITER
CEEEGGNORRRY	GREENGROCERY	CEEEIOPRRTTY	RECITE POETRY
CEEEGHINPRTT	EIGHT PER CENT	CEEEIOPTTUVX	TOP EXECUTIVE
CEEEGHISSTWX	EXCESS WEIGHT	CEEEIPPRSSTV	PERSPECTIVES
CEEEGHMOORTT	COME TOGETHER	CEEEIPRRSSUV	REPERCUSSIVE
CEEEGHNORSUY	REGENCY HOUSE	CEEEKLNOOOPS	KEEP ONE'S COOL
CEEEGHOPRSTT	GOT THE CREEPS	CEEEKLNOPSSU	KEEPS COUNSEL
CEEEGIIKNNOP	KEEPING ON ICE	CEEEKLNORSTW	SKELETON CREW
CEEEGIILLNNT	INTELLIGENCE	CEEEKLNRSSSS	RECKLESSNESS
CEEEGIINNPRX	EXPERIENCING	CEEEKLOPPRTT	COPPER KETTLE
CEEEGIKLNOPS	KEEPING CLOSE	CEEEKLORRSTV	CLEVER STROKE
CEEEGIKNOPRS	KEEPING SCORE	CEEEKORRRSUW	RESCUE WORKER
CEEEGINNNOPS	OPENING SCENE	CEEELLORSTTY	ELECTROLYTES
CEEEGINNPRRT	PRINCE REGENT	CEEELMNOPSST	COMPLETENESS
CEEEGINOOPST	GONE TO PIECES	CEEELMOORTTW	TELECOM TOWER
CEEEGINORSTV	EIGENVECTORS	CEEELNOSTUVW	TWELVE OUNCES
CEEEGIOOPSST	GOES TO PIECES	CEEELOPRRSST	PRESELECTORS
CEEEGJLLOSSU	JESUS COLLEGE	CEEELOPRRTTY	ELECTROTYPER
CEEEGLMOSTUW	WELCOME GUEST	CEEELOPRSTTY	ELECTROTYPES
CEEEGLNNNOST	LONG SENTENCE	CEEEMNNNORTU	RENOUNCEMENT
CEEFGINRSTYY	REGENCY STYLE	CEEEMOPRRSTT	SPECTROMETER
CEEEHHIINSTW	CHINESE WHITE	CEEENNNOOSST	NOT ONE'S SCENE
CEEEHHIRSTTW	THREE WITCHES	CEEENNORSTTT	TEN-CENT STORE
CEEEHIILNNST	LIECHENSTEIN	CEEENNPRTUUV	VENEPUNCTURE
CEEEHIIMRSTU	EUHEMERISTIC	CEEENORRRSTT	STREET CORNER
CEEEHIIPRRSV	RECEIVERSHIP	CEEEOOPRRTTX	EXTEROCEPTOR
CEEEHIISTTWZ	TWICE THE SIZE	CEEEOOPRSSST	STEREOSCOPES
CEEEHIKNSTTT	KITCHENETTES	CEEFFFHIPRTT	PERFECT FIFTH
CEEEHIKRSTTW	THREE WICKETS	CEEFFFIMOORT	TERM OF OFFICE
CEEEHILLOPRT	ELECTROPHILE	CEEFFFINORST	FIRST OFFENCE
CEEEHIMNPSWY	CHIMNEY SWEEP	CEEFFGIIOPUV	GIVE UP OFFICE
CEEEHIMNRSTU	HERMENEUTICS	CEEFFGILNORS	EFFLORESCING
CEEEHINNQTUW	NEW TECHNIQUE	CEEFFHKLOOPS	FLOCK OF SHEEP
CEEEHINOPTTX	THE EXCEPTION	CEEFFHLNNRTU	FLUENT FRENCH
CEEEHINOSSSV	COHESIVENESS	CEEFFHLNOOSU	OUNCE OF FLESH
CEEEHINQSTTU	QUIT THE SCENE	CEEFFHNOOSST	OFF ONE'S CHEST
CEEEHKKMNOYY	CHEEKY MONKEY	CEEFFIKOSTTY	STICKY TOFFEE
CEEEHKRSTTUY	STRUCK THE EYE	CEEFFIMNNOOR	MINOR OFFENCE
CEEEHLLPSSSY	SPEECHLESSLY	CEEFFIMORSSS	OFFICERS MESS
CEEEHLMMOOSW	WELCOMES HOME	CEEFFINPRTTY	FIFTY PER CENT
CEEEHLMOORSW	HEROS WELCOME	CEEFFIOPRRSS	PRESS OFFICER
CEEEHLNOOPPS	CHOSEN PEOPLE	CEEFFIOPRTTY	PETTY OFFICER
CEEEHLNOSSST	CLOTHES SENSE	CEEFFLLMOOSW	COMES OFF WELL
CEEEHLNOSSTT	LOSE THE SCENT	CEEFFLNORSSU	FORCEFULNESS
CEEEHMNNNRTT	ENTRENCHMENT	CEEFGGILNNTU	GENUFLECTING
CEEEHMNNRRTT	RETRENCHMENT	CEEFGHIINPSY	SPEECHIFYING
CEEEHNOPRRST	CENTROSPHERE	CEEFGHIIORRU	HEROIC FIGURE
CEEEHNOSTTTU	CUT ONES TEETH	CEEFGHIPRSTT	PERFECT SIGHT
CEEEHNRSTTTU	CHESTNUT TREE	CEEFGIILNRTY	ELECTRIFYING
CEEEHORRSSTU	THREE COURSES	CEEFGIINNSTT	FENCE-SITTING
CEEEHPPRSTTY	PRETTY SPEECH	CEEFGILNNOTU	GENUFLECTION
CEEEIILLNTTV	INTELLECTIVE	CEEFGIMOORST	COMES TO GRIEF
CEEEIIMNNPRT	IMPERTINENCE	CEEFGLLLNTUY	NEGLECTFULLY
CEEEIIMORRST	METEORIC RISE	CEEFHIIKPPRS	CHIEF SKIPPER
CEEEIINPRSST	INTERSPECIES	CEEFHIINSSTW	CHIEF WITNESS
CEEEIIPRRSTV	IRRESPECTIVE	CEEFHILOPRRS	CRIES FOR HELP
CEEEIKLNRSTV	ELEVEN TRICKS	CEEFHIMNORRU	CHIEF MOURNER
CEEEIKNSSTVW	SEVEN WICKETS	CEEFHKNNOPRS	FRENCH SPOKEN
CEEEILLNOPQU	EQUIPOLLENCE		SPOKEN FRENCH
CEEEILNOSSUV	USES VIOLENCE	CEEFHLNNORSS	FRENCH LESSON
CEEEILNRRSSV	SILVER SCREEN	CEEFHLOOPSSS	LOSS OF SPEECH
CEEEILPPRTVY	PERCEPTIVELY	CEEFHLOOPSSW	SLOW OF SPEECH
CEEEIMMMNOTT	COMMITTEEMEN	CEEFHNOOSSTU	SENSE OF TOUCH
CEEEIMNNOPRS	OMNIPRESENCE	CEEFIIIILNST	INFELICITIES
CEEEIMNNORUY	YOUR EMINENCE	CEEFIIILNORSS	LEIF ERICSSON
CEEEINNOPRST	IN ONE RESPECT	CEEFIILRTTVY	REFLECTIVITY
CEEEINNQSSTU	QUINTESSENCE	CEEFIIMNOPRT	IMPERFECTION
CEEEINOOSTUY	NICE TO SEE YOU	CEEFIINOPRST	FRONTISPIECE
CEEEINOPSTTW	WENT TO PIECES	CEEFIIPRTTVY	PERFECTIVITY

CEEFIIRRSSTV	FIRST SERVICE
CEEFIKKLNOSS	KICKS ONESELF
CEEFIKOOPRSW	PIECES OF WORK
CEEFILMNOSUU	COME IN USEFUL
CEEFILMNRSSU	MERCIFULNESS
CEEFILMSSUXY	FLIMSY EXCUSE
CEEFILNNOORT	ON REFLECTION
CEEFILNNORST	INFLORESCENT
CEEFILNOOSVW	VOW OF SILENCE
CEEFIMNNNNOST	CONFINEMENTS
CEEFIMNOOORV	MOOR OF VENICE
CEEFIMNOOPRY	PRICE OF MONEY
CEEFIMOORSTU	COURSE OF TIME
CEEFINOPPRST	FINE PROSPECT
CEEFINOPRRTY	PRINCE OF TYRE
CEEFINORSTTU	COUNTERFEITS
CEEFIOORSTUV	OUT OF SERVICE
CEEFIOPRSSTX	EXCESS PROFIT
CEEFKLLOORSS	RECKLESS FOOL
CEEFKOOPPSTU	COST OF UPKEEP
CEEFLLMOOOOPT	COMPLETE FOOL
CEEFLLPRSTUY	RESPECTFULLY
CEEFLMOPRSTU	CLUMP OF TREES
CEEFLNOOOORTT	REEL OF COTTON
CEEFLNOORSSS	CROSS ONESELF
CEEFLNOQRUWY	LOW FREQUENCY
CEEFLOOOORRUY	EYE FOR COLOUR
CEEFLOOORSUV	COURSE OF LOVE
CEEFNNOOOOTT	ONCE TOO OFTEN
CEEFNNOOOSST	STONE OF SCONE
CEEFNOOOQSSTU	QUEEN OF SCOTS
CEEFNOPRRTTY	FORTY PER CENT
CEEGGIKLLNOS	KINGS COLLEGE
CEEGGILNOSSY	GLYCOGENESIS
CEEGGLNORSST	GROSS NEGLECT
CEEGHHIIKTTW	EIGHTH WICKET
CEEGHHINOPTV	GIVEN THE CHOP
CEEGHHIOPRSTV	GIVES THE CHOP
CEEGHHIORSST	HIGHEST SCORE
CEEGHHISTTTT	GET THE STITCH
CEEGHIIKSTTW	EIGHT WICKETS
CEEGHILMNOOT	COMING TO HEEL
CEEGHILMOSTW	WELCOME SIGHT
CEEGHILNOOST	TECHNOLOGIES
CEEGHILNOPTY	PHYLOGENETIC
CEEGHILOOPRT	HERPETOLOGIC
CEEGHIMNOPSV	MOVING SPEECH
CEEGHINNOPTY	HYPNOGENETIC
CEEGHINOORTT	ORTHOGENETIC
CEEGHINORRSU	ROUSING CHEER
CEEGHINPRSTU	PETER CUSHING
CEEGHKNORSTT	G.K.CHESTERTON
CEEGIIIKLPRV	VICE-LIKE GRIP
CEEGIIIMNPSS	MISSING PIECE
CEEGIIJNNRTT	INTERJECTING
CEEGIIKLNSTT	SINGLE TICKET
CEEGIIKLNSTW	SINGLE WICKET
CEEGIILLNPRS	SELLING PRICE
CEEGIIINNOPPR	OPENING PRICE
CEEGIIMNNOPRT	PIERCING NOTE
CEEGIINNPRTT	INTERCEPTING
CEEGIINNRSTT	INTERSECTING
CEEGIINNSTWX	EXCITING NEWS
CEEGIINOPRTV	PRECOGNITIVE
CEEGIINRSTTT	SITTING ERECT
CEEGIKKNOPST	KEEPING STOCK
CEEGIKKNOSST	GET ONE'S KICKS
CEEGIKLLNOPS	GLOCKENSPIEL
CEEGIKNNOPTU	KEEPING COUNT
CEEGIKOPRRTY	GREEK CYPRIOT
CEEGILLNNNOR	LINCOLN GREEN

CEEGILMOOORT	METEOROLOGIC
CEEGILRSTTUY	GUILTY SECRET
CEEGIMNNNOPRS	RECOMPENSING
CEEGIMNNOSTV	COMING EVENTS
CEEGINNNNORTU	ENCOUNTERING
CEEGINRRRSTU	RESURRECTING
CEEGMNOORRST	COSTERMONGER
CEEGOORRRSTY	GROCERY STORE
CEEHHHIOPRSS	CHERISH HOPES
CEEHHIIKNNTT	IN THE KITCHEN
CEEHHIKLLNST	HELL'S KITCHEN
CEEHHILNRSTT	THE CHILTERNS
CEEHHIMNPTUY	UP THE CHIMNEY
CEEHHIMPRRTY	HYPERTHERMIC
CEEHHINPRSTY	HYPERSTHENIC
CEEHHKLLOOSW	HOLLOW CHEEKS
CEEHHLOORSST	CLOTHES HORSE
	CLOTHESHORSE
CEEHHMOOPRRS	CHROMOSPHERE
CEEHHOOPPRSS	PHOSPHORESCE
CEEHIIKNPRTY	HYPERKINETIC
CEEHIIKRSTTT	STICK IT THERE!
CEEHIILLNPRS	SPINE-CHILLER
CEEHIILPPPR	CHILLI PEPPER
CEEHIIMNORSU	HEINOUS CRIME
CEEHIINOOTVW	WITH ONE VOICE
CEEHIINPRTTU	IN THE PICTURE
CEEHIKMNOSSS	HOMESICKNESS
CEEHIKNOPSTU	KEEPS IN TOUCH
CEEHIKNOSTTV	KITCHEN STOVE
CEEHIKOPRSTU	SOPHIE TUCKER
CEEHILLNOSST	CLOTHESLINES
CEEHILMOORTV	MOTOR VEHICLE
CEEHILNNORTY	INCOHERENTLY
CEEHILNOOSSS	COHESIONLESS
CEEHILNORSST	CROSS THE LINE
CEEHILORSSTT	SCOTTISH REEL
CEEHILPRSSTU	LECTURESHIPS
CEEHIMMORRTT	THERMOMETRIC
CEEHIMNOOSTU	HOME COUNTIES
CEEHIMNORSTU	NEUROCHEMIST
CEEHIMRSSTTY	CHEMISTRY SET
CEEHINNNOTTT	THE CONTINENT
CEEHINOOPRST	STEREOPHONIC
CEEHINOOORRSS	RHINOCEROSES
CEEHINOPRSTV	THE PROVINCES
CEEHINRRSTTU	STREET URCHIN
CEEHIOOPRRTY	HEROIC POETRY
CEEHIOOPSSTT	SHOT TO PIECES
CEEHIOPRSTUU	PICTURE HOUSE
CEEHIORSSTVW	SWITCHES OVER
CEEHJLMNNOST	JOHN CLEMENTS
CEEHKMNNORWY	MONKEY WRENCH
CEEHKNOORSTW	KNOW THE SCORE
CEEHLLMOORWY	CHROME YELLOW
CEEHLLNPRRUY	HENRY PURCELL
CEEHLLOOOSST	LOOSE CLOTHES
CEEHLMOOPRTU	THERMOCOUPLE
CEEHLOORRSTU	THREE COLOURS
CEEHMMOOPRTU	HOME COMPUTER
CEEHMNOORRST	CHRONOMETERS
CEEHMOPRRSTY	PSYCHROMETER
CEEHMORSTTYY	HYSTERECTOMY
CEEHNNOORTTU	ON THE COUNTER
CEEHNNRTTTUY	TENTH CENTURY
CEEHNOOQRRTU	THE CONQUEROR
CEEHNOPRSSTW	SHOWN RESPECT
CEEHNRRSTTUW	TURN THE SCREW
CEEHOOPSSSTT	STETHOSCOPES
CEEHOPRSSSTW	SHOWS RESPECT
CEEHORRSTTYY	ERYTHROCYTES

CEEHORSSSSTT	CROSSES THE T'S	CEEINNOORRST	RECONNOITRES
CEEHORSSTTTU	OUTSTRETCHES	CEEINNORSSTT	CONTRITENESS
	STRETCHES OUT	CEEINNPRTUUV	VENIPUNCTURE
CEEIIIMNPPRT	IMPERCIPIENT	CEEINNRRRTTU	INTERCURRENT
CEEIIINNPRRS	RISEN IN PRICE	CEEINOOPPRRS	PIONEER CORPS
CEEIIINNSSSV	INCISIVENESS	CEEINOOPRSTU	COUNTERPOISE
CEEIIINPRRSS	RISES IN PRICE	CEEINOPRRSSU	REPERCUSSION
CEEIIJNNORTT	INTERJECTION	CEEINOPRRSTT	IN RETROSPECT
CEEIIKKLNPRW	WINKLE-PICKER		INTERCEPTORS
CEEIIKLLNRSV	NICKEL SILVER	CEEINOPRSSSU	PRECIOUSNESS
CEEIILLNNOTT	INTELLECTION	CEEINOPSSSSU	SPECIOUSNESS
CEEIILLNORVV	LIVE IN CLOVER	CEEINORRRSTU	RESURRECTION
CEEIILMNNOOT	COME INTO LINE	CEEINORRSSST	INTERCROSSES
CEEIILMNNORT	INCLINOMETER	CEEINORRSSTY	INTERCESSORY
CEEIILMOPPRT	POLICE PERMIT	CEEINORSTTTU	RECONSTITUTE
CEEIILNNPRSS	PRINCELINESS	CEEINPPRRRTU	PRINCE RUPERT
CEEIILNPSSTX	EXPLICITNESS	CEEINPRSTTXY	SIXTY PER CENT
CEEIIMNOOTVW	COME INTO VIEW	CEEINRRSSTUU	CURRENT ISSUE
CEEIIMNOSSSS	SECESSIONISM	CEEIOOPRRSTT	PROTECTORIES
CEEIIMNOSTTU	CEMENTITIOUS	CEEKKLNORSSU	SORE KNUCKLES
CEEIIMOPRSSU	SEMIPRECIOUS	CEEKLLMNOUWY	WEEKLY COLUMN
CEEIIMORRSTU	MERETRICIOUS	CEEKLMNNOSUY	MONKEY'S UNCLE
CEEIIMORSSTV	VISCOSIMETER	CEEKLNOOOPST	KEPT ONE'S COOL
CEEIINNNNOTV	INCONVENIENT	CEEKLNRTUUVY	LUCKY VENTURE
CEEIINNOPRTT	INTERCEPTION	CEEKLOOPRSST	ROCKS TO SLEEP
CEEIINNORSST	INTERCESSION	CEEKNNOOPSTU	UP TO ONES NECK
CEEIINNORSTT	INTERSECTION	CEEKNOOPSSTY	KEYSTONE COPS
CEEIINOPRSTT	RECEPTIONIST	CEEKNORRSUVW	NERVOUS WRECK
CEEIINORSSTV	INSECTIVORES	CEEKOOPRRSSU	PRESSURE-COOK
CEEIINOSSSST	SECESSIONIST	CEEKOORRRSTT	RETRO-ROCKETS
CEEIIOPSTTUW	TWO-PIECE SUIT	CEEKORSSTTTU	TRUSTEE STOCK
CEEIIPPRRSTV	PRESCRIPTIVE	CEELLMOOSTUW	COMES OUT WELL
CEEIIPPRTTVY	PERCEPTIVITY	CEELLNOOOOSS	LOSE ONE'S COOL
CEEIIJLOPRTVY	PROJECTIVELY	CEELMMNOOOPP	COMMON PEOPLE
CEEIIJNORRTTY	INTERJECTORY	CEELNNOQSTUY	CONSEQUENTLY
CEEIKKNNORSS	RISK ONES NECK	CEELOOOPRSTU	COLEOPTEROUS
CEEIKKNOPSST	KEEPS IN STOCK	CEEMMOOPRSTT	COMPTOMETERS
CEEIKKNOPSTV	POCKET-KNIVES	CEEMMOORSSTT	COMES TO TERMS
CEEIKLLSSSTT	SELLS TICKETS	CEEMNOORSTUV	COUNTERMOVES
CEEIKLMNPPRU	PUMPERNICKEL	CEEMOOOPRSTW	COMES TO POWER
CEEIKLNOSSSV	LOVESICKNESS	CEEMOOPRSSSU	COMES UP ROSES
CEEIKLRSTTVW	TWELVE TRICKS	CEEMOPRRSTTY	SPECTROMETRY
CEEIKMNOORYY	MICKEY ROONEY	CEEMOPRRSTUU	SUPREME COURT
CEEIKMNOSSUU	QUEENS MUSICK	CEENNOOQRSTU	QUEEN CONSORT
CEEIKNNOOPSS	PICK ONES NOSE	CEENNOORRSST	CORNERSTONES
CEEIKNNOOPST	IN ONE'S POCKET	CEENNOORRTTU	COUNTERTENOR
CEEIKNRRSSTU	TINKERS CURSE	CEENOORRRTTV	CONTROVERTER
CEEIKNRRTTTU	RETURN TICKET	CEENOOSSSTUV	COVETOUSNESS
CEEILLMNNOPTY	INCOMPLETELY	CEEOOPRRRSSS	COREPRESSORS
CEEILLMOPSTT	COMPLETE LIST	CEEOPPRSSSTU	PROSPECTUSES
CEEILLNOPQUY	EQUIPOLLENCY	CEERRRSSTTUU	RESTRUCTURES
CEEILLOPPSTU	PULL TO PIECES	CEFFFIIORRST	FIRST OFFICER
CEEILLORSSTY	ELECTROLYSIS	CEFFFINOORRU	RUN FOR OFFICE
CEEILLPRSUVY	PRECLUSIVELY	CEFFGHIOOSTU	SOUGHT OFFICE
CEEILMOOPRSY	COPOLYMERISE	CEFFGILMOOUX	GULF OF MEXICO
CEEILMOOPRYZ	COPOLYMERIZE	CEFFHIJLNOWY	JOHN WYCLIFFE
CEEILMOORRST	COLORIMETERS	CEFFHIKOORRS	OFF HIS ROCKER
CEEILMOQSTUY	COMES QUIETLY	CEFFHINRTTUY	FIFTH CENTURY
CEEILNNNOTVY	CONVENIENTLY	CEFFHIRSSSTT	FESTSCHRIFTS
CEEILOOPRSTT	COLEOPTERIST	CEFFHMNOOPSU	OFF ONES CHUMP
CEEILOPRTTVY	PROTECTIVELY	CEFFIIINNSTU	INSUFFICIENT
CEEIMMNORTTT	TRITE COMMENT	CEFFIILNSTUY	SUFFICIENTLY
CEEIMMRSSTTY	METRIC SYSTEM	CEFFIOORSSST	CROSSES IT OFF
CEEIMNNORSTU	COUNTERMINES	CEFFMOOORSTW	COME OFF WORST
CEEIMNOOPPRS	POOR SPECIMEN	CEFGGIINNRTU	CENTRIFUGING
CEEIMNOORSTT	ECONOMETRIST	CEFGHHISTTTU	FIGHT THE CUTS
CEEIMOPRSSTU	COMPUTERISES	CEFGIIILMNTX	EXCITING FILM
CEEIMOPRSTUZ	COMPUTERIZES	CEFGIIKLLNRY	FLICKERINGLY
CEEIMPPRSSTU	PRIME SUSPECT	CEFGIIKLNPTY	FLYING PICKET
CEEINNNOOPPT	POPE INNOCENT	CEFGIILMNOOT	COMING TO LIFE
CEEINNNOQSTU	INCONSEQUENT	CEFGINNORRTY	FORCING ENTRY

CEFHHILNOPRS	FRENCH POLISH
	FRENCH-POLISH
CEFHIKORTTUW	FOURTH WICKET
CEFHILLOPRTU	CURL OF THE LIP
CEFHILMNORTU	TIME FOR LUNCH
CEFHIOORSTUV	VOUCHES FOR IT
CEFHLLLOOOSW	SCHOOLFELLOW
CEFHLMOOOORRS	REFORM SCHOOL
CEFHMMOOOORST	HOME COMFORTS
CEFIIILNOSTU	INFELICITOUS
CEFIIILLOSTUY	FELICITOUSLY
CEFIILMNNTUY	MUNIFICENTLY
CEFIILMORRTU	FLUORIMETRIC
CEFIILNOPRSS	PROLIFICNESS
CEFIILNOPRTY	PROFICIENTLY
CEFIILNORSST	FRICTIONLESS
CEFIILNOSTUY	INFECTIOUSLY
CEFIIMNORSST	COMES IN FIRST
CEFIKLOPRSSW	PICKS FLOWERS
CEFILNNOSSTU	FUNCTIONLESS
CEFILNOORSTU	COUNTERFOILS
CEFILOOORSUVY	VOCIFEROUSLY
CEFINOOPRTTU	PUT INTO FORCE
CEFINRRSTTUW	SWIFT CURRENT
CEFINRRSTTUY	FIRST CENTURY
CEFKKLOORRSW	CLERK OF WORKS
CEFKKLOORSTU	STROKE OF LUCK
CEFLLNOORSST	SELF-CONTROLS
CEFLNORSSUUU	FURUNCULOSES
CEFLOOOPRSSU	FLUOROSCOPES
CEFNOOOTTTUX	OUT OF CONTEXT
CEFNOORRRSUV	RUNS FOR COVER
CEGGGIIINPRR	PRICE RIGGING
CEGGIIILNNNV	CLINGING VINE
CEGGIIINNOSV	SINGING VOICE
CEGGIIINNOTV	GIVING NOTICE
CEGGIKLNTTUY	GETTING LUCKY
CEGGIKNSTTTU	GETTING STUCK
CEGGILNOOORT	GERONTOLOGIC
CEGGINORSSTT	GETTING CROSS
CEGHHIILOPRY	HIEROGLYPHIC
CEGHHIILOTVY	HIGH VELOCITY
CEGHHIIMNORT	COMING HITHER
CEGHHIIMNSTT	HEMSTITCHING
CEGHHIINRSTT	ETHNIC RIGHTS
CEGHHILLOSTT	LIGHT CLOTHES
CEGHHILNOSTT	NIGHT CLOTHES
CEGHHIOSTTTT	GOT THE STITCH
CEGHHIOTTTUW	THOUGHT TWICE
CEGHHIRSTTTT	STRETCH TIGHT
CEGHHMOORSTU	COMES THROUGH
CEGHIIKLNOPS	PICKING HOLES
CEGHIIKNPRSW	SHIPWRECKING
CEGHIILNPSTW	CLIP THE WINGS
CEGHIILNTTWY	TWICE NIGHTLY
CEGHIILRRSTU	LIGHT CRUISER
CEGHIINNRSST	CHRISTENINGS
CEGHIINOPRTV	OVERPITCHING
CEGHIIOPSSTY	GEOPHYSICIST
CEGHIJORSTUU	ROUGH JUSTICE
CEGHIKNOORRS	ROCKING HORSE
CEGHILMOOSTT	COMES TO LIGHT
CEGHILNOOORS	CHRONOLOGIES
CEGHILNOOORZ	CHRONOLOGIZE
CEGHILNOOSTT	TECHNOLOGIST
CEGHILOOPSSY	PSYCHOLOGISE
CEGHILOOPSYZ	PSYCHOLOGIZE
CEGHIMNOOSTT	THINGS TO COME
CEGHIMNORSUZ	ZURICH GNOMES
CEGHIMNORSWY	SHOWING MERCY
CEGHIMORTUUX	COUGH MIXTURE
CEGHINPRSTTU	STRETCHING UP
CEGHKMOORSSU	SMOKERS COUGH
CEGHLNOOOOST	GONE TO SCHOOL
CEGHLNOOOORRS	CHRONOLOGERS
CEGHLOOOOSST	GOES TO SCHOOL
CEGIIIKLLNVY	CLING LIKE IVY
CEGIIILLNNNP	PENCILLING IN
CEGIIIILMNOPS	POLEMICISING
CEGIIIILMNOPZ	POLEMICIZING
CEGIIINOTTXY	TOXIGENICITY
CEGIIINPRRSS	RISING PRICES
CEGIIJNNORTT	INTROJECTING
CEGIIKLLMNRY	MERCY KILLING
CEGIIKLLNUVY	CLUNG LIKE IVY
CEGIIKLLORSV	LOVESICK GIRL
CEGIIKLNNORT	INTERLOCKING
CEGIIKNNOPRR	RON PICKERING
CEGIILLOOSTX	LEXICOLOGIST
CEGIILMOOSSU	MUSICOLOGIES
CEGIILNOPRSV	PIGS IN CLOVER
CEGIIMNNNOOY	COINING MONEY
CEGIIMNNPSST	MINCING STEPS
CEGIINNNORSW	WINNING SCORE
CEGIINNOOPRT	PRECOGNITION
CEGIINNORTTU	TURNING TO ICE
CEGIINOPRTYY	PYROGENICITY
CEGIKKNNOORV	KNOCKING OVER
CEGIKKNOOSST	GOT ONE'S KICKS
CEGIKKNORSTY	SKYROCKETING
CEGIKLNNOSSU	KINGS COUNSEL
CEGIKLNOORSV	OVERLOCKINGS
CEGILLLMNOPY	COMPELLINGLY
CEGILLMOPTUX	GUILT COMPLEX
CEGILLNNOSSU	COUNSELLINGS
CEGILLNOOPUV	LOVING COUPLE
CEGILNNNOSTY	CONSENTINGLY
CEGILNNNOTTY	CONTINGENTLY
CEGILNOOORTW	COOLING TOWER
CEGILNOOPRSU	SUPERCOOLING
CEGILNOOPRTY	GLYCOPROTEIN
CEGILNOOSTTU	CUTTING LOOSE
CEGIMNNNOSST	CONSIGNMENTS
CEGIMNNOORRY	CRYING NO MORE
CEGIMNOORSTT	COME IT STRONG
	COMING TO REST
CEGIMOOPRSST	COMES TO GRIPS
CEGIMORRRSUY	MICROSURGERY
CEGINNOOPSST	COPINGSTONES
CEGINNORSSTU	COUNTERSIGNS
CEGINNPSSTUU	UNSUSPECTING
CEGINOOORSSV	CROSSING OVER
	CROSSING-OVER
CEGINPRSSTTU	PRESS CUTTING
CEGLMORSTUUY	UGLY CUSTOMER
CEGMNNOOORST	COME ON STRONG
CEHHILLOSTV	CHEVIOT HILLS
CEHHIILMOPRT	THERMOPHILIC
CEHHIIRSTTTW	SWITCH HITTER
CEHHILLOPRTT	ROLL THE PITCH
CEHHILNRSSSU	CHURLISHNESS
CEHHIMOOPSTT	PHOTOCHEMIST
CEHHIMOPSSST	CHEMISTS SHOP
CEHHINRSTTUW	WITCH-HUNTERS
CEHHIOOPPRST	PHOTOSPHERIC
CEHHIOOPRSTT	HOPE TO CHRIST
CEHHIOPPRRTY	HYPERTROPHIC
CEHHLOOOSSSU	SCHOOLHOUSES
CEHIIIKRRSTT	STRIKE IT RICH
CEHIIIKSSTTV	VISIT THE SICK
CEHIIILNOOPS	EOSINOPHILIC
CEHIIILNPPPR	PRINCE PHILIP

CEHIIIMNSTTT	STITCH IN TIME
CEHIIJLLMNOT	JONI MITCHELL
CEHIIJORSTWY	CRIES WITH JOY
CEHIIKLNOPSS	PICKS HOLES IN
CEHIIKLNSSST	TICKLISHNESS
CEHIIKMRSTTW	TRIMS THE WICK
CEHIIKNNOPSS	PHONES IN SICK
CEHIIKNRSTTW	WINS THE TRICK
CEHIILLNOSTY	LYSOLECITHIN
CEHIILMNOPRS	NECROPHILISM
CEHIILNOPRTU	NEUTROPHILIC
CEHIILNQSSSU	CLIQUISHNESS
CEHIILOPSTTY	POLYTHEISTIC
CEHIIMNOOSTT	MONOTHEISTIC
CEHIIMOORSTT	TRICHOTOMIES
CEHIINOPRSTT	IN THE TROPICS
CEHIIOPRTTUW	WITHOUT PRICE
CEHIJNOSSTTU	JUST THIS ONCE
CEHIKKMOOTTY	TOOK THE MICKY
CEHILLNNOPSU	PUNCHINELLOO
CEHILLOPPTYY	POLYPHYLETIC
CEHILMNOPPTY	NYMPHOLEPTIC
CEHILNNOSSSW	CLOWNISHNESS
CEHILNOOORSS	SENIOR SCHOOL
CEHILOOPRTTU	LUTEOTROPHIC
CEHILORRTTUU	HORTICULTURE
CEHIMMNNOOST	IN THE COMMONS
CEHIMMOOPRST	CHEMOTROPISM
CEHIMNNOOSTT	MONTHS NOTICE
CEHIMNOPRSSU	CONSUMERSHIP
CEHIMNORRTYY	ERYTHROMYCIN
CEHIMOOPRRTT	THERMOTROPIC
CEHIMOOSSSST	SCHISTOSOMES
CEHIMOPPRSST	COPPERSMITHS
CEHINNNRTTUY	NINTH CENTURY
CEHINNORRSSY	SYNCHRONISER
CEHINNORRSYZ	SYNCHRONIZER
CEHINNORSSSY	SYNCHRONISES
CEHINNORSSYZ	SYNCHRONIZES
CEHINNORTTUY	IN THE COUNTRY
CEHINOPRSTTY	PYROTECHNIST
CEHINOSSSSTT	SCOTTISHNESS
CEHINRSTTUXY	SIXTH CENTURY
CEHIOOPPRRST	TROPOSPHERIC
CEHKLNOPSSUU	PUSH ONES LUCK
CEHKMMOOOSTU	SMOKE TOO MUCH
CEHLMMOORSSU	SUMMER SCHOOL
CEHLNOOOSSTT	SENT TO SCHOOL
CEHLNOOOSTTW	WENT TO SCHOOL
CEHLOOOOPPST	SCOOP THE POOL
CEHLOOOPRRST	SCHOOL REPORT
CEHMNNOORSWY	SHOWN NO MERCY
CEHMNOORSSWY	SHOWS NO MERCY
CEHMNOPRSSTU	CHOSEN TRUMPS
CEHMOOOOPPST	PHOTOCOMPOSE
CEHMOOOPRTUV	PROVE TOO MUCH
CEHMOOPRSSTU	CHOOSE TRUMPS
CEHMOOSSSTUU	CUSTOMSHOUSE
CEHMOPRRSTYY	PSYCHROMETRY
CEHNOORSTUUY	COUNTRY HOUSE
CEHOORSSTUWY	SHOW COURTESY
CEHPRRRSSUYY	CYPRUS SHERRY
CEIIIILNSTV	INCIVILITIES
CEIIILMNPSST	IMPLICITNESS
CEIIILOPRSTV	PROCLIVITIES
CEIIIMMMNPRU	MINIMUM PRICE
CEIIINOPRSST	PRECISIONIST
CEIIINORTTWZ	ZWITTERIONIC
CEIIINOSSTVV	VIVISECTIONS
CEIIJNNOORTT	INTROJECTION
CEIIKLLNOPSS	LICK ONES LIPS

CEIIKRRSSTUY	SECURITY RISK
CEIILLLNOSSW	LEWIS COLLINS
CEIILLNOSTUY	LICENTIOUSLY
CEIILLRSTUUV	SILVICULTURE
CEIILMNNOSTY	OMNISCIENTLY
CEIILNOPRSUY	PERNICIOUSLY
CEIILOPRSSUU	SUPERCILIOUS
CEIIMMNOORSS	COMMISSIONER
CEIIMMNOPRTU	MINICOMPUTER
CEIIMNOPPSTT	COMPETITIONS
CEIIMNRSTTUW	WRITTEN MUSIC
CEIINNNNOOTT	IN CONTENTION
CEIINNNOSSTT	INCONSISTENT
CEIINNORRSTU	INSURRECTION
CEIINNPQRSTU	QUENTIN CRISP
CEIINOOPRRTY	INCORPOREITY
CEIINOPPRRST	PRESCRIPTION
CEIINORRSSTT	RESTRICTIONS
CEIINORSSTUX	EXCURSIONIST
CEIINOSTTTUV	CONSTITUTIVE
CEIINRRSSTUZ	SCRUTINIZERS
CEIIOPPRRSTV	PROSCRIPTIVE
CEIIPRRRSTTW	SCRIPTWRITER
CEIIPSSTTUVY	SUSCEPTIVITY
CEIKKLRSSTUY	STRIKES LUCKY
CEIKKMNORSTY	MONKEY TRICKS
CEIKLMOQSUVY	MOVES QUICKLY
CEIKLNOOSSST	STICK ON SOLES
CEIKLORSTTTU	TICKLES TROUT
CEILLLNOOOSV	VIOLONCELLOS
CEILLMOPSUVY	COMPULSIVELY
CEILLMOSTUUY	METICULOUSLY
CEILLNOPRSSU	CURLS ONES LIP
CEILLNOSUVVY	CONVULSIVELY
CEILLOPRSTSU	PORTCULLISES
CEILMNOOOSUY	MONOECIOUSLY
CEILMNOOSTUU	CONTUMELIOUS
CEILMOOOPSST	COSMOPOLITES
CEILNNOORSTU	CONTOUR LINES
CEILNNOSSTTY	CONSISTENTLY
CEILNOORRTTU	INTERLOCUTOR
CEILNOORSSUY	CENSORIOUSLY
CEILNOORSTUW	LOW COUNTRIES
CEILNOSSSSUU	LUSCIOUSNESS
CEILNOSSTUUY	INCESTUOUSLY
CEILRRSTTTUY	STRICTLY TRUE
CEILRRSUUUXY	LUXURY CRUISE
CEIMMNOOPSST	COMPOS MENTIS
CEIMMOOPRRSS	COMPROMISERS
CEIMNNOOPRSU	MISPRONOUNCE
CEIMNOOPRSSS	COMPRESSIONS
CEIMNOORRRVX	CONVEX MIRROR
CEIMNOPRSTTY	STREPTOMYCIN
CEIMNORSSSTU	CONSUMERISTS
	MISCONSTRUES
CEINNOOPRTTU	COUNTERPOINT
CEINNOORSSSU	CONNOISSEURS
CEINNORSSTWW	CROWN WITNESS
CEINNOSSTTTU	CONSTITUENTS
CEINOOOPSSTU	COPIOUS NOTES
CEINOOPRSSTU	PROSECUTIONS
CEINORRSSTUU	RUN ITS COURSE
CEINPSSSTTUU	INTUSSUSCEPT
CEIOOORSSTTU	CROSSES IT OUT
CEIOPRRSTTUY	PICTURE STORY
CEIPPRRSSSTU	SUPERSCRIPTS
CEJNOORRRSUY	CORONERS JURY
CEKORRRRSTTU	STRUCK TERROR
	TERROR-STRUCK
CELLLOORSSUY	COLOURLESSLY
CELLMOOPRRST	COMPTROLLERS

CELLNOOOOSST	LOST ONE'S COOL
CELLNOOORSST	LOSES CONTROL
CELLOORSSSWY	SCORES SLOWLY
CELNOOOORRTTW	CONTROL TOWER
CEMMNNNOOSSU	UNCOMMONNESS
CEMMNNOOOPRS	COMMON PERSON
CEMMOOSTUXYY	MYXOMYCETOUS
CEMMOPPRSTUU	COME UP TRUMPS
CEMNOOOOPTTU	COME OUT ON TOP
CEMNOOPSTTUU	CONTEMPTUOUS
CEMNOORSTUUY	COUNTRY MOUSE
CEMOOOORRSTT	MOTOR SCOOTER
CENNOOPTTTUU	COUNT UP TO TEN
CENNOORRTTUU	RUN COUNTER TO
CENNOSSSTUUU	UNCTUOUSNESS
CEOOPPRRSSTY	ROSY PROSPECT
CFFFHINNOPSU	PINCH OF SNUFF
CFFGHIINOSTW	SWITCHING OFF
CFFGIINOTTTU	CUTTING IT OFF
CFFGILNOSTTU	SCUTTLING OFF
CFFHKLNOPSUU	SUFFOLK PUNCH
CFFHOOORSTTU	TOUCH OF FROST
CFFKKKNOOORW	KNOCK OFF WORK
CFGHIIKNOPRT	PITCHFORKING
CFGHIMNOORTU	COMING FOURTH
CFGIIIKNPRTU	PICKING FRUIT
CFGIILNOOSTV	COST OF LIVING
	COST-OF-LIVING
CFGIJNOORRYY	CRYING FOR JOY
CFGIKKLNNOSY	KNOCKS FLYING
CFGIKLLNOOSW	FLOWING LOCKS
CFGILLMNNOUY	FLYING COLUMN
CFGILMNOORTY	COMFORTINGLY
CFHHIKMNOSTU	THINKS MUCH OF
CFIIILOSTTUY	FICTITIOUSLY
CFIILLNOOSTU	SOLIFLUCTION
CFIKKNOORSSX	KNOCKS FOR SIX
CFILNORSSUUU	FURUNCULOSIS
CFILOOOORRTU	RIOT OF COLOUR
CFIMNNOORTUY	UNCONFORMITY
CFLNOOOORTTU	OUT OF CONTROL
CFMOPRRSTTUU	CUT FOR TRUMPS
CGGHIINOPRTY	COPYRIGHTING
CGGHILNNOOTU	GOING TO LUNCH
CGHHIINNTTUW	WITCH-HUNTING
CGHHIINOPSTT	HITCHING POST
CGHHIINORTUW	WITCHING HOUR
CGHIIIMNNOPS	INCOMING SHIP
CGHIIINNOPTT	PITCHING INTO
CGHIIKKKNNOPS	SHOCKING PINK
CGHIILOORSTT	TRICHOLOGIST
CGHIIMNOOPSY	PHYSIOGNOMIC
CGHIINNORSSU	SING IN CHORUS
CGHIINOPPSTY	SHOPPING CITY
CGHIINORSTUU	CURIOUS THING
CGHIIORSSTUU	CURIOUS SIGHT
CGHIKLNNOORS	LOCKING HORNS
CGHIKLNNORUW	WORKING LUNCH
CGHILNOOORST	CHRONOLOGIST
CGHILNOOOSTU	SCHOOL OUTING
CGHILOOPSSTY	PSYCHOLOGIST
CGHIMNOORSST	SHORTCOMINGS
CGHINNOOPTUU	TOUCHING UPON
CGHINOOOOPPTY	PHOTOCOPYING
CGHINORSTTTU	CUTTING SHORT
CGIIIILNOPST	POLITICISING
CGIIIILNOPTZ	POLITICIZING
CGIIKNNOSTT	STICKING IT ON
CGIIIKNOSTTT	STICKING TO IT
CGIIIMNOSSTY	MISOGYNISTIC
CGIIIMNRSTUW	WRITING MUSIC
CGIIINNRSTUZ	SCRUTINIZING
CGIIKKLNOSST	SILK STOCKING
CGIIKNORRSWY	WORRYING SICK
CGIILMOOSSTU	MUSICOLOGIST
CGIILOOOSSST	SOCIOLOGISTS
CGIILOOOSTTX	TOXICOLOGIST
CGIIMMNNOOOR	COMMON ORIGIN
CGIIMMNOOPRS	COMPROMISING
CGIINNNOOTTU	COUNTING ON IT
CGIINNOSTTTU	CONSTITUTING
CGIINNOTTTUW	CUTTING IN TWO
CGIINOTTTTUU	CUTTING IT OUT
CGIKLLNOORST	ROLLING STOCK
CGIKMNNOOOTW	COMING TO KNOW
CGIKNOOPRRST	KINGS PROCTOR
CGILLNOOORSU	LOSING COLOUR
CGILLOOOPSWY	GO-SLOW POLICY
CGILMNOOPSSU	GOSSIP COLUMN
CGILMOOOSSST	COSMOLOGISTS
CGILNOOSTUUY	CONTIGUOUSLY
CGILOOOPPSTY	STOP-GO POLICY
CGILOOOPRSTT	PROCTOLOGIST
CGIMMNOOOPSS	COMMON GOSSIP
CGIMNOOOSSST	COSMOGONISTS
CGINNNOOPPUU	POUNCING UPON
CGINNNOOPTUU	COUNTING UPON
CGINNNORSSTU	RUNNING COSTS
CHHIIOOPPRST	PHOSPHORITIC
CHHILMOPRTYY	POLYRHYTHMIC
CHHIOOPRRTTY	THYROTROPHIC
CHHLOOOPRSUY	HYPOCHLOROUS
CHIIKKLNQTUY	THINK QUICKLY
CHIINOOPTTYY	HYPOTONICITY
CHIJLNOOORSU	JUNIOR SCHOOL
CHILLNORTUYY	HILLY COUNTRY
CHIMMNOOOORST	MONOCHROMIST
CHIMNOPRSTYY	CHYMOTRYPSIN
CHIMOOOORSTTU	TRICHOTOMOUS
CHINOOPPSTYY	POSTHYPNOTIC
CHIOOOPPRRTT	PROTOTROPHIC
CHKMNNOOOOTUW	KNOWN TOO MUCH
CHKMNOOOOSTUW	KNOWS TOO MUCH
CHKOORRRRSTU	HORROR-STRUCK
CHMMNOOOORSST	SHORT COMMONS
CHNNOORRTTUY	NORTH COUNTRY
CHNOOORSSTUU	SCOUTS HONOUR
CIIILLLLSTT	ILLICIT STILL
CIIIIOPSSTTV	POSITIVISTIC
CIIILLMPTTUY	MULTIPLICITY
CIIINNOPRSST	INSCRIPTIONS
CIIKORSSTTTW	STICK OR TWIST
	TWIST OR STICK
CIILLOOSSTUY	SOLICITOUSLY
CIILMNOOOPST	MONOPOLISTIC
CIILOORSTUVY	VICTORIOUSLY
CIILOPSSSUUY	SUSPICIOUSLY
CIIMNOOOPSST	COMPOSITIONS
CIIMNOPRSTTY	NYCTITROPISM
CIINNOOSTTTU	CONSTITUTION
CIINNORSSTTU	INSTRUCTIONS
CIINOOPPRRST	PROSCRIPTION
CIJLNORSSTUU	JURISCONSULT
CIJMMNNOORSY	JIMMY CONNORS
CILLMOOPRSUY	COMPULSORILY
CILLORRSSUUY	SCURRILOUSLY
CILNNOOOSTUV	CONVOLUTIONS
CILNNOOSTUUY	CONTINUOUSLY
CILOPRSSTUUY	SCRUPULOSITY
CIMNNOOPSSTU	CONSUMPTIONS
CIMNNOOSSTUU	CUSTOMS UNION
CIMNNORRSSTU	TURNS CRIMSON

CINOPRRSTTTU	P.T.INSTRUCTOR
CKLOPRSSSTUU	SURPLUS STOCK
CKLORSSTTTUU	TRUSTS TO LUCK
CLLOPRSSUUUY	SCRUPULOUSLY
CLNOPRSSUUUU	UNSCRUPULOUS
CMMNOORSSTUU	COURT SUMMONS
CNOOPRRSTTUY	COUNTRY SPORT
DDDDDEFISUUY	FUDDY-DUDDIES
DDDEEEFIINNR	FRIEND INDEED
DDDEEEGHINOT	DOING THE DEED
DDDEEEINNTUU	DUNDEE UNITED
DDDEEEINRRSS	DRESSED IN RED
DDDEEEENRRSSU	UNDERDRESSED
DDDEEFFILLNO	FLODDEN FIELD
DDDEEFHIIIMU	DEHUMIDIFIED
DDDEEGILNOPP	PEDDLING DOPE
DDDEEGINRSSW	WEDDING DRESS
DDDEEHHINPST	HIDDEN DEPTHS
DDDEEIIIMPSY	EPIDIDYMIDES
DDDEEINOPRUW	WOUNDED PRIDE
DDDEEINRSTUU	UNDERSTUDIED
DDDEHINORSTU	DID THE ROUNDS
DDDEHNNOOORR	RHODODENDRON
DDDEIIIKRSTV	DIVIDED SKIRT
DDEEEEGLLNNO	GOLDEN NEEDLE
DDEEEEHINNPT	IN THE DEEP END
DDEEEEHIRSTY	DRIED THE EYES
DDEEEEHOSSTW	SOWED THE SEED
DDEEEEELLRSVW	WELL DESERVED
DDEEEEMNNSST	DEMENTEDNESS
DDEEEENNSSTX	EXTENDEDNESS
DDEEEENORTVX	OVEREXTENDED
DDEEEFGINNRU	UNDERFEEDING
DDEEEFIINNNR	FRIEND IN NEED
DDEEEFILNORS	DRIED ONESELF
DDEEEGHILPSY	SIGHED DEEPLY
DDEEEGHISSTW	DIGS THE WEEDS
DDEEEGMOOPRT	GOOD-TEMPERED
DDEEEHHNRRTU	THREE HUNDRED
DDEEEHNNRSUV	SEVEN HUNDRED
DDEEEHOPRTTT	POTTED THE RED
DDEEEIINOSVW	ONE-SIDED VIEW
DDEEEIINSSST	DESENSITISED
DDEEEIINSSTZ	DESENSITIZED
DDEEEIKMNNOS	ENDED IN SMOKE
DDEEEIKNRTWY	DIRTY WEEK-END
DDEEEILMNRTY	DETERMINEDLY
DDEEEILOPRWW	WIELDED POWER
DDEEEIMNRRU	RUDE REMINDER
DDEEEINNNPST	INDEPENDENTS
DDEEEINNOSSS	ONE-SIDEDNESS
DDEEEINNPRST	INTERDEPENDS
DDEEEINNRRSV	SERVED DINNER
DDEEEINOORTV	TIDED ONE OVER
DDEEEINRRSSS	DRESSES IN RED
DDEEEKLNORWW	WEEKEND WORLD
DDEEELNOPRRT	OLD PRETENDER
DDEEELNRSUVY	UNDESERVEDLY
DDEEENOPRSUX	UNDEREXPOSED
DDEEENRRSSSU	UNDERDRESSES
DDEEFFGLLLUY	FULLY-FLEDGED
DDEEFGGIILNY	FEELING GIDDY
DDEEFGHINORU	DIED OF HUNGER
DDEEFGIIILNS	FIELDING SIDE
DDEEFGIILMNR	MIDDLE FINGER
DDEEFHIIIMRU	DEHUMIDIFIER
DDEEFHIIIMSU	DEHUMIDIFIES
DDEEFHIOOOPV	DEVOID OF HOPE
DDEEFIIINNTU	UNIDENTIFIED
DDEEFIILLMRS	FREDDIE MILLS
DDEEFIILRTUY	YIELDED FRUIT

DDEEFIILSSTU	FIELD STUDIES
DDEEFLLRSSUY	FULLY DRESSED
DDEEFMNNOORT	FROM END TO END
DDEEFNOOPSSU	SPEED OF SOUND
DDEEGGINSTUW	WEDDING GUEST
DDEEGHHINRTU	EIGHT HUNDRED
DDEEGHHOOPRS	GOOD SHEPHERD
DDEEGHHOPRSS	SHEPHERDS DOG
DDEEGHIILMTW	MIDDLEWEIGHT
DDEEGHIINTWW	WHITE WEDDING
DDEEGHILLNOP	HOLD IN PLEDGE
DDEEGIILMNNS	SINGLE-MINDED
DDEEGIINQTUW	QUIET WEDDING
DDEEGIINRSTW	WEDDING RITES
DDEEGLLNORUW	WELL GROUNDED
DDEEGMNOOOOS	DONE SOME GOOD
DDEEGMOOOOSS	DOES SOME GOOD
DDEEHHKLOSTY	HOLDS THE DYKE
DDEEHHIINNRST	DISINHERITED
DDEEHIKORSST	KISSED THE ROD
DDEEHILMNRSU	HUNDRED MILES
DDEEHINORTTY	DONE THE DIRTY
DDEEHIORSTTY	DOES THE DIRTY
DDEEHKNNORUW	HUNKERED DOWN
DDEEHNNOORTU	HUNDRED TO ONE
DDEEIIJNPRRU	INJURED PRIDE
DDEEIIKLLMNY	LIKE-MINDEDLY
DDEEIIKLNOOS	LOOKED INSIDE
DDEEIILMMNPS	SIMPLEMINDED
DDEEIILMNPST	SPLENDID TIME
DDEEIIQSSTUU	DISQUIETUDES
DDEEIIRRSSST	DIRE DISTRESS
DDEEIIKLMOPRW	POWDERED MILK
DDEEIKNNRRUW	WUNDERKINDER
DDEEILLOPSSW	WELL DISPOSED
	WELL-DISPOSED
DDEEILMNNOPY	OPEN-MINDEDLY
DDEEILNNPSSS	SPLENDIDNESS
DDEEILNOPSSS	LOPSIDEDNESS
DDEEILOORRTV	LORDED IT OVER
DDEEIMMNORSW	SIMMERED DOWN
DDEEIMNNOSTW	DISENDOWMENT
DDEEINNORRRS	ORDERS DINNER
DDEEINNRRSUU	UNDERINSURED
DDEEINOOSSTT	DOTTED ONE'S I'S
DDEEINRSSTUU	UNDERSTUDIES
DDEEIOPSSSSS	DISPOSSESSED
DDEELNNOPSTY	DESPONDENTLY
DDEENNOOOPRU	DONE ONE PROUD
DDEENNOOSTUY	DONE ONE'S DUTY
DDEENOOOPRSU	DOES ONE PROUD
DDEENOOSSTUY	DOES ONE'S DUTY
DDEFFGHIIORT	DIED OF FRIGHT
DDEFFILLNORU	LORD NUFFIELD
DDEFFINOSSTU	DID ONE'S STUFF
DDEFGGHIIINT	DIED FIGHTING
DDEFGHNOORTU	GOD OF THUNDER
DDEFGIMNOORY	MY GOOD FRIEND
DDEFGIMNRSUU	SIGMUND FREUD
DDEFHIIORSTT	DIED OF THIRST
DDEFILNORRWY	FRIENDLY WORD
DDEFINOORTUX	OXFORD UNITED
DDEFNOOOPRSU	SOUNDPROOFED
DDEGGHHIISTY	GIDDY HEIGHTS
DDEGGIOOOOSY	GOODY-GOODIES
DDEGGJMNOOTU	GOOD JUDGMENT
DDEGHHIILMNY	HIGH-MINDEDLY
DDEGHHIISSTT	DID THE SIGHTS
DDEGHHLOOOSU	HOUSEHOLD GOD
DDEGHIINNOST	DID ONE'S THING
DDEGHIRRSUUY	HURDY-GURDIES

DDEGHMOOORUU	GOOD-HUMOURED
DDEGIIKNORUY	YOU'RE KIDDING!
DDEGIKLLOSTU	LIKE GOLD DUST
DDEGILLNNOWY	LONG-WINDEDLY
DDEGILMNNOPU	LEMON PUDDING
DDEGIMNNORST	NODDING TERMS
	STRONG-MINDED
DDEGINNNOOOW	DOING ONE DOWN
DDEGINNOORSW	DOING WONDERS
DDEGINNORSSW	DRESSING DOWN
DDEGLNOORTTU	TURNED TO GOLD
DDEHHOOSSTTU	SHOUT THE ODDS
DDEHIIIMNNSU	UNDIMINISHED
DDEHIILPSSTT	DID THE SPLITS
DDEHIKLNORSU	HUNDRED KILOS
DDEHILNNOOPR	PHILODENDRON
DDEHILNORRUW	WHIRLED ROUND
DDEHILNOTTWW	WHITTLED DOWN
DDEHINOORSTU	RIDE TO HOUNDS
DDEHLLOORSSU	OLD SHOULDERS
DDEHMNOOOSTW	SMOOTHED DOWN
DDEHOOPPRRST	DROPPED SHORT
DDEIIILNSTTY	DID IT IN STYLE
DDEIIILPRSTY	DISPIRITEDLY
DDEIIJLNOSTY	DISJOINTEDLY
DDEIIKNORRTV	DRIVE TO DRINK
DDEIIMNOSUVV	MODUS VIVENDI
DDEIJNOOTTTW	JOTTED IT DOWN
DDEIKNOORRTV	DROVE TO DRINK
DDEIKNOORRTW	RIDDEN TO WORK
DDEIKNORRSTU	SKIRTED ROUND
DDEILNNOOORT	LONDON EDITOR
DDEILNORRTUW	TWIRLED ROUND
DDEIMNOORRWW	DORMER WINDOW
DDEIMOOPPSUU	PSEUDOPODIUM
DDEINNORTTUW	TURNED IT DOWN
DDEINOORSSTW	DID ONE'S WORST
DDEKLNNOOOOW	LOOKED DOWN ON
DDENORSTTTUU	TURNED TO DUST
DDFGHILNOOPS	GOLDFISH POND
DDFGIINNORSW	FINDING WORDS
DDFGILNOOORS	FOLDING DOORS
DDFIILOOPQRU	DROP OF LIQUID
DDGGIINNNORW	GRINDING DOWN
DDGHINNNOOUW	HOUNDING DOWN
DDGIILNOORSS	SLIDING DOORS
DDGINNOOPPRW	DROPPING DOWN
DDGINORSSTTU	GRINDS TO DUST
DDGLLOOORSWY	WORLDLY GOODS
DDGMNOOORSUU	GOOD ROUND SUM
DDGNOORSTTUU	GROUND TO DUST
DEEEEEFHLNST	FEELS THE NEED
DEEEEEFILLRV	FEEL RELIEVED
DEEEEEGHLNTT	GET THE NEEDLE
DEEEEEGHRRST	THREE DEGREES
DEEEEFFLNORS	FREED ONESELF
DEEEEFGILNPS	DEEP FEELINGS
DEEEEFHKNOTW	END OF THE WEEK
DEEEEFILRRVY	FREE DELIVERY
DEEEEGGHHIRR	HIGHER DEGREE
DEEEEGGHINTV	GIVEN THE EDGE
DEEEEGHHNRTT	THE NTH DEGREE
DEEEEGHLNOTT	GOT THE NEEDLE
DEEEEGIILNNS	DIESEL ENGINE
DEEEEGNNRRTU	NEUTER GENDER
DEEEEHHLNRTU	UNDER THE HEEL
DEEEEHHPRRSS	SHEEPHERDERS
DEEEEHILNOST	ON THE LEE SIDE
DEEEEHIPSTWY	WIPED THE EYES
DEEEEHIRSSTY	DRIES THE EYES
DEEEEHKMOSTW	SMOKE THE WEED
DEEEEHLNSSSS	HEEDLESSNESS
DEEEEIKNQTUW	QUIET WEEKEND
DEEEEIMNPRRT	PREDETERMINE
DEEEEINPRSTT	DEEP INTEREST
DEEEELMNORTV	LOVE ME TENDER
DEEEELNNSSSS	NEEDLESSNESS
DEEEEMNNOSST	MEETS ONE'S END
DEEEEMOPRSST	SPEEDOMETERS
DEEEENOPRSVX	EXPOSED NERVE
DEEEENOSSSUY	USED ONE'S EYES
DEEEENRRRVVY	VERY REVEREND
DEEEENRSSSSV	RESERVEDNESS
DEEEEORRRRSV	REVERSE ORDER
DEEEEPPRSSSX	EXPRESS SPEED
DEEEFFINNOST	FIND ONES FEET
DEEEFGIILNRT	FEELING TIRED
DEEEFGINRRYZ	FREEZE-DRYING
DEEEFGLLNNOT	LONG-FELT NEED
DEEEFGLNORSV	SELF-GOVERNED
DEEEFHIKOPRT	POKED THE FIRE
DEEEFHILNNOP	IN NEED OF HELP
DEEEFHILNNOT	END OF THE LINE
DEEEFHILNSTW	FEELS THE WIND
DEEEFHINOSTV	DEN OF THIEVES
DEEEFHOOPRST	FOSTERED HOPE
DEEEFIIIMNTT	DEFINITE TIME
DEEEFIINNSST	DEFINITENESS
DEEEFILNNOSS	ENDS ONE'S LIFE
DEEEFILNOPRS	PRIDE ONESELF
DEEEFILNORSS	DRIES ONESELF
DEEEFILORRVV	LIVED FOR EVER
DEEEFINOSTTV	TIDE OF EVENTS
DEEEFINRRRTU	RETURNED FIRE
DEEEFINRSTUX	SIX FEET UNDER
DEEEFLLMOPSY	SELF-EMPLOYED
DEEEFNNQRTUU	UNFREQUENTED
DEEEGGLNORRS	GOLDERS GREEN
DEEEGHIIRRTT	RIDE THE TIGER
DEEEGHIKLNRT	KING ETHELRED
DEEEGHILNOST	ON THE LEG-SIDE
DEEEGHINNPRR	REPREHENDING
DEEEGHIORRTT	RODE THE TIGER
DEEEGHIORTVW	OVERWEIGHTED
DEEEGHNNRSTT	STRENGTHENED
DEEEGIINNRRV	ENGINE DRIVER
DEEEGIKMOOPT	KEEP GOOD TIME
DEEEGIKNNNOY	DONKEY ENGINE
DEEEGIKNNPRU	KEEPING UNDER
DEEEGIKNOPRR	KEEPING ORDER
DEEEGILLOTVW	GET WELL-OILED
DEEEGILNOPRV	REDEVELOPING
DEEEGINNPRSS	PRESSING NEED
DEEEGINNRSSS	RESIGNEDNESS
DEEEGINNRSSV	EVENING DRESS
DEEEGINPRRSS	DEREPRESSING
DEEEGLLMNOPS	SOLEMN PLEDGE
DEEEGLORRSSV	GOLD RESERVES
DEEEGORRRSST	RETROGRESSED
DEEEHHIORSTT	THE OTHER SIDE
DEEEHHIPPRSS	SHEPHERDS PIE
DEEEHHNOOSTU	DONE THE HOUSE
DEEEHHNOPSTU	USED THE PHONE
DEEEHHOOSSTU	DOES THE HOUSE
DEEEHHOPSTTU	THE DEEP SOUTH
DEEEHIIKLLTV	LIKE THE DEVIL
DEEEHIILRTVW	WHITE-LIVERED
DEEEHIKNRSST	REND THE SKIES
DEEEHILMNOST	HOLD IN ESTEEM
DEEEHILPRTTT	PITT THE ELDER
DEEEHILRTVVY	THE VERY DEVIL
DEEEHIMSSTTT	STEMS THE TIDE

DEEEHKNRTTUY	TURNED THE KEY
DEEEHLNNORST	HELDENTENORS
DEEEHLNORSTW	SEEN THE WORLD
DEEEHLORSSTW	SEES THE WORLD
DEEEHLRRSSSW	WELSH DRESSER
DEEEHMNNORTT	DETHRONEMENT
DEEEHMNORRTU	RETURNED HOME
DEEEHNNOOPRT	OPEN OTHER END
DEEEHNORRSTU	UNDER THE ROSE
DEEEHNRSSTTT	SETS THE TREND
DEEEIIKLOSSW	DOES LIKEWISE
DEEEIILLLNNS	DENNIS LILLEE
DEEEIINRSSST	DESENSITISER
DEEEIINRSSTZ	DESENSITIZER
DEEEIINSSSST	DESENSITISES
DEEEIINSSSTZ	DESENSITIZES
DEEEIKLNOSST	SKELETONISED
DEEEIKLNOSTZ	SKELETONIZED
DEEEILLNRSVW	WELL VERSED IN
DEEEILMMPRSY	SIMPLE REMEDY
DEEEILNNOPST	NEEDLEPOINTS
DEEEILNORTVY	DELIVERY NOTE
DEEEILNRSTTY	INTERESTEDLY
DEEEILNSSSUV	DELUSIVENESS
DEEEILPRSSVY	DEPRESSIVELY
DEEEILRSSSTT	ELDEST SISTER
DEEEILRSTTUY	ERUDITE STYLE
DEEEIMNNOSSY	MINDS ONE'S EYE
	ONES MINDS EYE
DEEEIMNOORTV	DONE OVERTIME
DEEEIMNRSSTV	DISSEVERMENT
DEEEIMOORSTV	DOES OVERTIME
DEEEIMOPRSTX	EXTEMPORISED
DEEEIMOPRTXZ	EXTEMPORIZED
DEEFINNRRSSV	SERVES DINNER
DEEEINNRSTTU	UNINTERESTED
DEEEINOORSTV	TIDES ONE OVER
DEEEINOPRRSS	DEREPRESSION
DEEEINORRRSV	INVERSE ORDER
DEEEINORRTVW	OVERWINTERED
DEEEINORSTVW	STEVIE WONDER
DEEEINPRRSST	INTERSPERSED
DEEEINPRSTUX	EXPENDITURES
DEEEJLLOPPRT	JET-PROPELLED
DEEEKLNNOOST	ENDOSKELETON
DEEEKNOOPRSW	KEEP ONES WORD
DEEELLNORVWY	DONE VERY WELL
DEEELLORSVWY	DOES VERY WELL
DEEELMNNORSY	MONEYLENDERS
DEEELMNOPRTY	REDEPLOYMENT
DEEELMNOPSTV	DEVELOPMENTS
DEEELMNPPSTU	SUPPLEMENTED
DEEELNNOPSUV	ELEVEN POUNDS
DEEELNOPRSSU	SOUND SLEEPER
DEEELNOPSSST	SENDS TO SLEEP
DEEELNRRSUVY	UNRESERVEDLY
DEEEMNORRSTV	MOST REVEREND
DEEENNORSSVW	SEVEN WONDERS
DEEENOOOPRRV	EVER-OPEN DOOR
DEEENOOPRSSY	DROP ONE'S EYES
DEEENOPRSSUX	UNDEREXPOSES
DEEENORRSTTV	STREET VENDOR
DEEENPRSSTUW	STEWED PRUNES
DEEENRRSSTTT	TRENDSETTERS
DEEEOORRRRST	RESTORE ORDER
DEEEOPPRSSSS	PREPOSSESSED
DEEFFGGIORRT	TRIGGERED OFF
DEEFFHINOOST	ON THE OFF-SIDE
DEEFFILNNOSS	FINDS ONESELF
DEEFFILOSTUV	STUFFED OLIVE
DEEFFINNOOPS	PENSIONED OFF

DEEFFINNORTU	ROUND FIFTEEN
DEEFFLMNOSTU	MUFFLED TONES
DEEFFLNNOOSU	FOUND ONESELF
DEEFFLORSSSU	SUFFERED LOSS
DEEFFMOORRSU	FOUR FREEDOMS
DEEFGHILOPST	SPEED OF LIGHT
DEEFGHINORSU	DIES OF HUNGER
DEEFGIIKNNRR	KNIFE GRINDER
DEEFGIILNNOS	DIG ONESELF IN
DEEFGIKLNNRU	FEELING DRUNK
DEEFGILNNOSS	FIND ONES LEGS
DEEFGILNNOSU	DUG ONESELF IN
DEEFGILNOOTT	IN GOOD FETTLE
DEEFGINNOOPS	SPOON FEEDING
	SPOON-FEEDING
DEEFHIIMNSTT	FINDS THE TIME
DEEFHIINNSSS	FIENDISHNESS
DEEFHILNRSST	FINDS SHELTER
DEEFHIMNNQTY	FIND THE MONEY
DEEFHIMNOTTU	FOUND THE TIME
DEEFHINORRTU	ROUND THE FIRE
DEEFHIOPRTVY	TYPHOID FEVER
DEEFIIJKNNNOY	JOHN F.KENNEDY
DEEFHKOOORTY	KEY OF THE DOOR
DEEFHLLORSTU	LEFT SHOULDER
DEEFHLNOPRSS	SENDS FOR HELP
DEEFHLNORSTU	FOUND SHELTER
DEEFHOOONOWW	HEWERS OF WOOD
DEEFIIILNST	INFIDELITIES
DEEFIIIKLLRW	LIKE WILDFIRE
DEEFIIILLMNT	FILLED IN TIME
DEEFIIILNNTY	INDFFINITELY
DEEFIIILNTVY	DEFINITIVELY
DEEFIILNNRSS	FRIENDLINESS
DEEFIILPPRTT	FILTER-TIPPED
DEEFIIMOOPRT	PERIOD OF TIME
DEEFIIORRSTZ	TRIED FOR SIZE
DEEFILLMNORW	WELL-INFORMED
DEEFILLNOSSU	SELF-DELUSION
DEEFILNORSSS	LOSES FRIENDS
DEEFILOSSTTU	OUTSIDE LEFTS
DEEFIMOORRRT	ORDER OF MERIT
DEEFLNNOORSW	DROWN ONESELF
DEEFLOORSTUY	SUREFOOTEDLY
DEEFMNNNOOOY	NO END OF MONEY
DEEFNNOOORRU	UNDER ONE ROOF
DEEFNOPRSTUY	TYPEFOUNDERS
DEEFOORRSTTX	OXFORD STREET
DEEGGHHINOPP	HEDGEHOPPING
DEEGGHHLOOTT	HOGGED THE LOT
DEEGGHIOOSTY	GOOD EYESIGHT
DEEGGHIRSSTU	GUESSED RIGHT
DEEGGIINPRST	PREDIGESTING
DEEGGIINRTTT	GETTING TIRED
DEEGGIJMNTUV	GIVE JUDGMENT
DEEGGILNOPSS	SLEEPING DOGS
DEEGGILNORTT	GETTING OLDER
DEEGGNORSSUW	GUESSED WRONG
DEEGHHIIMMTU	MEDIUM HEIGHT
DEEGHHINNOTT	THE DONE THING
DEEGHHLOORTT	HOLD TOGETHER
DEEGHHOPSTTU	DEEP THOUGHTS
DEEGHIILLNSV	DISHEVELLING
DEEGHIINNSTW	WINDING-SHEET
DEEGHIINSTUX	EXTINGUISHED
DEEGHILOOTTV	GO TO THE DEVIL
DEEGHILORTVW	GIVE THE WORLD
DEEGHINORTVW	GIVEN THE WORD
DEEGHINPTTUW	GET THE WIND UP
DEEGHINRSSST	NIGHTDRESSES
DEEGHIORSTVW	GIVES THE WORD

DEEGHJMNPTUU	JUMPED THE GUN	DEEHIMORRSTT	RIDE THE STORM
DEEGHKOORSTT	STROKE THE DOG	DEEHINNSSTUY	THE SUNNY SIDE
DEEGHNORSSTU	GROUNDSHEETS	DEEHINOOSTTU	ON THE OUTSIDE
DEEGIILLNSTT	LETTING SLIDE	DEEHINORRSST	TORE IN SHREDS
DEEGIILMNNRT	INTERMINGLED	DEEHINORRTVW	DOWN THE RIVER
DEEGIILMOOPY	EPIDEMIOLOGY	DEEHINOSTTTW	DONE THE TWIST
DEEGIIMNNOST	DEMONETISING	DEEHINRSTTTU	TURNS THE TIDE
DEEGIIMNNOTZ	DEMONETIZING	DEEHIOPPRTTY	PTERIDOPHYTE
DEEGIIMNNPST	SPENDING TIME	DEEHIOSSTTTW	DOES THE TWIST
DEEGIIMNPRST	DISTEMPERING	DEEHKOOORTTY	KEY TO THE DOOR
DEEGIIMNSSTU	DISGUISEMENT	DEEHKOOPRSTW	SPOKE THE WORD
DEEGIINNPRST	PREDESTINING	DEEHLLLORTTW	TELL THE WORLD
DEEGIINOPRST	PREDIGESTION	DEEHLNOOOTTW	THE OLD ONE-TWO
DEEGIINPPSST	SIDESTEPPING	DEEHLNORTTWX	THE NEXT WORLD
DEEGIINPPSTU	SPEEDING IT UP	DEEHLOOPRTWY	THREE-PLY WOOD
DEEGIINPRSTW	SPEED WRITING	DEEHLOPSSTTW	LOWEST DEPTHS
DEEGIKLNNNOW	KNEELING DOWN	DEEHMOOOORSTV	SMOOTHED OVER
DEEGIKLNOOSS	GOOD LIKENESS	DEEHNNORSTUV	SEVENTH ROUND
DEEGILLLOOTW	GOT WELL-OILED	DEEHNOOOPRST	OPENS THE DOOR
DEEGILLMNOSU	MOLLIE SUGDEN	DEEHOOSSTTTT	STOOD THE TEST
DEEGILLNNRSU	UNDERSELLING	DEEIIIMNORVV	DRIVE-IN MOVIE
DEEGILLNRSSW	DRESSING WELL	DEEIIIMNRTTV	DIVERTIMENTI
DEEGILMNNNOY	LENDING MONEY	DEEIIINSSSVV	DIVISIVENESS
DEEGILMOOSTY	ETYMOLOGISED	DEEIIJLLMSTT	ILL-TIMED JEST
DEEGILMOOTYZ	ETYMOLOGIZED	DEEIIILLNSTVY	LIVED IN STYLE
DEEGILNNORUV	ENDURING LOVE	DEEIILNNSSUW	UNWIELDINESS
DEEGILNOORST	GOOD LISTENER	DEEIILPRSSVY	DISPERSIVELY
DEEGILNOSTTY	GENTLY DOES IT	DEEIIMMOSTVX	MIXED MOTIVES
DEEGILNOSTVV	GETS INVOLVED	DEEIIMNNRSTT	DISINTERMENT
DEEGILNPRSSY	DEPRESSINGLY	DEEIIMNORTTV	DIVERTIMENTO
DEEGINNOPRSV	OVERSPENDING	DEEIIMNRSSTT	DETERMINISTS
DEEGINNOPSWW	SWEEPING DOWN	DEEIINNORSST	IN ONES STRIDE
DEEGINNORRUV	VEERING ROUND	DEEIINNSSSTT	DISSENTIENTS
DEEGINNRRRSU	SURRENDERING	DEEIINOQRRTU	QUITE IN ORDER
DEEGINNRSTTT	TRENDSETTING	DEEIINPRSSST	SPIRITEDNESS
DEEGINOORSVW	GIVE ONES WORD	DEEIIOOPPSST	OPPOSITE SIDE
DEEGINORRSST	STRONG DESIRE	DEEIIOOPRSST	DEPOSITORIES
DEEGINORRSSV	OVERDRESSING	DEEIIRRSSSTW	WEIRD SISTERS
DEEGINQRSUYZ	SQUEEZING DRY	DEEIJNORRRSU	SURREJOINDER
DEEGKMNOOSTU	SMOKED TONGUE	DEEIKNOOOSST	TOOK ONE'S SIDE
DEEGLLNNOOWW	GONE DOWN WELL	DEEILLMOPRSW	PROMISED WELL
DEEGLLNOOSWW	GOES DOWN WELL	DEEILLNNQTUY	DELINQUENTLY
DEEGLNNOOSUY	ENDOGENOUSLY	DEEILLNORTTW	LITTLE WONDER
DEEGLNNOSSTU	GOLDEN SUNSET	DEEILLOPSTTU	SPELLED IT OUT
DEEGLOOPRRST	PORTERS LODGE	DEEILMNNSSSS	MINDLESSNESS
DEEGMOOPRSTT	GETS PROMOTED	DEEILNNOOPRS	PREDNISOLONE
DEEHHHIRTTTU	HIDE THE TRUTH	DEEILNNSSSSW	WINDLESSNESS
DEEHHIJNRTTU	JUNE THE THIRD	DEEILNOOPPRT	LEPIDOPTERON
DEEHHILLNOST	HOLDS THE LINE	DEEILNOPRSTT	TITLED PERSON
DEEHHILNORST	HOLD THE REINS	DEEILNRSTWWY	WESTERLY WIND
DEEHHIOPPRSW	HORSEWHIPPED	DEEILOPPPSTY	POLYPEPTIDES
DEEHHIOPSSTY	HYPOTHESISED	DEEILOPRSSTY	PROSELYTISED
DEEHHIOPSTYZ	HYPOTHESIZED	DEEILOPRSTYZ	PROSELYTIZED
DEEHHLOORSSU	HOUSEHOLDERS	DEEIMMNORUVY	NEVER YOU MIND!
DEEHIIKNRTTW	TINKERED WITH	DEEIMNNRSTTU	INSTRUMENTED
DEEHIIKRSSSW	SIDE-WHISKERS	DEEIMNORUUYY	MUD IN YOUR EYE
DEEHIILNQRSU	RELINQUISHED	DEEIMOPPRSSU	SUPERIMPOSED
DEEHIIMOPRSV	IMPOVERISHED	DEEINNNORSST	NONRESIDENTS
DEEHIINOPSST	OPEN THIS SIDE	DEEINNOOPSTU	PUT ON ONE SIDE
DEEHIINPSSTW	DISPENSE WITH	DEEINNOQSTUU	UNQUESTIONED
DEEHIINRSSTW	DRESS IN WHITE	DEEINNPRSSTU	SUPERINTENDS
DEEHIKMNRRST	METHS DRINKER	DEEINNQRRUUY	UNDER ENQUIRY
DEEHIKNNRSTU	UNDER THE SKIN	DEEINNRRTTUV	INVERTED TURN
DEEHIKORSSST	KISSES THE ROD	DEEINNRWTTUW	UNDERWRITTEN
DEEHILLNORTT	ROTTED IN HELL	DEEINOOPSTTU	PUT TO ONE SIDE
DEEHILLPRSUV	SHRIVELLED UP	DEEINORRRTTW	WRITTEN ORDER
DEEHILMOOSTT	THE DOLOMITES	DEEINOSSSTUW	USED ONE'S WITS
DEEHILNOSTVW	THE DEVILS OWN	DEEINRRRSTUW	UNDERWRITERS
DEEHILOORRSS	HORSE SOLDIER	DEEINSSSSUXY	SIDNEY SUSSEX
DEEHILRSTTWW	WRESTLED WITH	DEEIOPSSSSSS	DISPOSSESSES
DEEHIMNOORTU	TIME-HONOURED	DEEIOPSSSTTU	STEPS OUTSIDE

DEEKLOORRTUW	WORKED TO RULE
DEEKMNOOPRWY	POWDER MONKEY
DEEKNOORRRWW	WONDER-WORKER
DEELLNNOTWWW	WENT DOWN WELL
DEELLNOPSSUY	SLEEP SOUNDLY
DEELLNORTUWY	TURNED YELLOW
DEELMNORSTUY	TREMENDOUSLY
DEELNOPSTUVW	TWELVE POUNDS
DEELNORRSTWW	WESTERN WORLD
DEELNORSSTUW	TWELVE ROUNDS
DEELNOSSSSUU	SEDULOUSNESS
DEELNPPRRTUU	TURNED PURPLE
DEELNRRTTTUU	TURNED TURTLE
DEEMNOOPRSST	MODEST PERSON
DEEMNOOPRSSU	ENDOSPERMOUS
DEENNNOOOPUW	ONE-UP ONE-DOWN
DEENNNOOPTTU	TEN-POUND NOTE
DEENNNOSSTUW	UNWONTEDNESS
DEENNOPRSTUU	TURNED-UP NOSE
DEENNRSSTTUU	STUDENT NURSE
DEENOOPRSSST	DESSERT SPOON
	DESSERTSPOON
DEENOPRRSTTU	UNDER PROTECT
DEFFFHHNOORSU	OFFSHORE FUND
DEFFGHIIORST	DIES OF FRIGHT
DEFFGHNOORTU	OFF THE GROUND
DEFFHIRSSTTU	STUFFED SHIRT
DEFFHLNOOPSU	POUND OF FLESH
DEFFIIORRSTW	WORRIED STIFF
DEFFILNNOOOR	FIRE OF LONDON
DEFGGHIIINST	DIES FIGHTING
DEFGGIINORTT	GETTING RID OF
DEFGHHIIILTY	HIGH FIDELITY
	HIGH-FIDELITY
DEFGHILLLTUY	DELIGHTFULLY
DEFGHINNORST	SENDING FORTH
DEFGIIIMMNNNY	INDEMNIFYING
DEFGIIINNRTY	DENITRIFYING
DEFGIIINNSST	DISINFESTING
DEFGIIINRSVY	DIVERSIFYING
DEFGIILMNOOV	MODE OF LIVING
DEFGIIMNSTYY	DEMYSTIFYING
DEFGIIORTTUU	FIGURED IT OUT
DEFGILNOORVY	DYING FOR LOVE
DEFGINNOPTUY	TYPEFOUNDING
DEFGINORRSUU	ROUND FIGURES
DEFHHLOORSTT	HOLDS THE FORT
DEFHIIKNORSW	FINISHED WORK
DEFHIILOOPRS	FOOLISH PRIDE
DEFHIIORSSTT	DIES OF THIRST
DEFHILLOSTWW	WOLF-WHISTLED
DEFHINOOTTUW	OUT OF THE WIND
DEFHINORSTUW	THE FOUR WINDS
DEFHINPRSSTT	SPENDTHRIFTS
DEFHIOORRTTW	THE WORD FOR IT
DEFHKLLMOOOS	OLD FOLKS HOME
DEFHLOOORSSU	HOUSE OF LORDS
DEFHLOORSTTU	DUST THE FLOOR
DEFHOOOOTTUW	OUT OF THE WOOD
DEFHOOORSTUU	HOUSE OF TUDOR
DEFIIINORSTT	FIRST EDITION
DEFIILNOOPRS	PRIDE OF LIONS
DEFIILOPRSUY	PERFIDIOUSLY
DEFIINOPRSTU	PROFUNDITIES
DEFILLMRRUUW	WILFUL MURDER
DEFILLOOSTUW	FOLLOWED SUIT
DEFILLOPSTUW	STUPID FELLOW
DEFILMOORRTY	FIRMLY ROOTED
DEFILOOPPSSU	FOOD SUPPLIES
DEFILOORSTUY	DO IT YOURSELF
	DO-IT-YOURSELF

DEFIMNOOSTTU	SIDE OF MUTTON
DEFIMNORRSSU	DRESS UNIFORM
DEFINNORRSSW	SWORN FRIENDS
DEFINOOOPRRT	POINT OF ORDER
DEFINOORRRWW	WORRIED FROWN
DEFINRRSTTUY	TRUSTY FRIEND
DEFIOOORRSSUU	SUDORIFEROUS
DEFIOORSSSST	TOSS FOR SIDES
DEFJJMOOPRUY	JUMPED FOR JOY
DEFLNORSTTUW	FLUTTERS DOWN
DEFMORRRRTUY	TRY FOR MURDER
DEFNNOOPRSSU	PROFOUNDNESS
DEGGGINNORRU	GROUND GINGER
DEGGHIILNOTW	WEIGHT IN GOLD
DEGGHIINNOWW	WEIGHING DOWN
DEGGHILNNOTU	HUNTING LODGE
DEGGHILNOOSU	LODGING HOUSE
DEGGHLNOORSW	HORNSWOGGLED
DEGGIILMOORT	GOOD-TIME GIRL
DEGGIILNNNSW	LENDING WINGS
DEGGIINOOSTU	GOING OUTSIDE
DEGGIINOOTTU	OUTGOING TIDE
DEGGIINORRSV	GIVING ORDERS
DEGGIINORRTW	GROWING TIRED
DEGGIINRTTTY	GETTING DIRTY
DEGGIKNNRTTU	GETTING DRUNK
DEGGILNOORRW	GROWING OLDER
DEGGINNORSSW	DRESSING GOWN
DEGGINNORTTU	GETTING ROUND
DEGGLNOOORST	GOOD LONG REST
DEGGNNOOORTU	GONE TO GROUND
DEGGNOOORSTU	GOES TO GROUND
DEGGOOOOPRSS	GOOD PROGRESS
DEGHHIIIPRST	HIGH-SPIRITED
DEGHHIINOPST	DIPHTHONGISE
DEGHHIINOPTZ	DIPHTHONGIZE
DEGHHIISTYZZ	DIZZY HEIGHTS
DEGHHILNOSST	SHEDS LIGHT ON
DEGHHILORTUV	LIVED THROUGH
DEGHHINOOTTT	THE THING TO DO
DEGHHIORRTUV	DRIVE THROUGH
DEGHHIORSSTT	SHORTSIGHTED
DEGHHOOORRTUV	DROVE THROUGH
DEGHIINNRSST	INSIDE RIGHTS
DEGHIIINNRSTV	DIVINE RIGHTS
DEGHIIINNSSTU	THIN DISGUISE
DEGHIILLLPST	GILDS THE PILL
DEGHIILLLSTY	GILDS THE LILY
DEGHIILNORTW	DOWNRIGHT LIE
DEGHIINNNOST	NO END IN SIGHT
DEGHIINOSTTT	DOTTING THE I'S
DEGHIIORSTTU	OUTSIDE RIGHT
	OUTSIDE-RIGHT
DEGHILLNNOOW	GONE DOWNHILL
DEGHILLNOOSW	GOES DOWNHILL
DEGHILLOORRT	GOOD THRILLER
DEGHILMNOOST	SOMETHING OLD
DEGHILMOOSTY	MYTHOLOGISED
DEGHILMOOTYZ	MYTHOLOGIZED
DEGHILNNRTUY	THUNDERINGLY
DEGHILNSSTUY	STUDY ENGLISH
DEGHINNOOSSW	SHOWED NO SIGN
DEGHINNOOTTW	DOING THE TOWN
DEGHINNORWWY	WONDERING WHY
DEGHINOPSTUY	EIGHTY POUNDS
DEGHINOPTTUW	GOT THE WIND UP
DEGHIOOPQSUY	GOOD PHYSIQUE
DEGHIOORTUWY	WOODY GUTHRIE
DEGHLNOOPSUW	SNOWPLOUGHED
DEGHNNOOSTUU	HOUND'S-TONGUE
DEGIIIKNNNRW	DRINKING WINE

DEGIIILMMNST	SLIMMING DIET
DEGIIILNPPSS	SIDESLIPPING
DEGIIIMNNNOS	DIMENSIONING
DEGIIINNORST	DISORIENTING
DEGIIINNRRST	DISINTERRING
DEGIIKLNOORT	LOOKING TIRED
DEGIILLNNUYY	UNYIELDINGLY
DEGIILLNOTTT	LITTLE TIN GOD
DEGIILNNOORS	SOLDIERING ON
DEGIILNNORSS	RIDING LESSON
DEGIILNNOSUY	INDIGENOUSLY
DEGIILNOPSSS	SLOPING SIDES
DEGIILNOQUXY	LIQUID OXYGEN
DEGIINNNNOOW	DOWNING IN ONE
DEGIINNNNPRU	UNDERPINNING
DEGIINNOSSUU	DISINGENUOUS
DEGIINNRRTUW	UNDERWRITING
DEGIINOOPPSS	OPPOSING SIDE
DEGIINOPPRSS	PREDISPOSING
DEGIKLMNOORW	WORKING MODEL
DEGIKNOORRRW	WORKING ORDER
DEGILLLMNSUW	SLUM DWELLING
DEGILLNNOPUW	DWELLING UPON
DEGILLORRTTU	GRILLED TROUT
DEGILMNOPRTU	MULTIPRONGED
DEGILNNNOSTW	NESTLING DOWN
DEGILNNORSUY	RESOUNDINGLY
DEGILNNOSTTW	SETTLING DOWN
DEGILNOOOOST	ODONTOLOGIES
DEGILNOOOSTT	DEONTOLOGIST
DEGILNOORRTX	GIRL NEXT DOOR
DEGILOOPRSTT	PROGLOTTIDES
DEGILOPRTUVY	PROVED GUILTY
DEGIMNNORRSS	MORNING DRESS
DEGIMNOORRSS	DRESSING ROOM
DEGIMNRSSTTU	MUTED STRINGS
DEGINNNNOOSTU	DOING ONE'S NUT
DEGINNOPPSTW	STEPPING DOWN
DEGINNOPRSSW	PRESSING DOWN
DEGINNOQRTUU	UNDERQUOTING
DEGINOOOQSTU	GOOD QUESTION
DEGINOOPPRRV	DROPPING OVER
DEGINOOSTTTW	GETS DOWN TO IT
DEGLLNORSSUY	GROUNDLESSLY
DEGMNOORRRUY	MERRY-GO-ROUND
DEGNNOORTTUW	WENT TO GROUND
DEGNOOOOORSTU	GONE OUTDOORS
DEGOOOOORSSTU	GOES OUTDOORS
DEGOOOPSTTUU	PUT TO GOOD USE
DEHHHMMORTTY	RHYTHM METHOD
DEHHIJLRTTUY	JULY THE THIRD
DEHHILNORSST	NORTH SHIELDS
DEHHILOSSSTU	SOUTH SHIELDS
DEHHIOPRRTYY	HYPERTHYROID
DEHHLNOSSTUU	SLEUTHHOUNDS
DEHHLOOOPSTU	HOLD OUT HOPES
	HOLDS OUT HOPE
DEHHNOOORSTU	DO THE HONOURS
DEHHNOOORSTW	SHOWN THE DOOR
DEHHOOORSSTW	SHOWS THE DOOR
DEHHOOORSSTTU	SHUTS THE DOOR
DEHIIILNPPSY	PHILIP SIDNEY
DEHIIIMMNNST	DIMINISHMENT
DEHIIIRRSTUV	HURRIED VISIT
DEHIIKLLNOOU	UNLIKELIHOOD
DEHIILOPRSVW	DEVIL WORSHIP
DEHIIOPRSSTW	SHOWED SPIRIT
DEHIKLLNORTW	KNOW THE DRILL
DEHIKNRRRSSY	DRINKS SHERRY
DEHILLNNOTWW	WENT DOWNHILL
DEHILNOORRSY	IN HOLY ORDERS
DEHILNOPSTTU	PUTS THE LID ON
DEHILNOSTTWW	WHITTLES DOWN
DEHILOOPPRTT	DROP THE PILOT
DEHILOOPRRSV	OVERLORDSHIP
DEHILOSSTWWW	WILD-WEST SHOW
DEHIMMNOOPRS	ENDOMORPHISM
DEHIMMNOOOTT	NOT IN THE MOOD
DEHIMNOOOORTY	DOMINO THEORY
DEHIMNORSTUY	HOME INDUSTRY
DEHINNOOQRUY	HYDROQUINONE
DEHINNORRSST	TORN IN SHREDS
DEHINOOPRSST	SPINSTERHOOD
DEHINOOPSTWY	SHOWED NO PITY
DEHINOORRSTW	IN OTHER WORDS
DEHINOORRSWY	SIR HENRY WOOD
DEHINPPTTUUW	PUT THE WIND UP
DEHIOOOPPRST	PHOTOPERIODS
DEHLLOORRTWY	OTHERWORLDLY
DEHLNNOOOSSW	HOLDS ONE'S OWN
DEHLNOORRSUY	HORRENDOUSLY
DEHLNORSTUUY	THUNDEROUSLY
DEHMOOPPRSSU	PSEUDOMORPHS
DEHNNOORTTUW	ROUND THE TOWN
DEHNOOOORSTUW	SOUTHERNWOOD
DEHNOOPSTTUW	DOWN THE SPOUT
DEHNOORRSSTT	TORN TO SHREDS
DEHOOPPRSSTT	STOPPED SHORT
DEIIILLNOPRR	PILLION RIDER
DEIIILMNTUVY	DIMINUTIVELY
DEIIKLNOOOTT	LOOKED INTO IT
DEIILLOOQSUZ	SOLILOQUIZED
DEIILLORRTTT	LITTLE DORRIT
DEIILMNNOPSS	SLIP ONES MIND
DEIILPRSTUVY	DISRUPTIVELY
DEIIMNNOOSSW	IN ONES WISDOM
DEIINOOPRSTT	PERIODONTIST
DEIINORSTTWW	WRITES IT DOWN
DEIIOOPPRRST	POOR-SPIRITED
DEIKLLMNOPSY	SPOKEN MILDLY
DEIKLLOOPPSY	LOOKED SLIPPY
DEIKLNOOUVWY	DEVIL YOU KNOW
DEIKLOOORRSW	LOOKS WORRIED
DEIKLOOOSSTU	LOOKS OUTSIDE
DEIKMNNNOOSW	KNOW ONES MIND
DEIKNOORRTVW	DRIVEN TO WORK
DEIKOOORRSTVW	DRIVES TO WORK
DEILLNORSVWY	DRIVEN SLOWLY
DEILLORSSVWY	DRIVES SLOWLY
DEILNNOORSTW	LOST IN WONDER
DEILOPTTUUZZ	PUZZLED IT OUT
DEIMMNORRTTY	TOMMY TRINDER
DEIMNOPRSTUY	MIND YOUR STEP
DEIMOPPRSTTU	PROMPTITUDES
DEINNNOPSTUY	NINETY POUNDS
DEINNOOPRSST	SEND TO PRISON
DEINOOOOPPRRT	PROPORTIONED
DEINOOOPRTTU	PORTIONED OUT
DEINOORSSUUW	SERIOUS WOUND
DEINOSSSSTUU	STUDIOUSNESS
DEIOOOOPRSTV	VOODOO PRIEST
DEIOOPRRSSTT	SPORTS EDITOR
DEIOOPRSSSSS	DISPOSSESSOR
DEIOOPSSSTTU	STOPS OUTSIDE
DEIOORTTTTTU	TROTTED IT OUT
DEKNOORRSSWW	WORKS WONDERS
DELLMOORRSUY	MERRY OLD SOUL
DELLNOPSSTUY	SLEPT SOUNDLY
DELNNNOORSTY	LORD TENNYSON
DELNOOORSSSU	DOLOROUSNESS
DELNOPPRSSTU	LENDS SUPPORT
DELNOPSSTUUY	STUPENDOUSLY

DEMNOOOSSTTU	DO ONES UTMOST
DEMNOOPSSUUY	PSEUDONYMOUS
DENNOORSSSUW	WONDROUSNESS
DENNOPSTTUWY	TWENTY POUNDS
DENOOORSTTUW	WENT OUTDOORS
DFFGGINOOTUY	GOING OFF DUTY
DFFHNOORSSTU	SHORT OF FUNDS
DFGGGINOOOOR	GOING FOR GOOD
DFGGIILNNNOW	FLINGING DOWN
DFGHHILNOORT	HOLDING FORTH
DFGIINOOPRRV	PROVIDING FOR
DFGIKLNNOOOW	KNOWING OF OLD
DFGILLNOOOST	FOLDING STOOL
DFGILLOOOORR	FOR GOOD OR ILL
DFGIMNNOORRU	ON FIRM GROUND
DFGIMNORSTUY	STUDYING FORM
DFGINNOOOSTU	SOUND FOOTING
DFHIKOOPRSWY	DROP OF WHISKY
DFHILNOOORSU	POUND FOOLIGH
DFIINOOOORRUW	WORD OF HONOUR
DFIIINOORSUV	DIVISION FOUR
DFIILMNRSTUY	FILM INDUSTRY
DFINNOOORSTT	STOOD IN FRONT
DFLLNNOOOOOP	POOL OF LONDON
DFLNNOOOOPRT	PORT OF LONDON
DFLOOOPRRSTW	WORLD OF SPORT
DFLOOORRSSTW	LOST FOR WORDS
DGGGHIIILNTU	GUIDING LIGHT
DGGGIINNORUV	GIVING GROUND
DGGGILNNRUUY	UNGRUDGINGLY
DGGHHIILNOTT	HOLDING TIGHT
DGGHHIINNOSU	HIGH-SOUNDING
DGGHIINNOOT	GO INTO HIDING
DGGHIIKNNOOT	GOOD THINKING
DGGHIILNNORT	LIGHTNING ROD
DGGHIINNNOOT	DOING NOTHING
	NOTHING DOING
DGGHINOOOOST	GOOD SHOOTING
DGGIIIILNNSV	LIVING IN DIGS
DGGIIKLNORST	STRIKING GOLD
DGGIIKNNNORS	DRINKING SONG
DGGIIKNNORRY	DRINKING ORGY
DGGIINNNORRU	RINGING ROUND
DGGIINNNORSU	RINGING SOUND
DGGIINNOOORS	GOING INDOORS
DGGIINNORRSU	RISING GROUND
DGGILNNOORSU	LOSING GROUND
DGGINNNOOPSW	SPONGING DOWN
DGHHIIMNORTU	MIDNIGHT HOUR
DGHHILNOOSTT	HOLDS ON TIGHT
DGHIIJLNNOOT	JOINT HOLDING
DGHIILLLNOST	HOLDING STILL
DGHIINNOORSU	DISHONOURING
DGHIINOOTTUW	DOING WITHOUT
DGHIMMNNOSUU	HUMMING SOUND
DGHIMNOOORUU	IN GOOD HUMOUR
DGHIMNOOOUWY	MIND HOW YOU GO
DGHINNOOOSTW	SHOOTING DOWN
DGHINNOOOSTW	SHOWING ROUND
DGHINNOORSUW	THROWING DOWN
DGHINNOORTWW	THROWING DOWN
DGHINNOOSTUW	SHOUTING DOWN
DGHINNORRUWY	HURRYING DOWN
DGHINNOSTTUW	SHUTTING DOWN
DGHIOOPRSTTU	STOOD UPRIGHT
DGHNNOOSTUUW	GUNSHOT WOUND
DGIIIINNOSSV	DIVISION SIGN
DGIIILLNNOOSV	LONG DIVISION
DGIIILLNNOTVW	LIVING IT DOWN
DGIIKNNOOPRST	STOP DRINKING
DGIIKNNORSTW	STRIKING DOWN
DGIIKNOORRTW	RIDING TO WORK

DGIILOOPRSUY	PRODIGIOUSLY
DGIIMNNOPRST	SPRING TO MIND
DGIKLNNOOORU	LOOKING ROUND
DGILNNOORTTU	TURN INTO GOLD
DGILNOOOOSTT	ODONTOLOGIST
DGILNOOPPSUY	IN GOOD SUPPLY
DGIMNNOPRSTU	SPRUNG TO MIND
DGINNNNORRUU	RUNNING ROUND
DGINNNORRTUU	TURNING ROUND
DGINNOOOPSTW	STOOPING DOWN
DGINNOOOPSWW	SWOOPING DOWN
DGINNORRSSUU	SURROUNDINGS
DGLOOPRSSSUU	SURPLUS GOODS
DGNNOORRSTUU	RUNS TO GROUND
DGNOOPRRSSTU	SPORTS GROUND
DHHLOOOOOTTT	TOO HOT TO HOLD
DHIIKKNRSSWY	DRINKS WHISKY
DHILNORSSTTU	HOLDS IN TRUST
DIIILOOFRRSUU	YOUR LORDSHIP
DHIMOOPRRSTY	HYDROTROPISM
DHINOOORSTTT	ORTHODONTIST
DHINOPRSTTUY	THIRTY POUNDS
DHLLOOOPPSUY	PHYLLOPODOUS
DHLNOOORTUXY	UNORTHODOXLY
DHMMPPTTUUYY	HUMPTY DUMPTY
DIIIINOQSSTU	DISQUISITION
DIIILLNOSSSU	DISILLUSIONS
DIIINOOPSSST	DISPOSITIONS
DIILLMPSTTUY	PUTS IT MILDLY
DIILNOOSSSTU	DISSOLUTIONS
DINOOOPRRSST	INDOOR SPORTS
DINOOPRSTTUW	PUT INTO WORDS
DKLNNOOOOPUW	LOOK DOWN UPON
DLLMNNOOOTUY	DULL MONOTONY
DNOOOPRSTTUW	PUT DOWN ROOTS
DNOOOPTTUWWW	TWO-UP TWO-DOWN
DOOOOPRRSTTU	OUTDOOR SPORT
EEEEEENOSTYY	SEEN EYE TO EYE
EEEEEEOSSTYY	SEES EYE TO EYE
EEEEEFFLNOST	FEEL ONES FEET
EEEEEGNRSTVW	SWEET REVENGE
EEEEEFFLLNOSS	FEELS ONESELF
EEEEEFFLNORSS	FREES ONESELF
EEEEFGHILNRW	FREEWHEELING
EEEEFGHLRSTU	FEELS THE URGE
EEEEFGHORTTT	FEET TOGETHER
EEEEFGIINRRV	GIVE FREE REIN
EEEEFGIKNOSS	SKEIN OF GEESE
EEEEFGLLNOSS	FEEL ONE'S LEGS
EEEEFHLLLPSS	FEEL HELPLESS
EEEEFILNOTVV	FIVE TO ELEVEN
EEEEFINOPSTW	WIPE ONES FEET
EEEEFINRRSTT	INTEREST FREE
EEEEFLLNOSST	STEEL ONESELF
EEEEFLMORRSS	FEELS REMORSE
EEEEFLNNOPRS	PREEN ONESELF
EEEEFLNORSTX	EXERT ONESELF
EEEEFMPRSTUW	SWEET PERFUME
EEEEGHINORTV	OVER EIGHTEEN
EEEEGHLNSTTX	THE GENTLE SEX
EEEEGHRSSSTU	THREE GUESSES
EEEEGIILNPSS	SPIEGELEISEN
EEEEGIINOPRS	EPEIROGENIES
EEEEGINNOSTY	GET ONES EYE IN
EEEEGNRRSTTT	REGENT STREET
EEEEHHHLLRTW	WHERE THE HELL
EEEEHIKNOPTY	POKE IN THE EYE
EEEEHIKRSTTY	STRIKE THE EYE
EEEEHIMNRSTW	THREE WISE MEN
EEEEHIMNRTTX	IN THE EXTREME
EEEEHINSSTTV	THE SEVENTIES

EEEEHIPSSTWY	WIPES THE EYES	EEEFILNRSSTT	SELF-INTEREST
EEEEHKOPRSSU	HOUSEKEEPERS	EEEFILNSSTTX	SELF-EXISTENT
EEEEHLNRRSTW	STERN-WHEELER	EEEFILORRSVV	LIVES FOR EVER
EEEEHLNRSSTV	NEVERTHELESS	EEEFILOTTVVW	FIVE TO TWELVE
EEEEHNNPSSTV	EVEN STEPHENS	EEEFIRRRSSTV	FIRST RESERVE
EEEEHNOPSSTY	OPENS THE EYES	EEEFJLNNOOSY	ENJOY ONESELF
EEEEHNOSSTTT	SET ONES TEETH	EEEFKLNOPRSY	SPOKEN FREELY
EEEEIKNNRSTT	KEEN INTEREST	EEEFLLLORRSW	FLOWER SELLER
EEEEIMNPRRTX	EXPERIMENTER	EEEFLLMNOSSS	SENSE OF SMELL
EEEEIMNPRSSW	MINESWEEPERS	EEEFLLNOORSW	LOWER ONESELF
EEEEIMRSTVWX	EXTREME VIEWS	EEEFLLNOOSSS	LOSES ONESELF
EEEEINOPSSWY	WIPE ONES EYES	EEEFLLNSSSSS	SELFLESSNESS
EEEEINRRSTVW	SEVERE WINTER	EEEFLNNSSTUV	EVENTFULNESS
EEEEINSSSTWY	EYEWITNESSES	EEEFMOORSTUV	REFUSE TO MOVE
EEEEINSSSTTWX	SWEET SIXTEEN	EEEFNOORSTVY	EVERY SO OFTEN
EEEEKNNRTTVY	KENNY EVERETT	EEEFNRSTTUUV	FUTURE EVENTS
EEEEKOPRRSST	STOREKEEPERS	EEEGGGILLNPV	LEVEL PEGGING
EEEELLNORTVY	TELL EVERYONE	EEEGGHINRTTT	GETTING THERE
EEEELLPRRSST	PETER SELLERS	EEEGGHLORSTT	LEGS TOGETHER
EEEELLPSSTWY	SLEEP SWEETLY	EEEGGHNOORTT	GONE TOGETHER
EEEELNOPRRTT	LETTER OPENER	EEEGGHOORSTT	GOES TOGETHER
EEEELNOPSSUV	UP ONES SLEEVE	EEEGGHORSTTT	GETS TOGETHER
EEEELNPRSSSS	PEERLESSNESS	EEEGGLLOORRW	GEORGE ORWELL
EEEEMNOPRRTT	PENETROMETER	EEEGHHHIRSTT	THREE EIGHTHS
EEEEMNORSTTX	EXTENSOMETER	EEEGHHILNSTT	SEEN THE LIGHT
EEEENNOOPSSY	OPEN ONES EYES	EEEGHHILSSTT	SEES THE LIGHT
EEEENNPRRRTU	ENTREPRENEUR	EEEGHHINNSSTV	SEVEN EIGHTHS
EEEENNPRSSTT	PRESENT TENSE	EEEGHHISSSTT	SEE THE SIGHTS
EEEENORSSSTY	REST ONES EYES	EEEGHHLNRSTT	THREE LENGTHS
EEEENOSSSSUY	USES ONE'S EYES	EEEGHHOORSTW	WHO GOES THERE?
EEEENPRRSSSV	PERVERSENESS	EEEGHIINNNTV	IN THE EVENING
EEEEORRTTTTT	TEETER TOTTER	EEEGHIKNOPSU	HOUSEKEEPING
EEEFFGHOORWY	GEOFFREY HOWE		KEEPING HOUSE
EEEFFGIILNNR	FINER FEELING	EEEGHIKNRSTW	WE THREE KINGS
EEEFFHILRSTW	WHIFFLETREES	EEEGHILLPRST	LIGHT SLEEPER
EEEFFIILMNST	FIFTEEN MILES	EEEGHILNRSSV	ENGLISH VERSE
EEEFFIILNNTT	IN FINE FETTLE	EEEGHILORTTV	LIVE TOGETHER
EEEFFINORRST	EFFRONTERIES	EEEGHILRTTWW	WELTERWEIGHT
EEEFFINSSSUV	EFFUSIVENESS	EEEGHIMNOSTU	MEETING HOUSE
EEEFGGINNRRS	GREEN FINGERS		MEETINGHOUSE
EEEFGHIKNPRS	KEEPING FRESH	EEEGHIMRSTTY	EIGHTY METRES
EEEFGHILNOSW	WEIGH ONESELF	EEEGHINNRSSS	GREENISHNESS
EEEFGHIRRSTU	THREE FIGURES	EEEGHINNORSTV	SEVEN OR EIGHT
EEEFGIILNNVW	GIVEN NEW LIFE	EEEGHINSTTVW	GETS EVEN WITH
EEEFGIILNOSV	GIVE ONES LIFE	EEEGHINSTTVY	SEVENTY-EIGHT
EEEFGIILNSVW	GIVES NEW LIFE	EEEGHIQSTTUZ	TIGHT SQUEEZE
EEEFGILMNPTY	EMPTY FEELING	EEEGHLLNOPST	THE LONG SLEEP
EEEFGILNNSST	FLEETINGNESS	EEEGHNNRRSTT	STRENGTHENER
EEEFGILNRSTU	TRUE FEELINGS	EEEGHNOPRSTT	POTS THE GREEN
EEEFGINORRVZ	FREEZING OVER	EEEGHNORSSTT	TOGETHERNESS
EEEFGLLNOOST	LET ONESELF GO	EEEGHNORTTTW	WENT TOGETHER
EEEFGLLNOSST	FELT ONE'S LEGS	EEEGHOORSSTT	THREE STOOGES
EEEFGLNNSSUV	VENGEFULNESS	EEEGHOORTTYZ	HETEROZYGOTE
EEEFHIKNRRST	FREETHINKERS	EEEGIIKNPQTU	KEEPING QUIET
EEEFHIKOPRST	POKES THE FIRE	EEEGIILMNNTV	INVEIGLEMENT
EEEFHINRSSSV	FEVERISHNESS	EEEGIIMNNPSW	MINESWEEPING
EEEFHINSSTVV	FIVE SEVENTHS	EEEGIINNORRT	ORIENTEERING
EEEFHLLNOPSS	HELPS ONESELF	EEEGILLLNPSW	SLEEPING WELL
EEEFHMNRRSST	REFRESHMENTS	EEEGILRRSSVY	REGRESSIVELY
EEEFHNORSTTW	THE NEW FOREST	EEEGIMNPRRSU	REIGN SUPREME
EEEFHOOPRSSU	HOUSE OF PEERS	EEEGINNNOOSTY	GOT ONE'S EYE IN
EEEFHOOPRTTT	TOP OF THE TREE	EEEGINNOPRSV	OPENING VERSE
EEEFHORRSSTT	REST OF ESTHER	EEEGINNPRRST	REPRESENTING
EEEFIILLNOSV	LIVE ONES LIFE	EEEGINNPSSSW	SWEEPINGNESS
EEEFIILMMPRR	FILM PREMIERE	EEEGINNPSTUW	SWEETENING UP
EEEFIILNRSTT	LIFE INTEREST	EEEGINQRSSTU	SEQUESTERING
EEEFIIMNNNSS	FEMININENESS	EEEGINRRSSTT	STREET SINGER
EEEFIKLORRRW	RELIEF WORKER	EEEGIOORRSTU	GROTESQUERIE
EEEFILLNOOSS	LOSE ONES LIFE	EEEGKNORSTTU	TOKEN GESTURE
EEEFILLNSSSS	LIFELESSNESS	EEEGLNORSSST	REST ONES LEGS
EEEFILMNOOST	FEELS EMOTION	EEEGMNORSSSU	GRUESOMENESS

Word	Clue	Word	Clue
EEEGMOORSTTX	GO TO EXTREMES	EEEILLORSTTV	EVER SO LITTLE
EEEGNNORSSSU	GENEROUSNESS	EEEILLPRSSVY	ELVIS PRESLEY
EEEGNOOPRRST	PROGESTERONE	EEEILMNNPRTY	PREEMINENTLY
EEEGOOPPRSST	GOOSE-STEPPER	EEEILMNORSTU	SON ET LUMIERE
EEEGORRRSSST	RETROGRESSES	EEEILMNSSSST	TIMELESSNESS
EEEHHILLOSTW	OIL THE WHEELS	EEEILMNSSTVY	SEVENTY MILES
EEEHHILMOTTW	THE WHOLE TIME	EEEILMPPRTVY	PREEMPTIVELY
EEEHHILNPSTW	SPIN THE WHEEL	EEEILNNPRTVY	PREVENIENTLY
EEEHHINPSSSS	SHEEPISHNESS	EEEILNORSSTT	LOSE INTEREST
EEEHHIPRRSST	THE PERISHERS	EEEILNPRRSTT	TELEPRINTERS
EEEHHJNNTTTU	JUNE THE TENTH	EEEILNPRTVVY	PREVENTIVELY
EEEHHKLOOTTW	TOOK THE WHEEL	EEEILNRRRTVY	IRREVERENTLY
EEEHHKNNNORT	KENNETH HORNE	EEEILNRSSSST	TIRELESSNESS
EEEHHKRSTTTU	SEEK THE TRUTH	EEEILNRSSSTW	WESTERN ISLES
EEEHHLNORTUV	ELEVENTH HOUR	EEEILPRSSVXY	EXPRESSIVELY
	ELEVENTH-HOUR	EEEILRRRTTTW	LETTER WRITER
EEEHHMOPRRST	THERMOSPHERE	EEEIMMNPSTTU	UMPTEEN TIMES
EEEHIINRSTTU	THREE UNITIES	EEEIMNNORSSW	SWORN ENEMIES
EEEHIJMNNOTY	JOIN THE ENEMY	EEEIMNNPRSTT	PRESENTIMENT
EEEHIJNOQTUU	JOIN THE QUEUE	EEEIMNNRSTTV	REINVESTMENT
EEEHIKLNOOTY	LOOK IN THE EYE	EEEIMNNRSTTY	NINETY METRES
EEEHIKNRSSTT	RENT THE SKIES	EEEIMNNSSTUV	SEVEN MINUTES
EEEHILLMSTTT	TELLS THE TIME	EEEIMNORSSST	TIRESOMENESS
EEEHILPPRSTW	WHIPPLETREES	EEEIMNPRRSST	MISREPRESENT
EEEHILRRRSTW	WELSH TERRIER	EEEIMOORRSST	STEREOISOMER
EEEHILRSSSTV	SHIRT SLEEVES	EEEIMOPRRSTX	EXTEMPORISER
EEEHIMNNNRST	ENSHRINEMENT	EEEIMOPRRTXZ	EXTEMPORIZER
EEEHIMNRSTTU	THREE MINUTES	EEEIMOPRRSTX	EXTEMPORISES
EEEHINNOPSTT	SEEN THE POINT	EEEIMOPRSTUX	TIME EXPOSURE
EEEHINNORSTW	NONE THE WISER	EEEIMOPRSTXZ	EXTEMPORIZES
EEEHINOPSSTT	SEES THE POINT	EEEIMORSVWWY	WORMS EYE VIEW
EEEHINPRSTVY	HYPERTENSIVE	EEEINNNOSSSS	IN ONES SENSES
EEEHIOPRSTTT	THE POTTERIES	EEEINNOSSTTT	TEN-TON TESSIE
EEEHIPRRSSTT	THREE STRIPES	EEEINNPRSSTX	INEXPERTNESS
EEEHIRRSSSTT	THREE SISTERS	EEEINNPRSTUV	SUPERVENIENT
EEEHJMOPRRTY	JEREMY THORPE	EEEINORRRSSV	REVERSIONERS
EEEHJMPQTUUU	JUMP THE QUEUE	EEEINPRRSTTT	INTERPRETERS
EEEHLLNOPTYY	POLYETHYLENE	EEEINPRRSSST	INTERSPERSES
EEEHLLNPSSSS	HELPLESSNESS	EEEINRRSTTVW	WRITTEN VERSE
EEEHLMNNOSTV	ELEVEN MONTHS	EEEINRSSSSTV	SEVEN SISTERS
EEEHLMNOSSSS	HOMELESSNESS	EEEIOOPSTVWX	EXPOSE TO VIEW
EEEHLNOPSSSS	HOPELESSNESS	EEEJMNRRSTTY	JERMYN STREET
EEEHLOOSSTTV	LOSES THE VOTE	EEEKLNOOSSTX	EXOSKELETONS
EEEHLOPRRTUV	PROVE THE RULE	EEEKLNRRTUWY	WEEKLY RETURN
EEEHLOPRSTTW	POTTERS WHEEL	EEEKLOPRRTWY	WEEKLY REPORT
EEEHMMORRSTT	THERMOMETERS	EEEKLORRSSTW	STEELWORKERS
EEEHMNNNORTT	ENTHRONEMENT	EEELLLNRSSTY	RELENTLESSLY
EEEHMOORRSTW	METEOR SHOWER	EEELLNOORSSY	ROLL ONES EYES
EEEHMOPRRSST	SPHEROMETERS	EEELLNOSSSSV	LOVELESSNESS
EEEHMORTTUXY	EXTREME YOUTH	EEELLPSSTTWY	SLEPT SWEETLY
EEEHNNOOORTT	THREE TO ONE ON	EEELMNNOOSSS	LONESOMENESS
EEEHNNOORSTW	NONE THE WORSE	EEELMNNOOSTT	ON ONES METTLE
EEEHNORSSTTT	ON THE STREETS	EEELMNNRSTUY	MERSEY TUNNEL
EEEHNOSSSTUY	SHUT ONES EYES	EEELMNPPRSTU	SUPPLEMENTER
EEEHORRRSTTU	SHEER TORTURE	EEELMOPPRRTT	TELEPROMPTER
EEEIIINNNNNN	NINE NINE NINE	EEELNNOSSSST	TONELESSNESS
EEEIILMNSSTX	SIXTEEN MILES	EEELNNSSSSTU	TUNELESSNESS
EEEIILPPRSTX	PERPLEXITIES	EEELNORSSSTU	RESOLUTENESS
EEEIILPRTTVY	REPETITIVELY	EEELNRSSSSST	RESTLESSNESS
EEEIINPRRTTV	INTERPRETIVE	EEEMNNPRSSTT	PRESENTMENTS
EEEIINPRSSVX	INEXPRESSIVE	EEEMNORSTTUV	MOUNT EVEREST
EEEIINRRSTVW	INTERVIEWERS	EEEMNNRSTTTWY	TWENTY METRES
EEEIIPPRSTTU	PERPETUITIES	EEEMOPPRRSUW	SUPREME POWER
EEEIIPQRRSTU	PREREQUISITE	EEEMPRSSSSST	SEMPSTRESSES
EEEIKLMNOORT	ONE KILOMETRE	EEENNNOPRSSU	PURE NONSENSE
EEEIKLNOSSST	SKELETONISES	EEENOOPSSTUY	UP TO ONES EYES
EEEIKLNOSSTZ	SKELETONIZES	EEENOORSSTTT	TESTOSTERONE
EEEIKNOPPRRS	KEEP PRISONER	EEENOPRSSTTU	UP ONES STREET
EEEILLLOPPTT	LITTLE PEOPLE	EEENOPSSSTUY	SETS EYES UPON
EEEILLMSSTWY	SMILE SWEETLY	EEEOPPRSSSSS	PREPOSSESSES
EEEILLNRSTTT	SILENT LETTER	EEEOPRRSSTTY	STEREOTYPERS

EEEOPRRTTTVY	REVERT TO TYPE
EEEPRRRSSTUY	TYRE PRESSURE
EEFFFILORTTU	FUTILE EFFORT
EEFFFINORTTY	FIFTEEN FORTY
	FORTY FIFTEEN
EEFFFLNOSSTU	STUFF ONESELF
EEFFGHIILNST	FISHING FLEET
EEFFGHIILORS	SIGH OF RELIEF
EEFFGILLLNOV	LEVELLING OFF
EEFFGILNNNUY	FEELING FUNNY
	FUNNY FEELING
EEFFGILNRSSU	GLUE-SNIFFERS
EEFFGLLNORUY	FULL OF ENERGY
EEFFHHIJNTTU	JUNE THE FIFTH
EEFFHIKLOSTT	KETTLE OF FISH
EEFFHILOPSST	FLEET OF SHIPS
EEFFHILSTTVW	FIVE TWELFTHS
EEFFHINORSTU	FIFTEEN HOURS
EEFFHIOORRST	FIT FOR HEROES
EEFFHIORRSTT	FIRST OF THREE
EEFFHLORRSSW	FRESH FLOWERS
EEFFHMNOOORT	OFFER THE MOON
EEFFHNOOOPRS	OFFERS NO HOPE
EEFFIIILLORX	ELIXIR OF LIFE
EEFFIIKLNOST	FIFTEEN KILOS
EEFFIILMMOTY	MY TIME OF LIFE
EEFFILLLOOST	FILLET OF SOLE
EEFFINOOTTUV	FIVE OUT OF TEN
EEFFIOORRSSU	SERIOUS OFFER
EEFFLLOOSTUU	FELL OUT OF USE
EEFFLLORSSTY	EFFORTLESSLY
EEFFNRRSSTTU	STERNER STUFF
EEFGGHIILNRT	FEELING RIGHT
EEFGGHINRSTT	GETTING FRESH
EEFGGHORSTUU	SOUGHT REFUGE
EEFGGIILNRVY	GIVING FREELY
EEFGGINOORRV	GOING FOR EVER
EEFGGIOPRTTY	PETTIFOGGERY
EEFGHHIIILNR	IN HIGH RELIEF
EEFGHHIJNOTU	EIGHTH OF JUNE
EEFGHIIKNNRT	FREE THINKING
	FREETHINKING
EEFGHIILNRRT	FREIGHTLINER
EEFGHIILRTTW	WEIGHT-LIFTER
EEFGHIIPRRTZ	PRIZEFIGHTER
EEFGHIKOPSST	KEEPS SIGHT OF
EEFGHILMNOTT	LENGTH OF TIME
EEFGHILNNOST	FEELS NOTHING
EEFGHILNNOSW	SHOWN FEELING
EEFGHILNOSSW	SHOWS FEELING
EEFGHILNRRSY	REFRESHINGLY
EEFGHINNPRSU	FRESHENING UP
EEFGHINOSSST	SENSE OF SIGHT
EEFGHOOPRRTU	GROUP OF THREE
EEFGIIILLNNS	IN SINGLE FILE
EEFGIIJLNNOY	ENJOYING LIFE
EEFGIILLLNSY	FEELING SILLY
EEFGIILLNRTT	LITTLE FINGER
EEFGIILLNRUV	GIVE FULL REIN
EEFGIILMNPXY	EXEMPLIFYING
EEFGIIMMNRSW	FREE-SWIMMING
EEFGIIMNNNRT	INFRINGEMENT
EEFGIINNSSSU	USING FINESSE
EEFGIINSSTUV	FUGITIVENESS
EEFGIKNNOORT	FORETOKENING
EEFGIKNOOPTU	OUT OF KEEPING
EEFGILLORUVY	LOVELY FIGURE
EEFGILNOOTTU	GET OUT OF LINE
EEFGILNORRSY	FEELING SORRY
EEFGILNOSSTU	SENSE OF GUILT
EEFGIMNNOORY	FOREIGN MONEY

EEFGIMNOORTT	FOOT REGIMENT
EEFGINNORTUY	UNIT OF ENERGY
EEFGINORRSUU	FERRUGINEOUS
EEFGINORRTTU	FERRETING OUT
EEFGINORSSTU	REFUSE TO SIGN
EEFGLLNORSTY	FEEL STRONGLY
EEFGMNOORSTT	FORGET-ME-NOTS
EEFHHMMMOOOR	HOME FROM HOME
EEFHIILLSTTV	LIFTS THE VEIL
EEFHIJNRSTTU	JUNE THE FIRST
EEFHILNNORTT	THE FRONT LINE
EEFHILNOPPST	SLIP OF THE PEN
EEFHILOOPRTW	WIPE THE FLOOR
EEFHILRRRSTY	SHERRY TRIFLE
EEFHIMMNOORT	MOTHER OF MINE
EEFHIORSTTVY	FORTY THIEVES
EEFHLLNOOSTW	HONEST FELLOW
EEFHLLOPRSUY	HELP YOURSELF
EEFHLNNOOSSW	SHOWN ONESELF
EEFHLNOOOSST	SHOOT ONESELF
EEFHLNOORSUW	ON FOUR WHEELS
EEFHLNOOSSSW	SHOWS ONESELF
EEFHLORRTTTU	FOURTH LETTER
EEFHMMNOORSW	NEWS FROM HOME
EEFHMMNOORTT	FOR THE MOMENT
EEFHMOORRSTT	FOSTER MOTHER
EEFHNOORRSST	FORESHORTENS
EEFHNORRTTUV	VENTURE FORTH
EEFHNNORSSTUV	FOUR SEVENTHS
EEFHOOOPPRTW	PROPHET OF WOE
EEFIIILLNNTV	NINE TILL FIVE
EEFIIINNNSST	INFINITENESS
EEFIIINNRSST	INTENSIFIERS
EEFIIKLNORSS	RISK ONES LIFE
EEFIILOSSSTU	TISSUE OF LIES
EEFIIMNORSSU	SEMINIFEROUS
EEFIIORRSSTZ	TRIES FOR SIZE
EEFIKLLLNOSS	KILLS ONESELF
EEFIKOOPSTTU	KEEPS OUT OF IT
EEFILLNOOPSS	SPOIL ONESELF
EEFILMNOPTTY	PLENTY OF TIME
EEFILMOOORST	TOMFOOLERIES
EEFILMORRSTU	FLUORIMETERS
EEFILNNORSSU	RUINS ONESELF
EEFILNNQRTUY	INFREQUENTLY
EEFILNOORRTX	RETROFLEXION
EEFILNOSSSTU	SUITS ONESELF
EEFILOOPRRST	PROFITEROLES
EEFIMNNORRST	FRONTIERSMEN
EEFIMPRRRSSU	FIRM PRESSURE
EEFINNNOOTTU	NINE OUT OF TEN
EEFINOTTTVWY	TWENTY-FIVE TO
EEFIORRRSSTT	FOSTER SISTER
EEFKOORRSTUW	REFUSE TO WORK
EEFLLLOORWWY	YELLOW FLOWER
EEFLLMOORSSS	SMELL OF ROSES
EEFLLMORRSUY	REMORSEFULLY
EEFLLNNOOTUV	TUNNEL OF LOVE
EEFLLNNTUUVY	UNEVENTFULLY
EEFLLNOOOPSW	ONE FELL SWOOP
EEFLLORSTWYY	FLOWERY STYLE
EEFLLPRRSSUU	FULL PRESSURE
EEFLMNOOORSS	LOSE ONES FORM
EEFLMNOOPRTW	FLOWERPOT MEN
EEFLMNORSSSS	FORMLESSNESS
EEFLNNOOSSTU	FOUL ONE'S NEST
EEFLNOOPPRTY	PLENTY OF ROPE
EEFLNOOPSSTT	LEFT ONE'S POST
EEFLOORRRRTU	RULE OF TERROR
EEFLPRSTTUUY	PRETTY USEFUL
EEFMNOOOPRRY	MONEY FOR ROPE

EEFMNOPRTTTU	TEMPT FORTUNE	EEGHIMMOOOTT	TIME TO GO HOME
EEFNNNOOPRUY	FOURPENNY ONE	EEGHIMNNOSTW	SOMETHING NEW
EEFNNOOOPRST	PERSON OF NOTE	EEGHIMNOPRSS	PRESSING HOME
EEFNNORRSTTW	WESTERN FRONT	EEGHINNNRTUW	RUNG IN THE NEW
EEFNNORSTTUV	TURN OF EVENTS	EEGHINNOPSSY	HYPNOGENESIS
EEFNOOORSSST	FOOTSORENESS	EEGHINNPSTWY	PENNYWEIGHTS
EEGGGGHMRRUU	HUGGER-MUGGER	EEGHINOORSST	ORTHOGENESIS
EEGGGIIKNNOP	KEEPING GOING	EEGHINOPSTTT	GETS THE POINT
EEGGGINORRRS	GINGER ROGERS	EEGHINOSSSTW	GETS ONE'S WISH
EEGGHIIILNTV	GIVING THE LIE	EEGHJMMOORTY	JOG THE MEMORY
EEGGHIIKNPST	KEEPING SIGHT	EEGHKOORRTTW	WORK TOGETHER
EEGGHIILNNNT	ENLIGHTENING	EEGHKORSSTTW	GETS THE WORKS
EEGGHIINNSST	SEEING THINGS	EEGHLLOOPRST	HOT GOSPELLER
EEGGHIINNSTV	GIVEN THE SIGN	EEGHLLOPRTTU	PULL TOGETHER
EEGGHIINRRTV	VEERING RIGHT	EEGHLMNNOORS	LONGSHOREMEN
EEGGHIINSSTV	GIVES THE SIGN	EEGHLMOPRTTU	LUMP TOGETHER
EEGGHIINTTUV	GIVE IT THE GUN	EEGHLNORSSTT	LOSE STRENGTH
EEGGHIKNOTTT	GETTING THE O.K.	EEGHLNRSSSTT	STRENGTHLESS
EEGGIIINOOOTU	GUESSES RIGHT	EEGHLOOORSTU	HETEROLOGOUS
EEGGHOORRTTW	GROW TOGETHER	EEGHMMNOORRSW	WHOREMONGERS
EEGGIIIKLNPV	KEEPING VIGIL	EEGHMNOORTTU	MOTHER TONGUE
EEGGIIKNOPST	KEEPS IT GOING	EEGHNOOOOTTZ	GONE TO THE ZOO
EEGGIILNNRSS	GINGERLINESS	EEGHNOORSSUU	HOUSE SURGEON
EEGGILNOOPST	GOING TO SLEEP	EEGHOOOOSTTZ	GOES TO THE ZOO
EEGGILSSTUVY	SUGGESTIVELY	EEGHOOOPRTTV	GO OVER THE TOP
EEGGINNNRRTU	TURNING GREEN	EEGHOOPSTTTT	GETS TO THE TOP
EEGGINNPRRSS	SPRING GREEN	EEGHOORSSTTY	THE STORY GOES
EEGGINNPRTTU	PUTTING GREEN	EEGHOORSTUYZ	HETEROZYGOUS
EEGGINORSTTW	GETTING WORSE	EEGHOPPPRSST	PEPPERS GHOST
EEGGINPSTTTU	GETTING UPSET	EEGHOPRSTTTU	PUTS TOGETHER
EEGGNOORSSSU	GORGEOUSNESS	EEGIIILLNTTT	LETTING IT LIE
EEGGNORSSSUW	GUESSES WRONG	EEGIIINNRTVW	INTERVIEWING
EEGHHHORRTUW	WHERETHROUGH	EEGIIKLLNPST	KEEPING STILL
EEGHHHORSSTU	HUGS THE SHORE	EEGIIKLMNPSS	KEEPS SMILING
EEGHHIILLMTT	THE LIMELIGHT	EEGIIKNNNOPT	NOT IN KEEPING
EEGHHIINPRSS	SHEEPISH GRIN	EEGIIKNOPTTU	KEEPING IT OUT
EEGHHIINRSTT	HIGH INTEREST	EEGIILLLNNOT	TELLING NO LIE
EEGHHILNOTTV	LIGHT THE OVEN	EEGIILLLNPPS	SLEEPING PILL
EEGHHILRSTWW	WHEELWRIGHTS	EEGIILMMNNPT	IMPLEMENTING
EEGHHIMNPTUV	GIVEN THE HUMP	EEGIILMNNRST	INTERMINGLES
EEGHHIMPSTUV	GIVES THE HUMP	EEGIILNNOPST	SLEEPING ON IT
EEGHHINPSTUV	GIVEN THE PUSH	EEGIIMNNNOTU	UNION MEETING
EEGHHINRTTVY	THE VERY THING	EEGIIMNNNRSS	MINNESINGERS
EEGHHIORSTTU	SEE IT THROUGH	EEGIIMNNORST	REMONETISING
EEGHHIPRRSSU	HIGH PRESSURE	EEGIIMNNORTZ	REMONETIZING
	HIGH-PRESSURE	EEGIINNNORTT	ENTERING INTO
EEGHHIPSSTUV	GIVES THE PUSH	EEGIINNPRRST	ENTERPRISING
EEGHHOPRSTUW	SWEEP THROUGH	EEGIINNPRRTT	INTERPRETING
EEGHIIKNPSST	KEEPS IN SIGHT	EEGIINNRRTTY	ETERNITY RING
EEGHIILMNOTT	GONE THE LIMIT	EEGIINNRSSTW	WESTERNISING
EEGHIILMOSTT	GOES THE LIMIT	EEGIINNRSTWZ	WESTERNIZING
EEGHIILNNPRS	REPLENISHING	EEGIINOPRSWZ	SEIZING POWER
EEGHIILNPSTV	GIVEN THE SLIP	EEGIINRRSTVW	WRITING VERSE
EEGHIILPSSTV	GIVES THE SLIP	EEGIIOSSTTTW	GETS WISE TO IT
EEGHIIMNSTTU	EIGHT MINUTES	EEGIJMNPQUUU	QUEUE JUMPING
EEGHIINNNRTW	RING IN THE NEW		QUEUE-JUMPING
EEGHIINRSSST	TIGERISHNESS	EEGIKNNOORST	GONE ON STRIKE
EEGHIINRSTUX	EXTINGUISHER	EEGIKNNOPRTY	KEEP ON TRYING
EEGHIINSSTUX	EXTINGUISHES	EEGIKNOORSST	GOES ON STRIKE
EEGHIJNOORTT	JOIN TOGETHER	EEGILLLNOTUV	LEVELLING OUT
EEGHIKLNOPSS	SPOKE ENGLISH	EEGILLNNNOOT	TELLING NO ONE
EEGHIKLNORTT	LINK TOGETHER	EEGILLNOOSST	SELENOLOGIST
EEGHIKNNQSTU	QUEENS KNIGHT	EEGILLNOOSTT	LETTING LOOSE
EEGHIKNOPRST	KEEPS RIGHT ON	EEGILLNPPRXY	PERPLEXINGLY
EEGHIKNORTTT	KNIT TOGETHER	EEGILLNRSTWY	SWELTERINGLY
EEGHIKNPRSSU	SHEEPSKIN RUG	EEGILLOOPSST	SPELEOLOGIST
EEGHIKNPSSTU	SPIKE THE GUNS	EEGILLOOSSTT	TELEOLOGISTS
EEGHIKNRRSTU	HUNGER STRIKE	EEGILMNORTVW	LONG-TERM VIEW
EEGHILLSSTWY	WEIGHTLESSLY	EEGILMOOPSTY	EPISTEMOLOGY
EEGHILMNORVW	OVERWHELMING	EEGILMOOSSTY	ETYMOLOGISES
EEGHILNOPSSY	PHYLOGENESIS	EEGILMOOSTYZ	ETYMOLOGIZES

EEGILNNOPRSS	SINGLE PERSON
EEGILNNORTUV	VOLUNTEERING
EEGILNNOSSSV	GIVEN LESSONS
EEGILNOOPRSS	LOSE ONES GRIP
EEGILNOORRSW	LOWER REGIONS
EEGILNOOSSTT	SETTING LOOSE
EEGILNOPRTTU	TRIPLE-TONGUE
EEGILNOPSSTY	POLYGENESIST
EEGILNOSSSSV	GIVES LESSONS
EEGILOPRSSTT	POLTERGEISTS
EEGILQRRRSUY	GREY SQUIRREL
EEGIMNNORRVY	EVERY MORNING
EEGINNOOOPTT	GONE ON TIPTOE
EEGINOOOPRTU	GO INTO EUROPE
EEGINOOOPSTT	GOES ON TIPTOE
EEGINOOPRRVW	OVERPOWERING
EEGINOOPRSSS	SPOROGENESIS
EEGINOPPRRSU	UPPER REGIONS
EEGINOPPRSTV	OVERSTEPPING
	STEPPING OVER
EEGINOPRSSSS	REPOSSESSING
EEGINOPRSTTY	STEREOTYPING
EEGINOPSSTTT	GETS INTO STEP
EEGINOQSTUUZ	SQUEEZING OUT
EEGINORSSSUV	GRIEVOUSNESS
EEGINORSSTTT	SETTING STORE
EEGINOSSSUUX	EXIGUOUSNESS
EEGINPRRSSST	PRESTRESSING
EEGINPRSSTTU	GUTTERSNIPES
EEGIOPRRSSSV	PROGRESSIVES
EEGLLLNOPSSU	PULLS ONE'S LEG
EEGLMNNOOOPR	PROLEGOMENON
EEGLNNORSUUY	UNGENEROUSLY
EEGNNOORRSTW	GROWN ON TREES
EEGNNORRSSTV	STRONG NERVES
EEHHHIIRTTTT	THE THIRTIETH
EEHHIINSSSTV	THIEVISHNESS
EEHHIJNNNTTU	JUNE THE NINTH
EEHHIJNSTTUX	JUNE THE SIXTH
EEHHIKLOOPSS	LOOK SHEEPISH
EEHHILLNOPTY	THEOPHYLLINE
EEHHILLORSTV	OVER THE HILLS
EEHHINRSSSSW	SHREWISHNESS
EEHHIOPSSSTY	HYPOTHESISES
EEHHIOPSSTYZ	HYPOTHESIZES
EEHHJLNTTTUY	JULY THE TENTH
EEHHLLRTTTTU	TELL THE TRUTH
EEHHLOOSSTTW	STOLE THE SHOW
EEHHMOORSSTU	HOUSEMOTHERS
EEHHNOORRTTW	WHETHER OR NOT
EEHHNORSTTTW	THE NORTH-WEST
EEHHOOORRSST	SHORE TO SHORE
EEHHOOOSSTUU	HOUSE TO HOUSE
	HOUSE-TO-HOUSE
EEHHOOPRSSTW	SHOW THE ROPES
EEHHOOSSUUYY	HOUSEY HOUSEY
EEHHOSSTTTUW	THE SOUTH-WEST
EEHIIIMNNRTT	IN THE INTERIM
EEHIIIRRRRST	IRISH TERRIER
EEHIIKNPRSSY	HYPERKINESIS
EEHIIKNRSSSW	WHISKERINESS
EEHIIILLLRTTT	LITTLE HITLER
EEHIIILMNORT	THREE MILLION
EEHIILMNTTTW	WENT THE LIMIT
EEHIILMORTTV	OVER THE LIMIT
EEHIILNOSTTU	IN SILHOUETTE
EEHIILNPRSTY	PREHENSILITY
EEHIILNQRSSU	RELINQUISHES
EEHIILNRSSSV	LIVERISHNESS
EEHIILNRSTVW	WIN THE SILVER
EEHIILNSTTTW	WINS THE TITLE

EEHIIMOPRRSV	IMPOVERISHER
EEHIIMOPRSSV	IMPOVERISHES
EEHIINNPRTTW	TIP THE WINNER
EEHIINOQTUVV	ON THE QUI VIVE
EEHIINPRSTWZ	WINS THE PRIZE
EEHIINRSTTTW	WITH INTEREST
EEHIKLNNRRWY	HENRY WINKLER
EEHIKMNORRSY	YORKSHIREMEN
EEHIKNOSTTTW	WET TO THE SKIN
EEHILMNORSST	MOTHERLINESS
EEHILMOPRRSU	MILES PER HOUR
EEHILNNNORRT	NORTHERN LINE
EEHILNNPSTWY	PENNY WHISTLE
EEHILNNSSTTU	LETS IN THE SUN
EEHILNOPRSTT	PETER SHILTON
EEHILNOPSSTT	TELEPHONISTS
EEHILNORSTVW	WON THE SILVER
EEHILOPRSSST	HOSTILE PRESS
EEHILOPSTTTV	SPLIT THE VOTE
EEHILORRSSUU	LEISURE HOURS
EEHILRSSTTWW	WRESTLES WITH
EEHIMOPRSTTY	MORES THE PITY
EEHIMRRSTTTY	THIRTY METRES
EEHINNOOPPSS	PIN ONES HOPES
EEHINNOOPTTU	OUT IN THE OPEN
EEHINNOPRSTY	HYPERTENSION
EEHINNOPSTTU	UP TO THE NINES
EEHINOPPRSST	THE PIPERS SON
EEHINORSSTTT	THE ROT SETS IN
EEHINORSSTTW	SHOW INTEREST
EEHINRSSSSTY	SYNTHESISERS
EEHINRSSSTYZ	SYNTHESIZERS
EEHIOOPRSTTT	RISE TO THE TOP
EEHKMNORSSUY	RHESUS MONKEY
EEHKNOOPRSTW	KNOW THE ROPES
EEHKNOORUWWY	YOU-KNOW-WHERE
EEHLLMOORTVY	MOTHERLY LOVE
EEHLLOOPTTWY	POT THE YELLOW
EEHLMNOOPRSY	HOMELY PERSON
EEHLMNOSTTVW	TWELVE MONTHS
EEHLNRSSSSTU	RUTHLESSNESS
EEHLOORRSTTU	RULE THE ROOST
EEHLOOSSSSTT	LOSES THE TOSS
EEHMMORSSSUU	SUMMERHOUSES
EEHMNOOORSTU	HETERONOMOUS
EEHMNOORSTUY	HETERONYMOUS
EEHMNRRRSUYY	NURSERY RHYME
EEHNNOOORSTW	ONE-HORSE TOWN
EEHNNORRSTTW	NORTHWESTERN
EEHNOOOTTTWZ	WENT TO THE ZOO
EEHNORSSTTUW	SOUTHWESTERN
EEHOOOPRSTTT	ROSE TO THE TOP
EEHOOPPRSTTU	TO THE PURPOSE
EEHOOPTTTTUV	PUT TO THE VOTE
EEHOORRSTTVW	OVER THE WORST
EEHOPSTTTTTU	PUT TO THE TEST
EEHORSSSTTUW	SOUTHWESTERS
EEIIILMMNNTT	TEN-MILE LIMIT
EEIIINRSSTUV	UNIVERSITIES
EEIIKKLLNOTU	LIKE UNTO LIKE
EEIIKKMNPRST	STRIKE ME PINK!
EEIIKLLNNSSU	UNLIKELINESS
EEIIKMNRRSST	MINERS STRIKE
EEIIKNNOPPRS	KEEP IN PRISON
EEIIILLLMTTW	TIME WILL TELL
EEIIILMMNOPU	MILE UPON MILE
EEIIILMNTTTX	TILL NEXT TIME
EEIIILNNNOPU	LINE UPON LINE
EEIIILNSSTVY	LIVES IN STYLE
EEIIILLOPTVXY	EXPLOITIVELY
EEIIILLPPRSST	PIPISTRELLES

EEIILLRSSTTT	LITTLE SISTER	EEIMNNNORSTV	ENVIRONMENTS
EEIILMMNOSSW	WINSOME SMILE	EEIMNNOOTTTX	NEXT TO NO TIME
EEIILMNNSSTU	UNTIMELINESS	EEIMOPPRSSSU	SUPERIMPOSES
EEIILMNOPSST	IMPOLITENESS	EEIMOPRRSSUV	SURPRISE MOVE
EEIILMOORVZZ	MEZZO-RILIEVO	EEINNOOPQSTU	OPEN QUESTION
EEIILMPRSSVY	IMPRESSIVELY	EEINNOOPTTTW	WENT ON TIPTOE
	PERMISSIVELY	EEINNOPRSSUV	UNRESPONSIVE
EEIILNNOOSTV	ON TELEVISION	EEINNOPRRSTUV	SUPERVENTION
EEIILNNOPSTT	STEP INTO LINE	EEINNOQSTTUX	NEXT QUESTION
EEIILNORRSTV	RISE IN REVOLT	EEINOOPPSSST	OPPOSITENESS
EEIILNPPRSSS	SLIPPERINESS	EEINOOPRRSSS	RESPONSORIES
EEIILNPSSSST	PITILESSNESS	EEINOOPRRSTW	RISEN TO POWER
EEIIMMMMNNOTT	MOMENT IN TIME	EEINOOPRSSSS	REPOSSESSION
EEIIMMNNNSST	IMMINENTNESS	EEINOORRRSTV	RETROVERSION
EEIIMNNRTTTT	INTERMITTENT	EEINOORRSTVX	EXTROVERSION
EEIIMNOQSTTU	QUESTION TIME	EEINOPRRRSSU	SENIOR PURSER
EEIIMNPRRSTT	MISINTERPRET	EEINOPRSSSSU	SUPERSESSION
EEIIMNRSSSUV	MISS UNIVERSE	EEINOPRSSSTV	SPORTIVENESS
EEIINNNNOTVW	NEW INVENTION	EEINOPRSSSUV	PERVIOUSNESS
EEIINNNORTTV	INTERVENTION		PREVIOUSNESS
EEIINNRSSSST	SINISTERNESS	EEINOPRSTTUV	PETER USTINOV
EEIINOPPRSST	PROPENSITIES	EEINORSSSTUV	VITREOUSNESS
EEIINOPSSSTV	POSITIVENESS	EEINOSSSSTUW	USES ONE'S WITS
EEIINPRRTTUV	INTERRUPTIVE	EEINRRSSTTUV	SERVE ITS TURN
EEIINRSSTTUV	INVESTITURES	EEIOOPRRSSTW	RISES TO POWER
EEIIOOPRRSST	REPOSITORIES	FFIOPRRSTTWY	WRITES POETRY
EEIIPRSSTVXY	EXPRESSIVITY	EEKKOORRRSTV	VOORTREKKERS
EEIJKNNOPSST	SPOKEN IN JEST	EEKLMNOPUYZZ	MONKEY PUZZLE
EEIJLMNSTTUY	UNTIMELY JEST	EEKLMOOPSSUV	SPOKE VOLUMES
EEIJLNNOPSUU	JULIENNE SOUP	EEKLNNOOPPSY	SPOKEN OPENLY
EEIJNORSTTTU	JOINT TRUSTEE	EEKMOOORRTWW	TOMORROW WEEK
EEIKKLLNOOSW	LOOKS LIKE NEW	EEKNNOORSTTT	STOKE ON TRENT
EEIKLLMNOTTY	LITTLE MONKEY	EEKNNOORUVWY	YOU NEVER KNOW
EEIKLMNNOSTY	MILTON KEYNES	EEKNOOPPRSSS	SPOKESPERSON
EEIKLNOOPRSS	POOR LIKENESS	EEKNOORRSSTW	STONEWORKERS
EEIKLNOSSTVY	SEVENTY KILOS	EELLLNOOSSSU	SELL ONES SOUL
EEIKMNORSTWY	NEW YORK TIMES	EELLNNOORSSV	LOVELORNNESS
EEIKMOORRTVW	WORK OVERTIME	EELLNOOOOSSW	LOSE ONE'S WOOL
EEIKNNORSTTW	WENT ON STRIKE	EELLNOPSSSST	PLOTLESSNESS
EEIKOPRRRSTW	WORKER-PRIEST	EELLNOSSSSSU	SOULLESSNESS
EEIKORRRRSTT	STRIKE TERROR	EELLORRSSTTY	STORYTELLERS
EEIILLMOPRSSW	PROMISES WELL	EELMMMNOOSTU	LOSE MOMENTUM
EEIILLNNOSSSV	SLOVENLINESS	EELMMNNOPTUY	UNEMPLOYMENT
EEIILLNOSSUV	UNLOVELINESS	EELMMNOOSTVW	SLOW MOVEMENT
EEIILLNOPRSVY	LIVELY PERSON	EELMOPRRSTTY	STORMY PETREL
EEIILLNSSSSST	LISTLESSNESS	EELNNNOOORWY	ONLY ONE OWNER
EEIILLORRRTTT	LITTLE TERROR	EELNOPSSSSST	SPOTLESSNESS
EEIILLORRSTUY	IRRESOLUTELY	EELOPPRRSSTY	PROPERTYLESS
EEIILLRSSSSTY	RESISTLESSLY	EEMMORRRSSTU	SUMMER RESORT
EEIILMNOOOSTT	NO TIME TO LOSE	EEMNNOOPPSTT	POSTPONEMENT
EEIILMNOPPRSS	SIMPLE PERSON	EEMNNOORSSSU	ENORMOUSNESS
EEIILMOPPRRTY	PEREMPTORILY	EEMNNOOSSSUV	VENOMOUSNESS
EEIILNNOOPRTV	IN OPEN REVOLT	EEMNNORSSSUU	NUMEROUSNESS
EEIILNOOOORSSU	OLEORESINOUS	EENNOOPPRSSU	ON ONE'S UPPERS
EEIILNOOSSSTW	LOSE ONES WITS	EENNOSSSSTUU	SENSUOUSNESS
EEIILNOPRSSSU	PERILOUSNESS	EENNTTTTWWYY	TWENTY-TWENTY
EEIILNOPRSSVY	RESPONSIVELY	EENOOPPPRRRS	PROPER PERSON
EEIILNOPSSSTW	WETS ONE'S LIPS	EENOOPRRSTUU	NEUROPTEROUS
EEIILNPRRTTWY	WRITTEN REPLY	EENORRRRSTUV	ROVER'S RETURN
EEIILNPRSSTTY	PERSISTENTLY	EEOOPPRRSSTU	PREPOSTEROUS
EEIILNPRTTTWY	TRIPLE TWENTY	EEOPRRRSSSTU	TROUSER PRESS
EEIILNPSSSUVY	SUSPENSIVELY	EEPPRRTTTTYY	PRETTY-PRETTY
EEIILOPPRSSVY	OPPRESSIVELY	EFFFGHIILORT	FIGHT FOR LIFE
EEIILOPRRSSTY	PROSELYTISER	EFFFGHINORST	FRIGHTENS OFF
EEIILOPRRSTYZ	PROSELYTIZER	EFFGHIIINRT	FIGHTING FIRE
EEIILOPRSSSTY	PROSELYTISES	EFFGGIILNNSU	GLUE SNIFFING
EEIILOPRSSTYZ	PROSELYTIZES		GLUE-SNIFFING
EEIILOPSSSSVY	POSSESSIVELY		SNIFFING GLUE
EEIIMMNNNOOPST	EMPOISONMENT	EFFGHIMORTTY	MIGHTY EFFORT
EEIIMMNOPRSTV	IMPROVEMENTS	EFFGIINOOPRR	FIREPROOFING
EEIIMNNNOPRSY	MONEY-SPINNER	EFFGIKLOPRSU	SKIFFLE GROUP

EFFGINORSTUV	OVERSTUFFING
EFFHHIJLTTUY	JULY THE FIFTH
EFFHIMORRSTT	FROM THE FIRST
EFFHINOOPSTT	IN OFF THE POST
EFFHJNOORTUU	FOURTH OF JUNE
EFFHLLNOORSW	FLESH NOR FOWL
EFFHMOOOPRTT	TOP OF THE FORM
EFFHNOOORSTU	FRONT-OF-HOUSE
EFFIILNORRSU	RUINS FOR LIFE
EFFIIMNSTTUY	FIFTY MINUTES
EFFIINORTTTW	WRITTEN IT OFF
EFFIIORRSSTW	WORRIES STIFF
EFFILLORUUXY	LIFE OF LUXURY
EFFILNRSSTUU	FRUITFULNESS
EFFIMOPRSTUV	FIVE OF TRUMPS
EFGGGIINOPTT	PETTIFOGGING
EFGGHHIINRTT	NIGHT FIGHTER
EFGGHIILNRST	LIGHT FINGERS
	SELF-RIGHTING
EFGGHILNOOPR	GOING FOR HELP
EFGGHINORRTU	GOING FURTHER
EFGGIIMNNORV	MOVING FINGER
EFGGIINORTTT	FORGETTING IT
EFGGINOORSTU	REFUSING TO GO
EFGGNNOOORSU	GO FOR ONE'S GUN
EFGHHIILRRTU	RIGHTFUL HEIR
EFGHHIINSTTW	WINS THE FIGHT
EFGHHIJLOTUY	EIGHTH OF JULY
EFGHHILNTTTW	TWELFTH NIGHT
EFGHHIOPSTTT	STOP THE FIGHT
EFGHHOORSTTU	FORETHOUGHTS
EFGHIILNPRST	FIRST HELPING
EFGHIILOPRTT	FIGHTER PILOT
EFGHIINOTTUW	UNIT OF WEIGHT
EFGHIKLNOORS	LOOKING FRESH
EFGHILLNOOTW	THE FOLLOWING
EFGHILNNOTTU	UNIT OF LENGTH
EFGHILNRSSTU	RIGHTFULNESS
EFGHILOOSSST	LOSES SIGHT OF
EFGHILOOSSTW	LOSS OF WEIGHT
EFGHINORRTTY	RIGHT OF ENTRY
EFGHINORSTTT	SETTING FORTH
EFGHLLNRSTTU	FULL STRENGTH
EFGHLNOOPUUY	YOUNG HOPEFUL
EFGHNOOORTTT	GO TO THE FRONT
EFGIIINNNSTY	INTENSIFYING
EFGIIKLLLMNO	LONG-LIFE MILK
EFGIIKNNNPRU	PRUNING KNIFE
EFGIILMNSSTT	FILMSETTINGS
EFGIILMNSSTY	FILING SYSTEM
EFGIILNOPRST	SPORTING LIFE
EFGIILNORSST	STRING OF LIES
EFGIILNORSUV	GRISEOFULVIN
EFGIILNRRTYY	TERRIFYINGLY
EFGIINNOPRSY	PERSONIFYING
EFGIINNPRRST	FINGERPRINTS
EFGIINOPRRST	RITE OF SPRING
EFGIINORRSTV	VIRGIN FOREST
EFGIINORRTTT	RETROFITTING
EFGIIORSTTUU	FIGURES IT OUT
EFGILLLORSWY	GILLYFLOWERS
EFGILNOOOTTU	GOT OUT OF LINE
EFGILOOORSTUU	FUTUROLOGIES
EFGILOPRRTUY	PORTLY FIGURE
EFGLNNORSSUW	WRONGFULNESS
EFHHILLOOOSY	HOLY OF HOLIES
EFHHILLOOPTT	TOP OF THE HILL
EFHHLOOPRSTU	SHOUT FOR HELP
EFHHMNOORRTT	FROM THE NORTH
EFHHMOORSTTU	FROM THE SOUTH
EFHIIIMNOTTT	THIN TIME OF IT

EFHIIJNNNOTU	JOIN IN THE FUN
EFHIIKLLNORT	IN FOR THE KILL
EFHIILMNNOOS	NO FLIES ON HIM
EFHIILORSTTW	WHISTLE FOR IT
EFHIJLRSTTUY	JULY THE FIRST
EFHIKLMOOPTT	TOP OF THE MILK
EFHILLMNORTU	RUN OF THE MILL
	RUN-OF-THE-MILL
EFHILLOSSTWW	WOLF-WHISTLES
EFHILMNRSSTU	MIRTHFULNESS
EFHILNOPSSTU	SPOILS THE FUN
EFHIMOOSTTUW	OUT OF THE SWIM
EFHIMORRSSTX	SIXTH-FORMERS
EFHINNOORSSU	SUNSHINE ROOF
EFHIOORSTTTW	THE WORST OF IT
EFHKLOOORSTU	FRESH OUTLOOK
EFHLLNOSSSTU	SLOTHFULNESS
EFHLLPRSSSUU	SURPLUS FLESH
EFHLMOOOPRST	MOPS THE FLOOR
EFHLNNOOPRTY	HORN OF PLENTY
EFHLNOSSTUUY	YOUTHFULNESS
EFHLNRSSTTUU	TRUTHFULNESS
EFHLOOPSSTTW	STOPS THE FLOW
EFHMNOOORSTY	SHORT OF MONEY
EFHMOOOORTTU	OUT OF THE ROOM
EFHOOOPPPSTT	TOP OF THE POPS
EFHOORRSTTUY	FOURTH STOREY
EFIIILNNOOSV	LINE OF VISION
EFIIILOPRSTV	SPIRIT OF EVIL
EFIILLMSSTUW	WISTFUL SMILE
EFIILMNORSUU	LUMINIFEROUS
EFIILMOPRSVY	OVERSIMPLIFY
EFIIMOOPRTTV	PROFIT MOTIVE
EFIINOOPSSTU	POINT OF ISSUE
EFIIORRSTTYZ	TRY IT FOR SIZE
EFILMNOOTUUV	UNIT OF VOLUME
EFILNNOOOPTT	LEFT NO OPTION
EFILOPPRSSTU	SUPPORTS LIFE
EFILORSSTUUY	SUIT YOURSELF
EFIMMORRSSST	FORM MISTRESS
EFIMNNOPRSTU	NINE OF TRUMPS
EFIMNOOPRRRS	PRISON REFORM
EFIMNOPRSTUV	FIVE NO-TRUMPS
EFIMNORSTTUY	FORTY MINUTES
EFIMOOORSSTU	SUITE OF ROOMS
EFINOOPRRSTT	FRONTIER POST
EFISUUWYZZZZ	FUZZY-WUZZIES
EFKKOOORRSTW	STROKE OF WORK
EFKLLLLNOUWW	KNOW FULL WELL
EFKLNOOPSSTY	SOFTLY SPOKEN
	SPOKEN SOFTLY
EFLLNOORRUWY	LONELY FURROW
EFLLOPPRSUUY	PURPOSEFULLY
EFLMMOOORSSY	LOSS OF MEMORY
EFLMNNORSSUU	MOURNFULNESS
EFLMNOOOPRTY	PLENTY OF ROOM
EFLOOPRRSTUW	LUST FOR POWER
EFMNNOOSTUUV	MOUNT OF VENUS
EFMOOOOPRTTT	FROM TOP TO TOE
EFNNNORRRSTU	FRONT-RUNNERS
EFNOOPRRSTTU	RETURN OF POST
EGGGGIINNOTT	GETTING GOING
EGGGHIINRTTT	GETTING RIGHT
EGGGHINORTTU	GETTING ROUGH
EGGGHINOTTTU	GETTING TOUGH
EGGGIIKNNNR	REIGNING KING
EGGGIINNOTUV	GIVING TONGUE
EGGGINNORTTW	GETTING WRONG
EGGHHHHINOOT	HIGH ON THE HOG
EGGHHIIINRRS	RISING HIGHER
EGGHHIILNOST	LOSING HEIGHT

EGGHHIILSTTW	LIGHTWEIGHTS	EGHIINNSSSTY	SYNTHESISING
EGGHHIINPPST	HIGH-STEPPING	EGHIINNSSTYZ	SYNTHESIZING
EGGHIIINPPTV	GIVING THE PIP	EGHIINOSTTTW	GETS ON WITH IT
EGGHIIKLNNSS	KINGS ENGLISH	EGHIINRRRTTU	RETIRING HURT
EGGHIILNNNOT	NEON LIGHTING	EGHILLNORSST	SELLING SHORT
EGGHIILNNOOP	PIGEONHOLING	EGHILMOORSTY	MYTHOLOGISER
EGGHIILNOSTW	LOSING WEIGHT	EGHILMOORTYZ	MYTHOLOGIZER
EGGHIIMNNOOP	HOMING PIGEON	EGHILMOOSSTY	MYTHOLOGISES
EGGHIIMNNOOS	HOMOGENISING	EGHILMOOSTYZ	MYTHOLOGIZES
EGGHIIMNNOOZ	HOMOGENIZING	EGHILNNNORTU	IN THE LONG RUN
EGGHIINNNOPT	OPENING NIGHT	EGHILNOOPRST	PHRENOLOGIST
EGGHIINNPTTU	TIGHTENING UP	EGHILNOORTUU	ROUGH OUTLINE
EGGHIINOPPUV	GIVING UP HOPE	EGHILNOPRSTU	UPHOLSTERING
EGGHIINPRSSS	PRIGGISHNESS	EGHILNOPRTTY	TRYING TO HELP
EGGHIINRRSTV	SERVING RIGHT	EGHILNOSSTWY	SHOWING STYLE
EGGHIINRSTTT	SETTING RIGHT	EGHILNPPTTUU	PUT THE PLUG IN
EGGHILNNOSTT	LONGEST NIGHT	EGHILOOPPSST	PSEPHOLOGIST
EGGHILNSSSSU	SLUGGISHNESS	EGHIMNOOORSU	ROOMING HOUSE
EGGHINNOOOST	GONE SHOOTING	EGHIMNOOPPST	STOPPING HOME
EGGHINNOOPPS	CONE SHOPPING	EGHIMNORSSIW	WOMENS RIGHTS
EGGHINNOPTUU	TOUGHENING UP	EGHINNOOPRSU	OPENING HOURS
EGGHINOOOSST	GOES SHOOTING	EGHINNOOPRTW	THROWING OPEN
EGGHINOOPPSS	GOES SHOPPING	EGHINNOOSTTW	WENT SHOOTING
EGGHLNOORSSW	HORNSWOGGLES	EGHINNOPPSTW	WENT SHOPPING
EGGIIINORSTV	GIVING RISE TO	EGHINOOORSTV	OVERSHOOTING
EGGIILLNRTTY	GLITTERINGLY	EGHINOOPRRSV	GOVERNORSHIP
EGGIILNOOTUY	GOING QUIETLY	EGHINOOPSTTT	PHOTOSETTING
EGGIIMMNNOSW	GONE SWIMMING	EGHINOORRTVW	THROWING OVER
EGGIIMMNOSSW	GOES SWIMMING	EGHINOOTTUWY	GET ON WITH YOU!
EGGIIMNNORSV	MISGOVERNING	EGHINOPSTTUW	PUTS ON WEIGHT
EGGIINNOTTVV	GIVING VENT TO	EGHINORSTTTW	GHOSTWRITTEN
EGGIINPRTUVY	GIVE UP TRYING	EGHIOOOSTTVW	GIVE TWO HOOTS
EGGILLLNORVY	GROVELLINGLY	EGHIORSSSTTT	SETS TO RIGHTS
EGGILMNORSTW	GLOWING TERMS	EGHLLOOOPSTT	GO TO THE POLLS
EGGILNOORSSV	GLOSSING OVER	EGHMNOOOSTTU	SMOOTH TONGUE
EGGILNORSTUY	YOUNGEST GIRL	EGHMNOORSTTU	GUNS THE MOTOR
EGGILOOPSTTY	EGYPTOLOGIST	EGHNNOOPRTTU	ON THE TOP RUNG
EGGINNOOPTTT	GETTING ON TOP	EGHNOPRSTTTU	UP TO STRENGTH
EGGINNOOSSTU	OUTGOINGNESS	EGHOOORSSSTU	SHOOTS GROUSE
EGGINOOPRSST	GOING TO PRESS	EGHORRRSSUUY	SURGERY HOURS
EGGLNNOOORTY	RONTGENOLOGY	EGIIIIMNSTTV	VISITING TIME
EGGNNOORRUWY	GROWN YOUNGER	EGIIIJNNOSSU	JOINING ISSUE
EGHHIJNSTTTU	JUST THE THING	EGIIILLNNRSV	SILVER LINING
EGHHII NORTTW	THREW LIGHT ON	EGIIILMNNNSW	WINNING SMILE
EGHHILNOSSSU	GHOULISHNESS	EGIIILNORSST	RELIGIONISTS
EGHHILORSTUV	LIVES THROUGH	EGIIILNPRTTT	LETTING IT RIP
EGHHILOSTTWY	GHOSTLY WHITE	EGIIILNSSTUV	LIVING TISSUE
EGHHIMNORRUY	HURRYING HOME	EGIIIMNNRTTT	INTERMITTING
EGHHINOPSTTT	STOP THE NIGHT	EGIIIMNOPSTU	IMPETIGINOUS
EGHHINORSSUY	YOUR HIGHNESS	EGIIINNNPRWZ	PRIZEWINNING
EGHHNOORSSTU	THOROUGHNESS	EGIIINNNRTTW	INTERTWINING
EGHHOPRSTTUW	SWEPT THROUGH	EGIIINOPSSTV	POSITIVE SIGN
EGHIIILNNOPV	LIVING IN HOPE	EGIIKLNPPRRS	KLIPSPRINGER
EGHIIILNNPPS	SHIPPING LINE	EGIIKMMNORSV	SKIMMING OVER
EGHIIKLNSSWY	SINGLE WHISKY	EGIIKNOPPPRS	SKIPPING ROPE
EGHIIKMNORST	STRIKING HOME		SKIPPING-ROPE
EGHIIKNNORTV	THINKING OVER	EGIIKNOPPRSV	SKIPPING OVER
EGHIIKNORSTU	SHRIEKING OUT	EGIILLMNPTUX	MULTIPLEXING
EGHIILLNNSST	TEN SHILLINGS	EGIILLNOPRSV	SPILLING OVER
EGHIILLNORSW	WILLING HORSE	EGIILLNPRSUW	PULLING WIRES
EGHIILLNSTTT	LITTLE THINGS	EGIILMMNORVY	LIVING MEMORY
EGHIILNNOSTV	HONEST LIVING	EGIILMNNOOST	LOSING NO TIME
EGHIILNOSTTU	SILHOUETTING	EGIILMNNOPTT	MELTING POINT
EGHIILNPRSTT	LET THINGS RIP	EGIILMOORSTU	GLORIOUS TIME
EGHIILOOPSSY	PHYSIOLOGIES	EGIILMOOSSST	SEISMOLOGIST
EGHIIMNNNORT	IN THE MORNING	EGIILNNOPSTT	SLITTING OPEN
EGHIIMNNPRST	SHRIMPING NET	EGIILOORSUVW	GLORIOUS VIEW
EGHIINNNNRTU	IN THE RUNNING	EGIIMMNNSTWW	WENT SWIMMING
EGHIINNNORSW	WINNING HORSE	EGIIMNNNNOWY	WINNING MONEY
EGHIINNOSSST	IN ONE'S SIGHTS	EGIIMNOOPRRT	PRIMOGENITOR
EGHIINNRTTUW	TURNING WHITE	EGIIMNOORRST	RISORGIMENTO

EGIIMNOPRRST	MISREPORTING
EGIIMNORRTWY	WORRYING TIME
EGIINNNORTVY	INVENTORYING
EGIINNNPRTTU	TURPENTINING
EGIINNNSTUVW	STUNNING VIEW
EGIINNOPPSTT	STEPPING INTO
	STEPPING ON IT
EGIINNORRTTV	INTROVERTING
EGIINNPRRTTU	INTERRUPTING
EGIINNRRSSTW	STIRRING NEWS
EGIINOPPRRTV	TRIPPING OVER
EGIINPRRSSSU	PRESSURISING
EGIINPRRSSUZ	PRESSURIZING
EGIIOPRRSSTW	GOSSIP WRITER
EGIKLLMNOORY	KREMLINOLOGY
EGIKLNOOORSW	WORKING LOOSE
EGILLNNOORST	ROLLING STONE
EGILLNNSTTUY	UNSETTLINGLY
EGILMNOOOSTT	ENTOMOLOGIST
EGILMNOORSTU	NUMEROLOGIST
EGILNNOORSTU	TURNING LOOSE
EGILNOOPPRSV	SLOPPING OVER
EGILNOOPPRTV	TOPPLING OVER
EGILNOOPRSUY	PYROLIGNEOUS
EGILNOORSSSU	GLORIOUSNESS
EGILNOPRSTUY	GUILTY PERSON
EGILNOPRTUVY	PROVEN GUILTY
EGILNOPRUVZZ	PUZZLING OVER
EGILOPRSTUVY	PROVES GUILTY
EGIMNOOOPRTT	GET PROMOTION
EGIMNOORRTTY	TRIGONOMETRY
EGIMNOPRRTUV	OVERTRUMPING
EGIMNOQRSTTU	QUOTING TERMS
EGIMNORRRSUY	MINOR SURGERY
EGINNOOOPRST	GONE TO PRISON
EGINNOPPSSWW	SWOPPING NEWS
EGINNORSSTWY	TRY ONE'S WINGS
EGINNORTTUUV	VENTURING OUT
EGINOOOOPRSST	GOES TO PRISON
EGINOOPPRSTV	STOPPING OVER
EGINOOPPRSVW	SWOPPING OVER
EGINOOPRRSSS	PROGRESSIONS
EGINOORSSSUV	VIGOROUSNESS
EGINOPPPRSSU	PRESUPPOSING
EGINOPPRSTUV	GIVEN SUPPORT
EGINOPSTTTUU	PUTTING TO USE
EGINPRRSSSTU	PURSE STRINGS
EGIOPPRSSTUV	GIVES SUPPORT
EGIOPRRSSTTT	PIGS TROTTERS
EGLNOORRSSTU	LONG TROUSERS
EGLOOPRRSSSW	SLOW PROGRESS
EGMNOOOORRTW	GONE TOMORROW
EHHIIIKRSSWY	IRISH WHISKEY
EHHIILLOTTTW	TO HELL WITH IT!
EHHIILOOPPSS	PHILOSOPHIES
	PHILOSOPHISE
EHHIILOOPPSZ	PHILOSOPHIZE
EHHIILOPPSST	SPOIL THE SHIP
EHHIJLNNTTUY	JULY THE NINTH
EHHIJLSTTUXY	JULY THE SIXTH
EHHILOOPPRSS	PHILOSOPHERS
EHHILOPPSTUY	HYPOSULPHITE
EHHIMMOOOORST	HOMOIOTHERMS
EHHIMMOOOORTY	HOMOIOTHERMY
EHHIMPSSTTTU	HIT THE STUMPS
EHHINNOOOORTZ	ON THE HORIZON
EHHINOOOOPPRS	SIPHONOPHORE
EHHINPSTTUUW	UP WITH THE SUN
EHHIOOPSSSTT	THEOSOPHISTS
EHHKNORTTTUW	KNOW THE TRUTH
EHHMOOOORSTTW	THE MOTOR SHOW
EHHNOPRRTTUY	TROPHY HUNTER
EHHOOORRRSSTU	SHORTER HOURS
EHHOPSSTTTTU	PUTTS THE SHOT
EHIIMNPRSST	MINISTERSHIP
EHIIKLMOOPRT	POIKILOTHERM
EHIIKLMSSTTY	SKY'S THE LIMIT
EHIIKNORSTTV	THINKS IT OVER
EHIIKNSSSSTT	SKITTISHNESS
EHIILLLOSSTT	TILLS THE SOIL
EHIILLMNPSTU	PHILLUMENIST
EHIILLNOTTWW	THE WILL TO WIN
EHIILLOPSTWW	WILL O' THE WISP
	WILL-O'-THE-WISP
EHIILMOOPRST	HELIOTROPISM
EHIILMRSSSTV	SILVERSMITHS
EHIIMNOOSSSU	MISSION HOUSE
EHIIMNOPSSTT	MISS THE POINT
EHIIMNPRSTUX	XIPHISTERNUM
EHIINNOPSTTW	WINS THE POINT
EHIINORSTTUY	TRINITY HOUSE
EHIKLORSTTUW	TURKISH TOWEL
EHILMMOOPPRS	PLEOMORPHISM
EHILMNORSSTW	MINSTREL SHOW
EHILNOOPRTTU	LUTEOTROPHIN
EHILNOOPSSTW	WINS THE POOLS
EHILNOOPSUUY	EUPHONIOUSLY
EHILNOORTTWY	NOTEWORTHILY
EHILNOPSTTTU	PUT ON THE LIST
EHILNSSSSTTU	SLUTTISHNESS
EHIMMMOOPRSS	MESOMORPHISM
EHIMMNNOORSTU	MOTHERS UNION
EHIMNNORSTTW	WINTER MONTHS
EHIMNOOPPRRT	MINOR PROPHET
EHIMNOOPRSSW	SHOWN PROMISE
EHIMNOORSUUV	HUMOROUS VEIN
EHIMOOPRSSSW	SHOWS PROMISE
EHIMOORRSTVY	THIS VERY ROOM
EHIMOPRRSTUV	TRIUMPHS OVER
EHINNORSSTUW	UNWORTHINESS
EHINOORRSSTV	SHORT VERSION
EHINOORSSSST	SHORT SESSION
EHINOPRTTTUZ	PUT ON THE RITZ
EHIOOPPQRSUY	POOR PHYSIQUE
EHJNNNOORTTY	JOHNNY ROTTEN
EHJNOORRSTUY	SHORT JOURNEY
EHKLNOOOOTTU	ON THE LOOK-OUT
EHKNOORSTTWW	KNOW THE WORST
EHLLMOOPSSUY	MESOPHYLLOUS
EHLLOOOOPPST	LOOPS THE LOOP
EHLMOOOPPRTY	PHOTOPOLYMER
EHLNORSSSTUW	SHOWN RESULTS
EHLORSSSSTUW	SHOWS RESULTS
EHMMMNORSSTU	SUMMER MONTHS
EHMNNOORRSTT	NORTHERNMOST
EHMNOORSSSTY	HONORS SYSTEM
EHMNOORSSSUU	HUMOROUSNESS
EHMNOORSSTTU	SOUTHERNMOST
EHNNNOOOORSU	ON ONES HONOUR
EHNNOOOORSTT	TOOT ONES HORN
EHNNOOOTTTUW	OUT ON THE TOWN
EHNNOOPRSTTU	RUN ON THE SPOT
EHNNOORSSTTW	THROWN STONES
EHNOOPPSTTTU	PUT ON THE SPOT
EHNOORSSSTTW	THROWS STONES
EHOOOPRRSTTU	ORTHOPTEROUS
EIIIKNNNRTTW	WRITTEN IN INK
EIIILLLMMNOS	MILLION MILES
EIIILLNOPSTT	POINTILLISTE
EIIIMNNORSST	INTERMISSION
EIIIMPRTTTVY	PERMITTIVITY
EIIINOQRSSTU	REQUISITIONS

TWELVE-LETTER WORDS FGI

EIIINORSSSTV	REVISIONISTS
EIIKNNOPSTTU	TIE UP IN KNOTS
EIIKNSSSTTTV	ST. KITTS-NEVIS
EIILLLLMNOPS	PLIMSOLL LINE
EIILLLORSSUY	SERIOUSLY ILL
EIILLMNNOOOT	MILLION TO ONE
EIILLNORSSSU	ILLUSORINESS
EIILLNRUUVXY	LIVE IN LUXURY
EIILLOOQSSUZ	SOLILOQUIZES
EIILLQRSTTTU	LITTLE SQUIRT
EIILMNNORRTU	INNER TURMOIL
EIILMNOOSTUV	EVOLUTIONISM
EIILMOPRSUVY	IMPERVIOUSLY
EIILMRSTTUVY	MULTIVERSITY
EIILNNNOSTUV	TUNNEL VISION
EIILNOOOPPST	POLE POSITION
EIILNOORRSTU	IRRESOLUTION
EIILNOOSTTUV	EVOLUTIONIST
EIILNOPRSTUY	POLYNEURITIS
EIIMMNNOPRST	IMPRISONMENT
EIIMNNNQQUUU	QUINQUENNIUM
EIIMNNOOPRST	PREMONITIONS
EIIMNNOOSOTT	SETS IN MOTION
EIIMNNORTTTT	INTROMITTENT
EIIMNOORTTVY	MINORITY VOTE
EIIMNSSTTUXY	SIXTY MINUTES
EIINNOOPSSSS	IN POSSESSION
EIINNOORRSTV	INTROVERSION
EIINNOPRRTTU	INTERRUPTION
EIINOOPPRSST	PREPOSITIONS
EIINOORSTTTX	EXTORTIONIST
EIINOPRSSTTU	SUPERSTITION
EIINOPSSSTTW	PITS ONE'S WITS
EIINORSSTTTU	RESTITUTIONS
EIIOOPPSSTTV	POSTPOSITIVE
EIIOOPRRSTTY	POSTERIORITY
EIKLLNORSSTY	TRY ONES SKILL
EIKLOOOPRRSU	LOOK SUPERIOR
EIILLLRSSUWY	WILLY RUSSELL
EILLNNNOOTVY	NONVIOLENTLY
EILLNNOOORST	ROLLS INTO ONE
EILMNNOOPTTY	OMNIPOTENTLY
EILMNNOSSSUU	LUMINOUSNESS
EILMNOORSTTV	VIOLENT STORM
EILMOPPRSTUU	MULTIPURPOSE
EILMORSSTUYY	MYSTERIOUSLY
EILOORRSSUVV	SOLE SURVIVOR
EILOPSTTUUZZ	PUZZLES IT OUT
EIMNNNOOOTTT	NOT TO MENTION
EIMNNOSSSTUU	MUTINOUSNESS
EIMNOOOPRRST	PROMONTORIES
EIMNOOOQSTTU	MOOT QUESTION
EIMNOORSSSTU	TIMOROUSNESS
EIMNOPPRSSTU	PRESUMPTIONS
EIMNOPRSSSTY	PRISON SYSTEM
EIMNOPSSSTTY	POINTS SYSTEM
EINNOOPRSTTW	WENT TO PRISON
EINNOPRSSSUW	WIN ONES SPURS
EINNOPSTTTWY	TWENTY POINTS
EINOOPQSSTTU	QUIT ONES POST
EINOORSSSUUX	UXORIOUSNESS
EINOPRRSSTTW	WINTER SPORTS
EINOPRSSSSUU	SPURIOUSNESS
EINORSSSTUUV	VIRTUOUSNESS
EIOPRRRSSTTY	TYPISTS ERROR
EJLLMOOPRUWY	WOOLLY JUMPER
EKLLNOOPSSWY	SPOKEN SLOWLY
ELLNORSTTUUW	TURNS OUT WELL
ELMNOOOPRTUW	ONE LUMP OR TWO?
ELNOOPPSSSUU	POPULOUSNESS
ELNOOPRSTTUY	PORTENTOUSLY

ELOOPPRRSSUY	PROSPEROUSLY
ELOOPPRRSTTY	LOST PROPERTY
ELOORRSSTTUY	STERTOROUSLY
EMOOOPRRRSTT	STORM TROOPER
EMOOOPRRSSST	MOSS-TROOPERS
EMOOPPRRRTTT	PROMPT RETORT
EMOPPRSSTUUU	PRESUMPTUOUS
EMORRSSTTYYY	MYSTERY STORY
ENNOOORSSSSU	SONOROUSNESS
ENNOOPRSSSUW	WON ONE'S SPURS
ENNOORSSTTTU	TURNS TO STONE
ENOORSSSTTUU	TORTUOUSNESS
ENORRRSSTUYY	NURSERY STORY
FFFFGHILNOSU	SHUFFLING OFF
FFFFGIIOTTYY	GO FIFTY-FIFTY
FFFGHIIINNOS	FINISHING OFF
FFFHHIIOORRTT	FIRTH OF FORTH
FFFIOORRTTYY	FORTY OR FIFTY
FFGGGHINOREU	GIIRUGGING OFF
FFGGHHIIINST	FIGHTING FISH
FFGHIIINOTTT	HITTING IT OFF
FFGHIILNOOPS	POLISHING OFF
FFGIIINORTTW	WRITING IT OFF
FFGIILLNOPTU	PULLING IT OFF
FFGIINNORTTU	TURNING IT OFF
FFGIINOPPRST	STRIPPING OFF
FFGILOOOPRTU	PROOF OF GUILT
FFGIMNOORRSU	FORMING FOURS
FFGLNOORRSUU	FOUR FURLONGS
FFHHLOOSTUUY	FLUSH OF YOUTH
FFHJLOORTUUY	FOURTH OF JULY
FFIILLOPRSTU	FULL OF SPIRIT
FFIKNOORRTUW	UNFIT FOR WORK
FFIMNOOORTUU	OUT OF UNIFORM
FFLLOOORRSUW	FULL OF SORROW
FFMOOPRRSTUU	FOUR OF TRUMPS
FGGGHIIIINNOS	GOING FISHING
FGGGILNOOOST	FOOTSLOGGING
FGGHHIIINTTW	FIGHTING WITH
FGGHHIINOSTW	SHOWING FIGHT
FGGHIIILNTTT	LIGHT FITTING
FGGHIILMPSTY	PIGS MIGHT FLY
FGGHIINNNRTU	RUNNING FIGHT
FGGHIINOPSTT	STOP FIGHTING
FGGHINNOOORT	GO FOR NOTHING
FGGIINNNOORT	GOING IN FRONT
FGGIINNORRTU	GROWING FRUIT
FGGINNOOORTW	WRONG-FOOTING
FGGNOOORRUUY	GO FOR YOUR GUN
FGHHIINNORST	SHINING FORTH
FGHHILORRTTY	FORTHRIGHTLY
FGHHIORSTTTU	FIRST THOUGHT
FGHHLLOTTUUY	THOUGHTFULLY
FGHHLOORSTUW	FLOWS THROUGH
FGHIIIKNNSST	STINKING FISH
FGHIIILNRTTW	FLIRTING WITH
	TRIFLING WITH
FGHIILLNOSTT	STILL OF NIGHT
FGHIILNORRYY	HORRIFYINGLY
FGHIILNORSTW	WHISTLING FOR
FGHIINNOORTT	NOTHING FOR IT
FGHIINORRSTT	THIRSTING FOR
FGHIINORSSTU	ISSUING FORTH
FGHIINORSTTU	TROUT FISHING
FGHILNNNRSUU	RUNNING FLUSH
FGHILOPSTTTU	PUTS TO FLIGHT
FGHIMNOOOPRT	MOTHPROOFING
FGHINNOOSSTT	SOFT NOTHINGS
FGHINOOPRRTU	POURING FORTH
FGIIIMMNNORS	MISINFORMING
FGIIINNNNRSST	FIRST INNINGS

819

FGIILLNOSUUY	FULIGINOUSLY	GHHLLOPRSTUU	PULLS THROUGH
FGIILMNSTYYY	MYSTIFYINGLY		PULLTHROUGHS
FGIINNNORRTU	RUNNING FOR IT	GHIIIKNNNOTT	THINKING ON IT
FGIINOORSSTT	TOSSING FOR IT	GHIIILLNOPSY	LYOPHILISING
FGIINPRSTTTU	PUTTING FIRST	GHIIILLNOPYZ	LYOPHILIZING
FGIJNOOPRSSY	JOYS OF SPRING	GHIIJLNRSTUY	SLIGHT INJURY
FGIKMNOPRSTU	KING OF TRUMPS	GHIIJNOSSTWY	SINGS WITH JOY
FGIKNOOPRSST	SPORT OF KINGS	GHIIKLLORTTU	KILL OUTRIGHT
FGILOORSTTUU	FUTUROLOGIST	GHIIKLNNNTUY	UNTHINKINGLY
FGINNNOOPRUW	FROWNING UPON	GHIILLNNOSWW	SHOWN WILLING
FGINOOPSSTUY	PUSSYFOOTING	GHIILLNOSSTW	TWO SHILLINGS
FHIKLLOOOOSS	LOOKS FOOLISH	GHIILLNOSSWW	SHOWS WILLING
FHILLOPRSUWY	WORSHIPFULLY	GHIILLPRSTTY	TRIPS LIGHTLY
FHJOOORSSTUY	SHOUTS FOR JOY	GHIILMNNOOTT	MOONLIT NIGHT
FHLLNOOOORRU	ROLL OF HONOUR	GHIILNOPPSST	SHOPPING LIST
FHLLNRTTUUUY	UNTRUTHFULLY	GHIILNORSSTT	SHORT-LISTING
FHLNOOOORSSU	LOSS OF HONOUR	GHIILNPRSSUU	SULPHURISING
FHLNOOOORSUU	SOUL OF HONOUR	GHIILNPRSUUZ	SULPHURIZING
FIIILLOOORTV	OIL OF VITRIOL	GHIILOOPSSTY	PHYSIOLOGIST
FIIILNORSSTV	FIRST VIOLINS	GHIINOOPPTUW	WHOOPING IT UP
FIIILLMMNOORY	MONILIFORMLY	GHIINOPPPSTW	WHIPPING POST
FIILMMORTTUY	MULTIFORMITY	GHIINORSTTUW	WINS OUTRIGHT
FIILNOOOSSSV	LOSS OF VISION	GHIKNNNNOOTW	KNOWN NOTHING
FILLNOORSUUY	RUINOUS FOLLY	GHIKNNNOOSTW	KNOWS NOTHING
FILNOOORSTUU	RUNS OUT OF OIL	GHIKNOORRSUW	WORKING HOURS
FILOORSTTUUY	FORTUITOUSLY	GHILLNOOOTUW	HOLLOWING OUT
FIMNNOORRSTU	RUNS INTO FORM	GHILMOOOPRST	MORPHOLOGIST
FKKLOOOORRSW	LOOKS FOR WORK	GHILNOOOOPST	SHOOTING POOL
FMNOOPRRSTUU	FOUR NO-TRUMPS	GHILNOPRSTTU	PORT SUNLIGHT
GGGHHHIIILNT	HIGHLIGHTING	GHIMMOOPRSYZ	ZYGOMORPHISM
GGGHHINOORTU	GOING THROUGH	GHIMNOOOSTTU	SMOOTHING OUT
GGGIIIMNNOSS	GOING MISSING	GHIMOOOOSTYYZ	HOMOZYGOSITY
GGGIILNORTUW	WRIGGLING OUT	GHINNNORRSTU	RUNNING SHORT
GGGILMNOSTUU	SMUGGLING OUT	GHIOPRSSTTTU	PUTS TO RIGHTS
GGGILNNORSTU	STRUGGLING ON	GIIIKNNNRTW	WRITING IN INK
GGHHHIORRTTU	RIGHT THROUGH	GIIIKLLLMNPS	SPILLING MILK
GGHHIIILNNST	SHINING LIGHT	GIIILLNSSTTT	SITTING STILL
GGHHIIIMRSTT	MIGHT IS RIGHT	GIIILNNNRSUY	LYING IN RUINS
GGHHILNRSTUY	HIGHLY STRUNG	GIIILNNOPPST	SLIPPING INTO
	HIGHLY-STRUNG	GIIILNNORSTV	VIOLIN STRING
GGHIIIMNNNRST	MINING RIGHTS	GIIILNOPTTUV	LIVING UP TO IT
GGHIIINSTTTT	SITTING TIGHT	GIIIMNNORTTT	INTROMITTING
GGHIIKLNOORT	LOOKING RIGHT	GIIIMNOPRSTV	MOVING SPIRIT
GGHIILLNPTTU	PULLING TIGHT	GIIIMNORSSTU	MOISTURISING
GGHIILNOPSTT	SPOTLIGHTING	GIIIMNORSTUZ	MOISTURIZING
GGHIIINNOSSSW	SHOWING SIGNS	GIIINNNNOSSU	SING IN UNISON
GGHIINNRRTTU	TURNING RIGHT	GIIINNOOPRSV	PROVISIONING
GGHIINOOPSTU	OUTGOING SHIP	GIIINNPRTTUW	PUT IN WRITING
GGHIINOOTTUW	GOING WITHOUT	GIIINOSTTTTU	SITTING IT OUT
GGHIINORSTTV	VOTING RIGHTS	GIIINPRRSTTU	STIRRING IT UP
GGHIINPRTTTU	PUTTING RIGHT	GIIKLLLNOOSY	LOOKING SILLY
GGHINOORRRTW	RIGHT OR WRONG	GIIKLLMNOOST	MILKING STOOL
GGIIILNNRTUY	INTRIGUINGLY	GIIKLNNOOPPY	LOOKING NIPPY
GGIIKNOPRUVW	GIVING UP WORK	GIIKLNOSTTTU	SKITTLING OUT
GGIILMMNOSWY	GO SWIMMINGLY	GIIKNNNOSTTY	TYING IN KNOTS
GGIINNOPRSTU	SPRINGING OUT	GIIKNOORTTUW	WORKING IT OUT
GGIINNORSTTU	STRINGING OUT	GIIILNOORSSUY	INGLORIOUSLY
GGILMNNOORRY	MORNING GLORY	GIILMMNOOPSW	SWIMMING POOL
GGINNNORRTUW	WRONG TURNING	GIILMMNOOSTU	IMMUNOLOGIST
GHHHIKNORTTU	THINK THROUGH	GIILMNNOOOPS	MONOPOLISING
GHHHOOORSTTU	SHOOT THROUGH	GIILMNNOOOPZ	MONOPOLIZING
GHHIIINOOPST	HIGH POSITION	GIILMNORSSST	STIRLING MOSS
GHHIIINRSTTW	WITH THIS RING	GIILNPRRSSUY	SURPRISINGLY
GHHIKMORSSTU	SKIMS THROUGH	GIINNNNOOPRSS	SPRING ONIONS
GHHILNOORTTW	THROW LIGHT ON	GIINNNOPRTTU	TURNING POINT
GHHILOOPRSUY	HYGROPHILOUS	GIINOORSTTTU	SORTING IT OUT
GHHILOPRSSTU	SLIPS THROUGH	GIINOPPRSTTU	OUTSTRIPPING
GHHINNOORTTW	WORTH NOTHING	GIINOPRSTTTU	PROSTITUTING
GHHIOOTTTTUU	THOUGHT IT OUT	GIINOSSSTTUU	SUSSING IT OUT
GHHKLOOOORSTU	LOOKS THROUGH	GIKMNOOPSSST	STOPS SMOKING
		GIKNOOPPRSTW	STOPPING WORK

GIKNOOPRSSTW	STOPS WORKING
GILLMNOOSVWY	MOVING SLOWLY
GILLNPRSSSTU	PULLS STRINGS
GIMNOOOOPRTT	GOT PROMOTION
GIMNOOOOPRSS	MOSS-TROOPING
GINOOPRRSTWY	STOP WORRYING
GINOOPRSTTTY	TRYING TO STOP
GLOOOOOPRTYZ	PROTOZOOLOGY
HHIMMMOOOPRS	HOMOMORPHISM
HHINOOPRRTTY	THYROTROPHIN
HHMMOOOTTTUU	MOUTH TO MOUTH
HHNOOORSTTTU	NORTH TO SOUTH
HIIIILMNPSST	PHILISTINISM
HIIIILMNSTTW	WITHIN LIMITS
HIIILMOTTTUW	WITHOUT LIMIT
HIIIMNPTTUWY	WITH IMPUNITY
HIILLOOPPRWW	WHIPPOORWILL
HIINOPRSTTUU	IN HOT PURSUIT
HIJJMOPSTUWY	JUMPS WITH JOY
HIKLLUOOSSTT	SHOOTS TO KILL
HIKNOOPSSTTT	STOPS TO THINK
HILLORTTTUUW	TRUTH WILL OUT
HILMMOOPPRSY	POLYMORPHISM
HILNOOPSSTXY	XYLOPHONISTS
HIMOOOPPRSTT	PHOTOTROPISM
HLLOPPRSSTUU	PULLS UP SHORT
HLMMNOOOSUYY	HOMONYMOUSLY
HLMNOORSSTUY	RUNS SMOOTHLY
HLMOOPSSTUUY	POSTHUMOUSLY
HMMOOOOPRSSUU	MUSHROOM SOUP
HMNNOOOOPRUUY	UPON MY HONOUR
HOOPPRRSSTTY	SPORTS TROPHY
IIIIMMMNNNPYY	NIMINY-PIMINY
IIIINNNOQSSTU	INQUISITIONS
IIILNOPRSSTW	IN LOW SPIRITS
IIIMMNNOORSST	INTROMISSION
IIINNNNOOOPRU	IN OUR OPINION
IIINNOOOOPPST	IN OPPOSITION
IIINNORSTTTU	NUTRITIONIST
IIINNOSSTTTU	INSTITUTIONS
IIINOOOPPRRST	POOR IN SPIRIT
IIKMNORSSSSW	SINKS OR SWIMS
IIKNNOORTTTU	TOOK IT IN TURN
IILLOOOQSSSTU	SOLILOQUISTS
IILMNNOOOSTW	IN SLOW MOTION
IILMNOOSTUVY	VOLUMINOSITY
IILNORSTTUUY	NUTRITIOUSLY
IILOOPPRSTUY	PROPITIOUSLY
IINNNOOPSSTW	WINS ON POINTS
IINNOOOOPPRRT	IN PROPORTION
IINNOOOOPPTTT	POINT TO POINT
	POINT-TO-POINT
IINNOPPRSSTU	PUTS IN PRISON
IINOOOOPPRSST	PROPOSITIONS
IINOOOPSSSTU	SUPPOSITIONS
IINOOPRSTTTU	PROSTITUTION
ILLMNOOSUUVY	VOLUMINOUSLY
ILMNOOORSUVY	OMNIVOROUSLY
ILOPRSTTUVYY	TOPSY-TURVILY
INOOPPRSSTTU	OPPORTUNISTS
LLMOSTTUUUUY	TUMULTUOUSLY
LLOOPSTUUUVY	VOLUPTUOUSLY
LMMNOOPSTUUY	MOUNT OLYMPUS
LMNNOOOOSTUY	MONOTONOUSLY
LMNNOOSSUYYY	SYNONYMOUSLY
LOOPPPRSSTUY	SUPPLY TROOPS
MNPPRRSTTUUU	TURN UP TRUMPS

AAAAADEGNNTTV	AT AN ADVANTAGE	AAAAEHILNPPRR	PARAPHERNALIA
AAAAADGGIINNN	AGAIN AND AGAIN	AAAAEILMNSSSU	ASSUME AN ALIAS
AAAABBDEGGGGN	BAG AND BAGGAGE	AAAAFILNNOSTT	SONATA IN A FLAT
AAAABBDILNSST	AS BLIND AS A BAT	AAAAGIKMNPSST	MAKING A PASS AT
AAAABCCEELRTU	BACCALAUREATE	AAAAGILLNNOUV	GALINA ULANOVA
AAAABCCEGIKMN	CAME BACK AGAIN	AAAAGILMMNOST	AMALGAMATIONS
AAAABCDEEKRST	ACTED AS A BRAKE	AAAAGINNRSTTT	STRAIN AT A GNAT
AAAABCDIILLTY	ADIABATICALLY	AAAAHHILNSSTT	AS THIN AS A LATH
AAAABCDLOOSST	AS BALD AS A COOT	AAAAHOPRRRSSZ	SHARP AS A RAZOR
AAAABCEEKKSTT	TAKE A BACK SEAT	AAAAILNRSSSTU	AUSTRALASIANS
AAAABDDEMRSTT	MADE A BAD START	AAAAMORSSSTTW	AS WARM AS TOAST
AAAABDDINQRTU	QATAR AND DUBAI	AAAAPPRRSTUXY	X-RAY APPARATUS
AAAABDEELLLNS	ALAN BLEASDALE	AAABBDEKNNRSS	BANKS AND BRAES
AAAABDEKMRSTT	MAKE A BAD START	AAABBDELLOORV	ALL ABOVE BOARD
AAAABDILMORSS	AMBASSADORIAL	AAABBDLORSSSS	AS BOLD AS BRASS
AAAABEEKLMMSS	AS MEEK AS A LAMB	AAABBHMMOORSS	ABRAHAMS BOSOM
AAAABEGIKMNRS	MAKES A BARGAIN	AAABBIINORRST	BARBARISATION
AAAABEGILNRSS	SEALS A BARGAIN	AAABBIINORRTZ	BARBARIZATION
AAAABEHLPPRRS	PARAPHRASABLE	AAABCCCGHINRT	CATCHING A CRAB
AAAACCDELNSSU	CAUSE A SCANDAL	AAABCCDEEKMMO	MADE A COME-BACK
AAAACCDIIKLLS	LACKADAISICAL	AAABCCEEKKMMO	MAKE A COME-BACK
AAAACCEELNPRV	CAPE CANAVERAL	AAABCCEGIKMNO	COME BACK AGAIN
AAAACCHIMNRST	ACT AS CHAIRMAN	AAABCCEMORRSU	CAMERA OBSCURA
AAAACCLMNORST	MALACOSTRACAN	AAABCCGHILLNT	CATCHING A BALL
AAAACDDEEMNNV	MADE AN ADVANCE	AAABCCILLORTY	ACROBATICALLY
AAAACDEEKMNNV	MAKE AN ADVANCE	AAABCDDEEMNOT	CAME TO A BAD END
AAAACEFGILMSS	FACIAL MASSAGE	AAABCDEEFILRR	BARE-FACED LIAR
AAAACEFLPRSWY	FARAWAY PLACES		BAREFACED LIAR
AAAACEGHMNRRT	ARRANGE A MATCH	AAABCDEGHIRTW	WITH A BAD GRACE
AAAACEILNNPSS	AS CLEAN AS A PIN	AAABCDEHKNOST	HAD AT ONE'S BACK
AAAACEILNPSST	AT A SNAIL'S PACE	AAABCDEKLNRSW	LEAN BACKWARDS
AAAACEINRRSSV	CARAVANSERAIS	AAABCDELNRRST	BARNARD CASTLE
AAAACENNRRSTV	RENTS A CARAVAN	AAABCDHHIPSTT	HITS A BAD PATCH
AAAACFLLSTTUY	FATAL CASUALTY	AAABCDIKNORTW	BACKWARDATION
AAAACGHHMMNPR	GRAHAM CHAPMAN	AAABCDKKLRSWW	WALK BACKWARDS
AAAACIMNRSSST	ANTIMACASSARS	AAABCEEEMMNNW	BECAME A NEW MAN
AAAADDDDEOOSS	AS DEAD AS A DODO	AAABCEEHLLMPT	LAMBETH PALACE
AAAADDEEGNRRT	ARRANGED A DATE	AAABCEEILNRST	ASCERTAINABLE
AAAADDEGMRSSW	AWARDS DAMAGES	AAABCEELLMNNT	MENTAL BALANCE
AAAADEEGKNTTV	TAKE ADVANTAGE	AAABCEENRSSSU	AS SURE AS CAN BE
AAAADEEGNRRST	ARRANGES A DATE	AAABCEGILLLRY	ALGEBRAICALLY
AAAADEEHLPSST	AS PALE AS DEATH	AAABCEHKNOSST	HAS AT ONE'S BACK
AAAADEEHLSSVY	AS HEAVY AS LEAD	AAABCEHORSTTV	THE COSTA BRAVA
AAAADEFGIIPRW	PAID A FAIR WAGE	AAABCEIILNPTT	ANTICIPATABLE
AAAADEFOPSSST	AS DEAF AS A POST	AAABCEILLNORY	ANAEROBICALLY
AAAADEGHLMNOP	ALPHA AND OMEGA	AAABCEILNOOPT	PALAEOBOTANIC
AAAADEGHLNOWY	A LONG WAY AHEAD	AAABCEILNPSTT	CAPTAINS TABLE
AAAADEJMMRSTX	AJAX AMSTERDAM	AAABCEKKOOSTT	TOOK A BACK SEAT
AAAADELLLPRRW	DRAW A PARALLEL	AAABCGIINNRST	CANTABRIGIANS
AAAADFFLNNORU	FLORA AND FAUNA	AAABCIINNSSTY	ABYSSINIAN CAT
AAAADGHHIMMNT	MAHATMA GANDHI	AAABCILLLOPRY	PARABOLICALLY
AAAADHILNRSSS	AS HARD AS NAILS	AAABDDDLMNNOR	DONALD BRADMAN
AAAADHIMNPRSS	SPANISH ARMADA	AAABDDEENRRTW	BREAD AND WATER
AAAADHLNRRTUZ	NATURAL HAZARD	AAABDDELNTTUW	WATTLE AND DAUB
AAAAEEEGKNRTV	TAKE AN AVERAGE	AAABDEEFIRRSS	AS FREE AS A BIRD
AAAAEEFILRRRW	AERIAL WARFARE	AAABDEEFLSTTT	LEFT A BAD TASTE
AAAAEEGKMSTWY	MAKES A GETAWAY	AAABDEEGHINRT	BREATHED AGAIN
AAAAEFGIPRSWY	PAYS A FAIR WAGE	AAABDEEGIKNRT	BREAKING A DATE
AAAAEFKMPSSUX	MAKES A FAUX PAS	AAABDEEGMMNNT	BAD MANAGEMENT
AAAAEGIMMNRST	ANAGRAMMATISE	AAABDEEHIOTTT	HAD A BITE TO EAT
AAAAEGIMMNRTZ	ANAGRAMMATIZE	AAABDEEILTTTW	WAITED AT TABLE
AAAAEGNRSTVXZ	EXTRAVAGANZAS	AAABDEEINRRSS	ARABIAN DESERT
AAAAEHIKNRSST	AS THIN AS A RAKE	AAABDEGHHINTV	HAVE A BAD NIGHT

AAABDEGHHHNRTY	HANG BY A THREAD
AAABDEGIINRRV	DRIVE A BARGAIN
AAABDEGINORRV	DROVE A BARGAIN
AAABDEGMNNNOR	RAG-AND-BONE MAN
AAABDEHKNNSTU	TAKEN A HUSBAND
AAABDEHKNSSTU	TAKES A HUSBAND
AAABDELLNPSTU	SPANDAU BALLET
AAABDELORRSTV	TRAVELS ABROAD
AAABDEORRSTWY	BAYSWATER ROAD
AAABDFFIORSST	STIFF AS A BOARD
AAABDGIKLNNRW	DRAWING A BLANK
AAABDILLNOOSS	AS BOLD AS A LION
AAABDLLLOPPRU	POPULAR BALLAD
AAABEEEHHRRTV	HAVE A BREATHER
AAABEEEHKRRTT	TAKE A BREATHER
AAABEEELLRTUV	RATEABLE VALUE
AAABEEERRSTTT	BEATS A RETREAT
AAABEEFHKRSTV	HAVE BREAKFAST
AAABEEFKLRSTT	LATE BREAKFAST
AAABEEGHINRST	BREATHES AGAIN
AAABEEGIKNNTT	TAKEN A BEATING
AAABEEGIKNSTT	TAKES A BEATING
AAABEEGLLMNST	GENTLE AS A LAMB
AAABEEGLNSSTU	AUGEAN STABLES
AAABEEHIOSTTT	HAS A BITE TO EAT
AAABEEILLNSSV	AVAILABLENESS
AAABEEKLMMNRR	REMARKABLE MAN
AAABEEKPRRSTT	BATTERSEA PARK
AAABEELLNPSST	PALATABLENESS
AAABEEELMNNORS	REASONABLE MAN
AAABEENOOTTTT	BEATEN A TATTOO
AAABEFGIKLLNR	BREAKING A FALL
AAABEFILRRRTW	TRIBAL WARFARE
AAABEFINNRRTT	BANANA FRITTER
AAABEGIKMMNNRR	BREAKING AN ARM
AAABEGIKNPRRT	BREAKING APART
AAABEGKOOPSSS	BOOKS A PASSAGE
AAABEHLMNOPRT	ROMAN ALPHABET
AAABEIILLPPTY	APPEALABILITY
AAABEILLMNPTU	MANIPULATABLE
AAABEKLNRSTUW	BREAKS A WALNUT
AAABELNRTTUUY	NATURAL BEAUTY
AAABEMNOOSSSY	AS SOON AS MAYBE
AAABGHIINNRST	ARABIAN NIGHTS
AAABGIILLNRTZ	BLAZING A TRAIL
AAABHHOTTTTUW	WHAT ABOUT THAT?
AAABIIILLNOST	LABIALISATION
AAABIIILLNOTZ	LABIALIZATION
AAABIIILNTTTY	ATTAINABILITY
AAABIIKLNNOST	BALKANISATION
AAABIIKLNNOTZ	BALKANIZATION
AAABIILNORRTT	ARBITRATIONAL
AAACCCGHILOPR	CACOGRAPHICAL
AAACCDEEHNORT	ARCHDEACONATE
AAACCDEFGHLNO	GLAD OF A CHANCE
AAACCDEFILNTT	FATAL ACCIDENT
AAACCDEGHILNR	RADICAL CHANGE
AAACCDEHIILMN	MECHANICAL AID
AAACCDEIIMNNO	NADIA COMANECI
AAACCDEIINPTT	INCAPACITATED
AAACCDEIRRRST	CARDIAC ARREST
AAACCDHHINNTW	WATCH AND CHAIN
AAACCEEEELLNRS	CLEARANCE SALE
AAACCEEGHINTV	GAVE IT A CHANCE
AAACCEEHHLSTW	CATCHES A WHALE
AAACCEEHKRRTW	WEAK CHARACTER
AAACCEEHLNPST	CATCHES A PLANE
AAACCEEMRTUUV	CREATE A VACUUM
AAACCEFILNRRT	CENTRAL AFRICA
AAACCEGHHINNV	HAVING A CHANCE
AAACCEGHIKNNT	TAKING A CHANCE

AAACCEGHKMRRR	GRAHAM CRACKER
AAACCEGHLRRVY	CAVALRY CHARGE
AAACCEGNNOTUV	GAVE AN ACCOUNT
AAACCEHIMNRRT	MAIN CHARACTER
AAACCEHINRSTT	CATCHES A TRAIN
AAACCEHNRSTUW	CATCH UNAWARES
AAACCEHPRRRTT	CHARACTER PART
AAACCEIINPSTT	INCAPACITATES
AAACCEILMMOTX	CAME TO A CLIMAX
AAACCEILNNOTT	ATLANTIC OCEAN
AAACCEINNNQSTU	ACQUAINTANCES
AAACCELLPRSTY	CRYSTAL PALACE
AAACCELNORTYY	CYANOACRYLATE
AAACCFILLNSVY	FILLS A VACANCY
AAACCGILLLMOO	MALACOLOGICAL
AAACCIILMSSTT	SALAMI TACTICS
AAACCILLRSSTY	SARCASTICALLY
AAACCKLNRSTUW	CRACKS A WALNUT
AAACDDDEEEHNR	REACH A DEAD END
AAACDDDEGNRUV	ADVANCED GUARD
AAACDDEEEELNNO	LEAD ONE A DANCE
AAACDDEEGILNN	LEADING A DANCE
AAACDDEENNORW	DONE A WAR-DANCE
AAACDDEENORSW	DOES A WAR-DANCE
AAACDDEENSTVY	STEADY ADVANCE
AAACDDEIINNPV	PAID IN ADVANCE
AAACDDINNORSU	ISADORA DUNCAN
AAACDDKLNORVY	NAVAL DOCKYARD
AAACDEEEPPRRS	PREPARED A CASE
AAACDEEEQSTUU	ADEQUATE CAUSE
AAACDEEHHLLST	HAD ALL THE ACES
AAACDEEIMMNRR	AMERICAN DREAM
AAACDEEINPPRS	DISAPPEARANCE
AAACDEEKMNSSV	MAKES ADVANCES
AAACDEFIKRRST	DARKEST AFRICA
AAACDEGGIMNSU	CAUSING DAMAGE
AAACDEGILMMSS	CLAIMS DAMAGES
AAACDEGINRRSS	AIRS AND GRACES
AAACDEGLLNOTT	TOLD AT A GLANCE
AAACDEGLNNORS	ON A GRAND SCALE
AAACDEHHNORTU	REACH OUT A HAND
AAACDEHILMMSY	MICHAELMAS DAY
AAACDEHIMORTW	ATOMIC WARHEAD
AAACDEHINNPSS	ACHES AND PAINS
AAACDEHIPRSST	AS CHEAP AS DIRT
AAACDEHILLLOTT	CALLED TO A HALT
AAACDEHNNPSTY	CHEAP AND NASTY
AAACDEHORRTTW	COWARD AT HEART
AAACDEIIINPRT	PAEDIATRICIAN
AAACDEINNPSVY	PAYS IN ADVANCE
AAACDEKORSSTY	STEADY AS A ROCK
AAACDELNPPRRT	PART AND PARCEL
AAACDFNRRSSTT	ARTS AND CRAFTS
AAACDGGINNNOT	DANCING A TANGO
AAACDGHIIMPRT	DIAPHRAGMATIC
AAACDGIILLNTY	CALLING IT A DAY
AAACDGILMRRTU	DRAMATURGICAL
AAACDGILNNTWZ	DANCING A WALTZ
AAACDHIILOPRS	APHRODISIACAL
AAACDHIINOPRS	ANAPHRODISIAC
AAACDHIKPRSST	AS DARK AS PITCH
AAACDHILNOPTY	ANAPHYLACTOID
AAACDIILMNOPS	DIPSOMANIACAL
AAACDIINNNSSV	SCANDINAVIANS
AAACDILLOPRXY	PARADOXICALLY
AAACDILLQRTUY	QUADRATICALLY
AAACDILMNNSSY	CAYMAN ISLANDS
AAACDILNNRSSY	CANARY ISLANDS
AAACDKLLLMNOR	LOCAL LANDMARK
AAACDMMNNOSTU	MUSCAT AND OMAN
AAACEEEGILMNR	AMERICAN EAGLE

AAACEEEGKRRTT	TAKE GREAT CARE	AAACGIILMRSTT	MAGISTRATICAL
AAACEEEGLNNST	SEEN AT A GLANCE	AAACGILLMMRTY	GRAMMATICALLY
AAACEEEGLNSST	SEES AT A GLANCE	AAACGILLMPRTY	PRAGMATICALLY
AAACEEEIMNPRT	REMAIN AT PEACE	AAACGILNNOTTU	ANTICOAGULANT
AAACEEEKMRRTT	CREATE A MARKET	AAACGINPPRSSS	SCRAPING A PASS
AAACEEEPPRRSS	PREPARES A CASE	AAACHILLMSTTY	ASTHMATICALLY
AAACEEFGOPRSS	FORCE A PASSAGE	AAACHILLNOPRY	ANAPHORICALLY
AAACEEGIINRRV	AIR A GRIEVANCE	AAACIILLMOTXY	AXIOMATICALLY
AAACEEGILNPSV	LEAVING A SPACE	AAACIILLPRSTY	PARASITICALLY
AAACEEGLLLNTT	TELL AT A GLANCE	AAACIILLSTTVY	ATAVISTICALLY
AAACEEGLLMPRS	LARGE-SCALE MAP	AAACIILNOOSST	ASSOCIATIONAL
AAACEEGLNSTWY	GETS CLEAN AWAY	AAACIILNOSTTU	ACTUALISATION
AAACEEGLRSTWY	GETS CLEAR AWAY	AAACIILNOTTUZ	ACTUALIZATION
AAACEEGNRSTVX	EXTRAVAGANCES	AAACIIMNRRSTT	TRACTARIANISM
AAACEEHHLLSST	HAS ALL THE ACES	AAACIIORSSTTU	AUSTROASIATIC
AAACEEHLNPRRT	CHARTER A PLANE	AAACIKOPRRSST	SICK AS A PARROT
AAACEEINRSTTV	SET AT VARIANCE	AAACILLLNOTTY	LACTATIONALLY
AAACEEKLLMNOW	MAKE ALLOWANCE	AAACILLMNOPRY	PANORAMICALLY
AAACEEKLNPRTT	REPEL AN ATTACK	AAACILLMOTTUY	AUTOMATICALLY
AAACEELOPPRSS	PALE AS A CORPSE	AAACILLNOOTVY	AVOCATIONALLY
AAACEEMMNNRRST	ARMAMENTS RACE	AAACILLOPTTUY	CAPITAL OUTLAY
AAACEFGIILNNP	FINANCIAL PAGE	AAACILNNORSTT	TRANSACTIONAL
AAACEFIILNNRY	FINANCIAL YEAR	AAACILNNRSTTT	TRANSATLANTIC
AAACEFILLMNST	FALSE CLAIMANT	AAACILNORSTTU	ASTRONAUTICAL
AAACEFILNORRT	RAREFACTIONAL	AAACILNRRSTUV	INTRAVASCULAR
AAACEFILNPPRT	FRANTIC APPEAL	AAADDDDHINNST	DID A HANDSTAND
AAACEFIMORRTW	ATOMIC WARFARE	AAADDDEELTUVX	VALUE ADDED TAX
AAACEFIRRSTTW	STATIC WARFARE	AAADDDEENNWWX	WAXED AND WANED
AAACEFLMORRSU	CAUSE FOR ALARM	AAADDDEGINSTV	DISADVANTAGED
AAACEGGHIKMNN	MAKING A CHANGE	AAADDDEINRSWY	EDWARDIAN DAYS
AAACEGGIMNNRT	ACTING MANAGER	AAADDDDNRRSSYY	YARDS AND YARDS
AAACEGGINNSTT	ACTING AS AGENT	AAADDEEEHHLLV	HAD A LEVEL HEAD
AAACEGHHNNOTT	CHAETOGNATHAN	AAADDEEEHKNTW	AWAKEN THE DEAD
AAACEGHIKNPTT	TAKE A NIGHTCAP	AAADDEEEHKSTW	AWAKES THE DEAD
AAACEGIKKMNPT	MAKING A PACKET	AAADDEEEKMSST	MAKES A DEAD SET
AAACEGIKNPSTU	TAKING UP A CASE	AAADDEEEPRRRW	REAPED A REWARD
AAACEGILLNPSY	PLAYING A SCALE	AAADDEEFHILVY	HAVE A FIELD DAY
AAACEGILMNNOR	ANGLO-AMERICAN	AAADDEGGNRSTU	STANDARD GAUGE
AAACEGILMNNRS	AMERICAN SLANG	AAADDEGHINSTY	THIS DAY AND AGE
AAACEGIMMNPRS	SMEAR CAMPAIGN	AAADDEGINSSTV	DISADVANTAGES
AAACEGINRSSTT	REACTS AGAINST	AAADDEIINRRRW	AIR-RAID WARDEN
AAACEHIILLMNV	MACHIAVELLIAN	AAADDEILNORRV	DEAD ON ARRIVAL
AAACEHIIMNNNS	MANICHAEANISM	AAADDELLNSSSS	LADS AND LASSES
AAACEHIIMMNTT	MATHEMATICIAN	AAADDEMMSSTUU	MADAME TUSSAUD
AAACEHILLPTTY	APATHETICALLY	AAADDENNRSSTT	STAND AND STARE
AAACEHIMOOPPR	PHARMACOPOEIA	AAADDENRSSSTT	SETS A STANDARD
AAACEHLLLNRST	ANCESTRAL HALL	AAADDHILMOYYY	MAY DAY HOLIDAY
AAACEHLMNORST	STEAL A MARCH ON	AAADDLNORRSTY	ROYAL STANDARD
AAACEHLORRSTT	SCARLETT OHARA	AAADEEEEFRRRT	FREE TRADE AREA
AAACEHNRNRRSTW	SEARCH WARRANT	AAADEEEFLLMMN	MALE AND FEMALE
AAACEIILMNNRT	LATIN AMERICAN	AAADEEEHHLLSV	HAS A LEVEL HEAD
AAACEIKLMNOPS	ASK A POLICEMAN	AAADEEELMMNPX	MADE AN EXAMPLE
AAACEILMOOSST	OSTEOMALACIAS	AAADEEELMNORV	EAMON DE VALERA
AAACEKNRSTTUY	TAKE SANCTUARY	AAADEEELMPPRR	PREPARED A MEAL
AAACELLLMNOSS	ON A SMALL SCALE	AAADEEEMRRSTU	TREAD A MEASURE
AAACELLLMOSWW	SWALLOW A CAMEL	AAADEEFGILLSY	LEADS A GAY LIFE
AAACELLMNRSTY	SACRAMENTALLY	AAADEEFGIMRTV	GAVE A FIRM DATE
AAACELLNORRTT	CONTRALATERAL	AAADEEFHHLNRT	THREE AND A HALF
AAACELNRSSTUU	NATURAL CAUSES	AAADEEFHLNNSV	SEVEN AND A HALF
AAACELORSSTTW	COASTAL WATERS	AAADEEFHNRRTT	TAR AND FEATHER
AAACENRRRSTTU	RESTAURANT CAR	AAADEEFNNORWW	DAWN OF A NEW ERA
AAACFHIKLQSSU	QUICK AS A FLASH	AAADEEFNRRSTU	TURNS A DEAF EAR
AAACFIIILMRRT	ARTIFICIAL ARM	AAADEEGIKNNRT	TAKEN A READING
AAACFILLNSTTY	FANTASTICALLY	AAADEEGILMNNS	LEADING SEAMAN
AAACFKLNORTTT	FRONTAL ATTACK	AAADEEGILNNST	LEANED AGAINST
AAACFLMNOOPTY	FLOAT A COMPANY	AAADEEGIMNRTZ	TRADE MAGAZINE
AAACGHIILNSTY	SAILING A YACHT	AAADEEGLLNOPP	LODGE AN APPEAL
AAACGHINNSTWY	SNATCHING AWAY	AAADEEGLLNOPR	EDGAR ALLAN POE
AAACGHINPRTTU	CAUGHT IN A TRAP	AAADEEGLMMNRY	MARY MAGDALENE
AAACGIIKLMNPT	MAKING CAPITAL	AAADEEGMRRRSU	DEMERARA SUGAR
AAACGIIKLMNST	STAKING A CLAIM	AAADEEHHLNRTY	HALE AND HEARTY

AAADEEHIKLNRT	TAKE A HARD LINE
AAADEEHILMNPV	VEAL AND HAM PIE
AAADEEHIMNSTY	HAD AN EASY TIME
AAADEEIKNRSTT	TAKEN IT AS READ
AAADEEIKRSSTT	TAKES IT AS READ
AAADEEILNPWXY	EXPLAINED AWAY
AAADEEIMNOTTY	ONE DAY AT A TIME
AAADEEKMORSTW	WORKED AS A TEAM
AAADEEKMPRRSS	PASSED A REMARK
AAADEELLLPRRW	DREW A PARALLEL
AAADEELNORSTY	LEAD ONE ASTRAY
AAADEEMMNPTTT	MADE AN ATTEMPT
AAADEEMNRSTTW	MADE A NEW START
AAADEENNSSWWX	WAXES AND WANES
AAADEENRRSSYY	YEARS AND YEARS
AAADEFFHLLORS	HEADS FOR A FALL
AAADEFFNNORSU	SOUND A FANFARE
AAADEFGHHILNT	EIGHT AND A HALF
AAADEFHHILMNV	HAVE HALF A MIND
AAADEFIIIIMOST	MADE A HASH OF IT
AAADEFHINOPRS	FASHION PARADE
AAADEFHIRSSSY	FRESH AS A DAISY
AAADEFIKMOSTY	MAKES A DAY OF IT
AAADEFIKOPRST	AFRAID TO SPEAK
AAADEFILLRSST	AFTER ALL'S SAID
AAADEFILMRSTV	DRAMA FESTIVAL
AAADEFINQRRSU	FAIR AND SQUARE
AAADEFKLNOORS	ASKED FOR A LOAN
AAADEGGHLNRTU	LAUGH AT DANGER
AAADEGGILLNRU	LEGAL GUARDIAN
AAADEGGILNNRU	GUARDIAN ANGEL
AAADEGGIMNPSY	PAYING DAMAGES
AAADEGHIHIMNRT	HAD A NIGHTMARE
AAADEGHHIRSTT	STRAIGHT AHEAD
AAADEGHIKMNWY	MAKING HEADWAY
AAADEGHILNNNP	PLANNING AHEAD
AAADEGHINRRST	HARD AS GRANITE
AAADEGIIRQOOUE	HAZARDS A GUESS
AAADEGIIKMNNS	MAKING AN ASIDE
AAADEGIILNPTY	PLAYED IT AGAIN
AAADEGIIMMRST	DIAGRAMMATISE
AAADEGIIMMRTZ	DIAGRAMMATIZE
AAADEGILMOOSS	AS GOOD AS A MILE
AAADEGILNPRTY	LEADING A PARTY
AAADEGILNPSTY	PLAYED AGAINST
AAADEGILNRSTY	LEADING ASTRAY
AAADEGINNRWWY	WANDERING AWAY
AAADEGINPRRWY	PAYING A REWARD
AAADEGKNOOTTV	TOOK ADVANTAGE
AAADEGLLLMNRS	LARGE AND SMALL
AAADEGLLMNRST	GREAT AND SMALL
AAADEGLNNPRRT	GRANDPARENTAL
AAADEGNRRRSTT	STAR AND GARTER
AAADEGOORSSST	AS GOOD AS A REST
AAADEHHIMNNRT	RHADAMANTHINE
AAADEHHKMNRSW	WARM HANDSHAKE
AAADEHHNPRSSZ	HAPHAZARDNESS
AAADEHIKLNOTY	TAKEN A HOLIDAY
AAADEHIKLOSTY	TAKES A HOLIDAY
AAADEHLLNNOPY	PLAY A LONE HAND
AAADEHMMNNRST	ARMS AND THE MAN
AAADEILLQRRTU	QUADRILATERAL
AAADEKLLLMMST	MADE SMALL TALK
AAADEKNNPRTTT	PARK ATTENDANT
AAADEKNNPSTTU	TAKEN UP A STAND
AAADEKNPSSTTU	TAKES UP A STAND
AAADELMMOPSST	PLASMODESMATA
AAADELMOOPPRS	MADE A PROPOSAL
AAADENNRRSSTV	RANTS AND RAVES
AAADFFGIKNOTY	TAKING A DAY OFF
AAADFGINNORST	FOR AND AGAINST

AAADFILNOPRSS	PAIR OF SANDALS
AAADGGINRSSTU	GUARDS AGAINST
AAADGHHIINORV	HAVING A HAIR-DO
AAADGHIKNRSST	AS DARK AS NIGHT
AAADGHILNNNOY	LAYING A HAND ON
AAADGHIMRRSTT	STRAIGHT DRAMA
AAADGIKNOOSSW	AS GOOD AS A WINK
AAADGILLNORTY	GRADATIONALLY
AAADGILNNNORT	GRAND NATIONAL
AAADGILNNORTU	NATIONAL GUARD
AAADGIMNOORST	GOOD SAMARITAN
AAADGINNPRSTT	STANDING APART
AAADGINNSSSTT	STANDS AGAINST
AAADHILLNNOUY	ANNUAL HOLIDAY
AAADHILNOOWYY	AWAY ON HOLIDAY
AAADHIMMMMNSU	MUHAMMADANISM
AAADIIMNORSTT	DRAMATISATION
AAADIIMNORTTZ	DRAMATIZATION
AAADILLNSSTTT	AT A STANDSTILL
AAAEEEEGLMSSV	LEAVE A MESSAGE
AAAEEEFFRRRTYY	YEAR AFTER YEAR
AAAEEEGLMNPVX	GAVE AN EXAMPLE
AAAEEEGMNRSTT	ESTATE MANAGER
AAAEEEHKNPRSS	SHAKESPEAREAN
AAAEEEKLMMNPX	MAKE AN EXAMPLE
AAAEEEELLOPPTV	LEAVE TO APPEAL
AAAEEEELMPPRRS	PREPARES A MEAL
AAAEEFFGILLNGG	AS LARGE AS LIFE
AAAEEFFGIMRRST	MARRIAGE FEAST
AAAEEFGLORSVW	LAW OF AVERAGES
AAAEEFHILMOTW	A WHALE OF A TIME
AAAEEGGIMNRSSU	GERMAN SAUSAGE
AAAEEGHLOPPRR	PALAEOGRAPHER
AAAEEGINNRSSX	SEXAGENARIANS
AAAEEGKLLRSTT	GREAT SALT LAKE
AAAEEGKNOORTV	TOOK AN AVERAGE
AAAEEHILMRRST	RAISE THE ALARM
AAAEEHIMNSSTY	HAS AN EASY TIME
AAAEEHLLRSSVW	WALLS HAVE EARS
AAAEEIKKMMSST	MAKES A MISTAKE
AAAEEIKKNSTTW	WEAK AS A KITTEN
AAAEEINNNPSTW	NEAT AS A NEW PIN
AAAEEKLNNPTTY	TAKEN A PENALTY
AAAEEKLNPSTTY	TAKES A PENALTY
AAAEEKMMMNPTTT	MAKE AN ATTEMPT
AAAEEKMNNRSTTW	MAKE A NEW START
AAAEEKMPRRSSS	PASSES A REMARK
AAAEEKNNRSTUW	TAKEN UNAWARES
AAAEEKNRSSTUW	TAKES UNAWARES
AAAEELMPRRTUY	AMATEUR PLAYER
AAAEENORSSUVY	SAVE AS YOU EARN
	SAVE-AS-YOU-EARN
AAAEFFGNNOTTT	OFF AT A TANGENT
AAAEFFHINORST	AFTER A FASHION
AAAEFFIIPRRTV	PRIVATE AFFAIR
AAAEFGILNPSTV	PAGAN FESTIVAL
AAAEFGIORSSST	AS FAR AS IT GOES
AAAEFGMOPRSSS	PASSAGE OF ARMS
AAAEFHHIKMOST	MAKE A HASH OF IT
AAAEFHIKNPRSS	SHARP AS A KNIFE
AAAEFHILLNRVY	HEAVY RAINFALL
AAAEFIILMMRST	MATERFAMILIAS
AAAEFIILMPRST	PATERFAMILIAS
AAAEFILOPPRST	FAILS TO APPEAR
AAAEFINRSSTTW	AS FAR AS IT WENT
AAAEGGGILNORT	AGGREGATIONAL
AAAEGGGIMNNST	STAGE MANAGING
AAAEGGHIINNRS	GAINS A HEARING
AAAEGGILLNNPU	PLAIN LANGUAGE
AAAEGHHIMNRST	HAS A NIGHTMARE
AAAEGHHINRTTV	HAVING AT HEART

AAAEGHILNNPPV	HAVING AN APPLE
AAAEGHILNNTTV	HAVING A TALENT
AAAEGHILNSTTW	AGAINST THE LAW
AAAEGHIMMNRWY	HAMMERING AWAY
AAAEGHIMPPRRY	HAPPY MARRIAGE
AAAEGHLPSSTTT	AT THE LAST GASP
AAAEGIILLNRTV	LEAVING A TRAIL
AAAEGIKKLLNRS	SANG LIKE A LARK
AAAEGIKKMMNRR	MAKING A REMARK
AAAEGILLOPRRT	ALLIGATOR PEAR
AAAEGILMORRRY	ROYAL MARRIAGE
AAAEGILNNOPRY	REPAYING A LOAN
AAAEGIMMNPRST	PARAMAGNETISM
AAAEGINNNNORS	NONAGENARIANS
AAAEGINPRRSYY	SAYING A PRAYER
AAAEGINRSTTVX	EXTRAVASATING
AAAEGLLLMOPRR	PARALLELOGRAM
AAAEGLLRRRSUY	REGULAR SALARY
AAAEGLNRTTVXY	EXTRAVAGANTLY
AAAEHILMNPRST	MARSHAL PETAIN
AAAEHILNSSSTW	THE LAW IS AN ASS
AAAEHKNOPSSTT	TAKE A SNAPSHOT
AAAEHLMRTTTUW	WALTER MATTHAU
AAAEIIKLNPSST	SPEAKS ITALIAN
AAAEIILMNNOTX	EXAMINATIONAL
AAAEIILMNNRRT	ANIMAL TRAINER
AAAEIILMNORTX	EXAMINATORIAL
AAAEIILNQRSTU	EQUALITARIANS
AAAEILMNPRRTY	PARLIAMENTARY
AAAEILNNOPTTT	TEA PLANTATION
AAAEIMMMNRRTU	ARMAMENTARIUM
AAAEIMNPSTTWY	AWAITS PAYMENT
AAAEINORSTTVX	EXTRAVASATION
AAAEKKLLLMMST	MAKE SMALL TALK
AAAEKLMOOPPRS	MAKE A PROPOSAL
AAAELLNNRTTTU	NATURAL TALENT
AAAELLOPPPPRU	POPULAR APPEAL
AAAELMOPPRSST	APPEALS TO ARMS
AAAELNORTTTWY	ATTORNEY AT LAW
AAAELORRSSSTT	AS A LAST RESORT
AAAELQRRRSTTU	START A QUARREL
AAAEMMRRSSSTT	MASTERS-AT-ARMS
AAAEMRSSTTTUU	AMATEUR STATUS
AAAENORSSTUWY	RUNS AWAY TO SEA
AAAFFHIMORSTX	THOMAS FAIRFAX
AAAFGIKNORSUV	ASKING A FAVOUR
AAAFHHINPRSTT	PARTHIAN SHAFT
AAAFIJMOPPRSY	PAIR OF PYJAMAS
AAAFILLMORTWY	AWAY FROM IT ALL
AAAFILLNOPRTT	FALL INTO A TRAP
AAAFLLNOOPPRY	APPLY FOR A LOAN
AAAGGHIILNRSU	RAISING A LAUGH
AAAGGHLNOPPRR	LONG PARAGRAPH
AAAGGIIKLMNNS	MAKING A SIGNAL
AAAGGIILNRSSS	RAISING A GLASS
AAAGGIINNNRSTT	STARTING AGAIN
AAAGHIILNTTTU	TAUGHT ITALIAN
AAAGHIINRRSST	AS RIGHT AS RAIN
AAAGHIKLMNPSS	MAKING A SPLASH
AAAGHMNNNORUV	NORMAN VAUGHAN
AAAGIIILNRTTW	AWAITING TRIAL
AAAGIILLNRSWY	RAILWAY SIGNAL
AAAGIILNNOSST	ASSIGNATIONAL
AAAGIILNNOSTV	GALVANISATION
AAAGIILNNOTVZ	GALVANIZATION
AAAGIILNORTTV	GRAVITATIONAL
AAAGIINNPRTUU	TUPI-GUARANIAN
AAAGIINNSSSST	ASSASSINATING
AAAGIKLNNPPRY	PLAYING A PRANK
AAAGIKLNRSSUV	SUNIL GAVASKAR
AAAGILLNPTWYZ	PLAYING A WALTZ
AAAGILNOOPPRT	PROPAGATIONAL
AAAGIMNNOPRSY	PAYING A RANSOM
AAAGIPPRSSSTU	ASPARAGUS TIPS
AAAGKNORRSTTU	SARATOGA TRUNK
AAAGLMMNORSSY	AS LONG AS MY ARM
AAAHIIMNNRSTU	HUMANITARIANS
AAAHIINORRTTU	AUTHORITARIAN
AAAHIMNOQSSTU	THOMAS AQUINAS
AAAIIILMNNOST	ANIMALISATION
AAAIIILMNNOTZ	ANIMALIZATION
AAAIILLLLNPUV	ALLUVIAL PLAIN
AAAIILLNORTVY	VARIATIONALLY
AAAIIMNOORSTT	AROMATISATION
AAAIIMNOORTTZ	AROMATIZATION
AAAIINNOSSSST	ASSASSINATION
AAAIKLNOPRTTW	WALK INTO A TRAP
AAAIILLLNOTUVY	VALUATIONALLY
AAAILLNNORSTT	TRANSLATIONAL
AAAILMNOPRRTY	PARANORMALITY
AAAILMNORSTVY	SALVATION ARMY
AAAILNNNORSTT	TRANSNATIONAL
AAAILNNOPRSTU	SUPRANATIONAL
AAAINORSSSSST	ASSASSINATORS
AAAKLNOOPRTVY	ANATOLY KARPOV
AAALOOPRRSSUZ	POOR AS LAZARUS
AABBBCDEGIORR	CRIBBAGE BOARD
AABBBDEFJOOST	BEST OF A BAD JOB
AABBBIILORSTY	ABSORBABILITY
AABBCDEEEPTXY	EXPECTED A BABY
AABBCDEEIKRRR	BAREBACK RIDER
AABBCDEFKNOSU	BACK END OF A BUS
AABBCEEEEMMMR	BECAME A MEMBER
AABBCEEHILNOS	BELISHA BEACON
AABBCEEHKKRST	BREAKS THE BACK
AABBCEEKKNORS	BREAK ONES BACK
AABBCEEPRRTUY	BARBECUE PARTY
AABBCEHIKNSTT	STAB IN THE BACK
AABBCEHLLMOTX	MATCH-BOX LABEL
	MATCHBOX LABEL
AABBCEKKOOPPR	PAPERBACK BOOK
AABBCHILNRRRY	BRANCH LIBRARY
AABBCILLMOSTY	BOMBASTICALLY
AABBCILMORTTY	TRIAL BY COMBAT
AABBDDDINRRSS	DRIBS AND DRABS
AABBDDEEGILOR	BIODEGRADABLE
AABBDDEENNRRR	BERNARD BRADEN
AABBDDEERSSST	BRASS BEDSTEAD
AABBDEEEHKRRT	BREAK THE BREAD
AABBDEEEHNNTT	BEATEN THE BAND
AABBDEEFGLRST	FLABBERGASTED
AABBDEEGHHSTT	GET THE HABDABS
AABBDEEGIKNRR	BREAKING BREAD
AABBDEEHILTWY	ABIDE BY THE LAW
AABBDEGHHOSTT	GOT THE HABDABS
AABBDEGHILNVY	BEHAVING BADLY
AABBDEGINRSTU	RUBBED AGAINST
AABBDEIILLRT	BILLIARD TABLE
AABBEEGIKNNOR	BREAKING A BONE
AABBEEHHIKRTT	BREAK THE HABIT
AABBEEHILLSST	ESTABLISHABLE
AABBEEHILNSST	HABITABLENESS
AABBEEHKKNRST	BREAKS THE BANK
AABBEEIMNRSSU	SUBMARINE BASE
AABBEEKLMORRY	REMARKABLE BOY
AABBEEKLORSTT	BREAKS A BOTTLE
AABBEFLLLOOTT	TABLE FOOTBALL
AABBEFLOSSTTU	FABULOUS BEAST
AABBEGHINTTUY	BATHING BEAUTY
AABBEGIKLNOOT	BOOKING A TABLE
AABBEGNOPPRRW	BROWN PAPER BAG
AABBEIILLOSSU	BOUILLABAISSE

AABBEIINORSTV	ABBREVIATIONS
AABBEIKKNRSST	BREAK ITS BANKS
AABBENORRSSSU	BARBAROUSNESS
AABBIIILNOTTY	OBTAINABILITY
AABBIMMMNPSYY	NAMBY-PAMBYISM
AABCCCCIIPTUY	CUBIC CAPACITY
AABCCCHKMRSTY	SCRATCH MY BACK
AABCCDDHIKLRW	BACKWARD CHILD
AABCCDEEILNRT	CREDIT BALANCE
AABCCDEEINRRS	DESCRIBE AN ARC
AABCCDEHLLORU	CLAUDE CHABROL
AABCCDHINNOSW	BACON SANDWICH
AABCCDILLNPSU	PUBLIC SCANDAL
AABCCEEHKKTUW	BUCKWHEAT CAKE
AABCCEEHLMRRT	CHARM BRACELET
AABCCEEIRRSUU	BUREAUCRACIES
AABCCEEKLRRRR	CRACKER BARREL
AABCCEFKNNOSY	BACK ONES FANCY
AABCCEHHLPRYY	BRACHYCEPHALY
AABCCEHILNPRS	SPECIAL BRANCH
AABCCEHKLNOPT	CLAP ON THE BACK
AABCCEHLORTVY	TRAVEL BY COACH
AABCCEIIKLLMT	CLIMB LIKE A CAT
AABCCEIILMPRT	IMPRACTICABLE
AABCCEIILPTTY	ACCEPTABILITY
AABCCEKLORSTT	CRACKS A BOTTLE
AABCCEKNORSTT	BREAKS CONTACT
AABCCELNNOTUU	UNACCOUNTABLE
AABCCIILNNST	CANNIBALISTIC
AABCCIILLLTUY	CALCULABILITY
AABCCIILMPRTY	IMPRACTICABLY
AABCCIKLLOPST	BLOCK CAPITALS
AABCCKLNRRSTU	BLACKCURRANTS
AABCCLLNOSTUY	BY ALL ACCOUNTS
AABCCLNNOTUUY	UNACCOUNTABLY
AABCDDEEMNOOT	COME TO A BAD END
AABCDEEEEGGMN	BECAME ENGAGED
AABCDEEEEFNRSS	BAREFACEDNESS
AABCDEEEHLORV	OVERHEAD CABLE
AABCDEEEHLRRT	CEREBRAL DEATH
AABCDEEEINOQU	QUEEN BOADICEA
AABCDEEEENORRT	BEATEN A RECORD
AABCDEEFIPRRT	PREFABRICATED
AABCDEEGHILRS	DISCHARGEABLE
AABCDEEGILNNS	SENDING A CABLE
AABCDEEHHKLTT	THE BLACK DEATH
AABCDEEHIKLVY	BACKED HEAVILY
AABCDEEHLMPTY	PLAYED MACBETH
AABCDEEHLOUWY	EACH-WAY DOUBLE
AABCDEEIKNNRW	BACKED A WINNER
AABCDEELLLSSY	DECASYLLABLES
AABCDEENNORUV	OVERABUNDANCE
AABCDEFHHKNOT	BACK OF THE HAND
AABCDEFHLOOSW	SHOW A BOLD FACE
AABCDEFILMNNO	BALANCE OF MIND
AABCDEGIKLLNP	BACKPEDALLING
AABCDEGILLNNT	BALLET DANCING
AABCDEGKNORSW	GONE BACKWARDS
AABCDEGKORSSW	GOES BACKWARDS
AABCDEHHNOSSU	CHOSE A HUSBAND
AABCDEHIILTTY	DETACHABILITY
AABCDEHIIMORT	THIOCARBAMIDE
AABCDEHIKLNTW	BLACK AND WHITE
	BLACK-AND-WHITE
AABCDEHINOSTW	SHADOW CABINET
AABCDEHIRRRTU	RICHARD TAUBER
AABCDEHKLLNOT	TO HELL AND BACK
AABCDEHKLNOTT	BACK TO THE LAND
AABCDEHORRSTY	CARBOHYDRATES
AABCDEIKLLORY	LOCKABLE DIARY
AABCDEILNNORV	LIVER AND BACON
AABCDEILORSTV	LIVE BROADCAST
AABCDEKKNRSWW	KNEW BACKWARDS
AABCDEKLLNOST	BALL-AND-SOCKET
AABCDEKNRSTWW	WENT BACKWARDS
AABCDEKPRSSTW	STEP BACKWARDS
AABCDELMNORRU	RECORD AN ALBUM
AABCDELOPPRRS	CLAPPER-BOARDS
AABCDEMMNORTU	UNARMED COMBAT
AABCDGGIKNORW	GOING BACKWARD
AABCDGIILMOPT	DIPLOMATIC BAG
AABCDGIKLMRSU	BLACKGUARDISM
AABCDHINNOOPR	BRANCHIOPODAN
AABCDHIRRRRSY	BARRY RICHARDS
AABCDHNNOORRT	ROOT AND BRANCH
	ROOT-AND-BRANCH
AABCDIKNOPRTW	BACKWARD POINT
AABCDINOPRRTY	APRICOT BRANDY
AABCDINRRSTUY	BIRD SANCTUARY
AABCDKKNORSWW	KNOW BACKWARDS
AABCEEEEHKPRT	BREAK THE PEACE
AABCEEEELNPSS	PEACEABLENESS
AABCEEEFLLLNR	LA BELLE FRANCE
AABCEEFGGGSSX	EXCESS BAGGAGE
AABCEEEHHHLRT	HEAL THE BREACH
AABCEEEHLLRTT	CLEAR THE TABLE
AABCEEEHLNSST	TEACHABLENESS
AABCEEEILLPRR	IRREPLACEABLE
AABCEEEIRRRRT	ERECT A BARRIER
AABCEEEMMNNOW	BECOME A NEW MAN
AABCEEFFILTUU	BEAUTIFUL FACE
AABCEEFHHITTT	CHAFE AT THE BIT
AABCEEFHKORSS	BRACE OF SHAKES
AABCEEFIPRRST	PREFABRICATES
AABCEEFKRRSSU	BREAKS SURFACE
AABCEEFLORSTU	BEAUFORT SCALE
AABCEEGGPRRST	CARPET BAGGERS
	CARPETBAGGERS
AABCEEGHIOPRT	BACTERIOPHAGE
AABCEEGIILMNR	BEARING MALICE
AABCEEGIILNOT	ABIOGENETICAL
AABCEEGIMNORW	BECOMING AWARE
AABCEEGINRRST	CABARET SINGER
AABCEEHHLLRTW	BREACH THE WALL
AABCEEHHMMOST	THOMAS BEECHAM
AABCEEHHRSTUV	HAVE A BUTCHER'S
AABCEEHILMNPU	UNIMPEACHABLE
AABCEEHILNPTT	TIP THE BALANCE
AABCEEHKMOSTT	THOMAS A BECKET
AABCEEHLMRRTY	CARRY THE BLAME
AABCEEHOOPRRV	ABOVE REPROACH
AABCEEIILNPPR	INAPPRECIABLE
AABCEEIKMNRST	CABINETMAKERS
AABCEEILLMNRT	MENTAL CALIBRE
AABCEEILLPRRY	IRREPLACEABLY
AABCEEILMNOTX	TAXABLE INCOME
AABCEEILNNPSS	INCAPABLENESS
AABCEEIRRSTUU	BUREAUCRATISE
AABCEEIRRTUUZ	BUREAUCRATIZE
AABCEELLMORST	BEAT ALL-COMERS
AABCEELNRSSTT	TRACTABLENESS
AABCEENNOOSSV	SAVE ONES BACON
AABCEENRRSTTY	CARNABY STREET
AABCEFFHHIORT	BREACH OF FAITH
AABCEFFHLNOOT	ACT ON BEHALF OF
AABCEFHLLOORW	BACHELOR OF LAW
AABCEFHNOORRS	RASHER OF BACON
AABCEFIIINOTT	BEATIFICATION
AABCEFIINORTT	ABORTIFACIENT
AABCEFIINOSTY	FABIAN SOCIETY
AABCEFIOPRRRT	PREFABRICATOR
AABCEFLLNOOSS	LOSS OF BALANCE

AABCEGGIINNRS	BRINGING A CASE
AABCEGHHLLTTU	CAUGHT THE BALL
AABCEGHIILNTY	CHANGEABILITY
AABCEGHIKNORS	BACKING A HORSE
AABCEGHIOPRTY	BACTERIOPHAGY
AABCEGIIKMNNT	CABINETMAKING
AABCEGIKLNORS	BACKING A LOSER
AABCEGIKNNRSW	ANSWERING BACK
AABCEGILLMNNY	CALLING BY NAME
AABCEGILNNORV	OVERBALANCING
AABCEGILNNPRS	SPRING BALANCE
AABCEGINORRSS	BEARING A CROSS
AABCEGJLOOPTY	ABJECT APOLOGY
AABCEHHIKNNST	CASH IN THE BANK
AABCEHHIMPTTT	CHAMP AT THE BIT
AABCEHIKNNRSS	BACK IN HARNESS
AABCEHIKSSTTT	SITS AT THE BACK
AABCEHILLLMNR	LAMELLIBRANCH
AABCEHILMNPUY	UNIMPEACHABLY
AABCEHILMNRST	RICH MANS TABLE
AABCEHILMSTTU	SUITABLE MATCH
AABCEHINORSSW	CHASE RAINBOWS
AABCEHIRRRRSS	CRASH BARRIERS
AABCEHKLLOTTW	BACK TO THE WALL
AABCEHKLNOPST	SLAP ON THE BACK
AABCEHLLORSTT	CALLS TO THE BAR
AABCEIILNPPRY	INAPPRECIABLY
AABCEIKNNORRS	RACK ONES BRAIN
AABCEILLNNSUY	BALLY NUISANCE
AABCEILLOORTV	COLLABORATIVE
AABCEILMNNOOP	COMPANIONABLE
AABCEILNOSTUY	SALE BY AUCTION
AABCEINNRSTWY	WINS BY A CANTER
AABCEINOORRST	SERBO-CROATIAN
AABCEINRRSSTT	SCATTERBRAINS
AABCEKLNNOOSY	LAY ON ONE'S BACK
AABCELLNNOOST	BALLOON ASCENT
AABCELNRRSTTU	BURT LANCASTER
AABCEMRRSSTTT	ABSTRACT TERMS
AABCFFIILPRSU	PUBLIC AFFAIRS
AABCFFLLOORST	FOOTBALL SCARF
AABCFGIKLLNNO	FALLING BACK ON
AABCFGILNNOTU	CONFABULATING
AABCFHLLMOOTT	FOOTBALL MATCH
AABCFIKMNOORT	BACK-FORMATION
AABCFILNNOOTU	CONFABULATION
AABCFLNOORTUY	CONFABULATORY
AABCGIIILNNNS	CANNIBALISING
AABCGIIILNNNZ	CANNIBALIZING
AABCGIIKLNNRS	LACKING BRAINS
AABCGIILLOTUY	COAGULABILITY
AABCGIIMNRSST	BITING SARCASM
AABCGIINNNORT	BRING AN ACTION
AABCGILLNOORT	COLLABORATING
AABCGILMNRUWY	CRUMBLING AWAY
AABCGILNORTUW	CRAWLING ABOUT
AABCGILNORTXY	CARBOXYLATING
AABCGINNOPRTU	PRANCING ABOUT
AABCGINORRTUY	CARRYING ABOUT
AABCHKLMNNOOR	HONOR BLACKMAN
AABCIIILLMPTY	IMPLACABILITY
AABCIIILLNSTT	ANTIBALLISTIC
AABCIIILLPPTY	APPLICABILITY
AABCIIILNORST	CAST-IRON ALIBI
AABCIIILOSSTY	ASSOCIABILITY
AABCIILLLLSTY	BALLISTICALLY
AABCIILMNNOOT	COMBINATIONAL
AABCIILMNOORT	COMBINATORIAL
AABCIILMOPRTY	COMPARABILITY
AABCIINNOORST	CARBONISATION
AABCIINNOORTZ	CARBONIZATION
AABCILLNOOORT	COLLABORATION
AABCILLNOOSTV	BALTO-SLAVONIC
AABCILMNNOOPY	COMPANIONABLY
AABCILNOORTXY	CARBOXYLATION
AABCLLOOORRST	COLLABORATORS
AABCMNNNOOSTT	NONCOMBATANTS
AABCNNOOORSST	CONTRABASSOON
AABDDDDEEINRU	DEAD AND BURIED
AABDDDEEHNNRS	NABS RED-HANDED
AABDDDEEIORRS	RESIDED ABROAD
AABDDDEENSSUU	USED AND ABUSED
AABDDEEEHMMOR	HOME-MADE BREAD
AABDDEEHHLNTY	LEAD BY THE HAND
AABDDEEHNNOOP	ABANDONED HOPE
AABDDEEINRRRT	RETARDED BRAIN
AABDDEEIORRSS	RESIDES ABROAD
AABDDEEKLOOTU	DO A DOUBLE TAKE
AABDDEENORTUW	WANDERED ABOUT
AABDDEGIIMSTU	DISAMBIGUATED
AABDDEHINNOPS	ABANDONED SHIP
AABDDEIKORRST	DO A BRISK TRADE
AABDDEIORRSST	STARBOARD SIDE
AABDDELNORSTW	BELOW STANDARD
AABDDFHINNSSU	FINDS A HUSBAND
AABDDFHNNOSUU	FOUND A HUSBAND
AABDDGHILORTY	BROAD DAYLIGHT
AABDDGHORRSTU	DRAUGHTBOARDS
AABDDGIINNORR	DRAINING BOARD
AABDDGINNORTU	DOING A BAD TURN
AABDDIMNNORRS	SIR DON BRADMAN
AABDDIOORRSVY	ADVISORY BOARD
AABDDNNOORTUU	ROUND AND ABOUT
AABDEEEHIPRRT	PAID THE BEARER
AABDEEEHLPRTY	PLAYED THE BEAR
AABDEEEHNOOSV	ABOVE ONES HEAD
AABDEEEHNOPSU	HEAPED ABUSE ON
AABDEEEILLLRR	LIBERAL LEADER
AABDEEELRSTTV	SERVED AT TABLE
AABDEEFGGORUV	BEGGED A FAVOUR
AABDEEFGIILNT	INDEFATIGABLE
AABDEEFIMRSST	MADE FIRST BASE
AABDEEFKNORRT	TANKARD OF BEER
AABDEEGGINOOV	GIVE A DOG A BONE
AABDEEGHHNNOT	BANG ON THE HEAD
AABDEEGHLORTT	ALTOGETHER BAD
AABDEEGHORRST	BREAD SHORTAGE
AABDEEGJORSSU	SOBER AS A JUDGE
AABDEEHHKNTTY	TAKE BY THE HAND
AABDEEHIILRTT	REHABILITATED
AABDEEHIPRTTT	BAITED THE TRAP
AABDEEHLLLPTY	PLAYED THE BALL
AABDEEHLLPSST	PASSED THE BALL
AABDEEHORRSTW	WEATHERBOARDS
AABDEEIKKLOOR	READ LIKE A BOOK
AABDEEIKLNNPY	LIKE A BAD PENNY
AABDEEILMNRSS	ADMIRABLENESS
AABDEEILPRTYY	PLAYED IT BY EAR
AABDEEJKLOORU	LABOURED A JOKE
AABDEEKORRSST	SKATEBOARDERS
AABDEELLMPRSY	PLAYED MARBLES
AABDEELMNNSST	STEELBANDSMAN
AABDEELMNSTTT	BALD STATEMENT
AABDEELMRRSSY	EMBARRASSEDLY
AABDEELORRSST	RED AS A LOBSTER
AABDEELORRTWY	ORDEAL BY WATER
AABDEENSSSSUU	USES AND ABUSES
AABDEFFKOORST	BREAKFAST FOOD
AABDEFGIILNTY	INDEFATIGABLY
AABDEFGIOPRSS	BIRD OF PASSAGE
AABDEFGKLNNNO	BANK OF ENGLAND
AABDEFHIIORRY	FAIR-HAIRED BOY

AABDEFHIKRSST	BREAKFAST DISH
AABDEFIKLNNOR	BANK OF IRELAND
AABDEFKNORRTV	BANK OVERDRAFT
AABDEFLLOORRV	FALL OVERBOARD
AABDEGGINORRW	GROWING A BEARD
AABDEGHHINRRT	BREATHING HARD
AABDEGHHNRTUY	HUNG BY A THREAD
AABDEGHINORST	BRINGS TO A HEAD
AABDEGHINRRTW	DRAWING BREATH
AABDEGIIKLNRS	SANG LIKE A BIRD
AABDEGIILRRWY	RAILWAY BRIDGE
AABDEGIIMSSTU	DISAMBIGUATES
AABDEGIINNRRT	GRIN AND BEAR IT
AABDEGIKNORST	SKATEBOARDING
AABDEGILNRTTY	TREATING BADLY
AABDEGLLORRTU	RED RAG TO A BULL
AABDEHHORSTTU	THRASHED ABOUT
AABDEHINORRTT	BOARD THE TRAIN
AABDEHIRRTTTY	BIRTHDAY TREAT
AABDEHOPRRSUY	HARBOURED A SPY
AABDEIIILLNRT	BRILLIANT IDEA
AABDEIILMNRST	ADMINISTRABLE
AABDEIILNORTY	LIBERATION DAY
AABDEIILNRSVW	VARIABLE WINDS
AABDEIILPRSTY	SPREADABILITY
AABDEIINOOTTX	BETA-OXIDATION
AABDEILLNPRSY	PLAYS A BLINDER
AABDEILLNPSST	BEST LAID PLANS
AABDEILLORRTY	TRIAL BY ORDEAL
AABDEILMRTUVY	ADUMBRATIVELY
AABDCILOOPRRT	PORTABLE RADIO
AABDEINOPRTTU	BAD REPUTATION
AABDEINORRSTW	WINTERS ABROAD
AABDEINSSTTTU	SUBSTANTIATED
AABDEKLNRSTUY	LAUNDRY BASKET
AABDELLMNRSTU	UMBRELLA STAND
AABDELLNRSTVY	TRAVELS BY LAND
AABDEMNOPSTUY	UP BOYS AND AT EM!
AABDEMNORRTXY	RAYMOND BAXTER
AABDENNPROTUU	SUPERABUNDANT
AABDENORSTTUY	STATE BOUNDARY
AABDFGLNORSSY	GLASS OF BRANDY
AABDGIKNNOORT	TAKING ON BOARD
AABDGINNOSTTU	STANDING ABOUT
AABDGINOPRRTY	BOARDING PARTY
AABDHHIOSTTWY	HAD IT BOTH WAYS
AABDHHIPPRTYY	HAPPY BIRTHDAY
AABDHIMRRRTUU	ARTHUR RIMBAUD
AABDHINORSTUY	HITS A BOUNDARY
AABDHIPRRTTYY	BIRTHDAY PARTY
AABDIIJLSTTUY	ADJUSTABILITY
AABDIILLLPRSY	PLAY BILLIARDS
AABDNOORTUUWY	ROUND-ABOUT WAY
	ROUNDABOUT WAY
AABEEEEGLLMRT	MERE BAGATELLE
AABEEEEGLNRSS	AGREEABLENESS
AABEEEEHNRTTW	WEATHER-BEATEN
AABEEEEIKLMNS	MAKES A BEE-LINE
AABEEEEELLOSVV	ABOVE SEA-LEVEL
AABEEEGHKLPRT	GREEK ALPHABET
AABEEEGILLNRS	GENERALISABLE
AABEEEGILLNRZ	GENERALIZABLE
AABEEEGKNNOTW	BEGAN TO WEAKEN
AABEEEHHLMRST	SHARE THE BLAME
AABEEEHHKLRSST	BREAKS THE SEAL
AABEEEHHNORRST	BARE ONE'S HEART
AABEEEHPRRSTY	PAYS THE BEARER
AABEEEHPRSTTT	BREAST THE TAPE
AABEEEHRRTUUW	WEATHER BUREAU
AABEEEILLNORS	RELEASE ON BAIL
AABEEEKMQSSTU	MAKES A BEQUEST

AABEEEELLLMNSS	MALLEABLENESS
AABEEELNORSST	ELABORATENESS
AABEEELNPRSSS	SEPARABLENESS
AABEEELRSSTTV	SERVES AT TABLE
AABEEFHHLLTTT	HALF THE BATTLE
AABEEFHINRRST	FEATHERBRAINS
AABEEFHORSTTW	WASTE OF BREATH
AABEEFIKMNORS	MAKES A BONFIRE
AABEEFIKMRSST	MAKE FIRST BASE
AABEEFIKMRSTT	BREAKFAST TIME
AABEEFKLLNORS	BREAK ONES FALL
AABEEFLLLMORT	ALL OF A TREMBLE
AABEEFLNRRRST	TRANSFERRABLE
AABEEGHIINRTT	BEATING THE AIR
AABEEGHIKNRRT	HEARTBREAKING
AABEEGHLLNSSU	LAUGHABLENESS
AABEEGHLORTTW	WALTER BAGEHOT
AABEEGHMMRRTU	HAMBURGER MEAT
AABEEGIKLNRRU	BREAKING A RULE
AABEEGIKNNOPT	KEEPING A TAB ON
AABEEGILLMRRS	MARRIAGE BELLS
AABEEGILLTUVY	VILLAGE BEAUTY
AABEEGILNNSSV	NAVIGABLENESS
AABEEGILNSSTT	TANGIBLE ASSET
AABEEGIRRSSTT	GASTARBEITERS
AABEEGMNNRRTY	BY ARRANGEMENT
AABEEHHLSTTWZ	WHAT THE BLAZES
AABEEHIILRSTT	REHABILITATES
AABEEHILLRTTZ	BLAZE THE TRAIL
AABEEHILMRSTW	WHITE AS MARBLE
AABEEHIMNOSTT	IN THE SAME BOAT
AABEEHIMRRRST	THAMES BARRIER
AABEEHKOORRTT	TOOK A BREATHER
AABEEHLLPSSST	PASSES THE BALL
AABEEHLNRRTTY	LEARNT BY HEART
AABEEHLRRSSTY	BREATHALYSERS
AABEEHLRRSTYZ	BREATHALYZERS
AABEEHOPSTTTT	BEAT AT THE POST
AABEEIILPRTTY	REPEATABILITY
AABEEIKLNRTTY	TAKEN A LIBERTY
AABEEIKLRSTTY	TAKES A LIBERTY
AABEEIKMOPRRS	BREAK A PROMISE
AABEEILLLPSTU	PLAUSIBLE TALE
AABEEILLNRSST	BILATERALNESS
AABEEKMNNSTTT	BANK STATEMENT
AABEEKMNORSSS	BREAKS ONE'S ARM
AABEELNNOOTTW	WANT TO BE ALONE
AABEELNNORRST	NONARRESTABLE
AABEELNNPRSUU	SUPERANNUABLE
AABEELNOPRSSU	PERSONAL ABUSE
AABEELNRSTTXY	STANLEY BAXTER
AABEEMMNRRSST	EMBARRASSMENT
AABEENOORSSTU	ABOUT ONES EARS
AABEENRSTTTTY	TEST-BAN TREATY
AABEFGHIIKNRT	BREAKING FAITH
AABEFGHOPRRST	GASP FOR BREATH
AABEFGIKPRSST	PIG'S BREAKFAST
AABEFHLLSTWYY	FALLS BY THE WAY
AABEFHLMNNRSU	BASHFUL MANNER
AABEFIILLMRSY	FAIL MISERABLY
AABEFIKLNNRRU	BRIAN FAULKNER
AABEFKOORRTUW	OUTBREAK OF WAR
AABEFLMNORRST	TRANSFORMABLE
AABEGGIKMNRTU	TAKING UMBRAGE
AABEGGIMMNNRR	INGMAR BERGMAN
AABEGHIIKNTTT	TAKING THE BAIT
AABEGHIILNPST	ALPHABETISING
AABEGHIILNPTZ	ALPHABETIZING
AABEGHILNRSTY	BREATHALYSING
AABEGHILNRTYZ	BREATHALYZING
AABEGHILRRSTU	REGULAR HABITS

AABEGHIMNSTTW	BANTAMWEIGHTS
AABEGHINNRRTU	BARGAIN HUNTER
AABEGHINQRSSU	SQUARE BASHING
	SQUARE-BASHING
AABEGHINRRTWY	BARRING THE WAY
AABEGIILNORTY	GAY LIBERATION
AABEGIKKNNRRS	BREAKING RANKS
AABEGIKLMNTTU	TAKING A TUMBLE
AABEGIKMNNRTU	TAKING A NUMBER
AABEGIKNNOSTU	SNEAKING ABOUT
AABEGILLNRRUU	URBAN GUERILLA
AABEGILMNPRTU	PERAMBULATING
AABEGILNNORTU	LEARNING ABOUT
AABEGILNORRTU	GUBERNATORIAL
AABEGIMNORTUX	AMATEUR BOXING
AABEGOOOOSSTY	SAY BO TO A GOOSE
AABEHHORSSTTU	THRASHES ABOUT
AABEHILLORUVY	BEHAVIOURALLY
AABEHIOPRSTUV	PAST BEHAVIOUR
AABEHKMNRSSSY	BY SHANKS'S MARE
AABEHLMNNOORU	HONOURABLE MAN
AABEHMNOOSTTY	BAYS AT THE MOON
AABEHMORRRSTU	HARBOUR MASTER
	HARBOURMASTER
AABEIIILNNTTY	INNATE ABILITY
AABEIIILPRRTY	REPAIRABILITY
AABEIIKLMRTTY	MARKETABILITY
AABEIILLLOSTV	VOLATILISABLE
AABEIILLLOTVZ	VOLATILIZABLE
AABEIILMNORST	ABNORMALITIES
AABEIILMNTTTV	VITAMIN TABLET
AABEIILMSTTTY	METASTABILITY
AABEIILNNRRTU	RULE BRITANNIA
AABEIILNORSTV	VERBALISATION
AABEIILNORTVZ	VERBALIZATION
AABEIILNRSTWY	ANSWERABILITY
AABEIILRRUVXY	AUXILIARY VERB
AABEIINRRRSST	ARBITRARINESS
AABEIKNNORRTU	BREAK INTO A RUN
AABEILLNRSSTU	RUSSIAN BALLET
AABEILMNNOTTU	TABLE MOUNTAIN
AABEILMNOPRTU	PERAMBULATION
AABEILMNRSTTT	TRANSMITTABLE
AABEILNOORSTV	OBSERVATIONAL
AABEILNOSTTTT	BATTLE STATION
AABEILNRRTTVY	TRAVEL BY TRAIN
AABEINSSSTTTU	SUBSTANTIATES
AABEJMRRRSTWY	STRAWBERRY JAM
AABEKLNNORTUW	BROKEN A WALNUT
AABELMOPRRSTU	PERAMBULATORS
AABELMOPRRTUY	PERAMBULATORY
AABELNOPRRSTT	TRANSPORTABLE
AABELNPRSSSUU	UNSURPASSABLE
AABELOPRRTUUY	BEAUTY PARLOUR
AABEMNNNOSTYY	NOT BY ANY MEANS
AABEPRRRRSTTY	RASPBERRY TART
AABFGHINRRSST	BRASS FARTHING
AABFGILNOOTTU	FLOATING ABOUT
AABFHLORRRTUU	ARTHUR BALFOUR
AABGGHILNOTUU	LAUGHING ABOUT
AABGHIOOPRTUY	AUTOBIOGRAPHY
AABGHKOOOPRTU	AUTOGRAPH BOOK
AABGIIILNSSTY	ASSIGNABILITY
AABGIILLNOOST	GLOBALISATION
AABGIILLNOOTZ	GLOBALIZATION
AABGIILNRSTUW	BRING A LAWSUIT
AABHHIOSSTTWY	HAS IT BOTH WAYS
AABHIIILNPRRS	LIBRARIANSHIP
AABIIIILNRTVY	INVARIABILITY
AABIIIILNSTTY	INSATIABILITY
AABIIILLMPPTY	IMPALPABILITY

AABIIILMPSSTY	IMPASSABILITY
AABIIILNOSSTT	STABILISATION
AABIIILNOSTTZ	STABILIZATION
AABIILLLNNPRT	BRILLIANT PLAN
AABIILNNORSUV	LABOURS IN VAIN
AABIILNNSSTTU	INSUBSTANTIAL
AABIILNORSTTU	BRUTALISATION
AABIILNORTTUZ	BRUTALIZATION
AABILLNOOPRTY	PROBATIONALLY
AABILLNSSTTUY	SUBSTANTIALLY
AABILMNOOPRST	MALABSORPTION
AABLNOOPPRUVY	BUY ON APPROVAL
AABOOOOPRRSTX	SOAP-BOX ORATOR
AACCCDDEIINOT	COCAINE ADDICT
AACCCDEEIPSTV	ACCEPTS ADVICE
AACCCDEGIKNOR	CRACKING A CODE
AACCCDGHILNOT	CATCHING A COLD
AACCCDIOPRTWY	CAPACITY CROWD
AACCCEEELPSST	SPECTACLE CASE
AACCCEEHKLOOT	CHOCOLATE CAKE
AACCCEEILNRRT	RECALCITRANCE
AACCCEEKLLNOR	CORAL NECKLACE
AACCCEGHNORTU	CHARGE ACCOUNT
AACCCEHHILLST	CATCHES A CHILL
AACCCEHHINTTT	CATCH IN THE ACT
AACCCEHIJQRSU	JACQUES CHIRAC
AACCCEHILSSST	TEACH CLASSICS
AACCCEIMNNOTT	CAME IN CONTACT
AACCCFIIILNOT	CALCIFICATION
AACCCIIILMNTT	ANTICLIMACTIC
AACCCIILLLMTY	CLIMACTICALLY
AACCCLLNOOTTU	CALL TO ACCOUNT
AACCDDDDEIILO	ADDED A CODICIL
AACCDDEEHILLN	CLINCHED A DEAL
AACCDDEEIILMV	MEDICAL ADVICE
AACCDDEEINOTV	ACTED ON ADVICE
AACCDDEHIIRSS	DISACCHARIDES
AACCDDEHNNORS	SECOND-HAND CAR
AACCDDEHOPPRT	DROPPED A CATCH
AACCDDEILMNNT	MIDLAND ACCENT
AACCDDELLOORT	CALLED A DOCTOR
AACCDDENSSSTU	STANDS ACCUSED
AACCDDHNOOSST	SCOTCH AND SODA
AACCDDILLMMUV	DAVID MCCALLUM
AACCDEEEENRST	CREATED A SCENE
AACCDEEEFPSTT	ACCEPTS DEFEAT
AACCDEEEHHQSU	CASHED A CHEQUE
AACCDEEFHMNRY	FRENCH ACADEMY
AACCDEEGHLNPS	CHANGED PLACES
AACCDEEGIRRST	CARTRIDGE CASE
AACCDEEGIRRTT	CIGARETTE CARD
AACCDEEGKLORU	LACKED COURAGE
AACCDEEGNRSST	GRANTED ACCESS
AACCDEEHILLNS	CLINCHES A DEAL
AACCDEEHINRRT	CARRIED THE CAN
AACCDEEHIRRST	CHARACTERISED
AACCDEEHIRRTV	REACH A VERDICT
AACCDEEHIRRTZ	CHARACTERIZED
AACCDEEINNOTV	ADVANCE NOTICE
AACCDEFHNRRTY	FETCH AND CARRY
AACCDEGHHNNOP	CHOP AND CHANGE
AACCDEGHOORRT	GOOD CHARACTER
AACCDEHIILMOR	RADIOCHEMICAL
AACCDEHILRTTY	CATHEDRAL CITY
AACCDEHINPPTY	HAPPY ACCIDENT
AACCDEHIORRRT	CARRIED A TORCH
AACCDEHKRSSTT	STACK THE CARDS
AACCDEIIILNST	DIALECTICIANS
AACCDEIILLLTY	DIALECTICALLY
AACCDEIILPRTY	DAILY PRACTICE
AACCDEIINORTT	ACCREDITATION

AACCDEIKKMNRS	KICK AND SCREAM
AACCDEILLMSTU	MISCALCULATED
AACCDEILNOOTU	COEDUCATIONAL
AACCDEIMNNOPU	UNACCOMPANIED
AACCDEIORRRSS	CARRIED ACROSS
AACCDFIIIINOT	ACIDIFICATION
AACCDFIIILNPS	PACIFIC ISLAND
AACCDGIMMNOOT	ACCOMMODATING
AACCDHILORSTY	COLD AS CHARITY
AACCDHIMRRSST	CHRISTMAS CARD
AACCDIILLOPTY	APODICTICALLY
AACCDILNORTTV	VALID CONTRACT
AACCDIMMNOOOT	ACCOMMODATION
AACCEEEENRSST	CREATES A SCENE
AACCEEEFHNRSU	REFUSE A CHANCE
AACCEEEFIMRRW	ICE-CREAM WAFER
AACCEEEGIRSTT	CIGARETTE CASE
AACCEEEHHQSSU	CASHES A CHEQUE
AACCEEEEHLNOTV	LEAVE TO CHANCE
AACCEEEKLLNPR	PEARL NECKLACE
AACCEEEELNPRRT	CARPET CLEANER
AACCEEFFNOPRT	ACCEPT AN OFFER
AACCEEFGHLNOP	CHANCE OF PLACE
AACCEEFHHISTT	CATCHES A THIEF
AACCEEFHINRRT	FINE CHARACTER
AACCEEFIRSTUV	SURFACE-ACTIVE
AACCEEFLLSSUY	ACCUSE FALSELY
AACCEEGHIINTV	GIVE IT A CHANCE
AACCEEGHILMNT	CHEMICAL AGENT
AACCEEGHLNPSS	CHANGES PLACES
AACCEEGINNSSU	CAUSING A SCENE
AACCEEHHIMNNT	THE MAIN CHANCE
AACCEEHHLLRST	HARLECH CASTLE
AACCEEHHHNNORT	ANOTHER CHANCE
AACCEEHILMNOT	CATECHOLAMINE
AACCEEHILNNOT	COELACANTHINE
AACCEEHIMNSSS	MISSES A CHANCE
AACCEEHINRRST	CARRIES THE CAN
AACCEEHIRRSST	CHARACTERISES
AACCEEHIRRSTZ	CHARACTERIZES
AACCEEHKNNOST	TAKE NO CHANCES
AACCEEHLLOPRR	LOCAL PREACHER
AACCEEHLRRSST	CHARACTERLESS
AACCEEHMMNNORS	CHANCE ONES ARM
AACCEEHMORRST	SACCHAROMETER
AACCEEIILLPRS	CAPERCAILLIES
AACCEEIKMNPRT	PATRICK MACNEE
AACCEEILNORST	ACCELERATIONS
AACCEEILPPRTU	PICTURE PALACE
AACCEELLMNRSU	SLUM CLEARANCE
AACCEELMNRUUV	VACUUM CLEANER
AACCEEMNPPTTY	ACCEPT PAYMENT
AACCEFFILLRST	CLERICAL STAFF
AACCEFGKLOORU	LACK OF COURAGE
AACCEFHHIOTTT	TO CATCH A THIEF
AACCEFIIINOTT	ACETIFICATION
AACCEFINOPRSU	CAUSE FOR PANIC
AACCEFKNOOTTU	TAKE ACCOUNT OF
AACCEGGHIINNV	GIVING A CHANCE
AACCEGGIINNSS	GAINING ACCESS
AACCEGGIKNRTT	GETTING A CRACK
AACCEGHHIINOV	HAVING A CHOICE
AACCEGHIIKMNO	MAKING A CHOICE
AACCEGHIJKKNT	HACKING JACKET
AACCEGHIKNNST	TAKING CHANCES
AACCEGHILMPST	CATCH A GLIMPSE
AACCEGHILNNOS	LOSING A CHANCE
AACCEGHILNSST	TEACHING CLASS
AACCEGHINOOPR	OCEANOGRAPHIC
AACCEGHINORTV	CREATING HAVOC
AACCEGIILLNRT	CRITICAL ANGLE

AACCEGIILRSTT	CRITICAL STAGE
AACCEGIINNRRT	INCARCERATING
AACCEGIJKKNOR	CRACKING A JOKE
AACCEGILLNRTU	CALLING A TRUCE
AACCEGILLORTY	CATEGORICALLY
AACCEGINNNOTT	CONCATENATING
AACCEGINNOTUV	GIVE AN ACCOUNT
AACCEGINOORST	GREAT OCCASION
AACCEGINPRTTU	CUTTING A CAPER
AACCEHHINRTT	CATCH THE TRAIN
AACCEHHHNORTTW	CATCH ON THE RAW
AACCEHHOPPRTW	CATCH A WHOPPER
AACCEHIINNORT	CHAIN REACTION
AACCEHIINOSTT	CATECHISATION
AACCEHIINOTTZ	CATECHIZATION
AACCEHIKMRSST	CHRISTMAS CAKE
AACCEHILLLNTY	CHANTILLY LACE
AACCEHILLMSTY	SCHEMATICALLY
AACCEHILMNORS	HARMONIC SCALE
AACCEHILRRTTU	ARCHITECTURAL
AACCEHIMPRSTU	PHARMACEUTICS
AACCEHIOPSTUY	CAPACITY HOUSE
AACCEHIORRRST	CARRIES A TORCH
AACCEHIPPRRST	SHARP PRACTICE
AACCEHLLOSSTU	CASUAL CLOTHES
AACCEHLNOOSTU	COELACANTHOUS
AACCEHMNPRRST	SCRAP MERCHANT
AACCEHMOOPRSU	CAMPHORACEOUS
AACCEIIKLNOTT	ACT LIKE A TONIC
AACCEIILLMNTY	CINEMATICALLY
AACCEIILLMSSS	SEMICLASSICAL
AACCEIILLNRST	ANTICLERICALS
AACCEIINNORRT	INCARCERATION
AACCEIIOPRSTT	ECTOPARASITIC
AACCEIIORRSST	ARISTOCRACIES
AACCEIJKLOPRT	PRACTICAL JOKE
AACCEIKMRRSTU	CAUSTIC REMARK
AACCEILLMMORW	COMMERCIAL LAW
AACCEILLMRTUV	CIRCUMVALLATE
AACCEILLMSSTU	MISCALCULATES
AACCEILLNNOST	CANCELLATIONS
AACCEILMMOOTX	COME TO A CLIMAX
AACCEILMMORRT	COMMERCIAL ART
AACCEILNOOTVV	ACTIVE VOLCANO
AACCEILNPRSST	PRACTICALNESS
AACCEILPRSTTT	PRACTICAL TEST
AACCEILRSTUVY	SCARCITY VALUE
AACCEIMMNNOPT	ACCOMPANIMENT
AACCEIMOORRTT	ATOMIC REACTOR
AACCEINNNOOTT	CONCATENATION
AACCEINOOSSTT	STATE OCCASION
AACCEINOPSSSU	CAPACIOUSNESS
AACCEIORRRSSS	CARRIES ACROSS
AACCEKNORTTTU	COUNTERATTACK
AACCELLNOOPRR	LANCE CORPORAL
AACCELLPRSTUY	SPECTACULARLY
AACCELMNPRTUY	PAUL MCCARTNEY
AACCENNNOOPTU	OPEN AN ACCOUNT
AACCFGHHIINST	CATCHING A FISH
AACCFHHIILOTT	CATHOLIC FAITH
AACCFIIILLRSY	SACRIFICIALLY
AACCFIIILNORT	CLARIFICATION
AACCFIIINORST	SCARIFICATION
AACCFIIILNOSTU	FASCICULATION
AACCFIKLNOOTU	LACK OF CAUTION
AACCFLNOORTTW	LAW OF CONTRACT
AACCGGIILLLOO	GLACIOLOGICAL
AACCGHIIINNPV	HAVING A PICNIC
AACCGHIIMNSST	MISSING A CATCH
AACCGHIKNNPPU	PACKING A PUNCH
AACCGHILLNOOT	ANGLO-CATHOLIC

AACCGHILMOOPR	PHARMACOLOGIC	AACDDEGIKLNOT	LIKE CAT AND DOG
AACCGHINNORST	CASTING ANCHOR	AACDDEGJLNORU	JEAN-LUC GODARD
AACCGIIILMNST	ACCLIMATISING	AACDDEHHOSSSW	CHASED SHADOWS
AACCGIIILMNTZ	ACCLIMATIZING	AACDDEIIOSSST	DISASSOCIATED
AACCGIIILLNOOT	LOGICAL ACTION	AACDDEILNPPUV	ADVANCED PUPIL
AACCGIKMNNOTT	MAKING CONTACT	AACDDEINORTTY	TORY CANDIDATE
AACCGIKNNOTTU	TAKING ACCOUNT	AACDDEINPRRST	STANDARD PRICE
AACCGILLLNTUY	CALCULATINGLY	AACDDEKLLOOTT	TOTAL DEADLOCK
AACCGILNORTUY	AGRANULOCYTIC	AACDDENNOPPUW	PACE UP AND DOWN
AACCGILNOSTTU	CASTING A CLOUT	AACDDENOPRSST	SEND A POSTCARD
AACCHIILMNOOT	MACHICOLATION	AACDDFIIINNOT	DANDIFICATION
AACCHIILMRSSU	MUSICAL CHAIRS	AACDDIIJNOSTU	ADJUDICATIONS
AACCHIIMORTTY	ACHROMATICITY	AACDDIIMNORSS	ADMISSION CARD
AACCHIINNNOST	CACHINNATIONS	AACDDORSSTUWY	AWARDS CUSTODY
AACCHIINNORST	ANACHRONISTIC	AACDEEEEMNOPS	MADE ONE'S PEACE
AACCHILLLLOOY	ALCOHOLICALLY	AACDEEEFHRSTY	REACHED SAFETY
AACCHILLMORTY	CHROMATICALLY	AACDEEEFINRTT	CERTAIN DEFEAT
AACCHILLMOSTY	STOMACHICALLY	AACDEEEGHINSX	EXCHANGE IDEAS
AACCHILMNOORT	ROMAN CATHOLIC	AACDEEEGHRSTU	ARGUED THE CASE
AACCHLMMMNOOP	CLAPHAM COMMON	AACDEEEGILNRU	LARGE AUDIENCE
AACCIIINORSTT	CICATRISATION	AACDEEEGINNRT	CREATING A NEED
AACCIIINORTTZ	CICATRIZATION	AACDEEEGINNRSW	INCREASED WAGE
AACCIIKOSTTUV	VICIOUS ATTACK	AACDEEEHILNRS	SCARE HEADLINE
AACCIILLMNRSS	CRIMINAL CLASS	AACDEEEHILRRT	CLEARED THE AIR
AACCIILLMOPTY	APOMICTICALLY	AACDEEEHKLOOP	KEEP A COOL HEAD
AACCIILLMPRTY	IMPRACTICALLY	AACDEEEHLPSTU	PLEAD THE CAUSE
AACCIILLSSSST	CLASSICALISTS	AACDEEEHLRTWY	CLEARED THE WAY
AACCIIRRSSTTU	CARICATURISTS	AACDEEEHORSTT	TEACHES TO READ
AACCIKLMOOTTU	AUTOMATIC LOCK	AACDEEEHPSTTY	STAYED THE PACE
AACCIKLNOPRTW	PRAWN COCKTAIL	AACDEEEIMMMNT	MADE MINCEMEAT
AACCIKLOPRTTY	COCKTAIL PARTY	AACDEEEINPQTU	PEACE AND QUIET
AACCIKMNNOORRY	ROCKY MARCIANO	AACDEEELNORSV	LEAVE ONES CARD
AACCILLLNOOOT	COLLOCATIONAL	AACDEEENNRRTT	TRADE ENTRANCE
AACCILLMNORYY	ACRONYMICALLY	AACDEEFFHLTTT	THE FATTED CALF
AACCILLNSTTYY	SYNTACTICALLY	AACDEEFGHINTV	HAVING A DEFECT
AACCILLOPSSST	POSTCLASSICAL	AACDEEFIKLRVV	DAVE CLARK FIVE
AACCILMNOSTUU	ACCUMULATIONS	AACDEEFILNNOV	LINE OF ADVANCE
AACCILNNOOOTV	CONVOCATIONAL	AACDEEGHHINTT	CHEATING DEATH
AACCILNNOORTT	CONTRACTIONAL	AACDEEGHINPST	ESCAPING DEATH
AACCILNOOORSY	ROYAL OCCASION	AACDEEGHINRTW	DANCE WITH RAGE
AACCILNORTTUU	ACCULTURATION	AACDEEGHLNNPS	CHANGED PLANES
AACCILOOSSTTU	SOCIAL OUTCAST	AACDEEGHNNOTT	DANCE THE TANGO
AACCIMNNOORSTU	CARCINOMATOUS	AACDEEGINRRRU	UNDERCARRIAGE
AACCIMNOOSTTU	ACCUSTOMATION	AACDEEGINRSTT	GREAT DISTANCE
AACCINORSSTTY	SACROSANCTITY	AACDEEGLORRTV	CRADLE TO GRAVE
AACCLLNORTTUY	CONTRACTUALLY	AACDEEGNNNRRT	GRAND ENTRANCE
AACDDDEHILOPT	ADOPTED A CHILD	AACDEEGNRRTTU	GRANTED A TRUCE
AACDDEEEFFINT	DECAFFEINATED	AACDEEHHIINRS	CHERISH AN IDEA
AACDDEEEHILST	DELICATE SHADE	AACDEEHHIRSST	RAISED THE CASH
AACDDEEEHLLRY	CLEARHEADEDLY	AACDEEHHMRTTY	THREE-DAY MATCH
AACDDEEELLNVV	ADVANCED LEVEL	AACDEEHINNORT	DANCE ON THE AIR
AACDDEEGIINST	DECIDE AGAINST	AACDEEHINOPRS	COINED A PHRASE
AACDDEEGJOTUV	JUDGE ADVOCATE	AACDEEHINTTTU	AUTHENTICATED
AACDDEEHIRRTY	CARRIED THE DAY	AACDEEHIRRSTY	CARRIES THE DAY
AACDDEEHMNSST	DEAD MANS CHEST	AACDEEHISSTTW	THE DIE WAS CAST
AACDDEEHORSTT	SCARED TO DEATH	AACDEEHKLNOPT	DANCE THE POLKA
AACDDEEIILMMR	MIDDLE AMERICA	AACDEEHKLOOPT	KEPT A COOL HEAD
AACDDEEIIMNOS	MADE A DECISION	AACDEEHLLLOPW	HALLOWED PLACE
AACDDEEIILLMNR	RECLAIMED LAND	AACDEEHLORRST	CLEARS THE ROAD
AACDDEEIILNOTY	DELAYED ACTION	AACDEEHNPSSTT	STANDS THE PACE
AACDDEEIILPRTY	DIRECTED A PLAY	AACDEEIIKMNOS	MAKE A DECISION
AACDDEEINOSTW	WAITED A SECOND	AACDEEIIINRSST	SECTARIANISED
AACDDEEINRTTY	DEAD CERTAINTY	AACDEEIIINRSTZ	SECTARIANIZED
AACDDEELNOPRR	PLACED AN ORDER	AACDEEIKNNNVW	KNEW IN ADVANCE
AACDDEELOPRRY	PLAYED A RECORD	AACDEEIKNRSTT	CREATED A STINK
AACDDEFGILNOT	CAT-AND-DOG LIFE	AACDEEILLRTUV	LUCRATIVE DEAL
AACDDEFIKLNRT	TRACK AND FIELD	AACDEEILLRTVY	DECLARATIVELY
AACDDEFIMNNOOS	ACE OF DIAMONDS	AACDEEILLTUVV	VAUDEVILLE ACT
AACDDEGHIIMNN	ADDING MACHINE	AACDEEILMPRSS	PRESSED A CLAIM
AACDDEGHLNOOT	TEACH AN OLD DOG	AACDEEILNNRTV	VALENTINE CARD
AACDDEGHNNORU	CHANGED AROUND	AACDEEILPRTTU	RECAPITULATED

AACDEEIMNNOTT	DECONTAMINATE
AACDEEINNNRTV	RENT IN ADVANCE
AACDEEINPRSSV	SPACE INVADERS
AACDEEIORRTTV	DECORATIVE ART
AACDEEIQRSTTU	ACQUIRED TASTE
AACDEEKKLLPRS	LACKED SPARKLE
AACDEEKKLNOOS	LOOKED ASKANCE
AACDEEKLMNNNRS	LACKED MANNERS
AACDEEKNPPSST	SPENDS A PACKET
AACDEEKPRSTWY	SPEEDWAY TRACK
AACDEELLNNNOO	DONE ALL ONE CAN
AACDEELLNNOOS	DOES ALL ONE CAN
AACDEELLNRRTU	RETURNED A CALL
AACDEELNOPRRS	PLACES AN ORDER
AACDEELPRRRST	RED STAR PARCEL
AACDEEMNOQSTU	MADE A CONQUEST
AACDEENRRSSUW	CURSE AND SWEAR
AACDEFFIIMNRS	DISAFFIRMANCE
AACDEFFINRRTW	TRAFFIC WARDEN
AACDEFFIOOPRS	PAID OFF A SCORE
AACDEFGHIRSTT	STRAIGHT-FACED
AACDEFGIILNNP	FINDING A PLACE
AACDEFGIRSTUU	CUT A SAD FIGURE
AACDEFGLLNOOY	COLONEL GADAFY
AACDEFHHMOTTY	MATCH OF THE DAY
AACDEFHNOORTW	THANE OF CAWDOR
AACDEFIILNOST	FATAL DECISION
AACDEFIINPRTU	RAN UP A DEFICIT
AACDEFIKORSSV	ASKS FOR ADVICE
AACDEFILMORRR	RADICAL REFORM
AACDEFILMORRT	MODEL AIRCRAFT
AACDEFIMNORST	FROM A DISTANCE
AACDEFIMNRRTU	FRUIT AND CREAM
AACDEFIOORRRT	CARRIED TOO FAR
AACDEFLLNNOOR	ONCE AND FOR ALL
AACDEGGIINSTU	ACTING AS GUIDE
AACDEGGILLMOY	DEMAGOGICALLY
AACDEGGINNOOT	GOING TO A DANCE
AACDEGHIILPRT	GRAPHIC DETAIL
AACDEGHILRSTT	STRAIGHTLACED
AACDEGHIMNOOT	COMING TO A HEAD
AACDEGHINNNRST	CHANGED TRAINS
AACDEGHINRRRW	RICHARD WAGNER
AACDEGHNNORSU	CHANGES AROUND
AACDEGIIKKNST	KICKED AGAINST
AACDEGIIMMORT	IDEOGRAMMATIC
AACDEGIINRTTU	EDUCATING RITA
AACDEGIKMNORR	MAKING A RECORD
AACDEGILMNOPR	OLD CAMPAIGNER
AACDEGILNNRST	STANDING CLEAR
AACDEGIMNNRST	DANCING MASTER
AACDEGINORRTV	GRANT A DIVORCE
AACDEGINPRSSU	SUGAR AND SPICE
AACDEGIORRTTT	GREAT DICTATOR
AACDEGJKLNNOS	GLENDA JACKSON
AACDEGLMNNORS	SCANDALMONGER
AACDEGLNOPRRS	DROPS A CLANGER
AACDEGLNORTTU	CONGRATULATED
AACDEHHILLOTY	HOLIDAY CHALET
AACDEHHOSSSSW	CHASES SHADOWS
AACDEHIIMNRRT	ARCHIMANDRITE
AACDEHIKNPSST	STEAK AND CHIPS
AACDEHILNRRSW	CHARLES DARWIN
AACDEHLLOPSTT	THE OLD PALS ACT
AACDEHLMNNORT	CALENDAR MONTH
AACDEHLNNOPSS	CLAP ONES HANDS
AACDEHOORRSST	ACROSS THE ROAD
AACDEIIJLRIUX	EXTRAJUDICIAL
AACDEIILLMRTY	DIAMETRICALLY
AACDEIILLNNOT	DECLINATIONAL
AACDEIIILLOPRY	APERIODICALLY
AACDEIILNOORR	RADIO CAROLINE
AACDEIILORTVY	RADIOACTIVELY
AACDEIILPRRST	PRACTISED LIAR
AACDEIILPSSTU	ISSUED CAPITAL
AACDEIILRSTTU	DISARTICULATE
AACDEIINNPRSS	PRINCESS DIANA
AACDEIINNPTTU	UNANTICIPATED
AACDEIIOSSSST	DISASSOCIATES
AACDEIKLLNPST	SLAP AND TICKLE
AACDEIKNNNOVW	KNOW IN ADVANCE
AACDEILLNOTUY	EDUCATIONALLY
AACDEILMMORST	MELODRAMATICS
AACDEILMORSST	SACERDOTALISM
AACDEILNNORST	SLANDER ACTION
AACDEILNOSSTT	ANECDOTALISTS
AACDEILORSSTT	SACERDOTALIST
AACDEILPQRTUU	QUADRUPLICATE
AACDEIMMMNORRS	COMRADE IN ARMS
AACDEIMNPRSSV	SCRIMP AND SAVE
AACDEINOSSSUU	AUDACIOUSNESS
AACDEINPRRTUW	DRAWN A PICTURE
AACDEIOPRRTVY	VICTORY PARADE
AACDEIPRRSTUW	DRAWS A PICTURE
AACDEJKNNORSW	ANDREW JACKSON
AACDELNOOPRSY	PAY AN OLD SCORE
AACDELNOORSTW	DRAWN TO A CLOSE
AACDELNOPRSSY	PLAY ONES CARDS
AACDELOORSSTW	DRAWS TO A CLOSE
AACDEMMMNORRY	ARMY COMMANDER
AACDEMMMNOSSU	ASSUME COMMAND
AACDEMNOPPRTY	PARTED COMPANY
AACDENOPRSSTT	SENT A POSTCARD
AACDFFIILNRST	TRAFFIC ISLAND
AACDFHIKNRRRS	FRANK RICHARDS
AACDFLLMNNOOPST	MAP OF SCOTLAND
AACDGGIIIHINNNS	CHANGING HANDS
AACDGHIILLPRY	DIGRAPHICALLY
AACDGHIKMMNOU	MAKING MUCH ADO
AACDGHILNNPPS	CLAPPING HANDS
AACDGHILNNPSS	CLASPING HANDS
AACDGHILNOPRY	PLAYING A CHORD
AACDGIINNNNR	INCARNADINING
AACDGIINNNOST	DIAGNOSTICIAN
AACDGIKMMNNQT	TAKING COMMAND
AACDHHIIKKNST	HAD A THICK SKIN
AACDHILLLRUYY	HYDRAULICALLY
AACDHILLOPRSY	RHAPSODICALLY
AACDHILMNOORT	TRICHOMONADAL
AACDHIMMOOSSS	SADOMASOCHISM
AACDHIMNOOPSS	HAD COMPASSION
AACDHIMNOPRST	DARTS CHAMPION
AACDHIMOOSSST	SADOMASOCHIST
AACDHINOPQRSU	QUADRAPHONICS
AACDHLMMNOOSY	CHLAMYDOMONAS
AACDIIILLMOTY	IDIOMATICALLY
AACDIIIORRTTVY	RADIOACTIVITY
AACDIIJORSSTU	JUDAS ISCARIOT
AACDIILLLSTUY	DUALISTICALLY
AACDIILLORTTY	DICTATORIALLY
AACDIKPRSSTTY	ST.PATRICKS DAY
AACDILLLORSTY	CRYSTALLOIDAL
AACDILLMOPSSY	SPASMODICALLY
AACDKNNNNOORY	NOOK AND CRANNY
AACEEEEKMNOPS	MAKE ONES PEACE
AACEEEFHRSSTY	REACHES SAFETY
AACEEEFINRRSS	INCREASE FARES
AACEEEFMNOPSS	MEANS OF ESCAPE
AACEEEGGLLORW	GEORGE WALLACE
AACEEEGGHHLLNR	ALL CHANGE HERE
AACEEEGHLNUVX	EXCHANGE VALUE
AACEEEGHMNRST	TEACHES GERMAN

833

AACEEEGHRSSTU	ARGUES THE CASE
AACEEEGINPRTT	GREAT PATIENCE
AACEEEGNORSSU	ARGUE ONES CASE
AACEEEGNRTTUV	GAVE UTTERANCE
AACEEEGPRSSST	SECRET PASSAGE
AACEEEHJKLRTT	LEATHER JACKET
	LEATHERJACKET
AACEEEHLLNSTT	CLEAN THE SLATE
AACEEEHNORRSS	REACH ONE'S EARS
AACEEEIKMMMNT	MAKE MINCEMEAT
AACEEEILNRSVX	NAVAL EXERCISE
AACEEEKLNOPST	TAKE ONES PLACE
AACEEELMNNORS	CLEAR ONES NAME
AACEEELNORSTV	LEAVES NO TRACE
AACEEEMNNORSV	CARVE ONES NAME
AACEEENORSTVY	CAST AN EYE OVER
AACEEENOSSSTT	STATE ONES CASE
AACEEEOPRRSTV	SEPARATE COVER
AACEEFFGIMNOR	OFFICE MANAGER
AACEEFFGOORTU	FEAT OF COURAGE
AACEEFFKLRRTU	FEARFUL RACKET
AACEEFFNNRSTT	STAFF ENTRANCE
AACEEFGHHNORT	CHANGE OF HEART
AACEEFGHILNST	FALSE TEACHING
AACEEFGHNOPRX	PAR OF EXCHANGE
AACEEFGHNOSTT	STATE OF CHANGE
AACEEFGHSTTTT	GET AT THE FACTS
AACEEFGLNNORR	GENERAL FRANCO
AACEEFHHILNRT	REACH THE FINAL
AACEEFHILNPST	SLAP IN THE FACE
AACEEFHIMORTT	CAME TO THE FAIR
AACEEFHLLMSST	THE SMALL FACES
AACEEFHMSSTTY	SAFETY MATCHES
AACEEFHNNRRTW	TRENCH WARFARE
AACEEFILLLNNP	FALLEN IN PLACE
AACEEFILLORSW	SOCIAL WELFARE
AACEEFILNRSSU	LIFE ASSURANCE
AACEEFIMNRRTY	ENEMY AIRCRAFT
AACEEFIMPRRTU	FRAME A PICTURE
AACEEFINNOPST	PAINT ONES FACE
AACEEFJMNNOOS	JAM ON ONE'S FACE
AACEEFKNNOSTY	TAKE ONES FANCY
AACEEFLLMNOST	MALTESE FALCON
AACEEFLNRSSSU	SELF-ASSURANCE
AACEEFLRSTTUU	CAUSE A FLUTTER
AACEEGGINNOST	ACTING ONE'S AGE
AACEEGHHHINRW	REACH A NEW HIGH
AACEEGHHINSTV	HAVING THE ACES
AACEEGHHMRRTT	THE GREAT MARCH
AACEEGHHRRSST	CRASH THE GEARS
AACEEGHHRRSTT	THE GREAT CRASH
AACEEGHIINRRS	RAISING A CHEER
AACEEGHIKKNTT	TAKING THE CAKE
AACEEGHIKMNPS	MAKING A SPEECH
AACEEGHIKMNPT	MAKING THE PACE
AACEEGHILOPRS	ARCHIPELAGOES
AACEEGHINRSTV	HAVING A SECRET
AACEEGHLMNOPR	ENCEPHALOGRAM
AACEEGHLNNPSS	CHANGES PLANES
AACEEGHLNOORS	REACH ONES GOAL
AACEEGHNOOPRR	OCEANOGRAPHER
AACEEGHNORRTX	NO EXTRA CHARGE
AACEEGHNPRSTX	PART-EXCHANGES
AACEEGIIPRVWY	GIVEAWAY PRICE
AACEEGILLLNVY	EVANGELICALLY
AACEEGILLMMRT	TELEGRAM CLAIM
AACEEGILLMNST	CALLS A MEETING
AACEEGILMNSTU	CASUAL MEETING
AACEEGILNPRTW	WATERING PLACE
AACEEGILNRRSV	VICARS-GENERAL
AACEEGIMNNORR	AMERICAN NEGRO
AACEEGKOORRTT	TOOK GREAT CARE
AACEEGNORSTTT	RENTS A COTTAGE
AACEEHHILMRSV	MICHAEL HAVERS
AACEEHHIRSSST	RAISES THE CASH
AACEEHHLMNPST	CHELTENHAM SPA
AACEEHHLMRSSW	CASHMERE SHAWL
AACEEHHLPRSTT	CLEARS THE PATH
AACEEHIJQSTTU	HATTIE JACQUES
AACEEHIKLPRRR	CHARLIE PARKER
AACEEHIKNOQUV	HAVE A QUICK ONE
AACEEHILLMMNY	MICHAEL MANLEY
AACEEHILLSTTY	AESTHETICALLY
AACEEHILMSTTT	ATHLETICS TEAM
AACEEHILNOSST	CHASE ONES TAIL
AACEEHILNPRTT	PARENTHETICAL
AACEEHIMMNPST	IN THE SAME CAMP
AACEEHINPRRRT	CATHERINE PARR
AACEEHINSTTTU	AUTHENTICATES
AACEEHIRRTTTW	TREAT WITH CARE
AACEEHKLNRSTU	HERCULEAN TASK
AACEEHLMNNORST	ANCESTRAL HOME
AACEEHLOPPRRT	ALPHA-RECEPTOR
AACEEHMNRRTUU	HUMAN CREATURE
AACEEHOPRRTXY	ARCHAEOPTERYX
AACEEIILLNNOPT	NEAPOLITAN ICE
AACEEIINORRST	REACTIONARIES
AACEEIINOSTVV	EVASIVE ACTION
AACEEIINRSSST	SECTARIANISES
AACEEIINRSSTZ	SECTARIANIZES
AACEEIJKRSTTW	JACKIE STEWART
AACEEIKNRSSTT	CREATES A STINK
AACEEILLMMRTY	METAMERICALLY
AACEEILLNPRTV	VERTICAL PLANE
AACEEILLPRTTT	CAPITAL LETTER
AACEEILMMNNORT	ANEMOMETRICAL
AACEEILMOSTUY	CAME OUT EASILY
AACEEILMPRSSS	PRESSES A CLAIM
AACEEILNNOPPU	PANLEUCOPENIA
AACEEILNNQRUV	CARNIVAL QUEEN
AACEEILNNRSTW	SAINT LAWRENCE
AACEEILNOPTTT	PETTICOAT LANE
AACEEILNRRRTV	RECENT ARRIVAL
AACEEILORSTVV	CAST A VEIL OVER
AACEEILPRSTTU	RECAPITULATES
AACEEIMMNNRTT	REMITTANCE MAN
AACEEIMNPRSSU	PANIC MEASURES
AACEEINPRRRST	PERSIAN CARPET
AACEEINPRRTTV	ACTIVE PARTNER
AACEEIOPRSSTT	ECTOPARASITES
AACEEKLLPRSSY	SPEAKS CLEARLY
AACEEKMNOQSTU	MAKE A CONQUEST
AACEEKMNRSTUY	MAKES A CENTURY
AACEEKMRSSTUY	MAKES A CURTSEY
AACEEKNNPRRTU	PANCAKE TURNER
AACEEKNPPRRSW	NEWSPAPER RACK
AACEELLLRRTUX	EXTRACELLULAR
AACEELLNPSTUY	PENALTY CLAUSE
AACEELNNOPRUW	NUCLEAR WEAPON
AACEEMNPRTVYZ	CRAZY PAVEMENT
AACEEMPRRSTUU	CREATE A RUMPUS
AACEENNPPRSTU	APPURTENANCES
AACEFFFILNORT	LANE OF TRAFFIC
AACEFFGHINSTT	TEACHING STAFF
AACEFFGLLMORR	FALL FROM GRACE
AACEFFILLNOTY	AFFECTIONALLY
AACEFFINORTWY	ONE-WAY TRAFFIC
AACEFFOOPRSSY	PAYS OFF A SCORE
AACEFGHILORVY	AGE OF CHIVALRY
AACEFGHMMNRRR	FRENCH GRAMMAR
AACEFGHOSTTTT	GOT AT THE FACTS
AACEFGIIILLRT	ARTIFICIAL LEG

AACEFGIILNRTY	FACING REALITY	AACEGILLLLORY	ALLEGORICALLY
AACEFGIKLMNNO	LACK OF MEANING	AACEGILLLMRTU	METALLURGICAL
AACEFGLLLNOPU	PULL A LONG FACE	AACEGILLMNTUY	MUTAGENICALLY
AACEFHHOPPRRS	FRESH APPROACH	AACEGILLNPRYY	PANEGYRICALLY
AACEFIIILMORV	FAMILIAR VOICE	AACEGILLNPSST	CASTING A SPELL
AACEFIILNNNSW	FINANCIAL NEWS	AACEGILLOORTT	TERATOLOGICAL
AACEFIILNRRTY	FAIRLY CERTAIN	AACEGILLRSTTY	STRATEGICALLY
AACEFIKLLOOST	ACTS LIKE A FOOL	AACEGILMNORTV	GALVANOMETRIC
AACEFIKLMNRST	CRAFTSMANLIKE	AACEGILNNPSTU	ENCAPSULATING
AACEFILLLNOPT	FALL INTO PLACE	AACEGIMNORRTT	ORGANIC MATTER
AACEFILLLOPTW	CAPITAL FELLOW	AACEGIMNPPRSS	PRESS CAMPAIGN
AACEFILLTTUVY	FACULTATIVELY	AACEGIMNPRSUY	GAIN SUPREMACY
AACEFILOORRRY	ROYAL AIR FORCE	AACEGINNOORST	OCTOGENARIANS
AACEFILORRSTW	ARTICLES OF WAR	AACEGINNOORTT	GO INTO A TRANCE
AACEFIMNORSTU	MANUFACTORIES	AACEGINOSSSSU	SAGACIOUSNESS
AACEFINRSTTUY	SAFETY CURTAIN	AACEGLLMMORRU	GRAM MOLECULAR
AACEFIOORRRST	CARRIES TOO FAR	AACEGLLNRRTUY	RECTANGULARLY
AACEFLLMMORRS	MALCOLM FRASER	AACEGLMNOOSWY	COMES A LONG WAY
AACEFLOOPPPRS	FOOLSCAP PAPER	AACEGLNORSTTU	CONGRATULATES
AACEFLOOPPRTU	COURT OF APPEAL	AACEGMORRRTTU	MARGARET COURT
AACEFMNRRSTUU	MANAFACTURERS	AACEGNNOSSTTU	CONSTANT USAGE
AACEFNOPRRSTT	TRANSPORT CAFE	AACEHHIILMOPS	HAEMOPHILIACS
AACEGGGHHINNT	HATCHING AN EGG	AACEHIIILLNNOST	CASH ON THE NAIL
AACEGGHIKMNNS	MAKING CHANGES	AACEHHLOOPRTX	CEPHALOTHORAX
AACEGGHINOTTT	ACTING THE GOAT	AACEHIIMNRTTT	ARITHMETICIAN
AACEGGIKNORTU	TAKING COURAGE	AACEHIILLNTUV	HALLUCINATIVE
AACEGGILNNNRW	WARNING GLANCE	AACEHIILLSTTY	ATHEISTICALLY
AACEGGILNNPSS	PASSING GLANCE	AACEHIILMRSTT	THEATRICALISM
AACEGHHIIKKNS	CHIANG KAI SHEK	AACEHIILNPSTT	PANTHEISTICAL
AACEGHHIMNSTT	TEACHING MATHS	AACEHIILRTTTY	THEATRICALITY
AACEGHHINRSTW	WASHING THE CAR	AACEHIIMNNOST	MECHANISATION
AACEGHIILNRSV	LAVISHING CARE	AACEHIIMNNOTZ	MECHANIZATION
AACEGHIILNTTW	WIGAN ATHLETIC	AACEHIIMNNRST	CHRISTIAN NAME
AACEGHIINNSTT	ACTING IN HASTE	AACEHIIMNPSTY	METAPHYSICIAN
AACEGHIIKMNNPP	PINK CHAMPAGNE	AACEHIIOPSSST	ASSOCIATESHIP
AACEGHIKNORVW	WREAKING HAVOC	AACEHIKMRSSTT	STRIKES A MATCH
AACEGHILLLRTY	LETHARGICALLY	AACEHILLMRTUY	RHEUMATICALLY
AACEGHILLMPRY	GRAPHEMICALLY	AACEHILLNTTUY	AUTHENTICALLY
AACEGHILLPRRS	CALLIGRAPHERS	AACEHILMNPRRU	HURRICANE LAMP
AACEGHILMNNOR	NOMINAL CHARGE	AACEHILMOPTYY	POLYCYTHAEMIA
AACEGHILMOPYY	HYPOGLYCAEMIA	AACEHIMNNORRT	NORTH AMERICAN
AACEGHILOORST	ARCHAEOLOGIST	AACEHIMNOORRT	RHAETO ROMANIC
AACEGHILRSSTW	GLASS WITH CARE	AACEHIMNNORSTU	SOUTH AMERICAN
AACEGHIMMMRUX	MAXIMUM CHARGE	AACEHIMRRTTUY	REACH MATURITY
AACEGHIMNOPRT	CINEMATOGRAPH	AACEHINOOPRST	TO COIN A PHRASE
AACEGHINNRSST	CHANGES TRAINS	AACEHINORTTTU	AUTHENTICATOR
AACEGHINPRTTT	ACTING THE PART	AACEHJMPPRTUU	PARACHUTE JUMP
AACEGHLNOOSTT	ALONG THE COAST	AACEHKORSTTTU	TAKE A SHORT CUT
AACEGHOPRRRST	CARTOGRAPHERS	AACEHKQRSSSTU	SQUASH RACKETS
AACEGHOPRSSSU	SARCOPHAGUSES	AACEHLLNNSSUU	USUAL CHANNELS
AACEGIIIMNNRS	AMERICANISING	AACEHLMNOORST	STOLE A MARCH ON
AACEGIIIMNNRZ	AMERICANIZING	AACEHLMNOPRRS	PERSONAL CHARM
AACEGIIKKNTTW	TAKING A WICKET	AACEHLNOPSSYY	PSYCHOANALYSE
AACEGIIKLMNRT	MAKING IT CLEAR	AACEHLOOPSTUU	AUTOCEPHALOUS
AACEGIIKMNNRT	MAKING CERTAIN	AACEHLPRRSSTY	REACTS SHARPLY
AACEGIIKNPTTV	TAKING CAPTIVE	AACEHMMNORRST	THOMAS CRAMNER
AACEGIIKNRSTU	TAKING A CRUISE	AACEHMSSSSTTU	MASSACHUSETTS
AACEGIILLMNOR	MINERALOGICAL	AACEHNOPRSSTT	PHASE-CONTRAST
AACEGIILLMNTY	ENIGMATICALLY	AACEHOORTTTTX	EXTRACT A TOOTH
AACEGIILLNNTY	ANTIGENICALLY	AACEIIILMRSTT	MATERIALISTIC
AACEGIILMMNNR	REMAINING CALM	AACEIIINORTTV	RATIOCINATIVE
AACEGIILNNRTT	INTERCALATING	AACEIIJKNOSSS	JACKIE ONASSIS
AACEGIILNPRSV	SCRAPE A LIVING	AACEIIKLLMNTY	KINEMATICALLY
AACEGIINNNRRT	REINCARNATING	AACEIIKLOORST	ALISTAIR COOKE
AACEGIINNRRRT	RACING TRAINER	AACEIIKLRTTWY	RAILWAY TICKET
AACEGIINPRRTV	PREVARICATING	AACEIIILLLRSTY	REALISTICALLY
AACEGIINRRSTT	CREATING A STIR	AACEIIILLMNPTT	METALLIC PAINT
AACEGIKLNOPST	LOSING A PACKET	AACEIIILLNNPTT	ATLANTIC LINER
AACEGIKNNORRT	TAKING A CORNER	AACEIILMNNTTX	EXTINCT ANIMAL
AACEGIKNNSSTU	TAKING A CENSUS	AACEIILMNRSTT	STATE CRIMINAL
AACEGIKNORSTU	TAKING A COURSE	AACEIILNNORST	RACIAL TENSION

AACEIILNNORTT	INTERCALATION	AACFIINNOORTT	FRACTIONATION
AACEIILNNOSTT	CAT O' NINE TAILS	AACFIINOORSTT	FACTORISATION
	CAT-O'-NINE-TAILS	AACFIINOORTTZ	FACTORIZATION
AACEIILNNPSST	CASTLE IN SPAIN	AACFILLLMORUY	FORMULAICALLY
AACEIILNPRSTT	ANTIPARTICLES	AACGGHILLOOPR	GRAPHOLOGICAL
	PATERNALISTIC	AACGGHILMNNST	SLANGING MATCH
AACEIILOSSTVY	ASSOCIATIVELY	AACGGHINNPPTU	CAUGHT NAPPING
AACEIILPRRSTU	PARTICULARISE	AACGGIIKMNORS	SMOKING A CIGAR
AACEIILPRRTUZ	PARTICULARIZE	AACGGILMMOORT	LOGOGRAMMATIC
AACEIIMMOSTTU	SEMIAUTOMATIC	AACGHHILNOPTT	HATCHING A PLOT
AACEIIMNNOTTV	CONTAMINATIVE	AACGHHIMNNTTW	NIGHT WATCHMAN
AACEIIMNORSST	RACEMISATIONS	AACGHHIOPPRRT	RIGHT APPROACH
AACEIIMNORSTZ	RACEMIZATIONS	AACGHHMOOPRRT	CHROMATOGRAPH
AACEIINNNORRT	REINCARNATION	AACGHIILLNNTU	HALLUCINATING
AACEIINOPPRST	APPRECIATIONS	AACGHIILLNSTT	CALLS IT A NIGHT
AACEIINOPRRTV	PREVARICATION	AACGHIILLPRST	CALLIGRAPHIST
AACEIINORSTTU	CAUTERISATION	AACGHIIMNNNTW	WINNING A MATCH
AACEIINORTTUZ	CAUTERIZATION	AACGHIIPRRSTT	STRATIGRAPHIC
AACEIINPPRTTU	PAINT A PICTURE	AACGHIKNOOPTT	TOOK A NIGHTCAP
AACEIINRRRSTU	CURTAIN RAISER	AACGHILLOPRXY	XYLOGRAPHICAL
AACEIJKRSSTTT	STRAITJACKETS	AACGHILMNOOTT	COMING TO A HALT
AACEIKLMORRSW	WORKS A MIRACLE	AACGHILNNORTY	LYING AT ANCHOR
AACEIKLNOTTTV	VIOLENT ATTACK	AACGHILOOPPRT	TOPOGRAPHICAL
AACEIKLPQRRSU	PICKS A QUARREL	AACGHILOPPRTY	TYPOGRAPHICAL
AACEILLLNRRTU	INTRACELLULAR	AACGHIMNNOPVY	HAVING COMPANY
AACEILLLORTTY	COLLATERALITY	AACGHIMNNORRTW	MARCHING TO WAR
AACEILLMNPTUY	PNEUMATICALLY	AACGHINOOPPTT	CAPPING A TOOTH
AACEILLMNTYYZ	ENZYMATICALLY	AACGHIORRSTTT	STRAIGHT ACTOR
AACEILLNOORRT	CORRELATIONAL	AACGHLMMOORRS	GRAMMAR SCHOOL
AACEILMNRRSUV	VERNACULARISM	AACGHMMOORRST	CHROMATOGRAMS
AACEILMNRSSTU	STRAIN A MUSCLE	AACGHNOOPPRRW	WRONG APPROACH
AACEILMOPRTVY	COMPARATIVELY	AACGIIILLMSTY	IMAGISTICALLY
AACEILNNOPSTU	ENCAPSULATION	AACGIIILLNOST	GALLICISATION
AACEILNNPRTUY	INCUR A PENALTY	AACGIIILLNOTZ	GALLICIZATION
AACEILNOORSTT	TRAIL ONE'S COAT	AACGIIILLNNOST	ANGLICISATION
AACEILNOSSSSU	SALACIOUSNESS	AACGIIILLNNOTZ	ANGLICIZATION
AACEIMNOOPSST	COMPASSIONATE	AACGIIINNORTT	RATIOCINATING
AACEINOPPRRTU	APPEAR IN COURT	AACGIIINPPRTT	PARTICIPATING
AACEINOPRRSTT	PROCRASTINATE	AACGIIKLNPRTY	PLAYING A TRICK
AACEINOPRRTUY	PRECAUTIONARY	AACGIIILLLNTVY	VACILLATINGLY
AACEINOPRSSSU	RAPACIOUSNESS	AACGIIILLMNOTY	LAYING CLAIM TO
AACEJKLNNORST	JACK-O'-LANTERNS	AACGIIILLMSTTY	STIGMATICALLY
AACEJOPRRRSTT	JASPER CARROTT	AACGIIILLNNORY	INORGANICALLY
AACELLMNNORTU	NOMENCLATURAL	AACGIIILLNOSTY	AGONISTICALLY
AACELLMNORSSW	LOWERCLASSMAN	AACGIIILLMNRTTU	MATRICULATING
AACELMMNOPRTT	COMPARTMENTAL	AACGIIILNNRTUV	RAVING LUNATIC
AACELMNOPRWYY	COMPANY LAWYER	AACGIIILNORSTU	CARTILAGINOUS
AACELNORRSTUU	NATURAL COURSE	AACGIIILNPRSTW	PRACTISING LAW
AACELOORRSSTT	COASTAL RESORT	AACGIIILNPTTVY	CAPTIVATINGLY
AACEMNNOORSTT	ENTOMOSTRACAN	AACGIIILNRSSUV	VASCULARISING
AACFFGHIINNRS	AFFRANCHISING	AACGIIILNRSUVZ	VASCULARIZING
AACFFGIILNRST	TRAFFIC SIGNAL	AACGIIMNNNOTT	CONTAMINATING
AACFFIIILNOST	FALSIFICATION	AACGIINNORSTVY	GAINS A VICTORY
AACFFIORTTWWY	TWO-WAY TRAFFIC	AACGIJLNNOOTU	CONJUGATIONAL
AACFFLORSTTUY	FACULTY OF ARTS	AACGIKKNNOSST	KNOCKS AGAINST
AACFGIIIMNNOT	MAGNIFICATION	AACGIKLNORSSW	WALKING ACROSS
AACFGIIINORTT	GRATIFICATION	AACGIKNPRSSTT	STARTS PACKING
AACFGIILNNSTY	FASCINATINGLY	AACGILLLNOOPY	PALYNOLOGICAL
AACFGIINNORTT	FRACTIONATING	AACGILLLNOSTY	NOSTALGICALLY
AACFGIINNORWY	FORCING A WAY IN	AACGILLMMNOORY	AGRONOMICALLY
AACFGILNNOORT	CONFLAGRATION	AACGILLMNORST	CALLING TO ARMS
AACFGIMNNRTUU	MANUFACTURING	AACGILMNOOPST	CAMPANOLOGIST
AACFHIMNPRSST	CRAFTSMANSHIP	AACGILMNOORST	GASTRONOMICAL
AACFIIILRTTY	ARTIFICIALITY	AACGIMMMNOORT	MONOGRAMMATIC
AACFIIILMNOPT	AMPLIFICATION	AACGLNOORRTTU	CONGRATULATOR
AACFIIILNNNRU	FINANCIAL RUIN	AACHHIIKKNSST	HAS A THICK SKIN
AACFIIILNOQTU	QUALIFICATION	AACHHILMPRRTU	TRIUMPHAL ARCH
AACFIIIMNORST	RAMIFICATIONS	AACHHNORRSSTT	HARSH CONTRAST
AACFIILLORSTV	VICTORIA FALLS	AACHIILLNNOTU	HALLUCINATION
AACFIILMOTTTU	AUTOMATIC LIFT	AACHIILLRRTTY	ARTHRITICALLY
AACFIIILNORSTV	RIVAL FACTIONS	AACHIILNNOSST	SAINT NICHOLAS

AACHIIMNTTUVY	HUMAN ACTIVITY	AACLMMNOOSSTU	COMMON ASSAULT
AACHILLMRSSTU	MUSIC-HALL STAR	AACLMMPRSSSUU	MUSCULAR SPASM
AACHILLNORTUY	HALLUCINATORY	AACLQRRSTTUYZ	QUARTZ CRYSTAL
AACHILMNORSTY	LACHRYMATIONS	AADDDDEELRSTY	DASTARDLY DEED
AACHILMRSSSTT	LAST CHRISTMAS	AADDDDEIIINPV	PAID A DIVIDEND
AACHILNNOORRT	NORTH CAROLINA	AADDDDMMMNUYY	MUMMY AND DADDY
AACHILNNORTTT	NORTH ATLANTIC	AADDDEEEFIOTV	AVOIDED DEFEAT
AACHILNOORSTU	SOUTH CAROLINA	AADDDEEEFNRTW	FED AND WATERED
AACHILOPRSSTY	ASTROPHYSICAL	AADDDEEEHIRST	RAISED THE DEAD
AACHIMNOOPSSS	HAS COMPASSION	AADDDEEELPRSU	ADDED PLEASURE
AACHINOORSTTV	SHORT VACATION	AADDDEEGILMMN	MIDDLE-AGED MAN
AACHLNNOORSUY	ANACHRONOUSLY	AADDDEEIINNRV	EARN A DIVIDEND
AACHLNOPSSTYY	PSYCHOANALYST	AADDDEEILNNOR	DANIEL DERONDA
AACHNOPRRSSTT	SHARP CONTRAST	AADDDEEIMNNRT	RIDDEN A TANDEM
AACIIIILNOSTT	ITALICISATION	AADDDEEKLLTTW	TALKED TWADDLE
AACIIIILNOTTZ	ITALICIZATION	AADDDEEKMMNNO	MAKE DO AND MEND
AACIIIILNOTVV	CIVIL AVIATION	AADDDEEMMNNOS	MADE DEMANDS ON
AACIIILLMNRRT	CRIMINAL TRIAL		MADE NO DEMANDS
AACIIILLNNNOT	INCLINATIONAL	AADDDEEMNNRTU	MADE REDUNDANT
AACIIILLNPSTY	PIANISTICALLY	AADDDEFORRRTW	DARTED FORWARD
AACIIILLNNOSTT	NATIONALISTIC	AADDDEFORSSWW	ADDS A FEW WORDS
AACIIILNOOSST	SOCIALISATION	AADDDEHNOSSST	DOTS AND DASHES
AACIIILNOOSTZ	SOCIALIZATION	AADDDEIINPGVY	PAYS A DIVIDEND
AACIIILNOQSTU	ACQUISITIONAL	AADDDELLNRRUY	DULL AND DREARY
AACIIILNORSTT	RATIONALISTIC	AADDDELMNORST	STANDARD MODEL
AACIIINNOORTT	RATIOCINATION	AADDDGIOOORSW	SAID A GOOD WORD
AACIIINOPPRTT	PARTICIPATION	AADDDHINNRSTU	DID A HAND'S TURN
AACIIIOSSTTVY	ASSOCIATIVITY	AADDEEEEFFHHRT	FEATHERHEADED
AACIIKLMNPPRU	MUNICIPAL PARK	AADDEEEEHLNRT	THREAD A NEEDLE
AACIIILLMNOTWX	WILLIAM CAXTON	AADDEEEEILMNT	MEET A DEADLINE
AACIIILLMOSTTY	ATOMISTICALLY	AADDEEEEPRRSS	DEPRESSED AREA
AACIIILLMPRSTY	PRISMATICALLY	AADDEEEFHNSST	FATHEADEDNESS
AACIIILLOPRTTY	PATRIOTICALLY	AADDEEEFLORSV	LEAVES FOR DEAD
AACIIILLSSTTTY	STATISTICALLY	AADDEEEFORRTT	FEARED TO TREAD
AACIIILMNORTTU	MATRICULATION	AADDEEEHIRRST	REARED ITS HEAD
AACIIILMPRRSTU	PARTICULARISM	AADDEEEHIRSST	RAISES THE DEAD
AACIIILNNOSTUV	VULCANISATION	AADDEEEHKNOTW	AWOKEN THE DEAD
AACIIILNNOTUVZ	VULCANIZATION	AADDEEEHLLPTY	PLAYED THE LEAD
AACIIILNOPSTTU	CAPITULATIONS	AADDEEEINNRST	IN DEAD EARNEST
AACIIILNORSTTU	ARTICULATIONS	AADDEEEELMPRST	PADDLE STEAMER
AACIIILNPPPRRT	PRINCIPAL PART	AADDEEELNORRT	LEARNED TO READ
AACIIILORSCTUV	CASUAL VISITOR	AADDEEEMRRSTU	MEASURED TREAD
AACIIILPRRSTTU	PARTICULARIST	AADDEEFGILLOS	LEAD A DOGS LIFE
AACIIILPRRTTUY	PARTICULARITY	AADDEEFGIMOQW	MADE A GOOD WIFE
AACIIMMNNORTU	COMMUNITARIAN	AADDEEFIILNST	INFLATED IDEAS
AACIIMNNNOOTT	CONTAMINATION	AADDEEFLLLOOW	FOLLOWED A LEAD
AACIIINNNNOSTU	ANNUNCIATIONS	AADDEEFLLNOTU	UNFOLDED A TALE
AACIIINNOPSSTT	PANIC STATIONS	AADDEEFLNORRW	LEANED FORWARD
AACIIOPPRRTTY	PARTICIPATORY	AADDEEFLRSTTU	DREADFUL STATE
AACIKLLMNSTUY	LUCKY TALISMAN	AADDEEGHINRST	SHEDDING A TEAR
AACILLMMNOOTY	MONATOMICALLY	AADDEEGHRRSTW	GARETH EDWARDS
AACILLMNOOTUY	AUTONOMICALLY	AADDEEGILMNNN	MADE IN ENGLAND
AACILLMNOOTXY	TAXONOMICALLY	AADDEEGIMNNRT	IN GREAT DEMAND
AACILLMNOPSTY	COMPLAISANTLY	AADDEEGNNRRRW	ANDREW GARDNER
AACILLMNSTUUY	LUNATIC ASYLUM	AADDEEGNRRTUU	UNDERGRADUATE
AACILLNOPPRTT	TROPICAL PLANT	AADDEEGORSTYY	READY STEADY GO
AACILMNOOPRST	PROCLAMATIONS	AADDEEHHINNST	HEAD IN THE SAND
AACILMNOOPTTU	COMPUTATIONAL	AADDEEHHLNVYY	HEAVY-HANDEDLY
AACILMNRRSTUU	INTRAMUSCULAR	AADDEEHHLORST	SHARED THE LOAD
AACILMOOPSSTT	SOMATOPLASTIC	AADDEEHHLRRTY	HARDHEARTEDLY
AACILMORRSTTU	COURT-MARTIALS	AADDEEHILLOVY	HEAVILY LOADED
	COURTS-MARTIAL	AADDEEHILRRRT	RAID THE LARDER
AACILNNNOOOTT	CONNOTATIONAL	AADDEEHKMNRSU	MAKES A HUNDRED
AACILNNOORSTT	TRANSLOCATION	AADDEEHKNNNSS	HANDS AND KNEES
AACILOOPRRRTU	PROCURATORIAL	AADDEEHLOPRST	SPREAD THE LOAD
AACIMNNOOPSWY	COMPANIONWAYS	AADDEEHMNOSSS	DEAD MANS SHOES
AACIMNNOORSTT	CONTAMINATORS	AADDEEHMPRTUW	DEATH WARMED UP
AACIOPQRSSTTU	AQUATIC SPORTS	AADDEEHRSTTTY	STARTED THE DAY
AACKKLLMOOORT	CLOAKROOM TALK	AADDEEIILMNRV	LIVED IN A DREAM
AACKNOORSTTUY	TOOK SANCTUARY	AADDEEIMNRRRT	ARDENT ADMIRER
AACKNORRSSTTT	STARK CONTRAST	AADDEEIMQRSSU	MARQUIS DE SADE

AADDEEEIMRSTUY	READY-MADE SUIT
AADDEEKMMNNOS	MAKE DEMANDS ON
	MAKE NO DEMANDS
AADDEEKMNNRTU	MAKE REDUNDANT
AADDEELNORSTW	LEANED TOWARDS
AADDEELNRTTUU	UNADULTERATED
AADDEELNSSTWY	LAST WEDNESDAY
AADDEEMMNNPTY	DEMAND PAYMENT
AADDEEMNNOSST	MADE ONE'S STAND
AADDEENNOSVWW	WAVED ONE'S WAND
AADDEFFIIILST	DISAFFILIATED
AADDEFHHOOSTW	SHADOW OF DEATH
AADDEFINOORUV	DID ONE A FAVOUR
AADDEFIORSSWW	SAID A FEW WORDS
AADDEGGHNRRTU	GRANDDAUGHTER
AADDEGHHILNST	LIGHT AND SHADE
AADDEGHHIORRU	HAD A ROUGH RIDE
AADDEGHIMNOOV	HAVE A GOOD MIND
AADDEGHLNORTY	DEATH AND GLORY
AADDEGHNORRUY	ROUGH AND READY
	ROUGH-AND-READY
AADDEGHOPRRSS	ADDRESSOGRAPH
AADDEGIILLLNN	ALLIED LANDING
AADDEGIIMNNRT	RIDING A TANDEM
AADDEGIINNSST	STANDING ASIDE
AADDEGIKMMNNS	MAKING DEMANDS
AADDEGILNRSSS	SALAD DRESSING
AADDEGINNRSTY	STANDING READY
AADDEGINOPPRS	PROPAGANDISED
AADDEGINOPPRZ	PROPAGANDIZED
AADDEGLLOOOTT	TOLD A GOOD TALE
AADDEGLMNORSU	SUGARED ALMOND
AADDEHHNNORSU	HARE AND HOUNDS
AADDEHINOPPRR	HEARD A PIN DROP
AADDEHLLNORVY	RHONDDA VALLEY
AADDEIKNNRSST	EATS AND DRINKS
AADDEILMRRSSY	MRS.DALES DIARY
AADDEILNRSSST	DASTARDLINESS
AADDEKLORSTWW	WALKED TOWARDS
AADDELMNOPPRU	POPULAR DEMAND
AADDELMNORRST	LORD AND MASTER
AADDELNOSSTWY	SLOW AND STEADY
AADDELOPRSSST	POSTAL ADDRESS
AADDFGHINNSTT	STAND AND FIGHT
AADDFGLLNOOOR	FOR GOOD AND ALL
AADDFHMNOORTW	FOOD AND WARMTH
AADDGGHHINOOT	HAD A GOOD NIGHT
AADDGGINNRSTU	STANDING GUARD
AADDGGNOORRSU	DRAGOON GUARDS
AADDGHHINRSST	HIGH STANDARDS
AADDGHHINRSTY	HARD DAYS NIGHT
AADDGHINNSSTY	DAYS AND NIGHTS
AADDGIILNNNWWY	DWINDLING AWAY
AADDGIINNRSST	STANDARDISING
AADDGIINNRSTZ	STANDARDIZING
AADDGINORRSWW	DRAWING A SWORD
AADDGLNOOORTY	TOLD A GOOD YARN
AADDGLNOPRRTY	GRAND OLD PARTY
AADDGOOORSSWY	SAYS A GOOD WORD
AADDHHINOPRUW	HAD A WHIP-ROUND
AADDHHLLLNOOT	ALL HOT AND HOLD
AADDHIILMNOTV	DAVID HAMILTON
AADDHIKNOSSWY	WHISKY AND SODA
AADDHIMNOOSST	THOMAS ADDISON
AADDKLNNOPUWW	WALK UP AND DOWN
AADEEEEELNRSW	RENEWED A LEASE
AADEEEEGLLNRR	GENERAL DEALER
AADEEEEHNPRST	ENTERED A PHASE
AADEEEEFGILORT	FAILED TO AGREE
AADEEEEFHKNRRT	HANKERED AFTER
AADEEEEFLRSSTT	FEDERAL STATES
AADEEEEGGIKNRT	TAKING A DEGREE
AADEEEEGGINNRT	ENGAGE IN TRADE
AADEEEEGGLRTXY	EXAGGERATEDLY
AADEEEEGHILNRT	REGAIN THE LEAD
AADEEEEGHIPTUV	GAVE UP THE IDEA
AADEEEEGHLMPTY	PLAYED THE GAME
AADEEEEGIJLNRT	DARJEELING TEA
AADEEEEGLMNRST	SEND A TELEGRAM
AADEEEEGLRRRRU	REGULAR READER
AADEEEEGMNSSSS	SENDS A MESSAGE
AADEEEEHHHKNST	SHAKEN THE HEAD
AADEEEEHHHKSST	SHAKES THE HEAD
AADEEEEHHIKNTW	WEAK IN THE HEAD
AADEEEEHHKNNTV	THANKED HEAVEN
AADEEEEHHKNOSS	SHAKE ONES HEAD
AADEEEEHHLLNNV	HEAVEN AND HELL
AADEEEEHINRSTT	RAISED THE ANTE
AADEEEEHINSSTT	ANAESTHETISED
AADEEEEHINSTTZ	ANAESTHETIZED
AADEEEEHLNORTT	LEARNED TO HATE
AADEEEEHLQRRTU	HEATED QUARREL
AADEEEEHMNNOST	ONE AND THE SAME
AADEEEEHMNNOSTX	DEXAMETHASONE
AADEEEEHPRRRTW	REAP THE REWARD
AADEEEEIILMRST	DEMATERIALISE
AADEEEEIILMRTZ	DEMATERIALIZE
AADEEEEIILLPSSY	EASILY PLEASED
AADEEEEIILMNSST	MENTAL DISEASE
AADEEEEIILMOPST	AIMED TO PLEASE
AADEEEEIILNQRTU	ANTIQUE DEALER
AADEEEEIMNNRRT	MEDITERRANEAN
AADEEEEIMNNRST	REMAINS SEATED
AADEEEEIMPRRST	PARAMETERISED
AADEEEEIMPRRTZ	PARAMETERIZED
AADEEEELMORSSV	SERVE AS A MODEL
AADEEEELPRSTXY	EXASPERATEDLY
AADEEEEMMORSTU	MADE TO MEASURE
	MADE-TO-MEASURE
AADEEEORRSSTV	OVERSEAS TRADE
AADEEFFGMRSSU	SUFFERS DAMAGE
AADEEFFHKORRT	FEAR OF THE DARK
AADEEFFHKOTTY	TAKE THE DAY OFF
AADEEFGHILRST	RAISED THE FLAG
AADEEFGIIMRTV	GIVE A FIRM DATE
AADEEFGIJLMRS	JAMES GARFIELD
AADEEFGIKMOOW	MAKE A GOOD WIFE
AADEEFGIMMNOR	FORMED AN IMAGE
AADEEFGINPRRS	SPREADING FEAR
AADEEFGMORSSU	SUE FOR DAMAGES
AADEEFHHHIORT	HAIR OF THE HEAD
AADEEFHHHLRTY	HALFHEARTEDLY
AADEEFHHHNOTVW	WAVE OF THE HAND
AADEEFHILLMSS	FLASHED A SMILE
AADEEFHILMNST	FED THE ANIMALS
AADEEFHILNORS	FASHION LEADER
AADEEFHKLLOTY	LADY OF THE LAKE
AADEEFHLLLOST	LEASEHOLD FLAT
AADEEFHLLOTVY	VALLEY OF DEATH
AADEEFHRRSSTT	STARTED AFRESH
AADEEFIKNORRT	TAKEN FOR A RIDE
AADEEFIKORRSS	ASKED FOR A RISE
AADEEFILMNOOR	REMAINED ALOOF
AADEEFILMNOPT	TEMPLE OF DIANA
AADEEFIMMOOSST	MADE A MESS OF IT
AADEEFIOPPRRT	REAPED A PROFIT
AADEEFIRRTTWY	FRITTERED AWAY
AADEEFKMMNOOY	MADE A MONKEY OF
AADEEFKNOPSSV	KNAVE OF SPADES
AADEEFLMNORSU	MEASURE OF LAND
AADEEFMMOORSU	MADE A FOURSOME
AADEEFMNORRRW	MODERN WARFARE

AADEEFNSSSSTT	STEADFASTNESS
AADEEFORRRTWW	DRAWER OF WATER
AADEEGGHLORST	AT LOGGERHEADS
AADEEGGIINNTT	GETTING AN IDEA
AADEEGGIKLMNP	MAKING A PLEDGE
AADEEGGILNPRS	SPREAD-EAGLING
AADEEGGMNORSU	DANGEROUS GAME
AADEEGHHLOSST	HELD AS HOSTAGE
AADEEGHHNPRTT	THE GARDEN PATH
AADEEGHIKLNTT	TAKING THE LEAD
AADEEGHILNNTV	LEADING THE VAN
AADEEGHILNTVW	EVADING THE LAW
AADEEGHILNTWY	LEADING THE WAY
AADEEGHIMOOTV	HAVE A GOOD TIME
AADEEGHINPRSS	PRESSING AHEAD
AADEEGIIKNPRY	KEEPING A DIARY
AADEEGIILNNRV	EARNED A LIVING
AADEEGIILNNUV	GAINED IN VALUE
AADEEGIIMMRRX	MIXED MARRIAGE
AADEEGIKLNORT	TAKE IN A LODGER
AADEEGIKNNRUW	RUDE AWAKENING
AADEEGILMNORR	ORDERING A MEAL
AADEEGILNNPST	PLANTING A SEED
AADEEGILNNSTV	LEAVE STANDING
AADEEGIMMNNRY	MADE IN GERMANY
AADEEGIMNOSST	ADMITS ONE'S AGE
AADEEGIMNPRST	DISPARAGEMENT
AADEEGIMNRRTT	READING MATTER
AADEEGIMNRSTY	GAINED MASTERY
AADEEGIMORSSU	SERIOUS DAMAGE
AADEEGINNSTUX	EXSANGUINATED
AADEEGINRRTTW	TREADING WATER
AADEEGINRSSTT	EAST GRINSTEAD
AADEEGINRSTTT	TRADING ESTATE
AADEEGKNNOPTW	TAKEN DOWN A PEG
AADEEGLLLOOTT	TELL A GOOD TALE
AADEEGLNNOPRR	GENERAL PARDON
AADEEGMNOTTVW	MEAT AND TWO VEG
AADEEHHHMNORT	HEARTH AND HOME
AADEEHHLORSST	SHARES THE LOAD
AADEEHHNOPSTT	TAPS ON THE HEAD
AADEEHHNSSTTT	STANDS THE HEAT
AADEEHHORTTTW	WAR TO THE DEATH
AADEEHIILRRTW	TARRIED AWHILE
AADEEHIKLNPRT	LEAP IN THE DARK
AADEEHILLOOST	HAD A TILE LOOSE
AADEEHILNQRSU	HARLEQUINADES
AADEEHILNRTYY	EARLY IN THE DAY
AADEEHINNORSS	RAISE ONES HAND
AADEEHINOPRSS	PAID ONE'S SHARE
AADEEHINORSST	RAISED ONE'S HAT
AADEEHJNNORSY	SHARE AND ENJOY
AADEEHKKNNNTU	KENNETH KAUNDA
AADEEHKOORTTT	TAKE TO THE ROAD
AADEEHLLORTTT	LED TO THE ALTAR
AADEEHLMRRTWY	WARMHEARTEDLY
AADEEHLPPRTTY	PLAYED THE PART
AADEEHLPSSSTT	PASSED THE SALT
AADEEHNPPRRWY	HAPPY WANDERER
AADEEHORRRSTW	HARDWARE STORE
AADEEHORSTTTV	STARVE TO DEATH
AADEEIIKMNTVW	TAKEN A DIM VIEW
AADEEIIKMSTVW	TAKES A DIM VIEW
AADEEIIILLMPPT	LIMITED APPEAL
AADEEIILMNRSV	LIVES IN A DREAM
AADEEIILNNOST	DENATIONALISE
AADEEIIMNTTUW	WAITED A MINUTE
AADEEIKLNNPRS	SPRAINED ANKLE
AADEEIKMMNOST	MADE NO MISTAKE
AADEEILMMORST	MELODRAMATISE
AADEEILMMORTZ	MELODRAMATIZE
AADEEILMRRSST	DRESS MATERIAL
AADEEILNNSTVY	VALENTINES DAY
AADEEILOOPRRT	AERIAL TORPEDO
AADEEILORRVVW	DRAW A VEIL OVER
AADEEILORSSUY	EASILY AROUSED
AADEEILRSTVVY	ADVERSATIVELY
AADEEIMMNNOTTW	WAITED A MOMENT
AADEEIMNNOSUV	MADISON AVENUE
AADEEIMNPRRSY	MAIDEN'S PRAYER
AADEEINNOTUVW	WEAVE IN AND OUT
AADEEINOPRSST	ENDOPARASITES
AADEEINPRSSST	DISPARATENESS
AADEEINPSSSTW	PISSED AS A NEWT
AADEEJMNORTVY	NEVER JAM TODAY
AADEEKLLNORTT	LEARNED TO TALK
AADEEKLLNORTW	LEARNED TO WALK
AADEEKLNORTWW	WALKED ON WATER
AADEEKMNNOSST	MAKE ONES STAND
AADEEKMNRSSTU	KEEN AS MUSTARD
AADEEKNNOSSTT	TAKE ONE'S STAND
AADEEKNPRRTTW	PEWTER TANKARD
AADEELLMNORTW	WALTER MONDALE
AADEELNPPPRST	PEPPER AND SALT
	PEPPER-AND-SALT
	SALT AND PEPPER
AADEELNPSSTTU	SALTED PEANUTS
AADEELNRSTTUY	STAYED NEUTRAL
AADEELOOPSSUY	DO AS YOU PLEASE
AADEEMNNNOR3W	EAMONN ANDREWS
AADEEMNPRRTTW	WAR DEPARTMENT
AADEENNOSSVWW	WAVES ONE'S WAND
AADEENNOTTTTX	ANNOTATED TEXT
AADEENNPRSTUU	SUPERANNUATED
AADEENOPSSSWY	PASSED ONE'S WAY
AADEERRSTUVYY	EVERY SATURDAY
AADEFFFIIORST	TIDE OF AFFAIRS
AADEFFHHLNOTT	FLAT OF THE HAND
AADEFFHMNNNOR	OFF-HAND MANNER
	OFFHAND MANNER
AADEFFIIILSST	DISAFFILIATES
AADEFFIILMNWY	WIFE AND FAMILY
AADEFFLNNORSW	SAFFRON WALDEN
AADEFGHHINORR	HARD OF HEARING
	HARD-OF-HEARING
AADEFGHHIOORT	A HAIR OF THE DOG
AADEFGHIRSTTT	STARTED A FIGHT
AADEFGHLNRRTY	GRANDFATHERLY
AADEFGIILNNOR	LAID A FINGER ON
AADEFHHIKMNRS	FIRM HANDSHAKE
AADEFHHILMORV	HAVE A FIRM HOLD
AADEFHHOOPRTT	THE DROP OF A HAT
AADEFHIKLMORT	TAKE A FIRM HOLD
AADEFHINNOOPT	ON PAIN OF DEATH
AADEFHINNOSTU	FOUNTAINHEADS
AADEFHLLMOPTY	LADY OF THE LAMP
AADEFIILLMRSU	DISMAL FAILURE
AADEFIILLSTUW	FILED A LAWSUIT
AADEFIILNOSTU	FEUDALISATION
AADEFIILNOTUZ	FEUDALIZATION
AADEFILLNPRYY	PLAY A FRIENDLY
AADEFILMNOORS	MAID OF ORLEANS
AADEFILMNOORT	DEFORMATIONAL
AADEFILOOPRSS	FOOLS PARADISE
AADEFINOPRRRY	PRAYED FOR RAIN
AADEFLLLNOOPW	FOLLOWED A PLAN
AADEFLLMNNTUY	FUNDAMENTALLY
AADEFLNORRTUW	FLOUR AND WATER
AADEFORSSSWWY	SAYS A FEW WORDS
AADEGGGGIINRV	DIGGING A GRAVE
AADEGGGHINNNR	HANGING GARDEN
AADEGGHHILMNS	HIGHLAND GAMES

AADEGGHHIINNTY	GAINING THE DAY
AADEGGNNORTUV	VANTAGE GROUND
AADEGHHHLNOTU	HAD THE LAUGH ON
AADEGHHIIKNNT	THINKING AHEAD
AADEGHHIKMNST	HAD THE MAKINGS
AADEGHHIMORTU	HAD A ROUGH TIME
AADEGHHINOOST	SHOOTING AHEAD
AADEGHHIORRSU	HAS A ROUGH RIDE
AADEGHHLOOSST	HOLD AS HOSTAGE
AADEGHIIMNORT	HARD TO IMAGINE
AADEGHIINPTTV	HAVING IT TAPED
AADEGHILNRTUW	DAUGHTER-IN-LAW
AADEGHIMNORTW	DRAWING AT HOME
AADEGHINNOSVY	HAVING ONE'S DAY
AADEGHINNRRRW	WARREN HARDING
AADEGHINNRTUV	IN THE VANGUARD
AADEGHIOPRRRS	RADIOGRAPHERS
AADEGHLNNNRUY	LEAN AND HUNGRY
AADEGHLOPRTTY	PLAY HARD TO GET
AADEGIILMPRRU	IMPERIAL GUARD
AADEGIILNNSUV	LEAVING UNSAID
AADEGIILNRSTT	LEADING ARTIST
AADEGIIMNNRTV	ANIMADVERTING
AADEGIIMNRTYZ	DIRTY MAGAZINE
AADEGIINNNSTW	STANDING IN AWE
AADEGIINNORRT	TREADING ON AIR
AADEGIINPRRWZ	DRAWING A PRIZE
AADEGIKLNOPSU	SPEAKING ALOUD
AADEGIKMNNOSY	MAKING ONE'S DAY
AADEGIKMNORTU	MAKING A DETOUR
AADEGIKNORSTW	WORKED AGAINST
AADEGILMNPRTU	LEADING A TRUMP
AADEGILMOORST	MATERIAL GOODS
AADEGILNNNOST	STANDING ALONE
AADEGILNSTTVY	DEVASTATINGLY
AADEGIMNPRTTT	DARING ATTEMPT
AADEGIMNRRSTT	TRANSMIGRATED
AADEGIMNRRSTW	DRAWING MASTER
AADEGINNNOOSS	SAGE AND ONIONS
AADEGINNNORRT	RAN INTO DANGER
AADEGINNRSTTT	STANDING TREAT
AADEGINNRSTTU	TURNED AGAINST
AADEGINNRSTTW	STANDING WATER
AADEGINOPPRSS	PROPAGANDISES
AADEGINOPPRSZ	PROPAGANDIZES
AADEGINORRSTY	READING A STORY
AADEGINRSSTTV	AVENT-GARDISTS
	STARTED SAVING
AADEGLLNOORTY	TELL A GOOD YARN
AADEGLMNRSTUY	GRANTED ASYLUM
AADEGLNOPRSTT	PROSTATE GLAND
AADEGMNOORSTW	GO AND EAT WORMS
AADEGOPRSSTTU	POSTGRADUATES
AADEHHIKLMNPS	LIMP HANDSHAKE
AADEHHILMOORR	HAEMORRHOIDAL
AADEHHIORTVWW	HAVE A WORD WITH
AADEHHKNORSTT	TAKE SHORTHAND
AADEHHNNOSSSW	WASH ONES HANDS
AADEHIILLNSSW	WHEN ALL IS SAID
AADEHIILMOSSY	HAEMODIALYSIS
AADEHIILNNOPT	PAID ON THE NAIL
AADEHIINOTTWY	TOY WITH AN IDEA
AADEHIINRSSSS	HIRED ASSASSIN
AADEHIKLMORSY	HOLIDAYMAKERS
AADEHIKLNOORT	TOOK A HARD LINE
AADEHILNOOSSY	HOLIDAY SEASON
AADEHILNOPSTU	HAD ONE'S TAIL UP
AADEHIMNNORSTU	DIATHERMANOUS
AADEHINNSTTWY	STAND IN THE WAY
AADEHINOPPRRS	HEARS A PIN DROP
AADEHINORRRSY	ORDINARY SHARE
AADEHINORRSSV	SHARRON DAVIES
AADEHIPSSSTWY	PASSED THIS WAY
AADEHLLNOTWWY	LAY DOWN THE LAW
AADEHLMNORSTU	SOUND THE ALARM
AADEHLNNNOOSY	LAY ONE'S HAND ON
AADEHMNNOOOTY	HAD ONE TOO MANY
AADEHMNNOOPSST	SHAMPOO AND SET
AADEHMNOORSST	DO AS THE ROMANS
AADEHNNOORRTW	ETON AND HARROW
AADEHNNOORSTT	NOSE AND THROAT
AADEHNNOOSWWY	HAD ONE'S OWN WAY
AADEHNNOSSSTY	STAYS ONE'S HAND
AADEHNOPPRSSY	HOPES AND PRAYS
AADEHNORRSTTW	NORTHEASTWARD
AADEHNORSSSUZ	HAZARDOUSNESS
AADEHNORSSTUY	THOUSAND YEARS
AADEHOOPRSTTT	TAPS AT THE DOOR
AADEHORSSTTUW	SOUTHEASTWARD
AADEIILMMNRST	MALADMINISTER
AADEIILNNOPRT	NATIONAL PRIDE
AADEIIMMOSSTU	TIMID AS A MOUSE
AADEIIMMNNORSV	ANIMADVERSION
AADEIINNOPTTT	PAID ATTENTION
AADEIINOPSSST	DISPASSIONATE
AADEIIPQRRTTU	QUADRIPARTITE
AADEIJMNNOTTW	WANTED JAM ON IT
AADEIJMORRSST	MAJOR DISASTER
AADEIKKMNPSSU	KISS AND MAKE UP
AADEIKLNNOPRR	LEONARD PARKIN
AADEIKLNRRSTV	SILVER TANKARD
AADEIKLPPRSSY	SPEAKS RAPIDLY
AADEILLLOSTWW	SWALLOW-TAILED
AADEILLMMNORS	ADMIRAL NELSON
AADEILLNNQRUY	QUADRENNIALLY
AADEILLNOSSSY	ALL-DAY SESSION
AADEILMMORSTT	MELODRAMATIST
AADEILMNOSTTU	STAND OUT A MILE
AADEILNNORSST	NATIONAL DRESS
AADEILNORRRRT	TRIAL AND ERROR
AADEILNORSTTU	ADULTERATIONS
AADEILPPRSTTY	PLAYED ITS PART
AADEIMNNOORRS	MOIRA ANDERSON
AADEIMNOQRSSU	MADISON SQUARE
AADEIMNRRTTWY	MATERNITY WARD
AADEINNNOPRSW	DRAWN A PENSION
AADEINNOPPRSS	SPARED NO PAINS
AADEINNOPRSSW	DRAWS A PENSION
AADEINNORTTTW	DRAW ATTENTION
AADEINNPRSTUV	UNPAID SERVANT
AADEINOOPPSTW	TWO PEAS IN A POD
AADEINORRRTXY	EXTRAORDINARY
AADEIOOOPRRRT	RADIO OPERATOR
AADEJLMMNSTTU	MALADJUSTMENT
AADEKLNORSSTT	TOTAL DARKNESS
AADEKMNORRTTY	MARKET DRAYTON
AADELLOQRRRTU	QUARTER DOLLAR
AADELNOORSTY	LAY AT ONE'S DOOR
AADEMMNORSSYY	RAYMOND MASSEY
AADEMNOPPRSTU	PUTS A DAMPER ON
AADEMNORRTUWY	MANY A TRUE WORD
AADEMOPRRRSUU	SPREAD A RUMOUR
AADENNOORSSTT	STAND TO REASON
AADFFILMNORSU	FINDS A FORMULA
AADFFLMNOORUU	FOUND A FORMULA
AADFGGHLOOORU	GOOD FOR A LAUGH
AADFGIINPRRTT	DRIFTING APART
AADFGILNNOOST	STANDING ALOOF
AADFHLLOOSTTY	LADY OF SHALOTT
AADFIILNNOSTV	FIND SALVATION
AADFIKLLMOORW	MAID OF ALL WORK
AADFILLOOPRSY	APRIL FOOLS DAY

AADFILOOPRSTT	SOLD AT A PROFIT
AADFINRSSSTTT	FITS AND STARTS
AADFKMMNOORSW	KNOWS FROM ADAM
AADFLLNORSSST	STANDS OR FALLS
AADFNOORSSTWY	SWAYS TO AND FRO
AADGGHHINOOST	HAS A GOOD NIGHT
AADGGHINNNORU	HANGING AROUND
AADGGIIILNNOS	DIAGONALISING
AADGGIIILNNOZ	DIAGONALIZING
AADGGIIINNSST	SIDING AGAINST
AADGGIILNPRSY	DISPARAGINGLY
AADGHIIMNOTTV	HAVING TO ADMIT
AADGHIINNNRWZ	WINNING HAZARD
AADGHIINOTWWY	DOING AWAY WITH
AADGHILNNNOSS	NO HAND SIGNALS
AADGHILNNNOSY	LAYING HANDS ON
AADGHILNNPPSY	HAPPY LANDINGS!
AADGHILNOPRTY	HOLDING A PARTY
AADGHINRSTTUY	SATURDAY NIGHT
AADGIIIJLLNNN	LANDING IN JAIL
AADGIIILNNTWY	LADY IN WAITING
	LADY-IN-WAITING
AADGIIILNRSWY	RAILWAY SIDING
AADGIIIMNNUSS	GAIN ADMISSION
AADGIIINNRRTV	DRIVING A TRAIN
AADGIIKLMMNNO	ANIMAL KINGDOM
AADGIIKMNNORS	MAKING INROADS
AADGIILNNRSTT	STANDING TRIAL
AADGIIMNOOTTZ	DOGMATIZATION
AADGIINNNORTUW	WAITING AROUND
AADGIKLNNNORUW	WALKING AROUND
AADGILLPRSUVY	VULGAR DISPLAY
AADGILNNOPRST	PROSTAGLANDIN
AADGILNNUPRUY	PLAYING AROUND
AADGIMNPRSSTT	TRADING STAMPS
AADGINNRSSTTT	STANDING START
AADHHIKOOTTTW	HAD WHAT IT TOOK
AADHHINOPRSUW	HAS A WHIP-ROUND
AADHLLMRRRTUU	ARTHUR MULLARD
AADHLLOORSTWW	HARD TO SWALLOW
AADHNOOORSTWW	WORN TO A SHADOW
AADIIKLNNNORT	NATIONAL DRINK
AADIILLLNTTUY	LATITUDINALLY
AADIILLNORTTY	TRADITIONALLY
AADIILLNPTTUY	APTITUDINALLY
AADIILNOORSTW	ISOLATION WARD
AADIIMNNRSSTT	ADMINISTRANTS
AADIIMNORRSTT	ADMINISTRATOR
AADILLLNNOORS	RONALD ALLISON
AADILNOPSSTTW	PISTOLS AT DAWN
AADILNRSSTTUV	ALVIN STARDUST
AADNOOPRRRSTT	ROAD TRANSPORT
AAEEEEFGILNST	FEELING AT EASE
AAEEEEFNNORYY	AN EYE FOR AN EYE
AAEEEEGIPRRVV	GAVE A REPRIEVE
AAEEEEGLOPRST	EAGER TO PLEASE
AAEEEEHNNOPVY	HAVE AN EYE OPEN
AAEEEEKLNOSTV	TAKE ONES LEAVE
AAEEEENOSSSTT	SETS ONE AT EASE
AAEEEFFKKNOTW	TAKEN A WEEK OFF
AAEEEFFKKOSTW	TAKES A WEEK OFF
AAEEEFGGIRRUV	AVERAGE FIGURE
AAEEEFGHMMNOT	NAME OF THE GAME
AAEEEFHLMOSVV	VALE OF EVESHAM
AAEEEFILNNORS	FLEA IN ONES EAR
AAEEEFLNORTUV	LEAVE A FORTUNE
AAEEEFLNOSSST	SEALS ONE'S FATE
AAEEEFMRSSTUY	SAFETY MEASURE
AAEEEGGGKLNRU	GREEK LANGUAGE
AAEEEGGHHIRTV	AVERAGE HEIGHT
AAEEEGGHIRTVW	AVERAGE WEIGHT

AAEEEGHKMOSTW	TAKE-HOME WAGES
AAEEEGHLMPRST	GREASE THE PALM
AAEEEGHLNRTTY	HENLEY REGATTA
AAEEEGIIKLNPT	EATEN LIKE A PIG
AAEEEGIILLMPR	IMPERIAL EAGLE
AAEEEGILLMNTW	WELL MEET AGAIN
AAEEEGILMNPVX	GIVE AN EXAMPLE
AAEEEGILNRSWY	SEEING A LAWYER
AAEEEGILNSSYZ	EYELESS IN GAZA
AAEEEGILPSVWY	PLEASE GIVE WAY
AAEEEGINSSTTT	SETTING AT EASE
AAEEEGKMRSSTU	MAKES A GESTURE
AAEEEGLMMNRSS	GERMAN MEASLES
AAEEEGLMNRSTT	SENT A TELEGRAM
AAEEEGLPRRSTU	GREAT PLEASURE
AAEEEGMMMNNNTW	NEW MANAGEMENT
AAEEEGMNQRRTU	QUEEN MARGARET
AAEEEGNOPRRSV	AVERAGE PERSON
AAEEEHHISSTTW	WHITE AS A SHEET
AAEEEHHISTTVY	THE AYES HAVE IT
AAEEEHHLMNTTW	MAN AT THE WHEEL
AAEEEHHNNORTV	HEAVEN ON EARTH
AAEEEHIINRSTVW	HAVE THE ANSWER
AAEEEHIILLSSS	HAILE SELASSIE
AAEEEHIILNRTV	LEAVE IN THE AIR
AAEEEHIKKLSWY	EYES LIKE A HAWK
AAEEEHIKLORST	ATE LIKE A HORSE
	EAT LIKE A HORSE
AAEEEHIILNPSST	ELEPHANTIASES
AAEEEHILPPRRT	PRE-RAPHAELITE
AAEEEHIMMNRST	REMAIN THE SAME
AAEEEHIMMSTTT	AT THE SAME TIME
AAEEEHIMNNNOV	IN HEAVEN'S NAME
AAEEEHINRSSTT	RAISES THE ANTE
AAEEEHINSSSTT	ANAESTHETISES
AAEEEHINSSTTZ	ANAESTHETIZES
AAEEEHKLSTTTU	TAKE THE SALUTE
AAEEEHKRSTTTW	TAKE THE WATERS
AAEEEHLNPRTTT	PATENT LEATHER
AAEEEHMNRTTTT	HEAT TREATMENT
AAEEEHMNRTTTV	HAVE TREATMENT
AAEEEHNNOORST	NEAR ONE'S HEART
AAEEEHPPRRTWY	PREPARE THE WAY
AAEEEILLNOSTV	LEAVES IT ALONE
AAEEEILLRTUVV	RELATIVE VALUE
AAEEEILMNRRSU	LINEAR MEASURE
AAEEEIMPRRSST	PARAMETERISES
AAEEEIMPRRSTZ	PARAMETERIZES
AAEEEINRSSVVW	EVASIVE ANSWER
AAEEEKKLNOOST	TAKEN A LOOK-SEE
AAEEEKKLOOSST	TAKES A LOOK-SEE
AAEEEKLMNORSV	LEAVE ONE'S MARK
AAEEEKLQRRSSU	SEEKS A QUARREL
AAEEEKMMORSTU	MAKE TO MEASURE
AAEEEKMQRSSTU	MAKES A REQUEST
AAEEELMMNPRTT	TEMPERAMENTAL
AAEEELMNPSSTX	SETS AN EXAMPLE
AAEEELNNOSSTT	EATEN ONE'S SALT
AAEEEMNNNNTTW	NANETTE NEWMAN
AAEEEMNNPRTVW	PERMANENT WAVE
AAEEEMQRRSSUU	SQUARE MEASURE
AAEEENRRSSVWY	SEVEN YEARS WAR
AAEEFFGNRSSTT	STAFF SERGEANT
AAEEFFHLMNSST	FANS THE FLAMES
AAEEFFKNORRTU	FREAK OF NATURE
AAEEFFMNOSSTY	MEANS OF SAFETY
AAEEFFNOORSST	OFF-SEASON RATE
AAEEFGHILRSST	RAISES THE FLAG
AAEEFGHLLSTTU	SALUTE THE FLAG
AAEEFGHLRRTTU	GRATEFUL HEART
AAEEFGIKLNOPT	KEEPING AFLOAT

AAEEFGILLLNPS	FALLING ASLEEP
AAEEFGILLLNSV	FALLING LEAVES
AAEEFGILMNTTU	MENTAL FATIGUE
AAEEFGILNORTW	FLEW INTO A RAGE
AAEEFGIMOPSST	PASSAGE OF TIME
AAEEFGIMORSTV	RAVAGES OF TIME
AAEEFGJLNRRUW	JUNGLE WARFARE
AAEEFGLMORRTU	AMATEUR GOLFER
AAEEFHHIKRSTW	SHAKE WITH FEAR
AAEEFHHILNTWY	WITH HALF AN EYE
AAEEFHHORRSTT	HEART OF HEARTS
AAEEFHILLMSSS	FLASHES A SMILE
AAEEFHKNORSTV	KNAVE OF HEARTS
AAEEFHLLNORTT	FALLEN TO EARTH
AAEEFHLLOPPPR	APPEAL FOR HELP
AAEEFHORSTTTT	STATE OF THE ART
	STATE-OF-THE-ART
AAEEFHPRRSSTU	SHARP FEATURES
AAEEFIIKLMNRT	TAKE A FIRM LINE
AAEEFIILLMSTT	LAST A LIFETIME
AAEEFIILMNSTT	FINAL ESTIMATE
AAEEFIKMMOSST	MAKE A MESS OF IT
AAEEFILLLNNUV	FALLEN IN VALUE
AAEEFILNPRSTU	PLAIN FEATURES
AAEEFIMNRRTTT	FAIR TREATMENT
AAEEFIOPRRSTT	STATE OF REPAIR
AAEEFKKMMNOOY	MAKE A MONKEY OF
AAEEFKMNORSTU	MAKES A FORTUNE
AAEEFLLOPPRVY	APPLY FOR LEAVE
AAEEFLLPRRTWY	FAREWELL PARTY
AAEEFLNNOORTT	LATE AFTERNOON
AAEEFLNNRSTUW	TURNS A NEW LEAF
AAEEFMORRSTTW	STREAM OF WATER
AAEEFNORSTTTU	STATE OF NATURE
AAEEFOPPRRRRW	PREPARE FOR WAR
AAEEGGGILNNNV	AVENGING ANGEL
AAEEGGGMORSTT	GETS A MORTGAGE
AAEEGGHILNSTV	GAVE THE SIGNAL
AAEEGGHINORTT	TOGETHER AGAIN
AAEEGGHLLNSUW	WELSH LANGUAGE
AAEEGGHLNRTTT	AT GREAT LENGTH
AAEEGGIKNNOPT	KEEPING A TAG ON
AAEEGGILMORTV	AGGLOMERATIVE
AAEEGGINNOPRT	GENERATION GAP
AAEEGGINORSTT	GETS INTO A RAGE
AAEEGGMORRSTT	MORTGAGE RATES
AAEEGHHIKNRST	HANG THE KAISER
AAEEGHHLNOPST	ON THE SLAGHEAP
AAEEGHIIKNSTV	GIVEN IT A SHAKE
AAEEGHIIKSSTV	GIVES IT A SHAKE
AAEEGHILLRRTW	WALTER RALEIGH
AAEEGHILNRTVY	LAY IN THE GRAVE
AAEEGHIMNNPTW	PAWN IN THE GAME
AAEEGHIMNOSUZ	HOUSE MAGAZINE
AAEEGHINNNOVY	HAVING AN EYE ON
AAEEGHINNOSTT	EATING ONE'S HAT
AAEEGHKLNPSTT	SPEAK AT LENGTH
AAEEGHKNORSST	NO GREAT SHAKES
AAEEGHKNOSSTT	TAKEN HOSTAGES
AAEEGHKOSSSTT	TAKES HOSTAGES
AAEEGHLLNOTWY	GONE ALL THE WAY
AAEEGHLLOPPUV	GAVE UP ALL HOPE
AAEEGHLLOSTWY	GOES ALL THE WAY
AAEEGHORRSTTW	WATER SHORTAGE
AAEEGIIKLPSTW	SWEAT LIKE A PIG
AAEEGIILMNRRS	MARRIAGE LINES
AAEEGIILMPRTX	EXEMPLI GRATIA
AAEEGIILNNRWY	RAILWAY ENGINE
AAEEGIIMMPRTZ	EPIGRAMMATIZE
AAEEGIIMNRRRT	INTERMARRIAGE
AAEEGIIMNRSTV	VEGETARIANISM
AAEEGIIMRRRST	MARRIAGE RITES
AAEEGIKLMNOTT	TAKE A LONG TIME
AAEEGIKLNOTVW	TAKE A LONG VIEW
AAEEGIKLNRTTT	TAKING A LETTER
AAEEGIKMNPRUW	WEARING MAKE-UP
AAEEGILLNPSVW	WEAVING A SPELL
AAEEGILMNNNTU	ANNUAL MEETING
AAEEGILNNPRTT	PLANTING A TREE
AAEEGILNRRTTY	LITERARY AGENT
AAEEGIMMMNNST	MISMANAGEMENT
AAEEGIMNPRRST	SPARTAN REGIME
AAEEGIMNPRSTU	MEASURING TAPE
AAEEGIMNRTTUV	ARGUMENTATIVE
AAEEGINNSSTUX	EXSANGUINATES
AAEEGINPSTTTU	PUTTING AT EASE
AAEEGJMNORRST	SERGEANT MAJOR
AAEEGKLNOPSST	TAKEN AS GOSPEL
AAEEGKLOPSSST	TAKES AS GOSPEL
AAEEGLMNORSTV	GALVANOMETERS
AAEEGLOOPSSUY	GO AS YOU PLEASE
AAEEGLPPPRSSU	PURPLE PASSAGE
AAEEGMMMNRRSST	GERMAN MASTERS
AAEEGMNNNRRST	STRANGE MANNER
AAEEGNOQRRTUV	GAVE NO QUARTER
AAEEGNQRRSTTU	GRANT A REQUEST
AAEEGOSSSTTWY	TWO EASY STAGES
AAEEHHIIMNTTV	HAVE A THIN TIME
AAEEHHILNRTTW	WHITE HART LANE
AAEEHHIMPRSTT	AMPHITHEATRES
AAEEHHORRSTTT	HEART-TO-HEARTS
AAEEHIILNPRST	LEAPS IN THE AIR
AAEEHIILNPRTT	LEAPT IN THE AIR
AAEEHIILNPSST	ELEPHANTIASIS
AAEEHIILRRSTW	TARRIES AWHILE
AAEEHIINNPRST	PAIN IN THE ARSE
AAEEHIKLNRRSU	RUNS LIKE A HARE
AAEEHIKNORTTT	TAKEN TO THE AIR
AAEEHIKNRSTTT	TAKE THE STRAIN
AAEEHIKORSTTT	TAKES TO THE AIR
AAEEHIKORTTTT	TAKE IT TO HEART
AAEEHILLNNNPY	PHENYLALANINE
AAEEHILLNRSTW	IN ALL WEATHERS
AAEEHILLOOSST	HAS A TILE LOOSE
AAEEHILLOPSTV	LEAVE HOSPITAL
AAEEHILLOTTVW	VIOLATE THE LAW
AAEEHILLRSTTW	WHERE IT'S ALL AT
AAEEHIMMNORST	REMAINS AT HOME
AAEEHINORSSST	RAISES ONE'S HAT
AAEEHINOSTVWY	HAVE IT ONE'S WAY
AAEEHINRRSTVW	HITS A RAW NERVE
AAEEHINSSSTTT	ANAESTHETISTS
AAEEHKLMPRTTY	PLAY THE MARKET
AAEEHKMNNSSUW	HUMAN WEAKNESS
AAEEHKPPRSTTU	RAKE UP THE PAST
AAEEHLLLLOSVW	ALL HALLOWS EVE
AAEEHLLNRSSTW	ALL THE ANSWERS
AAEEHLLNTTWWY	WENT ALL THE WAY
AAEEHLLPPRSTW	PAPER THE WALLS
	PAPERS THE WALL
AAEEHLMNPRTTY	MENTAL THERAPY
AAEEHLMOORRRS	REHEARSAL ROOM
AAEEHLMRSTTUU	AMATEUR SLEUTH
AAEEHLNPPTTYY	PAY THE PENALTY
AAEEHLOSSTTYY	TO SAY THE LEAST
AAEEHLPSSSSTT	PASSES THE SALT
AAEEHMNORRTTT	ANOTHER MATTER
AAEEHMNRSSTTT	RASH STATEMENT
AAEEHNNOPPSWY	HAPPEN ONE'S WAY
AAEEHNOPRSSSY	PAYS ONE'S SHARE
AAEEHNOQRRSUV	HANOVER SQUARE
AAEEHNORSSTTT	EAST-NORTHEAST

AAEEHNPRSSTTW	WEARS THE PANTS	AAEFFINOPRSTV	PARAFFIN STOVE
AAEEHOSSSTTTU	EAST-SOUTHEAST	AAEFFIOPRRSTT	TEAR A STRIP OFF
AAEEIIILMMRST	IMMATERIALISE		TEAR OFF A STRIP
AAEEIIILMMRTZ	IMMATERIALIZE	AAEFFLLLORTTU	ALL OF A FLUTTER
AAEEIIKKLLSTW	WALKIE-TALKIES	AAEFGGILNRRUU	ANGULAR FIGURE
AAEEIIMNNNSST	INANIMATENESS	AAEFGGILNRSTU	FIRST LANGUAGE
AAEEIINNRRSSV	ANNIVERSARIES	AAEFGHHIILLNT	FAILING HEALTH
AAEEIINNRRSTV	VETERINARIANS	AAEFGHIILNNRT	TEARING IN HALF
AAEEIKKMMNOST	MAKE NO MISTAKE	AAEFGHILOPPRT	RIGHT OF APPEAL
AAEEIKLMNNRRW	WARLIKE MANNER	AAEFGHINRSTWY	FRIGHTENS AWAY
AAEEIKLMNSSTT	STATESMANLIKE	AAEFGHOPRRSTW	GRAPES OF WRATH
AAEEIKLMRSSTV	LEAVES ITS MARK	AAEFGIIKLNNRW	WALKING IN FEAR
AAEEIKLNSSTTV	TALKATIVENESS	AAEFGIILLMRSU	GALLIMAUFRIES
AAEEIKMMOPRSS	MAKES A PROMISE	AAEFGIILLNRSU	SIGNAL FAILURE
AAEEIKNRSSTTW	KNITS A SWEATER	AAEFGIILNPSTY	PLAYING IT SAFE
AAEEILLLLLNPRS	PARALLEL LINES	AAEFGIINRRSTT	STARTING A FIRE
AAEEILLLPPTVY	APPELLATIVELY	AAEFGIKLLMNRT	FALLING MARKET
AAEEILLNPTVXY	EXPLANATIVELY	AAEFGILLLMNST	FLAGELLANTISM
AAEEILLNRTTVY	ALTERNATIVELY	AAEFGILLLNOVW	LEAVING FALLOW
AAEEILMMNNPRU	MAURFFN LIPMAN	AAEFGILLLNSUV	FALLING VALUES
AAEEILMNNPTTT	MENTAL PATIENT	AAEFGILMNNNOR	MAN OF LEARNING
AAEEILMNNRRTU	REMAIN NEUTRAL	AAEFGILMNRRTY	FRAGMENTARILY
AAEEILMPRTTXY	PLAY EXTRA TIME	AAEFGII NNORSY	LAYS A FINGER ON
AACCILNNORTTV	NO ALTERNATIVE	AAEFGILNRSTUV	SERVING A FAULT
AAEEILNPRSSTT	ESSENTIAL PART	AAEFGILOPRSSS	PAIR OF GLASSES
AAEEILNRRSTTT	TRANSLITERATE	AAEFGIMNNORTT	FRAGMENTATION
AAEEILNSTTUUV	UNVEIL A STATUE	AAEFGIOPRRRST	PAIR OF GARTERS
AAEEILOPRTIVX	EXTRAPOLATIVE	AAEFGLLLMNORS	FROM ALL ANGLES
AAEEILRRRSTTU	TREASURE TRAIL	AAEFGLLMNRRST	FRAGRANT SMELL
AAEEIMMNRRRST	MASTER MARINER	AAEFGLNOORRUV	ORANGE FLAVOUR
AAEEIMNOPRRTV	NARRATIVE POEM	AAEFHHILLNOST	ALL THE FASHION
AAEEIMOQSSTUU	QUIET AS A MOUSE	AAEFHHILNNPST	FLASH IN THE PAN
AAEEIMPRRTTTV	PRIVATE MATTER	AAEFHIIKLMSSW	SWAM LIKE A FISH
AACCINNPR3TTY	SPINY ANTEATER	AAEFHIILMPPSY	HAPPY FAMILIES
AAEEINNRRRRST	RENT IN ARREARS	AAEFHILNOSSTT	LATEST FASHION
AAEEINOPRRSTV	PRIVATE REASON	AAEFHILRSSTTW	SALT-WATER FISH
AAEEINORRTUYY	YEAR IN YEAR OUT	AAEFHLNOPPRTT	PART OF THE PLAN
AAEEINORSSSTV	ASSEVERATIONS	AAEFHMORRTTTT	FOR THAT MATTER
AAEEINQRRTTUV	NATIVE QUARTER	AAEFHNORSTTTT	SAT AT THE FRONT
AAEEINRSSSTWY	WRITES AN ESSAY	AAEFHOOPSSTTV	HAVE A SOFT SPOT
AAEEIPRRSTTTZ	TRAPEZE ARTIST	AAEFIIIILMRST	FAMILIARITIES
AAEEKLMNOPSSY	MAKES ONE'S PLAY	AAEFIIILLOTTV	OF LITTLE AVAIL
AAEEKLMNORSSW	MORAL WEAKNESS	AAEFIIILLMRSTY	FAMILIAR STYLE
AAEEKLMRRTUWW	LUKEWARM WATER	AAEFIILLNNRSS	IN ALL FAIRNESS
AAEEKMMNORSTT	MAKES NO MATTER	AAEFIILLNNTTU	FLUENT ITALIAN
AAEEKMMNPRSTU	AMUSEMENT PARK	AAEFIILLSSTUW	FILES A LAWSUIT
AAEEKMOPRSSTT	MAKES A PROTEST	AAEFIILMORRTV	TIME OF ARRIVAL
AAEEKNNOPRSTT	TAKEN ONE'S PART	AAEFIIMNNOSTT	MANIFESTATION
AAEEKNOPRSSTT	TAKES ONE'S PART	AAEFILLMQRRUY	FAMILY QUARREL
AAEELLLLMNRTTY	MENTALLY ALERT	AAEFILLNOPRTT	FELL INTO A TRAP
AAEELMNORTUVY	MONETARY VALUE	AAEFILLOPRSTT	SELL AT A PROFIT
AAEELNORSSTTT	LONE-STAR STATE	AAEFILMMRSTTY	FAMILY MATTERS
AAEELNPRRRTTU	PRETERNATURAL	AAEFILMNNOORRT	REFORMATIONAL
AAEEMNRRSTTTT	STAR TREATMENT	AAEFILNNRTUUX	ANNUAL FIXTURE
AAEEMOOPRRSST	SEPARATE ROOMS	AAEFILNQRRSTU	QUARTERFINALS
AAEEMQRRRSTTU	QUARTERMASTER	AAEFLLNOPRRTT	FLORAL PATTERN
AAEENNPRSSTUU	SUPERANNUATES	AAEFLLNOPSSTU	PULLS A FAST ONE
AAEENOPRSTUYY	PAY AS YOU ENTER	AAEFMNOORSTTU	RAN OUT OF STEAM
AAEENOPSSSSWY	PASSES ONE'S WAY	AAEFMNORRRTUY	MARRY A FORTUNE
AAEENRRRSTTUU	RESTAURANTEUR	AAEFNORRRTUUV	RETURN A FAVOUR
AAEEOOPSSTTTU	SAUTE POTATOES	AAEGGGILMNORT	AGGLOMERATING
AAEEPRRSSTTUU	SUPERSATURATE	AAEGGHHIIOPRS	HAGIOGRAPHIES
AAEEQRRSSTTUV	QUARTERSTAVES	AAEGGHHILNNUY	LAUGHING HYENA
AAEERRRSSTTUU	RESTAURATEURS	AAEGGHIKNOSTT	TAKING HOSTAGE
AAEFFGIKNNORT	TAKING AN OFFER	AAEGGHILLNOOW	A LONG WHILE AGO
AAEFFHLLLOSWY	WAY OF ALL FLESH	AAEGGHILNRSTT	AT RIGHT-ANGLES
AAEFFIILMNORR	FORAMINIFERAL	AAEGGHIMNNRTT	HANGING MATTER
AAEFFIILMRTVY	AFFIRMATIVELY	AAEGGIILNTTUV	AGGLUTINATIVE
AAEFFIKOPRSST	STIFF AS A POKER	AAEGGIINNORSV	GIVING A REASON
AAEFFILNORTTV	VALIANT EFFORT	AAEGGILMNOORT	AGGLOMERATION
AAEFFINOORSTT	AFFORESTATION	AAEGGINRSTTTT	GETTING A START

AAEGGGLMNORSTW	WEST GLAMORGAN
AAEGHHHLNOSTU	HAS THE LAUGH ON
AAEGHHIKMNSST	HAS THE MAKINGS
AAEGHHIKMRRTW	HIGH-WATER MARK
AAEGHHIKNOTTT	TAKING THE OATH
AAEGHHIMORSTU	HAS A ROUGH TIME
AAEGHHINNORTV	HAVING ANOTHER
AAEGHHINORSVW	HAVING A SHOWER
AAEGHHINORTVY	HAVING A THEORY
AAEGHHINPSSTT	PASSING THE HAT
AAEGHHIOSSTTW	WHITE AS A GHOST
AAEGHHNNOPSTU	HANG ONES HAT UP
	HANG UP ONES HAT
AAEGHHOPPRRSS	PHRASEOGRAPHS
AAEGHHOPRSTTU	SPARE A THOUGHT
AAEGHIIILNTWW	WAITING AWHILE
AAEGHIIKNNSTW	TAKE IN WASHING
AAEGHIILNSTWY	STAYING AWHILE
AAEGHIINRTWWY	WITHERING AWAY
AAEGHIITTTWWY	GET AWAY WITH IT
AAEGHIKNORSTV	HAVING A STROKE
AAEGHIKNORTTT	TAKING TO HEART
AAEGHILLMNPTY	PLAYING HAMLET
AAEGHILMNOPTY	PLAYING AT HOME
AAEGHILNORRTW	HARROWING TALE
AAEGHILPRTTUY	PLAY THE GUITAR
AAEGHIMMNNNOR	MEANING NO HARM
AAEGHIMNOSTTY	STAYING AT HOME
AAEGHINNOOSVZ	HAVING A SNOOZE
AAEGHINNOSSVY	HAVING ONE'S SAY
AAEGHINNOSVWY	HAVING ONE'S WAY
AAEGHINORRRTW	ROAR WITH ANGER
AAEGHLLMOPRTY	METALLOGRAPHY
AAEGHLNOOSTWY	ALWAYS ON THE GO
AAEGHLNOSSTTU	TAUGHT A LESSON
AAEGHMNNNOOSS	HANGMANS NOOSE
AAEGHMNOOPRSU	PHANEROGAMOUS
AAEGHMOOPSSST	SMOOTH PASSAGE
AAEGHMORRTTUY	GREAT YARMOUTH
AAEGHMORSTUWY	WHATS YOUR GAME?
AAEGHNOPRRSTW	NARROWS THE GAP
AAEGHNPPRRSTT	SPRANG THE TRAP
AAEGIIILMNNRY	IMAGINARY LINE
AAEGIIILMNRST	MATERIALISING
AAEGIIILMNRTZ	MATERIALIZING
AAEGIIILMNTVY	IMAGINATIVELY
AAEGIIILNRRST	ARTERIALISING
AAEGIIILNRRTZ	ARTERIALIZING
AAEGIIILNSSTT	INITIAL STAGES
AAEGIIIMMNNRSS	IMAGINARINESS
AAEGIIIMNNTUV	UNIMAGINATIVE
AAEGIIINNRRTVW	VIRGINIA WATER
AAEGIIKKLLMNS	MAKES A KILLING
AAEGIIKKLLNRS	SING LIKE A LARK
AAEGIIKKLNOTT	TAKE A LIKING TO
AAEGIIKLNNPPS	PLAIN SPEAKING
AAEGIIKLNSSST	STEALING A KISS
AAEGIILLLORST	LEGISLATORIAL
AAEGIILLMRSTY	MAGISTERIALLY
AAEGIILLNNRTW	RETAINING WALL
AAEGIILMNORRS	RAISING MORALE
AAEGIILMNRSST	SAILING MASTER
AAEGIILNORSTV	ROASTING ALIVE
AAEGIIILNRRRVY	ARRIVING EARLY
AAEGIIMMMPRST	EPIGRAMMATISM
AAEGIIMMPRSTT	EPIGRAMMATIST
AAEGIIMNNOSTT	MAGNETISATION
AAEGIIMNNOTTZ	MAGNETIZATION
AAEGIIMNQQSUU	QUINQUAGESIMA
AAEGIINNNOOPV	GAVE AN OPINION
AAEGIINNRSSUW	ISSUE A WARNING
AAEGIINNRSTTU	GAIN IN STATURE
AAEGIJKLNOPRY	PLAYING A JOKER
AAEGIJLMORRTY	LARGE MAJORITY
AAEGIJMORRTTY	GREAT MAJORITY
AAEGIKKLLNRSU	SUNG LIKE A LARK
AAEGIKLNOORTT	LOOKING A TREAT
AAEGIKLNOPPST	STOPPING A LEAK
AAEGIKLNPPRSW	WALKING PAPERS
AAEGIKLNPRUWY	WAKING UP EARLY
AAEGIKMNNNRTY	MAKING AN ENTRY
AAEGIKMNNORRR	MAKING AN ERROR
AAEGIKMNNOSWY	MAKING ONE'S WAY
AAEGIKMNPRRSS	PASSING REMARK
AAEGIKNPRSSTT	STREAKING PAST
AAEGILLLLNPRY	LYING PARALLEL
AAEGILLLOTWWY	YELLOW WAGTAIL
AAEGILLMNOOPT	MEGALOPOLITAN
AAEGILMNNOPST	LEAMINGTON SPA
AAEGILMNORSSU	ASSUMING A ROLE
AAEGILNNRRSTT	RETRANSLATING
AAEGILNOPRTTX	EXTRAPOLATING
AAEGILNORSTTV	REVOLT AGAINST
AAEGILNPSTTUY	STAYING UP LATE
AAEGILNQRTTUY	LARGE QUANTITY
AAEGILOPRRTUX	EXPURGATIONAL
AAEGIMMMNNNNOS	NAMING NO NAMES
AAEGIMMNRSUVY	GIVEN A SUMMARY
AAEGIMMRSSUVY	GIVES A SUMMARY
AAEGIMNNNORTU	MOUNTAIN RANGE
AAEGIMNNORTTU	ARGUMENTATION
AAEGIMNOOPRST	SPERMATOGONIA
AAEGIMNORSTYZ	MAGAZINE STORY
AAEGIMNRRSSTT	TRANSMIGRATES
AAEGINNNNPPRSY	SPARING A PENNY
AAEGINNOPSWYY	PAYING ONE'S WAY
AAEGINNOSSSYY	SAYING ONE'S SAY
AAEGINOORSTTY	GEOSTATIONARY
AAEGINPPPPRRW	WRAPPING PAPER
AAEGLLMNOOPTY	PALAEONTOLOGY
AAEGLMNRRTTUY	TRULY GREAT MAN
AAEGLNNOOSSSU	ANALOGOUSNESS
AAEGMMMOPRRRS	ARMS PROGRAMME
AAEGMOPRSSSTY	STORMY PASSAGE
AAEHHIIKNNSTV	HAVE A THIN SKIN
AAEHHKNSTTWWW	KNEW WHAT'S WHAT
AAEHHOOOTTTUV	HAVE A TOOTH OUT
AAEHIIILMNSSS	LEISHMANIASIS
AAEHIIIMNNSTT	ANTIHISTAMINE
AAEHIILMMPSTU	EPITHALAMIUMS
AAEHIIORTTTUV	AUTHORITATIVE
AAEHIKNOSSTTV	STAKHANOVITES
AAEHIKNPPSSSS	SPEAKS SPANISH
AAEHILLNPSTTW	PAINTS THE WALL
AAEHILNNOPSTY	PAYS ON THE NAIL
AAEHILNNOSSST	THESSALONIANS
AAEHILNOPSSTU	HAS ONE'S TAIL UP
AAEHILNSTUUWY	IN THE USUAL WAY
AAEHIMMNOOSTT	AIMS AT THE MOON
AAEHIMNPSSSTT	STATESMANSHIP
AAEHIMOORSSTT	ATHEROMATOSIS
AAEHIPSSSSTWY	PASSES THIS WAY
AAEHKKLNSSSTT	THANKLESS TASK
AAEHKLOPRRTUW	WORK UP A LATHER
AAEHKMNNORSSS	ON SHANKS'S MARE
AAEHKMORSTTTW	WARM TO THE TASK
AAEHKNOOPSTTT	TAKEN A POT-SHOT
AAEHKOOPSSTTT	TAKES A POT-SHOT
AAEHLMNNSSTTY	LYTHAM ST.ANNES
AAEHLMOPRRTTY	TEMPORARY HALT
AAEHLMPRRTTYY	PLAY THE MARTYR
AAEHLNNOOQTUYY	ANTHONY QUAYLE

AAEHMNNOOOSTY	HAS ONE TOO MANY
AAEHMNORRRSTU	ARTHUR RANSOME
AAEHMNORSTUWY	WHATS YOUR NAME?
AAEHMNRRTTTUW	THREW A TANTRUM
AAEHNNOOSSWWY	HAS ONE'S OWN WAY
AAEIIILMMRTTY	IMMATERIALITY
AAEIIILMNNNRT	MAIN LINE TRAIN
AAEIIILMNOPTT	PALE IMITATION
AAEIIILNNOSTT	NATIONALITIES
AAEIIILNORSST	SERIALISATION
AAEIIILNORSTZ	SERIALIZATION
AAEIIKLLMMNOS	MAKES A MILLION
AAEIIKLNNOPST	ITALIAN SPOKEN
	SPOKEN ITALIAN
AAEIILLLMNRTY	MATRILINEALLY
AAEIILLLPRSTY	IPSILATERALLY
AAEIILLMNNOTT	IN NO TIME AT ALL
AAEIILLMNOSTT	METALLISATION
AAEIILLMNOTTZ	METALLIZATION
AAEIILLNOPOTT	PALLETISATION
AAEIILLNOPTTZ	PALLETIZATION
AAEIILLNORSTT	ALLITERATIONS
AAEIILLQTTUVY	QUALITATIVELY
AAEIILMNOPRTT	MATERIAL POINT
AAEIILMRRTTTV	TRIVIAL MATTER
AAEIILNNNORTT	INTERNATIONAL
AAEIILNNOORTT	ORIENTATIONAL
AAEIILNNORSTV	VERNALISATION
AAEIILNNORTVZ	VERNALIZATION
AAEIILNOPRRST	RESPIRATIONAL
AAEIILNPTTTWY	WAIT PATIENTLY
AAEIIMOPPRTVX	APPROXIMATIVE
AAEIINNNO8TTX	ANNEXATIONIST
AAEIINNNSTTTY	INSTANTANEITY
AAEIINOPPPRRT	INAPPROPRIATE
AAEIIOPPPRRTV	APPROPRIATIVE
AAEIIRRSTTTVY	VARIETY ARTIST
AAEIKLLNOSSTY	AS LIKELY AS NOT
AAEIKLLNPPSSY	SPEAKS PLAINLY
AAEIKLLPRTTVY	TALK PRIVATELY
AAEIKNOOPRSTV	PROVOKE A SAINT
AAEIKNOQSSSTU	ASKS A QUESTION
AAEIKNPRSSSSU	SPEAKS RUSSIAN
AAEILLNNOSSTY	SENSATIONALLY
AAEILLNNRTUWY	RAILWAY TUNNEL
AAEILLNOOPRTY	OPERATIONALLY
AAEILLNOPRTXY	EXPLANATORILY
AAEILMMNNPRUU	ANNUAL PREMIUM
AAEILMMNORRST	MORTAL REMAINS
AAEILMNOPRTTU	PERMUTATIONAL
AAEILMOPPRTXY	APPROXIMATELY
AAEILMORRTTTY	MORTALITY RATE
AAEILMRSSTWYY	RAILWAY SYSTEM
AAEILNNORRSTT	RETRANSLATION
AAEILNNRSTUUV	UNIVERSAL AUNT
AAEILNOOORTTV	LAEVOROTATION
AAEILNOOPRTTX	EXTRAPOLATION
AAEILNORSTTWY	SANITARY TOWEL
AAEILNQQTTUUY	EQUAL QUANTITY
AAEILOPPPRRTY	APPROPRIATELY
AAEILOPPRRRTY	PREPARATORILY
AAEIMNNNOORTT	ORNAMENTATION
AAEIMNORSSTTT	STATION MASTER
	STATIONMASTER
AAEIMNRSTTTUV	TRANSMUTATIVE
AAEINNNOSSTTU	INSTANTANEOUS
AAEINNOPPRSSS	SPARES NO PAINS
AAEINNOPRTTTT	RAPT ATTENTION
AAEINNOPSTTTY	PAYS ATTENTION
AAEINORRSSTTY	IN A SORRY STATE
AAEKNOQRRSSTU	ASKS NO QUARTER

AAELLMOOPSSTT	SMALL POTATOES
AAELLNNOOSWWY	ALL ONE'S OWN WAY
AAELMMNNORRSU	ROMAN NUMERALS
AAELMNNOOSSSU	ANOMALOUSNESS
AAELMNNOPSTTU	MOUNT PLEASANT
AAELMNOOPRRTY	TEMPORARY LOAN
AAELNNNRSSTUU	UNNATURALNESS
AAELNNPRRSSTT	TRANSPLANTERS
AAELNNPRRSTTY	TRANSPARENTLY
AAELOOORRTTVY	LAEVOROTATORY
AAELOORSSTTTT	STARTS TOO LATE
AAEMRRSSSTTTW	STRAW MATTRESS
AAEOOOPPRSSTT	PROPOSE A TOAST
AAEOOOPRSSTTT	ROAST POTATOES
AAEOPRRSTTTUY	STATUTORY RAPE
AAFFGIIILLMNY	FAMILY FAILING
AAFFGIKLMNOOO	MAKING A FOOL OF
AAFFGIKMNOSSU	MAKING A FUSS OF
AAFFHILOPSSTT	HOSPITAL STAFF
AAFFIILMRSTTV	MILITARY STAFF
AAFGGHHIINRTV	HAVING A FRIGHT
AAFGGHIILNNOS	GOING IN A FLASH
AAFGGIIIINOOTT	FIGHTS AGAINST
AAFGGHINOSTTU	FOUGHT AGAINST
AAFGGIIKMNOOT	MAKING A GO OF IT
AAFGGIILLLNSS	FILLING A GLASS
AAFGGIINNORUV	GAINING FAVOUR
AAFGGIKLNOORW	GOING FOR A WALK
AAFGHIIILMRST	FAMILIAR SIGHT
AAFGHIIKNNSST	SINKING A SHAFT
AAFGHJLORSTUU	JUST FOR A LAUGH
AAFGIIIILMNRS	FAMILIARISING
AAFGIIIILMNRZ	FAMILIARIZING
AAFGIIKMNOPRT	MAKING A PROFIT
AAFGIILNNOORT	FLOATING ON AIR
AAFGIILNNSTWY	STIFLING A YAWN
AAFGIILNOPSST	FAILING TO PASS
AAFGIIMNNORST	INFORM AGAINST
AAFGINNOOORTW	ON A WAR FOOTING
AAFHIINOPRSSS	PARIS FASHIONS
AAFHIJNNOSTTW	JONATHAN SWIFT
AAFHINOOPRRST	PARROT FASHION
AAFHKLLLOSSTT	THATS ALL FOLKS
AAFHMOORSTUWY	OUT OF HARMS WAY
AAFIIILMNRTUY	UNFAMILIARITY
AAFIILMMNNOST	INFLAMMATIONS
AAFIILMNNOORT	INFORMATIONAL
AAFIILMNOORST	FORMALISATION
AAFIILMNOORTZ	FORMALIZATION
AAFILMMNOORST	MALFORMATIONS
AAFILMNOPRRTY	INFORMAL PARTY
AAFILNNNOORTT	NATIONAL FRONT
AAFIMMNOORSST	MASS FORMATION
AAFKNOORSSSUV	ASKS NO FAVOURS
AAGGGIIILNNSV	GIVING A SIGNAL
AAGGGIILNNTTU	AGGLUTINATING
AAGGGILNNOOWY	GOING A LONG WAY
AAGGHIIIKNNNT	THINKING AGAIN
AAGGHIINNRSTW	GRANTING A WISH
AAGGHIILLNORT	RIGHT ALL ALONG
AAGGIIIKLMNNV	MAKING A LIVING
AAGGIIINNRSST	RISING AGAINST
AAGGIIKNNNRTW	TAKING WARNING
AAGGIILNNNRSW	WARNING SIGNAL
AAGGIILNNOTTU	AGGLUTINATION
AAGGIILNNRTTU	TRIANGULATING
AAGGIIINNORRST	AIR ON A G STRING
AAGGIINNOSTTV	VOTING AGAINST
AAGGIINNPRSWY	SPRINGING AWAY
AAGGILNNRSTTU	STRANGULATING
AAGGMNNNORUYY	ANGRY YOUNG MAN

AAGHHIILNOTUV	HIGH VALUATION
AAGHHIINRSTTV	HAVING A THIRST
AAGHHILLRSTTT	THAT'S ALL RIGHT
AAGHHILOPRTWY	HIGHWAY PATROL
AAGHHINOOPPRT	ANTHROPOPHAGI
AAGHHINPSSTTU	TAUGHT SPANISH
AAGHHNOOPPRTY	ANTHROPOPHAGY
AAGHHORRSTTUW	THROUGH A STRAW
AAGHIIILNRRSY	HAIR-RAISINGLY
AAGHIIKNNRSWY	SHRINKING AWAY
AAGHIILMNORTT	ANTILOGARITHM
AAGHIINNQSTUV	HAVING A SQUINT
AAGHIINPRSSTU	SPANISH GUITAR
AAGHIIOTTTWWY	GOT AWAY WITH IT
AAGHILLNPPRSU	APPALLING RUSH
AAGHILNPQSSUY	PLAYING SQUASH
AAGHIMNNNNORSY	SANG IN HARMONY
AAGHIMNOOSTWY	SMOOTHING AWAY
AAGHIMRSTTTUU	THAUMATURGIST
AAGHINRSSTTUU	TAUGHT RUSSIAN
AAGHLMOOSSSST	SMOOTH AS GLASS
AAGHOOSTTUUWY	SOUGHT A WAY OUT
AAGIIIKLMNNPT	MAKING IT PLAIN
AAGIIIKNNRSST	RAISING A STINK
AAGIIILMMNORT	IMMIGRATIONAL
AAGIIILNNNOST	NATIONALISING
AAGIIILNNNOTZ	NATIONALIZING
AAGIIILNNORST	RATIONALISING
AAGIIILNNORTZ	RATIONALIZING
AAGIIILNNOSST	SIGNALISATION
AAGIIILNNOSTZ	SIGNALIZATION
AAGIIINNNOSTV	INVAGINATIONS
AAGIIINNNSTTT	INSTANTIATING
AAGIIINPRSTWY	SPIRITING AWAY
AAGIIKKMMNRST	MAKING ITS MARK
AAGIIKLLNORST	ALLIGATOR SKIN
AAGIIKLNNPSTY	PAINSTAKINGLY
AAGIILNNORTTU	TRIANGULATION
AAGIILNORTUVZ	VULGARIZATION
AAGIILNRRTTUY	TRIANGULARITY
AAGIIMNNPRSTY	PRAYING MANTIS
AAGIIMNOPPRTX	APPROXIMATING
AAGIINNNNPRSY	SPINNING A YARN
AAGIINNOORSST	ORGANISATIONS
AAGIINNOORSTZ	ORGANIZATIONS
AAGIINNRSTTUY	STAYING IN A RUT
AAGIINOPPPRRT	APPROPRIATING
AAGIINORRSTTT	STARTING A RIOT
AAGIKLLNORSTT	TAKING A STROLL
AAGIKLNOPRRTT	TALKING PARROT
AAGILMMNNOSUY	MAGNANIMOUSLY
AAGILNNNPRSTT	TRANSPLANTING
AAGILNNOORSSW	GLORIA SWANSON
AAGILNNORSTTU	STRANGULATION
AAGILNNPRTTUY	PLAYING TRUANT
AAGIMNNNNOORTW	IGNORANT WOMAN
AAGIMNORRRSTT	TRANSMIGRATOR
AAGINSSSTTUUU	SAINT AUGUSTUS
AAHHILLLOSTTY	ALL THAT IS HOLY
AAHHKNOSTTWWW	KNOW WHATS WHAT
AAHIIMNNOORST	HARMONISATION
AAHIIMNNOORTZ	HARMONIZATION
AAHIINOORSTTU	AUTHORISATION
AAHIINOORTTUZ	AUTHORIZATION
AAHINOPSSSSTT	SHOP ASSISTANT
AAHJNNORSSSTU	JOHANN STRAUSS
AAHKNOOOPSSTT	TOOK A SNAPSHOT
AAHLLMNORSTYY	MONTHLY SALARY
AAHMNORRTTTUW	THROW A TANTRUM
AAIIILLMMNNNO	MAN IN A MILLION
AAIIILLNOTTUY	INITIAL OUTLAY

AAIIILMNORRST	IRRATIONALISM
AAIIILMNOSSST	ASSIMILATIONS
AAIIILMNPRSST	ANIMAL SPIRITS
AAIIILNNOPRST	INSPIRATIONAL
AAIIILNORRSTT	IRRATIONALIST
AAIIILNORRTTY	IRRATIONALITY
AAIIILNORSTTU	RITUALISATION
AAIIILNORTTUZ	RITUALIZATION
AAIIILNOSSTUV	VISUALISATION
AAIIILNOSTUVZ	VISUALIZATION
AAIIIMMNNNOST	ANTINOMIANISM
AAIIINNNOSTTT	INSTANTIATION
AAIIINOPRSTTV	PRIVATISATION
AAIIINOPRTTVZ	PRIVATIZATION
AAIIILMMNORTY	MATRIMONIALLY
AAIIILMNNOTTU	MULTINATIONAL
AAIIILNNOSSTT	INSTALLATIONS
AAIIILMNNOORST	NORMALISATION
AAIIILMNNOORTZ	NORMALIZATION
AAIIILNNNOTTUY	NATIONAL UNITY
AAIILNOSSSTTV	SALVATIONISTS
AAIIMMMNORSSTU	SUMMARISATION
AAIIMMNORSTUZ	SUMMARIZATION
AAIIMNOOPPRTX	APPROXIMATION
AAIIMNORRSTTY	MARTYRISATION
AAIIMNORRTTYZ	MARTYRIZATION
AAIINNOPRSSTT	STRAINS A POINT
AAIINNORSSTTU	INSTAURATIONS
AAIINOOPPPRRT	APPROPRIATION
AAIKLMNNOOPRS	ROMAN POLANSKI
AAIKLNNOPRSSW	PARKINSONS LAW
AAIKMNOOQRTTU	QUOTATION MARK
AAIKNNNOORSTW	ROWAN ATKINSON
AAILLMNQSTTUY	SMALL QUANTITY
AAILLMOOPPSTU	PAPILLOMATOUS
AAILLNOOPSTTU	POSTULATIONAL
AAILNNOOPRSTT	NATIONAL SPORT
AAILNNOPPSTTU	SUPPLANTATION
AAILNNORSRTTY	NATIONAL TRUST
AAILNOSSSSSTU	SUSTAINS A LOSS
AAIMMMMNOTUUX	MAXIMUM AMOUNT
AAIMMNNORSTTTU	TRANSMUTATION
AAIOOPPPRRRST	APPROPRIATORS
AALMNORRTUVYY	VOLUNTARY ARMY
ABBBBGIKLNOOR	BABBLING BROOK
ABBBCHLNOORTY	BOBBY CHARLTON
ABBBDEFNOORRS	BAND OF ROBBERS
ABBBEEILLQRUV	VERBAL QUIBBLE
ABBBEHLMORSTU	BLABBERMOUTHS
ABBCDEEGILMRU	CAMBRIDGE BLUE
ABBCDEEIILNRS	INDESCRIBABLE
ABBCDEGIMNRRU	BREADCRUMBING
ABBCDEIILNRSY	INDESCRIBABLY
ABBCDEMMMNOOR	BOMBER COMMAND
ABBCEEEEMMMOR	BECOME A MEMBER
ABBCEEEIMMNRT	CABINET MEMBER
ABBCEEGIILNOS	BEING SOCIABLE
ABBCEEHKKNORT	BROKEN THE BACK
ABBCEEHKNOOTT	TO THE BACKBONE
ABBCEEIJLNOOT	OBJECTIONABLE
ABBCEEIKLPRRY	BLACKBERRY PIE
ABBCEEKKNOORS	BROKE ONE'S BACK
ABBCEELNNORTY	ENTRANCE LOBBY
ABBCEGILNOPUU	BUBONIC PLAGUE
ABBCEHKOORRSS	SHOCK ABSORBER
ABBCEIILRRSTU	BISCUIT BARREL
ABBCEIJLNOOTY	OBJECTIONABLY
ABBCEILNORRST	SCARLET RIBBON
ABBCGHIIILOPR	BIBLIOGRAPHIC
ABBCIIILMNOTY	COMBINABILITY
ABBCIIILOPRST	PROBABILISTIC

ABBCIILLPRRUY	PUBLIC LIBRARY
ABBCKLNNORTUY	TONY BLACKBURN
ABBDDDEIILMVY	DAVID DIMBLEBY
ABBDDEEEIRRRT	BARTERED BRIDE
ABBDDEEHIMNTY	MINDED THE BABY
ABBDDNNOOPSUW	BOBS UP AND DOWN
ABBDEEEEELNRV	VENERABLE BEDE
ABBDEEEEHKORRT	BROKE THE BREAD
ABBDEEEEHLNTUU	THE BLUE DANUBE
ABBDEEEHNRRTU	BEAR THE BURDEN
ABBDEEFNORSTU	BEAST OF BURDEN
ABBDEEHLLOOUV	HAVE BLUE BLOOD
ABBDEEMPRRSTU	RUBBER-STAMPED
ABBDEFGHILOTW	THE BIG BAD WOLF
ABBDEFILOTUUY	BEAUTIFUL BODY
ABBDEGIMNNOPS	SPENDING A BOMB
ABBDEGMNNOOOW	GONE DOWN A BOMB
ABBDEGMNOOOSW	GOES DOWN A BOMB
ABBDEHHMORRTU	MOTHER HUBBARD
ABBDFHIKLRSTU	TALKED RUBBISH
ABBDEIJLLLNOY	BLIND-ALLEY JOB
ABBDEKOOOORRW	BORROWED A BOOK
ABBDELNOOOSSU	DOUBLE BASSOON
ABBDEMNNOOTWW	WENT DOWN A BOMB
ABBDEMNOPRTUU	PUT A BOMB UNDER
ABBDFFILMNNSU	BLINDMANS BUFF
ABBDFHILOORSU	LOAD OF RUBBISH
ABBDGGIINNPRU	BAD UPBRINGING
ABBDGIMNOOPPR	DROPPING A BOMB
ABBDHINOOORSY	ROBIN HOODS BAY
ABBEEEEHNSTTT	BEATEN THE BEST
ABBEEEGLLPSSS	PEBBLE GLASSES
ABBEEEKNNOORS	BREAK ONE'S BONE
ABBEEFHLLLMTU	FUMBLE THE BALL
ABBEEGIKLMNOO	GONE LIKE A BOMB
ABBEEGIKLMOOS	GOES LIKE A BOMB
ABBEEGNORRRSU	BARBER SURGEON
ABBEEHHIKORTT	BROKE THE HABIT
ABBEEHIORSTUV	BEST BEHAVIOUR
ABBEEHKKNNORT	BROKEN THE BANK
ABBEEIKLMNOTW	WENT LIKE A BOMB
ABBEEILMPRRTU	IMPERTURBABLE
ABBEEILNORSTT	ISOBEL BARNETT
ABBEEKLNOORTT	BROKEN A BOTTLE
ABBDELLMMNOOTZ	BAMBOOZLEMENT
ABBEELNPRRRTU	RUBBER PLANTER
ABBEELORRRSSU	RABBLE-ROUSERS
ABBEFGGNOORRS	GANG OF ROBBERS
ABBEFIIMPRSTY	BAPTISM BY FIRE
ABBEGHHIORRWY	HIGHWAY ROBBER
ABBEGHIIKLRST	TALK GIBBERISH
ABBEGHIILOPRR	BIBLIOGRAPHER
ABBFGHOORRTTU	BROUGHT TO BEAR
ABBEHILLLOOST	BOLSHOI BALLET
ABBEHNORSSUUU	SUBURBAN HOUSE
ABBEIIILOPRST	PROBABILITIES
ABBEIILLMORRY	MOBILE LIBRARY
ABBEIILMNNOOT	NOBLE AMBITION
ABBEIKKNORSST	BROKE ITS BANKS
ABBEILLMNOTUY	BILLY BEAUMONT
ABBEILMPRRTUY	IMPERTURBABLY
ABBEILSSTTTUU	SUBSTITUTABLE
ABBEIMMNNORTTT	NORMAN TEBBITT
ABBEINOORRSTT	TEAR TO RIBBONS
ABBELLNOOSTWZ	BLOWN TO BLAZES
ABBELLOORRTUU	LABOUR TROUBLE
ABBELLOOSSTWZ	BLOWS TO BLAZES
ABBENNOORSSTU	BURN ONES BOATS
ABBFGLLOORTUY	RUGBY FOOTBALL
ABBFLLOOOOSTT	FOOTBALL BOOTS
ABBGGIINNRTU	BRINGING ABOUT
ABBGIILNNRSTU	RUBBING SALT IN
ABBGIINNRSSUU	SUBURBANISING
ABBGIINNRSUUZ	SUBURBANIZING
ABBHIMNNOORST	BOSTON BRAHMIN
ABBIIILMOPRTY	IMPROBABILITY
ABCCCEEEILLRT	ELECTRIC CABLE
ABCCDEEEGINNR	CANDICE BERGEN
ABCCDEEHMNORS	SECOND CHAMBER
ABCCDEEIILRSY	RIDES A BICYCLE
ABCCDEEKOPRTU	CRACKED UP TO BE
ABCCDEHILORSU	COACHBUILDERS
ABCCDEIKKKNOT	KNOCKED IT BACK
ABCCDEINNNOOT	BAD CONNECTION
ABCCDENORSTTU	SUBCONTRACTED
ABCCDHINOORRY	HYDROCARBONIC
ABCCEEEHNOOUU	BOUNCE A CHEQUE
ABCCEEEIJOSTV	OBJECTIVE CASE
ABCCEEEIMMORR	ERIC MORECAMBE
ABCCEEEIMNTTX	BECAME EXTINCT
ABCCEEFHKKNOT	BACK OF THE NECK
ABCCEEHHSSTTU	CATCHES THE BUS
ABCCEEIILNNOV	INCONCEIVABLE
ABCCEEIKMNORT	INCOME BRACKET
ABCCEEIMOPRUU	MERCI BEAUCOUP
ABCCEFKOORRSX	BOX OF CRACKERS
ABCCEGIILOORT	BACTERIOLOGIC
ABCCEGIKLMNOW	WELCOMING BACK
ABCCEHIILLMUY	DIOCHEMICALLY
ABCCEIIILMPTY	IMPECCABILITY
ABCCEIIILSSTY	ACCESSIBILITY
ABCCEIILLMORS	SOCIAL CLIMBER
ABCCEIILNNOVY	INCONCEIVABLY
ABCCEIILORTTY	BACTERIOLYTIC
ABCCEKNNOORTT	BROKEN CONTACT
ABCCFFHILNOOT	FLITCH OF BACON
ABCCHHIIOPRRS	ARCHBISHOPRIC
ABCCHHIPRSTTU	BAPTIST CHURCH
ABCCIIINNSSTT	BASIC INSTINCT
ABCCIILLLNSUY	SUBCLINICALLY
ABCCIILNOPTUU	PUBLIC AUCTION
ABCCIILORRTXY	TRICARBOXYLIC
ABCCIILLORSTUY	SCORBUTICALLY
ABCCILMNOPPUY	PUBLIC COMPANY
ABCCKKLLOOOPR	BLACKPOOL ROCK
ABCCNOORRSTTU	SUBCONTRACTOR
ABCDDEEIILRST	DISCREDITABLE
ABCDDEELSSUUY	CLAUDE DEBUSSY
ABCDDEHNNOSSU	SECOND HUSBAND
ABCDDEIILRSTY	DISCREDITABLY
ABCDDEIINOORX	CARBON DIOXIDE
ABCDDEIKOPPRR	DROPPED A BRICK
ABCDDEILPRSSU	PUBLIC ADDRESS
	PUBLIC-ADDRESS
ABCDDHIMNOOOR	DIAMOND BROOCH
ABCDEEEEGGMNO	BECOME ENGAGED
ABCDEEEELRRTT	CATTLE BREEDER
ABCDEEEFIMNRS	BECAME FRIENDS
ABCDEEEFLNORS	BRACED ONESELF
ABCDEEEGHILRS	CHELSEA BRIDGE
ABCDEEEGINRRT	DECEREBRATING
ABCDEEEHLORRS	BREECHLOADERS
ABCDEEEHORRTT	BEAT THE RECORD
ABCDEEEINORRT	DECEREBRATION
ABCDEEEKORRRR	RECORD BREAKER
ABCDEEELMMNOR	RECOMMENDABLE
ABCDEEFFFGIOO	BADGE OF OFFICE
ABCDEEFIMNNOS	ABSENCE OF MIND
ABCDEEFNNORUY	BOUNDARY FENCE
ABCDEEGGLMRSS	SCRAMBLED EGGS
ABCDEEGHILNOR	BREECH-LOADING
ABCDEEHHINSTY	DEATH BY INCHES

ABCDEEHIINRTU	RITCHIE BENAUD
ABCDEEHILLLST	SLICED THE BALL
ABCDEEHILPTTT	PITCHED BATTLE
ABCDEEHKLOTWY	BLOCKED THE WAY
ABCDEEHKOORTT	ROCKED THE BOAT
ABCDEEHKPSSTU	PASSED THE BUCK
ABCDEEHLNNRTU	BURN THE CANDLE
ABCDEEHLRRRTU	ALBRECHT DURER
ABCDEEHOORTVW	ABOVE THE CROWD
ABCDEEIILLTTY	DELECTABILITY
ABCDEEIILTTTY	DETECTABILITY
ABCDEEIIMOSTY	BASIDIOMYCETE
ABCDEEIINPSST	BITS AND PIECES
ABCDEEILLOSTY	CELESTIAL BODY
ABCDEEILNPRTU	UNPREDICTABLE
ABCDEEINORRSS	DECARBONISERS
ABCDEEINORRSZ	DECARBONIZERS
ABCDEEIRRRSTY	SECRETARY BIRD
ABCDEEKKNORSU	BREAK ONES DUCK
ABCDEEKORRRSS	BREAKS RECORDS
ABCDEELORSTUU	CAUSED TROUBLE
ABCDEEMNOOPRY	BEYOND COMPARE
ABCDEENOPRRST	ORB AND SCEPTRE
ABCDEENPRSTTU	ABRUPT DESCENT
ABCDEFHIKLNOT	BACK IN THE FOLD
ABCDEFLNOOTUU	FLOUNCED ABOUT
ABCDEGHILLNTY	BY CANDLELIGHT
ABCDEGIILNPRU	READING PUBLIC
ABCDEGIINNORS	DECARBONISING
ABCDEGIINNORZ	DECARBONIZING
ABCDEGIINORTU	AUCTION BRIDGE
ABCDEHHIRTTWY	WATCH THE BIRDY
ABCDEHIIRRRRS	RICHARD BRIERS
ABCDEIIILLNPS	DISCIPLINABLE
ABCDEIILNNOOT	CONDITIONABLE
ABCDEIKNSTTTY	STAND-BY TICKET
ABCDEINNORRTU	BURN TO A CINDER
ABCDELOOPSWYY	PLAYED COWBOYS
ABCDEMOPPRTUY	EMPTY CUPBOARD
ABCDEMOPRRSTU	BROAD-SPECTRUM
ABCDEOOOPRRTY	BODY CORPORATE
	CORPORATE BODY
ABCDFIIIILOTY	CODIFIABILITY
ABCDGHIINRSTW	BIRD-WATCHINGS
ABCDGIIMNORRV	MORBID CRAVING
ABCDHIILLOPUY	PUBLIC HOLIDAY
ABCDHINORRRTU	RICHARD BURTON
ABCDIIIILNTVY	VINDICABILITY
ABCDIINRRSTTU	URBAN DISTRICT
ABCDILNOOSTUY	SOLD BY AUCTION
ABCDLNNNOOSTY	BONNY SCOTLAND
ABCEEEEHKOPRT	BROKE THE PEACE
ABCEEEFFHORTT	BEFORE THE FACT
ABCEEEFHILNTU	BLUE IN THE FACE
ABCEEEFIIINRS	BENEFICIARIES
ABCEEEFILNORR	REINFORCEABLE
ABCEEEFLNNORU	UNENFORCEABLE
ABCEEEFLNORSS	BRACES ONESELF
ABCEEEHINNOTT	BENEATH NOTICE
ABCEEEHKRRTTU	BREAK THE TRUCE
ABCEEEHMMRRRT	CHARTER MEMBER
ABCEEEIILNRST	BEEN REALISTIC
ABCEEEILMNNOT	MOBILE CANTEEN
ABCEEEILNOPTX	EXCEPTIONABLE
ABCEEEILNRSUV	UNSERVICEABLE
ABCEEEILNSSTX	EXCITABLENESS
ABCEEEILORRRV	IRRECOVERABLE
ABCEEEINRSSTY	BARE NECESSITY
ABCEEEKKKNNORS	BREAK ONES NECK
ABCEEEKLMSTTU	SAMUEL BECKETT
ABCEEEMMNNRRRS	REMEMBRANCERS

ABCEEEEOPRRSTT	BETA-RECEPTORS
ABCEEFGIIINNT	BENEFICIATING
ABCEEFHHILLRT	FILL THE BREACH
ABCEEFIIINNOT	BENEFICIATION
ABCEEFIJNOOPT	PATIENCE OF JOB
ABCEEFKNORRSU	BROKEN SURFACE
ABCEEFKORTTUW	BUCKET OF WATER
ABCEEFLMMRTUY	FACULTY MEMBER
ABCEEGHHKNNTY	HANG BY THE NECK
ABCEEGHHTTTUU	CAUGHT THE TUBE
ABCEEGHILLNTT	BELLING THE CAT
ABCEEGHIMNNRT	BRANCH MEETING
ABCEEGHLNOSWX	EXCHANGE BLOWS
ABCEEGIILMNRT	CLIMBING A TREE
ABCEEGIIMNNOT	CAME INTO BEING
ABCEEGIKNORRV	BREAKING COVER
ABCEEGILLNPRU	GENERAL PUBLIC
ABCEEGILNORSW	BOWLING CREASE
ABCEEGKNOPSTU	GET ONE'S BACK UP
ABCEEHHINORTT	INTO THE BREACH
ABCEEHIILLLOR	HILAIRE BELLOC
ABCEEHIKNNRTW	BACK THE WINNER
ABCEEHILLLSST	SLICES THE BALL
ABCEEHILORRTV	TERRIBLE HAVOC
ABCEEHKLOSSTT	CLOTHES BASKET
ABCEEHKPSSSTU	PASSES THE BUCK
ABCEEHLLNNOTU	LUNCHEON TABLE
ABCEEHMMNNNRST	EMBRANCHMENTS
ABCEEHNRRSTUY	TREASURY BENCH
ABCEEIIKRRRTT	TICKET BARRIER
ABCEEIILNRSSS	IRASCIBLENESS
ABCEEIILPRSTT	SPECIAL BITTER
ABCEEIILRRSUV	BURIAL SERVICE
ABCEEIILRSTTY	RESECTABILITY
ABCEEIKLNNOOS	LIE ON ONES BACK
ABCEEIKLPPRSU	PUBLIC SPEAKER
ABCEEILNNOSTT	INCONTESTABLE
ABCEEILNOPRRS	CEREBROSPINAL
ABCEEILNOPTXY	EXCEPTIONALLY
ABCEEILORRRVY	IRRECOVERABLY
ABCEEIMNOSSTV	COMBATIVENESS
ABCEEIMNRRSUW	SUBMARINE CREW
ABCEEIRRRSTWY	STRAWBERRY ICE
ABCEEJMRSTTTU	SUBJECT MATTER
ABCEEJOPRTTVY	ABJECT POVERTY
ABCEEKKLNOORV	NEVER LOOK BACK
ABCEEKMNNOORR	BROKEN ROMANCE
ABCEEKNNOOSTU	ABOUT ONE'S NECK
ABCEELMMNORSU	COMMENSURABLE
ABCEELNNOOPRU	PRONOUNCEABLE
ABCEELNNOQRUU	UNCONQUERABLE
ABCEELNORRSTY	ARBORESCENTLY
ABCEELORSSTUU	CAUSES TROUBLE
ABCEELRTTUUUY	BEAUTY CULTURE
ABCEENOOORRSSS	BEAR ONE'S CROSS
ABCEENOSTTTUY	BEAUTY CONTEST
ABCEEOPRRSUVX	PROCES-VERBAUX
ABCEFFLLLNOSU	CALL ONE'S BLUFF
	CALL ONES BLUFF
ABCEFGHIINRTW	WATCHING BRIEF
ABCEFGHNOPRSU	BUNCH OF GRAPES
ABCEFGIIILNNT	FILING CABINET
ABCEFGIILMMNR	CLIMBING-FRAME
ABCEFGIKNORTY	TAKING BY FORCE
ABCEFHIILLMRU	LIEBFRAUMILCH
ABCEFHILMRTUY	FAMILY BUTCHER
ABCEFHNRRSTUZ	FRANZ SCHUBERT
ABCEFHOORSSUU	CHORUS OF ABUSE
ABCEFHORRSTTU	BREACH OF TRUST
ABCEFIILLMMOR	MICROFILMABLE

ABCEFINOORRSU	CARBONIFEROUS
ABCEFLLOOORUZ	BLAZE OF COLOUR
ABCEFLMNNOORU	UNCONFORMABLE
ABCEFLMNOORTU	UNCOMFORTABLE
ABCEFLNOOSTUU	FLOUNCES ABOUT
ABCEGGHINNSSU	CHANGING BUSES
ABCEGGHINRRSS	BRINGS CHARGES
ABCEGHHLOPTUY	BOUGHT CHEAPLY
ABCEGHIILMNOO	HAEMOGLOBINIC
ABCEGHILNPUYY	BUYING CHEAPLY
ABCEGHIMNNSUU	SUB-MACHINE GUN
ABCEGHORRRSTU	TURBOCHARGERS
ABCEGIIKNTTTW	BATTING WICKET
ABCEGIILLOOOX	EXOBIOLOGICAL
ABCEGIILLOOPR	PREBIOLOGICAL
ABCEGIKKNORRS	BREAKING ROCKS
ABCEGIKLNNOSY	LOSING BY A NECK
ABCEGIKNOPRRT	REPORTING BACK
ABCEGILLLPRUY	PUBLIC GALLERY
ABCEGILLMUURY	EMBRYOLOGICAL
ABCEGILNOORST	BRING TO A CLOSE
ABCEGINORRSSZ	ZEBRA CROSSING
ABCEGKNOOPSTU	GOT ONE'S BACK UP
ABCEHIIKNSSTT	SITS IN THE BACK
ABCEHIKLLPTTU	THE BLACK TULIP
ABCEHIKLNSTTT	BLANKET-STITCH
ABCEHIKPPSTTU	PICKS UP THE TAB
ABCEHILOPSTTU	ABSOLUTE PITCH
ABCEHIMNOOPRX	CHAMPION BOXER
ABCEHIRRRRSSU	CRUSH BARRIERS
ABCEHJLNNOOST	JOHN CONSTABLE
ABCEHKLLRSTTU	STRUCK THE BALL
ABCEHKLRSSSUW	SWASHBUCKLERS
ABCEIIILLLMNR	CRIMINAL LIBEL
ABCEIIILLPRTY	REPLICABILITY
ABCEIIKLRRTTY	LIBRARY TICKET
ABCEIIILLMPTU	MULTIPLICABLE
ABCEIILMNPRSU	REPUBLICANISM
ABCEIILORSSTY	BACTERIOLYSIS
ABCEIIMNNOORT	RECOMBINATION
ABCEIINNNORTT	ANCIENT BRITON
ABCEIINORSSTT	OBSTETRICIANS
ABCEIKLLNORSS	CROSS-LINKABLE
ABCEILLLMORUY	BIMOLECULARLY
ABCEILLMNORYY	EMBRYONICALLY
ABCEILLMOOPRS	SOCIAL PROBLEM
ABCEILLNOSTUY	SELL BY AUCTION
ABCEILLORSTTY	OBSTETRICALLY
ABCEILNNOSTTY	INCONTESTABLY
ABCEILNPRSTUV	PUBLIC SERVANT
ABCEILORRRTUU	ARBORICULTURE
ABCEINRSSSUYZ	CRAZY BUSINESS
ABCEIOOORRRTV	CORROBORATIVE
ABCEKLNOOSSTW	BLOW ONE'S STACK
ABCEKNOPPSTUU	PUT ONES BACK UP
ABCELLLOOSSTY	OCTOSYLLABLES
ABCELMMNORSUY	COMMENSURABLY
ABCELMORSSSTU	STUMBLE ACROSS
ABCELNNOQRUUY	UNCONQUERABLY
ABCELNORSSTTU	COUNTERBLASTS
ABCENOORRSSYZ	BARONESS ORCZY
ABCFHILLOOPTT	FOOTBALL PITCH
ABCFHLLOOOTTU	TOUCH FOOTBALL
ABCFLMNNOORUY	UNCONFORMABLY
ABCFLMNOORTUY	UNCOMFORTABLY
ABCFLNOOORRSU	FLUOROCARBONS
ABCGGHIILNNPU	PUBLIC HANGING
ABCGGHIKLNOPU	PLOUGHING BACK
ABCGGIIKNNPRS	SPRINGING BACK
ABCGHHIILPUWY	PUBLIC HIGHWAY
ABCGHIIILLLMN	CLIMBING A HILL
ABCGHIIKKNNRS	SHRINKING BACK
ABCGHIIKLMNST	BLACKSMITHING
ABCGHIKLNSSUW	SWASHBUCKLING
ABCGIILLMNNPT	CLIMBING PLANT
ABCGIILNNPRUW	PUBLIC WARNING
ABCGIKKNNOOTU	KNOCKING ABOUT
ABCGINOOORRRT	CORROBORATING
ABCHILOOPRSTT	TROPHOBLASTIC
ABCIIILMOPTTY	COMPATIBILITY
ABCIIILNOSTUY	UNSOCIABILITY
ABCIILLMRSTUU	BICULTURALISM
ABCIILMOPTTUY	COMPUTABILITY
ABCIKMNOOORST	ON A BROOMSTICK
ABCILOORRTUVY	LABOUR VICTORY
ABCIMNNNOOOOP	BOON COMPANION
ABCINOOOOORRRT	CORROBORATION
ABCKKNOPRSTTU	BANKRUPT STOCK
ABCLRRSSTTUUU	SUBSTRUCTURAL
ABCOOOORRRRST	CORROBORATORS
ABCOOOORRRRTY	CORROBORATORY
ABDDDEEEEFHRT	FEATHERBEDDED
ABDDDEILMNORY	BROAD-MINDEDLY
ABDDEEEFFORTI	BETTER OFF DEAD
ABDDEEEHILTTW	WIELDED THE BAT
ABDDEEEHLORSU	DOUBLEHEADERS
ABDDEEEHNOOSW	BOWED ONE'S HEAD
ABDDEEEIMNNRS	BEDSIDE MANNER
ABDDEEELLORVY	DEARLY BELOVED
ABDDEEEMNOSTU	MADE ONE'S DEBUT
ABDDEFFFLNPUW	PUFFED AND BLEW
ABDDEEFIILLRT	DEFIBRILLATED
ABDDEEGGHILOR	HARD-BOILED EGG
ABDDEEGGHIPRT	BRIDGED THE GAP
ABDDEEGHILNNO	HELD IN BONDAGE
ABDDEEGHILORT	THE OLD BRIGADE
ABDDEEGHMNRTU	BANGED THE DRUM
ABDDEEGILLNOU	DOUBLE DEALING
	DOUBLE-DEALING
ABDDEEGNNORSU	DANGEROUS BEND
ABDDEEHIILNRT	TRAILED BEHIND
ABDDEEHILNRVY	DELIVER BY HAND
ABDDEEHINNORT	BEND IN THE ROAD
ABDDEEHLLORSU	SHOULDER BLADE
ABDDEEIILNPTY	DEPENDABILITY
ABDDEENOORTUW	WONDERED ABOUT
ABDDEFHIMNORT	BREADTH OF MIND
ABDDEFHLLNOOS	FLESH AND BLOOD
ABDDEGHHINNRT	RIGHT-HAND BEND
ABDDEGHILNNOO	HOLD IN BONDAGE
ABDDEGHINNNSY	SENDING BY HAND
ABDDEGIMNOORR	BRIDE AND GROOM
ABDDEGINPRTTU	BATTER PUDDING
ABDDEGLNNOOWY	GONE DOWN BADLY
ABDDEGLNOOSWY	GOES DOWN BADLY
ABDDEHHIINNRT	BIRD IN THE HAND
ABDDEHILNRSTW	DRAW THE BLINDS
ABDDEHLNOORRS	NO HOLDS BARRED
ABDDEHMNOORUW	HOMEWARD BOUND
ABDDEHNOOSSTU	HAD ONE'S DOUBTS
ABDDEIOOORRUW	BORROWED A QUID
ABDDELNNOTWWY	WENT DOWN BADLY
ABDDELNORSUUY	ROUNDLY ABUSED
ABDDFGIILNOTU	FIDDLING ABOUT
ABDDFHOOOSTUW	SHADOW OF DOUBT
ABDDGGIJNOOOO	DOING A GOOD JOB
ABDDGHINNOSTU	DOTING HUSBAND
ABDDGHINORTUU	BUDDING AUTHOR
ABDDGHLNOOSTU	BOUGHT AND SOLD
ABDDGINNOORSU	SOUNDING BOARD
ABDDGINNORSWY	BANDYING WORDS
ABDDIIILMNNNW	IN WIND AND LIMB

ABDEEEEGILTTV	VEGETABLE DIET
ABDEEEEHLPRTY	BREATHE DEEPLY
ABDEEEEHNRSTU	EASE THE BURDEN
ABDEEEEIILLRT	DELIBERATE LIE
ABDEEEEIILLOTV	LEAD TO BELIEVE
ABDEEEELRRSTV	RESERVED TABLE
ABDEEEEFFLORTT	BELATED EFFORT
ABDEEEEFGINRST	BREAST-FEEDING
ABDEEEEFIIMNTY	DEFINITE MAYBE
ABDEEEEFKLNORS	BARKED ONESELF
ABDEEEEFLNOSSU	ABUSED ONESELF
ABDEEEEGGMNNRU	NUMBER ENGAGED
ABDEEEEGHILNRT	BLEEDING HEART
ABDEEEEGHILSTV	VEGETABLE DISH
ABDEEEEGHIMPTT	EMPTIED THE BAG
ABDEEEEGHINPRT	DEEP BREATHING
ABDEEEEGINPPRR	BEING PREPARED
ABDEEEEGKLLNOW	KNOWLEDGEABLE
ABDEEEEGLNOOTT	GONE TO BED LATE
ABDEEEEGLOOSTT	GOES TO BED LATE
ABDEEEEGNNOORS	GOES ON A BENDER
ABDEEEEHHINRST	BEHIND THE EARS
ABDEEEEHIKMRST	BESIDE THE MARK
ABDEEEEHILORTV	HARD TO BELIEVE
ABDEEEEHKNORRT	BROKENHEARTED
ABDEEEEHLNOPTY	BEYOND THE PALE
ABDEEEEHLNOSTY	LEAD BY THE NOSE
ABDEEEEHLNRTTU	UNDER THE TABLE
ABDEEEEHMNRTTU	BEATEN THE DRUM
ABDEEEEHOPRSTW	SWEEP THE BOARD
ABDEEEEILNRSSS	DESIRABLENESS
ABDEEEEKMNOSTU	MAKE ONES DEBUT
ABDEEEEKNOOSTT	TAKE TO ONES BED
ABDEEEELMNNSST	STEELBANDSMEN
ABDEEEELNOOPTT	OPENED A BOTTLE
ABDEEEELNOTTTW	WENT TO BED LATE
ABDEEEELOPRRRS	REPEL BOARDERS
ABDEEEEMMORRTY	DAY TO REMEMBER
ABDEEEEMNORSUY	BEYOND MEASURE
ABDEEEENNNORTW	WENT ON A BENDER
ABDEEEENNSSTTW	STANDS BETWEEN
ABDEEFFILLOTT	FIELD OF BATTLE
ABDEEFFLORSUW	SUFFERED A BLOW
ABDEEFGHOOORT	BE OF GOOD HEART
ABDEEFGIILNOR	OBLIGE A FRIEND
ABDEEFGIMNNOR	MAN OF BREEDING
ABDEEFGLNOTUY	GONE BY DEFAULT
ABDEEFGLOSTUY	GOES BY DEFAULT
ABDEEFIIILSTY	DEFEASIBILITY
ABDEEFIIKLLRW	FLEW LIKE A BIRD
ABDEEFIILLRST	DEFIBRILLATES
ABDEEFINNRSST	ABSENT FRIENDS
ABDEEFINOSTXY	FIXED BAYONETS
ABDEEFLLOORRV	FELL OVERBOARD
ABDEEFLNTTUWY	WENT BY DEFAULT
ABDEEFLOORRTT	ORDER OF BATTLE
ABDEEFNNORRST	BRENDAN FOSTER
ABDEEGGHIMNTU	HUNTED BIG GAME
ABDEEGGHIPRST	BRIDGES THE GAP
ABDEEGHIILNNV	LEAVING BEHIND
ABDEEGIKMNNOS	MAKING ONE'S BED
ABDEEGILMNNOU	DOUBLE MEANING
ABDEEGILNRSST	DRESSING TABLE
ABDEEGKLLNOWY	KNOWLEDGEABLY
ABDEEGLOPRRRT	GARBLED REPORT
ABDEEGNNOOPRS	BEG ONES PARDON
ABDEEGNNOORSU	BE ON ONES GUARD
ABDEEGNOOORRV	GONE OVERBOARD
ABDEEGOOOORRSV	GOES OVERBOARD
ABDEEHHILORRT	HORRIBLE DEATH
ABDEEHHIORSST	HEAR BOTH SIDES

ABDEEHIINOSTT	A BIT ON THE SIDE
ABDEEHILMMRRU	HUMBLE ADMIRER
ABDEEHILMNRTU	DIAL THE NUMBER
ABDEEHILNORST	BEARDS THE LION
ABDEEHILNOTTW	WIELD THE BATON
ABDEEHIMOSSTT	MISSED THE BOAT
ABDEEHLNORSSU	DOUBLE HARNESS
ABDEEHLNORTTU	ROUND THE TABLE
ABDEEHNNOSTWW	NOW THE BAD NEWS
ABDEEHNOPSTTU	POUNDS THE BEAT
ABDEEHNORSSTU	BURNED TO ASHES
ABDEEHNPRRUUY	AUDREY HEPBURN
ABDEEHOPRSTTW	SWEPT THE BOARD
ABDEEIILMMSSY	MISSED BY A MILE
ABDEEIILNNNTV	VENETIAN BLIND
ABDEEIILNNPSS	INDISPENSABLE
ABDEEIILNORST	DELIBERATIONS
ABDEEIILNPTXY	EXPENDABILITY
ABDEEIIMRTTXY	AMBIDEXTERITY
ABDEEIILNORRS	BANDERILLEROS
ABDEEILMNOPRS	IMPONDERABLES
ABDEEILMORSST	MOST DESIRABLE
ABDEEILMRRSTU	MASTER BUILDER
ABDEEIILNNRTUY	TURN A BLIND EYE
ABDEEINNORSSU	USED ONE'S BRAIN
ABDEEINORTTUZ	BRAZENED IT OUT
ABDEEKLMNOOSS	MAKES OLD BONES
ABDEEKLOORRWY	BOWLED A YORKER
ABDEEKMNOOTUY	MONKEYED ABOUT
ABDEEKNOORRSW	BREAK ONES WORD
ABDEEELMOOPPRS	POSED A PROBLEM
ABDEELMORRSTT	LOMBARD STREET
ABDEELNNNORTT	ARNOLD BENNETT
ABDEELNOORSSU	BARED ONE'S SOUL
ABDEELNOOSTUV	LEAVES NO DOUBT
ABDEELNORRTUW	RETURNED A BLOW
ABDEELNORRVWW	BRAVE NEW WORLD
ABDEENOORRTVW	WENT OVERBOARD
ABDEENORRSTYY	BORN YESTERDAY
ABDEEOOPRTTTU	POTTERED ABOUT
ABDEEOORTTTTU	TOTTERED ABOUT
ABDEEORSTTTTU	BUTTERED TOAST
ABDEFFILLLOOT	FOOTBALL FIELD
ABDEFGHIILLNN	FALLING BEHIND
ABDEFGHIILNOR	HOLDING A BRIEF
ABDEFGHIKLOOT	BOOKED A FLIGHT
ABDEFGHNOOORU	BADGE OF HONOUR
ABDEFGINORSST	STRING OF BEADS
ABDEFHIIORRST	BIRDS OF THE AIR
ABDEFHNORSSTU	FUSS AND BOTHER
ABDEFHNRSTUUU	FUTURE HUSBAND
ABDEFIILLORRT	DEFIBRILLATOR
ABDEFILNOOTTW	BIT OF A LET-DOWN
ABDEFJKLOOOOR	LOOKED FOR A JOB
ABDEFLNSSTUUY	USEFUL STAND-BY
ABDEFLOORSTTW	BATTLE OF WORDS
ABDEGGGHIILNN	LAGGING BEHIND
ABDEGGGINNOPR	BEGGING PARDON
ABDEGGHHILNOT	HOLDING THE BAG
ABDEGGHINOOTT	GOING TO THE BAD
ABDEGGIILNPRY	PLAYING BRIDGE
ABDEGGIIMNNRR	INGRID BERGMAN
ABDEGGINNOPRW	BRING DOWN A PEG
ABDEGGINOOSYY	SAYING GOODBYE
ABDEGGINOOVWY	WAVING GOODBYE
ABDEGGLLOOOWY	BOWLED A GOOGLY
ABDEGHIIINRST	RAISING THE BID
ABDEGHIIKLNNW	WALKING BEHIND
ABDEGHIIMNRTU	THUMBING A RIDE
ABDEGHIINNSTY	STAYING BEHIND
ABDEGHIINRSSU	BRUSHING ASIDE

ABDEGHILNNOWY	LONG WAY BEHIND
ABDEGHINOORSU	BOARDING HOUSE
	BOARDINGHOUSE
ABDEGHINOORTT	BORING TO DEATH
ABDEGHIOOORUV	GOOD BEHAVIOUR
ABDEGIIKLNRS	SING LIKE A BIRD
ABDEGIIIMNNNR	BEARING IN MIND
ABDEGIIKLNRSU	SUNG LIKE A BIRD
ABDEGIILMNNSY	SENDING BY MAIL
ABDEGIILMNSSS	DISASSEMBLING
ABDEGIILNNRSW	SWEARING BLIND
ABDEGIILNNTTY	DYING IN BATTLE
ABDEGIINNOPTT	DEBATING POINT
ABDEGIKLNOPRU	DOUBLE-PARKING
ABDEGILNOOSTW	SWEATING BLOOD
ABDEGINNNOORW	BEARING DOWN ON
ABDEGINNNOTTW	BATTENING DOWN
ABDEGINOPRTTU	BRING UP TO DATE
ABDEGLLOORRTU	ROBERT DOUGALL
ABDEGNOCOOUVV	ANYBODY'S GUESS
ABDEHHIOPRTUY	PAID BY THE HOUR
ABDEHHKNOOTTY	TOOK BY THE HAND
ABDEHIIIILLLOY	BILLIE HOLIDAY
ABDEHIILOSTWY	SHOWED ABILITY
ABDEHILLOOPRY	HYPERBOLOIDAL
ABDEHILMNNSST	BLANDISHMENTS
ABDEHILNNOORT	RAN IN THE BLOOD
ABDEHILNOORSU	DISHONOURABLE
ABDEHINNOSSSU	HAD NO BUSINESS
ABDEHINSSSSUY	SHADY BUSINESS
ABDEHMORRSSTU	BERMUDA SHORTS
ABDEHNNOOORTY	NOBODY ON EARTH
ABDEHNNOOORUY	HONOUR AND OBEY
ABDEHNNORSSSU	RUBS ONE'S HANDS
ABDEHNOOSSSTU	HAS ONE'S DOUBTS
ABDEHNORRSUYY	SYDNEY HARBOUR
ABDEIILLORSTY	SOLDERABILITY
ABDEIILNNPSSY	INDISPENSABLY
ABDEIILRTTUXY	EXTRUDABILITY
ABDEIIMNOPRSS	BAD IMPRESSION
ABDEIINNORSTU	INSUBORDINATE
ABDEIINORSTUV	SUBORDINATIVE
ABDEIIOOPRSSS	BASIDIOSPORES
ABDEIKLLLORSU	SKILLED LABOUR
ABDEIKLNNOOOR	BROOK NO DENIAL
ABDEILLLLNORT	TEN-DOLLAR BILL
ABDEILLNOOORT	BLOOD RELATION
	BLOOD-RELATION
ABDEILMNNORRU	ORDINAL NUMBER
ABDEILNORSTUY	SUBORDINATELY
ABDEILNQRRUUY	LIQUEUR BRANDY
ABDEILOOSSSYZ	BLOODY ASSIZES
ABDEIMNNORSUU	DUBIOUS MANNER
ABDEINORRRSTT	TERRORIST BAND
ABDEJMOOPRRUV	JUMP OVERBOARD
ABDELLNORRTTU	ROLL AND BUTTER
ABDELNNOPTUUW	UNPUTDOWNABLE
ABDFFLNOPSSUW	PUFFS AND BLOWS
ABDFGHLOOOOTY	TOO GOOD BY HALF
ABDFGINORRRSW	BRINGS FORWARD
ABDFHIIRRSTTY	FIRST BIRTHDAY
ABDFILLNOTUUY	LADY BOUNTIFUL
ABDFKLNOOORRS	NORFOLK BROADS
ABDFNOOOPRSSU	BASSO PROFUNDO
ABDGHIIKNRSTY	KINGS BIRTHDAY
ABDGHILNNOSUV	LOVING HUSBAND
ABDGHINNOOTUV	HAVING NO DOUBT
ABDGIIKNORRST	SKIRTING BOARD
ABDGIILNNOORV	LIVING ON BOARD
ABDGIINNOOPPR	PIPING ON BOARD
ABDGIINNORSTU	SUBORDINATING

ABDGIMMNNORUU	BUMMING AROUND
ABDGINNORSSSU	SOUNDING BRASS
ABDHHHINOSTTW	WITH BOTH HANDS
ABDHIIINORSTY	HYBRIDISATION
ABDHIIINORTYZ	HYBRIDIZATION
ABDHILNOORSUY	DISHONOURABLY
ABDHIOOTTTUUW	WITHOUT A DOUBT
ABDIIIILMSSTY	ADMISSIBILITY
ABDIIILLMNNRT	BRILLIANT MIND
ABDIIILOPSSTY	DISPOSABILITY
ABDIIINOSSSTU	SUBSIDISATION
ABDIIINOSSTUZ	SUBSIDIZATION
ABDIINNOORSTU	SUBORDINATION
ABDINNORSTUWY	IN A BROWN STUDY
ABDMOOOORRTTU	OUTBOARD MOTOR
ABDNOOOPRRSUW	BORROWS A POUND
ABEEEEFHLNOSV	BEHAVE ONESELF
ABEEEEFHLRRTY	BREATHE FREELY
ABEEEEFLMPTTT	FEEBLE ATTEMPT
ABEEEEFLNORSU	UNFORESEEABLE
ABEEEEGKPRRSU	BURKES PEERAGE
ABEEEEHHRRSTT	THE THREE BEARS
ABEEEEHNORSTT	BARE ONES TEETH
ABEEEEILMMPRS	SEMIPERMEABLE
ABEEEEIRRRTVV	REVERBERATIVE
ABEEEEELLLOSVW	BELOW SEA-LEVEL
ABEEEELMNPRSS	PERMEABLENESS
ABEEEELNNORCCV	VENERABLENESS
ABEEEELNPRRST	REPRESENTABLE
ABEEEEMRTTUXY	EXTREME BEAUTY
ABEEEFFLMMORR	FREE FROM BLAME
ABEEEFHHOSTTV	HAVE THE BEST OF
ABEEEFHMNRSST	FANS THE EMBERS
ABEEEFHMORSTT	BEFORE THE MAST
ABEEEFINORTTX	EXORBITANT FEE
ABEEEFLNOSSSU	ABUSES ONESELF
ABEEEGHIMPSTT	EMPTIES THE BAG
ABEEEGHLLTTUV	GAVE THE BULLET
ABEEEGIIKLMNV	MAKING BELIEVE
ABEEEGIKNNOTW	BEGIN TO WEAKEN
ABEEEGINRRRTV	REVERBERATING
ABEEEGKLNORSS	BREAKS ONE'S LEG
ABEEEGKMNNRSS	BANK MESSENGER
ABEEEGKNNOTUW	BEGUN TO WEAKEN
ABEEEGLOORRTV	ROOT VEGETABLE
ABEEEGLOPSTUV	VEGETABLE SOUP
ABEEEHHLLSTYY	LAY BY THE HEELS
ABEEEHHLRRSST	BLESS HER HEART
ABEEEHIILNTTV	THE INEVITABLE
ABEEEHIKLLSTZ	LIKE THE BLAZES
ABEEEHILMPSTU	EATS HUMBLE PIE
ABEEEHILNPPRS	APPREHENSIBLE
ABEEEHJMMNRTY	JEREMY BENTHAM
ABEEEHKLLPRST	BREAK THE SPELL
ABEEEHKLNORST	BROKEN THE SEAL
ABEEEHKLRRSTU	BREAK THE RULES
ABEEEHKMMNNTT	THE EMBANKMENT
ABEEEHKNRSSTW	BREAKS THE NEWS
ABEEEHKORRRSS	HORSEBREAKERS
ABEEEHLLNRSTW	ANSWER THE BELL
ABEEEHLLOSTTT	LOSE THE BATTLE
ABEEEHNNORTTT	BETTER THAN ONE
ABEEEIIKLMNRS	BERKELEIANISM
ABEEEIIKLRSTT	TAKE LIBERTIES
ABEEEIIKKRRRST	STRIKEBREAKER
ABEEEIILMRSSS	LES MISÉRABLES
ABEEEILMNNTVY	BE MY VALENTINE
ABEEEILMNRSSS	MISERABLENESS
ABEEEILMNSSST	ESTIMABLENESS
ABEEEILNPRRTT	INTERPRETABLE

ABEEEEILNQSSTU	EQUITABLENESS
ABEEEILNRSSTV	VERITABLENESS
ABEEEIMMPRRTV	PRIVATE MEMBER
ABEEEIMORSSTT	SOBER ESTIMATE
ABEEEINORRRTV	REVERBERATION
ABEEEJLNNOSSY	ENJOYABLENESS
ABEEEKLOOPRSS	BOOKS A SLEEPER
ABEEEKNNOORSS	BREAK ONE'S NOSE
ABEEELLMNSSSS	BLAMELESSNESS
ABEEELLORTTTU	ROULETTE TABLE
ABEEELMNORSSV	REMOVABLENESS
ABEEELMPRSSTT	LAST SEPTEMBER
ABEEENOSSSTUU	BEAUTEOUSNESS
ABEEEORRRRTVY	REVERBERATORY
ABEEFFILLORTT	BATTLE FOR LIFE
ABEEFGGILNRTU	BEING GRATEFUL
ABEEFGHIINRRT	BREATHING FIRE
ABEEFGHLLRSTU	THREE BAGS FULL
ABEEFGIILNRRR	IRREFRANGIBLE
ABEEFGLNORTTU	UNFORGETTABLE
ABEEFHHILMSTT	SHIFT THE BLAME
ABEEFHHLMNRTU	HALF THE NUMBER
ABEEFHJOORRTT	RATE FOR THE JOB
ABEEFHKOOOORTY	BOOK OF THE YEAR
ABEEFHLLOOTTU	BEAT HELL OUT OF
ABEEFHLLORSTT	ALL FOR THE BEST
ABEEFHLOOPTTT	TOP OF THE TABLE
ABEEFIILNRRTV	BRIEF INTERVAL
ABEEFIILTUUVW	BEAUTIFUL VIEW
ABEEFILMNTTUU	MUTUAL BENEFIT
ABEEFILNSSTUU	BEAUTIFULNESS
ABEEFKLLNOORS	BROKE ONE'S FALL
ABEEFLOORSSTU	SEA OF TROUBLES
ABEEFLOORTTTW	BOTTLE OF WATER
ABEEGGHIMNRTU	BIG-GAME HUNTER
ABEEGGILLNNRS	ALLEN GINSBERG
ABEEGHHLPRSTU	BUSH TELEGRAPH
ABEEGHIKNORSU	HOUSEBREAKING
ABEEGHINNORRU	NEAR NEIGHBOUR
ABEEGHLLNOOTT	GONE TO THE BALL
ABEEGHLLOOSTT	GOES TO THE BALL
ABEEGIIKMNNST	BEING MISTAKEN
ABEEGIILMMNST	EMBLEMATISING
ABEEGIILMMNTZ	EMBLEMATIZING
ABEEGIINOSTTU	SEEING ABOUT IT
ABEEGIKLNOORS	BREAKING LOOSE
ABEEGIKLNORST	SERGEANT BILKO
ABEEGIKLNRRSU	BREAKING RULES
ABEEGIKLNRTTY	BREAK IT GENTLY
ABEEGIKNNOORW	RENEWING A BOOK
ABEEGIKNNOPST	KEEPING TABS ON
ABEEGILNNOOTT	NOT NEGOTIABLE
ABEEGILNORRVY	OVERBEARINGLY
ABEEGILRRRRUV	IRREGULAR VERB
ABEEGINORRSTT	ORANGE BITTERS
ABEEGJMOORRSY	GOOSEBERRY JAM
ABEEGJNOOPSUV	GAVE UP ONE'S JOB
ABEEGLNOORTUV	GAVE NO TROUBLE
ABEEHHILRSSST	BLESS HIS HEART
ABEEHHINORTTW	WITH ONE BREATH
ABEEHHLMPTTTU	THUMP THE TABLE
ABEEHIILNSTUX	INEXHAUSTIBLE
ABEEHIIORSTTT	RISE TO THE BAIT
ABEEHIKLLRSTT	STRIKE THE BALL
ABEEHILLNPSST	SPILL THE BEANS
ABEEHILMNSSTT	ESTABLISHMENT
ABEEHILNPPRSY	APPREHENSIBLY
ABEEHILNSTTTW	WINS THE BATTLE
ABEEHILOPRTTZ	PORT ELIZABETH
ABEEHILRSSSYY	SHIRLEY BASSEY
ABEEHIMOSSSTT	MISSES THE BOAT
ABEEHIOORSTTT	ROSE TO THE BAIT
ABEEHJKLOORTU	LABOUR THE JOKE
ABEEHKNOPRTTU	PUT ON THE BRAKE
	PUT THE BRAKE ON
ABEEHLLNOOOTW	BEAT ONE HOLLOW
ABEEHLLNOTTTW	WENT TO THE BALL
ABEEHLLOSTTTT	LOST THE BATTLE
ABEEHLMNRSTUV	HUMBLE SERVANT
ABEEHLNOORTUV	HAVE NO TROUBLE
ABEEHLNRSTTTU	TURN THE TABLES
ABEEHMOOORRTT	ROOM TO BREATHE
ABEEHMPRRSTUV	BUMPER HARVEST
ABEEHPRSSTTTU	PASS THE BUTTER
ABEEIIILLMNRS	BIMILLENARIES
ABEEIIILMNRSV	REMAIN VISIBLE
ABEEIIILLNRSS	ILLIBERALNESS
ABEEIILMMSSSY	MISSES BY A MILE
ABEEIILMNRTUY	ENUMERABILITY
ABEEIILNNOSST	BITE ONES NAILS
ABEEIILNPRTTY	PENETRABILITY
ABEEIILNRRSST	IRRITABLENESS
ABEEIKMOOPRRS	BROKE A PROMISE
ABEEIILLMMNRST	LAMBERT SIMNEL
ABEEIILLNPSSSU	PLAUSIBLENESS
ABEEIILLORRSTV	LIBERAL VOTERS
ABEEIILMMNOSSV	IMMOVABLENESS
ABEEIILMMNSSTU	IMMUTABLENESS
ABEEIILMNNNOTU	UNMENTIONABLE
ABEEIILMNNOSSW	SENSIBLE WOMAN
ABEEIILMNOPSUY	OBEY AN IMPULSE
ABEEIILNNRSSSS	BRAINLESSNESS
ABEEIILNNSTTUU	SUBLIEUTENANT
ABEEIILQRRRTTU	BITTER QUARREL
ABEEIILRSSTTTY	SETS AT LIBERTY
ABEEIINNORSSSU	USE ONES BRAINS
	USES ONE'S BRAIN
ABEEIINOPRRSSS	PRISONERS BASE
ABEEIINPRRSSTY	PRESBYTERIANS
ABEEIIOORRSSTV	OBSERVATORIES
ABEEIIOPRRTTTX	BEATRIX POTTER
ABEEKLMORRSTU	TROUBLEMAKERS
ABEEKMNNOORRS	BROKEN ONE'S ARM
ABEEKMNNORTUY	MOUNTEBANKERY
ABEEKORRRSSTT	BREASTSTROKER
ABEEKORRRSSTT	BREASTSTROKES
ABEELLMNORTTU	MENTAL TROUBLE
ABEELLMOOPRSV	SOLVE A PROBLEM
ABEELLMORRTWX	ROBERT MAXWELL
ABEELLOOPRRTW	ROBERT WALPOLE
ABEELMOOPPRSS	POSES A PROBLEM
ABEELNNNORRTU	NONRETURNABLE
ABEELNNOORSSSU	BARES ONE'S SOUL
ABEELNOOSSWWY	ELBOWS ONE'S WAY
ABEELOOPRSTUW	ABSOLUTE POWER
ABEEMMRRSSSTU	BREASTSUMMERS
ABEEMMNNOQRRSUU	BRUSQUE MANNER
ABEENORRSSTTU	RETURNS TO BASE
ABEFFGIIKNORT	BREAKING IT OFF
ABEFFGOORRSUV	BEG FOR FAVOURS
ABEFFIIMOPRST	BAPTISM OF FIRE
ABEFFLMOPRSST	STAFF PROBLEMS
ABEFFNNOOOSTW	OFF ONES OWN BAT
ABEFGHIILLNOT	LIFELONG HABIT
ABEFGHIILMNRT	HALF-TIMBERING
ABEFGHIILNORT	LIGHT A BONFIRE
ABEFGHINOTTUY	THING OF BEAUTY
ABEFGIOORTTTU	FORGET ABOUT IT
ABEFGLNORTTUY	UNFORGETTABLY
ABEFGNORSTTUY	BATTERY OF GUNS
ABEFHHOORRSTT	SHORT OF BREATH
ABEFHILLLOSTU	HAIL OF BULLETS

ABEFHKLOOOPTY	BOOK OF THE PLAY	ABEHILLNOSTWW	BLOWN A WHISTLE
ABEFIIILLRTTY	FILTERABILITY	ABEHILLOSSTWW	BLOWS A WHISTLE
ABEFIIJLNSTUU	UNJUSTIFIABLE	ABEHILMNOSTTU	HUMBLE STATION
ABEFILLOOPRSW	PAIR OF BELLOWS	ABEHILNORRSTW	BROTHERS-IN-LAW
ABEFILLORRTTU	FLORAL TRIBUTE	ABEHINNOSSSSU	HAS NO BUSINESS
ABEFILLSSSTTU	BLISSFUL STATE	ABEHJMNOORRRY	JOHN BARRYMORE
ABEFILMOOORTT	MOTOR LIFEBOAT	ABEHLLMOPSSUY	BLASPHEMOUSLY
ABEFILORRTTUV	BITTER FLAVOUR	ABEHLLRSTTUUU	TAURUS THE BULL
ABEFIMNNOSSSU	MAN OF BUSINESS	ABEHLNOORSTTU	BATTLE HONOURS
ABEFIOORRRSVW	BORROWS A FIVER	ABEHLORRSSTTY	ERYTHROBLASTS
ABEFKLNNOOSTW	BLANKET OF SNOW	ABEHOPPPRRSTU	PROPS UP THE BAR
ABEFKLOORRSTU	ASK FOR TROUBLE	ABEIIIILNTTVY	INEVITABILITY
ABEFLLLORSSUY	FOUR SYLLABLES	ABEIIILNOQRTU	EQUILIBRATION
ABEFLLNOOPSTU	TABLESPOONFUL	ABEIIILNORSTT	LIBERATIONIST
ABEFLOOOPRSTU	ABSOLUTE PROOF	ABEIIILNORTXY	INEXORABILITY
ABEFLOOPRRRSY	RASPBERRY FOOL	ABEIIILNPSTXY	EXPANSIBILITY
ABEGGGHILNOTT	BAGGING THE LOT	ABEIIILNRSTTY	SINTERABILITY
ABEGGHINOORTT	GOING TO THE BAR	ABEIIILMOPTYY	EMPLOYABILITY
ABEGGIIILNNRV	BRINGING ALIVE	ABEIIILNRTUVY	VULNERABILITY
ABEGGIIMNNOPI	OPENING GAMBIT	ABEIILMNRSSST	TRANSMISSIBLE
ABEGGILNNOPPT	PING-PONG TABLE	ABEIILNORSSTV	VIBRATIONLESS
ABEGGINNOSTTU	GETTING ON A BUS	ABEIILNRSSSUV	RIVAL BUSINESS
ABEGGORRSSTUY	BAGGY TROUSERS	ABEIILOPRTTXY	EXPORTABILITY
ABEGHHHIIRRTT	HIGH BIRTH-RATE	ABEIILOQRRTUY	EQUILIBRATORY
ABEGHHIINRTTT	HITTING THE BAR	ABEIILRTTTUVY	ATTRIBUTIVELY
ABEGHHKORRSTU	BREAKS THROUGH	ABEIIMNOSSSTU	AMBITIOUSNESS
	BREAKTHROUGHS	ABEIINSSSTTUV	SUBSTANTIVISE
ABEGHIIILLNPTY	PAYING THE BILL	ABEIINSSTTUVZ	OUDSTANTIVIZE
ABEGHIKNOORST	SHOOTING BRAKE	ABEIKLLMNORTU	BULLION MARKET
ABEGHIKNORRST	BREAKING SHORT	ABEIKNNOORRTU	BROKE INTO A RUN
ABEGHILLNOOTW	BEATING HOLLOW	ABEILLMNSSSSU	SMALL BUSINESS
ABEGHILNNSTWY	WINS BY A LENGTH	ABEILLNOOSSSY	OBSESSIONALLY
ABEGHILNORTUV	HAVING TROUBLE	ABEILMNNSSTTY	BY INSTALMENTS
ABEGHIMNNNOOTY	BAYING THE MOON	ABEILNOORSSSU	LABORIOUSNESS
ABEGHIMNOORRT	BREATHING ROOM	ABEILNOPPRSTU	INSUPPORTABLE
ABEGHINNRRTUW	BURN WITH ANGER	ABEILNORSSSUY	BYELORUSSIANS
ABEGHINOORTUV	HOVERING ABOUT	ABEILNSSTTUVY	SUBSTANTIVELY
ABEGHINOPRSTT	STOP BREATHING	ABEIMNNOPPTTY	BY APPOINTMENT
ABEGHLLMOOPUY	HUMBLE APOLOGY	ABEIMOPRRSTTU	SUBMIT A REPORT
ABEGIIILNOTTY	NEGOTIABILITY	ABEINNNORRSTU	TURN ONE'S BRAIN
ABEGIIILNQRTU	EQUILIBRATING	ABEINNORSTUVY	SUBVENTIONARY
ABEGIIILNRTTY	INTEGRABILITY	ABEINNSSSSTUY	NASTY BUSINESS
ABEGIIJLNNOTT	JOINING BATTLE	ABEINORRSSUVY	SUBVERSIONARY
ABEGIIKNNOPRT	BREAKING POINT	ABELLLLOPSSYY	POLYSYLLABLES
ABEGIIKNNORTW	BREAKING IN TWO	ABELLLMNOOSSY	MONOSYLLABLES
ABEGIIILLNORTV	VOTING LIBERAL	ABELMMNOORTWY	MELTON MOWBRAY
ABEGIIINORSTTT	TEARING TO BITS	ABELMMOORSSSY	ASSEMBLY ROOMS
ABEGIINPPRRST	STRIPPING BARE	ABELNPRRSTTUY	BUTLERS PANTRY
ABEGIINPRTTUY	PAYING TRIBUTE	ABELORSSTTTUU	ABSOLUTE TRUST
ABEGIKLMNORTU	MAKING TROUBLE	ABENNNOOSTTUW	SEWN ON A BUTTON
ABEGIKMMNOORT	BOOMING MARKET	ABENNOOOOPSSX	ON ONE'S SOAPBOX
ABEGIKMNNNOOS	MAKING NO BONES	ABENNOOSSTTUW	SEWS ON A BUTTON
ABEGIKNNOORST	BREAK INTO SONG	ABFGHIILLORTT	BIT OF ALL RIGHT
ABEGILNNNORTU	BORING A TUNNEL	ABFGHIILMNTTU	THUMBING A LIFT
ABEGILNNNRTTU	RUNNING BATTLE	ABFGHILLNOSTW	SNOWBALL FIGHT
ABEGILNOPPRTT	BLOTTING PAPER	ABFGIILLNOSTT	FALLING TO BITS
ABEGIMNNOSSSU	AMBIGUOUSNESS	ABFGIILNOTTTU	FLITTING ABOUT
ABEGINNOSSSUU	PAYING ONE'S SUB	ABFGIJNOORRTY	TRYING FOR A JOB
ABEGINOORRSTT	BORING TO TEARS	ABFGIOOORTTTU	FORGOT ABOUT IT
ABEGINRRSTTUY	BURSTING A TYRE	ABFIIILLLNTY	INFALLIBILITY
ABEGLMNOOORSS	ORANGE BLOSSOM	ABFIIIILLNORST	FIBRILLATIONS
ABEHHIIJRRSTT	THE BRITISH RAJ	ABFIIILOPRTTY	PROFITABILITY
ABEHHINNOORST	HEATH ROBINSON	ABFIILMNOOTTY	LOFTY AMBITION
ABEHHINORRSSU	BRUSH ONES HAIR	ABFIINOORRTTU	TOUR OF BRITAIN
ABEHHOPRSTUYY	PAYS BY THE HOUR	ABFLLLOOOOPST	FOOTBALL POOLS
ABEHIIIILPRSTY	PERISHABILITY	ABFLOORSSTUUY	FABULOUS STORY
ABEHIIINORTTX	ART EXHIBITION	ABGGIIMNNNTW	WINNING GAMBIT
ABEHIILNOPSTT	SHIP IN A BOTTLE	ABGGIIINNRSTU	BRINGING A SUIT
ABEHIILNSTUXY	INEXHAUSTIBLY	ABGGIKNNOPRTU	GOING BANKRUPT
ABEHIKNNSSSTU	BASKS IN THE SUN	ABGGILNNOOTUU	LOUNGING ABOUT
ABEHILLLPSTTU	UPHILL BATTLES	ABGHHILORRSTU	HARBOUR LIGHTS

ABGHIIKNNOTTU	THINKING ABOUT
ABGHIILMNNSUY	LYING IN AMBUSH
ABGHIIMMNSSTW	SWIMMING BATHS
ABGHIKNNRSTTU	BATHING TRUNKS
ABGHINOORTTUW	THROWING ABOUT
ABGIIIILNNTTY	INTANGIBILITY
ABGIIKLNORSTW	STRIKING A BLOW
ABGIILNNOPRTY	BRING INTO PLAY
ABGIILNPPTTUU	PUTTING UP BAIL
ABGIIMNNORRST	BRAINSTORMING
ABGIKMNORSTTY	TAKING BY STORM
ABGILNOOPRTUW	PROWLING ABOUT
ABHIIKNOSTTTU	THINKS ABOUT IT
ABHIINOPRSSTV	VIBRAPHONISTS
ABHIJNNNOORST	BRIAN JOHNSTON
ABHIMNNORRSTU	NORTHUMBRIANS
ABHKNNOPSSSYY	BY SHANKS'S PONY
ABIIIILLNOTVY	INVIOLABILITY
ABIIIILMPSSTY	IMPASSIBILITY
ABIIILMOPRTVY	IMPROVABILITY
ABIIILNOOSSTT	ABOLITIONISTS
ABIIILNSTTUUY	UNSUITABILITY
ABIIILRSTUVVY	SURVIVABILITY
ABIILMNOOSSTY	SYMBOLISATION
ABIILMNOOSTYZ	SYMBOLIZATION
ABIILMOOSSTTU	AUTOMOBILISTS
ABIJLNOOPPSSU	SLIPS UP ON A JOB
ABILMMNOSSSTU	SOMNAMBULISTS
ABILNOPPRSTUY	INSUPPORTABLY
ABLMNOOPRSTUW	BLOWN UP A STORM
ABLMOOPRSSTUW	BLOWS UP A STORM
ACCCCEEKNNOTY	COCKNEY ACCENT
ACCCDEEEINNNS	INCANDESCENCE
ACCCDEEHILMRR	CHARMED CIRCLE
ACCCDEEHKORST	CRACKS THE CODE
ACCCDEIMNRSTU	CIRCUMSTANCED
ACCCDEINORTTT	DIRECT CONTACT
ACCCDEINORTTU	CREDIT ACCOUNT
ACCCDEKLOORRS	OLD CROCKS RACE
ACCCEEELNNOSV	CONVALESCENCE
ACCCEEFFIOPST	ACCEPTS OFFICE
ACCCEEHIILRRT	ELECTRIC CHAIR
ACCCEEHKLSTTU	CUTS THE CACKLE
ACCCEEIILNOSS	SOCIAL SCIENCE
ACCCEEIILSSST	ECCLESIASTICS
ACCCEEILLNRTY	ECCENTRICALLY
ACCCEFFIILRRT	TRAFFIC CIRCLE
ACCCEFKNORTYY	CRAFTY COCKNEY
ACCCEHIILMOPR	MICROCEPHALIC
ACCCEHIILNNOR	CHILI CON CARNE
ACCCEHIINORTT	ARCHITECTONIC
ACCCEHIIOPRRT	CHOIR PRACTICE
ACCCEHKLORSTW	CLOCK-WATCHERS
ACCCEHLNOORRT	CHORAL CONCERT
ACCCEIMMNOOOR	MACROECONOMIC
ACCCEIMNNOOTT	COME IN CONTACT
ACCCEIMNRSSTU	CIRCUMSTANCES
ACCCEINNORSTT	ACTS IN CONCERT
ACCCEKLNORSTU	ACCOUNTS CLERK
ACCCELLNORRUY	LOCAL CURRENCY
ACCCELOOPRSTT	STREPTOCOCCAL
ACCCENNOOOVVX	CONCAVO-CONVEX
ACCCGHIKLNOTW	CLOCK-WATCHING
ACCCGHIKNOPST	SPATCHCOCKING
ACCCHILOOPSTY	STAPHYLOCOCCI
ACCCIILMMORT	MICROCLIMATIC
ACCCIIKKLOSTT	COCKTAIL STICK
ACCDDEEEEFNOT	CONCEDE DEFEAT
ACCDDEEEEHHRS	CHEDDAR CHEESE
ACCDDEEEFIIRS	SACRED EDIFICE
ACCDDEEEHHKLU	CHUCKLEHEADED

ACCDDEEFHINNO	HAD CONFIDENCE
ACCDDEEHIILLT	DELICATE CHILD
ACCDDEEIORRST	CREATE DISCORD
ACCDDFKLLOOOO	LOAD OF OLD COCK
ACCDEEEEMNSUX	EXCUSE-ME DANCE
ACCDEEEFFIOTV	AFFECTED VOICE
ACCDEEEFFNOSU	CAUSED OFFENCE
ACCDEEEFHOPRT	FORCED THE PACE
ACCDEEEFIIOPV	PIECE OF ADVICE
ACCDEEEFINNRT	REFINED ACCENT
ACCDEEEFINORS	CONFEDERACIES
ACCDEEEHKLRST	CLEAR THE DECKS
	CLEARS THE DECK
ACCDEEEHLNNRS	SLENDER CHANCE
ACCDEEEIJPRRU	RACE PREJUDICE
ACCDEEEINOPST	ESCAPED NOTICE
ACCDEEENNNRST	TRANSCENDENCE
ACCDEEFHINNOS	HAS CONFIDENCE
ACCDEEFIMNORS	CONFIRMED CASE
ACCDEEFINNOPS	CONFINED SPACE
ACCDEEGHNORSU	CHANGED COURSE
ACCDEEGINNSSY	DENYING ACCESS
ACCDEEHHILLNT	CLINCH THE DEAL
ACCDEEHHORRST	SCORCHED EARTH
ACCDEEHHRSSSU	ARCHDUCHESSES
ACCDEEHILLOPR	DELPHIC ORACLE
ACCDEEHILOTTU	DELICATE TOUCH
ACCDEEHINOSTU	OUTSIDE CHANCE
ACCDEEHKLORRT	ROCK THE CRADLE
ACCDEEHKLPRST	DESPATCH CLERK
ACCDEEHNOPRST	SECOND CHAPTER
ACCDEEHPRTTTU	ACCEPTED TRUTH
ACCDEEIILLSWY	CECIL DAY LEWIS
ACCDEEIILNOST	OCCIDENTALISE
ACCDEEIILNOTZ	OCCIDENTALIZE
ACCDEEIILRRTY	RIDE A TRICYCLE
ACCDEEIKKOPPT	PICKED A POCKET
ACCDEEIKLLRRT	ARTICLED CLERK
ACCDEEIKLPRTY	PLAYED CRICKET
ACCDEEILLRRSS	CLERICAL DRESS
ACCDEEILNOPSY	ENCYCLOPEDIAS
ACCDEEILORRTY	RODE A TRICYCLE
ACCDEEINNOOPT	CONCEDE A POINT
ACCDEEINNOPRT	ACCIDENT PRONE
	ACCIDENT-PRONE
ACCDEELNOOPRR	PLACE ON RECORD
ACCDEEMORSSTY	COMEDY ACTRESS
ACCDEENNNRSTY	TRANSCENDENCY
ACCDEFFIILSTU	DIFFICULT CASE
ACCDEFHMNOORS	SECOND OF MARCH
ACCDEFILMNORT	ARMED CONFLICT
ACCDEGHLNOORU	CHANGED COLOUR
ACCDEGIINORTT	DECORTICATING
ACCDEHHIKLLTY	LATCHKEY CHILD
ACCDEHHILOPRY	HYDROCEPHALIC
ACCDEHHNRRSUW	CHURCH WARDENS
	CHURCHWARDENS
ACCDEHHNRSTTU	ATTENDS CHURCH
ACCDEHHORRRRY	CHERRY ORCHARD
ACCDEHIIKLLRY	CRY LIKE A CHILD
ACCDEHIKNOOPS	PICK AND CHOOSE
ACCDEHILLMOOS	MEDICAL SCHOOL
ACCDEHINOORTW	WITH ONE ACCORD
ACCDEHKLLOORU	COLOURED CHALK
ACCDEHLLOORTT	CALL THE DOCTOR
ACCDEHLNOOTTU	HELD TO ACCOUNT
ACCDEHLOOOPRT	CHOCOLATE DROP
ACCDEIIKLOOPS	KALEIDOSCOPIC
ACCDEIILMNOST	OCCIDENTALISM
ACCDEIILOPRRU	CRUCIAL PERIOD
ACCDEIINOORTT	DECORTICATION

ACCDEIKLORSST	COCKTAIL DRESS	ACCEEGINNORTV	GIVEN A CONCERT
ACCDEILLMOPTY	COMPLICATEDLY	ACCEEGINORSTV	GIVES A CONCERT
ACCDEILMMOSUY	MUSICAL COMEDY	ACCEEGINPRRSS	PRINCESS GRACE
ACCDEILMNOPTU	UNCOMPLICATED	ACCEEGLLNRRUY	LEGAL CURRENCY
ACCDEINOPRRTU	PRACTICE ROUND	ACCEEHHLOORST	SCHOOLTEACHER
ACCDEIOORRSTT	DECORTICATES	ACCEEHHMMOOTY	CATHY COME HOME
ACCDEMOOPPRTW	POWDER COMPACT	ACCEEHHNRRSTU	EASTERN CHURCH
ACCDENNORRTTU	UNDER CONTRACT	ACCEEHHNSSTTU	CATCHES THE SUN
ACCDENOORTTTU	CONTRACTED OUT	ACCEEHHPRSTTU	CUP THAT CHEERS
ACCDEOORSSSTU	ROAD TO SUCCESS	ACCEEHIKMNTT	TICKET MACHINE
ACCDGIINNORTT	CONTRADICTING	ACCEEHIIRRTTT	THEATRE CRITIC
ACCDHHINOOPRY	HYPOCHONDRIAC	ACCEEHILLLOPT	CALL THE POLICE
ACCDHIILORSTV	CLAVICHORDIST	ACCEEHILLNOTY	ACETYLCHOLINE
ACCDHIILPRSUU	SULPHURIC ACID	ACCEEHILMNORU	NEUROCHEMICAL
ACCDHIMNOPSYY	PSYCHODYNAMIC	ACCEEHILMNRTT	TECHNICAL TERM
ACCDHILNOOOTTU	HOLD TO ACCOUNT	ACCEEHILMOPRT	PETROCHEMICAL
ACCDIIINORSTY	IDIOSYNCRATIC	ACCEEHILNNSST	TECHNICALNESS
ACCDIIJLORTUU	JUDICIAL COURT	ACCEEHILNPRRS	PRINCE CHARLES
ACCDIILLLNRYY	CYLINDRICALLY	ACCEEHIPPRRSU	PURCHASE PRICE
ACCDIIMMNNOOU	INCOMMUNICADO	ACCEEHNOORSST	CROSS THE OCEAN
ACCDIINNOORTT	CONTRADICTION	ACCEEHORRSTTY	OYSTERCATCHER
ACCDINOORRSTT	CONTRADICTORS	ACCEEIILLSTTY	CELESTIAL CITY
ACCDINOORRTTY	CONTRADICTORY	ACCEEILMMNSU	ECUMENICALISM
ACCDINOPSSSTT	PICTS AND SCOTS	ACCEEIILMMORS	COMMERCIALISE
ACCDMNOORRTTU	TRAM CONDUCTOR	ACCEEIILMMORZ	COMMERCIALIZE
ACCEEEEFHLNRT	CLEAR THE FENCE	ACCEEIILNOPRT	ELECTRIC PIANO
ACCEEEEGHOSTT	COTTAGE CHEESE	ACCEEIILNRRTT	ELECTRIC TRAIN
ACCEEEEGINNRT	ANCIENT GREECE	ACCEEIILORSSV	SOCIAL SERVICE
ACCEEEELLNPRX	PAR EXCELLENCE	ACCEEIIOPRRTV	RECIPROCATIVE
ACCEEEELMORRT	ACCELEROMETER	ACCEEIKLNOPRS	COCKER SPANIEL
ACCEEEFFILNOR	OFFICE CLEANER	ACCEEIKNORSST	CRICKET SEASON
ACCEEEFFNOSSU	CAUSES OFFENCE	ACCEEIILLNOOT	LOCAL ELECTION
ACCEEEFGIINNOO	CHANGE OF SCENE	ACCEEIILLORRRR	CLERICAL ERROR
ACCEEEFHHNRRT	FRENCH TEACHER	ACCEEILMNOOUV	ECONOMIC VALUE
ACCEEEFHHNRST	TEACHES FRENCH	ACCEEILNOPSTU	CONCEPTUALISE
ACCEEEFHOPRST	FORCES THE PACE	ACCEEILNOPTTT	PLATETECTONIC
ACCEEEFIMORRR	CAREER OF CRIME	ACCEEILNOPTUZ	CONCEPTUALIZE
ACCEEEGHIMNNT	CHANCE MEETING	ACCEEILNOSTTU	COUNCIL ESTATE
ACCEEEGHIRRSV	SERVICE CHARGE	ACCEEILNQSTUY	ACQUIESCENTLY
ACCEEEGLLMNRY	EMERGENCY CALL	ACCEEILORRRTZ	ELECTRIC RAZOR
ACCEEEHHHIOTV	HAVE THE CHOICE	ACCEEILORSTTT	ELECTROSTATIC
ACCEEEHILLNPT	TELENCEPHALIC	ACCEEIMMMNOTUX	EXCOMMUNICATE
ACCEEEHILMNPS	MESENCEPHALIC	ACCEEIMOPPRRS	COMPARE PRICES
ACCEEEHILNOOV	LEAVE NO CHOICE	ACCEEINNORTTV	CONCENTRATIVE
ACCEEEHMNNOOR	ONE MORE CHANCE	ACCEEINOPRTTV	CONTRACEPTIVE
ACCEEEHRRSSTT	STRETCHER CASE	ACCEEINORRTTUV	COUNTERACTIVE
ACCEEEIINPRRS	PRICE INCREASE	ACCEELLMMOORU	MACROMOLECULE
ACCEEEIIRSTVV	ACTIVE SERVICE	ACCEELLOORRTT	RATE COLLECTOR
ACCEEEIMNRSST	SCIENCE MASTER	ACCEELLOSSTTX	COLLECTS TAXES
ACCEEEINOPSST	ESCAPES NOTICE	ACCEELMNOPSTY	SELECT COMPANY
ACCEEFFIILRSS	SELF-SACRIFICE	ACCEELMOOOSST	COMES TO A CLOSE
ACCEEFFILNORT	CENTRAL OFFICE	ACCEELNNOSSTT	CONTACT LENSES
ACCEEFGIIINST	SCIENTIFIC AGE	ACCEELNNOSSTV	CONVALESCENTS
ACCEEFGIKMORT	GAME OF CRICKET	ACCEELOPRRSSY	SOCCER PLAYERS
ACCEEFGINNORT	FOREIGN ACCENT	ACCEEMNORRSTT	CONCERT MASTER
ACCEEFHIKMNRR	CHICKEN FARMER		CONCERTMASTER
ACCEEFILNOOTV	ACT OF VIOLENCE	ACCEEMNORSTTU	ACCOUTREMENTS
ACCEEFIMNOORT	CAME INTO FORCE	ACCEEMOOPPRRS	COMES A CROPPER
ACCEEFKLOPRST	LACK OF RESPECT	ACCEENORRRSTW	CORRECT ANSWER
ACCEEGHHIKMNW	CHECKWEIGHMAN	ACCEENORRSTUY	SCORE A CENTURY
ACCEEGHHKLNOT	CHANGE THE LOCK	ACCEENPPRRRUY	PAPER CURRENCY
ACCEEGHILNNST	ENGLISH ACCENT	ACCEFFFHIINOO	CHAIN OF OFFICE
ACCEEGHINSTTU	TAUGHT SCIENCE	ACCEFFIILOSUY	EFFICACIOUSLY
ACCEEGHKNOSTX	STOCK EXCHANGE	ACCEFFNOORRTU	CUT OFF A CORNER
ACCEEGHNNORTU	COUNTERCHANGE	ACCEFGHIORSST	RIGHT OF ACCESS
ACCEEGHNORRTU	COUNTERCHARGE	ACCEFGIIINRTT	CERTIFICATING
ACCEEGHNORSSU	CHANGES COURSE	ACCEFHKKLOOTW	COCK OF THE WALK
ACCEEGIKMNRRT	CRACK REGIMENT	ACCEFIIINOPST	SPECIFICATION
ACCEEGILNORRT	ELECTRIC ORGAN	ACCEFIIINORTT	CERTIFICATION
ACCEEGINNORSS	RECOGNISANCES		RECTIFICATION
ACCEEGINNORSZ	RECOGNIZANCES	ACCEFIIINPRST	INTRASPECIFIC

855

ACCEFIIKLNSTT	IN A CLEFT STICK
ACCEFIINNNORS	CONNIE FRANCIS
ACCEFIIORRTTY	CERTIFICATORY
ACCEFILMNNORY	FAMILY CONCERN
ACCEFILNNOOTT	FAIL TO CONNECT
ACCEFINNOORTY	CONFECTIONARY
ACCEFIOOPRTTU	OUT OF PRACTICE
ACCEFLMNSSSUU	SUCCESSFUL MAN
ACCEFOORSTTUY	ACT OF COURTESY
ACCEGGIKNORRS	GOING CRACKERS
ACCEGGILLOSTW	GLASGOW CELTIC
ACCEGHHILLRUV	VILLAGE CHURCH
ACCEGHHIOOPRR	CHOREOGRAPHIC
ACCEGHHMOORTU	CHARGE TOO MUCH
ACCEGHIILOPRX	LEXICOGRAPHIC
ACCEGHIIMNORT	MICRO-TEACHING
ACCEGHIIMNTTX	EXCITING MATCH
ACCEGHILLNOOT	TECHNOLOGICAL
ACCEGHILMOPYY	HYPOGLYCAEMIC
ACCEGHLNOORSU	CHANGES COLOUR
ACCEGIIINNNORT	CONCERTINAING
ACCEGIINNOOPS	GOES ON A PICNIC
ACCEGIINOPRRT	RECIPROCATING
ACCEGIINORRST	ARCTIC REGIONS
ACCEGILLNNOOY	ONCOGENICALLY
ACCEGILLNNOTU	CANCELLING OUT
ACCEGILLNORYY	CRYOGENICALLY
ACCEGILMNOORT	CONGLOMERATIC
ACCEGILNOPRSY	PLAYING SOCCER
ACCEGILNSSSSU	SIGNAL SUCCESS
ACCEGINNNNOTU	COUNTENANCING
ACCEGINNNORTT	CONCENTRATING
ACCEGINNORTTU	COUNTERACTING
ACCEGINNRRSUY	GAINS CURRENCY
ACCEGINOORRTT	GERONTOCRATIC
ACCEGINOPRRST	CATERING CORPS
ACCEGINPRSTTU	CUTTING CAPERS
ACCEGLNORRSUY	CURSORY GLANCE
ACCEHHHNOOPTT	CATCH ON THE HOP
ACCEHHIILMOST	HISTOCHEMICAL
ACCEHHIKPRSTW	CRACKS THE WHIP
ACCEHHILMOOPT	PHOTOCHEMICAL
ACCEHHILOOPRT	ORTHOCEPHALIC
ACCEHHILOSSTZ	ESCHSCHOLTZIA
ACCEHHIMNOPSS	CHESS CHAMPION
ACCEHHLLRSSUZ	CHARLES SCHULZ
ACCEHIIILMMNO	MICHAEL CIMINO
ACCEHIILLNSST	CALLISTHENICS
ACCEHIINNOOST	CHOSE IN ACTION
ACCEHIKLLMOOT	MILK CHOCOLATE
ACCEHIKLPRSWY	PHYSICAL WRECK
ACCEHILLOOPSS	SPECIAL SCHOOL
ACCEHILMNORTW	CLAIM THE CROWN
ACCEHILMOPRSS	ACCOMPLISHERS
ACCEHILMOPTYY	POLYCYTHAEMIC
ACCEHILOOPPRU	POPULAR CHOICE
ACCEHILOORSTY	CHORAL SOCIETY
ACCEHIMMNOORT	MOTOR MECHANIC
ACCEHINNNOPST	PANTECHNICONS
ACCEHIOOPSSTT	TACHISTOSCOPE
ACCEHIORRSSSU	RICH AS CROESUS
ACCEHKNNOOOST	TOOK NO CHANCES
ACCEHNORSTTTU	TRUST TO CHANCE
ACCEIIILLNRSV	CLIVE SINCLAIR
ACCEIIKLNOSTW	ANTICLOCKWISE
ACCEIIKNNPRST	PANIC-STRICKEN
ACCEIILMMMORS	COMMERCIALISM
ACCEIILMMORST	COMMERCIALIST
ACCEIILMNOSSS	NEOCLASSICISM
ACCEIILNOSSST	NEOCLASSICIST
ACCEIILPRRSTU	SUPERCRITICAL

ACCEIIMMMORST	COMMITS A CRIME
ACCEIIMMNNOTUV	COMMUNICATIVE
ACCEIIMNNOPRS	COPERNICANISM
ACCEIINNNOPTW	WENT ON A PICNIC
ACCEIINOOPRRT	RECIPROCATION
ACCEIINOPRTTU	ACTION PICTURE
ACCEIIOPPRSSU	PERSPICACIOUS
ACCEIKPRSSTTU	SUSPECT A TRICK
ACCEILLNOORTT	ART COLLECTION
ACCEILLNOTTTU	LITTLE ACCOUNT
ACCEILMMNORTU	CRUCIAL MOMENT
ACCEILMNORSTU	COUNTERCLAIMS
ACCEIMNNOSTTU	ANCIENT CUSTOM
ACCEINNNOORTT	CONCENTRATION
ACCEINNOOOPRT	PIANO CONCERTO
ACCEINNOOPRTT	CONTRACEPTION
ACCEINNOORRTY	CONCRETIONARY
ACCEINNOORSSY	CONCESSIONARY
ACCEINNOORTTU	COUNTERACTION
ACCEINNOOSSTX	TAX CONCESSION
ACCEINOOPPRTU	PREOCCUPATION
ACCEINOPPRSSU	PERCUSSION CAP
ACCEJLLNORTUY	CONJECTURALLY
ACCELLMOPSSTT	COLLECT STAMPS
ACCENNOORRSTT	CONCENTRATORS
ACCENOPRRSSTU	COUNTERSCARPS
ACCFFGHINORST	SCRATCHING OFF
ACCFFIINOORTT	FACT OR FICTION
ACCFHIIMNORTT	FRICTION MATCH
ACCFKNOOOOTTU	TOOK ACCOUNT OF
ACCGGHHIINSTT	CATCHING SIGHT
ACCGHHHHIMNRU	HIGH CHURCHMAN
ACCGHHINOOPRR	CHRONOGRAPHIC
ACCGHHINORSST	CROSS-HATCHING
	CROSSHATCHING
ACCGHIIILNOTZ	CATHOLICIZING
ACCGHIIINPRST	SCINTIGRAPHIC
ACCGHILLMNOPS	ACCOMPLISHING
ACCGHILLNOOOR	CHRONOLOGICAL
ACCGHILLOOPSY	PSYCHOLOGICAL
ACCGHINORSTTU	SCRATCHING OUT
ACCGHIOPPRRTY	CRYPTOGRAPHIC
ACCGIIILNRRSU	CIRCULARISING
ACCGIIILNRRUZ	CIRCULARIZING
ACCGIILLMOOSU	MUSICOLOGICAL
ACCGIILLOOOTX	TOXICOLOGICAL
ACCGIILMORRSU	MICROSURGICAL
ACCGIIMMNNOTU	COMMUNICATING
ACCGIINNNORTT	CONTRACTING IN
ACCGIKKNNOOOS	COCKING A SNOOK
ACCGILLLMOOYY	MYCOLOGICALLY
ACCGILLLOOTYY	CYTOLOGICALLY
ACCGILLOOOPRT	PROCTOLOGICAL
ACCGIMMOPRRTY	CRYPTOGRAMMIC
ACCGINORSSTTU	CUTTING ACROSS
ACCHIILMOSSST	SCHOLASTICISM
ACCHIILNOPRSU	PARISH COUNCIL
ACCHIIMNOOPRT	ACTINOMORPHIC
ACCHILLOPSTYY	PSYCHOTICALLY
ACCHILMOOPRTY	POLYCHROMATIC
ACCHIMMNOOORT	MONOCHROMATIC
ACCHIMOOPSSTY	PSYCHOSOMATIC
ACCHIOOPRRRST	CHIROPRACTORS
ACCIIILLLLRTY	CRITICALLY ILL
ACCIIILLNOOST	COLONIALISTIC
ACCIIILNNORTU	IN CIRCULATION
ACCIIILNOPTYY	PINOCYTICALLY
ACCIILMNOOPST	COMPLICATIONS
ACCIILMNOORRTU	CRIMINAL COURT
ACCIILNORTTTY	CONTRACTILITY
ACCIIMMNNOOTU	COMMUNICATION

ACCIIMMNORSTU	ROMANTIC MUSIC	ACDDELLLNOOOU	ALL ONE COULD DO
ACCIINNOOOSST	CONSOCIATIONS	ACDDENOORSTUU	SCOUTED AROUND
ACCIIOORRSSTV	VICTORIA CROSS	ACDDENORRUVWW	DOWNWARD CURVE
ACCIJLNNNOOTU	CONJUNCTIONAL	ACDDFMMNOOORW	WORD OF COMMAND
ACCILLOORSTUU	SOCIOCULTURAL	ACDDHIMNORSYY	HYDRODYNAMICS
ACCILMNNOOTTY	CONCOMITANTLY	ACDDIIINNNOOP	CANDID OPINION
ACCILMORRSSTY	MICROCRYSTALS	ACDDILMNNOTUY	MIDLAND COUNTY
ACCIMMNOORSTU	COMMUNICATORS	ACDDIMNORSSUW	WORDS AND MUSIC
ACCIMMNOORTUY	COMMUNICATORY	ACDDIOPRRSTTY	DIRTY POSTCARD
ACCINPRSTTUUU	ACUPUNCTURIST	ACDEEEEFILNSV	FALSE EVIDENCE
ACCLLORRSSTUU	CROSS-CULTURAL	ACDEEEEHHNRST	REACHES THE END
ACCNNOORTTTUU	TURN TO ACCOUNT	ACDEEEEHINNSW	CHEESE AND WINE
ACCNOOPSTTTUU	PUTS TO ACCOUNT	ACDEEEEHLNOPS	HELD ONE'S PEACE
ACCNOORRSSTUY	ACROSS COUNTRY	ACDEEEEHNNSTT	DEATH SENTENCE
ACDDDEEEHILOT	LOADED THE DICE	ACDEEEEHNOPST	OPENED THE CASE
ACDDDEEHILRRT	RETARDED CHILD	ACDEEEEHOSSTT	TOASTED CHEESE
ACDDDEEHNOORS	DODECAHEDRONS	ACDEEEEILRUVV	VALUE RECEIVED
ACDDDEHKKMOOS	SMOKED HADDOCK	ACDEEEEINPRSS	INCREASE SPEED
ACDDDEIKLNSSU	KISS AND CUDDLE	ACDEEEEINPRST	RESTED IN PEACE
ACDDDHIIILOOOV	CHILDHOOD DAYS	ACDEEEEMNQRSU	DREAM SEQUENCE
ACDDEEEEHHNRT	REACHED THE END	ACDEEEENRRSST	RENE DESCARTES
ACDDEEEEFFIORV	OFFERED ADVICE	ACDEEEEOPRRST	RESTORED PEACE
ACDDEEEEFHNRSU	SCHADENFREUDE	ACDEEEEFFIOPRR	OFFERED A PRICE
ACDDEEEHHOSTU	DETACHED HOUSE	ACDEEEFGHINTT	FEEDING THE CAT
ACDDEEEILNRST	DECENTRALISED	ACDEEEFHKLOST	LOCKED THE SAFE
	LICENSED TRADE	ACDEEEFIMNRRU	CAME UNDER FIRE
ACDDEEEILNRSU	DENUCLEARISED	ACDEEEFINORTV	CONFEDERATIVE
ACDDEEEILNRTZ	DECENTRALIZED	ACDEEEGGLNOPU	ENGAGED COUPLE
ACDDEEEILNRUZ	DENUCLEARIZED	ACDEEEGHHNRTY	DENY THE CHARGE
ACDDEEEILRSTV	SEALED VERDICT	ACDEEEGHIRTTV	GAVE THE CREDIT
ACDDEEEINNNRT	NICE AND TENDER	ACDEEEGHLOSTT	CLOSED THE GATE
ACDDEEEKMNOPR	PROMENADE DECK	ACDEEEGHORTTT	ACTED TOGETHER
ACDDEEEELNNOPT	PLACE END TO END	ACDEEEGIIKNSV	SEEKING ADVICE
ACDDEEEFFNOOPS	DOFFED ONE'S CAP	ACDEEEGINRSSV	DESERVING CASE
ACDDEEGIKNNOR	DEAD RECKONING	ACDEEEGMNRRWY	EMERGENCY WARD
ACDDEEGINNORS	SECOND READING	ACDEEEHIIIKLST	HEALED THE SICK
ACDDEEGNOPRRU	GARDEN PRODUCE	ACDEEEHHLLSST	HELD THE SCALES
ACDDEEHHIITTW	DICE WITH DEATH	ACDEEEHHOPRTT	REACHED THE TOP
ACDDEEHHILNOT	COLD IN THE HEAD	ACDEEEHIINNTU	IN THE AUDIENCE
ACDDEEHIPRRST	DESPATCH RIDER	ACDEEEHIKMPTT	PICKED THE TEAM
ACDDEEHNORRSU	SCORE A HUNDRED	ACDEEEHIKPRST	ASKED THE PRICE
ACDDEEIIJNUVW	JAUNDICED VIEW	ACDEEEHIKRTTT	TAKE THE CREDIT
ACDDEEIJMNSTU	DEMAND JUSTICE	ACDEEEHINNPST	TINNED PEACHES
ACDDEEILLMSSS	MIDDLE CLASSES	ACDEEEHINNSTT	INDECENT HASTE
ACDDEEILLORTW	ALLOWED CREDIT	ACDEEEHINRRUV	UNDERACHIEVER
ACDDEEILNOPRR	PLACED IN ORDER	ACDEEEHIORSTT	TEACHES TO RIDE
ACDDEEIMORSTT	DOMESTIC TRADE	ACDEEEHLLNTTU	CALLED THE TUNE
ACDDEEIMRRSTY	DRASTIC REMEDY	ACDEEEHLNOOPS	HOLD ONES PEACE
ACDDEEIMRSTTT	DICTATED TERMS	ACDEEEHMNNPRST	SPEED MERCHANT
ACDDEELLNORUU	DUODENAL ULCER	ACDEEEHNORSTT	THE SECOND-RATE
ACDDEELLOORRT	CALLED TO ORDER	ACDEEEHNPRSTX	CHEST EXPANDER
ACDDEEMNNORTU	COUNTERMANDED	ACDEEEHOPTTUY	THE DEUCE TO PAY
ACDDEFGHINOST	FACING THE ODDS	ACDEEEHORRSTU	TERRACED HOUSE
ACDDEFGILNNOR	FORCED LANDING	ACDEEEHORSSST	CROSSED THE SEA
ACDDEFGINORSY	SCARED OF DYING	ACDEEEHORSSTU	REDUCE TO ASHES
ACDDEFHIINRSS	DISFRANCHISED	ACDEEEIINOPSS	SAID ONE'S PIECE
ACDDEGHILNNRR	GRANDCHILDREN	ACDEEEIIORRRV	RADIO RECEIVER
ACDDEGHILNORS	HOLDING SACRED	ACDEEEILNRSST	DECENTRALISES
ACDDEHIJNOTWY	DANCED WITH JOY	ACDEEEILNRSSU	DENUCLEARISES
ACDDEHILNNTUW	UNWANTED CHILD	ACDEEEILNRSTZ	DECENTRALIZES
ACDDEHILSSTUY	TUESDAYS CHILD	ACDEEEILNRSUZ	DENUCLEARIZES
ACDDEHINOOPST	DODECAPHONIST	ACDEEEILNSSST	DELICATESSENS
ACDDEHNOOPPRR	DROPPED ANCHOR	ACDEEEIMMNNOOS	MADE ECONOMIES
ACDDEIIIMNRST	DISCRIMINATED	ACDEEEIMOPRRT	MODERATE PRICE
ACDDEIIILLNRTY	DENDRITICALLY	ACDEEEIMRSTTU	CRUDE ESTIMATE
ACDDEIIINNORTT	INDOCTRINATED	ACDEEEKLNPSSS	SLACKENS SPEED
ACDDEIKKPSTUU	KICKED UP A DUST	ACDEEEKNORRTV	COVERED MARKET
ACDDEIKLOORRT	DOCTOR KILDARE	ACDEEEKNORRRY	READY RECKONER
ACDDEIMNORTTU	DIAMOND CUTTER	ACDEEELLNOOSV	LEAVES ONE COLD
ACDDEINORSTTU	TRADE DISCOUNT	ACDEEELLOPRTT	ELECTROPLATED
ACDDEKKNNOORU	KNOCKED AROUND	ACDEEELMNOPSS	COMPASS NEEDLE

ACDEEEELMOOPST	PLEASED TO COME	ACDEEHIINNSTT	IN THE DISTANCE
ACDEEEELMORTTT	METAL DETECTOR	ACDEEHIIRRTVW	DRIVE WITH CARE
ACDEEEELNOPPSY	CLAPPED EYES ON	ACDEEHILLOPTT	COATED THE PILL
ACDEEEELNPRRSU	SUPERCALENDER	ACDEEHILORRTT	TETRACHLORIDE
ACDEEEELOPPRRU	POPULAR DECREE	ACDEEHIMMNORT	TIME MARCHED ON
ACDEEELOPRSST	APOSTLES CREED	ACDEEHIMNOPST	MADE ONE'S PITCH
ACDEEELORRSTU	ALTERED COURSE	ACDEEHIMNPRST	MARCHED IN STEP
ACDEEEELORSSTT	SETTLED A SCORE	ACDEEHIMOPRRT	ARC DE TRIOMPHE
ACDEEENNOPPRR	PREPONDERANCE	ACDEEHINNRSST	DISENCHANTERS
ACDEEENNRSTTU	ENDURANCE TEST	ACDEEHINRRSTT	THIRTEEN CARDS
ACDEEENORRSTW	SET A NEW RECORD	ACDEEHKORSTTT	STROKED THE CAT
ACDEEEORRSTTU	REDUCE TO TEARS	ACDEEHLNNOORR	HOLE AND CORNER
ACDEEFGIILMNT	MAGNETIC FIELD	ACDEEHLORTUWY	CLOUDY WEATHER
ACDEEFGILNORW	GALE-FORCE WIND	ACDEEHMNORTWW	WRETCHED WOMAN
ACDEEFGINNORT	CONFEDERATING	ACDEEIIIMNNRV	DRIVE-IN CINEMA
ACDEEFHHIKNRS	HANDKERCHIEFS	ACDEEIIKNNPRW	PICKED A WINNER
ACDEEFHIIMNOS	DONE A MISCHIEF	ACDEEIILLNNNP	INCLINED PLANE
ACDEEFHIIMOSS	DOES A MISCHIEF	ACDEEIILNOPTT	DELICATE POINT
ACDEEFHILLPUV	HELPFUL ADVICE	ACDEEIILNORSY	EARLY DECISION
ACDEEFHLMORRT	FROM THE CRADLE	ACDEEIILNOSTZ	SECTIONALIZED
ACDEEFHLNRSTW	LEFT-HAND SCREW	ACDEEIILPRTUV	REDUPLICATIVE
ACDEEFHLORTTU	CUT FOR THE LEAD	ACDEEIILPRTVY	PREDICATIVELY
ACDEEFHNNOORS	FORCE ONES HAND	ACDEEIIMNNRTY	INDETERMINACY
ACDEEFHNORRTW	THENCEFORWARD	ACDEEIINNORST	CONTAINERISED
ACDEEFHORSTTY	DEFRAY THE COST		INCONSIDERATE
ACDEEFIILNPRS	SPECIAL FRIEND	ACDEEIINNORTZ	CONTAINERIZED
ACDEEFIILNPRT	INFLATED PRICE	ACDEEIINOPRTT	DECREPITATION
ACDEEFIKLOPRW	PICKED A FLOWER	ACDEEIJNSTUWY	SWEET AND JUICY
ACDEEFILNNOST	SELF-CONTAINED	ACDEEIKLOOPSS	KALEIDOSCOPES
ACDEEFILNORST	CONFEDERALIST	ACDEEILLMORRT	ALL-TIME RECORD
ACDEEFILOORST	FAILED TO SCORE	ACDEEILLNNSTY	CLANDESTINELY
ACDEEFILRRRUV	CAREFUL DRIVER	ACDEEILLOTTTW	TWICE-TOLD TALE
ACDEEFINNOORT	CONFEDERATION	ACDEEILMMSSTY	DECIMAL SYSTEM
ACDEEFKMORRSY	ASKED FOR MERCY	ACDEEILMNORSS	COMRADELINESS
ACDEEFLMOPRRY	PLEAD FOR MERCY	ACDEEILMNPSST	DISPLACEMENTS
ACDEEFLOORTTV	DROVE OF CATTLE	ACDEEILMOPRRU	MARRIED COUPLE
ACDEEFMNORRRY	ERRAND OF MERCY	ACDEEILNNNOPT	PLEAD INNOCENT
ACDEEFNNORRTY	FORCED AN ENTRY	ACDEEILNNORWW	WINDOW CLEANER
ACDEEFNOORSWY	FORCED ONE'S WAY	ACDEEILNOPRRS	PLACES IN ORDER
ACDEEFNORRRTW	CENTRE FORWARD	ACDEEILNORSTY	CONSIDERATELY
	CENTRE-FORWARD	ACDEEILNORTUV	COUNTERVAILED
ACDEEFOOPPRRR	PAPER OF RECORD	ACDEEILNPPRRU	PERPENDICULAR
ACDEEGGINRRST	GREETINGS CARD	ACDEEILOPPRSU	PILED UP A SCORE
ACDEEGHHINORW	WEIGHED ANCHOR	ACDEEILOPRRTY	DEPRECATORILY
ACDEEGHHNORSS	CHANGED HORSES	ACDEEIMMNRSTT	MINCED MATTERS
ACDEEGHHOOPRR	CHOREOGRAPHED	ACDEEIMMNORSSX	CROSS-EXAMINED
ACDEEGHIIRRTW	CARRIED WEIGHT	ACDEEIMNORSTU	DOCUMENTARIES
ACDEEGHILNRRU	HURRIED GLANCE	ACDEEIMOPRSS	COMPRESSED AIR
ACDEEGHINOSTT	GO THE DISTANCE	ACDEEIMORRSST	DEMOCRATISERS
ACDEEGHNOPRS	CHANGED PERSON	ACDEEIMORRSTZ	DEMOCRATIZERS
ACDEEGHNORRUY	GREYHOUND RACE	ACDEEIMOSSTTT	ESTIMATED COST
ACDEEGHOORSUW	SHOWED COURAGE	ACDEEIMRSSTTT	DICTATES TERMS
ACDEEGIILMNSS	MEDICINE GLASS	ACDEEINNORSSS	SECONDARINESS
ACDEEGIIMORST	TRAGICOMEDIES	ACDEEINRSSUVY	SUNDAY SERVICE
ACDEEGIINORSV	GRAVE DECISION	ACDEEIRSSSTTU	ACUTE DISTRESS
ACDEEGIINPRTT	DECREPITATING	ACDEEKNORSSTX	DRANK TO EXCESS
ACDEEGIILNNPRS	SPRING-CLEANED	ACDEELLMPSUU	PULLED A MUSCLE
ACDEEGILNPRTY	DEPRECATINGLY	ACDEELNNORSUU	UNSECURED LOAN
ACDEEGIMMNNOR	COMMANDEERING	ACDEELOPRRTVY	PARTLY COVERED
ACDEEGIMNNRYY	DYNAMIC ENERGY	ACDEEMMNOPSST	PASSED COMMENT
ACDEEGINNRSTT	STANDING ERECT	ACDEEMNNORRUV	UNDER-COVER MAN
ACDEEGINOORST	SEEING A DOCTOR		UNDERCOVER MAN
ACDEEGINOPRRT	TAPE RECORDING	ACDEEMNNPRTUU	MEND A PUNCTURE
	TAPE-RECORDING	ACDEEMNOOPRST	COMPARED NOTES
ACDEEGLLMNOTU	LEGAL DOCUMENT	ACDEEMNOPSTTT	SECOND ATTEMPT
ACDEEGLMNOORT	CONGLOMERATED	ACDEEMOPRRTTT	RECORD ATTEMPT
ACDEEGNNOSSTT	DECONGESTANTS	ACDEENOOPRTUY	READY TO POUNCE
ACDEEGNORSSST	GETS ONE'S CARDS	ACDEENORRTTVY	CONVERTED A TRY
ACDEEHHLLOSST	HOLD THE SCALES	ACDEFFHLNOOST	ON THE SCAFFOLD
ACDEEHIILLOPT	DIAL THE POLICE	ACDEFFIILNOOT	FIELD OF ACTION
ACDEEHIILNRRS	RAISE CHILDREN	ACDEFGHHHIILN	HIGHLAND CHIEF

ACDEFGIILNSSY	DECLASSIFYING	ACDEHIINRSSTT	DENTISTS CHAIR
ACDEFGILLRSUY	DISGRACEFULLY	ACDEHIIOPSSTT	SOPHISTICATED
ACDEFHIINRSSS	DISFRANCHISES	ACDEHIJNOSTWY	DANCES WITH JOY
ACDEFHIINRTUW	FACED WITH RUIN	ACDEHIKLNOPSV	PICK AND SHOVEL
ACDEFHILLLOTW	CALL OF THE WILD	ACDEHIKNPRSST	PITCH DARKNESS
ACDEFHILMNRTY	FRIENDLY MATCH	ACDEHIKORRSST	STRIKES A CHORD
ACDEFHILNORTU	CHILD OF NATURE	ACDEHILMNOPTY	ENDOLYMPHATIC
ACDEFHKLORTUW	LUCK OF THE DRAW	ACDEHILMORRTY	HYDROMETRICAL
ACDEFHLNOPRTU	CLAP OF THUNDER	ACDEHILOOPRST	POLISHED ACTOR
ACDEFHMNRRSTU	FRENCH MUSTARD	ACDEHIMMNOPRS	COMMANDERSHIP
ACDEFHOORRSTT	STRETCH OF ROAD	ACDEHIMMNORTY	THERMODYNAMIC
ACDEFHSSTTTUY	STUDY THE FACTS	ACDEHINORSSTT	SHORT DISTANCE
ACDEFIIILNNOS	FINAL DECISION	ACDEHKLMOOTTU	TALKED TOO MUCH
ACDEFIILMNORR	CONFIRMED LIAR	ACDEHLLMNOOST	OLD-CLOTHES MAN
ACDEFIINNSSTT	DISINFECTANTS	ACDEHLNOPRSSU	HAD NO SCRUPLES
ACDEFIINPRTUU	RUN UP A DEFICIT	ACDEHLNOSSTUY	SUNDAY CLOTHES
ACDEFIINRRTUV	UNFAIR VERDICT	ACDEHLNOSTTUY	STAYED TO LUNCH
ACDEFIKKPSSUU	KICKED UP A FUSS	ACDEHNNOPSSSU	CUPS ONE'S HANDS
ACDEFIKNNOSST	ACT OF KINDNESS	ACDEHNOOORTTW	CROWNED A TOOTH
ACDEFIKORRSST	ASKS FOR CREDIT	ACDEHNOORSSSW	SHOW ONES CARDS
ACDEFILLOOSVW	FOLLOWS ADVICE	ACDEHNOSSTTUY	COUNTS THE DAYS
ACDEFILMNNOTU	MALFUNCTIONED	ACDEHOOOPRRTT	PROTOCHORDATE
ACDEFILNNRTUY	UNFRIENDLY ACT	ACDEHOOORSTTW	CARED TWO HOOTS
ACDEFILNOOPRS	SECOND OF APRIL	ACDEIIILMNPSU	MUNICIPALISED
ACDEFINORRTTU	FRIEND AT COURT	ACDEIIILMNPUZ	MUNICIPALIZED
ACDEFIORRRUUV	CURRIED FAVOUR	ACDEIIILNNTTW	IDENTICAL TWIN
ACDEFKLLLOUWW	LAWFUL WEDLOCK	ACDEIIILNRSSV	CIVILIAN DRESS
ACDEFNNOOORST	NOT FOR A SECOND	ACDEIIIMMNOST	NICOTINAMIDES
ACDEGGGKNOSSU	GO AND SUCK EGGS	ACDEIIIMNRSST	DISCRIMINATES
ACDEGGHINNRRU	UNDERCHARGING	ACDEIIJLLPRUY	PREJUDICIALLY
ACDEGGHIOORTW	WITH GOOD GRACE	ACDEIIJMNNORT	MAJOR INCIDENT
ACDEGGIKLNNOW	ACKNOWLEDGING	ACDEIIKLRSTTW	WILD-CAT STRIKE
ACDEGGILLOOPY	PEDOGOGICALLY		WILDCAT STRIKE
ACDEGGINORRSS	GRADE CROSSING	ACDEIIILLQSTTU	CALLED IT QUITS
ACDEGHIILNNOP	NO HIDING PLACE	ACDEIILLNOPRTU	REDUPLICATION
ACDEGHIIMNNRS	MERCHANDISING	ACDEIILNOTTWW	LATTICE WINDOW
ACDEGHIIMNNRY	DRYING MACHINE	ACDEIILNOTTXY	INTOXICATEDLY
ACDEGHIINNNST	DISENCHANTING	ACDEIIMNNOSTW	ANCIENT WISDOM
ACDEGHIIOPRSS	DISCOGRAPHIES	ACDEIIMNOOSTT	DOMESTICATION
ACDEGHIINNOSTU	COUNTING HEADS	ACDEIINNNOSTU	ACTED IN UNISON
ACDEGHINORSTT	DOING A STRETCH		DENUNCIATIONS
ACDEGHIOPRRSS	DISCOGRAPHERS	ACDEIINNOORST	CONSIDERATION
ACDEGHLLNOOSU	SLOUCHED ALONG	ACDEIINNORSTT	INDOCTRINATES
ACDEGIIKLLNST	SLIDING TACKLE	ACDEIINORRSTY	DISCRETIONARY
ACDEGIILLLOOY	IDEOLOGICALLY	ACDEIINOSSTTU	EDUCATIONISTS
ACDEGIILLMRUY	DEMIURGICALLY	ACDEIINRSTTUV	ADVENTURISTIC
ACDEGIILNORST	DOING ARTICLES	ACDEIKKLLQUWY	WALKED QUICKLY
ACDEGIILPQRSU	QUADRIPLEGICS	ACDEIKKNOSSWY	KNOCK SIDEWAYS
ACDEGIIMNORST	DEMOCRATISING	ACDEIKLMPRSTU	MUSTARD PICKLE
ACDEGIIMNORTZ	DEMOCRATIZING	ACDEIKNNNORTT	DARK CONTINENT
ACDEGIIMNOSTT	DOMESTICATING	ACDEILLMNORST	RECALLS TO MIND
ACDEGILLLMNOY	MODELLING CLAY	ACDEILLMNOSTU	METALLIC SOUND
ACDEGILLNOOOT	DEONTOLOGICAL	ACDEILLOORTWY	LOW-CALORY DIET
ACDEGILMNORST	STREAMING COLD	ACDEILLPPSTYY	DYSPEPTICALLY
ACDEGILMNRTUU	LUCID ARGUMENT	ACDEILMNORTUY	DOCUMENTARILY
ACDEGILNNNOSS	DANCING LESSON	ACDEILNNORSTY	CONSTRAINEDLY
ACDEGILNNOORT	GAINED CONTROL	ACDEILNOORRSW	SIR NOEL COWARD
ACDEGILNOORST	IN COLD STORAGE	ACDEILNOOSTTW	CLINT EASTWOOD
ACDEGIMMNNORW	WING COMMANDER	ACDEILNORRSSU	INCURRED A LOSS
ACDEGIMNNNOOT	COMING TO AN END	ACDEILNORSSTW	WINDSOR CASTLE
ACDEGLLLOOORV	GO COLD ALL OVER	ACDEILOOORRRV	COLORADO RIVER
ACDEGLNNOOTUY	COUNTY DONEGAL	ACDEILOOPRRTU	PARTI-COLOURED
ACDEGNNORRTUY	COUNTRY GARDEN	ACDEIMMNNOOST	COMMENDATIONS
ACDEHHHIMRRTT	MARCH THE THIRD	ACDEIMMNNOOST	CONDEMNATIONS
ACDEHHIINORSS	HARSH DECISION	ACDEIMNNOOTTU	DOCUMENTATION
ACDEHHLOPRSUY	HYDROCEPHALUS	ACDEIMNORSTTU	DOCUMENTARIST
ACDEHIIINPRTW	CRIED WITH PAIN	ACDEINNOPSSTU	PASS UNNOTICED
ACDEHIIINRSTZ	CHRISTIANIZED	ACDEINSSSTTUV	ST.VITUSS DANCE
ACDEHIILLRRTT	LITTLE RICHARD	ACDEIORRSSTTU	COURT DISASTER
ACDEHIILNOPRR	PERICHONDRIAL	ACDEKNNORTTUW	WANTED NO TRUCK
ACDEHIINOSSTY	HASTY DECISION	ACDEKNOOORTTU	COOKED TO A TURN

ACDELLNNNOORT	CENTRAL LONDON
ACDEMNOPRRSTU	ONE'S TRUMP CARD
ACDEOPRRSSTUY	DROPS A CURTSEY
ACDFFIIKLSTTU	DIFFICULT TASK
ACDFGIINRTTTU	CUTTING ADRIFT
ACDFGIJNNOORY	DANCING FOR JOY
ACDFGIMNOORRW	COMING FORWARD
ACDFHIILLRTUY	HYDRAULIC LIFT
ACDFHIKOORRRY	RICHARD OF YORK
ACDFIIIMNOOST	MODIFICATIONS
ACDFIIINNOORT	FAIR CONDITION
ACDFILNNOSTUY	DYSFUNCTIONAL
ACDFJMNOOOORTY	COMFORT AND JOY
ACDGGHINNNORU	CHANGING ROUND
ACDGGIMNNOPRU	CAMPING GROUND
ACDGHIIMNNNOY	COMING IN HANDY
ACDGHINNNOSTU	COUNTING HANDS
ACDGHINOOOOPRT	GONADOTROPHIC
ACDGHJLLOOOOPY	JOLLY GOOD CHAP
ACDGIIILNPPSS	SLIPPING A DISC
ACDGIILLMNNOT	CALLING TO MIND
ACDGIILNNOOST	CONSOLIDATING
ACDGIILNRSTTY	DISTRACTINGLY
ACDGIINNOSTTU	OUTDISTANCING
ACDGIJNNNORTU	GRAND JUNCTION
ACDGIKNOSTTUY	TAKING CUSTODY
ACDGILLNOOOOT	ODONTOLOGICAL
ACDGIMNNOOOOPY	IN GOOD COMPANY
ACDGIMNOPRSSU	MASS-PRODUCING
ACDGJKNNOOOORS	GORDON JACKSON
ACDGLOOSTUYYZ	ZYGODACTYLOUS
ACDHHIIKLNPRS	CHILDISH PRANK
ACDHHILLOOOSY	SCHOOL HOLIDAY
ACDHIIIKLNOTT	LAID IT ON THICK
ACDHIIINORRST	CHRISTIAN DIOR
ACDHIIKKNPSUY	KICK UP A SHINDY
ACDHIILMNOORT	MITOCHONDRIAL
ACDHIINOPSSTU	CUSTODIANSHIP
ACDHIIOPRSSTT	DICTATORSHIPS
ACDHILMNOOPRW	WORLD CHAMPION
ACDHKLORRSTUY	HARD-LUCK STORY
ACDIIILNORSSV	SIR COLIN DAVIS
ACDIIIMNNRSST	DISCRIMINANTS
ACDIIIMNORRST	DISCRIMINATOR
	DOCTRINAIRISM
ACDIIINOOSSST	DISSOCIATIONS
ACDIIIOOOPRST	RADIOISOTOPIC
ACDIILLLNSSSY	SCILLY ISLANDS
ACDIILLMNORRW	CRIMINAL WORLD
ACDIILLMNPSTU	MULTIPLICANDS
ACDIILLNNOOTY	CONDITIONALLY
ACDIILLQRSTUY	LIQUID CRYSTAL
ACDIILNNNOOTU	UNCONDITIONAL
ACDIILNOOOORST	DISCOLORATION
ACDIILPQRTUUY	QUADRUPLICITY
ACDIILRRRSTTU	RURAL DISTRICT
ACDIINNOORRTT	INDOCTRINATOR
ACDIINNOSSTTU	DISTANT COUSIN
ACDIINPRSSSTY	ST.CRISPINS DAY
ACDILMNOOORSS	COMORO ISLANDS
ACDILNOOORSST	CONSOLIDATORS
ACDILNOORRUVY	VINDALOO CURRY
ACDINOOQRSSTU	CONQUISTADORS
ACDLMNOOOSTUY	CONDYLOMATOUS
ACEEEEFFIRTTV	EFFECTIVE RATE
ACEEEEFFLORTT	TREACLE TOFFEE
ACEEEEFIILNRS	CEASE-FIRE LINE
ACEEEEGHHKNPT	KEEP THE CHANGE
ACEEEEHIMNRWW	WHERE WE CAME IN
ACEEEEHKPPPTU	KEEP UP THE PACE
ACEEEEHLPRSST	STEEPLECHASER
ACEEEEHLPSSST	STEEPLECHASES
ACEEEEHNNSTVY	HEAVY SENTENCE
ACEEEELLMNTTT	CLEMENT ATTLEE
ACEEEELNSSSSS	CEASELESSNESS
ACEEEEMMNOPTV	PEACE MOVEMENT
ACEEEENNPPPRY	CAYENNE PEPPER
ACEEEENPRRSSV	PERSEVERANCES
ACEEEEOPRRSST	RESTORES PEACE
ACEEEEPPRRSTW	CARPET SWEEPER
ACEEEFFGINOPR	PEACE OFFERING
ACEEEFFGLOPRU	PLACE OF REFUGE
ACEEEFFGLORRU	REGULAR COFFEE
ACEEEFFHILNTW	FLEW IN THE FACE
ACEEEFFHJRRRY	JEFFREY ARCHER
ACEEEFFJNORRT	REJECT AN OFFER
ACEEEFFLNOPRT	COFFEE PLANTER
ACEEEFFLNSSTU	EFFECTUALNESS
ACEEEFGGNNOOS	EGG ON ONE'S FACE
ACEEEFGHNNOUV	CHANGE OF VENUE
ACEEEFHHKLLOT	OF ALL THE CHEEK
ACEEEFHLNORTW	ENFORCE THE LAW
ACEEEFHLORSUV	CHEESE FLAVOUR
ACEEEFHMOORTT	CAME TO THE FORE
ACEEEFHNNOSTT	SAT ON THE FENCE
ACEEEFIKLOTTV	TICKET OF LEAVE
	TICKET-OF-LEAVE
ACEEEFILNOOST	LIE TO ONES FACE
ACEEEFINOPSST	SPITE ONES FACE
ACEEEFLLNORSS	CLEARS ONESELF
ACEEEFLMNOOST	CAME TO ONESELF
ACEEEFLORRSST	STEERS CLEAR OF
ACEEEFMORRRTT	REFRACTOMETER
ACEEEFNNRSUUV	UNEVEN SURFACE
ACEEEFPQRRSTU	PERFECT SQUARE
ACEEEGGGLSSUX	EXCESS LUGGAGE
ACEEEGGHRSTTU	THE CURATE'S EGG
ACEEEGHHKNPTT	KEPT THE CHANGE
ACEEEGHHLLNRT	THE CHALLENGER
ACEEEGHIMORTT	HETEROGAMETIC
ACEEEGHINSVWX	EXCHANGE VIEWS
ACEEEGHJKNOSX	EXCHANGE JOKES
ACEEEGHLOSSTT	CLOSES THE GATE
ACEEEGHNOSTUY	CAUGHT ONE'S EYE
ACEEEGILLNRSY	SEEING CLEARLY
ACEEEGILLNRTY	ENERGETICALLY
ACEEEGILNNPSW	SWEEPING CLEAN
ACEEEGILNRRST	STEERING CLEAR
ACEEEGILNRTUV	GIVEN A LECTURE
ACEEEGILRSTUV	GIVES A LECTURE
ACEEEGIMNNNRY	IN AN EMERGENCY
ACEEEGINRSTTT	TEN CIGARETTES
ACEEEGINRTTUV	GIVE UTTERANCE
ACEEEGLMNORTT	ELECTROMAGNET
ACEEEGLNNRRUY	NUCLEAR ENERGY
ACEEEGLNNRRUY	GENERAL CUSTER
ACEEEGLNRRSTU	GENERAL CUSTER
ACEEEGLNRSSSS	GRACELESSNESS
ACEEEGMNNORTU	ENCOURAGEMENT
ACEEEHHHLOPRT	HELP EACH OTHER
ACEEEHHILRSTV	HEALTH SERVICE
ACEEEHHNNRSST	HARSH SENTENCE
ACEEEHHOPRSTT	REACHES THE TOP
ACEEEHHPPRSTY	SPEECH THERAPY
ACEEEHIIPRRST	RAISE THE PRICE
ACEEEHIKKMTTY	TAKE THE MICKEY
ACEEEHIKMNSTY	SMACK IN THE EYE
ACEEEHIKRTTTT	THEATRE TICKET
ACEEEHILMNRTU	HERMENEUTICAL
ACEEEHINNORST	ON THE INCREASE
ACEEEHINRSSTT	THE RESISTANCE
ACEEEHINRSTVY	SEVEN-YEAR ITCH
ACEEEHJLMNRTW	JEWEL MERCHANT

ACEEEHKPPPTTU	KEPT UP THE PACE
ACEEEHLLLNOPT	TELEPHONE CALL
ACEEEHLLNNOPT	TELENCEPHALON
ACEEEHLMNNOPS	MESENCEPHALON
ACEEEHLMORTWY	HEARTY WELCOME
ACEEEHLMPSSSY	CHAMPS ELYSEES
ACEEEHLOPSSSU	HOPELESS CAUSE
ACEEEHLPRSTTW	RESPECT THE LAW
ACEEEHMMNOSTT	MEET ONES MATCH
ACEEEHMORRSTY	HOME SECRETARY
ACEEEHNNRSSST	ENCHANTRESSES
ACEEEHNOOSSTT	CHEESE ON TOAST
ACEEEHNORSSTV	HAVE NO SECRETS
ACEEEHNPRRSTT	THE CARPENTERS
ACEEEHORSSSST	CROSSES THE SEA
ACEEEHRRSSTTU	TREASURE CHEST
ACEEEIILLNNOP	ALL IN ONE PIECE
ACEEEIKLNSSTX	EXACT LIKENESS
ACEEEIKLPSSTT	TICKETS PLEASE
ACEEEIKMMNOOS	MAKE ECONOMIES
ACEEEIKNOPTTX	TAKE EXCEPTION
ACEEEIILNPSST	LICENSE PLATES
ACEEEIILLORSTV	CLOSE RELATIVE
ACEEEILMNNRTT	INTERLACEMENT
ACEEEILNNNRTT	TERCENTENNIAL
ACEEEILNRSSVY	NECESSARY EVIL
ACEEEIMMNNRTT	REMITTANCE MEN
ACEEEIMMRRSTU	METRIC MEASURE
ACEEEIMNNOPRS	NAME ONES PRICE
ACEEEIMNNRRSS	MERCENARINESS
ACEEEIMNNRSTY	SEMICENTENARY
ACEEEIMNORSVY	YEOMAN SERVICE
ACEEEINOPSSSY	SAYS ONE'S PIECE
ACEEEINRRSTTY	IN CAREY STREET
ACEEEKLNNOPSW	KNEW ONE'S PLACE
ACEEELLNORTTV	ELECTROVALENT
ACEEELLOPRSTT	ELECTROPLATES
ACEEELNOPRRTU	CENTRAL EUROPE
ACEEELORSSSTT	SETTLES A SCORE
ACEEELORSSTTU	LET OUT A SECRET
ACEEEMNNNORTY	ENTRANCE MONEY
ACEEENOOPRSSV	PROVE ONES CASE
ACEEFFGIKNNOT	TAKING OFFENCE
ACEEFFGLLMORR	FELL FROM GRACE
ACEEFFHHILORT	HEALTH OFFICER
ACEEFFHILLNTU	FULL IN THE FACE
ACEEFFHINOOTT	ON THE FACE OF IT
ACEEFFIIMNORR	MARINE OFFICER
ACEEFFILLNTUY	INEFFECTUALLY
ACEEFFINNOSTT	INSTANT COFFEE
ACEEFGHHINTTW	CHEWING THE FAT
ACEEFGHILMTTU	THE MAGIC FLUTE
ACEEFGHIMNSST	GEMEINSCHAFTS
ACEEFGHKLMOTU	LUCK OF THE GAME
ACEEFGHLNNSSU	CHANGEFULNESS
ACEEFGIIMNRRT	FERRIMAGNETIC
ACEEFGIIMRSST	FASCIST REGIME
ACEEFGIINNOPR	PIGEON FANCIER
ACEEFGILNRRTU	CENTRAL FIGURE
ACEEFGIMNNRST	FENCING MASTER
ACEEFGIMNORRT	FERROMAGNETIC
ACEEFGINOPRSU	SUING FOR PEACE
ACEEFGLLMOORS	COLLEGE OF ARMS
ACEEFGLLNNOST	FALCON-GENTLES
ACEEFGLORRRSU	REGULAR FORCES
ACEEFHHIINRST	FINISH THE RACE
ACEEFHHIRSTTT	FEATHERSTITCH
ACEEFHIIMMNNR	FEMININE CHARM
ACEEFHIINORRT	IN THE AIR FORCE
ACEEFHIKLNOOT	LOOK IN THE FACE
ACEEFHIKOPSTV	PACK OF THIEVES

ACEEFHILMORST	HALF-TIME SCORE
ACEEFHIMOORTT	COME TO THE FAIR
ACEEFHIMORRRU	CHIEF ARMOURER
ACEEFHINNOSTV	CHAIN OF EVENTS
ACEEFHLOOPSTT	TOP OF THE SCALE
ACEEFHLOPRTTU	FOUL THE CARPET
ACEEFHMNOSTUV	VOUCHSAFEMENT
ACEEFHOSSTTUW	SOUTH-WEST FACE
ACEEFHRSSSTTT	STRESS THE FACT
ACEEFIIINNPST	INFINITE SPACE
ACEEFIILLNNPR	FALLEN IN PRICE
ACEEFIILNNRSU	LIFE INSURANCE
ACEEFIINNRRSU	FIRE INSURANCE
ACEEFILLLNOPT	FELL INTO PLACE
ACEEFILLLORST	RECALLS TO LIFE
ACEEFILNOPRSW	PRINCE OF WALES
ACEEFILNOOSTU	ACQUIT ONESELF
ACEEFILOOSTTV	FALSETTO VOICE
ACEEFINOOORSV	VOICE OF REASON
ACEEFINOOPTTU	OUT OF PATIENCE
ACEEFINOSSSTU	FACETIOUSNESS
ACEEFINPRRRST	TRANSFER PRICE
ACEEFKMOPRRST	MARK OF RESPECT
ACEEFKMORRSSY	FOR MERCYS SAKE
ACEEFLMORRSTU	SECRET FORMULA
ACEEFMMNOORTU	COMMON FEATURE
ACEEFMMOOPRRU	CAME UP FOR MORE
ACEEFMORRRTTY	REFRACTOMETRY
ACEEFNNNORRTT	FRONT ENTRANCE
ACEEFNNORRSTY	FORCES AN ENTRY
ACEEFNOORSSWY	FORCES ONE'S WAY
ACEEGGGINNNOR	GEORGE CANNING
ACEEGGHHINRTW	CHEWING THE RAG
ACEEGGHIINNRV	GIVEN IN CHARGE
ACEEGGHIINNTV	GIVING THE CANE
ACEEGGIILRRTT	CIGARETTE GIRL
ACEEGGILLNPRU	GRUELLING PACE
ACEEGGILLNRU	GRUELLING RACE
ACEEGGHHILNPST	HALTING SPEECH
ACEEGGHHILRSSS	HIGHER CLASSES
ACEEGGHHIRTTWW	WEIGHTWATCHER
ACEEGGHHINORSS	CHANGES HORSES
ACEEGGHHNOSSTX	EXCHANGE SHOTS
ACEEGGHHOOPRRR	CHOREOGRAPHER
ACEEGGHIIMNNSW	SEWING MACHINE
ACEEGGHIINORSV	HEARING VOICES
ACEEGGHIINRSTT	CATHETERISING
ACEEGGHIINRTTZ	CATHETERIZING
ACEEGGHIIRRSTW	CARRIES WEIGHT
ACEEGGHILNOPRS	SELENOGRAPHIC
ACEEGGHILNORST	LOSING THE RACE
ACEEGGHILNORSU	CLEARING HOUSE
	CLEARINGHOUSE
ACEEGGHILOPRRX	LEXICOGRAPHER
ACEEGGHIMNNNRU	MACHINE GUNNER
ACEEGGHIMNOOTT	GO TO THE CINEMA
ACEEGGHINNOTTT	GET IN ON THE ACT
ACEEGGHINORSTV	OVERNIGHT CASE
ACEEGGHINOTTTT	GET INTO THE ACT
ACEEGGHIOPRRST	STEREOGRAPHIC
ACEEGGHIORRSSU	SERIOUS CHARGE
ACEEGGHPRRRSSU	SUPERCHARGERS
ACEEGIIILLNNPV	LIVING IN PEACE
ACEEGIIKNOPSV	SPEAKING VOICE
ACEEGIILLNRTY	ALLERGENICITY
ACEEGIILLMNPSW	SWEEPING CLAIM
ACEEGIILLNNOSV	SOCIAL EVENING
ACEEGIILLNORSV	SILVER COINAGE
ACEEGIILLNOSTV	CEASING TO LIVE
ACEEGIILSTTUV	GESTICULATIVE
ACEEGIIMMNNOST	MISCEGENATION

ACEEGIINNNRST	INTRANSIGENCE	ACEEHKLOORRTW	WORK THE ORACLE
ACEEGIINNSSTT	NECESSITATING	ACEEHKORSSTTT	STROKES THE CAT
ACEEGIINOPRRR	CARRIER PIGEON	ACEEHLLNNNNTU	CHANNEL TUNNEL
ACEEGIKLLRRTY	LEGAL TRICKERY	ACEEHLLOORSSV	SCHOOL-LEAVERS
ACEEGIKLMMNOW	MAKING WELCOME	ACEEHLMNORRTU	THERMONUCLEAR
ACEEGIKLNNSSW	KING WENCESLAS	ACEEHLNRSSTTU	TURN THE SCALES
ACEEGIKMNRSTT	TRACK MEETINGS		TURNS THE SCALE
ACEEGIKMNSSUX	MAKING EXCUSES	ACEEHLORRSTUY	TREACHEROUSLY
ACEEGIKNNOSTU	TAKING ONE'S CUE	ACEEHLOSTTTTU	LETS THE CAT OUT
ACEEGILLNOOS	SELENOLOGICAL	ACEEHLPPRSTUY	SUPPLY TEACHER
ACEEGILLLOOPS	SPELEOLOGICAL	ACEEHMNOPPRRT	RAPPROCHEMENT
ACEEGILLMORTY	GEOMETRICALLY	ACEEHNNORSTTT	HEARTS CONTENT
ACEEGILLOOPST	GO ALL TO PIECES	ACEEHNOOPSSSW	SHOW ONES PACES
ACEEGILMNNOQU	MAGNILOQUENCE	ACEEHNOPSSTTW	WATCH ONES STEP
ACEEGILMNORRU	REGULAR INCOME	ACEEHOOPRRTTT	ROTATE THE CROP
ACEEGILORTTUV	GUTTERAL VOICE	ACEEHOPPRRRSS	SHARECROPPERS
ACEEGIMMNORTT	MAGNETOMETRIC	ACEEHORSSTTUY	STAY THE COURSE
ACEEGIMNOPRST	SPERMATOGENIC	ACEEIIILPRSTU	PECULIARITIES
ACEEGINOORSSU	GOES ON A CRUISE	ACEEIIIPPRRTTV	PRECIPITATIVE
ACEEGINOPPPRS	POPPING CREASE	ACEEIILLLPPTY	EPILEPTICALLY
ACEEGINOPRTTX	EXPECTORATING	ACEEIILLMPSTY	EPISTEMICALLY
ACEEGJNNOSSTU	CONJUGATENESS	ACEEIILLNRRTY	RECTILINEARLY
ACEEGLLNNORSU	CONSUL GENERAL	ACEEIILMMNORS	CEREMONIALISM
ACEEGLMNOORST	CONGLOMERATES	ACEEIILMNORST	CEREMONIALIST
ACEEGNPRSTTUU	GETS A PUNCTURE	ACEEIILNOPTTT	PETTICOAT LINE
ACEEHHHMNRTTT	MARCH THE TENTH	ACEEIILNOSSTZ	SECTIONALIZES
ACEEHHHORTTTU	TOUCH THE HEART	ACEEIILPPRSVY	PAY LIP-SERVICE
ACEEHHIILMPRS	HEMISPHERICAL	ACEEIILPPRTTY	PRECIPITATELY
ACEEHHIKNNOTT	TAKE ON THE CHIN	ACEEIIMMORSTV	COMMISERATIVE
ACEEHHILNORVY	HEAVENLY CHOIR	ACEEIIMNNOSST	AMNIOCENTESIS
ACEEHHINOPSSV	HAVE ONE'S CHIPS	ACEEIIMNOPRTV	PRIVATE INCOME
ACEEHHIRSSTVY	HAVE HYSTERICS	ACEEIIMNORRST	MERCERISATION
ACEEHHIRVWWYY	EVERY WHICH WAY	ACEEIIMNORRTZ	MERCERIZATION
ACEEHHLLTTTWY	WATCH THE TELLY	ACEEIINNORSST	CONTAINERISES
ACEEHHLNORSTT	THE CHARLESTON	ACEEIINNORSTZ	CONTAINERIZES
ACEEHHORRSSTU	CHARTERHOUSES	ACEEIINNOSSTT	NECESSITATION
ACEEHHORSSTTW	WHAT'S THE SCORE?	ACEEIINNRSTTU	UNCERTAINTIES
ACEEHIIKNNNPT	PAIN IN THE NECK	ACEEIINOQRTUV	QUEEN VICTORIA
ACEEHIILMRRST	MISTER CHARLIE	ACEEIINORSSVV	VARICOSE VEINS
ACEEHIILNPSST	SISTINE CHAPEL	ACEEIIRSSTTUV	RESUSCITATIVE
ACEEHIILNRSTT	ELAINE STRITCH	ACEEIKLMORRRW	MIRACLE WORKER
ACEEHIIMSSSTT	AESTHETICISMS	ACEEIKORSSTTU	TAKE ITS COURSE
ACEEHIINORSTT	THEORETICIANS	ACEEILLLMPRSU	PECULIAR SMELL
ACEEHIJKPPRRT	JACK THE RIPPER	ACEEILLLNPSTY	SPLENETICALLY
ACEEHIJNORTTV	CARVE THE JOINT	ACEEILLLNRRTU	INTERCELLULAR
ACEEHIKKMNTTY	TAKEN THE MICKY	ACEEILLLNSTTU	INTELLECTUALS
ACEEHIKKMSTTY	TAKES THE MICKY	ACEEILLMNNRTY	INCREMENTALLY
ACEEHIKLLLOSV	HAVELOCK ELLIS	ACEEILLMNOSSU	MISCELLANEOUS
ACEEHIKMNOPST	MAKE ONE'S PITCH	ACEEILLNNORST	CRENELLATIONS
ACEEHIKNOPSST	SHEEPSKIN COAT	ACEEILLNOPTXY	EXCEPTIONALLY
ACEEHIKNRSSST	HEARTSICKNESS	ACEEILLNPRSST	IN ALL RESPECTS
ACEEHILLORTTY	THEORETICALLY	ACEEILLNPRTTY	CENTRIPETALLY
ACEEHILLSSTTT	TILT THE SCALES	ACEEILLORRTVY	CORRELATIVELY
	TILTS THE SCALE	ACEEILLPSTUVY	SPECULATIVELY
ACEEHILNNPSTU	PLACE IN THE SUN	ACEEILMNNSSSU	MASCULINENESS
ACEEHILOPPRRR	PROPER CHARLIE	ACEEILMNOPTTV	CONTEMPLATIVE
ACEEHILPRSTVY	THIS VERY PLACE	ACEEILMNORRSV	NORMAL SERVICE
ACEEHILPSSSTT	TIPS THE SCALES	ACEEILMNPRTTU	MENTAL PICTURE
ACEEHIMMNORST	TIME MARCHES ON	ACEEILMOOSTUY	COME OUT EASILY
ACEEHIMNOPSTU	UTOPIAN SCHEME	ACEEILMOPRSTU	PRECIOUS METAL
ACEEHIMNORSSS	MARCHIONESSES	ACEEILNNOPTUX	UNEXCEPTIONAL
ACEEHIMNOSTTW	WATCH ONE'S TIME	ACEEILNNOQSTU	CONSEQUENTIAL
ACEEHIMNOSTUY	HUMANE SOCIETY	ACEEILNNQRSTU	TRANQUIL SCENE
ACEEHIMNPRSST	MARCHES IN STEP	ACEEILNNRSSUY	UNNECESSARILY
ACEEHIMOPSSST	SMASH TO PIECES	ACEEILNOQSSUV	EQUIVOCALNESS
ACEEHIMOSSTTW	TEACHES TO SWIM	ACEEILNRSSTUV	LUCRATIVENESS
ACEEHIMRRSSTT	CHRISTMAS TREE	ACEEILOOPPRTVY	COOPERATIVELY
ACEEHINOPRRST	TERPSICHOREAN	ACEEILOPPRSSU	PILES UP A SCORE
ACEEHIPRRSSTY	SECRETARYSHIP	ACEEILOPRSTTY	STEREOTYPICAL
ACEEHJNNOPRRT	JOHN CARPENTER	ACEEILORRTTVY	RETROACTIVELY
ACEEHKLNORSST	CLOSE THE RANKS	ACEEIMMMOORTV	COMMEMORATIVE

ACEEIMMNNOOTY	CAME INTO MONEY	ACEFGHIILMNNY	FLYING MACHINE
ACEEIMMNRSSTT	MINCES MATTERS	ACEFGHIINNNRS	ENFRANCHISING
ACEEIMNNNOSTU	CEMENTS A UNION	ACEFGHIINOOSW	CHOOSING A WIFE
ACEEIMNNOOPTU	ONCE UPON A TIME	ACEFGHIINORSS	COARSE FISHING
ACEEIMNOPRRTW	WARM RECEPTION	ACEFGHILLNORU	LEN FAIRCLOUGH
ACEEIMNORRSSX	CROSS-EXAMINER	ACEFGIIIINSTV	SIGNIFICATIVE
ACEEIMNORSSSX	CROSS-EXAMINES	ACEFGIIKLNRSU	SURGICAL KNIFE
ACEEIMNPRTTUY	PNEUMATIC TYRE	ACEFGIILLNPRS	FALLING PRICES
ACEEINNNORSST	NONRESISTANCE	ACEFGIILMNNTY	MAGNIFICENTLY
ACEEINNNQRTUY	QUINCENTENARY	ACEFGIILNNRTU	LUNATIC FRINGE
ACEEINNNRSSTU	UNCERTAINNESS	ACEFGIINORTUV	CONFIGURATIVE
ACEEINNOOPTTX	NO EXPECTATION	ACEFGINORSTTU	REFUSING TO ACT
ACEEINNOORSVZ	CONVERSAZIONE	ACEFGLNOOOORRU	RANGE OF COLOUR
ACEEINNOPRRST	CERTAIN PERSON	ACEFHHIIINPST	CHIEFTAINSHIP
ACEEINNORSTUW	WENT ON A CRUISE	ACEFHHIMRRSTT	MARCH THE FIRST
ACEEINNOSSSTU	TENACIOUSNESS	ACEFHHLNNORTU	FOURTH CHANNEL
ACEEINOOPRSTU	PROTEINACEOUS	ACEFHIIKNTTUW	CUT WITH A KNIFE
ACEEINOOPRTTX	EXPECTORATION	ACEFHLLOOORST	LATE FOR SCHOOL
ACEEINOOPRTUV	UNCOOPERATIVE	ACEFHLLOPRRUY	REPROACHFULLY
ACEEINOORRSTV	OBSERVATOIRE	ACEFHLLHSTTTU	AT FULL STRETCH
ACEEINOPPPHST	APPERCEPTIONS	ACEFHLNOOOPRU	PLACE OF HONOUR
ACEEINORSSSUV	VERACIOUSNESS	ACEFHLOOPSSTT	TOP OF THE CLASS
ACEEINORSSTVV	CONSERVATIVES	ACEFHMOORSSTU	SMOOTH SURFACE
ACEEIOPRRSTTV	PRIVATE SECTOR	ACEFHNORSSTTU	COUNTERSHAFTS
ACEEIOPRRSTUV	PRIVATE SOURCE	ACEFHOOORRRST	ROOF ORCHESTRA
ACEEIORRSTUVY	AT YOUR SERVICE	ACEFHOORSSTWY	WAY OF THE CROSS
ACEEKLLNOPRSY	SPOKEN CLEARLY	ACEFIIINOPRTT	PETRIFICATION
ACEEKLNNOOPSW	KNOW ONES PLACE	ACEFIIINORSTV	VERSIFICATION
ACEEKLNOOOPST	TOOK ONE'S PLACE	ACEFIILLPRSUY	SUPERFICIALLY
ACEEKLNOOPTTX	LOOK EXPECTANT	ACEFIILMORRTY	MILITARY FORCE
ACEELLLLOORRT	ELECTORAL ROLL	ACEFIILMSSTUV	MUSIC FESTIVAL
ACEELLMNORSSW	LOWERCLASSMEN	ACEFIINNORSTU	FUNCTIONARIES
ACEELLMNRTTUY	MENTAL CRUELTY	ACEFIINPRRSSY	FAIRY PRINCESS
ACEELLMOQRTTU	CROQUET MALLET	ACEFIJNORSUUY	CAUSE OF INJURY
ACEELLNOOPRSU	PORCELLANEOUS	ACEFIKMOPRRRT	PERFORM A TRICK
ACEELLNSSSSSS	CLASSLESSNESS	ACEFILLORSTUY	COSTLY FAILURE
ACEELLOORRRST	ROLLER COASTER	ACEFILMMNOOTY	COMMIT A FELONY
ACEELMMNOPPTY	COMPLEMENTARY	ACEFILNNOOSSS	CONFESSIONALS
ACEELMNOPRSST	MENTAL PROCESS	ACEFILNNORSUU	NUCLEAR FUSION
ACEELMOORSTUW	TWO-COURSE MEAL	ACEFILNNPRUUY	FUNNY PECULIAR
ACEELMPRSTTUU	MUTUAL RESPECT	ACEFIMMNOORTX	INCOME-TAX FORM
ACEELNNOSTTTT	TALENT CONTEST	ACEFIMOOPRRSU	COMES UP FOR AIR
ACEELNNRRRSTU	SCARLET RUNNER	ACEFINNORRTTY	CONFRATERNITY
ACEELNOOPRRSS	CORPOREALNESS	ACEFINNOSTTTU	STATE FUNCTION
ACEELNOORSTTU	CLOSE TO NATURE	ACEFINORRRSTV	TREVOR FRANCIS
ACEELOQRRSSTU	CLOSE QUARTERS	ACEFINORSSSTU	FRACTIOUSNESS
ACEEMMMNOORSU	COMMON MEASURE	ACEFIORRRSUUV	CURRIES FAVOUR
ACEEMMMNNOPSST	ENCOMPASSMENT	ACEFJKKLNOORT	NORFOLK JACKET
ACEEMMNOORSST	COMES ON STREAM	ACEFKMNOOSSTY	STACKS OF MONEY
ACEEMMNOPSSST	PASSES COMMENT	ACEFKNNOOOSTY	TOOK ONE'S FANCY
ACEEMNNNNOSTU	ANNOUNCEMENTS	ACEFKOORRRTWY	FACTORY WORKER
ACEEMNNORRSST	REMONSTRANCES	ACEFMNOOPTTUY	NOT MY CUP OF TEA
ACEEMNOOPRSST	COMPARES NOTES	ACEGGHIIKNSTV	GIVING THE SACK
ACEEMOPRSSTTY	SPERMATOCYTES	ACEGGHIILLNTT	GETTING A CHILL
ACEENOOPRRTUU	EUROPEAN COURT	ACEGGHIKNOSTT	GETTING A SHOCK
ACEENRRSSSTTU	CURRENT ASSETS	ACEGGHILLLNNY	CHALLENGINGLY
ACEEOOPRRSTTT	PROTECTORATES	ACEGGHILNOPST	CLOSING THE GAP
ACEFFGHOSSTTU	CUTS OFF THE GAS	ACEGGHINPRRSU	SUPERCHARGING
ACEFFGIINORRT	RATING OFFICER	ACEGGHIOOOPRZ	ZOOGEOGRAPHIC
ACEFFGIKLNNOS	SLACKENING OFF	ACEGGIILNNPSS	SINGLE-SPACING
ACEFFGIMNOPRS	SCAMPERING OFF	ACEGGIILNSTTU	GESTICULATING
ACEFFHHHIMRTT	MARCH THE FIFTH	ACEGGIKLNNNOW	KNOWING GLANCE
ACEFFHIJLLOOR	FALL OF JERICHO	ACEGGILNNORUY	ENCOURAGINGLY
ACEFFHNOORSTU	SOUTH OF FRANCE	ACEGGILNOOSTY	GYNAECOLOGIST
ACEFFIILOPTTY	PETTY OFFICIAL	ACEGGILNOSSST	CLOSING STAGES
ACEFFINOOPSTV	POST OFFICE VAN	ACEGGINNOORST	CONGREGATIONS
ACEFGHNOPRSTY	PEGGY ASHCROFT	ACEGGINNORSST	GETTING ACROSS
ACEFGHHHIMORT	EIGHTH OF MARCH	ACEGGLLRSSSTU	CLASS STRUGGLE
ACEFGHHILRRTT	CHARTER FLIGHT	ACEGHHIIIMNNV	GIVE HIM AN INCH
ACEFGHHNOORST	SHORT OF CHANGE	ACEGHHIIPSTTT	PATHETIC SIGHT
ACEFGHIIKLNST	FISHING TACKLE	ACEGHHIMOPRRT	THERMOGRAPHIC

ACEGHHINOSTTT	ACTING THE HOST
ACEGHHIOPRRRS	CHIROGRAPHERS
ACEGHHIORTTUW	WITHOUT CHARGE
ACEGHHNORSSTU	SANG THE CHORUS
ACEGHHOPRRSTU	SCRAPE THROUGH
ACEGHHOPSTTTU	CAUGHT THE POST
ACEGHIILLNNST	ALL THINGS NICE
ACEGHIILMNRSU	CHARLIE MINGUS
ACEGHIILNNSTT	ANCIENT LIGHTS
ACEGHIILNNSTU	LAUNCHING SITE
ACEGHIMMMMNRU	MINIMUM CHARGE
ACEGHIIMNOSTT	CAME INTO SIGHT
ACEGHIIMNPPRW	WHIPPING CREAM
ACEGHIIMOPRSS	SEISMOGRAPHIC
ACEGHIINNPTTT	PITCHING A TENT
ACEGHIINOPTTY	PATHOGENICITY
ACEGHIKLNOPYY	PLAYING HOCKEY
ACEGHIKNOSSTT	SHOCKING STATE
ACEGHILLLOORY	RHEOLOGICALLY
ACEGHILLLOOSV	VILLAGE SCHOOL
ACEGHILLNNOSU	HALLUCINOGENS
ACEGHILLNOOPR	PHRENOLOGICAL
ACEGHILLNOOSV	LEAVING SCHOOL
ACEGHILLNTTWY	WATCHING TELLY
ACEGHILLOOPPS	PSEPHOLOGICAL
ACEGHILLOPSYY	GEOPHYSICALLY
ACEGHILNNORST	CHARLESTONING
ACEGHILNOPRRY	REPROACHINGLY
ACEGHILNORSSU	SOUL-SEARCHING
ACEGHIMNNOOTT	CAME TO NOTHING
ACEGHIMNNORTT	MAGNETIC NORTH
ACEGHIMNNORVY	HAVING NO MERCY
ACEGHIMNOORTT	COMING TO EARTH
ACEGHINNNRRTU	RUNNING THE CAR
ACEGHINNOOTTT	GOT IN ON THE ACT
ACEGHINOOPRRS	ICONOGRAPHERS
ACEGHINOOTTTT	GOT INTO THE ACT
ACEGHINORRSTT	ORCHESTRATING
ACEGHLLNOOSSU	SLOUCHES ALONG
ACEGHMOOPRRSS	COSMOGRAPHERS
ACEGHOPPRRRTY	CRYPTOGRAPHER
ACEGHOPPRRSST	SPECTROGRAPHS
ACEGHOPPRRSTY	SPECTROGRAPHY
ACEGHOPRRRSST	PROGRESS CHART
ACEGIIIMNNRRT	RECRIMINATING
ACEGIIINNORTV	VOICE TRAINING
ACEGIIINPPRTT	PRECIPITATING
ACEGIIINPRRSS	RAISING PRICES
ACEGIIKKLMORW	WORK LIKE MAGIC
ACEGIIILLLNOSS	ILLOGICALNESS
ACEGIILLLOOTY	ETIOLOGICALLY
ACEGIILLMOOSS	SEISMOLOGICAL
ACEGIILLNNSSW	LICENSING LAWS
ACEGIILLOSTTY	EGOTISTICALLY
ACEGIILMMNPSU	CAME UP SMILING
ACEGIILMNNRSU	LEARNING MUSIC
ACEGIILMNPRSS	PRESSING CLAIM
ACEGIILNOSTTU	GESTICULATION
ACEGIIMMNORST	COMMISERATING
ACEGIIMNOSSTV	VASECTOMISING
ACEGIIMNOSTVZ	VASECTOMIZING
ACEGIINOPRRSS	SOARING PRICES
ACEGIINOPRSTY	SAPROGENICITY
ACEGIINPRRSTT	RACING TIPSTER
	STARTING PRICE
ACEGIINRSSTTU	RESUSCITATING
ACEGIJKKMNOST	SMOKING JACKET
ACEGIKKLNOORW	LOOKING A WRECK
ACEGIKLMNNOSU	SUCKING A LEMON
ACEGIKLNNOSTU	TAKING COUNSEL
ACEGIKMNRRTTU	CUTTING REMARK

ACEGILLLORSTU	LOGICAL RESULT
ACEGILLLRSTTY	STRICTLY LEGAL
ACEGILLMNOOOT	ENTOMOLOGICAL
ACEGILLMNOORU	NUMEROLOGICAL
ACEGILLNOPTYY	GENOTYPICALLY
ACEGILLNRSSSU	RULING CLASSES
ACEGILLOOPRTY	GEOTROPICALLY
ACEGILMMNOSUV	MOVING A MUSCLE
ACEGILMNNOPTT	CONTEMPLATING
ACEGILMNOPRRU	COMING A PURLER
ACEGILMNOORRT	REGAIN CONTROL
ACEGILNNOORSS	CONGRESSIONAL
ACEGILNOPPPST	STOPPING PLACE
ACEGILORSTTUY	GESTICULATORY
ACEGIMMMNOORT	COMMEMORATING
ACEGIMMNORSTT	MAGNETIC STORM
ACEGIMNNOOSWY	COMING ONE'S WAY
ACEGIMNOPRSTU	PNEUMOGASTRIC
ACEGIMNPPSTTU	SETTING UP CAMP
ACEGINOOPRSTT	PROGNOSTICATE
ACEGINORSTTUY	TOURIST AGENCY
ACEGLMNOOORRT	CONGLOMERATOR
ACEGMNNOORSSW	CONGRESSWOMAN
ACEGMOOPRSSSY	GYROCOMPASSES
ACEGNOPRRSSTY	CONGRESS PARTY
ACEHHHIMMNRTT	MARCH THE NINTH
ACEHHHIMRSTTX	MARCH THE SIXTH
ACEHHIINOPRSZ	SCHIZOPHRENIA
ACEHHIJKOPTTT	HIT THE JACKPOT
ACEHHILPPRSYY	HYPERPHYSICAL
ACEHHIMNORTTW	NO MATTER WHICH
ACEHHLLOSSSTT	CALLS THE SHOTS
ACEHHMMNRSTUY	CHRYSANTHEMUM
ACEHHMOOOPRRT	CHROMATOPHORE
ACEHHNOORTTUW	TOUCH ON THE RAW
ACEHHOPPRSTYY	PSYCHOTHERAPY
ACEHIIIMNSTTT	A STITCH IN TIME
ACEHIIINPRSTW	CRIES WITH PAIN
ACEHIIINRSSTZ	CHRISTIANIZES
ACEHIIKLNOPST	LICK INTO SHAPE
ACEHIILLPPTYY	EPIPHYTICALLY
ACEHIILLRSTUY	HEURISTICALLY
ACEHIILMNSSSW	WHIMSICALNESS
ACEHIILMOTTUW	WITHOUT MALICE
ACEHIIMNNRSST	IN CHRIST'S NAME
ACEHIINRTTTWY	WITH CERTAINTY
ACEHIIOPSSSTT	SOPHISTICATES
ACEHIJKLLMOSU	MUSIC-HALL JOKE
ACEHIJKLOORSU	JAILHOUSE ROCK
ACEHIJKLPRSSY	PHYSICAL JERKS
ACEHIJKNOPTTW	WIN THE JACKPOT
ACEHILLLMOOPR	ALLELOMORPHIC
ACEHILLNNRTUV	LUNCH INTERVAL
ACEHILLNSTTYY	SYNTHETICALLY
ACEHILLOPPRTY	PROPHETICALLY
ACEHILMOPRSTT	THERMOPLASTIC
ACEHILNOOPPRS	CEPHALOSPORIN
ACEHILOOPRSTV	PRIVATE SCHOOL
ACEHILOPPRSWY	PHYSICAL POWER
ACEHIMMRRSSTT	CHRISTMAS TERM
ACEHIMMNPSTTUY	UNSYMPATHETIC
ACEHIMNRSSTTX	NEXT CHRISTMAS
ACEHIMORRSSST	CHRISTMAS ROSE
ACEHINOORRSTT	ORCHESTRATION
ACEHINOORSTTT	AT SHORT NOTICE
ACEHINOPPRRST	COPARTNERSHIP
ACEHINOPRSTTT	STRETCH A POINT
ACEHIOPRRSSTT	STRATOSPHERIC
ACEHJKNOOPTTW	WON THE JACKPOT
ACEHKMOOPTTTU	TOMATO KETCHUP
ACEHKNOPRSTTU	PUTS ON THE RACK

ACEHLMOORSSST	SCHOOLMASTERS
ACEHLNOOPRSTU	PERSONAL TOUCH
ACEHLNOORSTTT	AT THE CONTROLS
ACEHLNOPRSSSU	HAS NO SCRUPLES
ACEHMMNOOORST	COMES TO NO HARM
ACEHNNOORRTTY	ON THE CONTRARY
ACEHNOOPRSSST	CROSS ONES PATH
ACEHNOORSTTTU	CUT ONES THROAT
ACEHNORSSTTTU	ROAST CHESTNUT
ACEHNORSTUUWY	UNWORTHY CAUSE
ACEHOOORSSTTW	CARES TWO HOOTS
ACEHOPRSTTUWY	WATCH YOUR STEP
ACEHOPSTTTTUU	PUTS OUT THE CAT
	PUTS THE CAT OUT
ACEIIIILMPRST	IMPERIALISTIC
ACEIIILLMNPRW	PRINCE WILLIAM
ACEIIILLNORTV	VIOLIN RECITAL
ACEIIILLNOSTV	IN A STILL VIEW
ACEIIILLOPTVW	POLITICAL VIEW
ACEIIILLPSTTY	PIETISTICALLY
ACEIIILMNPSSU	MUNICIPALISES
ACEIIILMNPSUZ	MUNICIPALIZES
ACEIIILNOPRSV	PROVINCIALISE
ACEIIILNOPRVZ	PROVINCIALIZE
ACEIIILNOSTVV	VIVISECTIONAL
ACEIIILQSTUVY	ACQUISITIVELY
ACEIIIMNNORRT	RECRIMINATION
ACEIIINOPPRTT	PRECIPITATION
ACEIIKLMOSTTU	STICK OUT A MILE
ACEIIKNNRRSSU	INSURANCE RISK
ACEIIILLMOPRWW	WILLIAM COWPER
ACEIIILLMORSTY	ISOMETRICALLY
ACEIIILLNOORSW	LOW IN CALORIES
ACEIIILLNOPPST	SLIP INTO PLACE
ACEIIILLNOPSTW	POLITICAL NEWS
ACEIIILLNORRTY	ACRYLONITRILE
ACEIIILLNRRUVY	CURVILINEARLY
ACEIIILLNRSTXY	EXTRINSICALLY
ACEIIILLOOPTYZ	EPIZOOTICALLY
ACEIIILMNOPRRW	IMPERIAL CROWN
ACEIIILMNORTUV	VERMICULATION
ACEIIILMNOSSSU	MALICIOUSNESS
ACEIIILNOOPSTT	POLICE STATION
ACEIIILNOPRSST	PICTORIALNESS
ACEIIILNPPRTTY	PRECIPITANTLY
ACEIIILNPQTTUU	QUINTUPLICATE
ACEIIILNRRTTWY	WRITTEN A LYRIC
ACEIIILNRSSTTT	CLARINETTISTS
ACEIIIMMNOORST	COMMISERATION
ACEIIIMMNRSTTY	ANTISYMMETRIC
ACEIIIMNORRRTY	RECRIMINATORY
ACEIIINNOORSVZ	CONVERSAZIONI
ACEIIINOPRRSTT	PRACTITIONERS
ACEIIINORSSSUV	VICARIOUSNESS
ACEIIINORSSTTU	RESUSCITATION
ACEIIINOSSSUVV	VIVACIOUSNESS
ACEIIORRTTTVY	RETROACTIVITY
ACEIKLMNOPSSS	SMACK ONES LIPS
ACEIKLMOSTTUU	STUCK OUT A MILE
ACEIKLOOPRRST	SLICK OPERATOR
ACEIKLOOPRSTW	POETICAL WORKS
ACEIKMMMNOOST	COMMON MISTAKE
ACEIKOORTTTTU	TAKE IT TO COURT
ACEILLLMOPRYY	POLYMERICALLY
ACEILLLNOOSTY	COLONIAL STYLE
ACEILLMMRSTYY	SYMMETRICALLY
ACEILLMNOOPST	POLICEMANS LOT
ACEILLNNNOSSY	NONSENSICALLY
ACEILLNNNOTTY	CONTINENTALLY
ACEILLNNOOSTT	CONSTELLATION
ACEILLNOOPRRY	INCORPOREALLY
ACEILLNOQUUVY	UNEQUIVOCALLY
ACEILLNOSSTTW	CALL TO WITNESS
ACEILLOPRRTYY	LYRICAL POETRY
ACEILLRRSSSTY	CRYSTALLISERS
ACEILLRRSSTYZ	CRYSTALLIZERS
ACEILMMNOPRTY	COMPLIMENTARY
ACEILMMNNOOPTT	CONTEMPLATION
ACEILMMNNOORTV	ROMANTIC NOVEL
ACEILMNOOPPTY	POLITE COMPANY
ACEILMNOOPRSS	COMPRESSIONAL
ACEILMNOPRVYY	LIVERY COMPANY
ACEILMNOPSSTU	ACTS ON IMPULSE
ACEILNNOOSSTT	CAST IN ONE'S LOT
ACEILNNOSSSTU	CUTS ONE'S NAILS
ACEILNOOPRSSS	PROCESSIONALS
ACEILNOORRSTV	CONTROVERSIAL
ACEILNOPRRSSY	PRINCESS ROYAL
ACEILNOPRSSUY	PECUNIARY LOSS
ACEILNORSTTVY	CONTRASTIVELY
ACEILOOPRTVVY	PROVOCATIVELY
ACEIMMMNOOORT	COMMEMORATION
ACEIMMMNOORRRT	COMMIT AN ERROR
ACEIMMOOPPRTT	COMMIT TO PAPER
ACEIMNNOOPSST	COMPENSATIONS
ACEIMNNORRTTU	MACRONUTRIENT
ACEIMNOOOPSTT	COMES TO A POINT
ACEIMNORSSSTU	CUSTOMARINESS
ACEIMOOPPPSST	OPPOSITE CAMPS
ACEINNNOORSTT	CONSTERNATION
ACEINNNOORTTV	CONTRAVENTION
ACEINNNOPRTTY	INNOCENT PARTY
ACEINNOOORSSTV	CONVERSATIONS
ACEINNOORSTTW	CONISTON WATER
ACEINNORSSTTU	ENCRUSTATIONS
ACEINOORSSSTU	ATROCIOUSNESS
ACEINOORSSSUV	VORACIOUSNESS
ACEKNPRSTTUUU	STRUCK UP A TUNE
ACELLMMNOOORU	MONOMOLECULAR
ACELLNNRSTTUY	TRANSLUCENTLY
ACELLNOORRTUU	NEUTRAL COLOUR
ACELLNOORSTTY	CONSTELLATORY
ACELLOOPRSSTU	PASTEL COLOURS
ACELMNNOSTTUU	MUTUAL CONSENT
ACELMNOOPRSSS	CROSS ONES PALM
ACELMNOORRSUU	NEUROMUSCULAR
ACELNNOOPRTTT	COTTON PLANTER
ACEMNNOOPPRRTY	COMPANY REPORT
ACENNOOOOPRRT	NONCOOPERATOR
ACENNOORSSTTU	TURNS ONE'S COAT
ACENOOQRSTTTU	QUATTROCENTOS
ACFFFFILOORTW	FLOW OF TRAFFIC
ACFFFGHILNOTY	FLIGHT OF FANCY
ACFFGHIILRSTT	TRAFFIC LIGHTS
ACFFGIIILNPST	SPIFFLICATING
ACFFGIINORRTY	CARRYING IT OFF
ACFFGILNOSTUY	SUFFOCATINGLY
ACFFHHMOORRTU	FOURTH OF MARCH
ACFFIIINOORTT	FORTIFICATION
ACFFIINNOOPTT	IN POINT OF FACT
ACFGGHHIOSTTU	CAUGHT SIGHT OF
ACFGGHIIKNPT	PICKING A FIGHT
ACFGHHIIILNTT	HITCHING A LIFT
ACFGHIIIKLNNS	LACKING FINISH
ACFGHIILNNTTU	CUTTING IN HALF
ACFGHIIMRSSTT	CHRISTMAS GIFT
ACFGHILMNOOPS	GOLF CHAMPIONS
ACFGIIIILNNOT	LIGNIFICATION
ACFGIIIINNNST	INSIGNIFICANT
ACFGIIINNNOST	SIGNIFICATION
ACFGIIIKNOSTW	SICK OF WAITING
ACFGIIILLMNTV	FALLING VICTIM

ACFGIIILNNOPP	FLIPPING A COIN	ACGIIKLNNOSTY	LAYING IN STOCK
ACFGIIILNNSTY	SIGNIFICANTLY	ACGIIKLNPPSSS	SKIPPING CLASS
ACFGIIILNOORT	GLORIFICATION	ACGIIKLNPRSTY	PLAYING TRICKS
ACFGIIINNOPTT	PONTIFICATING	ACGIIKMNNOTTU	MAKING IT COUNT
ACFGIINNOORTU	CONFIGURATION	ACGIIKNPRSSTW	PICKING STRAWS
ACFGIKMNNOORTT	TAKING COMFORT	ACGIILLLOORVY	VIROLOGICALLY
ACFHIILLNOORY	HONORIFICALLY	ACGIILLMMNOOU	IMMUNOLOGICAL
ACFHIILLPSTYY	PHYSICALLY FIT	ACGIILLMNNOPY	COMPLAININGLY
ACFHILLOOSSTY	ACTS FOOLISHLY	ACGIILLMOOSTT	CLIMATOLOGIST
ACFHIMORRRTTY	CROMARTY FIRTH	ACGIILLNNORTW	CROWNING IT ALL
ACFIIIINNORTT	NITRIFICATION	ACGIILLNOOPTY	PLAYING IT COOL
ACFIIIINORTTV	VITRIFICATION	ACGIILLNRSSTY	CRYSTALLISING
ACFIIIJLLNOOT	JOLLIFICATION	ACGIILLNRSTYZ	CRYSTALLIZING
ACFIIIJNOSTTU	JUSTIFICATION	ACGIILMMNNOSU	COMMUNALISING
ACFIIILLMNOOT	MOLLIFICATION	ACGIILMMNNOUZ	COMMUNALIZING
ACFIIILLNNOTU	NULLIFICATION	ACGIILNORSTVY	SIGNAL VICTORY
ACFIIIMMMNOTU	MUMMIFICATION	ACGIILRRSTTUU	AGRICULTURIST
ACFIIIMNOORTT	MORTIFICATION	ACGIIMMNOORRS	MICROORGANISM
ACFIIIMNOOSST	ATOMIC FISSION	ACGIINNNOSTUY	CONSANGUINITY
ACFIIIMNOSTTY	MYSTIFICATION	ACGIINNOOPRRT	INCORPORATING
ACFIIINNOOPTT	PONTIFICATION	ACGIINNOOPRST	SCORING A POINT
ACFIIINNOOSTT	NOTIFICATIONS	ACGIINOOPRSTT	PATRIOTIC SONG
ACFIIJORSTTUY	JUSTIFICATORY	ACGIIOPRTTUVY	GROUP ACTIVITY
ACFILMNNOSTU	FUNCTIONALISM	ACGIKKLNOPTTU	TAKING POT LUCK
ACFIILNNOSTTU	FUNCTIONALIST	ACGIKLNNOORTT	TAKING CONTROL
ACFIILOPRRTTU	TROPICAL FRUIT	ACGIKNOORTTTU	TAKING TO COURT
ACFIMNNOORST	CONFIRMATIONS	ACGILLLMOOOPY	POMOLOGICALLY
ACFILNNOORTUY	ROYAL FUNCTION	ACGILLLNOOOSY	NOSOLOGICALLY
ACFILNOOSSSTW	CLASS OF ITS OWN	ACGILLLNOOOTY	ONTOLOGICALLY
ACFIMOORSTUVY	FAMOUS VICTORY	ACGILLMNPRSTU	CALLING TRUMPS
ACFINNNOOORTT	CONFRONTATION	ACGILLNOOOSTV	VOLCANOLOGIST
ACFLNNOOOORSTU	NON-FAST COLOUR	ACGILLNOOSTUV	VULCANOLOGIST
ACGGHHINNORST	SHORTCHANGING	ACGIMNOOOPSTT	COMING TO A STOP
ACGGHIILNNORS	CHORAL SINGING	ACGINNNORRSSU	RUNNING ACROSS
ACGGHIKLNOSTU	LAUGHING STOCK	ACHHHIIOTTTUW	WITHOUT A HITCH
	LAUGHINGSTOCK	ACHHIILLOOPPS	PHILOSOPHICAL
ACGGHHIIOPPRSY	PHYSIOGRAPHIC	ACHHIILNOPPRT	PHILANTHROPIC
ACGGHHIMNOOSTT	SHOOTING MATCH	ACHHIIMNOPPSS	CHAMPIONSHIPS
ACGGHHIMNOSTTU	SHOUTING MATCH	ACHHIINOOSTTW	IN CAHOOTS WITH
ACGGHIIIMNSSST	SCHISMATISING	ACHHILLNOPTXY	XANTHOPHYLLIC
ACGGHIIIMNSSTZ	SCHISMATIZING	ACHHIMNOOSTTU	AUTOCHTHONISM
ACGGHIIINPSTUV	CHAUVINIST PIG	ACHHLLNOOOSTU	ALLOCHTHONOUS
ACGGHIIKLLNOPS	LACKING POLISH	ACHHNOOOSTTUU	AUTOCHTHONOUS
ACGGHIIKMNNOPS	KINGS CHAMPION	ACHIIILNPPPRS	PRINCIPALSHIP
ACGGHIIKMNNRSS	SCRIMSHANKING	ACHIIKKNRSSTV	KNAVISH TRICKS
ACGGHIIILLOOPSY	PHYSIOLOGICAL	ACHIIKLNOSTTY	LAYS IT ON THICK
ACGGHIKMNOOSTU	ASKING TOO MUCH	ACHIILLOPSSTY	SOPHISTICALLY
ACGGHIKMNOOTTU	TAKING TOO MUCH	ACHIILMRSSSTT	CHRISTMAS LIST
ACGGHIKNNORTUV	HAVING NO TRUCK	ACHIIMMORRSTT	TRICHROMATISM
ACGGHILLMOOOPR	MORPHOLOGICAL	ACHIIMNNOOPPS	COMPANIONSHIP
ACGGHILLOOPRSS	OSCILLOGRAPHS	ACHIINOPSSTTU	PISTACHIO NUTS
ACGGHILLOOPRSY	OSCILLOGRAPHY	ACHIIPRSSSTTY	PSYCHIATRISTS
ACGGHILNOPSTTU	CAST LIGHT UPON	ACHILLMNNOPSYY	SYMPHONICALLY
ACGGHINOOTTTTU	CUTTING A TOOTH	ACHILLMNRSTUU	MUSIC-HALL TURN
ACGGHLNOORSSTU	LAUGHS TO SCORN	ACHILLNOOPTYY	HYPOTONICALLY
ACGGHMNOORSSTT	STRONG STOMACH	ACHILLORRTTUU	HORTICULTURAL
ACGIIIILLNNVZ	CIVILIANIZING	ACHILMOOPRRSY	PRIMARY SCHOOL
ACGIIIIMNNNRT	INCRIMINATING	ACHILNOORSSUU	UNSOCIAL HOURS
ACGIIKKMNQTU	MAKING IT QUICK	ACHILNOSSSTTU	SANSCULOTTISH
ACGIIIKKMNSTT	MAKING IT STICK	ACHILOOPPRRSS	SHIPS CORPORAL
ACGIIIKLNPRST	LACKING SPIRIT	ACHIMOOOPRSTT	SOMATOTROPHIC
ACGIIIKMNRSST	MISSING A TRICK	ACHKOOORSTTTU	TOOK A SHORT CUT
ACGIIIKNNNRTW	WINNING A TRICK	ACHLLMMOOORSY	CHROMOSOMALLY
ACGIIILLNNOOS	COLONIALISING	ACIIIILNOSSTV	CIVILISATIONS
ACGIIILLNNOOZ	COLONIALIZING	ACIIIILNOSTVZ	CIVILIZATIONS
ACGIIILLNNSTT	SCINTILLATING	ACIIIIMMNNNORT	INCRIMINATION
ACGIIILNRRTWY	WRITING A LYRIC	ACIIIMNNOSTTV	VICTIMISATION
ACGIIIMMNNORST	ROMANTICISING	ACIIIMNNOTTVZ	VICTIMIZATION
ACGIIIMMNNORTZ	ROMANTICIZING	ACIIILLNNOSTT	SCINTILLATION
ACGIIINNNNOPS	SPINNING A COIN	ACIIILLNNRSTY	INTRINSICALLY
ACGIIKKKNOPRUW	KICKING UP A ROW	ACIIILMMRSTUY	MILITARY MUSIC

ACIIILMNOPRSV	PROVINCIALISM
ACIIILNNOPRST	INSCRIPTIONAL
ACIIILNOOSSTT	COALITIONISTS
ACIIIMMNNORRTY	INCRIMINATORY
ACIIKKKNPSSTU	KICKS UP A STINK
ACIIKNOPSSTTU	PUTS A SOCK IN IT
ACIILLMOOOQSU	COLLOQUIALISM
ACIILLLOOQTUY	COLLOQUIALITY
ACIILLLRSTUUV	SILVICULTURAL
ACIILLLSSTTYY	STYLISTICALLY
ACIILLNRSTTYY	CRYSTALLINITY
ACIILMNOOOPST	COMPOSITIONAL
ACIILMNOORSUY	ACRIMONIOUSLY
ACIILMNOORTTY	MICROTONALITY
ACIILMNOORTVY	VOCAL MINORITY
ACIILMORRSSTY	MILITARY CROSS
ACIILNNOPPRTW	PRINCIPAL TOWN
ACIILNNORSTTU	INSTRUCTIONAL
ACIILNORSTTUV	VOLUNTARISTIC
ACIILOPPRSTTY	PARTY POLITICS
ACIILPRSSTTUU	APICULTURISTS
ACIIMMNNOOSTU	COMMUNISATION
ACIIMMNNOOTUZ	COMMUNIZATION
ACIIMNNOOSSTU	SANCTIMONIOUS
ACIINNNOOPRTU	PRONUNCIATION
ACIINNOOOPRRT	INCORPORATION
ACIINNOPRRSTT	TRANSCRIPTION
ACIINNORSSTTU	INCRUSTATIONS
ACIKLNNOOOPTZ	ZOOPLANKTONIC
ACILLMNNOOOTY	MONOTONICALLY
ACILLNNOOOTUV	CONVOLUTIONAL
ACILMNOOOPSST	COSMOPOLITANS
ACILMNOSSSTTU	SANSCULOTTISM
ACILMOOPRRRUY	PRIMARY COLOUR
ACILMOOPRRSTT	TROPICAL STORM
ACILMRRSSTTUU	STRUCTURALISM
ACILNNOORSUVY	CONVULSIONARY
ACILNNOOSSTTU	CONSULTATIONS
ACILNOORRSUVY	CARNIVOROUSLY
ACILRRSSTTTUU	STRUCTURALIST
ACIMMNNOOSSTU	CONSUMMATIONS
ACIMNOORRSTTY	ROMANTIC STORY
ACINOORRRTVWY	NARROW VICTORY
ACKKMNNOOPSST	POSTMANS KNOCK
ACKOOOPRSSTUY	COOKS UP A STORY
ACLMNOORSTUUU	AUTUMN COLOURS
ACLMORSSTTUUU	CUMULOSTRATUS
	STRATOCUMULUS
ADDDDEEEHHNNOT	NODDED THE HEAD
ADDDDEEIINNNW	WINED AND DINED
ADDDDEENNOSTU	DONE AND DUSTED
ADDDDEIIINPSV	PAID DIVIDENDS
ADDDEEEFLRSSS	SELF-ADDRESSED
ADDDEEEHHRSTW	SHREDDED WHEAT
ADDDEEEKNNRWY	EDWARD KENNEDY
ADDDEEEMMNNORT	DREADED MOMENT
ADDDEEENNOSSY	ENDED ONE'S DAYS
ADDDEEFIILLVW	DIVIDED WE FALL
ADDDEEFMOORSS	MODE OF ADDRESS
ADDDEEGHNRSTT	ADDED STRENGTH
ADDDEEHNNNORU	HUNDRED AND ONE
ADDDEEHNNNRTU	HUNDRED AND TEN
ADDDEEIKNORRR	ORDERED A DRINK
ADDDEGGLLNOSY	DADDY LONG-LEGS
ADDDEGINNOOTU	DODGE IN AND OUT
ADDDEHINNRSUX	HUNDRED AND SIX
ADDDEHNNORTUW	HUNDRED AND TWO
ADDDEIIKNNRRV	DRINK AND DRIVE
ADDDEIILLMNSV	SMALL DIVIDEND
ADDDEIILORSST	SORDID DETAILS
ADDDEIIMNNNOT	DANDIE DINMONT

ADDDEIINPSSVY	PAYS DIVIDENDS
ADDDENNORRTWW	DOWNWARD TREND
ADDDNNNOORRUU	ROUND AND ROUND
ADDEEEEEGLMPR	REDEEM A PLEDGE
ADDEEEEFILSST	ADESTE FIDELES
ADDEEEEGHNRTW	WEED THE GARDEN
ADDEEEEGHPRST	GATHERED SPEED
ADDEEEEHNRRTT	TENDERHEARTED
ADDEEEEKNSWWY	WEDNESDAY WEEK
ADDEEEEMOPRST	MODERATE SPEED
ADDEEEENNNORS	NEARED ONE'S END
ADDEEEEFFORRRW	REWARD OFFERED
ADDEEEEFHHMOOR	HEADED FOR HOME
ADDEEEFIINNNR	A FRIEND IN NEED
ADDEEEFILMRSU	DIE FLEDERMAUS
ADDEEEFILNNRR	LEARNED FRIEND
ADDEEEGHINPSS	PIGHEADEDNESS
ADDEEEGHINPTW	WIDENED THE GAP
ADDEEEGHLRRTU	ELDER DAUGHTER
ADDEEEGHNORSY	DEHYDROGENASE
ADDEEEGIINPSV	DEEP-SEA DIVING
ADDEEEGINNNOS	GAINED ONE'S END
ADDEEEGIPATTU	DEEP GRATITUDE
ADDEEEGIRRSST	READERS DIGEST
ADDEEEGLLMNRS	SMELLED DANGER
ADDEEEGLLNPRS	SPELLED DANGER
ADDEEEGMNRRRY	GERRYMANDERED
ADDEEEHHILSTT	HEADED THE LIST
ADDEEEHHNOSST	HOTHEADEDNESS
ADDEEEHILMSTT	THE MIDDLE EAST
ADDEEEHINNPSS	PINHEADEDNESS
ADDEEEHIPSTTU	HEATED DISPUTE
ADDEEEHMNOSSS	DEAD MEN'S SHOES
ADDEEEIILMNRZ	DEMINERALIZED
ADDEEEIINSTTT	DIED INTESTATE
ADDEEEILNNORT	LEARNED TO RIDE
ADDEEEIMNNRRS	SEND A REMINDER
ADDEEEINPRSTT	PREDESTINATED
ADDEEEKLLOOPS	LOOKED PLEASED
ADDEEENNOSWWY	WENDED ONE'S WAY
ADDEEENNSTWXY	NEXT WEDNESDAY
ADDEEENOPPRRT	PREPONDERATED
ADDEEERRSSSTU	RESTED ASSURED
ADDEEFFHNNOSS	OFFHANDEDNESS
ADDEEFFHNOOST	DOFFED ONE'S HAT
ADDEEFFLRRSUY	ALFRED DREYFUS
ADDEEFHILLPTY	PLAY THE FIDDLE
ADDEEFHILNRTV	LEFT-HAND DRIVE
ADDEEFHOORRTY	ORDER OF THE DAY
ADDEEFILLNORR	FILLED AN ORDER
ADDEEFILMORWW	WORLD-WIDE FAME
ADDEEFINPRRST	PARTED FRIENDS
ADDEEFLNNPRUY	PENNY DREADFUL
ADDEEFLNORSST	LEFT NO ADDRESS
ADDEEGGHINRST	DIGS THE GARDEN
ADDEEGGKLOORS	LOOKED DAGGERS
ADDEEGHILLTY	LIGHT-HEADEDLY
ADDEEGHHINTTY	DYING THE DEATH
ADDEEGHHKNOTU	KNEAD THE DOUGH
ADDEEGHIIMMNN	HIDDEN MEANING
ADDEEGHIIRSTW	DISAGREED WITH
ADDEEGHINRRST	DRAIN THE DREGS
ADDEEGHINRSST	SHEDDING TEARS
ADDEEGHLLNNTY	HANDLED GENTLY
ADDEEGHLNORWY	WRONGHEADEDLY
ADDEEGHLOORTY	GOOD-HEARTEDLY
ADDEEGHNORRTU	GATHERED ROUND
ADDEEGIINRSTT	DISINTEGRATED
ADDEEGILLPTUY	PLEADED GUILTY
ADDEEGIMNRSTU	STUDIED GERMAN
ADDEEGINRRSSS	DRESSED IN RAGS

ADDEEGNNRSSUU	UNGUARDEDNESS	ADDEGILLNORSV	GOLD AND SILVER
ADDEEGNORSSTU	ADDER'S-TONGUES		SILVER AND GOLD
ADDEEGOPRRSUW	POWDERED SUGAR	ADDEGILNNNOPU	LENDING A POUND
ADDEEHHNORSTU	THE ROUNDHEADS	ADDEGINNNNOST	STANDING ON END
ADDEEHIINNTTU	UNITED IN DEATH	ADDEGINNNOSST	NODDING ASSENT
ADDEEHIINRSTW	RAISED THE WIND	ADDEGINNNRSTU	UNDERSTANDING
ADDEEHIKLNRTY	KINDHEARTEDLY	ADDEGINNORRST	STANDING ORDER
ADDEEHILLNPTU	DULLED THE PAIN	ADDEGINOSSTTT	SETTING AT ODDS
ADDEEHIMNORST	THREE DIAMONDS	ADDEGLNOORTUY	GOODNATUREDLY
ADDEEHINNNORU	ONE IN A HUNDRED	ADDEGNOOOORTU	DONE A GOOD TURN
ADDEEHINNORST	TRIED ONE'S HAND	ADDEGNOOOPPRR	GOOD AND PROPER
ADDEEHINNOSST	TIED ONE'S HANDS	ADDEGNOOORSTU	DOES A GOOD TURN
ADDEEHINSSTWY	THIS WEDNESDAY	ADDEGNOOPRRSU	DROP ONES GUARD
ADDEEHIRSSTTU	RAISED THE DUST	ADDEGNORRSWWW	GREW DOWNWARDS
ADDEEHJKLLNYY	JEKYLL AND HYDE	ADDEHHIINOTTW	HAD DONE WITH IT
	JEKYLL-AND-HYDE	ADDEHHLNNOOSS	HOLDS ONE'S HAND
ADDEEHKOORTTW	WORKED TO DEATH	ADDEHHNNOOSTTU	HOUNDS TO DEATH
ADDEEHLNORTWY	DOWNHEARTEDLY	ADDEHILLMNRUY	EDMUND HILLARY
ADDEEHMNNOOOS	DO ONE HANDSOME	ADDEHILNORTUY	THE DAILY ROUND
ADDEEHMNORSTU	MADE THE ROUNDS	ADDEHILOSSTTT	ADDS TO THE LIST
ADDEEHNNOSSSU	USED ONE'S HANDS	ADDEHLLMNORUU	ROD HULL AND EMU
ADDEEHNOOSTTT	STONED TO DEATH	ADDEHLNNOOSSW	LOSE HANDS DOWN
ADDEEIIILMRST	DEMILITARISED	ADDEHNOOPRSTW	POWDER AND SHOT
ADDEEIIILMRTZ	DEMILITARIZED	ADDEIIIILNSUV	INDIVIDUALISE
ADDEEIIILORST	EDITORIALISED	ADDEIIIILNUVZ	INDIVIDUALIZE
ADDEEIIILORTZ	EDITORIALIZED	ADDEIIINSTTTU	ATTITUDINISED
ADDEEIILLRVYY	DAILY DELIVERY	ADDEIIINTTTUZ	ATTITUDINIZED
ADDEEIILLSTUY	IDEALLY SUITED	ADDEIIKLLNRST	TALK IN RIDDLES
ADDEEIILNNNOW	DANDELION WINE	ADDEIINOOORST	DEODORISATION
ADDEEIILNOPTY	YIELDED A POINT	ADDEIINOOORTZ	DEODORIZATION
ADDEEIINNNSSW	WINES AND DINES	ADDEIINOORRSV	ROAD DIVERSION
ADDEEIINNRSST	END IN DISASTER	ADDEIINOPRSTU	SUPERADDITION
ADDEEIINORSTT	DISORIENTATED	ADDEILLLMMNSY	SMALL-MINDEDLY
ADDEEIILNORRSW	OLDER AND WISER	ADDEILLMNOUWW	WALLOWED IN MUD
ADDEEIMNNOSSV	SEVEN DIAMONDS	ADDEILLSSSTUY	STUDY ALL SIDES
ADDEEIMNNSSSY	MANY-SIDEDNESS	ADDEILNORRTWY	TRODDEN WARILY
ADDEEIMORRTUV	DEVOUT ADMIRER	ADDEILOOSSTWW	SOWED WILD OATS
ADDEEINNOPRSW	OPENED INWARDS	ADDEIMMMRSSUY	MIDSUMMERS DAY
ADDEEINNSTTUW	UNITED WE STAND	ADDEIMNNRSSTU	MISUNDERSTAND
ADDEEIOSSTTUY	STAYED OUTSIDE	ADDEIMNOOPRSU	MODUS OPERANDI
ADDEENOPRRSSW	PRESSED ONWARD	ADDEINOORSSTY	STAYED INDOORS
ADDEFFMOORRSS	FORM OF ADDRESS	ADDELNOOPRSSW	DOWNWARD SLOPE
ADDEFGGILNOOY	DYING OF OLD AGE	ADDENOORRSSWW	DRAW ONES SWORD
ADDEFGHILRSTU	DREADFUL SIGHT	ADDFIIMNOOSSX	SIX OF DIAMONDS
ADDEFGJMNOTUY	DAY OF JUDGMENT	ADDFIMNOOOSTW	TWO OF DIAMONDS
ADDEFGORRRSUW	SURGED FORWARD	ADDGGHIINOOST	SAID GOODNIGHT
ADDEFHOPRRSUW	PUSHED FORWARD	ADDGGILLNNOOP	PLODDING ALONG
ADDEFHORRRSUW	RUSHED FORWARD	ADDGGILNNNORU	LANDING GROUND
ADDEFIINORRSW	INSIDE FORWARD	ADDGHIILMNOOT	DID A MOONLIGHT
ADDEFIMNNOOST	TEN OF DIAMONDS	ADDGIIINNTUV	INDIVIDUATING
ADDEFINORRRVW	DRIVEN FORWARD	ADDGIIKKNNORV	DRINKING VODKA
ADDEFIORRRSVW	DRIVES FORWARD	ADDGIILLLLNYY	DILLY DALLYING
ADDEFLOORSTWW	FLOWED TOWARDS		DILLYDALLYING
ADDEFLORRSTUY	DREADFUL STORY	ADDGIINNORRUV	DRIVING AROUND
ADDEGGHHLRRSTU	STRUGGLED HARD	ADDGIMNNNOORW	DID NO MAN WRONG
ADDEGGIIKLNOY	DYING LIKE A DOG	ADDGNOORRSWWW	GROW DOWNWARDS
ADDEGGNORRSUU	DANGEROUS DRUG	ADDHILORRTWW	THIRD WORLD WAR
ADDEGHHHORSTU	DASHED THROUGH	ADDHINNNOSSWW	WINS HANDS DOWN
ADDEGHHIINRST	RIGHT-HAND SIDE	ADDHLNNOOSSTW	LOST HANDS DOWN
ADDEGHHIINSTW	DID THE WASHING	ADDIIIILMNSUV	INDIVIDUALISM
ADDEGHHILNRSS	HIGHLAND DRESS	ADDIIIILNSTUV	INDIVIDUALIST
ADDEGHHILNRTY	RIGHT-HANDEDLY	ADDIIIILNTUVY	INDIVIDUALITY
ADDEGHILNOOTU	GO INTO A HUDDLE	ADDIIIINNOTUV	INDIVIDUATION
ADDEGHILNOSTY	LAYING THE ODDS	ADDILLLNOOWWY	WILD AND WOOLLY
ADDEGHILOPTVW	PAVED WITH GOLD	ADDKLNNOOOPUW	LOOK UP AND DOWN
ADDEGIILNNRRV	LIVING IN DREAD	ADEEEEEGHLNTV	GAVE THE NEEDLE
ADDEGIIMNNNPX	MIND-EXPANDING	ADEEEEEHLLRRW	WHEELER-DEALER
ADDEGIIMNNNRW	WANDERING MIND	ADEEEEFGLNRST	SELF-GENERATED
ADDEGIIMNNORV	DRIVING ONE MAD	ADEEEEFHIKLLT	FEEL LIKE DEATH
ADDEGILLLMOST	GOLD MEDALLIST	ADEEEEFHLSTUX	FEEL EXHAUSTED
		ADEEEEFHNOPST	OPENED THE SAFE

ADEEEEFHORTTZ	FREEZE TO DEATH
ADEEEEFLNOSST	SEATED ONESELF
ADEEEEGGLRSTT	GETS RELEGATED
ADEEEEGHKLPTT	TAKE THE PLEDGE
ADEEEEGHNOPTT	OPENED THE GATE
ADEEEEGLMORTX	EXTREME OLD AGE
ADEEEEGLPQRSU	DEEP SQUARE LEG
ADEEEEGMNRRTX	EXTREME DANGER
ADEEEEGPRRSTW	GREW DESPERATE
ADEEEEHHLORSV	HEAD OVER HEELS
ADEEEEHISSTUV	EVADE THE ISSUE
ADEEEEHMRRTTX	EXTREME HATRED
ADEEEEHNNORST	ENTER ONE'S HEAD
ADEEEEKKNSSWW	WEEKS AND WEEKS
ADEEEELNOPRTT	OPENED A LETTER
ADEEEELNQRSUV	ELEVEN SQUARED
ADEEEELNRSTVW	SWEET LAVENDER
ADEEEEMOPRSTV	DESPERATE MOVE
ADEEEEENPRSSST	DESPERATENESS
ADEEEEEFRSSTU	SUFFERS DEFEAT
ADEEEEFFGILNST	SELF-DEFEATING
ADEEEFFGIORRT	AGREE TO DIFFER
ADEEEFFHINNRT	FANNED THE FIRE
ADEEEFFHLNORT	LAND OF THE FREE
ADEEEFFHMORTT	MADE THE EFFORT
ADEEEFFIINRTT	DIFFERENTIATE
ADEEEFGHLNNOS	HANGED ONESELF
ADEEEFGLNOSSS	GASSED ONESELF
ADEEEFGNNORSS	SENSE OF DANGER
ADEEEFHIKLLTT	FELT LIKE DEATH
ADEEEFHILSTTT	FAILED THE TEST
ADEEEFHINOSST	ON THE SAFE SIDE
ADEEEFHINRSTW	FREE AS THE WIND
ADEEEFHLNNORS	HARDEN ONESELF
ADEEEFHLSTTUX	FELT EXHAUSTED
ADEEEFHOPRSST	THREE OF SPADES
ADEEEFHRRSTTU	FEATHER DUSTER
ADEEEFHRRTTUU	READ THE FUTURE
ADEEEFILLNRTY	DEFERENTIALLY
ADEEEFILNRSTY	SEDENTARY LIFE
ADEEEFIMNRSST	MEET AS FRIENDS
ADEEEFINQRRTU	ENQUIRED AFTER
ADEEEFLMNOSSU	AMUSED ONESELF
ADEEEFMNPRSTY	DEFERS PAYMENT
ADEEEFNOPQSSU	QUEEN OF SPADES
ADEEEFNOPSSSV	SEVEN OF SPADES
ADEEEFORRRRTW	REFER TO DRAWER
ADEEEGGGINNTT	GETTING AN EDGE
ADEEEGGGINRST	DESEGREGATING
ADEEEGGHHINTV	HAVING THE EDGE
ADEEEGGHHIORT	TO A HIGH DEGREE
ADEEEGGILNRST	TEENAGED GIRLS
ADEEEGGIMNNST	DISENGAGEMENT
ADEEEGGINNRRU	GENUINE REGARD
ADEEEGGINORST	DESEGREGATION
ADEEEGGNORRSS	GEORGE SANDERS
ADEEEGHHIMTTW	MADE THE WEIGHT
ADEEEGHHORSTT	HEADS TOGETHER
ADEEEGHIIPTUV	GIVE UP THE IDEA
ADEEEGHLMMRSS	SLEDGEHAMMERS
ADEEEGHLNORSS	DRAG ONE'S HEELS
ADEEEGHNOOSSW	SHOWED ONE'S AGE
ADEEEGHNPRTTU	TURNED THE PAGE
ADEEEGHORRSST	GATHERED ROSES
ADEEEGIINPSSW	SWEEPING ASIDE
ADEEEGILMNNRR	MERRIE ENGLAND
ADEEEGIMNRSST	DEMAGNETISERS
	DISAGREEMENTS
ADEEEGIMNRSTZ	DEMAGNETIZERS
ADEEEGIRRSTTV	TERGIVERSATED
ADEEEGKLNOOOS	LOOKED ONE'S AGE

ADEEEGLLNORTU	OUTGENERALLED
ADEEEGLPRSSTT	GETS PLASTERED
ADEEEGMPSSTTU	GETS STEAMED UP
ADEEEGOPRRSTW	GROW DESPERATE
ADEEEGOPRRTUY	DAGUERREOTYPE
ADEEEHHHILNOT	HOLE IN THE HEAD
ADEEEHHHLOOTV	THE OLD HEAVE-HO
ADEEEHHILMSTV	SHAME THE DEVIL
ADEEEHHLOPRTY	PLAYED THE HERO
ADEEEHHLORSTT	LOSE THE THREAD
ADEEEHHNOOPTV	HOPED TO HEAVEN
ADEEEHIKKNPRT	KEEP IN THE DARK
ADEEEHIKNRSST	SEES IN THE DARK
ADEEEHILMPRST	SIMPLE-HEARTED
ADEEEHILNPPTT	TAPPED THE LINE
ADEEEHIMNRSTT	HEREDITAMENTS
ADEEEHIMPSSTT	PASSED THE TIME
ADEEEHINNORST	ON THE NEAR-SIDE
ADEEEHINPRSST	PARENTHESISED
ADEEEHINPRSTZ	PARENTHESIZED
ADEEEHIORRSVW	OVERHEAD WIRES
ADEEEHLLOPPST	PLEASED TO HELP
ADEEEHLNOPRTY	OPENHEARTEDLY
ADEEEHLNSSSST	DEATHLESSNESS
ADEEEHIMNORRST	READ THE SERMON
ADEEEHNNOSTWW	DOWN THE SWANEE
ADEEEHNOPRRTW	OPEN THE DRAWER
ADEEEHNPRRTTT	THE TENDER TRAP
ADEEEHNPRSSTW	SPREAD THE NEWS
ADEEEHOPPRSST	STEPPED ASHORE
ADEEEHORRTVYY	EVERY OTHER DAY
ADEEEHPSSSTTT	PASSED THE TEST
ADEEEIILMNRRS	DEMINERALISER
ADEEEIILMNRRZ	DEMINERALIZER
ADEEEIILMNRSS	DEMINERALISES
ADEEEIILMNRSZ	DEMINERALIZES
ADEEEIILNOSTV	SIDE ELEVATION
ADEEEIILNRTVY	IN EVERY DETAIL
ADEEEIIMMNNSST	IMMEDIATENESS
ADEEEIIMMSTTT	ESTIMATED TIME
ADEEEIIMNNRTT	INDETERMINATE
ADEEEIIMNORSU	MADE ENQUIRIES
ADEEEIIMNRSTT	INTERMEDIATES
ADEEEIIMNRTTV	DETERMINATIVE
ADEEEIIMPRTTV	PREMEDITATIVE
ADEEEIINPRSST	PEDESTRIANISE
ADEEEIINPRSTZ	PEDESTRIANIZE
ADEEEIINSSTTT	DIES INTESTATE
ADEEEIIORRTTV	DETERIORATIVE
ADEEEIKNNOOST	TAKE ON ONE SIDE
ADEEEIKNNOSST	TAKEN ONE'S SIDE
ADEEEIKNOOSTT	TAKE TO ONE SIDE
ADEEEIKNOSSST	TAKES ONE'S SIDE
ADEEEIILLMMOSS	MADEMOISELLES
ADEEEIILLNPRTT	INTERPELLATED
ADEEEIILMNORST	RADIOELEMENTS
ADEEEIILMNRSTT	MELTED IN TEARS
ADEEEIILMNRTTY	DETERMINATELY
ADEEEIILNNNRUV	INLAND REVENUE
ADEEEIILNOPRSS	DEPERSONALISE
ADEEEIILNOPRSZ	DEPERSONALIZE
ADEEEIILNPRRST	INTERPLEADERS
ADEEEIILNRRRRV	LEARNER DRIVER
ADEEEIILOPPPRR	APPLE-PIE ORDER
ADEEEIILOPRSTT	TRIED TO PLEASE
ADEEEIILORRVVW	DREW A VEIL OVER
ADEEEIILOSSTUV	LEAVES OUTSIDE
ADEEEIIMNNRRST	SENT A REMINDER
ADEEEIIMNRSTTU	UNDERESTIMATE
ADEEEIIMNRSTTV	ADVERTISEMENT
ADEEEIIMORSTTV	OVERESTIMATED

ADEEEIMORSTVW	MODERATE VIEWS
ADEEEINPRSSTT	PREDESTINATES
ADEEEIORRSSST	SEASIDE RESORT
ADEEEIPRRRTUU	PIERRE TRUDEAU
ADEEEKOPPSTTU	KEEPS UP-TO-DATE
ADEEELLMNOPTV	DEVELOPMENTAL
ADEEELLMORRST	STEAMROLLERED
ADEEEELLNOORTV	LEARNED TO LOVE
ADEEELMNNNOSS	LENDS ONE'S NAME
ADEEELMNRSSSS	DREAMLESSNESS
ADEEELMNSTTTY	SETTLEMENT DAY
ADEEELNOSSSTY	NEEDLESS TO SAY
ADEEELOPRSTTT	POSTED A LETTER
ADEEELQRSTUVW	TWELVE SQUARED
ADEEEMNORSTUV	ADVENTURESOME
ADEEEMNPRRSST	PRESENTED ARMS
ADEEENOPPRRST	PREPONDERATES
ADEEENOPRRSSY	READY RESPONSE
ADEEFFGHNOOOS	GO OFF ONES HEAD
ADEEFFGIILNRT	LIFTED A FINGER
ADEEFFHHINOTT	TAN THE HIDE OFF
ADEEFFHHMOORT	HEAD OF THE FORM
ADEEFFHIINRRS	FRESH-AIR FIEND
ADEEFFHIKLOTT	TAKE THE LID OFF
ADEEFFHLMRTUY	MADE THE FUR FLY
ADEEFFHLOORTT	AFTER THE FLOOD
ADEEFFHMNOORS	HANDSOME OFFER
ADEEFFIILMMOR	MAIMED FOR LIFE
ADEEFFIILNRST	DIFFERENTIALS
ADEEFFIILSSST	SELF-SATISFIED
ADEEFFLLOORTW	FOLLOWED AFTER
ADEEFFLORSSSU	SUFFERED A LOSS
ADEEFFNOORRST	FOREST OF ARDEN
ADEEFGGILNRRS	SELF-REGARDING
ADEEFGHHLOSTW	SHOWED THE FLAG
ADEEFGHIINTTX	FIXING THE DATE
ADEEFGHIOPSST	EIGHT OF SPADES
ADEEFGIINNRVY	FRIDAY EVENING
ADEEFGJLNOPSU	PANEL OF JUDGES
ADEEFGLNOOORS	OLD FOR ONES AGE
ADEEFHHILNOST	LED THE FASHION
ADEEFHHILOSTU	HATFIELD HOUSE
ADEEFHHINOSTT	SOFT IN THE HEAD
ADEEFHHLOOTWY	WHOLE OF THE DAY
ADEEFHIILMSTT	THE MAILED FIST
ADEEFHIILNRSY	FINISHED EARLY
ADEEFHIJLMNOS	JOHN MASEFIELD
ADEEFHIKLNRTT	LEFT IN THE DARK
ADEEFHIKMORTW	WIDE OF THE MARK
ADEEFHIKNORRW	FRANKIE HOWERD
ADEEFHILMORTT	OLD FATHER TIME
ADEEFHILORTVY	LIVE FOR THE DAY
ADEEFHIMMNOST	OF THE SAME MIND
ADEEFHINRSSTU	RAISE THE FUNDS
ADEEFHIOORRST	RAISED THE ROOF
ADEEFHIRRSTTT	THIRSTED AFTER
ADEEFHLLOOPTY	PLAYED THE FOOL
ADEEFHLNOPRTU	PEAL OF THUNDER
ADEEFHLOORRTU	RULE OF THE ROAD
ADEEFHLORSTTY	SOFTHEARTEDLY
ADEEFHMMOOSTT	MADE THE MOST OF
ADEEFHMOOORTT	FROM HEAD TO TOE
ADEEFHMORRSTT	STREAMED FORTH
ADEEFHNOOOPST	TOP OF ONES HEAD
ADEEFHNOOORRT	ONE FOR THE ROAD
ADEEFHNOOOSTU	OUT OF ONES HEAD
ADEEFHNOORTTZ	FROZEN TO DEATH
ADEEFHNORRTXY	REYNARD THE FOX
ADEEFIILLNSSY	ELYSIAN FIELDS
ADEEFIILNNRSU	ENDS IN FAILURE
ADEEFIILNSTTY	FALSE IDENTITY

ADEEFIIMNORSS	ADMISSION FREE
	FREE ADMISSION
ADEEFILLOPRTY	FAILED TO REPLY
ADEEFILLORSUY	LADY OF LEISURE
ADEEFILMNOYZZ	FIZZY LEMONADE
ADEEFILMNOPRTY	PLAYED FOR TIME
ADEEFILNNORRT	LATE FOR DINNER
ADEEFILNSSSTU	SELF-SUSTAINED
ADEEFIMOORSTT	FRIED TOMATOES
ADEEFINNNORST	DANTES INFERNO
ADEEFINOORSTT	DEFORESTATION
ADEEFIOOPRSTT	FRIED POTATOES
ADEEFKMNOORSY	ASKED FOR MONEY
ADEEFLLPPRRUY	FULLY PREPARED
ADEEFLNORRSSU	SUE FOR SLANDER
ADEEFLOPRSTUY	REFUSED TO PLAY
ADEEFNNOPRSTU	SPEND A FORTUNE
ADEEGGHILNNRS	ENGLISH GARDEN
ADEEGGHLRSTTU	DEATH STRUGGLE
ADEEGGHOOSTTV	GAVE TO THE DOGS
ADEEGGIIMNNST	DEMAGNETISING
ADEEGGIIMNNTZ	DEMAGNETIZING
ADEEGGILLNNTY	DEALING GENTLY
ADEEGGINNOSWY	EDGING ONE'S WAY
ADEEGGINNOTXY	DEOXYGENATING
ADEEGGINORSSV	DIGS ONE'S GRAVE
ADEEGGLNNOORR	GENERAL GORDON
ADEEGGLNOPPRS	DOPPELGANGERS
ADEEGHHINRTTT	RIGHT AT THE END
ADEEGHIIKLMRT	LIKE GRIM DEATH
ADEEGHIINNRRT	RENDING THE AIR
ADEEGHIINNRST	DISHEARTENING
ADEEGHIINRSTT	AT THE RINGSIDE
ADEEGHIIRSSTW	DISAGREES WITH
ADEEGHILMNOST	HOLDS A MEETING
ADEEGHILNRSTY	NEARSIGHTEDLY
ADEEGHILNSSTW	SWINGS THE LEAD
ADEEGHIMMNOST	MADE SOMETHING
ADEEGHINNNOST	GET ONE'S HAND IN
ADEEGHINNOSSU	USING ONE'S HEAD
ADEEGHINNOSSV	HAVE DESIGNS ON
ADEEGHLLNNSTY	HANDLES GENTLY
ADEEGHLMNORST	GOLDEN HAMSTER
ADEEGHLNOSTTY	THE LONGEST DAY
ADEEGHMNNNSTU	MANNED THE GUNS
ADEEGHNNORRTU	NEAR THE GROUND
ADEEGHNORSTTT	STAND TOGETHER
ADEEGHOPPPSTT	STOPPED THE GAP
ADEEGHORSSTTU	ARGUED THE TOSS
ADEEGHPRSSTTU	STEPDAUGHTERS
ADEEGIIKKNPRT	KEEPING IT DARK
ADEEGIILMNNTY	DEMYELINATING
ADEEGIILNSSUX	DESEXUALISING
ADEEGIILNSUXZ	DESEXUALIZING
ADEEGIIMNPRTT	PREMEDITATING
ADEEGIINNNRST	ENDING IN TEARS
ADEEGIINNRRST	TRAINED SINGER
ADEEGIINORRTT	DETERIORATING
ADEEGIINPPSST	STEPPING ASIDE
ADEEGIINRSSTT	DISINTEGRATES
ADEEGIKLNORST	LEADING STOKER
	TAKE IN LODGERS
ADEEGIKMNOOST	TAKE SOME DOING
ADEEGIKNNRRST	KINDERGARTENS
ADEEGIKNNRSST	GREAT KINDNESS
ADEEGILLMNNOR	NOMINAL LEDGER
ADEEGIILLNORSW	WELL ORGANISED
ADEEGILLNRRST	DRILL SERGEANT
ADEEGILMOORST	DERMATOLOGIES
ADEEGILMRSSTY	GREATLY MISSED
ADEEGILNNNNOO	LONNIE DONEGAN

ADEEGILNNNOUV	LEAVING UNDONE	ADEEHILOPTTVY	THE DEVIL TO PAY
ADEEGILNNOOPS	OLD-AGE PENSION	ADEEHILOSTTUW	OUTSIDE THE LAW
ADEEGIMNNNOVY	MONDAY EVENING	ADEEHIMMOPRTX	MIXED METAPHOR
ADEEGIMNNOOPRT	IN A GOOD TEMPER	ADEEHIMNPPRSS	MISAPPREHENDS
ADEEGIMNOORTV	MOVED INTO GEAR	ADEEHIMNSTTUW	WEST HAM UNITED
ADEEGIMNRSSTU	STUDIES GERMAN	ADEEHINNOPSSW	WIPE ONES HANDS
ADEEGINNNPPTT	PATENT PENDING	ADEEHINNORSST	TRIES ONE'S HAND
ADEEGINNNSUVY	SUNDAY EVENING	ADEEHINNOSSST	TIES ONE'S HANDS
ADEEGINNOOTXY	DEOXYGENATION	ADEEHINOPPSTT	TIPPED ONE'S HAT
ADEEGINNORRVW	WANDERING OVER	ADEEHINOPTTWY	POINTED THE WAY
ADEEGINNORSSS	GRANDIOSENESS	ADEEHINORTWWW	WEATHER WINDOW
ADEEGINNORSSX	GRINDS ONE'S AXE	ADEEHINRRSSST	TEARS IN SHREDS
ADEEGINNOSWWY	WINGED ONE'S WAY	ADEEHIRSSSTTU	RAISES THE DUST
ADEEGINNRRSTW	WINTER GARDENS	ADEEHIRSSTWWY	THREW SIDEWAYS
ADEEGINOPPRSV	EAVESDROPPING	ADEEHKLOOPRTT	LOOKED THE PART
ADEEGINOPRRTY	POETRY READING	ADEEHKMNORSTU	MAKE THE ROUNDS
ADEEGINORRSSU	SERIOUS DANGER	ADEEHKMOPRSTT	MARKED THE SPOT
ADEEGINRRRVWY	VERY REWARDING	ADEEHKNNRRSST	RENDERS THANKS
ADEEGINRRSSSS	DRESSES IN RAGS	ADEEHKOPRSSTW	SPEAKS THE WORD
ADEEGLNNOORRT	GREATER LONDON	ADEEHLLLLSUVY	SHELLEY DUVALL
ADEEGLNNORSTU	DENTAL SURGEON	ADEEHLLNPSTUW	SEND UP THE WALL
ADEEGLNRRSTUY	DENTAL SURGERY	ADEEHLNNNOOTY	THE ONE AND ONLY
ADEEGMNNOOORY	EARN GOOD MONEY	ADEEHLNORSSTU	DAUNTLESS HERO
ADEEGMNNRRSTU	UNDERGARMENTS	ADEEHLORRRTWW	WORLD WAR THREE
ADEEGNNOOOORS	ONE GOOD REASON	ADEEHMMOOPRST	METAMORPHOSED
ADEEGNNOORSUX	GROUND ONE'S AXE	ADEEHMMNNOOORS	HARD ON SOMEONE
ADEEGNNORSSSU	DANGEROUSNESS	ADEEHMNNOORRSY	DYSMENORRHOEA
ADEEGNNRRRSUY	NURSERY GARDEN	ADEEHMNOORSTU	MOUNTED A HORSE
ADEEGNOOPRSWY	GROPED ONE'S WAY	ADEEHMOOPPSTT	STOPPED AT HOME
ADEEHHHINOSTT	HITS ON THE HEAD	ADEEHNNNOOOSW	ON ONE'S OWN HEAD
ADEEHHHIRSSTV	HAD THE SHIVERS	ADEEHNNOOOPRT	ON THE OPEN ROAD
ADEEHHHISSSTW	WASH THE DISHES	ADEEHNNOSSSSU	USES ONE'S HANDS
ADEEHHIILLSTW	HAD THE WILLIES	ADEEHNNOSSTUV	SEVEN THOUSAND
ADEEHHIKNRRSS	HEADSHRINKERS	ADEEHNOORRSTW	ANSWER THE DOOR
ADEEHHILNOORT	HOLE IN THE ROAD	ADEEHNOOSSTTT	STONES TO DEATH
ADEEHHILNOOTT	TOAD IN THE HOLE	ADEEHNORSSTTU	TURNED TO ASHES
	TOAD IN THE HOLE	ADEEHNORSSTTW	SHORT AND SWEET
ADEEHHIMNNPST	MANNED THE SHIP		TWOS AND THREES
ADEEHHIMOPRRT	HERMAPHRODITE	ADEEHNORTTTUU	TRUE UNTO DEATH
ADEEHHIMRSSTT	MISS THE THREAD	ADEEHNOSSTTTY	STAYS TO THE END
ADEEHHINPSTTU	PUT IN THE SHADE	ADEEHNSSSTTTT	STANDS THE TEST
ADEEHHIORRSSS	HORSERADISHES	ADEEHOORTUVWY	WHATEVER YOU DO
ADEEHHKNOOOSS	SHOOK ONE'S HEAD	ADEEHORSSTUVY	SHROVE TUESDAY
ADEEHHKORRRSTW	SHARED THE WORK	ADEEHRRSTUVYY	EVERY THURSDAY
ADEEHHLLNOSTW	THE SHALLOW END	ADEEIIILMRSST	DEMILITARISES
ADEEHHLLOORTT	THE ROAD TO HELL	ADEEIIILMRSTZ	DEMILITARIZES
ADEEHHLMNOOSU	HOUSEHOLD NAME	ADEEIIILORRST	EDITORIALISER
ADEEHHLLOORSTT	SHARED THE LOOT	ADEEIIILORRTZ	EDITORIALIZER
ADEEHHLOPSTTY	PLAYED THE HOST	ADEEIIILORSST	EDITORIALISES
ADEEHHLORSTTT	LOST THE THREAD	ADEEIIILORSTZ	EDITORIALIZES
ADEEHHMNOSTTW	DOWN THE THAMES	ADEEIIIMNQRSU	MADE INQUIRIES
ADEEHHNOOPSSS	DASH ONES HOPES	ADEEIIINPRSST	STIPENDIARIES
ADEEHHNORRTTU	ROUND THE EARTH	ADEEIIKLRRTTT	TREAT LIKE DIRT
ADEEHHNORSTTU	THREE THOUSAND	ADEEIIKMNOSSS	SEEK ADMISSION
ADEEHIIKLRSTY	HEARTY DISLIKE	ADEEIILLMMNSS	MILES AND MILES
ADEEHIILLNNOT	LAID ON THE LINE	ADEEIILLNRSTY	RESIDENTIALLY
ADEEHIINOPRRV	PROVIDE AN HEIR	ADEEIILMNNOTY	DEMYELINATION
ADEEHIINRSSTW	RAISES THE WIND	ADEEIILMQRSUU	LIQUID MEASURE
ADEEHIIOSSTUV	AVOID THE ISSUE	ADEEIILNOSTTT	LATEST EDITION
ADEEHIJMNORTY	JOINED THE ARMY	ADEEIILNRSSUV	UNIVERSALISED
ADEEHIJNNOTVY	JOINED THE NAVY	ADEEIILNRSUVZ	UNIVERSALIZED
ADEEHIKKNPRTT	KEPT IN THE DARK	ADEEIIMNNORTT	DETERMINATION
ADEEHIKMMRSST	MISSED THE MARK	ADEEIIMNNOSTT	SEDIMENTATION
ADEEHILLMOSTW	WELL-AIMED SHOT	ADEEIIMNNPRST	PRESIDENT AMIN
ADEEHILLNSSST	SHETLAND ISLES	ADEEIIMNOPPTT	APPOINTED TIME
ADEEHILLOPPPS	APPLE-POLISHED	ADEEIIMNOPRTT	PREMEDITATION
ADEEHILMNORTT	OLDER THAN TIME	ADEEIIMNORRTV	ARRIVED ON TIME
ADEEHILMNTTUY	UNTIMELY DEATH	ADEEIIMNPRSST	PEDESTRIANISM
ADEEHILNNORUY	HELD AN ENQUIRY	ADEEIIMRSSSTT	MISSED A SITTER
ADEEHILNNQSTU	HELD AN INQUEST	ADEEIINNOPRST	IN DESPERATION
ADEEHILNOSSUV	HAVE DELUSIONS	ADEEIINNORSTT	TENDERISATION

ADEEIINNORTTZ	TENDERIZATION
ADEEIINNPPRTW	TIPPED A WINNER
ADEEIINOORRTT	DETERIORATION
ADEEIINOPRTXY	EXPEDITIONARY
ADEEIINORSSTT	DISORIENTATES
ADEEIINRRSTVW	WATER-DIVINERS
ADEEIIOPSSSTU	ADIPOSE TISSUE
ADEEIKLLMORST	MODERATE SKILL
ADEEIKLLQTTUY	TALKED QUIETLY
ADEEIKLNOSSSV	LOVE AND KISSES
ADEEIKMNNOPSS	SPEAK ONES MIND
ADEEIKMNOPRRT	POINTED REMARK
ADEEILLLMNOST	STILL LEMONADE
ADEEILLMNOOPS	OILED ONE'S PALM
ADEEILLMNRTTY	DETRIMENTALLY
ADEEILLNOPPTW	WELL-APPOINTED
ADEEILLNORRVY	ORDINARY LEVEL
ADEEILLOSSTVW	OLD WIVES TALES
ADEEILLPRSSST	SPELL DISASTER
ADEEILLTTTTTT	TITTLE-TATTLED
ADEEILMMNNSTT	DISMANTLEMENT
ADEEILMNOORTZ	METRONIDAZOLE
ADEEILMNPPRSU	PURE AND SIMPLE
ADEEILNNRTTVY	INADVERTENTLY
ADEEILNOPPRRS	PERSONAL PRIDE
ADEEILNOQRRSU	RED LION SQUARE
ADEEILNORRSTV	LEARNS TO DRIVE
ADEEILNORRTTV	LEARNT TO DRIVE
ADEEILPRSSSTT	SPELT DISASTER
ADEEIMMNNOSSU	ONE'S NAME IS MUD
ADEEIMMNORSSU	MISDEMEANOURS
ADEEIMNNOOPST	MADE ONE'S POINT
ADEEIMNNOPRRT	MODERN PAINTER
	PREORDAINMENT
ADEEIMNNORSUV	DEVIOUS MANNER
ADEEIMNNORSTTV	DEMONSTRATIVE
ADEEIMNPRRTTT	PRINTED MATTER
ADEEINNOORRSW	WORD IN ONES EAR
ADEEINNOPRSST	TENDER PASSION
ADEEINNORTTTW	DREW ATTENTION
ADEEINNOSSTTU	SUSTAINED NOTE
ADEEINNOSSTTW	AT ONES WITS END
ADEEINOOPSSTT	DIE AT ONES POST
ADEEINOPRRSTT	PREDESTINATOR
ADEEINOPRRSTU	SUPERORDINATE
ADEEINRSTTTUW	TWISTED NATURE
ADEEIOOPRRTVW	OPERATIVE WORD
ADEEKLNOOPRSY	PLAYED SNOOKER
ADEEKNOORSWWY	WORKED ONE'S WAY
ADEELLLORSTVW	TWELVE DOLLARS
ADEELLMORSUZZ	MUZZLE-LOADERS
ADEELLNOORRWW	LOWER AND LOWER
ADEELLNOPPRUY	ROPE AND PULLEY
ADEELMNNORRRY	ORDERLY MANNER
ADEELNNSSSSTU	DAUNTLESSNESS
ADEELNOORRTUV	OVERLAND ROUTE
ADEELOOPPRTUV	OVERPOPULATED
ADEELOPPRSTVY	PLEADS POVERTY
ADEEMMMMNRSSSU	SUMMER MADNESS
ADEEMNOORSWWY	WORMED ONE'S WAY
ADEEMNOORTUUV	OUTMANOEUVRED
ADEEMNRSTTTUU	MATURE STUDENT
ADEENNNORSUVY	NEVER ON SUNDAY
ADEENNOOPSSTT	STEPTOE AND SON
ADEENNOSTTWYY	TWENTY-ONE DAYS
ADEENOOOSSSTW	SOWED ONE'S OATS
ADEENOORRSSWW	WORSE AND WORSE
ADEENOORSSSTW	EATS ONE'S WORDS
ADEENOPRRSSSW	PRESSES ONWARD
ADEENORSTTUVY	VENTURED TO SAY
ADEENPRSSSUXY	SUNDAY EXPRESS

ADEEORRRSTTUW	WARDOUR STREET
ADEFFHIKLOTWW	WALKED OFF WITH
ADEFFHILNRSTU	FURNISHED FLAT
ADEFFHKOOOTTY	TOOK THE DAY OFF
ADEFFIILLMNOR	FILLED IN A FORM
ADEFFMNOORSWW	MAN OF FEW WORDS
ADEFGGHIILNOU	DIE OF LAUGHING
ADEFGGHIILNTU	FIGHTING A DUEL
ADEFGGHIINNRSU	DASHING FIGURE
ADEFGGHINOORT	GATHERING FOOD
ADEFGGIIILNNS	FLINGING ASIDE
ADEFGGIINOORR	GOING FOR A RIDE
ADEFGGIKLNNNO	KING OF ENGLAND
ADEFGGIOORSTU	GOOD AT FIGURES
ADEFGHHILNOST	SLEIGHT OF HAND
ADEFGHIILNRRT	INFRARED LIGHT
ADEFGHIIMNRTT	AFTER MIDNIGHT
ADEFGHIINNRSV	HAVING FRIENDS
ADEFGHIINNTWY	FINDING THE WAY
ADEFGHIKLOORT	LOOKED A FRIGHT
ADEFGHINOORSW	FORESHADOWING
ADEFGHLLOOORT	ALL FOR THE GOOD
ADEFGHNOOSTTU	GETS OUT OF HAND
ADEFGGIIKMNNRS	MAKING FRIENDS
ADEFGIINNOORR	FOREORDAINING
ADEFGIJLMNNTU	FINAL JUDGMENT
ADEFGIJLNSSTU	SELF-ADJUSTING
ADEFGIKKMNNOR	KING OF DENMARK
ADEFGILLNOPST	SOFT-PEDALLING
ADEFGNNOOOORT	GOOD AFTERNOON
ADEFGORRRSSUW	SURGES FORWARD
ADEFHIILLOPST	FIELD HOSPITAL
ADEFHILLNOOOP	FIND A LOOPHOLE
ADEFHILNNPRTT	PENTLAND FIRTH
ADEFHILNOORSS	FOOLHARDINESS
ADEFHIMNNOORS	MODERN FASHION
ADEFHIOOPRSTW	SHOWED A PROFIT
ADEFHIOORTWZZ	THE WIZARD OF OZ
ADEFHLLOOORTW	FOLLOW THE ROAD
ADEFHLMNOORTW	MAN OF THE WORLD
ADEFHLMOOPRTW	MAP OF THE WORLD
ADEFHLOOORTTW	WOLF AT THE DOOR
ADEFHLOOPRTWY	WAY OF THE WORLD
ADEFHMNNOORTW	DOWN ON THE FARM
ADEFHNNOOOSTU	OUT OF ONES HAND
ADEFHOPRRSSUW	PUSHES FORWARD
ADEFHORRRSSUW	RUSHES FORWARD
ADEFIILLNQUUY	UNQUALIFIEDLY
ADEFIIINNORSST	TIN OF SARDINES
ADEFIKLLNNORS	DRANK ONE'S FILL
ADEFIKLNNORTW	WALKED IN FRONT
ADEFILLSSTTUY	DISTASTEFULLY
ADEFILMNNOSTW	MANSFIELD TOWN
ADEFILMNNORRSS	INFORMAL DRESS
ADEFILMNRSTUU	MUTUAL FRIENDS
ADEFILMOOPRSW	PEARL OF WISDOM
ADEFIINRSTTTUU	DISTANT FUTURE
ADEFIOORRRSTW	WAIT FOR ORDERS
ADEFLNOOPPPSU	POUND OF APPLES
ADEFMNOOOORTWY	END OF MOTORWAY
ADEFMORSSTUXY	STUDY FOR EXAMS
ADEFNNORTTUWY	FOUR AND TWENTY
ADEFNOOOOORSTU	OUT OF ONE'S ROAD
ADEGGGIIINNRS	SINGING A DIRGE
ADEGGHIINNNOT	NOTHING GAINED
ADEGGHIINNSSV	HAVING DESIGNS
ADEGGHIKLNOTW	WALKING THE DOG
ADEGGHINNOOTT	DOING THE TANGO
ADEGGHINNORTY	HYDROGENATING
ADEGGHINORRTW	RIGHTED A WRONG
ADEGGHLRRSSTU	STRUGGLES HARD

ADEGGGHHNOORSTY	THE GAY GORDONS
ADEGGIIILNSTV	GIVING DETAILS
ADEGGIILNNNST	DISENTANGLING
ADEGGIILNNRSS	NIGGARDLINESS
ADEGGIILNNORRV	GIVING AN ORDER
ADEGGINNOORVW	WOOD ENGRAVING
ADEGGINNORRRS	ORGAN-GRINDERS
ADEGGINNORTTU	GETTING AROUND
ADEGHHHORSSTU	DASHES THROUGH
ADEGHHIILNTTY	IN THE DAYLIGHT
ADEGHHIINNNTW	HANG IN THE WIND
ADEGHHILLNOST	DOING THE HALLS
ADEGHHIMMNSTU	MADE THINGS HUM
ADEGHHIMNNOST	HANDSOME THING
ADEGHHIMNOSTT	MADE THINGS HOT
ADEGHHINOSTTU	EIGHT THOUSAND
ADEGHHINSSTTT	STAND THE SIGHT
ADEGHHLLNOPTU	PLOUGH THE LAND
ADEGHHLLNORUY	HANDLE ROUGHLY
ADEGHHLNOPSTU	PLOUGH THE SAND
ADEGHHOPRSSTU	PASSED THROUGH
ADEGHIIILRTVW	LIVID WITH RAGE
ADEGHIILLNTTY	LET IN DAYLIGHT
ADEGHIILNPSTW	PIG AND WHISTLE
ADEGHIIMNOSST	SAID SOMETHING
ADEGHIINNNTWY	WINNING THE DAY
ADEGHIINNOORS	DOING ONE'S HAIR
ADEGHIINNORTV	HANDING IT OVER
ADEGHIINSSTTY	STAYED IN SIGHT
ADEGHIIRRSTTV	STRAIGHT DRIVE
ADEGHIKLLNNSY	KENNY DALGLISH
ADEGHIKLNOOPT	DOING THE POLKA
ADEGHIKNNORRW	WORK-HARDENING
ADEGHIKNRSTTY	RED SKY AT NIGHT
ADEGHILLORSTY	EIGHTY DOLLARS
ADEGHILLRSTTY	TREADS LIGHTLY
ADEGHILNNOOOY	GONE ON HOLIDAY
ADEGHILNOOOSY	GOES ON HOLIDAY
ADEGHILNOTTWZ	DOING THE WALTZ
ADEGHILNSTTUY	LAYING THE DUST
ADEGHINNNOOST	GOT ONE'S HAND IN
ADEGHINNNOSTT	ONE NIGHT STAND
ADEGHINNOORTY	HYDROGENATION
ADEGHINNOPRTU	POUNDING HEART
ADEGHINNOSTTW	WASTED NOTHING
ADEGHINOORSVW	OVERSHADOWING
ADEGHINOPRRST	SPARING THE ROD
ADEGHINOPRSWW	WASHING POWDER
ADEGHINORSTWY	SAYING THE WORD
ADEGHIOPRTTTU	RIGHT UP TO DATE
ADEGHIORRRTTU	WITHOUT REGARD
ADEGHIORSTTUW	SHOW GRATITUDE
ADEGHIPPSSTTU	DIGS UP THE PAST
ADEGHKLLOOSTY	LOOKED GHASTLY
ADEGHKNNOOSST	THANK GOODNESS!
ADEGHLMNORRTY	GRANDMOTHERLY
ADEGHLNOORTTU	RANG OUT THE OLD
ADEGHMNOOORRS	HORSE AND GROOM
ADEGHNOPRSTUW	PAWS THE GROUND
ADEGIIILNNSST	DESTALINISING
ADEGIIILNNSTZ	DESTALINIZING
ADEGIIIMNNRST	ADMINISTERING
ADEGIIIMNNSST	DISSEMINATING
ADEGIIIMNOPRS	PROMISING IDEA
ADEGIIINNNRSV	DRIVING INSANE
ADEGIIINNSSTY	STAYING INSIDE
ADEGIIKMNRSST	MAKING STRIDES
ADEGIIKNNRRTW	DRINKING WATER
ADEGIILLMNOOR	ORIGINAL MODEL
ADEGIILLMNOOT	ALL IN GOOD TIME
ADEGIILLMNSZZ	DAZZLING SMILE
ADEGIIILLRRTUY	LITERARY GUILD
ADEGIILMNTTUY	UNMITIGATEDLY
ADEGIILNNOOPS	LEAD POISONING
ADEGIILNNOPPR	DROPPING A LINE
ADEGIILNOOSTT	GO INTO DETAILS
ADEGIILOOOQSTU	GOOD QUALITIES
ADEGIIMMNNNRST	MASTERMINDING
ADEGIIMNNOPRT	PREDOMINATING
ADEGIIMNNOTUU	MOUNTAIN GUIDE
ADEGIIMNPRRSU	ARMED UPRISING
ADEGIINNNRRTU	UNDER TRAINING
ADEGIINORRSSY	DIGRESSIONARY
ADEGIINORRSTT	DISINTEGRATOR
ADEGIJMNNSTTU	SAT IN JUDGMENT
ADEGIKLNOOORT	TOOK IN A LODGER
ADEGIKNNOSSTU	TAKE SOUNDINGS
ADEGILLMMNSUY	SELLING A DUMMY
ADEGILLMNPPPU	APPLE DUMPLING
ADEGILLMOORTT	GRILLED TOMATO
ADEGILMNPRSTU	LEADING TRUMPS
ADEGILMOORSTT	DERMATOLOGIST
ADEGILNNOOQRTU	GRANDILOQUENT
ADEGILNOOPRTT	PROGLOTTIDEAN
ADEGIMNNORSTT	DEMONSTRATING
ADEGIMNNPRSSS	SPRING MADNESS
ADEGINNNORRTU	RUN INTO DANGER
ADEGINNOOPRST	DOING ONE'S PART
ADEGINNOPRSTT	DOTING PARENTS
ADEGINOPRRSSS	PASSING ORDERS
ADEGINOPRRSTY	READY TO SPRING
ADEGIOPPRRRSS	RAPID PROGRESS
ADEGKLNOOORSU	LOOK DANGEROUS
ADEGKNOORRSUW	DANGEROUS WORK
ADEGLLNNORSTU	TRUNDLES ALONG
ADEGLNNORRTUU	NEUTRAL GROUND
ADEGLNOOOSTTY	STAYED TOO LONG
ADEGLNOOPRRWY	POWER AND GLORY
ADEGMNNORSTUU	SOUND ARGUMENT
ADEGNORSSTTUY	SOUND STRATEGY
ADEHHIILPRRTT	APRIL THE THIRD
ADEHHIINOSTTW	HAS DONE WITH IT
ADEHHIKNORSTT	SHOT IN THE DARK
ADEHHILLLOSST	OLD AS THE HILLS
ADEHHINPTTUWW	UP WITH THE DAWN
ADEHHIOPRSSTT	SHOT THE RAPIDS
ADEHHIORSTTTU	THRASHED IT OUT
ADEHHIORSTVWW	HAVE WORDS WITH
ADEHIINNPRTW	WRITHED IN PAIN
ADEHIIKLNRSVY	DRINKS HEAVILY
ADEHIILNNNOOP	HELD AN OPINION
ADEHIILNNQRUY	HELD AN INQUIRY
ADEHIILNORTWY	WINTER HOLIDAY
ADEHIINNPRSTU	HUNTED IN PAIRS
ADEHIINNSTWWY	SWAY IN THE WIND
ADEHIKMNNNSSU	HUMAN KINDNESS
ADEHIKNPPRRSW	SHRINK-WRAPPED
ADEHILLLLORSW	HEADS WILL ROLL
ADEHILMMORSUY	SUMMER HOLIDAY
ADEHILMNOSSTU	THOUSAND MILES
ADEHILNNOOSSS	SOIL ONES HANDS
ADEHILNNOOTWY	WENT ON HOLIDAY
ADEHILNNOPSTU	LAND IN THE SOUP
ADEHILNNOQRUY	HOLD AN ENQUIRY
ADEHILNNOQSTU	HOLD AN INQUEST
ADEHILNPRSSTY	SPREADS THINLY
ADEHILOORRSTY	HOLIDAY RESORT
ADEHIMMNNOSST	ADMONISHMENTS
ADEHIMOOPRRST	MODERATORSHIP
ADEHINNORSTTU	TURN ON ITS HEAD
ADEHINNORSTTW	NORTHEAST WIND
ADEHINNOSSTTU	THE INS AND OUTS

873

ADEHINNRSSTWW	WITHDRAWNNESS
ADEHINOORRTTU	THE ROAD TO RUIN
ADEHINOOSTTWY	STOOD IN THE WAY
ADEHINORSSTTW	DOWN THE STAIRS
ADEHINORSTTUW	ROUND THE WAIST
ADEHINORSTTYY	THIRTY-ONE DAYS
ADEHINOSSTTUW	SOUTHEAST WIND
ADEHINRSTUVYY	HEAVY INDUSTRY
ADEHIORSSTWWY	THROW SIDEWAYS
ADEHIORSTTVYY	TO THIS VERY DAY
ADEHJNNNOORSW	ANDREW JOHNSON
ADEHKMOORRSTW	MADE SHORT WORK
ADEHKOOOORTTT	TOOK TO THE ROAD
ADEHLMNNNOOOT	LAND ON THE MOON
ADEHLMORRSSSU	SHOULDERS ARMS
ADEHLNOPSTTUY	SPY OUT THE LAND
ADEHLNPSSTTUY	STUDY THE PLANS
ADEHLOPRRSSTU	SHOULDER STRAP
ADEHMNNOOOSST	NOT SO HANDSOME
ADEHMRRRSTTUY	MUST TRY HARDER
ADEHNNOOOOSSWW	ONE'S OWN SHADOW
ADEHNNOOOSTTU	THOUSAND TO ONE
ADEHNNOORTTUW	AROUND THE TOWN
ADEHNNOPPSTUU	PUT ONE'S HAND UP
ADEHNOORRTUWY	OTHER WAY ROUND
ADEHNORRSTTWW	NORTHWESTWARD
ADEHORSSTTUWW	SOUTHWESTWARD
ADEHRSSSTTTUY	STUDY THE STARS
ADEIIILNNOPST	PAINTED IN OILS
ADEIIILNOQSUV	EQUAL DIVISION
ADEIIILNPSTTU	PLATITUDINISE
ADEIIILNPTTUZ	PLATITUDINIZE
ADEIIILNRSSTU	INDUSTRIALISE
ADEIIILNRSTUZ	INDUSTRIALIZE
ADEIIILPRSSTU	SPIRITUALISED
ADEIIILPRSTUZ	SPIRITUALIZED
ADEIIIMNNOSST	DISSEMINATION
ADEIIINNOPRTT	IN TREPIDATION
ADEIIINOSSTTV	DEVIATIONISTS
ADEIIINRRSSTT	IN DIRE STRAITS
ADEIIINSSTTTU	ATTITUDINISES
ADEIIINSTTTUZ	ATTITUDINIZES
ADEIIKMNNNPTY	PAYMENT IN KIND
ADEIIILLMNNNOO	MILLION AND ONE
ADEIIILLMNNNOS	ALL IN ONES MIND
ADEIIILLMNNOSY	DIMENSIONALLY
ADEIIILLNPRSUV	LIVERPUDLIANS
ADEIIILLNQRSTU	TRANQUILLISED
ADEIIILLNQRTUZ	TRANQUILLIZED
ADEIIILMMNOTTU	LIMITED AMOUNT
ADEIIILMMQTUUY	MEDIUM QUALITY
ADEIIILMNRRTUY	RUDIMENTARILY
ADEIIILMRRSSTY	MILITARY DRESS
ADEIIILNNOOPTY	OPINIONATEDLY
ADEIIILNOOPSST	DESPOLIATIONS
ADEIIILNORSTT	TRADITIONLESS
ADEIIILNQSTTUY	EQUIDISTANTLY
ADEIIIMMNNOOTT	TIME AND MOTION
ADEIIIMNNNOOST	DENOMINATIONS
ADEIIIMNNOOPRT	PREDOMINATION
ADEIIIMNNOORST	MODERNISATION
ADEIIIMNNOORTZ	MODERNIZATION
ADEIIIMNOOPRSV	MADE PROVISION
ADEIIINNNOSTTU	UNITED NATIONS
ADEIIINNOOPRRT	PREORDINATION
ADEIIINNOPPSTT	SNAPPED INTO IT
ADEIIINNOPSSST	DISPENSATIONS
ADEIIINNORSTTU	TRADE UNIONIST
ADEIIINOPPSTTU	DISPUTE A POINT
ADEIIINORSSSTT	DISSERTATIONS
ADEIIINRSSTTTU	UNITED ARTISTS
ADEIIOOOPRSST	RADIOISOTOPES
ADEIJNOPPRTUY	PUT IN JEOPARDY
ADEIKKNNNPPRYY	PINKY AND PERKY
ADEIKLNNNORRSU	DRUNKEN SAILOR
ADEIKLNNORSSY	ORKNEY ISLANDS
ADEIKLNOPPRSY	SPOKEN RAPIDLY
ADEILLMMOPRRU	DOLLAR PREMIUM
ADEILLNNORSTY	NINETY DOLLARS
ADEILLNOOOTVY	LOYAL DEVOTION
ADEILLNOOPRTY	PERIODONTALLY
ADEILLOPPSTTW	STOPPED AT WILL
ADEILLOPRRSVY	LORD PRIVY SEAL
ADEILLORRRTWY	LITERARY WORLD
ADEILMNMNOPRTY	PREDOMINANTLY
ADEILMNOPRSTT	PERMITS TO LAND
ADEILMOOOSTTU	STOOD OUT A MILE
ADEILNOOPRSST	DRESS OPTIONAL
ADEILNOORTUVY	DEVOLUTIONARY
ADEIMMMNORSTTY	DISTANT MEMORY
ADEIMNNOORSTT	DEMONSTRATION
ADEIMNOPPPRRR	PRIM AND PROPER
ADEIMOOOPPRSTY	PROMISED TO PAY
ADEIMOOPRSSTZ	SPERMATOZOIDS
ADEINNOOPSTTT	STAND ON TIPTOE
ADEINNOPSTTTU	PUTS AN END TO IT
ADEINOOOPRRSW	POISONED ARROW
ADEINOPRRRTUV	RAPID TURNOVER
ADEINOQRTTUUY	TORQUAY UNITED
ADEINORRRTTTU	TURNED TRAITOR
ADEINOSSSSSSUU	ASSIDUOUSNESS
ADEKNNOOOSSTT	TOOK ONE'S STAND
ADELLMNNOSTUY	MENTALLY SOUND
ADELLMOOPRRST	LORDS TEMPORAL
ADELLMORSTUWY	MUSTARD YELLOW
ADELLNORSTTWY	TWENTY DOLLARS
ADELMNNOPPSTY	OLD PENNY STAMP
ADELNNOOOPPTY	PLAYED PONTOON
ADELNNOOPRSTT	PORTLAND STONE
ADELNNOORSSSV	SONS AND LOVERS
ADELNORSTUUVY	ADVENTUROUSLY
ADELOOPPRSSST	LEOPARDS SPOTS
ADEMNOORRSSTT	DEMONSTRATORS
ADENNNOOPPTUY	POUND TO A PENNY
ADENNORSTUUUV	UNADVENTUROUS
ADENOOOORSSTT	STOOD TO REASON
ADFFFFHNPSSUU	HUFFS AND PUFFS
ADFFGIINNORUV	FINDING FAVOUR
ADFFHILNOSSTY	STANDOFFISHLY
ADFFHIMNNOSTU	DUSTIN HOFFMAN
ADFFHINOSTTUY	FIFTY THOUSAND
ADFFNNOORSTUU	RAN OUT OF FUNDS
ADFGGHHIILLNN	HIGHLAND FLING
ADFGGIILNNORT	DRIFTING ALONG
ADFGHILNNOST	IN SIGHT OF LAND
ADFGHIINNSSST	SHIFTING SANDS
ADFGHIORSTTUU	THIRD OF AUGUST
ADFGHNOOOORRUU	GUARD OF HONOUR
ADFGIIILNQSUY	DISQUALIFYING
ADFGIIINSSSTY	DISSATISFYING
ADFGIIMNNORRY	FRIDAY MORNING
ADFGIINNOPRTY	INFANT PRODIGY
ADFGIINNORSTT	STANDING FOR IT
ADFGILNNOOORU	FOOLING AROUND
ADFGIMNNOORUY	DAY OF MOURNING
ADFGIMNOORRVW	MOVING FORWARD
ADFGINNOORRWW	WORD OF WARNING
ADFGINNOPRSTU	STANDING UP FOR
ADFHHKLLNOOOO	HOOK OF HOLLAND
ADFHIKLMOOORT	TOOK A FIRM HOLD
ADFHIKNORSTWY	HAD FORTY WINKS
ADFHNOORSTTUY	FORTY THOUSAND

ADFIILNNOOSTU	FIND A SOLUTION
ADFILNOOPRSST	PROFIT AND LOSS
ADFILORRRSTWW	FIRST WORLD WAR
ADFINNNORSSTT	STANDS IN FRONT
ADFINOOPRRTUW	PUT IN A WORD FOR
ADFKLOOOORRTW	LOOK FORWARD TO
ADGGGHIILNNUY	DYING LAUGHING
ADGGGIINNNORU	GAINING GROUND
ADGGHHHIIMNTY	HIGH AND MIGHTY
	HIGH-AND-MIGHTY
ADGGHHILNNORU	ROUGH HANDLING
ADGGHHINOORST	GOOD THRASHING
ADGGHHINORTUW	WADING THROUGH
ADGGHIIIMNSSV	HAD MISGIVINGS
ADGGHILLNOOST	ALL GOOD THINGS
ADGGHINNORRTW	RIGHT AND WRONG
ADGGHINOOOOTT	A GOOD THING TOO
ADGGHINOOSSTY	SAYS GOODNIGHT
ADGGIIINNNORSS	DISORGANISING
ADGGIIINNNORSZ	DISORGANIZING
ADGGIINNNOOTU	GOING IN AND OUT
ADGGIINNNORSU	SINGING A ROUND
ADGGIINOPRSST	TRADING GOODIR
ADGGIKLNOOOTT	GOOD TALKING-TO
ADGGILLNOOOPW	GOOD WALLOPING
ADGGIMNNORTUU	MOUNTING GUARD
ADGHHINNRRTTU	RIGHT-HAND TURN
ADGHHINRSTTUY	THURSDAY NIGHT
ADGHHNOOORRTU	NO THROUGH ROAD
ADGHIIIKLNOSY	SKIING HOLIDAY
ADGHIIKLNNOTU	THINKING ALOUD
ADGHIILMNNOSY	ADMONISHINGLY
ADGHIILNORRTW	DOWNRIGHT LIAR
ADGHIIMNNOSTT	ADMITS NOTHING
ADGHIINNNPTTU	PUTTING IN HAND
ADGHIINNOPPRT	DROPPING A HINT
ADGHILLLMNOSS	SMALLHOLDINGS
ADGHIMNSSTTUY	STUDYING MATHS
ADGHINNOOOOPRT	GONADOTROPHIN
ADGHINNOPRSUU	PUSHING AROUND
ADGHINPRSSTTU	STANDS UPRIGHT
ADGHIOOOORTTUY	GOOD AUTHORITY
ADGHLLOOSTUUU	LAUGHS OUT LOUD
ADGHMNNOOPRRY	GYNANDROMORPH
ADGIIILMNSSTU	DISSIMULATING
ADGIIILNNRSSV	VIRGIN ISLANDS
ADGIIILNPRSSY	DISPRAISINGLY
ADGIIINNOPPST	DISAPPOINTING
ADGIIINNRSSTW	WINDING STAIRS
ADGIIJNNORUY	DOING AN INJURY
ADGIIKKNNORTT	TAKING TO DRINK
ADGIIKNNPRRTY	DRINKING PARTY
ADGIIKNNRRSTW	DRINKING STRAW
ADGIIILLNNSSTT	STANDING STILL
ADGIIMNNOSTWW	WANTING WISDOM
ADGIIMNOPSTUY	IMPOSING A DUTY
ADGIINNOSTTW	STANDING TO WIN
ADGIINNORSTTU	SITTING AROUND
ADGIINOPPTTTU	PUTTING PAID TO
ADGIKLNNOOORU	LOOKING AROUND
ADGIKMNNNOOSU	MAKING NO SOUND
ADGILLNNORRUY	RALLYING ROUND
ADGILMNNOPRTW	TRAMPLING DOWN
ADGILNNOSTTUY	OUTSTANDINGLY
ADGIMMNNNOORY	MONDAY MORNING
ADGIMNNNORSUY	SUNDAY MORNING
ADGIMNOORSTVW	MOVING TOWARDS
ADGIMNPRSSTUW	DRAWING STUMPS
ADGINNNNORRUU	RUNNING AROUND
ADGINNNNORRSU	RAN RINGS ROUND
ADGINNNNORRTUU	TURNING AROUND
ADGINNOPPRRUW	WRAPPING ROUND
ADGINNOPPRSTW	STRAPPING DOWN
ADGLOOOOOSTTT	TOO GOOD TO LAST
ADGMNOOOPRSST	GOOD SPORTSMAN
ADGNNOORRUWWY	WRONG WAY ROUND
ADHHKNOOORSTT	TOOK SHORTHAND
ADHHNNOORSTTU	NORTH AND SOUTH
ADHHNOORRSSUU	HOURS AND HOURS
ADHIILLNOQRTU	QUADRILLIONTH
ADHIILNNNOOOP	HOLD AN OPINION
ADHIILNNOQRUY	HOLD AN INQUIRY
ADHIILNOPPSST	SPIT AND POLISH
ADHIIMNOORSSU	DISHARMONIOUS
ADHIINSSSTTWY	ST.SWITHINS DAY
ADHILLORRSTTY	THIRTY DOLLARS
ADHILLORUUXYY	LUXURY HOLIDAY
ADHIMNOPRSSSW	SWORDSMANSHIP
ADHINOSSTTTUW	TWIST AND SHOUT
ADHINOSSTTIIXY	SIXTY THOUSAND
ADHKNOOOTUWWY	WHAT DO YOU KNOW?
ADIIIILMRSSTY	DISSIMILARITY
ADIIIILNNOQTU	IN LIQUIDATION
ADIIILLNOSSTT	DISTILLATIONS
ADIIILMNOSSTU	DISSIMULATION
ADIIILMNRSSTU	INDUSTRIALISM
ADIIILNRSSTTU	INDUSTRIALIST
ADIILNOOOPSST	PODSOLISATION
ADIILNOOOPSTZ	PODZOLISATION
ADIILNOOOPTZZ	PODZOLIZATION
ADIILNOPSTTUU	PLATITUDINOUS
ADIINNRSTTUYY	TRINITY SUNDAY
ADIIORSSSTTTU	ARTISTS STUDIO
ADILNNOOOPRRT	LONDON AIRPORT
ADILNRRRSTUUY	RURAL INDUSTRY
ADIMNNOORSSWY	IN SO MANY WORDS
ADIMOPRSSSTTU	SPORTS STADIUM
ADINOOOPRSSTU	POISONOUS DART
ADLNOOPPRSUWY	PLAY UPON WORDS
AEEEEEFKKRTWW	WEEK AFTER WEEK
AEEEEEHLNRSTW	RENEW THE LEASE
AEEEEEHRRSTVW	SEVERE WEATHER
AEEEEEINPRRRS	ARRIERE-PENSEE
AEEEEEKNNOPPY	KEEP AN EYE OPEN
AEEEEFFHILRRT	LIFE HEREAFTER
AEEEEFGGGGLOS	GAGGLE OF GEESE
AEEEEFGGGNRRS	FREE-RANGE EGGS
AEEEEFHLLRTTT	THREE FEET TALL
AEEEEFHLOPPTY	APPLE OF THE EYE
AEEEEFHNRTTTV	AFTER THE EVENT
AEEEEFJKLLRWY	FAKE JEWELLERY
AEEEEFKNRTTWX	WEEK AFTER NEXT
AEEEEFLLNOPSS	PLEASE ONESELF
AEEEEFLNOPRST	REPEAT ONESELF
AEEEEFNOSSSTY	FEAST ONES EYES
AEEEEFRRSVWYY	EVERY FEW YEARS
AEEEEGGHMSSTT	GET THE MESSAGE
AEEEEGHILNOTV	GAVE ONE THE LIE
AEEEEGHINRSTY	EIGHTEEN YEARS
AEEEEGIIPRRVV	GIVE A REPRIEVE
AEEEEHHKLNTTW	TAKEN THE WHEEL
AEEEEHHKLSTTW	TAKES THE WHEEL
AEEEEHHNNSTVV	SEVENTH HEAVEN
AEEEEHHPRRSSS	SHEEPSHEARERS
AEEEEHLNSSTTV	LEAVES THE NEST
AEEEEHMNORRSW	SOMEWHERE NEAR
AEEEEHNNOOSVY	HAVE ONE'S EYE ON
AEEEEHNPSSVXY	HEAVY EXPENSES
AEEEEHPRRTTWX	WEATHER EXPERT
AEEEEIMNPRSST	PASSEMENTERIE
AEEEEINNNRSTY	NINETEEN YEARS
AEEEEKMMNORST	MEET ONES MAKER

AEEEEKNNOPPTY	KEPT AN EYE OPEN	AEEEGIIKMMMNNS	MAKING ENEMIES
AEEEELNNPSTTV	TEN PAST ELEVEN	AEEEGIKLLLOPS	SLEEP LIKE A LOG
AEEEEMNOPRTTZ	TEMPERATE ZONE	AEEEGIKLLMNNT	GENTLEMANLIKE
AEEEEMNPRSSTT	TEMPERATENESS	AEEEGIKLNRRST	GENERAL STRIKE
AEEEENOPRRSTU	EASTERN EUROPE	AEEEGILLMORTV	REMOTE VILLAGE
AEEEENORSSTVY	AVERT ONES EYES	AEEEGILLNORSV	SEVILLE ORANGE
AEEEENRRRSTUV	NATURE RESERVE	AEEEGILLRSTTV	VILLAGE STREET
AEEEFFFNORRSU	REFUSE AN OFFER	AEEEGILNORRTX	EXTERIOR ANGLE
AEEEFFGHNORUV	HAVEN OF REFUGE	AEEEGILNPRTVY	NEGATIVE REPLY
AEEEFFHIINNRT	IN FINE FEATHER	AEEEGIMNPRRTY	PRAYER MEETING
AEEEFFHKMORTT	MAKE THE EFFORT	AEEEGINNOSSWY	SEEING ONE'S WAY
AEEEFGGMNOORR	GEORGE FOREMAN	AEEEGINNPRRVY	EVENING PRAYER
AEEEFGHHIRTTW	FEATHERWEIGHT	AEEEGINNPRSTV	GIVEN A PRESENT
AEEEFGHILMNOT	FEELING AT HOME	AEEEGINORSSST	TERATOGENESIS
AEEEFGHLMOOTV	LOVE OF THE GAME	AEEEGINPRSSTV	GIVES A PRESENT
AEEEFGIIKNNPS	IN SAFE KEEPING	AEEEGINRRSTTT	GREAT INTEREST
AEEEFGIILNNRU	ENGINE FAILURE	AEEEGIRRSSTTV	TERGIVERSATES
AEEEFGILNNSUY	UNEASY FEELING	AEEEGKMNORSSY	GREASE MONKEYS
AEEEFGLNOPSUV	GAVE ONESELF UP	AEEEGLMNNNRST	GENTLE MANNERS
AEEEFGLNOSSSS	GASSES ONESELF	AEEEGLMNNNSTT	ENTANGLEMENTS
AEEEFHHIRSSTV	FEVERISH HASTE	AEEEGLNORRSST	GENERAL STORES
AEEEFHHORRSTT	THREE OF HEARTS	AEEEGMMNORSTT	MAGNETOMETERS
AEEEFHINRSTTW	THE WATER'S FINE	AEEEGNNNORSTV	VENT ONE'S ANGER
AEEEFHIPRSTTV	FIVE PAST THREE	AEEEGNNRSSSST	STRANGENESSES
AEEEFHIRSSTTV	FEVERISH STATE	AEEEGNPRRSSTU	GREEN PASTURES
AEEEFHLMNOTVY	ELEVENTH OF MAY	AEEEHHILNPTTW	WHITE ELEPHANT
AEEEFHNOQRSTU	QUEEN OF HEARTS	AEEEHHINOSTTV	THE NOES HAVE IT
AEEEFHNORSSTV	SEVEN OF HEARTS	AEEEHHLPPRRTU	PURPLE HEATHER
AEEEFHNRRTTUU	THE NEAR FUTURE	AEEEHHMNSTTVY	MAY THE SEVENTH
AEEEFIILLMMRT	MILE AFTER MILE	AEEEHHMORRSTT	MOTHER THERESA
AEEEFIIMMRTTT	TIME AFTER TIME	AEEEHHNOOPSTV	HOPES TO HEAVEN
AEEEFIKLNOSST	STAKE ONES LIFE	AEEEHHNOOPSUV	HAVE OPEN HOUSE
AEEEFILLNNOST	EATEN ONE'S FILL	AEEEHIIMMMNNTT	IN THE MEANTIME
AEEEFILLNOSUV	VALUE ONES LIFE	AEEEHIKLLRTTT	TAKE THE TILLER
AEEEFILRSSSTV	SELF-ASSERTIVE	AEEEHILMNNOPP	EPIPHENOMENAL
AEEEFIMNNORRSS	FREEMASONRIES	AEEEHILNORTTV	THE REVELATION
AEEEFINOSSSTV	FESTIVE SEASON	AEEEHILNSSTWW	SWANEE WHISTLE
AEEEFINPSSTVV	FIVE PAST SEVEN	AEEEHILPRRTTV	THE RIVER PLATE
AEEEFINQRRSTU	ENQUIRES AFTER	AEEEHIMNORSTY	RAISE THE MONEY
AEEEFINQRTTUV	FREQUENTATIVE	AEEEHIMOPRSTT	RAISE THE TEMPO
AEEEFKLORRRWW	WELFARE WORKER	AEEEHIMPSSSTT	PASSES THE TIME
AEEEFKOPRSSTU	REFUSE TO SPEAK	AEEEHINPRSSST	PARENTHESISES
AEEEFILLLNOTW	LEFT WELL ALONE	AEEEHINPRSSTZ	PARENTHESIZES
AEEEFLMNOSSSU	AMUSES ONESELF	AEEEHINRRSTTY	THIRTEEN YEARS
AEEEFLNORSSST	ASSERT ONESELF	AEEEHINRRTTWW	WINTER WEATHER
AEEEFLNOSSSUV	SENSE OF VALUES	AEEEHINRSSTTY	STRAIN THE EYES
AEEEFLOPRTTUU	PUT OUT A FEELER	AEEEHKLOPRSTU	KEEP LATE HOURS
AEEEFMNOPSSTT	STAMP ONE'S FEET	AEEEHKNNOOPST	KEEP ONES HAT ON
AEEEFMNPRSTUY	REFUSE PAYMENT	AEEEHKNNORSTW	KNEW THE REASON
AEEEFMOPRSTTX	TEAM OF EXPERTS	AEEEHKNNRSTWW	KNEW THE ANSWER
AEEEFNORRSTTW	WATER SOFTENER	AEEEHLLMNORTT	TELL ME ANOTHER
	WATER-SOFTENER	AEEEHLLMNOSSW	MEALS ON WHEELS
AEEEFNORRSTUY	FOURTEEN YEARS	AEEEHLLMNSSTV	MANTLESHELVES
AEEEGGHMOSSTT	GOT THE MESSAGE	AEEEHLLORTVWY	LOVELY WEATHER
AEEEGGPRRSSUU	PRESSURE GAUGE	AEEEHLMOORSTV	LEAVES THE ROOM
AEEEGHHIKMTTW	MAKE THE WEIGHT	AEEEHLNOORSST	LOSE ONES HEART
AEEEGHHINPRSS	SHEEPSHEARING	AEEEHLNOPRRST	LEARN THE ROPES
AEEEGHHLORTTT	THE ALTOGETHER	AEEEHLNOSSSTT	SETS THE SEAL ON
AEEEGHIINNTTV	IN THE NEGATIVE	AEEEHLNPSSSSS	SHAPELESSNESS
AEEEGHIKLLPTU	LIKE THE PLAGUE	AEEEHLNRSSSST	HEARTLESSNESS
AEEEGHILPRRTW	TELEGRAPH WIRE	AEEEHLOPSSSTT	HOPELESS STATE
AEEEGHINOPPTV	GAVE ONE THE PIP	AEEEHLPPRRSTU	LEATHER UPPERS
AEEEGHKLNPTTU	TAKE THE PLUNGE	AEEEHLRSTTTVY	THE VERY LATEST
AEEEGHLLMRRVY	GAVE MERRY HELL	AEEEHMMMNNOPRT	PERMANENT HOME
AEEEGHLLOPPRT	TELEGRAPH POLE	AEEEHMNOORSTV	REMOVE ONES HAT
AEEEGHLLORSTV	LEATHER GLOVES	AEEEHMNORRTTW	NO MATTER WHERE
AEEEGHLNOPRRS	SELENOGRAPHER	AEEEHNNOOPRST	OPEN ONES HEART
AEEEGHLNOPRTU	ROGUE ELEPHANT	AEEEHNNRRSTTZ	ESTHER RANTZEN
AEEEGHMNOPRST	MAGNETOSPHERE	AEEEHNORRSTVW	WORSE THAN EVER
AEEEGHNORRSSU	GENEROUS SHARE	AEEEHOPRRRTTW	WEATHER REPORT
AEEEGHNORRSTV	HAVE NO REGRETS	AEEEHPPPRTTTU	PUPPET THEATRE

AEEEHPSSSSTTT	PASSES THE TEST
AEEEHQRRRSTTU	THREE QUARTERS
AEEEIIKMNQRSU	MAKE ENQUIRIES
AEEEIILNSTTUV	EVENTUALITIES
AEEEIILRRTTVY	REITERATIVELY
AEEEIKLLOPPRW	WARLIKE PEOPLE
AEEEIKLLOPPST	SLEEP LIKE A TOP
AEEEIKLRSSSTY	EYES LIKE STARS
AEEEIKMOPPRSS	KEEPS A PROMISE
AEEEILLNNOPPV	PLAIN ENVELOPE
AEEEILLNPRSTT	INTERPELLATES
AEEEILLNRRTVY	REVERENTIALLY
AEEEILMMORSTT	SOME TIME LATER
AEEEILMNPRSSX	EXEMPLARINESS
AEEEILMNPRTTY	INTEMPERATELY
AEEEILNNSSSST	ESSENTIALNESS
AEEEILNN3TVWZ	VIENNESE WALTZ
AEEEILNORSSTU	AT ONES LEISURE
AEEEILNORSSTV	ONES RELATIVES
AEEEILNRSSSTV	VERSATILENESS
AEEEILOPRSSTT	TRIES TO PLEASE
AEEEILRSSSVWW	WIRELESS WAVES
AEEEIMMNNPRST	SEMIPERMANENT
AEEEIMMNORSSU	IN SOME MEASURE
AEEEIMNNNRTTT	ENTERTAINMENT
AEEEIMNNORSTW	WRITE ONES NAME
AEEEIMNNRSTTT	REINSTATEMENT
AEEEILMNORSSSW	WEARISOMENESS
AEEEIMORSSTTV	OVERESTIMATES
AEEEINNPSSSVX	EXPANSIVENESS
AEEEINNSSTTTV	ATTENTIVENESS
AEEEINOPRRSTV	PERSEVERATION
AEEEINOPRSSTV	OPERATIVENESS
AEEEINPHSSSVV	PERVASIVENESS
AEEEINRRSSTTT	INTEREST RATES
AEEEINRSSSSTV	ASSERTIVENESS
AEEEIPRRSSTVV	PRESERVATIVES
AEEEKLLMRRSST	SELLERS MARKET
AEEEKLLNSSSST	SENSELESS TALK
AEEEKLMNPTWYY	WEEKLY PAYMENT
AEEEKLNOOOSTV	TOOK ONE'S LEAVE
AEEEKLRRSSTTW	STREETWALKERS
AEEEKNOPRSSST	SPEAKERS NOTES
AEEEELLLLNOSTW	LETS WELL ALONE
AEEEELLLNOPRSV	PERSONAL LEVEL
AEEEELLNSSSSUV	VALUELESSNESS
AEEELMNPRRSST	ERNEST MARPLES
AEEEELMPPRSTUY	EMPTY PLEASURE
AEEELNOOPSSTV	LEAVE ONES POST
AEEELNPRSTTTT	LETTERS PATENT
AEEEELNPSTTTVW	TEN PAST TWELVE
AEEEELNSSSSSTT	STATELESSNESS
	TASTELESSNESS
AEEEMNNOORSTW	WROTE ONE'S NAME
AEEEMNORSTTTV	OVERSTATEMENT
AEEEMNPRRSSTU	PREMATURENESS
AEEEMNRRSSSTU	STERN MEASURES
AEEEMNRSTTTTU	TRUE STATEMENT
AEEENNORRSUVY	RUNS AN EYE OVER
AEEENOPRSSTTT	POSTE RESTANTE
AEEEOOPSSTTTW	SWEET POTATOES
AEEEOPPRRSSUV	SERVE A PURPOSE
AEEEORRRSTTUV	TREASURE TROVE
AEEFFFHILOTVW	WE HAVE LIFT-OFF
AEEFFFLMORRTU	FREE FROM FAULT
AEEFFFLOORRSS	OFFERS FOR SALE
AEEFFFOORSTTW	WASTE OF EFFORT
AEEFFGHHIORST	FEAR OF HEIGHTS
AEEFFGINORRST	REAFFORESTING
AEEFFHILLNRTU	IN FULL FEATHER
AEEFFHIMOPPTW	WIPE OFF THE MAP
AEEFFHKLMRTUY	MAKE THE FUR FLY
AEEFFIKLLOSTT	FILLET OF STEAK
AEEFFKLNOSSTT	SKELETON STAFF
AEEFFKORRSSTU	SUFFER A STROKE
AEEFFLNOORSSW	SAW FOR ONESELF
AEEFFNOOPRRST	SPARE NO EFFORT
AEEFFNORSTTYZ	STATE OF FRENZY
AEEFGGHINORRT	FOREGATHERING
AEEFGGHINOSTV	GANG OF THIEVES
AEEFGGHINRSTW	WAGS THE FINGER
AEEFGGIINRRRT	REFRIGERATING
AEEFGGINNORSW	WAG ONES FINGER
AEEFGGINRTTTT	GETTING FATTER
AEEFGHHHIINRT	IN HIGH FEATHER
AEEFGHHIORSTT	EIGHT OF HEARTS
AEEFGHIINGTTT	SETTING A THIEF
AEEFGHIIPSTTV	FIVE PAST EIGHT
AEEFGHILNNOSV	HAVE ONES FLING
AEEFGHILNQRSV	HALF SOVEREIGN
AEEFGHILPRSUY	SHAPELY FIGURE
AEEFGHINOORTT	GONE TO THE FAIR
AEEFGHINORSVY	HAVING EYES FOR
AEEFGHIOORSTT	GOES TO THE FAIR
AEEFGHLLORSTW	LOWERS THE FLAG
AEEFGHLORRSTW	GATHER FLOWERS
AEEFGHNOOORSU	HOUSE OF ORANGE
AEEFGIIKLLOTV	FIT LIKE A GLOVE
AEEFGIILMNOTT	FAILING TO MEET
AEEFGIINORRRT	REFRIGERATION
AEEFGIIPRRTUV	PREFIGURATIVE
AEEFGIKMNORRT	FOREIGN MARKET
AEEFGILLLLOSW	IF ALL GOES WELL
AEEFGILLNNOSS	ALIGNS ONESELF
AEEFGILNNOSSV	SAVING ONESELF
AEEFGILNORRTV	FOREIGN TRAVEL
AEEFGILNPRTYZ	FLYING TRAPEZE
AEEFGIMNQQRUU	FORMING A QUEUE
AEEFGINRRRSUY	SUGAR REFINERY
AEEFGIORRRRST	REFRIGERATORS
AEEFGKLOOPRST	TAKE FOR GOSPEL
AEEFGMNOOPRRS	PANG OF REMORSE
AEEFGMOOPSSTT	MESS OF POTTAGE
AEEFGNNOPRSTW	FRONT-PAGE NEWS
AEEFHHINOSSTT	SET THE FASHION
AEEFHHLMTTTWY	MAY THE TWELFTH
AEEFHIILNRSSY	FINISHES EARLY
AEEFHIJMRSSTT	JAMES THE FIRST
AEEFHIKNOSSST	SHAKE ONES FIST
AEEFHILLNNSTW	WHITE FLANNELS
AEEFHILLOPRTW	FEATHER PILLOW
AEEFHILMNOPRU	REMAIN HOPEFUL
AEEFHILNOOSST	LOSE ONES FAITH
AEEFHILNORSTT	LIFT ONE'S HEART
AEEFHILNSSSST	FAITHLESSNESS
AEEFHILORSTTV	FIVE-STAR HOTEL
AEEFHIMOPRTTT	PART OF THE TIME
AEEFHINNORTTW	WENT TO THE FAIR
AEEFHIOORRSST	RAISES THE ROOF
AEEFHKMMOOSTT	MAKE THE MOST OF
AEEFHLMOOPRRT	MOTHER OF PEARL
	MOTHER-OF-PEARL
AEEFHLMORRSTW	FLAMETHROWERS
AEEFHLNORRRST	RAN FOR SHELTER
AEEFHLOOPRTWW	POWER OF THE LAW
AEEFHLOPSTTTT	LEFT AT THE POST
AEEFHMNOORRST	FROM ONES HEART
AEEFHMORRSTTT	AFTER THE STORM
AEEFHOOPPRRSUY	HOUSE OF PRAYER
AEEFHORRSTTWY	FROSTY WEATHER
AEEFIILLMNOOT	EMOTIONAL LIFE
AEEFIILLRRRTY	ARTILLERY FIRE

AEEFIILMNNRTY	EMINENTLY FAIR
AEEFIILMPPRRS	PREAMPLIFIERS
AEEFIILOPRRTV	PROLIFERATIVE
AEEFIINOQRSTU	FIRE A QUESTION
AEEFIJLNSSSTUW	JUST A FEW LINES
AEEFIKLLORTWW	FLOW LIKE WATER
AEEFILLMNRSUU	IN FULL MEASURE
AEEFILLMORSTU	METALLIFEROUS
AEEFILLNRRTTU	IN FULL RETREAT
AEEFILLOPPSTU	EPISTLE OF PAUL
AEEFILLOPRSTU	POLITE REFUSAL
AEEFILLORRSTY	REAL-LIFE STORY
AEEFILMPTTTTU	FUTILE ATTEMPT
AEEFILNNORSST	STRAIN ONESELF
AEEFILNORSSST	SELF-ASSERTION
AEEFILNRRSSTT	SELF-RESTRAINT
AEEFIMNNORSTT	FERMENTATIONS
AEEFIMOOORRRST	REFORMATORIES
AEEFINNOQRTTU	FREQUENTATION
AEEFINNORSSSU	NEFARIOUSNESS
AEEFINNORSTTV	TRAIN OF EVENTS
AEEFINOPRSTTU	SUPERFETATION
AEEFINORTTUUV	FAVOURITE TUNE
AEEFIOOPRRSST	PROFESSORIATE
AEEFIOQRRTTUV	QUARTER TO FIVE
AEEFKLLNOOSTT	TALK TO ONESELF
AEEFKLOOORRSVW	LEAVES FOR WORK
AEEFLLMNORSTT	FORESTALLMENT
AEEFLLMNRTTTU	FULL TREATMENT
AEEFLLNSSSSTU	FAULTLESSNESS
AEEFLMMOOPRSY	LAPSE OF MEMORY
AEEFLMNNORRSU	FUNERAL SERMON
AEEFLMNOORUVY	VALUE FOR MONEY
AEEFLMNORSSUV	ROMANS-FLEUVES
AEEFLMNRSSSTU	MASTERFULNESS
AEEFLMOQRRSTU	FORMAL REQUEST
AEEFLOPQRSSUW	PASQUEFLOWERS
AEEFLOPRSSTUY	REFUSES TO PLAY
AEEFMOPRRRRST	STAR PERFORMER
AEEFNNOOPPRRS	PROFANE PERSON
AEEFNNOORRSTT	AFTERNOON REST
AEEFNNOPRSTTU	SPENT A FORTUNE
AEEFNNORSSTTU	FORTUNATENESS
AEEFNORSSTTTU	STATE OF UNREST
AEEGGGIILMNNS	ENGAGING SMILE
AEEGGGNNORSTU	GONE GREAT GUNS
AEEGGGNORSSTU	GOES GREAT GUNS
AEEGGHHHLNOTTU	GET THE LAUGH ON
AEEGGHIILNSTV	GIVE THE SIGNAL
AEEGGHIILNRTU	GRUELLING HEAT
AEEGGHINNOOTV	GOING TO HEAVEN
AEEGGHINOORSU	GEORGIAN HOUSE
AEEGGHINORTTT	GETTING TO HEAR
AEEGGHINRRSTV	HAVING REGRETS
AEEGGHNNOOTTW	GET ON THE WAGON
AEEGGHNRRSTTT	GREAT STRENGTH
AEEGGHOOOOPRRZ	ZOOGEOGRAPHER
AEEGGIILNOSTY	LAYING SEIGE TO
AEEGGILNNOPSW	SWEEPING ALONG
AEEGGILNPTTTU	GETTING UP LATE
AEEGGIMNPRSTT	RAGING TEMPEST
AEEGGINNOOPRS	GOING ON A SPREE
AEEGGINNOSSSY	EASYGOINGNESS
AEEGGINOORSSV	GOING OVERSEAS
AEEGGIQRRRSSU	SQUARE-RIGGERS
AEEGGLLORRSUY	ROGUES GALLERY
AEEGGMNNOORRT	ROENTGENOGRAM
AEEGGNNRSTTUW	WENT GREAT GUNS
AEEGGNOORSTTU	GET ONE'S RAG OUT
AEEGGNOPRSSTU	GETS ONE'S RAG UP
AEEGHHHINOSST	ON THE HIGH SEAS
AEEGHHIILSVWY	WEIGHS HEAVILY
AEEGHHIIRTTWW	WHITE WITH RAGE
AEEGHHIMMMNOR	HAMMERING HOME
AEEGHHINOTTVV	HAVING THE VOTE
AEEGHHIOPPRTT	HEIGHT-TO-PAPER
AEEGHHIRSTTTT	HITS THE TARGET
AEEGHHRTTTTU	GET AT THE TRUTH
AEEGHIIKLNTTV	TAKING THE VEIL
AEEGHIIKNRSTT	TAKING THE RISE
AEEGHIIKNTTVW	TAKING THE VIEW
AEEGHIILNNORV	HEARING NO EVIL
AEEGHIILNRSTW	RESTING AWHILE
AEEGHIILNRTTV	LIVING THEATRE
AEEGHIIMMNNRTT	MATING IN THREE
AEEGHIINNORST	GET IN ONE'S HAIR
AEEGHIINNRTTV	HITTING A NERVE
AEEGHIINNSTTZ	ANESTHETIZING
AEEGHIKLNPSSS	SPEAKS ENGLISH
AEEGHIKLNPSSW	SPEAKING WELSH
AEEGHIKLNRSTT	TAKING SHELTER
AEEGHIKMMNOST	MAKE SOMETHING
AEEGHIKMNNSTW	MAKING THE NEWS
AEEGHIKMNOOPW	MAKING WHOOPEE
AEEGHIKMRRSTT	RIGS THE MARKET
AEEGHIKNSTTTT	TAKING THE TEST
AEEGHILLNRSSS	SELLING SHARES
AEEGHILLOPPUV	GIVE UP ALL HOPE
AEEGHILLOTWWY	YELLOW WITH AGE
AEEGHILMNRSST	ENGLISH MASTER
AEEGHILNNRTTY	THREATENINGLY
AEEGHILNNSTTW	LATE-NIGHT NEWS
AEEGHILNRTTTW	WRITE AT LENGTH
AEEGHILPRSSTT	TELEGRAPHISTS
AEEGHIMOPRRSS	SEISMOGRAPHER
AEEGHIMORSTTU	ROUGH ESTIMATE
AEEGHIMRRSSTT	MISS THE TARGET
AEEGHIMRTTTWY	WEIGHTY MATTER
AEEGHINNORSTU	RENTING A HOUSE
AEEGHINNPPTTU	UPPING THE ANTE
AEEGHINNPRSST	SHERPA TENSING
AEEGHINNPRTTY	PAYING THE RENT
AEEGHINOPRTTU	ARGUE THE POINT
	POURING THE TEA
AEEGHINOSSTTU	HOUSING ESTATE
AEEGHINPPRSSS	PASSENGER SHIP
AEEGHINNRRSSTT	STRAIGHTENERS
AEEGHKLNOPSTT	SPOKE AT LENGTH
AEEGHLLNOOTTW	GONE TO THE WALL
AEEGHLLNOPTUW	GONE UP THE WALL
AEEGHILNORRST	HELLO STRANGER
AEEGHLLOOSTTW	GOES TO THE WALL
AEEGHLLOPSTUW	GOES UP THE WALL
AEEGHLNOORTZZ	GO ON THE RAZZLE
AEEGHLNORTTTW	WROTE AT LENGTH
AEEGHLOORRSTW	WOOLGATHERERS
AEEGHLOPPRSTT	TELEGRAPH POST
AEEGHMMMOOPRR	HOME PROGRAMME
AEEGHNOOPRRTV	PHOTOENGRAVER
AEEGHNOORSTTW	GONE TO THE WARS
AEEGHNOPRRSST	STENOGRAPHERS
AEEGHNOPSSSTT	STEPS ON THE GAS
AEEGHNOPSTTTU	PUT ON THE STAGE
AEEGHOORSSTTW	GOES TO THE WARS
AEEGHORRSTTTT	START TOGETHER
AEEGHORSSSTTU	ARGUES THE TOSS
AEEGIIIJKLNNP	KEEPING IN JAIL
AEEGIIINSTTVV	INVESTIGATIVE
AEEGIIKLNNPPY	KEEPING IN PLAY
AEEGIILLLSTVY	LEGISLATIVELY
AEEGIILLNSSSV	SAILING VESSEL
AEEGIILMNNRSS	REMAINS SINGLE

AEEGIILMNORSS	GENERALISSIMO
AEEGIILNNRRTT	INTERRELATING
AEEGIILNNRSTX	EXTERNALISING
AEEGIILNNRTXZ	EXTERNALIZING
AEEGIIMMNRSTU	MEASURING TIME
AEEGIIMNNORTT	REGIMENTATION
AEEGIIMNNRRTTX	EXTERMINATING
AEEGIIMNSTTVW	EMITTING WAVES
AEEGIINNOPRRT	PEREGRINATION
AEEGIINORRTTV	INTERROGATIVE
AEEGIKLLLOPST	SLEPT LIKE A LOG
AEEGIKLMNSSUY	SEEKING ASYLUM
AEEGIKLNPRSSU	KINGS PLEASURE
AEEGIKLNRSTTW	STREETWALKING
AEEGIKMNPRSST	SPEAKING TERMS
AEEGILLLNPRST	SELLING PLATER
AEEGILLMNNSSY	MEANINGLESSLY
AEEGILLNRSTVY	EVERLASTINGLY
AEEGILMMOPRRV	LIVE PROGRAMME
AEEGILNNORTUW	NEW REGULATION
AEEGILNNPRTTY	PENETRATINGLY
AEEGILNPRSSST	PASSENGER LIST
AEEGILNPRTTTY	TYPING A LETTER
AEEGILNRSTTTW	WATLING STREET
AEEGIMMRSSSST	GAMES MISTRESS
AEEGIMNNRTTUY	INTEGUMENTARY
AEEGIMNOORSTV	MOVES INTO GEAR
AEEGIMNORROTV	OVERMASTERING
AEEGIMNOSSSTT	GETS INTO A MESS
AEEGINNNORTUV	GIVEN ONE A TURN
AEEGINNNOSSST	NESTING SEASON
AEEGINNOPRSTW	NEWGATE PRISON
AEEGINNORSSSU	USING ONE'S EARS
AEEGINNORSTUV	GIVES ONE A TURN
AEEGINNRSTTUU	SIGNATURE TUNE
AEEGINOQRRTUV	GIVE NO QUARTER
AEEGINOSSTTTW	GETS INTO A STEW
AEEGINQRSSTTU	SEQUESTRATING
AEEGINRRSSSTV	TRANSGRESSIVE
AEEGINRSSTTTT	SETTING AT REST
AEEGIORRRSTTV	TERGIVERSATOR
AEEGKOPRRRSSS	RAKES PROGRESS
AEEGLLLLNOPSST	LONG LAST SLEEP
AEEGLLMNNNTUY	UNGENTLEMANLY
AEEGLLMNRSUWZ	MANGEL-WURZELS
AEEGLNOPRRRSU	REGULAR PERSON
AEEGLNOPRSSTU	PERSONAL GUEST
AEEGLNORRRTUV	LARGE TURNOVER
AEEGNNOOSTWWY	GET ONES OWN WAY
AEEGNOOPRSSWY	GROPES ONE'S WAY
AEEGORSSSSTUU	STEGOSAURUSES
AEEHHHIRSSSTV	HAS THE SHIVERS
AEEHHHNOORTUV	HAVE THE HONOUR
AEEHHIILLSSTW	HAS THE WILLIES
AEEHHIINNOPTZ	PHENOTHIAZINE
AEEHHIINRRTTW	THREW IN THE AIR
AEEHHILNNSSTU	UNHEALTHINESS
AEEHHILNORSST	THE LIONS SHARE
AEEHHILNPRTTT	APRIL THE TENTH
AEEHHIMRSTTTW	WITH THE STREAM
AEEHHINOOPTTV	HAVE THE OPTION
AEEHHKORRSSTW	SHARES THE WORK
AEEHHKPRSTTTU	SPEAK THE TRUTH
AEEHHLLNOPRTU	HELL UPON EARTH
AEEHHLLNRRTTU	LEARN THE TRUTH
AEEHHLLOORSSTT	SHARES THE LOOT
AEEHHLLORRSTUY	THE EARLY HOURS
AEEHHLLOSSSTTW	STEALS THE SHOW
AEEHHMMNOORTTW	THE OTHER WOMAN
AEEHHMMNORRTTT	THE MATTERHORN
AEEHHHNNORTTTU	TURN ON THE HEAT
	TURN THE HEAT ON
AEEHHNOPSTTTU	PUTS THE HEAT ON
AEEHIIKLLMRSW	KAISER WILHELM
AEEHIILNNRTTV	IN THE INTERVAL
AEEHIILNPSTTV	LIVE IN THE PAST
AEEHIJKLMNPTU	JUMP IN THE LAKE
AEEHIJLMRSSTW	JAMES WHISTLER
AEEHIJMNPSSTU	JUMPS IN THE SEA
AEEHIKLORRSWY	KILROY WAS HERE
AEEHIKMMRSSST	MISSES THE MARK
AEEHIKNNSSSTV	SHAKIN' STEVENS
AEEHILLNNOSTY	LAYS ON THE LINE
AEEHILLOPPPRS	APPLE POLISHER
	APPLE-POLISHER
AEEHILLORTWWW	WEAR THE WILLOW
AEEHILMMNNOPS	PHENOMENALISM
AEEHILMMOOSST	MESOTHELIOMAS
AEEHILMNNOPST	PHENOMENALIST
AEEHILMNNORST	HOSTILE MANNER
AEEHILNNOSTTT	NOT IN THE LEAST
AEEHILNNRSSTU	UNEARTHLINESS
AEEHILORRTTVW	RELATIVE WORTH
AEEHIMMOPPRSY	HAPPY MEMORIES
AEEHIMMNOPSTU	MOUNTAIN SHEEP
AEEHIMMNNRSTTU	HUMAN INTEREST
AEEHIMNQSSSSU	SQUEAMISHNESS
AEEHIIMOPPRRTY	HYPERMETROPIA
AEEHINNOPPRSS	APPREHENSIONS
AEEHINNORSSTW	WINS ONE'S HEART
AEEHINORSSSTW	SEAWORTHINESS
AEEHINRRTTWWY	WINTRY WEATHER
AEEHIORRSSTTU	SERIOUS THREAT
AEEHIPRRRSSTU	TREASURERSHIP
AEEHJLLMOPSWX	MAXWELL JOSEPH
AEEHKLLNRSSTW	SWELL THE RANKS
AEEHKLNNSSSST	THANKLESSNESS
AEEHKLNOPSTTU	UP TO THE ANKLES
AEEHKLNPSSTTU	ELEPHANTS TUSK
AEEHKLOOSTTTU	TOOK THE SALUTE
AEEHKLOPRSTTU	KEPT LATE HOURS
AEEHKNNOOPSTT	KEPT ONE'S HAT ON
AEEHKNNOORSTW	KNOW THE ANSWER
AEEHKNNORSTWW	KNOW THE ANSWER
AEEHKOORSTTTW	TOOK THE WATERS
AEEHLLLMPRRYY	PLAY MERRY HELL
AEEHLLLOSSSVV	SHALLOW VESSEL
AEEHLLMMORSWY	YELLOWHAMMERS
AEEHLLMNOPSTT	SHEPTON MALLET
AEEHLLMORSSUW	WEE SMALL HOURS
AEEHLLNOTTTWW	WENT TO THE WALL
AEEHLLNPSTTUW	SENT UP THE WALL
AEEHLLNPTTUWW	WENT UP THE WALL
AEEHLLOPPRSTW	TELLS A WHOPPER
AEEHLMMNOSTTT	THE LAST MOMENT
AEEHLMNOOSSST	LOATHSOMENESS
AEEHLMPSSTTYY	PLAY THE SYSTEM
AEEHLNNNOTWYY	ANTHONY NEWLEY
AEEHLNOORSSTT	LOST ONE'S HEART
AEEHLNOPSSTTU	PUTS THE SEAL ON
AEEHLNORRSTTY	NORTHEASTERLY
AEEHLNOSSTUWW	NEW SOUTH WALES
AEEHLORRSTTYY	ROY HATTERSLEY
AEEHLORSSTTUY	SOUTHEASTERLY
AEEHLORSTTTTU	TRUE TO THE LAST
AEEHLPPRSSTTU	THE LAST SUPPER
AEEHMMMNORRSSY	ROMNEY MARSHES
AEEHMMOOPRRTY	TEMPORARY HOME
AEEHMMOOPRSST	METAMORPHOSES
AEEHMNOOPPRTU	PNEUMATOPHORE
AEEHMNOORRRSY	RHYME OR REASON

AEEHMNOPSTTTT	HONEST ATTEMPT	AEEILMNNNSTTU	UNSENTIMENTAL
AEEHMOOPPPRRST	PAPERS THE ROOM	AEEILMOPRRTXY	EXTEMPORARILY
	SPERMATOPHORE	AEEILNNNOPRST	ANTIPERSONNEL
AEEHMOPPRSTTY	SPERMATOPHYTE	AEEILNNOOOOPTV	LEAVE NO OPTION
AEEHMORRSTTWY	STORMY WEATHER	AEEILNNOQRUVX	VERNAL EQUINOX
AEEHNORRRTTTU	RETURN TO EARTH	AEEILNNORTTUV	VIOLENT NATURE
AEEHNORSSTTTU	SOUTHERN STATE	AEEILNNORTTVW	WRITTEN A NOVEL
AEEHNORSTTTWW	WENT TO THE WARS	AEEILNNPRRSTT	SILENT PARTNER
AEEHOOPRTTTUU	POUR OUT THE TEA	AEEILNNRSSSUV	UNIVERSALNESS
AEEHPPRRSSTUV	HARVEST SUPPER	AEEILNOOPRTTT	TELEPORTATION
AEEHRRSSTTTTU	UTTERS THREATS	AEEILNOPRSSTV	PRIVATE LESSON
AEEIIIKMNQRSU	MAKE INQUIRIES	AEEILNORRSTTW	LEARNS TO WRITE
AEEIIIILLNRTTT	INITIAL LETTER	AEEILNORRTTTW	LEARNT TO WRITE
AEEIIILMNPRRS	PRELIMINARIES	AEEILOPRRSSTT	LIES PROSTRATE
AEEIIIMNSSTTV	IMITATIVENESS	AEEILORRSTTVY	RESTORATIVELY
AEEIIKLMNPRSS	MARLINESPIKES	AEEILQRSTTTUY	QUALITY STREET
AEEIIILLLMNNPR	PREMILLENNIAL	AEEIMMNNORSST	MOMENTARINESS
AEEIIILMMPRSV	PRIMEVAL SLIME	AEEIMMNOOPRTT	OTTOMAN EMPIRE
AEEIIILLMRSSTU	MITRAILLEUSES	AEEIMNNNNOOSW	IN ONES OWN NAME
AEEIIILLNNPTTY	PENITENTIALLY	AEEIMNNORSSTV	NORMATIVENESS
AEEIIILLNSTTXY	EXISTENTIALLY	AEEIMNOPPRSST	PAST ONES PRIME
AEEIIILMNNRSST	REMAINS SILENT	AEEIMNOPRRSST	TEMPORARINESS
AEEIIILMNOPRSS	IMPERSONALISE	AEEIMNOPRSSTX	PROXIMATENESS
AEEIIILMNOPRSZ	IMPERSONALIZE	AEEIMNORRSTTV	REMONSTRATIVE
AEEIIILNNORRTT	INTERRELATION	AEEIMNORRTTTU	ROUTINE MATTER
AEEIIILNNOOSTV	INVIOLATENESS	AEEIMNORRTTXY	EXTERMINATORY
AEEIIILNNPRSST	PAINTERLINESS	AEEIMORRSSTTU	SERIOUS MATTER
AEEIIILNNPSSTV	PLAINTIVENESS	AEEIMRSSSSTTY	SYSTEMATISERS
AEEIIILNOPQTTU	EQUIPOTENTIAL	AEEIMRSSSTTYZ	SYSTEMATIZERS
AEEIIILNOPRSST	PERSONALITIES	AEEINNOPRRRST	SENIOR PARTNER
AEEIIILNOPRTTV	INTERPOLATIVE	AEEINNOPRSSTT	PRESENTATIONS
AEEIIILNRSSSUV	UNIVERSALISES	AEEINNOQRRTTU	QUARTER TO NINE
AEEIIILNRSSUVZ	UNIVERSALIZES	AEEINNOSSSTWY	SET IN ONE'S WAYS
AEEIIILORRRTTX	EXTERRITORIAL	AEEINNRRSTTWW	WRITTEN ANSWER
AEEIIMMNNRSTTT	INTIMATE TERMS	AEEINOOPQSSTU	POSE A QUESTION
AEEIIMMNNORTTX	EXTERMINATION	AEEINOPPRRSTV	PRIVATE PERSON
AEEIIMNORRSTV	ARRIVES ON TIME	AEEINOPRRSSTT	STATE PRISONER
AEEIIMNPSSSSV	IMPASSIVENESS	AEEINOQRSSTTU	SEQUESTRATION
AEEIIMNQRSSTU	EQUESTRIANISM	AEEINOSSSTUVX	VEXATIOUSNESS
AEEIIMRSSSSTT	MISSES A SITTER	AEEIOOPRSTTV	POSTOPERATIVE
AEEIINNOQRSTU	QUESTIONNAIRE	AEEIPPRRSTTTT	PITTER-PATTERS
AEEIINORSSSVW	AIRS ONE'S VIEWS	AEEJLLORRSTVY	TRAVELLERS JOY
AEEIIOPPRRRST	PROPRIETARIES	AEEKKLOOOPSTU	KEEPS A LOOK-OUT
AEEIIOPRRRSTY	PRAIRIE OYSTER	AEEKLMOPSSSUV	SPEAKS VOLUMES
AEEIKLLOPPSTT	SLEPT LIKE A TOP	AEEKLNOOPRRSY	SNOOKER PLAYER
AEEIKLNOOSSTU	SEEK A SOLUTION	AEEKMNNOOSSUV	VENOMOUS SNAKE
AEEIKLORSSTUY	TAKE SERIOUSLY	AEEKMORRSSSTT	MASTERSTROKES
AEEIKMNNOOPST	MAKE ONES POINT	AEELLMOORRTTW	MARTELLO TOWER
AEEIKMNNRSTTT	SKIN TREATMENT	AEELLMOQRRSUY	QUARRELSOMELY
AEEIKNNOPRRST	TAKEN PRISONER	AEELLNOPRSSTY	PERSONAL STYLE
AEEIKNOPRSSTT	STREPTOKINASE	AEELLOOPPRRRX	POLAR EXPLORER
AEEIKNPRSTTUU	STRIKE UP A TUNE	AEELLOORSTWWY	WOOLLY SWEATER
AEEILLLMNNSST	MENTAL ILLNESS	AEELMMNNORTTT	MENTAL TORMENT
AEEILLLNRRSTW	ALL-IN WRESTLER	AEELMNORRTTTU	MENTAL TORTURE
AEEIILLMNNSTTY	SENTIMENTALLY	AEELMNORRTUVY	VOLUNTEER ARMY
AEEILLMNPRSTY	SEMPITERNALLY	AEELMNPPRSTUY	SUPPLEMENTARY
AEEILLMNPTTUY	PENULTIMATELY	AEELMOPRRRSSU	MORAL PRESSURE
AEEILLNOPRRTT	INTERPELLATOR	AEELMPPRRTTUY	TRUMPET PLAYER
AEEILLNOSTTTW	SATELLITE TOWN	AEELNOOOORRST	SOONER OR LATER
AEEILLNRRSSUV	UNIVERSAL RULE	AEELNOPPRRTUV	APPLE TURNOVER
AEEILLNRSTUXY	INTERSEXUALLY	AEELNOPPRSTTY	PLENTY TO SPARE
AEEILLOPRSTTT	LITTLE TO SPARE	AEELNOPRSTTTT	TALENT SPOTTER
AEEILLOPRTVXY	EXPLORATIVELY	AEELNQRRRTTUY	QUARTERLY RENT
AEEILLPRRSTTV	SILVER PLATTER	AEELPPPRRSSUY	APPLY PRESSURE
AEEILLPRSTUVY	SUPERLATIVELY	AEEMMNNNPPSTTY	TENPENNY STAMP
AEEILLRRRSTTY	TERRESTRIALLY	AEEMMNNOORSSTW	ONE'S OWN MASTER
AEEILLRRSTTYY	LITERARY STYLE	AEEMMNNOOPRSTT	PERMANENT POST
AEEILLSTTTTTT	TITTLE-TATTLES	AEEMMNOOPRSTTU	TREPONEMATOUS
AEEILMMNNPRTY	IMPERMANENTLY	AEEMMNOORSTUUV	OUTMANOEUVRES
AEEILMMNOORST	MEMORIAL STONE	AEEMNPRRRSUUY	SUPERNUMERARY
AEEILMNNNORTV	ENVIRONMENTAL	AEENNOOPPRSST	OPENS ONE'S TRAP

AEENNORSTTTWW	NEWTON STEWART
AEENOOPRSSSST	STOPS ONE'S EARS
AEENOPPPPRTTU	PUT PEN TO PAPER
AEENORSSTTUVY	VENTURES TO SAY
AEEOOPRRSSTTT	STATE TROOPERS
AEFFFILLLORWY	FAIRLY WELL OFF
AEFFGGGINORST	STAGGERING OFF
AEFFGGHILLNTY	FLYING THE FLAG
AEFFGGIINOSTU	SIGN OF FATIGUE
AEFFGGIINRSTU	REFUSING A GIFT
AEFFGHILNOSSU	FLASH OF GENIUS
AEFFGHILOORST	GO OFF THE RAILS
AEFFGHILORTTU	FIT OF LAUGHTER
AEFFGHLLLOOTW	FOLLOW THE FLAG
AEFFGHLLNRTUU	UNFURL THE FLAG
AEFFGHNORSTTU	TURN OFF THE GAS
AEFFGIIKMNOTT	TAKING TIME OFF
AEFFGIILNORSU	SIGN OF FAILURE
AEFFGILLMNNOU	FULL OF MEANING
AEFFGINOOPRTY	OFFERING TO PAY
AEFFHHIILPRTT	APRIL THE FIFTH
AEFFHHSSTTTTU	THAT'S THE STUFF
AEFFHKNOPRRST	PROFFER THANKS
AEFFHNOPRTTTU	TURN OFF THE TAP
AEFFIILLOQTUY	QUALITY OF LIFE
AEFFIIMORRTUV	FIRM FAVOURITE
AEFFILMNORTUY	FAMILY FORTUNE
AEFFIOOPRRSTT	TORE A STRIP OFF
	TORE OFF A STRIP
AEFFLLLOOSSTUU	FALLS OUT OF USE
AFFFNNOPRRSSU	SPURNS AN OFFER
AEFFNORRSSTUY	RUNS FOR SAFETY
AEFGGHIIILNRT	LIGHTING A FIRE
AEFGGHIILLNPT	FILLING THE GAP
AEFGGHNNOPRSU	PANGS OF HUNGER
AEFGGIIKNRSTU	FIGURE SKATING
AEFGGIINRSTTT	GETTING A FIRST
AEFGGLOOOSTTU	GETS OUT OF GAOL
AEFGHHIILOPRT	EIGHTH OF APRIL
AEFGHHILOSSTT	HOISTS THE FLAG
AEFGHHOORRSTU	THOROUGHFARES
AEFGHHORSTTTU	AFTERTHOUGHTS
AEFGHIIILLNRT	FILLING THE AIR
AEFGHIIKLNTTT	TAKING THE LIFT
AEFGHIILLMNSS	FLASHING SMILE
AEFGHIILMOPRS	FILMOGRAPHIES
AEFGHIINORSTT	SHIFT INTO GEAR
AEFGHIKLNOPRS	ASKING FOR HELP
AEFGHILMORSTT	STREAM OF LIGHT
AEFGHILNOORSS	LOSS OF HEARING
AEFGHINNNPRTY	PENNY FARTHING
	PENNY-FARTHING
AEFGHINOSSTWY	FIGHTS ONE'S WAY
AEFGHLNPRSTUU	RUNS UP THE FLAG
AEFGHLORRSSSY	GLASS OF SHERRY
AEFGHNOOSTUWY	FOUGHT ONE'S WAY
AEFGHNOSTTTUU	TENTH OF AUGUST
AEFGIIILLLNNN	FALLING IN LINE
AEFGIIILLLNNOV	FALLING IN LOVE
AEFGIIILLLNNST	FALLING SILENT
AEFGIILLNORVY	FIRING A VOLLEY
AEFGIILMNOOTV	FAILING TO MOVE
AEFGIILNNNNSSU	UNFAILINGNESS
AEFGIILNOPRRT	PROLIFERATING
AEFGIINNOPRST	POINTS A FINGER
AEFGIINNSSSTY	SIGNIFY ASSENT
AEFGIINOPRRTU	PREFIGURATION
AEFGIJLNOOPRY	LEAPING FOR JOY
AEFGIJLOOSTTU	GETS OUT OF JAIL
AEFGIKMNOORRS	ASKING FOR MORE
AEFGILLLNOSSS	FILL ONES GLASS

AEFGILLNNORTY	LEARNING TO FLY
AEFGILLNNRTUY	UNFALTERINGLY
AEFGILNNOOSSU	USING ONE'S LOAF
AEFGILNNOTTTU	FLATTENING OUT
AEFGILNOORTTV	FLOATING VOTER
AEFGILOPPRRUU	POPULAR FIGURE
AEFGIMMNNORSST	STRING OF NAMES
AEFGIMNOORRRR	MARGIN OF ERROR
AEFGINNNOORTW	NOTE OF WARNING
AEFGINOOPRRTW	WATERPROOFING
AEFGINOOPRSSS	SONGS OF PRAISE
AEFGINOORSTUV	FAVOURITE SONG
AEFGINOPRSTUY	REFUSING TO PAY
AEFGLLMMOPRRU	FULL PROGRAMME
AEFGLLRRTTUUY	TRULY GRATEFUL
AEFGMNNOORTTY	MARGOT FONTEYN
AEFGMOOTTUWYY	GET OUT OF MY WAY
AEFGNOOORSTTW	SET A FOOT WRONG
AEFHHIIINNSTT	IN AT THE FINISH
AEFHHIKOORSTW	SHOOK WITH FEAR
AEFHHOOPRSTTW	PART OF THE SHOW
AEFHHOORRRTUU	HOUR AFTER HOUR
AEFHHOORSSTTW	STAR OF THE SHOW
AEFHIIIKLMSSW	SWIM LIKE A FISH
AEFHIIKLMSSUW	SWUM LIKE A FISH
AEFHIILPRRSTT	APRIL THE FIRST
AEFHIINNOPSST	PINS ONE'S FAITH
AEFHIJNOOPTTW	POINT OF THE JAW
AEFHILNNPSSTU	FLUENT SPANISH
AEFHILNOOSSTT	LOST ONE'S FAITH
AEFHIMNNOOSTT	TIMON OF ATHENS
AEFHINNORSSUY	RAY OF SUNSHINE
AEFHINNORSTTT	SAT IN THE FRONT
AEFHINOORSTUV	THOSE IN FAVOUR
AEFHINOPRSTTT	FARTHEST POINT
AEFHINORSTTTT	SIT AT THE FRONT
AEFHKLNOOTTTW	TALK OF THE TOWN
AEFHKMNOOORST	ASK FOR THE MOON
AEFHKNOPRSSTU	PROFUSE THANKS
AEFHLNOOOORSTT	SAT ON THE FLOOR
AEFHMMOORRSTY	STRAY FROM HOME
AEFHNOORRTTUW	WORTH A FORTUNE
AEFHOORSSTTUU	HOUSE OF STUART
AEFIIIILMNNST	INFINITESIMAL
AEFIIILLPRSTU	SPIRITUAL LIFE
AEFIIILMNSSST	SEMIFINALISTS
AEFIIILNNOSTT	STATION IN LIFE
AEFIIILNORSTT	FERTILISATION
AEFIIILNORTTZ	FERTILIZATION
AEFIIINNOSTTU	FINE SITUATION
AEFIIKLMNOORT	TOOK A FIRM LINE
AEFIILLLNNTUY	INFLUENTIALLY
AEFIILLNNNNRSU	FALLEN IN RUINS
AEFIILLPRSSTU	SPIRITUAL SELF
AEFIILMMOPSST	FALSE OPTIMISM
AEFIILMNNORUY	FAMILY REUNION
AEFIILMNORTVY	INFORMATIVELY
AEFIILNOOPRRT	PROLIFERATION
AEFIIMNORRSTW	MINISTER OF WAR
AEFIINNOOOPTT	TOO FINE A POINT
AEFIINOPRRSTU	PUT IN FOR A RISE
AEFIKLRSSSTTU	FRUITLESS TASK
AEFIKOPRRRTWY	FIREWORK PARTY
AEFILLLOOORTV	ROOT OF ALL EVIL
AEFILLMORSSTT	STALLS FOR TIME
AEFILLNOORRRT	FALL INTO ERROR
AEFILMMNNOOST	MONOFILAMENTS
AEFILMNOPRSTT	SELF-IMPORTANT
AEFILNNRSSTUU	FLUENT RUSSIAN
AEFILNOOPRSSS	PROFESSIONALS

AEFILNOOPRSSW	PASSION FLOWER	AEGGILNOPPRSW	GROWING APPLES
	PASSIONFLOWER	AEGGIMNNOORST	GOING ON STREAM
AEFILOPRRSSTT	SELF-PORTRAITS	AEGGIMNNOORTV	MOVING TO ANGER
AEFIMNNOORTTU	NOT FOR A MINUTE	AEGGINNORRRTT	RAGING TORRENT
AEFINNOORRRTT	TORRENT OF RAIN	AEGGINNRRSSST	TRANSGRESSING
AEFINOOPRRRSW	PRISONER OF WAR	AEGGMNNOORRST	RONTGENOGRAMS
AEFINOPRRRTTU	RETURN A PROFIT	AEGGNOOORSTTU	GOT ONE'S RAG OUT
AEFIOPPRSSTUW	SUPPORTS A WIFE	AEGHHHIINTTTY	HITTING THE HAY
AEFKMNOPRSTUV	KNAVE OF TRUMPS	AEGHHHIIINNRTW	WITHIN HEARING
AEFLLLNOOOSTT	FALL TO ONE'S LOT	AEGHHIIKNNTTT	TAKING THE HINT
AEFLLMOOPRSST	PLATFORM SOLES	AEGHHIINRSTTT	IN THE STRAIGHT
AEFLLNNRTUUWY	UNLAWFUL ENTRY	AEGHHIKMMNSTU	MAKE THINGS HUM
AEFLMOOPRRSTT	FORMAL PROTEST	AEGHHIKMNOSTT	MAKE THINGS HOT
AEFLMOPRRRTUY	POULTRY FARMER	AEGHHILLMPSTT	LIGHTS THE LAMP
AEFLNNORTTUUY	UNFORTUNATELY	AEGHHILNORSSY	ROYAL HIGHNESS
AEFLNPRSSTUVY	VENUS'-FLYTRAPS	AEGHHILNRSTTY	EARTHLY THINGS
AEFLOOPPRRTWY	LAW OF PROPERTY	AEGHHINNNOOTV	HAVE NOTHING ON
AEFLOPPRSSTUU	PUTS UP FOR SALE	AEGHHINOSTWWY	SHOWING THE WAY
AEFMMMNNOOORTT	NOT FOR A MOMENT	AEGHHIOPPRRSY	PHYSIOGRAPHER
AEFMNNOOOORTUY	RAN OUT OF MONEY	AEGHHIPRSSUWY	SUPERHIGHWAYS
AEFMNOOOPSSTT	STAMP ONE'S FOOT	AEGHHMMORTTTUU	MATURE THOUGHT
AEFMNOOPPRRTY	MAN OF PROPERTY	AEGHHNNOPSTUU	HUNG ONE'S HAT UP
AEFMNOORSTTUU	RUN OUT OF STEAM		HUNG UP ONE'S HAT
AEFMNOPRRSTTU	PERFORM A STUNT	AEGHHNOORSTUW	SAW ONE THROUGH
AEFOOORRRSSTW	TEARS OF SORROW	AEGHHOOPPRRST	PHOTOGRAPHERS
AEFOOQRRRTTUU	QUARTER TO FOUR	AEGHHOOPTTTTU	TOUGH AT THE TOP
AEGGGGINNNOTU	NAGGING TONGUE	AEGHHOPRSSSTU	PASSES THROUGH
AEGGGGINNOTUW	WAGGING TONGUE	AEGHHORTTTTTU	GOT AT THE TRUTH
AEGGGHHIIINNNT	GAINING HEIGHT	AEGHIIIKKLNNT	THINKING ALIKE
AEGGGHIIINNTW	GAINING WEIGHT	AEGHIIILNPRST	HEALING SPIRIT
AEGGGIINRRTTU	REGURGITATING	AEGHIIILNRTVW	GIVEN IT A WHIRL
AEGGGILNORRRW	GROWING LARGER	AEGHIIILRSTVW	GIVES IT A WHIRL
AEGGGILNPRRUY	PLAYING RUGGER	AEGHIIKKLNSTT	TAKING THE SILK
AEGGGLLNORSTU	STRUGGLE ALONG	AEGHIIKLLNPTT	TAKING THE PILL
AEGGHHIKLLSTU	HUGH GAITSKELL	AEGHIIKLLOTTU	OUT LIKE A LIGHT
AEGGHHILLNOTW	GLOWING HEALTH	AEGHIIKLRSSTT	STRIKES A LIGHT
AEGGHHILNSTTU	TAUGHT ENGLISH	AEGHIIKNNSSTV	HAVING KITTENS
AEGGHHLNOOTTU	GOT THE LAUGH ON	AEGHIIKNPSSTT	TAKING THE PISS
AEGGHHORSTTTU	GREAT THOUGHTS	AEGHIILLMSTVY	VILLAGE SMITHY
AEGGHIIILNPPT	LIGHTING A PIPE	AEGHIILNNOOST	SHOOTING A LINE
AEGGHIIKNOTVY	GIVING THE OKAY	AEGHIILNNRSTU	IN THE SINGULAR
AEGGHIILMNPTV	GIVING THE PALM	AEGHIIMNPRRTU	REMAIN UPRIGHT
AEGGHIILNSTTT	SETTING ALIGHT	AEGHIINNNRTWW	WINNING THE WAR
AEGGHIIINNPPST	SHIPPING AGENT	AEGHIINNOORST	GOT IN ONE'S HAIR
AEGGHIINNRSTT	STRAIGHTENING	AEGHIINNORSTU	HOUSETRAINING
AEGGHIIRSTTTT	GET IT STRAIGHT	AEGHIINNORSTV	HAVING IN STORE
AEGGHILLMNOOP	GALLOPING HOME	AEGHIINNORTWY	WRITHE IN AGONY
AEGGHILNOORTW	WOOLGATHERING	AEGHIINRSSSSU	ISSUING SHARES
AEGGHILNORUUY	YOU'RE LAUGHING	AEGHIKLNOOPYY	PLAYING HOOKEY
AEGGHINNOORST	SHOOTING RANGE	AEGHIKLNORSST	STALKING HORSE
AEGGHHNNOOOTTW	GOT ON THE WAGON		STALKING-HORSE
AEGGHHNNOOPRRT	RONTGENOGRAPH	AEGHIKNNRRSTT	KNIGHTS-ERRANT
AEGGIIILLNNTTV	GIVING A LITTLE	AEGHILLPRSSTU	SUGARS THE PILL
AEGGIIILNNORS	REGIONALISING	AEGHILLRSTTTY	TREATS LIGHTLY
AEGGIIILNNORZ	REGIONALIZING	AEGHILMNNOTWW	MOWING THE LAWN
AEGGIIIMNPSTT	SPITTING IMAGE	AEGHILNORSTUV	VAULTING HORSE
AEGGIIINNSTTV	INVESTIGATING	AEGHIMMNNOOPTY	PAYING THE MOON
AEGGIIINRSTTV	GIVING IT A REST	AEGHIMNNORTTUW	MOUTH-WATERING
AEGGIILLMNOST	GLOATING SMILE	AEGHIMNOSSSTY	SAYS SOMETHING
AEGGIILLNNOSV	GIVING ONE'S ALL	AEGHINNNNORRSU	RUNNING ASHORE
AEGGIILNNOSSV	GIVING A LESSON	AEGHINNNOSSTU	HUNTING SEASON
AEGGIIINNORRTT	INTERROGATING	AEGHINNOORSST	ON A SHOE-STRING
AEGGIIINNPRTTU	PUTTING IN GEAR		ON A SHOESTRING
AEGGIIINORRTTU	REGURGITATION	AEGHINNOORTTW	NOTHING TO WEAR
AEGGIIINORRTUV	GIVING QUARTER	AEGHINNOORSSTV	HAVE NO STRINGS
AEGGIINRSTTTT	SITTING TARGET	AEGHINNOSSTTT	SETS AT NOTHING
AEGGIKMNOPSUV	GAVE UP SMOKING	AEGHINNOSSTTW	WASTES NOTHING
AEGGILLNORRTW	GROWING TALLER	AEGHINORSTTTU	STRAIGHTEN OUT
AEGGILLNORTTW	GET IT ALL WRONG	AEGHINORSTTVY	STAY OVERNIGHT
AEGGILNNNOPRU	ENLARGING UPON	AEGHINPPRRSTT	SPRING THE TRAP
AEGGILNNOORSS	LOSING ONE'S RAG	AEGHINPRSSTTU	STRAIGHTENS UP

AEGHLMMOORTTY	THREMMATOLOGY
AEGHLMNORRSTT	MORAL STRENGTH
AEGHMNOOOPSTU	ENTOMOPHAGOUS
AEGHMNOORSSST	GATHERS NO MOSS
AEGHMNOPRRSSU	HUMAN PROGRESS
AEGHNNOOPTTUY	PUT ON THE AGONY
AEGHNNORSSTTU	TURNS ON THE GAS
AEGHNOOPPRRRS	PORNOGRAPHERS
AEGHNPPRRSTTU	SPRUNG THE TRAP
AEGIIILLNNNTW	WAITING IN LINE
AEGIIIKLLMNPS	SPIKE MILLIGAN
AEGIIILNNNRST	INTERNALISING
AEGIIILNNNRTZ	INTERNALIZING
AEGIIILNNNSWY	WINNING EASILY
AEGIIILNORRST	SOLITAIRE RING
AEGIIINNNOOPV	GIVE AN OPINION
AEGIIINNNPRWZ	WINNING A PRIZE
AEGIIINNOSTTV	INVESTIGATION
AEGIIINSTTTVW	GIVEN IT A TWIST
AEGIIISSTTTVW	GIVES IT A TWIST
AEGIIKLNNPRSW	SPARKLING WINE
AEGIIKLNNPSTW	WALKING IN STEP
AEGIIKLNORTTV	TALKING IT OVER
AEGIIKMNNNOOS	MAKING NO NOISE
AEGIIKMNORSTW	MAKING IT WORSE
AEGIIKMNOTTTU	TAKING TIME OUT
AEGIIKNNNRSTW	WINNING STREAK
AEGIIKNNORSTT	STRIKING A NOTE
AEGIIKNOPRSST	RISING TO SPEAK
	STRIKING A POSE
AEGIIILLLLNRTY	LILLIE LANGTRY
AEGIIILNOOPST	LEGAL POSITION
AEGIIILMNNNRTWY	TIMELY WARNING
AEGIIILMNORRTY	LARGE MINORITY
AEGIIILMNORSST	MINERALOGISTS
AEGIIILMNPRSST	SLIPSTREAMING
AEGIIILNNNPSTY	PLAYING TENNIS
AEGIIILNNNPTUY	PLAYING IN TUNE
AEGIIILNNOPRSS	PERSONALISING
AEGIIILNNOPRSZ	PERSONALIZING
AEGIILNNOPRTT	INTERPOLATING
AEGIILNNORTVW	WRITING A NOVEL
AEGIILNRSSTVV	VESTAL VIRGINS
AEGIILRRSSTUV	REGULAR VISITS
AEGIIMMNNOPRST	IMPERSONATING
AEGIIMMNNOPSTT	PIGMENTATIONS
AEGIIMMNNRRRTY	INTERMARRYING
AEGIIMNSSSTTY	SYSTEMATISING
AEGIIMNSSTTYZ	SYSTEMATIZING
AEGIINNNSTTTT	SITTING TENANT
AEGIINNOORRTT	INTERROGATION
AEGIINNOORTTY	GAIN NOTORIETY
AEGIINNORRTUY	GENITOURINARY
AEGIINNPRRSUV	NURSING A VIPER
AEGIINNQRSTUY	INQUIRY AGENTS
AEGIINOORSTTT	GIANT TORTOISE
AEGIINOPPRRTX	EXPROPRIATING
AEGIINORRSSTT	REGISTRATIONS
AEGIINORSTTVY	INVESTIGATORY
AEGIINOSTTTUW	SWEATING IT OUT
AEGIINRRSTUVY	UNIVERSITY RAG
AEGIKKLNRTTUY	TALKING TURKEY
AEGIKLLNORRST	ROLLER SKATING
	ROLLER-SKATING
AEGIKLMNOOOTT	TOOK A LONG TIME
AEGIKLNNOSSST	TAKING LESSONS
AEGIKLNOOOTVW	TOOK A LONG VIEW
AEGILLLMNSSST	SMELLING SALTS
AEGIILLNNOOSS	LOSING ONE'S ALL
AEGILLMRSSTTU	METALLURGISTS
AEGILLNORSTTY	TELLING A STORY
AEGILLNOSSSTT	ON ITS LAST LEGS
AEGILMNNNORSW	SOLEMN WARNING
AEGILMNNORRST	NEIL ARMSTRONG
AEGILMNOOORTU	OUTER MONGOLIA
AEGILNNNORSUY	UNREASONINGLY
AEGILNNOOSSWY	LOSING ONE'S WAY
AEGILNNOPSTTU	PUTTING ON SALE
AEGILNNRSSTTW	STARTLING NEWS
AEGILNOOPRRSS	PROGRESSIONAL
AEGILNOOPRRTU	AIRPORT LOUNGE
AEGILNOPPRRSU	POPULAR SINGER
AEGILNOPSTTUX	EXPOSTULATING
AEGILOORRSSUY	GLORIOUS YEARS
AEGILOORSSTTT	TERATOLOGISTS
AEGIMMMMNPTUYY	EGYPTIAN MUMMY
AEGIMMOPORRUZ	QUIZ PROGRAMME
AEGIMNNNRRSTU	RUNNING STREAM
AEGIMNNOPRRRY	MORNING PRAYER
AEGIMNNORRSTT	REMONSTRATING
AEGIMNNORSSSW	SWING ONE'S ARMS
AEGIMNNRRSSTWY	WARNING SYSTEM
AEGIMNOOPRSSU	ANGIOSPERMOUS
AEGIMNOOORSTTV	MOVING TO TEARS
AEGIMNPRSSSTU	PASSING MUSTER
AEGINNOPPTTTU	PUTTING ON TAPE
AEGINNOPRSSSU	GAIN ONE'S SPURS
AEGINNORRSSST	TRANSGRESSION
AEGINOORRRSTT	INTERROGATORS
AEGINOORRRTTY	INTERROGATORY
AEGINQRRSTTTU	STRING QUARTET
AEGLNOOOPTTUY	GONE OUT TO PLAY
AEGLNORRSSSUU	GARRULOUSNESS
AEGLOOOPSTTUY	GOES OUT TO PLAY
AEGLOOPRRRSTU	REGULAR TROOPS
AEGMMNNORSSSUW	SWUNG ONE'S ARMS
AEGNNOOOSTWWY	GOT ONE'S OWN WAY
AEGNORRRSSSST	TRANSGRESSORS
AEHHIILMSTTTT	THATS THE LIMIT
AEHHIILNNPRTT	APRIL THE NINTH
AEHHIILORSTTV	HEALTH VISITOR
AEHHIILPRSTTX	APRIL THE SIXTH
AEHHIINORRTTW	THROW IN THE AIR
AEHHIINORSTTW	WITHIN EARSHOT
AEHHIKLPRTTUW	UP WITH THE LARK
AEHHILLMNPTTY	PLATYHELMINTH
AEHHILMMOOORT	HOMOIOTHERMAL
AEHHILNOORTTT	HOT ON THE TRAIL
AEHHILOPSSTTU	THIOSULPHATES
AEHHIMNNNORTT	AN R IN THE MONTH
AEHHINOPSTTTW	WHATS THE POINT?
AEHHIOPPRSTYY	PHYSIOTHERAPY
AEHHIORSSTTTU	THRASHES IT OUT
AEHHLLMORSSTU	THE SMALL HOURS
AEHHLLOPSTTUW	PUSH TO THE WALL
AEHHLNOOPSTTU	HOTHOUSE PLANT
AEHHLOOPPRSTY	PHOSPHORYLATE
AEHHMMNOOOPPST	MONOPHOSPHATE
AEHHMOOSSTTWY	SMOOTHS THE WAY
AEHHOOPRRSSST	SHARPSHOOTERS
AEHIIILOPSSTT	HOSPITALITIES
AEHIIINNPRSTW	WRITHES IN PAIN
AEHIIJLNORTTW	THREW INTO JAIL
AEHIIJMNORTTY	IN THE MAJORITY
AEHIIKOTTTUWY	TAKE IT WITH YOU
AEHIILLNOPTVY	PLAY THE VIOLIN
AEHIILLNPSTTY	PAINTS THE LILY
AEHIILMNNORVY	LIVE IN HARMONY
AEHIILNOPRSST	RELATIONSHIPS
AEHIILNORSSSU	HILARIOUSNESS
AEHIIMOOORTVWW	ROOM WITH A VIEW
AEHIINORRSSTW	AIRWORTHINESS

883

AEHIINRRSTTTW	WITH RESTRAINT
AEHIIRRSSSTTW	SHIRTWAISTERS
AEHIKNNOPPSSS	SPANISH SPOKEN
	SPOKEN SPANISH
AEHIKNOORSTTT	TOOK THE STRAIN
AEHIKOOORTTTT	TOOK IT TO HEART
AEHILLLPSSSTT	SPILLS THE SALT
AEHILLNOPPSTU	PULL INTO SHAPE
AEHILMOOSTUXY	HOMOSEXUALITY
AEHILMOPSSTTT	SPLITS THE ATOM
AEHILNNOOOORST	HORATIO NELSON
AEHILNOPRSSTU	HOSPITAL NURSE
AEHIMMNOPRTUY	IMMUNOTHERAPY
AEHIMMOOPRSST	METAMORPHOSIS
AEHIMMOORRSST	SIR THOMAS MORE
AEHIMNNOOPRST	ENANTIOMORPHS
AEHIMMNOPTTUU	UP THE MOUNTAIN
AEHIMNNPRSSTT	TRANSSHIPMENT
AEHIMNOOPRSTT	PAINTS THE ROOM
AEHIMNPRSTUUY	SUPERHUMANITY
AEHIMORRSSTTY	HISTORY MASTER
AEHINNOPTTUWY	WITHOUT A PENNY
AEHINOORSTTUW	WITHOUT REASON
AEHINOPPSSTTU	PUTS INTO SHAPE
AEHINORRSSTTW	SHOW RESTRAINT
AEHIOPPPSSTTT	PIPS AT THE POST
AEHJJLNNOOPSU	JOHN PAUL JONES
AEHJLMNNOOSSU	SAMUEL JOHNSON
AEHKKMOORRSTW	MAKE SHORT WORK
AEHKLMNNOOOTW	WALK ON THE MOON
AEHKMOPRSSTTX	X MARKS THE SPOT
AEHLLLOOSSWWW	SWALLOWS WHOLE
AEHLLNOPRSUUY	SULPHONYLUREA
AEHLMNOORRSTT	SHORT-TERM LOAN
AEHLNOORSSTTW	WORTH ONES SALT
AEHMMNOOPRRTTY	ANTHROPOMETRY
AEHMNOOPRSSSU	AMORPHOUSNESS
AEHMNOORSSTTW	SHORTEST WOMAN
AEHMNOQRTTUUY	QUANTUM THEORY
AEHNNOPRSTTTU	TURNS ON THE TAP
AEHNOOPRRSSSU	SARRUSOPHONES
AEHNOPRSSSTTU	SHUTS ONE'S TRAP
AEHNOPRSTTTWY	NATWEST TROPHY
AEIIILLMNNNOO	ONE IN A MILLION
AEIIILLMNORSS	MILLIONAIRESS
AEIIILLMNPRRY	PRELIMINARILY
AEIIILLMNRSTY	MINISTERIALLY
AEIIILLMRRSTT	TRILITERALISM
AEIIILMNPRTTY	AMITRIPTYLINE
AEIIILNNOSTTU	LUTEINISATION
AEIIILNNOTTUZ	LUTEINIZATION
AEIIILNORSSTT	STERILISATION
AEIIILNORSTTZ	STERILIZATION
AEIIILPRSSSTU	SPIRITUALISES
AEIIILPRSSTUZ	SPIRITUALIZES
AEIIIMNOORSST	ISOMERISATION
AEIIIMNOORSTZ	ISOMERIZATION
AEIIINNNRSTVV	STRIVEN IN VAIN
AEIIINNORSSSV	VISIONARINESS
AEIIINNORSTTW	WINTERISATION
AEIIINNORSTVV	IN VINO VERITAS
AEIIINNORTTWZ	WINTERIZATION
AEIIINNOSSSTT	SENSITISATION
AEIIINNOSSTTZ	SENSITIZATION
AEIIINNRSSTVV	STRIVES IN VAIN
AEIIKLLMMNOSS	MAKES MILLIONS
AEIIKLLNOPRSS	PASSION KILLER
AEIIKMNOOPRSV	MAKE PROVISION
AEIIKMNOPRSSS	ASK PERMISSION
AEIIKNNNRTTTU	TAKEN IT IN TURN
AEIIKNNRSTTTU	TAKE IT IN TURNS
AEIIILLLLMOPWW	WILLIAM POWELL
AEIIILLMNOPRRT	IN MORTAL PERIL
AEIIILLNNNOTTY	INTENTIONALLY
AEIIILLNOQRSUV	LIVE IN SQUALOR
AEIIILLNOQRTUV	VENTRILOQUIAL
AEIIILLNQRRSTU	TRANQUILLISER
AEIIILLNQRRTUZ	TRANQUILLIZER
AEIIILLNQRSSTU	TRANQUILLISES
AEIIILLNQRSTUZ	TRANQUILLIZES
AEIIILLORRRTTY	TERRITORIALLY
AEIIILMNNNSSTT	IN INSTALMENTS
AEIIILMNNOOSST	SOLEMNISATION
AEIIILMNNOPSTU	EMULSION PAINT
AEIIILMNOPRSTY	IMPERSONALITY
AEIIILMNORSSST	TRIM ONE'S SAILS
AEIIILNNNNOTTU	UNINTENTIONAL
AEIIILNNOOPRTT	INTERPOLATION
AEIIILNNORSSTT	LOSE IN TRANSIT
AEIIILNOOPPRST	PREPOSITIONAL
AEIIILNOOPSTTX	EXPLOITATIONS
	SEXPLOITATION
AEIIILNOPPSSTU	PONTIUS PILATE
AEIIILNOPRSTUV	PULVERISATION
AEIIILNOPRTUVZ	PULVERIZATION
AEIIILNOQSTTUV	VITAL QUESTION
AEIIILNOSSTTTW	TWIST ONE'S TAIL
AEIIILNPRSSSTU	SPIRITUALNESS
AEIIILNRSSSTUV	UNIVERSALISTS
AEIIILOOPPRRRT	PROPRIETORIAL
AEIIILORSSTUVW	SAVILE ROW SUIT
AEIIIMNNOOPRST	IMPERSONATION
AEIIIMNNPRRSSU	RISEN UP IN ARMS
AEIIIMNOOPRSTT	TEMPORISATION
AEIIIMNOOPRTTZ	TEMPORIZATION
AEIIIMNOSSSTTY	SYSTEMISATION
AEIIIMNOSSTTYZ	SYSTEMIZATION
AEIIIMOOPPRSTY	I PROMISE TO PAY
AEIIINOOPPRRTX	EXPROPRIATION
AEIIINOORRRTTZ	TERRORIZATION
AEIIINORRSSSTT	TRANSISTORISE
AEIIINORRSSTTZ	TRANSISTORIZE
AEIIINPRSTTTUY	PATERNITY SUIT
AEIIINRRSSTTUV	RETURNS A VISIT
AEIJKLOSSTUUY	JUST AS YOU LIKE
AEIJNNOPRRRTU	JUNIOR PARTNER
AEIJNNOPRRSTT	JOINT PARTNERS
AEIKLLNNOORTW	WINNER TOOK ALL
AEIKLLNNOPPSY	SPOKEN PLAINLY
AEIKLMNOPRSST	SPORTSMANLIKE
AEIKLORRRSTWY	LITERARY WORKS
AEIKNNOORSSTW	AT ONES OWN RISK
AEIKNNOPRSSSU	RUSSIAN SPOKEN
	SPOKEN RUSSIAN
AEIKNOQSSSSTU	ASKS QUESTIONS
AEIILLLMNOOSSS	SALMONELLOSIS
AEIILLNOTTTUW	TALENT WILL OUT
AEIILLMNORSSTV	SMALL INVESTOR
AEIILLNOPRTTWW	WILLOW PATTERN
AEILMMMMOUUVX	MAXIMUM VOLUME
AEILMMNNOORRY	MARILYN MONROE
AEILMMNNOOPSTU	MOUNTAIN SLOPE
AEILMNNRSSTTU	INSTRUMENTALS
AEILMNOOOSSSW	WISE AS SOLOMON
AEILMNOOPRSTT	METROPOLITANS
AEILMNOPRTTUY	IMPORTUNATELY
AEILMORSTTTUY	STATUTORY MILE
AEILNNORSSTUV	VOLUNTARINESS
AEILNNORSTUVY	INTRAVENOUSLY
AEILNOOPRSTTT	PETROL STATION
AEILNOOPSTTUX	EXPOSTULATION
AEILNOORRTUVY	REVOLUTIONARY

AEILNPPRRSTTY	SPLINTER PARTY	AFGHIIILNNSST	FINISHING LAST
AEILOOQRSTUUZ	LOUIS QUATORZE	AFGHIIKNNOTWY	WAY OF THINKING
AEIMMNNOOSTUV	MOVE MOUNTAINS	AFGHIILMNNOSS	SALMON FISHING
AEIMMNNOOSTUX	ANXIOUS MOMENT	AFGHIILNNRTTY	LIGHT INFANTRY
AEIMMNNOSSSSUU	ISSUE A SUMMONS	AFGHIINOPRRST	PROFIT SHARING
AEIMMNQRTTUUU	QUANTUM MERUIT	AFGHIKLOSSSWY	GLASS OF WHISKY
AEIMNNOOPPRTT	APPORTIONMENT	AFGHIKNNOORST	ASK FOR NOTHING
AEIMNNOORRSTT	REMONSTRATION	AFGHILLNORSTY	SALLYING FORTH
AEIMNNOOSTUUV	UNANIMOUS VOTE	AFGHINNOSTTUU	NINTH OF AUGUST
AEIMNNORSSTTU	MENSTRUATIONS	AFGHINOOPRSTU	PUSHING TOO FAR
AEIMNOPRRTTVY	VERY IMPORTANT	AFGHINOORSSTT	STRING OF OATHS
AEIMNOPRSSTTT	PROTESTANTISM	AFGHINOORSUVW	SHOWING FAVOUR
AEIMNORSSSTTW	TWISTS ONE'S ARM	AFGHIOSSTTUUX	SIXTH OF AUGUST
AEIMOOPPRSSTY	PROMISES TO PAY	AFGHLOOPRRUUW	PLOUGH A FURROW
AEIMORRRRSTTY	TERRORIST ARMY	AFGIIILNNRTUY	INFURIATINGLY
AEINNOOPRSSTU	PUTS IN ONE'S OAR	AFGIIILNOORVW	VIRGINIA WOOLF
	PUTS ONE'S OAR IN	AFGIIKMNOPRTU	MAKING UP FOR IT
AEINNOOSSTTTU	EUSTON STATION	AFGIILMNORRSU	FORMULARISING
AEINNORSSTTTU	STERNUTATIONS	AFGIILMNORRUZ	FORMULARIZING
AEINOOUUPPRTT	PROPORTIONATE	AFGIILNNOOPTT	FLOATING-POINT
AEINOOOPRRSTT	PROTONOTARIES	AFGIINNNNORUVW	WINNING FAVOUR
AEINOOPRSSSUV	OVIPAROUSNESS	AFGIINNOORTTU	OUT OF TRAINING
AFINOOPRSSTTT	PROTECTIONS	AFGIKMNOOPRST	MAKING SPORT OF
AEINOORSSSTTU	TOURIST SEASON	AFGILNRRSSTTUY	FRUSTRATINGLY
AEINOPQSSTTUU	PUTS A QUESTION	AFGIMNNOOSTUY	ANONYMOUS GIFT
AEINORRSTTTWY	WRITTEN A STORY	AFGNOOOPRTTUW	PUT A FOOT WRONG
AEIPPRRRSSTUY	SURPRISE PARTY	AFHHIILORSTUW	WITH A FLOURISH
AEKLLNNOPRSSU	PULLS ONE'S RANK	AFHIIINOPSSTTU	PUTS A FINISH TO
AEKLLPPSSSTUU	PULLS UP STAKES	AFHIINORSSTTT	START TO FINISH
AEKLNNOOPRSTT	NON-STOP TALKER	AFHIKNORSSTWY	HAS FORTY WINKS
AEKNOOPRSUWWY	WORK ONES WAY UP	AFHILLMOORRRS	HALL OF MIRRORS
AELLMNOPRRSUY	SUPERNORMALLY	AFHIOOPRRSTTY	PART OF HISTORY
AELMNOOOPSTTY	STATE MONOPOLY	AFHMNNOOOORRT	MATRON OF HONOR
AELMOOOPSSSTX	TOXOPLASMOSES	AFHMOOPSTTUYY	OUT OF SYMPATHY
AELNNOOPSSTUY	SPONTANEOUSLY	AFIIILLMMNOUU	ALUMINIUM FOIL
AELNOOPTTTUWY	WENT OUT TO PLAY	AFIIILNOOSSST	FOSSILISATION
AELOOPPRRRSTU	POPULAR RESORT	AFIIILNOOSSTZ	FOSSILIZATION
AEMMNNOOPPRSU	POMPOUS MANNER	AFIILLORSTTUY	FLIRTATIOUSLY
AEMMNOOORSTTU	MONOTREMATOUS	AFIILOPRSSSUY	FISSIPAROUSLY
AEMMNOPPPRTTY	PROMPT PAYMENT	AFIIMNNNOOOPR	FORM AN OPINION
AEMNNNOOSSSUY	ANONYMOUSNESS	AFIINNOOPRTUV	POINT IN FAVOUR
AEMNNOPPSTTWY	TWOPENNY STAMP	AFINNOORTTUWY	WAY OUT IN FRONT
AEMNOOOPRSSZZ	MEZZO-SOPRANOS	AFKLNOORTTTUU	TALK OUT OF TURN
AEMNOOPPRRSSU	PROSPEROUS MAN	AGGGHIINORSTT	GOING STRAIGHT
AEMOOPPRRSTTY	TEMPORARY STOP	AGGGHINNOTUYY	GAY YOUNG THING
AEMOORRRSSSTT	RESORTS TO ARMS	AGGGIIILNNRUV	GIVING A RULING
AEMORRRSSSTTU	SMART TROUSERS	AGGGIIINNNRVW	GIVING WARNING
AENOOPPPRSTTU	PUT A STOPPER ON	AGGGIIINNRTTU	INGURGITATING
AENOPRRSSSTUU	RAPTUROUSNESS	AGGGIILNNNOSW	SWINGING ALONG
AENRRSSTTTUVY	TRUSTY SERVANT	AGGHHIIILNNST	SHINING A LIGHT
AFFFGHIOSTTUU	FIFTH OF AUGUST	AGGHHIIIMNOOT	AIMING TOO HIGH
AFFFGILLLNOOU	FALLING FOUL OF	AGGHHIIINNORS	RAISING ON HIGH
AFFFGINNORSSU	GRAINS OF SNUFF	AGGHHIILNOPRT	LITHOGRAPHING
AFFGGHIILNOTU	LAUGHING IT OFF	AGGHHIIRRSTTT	STRAIGHT RIGHT
AFFGHINORRSTU	FOUR FARTHINGS	AGGHHIIKMNRTT	MAKING IT RIGHT
AFFGIORSSTTUU	FIRST OF AUGUST	AGGHIIIMNSSSV	HAS MISGIVINGS
AFFHILOOPRRTU	FOURTH OF APRIL	AGGHIIKLLNTTY	TAKING LIGHTLY
AFFINOOPRRSTT	TORN A STRIP OFF	AGGHIILLNNSUY	LANGUISHINGLY
	TORN OFF A STRIP	AGGHIILNNOOST	ANTHOLOGISING
AFGGGINNOOORS	GOING FOR A SONG	AGGHIILNNOOTZ	ANTHOLOGIZING
AFGGHHIIRSTTT	STRAIGHT FIGHT	AGGHIINNNOOTT	NOTHING TO GAIN
AFGGHIIINNNTW	WINNING A FIGHT	AGGHIINNNOSTV	SAVING NOTHING
AFGGHIIKLMNOT	MAKING LIGHT OF	AGGHIINNNOSTY	SAYING NOTHING
AFGGIIMNOORSW	GOING FOR A SWIM	AGGHIIORSTTTT	GOT IT STRAIGHT
AFGGIINNOOPRS	GOING FOR A SPIN	AGGHILNNORRUY	HURRYING ALONG
AFGGIINNRRSTU	TRANSFIGURING	AGGIIIIMNSSTV	GIVING IT A MISS
AFGGIINOOPRRT	GOING FOR A TRIP	AGGIIILNNRSSU	SINGULARISING
AFGGILLNNNOUY	GOING ALL FUNNY	AGGIIILNNRSUZ	SINGULARIZING
AFGHHILRSSTTU	STRAIGHT FLUSH	AGGIIINNORTTU	INGURGITATION
AFGHHNOOTTTUW	WANT OF THOUGHT	AGGIILNNOPPRR	GRAPPLING IRON
AFGHIIILLNNTW	FALLING IN WITH	AGGIILNPPRRST	STRAPPING GIRL

AGGIINOPRSSTU	GOING UPSTAIRS
AGGILLNOOOPTT	GOING ALL TO POT
AGGILLNOORTTW	GOT IT ALL WRONG
AGGIMNNORRUYY	MARRYING YOUNG
AGGINNORSTTUY	STARTING YOUNG
AGGINNPRSSWYY	GYPSYS WARNING
AGHHIIKNRSTTY	THINK STRAIGHT
AGHHIILMNRSTY	NIGHTMARISHLY
AGHHINOOPRSST	SHARPSHOOTING
AGHHIOORSSTTT	SHOOT STRAIGHT
AGHHLLMOOOPTY	OPHTHALMOLOGY
AGHHLMNNOOOPT	MONOPHTHONGAL
AGHIIIINNNSVW	WISHING IN VAIN
AGHIIILNOPSST	HOSPITALISING
AGHIIILNOPSTZ	HOSPITALIZING
AGHIIILNPRSTT	HAIRSPLITTING
AGHIIKMNORSTY	MAKING HISTORY
AGHIIKNNOOSTW	TOOK IN WASHING
AGHIIKNNRSTTT	START THINKING
AGHIIKNORSSTW	THROWING A KISS
AGHIILMNOOSST	SMOOTH SAILING
AGHIILNNOSSTY	ASTONISHINGLY
AGHIIMNNNORSY	SING IN HARMONY
AGHIIMNNORRSU	SHINING ARMOUR
AGHIINOPSSTTY	HYPOSTATISING
AGHIINOPSTTYZ	HYPOSTATIZING
AGHIKNOPRSTTU	TAKING UP SHORT
AGHILNOORSUVW	SHOWING VALOUR
AGHIMNNNORSUY	SUNG IN HARMONY
AGHINNOOPSTTT	STOP AT NOTHING
AGHINNOOPTTTU	PUTTING ON OATH
AGHINOOPRSTTY	SHOOTING PARTY
AGHINPRSSTTTU	THRUSTING PAST
AGIIIIMNNRTUZ	MINIATURIZING
AGIIIJLNNPTTU	PUTTING IN JAIL
AGIIIKLLLNRTU	RITUAL KILLING
AGIIILLLNTTTY	TITILLATINGLY
AGIIINNNNOPTW	WINNING A POINT
AGIIINNPRSSSU	PRUSSIANISING
AGIIINNPRSSUZ	PRUSSIANIZING
AGIKKKLNOOOTT	TOOK A LIKING TO
AGIKKMNNNOTW	MAKING IT KNOWN
AGIKKKNNORSST	TAKING NO RISKS
AGIIKLLNOSTTT	TAKING ITS TOLL
AGIIILLNNOPRTY	RALLYING POINT
AGIILMOOPRSTT	PRIMATOLOGIST
AGIILNNOPRSSU	RULING PASSION
AGIILNNOPRSTY	PATRONISINGLY
AGIILNNOPRTYZ	PATRONIZINGLY
AGIILNOSTTUUY	UGLY SITUATION
AGIILOORSSSTY	ASSYRIOLOGIST
AGIIMMMNNRTTUY	GRANT IMMUNITY
AGIIMMNNRSTTWY	TWISTING MY ARM
AGIINNOOPPRTV	PROVING A POINT
AGIINNOPRSTTT	STARTING POINT
	TRAIN SPOTTING
AGIINNOPRSTTU	PUTTING ON AIRS
AGIINORRSTTWY	WRITING A STORY
AGIKLLLNOSWWY	WALKING SLOWLY
AGIKNNORSTTTU	TAKING ON TRUST
AGILMNOPPSSUY	PLAYING POSSUM
AGILMNPPRSTUY	PLAYING TRUMPS
AGILMOOOSSTTT	STOMATOLOGIST
AGILMOORRSTTY	MARTYROLOGIST
AGLLOOOSTTUUY	TAUTOLOGOUSLY
AGOOPRSSTTTUU	PUT OUT TO GRASS
AHHIIORTTTUWY	WITH AUTHORITY
AHIIILNNOOTTW	ANOINT WITH OIL
AHIIILNOPSTTY	INHOSPITALITY
AHIIJLNOORTTW	THROW INTO JAIL
AHIIKLLORTWWW	WORK WITH A WILL
AHIILLMNOORTW	WORTH A MILLION
AHIIMNOOSSTWY	SHOW ANIMOSITY
AHIINNOOPSTTY	HYPNOTISATION
AHIINNOOPTTYZ	HYPNOTIZATION
AHIJOSSSTUUWY	JUST AS YOU WISH
AHIKLOORSTTUW	KILOWATT-HOURS
AHILMMNNOORTYY	HOLY MATRIMONY
AHIMNOPPRSSST	SPORTSMANSHIP
AHKLNNOOPPTTY	PHYTOPLANKTON
AHKNNNOOPSSSY	ON SHANKS'S PONY
AHLLOOOPTTTUU	PULL A TOOTH OUT
AIIIILNNOQSTU	INQUISITIONAL
AIIIILNOQRSTU	INQUISITORIAL
AIIILLMMORRSW	WILLIAM MORRIS
AIIILLMNNOSTU	ILLUMINATIONS
AIIILLMNPSTUY	PUSILLANIMITY
AIIILNNOSTTTU	INSTITUTIONAL
AIIILPRSSSTTU	SPIRITUALISTS
AIIIMNNORSSTT	MINISTRATIONS
AIIIMNOOPRSTV	IMPROVISATION
AIIIOOPRTVVVY	OVOVIVIPARITY
AIIJNOOPSTTUX	JUXTAPOSITION
AIIILLMNNOORST	RAN TO MILLIONS
AIILLMNOPSSUU	PUSILLANIMOUS
AIILLNNORTTUY	NUTRITIONALLY
AIILLNNORTUVY	INVOLUNTARILY
AIILLNOOPRSVY	PROVISIONALLY
AIILLNORSSTTU	ILLUSTRATIONS
AIILMNNOPSTUU	LUMINOUS PAINT
AIILNNORSSTTT	LOST IN TRANSIT
AIILNOOOOPPRST	PROPOSITIONAL
AIILNOOPPSSTU	SUPPOSITIONAL
AIIMMMMNNOTUU	MINIMUM AMOUNT
AIIMMMNOPSTUX	MAXIMUM POINTS
AIIMNNORSSSST	TRANSMISSIONS
AIIMOOPRRSTVY	IMPROVISATORY
AIINNOOPRSSTT	TRANSPOSITION
AIINNOPRSTTUY	UNIONIST PARTY
AIIOOOPRSUVVV	OVOVIVIPAROUS
AILLMNORRTUWW	A WORM WILL TURN
AILLNOPPSTTUY	POSTNUPTIALLY
AILMNNOOSTUUY	MOUNTAINOUSLY
AILMOOOPSSSTX	TOXOPLASMOSIS
AILNOOOOPPRRST	PROPORTIONALS
AILNORSSTTUVY	VOLUNTARYISTS
AIMNOOPPRSTTT	IMPORTANT POST
AIOOOPPSSTTTTU	PUTS A STOP TO IT
AKLNOOOORRTUW	NARROW OUTLOOK
AKLNOORRTUVWY	VOLUNTARY WORK
ANOOOORSSSTTT	STARTS TOO SOON
BBBBBEEHLLSUU	HUBBLE-BUBBLES
BBBEEEKLRSUYY	BUSBY BERKELEY
BBCCCEEHHKRUY	CHUBBY CHECKER
BBCCEEILMOPSU	BECOMES PUBLIC
BBCCGIKNNOORU	BUCKING BRONCO
BBCDEEELORSTT	COBBLED STREET
BBCDEEELORTTU	COULD BE BETTER
BBCDEEILNORST	SCRIBBLED NOTE
BBCDGIIIKLNRU	BUILDING BRICK
BBCDGIIKLLNOU	BUILDING BLOCK
BBCDGINNORSUW	SCRUBBING DOWN
BBCEEGIKNNRRU	RUBBERNECKING
BBCEEHKOSSTYZ	SKETCHES BY BOZ
BBCEEHLORRRSY	SHERRY COBBLER
BBCEEHLORRTTT	BERTOLT BRECHT
BBCEEIORRSSUV	OVERSUBSCRIBE
BBCEHMOORRSTU	BUTCHER'S-BROOM
BBCEIILMNOSTU	INCOMBUSTIBLE
BBCELNOORSUUY	BOBS YOUR UNCLE!
BBCFIIOOSSTUX	BOX OF BISCUITS
BBCGIKKLNOOOS	BLOCK-BOOKINGS

BBCHIIILPRSTU	BRITISH PUBLIC
BBCINOORSSTTU	CUTS TO RIBBONS
BBDDEEGILNNOU	BENDING DOUBLE
BBDEEEHILRSST	BLESS THE BRIDE
BBDEEEHINNORT	BRED IN THE BONE
BBDEEEHNORRTU	BORE THE BURDEN
BBDEEELNNOOSW	BEND ONE'S ELBOW
BBDEEGILMOPRR	BRIDGE PROBLEM
BBDEEHILLORTT	ROBBED THE TILL
BBDEELLOORTUU	DOUBLE TROUBLE
BBDEELNRSSSUU	BLUNDERBUSSES
BBDEEMOOOPRRT	TORPEDO BOMBER
BBDEGHIILNRSU	BLUSHING BRIDE
BBDEHLOOOORRST	BLOOD BROTHERS
BBDIIILNOOSVY	DIVISION LOBBY
BBDLNNOORSSUU	LONDON SUBURBS
BBEEEEEEHIIJS	HEEBIE-JEEBIES
BBEEEEFFIKORST	BRISKET OF BEEF
BBEEEGIILNNSS	BEING SENSIBLE
BBEEFFHILLTTTU	BITE THE BULLET
BBEEEHLORRSTU	LOSE THE RUBBER
BBEEEEINORRSSY	BOYSENBERRIES
BBEEEKNNOOORS	BROKE ONE'S BONE
BBEEELNNOOSTW	BENT ONE'S ELBOW
BBEEGHILLNORT	BRIGHTON BELLE
BBEEGHKNOOOTY	GONE BY THE BOOK
BBEEGHKOOOSTY	GOES BY THE BOOK
BBEEHKNOOTTWY	WENT BY THE BOOK
BBEEHLORRSTTU	LOST THE RUBBER
BBEEILLLOTTUY	LITTLE BOY BLUE
BBEEENOOOORTTT	TO BE OR NOT TO BE
BBEFHIIORSSTT	BEST OF BRITISH
BBEGGILNNRTUY	RUBBING GENTLY
BBEGGIMMNNORUY	MONEY-GRUBBING
BBEINOOOORRST	TORE TO RIBBONS
BBGHHIIORSTTU	BOUGHT BRITISH
BBGHIIINRSTUY	BUYING BRITISH
BBGHKOOOOORTTU	BROUGHT TO BOOK
BBHIIIILLMOPS	BIBLIOPHILISM
BBHIIIILLOPST	BIBLIOPHILIST
BBINNOOOORRST	TORN TO RIBBONS
BCCCDEIIMRRSU	CIRCUMSCRIBED
BCCCEIIMRRSSU	CIRCUMSCRIBES
BCCCEINNOSTTU	CUBIC CONTENTS
BCCDEEEIILLLM	CECIL B.DE MILLE
BCCDEELLOORTT	DEBT COLLECTOR
BCCDEILOPRRSU	PUBLIC RECORDS
BCCEEEEHIISSTU	CHEESE BISCUIT
BCCEEEIMNOTTX	BECOME EXTINCT
BCCEEFIMNOORS	COMBINE FORCES
BCCEEHIKKKTTU	KICK THE BUCKET
BCCEEHNORRSSS	CROSSBENCHERS
BCCEEIILORRTT	TRIBOELECTRIC
BCCEEIILPRSUV	PUBLIC SERVICE
BCCEEIKKKNORR	KNICKERBOCKER
BCCEEIILLSUUVX	EXCLUSIVE CLUB
BCCEFJNOOORST	OBJECT OF SCORN
BCCEGIKNRSTUY	CRYING BUCKETS
BCCEHHINOOOSS	HOBSONS CHOICE
BCCEIIIJOSTTV	OBJECTIVISTIC
BCCEILLNOOOTX	COLLECTION BOX
BCCEILMMNOPTU	PUBLIC COMMENT
BCCEILNORSTTU	CONSTRUCTIBLE
BCCELMOSSSSUY	SUCCESS SYMBOL
BCCGHIKLNOOPP	CHOPPING BLOCK
BCCGIIILMOOOR	MICROBIOLOGIC
BCCILMMNOOSTU	COMMUNIST BLOC
BCDDDELLLOOOY	COLD-BLOODEDLY
BCDDEEEEINOOW	OWED OBEDIENCE
BCDDEEEIMNRSU	DISENCUMBERED
BCDDEEEEKLORSU	DOUBLE-DECKERS
BCDDEEENRSTUU	UNSECURED DEBT
BCDDEEFINNOOT	CONFINED TO BED
BCDDEELNOOTUU	COUNTED DOUBLE
BCDDEELOORSSU	DOUBLE-CROSSED
BCDDEIIILTTUY	DEDUCTIBILITY
BCDDEKNOOORTW	DOWN TO BEDROCK
BCDDGILLNOORU	BLOODCURDLING
BCDEEEEINOOSW	OWES OBEDIENCE
BCDEEEFGHOOOR	BE OF GOOD CHEER
BCDEEEFIMNORS	BECOME FRIENDS
BCDEEEHIKPSTT	PICKED THE BEST
BCDEEEEHNOSSTT	THE SECOND BEST
BCDEEEEILLLNPU	BLUE-PENCILLED
BCDEEEKORRSST	STOCKBREEDERS
BCDEEFFIILNTU	BEEN DIFFICULT
BCDEEFINNOOST	CONFINES TO BED
BCDEEGIKNORST	STOCKBREEDING
BCDEEHIILLRRT	TERRIBLE CHILD
BCDEEHIJLLNOTU	JOINED THE CLUB
BCDEEIIILLNNRS	INDISCERNIBLE
BCDEEIIJSSTUV	SUBJECTIVISED
BCDEEIIJSTUVZ	SUBJECTIVIZED
BCDEEIKLNORTU	CRUEL TO BE KIND
BCDEEILMNNOSU	DUMB INSOLENCE
BCDEEINNOOTTU	TO BE CONTINUED
BCDEEKKNOORSU	BROKE ONE'S DUCK
BCDEEKKNRTUYY	KENTUCKY DERBY
BCDEEKNOORRRS	BROKEN RECORDS
BCDEELMRRRUUY	CRY BLUE MURDER
BCDEELNORTUUY	DOUBLE CENTURY
BCDEELOORRSSU	DOUBLE CROSSER
	DOUBLE-CROSSER
BCDEELOORSSSU	DOUBLE-CROSSES
BCDEGHILOOPTU	THE PUBLIC GOOD
BCDEHHILLLOOT	CHILL THE BLOOD
BCDEHIKLNOORS	CHILDRENS BOOK
BCDEHKLNOORTU	ROUND THE BLOCK
BCDEHMOOOTTTU	TOUCHED BOTTOM
BCDEIIIILNRTY	INCREDIBILITY
BCDEIILMOSSST	DOMESTIC BLISS
BCDEIKLNNOORW	BORN IN WEDLOCK
BCDELLOOOPSSU	BLOODLESS COUP
BCDELNNOOORTY	BEYOND CONTROL
BCDENOOORRRTUY	BORDER COUNTRY
BCEEEEFINORSV	BEEN OF SERVICE
BCEEEEFKNOORR	REFERENCE BOOK
BCEEEFFIILSTV	VISIBLE EFFECT
BCEEEFGIINNRR	BIREFRINGENCE
BCEEEGIINORST	BIOENERGETICS
BCEEEGILNOORZ	COOLING BREEZE
BCEEEGIMNNOTW	COMING BETWEEN
BCEEEGIMNORTY	EMBRYOGENETIC
BCEEEHIKLRRSU	HUCKLEBERRIES
BCEEEHKORRTTU	BROKE THE TRUCE
BCEEEIILMPPRT	IMPERCEPTIBLE
BCEEEIILMRRRT	TERRIBLE CRIME
BCEEEIJNOSSTV	OBJECTIVENESS
BCEEEIILLNOSSS	BELLICOSENESS
BCEEEILMNOSST	BECOMES SILENT
BCEEEILMRSSTV	CLIMBS EVEREST
BCEEEILNOPRWY	EYEBROW PENCIL
BCEEEKKNNOORS	BROKE ONE'S NECK
BCEEFFHJOSTTU	OFF THE SUBJECT
BCEEFGHHIIITW	BIG WHITE CHIEF
BCEEFGIILMNRU	BEING MERCIFUL
BCEEFHKLOSTTU	THE BEST OF LUCK
BCEEFLNOOSSTT	BOTTLE OF SCENT
BCEEGIILMNPTU	PUBLIC MEETING
BCEEGIIMNNOOT	COME INTO BEING
BCEEGIKLNNRSU	BEGINNERS LUCK
BCEEGINORSTTU	COURSE BETTING

BCEEHIILMORRR	HORRIBLE CRIME
BCEEHIJKNNOST	JOHN STEINBECK
BCEEHILOORRTZ	HECTOR BERLIOZ
BCEEHILOPSTTY	THE BEST POLICY
BCEEHKOPRSSTU	BUCK STOPS HERE
BCEEHMNNORRSU	MOURNERS' BENCH
BCEEHNOOSTTTU	CUTS TO THE BONE
BCEEIIJSSSTUV	SUBJECTIVISES
BCEEIIJSSTUVZ	SUBJECTIVIZES
BCEEIILMPPRTY	IMPERCEPTIBLY
BCEEIILNNORTV	INCONVERTIBLE
BCEEIKLORSTWW	BOWLERS WICKET
BCEEILMNOPSTT	CONTEMPTIBLES
BCEEILNOOPSTW	BLOWN TO PIECES
BCEEILOOPSSTW	BLOWS TO PIECES
BCEEILPRSTTUU	PUBLIC TRUSTEE
BCEEIMMOSSTTU	SUBCOMMITTEES
BCEEINNOORRTT	RONNIE CORBETT
BCEEJMNNOOOTY	MONEY NO OBJECT
BCEELMMNOPRUX	COMPLEX NUMBER
BCEENOOORRSSS	BORE ONE'S CROSS
BCEEOOPRRSSTU	SOP TO CERBERUS
BCEFFGIIKNOOO	BOOKING OFFICE
BCEFFGIMNOOST	COMING OFF BEST
BCEFFIOOOPSTX	POST OFFICE BOX
BCEFHIJMOORTT	OBJECT OF MIRTH
BCEFHIMNOOOTT	FINE TOOTH-COMB
	FINE TOOTHCOMB
	FINE-TOOTH COMB
BCEFIIKLOPRSS	PILES OF BRICKS
BCEFIKKOOOSTT	BOOK OF TICKETS
BCEFJMOOORRST	JOBS COMFORTER
BCEGIIILNPUVW	VIEWING PUBLIC
BCEGIINPRRSSU	SUPERSCRIBING
BCEGIKLNOSSTU	BLUESTOCKINGS
BCEGIMNOOSTTU	COMING OUT BEST
BCEHIIILPRRSU	IRISH REPUBLIC
BCEHILMOOPTTT	CLIMB TO THE TOP
BCEHILNNSSSUU	BUSINESS LUNCH
BCEHIMMORRTTU	ROBERT MITCHUM
BCEHJNORSTTUY	THORNY SUBJECT
BCEHKMNIOSSTUU	SUCK ONES THUMB
BCEHLMOORRSSY	CHERRY BLOSSOM
BCEHMOOOSTTTU	TOUCHES BOTTOM
BCEHNNORSTTUW	CHESTNUT BROWN
BCEIIJSSSTTUV	SUBJECTIVISTS
BCEIILNNORTVY	INCONVERTIBLY
BCEIILNOPRRTU	INCORRUPTIBLE
BCEIILNPQRRUU	PUBLIC ENQUIRY
BCEIIMNSSSSUU	MUSIC BUSINESS
BCEIKLMOPRRTY	TRICKY PROBLEM
BCEIKLNOOOSST	LICK ONE'S BOOTS
BCEILMOOPRSTW	CLIMBS TO POWER
BCEILORSTTUVY	OBSTRUCTIVELY
BCEINNNOSSTTU	SUBCONTINENTS
BCEKLMNNRUUUY	UNLUCKY NUMBER
BCELLMOOOPRRU	COLOUR PROBLEM
BCELLNNOOOOSW	BLOWN ONE'S COOL
BCELLNOOOOSSW	BLOWS ONE'S COOL
BCELLORSTUUUY	TUBERCULOUSLY
BCERRSSSTTUUU	SUBSTRUCTURES
BCGHNOOOORTUUY	COUNTY BOROUGH
BCGIIILMNNORS	CLIMBING IRONS
BCGIIILOOOSST	SOCIBIOLOGIST
BCGIILLNOPPRW	CRIPPLING BLOW
BCGILMNOOOSTW	COMING TO BLOWS
BCHIIIOPSSSTY	BIOPHYSICISTS
BCHIILNOORSTY	BRITISH COLONY
BCHIILNORSSTU	BRITISH CONSUL
BCHIILOPPRSUW	PUBLIC WORSHIP
BCHIKMOOOORTTT	HIT ROCK-BOTTOM
BCIIIIILMMSTY	IMMISCIBILITY
BCIIIIILNNTVY	INVINCIBILITY
BCIIILNNOOPPU	PUBLIC OPINION
BCIIILNPQRUUY	PUBLIC INQUIRY
BCIILNOPRRTUY	INCORRUPTIBLY
BCIINNOORSTTU	CONTRIBUTIONS
BCIINOPRSSSTU	SUBSCRIPTIONS
BCILLLLNNOOYY	BILLY CONNOLLY
BDDDEEEIINNOS	DIED IN ONE'S BED
BDDDEEFIIIVVY	DIVIDED BY FIVE
BDDDEEEGILNOUW	DOUBLE WEDDING
BDDDEEHINOPPR	DROPPED BEHIND
BDDDEEIIINNVY	DIVIDED BY NINE
BDDDEFIIORUVY	DIVIDED BY FOUR
BDDDEGHILNOOS	SHEDDING BLOOD
BDDDEGIINNOOS	DO ONES BIDDING
BDDDEIIMNRSTU	DISTURBED MIND
BDDEEEEIMMRRS	DISREMEMBERED
BDDEEEEKNNNOS	ON BENDED KNEES
BDDEEEHIIRTVY	DIVIDE BY THREE
BDDEEEIINNOSS	DIES IN ONE'S BED
BDDEEEIINSVVY	DIVIDE BY SEVEN
BDDEEEIILLMOSW	DISEMBOWELLED
BDDEEEEILNRSSU	DRESSED IN BLUE
BDDEEFFIMOORR	BID FOR FREEDOM
BDDEEFIIISVVY	DIVIDES BY FIVE
BDDEEFOORRRRT	ROBERT REDFORD
BDDEEGGGNOOTW	GET BOGGED DOWN
BDDEEGHHIIRST	HIGHEST BIDDER
BDDEEGHIIITVY	DIVIDE BY EIGHT
BDDEEGLNOOTUU	DOUBLE-TONGUED
BDDEEHILNRSTW	DREW THE BLINDS
BDDEEHLOOORTT	BOLTED THE DOOR
BDDEEIIINNSVY	DIVIDES BY NINE
BDDEEIILNOSTY	DISOBEDIENTLY
BDDEEIJLNOOTU	DOUBLE-JOINTED
BDDEEILMOORVY	REMOVED BODILY
BDDEEIMNNRSTU	DISBURDENMENT
BDDEEINOPSTUY	BEYOND DISPUTE
BDDEEIOOORRSSY	DISOBEY ORDERS
BDDEENNNOSSUU	UNBOUNDEDNESS
BDDEFIIORSUVY	DIVIDES BY FOUR
BDDEGGGNOOOTW	GOT BOGGED DOWN
BDDEGGIINNSUU	BUDDING GENIUS
BDDEGHILNORSU	BURNISHED GOLD
BDDEGIINNNTVY	DIVIDING BY TEN
BDDEGIILMNNNY	MINDBENDINGLY
BDDEGIINRRTUW	BUDDING WRITER
BDDEIISSTTTUU	DISUBSTITUTED
BDDEILNNORSSW	WORD-BLINDNESS
BDDEMNRSSTUUY	BURY ST. EDMUNDS
BDDGIIIINSVXY	DIVIDING BY SIX
BDDGIIINOTVWY	DIVIDING BY TWO
BDEEEEFIINRTV	DERIVE BENEFIT
BDEEEEFILNOSS	BESIDE ONESELF
BDEEEEGHNOSST	HEDGE ONE'S BETS
BDEEEEMNNNORSU	NUMBER ONE SEED
BDEEEFFILNOTU	DOUBLE FIFTEEN
BDEEEFGGMOORR	BEGGED FOR MORE
BDEEEFGILNOTT	FEEDING BOTTLE
BDEEEFGIMNNOR	MEN OF BREEDING
BDEEEFHINORTW	BEFORE THE WIND
BDEEEFILNORSU	BURIED ONESELF
BDEEEFLLNOOSS	BE ONE'S OLD SELF
BDEEEFMMNORRU	FOUNDER MEMBER
BDEEEGHIILNTW	BLEEDING WHITE
BDEEEGHINNSST	BENIGHTEDNESS
BDEEEGIJLLNOU	GOLDEN JUBILEE
BDEEEGIKLLRSY	KILL BY DEGREES
BDEEEGNOOQSSU	GOOD QUEEN BESS
BDEEEHHIILNTV	BEHIND THE VEIL

BDEEEHHLLPSTU	PUSHED THE BELL	BDEGGHIIINRTV	GIVING THE BIRD
BDEEEHHNOORSS	HORSESHOE BEND	BDEGGHINOOORU	GOOD NEIGHBOUR
BDEEEHIINNRRS	INNER HEBRIDES	BDEGGINNOORVY	GOVERNING BODY
BDEEEHINOSSTT	BETS ON THE SIDE	BDEGHHINOOORU	NEIGHBOURHOOD
BDEEEHLLLLOTT	TOLLED THE BELL	BDEGHHOORRSTU	THOROUGHBREDS
BDEEEHLOPTTTU	POTTED THE BLUE	BDEGHIIINRSST	DIGS IN THE RIBS
BDEEEHLORRSTT	ELDEST BROTHER	BDEGHIINNORTW	BIRD ON THE WING
BDEEEHMOORRST	THREE BEDROOMS	BDEGHIINSTTTU	BITING THE DUST
BDEEEIILNNNOY	BLIND IN ONE EYE	BDEGHINOOSTTT	BEST THING TO DO
BDEEEIILNOTTV	DONT BELIEVE IT	BDEGIIILSTTY	DIGESTIBILITY
BDEEEIILNOSTUX	DOUBLE SIXTEEN	BDEGIIILMNORS	DISEMBROILING
BDEEEIILNRSSSU	DRESSES IN BLUE	BDEGIILNNNOUW	WINNING DOUBLE
BDEEEIMMMNRST	DISMEMBERMENT	BDEGIINNOPPST	STOPPING IN BED
BDEEEINORSSTT	TRIED ONE'S BEST	BDEGIINNOSSSU	DOING BUSINESS
BDEEEKNNNOOSY	BEYOND ONES KEN	BDEGILLNNOOTY	TELLING NOBODY
BDEEEKNNNORRTY	ROBERT KENNEDY	BDEGINNOOOPRT	PONTOON BRIDGE
BDEEEELNNORSTU	UNDER ONE'S BELT	BDEGINNOPSSTY	SENDING BY POST
BDEEEELNPRSSTU	SUSPENDER BELT	BDEHHMNOOORRS	RHOMBOHEDRONS
BDEEEENNOPSSST	BEND ONE'S STEPS	BDEHIIILNNTUY	UNINHIBITEDLY
BDEEEENNORSTTW	NEW BOND STREET	BDEHIKLOPRSUW	PUBLISHED WORK
BDEEFFINOORST	BORED ONE STIFF	BDEHILNNOORTU	RUN IN THE BLOOD
BDEEFFINORSST	BEST OF FRIENDS	BDEHLNOOOORTTU	UNBOLT THE DOOR
BDEEFFGILORSUU	DOUBLE FIGURES	BDEHLONRCCCUU	RUBS SHOULDERS
BDEEFHIILLLLT	FILLED THE BILL	BDEIIIRSSTTUV	DISTRIBUTIVES
BDEEFHIILLTTT	FITTED THE BILL	BDEIIJLMNOOOT	DEMOLITION JOB
BDEEFHILLOOTT	FOOTED THE BILL	BDEILMNNNOOSW	BLOWN ONE'S MIND
BDEEFHLOOORTZ	FROZE THE BLOOD	BDEILMNNOOSSW	BLOWS ONE'S MIND
BDEEFIIILNSTY	DEFENSIBILITY	BDEILNOOOPRTU	DOUBLE PORTION
BDEEFOOPRRSTU	FOUR-POSTER BED	BDEILOOOQRSTUU	DOUBLE OR QUITS
BDEEGGHIINNTT	GETTING BEHIND	BDEINOOPRRSST	DEBTORS PRISON
BDEEGHHIIRSTT	THE BRIGHT SIDE	BDEINOPRSSSTU	BIRDS-NEST SOUP
BDEEGHILLNOPU	DOUBLE HELPING	BDEKLNOOORTWY	OLD BOY NETWORK
BDEEGIIILLNRWY	BEWILDERINGLY	BDFFGHIILORST	FLIGHT OF BIRDS
BDEEGIILMNSSX	MIXED BLESSING	BDFHINORSTUUY	HUB OF INDUSTRY
BDEEGIINNRRSU	BURNING DESIRE	BDFHMOOORTUWY	BY WORD OF MOUTH
BDEEGILNOPPRY	PROBING DEEPLY	BDFIINNOOOOPY	BODY OF OPINION
BDEEGINNOOSST	DOING ONE'S BEST	BDGGHIIILLNNT	BLINDING LIGHT
BDEEGINNORRUV	OVERBURDENING	BDGHIMNOORTTU	BRINGING ROUND
BDEEGINOORRSY	OBEYING ORDERS	BDGIIIKLNNRST	STRIKING BLIND
BDEEGLNOOSTUU	DOUBLE-TONGUES	BDGIILLLNOOPS	SPILLING BLOOD
BDEEHHHPRSSSU	SHEPHERDS BUSH	BDGIILNNOOOTW	BOILING DOWN TO
BDEEHHMNRTTUU	UNDER THE THUMB	BDHINOOORSUUU	DUBIOUS HONOUR
BDEEHIILRRSTV	THE LIVER BIRDS	BDHLLLOOOOWWY	HOLLYWOOD BOWL
BDEEHILLOPPTT	TOPPED THE BILL	BDIIILLOSSTUY	DISSOLUBILITY
BDEEHINSTTTTU	BITTEN THE DUST	BDIIINORSSTTU	DISTRIBUTIONS
BDEEHLOOOSSTY	BLOODSHOT EYES	BDIIKLLORSSTW	KILLS TWO BIRDS
BDEEHOPPSSTTU	STOPPED THE BUS	BEEEEEFGLRSTU	FEEBLE GESTURE
BDEEIILMMNRTU	LIMITED NUMBER	BEEEEFGILNRTT	FEELING BETTER
BDEEIILNORRTU	IN DIRE TROUBLE	BEEEEFGILORRS	FOLIES BERGERE
BDEEIILMOORSVY	REMOVES BODILY	BEEEEFLNORSTT	BETTER ONESELF
BDEEILNNOOPWW	BLOWN WIDE OPEN	BEEEEGNNOORTT	GONE ONE BETTER
BDEEILNOOPSWW	BLOWS WIDE OPEN	BEEEEGNOOORTT	GOES ONE BETTER
BDEEIMNRSSSTU	DISBURSEMENTS	BEEEEHHLSSTTY	SET BY THE HEELS
BDEEJMNOORSTU	TREMENDOUS JOB		SETS BY THE HEEL
BDEEKNOOOOSTT	TOOK TO ONE'S BED	BEEEEHILNPRRS	REPREHENSIBLE
BDEEKNOOORRSW	BROKE ONE'S WORD	BEEEEHILNSTWW	BETWEENWHILES
BDEEELLNOOSSSS	BLOODLESSNESS	BEEEEHLOPPSTT	THE BEST PEOPLE
BDEEELNNOSSSSU	BOUNDLESSNESS	BEEEEILNNNNTT	LENNIE BENNETT
BDEEELOOPRRSSU	BLOOD PRESSURE	BEEEELLLRSSTT	BELLES LETTRES
BDEEMNOOORRWY	BORROWED MONEY	BEEEELLNOSSTV	ONES LEVEL BEST
BDEFFNOOOOPRRU	BURDEN OF PROOF	BEEEEMNPRSTTX	NEXT SEPTEMBER
BDEFGGHIIORSS	BRIDGE OF SIGHS	BEEEENNORTTTW	WENT ONE BETTER
BDEFGILNORTUU	BURDEN OF GUILT	BEEEFFGIINNRT	FRINGE BENEFIT
BDEFHILOORSTW	BOSWORTH FIELD	BEEEFGHNORRTU	RUB OF THE GREEN
BDEFHIMOORSST	FROM BOTH SIDES	BEEEFGHOSSTTT	GETS THE BEST OF
BDEFIIKNOSSTT	BEST OF ITS KIND	BEEEFGILNORWZ	BELOW FREEZING
BDEFIILLMNOOR	BIRD OF ILL OMEN	BEEEFILNORSSU	BURIES ONESELF
BDEFIIMNNOOST	BIT OF ONE'S MIND	BEEEFINORRSSU	BEFORE SUNRISE
BDEFNOOPRTTUU	POUND OF BUTTER	BEEEGGGILNRTT	BEGGING LETTER
BDEGGGIINNNOO	GOOD BEGINNING	BEEEGHIKNNOTW	BOWING THE KNEE

889

BEEEGHILLTTUV	GIVE THE BULLET
BEEEGHILNOTVW	GIVEN THE ELBOW
BEEEGHILNPRST	SLEEPING BERTH
BEEEGHILOSTVW	GIVES THE ELBOW
BEEEGILLLNRTY	BELLIGERENTLY
BEEEGILNNORTU	ENGINE TROUBLE
BEEEGIMNORSSY	EMBRYOGENESIS
BEEEGKLNNOORS	BROKEN ONE'S LEG
BEEEGMNNORSTU	GET ONE'S NUMBER
BEEEHHLLPSSTU	PUSHES THE BELL
BEEEHHOORRRTV	HERBERT HOOVER
BEEEHILLLNOPT	TELEPHONE BILL
BEEEHILLMMNST	EMBELLISHMENT
BEEEHILNPRRSY	REPREHENSIBLY
BEEEHINNPRTTY	THREEPENNY BIT
BEEEHJLNOOPST	SLEEP ON THE JOB
BEEEHKLLOPRST	BROKE THE SPELL
BEEEHKLNOOOPT	TELEPHONE BOOK
BEEEHKLNORRTU	BROKEN THE RULE
BEEEHKLORRSTU	BROKE THE RULES
BEEEHKNNORSTW	BROKEN THE NEWS
BEEEHNORRSSTV	SEVEN BROTHERS
BEEEIIJLLRSUV	SILVER JUBILEE
BEEEIIJOPRTTV	REPETITIVE JOB
BEEEIILNPRSSX	INEXPRESSIBLE
BEEEIILPRRRSS	IRREPRESSIBLE
BEEEIILLNNOOPR	OPEN REBELLION
BEEEILOPRRRST	SIR ROBERT PEEL
BEEEILRSTTTWY	BITTERSWEETLY
BEEEIMMNNRRSTU	REIMBURSEMENT
BEEEIMNORRSTZ	ROBERT MENZIES
BEEEIMORRRSTT	BITTER REMORSE
BEEEINORSSSTT	TRIES ONE'S BEST
BEEEINOSSSSSV	OBSESSIVENESS
BEEEINOSSSTUY	EYE TO BUSINESS
BEEEIOORRSTTW	BERTIE WOOSTER
BEEEKNNOOORSS	BROKE ONE'S NOSE
BEEELMNNOOSWY	BLEW ONE'S MONEY
BEEELNNOOPRVW	BROWN ENVELOPE
BEEENNNNOOOSW	BEEN ON ONE'S OWN
BEEENNOORSSST	REST ONES BONES
BEEENNOPSSSTT	BENT ONE'S STEPS
BEEEOORRRSTTW	BETTER OR WORSE
BEEFFIILNOORS	SIRLOIN OF BEEF
BEEFFINOORSST	BORES ONE STIFF
BEEFGIIINNORR	BEING INFERIOR
BEEFGIILMNNRS	NIMBLE FINGERS
BEEFGIINORTUW	WEB OF INTRIGUE
BEEFGIKNOOOSS	BOOK OF GENESIS
BEEFGILNORSUY	BEING YOURSELF
BEEFGINRRSTTU	BUTTERFINGERS
BEEFGNOORSTTT	BEST FORGOTTEN
BEEFGNORRSTUY	BURST OF ENERGY
BEEFHIMNRRSTU	REFURBISHMENT
BEEFHLNOOSTTW	SOFTEN THE BLOW
BEEFHLOORRSTY	SHORTLY BEFORE
BEEFHOORRRSTT	FOSTER BROTHER
BEEFIIJNNOOTV	NINE TO FIVE JOB
BEEFILLMORSUU	UMBELLIFEROUS
BEEFIMOOSSTTV	BEST OF MOTIVES
BEEFINNNOOSST	BIT OF NONSENSE
BEEFNNOOOPSTT	TOP OF ONE'S BENT
BEEGGHINTTTU	GETTING THE BUG
BEEGGHIILMRRT	THIMBLERIGGER
BEEGGHINORRTT	BRING TOGETHER
BEEGGIILLNNNW	BEGINNING WELL
BEEGGIILNNSSV	GIVEN BLESSING
BEEGGIILNSSSV	GIVES BLESSING
BEEGGILMNORSW	GLOWING EMBERS
BEEGGINORRTTW	GROWING BETTER
BEEGGHHILLSTTU	THE LIGHT BLUES
BEEGHHLOORTTU	BROUGHT TO HEEL
BEEGHIILRRSTT	TERRIBLE SIGHT
BEEGHIKLNNORS	BROKEN ENGLISH
BEEGHILMNOSTU	SOMETHING BLUE
BEEGHINNOOPTX	OPENING THE BOX
BEEGHINNSTTTX	NEXT BEST THING
BEEGHJKLNOOTU	THE JUNGLE BOOK
BEEGHLNORSTTW	BELOW STRENGTH
BEEGHNRRSTTTU	BRUTE STRENGTH
BEEGIIILLNNUVY	UNBELIEVINGLY
BEEGIILNNNRTW	WINNING TREBLE
BEEGIIMMNRSTT	SITTING MEMBER
BEEGIIMNOPRSS	BEG PERMISSION
BEEGIINOPRRSU	BEING SUPERIOR
	SUPERIOR BEING
BEEGIJLNNNSUU	JUNGLE BUNNIES
BEEGIJNOOPSUV	GIVE UP ONES JOB
BEEGIKLNORTTY	BROKE IT GENTLY
BEEGIKNNORTTW	KNOWING BETTER
BEEGILNNOOPRW	OPENING BOWLER
BEEGILNOORTUV	GIVE NO TROUBLE
BEEGINNOOSTTU	BIT ONE'S TONGUE
BEEGLOOORRSTTT	GLOBE-TROTTERS
BEEGMNNOORSTU	GOT ONE'S NUMBER
BEEHHILOSTTTT	HITS THE BOTTLE
BEEHHINORSTTW	BEEN SHORT WITH
BEEHIIIMPRRST	BRITISH EMPIRE
BEEHIIINORSTX	EXHIBITIONERS
BEEHIIKNOPRST	POKE IN THE RIBS
BEEHIILNOORRS	HORRIBLE NOISE
BEEHIINNSSSTU	IN THE BUSINESS
BEEHILLORRTTT	LITTLE BROTHER
BEEHILMNOOTTT	THE BOTTOM LINE
BEEHILNORRSST	BROTHERLINESS
BEEHINNORSTWZ	WINS THE BRONZE
BEEHJLNOOPSTT	SLEPT ON THE JOB
BEEHLLOORRTVY	BROTHERLY LOVE
BEEHLOOPSTTUW	UP TO THE ELBOWS
BEEHLOQRSSUUW	BURLESQUE SHOW
BEEHMMNOOSSTU	THUMB ONES NOSE
BEEHOORRSTTUY	ROBERT SOUTHEY
BEEHORSSTTTUW	SHORT BUT SWEET
BEEIIIILNSSST	SENSIBILITIES
BEEIIILNNSSSV	INVISIBLENESS
BEEIIILNSTTXY	EXTENSIBILITY
BEEIIILRRSTVY	REVERSIBILITY
BEEIIKLOORSTT	TOOK LIBERTIES
BEEIILNOPRRSS	IRRESPONSIBLE
BEEIILNPRRTTU	INTERRUPTIBLE
BEEIILNPRSSXY	INEXPRESSIBLY
BEEIILNRRSTTW	TERRIBLE TWINS
BEEIILOPQSSTU	QUITE POSSIBLE
BEEIILPRRRSSY	IRREPRESSIBLY
BEEIILRRTTUVY	RETRIBUTIVELY
BEEIKMNNOOPRRS	BROKEN PROMISE
BEEILLMMOPPRS	SIMPLE PROBLEM
BEEILLNNOSSSU	INSOLUBLENESS
BEEILNOOPSSTW	TIPS ONE'S ELBOW
BEEILNRSSTUVY	SUBSERVIENTLY
BEEIMNRSSSSTU	BUSINESS TERMS
BEEIMNSSSSSUY	MESSY BUSINESS
BEEINOOORRRST	BOSTON TERRIER
BEEINORRSSSTT	BRONTE SISTERS
BEEINORSSSTUV	OBTRUSIVENESS
BEELLMOORSTUY	TROUBLESOMELY
BEELMNNOOOSWY	BLOW ONE'S MONEY
BEELNPRRRTUYY	REPLY BY RETURN
BEENNOOSSSTUU	BOUNTEOUSNESS
BEFFGHILORRTU	FRIGHTFUL BORE
BEFFGINNORRTU	BURNT OFFERING

BEFFHIKLMOOOT	BOOK OF THE FILM
	FILM OF THE BOOK
BEFGGIINORRST	BRINGS TO GRIEF
BEFGHILOORTTU	BROUGHT TO LIFE
BEFGIIILNRSTU	FILIBUSTERING
BEFGIILLNORSU	SUING FOR LIBEL
BEFHIILLMORTT	FILL TO THE BRIM
BEFHILLMORTTU	FULL TO THE BRIM
BEFIIIILLNTXY	INFLEXIBILITY
BEFILLNOOSSTU	BOUT OF ILLNESS
BEFILNNOSSTUU	BOUNTIFULNESS
BEFINNNSSSUUY	FUNNY BUSINESS
BEFINOOSSSTUU	OUT OF BUSINESS
BEFKNNNOORRTU	UNBROKEN FRONT
BEFLOOOPRSTTU	SPOT OF TROUBLE
BEFLOOOSTTTTU	BOTTLE OF STOUT
BEGGGGIINORRW	GROWING BIGGER
BEGGGHIINOTVY	GIVING THE GO-BY
BEGGHIINNNORR	HERRINGBONING
BEGGHIINNPRTU	BRIGHTENING UP
BEGGHIINOOTTV	GIVING THE BOOT
BEGGIIIILLNTY	NEGLIGIBILITY
BEGGIIKNNNONW	BEGINNING WORK
BEGGIILNORTUV	GIVING TROUBLE
BEGGILNOORTTT	GLOBE-TROTTING
BEGGINOOSSTUX	SUGGESTION BOX
BEGHHKNOORRTU	BROKEN THROUGH
BEGHIIILNORST	BRITISH LEGION
BEGHIILLNORTT	LITTLE BIGHORN
BEGHIIMNSSSTU	MISSING THE BUS
BEGHILLNOOTTW	BLOWING THE LOT
BEGHIMMORRRST	BROTHERS GRIMM
BEGHLLOPRTUUW	WELL BROUGHT UP
BEGHMOOOOTTTT	GO TO THE BOTTOM
BEGHNOOORRTTU	ROTTEN BOROUGH
BEGIIOORRSTTTU	BROUGHT TO REST
BEGIIIIILLNTY	INFLIGIBILITY
BEGIIILNNNORT	BRING INTO LINE
BEGIIILNNOPST	BITING ONE'S LIP
BEGIIKLLLNNSU	SELLING IN BULK
BEGIILNNNOPTW	TEN-PIN BOWLING
	TENPIN BOWLING
BEGIIMNNNNRUW	WINNING NUMBER
BEGIINNNOOORTT	GONE INTO ORBIT
BEGIINOOORSTT	GOES INTO ORBIT
BEGIKNNOOORST	BROKE INTO SONG
BEGILLNNOTUWY	YELLOW BUNTING
BEGILMNORSTUV	STUMBLING OVER
BEHHILOOPRSTT	SPOIL THE BROTH
BEHIIIMMNOSTX	EXHIBITIONISM
BEHIIIINOSTTX	EXHIBITIONIST
BEHIIILOPRTVY	PROHIBITIVELY
BEHIILMNNOOPU	HUMBLE OPINION
BEHIIMMRSSTUU	BRITISH MUSEUM
BEHILNOOSTWWY	THE WINSLOW BOY
BEHIMNOOSSSTY	TOMBOYISHNESS
BEHIMNORTTUUW	WITHOUT NUMBER
BEHINOOPSTTTU	PUTS THE BOOT IN
BEHINORSSSSUU	BUSINESS HOURS
BEHLNOOOOSSTT	SHOOT ONES BOLT
BEHNOOOPRSTTU	POOR BUT HONEST
BEIIIILNNSSTY	INSENSIBILITY
BEIIIILOPSSST	POSSIBILITIES
BEIIILRSSTTY	RESISTIBILITY
BEIIKNRSSSSUY	RISKY BUSINESS
BEIILMNOOPSST	NOT IMPOSSIBLE
BEIILNOOSSSUV	OBLIVIOUSNESS
BEIILNOPRRSSY	IRRESPONSIBLY
BEIINNOORTTTW	WENT INTO ORBIT
BEIKMOORSSTTT	STRIKES BOTTOM
BEIKNNOORSSTW	KNIT ONES BROWS
BEIKNOOOSSSTU	SUITS ONE'S BOOK
BEILLMNPTTUYY	MULTIPLY BY TEN
BEILMMNOOSUUV	OMNIBUS VOLUME
BEILMOOPSSTTT	BOTTOMLESS PIT
BEILNNOOPSTTU	BUTTON ONE'S LIP
BEILNNOQSTTUU	BLUNT QUESTION
BEILNORSTUUVY	UNOBTRUSIVELY
BEILOOPRSSSTW	WORST POSSIBLE
BEILOORRRSSTV	BRISTOL ROVERS
BEILOPRRSTTUU	STIR UP TROUBLE
BEIMNOPSSSTUU	BUMPTIOUSNESS
BEINNOOOSSSUX	OBNOXIOUSNESS
BEKLMNOOPRTTY	KNOTTY PROBLEM
BEMNOPRRSUUUY	YOUR NUMBERS UP
BENNNOOORRTTU	BURTON ON TRENT
BENOORRSTTTUU	TROUSER BUTTON
BFFGGIIINNORT	BRINGING IT OFF
BFGGHIINNORRT	BRINGING FORTH
BFGHINORRSTTU	BURSTING FORTH
BCCHHINORRSTU	BRINGS THROUGH
BGHHNOORTTTUU	BUTTON-THROUGH
BGHIIILLSTTUY	SLIGHTLY BUILT
BGHIINNRRSTTU	BURNING THIRST
BGHILLNOORTUY	THYROGLOBULIN
BGHINOPRRSSTU	BRINGS UP SHORT
BGILMNNOPSTUU	STUMBLING UPON
BGILMNOOPRSSS	SPRING BLOSSOM
BGINOOOPRTVXYY	VOTING BY PROXY
BIIIILLOSTVWY	LOW VISIBILITY
BIIIILMOPSSTY	IMPOSSIBILITY
BIILLMPSTUXYY	MULTIPLY BY SIX
BIINOSSSTTTUU	SUBSTITUTIONS
BILLMOPTTUWYY	MULTIPLY BY TWO
BILLNPSTTTUUY	PUTS IT BLUNTLY
BILNNNOORSTUU	SUNBURN LOTION
BILNOOPRTTUUY	BUTTON YOUR LIP
BILOOOPPRRSUY	OPPROBRIOUSLY
BJMNNOOOOOSTU	MONOTONOUS JOB
CCCCEEIKLLORT	ELECTRIC CLOCK
CCCCEEINNOPSU	CONCUPISCENCE
CCCCEIIKKLLTY	CLICKETY CLICK
CCCCEIOOPRSTT	STREPTOCOCCIC
CCCDDEFNOOOTU	CODE OF CONDUCT
CCCDEEEEENRRSU	RECRUDESCENCE
CCCDEIILORSTU	CLOSED CIRCUIT
	CLOSED-CIRCUIT
CCCDEIIMNRSUU	UNCIRCUMCISED
CCCEEEEFILNRT	ELECTRIC FENCE
CCCEEEFILPRRT	PERFECT CIRCLE
CCCEEEFIMNRRU	CIRCUMFERENCE
CCCEEEHOPRRST	CORRECT SPEECH
CCCEEEIILNOPT	POETIC LICENCE
CCCEEEIILLRSST	SELECT CIRCLES
CCCEEFHIKNRRT	FRENCH CRICKET
CCCEEHHIRRSUV	CHURCH SERVICE
CCCEEHIKLORST	ELECTRIC SHOCK
CCCEEHIKRSTUY	SECURITY CHECK
CCCEEIKKNNORS	CRICK ONES NECK
CCCEEIKNORTTT	CONCERT TICKET
CCCEEILOOPRST	ELECTROSCOPIC
CCCEEGHIKNORSS	CROSS-CHECKING
CCCEHIKLNOUUY	UNLUCKY CHOICE
CCCEIIILORSUV	VICIOUS CIRCLE
CCCEIILORTTUY	RETICULOCYTIC
CCCEIIMMNOOOR	MICROECONOMIC
CCCEIIMNOOOOS	SOCIOECONOMIC
CCCEIINNNORTTY	CONCENTRICITY
CCCEIKNORTTUY	COUNTY CRICKET
CCCEIILMPRSTUY	CIRCUMSPECTLY
CCCEIOOPPRSST	SPECTROSCOPIC
CCCEOOOPRSSTTU	STREPTOCOCCUS

CCCFHJKNOOOORT	JOHN COCKCROFT
CCCIIIMNORSSU	CIRCUMCISIONS
CCCIIIMORRSTU	MICROCIRCUITS
CCCIILLOOOPSS	OSCILLOSCOPIC
CCCILNNOOTUUY	COUNTY COUNCIL
CCDDEEEEIORRV	DIVORCE DECREE
CCDDEEEINRSTT	DIRECT DESCENT
CCDDEEELLMNNO	CONDEMNED CELL
CCDDEEGINNNOS	CONDESCENDING
CCDDEELLOSTTU	COLLECTED DUST
CCDDEGHHINRUW	CHURCH WEDDING
CCDDENOORRTTUU	CONDUCTED TOUR
CCDDGNOOOORTU	GOOD CONDUCTOR
CCDEEEEHHLNTT	CLENCHED TEETH
CCDEEEEHLNORT	CROCHET NEEDLE
CCDEEEEILNQSU	DELIQUESCENCE
CCDEEEEMNSSTU	DETUMESCENCES
CCDEEEFLLLOST	SELF-COLLECTED
CCDEEEGKLNOOS	COCKED ONE'S LEG
CCDEEEHIIMNST	MEDICINE CHEST
CCDEEEHILLNOR	LICENCE HOLDER
CCDEEEHILPPPS	CLIPPED SPEECH
CCDEEEHOQRSSU	CROSSED CHEQUE
CCDEEEINNOSST	CONCEITEDNESS
CCDEEEELLNNOTW	WELL-CONNECTED
CCDEEELLNOSST	COLLECTEDNESS
CCDEEENNNOSST	CONNECTEDNESS
CCDEEENNORSST	CONCERTEDNESS
CCDEEFFINOORS	SECOND OFFICER
CCDEEGHHINTUW	CHEWING THE CUD
CCDEEHIIILMOT	LIMITED CHOICE
CCDEEHIKKLOPT	PICKED THE LOCK
CCDEEHILORRTY	HYDROELECTRIC
CCDEEIILLLRRT	ELECTRIC DRILL
CCDEEIILLOSTV	COLLECTIVISED
CCDEEIILLOTVZ	COLLECTIVIZED
CCDEEIINOPRTU	OPEN-CIRCUITED
CCDEEIKKOPPST	PICKED POCKETS
CCDEEILMNOPSY	ENCYCLOPEDISM
CCDEEILNOOPRT	COLD RECEPTION
CCDEEILNOPSTY	ENCYCLOPEDIST
CCDEEINNNOOSS	CONDESCENSION
CCDEEINRRRTTU	DIRECT CURRENT
CCDEELNNNORUY	UNCONCERNEDLY
CCDEELOPRRSSU	RED CORPUSCLES
CCDEENNORSTUY	SECOND CENTURY
CCDEENORRSTTU	RECONSTRUCTED
CCDEENORSSSTU	CONDUCTRESSES
CCDEFHIOOORSW	CHOICE OF WORDS
CCDEGIINNNOST	DISCONNECTING
CCDEGIINNORST	DISCONCERTING
CCDEGIKNORRTU	CRICKET GROUND
CCDEGINNNOORT	CONNECTING ROD
CCDEHIMNOPTUY	OCCUPY THE MIND
CCDEHKLNOORTU	ROUND THE CLOCK
	ROUND-THE-CLOCK
CCDEHLMMNOOOT	THE COMMON COLD
CCDEIIIMMOSTU	COMMIT SUICIDE
CCDEIINNNOOST	DISCONNECTION
CCDEIINOPRSTU	DISCOUNT PRICE
CCDEILMOOPRRY	OLYMPIC RECORD
CCDEILNOORRTT	CREDIT CONTROL
CCDEIMMOOPSSU	COMPOSED MUSIC
CCDEIMNOORSTU	SEMICONDUCTOR
CCDEKLLMNOPUU	PENDULUM CLOCK
CCDFIMOOORSTU	DOCTOR OF MUSIC
CCDGHINNOORUW	CROUCHING DOWN
CCDIIORRSTTTU	DISTRICT COURT
CCDNNNOOORSTU	NONCONDUCTORS
CCDNOOOORRTTUU	TOUR CONDUCTOR
CCEEEEEFFNRSV	EFFERVESCENCE
CCEEEEEFFLNORS	EFFLORESCENCE
CCEEEEEHIKNRSV	NECKERCHIEVES
CCEEEEEHLLNRXY	HER EXCELLENCY
CCEEEEIINORTV	RECEIVE NOTICE
CCEEEEIKLNRTV	CRICKET ELEVEN
CCEEEEEILMRRTT	ELECTRIC METER
CCEEEEIRRSSTV	SECRET SERVICE
CCEEEFFIOSTTV	COST-EFFECTIVE
CCEEEFHHIOORT	CHOICE OF THREE
CCEEEFIKPRTTW	PERFECT WICKET
CCEEEFILNNORS	INFLORESCENCE
CCEEEFILORRRT	FERROELECTRIC
CCEEEFILORSVY	VEIL OF SECRECY
CCEEEHHLPRSTU	CHURCH STEEPLE
CCEEEHIIMNPSY	CHIMNEYPIECES
CCEEEHILLNSXY	HIS EXCELLENCY
CCEEEHMOOPRRT	CHEMORECEPTOR
CCEEEIIIMNPPR	IMPERCIPIENCE
CCEEEIILOPRTZ	PIEZOELECTRIC
CCEEEIILRSTTY	LEICESTER CITY
CCEEEIIMNNRSS	REMINISCENCES
CCEEEIINNNNOV	INCONVENIENCE
CCEEEIKRRSTTT	TEST CRICKETER
CCEEEILMNNORT	RECONCILEMENT
CCEEEILNNORST	SELENOCENTRIC
CCEEEILNNOSSS	SCIENCE LESSON
CCEEEILORSTTV	ELECTRIC STOVE
CCEEEIMMNSSUU	SCIENCE MUSEUM
CCEEEINNNOQSU	IN CONSEQUENCE
	INCONSEQUENCE
CCEEEIORSSTTY	SECRET SOCIETY
CCEEELOOPRSST	ELECTROSCOPES
CCEEEMMMNNOST	COMMENCEMENTS
CCEEFFHIILOOP	CHIEF OF POLICE
CCEEFFIILOOPR	POLICE OFFICER
CCEEFFIORSTUU	CURIOUS EFFECT
CCEEFHIINNRSU	FRENCH CUISINE
CCEEFHILLRRTY	CYRIL FLETCHER
CCEEFHLOOPRST	SCHOOL PREFECT
CCEEFIIINPRST	INTERSPECIFIC
CCEEFIKLORSTY	STICK OF CELERY
CCEEFIMNOOORT	COME INTO FORCE
CCEEFINNOORST	CONFECTIONERS
CCEEFINNOORTY	CONFECTIONERY
CCEEFORSSSSUU	SURE OF SUCCESS
CCEEGGILNNOOU	GLUCONEOGENIC
CCEEGHIILLRTT	ELECTRIC LIGHT
CCEEGHILNOPSS	CLOSING SPEECH
CCEEGHINNOSTU	TOUCHING SCENE
CCEEGIINNNOST	CONTINGENCIES
CCEEGIINNOPRV	PRECONCEIVING
CCEEGIINORTTY	EGOCENTRICITY
CCEEGILNORTTU	ELECTROCUTING
CCEEGINNOPRRT	PRECONCERTING
CCEEHHIIKLLSTT	CHECKS THE TILL
CCEEHHNNRRSTUW	WESTERN CHURCH
CCEEHIIKLNOPT	KITCHEN POLICE
CCEEHIILLLOPRT	ELECTROPHILIC
CCEEHIINORSST	HISTORIC SCENE
CCEEHIILLLMOWY	CHILLY WELCOME
CCEEHILOOPRTT	PHOTOELECTRIC
CCEEHIMMNOOOS	HOME ECONOMICS
CCEEHIMNNORRY	CHIMNEY CORNER
CCEEHINORSSTT	CROTCHETINESS
CCEEHIOPRSSTU	CRUSH TO PIECES
CCEEHIORRRSTT	SCOTCH TERRIER
CCEEHMOOPTTUX	EXPECT TOO MUCH
CCEEHNNORRSTU	CUTS THE CORNER
CCEEHOORSSTTV	COVERS THE COST
CCEEIIJOPSTTU	POETIC JUSTICE
CCEEIIKOPPSST	PICKS TO PIECES

892

CCEEIIILNOPST	PILOTS LICENCE	CCEMMNNNOOOST	COMMON CONSENT
CCEEIILLOSSTV	COLLECTIVISES	CCENORRRSSSTU	CROSSCURRENTS
CCEEIILLOSTVZ	COLLECTIVIZES	CCFGIIILLNNOTY	CONFLICTINGLY
CCEEIINNNOSST	INCONSISTENCE	CCFHLOOOORTUU	TOUCH OF COLOUR
CCEEIINNQSTTU	CINQUECENTIST	CCFKKKKNNOOOR	KNOCK-FOR-KNOCK
CCEEIKKLLNOOO	LIKE ONE O'CLOCK	CCGGHHINOORTU	GOING TO CHURCH
CCEEIKOQRRUVY	QUICK RECOVERY	CCGHIIKNOTTUU	CHUCKING IT OUT
CCEEILMOORRTT	ELECTRIC MOTOR	CCGHILNOOOSST	CONCHOLOGISTS
CCEEILNNORSTV	CONVENTICLERS	CCGIIKKLNORST	STRIKING CLOCK
CCEEILNOOOPRT	COOL RECEPTION	CCGIINORRSSSS	CRISSCROSSING
CCEEILNOORTTU	ELECTROCUTION	CCGIKLNOORTWY	CYCLING TO WORK
CCEEILNOSTUVY	CONSECUTIVELY	CCGIKMNNOSTUU	COMING UNSTUCK
CCEEIMOPRRSTT	SPECTROMETRIC	CCHHIOPPSSSYY	PSYCHOPHYSICS
CCEEINNNORSTT	INTERCONNECTS	CCHIIKKNOOTTU	KICK INTO TOUCH
CCEEINNOOPPRT	PRECONCEPTION	CCHIINNORSSTY	SYNCHRONISTIC
CCEEINNORRSST	INCORRECTNESS	CCHIIOPRRSSTU	CORPUS CHRISTI
CCEEINOOPRRUW	OWNER OCCUPIER	CCHIIORRSSTTU	SHORT-CIRCUITS
	OWNER-OCCUPIER	CCHKKNNOOPTUU	KNOCKOUT PUNCH
CCEEKLNNOOSTW	TEN O CLOCK NEWS	CCIIILNNOSSTU	SITS IN COUNCIL
CCEELLNOORRTT	RENT COLLECTOR	CCIINNOOPSSUU	INCONSPICUOUS
CCEEOOPPRSSST	SPECTROSCOPES	CCIINNOORSSTT	CONSTRICTIONS
CCEFFIIINNSUY	INSUFFICIENCY	CCIINOOOOPRRT	CORTICOTROPIN
CCEFGHHIIOORT	RIGHT OF CHOICE	CCIKKLNRSTTUUY	STRUCK IT LUCKY
CCEFGINOOOSSU	SIGN OF SUCCESS	CCILMOORSSTTY	MOTORCYCLISTS
CCEFIILMRSST	SELF-CRITICISM	CCILNNOOSSUUY	UNCONSCIOUSLY
CCEFIILNNNORT	INNER CONFLICT	CCILNOOPSSUUY	CONSPICUOUSLY
CCEFILNOOSSSU	SELF-CONSCIOUS	CCINNOORSSTTU	CONSTRUCTIONS
CCEFKLOOOORSUW	CUCKOOFLOWERS	CCINNOORSTUUY	COUNTRY COUSIN
CCEGIIIKNNPRS	SPRING CHICKEN	CCMNOORSTTUUY	COUNTRY CUSTOM
CCEGHIIKQRSTU	GETS RICH QUICK	CDDDEEEINNSSU	UNDECIDEDNESS
CCEGIIIMMNNOSV	MISCONCEIVING	CDDDEEORSTTUU	REDUCED TO DUST
CCEGIIKKNNOTW	KNOCKING TWICE	CDDEEEEFFIRST	DESIRED EFFECT
CCEGIIMNNRTUV	CIRCUMVENTING	CDDEEEENNPRTU	UNPRECEDENTED
CCEHHIINOPRSZ	SCHIZOPHRENIC	CDDEEEFIIOPSS	SPECIFIED DOSE
CCEHHIMOOPRRS	CHROMOSPHERIC	CDDEEEFIRRSTU	REFUSED CREDIT
CCEHIIILORSTT	HOSTILE CRITIC	CDDEEEGINPRSU	REDUCING SPEED
CCEIIIIKNOPSTY	PSYCHOKINETIC	CDDEEEHHLORRT	HELD THE RECORD
CCEHIILOSSTTY	CHOLECYSTITIS	CDDEEEHIKNSTT	TENDED THE SICK
CCEHIIMORSSTW	MICROSWITCHES	CDDEEEHIORRTT	OTHER-DIRECTED
CCEHIKLNOOPSS	LICK ONES CHOPS	CDDEEEHLOPTUY	DEEPLY TOUCHED
CCEHIKOQTTTUU	CUT TO THE QUICK	CDDEEEIKPPPSU	PICKED UP SPEED
CCEHILLOOPRST	COLLECTORSHIP	CDDEEEINRSTTX	EXTENDS CREDIT
CCEHILMNOORTY	CHLOROMYCETIN	CDDEEEIOORRRV	VIDEO RECORDER
CCEHIMOPRRSTY	PSYCHROMETRIC	CDDEEEIORSTUU	DECIDUOUS TREE
CCEHIMOPRSSTY	PSYCHOMETRICS	CDDEEEIORSTUZ	REDUCED TO SIZE
CCEHIORSSSSTT	CROSS-STITCHES	CDDEEEORRSTTW	CROWDED STREET
CCEHLNNOOOSTV	CONVENT SCHOOL	CDDEEFHINRSTU	STUDIED FRENCH
CCEHNOOSSTTTU	COUNTS THE COST	CDDEEFIIILMOX	FIXED DOMICILE
CCEIIIMORSSTV	VISCOSIMETRIC	CDDEEFMNNOORS	CONDENSED FORM
CCEIIKNORSTTT	ITS NOT CRICKET	CDDEEGNOORRUV	COVERED GROUND
CCEIILLOSSTTV	COLLECTIVISTS	CDDEEHHLOORRT	HOLD THE RECORD
CCEIILMNOOPSY	INCOMES POLICY	CDDEEHIKLSTTU	LICKED THE DUST
CCEIIMNNOOPST	MISCONCEPTION	CDDEEHKLOOORT	LOCKED THE DOOR
CCEIIMNNORTUV	CIRCUMVENTION	CDDEEHLOOORST	CLOSED THE DOOR
CCEIIMNOOSSSU	SEMICONSCIOUS	CDDEEIIILOPST	DEPOLITICISED
CCEIINNNOSSTY	INCONSISTENCY	CDDEEIIILOPTZ	DEPOLITICIZED
CCEIINNOOSSTU	CONSCIENTIOUS	CDDEEIILNOSTU	DINUCLEOTIDES
CCEIJLNNOTUVY	CONJUNCTIVELY	CDDEEIIMNSTUY	STUDY MEDICINE
CCEIKKKLLOORW	LIKE CLOCKWORK	CDDEEIIINNOORT	RECONDITIONED
CCEIKLNOOSSWX	SIX O CLOCK NEWS	CDDEEIINNOOST	SECOND EDITION
CCEIKLNORSTUW	TURN CLOCKWISE	CDDEEIKLMNNOS	CONDENSED MILK
CCEIKMPRSSTTU	CRICKET STUMPS	CDDEEIMNNNOTT	CONTENTED MIND
CCEILLOOOPSSS	OSCILLOSCOPES	CDDEEINOSSSUU	DECIDUOUSNESS
CCEILMNOOSTUY	SOCIETY COLUMN	CDDEEKKLNNRUU	KNUCKLED UNDER
CCEILOOPRRTUU	COLOUR PICTURE	CDDEELOPPRTUU	REDUCED TO PULP
CCEIMMOOPRRTU	MICROCOMPUTER	CDDEFHIIILLOR	LORD LICHFIELD
CCEIMMOOPSSSU	COMPOSES MUSIC	CDDEGHNOORTUU	TOUCHED GROUND
CCEINNOOPRRST	PRINCE CONSORT	CDDEGIIJRSTTU	DISTRICT JUDGE
CCEINNOOSSSSU	CONSCIOUSNESS	CDDEHHILOORRY	HYDROCHLORIDE
CCEINNPPRSUUW	CUP-WINNERS CUP	CDDEHLNORSTUU	THUNDERCLOUDS
CCEINOORSSSST	CROSS-SECTIONS	CDDEIIIILNNPS	INDISCIPLINED

CDDEIINNNOOTU	UNCONDITIONED
CDDEINNOORSTU	SOUND DOCTRINE
CDDEKKNNNOOOOW	KNOCKED ON WOOD
CDDEOOOORRRSST	DOCTORS ORDERS
CDDEOOORRSSSSW	CROSSED SWORDS
CDDGIINNOOOOT	GOOD CONDITION
CDDGILLLMNOOY	MOLLYCODDLING
CDDGINNOORRUW	CROWDING ROUND
CDEEEEEHMMNNRT	CREME DE MENTHE
CDEEEEEILNORT	ELECTIONEERED
CDEEEEFFILNNO	LINE OF DEFENCE
CDEEEEFFILNNS	IN SELF-DEFENCE
CDEEEEFHINRSV	FRESH EVIDENCE
CDEEEEFHNORSW	SHOW DEFERENCE
CDEEEEFINSSTV	DEFECTIVENESS
CDEEEEFLLNSSY	DEFENCELESSLY
CDEEEEEHIKORTV	RECEIVED THE O.K.
CDEEEEEHKPSSTW	SWEEPS THE DECK
CDEEEEHNPTTUX	THE UNEXPECTED
CDEEEEIINNPRX	INEXPERIENCED
CDEEEEIMNRRST	TENDER MERCIES
CDEEEEINPSSTV	DECEPTIVENESS
CDEEEEIORRRSV	RECEIVE ORDERS
CDEEEEIQRSTUZ	CREDIT SQUEEZE
CDEEEENNNRSTU	UNDER SENTENCE
CDEEEFFFNOORT	DONE FOR EFFECT
CDEEEFFGINORR	COFFEE GRINDER
CDEEEFFIINNRS	INDIFFERENCES
CDEEEFFLNOSSS	SELF-CONFESSED
CDEEEFGNNORST	STRONG DEFENCE
CDEEEFHIIPRTX	FIXED THE PRICE
CDEEEFHILLOST	CLOSED THE FILE
CDEEEFHILRSST	CHESTERFIELDS
CDEEEFIKKLNOS	KICKED ONESELF
CDEEEFILNNOST	LINE OF DESCENT
CDEEEFILNOPST	SELF-DECEPTION
CDEEEFILNSSTU	DECEITFULNESS
CDEEEFIMNORRU	COME UNDER FIRE
CDEEEFIRRSSTU	REFUSES CREDIT
CDEEEFORRRRSS	CROSS-REFERRED
CDEEEGHIIRTTV	GIVE THE CREDIT
CDEEEGHIRSTTT	GETS THE CREDIT
CDEEEGHMRRTTU	MUCH REGRETTED
CDEEEGIIKNNSV	KINGS EVIDENCE
CDEEEHHIPRRSU	HURRIED SPEECH
CDEEEHIOPSTTV	SHOP DETECTIVE
CDEEEHJNNOSTU	JUNE THE SECOND
CDEEEHMNOOSTT	COMES TO THE END
CDEEEHOPRSSTW	SHOWED RESPECT
CDEEEIIINRSVV	DIVINE SERVICE
CDEEEIIMNPRTV	RECEPTIVE MIND
CDEEEIINNRRSV	DINNER SERVICE
CDEEEIINRSSTY	DIRE NECESSITY
CDEEEIJNOORRT	EJECTION ORDER
CDEEEIKMPQRTU	QUICK-TEMPERED
CDEEEIKNOPRST	RECEPTION DESK
CDEEEIKORTTVW	DETECTIVE WORK
CDEEEILMNORST	DECLINOMETERS
CDEEEINNORSST	RECONDITENESS
CDEEEINNORSVW	SWORN EVIDENCE
CDEEEINNPRRST	SCREEN-PRINTED
CDEEEINSSSTUV	SEDUCTIVENESS
CDEEEIOPRRTTY	RECITED POETRY
CDEEEIORSSTUZ	REDUCES TO SIZE
CDEEEKLOOPRST	ROCKED TO SLEEP
CDEEEENNNOSSTT	CONTENTEDNESS
CDEEFFGNOORSU	COFFEE GROUNDS
CDEEFFILNNOST	SELF-CONFIDENT
CDEEFFIOOPRST	POST-OFFICE RED
CDEEFGILNNOOU	GOOD INFLUENCE
CDEEFGILNORRS	SELF-RECORDING

CDEEFHIIINORT	EDITOR IN CHIEF
CDEEFHIKNOSTT	END OF THE STICK
CDEEFHINRSSTU	STUDIES FRENCH
CDEEFHKNOSSTU	DUCHESS OF KENT
CDEEFHLLOORSU	FLESH-COLOURED
CDEEFHNOOORTW	ONE OF THE CROWD
CDEEFIINNOOSV	FIND ONE'S VOICE
CDEEFIKLOPRSW	PICKED FLOWERS
CDEEFILLLNSUY	FULLY LICENSED
CDEEFILPRSSTU	DISRESPECTFUL
CDEEFIMNNORSS	CONFIRMEDNESS
CDEEFIOOPRRSU	SOURCE OF PRIDE
CDEEFIOORRSUV	SUE FOR DIVORCE
CDEEFLOOOPPRW	CROWD OF PEOPLE
CDEEFLRSSSTTU	SELF-DESTRUCTS
CDEEGHILNNOPS	SECOND HELPING
CDEEGHIMNNOPR	COMPREHENDING
CDEEGHOORRTTW	CROWD TOGETHER
CDEEGIIILMOOP	EPIDEMIOLOGIC
CDEEGIILNORRV	LIVE RECORDING
CDEEGIINNORRS	RECONSIDERING
CDEEGIINOPRST	GRIND TO PIECES
CDEEGIINPRSSU	CRUISING SPEED
CDEEGIINRRSTT	DERESTRICTING
CDEEGIMNOPRSS	DECOMPRESSING
CDEEGINNNORSTU	COUNTERSIGNED
CDEEGINOOOPRT	GOOD RECEPTION
CDEEHHHIIRRTT	THE THIRD REICH
CDEEHHILMNNORS	CHILDRENS HOME
CDEEHHMMNOORT	THE COMMON HERD
CDEEHIIKLNOPS	PICKED HOLES IN
CDEEHIIKLNSTV	DEVILS KITCHEN
CDEEHIKOORTTT	TOOK THE CREDIT
CDEEHILLNSSSS	CHILDLESSNESS
CDEEHILOSSTUU	CLOUD THE ISSUE
CDEEHJLNOSTUY	JULY THE SECOND
CDEEHLOOORSST	CLOSES THE DOOR
CDEEHMNOORSWY	SHOWED NO MERCY
CDEEIIIILOPSST	DEPOLITICISES
CDEEIIILOPSTZ	DEPOLITICIZES
CDEEIIIMNRSTT	DETERMINISTIC
CDEEIIIMOSSTT	DOMESTICITIES
CDEEIIINNSSTV	DISINCENTIVES
CDEEIIKNOOPTT	POCKET EDITION
CDEEIILMOOPTT	COMPLETE IDIOT
CDEEIILNOPRST	PREDILECTIONS
CDEEIILNORTTU	TRINUCLEOTIDE
CDEEIILNOSSSU	DELICIOUSNESS
CDEEIILPRSTVY	DESCRIPTIVELY
CDEEIINNSSTUV	INDUCTIVENESS
CDEEIINNORRTTU	INDIRECT ROUTE
CDEEIIORSSSTU	DISCOURTESIES
CDEEIJNPRRSUU	JURISPRUDENCE
CDEEIKLNORSTU	TRIED ONE'S LUCK
CDEEIKNNOOTWW	ONE WICKET DOWN
CDEEIKNOPSTUY	KEEP IN CUSTODY
CDEEIKNORSSTX	DRINK TO EXCESS
CDEEILLNOPRSU	CURLED ONE'S LIP
CDEEILMNOOPTU	MOUNTED POLICE
CDEEILMNORSUV	UNSOLVED CRIME
CDEEILMNOOPRSY	COPOLYMERISED
CDEEILMOOPRYZ	COPOLYMERIZED
CDEEILOORRSSU	DECOLOURISERS
CDEEILOORRSUZ	DECOLOURIZERS
CDEEILRSTTUVY	DESTRUCTIVELY
CDEEIMNOOPRSS	DECOMPRESSION
CDEEIMNOORSTY	MODERN SOCIETY
CDEEIMOOPRSTU	PERIOD COSTUME
CDEEINOORRSSS	RECORD SESSION
CDEEINORSTTTU	RECONSTITUTED
CDEEIOPPRRSST	ESPRIT DE CORPS

CDEEKKLLNNRSUU	KNUCKLES UNDER
CDEEKKLLNRSTUU	KNUCKLE-DUSTER
CDEEKNORSSTUX	DRUNK TO EXCESS
CDEELNORSSSUU	CREDULOUSNESS
CDEELOPPRSTUU	REDUCES TO PULP
CDEEMMNOORSTU	MODERN COSTUME
CDEEMNOOORSUY	COME ON YOU REDS
CDEENNOOPRRST	CORRESPONDENT
CDEENNOOPRSST	CO-RESPONDENTS
CDEENNOSSTTWY	TWENTY SECONDS
CDEENNRRRSTUU	UNDERCURRENTS
CDEEORRRSSSSSS	CROSS-DRESSERS
CDEFFFILOORSV	CLIFFS OF DOVER
CDEFFGHIILNOO	HOLDING OFFICE
CDEFFHIIOSTTW	SWITCHED IT OFF
CDEFFIIILMTTU	DIFFICULT TIME
CDEFGIKKLNNOY	KNOCKED FLYING
CDEFHILMNOORT	IN FROM THE COLD
CDEFHINNORSWW	FRENCH WINDOWS
CDEFIIILMNOSTU	SELF-INDUCTION
CDEFIINOORRSY	CRY OF DERISION
CDEFIKKNOORSX	KNOCKED FOR SIX
CDEFFILNNOOORS	CRIES OF LONDON
CDEFOORSSTUUY	COURSE OF STUDY
CDEGGINNOOORR	GOING ON RECORD
CDEGHIIINORST	RIGHT DECISION
CDEGHIIKNORTT	DOING THE TRICK
CDEGHIILNOPRS	PERISHING COLD
CDEGHILNNORRU	ORDERING LUNCH
CDEGHILNNORTU	UNDERCLOTHING
CDEGHILNNORUY	YOUNG CHILDREN
CDEGHILNOOORZ	CHRONOLOGIZED
CDEGHILNOSTUY	YOUNGEST CHILD
CDEGHILOOPSSY	PSYCHOLOGISED
CDEGHILOOPSYZ	PSYCHOLOGIZED
CDEGHNOORSTUU	TOUCHES GROUND
CDEGIILLNPRSU	REDUCING PILLS
CDEGIILNOORSU	DECOLOURISING
CDEGIILNOORUZ	DECOLOURIZING
CDEGIIMNNOOSTU	COMING OUTSIDE
CDEGIINNNNOSS	SECOND INNINGS
CDEGIINNNOSTT	DISCONTENTING
CDEGIINNOORSW	WRONG DECISION
CDEGIINNORSUW	WINDING COURSE
CDEGIINORTVWY	WINGED VICTORY
CDEGIKNNNNORUW	UNCROWNED KING
CDEGILNNOOORY	ENDOCRINOLOGY
CDEGINNNOOPRRS	CORRESPONDING
CDEGINOOPRRUV	OVERPRODUCING
CDEGINOPPRSTY	STOPPED CRYING
CDEGMNOOOOOST	COMES TO NO GOOD
CDEGMNOOORSSU	CONSUMER GOODS
CDEGOOOPPRSST	GOOD PROSPECTS
CDEHHIILLOPST	SPOIL THE CHILD
CDEHHILNORRSU	CHILDRENS HOUR
CDEHHIOOPRSTT	HOPED TO CHRIST
CDEHIIKMNSTTU	STICK IN THE MUD
	STICK-IN-THE-MUD
CDEHIILNOOOST	SCHOOL EDITION
CDEHIIMNOPRRU	PERICHONDRIUM
CDEHIINOORRRT	IN THE CORRIDOR
CDEHIIOOOPPRT	PHOTOPERIODIC
CDEHIIOPPRTTY	PTERIDOPHYTIC
CDEHILLOOPRSY	POLICYHOLDERS
CDEHILNOPSTUU	UP IN THE CLOUDS
CDEHIMNOPRSTU	PITCHER'S MOUND
CDEHIMOOOPPRSU	PSEUDOMORPHIC
CDEHIMOORTTYY	THYROIDECTOMY
CDEHINOOSSTUU	DISCOUNT HOUSE
CDEHINORSSTTY	THIRTY SECONDS
CDEHKLNOOORTU	UNLOCK THE DOOR
CDEHKMMOOOSTU	SMOKED TOO MUCH
CDEHKNRRSTTUU	THUNDERSTRUCK
CDEHMMOORTTYY	TOMMY DOCHERTY
CDEHMOOOPRTUV	PROVED TOO MUCH
CDEHMOPRRRTUU	RUPERT MURDOCH
CDEIIIILLNNPSS	INDISCIPLINES
CDEIIIINNSTTV	INDISTINCTIVE
CDEIIILNOPSST	SPLIT DECISION
CDEIIILNSTTVY	DISTINCTIVELY
CDEIIIMMNNNORT	MINOR INCIDENT
CDEIIINNORSST	INDISCRETIONS
CDEIIINORRSTT	DERISTRICTION
CDEIIJLNSTUVY	DISJUNCTIVELY
CDEIIJNOSSSUU	JUDICIOUSNESS
CDEIIKLQTTUWY	QUICK-WITTEDLY
CDEIIMMNOOSSS	DECOMMISSIONS
CDEIIMNOOOPST	DECOMPOSITION
CDEIINNNOOOPS	SECOND OPINION
CDEIINNOOPRST	PRECONDITIONS
CDEIINRRSSTTU	DISTRICT NURSE
CDEIIRSTTTUVY	DESTRUCTIVITY
CDEIKNOPSTTUY	KEPT IN CUSTODY
CDEILLMOORTUU	MULTICOLOURED
CDEILLNORSUUY	INCREDULOUSLY
CDEILMMNOOOR3	COMMON SOLDIER
CDEILMNOOPSUY	COMPENDIOUSLY
CDEILNORSSSUU	LUDICROUSNESS
CDEILPRSTTUUY	PUTS IT CRUDELY
CDEIMMMNORRSTU	COMMITS MURDER
CDEIMNNNOOPST	DENNIS COMPTON
CDEIMNNOOPRSU	MISPRONOUNCED
CDEIMNNOORSSS	CROSS ONES MIND
CDEIMNNORRSTU	TURNED CRIMSON
CDEINNOOPRTUV	NONPRODUCTIVE
CDEINOOPRRSTU	REPRODUCTIONS
CDEINOOSTTUWZ	CUT DOWN TO SIZE
CDEKLORSTTTUU	TRUSTED TO LUCK
CDELMNOOOOTY	MONOCOTYLEDON
CDELOOOPPRRTT	LORD PROTECTOR
CDEOORRSSSSSW	CROSSES SWORDS
CDFFMOOOORRTW	WORD OF COMFORT
CDFGHILNOOOPP	COPPING HOLD OF
CDFGIIMNOORST	DISCOMFORTING
CDFGIIOORRTVY	DIG FOR VICTORY
CDFGIOORRTUVY	DUG FOR VICTORY
CDGHIIIMNNORT	COMING IN THIRD
CDGHIILNOORSV	DRIVING SCHOOL
CDGIIINNNOSTU	DISCONTINUING
CDGIIMNSSTUUY	STUDYING MUSIC
CDGIKKLNNNOUW	KNUCKLING DOWN
CDGILNOORTUUY	CRYING OUT LOUD
CDGINNOORSTUU	SCOUTING ROUND
CDGLNNOOORRTU	GROUND CONTROL
CDGMMNNOOORSU	COMMON GROUNDS
CDHIIMNNOOORT	MITOCHONDRION
CDHILLLOOSSTW	COTSWOLD HILLS
CDHILMOOOSTUY	DICHOTOMOUSLY
CDHJNNOOOORST	DOCTOR JOHNSON
CDHLMMOOORSUU	MUSHROOM CLOUD
CDIIIJLNOSUUY	INJUDICIOUSLY
CDIIIJNORSSTU	JURISDICTIONS
CDIIIMNNNOOTT	MINT CONDITION
CDIIINNOSTTUY	DISCONTINUITY
CDIILLOPSTUUY	DUPLICITOUSLY
CDIINNOOOOPRT	POOR CONDITION
CDIINNOORSTTU	INTRODUCTIONS
CDIINNOOSSTUU	DISCONTINUOUS
CEEEEEGHINNPT	EIGHTEEN PENCE
CEEEEEGHRRSUY	GRUYERE CHEESE
CEEEEEHNNPRTW	THREE NEW PENCE
CEEEEEIMNRSTX	MERE EXISTENCE

895

CEEEEEINNNNPT	NINETEEN PENCE	CEEEFNNOORSTU	NOTE OF CENSURE
CEEEEELNNPRTV	ELEVEN PER CENT	CEEEFNOORSTUV	VOTE OF CENSURE
CEEEEFFINSSTV	EFFECTIVENESS	CEEEGHHILNOTW	COG IN THE WHEEL
CEEEEFGHIINNR	CHIEF ENGINEER	CEEEGHIILMNTT	MELTING THE ICE
CEEEEFGILNRSU	FEELING SECURE	CEEEGHIINRSTX	NIGHT EXERCISE
CEEEEFILLMORW	WELCOME RELIEF	CEEEGHIKNNOTU	TONGUE IN CHEEK
CEEEEFILNSSTX	SELF-EXISTENCE		TONGUE-IN-CHEEK
CEEEEFINNRRST	INTERFERENCES	CEEEGHILNNSTT	LIGHT SENTENCE
CEEEEFLLNOSSX	EXCELS ONESELF	CEEEGHINPRTTY	EIGHTY PER CENT
CEEEEFLNOSSUX	EXCUSE ONESELF	CEEEGHIPRTTTU	GET THE PICTURE
CEEEEFNNOPRTU	FOURTEEN PENCE	CEEEGHLOORSTT	CLOSE TOGETHER
CEEEEGHINORTT	HETEROGENETIC	CEEEGHOORSTTU	GO TO THE RESCUE
CEEEEGHIOPRTT	PIECE TOGETHER	CEEEGIIILNNRV	CIVIL ENGINEER
CEEEEGHPRSSTT	GETS THE CREEPS	CEEEGIIKKNPTW	KEEPING WICKET
CEEEEGIINRSSV	SEEING SERVICE		WICKETKEEPING
CEEEEGIKNPRST	KEEPING SECRET	CEEEGIIKNNRTY	KINETIC ENERGY
CEEEEGIMNRSTT	SECRET MEETING	CEEEGIILLNNRT	INTELLIGENCER
CEEEEGIMNRTXY	EMERGENCY EXIT	CEEEGIILLNNST	INTELLIGENCES
CEEEEGINNOOSU	EUGENE IONESCO	CEEEGIKNNRSSS	GREENSICKNESS
CEEEEGLLNOQSU	QUEENS COLLEGE	CEEEGILOPRRSV	PERVERSE LOGIC
CEEEEHHHKORTT	THE OTHER CHEEK	CEEEGINOSSTVX	GIVEN TO EXCESS
CEEEEHIKORSTV	RECEIVES THE O.K.	CEEEGLLMNOORT	MERTON COLLEGE
CEEEEHINNPRTT	THIRTEEN PENCE	CEEEGMNOPRSTY	EMERGENCY STOP
CEEEEHLLORSTV	LEVEL THE SCORE	CEEEHHINNRSTT	IN THE TRENCHES
CEEEEHLNRSSSS	CHEERLESSNESS	CEEEHHIPQRTTU	QUEER THE PITCH
CEEEEIKKPRSTW	WICKETKEEPERS	CEEEHIKKLNOSS	KICK ONES HEELS
CEEEEILNSSSTV	SELECTIVENESS	CEEEHIKNSTTVW	SEVENTH WICKET
CEEEEIMNNORTT	ONE CENTIMETRE	CEEEHIKORTTVW	OVER THE WICKET
CEEEEINNNPPTY	TENPENNY PIECE	CEEEHILLMOSU	HEMICELLULOSE
CEEEEINNPRSUV	SUPERVENIENCE	CEEEHILLOPRST	ELECTROPHILES
CEEEEINPRSSTV	RECEPTIVENESS	CEEEHILNOSSTT	STILTON CHEESE
CEEEEINRSSSTV	SECRETIVENESS	CEEEHILOPRRTW	LOWER THE PRICE
CEEEEINSSSSVX	EXCESSIVENESS	CEEEHIMNNOPSS	PENSION SCHEME
CEEEEIOPRRSWX	EXERCISE POWER	CEEEHIMNOPRSV	COMPREHENSIVE
CEEEEIOPRTTVX	EXTEROCEPTIVE	CEEEHIMOORRST	TIRESOME CHORE
CEEEEJNNRSTUV	REJUVENESCENT	CEEEHINORSTWZ	SEIZE THE CROWN
CEEEELMORRSTT	ELECTROMETERS	CEEEHLLNOOOSS	COOL ONES HEELS
CEEEELNOOSSSY	CLOSE ONES EYES	CEEEHLLNOSTTX	EXCELLENT SHOT
CEEEELNPRTTVW	TWELVE PER CENT	CEEEHLORSSTTT	STREET CLOTHES
CEEEENRRTTUUV	REVENUE CUTTER	CEEEHNNORSSTT	SHORT SENTENCE
CEEEFFGIIKNOS	SEEKING OFFICE	CEEEHNOSSTTTU	CUTS ONE'S TEETH
CEEEFFGILLNTT	TELLING EFFECT	CEEEHNSSTTTUW	SWEET CHESTNUT
CEEEFFHMNPRRU	FRENCH PERFUME	CEEEIILNRSSTV	SILENT SERVICE
CEEEFFIILNTVY	INEFFECTIVELY	CEEEIIMNNRTTT	INTERMITTENCE
CEEEFFIINNOPTY	FIFTY-ONE PENCE	CEEEIIMNPPRSZ	PRIZE SPECIMEN
CEEEFFIINNOSTU	FIFTEEN OUNCES	CEEEIINNPPSXY	SIXPENNY PIECE
CEEEFFINNPTWY	FIFTY NEW PENCE	CEEEIINOPRTTV	INTEROCEPTIVE
CEEEFFINNSSTT	STIFF SENTENCE	CEEEIINORRSSV	SENIOR SERVICE
CEEEFFPRRTTUU	FUTURE PERFECT	CEEEIINPPRSTV	IN PERSPECTIVE
CEEEFGHIIOPST	PIECES OF EIGHT	CEEEIJLOPRSUW	PRECIOUS JEWEL
CEEEFGILNSTUX	SELF-EXECUTING	CEEEILLMNOPSST	SPLENECTOMIES
CEEEFGJLLNORY	JOYCE GRENFELL	CEEEILMNRSSSS	MERCILESSNESS
CEEEFHIIPRSTX	FIXES THE PRICE	CEEEILMOORTTV	ELECTROMOTIVE
CEEEFHILLOSST	CLOSES THE FILE	CEEEILNOOOSSV	LOSE ONES VOICE
CEEEFHINNOSTT	SIT ON THE FENCE	CEEEILNOSSSSV	VOICELESSNESS
CEEEFHINRSSST	SCENESHIFTERS	CEEEILNOSTVXY	COEXTENSIVELY
CEEEFHIORSSTU	FORCE THE ISSUE	CEEEILNSSSSUV	SECLUSIVENESS
CEEEFHLOORSSY	CHOOSES FREELY	CEEEILNSSSUVX	EXCLUSIVENESS
CEEEFHLOPRSWY	FLOWERY SPEECH	CEEEILPPRSTVY	PERSPECTIVELY
CEEEFHMOOORTT	COME TO THE FORE	CEEEIMMNOPRST	PRECISE MOMENT
CEEEFHOOPPRSW	POWER OF SPEECH	CEEEIMMNRTTUX	CEMENT MIXTURE
CEEEFIILLNNUV	EVIL INFLUENCE	CEEEIMOPRRRRT	CRIME REPORTER
CEEEFIILLNRUV	RECEIVE IN FULL	CEEEIINNPRTTY	NINETY PER CENT
CEEEFILLNRSTY	SINCERELY FELT	CEEEIINNOPPTWY	TWOPENNY PIECE
CEEEFILOPRSTT	TOP-SECRET FILE	CEEEIINNOPSTXY	SIXTY-ONE PENCE
CEEEFIMNNORRT	REINFORCEMENT	CEEEIINNORRSSV	SCREEN VERSION
CEEEFIMNPRSST	IMPERFECTNESS	CEEEIINNOSTUX	SIXTEEN OUNCES
CEEEFINORRTTU	COUNTERFEITER	CEEEINNPRRSTT	PRINCES STREET
CEEEFKLLMNOTU	ELEMENT OF LUCK	CEEEINRRRSSTW	SCREENWRITERS
CEEEFLMNOOOST	COME TO ONESELF	CEEEINRRRSTUV	RETURN SERVICE
CEEEFNNOOPRTY	FORTY-ONE PENCE	CEEEINRSSSUVX	EXCURSIVENESS

CEEEIOPRRSTTV	RETROSPECTIVE	CEEGHIIRRSTUW	CRUISERWEIGHT
CEEEIOPRRSTTY	RECITES POETRY	CEEGHIKORSTTT	STICK TOGETHER
CEEEKLNOOOPSS	KEEPS ONE'S COOL	CEEGHILMMNNOOW	WELCOMING HOME
CEEELLMNOSTTX	MOST EXCELLENT	CEEGHIMNOOPRT	MORPHOGENETIC
CEEEELNNOQSSUU	QUEENS COUNSEL	CEEGHINORRSSU	ROUSING CHEERS
CEEELNOOORSTU	ENTEROCOELOUS	CEEGHINORTTUW	COUNTERWEIGHT
CEEEMOPRRSSTT	SPECTROMETERS	CEEGHIOPRTTTU	GOT THE PICTURE
CEEEMOQRRSTUU	QUEER CUSTOMER	CEEGHKORSTTTU	STUCK TOGETHER
CEEENNNOSTTUV	UNEVEN CONTEST	CEEGIIKKLLSTU	STICK LIKE GLUE
CEEENNPRTTTWY	TWENTY PER CENT	CEEGILNNOSUV	USING VIOLENCE
CEEENNRRSTTUV	CURRENT EVENTS	CEEGIINNORSTV	SERVING NOTICE
CEEFFFGIINOOR	FOREIGN OFFICE	CEEGIJLLNOORU	JUNIOR COLLEGE
CEEFFGGIINNOV	GIVING OFFENCE	CEEGIKKLLSTUU	STUCK LIKE GLUE
CEEFFGHIOOOTT	GO TO THE OFFICE	CEEGIKKNOSSST	GETS ONE'S KICKS
CEEFFGHIPRRTT	PERFECT FRIGHT	CEEGIKLLNOPSS	GLOCKENSPIELS
CEEFFGIMNNOOR	MORNING COFFEE	CEEGIKNNOOSTW	GET ON ONE'S WICK
CEEFFHIKLOOPR	FLICKER OF HOPE	CEEGIKOPRRSTY	GREEK CYPRIOTS
CEEFFHINRSSTT	FESTSCHRIFTEN	CEEGILLNORSSV	LEVEL CROSSING
CEEFFHIOTTTUW	WITHOUT EFFECT	CEEGILMMNNOPT	COMPLEMENTING
CEEFFIIILNNTY	INEFFICIENTLY	CEEGILNOPRTTY	ELECTROTYPING
CEEFFIINOORTU	OFFICE ROUTINE	CEEGINORSSTTU	SETTING COURSE
CEEFFIINPSTXY	FIFTY-SIX PENCE	CEEGIOPRRSSST	GROSS RECEIPTS
CEEFFINOPTTWY	FIFTY-TWO PENCE	CEEGKNOOOOOCC	COOK ONE'S GOOSE
CEEFFKLORSTTU	FLEET OF TRUCKS	CEEGLNOORSSSS	CROSS ONES LEGS
CEEFFKNOOORRS	OFF ONES ROCKER	CEEGMNNOORSSW	CONGRESSWOMEN
CEEFGGINOORST	GOING SCOT-FREE	CEEGMNOORRSST	COSTERMONGERS
CEEFGHHILRSTU	CHEERFUL SIGHT	CEEHIIIMMORSTT	THERMOCHEMIST
CEEFGHHINQRUY	HIGH FREQUENCY	CEEHHIMOOPRRT	HETEROMORPHIC
CEEFGHKLOORTT	FLOCK TOGETHER	CEEHHIOOPRRTT	HETEROTROPHIC
CEEFGIIILMNNO	FEMININE LOGIC	CEEHHLOORSSST	CLOTHESHORSES
CEEFGIIKNNSSS	FEIGN SICKNESS	CEEHHNNOOSTTT	HOT ON THE SCENT
CEEFGIIMNPRTT	PERFECT TIMING	CEEHHNNORSSTTU	HORSE CHESTNUT
CEEFGIINOPRST	PIECE OF STRING	CEEHIIIJLRSTU	JULIE CHRISTIE
CEEFGILNORRSY	SCORING FREELY	CEEHIIKNNPRTW	PICK THE WINNER
CEEFGINOORSTU	SECURE FOOTING	CEEHIILLNPRSS	SPINE-CHILLERS
CEEFHIIKMNOTT	THE NICK OF TIME	CEEHIILLLOPSTW	POLICE WHISTLE
CEEFHIKOSTTYY	KEYS OF THE CITY	CEEHIIMNSSTTY	SEMISYNTHETIC
CEEFHINORRTTU	FURTHER NOTICE	CEEHIINORSSTT	HISTORIC TENSE
CEEFHKMNOPRTU	FROM THE NECK UP	CEEHIJKSTTTTU	JUST THE TICKET
CEEFIILLNOTWZ	FELLOW CITIZEN	CEEHIKKMOOTTY	TOOK THE MICKEY
CEEFIIMNOPRST	IMPERFECTIONS	CEEHIKLLORTTW	ROLL THE WICKET
	PERFECTIONIST	CEEHIKORSSTTV	OVER THE STICKS
CEEFIINOPRSTT	PERFECTIONIST	CEEHILOOPRRTU	HERCULE POIROT
CEEFILMMNOOST	COMMIT ONESELF	CEEHIMNNOOPRS	COMPREHENSION
CEEFILNOORRTT	RETROFLECTION	CEEHIMNNORSTT	ETHNOCENTRISM
CEEFIILOOPRUVW	POWERFUL VOICE	CEEHIMOPPRRTY	HYPERMETROPIC
CEEFIMORRSSTY	SISTER OF MERCY	CEEHINNOPSTTT	PITCH ONE'S TENT
CEEFINOORSSSU	FEROCIOUSNESS	CEEHINOPPRRST	PRECENTORSHIP
CEEFINOPRSTXY	FORTY-SIX PENCE	CEEHINORRSTTY	RECENT HISTORY
CEEFIOOPRRRSU	SUPERIOR FORCE	CEEHINPRRTTTY	THIRTY PER CENT
CEEFIOPRSSSTX	EXCESS PROFITS	CEEHIOOOPSSTT	SHOOT TO PIECES
CEEFLLORRSUUY	RESOURCEFULLY	CEEHIPPPRRTTUU	PUT UP THE PRICE
CEEFLMOORSTWY	FROSTY WELCOME	CEEHKLORSSTUY	RECKLESS YOUTH
CEEFMMOOOPRRU	COME UP FOR MORE	CEEHLNOOOPRTT	PHOTOELECTRON
CEEFNOOOPRTTWY	FORTY-TWO PENCE	CEEHLNOOOSSTU	LOSE ONES TOUCH
CEEFOOOOPRRSUW	SOURCE OF POWER	CEEHMMOOOPRSTU	HOME COMPUTERS
CEEFOOOORRRSTT	RESORT TO FORCE	CEEHMOPRRSSTY	PSYCHROMETERS
CEEGGHIKLNOSW	GLOWING CHEEKS	CEEHNNORRRTTU	TURN THE CORNER
CEEGGHILNORTT	CLING TOGETHER	CEEHNOOOSSTTU	TOUCH ONES TOES
CEEGGHLNORTTU	CLUNG TOGETHER	CEEHNOOPRSSSW	SHOW NO RESPECT
CEEGGIINOOPST	GOING TO PIECES	CEEHNOORSSTTW	STONE THE CROWS!
CEEGGILLNOORT	GIRTON COLLEGE	CEEHOOOPPRRTT	PHOTORECEPTOR
CEEGHHIIILNTT	HIT THE CEILING	CEEHPPRRSTTUU	THE UPPER CRUST
CEEGHHIMNOSSU	HOUSING SCHEME	CEEIIILNNPRTW	WRITE IN PENCIL
CEEGHHINRTTUY	EIGHTH CENTURY	CEEIIINNORSTZ	SENIOR CITIZEN
CEEGHHISSTTTT	GETS THE STITCH	CEEIIJLNOPRST	REJECTION SLIP
CEEGHHORSTTTU	SECRET THOUGHT	CEEIIJNNORSTT	INTERJECTIONS
CEEGHIIILLNPS	SHILLING PIECE	CEEIIKKLNPRSW	WINKLE-PICKERS
CEEGHIILNNOTT	ELECTION NIGHT	CEEIILMNNORST	INCLINOMETERS
CEEGHIIMNNOST	SOMETHING NICE	CEEIILMOPTTVY	COMPETITIVELY
CEEGHIINORTVW	CHEWING IT OVER	CEEIILNNOPRTW	WROTE IN PENCIL

CEEIILNNSSSUV	INCLUSIVENESS
CEEIILOOPSTTY	POLITE SOCIETY
CEEIILRRSTTVY	RESTRICTIVELY
CEEIIMNORSSST	SECRET MISSION
CEEIIMORSSSTV	VISCOSIMETERS
CEEIINNORSSTT	INTERSECTIONS
CEEIINOPRSSTT	RECEPTIONISTS
CEEIINOPRSTTV	INTROSPECTIVE
CEEIINOSSSSST	SECESSIONISTS
CEEIINPSSTXXY	SIXTY-SIX PENCE
CEEIINQRRSTUY	SECRET INQUIRY
CEEIINRSTTVVY	IN CIVVY STREET
CEEIJLNORTUUV	JUVENILE COURT
CEEIKLNORSSTU	TRIES ONE'S LUCK
CEEIKLORTTTTY	LOTTERY TICKET
CEEIKMMNOQTUV	QUICK MOVEMENT
CEEIKNOOOPTTX	TOOK EXCEPTION
CEEILLLOOSSTV	ELVIS COSTELLO
CEEILMNNOPTTY	INCOMPETENTLY
CEEILMNOORSUY	CEREMONIOUSLY
CEEILMOOPRSSY	COPOLYMERISES
CEEILMOOPRSYZ	COPOLYMERIZES
CEEILNNOOPRTU	NUCLEOPROTEIN
CEEILNOOOSSTV	LOST ONE'S VOICE
CEEILNOSSSTUY	NECESSITOUSLY
CEEILOOPRSSTT	COLEOPTERISTS
CEEILOPPRSTVY	PROSPECTIVELY
CEEILORSTTTUY	COURTESY TITLE
CEEILPQRSTUUY	PICTURESQUELY
CEEIMMNNOOOTY	COME INTO MONEY
CEEIMNNNOORSUU	UNCEREMONIOUS
CEEIMNOOOPRRT	RECEPTION ROOM
CEEIMOPPRRSTV	PROMPT SERVICE
CEEINNNOOPRTV	PROVE INNOCENT
CEEINOOOOPPRRT	POOR RECEPTION
CEEINOOPRRSTT	RETROSPECTION
CEEINOOPRSSTU	PRECIOUS STONE
CEEINOOPRSSTY	SOCIETY PERSON
CEEINOORRSSSV	CORROSIVENESS
CEEINOORRSSTV	CONTROVERSIES
CEEINOPRRSSSU	REPERCUSSIONS
CEEINOPSTTWXY	SIXTY-TWO PENCE
CEEINORRRSSTU	RESURRECTIONS
CEEINORSSTTTU	RECONSTITUTES
CEEINOSSSSTUV	VISCOUNTESSES
CEEIPPRRTTTUY	PRETTY PICTURE
CEEKLMOOPRSTW	COMPLETE WORKS
CEEKLNOOORSSY	COOKERY LESSON
CEEKNNNOOOSTU	OUT ON ONE'S NECK
CEEKOOPRRSTTU	TROUSER POCKET
CEEELLNOOOSSSS	LOSES ONE'S COOL
CEEELMMOPSSTXY	COMPLEX SYSTEM
CEEELMNOOORRTT	REMOTE CONTROL
CEEELNOOSSSSTU	CUT ONES LOSSES
CEEELNORSTTUVY	COSTLY VENTURE
CEEELOOOPRRSSU	POOL RESOURCES
CEEELPQRSSTUUU	SCULPTURESQUE
CEEELRRSSSTTUU	STRUCTURELESS
CEEEMMNNOOPTUY	PNEUMONECTOMY
CEEEMNNNOOPRTU	PRONOUNCEMENT
CEEEMNOPRTTTTU	UTTER CONTEMPT
CEEENNOORRSTTU	COUNTERTENORS
CEEENOORRSSTTV	CONTROVERTERS
CEEENOORSSSTUU	COURTEOUSNESS
CEEENOPRRRRTTU	CURRENT REPORT
CEEEOOPRRRRTTU	COURT REPORTER
CEEFFFGIILNORY	FLYING OFFICER
CEEFFFGIILNSSU	SELF-SUFFICING
CEEFFFHIIOORRTU	FOURTH OFFICER
CEEFFFINOORRSU	RUNS FOR OFFICE
CEEFFGGHIINORT	FIGHTING FORCE
CEEFFGIINOORST	SORTING OFFICE
CEEFFGILLMNOOW	COMING OFF WELL
CEEFFHIIMOOSTU	OUT OF MISCHIEF
CEEFFHIIOSSTTW	SWITCHES IT OFF
CEEFFIINOOSSSU	OFFICIOUSNESS
CEEFGGHIILNOST	CLOSE FIGHTING
CEEFGGIIMNNOORT	COMING TO GRIEF
CEEFGHILNOPRRY	CRYING FOR HELP
CEEFGHILNOSTTY	THE FLYING SCOT
CEEFGHILOORSTU	SOURCE OF LIGHT
CEEFGHINOOSTUU	TOUCH OF GENIUS
CEEFGIIINNTTTU	CUTTING IT FINE
CEEFGIIJNNOORS	JOINING FORCES
CEEFGIIKLNPSTY	FLYING PICKETS
CEEFGIIKNORRST	STRIKING FORCE
CEEFGIILNOOPRY	FOREIGN POLICY
CEEFGILLNNNOUW	CUNNING FELLOW
CEEFHHNOOSTTUU	TOUCH OF THE SUN
CEEFHILOOSSTTU	SUIT OF CLOTHES
CEEFHLLLOOOSSW	SCHOOLFELLOWS
CEEFHLOOOORRSST	CROSS THE FLOOR
CEEFHMNOOOORRTY	CRY FOR THE MOON
CEEFHNORRTTUUY	FOURTH CENTURY
CEEFIIILMNPPRR	FIRM PRINCIPLE
CEEFIIINORRTTW	FICTION WRITER
CEEFIILMNOORTV	LIVE IN COMFORT
CEEFIILOPRSSUU	SPICULIFEROUS
CEEFIJLMOOPRRT	FILM PROJECTOR
CEEFILLMOORTTT	LITTLE COMFORT
CEEFILNNOORTUY	LINE OF COUNTRY
CEEFILNOPRRTUY	PERFUNCTORILY
CEEFINOOPRSTTU	PUTS INTO FORCE
CEEFKLMMNOOOSU	COLUMN OF SMOKE
CEEFLLNOORSSUU	COLOURFULNESS
CEEFOOOORRSUWY	SOURCE OF WORRY
CEEGGHHIIINOPTV	GIVING THE CHOP
CEEGGHLNOOOORY	GEOCHRONOLOGY
CEEGGIIILNNNSV	CLINGING VINES
CEEGGIINNOOSSV	SING-SONG VOICE
CEEGGILNNOOORT	RONTGENOLOGIC
CEEGHHIILOPRSY	HIEROGLYPHICS
CEEGHHINNORSSU	SING THE CHORUS
CEEGHHNORSSTUU	SUNG THE CHORUS
CEEGHIIIKNNTTW	THINKING TWICE
CEEGHIIILLNNPS	SPINE-CHILLING
CEEGHIIMNNOOSTT	COME INTO SIGHT
CEEGHIINNNNPPY	PENNY PINCHING
	PENNY-PINCHING
CEEGHIINNNPTUW	WINNING THE CUP
CEEGHIINORSTVW	SWITCHING OVER
CEEGHIIRSTTTUY	TIGHT SECURITY
CEEGHIKNNNOORT	NECK OR NOTHING
CEEGHIKNOORRSY	COOKING SHERRY
CEEGHILLNNOOST	IN LONG CLOTHES
CEEGHILNNORSTU	CLOSE-RUN THING
CEEGHILNOOORSZ	CHRONOLOGIZES
CEEGHILNOOSSTT	TECHNOLOGISTS
CEEGHILOOPSSSY	PSYCHOLOGISES
CEEGHILOOPSSYZ	PSYCHOLOGIZES
CEEGHIMNNOOOTT	COME TO NOTHING
CEEGHINNOOSTUU	COUNTINGHOUSE
CEEGHINORSSSTT	CROSSING THE T'S
CEEGHINORSTTTU	OUTSTRETCHING
	STRETCHING OUT
CEEGHMOORRSTUU	ROUGH CUSTOMER
CEEGHMOORSTTUU	TOUGH CUSTOMER
CEEGHOPRRSSUYY	PSYCHOSURGERY
CEEGIIIINNPRRS	RISING IN PRICE
CEEGIIIKLLNSVY	CLINGS LIKE IVY
CEEGIIIKNNNTTW	WINNING TICKET
CEEGIIKLLORSSV	LOVESICK GIRLS

CEGIIKNOPRRST	REPORTING SICK	CEHNOORRSSSTU	SOUTHERN CROSS
CEGIILMMNNOPT	COMPLIMENTING	CEIIIKLLLNOSW	WILKIE COLLINS
CEGIILMMNOPSU	COME UP SMILING	CEIIILLMOOPTY	POLIOMYELITIC
CEGIILMNOQTUY	COMING QUIETLY	CEIIILNNSTTVY	INSTINCTIVELY
CEGIILNNOPSSW	CLIP ONES WINGS	CEIIIMNNOOPTT	IN COMPETITION
CEGIIMMNNOSTU	TIME-CONSUMING	CEIIIMNOPSTUY	IMPECUNIOSITY
CEGIIMNNNORTU	COUNTERMINING	CEIIJNOOPRSTT	PROJECTIONIST
CEGIIMNOORRTT	TRIGONOMETRIC	CEIIKKLRSTTUY	STRIKE IT LUCKY
CEGIIMNOPRSTU	COMPUTERISING	CEIIKNOQRSTTU	TRICK QUESTION
CEGIIMNOPRTUV	MOVING PICTURE	CEIILLLNOOSTV	VIOLONCELLIST
CEGIIMNOPRTUZ	COMPUTERIZING	CEIILMNOPSUUY	IMPECUNIOUSLY
CEGIINNNOORRT	RECONNOITRING	CEIILNNNNOTTY	INCONTINENTLY
CEGIINNOPPRRT	INTERCROPPING	CEIILNNOORTTU	INTERLOCUTION
CEGIINNOPRSTT	INTROSPECTING	CEIILNOOOPRST	PRECISION TOOL
CEGIINORRTTUU	COURT INTRIGUE	CEIILNOPRRTUV	PROVENTRICULI
CEGIINORSTTXY	EXCITING STORY	CEIILNRSTTUVY	INSTRUCTIVELY
CEGIIOOPSSSTY	SOCIETY GOSSIP	CEIILOOPPRSTW	POWER POLITICS
CEGIKNNOOOSTW	GOT ON ONE'S WICK	CEIILOPPRSTUY	PRECIPITOUSLY
CEGIKNOQRRSST	SCORING STROKE	CEIILRRSSTTUU	SERICULTURIST
CEGILLMNOOTUW	COMING OUT WELL	CEIIMMNNOORSSS	COMMISSIONERS
CEGILMOOOSSTT	COSMETOLOGIST	CEIIMMNOPRSTU	MINICOMPUTERS
CEGILMOOPRTUY	GLOOMY PICTURE	CEIIMMRSSSSTU	MUSIC MISTRESS
CEGIMMNOORSTT	COMING TO TERMS	CEIIMNNOORSTU	MINOR COUNTIES
CEGIMNOOOPRTW	COMING TO POWER	CEIIMNNORRTTU	MICRONUTRIENT
CEGIMNOOPRSSU	COMING UP ROSES	CEIIMNOOPRSTT	PROTECTIONISM
CEGINNOORRTTV	CONTROVERTING	CEIIMNOOPRTTU	MOTION PICTURE
CEGINORRTTTTU	CUTTING RETORT	CEIINNOOPRSTT	INTROSPECTION
CEGINPRSSSTTU	PRESS CUTTINGS	CEIINNORRSSTU	INSURRECTIONS
CEGINRRRSTTUU	RESTRUCTURING	CEIINOOPRSTTT	PROTECTIONIST
CEGLNNNOOOUYY	ONLY YOUNG ONCE	CEIINOPPRRSST	PRESCRIPTIONS
CEGNNOORSSSUU	CONGRUOUSNESS	CEIINOPRSSSTU	PERCUSSIONIST
CEGNNORRRSTTU	STRONG CURRENT	CEIINORSSSTUX	EXCURSIONISTS
CEIIIIILLLNRST	CHILTERN HILLS	CEIIPRRRSSTTW	SCRIPTWRITERS
CEHHIIMMOOORT	HOMOIOTHERMIC	CEIJMMOPRRTUY	COMMIT PERJURY
CEHHIKNNOOOTT	TOOK ON THE CHIN	CEIKLLNNOUUVY	UNLUCKY IN LOVE
CEHHIOOPRSSTI	HOPES TO CHRIST	CEIKNOOQSSTTU	STOCK QUESTION
CEHHKORRSTTUU	STRUCK THE HOUR	CEIKOOORSSTTU	TOOK ITS COURSE
CEHHNOORSTTUU	COUNT THE HOURS	CEILLMNOOSTTY	TONSILLECTOMY
CEHIIIINNTTVY	IN THE VICINITY	CEILMNNOOOSSU	MONONUCLEOSIS
CEHIIIKLNOPTT	PILE IT ON THICK	CEILMNOORSTUY	COTERMINOUSLY
CEHIIIKRRSSTT	STRIKES IT RICH	CEILMNOPSTUVY	CONSUMPTIVELY
CEHIIIKSSSTTV	VISITS THE SICK	CEILNNOOSTTUY	CONTENTIOUSLY
CEHIIKLNOSSTT	ON THE SICK LIST	CEILNNOSTTTUY	CONSTITUENTLY
CEHIIKNOPSSSY	PSYCHOKINESIS	CEILNOORRSTTU	INTERLOCUTORS
CEHIILMOSSUVY	MISCHIEVOUSLY	CEILNOORRTTUY	INTERLOCUTORY
CEHIILNNOOSTT	COIN IN THE SLOT	CEILOPPRSSUUY	PERSPICUOUSLY
CEHIIMNOOPRST	CHEMISORPTION	CEIMMMNOORSSU	EUROCOMMUNISM
CEHIIMOORSTTY	STOICHIOMETRY	CEIMMNOORSTUU	EUROCOMMUNIST
CEHIINOOTTTUW	WITHOUT NOTICE	CEIMNNOOPRSSU	MISPRONOUNCES
CEHIINOPPRSST	INSPECTORSHIP	CEINNNOOSSSUU	INNOCUOUSNESS
CEHIINOPRTTYY	HYPERTONICITY	CEINNOOPRSTTU	COUNTERPOINTS
CEHILNNOORTTV	CLIVE THORNTON	CEINOORRSTUUY	COUNTRY SQUIRE
CEHIMNOOOPRRT	CHROMOPROTEIN	CEINORRSSSTUU	RUNS ITS COURSE
CEHIMNOOOPRST	CHEMOSORPTION	CEIOOOPPPRRRT	PROPRIOCEPTOR
CEHIMOPRSSTTY	PSYCHOMETRIST	CEIOOPRRRSTUU	SUPERIOR COURT
CEHINNORRSSSY	SYNCHRONISERS	CELLMNNNOOSSU	NELSONS COLUMN
CEHINNORRSSYZ	SYNCHRONIZERS	CELLMNOOORTUV	VOLUME CONTROL
CEHINORSTTUVW	NERVOUS TWITCH	CELLNOOSSUUVV	CONVOLVULUSES
CEHIOOPPRRSTT	PROTECTORSHIP	CELOOOPRRSSTU	POSTER COLOURS
CEHKLLMOOORWY	HOLLOW MOCKERY	CELOOPRRSTTUY	PRETTY COLOURS
CEHKMMOOOSSTU	SMOKES TOO MUCH	CEMMMOOOPPRSU	COMMON PURPOSE
CEHLLNNOPPSUU	PULL NO PUNCHES	CEMNORRRRTUUU	CURRENT RUMOUR
CEHLNOOOSSTTU	LOST ONE'S TOUCH	CENNOOPRTTUWY	NEWPORT COUNTY
CEHLNOORRSSUY	NURSERY SCHOOL	CENNOORRSTTUU	RUNS COUNTER TO
CEHLOOOOPPSST	SCOOPS THE POOL	CEOOOOPPPRRSST	POOR PROSPECTS
CEHMNOORRTTUY	MOTHER COUNTRY	CEOOPPRRSSSSU	CROSS PURPOSES
CEHMOOOOPPRST	PHOTOCOMPOSER		CROSS-PURPOSES
CEHMOOOPRSTUV	PROVES TOO MUCH		
CEHMOOPRSSSTU	CHOOSES TRUMPS	CFFGGHIINOOTU	FIT OF COUGHING
CEHMOOSSSSTUU	CUSTOMSHOUSES	CFFGIIKKNNOOT	KNOCKING IT OFF
CEHNNOORRRSST	NORTHERN CROSS	CFFGIINOORSST	CROSSING IT OFF
		CFFIIKNOOORTW	WORK OF FICTION

CFFKKKNOOOORSW	KNOCKS OFF WORK
CFFKKNOOOPSST	KNOCK SPOTS OFF
CFGHHHMOOTTUU	THOUGHT MUCH OF
CFGHIILLNNNUY	UNFLINCHINGLY
CFGHIINOORTUV	VOUCHING FOR IT
CFGHILMNOOORR	CHLOROFORMING
CFGIIIMNNORST	COMING IN FIRST
CFGIIKNOPRSTU	STICKING UP FOR
CFGILLNOORSUY	FLYING COLOURS
CFHILMNOOORSU	SCHOOL UNIFORM
CFHNNOOOORRSTW	CROWN OF THORNS
CFIMMNNNOOORS	NONCONFORMISM
CFIMNNNOOORST	NONCONFORMIST
CFIMNNNOOORTY	NONCONFORMITY
CFLLNOOOORSST	LOSS OF CONTROL
CFMOOOORSTTTUU	TOUT FOR CUSTOM
CFMOPRRSSTTUU	CUTS FOR TRUMPS
CFOOOPRTTTUUU	PUT OUT OF COURT
CGGGIIMNNOOOR	COMING OR GOING
CGGHHIMNOORTU	COMING THROUGH
CGGHHNOOOPUW	WHOOPING COUGH
CGGHIIIKNSTTT	STICKING TIGHT
CGGHIILMNOOTT	COMING TO LIGHT
CGGHILNOOOOST	GOING TO SCHOOL
CGGHINOORRSSU	ROUGH CROSSING
CGGIIMNOOPRST	COMING TO GRIPS
CGGILNNOORRWY	CROWNING GLORY
CGHHINOOOSTTU	SOOTHING TOUCH
CGHIIIKKNNQTU	QUICK THINKING
CGHIIIKNNNOPS	PHONING IN SICK
CGHIIJNORTWYY	CRYING WITH JOY
CGHIILOORSSTT	TRICHOLOGISTS
CGHIIMNOOSSTU	SOOTHING MUSIC
CGHIINNNORSSY	SYNCHRONISING
CGHIINNNORSYZ	SYNCHRONIZING
CGHILMNOORSTY	COMING SHORTLY
CGHILNOOOORSST	CHRONOLOGISTS
CGHILOOPSSSTY	PSYCHOLOGISTS
CGHINOORRSSUU	ROUSING CHORUS
CGIIIKNNOPSTT	STICKING POINT
CGIIIKNOSTTTU	STICKING IT OUT
CGIIILLOOOPST	OLIGOPOLISTIC
CGIIILMNOORST	CRIMINOLOGIST
CGIIILNOOSSTU	SOCIOLINGUIST
CGIIIMMNNOOSS	COMMISSIONING
CGIIIMNRRSSTU	STIRRING MUSIC
CGIIIOOPSSSUV	VICIOUS GOSSIP
CGIIKKLLNOOSY	LOOKING SICKLY
CGIIKKLNOSSST	SILK STOCKINGS
CGIIKKLNRSTUY	STRIKING LUCKY
CGIIKLMNOQUVY	MOVING QUICKLY
CGIIKLNORTTTU	TICKLING TROUT
CGIILMOORSSUU	GLORIOUS MUSIC
CGIILOOOSSTTX	TOXICOLOGISTS
CGIIMNNORSSTU	MISCONSTRUING
CGIINOOORSSTTU	CROSSING IT OUT
CGIINOPPPRRST	STRIP-CROPPING
CGILLNNOOORST	LOSING CONTROL
CGILLNOORSSWY	SCORING SLOWLY
CGILNNOORSUUY	INCONGRUOUSLY
CGIMMNOOOOOPRS	COMPOSING ROOM
CHHIMMOOOOPRST	PHOTOCHROMISM
CHIIILOOPRSST	SOLICITORSHIP
CHIIKKLNQSTUY	THINKS QUICKLY
CHIIOOPRSSTUY	CURIOSITY SHOP
CHIIOOPTTTXYY	PHYTOTOXICITY
CHILLOOORTVWY	HOLLOW VICTORY
CHILMMNNOOOUY	HOLY COMMUNION
CHILNOOOPPRSSU	PROCONSULSHIP
CHLNNOORSSUYY	SYNCHRONOUSLY
CIIIIIMPRSTTV	PRIMITIVISTIC
CIIILRSTTTUUV	VITICULTURIST
CIILLNOPSTUUY	PUNCTILIOUSLY
CIILMMOOOPSST	COSMOPOLITISM
CIINNOOORSTTT	CONTORTIONIST
CIINNOOSSTTTU	CONSTITUTIONS
CIINOOPPRRSST	PROSCRIPTIONS
CIJLNORSSSTUU	JURISCONSULTS
CIKNOOORSTUUW	CURIOUS TO KNOW
CIKOOOORTTTTU	TOOK IT TO COURT
CILMOOPRSSUUY	PROMISCUOUSLY
CILMOPRSSTUUY	SCRUMPTIOUSLY
DDDEEEEINNPRT	INTERDEPENDED
DDDEEEFHIOSTT	THE EISTEDDFOD
DDDEEEFIKLNOS	KIDDED ONESELF
DDDEEEINNORRR	ORDERED DINNER
DDDEEGGILNNOW	GOLDEN WEDDING
DDDEEGOORSTWW	TWO-EDGED SWORD
DDDEEINORSSWW	WINDOW-DRESSED
DDDEFIIINRSTV	FIRST DIVIDEND
DDDEGHIINOORR	RED RIDING HOOD
DDDEHNNOOOORRS	RHODODENDRONS
DDDEHNNOPRSUU	HUNDRED POUNDS
DDDEILLMNORWY	WORLDLY-MINDED
DDEEEEFFHNOPT	OFF THE DEEP END
DDEEEEFFLNNOS	DEFEND ONESELF
DDEEEEFILNNOS	ENDED ONE'S LIFE
DDEEEEFLLNOSU	DELUDE ONESELF
DDEEEEHILRSST	SHELTERED SIDE
DDEEEEHINRRSV	HIDDEN RESERVE
DDEEEEHKMOSTW	SMOKED THE WEED
DDEEEEIMNNOSY	MINDED ONE'S EYE
DDEEEEIMNPRRT	PREDETERMINED
DDEEEEINORSSY	DRIED ONE'S EYES
DDEEEEENNOPSS	OPEN-ENDEDNESS
DDEEEEFGGHINOT	FEEDING THE DOG
DDEEEFHHIIPTW	DEFIED THE WHIP
DDEEEFHILRRST	FIDDLERS THREE
DDEEEFHIMNRTY	FIND THE REMEDY
DDEEEFILNOPRS	PRIDED ONESELF
DDEEEFINOOSSV	DEVOID OF SENSE
DDEEEGHILNSST	DELIGHTEDNESS
DDEEEGHIOSSTU	DODGE THE ISSUE
DDEEEGIKLNOWW	WIDE KNOWLEDGE
DDEEEGINRRSSS	DRESS DESIGNER
DDEEEHHMOPPRT	DROPPED THE HEM
DDEEEHILNOTTT	THE DOTTED LINE
DDEEEHINRTTTU	TURNED THE TIDE
DDEEEHMNRRSTU	HUNDRED METRES
DDEEEHNOOOPRT	OPENED THE DOOR
DDEEEIILNOTUX	DE-LUXE EDITION
DDEEEIINPPSST	STEPPED INSIDE
DDEEEIINRSSTT	DISINTERESTED
DDEEEILNNNPTY	INDEPENDENTLY
DDEEEINNPRSTU	SUPERINTENDED
DDEEEELMNOPRUY	UNDEREMPLOYED
DDEEEMNNOOSST	SOONEST MENDED
DDEEEOOORRRRST	RESTORED ORDER
DDEEFFIIKNNRT	DIFFERENT KIND
DDEEFGHILLOPU	PLOUGHED FIELD
DDEEFGLOOOSSV	GODDESS OF LOVE
DDEEFHIIIMRSU	DEHUMIDIFIERS
DDEEFHLNOORTW	END OF THE WORLD
DDEEFINOPRRST	PRESIDENT FORD
DDEEFINRRSTTU	TRUSTED FRIEND
DDEEFLNORTTUW	FLUTTERED DOWN
DDEEGHHINRTUW	HUNDREDWEIGHT
DDEEGHIILLLPT	GILDED THE PILL
DDEEGHIILLLTY	GILDED THE LILY
DDEEGHIILMSTW	MIDDLEWEIGHTS
DDEEGHKOORSTT	STROKED THE DOG
DDEEGIIILMSSU	GUIDED MISSILE

DDEEGIILNRSVW	SILVER WEDDING
DDEEGIIMNSSSU	MISGUIDEDNESS
DDEEGIINNRRSS	DRESSING IN RED
DDEEGINNNRRSSU	UNDERDRESSING
DDEEHHNNOORTU	HOT ONE HUNDRED
DDEEHHOOOORRTU	OUT-HEROD HEROD
DDEEHHOOOORSTW	SHOWED THE DOOR
DDEEHIINPSSTW	DISPENSED WITH
DDEEHIKSSSTTU	KISSED THE DUST
DDEEHILNOOTWY	DYED IN THE WOOL
	DYED-IN-THE-WOOL
DDEEHLNORRTUW	THE UNDERWORLD
DDEEHMMNOORST	MODERN METHODS
DDEEHNNOORSTU	DONE THE ROUNDS
DDEEHNOORSSTU	DOES THE ROUNDS
DDEEIIILMOPRT	LIMITED PERIOD
DDEEIIKMNRRST	KIDDERMINSTER
DDEEIIMNORSSU	SERIOUS-MINDED
DDEEIIMNSSTTW	DIM-WITTEDNESS
DDEEIJNNOUSWX	DOW-JONES INDEX
DDEEIKLLORSST	DRESSED TO KILL
DDEEIKLOOORRW	LOOKED WORRIED
DDEFFIKIOOOSTU	LOOKED OUTSIDE
DDEEILMNPSSUU	SUDDEN IMPULSE
DDEEILNOPRRST	LORD PRESIDENT
DDEEIMNNOSSTW	DISENDOWMENTS
DDEEINORRSSWW	WINDOW DRESSER
DDEEINORSSSWW	WINDOW-DRESSES
DDEEKNOORRSWW	WORKED WONDERS
DDEELOOPRRSSY	POORLY DRESSED
DDEENOORRSSWW	DREW ONE'S SWORD
DDEFFGHIILSTU	DIFFUSED LIGHT
DDEFGHIIIIMNUY	DEHUMIDIFYING
DDEFHHIIINRST	FINISHED THIRD
DDEFHIOOORTTUV	DEVOID OF TRUTH
DDEFIKNOORSUW	DUKE OF WINDSOR
DDEFLNOORSTTY	TRODDEN SOFTLY
DDEFNOOOORRTTU	TROD UNDERFOOT
DDEGGHHIILNST	SHEDDING LIGHT
DDEGGHHIIINNOU	IN HIGH DUDGEON
DDEGGIMNOOOOS	DOING SOME GOOD
DDEGGINNOPPSU	SPONGE PUDDING
DDEGGNNOOORRUU	GO UNDERGROUND
DDEGHHIINOPST	DIPHTHONGISED
DDEGHHIINOPTZ	DIPHTHONGIZED
DDEGHHIOORRSU	RIDE ROUGH-SHOD
	RIDE ROUGHSHOD
DDEGHHLMORTUU	MUDDLE THROUGH
DDEGHHNOSTTUU	SUDDEN THOUGHT
DDEGHHOOOORRSU	RODE ROUGH-SHOD
	RODE ROUGHSHOD
DDEGHIIILMTTY	THE GIDDY LIMIT
DDEGHIIINSSTU	DISTINGUISHED
DDEGHIIINORTTY	DOING THE DIRTY
DDEGIIKMNNOTU	UNITED KINGDOM
DDEGIIMMNNOOP	IMPENDING DOOM
DDEGINNOOOPRU	DOING ONE PROUD
DDEGINNOOSTUY	DOING ONE'S DUTY
DDEGINNRSTUUY	UNDERSTUDYING
DDEGINOOPRRTW	GRIND TO POWDER
DDEGINOPRSTUW	DUSTING POWDER
DDEGJMNNOSTUU	SOUND JUDGMENT
DDEHHINOORSTU	DID THE HONOURS
DDEHHLOOORSUW	HOUSEHOLD WORD
DDEHHOOSSSTTU	SHOUTS THE ODDS
DDEHILMNORSTU	IN THE DOLDRUMS
DDEHILNNOOPRS	PHILODENDRONS
DDEHILOPSTTUY	HOTLY DISPUTED
DDEHINOOPPSWW	WINDOW-SHOPPED
DDEHLNOORRTUW	ROUND THE WORLD
DDEIIIILMSSTU	DISSIMILITUDE
DDEIIIKNPRRST	KINDRED SPIRIT
DDEIIILLNOSSU	DISILLUSIONED
DDEIIKNNORRTV	DRIVEN TO DRINK
DDEIIKNORRSTV	DRIVES TO DRINK
DDEIILLNRSSTT	DENTISTS DRILL
DDEIINOPPSTTU	DISPUTED POINT
DDEIINOPRRSSW	INSPIRED WORDS
DDEIKLMNOORUW	UNDER MILK WOOD
DDEIMMNNOORRSS	DESMOND MORRIS
DDEIMNOORSSTU	MISUNDERSTOOD
DDEIMNOOSSTTU	DID ONE'S UTMOST
DDFGGGHIINNOT	DING-DONG FIGHT
DDFGIIKNOOOST	GOOD OF ITS KIND
DDFIIMNNOOTUY	IF YOU DONT MIND
DDFIKNNOORRSU	ROUND OF DRINKS
DDFIMOOORSSWW	WORDS OF WISDOM
DDGGGINNOOORU	GOOD GROUNDING
DDGIINNORSTU	GRIND INTO DUST
DDGILNNOOORSU	ON SOLID GROUND
DDHIIIINORSTV	THIRD DIVISION
DDILLMOORSWWY	WORLDLY WISDOM
DEEEEEGHILNTV	GIVE THE NEEDLE
DEEEEEGHKLPPT	KEEP THE PLEDGE
DEEEEEGHLNSTT	GETS THE NEEDLE
DEEEEEHNOPSTY	OPENED THE EYES
DEEEEEFFGIRRRZ	FRIDGE FREEZER
DEEEEFFILNSSV	SELF-DEFENSIVE
DEEEEFGIINNRR	GREEN-FINGERED
DEEEEFGILLNPY	FEELING DEEPLY
DEEEEFGILNNRT	TENDER FEELING
DEEEEFGLLNOPS	PLEDGE ONESELF
DEEEEFHILLRST	SHELTERED LIFE
DEEEEFHLLNOPS	HELPED ONESELF
DEEEEFINNSSSV	DEFENSIVENESS
DEEEEFINRRSTV	FERVENT DESIRE
DEEEEFNNORSTU	UNDER ONE'S FEET
DEEEEGHKLPPTT	KEPT THE PLEDGE
DEEEEGINNRSTY	NINETY DEGREES
DEEEEGNNOORRTW	GREENWOOD TREE
DEEEEHIKNOPTY	POKED IN THE EYE
DEEEEHKMOSSTW	SMOKES THE WEED
DEEEEHLNNORSU	UNDER ONE'S HEEL
DEEEEILOPPRRT	RETIRED PEOPLE
DEEEEIMNPRRST	PREDETERMINED
DEEEEIMNPRRST	PREDETERMINES
DEEEEINORSSSY	DRIES ONE'S EYES
DEEEEKNNOPPSU	KEEP ONES END UP
DEEEEKNOOPPST	KEEP ONE POSTED
DEEEELLPRRSVW	WELL PRESERVED
	WELL-PRESERVED
DEEEELMNOPRTV	REDEVELOPMENT
DEEEENPRRSSTV	PERVERTEDNESS
DEEEFFGJJRSUY	JUDGE JEFFREYS
DEEEFFHNOOOPR	OFFERED NO HOPE
DEEEFFIILOPRV	DEPRIVE OF LIFE
DEEEFFIINRTVW	DIFFERENT VIEW
DEEEFFINNRSST	DIFFERENTNESS
DEEEFFINRRTVY	VERY DIFFERENT
DEEEFGHILNOSW	SHOWED FEELING
DEEEFGIIILNRS	SIEGFRIED LINE
DEEEFGIILMNSX	MIXED FEELINGS
DEEEFGIKLLORS	DEGREE OF SKILL
DEEEFGKLLNOSW	SELF-KNOWLEDGE
DEEEFGKLNOORW	FOREKNOWLEDGE
DEEEFHHIIPSTW	DEFIES THE WHIP
DEEEFHIILLTTV	LIFTED THE VEIL
DEEEFHIKNNRTU	UNDER THE KNIFE
DEEEFHILNOSTT	ON THE LEFT SIDE
DEEEFHIMRSTTX	FIXED THE TERMS
DEEEFHLNOOSSW	SHOWED ONESELF
DEEEFHNOORRST	FORESHORTENED

901

DEEEFIKLLLNOS	KILLED ONESELF
DEEEFILLNNOSV	FIND ONES LEVEL
DEEEFILLNSTVY	SELF-EVIDENTLY
DEEEFILNNORSU	RUINED ONESELF
DEEEFILNOPRSS	PRIDES ONESELF
DEEEFIMORRSVY	FROM EVERY SIDE
DEEEFIOOPRSUX	DIE OF EXPOSURE
DEEEFLLLNOOSW	DO ONESELF WELL
DEEEFLLLLOPPRS	SELF-PROPELLED
DEEEFLOPRRSSW	PRESSED FLOWER
DEEEFLOPSSSSS	SELF-POSSESSED
DEEEFMOORSTUV	REFUSED TO MOVE
DEEEFNNNOOOSS	END OF ONE'S NOSE
DEEEGGGHIINTV	GIVING THE EDGE
DEEEGGHHILNPST	SIGN THE PLEDGE
DEEEGGINNOSTT	SETTING ON EDGE
DEEEGHHINRTTT	GRIND THE TEETH
DEEEGHIINNRRT	THIRD ENGINEER
DEEEGHIIRRSTT	RIDES THE TIGER
DEEEGHINORTTT	GET INTO THE RED
DEEEGHINOSSTW	SOWING THE SEED
DEEEGHINRRRTV	RIGHT REVEREND
DEEEGHINRSTYY	DRYING THE EYES
DEEEGHKLOOPTT	TOOK THE PLEDGE
DEEEGHLLNORTU	THE GOLDEN RULE
DEEEGHLNNOOOT	GONE ON THE DOLE
DEEEGHLNOOOST	GOES ON THE DOLE
DEEEGHNOORRSU	HONOURS DEGREE
DEEEGIIMNNRSSS	MESSINES RIDGE
DEEEGIINSSSTV	DIGESTIVENESS
DEEEGIIPPRSUV	GIUSEPPE VERDI
DEEEGIKNOPPST	KEEPING POSTED
DEEEGINNORTVX	OVEREXTENDING
DEEEGINNPPRSS	SPENDING SPREE
DEEEGINORRUVW	RENEWED VIGOUR
DEEEGINRRSTTU	GERTRUDE STEIN
DEEEGLLLNOPSU	PULLED ONE'S LEG
DEEEGLMNOOTVW	TWELVE GOOD MEN
DEEEGLMOORTXY	EXTREMELY GOOD
DEEEGLNNOORWW	OWEN GLENDOWER
DEEEGLNORSSST	GOLDEN TRESSES
DEEEGOPRRSSUV	GOD PRESERVE US!
DEEEHIIMNNSTY	IN THE MINDS EYE
DEEEHIINNRRTW	RIDE THE WINNER
DEEEHIKNRSSST	RENDS THE SKIES
DEEEHILMPTTTV	TEMPT THE DEVIL
DEEEHILNRSSTW	THE WILDERNESS
DEEEHINNORRTW	RODE THE WINNER
DEEEHINOOPRST	OPEN OTHER SIDE
DEEEHLMNNOOWY	HONEYDEW MELON
DEEEHLNNOOTTW	WENT ON THE DOLE
DEEEHLNNORTUV	ELEVENTH ROUND
DEEEHLOPRRTUV	PROVED THE RULE
DEEEHLOPRSSTT	SHELTERED SPOT
DEEEHMOPRRSTT	SHORT-TEMPERED
DEEEHNNOPSTTW	PETE TOWNSHEND
DEEEHNORSTTTW	DOWN THE STREET
DEEEIILLMPTVX	MILD EXPLETIVE
DEEEIINNRSTTV	INVITE TENDERS
DEEEIINRSSTTW	WIDE INTERESTS
DEEEIKKLLNOOW	LOOKED LIKE NEW
DEEEIILLLMPRTY	ILL-TEMPEREDLY
DEEEIILLMSSTWY	SMILED SWEETLY
DEEEIILLORSTUY	DELETERIOUSLY
DEEEIILLPPSTVY	STEPPED LIVELY
DEEEIILMOPRRRW	WORLD PREMIERE
DEEEILNPRRTTT	PRINTED LETTER
DEEEIMPPRRTUY	DEPUTY PREMIER
DEEEINNOOPRRR	OPENED IN ERROR
DEEEINNPRRSUV	SERVE UP DINNER
DEEEINOPRRRST	RETIRED PERSON

DEEEINOQSTUVX	VEXED QUESTION
DEEEIIOOPSTVWX	EXPOSED TO VIEW
DEEEKNNOPPSTU	KEPT ONE'S END UP
DEEEKNOOPPSTT	KEPT ONE POSTED
DEEELLNNPRSTY	RESPLENDENTLY
DEEELNNSSSTTU	UNSETTLEDNESS
DEEENNNOORSSU	UNDER ONES NOSE
DEEENOOPRSSSY	DROPS ONE'S EYES
DEEENOPRRSUUX	UNDEREXPOSURE
DEEENOPSSSSSS	POSSESSEDNESS
DEEENPRRRSSUU	UNDER PRESSURE
DEEEOORRRRSST	RESTORES ORDER
DEEEORRSSTTUW	TWEED TROUSERS
DEEFFFGHINORT	FRIGHTENED OFF
DEEFFFGNOORTU	FEET OFF GROUND
DEEFFFINORRST	FIRST OFFENDER
DEEFFGGIINNRU	FINDING REFUGE
DEEFFGIIILNNR	FINDING RELIEF
DEEFFGNNOORUY	YOUNG OFFENDER
DEEFFHIPRSTUY	DEPUTY SHERIFF
DEEFFIILLNRTY	INDIFFERENTLY
DEEFFIILNORRU	RUINED FOR LIFE
DEEFFIINOOPRT	DEFINITE PROOF
DEEFFIKLNOORT	LOOK DIFFERENT
DEEFFILOSSTUV	STUFFED OLIVES
DEEFFINNOPSTU	FIFTEEN POUNDS
DEEFFINNORSTU	FIFTEEN ROUNDS
DEEFFKRSTTUUY	STUFFED TURKEY
DEEFFLMOOORSS	LOSS OF FREEDOM
DEEFFNNOOSSTU	DONE ONE'S STUFF
DEEFFNOOSSSTU	DOES ONE'S STUFF
DEEFGGHIILNRT	LIGHT-FINGERED
DEEFGHIILNNRY	HENRY FIELDING
DEEFGHILORSTY	FORESIGHTEDLY
DEEFGHIOOOSUW	GOOD HOUSEWIFE
DEEFGIIILNNSS	DIGS ONESELF IN
DEEFGIIMNRSTU	DISFIGUREMENT
DEEFGIINOORRT	FOREIGN EDITOR
DEEFGILLNNSTU	SELF-INDULGENT
DEEFGILNNORSY	DRYING ONESELF
DEEFGILNORRTU	FERTILE GROUND
DEEFGINORSSTU	REFUSED TO SIGN
DEEFHHLLOORTU	FOLLOW THE HERD
DEEFHHMMNNOOTT	END OF THE MONTH
DEEFHIIJLNTUW	JUNE WHITFIELD
DEEFHILNOPSTU	SPOILED THE FUN
DEEFHIMOPRSTU	PUSHED FOR TIME
DEEFHINORTTTU	TURN OF THE TIDE
DEEFHLMOOOOSW	WHOLESOME FOOD
DEEFHNOORSTTY	END OF THE STORY
DEEFHNORRTTUV	VENTURED FORTH
DEEFIIMNNORRT	TIME FOR DINNER
DEEFILLLOORSW	FELLOW SOLDIER
DEEFILLPPQUUY	FULLY EQUIPPED
DEEFILMNORTUW	WONDERFUL TIME
DEEFILMNRRSTY	FRIENDLY TERMS
DEEFILNOPRSSU	SPLENDIFEROUS
DEEFILOPPRSTU	SUPPORTED LIFE
DEEFINNOOPTUV	FIVE-POUND NOTE
DEEFKOORRSTUW	REFUSED TO WORK
DEEFLLORRSTUY	FULLY RESTORED
DEEFLNNOORSSW	DROWNS ONESELF
DEEFLNNORSSUW	WONDERFULNESS
DEEFLNNOSUWW	WONDERFUL NEWS
DEEFLNOOPPRSU	PROFOUND SLEEP
DEEFMNOORSTTU	MODEST FORTUNE
DEEGGHIILLNNTW	LENDING WEIGHT
DEEGGHIILLNPSY	SIGHING DEEPLY
DEEGGHIOOSTTV	GIVE TO THE DOGS
DEEGGHNOOOSTT	GONE TO THE DOGS
DEEGGHOOOSSTT	GOES TO THE DOGS

DEEGGIIKLLNTT	GETTING KILLED	DEEHIKMNRRSST	METHS DRINKERS
DEEGHHIIOTTTW	GO WITH THE TIDE	DEEHIKNOPPTTT	POTTED THE PINK
DEEGHHIKLNOTY	HOLDING THE KEY	DEEHIKSSSSTTU	KISSES THE DUST
DEEGHHINOOSTU	DOING THE HOUSE	DEEHILNOPSSTT	DONE THE SPLITS
	IN THE DOG-HOUSE	DEEHILOPSSSTT	DOES THE SPLITS
	IN THE DOGHOUSE	DEEHIMOOPRSSW	SHOWED PROMISE
DEEGHHINOPTTU	DEEP IN THOUGHT	DEEHIMOPRRTUV	TRIUMPHED OVER
DEEGHHINORTTT	RIGHT TO THE END	DEEHIMORRTWWY	THE MERRY WIDOW
DEEGHHINOSSTT	DONE THE SIGHTS	DEEHINNOOPTWW	OPEN THE WINDOW
DEEGHHIOSSSTT	DOES THE SIGHTS	DEEHINOPRRSTU	HURT ONES PRIDE
DEEGHIIKLNOTW	GO LIKE THE WIND	DEEHIOORSTTWW	WORD TO THE WISE
DEEGHIINNSSTW	WINDING-SHEETS	DEEHIOPPRSTTY	PTERIDOPHYTES
DEEGHIKNPSSTU	SPIKED THE GUNS	DEEHIOPRRSTTT	STIRRED THE POT
DEEGHILLNOSUW	DWELLING HOUSE	DEEHKNOOPRSTW	THE SPOKEN WORD
DEEGHILMNNORS	MODERN ENGLISH	DEEHLLOOOOPPT	LOOPED THE LOOP
DEEGHILMOOSTY	DEMYTHOLOGISE	DEEHLORSSSTUW	SHOWED RESULTS
DEEGHILMOOTYZ	DEMYTHOLOGIZE	DEEHNNOPPRSTY	THE PENNY DROPS
DEEGHILNOORST	THE GONDOLIERS	DEEHNNORSTTUW	WENT THE ROUNDS
DEEGHILNORTVW	GIVEN THE WORLD	DEEHNOOOPRSTT	ON THE DOOR-STEP
DEEGHILORSTVW	GIVES THE WORLD		ON THE DOORSTEP
DEEGHINNNOOST	DONE ONE'S THING	DEEHOOPPRSTTT	STOPPED THE ROT
DEEGHINNOOSST	DOES ONE'S THING	DEEIIMMNNRST	INDETERMINISM
DEEGHINOORTTT	GOT INTO THE RED	DEEIIMNNRSTT	INDETERMINIST
DEEGHINOPRTTT	POTTING THE RED	DEEIIKNNOSTUW	KNEW INSIDE OUT
DEEGHINPSTTUW	GETS THE WIND UP	DEEIILMNNOSSS	DIMENSIONLESS
DEEGHKOOOORRTX	GREEK ORTHODOX	DEEIILNNOSTTY	DONE IT IN STYLE
DEEGHKOORSSTT	STROKES THE DOG	DEEIILNORSSSU	DELIRIOUSNESS
DEEGHNNOORSTU	GONE THE ROUNDS	DEEIILNOSSTTY	DOES IT IN STYLE
DEEGHNNRRSTTU	UNDER STRENGTH	DEEIILNPRRSTV	PRINTERS DEVIL
	UNDERSTRENGTH	DEEIILOPPRSTT	LEPIDOPTERIST
DEEGHNOORSSTU	GOES THE ROUNDS	DEEIILOPSTUXY	EXPEDITIOUSLY
DEEGHNOORSTUU	HONOURED GUEST	DEEIILPPRRSTY	SPIRITED REPLY
DEEGHNOOSTTTW	WENT TO THE DOGS	DEEIIMMRSSSTY	DISSYMMETRIES
DEEGHOOOORSTTT	STOOD TOGETHER	DEEIIMNNSSTTV	DISINVESTMENT
DEEGIIIKLNOSW	DOING LIKEWISE	DEEIIMNOPPSTT	STOPPED IN TIME
DEEGIIIKMNNNP	KEEPING IN MIND	DEEIIMNORSTTV	DIVERTIMENTOS
DEEGIIINNSSST	DESENSITISING	DEEIINOPRSSTU	SERENDIPITOUS
DEEGIIINNSSTZ	DESENSITIZING	DEEIINOPRSTTT	PRESIDENT TITO
DEEGIIKMNNNOS	ENDING IN SMOKE	DEEIINOSSSSTU	SEDITIOUSNESS
DEEGIILMNNORY	DOMINEERINGLY	DEEIIOOPPSSST	OPPOSITE SIDES
DEEGIILNOPRWW	WIELDING POWER	DEEIJNORRRSSU	SURREJOINDERS
DEEGIIMNOORTV	DOING OVERTIME	DEEIKKLLORRSW	SKILLED WORKER
DEEGIINNNRRSV	SERVING DINNER	DEEIKLLORSSST	DRESSES TO KILL
DEEGIINNOORTV	TIDING ONE OVER	DEEIKLNNOOSVW	DEVIL ONE KNOWS
DEEGIINNOOSST	DIG IN ONES TOES	DEEIKMNNOOPSS	SPOKE ONE'S MIND
	DIG ONES TOES IN	DEEIKMNNORSSU	UNDER ONES SKIN
DEEGIINPRSSSU	INSPIRED GUESS	DEEIKNNOOOOST	TOOK ON ONE SIDE
DEEGIKLLNNOTU	DUKE ELLINGTON	DEEIKNOOOOSTT	TOOK TO ONE SIDE
DEEGILLNNOSSV	LONG-LIVEDNESS	DEEILLNNOOORT	ROLLED INTO ONE
DEEGILNORVWY	DOING VERY WELL	DEEILMMORRSSU	SUMMER SOLDIER
DEEGILNOPRTTU	TRIPLE-TONGUED	DEEILMNOOPRRS	MODEL PRISONER
DEEGIMNNNOPSY	SPENDING MONEY	DEEILMNOOSSSU	MELODIOUSNESS
DEEGIMNOPRTUU	IMPUDENT ROGUE	DEEILNNOSTTUY	TENDENTIOUSLY
DEEGINNNORSTU	RUNNING TO SEED	DEEILNORSSSTU	DESULTORINESS
DEEGINNNORSUW	UNDER ONES WING	DEEILNOSSSSTU	DISSOLUTENESS
DEEGINNOOSSTU	DUG IN ONE'S TOES	DEEILNRSSTTUY	STEEL INDUSTRY
	DUG ONE'S TOES IN	DEEILOOPPRSTU	LEPIDOPTEROUS
DEEGINNOPPRSW	SPENDING POWER	DEEIMOOOORRTWW	TOMORROW WE DIE
DEEGINNOPRSUX	UNDEREXPOSING	DEEINNOOPSSTU	PUTS ON ONE SIDE
DEEGINNORSTTW	DOWNING STREET	DEEINNOPSSTUX	SIXTEEN POUNDS
DEEGINOOPRRSV	DESERVING POOR	DEEINNPRRTTUU	UNINTERRUPTED
DEEHHHINRRTTY	HENRY THE THIRD	DEEINOOPSSTTU	PUTS TO ONE SIDE
DEEHHIIMNNUUY	YEHUDI MENUHIN	DEEINOORTTTUV	UTTER DEVOTION
DEEHHIOPPRRTY	HYPERTROPHIED	DEEINRRSSTTUV	SERVED ITS TURN
DEEHHLLOORTWW	THE WHOLE WORLD	DEEIORSSSTTWY	WEST SIDE STORY
DEEHHLLOOSSTU	THE DOLLS HOUSE	DEEKNOORRRSWW	WONDER-WORKERS
DEEHIIIINORSTV	DIVISION THREE	DEFLLNOPSSSUY	SLEEPS SOUNDLY
DEEHIIKNPPTTW	TIPPED THE WINK	DEELLNORTTUUW	TURNED OUT WELL
DEEHIILLLOSTT	TILLED THE SOIL		WELL TURNED OUT
DEEHIILNNNOST	IN THE LIONS DEN	DEELOORRTTTWW	TWO-LETTER WORD
DEEHIINPSSSTW	DISPENSES WITH	DEEMMRRRSTUYY	MURDER MYSTERY

DEEMNORRSSSUU	MURDEROUSNESS	DEGHIILLNOSWW	SHOWED WILLING
DEENNOOOORSSTW	DONE ONE'S WORST	DEGHIILOPRTWW	GLOW WITH PRIDE
DEENNOOPRSSSU	PONDEROUSNESS	DEGHIIMMNNORST	ONES RIGHT MIND
DEENNOORSTTTU	TURNED TO STONE	DEGHIIMMNNOSST	MISSED NOTHING
DEENNOPSSTUVY	SEVENTY POUNDS	DEGHIINOSTTTW	DOING THE TWIST
DEENOOORSSSTW	DOES ONE'S WORST	DEGHIKNNNORUW	HUNKERING DOWN
DEENOOPRSSSST	DESSERTSPOONS	DEGHIKNORSSTU	KISS THE GROUND
DEENORRSSSUUV	VERDUROUSNESS	DEGHILMOOOSTT	METHODOLOGIST
DEFFFHIILLOTT	LIFT THE LID OFF	DEGHILNOORTTU	RING OUT THE OLD
DEFFFHNOORSSU	OFFSHORE FUNDS	DEGHIMMNOOOSTT	SOMETHING TO DO
DEFFGHIOORSTT	FIT FOR THE GODS	DEGHINNOORSTU	UNDERSHOOTING
DEFFHIIINRSST	FINISHED FIRST	DEGHINNORSSTW	DOWNRIGHTNESS
DEFFHINOORSST	HOST OF FRIENDS	DEGHLNOORTTUU	RUNG OUT THE OLD
DEFFIIILNOOSV	FIELD OF VISION	DEGHMMNOOSTTU	SMOOTH-TONGUED
DEFFIINOORTTW	FORTIFIED TOWN	DEGHNORSTTTUW	STUNTED GROWTH
DEFFINOORSSTU	FUND OF STORIES	DEGHOOOOSSTWY	GOODY TWO-SHOES
DEFFKKLNOOORU	DUKE OF NORFOLK	DEGIIKLNNOOS	LOOKING INSIDE
DEFGGHINNORUY	DYING OF HUNGER	DEGIIILNPSSTT	SIDESPLITTING
DEFGGIILNNNSY	SENDING FLYING	DEGIIILNQSTUY	DISQUIETINGLY
DEFGGIINNOTTW	GETTING WIND OF	DEGIIIMMNNNQRU	ENQUIRING MIND
DEFGHILLMOOST	THE MILLS OF GOD	DEGIIJMNNSTTU	SIT IN JUDGMENT
DEFGHILNOORSX	OXFORD ENGLISH	DEGIIKLNORSST	STRONG DISLIKE
DEFGHINOOORRST	ORDER OF THINGS	DEGIIKNNNORRW	WORKING DINNER
DEFGHMOOORRTW	FROM THE WORD GO	DEGIILNNORSSV	DRIVING LESSON
DEFGIIILNORTV	TIRED OF LIVING	DEGIILNNORSTV	DR.LIVINGSTONE
DEFGIIILNRTUY	YIELDING FRUIT	DEGIILNOORRTV	LORDING IT OVER
DEFGIILNNORSS	LOSING FRIENDS	DEGIILNRSSSTY	DISTRESSINGLY
DEFGIINOOORRS	INFERIOR GOODS	DEGIILOOPRSTT	PTERIDOLOGIST
DEFHHIIINRSST	FINISHES THIRD	DEGIIMMNNORSW	SIMMERING DOWN
DEFHHMOOOOOPPT	PHOPHET OF DOOM	DEGIINNNOOOTT	GOOD INTENTION
DEFHIILORSTTW	WHISTLED FOR IT	DEGIINNOOSSTT	DOTTING ONE'S I'S
DEFHIKLLOOOOS	LOOKED FOOLISH	DEGIINOPSSSSS	DISPOSSESSING
DEFHILMRRTTYY	MERTHYR TYDFIL	DEGIKLNOOORST	TOOK IN LODGERS
DEFHINOOOORTT	FOOT IN THE DOOR	DEGIKMNOOOOST	TOOK SOME DOING
DEFHJOOORSTUY	SHOUTED FOR JOY	DEGIKNNOORRWW	WONDER-WORKING
DEFHLOOOOPRTTW	TOP OF THE WORLD	DEGILLMNOOOTW	GOODWILL TO MEN
DEFHLOORSSTTU	DUSTS THE FLOOR	DEGILLNPRSSTU	PULLED STRINGS
DEFIIINNOQTUY	DEN OF INIQUITY	DEGILNNOPRSTU	POUND STERLING
DEFIIKLLNNORS	DRINK ONES FILL	DEGILNOOORRVV	REVOLVING DOOR
DEFIIMMNOOTTU	TIME OUT OF MIND	DEGILNOOOSSTT	DEONTOLOGISTS
DEFIKLLNNORSU	DRUNK ONE'S FILL	DEGKNNOOOSSSW	GOODNESS KNOWS!
DEFIKNNOOSSTU	OUT OF KINDNESS	DEGLNOOOPRTUW	GUNPOWDER PLOT
DEFILOOOORRSUY	ODORIFEROUSLY	DEGMNOOORRRSUY	MERRY-GO-ROUNDS
DEFIMNNNOOOSW	MIND OF ONES OWN	DEGOOOOPSSTTUU	PUTS TO GOOD USE
DEFIMNNOOOSTU	OUT OF ONES MIND	DEHHHILNOOSTU	HOUSEHOLD HINT
DEFKKLOOOOORRW	LOOKED FOR WORK	DEHHIILOOPSSD	PHILOSOPHISED
DEFLNNOOOORTW	TOWER OF LONDON	DEHHIILOOPPSZ	PHILOSOPHIZED
DEFOOPRRRTTUY	REPORT FOR DUTY	DEHHILNORTTUW	HURL TO THE WIND
DEGGHIINORTVW	GIVING THE WORD	DEHHNOOSSTTUW	THE SOUTH DOWNS
DEGGHIMNOOOST	SOMETHING GOOD	DEHIILNOPTTTU	PUT THE LID ON IT
DEGGHNNOOOOTU	NOT GOOD ENOUGH	DEHIILOPPPSTW	PISTOL-WHIPPED
DEGGIINNOTTTW	GETTING IT DOWN	DEHIJJMOPTUWY	JUMPED WITH JOY
DEGGILLNNOOWW	GOING DOWN WELL	DEHILLNORSTTU	ROLL IN THE DUST
DEGHHHOPRSTUU	PUSHED THROUGH	DEHILNNORRTWY	NORTHERLY WIND
DEGHHHORRSTUU	RUSHED THROUGH	DEHILOOPPRSTT	DROPS THE PILOT
DEGHHIINNNTUW	HUNG IN THE WIND	DEHIMNOORRSTY	MODERN HISTORY
DEGHHIINOPSST	DIPHTHONGISES	DEHIMOPPRSSTT	POTTED SHRIMPS
DEGHHIINOPSTZ	DIPHTHONGIZES	DEHINNORSTTWW	NORTHWEST WIND
DEGHHIINOTTWW	GO WITH THE WIND	DEHINOOPPRSWW	WINDOW SHOPPER
DEGHHILNOPSTU	SHED LIGHT UPON		WINDOW-SHOPPER
DEGHHILORRSTU	RIGHT SHOULDER	DEHINORSTTTUW	ROUND THE TWIST
DEGHHINOORTTT	RIGHT ON THE DOT	DEHINOSSTTUWW	SOUTHWEST WIND
DEGHHINORRTUV	DRIVEN THROUGH	DEHINPPSTTUUW	PUTS THE WIND UP
DEGHHIOOSSTTT	STOOD THE SIGHT	DEHLLOPPRRSTU	PULLED UP SHORT
DEGHHIORRSTUV	DRIVES THROUGH	DEHMNORRSSTTU	THUNDERSTORMS
DEGHHKLOOORTU	LOOKED THROUGH	DEHNNNOOORSSU	SOUND ONES HORN
DEGHHLLOPRTUU	PULLED THROUGH	DEHOOPRSTTTUW	PUT TO THE SWORD
DEGHIIIINNRST	DISINHERITING	DEIIILMNOOSTT	DEMOLITIONIST
DEGHIIINSSSTU	DISTINGUISHES	DEIIINNOSSSSU	INSIDIOUSNESS
DEGHIIKNORSST	KISSING THE ROD	DEIIINNOSSSUV	INVIDIOUSNESS
		DEIIKNNOOSTUW	KNOW INSIDE OUT

DEIIKNNOPSTTU	TIED UP IN KNOTS	DHHIMNOPRSTYY	THIRD SYMPHONY
DEIIKNORSSTTW	SIT-DOWN STRIKE	DHJLNNNNOOOSY	LYNDON JOHNSON
DEIILLMPPSTUY	LIMITED SUPPLY	DIIIINNOOPSST	INDISPOSITION
DEIILLOPRSTWY	LOW-SPIRITEDLY	DIIIINOQSSSTU	DISQUISITIONS
DEIILMNOPRTVY	IMPROVIDENTLY	DIILLMNNOOPSU	MILLION POUNDS
DEIILNOOSTTUV	DEVOLUTIONIST	DIILLMOPTTTUY	TO PUT IT MILDLY
DEIIMNNNOOTTT	DONT MENTION IT	DIILMNOSTTUUU	MULTITUDINOUS
DEIINNOOPSSWW	WIDOWS PENSION	DIILNORSSTUUY	INDUSTRIOUSLY
DEIINNORSTTUU	TURN INSIDE OUT	DIINOOOOPPRRST	DISPROPORTION
DEIINNORTTTWW	WRITTEN IT DOWN	DILNOOOORSWWW	WOODROW WILSON
DEIINOOOPPRST	PROPOSITIONED	DIMNOOORRTTWY	DORMITORY TOWN
DEIINOOPRSSTT	SPORTS EDITION	DINOOPRSSTTUW	PUTS INTO WORDS
DEIINOOPSSSSS	DISPOSSESSION	DMOOPRSTTUVYY	TOPSY-TURVYDOM
DEIKKLLNORSUW	UNSKILLED WORK	DNOOOPRSSTTUW	PUTS DOWN ROOTS
DEIKLOOPRRSSU	LOOK SURPRISED	EEEEEEEGNRRRTV	EVERGREEN TREE
DEILLLOOOPRRV	LORD LIVERPOOL	EEEEEEELNRRSVV	RESERVE ELEVEN
DEILLMORRTUUW	MURDER WILL OUT	EEEEEFKRSVWWY	EVERY FEW WEEKS
DEILLNNORSSUW	UNWORLDLINESS	EEEEEGHIMNTTY	MEETING THE EYE
DEILLNOOOPSUX	LOUD EXPLOSION	EEEEEHLMORSSW	SOMEWHERE ELSE
DEILOOROOTVWY	OLD WIVES' STORY	EFEEEIKNNOPSY	KEEP ONES EYE IN
DEIMNNOOPSTTU	PUT ONES MIND TO	EEEEEIKNPRRSV	KEEP IN RESERVE
DEINOOOOPSTTT	STOOD ON TIPTOE	EEEEEKNNOOPSY	KEEP ONES EYE ON
DEKNNOPRRSTUU	DRUNKEN STUPOR	EEEEEFFGIILLNR	FEELING RELIEF
DEMNOOOOPRSTTU	MOUNTED TROOPS	EEEEEFFILNORSS	SENSE OF RELIEF
DFFGGHIIINORTY	DYING OF FRIGHT	EEEEFFIMNRSTT	FIFTEEN METRES
DFFIMNOOOSTUW	FOUNT OF WISDOM	EEEEEFFLNOORSS	SEE FOR ONESELF
DFFNNOORSTUUU	RUN OUT OF FUNDS	EEEEEFGGIKNRSU	SEEKING REFUGE
DFGGGHIIINNTY	DYING FIGHTING	EEEEEFGIINNRRV	GIVEN FREE REIN
DFGGHIIKNNRTU	FIGHTING DRUNK	EEEEEFGIINRRSV	GIVES FREE REIN
DFGGIIILLNNTUY	FINDING GUILTY	EEEEEFGILLNPSY	FEELING SLEEPY
DFGHIIINORSTTY	DYING OF THIRST	EEEEEFGLLNOSSS	FEELS ONE'S LEGS
DFGIILLNNOOWW	FOLLOWING WIND	EEEEEFGNOOSTTT	GET TO ONES FEET
DFGIINNOOOOPS	FOOD POISONING	EEEEFGNOPSTTU	GET ONE'S FEET UP
DFGINNOOOPRSU	SOUNDPROOFING	EEEEEFHHIOTTWY	WHITE OF THE EYE
DFIIIINORSSTV	FIRST DIVISION	EEEEEFHKLOPTTT	KEEP TO THE LEFT
DFILLRSSTTUUY	DISTRUSTFULLY	EEEEEFHLORTTTV	VEER TO THE LEFT
DGGGINNOOORTU	GOING TO GROUND	EEEEEFHNNORSTU	THE UNFORESEEN
DGGHIILLNNOOW	GOING DOWNHILL	EEEEEFILPRRRSV	LIFE PRESERVER
DGGHIILLNOTUY	HOLDING GUILTY	EEEEEFKLNOOPST	KEEP TO ONESELF
DGGHINNNNORTUU	HUNTING GROUND	EEEEEFKMNOOSTT	TOKEN OF ESTEEM
DGGIINNNNORSUW	SWINGING ROUND	EEEEEFLLNOPSSU	FEEL ONES PULSE
DGGILNNOOPRSU	SLOPING GROUND	EEEEEFLLNOSSST	STEELS ONESELF
DGGILNNOORTTU	TURNING TO GOLD	EEEEEFLNNOPRSS	PREENS ONESELF
DGGINOOOORSTU	GOING OUTDOORS	EEEEEFLNORSSTV	NERVES OF STEEL
DGGINOOOPRSST	SPORTING GOODS	EEEEEFLNORSSTX	EXERTS ONESELF
DGHHIKNNOTTUU	UNKIND THOUGHT	EEEEEGHHILNOST	EIGHTEEN HOLES
DGHIILNNORRUW	WHIRLING ROUND	EEEEEGHHIMSSTT	HIGHEST ESTEEM
DGHIILNNOTTWW	WHITTLING DOWN	EEEEEGHIILMNST	EIGHTEEN MILES
DGHIILNRSTTUY	LIGHT INDUSTRY	EEEEEGHIILNOTV	GIVE ONE THE LIE
DGHIMNNOOOSTW	SMOOTHING DOWN	EEEEEGHIJKNOST	SEEING THE JOKE
DGHINOOORSSTW	SOOTHING WORDS	EEEEEGHILMORST	EIGHTSOME REEL
DGHINOOPPRRST	DROPPING SHORT	EEEEEGHILNRSTW	STEERING WHEEL
DGIIIIMNNNQRU	INQUIRING MIND	EEEEEGHINNORSST	HETEROGENESIS
DGIIIMNNNPTTU	PUTTING IN MIND	EEEEEGHINORTTY	HETEROGENEITY
DGIIIMNORRRRV	DRIVING MIRROR	EEEEEGHNOORSTU	HETEROGENEOUS
DGIIINNORTTWW	WRITING IT DOWN	EEEEEGINNOSSTY	GETS ONE'S EYE IN
DGIIJNNOOTTTW	JOTTING IT DOWN	EEEEEGPRRRSSTX	EXPRESS REGRET
DGIIKNNORRSTU	SKIRTING ROUND	EEEEEHHMMOOSTW	HOME SWEET HOME
DGIIKNOORRTVW	DRIVING TO WORK	EEEEEHHNNRSSTTV	THREE SEVENTHS
DGIILLNORSVWY	DRIVING SLOWLY	EEEEEHIKLNOPPT	PENELOPE KEITH
DGIILNNORRTUW	TWIRLING ROUND	EEEEEHIKNOPSTY	POKES IN THE EYE
DGIIMNNOPRSST	SPRINGS TO MIND	EEEEEHIKNRSTTW	THIRTEEN WEEKS
DGIINNNNOPRSU	SPINNING ROUND	EEEEEHIKRSSTTY	STRIKES THE EYE
DGIINNNORTTUW	TURNING IT DOWN	EEEEEHILLNNOPT	TELEPHONE LINE
DGIINNOPTTTUW	PUTTING IT DOWN	EEEEEHINNPRSTT	THE SERPENTINE
DGIKNNOOOSSTU	TOOK SOUNDINGS	EEEEEHINRRSSTV	IN THE RESERVES
DGILNOOPRRSTW	SPORTING WORLD	EEEEFHKLLRRSTT	HELTER SKELTER
DGINNNORRRSUU	RUN RINGS ROUND		HELTER-SKELTER
DGINNORSTTTUU	TURNING TO DUST	EEEEEHKNOOPPSU	KEEP OPEN HOUSE
DGLMNNOOOORSUY	SOLOMON GRUNDY	EEEEEHLLORTTUW	ROULETTE WHEEL
DGLMNOOOOSSTU	ODONTOGLOSSUM	EEEEEHLNRRSSTW	STERN-WHEELERS

EEEEHMNNNOSTTU	TENEMENT HOUSE
EEEEHNNNORSSS	SHEER NONSENSE
EEEEHNNPSSSTV	EVENS STEPHENS
EEEEEHNOSSSTTT	SETS ONE'S TEETH
EEEEIIKKLLMST	LIKE MEETS LIKE
EEEEIILMNNNST	NINETEEN MILES
EEEEEIILNNPSVX	EXPENSIVE LINE
EEEEIIMNPSTVX	EXPENSIVE ITEM
EEEEIJLLRRSWY	JERRY LEE LEWIS
EEEEIKKNOTUWW	WEEK IN,WEEK OUT
EEEEIKNNOPSTY	KEPT ONE'S EYE IN
EEEEIKNPRRSTV	KEPT IN RESERVE
EEEEIILLNRSSSV	SEVERE ILLNESS
EEEEIILMNNNOST	IN ONES ELEMENT
EEEEIILMNNSTUV	ELEVEN MINUTES
EEEEIMNORSSTV	SERVE ONES TIME
EEEEIMNPRRSTX	EXPERIMENTERS
EEEEINNPSSSVX	EXPENSIVENESS
EEEEINNRSSTTV	RETENTIVENESS
EEEEINNSSSTVX	EXTENSIVENESS
EEEEINQRRSTTU	IN QUEER STREET
EEEEJJKMMOORR	JEROME K.JEROME
EEEEKLORRSSSS	LOSERS SEEKERS
EEEEKNNOOPSTY	KEPT ONE'S EYE ON
EEEEELLNPSSSSS	SLEEPLESSNESS
EEEEELLPSSSTWY	SLEEPS SWEETLY
EEEEELMNNOOSVY	LOVE ONES ENEMY
EEEEELMNOORSUZ	LEMON SQUEEZER
EEEEELNNOORSSV	LOSE ONES NERVE
EEEEELNNRSSSSV	NERVELESSNESS
EEEEELNNSSSSSS	SENSELESSNESS
EEEEELPRRSSSTT	LETTERPRESSES
EEEEELPRRSSTTX	EXPRESS LETTER
EEEEEMNOPRRSTT	PENETROMETERS
EEEEEMNORSSTTX	EXTENSOMETERS
EEEEEMNRSSTTVY	SEVENTY METRES
EEEEENNNORSSSV	NONSENSE VERSE
EEEEENNPRRRSTU	ENTREPRENEURS
EEEEENNPRSSTTV	PRESENT EVENTS
EEEEENOPRRSTUW	WESTERN EUROPE
EEEEEPRRRSSTUX	EXERT PRESSURE
EEEEFFGHOORTTW	WHERE TO GET OFF
EEEEFFGIILNNRS	FINER FEELINGS
EEEEFFGIILLLNOW	FELLOW FEELING
EEEEFFGLNOORST	FORGET ONESELF
EEEEFFGNOORRSU	GENEROUS OFFER
EEEEFFIILLORSU	LIFE OF LEISURE
EEEEFFIINNNTTY	NINETEEN FIFTY
EEEEFFILORRSTT	LETTERS OF FIRE
EEEEFFINNOSSSV	OFFENSIVENESS
EEEEFFLLNOOSTT	LEFT TO ONESELF
EEEEFFLNOORSSU	SURE OF ONESELF
EEEEFGHILNOSSW	WEIGHS ONESELF
EEEEFGHIRRSTTT	GET THERE FIRST
EEEEFGHNNORRTU	RUN OF THE GREEN
EEEEFGIILNORRT	FERTILE REGION
EEEEFGILLMNNOY	LIFELONG ENEMY
EEEEFGILNNNSSU	UNFEELINGNESS
EEEEFGILNNORSS	RESIGN ONESELF
EEEEFGILNOPSUV	GIVE ONESELF UP
EEEEFGIMNPRRTU	PREFIGUREMENT
EEEEFGLLNOOSST	LETS ONESELF GO
EEEEFGILNRRSSTU	REGRETFULNESS
EEEEFGNNOOOORRV	GONE ON FOR EVER
EEEEFGNOOORRSV	GOES ON FOR EVER
EEEEFGNOOOSTTT	GOT TO ONE'S FEET
EEEEFGNOOPSTTU	GOT ONE'S FEET UP
EEEEFHIILLMPST	THE SIMPLE LIFE
EEEEFHILMNOSTW	NOW SEE THE FILM
EEEEFHIMMOOSTT	SOME OF THE TIME
EEEEFHIMOSTTTT	THE TEST OF TIME
EEEEFHIMRSSTTX	FIXES THE TERMS
EEEEFHJNNOSTUV	SEVENTH OF JUNE
EEEEFHKLOPTTTT	KEPT TO THE LEFT
EEEEFHLLOORTTW	WELL TO THE FORE
EEEEFHLNSSTTVW	SEVEN TWELFTHS
EEEEFHLOOPRSTW	SWEEP THE FLOOR
EEEEFHLOORRTTU	THREE-FOOT RULE
EEEEFHNOPRRSTT	FOR THE PRESENT
EEEEFIIILMNNSW	FEMININE WILES
EEEEFIKLMNORST	ELEMENT OF RISK
EEEEFILMNNOOOT	FEEL NO EMOTION
EEEEFILMNOOPSS	IMPOSE ONESELF
EEEEFILMNORSTU	FOURTEEN MILES
EEEEFILOORRSTT	RESTORE TO LIFE
EEEEFINNNORTTY	NINETEEN FORTY
EEEEFJLNNOOSSY	ENJOYS ONESELF
EEEEFKLLMOSSSU	SMOKELESS FUEL
EEEEFKLNOOPSTT	KEPT TO ONESELF
EEEEFLLNOORSSW	LOWERS ONESELF
EEEEFLLNOPSSTU	FELT ONE'S PULSE
EEEEFLLNORRTTU	FORTUNE TELLER
	FORTUNE-TELLER
EEEEFLNNRSSSTU	RESENTFULNESS
EEEEFLNOORSTTU	TRUE TO ONESELF
EEEEFLOPRSTTUU	PUT OUT FEELERS
EEEEFMOORSSTUV	REFUSES TO MOVE
EEEEFNNNOOOSTW	ON ONES OWN FEET
EEEEFNNOOOSTTU	OUT ON ONES FEET
EEEEFNNOORRTVW	WENT ON FOR EVER
EEEEFNNOOSTTUV	SEVEN OUT OF TEN
EEEEFNOOORSTTU	OUT OF ONE'S TREE
EEEEFNOPPSTTUU	PUT ONES FEET UP
EEEEGGGGHILSTT	GET THE GIGGLES
EEEEGGHHHILNRTT	THE GREEN LIGHT
EEEEGGHIORTTTT	GET IT TOGETHER
EEEEGGHNOORTTT	GET ON TOGETHER
EEEEGGIINNNQRU	REIGNING QUEEN
EEEEGGINORRSUV	GENEROUS GIVER
EEEEGGINORSSSU	EGREGIOUSNESS
EEEEGHHHIJNTTU	JUNE THE EIGHTH
EEEEGHHHIRSTTT	THE HIGH STREET
EEEEGHHINSSSTT	SEEN THE SIGHTS
EEEEGHHIRSSTTV	GET THE SHIVERS
EEEEGHHISSSSTT	SEES THE SIGHTS
EEEEGHHNOORSTU	SEE ONE THROUGH
EEEEGHIILLSTTW	GET THE WILLIES
EEEEGHIILNNOTT	TOEING THE LINE
EEEEGHIINOPPTV	GIVE ONE THE PIP
EEEEGHIINPSTWY	WIPING THE EYES
EEEEGHIJRSTTTT	GET THE JITTERS
EEEEGHILLMRRVY	GIVE MERRY HELL
EEEEGHILMNNNTT	ENLIGHTENMENT
EEEEGHILMNOSST	SOMETHING ELSE
EEEEGHILMNRSTW	WELSH REGIMENT
EEEEGHILNNQSSU	QUEENS ENGLISH
EEEEGHILNORRST	LET GO THE REINS
EEEEGHILNRSSTT	ENGLISH SETTER
EEEEGHILRSTTWW	WELTERWEIGHTS
EEEEGHIMNOSSTU	MEETINGHOUSES
EEEEGHINNORRST	NETHER REGIONS
EEEEGHINNRTVWY	GREEN WITH ENVY
EEEEGHINORRSTV	SERVE ONE RIGHT
EEEEGHINORSTTT	GRIT ONES TEETH
EEEEGHINOSSTUW	USE ONES WEIGHT
EEEEGHINSSTTVY	SEVENTY-EIGHTS
EEEEGHMNNORTTV	THE GOVERNMENT
EEEEGHNNRRSSTT	STRENGTHENERS
EEEEGHOORSTTYZ	HETEROZYGOTES
EEEEGIIIKNNPVW	KEEPING IN VIEW
EEEEGIIKLNNPST	KEEPING SILENT
EEEEGIIKNNNPTU	KEEPING IN TUNE

EEEGIIKNNPPST	KEEPING IN STEP
EEEGIILNNOOTX	GONE INTO EXILE
EEEGIILNOOSTX	GOES INTO EXILE
EEEGIINRRSTTV	SERVIETTE RING
EEEGILMMNNORU	LEMON MERINGUE
EEEGILMNNOOST	LONG TIME NO SEE
EEEGILNOORSTV	VENEREOLOGIST
EEEGILORRRSTW	LOWER REGISTER
EEEGIMNPRRSSU	REIGNS SUPREME
EEEGINNOSSSUY	USING ONE'S EYES
EEEGINNOSSTTY	SETTING EYES ON
EEEGIORRRSSTV	RETROGRESSIVE
EEEGIPPRRRSTU	UPPER REGISTER
EEEGNNOOPSSTU	GET UP ONE'S NOSE
EEEGNNORRSUVY	NERVOUS ENERGY
EEEGNOQRSSSTU	GROTESQUENESS
EEEHHHIOSTTUW	THE WHITE HOUSE
EEEHHIILNPRTW	THREE-LINE WHIP
EEEHHILLOSSTW	OILS THE WHEELS
FFFHHIORRSTVW	WHITHERSOEVER
EEEHHLNOOSSUW	HOUSE ON WHEELS
EEEHHNOOORRTT	ONE OR THE OTHER
EEEHHNOOSSTTW	SHOW ONES TEETH
EEEHHNORSTUWY	SEE HOW THEY RUN
EEEHIIILNNPPT	IN THE PIPELINE
EEEHIIIMPRSTT	THE TIME IS RIPE
EEEHIILMNRSTT	THIRTEEN MILES
EEEHIKLNOOSTY	LOOK IN THE EYES
EEEHILLMPRSTY	SHIRLEY TEMPLE
EEEHILLOSSTTT	STILETTO HEELS
EEEHILMNNPRST	REPLENISHMENT
EEEHILMOPRRTY	PYRHELIOMETER
EEEHILNORSSTW	ON THE WIRELESS
EEEHILNRSSTTT	ENTER THE LISTS
EEEHIMMOORSTT	SOME OTHER TIME
EEEHIMNNNOOPP	EPIPHENOMENON
EEEHIMNOPRSST	ON THE PREMISES
EEEHJLLOPRSSW	JEWELLERS SHOP
EEEHKLOOORRTV	LOOK OVER THERE
EEEHKNOOPPSTU	KEPT OPEN HOUSE
EEEHLLNOOPSTT	TELEPHOTO LENS
EEEHLMNOOSSSW	WHOLESOMENESS
EEEHLOPRRSTUV	PROVES THE RULE
EEEHMNNORSTUY	SOUTHERN YEMEN
EEEHMOORSSSTU	SOMERSET HOUSE
EEEHNNOPRSTTX	THE NEXT PERSON
EEEIILLNRSSSU	LEISURELINESS
EEEIILNNOTTWX	WENT INTO EXILE
EEEIIILNNPSVXY	INEXPENSIVELY
EEEIILNOSSTTV	TELEVISION SET
EEEIINNNSSTVV	INVENTIVENESS
EEEIINNNSTTXY	NINETEEN SIXTY
EFFHINNSSSSTV	SENSITIVENESS
EEEIINORSSTVV	OVERSENSITIVE
EEEIINQRSSSTU	REQUISITENESS
EEEIINQSSSTUX	EXQUISITENESS
EEEIINRSSSSTV	RESISTIVENESS
EEEIIPQRRSSTU	PREREQUISITES
EEEIKLMNORSTT	TEN KILOMETRES
EEEILLMSSSTWY	SMILES SWEETLY
EEEILMNOPRTTV	VIOLENT TEMPER
EEEILMNSTTUVW	TWELVE MINUTES
EEEILMPQRSSTU	SIMPLE REQUEST
EEEILNNPSSSSS	SPINELESSNESS
EEEILNOPRSSUV	ELUSIVE PERSON
EEEILNOPSSSVX	EXPLOSIVENESS
EEEILNPRSSSUV	REPULSIVENESS
EEEIMMNNNOOTV	IN ONE MOVEMENT
EEEIMNNPRSSTT	PRESENTIMENTS
EEEIMNOOPRTTT	POTENTIOMETER
EEEIMNPRRSSST	MISREPRESENTS

EEEIMOORRSSST	STEREOISOMERS
EEEINNOPSSTTV	VENT ONE'S SPITE
EEEINPRSSTTWX	EXPERT WITNESS
EEEIOOPSSTVWX	EXPOSES TO VIEW
EEEKLMNOOSSSZ	SMOKELESS ZONE
EEEKLMOOPRRTT	OTTO KLEMPERER
EEEKNNOOPSSTU	UP TO ONES KNEES
EEELLMORRSSSY	REMORSELESSLY
EEELMNNOOOSSY	LOSE ONES MONEY
EEELMNORSTUVY	VENTURESOMELY
EEELMNPPRSSTU	SUPPLEMENTERS
EEELNNOORSSTV	LOST ONE'S NERVE
EEELNNOPSSSTU	PLENTEOUSNESS
EEELNOPRSSSSW	POWERLESSNESS
EEEMMMNNOPRSTT	PRESENT MOMENT
EEENNNORSSTTU	UTTER NONSENSE
EEENNOORRSSSU	ERRONEOUSNESS
EEENNOORTTVWY	OVER TWENTY-ONE
EEENNORRSSTUV	SERVE ONE'S TURN
EEENOPRRSSTWW	WESTERN POWERS
EEEOPRRSTTTVY	REVERTS TO TYPE
EEFFFLLLNOOSU	FULL OF ONESELF
EEFFFLNOSSSIU	STUFFS ONESELF
EEFFGGHIIORTU	FIGURE OF EIGHT
EEFFGHIOPSTTU	OFF-THE-PEG SUIT
EEFFGIILNOPST	SLEEPING IT OFF
EEFFGILMORRTU	FREE FROM GUILT
EEFFGIMNOPRTT	TEMPTING OFFER
EEFFGLLORRSTU	FULL OF REGRETS
EEFFGLNOOORST	FORGOT ONESELF
EEFFGLNORSSTU	FORGETFULNESS
EEFFHHHINRTTY	HENRY THE FIFTH
EEFFHIINRTTTY	FIFTEEN THIRTY
	THIRTY FIFTEEN
EEFFHJLNOTTUW	TWELFTH OF JUNE
EEFFHMNOOORST	OFFERS THE MOON
EEFFIILLRSTTY	SELF-FERTILITY
EEFFIILNNOSVY	INOFFENSIVELY
EEFFIKOSTTWWY	FIFTY-TWO WEEKS
EEFFILNOOOSTU	OUT OF ONE'S LIFE
EEFFILNOORTTV	VIOLENT EFFORT
EEFFKNNOSSTUW	KNEW ONE'S STUFF
EEFFMNORSTTU	SUFFER TORMENT
EEFGCGGILNORY	FEELING GROGGY
EEFGGGIINRRRT	TRIGGER FINGER
EEFGGHILNNRUY	FEELING HUNGRY
EEFGGIIILNNVW	GIVING NEW LIFE
EEFGGIILLNTUY	FEELING GUILTY
	GUILTY FEELING
EEFGGIILNNOOR	FOREIGN LEGION
EEFGGILLMNNOR	FELLMONGERING
EEFGGILNNORST	STRONG FEELING
EEFGGILNNORSV	SELF-GOVERNING
EEFGGINNOORTU	FOREIGN TONGUE
EEFGHIIKNOPRT	POKING THE FIRE
EEFGHIILNRRST	FREIGHTLINERS
EEFGHIILRSTTW	WEIGHT-LIFTERS
EEFGHIJKNOSTW	KING OF THE JEWS
EEFGHIKMORRTT	KERMIT THE FROG
EEFGHILLLNOOW	HOLLOW FEELING
EEFGHILLNNSTU	FLUENT ENGLISH
EEFGHILMMOOPR	GLIMMER OF HOPE
EEFGHILORSSTU	SELF-RIGHTEOUS
EEFGHINOOPRST	FOSTERING HOPE
EEFGHINOORRSS	FOREIGN SHORES
EEFGHINOOTTTU	EIGHT OUT OF TEN
EEFGHIORRSTTT	GOT THERE FIRST
EEFGHLNORRSTU	THREE FURLONGS
EEFGIIKLNNTTW	TWINKLING FEET
EEFGIILLNNRUV	GIVEN FULL REIN
EEFGIILLNRSUV	GIVES FULL REIN

EEFGIILNNOPTY	FEELING NO PITY
EEFGIILNOPTTU	FEELING UP TO IT
EEFGIILNORRVV	LIVING FOR EVER
EEFGIIMNNOSST	SENSE OF TIMING
EEFGIINNOPRTZ	FREEZING POINT
EEFGIINNORSTT	SETTING ON FIRE
EEFGIINNRRRTU	RETURNING FIRE
EEFGIINORSTTT	SETTING FIRE TO
EEFGIJNOOPRWY	WEEPING FOR JOY
EEFGIKNNORSSU	SURGEONS KNIFE
EEFGILLNNOOSS	LOSING ONESELF
EEFGILMMORSUU	GEMMULIFEROUS
EEFGILNOOSTTU	GETS OUT OF LINE
EEFGINNOORSST	FRONTOGENESIS
EEFGINOORRRRT	REIGN OF TERROR
EEFGINORSSSTU	REFUSES TO SIGN
EEFGLOOOPPPRU	GROUP OF PEOPLE
EEFHHIILNOPST	SHIP OF THE LINE
EEFHHINRRSTTY	HENRY THE FIRST
EEFHHJNORTTUU	JUNE THE FOURTH
EEFHHNOORSTUU	RUN OF THE HOUSE
EEFHHOOOSTTUU	OUT OF THE HOUSE
EEFHIILMOSSTV	SELFISH MOTIVE
EEFHIILNRTTTU	RIFT IN THE LUTE
EEFHILNNSSSSU	UNSELFISHNESS
EEFHILNSSSSST	SHIFTLESSNESS
EEFHINNOORRTT	ON THE FRONTIER
EEFHJLNOSTUVY	SEVENTH OF JULY
EEFHKOORRTUWY	FORTY-HOUR WEEK
EEFHLNOOOSSST	SHOOTS ONESELF
EEFHLNORRRSTU	RUN FOR SHELTER
EEFHLNORTTTTU	TURN TO THE LEFT
EEFHLOOPRSTTW	SWEPT THE FLOOR
EEFHMNOORSSUU	SENSE OF HUMOUR
EEFHMOORSTTTU	FROM THE OUTSET
EEFHMOPRRSTTU	THREE OF TRUMPS
EEFHNNORRTTUU	FORTUNE HUNTER
EEFHNOORRSTUU	FOURTEEN HOURS
EEFHNORRSTTUV	VENTURES FORTH
EEFIIIILLMMTV	FIVE-MILE LIMIT
EEFIIIPRSSTTV	FESTIVE SPIRIT
EEFIIKLMORSTW	LIFETIMES WORK
EEFIILLRSSTTY	SELF-STERILITY
EEFIIMNOORSTY	IN TIMES OF YORE
EEFIINOQRSSTU	FIRE QUESTIONS
EEFILLLLMNTUY	MELLIFLUENTLY
EEFILLNNPSSTU	PLENTIFULNESS
EEFILLNOOPSSS	SPOILS ONESELF
EEFILLNOORRRT	FELL INTO ERROR
EEFILMNNOOOTT	FELT NO EMOTION
EEFILNOOPSTTU	STEP OUT OF LINE
EEFILNRSSSSTU	FRUITLESSNESS
EEFILOPRSSTUY	PESTIFEROUSLY
EEFILORRSTTUY	TRUE-LIFE STORY
EEFIMOPPRRSTU	TIME FOR SUPPER
EEFIMOPRRSTUU	FURIOUS TEMPER
EEFIMORSSSSTT	TIMES OF STRESS
EEFINOORSTTTU	OUT OF INTEREST
EEFKOORRSSTUW	REFUSES TO WORK
EEFLLLNOOOSTT	FELL TO ONE'S LOT
EEFLLLNOPPSUU	PULL ONESELF UP
EEFLMNNOOPTYY	PLENTY OF MONEY
EEFLNNOOSSSTU	FOULS ONE'S NEST
EEFLNOOPSTTUU	PUT ONESELF OUT
EEFLOPPRSSUUU	USEFUL PURPOSE
EEFMNOOORSTVW	VOTES FOR WOMEN
EEFMNOPQRSTU	QUEEN OF TRUMPS
EEFMNOPRSSTUV	SEVEN OF TRUMPS
EEFMNOPRSTTTU	TEMPTS FORTUNE
EEGGGGHILOSTT	GOT THE GIGGLES
EEGGGHINOORTT	GOING TOGETHER
EEGGHHHLOOOTW	GO THE WHOLE HOG
EEGGHHINORSTU	SEEING THROUGH
EEGGHHNNOOSUU	ENOUGHS ENOUGH
EEGGHHIINNNOST	SEEING NOTHING
EEGGHIINNTTUV	GIVEN IT THE GUN
EEGGHIINORTVW	OVERWEIGHTING
EEGGHIINPPTTT	GETTING THE PIP
EEGGHIINSTTUV	GIVES IT THE GUN
EEGGHILNOPRSU	SLEEPING ROUGH
EEGGHINNNRSTT	STRENGTHENING
EEGGHIOORTTTT	GOT IT TOGETHER
EEGGHNOOORTTT	GOT ON TOGETHER
EEGGIIILLNNNTT	GETTING IN LINE
EEGGIIKMNNOPV	KEEPING MOVING
EEGGIIKNNPRTY	KEEPING TRYING
EEGGIIMNNPRST	SPRING MEETING
EEGGIJKOPRRYY	JIGGERY-POKERY
EEGGILLNNOTTW	GETTING ON WELL
EEGGILOPRSTTT	LESTER PIGGOTT
EEGGINOOPPSST	GOOSE-STEPPING
EEGGINORRRSST	RETROGRESSING
EEGHHHIJLTTUY	JULY THE EIGHTH
EEGHHHINOORSS	ONES HIGH HORSE
EEGHHIILNNRSTT	THE RIGHT LINES
EEGHHIILOPSVX	HIGH EXPLOSIVE
EEGHHIINQTTTU	QUITE THE THING
EEGHHILNOSTTV	LIGHTS THE OVEN
EEGHHILOSTTTV	LIGHT THE STOVE
EEGHHINNOPSTU	USING THE PHONE
EEGHHINORSTTU	SEEN IT THROUGH
EEGHHIORSSTTU	SEES IT THROUGH
EEGHHIORSSTTV	GOT THE SHIVERS
EEGHHNOORRSTW	THE WRONG HORSE
EEGHHOPRSSTUW	SWEEPS THROUGH
EEGHHOSSTTTUW	SWEET THOUGHTS
EEGHIIIMNRRST	IRISH REGIMENT
EEGHIIKLMNOST	SOMETHING LIKE
EEGHIIKNPPTUW	KEEPING UP WITH
EEGHIILLLNPRW	WILLING HELPER
EEGHIILLNOTTU	THE GUILLOTINE
EEGHIILLOSTTW	GOT THE WILLIES
EEGHIILNNNOST	SIGN ON THE LINE
EEGHIILNNNPSW	SPINNING WHEEL
EEGHIILNNOTVW	IN THE LONG VIEW
EEGHIIMNNOOTY	INHOMOGENEITY
EEGHIINNNRSTW	RINGS IN THE NEW
EEGHIIORTTTVW	GET IT OVER WITH
EEGHIIPRRSSST	SHIPS REGISTER
EEGHIJORSTTTT	GOT THE JITTERS
EEGHIKLNNOPSS	ENGLISH SPOKEN
	SPOKEN ENGLISH
EEGHIKNNRTTUY	TURNING THE KEY
EEGHIKNOOSSTT	SKEET SHOOTING
EEGHIKNORSTVW	GIVEN THE WORKS
EEGHIKNPSSSTU	SPIKES THE GUNS
EEGHILLNNOSSS	ENGLISH LESSON
EEGHILLOPRRTT	PETROL LIGHTER
EEGHILMNNORTT	IN THE LONG TERM
EEGHILNOOSSST	LOSE ONES SIGHT
EEGHILNOOSTTV	LOSING THE VOTE
EEGHILNRSSSTT	RESTLESS NIGHT
EEGHILNSSSSST	SIGHTLESSNESS
EEGHILOOPRSTT	HERPETOLOGIST
EEGHIMNNOOOSU	INHOMOGENEOUS
EEGHIMNNORRTU	RETURNING HOME
EEGHIMNOOPRSS	MORPHOGENESIS
EEGHIMNOPSTTU	SETTING UP HOME
EEGHIMNORSTTT	THERMOSETTING
EEGHIMNPSTTTU	SETTING THEM UP
EEGHIMOOOSTTV	GO TO THE MOVIES

EEGHINNOSSTTW	SWEET NOTHINGS	EEHIILNRSSTVW	WINS THE SILVER
EEGHINNOSTTUV	EVEN THINGS OUT	EEHIIMOOPSSTV	PHOTOEMISSIVE
EEGHINOOPTTTT	GET TO THE POINT	EEHIINNPRSTTW	TIPS THE WINNER
EEGHINOPPPRSS	SHOPPING SPREE	EEHIINOPSSTYZ	HYPOSENSITIZE
EEGHINORSSSTU	RIGHTEOUSNESS	EEHIKLLOORTTT	TOOK THE TILLER
EEGHINOSSSSTT	SET ONES SIGHTS	EEHIKORRSSTWY	WEST YORKSHIRE
EEGHIOORRRTUX	ROUGH EXTERIOR	EEHILLOORSSTT	TORTOISESHELL
EEGHIOORSSTYZ	HETEROZYGOSIS	EEHILMOOPRSTT	THE METROPOLIS
EEGHIOPRTTTTU	PUT IT TOGETHER	EEHILNNOSTTTX	NEXT ON THE LIST
EEGHJMMOORSTY	JOGS THE MEMORY	EEHILNOOPRSSW	SOLE OWNERSHIP
EEGHKLNOOPTTU	TOOK THE PLUNGE	EEHILNOORSSST	LOSE ONES SHIRT
EEGHLMNNOOOPY	PHENOMENOLOGY	EEHILNOOSTTTU	OUT ON THE TILES
EEGHLMNOOOSUY	HOMOGENEOUSLY	EEHILOPSSSTTX	THE SEX PISTOLS
EEGHMNNOOOOTT	GONE TO THE MOON	EEHILOPSSTTTV	SPLITS THE VOTE
EEGHMNOOOOSTT	GOES TO THE MOON	EEHIMNOPTTTUU	UP TO THE MINUTE
EEGIIINNOSSSV	SEEING VISIONS		UP-TO-THE-MINUTE
EEGIIKLNNOSST	SKELETONISING	EEHIMORRSTTVW	SHORT-TERM VIEW
EEGIIKLNNOSTZ	SKELETONIZING	EEHINNOOPPSSS	PINS ONE'S HOPES
EEGIIKLNNSTWY	TWINKLING EYES	EEHINNOOPRSTTW	THE TWO RONNIES
EEGIILLLNNOST	TELLING NO LIES	EEHINNOSSTTTU	INTO THE SUNSET
EEGIILLLNNTTY	INTELLIGENTLY	EEHINOOPRSTTT	RISEN TO THE TOP
EEGIILLNOPWWW	WEEPING WILLOW	EEHIOOPRSSTTT	RISES TO THE TOP
EEGIILNNRSTTY	INTERESTINGLY	EEHKNNOOOORSTT	ON TENTERHOOKS
EEGIILNORSSSU	RELIGIOUSNESS	EEHLLOOPSTTWY	POTS THE YELLOW
EEGIIMMMNSTTU	SUMMIT MEETING	EEHLNORRSTTWY	NORTHWESTERLY
EEGIIMNOPRRTU	PRIMOGENITURE	EEHLNORSSSSTW	WORTHLESSNESS
EEGIIMNOPRSTX	EXTEMPORISING	EEHLORSSTTUWY	SOUTHWESTERLY
EEGIIMNOPRTXZ	EXTEMPORIZING	EEHMMNOOTTUVY	YOUTH MOVEMENT
EEGIINNNRSTTU	UNINTERESTING	EEHMMNOOOPSTU	OPEN ONES MOUTH
EEGIINNORRTVW	OVERWINTERING	EEHMMNOOOTTTW	WENT TO THE MOON
EEGIINNPRRSST	INTERSPERSING	EEHMNOOOSSSTT	TOOTHSOMENESS
EEGIKMNOOPSSU	GOES UP IN SMOKE	EEHMNOPPTTUUY	PUT UP THE MONEY
EEGIKNNOPSSSU	SPIKE ONES GUNS	EEHMNOPRRSTTU	THREE NO-TRUMPS
EEGIKNOOPRUWY	KEEP YOUR WIG ON!	EEHMOORSTTTUX	SMOOTH TEXTURE
EEGILLNNNRTUY	UNRELENTINGLY	EEHNOOPRSSTTT	SERPENTS TOOTH
EEGILLNOOSSST	SELENOLOGISTS	EEHNORSSTTTWW	WEST-NORTHWEST
EEGILLNOPRRRS	SPELLING ERROR	EEHOOPSTTTTUV	PUTS TO THE VOTE
EEGILLOOPSSST	SPELEOLOGISTS	EEHOORRSSTTTU	SHORTEST ROUTE
EEGILMNNPPSTU	SUPPLEMENTING	EEHOPSSTTTTTU	PUTS TO THE TEST
EEGILMOOORSTT	METEOROLOGIST	EEHOSSSTTTUWW	WEST-SOUTHWEST
EEGILNNRSSTUW	SWELTERING SUN	EEIIILNNSSTVY	INSENSITIVELY
EEGILNOPRSTTU	TRIPLE-TONGUES	EEIIIMMNPRRST	PRIME MINISTER
EEGIMMNNORSTV	MISGOVERNMENT	EEIIIMNPRSSTV	PRIMITIVENESS
EEGIMMNOOPRRT	OTTO PREMINGER	EEIIIMOPPRRST	IMPROPRIETIES
EEGINNNOSSSUU	INGENUOUSNESS	EEIIINOPPRRST	PIONEER SPIRIT
EEGINNOPPSSTT	STEPPING STONE	EEIIKLMORSSTX	SIX KILOMETRES
	STEPPING-STONE	EEIILLMNSSSST	LIMITLESSNESS
EEGINNOPRSTTV	SPORTING EVENT	EEIILMNNPRTTY	IMPERTINENTLY
EEGINOORRRSST	RETROGRESSION	EEIILMNNTTTUX	UNTIL NEXT TIME
EEGINOPPRSSSS	PREPOSSESSING	EEIILMNPSSSUV	IMPULSIVENESS
EEGINORRSSTUY	YOUNGER SISTER	EEIILMOOSSTTY	OSTEOMYELITIS
EEGINORSTTTUW	TONGUE TWISTER	EEIILNOORSTUV	REVOLUTIONISE
EEGJMMNOOORSY	JOG ONES MEMORY	EEIILNOORTUVZ	REVOLUTIONIZE
EEGLLLNOOOSVW	WOOLLEN GLOVES	EEIILNOPRTVVY	LIVE IN POVERTY
EEGLMNOOOPRSU	PROLEGOMENOUS	EEIILOPPRSTVY	PREPOSITIVELY
EEGLNPRRSSUUY	SURPLUS ENERGY	EEIILOPRSTTUY	REPETITIOUSLY
EEGNNOOOPSSTU	GOT UP ONE'S NOSE	EEIILPPRRTUZZ	PULITZER PRIZE
EEGOPPRRRSSUU	PRESSURE GROUP	EEIIMMNNSTTUY	NINETY MINUTES
EEHHHINRSTTXY	HENRY THE SIXTH	EEIIMNOPRRRTT	INTERIM REPORT
EEHHHLORTTTUW	THE WHOLE TRUTH	EEIIMNOPRSSSU	IMPERIOUSNESS
EEHHIINNNSSTU	IN THE SUNSHINE	EEIIMNOPSSSSX	EXPRESSIONISM
EEHHIINNOOPTW	WINNIE THE POOH	EEIIMNPRRSSTT	MISINTERPRETS
EEHHIIORSSTWW	WISH OTHERWISE	EEIIMNPRRTTTW	WRITTEN PERMIT
EEHHIKORRSTTU	STRIKE THE HOUR	EEIINNOOPPRTX	EXPERT OPINION
EEHHINNORRSTTU	THIRTEEN HOURS	EEIINNOPPRRST	INTERSPERSION
EEHHKLOORSTWW	THE WHOLE WORKS	EEIINOPRSSSTX	EXPRESSIONIST
EEHHKOPRSTTTU	SPOKE THE TRUTH	EEIINOPRTTTUX	EXPERT TUITION
EEHHLNOOSSTTW	STOLEN THE SHOW	EEIIOOPSSSTVW	OPPOSITE VIEWS
EEHHOOPRSSSTW	SHOWS THE ROPES	EEIKLMOORSTTW	TWO KILOMETRES
EEHIIILLLOTTVW	THE WILL TO LIVE	EEIKMNNOORSSY	RISK ONES MONEY
EEHIIILLMMNNTU	THE MILLENNIUM	EEIKMNNOPSTUW	WENT UP IN SMOKE

EEIKOPRRRSSTW	WORKER-PRIESTS
EEIKORRRRSSTT	STRIKES TERROR
EEILLMOPRSTTU	MULTIPLE STORE
EEILLNOOSSWYY	LINSEY-WOOLSEY
EEILLOPPPRSSY	SLIPPERY SLOPE
EEILMMNNOOPRSS	SOLEMN PROMISE
EEILMPPRSTUVY	PRESUMPTIVELY
EEILNNOORSTUW	NEW RESOLUTION
EEILNNOPSSSSST	POINTLESSNESS
EEILNNOSSTTUY	SENTENTIOUSLY
EEILNOPPRSSSU	PURSE ONES LIPS
EEILNOPRSSTTT	SILENT PROTEST
EEILNOPRSTTUY	PRETENTIOUSLY
EEILPPRSSSUVY	SUPPRESSIVELY
EEIMMOPPRSSTY	EMPTY PROMISES
EEIMNNNOPRSSY	MONEY-SPINNERS
EEIMNNSTTTUWY	TWENTY MINUTES
EEIMNOORRSSSW	WORRISOMENESS
EEIMNOPSSSTUU	IMPETUOUSNESS
EEIMRRRSTTWYY	MYSTERY WRITER
EEINNOORRSTVW	IT'S NOW OR NEVER
EEINNOPRSSSUU	PENURIOUSNESS
EEINNOPRSTTUU	UNPRETENTIOUS
EEINOOPPRSSSS	PREPOSSESSION
EEINOOPPRSSSU	SERIOUS PERSON
EEINOORRRSSTV	RETROVERSIONS
EEINOPPRSSSUV	PURPOSIVENESS
EEINOPRRRRRST	PRINTERS ERROR
EEINOPRRTTTWY	WRITTEN POETRY
EEINOPRSSSSTU	PRESS ONES SUIT
EEINOPSSSSTTY	PETTY SESSIONS
EEINRRSSSTTUV	SERVES ITS TURN
EEJMMNNOOSTTU	JUST ONE MOMENT
EEJNNORRRTUUY	RETURN JOURNEY
EEKLLNOOOOSSS	LOSE ONES LOOKS
EEKLMNOOPSSUV	SPOKEN VOLUMES
EEKLMNOPSUYZZ	MONKEY-PUZZLES
EEKNNOOPSSSSTU	OUTSPOKENNESS
EEKNOOPPRSSSS	SPOKESPERSONS
EELLNOOPPPRYY	POLYPROPYLENE
EELMNNOOOSSTY	LOST ONE'S MONEY
EELMNORSSSTUU	TREMULOUSNESS
EELMOPSSTTUUY	TEMPESTUOUSLY
EELNOQRSSSUUU	QUERULOUSNESS
EEMMNNOOSSSTU	MOMENTOUSNESS
EEMNNOPRSSTUV	SEVEN NO-TRUMPS
EEMNORSSSTUVY	NERVOUS SYSTEM
EEMOOOOPPRSSTU	TO SOME PURPOSE
EENNOOPPRSSTU	OPPORTUNENESS
EENNORSSSSTUU	STRENUOUSNESS
EENNORSSSTUUV	VENTUROUSNESS
EENOOPPRRRTWY	PROPERTY OWNER
EENOPPRRSSTUU	PUT ON PRESSURE
EENOPPRSSSSTW	STOP-PRESS NEWS
EEOOPRRRSSSWX	EXPRESS SORROW
EFFGGGIINORRT	TRIGGERING OFF
EFFGGHHHHIOOT	HIGH OFF THE HOG
EFFGGHILLOTTY	GET OFF LIGHTLY
EFFGGILNNORSU	LONG-SUFFERING
EFFGHHILLOOTY	HEIGHT OF FOLLY
EFFGHIILLMOTY	LIGHT OF MY LIFE
EFFGHIILMNNSU	ENGLISH MUFFIN
EFFGHIILMRTTU	FRIGHTFUL TIME
EFFGHILOPSSTT	FLIGHT OF STEPS
EFFGHIOOTTUWY	GET OFF WITH YOU
EFFGIINNNOOPS	PENSIONING OFF
EFFGILNORSSU	SUFFERING LOSS
EFFGKOOOORTWW	OFF TO WORK WE GO
EFFHIIINRSSST	FINISHES FIRST
EFFHJLLOTTUWY	TWELFTH OF JULY
EFFHLOOORTUWY	FLOWER OF YOUTH

EFFIILOORSSSU	FOSSILIFEROUS
EFFIILPPPRSTU	STIFF UPPER LIP
EFFILLMOOPRSU	FULL OF PROMISE
EFFKNNOOSSTUW	KNOW ONES STUFF
EFGGHIIILNTTW	WEIGHT-LIFTING
EFGGHIIINPRTZ	PRIZEFIGHTING
EFGGHIILNNRTY	FRIGHTENINGLY
EFGGHILNORSTU	EIGHT FURLONGS
EFGGHIOOSTTTU	GET OUT OF SIGHT
EFGHHIIMNORTU	UNIFORM HEIGHT
EFGHHIINRSTTT	THE FIRST THING
EFGHHILNOOTTU	LINE OF THOUGHT
EFGHHILOOSTTT	THE FOOTLIGHTS
EFGHHILORRTTU	FILTER THROUGH
EFGHHLLOOTTUW	WELL THOUGHT OF
	WELL-THOUGHT-OF
EFGHIIILLNSSV	FIVE SHILLINGS
EFGHIILNORSTT	FORTNIGHTLIES
EFGHIIMNORTUW	UNIFORM WEIGHT
EFGHILLOPRTUW	UPRIGHT FELLOW
EFGHILMNNORTU	UNIFORM LENGTH
EFGHILNORRTUW	RIGHTFUL OWNER
EFGHIMMNOORRT	THERMOFORMING
EFGHIMOOPRRTT	FIGHT PROMOTER
EFGHIMOPRSTTU	EIGHT OF TRUMPS
EFGHINOORRRTT	NIGHT OF TERROR
EFGHNOOORSTUU	GUEST OF HONOUR
EFGIIIILLMNNT	FILLING IN TIME
EFGIILNORRRRT	TRIFLING ERROR
EFGIIMNNOOOST	SIGN OF EMOTION
EFGIINORRSTYZ	TRYING FOR SIZE
EFGINNOOOSTTT	SETTING ON FOOT
EFGKLOOOOPRST	TOOK FOR GOSPEL
EFGNNOOOORSTT	SOON FORGOTTEN
EFHHJLORTTUUY	JULY THE FOURTH
EFHHLOOPRSSTU	SHOUTS FOR HELP
EFHIIJNNNOSTU	JOINS IN THE FUN
EFHIIKLLNOTTT	THINK LITTLE OF
EFHIILORSSTTW	WHISTLES FOR IT
EFHIIINNORSTTT	SIT IN THE FRONT
EFHIKNOOOSSST	SHOOK ONE'S FIST
EFHILLOORSTTT	LITTLE SHORT OF
EFHILLOORTTTW	OF LITTLE WORTH
EFHILNOOOPRSS	FOOLISH PERSON
EFHILNOOORSTT	SIT ON THE FLOOR
EFHIMNOOPRTTU	NOTE OF TRIUMPH
EFHIOOPPRRSSS	PROFESSORSHIP
EFHMMNOORTTTU	MOMENT OF TRUTH
EFHNOOOOPRSTT	ON THE ROOF-TOPS
EFIIMMOPRRTV	PRIMITIVE FORM
EFIIINPRRSTWZ	WIN FIRST PRIZE
EFIILLNOOPRSU	POLLINIFEROUS
EFIINOPRRSTWZ	WON FIRST PRIZE
EFIIOOOPPRSTV	POSITIVE PROOF
	PROOF POSITIVE
EFIKLLMNORTUY	MULL OF KINTYRE
EFIKNNOOOSSTU	OUT OF ONE'S SKIN
EFILLLLMOSUUY	MELLIFLUOUSLY
EFILLNNOOOSWW	WILL OF ONES OWN
EFILLOOPRRSUY	PROLIFEROUSLY
EFILMNOOOSTUV	MOUNT OF OLIVES
EFILMNOORSSUY	SOMNIFEROUSLY
EFILNNOOOORTUY	NOT ON YOUR LIFE
EFILNNORRSSTU	LIST OF RUNNERS
EFILNOOORSSTU	STOLONIFEROUS
EFILNOORSSSUV	FRIVOLOUSNESS
EFINOOOSSTTUW	OUT OF ONE'S WITS
EFKLOOORTTUUU	FUTURE OUTLOOK
EFLNOORRSSSUW	SORROWFULNESS
EFMNNOOOORTUUY	RUN OUT OF MONEY
EGGGHHHILNOOTT	HOGGING THE LOT

EGGGHIIINNNSTV	GIVING THE SIGN
EGGGHIINRSSTU	GUESSING RIGHT
EGGGINNORSSUW	GUESSING WRONG
EGGHHIIMNPTUV	GIVING THE HUMP
EGGHHIINPSTUV	GIVING THE PUSH
EGGHHILNOSTTU	SINGLE THOUGHT
EGGHIIIKLLNNT	LIKE LIGHTNING
EGGHIIILMNOTT	GOING THE LIMIT
EGGHIIILMNTTT	LIGHT-EMITTING
EGGHIIILNPSTV	GIVING THE SLIP
EGGHIIINNSTUX	EXTINGUISHING
EGGHIIINTTTTW	GETTING WITH IT
EGGHIILMNNOTV	LIGHTNING MOVE
EGGHIJMNNPTUU	JUMPING THE GUN
EGGHLMOOOOPRY	GEOMORPHOLOGY
EGGIIILMNNNRT	INTERMINGLING
EGGIIINNNNSTU	SINGING IN TUNE
EGGIIKLLNNOOR	LINGERING LOOK
EGGIIKMNOPSUV	GIVE UP SMOKING
EGGIIKNNOORST	GOING ON STRIKE
EGGIILMNOOSTY	ETYMOLOGISING
EGGIILMNOOTYZ	ETYMOLOGIZING
EGGIILNNOSSSV	GIVING LESSONS
EGGIILNOORRSU	GLORIOUS REIGN
EGGIINNNOPPRS	SPRINGING OPEN
EGGIINNOOOPTT	GOING ON TIPTOE
EGGIINNOPRRSV	SPRINGING OVER
EGGIKNNOOTTTW	GETTING TO KNOW
EGGILNOOORSTT	GERONTOLOGIST
EGGILNOOPRRTW	GLOWING REPORT
EGHHHIIINORSTU	THE HOUR IS NIGH
EGHHHOPRSSTUU	PUSHES THROUGH
EGHHHORRSSTUU	RUSHES THROUGH
EGHHIINOPPRSW	HORSEWHIPPING
EGHHIINOPSSTY	HYPOTHESISING
EGHHIINOPSTYZ	HYPOTHESIZING
EGHHILNOPTTTU	PUT ON THE LIGHT
EGHHINOPRTTUU	PURE IN THOUGHT
EGHHINORSSTTT	SHORTEST NIGHT
EGHHIOORTTTUV	THOUGHT IT OVER
EGHHLLOSSTTUY	THOUGHTLESSLY
EGHHLNNORTTUU	TUNNEL THROUGH
EGHIIIKLNNOTT	NOTHING LIKE IT
EGHIIIKNNRSST	KISS IN THE RING
EGHIIIKNNRTTW	TINKERING WITH
EGHIIILLPSTTT	THIS LITTLE PIG
EGHIIILNNQRSU	RELINQUISHING
EGHIIIMNOPRSV	IMPOVERISHING
EGHIIINRSTTTW	TIE WITH STRING
EGHIIKLNOORTW	WITHERING LOOK
EGHIILLNNORTT	ROTTING IN HELL
EGHIILLNPRSUV	SHRIVELLING UP
EGHIILLNPSSTT	LET THINGS SLIP
EGHIILLORRTVW	ORVILLE WRIGHT
EGHIILNNPSTUV	LIVEN THINGS UP
EGHIILNPRSSST	SPRIGHTLINESS
EGHIILNPRSSTT	LETS THINGS RIP
EGHIILNRSTTWW	WRESTLING WITH
EGHIIMNNOSSST	MISSES NOTHING
EGHIIMNOOPSSY	PHYSIOGNOMIES
EGHIIOORTTTVW	GOT IT OVER WITH
EGHIKLNNOOOSS	SLING ONE'S HOOK
EGHILMNNOOSST	MOONLESS NIGHT
EGHILNNOOOSTT	NOTHING TO LOSE
EGHILNOOSSSTT	LOSING THE TOSS
	LOST ONE'S SIGHT
EGHILNORRSTTW	STERLING WORTH
EGHILNPPSTTUU	PUTS THE PLUG IN
EGHIMNOOORSTV	SMOOTHING OVER
EGHIMNOOPSTTU	UP TO SOMETHING
EGHINNNOOTTTX	NEXT TO NOTHING
EGHINNOPRSTTU	THRUSTING OPEN
EGHINOOOSTTVW	GIVEN TWO HOOTS
EGHINOOPRSSTU	SPORTING HOUSE
EGHINOOPSSTTT	PHOTOSETTINGS
EGHINOPPRRSTU	UPRIGHT PERSON
EGHINOPPSSTTU	SETTING UP SHOP
EGHIOOOSSTTVW	GIVES TWO HOOTS
EGHKLNNOOOSSU	SLUNG ONE'S HOOK
EGHKLNOOPRSUY	ROUGHLY SPOKEN
EGHKMOPRSTUUW	GUM UP THE WORKS
EGIIIILNORRST	IRRELIGIONIST
EGIIILLNNSTVY	LIVING IN STYLE
EGIIIILLORRSUY	IRRELIGIOUSLY
EGIIILNOSSSTU	LITIGIOUSNESS
EGIIIMNNRSSTT	STIRRING TIMES
EGIIJNNNNNPSY	SPINNING JENNY
EGIIKLLNORRWW	WILLING WORKER
EGIIKNNNORSTW	WINNING STROKE
EGIIKNOPPPRSS	SKIPPING ROPES
EGIILLMNOPRSW	PROMISING WELL
EGIILLNNNSSUW	UNWILLINGNESS
EGIILLNOPSTTU	SPELLING IT OUT
EGIILLNOSTUUW	GENIUS WILL OUT
EGIILMNNRTTUY	UNREMITTINGLY
EGIILMOOSSSST	SEISMOLOGISTS
EGIILNNOOSTTT	SETTING LOTION
EGIILNNOPPSTT	SPLITTING OPEN
EGIILNNOPSSTT	LISTENING POST
EGIILNOPRSSTY	PROSELYTISING
EGIILNOPRSTYZ	PROSELYTIZING
EGIILNORSTUVY	VERTIGINOUSLY
EGIILOPRSSTUY	PRESTIGIOUSLY
EGIIMNNNNOPSY	MONEY-SPINNING
EGIIMNNNRSTTU	INSTRUMENTING
EGIIMNNOPRSSS	MISSING PERSON
EGIIMNOOPRRST	PRIMOGENITORS
EGIIMNOORRSST	RISORGIMENTOS
EGIIMNOPPRSSU	SUPERIMPOSING
EGIIMOPRRSSSV	PROGRESSIVISM
EGIINNNNNORWW	WINNING RENOWN
EGIINNNOQSTUU	UNQUESTIONING
EGIINNOPRRRRT	PRINTING ERROR
EGIINNOSSSTUW	USING ONE'S WITS
EGIINNPPRRSST	PRINTING PRESS
EGIINNRRSSSTU	NURSING SISTER
EGIINOOPRRSTW	RISING TO POWER
EGIINOPRRTTWY	WRITING POETRY
EGIINOPRTTTUV	PUTTING IT OVER
EGIINPRSTTTTY	SITTING PRETTY
EGIIOPRRSSSTV	PROGRESSIVIST
EGIKLNOORRTUW	WORKING TO RULE
EGIKNOOORSTTU	GO OUT ON STRIKE
EGIKNOORSTTTW	SETTING TO WORK
EGILLNNOORSST	ROLLING STONES
EGILLNNORTUWY	TURNING YELLOW
EGILNNOSSSTUU	GLUTINOUSNESS
EGILNNPRRTUUU	TURNING PURPLE
EGILNNRRTTTUU	TURNING TURTLE
EGILNOPPRRSTU	SPLINTER GROUP
EGIMMNORRSSTW	STRONG SWIMMER
EGIMMNOOORSTT	STRONG EMOTION
EGIMNNOORRSSU	ROUSING SERMON
EGIMNOOOPRSTT	GETS PROMOTION
EGINOPPRRSSST	SPORTING PRESS
EGKNOOOORTTUW	GONE OUT TO WORK
EGKOOOORSTTUW	GOES OUT TO WORK
EGMMNOOPRSSUY	GYMNOSPERMOUS
EGNOOPRRSSTTT	STRONG PROTEST
EHHIILOOPPSSS	PHILOSOPHISES
EHHIILOOPPSSZ	PHILOSOPHIZES
EHHIILOPPSSST	SPOILS THE SHIP

911

EHHIKNORSTTTW	THINK THE WORST
EHHIMNOOPRSTT	MOTHER SHIPTON
EHHIMPSSSTTTU	HITS THE STUMPS
EHHMNOOSSTTUU	SHUT ONE'S MOUTH
EHHNNOOOORSSSW	SHOW ONE'S HORNS
EHIIILLOSTTTW	TELL IT HOW IT IS
EHIIIMNNORTTY	IN THE MINORITY
EHIIKLQRSUUWY	LIQUEUR WHISKY
EHIILLMNPSSTU	PHILLUMENISTS
EHIILLNORSTUW	WILLIE RUSHTON
EHIILLOPSSTWW	WILL O' THE WISPS
	WILL-O'-THE-WISPS
EHIILNOOPSTTY	OPEN HOSTILITY
EHIIMNOOOOPSST	PHOTOEMISSION
EHIIMNRSTTTUY	THIRTY MINUTES
EHIINOOOOPPSTT	THE OPPOSITION
EHIINOOSSTTTU	SIT THIS ONE OUT
EHILMNOOOOPSTU	ENTOMOPHILOUS
EHILNNOOOOPSTW	WIN ON THE POOLS
EHILNOOPSSTTT	LOST IN THE POST
EHILNOORSSSTT	LOST ONE'S SHIRT
EHILNOORSSSTY	HISTORY LESSON
EHILNOPSSTTTU	PUTS ON THE LIST
EHILORRSSTUUY	SERIOUSLY HURT
EHIMMOOPRRSTT	THERMOTROPISM
EHIMNOPSSTTUY	MISSPENT YOUTH
EHINOPRSTTTUZ	PUTS ON THE RITZ
EHJKLNORSSTUW	WORTHLESS JUNK
EHLMNOOPRRTTY	MONTHLY REPORT
EHLMOOOOPPRSTY	PHOTOPOLYMERS
EHLNNOOOOPSTW	WON ON THE POOLS
EHMNOORSSSTUY	HONOURS SYSTEM
EHNNOOPRSSTTU	RUNS ON THE SPOT
EHNOOPPSSTTTU	PUTS ON THE SPOT
EHOORRRSSSTTU	SHORT TROUSERS
EIIIILNQSTUVY	INQUISITIVELY
EIIIINNSSTTVY	INSENSITIVITY
EIIILLMOOPSTY	POLIOMYELITIS
EIIIMMNOPRSSS	IMPRESSIONISM
EIIIMNNORSSST	INTERMISSIONS
EIIIMNOPRSSST	IMPRESSIONIST
EIIINNOOPRSTT	INTERPOSITION
EIIINOPPQRSTU	PROPINQUITIES
EIIINPPRSSTTU	PIN-STRIPE SUIT
EIIIPRRSSSTUV	SURPRISE VISIT
EIIJMMNNOTUYY	ENJOY IMMUNITY
EIIJNNORSSSUU	INJURIOUSNESS
EIIJNORRSSUUY	SERIOUS INJURY
EIIKNNOPSSTTU	TIES UP IN KNOTS
EIILLMNNOSUVY	VINYL EMULSION
EIILLNOQSSTUY	SILLY QUESTION
EIILMNOQRSTUV	VENTRILOQUISM
EIILMOORRSTUY	MERITORIOUSLY
EIILNOORSTTUV	REVOLUTIONIST
EIILNOQRSTTUV	VENTRILOQUIST
EIILOOPRSSSST	LEPTOSPIROSIS
EIILOPPSSTUVY	SUPPOSITIVELY
EIIMMNNOOOTTT	OMIT TO MENTION
EIIMMORRSSTUV	SUMMER VISITOR
EIIMNNNQQSUUU	QUINQUENNIUMS
EIIMNOORSSSTT	MONSTROSITIES
EIINOOPPRSSTU	SUPERPOSITION
EIINOOPPRSTTU	OPPORTUNITIES
EIINOPRSSSTTU	SUPERSTITIONS
EIIOOPPRSSSTU	SUPPOSITORIES
EIIOPRRSSTTUU	SURREPTITIOUS
EIIOPRSSSTTUU	SUPERSTITIOUS
EIJLNOOPPRSTU	JET PROPULSION
EIJOORSSSSTTU	JUST-SO STORIES
EIKLOOORSSTUY	TOOK SERIOUSLY
EIKNNOOOOPSTT	TOOK ONE'S POINT

EILLMNNNOPSTU	SIMPLON TUNNEL
EILLMOOOORTTT	TOO LITTLE ROOM
EILNNOOPPRTUY	INOPPORTUNELY
EILNORSSSUUUX	LUXURIOUSNESS
EIMNOORSSSSTY	STORMY SESSION
EIMNOSSTUUUVV	MOUNT VESUVIUS
EINNOPRSSSSUW	WINS ONE'S SPURS
EKLLNOOOOOSSST	LOST ONE'S LOOKS
EKNOOORTTTUWW	WENT OUT TO WORK
EMNNOORSSSSTU	MONSTROUSNESS
EMNOPSSSSTUUU	SUMPTUOUSNESS
FFGGHHIINOSTY	FIGHTING SHY OF
FFGGHIIINORTT	FIGHTING FOR IT
FFGGHILLOOTTY	GOT OFF LIGHTLY
FFGHIINNOORTT	FIT FOR NOTHING
FFGIINORRSTWY	WORRYING STIFF
FFHHIMNOPSTYY	FIFTH SYMPHONY
FGGHHIIINRSST	FISHING RIGHTS
FGGHIIINOTTTU	FIGHTING IT OUT
FGGHIIKLNNORT	FORK LIGHTNING
FGGHIILNOOSST	LOSING SIGHT OF
FGGHIINNORTTY	FRYING TONIGHT
FGGHIOOOSTTTU	GOT OUT OF SIGHT
FGGIINNORSTW	SWINGING FOR IT
FGGIIINORTTUU	FIGURING IT OUT
FGGIIJNNOORSY	SINGING FOR JOY
FGGINNNOOOSSW	ON WINGS OF SONG
FGHHIORSSTTTU	FIRST THOUGHTS
FGHHLLOOOORTUW	FOLLOW THROUGH
	FOLLOW-THROUGH
FGHHLOOOOSTTUW	SLOW OF THOUGHT
FGHIIILNOORSV	FOOLISH VIRGIN
FGHIIINNOPSST	FINISHING POST
FGHIIINORSTTX	HITTING FOR SIX
FGHIILLMNOOTT	MOONLIGHT FLIT
FGHIILLNORSSU	FOUR SHILLINGS
FGHIILLNOSTWW	WOLF-WHISTLING
FGIILLNOOSTUW	FOLLOWING SUIT
FGIJJMNOOPRUY	JUMPING FOR JOY
FGLMNNOOOOOSS	SONG OF SOLOMON
FHHIMOOPRRTUU	HOUR OF TRIUMPH
FHIIOOPRSTTUY	SPIRIT OF YOUTH
FHILLOORRSTTU	OUT FOR THRILLS
FHIMNOPRSSTYY	FIRST SYMPHONY
FHINNOOOOPRTU	POINT OF HONOUR
FHIOORRRTTTYY	THIRTY OR FORTY
FIILMOPRSSUUY	SIMPLY FURIOUS
FIINNOOOPPRTT	POINT FOR POINT
FIJNOOOPTTTUU	PUT OUT OF JOINT
FILLMRSSTTUUY	MISTRUSTFULLY
GGGHHINOOORTU	THOROUGHGOING
GGGHIINNOOOST	GOING SHOOTING
GGGHIINNOOPPS	GOING SHOPPING
GGGHILNNOORSW	HORNSWOGGLING
GGGIIMMNNNOSW	GOING SWIMMING
GGHHIIKNNNST	SHINING KNIGHT
GGHHIILNORTUV	LIVING THROUGH
GGHHIINSTTTTU	SHUTTING TIGHT
GGHIIIKLLNNSS	KINGS SHILLING
GGHIIILNPRSTT	STRIP LIGHTING
GGHIILMNOOSTY	MYTHOLOGISING
GGHIILMNOOTYZ	MYTHOLOGIZING
GGHIINNNOOSSW	SHOWING NO SIGN
GGHILNNOOPSUW	SNOWPLOUGHING
GGHINNNOOOOTT	NOTHING TO GO ON
GGIILNOPRTUVY	PROVING GUILTY
GGIINNOOOPRST	GOING TO PRISON
GGIINOPPRRSTY	GRIPPING STORY
GGIINOPPRSTUV	GIVING SUPPORT
GHHHIKNORSTTU	THINKS THROUGH
GHHHOOOORSSTTU	SHOOTS THROUGH

GHHIIIINPRSST	IN HIGH SPIRITS
GHHILNNOORTTW	THROWN LIGHT ON
GHHILNOORSTTW	THROWS LIGHT ON
GHHILNOOSTTTU	LOST IN THOUGHT
GHIIIKNNOTTTU	THINKING IT OUT
GHIIINOPRSSTW	SHOWING SPIRIT
GHIIINORSSTUV	VISITING HOURS
GHIIKNNOPRSUW	PUNISHING WORK
GHIILNOOOORSTT	ORNITHOLOGIST
GHIIMNNOOOORST	SMOOTHING IRON
GHIINNNOOTTTW	IN TOWN TONIGHT
GHIINNOOPSTWY	SHOWING NO PITY
GHIINNORSSTTW	WITH NO STRINGS
GHIINOOOSTTTU	SHOOTING IT OUT
GHIINPPTTTUUW	PUTTING UP WITH
GHIMNOOOORRTTW	TOMORROW NIGHT
GHINNOOPSTTUW	PUTTING ON SHOW
GHINOOPPRSSTT	STOPPING SHORT
GHINOORSSTTTU	SORT THINGS OUT
GIIIKLNNOOOTT	LOOKING INTO IT
GIIILLNOOOSUZ	SOLILOQUIZING
GIIILMNNOOSUY	IGNOMINIOUSLY
GIIILNOORSTUV	RIOTOUS LIVING
GIIINNPPROTTUW	PUTS IN WRITING
GIIINOPSTTTTU	SPITTING IT OUT
GIIKLLNOOPPSY	LOOKING SLIPPY
GIIKNNNNOORUW	UNKNOWN ORIGIN
GIIKNNOPRRSTW	PRINTING WORKS
GIILNOPTTUUZZ	PUZZLING IT OUT
GIINNOOOOPPRRT	PROPORTIONING
GIINNOOOOPRTTU	PORTIONING OUT
GIINNOPPRRSTT	SPORTING PRINT
GIINOORTTTTTU	TROTTING IT OUT
GIKNOOPRTTTUW	PUTTING TO WORK
GINOOPRTTTTUU	PUTTING TO ROUT
GKLLMOOOOOTUY	GLOOMY OUTLOOK
HHHIILMORTTWW	HOWL WITH MIRTH
HHIIOORTTTUWW	WITH OR WITHOUT
HHIMNNNOPSTYY	NINTH SYMPHONY
HHIMNOPSSTXYY	SIXTH SYMPHONY
HHMOORSTTUUUY	SHUT YOUR MOUTH!
HIILLMNOORSTW	WORTH MILLIONS
HIILLOOPPRSWW	WHIPPOORWILLS
HIINNOPRRSTTU	RUSH INTO PRINT
HILNOPPRSSTUY	IN SHORT SUPPLY
HILORRSTTTUWY	TRUSTWORTHILY
HINNOOOOPRSTUW	WIN TOP HONOURS
HINOOPRSSSSTY	SHORT SYNOPSIS
HLLNOOOOPPSUYY	POLYPHONOUSLY
HNNOOOOOPRSTUW	WON TOP HONOURS
HNORRSTTTUUWY	UNTRUSTWORTHY
IIIMNNOORSSST	INTROMISSIONS
IIKNNOORSTTTU	TOOK IT IN TURNS
IILLLORSSTUUY	ILLUSTRIOUSLY
IILLMNNOORSTU	RUN TO MILLIONS
IINNOOOPPSTTT	POINT-TO-POINTS

AAAAACEFKLNPST	FLAT AS A PANCAKE	AAAAEGGIKMNTWY	MAKING A GETAWAY
AAAAACGILMMNRT	ANAGRAMMATICAL	AAAAEGHLOPSSST	AS PALE AS A GHOST
AAAAACHKPRSSST	AS SHARP AS A TACK	AAAAEGIMMNRSST	ANAGRAMMATISES
AAAAADEHMRSSTT	AS MAD AS A HATTER	AAAAEGIMMNRSTZ	ANAGRAMMATIZES
AAAAAHKLPPRSSY	AS HAPPY AS A LARK	AAAAEILMNSSSSU	ASSUMES AN ALIAS
AAAAABBCEILRSTY	SABBATICAL YEAR	AAAAFGIKMNPSUX	MAKING A FAUX PAS
AAAAABBIIMNRSST	SABBATARIANISM	AAAAFIIMNRRSST	RASTAFARIANISM
AAAABCEEKKNSTT	TAKEN A BACK SEAT	AAAAGHIMNOPRST	PHANTASMAGORIA
AAAABCEEKKSSTT	TAKES A BACK SEAT	AAAAGIILMNPSTY	PLAY IT AGAIN,SAM
AAAABCEELLLRSS	AS CLEAR AS A BELL	AAAAGINNRSSTTT	STRAINS AT A GNAT
AAAABCEGIKNRST	ACTING AS A BRAKE	AAAAHLPPRRSSYY	AS HAPPY AS LARRY
AAAABDEEELSTTV	LEAVE A BAD TASTE	AAAAIILLNOPSTT	PALATALISATION
AAAABDEEGILNRS	SEALED A BARGAIN	AAAAIILLNOPTTZ	PALATALIZATION
AAAABDEKMRSSTT	MAKES A BAD START	AAABBCDIKNORRS	BARBARA DICKSON
AAAABDFHRSSSTU	AS DAFT AS A BRUSH	AAABBCEINOSSTT	SEBASTIAN CABOT
AAAABEILNORSSV	AS BRAVE AS A LION	AAABBCFHNNNOSU	BUNCH OF BANANAS
AAAABGGIIKMNNR	MAKING A BARGAIN	AAABBEEFKLRSTT	BREAKFAST TABLE
AAAACCDDELNSSU	CAUSED A SCANDAL	AAABBEEKLLMSTT	BASKETBALL TEAM
AAAACCDEELNRST	CREATE A SCANDAL	AAABBEGHIIKNRT	BREAKING A HABIT
AAAACCDELLLLMO	MADE A LOCAL CALL	AAABBEGLLNOORR	BARRAGE BALLOON
AAAACCDELNSSSU	CAUSES A SCANDAL	AAABCCCILMNOOY	CYANOCOBALAMIC
AAAACCEIKNOPSV	VAIN AS A PEACOCK	AAABCCDEGKLNRW	BACKWARD GLANCE
AAAACCEKLLLLMO	MAKE A LOCAL CALL	AAABCCEEGKMOST	STAGE A COMEBACK
AAAACCGHINNVVY	HAVING A VACANCY	AAABCCEEHKKORT	CHOKE BACK A TEAR
AAAACCHIMNRSST	ACTS AS CHAIRMAN	AAABCCEEKKMMOS	MAKES A COME-BACK
AAAACCHKLNNTTU	LAUNCH AN ATTACK	AAABCCEGIKMNOS	COMES BACK AGAIN
AAAACDEEHRSTTY	A DAY AT THE RACES	AAABCCEKLNRSTU	STRUCK A BALANCE
AAAACDEEILMNPT	A TIME AND A PLACE	AAABCCEKNORRTT	BREAK A CONTRACT
AAAACDEEKMNNSV	MAKES AN ADVANCE	AAABCCHIKLPSST	AS BLACK AS PITCH
AAAACDEENNRRTV	RENTED A CARAVAN	AAABCCILMNNOOY	CYANOCOBALAMIN
AAAACDEGHMMNRRT	ARRANGED A MATCH	AAABCDEEFLNORT	BALANCE OF TRADE
AAAACDGIILMMRT	DIAGRAMMATICAL	AAABCDEHILNRST	TABLE AND CHAIRS
AAAACDHILNORVY	CARAVAN HOLIDAY	AAABCDEKLNRSSW	LEANS BACKWARDS
AAAACEEELNPPRST	LAST APPEARANCE	AAABCDEKLNRSTW	LEANT BACKWARDS
AAAACEGHJLLMNS	JAMES CALLAGHAN	AAABCDELLMORSS	AS COLD AS MARBLE
AAAACEGHMNNRST	ARRANGES A MATCH	AAABCDIKNORSTW	BACKWARDATIONS
AAAACEGILLMMNO	MEGALOMANIACAL	AAABCDKKLRSSWW	WALKS BACKWARDS
AAAACFNOSSSTUY	AS FAST AS YOU CAN	AAABCEEEHMSSTY	AS THE CASE MAY BE
AAAACGNORRSTTU	ACT AS GUARANTOR	AAABCEEFGLLMOU	CAMOUFLAGEABLE
AAAADDDEEGMRSW	AWARDED DAMAGES	AAABCEEFHORSVW	SHOW A BRAVE FACE
AAAADDEHJMOORR	MAJOR ROAD AHEAD	AAABCEEGIMNPRR	PRE-CAMBRIAN AGE
AAAADDEHMNNSTT	ADAM AND THE ANTS	AAABCEEHKNOSTV	HAVE AT ONE'S BACK
AAAADEEGKNNTTV	TAKEN ADVANTAGE	AAABCEEIKLNRST	STRIKE A BALANCE
AAAADEEGKNSTTV	TAKES ADVANTAGE	AAABCEFGHLNRRT	FLAGRANT BREACH
AAAADEFGOOSSST	AS GOOD AS A FEAST	AAABCEHILLLPTY	ALPHABETICALLY
AAAADEFJLMMORR	JAR OF MARMALADE	AAABCEHILMRRTT	MICHAEL BARRATT
AAAADEGGINNRRT	ARRANGING A DATE	AAABCEHLNOPPRU	UNAPPROACHABLE
AAAADEGHMNNSSSU	SAUSAGE AND MASH	AAABCEILMNRRSU	ARABIC NUMERALS
AAAADEGIMMNRST	ANAGRAMMATISED	AAABCELLLMORST	BALMORAL CASTLE
AAAADEGIMMNRTZ	ANAGRAMMATIZED	AAABCELLORRSUU	CASUAL LABOURER
AAAADEHNORSSST	AS HARD AS A STONE	AAABCGHIKLNSST	AS BLACK AS NIGHT
AAAADEILMNSSSU	ASSUMED AN ALIAS	AAABCGIKNRRSTU	STRUCK A BARGAIN
AAAADELLLLNPRRW	DRAWN A PARALLEL	AAABCHILLMNNOR	ABRAHAM LINCOLN
AAAADELLLLPRRSW	DRAWS A PARALLEL	AAABCHLNOPPRUY	UNAPPROACHABLY
AAAADGILNRRSWY	DRAWING A SALARY	AAABCIILLOPRTY	PARABIOTICALLY
AAAADHJLLNTTZZ	AND ALL THAT JAZZ	AAABDDEEHLLOTW	DEAL A DEATH BLOW
AAAADILLNOPTTY	ADAPTATIONALLY	AAABDDEELLLLNN	BE-ALL AND END-ALL
AAAAEEEGKNNRTV	TAKEN AN AVERAGE	AAABDDEENRRRST	STANDARD BEARER
AAAAEEEGKNRSTV	TAKES AN AVERAGE		STANDARD-BEARER
AAAAEEEEHKNPRSS	SHAKESPEAREANA	AAABDDEHILNNSU	AN IDEAL HUSBAND
AAAAEEGLNNORTU	GUARANTEE A LOAN	AAABDDNNOORTUU	AROUND AND ABOUT
AAAAEEHIKNPRSS	SHAKESPEARIANA	AAABDEEEGLLSTV	VEGETABLE SALAD
AAAAEEKNORRSSZ	AS KEEN AS A RAZOR	AAABDEEEHORTVW	HEAD ABOVE WATER

AAABDEEEELMPSTX	SET A BAD EXAMPLE
AAABDEEFHLNPRS	PHRASE AND FABLE
AAABDEEGKOOPSS	BOOKED A PASSAGE
AAABDEEHLORRRV	HAD OVER A BARREL
AAABDEEMRSSSSS	AMBASSADRESSES
AAABDEGHHNRSTY	HANGS BY A THREAD
AAABDEGHIIMNTV	HAVING A BAD TIME
AAABDEGHILMPSS	MADE A BIG SPLASH
AAABDEGHMNNRSS	BANGERS AND MASH
AAABDEGIINRRRV	DRIVEN A BARGAIN
AAABDEGIINRRSV	DRIVES A BARGAIN
AAABDEHHNRRRST	SARAH BERNHARDT
AAABDEHLLNNOOP	ABANDON ALL HOPE
AAABDEILLMNOSS	AS BLIND AS A MOLE
AAABDEILLORTTU	READ ALL ABOUT IT
AAABDELLNOSSSU	AS SOUND AS A BELL
AAABDELNNORRWW	ANDREW BONAR LAW
AAABDGHIKNNSTU	TAKING A HUSBAND
AAABDHIMOPRSSS	AMBASSADORSHIP
AAABDIINORSSTT	BASTARDICATION
AAABDIINORSTTZ	BASTARDIZATION
AAABEEEENRRTTT	BEATEN A RETREAT
AAABEEEGHILNTZ	ELIZABETHAN AGE
AAABDEEEGHILNRTZ	ELIZABETHAN ERA
AAABEEEHIOTTTV	HAVE A BITE TO EAT
AAABEEEHKNRRTT	TAKEN A BREATHER
AAABEEEHKRRSTT	TAKES A BREATHER
AAABEEELPRSSTT	SEPARATE TABLES
AAABEEFFKHRSTT	AFTER BREAKFAST
AAABEEFKLRRSTY	EARLY BREAKFAST
AAABEEGGINRTTV	BATTING AVERAGE
AAABEEGIMRRRUU	MARRIAGE BUREAU
AAABEEHLORRRSV	HAS OVER A BARREL
AAABEEILNNSSTT	ATTAINABLENESS
AAABEGGHIINNRT	BREATHING AGAIN
AAABEGGIIKNNTT	TAKING A BEATING
AAABEGGIILNNPR	PLEA BARGAINING
AAABEGHIKLMPSS	MAKE A BIG SPLASH
AAABEGIIKNRRST	STRIKE A BARGAIN
AAABEGIILLNOUV	BOUGAINVILLAEA
AAABEGIILLSTVY	SALVAGEABILITY
AAABEGIILNTTTW	WAITING AT TABLE
AAABEGINOOTTTT	BEATING A TATTOO
AAABEIILLMNPRR	PRIMA BALLERINA
AAABEILNOOPSTT	PALAEOBOTANIST
AAABEILOORRRSU	AURORA BOREALIS
AAABELLMNORRUU	MANUAL LABOURER
AAABELLNNPRSTT	TRANSPLANTABLE
AAABGHLMOPRTUU	AUTOGRAPH ALBUM
AAABHLNORRRTUU	NATURAL HARBOUR
AAABIILLNPTTUY	UNPALATABILITY
AAACCCEEEFFMOT	CAME FACE TO FACE
AAACCCEEHKLMRT	CATCH A MACKEREL
AAACCCEEIMNNRT	AMERICAN ACCENT
AAACCCEEISSTUV	ACCUSATIVE CASE
AAACCCEHILRSTT	CATACHRESTICAL
AAACCCEHORRRTT	CHARACTER ACTOR
AAACCCEINNORTT	ANTARCTIC OCEAN
AAACCDDEEIIRSS	CARDIAC DISEASE
AAACCDDEGIMNNY	DANCING ACADEMY
AAACCDEEMRTUUV	CREATED A VACUUM
AAACCDEFHINNNR	FRENCH CANADIAN
AAACCDEFILLNVY	FILLED A VACANCY
AAACCDEGILNNRR	RACING CALENDAR
AAACCDEHHRRSTY	SHADY CHARACTER
AAACCDEKLNRTUW	CRACKED A WALNUT
AAACCDFFIORRTT	ROAD TRAFFIC ACT
AAACCDILORRSUV	CARDIOVASCULAR
AAACCDLMMNOOST	COASTAL COMMAND
AAACCDMMMMNOPT	CAMP COMMANDANT
AAACCEEEELLLLNV	CANCEL ALL LEAVE

AAACCEEILMNRRT	CENTRAL AMERICA
AAACCEEINNSSUU	CAUSE A NUISANCE
AAACCEEMRSTUUV	CREATES A VACUUM
AAACCEFHMNORRT	MAN OF CHARACTER
AAACCEGGILNNST	CASTING A GLANCE
AAACCEGHHILNTW	CATCHING A WHALE
AAACCEGHILLOOR	ARCHAEOLOGICAL
AAACCEGHILNNPT	CATCHING A PLANE
AAACCEHILMPRTU	PHARMACEUTICAL
AAACCEHLMORRRT	MORAL CHARACTER
AAACCEIILOPRTV	VICTORIA PALACE
AAACCEIKLMNRRS	ANIMAL CRACKERS
AAACCEILMNPTTY	MENTAL CAPACITY
AAACCEILNOPTTW	TACTICAL WEAPON
AAACCELLRRSSTY	CLEAR AS CRYSTAL
AAACCELNORSTYY	CYANOACRYLATES
AAACCGHHILPRTY	TACHYGRAPHICAL
AAACCGHIINNRTT	CATCHING A TRAIN
AAACCGHIKNSTTT	SCATHING ATTACK
AAACCGHILOPRRT	CARTOGRAPHICAL
AAACCGIIINNPTT	INCAPACITATING
AAACCGILLLLNRS	CALLING ALL CARS
AAACCHILLMORTY	ACHROMATICALLY
AAACCHLRSTTTUW	CLUTCH AT A STRAW
AAACCIIINNOPTT	INCAPACITATION
AAACCILLORTTUY	AUTOCRATICALLY
AAACCNNNOPRTUU	RAN UP AN ACCOUNT
AAACDDDEEEMNOT	CAME TO A DEAD END
AAACDDEEEELNNOS	LEADS ONE A DANCE
AAACDDEEGILMMS	CLAIMED DAMAGES
AAACDDEEGLRSTU	GRADUATED SCALE
AAACDDEGGKLNOR	CLOAK AND DAGGER
	CLOAK-AND-DAGGER
AAACDDEGINNORW	DOING A WAR-DANCE
AAACDDEHINNPRU	UNDER A HANDICAP
AAACDDFLLMNOOR	FLORA MACDONALD
AAACDEEEEHKLPR	KEEP A CLEAR HEAD
AAACDEEEGINNUV	GAVE AN AUDIENCE
AAACDEEEHKLPRT	KEPT A CLEAR HEAD
AAACDEEEKMRRTT	CREATED A MARKET
AAACDEEEKOSTTT	TOASTED TEA-CAKE
AAACDEEELNRRWX	CREWE ALEXANDRA
AAACDEEEMNNNRT	MADE AN ENTRANCE
AAACDEEFGOPRSS	FORCED A PASSAGE
AAACDEEGGHHINR	RAGING HEADACHE
AAACDEEGINRSTT	REACTED AGAINST
AAACDEEHILNNNR	CARDINAL HEENAN
AAACDEEKNOPSST	TOSSED A PANCAKE
AAACDEEKNPSTUY	PANCAKE TUESDAY
AAACDEELLMNOSW	MADE ALLOWANCES
AAACDEFHJKLOTY	DAY OF THE JACKAL
AAACDEGHIKLOPY	PACKAGE HOLIDAY
AAACDEGIIMNNTT	GAIN ADMITTANCE
AAACDEGIKMNNSV	MAKING ADVANCES
AAACDEGIMNNORU	CAME ROUND AGAIN
AAACDEGINNRSVY	ADVANCING YEARS
AAACDEHLLRSSTT	ALL THAT'S SACRED
AAACDEIIIMNNNR	AMERICAN INDIAN
AAACDEIJLLNNRU	JULIAN CALENDAR
AAACDEILMMNOPT	MADE A COMPLAINT
AAACDEKLLMNRTU	MADE A TRUNK CALL
AAACDFHIIILNRT	ARTIFICIAL HAND
AAACDGHINOSSTW	CASTING A SHADOW
AAACDHIINOPRSS	ANAPHRODISIACS
AAACDHILMRRTTY	ADMIRALTY CHART
AAACDHINNRSTTU	TRISTAN DA CUNHA
AAACDIIILNORST	RADICALISATION
AAACDIIILNORTZ	RADICALIZATION
AAACDIILNNOSST	SCANDALISATION
AAACDIILNNOSTZ	SCANDALIZATION
AAACDIILRTUVWY	RAILWAY VIADUCT

AAACEEEGKNRRTT	TAKEN GREAT CARE
AAACEEEGKRRSTT	TAKES GREAT CARE
AAACEEEHHLLSTV	HAVE ALL THE ACES
AAACEEEIMNPRST	REMAINS AT PEACE
AAACEEEKMNNNRT	MAKE AN ENTRANCE
AAACEEEKMRRSTT	CREATES A MARKET
AAACEEENOSSTTV	VACATE ONES SEAT
AAACEEFGOPRSSS	FORCES A PASSAGE
AAACEEFLNRRRUW	NUCLEAR WARFARE
AAACEEGGGILLNU	GAELIC LANGUAGE
AAACEEGGHLNSTU	TEACH LANGUAGES
AAACEEGGLNORSU	COARSE LANGUAGE
AAACEEGIINRRSV	AIRS A GRIEVANCE
AAACEEGINPPRRS	PREPARING A CASE
AAACEEGINSSSTV	GAVE ASSISTANCE
AAACEEGLLLNSTT	TELLS AT A GLANCE
AAACEEGNRSSSUV	GAVE ASSURANCES
AAACEEGOPPSSTU	CAUSE A STOPPAGE
AAACEEHIILNSTT	TEACHES ITALIAN
AAACEEHLNPRRST	CHARTERS A PLANE
AAACEEHMMNNRST	MERCHANT SEAMAN
AAACEEILLNORRS	ALSACE LORRAINE
AAACEEILNNNPSW	CLEAN AS A NEW PIN
AAACEEINORSTTV	EASTER VACATION
AAACEEINRSSTTV	SETS AT VARIANCE
AAACEEJLMPSSST	ST.JAMESS PALACE
AAACEEKLLMNOSW	MAKE ALLOWANCES
	MAKES ALLOWANCE
AAACEEKLNPRSTT	REPELS AN ATTACK
AAACEEKNOPSSST	TOSSES A PANCAKE
AAACEENOPRRRTU	CREATE AN UPROAR
AAACEFIIIKLLRT	ARTIFICIAL LAKE
AAACEGGHLMNPSS	CHAMPAGNE GLASS
AAACEGHHIIRSTT	AGATHA CHRISTIE
AAACEGHIKNNPTT	TAKEN A NIGHTCAP
AAACEGHIKNPSTT	TAKES A NIGHTCAP
AAACEGHILLMOOT	HAEMATOLOGICAL
AAACEGHILMNRST	STEALING A MARCH
AAACEGHNRSTUUW	CAUGHT UNAWARES
AAACEGIILMMPRT	EPIGRAMMATICAL
AAACEGILMNNORS	ANGLO-AMERICANS
AAACEGINSSTUWY	GIANTS CAUSEWAY
AAACEGRSSSTUUU	AUGUSTUS CAESAR
AAACEHHIKKLTWW	WATCH LIKE A HAWK
AAACEHHMMNORTT	MORE THAN A MATCH
AAACEHIILMRRSV	AIR VICE-MARSHAL
AAACEHILLMMTTY	MATHEMATICALLY
AAACEHILMOOPPR	PHARMACOPOEIAL
AAACEHLMNORSST	STEALS A MARCH ON
AAACEIILLLLMWW	WILLIAM WALLACE
AAACEIJMNSSTTY	SATANIC MAJESTY
AAACEIKLMMNOPT	MAKE A COMPLAINT
AAACEIKLMNOPSS	ASKS A POLICEMAN
AAACEILLMOPSTY	APOSEMATICALLY
AAACEILLMPRRTY	PARAMETRICALLY
AAACEILLMSTTTY	METASTATICALLY
AAACEILLNORTUY	AERONAUTICALLY
AAACEILMMNRSST	SACRAMENTALISM
AAACEILMNOPRRT	AMERICAN PATROL
AAACEILNORTTUY	CAUTIONARY TALE
AAACEKLNOPRSTT	PERSONAL ATTACK
AAACEKNNRSTTUY	TAKEN SANCTUARY
AAACEKNRSSTTUY	TAKES SANCTUARY
AAACELLLMOSSWW	SWALLOWS A CAMEL
AAACEMMNOPRTUY	AMATEUR COMPANY
AAACENNNOOOSSS	AS SOON AS ONE CAN
AAACFGILMNNOPP	PLAN OF CAMPAIGN
AAACFHLMOOPPRR	FORMAL APPROACH
AAACFIIINNORST	AFRICANISATION
AAACFIIINNORTZ	AFRICANIZATION
AAACFIILLSTTY	FATALISTICALLY
AAACFIILLOPTTY	CAPITAL OF ITALY
AAACFIILNOPPST	CAPITAL OF SPAIN
AAACFIILNSTTTY	FANTASTICALLY
AAACFIJNNOORST	SAINT JOAN OF ARC
AAACFILNOPRRTT	FRACTIONAL PART
AAACFIMMOPSTUX	COMMIT A FAUX PAS
AAACFLMNOOPSTY	FLOATS A COMPANY
AAACGGHHIILOPR	HAGIOGRAPHICAL
AAACGHHIINRTUV	HAVING A HAIRCUT
AAACGHILLLNOTT	CALLING TO A HALT
AAACGHILNOPRRU	URANOGRAPHICAL
AAACGHIMNOPRST	PHANTASMAGORIC
AAACGIILLMSTTY	ASTIGMATICALLY
AAACGIILMMRTTY	GRAMMATICALITY
AAACGILLMNORTY	MORGANATICALLY
AAACGILNNOSTTU	ANTICOAGULANTS
AAACHIIKNSSSTT	AS THIN AS A STICK
AAACHILLLLOPTY	ALLOPATHICALLY
AAACHILMMNNOPY	NYMPHOMANIACAL
AAACIILNOPPSTT	CAPITALISATION
AAACIIILNOPTTZ	CAPITALIZATION
AAACIILLLMNSTY	TALISMANICALLY
AAACIILLMNNOPT	NOMINAL CAPITAL
AAACIILLNNRRTY	INTRACRANIALLY
AAACIILNOSSTTU	ACTUALISATIONS
AAACIILNOSTTUZ	ACTUALIZATIONS
AAACIIMNNORTTT	MAIN ATTRACTION
AAACILMNOPRWYY	RAILWAY COMPANY
AAACINORRSTTTT	STAR ATTRACTION
AAADDDEEHLMNNS	DEAD MANS HANDLE
AAADDDEEMNNRSS	NAME AND ADDRESS
AAADDDEEENNRRTV	RANTED AND RAVED
AAADDDEHNNNOST	DONE A HANDSTAND
AAADDDEHNNNOSST	DOES A HANDSTAND
AAADDDIINSSTVY	SAINT DAVIDS DAY
AAADDDINNOTUYY	DAY IN AND DAY OUT
AAADDEEEFNRRTU	TURNED A DEAF EAR
AAADDEEFNORRVY	FOR EVER AND A DAY
	FOREVER AND A DAY
AAADDEEGHIKNTW	AWAKING THE DEAD
AAADDEEGHIMNNR	DEMAND A HEARING
AAADDEEGHRSSUZ	HAZARDED A GUESS
AAADDEEGIKMNST	MAKING A DEAD SET
AAADDEEGLLNOPP	LODGED AN APPEAL
AAADDEELMNRSUX	ALEXANDRE DUMAS
AAADDEFFIILSST	AS FIT AS A FIDDLE
AAADDEFHIMORST	MADE A DASH FOR IT
AAADDEGGINRSTU	GUARDED AGAINST
AAADDEGGNRRSTW	AT DAGGERS DRAWN
AAADDEGIIMMRST	DIAGRAMMATISED
AAADDEGIIMMRTZ	DIAGRAMMATIZED
AAADDEGMOORSTT	MADE A GOOD START
AAADDEHLLNRRUY	LAUREL AND HARDY
AAADDEIILNPRSS	ISLAND PARADISE
AAADDEIMMORRRS	DEAR SIR OR MADAM
AAADDEMNOSSTTU	AS DEAD AS MUTTON
AAADDFHHILLOYY	HALF-DAY HOLIDAY
AAADDFHLLOOOTT	TOAD OF TOAD HALL
AAADDGGIINNSTV	DISADVANTAGING
AAADDGILLNOSST	AGAINST ALL ODDS
AAADDGLNNPRSTY	GRANDSTAND PLAY
AAADDHHIKLNNNW	WALK HAND IN HAND
AAADDKLNORRSSU	AS DRUNK AS A LORD
AAADEEEEHHLLVV	HAVE A LEVEL HEAD
AAADEEEHHNNRTV	HEAVEN AND EARTH
AAADEEEHLNPRSS	SHARP AS A NEEDLE
AAADEEEIMMNSTT	MADE AN ESTIMATE
AAADEEELLMRRTW	WALTER DE LA MARE
AAADEEEMMNSTTT	MADE A STATEMENT
AAADEEEMRRSSTU	TREADS A MEASURE
AAADEEENOQRSTU	ADEQUATE REASON

AAADEEFFLLNORS	FALL ON DEAF EARS
AAADEEFHLLMSTU	FULL STEAM AHEAD
AAADEEFILOPPRT	FAILED TO APPEAR
AAADEEGGHIINNR	GAINED A HEARING
AAADEEGHHMSTTW	WHATS THE DAMAGE?
AAADEEGILLNPPR	PILLAGE AND RAPE
	RAPE AND PILLAGE
AAADEEGILNNRRT	LEARNING A TRADE
AAADEEGINNSSTT	STANDING AT EASE
AAADEEGINPRRRW	REAPING A REWARD
AAADEEGLLNOPPS	LODGES AN APPEAL
AAADEEHHHMPSTT	HAMPSTEAD HEATH
AAADEEHIKLNNRT	TAKEN A HARD LINE
AAADEEHIKLNRST	TAKES A HARD LINE
AAADEEHILMRRST	RAISED THE ALARM
AAADEEHLLOOSST	HAD A SLATE LOOSE
AAADEEHLLORTTT	LEAD TO THE ALTAR
AAADEEHLMNNNRT	NEANDERTHAL MAN
AAADEEIMNPTTWY	AWAITED PAYMENT
AAADEELMNPRSST	PLEASANT DREAMS
AAADEELMOPPRST	APPEALED TO ARMS
AAADEELMPQRRUU	MADE UP A QUARREL
AAADEELNORSSTY	LEADS ONE ASTRAY
AAADEELNPPPRSS	APPLES AND PEARS
AAADEENNOQRRTU	ONE AND A QUARTER
AAADEFFNNORSSU	SOUNDS A FANFARE
AAADEFHIKMORST	MAKE A DASH FOR IT
AAADEFIILLRSST	AFTER ALL IS SAID
AAADEFLMMOOPRT	POT OF MARMALADE
AAADEGGHINOORV	HAVING A GOOD EAR
AAADEGGHLNRSTU	LAUGHS AT DANGER
AAADEGGIIKNNRT	TAKING A READING
AAADEGHIIRSSTT	STRAIGHT AS A DIE
AAADEGIIKNRSTT	TAKING IT AS READ
AAADEGIIMMRSST	DIAGRAMMATISES
AAADEGIIMMRSTZ	DIAGRAMMATIZES
AAADEGILMMNNOS	NOMINAL DAMAGES
AAADEGILNNRSTV	SALT AND VINEGAR
AAADEGIMNNNORR	MANDARIN ORANGE
AAADEGKMOORSTT	MAKE A GOOD START
AAADEGLNOSTUVY	ADVANTAGEOUSLY
AAADEGNRRSSTTT	RAGS AND TATTERS
AAADEHHHINTVWY	WITH A HEAVY HAND
AAADEHHINOTWWY	HAD A WAY WITH ONE
AAADEHKMRRSSTT	HARD TASKMASTER
AAADEHLLNNOPSY	PLAYS A LONE HAND
AAADEHLLNPRSTT	LATH AND PLASTER
AAADEHLMNORSSY	HANDSOME SALARY
AAADEHMNPSTTYY	TEA AND SYMPATHY
AAADEIILMPRRTY	MILITARY PARADE
AAADEIILNNRTUV	VALETUDINARIAN
AAADEIILNRRSTU	INDUSTRIAL AREA
AAADEILLQRRSTU	QUADRILATERALS
AAADEILNNRTWWY	INLAND WATERWAY
AAADEILNRSTTTY	LATTER-DAY SAINT
AAADEIMNNORRSY	ORDINARY SEAMAN
AAADEMMNNNPRSU	MAN AND SUPERMAN
AAADENOQRRTTUW	TWO AND A QUARTER
AAADFFIMORRSST	STIFF AS A RAMROD
AAADFGIIKMNOTY	MAKING A DAY OF IT
AAADFINRSSSTWY	WAIFS AND STRAYS
AAADGGHINNSSTT	STANDING AGHAST
AAADGHIIKLNOTY	TAKING A HOLIDAY
AAADGHIOOPRRTU	AUTORADIOGRAPH
AAADGIIINNRRRW	AIR-RAID WARNING
AAADGIKMNRRSTV	STARK RAVING MAD
AAADGIKNNPSTTU	TAKING UP A STAND
AAADGILNNPPRUW	DRAWING UP A PLAN
AAADGINNNRRTTYY	TRY AND TRY AGAIN
AAADHIMNNNOSTU	MAN IN A THOUSAND
AAADIIILLNNRTTU	LATITUDINARIAN

AAADIILLMMNNRWY	WILLIAM AND MARY
AAADIKLLNORSWY	ALL IN A DAYS WORK
AAADKKMNPRRSSS	MARKS AND SPARKS
AAAEEEEGHKRTTV	TAKE THE AVERAGE
AAAEEEEGLMSSSV	LEAVES A MESSAGE
AAAEEEEFHIKKLLS	SHAKE LIKE A LEAF
AAAEEEGGLMNNNR	GENERAL MANAGER
AAAEEEGLLNRRSU	AS A GENERAL RULE
AAAEEEHIMNSTVY	HAVE AN EASY TIME
AAAEEEHKNPRSSS	SHAKESPEAREANS
AAAEEEIKMMNSTT	MAKE AN ESTIMATE
AAAEEEKLMMNPSX	MAKES AN EXAMPLE
AAAEEEKMMNSTTT	MAKE A STATEMENT
AAAEEFHOSSSSSU	AS SAFE AS HOUSES
AAAEEFLORRTWZZ	WEAR TO A FRAZZLE
AAAEFGGGLMNNRU	GERMAN LANGUAGE
AAAEEGGILNNTUV	NATIVE LANGUAGE
AAAEEGGLMNRSTU	LANGUAGE MASTER
AAAEEGGMOPRRTY	REPAY A MORTGAGE
AAAEEGGNRRSSSS	AS GREEN AS GRASS
AAAEEGHIMNNRTV	HAVE A NIGHTMARE
AAAEEGHILNPRSV	HAVING A RELAPSE
AAAEECGIIIMRTTTT	AIM AT THE TARGET
AAAEEGIIKMNNRRT	TAKE IN MARRIAGE
AAAEEGILMNPPRR	PREPARING A MEAL
AAAEEGINNPPUUW	PAPUA NEW GUINEA
AAAEEGINNPRSTU	SEPTUAGENARIAN
AAAEEGLOSSEUVV	DAVELOV SAUSAGE
AAAEFGMNRRSSTT	SERGEANT-AT-ARMS
AAAEEGMNRSSTTT	GREAT STATESMAN
AAAEEGRSSSSTUW	AS SWEET AS SUGAR
AAAEEHHIINRRTV	HEAVIER THAN AIR
	HEAVIER-THAN-AIR
AAAEEHILLMRTTW	MATERIAL WEALTH
AAAEEHILMRRSST	RAISES THE ALARM
AAAEEHLLOOSSST	HAS A SLATE LOOSE
AAAEEJLNPRRSTU	JEAN-PAUL SARTRE
AAAEEKLMPQRRUU	MAKE UP A QUARREL
AAAEEKMMNPSTTT	MAKES AN ATTEMPT
AAAEEKMNRSSTTW	MAKES A NEW START
AAAEELLNOPPPRS	PERSONAL APPEAL
AAAEELMNNNPHST	PLEASANT MANNER
AAAEELNOOPPRST	APPEAL TO REASON
AAAEFFFFIORSSTT	AFFAIRS OF STATE
	STATE OF AFFAIRS
AAAEFGHIKNNRUV	FRANKIE VAUGHAN
AAAEFHHIKMOSST	MAKES A HASH OF IT
AAAEFHIKLNNRRT	ARETHA FRANKLIN
AAAEFHINPRSSST	AS FRESH AS PAINT
AAAEFIILMMNNRR	FAMILIAR MANNER
AAAEFIILMPRSST	PATRESFAMILIAS
AAAEFKNOORSTTT	AT A RATE OF KNOTS
AAAEFKRORRRSST	ART FOR ARTS SAKE
AAAEFLLOOPPRSV	SEAL OF APPROVAL
AAAEGGGLLNRUUV	VULGAR LANGUAGE
AAAEGGIILNNNST	LEANING AGAINST
AAAEGHIKMNNRST	MAN-EATING SHARK
AAAEGHILLNSTTW	AGAINST THE WALL
AAAEGHINNNORSTW	SWEARING AN OATH
AAAEGHNOOTTTWY	ONE THAT GOT AWAY
AAAEGIIILMNRST	EGALITARIANISM
AAAEGIIKKMMNST	MAKING A MISTAKE
AAAEGIILLNNPWXY	EXPLAINING AWAY
AAAEGIKLNNPTTY	TAKING A PENALTY
AAAEGIKMNORSTW	WORKING AS A TEAM
AAAEGIKMNPRRSS	PASSING A REMARK
AAAEGIKMNRSTUW	TAKING UNAWARES
AAAEGILLMNRSTT	MAGELLAN STRAIT
AAAEGILNNPPTYY	PAYING A PENALTY
AAAEGINORSTTVW	STARVATION WAGE
AAAEGLLLMOPRRS	PARALLELOGRAMS

AAAEGLMOPRRSSU	MASSAGE PARLOUR
AAAEGMMNNORRTTT	TETRAGRAMMATON
AAAEGMNNNORRRT	ARROGANT MANNER
AAAEHHIKSSTTTW	HAS WHAT IT TAKES
AAAEHHILLNNOTT	NATIONAL HEALTH
AAAEHHINOSTWWY	HAS A WAY WITH ONE
AAAEHIKRSTTTWW	WAKE WITH A START
AAAEHILLNNOTTW	NATIONAL WEALTH
AAAEHILMNNNOTT	NATIONAL ANTHEM
AAAEHILORSSTUU	AUSTRALIA HOUSE
AAAEHKNNOPSSTT	TAKEN A SNAPSHOT
AAAEHKNOPSSSTT	TAKES A SNAPSHOT
AAAEKKLLLMMSST	MAKES SMALL TALK
AAAEKLMOOPPRSS	MAKES A PROPOSAL
AAAELQRRRSSTTU	STARTS A QUARREL
AAAFGIKLNNOORS	ASKING FOR A LOAN
AAAFILLLNORUVV	VANILLA FLAVOUR
AAAFILLNOPRSTT	FALLS INTO A TRAP
AAAFINORRSSTWW	SWIFT AS AN ARROW
AAAFMMNNOPRSTY	MAN OF MANY PARTS
AAAGGIIILNNPTY	PLAYING IT AGAIN
AAAGGIILNNPSTY	PLAYING AGAINST
AAAGHHIINTVWWY	HAVING A WAY WITH
AAAGHHOPPRRRST	SHORT PARAGRAPH
AAAGHILNOSSSTU	AS TOUGH AS NAILS
AAAGIILLNNOTVY	NAVIGATIONALLY
AAAGIILNNOORST	ORGANISATIONAL
AAAGIILNNOORTZ	ORGANIZATIONAL
AAAHILNORRSTTU	NORTH AUSTRALIA
AAAHILORSSTTUU	SOUTH AUSTRALIA
AAAIIIMMNNQRSTU	ANTIQUARIANISM
AAAIILNNORSTTU	NATURALISATION
AAAIILNNORTTUZ	NATURALIZATION
AAAIILNORSTTWY	RAILWAY STATION
AAAIINNOSSSSST	ASSASSINATIONS
AAAIINOPPRRTTT	PAINT A PORTRAIT
AAAIKLNOPRSTTW	WALKS INTO A TRAP
AABBCCEINSSSTU	BASIC SUBSTANCE
AABBCDDEEGLNTU	BALANCED BUDGET
AABBCDEEIIKLRY	CRIED LIKE A BABY
AABBCDEGIIKNRR	BARE-BACK RIDING
	BAREBACK RIDING
AABBCEEEIMNORR	BECAME AIRBORNE
AABBCCEEGINPTXY	EXPECTING A BABY
AABBCEEIIKLRSY	CRIES LIKE A BABY
AABBCEEKKNORSS	BREAKS ONE'S BACK
AABBCEHIKNSSTT	STABS IN THE BACK
AABBCGIIIKNNRT	BACKING BRITAIN
AABBDDEEHILTWY	ABIDED BY THE LAW
AABBDDEEHOSTTT	STABBED TO DEATH
AABBDDEENNOOVY	ABOVE AND BEYOND
AABBDDEENRRTTU	BREAD AND BUTTER
	BREAD-AND-BUTTER
AABBDEEEHKRRST	BREAKS THE BREAD
AABBDEEFIKNRST	BREAKFAST IN BED
AABBDEEGHHSSTT	GETS THE HABDABS
AABBDEEGHINNTT	BEATING THE BAND
AABBDEEHILSTWY	ABIDES BY THE LAW
AABBDEEHIMNORT	BROAD IN THE BEAM
AABBDEEIKMOOTT	A BOOK AT BEDTIME
AABBDEEILNOPTT	DEBATABLE POINT
AABBDEHMOOTTUY	MAD ABOUT THE BOY
AABBDEIIMNNRRU	INDIA-RUBBER MAN
AABBDEILNNOSTY	BABES IN TOYLAND
AABBDGGIINNNOR	BROBDINGNAGIAN
AABBEEEHIRSTTW	THE WATER BABIES
AABBEEEIKLLPSY	SLEEP LIKE A BABY
AABBEEEENORSSTT	BEAT ONES BREAST
AABBEEEHHIKRSTT	BREAKS THE HABIT
AABBEEIKLLPSTY	SLEPT LIKE A BABY
AABBEEINNORSST	BEAT ONES BRAINS

AABBEFGGILNRST	FLABBERGASTING
AABBEIKKNRSSST	BREAKS ITS BANKS
AABBGGIIINNRSTU	RUBBING AGAINST
AABCCCCEHHILPRY	BRACHYCEPHALIC
AABCCDDEEINRRS	DESCRIBED AN ARC
AABCCDEEILLNNY	NICELY BALANCED
AABCCDDEEINRRSS	DESCRIBES AN ARC
AABCCDEEKLORTT	CRACKED A BOTTLE
AABCCDEIILLRTY	BACTERICIDALLY
AABCCDEILNORTT	CONTRADICTABLE
AABCCDEKKLLNOT	BLOCK AND TACKLE
AABCCDKLNNOORW	ALCOCK AND BROWN
AABCCEEELNPSST	ACCEPTABLENESS
AABCCEEFHIKLNT	BLACK IN THE FACE
AABCCEEFIKLMOT	CAME BACK TO LIFE
AABCCEEGHILNTX	BALTIC EXCHANGE
AABCCEEHHLLSTT	CATCHES THE BALL
AABCCEEHIMMNOP	BECAME CHAMPION
AABCCEELNNORTU	COUNTERBALANCE
AABCCEENNRRSUY	CRANBERRY SAUCE
AABCCEFHLOOORT	BAR OF CHOCOLATE
AABCCEFKNNOSSY	BACKS ONE'S FANCY
AABCCEGHIIOPRT	BACTERIOPHAGIC
AABCCEGIILMNRT	BRACING CLIMATE
AABCCEGIKNRSTT	BACKSCATTERING
AABCCEHILLMOPS	ACCOMPLISHABLE
AABCCEHKLNOPST	CLAPS ON THE BACK
AABCCEHLNORRRU	CHARCOAL BURNER
AABCCEHLORSTVY	TRAVELS BY COACH
AABCCEIIKLLMST	CLIMBS LIKE A CAT
AABCCEILMMRTUU	CIRCUMAMBULATE
AABCCEKNOORRTT	BROKE A CONTRACT
AABCCELNOOPRTT	TOBACCO PLANTER
AABCCELNORRTTV	VERBAL CONTRACT
AABCCFHLLMOSSY	CLASH OF CYMBALS
AABCCGIIKLNNRT	BALANCING TRICK
AABCCGIIKRRSTY	CARRY A BIG STICK
AABCCHILORRUVY	RICH VOCABULARY
AABCCIIILLPRTTY	PRACTICABILITY
AABCCIILNOTTUY	ACCOUNTABILITY
AABCDDEEEEHNRS	BREAD AND CHEESE
AABCDDEEEGINOS	DEBASED COINAGE
AABCDDEEGHIRST	DISCHARGE A DEBT
AABCDDEEKNPSTU	BUCKET AND SPADE
AABCDDEEMNOOST	COMES TO A BAD END
AABCDDEILMNNNU	UNBALANCED MIND
AABCDDELLLMNOP	DONALD CAMPBELL
AABCDDNOOORRRT	DOCTOR BARNARDO
AABCDEEEGHNRUU	BUREAU DE CHANGE
AABCDEEEGINRRT	BETA-ADRENERGIC
AABCDEEEHILNNY	HELD IN ABEYANCE
AABCDEEEMMNNRY	REMEMBRANCE DAY
AABCDEEFGGOORU	BADGE OF COURAGE
AABCDEEFILLMNU	FIELD AMBULANCE
AABCDEEGINORRT	BEATING A RECORD
AABCDEEHIHLNNOY	HOLD IN ABEYANCE
AABCDEEHLLORTT	CALLED TO THE BAR
AABCDEEHLNOORZ	HONORE DE BALZAC
AABCDEEHORTTUY	CATHODE-RAY TUBE
AABCDEEIKRRSTV	BACK-SEAT DRIVER
AABCDEEINORRST	CARRIED ONE'S BAT
AABCDEEINRRSTT	SCATTERBRAINED
AABCDEENNOOSSV	SAVED ONE'S BACON
AABCDEENNPRSUU	SUPERABUNDANCE
AABCDEENRSSSTT	ABSTRACTEDNESS
AABCDEFGINNORS	SENDING FOR A CAB
AABCDEFHKNNOOS	BACK OF ONE'S HAND
AABCDEFHLNOOSW	SHOWN A BOLD FACE
AABCDEFHLOOSSW	SHOWS A BOLD FACE
AABCDEFLLNRSSY	FANCY-DRESS BALL
AABCDEFLNOOPTU	PUT ON A BOLD FACE

AABCDEGIKLNRRT	BLANK CARTRIDGE
AABCDEGIKNNOOV	ADVANCE BOOKING
AABCDEGINRSSTT	ABSTRACT DESIGN
AABCDEHHNNOSSU	CHOSEN A HUSBAND
AABCDEHHNOOSSU	CHOOSE A HUSBAND
AABCDEHIINNRTU	NUDIBRANCHIATE
AABCDEHIKNOOPT	HAD A BONE TO PICK
AABCDEHILMPSTY	DESPATCH BY MAIL
AABCDEHINORSSW	CHASED RAINBOWS
AABCDEHKLNRSTU	BLACK AS THUNDER
AABCDEHOORRSST	ACROSS THE BOARD
	ACROSS-THE-BOARD
AABCDEIILLNOSS	DIABOLICALNESS
AABCDEIINSSTTU	TEA AND BISCUITS
AABCDEIKNNORSY	IN ONE'S BACK YARD
AABCDEILMNNRRU	CARDINAL NUMBER
AABCDEILORUVWY	WIDE VOCABULARY
AABCDEINNNOORT	INNOCENT ABROAD
AABCDEKPRSSSTW	STEPS BACKWARDS
AABCDELMNORRSU	RECORDS AN ALBUM
AABCDENOPRSSSW	BOWS AND SCRAPES
AABCDFFILLORRT	TRAFFIC BOLLARD
AABCDFKLNNOOST	BANK OF SCOTLAND
AABCDGGIKNORSW	GOING BACKWARDS
AABCDGIINOPRRU	AIRING CUPBOARD
AABCDHIKLNOPSU	BISHOP AUCKLAND
AABCDKKNNORSWW	KNOWN BACKWARDS
AABCDKKNORSSWW	KNOWS BACKWARDS
AABCEEEEFLNOSV	LEAVE OF ABSENCE
AABCEEEEHKPRST	BREAKS THE PEACE
AABCEEEFLNNOSS	SENSE OF BALANCE
AABCEEEGHLNNSS	CHANGEABLENESS
AABCEEEHHHLRST	HEALS THE BREACH
AABCEEEHILLMNP	BLENHEIM PALACE
AABCEEEHKNRTTT	THE BEATEN TRACK
AABCEEEHLLRSTT	CLEARS THE TABLE
AABCEEEILLMQTU	EQUABLE CLIMATE
AABCEEEILSTTTX	EXCITABLE STATE
AABCEEEIRRRRST	ERECTS A BARRIER
AABCEEEMMNNOSW	BECOMES A NEW MAN
AABCEEFHIRRSST	REACH FIRST BASE
AABCEEFINOSSST	BE OF ASSISTANCE
AABCEEFLNOOPRW	BALANCE OF POWER
AABCEEGGHILNNT	BLEACHING AGENT
AABCEEGHINPRST	BREATHING SPACE
AABCEEGHLNORUX	LABOUR EXCHANGE
AABCEEHHMMRRSTT	THE STAR CHAMBER
AABCEEHILNPSTT	TIPS THE BALANCE
AABCEEHILNRSST	CHARITABLENESS
AABCEEHILOPRRR	IRREPROACHABLE
AABCEEHKMNNRRT	MERCHANT BANKER
AABCEEHLMNORSS	ELASMOBRANCHES
AABCEEHNNRRRTY	CARRY THE BANNER
AABCEEIKMNPRTU	PNEUMATIC BRAKE
AABCEEILLLMMTY	EMBLEMATICALLY
AABCEEILLMMNPSS	IMPLACABLENESS
AABCEEILMNOPST	POLICEMANS BEAT
AABCEEINORRSST	CARRIES ONE'S BAT
AABCEEKQRRSSTU	SQUARE BRACKETS
AABCEELMNOPRSS	COMPARABLENESS
AABCEELNNRSTTU	NUCLEAR TEST BAN
AABCEENNOOSSSV	SAVES ONE'S BACON
AABCEFFHLNOOST	ACTS ON BEHALF OF
AABCEFGHIILRTT	CHARITABLE GIFT
AABCEFGIINPRRT	PREFABRICATING
AABCEFHKLLMOST	SMALL OF THE BACK
AABCEFHLOORRST	BACHELOR OF ARTS
AABCEFIIINOTTU	BEAUTIFICATION
AABCEFIINNOSTU	BIT OF A NUISANCE
AABCEFIINOPRRT	PREFABRICATION
AABCEFKLNNOOST	FLAT ON ONES BACK
AABCEFMNNOSSTU	MAN OF SUBSTANCE
AABCEGHHIIMNNT	BATHING MACHINE
AABCEGHIIKLNVY	BACKING HEAVILY
AABCEGHILMNPTY	PLAYING MACBETH
AABCEGIIKNNNRW	BACKING A WINNER
AABCEGINNORRTU	BARGAIN COUNTER
AABCEHHIMPSTTT	CHAMPS AT THE BIT
AABCEHIILLRSTY	HEBRAISTICALLY
AABCEHIKNOOPST	HAS A BONE TO PICK
AABCEHILLLMNRS	LAMELLIBRANCHS
AABCEHILLPRRYY	HYPERBARICALLY
AABCEHILOPRRRY	IRREPROACHABLY
AABCEHILPSTUYY	PHYSICAL BEAUTY
AABCEHINORSSSW	CHASES RAINBOWS
AABCEHKLLOSTTW	BACKS TO THE WALL
AABCEHKLNOPSST	SLAPS ON THE BACK
AABCEHKMNNOORS	MAN ON HORSEBACK
AABCEHLMOORSST	BATHROOM SCALES
AABCEIIINNNRTT	ANCIENT BRITAIN
AABCEIILNPPRU	APPEAR IN PUBLIC
AABCEIILRTTTXY	EXTRACTABILITY
AABCEIKKKLLORW	WORK LIKE A BLACK
AABCEIKNNORRSS	RACK ONE'S BRAINS
AABCEIKNNORRSS	RACKS ONE'S BRAIN
AABCEILLLRSTYZ	CRYSTALLIZABLE
AABCEILLMORRTY	BAROMETRICALLY
AABCEILMNPPRUY	REPUBLICAN ARMY
AABCEILNORSSTU	CONSTABULARIES
AABCEINOORRSTV	OBSERVATION CAR
AABCEKLLNOSSTT	TOTAL BLACKNESS
AABCFIIILLMRT	ARTIFICIAL LIMB
AABCFIKMNOORST	BACK-FORMATIONS
AABCGHIILLOPRY	BIOGRAPHICALLY
AABCGHIIOOPRTU	AUTOBIOGRAPHIC
AABCGIINNNORST	BRINGS AN ACTION
AABCHILOOPRSTU	CLAUSTROPHOBIA
AABCIIILLMSTUY	MUSICAL ABILITY
AABCIIILLNOTTY	ANTIBIOTICALLY
AABCIIILNRTTTY	INTRACTABILITY
AABCIILMMNNOTU	CLIMB A MOUNTAIN
AABCIIMNNORSST	ABSTRACTIONISM
AABCIINORSSTTT	ABSTRACTIONIST
AABCIKNNNOOTUY	YOU CAN BANK ON IT
AABCILLNOOOORST	COLLABORATIONS
AABCILMMNOORTT	IN MORTAL COMBAT
AABCILNNOSSTTU	CONSUBSTANTIAL
AABCLOOOPRRUVY	POOR VOCABULARY
AABCNNOOORSSST	CONTRABASSOONS
AABDDDEEIKLOTU	DID A DOUBLE TAKE
AABDDDEGGGNNOU	BOUND AND GAGGED
AABDDDEGMORRUY	ARMED BODYGUARD
AABDDDEIIKRRST	DID A BRISK TRADE
AABDDDELNORSTU	DOUBLE STANDARD
AABDDEEEEHNRSS	BAREHEADEDNESS
AABDDEEEILNTTY	BATTED AN EYELID
AABDDEEFHILLOU	HAD A DOUBLE LIFE
AABDDEEFIIORRS	FIRE A BROADSIDE
AABDDEEHHLLLNT	HANDLED THE BALL
AABDDEEHHLNSTY	LEADS BY THE HAND
AABDDEEHORRSTT	TREAD THE BOARDS
AABDDEEILLMNRU	DIALLED A NUMBER
AABDDEEILLNPRY	PLAYED A BLINDER
AABDDEEIMMNNUVW	MEDIUM WAVEBAND
AABDDEEIMNNORT	ONE-ARMED BANDIT
AABDDEEINORRST	RESIDENT ABROAD
AABDDEELNNRSTU	UNDERSTANDABLE
AABDDEFFGHHIOT	THIEF OF BAGHDAD
AABDDEFHINNSUW	HUSBAND AND WIFE
AABDDEFIIOPRRS	BIRD OF PARADISE
AABDDEGIINOORT	BIODEGRADATION
AABDDEGIINORRS	RESIDING ABROAD

AABDDEGINNOPRT	PADDINGTON BEAR	AABDEGILNTUYZZ	DAZZLING BEAUTY
AABDDEHHIINNRT	A BIRD IN THE HAND	AABDEGIMNNNNRR	BERNARD MANNING
AABDDEIIINRRST	ARISTIDE BRIAND	AABDEGINNORTUW	WANDERING ABOUT
AABDDELNNOPSSU	LEAPS AND BOUNDS	AABDEGIOOOOSST	SAID BO TO A GOOSE
AABDDELNNRSTUY	UNDERSTANDABLY	AABDEGMNOORRUV	AVOGADRO NUMBER
AABDDFHOOOSTUW	SHADOW OF A DOUBT	AABDEHINORRSTT	BOARDS THE TRAIN
AABDDFINOOORYY	DIARY OF A NOBODY	AABDEHJLNOSSUU	JEALOUS HUSBAND
AABDDGGIIINNST	BIDDING AGAINST	AABDEIILLORSV	BASIL DOLIVEIRA
AABDDGHIINNRTW	BAD HANDWRITING	AABDEIIKLLMRRR	BILLIARD MARKER
AABDDHLNORSWWY	WASH AND BLOW-DRY	AABDEIIKMNORST	DISEMBARKATION
AABDEEEEELPSST	PLEASE BE SEATED	AABDEIIILLPRRY	BILLIARD PLAYER
AABDEEEFFNORRT	BEFORE AND AFTER	AABDEIILNNORUV	LABOURED IN VAIN
AABDEEEFGIRRTV	FIVE-BARRED GATE	AABDEIINOOSTTU	AUTOANTIBODIES
AABDEEEFHHLOTT	HEAD OF THE TABLE	AABDEILLNNSTWY	STANLEY BALDWIN
AABDEEEFHINRRT	FEATHERBRAINED	AABDELNNNOOPRY	NAPOLEON BRANDY
AABDEEEGGLMRSS	GARBLED MESSAGE	AABDFFFFOOORWY	OFF-OFF-BROADWAY
AABDEEEGHIRTVW	GAVE A WIDE BERTH	AABDGGIIIMNSTU	DISAMBIGUATING
AABDEEEGKLOOPT	KEEP A GOOD TABLE	AABDGHIILNPTTU	PUT IN A BAD LIGHT
AABDEEEHHIRRSS	HABERDASHERIES	AABDGHIINNNOPS	ABANDONING SHIP
AABDEEEHHKRRTT	BREAK THE THREAD	AABDGIIIMNOSTU	DISAMBIGUATION
AABDEEEHHLMRST	SHARED THE BLAME	AABDGILNOORSST	BROAD AS IT'S LONG
AABDEEEHILNNNR	BANNER HEADLINE	AABDHHNPRSSUUW	WASH AND BRUSH-UP
AABDEEEHLLMORW	WHOLEMEAL BREAD	AABDHILMNOSSUY	BUSMANS HOLIDAY
AABDEEEHLNRRTY	LEARNED BY HEART	AABDIILLLPRSSY	PLAYS BILLIARDS
AABDEEEHNORRST	BARED ONE'S HEART	AABDIILNORRSTU	SIR ADRIAN BOULT
AABDEEEHNNRRSST	THREADBARENESS	AABDIINOOPPRST	DISAPPROBATION
AABDEEEILLNORS	RELEASED ON BAIL	AABEEEGGILNNTT	ENGAGE IN BATTLE
AABDEEEILRSSST	DESIRABLE ASSET	AABEEEGHIMNNRT	BEARING THE NAME
AABDEEEELLRSTVY	TRAVELLED BY SEA	AABEEEGIIKLMNN	MAKING A BEE-LINE
AABDEEEOORRSTT	RED AS A BEETROOT	AABEEEGIKNPRST	KEEPING ABREAST
AABDEEFHILLOSU	HAS A DOUBLE LIFE	AABEEEGILNNOPS	PENSIONABLE AGE
AABDEEFLORRTTY	READY FOR BATTLE	AABEEEGINNORTT	BEAT GENERATION
AABDEEGGGINRRU	BEARING A GRUDGE	AABEEEHHILRTVY	BREATHE HEAVILY
AABDEEGGIIMNNN	MADE A BEGINNING	AABEEEHHLMRSST	SHARES THE BLAME
AABDEEGGIMNNRR	GINGERBREAD MAN	AABEEEHKNORRST	BREAK ONES HEART
AABDEEGIILLNRR	READING BRAILLE	AABEEEHLRRSTTT	RATTLE THE SABRE
AABDEEGILMNNRT	REGIMENTAL BAND	AABEEEHNORRSST	BARES ONE'S HEART
AABDEEGKLOOPTT	KEPT A GOOD TABLE	AABEEEHNORSSTV	SAVE ONES BREATH
AABDEEHHKNNTTY	TAKEN BY THE HAND	AABEEEHPRSSTTT	BREASTS THE TAPE
AABDEEHHKNSTTY	TAKES BY THE HAND	AABEEEILLNORSS	RELEASES ON BAIL
AABDEEHHLLTTTY	THAT'LL BE THE DAY	AABEEEILMNORST	REASONABLE TIME
AABDEEHILLRTTZ	BLAZED THE TRAIL	AABEEEILNRSSST	BARE ESSENTIALS
AABDEEHLLORTUV	A TROUBLE HALVED	AABEEEIMNNOSTT	NOISE ABATEMENT
AABDEEHLNORTTU	AROUND THE TABLE	AABEEEINORRSWY	RAISE AN EYEBROW
AABDEEHLNTTWWY	WANTED BY THE LAW	AABEEEKLMNRRSS	REMARKABLENESS
AABDEEHLORRSTU	A TROUBLE SHARED	AABEEELLMNNSST	LAMENTABLENESS
AABDEEHMNOOTTY	BAYED AT THE MOON	AABEEELLORSTTY	ELABORATE STYLE
AABDEEHNOORSTT	SEAT ON THE BOARD	AABEEELNNOORSS	REASONABLENESS
AABDEEIKKLOORS	READS LIKE A BOOK	AABEEELNNOSSSS	SEASONABLENESS
AABDEEILLRRTVY	TRAVELLED BY AIR	AABEEFGGILNNST	SELF-ABNEGATING
AABDEEILLORTTUV	TRAVELLED ABOUT	AABEEFGIKNORRT	BREAKING FOR TEA
AABDEEMOOPRRTY	TEMPORARY ABODE	AABEEFGILNNOST	SELF-ABNEGATION
AABDEFGHMNNOOU	OF HUMAN BONDAGE	AABEEFGILNOSST	SEASONABLE GIFT
AABDEFHIIORRSY	FAIR-HAIRED BOYS	AABEEFGLLLOOTU	FOOTBALL LEAGUE
AABDEFIILLOPPR	APPLIED FOR BAIL		LEAGUE FOOTBALL
AABDEFIJLOOPPR	APPLIED FOR A JOB	AABEEFHLLNTWYY	FALLEN BY THE WAY
AABDEFIKLMORST	FORMIDABLE TASK	AABEEFHLNORRTY	HARRY BELAFONTE
AABDEFILMOORTT	MADE A BOLT FOR IT	AABEEFHOPRRSTU	PAUSE FOR BREATH
AABDEFILNORUVW	FAVOURABLE WIND	AABEEFIKMRSSST	MAKES FIRST BASE
AABDEFLLOORRSV	FALLS OVERBOARD	AABEEFIORRSTTT	ARBITER OF TASTE
AABDEFLMMRTTUY	MADAM BUTTERFLY	AABEEFKLLNORSS	BREAKS ONE'S FALL
AABDEFMNOORRSW	NEWS FROM ABROAD	AABEEGGHRSTTTY	THE GREAT GATSBY
AABDEGHHOORTTU	BROUGHT TO A HEAD	AABEEGGIIKMNNN	MAKE A BEGINNING
AABDEGHIIINNNWY	WINNING BY A HEAD	AABEEGGILNORVW	BOWLING AVERAGE
AABDEGHILNRRTY	BRIGHT AND EARLY	AABEEGHIKLNRTW	BREAKING THE LAW
AABDEGHINNNOOP	ABANDONING HOPE	AABEEGHILLNTTY	LAYING THE TABLE
AABDEGHINRSSTU	BRUSHED AGAINST	AABEEGHILNPRTY	PLAYING THE BEAR
AABDEGHNNNOOTW	ON THE BAND-WAGON	AABEEGHILOPRTW	WITH A BARGEPOLE
	ON THE BANDWAGON	AABEEGHINNOPSU	HEAPING ABUSE ON
AABDEGIIILLLNNW	WILLING AND ABLE	AABEEGIILMNNSS	IMAGINABLENESS
AABDEGIKMNORRT	MARKETING BOARD	AABEEGIKLLMRRR	REMARKABLE GIRL

AABEEGIKMNORRR	BROKEN MARRIAGE	AABEIIILLNORTZ	LIBERALIZATION
AABEEGIKMNQSTU	MAKING A BEQUEST	AABEIIILMNRRST	LIBERTARIANISM
AABEEGIKMORRRR	MARRIAGE BROKER	AABEIIILNPRSTY	INSEPARABILITY
AABEEGILNOPRTT	OPERATING TABLE	AABEIILLPRSTUY	PLEASURABILITY
AABEEGILNRSTTV	SERVING AT TABLE	AABEIILNSSSTTU	SUBSTANTIALISE
AABEEGLMNRRTUV	VERBAL ARGUMENT	AABEIILNSSTTUZ	SUBSTANTIALIZE
AABEEHIIILRTTV	REHABILITATIVE	AABEIINSSTTTUV	SUBSTANTIATIVE
AABEEHILLRSTTZ	BLAZES THE TRAIL	AABEIKNNORRSTU	BREAKS INTO A RUN
AABEEHJKMNORST	JAM ON THE BRAKES	AABEIKNOORRTTT	BREAK INTO A TROT
AABEEHKLPPRSTY	APPLY THE BRAKES	AABEILNOPRRTTU	PERTURBATIONAL
AABEEHKNRSTTTU	BURN AT THE STAKE	AABEILNOSSTTTT	BATTLE STATIONS
AABEEHLLNOORTW	WEATHER BALLOON	AABEILNRRSTTVY	TRAVELS BY TRAIN
AABEEHOPSSTTTT	BEATS AT THE POST	AABEIMNNRRSTTUW	BURST WATER MAIN
AABEEIILMNOTTT	ANTIMETABOLITE	AABEINNOSSSUWY	AWAY ON BUSINESS
AABEEIILNNRSSV	INVARIABLENESS	AABEKMRRRRSTWY	STRAWBERRY MARK
AABEEIKMOPRRSS	BREAKS A PROMISE	AABELLLNOORTTU	NO TROUBLE AT ALL
AABEEILLMMNNOT	NATIONAL EMBLEM	AABENOOPRSTTTY	BOSTON TEA PARTY
AABEEILLMMORRT	ALBERT MEMORIAL	AABERRRRSTTTWY	STRAWBERRY TART
AABEEILMNPSSSS	IMPASSABLENESS	AABFFGGHINOOTW	GO OFF WITH A BANG
AABEEILNNQQTTW	I WANT TO BE ALONE	AADFQIIIILLORTT	A BIT OF ALL RIGHT
AABEEILNNSTTTU	SUITABLE TENANT	AABFIIILLMMNTY	INFLAMMABILITY
AABEELMNNOSSTY	BY NO MEANS LEAST	AABFIILLNPPTUY	UNFLAPPABILITY
AABEELMORSSTTU	ABSOLUTE MASTER	AABGGIILNNNOWY	WINNING BY A GOAL
AABEELNNOOSTTW	WANTS TO BE ALONE	AABGHHINORSTTU	THRASHING ABOUT
AABEELNNRRSTUY	SUBTERRANEANLY	AABGHINOPRRSUY	HARBOURING A SPY
AABEEPRSTTUXYY	BAYEUX TAPESTRY	AABGIILNRSSTUW	BRINGS A LAWSUIT
AABEFFGLLMOOOT	GAME OF FOOTBALL	AABGIINNSSTTTU	SUBSTANTIATING
AABEFGGGINORUV	BEGGING A FAVOUR	AABGILLNNQQOQPU	GO UP IN A BALLOON
AABEFGIIIKLRSTT	LIGHT BREAKFAST	AABHHLLLOSTTYY	BY ALL THAT'S HOLY
AABEFGHOPRRSST	GASPS FOR BREATH	AABHIIRRROOTWY	BRITISH AIRWAYS
AABEFGIIKMNNOR	MAKING A BONFIRE	AABHILNOORRSTZ	HORIZONTAL BARS
AABEFHLLOSTUUW	FABULOUS WEALTH	AABIIILLOPRSTY	POLARISABILITY
AABEFIILLMRSSY	FAILS MISERABLY	AABIIILLOPRTYZ	POLARIZABILITY
AABEFIILLOPPRS	APPLIES FOR BAIL	AABIIILMNNRSSU	ANNUS MIRABILIS
AABEFIJLOOPPRS	APPLIES FOR A JOB	AABIILLNPRSSUY	SALISBURY PLAIN
AABEFIKLMOORTT	MAKE A BOLT FOR IT	AABIILNSSTTTUY	SUBSTANTIALITY
AABEFILMNOTUUW	BEAUTIFUL WOMAN	AABIINNOSSTTTU	SUBSTANTIATION
AABEFIRRRRSTWY	STRAWBERRY FAIR	AABIJLMOORRTUY	LABOUR MAJORITY
AABEFLLLOOPRTY	FOOTBALL PLAYER	AABILMNSSSTTUU	SUBSTANTIAL SUM
AABEFLLNOOOSST	FOOTBALL SEASON	AABLNOOPPRSUVY	BUYS ON APPROVAL
AABEFLNORRTUZZ	BURN TO A FRAZZLE	AABMNNOOOTTUWW	WOMAN ABOUT TOWN
AABEFORSSSTTTU	AS SOFT AS BUTTER	AACCCCENNOOOVV	CONCAVO-CONCAVE
AABEGGGIIINNNN	BEGINNING AGAIN	AACCCDDEEEIPTV	ACCEPTED ADVICE
AABEGHIIILNRTT	REHABILITATING	AACCCDEHNORSTU	CONDUCT A SEARCH
AABEGHIINNORTT	INTO THE BARGAIN	AACCCDGILNORTY	ACT ACCORDINGLY
AABEGHIINPRTTT	BAITING THE TRAP	AACCCDIIIMRRTT	DRAMATIC CRITIC
AABEGHIKLNRTTY	BREATHTAKINGLY	AACCCEEEFFMOOT	COME FACE TO FACE
AABEGHILLLNPTY	PLAYING THE BALL	AACCCEEGHHILMN	CHEMICAL CHANGE
AABEGHILLNNQTU	BANQUETING HALL	AACCCEEHLMOORT	CHOCOLATE CREAM
AABEGHILLNPSS	PASSING THE BALL	AACCCEEIILLSST	ECCLESIASTICAL
AABEGHINRSSSTU	BRUSHES AGAINST	AACCCEFHNNOSTY	CATCH ONE'S FANCY
AABEGHIOOPRRTU	AUTOBIOGRAPHER	AACCCEFIKLOPRT	LACK OF PRACTICE
AABEGIIILLLLTY	LEGAL LIABILITY	AACCCEIIIRRSTT	CHARACTERISTIC
AABEGIIKLNRTTY	TAKING A LIBERTY	AACCCEHILMORST	CHROMATIC SCALE
AABEGIIKNOPPUY	BUY A PIG IN A POKE	AACCCGHHIILLNT	CATCHING A CHILL
AABEGIILNPRTYY	PLAYING IT BY EAR	AACCCGHHILNNRU	ANGLICAN CHURCH
AABEGIJKLNOORU	LABOURING A JOKE	AACCCGHINOPRTU	GRAPHIC ACCOUNT
AABEGILLMNPRSY	PLAYING MARBLES	AACCCGIKNORRST	STOCK-CAR RACING
AABEGILLNRRRUU	URBAN GUERRILLA	AACCCHIIMRRRT	ARMCHAIR CRITIC
AABEGILMNRRSSY	EMBARRASSINGLY	AACCCHLLOOPSTY	STAPHYLOCOCCAL
AABEGILNNOOTUY	LAYING ABOUT ONE	AACCCIILLMSSU	CLASSICAL MUSIC
AABEGIMNNNNOPST	OPENING BATSMAN	AACCCIILNNOTUV	VATICAN COUNCIL
AABEGINNNRRSTU	RUNNING ABREAST	AACCCLLNOOSTTU	CALLS TO ACCOUNT
AABEGOOOOOSSTY	SAY 'BOO' TO A GOOSE	AACCDDDEEHHNRT	CATCH RED-HANDED
AABEGOOOOSSSTY	SAYS BO TO A GOOSE	AACCDDDELLOSTU	CALCULATED ODDS
AABEHHIOSTTVWY	HAVE IT BOTH WAYS	AACCDDDGIIILNO	ADDING A CODICIL
AABEHIIILNORTT	REHABILITATION	AACCDDEEEEFPTT	ACCEPTED DEFEAT
AABEHILLOSTTWW	SWALLOW THE BAIT	AACCDEEEELLLNV	CANCELLED LEAVE
AABEHLMMOORSST	SMOOTH AS MARBLE	AACCDEEEFFNSTU	CAUSE AND EFFECT
AABEHMORRRSSTU	HARBOURMASTERS	AACCDEEEFHNRSU	REFUSED A CHANCE
AABEIIIILLNNNTY	INALIENABILITY	AACCDEEEHHKLNS	CHALK AND CHEESE

AACCDEEEIMNRSU	ICE-CREAM SUNDAE
AACCDEEFFIMRTT	DRAMATIC EFFECT
AACCDEEFIIMRSS	MADE SACRIFICES
AACCDEEFLLSSUY	ACCUSED FALSELY
	FALSELY ACCUSED
AACCDEEGIILMNO	DECIMAL COINAGE
AACCDEEHHNOSTT	CATCH ONES DEATH
AACCDEEHIINORS	REACH A DECISION
AACCDEEHLNRRST	CRADLE SNATCHER
AACCDEEHMNNORS	CHANCED ONE'S ARM
AACCDEEILNNSST	ACCIDENTALNESS
AACCDEEILNPRTT	DENTAL PRACTICE
AACCDEELLNSSTU	CALCULATEDNESS
AACCDEFHKNORTW	THE CRACK OF DAWN
AACCDEGHIILLNN	CLINCHING A DEAL
AACCDEGIILNRRW	DRAWING A CIRCLE
AACCDEGIINNOTV	ACTING ON ADVICE
AACCDEHHNOORSS	COACH AND HORSES
AACCDEHIIKLLST	ACTS LIKE A CHILD
AACCDEHIILNPPS	PLAICE AND CHIPS
AACCDEHIKNOOTT	INTO A COCKED HAT
AACCDEHILLLNOW	CHILD ALLOWANCE
AACCDEHILOPRSY	POLYSACCHARIDE
AACCDEHIMNNORS	MONOSACCHARIDE
AACCDEHINNPPRS	PINCH AND SCRAPE
AACCDEHIOPPRRT	DIRECT APPROACH
AACCDEHKRSSSTT	STACKS THE CARDS
AACCDEHNORRSTU	SOUND CHARACTER
AACCDEHNORSTTW	SCOTCH AND WATER
AACCDEHRRSTTUY	CHARACTER STUDY
AACCDEIINNORTT	CONTRAINDICATE
AACCDEIINORSTT	ACCREDITATIONS
AACCDEIKLLRSTU	CALCULATED RISK
AACCDEILLMORTY	DEMOCRATICALLY
AACCDEILMOORRW	MORAL COWARDICE
AACCDEILMOORST	SOCIAL DEMOCRAT
AACCDELOORSTUV	CAST A CLOUD OVER
AACCDFFIINNOTT	FACT AND FICTION
AACCDFHIMMNNOO	CHAIN OF COMMAND
AACCDGHIILOPRS	DISCOGRAPHICAL
AACCDGHINOPPRT	DROPPING A CATCH
AACCDGILLNOORT	CALLING A DOCTOR
AACCDGILNOORTW	ACCORDING TO LAW
AACCDHIILLNORY	DIACHRONICALLY
AACCDHKNORRTTU	HARD NUT TO CRACK
AACCDHNNNOORRW	CROWN AND ANCHOR
AACCDIILNOSTUW	WILD ACCUSATION
AACCDIKNORSSTU	TURKS AND CAICOS
AACCDIMMNOOOST	ACCOMMODATIONS
AACCEEEEFFNRTT	CREATE AN EFFECT
AACCEEEEGILRVY	RECEIVE A LEGACY
AACCEEEEFHNRSSU	REFUSES A CHANCE
AACCEEEGINNRST	CREATING A SCENE
AACCEEEEHHILMMR	MICHAEL MEACHER
AACCEEEEHIMNORS	MACARONI CHEESE
AACCEEEEHKMNOOST	TAKE ONES CHANCE
AACCEEEEHLNOSTV	LEAVES TO CHANCE
AACCEEFFHOSSTT	FACTS OF THE CASE
AACCEEFFILNOPT	CAPITAL OFFENCE
AACCEEFGHLORSS	SCALE OF CHARGES
AACCEEFGIIRRST	GREAT SACRIFICE
AACCEEFIIKMRSS	MAKE SACRIFICES
AACCEEFKNOPRTT	PONTEFRACT CAKE
AACCEEFLLSSSUY	ACCUSES FALSELY
AACCEEGHHINQSU	CASHING A CHEQUE
AACCEEGHIINNTV	GIVEN IT A CHANCE
AACCEEGHIINSTV	GIVES IT A CHANCE
AACCEEGHILLNRY	LEGAL CHICANERY
AACCEEGHIRRTTT	GREAT ARCHITECT
AACCEEGIPRRTTT	TARGET PRACTICE
AACCEEHKNNNOST	TAKEN NO CHANCES
AACCEEHKNNNOSST	TAKES NO CHANCES
AACCEEHHMNNORSS	CHANCES ONE'S ARM
AACCEEHHMORRSST	SACCHAROMETERS
AACCEEHHNOORSST	ACROSS THE OCEAN
AACCEEIILLMPSSX	CLASSIC EXAMPLE
AACCEEILNNRSTU	NATURAL SCIENCE
AACCEEINNNORSS	RECONNAISSANCE
AACCEEELNORRRTU	NUCLEAR REACTOR
AACCEEELNORSSSU	CALCAREOUSNESS
AACCEEMNPPSTTY	ACCEPTS PAYMENT
AACCEFFILLORSS	CLASSICAL OFFER
AACCEFFILORRVY	CAVALRY OFFICER
AACCEFGHHIINTT	CATCHING A THIEF
AACCEFGHHNOOST	GHOST OF A CHANCE
AACCEFGNOORTTU	OF GREAT ACCOUNT
AACCEFHIIMNRSU	HUMAN SACRIFICE
AACCEFHILLNTVY	FILL THE VACANCY
AACCEFHLLRTUWY	WATCH CAREFULLY
AACCEFHOORRTTU	OUT OF CHARACTER
AACCEFINOPRTTW	WANT OF PRACTICE
AACCEFKNNOOTTU	TAKEN ACCOUNT OF
AACCEFKNOOSTTU	TAKES ACCOUNT OF
AACCEGGHILNNPS	CHANGING PLACES
AACCEGGIKLNORU	LACKING COURAGE
AACCEGGILLNOOY	GYNAECOLOGICAL
AACCEGGINNRSST	GRANTING ACCESS
AACCEGHHINTTTU	CAUGHT IN THE ACT
AACCEGHHLMNNPU	CHAMPAGNE LUNCH
AACCEGHIIKKLNN	CHICKEN À LA KING
AACCEGHIILMNRR	CRIMINAL CHARGE
AACCEGHIIMNNSS	MISSING A CHANCE
AACCEGHIINRRST	CHARACTERISING
AACCEGHIINRRTZ	CHARACTERIZING
AACCEGHILLOOST	ESCHATOLOGICAL
AACCEGHINNPPST	CATCHES NAPPING
AACCEGHINNRRTY	CARRYING THE CAN
AACCEGIIMNRTUV	CIRCUMNAVIGATE
AACCEGIKNOPSTT	COSTING A PACKET
AACCEGINNNOTUV	GIVEN AN ACCOUNT
AACCEGINNORSS	CRASS IGNORANCE
AACCEGINNOSTUV	GIVES AN ACCOUNT
AACCEGLNRTTTUU	GUTTURAL ACCENT
AACCEHHIILLNPR	CHARLIE CHAPLIN
AACCEHHIILLRRY	HIERARCHICALLY
AACCEHHILLNPRS	CHARLES CHAPLIN
AACCEHHINOTTUW	WITHOUT A CHANCE
AACCEHHIPSSTTW	WATCH THIS SPACE
AACCEHIILOPPRS	ARCHIEPISCOPAL
AACCEHIILQRRSU	SQUIREARCHICAL
AACCEHIJKLMNOS	MICHAEL JACKSON
AACCEHIKKLORST	COCKTAIL SHAKER
AACCEHIKLOOSVZ	CZECHOSLOVAKIA
AACCEHILLNOOPT	PLAIN CHOCOLATE
AACCEHILLPRTYY	ARCHETYPICALLY
AACCEHKNNORRTW	KNOWN CHARACTER
AACCEHLMNOOPRSU	MACROCEPHALOUS
AACCEIIKLNOSTT	ACTS LIKE A TONIC
AACCEIILLNNPRT	PRE-NATAL CLINIC
AACCEIILMNNRSU	INSURANCE CLAIM
AACCEIJKLOPRRT	PRACTICAL JOKER
AACCEIILLLOPPTY	APOPLECTICALLY
AACCEIILLMTUUVY	ACCUMULATIVELY
AACCEIILLNORTTU	LITERAL ACCOUNT
AACCEILMMOOSTX	COMES TO A CLIMAX
AACCEILMRSSSST	CLASSICS MASTER
AACCEILNPRRSTU	PRACTICAL NURSE
AACCEILPRSSSTU	PARTIAL SUCCESS
AACCEIMMNNOPST	ACCOMPANIMENTS
AACCEKNORSTTTU	COUNTERATTACKS
AACCELLLMMMNOR	MALCOLM MCLAREN
AACCELLMMOORRU	MACROMOLECULAR

AACCELMMMNNOOPR	COMMON PARLANCE	AACDDEILLNTTUV	CULTIVATED LAND
AACCENNNOOPSTU	OPENS AN ACCOUNT	AACDDEILNOOPRS	PAID AN OLD SCORE
AACCENOORRSTWW	WARSAW CONCERTO	AACDDEILNOTTUU	ADULT EDUCATION
AACCENOQRSSTUU	SQUARE ACCOUNTS	AACDDEILPQRTUU	QUADRUPLICATED
AACCFGINNNORTY	CANNING FACTORY	AACDDEINOPRSSW	PASSED IN A CROWD
AACCFHOORRRRTY	CARRY A TORCH FOR	AACDDEMMMNNOSSU	ASSUMED COMMAND
AACCFIIILNOSST	CLASSIFICATION	AACDDEMNNOORSTT	DOCTORS MANDATE
AACCFIIINNOSTT	SANCTIFICATION	AACDDENNOORRTY	DOT AND CARRY ONE
AACCFIILORSSTY	CLASSIFICATORY	AACDDENNOPPSUW	PACES UP AND DOWN
AACCFILLOPTTUY	FULL TO CAPACITY	AACDDENOPRSSST	SENDS A POSTCARD
AACCFILMNOOORS	FORMAL OCCASION	AACDDFIJKMNOOS	JACK OF DIAMONDS
AACCFNNORTTTUU	TURF ACCOUNTANT	AACDDGHIILNOPT	ADOPTING A CHILD
AACCGHHIILOPRR	CHIROGRAPHICAL	AACDDGIINOPPTU	TAPIOCA PUDDING
AACCGHIILNOOPR	ICONOGRAPHICAL	AACDDHILRSSTUY	SATURDAYS CHILD
AACCGHIILNRSTV	SCRATCH A LIVING	AACDEEFFFGHHNTX	HEATED EXCHANGE
AACCGHILLOPTYY	PHAGOCYTICALLY	AACDEEEFFMNNRT	AFFECTED MANNER
AACCGHILMOOPRS	COSMOGRAPHICAL	AACDEEEFHMNSSS	SHAMEFACEDNESS
AACCGHILSSSTTU	TAUGHT CLASSICS	AACDEEEFHOPSST	THE ACE OF SPADES
AACCGHINORRRTY	CARRYING A TORCH	AACDEEEFIMNRTT	FREE ADMITTANCE
AACCGIILLLLMOOT	CLIMATOLOGICAL	AACDEEEFINRRSS	INCREASED FARES
AACCGIILLMNSTU	MISCALCULATING	AACDEEEGHINPRS	READING A SPEECH
AACCGINNOSSTUV	SAVINGS ACCOUNT	AACDEEEGHINSSX	EXCHANGES IDEAS
AACCGINORRRSSY	CARRYING ACROSS	AACDEEEGIINNUV	GIVE AN AUDIENCE
AACCHIILLMSSTY	SCHISMATICALLY	AACDEEEGILLMNT	CALLED A MEETING
AACCHIILMNOOST	MACHICOLATIONS	AACDLLCGINNRRW	ANDREW CARNEGIE
AACCHILLLOSSTY	SCHOLASTICALLY	AACDEEEGNORSSU	ARGUED ONE'S CASE
AACCHILLOSSTTY	STOCHASTICALLY	AACDEEEGNORTTT	RENTED A COTTAGE
AACCHILMORRSST	CHRISTMAS CAROL	AAODECCIIIIILLTT	DELICATE HEALTH
AACCHILNOPSTYY	PSYCHOANALYTIC	AACDEEEHHLLLST	HELD ALL THE ACES
AACCHLRSSTTTUW	CLUTCH AT STRAWS	AACDEEEHHLPRTT	CLEARED THE PATH
AACCIIILMPRTTY	IMPRACTICALITY	AACDEEEHIPRRTT	DEAR AT THE PRICE
AACCIIILOSTTVY	SOCIAL ACTIVITY	AACDEEEHKLOOPS	KEEPS A COOL HEAD
AACCIIILLMNOSTU	MISCALCULATION	AACDEEEHLPSSTU	PLEADS THE CAUSE
AACCIIILLQSSTUY	CLASSIC QUALITY	AACDEEEILRTTTT	DICTATE A LETTER
AACCIILMNRSTTU	CIRCUMSTANTIAL	AACDEEEIMNOQTU	ADEQUATE INCOME
AACCIILNNOOOST	CONSOCIATIONAL	AACDEEEINRSSTY	STEADY INCREASE
AACCILLNOOPTUY	OCCUPATIONALLY	AACDEEEIRRRSTT	RESTRICTED AREA
AACCILNORSTTUU	ACCULTURATIONS	AACDEEELNNPPTY	PEACE AND PLENTY
AACCKMMMNOOSSU	AS COMMON AS MUCK	AACDFFELNORSSV	LEAVES ONE'S CARD
AACCNNNOPRTUUU	RUN UP AN ACCOUNT	AACDEEEMNNORSV	CARVED ONE'S NAME
AACDDDEEEMNOOT	COME TO A DEAD END	AACDEEENOSSSTT	STATED ONE'S CASE
AACDDDEEGIINST	DECIDED AGAINST	AACDEEFGIMORRR	FORCED MARRIAGE
AACDDDEEINNNNR	DINNER AND DANCE	AACDEEFHORRRSW	REACHES FORWARD
AACDDDEKKNRSSU	DUCKS AND DRAKES	AACDEFFFIKILOOT	ACTED LIKE A FOOL
AACDDDENNOPPUW	PACED UP AND DOWN	AACDEEFILLNOWX	FIXED ALLOWANCE
AACDDDEORSTUWY	AWARDED CUSTODY	AACDEEFIMPRRTU	FRAMED A PICTURE
AACDDEEEGHINSX	EXCHANGED IDEAS	AACDEEFLRSTTUU	CAUSED A FLUTTER
AACDDEEEHHOPRW	HEADACHE POWDER	AACDEEGGLNNOSU	SECOND LANGUAGE
AACDDEEEHLORRT	CLEARED THE ROAD	AACDEEGHHINPRT	CHAPTER HEADING
AACDDEEEHMNNRT	DETACHED MANNER	AACDEEGHIKLNPT	DEALING THE PACK
AACDDEEELMNRRY	LED A MERRY DANCE	AACDEEGHINORTT	TEACHING TO READ
AACDDEEEMNNNOR	DEMAND AN ENCORE	AACDEEGHINRSTW	DANCES WITH RAGE
AACDDECFHORRRW	REACHED FORWARD	AACDEEGHNNOSTT	DANCES THE TANGO
AACDDEEFIKORSV	ASKED FOR ADVICE	AACDEEGIILLNRT	LEADING ARTICLE
AACDDEEFILLLNN	DECLINE AND FALL	AACDEEGILNNOPR	PLEAD IGNORANCE
AACDDEEGHINRTW	DANCED WITH RAGE	AACDEEGILNNPRS	SENDING A PARCEL
AACDDEEGHNNOTT	DANCED THE TANGO	AACDEEGILNRSST	LEADING ACTRESS
AACDDEEGIINSST	DECIDES AGAINST	AACDEEGIMNORRS	SECOND MARRIAGE
AACDDEEGILLNRU	GRADUAL DECLINE	AACDEEGINPRSWY	SPEEDWAY RACING
AACDDEEHIKNOST	CHAINED TO A DESK	AACDEEGINRRRSU	UNDERCARRIAGES
AACDDEEHKLNOPT	DANCED THE POLKA	AACDEEHHILNRTW	HANDLE WITH CARE
AACDDEEILOSTVV	DEVILS ADVOCATE	AACDEEHHINSSTT	CAST IN THE SHADE
AACDDEEIMNNOTT	DECONTAMINATED	AACDEEHHLLLOST	HOLD ALL THE ACES
AACDDEEIMORSVY	MADE A DISCOVERY	AACDEEHIILMNPT	EMPHATIC DENIAL
AACDDEEINNORRV	ORDER IN ADVANCE	AACDEEHIINNRSV	SEARCHED IN VAIN
AACDDEEMNNORTU	DEMAND A RECOUNT	AACDEEHILMRRTW	CLAIM THE REWARD
AACDDEFIORRRRW	CARRIED FORWARD	AACDEEHIMMNRSY	MECHANISED ARMY
AACDDEGHILLNNO	HOLDING A CANDLE	AACDEEHIMNRRRS	CHARRED REMAINS
AACDDEGILMMNNO	COMMANDING LEAD	AACDEEHINNNSTT	IN THE ASCENDANT
AACDDEHKLLNNOS	ALL HANDS ON DECK	AACDEEHINNORST	DANCES ON THE AIR
AACDDEIILRSTTU	DISARTICULATED	AACDEEHIORRTTT	READ THE RIOT ACT

AACDEEEHKLNOPST	DANCES THE POLKA
AACDEEHLLRTTYY	LADY CHATTERLEY
AACDEEHLNPPSSU	PLEASED AS PUNCH
AACDEEHLOORSSW	HAD A SCREW LOOSE
AACDEEHLPRRSTY	REACTED SHARPLY
AACDEEHNPRRTUY	CHEAP-DAY RETURN
AACDEEIIKMNOSS	MAKES A DECISION
AACDEEIILMMTTY	ACT IMMEDIATELY
AACDEEIILNNRTV	DEVIL INCARNATE
AACDEEIKLMORRW	WORKED A MIRACLE
AACDEEIKLNRSWW	AWKWARD SILENCE
AACDEEIKLPQRRU	PICKED A QUARREL
AACDEEIKMORSVY	MAKE A DISCOVERY
AACDEEILLNQTUW	WELL ACQUAINTED
AACDEEILNNPPPR	PENCIL AND PAPER
AACDEEILNNSSST	LEND ASSISTANCE
AACDEEIMNNOSTT	DECONTAMINATES
AACDEEKLORVVWY	COVERED WALKWAY
AACDEELLOPRRTY	CALLED TO PRAYER
AACDEELNNNRSTT	TRANSCENDENTAL
AACDEEMPRRSTUU	CREATED A RUMPUS
AACDEFGIRSSTUU	CUTS A SAD FIGURE
AACDEFGLOOOSST	SALE OF GOODS ACT
AACDEFIIINNOTZ	DENAZIFICATION
AACDEFINOORRTY	READY FOR ACTION
AACDEFIORRRRSW	CARRIES FORWARD
AACDEGGHIOORTW	WITH A GOOD GRACE
AACDEGHHILLNTT	HIGHLAND CATTLE
AACDEGHIILLNTT	CALLED IT A NIGHT
AACDEGHILOOTTY	HOLIDAY COTTAGE
AACDEGHINOPPRS	SHOPPING ARCADE
AACDEGHINRRTYY	CARRYING THE DAY
AACDEGIILNPRSV	SCRAPED A LIVING
AACDEGIILNPRTY	DIRECTING A PLAY
AACDEGIINNOSTW	WAITING A SECOND
AACDEGIINORTVY	GAINED A VICTORY
AACDEGIKKNNOST	KNOCKED AGAINST
AACDEGIKNPRSTT	STARTED PACKING
AACDEGILLMOORT	DERMATOLOGICAL
AACDEGILLNNNOO	DOING ALL ONE CAN
AACDEGILMNOSST	DOGMATICALNESS
AACDEGILNNOPRR	PLACING AN ORDER
AACDEGILNOPRRY	PLAYING A RECORD
AACDEGILNORSTW	DRAWING TO SCALE
AACDEGIMNNOORU	COME ROUND AGAIN
AACDEGIMNOPRSS	COMPASS READING
AACDEGINNNPRRT	DANCING PARTNER
AACDEGINORRSTV	GRANTS A DIVORCE
AACDEGKNOPPSSU	PACKS UP AND GOES
AACDEGLMNNORSS	SCANDALMONGERS
AACDEGMNOSSTUU	CUSTOM AND USAGE
AACDEHHILLMOTT	OLDHAM ATHLETIC
AACDEHIIKNPRTW	RACKED WITH PAIN
AACDEHILLNNNSS	CHANNEL ISLANDS
AACDEHIMNPRTUY	DEPUTY CHAIRMAN
AACDEHINRRTTUW	DRAW THE CURTAIN
AACDEHLNNOPSSS	CLAPS ONE'S HANDS
AACDEHLNOPSSYY	PSYCHOANALYSED
AACDEHMOPRSTUY	PACHYDERMATOUS
AACDEIIILLLSTY	IDEALISTICALLY
AACDEIIILMNNOST	DECIMALISATION
AACDEIIILMNOTZ	DECIMALIZATION
AACDEIIIKPRSTTT	SPIRITED ATTACK
AACDEIILMNNOOP	IDEAL COMPANION
AACDEIILNOSTTU	EDUCATIONALIST
AACDEIILNRRTUV	CARDINAL VIRTUE
AACDEIILPRRSTU	PARTICULARISED
AACDEIILPRRTUZ	PARTICULARIZED
AACDEIILRSSTTU	DISARTICULATES
AACDEIIMNORSTY	AERODYNAMICIST
AACDEIINORTTTX	DIRECT TAXATION
AACDEIKNNNNOVW	KNOWN IN ADVANCE
AACDEIKNNNOSVW	KNOWS IN ADVANCE
AACDEILLNORSWY	CARDINAL WOLSEY
AACDEILNNNOOST	CONDENSATIONAL
AACDEILNOOTTUY	EDUCATIONAL TOY
AACDEILPQRSTUU	QUADRUPLICATES
AACDEIMMNNORRSS	COMRADES IN ARMS
AACDEINNNOORRU	RADIO ANNOUNCER
AACDEINOPRRSTT	PROCRASTINATED
AACDEINOPRSSSW	PASSES IN A CROWD
AACDEKLORRSTWY	COWARDLY STREAK
AACDELNNOSSSSU	SCANDALOUSNESS
AACDELNOOPRSSY	PAYS AN OLD SCORE
AACDELNOPRSSSY	PLAYS ONE'S CARDS
AACDEMMMNOSSSU	ASSUMES COMMAND
AACDFFHIILORTY	HOLIDAY TRAFFIC
AACDFFIIILOORT	ARTIFICIAL FOOD
AACDFGHIINOOTT	ACT IN GOOD FAITH
AACDFHIIIMNRST	DRAMATIC FINISH
AACDFHIMORSSTY	DAY OF CHRISTMAS
AACDGGHINNNORU	CHANGING AROUND
AACDGHHINOSSSW	CHASING SHADOWS
AACDGHIILMNOPY	CAMPING HOLIDAY
AACDGHINNOPSWY	PAYING CASH DOWN
AACDGIIINOSSST	DISASSOCIATING
AACDGIILLNOSTY	DIAGNOSTICALLY
AACDGIILNNOSST	SOCIAL STANDING
AACDGIINOPPRST	PROPAGANDISTIC
AACDHIIILLOPTY	IDIOPATHICALLY
AACDHIMNOPRSST	DARTS CHAMPIONS
AACDHIRRRSSSTU	RICHARD STRAUSS
AACDIIIILLNNPRS	DISCIPLINARIAN
AACDIIILNNPRST	PITCAIRN ISLAND
AACDIIIINOOSSST	DISASSOCIATION
AACDIILLLMOPTY	DIPLOMATICALLY
AACDIILNNOPRST	CARDINAL POINTS
AACDIMMNOORSST	AS COMMON AS DIRT
AACDIMNNOPPUWY	WIND UP A COMPANY
AACEEEEGHMNRRT	REACH AGREEMENT
AACEEEEGKNNRVW	WREAK VENGEANCE
AACEEEEHKLMTTT	LET THEM EAT CAKE
AACEEEEHMNPRSS	PARMESAN CHEESE
AACEEEFFHHORTT	FACE OF THE EARTH
AACEEEFGHNORTX	RATE OF EXCHANGE
AACEEEFHHKORST	SHARE OF THE CAKE
AACEEEFHINRSTT	STARE IN THE FACE
AACEEEFILPRSTU	SPECIAL FEATURE
AACEEEFINRRSSS	INCREASES FARES
AACEEEGGHINRTV	NEGATIVE CHARGE
AACEEEGHHHRRTT	CHARGE THE EARTH
AACEEEGHINNTVW	WITH A VENGEANCE
AACEEEGHMNNNOS	CHANGE ONES NAME
AACEEEGIPPRRTT	CIGARETTE PAPER
AACEEEGKNOORTV	GAVE ONE A ROCKET
AACEEEGMOOSSYY	EASY COME,EASY GO
AACEEEGNORSSSU	ARGUES ONE'S CASE
AACEEEGNPRRSTT	STAGE CARPENTER
AACEEEHIIMNOSV	ACHIEVE ONES AIM
AACEEEHINNRSST	THE RENAISSANCE
AACEEEHIPRRTTV	PRIVATE TEACHER
AACEEEHISSTTTT	AESTHETIC TASTE
AACEEEHJKLRSTT	LEATHERJACKETS
AACEEEHKMRRRST	MARKET RESEARCH
AACEEEHKNRTTTW	RENEW THE ATTACK
AACEEEHLLNSSTT	CLEANS THE SLATE
AACEEEHLMNNRST	CHANNEL STEAMER
AACEEEHNNOOTVW	ON THE OCEAN WAVE
AACEEEIKKLNPRS	KEEP A SLACK REIN
AACEEEIKMMMNST	MAKES MINCEMEAT
AACEEEILNPRSUV	UNIVERSAL PEACE
AACEEEKLNNOPST	TAKEN ONE'S PLACE

AACEEEEKLNOPSST	TAKES ONE'S PLACE	AACEEHINRSSSTU	TEACHES RUSSIAN
AACEEEELLNNOPRS	LEARN ONE'S PLACE	AACEEHIPRRRSTT	CHARTERPARTIES
AACEEEELLPRRSTV	SPACE TRAVELLER	AACEEHIRRSTTTW	TREATS WITH CARE
AACEEEELMNNORSS	CLEARS ONE'S NAME	AACEEHKKLPSTTU	TAKE UP THE SLACK
AACEEEELMNRSTTT	CLEAR STATEMENT	AACEEHLLLNPRRS	CHARLES PARNELL
AACEEEMMNNOSSTU	CONSUMMATE EASE	AACEEHLLOPPRTT	APPLE CHARLOTTE
AACEEEMMNNORSSV	CARVES ONE'S NAME	AACEEHLNORSSTU	LANCASTER HOUSE
AACEEEMNNOORSST	CAME TO ONE'S EARS	AACEEHLOORSSSW	HAS A SCREW LOOSE
AACEEEENORSSTVY	CASTS AN EYE OVER	AACEEHLOPPRRST	ALPHA-RECEPTORS
AACEEENOSSSSTT	STATES ONE'S CASE	AACEEHNORRTUVW	TOUCH A RAW NERVE
AACEEFFIIKNPTT	KEEP-FIT FANATIC	AACEEHNPRRRRTY	HARRY CARPENTER
AACEEFFILNOTTY	AFFECTIONATELY	AACEEIIKLLNOTW	A TOWN LIKE ALICE
AACEEFFLNNOOST	FLAT ON ONES FACE	AACEEIIILLPPRST	PARTIAL ECLIPSE
AACEEFGGHLNNRU	FRENCH LANGUAGE	AACEEIIILMRRRTY	MILITARY CAREER
AACEEFGHSSTTTT	GETS AT THE FACTS	AACEEIILOPRSTV	OVERCAPITALISE
AACEEFHILNPSST	SLAPS IN THE FACE	AACEEIILOPRTVZ	OVERCAPITALIZE
AACEEFHLMOSSTU	FALSE MOUSTACHE	AACEEIILPPRTVY	APPRECIATIVELY
AACEEFILLORRUW	CAULIFLOWER EAR	AACEEIIMNNNRRT	ANCIENT MARINER
AACEEFILORRTUV	CLEAR FAVOURITE	AACEEIIMNNOSTV	NOMINATIVE CASE
AACEEFIMPRRSTU	FRAMES A PICTURE	AACEEIIRRSTTTV	CREATIVE ARTIST
AACEEFINNOPSST	PAINTS ONE'S FACE	AACEEIKKLNPRST	KEPT A SLACK REIN
AACEEFKNNNOSTY	TAKEN ONE'S FANCY	AACEEIKLMNOSST	STAKE ONES CLAIM
AACEEFKNNOSSTY	TAKES ONE'S FANCY	AACEEIILLMPPTXY	TYPICAL EXAMPLE
AACEEFKNORSTTV	ATTACK OF NERVES	AACEEIILLPRSTTT	CAPITAL LETTERS
AACEEFLLNOORRS	FOR ALL ONE CARES	AACEEILMMNSSTU	IMMACULATENESS
AACEEFLMOPPRRY	APPEAL FOR MERCY	AACEEILNNSSSTT	LENT ASSISTANCE
AACEEFLRSSTTUU	CAUSES A FLUTTER	AACEEILNRSSTTU	ARTICULATENESS
AACEEGGHHIMRTT	MAGGIE THATCHER	AACEEIILORSRTTV	VERSATILE ACTOR
AACEEGGHHNNNRST	RANG THE CHANGES	AACEEILORSSTVV	CASTS A VEIL OVER
AACEEGGHIMNNRT	TEACHING GERMAN	AACEEINNPRRSST	TRANSPARENCIES
AACEEGGHINRSTU	ARGUING THE CASE	AACEEINOPRSSTT	STARE INTO SPACE
AACEEGGILLLNOY	GENEALOGICALLY	AACEEINRSSTTTV	ATTRACTIVENESS
AACEEGGHHILLNRT	HEARING THE CALL	AACEEKMNOQSSTU	MAKES A CONQUEST
AACEEGGHHINRRST	HEART-SEARCHING	AACEELLLNPRSSU	PRUNELLA SCALES
AACEEGGHHLNOPPR	ENCEPHALOGRAPH	AACEELLLOPRRSU	PARALLEL COURSE
AACEEGGHIILNRRT	CLEARING THE AIR	AACEELLNOPPRSW	LOCAL NEWSPAPER
AACEEGGHIKNNOSV	HAVING ONE'S CAKE	AACEELNNOPRSUW	NUCLEAR WEAPONS
AACEEGGHILMPRYY	HYPERGLYCAEMIA	AACEEMPRRSSTUU	CREATES A RUMPUS
AACEEGGHILNNRTT	CENTRAL HEATING	AACEENNOORSSTW	NO CASE TO ANSWER
AACEEGGHILNRTWY	CLEARING THE WAY	AACEENOOPSSTTV	VACATE ONES POST
AACEEGGHINPSTTY	STAYING THE PACE	AACEFFGIILLLRT	ILLEGAL TRAFFIC
AACEEGGHLMNOPRS	ENCEPHALOGRAMS	AACEFFGLLMORRS	FALLS FROM GRACE
AACEEGGHNNOSSWY	CHANGE ONES WAYS	AACEFFINORRRTW	WARRANT OFFICER
AACEEGGHNNPRRST	CHANGE PARTNERS	AACEFFINRRRSTII	CURRENT AFFAIRS
AACEEGIIILLMNSV	EVANGELICALISM	AACEFFLMORTTTY	MATTER-OF-FACTLY
AACEEGIILMNNOR	AMERICAN LEGION	AACEFGGHILNORT	FLOATING CHARGE
AACEEGIINSSSTV	GIVE ASSISTANCE	AACEFGIILLLNNP	FALLING IN PLACE
AACEEGILLORRTT	ROLL A CIGARETTE	AACEFGIILNOPRT	FOREIGN CAPITAL
AACEEGILNNORTV	LEAVING NO TRACE	AACEFGLLLNOPSU	PULLS A LONG FACE
AACEEGILNOOTTV	LOVE IN A COTTAGE	AACEFHILNOOPPR	LINE OF APPROACH
AACEEGIMNNNOVY	CONVEY A MEANING	AACEFHIMRRSSTT	AFTER CHRISTMAS
AACEEGINNNRSTU	INSURANCE AGENT	AACEFHINORRSTU	SOUTHERN AFRICA
AACEEGINRSSSUV	GIVE ASSURANCES	AACEFHMNNOSTTY	NON-SAFETY MATCH
AACEEGLLMNOPRT	COMPLEAT ANGLER	AACEFIIILMNNST	FINANCIAL TIMES
AACEEGMMOPPRRS	SPACE PROGRAMME	AACEFIIILNRSST	ARTIFICIALNESS
AACEEHHHILMORST	CHAMOIS LEATHER	AACEFIILMORTTU	AUTOMATIC RIFLE
AACEEHHINPSSST	TEACHES SPANISH	AACEFIILOPPRRS	PAIR OF CALIPERS
AACEEHHLLORRST	HALLE ORCHESTRA	AACEFILLLNOPST	FALLS INTO PLACE
AACEEHHLMNNSTW	SWAM THE CHANNEL	AACEFILLNOSSSU	FALLACIOUSNESS
AACEEHHLORRTTT	CLEAR THE THROAT	AACEFIMNOORTUV	CAME INTO FAVOUR
AACEEHIILNRSTT	CASTLE IN THE AIR	AACEFIORRRSTTT	FIRST-RATE ACTOR
AACEEHIINNRSSV	SEARCHES IN VAIN	AACEFKOOOPSSTT	SACK OF POTATOES
AACEEHIJNORRTT	JOIN THE RAT-RACE	AACEFLLOOPRRRT	CALL FOR A REPORT
AACEEHIKKLNSTT	TAKE IN THE SLACK	AACEGGHHINOPRR	CHOREAGRAPHING
AACEEHILLMPTTY	EMPATHETICALLY	AACEGGHILLOPRY	GEOGRAPHICALLY
AACEEHILLMTTTY	METATHETICALLY	AACEGGHILMPSTU	CAUGHT A GLIMPSE
AACEEHILMMMRST	MICHAELMAS TERM	AACEGGHIINNNPS	CHANGING PLANES
AACEEHILMNSSST	IN THE SAME CLASS	AACEGGILNNOORT	CONGREGATIONAL
AACEEHILNNPSTU	A PLACE IN THE SUN	AACEGGINNRRTTU	GRANTING A TRUCE
AACEEHILNOSSST	CHASES ONE'S TAIL	AACEGHHIILSSTU	HIGH CASUALTIES
AACEEHILRRTUVX	EXTRAVEHICULAR	AACEGHHIIMNNSW	WASHING MACHINE

AACEGHHIINRSST	RAISING THE CASH	AACEHLMNNOORST	STOLEN A MARCH ON
AACEGHHILNOPRT	ETHNOGRAPHICAL	AACEHLNOPPRSSY	APOCRYPHALNESS
AACEGHHIMOPPTT	APOPHTHEGMATIC	AACEHLNOPSSSYY	PSYCHOANALYSES
AACEGHHINRTTTU	CAUGHT THE TRAIN	AACEHMNOPRSTUY	PARENCHYMATOUS
AACEGHHNORTTUW	CAUGHT ON THE RAW	AACEHOORSTTTTX	EXTRACTS A TOOTH
AACEGHHOPPRTUW	CAUGHT A WHOPPER	AACEHQQRSSSTUU	SQUASH RACQUETS
AACEGHIILLPPRY	EPIGRAPHICALLY	AACEIIILNOPSST	SPECIALISATION
AACEGHIIMNNRSV	VANISHING CREAM	AACEIIILNOPSTZ	SPECIALIZATION
AACEGHIINNOPRS	COINING A PHRASE	AACEIIILNPTTVY	ANTICIPATIVELY
AACEGHIINNTTTU	AUTHENTICATING	AACEIIILLMMNNOOT	CALAMINE LOTION
AACEGHIJKRSTTT	STRAIGHTJACKET	AACEIILLMNNRRWY	CRIMINAL LAWYER
AACEGHILLLMPTY	PHLEGMATICALLY	AACEIIILNPSTTY	ANTISEPTICALLY
AACEGHILLMOPRT	METALLOGRAPHIC	AACEIIILNRTTUY	INARTICULATELY
AACEGHILLNOPTY	PATHOGENICALLY	AACEIIILMNNNOOT	NATIONAL INCOME
AACEGHILLOOPRS	PHRASEOLOGICAL	AACEIIILMNNOTTT	CLAIM ATTENTION
AACEGHILMNOOSZ	SCHOOL MAGAZINE	AACEIILNNORSTT	CENTRALISATION
AACEGHILOPPRRT	PETROGRAPHICAL	AACEIILNNORTTZ	CENTRALIZATION
AACEGHIMMNNNNRR	CHARMING MANNER	AACEIILNNPSSST	CASTLES IN SPAIN
AACEGHIMNOPRST	CINEMATOGRAPHS	AACEIILNOOPPSU	PAPILIONACEOUS
AACEGHIMNOPRTY	CINEMATOGRAPHY	AACEIILNOPRTTU	RECAPITULATION
AACEGHLNNSTUUW	WELTANSCHAUUNG	AACEIILNORRTVY	EARLY VICTORIAN
AACEGIIINNRSST	SECTARIANISING	AACEIILNORSSTU	SECULARISATION
AACEGIIINNRSTZ	SECTARIANIZING	AACEIILNORSTUZ	SECULARIZATION
AACEGIIKNNRSTT	CREATING A STINK	AACEIILPPPRSTT	PAST PARTICIPLE
AACEGIILLLLSTY	LEGALISTICALLY	AACEIILPRRSSTU	PARTICULARISES
AACEGIILLLOOTY	AETIOLOGICALLY	AACEIILPRRSTUZ	PARTICULARIZES
AACEGIILLNOPTT	POLITICAL AGENT	AACEIINNORSSTW	SIR ISAAC NEWTON
AACEGIILLNORTY	IATROGENICALLY	AACEIINORSSSUV	AVARICIOUSNESS
AACEGIILMNPRSS	PRESSING A CLAIM	AACEIINPPRSTTU	PAINTS A PICTURE
AACEGIILNPRSSV	SCRAPES A LIVING	AACEIKLOOPTTUY	TAKE OUT A POLICY
AACEGIILNPRTTU	RECAPITULATING	AACEIKPRRSSTTU	SURPRISE ATTACK
AACEGIINOORSTT	CATEGORISATION	AACEIILLLORSTY	ALLOSTERICALLY
AACEGIINOORTTZ	CATEGORIZATION	AACEILLLNOPSTY	PLEONASTICALLY
AACEGIKKLLNPRS	LACKING SPARKLE	AACEILLMMNORTY	MANOMETRICALLY
AACEGIKKLNNOOS	LOOKING ASKANCE	AACEILLMMRSTYY	ASYMMETRICALLY
AACEGIKLMNNNRS	LACKING MANNERS	AACEILLMSSTTYY	SYSTEMATICALLY
AACEGIKMNNRTUY	MAKING A CENTURY	AACEILLOORTTUY	AUTOEROTICALLY
AACEGIKMNRSTUY	MAKING A CURTSEY	AACEILMMNOPPTY	PAY A COMPLIMENT
AACEGILLLOOPTY	APOLOGETICALLY	AACEILMNNOOPST	COMPENSATIONAL
AACEGILLNNRRTU	RETURNING A CALL	AACEILMNORRTTY	MORAL CERTAINTY
AACEGILMNOORUZ	COLOUR MAGAZINE	AACEILMNOSSSTU	CALAMITOUSNESS
AACEGILNNOORTT	TOTAL IGNORANCE	AACEILMNRSSSTU	STRAINS A MUSCLE
AACEGILNRRTTUY	RECTANGULARITY	AACEILNNOOPRSW	NAPOLEONIC WARS
AACEGIMNPRSSUY	GAINS SUPREMACY	AACEILNNOORSTV	CONSERVATIONAL
AACEGLLMMNORST	MALCOLM SARGENT		CONVERSATIONAL
AACEHHIIKKNSTV	HAVE A THICK SKIN	AACEILNNORSTTT	CENTRAL STATION
AACEHHIKNPRTTW	RAN WITH THE PACK	AACEILNNPRSTUY	INCURS A PENALTY
AACEHHINOORSTT	CHAIN TO THE OARS	AACEILNOORRSTV	CONSERVATORIAL
AACEHIIIMNRSTT	ARITHMETICIANS	AACEIMMNORSTUV	SUMMER VACATION
AACEHIILLLLPTY	PHILATELICALLY	AACEIMNOOPPRST	AMERICAN TROOPS
AACEHIILLMRTTY	ARITHMETICALLY	AACEIMNOPPRTVY	PRIVATE COMPANY
AACEHIILLNTTTY	ANTITHETICALLY	AACEIMNOPRSTTU	STORM IN A TEA-CUP
AACEHIILMNSTUV	MALE CHAUVINIST	AACEINNNRRSTUY	INNER SANCTUARY
AACEHIILLNNNOST	CHANNELISATION	AACEINOPPRRSTU	APPEARS IN COURT
AACEHIILNNNOTZ	CHANNELIZATION	AACEINOPRRSSTT	PROCRASTINATES
AACEHIIMNOSSTT	SCHEMATISATION	AACEINOPRSSSST	CAST ASPERSIONS
AACEHIIMNOSTTZ	SCHEMATIZATION	AACEKLNNORSTUY	CANTANKEROUSLY
AACEHIINNOTTTU	AUTHENTICATION	AACEKMOORRSTUU	MARK OUT A COURSE
AACEHIKKLMORRW	WORK LIKE A CHARM	AACELNOPRRSSTU	NATURAL PROCESS
AACEHILLMNNORY	ENHARMONICALLY	AACENORTTTTWWY	TWENTY-TWO CARAT
AACEHILLMNNTTW	CAN'T WIN THEM ALL	AACFGHIILNSTTT	LIGHT FANTASTIC
AACEHILLMNOPTY	PHONEMATICALLY	AACFGIIIMNNOST	MAGNIFICATIONS
AACEHILLMOPRTY	METAPHORICALLY	AACFGIIKLNNORT	LACK OF TRAINING
AACEHILLMPSTYY	METAPHYSICALLY	AACFGILLLNOOW	FOLLOW A CALLING
AACEHILMNNORSS	HARMONICALNESS	AACFGILNNOORST	CONFLAGRATIONS
AACEHILMNORRTT	MERCHANT TAILOR	AACFGILNORRTUV	VULGAR FRACTION
AACEHILNNORSST	IN ANOTHER CLASS	AACFGINOORRRTY	CARRYING TOO FAR
AACEHIMNOOPSSV	HAVE COMPASSION	AACFGMNNNOSUYY	YOUNG MANS FANCY
AACEHINORSTTTU	AUTHENTICATORS	AACFIIIKLLRST	ARTIFICIAL SILK
AACEHKNORSTTTU	TAKEN A SHORT CUT	AACFIIILMNOPST	AMPLIFICATIONS
AACEHKORSSTTTU	TAKES A SHORT CUT	AACFIIILNOQSTU	QUALIFICATIONS

AACFIIIMMNNOOT	AMMONIFICATION	AACIILLMMNSTUY	NUMISMATICALLY
AACFIIINNOOPST	SAPONIFICATION	AACIILLMQSTUUY	MUSICAL QUALITY
AACFIIINNOQTTU	QUANTIFICATION	AACIILLOPPRTTY	PARTY POLITICAL
AACFIIINORSTTT	STRATIFICATION		POLITICAL PARTY
AACFIILLMRSSST	FIRST CLASS MAIL	AACIILNOOPPRRST	CONSPIRATORIAL
AACFIILMNNOORT	CONFIRMATIONAL	AACIILNORSSTTY	CRYSTALISATION
AACFIILNNORRWY	FINANCIAL WORRY	AACIILNORSTTYZ	CRYSTALIZATION
AACFIILORSSTTY	SATISFACTORILY	AACIILOPRSSTTY	SOCIALIST PARTY
AACFIIMNOOPRRS	FAIR COMPARISON	AACIINNOOSSTTT	ACTION STATIONS
AACFILMNNOOOORT	CONFORMATIONAL	AACIKLOOOPRRSY	ALAS POOR YORICK
AACFINORSSTTUY	UNSATISFACTORY	AACILLLLOOPRTY	ALLOTROPICALLY
AACGGHHIILMNTT	LIGHTING A MATCH	AACILLLNORSTUY	ULTRASONICALLY
AACGGHIINNNRST	CHANGING TRAINS	AACILLMNOORSTY	ASTRONOMICALLY
AACGGIIKKNNST	KICKING AGAINST	AACILLMOPSTTYY	ASYMPTOTICALLY
AACGGILMNNOOWY	COMING A LONG WAY	AACILNNNOSTTUV	ANTICONVULSANT
AACGGILNNORTTU	CONGRATULATING	AACINNNORSSTTT	CONSTANT STRAIN
AACGHHINNORSUV	HAVING A CRUSH ON	AACINOOOPRRTTX	CORPORATION TAX
AACGHHMOOPRRTY	CHROMATOGRAPHY	AACINOOPRRRSTT	PROCRASTINATOR
AACGHIIJKLLMRT	I'M ALL RIGHT, JACK	AACINORRTUVWYY	RUNAWAY VICTORY
AACGHIIKMNRSTT	STRIKING A MATCH	AACKLNOOPRRSTY	ROYAL TANK CORPS
AACGHIILLPRSST	CALLIGRAPHISTS	AACLLNNOPRTTUY	CONTRAPUNTALLY
AACGHILLLOOPTY	PATHOLOGICALLY	AACLMOOPRRRSYY	ROYAL ARMY CORPS
AACGHILLRRRSTU	ARTHUR SCARGILL	AADDDDEEFORSWW	ADDED A FEW WORDS
AACGHILMOOPRST	PHARMACOLOGIST	AADDDDEEHINRSW	WASHED AND DRIED
AACGHLOOPPRSYY	PARAPSYCHOLOGY	AADDDEEEFIMTTT	ADMITTED DEFEAT
AACGIIINNNOPTT	ACTION PAINTING	AADDDEEEHHNRSS	HARDHEADEDNESS
AACGIIKLNNOSTY	LAYING IN A STOCK	AADDDEEHHMMNUW	HUMMED AND HAWED
AACGIIKLNOPRTW	WORKING CAPITAL	AADDDEEHNNNORU	A HUNDRED AND ONE
AACGIIKOPRRTTW	GATWICK AIRPORT	AADDDEEHNOPPRY	HOPED AND PRAYED
AACGIILLMOOPRT	PRIMATOLOGICAL	AADDDEEIINNRSV	EARNS A DIVIDEND
AACGIILLOORSSY	ASSYRIOLOGICAL	AADDDEILLNORSS	LORDS AND LADIES
AACGIILNRTTUWY	RAILWAY CUTTING	AADDDENOORSSTT	STOOD AND STARED
AACGIINNNNORSW	WINNING AN OSCAR	AADDDGHIMNOOOT	HAD A GOOD MIND TO
AACGIJKLNNORSU	KING JUAN CARLOS	AADDEEEEEHLNRST	THREADS A NEEDLE
AACGIILLOORSTY	ASTROLOGICALLY	AADDEEEEEILMNST	MEETS A DEADLINE
AACGILLLOOTTUY	TAUTOLOGICALLY	AADDEEEEIMNRST	REMAINED SEATED
AACGILLLRRTUUY	AGRICULTURALLY	AADDEEEFFGMRSU	SUFFERED DAMAGE
AACGILLMOOOSTT	STOMATOLOGICAL	AADDEEEFGILNNW	NEW-FANGLED IDEA
AACGILLMOORRTY	MARTYROLOGICAL	AADDEEEFHLLPSU	FULL SPEED AHEAD
AACGILMNOOPSST	CAMPANOLOGISTS	AADDEEEFNRSSTW	FEEDS AND WATERS
AACGILNNOORTTU	CONGRATULATION	AADDEEEGGINNRT	ENGAGED IN TRADE
AACGIMNNOPPRTY	PARTING COMPANY	AADDEEEHIMNSTV	DAME EDITH EVANS
AACGINNNOPTTTU	PUTTING ON AN ACT	AADDEEEHLLNRST	THE DARDANELLES
AACGLNOORRSTTU	CONGRATULATORS	AADDEEEHLLNSSW	WHEELS AND DEALS
AACGLNOORRTTUY	CONGRATULATORY	AADDEEEIILMRST	DEMATERIALISED
AACHHIINORSTUY	ICHTHYOSAURIAN	AADDEEEIILMRTZ	DEMATERIALIZED
AACHHILLMRRTYY	ARRHYTHMICALLY	AADDEEELMORSSV	SERVED AS A MODEL
AACHHIMPPRSSTY	HAPPY CHRISTMAS	AADDEEELMPRSST	PADDLE STEAMERS
AACHIIIMNNSTT	ANTIHISTAMINIC	AADDEEEELNORSSV	LEAVE NO ADDRESS
AACHIIKMMORRT	COMMIT HARA-KIRI	AADDEEERSSTTYY	YESTERDAYS DATE
AACHIILLMNSTUY	HUMANISTICALLY	AADDEEFGHLOORS	FLOG A DEAD HORSE
AACHIILLNNOSTU	HALLUCINATIONS	AADDEEFGIINOTV	AVOIDING DEFEAT
AACHIILLOPRSTY	APHORISTICALLY	AADDEEFGILLOSS	LEADS A DOG'S LIFE
	HISTORICAL PLAY	AADDEEFGILNORV	LEAVING FOR DEAD
AACHIKLNNOPTUW	WALK INTO A PUNCH	AADDEEFGMORSSU	SUED FOR DAMAGES
AACHILLOORTTUY	LOCAL AUTHORITY	AADDEEFILMNRRS	FIREMANS LADDER
AACHILLOPSTTYY	HYPOSTATICALLY	AADDEEFLLORRTU	FORT LAUDERDALE
AACHILNOPSSSYY	PSYCHOANALYSIS	AADDEEGGINRRRU	GRENADIER GUARD
AACHIMPRRSSTTY	CHRISTMAS PARTY	AADDEEGHIINRST	RAISING THE DEAD
AACHLNOPSSSTYY	PSYCHOANALYSTS	AADDEEGHLLRTYU	GLUTARALDEHYDE
AACHOORRRTTTUZ	CUT-THROAT RAZOR	AADDEEGILRRRSW	SIR EDWARD ELGAR
AACIIIINNNOPTT	IN ANTICIPATION	AADDEEGIMMNRRS	DREAMING DREAMS
AACIIILLMMRSTU	MULTIRACIALISM	AADDEEGNRRSTUU	UNDERGRADUATES
AACIIILLNRSTTY	INARTISTICALLY	AADDEEHILNNORT	NEANDERTHALOID
AACIIILMNOPPST	MISAPPLICATION	AADDEEHILRRRST	RAIDS THE LARDER
AACIIILNNORSST	NATIONAL CRISIS	AADDEEHIMNRSTY	MY HANDS ARE TIED
AACIIILNOPSSTT	PLASTICISATION	AADDEEHINNORSS	RAISED ONE'S HAND
AACIIILNOPSTTZ	PLASTICIZATION	AADDEEHINNRTWW	WIND AND WEATHER
AACIIIMNOOSSST	ASSOCIATIONISM	AADDEEHINORSUW	EDWARDIAN HOUSE
AACIIILLLMORSTY	MORALISTICALLY	AADDEEHINRSSSW	WASHES AND DRIES
AACIIILLLRSTTUY	ALTRUISTICALLY	AADDEEHMNOPRSS	HOPES AND DREAMS

927

AADDEEHNNOSSTY	STAYED ONE'S HAND
AADDEEHORSTTTV	STARVED TO DEATH
AADDEEIILNNOST	DENATIONALISED
AADDEEIILNNOTZ	DENATIONALIZED
AADDEEIINPRTTY	IDENTITY PARADE
AADDEEIKKNNSTY	STEAK AND KIDNEY
AADDEEILLNRSSW	LEEWARD ISLANDS
AADDEEINNOTUVW	WEAVED IN AND OUT
AADDEEIPRRSSTV	PRIVATE ADDRESS
AADDEEKMMMNNOSS	MAKES DEMANDS ON
	MAKES NO DEMANDS
AADDEEKMMNNRSTU	MAKES REDUNDANT
AADDEEKMOPPRRR	DROPPED A REMARK
AADDEELNOQRRSU	SQUADRON LEADER
AADDEEMMMNNPSTY	DEMANDS PAYMENT
AADDEFLLNOTUWY	FATALLY WOUNDED
AADDEFNOORSTWY	SWAYED TO AND FRO
AADDEGGHNRRSTU	GRANDDAUGHTERS
AADDEGHHINNNNO	GONE HAND IN HAND
AADDEGHHINNNOS	GOES HAND IN HAND
AADDEGHIKMNNRU	MAKING A HUNDRED
AADDEGHINOSSTT	AGAINST THE ODDS
AADDEGHINRSTTW	STANDARD WEIGHT
AADDEGHLMNNORT	THE GRAND OLD MAN
AADDEGHOPRRSSS	ADDRESSOGRAPHS
AADDEGIKLLNTTW	TALKING TWADDLE
AADDEGILLLNNOR	LENDING A DOLLAR
AADDEGIMNNNOPY	PAYING ON DEMAND
AADDEGINNNORTW	DRAWING TO AN END
AADDEGINNRSTVW	GRANDSTAND VIEW
AADDEGLLLLNOOW	ALL WELL AND GOOD
AADDEHHHHINPTW	HAD THE WHIP-HAND
AADDEHHINNNNTW	WENT HAND IN HAND
AADDEHHIORTTWY	DO IT THE HARD WAY
AADDEHHLORSTTW	HAD THE LAST WORD
AADDEHILNOTWW	LAID DOWN THE LAW
AADDEHILNNNOOS	LAID ONE'S HAND ON
AADDEHILOPTTUW	WITHOUT A PADDLE
AADDEHIMNORSST	DID AS THE ROMANS
AADDEHINNOSSTT	STAND ON ITS HEAD
AADDEHKNNOPSUW	SHAKE UP AND DOWN
AADDEHNNNOOSTU	THOUSAND AND ONE
AADDEHNNNORSTU	DONE A HAND'S TURN
AADDEHNNORSSTU	DOES A HAND'S TURN
AADDEIIILNSTTU	STUDIED ITALIAN
AADDEILLNNORTV	TORVILL AND DEAN
AADDEILNOOORST	LAID AT ONE'S DOOR
AADDEINNOPPRTW	POWDER AND PAINT
AADDFGINORRRTW	DARTING FORWARD
AADDFHHMMNNOORT	FROM HAND TO HAND
AADDGGHHLNOOTTU	TAUGHT AN OLD DOG
AADDGHIMNOOOST	HAS A GOOD MIND TO
AADDGIIKNNNRST	STANDING A DRINK
AADDGIILNNRSTV	LIVING STANDARD
AADDGINNNORSTU	STANDING A ROUND
	STANDING AROUND
AADDHILNNOSSTU	THOUSAND ISLAND
AADDHMNRSTUUYY	MAUNDY THURSDAY
AADDINPSSSTTUW	SPIT AND SAWDUST
AADDKLNNOPSUWW	WALKS UP AND DOWN
AADEEEEEHKLLPV	KEEP A LEVEL HEAD
AADEEEEEFLNOSST	SEALED ONE'S FATE
AADEEEEEGGHLTVY	GAVE THE GLAD EYE
AADEEEEEGGLORRT	TO A LARGE DEGREE
AADEEEEHIIKLSV	HEAD LIKE A SIEVE
AADEEEEEHKLLPTV	KEPT A LEVEL HEAD
AADEEEEELMMNOTT	MADE AN OMELETTE
AADEEEEPRSSTTT	DESPERATE STATE
AADEEEFFHLMNNT	FANNED THE FLAME
AADEEEFFHNOOST	ATE ONE'S HEAD OFF
	EAT ONE'S HEAD OFF

AADEEEEFFLLNORS	FELL ON DEAF EARS
AADEEEFGHILMNS	FEELING ASHAMED
AADEEEFGHLRRTT	ALFRED THE GREAT
AADEEEFGIOPRST	PATE DE FOIE GRAS
AADEEEFHHHKOST	SHAKE OF THE HEAD
AADEEEFHILMNST	FEED THE ANIMALS
AADEEEFLNNRTUW	TURNED A NEW LEAF
AADEEEGGINNRST	ENGAGES IN TRADE
AADEEEGHHINOSV	GAVE ONE HIS HEAD
AADEEEGHIKSTWY	EIGHT DAYS A WEEK
AADEEEGHILNRST	REGAINS THE LEAD
AADEEEGHLMPRST	GREASED THE PALM
AADEEEGHLRRTTY	GREATHEARTEDLY
AADEEEGHMNRTTU	HEATED ARGUMENT
AADEEEGHNNNRTT	THREATEN DANGER
AADEEEGHNNRTTW	WATER THE GARDEN
AADEEEGIINRTTV	VEGETARIAN DIET
AADEEEGKMNNRRT	MARKET GARDENER
AADEEEGLMNRSST	SENDS A TELEGRAM
AADEEEGNNOSTWY	GET ONE'S END AWAY
AADEEEGNNRRTUU	UNDER GUARANTEE
AADEEEHHILPRTT	ADELPHI THEATRE
AADEEEHHKNNOSS	SHAKEN ONE'S HEAD
AADEEEHHKNOSSS	SHAKES ONE'S HEAD
AADEEEHHLMORTT	MODERATE HEALTH
AADEEEHHLPRSTU	HAD THE PLEASURE
AADEEEHHLRTVYY	HEAVYHEARTEDLY
AADEEEHIKLNRTV	LEAVE IN THE DARK
AADEEEHIMMNORT	REMAINED AT HOME
AADEEEHIMMRRTT	MERMAID THEATRE
AADEEEHKLRRSTT	DEERSTALKER HAT
AADEEEHLLPPRTW	PAPERED THE WALL
AADEEEHLNNORSV	REVEAL ONE'S HAND
AADEEEHLRRRSSS	DRESS REHEARSAL
AADEEEHPPRRTWY	PREPARED THE WAY
AADEEEHPRRRSTW	REAPS THE REWARD
AADEEEIILMRSST	DEMATERIALISES
AADEEEIILMRSTZ	DEMATERIALIZES
AADEEEIILLPPPR	PARALLELEPIPED
AADEEEIILLNNRVW	WE LIVE AND LEARN
AADEEEINNQSSTU	INADEQUATENESS
AADEEELLMNOOPR	MODEL AEROPLANE
AADEEELMNORTTT	MODERATE TALENT
AADEEELMNRSSTT	ELDER STATESMAN
AADEEELMORSSSV	SERVES AS A MODEL
AADEEELNOPSSTT	SET ON A PEDESTAL
AADEEEMNORSTUW	WE ARE NOT AMUSED
AADEEFFHKNOTTY	TAKEN THE DAY OFF
AADEEFFHKOSTTY	TAKES THE DAY OFF
AADEEFFILNORRR	RAN FOR DEAR LIFE
AADEEFFMNNORTU	FAME AND FORTUNE
AADEEFGGHLNOSZ	HALF A DOZEN EGGS
AADEEFGHILNNOS	EASE OF HANDLING
AADEEFGHINRTWY	FRIGHTENED AWAY
AADEEFGHLLSTTU	SALUTED THE FLAG
AADEEFGHLNNORT	HEART OF ENGLAND
AADEEFGIIMMNRTV	GIVEN A FIRM DATE
AADEEFGIIMRSTV	GIVES A FIRM DATE
AADEEFGIKMOOSW	MAKES A GOOD WIFE
AADEEFGILLLRTZ	ELLA FITZGERALD
AADEEFGINORRTT	FEARING TO TREAD
AADEEFGKNORRTT	TAKE FOR GRANTED
AADEEFGMORSSSU	SUES FOR DAMAGES
AADEEFHHILNOST	LEAD THE FASHION
AADEEFHILNRTTY	FAINTHEARTEDLY
AADEEFHLMNOOST	OLD MAN OF THE SEA
AADEEFHMNNOOSTW	WHAT ONE'S MADE OF
AADEEFHMOPRRTT	MADE FOR THE PART
AADEEFIMOORRTT	FAIR TO MODERATE
AADEEFINNNPRRT	AFTER-DINNER NAP
AADEEFKMNORSTT	STATE OF DENMARK

AADEEFLLNOPSTU	PULLED A FAST ONE	AADEEIKNOQSSTU	ASKED A QUESTION
AADEEFMNNOOTTY	DAY OF ATONEMENT	AADEEILMNTTTTU	MENTAL ATTITUDE
AADEEFNNOOORUV	DONE ONE A FAVOUR	AADEEILNORRVVW	DRAWN A VEIL OVER
AADEEFNNOOSVWW	WAVE OF ONE'S WAND	AADEEILNPPRSWY	DAILY NEWSPAPER
AADEEFNOOORSUV	DOES ONE A FAVOUR	AADEEILNRRSSTU	TREASURE ISLAND
AADEEFOPPRRRRW	PREPARED FOR WAR	AADEEILNRRSTTT	TRANSLITERATED
AADEEFORRRSTWW	DRAWERS OF WATER	AADEEILORRSVVW	DRAWS A VEIL OVER
AADEEGGHHHINNT	HANGING THE HEAD	AADEEIMNNNRSTW	DENNIS WATERMAN
AADEEGGHIORRUV	GAVE A ROUGH RIDE	AADEEINNOORRSW	A WORD IN ONE'S EAR
AADEEGGILNRSSS	READING GLASSES	AADEEINNOSTUVW	WEAVES IN AND OUT
AADEEGGIMNNRST	AGGRANDISEMENT	AADEEINNPRSSTT	ANTIDEPRESSANT
AADEEGGIMNNRTZ	AGGRANDIZEMENT	AADEEKMNNOSSST	MAKES ONE'S STAND
AADEEGGLMNNORU	MODERN LANGUAGE	AADEEKNNNOSSTT	TAKEN ONE'S STAND
AADEEGGMMNNOOT	GOOD MANAGEMENT	AADEEKNNNOSSTT	TAKES ONE'S STAND
AADEEGHHHIKNST	SHAKING THE HEAD	AADEEKNOORSTTW	TAKE AT ONE'S WORD
AADEEGHHIORRUV	HAVE A ROUGH RIDE	AADEEKNOQRRSTU	ASKED NO QUARTER
AADEEGHIILNRTV	LAID IN THE GRAVE	AADEELLMNPRTTY	DEPARTMENTALLY
AADEEGHIIMNSUV	GIVE A MAN HIS DUE	AADEELNOPPSTTU	PUT ON A PEDESTAL
AADEEGHIINNRST	REARING ITS HEAD	AADEELOORSTTTT	STARTED TOO LATE
AADEEGHIINRSTV	VEGETARIAN DISH	AADEELPPQSTUUY	ADEQUATE SUPPLY
AADEEGHIINSTTT	AGAINST THE TIDE	AADEENNNNNORRTW	WENT ON AN ERRAND
AADEEGHILLNPTY	PLAYING THE LEAD	AADEENNPPRSSTT	PAST AND PRESENT
AADEEGHILLPRTY	DAILY TELEGRAPH	AADEEPRRSSTTUU	SUPERSATURATED
AADEEGHKMORSTV	GOD SAVE THE MARK	AADEFFIILORSTT	EDITORIAL STAFF
AADEEGHLNNOPST	GOLDEN PHEASANT	AADEFFLNOPPRSU	APPEAL FOR FUNDS
AADEEGHNOPRRTW	NARROWED THE GAP	AADEFGGHMORSTU	GAME OF DRAUGHTS
AADEEGIKLNNORT	TAKEN IN A LODGER	AADEFGHIIMNOTT	MADE A NIGHT OF IT
AADEEGIKLNORST	TAKES IN A LODGER	AADEFGHILOOSTT	GET A LOAD OF THIS!
AADEEGILLLNRTT	LITTLE AND LARGE	AADEFGILLLNOOW	FOLLOWING A LEAD
AADEEGILNNORHT	LEARNING TO READ	AADEFGILLNNOTU	UNFOLDING A TALE
AADEEGILNNSSTV	READING A LESSON	AADEFGILNNORRW	LEANING FORWARD
AADEEGILNNSSTV	LEAVES STANDING	AADEFGILNNOPRY	PLAY FOR ENGLAND
AADEEFGIMNNRST	DISARRANGEMENT	AADEFGLNOORRSS	GARLAND OF ROSES
AADEEGIMNOPRWZ	POWDER MAGAZINE	AADEFHIIKKLNRS	DRANK LIKE A FISH
AADEEGINNRRSTU	TEARING ASUNDER	AADEFHIKLMNORT	TAKEN A FIRM HOLD
AADEEGLLLNORTV	TRAVELLED ALONG	AADEFHIKLMORST	TAKES A FIRM HOLD
AADEEGLLLOOSTT	TELLS A GOOD TALE	AADEFHILMOORTT	FROM HEAD TO TAIL
AADEEGNNNNNOORR	GONE ON AN ERRAND	AADEFHINNOOPRS	ONE PAIR OF HANDS
AADEEGNNNOORRS	GOES ON AN ERRAND	AADEFHKNOOPSTW	THE AKOND OF SWAT
AADEEGNNOOSTWY	GOT ONE'S END AWAY	AADEFHLMNNOOPS	PALM OF ONES HAND
AADEEHHIKNRSSV	SHIVER AND SHAKE	AADEFIIMNOOPTT	MADE A POINT OF IT
AADEEHHILMNSSS	HANDELS MESSIAH	AADEFIIMNNORSTU	DIAMANTIFEROUS
AADEEHHIMPRSST	HEADMASTERSHIP	AADEFILLNPRSYY	PLAYS A FRIENDLY
AADEEHHNORRTTU	AROUND THE EARTH	AADEFILMMNNSTU	FUNDAMENTALISM
AADEEHHOOSTTTW	HAD A SWEET TOOTH	AADEFILMNNSTTU	FUNDAMENTALIST
AADEEHIILNNNPT	INDIAN ELEPHANT	AADEFILMOPPRST	RAISED PLATFORM
AADEEHIILPRSSV	LAVISHED PRAISE	AADEFILNOOORTW	NOT A WORD OF A LIE
AADEEHIILRRRST	AIR-RAID SHELTER	AADEFKNOORSSUV	ASKED NO FAVOURS
AADEEHIIMNNRST	MARRIED IN HASTE	AADEGGGHINNNRS	HANGING GARDENS
AADEEHIINNRTVW	HAD AN INTERVIEW	AADEGGHHINOOTV	HAVE A GOOD NIGHT
AADEEHIKNQRSUV	QUIVER AND SHAKE	AADEGGIILNNNSS	SENDING A SIGNAL
AADEEHILLNPTTW	PAINTED THE WALL	AADEGGIIMNNORT	MANAGING EDITOR
AADEEHILLOTTVW	VIOLATED THE LAW	AADEGGIMNOPRRT	DAMAGING REPORT
AADEEHILNPPTTY	PAID THE PENALTY	AADEGHHILNORST	SHARING THE LOAD
AADEEHILORSSTY	EASTER HOLIDAYS	AADEGHHLOOSSST	HOLDS AS HOSTAGE
AADEEHIMMNNOOTT	AIMED AT THE MOON	AADEGHHOPRSTTU	SPARED A THOUGHT
AADEEHINNORSSS	RAISES ONE'S HAND	AADEGHIILNNPPY	DAILY HAPPENING
AADEEHKNOORTTT	TAKEN TO THE ROAD	AADEGHIINNSTTW	AGAINST THE WIND
AADEEHKOORSTTT	TAKES TO THE ROAD	AADEGHILNNRSTT	STARTING HANDLE
AADEEHKPPRSTTU	RAKED UP THE PAST	AADEGHILNRSTUW	DAUGHTERS-IN-LAW
AADEEHLLMNNSTW	MANNED THE WALLS	AADEGHIMMMNNORS	HANDSOME MARGIN
AADEEHMNNORUUV	HUMAN ENDEAVOUR	AADEGHIMMNRSTW	MADE THINGS WARM
AADEEHMOOPSSTT	MASHED POTATOES	AADEGHINRSTTTY	STARTING THE DAY
AADEEHNORRSTUW	SWEAR UNDER OATH	AADEGHLOPRSTTY	PLAYS HARD TO GET
AADEEHORSSTTTV	STARVES TO DEATH	AADEGHMMMNNORST	HAMMER AND TONGS
AADEEIIKLNOPPS	LIKE PEAS IN A POD	AADEGHNOORRRTT	GREAT NORTH ROAD
AADEEIILNNOSST	DENATIONALISES	AADEGIIIKMNTVW	TAKING A DIM VIEW
AADEEIILNNOSTZ	DENATIONALIZES	AADEGIIILMNNRV	LIVING IN A DREAM
AADEEIILNPQSSU	SESQUIPEDALIAN	AADEGIILNNORVZ	GALVANIZED IRON
AADEEIINNPRRST	PREDESTINARIAN	AADEGIILNRRTWY	TREADING WARILY
AADEEIKLMOPRTV	EVAPORATED MILK	AADEGIIMNNORSSV	GRAVE ADMISSION

AADEGIIMNRSTYZ	DIRTY MAGAZINES
AADEGIINNORRTT	INTERGRADATION
AADEGIINNRSSUW	ISSUED A WARNING
AADEGIKLNNORTW	WALK INTO DANGER
AADEGIKLNRSTTT	STARTED TALKING
AADEGIKNOOPRTT	TAKE IN GOOD PART
AADEGILLLNORST	GALLANT SOLDIER
AADEGILNNORSTW	LEANING TOWARDS
AADEGIMMOOPRRR	RADIO PROGRAMME
AADEGINNNOSVWW	WAVING ONE'S WAND
AADEGINOORRRTT	RETROGRADATION
AADEGLLNOORSTY	TELLS A GOOD YARN
AADEGMMMNORRTTU	MARGARET DUMONT
AADEHHHHINPSTW	HAS THE WHIP-HAND
AADEHHINNNOPTW	WITH AN OPEN HAND
AADEHHINOPRUVW	HAVE A WHIP-ROUND
AADEHHKNNORSTT	TAKEN SHORTHAND
AADEHHKNORSSTT	TAKES SHORTHAND
AADEHHLNNORRST	LEARN SHORTHAND
AADEHHLORSSTTW	HAS THE LAST WORD
AADEHIILLMNPSU	SULPHANILAMIDE
AADEHIILMPPRRY	HAPPILY MARRIED
AADEHIIMMNPSSY	MIDSHIPMAN EASY
AADEHIIMNNOSTU	DEHUMANISATION
AADEHIIMNNOTUZ	DEHUMANIZATION
AADEHIINOSTTWY	TOYS WITH AN IDEA
AADEHIIOPRRSTT	RADIOTHERAPIST
AADEHINNNOOSTU	ONE IN A THOUSAND
AADEHINNOPSSSU	DIAPHANOUSNESS
AADEHINNRSSTTT	STAND THE STRAIN
AADEHINNSSTTWY	STANDS IN THE WAY
AADEHINORRRSSY	ORDINARY SHARES
AADEHINORSTTUW	AROUND THE WAIST
AADEHJLNNORSTU	JOAN SUTHERLAND
AADEHLLNOSTWWY	LAYS DOWN THE LAW
AADEHLMNORSSTU	SOUNDS THE ALARM
AADEHLNNNOOSSY	LAY ONE'S HANDS ON
	LAYS ONE'S HAND ON
AADEHLORSSTTWY	SAY THE LAST WORD
AADEHNNNOOSSST	SAT ON ONE'S HANDS
AADEHNORRSSTTW	NORTHEASTWARDS
AADEHORSSSTTUW	SOUTHEASTWARDS
AADEIIILNSSTTU	STUDIES ITALIAN
AADEIIIMNRSTTV	ADMINISTRATIVE
AADEIILLLLMNTWY	WILLIAM TYNDALE
AADEIILLMNNNOO	A MILLION AND ONE
AADEIILLMNNPPS	PLAIN AND SIMPLE
AADEIILMNNNOOT	DENOMINATIONAL
AADEIILMNOORST	DEMORALISATION
AADEIILMNOORTZ	DEMORALIZATION
AADEIILMORSTTU	TAILOR-MADE SUIT
AADEIILNNOPSST	DISPENSATIONAL
AADEIILNOOPRST	DEPOLARISATION
AADEIILNOOPRTZ	DEPOLARIZATION
AADEIIMNNORSSV	ANIMADVERSIONS
AADEIIMNOPRSST	ENDOPARASITISM
AADEIINNOPRSTT	STRAINED A POINT
AADEIINORSTTTV	STARVATION DIET
AADEIKNNNOOSST	STEAK AND ONIONS
AADEILLLOPRSSTY	PLAY AT SOLDIERS
AADEILMNOSSTTU	STANDS OUT A MILE
AADEILNNORTUUV	UNDERVALUATION
AADEILNOSSSSTU	SUSTAINED A LOSS
AADEIMMMNNORRUW	UNMARRIED WOMAN
AADEINNNNORTTTW	DRAWN ATTENTION
AADEINNNOSSTWY	STAND IN ONE'S WAY
AADEINNORSTTTW	DRAWS ATTENTION
AADEINOOPPPRST	ADOPTION PAPERS
AADELLLNOPRRUY	ALL-ROUND PLAYER
AADELLLNRRTUYY	REALLY AND TRULY
AADELMNNNOOPRT	ORNAMENTAL POND

AADELNNOOPRSTT	TREASON AND PLOT
AADELNNPSTTUUY	UNPLEASANT DUTY
AADEMOPRRRSSUU	SPREADS A RUMOUR
AADENNOORSSSTT	STANDS TO REASON
AADEOOOPPRSSTT	PROPOSED A TOAST
AADFFGIIIILNST	DISAFFILIATING
AADFFIIIILNOST	DISAFFILIATION
AADFFIIIMNORST	DISAFFIRMATION
AADFFINORSSTUU	FAST AND FURIOUS
AADFGHIILLNOOT	IN ALL GOOD FAITH
AADFGIINNOTUWY	FINDING A WAY OUT
AADFHIJNORRTUY	THIRD OF JANUARY
AADFIILLMNORRUW	UNFAMILIAR WORD
AADFIILNNOSSTV	FINDS SALVATION
AADFILLNNOOTUY	FOUNDATIONALLY
AADFILLNORSSTW	FALL DOWNSTAIRS
AADFILNNOOSTUV	FOUND SALVATION
AADGGHIILNSTVY	DAYLIGHT SAVING
AADGGIINNNOSTT	STANDING TO GAIN
AADGGIINNOPPRS	PROPAGANDISING
AADGGIINNOPPRZ	PROPAGANDIZING
AADGHHILNNRTYY	HARDLY ANYTHING
AADGHINNOOSTTW	SHOOTING AT DAWN
AADGIIIMNNOSSS	GAINS ADMISSION
AADGIIKNNRSTTT	DRINKING A TOAST
AADGIINNORSTTT	TRADING STATION
AADGIKLNORSTWW	WALKING TOWARDS
AADGILLNNSSSSU	SLUGS AND SNAILS
AADGILMMNNOPRS	RANDOM SAMPLING
AADGILNNPPRSUW	DRAWING UP PLANS
AADGINNNORRRSU	RAN RINGS AROUND
AADHHIINNNORTW	WITH AN IRON HAND
AADHIMNRRSSTTY	TRISTRAM SHANDY
AADHLMNNNOOORT	LONDON MARATHON
AADIIILLMNNORSW	DORIAN WILLIAMS
AADIIILMNORSTT	TRADITIONALISM
AADIIILNORSTTT	TRADITIONALIST
AADIIIIMNNORSTT	ADMINISTRATION
AADIIIMNRRSTTX	ADMINISTRATRIX
AADIIMNORRSSTT	ADMINISTRATORS
AADIINNNRSSSTU	NUTS AND RAISINS
AADILLLMORSSTW	ITS A SMALL WORLD
AADILNNNRRTTUU	TURN TAIL AND RUN
AADIMNOOORRSTY	RADIO ASTRONOMY
AADLLLOORSTTTY	TOLD A TALL STORY
AAEEEEEGLLNRRS	GENERAL RELEASE
AAEEEEFHLLSSSY	FALSE EYELASHES
AAEEEEGHHHOTVV	GAVE THE HEAVE-HO
AAEEEEGILNNRSW	RENEWING A LEASE
AAEEEEGNPRSTTX	AT GREAT EXPENSE
AAEEEEHKKNSTTW	WEAK AT THE KNEES
AAEEEEKLMMNOTT	MAKE AN OMELETTE
AAEEEEKLNNRSTV	TAKEN ONE'S LEAVE
AAEEEEKLNOSSTV	TAKES ONE'S LEAVE
AAEEEEELLLLNOVW	LEAVE WELL ALONE
AAEEEFFHHHKOTTT	TAKE THE HEAT OFF
AAEEEFGHINRRSU	REFUSE A HEARING
AAEEEFGMMNNOSSV	SEVEN AGES OF MAN
AAEEEFHKNORSSV	FOR HEAVENS SAKE!
AAEEEFIILMNNPP	FEMININE APPEAL
AAEEEFILNRSTTU	SALIENT FEATURE
AAEEEFIMRRTTTX	AFTER EXTRA TIME
AAEEEFLMNSSTTT	FALSE STATEMENT
AAEEEFLNORSTUV	LEAVES A FORTUNE
AAEEEFMRSSSTUY	SAFETY MEASURES
AAEEEGGHLPRTTU	THE GREAT PLAGUE
AAEEEGHHKMNNRT	KENNETH GRAHAME
AAEEEGHINNPRST	ENTERING A PHASE
AAEEEGHKOORTTV	TOOK THE AVERAGE
AAEEEGHLMPRSST	GREASES THE PALM
AAEEEGHLRSSSTW	WEATHERGLASSES

AAEEEGHMNOSTWY	GONE THE SAME WAY
AAEEEGHMOSSTWY	GOES THE SAME WAY
AAEEEGIKLMNNWYZ	WEEKLY MAGAZINE
AAEEEGILMNNPVX	GIVEN AN EXAMPLE
AAEEEGILMNPSVX	GIVES AN EXAMPLE
AAEEEGLLMNSTTT	LEGAL STATEMENT
AAEEEGLMNOPRSS	GREASE ONES PALM
AAEEEGLNNPPRSS	PASSENGER PLANE
AAEEEGMNNPRRRT	PREARRANGEMENT
AAEEEGMNRRSSTT	MASTER SERGEANT
AAEEEGMNRSTTTV	GRAVE STATEMENT
AAEEEGNNOSSSTV	GAVE ONE'S ASSENT
AAEEEGNOPSSTUV	GAVE UP ONE'S SEAT
AAEEEGNORTTTTX	TO A GREAT EXTENT
AAEEEHHIPRSSTY	HYPERAESTHESIA
AAEEEHHLPRSSTU	HAS THE PLEASURE
AAEEEHHNPPSSTW	SEE WHAT HAPPENS
AAEEEHHPRRSTTV	REAP THE HARVEST
AAEEEHIILNRSTV	LEAVES IN THE AIR
AAEEEHIKLORSST	EATS LIKE A HORSE
AAEEEHILLOOSTV	HAVE A TILE LOOSE
AAEEEHIMMNRSST	REMAINS THE SAME
AAFFFHINNOPRTT	ENTERTAIN A HOPE
AAEEEHIINOPRRTT	OPEN-AIR THEATRE
AAEEEHIPPRTTTY	HEARTY APPETITE
AAEEEHIRRTTTVY	VARIETY THEATRE
AAEEEHKLNSTTTU	TAKEN THE SALUTE
AAEEEHKLSSTTTU	TAKES THE SALUTE
AAEEEHKNRSTTTW	TAKEN THE WATERS
AAEEEHKORTTTTW	TAKE TO THE WATER
AAEEEHKRSSTTTW	TAKES THE WATERS
AAEEEHLNORSSTT	STEAL ONES HEART
AAEEEHLOPSTTTV	LEAVE AT THE POST
AAEEEHLRSTTTVY	AT THE VERY LEAST
AAEEEHMNSTTWWY	WENT THE SAME WAY
AAEEEHMOPRRRST	RARE ATMOSPHERE
AAEEEHNOSSSTWY	AS SWEET AS HONEY
AAEEEHPPRRSTWY	PREPARES THE WAY
AAEEEIILNRRTTV	INVETERATE LIAR
AAEEEIKNNRSTTT	TAKE AN INTEREST
AAEEEILLPRRSWY	RAILWAY SLEEPER
AAEEEILLSSTTTT	SATELLITE STATE
AAEEEILMNNRSTU	NATURAL ENEMIES
AAEEEINRRRSTVV	NARRATIVE VERSE
AAEEEKLMNNSSTW	MENTAL WEAKNESS
AAEEEKLMNORSSV	LEAVES ONE'S MARK
AAEEEKMMORSSTU	MAKES TO MEASURE
AAEEEELLQRRSTTU	SETTLE A QUARREL
AAEEEELMOPRRSTY	TEMPORARY LEASE
AAEEEELNOPRSSTT	PERSONAL ESTATE
AAEEEMNNNORSSW	ANSWER ONES NAME
AAEEFFGGINORRW	WAG A FOREFINGER
AAEEFFGIKKNOTW	TAKING A WEEK OFF
AAEEFFHKNOOSTT	TAKE ONES HAT OFF
AAEEFGGHIILNNV	HAVING A FEELING
AAEEFGGIILNORT	FAILING TO AGREE
AAEEFGHIKNNRRT	HANKERING AFTER
AAEEFGHILLNRRT	LARGER THAN LIFE
AAEEFGHILMNTWY	MEETING HALFWAY
AAEEFGHILNORSV	HALF A SOVEREIGN
AAEEFGHLLOPRTU	PEAL OF LAUGHTER
AAEEFGHLLSSTTU	SALUTES THE FLAG
AAEEFGHORSSTTY	THE FORSYTE SAGA
AAEEFGIILNORST	FLIES INTO A RAGE
AAEEFGILLNNTTU	FLAG LIEUTENANT
AAEEFGILNNORSS	FALSE REASONING
AAEEFGILNNORST	SEAT OF LEARNING
AAEEFGIORSTTTT	GET A TASTE FOR IT
AAEEFGLNNOORTU	GONE TO A FUNERAL
AAEEFGLNOORSTU	GOES TO A FUNERAL
AAEEFHHIKNRSTW	SHAKEN WITH FEAR
AAEEFHHIKRSSTW	SHAKES WITH FEAR
AAEEFHHLORSTTT	SALT OF THE EARTH
AAEEFHIKKLLOOS	SHOOK LIKE A LEAF
AAEEFHIKLLMORT	HALF A KILOMETRE
AAEEFHILOPRSUW	PAUSE FOR A WHILE
AAEEFHLLOPPPRS	APPEALS FOR HELP
AAEEFIIKLMNNRT	TAKEN A FIRM LINE
AAEEFIIKLMNRST	TAKES A FIRM LINE
AAEEFIILLMSSTT	LASTS A LIFETIME
AAEEFIKMMOPRTT	TAKE A TIP FROM ME
AAEEFIKMMOSSST	MAKES A MESS OF IT
AAEEFILNNRRSTT	TRANSFERENTIAL
AAEEFIMORRSTVY	FORMATIVE YEARS
AAEEFJMNOOPPRR	EMPEROR OF JAPAN
AAEEFKKMMNNOOSY	MAKES A MONKEY OF
AAEEFKMMOORSSU	MAKES A FOURSOME
AAEEFKMNNRSTTT	FRANK STATEMENT
AAEEFLLMORRSTW	FAREWELL TO ARMS
AAEEFLNNORTTUW	WENT TO A FUNERAL
AAEEFLOORRTWZZ	WORE TO A FRAZZLE
AAEEFMOORRRTYY	FROM YEAR TO YEAR
AAEEFFMORSSTTTT	MATTERS OF STATE
AAEEFOPPRRRRSW	PREPARES FOR WAR
AAEEGGGIMNNNNR	ENGAGING MANNER
AAEEGGHILMNPTY	PLAYING THE GAME
AAEEGGHMNOOPRT	GO ON THE RAMPAGE
AAEEGGIIIKLNPT	EATING LIKE A PIG
AAEEGGIIILMNRZ	GIRLIE MAGAZINE
AAEEGGIIMNNRTT	MAN-EATING TIGER
AAEEGGIKMNNPRS	SPEAKING GERMAN
AAEEGGIKMNRSTU	MAKING A GESTURE
AAEEGGILNRSTTT	SETTING AT LARGE
AAEEGGKLNNOPSU	SPOKEN LANGUAGE
AAEEGHHHLNOTUV	HAVE THE LAUGH ON
AAEEGHHIKMNSTV	HAVE THE MAKINGS
AAEEGHHIKNNNTV	THANKING HEAVEN
AAEEGHHILNNOPR	ON A HIGHER PLANE
AAEEGHHIMORTUV	HAVE A ROUGH TIME
AAEEGHHINPRTTY	PAYING THE EARTH
AAEEGHHLORSTTU	TOUGH AS LEATHER
AAEEGHHLRRTTUY	HEARTY LAUGHTER
AAEEGHIINNRSTT	RAISING THE ANTE
AAEEGHIINNSSTT	ANAESTHETISING
AAEEGHIINNSTTZ	ANAESTHETIZING
AAEEGHIINPRRTV	PRIVATE HEARING
AAEEGHIKNSSTTY	TAKE THINGS EASY
AAEEGHILNNORTT	LEARNING TO HATE
AAEEGHILNRSTVY	LAYS IN THE GRAVE
AAEEGHKLNPSSTT	SPEAKS AT LENGTH
AAEEGHLLMOPRRT	METALLOGRAPHER
AAEEGHLNNRTTTU	RAN THE GAUNTLET
AAFFGIIKLPSSTW	SWEATS LIKE A PIG
AAEEGIILLMNNRT	LITERAL MEANING
AAEEGIILLNNOTV	LEAVING IT ALONE
AAEEGIILMNOPST	AIMING TO PLEASE
AAEEGIILNNORST	GENERALISATION
AAEEGIILNNORTZ	GENERALIZATION
AAEEGIILNNOSTV	EVANGELISATION
AAEEGIILNNOTVZ	EVANGELIZATION
AAEEGIIMNPRRST	PARAMETERISING
AAEEGIIMNPRRTZ	PARAMETERIZING
AAEEGIKKLNOOST	TAKING A LOOK-SEE
AAEEGIKLMNNOTT	TAKEN A LONG TIME
AAEEGIKLMNOSTT	TAKES A LONG TIME
AAEEGIKLNNOOOV	GAVE ONE A LOOK IN
AAEEGIKLNNOTVW	TAKEN A LONG VIEW
AAEEGIKMNQRSTU	MAKING A REQUEST
AAEEGIKNOSTUWY	SEEKING A WAY OUT
AAEEGILLMNOPPS	ANGLEPOISE LAMP
AAEEGILLNOTTVY	VEGETATIONALLY
AAEEGILMMNORRT	ANGELA MORTIMER

AAEEGILNNORSTT	LAST GENERATION
AAEEGILNNOSSTT	EATING ONE'S SALT
AAEEGILNORSSSS	RAISE ONES GLASS
AAEEGILNPRSTXY	EXASPERATINGLY
AAEEGINNNORRSS	RANG IN ONE'S EARS
AAEEGINNPRRSST	PASSENGER TRAIN
AAEEGKMMNOORVW	MAKE A WRONG MOVE
AAEEGNQRRSSTTU	GRANTS A REQUEST
AAEEHHHINRRTTW	RAN WITH THE HARE
AAEEHHHIRTTVWY	WITH HEAVY HEART
AAEEHHMNRRSTTT	HARSH TREATMENT
AAEEHHMRSTTTTW	WHATS THE MATTER?
AAEEHHOOSSTTTW	HAS A SWEET TOOTH
AAEEHIILLNSSTY	LAY IN THE AISLES
AAEEHIILPRSSSV	LAVISHES PRAISE
AAEEHIIMNRRSST	MARRIES IN HASTE
AAEEHIINNRSTVW	HAS AN INTERVIEW
AAEEHIKNNRSTTT	TAKEN THE STRAIN
AAEEHIKNORTTTT	TAKEN IT TO HEART
AAEEHIKNRSSTTT	TAKES THE STRAIN
AAEEHIKORSTTTT	TAKES IT TO HEART
AAEEHIKORSTTVW	TAKE A SHORT VIEW
AAEEHILLOPSSTV	LEAVES HOSPITAL
AAEEHILLOSTTVW	VIOLATES THE LAW
AAEEHILLRRTVYY	HEAVY ARTILLERY
AAEEHILMMOOSTT	MESOTHELIOMATA
AAEEHILMNPRTTU	THE PLANETARIUM
AAEEHILNOPSTUV	HAVE ONE'S TAIL UP
AAEEHILNPRSSTV	SILVER PHEASANT
AAEEHILNPRSTTU	TARPAULIN SHEET
AAEEHIMNRSSSTU	AMATEURISHNESS
AAEEHINORSTTTW	WEATHER STATION
AAEEHKLMPRSTTY	PLAYS THE MARKET
AAEEHKLNORTTWW	WALK ON THE WATER
AAEEHKPPRSSTTU	RAKES UP THE PAST
AAEEHLLNOPRTWY	HALLOWEEN PARTY
AAEEHLLORSSTWY	ROSES ALL THE WAY
AAEEHLLPPRSSTW	PAPERS THE WALLS
AAEEHLMNOPRTTT	APARTMENT HOTEL
AAEEHLNPPSTTYY	PAYS THE PENALTY
AAEEHLNPRSTTWY	WEALTHY PARENTS
AAEEHMNNOOOTVY	HAVE ONE TOO MANY
AAEEHMNOPRSTTU	APARTMENT HOUSE
AAEEHMOPSTTTYY	STAY-AT-HOME TYPE
AAEEHNNOOSVWWY	HAVE ONES OWN WAY
AAEEHNNOPPSSWY	HAPPENS ONE'S WAY
AAEEHORSTUVWYY	WHATEVER YOU SAY
AAEEIILLLRRTVY	ALLITERATIVELY
AAEEIILMMNRSST	IMMATERIALNESS
AAEEIILNNOSSST	SENSATIONALISE
AAEEIILNNOSSTZ	SENSATIONALIZE
AAEEIILNOPRRST	PROLETARIANISE
AAEEIILNOPRRTZ	PROLETARIANIZE
AAEEIINOQRSSTU	RAISE A QUESTION
AAEEIKKLLORSVW	WORK LIKE A SLAVE
AAEEIKKLMNNOPS	SPOKEN LIKE A MAN
AAEEIKKLNNOSST	SANK LIKE A STONE
AAEEIKKMMNOSST	MAKES NO MISTAKE
AAEEIKLLNNRSTW	WINNER TAKES ALL
AAEEILMNNOPPRT	OPEN PARLIAMENT
AAEEILMPRSTTXY	PLAYS EXTRA TIME
AAEEILNNOPRSTT	PRESENTATIONAL
AAEEILNNPRRTTY	INTERPLANETARY
AAEEILNRRSSTTT	TRANSLITERATES
AAEEILNSSTTUUV	UNVEILS A STATUE
AAEEILPQRRRTUV	PRIVATE QUARREL
AAEEIMNPRSTTTV	PAVEMENT ARTIST
AAEEINNOPSSSST	PASSIONATENESS
AAEEINNRSSTTWY	WRITTEN AN ESSAY
AAEEINOPRRSSTV	PRIVATE REASONS
AAEEINQRRSTTUV	NATIVE QUARTERS
AAEEINRRSSTTTW	WATER-RESISTANT
AAEEKLMNOORTVW	MAKE LOVE NOT WAR
AAEEKLMNOPRRRS	PERSONAL REMARK
AAEELMNOPRRSTT	PERSONAL MATTER
AAEELMNOPRTTTT	APARTMENT TO LET
AAEELNNNPSSSTU	UNPLEASANTNESS
AAEELNNOOPRRSS	PERSONAL REASON
AAEELNNOPPRSST	PLEASANT PERSON
AAEEMMNNORRSUVY	ARMY MANOEUVRES
AAEEMNOOQRRSTU	ROOT-MEAN-SQUARE
AAEEMMORRRSSTTU	QUARTERMASTERS
AAEENOPQRRSTTU	QUARTER PAST ONE
AAEENOPRRSSSSYY	SAY ONES PRAYERS
AAEENPQRRSTTTU	QUARTER PAST TEN
AAEENRRRSSTTUU	RESTAURANTEURS
AAEEPRRSSSTTUU	SUPERSATURATES
AAEFFFGIINORRS	FOREIGN AFFAIRS
AAEFFGIIILMRRU	FAMILIAR FIGURE
AAEFFGIILNNNRW	WINNING A RAFFLE
AAEFFGIINOPRTY	PAYING A FORFEIT
AAEFFGIMNORSTY	MARGIN OF SAFETY
AAEFFHILMLOOPS	POLISH OFF A MEAL
AAEFFIIMNNORRS	FORAMINIFERANS
AAEFFILNOSTTUX	IN A STATE OF FLUX
AAEFFIOPRRSSTT	TEARS OFF A STRIP
AAEFGGHIILNRST	RAISING THE FLAG
AAEFGGHILLNTUY	FILTHY LANGUAGE
AAEFGGIIMMNNOR	FORMING AN IMAGE
AAEFGHIIKMNOTT	MAKE A NIGHT OF IT
AAEFGHIILLMNSS	FLASHING A SMILE
AAEFGHIILLNNTT	LATE NIGHT FINAL
AAEFGHILLNORTT	FALLING TO EARTH
AAEFGHILLRRRSY	GREYFRIARS HALL
AAEFGHILNRTTUV	HAVING A FLUTTER
AAEFGHINRRSSTT	STARTING AFRESH
AAEFGHLOORRRTU	ROAR OF LAUGHTER
AAEFGIIKLMMNOS	MILK OF MAGNESIA
AAEFGIIKNORRSS	ASKING FOR A RISE
AAEFGIILLLNNUV	FALLING IN VALUE
AAEFGIILMNNOOR	REMAINING ALOOF
AAEFGIILNNORTU	NATIONAL FIGURE
AAEFGIINOPPRRT	REAPING A PROFIT
AAEFGIINRRTTWY	FRITTERING AWAY
AAEFGIINSSTTTY	TESTIFY AGAINST
AAEFGIKMNNORTU	MAKING A FORTUNE
AAEFGILLLMORTY	LEGAL FORMALITY
AAEFGIOORSTTTT	GOT A TASTE FOR IT
AAEFHHMMOOTTTU	FOAM AT THE MOUTH
AAEFHIILMNNRTY	RAN IN THE FAMILY
AAEFHIILMNTWYY	IN THE FAMILY WAY
AAEFHILNOOSSTV	SLAVE TO FASHION
AAEFHIMNNRRSSY	FISHERMANS YARN
AAEFHJNNORTTUY	TENTH OF JANUARY
AAEFHLMNNPPSTY	HALFPENNY STAMP
AAEFIIKMNOOPTT	MAKE A POINT OF IT
AAEFIIMNNOSSTT	MANIFESTATIONS
AAEFIINNORRSTT	FRATERNISATION
AAEFIINNORRTTZ	FRATERNIZATION
AAEFILLOPRSSTT	SELLS AT A PROFIT
AAEFILNNOORRTU	FUNERAL ORATION
AAEFILOPPRRSST	PLASTER OF PARIS
AAEFIMNORRSTTV	TRANSFORMATIVE
AAEFLLNOOPRTTW	FOLLOW A PATTERN
AAEFLLNOPRRRUU	FUNERAL PARLOUR
AAEFLNOOPRRSUV	PERSONAL FAVOUR
AAEFLNOORRTWZZ	WORN TO A FRAZZLE
AAEFNORRRSTUUV	RETURNS A FAVOUR
AAEGGGILLNNUUV	LIVING LANGUAGE
AAEGGGLLNNORSTU	STRONG LANGUAGE
AAEGGGLNORRSSW	GLASGOW RANGERS
AAEGGHHIOTTTUV	GAVE IT A THOUGHT

AAEGGHIIIKNSTV	GIVING IT A SHAKE
AAEGGHIKNOSSTT	TAKING HOSTAGES
AAEGGHILLNOTWY	GOING ALL THE WAY
AAEGGHILMMNRRS	ENGLISH GRAMMAR
AAEGGHILMNRTTU	LAUGHING MATTER
AAEGGIIILNNNRV	EARNING A LIVING
AAEGGIIILNNNUV	GAINING IN VALUE
AAEGGIIKLMNRST	GLARING MISTAKE
AAEGGIIKLNNPRS	SPRINGING A LEAK
AAEGGIIMMNNRSTY	GAINING MASTERY
AAEGGIINNNNSTUX	EXSANGUINATING
AAEGGIKLNOPSST	TAKING AS GOSPEL
AAEGGILMNOORST	AGGLOMERATIONS
AAEGGILMNOSSYZ	GLOSSY MAGAZINE
AAEGHHIILNRRTT	LIGHTER THAN AIR
	LIGHTER-THAN-AIR
AAEGHHNNOPSSTU	HANGS ONE'S HAT UP
	HANGS UP ONE'S HAT
AAEGHHOPRSSTTU	SPARES A THOUGHT
AAEGHIIKNNNSTW	TAKEN IN WASHING
AAEGHIIKNNSSTW	TAKES IN WASHING
AAEGHIIKNORTTT	TAKING TO THE AIR
AAEGHIILNRRTWY	TARRYING AWHILE
AAEGHIINNNORSST	RAISING ONE'S HAT
AAEGHIIRRSTTTV	RIGHT AS A TRIVET
AAEGHIISTTTWWY	GETS AWAY WITH IT
AAEGHIKLMSSTTY	GHASTLY MISTAKE
AAEGHIKMMNRSTW	MAKE THINGS WARM
AAFGHILLORTTUY	LEGAL AUTHORITY
AAEGHILNPPRTTY	PLAYING THE PART
AAEGHILNPSSSTT	PASSING THE SALT
AAEGHILPRSTTUY	PLAYS THE GUITAR
AAEGHINNOORSTW	SWEARING ON OATH
AAEGHINNRRSSTW	WARREN HASTINGS
AAEGHINOPRRSSY	PHRASE OR SAYING
AAEGHINORRRSTW	ROARS WITH ANGER
AAEGHINRRSSTTW	STRAIGHT ANSWER
AAEGHIOTTUWWYY	GET AWAY WITH YOU!
AAEGHLOQRRSTUU	SOUGHT A QUARREL
AAEGIIIJMNNORR	JOIN IN MARRIAGE
AAEGIIILMNORSU	RELIGIOUS MANIA
AAEGIIILNNOSTT	GELATINISATION
AAEGIIILNNOTTZ	GELATINIZATION
AAEGIIIMMNNTTUW	WAITING A MINUTE
AAEGIIKKLLNRSS	SINGS LIKE A LARK
AAEGIIKKLNNOTT	TAKEN A LIKING TO
AAEGIIKKLNOSTT	TAKES A LIKING TO
AAEGIIKLMNRSTV	LEAVING ITS MARK
AAEGIIKMMNOPRS	MAKING A PROMISE
AAEGIIKMNOORRT	TOOK IN MARRIAGE
AAEGIIILLLMNOPR	IMPERIAL GALLON
AAEGIIILLNOORST	ALLEGORISATION
AAEGIIILLNOORTZ	ALLEGORIZATION
AAEGIILNNNSSUV	UNAVAILINGNESS
AAEGIILNORRSTU	REGULARISATION
AAEGIILNORRTUZ	REGULARIZATION
AAEGIIMMNNOTTW	WAITING A MOMENT
AAEGIIMMNNPPRUY	PAYING A PREMIUM
AAEGIINNNOSTUX	EXSANGUINATION
AAEGIINNRSSSUW	ISSUES A WARNING
AAEGIINNRSSTTU	GAINS IN STATURE
AAEGIINNRSSTWY	WRITING AN ESSAY
AAEGIINNSSTTUU	SAINT AUGUSTINE
AAEGIINORSTTUV	GRAVE SITUATION
AAEGIKLLNNORTT	LEARNING TO TALK
AAEGIKLLNNORTW	LEARNING TO WALK
AAEGIKLMNNOPSY	MAKING ONE'S PLAY
AAEGIKLNNORTWW	WALKING ON WATER
AAEGIKMMNNORTT	MAKING NO MATTER
AAEGIKMNOPRSTT	MAKING A PROTEST
AAEGIKNNOPRSTT	TAKING ONE'S PART

AAEGILLLNOSSST	SELLING AT A LOSS
AAEGILMNNOOPSS	MISS AN OPEN GOAL
AAEGILMNOOPRST	SPERMATOGONIAL
AAEGILNNRSTTUY	STAYING NEUTRAL
AAEGILNOOPRSTT	PROGESTATIONAL
AAEGILNORSSTTV	REVOLTS AGAINST
AAEGILNRSSTUUU	USUAL SIGNATURE
AAEGIMNNORSSST	IGNORANT MASSES
AAEGINNNPRSTUU	SUPERANNUATING
AAEGINNOPSSSWY	PASSING ONE'S WAY
AAEGINNPRSSTTY	ASSENTING PARTY
AAEGINOPRSSTTT	PROTEST AGAINST
AAEGKNNORRTTUW	TAKE A WRONG TURN
AAEGMMOPPRRRTY	PARTY PROGRAMME
AAEHHIILLMRTTWY	WITH ALL MY HEART
AAEHHIIMNPRSSSU	SUSAN HAMPSHIRE
AAEHIIIMNNSSTT	ANTIHISTAMINES
AAEHIIKLNPRSTW	TALK IN A WHISPER
AAEHIIILLLMNPRT	PARLIAMENT HILL
AAEHIIILLLNPTVY	PLAY THE VILLAIN
AAEHIIILLMNRSTW	WILLIAM SHATNER
AAEHIILNNNOTTW	WIN THE NATIONAL
AAEHIJLLMNNORT	JONATHAN MILLER
AAEHIKLOOOPTTT	LIKE A HOT POTATO
AAEHIKORSTTTWW	WOKE WITH A START
AAEHILLMNOPSTT	MENTAL HOSPITAL
AAEHILLOPRSTTT	THROAT PASTILLE
AAEHILMNNORSTU	HUMAN RELATIONS
AAFHILNNNOOTTW	WON THE NATIONAL
AAEHKLOPRRSTUW	WORKS UP A LATHER
AAEHKMORSSTTTW	WARMS TO THE TASK
AAEHKNNORSSSTT	THANK ONE'S STARS
AAEHLMPRRSTTYY	PLAYS THE MARTYR
AAEHMNNNORRRTU	MARATHON RUNNER
AAEHMNOOORTTTT	NOT MATTER A HOOT
AAEIIILLMMNNRS	MILLENARIANISM
AAEIIILMNNORST	MINERALISATION
AAEIIILMNNORTZ	MINERALIZATION
AAEIIILLNORSTTV	REVITALISATION
AAEIIILNORTTVZ	REVITALIZATION
AAEIIIMMNNNORTT	MARITIME NATION
AAEIILMNNOSSST	SENSATIONALISM
AAEIILNNNORSTT	INTERNATIONALS
AAEIILLNNORRRTT	TORRENTIAL RAIN
AAEIILNNORSTTU	NEUTRALISATION
AAEIILNNORTTUZ	NEUTRALIZATION
AAEIILNNOSSSTT	SENSATIONALIST
AAEIILNPSTTTWY	WAITS PATIENTLY
AAEIILNQTTTUVY	QUANTITATIVELY
AAEIIMOPPPRRST	MISAPPROPRIATE
AAEIINNNOSSTTX	ANNEXATIONISTS
AAFIINNPPRRSTT	ANTIPERSPIRANT
AAEIINOPRSSTTU	PASTEURISATION
AAEIINOPRSTTUZ	PASTEURIZATION
AAEIJLNORRUWYY	RAILWAY JOURNEY
AAEIJMNOOOPRRT	MAJOR OPERATION
AAEIKLLPRSTTVY	TALKS PRIVATELY
AAEIKNNOOPPTTU	TAKE UP AN OPTION
AAEILLLLMRTTUY	MULTILATERALLY
AAEIILLLORRRTYY	ROYAL ARTILLERY
AAEILLMNNNPSTT	INSTALMENT PLAN
AAEILLMNNSSTTT	LAST INSTALMENT
AAEILLORRTTUVY	ULTRAVIOLET RAY
AAEILMMNNPPRRTU	RUMP PARLIAMENT
AAEILMNRSSSTUX	TRANSSEXUALISM
AAEILMOOPPRSTT	SPATIOTEMPORAL
AAEIMMNNORSTTU	MOUNTAIN STREAM
AAEIMNNNOORSTT	ORNAMENTATIONS
AAEIMNORSSSTTT	STATIONMASTERS
AAEINNNOOPTTTY	PAY NO ATTENTION
AAEINNNOPRSTUU	SUPERANNUATION

AAEIPQRRSSTTUX	QUARTER PAST SIX
AAELLLLORSTTTY	TELL A TALL STORY
AAELLNORSSSTUY	SALUTARY LESSON
AAELLNPRRSTUUY	SUPERNATURALLY
AAELMNSSSSTTYY	SYSTEMS ANALYST
AAELNNNORRTUUV	ANNUAL TURNOVER
AAENORRRSSTTTU	TARTAN TROUSERS
AAEOOOOPPRSSSTT	PROPOSES A TOAST
AAEOPQRRSTTTUW	QUARTER PAST TWO
AAFFFFGGILLLNOO	FALLING OFF A LOG
AAFFFHIJNORTUY	FIFTH OF JANUARY
AAFFIJNORRSTUY	FIRST OF JANUARY
AAFGGHIINRSTTT	STARTING A FIGHT
AAFGIIILLNSTUW	FILING A LAWSUIT
AAFGIIILLMNNNPY	FAMILY PLANNING
AAFGIIMNNORSST	INFORMS AGAINST
AAFGIINNOPRRRY	PRAYING FOR RAIN
AAFGILLLNNOOPW	FOLLOWING A PLAN
AAFGILMPRRSUUY	SUGAR-PLUM FAIRY
AAFHIJNNNORTUY	NINTH OF JANUARY
AAFHIJNORSTUXY	SIXTH OF JANUARY
AAFIIIMNNORRTU	UNIFORMITARIAN
AAFIILMOPRRTTY	FAMILY PORTRAIT
AAFIINOORRTTTW	WAR OF ATTRITION
AAFILMOPPRSTUY	SUPPORT A FAMILY
AAFIMNNOORRSTT	TRANSFORMATION
AAGGHIIKLNOORT	LOOK RIGHT AGAIN
AAGGHLMNOORSTU	SOUTH GLAMORGAN
AAGGIIIKKLLMNN	MAKING A KILLING
AAGGIIILNNRTTY	INGRATIATINGLY
AAGGIIKNNORSTW	WORKING AGAINST
AAGGIIMNNRRSTT	TRANSMIGRATING
AAGGIINNNNRSTU	RUNNING AGAINST
AAGGIINNNRSTTU	TURNING AGAINST
AAGGIINNPPRRST	SPRINGING A TRAP
	SPRINGING APART
AAGGIINNRSSTTV	STARTING SAVING
AAGGIJLLMNOOPR	GALLOPING MAJOR
AAGGILMNNRSTUY	GRANTING ASYLUM
AAGHHIILLMORTW	WILLIAM HOGARTH
AAGHHNOOPPRRTY	ANTHROPOGRAPHY
AAGHHNOOPPRSTU	ANTHROPOPHAGUS
AAGHIILMNRSTT	ANTILOGARITHMS
AAGHIINPSSSTWY	PASSING THIS WAY
AAGHIKNOOPSTTT	TAKING A POT-SHOT
AAGHIMRSSTTTUU	THAUMATURGISTS
AAGHINOPRRTTWY	THROWING A PARTY
AAGIIIKLLMMNNO	MAKING A MILLION
AAGIIIMNNSSTUU	AUGUSTINIANISM
AAGIIIMNOSSTTT	STIGMATISATION
AAGIIIMNOSTTTZ	STIGMATIZATION
AAGIIJMNNNOTTW	WANTING JAM ON IT
AAGIIILLNQSTTUY	LASTING QUALITY
AAGIILNPPRSTTY	PLAYING ITS PART
AAGIILOOPRSSTT	PARASITOLOGIST
AAGIIMNNORRSTT	TRANSMIGRATION
AAGIINNNOPPRSS	SPARING NO PAINS
AAGILNNNORSSTU	RUNNING AT A LOSS
AAGIMNORRRSSTT	TRANSMIGRATORS
AAGIMNORRRSTTY	TRANSMIGRATORY
AAGINRRRTTTYYY	TRY,TRY,TRY AGAIN
AAHHIKNOSTTWWW	KNOW WHAT IS WHAT
AAHHKNNOSTTWWW	KNOWN WHAT'S WHAT
AAHHKNOSSTTWWW	KNOWS WHAT'S WHAT
AAHIIKLLMNNOST	THANKS A MILLION
AAHIINOORSSTTU	AUTHORISATIONS
AAHIINOORSTTUZ	AUTHORIZATIONS
AAHILMNOOPRSTT	HOSPITAL MATRON
AAHILNORRSTTUY	NATURAL HISTORY
AAHINNNOOPRRST	SHANNON AIRPORT
AAHLMMPSTTUUYY	MUTUAL SYMPATHY

AAHLMOOPRRSSTV	PROVOST MARSHAL
AAHMNNORRTTTUW	THROWN A TANTRUM
AAHMNNORRSTTTUW	THROWS A TANTRUM
AAHNOORRSSTTUY	HONORARY STATUS
AAHNOORRSTTTWW	NOT WORTH A STRAW
AAIIIILMNORSTT	MILITARISATION
AAIIIILMNORTTZ	MILITARIZATION
AAIIIILMNRSTTU	UTILITARIANISM
AAIIIILNORSTTV	TRIVIALISATION
AAIIIILNORTTVZ	TRIVIALIZATION
AAIIIIMNNOSTTV	VITAMINISATION
AAIIIIMNNOTTVZ	VITAMINIZATION
AAIIIIMNNRRSTT	TRINITARIANISM
AAIIIINOPRSTTV	AVIATION SPIRIT
AAIIIILLNOOSTTV	VOLATILISATION
AAIIIILLNOOTTVZ	VOLATILIZATION
AAIIJKLNNSSVVY	VASLAV NIJINSKY
AAIIILLNORSTTU	ILLUSTRATIONAL
AAIILLMNNOSTTU	MULTINATIONALS
AAIILLNNORSTTY	TRANSITIONALLY
AAIILLNOOPPSTY	APPOSITIONALLY
AAIILMOORTTTTY	MILITARY TATTOO
AAIILNOOPPRTUZ	POPULARIZATION
AAIIMNOOPPRSTX	APPROXIMATIONS
AAIIMNOORRSSTZ	ZOROASTRIANISM
AAIINOOPPPRRST	APPROPRIATIONS
AAIJMNOORRRTWY	NARROW MAJORITY
AAIKMNOOQRSTTU	QUOTATION MARKS
AAILMMNNORSTTU	ULTRAMONTANISM
AAIMNNORSSTTTU	TRANSMUTATIONS
AAINNOOPRRSTTT	TRANSPORTATION
AALNNOOPRRSTTY	LAY ON TRANSPORT
ABBBEEHLOSSTUU	SOUTH SEA BUBBLE
ABBCDDEEHLOTTU	CLUBBED TO DEATH
ABBCDEEEHNORTT	CAN'T BE BOTHERED
ABBCDEEHIKNNOS	BEHIND ONES BACK
ABBCDEFLLOOORS	LOAD OF COBBLERS
ABBCDEGHIKMPRU	HUMPBACK BRIDGE
ABBCDEIIMNNORY	INCENDIARY BOMB
ABBCDEILMOOSTU	DISCOMBOBULATE
ABBCDENOOPRRSS	COPS AND ROBBERS
ABBCEEEEMMMORS	BECOMES A MEMBER
ABBCEEEIMNOORR	BECOME AIRBORNE
ABBCEEEKLMPRST	BLACK SEPTEMBER
ABBCEEGIJLNOTT	TANGIBLE OBJECT
ABBCEEKKNNOORS	BROKEN ONE'S BACK
ABBCEELLNRRTUY	CANTERBURY BELL
ABBCEIIKNNSSSU	BACK IN BUSINESS
ABBCEIIILLMOTTW	WILLIAM COBBETT
ABBCEIKLLLOTTX	LITTLE BLACK BOX
ABBCFHIKORRSTU	STICK OF RHUBARB
ABBCGHILLNOORU	RUBBING ALCOHOL
ABBDDDEEEFLNOW	EBBED AND FLOWED
ABBDDEEELORSTU	DOUBLE-BREASTED
ABBDDELLNOOTUY	BEYOND ALL DOUBT
ABBDDHLLLNOSUU	OLD BULL AND BUSH
ABBDEEEHKNORRT	BROKEN THE BREAD
ABBDEEEHLLSTVY	SAVED BY THE BELL
ABBDEEEHNRRSTU	BEARS THE BURDEN
ABBDEEFHLLLMTU	FUMBLED THE BALL
ABBDEEGHNOORTY	GONE BY THE BOARD
ABBDEEGHOORSTY	GOES BY THE BOARD
ABBDEEHINOOSTW	BABES IN THE WOOD
ABBDEEHNORTTWY	WENT BY THE BOARD
ABBDEEINORRRST	ROBIN REDBREAST
ABBDEFINORSSSU	BAD FOR BUSINESS
ABBDEFLNOORTTY	BOTTLE OF BRANDY
ABBDEGHHILNOTY	HOLDING THE BABY
ABBDEGHINNRTUY	DEATH BY BURNING
ABBDEGIIORRTTT	BRIGITTE BARDOT
ABBDEHILNOOOST	HOB-NAILED BOOTS

ABBDEHINRRSSSU	BURNISHED BRASS
ABBDEIKNNOOOSS	IN ONES BAD BOOKS
ABBDEMNOPRSTUU	PUTS A BOMB UNDER
ABBDGGIMMNNOOOW	GOING DOWN A BOMB
ABBDIIIILNTTUY	INDUBITABILITY
ABBDINOOOTTTUU	NO DOUBT ABOUT IT
ABBDNNOOSSTTUW	BUTTONS AND BOWS
ABBEEEFHLLLLOT	BELLE OF THE BALL
ABBEEEFHMMORRT	MEMBER OF THE BAR
ABBEEEGHINSTTT	BEATING THE BEST
ABBEEEKNNOORSS	BREAK ONE'S BONES
	BREAKS ONE'S BONE
ABBEEFHLLLMSTU	FUMBLES THE BALL
ABBEEHHIKNORTT	BROKEN THE HABIT
ABBEEHINNOOPRT	PHENOBARBITONE
ABBEEILLOPRSSY	BARELY POSSIBLE
ABBEEINNOOPRTT	PENTOBARBITONE
ABBEGGIIKLMNOO	GOING LIKE A BOMB
ABBEGGIINNORRT	BRINGING TO BEAR
ABBEGHHIORRWYY	HIGHWAY ROBBERY
ABBEGHIIILOPRS	BIBLIOGRAPHIES
ABBEGHIIKLRSST	TALKS GIBBERISH
ABBEGHIILOPRRS	BIBLIOGRAPHERS
ABBEGIINNNRRUW	WINNING A RUBBER
ABBEGIMNPRRSTU	RUBBER-STAMPING
ABBEHIIMRSSSTY	BRITISH EMBASSY
ABBEIKKNNORSST	BROKEN ITS BANKS
ABBEINOORRSSTT	TEARS TO RIBBONS
ABBENNOORSSSTU	BURNS ONE'S BOATS
ABBGHIIKLNRSTU	TALKING RUBBISH
ABBGIKNOOOORRW	BORROWING A BOOK
ABBHOOOORRTTWW	WORTH A BOB OR TWO
ABCCCEGHINOOTW	CHEWING TOBACCO
ABCCCEHILMNORU	COUNCIL CHAMBER
ABCCDDEEIILNRY	RIDDEN A BICYCLE
ABCCDEEEHNOQUU	BOUNCED A CHEQUE
ABCCDEGIIILNRY	RIDING A BICYCLE
ABCCDEGIILPRSU	PUBLIC DISGRACE
ABCCDEGINORRTT	CONTRACT BRIDGE
ABCCDEHKOORRUV	CHUCK OVERBOARD
ABCCEEEHHSTTTU	CATCHES THE TUBE
ABCCEEEHNNNORT	BENEATH CONCERN
ABCCEEEHNNOQSUU	BOUNCES A CHEQUE
ABCCEEFHILNOST	CHIEF CONSTABLE
ABCCEEFIKLMOOT	COME BACK TO LIFE
ABCCEEFKKNNOOS	BACK OF ONE'S NECK
ABCCEEHIIKNNTT	KITCHEN CABINET
ABCCEEHIKLNPRT	THE BLACK PRINCE
ABCCEEHIMMNOOP	BECOME CHAMPION
ABCCEEIILLNORR	IRRECONCILABLE
ABCCEEILOPSSST	ACCESSIBLE SPOT
ABCCEEGHHINSTTU	CATCHING THE BUS
ABCCEHIINORSST	BRONCHIECTASIS
ABCCEIIILNOTVY	CONCEIVABILITY
ABCCEIIIMORSTV	ABOVE CRITICISM
ABCCEIIILNORRY	IRRECONCILABLY
ABCCEIILNNPSUU	PUBLIC NUISANCE
ABCCEIJLOPSTTU	TOPICAL SUBJECT
ABCCEILMNNOSTU	UNCLE TOMS CABIN
ABCCEILNNNOOSU	UNCONSCIONABLE
ABCCEKNNOORRTT	BROKEN CONTRACT
ABCCFIILLNORTT	TRIBAL CONFLICT
ABCCGIIKKKNNOT	KNOCKING IT BACK
ABCCGIKKLNOSST	BLACK STOCKINGS
ABCCGINNOORTTU	BRING TO ACCOUNT
ABCCGINNORSTTU	SUBCONTRACTING
ABCCHIKNOORSTT	CAT ON HOT BRICKS
ABCCHILOOPRSTU	CLAUSTROPHOBIC
ABCCILNNNOOSUY	UNCONSCIONABLY
ABCCINOOOORRSTT	BOA CONSTRICTOR
ABCCNOORRSSTTU	SUBCONTRACTORS
ABCDDDEEIINRTT	DEBIT AND CREDIT
ABCDDDEEILLNOO	BILLED AND COOED
ABCDDEEHILLMRT	CLIMB THE LADDER
ABCDDEEHIORRST	HARD TO DESCRIBE
ABCDDEEIKLNRSS	DRESSED IN BLACK
ABCDDEEILNNORT	BENEDICT ARNOLD
ABCDDEFIIMORW	WIDDICOMBE FAIR
ABCDDEHKNNOOOS	SECOND-HAND BOOK
ABCDDEHLLNOOTW	BLEW HOT AND COLD
ABCDDGGKNOOORU	GOOD BACKGROUND
ABCDDGINOPRRUY	DRYING CUPBOARD
ABCDDHLLNOOOTW	BLOW HOT AND COLD
ABCDEEEEGGMNOS	BECOMES ENGAGED
ABCDEEEEHLMRWY	REACHED WEMBLEY
ABCDEEEEKKNPRS	BREAKNECK SPEED
ABCDEEEELLNSST	DELECTABLENESS
ABCDEEEELNRSST	CELEBRATEDNESS
ABCDEEEELORSTU	ABSOLUTE DECREE
	DECREE ABSOLUTE
ABCDEEEGHHJKTY	JACK-BY-THE-HEDGE
ABCDEEEHHINRTW	WIDEN THE BREACH
ABCDEEEHILMSST	BEST LAID SCHEME
ABCDEEEHKORRRT	BREAK THE RECORD
ABCDEEEHORRSTT	BEATS THE RECORD
ABCDEEEHPRRTUY	REACHED PUBERTY
ABCDEEEILNORRS	BORDERLINE CASE
ABCDEEEILNPSSS	DESPICABLENESS
ABCDEEELLOOORT	COLORADO BEETLE
ABCDEEFFHIMMNOR	CAME FROM BEHIND
ABCDEEFHNPRSTU	PERFECT HUSBAND
ABCDEEGHLNOSWX	EXCHANGED BLOWS
ABCDEEHHIIRTTW	WATCH THE BIRDIE
ABCDEEHHKLNOOT	HEAD ON THE BLOCK
ABCDEEHIKPPTTU	PICKED UP THE TAB
ABCDEEHIMMPRRS	MEMBERSHIP CARD
ABCDEEHINPRSSS	HERBS AND SPICES
ABCDEEHKLOPTTT	POTTED THE BLACK
ABCDEEHLNNRSTU	BURNS THE CANDLE
ABCDEEHNNOOPRRY	BEYOND REPROACH
ABCDEEIILLNNOR	INCONSIDERABLE
ABCDEEIKLNRSSS	DRESSES IN BLACK
ABCDEEILNOORST	SELECTION BOARD
ABCDEEKKNORSSU	BREAKS ONE'S DUCK
ABCDEFIKMNNOOS	BACK OF ONE'S MIND
ABCDEFIMNOOOTW	BIT OF A COME-DOWN
ABCDEFOOOORRTT	BAREFOOT DOCTOR
ABCDEGIIIKLSTW	WIELD A BIG STICK
ABCDEGIILNNNOR	BLIND IGNORANCE
ABCDEHIOOPRRTV	PITCH OVERBOARD
ABCDEHKLNOORTU	AROUND THE BLOCK
ABCDEIIILPRTTY	PREDICTABILITY
ABCDEIILNNORSY	INCONSIDERABLY
ABCDEILNNNOOST	BONNIE SCOTLAND
ABCDEIMMNNOOORX	CARBON MONOXIDE
ABCDEINNORRSTU	BURNS TO A CINDER
ABCDEINNORRTTU	BURNT TO A CINDER
ABCDELMNORSSSTU	STUMBLED ACROSS
ABCDFLNOOOORRT	BOARD OF CONTROL
ABCDGHILNOOORS	BOARDING SCHOOL
ABCDGIIKNOPPRR	DROPPING A BRICK
ABCDHINOOOPRSU	BRANCHIOPODOUS
ABCDHNOOOORRSUY	HYDROCARBONOUS
ABCDIMNNOORTTU	BADMINTON COURT
ABCDIMNOOPSSUY	DUBIOUS COMPANY
ABCEEEEHKNOPRT	BROKEN THE PEACE
ABCEEEEHLMRSWY	REACHES WEMBLEY
ABCEEEFFGHLOOT	FACE OF THE GLOBE
ABCEEEFHIOPRRS	PAIR OF BREECHES
ABCEEEFIILNNSS	BENEFICIALNESS
ABCEEEFMOORRVY	OVERCOME BY FEAR
ABCEEEGHIIKNRT	BREAKING THE ICE

ABCEEEGIIMNNTT	CABINET MEETING
ABCEEEGKLLMRSS	RECKLESS GAMBLE
ABCEEEGLRRTUVY	VEGETABLE CURRY
ABCEEEHHKOTTTT	TO THE BACK TEETH
ABCEEEHIILMNNT	MICHAEL BENTINE
ABCEEEHIKKRTTW	BREAK THE WICKET
ABCEEEHKRRSTTU	BREAKS THE TRUCE
ABCEEEHMMMRRRST	CHARTER MEMBERS
ABCEEEHNRRTTTU	BETTER THAN CURE
ABCEEEHPRRSTUY	REACHES PUBERTY
ABCEEEIILLRRSTV	SILVER BRACELET
ABCEEEINRRSSSU	BUSINESS CAREER
ABCEEEKKNNORSS	BREAKS ONE'S NECK
ABCEEEELLORSSUY	SCORE A BULL'S-EYE
	SCORE A BULLS EYE
ABCEEENSSSTTUW	SWEET SUBSTANCE
ABCEEFGHILLNOX	BILL OF EXCHANGE
ABCEEFGILNNORS	BRACING ONESELF
ABCEEFHHILLRST	FILLS THE BREACH
ABCEEFHKLORSTT	THE BLACK FOREST
ABCEEFIILNORTY	ENFORCEABILITY
ABCEEFIILOTUUV	BEAUTIFUL VOICE
ABCEEFLLOORTTT	BOTTLE OF CLARET
ABCEEGHHKNNSTY	HANGS BY THE NECK
ABCEEGHINORSTT	BEARING THE COST
ABCEEGHINPQUYY	PAYING BY CHEQUE
ABCEEGHKRRSTTU	GRUB-STREET HACK
ABCEEGHLNOSSWX	EXCHANGES BLOWS
ABCEEGIIILNRST	BEING REALISTIC
ABCEEGILLLLLOO	BALLIOL COLLEGE
ABCEEGINNORRTU	BRUTE IGNORANCE
ABCEEGKKOORRST	STOCKBROKERAGE
ABCEEGKNNOOSTW	GET ONES OWN BACK
ABCEEGKNOPSSTU	GETS ONE'S BACK UP
ABCEEGLLMNNSTU	GENTLEMANS CLUB
ABCEEHHHRTTTUY	BURY THE HATCHET
ABCEEHHILNORTV	THE OLIVE BRANCH
ABCEEHHNOPTTTU	BEAT TO THE PUNCH
ABCEEHIIKSTTTU	TAKE THE BISCUIT
ABCEEHIJKNOSTX	JACK-IN-THE-BOXES
ABCEEHIKNNRSTW	BACKS THE WINNER
ABCEEHIMMNRRTT	TIMBER MERCHANT
ABCEEHKLNNOSTU	LUNCHEON BASKET
ABCEEHLORRRTUV	TRAVEL BROCHURE
ABCEEHMORRRTTU	TORTURE CHAMBER
ABCEEIIILRSTVY	SERVICEABILITY
ABCEEIIKRRRSTT	TICKET BARRIERS
ABCEEIILORRTVY	RECOVERABILITY
ABCEEIILPRSTTY	RESPECTABILITY
ABCEEIKLNNOOSS	LIES ON ONE'S BACK
ABCEEILMNOPSST	COMPATIBLENESS
ABCEEILNNOSSSU	UNSOCIABLENESS
ABCEEIMNOOPRST	BOSTON CREAM PIE
ABCEELPRRSSSTU	BRUSSELS CARPET
ABCEENOORRSSSS	BEARS ONE'S CROSS
ABCEFFILMOPRRT	TRAFFIC PROBLEM
ABCEFFLLLNOSSU	CALLS ONE'S BLUFF
ABCEFGIILMMNRS	CLIMBING-FRAMES
ABCEFIILLNOORT	ACTION FOR LIBEL
ABCEFIILLPSTUV	PUBLIC FESTIVAL
ABCEFLLOOPRRTU	BULLET-PROOF CAR
	BULLETPROOF CAR
ABCEGGHHORRSTU	BROUGHT CHARGES
ABCEGHIILLNST	SLICING THE BALL
ABCEGHIINNPPRT	CHIPPING BARNET
ABCEGHIKLNOOTT	GO INTO THE BLACK
ABCEGHIKLNOTWY	BLOCKING THE WAY
ABCEGHIKNOORTT	ROCKING THE BOAT
ABCEGHIKNPSSTU	PASSING THE BUCK
ABCEGHIMNOSTTU	BATHING COSTUME
ABCEGHLNORSTTY	BY A LONG STRETCH
ABCEGIIIJNORST	JACOBITE RISING
ABCEGIIKNNNNWY	WINNING BY A NECK
ABCEGIILNPTTUY	PUBLICITY AGENT
ABCEGIILOORSTT	BACTERIOLOGIST
ABCEGILNORSTUU	CAUSING TROUBLE
ABCEGKKNOOORTW	GONE BACK TO WORK
ABCEGKKOOOORSTW	GOES BACK TO WORK
ABCEGKNNOOOSTW	GOT ONE'S OWN BACK
ABCEHHIORRSSTT	HIT THE CROSSBAR
ABCEHIKLLNOSTT	ON THE BLACK LIST
ABCEHILLLMPTUW	CLIMB UP THE WALL
ABCEHILLLOPRYY	HYPERBOLICALLY
ABCEHILLNNORST	BRISTOL CHANNEL
ABCEHILORRSTTY	ERYTHROBLASTIC
ABCEHINOPRSSTU	PASS THE RUBICON
ABCEHJLNNOORRY	JOHN BARLEYCORN
ABCEHLMOORSTTU	STOMACH TROUBLE
ABCEIIILMNNRVY	INVINCIBLE ARMY
ABCEIIILORRTVY	IRREVOCABILITY
ABCEIILMRSTTUU	MUSICAL TRIBUTE
ABCEIINNNORSTT	ANCIENT BRITONS
ABCEIINOOPSSUV	ABOVE SUSPICION
ABCEIINOORTTUY	OBITUARY NOTICE
ABCEILLLMOORTY	BOLOMETRICALLY
ABCEILLNOSSTUY	SELLS BY AUCTION
ABCEILLORRSTYY	BAY CITY ROLLERS
ABCEILNNNOSTTU	SUBCONTINENTAL
ABCEIMORRRSSTU	CUSTOMS BARRIER
ABCEKKKNOORTTWW	WENT BACK TO WORK
ABCEKLLOOOPRTW	BLACKPOOL TOWER
ABCEKNOPPSSTUU	PUTS ONE'S BACK UP
ABCELLLNNOORTU	UNCONTROLLABLE
ABCELMORSSSSTU	STUMBLES ACROSS
ABCELMPRRSSTUU	CLUBS ARE TRUMPS
ABCELNOSSTUUUY	SUBCUTANEOUSLY
ABCFFFLMOOORTY	COMFORTABLY OFF
ABCFGILNNOOTUU	FLOUNCING ABOUT
ABCFHILOOPPTTU	PUBLIC FOOTPATH
ABCFIIILMNORTY	CONFIRMABILITY
ABCFLLNOOOOPTU	FOOTBALL COUPON
ABCGHIIIMMNRTY	BIRMINGHAM CITY
ABCGIIILLNORTU	LUBRICATING OIL
ABCGILNOOPSWYY	PLAYING COWBOYS
ABCHIILNOTTUUY	UNTOUCHABILITY
ABCHIMNORSSSTU	CHRISTMAS BONUS
ABCHIOSSTTTUWY	IT CUTS BOTH WAYS
ABCIIIIJLSTTUY	JUSTICIABILITY
ABCIIILLLOPSTY	COLLAPSIBILITY
ABCIIILNRSTTUY	INSCRUTABILITY
ABCIILMNNOSTUU	SOMNAMBULISTIC
ABCIILMNOOSTUU	BITUMINOUS COAL
ABCIJKKNNOOSTT	JOINT-STOCK BANK
ABCIKKNNOOTUWY	WIN BY A KNOCK-OUT
ABCILMNORSTUUY	RAMBUNCTIOUSLY
ABCIMNNNOOOOPS	BOON COMPANIONS
ABCKKNNOOOTUWY	WON BY A KNOCK-OUT
ABDDDEEHNORSTU	DEVOTED HUSBAND
ABDDDEEMOORVYY	OVER MY DEAD BODY
ABDDDEHILOOOSV	AVOID BLOODSHED
ABDDEEEEHLPRTY	BREATHED DEEPLY
ABDDEEEEHNRSTU	EASED THE BURDEN
ABDDEEEELNNPSS	DEPENDABLENESS
ABDDEEEFGHINRT	FEATHERBEDDING
ABDDEEEFILLLOU	LED A DOUBLE LIFE
ABDDEEEFILNRTY	FRIENDLY DEBATE
ABDDEEEGIIMNRT	BEDTIME READING
ABDDEEEHILNORT	BEARDED THE LION
ABDDEEEHLLNSSU	BULLHEADEDNESS
ABDDEEEHNNOOST	ON ONES DEATH-BED
ABDDEEEHNOPTTU	POUNDED THE BEAT
ABDDEEEMNRSSST	BEST DRESSED MAN

ABDDEEFGIILNOR	OBLIGED A FRIEND
ABDDEEGINORSUY	GUIDED BY REASON
ABDDEEHHIORSST	HEARD BOTH SIDES
ABDDEEHHNOORTT	HOT AND BOTHERED
ABDDEEHIILSSST	DISESTABLISHED
ABDDEEHILNRSVY	DELIVERS BY HAND
ABDDEEHIMNNORT	BROADEN THE MIND
ABDDEEIIJLMNOU	DIAMOND JUBILEE
ABDDEEILMNNSTY	ABSENTMINDEDLY
ABDDEELMORSUUY	MADE DOUBLY SURE
ABDDEFGIMORRST	STAMFORD BRIDGE
ABDDEFGINNORRW	BENDING FORWARD
ABDDEFHILLNNOT	LAND OF THE BLIND
ABDDEFILNOORSS	BAND OF SOLDIERS
ABDDEGGILNNOTT	DING-DONG BATTLE
ABDDEGHILNNOOS	HOLDS IN BONDAGE
ABDDEHILNNRSTW	DRAWN THE BLINDS
ABDDEHILNRSSTW	DRAWS THE BLINDS
ABDDEHLOORRSSU	BROAD SHOULDERS
ABDDENOOOPRRUW	BORROWED A POUND
ABDDFHLMNOOOSU	BAND OF HOODLUMS
ABDDFILOORRSTW	DRAW FIRST BLOOD
ABDDFMNOOORRWX	FORD MADOX BROWN
ABDDGGILNNOOWY	GOING DOWN BADLY
ABDDGIILNNNOSU	BUILDING ON SAND
ABDDGIMNNPRSSU	BUMPS AND GRINDS
ABDDLNNOOOSUWY	OWN BODY AND SOUL
ABDEEEEFHLNOSV	BEHAVED ONESELF
ABDEEEEEFHLRRTY	BREATHED FREELY
ABDEEEEGHKLPRT	BREAK THE PLEDGE
ABDEEEEEHLPRSTY	BREATHES DEEPLY
ABDEEEEHNORSTT	BARED ONE'S TEETH
ABDEEEEHNRSSTU	EASES THE BURDEN
ABDEEEEIILLOSTV	LEADS TO BELIEVE
ABDEEEEILNRSST	DELIBERATENESS
ABDEEEEKLOOPRS	BOOKED A SLEEPER
ABDEEEENRSSTTY	SEEN BETTER DAYS
ABDEEEFFIILNRT	DIFFERENTIABLE
ABDEEEFGHOORTW	BEWARE OF THE DOG
ABDEEEFGJOPRUU	UP BEFORE A JUDGE
ABDEEEFILLRSSU	BLUE-ARSED FLIES
ABDEEEGHIIRTVW	GIVE A WIDE BERTH
ABDEEEGHINORTV	GAVE ONE THE BIRD
ABDEEEGHINRSST	BIGHEARTEDNESS
ABDEEEGHNORTVY	BEYOND THE GRAVE
ABDEEEGILNOTUV	DOUBLE NEGATIVE
ABDEEEGILNRSST	SINGLE-BREASTED
ABDEEEGIMSTTTU	BUDGET ESTIMATE
ABDEEEGLNOORTY	GONE TO BED EARLY
ABDEEEGLOORSTY	GOES TO BED EARLY
ABDEEEHHILLSTY	LAID BY THE HEELS
ABDEEEHHKORRTT	BROKE THE THREAD
ABDEEEHHLNRSTT	HELD ONE'S BREATH
ABDEEEHHNOORST	BOTHER ONE'S HEAD
ABDEEEHILNNORT	ON THE BREADLINE
ABDEEEHLNOSSTY	LEADS BY THE NOSE
ABDEEEHNOOORTT	BORE ONE TO DEATH
ABDEEEHNOORSTX	BOXED ON THE EARS
ABDEEEHOPRSSTW	SWEEP THE BOARDS
	SWEEPS THE BOARD
ABDEEEIILLRTVY	DELIBERATIVELY
ABDEEEIILMNNRT	INDETERMINABLE
ABDEEEIINNOPZZ	BENZODIAZEPINE
ABDEEEILLORRRT	TERRIBLE ORDEAL
ABDEEEIMNNOOTV	ABOVEMENTIONED
ABDEEEIMNORSST	SEASONED TIMBER
ABDEEEIORRSSWY	RAISED EYEBROWS
ABDEEEIRRRSTUU	BURIED TREASURE
ABDEEEKMNOSSTU	MAKES ONE'S DEBUT
ABDEEEKNNOOSTT	TAKEN TO ONE'S BED
ABDEEEKNOOSSTT	TAKES TO ONE'S BED
ABDEEEELLNOPRSS	DEPLORABLENESS
ABDEEEELLNOPRUY	PALE BLUE YONDER
ABDEEEILNOOSWWY	ELBOWED ONE'S WAY
ABDEEEELNORTTWY	WENT TO BED EARLY
ABDEEEELOPRRRSS	REPELS BOARDERS
ABDEEEEMNNNOOSS	ON ONE'S BEAM ENDS
	ON ONES BEAM-ENDS
ABDEEEENORRSTTU	RETURNED TO BASE
ABDEEEENORSSTUV	BEST ENDEAVOURS
ABDEEFFHINOOST	BIT ONE'S HEAD OFF
ABDEEFFILLORTT	BATTLED FOR LIFE
ABDEEFGHILORTY	BEFORE DAYLIGHT
ABDEEFGHINRRST	FINGERS BREADTH
ABDEEFGIILNORS	OBLIGES A FRIEND
ABDEEFHHIOSTTT	HAD THE BEST OF IT
ABDEEFHHOORRTT	ORDER OF THE BATH
ABDEEFHILRSTTU	HAD BUTTERFLIES
ABDEEFIIIKLLRS	FLIES LIKE A BIRD
ABDEEFIIILLRTV	DEFIBRILLATIVE
ABDEEFILMNORSS	FORMIDABLENESS
ABDEEFIMNNRRST	MANS BEST FRIEND
ABDEEFIMOSTTTU	SUBMIT TO DEFEAT
ABDEEFIOOPSSTX	SAFE DEPOSIT BOX
ABDEEFIOORRRVW	BORROWED A FIVER
ABDEEGGILNOTT	GOING TO BED LATE
ABDEEGCCINNNOOR	GOING ON A BENDER
ABDEEGHIILNTTW	WIELDING THE BAT
ABDEEGHIIRSSST	BRIGHTS DISEASE
ABDEEGHILNORTW	LONG WHITE BEARD
ABDEEGHIMNRTTU	BEATING THE DRUM
ABDEEGHINNOOSW	BOWING ONE'S HEAD
ABDEEGHNOORTUV	ABOVE THE GROUND
ABDEEGILNORRSV	GARBLED VERSION
ABDEEGILOORRTW	WATERLOO BRIDGE
ABDEEGIOORSTVY	EVERY BIT AS GOOD
ABDEEGKNNORRUW	BREAK NEW GROUND
ABDEEGKOOPRTUX	EXPURGATED BOOK
ABDEEGLNOOOSTY	GET A BLOODY NOSE
ABDEEGNNOOPRSS	BEGS ONE'S PARDON
ABDEEHHIORSSST	HEARS BOTH SIDES
ABDEEHHLNOORST	HOLD ONES BREATH
ABDEEHIILSSSST	DISESTABLISHES
ABDEEHIKNNSSTU	BASKED IN THE SUN
ABDEEHILMNRSTU	DIALS THE NUMBER
ABDEEHILMOORUV	MODEL BEHAVIOUR
ABDEEHILNOSTTW	WIELDS THE BATON
ABDEEHILNOSTVY	DONE IT BY HALVES
ABDEEHILOSSTVY	DOES IT BY HALVES
ABDEEHINORSTUY	QUEENS BIRTHDAY
ABDEEHNOOSSTUV	HAVE ONES DOUBTS
ABDEEHIOORRRTVW	THREW OVERBOARD
ABDEEHOPRSSTTW	SWEPT THE BOARDS
ABDEEIIILNRSTV	INVISIBLE TRADE
ABDEEIILLLPSUV	PLAUSIBLE DEVIL
ABDEEIILMNRTUY	DENUMERABILITY
ABDEEIKLNOSSWY	BODILY WEAKNESS
ABDEEILMMSTUWY	WEMBLEY STADIUM
ABDEEILMNNORST	INDEMONSTRABLE
ABDEEILNNRSTUY	TURNS A BLIND EYE
ABDEEILOOOPSTT	BOILED POTATOES
ABDEEIMNOSSUVY	BY DEVIOUS MEANS
ABDEEINNORSSSU	USED ONE'S BRAINS
ABDEEKLMORSUUY	MAKE DOUBLY SURE
ABDEEKNOORRSSW	BREAKS ONE'S WORD
ABDEELLLLMORRU	ROLLED UMBRELLA
ABDEELLMOOPRSV	SOLVED A PROBLEM
ABDEELLOPPSTTU	STOPPED A BULLET
ABDEELNRSTTTUU	UNSALTED BUTTER
ABDEELORRSTTUW	TROUBLED WATERS
ABDEENNOOSTTUW	SEWED ON A BUTTON

ABDEFGGIILNORT	FLOATING BRIDGE	ABDGIINOOQRRUW	BORROWING A QUID
ABDEFGGILNOTUY	GOING BY DEFAULT	ABDGINNOOPRTTU	PUTTING ON BOARD
ABDEFGIIILLNRT	DEFIBRILLATING	ABDIIIILMNOTTY	INDOMITABILITY
ABDEFHLLMOORSU	SHOULDER OF LAMB	ABDIIILNORSTTU	DISTRIBUTIONAL
ABDEFIIILLNORT	DEFIBRILLATION	ABDIIOOOPRSSSU	BASIDIOSPOROUS
ABDEFIIKLLNORW	FLOWN LIKE A BIRD	ABEEEEEGGLNRTV	GREEN VEGETABLE
ABDEFIILLLLORV	FIVE-DOLLAR BILL	ABEEEEFHINPRTT	REAP THE BENEFIT
ABDEFIILLORRST	DEFIBRILLATORS	ABEEEEFHLNOSSV	BEHAVES ONESELF
ABDEFIILLORRTY	DEFIBRILLATORY	ABEEEEFHLRRSTY	BREATHES FREELY
ABDEFINOOQRRUY	BOARD OF ENQUIRY	ABEEEEGGLRSTVW	GREW VEGETABLES
ABDEFMOOOORRSTW	FROM BAD TO WORSE	ABEEEEHILMNPTU	EATEN HUMBLE PIE
ABDEGGGHIIINPRT	BRIDGING THE GAP	ABEEEEHILNQTUZ	QUEEN ELIZABETH
ABDEGGGHIILNRRT	GILBERT HARDING	ABEEEEEHNORSSTT	BARFS ONE'S TEETH
ABDEGGHIMNNRTU	BANGING THE DRUM	ABEEEEHNRRTTTV	BETTER THAN EVER
ABDEGGIILLLNNY	LEGALLY BINDING	ABEEEEFFNOORRST	BEREFT OF REASON
ABDEGGIKNNORRU	BREAKING GROUND	ABEEEEFHMNRRRST	REFRESHMENT BAR
ABDEGGINNOPRSW	BRINGS DOWN A PEG	ABEEEEFILNNRRTT	ENFANT TERRIBLE
ABDEGGINOOORRV	GOING OVERBOARD	ABEEEGGLORSTVW	GROW VEGETABLES
ABDEGHIIILLNNRT	TRAILING BEHIND	ABEEEGHILMNNOR	BLENHEIM ORANGE
ABDEGHIIJLNOOR	JOHN LOGIE BAIRD	ABEEEGHOOPTUVZ	GAVE UP THE BOOZE
ABDEGHIILNOSUU	BUILDING A HOUSE	ABEEEGIKNNOSTW	BEGINS TO WEAKEN
ABDEGHILMNNRST	TREMBLING HANDS	ABEEEGILLNPSTT	SLEEPING TABLET
ABDEGHINOORSSU	BOARDINGHOUSES	ABEEEGILNPSTUY	SLEEPING BEAUTY
ABDEGHLMNORTUU	ROUGH AND TUMBLE	ABEEEHHKLOSTTT	SHAKE THE BOTTLE
	ROUGH-AND-TUMBLE	ABEEEHHLLSSTYY	LAYS BY THE HEELS
ABDEGHLNOORTWW	DRAW THE LONGBOW	ABEEEHIJKNOPRS	JOSEPHINE BAKER
ABDEGIIIKLNRSS	SINGS LIKE A BIRD	ABEEEHIKLRTTTY	TAKE THE LIBERTY
ABDEGIILLNNRRY	LENDING LIBRARY	ABEEEHIMNNRTTU	THREE MEN IN A TUB
ABDEGIILLNRSST	GILBERT ISLANDS	ABEEEHKLLPRSST	BREAKS THE SPELL
ABDEGIJMNNOTTU	OBTAIN JUDGMENT	ABEEEHKLORTTTU	TAKE THE TROUBLE
ABDEGIKLMNNOOS	MAKING OLD BONES	ABEEEHKLRRSSTU	BREAKS THE RULES
ABDEGILNNOOTUV	LEAVING NO DOUBT	ABEEEHKMNNOSTTY	BY THE SAME TOKEN
ABDEGINNOOORTUW	WONDERING ABOUT	ABEEEHKNOORRST	BROKE ONE'S HEART
ABDEGINOOPRRUY	I BEG YOUR PARDON	ABEEEHLLLRSSTY	THREE SYLLABLES
ABDEGINOPRSTTU	BRINGS UP TO DATE	ABEEEHLLNRSSTW	ANSWERS THE BELL
ABDEGLNOOOOSTY	GOT A BLOODY NOSE	ABEEEHLLOOSSTT	LOSES THE BATTLE
ABDEGNOOOPRTTU	TORPEDO GUNBOAT	ABEEEHLMNORTTT	THREE-BOTTLE MAN
ABDEHIIILLNRSTY	BRITISH LEYLAND	ABEEEHLNRSSSST	BREATHLESSNESS
ABDEHILNOPRSUY	RHAPSODY IN BLUE	ABEEEHMOORSTUW	SOMEWHERE ABOUT
ABDEHINNNOSSSU	BUSINESS ON HAND	ABEEEHNOORSSTX	BOXES ON THE EARS
ABDEHLMNNOOTWW	BLOW THE MAN DOWN	ABEEEIIKLNRSTT	TAKEN LIBERTIES
ABDEHMNNOORTUY	HAD MONEY TO BURN	ABEEEIIKLRSSTT	TAKES LIBERTIES
ABDEHOOORRRTVW	THROW OVERBOARD	ABEEEIILLNPRSST	ALBERT EINSTEIN
ABDEIIILMNOOST	DEMOBILISATION	ABEEEIILNNSSTV	INEVITABLENESS
ABDEIIILMNOOTZ	DEMOBILIZATION	ABEEEIIKKRRRSST	STRIKEBREAKERS
ABDEIIIILNORRTY	LIBRARY EDITION	ABEEEIKNNOPRTV	BREAK-EVEN POINT
ABDEIIILNPSSTY	DISPENSABILITY	ABEEEIILLORSTUV	VIOLETS ARE BLUE
ABDEIIILNRSTUY	UNDESIRABILITY	ABEEEIILNNRRSST	TERMINABLENESS
ABDEIIIRRSSTTU	DISTRIBUTARIES	ABEEEIILNRRRTTV	INTERVERTEBRAL
ABDEIILNOORSTW	BOWDLERISATION	ABEEEKNNOORSSS	BREAKS ONE'S NOSE
ABDEIILNOORTWZ	BOWDLERIZATION	ABEEELLNNRSSUV	VULNERABLENESS
ABDEIINSSSTTUV	SUBSTANTIVISED	ABEEELNNOPRSSS	PERSONABLENESS
ABDEIINSSTTUVZ	SUBSTANTIVIZED	ABEEENOOORRSTT	BORE ONE TO TEARS
ABDEIKLNNOOORS	BROOKS NO DENIAL	ABEEENOOPRSSUW	ABUSE ONES POWER
ABDEIKLNORSSTU	BLOUSE AND SKIRT	ABEEFFHLOOOTTT	FOOT OF THE TABLE
ABDEILLMNNOPTU	PLATINUM BLONDE	ABEEFFILLOPSTU	ABSOLUTE PIFFLE
ABDEILLNOOOORST	BLOOD-RELATIONS	ABEEFFILLORSTT	BATTLES FOR LIFE
ABDEILLNOORTTU	TOIL AND TROUBLE	ABEEFGIKLNNORS	BARKING ONESELF
ABDEILMNNORRSU	ORDINAL NUMBERS	ABEEFGILNNOSSU	ABUSING ONESELF
ABDEILMNNORSTY	INDEMONSTRABLY	ABEEFGIMNOPRRR	PERFORMING BEAR
ABDEILMORSTUXY	AMBIDEXTROUSLY	ABEEFHHILMSSTT	SHIFTS THE BLAME
ABDEILNOQTTUUY	DOUBLE QUANTITY	ABEEFHHIOSSTTT	HAS THE BEST OF IT
ABDEINNNOORSSY	IN ONES BORN DAYS	ABEEFHILRSSTTU	HAS BUTTERFLIES
ABDEJMOOPRRSUV	JUMPS OVERBOARD	ABEEFHLLOOSTTU	BEATS HELL OUT OF
ABDENNOORSSTUU	ROUNDABOUTNESS	ABEEFHLMMOORRT	THERMOFORMABLE
ABDENORSSSTTUY	TRUSTS AND OBEYS	ABEEFHMOOOSTTT	BOTTOM OF THE SEA
ABDFGHOORRRTUW	BROUGHT FORWARD	ABEEFIIMMMNTUX	MAXIMUM BENEFIT
ABDFGIILMNOPRS	BAND OF PILGRIMS	ABEEFIILLNMORRS	SMALL-BORE RIFLE
ABDFGLLNOOORTU	FOOTBALL GROUND	ABEEFILNOPRSST	PROFITABLENESS
ABDFHLNOOORSTW	SHOW A BOLD FRONT	ABEEFKLLNNOORS	BROKEN ONE'S FALL
ABDGHIMNOOSTTU	DOUBTING THOMAS	ABEEFLMORRTTUW	TUMBLER OF WATER

ABEEFNOORRSTTU	TORRENT OF ABUSE
ABEEGGHIMNPTTY	EMPTYING THE BAG
ABEEGGGLNORRSUY	GEORGE LANSBURY
ABEEGHHILNSTUV	HAVING THE BLUES
ABEEGHIILLLNPR	LIBERAL HELPING
ABEEGHIILNSTUX	EXTINGUISHABLE
ABEEGHIKNORSSU	HOUSEBREAKINGS
ABEEGHINNOPTTT	OPEN THE BATTING
ABEEGHINNORRSU	NEAR NEIGHBOURS
ABEEGHINPRRRTU	BRING UP THE REAR
ABEEGIIIJKLLNN	BILLIE JEAN KING
ABEEGIIKKNRRST	STRIKEBREAKING
ABEEGIINNRSSTW	BEARING WITNESS
ABEEGIKLNRSTTY	BREAKS IT GENTLY
ABEEGILNNOOPTT	OPENING A BOTTLE
ABEEGILNNOOTTT	GONE INTO BATTLE
ABEEGILNOOSTTT	GOES INTO BATTLE
ABEEGINNORRRST	ROGER BANNISTER
ABEEGLOOPRRSYY	PLAY GOOSEBERRY
ABEEGMNORSSSUU	UMBRAGEOUSNESS
ABEEGNRRSTTTUU	STRANGE BUT TRUE
ABEEHHIQRRSTTU	HERBERT ASQUITH
ABEEHHLMPSTTTU	THUMPS THE TABLE
ABEEHIINORSTTT	RISEN TO THE BAIT
ABEEHIIORSSTTT	RISES TO THE BAIT
ABEEHIKLLRSSTT	STRIKES THE BALL
ABEEHIKLMORSTU	LIKE A SORE THUMB
ABEEHIKMNNNOTY	MONEY IN THE BANK
ABEEHILLNPSSST	SPILLS THE BEANS
ABEEHILMNSSSTT	ESTABLISHMENTS
ABEEHILNOSTTTT	NOT THE LEAST BIT
ABEEHIMOORTTUW	WRITE HOME ABOUT
ABEEHINNOSSSUV	HAVE NO BUSINESS
ABEEHINOORRTVW	OVER THE RAINBOW
ABEEHJKLOORSTU	LABOURS THE JOKE
ABEEHKNOPRSTTU	PUTS ON THE BRAKE
	PUTS THE BRAKE ON
ABEEHKOPRRRTTW	PETER BARKWORTH
ABEEHLLNOOOSTW	BEATS ONE HOLLOW
ABEEFHLMNNOPRRT	ROBERT HELPMANN
ABEEHLNNOPTUYZ	PHENYLBUTAZONE
ABEEHLNRSSTTTU	TURNS THE TABLES
ABEEHLOORTTTTW	HOT-WATER BOTTLE
ABEEHMMNOORRRY	HONORARY MEMBER
ABEEHMNORSTTTT	BETTER THAN MOST
ABEEHNORRRRSTW	WARNER BROTHERS
ABEEIIILMMPRTY	IMPERMEABILITY
ABEEIIILMNNSST	INIMITABLENESS
ABEEIIILMNRSSV	REMAINS VISIBLE
ABEEIIILRRTTVY	RETRIEVABILITY
ABEEIIILMNNOSSV	NO VISIBLE MEANS
ABEEIIILMNOPRSS	IMPRESSIONABLE
ABEEIIILNNOSSST	BITES ONE'S NAILS
ABEEIIILNPRSTTY	PRESENTABILITY
ABEEIIILNPRTTVY	PREVENTABILITY
ABEEIIINRRSTTVV	TRANSITIVE VERB
ABEEIKMNNOOPRRS	BROKEN A PROMISE
ABEEIKPRRSSTUY	TAKE BY SURPRISE
ABEEIILLLNSTTTU	LATEST BULLETIN
ABEEIILLMRSSSTT	BALLET MISTRESS
ABEEIILMNNNOSTU	UNMENTIONABLES
ABEEIILMNNOPRSS	RESPONSIBLE MAN
ABEEIILMNOPSSUY	OBEYS AN IMPULSE
ABEEIILMOPPRSSU	SUPERIMPOSABLE
ABEEIILNNOQSTUU	UNQUESTIONABLE
ABEEIILNNOTTTTW	WENT INTO BATTLE
ABEEIILNNSSTTUU	SUBLIEUTENANTS
ABEEIIMNNNOSSSU	ONE-MAN BUSINESS
ABEEIIMNRSSSTTU	BUSINESS MATTER
ABEEIIMOPRRRTTV	REPORT VERBATIM
	VERBATIM REPORT

ABEEIINNORSSSSU	USES ONE'S BRAINS
ABEEKORRRSSSTT	BREASTSTROKERS
ABEELLMOOPRSSV	SOLVES A PROBLEM
ABEELLNOPRSTUV	VULNERABLE SPOT
ABEELMMNOORTUV	LABOUR MOVEMENT
ABEELMNNSTTTTU	BLUNT STATEMENT
ABEELNNORSTTUY	BURY ONES TALENT
ABEFFGGHILNOTW	BLOWING THE GAFF
ABEFFGGHHIORRTT	FIGHT FOR BREATH
ABEFFGILNORSUW	SUFFERING A BLOW
ABEFFGOORRSSUV	BEGS FOR FAVOURS
ABEFFLLNOOOOST	BALL OF ONES FOOT
ABEFGHIILNORST	LIGHTS A BONFIRE
ABEFGHINOPRRST	BREATH OF SPRING
ABEFGIIILNRRTY	REFRANGIBILITY
ABEFGIILNNNORZ	BLAZING INFERNO
ABEFGIINNOSTXY	FIXING BAYONETS
ABEFGIOORSTTTU	FORGETS ABOUT IT
ABEFGNNOOORRTU	GONE FOR A BURTON
ABEFGNOORRSTU	GOES FOR A BURTON
ABEFHIKMNNORTU	THINK OF A NUMBER
ABEFIIIIILLQTUY	LIQUEFIABILITY
ABEFIIILRRTTUY	IRREFUTABILITY
ABEFIILMNSSSUY	FAMILY BUSINESS
ABEFILMNORSTTU	BURST INTO FLAME
ABEFIILMOOORSTT	MOTOR LIFEBOATS
ABEFILNOOPRSST	SELF-ABSORPTION
ABEFKLNOOOORRSU	BROOK NO REFUSAL
ABEFKLOORRSSTU	ASKS FOR TROUBLE
ABEFLLNOOPSSTU	TABLESPOONFULS
	TABLESPOONSFUL
ABEFNNOORRTTUW	WENT FOR A BURTON
ABEGGGHIIMNNTU	BIG-GAME HUNTING
	HUNTING BIG GAME
ABEGGGILNORSTW	STAGGERING BLOW
ABEGGHILLNOOTT	GOING TO THE BALL
ABEGHHINORSTTU	BAR THE SHOUTING
ABEGHHMOPRRTUY	HUMPHREY BOGART
ABEGHIIKNNOSTT	SINKING THE BOAT
ABEGHIILRRSSTV	BRIGHT AS SILVER
ABEGHIIMNOSSTT	MISSING THE BOAT
ABEGHIKNNORTWY	KNOWING BY HEART
ABEGHIKNOPPSST	SHOPPING BASKET
ABEGHILMNOOOSU	HAEMOGLOBINOUS
ABEGHILMNOOOXY	OXYHAEMOGLOBIN
ABEGHILNORSTTW	SHATTERING BLOW
ABEGHINNORSSTU	BURNING TO ASHES
ABEGHINNRRSTUW	BURNS WITH ANGER
ABEGHINOPRSSTT	STOPS BREATHING
ABEGHLMNRRSSTU	BREMSSTRAHLUNG
ABEGHNNORRTUWY	RUB THE WRONG WAY
ADCGIIILLLNRW	BEARING ILL-WILL
ABEGIIILMMNSSY	MISSING BY A MILE
ABEGIIILNMPRTY	IMPREGNABILITY
ABEGIINNNORSSU	USING ONE'S BRAIN
ABEGIINNORTTUZ	BRAZENING IT OUT
ABEGIKLMNOPPRR	PARKING PROBLEM
ABEGIKLNOORRWY	BOWLING A YORKER
ABEGIKMNNOOTUY	MONKEYING ABOUT
ABEGIKNNOORSST	BREAKS INTO SONG
ABEGILMNOOPPRS	POSING A PROBLEM
ABEGILMNOORRVV	OVERARM BOWLING
ABEGILNNOORSSU	BARING ONE'S SOUL
ABEGILNNOORRTUW	RETURNING A BLOW
ABEGINOOPRTTTU	POTTERING ABOUT
ABEGINOORTTTTU	TOTTERING ABOUT
ABEHHIJNOPSTTT	JOHN THE BAPTIST
ABEHHIMPRRRSUY	BARRY HUMPHRIES
ABEHHOOPSTTTUU	PUSH THE BOAT OUT
ABEHIIIILNRTTY	INHERITABILITY
ABEHIIILSTTUXY	EXHAUSTIBILITY

ABEHIILLMORTTY	THERMOLABILITY	ACCCEEIILSSSTU	ECCLESIASTICUS
ABEHIILNOOSSTV	BOLSHEVISATION	ACCCEENNOOOVVX	CONVEXO-CONCAVE
ABEHIILNOOSTVZ	BOLSHEVIZATION	ACCCEFINOOPRRT	TROPIC OF CANCER
ABEHIIMNOPSSSU	AMPHIBIOUSNESS	ACCCEHHHIILNTT	TECHNICAL HITCH
ABEHILLMMOOOST	HOLOMETABOLISM	ACCCEHHILOOPST	CHOCOLATE CHIPS
ABEHILNOOPRTTU	LABOUR THE POINT	ACCCEHIILLNOTY	ACETYLCHOLINIC
ABEHIMNORRRSST	BROTHERS IN ARMS	ACCCEHIINORSTT	ARCHITECTONICS
ABEHKMOORRSTTW	MARKET BOSWORTH	ACCCEHINOSSTTT	SCOTTISH ACCENT
ABEHILLMOOOOSTU	HOLOMETABOLOUS	ACCCEIIKLRRTTU	CIRCULAR TICKET
ABEHLMNOOORSTU	MOST HONOURABLE	ACCCEILLNNORTY	CONCENTRICALLY
ABEHLMNOOTTTUW	MATTHEW BOULTON	ACCCEIMMNOOORS	MACROECONOMICS
ABEHMNNOORSTUY	HAS MONEY TO BURN	ACCCEIMMNOOPRT	COMMON PRACTICE
ABEIIILLOPTTXY	EXPLOITABILITY	ACCCEIMMNOSTTU	CAUSTIC COMMENT
ABEIIKLMOPSSST	IMPOSSIBLE TASK	ACCCEIMNNOOSTT	COMES IN CONTACT
ABEIINSSSSTTUV	SUBSTANTIVISES	ACCCENNORRTTUU	CURRENT ACCOUNT
ABEIINSSSTTUVZ	SUBSTANTIVIZES	ACCCHIIOOPSSTT	TACHISTOSCOPIC
ABEIKNNNOORRTU	BROKEN INTO A RUN	ACCCHIKNOOQTTU	QUICK TO CATCH ON
ABEIKNOOORRTTT	BROKE INTO A TROT	ACCCHLOOPSSTUY	STAPHYLOCOCCUS
ABEILMNNORSTUU	INSURMOUNTABLE	ACCCILNOOSSSSU	CLASS CONSCIOUS
ABEILNNOORRTTU	RAN INTO TROUBLE		CLASS-CONSCIOUS
ABEILNNOQSTUUY	UNQUESTIONABLY	ACCDDDEEEEFNOT	CONCEDED DEFEAT
ABEILNORSSSSUU	SALUBRIOUSNESS	ACCDDDEEIORRST	CREATED DISCORD
ABEIMNNORTTTUU	BUTTER MOUNTAIN	ACCDDEEEEFNOST	CONCEDES DEFEAT
ABEIMOPRRSSTTU	SUBMITS A REPORT	ACCDDEEEEHKLRT	CLEARED THE DECK
ABEINNNORRSSTU	TURNS ONE'S BRAIN	ACCDDEEEHIILRV	HERALDIC DEVICE
ABEINOOOPRRRST	AIRBORNE TROOPS	ACCDDEEHHNRTTU	ATTENDED CHURCH
ABEINORRSSTTTU	BURST INTO TEARS	ACCDDEEHILNNPS	SPLENDID CHANCE
ABENOORRSSSTUU	BRONTOSAURUSES	ACCDDEEINNOOPT	CONCEDED A POINT
ABFGGHIIKLNOOT	BOOKING A FLIGHT	ACCDDEEIORRSST	CREATES DISCORD
ABFGIIIILNNRTY	INFRANGIBILITY	ACCDDEELNOOPRR	PLACED ON RECORD
ABFGIIIINNOPRRT	BRING IN A PROFIT	ACCDDEENORRSTT	STAND CORRECTED
ABFGIJKLNOOOOR	LOOKING FOR A JOB	ACCDDEFGIINORT	DECIDING FACTOR
ABFHIILNOORSST	BRISTOL FASHION	ACCDDEINNOSTTV	STAND CONVICTED
ABFIIIILNOSSTY	FISSIONABILITY	ACCDDHHIIMORRU	RICHARD MURDOCH
ABFIILMNOOSTTY	LOFTY AMBITIONS	ACCDEEEEKNPRT	TAKE PRECEDENCE
ABFIKNOORSSTWY	NASTY BIT OF WORK	ACCDEEEEFFHPST	AFFECTED SPEECH
ABGGGILLNOOOWY	BOWLING A GOOGLY	ACCDEEEFHINNOV	HAVE CONFIDENCE
ABGHHIIOOTTTTUU	THOUGHT ABOUT IT	ACCDEEEFIKLNOV	LACK OF EVIDENCE
ABGHIIILNOSTWY	SHOWING ABILITY	ACCDEEEGILLLMO	MEDICAL COLLEGE
ABGHINORRTTTUU	RIGHT ABOUT TURN	ACCDEEEHHIKNRT	CHICKENHEARTED
ABGHLNNOOOSTTY	NOT BY A LONG SHOT	ACCDEEEHHINSSW	CHEESE SANDWICH
ABGIIIILLNNORST	STIRLING ALBION	ACCDEEEHKLRSST	CLEARS THE DECKS
ABGIILLNNNPRUU	RUNNING UP A BILL	ACCDEEEIILNPPS	APPLIED SCIENCE
ABGIILNNOPRSTY	BRINGS INTO PLAY	ACCDEEEELLOSTTX	COLLECTED TAXES
ABGIINOPTTTTUU	PUTTING IT ABOUT	ACCDEEFFIILMOR	MEDICAL OFFICER
ABHIIIKLNNTTUY	UNTHINKABILITY	ACCDEEFGIINNNO	GAIN CONFIDENCE
ABIIIJLLNOTTY	JOINT LIABILITY	ACCDEEFIIORSTV	DECISIVE FACTOR
ABIIIILLMPSTUY	IMPLAUSIBILITY	ACCDEEFILNNSTU	SELF-INDUCTANCE
ABIIIILMMNOOTZ	IMMOBILIZATION	ACCDEEGHHKLNOT	CHANGED THE LOCK
ABIIIIMNNOSTTU	BITUMINISATION	ACCDEEGHIINSTT	CASTING THE DICE
ABIIIIMNNOTTUZ	BITUMINIZATION	ACCDEEGHNNORTU	COUNTERCHANGED
ABIILLNORSSUUY	INSALUBRIOUSLY	ACCDEEHHIKPRTW	CRACKED THE WHIP
ABIILNOSSTTTUU	SUBSTITUTIONAL	ACCDEEHHMMNORST	MARCH THE SECOND
ABILMNNORSTUUY	INSURMOUNTABLY	ACCDEEHIKLNRSS	CHARLES DICKENS
ACCCCHILOOPSTY	STAPHYLOCOCCIC	ACCDEEHIKOORRS	RIDE A COCK-HORSE
ACCCDEEEEHKORT	CRACKED THE CODE	ACCDEEHIKRRTT	THREE-CARD TRICK
ACCCDEEEFFIOPT	ACCEPTED OFFICE	ACCDEEHKLORRST	ROCKS THE CRADLE
ACCCDEEEIILMNS	MEDICAL SCIENCE	ACCDEEHLLOSTWY	WATCHED CLOSELY
ACCCDEEINNORTT	ACTED IN CONCERT	ACCDEEHNOOPSTU	TOUCHED ONE'S CAP
ACCCDEEINOPSTV	ESCAPED CONVICT	ACCDEEIILLRSTU	CLERICAL DUTIES
ACCCDEINORRTTU	ERRATIC CONDUCT	ACCDEEIILMMORS	COMMERCIALISED
ACCCDFFHIILTTU	DIFFICULT CATCH	ACCDEEIILMMORZ	COMMERCIALIZED
ACCCEEEEHINRST	SCIENCE TEACHER	ACCDEEIILRRSTY	RIDES A TRICYCLE
ACCCEEEEHINSST	TEACHES SCIENCE	ACCDEEIJLPRSSU	CLASS PREJUDICE
ACCCEEEGHILRRT	ELECTRIC CHARGE	ACCDEEILLMOORW	CORDIAL WELCOME
ACCCEEEIILLNPS	SPECIAL LICENCE	ACCDEEILMNORTY	ELECTRODYNAMIC
ACCCEEEIIMNORRT	ICE-CREAM CORNET	ACCDEEILNNNSTY	INCANDESCENTLY
ACCCEEEENORRRU	RARE OCCURRENCE	ACCDEEILNOPSTU	CONCEPTUALISED
ACCCEEFILLLMRU	CAME FULL CIRCLE	ACCDEEILNOPTUZ	CONCEPTUALIZED
ACCCEEHILLNORV	VICE-CHANCELLOR	ACCDEEILOORRST	CROCODILE TEARS
ACCCEEIILNOSSS	SOCIAL SCIENCES	ACCDEEIMMNNOTUX	EXCOMMUNICATED

ACCDEEIMNOPPTY	APPENDICECTOMY
ACCDEEIMOPPRRS	COMPARED PRICES
ACCDEEINNNOSTU	DISCOUNTENANCE
ACCDEEINNOOPST	CONCEDES A POINT
ACCDEEINPPRRSS	PARC DES PRINCES
ACCDEELNOOPRRS	PLACES ON RECORD
ACCDEEMMNOPRST	COMMAND RESPECT
ACCDEEMNOSSSTU	ACCUSTOMEDNESS
ACCDEENOORTUUV	OVERDUE ACCOUNT
ACCDEENORRSTUY	SCORED A CENTURY
ACCDEFHKMOOOORT	THE CRACK OF DOOM
ACCDEFIIILRTTY	CREDIT FACILITY
ACCDEGHHMOORTU	CHARGED TOO MUCH
ACCDEGIILLNOOV	CALVIN COOLIDGE
ACCDEGINORRTTU	CUTTING A RECORD
ACCDEHHIILLOOPY	DOLICHOCEPHALY
ACCDEHIILLNORY	DAILY CHRONICLE
ACCDEHKLNOORTU	AROUND THE CLOCK
ACCDEHILLLNOORR	LORD CHANCELLOR
ACCDEHLLOORSTT	CALLS THE DOCTOR
ACCDEIIILLLNPY	PICCADILLY LINE
ACCDEIILLOPRRT	CRITICAL PERIOD
ACCDEIILLNNOTY	COINCIDENTALLY
ACCDEIILMNORRR	CRIMINAL RECORD
ACCDEIINNNOSTU	DISCONTINUANCE
ACCDEILLNOOPSY	ENDOSCOPICALLY
ACCDEIMMNOORTY	ROMANTIC COMEDY
ACCDEINOOPSTTU	DEPOSIT ACCOUNT
ACCDELMNOSTUUY	UNACCUSTOMEDLY
ACCDGIILLLOSUY	GLUCOSIDICALLY
ACCDGIILLLOSYY	GLYCOSIDICALLY
ACCDHHINOOPRSY	HYPOCHONDRIACS
ACCDHIIILNNORV	CHRONIC INVALID
ACCDHIIKLLNOOR	ALCOHOLIC DRINK
ACCDHIILORSSTV	CLAVICHORDISTS
ACCDHINOPSSYY	PSYCHODYNAMICS
ACCDHLNOOOSTTU	HOLDS TO ACCOUNT
ACCDIINNOORSTT	CONTRADICTIONS
ACCDILMMNOORTU	IMMORAL CONDUCT
ACCEEEEFHIKOPT	PIECE OF THE CAKE
ACCEEEEFHLNRST	CLEARS THE FENCE
ACCEEEEFNNOPRR	CONFERENCE PEAR
ACCEEEEHHINSTZ	SEIZE THE CHANCE
ACCEEEEHILRRTT	ELECTRIC HEATER
ACCEEEEHLNOQSU	ENCLOSE A CHEQUE
ACCEEEEHMNOSTT	CAME TO THE SCENE
ACCEEEEHNOSSTY	CATCHES ONE'S EYE
ACCEEEELMORRST	ACCELEROMETERS
ACCEEEFFILPSST	SPECIAL EFFECTS
ACCEEEFGINNNOO	AGE OF INNOCENCE
ACCEEEFHIKLOST	SLICE OF THE CAKE
ACCEEEFILNPTXY	LIFE EXPECTANCY
ACCEEEGHILMNRY	CHEMICAL ENERGY
ACCEEEGHLMNOPT	COMPLETE CHANGE
ACCEEEHHILRRST	CHARLIE CHESTER
ACCEEEHHILRRTT	CIRCLE THE EARTH
ACCEEEHIKMNNOT	CHECKMATE IN ONE
ACCEEEHIKNOOST	TAKE ONES CHOICE
ACCEEEHILMORST	STEREOCHEMICAL
ACCEEEHILNOOSV	LEAVES NO CHOICE
ACCEEEHILRRSTV	ELECTRIC SHAVER
ACCEEEHKLNOPST	STEPHEN LEACOCK
ACCEEEIINPRRSS	INCREASE PRICES
ACCEEEILPRRSWY	CREEPY-CRAWLIES
ACCEEENNOPSTUX	EXPENSE ACCOUNT
	EXPENSE-ACCOUNT
ACCEEEORRSSTUW	WORCESTER SAUCE
ACCEEFFGINNOSU	CAUSING OFFENCE
ACCEEFFHHNNOOT	ON THE OFF CHANCE
ACCEEFFIILORST	OFFICIAL SECRET
ACCEEFFIIRSTTT	ARTISTIC EFFECT

ACCEEFGHHINNRT	TEACHING FRENCH
ACCEEFGHINOPRT	FORCING THE PACE
ACCEEFGHNOORSU	CHANGE OF COURSE
ACCEEFHILNOTTT	LEFT IT TO CHANCE
ACCEEFHIMOORTT	MATTER OF CHOICE
ACCEEFILLMNORT	CALM REFLECTION
ACCEEFILLMORTV	COLLECTIVE FARM
ACCEEFIMORRRTT	REFRACTOMETRIC
ACCEEGGIILNNPR	PIERCING GLANCE
ACCEEGHHKLNOST	CHANGES THE LOCK
ACCEEGHIIKNNOT	ICING ON THE CAKE
ACCEEGHIKNTTTU	CUTTING THE CAKE
ACCEEGHKLNNOSU	CHANGE ONES LUCK
ACCEEGHNNORSTU	COUNTERCHANGES
ACCEEGHNORRSTU	COUNTERCHARGES
ACCEEGIILRRTTU	ELECTRIC GUITAR
ACCEEGIINNOPST	ESCAPING NOTICE
ACCEEGIINNORSS	CARCINOGENESIS
ACCEEGILLNNORU	GENERAL COUNCIL
ACCEEGILLNORTY	EGOCENTRICALLY
	GEOCENTRICALLY
ACCEEGKLMOSTUU	COMSTUCK LFAGUF
ACCEEHHILMMORT	THERMOCHEMICAL
ACCEEHHIMRRSST	CHRISTMAS CHEER
ACCEEHHKNOSSTT	SCOTCH THE SNAKE
ACCEEHHLOORSST	SCHOOLTEACHERS
ACCEEHHOPSSTTT	CATCHES THE POST
ACCEEHIIILNSTT	TECHNICALITIES
ACCEEHIILMOORV	MALE VOICE CHOIR
ACCEEHIIORTVVY	ACHIEVE VICTORY
ACCEEHIKMNOTTW	CHECKMATE IN TWO
ACCEEHIKOORTUY	TAKE YOUR CHOICE
ACCEEHILLLOPST	CALLS THE POLICE
ACCEEHILMOPRST	PETROCHEMICALS
ACCEEHIMMOTTTW	WATCH COMMITTEE
ACCEEHIMMNOSSS	MISS ONES CHANCE
ACCEEHIMNNPRRT	MERCHANT PRINCE
ACCEEHIMNRSTTY	MANCHESTER CITY
ACCEEHINOPRSUX	CHEAP EXCURSION
ACCEEHKNNOOOST	TOOK ONE'S CHANCE
ACCEEHLLOSSTWY	WATCHES CLOSELY
ACCEEHLMOOORRT	MOROCCO LEATHER
ACCEEHMNNORRSTU	COUNTERMARCHES
ACCEEHMORSSTTT	TEST MATCH SCORE
ACCEEHNNNORRTT	NORTHERN ACCENT
ACCEEHNNORSTTU	SOUTHERN ACCENT
ACCEEHNOOPSSTU	TOUCHES ONE'S CAP
ACCEEHORRSSTTY	OYSTERCATCHERS
ACCEEIILLNNNNO	IN ALL INNOCENCE
ACCEEIILLNRTTU	ELECTRICAL UNIT
ACCEEIILMMORSS	COMMERCIALISES
ACCEEIILMMORSZ	COMMERCIALIZES
ACCEEIIMNNOOPP	COMPANION PIECE
ACCEEIIMMNNOORT	ECONOMETRICIAN
ACCEEIINNOORSS	CONCESSIONAIRE
ACCEEIKLLORRRW	CLERICAL WORKER
ACCEEIILLLNORTY	ELECTRONICALLY
ACCEEIILLLOPSTY	TELESCOPICALLY
ACCEEIILLRRRTTU	CIRCULAR LETTER
ACCEEIILNOPPRSU	POPULAR SCIENCE
ACCEEIILNOPRSSY	CONCEPTUALISES
ACCEEIILNOPSTUZ	CONCEPTUALIZES
ACCEEIILNRRTTUU	CURTAIN LECTURE
ACCEEIILORSSTTT	ELECTROSTATICS
ACCEEIIMMNOSTUX	EXCOMMUNICATES
ACCEEIMOPPRRSS	COMPARES PRICES
ACCEEINNOOPRRT	OPEN-AIR CONCERT
ACCEEINOPRSTTV	CONTRACEPTIVES
ACCEEIORRSTUVY	SECURE A VICTORY
ACCEELLMMOORSU	MACROMOLECULES
ACCEELNOSSTTTU	SETTLE ACCOUNTS

ACCEELOPRSSSTY	ROSY SPECTACLES	ACCEIILNOORRTY	RECONCILIATORY
ACCEEMMNNNOORT	COMMON ENTRANCE	ACCEIILORSSTUY	SOCIAL SECURITY
ACCEEMNORRSSTT	CONCERTMASTERS	ACCEIINNOPRSTT	CONCERT PIANIST
ACCEENORRSSTUY	SCORES A CENTURY	ACCEIINOPRSSSU	CAPRICIOUSNESS
ACCEFFIIILNOOT	OFFICIAL NOTICE	ACCEIINORRTTVY	CERTAIN VICTORY
ACCEFFIILLNOOO	COLONIAL OFFICE	ACCEIKLNOORSTY	ROCKY COASTLINE
ACCEFFIILNOSSU	OFFICIAL CENSUS	ACCEIKLOORSTTY	OYSTER COCKTAIL
ACCEFFIILOORSU	OFFICIAL SOURCE	ACCEIKNOPSTTUU	STUCK UP A NOTICE
ACCEFFNOORRSTU	CUTS OFF A CORNER	ACCEIKPRSSSTTU	SUSPECTS A TRICK
ACCEFGGHHIINNT	FIGHTING CHANCE	ACCEILLLNOOSTT	LAST COLLECTION
ACCEFGGIINNRSU	ACCUSING FINGER	ACCEILLNNOOSSY	CONCESSIONALLY
ACCEFGHHIILMNT	FLIGHT MECHANIC	ACCEILLNOOSSTU	ELOCUTION CLASS
ACCEFGIIIINNNS	INSIGNIFICANCE	ACCEILLNOSSSUY	SUCCESSIONALLY
ACCEFHHIKOPRTW	CRACK OF THE WHIP	ACCEILMMNNOOSS	COMMONSENSICAL
ACCEFHIINOOSTT	FIT THE OCCASION	ACCEILMMNNOOOP	SOLEMN OCCASION
ACCEFHIMNORTYY	FACTORY CHIMNEY	ACCEILNNOOTTVX	EXTINCT VOLCANO
ACCEFHIOPRRSTU	PAIR OF CRUTCHES	ACCEILNOOORTTV	CONTRALTO VOICE
ACCEFIIIILLNSTY	SCIENTIFICALLY	ACCEILNOORSSST	CROSS-SECTIONAL
ACCEFIIINOPSST	SPECIFICATIONS	ACCEIMMMNNNOOSU	COMMON NUISANCE
ACCEFIIKLNPTTU	CUP FINAL TICKET	ACCEIMNOOSTTUY	ACTINOMYCETOUS
ACCEFIKOPPRSST	PACKET OF CRISPS	ACCELLMOOPRSTT	STAMP COLLECTOR
ACCEFILLMNNOTT	MENTAL CONFLICT	ACCELLMOPSSSTT	COLLECTS STAMPS
ACCEFILNNOOSTT	FAILS TO CONNECT	ACCELNOOPPRRTU	POPULAR CONCERT
ACCEFINNOOSSUU	CAUSE CONFUSION	ACCEMMMNNOOORST	COMMON ANCESTOR
ACCEFINOOOORSTU	COURSE OF ACTION	ACCEMORRRSTTUU	MACROSTRUCTURE
ACCEGGHINNORSU	CHANGING COURSE	ACCFFIIINORTTU	FRUCTIFICATION
ACCEGGIINNORTV	GIVING A CONCERT	ACCFFILNOORRTT	TRAFFIC CONTROL
ACCEGHHIINNSTTU	CATCHING THE SUN	ACCFGIIIINNNSY	INSIGNIFICANCY
ACCEGHHMOORSTU	CHARGES TOO MUCH	ACCFHLLOOORSSU	CLASH OF COLOURS
ACCEGHIIIMMNNN	MINCING MACHINE	ACCFIIIIILNOST	SILICIFICATION
ACCEGHIIILLNNOU	HALLUCINOGENIC	ACCFINNOOOPTTT	POINT OF CONTACT
ACCEGHIIMNNPRR	PRINCE CHARMING	ACCGGHILNNOORU	CHANGING COLOUR
ACCEGHIKNPTTTU	CUTTING THE PACK	ACCGGIINNNOOP	GOING ON A PICNIC
ACCEGHINNOPRST	SPORTING CHANCE	ACCGGILNNOOTUW	GLOWING ACCOUNT
ACCEGHIOPPRRST	SPECTROGRAPHIC	ACCGHIILLOOPRS	OSCILLOGRAPHIC
ACCEGIIILMNTXX	EXCITING CLIMAX	ACCGHILOPRSSUY	PSYCHOSURGICAL
ACCEGIIKKNOPPT	PICKING A POCKET	ACCGIIIILLMNOOR	CRIMINOLOGICAL
ACCEGIIKLNPRTY	PLAYING CRICKET	ACCGILLLLOTYYY	GLYCOLYTICALLY
ACCEGIILNRTUXY	EXCRUCIATINGLY	ACCGILLLMOOOSY	COSMOLOGICALLY
ACCEGILLOOPRSS	LOGICAL PROCESS	ACCGILLOOPRSSY	GYROSCOPICALLY
ACCEGILMNOOOST	COMING TO A CLOSE	ACCGINNOORTTTU	CONTRACTING OUT
ACCEGIMNOOPPRR	COMING A CROPPER	ACCHHIILMNRTTU	CHURCH MILITANT
ACCEGINNORRTTU	CUTTING A CORNER	ACCHHILOPPSSYY	PSYCHOPHYSICAL
ACCEGINORRSSSU	ROARING SUCCESS	ACCHHIMOOORRTT	ORTHOCHROMATIC
ACCEGINRSSSUVY	VARYING SUCCESS	ACCHIILLOPRTYY	HYPOCRITICALLY
ACCEGKLOPPRUUU	PLUCK UP COURAGE	ACCHIIMMNNOSTU	COMMUNIST CHINA
ACCEGNOORTTTUY	COUNTRY COTTAGE	ACCHLMNNOOTTUY	MONTHLY ACCOUNT
ACCEHHILLNOPRS	CHANCELLORSHIP	ACCIIILLOOPPTT	POLITICAL TOPIC
ACCEHHLLMRSSUZ	CHARLES M. SCHULZ	ACCIIIMNORRSSU	ROSICRUCIANISM
ACCEHHOPRSTTTU	UP TO THE SCRATCH	ACCIIMMNNOOSTU	COMMUNICATIONS
ACCEHIIKLLLNST	TECHNICAL SKILL	ACCIKKLNOORRTW	CLOCKWORK TRAIN
ACCEHIIILLLMNOS	MICHAEL COLLINS	ACCILMNOOSTUUY	CONTUMACIOUSLY
ACCEHIJKMNOOPY	CHAMPION JOCKEY	ACCILNNOORSTTU	CONSTRUCTIONAL
ACCEHILMMNOPST	ACCOMPLISHMENT	ACCINPRSSTTUUU	ACUPUNCTURISTS
ACCEHILMNOORRT	CHRONOMETRICAL	ACCNNOORSTTTUU	TURNS TO ACCOUNT
ACCEHILMNORSTW	CLAIMS THE CROWN	ACDDDEEELNNOPT	PLACED END TO END
ACCEHILNPRSSUY	NUCLEAR PHYSICS	ACDDDEEHHIITTW	DICED WITH DEATH
ACCEHINNOPRTTY	HYPNOTIC TRANCE	ACDDDEEHILSSTT	SADDLE-STITCHED
ACCEHKMNOOPSSS	SMACK ONE'S CHOPS	ACDDDEEHNORRSU	SCORED A HUNDRED
ACCEHLLNNOOOTT	ALCOHOL CONTENT	ACDDDEEIILMNST	MIDDLE DISTANCE
ACCEHNORSSTTTU	TRUSTS TO CHANCE		MIDDLE-DISTANCE
ACCEHNOTTTTWWY	CATCH TWENTY-TWO	ACDDDEILLLNOOU	DID ALL ONE COULD
ACCEIIILLNNOORT	RECONCILIATION	ACDDEEEEINPRSS	INCREASED SPEED
ACCEIIILRRRTTY	LITERARY CRITIC	ACDDEEEEKLNPSS	SLACKENED SPEED
ACCEIIKKLMPSUW	SAMUEL PICKWICK	ACDDEEEFNNOOTV	DEED OF COVENANT
ACCEIIKKPPPRSW	PICKWICK PAPERS	ACDDEEEGHLLRYY	GLYCERALDEHYDE
ACCEIIKLNNOPRS	CECIL PARKINSON	ACDDEEEHIMNTTU	EDUCATE THE MIND
ACCEIIKNOPSTTU	STICK UP A NOTICE	ACDDEEEHOPPRST	DROPPED THE CASE
ACCEIIILLMOORSY	SERIOCOMICALLY	ACDDEEEHORSSTU	REDUCED TO ASHES
ACCEIIILMMNORTT	CRITICAL MOMENT	ACDDEEEELNNOPST	PLACES END TO END
ACCEIIILMMORSST	COMMERCIALISTS	ACDDEEEENORSVYY	EVERY SECOND DAY

ACDDEEEEOORRSTTU	REDUCED TO TEARS	ACDEEEEINPRSSS	INCREASES SPEED
ACDDEEEFHNNOORS	FORCED ONE'S HAND	ACDEEEEINRRRSV	RENDER A SERVICE
ACDDEEFIINORUV	DECIDE IN FAVOUR	ACDEEEEINSSTTV	STATE'S EVIDENCE
ACDDEEFIKLOOSV	DEVIL'S FOOD CAKE	ACDEEEEMMNOPSU	COME UP AND SEE ME
ACDDEEFIKORRST	ASKED FOR CREDIT	ACDEEEEOPRRTVX	DEEP EXTRA COVER
ACDDEEGHIILNOT	LOADING THE DICE	ACDEEEFFHNRSST	FARFETCHEDNESS
ACDDEEGHORSSUW	DOWAGER DUCHESS	ACDEEEFFILNNOS	FANCIED ONESELF
ACDDEEGILNPRTU	TREACLE PUDDING	ACDEEEFFINRSTV	VAST DIFFERENCE
ACDDEEGINNNORRS	ASCENDING ORDER	ACDEEEFFNNSSTU	UNAFFECTEDNESS
ACDDEEGKLLNOWY	ACKNOWLEDGEDLY	ACDEEEFGHINORT	GO RED IN THE FACE
ACDDEEGLLORSUY	CLOSELY GUARDED	ACDEEEFHLNORTW	ENFORCED THE LAW
ACDDEEHHIILLRS	HERALDIC SHIELD	ACDEEEFHMORRST	THE ARMED FORCES
ACDDEEHHIISTTW	DICES WITH DEATH	ACDEEEFIILLLPT	FILLETED PLAICE
ACDDEEHHORRSTW	SHOW THE RED CARD	ACDEEEFILLLORT	RECALLED TO LIFE
ACDDEEHIILNRRS	RAISED CHILDREN	ACDEEEFILNOOST	LIED TO ONE'S FACE
ACDDEEHIKLOTTT	TICKLED TO DEATH	ACDEEEFILORTTV	LETTER OF ADVICE
ACDDEEHMNNOOTT	CONDEMN TO DEATH	ACDEEEGHHINNRT	REACHING THE END
ACDDEEHNORRSSU	SCORES A HUNDRED	ACDEEEGHHNORRT	CHANGE THE ORDER
ACDDEEHNOSTTUY	COUNTED THE DAYS	ACDEEEGHINSVWX	EXCHANGED VIEWS
ACDDEEHOORRSST	CROSSED THE ROAD	ACDEEEGHJKNOSX	EXCHANGED JOKES
ACDDEEIINOPSTT	DICTATION SPEED	ACDEEEHHIKNRSV	HANDKERCHIEVES
ACDDEEIINOSTUU	STUDIO AUDIENCE	ACDEEEHIILNPST	ENCEPHALITIDES
ACDDEEIJMNSSTU	DEMANDS JUSTICE	ACDEEEHIIPRRST	RAISED THE PRICE
ACDDEEILLMNORT	RECALLED TO MIND	ACDEEEHIKNRTTT	TAKEN THE CREDIT
ACDDEEILMNSTTU	MEDICAL STUDENT	ACDEEEHIKRSTTT	TAKES THE CREDIT
ACDDEEMMNNORSU	CONSUMER DEMAND	ACDEEEHILLNNOT	HELD AN ELECTION
ACDDEENNNOPPSU	POUNDS AND PENCE	ACDEEEHILLSTTT	TILTED THE SCALE
ACDDEENORRSSUW	CURSED AND SWORE	ACDEEEHILPPSTT	TIPPED THE SCALE
ACDDEEILOOPPRS	APPLE OF DISCORD	ACDEEEHILPSTTU	DUPLICATE SHEET
ACDDEFINNORSST	FIRST AND SECOND	ACDEEEHINNNOOS	CHEESE AND ONION
ACDDEGHIINNRSV	DANCING DERVISH	ACDEEEHINRRSUV	UNDERACHIEVERS
ACDDEGHIORRRHS	RICHARD RODGERS	ACDEEEHJMNOSST	JAMES THE SECOND
ACDDEGHLNNOOOT	GONE HOT AND COLD	ACDEEEHLNOOPSS	HOLDS ONE'S PEACE
ACDDEGHLNOOOTV	GOES HOT AND COLD	ACDEEEHLNRSTTU	TURNED THE SCALE
ACDDEGIILMNNOT	OLD-TIME DANCING	ACDEEEHNPRRTTU	UNDER THE CARPET
ACDDEHHILMNORT	MOTHER AND CHILD	ACDEEEHORSSSTU	REDUCES TO ASHES
ACDDEHHNNOOPSS	SECOND-HAND SHOP	ACDEEEIILLNNUV	DECLINE IN VALUE
	SECONDHAND SHOP	ACDEEEIIMNNPTT	PATENT MEDICINE
ACDDEHIKNNOSTT	STAND IN THE DOCK	ACDEEEILNNRTTV	DECENT INTERVAL
ACDDEHIIOPPRSTT	DROPPED A STITCH	ACDEEEILNORRSY	ROYAL RESIDENCE
ACDDEHLNNOOTTW	WENT HOT AND COLD	ACDEEEILOOPRST	RADIO TELESCOPE
ACDDEIIIMNOOTV	INDICATIVE MOOD	ACDEEEIMMNOORT	MODERATE INCOME
ACDDEIIINNOORT	AIR CONDITIONED	ACDEEEIMNNNORU	UNEARNED INCOME
ACDDEIIJLMRRUU	JUDICIAL MURDER	ACDEEEIMNNNOTU	CEMENTED A UNION
ACDDEIILMNTTUV	CULTIVATED MIND	ACDEEEIMNNOPRS	NAMED ONE'S PRICE
ACDDEILMMOORST	DOCTORS DILEMMA	ACDEEEIMNOPPST	APPENDECTOMIES
ACDDEILNPRSSUU	CURLS UP AND DIES	ACDEEEINNNOPSX	ONE AND SIXPENCE
ACDDEINNOORSTT	DISCORDANT NOTE	ACDEEEINORRSSW	CRIED ONE'S WARES
ACDDEINNOOSTUU	SOUND EDUCATION	ACDEEEINORSSTV	DECORATIVENESS
ACDDEKMNOORRSS	MODS AND ROCKERS	ACDEEELLNNORSU	LEARNED COUNSEL
ACDDELMNOORRTV	TREVOR MCDONALD	ACDEEELNPRRSSU	SUPERCALENDERS
ACDDELNOORRSWW	SECOND WORLD WAR	ACDEEFFMNORRTY	ENDARTERECTOMY
ACDDENNORRSSUW	CURSED AND SWORN	ACDEEENNORSSST	SECOND-RATENESS
ACDDEOPPRRSTUY	DROPPED A CURTSY	ACDEEENOOPRSSV	PROVED ONE'S CASE
ACDDFGHILLOOTY	COLD LIGHT OF DAY	ACDEEENORRSSTW	SETS A NEW RECORD
ACDDFMMNOOORSW	COMMAND OF WORDS	ACDEEENRRRSTUY	UNDERSECRETARY
ACDDGHINOORRRS	GORDON RICHARDS	ACDEEEOORRSSTTU	REDUCES TO TEARS
ACDDGIILMNOOOP	PLACIDO DOMINGO	ACDEEFFGIINORV	OFFERING ADVICE
ACDDHHHILOOPPY	HAPPY CHILDHOOD	ACDEEFFHNOORSY	CRY ONE'S HEAD OFF
ACDDHHILRSSTUY	THURSDAYS CHILD	ACDEEFFILORRRS	SCARRED FOR LIFE
ACDDIINOORRTWY	DICTIONARY WORD	ACDEEFFIMNNORS	OFFICERS AND MEN
ACDEEEEEFMNRSU	DEFENCE MEASURE	ACDEEFGHINRSTU	CRUSHING DEFEAT
ACDEEEEFGILMRT	REFLECTED IMAGE	ACDEEFGHOOOOPP	CAPE OF GOOD HOPE
ACDEEEEFLLNORS	CLEARED ONESELF	ACDEEFGILNPRRT	PERFECT DARLING
ACDEEEEFLORRST	STEERED CLEAR OF	ACDEEFGNOORRSU	SOURCE OF DANGER
ACDEEEEGILMNNT	MAGNETIC NEEDLE	ACDEEFHHNOORTW	CROWN OF THE HEAD
ACDEEEEGILPRTT	PEDIGREE CATTLE	ACDEEFHIINNRSS	DISENFRANCHISE
ACDEEEEHILPRSV	DELIVER A SPEECH	ACDEEFHLORSTTU	CUTS FOR THE LEAD
ACDEEEEHINNOSV	ACHIEVE ONES END	ACDEEFHNNOORSS	FORCES ONE'S HAND
ACDEEEEHPPPRRS	PREPARED SPEECH	ACDEEFHORRSSTW	CHEST OF DRAWERS
		ACDEEFHORSSTTY	DEFRAYS THE COST

ACDEEFIIKLLNTY	FELICITY KENDAL
ACDEEFILLMOPRS	SELF-PROCLAIMED
ACDEEFILLRRUVY	DRIVE CAREFULLY
ACDEEFILNORSST	CONFEDERALISTS
ACDEEFINNOORST	CONFEDERATIONS
ACDEEFINOQRRUY	RADIO FREQUENCY
ACDEEFINRRRSTT	CREDIT TRANSFER
ACDEEFLLLLMOSU	FULL-SCALE MODEL
ACDEEFLLORRUVY	DROVE CAREFULLY
ACDEEFLMOPRRSY	PLEADS FOR MERCY
ACDEEFNORRRSTW	CENTRE-FORWARDS
ACDEEGGILNNORR	RECORDING ANGEL
ACDEEGHHHIOTWY	THE HIGHWAY CODE
ACDEEGHHILNOST	HOLDING THE ACES
ACDEEGHHNOSSTX	EXCHANGED SHOTS
ACDEEGHIIMNNNV	VENDING MACHINE
ACDEEGHIINORTT	TEACHING TO RIDE
ACDEEGHILLRSTY	CLEAR-SIGHTEDLY
ACDEEGHILOOSSW	WILD GOOSE CHASE
ACDEEGHIMNNNOS	CHANGE ONES MIND
ACDEEGHLLNNORU	CHALLENGE ROUND
ACDEEGHLNORRTU	CLEAR THE GROUND
ACDEEGIILNNOOT	GO INTO A DECLINE
ACDEEGIILNNRST	DECENTRALISING
ACDEEGIILNNRSU	DENUCLEARISING
ACDEEGIILNNRSY	DECLINING YEARS
ACDEEGIILNNRTZ	DECENTRALIZING
ACDEEGIILNNRUZ	DENUCLEARIZING
ACDEEGIINORSTT	STAGE DIRECTION
ACDEEGIKLLNSSS	CLINKED GLASSES
ACDEEGIKNNNOPS	SEND ONE PACKING
ACDEEGILLNNOOV	LEAVING ONE COLD
ACDEEGILNNOQRU	GRANDILOQUENCE
ACDEEGIMNORSTU	DISCOURAGEMENT
ACDEEGINORRSTT	SETTING A RECORD
ACDEEGINPRRSTT	SPENT CARTRIDGE
ACDEEGKLMNNOTW	ACKNOWLEDGMENT
ACDEEHHIKNSTTW	WHAT THE DICKENS?
ACDEEHHILMNORR	MICHAEL HORDERN
ACDEEHHINNOTTW	ON WITH THE DANCE
ACDEEHHKKNNOOT	KNOCK ON THE HEAD
ACDEEHHLLOSSST	HOLDS THE SCALES
ACDEEHHLLOSSTT	CALLED THE SHOTS
ACDEEHIIINNRST	DISINHERITANCE
ACDEEHIIILLOPST	DIALS THE POLICE
ACDEEHIILNRRSS	RAISES CHILDREN
ACDEEHIJNORTTV	CARVED THE JOINT
ACDEEHILLNNOOT	HOLD AN ELECTION
ACDEEHILLNNOST	ACHILLES TENDON
ACDEEHILMNOSST	METHODICALNESS
ACDEEHILNNRSUY	CHINESE LAUNDRY
ACDEEHILNOPRST	APRIL THE SECOND
ACDEEHILNORSVY	CASH ON DELIVERY
ACDEEHIMNNNSTT	DISENCHANTMENT
ACDEEHINNOOPRT	DROP IN THE OCEAN
ACDEEHINRRTTUW	DREW THE CURTAIN
ACDEEHKHLNORSST	CLOSED THE RANKS
ACDEEHKNOPRRRY	HYDE PARK CORNER
ACDEEHLLNORRTU	UNDER THE COLLAR
ACDEEHLOPPPRSY	CHOPPED PARSLEY
ACDEEHNNOORRTZ	HERNANDO CORTEZ
ACDEEHOOOORRSTU	HOUSE DECORATOR
ACDEEHOOPRRTTT	ROTATED THE CROP
ACDEEHOORRSSST	CROSSES THE ROAD
ACDEEIIILNOPST	SPECIAL EDITION
ACDEEIIILPPRSV	PAID LIP-SERVICE
ACDEEIIILLNRSTU	CARLISLE UNITED
ACDEEIILOSSTTU	DELICIOUS TASTE
ACDEEIJLLNOUWY	YELLOW JAUNDICE
ACDEEIJNOSSTUW	SAW JUSTICE DONE
ACDEEILMNOPSTU	ACTED ON IMPULSE

ACDEEILMNORRRU	NUMERICAL ORDER
ACDEEILMNRSSTU	STRAINED MUSCLE
ACDEEILNNNOPST	PLEADS INNOCENT
ACDEEILNOORSST	DO ONES ARTICLES
ACDEEILNPPRRSU	PERPENDICULARS
ACDEEIMMNNOORT	RECOMMENDATION
ACDEEIMMNORSTV	INVERTED COMMAS
ACDEEIMNOPRSTY	CRIME DOESNT PAY
ACDEEINNOORSST	COORDINATENESS
ACDEEINNOPSTWX	TWO AND SIXPENCE
ACDEEINNRRTTUV	RETURN A VERDICT
ACDEEELMNNNOOPY	PLANNED ECONOMY
ACDEEELMNNOPRTT	PORTLAND CEMENT
ACDEEELNNNRSTTY	TRANSCENDENTLY
ACDEEELOOPRSTTU	PLOTTED A COURSE
ACDEEMMMNOPRSU	SUPREME COMMAND
ACDEEMMNOORRTY	RECOMMENDATORY
ACDEEMMNOPRSSX	EXPRESS COMMAND
ACDEEMNNPRSTUU	MENDS A PUNCTURE
ACDEENNOORSTTU	TURNED ONE'S COAT
ACDEENNORRSUVY	ORDNANCE SURVEY
ACDEEOOORRRTVY	ROAD TO RECOVERY
ACDEFFGINNOOPS	DOFFING ONE'S CAP
ACDEFFIINRSTTY	TRAFFIC DENSITY
ACDEFGHIIIMNOS	DOING A MISCHIEF
ACDEFGHIMMNORT	FIGHTER COMMAND
ACDEFGIKNNOORY	DAY OF RECKONING
ACDEFGILNORTTU	CUTTING FOR DEAL
ACDEFGJKLMNOTU	LACK OF JUDGMENT
ACDEFGLNNNOORW	CROWN OF ENGLAND
ACDEFGNOOSSTUU	SECOND OF AUGUST
ACDEFHHNNORRSTU	CRASH OF THUNDER
ACDEFHILLOOSTY	ACTED FOOLISHLY
ACDEFHMNNOPRRY	PARDON MY FRENCH!
ACDEFHOORRTTUW	WARD OF THE COURT
ACDEFIIIINNOTT	IDENTIFICATION
ACDEFIIIINOOTTX	DETOXIFICATION
ACDEFIILLNNOTY	CONFIDENTIALLY
ACDEFIINPRSTUU	RUNS UP A DEFICIT
ACDEFILNOOORRT	LORD OF CREATION
ACDEFIOOPRRSSY	ROSES OF PICARDY
ACDEFLLRSTUUYY	STUDY CAREFULLY
ACDEGGGHIINNRT	DIGGING A TRENCH
ACDEGGIIKNNNPS	SENDING PACKING
ACDEGGIMOOORSU	GOOD GRACIOUS ME!
ACDEGHHHORRTTU	THROUGH THE CARD
ACDEGHHINRRSTW	RIGHT-HAND SCREW
ACDEGHHIORRRTU	CARRIED THROUGH
ACDEGHHOPRRSTU	SCRAPED THROUGH
ACDEGHIILNOPTV	HOLDING CAPTIVE
ACDEGHIILORRST	RICHARD STILGOE
ACDEGHILLMOOOT	METHODOLOGICAL
ACDEGHILLNOSSS	HOLDING CLASSES
ACDEGHIMNNORRS	MARCHING ORDERS
ACDEGHIMORSTTY	STRAIGHT COMEDY
ACDEGHINNNNOOT	DANCE ON NOTHING
ACDEGHKNORRTUY	GREYHOUND TRACK
ACDEGHLNOORSTU	LAUGHED TO SCORN
ACDEGIIILLNORTW	ALLOWING CREDIT
ACDEGIIILLOOPRT	PTERIDOLOGICAL
ACDEGIIILLOOSTT	DIALECTOLOGIST
ACDEGIILNNOPRR	PLACING IN ORDER
ACDEGIIMMNNOVW	COMMANDING VIEW
ACDEGIIMNNRSTT	DICTATING TERMS
ACDEGIIINRRSSTW	SACRED WRITINGS
ACDEGIILLNOORT	CALLING TO ORDER
ACDEGIMNNNORTU	COUNTERMANDING
ACDEGIMNOPRTTU	COMPUTER DATING
ACDEGINOOPRSTT	PROGNOSTICATED
ACDEGINOORRRTU	CORRUGATED IRON
ACDEGMMNNOOORR	COMMON OR GARDEN

ACDEHHIILOORTZ	CHLOROTHIAZIDE	ACDGIKNNNORTUY	KING AND COUNTRY
ACDEHHIIMOPRRT	HERMAPHRODITIC	ACDGILNNOORRRT	LORD CARRINGTON
ACDEHHIJLMRSTU	JUDITH CHALMERS	ACDGIMNNOOOOPS	GOOD COMPANIONS
ACDEHIILLNOSTY	HEDONISTICALLY	ACDGINNOORSTUU	SCOUTING AROUND
ACDEHIILMORSTY	MEDICAL HISTORY	ACDHHIIOPRRSST	HARPSICHORDIST
ACDEHIILPPPSSY	APPLIED PHYSICS	ACDHHILLOOOSSY	SCHOOL HOLIDAYS
ACDEHIIMORRSTY	RADIOCHEMISTRY	ACDHIIKKNPSSUY	KICKS UP A SHINDY
ACDEHIINNOORTT	HEART CONDITION	ACDHILLLORTYYY	HYDROLYTICALLY
ACDEHIKNOQRTUW	QUICK ON THE DRAW	ACDHILLNOOPRYY	HYDROPONICALLY
ACDEHILLLNOTTY	THAT'LL DO NICELY	ACDHKNOORSSTTY	SHORT AND STOCKY
ACDEHILLMOPRYY	HYPODERMICALLY	ACDIIIILNNNOST	DISINCLINATION
ACDEHILMOOPPRR	CHLORPROPAMIDE	ACDIIIMMNORST	DISCRIMINATION
ACDEHILNNNNRSY	CHILDRENS NANNY	ACDIIIJLNORSTU	JURISDICTIONAL
ACDEHILNPRRSTY	CHILDRENS PARTY	ACDIILLNNOOTTY	CONDITIONALITY
ACDEHILPRRSSUY	HYDRAULIC PRESS	ACDIIIMMNORRSST	DISCRIMINATORS
ACDEHIMMNORSTY	THERMODYNAMICS	ACDIIIMMNORRSTY	DISCRIMINATORY
ACDEHINOSSTTTW	CAST TO THE WINDS	ACDIIINNNOOORT	INCOORDINATION
ACDEHKKNOOOORTT	KNOCK AT THE DOOR	ACDIIINNNOORTT	INDOCTRINATION
ACDEHLOOOOPPRSV	APPROVED SCHOOL	ACDIILNNOUOOSST	DISCONSOLATION
ACDEHLOOPRTTWY	PLAY TO THE CROWD	ACDIILNPPTTUWX	TWIXT CUP AND LIP
ACDEHMNNNOPSUY	SHUNNED COMPANY	ACDIILOPRSSTTT	POSTAL DISTRICT
ACDEHNNOOPRSST	THE PROS AND CONS	ACDIIPRSSSTTUY	CRASS STUPIDITY
ACDEHNNOORSSSW	SHOWN ONE'S CARDS	ACDILLLMOOORXY	LOXODROMICALLY
ACDEHNOORSSSSW	SHOWS ONE'S CARDS	ACDIMNOOPRSSTU	MASS PRODUCTION
ACDEIIIIMMNNRST	INDISCRIMINATE	ACDKNOOOOORTTUU	OUT-AND-OUT CROOK
ACDEIIIIMMNRSTV	DISCRIMINATIVE	ACDMMNOOPPRSTU	COMMAND SUPPORT
ACDEIIIKLLNNOT	KILLED IN ACTION	ACDNNNNOORTTUWY	TOWN AND COUNTRY
ACDEIIILNNORTU	UNIDIRECTIONAL	ACEEEEEILRRTTV	RECEIVE A LETTER
ACDEIIILNNSTTW	IDENTICAL TWINS	ACEEEEENNRSSTV	SERVE A SENTENCE
ACDEIIILNORTTY	DIRECTIONALITY	ACEEEEFFFLMNST	SELF-EFFACEMENT
ACDEIIINORSSSY	IDIOSYNCRASIES	ACEEEEFHLLPRSW	FAREWELL SPEECH
ACDEIIKKKKNPSTU	KICKED UP A STINK	ACEEEEFLMPPRTX	PERFECT EXAMPLE
ACDEIIILMNPRTU	PNEUMATIC DRILL	ACEEEEFLNPRSST	FALSE PRETENCES
ACDEIILMMNOPTY	LIMITED COMPANY	ACEEEEGHHIKNPST	KEEPS THE CHANGE
ACDEIILMMOOPTV	DIPLOMATIC MOVE	ACEEEEGIINNPRX	GAIN EXPERIENCE
ACDEIILNNOOOST	DECOLONISATION	ACEEEEGIKNPRST	KEEPING A SECRET
ACDEIILNNOOOTZ	DECOLONIZATION	ACEEEEGILNRRSV	GENERAL SERVICE
ACDEIILNNOPPRS	CLAPPED IN IRONS	ACEEEEHHILNRTW	CATHERINE WHEEL
ACDEIILNOOORST	DECOLORISATION	ACEEEEHHLLRRSW	CHARLES WHEELER
ACDEIILNOOORTZ	DECOLORIZATION	ACEEEEHIKORTVY	RECEIVE THE OKAY
ACDEIILNPQTTUU	QUINTUPLICATED	ACEEEEHKPPPSTU	KEEPS UP THE PACE
ACDEIINNOORSST	CONSIDERATIONS	ACEEEEHLMNRTTW	CLEMENT WEATHER
ACDEIKKNOSSSWY	KNOCKS SIDEWAYS	ACEEEEHLNNOSTT	CLEAN ONES TEETH
ACDLIKLMNOOPRX	DARK COMPLEXION	ACEEEEHLPRSSST	STEEPLECHASERS
ACDEILLMNOOSTY	ENDOSMOTICALLY	ACEEEEHNPQRSTU	PRESENT A CHEQUE
ACDEILLNOOSSTY	DISCONSOLATELY	ACEEEEHPSSSSTY	CAST SHEEP'S EYES
ACDEILOPPRRTUV	POPULAR VERDICT	ACEEEEIKNOPPSS	SPEAK ONE'S PIECE
ACDEIMNNOOSTTU	DOCUMENTATIONS	ACEEEEILMNRSTX	MENTAL EXERCISE
ACDEIMNNORRTTU	TRUMAN DOCTRINE	ACEEEEINNRRSTT	TERCENTENARIES
ACDEINOOQRSSTU	CONQUISTADORES	ACEEEEINNPPRSTX	PAST EXPERIENCE
ACDEIOPRRSSTTW	POST-WAR CREDITS	ACEEEEINPRSTVX	VAST EXPERIENCE
ACDEIORRSSSTTU	COURTS DISASTER	ACEEEEMMNOPSTV	PEACE MOVEMENTS
ACDEKOOOOPRSTUY	COOKED UP A STORY	ACEEEENNPRRTTU	TRUE REPENTANCE
ACDFFIOPPRRSST	STAFFORD CRIPPS	ACEEEFFFOPRSTU	PAUSE FOR EFFECT
ACDFGHHIILNOST	THINGS OF A CHILD	ACEEEFFHIILNST	FLIES IN THE FACE
ACDFGHIIIINNRSS	DISFRANCHISING	ACEEEFFILNNOSS	FANCIES ONESELF
ACDFGHILMNNTUY	FLYING DUTCHMAN	ACEEEFFINORRST	COFFEE STRAINER
ACDFHIIIIMNOTU	HUMIDIFICATION	ACEEEFFJNORRST	REJECTS AN OFFER
ACDFIIIILNOOST	SOLIDIFICATION	ACEEEFGGILLNNT	FLEETING GLANCE
ACDFILMNOOOORTU	CLOUD FORMATION	ACEEEFGIILNNRT	FEELING CERTAIN
ACDGGGIIMNNNOO	COMING AND GOING	ACEEEFGORRRSTU	CAUSE FOR REGRET
ACDGHIIJNNOTWY	DANCING WITH JOY	ACEEEFHIMRRTUV	RHEUMATIC FEVER
ACDGHIIKNORRST	STRIKING A CHORD	ACEEEFHKOOPRTU	KEEP OUT OF REACH
ACDGHILLLOORYY	HYDROLOGICALLY	ACEEEFHLNORSTW	ENFORCES THE LAW
ACDGHILMNNOOPY	HOLDING COMPANY	ACEEEFHORSTTVW	CREST OF THE WAVE
ACDGHINNOOPPRR	DROPPING ANCHOR	ACEEEFIIOPRTUV	FAVOURITE PIECE
ACDGIIIIMMNNRST	DISCRIMINATING	ACEEEFIKLOSTTV	TICKETS OF LEAVE
ACDGIIINNNORTT	INDOCTRINATING		TICKETS-OF-LEAVE
ACDGIIKKNPSTUU	KICKING UP A DUST	ACEEEFILMORSUV	FIVE-COURSE MEAL
ACDGIILMOPRSUY	MUSICAL PRODIGY	ACEEEFILNOOSST	LIES TO ONE'S FACE
ACDGIKKNNNOORU	KNOCKING AROUND	ACEEEFILNOOVVW	WAVE OF VIOLENCE

ACEEEFINOPSTTT	TEST OF PATIENCE
ACEEEFLLORRTUW	FELLOW CREATURE
ACEEEFLMNNORTW	LAW ENFORCEMENT
ACEEEFMORRRSTT	REFRACTOMETERS
ACEEEGGHHINPRT	HIGH PERCENTAGE
ACEEEGHHILNRST	ENGLISH TEACHER
ACEEEGHHILNSST	TEACHES ENGLISH
ACEEEGHHLNRSTU	CHANGE THE RULES
ACEEEGHILNPSST	STEEPLECHASING
ACEEEGHINNOPST	OPENING THE CASE
ACEEEGHINPSTTT	SETTING THE PACE
ACEEEGHINSSVWX	EXCHANGES VIEWS
ACEEEGHJKNOSSX	EXCHANGES JOKES
ACEEEGHLLMNNOW	NEWNHAM COLLEGE
ACEEEGHLNNSSSS	CHANGELESSNESS
ACEEEGHNNNOSTU	CHANGE ONES TUNE
ACEEEGHNOORSTT	GONE TO THE RACES
ACEEEGHOORSSTT	GOES TO THE RACES
ACEEEGHOPRRSTT	SCRAPE TOGETHER
ACEEEGIILNNRTU	GENUINE ARTICLE
ACEEEGIILPRSVV	GAVE LIP SERVICE
ACEEEGIIMNNPRS	PRECISE MEANING
ACEEEGIINNPRST	RESTING IN PEACE
ACEEEGIINRSTUV	CREATIVE GENIUS
ACEEEGIKMORSTT	CIGARETTE SMOKE
ACEEEGIKNOORTV	GIVE ONE A ROCKET
ACEEEGILLNOORV	VENEREOLOGICAL
ACEEEGILNOPRST	POLICE SERGEANT
ACEEEGILRRRSUV	REGULAR SERVICE
ACEEEGIMMOSTTT	COMMITTEE STAGE
ACEEEGINNOOSTV	GAVE ONE'S NOTICE
ACEEEGINNRTTUV	GIVEN UTTERANCE
ACEEEGINOPRRST	RESTORING PEACE
ACEEEGINPRTTVY	PETTY GRIEVANCE
ACEEEGINRSTTUV	GIVES UTTERANCE
ACEEEGLMMNNPTU	GUN EMPLACEMENT
ACEEEGLMNORSTT	ELECTROMAGNETS
ACEEEGLNNNORST	GENERAL CONSENT
ACEEEHHHLOPRST	HELPS EACH OTHER
ACEEEHHIIMMNTT	THE TIME MACHINE
ACEEEHHLPRSTTY	HEALTHY RESPECT
ACEEEHIIPRRSST	RAISES THE PRICE
ACEEEHIKKMNTTY	TAKEN THE MICKEY
ACEEEHIKKMSTTY	TAKES THE MICKEY
ACEEEHIKRTTTWW	WATER THE WICKET
ACEEEHILLNRSTV	CLEAN THE SILVER
ACEEEHILLOPRSW	WHOLESALE PRICE
ACEEEHILNNNRST	CHINESE LANTERN
ACEEEHIMMPPRSU	MEERSCHAUM PIPE
ACEEEHKKLNNRTU	NEAR THE KNUCKLE
ACEEEHKORRRRSW	RESEARCH WORKER
ACEEEHLOPRRTTY	ELECTROTHERAPY
ACEEEHLPRSSTTW	RESPECTS THE LAW
ACEEEHMMNOSSTT	MEETS ONE'S MATCH
ACEEEHMMOORTTY	HAEMOCYTOMETER
ACEEEHMNNNORRT	COHERENT MANNER
ACEEEHNNOPRSTW	SHOW REPENTANCE
ACEEEHNORSTTTW	WENT TO THE RACES
ACEEEIIJLNPPPU	PINEAPPLE JUICE
ACEEEIILMNNNST	SEMICENTENNIAL
ACEEEIILNNNORS	INCLINE ONES EAR
ACEEEIIMNOPRTU	PEACE IN OUR TIME
ACEEEIIMNOPSTV	POSITIVE MENACE
ACEEEIINOORSSV	RAISE ONES VOICE
ACEEEIINOPRRSV	OPEN-AIR SERVICE
ACEEEIINRSTTTV	ACTIVE INTEREST
ACEEEIIRRRTTVW	CREATIVE WRITER
ACEEEIKMMNOOSS	MAKES ECONOMIES
ACEEEIKNNOPTTX	TAKEN EXCEPTION
ACEEEIKNOPSTTX	TAKES EXCEPTION
ACEEEILMNORTTU	ROMAINE LETTUCE

ACEEEILNRRSSTU	CREATURELINESS
ACEEEILPQRSSTU	SPECIAL REQUEST
ACEEEILPRRSSUU	PLEASURE CRUISE
ACEEEIMNNOPRSS	NAMES ONE'S PRICE
ACEEEINNNSTUVX	INVENT AN EXCUSE
ACEEEINORRSSSW	CRIES ONE'S WARES
ACEEEIOPSSSSSV	POSSESSIVE CASE
ACEEEKNOPRRRSS	SPEAKERS CORNER
ACEEELMNNOPSTY	ENCLOSE PAYMENT
ACEEELMNOPRSTW	COMPLETE ANSWER
ACEEELMNOPRTUX	COUNTEREXAMPLE
ACEEELORSSTTTU	LETS OUT A SECRET
ACEEELPRSTTUUY	EUCALYPTUS TREE
ACEEEMMNOOORSST	COME TO ONE'S EARS
ACEEEMMNOORRST	REMOTE ANCESTOR
ACEEEMNORRSTUU	COUNTERMEASURE
ACEEENOOPRSSSV	PROVES ONE'S CASE
ACEEFFFGILLNSY	SELF-EFFACINGLY
ACEEFFFHILOSTT	THE FACTS OF LIFE
ACEEFFFIOORSTT	OFFICER OF STATE
ACEEFFGIINOPRR	OFFERING A PRICE
ACEEFFGIINRTUU	CUT A FINE FIGURE
ACEEFFGIKNNOPR	PARKING OFFENCE
ACEEFFHHILMORS	EACH FOR HIMSELF
ACEEFFHHKLPSTU	SHUFFLE THE PACK
ACEEFFHILNNOTW	FLOWN IN THE FACE
ACEEFFHIOPRTTT	PATHETIC EFFORT
ACEEFFHORTTTUW	CUT OFF THE WATER
ACEEFFIILLLOPT	FILLET OF PLAICE
ACEEFFKLNPRRTY	PERFECTLY FRANK
ACEEFGHHILNOTU	HIGH-OCTANE FUEL
ACEEFGHIIMNNRU	MACHINE-GUN FIRE
ACEEFGHIKLNOST	LOCKING THE SAFE
ACEEFGHIKNNPRS	SPEAKING FRENCH
ACEEFGINNOOPRR	PRINCE OF ORANGE
ACEEFHHIORRSTT	OSTRICH FEATHER
ACEEFHHKORRSTY	REACH FOR THE SKY
ACEEFHHMMNORSTV	SEVENTH OF MARCH
ACEEFHHMMORSTTU	SCUM OF THE EARTH
ACEEFHIJKNOSTV	THE JACKSON FIVE
ACEEFHIKLNOOST	LOOKS IN THE FACE
ACEEFHILMNOORT	COIN OF THE REALM
ACEEFHILMNOPRS	INFORMAL SPEECH
ACEEFHILNPPPST	FLIPPANT SPEECH
ACEEFHILOPRSTT	RELIC OF THE PAST
ACEEFHILORSSTW	AS THE CROW FLIES
ACEEFHIMOORSTT	COMES TO THE FAIR
ACEEFHKOOPRTTU	KEPT OUT OF REACH
ACEEFHLOPRSTTU	FOULS THE CARPET
ACEEFHMNOORTTT	CAME TO THE FRONT
ACEEFIIINORSTT	ESTERIFICATION
ACEEFIKLNORSTT	LACK OF INTEREST
ACEEFIKLORRTTW	TRICKLE OF WATER
ACEEFIKNNORRTW	KNEW FOR CERTAIN
ACEEFILMNOPRST	SELF-IMPORTANCE
ACEEFILMPRRSTU	SIMPLE FRACTURE
ACEEFILNNNOOST	CONTAIN ONESELF
ACEEFILNOQSSTU	ACQUITS ONESELF
ACEEFIMMOPRTTU	PRIME CUT OF MEAT
ACEEFINNORSSTU	SURFACE TENSION
ACEEFINORRRSST	REFRACTORINESS
ACEEFKNOPTTTWY	PACKET OF TWENTY
ACEEFLMOORRSUU	FOUR-COURSE MEAL
ACEEFLNNOOPSTW	PLACE OF ONES OWN
ACEEFMOORRSTTU	MATTER OF COURSE
ACEEGGHHINNRST	RING THE CHANGES
ACEEGGHHNNRSTU	RUNG THE CHANGES
ACEEGGHHNORSTT	GET SHORT CHANGE
ACEEGGHIKNSTTT	GETTING THE SACK
ACEEGGHILNOSTT	CLOSING THE GATE
ACEEGGHINORTTT	ACTING TOGETHER

ACEEGGIILNRTUV	GIVING A LECTURE
ACEEGGIMNNORRS	SCAREMONGERING
ACEEGHHHHHIMRTT	MARCH THE EIGHTH
ACEEGHHIIKLNST	HEALING THE SICK
ACEEGHHILLNNNS	ENGLISH CHANNEL
ACEEGHHINOPRTT	REACHING THE TOP
ACEEGHHIRSTTWW	WEIGHTWATCHERS
ACEEGHHNOSSSTX	EXCHANGES SHOTS
ACEEGHHOOPRRRS	CHOREOGRAPHERS
ACEEGHIIKMNPTT	PICKING THE TEAM
ACEEGHIIKNPRST	ASKING THE PRICE
ACEEGHIINNNRTW	WINNING THE RACE
ACEEGHIINNPRST	SPEECH TRAINING
ACEEGHIINPPRTY	PAYING THE PRICE
ACEEGHIINSSTVX	EXCHANGE VISITS
ACEEGHIIOPRRST	PREHISTORIC AGE
ACEEGHIIOPRSTV	POSITIVE CHARGE
ACEEGHIKKLOOST	GO LIKE HOT CAKES
ACEEGHILLNNTTU	CALLING THE TUNE
ACEEGHILLOOPRT	HERPETOLOGICAL
ACEEGHILNORSSU	CLEARINGHOUSES
ACEEGHIMNOPRST	MAGNETOSPHERIC
ACEEGHINNOSTTT	GETS IN ON THE ACT
ACEEGHINORSSST	CROSSING THE SEA
ACEEGHINOSTTTT	GETS INTO THE ACT
ACEEGHINPTTTTU	CUTTING THE TAPE
ACEEGHLPRSTTUU	GUTTURAL SPEECH
ACEEGHMMMMNNOOR	GREENHAM COMMON
ACEEGIIJNRSTTU	GREAT INJUSTICE
ACEEGIIKLNNNSS	LACKING IN SENSE
ACEEGIIKLNOPTT	GET INTO A PICKLE
ACEEGIILMNNSUV	MUSICAL EVENING
ACEEGIILORRSST	SOCIAL REGISTER
ACEEGIINNNORTT	TRACTION ENGINE
ACEEGIINNOPSTW	SWEEPING ACTION
ACEEGIINORTTTY	TERATOGENICITY
ACEEGIKMNNOPPY	KEEPING COMPANY
ACEEGIKNNNOPST	SENT ONE PACKING
ACEEGILLMOOORT	METEOROLOGICAL
ACEEGILLNOPRTT	ELECTROPLATING
ACEEGILLPRRTUY	PICTURE GALLERY
ACEEGILMNOORTV	CONGLOMERATIVE
ACEEGILMNORSTY	LARYNGECTOMIES
ACEEGILNOOPPSY	CLAPPING EYES ON
ACEEGILNOOPRSY	SINCERE APOLOGY
ACEEGILNORRSTU	ALTERING COURSE
ACEEGILNORSSTT	SETTLING A SCORE
ACEEGIMMNNOPTY	COMPANY MEETING
ACEEGINORSSTTU	SETTING A COURSE
ACEEGKLMNNOORT	GENTLEMAN CROOK
ACEEGLNOORRSTU	COLOUR SERGEANT
ACEEGMMNNOORST	COMMON SERGEANT
ACEEHHIIKSSTTV	THICK AS THIEVES
ACEEHHIKNNNOTT	TAKEN ON THE CHIN
ACEEHHIKNNOSTT	TAKES ON THE CHIN
ACEEHHIKSTTTTT	THATS THE TICKET
ACEEHHILMNNSTW	SWIM THE CHANNEL
ACEEHHILMNORTT	CLAIM THE THRONE
ACEEHHIMOPRSTT	CHEMOTHERAPIST
ACEEHHIORRSTTY	HISTORY TEACHER
ACEEHHLMNNSTUW	SWUM THE CHANNEL
ACEEHHNOPRSTUY	RANCH-TYPE HOUSE
ACEEHIINPPPRST	APPRENTICESHIP
ACEEHIJMNNOPTU	JUMP IN THE OCEAN
ACEEHIJNORSTTV	CARVES THE JOINT
ACEEHIKMNOPSST	MAKES ONE'S PITCH
ACEEHILLMNRRTW	WARREN MITCHELL
ACEEHILLMORTXY	EXOTHERMICALLY
ACEEHILLSSSTTT	TILTS THE SCALES
ACEEHILMMMNNRSW	CHANNEL SWIMMER
ACEEHILNNOOSTV	VENETIAN SCHOOL
ACEEHILNOPRRST	SILENT REPROACH
ACEEHIMMMNNORSSV	SERVOMECHANISM
ACEEHIMNNOOPTTT	CAME TO THE POINT
ACEEHINNORRSTT	SAT IN THE CORNER
ACEEHINPPRRSST	SHIPS CARPENTER
ACEEHIORRRSSTV	ACROSS THE RIVER
ACEEHKLMOORSTT	CLOSE TO THE MARK
ACEEHKLNNORSST	CLOSES THE RANKS
ACEEHKLOORRSTW	WORKS THE ORACLE
ACEEHKMNORSTTT	SHOCK TREATMENT
ACEEHLNOPRSSUV	HAVE NO SCRUPLES
ACEEHLNRSSSTTU	TURNS THE SCALES
ACEEHLOPPPRSTU	COPPER SULPHATE
ACEEHLORRSSTTU	CHARLOTTE RUSSE
ACEEHMORRSSSTT	CROSS THE STREAM
ACEEHNNOOPSSSW	SHOWN ONE'S PACES
ACEEHNOOPSSSSW	SHOWS ONE'S PACES
ACEEHNOORRSSST	CROSS ONES HEART
ACEEHOOPPRRSTTT	ROTATES THE CROP
ACEEHORSSSTTUY	STAYS THE COURSE
ACEEIIIMMNNNSTT	IN ANCIENT TIMES
ACEEIIINPRTTVZ	PRIVATE CITIZEN
ACEEIIJLNNORTT	INTERJECTIONAL
ACEEIILMNNOPST	SPECIAL MENTION
ACEEIILMNORSST	CEREMONIALISTS
ACEEIILNNOPTTT	EPICONTINENTAL
ACEEIILNNORSST	INTERCESSIONAL
ACEEIILNOPTTXY	EXCEPTIONALITY
ACEEIILPPRSSVY	PAYS LIP-SERVICE
ACEEIIMNNPRRRT	PARTNER IN CRIME
ACEEIIMNRSSTTU	STREET MUSICIAN
ACEEIINNRSSTTU	RESISTANCE UNIT
ACEEIINORSSTTV	SERVICE STATION
ACEEIINRRSSTTZ	CITIZENS ARREST
ACEEIKLMNNSSST	MENTAL SICKNESS
ACEEIKLMNOORTW	EMOTIONAL WRECK
ACEEIKMNNNORRT	INNOCENT REMARK
ACEEIKNORSSTTU	TAKEN ITS COURSE
ACEEIKORSSSTTU	TAKES ITS COURSE
ACEEIKPPPRRSSTU	SURPRISE PACKET
ACEEIILLLLNTTUY	INTELLECTUALLY
ACEEILLMNORRTU	INTERMOLECULAR
ACEEILMMNNOSTT	SALIENT COMMENT
ACEEILMNOPRSSS	PRESS ONES CLAIM
ACEEILMNOPSSTT	PENTECOSTALISM
ACEEILMNSSTUUV	CUMULATIVENESS
ACEEILMOOSSTUY	COMES OUT EASILY
ACEEILNNOOSTTT	CLOSE ATTENTION
ACEEILNNOPPSTU	PUT IN ONES PLACE
ACEEILNOPPRRSU	PECULIAR PERSON
ACEEILNOPSSTTT	PENTECOSTALIST
ACEEILNORRRSTU	RESURRECTIONAL
ACEEILNORSTVVY	CONSERVATIVELY
ACEEILPPPRRSST	CARPET SLIPPERS
ACEEIMMMNNOOTTW	COMMITTEEWOMAN
ACEEIMMMNNNPRTT	INTERNMENT CAMP
ACEEIMMNNORSTU	INCOMMENSURATE
ACEEIMMNPRSSTY	IN MANY RESPECTS
ACEEIMNOOORRRT	RECREATION ROOM
ACEEIMNOOPRRST	CONTEMPORARIES
ACEEIMNORRSSST	MARTIN SCORSESE
ACEEIMMNORSSSX	CROSS-EXAMINERS
ACEEINNOOOPRTV	NONCOOPERATIVE
ACEEINNOORSSVZ	CONVERSAZIONES
ACEEINOORRSSTV	CONSERVATOIRES
	CONSERVATORIES
ACEEINOPRRSSSU	PRECARIOUSNESS
ACEEINOQRRSTTU	QUARTER SECTION
ACEEKLNNNOOPSW	KNOWN ONE'S PLACE
ACEEKLNNOOPSSW	KNOWS ONE'S PLACE
ACEEKLNOOPSTTX	LOOKS EXPECTANT

ACEELLNOORRSUY	ROYAL ENCLOSURE	ACEFLORRSSSTTU	CLUSTER OF STARS
ACEELMMNORSTUY	COMMENSURATELY	ACEFOOOOPRRSTTU	TROUPE OF ACTORS
ACEELMNOPRSSTY	CRAMP ONES STYLE	ACEGGHHIINNORW	WEIGHING ANCHOR
ACEELNNOQSTTUU	UNEQUAL CONTEST	ACEGGHHIINTTWW	WEIGHTWATCHING
ACEELNOPRSTUUY	PERCUTANEOUSLY	ACEGGHHINNORSS	CHANGING HORSES
ACEEMNNOPPRSTY	PRESENT COMPANY	ACEGGHHNOORSTT	GOT SHORT CHANGE
ACEENORRRTTTUY	COUNTRY RETREAT	ACEGGHIINRRTWY	CARRYING WEIGHT
ACEFFGIILNORSS	SIGNALS OFFICER	ACEGGHINNNOTVV	VINCENT VAN GOGH
ACEFFGIOOORRTVY	FORCE OF GRAVITY	ACEGGHINOORSUW	SHOWING COURAGE
ACEFFHHLMORTTW	TWELFTH OF MARCH	ACEGGIILNNNPRS	SPRING CLEANING
ACEFFIIIKLORST	OFFICIAL STRIKE		SPRING-CLEANING
ACEFFIIILLMOSY	SEMIOFFICIALLY	ACEGGIINNOORSU	GOING ON A CRUISE
ACEFFIIILNOORS	LIAISON OFFICER	ACEGGILLNOOORT	GERONTOLOGICAL
ACEFFIILNOORST	SORE AFFLICTION	ACEGGILMNNOORT	CONGLOMERATING
ACEFFJLLLOOSTY	CALFS-FOOT JELLY	ACEGGILNOOSSTY	GYNAECOLOGISTS
ACEFGGIINRTTUU	CUTTING A FIGURE	ACEGHHHNOOPTTU	CAUGHT ON THE HOP
ACEFGHHLORTTUU	CAREFUL THOUGHT	ACEGHHHOORRSTU	THOROUGH SEARCH
ACEFGHILLMNORW	CHARMING FELLOW	ACEGHHIIKNRTTT	HITTING THE RACK
ACEFGHILMNOOPR	CHAMPION GOLFER	ACEGHHIIKNSTTT	HITTING THE SACK
ACEFGHKLNORSTT	LACK OF STRENGTH	ACEGHHIKNORTTT	ON THE RIGHT TACK
ACEFGIIILLNNPR	FALLING IN PRICE	ACEGHHIORRRSTU	CARRIES THROUGH
ACEFGIIKLNNNOR	FINAL RECKONING	ACEGHHOPRRSSTU	SCRAPES THROUGH
ACEFGIIKLNOPRW	PICKING A FLOWER	ACEGHIIIKLMMNN	MILKING MACHINE
ACEFGIILNOORST	FAILING TO SCORE	ACEGHIIKKMNTTY	TAKING THE MICKY
ACEFGIINNORTTU	CENTRIFUGATION	ACEGHIIILLNOPTT	COATING THE PILL
ACEFGIKMNORRSY	ASKING FOR MERCY	ACEGHIIMMNNORT	TIME MARCHING ON
ACEFGILLNOORSU	FALSE COLOURING	ACEGHIIMNNPRST	MARCHING IN STEP
ACEFGINNOORSWY	FORCING ONE'S WAY	ACEGHIIMNOSTTW	TEACHING TO SWIM
ACEFGIOOPRRTUU	CUT A POOR FIGURE	ACEGHIINNORRTT	IN A TIGHT CORNER
ACEFGLMOOORSTY	GLOOMY FORECAST	ACEGHIINOSTTUW	WITHOUT CEASING
ACEFGNNOORRRSS	RAN FOR CONGRESS	ACEGHIKMNRRRSU	CRUSHING REMARK
ACEFHHHMORRTTU	MARCH THE FOURTH	ACEGHIKNORSTTT	STROKING THE CAT
ACEFHHLLOOOSSW	SCHOOL OF WHALES	ACEGHILLLLNORT	CALLING THE ROLL
ACEFHHOOPRSTTT	TOP OF THE CHARTS	ACEGHILLLNOOTY	ETHNOLOGICALLY
ACEFHHORRRSTTU	SEARCH FOR TRUTH	ACEGHILLNOOPTY	PHOTOGENICALLY
ACEFHIIIOTTVVY	HIVE OF ACTIVITY	ACEGHILMNRSTTW	WRESTLING MATCH
ACEFHIIKNSTTUW	CUTS WITH A KNIFE	ACEGHILNNTTTUW	CUTTING THE LAWN
ACEFHIJLLOORSW	WALLS OF JERICHO	ACEGHILNORSSSU	SOUL-SEARCHINGS
ACEFHIKLLNRTUY	THINK CAREFULLY	ACEGHIMNNOPSTU	MACHINE-GUN POST
ACEFHIKORRSSST	FOR CHRIST'S SAKE	ACEGHINOPSSTTT	CHANGE ITS SPOTS
ACEFHIKRRSTTUW	STRUCK WITH FEAR	ACEGHINOPSSTTY	PAYING THE COSTS
ACEFHILOOPPRSW	PLACE OF WORSHIP	ACEGHKNNOORTTW	ON THE WRONG TACK
ACEFHINNORRSTU	CURRENT FASHION	ACEGHOPPRRRSTY	CRYPTOGRAPHERS
ACEFHINOPPPSSU	CUP OF HAPPINESS	ACEGIIIKLNNOPS	LACKING IN POISE
ACEFHJOORSTTUU	JUST OUT OF REACH	ACEGIIIKNNNPRW	PICKING A WINNER
ACEFIIIINORTVV	REVIVIFICATION	ACEGIIILNNOSTZ	SECTIONALIZING
ACEFIIILMNOSTU	EMULSIFICATION	ACEGIIINNNORST	CONTAINERISING
ACEFIIILPRSTUY	SUPERFICIALITY	ACEGIIINNNORTZ	CONTAINERIZING
ACEFIIIMNOSTTU	FICTITIOUS NAME	ACEGIIKKLMORSW	WORKS LIKE MAGIC
ACEFIIIMNOPRTTT	PRETTIFICATION	ACEGIIKLLRSSTT	STRATEGIC SKILL
ACEFIIKPPPSTUW	PICK UP A FEW TIPS	ACEGIIKLNOOPTT	GOT INTO A PICKLE
ACEFIILMNOOPRX	FAIR COMPLEXION	ACEGIIKLNPRTTU	TALKING PICTURE
ACEFIILMNOPRST	SIMPLE FRACTION	ACEGIIKNOORSTV	STICK IN A GROOVE
ACEFIILNNORSSU	NUCLEAR FISSION	ACEGIILLLOOPTY	GEOPOLITICALLY
ACEFIIMNOOPRSS	CRIME OF PASSION	ACEGIILLLOSTUY	EULOGISTICALLY
ACEFIINOSSSTTU	FACTITIOUSNESS	ACEGIILLMNOORT	TERMINOLOGICAL
ACEFIKLMOPRTTT	PLATFORM TICKET	ACEGIILLOOORST	SOTERIOLOGICAL
ACEFIKMOPRRRST	PERFORMS A TRICK	ACEGIILLORSSUY	SACRILEGIOUSLY
ACEFIKNNOORRTW	KNOW FOR CERTAIN	ACEGIILNNNOTUY	UNCONGENIALITY
ACEFILLNNOOSSY	CONFESSIONALLY	ACEGIILNNORTUV	COUNTERVAILING
ACEFILMMNNOOSTY	COMMITS A FELONY	ACEGIILNNPPTTU	PUTTING IN PLACE
ACEFILMOQRTUYY	QUALITY OF MERCY	ACEGIILNOPPRSU	PILING UP A SCORE
ACEFIMNOOORTUV	COME INTO FAVOUR	ACEGIILORRSTTU	RELIGIOUS TRACT
ACEFIMNORSSSTW	SWARM OF INSECTS	ACEGIIMMNNNRST	MINCING MATTERS
ACEFINOOPPRRRT	PROPER FRACTION	ACEGIIMMNNNOPST	OPEN-CAST MINING
ACEFINOOPRRSST	PRESS FOR ACTION	ACEGIIMNNORSSX	CROSS-EXAMINING
ACEFINRRRSTTUU	INFRASTRUCTURE	ACEGIINNNOOOTT	GONE INTO ACTION
ACEFIOORSSSTUZ	COURT OF ASSIZES	ACEGIINNOOOSTT	GOES INTO ACTION
ACEFLLNOORRRSU	ALL FOUR CORNERS	ACEGIINOPRSSUV	GRAVE SUSPICION
ACEFLNNOOOSSSW	CLASS OF ONES OWN	ACEGIINOPSSUUV	VAGUE SUSPICION
ACEFLNOORSSSTU	COLOURFASTNESS	ACEGIKLNORSSSW	WORKING CLASSES

ACEGIKNOORSTUV	STUCK IN A GROOVE	ACEIIIMMNNORRST	RECRIMINATIONS
ACEGILLLMNPSUU	PULLING A MUSCLE	ACEIIINNNOOOOPV	VOICE AN OPINION
ACEGILLLMOOTYY	ETYMOLOGICALLY	ACEIIINNNOPSSTX	EXPANSIONISTIC
ACEGILLLNOORUY	NEUROLOGICALLY	ACEIIINNOPTTUV	PUNITIVE ACTION
ACEGILLLOOPRTY	PETROLOGICALLY	ACEIIINOOPSTTV	POSITIVE ACTION
ACEGILMNNOOOORT	CONGLOMERATION	ACEIIINOPPRSTT	PRECIPITATIONS
ACEGILNNNTTTUU	CUTTING A TUNNEL	ACEIIKLMOSSTTU	STICKS OUT A MILE
ACEGILNNOOORRST	REGAINS CONTROL	ACEIIKNNOORSST	STICK IN ONE'S OAR
ACEGILNOPRSSTU	PLASTIC SURGEON	ACEIILLLNNOPSU	PAULINE COLLINS
ACEGILPRRSSTUY	PLASTIC SURGERY	ACEIILLLLNRTUUY	UNICELLULARITY
ACEGIMMNNOORST	COMING ON STREAM	ACEIILLMNNOOOS	NEOCOLONIALISM
ACEGIMMNNOPSST	PASSING COMMENT	ACEIILLMNOPPRR	MORAL PRINCIPLE
ACEGIMNNOOPRST	COMPARING NOTES	ACEIILLNNNRTUY	INTERNUNCIALLY
ACEGINNNOOSSUU	CONSANGUINEOUS	ACEIILLNNOOOST	NEOCOLONIALIST
ACEGINNOOSSSTU	CONTAGIOUSNESS	ACEIILLNNOQSTU	CALL IN QUESTION
ACEGINNOPSSSUU	PUGNACIOUSNESS	ACEIILLNOPPSST	SLIPS INTO PLACE
ACEGINNORRTTVY	CONVERTING A TRY	ACEIILLNOPRSTY	ISENTROPICALLY
ACEGINNORSSSUU	UNGRACIOUSNESS	ACEIILLMORRSTTY	MILITARY ESCORT
ACEGINOQPRSSTT	PROGNOSTICATES	ACEIILNNOOPRNOT	IN LOCO PARENTIS
ACEGLMNOOORRST	CONGLOMERATORS	ACEIILNNORRSTU	INSURRECTIONAL
ACEHHIIIKLNNNT	LINK IN THE CHAIN	ACEIILNOPRSTUY	PERTINACIOUSLY
ACEHHIIMRSSTTW	WHITE CHRISTMAS	ACEIILNOSSSSUV	LASCIVIOUSNESS
ACEHHIIINOPPRTI	PITHECANTHROPI	ACEIILNPQSTTUU	QUINTUPLICATES
ACEHHIINOPSSUY	HOUSE PHYSICIAN	ACEIILOOPRRSSU	SOCIAL SUPERIOR
ACEHHIKNPRTTUW	RUN WITH THE PACK	ACEIIMMNOORSST	COMMISERATIONS
ACEHHILLOPTTYY	HYPOTHETICALLY	ACEIINNNOOTTTW	WENT INTO ACTION
ACEHHKMNRSTUVY	THANKS VERY MUCH	ACEIINOPSSSSUU	AUSPICIOUSNESS
ACEHHLMOOOPPST	OPHTHALMOSCOPE	ACEIJLNOORSTUY	SOCIETY JOURNAL
ACEHHLNNOORSTT	CHARLTON HESTON	ACEIJMMRSSTUUY	SUMMARY JUSTICE
ACEHIIIMMNRSSTUV	CHRYSANTHEMUMS	ACEIKLLMMOORST	SMALL-TIME CROOK
ACEHIIKLNOPSST	LICKS INTO SHAPE	ACEIKLMNOPSSSS	SMACKS ONE'S LIPS
ACEHIIKLPRSTTT	PARTICK THISTLE	ACEIKNNOORSSTU	STUCK IN ONE'S OAR
ACEHIILLPSTUUY	EUPHUISTICALLY	ACEIKNOORTTTTU	TAKEN IT TO COURT
ACEHIILNOPRSTY	PLACE IN HISTORY	ACEIKOORSTTTTU	TAKES IT TO COURT
ACEHIIMNNNOPST	TENNIS CHAMPION	ACEILLLMORTUVY	VOLUMETRICALLY
ACEHIIMNNOOPRT	ENANTIOMORPHIC	ACEILLNNNOOTVY	CONVENTIONALLY
ACEHIIMNOORSST	TRICHOMONIASES	ACEILLNNOOSSTT	CONSTELLATIONS
ACEHIINNORSTTY	ANCIENT HISTORY	ACEILLNOOPRSST	CROSS-POLLINATE
ACEHIINNSSTTUU	UNENTHUSIASTIC	ACEILLNOOPRSSY	PROCESSIONALLY
ACEHIINOOPRTTU	EUTROPHICATION	ACEILLNOPRSSUY	SUPERSONICALLY
ACEHIINOPPRSST	SPINTHARISCOPE	ACEILLNOSSSTTW	CALLS TO WITNESS
ACEHIIOORRSTTT	OSTEOARTHRITIC	ACEILMNNOOPSTT	CONTEMPLATIONS
ACEHIJKNOPSTTW	WINS THE JACKPOT	ACEILMNOOPRRTY	CONTEMPORARILY
ACEHIKKINOOSTT	TOOK IN THE SLACK	ACEILMNOOPSSSS	COMPASSIONLESS
ACEHIKKNNOOPST	KNOCK INTO SHAPE	ACEILMNORSSSUU	MIRACULOUSNESS
ACEHILLNOPPTYY	PHENOTYPICALLY	ACEILNNNNOOTUV	UNCONVENTIONAL
ACEHILLNOPRSYY	HYPERSONICALLY	ACEILNNOOSSTTT	CASTS IN ONE'S LOT
ACEHILLOPRSTTY	PROSTHETICALLY	ACEILNOOQSSSUU	LOQUACIOUSNESS
ACEHILMMNOSTTU	MOUNT ST. MICHAEL	ACEILORRSSTTTW	SIR WALTER SCOTT
ACEHILMNOOPRRZ	CHLORPROMAZINE	ACEIMMNNNOORSTU	COMMENSURATION
ACEHILNOOPRSWW	WIN, PLACE OR SHOW	ACEIMMNOORRRST	COMMITS AN ERROR
ACEHILNORSSSUV	CHIVALROUSNESS	ACEIMMOOPPRSTT	COMMITS TO PAPER
ACEHILOPRSSTTT	ATHLETIC SPORTS	ACEIMNNNOOPRTU	PRONUNCIAMENTO
ACEHIMMNRRSSTY	MERRY CHRISTMAS	ACEIMNNRRRSTTU	MACRONUTRIENTS
ACEHIMNOOPPRTU	PNEUMATOPHORIC	ACEIMNOOPSSTTU	CAME OUT IN SPOTS
ACEHIMNOOPRRTT	ANTHROPOMETRIC	ACEINNNOOOOPRT	NONCOOPERATION
ACEHIMOPPRSTTY	SPERMATOPHYTIC	ACEINNNOORSSTTV	CONTRAVENTIONS
ACEHINOORRSSTT	ORCHESTRATIONS	ACELLMNNOOPRSU	PERSONAL COLUMN
ACEHKKLOOPSTTU	TOOK UP THE SLACK	ACELMNOORSSSUU	CLAMOUROUSNESS
ACEHKNNOOOORSTT	HOT ON ONE'S TRACK	ACELNNORRTTUUY	NEUTRAL COUNTRY
ACEHLLMMOORSTW	THOMAS CROMWELL	ACELRRRSTTTUUU	ULTRASTRUCTURE
ACEHMMOOPTTTTU	ATTEMPT TOO MUCH	ACEMNNNOOQRSTU	NORMAN CONQUEST
ACEHNOORSSTTTU	CUTS ONE'S THROAT	ACEMNNOOPPRSTT	COMPONENT PARTS
ACEIIILMNPSTU	MUNICIPALITIES	ACEMNOOORSSTTU	ENTOMOSTRACOUS
ACEIIILLNPPRST	PRINCIPALITIES	ACFFGIMNOOORRT	GRAIN OF COMFORT
ACEIIILLMOPRTY	MILITARY POLICE	ACFFIIINOORSTT	FORTIFICATIONS
ACEIIILLMPTTUV	MULTIPLICATIVE	ACFGHHHINOOTTU	CHAIN OF THOUGHT
ACEIIILLNPPRTV	VITAL PRINCIPLE	ACFGIIKKNPSSUU	KICKING UP A FUSS
ACEIIILLNNRSTUV	INTRINSIC VALUE	ACFGIILMNNNOTU	MALFUNCTIONING
ACEIIILLNRRTUVY	CURVILINEARITY	ACFGIIMNOOPRRU	COMING UP FOR AIR
ACEIIIMMNOORSS	COMMISSIONAIRE	ACFGIINNOORSTU	CONFIGURATIONS

ACFGILMNNOSSTY	FLYING SCOTSMAN
ACFGINORRRUUVY	CURRYING FAVOUR
ACFHILORSSSSTT	FIRST-CLASS SHOT
ACFHIMNOOORSTT	NO STOMACH FOR IT
ACFIIIILMNOPST	SIMPLIFICATION
ACFIIIINNORSTT	NITRIFICATIONS
ACFIIIJLLNOOST	JOLLIFICATIONS
ACFIIIILLNNOSTU	NULLIFICATIONS
ACFIIILNOSTTTU	STULTIFICATION
ACFIIIMNOSSTTY	MYSTIFICATIONS
ACFIILLRSTTUUY	FUTURISTICALLY
ACFIILMMOORRTT	COMMIT FOR TRIAL
ACFIILMNNOSSTU	FUNCTIONALISMS
ACFIINOOPRRSTT	STRIP FOR ACTION
ACFIINOOPRRTTT	PATRIOTIC FRONT
ACFIIOOPRRSSSS	PAIR OF SCISSORS
ACFILOPRSSSSTT	FIRST CLASS POST
ACFIMNOOORSTTT	COMFORT STATION
ACFINNNOOORSTT	CONFRONTATIONS
ACFINOOOPTTTUU	PUT OUT OF ACTION
ACFLMOORSSSTUW	SWARM OF LOCUSTS
ACFLNNOOORSSTU	NON-FAST COLOURS
ACGGHHILMNOPTU	PLOUGHING MATCH
ACGGHIILNNOSTT	CASTING LIGHT ON
ACGGHIJLNORSTU	CONJUGAL RIGHTS
ACGGHILLNNOOSU	SLOUCHING ALONG
ACGGIIILNORSUV	GRACIOUS LIVING
ACGGIILNNNOORT	GAINING CONTROL
ACGHHHIIOOPSTUY	ICHTHYOPHAGOUS
ACGHHIKOQSTTUU	QUICK AS THOUGHT
ACGHHILLMOOOPT	OPHTHALMOLOGIC
ACGHHINNOPRTUW	THROWING A PUNCH
ACGHHIORRRTTUY	CARRY IT THROUGH
ACGHIIIINNRSTZ	CHRISTIANIZING
ACGHIIIKNNRSTV	VANISHING TRICK
ACGHIIINNPRTWY	CRYING WITH PAIN
ACGHIIINPSSTUV	CHAUVINIST PIGS
ACGHIIKNNOSTTT	STICK AT NOTHING
ACGHIILLLLOOPY	PHILOLOGICALLY
ACGHIILLLLOOTY	LITHOLOGICALLY
ACGHIILLLOOSTY	HISTOLOGICALLY
ACGHIILLNOOORT	ORNITHOLOGICAL
ACGHIILMNOOPSY	PHYSIOGNOMICAL
ACGHIKLMNOOTTU	TALKING TOO MUCH
ACGHIKNNOSTTTU	STUCK AT NOTHING
ACGHILLLMOOTYY	MYTHOLOGICALLY
ACGHILNNOSTTUY	STAYING TO LUNCH
ACGHILNOPSSTTU	CASTS LIGHT UPON
ACGHIMMNNOOOORT	COMING TO NO HARM
ACGHINNOOORTTW	CROWNING A TOOTH
ACGHINOOORSTTW	CARING TWO HOOTS
ACGIIIILMNNPSU	MUNICIPALISING
ACGIIIILMNNPUZ	MUNICIPALIZING
ACGIIIJLLNOSTY	JINGOISTICALLY
ACGIIIKNNRSTTU	STICKING IN A RUT
ACGIIILLLNSTUY	LINGUISTICALLY
ACGIIILLNQSTTU	CALLING IT QUITS
ACGIIILPRRSSTU	SURGICAL SPIRIT
ACGIIINNNNOSTU	ACTING IN UNISON
ACGIIINNRRSTTT	STRICT TRAINING
ACGIIKKLLNQUWY	WALKING QUICKLY
ACGIIILLLLMNOOY	LIMNOLOGICALLY
ACGIIILLMOOSSTT	CLIMATOLOGISTS
ACGIILNNORRSSU	INCURRING A LOSS
ACGIIMMNOORRSS	MICROORGANISMS
ACGIIMMNORSSSW	SWIMMING ACROSS
ACGIIMMNOOOPTT	COMING TO A POINT
ACGIKNNNORTTUW	WANTING NO TRUCK
ACGIKNNOOORTTU	COOKING TO A TURN
ACGILLNOOOSSTV	VOLCANOLOGISTS
ACGILLNOOSSTUV	VULCANOLOGISTS
ACGIMNNOOPRTUY	TOURING COMPANY
ACGIMNNOOPRTTUY	COMING-OUT PARTY
ACGINNNNORRSTUW	RUNNING TWO CARS
ACGINNPSTTTUUY	CUTTING UP NASTY
ACGINOOOPRRSTT	PROGNOSTICATOR
ACGINOPPRSSTTU	SUPPORTING CAST
ACHHIIOSTTTTUW	WITHOUT A STITCH
ACHHIMNNOOPRTWY	WORTHY CHAMPION
ACHHLMOOOOPPSTY	OPHTHALMOSCOPY
ACHIIIIMNNRSTV	RICH IN VITAMINS
ACHIIILLNORSTY	HISTRIONICALLY
ACHIIIMNNOORSST	TRICHOMONIASIS
ACHIIINOOPSSTT	SOPHISTICATION
ACHIIKLOORRSTW	HISTORICAL WORK
ACHIILLLMNOOTY	MONOLITHICALLY
ACHIILLMOOPRSY	ISOMORPHICALLY
ACHIILLMOORSTY	MILITARY SCHOOL
ACHIIOPRSSSTTY	ASTROPHYSICIST
ACHIKLOPQRTTUW	PATCHWORK QUILT
ACHILLLNOOPPYY	POLYPHONICALLY
ACHILLLOOPTTYY	PHOTOLYTICALLY
ACHILLMNNOOOOPY	MONOPHONICALLY
ACHILNNOPSSTTU	CONSULTANTSHIP
ACHIMNOOOPSSSW	SHOW COMPASSION
ACHLNNOORSSUYY	ASYNCHRONOUSLY
ACIIIILNOOPSTT	POLITICISATION
ACIIIILNOOPTTZ	POLITICIZATION
ACIIIILPRSSTTU	SPIRITUALISTIC
ACIIIILLMPSSTY	SIMPLISTICALLY
ACIIILLMNOPTTU	MULTIPLICATION
ACIIILLMOPSTTY	OPTIMISTICALLY
ACIIILLNNOSSTT	SCINTILLATIONS
ACIIILNOOOPSST	SOCIAL POSITION
ACIILLLMOOQSSU	COLLOQUIALISMS
ACIILNNOOPPRST	CLAP INTO PRISON
ACIILNNOOSSTTU	CONSTITUTIONAL
ACIINNNOOPRSTU	PRONUNCIATIONS
ACIINNOPRRSSTT	TRANSCRIPTIONS
ACIKLOOOOPTTUY	TOOK OUT A POLICY
ACIKMNNOORSTUY	ROCKY MOUNTAINS
ACILLMMNNOOTTY	NONCOMMITTALLY
ACILLNOOQRTTUY	QUALITY CONTROL
ACILOOORRSSUUV	VARIOUS COLOURS
ACILRRSSSTTTUU	STRUCTURALISTS
ACIMMNNOPRSTTUY	COMMUNIST PARTY
ACLNNOOPPSSTUY	CONSTANT SUPPLY
ADDDDEEEHHNNOOS	NODDED ONE'S HEAD
ADDDDEEEIILRSS	RIDE SIDE-SADDLE
ADDDDEEEILORSS	RODE SIDE-SADDLE
ADDDDEGIIMNNOW	DIAMOND WEDDING
ADDDDEGINNOOTU	DODGED IN AND OUT
ADDDDEHIIORSST	DID AS OTHERS DID
ADDDEEEEHHLLNOS	SOLED AND HEELED
ADDDEEEIMORRTV	DEVOTED ADMIRER
ADDDEEEINRSTTT	TRIED AND TESTED
ADDDEEFHILMOTY	MIDDLE OF THE DAY
ADDDEEFHINNRUV	HUNDRED AND FIVE
ADDDEEFINORSSX	NO FIXED ADDRESS
ADDDEEFLLLUWWY	LAWFULLY WEDDED
ADDDEEGHHINNOT	NODDING THE HEAD
ADDDEEGHHNOTTU	THOUGHT AND DEED
ADDDEEHHIRRTTW	EDWARD THE THIRD
ADDDEEHHNOOTTU	HOUNDED TO DEATH
ADDDEEHILNORRS	RHODE ISLAND RED
ADDDEEHILOSTTT	ADDED TO THE LIST
ADDDEEHIMNNOOS	DID ONE HANDSOME
ADDDEEHINNNNRU	HUNDRED AND NINE
ADDDEEHLOORTTW	DEAD TO THE WORLD
ADDDEEIIILLQUVY	EQUALLY DIVIDED
ADDDEEILLMOSTT	MADE LITTLE ODDS
ADDDEEIINNOOORS	ENDORADIOSONDE

ADDDEFHIIILTVW	DAVID WHITFIELD
ADDDEFHNNORRUU	HUNDRED AND FOUR
ADDDEGHHIIIVWY	DIVIDED HIGHWAY
ADDDEGHLOOOSTY	THE GOOD OLD DAYS
ADDDEGINNNOOSTU	DODGES IN AND OUT
ADDDEHILNORSSW	SWORD AND SHIELD
ADDDEHLLNORRSU	HUNDRED DOLLARS
ADDDEHNOORSTWW	TWO-HANDED SWORD
ADDDEIIIILNSUV	INDIVIDUALISED
ADDDEIIIILNUVZ	INDIVIDUALIZED
ADDDEIILLOTVYY	DIVIDED LOYALTY
ADDEEEEEGLMPRS	REDEEMS A PLEDGE
ADDEEEEEFFFRSTU	SUFFERED DEFEAT
ADDEEEEEFHRRRSS	DEFERRED SHARES
ADDEEEEGHNRSTW	WEEDS THE GARDEN
ADDEEEEEHINNPTT	IN AT THE DEEP END
ADDEEEEEHISSTUV	EVADED THE ISSUE
ADDEEEEHNNNSSV	EVENHANDEDNESS
ADDEEEEEIILMRSV	MADE DELIVERIES
ADDEEEEENRSVWYY	EVERY WEDNESDAY
ADDEEEEFFGIORRT	AGREED TO DIFFER
ADDEEEFFIINRTT	DIFFERENTIATED
ADDDEEEFIIIINOTTY	THE END OF THE DAY
ADDEEEFHLNNSST	LEFT-HANDEDNESS
ADDEEEFHNOSSST	SOFTHEADEDNESS
ADDEEEFIILNNRU	ENDED IN FAILURE
ADDEEEFIMNRRTU	FREDDIE TRUEMAN
ADDEEEGHIIDTTV	THE GREAT DIVIDE
ADDDEEGHLRSTTU	ELDEST DAUGHTER
ADDEEEHHILMSTV	SHAMED THE DEVIL
ADDEEEHHLNOPSU	HELD ONE'S HEAD UP
	HELD UP ONE'S HEAD
ADDEEEHHLOTTTU	DUEL TO THE DEATH
ADDEEEHIMNPPRS	MISAPPREHENDED
ADDEEEHINNNOST	TANNED ONE'S HIDE
ADDEEEHINNNRRS	HARDENED SINNER
ADDEEEHINRRSTU	HIDDEN TREASURE
ADDEEEHKNNRRST	RENDERED THANKS
ADDEEEHNNNOPSS	OPENHANDEDNESS
ADDEEEHNOSTTTY	STAYED TO THE END
ADDEEEIINPRSST	PEDESTRIANISED
ADDEEEIINPRSTZ	PEDESTRIANIZED
ADDEEEIKMNNSSW	WEAK-MINDEDNESS
ADDEEEILNNNPSS	NEEDLES AND PINS
	PINS AND NEEDLES
ADDEEEILNNRSTT	LANDED INTEREST
ADDEEEILNOPRSS	DEPERSONALISED
ADDEEEILNOPRST	PLIED ONE'S TRADE
ADDEEEILNOPRSZ	DEPERSONALIZED
ADDEEEILNORRTV	LEARNED TO DRIVE
ADDEEEILOPRRTT	DETAILED REPORT
ADDEEEIMNPRTTU	UNPREMEDITATED
ADDEEEIMNRSTTU	UNDERESTIMATED
ADDEEELLMNRSSW	WELL-DRESSED MAN
ADDEEELMNOOPRW	LEMONADE POWDER
ADDEEELOPPRTVY	PLEADED POVERTY
ADDEEEMOOOORSSS	DOES AS ROME DOES
ADDEEEENPRRSSST	PRESENT ADDRESS
ADDEEEFFHHIRTTW	EDWARD THE FIFTH
ADDEEEFGGHLOOTT	FLOGGED TO DEATH
ADDEEEFGHHINOTT	THE DEAD OF NIGHT
ADDEEEFGIIMNNRY	FINDING A REMEDY
ADDEEEFGINNNOSU	DEAFENING SOUND
ADDEEEFGJMNOTUY	DAY OF JUDGEMENT
ADDEEEFHILLPSTY	PLAYS THE FIDDLE
ADDEEEFHILORTVY	LIVED FOR THE DAY
ADDEEEFHINRSSTU	RAISED THE FUNDS
ADDEEEFHIRRSTTW	EDWARD THE FIRST
ADDEEEFHLOOPRTT	TOP OF THE LADDER
ADDEEEFHLOOSTTU	OUT OF THE SADDLE
ADDEEEFHMOOORRT	MADE FOR THE DOOR
ADDEEEFLNORRSSU	SUED FOR SLANDER
ADDEEEFNOORRTTU	TREAD UNDERFOOT
ADDEEEFOPPRRSTW	STEPPED FORWARD
ADDEEEFOPRRRSSW	PRESSED FORWARD
ADDEEEGGHNORRTU	GATHERED GROUND
ADDEEEGGINNOOTW	GONE TO A WEDDING
ADDEEEGGINOOSTW	GOES TO A WEDDING
ADDEEEGHHHINNSS	HIGH-HANDEDNESS
ADDEEEGHHILLNOT	HOLDING THE LEAD
ADDEEEGHHKNOSTU	KNEADS THE DOUGH
ADDEEEGHILLNNSY	SINGLE-HANDEDLY
ADDEEEGHINNRSUU	HUNDRED GUINEAS
ADDEEEGHINNSTWY	WEDNESDAY NIGHT
ADDEEEGHINRRSST	DRAINS THE DREGS
ADDEEEGHLORSTTU	OLDEST DAUGHTER
ADDEEEGHNNOORTW	ON THE DOWN GRADE
ADDEEEGHNOPRTUW	PAWED THE GROUND
ADDEEEGIIMORSTT	DISTORTED IMAGE
ADDEEEGIINNNNST	STANDING IN NEED
ADDEEEGINNNORRS	SENDING AN ORDER
ADDEEEGINNNOSSY	ENDING ONE'S DAYS
ADDEEEGINNOTTWW	WENT TO A WEDDING
ADDEEEGNNNORTUY	YOUNG AND TENDER
ADDEEEHHIRSTTWX	EDWARD THE SIXTH
ADDEEEHHHLNOOPSU	HOLD ONES HEAD UP
	HOLD UP ONES HEAD
ADDEEEHHNOPRSST	SHORTHAND SPEED
ADDEEEHIINOPRRV	PROVIDED AN HEIR
ADDEEEHILNORTUV	LIVE TO A HUNDRED
ADDEEEHINNOPSSW	WIPED ONE'S HANDS
ADDEEEHIOORRTTW	WORRIED TO DEATH
ADDEEEHLMMOORST	SLAMMED THE DOOR
ADDEEEHLMORRSSU	SHOULDERED ARMS
ADDEEEHMRSTTUWY	MUDDY THE WATERS
ADDEEEHOOORSSST	DOES AS OTHERS DO
ADDEEEHOOPRSTVY	PAY OVER THE ODDS
ADDEEEIIKLNPRSS	SPEAK IN RIDDLES
ADDEEEIILLRSTTW	DISTILLED WATER
ADDEEEIILNORRST	TRAINED SOLDIER
ADDEEEIINNRSSST	ENDS IN DISASTER
ADDEEEIINPSSSST	DISSIPATEDNESS
ADDEEEIIOPRRSTV	DRIVE TO DESPAIR
ADDEEEIIPPRRSTT	DEPARTED SPIRIT
ADDEEEIKLLMOSTT	MAKE LITTLE ODDS
ADDEEEILMNNPRSU	NIL DESPERANDUM
ADDEEEILNOOQSTU	LOADED QUESTION
ADDEEEIMMNNOPSU	MADE ONE'S MIND UP
	MADE UP ONE'S MIND
ADDEEEINNNORSWY	NINE DAYS WONDER
ADDEEEINOOPSSTT	DIED AT ONE'S POST
ADDEEEIOOPRRSTV	DROVE TO DESPAIR
ADDEEEIOPPRRSTT	DROPPED A SITTER
ADDEEEKNNOOOORRS	DARKEN ONES DOOR
ADDEEELNOOOSSST	DOES AS ONE'S TOLD
ADDEEENOPRRSSSW	PRESSED ONWARDS
ADDEEFFIIMNOOSV	FIVE OF DIAMONDS
ADDEFGGHIILNOU	DIED OF LAUGHING
ADDEFGHHILNRTY	LEFT HIGH AND DRY
ADDEFHILLNOOSY	OLD-FASHIONEDLY
ADDEFIILNNSSSU	DISDAINFULNESS
ADDEFIIMNNNOOS	NINE OF DIAMONDS
ADDEFIIMNOORSU	DIAMONDIFEROUS
ADDEFIIMNOTTTU	ATTITUDE OF MIND
ADDEFILMMORRRU	DIAL M FOR MURDER
ADDEFIOORRSTUW	OUTSIDE FORWARD
ADDEFLMNOOSTTU	SADDLE OF MUTTON
ADDEGGGHILNORU	HOLDING A GRUDGE
ADDEGHIINNRRTV	RIGHT-HAND DRIVE
ADDEGHHILNOORT	HOLDING THE ROAD
ADDEGHHLLNORUY	HANDLED ROUGHLY
ADDEGHIJOOOSWW	JOSIAH WEDGWOOD

ADDEGHINNNOTTU	NOTHING DAUNTED	ADEEEEEGHNNORSV	HAD ONE'S REVENGE
ADDEGHINNOORTW	GO DOWN THE DRAIN	ADEEEEEGMNNRSSS	SEND A MESSENGER
ADDEGHINNOPSSU	HAD DESIGNS UPON	ADEEEEHHINQRTU	QUEER IN THE HEAD
ADDEGHLLOOTUUU	LAUGHED OUT LOUD	ADEEEEHHLMMPST	HEMEL HEMPSTEAD
ADDEGIIKNNORRR	ORDERING A DRINK	ADEEEEHILLMRST	THE EMERALD ISLE
ADDEGINNNRSSTU	UNDERSTANDINGS	ADEEEEHIPRRRTY	HEREDITARY PEER
ADDEGINNORRSST	STANDING ORDERS	ADEEEEHISSSTUV	EVADES THE ISSUE
ADDEGNOOOORSSW	GOOD AS ONES WORD	ADEEEEHLRSTTTW	SETTLED WEATHER
ADDEGNOOPRSSU	DROPS ONE'S GUARD	ADEEEEHNNOOPSY	HAD ONE'S EYE OPEN
ADDEHHNNOORSSU	HORSE AND HOUNDS	ADEEEEHNNORSST	ENTERS ONE'S HEAD
ADDEHIINPSSSTU	STUDIED SPANISH	ADEEEEHOQSTTUZ	SQUEEZE TO DEATH
ADDEHINNORSSTY	DIRTY ONE'S HANDS	ADEEEEIIKLMRSV	MAKE DELIVERIES
ADDEHINOOOSSTT	STOOD ON ITS HEAD	ADEEEEIIKLMNRRW	LAKE WINDERMERE
ADDEHLNNOOSSSW	LOSES HANDS DOWN	ADEEEEIPRSSVWX	EXPRESSED A VIEW
ADDEHLNOORRTUW	AROUND THE WORLD	ADEEEEELLNRRSTW	WELL-EARNED REST
ADDEIIILNSSSUV	INDIVIDUALISES	ADEEEELNNNRRVV	NEVER-NEVER LAND
ADDEIIILNSUVZ	INDIVIDUALIZES	ADEEEENPPRRSSS	PREPAREDNESSES
ADDEIIILMNOPST	SIMPLE ADDITION	ADEEEFFFLOORRS	OFFERED FOR SALE
ADDEIIILNPSTTU	PLATITUDINISED	ADEEEFFFNORRSU	REFUSED AN OFFER
ADDEIIILNPTTUZ	PLATITUDINIZED	ADEEEFFGIORRST	AGREES TO DIFFER
ADDEIIILNRSSTU	INDUSTRIALISED	ADEEEEFFGMNORRR	FREE FROM DANGER
ADDEIIILNRSTUZ	INDUSTRIALIZED	ADEEEFFIINRSTT	DIFFERENTIATES
ADDEIIKLLNRSST	TALKS IN RIDDLES	ADEEEEFGGRRSTUU	RUGGED FEATURES
ADDEIILNOPPSTY	DISAPPOINTEDLY	ADEEEFGHHLRTTU	FEEL THE DRAUGHT
ADDEIINOPPSTTU	DISPUTED A POINT	ADEEEFGHIINPSS	DEEP-SEA FISHING
ADDEIINRSSSTUU	STUDIED RUSSIAN	ADEEEEFGHLLORTW	LOWERED THE FLAG
ADDEILMNNORRWY	NARROW-MINDEDLY	ADEEEFGIINNNOS	DEAFENING NOISE
ADDEILNNOORRRY	LONDONDERRY AIR	ADEEEFGILLNNOS	ALIGNED ONESELF
ADDEIMNNRSSSTU	MISUNDERSTANDS	ADEEEFGLNNNOQU	QUEEN OF ENGLAND
ADDEKNNNORSSUW	ADDRESS UNKNOWN	ADEEEFGLNNNSSW	NEWFANGLEDNESS
ADDEKNOORRSTWW	DOWNWARD STROKE	ADEEEFHHHOOSTU	HEAD OF THE HOUSE
ADDENNOORRSSWW	DRAWN ONE'S SWORD	ADEEEFHHINORTT	HEAR THE END OF IT
ADDENOORRSSSWW	DRAWS ONE'S SWORD	ADEEEFHHIORRTV	HEAD OF THE RIVER
ADDFFIMNOOORSU	FOUR OF DIAMONDS	ADEEEFHHNORSTT	ENDS OF THE EARTH
ADDFGHNOOOSTTU	STOOD AND FOUGHT	ADEEEFHHLNNORSS	HARDENS ONESELF
ADDFGIIILMNORT	FAIR TO MIDDLING	ADEEEFHMNORTTT	END OF THE MATTER
ADDFGIIKMNNOOS	KING OF DIAMONDS	ADEEEFHNOOSSTY	ONE OF THESE DAYS
ADDFGIIKNNORRY	DYING FOR A DRINK	ADEEEFHNRRSSTVW	THE SEVEN DWARFS
ADDFGIINORRRVW	DRIVING FORWARD	ADEEEFHRRSTTUU	READS THE FUTURE
ADDGGIINNOOORTU	DOING A GOOD TURN	ADEEEFIINRSSTV	NEVER SATISFIED
ADDGIIKLNPRRUY	RUDYARD KIPLING	ADEEEFIKLNOSST	STAKED ONE'S LIFE
ADDGINOOOPRTUW	PUT IN A GOOD WORD	ADEEEFILLNOPPS	APPLIED ONESELF
ADDGLOOOORSTTY	TOLD A GOOD STORY	ADEEEFILLNOSUV	VALUED ONE'S LIFE
ADDGNNOORRSWWW	GROWN DOWNWARDS	ADEEEFIMNNOORT	AFOREMENTIONED
ADDGNOORRSSWWW	GROWS DOWNWARDS	ADEEEFIMNPRRTT	FIRE DEPARTMENT
ADDHKNNOOOPSUW	SHOOK UP AND DOWN	ADEEEFIORRSTTU	FEATURES EDITOR
ADDHNNOOPSSTUU	THOUSAND POUNDS	ADEEEFKOPRSSTU	REFUSED TO SPEAK
ADDIIIILNSSTUV	INDIVIDUALISTS	ADEEEFLNNNOOST	LAND ON ONES FEET
ADDKLNNOOOPSUW	LOOKS UP AND DOWN	ADEEEFMNPRSTUY	REFUSED PAYMENT
ADEEEEEFHMNTTY	DEFEAT THE ENEMY	ADEEEGGGGINNTT	GETTING ENGAGED
ADEEEEEGHPRRST	THREE-SPEED GEAR	ADEEEGGHIINTTT	GETTING THE IDEA
ADEEEEEGNNRSST	DEGENERATENESS	ADEEEGGHINPRST	GATHERING SPEED
ADEEEEEHLLRRSW	WHEELER-DEALERS	ADEEEGHHIILVWY	WEIGHED HEAVILY
ADEEEEEHMPSSSY	MADE SHEEP'S EYES	ADEEEGHHIINOSV	GIVE ONE HIS HEAD
ADEEEEELLNOPSV	SEALED ENVELOPE	ADEEEGHHIMORTT	MODERATE HEIGHT
ADEEEEFFGHKOTT	TAKE THE EDGE OFF	ADEEEGHHMNPRRS	GERMAN SHEPHERD
ADEEEEFGHLRTTU	AFTER THE DELUGE	ADEEEGHHORRTTT	THREAD TOGETHER
ADEEEEFHIKLLST	FEELS LIKE DEATH	ADEEEGHIINPTUV	GIVEN UP THE IDEA
ADEEEEFHINRSUW	AUF WIEDERSEHEN	ADEEEGHIIPSTUV	GIVES UP THE IDEA
ADEEEEFHLSSTUX	FEELS EXHAUSTED	ADEEEGHILMNNRT	ENLARGE THE MIND
ADEEEEFHORSTTZ	FREEZES TO DEATH	ADEEEGHILNNORW	LEADING NOWHERE
ADEEEEFLLNOPSS	PLEASED ONESELF	ADEEEGHIMORTTW	MODERATE WEIGHT
ADEEEEFNOPPSTT	TAPPED ONE'S FEET	ADEEEGHIOOSSTT	GO TO THE SEASIDE
ADEEEEFNORRRVV	FOR EVER AND EVER	ADEEEGHLMORRTY	THE OLD GREY MARE
ADEEEEFNPRSSXY	DEFRAY EXPENSES	ADEEEGHLNORSSS	DRAGS ONE'S HEELS
ADEEEEGGHILNNT	ENLIGHTENED AGE	ADEEEGHNNOOOST	GONE TO ONE'S HEAD
ADEEEEGGHILTVY	GIVE THE GLAD EYE	ADEEEGHNOOOSST	GOES TO ONE'S HEAD
ADEEEEGHILLNRW	WHEELER-DEALING	ADEEEGHNOORRRY	HONORARY DEGREE
ADEEEEGHKLNPTT	TAKEN THE PLEDGE	ADEEEGIILMNNRS	ENDEARING SMILE
ADEEEEGHKLPSTT	TAKES THE PLEDGE	ADEEEGIILMNNST	REMAINED SINGLE
ADEEEEGHMNSSST	SEND THE MESSAGE	ADEEEGIILMRRST	REGISTERED MAIL

ADEEEGIINNSSTT	SEEING A DENTIST
ADEEEGILNNRSTT	SENDING A LETTER
ADEEEGILNRSSTU	GENERAL STUDIES
ADEEEGIMNNNNORT	NOD IN AGREEMENT
ADEEEGINNNNORS	NEARING ONE'S END
ADEEEGINNSTUVY	TUESDAY EVENING
ADEEEGLNRRSSSS	REGARDLESSNESS
ADEEEGNOOPRSTX	EXPOSE TO DANGER
ADEEEGNOPRRSTW	GROWN DESPERATE
ADEEEGOPRRRSTT	RETROGRADE STEP
ADEEEGOPRRSSTW	GROWS DESPERATE
ADEEEGOPRRSTUY	DAGUERREOTYPES
ADEEEHHHIORTTV	HIT OVER THE HEAD
ADEEEHHIILNNST	IN THE HEADLINES
ADEEEHHILMSSTV	SHAMES THE DEVIL
ADEEEHHLLOOSSU	LEASEHOLD HOUSE
ADEEEHHLLORTWY	WHOLEHEARTEDLY
ADEEEHHLNNRSTT	THE NETHERLANDS
ADEEEHHLORSSTT	LOSES THE THREAD
ADEEEHHMMNRRTU	UNDER THE HAMMER
ADEEEHHNOPPPTT	TAPPED THE PHONE
ADEEEHIJMNPSTU	JUMPED IN THE SEA
ADEEEHIKKNPRST	KEEPS IN THE DARK
ADEEEHIKLLNNPW	KEEP WELL IN HAND
ADEEEHIKMNOSSU	HOUSEMAIDS KNEE
ADEEEHIKNNNOPS	KEEP ONES HAND IN
ADEEEHILNOOPRT	RADIO TELEPHONE / RADIOTELEPHONE
ADEEEHIMNNRSTT	DISHEARTENMENT
ADEEEHIMNORSTY	RAISED THE MONEY
ADEEEHIMNRSTTU	READ THE MINUTES
ADEEEHIMOPRSTT	RAISED THE TEMPO
ADEEEHKKLLNNNT	KENNETH KENDALL
ADEEEHLLOPRSTT	ALLOTTED SPHERE
ADEEEHLNNOSTUV	ELEVEN THOUSAND
ADEEEHMMNOPRTT	HOME DEPARTMENT
ADEEEHMNOORSTV	REMOVED ONE'S HAT
ADEEEHMNORRSST	READS THE SERMON
ADEEEHMOOPPRRT	PAPERED THE ROOM
ADEEEHNNOOSTTW	WENT TO ONE'S HEAD
ADEEEHNNORSSTW	WHERE ONE STANDS
ADEEEHNOPRRSTW	OPENS THE DRAWER
ADEEEHNPRSSSTW	SPREADS THE NEWS
ADEEEHRRSTTTTU	UTTERED THREATS
ADEEEIIIKLMNSV	MIND LIKE A SIEVE
ADEEEIIIMNRRST	INTERMEDIARIES
ADEEEIIKLMNRSW	MIND LIKE A SEWER
ADEEEIILLLNTVV	LIVE AND LET LIVE
ADEEEIILMMPRTY	IMMEDIATE REPLY
ADEEEIILMNNRST	REMAINED SILENT
ADEEEIILMNRRSS	DEMINERALISERS
ADEEEIILMNRRSZ	DEMINERALIZERS
ADEEEIILMNRTTY	INTERMEDIATELY
ADEEEIIMMQRSUV	DEMISEMIQUAVER
ADEEEIIMNRSTTV	DETERMINATIVES
ADEEEIINORSSVW	AIRED ONE'S VIEWS
ADEEEIINPRSSST	PEDESTRIANISES
ADEEEIINPRSSTZ	PEDESTRIANIZES
ADEEEIKNNNOOST	TAKEN ON ONE SIDE
ADEEEIKNNOOSST	TAKES ON ONE SIDE
ADEEEIKNNOOSTT	TAKEN TO ONE SIDE
ADEEEIKNOOSSTT	TAKES TO ONE SIDE
ADEEEILMNORRSV	DELIVER A SERMON
ADEEEILNOPRSSS	DEPERSONALISES
ADEEEILNOPRSST	PLIES ONE'S TRADE
ADEEEILNOPRSSZ	DEPERSONALIZES
ADEEEILNORRTTW	LEARNED TO WRITE
ADEEEILNPRSTUV	PENAL SERVITUDE
ADEEEIMMNORSST	IMMODERATENESS
ADEEEIMNRSSTTU	UNDERESTIMATES
ADEEEIMNRSSTTV	ADVERTISEMENTS
ADEEEIINNSSSSVX	SIXES AND SEVENS
ADEEEINORRSSTT	STIRRED ONE'S TEA
ADEEEKNPPRRSUW	KEEP UNDER WRAPS
ADEEELLNNNOSWY	LESLEY ANNE DOWN
ADEEELMNORRSUY	LEND ME YOUR EARS
ADEEELNRRRSUUV	SURRENDER VALUE
ADEEEMMNNRRTTTU	UNDER TREATMENT
ADEEEMMNNRSTTTU	UNDERSTATEMENT
ADEEEMNNOOPPRST	OPENED ONE'S TRAP
ADEEEMNNOORSSTW	EATEN ONE'S WORDS
ADEEEOPPRRSSUV	SERVED A PURPOSE
ADEEFFGGIINNRU	FINDING A REFUGE
ADEEFFGHHLNOOT	GO OFF THE HANDLE
ADEEFFGHIORRSU	HEAD FOR FIGURES
ADEEFFHHHIORTW	OFF WITH HER HEAD
ADEEFFHHINOSTT	TANS THE HIDE OFF
ADEEFFHIKLNOTT	TAKEN THE LID OFF
ADEEFFHIKLOSTT	TAKES THE LID OFF
ADEEFFIIIMOPPTW	WIPED OFF THE MAP
ADEEFFIILLNRTY	DIFFERENTIALLY
ADEEFFIILNORRRU	RUN FOR DEAR LIFE
ADEEFFNNOOPRRSU	SPURNED AN OFFER
ADEEFFNOOPRRST	SPARED NO EFFORT
ADEEFGHHHIORST	HEAD FOR HEIGHTS
ADEEFGHHILOSTT	HOISTED THE FLAG
ADEEFGHHIMNOOR	HEADING FOR HOME
ADEEFGHHLRTTTU	FELT THE DRAUGHT
ADEEFGHILNNORS	NO HARD FEELINGS
ADEEFGHIMMNNOOT	IN THE NAME OF GOD
ADEEFGHINRSSST	FARSIGHTEDNESS
ADEEFGHORRSTTU	FOSTER DAUGHTER
ADEEFGIINNOPRT	POINTED A FINGER
ADEEFGIINRRRST	STIRRED A FINGER
ADEEFGILMOORSS	GAME OF SOLDIERS
ADEEFGINNORSST	FINGERS AND TOES
ADEEFGLNORRSSU	GROUNDLESS FEAR
ADEEFGMOOORRSU	FOR GOOD MEASURE
ADEEFHHLOOSTUY	LADY OF THE HOUSE
ADEEFHIILPRSTT	DEPART THIS LIFE
ADEEFHIKLLOTTV	TALK OF THE DEVIL
ADEEFHILLNOSTU	THE LIFE AND SOUL
ADEEFHILNOPSTU	LIFT UP ONES HEAD
ADEEFHILNSSTTW	HALF-WITTEDNESS
ADEEFHILORSTVY	LIVES FOR THE DAY
ADEEFHILRRSTTU	FURTHER DETAILS
ADEEFHIMNOSSTT	THE SANDS OF TIME
ADEEFHKMOOORRT	MAKE FOR THE DOOR
ADEEFHNOOOSSTY	ONE OF THOSE DAYS
ADEEFHNORRSSSU	FOUNDERS SHARES
ADEEFIILMNNRTT	INTIMATE FRIEND
ADEEFIIMNOOPRR	EMPEROR OF INDIA
ADEEFIINOQRSTU	FIRED A QUESTION
ADEEFIKMMNNNOY	ENEMY OF MANKIND
ADEEFILLMORSTT	STALLED FOR TIME
ADEEFILLNNOTTT	LITTLE AND OFTEN
ADEEFILOPRSSSU	REFUSE DISPOSAL
ADEEFIOPPRSTUW	SUPPORTED A WIFE
ADEEFLLLMOORWY	FOLLOW MY LEADER / FOLLOW-MY-LEADER
ADEEFLNNNORSTY	ALFRED TENNYSON
ADEEFLNNORRSSU	SUES FOR SLANDER
ADEEFLORRRSSTU	FLARED TROUSERS
ADEEFNNOPRSSTU	SPENDS A FORTUNE
ADEEFNOOOPPSTT	TAPPED ONE'S FOOT
ADEEFOPRRRSSSW	PRESSES FORWARD
ADEEGGHIILNNRT	LINGERING DEATH
ADEEGGHIILNSTY	SEEING DAYLIGHT
ADEEGGHIINNPTW	WIDENING THE GAP
ADEEGGHIIORRUV	GIVE A ROUGH RIDE
ADEEGGHIKNOSTV	GOD SAVE THE KING!
ADEEGGHILLNNNT	GENTLE HANDLING

ADEEGGHIMMNNORT	DOG IN THE MANGER
ADEEGGIIMNRRTT	GETTING MARRIED
ADEEGGIINNNNNOS	GAINING ONE'S END
ADEEGGIINPTTTT	GETTING IT TAPED
ADEEGGIILLMNNRS	SMELLING DANGER
ADEEGGIILLNNPRS	SPELLING DANGER
ADEEGGIILNRTTTT	GETTING RATTLED
ADEEGGIMNNRRRY	GERRYMANDERING
ADEEGGINNOOSVY	SAY GOOD EVENING
ADEEGGINPRSTTU	DEPARTING GUEST
ADEEGGINRSTTTT	GETTING STARTED
ADEEGHHHIINRTT	RIGHT IN THE HEAD
ADEEGHHHINPTTW	GET THE WHIP-HAND
ADEEGHHILNSTT	HEADING THE LIST
ADEEGHHIINPRST	HIGH-SPEED TRAIN
ADEEGHHILLNOTT	LIGHTEN THE LOAD
ADEEGHHILLRTTY	LIGHTHEARTEDLY
ADEEGHHILNOSSY	HIGHLY SEASONED
ADEEGHHILRSTTW	SAW THE RED LIGHT
ADEEGHHINNOSTW	DONE THE WASHING
ADEEGHHINOSSTW	DOES THE WASHING
ADEEGHIILNNRTW	DRAWING THE LINE
ADEEGHIILNPTVY	PAYING THE DEVIL
ADEEGHIINNORSY	DYEING ONE'S HAIR
ADEEGHIKNNOPRRT	GROPE IN THE DARK
ADEEGHILLLRTTV	TRAVELLED LIGHT
ADEEGHILLPRSTU	SUGARED THE PILL
ADEEGHILLRTTTY	TREATED LIGHTLY
ADEEGHILNNRRTY	HEARTRENDINGLY
ADEEGHILOPRSST	SHEEPDOG TRIALS
ADEEGHIMMNNNRTU	MADE THE RUNNING
ADEEGHIMNNRSTTYY	DON'T GIVE ME THAT
ADEEGHINNNOSST	GETS ONE'S HAND IN
ADEEGHINOPRTTU	ARGUED THE POINT
ADEEGHINPRSTTU	STRAIGHTENED UP
ADEEGHINRSTTYY	YESTERDAY NIGHT
ADEEGHLORSTTTW	GET THE LAST WORD
ADEEGHNNNOOSST	GET ONES HANDS ON
ADEEGHNNOORSTTU	TURNED ON THE GAS
ADEEGHNOORRTTU	EAR TO THE GROUND
ADEEGHNORSSTTT	STANDS TOGETHER
ADEEGIIILMNNRS	DEMINERALISING
ADEEGIIILMNNRZ	DEMINERALIZING
ADEEGIIIMNNNRT	MAIN INGREDIENT
ADEEGIIINRSTTV	DISINTEGRATIVE
ADEEGIIKNNOSST	TAKING ONE'S SIDE
ADEEGIILNNOOTT	GONE INTO DETAIL
ADEEGIILNNOPWY	LAYING WIDE OPEN
ADEEGIILNNORRT	LEARNING TO RIDE
ADEEGIILNOOSTT	GOES INTO DETAIL
ADEEGIILNOSTUV	LEAVING OUTSIDE
ADEEGIILRRSTTY	LITERARY DIGEST
ADEEGIIMMNNNRT	IMMINENT DANGER
ADEEGIINNPRSTT	PREDESTINATING
ADEEGIINNSTTTY	DYING INTESTATE
ADEEGIKLLNOOPS	LOOKING PLEASED
ADEEGIKLNNORST	TAKEN IN LODGERS
ADEEGIKLNORSST	TAKES IN LODGERS
ADEEGIKMNNOOST	TAKEN SOME DOING
ADEEGIKMNOOSST	TAKES SOME DOING
ADEEGILLORRRSU	REGULAR SOLDIER
ADEEGINNNNPPSY	SPENDING A PENNY
ADEEGINNNOSWWY	WENDING ONE'S WAY
ADEEGINNNRRSTU	RENTING ASUNDER
ADEEGINNOPPRRT	PREPONDERATING
ADEEGINOPRRRSU	UNDERGO REPAIRS
ADEEGINRRSSSTU	RESTING ASSURED
ADEEGLNOPRRSUU	PLEASURE GROUND
ADEEGLNORRSTUY	GOLDEN TREASURY
ADEEGMNNOOORSY	EARNS GOOD MONEY
ADEEGMNOOOSTWY	WASTE GOOD MONEY
ADEEGMNOOPRRSS	MADE NO PROGRESS
ADEEGMOORRRTTY	DEROGATORY TERM
ADEEGNNOPPRSTU	PSEUDOPREGNANT
ADEEGOPRRSSSTY	STEADY PROGRESS
ADEEHHHLORSTTT	AT THE THRESHOLD
ADEEHHHHNNOORTT	ON THE OTHER HAND
ADEEHHIINOTTVW	HAVE DONE WITH IT
ADEEHHILLNOSTW	HOW THE LAND LIES
ADEEHHILMORTTT	ARMED TO THE HILT
ADEEHHILOTTTTX	TAXED TO THE HILT
ADEEHHIMOPRRST	HERMAPHRODITES
ADEEHHINPSSTTU	PUTS IN THE SHADE
ADEEHHLMNOOSSU	HOUSEHOLD NAMES
ADEEHHMOOSTTWY	SMOOTHED THE WAY
ADEEHHORSSTTTY	THE SHORTEST DAY
ADEEHIIKLNNRTW	RAN LIKE THE WIND
ADEEHIILLNPTTY	PAINTED THE LILY
ADEEHIILNTTTW	WAIT TILL THE END
ADEEHIILNPSTTV	LIVED IN THE PAST
ADEEHIIINOPRRSV	PROVIDES AN HEIR
ADEEHIIOSSSTUV	AVOIDS THE ISSUE
ADEEHIJNOPRRRS	SHARP REJOINDER
ADEEHIKLLNNPTW	KEPT WELL IN HAND
ADEEHIKLORRSSY	YORKSHIRE DALES
ADEEHIKLOSSTTU	LAUD TO THE SKIES
ADEEHIKNNNOPST	KEPT ONE'S HAND IN
ADEEHILLLNNOTW	ALL DOWN THE LINE
ADEEHILLLPSSTT	SPILLED THE SALT
ADEEHILLMNOSST	ON THE SMALL SIDE
ADEEHILLORTTVW	DRIVE TO THE WALL
ADEEHILLOSUVVW	VAUDEVILLE SHOW
ADEEHILPRTUVW	DRIVE UP THE WALL
ADEEHILMMMPRTT	TRIMMED THE LAMP
ADEEHILNOOPRTY	RADIOTELEPHONY
ADEEHILNORSSTT	SEAT IN THE LORDS
ADEEHIMNOOPRTT	PAINTED THE ROOM
ADEEHINNOPSSSW	WIPES ONE'S HANDS
ADEEHIOOORSTTW	WORRIES TO DEATH
ADEEHKLOORRSTY	TAKE HOLY ORDERS
ADEEHKMNORSSTU	MAKES THE ROUNDS
ADEEHKMOPRSTTX	X MARKED THE SPOT
ADEEHKOOOSTTTW	TAKE TO THE WOODS
ADEEHLLLOOSWWW	SWALLOWED WHOLE
ADEEHLLNOPSTTW	DWELL ON THE PAST
ADEEHLLNPSSTUW	SENDS UP THE WALL
ADEEHLLOORTTVW	DROVE TO THE WALL
ADEEHLLOPRTUVW	DROVE UP THE WALL
ADEEHLLORRTTVW	TRAVEL THE WORLD
ADEEHLNOPSTTTW	DWELT ON THE PAST
ADEEHLNOSTTUVW	TWELVE THOUSAND
ADEEHLOPRRRSTY	THE LORDS PRAYER
ADEEHLORSTTTUY	STOUTHEARTEDLY
ADEEHMMNNOOSST	HAD ONE'S MOMENTS
ADEEHMMNNPPSTU	MANNED THE PUMPS
ADEEHMNORSSTTU	THOUSAND METRES
ADEEHNNOPRTTTU	TURNED ON THE TAP
ADEEHNNOORSSTW	ANSWERS THE DOOR
ADEEHNOORRSTUW	SWORE UNDER OATH
ADEEHNORRSSTTY	TRY ONES HARDEST
ADEEIIKLLMMRRT	ILL-TIMED REMARK
ADEEIIKLRRSTTT	TREATS LIKE DIRT
ADEEIIKMNOSSSS	SEEKS ADMISSION
ADEEIIILLLOOTTZ	ELIZA DOOLITTLE
ADEEIIILLNPRSTY	PRESIDENTIALLY
ADEEIIILMNNNOOS	ONE-DIMENSIONAL
ADEEIIILMNOPRST	MINERAL DEPOSIT
ADEEIIILNNOTTTW	WENT INTO DETAIL
ADEEIIILNPRSSTU	SPIRITUAL NEEDS
ADEEIIILOPRRSTV	PRIVATE SOLDIER
ADEEIIILORRRTTY	LITERARY EDITOR
ADEEIIIMMOOPRTV	IMPERATIVE MOOD

ADEEIIMNNNOSSY	EASY IN ONES MIND	ADEFHIIIKKLNRS	DRINK LIKE A FISH
ADEEIIMNNOOSTT	DEMONETISATION	ADEFHIIKKLNRSU	DRUNK LIKE A FISH
ADEEIIMNNOOTTZ	DEMONETIZATION	ADEFHIIMNPRRSW	WARM FRIENDSHIP
ADEEIIMNNORSST	ONE'S NAME IS DIRT	ADEFHILLNOOOPS	FINDS A LOOPHOLE
ADEEIIMNNOSSTT	SEDIMENTATIONS	ADEFHIMNOOPRST	HANDSOME PROFIT
ADEEIINNNOTVWW	VENETIAN WINDOW	ADEFHINOORRTTU	FOR THE DURATION
ADEEIINNOPRSTT	PREDESTINATION	ADEFHILLOORRTW	FOR ALL THE WORLD
ADEEIINRRSTTUV	RETURNED A VISIT	ADEFHLLNOOOOPU	FOUND A LOOPHOLE
ADEEIINSSSSSUV	DISSUASIVENESS	ADEFHLLOOORSTW	FOLLOWS THE ROAD
ADEEIJLMNOORTU	ROMEO AND JULIET	ADEFHLMNOOORRT	LORD OF THE MANOR
ADEEIKMMNNOPSU	MAKE ONES MIND UP	ADEFHLOORRSTWW	WAR OF THE WORLDS
	MAKE UP ONES MIND	ADEFHMNOORSSTU	MASTER OF HOUNDS
ADEEIKMNNOPSSS	SPEAKS ONE'S MIND	ADEFHNNOOOSSTU	OUT OF ONE'S HANDS
ADEEIKNOQSSSTU	ASKED QUESTIONS	ADEFIIINNOSSTT	DISINFESTATION
ADEEIILLNNORTTU	LORD LIEUTENANT	ADEFIILLNOSSTU	FALL INTO DISUSE
ADEEIILLOPRSTVY	POSTAL DELIVERY	ADEFIILNNNORTY	FRIENDLY NATION
ADEEIILLPRSSSST	SPELLS DISASTER	ADEFIILNNOSTUY	FAIL IN ONES DUTY
ADEEILNNRRSTUY	UNRESTRAINEDLY	ADEFIINNOOORRT	FOREORDINATION
ADEEILNORRSSWW	WORLD-WEARINESS	ADEFIINOSSSSTU	FASTIDIOUSNESS
ADEEIMMNNORRTTV	MIND OVER MATTER	ADEFIKKNNORSSV	KNIVES AND FORKS
ADEEIMNNORRSST	ARRONDISSEMENT	ADEFILLNORSSTW	FELL DOWNSTAIRS
ADEEIMNNORSSTTV	DEMONSTRATIVES	ADEFILMOOPRSSW	PEARLS OF WISDOM
ADEEIMNORSSTTW	TWISTED ONE'S ARM	ADEFILNNOOSSTU	FOUNDATIONLESS
ADEEINNOOPPRRT	PREPONDERATION	ADEFIMNNNOOOSW	A MIND OF ONE'S OWN
ADEEINNRRRSTTU	UNDER RESTRAINT	ADEFINOOPPSTTU	SNAPPED OUT OF IT
ADEEINOOPQSSTU	POSED A QUESTION	ADEFIOORRRSSTW	WAITS FOR ORDERS
ADEEINOOPSSSTT	DIES AT ONE'S POST	ADEFIOORRSSTTV	STRAITS OF DOVER
ADEEKLLNNOPRSU	PULLED ONE'S RANK	ADEFLLMNOOPRSW	NEW LAMPS FOR OLD
ADEEKLLPPSSTUU	PULLED UP STAKES	ADEFLNOOPRSTTY	FLOYD PATTERSON
ADEEKMMNOORTVW	MOVE DOWN-MARKET	ADEGGGIINPRRSU	GRUDGING PRAISE
ADEEKNPPRRSTUW	KEPT UNDER WRAPS	ADEGGGIKLNOORS	LOOKING DAGGERS
ADEELLNOOOPSTY	ONLY TOO PLEASED	ADEGGGLLNORSTU	STRUGGLED ALONG
ADEELLNORSSTVY	SEVENTY DOLLARS	ADEGGHHILNOOST	HOLDING HOSTAGE
ADEELMMNNOORWY	DOWN MEMORY LANE	ADEGGHHINORRTU	READING THROUGH
ADEELNNOPPRRTY	PREPONDERANTLY	ADEGGHIKMNNNOO	MADE IN HONG KONG
ADEELNNORSSSSU	SLANDEROUSNESS	ADEGGHILLNNNTY	HANDLING GENTLY
ADEELNNORSTUZZ	SNOZZLE DURANTE	ADEGGHINNORRTU	GATHERING ROUND
ADEELNORRRSSTV	LORDS TAVERNERS	ADEGGIIINNRSTT	DISINTEGRATING
ADEEMNNPPSSTUY	SUSPEND PAYMENT	ADEGGIIINPRVYZ	PRIZE-GIVING DAY
ADEEMNOPPPSTTY	STOPPED PAYMENT	ADEGGIIKNNPRUV	GAVE UP DRINKING
ADEEMOORRRSSTT	RESORTED TO ARMS	ADEGGIIILLNPTUY	PLEADING GUILTY
ADEENOORSSSTWW	WASTE ONES WORDS	ADEGGIILNRSSSV	DRIVING GLASSES
ADEENOPRRSSSSW	PRESSES ONWARDS	ADEGGIINNORTTW	GETTING A WORD IN
ADEENORRSTTUVY	ADVENTURE STORY	ADEGGIINNRRSSS	DRESSING IN RAGS
ADEENPRRRSTTUU	PUT UNDER ARREST	ADEGGILMNOOPRS	SPREADING GLOOM
ADEEORRRRSSSTT	STARTERS ORDERS	ADEGGIMNNNRSTUY	STUDYING GERMAN
ADEFFFHIILNRTU	FAITHFUL FRIEND	ADEGHHHINOPTTW	GOT THE WHIP-HAND
ADEFFGGHHNNORRU	GERARD HOFFNUNG	ADEGHHIINNNSTW	HANGS IN THE WIND
ADEFFGHINNOOST	DOFFING ONE'S HAT	ADEGHHIINNOTVW	HAVING DONE WITH
ADEFFGHINNORTU	FOUNDING FATHER	ADEGHHIINNORTTT	HITTING THE ROAD
ADEFFHHHIIOSTW	OFF WITH HIS HEAD	ADEGHHILLMNOPT	HOLDING THE PALM
ADEFFHILLNOSUY	FULLY-FASHIONED	ADEGHHILNOPSST	HOLDING THE PASS
ADEFFHMOOOORTT	FROM HEAD TO FOOT	ADEGHHINOPSTUW	DO THE WASHING-UP
ADEFGGHHILLNOT	HEADLONG FLIGHT	ADEGHHINOSTTUY	EIGHTY THOUSAND
ADEFGGHIILNOSU	DIES OF LAUGHING	ADEGHHINSSSTTT	STANDS THE SIGHT
ADEFGHHILNOTTY	LADY OF THE NIGHT	ADEGHHIRSTTTUU	AUGUST THE THIRD
ADEFGHHOORSTTW	WRATH OF THE GODS	ADEGHHLLNOPSTU	PLOUGHS THE LAND
ADEFGHILLNNOST	END OF ALL THINGS	ADEGHHLLNORSUY	HANDLES ROUGHLY
ADEFGHILNQSTUY	THE FLYING SQUAD	ADEGHHLNOPSSTU	PLOUGH THE SANDS
ADEFGHIMOORRTY	FAIRY GODMOTHER		PLOUGHS THE SAND
ADEFGHLNNNOORT	NORTH OF ENGLAND	ADEGHIINNNRSTW	RAISING THE WIND
ADEFGHLNNOOSTU	SOUTH OF ENGLAND	ADEGHIILLNNPTU	DULLING THE PAIN
ADEFGIIILLNNORR	FILLING AN ORDER	ADEGHIILLNSTTY	LETS IN DAYLIGHT
ADEFGIIMNORRST	TRANSMOGRIFIED	ADEGHIINNORTWY	WRITHED IN AGONY
ADEFGIIMNRSTTU	FIRST MAGNITUDE	ADEGHIINORSSTW	WHIGS AND TORIES
ADEFGIINNNOSWY	FINDING ONE'S WAY	ADEGHIINRSSTTU	RAISING THE DUST
ADEFGIINNPRRST	PARTING FRIENDS		THRUSTING ASIDE
ADEFGILNORSTTY	TREADING SOFTLY	ADEGHIKNOORTTW	WORKING TO DEATH
ADEFGIMNNORSST	AMONGST FRIENDS	ADEGHILMNNOOOT	DONE A MOONLIGHT
ADEFGKNOOORRTT	TOOK FOR GRANTED	ADEGHILMNNOTUY	HAUNTING MELODY
ADEFGLLNNOOOPU	PLAGUE OF LONDON	ADEGHILMNOOOST	DOES A MOONLIGHT

ADEGHILMNRSSTU	ENGLISH MUSTARD
ADEGHIMMOPRRRT	THIRD PROGRAMME
ADEGHINNNORSSW	WRING ONES HANDS
ADEGHINNNORSTY	TRYING ONE'S HAND
ADEGHINNNOSSSU	USING ONE'S HANDS
ADEGHINNNOSSTT	ONE-NIGHT STANDS
ADEGHINNNOSSTY	TYING ONE'S HANDS
ADEGHINNOOPTTY	PAYING ON THE DOT
ADEGHINNOOSTTT	STONING TO DEATH
ADEGHINNOPSSSU	HAS DESIGNS UPON
ADEGHINOPTTTTU	PUTTING TO DEATH
ADEGHINORSTTUW	SHOWN GRATITUDE
ADEGHIORSSTTUW	SHOWS GRATITUDE
ADEGHLOORSTTTW	GOT THE LAST WORD
ADEGHNNNOOOSST	GOT ONE'S HANDS ON
ADEGHNNOORSTTU	SAT ON THE GROUND
ADEGHNNORSTTUW	TURN DOWN THE GAS
ADEGIIIILMNRST	DEMILITARISING
ADEGIIIILMNRTZ	DEMILITARIZING
ADEGIIIILNORST	EDITORIALISING
ADEGIIIILNORTZ	EDITORIALIZING
ADEGIIILNNNNST	STANDING IN LINE
ADEGIIILNNOPTY	YIELDING A POINT
ADEGIIILNNPRVW	PREVAILING WIND
ADEGIIINNNORSTT	DISINTEGRATION
	DISORIENTATING
ADEGIIKLLMNNPSY	SPEAKING MILDLY
ADEGIIKLMNNNRU	RUNNING LIKE MAD
ADEGIILLMNORSY	DEMORALISINGLY
ADEGIILLMNORYZ	DEMORALIZINGLY
ADEGIILLMNPRSY	PYRAMID SELLING
ADEGIILNNSTTTT	LETTING IT STAND
ADEGIILNRSSSST	DISTRESS SIGNAL
ADEGIINNNNOPRSW	OPENING INWARDS
ADEGIINNNNOSWWY	WINDING ONE'S WAY
ADEGIINORRSSTT	DISINTEGRATORS
ADEGIINOSSTTUY	STAYING OUTSIDE
ADEGIKLNOPPSTT	STOPPED TALKING
ADEGIKNNNOSSTU	TAKEN SOUNDINGS
ADEGIKNNOSSSTU	TAKES SOUNDINGS
ADEGILLLNORSUY	DANGEROUSLY ILL
ADEGILLNOPTTUY	PLEAD NOT GUILTY
ADEGILMOORSSTT	DERMATOLOGISTS
ADEGILNNOOSSTT	STANDING TO LOSE
ADEGIMNNORSTUY	TUESDAY MORNING
ADEGINNNNRRRSU	RUNNING ERRANDS
ADEGINNNNOORSSU	SOUND REASONING
ADEGINNNNOPTTTU	PUTTING AN END TO
ADEGINNNNORRSTU	RUNS INTO DANGER
ADEGINNNPSSSTU	UPSTANDINGNESS
ADEGINNOORSSSTW	GONE DOWNSTAIRS
ADEGINNOPRRSSW	PRESSING ONWARD
ADEGINNPRSTTUU	PUTTING ASUNDER
ADEGINOOOOPRTTU	GOOD REPUTATION
ADEGKLNOOOORSSU	LOOKS DANGEROUS
ADEGLLOOORSTTY	TELL A GOOD STORY
ADEGMNNNNOOORW	DONE NO MAN WRONG
ADEGMNNNOOORSW	DOES NO MAN WRONG
ADEGNNOORSSTUY	STAY ONES GROUND
ADEGNOOOORTTUUU	OUT-AND-OUT ROGUE
ADEGNOORSSSTTU	SEND OUT TO GRASS
ADEHHIILLLLSSY	SHILLY-SHALLIED
ADEHHILNORTTWW	WHAT IN THE WORLD?
ADEHHIOOOPRSSTT	SHOOT THE RAPIDS
ADEHHLLMORRTYY	HYDROTHERMALLY
ADEHHLLOOOORSUY	ROYAL HOUSEHOLD
ADEHHLNOOOOTTT	TOO HOT TO HANDLE
ADEHIIIKLLNRWW	LIKE A WHIRLWIND
ADEHIILMNNORVY	LIVED IN HARMONY
ADEHIILNNNSSTU	ISLAND IN THE SUN
ADEHIIMNORSSTW	SHADOW MINISTER
ADEHIINNNOTTUW	NATION-WIDE HUNT
	NATIONWIDE HUNT
ADEHIINNRSTTWW	STRAW IN THE WIND
ADEHIINNSSTWWY	SWAYS IN THE WIND
ADEHIINPSSSSTU	STUDIES SPANISH
ADEHILMMORSSUY	SUMMER HOLIDAYS
ADEHILNNOORRTW	IN ANOTHER WORLD
ADEHILNNOOSSSS	SOILS ONE'S HANDS
ADEHILNNOPSSTU	LANDS IN THE SOUP
ADEHILNNOQRSUY	HOLDS AN ENQUIRY
ADEHILNNOQSSTU	HOLDS AN INQUEST
ADEHIMNOOORSTW	SHOW MODERATION
ADEHINNNOOSSST	SIT ON ONE'S HANDS
ADEHINNNOSTTUY	NINETY THOUSAND
ADEHINNORSSTTU	TURNS ON ITS HEAD
ADEHINOORRSSTW	ROADWORTHINESS
ADEHINOORSSTTT	STOOD THE STRAIN
ADEHINNORSSTWWY	THROWN SIDEWAYS
ADEHIORSSSTWWY	THROWS SIDEWAYS
ADEHJLNOORSSUY	JOSHUA REYNOLDS
ADEHLLNPPSSSUU	PUSHES AND PULLS
ADEHLMNNNOOOST	LANDS ON THE MOON
ADEHLOORRSSTYY	DOROTHY L.SAYERS
ADEHNNOOOORRTTW	NOT ANOTHER WORD!
ADEHNNOOORSTTW	DOWN ONE'S THROAT
ADEHNNOORRSTUW	SWORN UNDER OATH
ADEHNNOPPSSTUU	PUT ONE'S HANDS UP
	PUTS ONE'S HAND UP
ADEHNNNOSTTUWY	TWENTY THOUSAND
ADEHNORRSSTTWW	NORTHWESTWARDS
ADEHORSSSTTUWW	SOUTHWESTWARDS
ADEIIIKLNNSSTT	INSTANT DISLIKE
ADEIIILMNNNOSTY	DIMENSIONALITY
ADEIIILNPSSTTU	PLATITUDINISES
ADEIIILNPSTTUZ	PLATITUDINIZES
ADEIIILNRSSSTU	INDUSTRIALISES
ADEIIILNRSSTUZ	INDUSTRIALIZES
ADEIIINNOORSTT	DISORIENTATION
ADEIIINNNOPRSVZ	PANZER DIVISION
ADEIIILNOPRTVY	PROVIDENTIALLY
ADEIILLNOQRSUV	LIVED IN SQUALOR
ADEIILMNNNOOSX	MASON-DIXON LINE
ADEIILMNNOOSTW	TWO-DIMENSIONAL
ADEIILNNNOORSV	LIVER AND ONIONS
ADEIILNOOOPPRTU	POPULAR EDITION
ADEIILNOSTTUVY	ADVENTITIOUSLY
ADEIIMMNOPPSTT	DISAPPOINTMENT
ADEIIMNOOPRSSV	MADE PROVISIONS
ADEIINOPPSSTTU	DISPUTES A POINT
ADEIINORRSSSTT	TRANSISTORISED
ADEIINORRSSTTZ	TRANSISTORIZED
ADEIINRSSSSTUU	STUDIES RUSSIAN
ADEIJNOPPRSTUY	PUTS IN JEOPARDY
ADEIKKLLMNORSW	SKILLED WORKMAN
ADEILMOPRRTTUU	MORAL TURPITUDE
ADEILMOPRRSSSTU	IDOLATROUSNESS
ADEILNPRSSTTUY	STAPLE INDUSTRY
ADEIMMMNOOSTUV	MOVED MOUNTAINS
ADEIMMNOSSSSUU	ISSUED A SUMMONS
ADEIMNNOORSSTT	DEMONSTRATIONS
ADEINNNOOSSTWY	STOOD IN ONE'S WAY
ADEINNOOPSSTTT	STANDS ON TIPTOE
ADEINNORSSTTWW	WENT DOWNSTAIRS
ADEINOOOPPRRRTT	PROPORTIONATED
ADEINOOOORRTTTX	DEXTROROTATION
ADEKNOOOORSTTW	TOOK AT ONE'S WORD
ADELLMNOOPRRST	LORD PALMERSTON
ADELLOORRSSWWW	SWORD SWALLOWER
	SWORD-SWALLOWER
ADENNOOPPPRTUW	PUT DOWN ON PAPER
ADENNORSSSSTTU	TOSSES AND TURNS

ADENOOOORSSTTT	STARTED TOO SOON
ADENORSTTTWWYY	TWENTY-TWO YARDS
ADEOOOORRRTTTXY	DEXTROROTATORY
ADFFHILNOOORSW	WORLD OF FASHION
ADFFHNOOORRTTW	NORTH OF WATFORD
ADFFIIMNNOORTU	FIRM FOUNDATION
ADFGGINORRRSUW	SURGING FORWARD
ADFGHINOPRRSUW	PUSHING FORWARD
ADFGHINORRRSUW	RUSHING FORWARD
ADFGIKLNOOORRW	LOOKING FORWARD
ADFGILNOOPRSSU	GROUP OF ISLANDS
ADFGILNOORSTWW	FLOWING TOWARDS
ADFGINOPRRTTUW	PUTTING FORWARD
ADFHMNNOOSSTUY	MONTH OF SUNDAYS
ADFIILLMOOPRSW	PILLAR OF WISDOM
ADFIILNNOOSSTU	FINDS A SOLUTION
ADFILNNOOOSTUU	FOUND A SOLUTION
ADFINOOPRRSTUW	PUTS IN A WORD FOR
ADFNOORRSSTTTY	STONY STRATFORD
ADGGGHHILNHRSTU	STRUGGLING HARD
ADGGGHHOORSSTYY	SHAGGY-DOG STORY
ADGGHHHINORSTU	DASHING THROUGH
ADGGHIILNNOOOY	GOING ON HOLIDAY
ADGGHINNOOOOTT	ON TO A GOOD THING
ADGGHINNOPRTUY	HANGING UP TO DRY
ADGGIIILLLMNOW	WILLIAM GOLDING
ADGGIINNNNORRTU	TRAINING GROUND
ADGGILLNNNORTU	TRUNDLING ALONG
ADGGIMNNOOORSY	SAY GOOD MORNING
ADGGIMNNOPRSTU	STAMPING GROUND
ADGGINNNNORRUU	RUNNING AGROUND
ADGGINOPRRSUWW	GROWING UPWARDS
ADGHHHILNNOTUW	HUNT HIGH AND LOW
ADGHHIKLLNOOOW	LOOK HIGH AND LOW
ADGHIIKLNOORWY	WORKING HOLIDAY
ADUGHMNNOOPRRSY	GYNANDROMORPHS
ADGIIMNNOOPRRYY	GYNANDROMORPHY
ADGHOOOPPSTUUW	PUT UP A GOOD SHOW
ADGIIIINNSTTTU	ATTITUDINISING
ADGIIIINNTTTUZ	ATTITUDINIZING
ADGIILLLNNOTUY	LONGITUDINALLY
ADGIILLMNNOUWW	WALLOWING IN MUD
ADGIILNOOSSTWW	SOWING WILD OATS
ADGIILNOPPRSVY	DISAPPROVINGLY
ADGIINNOORSSTT	GOODS IN TRANSIT
ADGIINNOORSSTY	STAYING INDOORS
ADGIINNOPRTTUW	PUTTING IN A WORD
ADGIKNOOOOPRTT	TOOK IN GOOD PART
ADGILLLMOOTUUW	MUTUAL GOODWILL
ADGILOPPPSSTUY	PUPPY-DOGS TAILS
ADGINNNORRRSUU	RUN RINGS AROUND
ADHHIILNOSTUWY	WHITSUN HOLIDAY
ADHHIKNOOTTUWY	WHAT DO YOU THINK?
ADHHINORSTTTUY	THIRTY THOUSAND
ADHIIKPRRRSTTY	THIRD-PARTY RISK
ADHIILLLNORRSW	SIR ROWLAND HILL
ADHIILNNNOOOPS	HOLDS AN OPINION
ADHIILNNOQRSUY	HOLDS AN INQUIRY
ADHIINNOORSTTZ	DISTANT HORIZON
ADHILNNOPPRRTU	RANDOLPH TURPIN
ADHLMOOORRSSWY	LORD MAYORS SHOW
ADHNOPPRSTUUUY	PUT YOUR HANDS UP
ADIIILNRSSSTTU	INDUSTRIALISTS
ADIILLLLMNOORS	MILLION DOLLARS
ADIILLOPRRSSTU	LORDS SPIRITUAL
ADIILNOORSTTUW	WORLD SITUATION
ADIILOPSSTTUUY	DISPUTATIOUSLY
ADIIMMMNNOPTUU	AMMUNITION DUMP
ADIIMNNOOSSTTU	DOMINION STATUS
ADIIMNOOOPPRRT	RAPID PROMOTION
ADILLMNNOOOSSS	SOLOMON ISLANDS

ADIMNOOORRSSTW	DOWNSTAIRS ROOM
ADINNRSSSTTTUW	TWISTS AND TURNS
ADKMMOORRSUWYY	YOU MARK MY WORDS!
ADMNNNOOOORSUY	ANONYMOUS DONOR
AEEEEEGGHMMNNTY	ENGAGE THE ENEMY
AEEEEEGLNRRRSV	GENERAL RESERVE
AEEEEEHKMPSSSY	MAKE SHEEP'S EYES
AEEEEEHLNRSSTW	RENEWS THE LEASE
AEEEEEKLPRRSSU	PLEASURE SEEKER
AEEEEEKNNOPPSY	KEEPS AN EYE OPEN
AEEEEEMMRRSTUX	EXTREME MEASURE
AEEEEFFHKKOTTW	TAKE THE WEEK OFF
AEEEEEFFILLNOSW	NEW LEASE OF LIFE
AEEEEEFGGILNNOS	FEELING ONE'S AGE
AEEEEFGHHILNTT	FEELING THE HEAT
AEEEEFILLNNOSW	NEW LEASE ON LIFE
AEEEEFILNPSTVV	FIVE PAST ELEVEN
AEEEEEFLLNOPSSS	PLEASES ONESELF
AEEEEFLNOORPSY	APPLE OF ONE'S EYE
AEEEEEFLNOPPRRS	PREPARE ONESELF
AEEEEEFLNOPRSST	REPEATS ONESELF
AEEEEFFNOSSSSTY	FEASTS ONE'S EYES
AEEEEEGGHMSSSTT	GETS THE MESSAGE
AEEEEEGGILMNNRT	GENERAL MEETING
AEEEEEGGLNOSSST	GET ONE'S SEA LEGS
AEEEEGHHHIOTVV	GIVE THE HEAVE-HO
AEEEEGHHNNPSTX	HANG THE EXPENSE
AEEEEEGHMNSSSTT	SENT THE MESSAGE
AEEEEEGHHNORSSV	HAS ONE'S REVENGE
AEEEEGIINPRRVV	GIVEN A REPRIEVE
AEEEEGIIPRRSVV	GIVES A REPRIEVE
AEEEEGIKNNNOPY	KEEPING AN EYE ON
AEEEEGINSSTTVV	VEGETATIVENESS
AEEEEEGLMMNRSTU	LEG MEASUREMENT
AEEEEGLNNPRRTV	EVERGREEN PLANT
AEEEEGMMNNORSST	SENT A MESSENGER
AEEEEEGMNORSSTU	GET ONE'S MEASURE
AEEEEEHHLMNTTVY	MAY THE ELEVENTH
AEEEEEHLNORSSTT	STEEL ONE'S HEART
AEEEEEHNNOOPSSY	HAS ONE'S EYE OPEN
AEEEEIKLNOOPRS	KEEP A LOOSE REIN
AEEEEIKMNNPRST	EMINENT SPEAKER
AEEEEILMNNRSST	ELEMENTARINESS
AEEELLINNPRRTTT	INTERPENETRATE
AEEEEINPRRSTTV	REPRESENTATIVE
AEEEEIPRSSSVWX	EXPRESSES A VIEW
AEEEEKMMNORSST	MEETS ONE'S MAKER
AEEEEELLMNRRTUY	ELEMENTARY RULE
AEEEELMNPRTTXY	EXTREME PENALTY
AEEEEELNPQRSSUU	QUEENS PLEASURE
AEEEENNOORRSVY	RAN ONE'S EYE OVER
AEEFFFNNOPPRSSX	SPARE NO EXPENSE
AEEEENORSSSTVY	AVERTS ONE'S EYES
AEEEFFFKLNOOST	TAKE ONESELF OFF
AEEEEFFFNORRSSU	REFUSES AN OFFER
AEEEEFFGILMNOOS	GAME OF ONES LIFE
AEEEEFFHKMORSTT	MAKES THE EFFORT
AEEEEFFHNOPSSTT	FEAST OF STEPHEN
AEEEEFFLLNNOOST	FALL ON ONES FEET
AEEEEFFLLNORSTT	FLATTER ONESELF
AEEEEFFLOOPRRTW	FLOW OF REPARTEE
AEEEEFFNOORRRST	OR NEAREST OFFER
AEEEFGGILNNRST	FEELING STRANGE
	STRANGE FEELING
AEEEFGHHIRSTTW	FEATHERWEIGHTS
AEEEFGHIILNNPT	FEELING THE PAIN
AEEEFGHILMNNOS	FEELING NO SHAME
AEEEFGHILMNOPT	GENIE OF THE LAMP
AEEEFGHINNOPST	OPENING THE SAFE
AEEEFGHINNORSS	SENSE OF HEARING
AEEEFGHLMORSTU	RULES OF THE GAME

AEEEFGHLOOPTTU	TOP OF THE LEAGUE
AEEEFGIILNPRRT	REPEATING RIFLE
AEEEFGIKLNPRSY	SPEAKING FREELY
AEEEFGILNNOSST	SEATING ONESELF
AEEEFGILNNOSWY	FEELING ONE'S WAY
AEEEFGMORRRTTT	MATTER OF REGRET
AEEEFHHIKLSSTW	THE FLESH IS WEAK
AEEEFHHLLLORRT	HELL FOR LEATHER
	HELL-FOR-LEATHER
AEEEFHHOORRSTY	HORSE OF THE YEAR
AEEEFHIIRRSSTT	IRISH FREE STATE
AEEEFHIKMORRTT	TAKE IT FROM HERE
AEEEFHILMMNRST	FIREMANS HELMET
AEEEFHLLORTTTW	LETTER OF THE LAW
AEEEFHLMNOOPPT	MAN OF THE PEOPLE
AEEEFIILNNRRTT	INTERFERENTIAL
AEEEFIKLNOSSST	STAKES ONE'S LIFE
AEEEFILLNNOPSX	EXPLAIN ONESELF
AEEEFILLNOPPSS	APPLIES ONESELF
AEEEFILLNOSSUV	VALUES ONE'S LIFE
AEEEFILLNPRRTY	PREFERENTIALLY
AEEEFILNOOSSTV	TO SAVE ONE'S LIFE
AEEEFILPSTTVVW	FIVE PAST TWELVE
AEEEFINORRSTTT	RATE OF INTEREST
AEEEFINORSTTVW	FIVE TWOS ARE TEN
	TWO FIVES ARE TEN
AEEEFIOPRRSTWZ	PAIR OF TWEEZERS
AEEEFKOPRSSSTU	REFUSES TO SPEAK
AEEEFLLOOPRSUV	LOVE OF PLEASURE
AEEEFLMNORRSUW	MAUREEN FLOWERS
AEEEFLNORSSSST	ASSERTS ONESELF
AEEEFLOPRSTTUU	PUTS OUT A FEELER
AEEEFMNOPSSSTT	STAMPS ONE'S FEET
AEEEFMNPRSSTUY	REFUSES PAYMENT
AEEEFNORRSSTTW	WATER-SOFTENERS
AEEEGGGIMNNNRT	ENGAGEMENT RING
AEEEGGGLMNNNOT	LONG ENGAGEMENT
AEEEGGHHORRTTT	GATHER TOGETHER
AEEEGGHHINNOPTT	OPENING THE GATE
AEEEGGHHNNOOSTT	GONE ON THE STAGE
AEEEGGHNOOSSTT	GOES ON THE STAGE
AEEEGGILNNRSTV	STEEL ENGRAVING
AEEEGGILNOSSSV	SEA-GOING VESSEL
AEEEGGINRSSSSV	AGGRESSIVENESS
AEEEGGLMNNRRTTU	URGENT TELEGRAM
AEEEGGLNOOSSST	GOT ONE'S SEA LEGS
AEEEGGLNORSUVY	GAVE GENEROUSLY
AEEEGHHHIKLNTTW	TAKING THE WHEEL
AEEEGHHIKMSTTW	MAKES THE WEIGHT
AEEEGHHIOPRTTW	GREAT WHITE HOPE
AEEEGHHIRRSSTVV	GAVE THE SHIVERS
AEEEGHHMMNNOORT	HOME ON THE RANGE
AEEEGHHNNOSSTT	GNASH ONES TEETH
AEEEGGHHNOPSTUV	GAVE ONE THE PUSH
AEEEGHHOORTTTT	GO TO THE THEATRE
AEEEGHIIKNPRTT	KEEP A TIGHT REIN
AEEEGHIILLSTVW	GAVE THE WILLIES
AEEEGHIILLLNTTT	TELLING THE TALE
AEEEGHILNNSTTV	LEAVING THE NEST
AEEEGHILNOPSTV	GAVE ONE THE SLIP
AEEEGHIILRSTTW	SWELTERING HEAT
AEEEGHINRSSTUV	RHESUS NEGATIVE
AEEEGHKLNNPTTU	TAKEN THE PLUNGE
AEEEGHKLNPSTTU	TAKES THE PLUNGE
AEEEGHKNOOSTTT	GONE TO THE STAKE
AEEEGHKOOSSTTT	GOES TO THE STAKE
AEEEGHLMNNRSTU	GENTLEMAN USHER
AEEEGHLMORRTTU	THERMOREGULATE
AEEEGHLNOPRRSS	SELENOGRAPHERS
AEEEGHLNPRSTTT	GRASP THE NETTLE
AEEEGHNNOSTTTW	WENT ON THE STAGE

AEEEGHNOOOPRTT	GONE TO THE OPERA
AEEEGHNRSSSTUW	GUESS THE ANSWER
AEEEGHOOOPRSTT	GOES TO THE OPERA
AEEEGIIMMNNOPRT	OPEN-AIR MEETING
AEEEGIKLLLOPSS	SLEEPS LIKE A LOG
AEEEGIKMNPRRSW	SWEEPING REMARK
AEEEGILLMNNRTT	LITTLE GREEN MAN
AEEEGILNNOPRTT	OPENING A LETTER
AEEEGILNNORRSY	ROYAL ENGINEERS
AEEEGILNRSTTUV	NEGATIVE RESULT
AEEEGINNNORTTX	NEXT GENERATION
AEEEGINNNOSTTX	GET AN EXTENSION
AEEEGINNOSSSTV	GIVE ONES ASSENT
AEEEGINOPRRSSU	GENEROUS PRAISE
AEEEGINOPSSTVV	GIVE UP ONES SEAT
AEEEGINORSSTTV	SOVEREIGN STATE
AEEEGLMNNRTVWY	TWELVE ANGRY MEN
AEEEGMNOORSSTU	GOT ONE'S MEASURE
AEEEGNNNORSSTV	VENTS ONE'S ANGER
AEEEGNNORRSTUU	GENEROUS NATURE
AEEEHHHIOSSTTW	HE WHO HESITATES
AEEEHHHIRSSTVV	HAVE THE SHIVERS
AEEEHHHMMMRRTTW	THREW THE HAMMER
AEEEHHIILLSTVW	HAVE THE WILLIES
AEEEHHIILPSTVWY	HEAVY WITH SLEEP
AEEEHHIMMRRTTUX	HEATHER MIXTURE
AEEEHHINOSSTTU	SEAT IN THE HOUSE
AEEEHHHLNNOOPRT	HELP ONE ANOTHER
AEEEHHNNRRRTTTU	NEARER THE TRUTH
AEEEHHOPPRRTTW	WEATHER PROPHET
AEEEHHORRSSTTW	WATER THE HORSES
AEEEHIJKKLLLSY	SHAKE LIKE JELLY
AEEEHIJMSSSTTW	JESSIE MATTHEWS
AEEEHIKLLNRTTT	TAKEN THE TILLER
AEEEHIKLLRSTTT	TAKES THE TILLER
AEEEHIKMKNNORTY	RAKE IN THE MONEY
AEEEHIKNNOOPRS	KEEP ONES HAIR ON
AEEEHILLLMMNRV	HERMAN MELVILLE
AEEEHILNPPRSVY	APPREHENSIVELY
AEEEHILNQSTTTU	LAST IN THE QUEUE
AEEEHILNRSTTTW	THE WINTERS TALE
AEEEHILORRTVVW	THREW A VEIL OVER
AEEEHIMMNPRSTU	HIP MEASUREMENT
AEEEHIMNNRSTTT	MAN IN THE STREET
AEEEHIMNORSSTY	RAISES THE MONEY
AEEEHIMOPRSSTT	RAISES THE TEMPO
AEEEHINNPRPSTW	IN THE NEWSPAPER
AEEEHINRSSSTTY	STRAINS THE EYES
AEEEHINSSSTUVX	EXHAUSTIVENESS
AEEEHKLOPRSSTU	KEEPS LATE HOURS
AEEEHKNNOOPSST	KEEPS ONE'S HAT ON
AEEEHKNOSTTTTW	WENT TO THE STAKE
AEEEHLLORSTUXY	HETEROSEXUALLY
AEEEHLNOORSSST	LOSES ONE'S HEART
AEEEHLNOORSSTT	STOLE ONE'S HEART
AEEEHLNOPRRSST	LEARNS THE ROPES
AEEEHLNOPRRSTT	LEARNT THE ROPES
AEEEHMNNOORSSTV	REMOVES ONE'S HAT
AEEEHNNOOPRSST	OPENS ONE'S HEART
AEEEHNOOPRTTTW	WENT TO THE OPERA
AEEEHOOQRRRTTTU	QUARTER TO THREE
AEEEIIINNPRSTT	PENITENTIARIES
AEEEIIKMNQRSSU	MAKES ENQUIRIES
AEEEIIILLNPRTXY	EXPERIENTIALLY
AEEEIIILLNRSSTT	ILLITERATENESS
AEEEIIILMNNSSTT	SENTIMENTALISE
AEEEIIILMNNSTTZ	SENTIMENTALIZE
AEEEIIIMNNPRSTV	IMPERATIVENESS
AEEEIIINPPRSSTV	SENSITIVE PAPER
AEEEIIINPRRTTTV	INTERPRETATIVE
AEEEIIQSSTTTUX	EXQUISITE TASTE

AEEEIKLLOPPSST	SLEEPS LIKE A TOP	AEEFGIIKLLOSTV	FITS LIKE A GLOVE
AEEEIKLNOOPRST	KEPT A LOOSE REIN	AEEFGIILLNNOST	EATING ONE'S FILL
AEEEILLMNPRTXY	EXPERIMENTALLY	AEEFGIIMMNRRST	FERRIMAGNETISM
AEEEILLMPPRSSU	SIMPLE PLEASURE	AEEFGIINNQRRTU	ENQUIRING AFTER
AEEEILLNSSSSTT	STAINLESS STEEL	AEEFGIINRSSTUV	FIGURATIVENESS
AEEEILMNNPRSTT	PRESENTIMENTAL	AEEFGIKLMOSSTT	GAME OF SKITTLES
AEEEILNOPRSTUV	SUPERELEVATION	AEEFGIKLNORSST	STRIKE ONE'S FLAG
AEEEILOPPRRTVY	PREOPERATIVELY	AEEFGIKNNOSSSW	SIGN OF WEAKNESS
AEEEIMNNNNRSTTT	ENTERTAINMENTS	AEEFGIKNORSSSV	ASK FORGIVENESS
AEEEIMNNORSSTW	WRITES ONE'S NAME	AEEFGILMNNNSSU	MEANINGFULNESS
AEEEIMNNRRTUUV	UNREMUNERATIVE	AEEFGILMNNOPSU	GONE UP IN FLAMES
AEEEIMNOPRTTXY	EXTEMPORANEITY	AEEFGILMNNOSSU	AMUSING ONESELF
AEEEINNOPRRSTT	REPRESENTATION	AEEFGILMNOPRRS	PERFORMING SEAL
AEEEINNOPSSSTY	SPAT IN ONE'S EYES	AEEFGILMNOPSSU	GOES UP IN FLAMES
AEEEINNORSSSTY	STRAIN ONES EYES	AEEFGILNPRSSTT	FALTERING STEPS
AEEEINPRSSSSUV	PERSUASIVENESS	AEEFGIMMNNOPTY	EMPTY OF MEANING
AEEEKKNNORSWYY	NEW YORK YANKEES	AEEFGIMMNORRST	FERROMAGNETISM
AEEEELLNOORSTWW	WOOLLEN SWEATER	AEEFGKLNOOPRST	TAKEN FOR GOSPEL
AEEEILLNOPRRSTT	PERSONAL LETTER	AEEFGKLOOPNOOT	TAKES FOR GOSPEL
AEEFFILNOPRSTUV	PETER O'SULLEVAN	AEEFGLNNRSSTUU	UNGRATEFULNESS
AEEEELLOPSSTTVW	TWELVE APOSTLES	AEEFGOOPRRRSST	RATE OF PROGRESS
AEEEELMNNORSTTY	SOLEMN ENTREATY	AEEFHHINOSSSTT	SETS THE FASHION
AEEEELMNORRRSST	NAMELESS TERROR	AEEFHHLNNOPSVY	SHOVE-HALFPENNY
AEEEELMOPRRTTUW	LOW TEMPERATURE	AEEFHHNOOORSUV	HOUSE OF HANOVER
AEEEELNNOOORSSS	LOSE ONES REASON	AEEFHIIKRRSTTW	STRIKE WITH FEAR
AEEEELNOOPSSSTV	LEAVES ONE'S POST	AEEFHIKNNOSSST	SHAKEN ONE'S FIST
AEEEELNOPRRSTUV	PLEASE TURN OVER	AEEFHIKNOSSSST	SHAKES ONE'S FIST
AEEEELNRRSSSTTU	RESTLESS NATURE	AEEFHILMNOPRSU	REMAINS HOPEFUL
AEEEEMNNOOSSTWY	WASTE ONES MONEY	AEEFHILMORSTTT	FOR THE LAST TIME
AEEEEMNOOPRSTUX	EXTEMPORANEOUS	AEEFHILNNOPSTW	TWO HALFPENNIES
AEEEEMNORRRRSTV	TRANMERE ROVERS	AEEFHILNOOSSST	LOSES ONE'S FAITH
AEEEENNORSSSTUX	EXTRANEOUSNESS	AEEFHILNOPRSTV	SEVENTH OF APRIL
AEEEENNORSTTWYY	TWENTY-ONE YEARS	AEEFHILNORSSTT	LIFTS ONE'S HEART
AEEEENOQRRSTTUV	QUARTER TO SEVEN	AEEFHIMNOORRTT	THE REFORMATION
AEEEENQSSSSTTUU	STATUESQUENESS	AEEFHIMNOSTTXY	SIXTEENTH OF MAY
AEEEEOPPRRSSSUV	SERVES A PURPOSE	AEEFHIMNOTTTWY	TWENTIETH OF MAY
AEEFFFHHILTTUW	THE FAITHFUL FEW	AEEFHINNNOORTT	IN THE AFTERNOON
AEEFFFHIMNOTTY	FIFTEENTH OF MAY	AEEFHINOORRTTU	HEIR TO A FORTUNE
AEEFFFGHIINNNRT	FANNING THE FIRE	AEEFHKMMOOSSTT	MAKES THE MOST OF
AEEFFGHNORSTTT	FEAT OF STRENGTH	AEEFHLLLMMOPST	SMELL OF THE LAMP
AEEFFGILMNOPRR	PERFORMING FLEA	AEEFHLLORSSTUW	THESE FOUR WALLS
AEEFFGILMNPRRU	FAR-FLUNG EMPIRE	AEEFHLMNOSSSST	FATHOMLESSNESS
AEEFFGMNORSSUW	WOMENS SUFFRAGE	AEEFHMMMNNOOTT	MAN OF THE MOMENT
AEEFFHHIRRRSTW	FRESHWATER FISH	AEEFHNOORSSSTU	THE FOUR SEASONS
AEEFFHHKOOOTTT	TOOK THE HEAT OFF	AEEFHOORRSSSTW	WARS OF THE ROSES
AEEFFHHNNORTTTU	TURN OFF THE HEAT	AEEFIIKLLMNSSY	FAMILY LIKENESS
	TURN THE HEAT OFF	AEEFIIKPRRSTTZ	TAKE FIRST PRIZE
AEEFFHIIINRSTT	FAT IS IN THE FIRE	AEEFIILMNORTTV	INTERVAL OF TIME
AEEFFHILMNOOTY	ONE OF THE FAMILY	AEEFIILNNRRSTT	INTERNAL STRIFE
AEEFFHIMOPPSTW	WIPES OFF THE MAP	AEEFIINNORRRTU	INFERIOR NATURE
AEEFFHKLMRSTUY	MAKES THE FUR FLY	AEEFIINOQRSSTU	FIRES A QUESTION
AEEFFIKLOPRSST	SPEAK FOR ITSELF	AEEFIKLLMNOSTY	FAMILY SKELETON
AEEFFILNNOORRS	RAN FOR ONE'S LIFE	AEEFIKLLORSTWW	FLOWS LIKE WATER
AEEFFKORRSSSTU	SUFFERS A STROKE	AEEFILMNNOORZZ	MEZZANINE FLOOR
AEEFFLLNOOSTUU	FALLEN OUT OF USE	AEEFILMNNPSTUW	WENT UP IN FLAMES
AEEFFNOOPRRSST	SPARES NO EFFORT	AEEFILMNOPRTTY	FLY INTO A TEMPER
AEEFGGHHINOTTT	GET THE HANG OF IT	AEEFILNNOORTTV	FRONT ELEVATION
AEEFGGHILNNNOS	HANGING ONESELF	AEEFILNNORSSST	STRAINS ONESELF
AEEFGGHILNRSTT	FLIGHT SERGEANT	AEEFILNORSSSST	SELF-ASSERTIONS
AEEFGGIILLNRSTU	SELF-REGULATING	AEEFINPSTTTVWY	TWENTY-FIVE PAST
AEEFGGILLNNOSSS	GASSING ONESELF	AEEFKLLNOOSSTT	TALKS TO ONESELF
AEEFGGINNORSSW	WAGS ONE'S FINGER	AEEFLLMNNOOSTUW	LAW UNTO ONESELF
AEEFGHHINRRSTT	THREE FARTHINGS	AEEFLLNNOOOPSTW	AT ONE FELL SWOOP
AEEFGHHIOPRRST	SPRIG OF HEATHER	AEEFLLNOOSSTYY	SENSE OF LOYALTY
AEEFGHIILNNRTW	INFRINGE THE LAW	AEEFLLOOORRSTT	FOR SALE OR TO LET
AEEFGHIILNSTTT	FAILING THE TEST	AEEFLNNOORSUW	ONE'S OWN FUNERAL
AEEFFGHINOORTTV	FOOT IN THE GRAVE	AEEFLNNOOOPSTU	ONE TEASPOONFUL
AEEFGHIOPPRRTT	PREPARE TO FIGHT	AEEFMOORSSTTTW	FROM EAST TO WEST
AEEFGHJLLNOTUW	LAW OF THE JUNGLE	AEEFNOOPRRSSTW	WATERPROOFNESS
AEEFGHLORRSSTW	GATHERS FLOWERS	AEEGGGHHINNTTT	GETTING THE HANG
AEEFGHOOTTTUWY	GET OUT OF THE WAY	AEEGGHHHORSTTU	THROUGH THE AGES

959

AEEGGHHHLNOSTTU	GETS THE LAUGH ON
AEEGGHHNRRSTTT	GATHER STRENGTH
AEEGGHHOPSTTUV	GAVE UP THE GHOST
AEEGGHIIIMNPTV	THIEVING MAGPIE
AEEGGHIILNNSTV	GIVEN THE SIGNAL
AEEGGHIILNSSTV	GIVES THE SIGNAL
AEEGGHIIMNNNTW	WINNING THE GAME
AEEGGHIINRSSTT	SEEING STRAIGHT
AEEGGHIKNOTTTY	GETTING THE OKAY
AEEGGHIMNNNORR	HERMANN GOERING
AEEGGHINNOOSSW	SHOWING ONE'S AGE
AEEGGHINNPRRTTU	TURNING THE PAGE
AEEGGHINOORRRS	GEORGE HARRISON
AEEGGHINORRSST	GATHERING ROSES
AEEGGHLNNOOTWY	GONE THE LONG WAY
AEEGGHLNOOSTWY	GOES THE LONG WAY
AEEGGHNNOOPRRT	ROENTGENOGRAPH
AEEGGHNNOOSTTW	GETS ON THE WAGON
AEEGGIIIKNNPTW	KEEPING WAITING
AEEGGIILNNNOTT	GETTING A LINE ON
AEEGGIIMNNSSTT	GETTING IN A MESS
AEEGGIIINNPRSTV	GIVING A PRESENT
AEEGGIINNSTTTW	GETTING IN A STEW
AEEGGIINORSSTT	SEGREGATIONIST
AEEGGIINRRSTTV	TERGIVERSATING
AEEGGIKLNNOOOS	LOOKING ONE'S AGE
AEEGGILLNNORTU	OUTGENERALLING
AEEGGILNORSTVV	REVOLVING STAGE
AEEGGILNPRTTUY	GETTING UP EARLY
AEEGGIMNNOOTTV	GETTING A MOVE ON
AEEGGIMNPSTTTU	GETTING UP STEAM
AEEGGINNOSTTWY	GETTING ONE'S WAY
AEEGGINOOORTTV	GET INTO A GROOVE
AEEGGINORRSSSU	GREGARIOUSNESS
AEEGGMNNOORRST	ROENTGENOGRAMS
AEEGGNOORSSTTU	GETS ONE'S RAG OUT
AEEGHHHIILPRTT	APRIL THE EIGHTH
AEEGHHIIMRTTTT	AT THE RIGHT TIME
AEEGHHIKLLLSTV	HIGH-LEVEL TALKS
AEEGHHILNOPRTY	PLAYING THE HERO
AEEGHHINNOOPTV	HOPING TO HEAVEN
AEEGHHLORSSTUU	SLAUGHTERHOUSE
AEEGHHMMNNOORTU	MORE THAN ENOUGH
AEEGHHNSTTTTUU	AUGUST THE TENTH
AEEGHHRSTTTTTU	GETS AT THE TRUTH
AEEGHIIILMPRTW	IMPERIAL WEIGHT
AEEGHIIKNPRTTT	KEPT A TIGHT REIN
AEEGHIILMNNPSX	SHINING EXAMPLE
AEEGHIILNNPPTT	TAPPING THE LINE
AEEGHIIMNPSSTT	PASSING THE TIME
AEEGHIINNOPRTU	GONE UP IN THE AIR
AEEGHIINNORSST	GETS IN ONE'S HAIR
AEEGHIINNPRSST	PARENTHESISING
AEEGHIINNPRSTZ	PARENTHESIZING
AEEGHIINOPRSTU	GOES UP IN THE AIR
AEEGHIINPPPRTY	PAYING THE PIPER
AEEGHIINRRSTTW	WITHERING STARE
AEEGHIIPRRRSST	PARISH REGISTER
AEEGHIKLLMNNST	ALL THE KINGS MEN
AEEGHIKMMNOSST	MAKES SOMETHING
AEEGHIKMNNNRTU	MAKE THE RUNNING
AEEGHIKNOPRSTT	KEEP STRAIGHT ON
AEEGHIKORSTTVW	GAVE IT THE WORKS
AEEGHILLNOPPUV	GIVEN UP ALL HOPE
AEEGHILLNOPRSW	LEGAL OWNERSHIP
AEEGHILLNPSSST	SELLING THE PASS
AEEGHILLOPPSUV	GIVES UP ALL HOPE
AEEGHILMNOORTV	LEAVING THE ROOM
AEEGHILNNOOPTY	PILE ON THE AGONY
AEEGHILNRSTTTW	WRITES AT LENGTH
AEEGHIMNOOSTTT	SOMETHING TO EAT
AEEGHIMNORSTTX	SOMETHING EXTRA
AEEGHIMOPRRSSS	SEISMOGRAPHERS
AEEGHINOPPRSST	STEPPING ASHORE
AEEGHINPSSSTTT	PASSING THE TEST
AEEGHINRSSTTTW	WATERTIGHTNESS
AEEGHIOQRRTTTU	QUARTER TO EIGHT
AEEGHKLNNOPSTT	SPOKEN AT LENGTH
AEEGHLMOORTTUV	MOVE TO LAUGHTER
AEEGHLNNOTTWWY	WENT THE LONG WAY
AEEGHLNNRTTTUU	RUN THE GAUNTLET
AEEGHLOOPRRSTT	PETROL SHORTAGE
AEEGHLOQRRSSTU	SHORT SQUARE LEG
AEEGHMMMNORTTU	GATHER MOMENTUM
AEEGHMNORRTTTU	ROUGH TREATMENT
AEEGHNNORRSUUV	RAVENOUS HUNGER
AEEGHNOPSSTTTU	PUTS ON THE STAGE
AEEGIIILLLMTTY	ILLEGITIMATELY
AEEGIIIILLNNRST	INERTIA SELLING
AEEGIIILLNNSTT	INTELLIGENTSIA
AEEGIIILRRRSTU	IRREGULARITIES
AEEGIIJKNNPSST	SPEAKING IN JEST
AEEGIIKLNNOOOV	GIVE ONE A LOOK IN
AEEGIIKLNNOPSV	SPEAKING NO EVIL
AEEGIILLLNNRTT	LITTLE LEARNING
AEEGIILLMNRTTV	TRAVELLING TIME
AEEGIILLNNPRTT	INTERPELLATING
AEEGIILLNSSSSV	SAILING VESSELS
AEEGIILMNNNRSTT	MELTING IN TEARS
AEEGIILNNNNORSV	EARN ONES LIVING
AEEGIILNORSTUZ	REGULATION SIZE
AEEGIIMNNNNORTU	MOUNTAINEERING
AEEGIIMNOPRSSV	GAVE PERMISSION
AEEGIIMNOPRTVY	PAYING OVERTIME
AEEGIIMNORSTTV	OVERESTIMATING
AEEGIINNNORRSS	RING IN ONES EARS
AEEGIINNOPRRST	PEREGRINATIONS
AEEGIINNPRSTTY	PAYING INTEREST
AEEGIINORRSTTV	INTERROGATIVES
	TERGIVERSATION
AEEGIJNNOSSTTW	SETTING ONE'S JAW
AEEGIKLNNOPPSY	SPEAKING OPENLY
AEEGILLLMNOPRS	MILES PER GALLON
AEEGILLLNNOSTT	TELLING NO TALES
AEEGILLMNNORRST	STEAMROLLERING
AEEGILLNNOORTV	LEARNING TO LOVE
AEEGILLNNOPRSX	ROLLING EXPANSE
AEEGILNNOORSTT	LOST GENERATION
AEEGILNNOOSSSU	OLEAGINOUSNESS
AEEGILNNORRRSW	SENIOR WRANGLER
AEEGILNNOSSSTU	GELATINOUSNESS
AEEGILNOPRSTTT	POSTING A LETTER
AEEGILNOPRSTTY	TRYING TO PLEASE
AEEGIMMNNOPTVV	MOVING PAVEMENT
AEEGIMNNORSSSU	GRAMINEOUSNESS
AEEGIMNNPRRSST	PRESENTING ARMS
AEEGINNNOOSTTX	GOT AN EXTENSION
AEEGINNNORRSSU	RUNG IN ONE'S EARS
AEEGINNOOQRRTUV	GIVEN NO QUARTER
	NO QUARTER GIVEN
AEEGINNPPRRSTT	PARTING PRESENT
AEEGINOOPRRSTU	SUPEREROGATION
AEEGINOQRRSTUV	GIVES NO QUARTER
AEEGIORRRSSTTV	TERGIVERSATORS
AEEGKLLNOOORTU	GENERAL OUTLOOK
AEEGKMNOOOPRRSS	MAKE NO PROGRESS
AEEGLLMNNORTVY	GOVERNMENTALLY
AEEGLLNNOOSSST	ON ONES LAST LEGS
AEEGLMNNNOORTV	GOVERNMENT LOAN
AEEGMMMNNOOPRRY	MONEY PROGRAMME
AEEGMMNNOOPRTTU	OPEN TO ARGUMENT
AEEGMNNOORSTUU	GENEROUS AMOUNT

AEEGMNORRSSSTU	STRONG MEASURES
AEEGNNNOOOSWWY	GONE ONE'S OWN WAY
AEEGNNOOOSSWWY	GOES ONE'S OWN WAY
AEEGNNOOSSTWWY	GETS ONE'S OWN WAY
AEEGNOORSSSTUU	OUTRAGEOUSNESS
AEEGOOPRRRSTUY	SUPEREROGATORY
AEEHHHINRRTTUW	RUN WITH THE HARE
AEEHHHMMORRTTW	THROW THE HAMMER
AEEHHIKLLLOSTTT	TAKE TO THE HILLS
AEEHHILNOPRTUY	PHENYLTHIOUREA
AEEHHILOPRSSST	SHARE THE SPOILS
AEEHHIMMNRRSST	HERMAN'S HERMITS
AEEHHKPRSSTTTU	SPEAKS THE TRUTH
AEEHHLLOOPRSTV	ALL OVER THE SHOP
AEEHHLLOORSTVW	ALL OVER THE SHOW
AEEHHLNRRSTTTU	LEARNS THE TRUTH
AEEHHLNRRTTTTU	LEARNT THE TRUTH
AEEHHMOOSSTTWY	SMOOTHES THE WAY
AEEHHNNOORSTTT	SAT ON THE THRONE
AEEHHNNORSTTTU	TURNS ON THE HEAT
	TURNS THE HEAT ON
AEEHHOPPPRSSTU	SUPERPHOSPHATE
AEEHHIIILLLNTTW	IN A LITTLE WHILE
AEEHHIIILLLTWWW	WILLIE WHITELAW
AEEHHIIKLNOOPST	HATE LIKE POISON
AEEHHIILLNNOTTY	LAY IT ON THE LINE
AEEHIILNPSSTTV	LIVES IN THE PAST
AEEHIINNPRTTUW	WENT UP IN THE AIR
AEEHIIRRSTTVWW	SERVE WITH A WRIT
AEEHIJKLMNPSTU	JUMPS IN THE LAKE
AEEHIKKLOORRSW	WORK LIKE A HORSE
AEEHIKMNNPSTTU	TAKE PUNISHMENT
AEEHIIKNNOOPRST	KEPT ONE'S HAIR ON
AEEHIKNOOPRRUY	KEEP YOUR HAIR ON!
AEEHILOORRTVVW	THROW A VEIL OVER
AEEHIMNOPSTTTT	THE TEMPTATIONS
AEEHINNOOORSSV	SHOVE IN ONE'S OAR
AEEHINNOORRSTV	ANOTHER VERSION
AEEHINOORRSTTT	THE RESTORATION
AEEHINPPPPRRSW	WHIPPERSNAPPER
AEEHIORRTTTUXY	EXERT AUTHORITY
AEEHKLLLNRSSSTW	SWELLS THE RANKS
AEEHKLOOORTTUW	WEATHER OUTLOOK
AEEHKLORRRSTTU	ARTHUR KOESTLER
AEEHKMNOPRTTTU	PUT ON THE MARKET
AEEHKNNNOORSTW	KNOWN THE REASON
AEEHKNNNORSTWW	KNOWN THE ANSWER
AEEHKNNOORSSTW	KNOWS THE REASON
AEEHKNNORSSTWW	KNOWS THE ANSWER
AEEHKOOORTTTTW	TOOK TO THE WATER
AEEHLLLMPRRSYY	PLAYS MERRY HELL
AEEHLLNOPRRSWW	WELL-WORN PHRASE
AEEHLMNOOORRSS	NAMELESS HORROR
AEEHLMOOSSTTVV	SMOOTH AS VELVET
AEEHLMPSSSTTYY	PLAYS THE SYSTEM
AEEHLNOORTTUZZ	OUT ON THE RAZZLE
AEEHMMMNNOOSSST	HAS ONE'S MOMENTS
AEEHMNNOORRRSY	RHYME NOR REASON
AEEHMNNPRSSSUU	SUPERHUMANNESS
AEEHMNOOPPRSTU	PNEUMATOPHORES
AEEHMNOORRRSTY	RESTORE HARMONY
AEEHMNORSSTTTT	SHORT STATEMENT
AEEHMOOPPRRSST	SPERMATOPHORES
AEEHMOPPRSSTTY	SPERMATOPHYTES
AEEHMORSSSTTUW	ASSUME THE WORST
AEEHNNOORRSUWY	NEW YEAR HONOURS
AEEHNORRRSTTTU	RETURNS TO EARTH
AEEHNORSSSTTTU	SOUTHERN STATES
AEEHOOPRSTTTUU	POURS OUT THE TEA
AEEIIIINSTTTTV	INITIATIVE TEST
AEEIIIKMNORSSU	MAKES INQUIRIES

AEEIIILMMMMORT	TIME IMMEMORIAL
AEEIIILMNSSTTX	EXISTENTIALISM
AEEIIILNOPSTTT	POTENTIALITIES
AEEIIILNSSTTTX	EXISTENTIALIST
AEEIIKKLNNOSST	SINK LIKE A STONE
AEEIIKMORSSSTU	SERIOUS MISTAKE
AEEIILLLNPSTTY	PESTILENTIALLY
AEEIILLMPPPRRU	IMPERIAL PURPLE
AEEIILLNNOPRTT	INTERPELLATION
AEEIILLNOPSTVY	TELEVISION PLAY
AEEIILLOPTTVXY	EXPLOITATIVELY
AEEIILMMNNOPTT	IMPLEMENTATION
AEEIILMMNNSSTT	SENTIMENTALISM
AEEIILMNNSSTTT	SENTIMENTALIST
AEEIILMNNSTTTY	SENTIMENTALITY
AEEIILMNOPQSTU	SIMPLE EQUATION
AEEIILMNORSSTU	SERIOUS AILMENT
AEEIILMNOSSTTV	TELEVISION MAST
AEEIILNNNOPGTW	WIN ON PENALTIES
AEEIILNNQSSTTU	QUINTESSENTIAL
AEEIILNOPRTTUV	EVIL REPUTATION
AEEIILNORSSSTT	TELEVISION STAR
AEEIILNRSTTUXY	INTERSEXUALITY
AEEIILNRSTUVYY	YALE UNIVERSITY
AEEIIMNNOORSTT	REMONETISATION
AEEIIMNNOORTTZ	REMONETIZATION
AEEIIMNOORSTTV	OVERESTIMATION
AEEIIMORRRRRVW	REAR-VIEW MIRROR
AEEIINNOPRRTTT	INTERPRETATION
AEEIINNOQRSSTU	QUESTIONNAIRES
AEEIINNORSSTTW	WESTERNISATION
AEEIINNORSTTWZ	WESTERNIZATION
AEEIINNOSSTTTU	TENSE SITUATION
AEEIINNRSSSTTV	TRANSITIVENESS
AEEIINOQRSTTUU	QUEER SITUATION
AEEIKKLNNOSSTU	SUNK LIKE A STONE
AEEIKLLPRSSTTY	SKITTLES PLAYER
AEEIKLNOOSSSTU	SEEKS A SOLUTION
AEEIKLNORSSTUY	TAKEN SERIOUSLY
AEEIKLORSSSTUY	TAKES SERIOUSLY
AEEIKMNNOOPSST	MAKES ONE'S POINT
AEEIKNNNOOPSSW	WEAK ON ONES PINS
AEEIKNNNOOPSTT	TAKEN ONE'S POINT
AEEIKNNOOPSSTT	TAKES ONE'S POINT
AEEIKNNOORSTTT	TOOK AN INTEREST
AEEIKNOOPSSSST	TAKE POSSESSION
AEEIKNPRSSTTUU	STRIKES UP A TUNE
AEEIILLMRSTTTUU	ULTIMATE RESULT
AEEIILLNNRSSSTT	SLATTERNLINESS
AEEIILLNOQRRTUV	VIOLENT QUARREL
AEEIILMNNNNRSSU	UNMANNERLINESS
AEEIILNNNOOPSTW	WON ON PENALTIES
AEEIILNNOOOPSTV	LEAVES NO OPTION
AEEIILNNOORSSTT	LISTEN TO REASON
AEEIILNOORTTTXY	EXTORTIONATELY
AEEIIMMOPRRSTTV	IMPROVE MATTERS
AEEIIMNNOPRTTTV	IMPORTANT EVENT
AEEIIMNOQRSSTTU	QUESTION MASTER
	QUESTION-MASTER
AEEIIMOPRSSTTTU	SERIOUS ATTEMPT
AEEIINOOPQSSSTU	POSES A QUESTION
AEEIINOPPRRSSTX	RAPT EXPRESSION
AEEIINOPRRRSTUU	SUPERIOR NATURE
AEEIINQRRRSTTUW	WINTER QUARTERS
AEEILLMNORSSSUV	MARVELLOUSNESS
AEEILLMNPRRSTUY	PREMENSTRUALLY
AEEILNNOOOORSSST	LOST ONE'S REASON
AEEILOPPQRRSTUU	POPULAR REQUEST
AEEILOPPRRRTUWY	PERPETUAL WORRY
AEEINNNOOSTWWWY	WENT ONE'S OWN WAY
AEEINNOOORRSSST	REST ON ONES OARS

AEENOPPPPRSTTU	PUTS PEN TO PAPER
AEFFGGIIILNNRT	LIFTING A FINGER
AEFFGHHISTTTUU	AUGUST THE FIFTH
AEFFGHLLLOOSTW	FOLLOWS THE FLAG
AEFFGHLLNRSTUU	UNFURLS THE FLAG
AEFFGHNORSSTTU	TURNS OFF THE GAS
AEFFGILLNOORTW	FOLLOWING AFTER
AEFFGILNORSSSU	SUFFERING A LOSS
AEFFHILLOPRTTW	TWELFTH OF APRIL
AEFFHILNNSSTUU	UNFAITHFULNESS
AEFFHIMNNORSTTY	THE FIRST OF MANY
AEFFHIOORSTTUW	FISH OUT OF WATER
AEFFHKLMOORSTW	SLOW OFF THE MARK
AEFFHKNOOOOSTT	TOOK ONE'S HAT OFF
AEFFHKNOPRRSST	PROFFERS THANKS
AEFFHNOPRSTTTU	TURNS OFF THE TAP
AEFFIILLMOPRSU	FULFIL A PROMISE
AEFFIIMNOORRSU	FORAMINIFEROUS
AEFFIINNNOOOPR	OFFER AN OPINION
AEFFILMNORSTUY	FAMILY FORTUNES
AEFFLOOPRRSSWY	SPRAY OF FLOWERS
AEFGGGHIINRTTT	GETTING A FRIGHT
AEFGGHHIILNTTW	FIGHTING THE LAW
AEFGGHHILNOSTW	SHOWING THE FLAG
AEFGGHHINOOTTT	GOT THE HANG OF IT
AEFGGHHIOSTTUU	EIGHTH OF AUGUST
AEFGGHIIILLNSV	FISHING VILLAGE
AEFGGHIINOORTT	GOING TO THE FAIR
AEFGGHIKNSTUWY	GUY FAWKES NIGHT
AEFGGHINORTTTW	GETTING WHAT FOR
AEFGGORRRSSTTU	GUTS FOR GARTERS
AEFGHHILNRSTUW	FLUSH WITH ANGER
AEFGHHINOPSTTT	THING OF THE PAST
AEFGHHLMNOOOTT	GOAL OF THE MONTH
AEFGHHNOOORRTU	NO THOROUGHFARE
AEFGHIIILNNRSY	FINISHING EARLY
AEFGHIIILORSTU	RELIGIOUS FAITH
AEFGHIILMPRRST	PILGRIM FATHERS
AEFGHIINNNOOTV	HAVING NONE OF IT
AEFGHIINOORRST	RAISING THE ROOF
AEFGHIINORSSTT	SHIFTS INTO GEAR
AEFGHIINRRSTTT	THIRSTING AFTER
AEFGHILLNOOPTY	PLAYING THE FOOL
AEFGHIMNORRSTT	STREAMING FORTH
AEFGHINNNPRSTY	PENNY-FARTHINGS
AEFGHIRSSTTTUU	AUGUST THE FIRST
AEFGHLLNRSTTTU	AT FULL STRENGTH
AEFGHLOPSTTTUU	PUT THE FLAGS OUT
AEFGHOOOOTTTUWY	GOT OUT OF THE WAY
AEFGIILLNOPRTY	FAILING TO REPLY
AEFGIILMNOPRTY	PLAYING FOR TIME
AEFGIILMNRRTTT	TRIFLING MATTER
AEFGIILNNSSSTU	SELF-SUSTAINING
AEFGIIMNNORTTY	MAN OF INTEGRITY
AEFGIIMNNORRSST	TRANSMOGRIFIES
AEFGIINNOORSTT	FOREIGN STATION
AEFGIINOORRRST	ROARING FORTIES
AEFGIKLKNOORRVW	LEAVING FOR WORK
AEFGIKLNOPSSTY	SPEAKING SOFTLY
AEFGIKMNNOORSY	ASKING FOR MONEY
AEFGILLLNOSSSS	FILLS ONE'S GLASS
AEFGILLNNOPRTW	FLOWERING PLANT
AEFGILLNNRTTUY	UNFLATTERINGLY
AEFGILNOPRRSST	STRING OF PEARLS
AEFGILNOPRSTUY	REFUSING TO PLAY
AEFGLLLNOOOPRT	GALLON OF PETROL
AEFGLLNNOOORSU	GONE ON ALL FOURS
AEFGLLNOOORRST	GONE FOR A STROLL
AEFGLLNOOORSSU	GOES ON ALL FOURS
AEFGLLOOORRSST	GOES FOR A STROLL
AEFGLNORRRSTUW	WRONGFUL ARREST

AEFGMMNNOPRRUY	FUNNY PROGRAMME
AEFGNOOOOSTUWY	GO OUT OF ONES WAY
AEFGNOOORSSTTW	SETS A FOOT WRONG
AEFGNOOPRRSTTY	FRONT-PAGE STORY
AEFHHHLLNORTUY	HELL HATH NO FURY
AEFHHIIMORTTTY	THIRTIETH OF MAY
AEFHHILOPRRTTU	APRIL THE FOURTH
AEFHHLNNOPRTWY	HALFPENNYWORTH
AEFHHOORRSTUWY	HOW'S YOUR FATHER
AEFHIIIKLMSSSW	SWIMS LIKE A FISH
AEFHIILLMMOORY	FAMILY HEIRLOOM
AEFHIILMNNRTUY	RUN IN THE FAMILY
AEFHIILNNOPRTY	HYPERINFLATION
AEFHIILOPRSTTW	SPIRIT OF THE LAW
AEFHIINNNOSSTT	PIN ONES FAITH ON
AEFHIIORTUVVWW	VIEW WITH FAVOUR
AEFHIKNORSTVWY	HAVE FORTY WINKS
AEFHILLLOORTTW	FOLLOW THE TRAIL
AEFHINNORSSTTTT	SITS AT THE FRONT
AEFHIOOPRRSTWY	WORTHY OF PRAISE
AEFHIORRSTTTYZ	TRY THAT FOR SIZE
AEFHKMNOOORSST	ASKS FOR THE MOON
AEFHKMOORRSTUU	STREAK OF HUMOUR
AEFHLLOOPPSTUU	PULL OUT OF SHAPE
AEFHLLOPRTUUXY	THE LAP OF LUXURY
AEFHMMOOPRRSSU	ARMS OF MORPHEUS
AEFHMMOOPSSTUU	POSTHUMOUS FAME
AEFHMMOORRSSTY	STRAYS FROM HOME
AEFHMOOPRRSTTT	FOR THE MOST PART
AEFHNOOOSTTTTW	TOAST OF THE TOWN
AEFIIINNQTTTUY	FINITE QUANTITY
AEFIILLORRSSUY	ROYAL FUSILIERS
AEFIILOPPPRRSS	PAIR OF SLIPPERS
AEFIINOPRRSSTU	PUTS IN FOR A RISE
AEFIINORRSSTTU	INFERIOR STATUS
AEFIKLOPRSSSTT	PROFITLESS TASK
AEFILLNNOOOSWW	A WILL OF ONE'S OWN
AEFILLNOOPRSSY	PROFESSIONALLY
AEFILLNOOORRST	FALLS INTO ERROR
AEFILNOOPRSSSW	PASSIONFLOWERS
AEFINOPRRRSTTU	RETURNS A PROFIT
AEFIOOPRRRSSTU	PAIR OF TROUSERS
AEFKLLNNOOORSW	FOR ALL ONE KNOWS
AEFKNOOPRSTTUU	SPEAK OUT OF TURN
AEFLLLNOOOSSTT	FALLS TO ONE'S LOT
AEFLLNNOORSTUW	WENT ON ALL FOURS
AEFLLNOORRSTTW	WENT FOR A STROLL
AEFLNOOOPRRTTU	RAN OUT OF PETROL
AEFLNOOORRSTTW	LOT TO ANSWER FOR
AEFMNOOOPSSSTT	STAMPS ONE'S FOOT
AEFMNOOPPRSSTU	MEANS OF SUPPORT
AEFMNOORSSTTUU	RUNS OUT OF STEAM
AEFMNOPRRSSTTU	PERFORMS A STUNT
AEFMOPSSSTTUUU	SUMPTUOUS FEAST
AEFOOORRSTTUWW	TWO TWOS ARE FOUR
AEGGGGINNORSTU	GOING GREAT GUNS
AEGGGGINNOSTUW	WAGGING TONGUES
AEGGGHHIILNST	LIGHTING THE GAS
AEGGGLLNORSSTU	STRUGGLES ALONG
AEGGHHIILNTTWY	LIGHTING THE WAY
AEGGHHIINNNORT	HEARING NOTHING
AEGGHHIIOTTTUV	GIVE IT A THOUGHT
AEGGHHILNOSTTY	LAYING THE GHOST
AEGGHIIIMNSSVV	HAVE MISGIVINGS
AEGGHIINNRTTW	WEIGHT TRAINING
AEGGHIILLNRTTT	GETTING A THRILL
AEGGHIIMNNNNOT	MEANING NOTHING
AEGGHIINNNRSTT	GAIN IN STRENGTH
AEGGHIINNOSTWW	GONE WITH A SWING
AEGGHIINOSSTWW	GOES WITH A SWING
AEGGHIIRSSTTTT	GETS IT STRAIGHT

AEGGHILLNOOTTW	GOING TO THE WALL
AEGGHILLNOPTUW	GOING UP THE WALL
AEGGHILMMOPRRT	LIGHT PROGRAMME
AEGGHIMNNNNSTU	MANNING THE GUNS
AEGGHIMNORRSTT	GATHERING STORM
AEGGHINNOOPRTV	PHOTOENGRAVING
AEGGHINNRRSSTT	STRANGER THINGS
AEGGHINOORSTTW	GOING TO THE WARS
AEGGHINOPPPSTT	STOPPING THE GAP
AEGGHINORSSTTU	ARGUING THE TOSS
AEGGHLNNOOSTTY	GO TO ANY LENGTHS
AEGGHNNOOPRRST	RONTGENOGRAPHS
AEGGHNNOOPRRTY	RONTGENOGRAPHY
AEGGIIKLNNOOTT	GETTING A LOOK IN
AEGGIILLNNOSTT	ILL-GOTTEN GAINS
AEGGIIMNNOORTV	MOVING INTO GEAR
AEGGIINNNORTUV	GIVING ONE A TURN
AEGGIINNNOSWWY	WINGING ONE'S WAY
AEGGIINNORTWXY	GROWING ANXIETY
AEGGILLMNORRSW	GROWING SMALLER
AEGGILLNORSTTW	GETS IT ALL WRONG
AEGGINNOOPRSWY	GROPING ONE'S WAY
AEGGINNOSSSTUY	ANY SUGGESTIONS?
AEGGINOOOORTTV	GOT INTO A GROOVE
AECCINOOGGTTUU	AUTOSUGGESTION
AEGGLPPRSTTUUU	PUT UP A STRUGGLE
AEGGMNNOOSTUWY	GO WEST YOUNG MAN
AEGGMNNORRSTTU	STRONG ARGUMENT
AEGHHHIILRTTTW	WITH LIGHT HEART
AEGHHHILLOTTWW	GLOW WITH HEALTH
AEGHHIIKMNRTTT	HITTING THE MARK
AEGHHIIMNNNPST	MANNING THE SHIP
AEGHHIINNPSSTT	PASS IN THE NIGHT
AEGHHIKMMNSSTU	MAKES THINGS HUM
AEGHHIKMNOSSTT	MAKES THINGS HOT
AEGHHIKNORRSTW	SHARING THE WORK
AEGHHILNOORSTT	SHARING THE LOOT
AEGHHILNOPSTTY	PLAYING THE HOST
AEGHHINNNOORTT	NOTHING ON EARTH
AEGGHHINNSTTTUU	AUGUST THE NINTH
AEGHHISSTTTUUX	AUGUST THE SIXTH
AEGHHLLLOORTUW	HOLLOW LAUGHTER
AEGHIIILLNNNPS	IN PLAIN ENGLISH
AEGHIIIIINNSTTT	STING IN THE TAIL
AEGHIIINNPRRST	SPRING IN THE AIR
AEGHIIINNSTTWW	WAIT IN THE WINGS
AEGHIIJMNNORTY	JOINING THE ARMY
AEGHIIJNNNOTVY	JOINING THE NAVY
AEGHIIKMMNRSST	MISSING THE MARK
AEGHIILLLRRTTY	LIGHT ARTILLERY
AEGHIILLNOPPPS	APPLE-POLISHING
AEGHIIMNNNOOOST	HOMOGENISATION
AEGHIIMNNOOOTZ	HOMOGENIZATION
AEGHIIMNPRRSTU	REMAINS UPRIGHT
AEGHIINNOPPSTT	TIPPING ONE'S HAT
AEGHIINNOPTTWY	POINTING THE WAY
AEGHIINNORSTWY	WRITHES IN AGONY
AEGHIINNSTTWWW	WENT WITH A SWING
AEGHIINRSSSTTT	IN STRAIGHT SETS
AEGHIKLLNOOSST	LOOK IN THE GLASS
AEGHIKLNOOPRTT	LOOKING THE PART
AEGHIKLNORSSST	STALKING-HORSES
AEGHIKMNOPRSTT	MARKING THE SPOT
AEGHIKNNRRRTTY	KNIGHT-ERRANTRY
AEGHIKNOOSSTTY	TOOK THINGS EASY
AEGHIKNOPRSTTT	KEPT STRAIGHT ON
AEGHILMOORSTTU	RHEUMATOLOGIST
AEGHILNNNOOPSS	HANG ON ONE'S LIPS
AEGHIMMNOOPRST	METAMORPHOSING
AEGHIMNNOORSTU	MOUNTING A HORSE
AEGHIMNNORRSTT	STRONG IN THE ARM
AEGHIMNOOPPSTT	STOPPING AT HOME
AEGHIMNOOSSTTY	SOMETHING TO SAY
AEGHIMNOPSTTTU	PUTTING TO SHAME
AEGHIMNORSSTTT	START SOMETHING
AEGHINNNORRTTU	RUNNING TO EARTH
AEGHINNOOOSSST	SHOOTING SEASON
AEGHINNORSSTTU	TURNING TO ASHES
AEGHINOOOPPRRS	SPORANGIOPHORE
AEGHINORSSTTTU	STRAIGHTENS OUT
AEGHINORSSTTVY	STAYS OVERNIGHT
AEGHINPPRRSSTT	SPRINGS THE TRAP
AEGHJMNNOOPTUW	JUMP ON THE WAGON
AEGHLLMOPRTUYY	PLYMOUTH ARGYLE
AEGHMMOOPRRTTY	PHOTOGRAMMETRY
AEGHNNOOPSTTUY	PUTS ON THE AGONY
AEGIIIILMNOSTT	LEGITIMISATION
AEGIIIILMNOTTZ	LEGITIMIZATION
AEGIIILMNRSTUY	MILITARY GENIUS
AEGIIILNNRSSUV	UNIVERSALISING
AEGIIILNNRSUVZ	UNIVERSALIZING
AEGIIIMNNORRTV	ARRIVING ON TIME
AEGIIIMNRSSSTT	MISSING A SITTER
AEGIIINNNNOOPV	GIVEN AN OPINION
AEGIIINNNOOPSV	GIVES AN OPINION
AEGIIINNNPPRTW	TIPPING A WINNER
AEGIIINNORSTTT	INTEGRATIONIST
AEGIIKLLNNOTTW	KNOWING A LITTLE
AEGIIKLLNQTTUY	TALKING QUIETLY
AEGIILLLNNRSTW	ALL-IN WRESTLING
AEGIILLMNNOOPS	OILING ONE'S PALM
AEGIILLNTTTTTT	TITTLE-TATTLING
AEGIILMNNOORST	MONGRELISATION
AEGIILMNNOORTZ	MONGRELIZATION
AEGIILNNNRSTTY	INTRANSIGENTLY
AEGIILNNPPSTUY	UNAPPETISINGLY
AEGIILNNPPTUYZ	UNAPPETIZINGLY
AEGIILNOPRRSTU	NEGRO SPIRITUAL
AEGIILNQRRSTUV	LIVING QUARTERS
AEGIINNNPRRRSU	RUNNING REPAIRS
AEGIINNOOPSSSS	GAIN POSSESSION
AEGIINNOORSTTY	GAINS NOTORIETY
AEGIINPPRRSSTT	ASSET-STRIPPING
AEGIJKMNNOORTT	NO JOKING MATTER
AEGIKLLNOPGGWY	SPEAKING SLOWLY
AEGIKLNNOOPRSY	PLAYING SNOOKER
AEGIKNNNOOSWWY	KNOWING ONE'S WAY
AEGIKNNOORSWWY	WORKING ONE'S WAY
AEGILLMNNOOQTUY	MAGNILOQUENTLY
AEGILMNNOOTUYY	LAYING OUT MONEY
AEGILMNOOORSTU	OSMOREGULATION
AEGILNOOPRTTWY	WRITTEN APOLOGY
AEGILNOPRRSTTY	LYING PROSTRATE
AEGIMMNOOPRSTU	SPERMATOGONIUM
AEGIMNNNSSSSUU	UNASSUMINGNESS
AEGIMNNOORSWWY	WORMING ONE'S WAY
AEGIMNNOORTUUV	OUTMANOEUVRING
AEGIMNNORSSSSW	SWINGS ONE'S ARMS
AEGIMNPRRSSSTT	SPRING MATTRESS
AEGINNNOOPRRST	IGNORANT PERSON
AEGINNOOOSSSTW	SOWING ONE'S OATS
AEGINNOPPPRTTU	PUTTING ON PAPER
AEGINNOPRSSSSU	GAINS ONE'S SPURS
AEGINNORRSSSST	TRANSGRESSIONS
AEGINNORSTTUVY	VENTURING TO SAY
AEGINOOPRRSTTU	GO INTO RAPTURES
AEGINORSSSTTUU	GRATUITOUSNESS
AEGLNOOPPSSSTU	TOP UP ONES GLASS
AEGNOOORSSSTTU	SENT OUT TO GRASS
AEHHHILNOORTTU	HOLIER THAN THOU
	HOLIER-THAN-THOU
AEHHIILLLLSSSY	SHILLY-SHALLIES

AEHHIINNORRTTW	THROWN IN THE AIR
AEHHIINORRSTTW	THROWS IN THE AIR
AEHHIIPRSSTTTT	THATS THE SPIRIT
AEHHILLMNPSTTY	PLATYHELMINTHS
AEHHINNORSTTWW	WHITER THAN SNOW
AEHHKLLOOOTTUY	HEALTHY OUTLOOK
AEHHLORRRSTUUV	RUSH-HOUR TRAVEL
AEHHNNOORRSTTT	NORTH-NORTHEAST
AEHHOOSSSTTTUU	SOUTH-SOUTHEAST
AEHIILLNNOORTZ	HORIZONTAL LINE
AEHIILLNOPSTVY	PLAYS THE VIOLIN
AEHIILMNNORSVY	LIVES IN HARMONY
AEHIILNOPSTTUW	WITH ONE'S TAIL UP
AEHIILOPRRSTWY	PRAISEWORTHILY
AEHIIOORRSSTTT	OSTEOARTHRITIS
AEHIKMNOORRSWY	YORKSHIREWOMAN
AEHIKOOORSTTVW	TOOK A SHORT VIEW
AEHILLLLOPSTWW	SWALLOW THE PILL
AEHILLLMMOOPRS	ALLELOMORPHISM
AEHILLNOPPSSTU	PULLS INTO SHAPE
AEHILMNNOSSTUW	WELSH MOUNTAINS
AEHILNNOOORSTT	HOT ON ONES TRAIL
AEHILNOORSSTTT	SLIT ONE'S THROAT
AEHILOOPPRRSTT	HOSPITAL PORTER
AEHIMNNNNOOORTT	NO ROOM AT THE INN
AEHIMNNOORSSSU	HARMONIOUSNESS
AEHIMOOPPPSSTU	HIPPOPOTAMUSES
AEHIMOPPRSSSTT	POSTMASTERSHIP
AEHINNORRSSTTW	SHOWN RESTRAINT
AEHINOOPTTTUWY	POINT OUT THE WAY
AEHINORRSSSTTW	SHOWS RESTRAINT
AEHKKMOORRSSTW	MAKES SHORT WORK
AEHKLMNNOOOSTW	WALKS ON THE MOON
AEHLMMNNOPTTYY	MONTHLY PAYMENT
AEHLOPPRSTTUWY	HOT-WATER SUPPLY
AEHNNOOORSTTWY	NOT TO REASON WHY
AEHNOOPRRSSTTU	TRANSPORT HOUSE
AEIIILLNRSTTTY	INTERSTITIALLY
AEIIILMMNNOTUV	LIVE AMMUNITION
AEIIILNNRSTTVY	INTRANSITIVELY
AEIIILORRRTTTY	TERRITORIALITY
AEIIINNNOOOPRS	AIR ONES OPINION
AEIIINNOOPPRTV	PRIVATE OPINION
AEIIINOPRTTTUV	PRIVATE TUITION
AEIIJLMMOPRSTY	SIMPLE MAJORITY
AEIIJLMNORSTTY	SILENT MAJORITY
AEIIJLMNPRTUYY	PLAY INJURY TIME
AEIIJNNOOOPRTT	JOINT OPERATION
AEIIKLLNOPRSSS	PASSION KILLERS
AEIIKMNOOPRSSV	MAKE PROVISIONS
	MAKES PROVISION
AEIIKMNOPRSSSS	ASKS PERMISSION
AEIIKNNNRSTTTU	TAKEN IT IN TURNS
AEIIKNNRSSTTTU	TAKES IT IN TURNS
AEIILLLMNNOPST	POSTMILLENNIAL
AEIILLLRSTTUVY	ILLUSTRATIVELY
AEIILLMNORSWWY	WALLOW IN MISERY
AEIILLNNNQQUUY	QUINQUENNIALLY
AEIILLNNOOSSTU	SALINE SOLUTION
AEIILLNNOSSSUV	VILLAINOUSNESS
AEIILLNOORTUVY	EVOLUTIONARILY
AEIILLNOQRSSUV	LIVES IN SQUALOR
AEIILLNQRRSSTU	TRANQUILLISERS
AEIILLNQRRSTUZ	TRANQUILLIZERS
AEIILMNOOPRSTY	POLYMERISATION
AEIILMNOOPRTYZ	POLYMERIZATION
AEIILMNORSSSST	TRIMS ONE'S SAILS
AEIILNNRSSSTTT	LOSES IN TRANSIT
AEIILNNRRSTTUV	VIRULENT STRAIN
AEIILNOSSSTTTW	TWISTS ONE'S TAIL
AEIILOPPRRSTUW	SPIRITUAL POWER

AEIIMNNOOOPRRT	MINOR OPERATION
AEIIINNORRSSSTT	TRANSITORINESS
AEIINOPRRSSSTU	PRESSURISATION
AEIINOPRRSSTUZ	PRESSURIZATION
AEIINOPRSSSUVV	VIVIPAROUSNESS
AEIINORRSSSSTT	TRANSISTORISES
AEIINORRSSSTTZ	TRANSISTORIZES
AEIKNNOOOPSSSU	POISONOUS SNAKE
AEIKNNOOQSSSTU	ASK NO QUESTIONS
AEILLLLMMOPSSU	SAMUEL PLIMSOLL
AEILLMNNRSTTUY	INSTRUMENTALLY
AEILLMNOSSTUUY	SIMULTANEOUSLY
AEILMNOOOPRSST	SALES PROMOTION
AEILMNOPRRSTUY	SUPERNORMALITY
AEILNOOOPPRTUV	OVERPOPULATION
AEILNOOPRSTUUV	SUPEROVULATION
AEILNOOSSTTTUY	OSTENTATIOUSLY
AEILOPRRSSTUVY	VASTLY SUPERIOR
AEIMMNNOOSSTUV	MOVES MOUNTAINS
AEIMMNOSSSSSUU	ISSUES A SUMMONS
AEIMNNOOPPRSTT	APPORTIONMENTS
AEIMNNOORRSTTU	MOUNTAIN RESORT
AEIMNNOORSTTUY	MOUNTAIN OYSTER
AEIMNOOOOPPRST	PROPOSE A MOTION
AEINOOOPPPRRSTT	PROPORTIONATES
AEINOOPRRSSSUU	UPROARIOUSNESS
AEIOPRRSSSTTUU	SUPERIOR STATUS
AEKLLLOOOOTTVY	LOVELY TO LOOK AT
AEKLLNNOOORSWW	ALL ONES OWN WORK
AEKNOOPRSSUWWY	WORKS ONE'S WAY UP
AELLOOPPRRSTUY	LOYAL SUPPORTER
AELMNNOORRRTTU	RETURN TO NORMAL
AENOOPPPRSSTTU	PUTS A STOPPER ON
AFFFILLOORRSTT	FIRST-FLOOR FLAT
AFFGGHIIINORRT	FIGHTING FOR AIR
AFFGHHIIINNOSTT	FIGHT TO A FINISH
AFFGHHIIRRRTTU	ARTHUR GRIFFITH
AFFGHIIKLNOTWW	WALKING OFF WITH
AFFGHIILOOPRST	SPOIL FOR A FIGHT
AFFGHIILORSSTT	FLIGHT OF STAIRS
AFFGHOORSTTUUU	FOURTH OF AUGUST
AFFGIIILLMMNNOR	FILLING IN A FORM
AFFIILLLOTTUVY	FULL OF VITALITY
AFGGHHHIILNSST	FLASHING THIGHS
AFGGHHIILLNNST	LIGHTNING FLASH
AFGGHHILLNORTU	FALLING THROUGH
AFGGHIIKLNOORT	LOOKING A FRIGHT
AFGHHINOORTTTU	TRAIN OF THOUGHT
AFGHIINNOOSTTY	SAY NOTHING OF IT
AFGHIINOOPRSTW	SHOWING A PROFIT
AFGHIKNNOORSST	ASKS FOR NOTHING
AFGHINNNOORTTW	WANT FOR NOTHING
AFGHLOOPRRSUUW	PLOUGHS A FURROW
AFGIIILLNNNRSU	FALLING IN RUINS
AFGIIILLNNOSTT	FILLING STATION
AFGIIKLNNNORTW	WALKING IN FRONT
AFGIIKLNOORRVW	WORK FOR A LIVING
AFGIILMNNORTTU	TRIFLING AMOUNT
AFGNOOOPRSTTUW	PUTS A FOOT WRONG
AFHHMOOPSSTWYY	SHOW OF SYMPATHY
AFHHOOOOORTTTT	TOOTH FOR A TOOTH
AFHIIINOPSTTTU	PUT A FINISH TO IT
AFIIIMMNNOORST	MISINFORMATION
AFIILLMORSTUUY	MULTIFARIOUSLY
AFIIMNNNOOOOPRS	FORMS AN OPINION
AFKLNOORSTTTUU	TALKS OUT OF TURN
AGGGHIIINNORRTW	RIGHTING A WRONG
AGGGIILNNNORST	STRINGING ALONG
AGGHHIIILLNORY	HIGHLY ORIGINAL
AGGHHINOPRSSTU	PASSING THROUGH
AGGHHINOPSSTTU	PASSING THOUGHT

AGGHIIIILNRTVW	GIVING IT A WHIRL
AGGHIIIKLNRSTT	STRIKING A LIGHT
AGGHIIINNSSTTY	STAYING IN SIGHT
AGGHIILNPRSTUW	WALPURGIS NIGHT
AGGHIINNNOSTTW	WASTING NOTHING
AGGHIKLLNOOSTY	LOOKING GHASTLY
AGGIIIINSTTTVW	GIVING IT A TWIST
AGGIIILNNORTVY	INVIGORATINGLY
AGGILNNOOOSTTY	STAYING TOO LONG
AGGILNOOOPTTUY	GOING OUT TO PLAY
AGHHIIKNRSSTTT	THINKS STRAIGHT
AGHHIINORSTTTU	THRASHING IT OUT
AGHHIIOOPRRSTY	HISTORIOGRAPHY
AGHHILOOOPSTTY	HISTOPATHOLOGY
AGHHIIOORSSSTTT	SHOOTS STRAIGHT
AGHHJLNOORSTWY	JOHN GALSWORTHY
AGHIIIINNNPRTW	WRITHING IN PAIN
AGHIIILNPRSSTT	SPLITTING HAIRS
AGHIIINNNNORSTV	VANISHING POINT
AGHIIINNNPRSTU	HUNTING IN PAIRS
AGHIIKMNNNORRTU	KNIGHT IN ARMOUR
AGHIIKNNPPRRSW	SHRINK-WRAPPING
AGHIIKNNRSSTTT	STARTS THINKING
AGHIILLNORRTWY	RAY ILLINGWORTH
AGHIIILNOOOPSTT	GO INTO HOSPITAL
AGHIIMMNNNORSSY	SINGS IN HARMONY
AGHIINNORTTUWW	WITHOUT WARNING
AGHILNOOOPRSTT	ANTHROPOLOGIST
AGHINNOOPSSTTT	STOPS AT NOTHING
AGHINNOOPSSTTW	WASHINGTON POST
AGHINNOOPSTTUW	PUTTING ON A SHOW
AGIIIILLMMNNOR	GIRL IN A MILLION
AGIIIILNNNOPST	PAINTING IN OILS
AGIIIILNPRSSTU	SPIRITUALISING
AGIIIILNPRSTUZ	SPIRITUALIZING
AGIIIINNNRSTVV	STRIVING IN VAIN
AGIIIKLLMMNNOS	MAKING MILLIONS
AGIIIKNNNRTTTU	TAKING IT IN TURN
AGIIIILLLMNNTUY	ILLUMINATINGLY
AGIIIILLNNQRSTU	TRANQUILLISING
AGIIIILLNNQRTUZ	TRANQUILLIZING
AGIIIMMNNPRRSSU	RISING UP IN ARMS
AGIIINNNOPPSTT	SNAPPING INTO IT
AGIIKNORRSSTVY	IGOR STRAVINSKY
AGIILLLLLMNTUUY	MULTILINGUALLY
AGIILLNNOOPSTT	POLLING STATION
AGIILLNOORSUVY	VAINGLORIOUSLY
AGIILLNOPPSTTW	STOPPING AT WILL
AGIILNNOPRTTTU	PUTTING ON TRIAL
AGIILNOPRSSTTT	STARTING PISTOL
AGIILOORSSSSTY	ASSYRIOLOGISTS
AGIIMNOOPPRSTY	PROMISING TO PAY
AGIIMNOPRRSSTT	PROMISING START
AGIINNORRRTTTU	TURNING TRAITOR
AGILMNOORRSSTU	LOUIS ARMSTRONG
AGILMOOOSSSTTT	STOMATOLOGISTS
AGILNNNOOOPPTY	PLAYING PONTOON
AGINOOPPSTTTTU	PUTTING A STOP TO
AGINOPPPRRSTTU	SUPPORTING PART
AGKNNOOORRTTUW	TOOK A WRONG TURN
AGLMMOOOPSTTYY	SYMPTOMATOLOGY
AGNOORRSSTTTUU	TURN OUT TO GRASS
AGOOPRSSSTTTUU	PUTS OUT TO GRASS
AHHIILNNPPRSTT	PHILANTHROPIST
AHHLLNOOPSTUXY	XANTHOPHYLLOUS
AHIIILLNOOPSTY	LYOPHILISATION
AHIIILLNOOPTYZ	LYOPHILIZATION
AHIIILNNOOSTTW	ANOINTS WITH OIL
AHIIJLNNOORTTW	THROWN INTO JAIL
AHIIJLNOORSTTW	THROWS INTO JAIL
AHIIKLLORSTWWW	WORKS WITH A WILL

AHIILLMNORSTUW	WILLIAM RUSHTON
AHIILMNNOORSUY	INHARMONIOUSLY
AHIILNOPRSSTUU	SULPHURISATION
AHIILNOPRSTUUZ	SULPHURIZATION
AHIIMNNOOSSTWY	SHOWN ANIMOSITY
AHIIMNOOSSSTWY	SHOWS ANIMOSITY
AHIJLLMNORSTTU	JOHN STUART MILL
AHIJNNOORSSTTW	SAINT-JOHN'S-WORT
AHILLNOOOPRSWY	HOLLOWAY PRISON
AHKLNOOPRSSTTW	TWO SHORT PLANKS
AHLLOOOPSTTTUU	PULLS A TOOTH OUT
AIIKMNOORRSSWY	MISSIONARY WORK
AIILMNNOOOOPST	MONOPOLISATION
AIILMNNOOOOPTZ	MONOPOLIZATION
AIILMNOOPRSSUY	PARSIMONIOUSLY
AIILNOOPPRSSTV	SPORTS PAVILION
AIILNOOPPSSTUY	SUPPOSITIONALY
AIINNOOPRSSSTT	TRANSPOSITIONS
AIKNNNOORRRUWW	UNKNOWN WARRIOR
AIKNNOOOOPPTTU	TOOK UP AN OPTION
AILLLNORUUUWWXY	WALLOW IN LUXURY
AILLNOOOPPRRTY	PROPORTIONALLY
AILNNOOOPPSSTU	POISONOUS PLANT
BBBBEEHLRSTTUU	BURST THE BUBBLE
BBBBEGILLNO3UW	BLOWING BUBBLES
BBBCGHINRRSSUU	SCRUBBING BRUSH
BBBDEEILORSTTY	SOBBED BITTERLY
BBBDEHLLLMMNOOS	BLOND BOMBSHELL
BBBEEGHINTTTUY	BITTEN BY THE BUG
BBBEILLOOSSWYY	BOYS WILL BE BOYS
BBCCEGIILMNOPU	BECOMING PUBLIC
BBCDEEIORRSSUV	OVERSUBSCRIBED
BBCDGIIKLNRSU	BUILDING BRICKS
BBCEEEHORRRTTU	ROBERT THE BRUCE
BBCEEFFHHNOSTTU	BEST OF THE BUNCH
BBCEEHILMMPRSU	CLUB MEMBERSHIP
BBCEEIORRSSSUV	OVERSUBSCRIBES
BBCEHIIJRSSTTU	BRITISH SUBJECT
BBCEHMOOORRSSTU	BUTCHER'S-BROOMS
BBCELMNOORRUUY	COLOUR BY NUMBER
BBCGIKLLMNOSTU	STUMBLING BLOCK
BBCIIILMOSTTUY	COMBUSTIBILITY
BBDEEEGHORRTTU	RUBBED TOGETHER
BBDEEELLNNOOSSW	BENDS ONE'S ELBOW
BBDEEEENOOSSTTU	STUBBED ONE'S TOE
BBDEGIKLNOORRY	BROOKLYN BRIDGE
BBDGHIILLORSTU	BRITISH BULLDOG
BBDHJNNOOORSWY	JOHN BROWNS BODY
BBEEEGILLNOOSS	NOBLESSE OBLIGE
BBEEEHILLSTTTU	BITES THE BULLET
BBEEEEHLORRSSTU	LOSES THE RUBBER
BBEEEILLNOORRX	BOXER REBELLION
BBEEEKNNNOOORS	BROKEN ONE'S BONE
BBEEEKNNOOORSS	BROKE ONE'S BONES
BBEEGHOORRSSUY	GOOSEBERRY BUSH
BBEEGILNORRTUW	TROUBLE BREWING
BBEEHILLNOTTTU	BIT ON THE BULLET
BBEFHJOOORSSTY	JOBS FOR THE BOYS
BBEFKOOOOPRRSV	BOOK OF PROVERBS
BBEFLLNOORSTUW	STUBBORN FELLOW
BBEGGHIKNOOOTY	GOING BY THE BOOK
BBEGGIIINNNORT	BRING INTO BEING
BBEGHIIILLNORTT	ROBBING THE TILL
BBEGHIILNORTT	BRING TO THE BOIL
BBEGINNOORRRTW	ROBERT BROWNING
BBEHHLLNORSTUY	BULL BY THE HORNS
BBEHKOOORRRSST	BROOKS BROTHERS
BBEEINNOOORRRST	ROBERT ROBINSON
BBGGIIKNNOOORT	BRINGING TO BOOK
BBHIIIILLLOPSST	BIBLIOPHILISTS
BCCCEEEIJNSSTU	SCIENCE SUBJECT

BCCCEEFIIJOPST	SPECIFIC OBJECT
BCCCGIIIMNRRSU	CIRCUMSCRIBING
BCCCIIMOOPRSSU	SUBMICROSCOPIC
BCCDEEFHLNOORU	CORDON BLEU CHEF
BCCDEEFIMNOORS	COMBINED FORCES
BCCDEEHHIKLNOT	BEHIND THE CLOCK
BCCDEEIIJNORTT	INDIRECT OBJECT
BCCDHIIIKLLLOW	WILD BILL HICOCK
BCCDIIILNOTTUY	CONDUCTIBILITY
BCCEEEEGILRTTU	ICEBERG LETTUCE
BCCEEEHILRSSTT	THE BEST CIRCLES
BCCEEEIMNOSTTX	BECOMES EXTINCT
BCCEEFIMNOORSS	COMBINES FORCES
BCCEEHIKKKSTTU	KICKS THE BUCKET
BCCEEIKKKNORRS	KNICKERBOCKERS
BCCEEIKLNOOTUX	EXECUTION BLOCK
BCCEFHHIKNOPTU	PICK OF THE BUNCH
BCCEFHLOOOSTTT	BOTTLE OF SCOTCH
BCCFFMMOOOORRTU	CRUMB OF COMFORT
BCCGHILNOOORUU	BOROUGH COUNCIL
BCCHIIILNORSTU	BRITISH COUNCIL
BCDDEEEHHILNSU	BEHIND SCHEDULE
BCDDEEEHLLOORTU	CURDLE THE BLOOD
BCDEEEEILMRSTV	CLIMBED EVEREST
BCDEEEFGGMORRY	BEGGED FOR MERCY
BCDEEEFIJOORST	OBJECT OF DESIRE
BCDEEEGHIINRRS	RIDING BREECHES
BCDEEEGIINNOOW	OWING OBEDIENCE
BCDEEEHIILMNRT	THREE BLIND MICE
BCDEEEHILMNOPR	COMPREHENDIBLE
BCDEEEHJORSTUU	JUDE THE OBSCURE
BCDEEEHKOORRRT	BROKE THE RECORD
BCDEEEIIJNORSU	BIJOU RESIDENCE
BCDEEEIILMNOTT	MEDICINE BOTTLE
BCDEEEIKNORTWW	BERWICK ON TWEED
BCDEEEIMNNNRRUU	REDUCE IN NUMBER
BCDEEEIPRRSTTX	PRESCRIBED TEXT
BCDEEFFIMNOORT	COMBINED EFFORT
BCDEEFHIMMNOOR	COME FROM BEHIND
BCDEEGGHINOORR	BRING GOOD CHEER
BCDEEGIIMNNRSU	DISENCUMBERING
BCDEEHJOPRSTTU	DROP THE SUBJECT
BCDEEHOOORRRSST	CROSS THE BORDER
BCDEEIILNOORTU	RIBONUCLEOTIDE
BCDEEIILNRSTTU	INDESTRUCTIBLE
BCDEEILMOOPRTW	CLIMBED TO POWER
BCDEEKKNNOORSU	BROKEN ONE'S DUCK
BCDEELNOOORSST	STONE-COLD SOBER
BCDEELOOORRSSSU	DOUBLE CROSSERS
BCDEEMOOOPPRTT	COPPER-BOTTOMED
BCDEFFGIIILNOU	OFFICE BUILDING
BCDEFFGIIILNTU	BEING DIFFICULT
BCDEFGIINNNOOT	CONFINING TO BED
BCDEFHIOOORRTT	THIRD OF OCTOBER
BCDEFIKLLOOORT	TRICKLE OF BLOOD
BCDEFIKLNOSSTU	BUNDLE OF STICKS
BCDEGHIMOOPRSY	GOOD-BYE MR.CHIPS
	GOODBYE MR.CHIPS
BCDEGHINOORTTU	BOUGHT ON CREDIT
BCDEGIINNORTUY	BUYING ON CREDIT
BCDEGILNNOOTUU	COUNTING DOUBLE
BCDEGILNOORSSU	DOUBLE-CROSSING
BCDEHIILOOPTTY	THE BODY POLITIC
BCDEHILLLNOOOS	CHILL ONE'S BLOOD
BCDEHIOOORRSSTT	SCOTTISH BORDER
BCDEIIILRRTUY	IRREDUCIBILITY
BCDEIIILPPRSTU	PUBLIC SPIRITED
	PUBLIC-SPIRITED
BCDEIKNOORRSTU	DISCOUNT BROKER
BCDFHIILNORRST	FIRST-BORN CHILD
BCDGHIILLNOOSU	SCHOOL BUILDING

BCDHHIIOOPRTYY	HYDROPHOBICITY
BCDMOOOORRSSUWW	WORMWOOD SCRUBS
BCEEEEIIRRRSSV	SERVICEBERRIES
BCEEEFGIINORSV	BEING OF SERVICE
BCEEEFINNORRTU	BRIEF ENCOUNTER
BCEEEGHIKLNOOS	BESEECHING LOOK
BCEEEGILRSTTUY	GUEST CELEBRITY
BCEFFHIILNPTUY	IN THE PUBLIC EYE
BCEEEHIKKORTTW	BROKE THE WICKET
BCEEEHILMNOPRS	COMPREHENSIBLE
BCEEEHKNORRTTU	BROKEN THE TRUCE
BCEEEIKMNORRTZ	ROBERT MCKENZIE
BCEEEKKNNNOORS	BROKEN ONE'S NECK
BCEEEMMNORSSSU	CUMBERSOMENESS
BCEEEMNOPRRSTU	CURB ONES TEMPER
BCEEFHILOORRSW	BOWL OF CHERRIES
BCEEFHNOOOORTTT	TENTH OF OCTOBER
BCEEFIIILPRTTY	PERFECTIBILITY
BCEEGHIIKNPSTT	PICKING THE BEST
BCEEGIILLLNNPU	BLUE-PENCILLING
BCEEGIILMNNOST	BECOMING SILENT
BCEEGIILMNORTV	TREMBLING VOICE
BCEEGIIMNNOOST	COMES INTO BEING
BCEEGIMNNNOSSU	UNBECOMINGNESS
BCEEHIIILMNRST	BRITISH TELECOM
BCEEHILMNOPRSY	COMPREHENSIBLY
BCEEIIIILLRSTV	CIVIL LIBERTIES
BCEEIIILNNNSSV	INVINCIBLENESS
BCEEIIILPPRTTY	PERCEPTIBILITY
BCEEIILMNNOSTU	BIOLUMINESCENT
BCEEIILMNOPRSS	INCOMPRESSIBLE
BCEEIILNPRSTTU	PUBLIC INTEREST
BCEEIJORSSSTUU	SERIOUS SUBJECT
BCEEILNOORRTTV	CONTROVERTIBLE
BCEEILOPPRSUUX	PUBLIC EXPOSURE
BCEEIMMNPRSTUU	SUPERINCUMBENT
BCEELMNOOOSUUY	COME ON YOU BLUES
BCEEMNNOORRTUU	NUMBER ONE COURT
BCEFFFHIOOORTT	FIFTH OF OCTOBER
BCEFFGLLOOSSTU	SET OF GOLF-CLUBS
BCEFFHLNOORSUW	BUNCH OF FLOWERS
BCEFFIOOOORRSTT	FIRST OF OCTOBER
BCEFHINNOOORTT	NINTH OF OCTOBER
BCEFHIOOORSTTX	SIXTH OF OCTOBER
BCEGHIIJLNNOTU	JOINING THE CLUB
BCEGHIOPPRRSTT	BRIGHT PROSPECT
BCEGIIIJNSSTUV	SUBJECTIVISING
BCEGIIIJNSTUVZ	SUBJECTIVIZING
BCEGIIJNORSTTU	BRING TO JUSTICE
BCEGIMMNNOOOOY	BOOMING ECONOMY
BCEHIIILNORSV	CHOIR INVISIBLE
BCEHIIKOOSTTTU	TOOK THE BISCUIT
BCEHIILMPRSSUU	MUSIC PUBLISHER
BCEHILMOOPSTTT	CLIMBS TO THE TOP
BCEHKLNOOSTTUU	BLOCK OUT THE SUN
BCEHKMNOSSSTUU	SUCKS ONE'S THUMB
BCEIIILPSSTTUY	SUSCEPTIBILITY
BCEIIKNNNSTTWY	KNEW BY INSTINCT
BCEIILMNOPRSSY	INCOMPRESSIBLY
BCEIILNORTTUVY	CONTRIBUTIVELY
BCEIINNOORRSTTU	CONTRIBUTORIES
BCEIKLNOOOSSST	LICKS ONE'S BOOTS
BCEILOPPPRRTUY	PUBLIC PROPERTY
BCEINNNOOORRSSU	ROBINSON CRUSOE
BCEINNOOSSSTUY	BUSINESS TYCOON
BCELOPPRRSSTUU	SUPPORTERS CLUB
BCGHIMMNOOOTTU	TOUCHING BOTTOM
BCGIIILMOOORST	MICROBIOLOGIST
BCGIIILOOOSSST	SOCIOBIOLOGISTS
BCHIKMOOOORSTTT	HITS ROCK-BOTTOM
BCHNNOOOORWWWW	HOW NOW BROWN COW

BCIIILOPRRTTUY	CORRUPTIBILITY
BCIIKNNNOSTTWY	KNOW BY INSTINCT
BCIIMNOORSSTTU	OBSTRUCTIONISM
BCIINNOOPRSSTU	ON SUBSCRIPTION
BCIINOORSSTTTU	OBSTRUCTIONIST
BCIKMNNOPRTUUY	COUNTRY BUMPKIN
BDDDDEGIIINNOS	DID ONE'S BIDDING
BDDDEEEEHIIRTVY	DIVIDED BY THREE
BDDDEEEIINSVVY	DIVIDED BY SEVEN
BDDDEEGHIIITVY	DIVIDED BY EIGHT
BDDEEEEFIINRTV	DERIVED BENEFIT
BDDEEEEFILLMNY	FEEBLEMINDEDLY
BDDEEEEGHNOSST	HEDGED ONE'S BETS
BDDEEEEIILNVVY	DIVIDE BY ELEVEN
BDDEEEELNNORTU	DOUBLE ENTENDRE
BDDEEEFFGGIORT	BEGGED TO DIFFER
BDDEEEGHINRRTU	UNDER THE BRIDGE
BDDEEEHIIRSTVY	DIVIDES BY THREE
BDDEEEIILTVVWY	DIVIDE BY TWELVE
BDDEEEIINSSVVY	DIVIDES BY SEVEN
BDDEEELORRSSSY	SOBERLY DRESSED
BDDEEEFFIMOORRS	BIDS FOR FREEDOM
BDDEEGGGGNUUSTW	GETS BOGGED DOWN
BDDEEGGIINNOOV	BID GOOD EVENING
BDDEEGGINNORRU	BREEDING GROUND
BDDEEGHIIISTVY	DIVIDES BY EIGHT
BDDEEGHIIMNNNT	BENDING THE MIND
BDDEEGHIINNOPT	OPEN THE BIDDING
BDDEEGHHNNOORTU	GO ROUND THE BEND
BDDEEGHNORRUYY	GREYHOUND DERBY
BDDEEGIINNNOSY	DYING IN ONE'S BED
BDDEEHIINNPPTU	NIPPED IN THE BUD
BDDEEIINTTVWYY	DIVIDE BY TWENTY
BDDEEIOORRSSSY	DISOBEYS ORDERS
BDDEFFIINORRTU	FORBIDDEN FRUIT
BDDEFGIIIINVVY	DIVIDING BY FIVE
BDDEFGIINNORSS	FORBIDDINGNESS
BDDEFILOORRSTW	DREW FIRST BLOOD
BDDEGHIINNOPPR	DROPPING BEHIND
BDDEGIIIINNNVY	DIVIDING BY NINE
BDDEGIIILLNSTU	LISTED BUILDING
BDDEIIKLLORSTW	KILLED TWO BIRDS
BDDFGIIINORUVY	DIVIDING BY FOUR
BDDGGIIMNNOOOR	BID GOOD MORNING
BDDIMMNOORSWYY	MY WORD IS MY BOND
BDEEEEFHLOORTZ	FREEZE THE BLOOD
BDEEEEFIINRSTV	DERIVES BENEFIT
BDEEEEFINNRSTW	BETWEEN FRIENDS
BDEEEEGHIKNNNT	BENDING THE KNEE
BDEEEEGHILNOTU	DOUBLE EIGHTEEN
BDEEEEGHKLOPRT	BROKE THE PLEDGE
BDEEEEGHNOSSST	HEDGES ONE'S BETS
BDEEEEHHHILNTW	BEHIND THE WHEEL
BDEEEEHLLPRSST	PRESSED THE BELL
BDEEEEILNNNOTU	DOUBLE NINETEEN
BDEEEEILNRRRWY	ELDERBERRY WINE
BDEEEEFFHLOOORT	BEFORE THE FLOOD
BDEEEFGINRRTTU	BUTTERFINGERED
BDEEEFIILNRRTU	BRIEF INTERLUDE
BDEEEFLMNOOTTU	ELEMENT OF DOUBT
BDEEEFLNNNOTUV	BENEVOLENT FUND
BDEEEFLNNORSUV	BUNDLE OF NERVES
BDEEEFLNOORTUU	DOUBLE FOURTEEN
BDEEEGHIINORTV	GIVE ONE THE BIRD
BDEEEGIIMMNRRS	DISREMEMBERING
BDEEEGJMNRTTTU	BETTER JUDGMENT
BDEEEHHIIMNSTT	BEHIND THE TIMES
BDEEEHIINOPSTT	BESIDE THE POINT
BDEEEHILNNORVZ	LEONID BREZHNEV
BDEEEHILNORTTU	DOUBLE THIRTEEN
BDEEEHILOPPTTW	TIPPED THE ELBOW

BDEEEHINORTTTT	TO THE BITTER END
BDEEEHNNNORTTU	UNDER THE BONNET
BDEEEHORRRSSVW	SHREWD OBSERVER
BDEEEILMMNOSTW	DISEMBOWELMENT
BDEEEILMNOPRTX	BOLD EXPERIMENT
BDEEELLNORSSTU	ENDLESS TROUBLE
BDEEELOOPRSUUX	DOUBLE EXPOSURE
BDEEENNOPSSSST	BENDS ONE'S STEPS
BDEEFGHIIMNORT	BEFORE MIDNIGHT
BDEEFHHIIJNOST	FINISHED THE JOB
BDEEFHLNOOORTZ	FROZEN THE BLOOD
BDEEFHOOOORRTT	ORDER OF THE BOOT
BDEEFLNOOOORSZ	FROZE ONE'S BLOOD
BDEEGGHIINRTTT	GETTING THE BIRD
BDEEGGHILMNOST	THE MIND BOGGLES
BDEEGHILLLMNUW	HUMBLE DWELLING
BDEEGHLNOORTUW	BELOW THE GROUND
BDEEGHLNOORTWW	DREW THE LONGBOW
BDEEGIILLMNOSW	DISEMBOWELLING
BDEEGIILNNRSSU	DRESSING IN BLUE
BDEEGILLNRSTUW	TUNBRIDGE WELLS
BDEEGILNNOPTTU	PLUNGE INTO DEBT
BDEEGKNNOOHNUW	BROKE NEW GROUND
BDEEGLNOOOPSTU	GET ONE'S BLOOD UP
BDEEHHLMPPSTTU	PLUMB THE DEPTHS
BDEEHIIKNOPRST	POKED IN THE RIBS
BDEEHIILMNOTTY	BEYOND THE LIMIT
BDEEHINOORS3TU	BRUSH TO ONE SIDE
BDEEHMNNORSTUU	UNDER ONES THUMB
BDEEHNOOORTTXY	THE BUY NEXT DOOR
BDEEHNOOPRTTTW	POTTED THE BROWN
BDEEIILNOPSTTU	BOTTLE UP INSIDE
BDEEIKNOOOSSTU	SUITED ONE'S BOOK
BDEEIMNOOORRTW	ON BORROWED TIME
BDEEINNOOQSTUY	BEYOND QUESTION
BDEEINORSSSSTU	BURST ONE'S SIDES
BDEEKNNOOORRSW	BROKEN ONE'S WORD
BDEELMOOPRRSUW	BORROWED PLUMES
BDEELNNOOOSSY	BLOODY ONE'S NOSE
BDEEMNOOOPPRSW	MOPPED ONE'S BROW
BDEGGHINOOORSU	GOOD NEIGHBOURS
BDEGGILNNOOTUU	DOUBLE-TONGUING
BDEGHIIHNOOORSU	NEIGHBOURHOODS
BDEGHILNOOQRTT	BOLTING THE DOOR
BDEGHILNORSTTY	BODILY STRENGTH
BDEGIILMNOORVY	REMOVING BODILY
BDEGIIMNOORSTT	BED-SITTING ROOM
	BED-SITTING-ROOM
BDEGIINOOSSSSU	BUSINESS IS GOOD
BDEGLLMOOSSSUY	GOD BLESS MY SOUL!
BDEGLNOOOOPSTU	GOT ONE'S BLOOD UP
BDEHIIKLNORSTY	SYBIL THORNDIKE
BDEHIIKMORRRSS	BORDER SKIRMISH
BDEHIILLORSTTT	THRILLED TO BITS
BDEHIINOSSSTUW	DO BUSINESS WITH
BDEHILNNOORSTU	RUNS IN THE BLOOD
BDEHLNOOORSTTU	UNBOLTS THE DOOR
BDEIIIILMQRSUU	DISEQUILIBRIUM
BDEIIIILNSSTTY	DISTENSIBILITY
BDEIIILNNOSSSU	LIBIDINOUSNESS
BDEIIILRSTTUVY	DISTRIBUTIVELY
BDEIILMNNOOSTU	OMNIBUS EDITION
BDEILNNOOOORSUY	OLD BOYS REUNION
BDEIMNNNORRSUU	IN ROUND NUMBERS
BDEINNOOSSSTUW	DOWN TO BUSINESS
BDEKLNOOORSTWY	OLD BOYS' NETWORK
BDFGIIINOORTUU	DOUBTFUL ORIGIN
BDFHILOOORRSTT	THIRST FOR BLOOD
BDFMNOOOOORRTU	NO ROOM FOR DOUBT
BDGGGIINNOOPRU	GOOD UPBRINGING
BDGGIIIMNNNORT	BRINGING TO MIND

BDGGIIINNORSTT	GRINDING TO BITS
BDGHIMNNOSSTUW	THUMBS-DOWN SIGN
BDGIIIILOOSTVY	GOOD VISIBILITY
BDGIILNNOOOOPS	BLOOD POISONING
BDHIILLOORSTTY	BLOODTHIRSTILY
BDHJLNNNNOOOSY	LYNDON B.JOHNSON
BEEEEEEHNSTTWY	BETWEEN THE EYES
BEEEEEFFHILNTT	FEEL THE BENEFIT
BEEEEEFNOORSSY	BEFORE ONES EYES
BEEEEEGHPRTTUZ	GET THE BREEZE UP
BEEEEFFHILNTTT	FELT THE BENEFIT
BEEEEFGHORTTTT	GET THE BETTER OF
BEEEEFHHOORRST	BEFORE THE HORSE
BEEEEFIMNOORST	BEFORE ONES TIME
BEEEEFLNORSSTT	BETTERS ONESELF
BEEEEGHOPRTTUZ	GOT THE BREEZE UP
BEEEEHKOPRRRST	BROTHER'S KEEPER
BEEEEHLLPRSSST	PRESSES THE BELL
BEEEEHLNOPSTWX	BLOW THE EXPENSE
BEEEELNNNOSSTV	BENEVOLENTNESS
BEEEFFGIINNRST	FRINGE BENEFITS
BEEEFGGINORSSV	BEG FORGIVENESS
BEEEFGHIOSTTTT	GET THE BEST OF IT
BEEEFGHOORTTTT	GOT THE BETTER OF
BEEEFGILRSTTTU	GET BUTTERFLIES
BEEEFHHOOPRSTT	HOPE FOR THE BEST
BEEEFHIILMMPRS	LIFE MEMBERSHIP
BEEEFHIMOSSTTT	THE BEST OF TIMES
BEEEFINORSSSUY	EYE FOR BUSINESS
BEEEGGIIINNNOR	BIOENGINEERING
BEEEGGINNOORTT	GOING ONE BETTER
BEEEGHILLNTTUV	GIVEN THE BULLET
BEEEGHILLSTTUV	GIVES THE BULLET
BEEEGHINOQSTTU	BEG THE QUESTION
BEEEGHIOOPTUVZ	GIVE UP THE BOOZE
BEEEGIIILLNOSUY	I'LL BE SEEING YOU
BEEEGINNOOSTTU	BITE ONES TONGUE
BEEEGMNNORSSTU	GETS ONE'S NUMBER
BEEEHHILLSTTUY	HIT THE BULLS-EYE
BEEEHHILLSTTWW	BLEW THE WHISTLE
BEEEHHLNOOOPTT	TELEPHONE BOOTH
BEEEHHNORSSTTU	BRUSH ONES TEETH
BEEEHIKLOORSTT	STOKE THE BOILER
BEEEHILORRRSTW	WHORTLEBERRIES
BEEEHIMNNRRTTU	NUMBER THIRTEEN
BEEEHIRSSSTVWY	VERY BEST WISHES
BEEEHJLNOOPSST	SLEEPS ON THE JOB
BEEEHKLLNOPRST	BROKEN THE SPELL
BEEEHKLNORRSTU	BROKEN THE RULES
BEEEHLORRRSTVY	EVERLY BROTHERS
BEEEIILNOORTTV	BELIEVE IT OR NOT
BEEEIIMMORRSTT	BITTER MEMORIES
BEEEIKLLNOOSTT	LIKE ONE'S BOTTLE
BEEEILLNORSSSU	REBELLIOUSNESS
BEEEILNRSSSTTU	BUSINESS LETTER
BEEEINRSSSSUVV	SUBVERSIVENESS
BEEEKNNNOOORSS	BROKEN ONE'S NOSE
BEEENNOORSSSST	RESTS ONE'S BONES
BEEFGGGIMNOORR	BEGGING FOR MORE
BEEFGHINOORRTT	BRING TO THE FORE
BEEFGHIOOSTTTT	GOT THE BEST OF IT
BEEFGHLLNOORTU	GONE FOR THE BULL
BEEFGHLLOORSTU	GOES FOR THE BULL
BEEFGILNNOORST	BRING TO ONESELF
BEEFGILNNORSUY	BURYING ONESELF
BEEFGILORSTTTU	GOT BUTTERFLIES
BEEFHHIIJNOSST	FINISHES THE JOB
BEEFHILLMMPRSU	FULL MEMBERSHIP
BEEFHLLNORTTUW	WENT FOR THE BULL
BEEFHLNOOSSTTW	SOFTENS THE BLOW
BEEFIIIMNNNRTU	INFINITE NUMBER

BEEFIILNNOSSSU	LINE OF BUSINESS
BEEFILOORTUUYY	YOU BET YOUR LIFE!
BEEGGGHINOTTTY	GETTING THE GO-BY
BEEGGHIIINNNNT	IN THE BEGINNING
BEEGGHIILLNNRT	RINGING THE BELL
BEEGGHIILMRRST	THIMBLERIGGERS
BEEGGHIILNNORT	BRINGING TO HEEL
BEEGGHIILNOTVW	GIVING THE ELBOW
BEEGGHINOOTTTT	GETTING THE BOOT
BEEGGHINORRSTT	BRINGS TOGETHER
BEEGGIIKNNRSTU	STINGING REBUKE
BEEGGIILMNORTY	BOY MEETING GIRL
BEEGGILRRSTTTU	BITTER STRUGGLE
BEEGHHIILLNPSTU	PUSHING THE BELL
BEEGHHMPSTTTUU	GET THE THUMBS UP
BEEGHILLLLNOTT	TOLLING THE BELL
BEEGHILMOPRTWY	WEIGHTY PROBLEM
BEEGHILNOPTTTU	POTTING THE BLUE
BEEGHNOORRRTUY	YOUNGER BROTHER
BEEGIIIILLLNNTU	UNINTELLIGIBLE
BEEGIIMNNNORST	INNERMOST BEING
BEEGIIMNOPRSSS	BEGS PERMISSION
BEEGIJNNOOPSUV	GIVEN UP ONE'S JOB
BEEGIJNOOPSSUV	GIVES UP ONE'S JOB
BEEGIKLMNORSSW	BLEW SMOKE-RINGS
BEEGIKLNNORTTY	BROKEN IT GENTLY
BEEGILNNOORTUV	GIVEN NO TROUBLE
BEEGILNOORSTUV	GIVES NO TROUBLE
BEEGILNOORTTTU	GET INTO TROUBLE
BEEGINNNNOOOSW	BEING ON ONE'S OWN
BEEGINNORSSTTY	TRYING ONE'S BEST
BEEGINORSSTTTY	SETTING STORE BY
BEEHHHILMNTTTU	HUNT THE THIMBLE
BEEHHHOORRTTTW	WORTH THE BOTHER
BEEHHILLOSTTWW	BLOW THE WHISTLE
BEEHHILOSSSSTU	BLESS THIS HOUSE
BEEHHKLOOOSTTT	SHOOK THE BOTTLE
BEEHIIKNOPRSST	POKES IN THE RIBS
BEEHIKLOORTTTY	TOOK THE LIBERTY
BEEHILMNORRSUW	WHILE ROME BURNS
BEEHILMNORRTUW	WHILE ROME BURNT
BEEHILNOPRSSTU	PUBLISHERS NOTE
BEEHINOOPRSTTT	STRIP TO THE BONE
BEEHKLOOORTTTU	TOOK THE TROUBLE
BEEHLOOOORRSTTU	TROUBLESHOOTER
BEEHMMNNOOSSSTU	THUMBS ONE'S NOSE
BEEHNOPRSSTTTU	PRESS THE BUTTON
BEEIIIIMPRRTTV	PRIMITIVE TRIBE
BEEIIKLNNSSSUU	UNBUSINESSLIKE
BEEIILLLLTTTTY	LITTLE BY LITTLE
BEEIILNOSSTVWY	LIVE BY ONE'S WITS
BEEIILOPRSSTVX	VISIBLE EXPORTS
BEEIIMNSSSSUUV	SUBMISSIVENESS
BEEIINNNOSSTTT	BEST INTENTIONS
BEEIKMNNOSSSUY	MONKEY BUSINESS
BEEILLLNNOPSTU	PULL IN ONE'S BELT
BEEILNNOORRSTU	TROUBLE IN STORE
BEEILOORRSSTUU	SERIOUS TROUBLE
BEEIMNNOPRSSUU	ONE'S NUMBER IS UP
BEEIMNOOPPRSTU	OPPOSITE NUMBER
BEEINOOQSSSSUU	OBSEQUIOUSNESS
BEEINOORSSSSTU	BOISTEROUSNESS
BEELMNNNOOOSWY	BLOWN ONE'S MONEY
BEELMNNOOOSSWY	BLOWS ONE'S MONEY
BEELMNOOSSSSTT	BOTTOMLESSNESS
BEELNOOOPSSTUW	UP TO ONE'S ELBOWS
BEELOOOPRRSSTUY	OBSTREPEROUSLY
BEEMMNNOORRSUU	ENORMOUS NUMBER
BEFFGIINNOORST	BORING ONE STIFF
BEFGGHIOORRTTU	BROUGHT TO GRIEF
BEFGGIIILLNNORT	BRINGING TO LIFE

BEFGGIILNORSUW	BOWLING FIGURES
BEFGHIIILLLLNT	FILLING THE BILL
BEFGHIIILLNTTT	FITTING THE BILL
BEFGHIILLNOOTT	FOOTING THE BILL
BEFGHILNORRSUW	FLOWERING SHRUB
BEFGILLMNNORSU	SMELL OF BURNING
BEFGILNRSSTTUY	FLYING BUTTRESS
BEFHHKMNOOOOTT	BOOK OF THE MONTH
BEFHIILLMORSTT	FILLS TO THE BRIM
BEFHIKLOOSTTWY	BOTTLE OF WHISKY
BEFIILLMPTUVYY	MULTIPLY BY FIVE
BEFKLLOOOORRTU	LOOK FOR TROUBLE
BEFNOOPRRSTTUY	BY RETURN OF POST
BEGGGIILNNSSV	GIVING BLESSING
BEGGIIILSSTTUY	SUGGESTIBILITY
BEGGIINNORRSTT	BRINGING TO REST
BEGHHIILLNTTTU	HITTING THE BULL
BEGHHIIMNNPTTU	BUMP IN THE NIGHT
BEGHHIINORSTTW	BEING SHORT WITH
BEGHHIORRRSTTW	WRIGHT BROTHERS
BEGHHMOPSTTTUU	GOT THE THUMBS UP
BEGHIILLNOPPTT	TOPPING THE BILL
BEGHIILLNOSTUV	BLUSHING VIOLET
BEGHILMNNOOPRSU	HOUSING PROBLEM
BEGHINOPP33TTU	STOPPING THE BUS
BEGIIILNNNORST	BRINGS INTO LINE
BEGIINNOOSSSTU	GO INTO BUSINESS
BEGIJKNNNOOO3W	KNOWING ONE'O JOB
BEGIJLLNORTTUW	LITTLE BROWN JUG
BEGIKLMNOORSSW	BLOW SMOKE-RINGS
BEGIKNNNOOORST	BROKEN INTO SONG
BEGIKNOOORRRTV	TREVOR BROOKING
BEGILLNNOOOTTW	WELLINGTON BOOT
BEGILNNOOOPSTW	BLOWING ONE'S TOP
BEGILNOOORTTTU	GOT INTO TROUBLE
BEGILNORSSSUUU	LUGUBRIOUSNESS
BEHHIILMOSTTUW	WITHOUT BLEMISH
BEHHIKNOOPSTTU	PUT THE KIBOSH ON
BEHHILOOPRSSTT	SPOILS THE BROTH
BEHHMNOPRRTUUY	HUMPHREY BURTON
BEHIIIIMNOSSTX	EXHIBITIONISMS
BEHILLNOORSWWY	YELLOWISH BROWN
BEHLNOOOOSSSTT	SHOOTS ONE'S BOLT
BEHNORRSSTUWWY	SHREWSBURY TOWN
BEIIIILMPRSSTY	PERMISSIBILITY
BEIIILNOPRSSTY	RESPONSIBILITY
BEIIKNNOPRRSTU	UNBROKEN SPIRIT
BEIILLMNNPTUYY	MULTIPLY BY NINE
BEIINOQSSSTUUU	UBIQUITOUSNESS
BEIKNNOORSSSTW	KNITS ONE'S BROWS
BEIKOOPRRSSTUY	TOOK BY SURPRISE
BEILNNOOPSSTTU	BUTTON ONE'S LIPS
	BUTTONS ONE'S LIP
BEILNNOORRTTUU	RUN INTO TROUBLE
BEILOPRRSSTTUU	STIRS UP TROUBLE
BFGILLNORSTTUU	FULL TO BURSTING
BFILLMOPRTUUYY	MULTIPLY BY FOUR
BGGHHHOORRTTUU	BROUGHT THROUGH
BGGHHIIKLNOSWY	BLOWING SKY-HIGH
BGGHHILOORTTTU	BROUGHT TO LIGHT
BGGHHIOORTTTUU	BOUGHT OUTRIGHT
BGGHIIKNNOSTWY	KNOWING BY SIGHT
BGGHIINORTTUUY	BUYING OUTRIGHT
BGGIIINNOOORTT	GOING INTO ORBIT
BGHHOOPRRSTTUU	BROUGHT UP SHORT
BGIIKMNOORSTTT	STRIKING BOTTOM
BGIILLMMNNOOUU	IMMUNOGLOBULIN
BHIIIINOOPRSTT	PROHIBITIONIST
BIIIILOOPRSTVY	POOR VISIBILITY
CCCDEEEEFHIIKRT	CERTIFIED CHECK
CCCDEEGINNOOOS	GOOD CONSCIENCE

CCCDEEHIIKNRRU	CURRIED CHICKEN
CCCDEHHINORRTU	CHURCH DOCTRINE
CCCDGIILOOORTU	GLUCOCORTICOID
CCCEEEFIMNNRRSU	CIRCUMFERENCES
CCCEEEIIINRSTT	ECCENTRICITIES
CCCEEEIKLOORRT	ELECTRIC COOKER
CCCEEEILNNOSSS	CONSCIENCELESS
CCCEEFIIINNOST	SCIENCE FICTION
CCCEEFILLLMORU	COME FULL CIRCLE
CCCEEIIINOPRTV	CIVIC RECEPTION
CCCEEIILRTTTUY	ELECTRICITY CUT
CCCEEIKKNNORSS	CRICKS ONE'S NECK
CCCEFGINOOPRUY	OCCUPYING FORCE
CCCEGIILLNNOOT	COIN COLLECTING
CCCEIIILLOSTTV	COLLECTIVISTIC
CCCEIIIMNOORSS	ECONOMIC CRISIS
CCCEIIMMNNOORS	MICROECONOMICS
CCCEIIMNOPRSTU	CIRCUMSPECTION
CCCEIMMNOPRTTY	CRYPTIC COMMENT
CCCEMMNNOORRUY	COMMON CURRENCY
CCCHHHIORSSTTU	SCOTTISH CHURCH
CCCIIIMNNORSUU	UNCIRCUMCISION
CCCIIIMORRRTUY	MICROCIRCUITRY
CCCIILMNOORTUU	CIRCUMLOCUTION
CCCILMOORRTUUY	CIRCUMLOCUTORY
CCDDEEEELNORRSU	SECLUDED CORNER
CCDDEEIILNNOSTY	DISCONNECTEDLY
CCDDEEOUURRHVTI	STUCK COMMEL IFIT
CCDDEINOOOSTTV	STOOD CONVICTED
CCDDELNOORRTUY	ORDERLY CONDUCT
CCDEEEEFLNNOSU	DEFENCE COUNSEL
CCDEEEEFNNOSSY	SENSE OF DECENCY
CCDEEEEIILLRST	DIESEL-ELECTRIC
CCDEEEEIINORTV	RECEIVED NOTICE
CCDEEEEKNOOPRT	TOOK PRECEDENCE
CCDEEEFFIINRTT	INDIRECT EFFECT
CCDEEEFFILNNOS	SELF-CONFIDENCE
CCDEEEFIIMPRSY	SPECIFIC REMEDY
CCDEEEFILNNOOS	LOSE CONFIDENCE
CCDEEEGNOORRSS	GREEN CROSS CODE
CCDEEEHHIKLLTT	CHECKED THE TILL
CCDEEEHIIKLNRV	CHICKEN-LIVERED
CCDEEEHIIMNNUV	MUCH IN EVIDENCE
CCDEEEHIINPRST	INDIRECT SPEECH
CCDEEEHIIKLNOSS	SHOCKED SILENCE
CCDEEEHOORSSTTV	COVERED THE COST
CCDEEEIIKOPPST	PICKED TO PIECES
CCDEEEIIMNORTT	CRIME DETECTION
CCDEEEIINNNNOV	INCONVENIENCED
CCDEEEINNNORTT	INTERCONNECTED
CCDEEEILLMOOPST	COLLECTED POEMS
CCDEEENNOOPRRS	CORRESPONDENCE
CCDEEFFHIKNSTU	STUFFED CHICKEN
CCDEEFHHMORRRU	REFORMED CHURCH
CCDEEFILNNOOST	LOST CONFIDENCE
CCDEEGIIILNNRV	DRIVING LICENCE
CCDEEHIKLNNOOS	CHICKEN NOODLES
CCDEEHILNOORTU	TECHNICOLOURED
CCDEEHNOOSTTTU	COUNTED THE COST
CCDEEIILMNORTU	COMIC INTERLUDE
CCDEEIINOPRRTU	PRICE REDUCTION
CCDEEIMORRSTTU	CREDIT CUSTOMER
CCDEEKLLOORSTW	COLLECTED WORKS
CCDEEOOOPRRRTUU	COURT PROCEDURE
CCDEFIIILNRRTY	FRIENDLY CRITIC
CCDEGHHIIKLNNO	HOLDING IN CHECK
CCDEGIILNNOOOR	ENDOCRINOLOGIC
CCDEGIIMNNOSTU	SEMICONDUCTING
CCDEGILLNOSTTU	COLLECTING DUST
CCDEGINNNOORST	CONNECTING RODS
CCDEHHILLNOORS	SCHOOLCHILDREN

CCDEHIIORRSTTU	SHORT-CIRCUITED
CCDEIIIMMOSSTU	COMMITS SUICIDE
CCDEIIINORSTTU	REDUCTIONISTIC
CCDEIILMOOPSTY	DOMESTIC POLICY
CCDEIILNNORRSU	ROUND IN CIRCLES
CCDEIIOOORRSTT	CORTICOSTEROID
CCDEIKKNNOOPRW	KNOCK-DOWN PRICE
CCDEIMNOORSSTU	SEMICONDUCTORS
CCDENOOPRRSTUU	SUPERCONDUCTOR
CCDGHIIKNNORST	DRINKING SCOTCH
CCDHHHOOOORRTUX	ORTHODOX CHURCH
CCEEEEEEHHHIRSS	CHESHIRE CHEESE
CCEEEEEJNNRSUV	REJUVENESCENCE
CCEEEEEFHIITUVX	CHIEF EXECUTIVE
CCEEEEEFILNPRST	PERFECT SILENCE
CCEEEEEFNORRRSS	CROSS REFERENCE
	CROSS-REFERENCE
CCEEEEEHHHOORTT	CHEER TO THE ECHO
CCEEEEEHMNNOOST	COME ON THE SCENE
CCEEEEEIINORSTV	RECEIVES NOTICE
CCEEEEEIKLLRTTT	ELECTRIC KETTLE
CCEEEEFHILOOPRT	THE POLICE FORCE
CCEEEEFHMNRSUXY	EXCUSE MY FRENCH!
CCEEEEFMNNOOORR	CONFERENCE ROOM
CCEEEEGHIIKKNNP	KEEPING IN CHECK
CCEEEEGJLNNORTU	CONCRETE JUNGLE
CCEEEEHHHNNRRTTU	ENTER THE CHURCH
CCEEEEHIKLLNOSS	CLICK ONES HEELS
CCEEEEHILMORRTT	THERMOELECTRIC
CCEEEEHIMNOOPRT	CHEMORECEPTION
CCEEEEHMOOPRRST	CHEMORECEPTORS
CCEEEEIIKLNORTT	ELECTROKINETIC
CCEEEEIILOPSTVW	TELESCOPIC VIEW
CCEEEEIKLNOPRRT	RECEPTION CLERK
CCEEEEIILNOPSST	TELESCOPIC LENS
CCEEEEINSSSSSUV	SUCCESSIVENESS
CCEEEEJNOPRRTUU	PURE CONJECTURE
CCEEEELLNORUXYY	YOUR EXCELLENCY
CCEEEELNNOORSTU	CLOSE ENCOUNTER
CCEEEFGHIIILNNS	FISHING LICENCE
CCEEEFHIINOPRST	CHIEF INSPECTOR
CCEEEFHILNNOSST	CLENCH ONES FIST
CCEEEFIKLORRSTU	RULES OF CRICKET
CCEEEFIMNOOORST	COMES INTO FORCE
CCEEEFIMNOOORSU	SOURCE OF INCOME
CCEEEFLNSSSSSUU	SUCCESSFULNESS
CCEEEGGIKLNNOOS	COCKING ONE'S LEG
CCEEEGHHIILRSST	HIGHEST CIRCLES
CCEEEGHILLORSST	CHRISTS COLLEGE
CCEEEGIILMNNOTU	COUNCIL MEETING
CCEEEHIILLMOPTU	MULTIPLE-CHOICE
CCEEEHIKNOOOOST	TOOK ONE'S CHOICE
CCEEEHILMNORSTU	LUNCH-TIME SCORE
CCEEEHILOPRSTUW	WHITE CORPUSCLE
CCEEEHMOOPSTTUX	EXPECTS TOO MUCH
CCEEEIILNNORSTU	SILENCE IN COURT
CCEEEIINNOSSTTU	CONSTITUENCIES
CCEEEIINNQSSTTU	CINQUECENTISTS
CCEEEIKLNNNOOSW	NINE O CLOCK NEWS
CCEEEIKMMORTTTU	COMMUTER TICKET
CCEEEIILLMOORSTT	COLLECTORS ITEM
CCEEEIILLNNOOTUV	COLLECTIVE NOUN
CCEEEIILMNOPRSUU	SUPREME COUNCIL
CCEEEIILNNOSSSUV	CONCLUSIVENESS
CCEEEINNOOPPRST	PRECONCEPTIONS
CCEEEINOOPRRSUW	OWNER-OCCUPIERS
CCEEEINOOPRSSSU	PRECOCIOUSNESS
CCEEELNORRTTUUU	COUNTERCULTURE
CCEEENNORRRTTUU	COUNTERCURRENT
CCEEENOORRSSTWY	SWORN TO SECRECY
CCEFFHIIOOSSTT	SCOTTISH OFFICE

CCEFFIMOORSSTU	CUSTOMS OFFICER
CCEFHIIINORTUX	THE CRUCIFIXION
CCEFHIKOORSTTU	THE FIRST CUCKOO
CCEFIJOORSTTUU	COURT OF JUSTICE
CCEGGHILNOOOOR	GEOCHRONOLOGIC
CCEGHIIKKLNOPT	PICKING THE LOCK
CCEGHILNOSSSUW	HOWLING SUCCESS
CCEGHIMNOOORTW	ECONOMIC GROWTH
CCEGHINOSTTTTU	CUTTING THE COST
CCEGIIILLNOSTV	COLLECTIVISING
CCEGIIILLNOTVZ	COLLECTIVIZING
CCEGIIINNPRTTU	CUTTING IN PRICE
CCEGIIKKNOPPST	PICKING POCKETS
CCEGIILNOSTTTU	CUTTING IT CLOSE
CCEGIINNNNOSSV	CONVINCINGNESS
CCEGIKMNNOORST	SMOKING CONCERT
CCEGILNOOPRTUU	COURTING COUPLE
CCEGINNORRSTTU	CUTTING CORNERS
	RECONSTRUCTING
CCEHHMMNOOOTTU	THE COMMON TOUCH
CCEHIIIMOORSTT	STOICHIOMETRIC
CCEHIKLNOOPSSS	LICKS ONE'S CHOPS
CCEHIKOQSTTTUU	CUTS TO THE QUICK
CCEHIMMNOSTTUY	COMMUNITY CHEST
CCEHIMOOSSTUYZ	SCHIZOMYCETOUS
CCEHINOOPRSSUY	HYPERCONSCIOUS
CCEHINOOPRSTUY	PSYCHONEUROTIC
CCEHKLNOOPSTTU	PUT THE CLOCKS ON
CCEIIIJKMMNRTY	JIMMINY CRICKET
CCEIIIMMNNNOTTV	INNOCENT VICTIM
CCEIIILLNNOSUV	INCONCLUSIVELY
CCEIILNNNSSTUU	CUNNILINCTUSES
CCEIILNNOOORTV	VIOLIN CONCERTO
CCEIINORSSSTUU	CIRCUITOUSNESS
CCEIKLNORSSTUW	TURNS CLOCKWISE
CCEILNOOPRSSUY	PRECONSCIOUSLY
CCEILNORSTTUVY	CONSTRUCTIVELY
CCEIMMOOPRRSTU	MICROCOMPUTERS
CCEIMOOOPRRRSS	MICROPROCESSOR
CCEIMORRRSTTUU	MICROSTRUCTURE
CCEINNOORRSTTU	RECONSTRUCTION
CCEIOOPPRSSSTT	SPECTROSCOPIST
CCEMMNOOORSTUY	COMMON COURTESY
CCFIIIMNNOORTV	FIRM CONVICTION
CCFILLNOOSSUUY	FULLY CONSCIOUS
CCGHIILNNOOSUU	COUNCIL HOUSING
CCGHIIOOPRSTYY	HYGROSCOPICITY
CCGIIJKNNORRTU	CONJURING TRICK
CCGIIMMNOOPSSU	COMPOSING MUSIC
CCHIIKKNOOSTTU	KICKS INTO TOUCH
CCHIINOOOPRRTT	CORTICOTROPHIN
CCHIIOOPRRRTVYY	PYRRHIC VICTORY
CCIIIJJNNOSTTUV	CONJUNCTIVITIS
CCIIMNORSSTTUV	CONSTRUCTIVISM
CCIIINORSSTTTUV	CONSTRUCTIVIST
CCIKILLMNOORNSU	ROCK N ROLL MUSIC
CCILLNNOOORTUW	TOWN COUNCILLOR
CDDDEEEEINRTTX	EXTENDED CREDIT
CDDDEEGIMORSTU	DOMESTIC DRUDGE
CDDEEEEIORRRSV	RECEIVED ORDERS
CDDEEEENOPRSUW	REDUCE SPEED NOW
CDDEEEFIIMNOOS	DOSE OF MEDICINE
CDDEEEFLRSSTTU	SELF-DESTRUCTED
CDDEEEHIMNRUVY	VERY MUCH INDEED
CDDEEEHNNPRRTU	HUNDRED PER CENT
CDDEEEOOPRRTUW	REDUCE TO POWDER
CDDEEFHIINNOSS	FINISHED SECOND
CDDEEFIOORRSUV	SUED FOR DIVORCE
CDDEEGGILLNOPU	COLLEGE PUDDING
CDDEEGHLMNOOTU	DODGE THE COLUMN
CDDEEGIINOSTWY	SOCIETY WEDDING

CDDEEHHLOORRST	HOLDS THE RECORD
CDDEEIIMMNOOSS	DECOMMISSIONED
CDDEEIINNOORST	CONSIDER IT DONE
CDDEEIINOPPPRR	DROPPED IN PRICE
CDDEEIKLNNOUVY	LUDOVIC KENNEDY
CDDEEILLOSSTUY	STUDIED CLOSELY
CDDEEINOOPRRSV	DIVORCED PERSON
CDDEELNOORRRWW	NEW WORLD RECORD
CDDEGIIILLNRRT	DIRECT DRILLING
CDDEGIIILNOOPS	GOOD DISCIPLINE
CDDEGINNOORRSU	SOUND RECORDING
CDDEGINORSTTUU	REDUCING TO DUST
CDDEHIILMOORSU	SODIUM CHLORIDE
CDDEHIKNOOOSTT	STOOD IN THE DOCK
CDDEIIILLORVWZ	CIVILIZED WORLD
CDDEIIINNOOSSV	SECOND DIVISION
CDDEILLOOORTTT	DOCTOR DOLITTLE
CDDEILNOOOSTUY	DICOTYLEDONOUS
CDDEINOOOOPRTU	FOOD PRODUCTION
CDEEEEEFILNOSV	DECEIVE ONESELF
CDEEEEEINNQSUV	QUEENS EVIDENCE
CDEEEEFHNNORSW	SHOWN DEFERENCE
CDEEEEFHNORSSW	SHOWS DEFERENCE
CDEEEEFINNSSTW	DEFENCE WITNESS
CDEEEEFLNOSSUX	EXCUSED ONESELF
CDEEEEGGILNTTT	GETTING ELECTED
CDEEEEGHIOPRTT	PIECED TOGETHER
CDEEEEGINNNORS	SECOND ENGINEER
CDEEEEHIILMTTX	EXCEED THE LIMIT
CDEEEEHILOTTTV	HOTEL DETECTIVE
CDEEEEHIOSTTUV	HOUSE DETECTIVE
CDEEEEHOPPRRST	REPORTED SPEECH
CDEEEEIJNOSSTU	SEE JUSTICE DONE
CDEEEEILNOTTVV	DETECTIVE NOVEL
CDEEEEILNPRSTT	PRESIDENT ELECT
CDEEEEIOPRRSWX	EXERCISED POWER
CDEEEEIORRRSSV	RECEIVES ORDERS
CDEEEEIORSTTTV	STORE DETECTIVE
CDEEEELNOOSSSY	CLOSED ONE'S EYES
CDEEEEENNPSSTUX	UNEXPECTEDNESS
CDEEEEOPRRSVYY	SPEEDY RECOVERY
CDEEEFFINNOSST	FIFTEEN SECONDS
CDEEEEFGHILLNOT	FEELING THE COLD
CDEEEFGIKNOSTT	STOCKINGED FEET
CDEEEFGILLNNSU	SELF-INDULGENCE
CDEEEFGLLORRTY	REFLECTED GLORY
CDEEEFHIORSSTU	FORCED THE ISSUE
CDEEEFIILLNRUV	RECEIVED IN FULL
CDEEEFILMOORTV	REFLECTIVE MOOD
CDEEEFILNNNUUU	UNDUE INFLUENCE
CDEEEFILNOPSST	SELF-DECEPTIONS
CDEEEFFILORRTTT	LETTER OF CREDIT
CDEEEFIMNNOPRS	PRESENCE OF MIND
CDEEEFIMNORRSU	COMES UNDER FIRE
CDEEEFLNOORSSS	CROSSED ONESELF
CDEEEGGIINTTTX	GETTING EXCITED
CDEEEGHIINRTTV	GIVEN THE CREDIT
CDEEEGHIIRSTTV	GIVES THE CREDIT
CDEEEGHINNQSUU	UNSIGNED CHEQUE
CDEEEGIINORRRV	RECEIVING ORDER
CDEEEGLLNOSTTU	COLLEGE STUDENT
CDEEEHHHIOPRSS	CHERISHED HOPES
CDEEEHHNNORSTY	HENRY THE SECOND
CDEEEHIKNRRSST	KITCHEN DRESSER
CDEEEHILNORSST	CROSSED THE LINE
CDEEEHINORSTWZ	SEIZED THE CROWN
CDEEEHIPRSTTUW	WITH DUE RESPECT
CDEEEHKLOOPTTU	KEEP THE COLD OUT
CDEEEIIINNSSSV	INDECISIVENESS
CDEEEIILMNTTWX	WILD EXCITEMENT
CDEEEIINRSSTUV	UNITED SERVICES

CDEEEIINRSTTTY	SECRET IDENTITY
CDEEEIKLRRRSSV	RECKLESS DRIVER
CDEEEILMNOPSST	SPLENECTOMISED
CDEEEILMNOPSTZ	SPLENECTOMIZED
CDEEEIORSTTTVY	DETECTIVE STORY
CDEEEKMNOOSTYY	KEYSTONE COMEDY
CDEEFFFNOOPRTU	PROFOUND EFFECT
CDEEFFGHHHIILO	HELD HIGH OFFICE
CDEEFFILOORRRY	ORDERLY OFFICER
CDEEFGHINNRRSS	FRENCH DRESSING
CDEEFGIINRRSTU	REFUSING CREDIT
CDEEFGIMOOPRST	GIFTED COMPOSER
CDEEFGINORRSSS	CROSSED FINGERS
	FINGERS CROSSED
CDEEFGIOORSSTY	DREGS OF SOCIETY
CDEEFHHILNOPRS	FRENCH-POLISHED
CDEEFHHIOORTTW	THROW OF THE DICE
CDEEFHIINNOSSS	FINISHES SECOND
CDEEFHIKLLOTUV	LUCK OF THE DEVIL
CDEEFHLNORTTUY	FLED THE COUNTRY
CDEEFIIILLNPSS	SELF-DISCIPLINE
CDEEFIIKLLPRSW	WILFRED PICKLES
CDEEFIINNOOOOV	FINDS ONE'S VOICE
CDEEFINNOOOSUV	FOUND ONE'S VOICE
CDEEFIOORRSSUV	SUES FOR DIVORCE
CDEEFLLLNOORST	SELF-CONTROLLED
CDEEFMOOOORRRSY	COMEDY OF ERRORS
CDEEGGHHIINTTT	GETTING HITCHED
CDEEGGILLNNOOW	DOWNING COLLEGE
CDEEGHHIIKNTTT	HITTING THE DECK
CDEEGHHIRSTTTT	STRETCHED TIGHT
CDEEGHIIKNNSTT	TENDING THE SICK
CDEEGHIMNNOOTT	COMING TO THE END
CDEEGHNOORRTUV	COVER THE GROUND
CDEEGIIKNPPPSU	PICKING UP SPEED
CDEEGIINOPRSST	GRINDS TO PIECES
CDEEGIINORSTUZ	REDUCING TO SIZE
CDEEGILNNORXYY	OXYGEN CYLINDER
CDEEGINOOPRSTU	GROUND TO PIECES
CDEEHHIMNNOTWY	DOWN THE CHIMNEY
CDEEHHKOOPRRSS	SHEPHERDS CROOK
CDEEHIIKSSTTV	VISITED THE SICK
CDEEHIIKMMRRTTW	TRIMMED THE WICK
CDEEHIILLLNRTT	LITTLE CHILDREN
CDEEHIKNORTTUW	ROUND THE WICKET
CDEEHILMNNOPTT	HELD IN CONTEMPT
CDEEHILNOOSTTW	CLOSE TO THE WIND
CDEEHILNOOSTWW	CLOSE THE WINDOW
CDEEHILOSSSTUU	CLOUDS THE ISSUE
CDEEHKLOOPTTTU	KEPT THE COLD OUT
CDEEHKLOORSTUW	WORK TO SCHEDULE
CDEEHLNOOSTTTY	HOTLY CONTESTED
CDEEHLOOOOPPST	SCOOPED THE POOL
CDEEHLOOOOPPRRR	ROD,POLE OR PERCH
CDEEHNNOORRRTU	ROUND THE CORNER
CDEEHNOOORSSSW	CHOSE ONE'S WORDS
CDEEIIINNSSTVV	VINDICTIVENESS
CDEEIIKLOORSTT	COILED TO STRIKE
CDEEIILLMMNOPT	IDLE COMPLIMENT
CDEEIILMNNOPST	IMPLIED CONSENT
CDEEIILMNOPSTU	UNLIMITED SCOPE
CDEEIILNNORSS	CRINOLINE DRESS
CDEEIINNOPRSWZ	WIN SECOND PRIZE
CDEEIINNORRTTU	CURRENT EDITION
CDEEIINOQRSTTU	DIRECT QUESTION
CDEEIINRSSSSUV	DISCURSIVENESS
CDEEIIOOPPRSST	DIRECT OPPOSITE
CDEEIJLOOPRRST	SLIDE PROJECTOR
CDEEIKLLOSSSSU	CLOUDLESS SKIES
CDEEIKNOPSSTUY	KEEPS IN CUSTODY
CDEEIKNORSSSTX	DRINKS TO EXCESS

CDEEILLNOOPTUY	POLYNUCLEOTIDE
CDEEILLOSSSTUY	STUDIES CLOSELY
CDEEILMNNNOOOTU	MONONUCLEOTIDE
CDEEILMOOPPSUX	OEDIPUS COMPLEX
CDEEILNOORRSUX	EXCLUSION ORDER
CDEEIMNNNOSTTT	DISCONTENTMENT
CDEEIMNNOORSSW	MINCE ONES WORDS
CDEEINNOOPRSWZ	WON SECOND PRIZE
CDEEINNOOPRTTU	COUNTERPOINTED
CDEEINOPRSSTUV	PRODUCTIVENESS
CDEEKKLNRSSTUU	KNUCKLE-DUSTERS
CDEEKNNNNOOOSW	DOWN ON ONE'S NECK
CDEELLNNOORRTT	CONTROLLED RENT
CDEELOPRRSSTUU	PRODUCE RESULTS
CDEENNOOPRRSST	CORRESPONDENTS
CDEENNOORSTTVY	SEND TO COVENTRY
CDEENOOOORTTTW	COTTONWOOD TREE
CDEFFGHHHIILOO	HOLD HIGH OFFICE
CDEFFHILNOORTU	CHILD OF FORTUNE
CDEFFIIIILNSTU	IN DIFFICULTIES
CDEFFIIILMSTTU	DIFFICULT TIMES
CDEFFIILLNNOTU	FULL OF INCIDENT
CDEFFKKKKNOOORW	KNOCKED OFF WORK
CDEFGHINNRSTUY	STUDYING FRENCH
CDEFHIINOOORSU	HOUR OF DECISION
CDEFHLLOOORTWW	FOLLOW THE CROWD
CDEFIILMNOORTV	LIVED IN COMFORT
CDEFMNOOOORSWY	ECONOMY OF WORDS
CDEGGHHIJORTUU	HIGH COURT JUDGE
CDEGGINNOORRUV	COVERING GROUND
CDEGHHIOORTTWW	GO WITH THE CROWD
CDEGHHNOORTTUU	TOUCH THE GROUND
CDEGHHNOOSSTTU	SECOND THOUGHTS
CDEGHIIINORRTT	RIGHT DIRECTION
CDEGHIIKLNSTTU	LICKING THE DUST
CDEGHIKLNOOOORT	LOCKING THE DOOR
CDEGHILNOOORST	CLOSING THE DOOR
CDEGIIIIILNOPST	DEPOLITICISING
CDEGIIIILNOPTZ	DEPOLITICIZING
CDEGIIINNNOORT	RECONDITIONING
CDEGIIINNOORRTW	WRONG DIRECTION
CDEGIKKLNNNRUU	KNUCKLING UNDER
CDEGILNOPPRTUU	REDUCING TO PULP
CDEHHIILLOPSST	SPOILS THE CHILD
CDEHHNNOOOTTUW	ON THE TOUCHDOWN
CDEHIIIKLNOPTT	PILED IT ON THICK
CDEHIIKLMRTTUY	THIRD TIME LUCKY
CDEHIIKMNSSTTU	STICK-IN-THE-MUDS
CDEHILMNNOOPTT	HOLD IN CONTEMPT
CDEHILNOPRTUWW	WIN THE WORLD CUP
CDEHILNORRSSTY	CHILDRENS STORY
CDEHINOOOORRSTY	HYDROCORTISONE
CDEHKKNNOOOOORT	KNOCK ON THE DOOR
CDEHKLNOOOORSTU	UNLOCKS THE DOOR
CDEHKOOOORRRST	SHORT ORDER COOK
CDEHLNOOPRTUWW	WON THE WORLD CUP
CDEHMNNOOPSSYY	SECOND SYMPHONY
CDEIIIILRSTTUV	DIVERTICULITIS
CDEIIIKLMNNOSY	EMILY DICKINSON
CDEIIIMNNOOPRT	PRIME CONDITION
CDEIIINNNSSSTT	INDISTINCTNESS
CDEIIJLOPRSUUY	PREJUDICIOUSLY
CDEIIKNOSSTWWX	SIX WICKETS DOWN
CDEIILNNOOPRTU	PRODUCTION LINE
CDEIILNNOPPRSU	SOUND PRINCIPLE
CDEIILNORSSSUU	RIDICULOUSNESS
CDEIIMNNOOPPRST	PROMPT DECISION
CDEIINNNNOOOOT	ON ONE CONDITION
CDEIINNOOPSSSU	OPEN DISCUSSION
CDEIINNOPRSSUU	UNDER SUSPICION
CDEIKLLOOOPRSV	LIVERPOOL DOCKS

CDEIKLNNOOOSSUW	LICK ONES WOUNDS
CDEIKNOOSTTWWW	TWO WICKETS DOWN
CDEILNOOOOPPRY	OPEN-DOOR POLICY
CDEILOORSSTUUY	DISCOURTEOUSLY
CDEIMMNOOOSSSU	COMMODIOUSNESS
CDEINOOOPRRTUV	OVERPRODUCTION
CDEINOOSSTTUWZ	CUTS DOWN TO SIZE
CDEKLNNNOOOSUW	DOWN ON ONES LUCK
CDELMNNOOOOOSTY	MONOCOTYLEDONS
CDFFGIIMNNOORT	FINDING COMFORT
CDFGIIOORRSTVY	DIGS FOR VICTORY
CDFIINNOOOOTTU	OUT OF CONDITION
CDGGHINNOORTUU	TOUCHING GROUND
CDGGIMMNOOOOOT	COMING TO NO GOOD
CDGIKKNNNOOOOW	KNOCKING ON WOOD
CDGINOORRSSSSW	CROSSING SWORDS
CDHHIIILLOPRTYY	HYDROPHILICITY
CDHIINOOOOOPRSU	CONIDIOPHOROUS
CDHILNNOOOSSTT	LONDON SCOTTISH
CDIIIMNNOPSSSUU	SUSPICIOUS MIND
CDIILMMNOOOSUY	INCOMMODIOUSLY
CDIILNOORRTTUY	INTRODUCTORILY
CDIKKLNOOOQRUU	QUICK LOOK ROUND
CDINNOORSTTTUY	COTTON INDUSTRY
CEEEEEEHLMOSTT	CHEESE OMELETTE
CEEEEEENNNPSTV	SEVENTEEN PENCE
CEEEEEENNRSSTV	SEVERE SENTENCE
CEEEEFFINNPSTT	FIFTEEN PER CENT
CEEEEFFINORRUV	REVENUE OFFICER
CEEEEFFLNRSTVY	EFFERVESCENTLY
CEEEEFFOOPRSSS	ESPRESSO COFFEE
CEEEEFGIINRRSX	FINGER EXERCISE
CEEEEFHLLPSSST	LEFT SPEECHLESS
CEEEEFIINNPPVY	FIVEPENNY PIECE
CEEEEFILNNRTUX	EXERT INFLUENCE
CEEEEFILNRSSTV	REFLECTIVENESS
CEEEEFIMNPRSTT	IMPERFECT TENSE
CEEEEFLNOPRSST	RESPECT ONESELF
CEEEEFLNOSSSUX	EXCUSES ONESELF
CEEEEGHINNOPTY	EIGHTY-ONE PENCE
CEEEEGHIOPRSTT	PIECES TOGETHER
CEEEEGIILNNORT	ELECTIONEERING
CEEEEGINNPRSTU	GENUINE RESPECT
CEEEEHIIPRSTTU	THREE-PIECE SUIT
CEEEEHLLORSSTV	LEVELS THE SCORE
CEEEEHLNPSSSSS	SPEECHLESSNESS
CEEEEIISTTUUVX	EXECUTIVE SUITE
CEEEEIKNOOPPSS	SPOKE ONE'S PIECE
CEEEEIMNNNRSTT	TEN CENTIMETRES
CEEEEINNNNOPTY	NINETY-ONE PENCE
CEEEEINNPRSTTX	SIXTEEN PER CENT
CEEEEINPPRSSTV	PERCEPTIVENESS
CEEEEINPPRRSTV	IN EVERY RESPECT
CEEEEINPRSSSTV	RESPECTIVENESS
CEEEEIOPRRSSWX	EXERCISES POWER
CEEEEKLLPRSTTW	WELL-KEPT SECRET
CEEEELNOOSSSSY	CLOSES ONE'S EYES
CEEEENNNOPTTWY	TWENTY-ONE PENCE
CEEEENNNPTTWWY	TWENTY NEW PENCE
CEEEENNPRSTTVY	SEVENTY PER CENT
CEEEFFFGOORSTT	GET OFF SCOT-FREE
CEEEFFFIINPTVY	FIFTY-FIVE PENCE
CEEEFFGHIOPRSU	FIGURE OF SPEECH
CEEEFFHIILOPST	THE SPICE OF LIFE
CEEEFFHILOPSTT	SPOIL THE EFFECT
CEEEFFIINNNPTY	FIFTY-NINE PENCE
CEEEFFILPRSTTU	PETER SUTCLIFFE
CEEEFFINOORSSU	SERIOUS OFFENCE
CEEEFFINOPRTVY	FORTY-FIVE PENCE
CEEEFGHIIKLNPS	FEELING PECKISH
CEEEFGIINORRSV	FOREIGN SERVICE

CEEEFGILNPRSST	SELF-RESPECTING
CEEEFGINPRSTTT	PERFECT SETTING
CEEEFGLLNNSSTU	NEGLECTFULNESS
CEEEFHILMNNRST	SELF-ENRICHMENT
CEEEFHINNOSSTT	SITS ON THE FENCE
CEEEFHIORSSSTU	FORCES THE ISSUE
CEEEFHLNORTTUY	FLEE THE COUNTRY
CEEEFHLOPPRSUW	POWERFUL SPEECH
CEEEFHMOOORSTT	COMES TO THE FORE
CEEEFHNNORSSSU	RUSH ONES FENCES
CEEEFIILLNRSUV	RECEIVES IN FULL
CEEEFIILOPRSSV	PIECES OF SILVER
CEEEFIINPSTVXY	SIXTY-FIVE PENCE
CEEEFILNOPPRST	SELF-PERCEPTION
CEEEFINNNOPRTY	FORTY-NINE PENCE
CEEEFINOORRSTU	CONIFEROUS TREE
CEEEFINORRSTTU	COUNTERFEITERS
CEEEFKNOOPRSTT	TOKEN OF RESPECT
CEEEFLMNOOOPSS	COMPOSE ONESELF
CEEEFLMNOOOSST	COMES TO ONESELF
CEEEFLNOORSSSS	CROSSES ONESELF
CEEEFLNPRSSSTU	RESPECTFULNESS
CEEEFLOOOPPRSS	SCORES OF PEOPLE
CEEEFNNOORSTUU	FOURTEEN OUNCES
CEEEFNOORSSTUV	COURSE OF EVENTS
CEEEGGGMNOORRV	GEORGE MCGOVERN
CEEEGHHILNOSTW	COGS IN THE WHEEL
CEEEGHHLNOTTTU	THE GENTLE TOUCH
CEEEGHIIKNNTTT	GET IT IN THE NECK
CEEEGHIIKNORTV	RECEIVING THE O.K.
CEEEGHIINPSTXY	EIGHTY-SIX PENCE
CEEEGHILNNOSTV	EVENING CLOTHES
CEEEGHINOPTTWY	EIGHTY-TWO PENCE
CEEEGHIPRSTTTU	GETS THE PICTURE
CEEEGIIILPRSVV	GIVE LIP SERVICE
CEEEGIILLNNRST	INTELLIGENCERS
CEEEGIINNOOSTV	GIVE ONES NOTICE
CEEEGIKLNNOPSU	KEEPING COUNSEL
CEEEGILNORRTTV	COVERING LETTER
CEEEGLMNOSTUUW	UNWELCOME GUEST
CEEEGNOOORSSTU	GO TO ONE'S RESCUE
CEEEHHHIOPRSSS	CHERISHES HOPES
CEEEHHIIKKNTTT	KICK IN THE TEETH
CEEEHHIIKNSTTV	THIEVES KITCHEN
CEEEHHILOPRRST	CHRISTOPHER LEE
CEEEHHIPQRSTTU	QUEERS THE PITCH
CEEEHIJNOPSTTU	STEP ON THE JUICE
CEEEHIKKLNOSSS	KICKS ONE'S HEELS
CEEEHIKNNOPPSU	KEEP ONES CHIN UP
CEEEHILLORRSTW	LESLIE CROWTHER
CEEEHILNORSSST	CROSSES THE LINE
CEEEHILOPRRSTW	LOWERS THE PRICE
CEEEHILRSSTTUV	SHUTTLE SERVICE
CEEEHIMNOPRSSV	COMPREHENSIVES
CEEEHIMORSSTTY	HYSTERECTOMIES
	HYSTERECTOMISE
CEEEHIMORSTTYZ	HYSTERECTOMIZE
CEEEHINNOPRTTY	THIRTY-ONE PENCE
CEEEHINNORSTTU	THIRTEEN OUNCES
CEEEHINOPQRSTU	QUEER ONE'S PITCH
CEEEHINORRSTTU	CHINESE TORTURE
CEEEHINORSSTWZ	SEIZES THE CROWN
CEEEHIOOPPRTTV	PHOTORECEPTIVE
CEEEHJLNORSTWW	THE CROWN JEWELS
CEEEHLLNOOOSSS	COOLS ONE'S HEELS
CEEEHLLNOOPRTW	HOLLOW PRETENCE
CEEEHNNNRSTTUVY	SEVENTH CENTURY
CEEEHNOORRTTUV	OVER THE COUNTER
CEEEHORRSSSTTT	CROSS THE STREET
CEEEIILNPPPRRT	PETER PRINCIPLE

CEEEIIMNRSSTTX	SIX CENTIMETRES
CEEEIIMOORRSST	STEREOISOMERIC
CEEEIINNNPSTXY	NINETY-SIX PENCE
	SIXTY-NINE PENCE
CEEEIINPPRRSST	INSPIRE RESPECT
CEEEIILLNORSTTU	ELECTION RESULT
CEEEILMNNOPSST	INCOMPLETENESS
CEEEILNOOORSVW	LOWER ONES VOICE
CEEEILNOOOSSSV	LOSES ONE'S VOICE
CEEEIMMMNOOTTW	COMMITTEEWOMEN
CEEEIMMMNPSSUU	MUSEUM SPECIMEN
CEEEIMMNNOPRTV	PINCER MOVEMENT
CEEEIMNORSTTTW	TWO CENTIMETRES
CEEEINNNOPRSST	PRISON SENTENCE
CEEEINNNOPTTWY	NINETY-TWO PENCE
CEEEINNPSTTWXY	TWENTY-SIX PENCE
CEEEINOPRSSTTV	PROTECTIVENESS
CEEEINPSSSSTUV	SUSCEPTIVENESS
CEEEKOOPRRRSSU	PRESSURE COOKER
CEEENNOPPPRRRT	PEPPERCORN RENT
CEEENNOPTTTWWY	TWENTY-TWO PENCE
CEEENOORSSTUUY	CRY ONES EYES OUT
CEEFFFGOUOORSTT	GOT OFF SCOT-FREE
CEEFFFHIMORTTW	WITH EFFECT FROM
CEEFFFIILNSSTU	SELF-SUFFICIENT
CEEFFFINOPRTUY	FIFTY-FOUR PENCE
CEEFFGIIKNRSTT	STRIKING EFFECT
CEEFFGIIORRSTY	REGISTRY OFFICE
CEEFFHIILNNOOS	INCH OF ONE'S LIFE
CEEFFHNOPSTTTU	PUT OFF THE SCENT
CEEFFNNOOOSSTU	CUT OFF ONES NOSE
CEEFFNOOPRRTUY	FORTY-FOUR PENCE
CEEFGHHIMNUSST	SCHEME OF THINGS
CEEFGHIIINPRTX	FIXING THE PRICE
CEEFGHIILLNOST	CLOSING THE FILE
CEEFGHIKNOOORRT	CROOK THE FINGER
CEEFGHILNOORSY	CHOOSING FREELY
CEEFGIIKKLNNOS	KICKING ONESELF
CEEFGIIKNNSSSS	FEIGNS SICKNESS
CEEFGIINNORTTU	COUNTERFEITING
CEEFGINORRRRSS	CROSS-REFERRING
CEEFGLLLNOOOSW	WOLFSON COLLEGE
CEEFHHIILNRTTU	LEFT IN THE LURCH
CEEFHHILNOPRSS	FRENCH-POLISHES
CEEFHHMNORRTUV	FRENCH VERMOUTH
CEEFHIIOOPRSTY	PIECE OF HISTORY
CEEFHLLNOOSTTW	FOLLOW THE SCENT
CEEFHLNORTTTUY	LEFT THE COUNTRY
CEEFHLNRTTTUWY	TWELFTH CENTURY
CEEFHMNOOORTTT	COME TO THE FRONT
CEEFHNORRSTTUW	TURN OF THE SCREW
CEEFIILNOSSSTU	FELICITOUSNESS
CEEFIILORRSSST	CROSS-FERTILISE
CEEFIILORRSSTZ	CROSS-FERTILIZE
CEEFIIMNOORSTU	IN COURSE OF TIME
CEEFIINNOSSSTU	INFECTIOUSNESS
CEEFIINOOPRRTT	FIRE PROTECTION
CEEFIINOPRSSTT	PERFECTIONISTS
CEEFILMMNOOSST	COMMITS ONESELF
CEEFILNNOOPRTU	UPON REFLECTION
CEEFILNNOSSSTT	SELF-CONSISTENT
CEEFINNOORSSTU	TRUE CONFESSION
CEEFINOOOOPSTV	TOP OF ONES VOICE
CEEFINOORSSSUV	VOCIFEROUSNESS
CEEFINOPRSTUXY	SIXTY-FOUR PENCE
CEEFLLLMMNOPTU	FULL COMPLEMENT
CEEFLLNNOOORST	CONTROL ONESELF
CEEFMMMOOOPRRSU	COMES UP FOR MORE
CEEFOOORRRSSTT	RESORTS TO FORCE
CEEGGHHINOPTTT	GETTING THE CHOP
CEEGGHILNORSTT	CLINGS TOGETHER

973

CEEGHHIIILNSTT	HITS THE CEILING
CEEGHHILNOPSST	SHEEPS CLOTHING
CEEGHHIRSSTTTT	STRETCHES TIGHT
CEEGHIIKNNOPTU	KEEPING IN TOUCH
CEEGHIIKNNOTTT	GOT IT IN THE NECK
CEEGHIIINNPPRST	SHIPPING CENTRE
CEEGHIINPRRSST	STIRRING SPEECH
CEEGHIIRRSSTUW	CRUISERWEIGHTS
CEEGHIKMNOPRST	SHOCKING TEMPER
CEEGHIKORSSTTT	STICKS TOGETHER
CEEGHINNOOQRRU	CONQUERING HERO
CEEGHINNOPPRST	SHOPPING CENTRE
CEEGHINOPRSSTW	SHOWING RESPECT
CEEGHINORSTTUW	COUNTERWEIGHTS
CEEGHLNOOOORTTY	TEROTECHNOLOGY
CEEGIIKKLLSSTU	STICKS LIKE GLUE
CEEGIIKKNNOPST	KEEPING IN STOCK
CEEGIIKLLNSSTT	SELLING TICKETS
CEEGIIILNORTTY	TRINITY COLLEGE
CEEGIILNNORRTY	NITROGLYCERINE
CEEGIINOPRRTTY	RECITING POETRY
CEEGIKLNOOPRST	ROCKING TO SLEEP
CEEGIKNNOOSSTW	GETS ON ONE'S WICK
CEEGILMNNORSTU	STEERING COLUMN
CEEGKNOOOOOSSS	COOKS ONE'S GOOSE
CEEGNNOOPRRTUU	ENCOUNTER GROUP
CEEHHHIRSTTTWW	THREW THE SWITCH
CEEHHIIKKNNSTT	THE KITCHEN SINK
CEEHHIILRTTTTU	ELICIT THE TRUTH
CEEHHILNNOOTTU	ON THE TOUCH-LINE
CEEHHIMMORSSTT	THERMOCHEMISTS
CEEHHINRRTTTUW	WITH THE CURRENT
CEEHHKLLMOORSS	SHERLOCK HOLMES
CEEHHMOORSSTUW	SO MUCH THE WORSE
CEEHHNNNOOPSTU	PUNCH ON THE NOSE
CEEHHNOOPPRSST	PHOSPHORESCENT
CEEHIIKLNNSTTU	KITCHEN UTENSIL
CEEHIIKNNPRSTW	PICKS THE WINNER
CEEHIIKNRRSTTT	THIRTEEN TRICKS
CEEHIIILLMPSSTV	HELPLESS VICTIM
CEEHIIILLPRSTTT	LITTLE PITCHERS
CEEHIIILMOPRRTY	PYRHELIOMETRIC
CEEHIIINNORRSTT	SIT IN THE CORNER
CEEHIIINPRSTTXY	THIRTY-SIX PENCE
CEEHIIIOOPRRTTY	ERYTHROPOIETIC
CEEHIKLLORSTTW	ROLLS THE WICKET
CEEHIKNNOPPSTU	KEPT ONE'S CHIN UP
CEEHIKNOOSSTTW	SHOW ONES TICKET
CEEHILLOOOSTTT	LITTLE TO CHOOSE
CEEHIMMOPSSSTY	METEMPSYCHOSIS
CEEHIMNOOOPTTT	COME TO THE POINT
CEEHIMNORRSTUY	NEUROCHEMISTRY
CEEHIMOPRRSTTY	PETROCHEMISTRY
CEEHINNNNOOTTT	ON THE CONTINENT
CEEHINOOOPPRTT	PHOTORECEPTION
CEEHINOPQRSTTU	THE CINQUE PORTS
CEEHINOPRTTTWY	THIRTY-TWO PENCE
CEEHIOOOOPRRRRR	RICHER OR POORER
CEEHIOOOPSSSTT	SHOOTS TO PIECES
CEEHIOPRSTTTUW	WITHOUT RESPECT
CEEHIPPPRSTTUU	PUTS UP THE PRICE
CEEHLMNOOOSSTU	CLOSE ONES MOUTH
CEEHLNOOOPRSTT	PHOTOELECTRONS
CEEHLNOOOSSSTU	LOSES ONE'S TOUCH
CEEHNNORRRSTTU	TURNS THE CORNER
CEEHNOOPRSSSTW	SHOWS NO RESPECT
CEEHNOPRSSTTUW	PUT THE SCREWS ON
CEEHOOOOPPRRSTT	PHOTORECEPTORS
CEEIIILLNNPRSTW	WRITES IN PENCIL
CEEIIILLOPRSTTU	PRECIOUS LITTLE
CEEIILMNRSSTUV	INCLUSIVE TERMS
CEEIILMORRSTUY	MERETRICIOUSLY
CEEIILNNNNOTVY	INCONVENIENTLY
CEEIILNNOSSSTU	LICENTIOUSNESS
CEEIILPPRRSTVY	PRESCRIPTIVELY
CEEIIMNOOPRTTT	POTENTIOMETRIC
CEEIINNOPRSSSU	PERNICIOUSNESS
CEEIIOOPPPRRTV	PROPRIOCEPTIVE
CEEIKKNOORSTTW	WORK ONES TICKET
CEEIKNORRRRSTT	TERROR-STRICKEN
CEEIILLLMOORRVW	OLIVER CROMWELL
CEEIILLNOORSTU	NITROCELLULOSE
CEEIILLMOTUVYZZ	MUZZLE VELOCITY
CEEIILMNOPSSSUV	COMPULSIVENESS
CEEIILMNOSSSTTU	COUNTLESS TIMES
CEEIILMNOSSSTUU	METICULOUSNESS
CEEIILMORSTTTUY	UTMOST CELERITY
CEEIILNNNOQSTUY	INCONSEQUENTLY
CEEIILNNOSSSUVV	CONVULSIVENESS
CEEIILNNRRRTTUY	INTERCURRENTLY
CEEIILNORRSSUYY	YOURS SINCERELY
CEEIIMMNNOOOSTY	COMES INTO MONEY
CEEIIMMNNOORSTT	COMMON INTEREST
CEEIINNNNOOPRTV	PROVEN INNOCENT
CEEIINNNOOPRSTV	PROVES INNOCENT
CEEIINNNNORSTTW	WRITTEN CONSENT
CEEIINNOORSSSSU	CENSORIOUSNESS
CEEIINNOSSSSTUU	INCESTUOUSNESS
CEEKNNOOOSSTTT	STOCKTON ON TEES
CEELLNOORSSSSU	COLOURLESSNESS
CEELLRRTTUUUUV	CULTURE-VULTURE
CEELMNOOOPRRSTU	SUPREME CONTROL
CEELNOOOPRSSTU	PLOT ONES COURSE
CEELNOOPRRSTUV	VOLUNTEER CORPS
CEELNOOSSSSSTU	CUTS ONE'S LOSSES
CEELOOOPRRSSSU	POOLS RESOURCES
CEEMNNNOOOSTUY	COUNT ONES MONEY
CEEMNNNOOPRSTU	PRONOUNCEMENTS
CEENNOORSTTTVY	SENT TO COVENTRY
CEEPRRRSSTTUUU	SUPERSTRUCTURE
CEFFFHIIILLMOSU	FULL OF MISCHIEF
CEFFGHIIINOPPS	SHIPPING OFFICE
CEFFGIKLNOOOPS	FLOCK OF PIGEONS
CEFFIIILLNNSTUY	INSUFFICIENTLY
CEFGHHIIKOSSTT	SICK OF THE SIGHT
CEFGHIMNOORSUZ	GNOMES OF ZURICH
CEFGHINNOORSSST	SIGN OF THE CROSS
CEFGIIKLNOPRSW	PICKING FLOWERS
CEFGILMOOOPRTU	PICTURE OF GLOOM
CEFGINNOOOOSST	GO TO CONFESSION
CEFGINNOORRTUY	FOREIGN COUNTRY
CEFGNNOORRRSSU	RUN FOR CONGRESS
CEFHHIIIKNOTTT	IN THE THICK OF IT
CEFHHIIKLORSTU	LUCK OF THE IRISH
CEFHHIOPRRRSTY	CHRISTOPHER FRY
CEFHKLLNOOOTU	KNOCK HELL OUT OF
CEFHMMNOOOOSSU	HOUSE OF COMMONS
CEFHNNOOORTTUU	OUT FOR THE COUNT
CEFIIILLNOSTUY	INFELICITOUSLY
CEFIIILOPRRRTW	PROLIFIC WRITER
CEFIIINOSSSTTU	FICTITIOUSNESS
CEFIIKLMRSTTUY	FIRST TIME LUCKY
CEFIILMNOORSTV	LIVES IN COMFORT
CEFIILORSSSSTU	SCOTS FUSILIERS
CEFIIMMMMNNORTT	FIRM COMMITMENT
CEFIIMMNOORSSY	MISSION OF MERCY
CEFIMMNOOOORRT	COMMON FRONTIER
CEFKLMNOORSUUY	UNLUCKY FOR SOME
CEFLOOORRTTUUU	RULE OUT OF COURT
CEGGHIIIKNNSST	SICKENING SIGHT
CEGGHILMOOOOPR	GEOMORPHOLOGIC
CEGGIIKNNSTTTU	GETTING STUCK IN

CEGGIINNNORSTU	COUNTERSIGNING	CEIIMNNORRSTTU	MICRONUTRIENTS
CEGHHINORSSSTU	SINGS THE CHORUS	CEIIMORRSTUUUX	CURIOUS MIXTURE
CEGHIIIKLNNOPS	PICKING HOLES IN	CEIINNNOOPRRTU	CURRENT OPINION
CEGHIILNNORTTW	WINTER CLOTHING	CEIINNOORSTTTU	RECONSTITUTION
CEGHIIMNOOSSTT	COMES INTO SIGHT	CEIINOOOPPPRRT	PROPRIOCEPTION
CEGHIJNOOPRSTU	HOUSING PROJECT	CEIINOOPRSSTTT	PROTECTIONISTS
CEGHIKLNOORSTW	WORKING CLOTHES	CEIINOORSSSTUV	VICTORIOUSNESS
CEGHILMNOPRTUY	RHYMING COUPLET	CEIINOPPRSSSTU	SUPERSCRIPTION
CEGHIMNNOOOSTT	COMES TO NOTHING	CEIINOPRRSSTUY	SECURITY PRISON
CEGHIMNNOORSWY	SHOWING NO MERCY	CEIINOPRSSSSTU	PERCUSSIONISTS
CEGHINNOOSSTUU	COUNTINGHOUSES	CEIINOPSSSSSUU	SUSPICIOUSNESS
CEGHINORRRSTTU	CRUSHING RETORT	CEIJMMOPRRSTUY	COMMITS PERJURY
CEGHLNOOOOORRSV	SCHOOL GOVERNOR	CEILLMMMNOOPTU	COMMON MULTIPLE
CEGHNNOOORSSUY	GEOSYNCHRONOUS	CEILLMNOOSTUUY	CONTUMELIOUSLY
CEGHNOOORTTTUY	GO TO THE COUNTRY	CEILNOOOQRSTUU	COLOUR QUESTION
CEGIIJLNNOOTUV	JULIE COVINGTON	CEILNOPRRSTUUV	PROVENTRICULUS
CEGIIJNORSSSTU	GROSS INJUSTICE	CEILNORRSSSSUU	SCURRILOUSNESS
CEGIIKLNNOOSTU	COOKING UTENSIL	CEIMMMMOOOORTTY	COMMIT TO MEMORY
CEGIILLNNOPRSU	CURLING ONE'S LIP	CEIMNOOOPOOTTU	COME OUT IN SPOTS
CEGIILMMNOPSSU	COMES UP SMILING	CEINNNOOSSSTUU	CONTINUOUSNESS
CEGIILMNOOPRSY	COPOLYMERISING	CEIOOOPPPRRRST	PROPRIOCEPTORS
CEGIILMNOOPRYZ	COPOLYMERIZING	CEKLMOOPRSTTUU	MOCK TURTLE SOUP
CEGIILNNOPSSSW	CLIPS ONE'S WINGS	CELMNOOPSTTUUY	CONTEMPTUOUSLY
CEGIIMNOPRSTUV	MOVING PICTURES	CELNOPRSSSSUUU	SCRUPULOUSNESS
CEGIIMNOSSTTTU	SETTING TO MUSIC	CEMMNOOOPPRRTY	COMMON PROPERTY
CEGIINNORSTTTU	RECONSTITUTING	CFFGHIIINOSTTW	SWITCHING IT OFF
CEGIKLNNORSTUY	TRYING ONE'S LUCK	CFFKKNOOOPSSST	KNOCKS SPOTS OFF
CEGILLMNOOPRTY	LONG-TERM POLICY	CFGGIIKKLNNNOY	KNOCKING FLYING
CEGILLNNOOOOSS	LOSING ONE'S COOL	CFGHHIIINNOSTU	FINISHING TOUCH
CEGILMOOOSSSTT	COSMETOLOGISTS	CFGHHIIKMNNOTU	THINKING MUCH OF
CEGINNOOSSSTUU	CONTIGUOUSNESS	CFGIIKKNNOORSX	KNOCKING FOR SIX
CEGLMOOOPPRSTY	GLOOMY PROSPECT	CFHIINOOOPPRST	PORTION OF CHIPS
CEHHIORSTTTWW	THROW THE SWITCH	CFHLLNOOOORRSU	SCROLL OF HONOUR
CEHHIIMORSSTTY	HISTOCHEMISTRY	CFIMNNNOOORSST	NONCONFORMISTS
CEHHIMOOPRSTTY	PHOTOCHEMISTRY	CFMOOORSSTTTUU	TOUTS FOR CUSTOM
CEHHINOOPSTTTY	PHOTOSYNTHETIC	CFOOOPRSTTTUUU	PUTS OUT OF COURT
CEHHMOOPPSTYYY	HYPOPHYSECTOMY	CGGHHINORTTTUU	CUTTING THROUGH
CEHHNOORSSTTUU	COUNTS THE HOURS	CGGHIILNNOOORZ	CHRONOLOGIZING
CEHIIIKLMOOPRT	POIKILOTHERMIC	CGGHIILNOOPSSY	PSYCHOLOGISING
CEHIIIKLNOPSTT	PILES IT ON THICK	CGGHIILNOOPSYZ	PSYCHOLOGIZING
CEHIIIMNNORTTY	ETHNIC MINORITY	CGGHINOPRTTUUU	CUTTING UP ROUGH
CEHIILNOOORRRR	RECOIL IN HORROR	CGGIINNOPPRSTY	STOPPING CRYING
CEHIIMMNOORSTT	HISTORIC MOMENT	CGGILLNOOORSUW	GLOWING COLOURS
CEHIJLNOOORSTU	JOIN THE COLOURS	CGHHIIIMMNNOUSS	HIGH COMMISSION
CEHIKLORRSSTTY	STRICTLY KOSHER	CGHHIINOOPRSTT	HOPING TO CHRIST
CEHIKNOPSSTTTU	PUT IN THE STOCKS	CGHHIKLOQTTUUY	THOUGHT QUICKLY
CEHILLNOOPRRST	CONTROLLERSHIP	CGHIIIIKNRRSTT	STRIKING IT RICH
CEHILNOORSTTUY	HOSTILE COUNTRY	CGHIILNOPSSTUY	PSYCHOLINGUIST
CEHINOOPRSSSUY	PSYCHONEUROSIS	CGHIINNNOOPPRT	CHIPPING NORTON
CEHKLLOOPRTTUU	PULL THE CORK OUT	CGHIINORSTTTTU	CUTTING IT SHORT
CEHLLNNOOPPSSUU	PULLS NO PUNCHES	CGHIKMMNOOOSTU	SMOKING TOO MUCH
CEHLOOOOPRRTTU	TROOP THE COLOUR	CGIIIKMNNOOOTUW	KNOWING TOO MUCH
CEHMOOOOPRSTTU	PROTEST TOO MUCH	CGHIMNOOOPRTUV	PROVING TOO MUCH
CEHNNNOORRTTUY	NORTHERN COUNTY	CGHIMNOOORSSST	SMOOTH CROSSING
CEHNNOORSTTUUY	SOUTHERN COUNTY	CGHIMNOOPRSSTU	CHOOSING TRUMPS
CEHNOORRTTTUUY	TOUR THE COUNTRY	CGIIILMNOORSST	CRIMINOLOGISTS
CEIIIINOSSTTVV	VIVISECTIONIST	CGIIILNNORTTUY	CONTINUITY GIRL
CEIIIKLLNNRSTT	KILLER INSTINCT	CGIIILNOOSSSTU	SOCIOLINGUISTS
CEIIJNOOPRSSTT	PROJECTIONISTS	CGIIMMNNOOPRSU	UNCOMPROMISING
CEIIKKLRSSTTUY	STRIKES IT LUCKY	CGIIMNNNOOPRSU	MISPRONOUNCING
CEIIKNOQRSTTUY	TRICKY QUESTION	CGIIMNNNORRSTU	TURNING CRIMSON
CEIILLNOOSSSTV	VIOLONCELLISTS	CGIIMNOPSTTTUU	PUTTING TO MUSIC
CEIILLMMNNOOTT	LITTLE IN COMMON	CGIKLNNNOOSSTY	NYLON STOCKINGS
CEIILLOPRSSUUY	SUPERCILIOUSLY	CGIKLNORSTTTUU	TRUSTING TO LUCK
CEIILMOOPRSTXY	CLOSE PROXIMITY	CHIIINNRRSTTWW	INTRINSIC WORTH
CEIILNNNOSSTTY	INCONSISTENTLY	CHIIKOPRRSTTUY	TURKISH CYPRIOT
CEIILNOOSSSSTU	SOLICITOUSNESS	CHIILORRSTTTUU	HORTICULTURIST
CEIILNOSTTTUUY	CONSTITUTIVELY	CHIINOPRRSSTTU	INSTRUCTORSHIP
CEIILOPPRRSTVY	PROSCRIPTIVELY	CHIIOOORSSTTXY	THYROTOXICOSIS
CEIILRRSSSTTUU	SERICULTURISTS	CHMMNNOOOOORSST	ON SHORT COMMONS
CEIIMNNOOOPSSU	PNEUMOCONIOSIS	CIIILLRSSTTUUV	SILVICULTURIST

CIIILRSSTTTUUV	VITICULTURISTS
CIIKORSSSSTTTW	STICKS OR TWISTS
CIINNOOORSSTTT	CONTORTIONISTS
CKNNNNOORTUUWY	UNKNOWN COUNTRY
CLLNOPRSSUUUUY	UNSCRUPULOUSLY
DDDEEEEEFFLNOPY	DEEPLY OFFENDED
DDDEEEEFLLLNOSU	DELUDED ONESELF
DDDEEEEELNOPRUV	UNDERDEVELOPED
DDDEEEEGHIOSSTU	DODGED THE ISSUE
DDDEEEEKNOORRUW	DEREK UNDERWOOD
DDDEEHHOOSSTTU	SHOUTED THE ODDS
DDDEEILNOORSUW	WOUNDED SOLDIER
DDDEGHHLMORTUU	MUDDLED THROUGH
DDDEGHINNORRUU	HID UNDERGROUND
DDDEIIKLNOPSSY	KINDLY DISPOSED
DDDENNOOPRSUUW	SUDDEN DOWNPOUR
DDEEEEEGNNORRU	ONE DEGREE UNDER
DDEEEEFFLNNOSS	DEFENDS ONESELF
DDEEEEFGLLNOPS	PLEDGED ONESELF
DDEEEEFILMNRST	SELF-DETERMINED
DDEEEEFLLNOSSU	DELUDES ONESELF
DDEEEEHIMMSTTT	STEMMED THE TIDE
DDEEEEHINRRSSV	HIDDEN RESERVES
DDEEEEIMNNRSST	DETERMINEDNESS
DDEEEEINNNPRTT	INTERDEPENDENT
DDEEEEINOPPRSS	DEEP DEPRESSION
DDEEEFFIILOPRV	DEPRIVED OF LIFE
DDEEEFHIMNRSTY	FINDS THE REMEDY
DDEEEFHINORRTU	HEREFORD UNITED
DDEEEFHMNORTUY	FOUND THE REMEDY
DDEEEFILLLNOSW	DID ONESELF WELL
DDEEEFIOOPRSUX	DIED OF EXPOSURE
DDEEEFLLLOPUVY	FULLY DEVELOPED
DDEEEFLNNOORSW	DROWNED ONESELF
DDEEEGGINRSSTT	GETTING DRESSED
DDEEEGHHLORTTU	HUDDLE TOGETHER
DDEEEGHIINRRTT	RIDDEN THE TIGER
DDEEEGHINNRSTU	THE UNDERSIGNED
DDEEEGHIOSSSTU	DODGES THE ISSUE
DDEEEGIILMRRST	MIDDLE REGISTER
DDEEEGIINNNPRT	INTERDEPENDING
DDEEEGINNPRSTW	WEDDING PRESENT
DDEEEGLMOOPRTY	GOOD-TEMPEREDLY
DDEEEGLNOOPRSW	PLEDGE ONES WORD
DDEEEHIINRSSTW	DRESSED IN WHITE
DDEEEHILLORSTV	SOLVE THE RIDDLE
DDEEEHILMNOPTV	DEVELOP THE MIND
DDEEEHILNOSTTW	LET THE SIDE DOWN
DDEEEIIINORSTV	REVISED EDITION
DDEEEIIKLMNNSS	LIKE-MINDEDNESS
DDEEEIINNRRSSV	DINNER IS SERVED
DDEEEIINNRSTTV	INVITED TENDERS
DDEEEIMNNNOPSS	OPEN-MINDEDNESS
DDEEEIMNNNORTU	UNDERMENTIONED
DDEEEINNNORTTU	UNDER DETENTION
DDEEEINNOORRTT	DETENTION ORDER
DDEEEINNPRRSUV	SERVED UP DINNER
DDEEEIOPPSSTTU	STEPPED OUTSIDE
DDEEEMMNNOSTUV	SUDDEN MOVEMENT
DDEEFFIIILLOSW	WILD SIDE OF LIFE
DDEEFGIIKLNNOS	KIDDING ONESELF
DDEEFHLOORSTTU	DUSTED THE FLOOR
DDEEFIIMOORSST	FROM SIDE TO SIDE
DDEEFIKNRRSTUY	DUTY-FREE DRINKS
DDEEFIMORRRRTU	TRIED FOR MURDER
DDEEFINNORRRSS	DRESS FOR DINNER
DDEEFLNOOOPRSU	DO ONESELF PROUD
DDEEGGIIJNPRSU	PRESIDING JUDGE
DDEEGHHIKLNOTY	HOLDING THE DYKE
DDEEGHHINRSTUW	HUNDREDWEIGHTS
DDEEGHIIILMNPT	PIG IN THE MIDDLE

DDEEGHIILNSSTU	STUDIED ENGLISH
DDEEGHILMOOSTY	DEMYTHOLOGISED
DDEEGHILMOOTYZ	DEMYTHOLOGIZED
DDEEGHLNNOORSU	HELD ONE'S GROUND
DDEEGHNNORRTUU	THE UNDERGROUND
	UNDER THE GROUND
DDEEGIILLMNNSY	SINGLE-MINDEDLY
DDEEGIINNNNORR	ORDERING DINNER
DDEEGILNNNOSSW	LONG-WINDEDNESS
DDEEHHLLMOOOSU	MODEL HOUSEHOLD
DDEEHINNORRSUU	UNDERNOURISHED
DDEEHINNOSTTUU	SOUTHEND UNITED
DDEEIIIILMNOTT	LIMITED EDITION
DDEEIIINPRSSST	DISPIRITEDNESS
DDEEIIJNNOSSST	DISJOINTEDNESS
DDEEIIKLNOPRSS	SPOKE IN RIDDLES
DDEEIIILLMMNPSY	SIMPLEMINDEDLY
DDEEIILNORRSSS	DISORDERLINESS
DDEEIIMNOORTTU	DIEU ET MON DROIT
DDEEIOOPPSSTTU	STOPPED OUTSIDE
DDEFFLLOOOOOVY	FOOD,LOVELY FOOD
DDEFGHIMNOOORT	GOOD FOR THE MIND
DDEFGHLOOOORTW	THE WORLD OF GOOD
DDEFHLOORRRRTU	LORD RUTHERFORD
DDEFLLNOORRUWW	WONDERFUL WORLD
DDEGGHINNOSTUW	SHOT-GUN WEDDING
	SHOTGUN WEDDING
DDEGGIIMNNNORW	WEDDING MORNING
DDEGHHIOORRSSU	RIDES ROUGH-SHOD
	RIDES ROUGHSHOD
DDEGHHLMORSTUU	MUDDLES THROUGH
DDEGHHLOOOOSSU	HOUSEHOLD GOODS
DDEGHILLNORTTY	TRODDEN LIGHTLY
DDEGHINNOORSTU	DOING THE ROUNDS
DDEGHLMOOORUUY	GOOD-HUMOUREDLY
DDEGHLNNOOORSU	HOLD ONE'S GROUND
DDEGIINNORSSWW	WINDOW DRESSING
	WINDOW-DRESSING
DDEGILLMOORSUU	GLORIOUS MUDDLE
DDEGILMNNORSTY	STRONG-MINDEDLY
DDEGINOOPRRSTW	GRINDS TO POWDER
DDEGLNOORRSTWY	STRONGLY WORDED
DDEGNOOOPRRTUW	GROUND TO POWDER
DDEHIIIMNNORST	THIRD DIMENSION
DDEHIILOPRSUUX	SULPHUR DIOXIDE
DDEHILNNOORTWW	DOWN IN THE WORLD
DDEHIMNNOPSTUW	DOWN IN THE DUMPS
DDEHLLOOOORSTTY	THE OLD OLD STORY
DDEHLNOORRSSUU	ROUND SHOULDERS
DDEIIILMSSSSTU	DISSIMILITUDES
DDEINNOPRSTUUW	TURN UPSIDE DOWN
DDFGGGGIILNOOR	DIGGING FOR GOLD
DDFMOOOOOORRRT	FROM DOOR TO DOOR
DDGGIINNORSTTU	GRINDING TO DUST
DDGIIIKNNORRTV	DRIVING TO DRINK
DDGIINNORSSTTU	GRINDS INTO DUST
DDGINNOORSTTUU	GROUND INTO DUST
DEEEEEFGHILNNT	FEELING THE NEED
DEEEEEFLLNOSST	STEELED ONESELF
DEEEEEFLNNOPRS	PREENED ONESELF
DEEEEEFLNORSTX	EXERTED ONESELF
DEEEEEGHILNNTV	GIVEN THE NEEDLE
DEEEEEGHILNSTV	GIVES THE NEEDLE
DEEEEEGHKLPPST	KEEPS THE PLEDGE
DEEEEFFHILLSST	SHEFFIELD STEEL
DEEEEFFMMNOORY	ENEMY OF FREEDOM
DEEEEFGHILNOSW	WEIGHED ONESELF
DEEEEFGIILNRST	GREENFIELD SITE
DEEEEFGIIMMNNR	FEMININE GENDER
DEEEEFGILNNRST	TENDER FEELINGS
DEEEEFGLLNOPSS	PLEDGES ONESELF

DEEEEFHINNOSTV	ON THE DEFENSIVE
DEEEEFHNORSTTT	END OF THE STREET
DEEEEFIKNPRRSS	FINDERS KEEPERS
DEEEEFILNRSSTT	SELF-INTERESTED
DEEEEFJLNNOOSY	ENJOYED ONESELF
DEEEEFLLNOORSW	LOWERED ONESELF
DEEEEGGGHINTTT	GETTING THE EDGE
DEEEEGGHIMORRT	GEORGE MEREDITH
DEEEEGHHILMSTY	HIGHLY ESTEEMED
DEEEEGHHILRSTT	SEE THE RED LIGHT
DEEEEGHHNORTTT	TO THE NTH DEGREE
DEEEEGHNOPRTTT	POTTED THE GREEN
DEEEEGIIOPRSTV	POSITIVE DEGREE
DEEEEGIKMOOPRT	GOOD TIME-KEEPER
	GOOD TIMEKEEPER
DEEEEGILMNNRRT	GENTLE REMINDER
DEEEEGIMNNNOST	MEETING ONE'S END
DEEEEGIMNPRRSU	REIGNED SUPREME
DEEEEGNORSSSTT	GET ONES DESERTS
DEEEEHHILLOSTW	OILED THE WHEELS
DEEEEIIKLMRSTX	EXTREME DISLIKE
DEEEEILLMMUSSS	MESDEMOISELLES
DEEEEIMNORSSTV	SERVED ONE'S TIME
DEEEEIMNPRRSST	MISREPRESENTED
DEEEEINRSSTTTV	VESTED INTEREST
DEEEEKNNOPPSSU	KEEPS ONE'S END UP
DEEEEKNOOPPSST	KEEPS ONE POSTED
DEEEELMNNOOSVY	LOVED ONE'S ENEMY
DEEEEENNRRSSSUV	UNRESERVEDNESS
DEEEEENRRRSSTUW	SWEET SURRENDER
DEEEEOPRRTTTVY	REVERTED TO TYPE
DEEEFFFLNNOORS	FEND FOR ONESELF
DEEEFFFLNOSSTU	STUFFED ONESELF
DEEEFFGHILNOPT	DEPTH OF FEELING
DEEEFFGHIMORRT	FREEDOM FIGHTER
DEEEFFGHKOOOTT	TOOK THE EDGE OFF
DEEEFFGIIINRTU	DEFINITE FIGURE
DEEEFFGOORRSST	DEGREES OF FROST
DEEEFFHMNOOOORT	OFFERED THE MOON
DEEEFFIILLRSST	SELF-FERTILISED
DEEEFFIILLRSTZ	SELF-FERTILIZED
DEEEFFIILOPRSV	DEPRIVES OF LIFE
DEEEFFIINQRTTU	QUITE DIFFERENT
DEEEFGHIILNNTW	FEELING THE WIND
DEEEFGIILNNNOS	ENDING ONE'S LIFE
DEEEFHHINOTTTW	TEETH OF THE WIND
DEEEFHIMNOOTTT	TO THE END OF TIME
DEEEFHLNNNOTTU	END OF THE TUNNEL
DEEEFIIIMNNTT	INDEFINITE TIME
DEEEFIIINNNSST	INDEFINITENESS
DEEEFIIINNSSTV	DEFINITIVENESS
DEEEFILLNNOSSV	FINDS ONE'S LEVEL
DEEEFILLNOOPSS	SPOILED ONESELF
DEEEFILMNOOPSS	IMPOSED ONESELF
DEEEFILOORRSTT	RESTORED TO LIFE
DEEEFIMOPRRSST	PRESSED FOR TIME
DEEEFIOOPRSSUX	DIES OF EXPOSURE
DEEEFIPRRRSTUV	PRESERVED FRUIT
DEEEFLLNNOOSUV	FOUND ONE'S LEVEL
DEEEFLNNOOSSTU	FOULED ONE'S NEST
DEEEFLNOOOPPSZ	DOZENS OF PEOPLE
DEEEFMNOPRTTTU	TEMPTED FORTUNE
DEEEFNOORSSSTU	SUREFOOTEDNESS
DEEEGGHHHORSTU	HUGGED THE SHORE
DEEEGGHHIORRTT	GEORGE THE THIRD
DEEEGHHINRSTTT	GRINDS THE TEETH
DEEEGHHNORTTTU	GROUND THE TEETH
DEEEGHIILNNOSS	DIG IN ONES HEELS
	DIG ONES HEELS IN
DEEEGHIKMNOSTW	SMOKING THE WEED

DEEEGHILNNOSSU	DUG IN ONE'S HEELS
	DUG ONE'S HEELS IN
DEEEGHILNORSTW	SEEING THE WORLD
DEEEGHINNOPSTU	EIGHTEEN POUNDS
DEEEGHINNORSTT	GRIND ONE'S TEETH
DEEEGHINORRSTV	SERVED ONE RIGHT
DEEEGHINORSTTT	GETS INTO THE RED
DEEEGHINOSSTUW	USED ONE'S WEIGHT
DEEEGHLNNOOSTU	HELD ONE'S TONGUE
DEEEGIIKLNNNTT	KNITTING NEEDLE
DEEEGIIMNNNOSY	MINDING ONE'S EYE
DEEEGIIMNNPRRT	PREDETERMINING
DEEEGIINRSSSSV	DIGRESSIVENESS
DEEEGILNNOPSST	SENDING TO SLEEP
DEEEGINNORSSYY	DRYING ONE'S EYES
DEEEGINNPRSSSW	DEPRESSING NEWS
DEEEGIOPRRSSTT	REGISTERED POST
DEEEGNNOPRRTUY	YOUNG PRETENDER
DEEEGNOORSSSTT	GOT ONE'S DESERTS
DEEEHHIILNNRTT	THE THIN RED LINE
DEEEHHINOORSTT	ON THE OTHER SIDE
DEEEHHLNOORSSS	HELD ONE'S HORSES
DEEEHHOOPRSSTW	SHOWED THE ROPES
DEEEHHPPRRSSSU	SHEPHERDS PURSE
DEEEHIILNNOSST	ON THE SIDELINES
DEEEHIINNOOSSS	DIE IN ONES SHOES
DEEEHIINNRRSTW	RIDES THE WINNER
DEEEHIINRSSSTW	DRESSES IN WHITE
DEEEHILMPSTTTV	TEMPTS THE DEVIL
DEEEHILNNPSSSU	HELD IN SUSPENSE
DEEEHIORSTTUVY	THE VERY OUTSIDE
DEEEHLLMOOOPPS	OLD PEOPLES HOME
DEEEIIIKLNNSST	INTENSE DISLIKE
DEEEIILMMNRRTY	TIMELY REMINDER
DEEEIILMNNORST	EMINENT SOLDIER
DEEEIIMNNNOSSY	IN ONES MINDS EYE
DEEEIIMNPRRSTT	MISINTERPRETED
DEEEIIMNRSSTTV	DIVERTISSEMENT
DEEEIINNRSSTTV	INVITES TENDERS
DEEEIINORRSSVV	REVISED VERSION
DEEEIINPRSSSSV	DISPERSIVENESS
DEEEIKNNOOSSTU	OUTSIDE ONES KEN
DEEEILNNOOPVWW	WINDOW ENVELOPE
DEEEILNOPSSTTW	WETTED ONE'S LIPS
DEEEILNOQRTUUV	UNREQUITED LOVE
DEEEINNNNOPSTU	NINETEEN POUNDS
DEEEINNPRSTTU	SUPERINTENDENT
DEEEINNPRRSSUV	SERVES UP DINNER
DEEELOPRRRSSUV	LORD PRESERVE US!
DEEEMNNORSSSTU	TREMENDOUSNESS
DEEEENNNORTTUWY	UNDER TWENTY-ONE
DEEEENNOORSSTTW	DOWN ONE'S STREET
DEEEENNORRSTTU	RETURN TO SENDER
DEEEENNORRSSTUV	SERVED ONE'S TURN
DEEEENOOPRSSSTT	DESERT ONES POST
DEEFFGIILLNNOR	LIFELONG FRIEND
DEEFFGIILNNNOS	FINDING ONESELF
DEEFFGNNOORSUY	YOUNG OFFENDERS
DEEFFHIILNNSTU	LEFT UNFINISHED
DEEFFHILLOORST	LORD OF THE FLIES
DEEFFHINNORTTU	FIFTEENTH ROUND
DEEFFIILLNOTTU	OUT IN LEFT FIELD
DEEFFIKLNOORST	LOOKS DIFFERENT
DEEFFINORRSTTY	DIFFERENT STORY
DEEFFLOOOPPRST	DROP OFF TO SLEEP
DEEFGHHIIINPTWY	DEFYING THE WHIP
DEEFGHHOOPSTTU	SPEED OF THOUGHT
DEEFGHIIIMNNTT	FINDING THE TIME
DEEFGHIILNNRST	FINDING SHELTER
DEEFGHILLNSSTU	DELIGHTFULNESS
DEEFGHILNNOPRS	SENDING FOR HELP

DEEFGIILNNOPRS	PRIDING ONESELF
DEEFGIIMNNNNORW	WINNING FREEDOM
DEEFGIILLNORSUV	FUR-LINED GLOVES
DEEFGINNNNOOSTU	FIND ONE'S TONGUE
DEEFHHINORSSUU	FURNISHED HOUSE
DEEFHHLLOORSTW	FOLLOWS THE HERD
DEEFHHLOOOORSTU	HOUSE OF THE LORD
DEEFHHLOOPPRSTU	SHOUTED FOR HELP
DEEFHIIJNNNOTU	JOINED IN THE FUN
DEEFHIIKLNORTW	WORK IN THE FIELD
DEEFHILLOORSST	LORD OF THE ISLES
DEEFHIMOPRSSTY	DEPTHS OF MISERY
DEEFHLMOOOOPPRT	MOPPED THE FLOOR
DEEFHLMOOOORRTU	HELD OUT FOR MORE
DEEFHLNOORSTWW	NEWS OF THE WORLD
DEEFHLOOPPSTTW	STOPPED THE FLOW
DEEFHMNOOPRSUY	PUSHED FOR MONEY
DEEFHNOOOOPSTTU	OUT OF ONES DEPTH
DEEFHOOORRSSTW	SHERWOOD FOREST
DEEFIIILMOPRSV	OVERSIMPLIFIED
DEEFIIIORRSTTZ	TRIED IT FOR SIZE
DEEFIILLNOSSTU	FELL INTO DISUSE
DEEFIIMNOORRRT	IN ORDER OF MERIT
DEEFIINOPRSSSU	PERFIDIOUSNESS
DEEFIINOQRSSTU	FIRED QUESTIONS
DEEFILOORRSTUY	DO-IT-YOURSELFER
DEEFIMORRRRSTU	TRIES FOR MURDER
DEEFLOOORRRTUU	RULE OUT OF ORDER
DEEFLOORRRTTUW	FOUR-LETTER WORD
DEEFNNOOPRSTUU	FOURTEEN POUNDS
DEEGGHIIINNRRTT	RIDING THE TIGER
DEEGGHIILNNPST	LIGHTNING SPEED
DEEGGHILNNOOOT	GOING ON THE DOLE
DEEGGHINOOSTTV	GIVEN TO THE DOGS
DEEGGHIOOSSTTV	GIVES TO THE DOGS
DEEGGHNOOORTTW	GO DOWN TOGETHER
DEEGGIINORRTTW	GETTING WORRIED
DEEGHHIILLNNOT	HOLDING THE LINE
DEEGHHIINORSTT	ON THE RIGHT SIDE
DEEGHHILNORTVY	HOLD EVERYTHING
DEEGHHIMNOPPRT	DROPPING THE HEM
DEEGHHOORSTTTW	THREW TO THE DOGS
DEEGHIILLNSSTT	LET THINGS SLIDE
DEEGHIILMNNTTVW	TWELVE MIDNIGHT
DEEGHIILNSSSTU	STUDIES ENGLISH
DEEGHIIMNNNPSTT	MINDING THE STEP
DEEGHIIMNOPRSW	WHISPERING DOME
DEEGHIINNRTTTU	TURNING THE TIDE
DEEGHILMOOSSTY	DEMYTHOLOGISES
DEEGHILMOOSTYZ	DEMYTHOLOGIZES
DEEGHILNNNOOSS	ON ONES HIND LEGS
DEEGHILNORTTVY	TOLD EVERYTHING
DEEGHINNOOOOPRT	OPENING THE DOOR
DEEGHINNNOORSTW	ON THE WRONG SIDE
DEEGHINOORSSWW	WEIGH ONES WORDS
DEEGHINOPRRTVY	DROP EVERYTHING
DEEGHLNNOOOSTU	HOLD ONES TONGUE
DEEGHMNNOORTTU	GUNNED THE MOTOR
DEEGHNNOOOSTWW	NOW THE GOOD NEWS
DEEGHNOOOOPSST	HOPE TO GOODNESS
DEEGIIILLNSTT	LETTING IT SLIDE
DEEGIIIILLPSYZZ	DIZZY GILLESPIE
DEEGIIIILMNNRRV	LIVING REMINDER
DEEGIIIILMOOPST	EPIDEMIOLOGIST
DEEGIIINNPPSST	STEPPING INSIDE
DEEGIIKLNNRSSV	DRINKING VESSEL
DEEGIILOORRRSU	RELIGIOUS ORDER
DEEGIINNNPRSTU	SUPERINTENDING
DEEGIINNOOSSST	DIGS IN ONE'S TOES
	DIGS ONE'S TOES IN
DEEGIINNORRSTT	SETTING IN ORDER

DEEGIINNORSSTW	TRIED ONE'S WINGS
DEEGIINNSTTUUV	UNINVITED GUEST
DEEGIKNNOPSSSU	SPIKED ONE'S GUNS
DEEGILLORRSSTY	LLOYDS REGISTER
DEEGILNNNOOTTW	LETTING ONE DOWN
DEEGIMNNOOSTTV	GOOD INVESTMENT
DEEGIMNOOORTTU	OUTDOOR MEETING
DEEGINNOPPSTTU	PUTTING ON SPEED
DEEGINOOORRRST	RESTORING ORDER
DEEGLNNORSSSSU	GROUNDLESSNESS
DEEHHHLNOORSTT	ON THE THRESHOLD
DEEHHIILOPPSST	SPOILED THE SHIP
DEEHHIINNORSTT	THORN IN THE SIDE
DEEHHIINORSTTW	THE DIE IS THROWN
DEEHHILLNNOOSU	HOUSEHOLD LINEN
DEEHHINOPRRSTT	THE THIRD PERSON
DEEHHINORTTTWW	THREW TO THE WIND
DEEHHLNOOOORSSS	HOLD ONES HORSES
DEEHHNNOOORSTU	DONE THE HONOURS
DEEHHNOOOORSTW	SHOW ONE THE DOOR
DEEHHNOOORSSTU	DOES THE HONOURS
DEEHHNNOORSSTUU	ROUND THE HOUSES
DEEHIIKLNNRTUW	RUN LIKE THE WIND
DEEHIIKLOOSTUW	DO THOU LIKEWISE
DEEHIIILLLOTWWW	WIELD THE WILLOW
DEEHIILLPRSTWW	SWELL WITH PRIDE
DEEHIINOPSSTYZ	HYPOSENSITIZED
DEEHIIPRSSTTUY	SHEER STUPIDITY
DEEHILLMOORRTY	OLD MOTHER RILEY
DEEHILNNOPSSSU	HOLD IN SUSPENSE
DEEHILOPRRSTUV	SOLD UP THE RIVER
DEEHINNOOPSTWW	OPENS THE WINDOW
DEEHINNOPRSTTU	THIRTEEN POUNDS
DEEHINOPRRSSTU	HURTS ONE'S PRIDE
DEEHINORRTTTWW	THE WRITTEN WORD
DEEHKMNOOOORSW	DO ONE'S HOMEWORK
DEEHLNOPRRUUVY	RUDOLPH NUREYEV
DEEIIILLMRSTUV	VERISIMILITUDE
DEEIIIIMNSTUVZ	DIMINUTIVE SIZE
DEEIIIMNNSSTUV	DIMINUTIVENESS
DEEIIKLLNORSST	TRIED ONE'S SKILL
DEEIIKOOPRSSTT	POISED TO STRIKE
DEEIILNOORSTUV	REVOLUTIONISED
DEEIILNOORTUVZ	REVOLUTIONIZED
DEEIILNOPRTVVY	LIVED IN POVERTY
DEEIILNOPSSSST	SPLIT ONES SIDES
DEEIILOPPRSSTT	LEPIDOPTERISTS
DEEIINNNOPRSTX	PRESIDENT NIXON
DEEIINNSSTTUVY	INTENSIVE STUDY
DEEIINOPSSTTTW	PITTED ONE'S WITS
DEEIINPRSSSTUV	DISRUPTIVENESS
DEEIKMNNNOOPSS	SPOKEN ONE'S MIND
DEEILMMORRSSSU	SUMMER SOLDIERS
DEEILMOPPRRTVY	PROMPT DELIVERY
DEEILNOPPRSSSU	PURSED ONE'S LIPS
DEEIMNNNOOPRSY	PREY ON ONES MIND
DEEIMNOPRRSTUW	WORDS PER MINUTE
DEEINORSSSTTUU	SERIOUS STUDENT
DEEMNNOOOSSTTU	DONE ONE'S UTMOST
DEEMNOOOSSSTTU	DOES ONE'S UTMOST
DEENNOOOOPRSST	ON ONE'S DOORSTEP
DEENNOOOORSSTT	TROD ON ONE'S TOES
DEENNOPSSSSTUU	STUPENDOUSNESS
DEFFFHIILLOSTT	LIFTS THE LID OFF
DEFFGINNOOSSTU	DOING ONE'S STUFF
DEFFHILLNRSUUY	FULLY FURNISHED
DEFFHLOOOORRTW	ROOF OF THE WORLD
DEFFIILMNORRSU	MORRIS NUFFIELD
DEFGHHILNOORTT	HOLDING THE FORT
DEFGHIILLNNOTTW	FLING TO THE WIND
DEFGHILNNOTTUW	FLUNG TO THE WIND

DEFGHILNOORRST	LORD OF THE RINGS
DEFGHILNORSTUW	WONDERFUL SIGHT
DEFGHIMNNORSTT	STRENGTH OF MIND
DEFGHLOOOORSTU	GOOD FOR THE SOUL
DEFGIINNORRSSUU	IN ROUND FIGURES
DEFGILLNNOORST	LONG-LOST FRIEND
DEFGILMORRTUUY	GUILTY OF MURDER
DEFGILNNORTTUW	FLUTTERING DOWN
DEFGNNOOOOORSW	FOR ONES OWN GOOD
DEFHHMOOOOPPST	PHOPHETS OF DOOM
DEFHIIKNNORSUW	UNFINISHED WORK
DEFHIINORSTUVY	HIVE OF INDUSTRY
DEFHINOOORSSUW	HOUSE OF WINDSOR
DEFHINOORSTTUW	TO THE FOUR WINDS
DEFHKMMNOOOTUU	DUKE OF MONMOUTH
DEFHLMOOOORRTU	HOLD OUT FOR MORE
DEFIIIMNNORSST	FIRST DIMENSION
DEFIIKLLNNORSS	DRINKS ONE'S FILL
DEFIILLLSSTTUY	STILL-LIFE STUDY
DEFIIMNORRSTTU	FIRST TIME ROUND
DEFILLNORRSTUU	DOLLS FURNITURE
DEFIMNNNORSSUU	UNDRESS UNIFORM
DEFIMOOOOPRRSTU	ROOM FOR DISPUTE
DEFLMMOORRSTUU	MURDER MOST FOUL
DEFLNNOOOORSSW	WORLD OF ONES OWN
DEFOOPRRRSTTUY	REPORTS FOR DUTY
DEGGGIINOOOOTT	GOING TO THE DOGS
DEGGHHIINNRTTU	DURING THE NIGHT
DEGGHHIINOSSTT	DOING THE SIGHTS
DEGGHIIILLLNPT	GILDING THE PILL
DEGGHIIILLLNTY	GILDING THE LILY
DEGGHIIINNNOOT	GONE INTO HIDING
DEGGHIIINNNOOST	GOES INTO HIDING
DEGGHIIJLNORSU	SIR JOHN GIELGUD
DEGGHIILNNNOTW	WINNING THE GOLD
DEGGHIILNORTVW	GIVING THE WORLD
DEGGHIINNNOOST	DOING ONE'S THING
DEGGHIKNOORSTT	STROKING THE DOG
DEGGHINNOORSTU	GOING THE ROUNDS
DEGGIIIKNNPRUV	GIVE UP DRINKING
DEGHHIIIILLOPSY	HIGHLY POLISHED
DEGHHIIIILPRSTY	HIGH-SPIRITEDLY
DEGHHIIKLRSTTU	TURKISH DELIGHT
DEGHHIKMMORSTU	SKIMMED THROUGH
DEGHHILNOOOPTU	HOLDING OUT HOPE
DEGHHILNOPSSTU	SHEDS LIGHT UPON
DEGHHILOPPRSTU	SLIPPED THROUGH
DEGHHILORSSTTY	SHORTSIGHTEDLY
DEGHHINOOOORSTW	SHOWING THE DOOR
DEGHHOOOORSTTTW	THROW TO THE DOGS
DEGHIIINNNOTTW	WENT INTO HIDING
DEGHIIIINNPSSTW	DISPENSING WITH
DEGHIIINRSTTTW	TIED WITH STRING
DEGHIIKNNRRRSY	DRINKING SHERRY
DEGHIIKNSSSTTU	KISSING THE DUST
DEGHIIILLPPRTTY	TRIPPED LIGHTLY
DEGHIILNOPSSTT	DOING THE SPLITS
DEGHIILOPRSTWW	GLOWS WITH PRIDE
DEGHIIMMMMNRSTU	MIDSUMMER NIGHT
DEGHILLLNOTTWY	LET DOWN LIGHTLY
DEGHILLNOORTWW	WORTH DOING WELL
DEGHILNNNOOOSW	HOLDING ONE'S OWN
DEGHILNOOPRTUW	GO UP IN THE WORLD
DEGHILNOORSTTU	RINGS OUT THE OLD
DEGHINNNOOOSTW	DO ONE'S OWN THING
DEGHINNOORSTTU	SIT ON THE GROUND
DEGHLNOORSSUUY	YOUNG SHOULDERS
DEGIIILNNOSTTY	DOING IT IN STYLE
DEGIIJMNNSSTTU	SITS IN JUDGMENT
DEGIIKLLNORSST	DRESSING TO KILL
DEGIIKLNNNOSSV	LOVING KINDNESS

DEGIIKLNOOOORRW	LOOKING WORRIED
DEGIIKLNOOOSTU	LOOKING OUTSIDE
DEGIILLLNOPSTU	DUELLING PISTOL
DEGIILNNOORTVX	LIVING NEXT DOOR
DEGIILNNOSSUUY	DISINGENUOUSLY
DEGIILORSSTUUY	RELIGIOUS STUDY
DEGIIMMMNNOPRST	IMPENDING STORM
DEGIINNNOOOSTT	GOOD INTENTIONS
DEGIINNOPRRTTU	PUTTING IN ORDER
DEGIINOOPRSSSU	PRODIGIOUSNESS
DEGIKMMNOOPSST	STOPPED SMOKING
DEGIKNNOORRSWW	WORKING WONDERS
DEGIKNOOPPRSTW	STOPPED WORKING
DEGILNNOPPRSTU	LENDING SUPPORT
DEGILNOOOOPRTY	PERIODONTOLOGY
DEGILNOOORRSVV	REVOLVING DOORS
DEGILNOORSSTUY	SOUL-DESTROYING
DEGINNNOOORSSTW	DOING ONE'S WORST
DECLMMNOOOORRTY	LORD MONTGOMERY
DEHHILNORSTTUW	HURL TO THE WINDS
	HURLS TO THE WIND
DEHHIMNNOOTTUW	DOWN IN THE MOUTH
DEHHINOORTTTWW	THROW TO THE WIND
DEHIILNOPSTTTU	PUTS THE LID ON IT
DEHIIMOOOPPRST	PHOTOPERIODISM
DEHIKNOOPPSTTT	STOPPED TO THINK
DEHIMMOOPPRSSU	PSEUDOMORPHISM
DEHINOOPPRSSWW	WINDOW-SHOPPERS
DEHIOOPPRSTTUY	PTERIDOPHYTOUS
DEHKLOOOOORRSTY	TOOK HOLY ORDERS
DEHKOOOOOSTTTW	TOOK TO THE WOODS
DEHLLOOOORSTTTW	LOST TO THE WORLD
DEHMMOOOPPRSSUU	PSEUDOMORPHOUS
DEHNNNOOOORSSSU	SOUNDS ONE'S HORN
DEHOOPRSSTTTUW	PUTS TO THE SWORD
DEIIIINNOOPSST	INSIDE POSITION
DEIIILMNOOSSTT	DEMOLITIONISTS
DEIIINOOPPRSST	PREDISPOSITION
DEIIKNNNOOSTUW	KNOWN INSIDE OUT
DEIIKNNOOSSTUW	KNOWS INSIDE OUT
DEIILNOOSSTTUV	DEVOLUTIONISTS
DEIILOOPPRRSTY	POOR-SPIRITEDLY
DEIIMMNNRSTTUW	WIND INSTRUMENT
DEIINNORSSTTUU	TURNS INSIDE OUT
DEIINOPQSSTTUU	STUPID QUESTION
DEIKLNNNOORSUW	UNKNOWN SOLDIER
DEIKLOOPRRSSSU	LOOKS SURPRISED
DEILMNNNOORSTU	LONDON TERMINUS
DEIMNNOOPSSTTU	PUTS ONE'S MIND TO
DELMNOOPSSUUYY	PSEUDONYMOUSLY
DEMOPPRRSTTUUY	TRUMPED-UP STORY
DFFGHHOOOOORTTU	FOOD FOR THOUGHT
DFFIIMNOOOORSTY	MINISTRY OF FOOD
DFFNNOOORSSTUUU	RUNS OUT OF FUNDS
DFGGGHIINNOOTW	GO DOWN FIGHTING
DFGGHINNOOOORT	GOOD FOR NOTHING
	GOOD-FOR-NOTHING
DFGHHIIIINNRST	FINISHING THIRD
DFGHHLMOOOTTUU	THOUGHTFUL MOOD
DFGHIINOORSTTT	FIRST THING TO DO
DFGHILLNNOOOST	LIGHTS OF LONDON
DFHHIILNOORSUW	IRISH WOLFHOUND
DFHIIINOORSTUV	FOURTH DIVISION
DFHILOOORSTTUW	OUT OF THIS WORLD
DFIIIKNOOORSVW	DIVISION OF WORK
DGGHHIIIINNOPST	DIPHTHONGISING
DGGHHIIIINNOPTZ	DIPHTHONGIZING
DGGHHIILNNOOTT	HOLDING ON TIGHT
DGGHHIINORRTUV	DRIVING THROUGH
DGGHIIIINNSSTU	DISTINGUISHING
DGGHIIKNNORRTU	DRINKING TROUGH

DGGHINNNORSTUU	HUNTING GROUNDS
DGGIMNNOOPRSTU	STOMPING GROUND
DGHIIIKKNNRSWY	DRINKING WHISKY
DGHIIIKLLNNOSW	DOWNHILL SKIING
DGHIILNNORSTTU	HOLDING IN TRUST
DGHIINNOOPPSWW	WINDOW SHOPPING
	WINDOW-SHOPPING
DGHINNORRRTTUU	TURN RIGHT ROUND
DGIIIILLNNOSSU	DISILLUSIONING
DGIINNOPRSTTUW	PUTTING IN WORDS
DGINNNORRRSSUU	RUNS RINGS ROUND
DHHIIMOOPRSTYY	HYPOTHYROIDISM
DIIIINNOOPSSST	INDISPOSITIONS
DIINOOOPPRRSST	DISPROPORTIONS
EEEEEEGINOSTYY	SEEING EYE TO EYE
EEEEEFGNOSTTTW	GET ONES FEET WET
EEEEEFINPRRRST	FREE ENTERPRISE
EEEEEGINNQRUUV	QUEEN GUINEVERE
EEEEEGINRSSTVW	REVENGE IS SWEET
EEEEEIKNNOPSSY	KEEPS ONE'S EYE IN
EEEEEIKNPRRSSV	KEEPS IN RESERVE
EEEEEILMNNSSTV	SEVENTEEN MILES
EEEEEKMNOPPRST	KEEP ONES TEMPER
EEEEEKNNOOPSSY	KEEPS ONE'S EYE ON
EEEEELLNORTVVW	ELEVEN OR TWELVE
EEEEEFFGILLNNOS	FEELING ONESELF
EEEEEFFGILNNORS	FREEING ONESELF
EEEEEFFINORRSTT	FREE OF INTEREST
EEEEEFFLLNNOOST	FELL ON ONE'S FEET
EEEEEFFLNNOORSS	SEEN FOR ONESELF
EEEEEFFLNOORSSS	SEES FOR ONESELF
EEEEEFGGHILNRTU	FEELING THE URGE
EEEEEFGGHILNTTT	GETTING THE FEEL
EEEEEFGIILNNNST	INTENSE FEELING
EEEEEFGILMNORRS	FEELING REMORSE
EEEEEFGNOOSSTTT	GETS TO ONE'S FEET
EEEEEFGNOOSTTTW	GOT ONE'S FEET WET
EEEEEFGNOPSSTTU	GETS ONE'S FEET UP
EEEEEFHJLNNOTUV	ELEVENTH OF JUNE
EEEEEFHKLOPSTTT	KEEPS TO THE LEFT
EEEEEFHLLNSTTVW	ELEVEN TWELFTHS
EEEEEFHLNOOOOPPT	ONE OF THE PEOPLE
EEEEEFHLORSTTTV	VEERS TO THE LEFT
EEEEEFILPRSSSVX	SELF-EXPRESSIVE
EEEEEFIMNORRRTT	INTERFEROMETER
EEEEEFINOORSSTT	RISE TO ONES FEET
EEEEEFINORSSSTV	SERIES OF EVENTS
EEEEEFKLNOOPSST	KEEPS TO ONESELF
EEEEEFLLNOPSSSU	FEELS ONE'S PULSE
EEEEEFLNOPRSSSX	EXPRESS ONESELF
EEEEEFNOOORSSTT	ROSE TO ONE'S FEET
EEEEEGGLNOORSTV	GET ONE'S LEG OVER
EEEEEGHHHILNOTT	EIGHTEENTH HOLE
EEEEEGHHINNRSSS	SERENE HIGHNESS
EEEEEGHIILNNOTV	GIVEN ONE THE LIE
EEEEEGHIILNOSTV	GIVES ONE THE LIE
EEEEEGHIINNNTTY	NINETEEN EIGHTY
EEEEEGHINNOPSTY	OPENING THE EYES
EEEEEGMNOORSTTX	GONE TO EXTREMES
EEEEEGMOORSSTTX	GOES TO EXTREMES
EEEEEGPRRRSSSTX	EXPRESS REGRETS
EEEEEHHJNNSTTUV	JUNE THE SEVENTH
EEEEEHHLNNOOPTT	ON THE TELEPHONE
EEEEEHIILNNOOSTT	LIE IN ONE'S TEETH
EEEEEHILLNPSTTW	SWEETEN THE PILL
EEEEEHIMMORRRRT	MORE THE MERRIER
EEEEEHKLLRRSSTT	HELTER-SKELTERS
EEEEEHKLOPRSTTU	KEEP TO THE RULES
EEEEEHKNOOPPSSU	KEEPS OPEN HOUSE
EEEEEIINNNNNTTY	NINETEEN NINETY
EEEEEIINPRSSTTV	REPETITIVENESS

EEEEIKLMNORSST	REMOTE LIKENESS
EEEEEIKNNPPSSSU	KEEP IN SUSPENSE
EEEEEILPRRTTTWY	TELETYPEWRITER
EEEEIMMOPPRRRS	PROSPER MERIMEE
EEEEEIMNORSSSTV	SERVES ONE'S TIME
EEEEEINNNNTTTWY	NINETEEN TWENTY
EEEEEINNPRSSTVV	PREVENTIVENESS
EEEEEINPRSSSSVX	EXPRESSIVENESS
EEEEEKMNOPPRSTT	KEPT ONE'S TEMPER
EEEEELLNNRSSSST	RELENTLESSNESS
EEEEELMNNOOSSVY	LOVES ONE'S ENEMY
EEEEELMNOOPRSST	LOSE ONES TEMPER
EEEEELNNNOPSSTV	VENT ONE'S SPLEEN
EEEEELNNOORSSSV	LOSES ONE'S NERVE
EEEEMMNORSTTTWX	WENT TO EXTREMES
EEEEEMOPRRTTVXY	EXTREME POVERTY
EEEEEPRRRSSSTUX	EXERTS PRESSURE
EEEFFFHILMOORT	FOR THE LIFE OF ME
EEEEFFFNNOORSTU	RUN OFF ONE'S FEET
EEEEFFGGHHIORTT	GEORGE THE FIFTH
EEEEFFGLNOORSST	FORGETS ONESELF
EEEEFFHHIIMOTTT	THE THIEF OF TIME
EEEEFFHHLLNOSTT	LEFT ON THE SHELF
EEEEFFHIILLORTY	THE LIFE OF RILEY
EEEEFFHIMOPRSST	OFF THE PREMISES
EEEEFFHINNOOSTV	ON THE OFFENSIVE
EEEEFFHKKOOOOTTW	TOOK THE WEEK OFF
EEEEFFHLNOORTUW	WHEEL OF FORTUNE
EEEEFFIILMNOOST	TIME OF ONES LIFE
EEEEFFIIMNNSTTU	FIFTEEN MINUTES
EEEEFFIILLNOOOSV	LOVE OF ONES LIFE
EEEEFFLNORSSSST	EFFORTLESSNESS
EEEEFFLOORRSSUY	SEE FOR YOURSELF
EEEEFGGHIORRSTT	GEORGE THE FIRST
EEEFGHIIINNPRT	FINGER IN THE PIE
EEEEFGHILLNNOPS	HELPING ONESELF
EEEEFGHIRRSSTTT	GETS THERE FIRST
EEEEFGIILMNNOOT	FEELING EMOTION
EEEEFGILNNOPSUV	GIVEN ONESELF UP
EEEEFGILNNORSSS	RESIGNS ONESELF
EEEEFGILNOPSSUV	GIVES ONESELF UP
EEEFGLMNNORSTV	SELF-GOVERNMENT
EEEFHHJLNTTTUW	JUNE THE TWELFTH
EEEEFHJLLNOTUVY	ELEVENTH OF JULY
EEEEFHJLOPSSTTU	SLEEP OF THE JUST
EEEEFHKNOOPRSTT	STROKE OF THE PEN
EEEEFHLMNOOOTVY	THE LOVE OF MONEY
EEEEFHLOOPRSSTW	SWEEPS THE FLOOR
EEEEFHMOORSTTWY	WORTHY OF ESTEEM
EEEFIIKLMORSTV	FIVE KILOMETRES
EEEEFIILNNORSSU	INSURE ONES LIFE
EEEEFIKLLLMNOST	ELEMENT OF SKILL
EEEEFILMNNOOOST	FEELS NO EMOTION
EEEEFILMNNOOPRSV	IMPROVE ONESELF
EEEEFILMNOOPSSS	IMPOSES ONESELF
EEEEFILNNPSSSTU	LEFT IN SUSPENSE
EEEEFILNOPRSSSX	SELF-EXPRESSION
EEEFILOORRSSTT	RESTORES TO LIFE
EEEEFIMNORRRTTY	INTERFEROMETRY
EEEEFLLLMNSTTTU	FULL SETTLEMENT
EEEFLLMMNOPSTY	SELF-EMPLOYMENT
EEEFLLNORRSTTU	FORTUNE-TELLERS
EEEEFLOPRSSTTUU	PUTS OUT FEELERS
EEEFNNOOOSTTWW	ONE'S OWN TWO FEET
EEEFNOOPPRRSTU	PERSON OF REPUTE
EEEFNOOPPRSSSU	SENSE OF PURPOSE
EEEFNOPPSSTTUU	PUTS ONE'S FEET UP
EEEGGGGHILSSTT	GETS THE GIGGLES
EEEGGGHINORRSW	GEORGE GERSHWIN
EEEGGHHIILNSTT	SEEING THE LIGHT
EEEGGHHIORSTTX	GEORGE THE SIXTH

EEEGGHIMNRSTTV	GIVE ME STRENGTH!	EEEHKLOPRSTTTU	KEPT TO THE RULES
EEEGGHHINNORTTW	GETTING NOWHERE	EEEHLMNOOPRSSS	HOMELESS PERSON
EEEGGHINOOPRUV	GIVE ENOUGH ROPE	EEEHLNNNOORSTU	TURN ON ONES HEEL
EEEGGHINORSTVY	EVERYTHING GOES	EEEHNNOOPRTTVW	WENT OVER THE TOP
EEEGGHIORSTTTT	GETS IT TOGETHER	EEEIIKLMNNORST	NINE KILOMETRES
EEEGGHHNOORSTTT	GETS ON TOGETHER	EEEIIILLNRSTTTT	LITTLE INTEREST
EEEGGHGHOPRRTTUW	GREW UP TOGETHER	EEEIILMNPRSSTT	SIMPLE INTEREST
EEEGGIKMNNRSSS	KINGS MESSENGER	EEEIILNPRSSVXY	INEXPRESSIVELY
EEEGGILNORSUVY	GIVE GENEROUSLY	EEEIIMNNNRTTTW	INTERTWINEMENT
EEEGGIMNNOORSS	GEORGES SIMENON	EEEIIMNPRSSSSV	IMPRESSIVENESS
EEEGGINSSSSTUV	SUGGESTIVENESS		PERMISSIVENESS
EEEGGLNOOORSTV	GOT ONE'S LEG OVER	EEEIINNOPSSSTY	SPIT IN ONE'S EYES
EEEGHHHHINRTTY	HENRY THE EIGHTH	EEEIKLORRRSSTW	TIRELESS WORKER
EEEGHHIIRSSTVV	GIVE THE SHIVERS	EEEIKNNNOOOPSS	POKE ONES NOSE IN
EEEGHHIKIOPRTTT	KEEP TO THE RIGHT	EEEIKNNPRSSSTU	KEPT IN SUSPENSE
EEEGHHIMMNNOSTT	EIGHTEEN MONTHS	EEEIKNSSTTWWXY	TWENTY-SIX WEEKS
EEEGHHINOPSTUV	GIVE ONE THE PUSH	EEEILLNOPRSSTT	LITTLE RESPONSE
EEEGHHIORRTTTV	VEER TO THE RIGHT	EEEILNNOPRSSST	PRETENSIONLESS
EEEGHHIRSSSTTV	GETS THE SHIVERS	EEEILNPRRRTTY	PERTINENT REPLY
EEEGHHNNOORSTU	SEEN ONE THROUGH	EEEILNOPRSSSSX	EXPRESSIONLESS
EEEGHHNOORSSTU	SEES ONE THROUGH	EEEILNORRSSSTU	IRRESOLUTENESS
EEEGHIIILLSTVW	GIVE THE WILLIES	EEEILNRSSSSSST	RESISTLESSNESS
EEEGHIIKNNOPTY	POKING IN THE EYE	EEEIMNOOPRSTTT	POTENTIOMETERS
EEEGHIIKNRSTTY	STRIKING THE EYE	EEEIMNOPPRRSST	PEREMPTORINESS
EEEGHIIILLMNTTT	TELLING THE TIME	EEEIMNORRRTTYY	ENEMY TERRITORY
EEEGHIILLSSTTW	GETS THE WILLIES	EEEINNOOPRTTUW	WENT INTO EUROPE
EEEGHIILNOPSTV	GIVE ONE THE SLIP	EEEINNOPRSSSSV	RESPONSIVENESS
EEEGHIINNOPPTV	GIVEN ONE THE PIP	EEEINNOPRSSUUX	RUINOUS EXPENSE
EEEGHIINNOPSTT	SEEING THE POINT	EEEINNOPSSSTTV	VENTS ONE'S SPITE
EEEGHIINOPPSTV	GIVES ONE THE PIP	EEEINOPPRSSSSV	OPPRESSIVENESS
EEEGHILLMNRRVY	GIVEN MERRY HELL	EEEINOPSSSSSSV	POSSESSIVENESS
EEEGHILLMRRSVY	GIVES MERRY HELL	EEEJLLLMOPRTUY	PETROLEUM JELLY
EEEGHILLNPSSST	SLEEPLESS NIGHT	EEELLMNNOPSTWY	MONEY WELL SPENT
EEEGHILLNRTTVY	TELL EVERYTHING	EEELMMNOOORSSY	LOSE ONES MEMORY
EEEGHILNORSSTT	LETS GO THE REINS	EEELMNNOOOSSSY	LOSES ONE'S MONEY
EEEGHILNORSTVY	LOSE EVERYTHING	EEELMNOOPRSSTT	LOST ONE'S TEMPER
EEEGHILNSSSSTW	WEIGHTLESSNESS	EEEMMMNNOOSTVW	WOMEN'S MOVEMENT
EEEGHIMMNORSTT	MOTHERS MEETING	EEENNOOOPSSSTT	STEP ON ONE'S TOES
EEEGHINORRSSTV	SERVES ONE RIGHT	EEENNORRSSSTUV	SERVES ONE'S TURN
EEEGHINORSSTTT	GRITS ONE'S TEETH	EEEOOOPRRRSTTW	RESTORE TO POWER
EEEGHINOSSSTUW	USES ONE'S WEIGHT	EEFFFIILLLMNSTU	SELF-FULFILMENT
EEEGHNNOOORSST	GET ON ONES HORSE	EEFFFFKLNOOOOST	TOOK ONESELF OFF
EEEGHNOOOPRTTV	GONE OVER THE TOP	EEFFGHINNOOOPR	OFFERING NO HOPE
EEEGHNOPRRTTUW	UP THE WRONG TREE	EEFFGHINOOPTTT	GET OFF THE POINT
EEEGHOOOPRSTTV	GOES OVER THE TOP	EEFFGINOOPPRRY	GEOFFREY RIPPON
EEEGIIMNOPRSSS	SPERMIOGENESIS	EEFFGLNNOORSSU	RUN OFF ONE'S LEGS
EEEGILLMNORTUY	YOURE TELLING ME!	EEFFHHILLOORTT	FOR THE HELL OF IT
EEEGILNOORSSTV	VENEREOLOGISTS	EEFFHHILNOSSST	SINS OF THE FLESH
EEEGIMNOPRSTTT	PROTEST MEETING	EEFFHHOOPRSSTT	HOT OFF THE PRESS
EEEGINNOOOPRTU	GONE INTO EUROPE	EEFFHHOORRTTTW	WORTH THE EFFORT
EEEGINOOOPRSTU	GOES INTO EUROPE	EEFFHINNOORRTT	IN THE FOREFRONT
EEEGINOOPRRSVW	SOVEREIGN POWER	EEFFIKLOOPRSST	SPOKE FOR ITSELF
EEEGLNNOOOSSTU	LOSE ONES TONGUE	EEFFILLMNOSSTU	FULLNESS OF TIME
EEEGNNOOPSSSTU	GETS UP ONE'S NOSE	EEFFILNNOORSTU	RUN FOR ONES LIFE
EEEHHILMOPPSST	MEPHISTOPHELES	EEFFMNORRSSTTU	SUFFERS TORMENT
EEEHHJLNSTTUVY	JULY THE SEVENTH	EEFGGHHIINOSTU	HEIGHT OF GENIUS
EEEHHLNNOOOSST	HOT ON ONES HEELS	EEFGGHIIKNOPST	KEEPING SIGHT OF
EEEHHNNOOSSTTW	SHOWN ONE'S TEETH	EEFGGHIILNNNOT	FEELING NOTHING
EEEHHNOOSSSTTW	SHOWS ONE'S TEETH	EEFGGHIILNNOSW	SHOWING FEELING
EEEHIIINNNOPPRR	NOREPINEPHRINE	EEFGGHIIINRSTTT	STREET FIGHTING
EEEHIINNNRTTTY	NINETEEN THIRTY	EEFGGIIKLNNNS	SINKING FEELING
EEEHIINPRSSTVY	HYPERSENSITIVE	EEFGGILNNORSST	STRONG FEELINGS
EEEHIJLMNORRSU	JOHN LE MESURIER	EEFGGINNOOORRV	GOING ON FOR EVER
EEEHIKKLNOOPST	TELEPHONE KIOSK	EEFGGNNNOOOORSU	GONE FOR ONE'S GUN
EEEHIKLNOOSSTY	LOOKS IN THE EYES	EEFGGNNOOORSSU	GOES FOR ONE'S GUN
EEEHIKNOOPPTTT	KEEP TO THE POINT	EEFGHHIIILRSTW	SIGH WITH RELIEF
EEEHILLPRRSTUV	SELL UP THE RIVER	EEFGHHIMMORSTU	HEIGHT OF SUMMER
EEEHILMOPRRSTY	PYRHELIOMETERS	EEFGHIIILLNTTV	LIFTING THE VEIL
EEEHILNOSSTTWW	WET ONES WHISTLE	EEFGHIIILLTTTWY	FLYWEIGHT TITLE
EEEHIORRSSTTUVW	WITHOUT RESERVE	EEFGHIIMNOSSTT	SIGN OF THE TIMES
EEEHKLNOPTTTTU	PUT THE KETTLE ON	EEFGHIIMNRSTTX	FIXING THE TERMS

EEFGHIINNOPRTT	POINT THE FINGER	EEGGILLLNNOPSU	PULLING ONE'S LEG
EEFGHIKOOPSTTU	KEEP OUT OF SIGHT	EEGGINNOORRSTW	GROWING ON TREES
EEFGHILNNOOSSW	SHOWING ONESELF	EEGHHHNNOORSTTU	THROUGH THE NOSE
EEFGHINNOORRST	FORESHORTENING	EEGHHIIILLMNTT	IN THE LIMELIGHT
EEFGHINNOPRTTU	PUT THE FINGER ON	EEGHHIILLNRSST	THREE SHILLINGS
EEFGHINOOPTTTU	TIP OF THE TONGUE	EEGHHIIMOSTTTW	GO WITH THE TIMES
EEFGHNNOPRTUYY	PENNY FOR THE GUY	EEGHHILOSSTTTV	LIGHTS THE STOVE
EEFGHNOOORSTTT	GOES TO THE FRONT	EEGHHNNOORSTUW	ROUGH-HEWN STONE
EEFGHNORSSTTTT	TEST OF STRENGTH	EEGHIIKNNRRSSY	HENRY KISSINGER
EEFGIIKLLLNNOS	KILLING ONESELF	EEGHIIKNRRSTVY	RISK EVERYTHING
EEFGIIKNOOPTTU	KEEPING OUT OF IT	EEGHIIKORSTTVW	GIVE IT THE WORKS
EEFGIILNNNORSU	RUINING ONESELF	EEGHIILLNNQSSU	QUEENS SHILLING
EEFGIILNNOSSTU	SUITING ONESELF	EEGHIILNNNOSST	SIGNS ON THE LINE
EEFGIIMNMNNOOR	ONE FINE MORNING	EEGHIIMNNSTTUX	EXTINGUISHMENT
EEFGIKNOORSSTU	STROKE OF GENIUS	EEGHIINNNNOPST	OPEN THE INNINGS
EEFGILLNNORTTU	FORTUNE-TELLING	EEGHIIORSTTTVW	GETS IT OVER WITH
EEFGIMMNNORRTV	FIRM GOVERNMENT	EEGHILLMNORVWY	OVERWHELMINGLY
EEFGIMNNOORSTUV	REFUSING TO MOVE	EEGHILLNOPSTUW	PULL ONES WEIGHT
EEFGNNNOORSTUW	WENT FOR ONE'S GUN	EEGHILNOOSSSST	LOSES ONE'S SIGHT
EEFHHHNORRTTUY	HENRY THE FOURTH	EEGHILNOPRRTUV	PROVING THE RULE
EEFHHJLLTTTUWY	JULY THE TWELFTH	EEGHILNORSTTVY	LOST EVERYTHING
EEFHHMMNNOOORTT	ON THE HOME FRONT	EEGHIMNNOPRTVW	GOVERNMENT WHIP
EEFHHNOOOORTTT	ON THE OTHER FOOT	EEGHINNOORRSTU	SOUTHERN REGION
EEFHIIIINNORRST	IRONS IN THE FIRE	EEGHINNOSSTTUV	EVENS THINGS OUT
EEFHIILMOPSSST	HOPELESS MISFIT	EEGHINOOPSTTTT	GETS TO THE POINT
EEFHIKMOOOORRTT	TOOK IT FROM HERE	EEGHINOPRTTTUY	PITT THE YOUNGER
EEFHILNNOSSTTT	THE FLINTSTONES	EEGHINOPSSTTUU	SETTING UP HOUSE
EEFHINOORSSSSTY	SENSE OF HISTORY	EEGHINOSSSSTTT	SETS ONE'S SIGHTS
EEFHINOPRRSSTT	THE FIRST PERSON	EEGHIOORSTTYYZ	HETEROZYGOSITY
EEFHLLNOOOSSTU	OUT OF ONES SHELL	EEGHIOPRSTTTTU	PUTS IT TOGETHER
EEFHLNORRRSSTU	RUNS FOR SHELTER	EEGHLLNOOOPSTT	GONE TO THE POLLS
EEFHLNORSTTTTU	TURNS TO THE LEFT	EEGHLLOOOPSSTT	GOES TO THE POLLS
EEFHNNOOOOSSUW	HOUSE OF ONES OWN	EEGHLLOOORSTUY	HETEROLOGOUSLY
EEFHNNOORTTTTW	WENT TO THE FRONT	EEGHNNOOOORSST	GOT ON ONE'S HORSE
EEFIIILLMNOSTV	TELEVISION FILM	EEGHOOOORSSSTY	SO THE STORY GOES
EEFIIILMOPRSSV	OVERSIMPLIFIES	EEGIIMMNOPRSSV	GIVE PERMISSION
EEFIIIORRSSTTZ	TRIES IT FOR SIZE	EEGIIKKLLNNOOW	LOOKING LIKE NEW
EEFIILMMNORTUU	FOUR-MINUTE MILE	EEGIIKLNNNOSTV	KEN LIVINGSTONE
EEFIIMMMOORTTT	FROM TIME TO TIME	EEGIILLMNNSSTWY	SMILING SWEETLY
EEFIIMNOOQSTTU	QUESTION OF TIME	EEGIIILLNPPSTVY	STEPPING LIVELY
EEFIINOQRSSSTU	FIRES QUESTIONS	EEGIILLNRRSSTV	STERLING SILVER
EEFIKLMOORRSTU	FOUR KILOMETRES	EEGIILMOOPSSTT	EPISTEMOLOGIST
EEFILLNNOOOPSW	IN ONE FELL SWOOP	EEGIINNNPRRSTU	UNENTERPRISING
EEFILNOOPSSSSS	SELF-POSSESSION	EEGIINNNORSSTW	TRIES ONE'S WINGS
EEFILNOOPSSTTU	STEPS OUT OF LINE	EEGIINNPRSTTUV	PUTTING IN VERSE
EEFILNOORSSSTT	LOSS OF INTEREST	EEGIINOOPSTVWX	EXPOSING TO VIEW
EEFILNOPPRSSTU	SPITEFUL PERSON	EEGIKNNOPSSSSU	SPIKES ONE'S GUNS
EEFINORRRSTTUU	FURNITURE STORE	EEGILLLNNOPSSS	SPELLING LESSON
EEFKOOPRRRSSUW	PRESSURE OF WORK	EEGILLOPRRSSTT	LITTLE PROGRESS
EEFLLLMMNOPTUY	FULL EMPLOYMENT	EEGILMOOORSSTT	METEOROLOGISTS
EEFLLLNOPPSSUU	PULLS ONESELF UP	EEGILNNNSSTTUW	UNSETTLING NEWS
EEFLLNNOOOOSSW	FOLLOW ONES NOSE	EEGILNOOPRRVWY	OVERPOWERINGLY
EEFLMNOOOOORRVY	FOR LOVE OR MONEY	EEGILNOPPSTTTU	PUTTING TO SLEEP
EEFLNOOPSSTTUU	PUTS ONESELF OUT	EEGINNOOPRTTUV	PUTTING ONE OVER
EEFLNOPPRSSSUU	PURPOSEFULNESS	EEGINNOPPSSSTT	STEPPING-STONES
EEGGGGIIIKNNOPT	KEEPING IT GOING	EEGINOOPRRRRTV	ROVING REPORTER
EEGGHHIILNNSTT	SHEET LIGHTNING	EEGINOORRSSSST	RETROGRESSIONS
EEGGHHIMNPTTTU	GETTING THE HUMP	EEGINORSSSTTUY	YOUNGEST SISTER
EEGGHHINNOOSUU	ENOUGH IS ENOUGH	EEGJMMNOOOORSSY	JOGS ONE'S MEMORY
EEGGHHINPSTTTU	GETTING THE PUSH	EEGLNNOOOSSTTU	LOST ONE'S TONGUE
EEGGHHIOPSTTUV	GIVE UP THE GHOST	EEGMNNOOPRSTTV	GOVERNMENT POST
EEGGHIIIKNNPST	KEEPING IN SIGHT	EEGOOPPRRRRSST	PROGRESS REPORT
EEGGHIIKNNOPRT	KEEPING RIGHT ON	EEHHHMOORSSTTU	THE HORSE'S MOUTH
EEGGHIILNPSTTT	GETTING THE SLIP	EEHHIIILLNPSST	THE PHILLIPINES
EEGGHILLPRRTTU	PULL THE TRIGGER	EEHHIIJKOPRSST	SIR KEITH JOSEPH
EEGGHINORRSTTT	STRING TOGETHER	EEHHIINORSTTVW	IN THE SHORT VIEW
EEGGHOOPRRTTUW	GROW UP TOGETHER	EEHHIKORRSSTTU	STRIKES THE HOUR
EEGGIIKLMNNPS	KEEPING SMILING	EEHHILLLORTWWW	WELL WORTH WHILE
EEGGIIILNNOOTX	GOING INTO EXILE	EEHHILMMNOTTTU	MELT IN THE MOUTH
EEGGIILNNNSTTT	STINGING NETTLE	EEHHILNOORSTWW	WORTH ONES WHILE
EEGGIINNNOSSSW	SINGE ONE'S WINGS	EEHHILNPPRSTTU	HUNT THE SLIPPER

EEHHIMMOOPRRST	HETEROMORPHISM
EEHHIMNORRSTTT	IN THE SHORT TERM
EEHHINNOORSSTW	WIN ON THE HORSES
EEHHINNOORSTTT	SIT ON THE THRONE
EEHHIOOPPRRRSW	HERO-WORSHIPPER
EEHHJNNOOOSSTU	JOHN STONEHOUSE
EEHHKNOPRSTTTU	SPOKEN THE TRUTH
EEHHLLOORSTTUY	YOUTH-HOSTELLER
EEHHLLORTTTTTU	TO TELL THE TRUTH
EEHHLMNNOOOOTY	HONEYMOON HOTEL
EEHHMNNOORTTTU	MOUNT THE THRONE
EEHHNNOOORSSTW	WON ON THE HORSES
EEHHNOPRRSTTUU	USURP THE THRONE
EEHIIJMNPRRTUV	JUMP IN THE RIVER
EEHIILLRRRRTTW	THRILLER WRITER
EEHIILMNNQRSTU	RELINQUISHMENT
EEHIILNOSSSTTW	HOSTILE WITNESS
EEHIIMMNOPRSTV	IMPOVERISHMENT
EEHIINOOPRRTTY	ERYTHROPOIETIN
EEHIINOOPSSSTT	PHOTOSENSITISE
EEHIINOOPSSTTV	PHOTOSENSITIVE
EEHIINOOPSSTTZ	PHOTOSENSITIZE
EEHIINOPSSSTYZ	HYPOSENSITIZES
EEHIIOOPRRSSTY	ERYTHROPOIESIS
EEHIIOPRSTTTUW	WITHOUT RESPITE
EEHIJKKLLLOOSY	SHOOK LIKE JELLY
EEHIKMNOORRSWY	YORKSHIREWOMEN
EEHIKNOOPPTTTT	KEPT TO THE POINT
EEHILLOORSSSTT	TORTOISESHELLS
EEHILNNNOPSTTY	PENNY IN THE SLOT
EEHILNNOORSTTW	THREW IN ONE'S LOT
EEHILNOORSSSST	LOSES ONE'S SHIRT
EEHIMMNOOOOPRST	PROMISE THE MOON
EEHIMNOOOPRTTT	MORE TO THE POINT
EEHIMOOPRRRSTU	MOTHER SUPERIOR
EEHINNNOOOOPPSS	PIN ONES HOPES ON
EEHINNNOOPSSSU	PUSH ONE'S NOSE IN
EEHINNOOOPTTTU	OUT INTO THE OPEN
EEHINNOORSSTTW	NOTEWORTHINESS
EEHINOOPPQSTTU	POP THE QUESTION
EEHINOPQSTTTUU	PUT THE QUESTION
EEHIOOPTTTTTUV	PUT IT TO THE VOTE
EEHIOORRSSTTVW	THE WORST IS OVER
EEHIOPSTTTTTTU	PUT IT TO THE TEST
EEHKNNOOPSTTWW	KNEW WHEN TO STOP
EEHLLNOOPSTTTW	WENT TO THE POLLS
EEHLMNORSSSSUU	HUMOURLESSNESS
EEHMNNOOOPSSTU	OPENS ONE'S MOUTH
EEHMNOPPSTTUUY	PUTS UP THE MONEY
EEHNNOOPRRTTUW	TURN ON THE POWER
EEIIIKLLLSTTT	TELL IT LIKE IT IS
EEIIKKLLNNTTWW	TWINKLE TWINKLE
EEIIKLLNORSSTT	TRIES ONE'S SKILL
EEIILLNORSSSSU	SERIOUS ILLNESS
EEIILMNNRTTTTY	INTERMITTENTLY
EEIILMOORRTTUV	ULTERIOR MOTIVE
EEIILNNOOSSTVW	LIVE ON ONES WITS
EEIILNOORSSTUV	REVOLUTIONISES
EEIILNOORSTUVZ	REVOLUTIONIZES
EEIILNOPRSTVVY	LIVES IN POVERTY
EEIIMMMNNNORRSS	NINE MENS MORRIS
EEIIMNNNOOTTTX	IN NEXT TO NO TIME
EEIIMNOPRSSSUV	IMPERVIOUSNESS
EEIIMNORRSSSST	SENIOR MISTRESS
EEIIMNRRSTTUVY	UNIVERSITY TERM
EEIINNOPRSTUVY	OPEN UNIVERSITY
EEIKMNNOORSSSY	RISKS ONE'S MONEY
EEIKNNOOPPSSTU	PUT ONES SPOKE IN
EEIILLMOOPRRSWY	PRIMROSE YELLOW
EEIILMMNOOPRSSY	SLIP ONES MEMORY
EEIILMNNOOSSSST	MOTIONLESSNESS

EEIILNOOOPSSSSS	SOLE POSSESSION
EEIILNOPPRSSSSU	PURSES ONE'S LIPS
EEIILOOOPPRRRST	SOLE PROPRIETOR
EEIMNNOOPRSSTU	MINESTRONE SOUP
EEIMNORSSSSTUY	MYSTERIOUSNESS
EEINNNOORSSTUV	NERVOUS TENSION
EEINNOOOPPRSTV	PROVE ONES POINT
EEINNOOOPQSTTU	OPEN TO QUESTION
EEINOOPPRRRSSU	SUPERIOR PERSON
EEKLLNOOOOSSSS	LOSES ONE'S LOOKS
EELMMMNOOORSSY	LOST ONE'S MEMORY
EELNOOPPRRSTTY	STOLEN PROPERTY
EELOOPPRRSSTUY	PREPOSTEROUSLY
EEMNNNOOORSSTW	ON ONES OWN TERMS
EENNNOOPRSSTUU	TURN ONES NOSE UP
	TURN UP ONES NOSE
EENNOOOOPPRRSST	PERSON TO PERSON
EENNOOOPRSSTTU	PORTENTOUSNESS
EENNOOPRSSTTUU	TURN UP ONE'S TOES
EENOPPRRSSSTUU	PUTS ON PRESSURE
EEOOPPRRRRSSTT	SPORTS REPORTER
EFFFFGIIINOTTYY	GONE FIFTY-FIFTY
EFFFFGIIOSTTYY	GOES FIFTY-FIFTY
EFFFFIINTTTWYY	WENT FIFTY-FIFTY
EFFFGGHIINNORT	FRIGHTENING OFF
EFFFGIIILLLLNSU	SELF-FULFILLING
EFFGGHILLOSTTY	GETS OFF LIGHTLY
EFFGIIIIILRQTTT	THE FIRST FLIGHT
EFFGHIILMNNSSU	ENGLISH MUFFINS
EFFGHINNOOORTT	NOTHING TO OFFER
EFFGHINOOOPTTT	GOT OFF THE POINT
EFFGIIILNNNORRU	RUINING FOR LIFE
EFFGIIJLNSSTUY	SELF-JUSTIFYING
EFFGIINNOPRSTT	OFFSET PRINTING
EFFGILNORRSSTY	FLYING FORTRESS
EFFHHIOOORRSTY	OTHER FISH TO FRY
EFFHHMOOOORRTTU	ROOF OF THE MOUTH
EFFILNOOPRSTTT	LEFT FOOTPRINTS
EFFKNNNOOSSTUW	KNOWN ONE'S STUFF
EFFKNNOOSSSTUW	KNOWS ONE'S STUFF
EFFNORSSSTTTUU	STRUT ONES STUFF
EFGGHINNNOOOORT	GONE FOR NOTHING
EFGGHINNNOOORST	GOES FOR NOTHING
EFGGHINNNORSSTT	SIGN OF STRENGTH
EFGGHIIOOSSTTTU	GETS OUT OF SIGHT
EFGGHNNOOOSSST	THE SONG OF SONGS
EFGGIIILLNNRUV	GIVING FULL REIN
EFGGIIIMNOPRSU	IMPOSING FIGURE
EFGGIIINNNORTX	NITROGEN-FIXING
EFGGIIINNPRRT	FINGERPRINTING
EFGGIIINNRSTTT	GETTING IN FIRST
EFGGIINNORSSTU	REFUSING TO SIGN
EFGHHHIJMOPRTU	FOR THE HIGH JUMP
EFGHHIIMNOSSTY	SOMETHING FISHY
EFGHHIINOORTTT	HITTING THE ROOF
EFGHHILORRSTTU	FILTERS THROUGH
EFGHHINOOORTTT	ON THE RIGHT FOOT
EFGHHINORRSSTT	FORTHRIGHTNESS
EFGHHINORRTTTU	THE RING OF TRUTH
EFGHHIRRSSTTTT	GET SHORT SHRIFT
EFGHHLNOSSTTUU	THOUGHTFULNESS
EFGHHNNOORSSTTW	SHOW OF STRENGTH
EFGHIIIMRRSTTT	RIGHT FIRST TIME
EFGHIILNNOPSTU	SPOILING THE FUN
EFGHIKOOPSTTTU	KEPT OUT OF SIGHT
EFGHILLNORSTTW	STRENGTH OF WILL
EFGHILNNNOPRRU	RUNNING FOR HELP
EFGHILNNOOOORU	LEGION OF HONOUR
EFGHILNNOOTTTU	LEFT NOTHING OUT
EFGHIMNNNOORRU	RUNNING FOR HOME
EFGHINNNOORTTW	WENT FOR NOTHING

EFGHINNORRTTUV	VENTURING FORTH	EGHIIILLLNOSTT	TILLING THE SOIL
EFGHLNOORSSSTT	LOSS OF STRENGTH	EGHIIILNRSTTTU	IN ITS TRUE LIGHT
EFGHNNOOOORTTW	ON THE WRONG FOOT	EGHIIINNRRRSVY	SIR HENRY IRVING
EFGIILLNQRRSUY	FLYING SQUIRREL	EGHIIINRSSTTTW	TIES WITH STRING
EFGIILNOPPRSTU	SUPPORTING LIFE	EGHIIKNNNRRSTU	RUNNING THE RISK
EFGIKNOORRSTUW	REFUSING TO WORK	EGHIIKNNOPPTTT	POTTING THE PINK
EFGILNOPPRSSTU	SELF-SUPPORTING	EGHIILLMORSTTT	GRIST TO THE MILL
EFHHILMNOSTUWY	FLUSH WITH MONEY	EGHIILLNPSSSTT	l FTS THINGS SLIP
EFHIIIILORSSTUY	THIS IS YOUR LIFE	EGHIILNNPSSTUV	LIVENS THINGS UP
EFHIIKLLNOSTTT	THINKS LITTLE OF	EGHIIMNOOPRSSW	SHOWING PROMISE
EFHIILNORSSTTT	FIRST ON THE LIST	EGHIIMNOPRRTUV	TRIUMPHING OVER
EFHIINNORSSTTT	SITS IN THE FRONT	EGHIINNNOORSTW	IN ONES OWN RIGHT
EFHILLLMNOOSST	MILL ON THE FLOSS	EGHIINNNOSSTTW	WINNING THE TOSS
EFHILNOOORSSTT	SITS ON THE FLOOR	EGHIINOOPRSTTT	RISING TO THE TOP
EFHILNOPRSSSUW	WORSHIPFULNESS	EGHIINOPRRSTTT	STIRRING THE POT
EFHIOOPRRRSTTW	THIRST FOR POWER	EGHIJLLNNOORSV	LONG JOHN SILVER
EFHLNNRSSTTUUU	UNTRUTHFULNESS	EGHIKLNNOOOSSS	SLINGS ONE'S HOOK
EFIIINPRRSSTWZ	WINS FIRST PRIZE	EGHILLNOOOOPPT	LOOPING THE LOOP
EFIIKOOPRRSTTZ	TOOK FIRST PRIZE	EGHILLNPRSSTTU	PULL THE STRINGS
EFINOORSSSTTUU	FORTUITOUSNESS	EGHILNNNOOPSSU	HUNG ON ONE'S LIPS
EFIOOPPRRSTUUW	PURSUIT OF POWER	EGHILNORSSSTUW	SHOWING RESULTS
EFKNOOOPRSTTUU	SPOKE OUT OF TURN	EGHINNOOOORRTVW	ROW OVER NOTHING
EFLNOOOPRRTTUU	RUN OUT OF PETROL	EGHINNOORSSTTW	THROWING STONES
EFMNNOOORSTUUY	RUNS OUT OF MONEY	EGHINOOPPRSTTT	STOPPING THE ROT
EGGGGGIINNNOOO	GOING,GOING,GONE	EGHKMOPRSSTUUW	GUMS UP THE WORKS
EGGGHHIINORTTTU	GETTING THROUGH	EGIIILMMNNORVY	IN LIVING MEMORY
EGGGHIIIINNTTUV	GIVING IT THE GUN	EGIIIMNNNNORTW	WINNING ON MERIT
EGGGHIIINRTTTT	GETTING IT RIGHT	EGIIIMNNOPPSTT	STOPPING IN TIME
EGGGHIIINPTTTTU	GETTING UPTIGHT	EGIIKLLMNOORST	KREMLINOLOGIST
EGGGIINNORTTTW	GETTING IT WRONG	EGIIKNORRRRSTT	STRIKING TERROR
EGGGIINOPRSTTT	GETTING TO GRIPS	EGIIILLMNNNOORY	ROLLING IN MONEY
EGGGINNOORRUWY	GROWING YOUNGER	EGIILLNNNOOORT	ROLLING INTO ONE
EGGHHIIILNNTTW	WHITE LIGHTNING	EGIILMMNNOSSSW	SWIMMING LESSON
EGGHHIINRSSTTT	SET THINGS RIGHT	EGIILMMNNSTWWY	WENT SWIMMINGLY
EGGHIILMNPTTU	LIGHTING-UP TIME	EGIINNOPPRTTUW	PUTTING IN POWER
EGGHIIKNNPSSTU	SPIKING THE GUNS	EGIINNOPRRRSTU	INTERIOR-SPRUNG
EGGHILLLPRSTUU	UPHILL STRUGGLE	EGIINNRRSSTTUV	SERVING ITS TURN
EGGHIMNNOOOOTT	GOING TO THE MOON	EGIKNOOPRRRSSW	WORK IN PROGRESS
EGGHINOOORSSTU	GROUSE SHOOTING	EGILLNNORTTUUW	TURNING OUT WELL
	SHOOTING GROUSE	EGILMNNOOSSSTU	MOUNTING LOSSES
EGGIIKMNNOOPSU	GOING UP IN SMOKE	EGILNOOPPRRSTU	SUPPORTING ROLE
EGGIIKMNNOPSUV	GIVEN UP SMOKING	EGILNOORSSSTUU	GLORIOUS SUNSET
EGGIIKMNOPSSUV	GIVES UP SMOKING	EGINNNOORSTTTU	TURNING TO STONE
EGGIILMMNNOSWY	GONE SWIMMINGLY	EGINNOOOPRRRSV	PRISON GOVERNOR
EGGIILMMNOSSWY	GOES SWIMMINGLY	EGLNNOOSSSTTUU	GLUTTONOUSNESS
EGGIILNNOPRTTU	TRIPLE-TONGUING	EHHIKLLOOOSTTT	TOOK TO THE HILLS
EGGILNNOOOORSTT	RONTGENOLOGIST	EHHIKLMNOOOTTU	LOOK IN THE MOUTH
EGGINOPPRSTTTU	GETTING SUPPORT	EHHIKNOORRRSTY	NORTH YORKSHIRE
EGHHHIINNORSTU	THE SHINING HOUR	EHHIKNORSSTTTW	THINKS THE WORST
EGHHHILLMORTTU	THROUGH THE MILL	EHHIKOORRSSTUY	SOUTH YORKSHIRE
EGHHHIMNOPSTYY	EIGHTH SYMPHONY	EHHILNOORSSTTT	ON THE SHORT LIST
EGHHHNOORTTTUW	THROUGH THE TOWN	EHHINOOPSSSTTY	PHOTOSYNTHESIS
EGHHIILLNNOSST	HONEST SHILLING	EHHMNOOSSSTTUU	SHUTS ONE'S MOUTH
EGHHIILMNNOOTT	IN THE MOONLIGHT	EHHNNNOOOORSSSW	SHOWN ONE'S HORNS
EGHHIILNORSSTY	ENGLISH HISTORY	EHHNNOOORSSSSW	SHOWS ONE'S HORNS
EGHHIIINNOTTTTW	HITTING THE TOWN	EHHNNOORRSTTTW	NORTH-NORTHWEST
EGHHIINOPSTTTT	HITTING THE POST	EHHOOOSSSTTTUUW	SOUTH-SOUTHWEST
EGHHILNOOOTTT	LONG IN THE TOOTH	EHIIIINNOQSTTU	THE INQUISITION
EGHHILNNORRSTT	NORTHERN LIGHTS	EHIIIMNOPRSSTW	WITH PERMISSION
EGHHILNNORTTTU	TURN ON THE LIGHT	EHIIJNNOOPRSTW	JOINT OWNERSHIP
EGHHILNOPRTTUW	THREW LIGHT UPON	EHIINOOSSSTTTU	SITS THIS ONE OUT
EGHHILNOPSTTTU	PUTS ON THE LIGHT	EHIIOOPPPRRRST	PROPRIETORSHIP
EGHHIMOPRSTTUU	IMPURE THOUGHTS	EHIJMMNOSSTTTU	JUST THIS MOMENT
EGHHINNNOOTTTW	NIGHT ON THE TOWN	EHIKMMNOOPSTTU	TOOK PUNISHMENT
EGHHINNNORSTUW	RUNNING THE SHOW	EHIKMOOORRRSSY	YORKSHIRE MOORS
EGHHINOPSTTTTU	PUTTING THE SHOT	EHIKNOORSSTTTU	ON THE OUTSKIRTS
EGHHINORRTTTTU	TURN TO THE RIGHT	EHILNNOOOPSSTW	WINS ON THE POOLS
EGHHLNNORSTTUU	TUNNELS THROUGH	EHILNNOOORSTTW	THROW IN ONES LOT
EGHIIIKLMNNSST	THE MISSING LINK	EHINORRTTTTWYY	TWENTY OR THIRTY
EGHIIIKNNORTTV	THINKING IT OVER	EHIOOPPRSTTUUW	WITHOUT PURPOSE
EGHIIIKNNPPTTW	TIPPING THE WINK	EHKNNOOOPSTTWW	KNOW WHEN TO STOP

EHMNOOPSSSSTUU	POSTHUMOUSNESS
EHNNOOOPPRTTWY	WORTHY OPPONENT
EIIIMNOPRSSSST	IMPRESSIONISTS
EIIJMMNNOSTUYY	ENJOYS IMMUNITY
EIILLMNOOPSSTU	SIMPLE SOLUTION
EIILNNORSSTTUU	ULSTER UNIONIST
EIILNOORSSTTUV	REVOLUTIONISTS
EIILNOQRSSTTUV	VENTRILOQUISTS
EIILOOPPSSTTVY	POSTPOSITIVELY
EIIMMMNNOOOSTTT	OMITS TO MENTION
EIIMMNNOOOPRTTY	POETRY IN MOTION
EIINNORSSSTTUU	NUTRITIOUSNESS
EIINNORSTTUVWY	UNIVERSITY TOWN
EIINOOPPPRSSTU	PRESUPPOSITION
EIINOOPPRSSSTU	PROPITIOUSNESS
EIKNNNNOOOOSSW	KNOW ONES ONIONS
EIKNOOOOPSSSST	TOOK POSSESSION
EILMNNOOSSSUUV	VOLUMINOUSNESS
EIMMNOPPRSSSUU	IMMUNOSUPPRESS
EIMNNOOORSSSUV	OMNIVOROUSNESS
EIMNOOOPRRSSTY	PROMISSORY NOTE
FIMNOPRSSSSTTU	STIR ONES STUMPS
EKNNNNOOPRSSUW	PERSONS UNKNOWN
ELLNNNOOORTUYY	NOT ON YOUR NELLY!
ELMNOSSSTTUUUU	TUMULTUOUSNESS
ELMOPPRSSTUUUY	PRESUMPTUOUSLY
ELNOOPSSSTUUUV	VOLUPTUOUSNESS
EMNNNOOOOSSSTU	MONOTONOUSNESS
FFGGHHIILRSTTU	FRIGHTFUL SIGHT
FFGHIIIINNRSST	FINISHING FIRST
FFGHIINNORSSTU	SOFT FURNISHING
FFGHIINOORRTTU	HITTING FOR FOUR
FFGINOOOOPPRST	PROOF OF POSTING
FGGHHILNOORTUW	FLOWING THROUGH
FGGHIIIINPRSTT	FIGHTING SPIRIT
FGGHIMNOORRRTW	RIGHT FROM WRONG
FGHHIIKNNNOOTT	THINK NOTHING OF
FGHHINNOOORSTT	NOTHING SHORT OF
FGHHIOORRSSTTT	GOT SHORT SHRIFT
FGHHLLOOORSTUW	FOLLOWS THROUGH
FGHIIILNORSTTW	WHISTLING FOR IT
FGHIIKLLNOOOOS	LOOKING FOOLISH
FGHIJNOOORSTUY	SHOUTING FOR JOY
FGIINNNOOORSST	STRING OF ONIONS
FGIINNNNOPRTTTU	PUTTING IN FRONT
FGIKKLNOOOORRW	LOOKING FOR WORK
FGKLNOOOORRTTUW	GLUTTON FOR WORK
FHHMNOOPRSTUYY	FOURTH SYMPHONY
FIIIILNORSSTTV	FIRST VIOLINIST
FIIIMNOOOPPRST	FIRM OPPOSITION
FIJNOOOOPSTTTUU	PUTS OUT OF JOINT
GGHHHHOORTTTUU	THOUGHT THROUGH
GGHHHINOPRSTUU	PUSHING THROUGH
GGHHHINORRSTUU	RUSHING THROUGH
GGHHIILMNNOOTT	MOONLIGHT NIGHT
GGHHIINNNORTUW	WINNING THROUGH
GGHHIINOORSSTT	SHOOTING RIGHTS
GGHHIINPRSTTTU	PUT THINGS RIGHT
GGHHIKLNOOORTU	LOOKING THROUGH
GGHHILLNOPRTUU	PULLING THROUGH
GGHHINNNNORRTUU	RUNNING THROUGH
GGHHINOPRTTTUU	PUTTING THROUGH
GGHIIIJNNOSTWY	SINGING WITH JOY
GGHIIILLNNOSWW	SHOWING WILLING
GGHIIIMNNNOSST	MISSING NOTHING
GGHIIINPRSTTTU	SITTING UPRIGHT
GGHIIKNNNNOOTW	KNOWING NOTHING
GGHIINOOOOSTTVW	GIVING TWO HOOTS
GGIILLNNPRSSTU	PULLING STRINGS
GGIIMNNNNOOORTU	GO INTO MOURNING
GGIKNOOOORTTUW	GOING OUT TO WORK

GHHIIILNOOPPSS	PHILOSOPHISING
GHHIIILNOOPPSZ	PHILOSOPHIZING
GHHIIKNNOSTTTU	THINK THINGS OUT
GHHILNOOPRTTUW	THROW LIGHT UPON
GHHINOPPSSTTUU	SHUTTING UP SHOP
GHIIILNOPPPSTW	PISTOL-WHIPPING
GHIIJJMNOPTUWY	JUMPING WITH JOY
GHIIKLLNOOOSTT	SHOOTING TO KILL
GHIINNNNOORSUW	WINNING HONOURS
GHIINORSSTTTUW	WITHOUT STRINGS
GHILLNOPPRSTUU	PULLING UP SHORT
GHINOORSSSTTTU	SORTS THINGS OUT
GIIIINNPRTTTUW	PUT IT IN WRITING
GIIILMNOPPPRSU	PROMISING PUPIL
GIIILNNOPSTTTW	SPLITTING IN TWO
GIIIMNNNNOOPST	SPINNING MOTION
GIIINNNOPRSTTU	PUTTING IN IRONS
GIIINNOOOPPRST	PROPOSITIONING
GIIKMMNNRSSTUW	SWIMMING TRUNKS
GIIKNNNOPSTTUY	TYING UP IN KNOTS
GIINNOOOPRSSTT	STRONG POSITION
GILNNOOORSSTTU	STRONG SOLUTION
GILOOOOUPRSTTZ	PROTOZOOLOGIST
HHHIILMORSTTWW	HOWLS WITH MIRTH
HINNOOOOPRSSTUW	WINS TOP HONOURS
HLLMOOOOPPRSUYY	POLYMORPHOUSLY
IIIOOPPSSSTTUU	SUPPOSITITIOUS
IIJLNNORSTTUUY	INSULT TO INJURY
IILLMNNOORSSTU	RUNS TO MILLIONS

985

AAAAACDEELLNPRX	ALEXANDRA PALACE	AAAAEFGGIINPRWY	PAYING A FAIR WAGE
AAAAACDEHHMMRRS	MAD AS A MARCH HARE	AAAAEFGGNNRSTTU	GARGANTUAN FEAST
AAAAADDEGINSTTV	AT A DISADVANTAGE	AAAAEFGLQRRRSTU	TRAFALGAR SQUARE
AAAAADDEPRRRSTU	PER ARDUA AD ASTRA	AAAAEGIMNRRRUWY	RUNAWAY MARRIAGE
AAAAAHOPRRRSSSZ	AS SHARP AS A RAZOR	AAAAEHMNORSTTWY	WAY TO A MAN'S HEART
AAAABBDEGJOPSUV	GAVE UP AS A BAD JOB	AAAAEIILMNNPRRT	PARLIAMENTARIAN
AAAABCCELLLMNNU	CALL AN AMBULANCE	AAAAGGIIMMNNNRST	ANAGRAMMATISING
AAAABCEEHLLLMTV	BALACLAVA HELMET	AAAAGGIIMMNNNRTZ	ANAGRAMMATIZING
AAAABCEGIKKNSTT	TAKING A BACK SEAT	AAAAGHIIMMNNSTTT	ITS THAT MAN AGAIN
AAAABCEILLNOOPT	PALAEOBOTANICAL	AAAAGIILMNNSSSU	ASSUMING AN ALIAS
AAAABDEEELSSTTV	LEAVES A BAD TASTE	AAAALOOPPRRSSSUZ	AS POOR AS LAZARUS
AAAABDFFIORSSST	AS STIFF AS A BOARD	AAABBDDEEFKNRST	BED AND BREAKFAST
AAAABDGIKMNRSTT	MAKING A BAD START	AAABBDEGIJOPSUV	GIVE UP AS A BAD JOB
AAAABDHNOPPSSYY	HAPPY AS A SANDBOY	AAABBDEILMNNRUY	BARNUM AND BAILEY
AAAABEEEGGILMRR	MARRIAGEABLE AGE	AAABBDEINRRRSST	BARBRA STREISAND
AAAABEEFHILNORS	FASHIONABLE AREA	AAABBEEGIMNNSRT	BARGAIN BASEMENT
AAAABEEGLLMNSST	AS GENTLE AS A LAMB	AAABBEEHILLLPRT	BRAILLE ALPHABET
AAAABEGGIILNNRS	SEALING A BARGAIN	AAABBEEHHOPRRRTW	BARBARA HEPWORTH
AAAACCCCCHHNSTT	CATCH AS CATCH CAN	AAABCCCELNNOSTU	BALANCE ACCOUNTS
	CATCH-AS-CATCH-CAN	AAABCCDEEEILLNT	DELICATE BALANCE
AAAACCDDEELNRST	CREATED A SCANDAL	AAABCCDEEGKMOST	STAGED A COMEBACK
AAAACCDEELNRST	CREATES A SCANDAL	AAABCCDEEHKKORT	CHOKED BACK A TEAR
AAAACCDEHIMNRST	ACTED AS CHAIRMAN	AAABCCEEGKMOSST	STAGES A COMEBACK
AAAACCDEILLNNNO	CALEDONIAN CANAL	AAABCCEEHILRSTU	CHARITABLE CAUSE
AAAACCDGILNNSSU	CAUSING A SCANDAL	AAABCCEEHKKORST	CHOKES BACK A TEAR
AAAACCDIIKLLLSY	LACKADAISICALLY	AAABCCEEHKMORTT	CAME BACK TO EARTH
AAAACCEKLLLLMOS	MAKES A LOCAL CALL	AAABCCEEHLMNRSU	AMBULANCE CHASER
AAAACDDLMMNORSY	RAMSAY MACDONALD	AAABCCEGIKKMMNO	MAKING A COME-BACK
AAAACDEGIINPRRR	CARRIAGE AND PAIR	AAABCCEILLLSST	CLASSICAL BALLET
AAAACDEGIKMNNNV	MAKING AN ADVANCE	AAABCCEKNORRSTT	BREAKS A CONTRACT
AAAACDEGILRRUWY	DUAL CARRIAGE-WAY	AAABCCGGIIKMNNO	COMING BACK AGAIN
	DUAL CARRIAGEWAY	AAABCDDEILNORTU	LABOUR CANDIDATE
AAAACDEKORSSSTY	AS STEADY AS A ROCK	AAABCDDEKKLRSWW	WALKED BACKWARDS
AAAACEEGLLMNNNO	ALL ONE CAN MANAGE	AAABCDEEEHILMNR	MACHINE-READABLE
AAAACEFFMORSTTT	AS A MATTER OF FACT	AAABCDEFHLNORST	BREATH OF SCANDAL
AAAACEGIILRRRWY	RAILWAY CARRIAGE	AAABCDEGILNNORT	BOTANICAL GARDEN
AAAACEGINNNRRTV	RENTING A CARAVAN	AAABCDFNNOORRTW	CONTRABAND OF WAR
AAAACFGHHILMNSU	HALF AS MUCH AGAIN	AAABCEEEFKLRRST	BREAKFAST CEREAL
AAAACFGNOORSSUY	AS FAR AS YOU CAN GO	AAABCEEFHNORSVW	SHOWN A BRAVE FACE
AAAACFHIKLQSSSU	AS QUICK AS A FLASH	AAABCEEFHORSSVW	SHOWS A BRAVE FACE
AAAACFILNORTTTT	FATAL ATTRACTION	AAABCEEFNOPRTUV	PUT ON A BRAVE FACE
AAAACGGHIMMNNRT	ARRANGING A MATCH	AAABCEEIKLNRSST	STRIKES A BALANCE
AAAACGIILNPSTTX	CAPITAL GAINS TAX	AAABCEEIMMNRSSY	AMERICAN EMBASSY
AAAACGNORRSSTTU	ACTS AS GUARANTOR	AAABCEHIILLMSST	ESTABLISH A CLAIM
AAAACIKOPRRSSST	AS SICK AS A PARROT	AAABCEHIILTTTUV	CULTIVATE A HABIT
AAAADDDEILNOORS	DEAD AS A DOORNAIL	AAABCEINPRRSTTT	ABSTRACT PAINTER
AAAADDEGGIMNRSW	AWARDING DAMAGES	AAABCEIORRRSTTVY	VARSITY BOAT-RACE
AAAADEEFINRRRTW	FAIR WEAR AND TEAR	AAABCHIILLNNOTT	LOCAL INHABITANT
AAAADEEGLMMNORR	ORANGE MARMALADE	AAABCHIILOPPRTY	APPROACHABILITY
AAAADEEGLNNORTU	GUARANTEED A LOAN	AAABCIIILNNNOST	CANNIBALISATION
AAAADEFGINNRTUV	UNFAIR ADVANTAGE	AAABCIIILNNNOTZ	CANNIBALIZATION
AAAADEFHIRSSSSY	AS FRESH AS A DAISY	AAABDDDDEEEINTT	AIDED AND ABETTED
AAAADEGGIKNNTTV	TAKING ADVANTAGE	AAABDDEEHLLOSTW	DEALS A DEATH BLOW
AAAADEGHMNNSSSSU	SAUSAGES AND MASH	AAABDDEEHLLOTTW	DEALT A DEATH BLOW
AAAADEGINNNRSTTT	STRAINED AT A GNAT	AAABDDEELLORRTV	TRAVELLED ABROAD
AAAAEEEGGHMTVWY	GAVE THE GAME AWAY	AAABDDEELMNNOPY	PAYABLE ON DEMAND
AAAAEEGGIKNNRTV	TAKING AN AVERAGE	AAABDDEENNRRSST	STANDARD-BEARERS
AAAAEEGLLLPPRSS	PARALLEL PASSAGE	AAABDEEEEHHKPRT	TAKE A DEEP BREATH
AAAAEEGLNNORSTU	GUARANTEES A LOAN	AAABDEEEGIKLNRR	LIKE A BEAR GARDEN
AAAAEEIKKNSSTTW	AS WEAK AS A KITTEN	AAABDEEEGIMNOTV	GAVE ONE A BAD TIME
AAAAEEIKMNRSSTW	MAKE A SAINT SWEAR	AAABDEEEILLORTT	ELABORATE DETAIL
AAAAEEILNNRSTTV	AS AN ALTERNATIVE	AAABDEEELMPSSTX	SETS A BAD EXAMPLE
AAAAEEINNNPSSTW	AS NEAT AS A NEW PIN	AAABDEEFIKMORRT	MADE A BREAK FOR IT

AAABDEEFINRRSST	ABERFAN DISASTER
AAABDEEGGIMNNTT	GETTING A BAD NAME
AAABDEEGJORSSSU	AS SOBER AS A JUDGE
AAABDEHLLNNOOPS	ABANDONS ALL HOPE
AAABDGGHHIINNTV	HAVING A BAD NIGHT
AAABDGGIIINNRRV	DRIVING A BARGAIN
AAABEEEEGHORTVV	ABOVE THE AVERAGE
AAABEEEGINRRTTT	BEATING A RETREAT
AAABEEEHLORRRVV	HAVE OVER A BARREL
AAABEEFGGLNOSUU	ABUSE OF LANGUAGE
AAABEEFHKRRSTTY	HEARTY BREAKFAST
AAABEEFIKKMORRT	MAKE A BREAK FOR IT
AAABEFGGILNRRRU	LANGUAGE BARRIER
AAABEEGHHINRRTV	HAVING A BREATHER
AAABEEGHIKNRRTT	TAKING A BREATHER
AAABEEHILMPRRRR	IRREPARABLE HARM
AAABEEHLLNRTUVY	BEHAVE NATURALLY
AAABEEKLMMNORHW	REMARKABLE WOMAN
AAABEFGHIKNRSTV	HAVING BREAKFAST
AAABEFILOPRSSSS	AS FAR AS POSSIBLE
AAABEFLLMOONTTU	AMATEUR FOOTBALL
AAABEGGIKNOOPSS	BOOKING A PASSAGE
AAABEGHIKLMPSSS	MAKES A BIG SPLASH
AAABEGIIKNRRSST	STRIKES A BARGAIN
AAABEGIILLNOSUV	BOUGAINVILLAEAS
AAABEGIKLNNRTUW	BREAKING A WALNUT
AAABEHIILNOPSTT	ALPHABETISATION
AAABEHIILNOPTTZ	ALPHABETIZATION
AAABEHILNPRSSTU	RUSSIAN ALPHABET
AAABEHLLLLORRTY	ROYAL ALBERT HALL
AAABEILLMNOOTTU	SUBSTANTIAL MEAL
AAABEILMMNOSSUY	IMMUNOASSAYABLE
AAABEILNRRSTTTU	ALASTAIR BURNETT
AAABEILNSTTUVVX	TABLEAUX VIVANTS
AAABIIILLNSSTUY	UNASSAILABILITY
AAABIILLNNORRTY	NATIONAL LIBRARY
AAACCCIIILLMNTT	ANTICLIMACTICAL
AAACCDDEEHILNTT	ACCIDENTAL DEATH
AAACCDDEEIKLLST	LIKE A SCALDED CAT
AAACCDEEEHMNPRS	PEACHES AND CREAM
AAACCDEEINNSSUU	CAUSED A NUISANCE
AAACCDEGIMNNOTU	CUT AND COME AGAIN
AAACCDEIILNRTWY	RAILWAY ACCIDENT
AAACCDEILNNOQTU	OLD ACQUAINTANCE
AAACCDEKOOPPRSU	PROUD AS A PEACOCK
AAACCDHIIILMMNO	HOMICIDAL MANIAC
AAACCDHILORSSTY	AS COLD AS CHARITY
AAACCDILMMNOOOT	ACCOMMODATIONAL
AAACCDKKNSSSSTT	STACKS AND STACKS
AAACCEEEINPPRTY	PEACE AT ANY PRICE
AAACCEEELLLLNSV	CANCELS ALL LEAVE
AAACCEEFGHMNOPS	CASE OF CHAMPAGNE
AAACCEEFHILMRRW	CHEMICAL WARFARE
AAACCEEGHIKNRRY	HACKNEY CARRIAGE
AAACCEEHILMMNNS	MECHANICAL MEANS
AAACCEEHIQRRTTU	QUITE A CHARACTER
AAACCEEHNRSSTUW	CATCHES UNAWARES
AAACCEEIIILLMNRV	VANILLA ICE-CREAM
AAACCEEIILLNORRT	RACIAL TOLERANCE
AAACCEEINNSSSUU	CAUSES A NUISANCE
AAACCEFFILNOPRT	CAPITAL OF FRANCE
AAACCEFGHHNOOST	A GHOST OF A CHANCE
AAACCEFIIRRRRRT	AIRCRAFT CARRIER
AAACCEFILNOSSTU	FALSE ACCUSATION
AAACCEGHILNOOPR	OCEANOGRAPHICAL
AAACCEGIINNPRTY	EARNING CAPACITY
AAACCEGIINPSTTY	SEATING CAPACITY
AAACCEGIMNRTUUV	CREATING A VACUUM
AAACCEHILMPRSTU	PHARMACEUTICALS
AAACCEIILLNNNTT	ANTE-NATAL CLINIC
AAACCELOOPPPRST	ACCEPT A PROPOSAL
AAACCENNOQRSTUU	SQUARE AN ACCOUNT
AAACCFGIILLNNVY	FILLING A VACANCY
AAACCGHILLMOOPR	PHARMACOLOGICAL
AAACCGIKLNNRTUW	CRACKING A WALNUT
AAACCHILLLNOTUY	ANACOLUTHICALLY
AAACCHILMORRSST	A CHRISTMAS CAROL
AAACCHINNORSSTT	CASH TRANSACTION
AAACCIIILMNOSTT	ACCLIMATISATION
AAACCIIILMNOTTZ	ACCLIMATIZATION
AAACCILLLOPPTYY	APOCALYPTICALLY
AAACDDDDEEEEEHNR	REACHED A DEAD END
AAACDDDEEEEEHNRS	REACHES A DEAD END
AAACDDDEINORTTT	ADDED ATTRACTION
AAACDDEEEELMNRRY	LEAD A MERRY DANCE
AAACDDEEFILLOTV	DEAF TO ALL ADVICE
AAACDDEEHHNNORTU	REACHED OUT A HAND
AAACDDEEINNRSVY	ADVANCED IN YEARS
AAACDDEEELLNNOPS	DONALD PLEASANCE
AAACDDEEMOOPSTI	CAME TO A DEAD STOP
AAACDDEGMMNNNNOS	SONG AND DANCE MAN
AAACDDGINNORSST	RAIN CATS AND DOGS
AAACDEEEEHIKLRDG	KEEPS A CLEAR HEAD
AAACDEEEEIMNPRT	REMAINED AT PEACE
AAACDEEEELMNPSW	MADE A CLEAN SWEEP
AAACDEEEGIINRRV	AIRED A GRIEVANCE
AAACDEEEHLNPRRT	CHARTERED A PLANE
AAACDEEEIKNPSTT	KEEP AT A DISTANCE
AAACDEEEMMNRSTU	AMUSEMENT ARCADE
AAACDEEENOSSTTV	VACATED ONE'S SEAT
AAACDEEGHMMMNSTT	GAME,SET AND MATCH
AAACDEEGHMNNRTX	EXCHANGE AND MART
AAACDEEGOPPTOGTU	CAUSED A STOPPAGE
AAACDEEHHNORSTU	REACHES OUT A HAND
AAACDEEIKLMNOPS	ASKED A POLICEMAN
AAACDEEIKNPSTTT	KEPT AT A DISTANCE
AAACDEELLLMOSWW	SWALLOWED A CAMEL
AAACDEENOPRRRTU	CREATED AN UPROAR
AAACDEFJKLLORST	JACK OF ALL TRADES
	JACK-OF-ALL-TRADES
AAACDEFLMNOOPTY	FLOATED A COMPANY
AAACDEGGIILMMNS	CLAIMING DAMAGES
AAACDEGHILLRSTY	CLEAR AS DAYLIGHT
AAACDEGHINPSSSU	SAUSAGE AND CHIPS
AAACDEGIIILNRRV	INVALID CARRIAGE
AAACDEGIIMNNPSTT	GAINS ADMITTANCE
AAACDEGIINNNPVY	PAYING IN ADVANCE
AAACDEGIINPPRST	DISAPPEARING ACT
AAACDEGINORRRTU	REARGUARD ACTION
AAACDEHIILMMSSY	MICHAELMAS DAISY
AAACDEHIILLRSSTT	ALL THAT IS SACRED
AAACDEHNPRSSTWY	WATCHES AND PRAYS
AAACDEIILMMRTYY	MILITARY ACADEMY
AAACDEILLMNORYY	AERODYNAMICALLY
AAACDEILLNNOSTT	NO DISTANCE AT ALL
AAACDEILNNNORTY	ROYAL AND ANCIENT
AAACDEILNOPRSSX	PARADOXICALNESS
AAACDEILNPRSSTT	LANDSCAPE ARTIST
AAACDELMNOPSTUY	PLAY CAT AND MOUSE
AAACDFFFIKMPRRRS	CARDIFF ARMS PARK
AAACDFIIILNNRWZ	FINANCIAL WIZARD
AAACDGILLMRRTUY	DRAMATURGICALLY
AAACDGILNNNNORU	GRAND UNION CANAL
AAACDHILLLMMNOR	HAROLD MACMILLAN
AAACDILILLMMNOPS	CALM AS A MILL-POND
AAACDIMNOOPRRSW	DRAW A COMPARISON
AAACEEEEGKNPRTT	TAKE A PERCENTAGE
AAACEEEEKLMNPSW	MAKE A CLEAN SWEEP
AAACEEEGGHLNRTU	LANGUAGE TEACHER
AAACEEEGGILNNST	SEEING AT A GLANCE
AAACEEEGHILLRTV	GAVE THE ALL-CLEAR
AAACEEEGILLNRSW	SWEAR ALLEGIANCE

AAACEEEHIKNSTWY	CHINESE TAKEAWAY	AAADDDEILLNNOSS	ALL'S SAID AND DONE
AAACEEEKMNNNNRST	MAKES AN ENTRANCE	AAADDDGHIILLNOTV	DAVID AND GOLIATH
AAACEEEENOSSSTTV	VACATES ONE'S SEAT	AAADDDGHINNNOST	DOING A HANDSTAND
AAACEEEFGLMNOPRR	GALA PERFORMANCE	AAADDEEEEEGMNRV	DAME EDNA EVERAGE
AAACEEEFHILNNPRT	AFRICAN ELEPHANT	AAADDEEEEGGIRTX	EXAGGERATED IDEA
AAACEEFIMNOPSST	CAME TO A FINE PASS	AAADDEEFFNNORSU	SOUNDED A FANFARE
AAACEEFINPPRRST	FIRST APPEARANCE	AAADDEEGGGLNRUU	GUARDED LANGUAGE
AAACEEGGIKNRRTT	TAKING GREAT CARE	AAADDEEGGHHLNTV	GAVE THE GLAD HAND
AAACEEGGILNNNTU	ANCIENT LANGUAGE	AAADDEEGGHLNRTU	LAUGHED AT DANGER
AAACEEGHIILLOPT	PALAEOLITHIC AGE	AAADDEEGHIMNNRS	DEMANDS A HEARING
AAACEEGIILMNRTZ	MAGAZINE ARTICLE	AAADDEEGLLNNNSW	ENGLAND AND WALES
AAACEEGIIMMNRSTT	RACE AGAINST TIME	AAADDEEHLLNNOPY	PLAYED A LONE HAND
AAACEEGIIPRRRTV	PRIVATE CARRIAGE	AAADDEELLLNORSV	SALVADOR ALLENDE
AAACEEGIKMNRRTT	CREATING A MARKET	AAADDEFGHIILNVY	HAVING A FIELD DAY
AAACEEGILNORTTV	LACTO-VEGETARIAN	AAADDEFHLNRRSTU	HARD AND FAST RULE
AAACEEGINRSSSTT	GREAT ASSISTANCE	AAADDEGHIINNSTY	IN THIS DAY AND AGE
AAACEEGOPPSSSTU	CAUSES A STOPPAGE	AAADDEGHINNORTX	HAD AN AXE TO GRIND
AAACEEHHNSTTWWY	WHEN THE CATS AWAY	AAADDEGINOORRRT	DO A ROARING TRADE
AAACEEHILLNSSTW	CLEAN AS A WHISTLE	AAADDEGINOSSTUV	DISADVANTAGEOUS
AAACEEHILLNSTTW	WITH A CLEAN SLATE	AAADDEHNNNOOSTU	A THOUSAND AND ONE
AAACEEHILLNSTTY	ANAESTHETICALLY	AAADDENNRSSSSTT	STANDS AND STARES
AAACEEHILSSTUVY	HEAVY CASUALTIES	AAADDFIKLLLNNSS	FALKLAND ISLANDS
AAACEEHNPRRSTTU	CHEAP RESTAURANT	AAADDHHIKLNNNSW	WALKS HAND IN HAND
AAACEEINNOSSSTU	CAUSE A SENSATION	AAADDIINNORSSTT	STANDARDISATION
AAACEEKLLMNOSSW	MAKES ALLOWANCES	AAADDIINNORSTTZ	STANDARDIZATION
AAACEELNORSSWWY	SAW ONE'S WAY CLEAR	AAADEEEENNNRRRR	NEARER AND NEARER
AAACEENOPRRRSTU	CREATES AN UPROAR	AAADEEEFLMNNRSU	UNDER A FALSE NAME
AAACEFGGINOPRSS	FORCING A PASSAGE	AAADEEEGHIMPRRT	REPAIR THE DAMAGE
AAACEFHHIILMRRS	AIR CHIEF MARSHAL	AAADEEEGNRRSSVV	VANESSA REDGRAVE
AAACEFHMMNOOPPRS	MEANS OF APPROACH	AAADEEEKLLTVWWY	ELEVATED WALKWAY
AAACEFIILMMMNOT	MAIN CLAIM TO FAME	AAADEEFFLLNORSS	FALLS ON DEAF EARS
AAACEFILMNOPRTT	ACT OF PARLIAMENT	AAADEEFFNRRSSTT	FASTER AND FASTER
AAACEFILNNSSSTT	FANTASTICALNESS	AAADEEFGGIILLNY	LEADING A GAY LIFE
AAACEFILNPRRSTT	CAPITAL TRANSFER	AAADEEFGINNRRTU	TURNING A DEAF EAR
AAACEFMMNNRSSTT	MASTER CRAFTSMAN	AAADEEFHILLLNRW	HAIL AND FAREWELL
AAACEGGIINNRSTT	REACTING AGAINST	AAADEEFHMRRSSTT	MADE A FRESH START
AAACEGHIIILLNNTT	TEACHING ITALIAN	AAADEEFMNNSSTWY	SWEET FANNY ADAMS
AAACEGIILLMNRRT	CRIMINAL AT LARGE	AAADEEGIIMRRRSV	MARRIAGE ADVISER
AAACEGIKLLMNNOW	MAKING ALLOWANCE	AAADEEGIPSSSSST	ASSISTED PASSAGE
AAACEGIKNNOPSST	TOSSING A PANCAKE	AAADEEGJLNNRRTU	ADJUTANT GENERAL
AAACEGILMMNRSST	GRAMMATICALNESS	AAADEEHHHHLLNTTW	HEALTH AND WEALTH
AAACEGILPRRSTUV	GAVE PARTICULARS	AAADEEHHLNRRTWY	LEARN THE HARD WAY
AAACEHIILMRTTTY	MILITARY ATTACHE	AAADEEHHNPPSTWW	SAW WHAT HAPPENED
AAACEHIIMNNPRSS	SPANISH-AMERICAN	AAADEEHIKRSSTWW	WEAK AS DISHWATER
AAACEHIMMNOPRTU	AMATEUR DRAMATICS	AAADEEHLLLORSTT	LEADS TO THE ALTAR
AAACEHIMPPRSTTY	PARASYMPATHETIC	AAADEEILMNORSTT	MADE ALTERATIONS
AAACEHLPPQRRTUU	PATCH UP A QUARREL	AAADEEIMNNORSST	MADE AN ASSERTION
AAACEIIIMMNNORST	AMERICANISATION	AAADEEIMNQRRTTU	TIME AND A QUARTER
AAACEIIIMMNNORTZ	AMERICANIZATION	AAADEEINNNRRSTVY	ANNIVERSARY DATE
AAACEIIIMMNNPRRS	AMERICAN IN PARIS	AAADEEKMNRSSSTU	AS KEEN AS MUSTARD
AAACEIILMNRRTTU	CURTAIN MATERIAL	AAADEELQRRRSTTU	STARTED A QUARREL
AAACEIILPRRSSST	SPIRAL STAIRCASE	AAADEFFGHILLNOR	HEADING FOR A FALL
AAACEIKLMMNOPST	MAKES A COMPLAINT	AAADEFHHOOPRTTT	AT THE DROP OF A HAT
AAACEIKLMMNORTX	EXCLAMATION MARK	AAADEFHIKMORSST	MAKES A DASH FOR IT
AAACEIKLNNOPSST	SANK ONE'S CAPITAL	AAADEFIILNORRTT	TRADITIONAL FARE
AAACEKKLLMNRSTU	MAKES A TRUNK CALL	AAADEFIILNOOPPR	APPLIED FOR A LOAN
AAACFGIILLNOPTT	FLOATING CAPITAL	AAADEGGHINRSSUZ	HAZARDING A GUESS
AAACFGIINNRRTTU	ANTI-AIRCRAFT GUN	AAADEGGILLNNOPP	LODGING AN APPEAL
AAACFHINORRSTUW	SOUTH AFRICAN WAR	AAADEGGLNRRSTUU	GRANULATED SUGAR
AAACFIMMOPSSTUX	COMMITS A FAUX PAS	AAADEGHIIKLLNRU	LAUGH LIKE A DRAIN
AAACGGHIIKNNPTT	TAKING A NIGHTCAP	AAADEGHIIKLNNRT	TAKING A HARD LINE
AAACGGHIJKLNSSU	LAUGHING JACKASS	AAADEGHINNORSTX	HAS AN AXE TO GRIND
AAACGIKNNRSTTUY	TAKING SANCTUARY	AAADEGKMOORSSTT	MAKES A GOOD START
AAACHIILLLNNOTU	HALLUCINATIONAL	AAADEGMNPSSTUUY	GUY DE MAUPASSANT
AAACIILNORSSTUV	VASCULARISATION	AAADEGNNORTTTUV	TURN TO ADVANTAGE
AAACIILNORSTUVZ	VASCULARIZATION	AAADEHIMPRSTTTY	THE LADY IS A TRAMP
AAACIINNOSTTTUV	SITUATION VACANT	AAADEHIMNRRSTVY	MARTHAS VINEYARD
AAACILLMOOSTTUY	LOUISA MAY ALCOTT	AAADEIILNNRSTUV	VALETUDINARIANS
AAACILLNORSTTUY	ASTRONAUTICALLY	AAADEIKLNOPRTTW	WALKED INTO A TRAP
AAACILLNRRSTUVY	INTRAVASCULARLY	AAADEILNPRTTTUU	NATURAL APTITUDE
AAACILNOSSTTTUY	CASUALTY STATION	AAADFGGHLNORTUW	LAUGH AND GROW FAT

Word	Clue
AAADFGHHIILMNNV	HAVING HALF A MIND
AAADFGHINNRTUWY	FIGHT AND RUN AWAY
AAADFGLMNNOORYY	FOR MANY A LONG DAY
AAADFILOOPRRTTY	PORTRAIT OF A LADY
AAADFLLNOOSSSUY	AND SO SAY ALL OF US
AAADGGGIINNRSTU	GUARDING AGAINST
AAADGGIIIMMNRST	DIAGRAMMATISING
AAADGGIIIMMNRTZ	DIAGRAMMATIZING
AAADGGIINNNNWWX	WAXING AND WANING
AAADGGIINNNSSTT	STANDING AGAINST
AAADGHIOOPRRSTU	AUTORADIOGRAPHS
AAADGHIOOPRRTUY	AUTORADIOGRAPHY
AAADGIILLMNTTWZ	WALTZING MATILDA
AAADGIKMNNRRSSTT	STARK STARING MAD
AAADHIILLNNOOTY	NATIONAL HOLIDAY
AAADHIINNNOOPRZ	HAZARD AN OPINION
AAADIIILNNRSTTU	LATITUDINARIANS
AAADIIJLNORTTZZ	TRADITIONAL JAZZ
AAAEEEEGHKNRTTV	TAKEN THE AVERAGE
AAAEEEEGHKRSTTV	TAKES THE AVERAGE
AAAEEEEEGLNRSTTT	REAL ESTATE AGENT
AAAEEEGCLNOSVWY	GAVE ONESELF AWAY
AAAEEEFHIKKLLNS	SHAKEN LIKE A LEAF
AAAEEEEFHIKKLLSS	SHAKES LIKE A LEAF
AAAEEEEFLNORSTWY	TEAR ONESELF AWAY
AAAEEEGGHIMTVWY	GIVE THE GAME AWAY
AAAEEEGGILMNSSV	LEAVING A MESSAGE
AAAEEEFGGLMNNNTV	NAVAL ENGAGEMENT
AAAEEEGIMNOSTTT	ONE STAGE AT A TIME
AAAEEEEHHISSSTTW	AS WHITE AS A SHEET
AAAEEEEHLLOOSSTV	HAVE A SLATE LOOSE
AAAEEEEIKMMNNSSTT	MAKES AN ESTIMATE
AAAEEEEKMMNNSSTTT	MAKES A STATEMENT
AAAEEEMNPRRRTTU	RAN A TEMPERATURE
AAAEEEFGHHILRSTT	LIGHT AS A FEATHER
AAAEEEFGILLRRRUW	GUERILLA WARFARE
AAAEEEFHKMRRSSTT	MAKE A FRESH START
AAAEEEFHMMMNNNORV	MANNA FROM HEAVEN
AAAEEEFHNOPRSTTZ	TARZAN OF THE APES
AAAEEEFLORRSTWZZ	WEARS TO A FRAZZLE
AAAEEGGHILMNTTU	HAEMAGGLUTINATE
AAAEEGGMOPRRSTY	REPAYS A MORTGAGE
AAAEEGGHHIKLLNUY	LAUGH LIKE A HYENA
AAAEEGHHOSTVWWY	GAVE THE SHOW AWAY
AAAEEEGHILMPRTTY	PLAY THE GREAT I AM
AAAEEEGHIMRSTTTT	AIMS AT THE TARGET
AAAEEEGIIKMNNRRT	TAKEN IN MARRIAGE
AAAEEEGIKMNRRST	TAKES IN MARRIAGE
AAAEEEGIKLMMNNPX	MAKING AN EXAMPLE
AAAEEEGILMMNOPST	PALAEOMAGNETISM
AAAEEEGILMNNNPPR	APPEALING MANNER
AAAEEEGIMNPRRRRT	MARRIAGE PARTNER
AAAEEEGINNPRSSTU	SEPTUAGENARIANS
AAAEEEGLMMNNNRSTT	GENTLEMAN-AT-ARMS
AAAEEGMNRRSSSTT	SERGEANTS-AT-ARMS
AAAEEEHHHIRTTVWY	WITH A HEAVY HEART
AAAEEEHHIKSTTTVW	HAVE WHAT IT TAKES
AAAEEEHHINOTVWWY	HAVE A WAY WITH ONE
AAAEEEHILNNORTTT	NATIONAL THEATRE
AAAEEEHIMPSSTTWY	PASS AWAY THE TIME
AAAEEEHMNNOSSTWY	MEAN WHAT ONE SAYS
	SAY WHAT ONE MEANS
AAAEEEIKLMNORSTT	MAKE ALTERATIONS
AAAEEEIKMNNORSST	MAKE AN ASSERTION
AAAEEIILLNNPRTTV	ALTERNATIVE PLAN
AAAEEEILMNSTTWXY	ALWAYS A NEXT TIME
AAAEEIMOQSSSTUU	AS QUIET AS A MOUSE
AAAEEKLMPQRRSUU	MAKES UP A QUARREL
AAAEELNOOPPRSST	APPEALS TO REASON
AAAEFFGGNNOOTTT	GO OFF AT A TANGENT
AAAEEFFIILNNRRST	INTERNAL AFFAIRS
AAAEEFFIKOPRSSST	AS STIFF AS A POKER
AAAEFGIILNOPPRT	FAILING TO APPEAR
AAAEFGIINNNORST	SEAFARING NATION
AAAEFILLNNOPRTT	FALLEN INTO A TRAP
AAAEEFILLNOOPPRS	APPLIES FOR A LOAN
AAAEFLLNOPRSTUV	PLEASANT FLAVOUR
AAAEGGGHIIINNNR	GAINING A HEARING
AAAEGGGHLNSTTUU	TAUGHT LANGUAGES
AAAEGGHIINNRSTT	AGAINST THE GRAIN
AAAEGGHILNNPSSU	SPANISH LANGUAGE
AAAEGGILNNRSSUU	RUSSIAN LANGUAGE
AAAEGGLLNOPPRUU	POPULAR LANGUAGE
AAAEGHHKOOPPRTT	TAKE A PHOTOGRAPH
AAAEGHIILMNRRST	RAISING THE ALARM
AAAEGIIIKLNNPST	SPEAKING ITALIAN
AAAEGIILMMMMNNST	ANIMAL MAGNETISM
AAAEGIIMNNPTTWY	AWAITING PAYMENT
AAAEGIINNOPRTTU	GAIN A REPUTATION
AAAEGIKMMNNPTTT	MAKING AN ATTEMPT
AAAEGIKMNNRSTTW	MAKING A NEW START
AAAEGILLLNNORTY	NATIONAL GALLERY
AAAEGILMNOPPRST	APPEALING TO ARMS
AAAEGMNNRRSTTTU	START AN ARGUMENT
AAAEGNNNOOPRRST	PERSONA NON GRATA
AAAEHIKRSSTTTWW	WAKES WITH A START
AAAEHLNNPRRSTTT	HEART TRANSPLANT
AAAEIIILMNORSTT	MATERIALISATION
AAAEIIILMNORTTZ	MATERIALIZATION
AAAEIIILMNQRSTU	EQUALITARIANISM
AAAEIIILNORRSTT	ANTERIALISATION
AAAEIIILNORRTTZ	ARTERIALIZATION
AAAEIILMNNOORTX	ORAL EXAMINATION
AAAEIIMNNOPRRSTT	PARAMETRISATION
AAAEIIMNOPRRTTZ	PARAMETRIZATION
AAAEILMNNPRRTUY	UNPARLIAMENTARY
AAAEILNNOOPRSTV	NAVAL OPERATIONS
AAAEIMNNOORSTTU	MOUNTAINOUS AREA
AAAEIMNRSSSSTTT	ASSISTANT MASTER
AAAEMORRSSSSTTU	TARSOMETATARSUS
AAAFGHHIIKMNOST	MAKING A HASH OF IT
AAAFIIIILMNNRST	FAMILIARISATION
AAAFIIIILMNORTZ	FAMILIARIZATION
AAAFLMOOPPPRSTV	STAMP OF APPROVAL
AAAGHIILLMNSUVW	VAUGHAN WILLIAMS
AAAGHIKNNOPSSTT	TAKING A SNAPSHOT
AAAGIILLNORTTVY	GRAVITATIONALLY
AAAGIILNNNOSSTV	NATIONAL SAVINGS
AAAGIKKLLLMMNST	MAKING SMALL TALK
AAAGIKLMNOOPPRS	MAKING A PROPOSAL
AAAGILNNOPRSTTU	SUGAR PLANTATION
AAAHIIIMMNNRSTU	HUMANITARIANISM
AAAIIILMNORSTTT	TOTALITARIANISM
AAAIIILNNNOOSTT	NATIONALISATION
AAAIIILNNNOOTTZ	NATIONALIZATION
AAAIIILNNOORSTT	RATIONALISATION
AAAIIILNNOORTTZ	RATIONALIZATION
AAAIIILMNNORTUWY	MOUNTAIN RAILWAY
AAAIINOPPRRSTTT	PAINTS A PORTRAIT
AAAILNNNOPRSTTT	TRANSPLANTATION
AABBBBDDDINRRSSY	BY DRIBS AND DRABS
AABBBDEEKLNQSUU	BUBBLE AND SQUEAK
AABBCEEEELMNRRS	BEAR RESEMBLANCE
AABBCEEGGIMNORS	BAMBER GASCOIGNE
AABBCEEGHIKKNRT	BREAKING THE BACK
AABBCEEHKLNOOST	BALANCE THE BOOKS
AABBCEGIIKLNRYY	CRYING LIKE A BABY
AABBCGHIIILLOPR	BIBLIOGRAPHICAL
AABBCIILNOPRTWY	CAPABILITY BROWN
AABBDDDDEEEHNNR	NABBED RED-HANDED
AABBDDDEELNORRT	BARRED AND BOLTED
	BOLTED AND BARRED

AABBDDDIINNRRSS	IN DRIBS AND DRABS
AABBDEEEGIRRSTT	BATTERSEA BRIDGE
AABBDEEEHHSTTWY	WET THE BABY'S HEAD
AABBDEEEHKNRSTW	BREAK THE BAD NEWS
AABBDEEHHIRTTTW	WITH BATED BREATH
AABBDEELNOORSTU	REASONABLE DOUBT
AABBDEGHIILNTWY	ABIDING BY THE LAW
AABBDEGHINOSTTT	STABBING TO DEATH
AABBDEGILNNRSUY	BRING AND BUY SALE
AABBDEIILLNORRY	BODLEIAN LIBRARY
AABBEEEFFKORRST	BEFORE BREAKFAST
AABBEEEHIKRRRRT	BREAK THE BARRIER
AABBEEEIKLLPSSY	SLEEPS LIKE A BABY
AABBEEEENORSSSTT	BEATS ONE'S BREAST
AABBEEGHIKKNNRT	BREAKING THE BANK
AABBEEGIKLNORTT	BREAKING A BOTTLE
AABBEEHMNRSTTTY	SHABBY TREATMENT
AABBEEINNORSSST	BEATS ONE'S BRAINS
AABBEFIILNORTTT	BATTLE OF BRITAIN
AABBELMNORSSTUU	STUBBORN AS A MULE
AABBGHINORSTTTU	BRIGHT AS A BUTTON
AABBIINNORSSTUU	SUBURBANISATION
AABBIINNORSTUUZ	SUBURBANIZATION
AABCCCEHILPRRTU	PUBLIC CHARACTER
AABCCCEIIKLNOTT	COCKTAIL CABINET
AABCCCELMOORSUU	COOL AS A CUCUMBER
AABCCDEEFKNNOSY	BACKED ONE'S FANCY
AABCCDEEHILLNSY	HENDECASYLLABIC
AABCCDEEIIKLLMT	CLIMBED LIKE A CAT
AABCCDEELNNORTU	COUNTERBALANCED
AABCCDEGIINNRRS	DESCRIBING AN ARC
AABCCDEILMMRTUU	CIRCUMAMBULATED
AABCCDNOOPTTTUU	PUT TO BAD ACCOUNT
AABCCEEELOPPRTV	PROVE ACCEPTABLE
AABCCEEHHNORSTT	CATCH ONES BREATH
AABCCEEHKMOORTT	COME BACK TO EARTH
AABCCEEILNPRSST	PRACTICABLENESS
AABCCEELNNORSTU	COUNTERBALANCES
AABCCEELNNOSSTU	ACCOUNTABLENESS
AABCCEELORRRSUV	CEREBROVASCULAR
AABCCEFHLLOOOST	SLAB OF CHOCOLATE
AABCCEGHHILLNTT	CATCHING THE BALL
AABCCEGIILLOORT	BACTERIOLOGICAL
AABCCEGIKLNORTT	CRACKING A BOTTLE
AABCCEGIKNNORTT	BREAKING CONTACT
AABCCEIKLLMPPRT	PATRICK CAMPBELL
AABCCEILMMRSTUU	CIRCUMAMBULATES
AABCCEKNNOORRTT	BROKEN A CONTRACT
AABCCELLLLMMMOP	MALCOLM CAMPBELL
AABCCIIILLLNTUY	INCALCULABILITY
AABCDDDEEGHIRST	DISCHARGED A DEBT
AABCDDDEENOPRSW	BOWED AND SCRAPED
AABCDDEEFHLOOSW	SHOWED A BOLD FACE
AABCDDEEGHIRSST	DISCHARGES A DEBT
AABCDDEELMNORRU	RECORDED AN ALBUM
AABCDDEFFNNOOOU	ABUNDANCE OF FOOD
AABCDDEGHLNOTUW	CAUGHT AND BOWLED
AABCDDEGIMNNOOT	COMING TO A BAD END
AABCDEEEEHHHLRT	HEALED THE BREACH
AABCDEEEEHLLRTT	CLEARED THE TABLE
AABCDEEEEIRRRRT	ERECTED A BARRIER
AABCDEEEEMMNORU	BECAME ENAMOURED
AABCDEEEGKLLNOW	ACKNOWLEDGEABLE
AABCDEEEHHLLRTW	BREACHED THE WALL
AABCDEEEHILMRRT	CARRIED THE BLAME
AABCDEEEHLLLNSY	HENDECASYLLABLE
AABCDEEFFHLNOOT	ACTED ON BEHALF OF
AABCDEEGINOPRST	SPEED-BOAT RACING
AABCDEEHHIMPTTT	CHAMPED AT THE BIT
AABCDEEHIKLLSTV	BLACK AS THE DEVIL
AABCDEEHILNNOSY	HOLDS IN ABEYANCE
AABCDEEHLNORSTT	CARDS ON THE TABLE
AABCDEEIKNNORRS	RACKED ONE'S BRAIN
AABCDEEILMNRRUV	AMBULANCE DRIVER
AABCDEELMNNOOPT	COMPLETE ABANDON
AABCDEFLNOOPSTU	PUTS ON A BOLD FACE
AABCDEHIIKLNNTW	IN BLACK AND WHITE
AABCDEHILLMNORR	LORD CHAMBERLAIN
AABCDEIILNOORST	ANABOLIC STEROID
AABCDEILMNNRRSU	CARDINAL NUMBERS
AABCDEKNNOORSWY	ONE'S OWN BACK YARD
AABCDEMNNSSSTUU	SUM AND SUBSTANCE
AABCDGILLMNNOOR	BALLROOM DANCING
AABCDHIILLMRTYY	DITHYRAMBICALLY
AABCDIKMNORRRST	BRICKS AND MORTAR
AABCEEEEKLNNOPS	KEEP ONES BALANCE
AABCEEEFHORSTUV	ABOVE THE SURFACE
AABCEEEGHILNNRT	INTERCHANGEABLE
AABCEEEGINPRSST	PERCENTAGE BASIS
AABCEEEHHLLRSTW	BREACHES THE WALL
AABCEEEHILMRRST	CARRIES THE BLAME
AABCEEEHLPRRRST	SCRAPE THE BARREL
AABCEEEKLNNOPST	KEPT ONE'S BALANCE
AABCEEEILMNNORST	BEATEN ALL-COMERS
AABCEEEELLNNOOSS	LOSE ONES BALANCE
AABCEEFFHKNRRST	FRENCH BREAKFAST
AABCEEFFHLNORTW	THREW OFF BALANCE
AABCEEFGIKNRRSU	BREAKING SURFACE
AABCEEFHIORRTTU	CREATURE OF HABIT
AABCEEFIMNOTTUY	IF YOU CANT BEAT EM
AABCEEFLMOORSTT	COMFORTABLE SEAT
AABCEEGHIILNTXY	EXCHANGEABILITY
AABCEEGHILNNRTY	INTERCHANGEABLY
AABCEEGIILLNOTY	ABIOGENETICALLY
AABCEEGIMMNNNOW	BECOMING A NEW MAN
AABCEEGLMNORTUU	CATALOGUE NUMBER
AABCEEHIKNOOPTV	HAVE A BONE TO PICK
AABCEEHILNOPRSTU	HERBACEOUS PLANT
AABCEEILNNOSTTT	TOTAL ABSTINENCE
AABCEEILNNRSSTT	INTRACTABLENESS
AABCEEINNORTTTY	BET ON A CERTAINTY
AABCEEKNOOQRSTU	BACK TO SQUARE ONE
AABCEEELLNNOOSST	LOST ONE'S BALANCE
AABCEELNRRSTTUY	CANTERBURY TALES
AABCEFFHLNOORTW	THROW OFF BALANCE
AABCEFHKLOORRTY	THE BACK OF A LORRY
AABCEGGHIILOOPR	BIOGEOGRAPHICAL
AABCEGHHINRSTUV	HAVING A BUTCHER'S
AABCEGHILLNPSY	CABLE-LAYING SHIP
AABCEGHILLNORTT	CALLING TO THE BAR
AABCEGHIOOPRSTU	BACTERIOPHAGOUS
AABCEGIKKLLNOOR	LOOK BACK IN ANGER
AABCEGINNNOOSSV	SAVING ONE'S BACON
AABCEGINNNORRSTY	CARRYING ONE'S BAT
AABCEHILMOORSTU	AUTOMOBILE CRASH
AABCEIILMNNOORT	RECOMBINATIONAL
AABCEIILNPPPRSU	APPEARS IN PUBLIC
AABCEIKKKLLORSW	WORKS LIKE A BLACK
AABCEILLLMOPRTY	PROBLEMATICALLY
AABCEILMNNOOPST	STABLE COMPANION
AABCEILNPPRRTUY	REPUBLICAN PARTY
AABCEKLLLLNNTUW	BLACKWALL TUNNEL
AABCFGIKLOORRRT	ROCK OF GIBRALTAR
AABCFIIILLNOSTY	SYLLABIFICATION
AABCFNOORSTTWYY	BY WAY OF CONTRAST
AABCGHIINNORSSW	CHASING RAINBOWS
AABCGHINNOORTTU	BROUGHT AN ACTION
AABCGHKLLNNOOTY	NOT BY A LONG CHALK
AABCGIIMMNNNOST	INCOMING BATSMAN
AABCHILNOOOSTTW	SLOW BOAT TO CHINA
AABCIIIILRSTTTY	ARTISTIC ABILITY
AABCIIILMNOPRTY	INCOMPARABILITY

AABCIILLLLRSTYY	TRISYLLABICALLY
AABCIILMMNNOSTU	CLIMBS A MOUNTAIN
AABDDDEEEFIIORRS	FIRED A BROADSIDE
AABDDDELNORSSTU	DOUBLE STANDARDS
AABDDDFHINNNOOT	BIND HAND AND FOOT
AABDDDGGILNNOOR	BOARD AND LODGING
AABDDEEEELNNRUV	UNLEAVENED BREAD
AABDDEEEFHLNORT	LEADER OF THE BAND
AABDDEEEEFILLLOU	LEAD A DOUBLE LIFE
AABDDEEEKLNOOTU	DONE A DOUBLE TAKE
AABDDEEEKLOOSTU	DOES A DOUBLE TAKE
AABDDEEFIIORRSS	FIRES A BROADSIDE
AABDDEEEGHLNNORT	BEL AND THE DRAGON
AABDDEEHINORRTT	BOARDED THE TRAIN
AABDDEEHOORRSVW	WASHED OVERBOARD
AABDDEEIKNORRST	DONE A BRISK TRADE
AABDDEEIKORRSST	DOES A BRISK TRADE
AABDDEEELLLNRTVY	TRAVELLED BY LAND
AABDDEIILLLPRSY	PLAYED BILLIARDS
AABDDELMNOPPRUY	BY POPULAR DEMAND
AABDDFGHIINNNSU	FINDING A HUSBAND
AABDDGHIILNORTY	IN BROAD DAYLIGHT
AABDEEEEFGHNORR	AGREE BEFOREHAND
AABDEEEEGGGLLTT	GATE LEGGED TABLE
AABDEEEEGGLNRTV	VEGETABLE GARDEN
AABDEEEEHINPRSV	HEAVEN BE PRAISED
AABDEEEEHPRSTTT	BREASTED THE TAPE
AABDEEEEILLLMMN	DAME NELLIE MELBA
AABDEEEFHILLOUV	HAVE A DOUBLE LIFE
AABDEEEGGILMNRT	REGIMENTAL BADGE
AABDEEEGGILNNTT	ENGAGED IN BATTLE
AABDEEEGIIMNOTV	GIVE ONE A BAD TIME
AABDEEEGILNORST	ELABORATE DESIGN
AABDEEEGKLOOPST	KEEPS A GOOD TABLE
AABDEEEHHILRTVY	BREATHED HEAVILY
AABDEEEHHKRRSTT	BREAKS THE THREAD
AABDEEEHILNNNRS	BANNER HEADLINES
AABDEEEHKOOPRTT	TOOK A DEEP BREATH
AABDEEEHLRRSTTT	RATTLED THE SABRE
AABDEEEHNORSSTV	SAVED ONE'S BREATH
AABDEEEINORRSWY	RAISED AN EYEBROW
AABDEEELNNOOTTW	WANTED TO BE ALONE
AABDEEFFHIORRST	BIRDS OF A FEATHER
AABDEEFGHOPRRST	GASPED FOR BREATH
AABDEEFHOPRRSTU	PAUSED FOR BREATH
AABDEEFIILLMRSY	FAILED MISERABLY
AABDEEFLLNOORRV	FALLEN OVERBOARD
AABDEEFLMNNNOST	SELF-ABANDONMENT
AABDEEGHHIISTTW	WHAT'S THE BIG IDEA?
AABDEEGHHILSTTW	WHAT'S THE BIG DEAL?
AABDEEGHINORRTW	WEATHERBOARDING
AABDEEGIIILRSTY	DISAGREEABILITY
AABDEEGIILLNNTTY	BATTING AN EYELID
AABDEEGILMNRRTU	BERMUDA TRIANGLE
AABDEEGINNORRST	STARBOARD ENGINE
AABDEEHHILOSTYY	HOLIDAY BY THE SEA
AABDEEKLMNNORTW	MENTAL BREAKDOWN
AABDEEPPPRRRTTUU	ABRUPT DEPARTURE
AABDEFGHHLMOORU	FLAMBOROUGH HEAD
AABDEFGIILLMORS	GAME OF BILLIARDS
AABDEFLMNOOORRS	DAME FLORA ROBSON
AABDEGGHIINNORT	BRINGING TO A HEAD
AABDEGHHIKNNTTY	TAKING BY THE HAND
AABDEGHHILLLNNT	HANDLING THE BALL
AABDEGIILLMNNRU	DIALLING A NUMBER
AABDEGIILLNNPRY	PLAYING A BLINDER
AABDEGIINNORRTW	WINTERING ABROAD
AABDEGIINNRRSST	GRINS AND BEARS IT
AABDEGIKLNOPRSY	BROADLY SPEAKING
AABDEGILNOORRSU	ORGANISED LABOUR
AABDEHHINORSTWY	WIN BY A SHORT HEAD
AABDEHHNOORSTWY	WON BY A SHORT HEAD
AABDEIIKMNORSST	DISEMBARKATIONS
AABDEIILNSSSTTU	SUBSTANTIALISED
AABDEIILNSSTTUZ	SUBSTANTIALIZED
AABDEINNSSTTTUU	UNSUBSTANTIATED
AABDELNNPRSTUUY	SUPERABUNDANTLY
AABDENNNOOOPSST	ABANDON ONES POST
AABDFFHHILNSTUU	FAITHFUL HUSBAND
AABDFINRSSSTTTY	BY FITS AND STARTS
AABDGGIINNNSSUU	USING AND ABUSING
AABDGHIILNPSTTU	PUTS IN A BAD LIGHT
AABDIILLLNORTUY	ALL-ROUND ABILITY
AABEEEEELMNSTTW	ATE BETWEEN MEALS
	EAT BETWEEN MEALS
AABEEEEGKLMRTTV	VEGETABLE MARKET
AABEEEEGLMNRRTV	VERBAL AGREEMENT
AABEEEEGLMRTTTV	VEGETABLE MATTER
AABEEEFIILMNRTT	MATERIAL BENEFIT
AABEEEGGHOPRRST	THE BEGGARS OPERA
AABEEEGGILNNSTT	ENGAGES IN BATTLE
AABEEEGGLLNNORR	GENERAL BELGRANO
AABEEEGHIKLNRST	BREAKING THE SEAL
AABEEEGHINPRRTY	PAYING THE BEARER
AABEEEGLLMNRSSY	GENERAL ASSEMBLY
AABEEEHHILRSTVY	BREATHES HEAVILY
AABEEEHHIMMNRSTT	IN THE SAME BREATH
AABEEEHHKLORRTT	HEARTBREAK HOTEL
AABEEEHHKORRSTU	HEARTBREAK HOUSE
AABEEEHIKMNSSTT	IN THE SAME BASKET
AABEEEHIMNNNORTT	THREE MEN IN A BOAT
AABEEEHKNORRSST	BREAKS ONE'S HEART
AABEEEHLNORSSTT	BREATHE ONES LAST
AABEEEHLRRSSTTT	RATTLES THE SABRE
AABEEEHHNOPSTTTT	BEATEN AT THE POST
AABEEEHHNORSSSTV	SAVES ONE'S BREATH
AABEEEEHNORSSTTW	WASTE ONES BREATH
AABEEEIKLKLORRVW	WORK LIKE A BEAVER
AABEEEILNPRRRSS	IRREPARABLENESS
AABEEEINORRSSWY	RAISES AN EYEBROW
AABEEEELLNPRSSSU	PLEASURABLENESS
AABEEEELMNNRRSST	REASONABLE TERMS
AABEEEELNORHSSTT	RATTLE ONE'S SABRE
AABEEEEMNRTTTTUY	BEAUTY TREATMENT
AABEEFGILRSTTUUV	GUSTAVE FLAUBERT
AABEEFHILNNOSSS	FASHIONABLENESS
AABEEFHOPRRSSTU	PAUSES FOR BREATH
AABEEFILLMMNNSS	INFLAMMABLENESS
AABEEFLLOPRRUVY	FAVOURABLE REPLY
AABEEFLMORRSTUV	FAVOURABLE TERMS
AABEEGGIIKMNNNS	MAKES A BEGINNING
AABEEGGLLMNOPRU	LANGUAGE PROBLEM
AABEEGHHILMNRST	SHARING THE BLAME
AABEEGHIKLMRRST	REMARKABLE SIGHT
AABEEGHIKLNRRTY	HEARTBREAKINGLY
AABEEGHILNNRRTY	LEARNING BY HEART
AABEEGHILPPPSTY	PLAY THE BAGPIPES
AABEEGHINNORRST	BARING ONE'S HEART
AABEEGIILLNNORS	RELEASING ON BAIL
AABEEGIILNNSSTT	INTANGIBLE ASSET
AABEEGIKMNNORRS	BREAKING ONE'S ARM
AABEEGILLNRSTVY	TRAVELLING BY SEA
AABEEGIMNNRSSSU	BUSINESS MANAGER
AABEEHILLORTTYZ	ELIZABETH TAYLOR
AABEEHINNORRTTW	WATER ON THE BRAIN
AABEEHJKMNORSST	JAMS ON THE BRAKES
AABEEHKNRSSTTTU	BURNS AT THE STAKE
AABEEHKNRSTTTTU	BURNT AT THE STAKE
AABEEHMRSSSTTTU	BURST AT THE SEAMS
AABEEIILLOPRRSS	IRREPARABLE LOSS
AABEEILNPRRSTTU	SUITABLE PARTNER
AABEELMNNORTTTU	EARL MOUNTBATTEN

AABEFFIINRSSSSU	BUSINESS AFFAIRS	AACCCHILLORSSSS	CLASSICS SCHOLAR
AABEFGHILLNTWYY	FALLING BY THE WAY	AACCCHINNOOOORT	CORONATION COACH
AABEFGIIKMNRSST	MAKING FIRST BASE	AACCCILLMMOORSY	MACROCOSMICALLY
AABEFGILNORTTTY	FLOATING BATTERY	AACCCILLMOOPRSY	MACROSCOPICALLY
AABEFHILMOORRTW	BARTHOLOMEW FAIR	AACCDDEEEHIRRTV	REACHED A VERDICT
AABEFHNOORRSTVW	SHOW A BRAVE FRONT	AACCDDEEEILLNNR	CINDERELLA DANCE
AABEFIILNOOSTTT	LIFE-BOAT STATION	AACCDDEEHIIKLLT	ACTED LIKE A CHILD
AABEFIKLMOORSTT	MAKES A BOLT FOR IT	AACCDDEEHKRSSTT	STACKED THE CARDS
AABEFILNOOPPRST	SELF-APPROBATION	AACCDDEEIKLMNNO	DIAMOND NECKLACE
AABEFLNORRSTUZZ	BURNS TO A FRAZZLE	AACCDDEEILNOTTU	DETAILED ACCOUNT
AABEFLNORRTTUZZ	BURNT TO A FRAZZLE	AACCDDEGINNSSTU	STANDING ACCUSED
AABEFLOPPRSSTUU	BURST OF APPLAUSE	AACCDDEIINNORTT	CONTRAINDICATED
AABEGHIILLNRTTZ	BLAZING THE TRAIL	AACCDEEEEFFNRTT	CREATED AN EFFECT
AABEGHIIINNPRSTW	BRIGHT AS A NEW PIN	AACCDEEEEGILRVY	RECEIVED A LEGACY
AABEGHIIOOPRSTU	AUTOBIOGRAPHIES	AACCDEEEFFNOPRT	ACCEPTED AN OFFER
AABEGHIMNNOOTTY	BAYING AT THE MOON	AACCDEEEFGINPTT	ACCEPTING DEFEAT
AABEGHIOOPRRSTU	AUTOBIOGRAPHERS	AACCDEEEGILNRST	CENTIGRADE SCALE
AABEGIIILMNRRTY	MILITARY BEARING	AACCDEEEGIMNNPT	ACCEPTED MEANING
AABEGIIKNOPPSUY	BUYS A PIG IN A POKE	AACCDEEEHIRRSTV	REACHES A VERDICT
AABEGIIILLNRRTVY	TRAVELLING BY AIR	AACCDEEEIINPTUV	CAPTIVE AUDIENCE
AABEGIKLNNNOPRT	POINT-BLANK RANGE	AACCDEEEMNPPTTY	ACCEPTED PAYMENT
AABEGIKNNOPRTTU	PUTTING A BRAKE ON	AACCDEEGHHOTTTT	THATCHED COTTAGE
AABEGIILNORTTUV	TRAVELLING ABOUT	AACCDEEHHLOOPRT	CEPHALOCHORDATE
AABEGILLNRRRSUU	URBAN GUERRILLAS	AACCDEEHHNORSST	SCRATCH ONES HEAD
AABEHILLOSSTTWW	SWALLOWS THE BAIT	AACCDEEHLNOOSTU	CHOCOLATE SUNDAE
AABEHIILMNOORRUV	NORMAL BEHAVIOUR	AACCDEEIIJLPRRU	RACIAL PREJUDICE
AABEIILMNORTUVY	MANOEUVRABILITY	AACCDEEIIKLNOTT	ACTED LIKE A TONIC
AABEIILNSSSSTTU	SUBSTANTIALISES	AACCDEEIIMNOOST	CAME TO A DECISION
AABEIILNSSSTTUZ	SUBSTANTIALIZES	AACCDEEINNRSSST	ARTS AND SCIENCES
AABEIIMNNNORSTU	NURSE AN AMBITION	AACCDEEKNORTTTU	COUNTERATTACKED
AABEIKNOORRSTTT	BREAKS INTO A TROT	AACCDEEMMMMNOOSU	MADE COMMON CAUSE
AABEILLLMMRSTTY	MARYS LITTLE LAMB	AACCDEENNNOOPTU	OPENED AN ACCOUNT
AABEILLNNRSTUWY	UNANSWERABILLTY	AACCDEENNNORRTU	RENDER AN ACCOUNT
AABEILLNOORRSTU	LABOUR RELATIONS	AACCDEFHILMORRW	MICHAEL CRAWFORD
AABEILNSSSSSUUU	BUSINESS AS USUAL	AACCDEFIKLNOOTU	LACK OF EDUCATION
AABELLNOSSTTTTU	LAST BUT NOT LEAST	AACCDEGHHNNOPSS	CHOPS AND CHANGES
AABFGIILLNOPPRY	APPLYING FOR BAIL	AACCDEGIILLLOOT	DIALECTOLOGICAL
AABFGIJLNOOPPRY	APPLYING FOR A JOB	AACCDEGIILNSTTY	DELAYING TACTICS
AABFIILLMMNNOTY	NONFLAMMABILITY	AACCDEGIIMNRTUV	CIRCUMNAVIGATED
AABGGHIINNRSSTU	BRUSHING AGAINST	AACCDEHIILLMORY	RADIOCHEMICALLY
AABGGIIILLNTTUY	AGGLUTINABILITY	AACCDEHIKLMNNRY	CHICKEN MARYLAND
AABGHHLMOOPPRTU	PHOTOGRAPH ALBUM	AACCDEHILOPRSSY	POLYSACCHARIDES
AABGHIJNNNOORRT	JONAH BARRINGTON	AACCDEIIKLLOOPS	KALEIDOSCOPICAL
AABGHILORSTTUUW	BROUGHT A LAWSUIT	AACCDEIILMMOORR	COMMERCIAL RADIO
AABGIIILNNNORUV	LABOURING IN VAIN	AACCDEIIMORSTTY	DRAMATIC SOCIETY
AABGIILLMNOOORT	MORAL OBLIGATION	AACCDEIINNORSTT	CONTRAINDICATES
AABGIILLNNOSSWY	BOWLING ANALYSIS	AACCDEIKKMNRSSS	KICKS AND SCREAMS
AABGIILLMMOPRRTY	PROGRAMMABILITY	AACCDEILLMNOSSS	SECOND CLASS MAIL
AABGIINOOORRTTT	GO TO ARBITRATION	AACCDEILLNOOTUY	COEDUCATIONALLY
AABHHIILLLOSTTYY	BY ALL THAT IS HOLY	AACCDEIMNPPRRSS	SCRIMP AND SCRAPE
AABILNNOOPPRTUU	URBAN POPULATION	AACCDEIMOPRRTTY	DEMOCRATIC PARTY
AACCCCDEEIILMRS	ACADEMIC CIRCLES	AACCDELOORSSTUV	CASTS A CLOUD OVER
AACCCCEIILNRRTT	ANTARCTIC CIRCLE	AACCDENOOORSSTUU	SQUARED ACCOUNTS
AACCCDEEEKKNNNR	NECK-AND-NECK RACE	AACCDGIIKNRRRTT	DIRT-TRACK RACING
AACCCDEGIINPTV	ACCEPTING ADVICE	AACCDGIILLMNNTU	CALCULATING MIND
AACCCDEEIILMPRT	MEDICAL PRACTICE	AACCDGILMMNOOTY	ACCOMMODATINGLY
AACCCDEFIIILNOT	DECALCIFICATION	AACCDGILNNOOPRT	ACCORDING TO PLAN
AACCCDEHNORSSTU	CONDUCTS A SEARCH	AACCDHIIMOOSSST	SADOMASOCHISTIC
AACCCDELLNOOTTU	CALLED TO ACCOUNT	AACCDHIMNORRRSS	RICHARD CROSSMAN
AACCCDGILNORSTY	ACTS ACCORDINGLY	AACCDHLMOOOORRSY	LORD MAYORS COACH
AACCCEEEEFFMOOST	COMES FACE TO FACE	AACCDILNNOORSUW	DRAW A CONCLUSION
AACCCEEHHINSTTT	CATCHES IN THE ACT	AACCEEEEFFNNRSTT	CREATES AN EFFECT
AACCCEEHHKRRSTT	CHARACTER SKETCH	AACCEEEEFLNRRSU	CASUAL REFERENCE
AACCCEEHILLOORT	CHOCOLATE ECLAIR	AACCEEEEGILRSVY	RECEIVES A LEGACY
AACCCEEHILSSSST	TEACHES CLASSICS	AACCEEEFNNNORRT	FORCE AN ENTRANCE
AACCCEEOORRSSTU	ASCOT RACECOURSE	AACCEEEGGHLNNSX	EXCHANGE GLANCES
AACCCEFGHINOSTT	CHANGE OF TACTICS	AACCEEEGIIILMNRR	MARRIAGE LICENCE
AACCCEHIIRRSSTT	CHARACTERISTICS	AACCEEEGIKPRTTT	CIGARETTE PACKET
AACCCEHMOPRSSTU	CAME UP TO SCRATCH	AACCEEEGILLLNNV	CANCELLING LEAVE
AACCCEIILNOOPSS	SPECIAL OCCASION	AACCEEEGILNPRRT	GENERAL PRACTICE
AACCCEIMNNOOTTT	CAME INTO CONTACT	AACCEEEGNNNOTUV	GAVE COUNTENANCE

AACCEEEHHIPPRTT	CHEAP AT THE PRICE
AACCEEEHILNOTTV	LEAVE IT TO CHANCE
AACCEEEHKNNNOST	TAKEN ONE'S CHANCE
AACCEEEHKNNNOSST	TAKE ONE'S CHANCES
	TAKES ONE'S CHANCE
AACCEEEILNNPSTT	CAPITAL SENTENCE
AACCEEEIRRSSSTT	SECRET STAIRCASE
AACCEEEKLNNOPSS	SLACKEN ONES PACE
AACCEEFGHILMNOT	CHANGE OF CLIMATE
AACCEEFGHINNRSU	REFUSING A CHANCE
AACCEEFIIKMRSSS	MAKES SACRIFICES
AACCEEFILLLRTTU	ELECTRICAL FAULT
AACCEEFIMNOORRW	ECONOMIC WARFARE
AACCEEGGHILNNRS	SEARCHING GLANCE
AACCEEGHILMPSST	CATCHES A GLIMPSE
AACCEEGHILNNOTV	LEAVING TO CHANCE
AACCEEGILPRRRTU	REGULAR PRACTICE
AACCEEHHINRSTTT	CATCHES THE TRAIN
AACCEEFHHJMNPTTU	JUMP AT THE CHANCE
AACCEEHHNNORSTTW	CATCHES ON THE RAW
AACCEEHHOPPRSTW	CATCHES A WHOPPER
AACCEEHIIN3TTUV	IN THE ACCUCATIVE
AACCEEHIIOPPRST	ARCHIEPISCOPATE
AACCEEHILORSSTT	THE COAST IS CLEAR
AACCEEIIIMMNNRTZ	AMERICAN CITIZEN
AACCEEIIILLOPRRT	POLITICAL CAREER
AACCEEIILLRRTWY	ELECTRIC RAILWAY
AACCEEIIPPRRTTV	PRIVATE PRACTICE
AACCEEIKLLNOOTT	TAKE A COLLECTION
AACCEEIKMRRRSTY	MERRY AS A CRICKET
AACCEEIILLMORTT	COLLECT MATERIAL
AACCEEILLMMORUV	COMMERCIAL VALUE
AACCEEILMMOPPRR	COMMERCIAL PAPER
AACCEEILMOPRRRU	ICE-CREAM PARLOUR
AACCEEINNNORSSS	RECONNAISSANCES
AACCEEJOOSSTUUU	JACQUES COUSTEAU
AACCEEKMMMNOOSU	MAKE COMMON CAUSE
AACCEFLNNOSTTTU	SETTLE AN ACCOUNT
AACCEELNORSTTUV	NEVER CAST A CLOUT
AACCEEFGHNNOSTUY	CAUGHT ONE'S FANCY
AACCEFGILLNSSUY	ACCUSING FALSELY
AACCEEFHILLMMORU	CHEMICAL FORMULA
AACCEEFHILLNSTVY	FILLS THE VACANCY
AACCEEGGHIIINNTV	GIVING IT A CHANCE
AACCEEGHIILLOPRX	LEXICOGRAPHICAL
AACCEEGHIIMNOPRT	CINEMATOGRAPHIC
AACCEEGHIKLNOSTT	AGAINST THE CLOCK
AACCEEGHIKNNNOST	TAKING NO CHANCES
AACCEEGHIMNNNORS	CHANCING ONE'S ARM
AACCEEGIIMNRSTUV	CIRCUMNAVIGATES
AACCEEGIINNRRTTY	RACING CERTAINTY
AACCEEGIMMNOPSST	MAGNETIC COMPASS
AACCEEHIILLMNSTY	MECHANISTICALLY
AACCEEHIKMNOORST	MARK THE OCCASION
AACCEEHILLLLMNOY	MELANCHOLICALLY
AACCEEHILLRRTTUY	ARCHITECTURALLY
AACCEEHIORRSSSSU	AS RICH AS CROESUS
AACCEEIIIILLMNRST	ANTICLERICALISM
AACCEEIIILLNRSTT	ANTICLERICALIST
AACCEEIIILLMOPRTT	TROPICAL CLIMATE
AACCEEIILLRRSSTW	CLASSICAL WRITER
AACCEEIIMNRSTTTU	CIRCUMSTANTIATE
AACCEEIKNNOOTTTU	TAKE INTO ACCOUNT
AACCEEIKOOPSTTTW	WAISTCOAT POCKET
AACCEEILLMNNORTY	NECROMANTICALLY
AACCEEIILLMNOTYYZ	COENZYMATICALLY
AACCEEILLPRRSTTU	PRACTICAL RESULT
AACCEEILNNOOORST	CONSOLATION RACE
AACCEEILNOPRSSUY	ASSURANCE POLICY
AACCEEILRRRRTUUX	EXTRACURRICULAR
AACCELNNOOPRSTU	PERSONAL ACCOUNT
AACCENOQRSSSTUU	SQUARES ACCOUNTS
AACCENORRSSTUUY	CARRY OUT A CENSUS
AACCFFFGHKLOOOT	GO OFF AT HALF COCK
AACCFGIKNNOOTTU	TAKING ACCOUNT OF
AACCFHILMRSSSTT	FIRST-CLASS MATCH
AACCFIIIILNNRSS	FINANCIAL CRISIS
AACCFIIILNOSSST	CLASSIFICATIONS
AACCGGHIINNNPPT	CATCHING NAPPING
AACCGGIINNNNOTUV	GIVING AN ACCOUNT
AACCGHHIMOOPRRT	CHROMATOGRAPHIC
AACCGHIMMNOORRT	CHRONOGRAMMATIC
AACCGIILMMNOOTX	COMING TO A CLIMAX
AACCGIIMNNORTUV	CIRCUMNAVIGATOR
AACCHHIIOOPPRTT	HIPPOCRATIC OATH
AACCHHILLOOOPRS	PAROCHIAL SCHOOL
AACCHHIORSTTTUW	WITHOUT A SCRATCH
AACCHIIIILLMMPTY	AMPHIMICTICALLY
AACCHIILLMOSSTY	MASOCHISTICALLY
AACCHIIILLPRSTYY	PSYCHIATRICALLY
AACCHIJLMNNOPTU	CLAPHAM JUNCTION
AACCHIKLOPRTUVY	CHALK UP A VICTORY
AACCIIILLLNSTVY	CALVINISTICALLY
AACCIIIILLOSSTY	SOCIALISTICALLY
AACCIIILMRSTTTY	MILITARY TACTICS
AACCIIILNORRSTU	CIRCULARISATION
AACCIIILNORRTUZ	CIRCULARIZATION
AACCIIILPRRSTTU	PARTICULARISTIC
AACCIIILLMNORTUV	CIRCUMVALLATION
AACCIILMMNNOOTU	COMMUNICATIONAL
AACCIILLLMOPSTYY	CYTOPLASMICALLY
AACCILLLOPRTTUY	PLUTOCRATICALLY
AACCLMOPRRRSTTUU	MACROSTRUCTURAL
AACCNNNNOPRSTUUU	RUNS UP AN ACCOUNT
AACDDDEEEIMNNRS	INCREASED DEMAND
AACDDDEEEMNOOST	COMES TO A DEAD END
AACDDDECFIIILNTT	CAT AND THE FIDDLE
AACDDDEEGHHNRTU	CAUGHT RED-HANDED
AACDDDEEHIKNQTU	QUICK AND THE DEAD
AACDDDEEIKKLLUW	WADDLE LIKE A DUCK
AACDDDEENNSTTUV	ADVANCED STUDENT
AACDDEEEEHLNRSS	CLEARHEADEDNESS
AACDDEEEEHLPSTU	PLEADED THE CAUSE
AACDDEEEEMRSUXY	READY-MADE EXCUSE
AACDDEEEEFFIIKLL	FACE LIKE A FIDDLE
AACDDEEEFFHHLOSU	AHEAD OF SCHEDULE
AACDDEEEHHIINRS	CHERISHED AN IDEA
AACDDEEEHILMRSW	MICHAEL EDWARDES
AACDDEEEILNORTY	DELAYED REACTION
AACDDEEEILRTTTT	DICTATED A LETTER
AACDDEEEIMPRTTT	PREMEDITATED ACT
AACDDEEEMNNNORS	DEMANDS AN ENCORE
AACDDEEFGHNORSS	CHANGE OF ADDRESS
AACDDEEGHLNOOST	TEACHES AN OLD DOG
AACDDEEGINORRTV	GRANTED A DIVORCE
AACDDEEGLNOPPRR	DROPPED A CLANGER
AACDDEEHHILNRTW	HANDLED WITH CARE
AACDDEEHHLLLLRST	HELD ALL THE CARDS
AACDDEEIIMNOPRT	MADE A PREDICTION
AACDDEEIMMNNNOTX	INCOME-TAX DEMAND
AACDDEEINNORRSV	ORDERS IN ADVANCE
AACDDEEKNNPPTUW	PACKED UP AND WENT
AACDDEELNOPRSSY	PLAYED ONE'S CARDS
AACDDEEMNNORSTU	DEMANDS A RECOUNT
AACDDEEMOOOPSTT	COME TO A DEAD STOP
AACDDEGGHIOTTTY	ACT THE GIDDY GOAT
AACDDEGGIIINNST	DECIDING AGAINST
AACDDEGGIINRSST	GISCARD DESTAING
AACDDEEHHIINRRRS	RICHARD SHERIDAN
AACDDEHHLLLORST	HOLD ALL THE CARDS
AACDDEHIMMNNORT	DIAMOND MERCHANT
AACDDEHLNOORTTW	HOT AND COLD WATER

AACDDEIILNNOORV	LEONARDO DA VINCI
AACDDELLNNORSST	DOLLARS AND CENTS
AACDDELNNORSTWY	NEW SCOTLAND YARD
AACDDEMNRRSSSTU	MUSTARD AND CRESS
AACDDGINNNOPPUW	PACING UP AND DOWN
AACDDGINORSTUWY	AWARDING CUSTODY
AACDDHIILNNSSSW	SANDWICH ISLANDS
AACDDHIKMNORRTY	TOM,DICK AND HARRY
AACDEEEEFLLORTT	ELECTORAL DEFEAT
AACDEEEEHINRSVY	HEARSAY EVIDENCE
AACDEEEEHLLNSTT	CLEANED THE SLATE
AACDEEEEHNORRSS	REACHED ONE'S EARS
AACDEEEELMNNORS	CLEARED ONE'S NAME
AACDEEEEFHHILNRT	REACHED THE FINAL
AACDEEEEFHINRSTT	STARED IN THE FACE
AACDEEEFILNNNOT	NATIONAL DEFENCE
AACDEEEFIMMMNOT	MADE MINCEMEAT OF
AACDEEEFINNNRRW	DRAW AN INFERENCE
AACDEEEFINNOPST	PAINTED ONE'S FACE
AACDEEEGGLLLMNO	MAGDALEN COLLEGE
AACDEEEEGHHHINRW	REACHED A NEW HIGH
AACDEEEEGHHHRRTT	CHARGED THE EARTH
AACDEEEEGHHORRSV	OVERHEAD CHARGES
AACDEEEEGHHRRSST	CRASHED THE GEARS
AACDEEEEGHILMRRV	MICHAEL REDGRAVE
AACDEEEEGHLLLRSU	CHARLES DE GAULLE
AACDEEEGHLNOORS	REACHED ONE'S GOAL
AACDEEEGHMNNNOS	CHANGED ONE'S NAME
AACDEEEGIINNNUV	GIVEN AN AUDIENCE
AACDEEEGIINNSUV	GIVES AN AUDIENCE
AACDEEEGINORRTV	AGREE ON A VERDICT
AACDEEEEHHIINRSS	CHERISHES AN IDEA
AACDEEEEHHKNPRSY	HACKNEYED PHRASE
AACDEEEEHIIMLNSST	ACHIEVED ONE'S AIM
AACDEEEEHIRRTTTW	TREATED WITH CARE
AACDEEEEHNPRRSTV	CHAPTER AND VERSE
AACDEEEILRSTTTT	DICTATES A LETTER
AACDEEEIMNNOPTX	MADE AN EXCEPTION
AACDEEEMOOPRSTT	CREAMED POTATOES
AACDEEFGLLLNOPU	PULLED A LONG FACE
AACDEEFHHILNSTT	HALF THE DISTANCE
AACDEEFHILLMNRS	MICHAEL FLANDERS
AACDEEFHIMNORTT	AIR OF DETACHMENT
AACDEEFIMNNOOSS	MADE A CONFESSION
AACDEEFNRRRTTUW	UNDERWATER CRAFT
AACDEEGGHIINNSX	EXCHANGING IDEAS
AACDEEGGNNOOPRS	EGG-AND-SPOON RACE
AACDEEGHHNOSTTU	CAUGHT ONE'S DEATH
AACDEEGHIKNNSYY	HACKNEYED SAYING
AACDEEGHILMNRST	MADE THINGS CLEAR
AACDEEGHILNORRT	CLEARING THE ROAD
AACDEEGHINNPSTT	STANDING THE PACE
AACDEEGHIPPRRSS	DISCHARGE PAPERS
AACDEEGHLLMOOSU	ALEC DOUGLAS-HOME
AACDEEGHNNOSSWY	CHANGED ONE'S WAYS
AACDEEGHNNPRRST	CHANGED PARTNERS
AACDEEGIKNNPPST	SPENDING A PACKET
AACDEEGILNNOPRS	PLEADS IGNORANCE
AACDEEGILNNORSV	LEAVING ONE'S CARD
AACDEEGIMNPRSUY	GAINED SUPREMACY
AACDEEGIMRRSTTU	DRAMATIC GESTURE
AACDEEGOPPRRRTU	CORRUGATED PAPER
AACDEEHHINSSSTT	CASTS IN THE SHADE
AACDEEHHLLLOSST	HOLDS ALL THE ACES
AACDEEHIKLMMNRS	HAMMER AND SICKLE
AACDEEHILMRRSTW	CLAIMS THE REWARD
AACDEEHIMRRTTUY	REACHED MATURITY
AACDEEHINNOOPRT	A DROP IN THE OCEAN
AACDEEHIORRSTTT	READS THE RIOT ACT
AACDEEHMNOORTTW	CAME DOWN TO EARTH
AACDEEHNNOPSSTU	OPEN-AND-SHUT CASE
AACDEEHNOOSTUWY	SEE WHAT YOU CAN DO
AACDEEHOORTTTTX	EXTRACTED A TOOTH
AACDEEIIIMMMNOTT	IMMEDIATE ACTION
AACDEEIIKMNOPRT	MAKE A PREDICTION
AACDEEIILMMSTTY	ACTS IMMEDIATELY
AACDEEIILOPRSTV	OVERCAPITALISED
AACDEEIILOPRTVZ	OVERCAPITALIZED
AACDEEIINPPRTTU	PAINTED A PICTURE
AACDEEIKLMNOSST	STAKED ONE'S CLAIM
AACDEEIKMORSSVY	MAKES A DISCOVERY
AACDEEILLMOPPTY	CAPITAL EMPLOYED
AACDEEILMNRSSTU	STRAINED A MUSCLE
AACDEEILNNSSSST	LENDS ASSISTANCE
AACDEEILSTTTTUV	CULTIVATED TASTE
AACDEEIMRRSSSTU	DRASTIC MEASURES
AACDEEINOPPRRTU	APPEARED IN COURT
AACDEEINOPRSSTT	STARED INTO SPACE
AACDEEKKLNOOOST	TAKE A SECOND LOOK
AACDEEMPQRRRSTU	CRAMPED QUARTERS
AACDEENOOPSSTTV	VACATED ONE'S POST
AACDEENRRSSSSUW	CURSES AND SWEARS
AACDEFFGINRSSTU	FACTS AND FIGURES
AACDEFFIIMORSST	DOMESTIC AFFAIRS
AACDEFGHINORRRW	REACHING FORWARD
AACDEFGIIKNORSV	ASKING FOR ADVICE
AACDEFIIKNRRRSS	SIR FRANCIS DRAKE
AACDEFIKOSTTTTW	TWO-FISTED ATTACK
AACDEFIMNNOORTU	FOUNDATION CREAM
AACDEFJNNOORSUY	SECOND OF JANUARY
AACDEFKNOORRSSS	ASK FOR ONES CARDS
AACDEFNPRRSSTYY	FANCY-DRESS PARTY
AACDEGGHIINNRTW	DANCING WITH RAGE
AACDEGGHINNNOTT	DANCING THE TANGO
AACDEGHIILLNNST	HAILING DISTANCE
AACDEGHIILLOPRY	IDEOGRAPHICALLY
AACDEGHIINNNORT	DANCING ON THE AIR
AACDEGHIKLNNOPT	DANCING THE POLKA
AACDEGHILLMOPRY	DEMOGRAPHICALLY
AACDEGHIMORSTWY	SAY THE MAGIC WORD
AACDEGHINRSSTTT	STRINGS ATTACHED
AACDEGIIKKLNNV	ALIVE AND KICKING
AACDEGIIIKMNNOS	MAKING A DECISION
AACDEGIIKLNNSTW	WALKING DISTANCE
AACDEGIIMNNNOTT	DECONTAMINATING
AACDEGIIMNRSTTT	DRAMATIC SETTING
AACDEGIINPRRTUW	DRAWING A PICTURE
AACDEGIKNOTTTWW	TWO-WINGED ATTACK
AACDEGILLMNOOPT	LODGE A COMPLAINT
AACDEGILNNORSYY	EARLY CLOSING DAY
AACDEGILNOORSTW	DRAWING TO A CLOSE
AACDEGIMNNOORSU	COMES ROUND AGAIN
AACDEHINNRRTTUW	DRAWN THE CURTAIN
AACDEHINRRSTTUW	DRAW THE CURTAINS
	DRAWS THE CURTAIN
AACDEHKNNOORRST	HARD ON ONE'S TRACK
AACDEHKNORRSSST	STOCKS AND SHARES
AACDEHOORRSSSTT	AT THE CROSS-ROADS
AACDEIIJLLRTUXY	EXTRAJUDICIALLY
AACDEIIKLMNOPRS	LICK AND A PROMISE
AACDEIILMMNOPPT	PAID A COMPLIMENT
AACDEIILMNNOOPS	LADIES COMPANION
AACDEIILNORSSTT	DICTATORIALNESS
AACDEIILNOSSTTU	EDUCATIONALISTS
AACDEIIMNNNOOTT	DECONTAMINATION
AACDEIIMNOORSTT	DEMOCRATISATION
AACDEIIMNOORTTZ	DEMOCRATIZATION
AACDEIIMNORSSTY	AERODYNAMICISTS
AACDEILLMORRTTU	COURT-MARTIALLED
AACDEILMNNOOTTU	DOCUMENTATIONAL
AACDEIMMNOOPRSS	MADE COMPARISONS
AACDEIMNNOOPRSW	DREW A COMPARISON

AACDEIMNOORSSTX	XMAS DECORATIONS
AACDEIMNPRSSSSV	SCRIMPS AND SAVES
AACDEKMORRSTUWW	AWKWARD CUSTOMER
AACDFFIILMOPSTT	DIPLOMATIC STAFF
AACDFGHIINOOSTT	ACTS IN GOOD FAITH
AACDFGINORRRRWY	CARRYING FORWARD
AACDFHIMORSSSTY	DAYS OF CHRISTMAS
AACDFHNOOSSSTTU	CAST OF THOUSANDS
AACDFIIINOSSSTT	DISSATISFACTION
AACDFIIORSSSTTY	DISSATISFACTORY
AACDGIIILNRSTTU	DISARTICULATING
AACDGIILNPQRTUU	QUADRUPLICATING
AACDGIINNOPRSSW	PASSING IN A CROWD
AACDGIKNNOORRTU	GO TO RACK AND RUIN
AACDGIMMMMNNOSSU	ASSUMING COMMAND
AACDHHILLOPRTYY	HYDROPATHICALLY
AACDHHILNOPRRRS	RALPH RICHARDSON
AACDHIILLNOOPRY	RADIOPHONICALLY
AACDHIILLOPRSTY	DIASTROPHICALLY
	TAKE ONES COAT OFF
AACDHIILMNRSSST	CHRISTMAS ISLAND
AACDHIJMMNNOQSUY	JOHN QUINCY ADAMS
AACDIIIILNNPRSS	DISCIPLINARIANS
AACDIIILNORSTTU	DISARTICULATION
AACDIIILNOORSTU	RADICAL SOLUTION
AACDIILNOPQRTUU	QUADRUPLICATION
AACDIINOOORSSTW	WORD ASSOCIATION
AACDILNNOOPRTTU	NATIONAL PRODUCT
AACDIMNNOPPSUWY	WINDS UP A COMPANY
AACDLLNOOPRSTUX	CASTOR AND POLLUX
AACDMNNOOPPUUWY	WOUND UP A COMPANY
AACDMNOORRRSSTY	ROSS AND CROMARTY
AACEEEEEHKLNPST	KEEP A CLEAN SHEET
AACEEEEEFHKLNRTV	TAKE FRENCH LEAVE
AACEEEEGGLNPRRT	LARGE PERCENTAGE
AACEEEEGHLNRSTT	GEANETTE CHARLES
AACEEEEGKNNRSVW	WREAKS VENGEANCE
AACEEEEHKLNPSTT	KEPT A CLEAN SHEET
AACEEEEHNORRSSS	REACHES ONE'S EARS
AACEEEELNORSSWY	SEE ONES WAY CLEAR
AACEEEEMNNPRRST	PERMANENT CREASE
AACEEEFHINRLNRST	REACHES THE FINAL
AACEEEFHINRSSTT	STARES IN THE FACE
AACEEEFHORRSTTW	WEATHER FORECAST
AACEEEFHORSTTVW	THE CREST OF A WAVE
AACEEEFIKMMMNOT	MAKE MINCEMEAT OF
AACEEEGHHHINRSW	REACHES A NEW HIGH
AACEEEGHHHRRSTT	CHARGES THE EARTH
AACEEEGHHRRSSST	CRASHES THE GEARS
AACEEEGHILLLRTV	GIVE THE ALL-CLEAR
AACEEEGHILLNSSU	ISSUE A CHALLENGE
AACEEEGHILNOOSV	ACHIEVE ONES GOAL
AACEEEGHLNOORSS	REACHES ONE'S GOAL
AACEEEGHMNNNOSS	CHANGES ONE'S NAME
AACEEEGIKMNNOPS	MAKING ONE'S PEACE
AACEEEGIKMORSTT	SMOKE A CIGARETTE
AACEEEGILLMNTTY	METAGENETICALLY
AACEEEGILLNNRST	SCALENE TRIANGLE
AACEEEGILLNORSW	SWORE ALLEGIANCE
AACEEEGINNNOPRT	CREATE AN OPENING
AACEEEGINNRRSUV	NURSE A GRIEVANCE
AACEEEGINNRRTTT	TERENCE RATTIGAN
AACEEEGKNOOPRTT	TOOK A PERCENTAGE
AACEEEGLLMNPRST	SMALL PERCENTAGE
AACEEEGNNORSTTV	AVERAGE CONTENTS
AACEEEHHILNSTTW	WITH A CLEAN SHEET
AACEEEHHNORRSST	SEARCH ONES HEART
AACEEEHIIMNOSSV	ACHIEVES ONE'S AIM
AACEEEHIKLLPTTT	TICKLE THE PALATE
AACEEEHKNRSTTTW	RENEWS THE ATTACK
AACEEEHLLLOPRTV	ALL OVER THE PLACE
AACEEEHLOORSSVW	HAVE A SCREW LOOSE

AACEEEHOPRRSTXY	ARCHAEOPTERYXES
AACEEEIKKLNPRSS	KEEPS A SLACK REIN
AACEEEIKMNNOPTX	MAKE AN EXCEPTION
AACEEEILNRSSSST	SALES RESISTANCE
AACEEEILNRSSSTT	LEAST RESISTANCE
AACEEEIMNPRRSSX	AMERICAN EXPRESS
AACEEEINRRSSSTT	CREASE RESISTANT
AACEEELLMORRSTV	REMOVE ALL TRACES
AACEEELLNNOPRSS	LEARNS ONE'S PLACE
AACEEELLNNOPRST	LEARNT ONE'S PLACE
AACEEELNNPRRSTY	PLAYERS ENTRANCE
AACEEELPRRRSSTU	CARELESS RAPTURE
AACEEEMNPRRRSTT	MASTER CARPENTER
AACEEENNQRRTTUY	QUATERCENTENARY
AACEEFFGLLMNORR	FALLEN FROM GRACE
AACEEFFHMORTTTT	FACT OF THE MATTER
AACEEFFIILMORRT	OFFICER MATERIAL
AACEEFFKNOOOSTT	TAKE OFF ONES COAT
	TAKE ONES COAT OFF
AACEEFFMNOSTTTT	STATEMENT OF FACT
AACEEFGHIIMRSTT	CHIEF MAGISTRATE
AACEEFGHILNNOSU	LAUGH IN ONE'S FACE
AACEEFGHNORTWWY	FACE THE WRONG WAY
AACEEFGIINNRRSS	INCREASING FARES
AACEEFGLMNORTTU	GENERAL FACTOTUM
AACEEFHIIILRTTT	ARTIFICIAL TEETH
AACEEFHIILMNNNR	INFERNAL MACHINE
AACEEFHKMOORTTU	CAME OUT OF THE ARK
AACEEFIINOORSST	FREE ASSOCIATION
AACEEFIKMNNOOSS	MAKE A CONFESSION
AACEEFILLLNNOPT	FALLEN INTO PLACE
AACEEFILLMNSTTU	MENTAL FACULTIES
AACEEFIMNOOPSST	COME TO A FINE PASS
AACEEFJPRSTTTUY	JUST A PRETTY FACE
AACEEFLLOOPSSTT	STATE OF COLLAPSE
AACEEFLMOPPRRSY	APPEALS FOR MERCY
AACEEGGHHNORSTV	GAVE SHORT CHANGE
AACEEGGHLMORTTT	CHATTEL MORTGAGE
AACEEGGIILLMNNT	CALLING A MEETING
AACEEGGILLMNOTY	GEOMAGNETICALLY
AACEEGGINNNORSSU	ARGUING ONE'S CASE
AACEEGGINNNORTTT	RENTING A COTTAGE
AACEEGHHILNPRTT	CLEARING THE PATH
AACEEGHHINRRSST	HEART-SEARCHINGS
AACEEGHHLLOSTTW	CHEAT THE GALLOWS
AACEEGHHLNOPPRS	ENCEPHALOGRAPHS
AACEEGHHLNOPPRY	ENCEPHALOGRAPHY
AACEEGHIINPRTTV	PRIVATE TEACHING
AACEEGHIKLMNRST	MAKE THINGS CLEAR
AACEEGHILLLPRTY	TELEGRAPHICALLY
AACEEGHILMMNRRT	REGIMENTAL MARCH
AACEEGHILNNPRSUU	INAUGURAL SPEECH
AACEEGHIMNOPRRT	CINEMATOGRAPHER
AACEEGHMNPPPRSU	CHAMPAGNE SUPPER
AACEEGHNNNOSSSWY	CHANGES ONE'S WAYS
AACEEGHNNPRRSST	CHANGES PARTNERS
AACEEGIIKMMMNNT	MAKING MINCEMEAT
AACEEGIILMNNOST	MISCEGENATIONAL
AACEEGIINNSSSTV	GIVEN ASSISTANCE
AACEEGIINSSSSTV	GIVES ASSISTANCE
AACEEGIKLLNPRSY	SPEAKING CLEARLY
AACEEGIKLNNOPST	TAKING ONE'S PLACE
AACEEGILLLNORSS	ALLEGORICALNESS
AACEEGILLNNORSW	SWORN ALLEGIANCE
AACEEGILLORRSTT	ROLLS A CIGARETTE
AACEEGIMNNNNORSV	CARVING ONE'S NAME
AACEEGIMNNNOSVY	CONVEYS A MEANING
AACEEGIMNOPRRTT	GREAT IMPORTANCE
AACEEGINNNOORTT	GONE INTO A TRANCE
AACEEGINNOORSTT	GOES INTO A TRANCE
AACEEGINNOSSSTT	STATING ONE'S CASE

AACEEEGINNRSSSUV	GIVEN ASSURANCES	AACEGHIIINNNRSV	SEARCHING IN VAIN
AACEEGINRSSSSUV	GIVES ASSURANCES	AACEGHIIKNNOQUV	HAVING A QUICK ONE
AACEEEHHIINRSTWY	WITHIN EASY REACH	AACEGHIILNNOSST	CHASING ONE'S TAIL
AACEEEHHLORRSTTT	CLEARS THE THROAT	AACEGHIINNRSSTU	TEACHING RUSSIAN
AACEEHIIKLLSTTY	KIAESTHETICALLY	AACEGHIJKRSSTTT	STRAIGHTJACKETS
AACEEHIILNRSSTT	CASTLES IN THE AIR	AACEGHILNNOOTTV	THE LONG VACATION
AACEEEHIINRRSTTU	RAISE THE CURTAIN	AACEGHILNPRRSTY	REACTING SHARPLY
AACEEHIJNORRSTT	JOINS THE RAT-RACE	AACEGHILOOPSTTT	COTTAGE HOSPITAL
AACEEEHIKKLNNSTT	TAKEN IN THE SLACK	AACEGHIRRSSSTTT	STRAIGHT ACTRESS
AACEEHIKKLNSSTT	TAKES IN THE SLACK	AACEGHLNNSSTUUW	WELTANCSHAUUNGS
AACEEEHILLNPRTTY	PARENTHETICALLY	AACEGIIILMNORSU	RELIGIOUS MANIAC
AACEEHILLPRTTUY	THERAPEUTICALLY	AACEGIIKLMNORRW	WORKING A MIRACLE
AACEEHILMMSTUVY	HEAVY-METAL MUSIC	AACEGIIKLNPQRRU	PICKING A QUARREL
AACEEEHILNNRRTUV	IN THE VERNACULAR	AACEGIIILMRRTVY	GRAVIMETRICALLY
AACEEHIMMPRSTTU	PURE MATHEMATICS	AACEGIILPRRSTUV	GIVE PARTICULARS
AACEEEHIMPPTTTTT	PATHETIC ATTEMPT	AACEGIIMNNORSSTV	MOVING STAIRCASE
AACEEHIMRRSTTUY	REACHES MATURITY	AACEGIKKLNOSSTT	STOCKTAKING SALE
AACEEHKKLNPSTTU	TAKEN UP THE SLACK	AACEGIKMNNOQSTU	MAKING A CONQUEST
AACEEHKKLPSSTTU	TAKES UP THE SLACK	AACEGILLLLMRTUY	METALLURGICALLY
AACEEHKLNPPRSTU	PHEASANT PLUCKER	AACEGILLNOPPRRTY	CALLING TO PRAYER
AACEEEHLNOORRSTT	CLEAR ONES THROAT	AACEGILMMMMNNORT	MARGINAL COMMENT
AACEEEHMMNNORRTTT	TATTENHAM CORNER	AACEGIMNPRRSTUU	CREATING A RUMPUS
AACEEIIILLLNNOTT	I CANNOT TELL A LIE	AACEHHINOORSSTT	CHAINS TO THE OARS
AACEEIILLPPRTTY	PERIPATETICALLY	AACEHIILMNSSTUV	MALE CHAUVINISTS
AACEEIILNNORSTV	NATIONAL SERVICE	AACEHIIMNORRSTY	AMERICAN HISTORY
AACEEIILOPRSSTV	OVERCAPITALISES	AACEHIINNOSTTTU	AUTHENTICATIONS
AACEEIILOPRSTVZ	OVERCAPITALIZES	AACEHIKKLMORRSW	WORKS LIKE A CHARM
AACEEIIMNNNRRSU	MARINE INSURANCE	AACEHILLMMOPRTY	METAMORPHICALLY
AACEEIINNOPTTVX	VAIN EXPECTATION	AACEHILLMNNOPST	PLAIN-CLOTHES MAN
AACEEIKLMNOSSST	STAKES ONE'S CLAIM	AACEHILLMOPRSTY	ATMOSPHERICALLY
AACEEIKNOPRSTTU	TAKE PRECAUTIONS	AACEHILLMPSTTYY	SYMPATHETICALLY
AACEEIILLMMSTTUY	IMMACULATE STYLE	AACEHILLNOPRTUY	NEUROPATHICALLY
AACEEIMNNOOTTTT	CAME TO ATTENTION	AACEHIMNORSSSST	CHRISTMAS SEASON
AACEEIMNOPRSSTV	COMPARATIVENESS	AACEHLLORRSSSTT	ORCHESTRA STALLS
AACEEINNNORTTTW	WENT INTO A TRANCE	AACEHLMORSSTUUW	WALRUS MOUSTACHE
AACEEINOPRSSSTT	STARES INTO SPACE	AACEHOOPPRRSTTU	PARACHUTE TROOPS
AACEEIOPRRSSTTU	PRECARIOUS STATE	AACEIIILMNOPPSS	EPISCOPALIANISM
AACEELLLLRRTUXY	EXTRACELLULARLY	AACEIIIMNNOPSTT	EMANCIPATIONIST
AACEELNNNOPRSTT	PARENTAL CONSENT	AACEIIKLNNOPSST	SINK ONES CAPITAL
AACEELOQRRSSTTU	AT CLOSE QUARTERS	AACEIILLLPRSTTY	PERISTALTICALLY
AACEENOOPSSSTTV	VACATES ONE'S POST	AACEIILLNOOPPTW	POLITICAL WEAPON
AACEFFFIMORRSTT	STREAM OF TRAFFIC	AACEIILMNNOSTTT	CLAIMS ATTENTION
AACEFFGINOOPRSY	PAYING OFF A SCORE	AACEIILMNOPRRTT	MALPRACTITIONER
AACEFFHIILORSTT	ARTICLES OF FAITH	AACEIILNOPPPRRV	PROVINCIAL PAPER
AACEFFHLMOPRRTY	CARRY OFF THE PALM	AACEIINNNQRTTUY	CERTAIN QUANTITY
AACEFFILMNOTTUU	MUTUAL AFFECTION	AACEIKLNNOPSSTU	SUNK ONE'S CAPITAL
AACEFGGINOORSST	ACT OF AGGRESSION	AACEIKLNOOPTTUY	TAKEN OUT A POLICY
AACEFGHIILPSTUY	PHYSICAL FATIGUE	AACEIKLOOPSTTUY	TAKES OUT A POLICY
AACEFGHMMNNORTUY	COUNTY FERMANAGH	AACEIKMMNOOPRSS	MAKE COMPARISONS
AACEFGIIKLLNOOT	ACTING LIKE A FOOL	AACEIILLMNNOTUWY	YOU CAN'T WIN 'EM ALL
AACEFGIILMNNNSU	FLAMING NUISANCE	AACEIILLNNOOTTTT	CALL ATTENTION TO
AACEFGIIMNPRRTU	FRAMING A PICTURE	AACEIILLNPPRSTYY	PRESYNAPTICALLY
AACEFGIKNNNOSTY	TAKING ONE'S FANCY	AACEIILMMNOPPSTY	PAYS A COMPLIMENT
AACEFGILNRSTTUU	CAUSING A FLUTTER	AACEIILMNNOOSTTU	NATIONAL COSTUME
AACEFHHIMRRSSTT	FATHER CHRISTMAS	AACEILMNOOPSSTY	COMPASSIONATELY
AACEFHIORSSTTUW	SOUTHWEST AFRICA	AACEIMMNOOPPSTY	PAY COMPENSATION
AACEFIIILNORSTT	ARTIFICIAL STONE	AACEINNNOSTTTXY	CONSTANT ANXIETY
AACEFIILLMSSTUV	MUSICAL FESTIVAL	AACEINOPRSSSSST	CASTS ASPERSIONS
AACEFIILLOPPRRS	PAIR OF CALLIPERS	AACEKMOORRSSTUU	MARKS OUT A COURSE
AACEFIILORRSUXY	AUXILIARY FORCES	AACELLNNOOPRRTT	PARENTAL CONTROL
AACEFIMOOPPRSSS	PAIR OF COMPASSES	AACFFIIINORSSSS	FRANCIS OF ASSISI
AACEFLLMOOPSTTU	CAME TO A FULL STOP	AACFGGHHIINNNOS	CHANGING FASHION
AACEFLLOOPRRRST	CALLS FOR A REPORT	AACFGHIIILLRTT	ARTIFICIAL LIGHT
AACEFLNOOORRTTY	TREATY OF LOCARNO	AACFGIILNNOORTU	CONFIGURATIONAL
AACEFNORRTTTUWY	TWENTY-FOUR CARAT	AACFGILLLLNOOSW	FOLLOWS A CALLING
AACEGGHIILNORST	SOCIAL GATHERING	AACFIILMNOOOPPRT	APPLICATION FORM
AACEGGHIIPRRRTU	UPRIGHT CARRIAGE	AACFILLMMNOOPRT	FORMAL COMPLAINT
AACEGGHILOOOPRZ	ZOOGEOGRAPHICAL	AACFILNNNOOORTT	CONFRONTATIONAL
AACEGGILLMNORTU	LOGICAL ARGUMENT	AACGGHIIILLNNTT	CALLING IT A NIGHT
AACEGHHIIINNPSST	TEACHING SPANISH	AACGGHIKNNOPSTU	HANG UP A STOCKING
AACEGHHLLNORSTU	CHARLES LAUGHTON	AACGGIIILLNNPRSV	SCRAPING A LIVING

AACGGIIINNORTVY	GAINING A VICTORY
AACGGIIKKNNNOST	KNOCKING AGAINST
AACGGIIKNNPRSTT	STARTING PACKING
AACGHHIILOPPRSY	PHYSIOGRAPHICAL
AACGHHILLLOOPRY	HOLOGRAPHICALLY
AACGHIILLLMORTY	LOGARITHMICALLY
AACGHIKNORSTTTU	TAKING A SHORT CUT
AACGHILLMNOOPRY	PHONOGRAMICALLY
AACGHILLNOOOPRT	ANTHROPOLOGICAL
AACGHILLOOPPRTY	TOPOGRAPHICALLY
AACGHILLOPPRTYY	TYPOGRAPHICALLY
AACGHILNNOPSSYY	PSYCHOANALYSING
AACGHLLOPRRSTYY	CRYSTALLOGRAPHY
AACGIIILMNNPTTU	PUTTING IN A CLAIM
AACGIIILNPRRSTU	PARTICULARISING
AACGIIILNPRRTUZ	PARTICULARIZING
AACGIILLRRSTTUU	AGRICULTURALIST
AACGIINNOPRRSTT	PROCRASTINATING
AACGIJLLNNOOTUY	CONJUGATIONALLY
AACGILLLLNOOPYY	PALYNOLOGICALLY
AACGILLMNOORSTY	GASTRONOMICALLY
AACGILNNOORSTTU	CONGRATULATIONS
AACGIMNOOORSTTW	ROOM TO SWING A CAT
AACHHIILNOPRSSW	WIN A SCHOLARSHIP
AACHHILNOOPRSSW	WON A SCHOLARSHIP
AACHIIIKMMORRST	COMMITS HARA-KIRI
AACHIILNPRSSVW	SPANISH CIVIL WAR
AACHIILLMNORSTY	HARMONISTICALLY
AACHIILLMRSSTTU	MUSIC-HALL ARTIST
AACHIILNOORSSTU	ANTISOCIAL HOURS
AACHIIMNRRRSTTY	CHRISTIAN MARTYR
AACHIINNOSTTUVW	WHITSUN VACATION
AACHIKLNNOPSTUW	WALKS INTO A PUNCH
AACHILLOOPRTTUY	AUTOTROPHICALLY
AACHILLOPPRSTYY	SAPROPHYTICALLY
AACHILNNOOPRSSS	NICHOLAS PARSONS
AACHINNOPRRSSTT	IN SHARP CONTRAST
AACIIIILNNOTVZ	CIVILIANIZATION
AACIIILSSSTTTTV	VITAL STATISTICS
AACIIIMMNNOORSTT	ROMANTICISATION
AACIIIMNNOORTTZ	ROMANTICIZATION
AACIIINOORSTTTV	VICTORIA STATION
AACIIJLNNORTUWY	RAILWAY JUNCTION
AACIILLLLPRSTUY	PLURALISTICALLY
AACIILLLMOPSTUY	POLITICAL ASYLUM
AACIILLNOOPRSTY	ANISOTROPICALLY
AACIILLNORSSTTY	CRYSTALLISATION
AACIILLNORSTTYZ	CRYSTALLIZATION
AACIILMOOPSTTTU	AUTOMATIC PISTOL
AACIILNNNOOPRTU	PRONUNCIATIONAL
AACIILNNNRSTTTU	NATURAL INSTINCT
AACIILRNNOPRRSTT	TRANSCRIPTIONAL
AACIIMMNNNOOPRS	COMPANION IN ARMS
AACIINNOOPRRSTT	PROCRASTINATION
AACIKMNNOPRTTUU	PUNCTUATION MARK
AACILLLLMOPSTYY	PLASMOLYTICALLY
AACILLMMOPSTTYY	SYMPTOMATICALLY
AACILLMNRRSTUUY	INTRAMUSCULARLY
AACILLMOOPSTTYY	SOMATOTYPICALLY
AACILLNNOOORSTU	NATIONAL COLOURS
AADDDDDEEEMMNNO	MADE DO AND MENDED
AADDDDEEEIINNRV	EARNED A DIVIDEND
AADDDEEEEEHLNRT	THREADED A NEEDLE
AADDDEEEEHLNNRT	NEEDLE AND THREAD
AADDDEEEGILMPRS	MIDDLE-AGE SPREAD
AADDDEEEHILRRRT	RAIDED THE LARDER
AADDDEEEMMNNPTY	DEMANDED PAYMENT
AADDDEEEMMNNORST	MODERATE DEMANDS
AADDDEEGHOPRTTU	ADOPTED DAUGHTER
AADDDEEGILMMNOW	MIDDLE-AGED WOMAN
AADDDEEIKMNPSSU	KISSED AND MADE UP
AADDDEEIILNNRSTV	STAND AND DELIVER
AADDDEEEKMMNNOSS	MAKES DO AND MENDS
AADDDEFGINORSWW	ADDING A FEW WORDS
AADDDEGIIINNPVY	PAYING A DIVIDEND
AADDDEHHIIRTTWY	DID IT THE HARD WAY
AADDDEIINNORSTT	STANDARD EDITION
AADDDEIINNRRTVW	DIVIDEND WARRANT
AADDDEKLNNOPUWW	WALKED UP AND DOWN
AADDDELMNNPPSUY	DEMAND AND SUPPLY
	SUPPLY AND DEMAND
AADDEEEEGHILNRT	REGAINED THE LEAD
AADDEEEEHPRRRTW	REAPED THE REWARD
AADDEEEEILNNPSS	SEE NAPLES AND DIE
AADDEEEEFLLRRSSW	FAREWELL ADDRESS
AADDEEEEGILNORTT	TRADE DELEGATION
AADDEEEGIMNOSTT	ADMITTED ONE'S AGE
AADDEEEHHNNSSVY	HEAVY-HANDEDNESS
AADDEEEHHNOPPTT	TAPPED ON THE HEAD
AADDEEEHHNNRRSST	HARDHEARTEDNESS
AADDEEEHIKLNPSY	PLAY HIDE-AND-SEEK
AADDEEEHNNNORST	SEEN AND NOT HEARD
AADDEEELNORSSSV	I FAVES NO ADDRESS
AADDEEEMMNOOSSY	MADE SOMEONE'S DAY
AADDEEEMNNORRSTU	TRODDEN A MEASURE
AADDEEFGHINNRRW	FREEHAND DRAWING
AADDEEFGHLOORSS	FLOGS A DEAD HORSE
AADDEEFGIIMNTTT	ADMITTING DEFEAT
AADDEEFILLNPRYY	PLAYED A FRIENDLY
AADDEEGGHHILNTV	GIVE THE GLAD HAND
AADDEEGGINRRRSU	GRENADIER GUARDS
AADDEEGHHILNRVY	LEAVE HIGH AND DRY
AADDEEGHHKLNNOS	GOLDEN HANDSHAKE
AADDEEGHLOPRTTY	PLAYED HARD TO GET
AADDEEGINNNRSTV	EVENING STANDARD
AADDEEGKMNNRRUU	UNGUARDED REMARK
AADDEEHHNNOSSSW	WASHED ONE'S HANDS
AADDEEHHNNOORSTT	DEATH ON THE ROADS
AADDEEHIINOTTWY	TOYED WITH AN IDEA
AADDEEHIMNPRRUU	DAPHNE DU MAURIER
AADDEEHKNNNNOSS	ON HANDS AND KNEES
AADDEEHLMNORSTU	SOUNDED THE ALARM
AADDEEHNNNOOSST	STAND ON ONES HEAD
AADDEEHNRRRSUWY	HUNDRED YEARS WAR
AADDEEHOOPPRTTT	TAPPED AT THE DOOR
AADDEEIKLNORRTW	LIKE A DROWNED RAT
AADDEEIMNNNOTTT	DEMAND ATTENTION
AADDEELLNRTTUUY	UNADULTERATEDLY
AADDEENNORRTTTT	TATTERED AND TORN
AADDEFIKMNNOOSV	KNAVE OF DIAMONDS
AADDEFILLMNOSSW	FLAWLESS DIAMOND
AADDEGHIJNNORRT	DJANGO REINHARDT
AADDEGHILNNRSST	STANDARD ENGLISH
AADDEGHIMNNNOOS	ONE MAN AND HIS DOG
AADDEGHIMNOOOTV	HAVE A GOOD MIND TO
AADDEGHMNNOOPRRT	GRANDPARENTHOOD
AADDEGIIIMNNOSS	GAINED ADMISSION
AADDEGIILLNNRWY	READY AND WILLING
AADDEGIKMMNNNOS	MAKING DEMANDS ON
	MAKING NO DEMANDS
AADDEGIKMNNNRTU	MAKING REDUNDANT
AADDEHHLNOOOTTV	TO HAVE AND TO HOLD
AADDEHILLNNSSST	SHETLAND ISLANDS
AADDEHILNNNOOSS	LAID ONE'S HANDS ON
AADDEHILORSSTTW	SAID THE LAST WORD
AADDEHINNOSSSTT	STANDS ON ITS HEAD
AADDEHKNNNOPSSU	SHAKEN UP AND DOWN
AADDEHKNNOPSSUW	SHAKES UP AND DOWN
AADDEHMNOOORSST	DO AS THE ROMANS DO
AADDEINNORRSSTV	STANDARD VERSION
AADDFGHHHINNOTT	FIGHT HAND TO HAND
	HAND-TO-HAND FIGHT

Word	Clue
AADDFGHINNSSSTT	STANDS AND FIGHTS
AADDGGHHIINNNNO	GOING HAND IN HAND
AADDGGHIIMNNOOV	HAVING A GOOD MIND
AADDGGINOOORSWY	SAYING A GOOD WORD
AADDGHHIILLMORR	LORD HIGH ADMIRAL
AADDGHINNNORSTU	DOING A HAND'S TURN
AADDGIILLNNRSSTV	LIVING STANDARDS
AADDHLLNOORSSTU	THOUSAND DOLLARS
AADEEEEEHKLLPSV	KEEPS A LEVEL HEAD
AADEEEEEGGIORRST	AGREE TO DISAGREE
AADEEEEEGGLLLNRU	GENERAL DE GAULLE
AADEEEEEGGNRSSTX	EXAGGERATEDNESS
AADEEEEEGIMNSTVX	EXTENSIVE DAMAGE
AADEEEEEHHKRRTWW	HEREWARD THE WAKE
AADEEEEEHIMMNRST	REMAINED THE SAME
AADEEEEEHLLMNTTT	THE LATE-LAMENTED
AADEEEEEIILRRRRT	AIREDALE TERRIER
AADEEEEELMNOPRTV	DEVELOPMENT AREA
AADEEEEFFHLMNNST	FANNED THE FLAMES
AADEEEEFFHNOOSST	EATS ONE'S HEAD OFF
AADEEEEFGHINRRSU	REFUSED A HEARING
AADEEEEFHHLNRSST	HALFHEARTEDNESS
AADEEEEFHIINSTTT	THE FAINTEST IDEA
AADEEEEFHILMNSST	FEEDS THE ANIMALS
AADEEEEFHIMNOOST	AHEAD OF ONE'S TIME
AADEEEEFHINRSSTW	AS FREE AS THE WIND
AADEEEEFHKNOTWYY	ANY DAY OF THE WEEK
AADEEEEFHLLOPPPR	APPEALED FOR HELP
AADEEEEFIILLMSTT	LASTED A LIFETIME
AADEEEEFILLOPPRV	APPLIED FOR LEAVE
AADEEEEGGIMNNSSS	SENDING A MESSAGE
AADEEEEGHLLNNRST	HANSEL AND GRETEL
AADEEEEGHNNRRSTT	THREATENS DANGER
AADEEEEGHNRRSTTW	WATERS THE GARDEN
AADEEEEGIIKLPSTW	SWEATED LIKE A PIG
AADEEEEGIIMNNRST	REMAINING SEATED
AADEEEEGINNPRRST	PRESIDENT REAGAN
AADEEEEGLLMNPRTT	LEGAL DEPARTMENT
AADEEEEGLLMPSTTU	GET ALL STEAMED UP
AADEEEEGLMNOPRSS	GREASED ONE'S PALM
AADEEEEGLMOOPSTX	SET A GOOD EXAMPLE
AADEEEEGLNPRRSSU	PLEASURE GARDENS
AADEEEEGNNOSSTWY	GETS ONE'S END AWAY
AADEEEEGNQRRSTTU	GRANTED A REQUEST
AADEEEEHHHNNORRST	HARDEN ONES HEART
AADEEEEHHNNOSSTT	HASTEN ONES DEATH
AADEEEEHIKLNRSTV	LEAVES IN THE DARK
AADEEEEHKLMPRTTY	PLAYED THE MARKET
AADEEEEHLLORSVWY	LEE HARVEY OSWALD
AADEEEEHLLPPRSTW	PAPERED THE WALLS
AADEEEEHLNNORSSV	REVEALS ONE'S HAND
AADEEEEHMNNRSSTV	THAMES AND SEVERN
AADEEEEHMNNRRSSTW	WARMHEARTEDNESS
AADEEEEHNNOPPSWY	HAPPENED ONE'S WAY
AADEEEEIKNRSTTTW	KNITTED A SWEATER
AADEEEEIILLLPPPRS	PARALLELEPIPEDS
AADEEEEIILLMPRSSY	MY LIPS ARE SEALED
AADEEEEIILMNNRRTU	REMAINED NEUTRAL
AADEEEEILMNPRSTT	DEPARTMENTALISE
AADEEEEILMNPRTTZ	DEPARTMENTALIZE
AADEEEEILMPRTTXY	PLAYED EXTRA TIME
AADEEEEILNSTTUUV	UNVEILED A STATUE
AADEEEEKMMNOOSSY	MAKE SOMEONE'S DAY
AADEEEELLQRRSTTU	SETTLED A QUARREL
AADEEEELMNNRTTTT	DENTAL TREATMENT
AADEEEELNOPSSSTT	SETS ON A PEDESTAL
AADEEEEMNPRSTTTT	STATE DEPARTMENT
AADEEEEPPRRSSTYY	YESTERDAYS PAPER
AADEEFFGGIMNNRSU	SUFFERING DAMAGE
AADEEFFHHILMOTY	HEAD OF THE FAMILY
AADEEFFHHLNOTTT	THE FAT OF THE LAND
AADEEEFFHKLNOOST	TALK ONE'S HEAD OFF
AADEEEFFHNNOOPSS	SNAP ONE'S HEAD OFF
AADEEEFFHORRRTYY	READY FOR THE FRAY
AADEEEFGIILLNNOPT	FAN-TAILED PIGEON
AADEEEFGIILLLSTUV	GAVE FULL DETAILS
AADEEEFGIMNRSSTT	GAME AND FIRST SET
AADEEEFGKNNORRTT	TAKEN FOR GRANTED
AADEEEFGKNORRSTT	TAKES FOR GRANTED
AADEEEFGLLNRTUUY	FULLY GUARANTEED
AADEEEFHHILNOSST	LEADS THE FASHION
AADEEEFHHLMORSTT	OLD FATHER THAMES
AADEEEFHHHMNORRTT	FATHER AND MOTHER
	MOTHER AND FATHER
AADEEEFHILNOSSSV	LOAVES AND FISHES
AADEEEFHILOPRSUW	PAUSED FOR A WHILE
AADEEEFHIMNNOOSTW	WHAT ONE IS MADE OF
AADEEEFHLOORSTTU	UTTER A FALSEHOOD
AADEEEFHOPRRRTYY	PRAYER FOR THE DAY
AADEEEFIILPQRSU	QUALIFIED PRAISE
AADEEEFIKNNOPSSS	SPEAK AS ONE FINDS
AADEEEFIMNORRRTU	MARRIED A FORTUNE
AADEEEFLLLLNPRSU	FALL UNDER A SPELL
AADEEEFNORRRTUUV	RETURNED A FAVOUR
AADEEGGGIINNNRT	ENGAGING IN TRADE
AADEEGGILLRSSSU	GRILLED SAUSAGES
AADEEGGIMNOSSTU	MADE A SUGGESTION
AADEEGGINORSSTY	SAINT GEORGES DAY
AADEEGGNOOOSSST	AS GOOD AS ONE GETS
AADEEGHHIKNNOSS	SHAKING ONE'S HEAD
AADEEGHHINNSTTT	STANDING THE HEAT
AADEEGHHNNPPRRTU	UP THE GARDEN PATH
AADEEGHILOPRRTY	RADIOTELEGRAPHY
AADEEGHILPRTTUY	PLAYED THE GUITAR
AADEEGHILRRSTUY	REAR ITS UGLY HEAD
AADEEGHINORRRTW	ROARED WITH ANGER
AADEEGHLLORRTTW	THE WORLD AT LARGE
AADEEGHLNPRSTUY	SUNDAY TELEGRAPH
AADEEGHOPRSSTVW	GAVE THE PASSWORD
AADEEGIIILMNRST	DEMATERIALISING
AADEEGIIILMNRTZ	DEMATERIALIZING
AADEEGIIMMNNOSTT	DEMAGNETISATION
AADEEGIIMMNNOTTZ	DEMAGNETIZATION
AADEEGIIMSSSSUU	ASSUME A DISGUISE
AADEEGIINNRSTTU	GAINED IN STATURE
AADEEGILMNORSSV	SERVING AS A MODEL
AADEEGILNNOPRTT	POTENTIAL DANGER
AADEEGILNORSSSS	RAISED ONE'S GLASS
AADEEGILNORSTTV	REVOLTED AGAINST
AADEEGINNRSTUVY	SATURDAY EVENING
AADEEGNNOOPRSUW	DANGEROUS WEAPON
AADEEHHHHHINPTVW	HAVE THE WHIP-HAND
AADEEHHILTTTTUY	HEALTHY ATTITUDE
AADEEHHKLNNORST	DRANK ONE'S HEALTH
AADEEHHKNORTTTU	TAKE THE HAT ROUND
AADEEHHLLMOSSTU	OLD AS METHUSELAH
AADEEHHLORSTTVW	HAVE THE LAST WORD
AADEEHHNNOSSSSW	WASHES ONE'S HANDS
AADEEHIIKLSSSTW	SEALED WITH A KISS
AADEEHIILNNRSTW	SAIL NEAR THE WIND
AADEEHKLOPRRTUW	WORKED UP A LATHER
AADEEHKMORSTTTW	WARMED TO THE TASK
AADEEHLLLLMNORTW	MEAN ALL THE WORLD
AADEEHLLLNORTTU	ALL-ROUND ATHLETE
AADEEHLLMNOTUWY	YOU, ME AND THE WALL
AADEEHLLNORRTUY	ALL THE YEAR ROUND
AADEEHLMPRRTTYY	PLAYED THE MARTYR
AADEEHMNNOORSST	DONE AS THE ROMANS
AADEEHMNOORSSST	DOES AS THE ROMANS
AADEEHNORRRSSTUW	SWEARS UNDER OATH
AADEEIILNLNOSSST	SENSATIONALISED
AADEEIILNOSSTUX	DESEXUALISATION

AADEEIILNOSTUXZ	DESEXUALIZATION
AADEEIILNPTTTWY	WAITED PATIENTLY
AADEEIILNRSTTTV	DISTANT RELATIVE
AADEEIINNPRRSST	PREDESTINARIANS
AADEEIINOQRSSTU	RAISED A QUESTION
AADEEIJLNNORSTV	JOINT AND SEVERAL
AADEEIKLLPRTTVY	TALKED PRIVATELY
AADEEIILLNNORUVY	YOU LIVE AND LEARN
AADEEILMNOORSTU	MADE A RESOLUTION
AADEEILMNRRTTUY	ARMED NEUTRALITY
AADEEILNNSSTTVY	ST.VALENTINES DAY
AADEEIMQRRRRSTU	MARRIED QUARTERS
AADEEINNPRSSSTT	ANTIDEPRESSANTS
AADEEINOPRRSSSY	SAID ONE'S PRAYERS
AADEEKNNOORSTTW	TAKEN AT ONE'S WORD
AADEEKNOORSSTTW	TAKES AT ONE'S WORD
AADEELMNOPRRSTT	PESTLE AND MORTAR
AADEELMNPPRTTUX	DUPLEX APARTMENT
AADEELNOPPSSTTU	PUTS ON A PEDESTAL
AADEEMNNNORSTTWW	WENT AND ATE WORMS
AADEEMPPRRSSSTU	SPADES ARE TRUMPS
AADEENNPPRSSUWY	SUNDAY NEWSPAPER
AADEFFFGHIKNOTTY	TAKING THE DAY OFF
AADEFFHIIMOPRRT	FAIR MAID OF PERTH
AADEFFHLMNORSTY	LAND OF MY FATHERS
AADEFFINNOORRTY	FRIDAY AFTERNOON
AADEFFLNOPPNOOU	APPEALS FOR FUNDS
AADEFGGIIIMNRTV	GIVING A FIRM DATE
AADEFGGIIKMNOOW	MAKING A GOOD WIFE
AADEFGGIMNORSSU	SUING FOR DAMAGES
AADEFGGINNORRTW	FORWARDING AGENT
AADEFGIIMNNORST	INFORMED AGAINST
AADEFGINNOOORUV	DOING ONE A FAVOUR
AADEFGINORSSWWY	SAYING A FEW WORDS
AADEFGLLNNOPRSY	PLAYS FOR ENGLAND
AADEFHHILLMORTY	HALF-TERM HOLIDAY
AADEFHIKMMMNORW	KNEW HIM FROM ADAM
AADEFHILLMNORST	FALL ON HARD TIMES
AADEFHILMMNOORS	HORNS OF A DILEMMA
AADEFHNNORSSTTU	FASTER THAN SOUND
AADEFMNNNOOORTY	MONDAY AFTERNOON
AADEFNNNOORSTUY	SUNDAY AFTERNOON
AADEGGHIILNRSTT	STRAIGHT DEALING
AADEGGHIIMNOOTV	HAVING A GOOD TIME
AADEGGKNOOSTTV	GAVE THANKS TO GOD
AADEGGIIKLNNORT	TAKING IN A LODGER
AADEGGIILNNNSTV	LEAVING STANDING
AADEGGINNNNOORR	GOING ON AN ERRAND
AADEGGLOPRRRSSU	GRADUAL PROGRESS
AADEGHHLNNOTUYY	YOUNG AND HEALTHY
AADEGHIINNNORSS	RAISING ONE'S HAND
AADEGHIINNNRRSS	RESTRAINING HAND
AADEGHIINNNRTTW	NEAT HANDWRITING
AADEGHIINNOPPRR	HEARING A PIN DROP
AADEGHIKNOORTTT	TAKING TO THE ROAD
AADEGHINNNOSSTY	STAYING ONE'S HAND
AADEGHINNOSSTUU	THOUSAND GUINEAS
AADEGHINORSTTTV	STARVING TO DEATH
AADEGHLMNOOOPSY	HANDSOME APOLOGY
AADEGIIIILNNSTW	LADIES IN WAITING
	LADIES-IN-WAITING
AADEGIIILNNNOST	DENATIONALISING
AADEGIIILNNNOTZ	DENATIONALIZING
AADEGIIKLNPPRSY	SPEAKING RAPIDLY
AADEGIINNNNOPRSW	DRAWING A PENSION
AADEGIINNOTUVW	WEAVING IN AND OUT
AADEGIKLNNORSTW	WALKS INTO DANGER
AADEGIKMNNNOSST	MAKING ONE'S STAND
AADEGIKMNOOPRRR	DROPPING A REMARK
AADEGIKNNNOSSTT	TAKING ONE'S STAND
AADEGIKNNOOPRTT	TAKEN IN GOOD PART

AADEGIKNOOOPRSTT	TAKES IN GOOD PART
AADEGINNNNNRRRU	RUNNING AN ERRAND
AADEHHIJNRRTTUY	JANUARY THE THIRD
AADEHHIILLLOSSST	AS OLD AS THE HILLS
AADEHHLNNORRSST	LEARNS SHORTHAND
AADEHHLNNORRSTT	LEARNT SHORTHAND
AADEHHNOPRSSTTU	PASS ROUND THE HAT
	PASS THE HAT ROUND
AADEHILNNOORRST	HARD ON ONE'S TRAIL
AADEHILNOSSSSTU	SOUTH SEA ISLANDS
AADEHINNRSSSTTT	STANDS THE STRAIN
AADEHINOPRSTTUY	SHADY REPUTATION
AADEHLNNNOOOSSSY	LAYS ONE'S HANDS ON
AADEHLORSSSTTWY	SAYS THE LAST WORD
AADEHNOOPRSSTWY	SODA-WATER SYPHON
AADEHNNOORSTTUWY	YEAR TWO THOUSAND
AADEHORRRSTVWYY	WORTHY ADVERSARY
AADEIIIILNNOSSTT	DESTALINISATION
AADEIIIILNNOSTTZ	DESTALINIZATION
AADEIIILNOPSSSTY	DISPASSIONATELY
AADEIIILNORRRTXY	EXTRAORDINARILY
AADEIIMOPPPRRST	MISAPPROPRIATED
AADEIINNNOOPTTT	PAID NO ATTENTION
AADEIINNOSTTTUW	SITUATION WANTED
AADEIKNOORSTUWW	AWKWARD QUESTION
AADEILLNNOPTTTU	PUT AN END TO ALL
AADEILLNOPRSTUY	DUAL PERSONALITY
AADEILLOPRSSSTY	PLAYS AT SOLDIERS
AADEILMNNOORSTT	DEMONSTRATIONAL
AADEILNOPPPRSTY	RAIN STOPPED PLAY
AADEINNNOSSSTWY	STANDS IN ONE'S WAY
AADEINNOORSSSTT	SARDINES ON TOAST
AADEINNRRSSSSTT	STRESS AND STRAIN
AADEINPRRSSSSTT	STARS AND STRIPES
AADEKLNOPRRSTWY	WORK,REST AND PLAY
AADELMNNOORSSWY	LAY DOWN ONES ARMS
AADELNOPRSTTUUY	POLYUNSATURATED
AADFFGIILMNNORU	FINDING A FORMULA
AADFFGOOOORSTTT	OFF TO A GOOD START
AADFGHHIILMNORV	HAVING A FIRM HOLD
AADFGHHKNOORTTT	THANK GOD FOR THAT
AADFGHIIKLMNORT	TAKING A FIRM HOLD
AADFGHIORRRSTTW	STRAIGHTFORWARD
AADFGIKMMNNOORW	KNOWING FROM ADAM
AADFHIKMMMNOORW	KNOW HIM FROM ADAM
AADFHMNNOOSSTUY	A MONTH OF SUNDAYS
AADFIIILNNORSTY	DISINFLATIONARY
AADFIIINNORSSTTT	FIRST-AID STATION
AADFIINNRSSSTTT	IN FITS AND STARTS
AADFILLNORSSSTW	FALLS DOWNSTAIRS
AADFLMOORSSSTUW	FAMOUS LAST WORDS
AADFLOOOORRSSSTW	AT A LOSS FOR WORDS
AADFNNOOOORRSTTV	STRATFORD ON AVON
AADGGHIIKNNSTVY	THANKSGIVING DAY
AADGHHIIINORTVWW	HAVING A WORD WITH
AADGHHIKNNORSTT	TAKING SHORTHAND
AADGHINPRSSTTTU	STAND UP STRAIGHT
AADGIIILNNSTTUY	STUDYING ITALIAN
AADGIIINNNOORSST	DISORGANISATION
AADGIIIINNOORSTZ	DISORGANIZATION
AADGIINNNOOSTTV	STANDING OVATION
AADGIILNNORRSSSW	SLINGS AND ARROWS
AADGIMNNORRSTUY	SATURDAY MORNING
AADIIIKKLMNNPRT	DRINKA PINTA MILK
AADIIIILNORSSTTT	TRADITIONALISTS
AADIIIMMNNOSSTT	ADMINISTRATIONS
AADIIINNNOPRRSTW	DRAW INSPIRATION
AADIIJLMNOORRSU	RADIO JOURNALISM
AADIIKNOOPRSTWW	AWKWARD POSITION
AADIIILLNNPRSTTU	INDUSTRIAL PLANT
AADIINOORRRSSTT	TRANSISTOR RADIO

AADILMNNOOPRSTT	MORAL STANDPOINT
AADILNNOOPRRSTT	LAID ON TRANSPORT
AADMNNNOORSSSTU	SUN,MOON AND STARS
AAEEEEFGNORRSTT	ORANGE FREE STATE
AAEEEEGHRSSSTTY	THREE EASY STAGES
AAEEEEGLNOPRSUV	GAVE ONE PLEASURE
AAEEEEHHLPRSTUV	HAVE THE PLEASURE
AAEEEEHIKLNORST	EATEN LIKE A HORSE
AAEEEEILNRRSTTV	NEAREST RELATIVE
AAEEEEKLMMNOSTT	MAKES AN OMELETTE
AAEEEEKMNORSSTU	TAKE ONE'S MEASURE
AAEEEELLLNOSVW	LEAVES WELL ALONE
AAEEEELMPRRSSTU	PLEASURE STEAMER
AAEEEEFFHHKNOTTT	TAKEN THE HEAT OFF
AAEEEEFFHHKOSTTT	TAKES THE HEAT OFF
AAEEEFGHINRRSSU	REFUSES A HEARING
AAEEEEFGILLMNNRT	MATERNAL FEELING
AAEEEEFGILLNNPRT	PATERNAL FEELING
AAEEEEFGILMNRSTV	EVERLASTING FAME
AAEEEEFGILNNOSST	SEALING ONE'S FATE
AAEEEEFGILNORSSV	GAVE ONESELF AIRS
AAEEEEFGILNOSVWY	GIVE ONESELF AWAY
AAEEEEFGLMMNNRRT	GENTLEMAN FARMER
AAEEEEFGLMMNORRT	FORMAL AGREEMENT
AAEEEEFGLRRRSTUU	REGULAR FEATURES
AAEEEEFHIIKLORSU	LIKE A HOUSE AFIRE
AAEEEFHNNOORRTT	ONE AFTER ANOTHER
AAEEEEFILLOPPRSV	APPLIES FOR LEAVE
AAEEEEFLNOORSTWY	TORE ONESELF AWAY
AAEEEEGIILMSTTT	LEGITIMATE STAGE
AAEEEEGHINNNOPVY	HAVING AN EYE OPEN
AAEEEEGHLLNORRUV	GENERAL OVERHAUL
AAEEEEGIILLMNTTW	TILL WE MEET AGAIN
AAEEEGIILNRRWY	RAILWAY ENGINEER
AAEEEGIKLNNOSTV	TAKING ONE'S LEAVE
AAEEEGIKLNQRRSU	SEEKING A QUARREL
AAEEEGILLNNRRTT	ETERNAL TRIANGLE
AAEEEGILNNNPSTV	PLEASANT EVENING
AAEEEGKNRRRSTTU	GREEK RESTAURANT
AAEEEGLMMNNRSTT	GENTLEMEN-AT-ARMS
AAEEEGLMMNRTTUU	MUTUAL AGREEMENT
AAEEEGLMNOPRSSS	GREASES ONE'S PALM
AAEEEGLNNORRTTY	ATTORNEY GENERAL
AAEEEGLNORRSTTT	STRANGE TO RELATE
AAEEEHHILPPTTTY	HEALTHY APPETITE
AAEEEHHIMMMNPTT	METHAMPHETAMINE
AAEEEHHNNOPRTUV	HEAVEN UPON EARTH
AAEEEHHNPPSSSTW	SEES WHAT HAPPENS
AAEEEHHOOSTTTVW	HAVE A SWEET TOOTH
AAEEEHHPRRSSTTV	REAPS THE HARVEST
AAEEEHIILLMRSST	THE MARSEILLAISE
AAEEEHIILNORSTT	ETHEREALISATION
AAEEEHIILNORTTZ	ETHEREALIZATION
AAEEEHIINNRTVVW	HAVE AN INTERVIEW
AAEEEHIJKKLLLSY	SHAKE LIKE A JELLY
AAEEEHIKLLPRSSW	WILL SHAKESPEARE
AAEEEHINNOPRSTT	ENTERTAINS A HOPE
AAEEEHINNRSTWWY	SAW THE NEW YEAR IN
AAEEEHKNOORSTTT	TAKE TO ONE'S HEART
AAEEEHKNORTTTTW	TAKEN TO THE WATER
AAEEEHKORSTTTTW	TAKES TO THE WATER
AAEEEHLNORSSSTT	STEALS ONE'S HEART
AAEEEHLOPSSTTTV	LEAVES AT THE POST
AAEEEHMNNSSTTTW	THE NEW STATESMAN
AAEEEHNNOORRSTT	NEAR TO ONE'S HEART
AAEEEHNOORSTTTU	ATE ONE'S HEART OUT
AAEEEHORRSTUWYY	STAY WHERE YOU ARE
AAEEEIIKLLPPRUV	LIVE LIKE A PAUPER
AAEEEIIKLORTTTV	TAKE IT OR LEAVE IT
AAEEEIILMMPRRSU	IMPERIAL MEASURE
AAEEEIIMNNORTTT	MARIE ANTOINETTE
AAEEEIKNNNRSTTT	TAKEN AN INTEREST
AAEEEIKNNRSSTTT	TAKES AN INTEREST
AAEEEEILLLMNNOPV	MANILLA ENVELOPE
AAEEEEILLNPPRSSY	SLIPPERY AS AN EEL
AAEEEEILMNNPRRTT	ENTER PARLIAMENT
AAEEEEILNORTTTVV	ALTERNATIVE VOTE
AAEEEELLLRRSSTTV	TRAVELLERS TALES
AAEEEELLMMNPRTTY	TEMPERAMENTALLY
AAEEEELLQRRSSTTU	SETTLES A QUARREL
AAEEEELMMNNRTTTT	MENTAL TREATMENT
AAEEEMNNNNORSSSW	ANSWERS ONE'S NAME
AAEEEMNPRRRTTUU	RUN A TEMPERATURE
AAEEFFGGINORRSW	WAGS A FOREFINGER
AAEEFFGHILMNNNT	FANNING THE FLAME
AAEEEFFHKNNOOSTT	TAKEN ONE'S HAT OFF
AAEEEFFHKNOOSSTT	TAKES ONE'S HAT OFF
AAEEEFFINOORRSTT	REAFFORESTATION
AAEEFGGGILNNORU	FOREIGN LANGUAGE
AAEEFGHLORRSTTU	TEARS OF LAUGHTER
AAEEFGILNNNRTUW	TURNING A NEW LEAF
AAEEFGILNNOOSTU	LEAGUE OF NATIONS
AAEEFGILNNORTUV	LEAVING A FORTUNE
AAEEFGIMMNNRRSST	FRAGMENTARINESS
AAEEFGIORSSTTTT	GETS A TASTE FOR IT
AAEEFHHLNRRSTTU	THAT'S HER FUNERAL
AAEEFHILOPRSSUW	PAUSES FOR A WHILE
AAEEFHILRSSTTVV	HARVEST FESTIVAL
AAEEFHMNORRTTWY	AFTER MY OWN HEART
AAEEFIILLNORSST	SELF-REALISATION
AAEEFIILLNORSTZ	SELF-REALIZATION
AAEEFIILMNNOSTX	SELF-EXAMINATION
AAEEFILNOPRSTTU	FALSE REPUTATION
AAEEFIMNNRRTTTU	UNFAIR TREATMENT
AAEEFIMNNORRRSTU	MARRIES A FORTUNE
AAEEFINNOORSSTT	AFTERNOON SIESTA
AAEEFIPQRRSTTUV	QUARTER PAST FIVE
AAEEFLLNOPRSTXY	SELF-EXPLANATORY
AAEEFLMMNNORSTTT	FORMAL STATEMENT
AAEEFLNNOORSTWY	TORN ONESELF AWAY
AAEEFMMNNOOPRSTU	PAUSE FOR A MOMENT
AAEEGGGHILLNNSU	ENGLISH LANGUAGE
AAEEGGHHLLSTTTU	GET THE LAST LAUGH
AAEEGGHILMNPRST	GREASING THE PALM
AAEEGGHIMNOSTWY	GOING THE SAME WAY
AAEEGGHINOSSSTY	AS THE SAYING GOES
AAEEGGHMOPRRSTY	GEOGRAPHY MASTER
AAEEGGIIILMNRSZ	GIRLIE MAGAZINES
AAEEGGIILMNNPVX	GIVING AN EXAMPLE
AAEEGGIKMNOSSTU	MAKE A SUGGESTION
AAEEGGILNNNPRTT	GENERATING PLANT
AAEEGGILNNRTTUW	WRITTEN LANGUAGE
AAEEGHHINNRSTVV	HAVING THE ANSWER
AAEEGHHINOOPPST	HOPE AGAINST HOPE
AAEEGHHINOPRTTT	NIGHT AT THE OPERA
AAEEGGHHIOSTVVWWY	GIVE THE SHOW AWAY
AAEEGHIIILNNPRT	LEAPING IN THE AIR
AAEEGHIIILNNRTV	LEAVING IN THE AIR
AAEEGHIIMMMNNORT	REMAINING AT HOME
AAEEGHIIMMNNOTT	ONE THING AT A TIME
AAEEGHIKLNSTTTU	TAKING THE SALUTE
AAEEGHIKNNRSSST	SNAKE IN THE GRASS
AAEEGHIKNNSSSTTY	TAKEN THINGS EASY
AAEEGHIKNRSTTTW	TAKING THE WATERS
AAEEGHIKNSSSTTY	TAKES THINGS EASY
AAEEGHILLLLNNOT	ALL ALONG THE LINE
AAEEGHILLNOPRST	GENERAL HOSPITAL
AAEEGHILLNPPRTW	PAPERING THE WALL
AAEEGHILMNRSTTT	SETTING THE ALARM
AAEEGHILNRSSTTU	AGAINST THE RULES
AAEEGHIMNNRTTTV	HAVING TREATMENT
AAEEGHINNOPRSSY	PAYING ONE'S SHARE

AAEEGHINNPRSTTW	WEARING THE PANTS
AAEEGHINPPRRTWY	PREPARING THE WAY
AAEEGHMMMORSSTU	SOMERSET MAUGHAM
AAEEGHNNNORSTTU	SANG ANOTHER TUNE
AAEEGIIIMNNSSTV	IMAGINATIVENESS
AAEEGIILLLNNRTT	A LITTLE LEARNING
AAEEGIILNNORSST	GENERALISATIONS
AAEEGIILNNORSTZ	GENERALIZATIONS
AAEEGIILNPRSTTV	PREVAILING TASTE
AAEEGIKLMNNORSV	LEAVING ONE'S MARK
AAEEGIKMMNORSTU	MAKING TO MEASURE
AAEEGILMNRRTTUVY	ARGUMENTATIVELY
AAEEGILNORSSSSS	RAISES ONE'S GLASS
AAEEGIMOOPPRRRS	PROPOSE MARRIAGE
AAEEGINNOPRSSSS	SANG ONE'S PRAISES
AAEEGKNOOPRSSSW	WORK ONES PASSAGE
AAEEGLLMORSSSTY	ALL SYSTEMS ARE GO
AAEEHHIIMRSTTTTW	WHAT IS THE MATTER
AAEEHHJNNRTTTUT	JANUARY THE TENTH
AAEEHHNNPPSTTWX	WHAT HAPPENS NEXT?
AAEEHIIKNPPRSSW	SPEAK IN A WHISPER
AAEEHIILMNPRRTY	PRELIMINARY HEAT
AAEEHIILMPPRRST	PRE RAPHAELITISM
AAEEHIKNORSTTVW	TAKEN A SHORT VIEW
AAEEHIKORSSTTVW	TAKES A SHORT VIEW
AAEEHINOORRSTTU	TEAR ONE'S HAIR OUT
AAEEHKLNORSTTWW	WALKS ON THE WATER
AAEEHLMNSSTTTWY	STANLEY MATTHEWS
AAEEHLNPRRSTTUU	THE SUPERNATURAL
AAEEHLOOOPRRSUY	ROYAL OPERA HOUSE
AAEEHMNNOORSTWY	MORE WAYS THAN ONE
AAEEHMNNOOSTTTT	STATEMENT ON OATH
AAEEHMPRRRSSTTU	HEARTS ARE TRUMPS
AAEEHNNOOORRTWY	ONE WAY OR ANOTHER
AAEEHNORTTUVWWY	WHATEVER YOU WANT
AAEEIILNNORSTTX	EXTERNALISATION
AAEEIILNNORTTXZ	EXTERNALIZATION
AAEEIILNNOSSSST	SENSATIONALISES
AAEEIILNNOSSSTZ	SENSATIONALIZES
AAEEIINNOOPRSTU	EUROPEANISATION
AAEEIINNOOPRTUZ	EUROPEANIZATION
AAEEIINOQRSSSTU	RAISES A QUESTION
AAEEIKKLLORSSVW	WORKS LIKE A SLAVE
AAEEIKLMNOORSTU	MAKE A RESOLUTION
AAEEIKLNNNOPRSS	SPRAIN ONES ANKLE
AAEEILMNNOPPRST	OPENS PARLIAMENT
AAEEILNNNOSSSTW	SENSATIONAL NEWS
AAEEILNOOPSSTUX	ANXIOUS TO PLEASE
AAEEINNPQRRSTTU	QUARTER PAST NINE
AAEEINOPPPRRSST	APPROPRIATENESS
AAEEIPQRRRSTTUV	PRIVATE QUARTERS
AAEELLNNOOOPSTT	A LOT ON ONE'S PLATE
AAEELLNPRRRTTUY	PRETERNATURALLY
AAEELMNPRSSTTYY	PLANETARY SYSTEM
AAEELNNOOPRRSSS	PERSONAL REASONS
AAEEMNOOQRRSSTU	ROOT-MEAN-SQUARES
AAEENNNPRRSSSTT	TRANSPARENTNESS
AAEENOPRRSSSSYY	SAYS ONE'S PRAYERS
AAEFFFINOORSTTT	OFF TO A FINE START
AAEFFGHILNOPTTY	PLAYTHING OF FATE
AAEFFHHIJNRTTUY	JANUARY THE FIFTH
AAEFFHILNRSTTUV	FAITHFUL SERVANT
AAEFFILMNOORRSU	FAIR MEANS OR FOUL
AAEFGGHHLNOSTTU	HANG THE FLAGS OUT
AAEFGGHIILMNRTY	FAMILY GATHERING
AAEFGGHIINNRTWY	FRIGHTENING AWAY
AAEFGGHILLNSTTU	SALUTING THE FLAG
AAEFGGHIMNNORTY	GAME FOR ANYTHING
AAEFGGIILNNNORY	LAYING A FINGER ON
AAEFGGIILNNORTY	FLYING INTO A RAGE
AAEFGGILNNOORTU	GOING TO A FUNERAL
AAEFGGIMNORTTWY	GETTING AWAY FROM
AAEFGHHIIKNRSTW	SHAKING WITH FEAR
AAEFGHHIJNORTJY	EIGHTH OF JANUARY
AAEFGHHILNRSTTT	FASTER THAN LIGHT
AAEFGHIIKMNOSTT	MAKES A NIGHT OF IT
AAEFGHIINNNRRTU	HAUNTING REFRAIN
AAEFGHLLMNOORTW	LONG ARM OF THE LAW
AAEFGIIIKLMNNRT	TAKING A FIRM LINE
AAEFGIIKMMNOSST	MAKING A MESS OF IT
AAEFGIILLMNOORW	WILLIAM OF ORANGE
AAEFGIKKLNNPRSY	FRANKLY SPEAKING
AAEFGIKKMMNNOOY	MAKING A MONKEY OF
AAEFGIKMMNOORSU	MAKING A FOURSOME
AAEFGILLNNOPSTU	PULLING A FAST ONE
AAEFGINOOPRRTUV	PARAGON OF VIRTUE
AAEFGINOPPRRRRW	PREPARING FOR WAR
AAEFHHILNRSSTTU	THAT'S HIS FUNERAL
AAEFHHMMOOSTTTU	FOAMS AT THE MOUTH
AAEFHIJNRRSTTUT	JANUARY THE FIRST
AAEFHILNNOOSTTW	WEALTH OF NATIONS
AAEFHINOPRSTTTT	PROTESTANT FAITH
AAEFHNOOPRRSTTT	PATRON OF THE ARTS
AAEFHNOOQRRRTUU	QUARTER OF AN HOUR
AAEFIIILLNORSTT	FERTILISATIONAL
AAEFIIILLNORTTZ	FERTILIZATIONAL
AAEFIILLMNNRRTUY	MILITARY FUNERAL
AAEFIILNOOPRRSS	PROFESSIONAL AIR
AAEFIILNQRRSTTU	QUARTERFINALIST
AAEFILLLLNNOOPST	FALL INTO ONE'S LAP
AAEFILLLNNOPTUX	FULL EXPLANATION
AAEFILMNNOOPRSS	PROFESSIONAL MAN
AAEFLLLLOOPPRRW	ROLL OF WALLPAPER
AAEFLLNOOPRSTTW	FOLLOWS A PATTERN
AAEFLMOOPPRSSTU	STORM OF APPLAUSE
AAEFLNOOORRSTTW	A LOT TO ANSWER FOR
AAEFOPQRRRSTTUU	QUARTER PAST FOUR
AAEGGHHHOOPRSTU	GO THROUGH A PHASE
AAEGGHHLLOSTTTU	GOT THE LAST LAUGH
AAEGGHIIMNNPPST	SHIPPING MAGNATE
AAEGGHIMNORRSTU	SHOTGUN MARRIAGE
AAEGGHINNOPRRTW	NARROWING THE GAP
AAEGGHINNSTTTTU	SETTING AT NAUGHT
AAEGGHNNNOORSST	SANG ANOTHER SONG
AAEGGIIILMNNNOR	ORIGINAL MEANING
AAEGGIIKLMNNOTT	TAKING A LONG TIME
AAEGGIIKLNNOTVW	TAKING A LONG VIEW
AAEGGILLLLNNORTV	TRAVELLING ALONG
AAEGHHHIILRTTTW	WITH A LIGHT HEART
AAEGHHHLLOSSTUW	HE WHO LAUGHS LAST
AAEGHHIIIMNNTTV	HAVING A THIN TIME
AAEGHHNOOOPPRST	ORGANOPHOSPHATE
AAEGHHNNOPRRTUU	AUTOGRAPH HUNTER
AAEGHIIILNPRSSV	LAVISHING PRAISE
AAEGHIIKNNPPSSS	SPEAKING SPANISH
AAEGHIIKNNRRSTT	TAKING THE STRAIN
AAEGHIIKNORTTTT	TAKING IT TO HEART
AAEGHIILLNNPTTW	PAINTING THE WALL
AAEGHIILLNOPSTV	LEAVING HOSPITAL
AAEGHIIILLNOTTVW	VIOLATING THE LAW
AAEGHIILNNNOPTY	PAYING ON THE NAIL
AAEGHIIMMNNOOTT	AIMING AT THE MOON
AAEGHIIMMNNRRSTY	MARRYING IN HASTE
AAEGHIINNOSTVWY	HAVING IT ONE'S WAY
AAEGHIKMMNNRSSTW	MAKES THINGS WARM
AAEGHIKNPPRSSTU	RAKING UP THE PAST
AAEGHIILLLNOTTTU	LET IT ALL HANG OUT
AAEGHILLLRSSTTT	ALL THAT GLISTERS
AAEGHILLLRSTTTT	ALL THAT GLITTERS
AAEGHIILLMNNSTTW	MANNING THE WALLS
AAEGHILMMNNOTYZ	MONTHLY MAGAZINE
AAEGHILNNNOPSSU	SUSAN PENHALIGON

AAEGIIIJMNNORRS	JOINS IN MARRIAGE
AAEGIIILMNRRTTW	WRITING MATERIAL
AAEGIIILNNOORST	REGIONALISATION
AAEGIIILNNOORTZ	REGIONALIZATION
AAEGIIILNNOSTTV	INVESTIGATIONAL
AAEGIIKKMMNNOST	MAKING NO MISTAKE
AAEGIIKLLNNPPSY	SPEAKING PLAINLY
AAEGIIKNNOQSSTU	ASKING A QUESTION
AAEGIIKNNPRSSSU	SPEAKING RUSSIAN
AAEGIIILLNNOSSTW	AGAINST ONES WILL
AAEGIILNNRRSTTT	TRANSLITERATING
AAEGIIMNOOPRRRT	MARRIAGE PORTION
AAEGIINNNNOPTTTY	PAYING ATTENTION
AAEGIKNNOQRRSTU	ASKING NO QUARTER
AAEGILLLNNNPRRU	RUNNING PARALLEL
AAEGILLNOOOPSTT	PALAEONTOLOGIST
AAEGILLOPRRRTTY	PORTRAIT GALLERY
AAEGILNOORSTTTT	STARTING TOO LATE
AAEGILOPPRRTTUY	GREAT POPULARITY
AAEGIMNNOOSSSST	SAMSON AGONISTES
AAEGINNPPRRRRST	SPARRING PARTNER
AAEGINOPRSSSTTT	PROTESTS AGAINST
AAEGINPPRRRSSSU	SPRANG A SURPRISE
AAEGINPRRSSTTUU	SUPERSATURATING
AAEGKNNNORRTTUW	TAKEN A WRONG TURN
AAEGKNNORRSTTUW	TAKES A WRONG TURN
AAEHHIJNNNRTTUY	JANUARY THE NINTH
AAEHHIJNRSTTUXY	JANUARY THE SIXTH
AAEHHILNOSTTTTY	STAY AT THE HILTON
AAEHHIOOPRRRTTW	HEATHROW AIRPORT
AAEHIIKLNPRSSTW	TALKS IN A WHISPER
AAEHIILLLNPSTVY	PLAYS THE VILLAIN
AAEHIILMNORTTUV	ITALIAN VERMOUTH
AAEHIILNNNOSTTW	WINS THE NATIONAL
AAEHIILOPPRSTTV	PRIVATE HOSPITAL
AAEHIILORTTTUVY	AUTHORITATIVELY
AAEHIKNORSTTTWW	WOKEN WITH A START
AAEHILLLOPRTTUW	WITHOUT PARALLEL
AAEHILLMNOOPRST	HOSPITAL ALMONER
AAEHILLNNOOPRTZ	HORIZONTAL PLANE
AAEHINOPRTTTUWY	PUT IT ANOTHER WAY
AAEHKNNORSSSSTT	THANKS ONE'S STARS
AAEHLLLNOOSTWYY	STANLEY HOLLOWAY
AAEIIILMNNNOSTT	MAIN LINE STATION
AAEIIILMNORSSTT	ARISTOTELIANISM
AAEIIILNNNORSTT	INTERNALISATION
AAEIIILNNNORTTZ	INTERNALIZATION
AAEIILLMNNRSTTU	TRANSILLUMINATE
AAEIILLNNNORTTY	INTERNATIONALLY
AAEIILLOORRSTVW	SAVILE ROW TAILOR
AAEIILMNRRSTUWY	RAILWAY TERMINUS
AAEIILMOPPRTVXY	APPROXIMATIVELY
AAEIILMORRRRTTY	TERRITORIAL ARMY
AAEIILNNOOPRSST	PERSONALISATION
AAEIILNNOOPRSTZ	PERSONALIZATION
AAEIILNNORRSTTT	TRANSLITERATION
AAEIILNNOSSSSTT	SENSATIONALISTS
AAEIIMMNNNOOORTX	EXAMINATION ROOM
AAEIIMNNNOOPPRT	NOMINATION PAPER
AAEIIMNNOSSSTTTY	SYSTEMATISATION
AAEIIMNOSSTTTYZ	SYSTEMATIZATION
AAEIIMOPPPRRSST	MISAPPROPRIATES
AAEIINNNPQRTTUU	PUT IN QUARANTINE
AAEIINNPPRRSSTT	ANTIPERSPIRANTS
AAEIINOPPRRRTTT	PORTRAIT PAINTER
AAEIJKKLNOORRTW	WORK LIKE A TROJAN
AAEIJLLMOORRTVY	OVERALL MAJORITY
AAEIJLNORRSUWYY	RAILWAY JOURNEYS
AAEIKLLORSSSTTT	IT TAKES ALL SORTS
AAEIKNNNOOPPTTU	TAKEN UP AN OPTION
AAEIKNNOOPPSTTU	TAKES UP AN OPTION
AAEILLNNOORTTTY	NATIONAL LOTTERY
AAEILLORRSTTUVY	ULTRAVIOLET RAYS
AAEILMNNOQTUUUX	AUTUMNAL EQUINOX
AAEILMNPRRSSTUU	SUPERNATURALISM
AAEILNNNOSSTTUY	INSTANTANEOUSLY
AAEILNOOORSTTTW	WATERLOO STATION
AAEILNOOPRRSTTY	RESTORATION PLAY
AAEILNOOPRSSSTU	PASS A RESOLUTION
AAEIMMNOPRRTTTT	IMPORTANT MATTER
AAEINNNNOPSSSTT	ANTS IN ONE'S PANTS
AAEINNNOOPSTTTY	PAYS NO ATTENTION
AAEINOPRRSSTTUU	SUPERSATURATION
AAELLLLORSSTTTY	TELLS A TALL STORY
AAELMNNOORRTTUY	ROYAL TOURNAMENT
AAELMNOOORRRSTY	ASTRONOMER ROYAL
AAENNNNOOSTTTTWW	WASTE NOT,WANT NOT
AAFFHJNOORRTUUY	FOURTH OF JANUARY
AAFGGGGHIIINNSTT	FIGHTING AGAINST
AAFGGGIILMNNSSY	MAGNIFYING GLASS
AAFGHINOOPSSTTV	HAVING A SOFT SPOT
AAFGIIIMNNNNOORT	GAIN INFORMATION
AAFGIILNNOOPSTT	GO INTO A FLAT SPIN
AAFGIINNORRSTTU	TRANSFIGURATION
AAFGIKNNOORSSUV	ASKING NO FAVOURS
AAFHHOOOOORTTTT	A TOOTH FOR A TOOTH
AAFIIIMMNNORRSTU	UNIFORMITARIANS
AAFIIKLLLMMNNRWY	WILLIAM FRANKLYN
AAFIILMNNORTTTY	INFANT MORTALITY
AAFIILMNOORRSTU	FORMULARISATION
AAFIILMNOORRTUZ	FORMULARIZATION
AAFILMOPPRSSTUY	SUPPORTS A FAMILY
AAGGHHINOPRSTTU	SPARING A THOUGHT
AAGGHIIIKNNNSTW	TAKING IN WASHING
AAGGHILMNNORTTW	MALIGNANT GROWTH
AAGGIIINNNRSSUW	ISSUING A WARNING
AAGGIIKLNNRSTTT	STARTING TALKING
AAGGMMNNNOSSSUU	MAGNUS MAGNUSSON
AAGHHIIIKNNNSTV	HAVING A THIN SKIN
AAGHHINOOOTTTUV	HAVING A TOOTH OUT
AAGHHKOOOOOPPRTT	TOOK A PHOTOGRAPH
AAGHHNNOOOORTTUY	HANG ON TO YOUR HAT
AAGHHNOOOPPRSTU	ANTHROPOPHAGOUS
AAGHIIILNORSTTV	SLIGHT VARIATION
AAGHILMNOOOOSTT	MOONLIGHT SONATA
AAGIIINNNOPRSTT	STRAINING A POINT
AAGIILNNOSSSSTU	SUSTAINING A LOSS
AAGIILNORSTTTUU	GUTTURALISATION
AAGIILNORTTTUUZ	GUTTURALIZATION
AAGILNNNOPRTTUU	RUNNING UP A TOTAL
AAGINOOOOPPRSSTT	PROPOSING A TOAST
AAHIIILNOOPSSTT	HOSPITALISATION
AAHIIILNOOPSTTZ	HOSPITALIZATION
AAHIINOOPSSTTTTY	HYPOSTATISATION
AAHIINOOPSTTTYZ	HYPOSTATIZATION
AAIIIIMNNNORSTTU	MINIATURISATION
AAIIIIMNNORTTUZ	MINIATURIZATION
AAIIILLNNOPRSTY	INSPIRATIONALLY
AAIIILMNORSTTTY	MILITARY STATION
AAIIIINNOPRSSSTU	PRUSSIANISATION
AAIIIINNOPRSSTUZ	PRUSSIANIZATION
AAIIJLNOOPSTTUX	JUXTAPOSITIONAL
AAIILNNOOPRSSTT	TRANSPOSITIONAL
AAIILNOORRSSTTT	TONSORIAL ARTIST
AAIILOOPRRSTUXY	AUXILIARY TROOPS
AAIIMNOOPRSSSTY	TRYPANOSOMIASIS
AAIINNOOPRSTTTU	SATURATION POINT
AAIINNOPPQRTTTU	QUART IN A PINT POT
AAILLNOOPPRRTUU	RURAL POPULATION
AAIMMNNOOPRSTTY	ANY PORT IN A STORM
AALNNOOPRRSSTTY	LAYS ON TRANSPORT
ABBBDDDENNOOPUW	BOBBED UP AND DOWN

ABBCDDEHIILMRRY	RICHARD DIMBLEBY
ABBCDDEILMOOSTU	DISCOMBOBULATED
ABBCDEEEIJLORST	DESIRABLE OBJECT
ABBCDEEFHKNOOTY	THE BACK OF BEYOND
ABBCDEGHILNOTTU	CLUBBING TO DEATH
ABBCDEHIKNOORTY	IN BY THE BACK DOOR
ABBCDEILMOOSSTU	DISCOMBOBULATES
ABBCEEEEILMNORRS	BORE RESEMBLANCE
ABBCEEEGIMMMNOR	BECOMING A MEMBER
ABBCEEEIIILMNSV	BECAME INVISIBLE
ABBCEEEEIMNOORRS	BECOMES AIRBORNE
ABBCEEEINRSSSTU	BARE SUBSISTENCE
ABBCEEIJLMMOOTV	IMMOVABLE OBJECT
ABBCEEIKLLLLORRY	ROCKABILLY REBEL
ABBCEELLNRRSTUY	CANTERBURY BELLS
ABBCEFGIIKLNORT	BRING BACK TO LIFE
ABBCEKLNORRRSUV	BLACKBURN ROVERS
ABBCHIIILMORSTU	BRITISH COLUMBIA
ABBDDEEEHINRSST	BIRDS AND THE BEES
	THE BIRDS AND BEES
ABBDDEEEELLLORRU	DOUBLE-BARRELLED
ADDDDCCIINNONCCU	RUBBED ONE'S HANDS
ABBDDELLNNOOSUY	BEYOND ALL BOUNDS
ABBDEEEEENRRTTTT	BETTER AND BETTER
ABBDEEEGGINRRTT	BIGGER AND BETTER
ABBDEEEHKNORSTW	BROKE THE BAD NEWS
ABBDEEGGGGIINRR	BIGGER AND BIGGER
ABBDEFGGIJNNORR	JOBBING GARDENER
ABBDEEGHIIKLRST	TALKED GIBBERISH
ABBDEEGHINRRTYZ	BRIGHT AND BREEZY
ABBDEEHHIOORRSY	RIDE A HOBBY-HORSE
ABBDEEHHOOORRSY	RODE A HOBBY-HORSE
ABBDEEKLOOORRRV	LORD BEAVERBROOK
ABBDEENNOORSSTU	BURNED ONE'S BOATS
ABBDEGGHINOORTY	GOING BY THE BOARD
ABBDEGHILLNOOUV	HAVING BLUE BLOOD
ABBDEGHILORRTYY	DAYLIGHT ROBBERY
ABBDEGIKLMNOOOW	GO DOWN LIKE A BOMB
ABBEEEEFHLLORTUW	BEWARE OF THE BULL
ABBEEEFILLORRSV	BARBER OF SEVILLE
ABBEEEHIKORRRRT	BROKE THE BARRIER
ABBEEEEHILNORSTW	SWEAR ON THE BIBLE
ABBEEEEHLNOORSTW	BELOW ONE'S BREATH
ABBEEEHNNORTTUV	NONE BUT THE BRAVE
ABBEEEKNNOORSSS	BREAKS ONE'S BONES
ABBEEFHILNRSTTY	BATS IN THE BELFRY
ABBEEIIJMNNNRTT	BENJAMIN BRITTEN
ABBEEIKLLLLLOUW	BELLOW LIKE A BULL
ABBEFGHILLLMNTU	FUMBLING THE BALL
ABBEGILLNOOSTWZ	BLOWING TO BLAZES
ABBEILMOOPRRSTY	IMPROBABLE STORY
ABCCCDEEEIILRRS	DESCRIBE A CIRCLE
ABCCCDEGIIMRRSU	CAMBRIDGE CIRCUS
ABCCCEHKKLOPTTU	PUT BACK THE CLOCK
	PUT THE CLOCK BACK
ABCCCGIIKLLLOOO	BIOLOGICAL CLOCK
ABCCDEFHIINORTT	ACCIDENT OF BIRTH
ABCCDEHKOORRSUV	CHUCKS OVERBOARD
ABCCDEIILNOPTUU	PUBLIC EDUCATION
ABCCDGIINNNORTT	BINDING CONTRACT
ABCCDGIKMNORSUU	BACKGROUND MUSIC
ABCCEEEEEHMMRST	CAMEMBERT CHEESE
ABCCEEEEFLNNORT	CONFERENCE TABLE
ABCCEEEEHHLNRTT	THE TREBLE CHANCE
ABCCEEEHILRRTTU	CRUCIBLE THEATRE
ABCCEEEEIKLLNRTT	ELECTRIC BLANKET
ABCCEEEEILNNOSSV	CONCEIVABLENESS
ABCCEEFGHJNOSTU	CHANGE OF SUBJECT
ABCCEEFHIKNORST	BREAST OF CHICKEN
ABCCEEFIKLMOOST	COMES BACK TO LIFE
ABCCEEGHHINTTTU	CATCHING THE TUBE
ABCCEEGHINNOQUU	BOUNCING A CHEQUE
ABCCEEHIMMMNOOPS	BECOMES CHAMPION
ABCCEEIIILLNORRS	IRRECONCILABLES
ABCCEEIILNNORRT	ELECTRONIC BRAIN
ABCCEEIILLNNOOPST	POLICE CONSTABLE
ABCCEFHILMOORSU	BACHELOR OF MUSIC
ABCCEFHLOOOOSTX	BOX OF CHOCOLATES
ABCCEFIIIJNOOTT	OBJECTIFICATION
ABCCEHKLNORTTUY	THE BLACK COUNTRY
ABCCEHKMOOORRTT	REACH ROCK-BOTTOM
ABCCEIIILMRRSTV	VERBAL CRITICISM
ABCCEINNOSSSSTU	BUSINESS CONTACT
ABCCGIIIILLMOOOR	MICROBIOLOGICAL
ABCCGIIILLOOOOS	SOCIOBIOLOGICAL
ABCCGINNOORSTTU	BRINGS TO ACCOUNT
ABCCIILMMMNOTUY	COMMUNICABILITY
ABCCIIILNORTTTY	CONTRACTIBILITY
ABCCIIKLMNNOOOT	COMBINATION LOCK
ABCCKNOPRRTTUUY	BANKRUPTCY COURT
ABCDDDEEKLLNOOT	LOCKED AND BOLTED
ABCDDEEEEHLNNRTU	BURNED THE CANDLE
ABCDDEEEENNNORUY	BEYOND ENDURANCE
ABCDDEEGIIMNRTU	CAMBRIDGE UNITED
ABCDDEEHILLMRST	CLIMBS THE LADDER
ABCDDEEILLOOSTW	DISLOCATED ELBOW
ABCDDEEINNORRTU	BURNED TO A CINDER
ABCDDEHHNNOTUUY	UNTOUCHED BY HAND
ABCDDGHIIMMNNOPU	BUDDING CHAMPION
ABCDDHLLNNOOOTW	BLOWN HOT AND COLD
ABCDDHLLNOOOSTW	BLOWS HOT AND COLD
ABCDEEEEHNORRTT	BEATEN THE RECORD
ABCDEEEEMMNOORU	BECOME ENAMOURED
ABCDEEEFHHILLRT	FILLED THE BREACH
ABCDEEEFFILLPRRU	FEDERAL REPUBLIC
ABCDEEEEFHKLLNOS	HELD ONESELF BACK
ABCDEEEGGGGIMNNO	BECOMING ENGAGED
ABCDEEEGHHKNNTY	HANGED BY THE NECK
ABCDEEEHHINRSTW	WIDENS THE BREACH
ABCDEEEHIKNNRTW	BACKED THE WINNER
ABCDEEEHILMSSST	BEST LAID SCHEMES
ABCDEEEHINORRTU	DECENT BEHAVIOUR
ABCDEEEHIPRSTTU	DISTURB THE PEACE
ABCDEEEEHKORRRST	BREAKS THE RECORD
ABCDEEEHNNOOHSY	BEYOND ONES REACH
ABCDEEELLORSSUY	SCORED A BULL'S EYE
	SCORED A BULL'S-EYE
ABCDEEFFLLLNOSU	CALLED ONE'S BLUFF
ABCDEEFHIOOORUV	CODE OF BEHAVIOUR
ABCDEEFHKLLNOOS	HOLD ONESELF BACK
ABCDEEGHILNRSTU	EDINBURGH CASTLE
ABCDEEGIIINNNRST	BASIC INGREDIENT
ABCDEEGIKNORRRS	BREAKING RECORDS
ABCDEEILMNORSSU	CONSIDERABLE SUM
ABCDEFFGIINOORR	BOARDING OFFICER
ABCDEGHHIKLNNOT	HELD NOTHING BACK
ABCDEGHIKNNORTU	IN THE BACKGROUND
ABCDEGIIIKLSSTW	WIELDS A BIG STICK
ABCDEGIINNRRTV	BRING IN A VERDICT
ABCDEGIIKLNNRSS	DRESSING IN BLACK
ABCDEHKNPRSTTUU	STRUCK UP THE BAND
ABCDEIIKMOORRST	RIDE A BROOMSTICK
ABCDEIILMOOPSTY	DECOMPOSABILITY
ABCDEIIMOOSSTUY	BASIDIOMYCETOUS
ABCDEIKMOOORRST	RODE A BROOMSTICK
ABCDEILNOOORRUW	RAINBOW-COLOURED
ABCDGHHIKLNNOOT	HOLD NOTHING BACK
ABCDIIIILRSTTTY	DISTRACTIBILITY
ABCEEEEGLLMNRRW	CAMBERWELL GREEN
ABCEEEEHIKLNRST	BREAK THE SILENCE
ABCEEEEHRRRRSTT	STRETCHER BEARER
ABCEEEEHRRSTTTY	BETRAY THE SECRET

ABCEEEEEIILLRRSV	RELIABLE SERVICE
ABCEEEEEILNOPPRZ	NOBEL PEACE PRIZE
ABCEEEEEILNRSSSV	SERVICEABLENESS
ABCEEEEFFLLMOORT	FEEL COMFORTABLE
ABCEEEFHLORSTUW	BELOW THE SURFACE
ABCEEEGHILMNRWY	REACHING WEMBLEY
ABCEEEGINSSSTUW	SUBSISTENCE WAGE
ABCEEEHHIRRTTTY	BITE AT THE CHERRY
ABCEEEHIJRSSTTU	RAISE THE SUBJECT
ABCEEEHIKKRSTTW	BREAKS THE WICKET
ABCEEEHMMNNOPTTT	BENEATH CONTEMPT
ABCEEEIILLNOSTV	CABLE TELEVISION
ABCEEEILNNOPTUX	UNEXCEPTIONABLE
ABCEEEILNNSSSSUX	INEXCUSABLENESS
ABCEEELLORSSSUY	SCORES A BULL'S EYE
	SCORES A BULL'S-EYE
ABCEEELMOPRSSTT	MOST RESPECTABLE
ABCEEFFLLMOORTT	FELT COMFORTABLE
ABCEEFHIMOOPRRS	BREACH OF PROMISE
ABCEEFHIMORRSST	BEFORE CHRISTMAS
ABCEEFHLLOORTVY	TOO CLEVER BY HALF
ABCEEFILNOPSSSU	PLACE OF BUSINESS
ABCEEFLMMOOORRT	MORE COMFORTABLE
ABCEEFLNNOOSTTT	TABLE OF CONTENTS
ABCEEGHIKKNNOPT	KEEP NOTHING BACK
ABCEEGHIKLNOTTT	GET INTO THE BLACK
ABCEEGHINORSSTT	TOSSING THE CABER
ABCEEGHINPRRTUY	REACHING PUBERTY
ABCEEGKNNOOSSTW	GETS ONE'S OWN BACK
ABCEEHHIILLTTTW	HIT THE BALL TWICE
ABCEEHHLNOSTTUU	THE UNTOUCHABLES
ABCEEHHNOPSTTTU	BEATS TO THE PUNCH
ABCEEHIIKNSTTTU	TAKEN THE BISCUIT
ABCEEHIIKSSTTTU	TAKES THE BISCUIT
ABCEEHIIMMOSSTU	AMBITIOUS SCHEME
ABCEEHLNOORRTTT	CHARLOTTE BRONTE
ABCEEIIIMNNRSTT	CABINET MINISTER
ABCEEEIIJNOORSST	RAISE OBJECTIONS
ABCEEIIJNOPRSST	SIR JACOB EPSTEIN
ABCEEIIHNOPRRTTX	EXORBITANT PRICE
ABCEEIJLRRSTTUY	LITERARY SUBJECT
ABCEEIKNNORRRSU	INSURANCE BROKER
ABCEEILMMNNORSU	INCOMMENSURABLE
ABCEEILMNNNOOOU	ONCE IN A BLUE MOON
ABCEEILNNOORSTV	CONVERSION TABLE
ABCEEILNNOPTUXY	UNEXCEPTIONABLY
ABCEEILNNRSSSTU	INSCRUTABLENESS
ABCEELNNNOOPRUU	UNPRONOUNCEABLE
ABCEGGGHIINNRRS	BRINGING CHARGES
ABCEGGHILNNOSWX	EXCHANGING BLOWS
ABCEGHIIKNPPTTU	PICKING UP THE TAB
ABCEGHIKKNNOPTT	KEPT NOTHING BACK
ABCEGHIKLNOOTTT	GOT INTO THE BLACK
ABCEGHIKLNOPTTT	POTTING THE BLACK
ABCEGHLOOORSTTU	BROUGHT TO A CLOSE
ABCEGIIILNORSTY	RECOGNISABILITY
ABCEGIIILNORTYZ	RECOGNIZABILITY
ABCEGIILOORSSTT	BACTERIOLOGISTS
ABCEGIKLNNNOOSY	LYING ON ONE'S BACK
ABCEGILLLMOORYY	EMBRYOLOGICALLY
ABCEHHIKLMNSTTU	THUMBNAIL SKETCH
ABCEHHIORRSSSTT	HITS THE CROSSBAR
ABCEHIINNORSTTU	IAIN CUTHBERTSON
ABCEHILLLMPSTUW	CLIMBS UP THE WALL
ABCEHILNOORSSUU	UNSOCIABLE HOURS
ABCEIIIILLNPTXY	INEXPLICABILITY
ABCEIILLNOPRSTU	PUBLIC RELATIONS
ABCEILMMNNORSUY	INCOMMENSURABLY
ABCEINNOOOORRST	CORONATION ROBES
ABCGGIKKNOOORTW	GOING BACK TO WORK
ABCGHIKKLLNOOST	THINGS LOOK BLACK

ABCGHINOSTTTUWY	CUTTING BOTH WAYS
ABCGIIINNNOORTT	BRING INTO ACTION
ABCGIINNORSSTTU	SUBTRACTION SIGN
ABCGIKLMNNORSUW	WORKING-MANS CLUB
ABCGILMNORSSSTU	STUMBLING ACROSS
ABCHHIIIMNOPRST	BRITISH CHAMPION
ABCHHIILLMORTYY	BIORHYTHMICALLY
ABCIIIILMNOPTTY	INCOMPATIBILITY
ABCIILLLNOORTTY	CONTROLLABILITY
ABCIILORRRSTTUU	ARBORICULTURIST
ABCIKKNNOOSTUWY	WINS BY A KNOCK-OUT
ABCILNOPPRRSTTU	PUBLIC TRANSPORT
ABDDDEEEHILNRVY	DELIVERED BY HAND
ABDDDEEIINORRRS	DISORDERED BRAIN
ABDDDEEIMNNORSS	BROAD-MINDEDNESS
ABDDDEHILOOOSSV	AVOIDS BLOODSHED
ABDDDEHLNNOORTU	BLOOD AND THUNDER
ABDDEEEFLLRSSTU	FULL-DRESS DEBATE
ABDDEEEGILNRTTY	GREATLY INDEBTED
ABDDEEEHILNOTTW	WIELDED THE BATON
ABDDEEEHILNRTUW	RED,WHITE AND BLUE
ABDDEEEHNOOORTT	BORED ONE TO DEATH
ABDDEEEHNOORSUW	BONDED WAREHOUSE
ABDDEEEIILNORTU	DUE DELIBERATION
ABDDEEEIILNNRTUY	TURNED A BLIND EYE
ABDDEEEIILOORSTT	A LOT TO BE DESIRED
ABDDEEFGIILLNRW	BIDDING FAREWELL
ABDDEEFGIORTTTU	DEBT OF GRATITUDE
ABDDEEFINORSTYY	STEADY BOYFRIEND
ABDDEEGGIINNNNN	BEGINNING AND END
ABDDEEGIINORRSV	ABRIDGED VERSION
ABDDEEHIMNNORST	BROADENS THE MIND
ABDDEEHMNOOORRS	DR.BERNARDOS HOME
ABDDEEIKLNNOOOR	BROOKED NO DENIAL
ABDDEEIMNNNOORS	BROADEN ONES MIND
ABDDEEINRSSSSSU	BUSINESS ADDRESS
ABDDEEJMOOPRRUV	JUMPED OVERBOARD
ABDDEELLLNOOPRW	LORD BADEN-POWELL
ABDDEELMNOORSSW	WARM-BLOODEDNESS
ABDDEGHIINNRSTT	START THE BIDDING
ABDDEGHINNORTWY	DEATH BY DROWNING
ABDDEGILOOOPSSS	DISPOSABLE GOODS
ABDDEGINNOORRSW	EDWARD G.ROBINSON
ABDDEGINNOSTTTU	OUTSTANDING DEBT
ABDDFILNOORRSTW	DRAWN FIRST BLOOD
ABDDFILOORRSSTW	DRAWS FIRST BLOOD
ABDDLNNOOOSSUWY	OWNS BODY AND SOUL
ABDEEEEEGPRRSTT	DEBRETT'S PEERAGE
ABDEEEEEINRRRRT	ABERDEEN TERRIER
ABDEEEEFHINOSST	BE ON THE SAFE SIDE
ABDEEEEFHMNNRST	FANNED THE EMBERS
ABDEEEEGHKLPRST	BREAKS THE PLEDGE
ABDEEEEHLLNRSTW	ANSWERED THE BELL
ABDEEEEMMNNOTUWY	BETWEEN YOU AND ME
ABDEEEFFHINOOST	BITE ONES HEAD OFF
ABDEEEFGHNOOORT	BEEN OF GOOD HEART
ABDEEEFHHILMSTT	SHIFTED THE BLAME
ABDEEEFHIMOSTTT	MADE THE BEST OF IT
ABDEEEGHIINRTVW	GIVEN A WIDE BERTH
ABDEEEGHIIRSTVW	GIVES A WIDE BERTH
ABDEEEGHILNPRTY	BREATHING DEEPLY
ABDEEEGHINNRSTU	EASING THE BURDEN
ABDEEEGILRRRTTY	TERRIBLE TRAGEDY
ABDEEEGIMSSTTTU	BUDGET ESTIMATES
ABDEEEGINNNSTTW	STANDING BETWEEN
ABDEEEGNNNOORSU	BEEN ON ONE'S GUARD
ABDEEEHHKNORRTT	BROKEN THE THREAD
ABDEEEHHLMPTTTU	THUMPED THE TABLE
ABDEEEHILLNPSST	SPILLED THE BEANS
ABDEEEHIRRSSTTT	SHED BITTER TEARS
ABDEEEHJKLOORTU	LABOURED THE JOKE

ABDEEEEHKLOSSTTU	DOUBLE THE STAKES
ABDEEEEHLNOORSTU	TROUBLE ONE'S HEAD
ABDEEEEHLNRSTTTU	TURNED THE TABLES
ABDEEEEHNNORRSTU	UNDER ONES BREATH
ABDEEEEHNOOORSTT	BORES ONE TO DEATH
ABDEEEEHOOPRSSSTW	SWEEPS THE BOARDS
ABDEEEEHPRSSTTTU	PASSED THE BUTTER
ABDEEEIIIILMNRSV	REMAINED VISIBLE
ABDEEEIKLNRSSTT	BEER AND SKITTLES
ABDEEEILMNOPSUY	OBEYED AN IMPULSE
ABDEEEIINNORSTTV	OBEDIENT SERVANT
ABDEEEMNNNOOSSY	BEYOND ONES MEANS
ABDEEEMOPRRTTUY	BODY TEMPERATURE
ABDEEEENOOOORRSTT	BORED ONE TO TEARS
ABDEEEENOOPRSSUW	ABUSED ONE'S POWER
ABDEEFHIMOOORUV	MODE OF BEHAVIOUR
ABDEEFHINNOORTW	END OF THE RAINBOW
ABDEEFHINORSSSU	HEAD FOR BUSINESS
ABDEEFHINRSSTTW	FIRST THE BAD NEWS
ABDEEFIIIILNSTY	INDEFEASIBILITY
ABDEEFIMOSSTTTU	SUBMITS TO DEFEAT
ABDEEFKLOOHRSTU	ASKED FOR TROUBLE
ABDEEGGILNOORTY	GOING TO BED EARLY
ABDEEGHIILNNORT	BEARDING THE LION
ABDEEGHILOOPRSS	PERISHABLE GOODS
ABDEEGHINNOPTTU	POUNDING THE BEAT
ABDEEGHINNRRTUW	BURNED WITH ANGER
ABDEEGIIKKNPRRS	KERB SIDE PARKING
ABDEEGIIILLMORTT	GOTTLIEB DAIMLER
ABDEEGIIILLOSTVY	LEGISLATIVE BODY
ABDEEGIKMNNOSTU	MAKING ONE'S DEBUT
ABDEEGIKNNOOSTT	TAKING TO ONE'S BED
ABDEEGKNNORRSUW	BREAKS NEW GROUND
ABDEEGLNOOOOSSTY	GETS A BLOODY NOSE
ABDEEGNNOOPRSSY	BEYOND ONES GRASP
ABDEEGNOOOSSSYY	SAY ONES GOODBYES
ABDEEHHHINORRSSU	BRUSHED ONE'S HAIR
ABDEEHHLNOORSST	HOLDS ONE'S BREATH
ABDEEHIKNPRSTTU	STRIKE UP THE BAND
ABDEEHILNNORSSU	IN DOUBLE HARNESS
ABDEEHIMNNRSTUW	WHITE MANS BURDEN
ABDEEHIMOORSTUV	MODEST BEHAVIOUR
ABDEEHINPRRSTTY	BIRTHDAY PRESENT
ABDEEHLLNSSTTUU	HUSTLE AND BUSTLE
ABDEEHLNNOOSSSU	LOSE ONES HUSBAND
ABDEEHOPPPPRRTU	PROPPED UP THE BAR
ABDEEILLMNORSTZ	BRONZE MEDALLIST
ABDEEIINNNORRSTU	TURNED ONE'S BRAIN
ABDEEKLMORSSUUY	MAKES DOUBLY SURE
ABDEEKNNORSTTWY	KNOWN BETTER DAYS
ABDEELLNRRRSSTU	BERTRAND RUSSELL
ABDEELNNOORRSTW	BOLTON WANDERERS
ABDEELNORSSTUUV	SUNSET BOULEVARD
ABDEEMNNOOPSTUY	STOP ME AND BUY ONE
ABDEFFHIORRRTUY	THIRD OF FEBRUARY
ABDEFFOOORRSTTW	BEST FOOT FORWARD
ABDEFGGIIILNNOR	OBLIGING A FRIEND
ABDEFGHINOOORRT	GOOD FOR THE BRAIN
ABDEFGIIIKLLNRY	FLYING LIKE A BIRD
ABDEFHHILNORSTW	THE BIRD HAS FLOWN
ABDEFHIINOORSTV	BREADTH OF VISION
ABDEFLMNOOOORST	BLOOD FROM A STONE
ABDEFLORRRSTTUU	DOUBTFUL STARTER
ABDEGGHNOOPRTUW	BROUGHT DOWN A PEG
ABDEGHHINNOORTV	BRIGHTON AND HOVE
ABDEGIIIILNSSST	DISESTABLISHING
ABDEGHIIILNSSTU	DISTINGUISHABLE
ABDEGHIILNOSTVY	DOING IT BY HALVES
ABDEGHILNORTUZZ	LEIGHTON BUZZARD
ABDEGHINOORTTTU	EDINBURGH TATTOO
ABDEGHLMNORSTUU	ROUGH-AND-TUMBLES
ABDEGHLNNOORTWW	DRAWN THE LONGBOW
ABDEGHLNNOORSTWW	DRAWS THE LONGBOW
ABDEGHOOPRTTTUU	BROUGHT UP TO DATE
ABDEGIILMNNOORT	DINING-ROOM TABLE
ABDEGIILNNOORTU	UNDER OBLIGATION
ABDEGIJMNNOSTTU	OBTAINS JUDGMENT
ABDEGILMNNORRUW	UNDERARM BOWLING
ABDEHLNNOOSSSTU	LOST ONE'S HUSBAND
ABDEHNOOORRRTVW	THROWN OVERBOARD
ABDEHOOOORRRSTVW	THROWS OVERBOARD
ABDEIIILMNOPRTY	IMPONDERABILITY
ABDEIIILPRSTTUY	DISREPUTABILITY
ABDEIILMNORSTTY	DEMONSTRABILITY
ABDEIILNNORSTUY	INSUBORDINATELY
ABDEIJLNOOOPPPSU	SLIPPED UP ON A JOB
ABDEIKLLLNORSUU	UNSKILLED LABOUR
ABDELMNNOORTTTU	LORD MOUNTBATTEN
ABDENOOOORRTTUUU	ROUNDABOUT ROUTE
ABDFGGIINNORRRW	BRINGING FORWARD
ABDFHLNNOOORSTW	SHOWN A BOLD FRONT
ABDFHLNOOOORSSTW	SHOWS A BOLD FRONT
ADDFLNNOOOOPRTTU	PUT ON A BOLD FRONT
ABDGHIIILNSSTUY	DISTINGUISHABLY
ABDGHLOOOOOSSTTU	TOUGH AS OLD BOOTS
ABDGIIIIMNNORTV	DRIVING AMBITION
ABDGINNOOOPRRUW	BORROWING A POUND
ABDHHIINORRSSTU	BRITISH HONDURAS
ABDHHIINOORRSTUY	BIRTHDAY HONOURS
ABDIIINNNOORSTU	INSUBORDINATION
ABEEEEEILNORSSV	BELIEVE ONE'S EARS
ABEEEEFGLNOOSTV	GET ABOVE ONESELF
ADEEEEFHINPRSTT	REAPS THE BENEFIT
ABEEEEEHILRRRTTW	TERRIBLE WEATHER
ABEEEELNNPRSSST	PRESENTABLENESS
ABEEEEFGHILNNOSV	BEHAVING ONESELF
ABEEEEFGHILNRRTY	BREATHING FREELY
ABEEEEFGLNOOOSTV	GOT ABOVE ONESELF
ABEEEFHHHLOSTTT	THE BEST OF HEALTH
ABEEEFHHIOSTTTV	HAVE THE BEST OF IT
ABEEEFHHLMORSTT	STAR OF BETHLEHEM
	STAR-OF-BETHLEHEM
ABEEEFHIKMOSTTT	MAKE THE BEST OF IT
ABEEEFHIILMRRTTW	TREMBLE WITH FEAR
ABEEEFHILRSTTUV	HAVE BUTTERFLIES
ABEEEFHLLNOOTTU	BEATEN HELL OUT OF
ABEEEFIIILMNOTT	FEEBLE IMITATION
ABEEEGGIKLNNORS	BREAKING ONE'S LEG
ABEEEGGINNORSST	GET ONE'S BEARINGS
ABEEEGGLNORSTVW	GROWN VEGETABLES
ABEEEGGLORSSTVW	GROWS VEGETABLES
ABEEEGHIILMNPTU	EATING HUMBLE PIE
ABEEEGHIKLNRRTU	BREAKING THE RULE
ABEEEGHIKNNRSTW	BREAKING THE NEWS
ABEEEGHILLMNRST	THE ELGIN MARBLES
ABEEEGHILNSTTTT	SETTING THE TABLE
ABEEEGHINNNORSTT	BARING ONE'S TEETH
ABEEEGHINORTVVY	ABOVE EVERYTHING
ABEEEGIKLNOOPRS	BOOKING A SLEEPER
ABEEEHHILORRRTW	HORRIBLE WEATHER
ABEEEHHILORRRTW	HORRIBLE WEATHER
ABEEEHHKLNOSTTT	SHAKEN THE BOTTLE
ABEEEHHKLOSSTTT	SHAKES THE BOTTLE
ABEEEHHOPRSTTTW	THE POWERS THAT BE
ABEEEHIILNRTTVV	IVAN THE TERRIBLE
ABEEEHIKLNRTTTY	TAKEN THE LIBERTY
ABEEEHIKLRSTTTY	TAKES THE LIBERTY
ABEEEHKLNORTTTU	TAKEN THE TROUBLE
ABEEEHKLOOTTTTT	TAKE TO THE BOTTLE
ABEEEHKLORSTTTU	TAKES THE TROUBLE
ABEEEHKNNOORRST	BROKEN ONE'S HEART
ABEEEHLLNNOOOTW	BEATEN ONE HOLLOW
ABEEEHLLOPSTTUY	UP TO THE EYEBALLS

1005

ABEEEEHLNNORSTTY	THE BLARNEY STONE
ABEEEHPRSSSTTTU	PASSES THE BUTTER
ABEEEIILLNOSTTV	TELEVISION TABLE
ABEEEIILMNNRRSS	MISERABLE SINNER
ABEEEIIMNNPRTYZ	BYZANTINE EMPIRE
ABEEEEILLNNORSST	INTOLERABLENESS
ABEEEELLMNOORSSS	LOSE ONE'S MARBLES
ABEEEENOOORRSSTT	BORES ONE TO TEARS
ABEEEENOOPRSSSUW	ABUSES ONE'S POWER
ABEEFFGGHHIOTTT	THE GIFT OF THE GAB
ABEEFFGHHORSTUV	GAVE THE BRUSH-OFF
ABEEFFGIILRTUUU	BEAUTIFUL FIGURE
ABEEFFHKLMOOOTT	TAKE THE BLOOM OFF
ABEEFFHNOOPRSTT	BORE THE PANTS OFF
ABEEFFHNORRTTUY	TENTH OF FEBRUARY
ABEEFGHHINOSTTV	HAVING THE BEST OF
ABEEFGHIKNOSSTT	KING OF THE BEASTS
ABEEFGHILNORRSU	HARBOUR FEELINGS
ABEEFGILNOORTTV	BOTTLE OF VINEGAR
ABEEFILORSTTTUY	STATUE OF LIBERTY
ABEEFIOOORSSTTTY	STATE OF SOBRIETY
ABEEFNOOORSSTWW	SWEAT OF ONES BROW
ABEEGGINNOORSST	GOT ONE'S BEARINGS
ABEEGHHMPSTTUUV	GAVE THE THUMBS UP
ABEEGHIIINORTTX	GREAT EXHIBITION
ABEEGHILLNOSTTT	LOSING THE BATTLE
ABEEGHINNOORSTX	BOXING ON THE EARS
ABEEGHINNOPSTTT	OPENS THE BATTING
ABEEGHINPRRRSTU	BRINGS UP THE REAR
ABEEGHLNOOPSTTT	BELONG TO THE PAST
ABEEGIIIKLNRSTT	TAKING LIBERTIES
ABEEGIIILMMNNSST	IMMITIGABLENESS
ABEEGILMNOPRSTT	SETTING A PROBLEM
ABEEGILMNRRRSTU	NUREMBERG TRIALS
ABEEGILNNOOSWWY	ELBOWING ONE'S WAY
ABEEGILNOORSTUY	OBEY REGULATIONS
ABEEGINNOPSTTTY	ANTE POST BETTING
ABEEGINNORRSTTU	RETURNING TO BASE
ABEEGLOOPRRSSYY	PLAYS GOOSEBERRY
ABEEHHINORRSSSU	BRUSHES ONE'S HAIR
ABEEHHLMOPRSTTW	WHATS THE PROBLEM?
ABEEHHMORRRSTTX	THE MARX BROTHERS
ABEEHIIILMNNSTV	THE INVISIBLE MAN
ABEEHIJJMNNORST	SIR JOHN BETJEMAN
ABEEHILMNORSSTW	BLAMEWORTHINESS
ABEEHLMNOPSSSSU	BLASPHEMOUSNESS
ABEEHMNNNOORRTT	TO THE MANNER BORN
ABEEHMNNOORTUVY	HAVE MONEY TO BURN
ABEEIIILMNPRTTY	IMPENETRABILITY
ABEEIILNNNOSSTT	BITTEN ONE'S NAILS
ABEEIILNNORSTUV	LABOUR-INTENSIVE
ABEEIIMNPRRSSTY	PRESBYTERIANISM
ABEEIKNPRRSSTUY	TAKEN BY SURPRISE
ABEEIKPRRSSSTUY	TAKES BY SURPRISE
ABEEILLMNOORRRY	LIONEL BARRYMORE
ABEEILLNNOPRTUV	VULNERABLE POINT
ABEEIMOPRRRSSTTV	REPORTS VERBATIM
ABEEELLMNOORSSST	LOST ONE'S MARBLES
ABEENORRSSTTTUY	BETRAY ONES TRUST
ABEFFFFHIORRTUY	FIFTH OF FEBRUARY
ABEFFFIORRRSTUY	FIRST OF FEBRUARY
ABEFFGHHIORRSTT	FIGHTS FOR BREATH
ABEFFGHHOORRTTU	FOUGHT FOR BREATH
ABEEFFGIILLNORTT	BATTLING FOR LIFE
ABEFFHINNORRTUY	NINTH OF FEBRUARY
ABEFFHIORRSTUXY	SIXTH OF FEBRUARY
ABEFFILLOORTTUX	FOOTBALL FIXTURE
ABEFGHHHIKNOTTT	KNIGHT OF THE BATH
ABEFGHLORRSTTUU	BURST OF LAUGHTER
ABEFGIINOORRRVW	BORROWING A FIVER
ABEFHIKMNNORSTU	THINKS OF A NUMBER

ABEFHLNOOORSTTU	HONOURS OF BATTLE
ABEFILMNORSSTTU	BURST INTO FLAMES
	BURSTS INTO FLAME
ABEFKLNOOORRSSU	BROOKS NO REFUSAL
ABEFLLLOORSSTTU	FOOTBALL RESULTS
ABEGGHHIKNORRTU	BREAKING THROUGH
ABEGGIILLNNNOPT	BEGINNING TO PALL
ABEGGIILNNOOTTT	GOING INTO BATTLE
ABEGHHILNOORRTU	RIGHT HONOURABLE
ABEGHHINOPRTUYY	PAYING BY THE HOUR
ABEGHIIINORSTTT	RISING TO THE BAIT
ABEGHIIKLLNRSTT	STRIKING THE BALL
ABEGHIIKNNNSSTU	BASKING IN THE SUN
ABEGHIIILLNOSTWW	BLOWING A WHISTLE
	WITH A SINGLE BLOW
ABEGHIILORTUUVY	GUILTY BEHAVIOUR
ABEGHILNNOORTUV	HAVING NO TROUBLE
ABEGHJNOOSTTUUU	JUST ABOUT ENOUGH
ABEGHNNOOOOPSSTU	HANG UP ONE'S BOOTS
ABEGHNORRSTUWWY	RUBS THE WRONG WAY
ABEGIIILNNNOSST	BITING ONE'S NAILS
ABEGIILNNSTTUUY	GUILTY BUT INSANE
ABEGIINNNOORSSU	USING ONE'S BRAINS
ABEGIKNNOPRRSSW	PAWNBROKERS SIGN
ABEGILLMNOOPRSV	SOLVING A PROBLEM
ABEGILLNOPPSTTU	STOPPING A BULLET
ABEGINNNOOSTTUW	SEWING ON A BUTTON
ABEHHHIORRSSTTY	BY THE SHORT HAIRS
ABEHIIIILMPRSTY	IMPERISHABILITY
ABEHIILMORSTTTY	THERMOSTABILITY
ABEHILLMNOPSSUY	HUMANLY POSSIBLE
ABEHILNOOPRSTTU	LABOURS THE POINT
ABEHKMNOOOSTTTT	SANK TO THE BOTTOM
ABEIIIILMNNRRTY	INTERMINABILITY
ABEIIILLMNORRTY	LIBERAL MINORITY
ABEIIILLNNRTUVY	INVULNERABILITY
ABEIILMMMNOSTUU	ABSOLUTE MINIMUM
ABEIKLLNOORTTUW	WALK INTO TROUBLE
ABEIKLMOOORRTTY	TIM BROOKE-TAYLOR
ABEIKNNOOORRTTT	BROKEN INTO A TROT
ABEILNNOORRSTVY	BORN INTO SLAVERY
ABEILNOOPSTTUVY	PATENTLY OBVIOUS
ABEIMNNRRSSSTTU	BRASS INSTRUMENT
ABEINOOOOPRSSTTV	OBSERVATION POST
ABEINORRSSSTTTU	BURSTS INTO TEARS
ABELOOPPRRRSTUU	LABOUR SUPPORTER
ABFGGINNOOORRTU	GOING FOR A BURTON
ABFGIIINNOOPRRST	BRINGS IN A PROFIT
ABFHILLLPPSSUYY	BLISSFULLY HAPPY
ABGGHILNNOOSTTY	NOT BY A LONG SIGHT
ABGHIIIKNNOTTTU	THINKING ABOUT IT
ABGHILNOOPRTTUY	BROUGHT INTO PLAY
ABGIIINNSSSTTUV	SUBSTANTIVISING
ABGIIINNSSTTUVZ	SUBSTANTIVIZING
ABGILMNOOPRSTUW	BLOWING UP A STORM
ABHHLMOOOPRRTUUY	PLYMOUTH HARBOUR
ABHIIOPPRRSSSTT	BRITISH PASSPORT
ABIINORSSTTTUUY	SUBSTITUTIONARY
ACCCCEEEEILNNORS	CLEAR CONSCIENCE
ACCCCEEFHNOSSSU	CHANCE OF SUCCESS
ACCCCEEGHIKNNOTU	CHECKING ACCOUNT
ACCCDDKLLNOOOUU	CLOUD-CUCKOO LAND
ACCCDEEGHIKNORT	CRACKING THE CODE
ACCCDEEHINORSVY	CHANCE DISCOVERY
ACCCDEEILNORRUY	DAILY OCCURRENCE
ACCCDEEINNOORTT	CONCERTED ACTION
ACCCDEFHHIKLORT	ALFRED HITCHCOCK
ACCCDEHHIIKNNSW	CHICKEN SANDWICH
ACCCDEHHIILLOOP	DOLICHOCEPHALIC
ACCCEEEEEFNNOPR	PEACE CONFERENCE
ACCCEEEEHLLNNTX	EXCELLENT CHANCE

ACCCEEEGHIINNST	TEACHING SCIENCE
ACCCEEEHHNNNORTU	CHANCE ENCOUNTER
ACCCEEFFGIINOPT	ACCEPTING OFFICE
ACCCEEGIILLLOOS	ECCLESIOLOGICAL
ACCCEEHIILNPSSY	PHYSICAL SCIENCE
ACCCEEHILLNORSV	VICE-CHANCELLORS
ACCCEEHILMOPRSS	CHEMICAL PROCESS
ACCCEEIIILMSSST	ECCLESIASTICISM
ACCCEEIILLNNNOS	IN ALL CONSCIENCE
ACCCEEIILMMNOOR	ECONOMIC MIRACLE
ACCCEGIIINNORTY	CARCINOGENICITY
ACCCEGIINNNORTT	ACTING IN CONCERT
ACCCEHMOOPRSTTU	COME UP TO SCRATCH
ACCCEIIILMMORST	COMMERCIALISTIC
ACCCEILMMOORRTU	COMMERCIAL COURT
ACCCEILOOPPRSST	SPECTROSCOPICAL
ACCCEIMNNOOOTTT	COME INTO CONTACT
ACCCGIIMNNNOOTT	COMING IN CONTACT
ACCCIILLMOOPRSY	MICROSCOPICALLY
ACCCIINNOORRTVY	CARRY CONVICTION
ACCDDEEEEEHKLRST	CLEARED THE DECKS
ACCDDEEEEFGINNOT	CONCEDING DEFEAT
ACCDDEEEEHHILLNT	CLINCHED THE DEAL
ACCDDEEEENNORRTU	ACCOUNT RENDERED
ACCDDEEHIIIKLLR	CRIED LIKE A CHILD
ACCDDEEHLLOORTT	CALLED THE DOCTOR
ACCDDEEIILNRRTY	RIDDEN A TRICYCLE
ACCDDEEINNNOSTU	DISCOUNTENANCED
ACCDDEENORRSSTT	STANDS CORRECTED
ACCDDEGIINORRST	CREATING DISCORD
ACCDDEIMMNNNNOOS	SECOND IN COMMAND
	SECOND-IN-COMMAND
ACCDDEINNOSSTTV	STANDS CONVICTED
ACCDEEEEEFFHLNRT	CLEARED THE FENCE
ACCDEEEEEHQRRRU	CHEQUERED CAREER
ACCDEEEEEKNNPRT	TAKEN PRECEDENCE
ACCDEEEEEKNPRST	TAKES PRECEDENCE
ACCDEEEEHHINSTZ	SEIZED THE CHANCE
ACCDEEEEHIKLNPS	CHEESE AND PICKLE
ACCDEEEEHLNOQSU	ENCLOSED A CHEQUE
ACCDEEEEINOPSTT	ESCAPE DETECTION
ACCDEEEFFMOORSS	FREEDOM OF ACCESS
ACCDEEEGHIKLNRT	CLEARING THE DECK
ACCDEEEHHILLNST	CLINCHES THE DEAL
ACCDEEEHHILRRTT	CIRCLED THE EARTH
ACCDEEEHILLLOPT	CALLED THE POLICE
ACCDEEEHNOORSST	CROSSED THE OCEAN
ACCDEEEIINPRRSS	INCREASED PRICES
ACCDEEEMORSSSTU	MODERATE SUCCESS
ACCDEEFFINNOORR	ORDNANCE OFFICER
ACCDEEFGIINNNOS	GAINS CONFIDENCE
ACCDEEFILNNOOTT	FAILED TO CONNECT
ACCDEEFINOOPRTV	ACT OF PROVIDENCE
ACCDEEGHIINNORT	CHANGE DIRECTION
ACCDEEGHKLNNOSU	CHANGED ONE'S LUCK
ACCDEEHIIIKLLRS	CRIES LIKE A CHILD
ACCDEEHIIORTVVY	ACHIEVED VICTORY
ACCDEEHILMNORTW	CLAIMED THE CROWN
ACCDEEHNORSTTTU	TRUSTED TO CHANCE
ACCDEEIIILNRUVZ	UNCIVILIZED RACE
ACCDEEIIMMMORTT	COMMITTED A CRIME
ACCDEEIIMNOOOST	COME TO A DECISION
ACCDEEIINORSSTU	SERIOUS ACCIDENT
ACCDEEIKNOPRSTY	SECONDARY PICKET
ACCDEEIKPRSSTTU	SUSPECTED A TRICK
ACCDEEILLMNORSY	ELECTRODYNAMICS
ACCDEEIMNOORRST	MADE CORRECTIONS
ACCDEEINNNOSSTU	DISCOUNTENANCES
ACCDEEIORRSTUVY	SECURED A VICTORY
ACCDEELLMOORRRS	ALL-COMERS RECORD
ACCDEELLMOPSSTT	COLLECTED STAMPS

ACCDEELLNOORRSS	CLOSER AND CLOSER
ACCDEELLNORSSTU	COULDN'T CARE LESS
ACCDEELNOSSTTTU	SETTLED ACCOUNTS
ACCDEEMMNOPRSST	COMMANDS RESPECT
ACCDEFGHHLNNORU	CHURCH OF ENGLAND
ACCDEFHIINNORTT	FRENCH DICTATION
ACCDEFINNOOSSUU	CAUSED CONFUSION
ACCDEFLNOORSSTU	CURSE OF SCOTLAND
ACCDEGHHINNRTTU	ATTENDING CHURCH
ACCDEGHINRSTTTU	CUTTING THE CARDS
ACCDEGIIILNRRTY	RIDING A TRICYCLE
ACCDEGIIMMMNNOOV	COMMANDING VOICE
ACCDEGIINNNOOPT	CONCEDING A POINT
ACCDEGILNNOOPRR	PLACING ON RECORD
ACCDEHIKKLNNSUW	KNUCKLE SANDWICH
ACCDEHILNORSTUW	WITCHES CAULDRON
ACCDEHLNOOOORSSY	SECONDARY SCHOOL
ACCDEIIILLMNRSY	SEMICYLINDRICAL
ACCDEIIILMNNSTU	INCIDENTAL MUSIC
ACCDEIILMMORRSTU	MUSICAL DIRECTOR
ACCDEIINOPRSSSU	RAPID SUCCESSION
ACCDEIKLMOPSSTY	SLAPSTICK COMEDY
ACCDEILLNOOTTYY	ENDOCYTOTICALLY
ACCDEILMMORSTUY	COMMERCIAL STUDY
ACCDEILNNOORSUW	DREW A CONCLUSION
ACCDEIMNOOPRRTY	COMPANY DIRECTOR
ACCDEIOPPRRSTTU	PICTURE POSTCARD
	PICTURE-POSTCARD
ACCDELLLLMMMOOW	MALCOLM MCDOWELL
ACCDELNOOPSSSST	SECOND CLASS POST
ACCDENNOORTTTUU	TURNED TO ACCOUNT
ACCDFFLMMOOOORRT	COLD COMFORT FARM
ACCDFGHILNNOOOS	SCHOOL OF DANCING
ACCDFIMNNOOSTUU	INFAMOUS CONDUCT
ACCDIILNOORRTTY	CONTRADICTORILY
ACCCEECFHHLMMRZ	CHERCHEZ LA FEMME
ACCEEEEFHIKOPST	PIECES OF THE CAKE
ACCEEEEGHIRSSVX	EXCESSIVE CHARGE
ACCEEEEHHINSSTZ	SEIZES THE CHANCE
ACCEEEEHLNOQSSU	ENCLOSES A CHEQUE
ACCEEEEHMNNNOVY	EVEN MONEY CHANCE
ACCEEEEHMORSTTU	CAME TO THE RESCUE
ACCEEEEFFGHORRUY	GEOFFREY CHAUCER
ACCEEEEFGHNNORSY	CHANGE OF SCENERY
ACCEEEFHIKLOSST	SLICES OF THE CAKE
ACCEEEFILLNORRT	CLEAR REFLECTION
ACCEEEFIMNORSST	MASTER OF SCIENCE
ACCEEEFINNPRSTU	PERFECT NUISANCE
ACCEEEFNNOPRRTY	PARTY CONFERENCE
ACCEEEGHIIKLLLN	CLING LIKE A LEECH
ACCEEEGHIKLLLNU	CLUNG LIKE A LEECH
ACCEEEGHINNOSTY	CATCHING ONE'S EYE
ACCEEEGILLNOQSU	LOGICAL SEQUENCE
ACCEEEGILMNORTT	ELECTROMAGNETIC
ACCEEEGINNNOTUV	GIVE COUNTENANCE
ACCEEEHHILRRSTT	CIRCLES THE EARTH
ACCEEEHHIMRRSST	RESEARCH CHEMIST
ACCEEEHIIKKLLST	STICK LIKE A LEECH
ACCEEEHIKKLLSTU	STUCK LIKE A LEECH
ACCEEEHIKNNOOST	TAKEN ONE'S CHOICE
ACCEEEHIKNOOSST	TAKES ONE'S CHOICE
ACCEEEHNOORSSST	CROSSES THE OCEAN
ACCEEEIINORSTVV	ON ACTIVE SERVICE
ACCEEEIINPRRSSS	INCREASES PRICES
ACCEEEILNNNOPTV	CONVENIENT PLACE
ACCEEEILORRSTTT	ELECTRIC TOASTER
ACCEEEIMORRSTTT	CORRECT ESTIMATE
ACCEEELNNNOOSTU	LOSE COUNTENANCE
ACCEEEMOOPRRSSU	EPSOM RACECOURSE
ACCEEFFGHIINORR	OFFICER IN CHARGE
ACCEEFFIILMNNOR	CRIMINAL OFFENCE

ACCEEFFIILORSST	OFFICIAL SECRETS
ACCEEFFIINNORSU	INSURANCE OFFICE
ACCEEFFIINOSSSU	EFFICACIOUSNESS
ACCEEFFIMMNNOOT	COMMIT AN OFFENCE
ACCEEFGHHLNOOST	CHANGE OF CLOTHES
ACCEEFGHMNOOSTU	CHANGE OF COSTUME
ACCEEFHINOOOPSW	CHOICE OF WEAPONS
ACCEEFIIILNORTT	ELECTRIFICATION
ACCEEFIILMNRRTU	CIRCUMFERENTIAL
ACCEEFIINOOSSTV	FESTIVE OCCASION
ACCEEFIJLOSSSTU	SCALES OF JUSTICE
ACCEEFIKLNNOSTY	TICKLE ONES FANCY
ACCEEFJKLOOPRSY	JOCKEY FOR PLACES
ACCEEFMOORRRTTU	CREATURE COMFORT
ACCEEGHHHIINOTV	HAVING THE CHOICE
ACCEEGHHIIMNNOT	COG IN THE MACHINE
ACCEEGHIILNNOOV	LEAVING NO CHOICE
ACCEEGHKLNNOSSU	CHANGES ONE'S LUCK
ACCEEGHLNNOORTX	EXCHANGE CONTROL
ACCEEGHNNNOOSTU	COUNT ONES CHANGE
ACCEEGIILLMNNRT	CRIMINAL NEGLECT
ACCEEGIIMOPRSUV	AMERIGO VESPUCCI
ACCEEGILLNOSTTX	COLLECTING TAXES
ACCEEGILMNOPSTV	MOVING SPECTACLE
ACCEEGINOOPRTTU	CIGARETTE COUPON
ACCEEHHHNOOPSTT	CATCHES ON THE HOP
ACCEEHHIMOORRTT	HETEROCHROMATIC
ACCEEHHLNNORSST	CROSS THE CHANNEL
ACCEEHIILLLNOPT	CALL IN THE POLICE
ACCEEHIILLOPPST	POLITICAL SPEECH
ACCEEHIILMNPRSS	PRINCESS MICHAEL
ACCEEHIIORSTVVY	ACHIEVES VICTORY
ACCEEHILOORRSTT	ATHEROSCLEROTIC
ACCEEHINNNORSSU	RUIN ONES CHANCES
ACCEEHKNNOOOSST	TOOK ONE'S CHANCES
ACCEEHLMNORRSTY	CHERRYSTONE CLAM
ACCEEIILLRRRSTY	LITERARY CIRCLES
ACCEEIIMMNOTUVX	EXCOMMUNICATIVE
ACCEEIINNOORSSS	CONCESSIONAIRES
ACCEEIKMNOORRST	MAKE CORRECTIONS
ACCEEIKNRRSTTUU	NUTCRACKER SUITE
ACCEEILLLNOOPTT	COLLECTION PLATE
ACCEEILLMNOORTY	ECONOMETRICALLY
ACCEEINORRSSSST	CROSS-RESISTANCE
ACCEEIORRSSTUVY	SECURES A VICTORY
ACCEEKNOORRSSTV	COVER ONES TRACKS
ACCEELMMNNOOPSS	COMMONPLACENESS
ACCEELNNNOOSSTU	LOST COUNTENANCE
ACCEELNOSSSTTTU	SETTLES ACCOUNTS
ACCEENNOPSSSTUU	SUSPENSE ACCOUNT
ACCEFFGIIILNRSS	SELF-SACRIFICING
ACCEFFIIILLOOPT	POLITICAL OFFICE
ACCEFGIIIPRSTVY	SPECIFIC GRAVITY
ACCEFHHMMNOSSUU	MUCH OF A MUCHNESS
ACCEFHIIKLLNRST	FILL IN THE CRACKS
ACCEFHIINOOSSTT	FITS THE OCCASION
ACCEFHIKOSSTTTT	STICK TO THE FACTS
ACCEFHIOOPRRSTT	SHORT OF PRACTICE
ACCEFHKOSSTTTTU	STUCK TO THE FACTS
ACCEFIIKLMNOTUY	IF YOU CAN'T LICK 'EM
ACCEFILLNOOTTTU	OF LITTLE ACCOUNT
ACCEFINNOOSSSUU	CAUSES CONFUSION
ACCEFLMNOOPRRTT	CONCERT PLATFORM
ACCEFLMNOSSSUUW	SUCCESSFUL WOMAN
ACCEGGGIIKNNRTT	GETTING CRACKING
ACCEGGHHIKLNNOT	CHANGING THE LOCK
ACCEGGHINNNORTU	COUNTERCHANGING
ACCEGHHIIKNPRTW	CRACKING THE WHIP
ACCEGHHINNOPSTT	CATCHING THE POST
ACCEGHILLLNOOTY	TECHNOLOGICALLY
ACCEGHILLNOSTWY	WATCHING CLOSELY
ACCEGHILNNNORSS	CHANNEL CROSSING
ACCEGHILNSTTTUW	CUTTING THE CLAWS
ACCEGHINNOOPSTU	TOUCHING ONE'S CAP
ACCEGIIILMMNORS	COMMERCIALISING
ACCEGIIILMMNORZ	COMMERCIALIZING
ACCEGIILLNNOORU	REGIONAL COUNCIL
ACCEGIILNNOPRSS	PELICAN CROSSING
ACCEGIILNNOPSTU	CONCEPTUALISING
ACCEGIILNNOPTUZ	CONCEPTUALIZING
ACCEGIIMMNNOTUX	EXCOMMUNICATING
ACCEGIIMNOPPRRS	COMPARING PRICES
ACCEGIKLLLNORTV	TRAVELLING CLOCK
ACCEGILLMNOPSTT	STAMP COLLECTING
ACCEGINNOOSTTTU	CUTTING ONE'S COAT
ACCEGINNORRSTUY	SCORING A CENTURY
ACCEGKLOPPRSUUU	PLUCKS UP COURAGE
ACCEHHIINNOPSSS	CASH IN ONES CHIPS
ACCEHHILLMNOOPR	CHLORAMPHENICOL
ACCEHHILLMOOPTY	PHOTOCHEMICALLY
ACCEHIIILLNOSTV	CIVILIAN CLOTHES
ACCEHIILMORTTVY	CLAIM THE VICTORY
ACCEHIIMNNOOSUU	UNANIMOUS CHOICE
ACCEHIINOOSSTTU	SUIT THE OCCASION
ACCEHIKLMMNNOTU	COMMUNAL KITCHEN
ACCEHILLPRSTUUY	PHYSICAL CULTURE
ACCEHILMMNOPSST	ACCOMPLISHMENTS
ACCEHINNOOPRRTT	ANTHROPOCENTRIC
ACCEHLLMNOOSTUY	COLLENCHYMATOUS
ACCEIIIKLNOPRTV	CRICKET PAVILION
ACCEIIKKNOSTTWY	ON A STICKY WICKET
ACCEIIKNOPSSTTU	STICKS UP A NOTICE
ACCEIILMMNOTUVY	COMMUNICATIVELY
ACCEIILNNOPRSUY	INSURANCE POLICY
ACCEIILNOQRSTUU	CRUCIAL QUESTION
ACCEIILOPPRSSUY	PERSPICACIOUSLY
ACCEIIMMNNOOTUX	EXCOMMUNICATION
ACCEIIMMNNOTUUV	UNCOMMUNICATIVE
ACCEIINOPPRTTTU	PUT INTO PRACTICE
ACCEIKKLMOOORTT	CLOAK-ROOM TICKET
ACCEIKLLNOOOOTT	TOOK A COLLECTION
ACCEILLMNOOPSTT	STAMP COLLECTION
ACCEILMNNOOOPSS	CLOSE COMPANIONS
ACCEILMOOPRRSTU	ULTRAMICROSCOPE
ACCEIMMNOORTUXY	EXCOMMUNICATORY
ACCEINNORRTTTTW	WRITTEN CONTRACT
ACCEMORRRSSTTUU	MACROSTRUCTURES
ACCFFIIINORSTTU	FRUCTIFICATIONS
ACCFFIILMOOSSTU	CUSTOMS OFFICIAL
ACCFGGHHIINOSTT	CATCHING SIGHT OF
ACCFIIILLNNOSTTU	FUNCTIONALISTIC
ACCGGHHIMNOORTU	CHARGING TOO MUCH
ACCGHILLLNOOORY	CHRONOLOGICALLY
ACCGHILLLOOPSYY	PSYCHOLOGICALLY
ACCGHILLOOPRSYY	HYGROSCOPICALLY
ACCGHKNOORTTTUU	TOUGH NUT TO CRACK
ACCGIILLLOOOTXY	TOXICOLOGICALLY
ACCGINOORTTTUUY	CUTTING YOUR COAT
ACCHHILMOOOPPST	OPHTHALMOSCOPIC
ACCIIIILNNOOPRT	CRITICAL OPINION
ACCIILLNOOPTTYY	PINOCYTOTICALLY
ACCIINOOOPRRTTY	CITY CORPORATION
ACCIJLLNNNOOTUY	CONJUNCTIONALLY
ACCIKLLMOOOOTTV	MOLOTOV COCKTAIL
ACCIKNNOOOOTTTU	TOOK INTO ACCOUNT
ACCILLLOORSTUUY	SOCIOCULTURALLY
ACCILMMMNNOOOPT	COMMON COMPLAINT
ACCILMORRRSTTUU	MICROSTRUCTURAL
ACCINOOOORRSSTTV	VASOCONSTRICTOR
ACDDDDEEILNPRUU	CURLED UP AND DIED
ACDDDEEEEINNNPY	INDEPENDENCE DAY
ACDDDEEEHIMNTTU	EDUCATED THE MIND

ACDDDEEEHNORSTW	EDWARD THE SECOND
ACDDDEEEIJMNSTU	DEMANDED JUSTICE
ACDDDEEELNOPRRS	LAND SPEED RECORD
ACDDDEEFIINORUV	DECIDED IN FAVOUR
ACDDDEEHILNSSWY	WEDNESDAYS CHILD
ACDDEEEEGHHINRT	DENIED THE CHARGE
ACDDEEEEHINNOSV	ACHIEVED ONE'S END
ACDDEEEEELNPRRSU	SUPERCALENDERED
ACDDEEEFHORSTTY	DEFRAYED THE COST
ACDDEEEFLMOPRRY	PLEADED FOR MERCY
ACDDEEEGHHNORRT	CHANGED THE ORDER
ACDDEEEGIIMNNNV	DAMNING EVIDENCE
ACDDEEEHILMSSTU	DUTCH ELM DISEASE
ACDDEEEHIMNSTTU	EDUCATES THE MIND
ACDDEEEHOPQSTTU	POST-DATED CHEQUE
ACDDEEEIIIINNTUV	INVITED AUDIENCE
ACDDEEEIILLNNUV	DECLINED IN VALUE
ACDDEEEILNNNOPT	PLEADED INNOCENT
ACDDEEEEILNORSST	ELECTION ADDRESS
ACDDEEELNNNOOTT	NEEDLE AND COTTON
ACDDEEEMNNPRTUU	MENDED A PUNCTURE
ACDDEEFHIILNNRW	WIFE AND CHILDREN
ACDDEEFHIINNRSS	DISENFRANCHISED
ACDDEEFHISSTTTU	STUDIED THE FACTS
ACDDEEFIINORSUV	DECIDES IN FAVOUR
ACDDEEGHIMNNNOS	CHANGED ONE'S MIND
ACDDEEGHLRRTUUX	DRAUGHT EXCLUDER
ACDDEEGIILMNRSS	DECLARED MISSING
ACDDEEGIILNNNRS	INNINGS DECLARED
ACDDEEGILNNNOPT	PLACING END TO END
ACDDEEGLNORRSUU	UNDER CLOSE GUARD
ACDDEEHHILNOSTU	HEAD IN THE CLOUDS
ACDDEEHHNORRSTW	SHOWN THE RED CARD
ACDDEEHHORRSSTW	SHOWS THE RED CARD
ACDDEEHIINNOOPT	DETACHED OPINION
ACDDEEHMNNOOSTT	CONDEMNS TO DEATH
ACDDEEHNNOPPSSU	CUPPED ONE'S HANDS
ACDDEEHNOORSSSW	SHOWED ONE'S CARDS
ACDDEEIILNORSST	DID ONE'S ARTICLES
ACDDEEIKKNOSSWY	KNOCKED SIDEWAYS
ACDDEEILNOPPRSS	DISPLACED PERSON
ACDDEEINNOPSSTU	PASSED UNNOTICED
ACDDEEIORRSSTTU	COURTED DISASTER
ACDDEEKKLNNORUY	UNDER LOCK AND KEY
ACDDEEMNNOORRSY	SECONDARY MODERN
ACDDEEOPPRRSTUY	DROPPED A CURTSEY
ACDDEFIILOOQRTU	QUALIFIED DOCTOR
ACDDEFLMOOORSSW	SWORD OF DAMOCLES
ACDDEGHHIIINTTW	DICING WITH DEATH
ACDDEGHINNNNOOT	DANCED ON NOTHING
ACDDEGHINNORRSU	SCORING A HUNDRED
ACDDEHHHIIRRRTT	RICHARD THE THIRD
ACDDEHIIKKNPSUY	KICKED UP A SHINDY
ACDDEHIKNNOSSTT	STANDS IN THE DOCK
ACDDEHIMOORRSST	STOMACH DISORDER
ACDDEIIKMPRUXYZ	CRAZY MIXED-UP KID
ACDDEIILMNNOSTU	MIDLAND COUNTIES
ACDDFGHILLNOOTW	COLD LIGHT OF DAWN
ACDDGGHILNNOOOT	GOING HOT AND COLD
ACDDHIIMNORSTYY	HYDRODYNAMICIST
ACDDIIIIILNSTUV	INDIVIDUALISTIC
ACDDIILMNNOOOOT	CONDITIONAL MOOD
ACDDLLMMNNOOORSS	LORDS AND COMMONS
ACDEEEEEGGHLRRT	THREE-LEGGED RACE
ACDEEEEEGIMRSSV	MESSAGE RECEIVED
ACDEEEEEILRRTTV	RECEIVED A LETTER
ACDEEEEENNRSSTV	SERVED A SENTENCE
ACDEEEEFFJNORRT	REJECTED AN OFFER
ACDEEEEFGHINNRS	DEAFENING CHEERS
ACDEEEEFILMNTTV	MENTAL DEFECTIVE
ACDEEEEFINNNRRW	DREW AN INFERENCE
ACDEEEEGHHINRST	DENIES THE CHARGE
ACDEEEEHHHLOPRT	HELPED EACH OTHER
ACDEEEEHIKORTVY	RECEIVED THE OKAY
ACDEEEEHILPRSSV	DELIVERS A SPEECH
ACDEEEEHIMNNNST	DENNIS THE MENACE
ACDEEEEHINNOSSV	ACHIEVES ONE'S END
ACDEEEEHLPRSTTW	RESPECTED THE LAW
ACDEEEEHNNOSTTT	SENTENCE TO DEATH
ACDEEEEILNNORTT	ENTENTE CORDIALE
ACDEEEEINRRRSSV	RENDERS A SERVICE
ACDEEEEELLNOORSV	DECLARE ONES LOVE
ACDEEEFFFOPRSTU	PAUSED FOR EFFECT
ACDEEEFFHIINRTW	WITH A DIFFERENCE
ACDEEEEFGHINOORS	EDGE OF ONE'S CHAIR
ACDEFFFGILNPRST	SELF-DEPRECATING
ACDEEEFHHIINRST	FINISHED THE RACE
ACDEEEFHHNOPRTT	END OF THE CHAPTER
ACDEEEFHIKLNOOT	LOOKED IN THE FACE
ACDEEEFHIKLNRTU	FACE LIKE THUNDER
ACDEEEFHILLNORS	HALL OF RESIDENCE
ACDEEEFHLOPRTTU	FOULED THE CARPET
ACDEEEFHMMNNOSTT	THE DESCENT OF MAN
ACDEEEFHNNRRSTUU	UNDER THE SURFACE
ACDEEEFHRSSSTTT	STRESSED THE FACT
ACDEEEFIIILNRTT	DEFINITE ARTICLE
ACDEEEFILOORSTY	LEADER OF SOCIETY
ACDEEEHNNOORSTTU	TEST OF ENDURANCE
ACDEFFFOPPRRSSS	PRESSED FOR SPACE
ACDEEEEGHHLNRSTU	CHANGED THE RULES
ACDEEEGHHNORRST	CHANGES THE ORDER
ACDEEEGHILORRTT	CIGARETTE HOLDER
ACDEEEGHINNOSTT	GONE THE DISTANCE
ACDEEEGHINOSSTT	GOES THE DISTANCE
ACDEEEGHMNNNOSTU	CHANGED ONE'S TUNE
ACDEEEGHOPRRSTT	SCRAPED TOGETHER
ACDEEEGIINNPRSS	INCREASING SPEED
ACDEEEGIIPPRTTT	TIPPED CIGARETTE
ACDEEEGIKLNNPSS	SLACKENING SPEED
ACDEEEGILMNNRSU	MASCULINE GENDER
ACDEEEGILNORRRT	DIRECTOR GENERAL
ACDEEEGKLMNNOTW	ACKNOWLEDGEMENT
ACDEEEGLLNORRVV	GROVER CLEVELAND
ACDEEEGNNORRTUV	UNDER-COVER AGENT
	UNDERCOVER AGENT
ACDEEEHHHORTTTU	TOUCHED THE HEART
ACDEEEHHILNRSTV	SAVE THE CHILDREN
ACDEEEHHLLTTTWY	WATCHED THE TELLY
ACDEEEHHNNORSTT	ASCEND THE THRONE
ACDEEEHIILMNRRT	MARLENE DIETRICH
ACDEEEHIINPRRSX	SHARE PRICE INDEX
ACDEEEHILLSSTTT	TILTED THE SCALES
ACDEEEHILPPSSTT	TIPPED THE SCALES
ACDEEEHIMNORRSV	DEVONSHIRE CREAM
ACDEEEHIMNOSTTW	WATCHED ONE'S TIME
ACDEEEHIMOPSSST	SMASHED TO PIECES
ACDEEEHINNOOPRS	PRICE ON ONES HEAD
ACDEEEHINNSTTTW	WENT THE DISTANCE
ACDEEEHINORSTTY	SINCE THE YEAR DOT
ACDEEEHKLOORRTW	WORKED THE ORACLE
ACDEEEHLNRSSTTU	TURNED THE SCALES
ACDEEEHNOOPSSSW	SHOWED ONE'S PACES
ACDEEEHNOPSSTTW	WATCHED ONE'S STEP
ACDEEEHORSSTTUY	STAYED THE COURSE
ACDEEEIILLNNSUV	DECLINES IN VALUE
ACDEEEIILLPRSVY	SPECIAL DELIVERY
ACDEEEIILNNNORS	INCLINED ONE'S EAR
ACDEEEIILNNRSST	STRAINED SILENCE
ACDEEEIIMNPRSSV	MANIC DEPRESSIVE
	MANIC-DEPRESSIVE
ACDEEEIINOORSSV	RAISED ONE'S VOICE
ACDEEEIKNOPRSTZ	TAKE SECOND PRIZE

ACDEEEILLRSSSSU	LEISURED CLASSES
ACDEEEILNNSTTUW	NEWCASTLE UNITED
ACDEEEINNORSSST	CONSIDERATENESS
ACDEEEINOPPRRSS	ESCAPED PRISONER
ACDEEEINPRRRSTT	PRESIDENT CARTER
ACDEEEKLNOOPTTX	LOOKED EXPECTANT
ACDEEELMNNOPSTY	ENCLOSED PAYMENT
ACDEEEMNNOPRRRT	PERMANENT RECORD
ACDEEFFFHIOORTY	OFFICER OF THE DAY
ACDEEFFHHKLPSTU	SHUFFLED THE PACK
ACDEEFFHHLRSSTU	SHUFFLE THE CARDS
ACDEEFFMNOOORT	FREEDOM OF ACTION
ACDEEFGILLLRUYY	YIELD GRACEFULLY
ACDEEFGILNRSSSU	DISGRACEFULNESS
ACDEEFGKKLLNOOW	LACK OF KNOWLEDGE
ACDEEFHHHLOOOST	HEAD OF THE SCHOOL
ACDEEFHHILLRSST	FATHERLESS CHILD
ACDEEFHIINNRSSS	DISENFRANCHISES
ACDEEFHIKORRTTT	TRICK OF THE TRADE
ACDEEFHIPSSTTTU	DISPUTE THE FACTS
ACDEEFHISSSTTTU	STUDIES THE FACTS
ACDEEFHLOORRSTW	CARES OF THE WORLD
ACDEEFIKMNNOPRR	PRINCE OF DENMARK
ACDEEFIKMOPRRRT	PERFORMED A TRICK
ACDEEFILLNNOSTY	SELF-CONTAINEDLY
ACDEEFILLNRRUVY	DRIVEN CAREFULLY
ACDEEFILLRRSUVY	DRIVES CAREFULLY
ACDEEFILNORRRTU	FUNERAL DIRECTOR
ACDEEFINOORSTUV	SECOND FAVOURITE
ACDEEFMOOORRRSY	A COMEDY OF ERRORS
ACDEEGGIILNORRT	CORDIAL GREETING
ACDEEGGIINORTTV	GETTING A DIVORCE
ACDEEGHHIINORTU	HIGHER EDUCATION
ACDEEGHIIILLMTT	LEGITIMATE CHILD
ACDEEGHIIKNRTTT	TAKING THE CREDIT
ACDEEGHIINSSTVX	EXCHANGED VISITS
ACDEEGHIMNNNOSS	CHANGES ONE'S MIND
ACDEEGHINOPPRST	DROPPING THE CASE
ACDEEGHINORSSTU	REDUCING TO ASHES
ACDEEGHIORRSSTW	EIGHT SCORE-DRAWS
ACDEEGHLNORRSTU	CLEARS THE GROUND
ACDEEGHMPPRRTUU	TRUMPED-UP CHARGE
ACDEEGHNOSSTTUU	AUGUST THE SECOND
ACDEEGIIILLMOOP	EPIDEMIOLOGICAL
ACDEEGIIKKLMORW	WORKED LIKE MAGIC
ACDEEGIILNRRSSV	CARELESS DRIVING
ACDEEGIINORSSTT	STAGE DIRECTIONS
ACDEEGIKNNNOPSS	SENDS ONE PACKING
ACDEEGILLOORRTY	COLERIDGE TAYLOR
ACDEEGILNNOORRT	REGAINED CONTROL
ACDEEGIMNNORSSTU	DISCOURAGEMENTS
ACDEEGINORRSTTU	REDUCING TO TEARS
ACDEEGKLMNNOSTW	ACKNOWLEDGMENTS
ACDEEGLLLNOOORV	GONE COLD ALL OVER
ACDEEGLLLOOORSV	GOES COLD ALL OVER
ACDEEGNNOORRRSU	DANGEROUS CORNER
ACDEEGNNOPPRSUY	PSEUDOPREGNANCY
ACDEEHHHILRRSTT	CHARLES THE THIRD
ACDEEHHIKPPRRTU	PICK UP THE THREAD
ACDEEHHINOPRRST	CHRISTOPHER DEAN
ACDEEHHLNOORSTT	DO THE CHARLESTON
ACDEEHHNOORTTUW	TOUCHED ON THE RAW
ACDEEHIIKLNOPST	LICKED INTO SHAPE
ACDEEHIKNORSSUW	SHAKEDOWN CRUISE
ACDEEHILLNNOOST	HOLDS AN ELECTION
ACDEEHILNNOSTWW	CLEAN THE WINDOWS
ACDEEHIMNOORSTU	ECHINODERMATOUS
ACDEEHINOPRSTTT	STRETCHED A POINT
ACDEEHINRRSTTUW	DREW THE CURTAINS
ACDEEHIOOPPPSTT	CHIPPED POTATOES
ACDEEHMNOOOORTTW	COME DOWN TO EARTH
ACDEEHHNNOORRRTU	AROUND THE CORNER
ACDEEHNOOPRSSST	CROSSED ONE'S PATH
ACDEEIIJLNPRSSU	PREJUDICIALNESS
ACDEEIILMNNNORS	CLEAR IN ONES MIND
ACDEEIILNNORSTY	INCONSIDERATELY
ACDEEIIMNNOPRSS	MANIC DEPRESSION
ACDEEIIMNORSSSU	SECURE ADMISSION
ACDEEIINNOORRST	RECONSIDERATION
ACDEEIKLMNOPSSS	SMACKED ONE'S LIPS
ACDEEILLNOSSTTW	CALLED TO WITNESS
ACDEEILLNPPRRUY	PERPENDICULARLY
ACDEEIMMNNORSTUY	SEMIDOCUMENTARY
ACDEEIMNNORSSTTV	DOMESTIC SERVANT
ACDEEINNOPSSSTU	PASSES UNNOTICED
ACDEEINRRRSTTUV	RETURNS A VERDICT
ACDEEJKLNOORSVY	DAVY JONES LOCKER
ACDEEJLLNRRRTUY	RED-CURRANT JELLY
ACDEELLLNOORTVW	WENT COLD ALL OVER
ACDEELMNOOPRRRU	NORMAL PROCEDURE
ACDEELMNOOPRSSS	CROSSED ONE'S PALM
ACDEELNOORSTTUY	DESOLATE COUNTRY
ACDEEMMMNNNOSTT	TEN COMMANDMENTS
ACDEEMMNNOOPPRY	POMP AND CEREMONY
ACDEEMNNOORSTY	STAND ON CEREMONY
ACDEENNNOQRTUUY	QUEEN AND COUNTRY
ACDEENOORRRSSTV	DONCASTER ROVERS
ACDEENOORRRSSVW	NEVER A CROSS WORD
ACDEFFGHLOOOSTT	GO TO THE SCAFFOLD
ACDEFFHIINOPRST	ACT OF FRIENDSHIP
ACDEFFIIILOTTVY	FIELD OF ACTIVITY
ACDEFFIILMRTTTU	DIFFICULT MATTER
ACDEFGHIINOOSTZ	SIGN OF THE ZODIAC
ACDEFGHINNNOORS	FORCING ONE'S HAND
ACDEFGIIKNORRST	ASKING FOR CREDIT
ACDEFGIILLNOOVW	FOLLOWING ADVICE
ACDEFGIIMNNPORS	COMPARE FINDINGS
ACDEFGILORSTTTZ	SCOTT FITZGERALD
ACDEFHHIIRRRSTT	RICHARD THE FIRST
ACDEFHIORSSTTTT	DISTORT THE FACTS
ACDEFIIIMNNNNOT	INDEMNIFICATION
ACDEFIIIINNORTT	DENITRIFICATION
ACDEFIIIINNOSTT	IDENTIFICATIONS
ACDEFIIIINORSTV	DIVERSIFICATION
ACDEFIIILNNOTTY	CONFIDENTIALITY
ACDEFIIIMNOSTTY	DEMYSTIFICATION
ACDEFIIKMNOSTTY	STICK OF DYNAMITE
ACDEFIILMMNORTUY	DOCUMENTARY FILM
ACDEFLMNNOOOPUY	COMPOUND A FELONY
ACDEGGHILNORSTU	GATHERING CLOUDS
ACDEGGHINNORRUY	GREYHOUND RACING
ACDEGHHILMNOSTU	HIGHLAND COSTUME
ACDEGHIIILNNRRS	RAISING CHILDREN
ACDEGHIIINRSTTT	DISTRICT HEATING
ACDEGHIILNNNSTY	DISENCHANTINGLY
ACDEGHINNNNOOST	DANCES ON NOTHING
ACDEGHINNOSTTUY	COUNTING THE DAYS
ACDEGHINOORRSST	CROSSING THE ROAD
ACDEGHINOPSSSTT	CHANGED ITS SPOTS
ACDEGIIILNNOOTT	CONGENITAL IDIOT
ACDEGIILLMNNORT	RECALLING TO MIND
ACDEGIILLOOSSTT	DIALECTOLOGISTS
ACDEGIIMMNNRSST	DANCING MISTRESS
ACDEGILLNNOOSSW	CLOSING-DOWN SALE
ACDEGILNNNOSTTU	CONSENTING ADULT
ACDEGINORSTTTUY	COTTAGE INDUSTRY
ACDEHIILLNNOOOS	HEAD-ON COLLISION
ACDEHIILOPSSTTY	SOPHISTICATEDLY
ACDEHIIMMNNRRSST	CHRISTMAS DINNER
ACDEHILLNOOPRTY	POLYCHLORINATED
ACDEHILNORRSSTU	SHORT AND CURLIES
ACDEHINOOPRTTUW	WHEAT PRODUCTION

ACDEHINOSSSTTTW	CASTS TO THE WINDS	ACEEEFFGHILOPRT	TELEGRAPH OFFICE
ACDEHKKNOOOORSTT	KNOCKS AT THE DOOR	ACEEEFFGHINNORX	OFFER IN EXCHANGE
ACDEHLOOPRSTTWY	PLAYS TO THE CROWD	ACEEEFFILNNSSTU	INEFFECTUALNESS
ACDEIIIKNNOPRRT	INDIAN ROPE-TRICK	ACEEEFFIMNOORTX	FREE OF INCOME-TAX
ACDEIIILMNNOORT	OMNIDIRECTIONAL	ACEEEFFLNOPRSST	PERSONAL EFFECTS
ACDEIIINNNOOOPV	VOICED AN OPINION	ACEEEFGGHINNORX	FOREIGN EXCHANGE
ACDEIIINNNOORST	IN CONSIDERATION	ACEEEFGGLRRSTUU	GRACEFUL GESTURE
	INCONSIDERATION	ACEEEFGHINOSVWX	EXCHANGE OF VIEWS
ACDEIIINOOPRRTV	VICTORIAN PERIOD	ACEEEFGILLNNORS	CLEARING ONESELF
ACDEIIJMORRTTVY	MAJORITY VERDICT	ACEEEFGILNNOPRR	PEREGRINE FALCON
ACDEIIILLMNOORTU	EDITORIAL COLUMN	ACEEEFGILNORRST	STEERING CLEAR OF
ACDEIILMNNOOPSV	DEVILS COMPANION	ACEEEFGNPRRRSTT	PERFECT STRANGER
ACDEIILMNOOOPST	DECOMPOSITIONAL	ACEEEFHHIINRSST	FINISHES THE RACE
ACDEIILNNNNOSTT	ISLAND CONTINENT	ACEEEFHHIRSSTTT	FEATHERSTITCHES
ACDEIILNOOOORSTU	DECOLOURISATION	ACEEEFHHLMNORTV	ELEVENTH OF MARCH
ACDEIILNOOORTUZ	DECOLOURIZATION	ACEEEFHIMNNNRST	ENFRANCHISEMENT
ACDEIILNOOPPRSU	POPULAR DECISION	ACEEEFHKLNOORTV	TOOK FRENCH LEAVE
ACDEIIMNOOOTTUV	SITUATION COMEDY	ACEEEFHKOOPRSTU	KEEPS OUT OF REACH
ACDEIKNNOSSSSTT	STICKS AND STONES	ACEEEFHHSSSSITT	OTHEGGEE THE FACT
ACDEIKNOOSTTTUY	TAKE INTO CUSTODY	ACEEEFIIILMNNOT	ONCE IN A LIFETIME
ACDEKKLNOOOOOST	TOOK A SECOND LOOK	ACEEEFIILMNORTX	INCOME-TAX RELIEF
ACDELLOOOPRRRRY	ORDERLY CORPORAL	ACEEEFIKNOOPRTW	NEAT PIECE OF WORK
ACDFHHHIINOPPSS	FISH AND CHIP SHOP	ACEEEFILLMOPRTU	COMPLETE FAILURE
ACDGHIINOPPRSTT	DROPPING A STITCH	ACEEEFINOOPSSTT	TO SPITE ONES FACE
ACDGHIMMNNOOPRRY	GYNANDROMORPHIC	ACEEEFLLMOORRRT	ELECTORAL REFORM
ACDGIIIINNNNOORT	AIR CONDITIONING	ACEEEFLMNNORRUY	FUNERAL CEREMONY
	AIR-CONDITIONING	ACEEEFLMNOSTTTT	ACT OF SETTLEMENT
ACDGII NOOOPRSS	COLORADO SPRINGS	ACEEEFLNNNNOOSU	ANNOUNCE ONESELF
ACDHIILLMNOORTY	MITOCHONDRIALLY	ACEEEGGHINNPSSW	SWEEPING CHANGES
ACDHILLOOPRRTYY	HYDROTROPICALLY	ACEEEGGINNNORTT	GETTING AN ENCORE
ACDIIIILL MNOORS	MID-AIR COLLISION	ACEEEGGHHLNRSSTU	CHANGES THE RULES
ACDIIIILNNNOSST	DISINCLINATIONS	ACEEEGIIIHILOPPRST	PREACH THE GOSPEL
ACDIILLNNNOOTUY	UNCONDITIONALLY	ACEEEGHILLRRSTT	CALL THE REGISTER
ACDIINNORSSTTUU	TITUS ANDRONICUS	ACEEEGHILOPRSVX	EXPLOSIVE CHARGE
ACDIKLLNOSSSTTT	STAND STOCK-STILL	ACEEEGHIMNNOOTT	GONE TO THE CINEMA
ACDMMNOOPPRSSTU	COMMANDS SUPPORT	ACEEEGHIMNOOSTT	GOES TO THE CINEMA
ACEEEEEFFHNPRRRS	PREFERENCE SHARE	ACEEEGHINNOPRTT	PARTHENOGENETIC
ACEEEEEGLNRSSSY	CEASELESS ENERGY	ACEEEGHINNOSSVW	CHANGE ONES VIEWS
ACEEEEEHLLPSSSV	LEAVE SPEECHLESS	ACEEEGHNNNOSSTU	CHANGES ONE'S TUNE
ACEEEEEILRRSTTV	RECEIVES A LETTER	ACEEEGHOPRRSSTT	SCRAPES TOGETHER
ACEEEEEIMNPRTTX	EXTREME PATIENCE	ACEEEGIIINPRRRV	VIRGINIA CREEPER
ACEEEEELNOPSSUV	ACE UP ONE'S SLEEVE	ACEEEGIIKNNNOPR	KEEP IN IGNORANCE
ACEEEEELNNRSSSTV	SERVES A SENTENCE	ACEEEGIILLLMOPR	IMPERIAL COLLEGE
ACEEEEFIMNNOPRX	MAN OF EXPERIENCE	ACEEEGIILLNOPPRY	EPEIROGENICALLY
ACEEEEFNORSSTTV	ASCENT OF EVEREST	ACEEEGIILLNORTT	INTERCOLLEGIATE
ACEEEEFPRRRSTTU	PERFECT TREASURE	ACEEEGIIINNOPSSY	SAYING ONE'S PIECE
ACEEEEGHLNRSTTX	EXCHANGE LETTERS	ACEEEGIKNNOORTV	GIVEN ONE A ROCKET
ACEEEEGHNRRRSTU	GREEN CHARTREUSE	ACEEEGIKNOORSTV	GIVES ONE A ROCKET
ACEEEEGIIMNNNSV	VENGEANCE IS MINE!	ACEEEGILLNOOPST	GONE ALL TO PIECES
ACEEEEGIINNPRSX	GAINS EXPERIENCE	ACEEEGILLOOPSST	GOES ALL TO PIECES
ACEEEEGILLNNORT	GENERAL ELECTION	ACEEEGIMNNORRTY	EMERGENCY RATION
ACEEEEGILNORTTV	ELECTRONEGATIVE	ACEEEGIMNOPRSTT	SPERMATOGENETIC
ACEEEEGILRRRSUX	REGULAR EXERCISE	ACEEEGLMNORRSTW	WELCOME STRANGER
ACEEEEGIMNRTTTX	GREAT EXCITEMENT	ACEEEGNNNOOSSTV	GAVE ONE'S CONSENT
ACEEEEGLLLMMNOU	EMMANUEL COLLEGE	ACEEEHHHHMMNRSTTV	MARCH THE SEVENTH
ACEEEEGPRRSSTTT	GREATEST RESPECT	ACEEEHHHORSTTTU	TOUCHES THE HEART
ACEEEEHHILRSTXY	HEALTHY EXERCISE	ACEEEHHILLNRTUV	LEAVE IN THE LURCH
ACEEEEHHORRSSTV	RECOVER THE ASHES	ACEEEHHIPPRSSTT	SPEECH THERAPIST
ACEEEEHIKORSTVY	RECEIVES THE OKAY	ACEEEHHLLSTTTWY	WATCHES THE TELLY
ACEEEEHILLPRSST	CELESTIAL SPHERE	ACEEEHHMNOORTTT	CAME TO THE THRONE
ACEEEEHIMNNPRUX	HUMAN EXPERIENCE	ACEEEHIJKKNPSST	SHEEPSKIN JACKET
ACEEEEHLMNOPRTT	TEMPERANCE HOTEL	ACEEEHIKLLLMNOOP	NO PLACE LIKE HOME
ACEEEEHLMORRSTU	THREE-COURSE MEAL	ACEEEHIKLLPPRST	LIKE THE CLAPPERS
ACEEEEHLNNOSSTT	CLEANS ONE'S TEETH	ACEEEHIKRSTTTWW	WATERS THE WICKET
ACEEEEHNPQRSSTU	PRESENTS A CHEQUE	ACEEEHILLNRSSTV	CLEANS THE SILVER
ACEEEEHPSSSSSTY	CASTS SHEEP'S EYES	ACEEEHILNNPPRRS	PENCIL SHARPENER
ACEEEEIKLNNOPPS	KEEP IN ONE'S PLACE	ACEEEHIMNNOOPTT	CAME INTO THE OPEN
ACEEEEIKNOPPSSS	SPEAKS ONE'S PIECE	ACEEEHIMNNOTTTW	WENT TO THE CINEMA
ACEEEEILQRRSSTU	LEICESTER SQUARE	ACEEEHIMNOSSTTW	WATCHES ONE'S TIME
ACEEEENOORSSTVY	CAST ONE'S EYE OVER	ACEEEHIMOPSSSST	SMASHES TO PIECES
ACEEEFFFOPRSSTU	PAUSES FOR EFFECT	ACEEEHKMNORRRTT	CORNER THE MARKET

ACEEEEHLMMNOORTW	MORE THAN WELCOME	ACEEFIILOOSTTTW	TALE OF TWO CITIES
ACEEEEHLNOORSSTT	TEAR ONES CLOTHES	ACEEFILNNNNOOSST	CONTAINS ONESELF
ACEEEEHLNORTTUVY	LEAVE THE COUNTRY	ACEEFILNORSSSTU	LACTIFEROUSNESS
ACEEEHMMOORSTTY	HAEMOCYTOMETERS	ACEEFILPPRRSSUY	SLIPPERY SURFACE
ACEEEHNNNNOPRSTW	SHOWN REPENTANCE	ACEEFINOOSTTUXY	STAY OF EXECUTION
ACEEEHNNOPRSSTW	SHOWS REPENTANCE	ACEEFLMNOOOPRRS	SOLO PERFORMANCE
ACEEEHNORRSSSTU	TREACHEROUSNESS	ACEEFNNOOOPSTTU	NOT ONE'S CUP OF TEA
ACEEEHORRSSSTTT	ACROSS THE STREET	ACEEGGGHINNNOTT	GETTING NO CHANGE
ACEEEIILLLNSTTU	INTELLECTUALISE	ACEEGGHHIIIMNNW	WEIGHING MACHINE
ACEEEIILLLNTTUZ	INTELLECTUALIZE	ACEEGGHHIILNNST	TEACHING ENGLISH
ACEEEIILLNORRUV	LAURENCE OLIVIER	ACEEGGHHINNNRSST	RINGS THE CHANGES
ACEEEIILMMORRSV	MEMORIAL SERVICE	ACEEGGHHINORSTV	GIVE SHORT CHANGE
ACEEEIILNNNORSS	INCLINES ONE'S EAR	ACEEGGHHNORSSTT	GETS SHORT CHANGE
ACEEEIIMNNOSSST	AMNIOCENTESISES	ACEEGGHIINNSVWX	EXCHANGING VIEWS
ACEEEIINOORSSSV	RAISES ONE'S VOICE	ACEEGGHIJKNNOSX	EXCHANGING JOKES
ACEEEIINPPRSSTT	PRECIPITATENESS	ACEEGGHINOORSTT	GOING TO THE RACES
ACEEEIJNORSTVVW	CONSERVATIVE JEW	ACEEGGIILNNNOOR	OCEAN-GOING LINER
ACEEEIKLNNOPPST	KEPT IN ONE'S PLACE	ACEEGGIINNRTTUV	GIVING UTTERANCE
ACEEEIKMMOOPRSS	SEEK A COMPROMISE	ACEEGHHIILNPRTT	IN THE RIGHT PLACE
ACEEEIILLNOPSTTW	WENT ALL TO PIECES	ACEEGHHIKNORSTW	SHOCKING WEATHER
ACEEEIILNOPRRSSV	PERSONAL SERVICE	ACEEGHHINOSTTWW	WATCH ONES WEIGHT
ACEEEIMRRSSTUUY	SECURITY MEASURE	ACEEGHIIINPRRST	RAISING THE PRICE
ACEEEINNNSSTUVX	INVENTS AN EXCUSE	ACEEGHIIKKMNTTY	TAKING THE MICKEY
ACEEEINNOPRSTTY	TRY ONES PATIENCE	ACEEGHIILLNSTTT	TILTING THE SCALE
ACEEEINNORSSTTU	EASTERN COUNTIES	ACEEGHIILNPPSTT	TIPPING THE SCALE
ACEEEINNQRSSTUY	SESQUICENTENARY	ACEEGHIKLLNRSSY	CHARLES KINGSLEY
ACEEEINOOPRSSTV	COOPERATIVENESS	ACEEGHILLOORTTT	CHARGE TOO LITTLE
ACEEEELLMORSSTTY	ELECTORAL SYSTEM	ACEEGHILNNRSTTU	TURNING THE SCALE
ACEEELLNNORTUVY	YOU NEVER CAN TELL	ACEEGHINNOOPRTT	ANTHROPOGENETIC
ACEEELMNNOPSSTY	ENCLOSES PAYMENT	ACEEGHINNORSSTV	HAVING NO SECRETS
ACEEELMNOPRSTUX	COUNTEREXAMPLES	ACEEGHNNOOPSSST	CHANGE ONE'S SPOTS
ACEEELNNNOSRTTVW	NEWCASTLE ON TYNE	ACEEGIINNRRTTVW	CREATIVE WRITING
ACEEEMNOOORSSST	COMES TO ONE'S EARS	ACEEGIIKLNOPSTT	GETS INTO A PICKLE
ACEEEMNORRSSTUU	COUNTERMEASURES	ACEEGIIKMMNNOOS	MAKING ECONOMIES
ACEEEENOPPRSSSTY	PAY ONES RESPECTS	ACEEGIIKNNNOPRT	KEPT IN IGNORANCE
ACEEFFFHILOORTW	OFFICER OF THE LAW	ACEEGIIKNNOPTTX	TAKING EXCEPTION
ACEEFFGHIILNNTY	FLYING IN THE FACE	ACEEGIILLLMORTY	MILITARY COLLEGE
ACEEFFGIINRSTUU	CUTS A FINE FIGURE	ACEEGIILLMNORVW	WILLIAM CONGREVE
ACEEFFHHIKLLOTT	TAKE THE CHILL OFF	ACEEGIILLMOOPST	EPISTEMOLOGICAL
ACEEFFHHKLPSSTU	SHUFFLES THE PACK	ACEEGIILNNRSSSU	SIR ALEC GUINNESS
ACEEFFHIKMMORST	SKIM OFF THE CREAM	ACEEGIILNOPRRTU	PRICE REGULATION
ACEEFFHLLOPRRSU	SELF-REPROACHFUL	ACEEGIIMNNNNOTU	CEMENTING A UNION
ACEEFFHNOORRSST	FATHER CONFESSOR	ACEEGIIMNNNOPRS	NAMING ONE'S PRICE
ACEEFFHORSTTTUW	CUTS OFF THE WATER	ACEEGIINOOSSSTT	GO INTO ECSTASIES
ACEEFFILNOSTTUY	AFFLUENT SOCIETY	ACEEGILLLNOPTYY	POLYGENETICALLY
ACEEFFNOORSSSTU	SURE OF ONES FACTS	ACEEGILLNNOOTTY	ONTOGENETICALLY
ACEEFGGHINSTTTT	GETTING THE FACTS	ACEEGILLNOORSTY	OESTROGENICALLY
ACEEFGHIKLNOSTT	KING OF THE CASTLE	ACEEGINNOOPRSSV	PROVING ONE'S CASE
ACEEFGHILNNORTW	ENFORCING THE LAW	ACEEGINNOPSSTTU	PUTTING ONE'S CASE
ACEEFGHILNOPRRS	SELF-REPROACHING	ACEEGINNORRSSWY	CRYING ONE'S WARES
ACEEFGHNOOPPRSU	CHANGE OF PURPOSE	ACEEGLLLLLOOSSU	ALL SOULS COLLEGE
ACEEFGIIJPRRTUU	GRAPEFRUIT JUICE	ACEEGLLMNNOORTV	LOCAL GOVERNMENT
ACEEFGIILLLNORT	RECALLING TO LIFE	ACEEGLMORRRSTUU	REGULAR CUSTOMER
ACEEFGILNNOOSTY	LYING TO ONE'S FACE	ACEEGMOPRRSTUUU	MUSTER UP COURAGE
ACEEFGILNRRTTUU	ULTRACENTRIFUGE	ACEEHHIIKNNOTTT	TAKE IT ON THE CHIN
ACEEFGINORRTTVY	CENTRE OF GRAVITY	ACEEHHIKRSSSTTW	THE CAT'S WHISKERS
ACEEFHHILOPRTTU	PICTURE OF HEALTH	ACEEHHILMNNSSTW	SWIMS THE CHANNEL
ACEEFHHILRRSSTT	CHARLES THE FIRST	ACEEHHILMNORSTT	CLAIMS THE THRONE
ACEEFHHMMNOOORRT	REACH FOR THE MOON	ACEEHHIMNOORRTT	HETEROCHROMATIN
ACEEFHIIJNOORRT	JOIN THE AIR FORCE	ACEEHHIMOPRSSTT	CHEMOTHERAPISTS
ACEEFHIILNPRSTT	IN THE FIRST PLACE	ACEEHHINOOPRTUW	PEACE WITH HONOUR
ACEEFHILNNOPRSY	FRENCH POLYNESIA	ACEEHHLMMNOOTTW	THE COMMONWEALTH
ACEEFHILRRSSSTU	FRUITLESS SEARCH	ACEEHHMMMNORRRTY	THE MERRY MONARCH
ACEEFHKMOOORTTU	COME OUT OF THE ARK	ACEEHHNNOORSTTUW	TOUCHES ON THE RAW
ACEEFHLNOPRRSSU	REPROACHFULNESS	ACEEHIIILOQRSTU	HEROIC QUALITIES
ACEEFHMORRTTTUX	CRUX OF THE MATTER	ACEEHIIKLLNSTTY	KINESTHETICALLY
ACEEFHOOPRRRSTU	PAR FOR THE COURSE	ACEEHIIKLNORSST	ROCK IN THE AISLES
ACEEFIILLMNOPTX	EXEMPLIFICATION	ACEEHIIILLMNOPTWY	THE MICE WILL PLAY
ACEEFIIILNORRRT	INFERIOR ARTICLE	ACEEHIIILLMPSTUY	EUPHEMISTICALLY
ACEEFIIIMNNNRST	FINANCE MINISTER	ACEEHIILMNNOPST	PHENOMENALISTIC
ACEEFIILNPRSSSU	SUPERFICIALNESS	ACEEHIILNOSTTVW	WATCH TELEVISION

ACEEHIIMORSSSTV	HIS MASTERS VOICE	ACEFGIORRRSTUUY	CUT A SORRY FIGURE
ACEEHIINOOPRRRS	PRAIRIE SCHOONER	ACEFGLLOOPSSTUU	PLAGUE OF LOCUSTS
ACEEHIINPPPRRSST	APPRENTICESHIPS	ACEFHHIMOOPSTTT	PIT OF THE STOMACH
ACEEHIJMNNOPSTU	JUMPS IN THE OCEAN	ACEFHHINNNOOSUV	HAUNCH OF VENISON
ACEEHIKKLNNRRST	SIR KENNETH CLARK	ACEFHHINORRRSTTU	IN SEARCH OF TRUTH
ACEEHIKLMPRTTUY	PRETTY MUCH ALIKE	ACEFHIILNPSSSTY	PHYSICAL FITNESS
ACEEHILLOOPSSTT	ALL SHOT TO PIECES	ACEFHIKLLNRSTUY	THINKS CAREFULLY
ACEEHILMOPPRRTY	HYPERMETROPICAL	ACEFHILLORSSSTT	FIRST-CLASS HOTEL
ACEEHILNORRTTUW	LOWER THE CURTAIN	ACEFIIIINNNOSTT	INTENSIFICATION
ACEEHILOORRSSST	ATHEROSCLEROSIS	ACEFIIINNOOPRST	PERSONIFICATION
ACEEHIMMORSTTTW	CAME TO TERMS WITH	ACEFIIKPPPSSTUW	PICKS UP A FEW TIPS
ACEEHINOPRSSTTT	STRETCHES A POINT	ACEFIILLOOPRSTY	PILLAR OF SOCIETY
ACEEHKMMMNOORTT	THE COMMON MARKET	ACEFIILMNNOOSSS	CONFESSIONALISM
ACEEHILMOOPSTTUW	COMPLETE WASH-OUT	ACEFIILNNOOSSST	CONFESSIONALIST
ACEEHMMOOOOORSTT	CAME HOME TO ROOST	ACEFIIMNOPRRSTT	FIRST IMPORTANCE
ACEEHNOOPRSSSST	CROSSES ONE'S PATH	ACEFIKLLLOOPRWW	LACK OF WILL POWER
ACEEIIILMRRSTVY	MILITARY SERVICE	ACEFIKLLNNOTTTW	LITTLE-KNOWN FACT
ACEEIIINQSSSTUV	ACQUISITIVENESS	ACEFIKNNNOORRTW	KNOWN FOR CERTAIN
ACEEIIKMNNRRSSTV	NEVER MISS A TRICK	ACEFIKNNOORRSTW	KNOWS FOR CERTAIN
ACEEIILLLMNSTTU	INTELLECTUALISM	ACEFIILMNNOORRTTV	TRAVEL IN COMFORT
ACEEIILLLNSTTTU	INTELLECTUALIST	ACEFIMNOOORSTUV	COMES INTO FAVOUR
ACEEIILLLNTTTUY	INTELLECTUALITY	ACEFINRRRSSTTUU	INFRASTRUCTURES
ACEEIIILLNOPSTTV	POLITICAL EVENTS	ACEFLLMOOOOPSTTU	COME TO A FULL STOP
ACEEIILMNOPRRTY	PRIMARY ELECTION	ACEFLLOPPSSTUUY	SUSPECT FOUL PLAY
ACEEIILNNNOOSTV	CONVENTIONALISE	ACEGGHHINNOSSTX	EXCHANGING SHOTS
ACEEIILNNNOOTVZ	CONVENTIONALIZE	ACEGGHIIMNNNORR	REIGNING MONARCH
ACEEIILNNNOQSTU	INCONSEQUENTIAL	ACEGGHIINNPRTTU	PUTTING IN CHARGE
ACEEIILNNOORTTV	VIOLENT REACTION	ACEGGHINNOOPRRT	RONTGENOGRAPHIC
ACEEIILNOPRSTTT	TOPICAL INTEREST	ACEGGHINRSSTTTU	CUTTING THE GRASS
ACEEIIMNNPRRRST	PARTNERS IN CRIME	ACEGGIIKLLNNSSS	CLINKING GLASSES
ACEEFIINNOORSTV	STENTORIAN VOICE	ACEGGILLNNOOORT	RONTGENOLOGICAL
ACEEIINNPPRSSTT	PRECIPITANTNESS	ACEGHHIIKNNNOTT	TAKING ON THE CHIN
ACEEIKMNOORSTTU	CAME OUT ON STRIKE	ACEGHHIIMNNNTTW	WINNING THE MATCH
ACEEIKNOPPRRSSU	PRICK ONES EARS UP	ACEGHHINNOPSSV	HAVING ONE'S CHIPS
	PRICK UP ONES EARS	ACEGHHIINRSSTVY	HAVING HYSTERICS
ACEEIILLLMNOSSUY	MISCELLANEOUSLY	ACEGIIIIIKNORRTTT	ON THE RIGHT TRACK
ACEEILLMMNOPRTY	COMPLEMENTARILY	ACEGHHILLNOSSTT	CALLING THE SHOTS
ACEEIILLMNOPTTVY	CONTEMPLATIVELY	ACEGHHIIKMNNNTT	KNITTING MACHINE
ACEEILLNNOQSTUY	CONSEQUENTIALLY	ACEGHIIJNNORRTTV	CARVING THE JOINT
ACEEILMMNOPRTTY	COMPLEMENTARITY	ACEGHIIKMNNOPST	MAKING ONE'S PITCH
ACEEIILNNNNOSSSS	NONSENSICALNESS	ACEGHIINNORSTTU	CUTTING ONE'S HAIR
ACEEILNNOPPSSTU	PUTS IN ONE'S PLACE	ACEGHIINNRSTTTT	TITANIC STRENGTH
ACEEIMMNNNNOTTU	ANCIENT MONUMENT	ACEGHIKLNNORSST	CLOSING THE RANKS
ACEEIMNNNOOOSTW	CAME INTO ONE'S OWN	ACEGHIKNNOSTTTU	COUNT THE TAKINGS
ACEEIMNNOOOTTTT	COME TO ATTENTION	ACEGHILLLNOOPRY	PHRENOLOGICALLY
ACEEIMNNOOPRTTY	CONTEMPORANEITY	ACEGHILLOOPRSTY	GEOSTROPHICALLY
ACEEIMNNORRTTUX	INCOME-TAX RETURN	ACEGHIMMOOPRRTT	PHOTOGRAMMETRIC
ACEEIMNOORSSSTU	MUSIC TO ONES EARS	ACEGHINNNORTTYY	TRY ANYTHING ONCE
ACEEINOOPRSSTVV	PROVOCATIVENESS	ACEGHINOOPRRTTT	ROTATING THE CROP
ACEEIOPPRRSTTUV	ACTIVE SUPPORTER	ACEGHINOPPRRSUW	PURCHASING POWER
ACEELLLNOOORSUV	LOVE CONQUERS ALL	ACEGHINOPSSSSTT	CHANGES ITS SPOTS
ACEELLLNOPSSSTY	SPOTLESSLY CLEAN	ACEGHKNNOORRTTW	ON THE WRONG TRACK
ACEELLMNNNOORUY	MAUREEN CONNOLLY	ACEGIIKLNPRSSTT	STICKING PLASTER
ACEELMNOOPRSSSS	CROSSES ONE'S PALM	ACEGIIKLNPRSTTU	TALKING PICTURES
ACEELMNOPRSSSTY	CRAMPS ONE'S STYLE	ACEGIIKNORSSTTU	TAKING ITS COURSE
ACEEMMNNOORSTTW	NEWS COMMENTATOR	ACEGIILLLRSTTY	STRICTLY ILLEGAL
ACEEMNNOOOPRSTU	CONTEMPORANEOUS	ACEGIILMNOORRTT	TRIGONOMETRICAL
ACEEMNOOPRRRSTY	MERCENARY TROOPS	ACEGIILMNOOSTUY	COMING OUT EASILY
ACEFFGIJLMNOPPU	JUMPING-OFF PLACE	ACEGIILNNOORTTV	TRAVEL INCOGNITO
ACEFFHIIILNNNOT	NAIL IN THE COFFIN	ACEGIIMMNNOOSST	COMMISSION AGENT
ACEFFHIKKMOQRTU	QUICK OFF THE MARK	ACEGIINOOPRSTTV	PROGNOSTICATIVE
ACEFFHOOOPPRRSU	PROOF OF PURCHASE	ACEGILLLMNOOOTY	ENTOMOLOGICALLY
ACEFFKNOOOOOSTT	TOOK OFF ONE'S COAT	ACEGILLNNOORSSY	CONGRESSIONALLY
	TOOK ONE'S COAT OFF	ACEGILMNNOOORST	CONGLOMERATIONS
ACEFGHHMORSTTUU	MUCH SOUGHT AFTER	ACEGILMNOORRTTU	COLOURING MATTER
ACEFGHIIMNOORTT	COMING TO THE FAIR	ACEGILNOOPRSTTU	PLOTTING A COURSE
ACEFGHIINNNOOOP	CHANGE OF OPINION	ACEGINNNOORSTTU	TURNING ONE'S COAT
ACEFGHMOOPRRRSS	MARCH OF PROGRESS	ACEGINNNOPRRSUU	RUNNING UP A SCORE
ACEFGIIIILNSTVY	SIGNIFICANTLY	ACEGINNNOPRSTTY	CONSENTING PARTY
ACEFGIIIMNNOORTTV	MOTIVATING FORCE	ACEGLMMOOPRSSUY	COMPULSORY GAMES
ACEFGIOOPRRSTUU	CUTS A POOR FIGURE	ACEHHHIMORTTTWW	WATCH WITH MOTHER

ACEHHIILLMNPTTY	PLATYHELMINTHIC
ACEHHIKNPRSTTUW	RUNS WITH THE PACK
ACEHHILLPPRSYYY	HYPERPHYSICALLY
ACEHHILNOOPPRSS	OPEN SCHOLARSHIP
ACEHHINNPSSSTTU	SPANISH CHESTNUT
ACEHHINOPPRSTTU	PITHECANTHROPUS
ACEHHIOPPRSSTTY	PSYCHOTHERAPIST
ACEHHLMOOOPPSST	OPHTHALMOSCOPES
ACEHIIKLLLTTTUW	WITH A LITTLE LUCK
ACEHIILLLOOPRTY	HELIOTROPICALLY
ACEHIILLNOOPRSY	IONOSPHERICALLY
ACEHIILLNOORSTV	HISTORICAL NOVEL
ACEHIILLLOOPRTTY	POLITICAL THEORY
ACEHIILLOPRRSTY	PREHISTORICALLY
ACEHIILMMNNOSTT	MONT SAINT MICHEL
ACEHIIMMMOPSTTY	SYMPATHOMIMETIC
ACEHIIMNNNOPSST	TENNIS CHAMPIONS
ACEHIIMOOSSSSST	SCHISTOSOMIASES
ACEHIINOPPRSSST	SPINTHARISCOPES
ACEHIKKNNOOPSST	KNOCKS INTO SHAPE
ACEHILLMOOPRTTY	PHOTOMETRICALLY
ACEHILLNPRSTTUU	PULL THE CURTAINS
ACEHILOPSSTUXYY	PSYCHOSEXUALITY
ACEHMMOOPSTTTTU	ATTEMPTS TOO MUCH
ACEHMNNOORSSTTU	TURN ONE'S STOMACH
ACEHNOOORSSTTTW	NOT CARE TWO HOOTS
ACEIIILLMPSSSTY	PESSIMISTICALLY
ACEIIILLNOSTVVY	VIVISECTIONALLY
ACEIIILLOPRRTTW	POLITICAL WRITER
ACEIIIMMNNOORSSS	COMMISSIONAIRES
ACEIIINNNOOOPSV	VOICES AN OPINION
ACEIIKNNOORSSST	STICKS IN ONE'S OAR
ACEIIILLMOSSTTV	STILL,SMALL VOICE
ACEIIILLMMNOPRTY	COMPLIMENTARILY
ACEIIILLNNOQSSTU	CALLS IN QUESTION
ACEIIILLORSTUVYY	VOYEURISTICALLY
ACEIILMNNNOOSTV	CONVENTIONALISM
ACEIILNNNOOSTTV	CONVENTIONALIST
ACEIILNNNOOTTVY	CONVENTIONALITY
ACEIILNNOOPRSTT	CENTRAL POSITION
ACEIILNNOPPPRRS	PRINCIPAL PERSON
ACEIILPRRSTTTVY	STRICTLY PRIVATE
ACEIIMNNOORSSSU	ACRIMONIOUSNESS
ACEIIMNNOOPRSTTU	COMPUTERISATION
ACEIIMNOOPRTTUZ	COMPUTERIZATION
ACEIINNOORSSTTV	CONSERVATIONIST
ACEIINNORRRSTUY	INSURRECTIONARY
ACEIINNORRRTTTU	COUNTERIRRITANT
ACEIKKNOORRTTWW	KNEW A TRICK OR TWO
ACEIKLLMMNOSSTU	CONSUMMATE SKILL
ACEIKLNOOSSSTTT	STICK TO ONE'S LAST
ACEIKNOOOPRSTTU	TOOK PRECAUTIONS
ACEIILLLNOPRSTYY	POLYCRYSTALLINE
ACEIILLNOOORRSTVY	CONTROVERSIALLY
ACEIILLNOPRSTTUY	PERSONALITY CULT
ACEIILLNNRRSTTTUY	STRICTLY NEUTRAL
ACEILMMNNOOOPUV	COMPANION VOLUME
ACEILNNOORRSTUV	UNCONTROVERSIAL
ACEILNNOORSTTTV	VIOLENT CONTRAST
ACEIMNNNOOPRSTU	PRONUNCIAMENTOS
ACEINNOORRSSSUV	CARNIVOROUSNESS
ACELLLMMNOOORUY	MONOMOLECULARLY
ACELPRRRSSTTUUU	SUPERSTRUCTURE
ACELRRRSSTTTUUU	ULTRASTRUCTURES
ACFFIIIILNOQRUY	OFFICIAL INQUIRY
ACFFILLOOPRRSTT	FIRST PORT OF CALL
ACFGHIILLNOOSTY	ACTING FOOLISHLY
ACFGHLOOORTTUUU	LAUGH OUT OF COURT
ACFGIIILNNNSTY	INSIGNIFICANTLY
ACFGIIKNOOPRSST	PAIR OF STOCKINGS
ACFHIILNNOOOPSS	CLASH OF OPINIONS

ACFIIILLMOORSTY	FAMILY SOLICITOR
ACFIILMMOORRSTT	COMMITS FOR TRIAL
ACFIINOOPRRSSTT	STRIPS FOR ACTION
ACFINOOOPSTTTUU	PUTS OUT OF ACTION
ACFINOOPPRTTUUU	PUT UP FOR AUCTION
ACGGHHINOPRRSTU	SCRAPING THROUGH
ACGGHHINORRRTUY	CARRYING THROUGH
ACGGHIKNNOPSTUU	HUNG UP A STOCKING
ACGGHILNNOORSTU	LAUGHING TO SCORN
ACGGIIINNNOOOTT	GOING INTO ACTION
ACGGIINNOOPRSTT	PROGNOSTICATING
ACGHHIIOOPPRRST	HISTORIOGRAPHIC
ACGHHIMOOOOPPRRT	MICROPHOTOGRAPH
	PHOTOMICROGRAPH
ACGHHLMNOPSSUU	PLOUGHMANS LUNCH
ACGHHLOOOPPSTYY	PSYCHOPATHOLOGY
ACGHIIIKLNNOTTY	LAYING IT ON THICK
ACGHIIILLLMNRTX	THRILLING CLIMAX
ACGHIIKNNOSSTTT	STICKS AT NOTHING
ACGHIIMNNOPPPSY	SHIPPING COMPANY
ACGHIMNNNNOPSUY	SHUNNING COMPANY
ACGIIIKKKNNPSTU	KICKING UP A STINK
ACGIIILNNNOPPRS	CLAPPING IN IRONS
ACGIIILNNPQTTUU	QUINTUPLICATING
ACGIIKNOORTTTTU	TAKING IT TO COURT
ACGIIILLLMMNOOUY	IMMUNOLOGICALLY
ACGIINNOOOPRSTT	PROGNOSTICATION
ACGIINOPRSSTTTU	PUTTING IT ACROSS
ACGIKNOOOPRSTUY	COOKING UP A STORY
ACGILLOOOOPRTZ	PROTOZOOLOGICAL
ACGILMMNNOOOOPY	GLOOMY COMPANION
ACHHIMNOOOPPRRT	ANTHROPOMORPHIC
ACHHLNOOOSTTUUY	AUTOCHTHONOUSLY
ACHIIIMOOSSSSST	SCHISTOSOMIASIS
ACHIIIMPRRSSSTT	CHRISTMAS SPIRIT
ACHIINNNOORSSTY	SYNCHRONISATION
ACHIINNOORSTYZ	SYNCHRONIZATION
ACHIIOPRSSSSTTY	ASTROPHYSICISTS
ACHIKLNNOOPPTTY	PHYTOPLANKTONIC
ACHILLLMOOPPRYY	POLYMORPHICALLY
ACHILLLORRTTUUY	HORTICULTURALLY
ACHILLOOOPPRTTY	PHOTOTROPICALLY
ACHIMNNOOOPSSSW	SHOWN COMPASSION
ACHIMNOOOPSSSSW	SHOWS COMPASSION
ACIIIKNORSTTTUY	TRICKY SITUATION
ACIIIKNOSSTTTUY	STICKY SITUATION
ACIIILLMNOPSTTU	MULTIPLICATIONS
ACIILLMNOOOPSTY	COMPOSITIONALLY
ACIILMNNOOOPSST	COSMOPOLITANISM
ACIILMMNOOOORSSY	ROYAL COMMISSION
ACIILMNNNOOSSUY	SANCTIMONIOUSLY
ACIILMNOPSSTUUU	MUTUAL SUSPICION
ACIILNNOOPPRSST	CLAPS INTO PRISON
ACIILNNOOSSTTTU	CONSTITUTIONALS
ACIKKNOOORRTTWW	KNOW A TRICK OR TWO
ADDDDEEEIILRSSS	RIDES SIDE-SADDLE
ADDDEEEEEEGLMPR	REDEEMED A PLEDGE
ADDDEEEEEGHNRTW	WEEDED THE GARDEN
ADDDEEEFHILLPTY	PLAYED THE FIDDLE
ADDDEEEGHHKNOTU	KNEADED THE DOUGH
ADDDEEEGHINRRST	DRAINED THE DREGS
ADDDEEEHHNNRRTU	HUNDRED AND THREE
ADDDEEEHHNNNRSUV	HUNDRED AND SEVEN
ADDDEEEIINNRSST	ENDED IN DISASTER
ADDDEEENPRRSTUU	SUDDEN DEPARTURE
ADDDEEFFFFHNPUU	HUFFED AND PUFFED
ADDDEEFFHILMOORT	MIDDLE OF THE ROAD
	MIDDLE-OF-THE-ROAD
ADDDEEGHHINNRTU	HUNDRED AND EIGHT
ADDDEEGHINNNOOS	NODDING ONE'S HEAD
ADDDEEHILNORTUV	LIVED TO A HUNDRED

ADDDEEEHIOOPRSTV	PAID OVER THE ODDS
ADDDEEHLLNPPSUU	PUSHED AND PULLED
ADDDEEIIKLLNRST	TALKED IN RIDDLES
ADDDEEIILLSSSTU	STUDIED ALL SIDES
ADDDEEINNNOOORSS	ENDORADIOSONDES
ADDDEENNNOOSSZZ	DOZENS AND DOZENS
ADDDEENNORSSTTU	TOSSED AND TURNED
ADDDEFFHINNRTUY	HUNDRED AND FIFTY
ADDDEFGLNNNOOUW	NEWFOUNDLAND DOG
ADDDEFHNNORRTUY	HUNDRED AND FORTY
ADDDEGIIINNPSVY	PAYING DIVIDENDS
ADDDEHHNNORSTUU	HUNDRED THOUSAND
ADDDEHINNRSTUXY	HUNDRED AND SIXTY
ADDDEKLNNOOOPUW	LOOKED UP AND DOWN
ADDDGGIINNNOOTU	DODGING IN AND OUT
ADDEEEEEHLLNSSV	LEVELHEADEDNESS
ADDEEEEEHNNORST	ENTERED ONE'S HEAD
ADDEEEEEMPRRSTY	DESPERATE REMEDY
ADDEEEEFFHINRRT	FEATHERED FRIEND
ADDEEEEFFHNOPTT	OFF AT THE DEEP END
ADDEEEEFGHNNORT	THE GARDEN OF EDEN
ADDEEEEFHLNNORO	HARDENED ONESELF
ADDEEEEFMNPRRTY	DEFERRED PAYMENT
ADDEEEEHLNRRTTY	TENDERHEARTEDLY
ADDEEEEHNOPRRTW	OPENED THE DRAWER
ADDEEEEHOQSTTUZ	SQUEEZED TO DEATH
ADDEEEFHHINORTT	HEARD THE END OF IT
ADDEEEFHHNOORTT	THE END OF THE ROAD
ADDEEEFHIMORRST	RISE FROM THE DEAD
ADDEEEFHMOORRST	ROSE FROM THE DEAD
ADDEEEFILMNNRRY	MY LEARNED FRIEND
ADDEEEGHHHIRTTW	EDWARD THE EIGHTH
ADDEEEGHHILNSST	LIGHT-HEADEDNESS
ADDEEEGHILMNNRT	ENLARGED THE MIND
ADDEEEGHNNOOSTW	GET ONE'S HEAD DOWN
ADDEEEGHNNORSSW	WRONGHEADEDNESS
ADDEEEGHNOORSST	GOOD-HEARTEDNESS
ADDEEEGMNNOOOORY	EARNED GOOD MONEY
ADDEEEGNOOPRSTX	EXPOSED TO DANGER
ADDEEEHHHISSSTW	WASHED THE DISHES
ADDEEEHHIMRSSTT	MISSED THE THREAD
ADDEEEHHNOOPSSS	DASHED ONE'S HOPES
ADDEEEHIIOSSTUV	AVOIDED THE ISSUE
ADDEEEHIKNNRSST	KINDHEARTEDNESS
ADDEEEHILNPRSTW	SPLENDID WEATHER
ADDEEEHLNOPTUUV	DEVALUE THE POUND
ADDEEEHMNNNOOOS	DONE ONE HANDSOME
ADDEEEHMNNOOOSS	DOES ONE HANDSOME
ADDEEEHNNORSSTW	DOWNHEARTEDNESS
ADDEEEIIKLRRTTT	TREATED LIKE DIRT
ADDEEEIKMNORRRT	MODERATE DRINKER
ADDEEEEILLPRSSST	SPELLED DISASTER
ADDEEEILNNSSSVY	SEVEN DEADLY SINS
ADDEEEMMPRRTTTU	ATTEMPTED MURDER
ADDEEFFIIMNNNRT	DIFFIDENT MANNER
ADDEEFGHLORRTTU	THE ARTFUL DODGER
ADDEEFGHMNORRRU	HANGED FOR MURDER
ADDEEFGIIMNNOOV	DEVOID OF MEANING
ADDEEFHHORRTTUW	EDWARD THE FOURTH
ADDEEFHIIMNRSTW	MADE FRIENDS WITH
ADDEEFHIMNOORST	THREE OF DIAMONDS
ADDEEFHIOPPRSST	DEPTHS OF DESPAIR
ADDEEFHLLOOORTW	FOLLOWED THE ROAD
ADDEEFIMNNOOQSU	QUEEN OF DIAMONDS
ADDEEFIMNNOOSSV	SEVEN OF DIAMONDS
ADDEEFIMORSSTUX	STUDIED FOR EXAMS
ADDEEFIOORRRSTW	WAITED FOR ORDERS
ADDEEFMNORRRTUW	WANTED FOR MURDER
ADDEEFNOORSTTU	TREADS UNDERFOOT
ADDEEGGIIMNNNPR	IMPENDING DANGER

ADDEEGGIINNNOOSV	SAID GOOD EVENING
ADDEEGGINNNNOPRT	PADDINGTON GREEN
ADDEEGHHINNRSST	RIGHT-HANDEDNESS
ADDEEGHHLLNOPTU	PLOUGHED THE LAND
ADDEEGHHILNOPSTU	PLOUGHED THE SAND
ADDEEGHIKNOPRRT	GROPED IN THE DARK
ADDEEGHILNNOOTU	GONE INTO A HUDDLE
ADDEEGHILNOOSTU	GOES INTO A HUDDLE
ADDEEGHIORSTTUW	SHOWED GRATITUDE
ADDEEGHNNOOOOSTW	GOT ONE'S HEAD DOWN
ADDEEGHNOOOORST	DO ONE'S HEART GOOD
ADDEEGIIKLNNORS	LIKE A DOG'S DINNER
ADDEEGIMNOOORSS	DOING AS ROME DOES
ADDEEGKLNOOORSU	LOOKED DANGEROUS
ADDEEGMMNNORTUU	UNGUARDED MOMENT
ADDEEGMNOOOSTWY	WASTED GOOD MONEY
ADDEEGNNOORSSTU	GOOD-NATUREDNESS
ADDEEHHHHILNPTW	HELD THE WHIP-HAND
ADDEEHHILNNOOOTU	HELD ONE'S HAND OUT
	HELD OUT ONE'S HAND
ADDEEHHHLNOOPSSU	HOLDS ONE'S HEAD UP
	HOLDS UP ONE'S HEAD
ADDEEHHNNORSTTU	SEND THE HAT ROUND
ADDEEHIINNSTWWY	SWAYED IN THE WIND
ADDEEHILMNOOTWY	LOADED WITH MONEY
ADDEEHILMNOPRST	THE PROMISED LAND
ADDEEHILNNOOSSS	SOILED ONE'S HANDS
ADDEEHILNNOPSTU	LANDED IN THE SOUP
ADDEEHILNNOTTUW	WENT INTO A HUDDLE
ADDEEHILNOPSTTU	SPIED OUT THE LAND
ADDEEHILNORSTUV	LIVES TO A HUNDRED
ADDEEHILNPSSTTU	STUDIED THE PLANS
ADDEEHINNOORTVW	OVER AND DONE WITH
ADDEEHINNORSTTU	TURNED ON ITS HEAD
ADDEEHIRSSSTTTU	STUDIED THE STARS
ADDEEHLMNNNOOOT	LANDED ON THE MOON
ADDEEHNNOOOOSST	STOOD ON ONE'S HEAD
ADDEEHOOPRSSTVY	PAYS OVER THE ODDS
ADDEEIIINNOPRRT	INORDINATE PRIDE
ADDEEIIKLNPRSSS	SPEAKS IN RIDDLES
ADDEEIIILLSSSSTU	STUDIES ALL SIDES
ADDEEIIMNPPRRSST	DAMPENED SPIRITS
ADDEEIINOPRRSTV	DRIVEN TO DESPAIR
ADDEEIIOPRRSSTV	DRIVES TO DESPAIR
ADDEEIKLLMOSSTT	MAKES LITTLE ODDS
ADDEEILLMMNNSSS	SMALL-MINDEDNESS
ADDEEILMNOPRTTT	PERMITTED TO LAND
ADDEEKMMNOORTVW	MOVED DOWN-MARKET
ADDEEKNNOOORRSS	DARKENS ONE'S DOOR
ADDEENOORSSSTWW	WASTED ONE'S WORDS
ADDEFFILMNNOOOS	LOAD OFF ONES MIND
ADDEFGHIIMNOOST	EIGHT OF DIAMONDS
ADDEFHIILNORSWW	WORLD AND HIS WIFE
ADDEFINOOORSTUV	ODDS-ON FAVOURITE
ADDEFKLOOOORRTW	LOOKED FORWARD TO
ADDEGGGIINNOOTW	GOING TO A WEDDING
ADDEGHHIIINPSTUW	DID THE WASHING UP
ADDEGHHILNNNOOS	HOLDING ONE'S HAND
ADDEGHHINNOOTTU	HOUNDING TO DEATH
ADDEGHHNOORSTTU	DASH TO THE GROUND
ADDEGHIILNOSTTT	ADDING TO THE LIST
ADDEGHIIMNNOTTT	ADMITTED NOTHING
ADDEGHINOOORSST	DOING AS OTHERS DO
ADDEGIIILMNNOPSU	SEMOLINA PUDDING
ADDEGILNNNNRSTU	UNDERSTANDINGLY
ADDEGILNNOOOSST	DOING AS ONE'S TOLD
ADDEGNNNOORSSTU	STAND ONE'S GROUND
ADDEGNNORRSTUUY	STAY UNDERGROUND
ADDEHHHHILNOPTW	HOLD THE WHIP-HAND
ADDEHHLNNOOOSTU	HOLD ONE'S HAND OUT
	HOLD OUT ONE'S HAND

ADDEHLNOORRSTUW	LOUDER THAN WORDS
ADDEIIIIILNSTUV	INDIVIDUALITIES
ADDEIIIILLNSTUVY	INDIVIDUAL STYLE
ADDEIILMNNOOQSTU	DEMOLITION SQUAD
ADDEILMMNSTTUUU	SUDDEN ULTIMATUM
ADDEIMNNNOPQSSS	MIND ONES PS AND QS
ADDELLMNOORTUWY	MORTALLY WOUNDED
ADDFFFHOOPRRSTU	DROP OF HARD STUFF
ADDFIILNNOOOSTU	SOLID FOUNDATION
ADDGGHIINNOORTW	GOOD HANDWRITING
ADDGGHILLMOORTY	LORD GOD ALMIGHTY
ADDGGIIIINNNNNW	WINING AND DINING
ADDGGIIMNNOOORS	SAID GOOD MORNING
ADDGHILNNNOOSSW	LOSING HANDS DOWN
ADDGIIIILLNNSUV	INDIVIDUALISING
ADDGIIIILLNNUVZ	INDIVIDUALIZING
ADDGINOOOPRSTUW	PUTS IN A GOOD WORD
ADDHHLNOOPRSUUY	HOLD UP YOUR HANDS
ADDIMNNOPQRSSUY	MIND YOUR P'S AND Q'S
ADEEEEEEEHLNRSTW	RENEWED THE LEASE
ADEEEEEEFHMNSTTY	DEFEATS THE ENEMY
ADEEEEEEFLNOPRST	REPEATED ONESELF
ADEEEEEEFNOSSSTY	FEASTED ONE'S EYES
ADEEEEEEGGHMMNNTY	ENGAGED THE ENEMY
ADEEEEEEGLORRSST	TO A LESSER DEGREE
ADEEEEEIKKLNTWW	LIKE A WET WEEKEND
ADEEEEEENORSSTVY	AVERTED ONE'S EYES
ADEEEEEFFGHKNOTT	TAKEN THE EDGE OFF
ADEEEEEFFGHKOSTT	TAKES THE EDGE OFF
ADEEEEEFFLLMNOST	MADE ONESELF FELT
ADEEEEEFHPRRRRSS	PREFERRED SHARES
ADEEEEEFINNOPSVW	DEFENSIVE WEAPON
ADEEEEEFLNOPPRRS	PREPARED ONESELF
ADEEEEEFLNORSSST	ASSERTED ONESELF
ADEEEEEFMNOPSSTT	STAMPED ONE'S FEET
ADEEEEEFNPRSSSXY	DEFRAYS EXPENSES
ADEEEEEGGHILNTVY	GIVEN THE GLAD EYE
ADEEEEEGGHILSTVY	GIVES THE GLAD EYE
ADEEEEEGHMNSSSST	SENDS THE MESSAGE
ADEEEEEGHNOQSTUV	GOD SAVE THE QUEEN
ADEEEEEGMNNRSSSS	SENDS A MESSENGER
ADEEEEEGNNNORSTV	VENTED ONE'S ANGER
ADEEEEEHHMORTTTT	ARMED TO THE TEETH
ADEEEEEHHNRRTTUW	UNDER THE WEATHER
ADEEEEEHINRSSTTY	STRAINED THE EYES
ADEEEEEHLLNOORSS	RELEASE ONES HOLD
ADEEEEEHNNOOPRST	OPENED ONE'S HEART
ADEEEEEHNNOPRSST	OPENHEARTEDNESS
ADEEEEEHOQSSTTUZ	SQUEEZES TO DEATH
ADEEEEEIIKLMRSSV	MAKES DELIVERIES
ADEEEEEIMNNRSSTT	DETERMINATENESS
ADEEEEEINNPRRTTT	INTERPENETRATED
ADEEEEEKNPRRRSTU	KEEP UNDER ARREST
ADEEEEENNOPPRSSX	SPARED NO EXPENSE
ADEEEEFFFGINRSTU	SUFFERING DEFEAT
ADEEEEFFFHLRRSTU	RUFFLED FEATHERS
ADEEEEFFFMMOORRR	FREEDOM FROM FEAR
ADEEEEFFGHNNOOOS	GONE OFF ONE'S HEAD
ADEEEEFFGHNOOOSS	GOES OFF ONE'S HEAD
ADEEEEFFHNNOOSTW	WENT OFF ONE'S HEAD
ADEEEEFFINRSSTTT	DIFFERENT TASTES
ADEEEEFFKORRSSTU	SUFFERED A STROKE
ADEEEEFGGGHINRTW	WAGGED THE FINGER
ADEEEEFGGHIIOSTT	THE FOGGIEST IDEA
ADEEEEFGHHLRSTTU	FEELS THE DRAUGHT
ADEEEEFGHILNOSST	SIDE OF THE ANGELS
ADEEEEFGHINORTTZ	FREEZING TO DEATH
ADEEEEFGHLORRSTW	GATHERED FLOWERS
ADEEEEFGILNNOSSS	FIND ONE'S SEA LEGS
ADEEEEFHHINORSTT	HEARS THE END OF IT
ADEEEEFHIILNNSUV	LEAVE UNFINISHED
ADEEEEFHIKLOPSTV	SPEAK OF THE DEVIL
ADEEEEFHILMNOPRU	REMAINED HOPEFUL
ADEEEEFHILNORSTT	LIFTED ONE'S HEART
ADEEEEFHLLLOORTW	FOLLOW THE LEADER
	FOLLOW-THE-LEADER
ADEEEEFHLMPRRSTU	RUMPLED FEATHERS
ADEEEEFHLNOPRTTW	PETER AND THE WOLF
ADEEEEFHNORSSSTT	SOFTHEARTEDNESS
ADEEEEFIKLLORTWW	FLOWED LIKE WATER
ADEEEEFILNNORSST	STRAINED ONESELF
ADEEEEFIMOPRRTTU	TIME OF DEPARTURE
ADEEEEFKLLNOOSTT	TALKED TO ONESELF
ADEEEEFLLLLNPRSU	FELL UNDER A SPELL
ADEEEEFLLNPRSSTU	FULL SPEED ASTERN
ADEEEEFLNNNOOSST	LANDS ON ONE'S FEET
ADEEEEFLNOORSTTW	WORLD AT ONES FEET
ADEEEEFLNOORTUVV	LOVE OF ADVENTURE
ADEEEEFMNNOORSTU	MADE ONE'S FORTUNE
ADEEEEGGHIKLNPTT	TAKING THE PLEDGE
ADEEEEGGHIKMRRTT	RIGGED THE MARKET
ADEEEEGGIMORRRUU	GEORGE DU MAURIER
ADEEEEGHHIINNOSV	GIVEN ONE HIS HEAD
ADEEEEGHHIINOSSV	GIVES ONE HIS HEAD
ADEEEEGHHNPPRTTU	GET THE UPPER HAND
ADEEEEGHHORRSTTT	THREADS TOGETHER
ADEEEEGHIKNNNRST	SEEING IN THE DARK
ADEEEEGHIINSSTUV	EVADING THE ISSUE
ADEEEEGHILMNNRST	ENLARGES THE MIND
ADEEEEGHILPPRSTT	DESPERATE PLIGHT
ADEEEEGHIMRSSTTT	MISSED THE TARGET
ADEEEEGHINNOOSTT	GET INTO ONES HEAD
ADEEEEGHINNRSSST	NEARSIGHTEDNESS
ADEEEEGHLOPPRSST	SPREAD THE GOSPEL
ADEEEEGHNOPPSSTT	STEPPED ON THE GAS
ADEEEEGHORRSTTTT	STARTED TOGETHER
ADEEEEGIKNNNNRSV	NEVER-ENDING TASK
ADEEEEGIKNOPPTTU	KEEPING UP-TO-DATE
ADEEEEGILLLNNRTT	LITTLE ENGLANDER
ADEEEEGILMNNNNOS	LENDING ONE'S NAME
ADEEEEGILMNNNNST	DISENTANGLEMENT
ADEEEEGILNNOOPRS	OLD-AGE PENSIONER
ADEEEEGILNNOORRT	OLDER GENERATION
ADEEEEGIMNNNNORST	NODS IN AGREEMENT
ADEEEEGLMNNRSSTU	ENDLESS ARGUMENT
ADEEEEGLNOPRRTUU	DEPARTURE LOUNGE
ADEEEEGLNORRRSTY	ORDERLY SERGEANT
ADEEEEGNOOPRSSTX	EXPOSES TO DANGER
ADEEEEHHHIILNSTT	HIT THE HEADLINES
ADEEEEHHHINRSTTW	THREW IN THE SHADE
ADEEEEHHHIORSTTV	HITS OVER THE HEAD
ADEEEEHHHISSSSTW	WASHES THE DISHES
ADEEEEHHIMRSSSTT	MISSES THE THREAD
ADEEEEHHLNNOORSS	HARD ON ONE'S HEELS
ADEEEEHHLNRSTTTU	STEAL THE THUNDER
ADEEEEHHNNORTTTU	TURNED ON THE HEAT
	TURNED THE HEAT ON
ADEEEEHHNOOPSSSS	DASHES ONE'S HOPES
ADEEEEHIILLMMNRST	THREE MILE ISLAND
ADEEEEHIILRRTTTY	HEREDITARY TITLE
ADEEEEHIIMNPTTTT	DIE IN THE ATTEMPT
ADEEEEHIJKLMNPTU	JUMPED IN THE LAKE
ADEEEEHIKMNNORTY	RAKED IN THE MONEY
ADEEEEHIKNNNOPSS	KEEPS ONE'S HAND IN
ADEEEEHILNOOPRST	RADIOTELEPHONES
ADEEEEHIMNNRSSTTU	READS THE MINUTES
ADEEEEHINNNQSTTUU	STAND IN THE QUEUE
ADEEEEHKLLNNRSSTW	SWELLED THE RANKS
ADEEEEHLLLMMPPRYY	PLAYED MERRY HELL
ADEEEEHLLMORRSUW	WHOLESALE MURDER
ADEEEEHLMPSSTTYY	PLAYED THE SYSTEM
ADEEEEHLNOOPRTUV	ENDEAVOUR TO HELP

ADEEEHNNNORTVWY	EVERY NOW AND THEN	ADEEFHLOOORSTTT	TOOLS OF THE TRADE
ADEEEHNNOOTTTXY	ONE DAY TO THE NEXT	ADEEFHMMOORRSTY	STRAYED FROM HOME
ADEEEHNORRRTTTU	RETURNED TO EARTH	ADEEFHMNNOORSTU	HANDSOME FORTUNE
ADEEEHNORRSTTTU	SOUND THE RETREAT	ADEEFIILLMOSSTT	OLD AS TIME ITSELF
ADEEEHOOPRTTTUU	POURED OUT THE TEA	ADEEFIILNOPQRSU	QUALIFIED PERSON
ADEEEIILMNNRTTY	INDETERMINATELY	ADEEFIIMNNSSTTY	MANIFEST DESTINY
ADEEEIILMNNSSTT	SENTIMENTALISED	ADEEFIKLMOORSST	FOR OLD TIMES SAKE
ADEEEIILMNNSTTZ	SENTIMENTALIZED	ADEEFIKLMOPSSST	SELF-IMPOSED TASK
ADEEEIILMNRTTVY	DETERMINATIVELY	ADEEFILLNNOOSWY	LAY DOWN ONES LIFE
ADEEEIILNOPPPRR	IN APPLE-PIE ORDER	ADEEFILNSSSSTTU	DISTASTEFULNESS
ADEEEIIMMQRSSUV	DEMISEMIQUAVERS	ADEEFIMMORSSSTU	STUDIES FOR EXAMS
ADEEEIIMOSSTTTU	OUTSIDE ESTIMATE	ADEEFINNOOPRRSZ	PRISONER OF ZENDA
ADEEEIILMNORRSSV	DELIVERS A SERMON	ADEEFINNOPRRRST	RAN FOR PRESIDENT
ADEEEINNPRRSSST	PRESIDENT NASSER	ADEEFINOPRRRTTU	RETURNED A PROFIT
ADEEEINPRRSTTTY	INTERESTED PARTY	ADEEFLLMNOOOSTT	TOLD SOMEONE FLAT
ADEEEKNPPRRSSUW	KEEPS UNDER WRAPS	ADEEFMMMNNOOSST	MOMENT OF MADNESS
ADEEEKNPRRRSTTU	KEPT UNDER ARREST	ADEEFMMNOORRTVW	FORWARD MOVEMENT
ADEEELLLMNOPTVY	DEVELOPMENTALLY	ADEEFMNOOOPSSTT	STAMPED ONE'S FOOT
ADEEELMNPPRSTTU	TRADE SUPPLEMENT	ADEEFMNOPRRSTTU	PERFORMED A STUNT
ADEEEMMMNNNNORSS	MEND ONE'S MANNERS	ADEEGGHHHHIINRR	HIGHER AND HIGHER
ADEEEMMORRRSTUY	TREASURED MEMORY	ADEEGGHIIINPTUV	GIVING UP THE IDEA
ADEEEMMNNOOSSTWY	WASTED ONE'S MONEY	ADEEGGHIIINRSTW	DISAGREEING WITH
ADEEEEMNOPRRSTTT	DEPARTMENT STORE	ADEEGGHIILMNNOT	HOLDING A MEETING
ADEEEENNOOOORSSTT	TREAD ON ONE'S TOES	ADEEGGHIILNNSTW	SWINGING THE LEAD
ADEEEENOOPPRSSST	STOPPED ONE'S EARS	ADEEGGHIINORRUV	GIVEN A ROUGH RIDE
ADEEEOPRRRSSTTU	TAPERED TROUSERS	ADEEGGHIIORRSUV	GIVES A ROUGH RIDE
ADEEFFFHHHLLNOTY	FLY OFF THE HANDLE	ADEEGGHILNPRSTU	SLEEPING DRAUGHT
ADEEFFGHLLLLÖÖTW	FOLLOWED THE FLAG	ADEEGGHIIINNOOOST	GOING TO ONE'S HEAD
ADEEFFGHLLNTUU	UNFURLED THE FLAG	ADEEGGHNOOOOTTU	GOOD ENOUGH TO EAT
ADEEFFGHNORSTTU	TURNED OFF THE GAS	ADEEGGHNORRTUUY	YOUNGER DAUGHTER
ADEEFFGHOORSSTT	FEAST FOR THE GODS	ADEEGGIINNNORSX	GRINDING ONE'S AXE
ADEEFFGIIINNRTT	DIFFERENTIATING	ADEEGGINNOORSVW	DIG ONES OWN GRAVE
ADEEFFGIINRSSTT	DIFFERING TASTES	ADEEGGINNOOSSVY	SAYS GOOD EVENING
ADEEFFFHINNOSTTU	FIFTEEN THOUSAND	ADEEGGINNRTTUWY	GETTING UNDER WAY
ADEEFFHKNOPRRST	PROFFERED THANKS	ADEEGGMMNORRTTU	GOTTERDAMMERUNG
ADEEFFHNOPRTTTU	TURNED OFF THE TAP	ADEEGGNNOORSUVW	DUG ONE'S OWN GRAVE
ADEEFFIIINNORTT	DIFFERENTIATION	ADEEGHHHINPSTTW	GETS THE WHIP-HAND
ADEEFFIKMNNOOST	TAKE ONES MIND OFF	ADEEGHHIILMNSTV	SHAMING THE DEVIL
ADEEFFILNORRRSU	RUNS FOR DEAR LIFE	ADEEGHHIILNRRT	HIGHLAND TERRIER
ADEEFFINORSSTTU	SUSTAINED EFFORT	ADEEGHHIILRTTUW	DIE WITH LAUGHTER
ADEEFFMMNOORRTW	FREEDOM FROM WANT	ADEEGHHIINPRSST	HIGH-SPEED TRAINS
ADEEFGGINORRSTU	FORGED SIGNATURE	ADEEGHHILLNOSTT	LIGHTENS THE LOAD
ADEEFGHHHIOTTTT	FIGHT TO THE DEATH	ADEEGHHILLMNOSTT	THE SAME OLD THING
ADEEFGHHLLOOPSTT	THE LAP OF THE GODS	ADEEFGHHILNORSTT	LOSING THE THREAD
ADEEFGHIILNNRTW	INFRINGED THE LAW	ADEEGHHJLNOOOTY	ENJOY GOOD HEALTH
ADEEFGHIINORSTT	SHIFTED INTO GEAR	ADEEGHHNOPPRTTU	GOT THE UPPER HAND
ADEEFGHIKMNNOOV	KINGDOM OF HEAVEN	ADEEGHIIMMNNTT	MIDNIGHT MATINEE
ADEEFGHILNOORRT	ALONG FOR THE RIDE	ADEEGHIIKLNRTWW	WRINKLED WITH AGE
ADEEFGHIOPPRRTT	PREPARED TO FIGHT	ADEEGHIIILLNRTTT	DEAR LITTLE THING
ADEEFGHKLNOOORS	GOD-FORSAKEN HOLE	ADEEGHIILNNRSTY	DISHEARTENINGLY
ADEEFGHOOORTTTU	GET OUT OF THE ROAD	ADEEGHIIMNNPPRS	MISAPPREHENDING
ADEEFGIIILNNNRU	ENDING IN FAILURE	ADEEGHIIMNPRRTU	REMAINED UPRIGHT
ADEEFGIIINNSSST	SIGNIFIED ASSENT	ADEEGHIIMNRTTVY	ADMIT EVERYTHING
ADEEFGIIILLLSTUV	GIVE FULL DETAILS	ADEEGHIINNNNOST	TANNING ONE'S HIDE
ADEEFGIILLLNOSSS	FILLED ONE'S GLASS	ADEEGHIINNRRSST	TEARING IN SHREDS
ADEEFGILMOORSSS	GAMES OF SOLDIERS	ADEEGHIKNNNRRST	RENDERING THANKS
ADEEFGINNRRRTUU	GARDEN FURNITURE	ADEEGHIKNOPRRST	GROPES IN THE DARK
ADEEFGKNOOORSSS	FOR GOODNESS SAKE!	ADEEGHIKNOPRSTW	SPEAKING THE WORD
ADEEFHHHILLORST	HEAD FOR THE HILLS	ADEEGHILNNOOPTY	PILED ON THE AGONY
ADEEFHIIKMNRSTW	MAKE FRIENDS WITH	ADEEGHIMNORSSTW	MADE THINGS WORSE
ADEEFHIILPRSSTT	DEPARTS THIS LIFE	ADEEGHINNMOOOSTT	GOT INTO ONE'S HEAD
ADEEFHIINNNOPST	PINNED ONE'S FAITH	ADEEGHINNOPSSUV	HAVE DESIGNS UPON
ADEEFHIINNSSTTU	UNFINISHED STATE	ADEEGHINNOSTTTY	STAYING TO THE END
ADEEFHIKLLLOSTTV	TALKS OF THE DEVIL	ADEEGHINNNRSTUV	THURSDAY EVENING
ADEEFHIKNNORSST	KINDNESS OF HEART	ADEEGHINNSSTTTT	STANDING THE TEST
ADEEFHILLMNORST	FELL ON HARD TIMES	ADEEGHINORSTTTU	STRAIGHTENED OUT
ADEEFHILNOPSSTU	LIFTS UP ONE'S HEAD	ADEEGHINORSTTVY	STAYED OVERNIGHT
ADEEFHIMMOOSTTT	MADE THE MOST OF IT	ADEEGHINSTTTWWY	TWENTY-EIGHT DAYS
ADEEFHINNSSTUWY	SAW THE FUNNY SIDE	ADEEGHIOPRSSTVW	GIVE THE PASSWORD
ADEEFHKMNOOORST	ASKED FOR THE MOON	ADEEGHKMNORRTTU	DRUG ON THE MARKET
ADEEFHKMOOORRST	MAKES FOR THE DOOR	ADEEGHLMOORTTUV	MOVED TO LAUGHTER

ADEEGHLORSSTTTW	GETS THE LAST WORD
ADEEGHNNNOOSSST	GETS ONE'S HANDS ON
ADEEGHNNOORRVWY	HANG ON EVERY WORD
ADEEGHNNORRTTUU	GET THE RUNAROUND
ADEEGHNOORRTTUZ	RAZE TO THE GROUND
ADEEGIIINNPRSST	PEDESTRIANISING
ADEEGIIKNNNOOST	TAKING ON ONE SIDE
ADEEGIIKNNOOSTT	TAKING TO ONE SIDE
ADEEGIILLNNOSTV	LEADING NOVELIST
ADEEGIILNNOOSTT	GONE INTO DETAILS
ADEEGIILNNOPRSS	DEPERSONALISING
ADEEGIILNNOPRSZ	DEPERSONALIZING
ADEEGIILNNOQSTU	LEADING QUESTION
ADEEGIILNNORRTV	LEARNING TO DRIVE
ADEEGIILNOOSSTT	GOES INTO DETAILS
ADEEGIIMNNRSTTU	UNDERESTIMATING
ADEEGIINNOORTTY	GAINED NOTORIETY
ADEEGILLMOORSTT	GRILLED TOMATOES
ADEEGIILLNORSUVY	LIVE DANGEROUSLY
ADEEGILNNOPRSTY	PLYING ONE'S TRADE
ADEEGILNOPPRTVY	PLEADING POVERTY
ADEEGINNOORSSTW	EATING ONE'S WORDS
ADEEGINNOPRSSSU	GAINED ONE'S SPURS
ADEEGINNOPRSSSW	SPREAD ONE'S WINGS
	SPREAD ONES WINGS
ADEEGLNOPRRSSUU	PLEASURE GROUNDS
ADEEGMNNOOSSTWY	WASTES GOOD MONEY
ADEEGNNOOPRRSSU	DANGEROUS PERSON
ADEEHHHINORSTTW	THROW IN THE SHADE
ADEEHHIIMSTTTVW	SWAM WITH THE TIDE
ADEEHHIKLNNORST	DRINK ONES HEALTH
ADEEHHIKMNOSTTT	TAKE THE HINDMOST
ADEEHHILMNPTTWY	WITHHELD PAYMENT
ADEEHHILOPRSSST	SHARED THE SPOILS
ADEEHHIMMOPRSTU	HUMID ATMOSPHERE
ADEEHHIMNORRTTU	ROTHERHAM UNITED
ADEEHHINNNORSTW	THREW IN ONE'S HAND
	THREW ONE'S HAND IN
ADEEHHINOPSTTTU	PUT INTO THE SHADE
ADEEHHKLNNORSTU	DRUNK ONE'S HEALTH
ADEEHHLLOPSTTUW	PUSHED TO THE WALL
ADEEHHNNORSTTTU	SENT THE HAT ROUND
ADEEHIIILLNNOTT	LAID IT ON THE LINE
ADEEHIILLKNOOPST	HATED LIKE POISON
ADEEHIILLMNRTTW	WINDMILL THEATRE
ADEEHIILLNOPTVY	PLAYED THE VIOLIN
ADEEHIILLNSTTTW	WAITS TILL THE END
ADEEHIIRRSTTVWW	SERVED WITH A WRIT
ADEEHIKKNOOSSTT	SOAKED TO THE SKIN
ADEEHIKLOSSSTTU	LAUDS TO THE SKIES
ADEEHILLNNOORTW	ALONE IN THE WORLD
ADEEHILLNNOTVWY	DOWN IN THE VALLEY
ADEEHILLNOPPSTU	PULLED INTO SHAPE
ADEEHILLNORTTVW	DRIVEN TO THE WALL
ADEEHILLNPRTUVW	DRIVEN UP THE WALL
ADEEHILLORSTTVW	DRIVES TO THE WALL
ADEEHILLPRSTUVW	DRIVES UP THE WALL
ADEEHILMNNOPRSS	POLISHED MANNERS
ADEEHILNNNORRRT	NORTHERN IRELAND
ADEEHILNNOORSTW	LET DOWN ONES HAIR
	LET ONES HAIR DOWN
ADEEHILNOPSSTTU	SPIES OUT THE LAND
ADEEHILNPSSSTTU	STUDIES THE PLANS
ADEEHILOOSTTTTV	THE DEVIL'S TATTOO
ADEEHIMMNORRRTU	UNMARRIED MOTHER
ADEEHIMNNNOOSST	TIME ON ONES HANDS
ADEEHINNOOORSSV	SHOVED IN ONE'S OAR
ADEEHINNOPRTTTW	PAINT THE TOWN RED
ADEEHINNOSSTTUX	SIXTEEN THOUSAND
ADEEHINORRSSTTW	SHOWED RESTRAINT
ADEEHIOPPPPSTTT	PIPPED AT THE POST

ADEEHIRSSSSTTTU	STUDIES THE STARS
ADEEHJMNOORRUWY	HOMEWARD JOURNEY
ADEEHKLMNNOOOTW	WALKED ON THE MOON
ADEEHKLNOORRSTY	TAKEN HOLY ORDERS
ADEEHKLOORRSSTY	TAKES HOLY ORDERS
ADEEHKNOOOSTTTW	TAKEN TO THE WOODS
ADEEHKOOOSSTTTW	TAKES TO THE WOODS
ADEEHLLLOORRTVW	ALL THE WORLD OVER
ADEEHLLNOPSSTTW	DWELLS ON THE PAST
ADEEHLLORRSTTVW	TRAVELS THE WORLD
ADEEHLMOORSSTTY	THE SAME OLD STORY
ADEEHLOQRRSSSUU	SQUARE SHOULDERS
ADEEHMNOORRRSTY	RESTORED HARMONY
ADEEHMNOPPRSTTU	PUT THE DAMPERS ON
ADEEHMORSSSTTUW	ASSUMED THE WORST
ADEEHNNOSSTTUVY	SEVENTY THOUSAND
ADEEIIMMNNNORTT	INDETERMINATION
ADEEIIINNOSSSTT	DESENSITISATION
ADEEIIINNOSSTTZ	DESENSITIZATION
ADEEIIKLMPRSSTU	PASTEURISED MILK
ADEEIIKMNOPRSSS	ASKED PERMISSION
ADEEIILLLLMRSSTV	SILVER MEDALLIST
ADEEIILMNOOPRTU	MINIATURE POODLE
ADEEIILNNOSTTTW	WENT INTO DETAILS
ADEEIILNOOPPRTX	POLAR EXPEDITION
ADEEIILNOOPSTTX	EXALTED POSITION
ADEEIILNOSSTTTW	TWISTED ONE'S TAIL
ADEEIIMNNORSTTU	UNDERESTIMATION
ADEEIINNNOOPSST	OPINIONATEDNESS
ADEEIINOOPRTTVV	PRIVATE DEVOTION
ADEEIKMMNNOPSSU	MAKES ONE'S MIND UP
	MAKES UP ONE'S MIND
ADEEIILMNNORSTTVY	DEMONSTRATIVELY
ADEEILNOORRRSST	LEONARD ROSSITER
ADEEIMMOPRRSTTV	IMPROVED MATTERS
ADEEIMNNORSTTUV	UNDEMONSTRATIVE
ADEEKMMNOORSTVW	MOVES DOWN-MARKET
ADEEKNOOPRSUWWY	WORKED ONE'S WAY UP
ADEEMNNNOOPSTUW	PUT ONES NAME DOWN
ADEEMNNPPSSSTUY	SUSPENDS PAYMENT
ADEENNNNNOOSSST	STAND NO NONSENSE
ADEENNNOOOSSSTT	STAND ON ONES TOES
ADEENNORSSSTUUV	ADVENTUROUSNESS
ADEENOORSSSSTWW	WASTES ONE'S WORDS
ADEENPRRRSSTTUU	PUTS UNDER ARREST
ADEFFGHIIKLNOTT	TAKING THE LID OFF
ADEFFHILLNORSUV	HANDFUL OF SILVER
ADEFFHILNNNRSTUU	UNFURNISHED FLAT
ADEFGGGHILNOOTT	FLOGGING TO DEATH
ADEFGHHIIILLQUY	HIGHLY QUALIFIED
ADEFGHHIILNOTTY	IN THE LIGHT OF DAY
ADEFGHHIKNOORTT	KNIGHT OF THE ROAD
ADEFGHIILLNNOTV	LAND OF THE LIVING
ADEFGHIILNORTVY	LIVING FOR THE DAY
ADEFGHIINNRSSTU	RAISING THE FUNDS
ADEFGHIKNNOORST	ASKED FOR NOTHING
ADEFGHLLNOORTTU	FALL TO THE GROUND
ADEFGHLOOPRRUUW	PLOUGHED A FURROW
ADEFGHOOOORTTTU	GOT OUT OF THE ROAD
ADEFGIIKMNNNRTU	FIRM UNDERTAKING
ADEFGIJMNOPRSTU	JUDGMENT OF PARIS
ADEFGILNNOORRW	WORLD OF LEARNING
ADEFGILNNORRSSU	SUING FOR SLANDER
ADEFGINOPPRRSTW	STEPPING FORWARD
ADEFGINOPRRRSSW	PRESSING FORWARD
ADEFHHIOORSTTTW	HAD THE WORST OF IT
ADEFHIIIKKLNRSS	DRINKS LIKE A FISH
ADEFHIINRSSTTWY	STAY WITH FRIENDS
ADEFHILMNNOOOSY	FOOL AND HIS MONEY
ADEFHKMOOORRSTW	MADE SHORT WORK OF
ADEFHLMNOOOORTWW	WOMAN OF THE WORLD

ADEFIIKLOPRRSWY	FIREWORK DISPLAY
ADEFIIKMNNOORST	INFORMATION DESK
ADEFIILLNNSTUVW	STAND IN FULL VIEW
ADEFIILLNOSSSTU	FALLS INTO DISUSE
ADEFIILMNNOORSU	FOUR-DIMENSIONAL
ADEFIILNNOSSTUY	FAILS IN ONE'S DUTY
ADEFIIMNNNOOOPR	FORMED AN OPINION
ADEFILMNORRTUUU	OUR MUTUAL FRIEND
ADEFINNNOOOSTTU	FOUNDATION STONE
ADEFKLNOORTTTUU	TALKED OUT OF TURN
ADEFNOOOORSSTUW	WORD OUT OF SEASON
ADEGGHHIILLNORSY	HIGHLY ORGANISED
ADEGGHHIINNOSTW	DOING THE WASHING
ADEGGHIILLNRTTY	TREADING LIGHTLY
ADEGGHIIINNNOSSV	HAVING DESIGNS ON
ADEGGHIKNOOSTTV	GIVE THANKS TO GOD
ADEGGHINNOPRTUW	PAWING THE GROUND
ADEGGIIILNINOOTT	GOING INTO DETAIL
ADEGGIIKLNNORST	TAKING IN LODGERS
ADEGGIIKMNNOOST	TAKING SOME DOING
ADEGGIINNNORRTU	UNDERGO TRAINING
ADEGGIINNNORTTU	GETTING A ROUND IN
ADEGGIINNPRTTU	PUTTING IN DANGER
ADEGHHHLNOOPTTU	HAND TO THE PLOUGH
ADEGHHIIMNNNOST	SOMETHING IN HAND
ADEGHHINNRRSTTU	HUNGER AND THIRST
ADEGHHINORSTTTW	DOWN THE STRAIGHT
ADEGHHLNNOORSTT	LONG AND THE SHORT
ADEGHHLNOPSSSTU	PLOUGHS THE SANDS
ADEGHIILKLNNRVY	DRINKING HEAVILY
ADEGHIIIINNOPRRV	PROVIDING AN HEIR
ADEGHIIKNNRSTTT	STARTED THINKING
ADEGHIILNNOSSUV	HAVING DELUSIONS
ADEGHIILNNPRSTY	SPREADING THINLY
ADEGHIINNNOPSSW	WIPING ONE'S HANDS
ADEGHIKMNNORSTU	MAKING THE ROUNDS
ADEGHILMMNOORST	SLAMMING THE DOOR
ADEGHILMNORRSSU	SHOULDERING ARMS
ADEGHIMNNORSTUY	MOTHERING SUNDAY
ADEGHINNNORSSSW	WRINGS ONE'S HANDS
ADEGHINOORRTTWY	WORRYING TO DEATH
ADEGHJNNOOORSTY	STAGE-DOOR JOHNNY
ADEGHLNNOORTUWY	THE LONG WAY ROUND
ADEGHNNNOOOORSSW	HANG ON ONE'S WORDS
ADEGHNNOORRTTUU	GOT THE RUNAROUND
ADEGHNNORSSTTUW	TURNS DOWN THE GAS
ADEGIIIOPRRSTTT	PRESTIDIGITATOR
ADEGIIKLNNOTTWY	TAKE IT LYING DOWN
ADEGIINNORSSSTT	DRESSING STATION
ADEGIINNPRSSTTY	DISSENTING PARTY
ADEGIINOPPRRSTT	DROPPING A SITTER
ADEGILLNNOQRTUY	GRANDILOQUENTLY
ADEGILLNOPSTTUY	PLEADS NOT GUILTY
ADEGINNOOPSSTTY	DYING AT ONE'S POST
ADEGINNOPRRSSSW	PRESSING ONWARDS
ADEGLLOOORSSTTY	TELLS A GOOD STORY
ADEGNNOORSSSTUY	STAYS ONE'S GROUND
ADEGNOORSSSSTTU	SENDS OUT TO GRASS
ADEHHIIILLMRTTW	WILLIAM THE THIRD
ADEHHIILLNNOSTUY	HOLIDAY IN THE SUN
ADEHHIIMMOPRRST	HERMAPHRODITISM
ADEHHILMNOPTTWY	WITHHOLD PAYMENT
ADEHHIMPRRSUVYY	SIR HUMPHREY DAVY
ADEHHINNNOORSTW	THROW IN ONES HAND
	THROW ONE'S HAND IN
ADEHHINORRRSTTW	SHORTHAND WRITER
ADEHHIOOPRSSSTT	SHOOTS THE RAPIDS
ADEHHKNOOOORTTTU	TOOK THE HAT ROUND
ADEHIIILNNOOTTW	ANOINTED WITH OIL
ADEHIIILNNOSTTW	SAIL INTO THE WIND
ADEHIIKLLORTWWW	WORKED WITH A WILL
ADEHIIMNNOOSSTWY	SHOWED ANIMOSITY
ADEHIINNRRSSTTWW	STRAWS IN THE WIND
ADEHIMNNOOOORSTW	SHOWN MODERATION
ADEHIMNOOOORSSTW	SHOWS MODERATION
ADEHINNNOORRSSW	DRAW IN ONES HORNS
ADEHINNNOOSSSST	SITS ON ONE'S HANDS
ADEHINNOOOORRTTU	ON THE ROAD TO RUIN
ADEHLLOOOPTTTUU	PULLED A TOOTH OUT
ADEHNNNOPPSSSTUU	PUTS ONE'S HANDS UP
ADEIIIKLLOSTTTW	TOLD IT LIKE IT WAS
ADEIIINNOPRRSTW	DREW INSPIRATION
ADEIIINNPRSSSTW	WINES AND SPIRITS
ADEIIJLNPRRSTUU	JURISPRUDENTIAL
ADEIIMNNOPPSSTT	DISAPPOINTMENTS
ADEIINNOOOPRTTW	WOODEN PARTITION
ADEIKLLORRSTTUW	ILLUSTRATED WORK
ADEILLMNPPRSUYY	PURELY AND SIMPLY
ADEILLNOORSSTVY	SOLD INTO SLAVERY
ADEILNINOOOFFROT	DROP INTO ONE'S LAP
ADEILNOOOSSSTWW	SOW ONES WILD OATS
ADEIMNOOOOPPRST	PROPOSED A MOTION
ADEIMNOOPPRRTTX	EXPORT AND IMPORT
ADELLLNORSSUWWY	SLOWLY AND SURELY
ADELLOORRSSSWWW	SWORD-SWALLOWERS
ADELMMNORRSSUUU	ROMULUS AND REMUS
ADENNOOOPPPRSTUW	PUTS DOWN ON PAPER
ADFFGLLNOOOORRTU	GROUND-FLOOR FLAT
ADFGGGHIIILLNNOUY	DYING OF LAUGHING
ADFGGHIOOPPTTUU	PUT UP A GOOD FIGHT
ADFGGIINOOOPRSTTW	WAITING FOR GODOT
ADFGHIILNNOORRU	GLORIA HUNNIFORD
ADFGIINNNNORSTT	STANDING IN FRONT
ADFGIKLNOOOOOTT	TOOK A LOT OF DOING
ADFHIHMMNOOORTTU	FROM HAND TO MOUTH
ADFLLNOOOPRSSUW	SOUND-PROOF WALLS
ADGGHHIILLNNORUY	HANDLING ROUGHLY
ADGGHIIILLNSTVY	LIVING DAYLIGHTS
ADGGHIILMNNOOOT	DOING A MOONLIGHT
ADGGHIINNPRSTTU	STANDING UPRIGHT
ADGGHILLNOOTUUU	LAUGHING OUT LOUD
ADGGHINNORRSSTW	RIGHTS AND WRONGS
ADGGIINNOORSSTW	GOING DOWNSTAIRS
ADGGIMNNNNOOOORW	DOING NO MAN WRONG
ADGGIMNNOOOORSSY	SAYS GOOD MORNING
ADGHHHILNNOSTUU	HUNTS HIGH AND LOW
ADGHHIINORSTVWW	HAVING WORDS WITH
ADGHHIKLLNOOOSW	LOOKS HIGH AND LOW
ADGHIILLOOORSUY	GLORIOUS HOLIDAY
ADGHIILOOSTTTWW	DOG WITH TWO TAILS
ADGHIIMNOOSSSTU	SOUGHT ADMISSION
ADGHIINNNOSTTTW	NOTWITHSTANDING
ADGHIINNOOPRRTW	POOR HANDWRITING
ADGHIINNPSSSTUY	STUDYING SPANISH
ADGHILNOOPRSSTU	HOSPITAL GROUNDS
ADGHIMNNNORRSTU	THURSDAY MORNING
ADGHINOOOORTTUY	ON GOOD AUTHORITY
ADGHIOOPRSSTTTU	STOOD UP STRAIGHT
ADGHOOOOPPSSTUUW	PUTS UP A GOOD SHOW
ADGIIILNNPSTTU	PLATITUDINISING
ADGIIIILNNPTTUZ	PLATITUDINIZING
ADGIIIILNNRSSTU	INDUSTRIALISING
ADGIIIILNNRSTUZ	INDUSTRIALIZING
ADGIIILNNOPPSTY	DISAPPOINTINGLY
ADGIIINNOPPSTTU	DISPUTING A POINT
ADGIIINNOQRRSTU	GRAND INQUISITOR
ADGIINNRSSSTUUY	STUDYING RUSSIAN
ADGINNNORRRSSUU	RUNS RINGS AROUND
ADHHINOPRSSTTTY	SHORTHAND TYPIST
ADHHJKNNNOORTWY	JOHNNY DANKWORTH
ADHHLNOOOORTTUY	HOLD ON TO YOUR HAT
ADHHMMMNNNOOSSTT	MONTHS AND MONTHS

ADHIILLNOORRSSW	SIR HAROLD WILSON
ADIIILLMNSTTTW	TILT AT WINDMILLS
ADIIILLNOPSTTUUY	PLATITUDINOUSLY
ADIILNOOOOPPRRST	DISPROPORTIONAL
ADINOOOOPRRTTUWW	PUT IN A WORD OR TWO
ADLNNNOOOOPRRSTT	LONDON TRANSPORT
AEEEEEGGHMMNNSTY	ENGAGES THE ENEMY
AEEEEEGHHLRSSTW	GREASE THE WHEELS
AEEEEEGHNNORSVV	HAVE ONES REVENGE
AEEEEEHKMPSSSSY	MAKES SHEEP'S EYES
AEEEEEHNNOOPSVY	HAVE ONE'S EYE OPEN
AEEEEEMMRRSSTUX	EXTREME MEASURES
AEEEEFFHKKNOTTW	TAKEN THE WEEK OFF
AEEEEEFFHKKOSTTW	TAKES THE WEEK OFF
AEEEEEFFHLOSSTTT	SET OF FALSE TEETH
AEEEEEFFKLLMNOST	MAKE ONESELF FELT
AEEEEEFGILMNOSTV	GAVE ONESELF TIME
AEEEEEFHIKLNRRRT	KATHLEEN FERRIER
AEEEEEFHLORRTTUW	THREW OUT A FEELER
AEEEEEFHNNORSSTT	FEATHER ONES NEST
AEEEEEFINOORTTTX	EXTORTIONATE FEE
AEEEEEFLNOPPRRSS	PREPARES ONESELF
AEEEEEFLNOPRSSSU	SENSE OF PLEASURE
AEEEEEFNNOOSSSTY	FEAST ONE'S EYES ON
AEEEEEGGLNOSSSST	GETS ONE'S SEA LEGS
AEEEEEGHHHINOTVV	GIVEN THE HEAVE-HO
AEEEEEGHHHIOSTVV	GIVES THE HEAVE-HO
AEEEEEGILLNNOPPR	PEOPLE IN GENERAL
AEEEEEGILMRSSSSW	WIRELESS MESSAGE
AEEEEEGILNNRRSTT	GENERAL INTEREST
AEEEEEGILNOPRSUV	GIVE ONE PLEASURE
AEEEEEGLLLMNSTTT	LEGAL SETTLEMENT
AEEEEEGMNORRSSUU	GENEROUS MEASURE
AEEEEEGMNORSSSTU	GETS ONE'S MEASURE
AEEEEEHIMNOPPSTT	PEE IN THE SAME POT
AEEEEEHJLMNRSTUW	THE NEW JERUSALEM
AEEEEEHKLNOOSSTT	TAKE TO ONE'S HEELS
AEEEEEHLMRSTTTTT	SETTLE THE MATTER
AEEEEEHLNORSSSTT	STEELS ONE'S HEART
AEEEEEHMNOPRSSTT	TENSE ATMOSPHERE
AEEEEEHNNOPPRRTY	THREEPENNY OPERA
AEEEEEHOSSTTTTTW	SWEET TO THE TASTE
AEEEEEIIJNPRRRSV	JEAN-PIERRE RIVES
AEEEEEIKLNOOPRSS	KEEPS A LOOSE REIN
AEEEEEILNNPRRRTU	ENTREPRENEURIAL
AEEEEEILNNPSSSUV	LEAVE IN SUSPENSE
AEEEEEILNPRRSTTU	REPENT AT LEISURE
AEEEEEIMNNPRSSTT	INTEMPERATENESS
AEEEEEINNPRRSTTT	INTERPENETRATES
AEEEEEINPRRSSTTT	STATE ENTERPRISE
AEEEEEINPRRSSTTV	REPRESENTATIVES
AEEEEEINPSSSTTVX	EXPENSIVE TASTES
AEEEEEKLNPPRSWWY	WEEKLY NEWSPAPER
AEEEEELLNPPRRSSW	NEWSPAPER SELLER
AEEEEELNNPRSTTUV	NET PRESENT VALUE
AEEEEELNOQRRTTUV	QUARTER TO ELEVEN
AEEEEELNORSSTTTX	TO A LESSER EXTENT
AEEEEENNOPPRSSSX	SPARES NO EXPENSE
AEEEEFFFILNOORRS	FEAR FOR ONES LIFE
AEEEEFFFKLNNOOST	TAKEN ONESELF OFF
AEEEEFFFKLNOOSST	TAKES ONESELF OFF
AEEEEFFFKLNOOSTW	WALK OFF ONE'S FEET
AEEEEFFGGIIKMNOS	SIEGE OF MAFEKING
AEEEEFFGHKOPRSST	KEEP OFF THE GRASS
AEEEEFFHHIKNOSTT	TAKE THE SHINE OFF
AEEEEFFHHIMNTTTY	MAY THE FIFTEENTH
AEEEEFFIMNNNORSV	OFFENSIVE MANNER
AEEEEFFINNOOPSVW	OFFENSIVE WEAPON
AEEEEFFKLNOOPRSS	SPEAK FOR ONESELF
AEEEEFFLLLNOORSV	FALL OVER ONESELF
AEEEEFFLLNORSSTV	FLATTERS ONESELF
AEEEEFGHHIMNOTTY	EIGHTEENTH OF MAY
AEEEEFGHIMORSTUW	MEASURE OF WEIGHT
AEEEEFGHLMNORSTU	MEASURE OF LENGTH
AEEEEFGIILNORSSV	GIVE ONESELF AIRS
AEEEEFGIINORRSTT	REGISTRATION FEE
AEEEEFGIINRSSTUV	FIGURATIVE SENSE
AEEEEFGILLMNNRTU	IN FULL AGREEMENT
AEEEEFGILLNNOPSS	PLEASING ONESELF
AEEEEFGINNOPPSTT	TAPPING ONE'S FEET
AEEEEFFHHILPRRSST	THE PEARL FISHERS
AEEEEFFHHMMNOOTTT	HEAT OF THE MOMENT
AEEEEFFHHORSTTTTU	THE FOURTH ESTATE
AEEEEFFHIKMNORRTT	TAKEN IT FROM HERE
AEEEEFFHIKMORRSTT	TAKES IT FROM HERE
AEEEEFFHIKMORRTTT	TAKE IT FROM THERE
AEEEEFHILLNOPRTV	ELEVENTH OF APRIL
AEEEEFHILLOPRSSU	HOPELESS FAILURE
AEEEEFHIMNNNOTTY	NINETEENTH OF MAY
AEEEEFHIMNNORSST	ANOTHER FINE MESS
AEEEEFHINNNRRTTUU	IN THE NEAR FUTURE
AEEEEFHKOOPTTUWY	KEEP OUT OF THE WAY
AEEEEFHLOORRTTUW	THROW OUT A FEELER
AEEEEFHLORRSTTWW	WATER THE FLOWERS
AEEEEFHOORRRSTWW	THE WORSE FOR WEAR
AEEEEFIKLLOOPPRW	KEEP A LOW PROFILE
AEEEEFIKLNNOOSTW	TAKE ONES OWN LIFE
AEEEEFILLNNOPSSX	EXPLAINS ONESELF
AEEEEFILMNOPRTTW	FLEW INTO A TEMPER
AEEEEFILMOPRRRTY	TEMPORARY RELIEF
AEEEEFKMNNOORSTU	MAKE ONES FORTUNE
AEEEEFLLLLORRTVW	FELLOW TRAVELLER
AEEEEFLLLMNOOSTT	TELL SOMEONE FLAT
AEEEEGGHHORRSTTT	GATHERS TOGETHER
AEEEEGGHINSSTTTT	SETTING THE STAGE
AEEEEGGHINSTTTTT	GETTING THE TASTE
AEEEEGGHOORRSTUW	GORGEOUS WEATHER
AEEEEGGIIINPRRVV	GIVING A REPRIEVE
AEEEEGGIMNNOPRRT	PRIOR ENGAGEMENT
AEEEEGGLNNOOORRV	GOVERNOR GENERAL
	GOVERNOR-GENERAL
AEEEEGHHILNORTTT	IN THE ALTOGETHER
AEEEEGHHIMPRRTTU	HIGH TEMPERATURE
AEEEEGHHINRRSSTV	SEVERE THRASHING
AEEEEGHHMMNOORSST	HORSE-SHOE MAGNET
AEEEEGHIIKNPRSTT	KEEPS A TIGHT REIN
AEEEEGHIINQSTTUZ	IN A TIGHT SQUEEZE
AEEEEGHIKLNOTTVW	TAKE THE LONG VIEW
AEEEEGHIMNNRSTWY	ERNEST HEMINGWAY
AEEEEGHIMRSSSTTT	MISSES THE TARGET
AEEEEGHINNNOOSVY	HAVING ONE'S EYE ON
AEEEEGHINNOPRSST	PARTHENOGENESIS
AEEEEGHLNNOORTZZ	GONE ON THE RAZZLE
AEEEEGHLNNOPRSTU	GREENHOUSE PLANT
AEEEEGHLNOORSTZZ	GOES ON THE RAZZLE
AEEEEGHLNPRSSTTT	GRASPS THE NETTLE
AEEEEGIIKMNOPPRS	KEEPING A PROMISE
AEEEEGIILMNNRRST	MINISTER-GENERAL
AEEEEGIINPRSSVWX	EXPRESSING A VIEW
AEEEEGILLMNNNSST	GENTLEMANLINESS
AEEEEGILMNNNSSSS	MEANINGLESSNESS
AEEEEGILMPQRRSUU	SQUARE-LEG UMPIRE
AEEEEGILNNOPRTTY	POTENTIAL ENERGY
AEEEEGILNNPPRRST	SLEEPING PARTNER
AEEEEGILNNPRSSTV	EVERLASTINGNESS
AEEEEGIMNOPRSSST	SPERMATOGENESIS
AEEEEGINNNNOSSSTV	GIVEN ONE'S ASSENT
AEEEEGINNNOSSSTX	GETS AN EXTENSION
AEEEEGINNOPSSTUV	GIVEN UP ONE'S SEAT
AEEEEGINNNOSSSSTV	GIVES ONE'S ASSENT
AEEEEGINOPSSSTUV	GIVES UP ONE'S SEAT
AEEEEGKNNOOSSSTT	GET ONES SKATES ON

AEEEGLLMMOPRRRS	PROGRAMME SELLER
AEEEHHILMNOPPST	MEPHISTOPHELEAN
AEEEHHILNPRSTTV	APRIL THE SEVENTH
AEEEHHIMNSTTTXY	MAY THE SIXTEENTH
AEEEHHIMNTTTTWY	MAY THE TWENTIETH
AEEEHHLOORRSTTT	RESTORE TO HEALTH
AEEEHHMORRSTTTW	WEATHER THE STORM
AEEEHHORRSSSTTW	WATERS THE HORSES
AEEEHIIKLLMORSW	WILLIE SHOEMAKER
AEEEHIIMMNNORRST	IMMERSION HEATER
AEEEHIJKKLLLNSY	SHAKEN LIKE JELLY
AEEEHIJKKLLLSSY	SHAKES LIKE JELLY
AEEEHIKMNNNORSTY	RAKES IN THE MONEY
AEEEHIKNNNOOPRSS	KEEPS ONE'S HAIR ON
AEEEHILLMNNOPPY	EPIPHENOMENALLY
AEEEHILMNOPSSTT	SPANISH OMELETTE
AEEEHILMORSTTTV	VIOLATE THE TERMS
AEEEHILNORRSSTT	NORTHEASTERLIES
AEEEHILUUPPRSTY	FORGE THE SAILOR
AEEEHILORSSSTTU	SOUTHEASTERLIES
AEEEHILORSTTUXY	HETEROSEXUALITY
AEEEHIORRSSTTWX	THREE TWOS ARE SIX
	TWO THREES ARE SIX
AEEEHKMOPRRSTTV	OVERSTEP THE MARK
AEEEHLNNOORSSTT	STOLEN ONE'S HEART
AEEEHLNNORTTWZZ	WENT ON THE RAZZLE
AEEEHILORRRSSTTU	LEATHER TROUSERS
AEEEHLORSSSTVWY	SEAWORTHY VESSEL
AEEEHMMNNOOSSTV	HAVE ONE'S MOMENTS
AEEEHMNNPPRSTTY	THREEPENNY STAMP
AEEEHMPRRSTTTUU	PURSUE THE MATTER
AEEEHORRRSSTTUW	WEAR THE TROUSERS
AEEEIIKMNRSSTTV	SENSITIVE MARKET
AEEEIILLQRTTUVY	RELATIVELY QUIET
AEEEIILMMNPRSTX	EXPERIMENTALISM
AEEEIILMNNSESTT	SENTIMENTALISES
AEEEIILMNNSSTTZ	SENTIMENTALIZES
AEEEIIMNNOPRTTX	EXPERIMENTATION
AEEEIINNRSSTTUV	SENSITIVE NATURE
AEEEIINPRSSSTTV	PASSIVE INTEREST
AEEEIKLLNNOPSST	TALK IN ONES SLEEP
AEEEIKMNNPRRRTT	PERTINENT REMARK
AEEEILLNNOOPSST	LOSE ON PENALTIES
AEEEIILMMNNPRSTY	SEMIPERMANENTLY
AEEEILNPRSSSTUV	SUPERLATIVENESS
AEEEIILQRRRTUVWY	QUARTERLY REVIEW
AEEEIMNNNORSTTW	WRITTEN ONE'S NAME
AEEEIMNPRRRSSUU	SUPERNUMERARIES
AEEEINNOPRRSSTT	REPRESENTATIONS
AEEEINNORSSSSTY	STRAINS ONE'S EYES
AEEEKKKNNNOOSSST	SANK TO ONE'S KNEES
AEEEKLLNNOOSSTV	SANK TO ONE'S LEVEL
AEEEKMMMMNNOOSYY	MONEY MAKES MONEY
AEEEKMNOOORSSTU	TOOK ONE'S MEASURE
AEEELLNNNOORSSS	LEARN ONES LESSON
AEEELMNOQRRSSSU	QUARRELSOMENESS
AEEELMOORSTTUVY	SAVOURY OMELETTE
AEEELNNOOORSSSS	LOSES ONE'S REASON
AEEELOQRRTTTUVW	QUARTER TO TWELVE
AEEEMMOOPRRRTTU	ROOM TEMPERATURE
AEEEMMNNNOOPSTY	PENNY TO ONE'S NAME
AEEEMMNNOOSSSTWY	WASTES ONE'S MONEY
AEEEMMNNRSTTTTUU	UNTRUE STATEMENT
AEEEMORRSSSTTVW	SERVE TWO MASTERS
AEEENOPPPRRRSTW	NEWSPAPER REPORT
AEEFFFGILNOORRS	OFFERING FOR SALE
AEEFFFGINNORRSU	REFUSING AN OFFER
AEEFFFHHINORTTU	THE FUN OF THE FAIR
AEEFFGHIKMNORTT	MAKING THE EFFORT
AEEFFGHILNOORST	GONE OFF THE RAILS
AEEFFGHILOORSST	GOES OFF THE RAILS
AEEFFGILMNOPRRS	PERFORMING FLEAS
AEEFFGILMNOSTTT	LETTING OFF STEAM
AEEFFGKLLNOOSSW	WALK OFF ONE'S LEGS
	WALK ONE'S LEGS OFF
AEEFFHHNORSTTTU	TURNS OFF THE HEAT
	TURNS THE HEAT OFF
AEEFFHILNORSTTW	WENT OFF THE RAILS
AEEFFHIORRSTTTW	OF THE FIRST WATER
AEEFFHJMNOORSST	THOMAS JEFFERSON
AEEFFHMNOORTTUY	FOURTEENTH OF MAY
AEEFFIKLOPRSSST	SPEAKS FOR ITSELF
AEEFGGHHINOSTTT	GETS THE HANG OF IT
AEEFGGHILLNORTW	LOWERING THE FLAG
AEEFGGIILLNNNOS	ALIGNING ONESELF
AEEFGHILLNNRTSW	INFRINGES THE LAW
AEEFGHIMNNORRTT	THE MORNING AFTER
AEEFGHIMORSTTTT	GIST OF THE MATTER
AEEFGHNOSSTTUUV	SEVENTH OF AUGUST
AEEFGHOOSTTTUWY	GETS OUT OF THE WAY
AEEFGIIINNSSSST	SIGNIFIES ASSENT
AEEFGIIKLNNOSST	STAKING ONE'S LIFE
AEEFGIILLNNOSUV	VALUING ONE'S LIFE
AEEFGIILNNNNORRS	INFERNAL REGIONS
AEEFGIKNOPRSSTU	REFUSING TO SPEAK
AEEFGIKNORSSSSV	ASKS FORGIVENESS
AEEFGILLNNOPPSY	APPLYING ONESELF
AEEFGILLNOOPRSS	LEGAL PROFESSION
AEEFGILNNNOORSY	LAY ONE'S FINGER ON
AEEFGIMNNPRSTUY	REFUSING PAYMENT
AEEFGINNNOPRSSS	SNAP ONES FINGERS
AEEFGMMNNOORRTV	FORM A GOVERNMENT
AEEFGNQOOSTTUWY	GET OUT OF ONES WAY
AEEFHHHILLPRTTW	APRIL THE TWELFTH
AEEFHHIMNORTTTY	THIRTEENTH OF MAY
AEEFHHMNNOORSTTY	MONTHS OF THE YEAR
AEEFHHMNNOORTTWY	WORTHY OF THE NAME
AEEFHHMOORRSSTW	SWAM FOR THE SHORE
AEEFHIIKRRSSTTW	STRIKES WITH FEAR
AEEFHIKMMMOOSTTT	MAKE THE MOST OF IT
AEEFHILLLLOTVYY	LILY OF THE VALLEY
AEEFHILNOPRSTTU	LIFT UP ONES HEART
AEEFHKOOPTTTUWY	KEPT OUT OF THE WAY
AEEFHLLLOPRTUVY	TRAVEL HOPEFULLY
AEEFIIMOOORRTTTT	ROOT OF THE MATTER
AEEFIIKMNNOORST	SEEK INFORMATION
AEEFIIKNPRRSTTZ	TAKEN FIRST PRIZE
AEEFIIKPRRSSTTZ	TAKES FIRST PRIZE
AEEFIILLOPRRTVY	PROLIFERATIVELY
AEEFIILMNOPRSSS	FALSE IMPRESSION
AEEFIILNNRSTTTU	FIRST LIEUTENANT
AEEFIILNOOPRSSS	PROFESSIONALISE
AEEFIIINOOPRSSZ	PROFESSIONALIZE
AEEFIIMNNORSSTV	INFORMATIVENESS
AEEFIIMNNOORSSTT	MINISTER OF STATE
AEEFIKLLOOPPRTW	KEPT A LOW PROFILE
AEEFILLLNNOOPST	FELL INTO ONE'S LAP
AEEFILLNNOORRRT	FALLEN INTO ERROR
AEEFILLOOPPQTUY	PEOPLE OF QUALITY
AEEFILNOOPRSTTV	LEAVE FOOTPRINTS
AEEFINOOPRRSSTT	PRISONER OF STATE
AEEFKMMMNOOOORRSY	ASK FOR MORE MONEY
AEEFLLLLNNOOOSTT	FALLEN TO ONE'S LOT
AEEFMNOPPRRSSTY	PRESS FOR PAYMENT
AEEFNOOOPRRTTWY	POWER OF ATTORNEY
AEEGGGHINNOOSTT	GOING ON THE STAGE
AEEGGGINNOOSTTT	GETTING ONE'S GOAT
AEEGGGLNNNOOOOV	EVONNE GOOLAGONG
AEEGGHHHISTTTUU	AUGUST THE EIGHTH
AEEGGHHIIILNVWY	WEIGHING HEAVILY
AEEGGHHIIKMNTTW	MAKING THE WEIGHT
AEEGGHHILNRTTVW	RIGHT WAVELENGTH

1021

AEEGGHHINSTTTTU	SHUTTING THE GATE
AEEGGHHNRRSSTTT	GATHERS STRENGTH
AEEGGHIIKLNNPSS	SPEAKING ENGLISH
AEEGGHIINNTTTWY	GETTING IN THE WAY
AEEGGHIKLNNPTTU	TAKING THE PLUNGE
AEEGGHIKNOOSTTT	GOING TO THE STAKE
AEEGGHILMNORTTY	MOTLEY GATHERING
AEEGGHINNORRSTV	HAVING NO REGRETS
AEEGGHINOOOPRTT	GOING TO THE OPERA
AEEGGHLMNNRTTUY	LENGTHY ARGUMENT
AEEGGHLNNORTVWW	WRONG WAVE-LENGTH
AEEGGHLNOOPRSSY	GEOGRAPHY LESSON
AEEGGHLORRSSTTW	LET THE GRASS GROW
AEEGGHNNOOPRRST	ROENTGENOGRAPHS
AEEGGIIILMNNNRS	REMAINING SINGLE
AEEGGIIMNNNNOTTT	GETTING A MENTION
AEEGGIINORSSSTT	SEGREGATIONISTS
AEEGGINNNNOORTUY	YOUNG GENERATION
AEEGGINNNNORTUUY	ANNIE GET YOUR GUN
AEEGGINNOOSSTTT	GETTING ONE'S OATS
AEEGGINOOORSTTV	GETS INTO A GROOVE
AEEGGLLNQRSTUUU	UNEQUAL STRUGGLE
AEEGGMNNNORRTTV	GOVERNMENT GRANT
AEEGHHHILLORRTW	HELL OR HIGH WATER
AEEGHHHIMORSTTT	THE HOME STRAIGHT
AEEGHHHORRSTTUY	THROUGH THE YEARS
AEEGHHIIKLLNSTT	TAKE THE SHILLING
AEEGHHIINNNSSTW	WINNING THE ASHES
AEEGHHILMMNNOSS	ENGLISHMANS HOME
AEEGHHILNOSSTTW	STEALING THE SHOW
AEEGHHIMNNOSTTT	NOT THE SAME THING
AEEGHHIMORSTTTW	GO WITH THE STREAM
AEEGHHINNOOPSUV	HAVING OPEN HOUSE
AEEGHHINNOPPPTT	TAPPING THE PHONE
AEEGHHLOOPPRTTY	TELEPHOTOGRAPHY
AEEGHHLORSSSTUU	SLAUGHTERHOUSES
AEEGHIIILNNRTTT	LETTING IN THE AIR
AEEGHIIIMNNRTTW	TEEMING WITH RAIN
AEEGHIIJMNNPSTU	JUMPING IN THE SEA
AEEGHIIKLLNRTTT	TAKING THE TILLER
AEEGHIILLNNNOTY	LAYING ON THE LINE
AEEGHIILLRRTTTU	LIGHT LITERATURE
AEEGHIIMNNORSTY	RAISING THE MONEY
AEEGHIIMNOPRSST	RAISING THE TEMPO
AEEGHIINNNSTTUY	NAUGHTY NINETIES
AEEGHIINORSSSST	RAISE ONES SIGHTS
AEEGHIJKLMNOPTU	GO JUMP IN THE LAKE
AEEGHIKLNNOORTT	THREATENING LOOK
AEEGHIKLOPRRTTW	TIGHT-ROPE WALKER
AEEGHIKMNNNRSTU	MAKES THE RUNNING
AEEGHIKMNNORSSTW	MAKE THINGS WORSE
AEEGHIKNOPRSSTT	KEEPS STRAIGHT ON
AEEGHILLNOPPRTW	TELLING A WHOPPER
AEEGHILNNOOPSTY	PILES ON THE AGONY
AEEGHILNNOORSST	LOSING ONE'S HEART
AEEGHILNNOOTTUV	LEAVE NOTHING OUT
AEEGHILNNRTTTTW	WRITTEN AT LENGTH
AEEGHIMNNOORSTY	REMOVING ONE'S HAT
AEEGHIMNNORSTUV	NIGHT MANOEUVRES
AEEGHIMNOOPPRRT	PAPERING THE ROOM
AEEGHINNNORSTTU	SING ANOTHER TUNE
AEEGHINNOOPRSST	ANTHROPOGENESIS
AEEGHINOORTTTTW	GET INTO HOT WATER
AEEGHINRRSTTTTU	UTTERING THREATS
AEEGHLMOORSTTUV	MOVES TO LAUGHTER
AEEGHLNNRSTTTUU	RUNS THE GAUNTLET
AEEGHMMMNORSTTU	GATHERS MOMENTUM
AEEGHNNNORSTTUU	SUNG ANOTHER TUNE
AEEGHORRSSSTTUU	ROGETS THESAURUS
AEEGIIIKMNNQRSU	MAKING ENQUIRIES
AEEGIIILMNNNRST	REMAINING SILENT
AEEGIIINNORSSVW	AIRING ONE'S VIEWS
AEEGIIKLLLNNTTT	INTELLIGENT TALK
AEEGIIKLLMNPSST	SPELLING MISTAKE
AEEGIIKLNNNOOOV	GIVEN ONE A LOOK IN
AEEGIIKLNNOOOSV	GIVES ONE A LOOK IN
AEEGIIILLLNOPSTW	WILLING TO PLEASE
AEEGIILNNNORSSV	EARNS ONE'S LIVING
AEEGIILNNORRTTW	LEARNING TO WRITE
AEEGIILNNPPRRSS	SPRINGER SPANIEL
AEEGIILNORRTTVY	INTERROGATIVELY
AEEGIIMNNNNORSTW	WRITING ONE'S NAME
AEEGIIMNNNOOPPST	OPPOSITE MEANING
AEEGIINNNNORRSSS	RINGS IN ONE'S EARS
AEEGIINNOPRSSSS	SING ONE'S PRAISES
AEEGIINNORRSSTT	STIRRING ONE'S TEA
AEEGIINNPRSSSTT	PASSING INTEREST
AEEGIINOORRRSTT	INTERROGATORIES
AEEGIINORRSSTTT	GASTROENTERITIS
AEEGIKKLNOOOPTU	KEEPING A LOOK-OUT
AEEGIKLMNOPSSUV	SPEAKING VOLUMES
AEEGIKLNNOOPRTT	PENETRATING LOOK
AEEGIKMNNOPRSST	ON SPEAKING TERMS
AEEGIILNNOOPSSTV	LEAVING ONE'S POST
AEEGIILNNOPRSSSX	SLANG EXPRESSION
AEEGIILOPRRRSTUY	GREATLY SUPERIOR
AEEGINNNOOPPRST	OPENING ONE'S TRAP
AEEGINNNORRSTUV	TURN IN ONES GRAVE
AEEGINNOPRSSSSU	SUNG ONE'S PRAISES
AEEGINOPPRRSSUV	SERVING A PURPOSE
AEEGKMNNOOPRRSSS	MAKES NO PROGRESS
AEEGKNNOOOSSSTT	GOT ONE'S SKATES ON
AEEGKNOORSSTTUY	GET YOUR SKATES ON
AEEGMMNOPPRRSSTY	PROGRESS PAYMENT
AEEGNOOQRRRSSUV	GROSVENOR SQUARE
AEEHHHIIMRTTTTY	MAY THE THIRTIETH
AEEHHHIINRTTTWW	WHITER THAN WHITE
AEEHHHILLNNOPPT	PHENOLPHTHALEIN
AEEHHHINRRSTTUW	RUNS WITH THE HARE
AEEHHHMMNORRTTW	THROWN THE HAMMER
AEEHHHMMORRSTTW	THROWS THE HAMMER
AEEHHIIKLRRSTTW	RISE WITH THE LARK
AEEHHIILMNOPPST	MEPHISTOPHELIAN
AEEHHIILMNOPRTV	IMPROVE IN HEALTH
AEEHHIJMPRSSSTY	HER MAJESTYS SHIP
AEEHHIKLLNOSTTT	TAKEN TO THE HILLS
AEEHHIKLLOSSTTT	TAKES TO THE HILLS
AEEHHIKLORRSTTW	ROSE WITH THE LARK
AEEHHILOPRSSSST	SHARES THE SPOILS
AEEHHIMMMNNNOOTT	THE MAN IN THE MOON
AEEHHIMNNPSTUVY	HEAVY PUNISHMENT
AEEHHIMNNOSTTTTU	TASTE IN THE MOUTH
AEEHHKLOOORTTWY	LOOK THE OTHER WAY
AEEHHLLOPSSTTUW	PUSHES TO THE WALL
AEEHIIIMNNNOTTV	IN THE NOMINATIVE
AEEHIIKLMORSTTT	THAT'S MORE LIKE IT
AEEHIIKLNOOPSST	HATES LIKE POISON
AEEHIIKLNPRSSST	SLAP IN THE KISSER
AEEHIIKNOPPRSSW	SPOKE IN A WHISPER
AEEHIIILLLNORSST	ROLL IN THE AISLES
AEEHIILLNNOSTTY	LAYS IT ON THE LINE
AEEHIIMNNNOSSTW	WITHIN ONE'S MEANS
AEEHIIMNNOPPRSS	MISAPPREHENSION
AEEHIIRRSSTTVWW	SERVES WITH A WRIT
AEEHIJKKLLLOOSY	SHOOK LIKE A JELLY
AEEHIKKLOORRSSW	WORKS LIKE A HORSE
AEEHIKLNNOPRTUY	PHENYLKETONURIA
AEEHIKMNNNPSTTU	TAKEN PUNISHMENT
AEEHIKMNNPSSTTU	TAKES PUNISHMENT
AEEHIKNOQSSSTTU	ASK THE QUESTIONS
AEEHILLMNRSSTTW	WESTMINSTER HALL
AEEHILMMNOOPRRY	HOLY ROMAN EMPIRE

AEEHILNOORRTVVW	THROWN A VEIL OVER
AEEHIMMNNOPPRSUY	UNHAPPY MEMORIES
AEEHINNOOORSSSV	SHOVES IN ONE'S OAR
AEEHINNOPRSSSTW	SHARPEN ONES WITS
AEEHINOOORRSTTU	TORE ONE'S HAIR OUT
AEEHINPPPPRRSSW	WHIPPERSNAPPERS
AEEHIORRSTTTUXY	EXERTS AUTHORITY
AEEHKLLNNORSSTW	SWOLLEN THE RANKS
AEEHKLLOOPRRRSU	PARKERHOUSE ROLL
AEEHKLNOOPSTTUW	SLOW ON THE UPTAKE
AEEHKMMOOPRSSTY	SMOKY ATMOSPHERE
AEEHKMMNOPRSTTTU	PUTS ON THE MARKET
AEEHKNOOOORSTTT	TOOK TO ONE'S HEART
AEEHLMNNOOPSSSY	SPLASH ONES MONEY
AEEHMNOORRRSSTY	RESTORES HARMONY
AEEHMNOPRRSSTUW	THREW UP ONE'S ARMS
AEEHMORSSSSTTUW	ASSUMES THE WORST
AEEHNNOORRSSUWY	NEW YEARS HONOURS
AEEHNOPRRSTTTTU	RETURN TO THE PAST
AEEHOORRSSTTVVW	THE WORST WAS OVER
AEEIIILLMNORSSS	MILLIONAIRESSES
AEEIIILNSSSTTTX	EXISTENTIALISTS
AEEIIINOORRSTTX	EXTERIORISATION
AEEIIINOORRTTXZ	EXTERIORIZATION
AEEIIKKLNNOSSST	SINKS LIKE A STONE
AEEIIILLLLMNNPRY	PREMILLENNIALLY
AEEIILLLMNNRSST	TERMINAL ILLNESS
AEEIILMNNSSSTTT	SENTIMENTALISTS
AEEIIILMNPRSTUUV	IMPULSIVE NATURE
AEEIILMOPRRSTUY	MALE SUPERIORITY
AEEIILNNNOPSSTW	WINS ON PENALTIES
AEEIILNNNOSTTTV	LATEST INVENTION
AEEIILNNOPPRTTY	PLENIPOTENTIARY
AEEIILNOORRSTUV	REVOLUTIONARIES
AEEIIMMNNORSTTT	ON INTIMATE TERMS
AEEIIMNNOPRSSTT	PRESENTATIONISM
AEEIIMNNOOPRSTTX	EXTEMPORISATION
AEEIIMNOOPRTTXZ	EXTEMPORIZATION
AEEIIINNOPRRSTTT	INTERPRETATIONS
AEEIIINRSSSTTXXY	SIX TENS ARE SIXTY
AEEIIINRSSTTTUVY	STATE UNIVERSITY
AEEIIOOPPPRSSTT	OPPOSITE PARTIES
AEEIKLMOPRRSTWY	WORKERS PLAYTIME
AEEIKNNOOPSSSST	TAKEN POSSESSION
AEEIKNOOPSSSSST	TAKES POSSESSION
AEEIILLLNORSSTVY	SELL INTO SLAVERY
AEEILLMNNNORTVY	ENVIRONMENTALLY
AEEIILLNNOOPSSTT	LOST ON PENALTIES
AEEILMNNNPRSTTU	INSTRUMENT PANEL
AEEILMNNOOPPRUU	PLEUROPNEUMONIA
AEEILMNNOOPPSTTU	SUPPLEMENTATION
AEEILMNNOOPPRTTU	PERPETUAL MOTION
AEEILMNORRSTTVY	REMONSTRATIVELY
AEEILNNOOPRRTUV	RELATIVE PRONOUN
AEEILNNOORSSSTT	LISTENS TO REASON
AEEIILNORRSSTTUU	RUSSIAN ROULETTE
AEEIILOOPPRSTTVY	POSTOPERATIVELY
AEEIMMNOPRSTTVV	VAST IMPROVEMENT
AEEIMMOPRRSSTTV	IMPROVES MATTERS
AEEIMNOORSTTTUX	EXTORTIONATE SUM
AEEIMNOQRSSSTTU	QUESTION-MASTERS
AEEINNNOPRSSSTT	INSTANT RESPONSE
AEEINOORRSSTTTY	RESTORE TO SANITY
AEEIOQRRSSSSTU	QUARTER SESSIONS
AEEIOPPPRRHRTTV	PRIVATE PROPERTY
AEEKLLNOOPRSTWY	YELLOWSTONE PARK
AEEKNNOOPSSSSTTU	PUT ONES SKATES ON
AEELMMNNOPPTUYY	UNEMPLOYMENT PAY
AEELMNNOORSTTUY	ANONYMOUS LETTER
AEEMMNNNOOOTTWW	ONE MAN WENT TO MOW
AEEMMNNOOOORRTUV	ROOM TO MANOEUVRE
AEEENNNOOPSSSSTU	SPONTANEOUSNESS
AEEENNOOORRSSSST	RESTS ON ONE'S OARS
AEFFFFHHIIORRSW	WHIFF OF FRESH AIR
AEFFGHHHIINOOST	HEIGHT OF FASHION
AEFFGHIIMNOPPTW	WIPING OFF THE MAP
AEFFGHIKLMNRTUY	MAKING THE FUR FLY
AEFFGHLOSTTTUUW	TWELFTH OF AUGUST
AEFFGILLNOOSTUU	FALLING OUT OF USE
AEFFGINNNOPRRSU	SPURNING AN OFFER
AEFFGINNOOPRRST	SPARING NO EFFORT
AEFFHHMORRRTTTU	FAR FROM THE TRUTH
AEFFIILLMOPRSSU	FULFILS A PROMISE
AEFFIINNNOOOOPRS	OFFERS AN OPINION
AEFGGHHIILNOSTT	HOISTING THE FLAG
AEFGGHHIINNRTTT	NIGHT AFTER NIGHT
AEFGGHHLNOSTTUU	HUNG THE FLAGS OUT
AEFGGHIILNNNOSV	HAVING ONE'S FLING
AEFGGHIINNNOSTWY	FIGHTING ONE'S WAY
AEFGGIILNNNOPRT	POINTING A FINGER
AEFGGIIINNRRRST	STIRRING A FINGER
AEFGGIILMNNOPSU	GOING UP IN FLAMES
AEFGGIMNNOPRWY	MAGNIFYING POWER
AEFGGIINNORRTUV	FORGIVING NATURE
AEFGGIKLNOOPRST	TAKING FOR GOSPEL
AEFGHHIINNORSST	NORTH SEA FISHING
AEFGHHIINNORRTTT	FROG IN THE THROAT
AEFGHHIORRSSTTV	GAVE SHORT SHRIFT
AEFGHHMOORSTTTU	STREAM OF THOUGHT
AEFGHHORSTTTUUU	AUGUST THE FOURTH
AEFGHIIKNNOSSST	SHAKING ONE'S FIST
AEFGHIILNNOOSST	LOSING ONE'S FAITH
AEFGHIKMMNOOSTT	MAKING THE MOST OF
AEFGHILNORRSTTT	TRIAL OF STRENGTH
AEFGHLOPSSTTTUU	PUTS THE FLAGS OUT
AEFGIIIMMNNRSTV	VISITING FIREMAN
AEFGIIINNOQRSTU	FIRING A QUESTION
AEFGIILLMNORSTT	STALLING FOR TIME
AEFGIILNNOORRSV	REASON FOR LIVING
AEFGIINNNNORTUW	WINNING A FORTUNE
AEFGIINOPPRSTUW	SUPPORTING A WIFE
AEFGILLLNNOOOST	LIONS OF LONGLEAT
AEFGILLNOPPRSTW	STRAPPING FELLOW
AEFGINNOOOPPSTT	TAPPING ONE'S FOOT
AEFGMMNOOORRRTU	ROOM FOR ARGUMENT
AEFGNOOOOSTTUWY	GOT OUT OF ONE'S WAY
AEFHHIIOORSSTTTW	HAS THE WORST OF IT
AEFHHLNNOPRSTWY	HALFPENNYWORTHS
AEFHHMMNNOORTTT	MONTH AFTER MONTH
AEFHIIILLMRSTTW	WILLIAM THE FIRST
AEFHIIKLNRRSTTW	SIR FRANK WHITTLE
AEFHIILMNNRSTTU	RUNS IN THE FAMILY
AEFHIILNNOPRSTY	HYPERINFLATIONS
AEFHIIINNNOOPSST	PINS ONE'S FAITH ON
AEFHIIORSTUVVWW	VIEWS WITH FAVOUR
AEFHILLLOORSTTW	FOLLOWS THE TRAIL
AEFHKKMOOOORRSTW	MAKE SHORT WORK OF
AEFHLLNOOOORRSTW	FOR ALL ONES WORTH
AEFHLLOOPPSSTUU	PULLS OUT OF SHAPE
AEFHMMMMNOORRTYY	MERRY MONTH OF MAY
AEFHOOOPSTTTUWY	OUT-OF-THE-WAY SPOT
AEFIIIILLMNNSTY	INFINITESIMALLY
AEFIIILNOQRRTUY	INFERIOR QUALITY
AEFIILLLNNOOPST	SELF-POLLINATION
AEFIILMNOOPRSSS	PROFESSIONALISM
AEFIILNORSSSTTU	FLIRTATIOUSNESS
AEFIIMNNOOOPRTT	MATTER OF OPINION
AEFIIMNORSSTTTY	MINISTRY OF STATE
AEFIINOPRSSSSSU	FISSIPAROUSNESS
AEFKNOOPRSSTTUU	SPEAKS OUT OF TURN
AEGGGHIIILNNSTV	GIVING THE SIGNAL

AEGGGHHIINRSTTTT	GETTING STRAIGHT
AEGGGHILNNOOTWY	GOING THE LONG WAY
AEGGGIIIMNRSSVV	GRAVE MISGIVINGS
AEGGGINNNOORSST	STRANGE GOINGS-ON
AEGGHHIILLMNPTT	LIGHTING THE LAMP
AEGGHHIILLRRSTU	GIRLISH LAUGHTER
AEGGHHIINOTTTUV	GIVEN IT A THOUGHT
AEGGHHIIOSTTTUV	GIVES IT A THOUGHT
AEGGHHINOORSSTU	HOUSING SHORTAGE
AEGGHIIINNOPRTU	GOING UP IN THE AIR
AEGGHIIKLLOOTTU	GO OUT LIKE A LIGHT
AEGGHIIKMMNNOST	MAKING SOMETHING
AEGGHIILLLNRTTV	TRAVELLING LIGHT
AEGGHIILLNNOTTT	NOTTING HILL GATE
AEGGHIILLNOPPUV	GIVING UP ALL HOPE
AEGGHIILLNPRSTU	SUGARING THE PILL
AEGGHIILLNRTTTY	TREATING LIGHTLY
AEGGHIILLNNRTTTW	WRITING AT LENGTH
AEGGHIIMNNNOSSTY	SAYING SOMETHING
AEGGHIINNNRSSTT	GAINS IN STRENGTH
AEGGHIINNOPRTTU	ARGUING THE POINT
AEGGHIINNPRSTTU	STRAIGHTENING UP
AEGGHIINRSSTTTT	SETTING STRAIGHT
AEGGHIKLNOPRSUY	ROUGHLY SPEAKING
AEGGHILLNOORSTY	SHOOTING GALLERY
AEGGHILNOOTTUWY	GET ALONG WITH YOU!
AEGGHIMMNNOSSTTU	TOUGH ASSIGNMENT
AEGGHINNNOORSST	SING ANOTHER SONG
AEGGHINNNORSTTU	TURNING ON THE GAS
AEGGHINNOOPRSTV	PHOTOENGRAVINGS
AEGGHINOORRTTUW	WROUGHT-IRON GATE
AEGGHLNNOOOOPRTY	PROLONG THE AGONY
AEGGHNNNOORSSTU	SUNG ANOTHER SONG
AEGGIINNOORTTTW	GETTING INTO A ROW
AEGGIINNOQRRTUV	GIVING NO QUARTER
AEGGIINNORTTTTU	GETTING INTO A RUT
AEGGINNNOOOSWWY	GOING ONE'S OWN WAY
AEGGINOOSSSTTUU	AUTOSUGGESTIONS
AEGGLPPRSSTTUUU	PUTS UP A STRUGGLE
AEGHHHILLOSTTWW	GLOWS WITH HEALTH
AEGHHHILOOOPPRT	PHOTOHELIOGRAPH
AEGHHHINNOORTUV	HAVING THE HONOUR
AEGHHIIILNRTTTT	HITTING THE TRAIL
AEGHHIILNORRTTT	ON THE RIGHT TRAIL
AEGHHIINNOOPTTV	HAVING THE OPTION
AEGHHIIOOPRRRST	HISTORIOGRAPHER
AEGHHILNNNOSSTT	LESS THAN NOTHING
AEGHHIMMNOOSTTWY	SMOOTHING THE WAY
AEGHIIILLLNNPTTY	PAINTING THE LILY
AEGHIIILNNPSTTV	LIVING IN THE PAST
AEGHIIINNSSTTWW	WAITS IN THE WINGS
AEGHIILLNPSSTT	SPILLING THE SALT
AEGHIILLMMNRSTT	ALL THE TRIMMINGS
AEGHIILLNNOSSST	ALL-NIGHT SESSION
AEGHIILLNNOTTTT	TELL IT NOT IN GATH
AEGHIILMMMNPRTT	TRIMMING THE LAMP
AEGHIIMNNOOPRTT	PAINTING THE ROOM
AEGHIIINNOPRSSTW	WITHIN ONES GRASP
AEGHIINNPTTTUWY	PUTTING IN THE WAY
AEGHIKLLNOOSSST	LOOKS IN THE GLASS
AEGHIKLMNPRSSTT	KNIGHTS TEMPLARS
AEGHIKNKNNOORTTW	KNEW A THING OR TWO
AEGHILLLNOOSWWW	SWALLOWING WHOLE
AEGHILMNORTTUWY	MOUTH-WATERINGLY
AEGHILNLNNOOPSSS	HANGS ON ONE'S LIPS
AEGHIMMMNNPPSTU	MANNING THE PUMPS
AEGHIMMNNOPPTTTU	PUTTING ON THE MAP
AEGHIMNORSSSTTT	STARTS SOMETHING
AEGHINNNOOPRRST	HARP ON ONE STRING
AEGHINNNNOPRTTTU	TURNING ON THE TAP
AEGHINOOOOPPRRSS	SPORANGIOPHORES
AEGHINOOORTTTTW	GOT INTO HOT WATER
AEGHJMNNOOPSTUW	JUMPS ON THE WAGON
AEGIIIIKMNNQRSU	MAKING INQUIRIES
AEGIIILMNOOORST	OLIGOMERISATION
AEGIIILMNOOORTZ	OLIGOMERIZATION
AEGIIINNORSSTTT	INTEGRATIONISTS
AEGIIINNRRSTTUV	RETURNING A VISIT
AEGIIKLNORSSTUY	TAKING SERIOUSLY
AEGIIKMNNNOOPST	MAKING ONE'S POINT
AEGIIKNNNOOPSTT	TAKING ONE'S POINT
AEGIIKNNNPRTTTT	KNITTING PATTERN
AEGIIKNNOOSSSTU	ASKING QUESTIONS
AEGIIKNNPRSTTUU	STRIKING UP A TUNE
AEGIILNNNOOOPTV	LEAVING NO OPTION
AEGIILNNOOPRRTT	PETROL RATIONING
AEGIILNNRSSTUVY	UNIVERSITY SLANG
AEGIIMNNRSSTTW	TWISTING ONE'S ARM
AEGIINNOOPQSSTU	POSING A QUESTION
AEGIINNOOPRSSTW	TOWERING PASSION
AEGIINNOOPSSSSS	GAINS POSSESSION
AEGIINNRRSTTUVY	UNIVERSITY GRANT
AEGIINPPRRRSSSU	SPRING A SURPRISE
AEGIKLLNNNOPRSU	PULLING ONE'S RANK
AEGIKLLNPPSSTUU	PULLING UP STAKES
AEGIKLNNOORTUWY	NOW YOU'RE TALKING!
AEGILLLNOPRRSTY	STROLLING PLAYER
AEGILLMMNNOPSTUU	LEGUMINOUS PLANT
AEGILMMNNNOSTTU	LASTING MONUMENT
AEGILNNNORSSSTU	STRAIN ONES LUNGS
AEGILNNOOPPRRTU	PUTTING ON PAROLE
AEGIMNNOPPPSTTY	STOPPING PAYMENT
AEGIMNNORRSTTTX	EXTRA STRONG MINT
AEGIMNOORRRSSTT	RESORTING TO ARMS
AEGINNOPPPRSTTU	PUPPET ON A STRING
AEGINOOPSTTTTUU	PUTTING OUT TO SEA
AEGINPPRRRSSSUU	SPRUNG A SURPRISE
AEGLNOOPPSSSTUU	TOPS UP ONE'S GLASS
AEHHHILLNOORRTW	HARROW ON THE HILL
AEHHHIMNNPRSSTU	HARSH PUNISHMENT
AEHHIIJMPSSSSTY	HIS MAJESTYS SHIP
AEHHIIKLNPSTTTW	LINK WITH THE PAST
AEHHIIOPPRSSTTY	PHYSIOTHERAPIST
AEHHILLMNORSSTU	IN THE SMALL HOURS
AEHHILMNOPRTTTU	LUMP IN THE THROAT
AEHHILOOPPRSTVY	PHOSPHORYLATIVE
AEHIIILLLMRSSWY	SHIRLEY WILLIAMS
AEHIIILMNNORTTT	MELT INTO THIN AIR
AEHIIJJMNOORTTY	JOIN THE MAJORITY
AEHIILNOOPPRRSS	SAILORS HORNPIPE
AEHIIMMNNOOPRST	ENANTIOMORPHISM
AEHIIMNOPPRRSSS	SHARP IMPRESSION
AEHIINNOOPSTTUX	EXHAUSTION POINT
AEHIKNNOOPPRSWY	HAPPY IN ONES WORK
AEHILLLLOPSSTWW	SWALLOWS THE PILL
AEHILNOORSSSTTT	SLITS ONE'S THROAT
AEHIMNNOOOOPRSTU	ENANTIOMORPHOUS
AEHINNOOORRSTTU	TORN ONE'S HAIR OUT
AEHINOOPSTTTUWY	POINTS OUT THE WAY
AEHIOOOPPRSTTUW	WITHOUT A PURPOSE
AEHLLNNOOOOPRTY	ANTHONY TROLLOPE
AEHLMMNNOPSTTYY	MONTHLY PAYMENTS
AEHMMNOOPRRSSTUW	THROW UP ONE'S ARMS
AEIIIJNNRSSSTUU	SUSTAIN INJURIES
AEIIILLMNOORRSW	MILLIONAIRES ROW
AEIIILMMMNNRSSX	MARXISM-LENINISM
AEIIILMNNRSSTTX	MARXIST-LENINIST
AEIIJLMNPRSTUYY	PLAYS INJURY TIME
AEIIKMNOOPRSSSV	MAKES PROVISIONS
AEIILLMNOSSSWWY	WALLOWS IN MISERY
AEIILLNOOPPRSTY	PREPOSITIONALLY
AEIILLNOORRTUVY	REVOLUTIONARILY

AEIILMNNRSSTTTU	INSTRUMENTALIST
AEIILMNNRSTTTUY	INSTRUMENTALITY
AEIILMOPRSTTTWY	MILITARY TWO-STEP
AEIILNNNOOOOPPRS	PERSONAL OPINION
AEIILNNNORSSTUV	INVOLUNTARINESS
AEIILNOOPRSSTTY	PROSELYTISATION
AEIILNOOPRSTTYZ	PROSELYTIZATION
AEIILOPQRRSTUUY	SUPERIOR QUALITY
AEIIMNNNOOPSSSS	MAN IN POSSESSION
AEIIMNNNORSTTTU	INSTRUMENTATION
AEIINNPQRRSUUUY	PURSUE AN INQUIRY
AEIINOOORRRRSTT	TERORRORISATION
AEIKLMNNOPRSSTU	UNSPORTSMANLIKE
AEIKNNOOQSSSSTU	ASKS NO QUESTIONS
AEILNOOOPPRRTTY	PROPORTIONATELY
AEIMNNOOPPRRSTT	IMPORTANT PERSON
AEIMNOOOOPPRSST	PROPOSES A MOTION
AEINOOPPRRRTTUY	RARE OPPORTUNITY
AELMNNOORRRSTTU	RETURNS TO NORMAL
AELNNNOOOOPPRRSU	PERSONAL PRONOUN
AEMNNOOOOPRRSTUU	PUT ON ONES ARMOUR
AEMNOPRRSSSTTTY	TRANSPORT SYSTEM
AEOOPPRSTTTTUUU	PUT OUT TO PASTURE
AFFGHHIINOSSTT	FIGHTS TO A FINISH
AFFGHHIINOOSTTU	FOUGHT TO A FINISH
AFFGHIILOOPRSST	SPOILS FOR A FIGHT
AFFGINNOORRTTWY	FOR WANT OF TRYING
AFFGLNOOOPRSSUU	SPOONFUL OF SUGAR
AFFHILLORSTUUYY	YOURS FAITHFULLY
AFFHINNOOOTTUUY	FOUNTAIN OF YOUTH
AFFILMOORRSSTTT	FROM FIRST TO LAST
AFGGGIIILNPRSST	FLAGGING SPIRITS
AFGGHIINPPTTTUU	PUTTING UP A FIGHT
AFGGIIMNNOORRSTY	TRANSMOGRIFYING
AFGGILLNNOOORSU	GOING ON ALL FOURS
AFGGILLNOOORRST	GOING FOR A STROLL
AFGGINNNOORSTUU	RUNNING OUT OF GAS
AFGHIIKMNNOTWYY	MY WAY OF THINKING
AFGHINNNOORSTTW	WANTS FOR NOTHING
AFGIIKLNOORRSVW	WORKS FOR A LIVING
AFGIINNOOPPSTTU	SNAPPING OUT OF IT
AFGIMNNNOORRRUY	RUNNING FOR MAYOR
AFHHIOORR3TTTWW	FOR WHAT ITS WORTH
AFHIIINOPSSTTTU	PUTS A FINISH TO IT
AFHIIMOORSSTUVW	SHOW FAVOURITISM
AFIIMNOORRRSTY	AIR MINISTRY ROOF
AFIILLLMOOPPRSS	PAIR OF PLIMSOLLS
AGGGGILLNNORSTU	STRUGGLING ALONG
AGGGHIINNOSTWW	GOING WITH A SWING
AGGHHHIORSTTTTU	THOUGHT STRAIGHT
AGGHHIIKMMNNSTU	MAKING THINGS HUM
AGGHHIIKMNNOSTT	MAKING THINGS HOT
AGGHHIINNNNOOTV	HAVING NOTHING ON
AGGHIIIILLNNSTTT	ALL-NIGHT SITTING
AGGHIIILNNNOTTV	NOT A LIVING THING
AGGHIIINNNORTWY	WRITHING IN AGONY
AGGHIINNNORSSTV	HAVING NO STRINGS
AGGHIINNNNRRSTTU	RUNNING STRAIGHT
AGGHIINOOSTTUWY	GO WITHOUT SAYING
AGGHIINPRSTTTTU	PUTTING STRAIGHT
AGGHIINQRSSTTTU	SQUATTING RIGHTS
AGGIIIINNNNOOPV	GIVING AN OPINION
AGGIIILMNNOORSS	GLARING OMISSION
AGGIIKLNNOPPSTT	STOPPING TALKING
AGHHHILOOOPPRTT	PHOTOLITHOGRAPH
AGHHIIILLNSSYY	SHILLY-SHALLYING
AGHHILLMOOOPSTT	OPHTHALMOLOGIST
AGHHILOPTTTTTUU	PUT THAT LIGHT OUT
AGHHOOOPPPRTTYY	PHOTOTYPOGRAPHY
AGHIIILMNNNORVY	LIVING IN HARMONY
AGHIIINNOPRRTUW	POURING WITH RAIN
AGHIKKMNOORRSTW	MAKING SHORT WORK
AGHIKKNNOOORTTWW	KNOW A THING OR TWO
AGHILNOOOPRSSTT	ANTHROPOLOGISTS
AGHILNOOOSSTTUU	SOUGHT A SOLUTION
AGHILNORRTTUUWX	LUXURIANT GROWTH
AGIIIKMNNOOPRSV	MAKING PROVISION
AGIIIKNNNRSTTTU	TAKING IT IN TURNS
AGIIIILLLMMNSTUU	MULTILINGUALISM
AGIIILLNNOQRSUV	LIVING IN SQUALOR
AGIIILNNNNORSSTT	LOSING IN TRANSIT
AGIIINNORRSSSTT	TRANSISTORISING
AGIIINNORRSSTTZ	TRANSISTORIZING
AGIIJKMNOORRTWY	WORKING MAJORITY
AGIIMMNNNNOOSTUV	MOVING MOUNTAINS
AGIIMMNNOSSSSUU	ISSUING A SUMMONS
AGIINNOOOPPRRTT	PROPORTIONATING
AGIMNNOOPRSSTUW	WRONG ASSUMPTION
AGINNOOOORSSTTT	STARTING TOO SOON
AGINNOPPRSTTTUU	PUTTING ON A SPURT
AGNOOORRSSTTTUU	TURNS OUT TO GRASS
AHHIIJLNOOPPSSU	JOHN PHILIP SOUSA
AIIIIILLMOOOPPRSY	MORAL PHILOSOPHY
AHHILNOOOPPRSTY	PHOSPHORYLATION
AHHINOOPRSSSTUW	PASS WITH HONOURS
AHIIILMORRSTTYY	MILITARY HISTORY
AHIILMNOORRSTUY	MILITARY HONOURS
AHIJNNOOHSSSTTW	SAINT JOHN'S WORT'S
AHIKNOPPRRRSSTU	PARKHURST PRISON
AHINOOOPRSSTUWY	WHATS YOUR POISON?
AHMNNNOOOPRTTTW	NORTHAMPTON TOWN
AIIIILLNOOQRSTUY	INQUISITORIALLY
AIIIJMMNNNNOORTY	JOIN IN MATRIMONY
AIIIJNNOOPSTTUX	IN JUXTAPOSITION
AIIIMNNNOSSTTUU	WOMANS INTUITION
AIILLOPRSSSTTUU	ILLUSTRIOUS PAST
AIILNOOOPPRRTTY	PROPORTIONALITY
AIINOOOPPPRSTTY	OPPOSITION PARTY
AIKNNNNOQQTTUUWY	UNKNOWN QUANTITY
AILLLNORSUUWWXY	WALLOWS IN LUXURY
BBBBEEFGIIILRTT	FLIBBERTIGIBBET
BBBBEEHLRSSTTUU	BURSTS THE BUBBLE
BBDEGIILNORSTTY	SOBBING BITTERLY
BBCCHILLOOOPSUY	PUBLIC-SCHOOL BOY
BBCDEEEIKLNORTU	BE CRUEL TO BE KIND
BBCEEEIIILMNOSV	BECOME INVISIBLE
BBCEEHNNORRRTUU	RUBBER TRUNCHEON
BBCEGIINORRSSUV	OVERSUBSCRIBING
BBCELMNOORRSUUY	COLOUR BY NUMBERS
BBCHKKOOOOORRYY	BY HOOK OR BY CROOK
BBDDEEEEHILRSST	BLESSED THE BRIDE
BBDDEEHLORRSSUU	RUBBED SHOULDERS
BBDEEEEHILRSSST	BLESSES THE BRIDE
BBDEEGINNORRSSU	BURN ONES BRIDGES
BBDEGIILLNNOOWY	BODY-LINE BOWLING
BBDEINNOOSSSSUY	NOBODYS BUSINESS
BBDIMOORRRSTUUY	DORMITORY SUBURB
BBEEEEGGHIINNTU	BEGIN THE BEGUINE
BBEEEEINNNNOOST	BEE IN ONES BONNET
BBEEEGHIILLNSW	NEW ENGLISH BIBLE
BBEEEHHILLOTTTW	HIT BELOW THE BELT
BBEEEHILLNOTTTU	BITE ON THE BULLET
BBEEEHILLNTTTTU	BITTEN THE BULLET
BBEEEHILNOORRSU	SWORE ON THE BIBLE
BBEEEKNNNOOOORSS	BROKEN ONE'S BONES
BBEEFHHILORSTTU	BIRTH OF THE BLUES
BBEFFHLLMOORTTU	BOLT FROM THE BLUE
BBEEGGHINORRTTU	RUBBING TOGETHER
BBEEGHIILLNTTTU	BITING THE BULLET
BBEEGHILNORRSTU	LOSING THE RUBBER
BBEEGHINORSTTTU	BRING OUT THE BEST
BBEEGINNOOSSTTU	STUBBING ONE'S TOE

BBEEHHLMRRSTUUY	THE MULBERRY BUSH
BBEEHILNNOORSTW	SWORN ON THE BIBLE
BBEFGINOOOORSST	BIG FOR ONE'S BOOTS
BBEGGIIINNNORST	BRINGS INTO BEING
BBEGHIILNOORSTT	BRINGS TO THE BOIL
BCCCEEEIIMNRTTU	CUBIC CENTIMETRE
BCCDEEEHIKKKTTU	KICKED THE BUCKET
BCCDEEFNOOOORST	SECOND OF OCTOBER
BCCDEFHIKNOOORS	BROOD OF CHICKENS
BCCDEIIIMNORSTY	BEYOND CRITICISM
BCCEEEIILMNNOSU	BIOLUMINESCENCE
BCCEEGIIMNNOTTX	BECOMING EXTINCT
BCCEEIIILLLRTTY	ELECTRICITY BILL
BCCEEIILNOPTUUX	PUBLIC EXECUTION
BCCEEIILLNOPRSUU	PUBLIC ENCLOSURE
BCCEEILNORRSTTU	RECONSTRUCTIBLE
BCCEFGIIMNNOORS	COMBINING FORCES
BCCEHINOORRSSTU	CROSS THE RUBICON
BCCEHINOOSSSTUU	THE SUBCONSCIOUS
BCCEIKMOOOPRRTT	ROCK-BOTTOM PRICE
BCCHKMOOOORTTTU	TOUCH ROCK-BOTTOM
BCDDDEEHLLOORTU	CURDLED THE BLOOD
BCDDDEELLNOOOSS	COLD-BLOODEDNESS
BCDDEEEFHIMOORRT	THIRD OF DECEMBER
BCDDEEEHIMORSTU	MUCH TO BE DESIRED
BCDDEEEILMRRRUU	CRIED BLUE MURDER
BCDDEEEIMNNRRUU	REDUCED IN NUMBER
BCDDEEHHILLLOOT	CHILLED THE BLOOD
BCDDEEHLLOORSTU	CURDLES THE BLOOD
BCDDEELLNOOORSU	CURDLE ONE'S BLOOD
BCDDGILLLNOORUY	BLOODCURDLINGLY
BCDDIIKLLLLNOOO	KILL IN COLD BLOOD
BCDEEEEFGHNOOOR	BEEN OF GOOD CHEER
BCDEEEEFHMNORTT	TENTH OF DECEMBER
BCDEEEEHHINNSST	BEHIND THE SCENES
	BEHIND-THE-SCENES
BCDEEEEHIIMNSTT	THE BEST MEDICINE
BCDEEEENOOPTTTX	NOT TO BE EXPECTED
BCDEEEEFFFHIMORT	FIFTH OF DECEMBER
BCDEEEEFFGIILNOR	FORCIBLE FEEDING
BCDEEEEFFIMORRST	FIRST OF DECEMBER
BCDEEEFHIMNNORT	NINTH OF DECEMBER
BCDEEEFHIMORSTX	SIXTH OF DECEMBER
BCDEEEEHKNOORRRT	BROKEN THE RECORD
BCDEEEIIILLLNNP	INDELIBLE PENCIL
BCDEEEILMRRRSUU	CRIES BLUE MURDER
BCDEEEIMNNRRSUU	REDUCES IN NUMBER
BCDEEFGIIMNNORS	BECOMING FRIENDS
BCDEEFHIMMNOORS	COMES FROM BEHIND
BCDEEFIIJKLOOST	OBJECT OF DISLIKE
BCDEEFILLOORRRW	LORD WILBERFORCE
BCDEEGGHINOORRS	BRINGS GOOD CHEER
BCDEEGIKLLNOPUW	PUBLIC KNOWLEDGE
BCDEEHHIOORRTTT	OCTOBER THE THIRD
BCDEEHIKNOPRTTU	DROP IN THE BUCKET
BCDEEHILLMNOPRR	PROBLEM CHILDREN
BCDEEHILMOOPTTT	CLIMBED TO THE TOP
BCDEEHJOPRSSTTU	DROPS THE SUBJECT
BCDEEHKMNOSSTUU	SUCKED ONE'S THUMB
BCDEEIKLNOOOSST	LICKED ONE'S BONES
BCDEEIILLMNOOPTT	OLD CONTEMPTIBLE
BCDEEILMMOOPRST	DOMESTIC PROBLEM
BCDEHILLNOOOSS	CHILLS ONE'S BLOOD
BCDEHILLNOPSUVW	DEVILS PUNCH BOWL
	DEVILS PUNCHBOWL
BCDEIIILOPRRTUY	REPRODUCIBILITY
BCDEIIILRSTTTUY	DESTRUCTIBILITY
BCDEIJMNOOSTUUV	SUBJUNCTIVE MOOD
BCDEILLNNOORSSU	COLOUR BLINDNESS
BCDEILMMMNNOOOW	WIMBLEDON COMMON
BCDGHIINOPPRSUY	CHIPPING SODBURY

BCDIIIMOORRSTUY	MORBID CURIOSITY
BCEEEEEGNOORRSZ	EBENEZER SCROOGE
BCEEEEEFFKNOOORR	BOOK OF REFERENCE
BCEEEEEFGIKLORTW	LEG BEFORE WICKET
BCEEEEEFHORRRSTU	SHEER BRUTE FORCE
BCEEEEGHILMRRSU	LIMBURGER CHEESE
BCEEEEEGKLLMOOPR	PEMBROKE COLLEGE
BCEEEEHIKLNORST	BROKE THE SILENCE
BCEEEEJNNOOPSTX	EXPENSE NO OBJECT
BCEEEEFFGILNORTY	BENEFIT OF CLERGY
BCEEEEFGHIIOPRTT	TIP OF THE ICEBERG
BCEEEEFGIMOORRVY	OVERCOME BY GRIEF
BCEEEFFHHIORRTTY	BITE OF THE CHERRY
BCEEEFIIKNNSSST	SICKNESS BENEFIT
BCEEEFIMMOORSTY	MEMBER OF SOCIETY
BCEEEGIILMNRSTV	CLIMBING EVEREST
BCEEEHHMORSTTTU	SO MUCH THE BETTER
BCEEEHHNOORTTTT	OCTOBER THE TENTH
BCEEEHIKKNORTTW	BROKEN THE WICKET
BCEEEILLOPPPRSU	PEOPLES REPUBLIC
BCEEEILNNORSSTV	CONVERTIBLENESS
BCEEEILNPSSSSTU	SUSCEPTIBLENESS
BCEEEMNOPRRSSTU	CURBS ONE'S TEMPER
BCEEFFGOOORTTYY	GEOFFREY BOYCOTT
BCEEFFHHIOORTTT	OCTOBER THE FIFTH
BCEEFGGGIMNORRY	BEGGING FOR MERCY
BCEEFGHHIOOORTT	EIGHTH OF OCTOBER
BCEEFHIJNOOSTTU	THE CUT OF ONE'S JIB
BCEEFHIKLNNRRUY	HUCKLEBERRY FINN
BCEEFHIOORRSTTT	OCTOBER THE FIRST
BCEEFLOOOORRSTUU	SOURCE OF TROUBLE
BCEEGIILNOOPSTW	BLOWING TO PIECES
BCEEGINNNOORSTTU	ON-COURSE BETTING
BCEEHHINNOORTTT	OCTOBER THE NINTH
BCEEHHIOORSTTTX	OCTOBER THE SIXTH
BCEEHIILNOORTVW	ROB WITH VIOLENCE
BCEEHILNOOPPTTU	OPEN TO THE PUBLIC
BCEEIIILMPPRRST	IMPRESCRIPTIBLE
BCEEINORSSSTTUV	OBSTRUCTIVENESS
BCEEKLMNNORSUUY	ONE'S LUCKY NUMBER
BCEFFHOOOORRTTU	FOURTH OF OCTOBER
BCEFHIJOOOPRSTW	OBJECT OF WORSHIP
BCEFIJLMOOSSTUY	SYMBOL OF JUSTICE
BCEGGIIIMNNNOOT	COMING INTO BEING
BCEGIIJNORSSTTU	BRINGS TO JUSTICE
BCEGIILMNOOPRTW	CLIMBING TO POWER
BCEGIJNNOOORSTT	STRONG OBJECTION
BCEGILLNNOOOOSW	BLOWING ONE'S COOL
BCEHHIMNOORSSUY	HIERONYMUS BOSCH
BCEHHLLOOOORSWY	SCHOOLBOY HOWLER
BCEHIIIIINOSTTX	EXHIBITIONISTIC
BCEHIILNOPPRSUW	PUBLIC OWNERSHIP
BCEHIINNOOOPPST	OPPOSITION BENCH
BCEHKLNOOSSTTUU	BLOCKS OUT THE SUN
BCEIIILMOPRSSTY	COMPRESSIBILITY
BCEIIKNOORSSSTT	STICK TO ONE'S RIBS
BCGHIINNNNOORST	CHRIS BONNINGTON
BCGIIIIILNORRTY	INCORRIGIBILITY
BCIIKNNNOSTTWY	KNOWN BY INSTINCT
BCIIKNNNOSSTTWY	KNOWS BY INSTINCT
BDDDEEEEHNRRSTU	REDS UNDER THE BED
BDDDEEEEIILNVVY	DIVIDED BY ELEVEN
BDDDEEEIILTVVWY	DIVIDED BY TWELVE
BDDDEEEIOORRSSY	DISOBEYED ORDERS
BDDDEEGIINNNOOS	DONE ONE'S BIDDING
BDDDEEGIINNNOOSS	DOES ONE'S BIDDING
BDDDEEIINTTVWYY	DIVIDED BY TWENTY
BDDEEEEGIKLLRSY	KILLED BY DEGREES
BDDEEEEIILNSVVY	DIVIDES BY ELEVEN
BDDEEEIILSTVVWY	DIVIDES BY TWELVE
BDDEEFGHIKNORUU	DUKE OF EDINBURGH

BDDEEFGKLNOOOWY	BODY OF KNOWLEDGE
BDDEEFLLLNOOSSU	FULL-BLOODEDNESS
BDDEEGGIINNOOSV	BIDS GOOD EVENING
BDDEEGHIIINRTVY	DIVIDING BY THREE
BDDEEGHIIINNOPST	OPENS THE BIDDING
BDDEEGIIINNSVVY	DIVIDING BY SEVEN
BDDEEGILNNOPTTU	PLUNGED INTO DEBT
BDDEEGILNNORTUU	UNBRIDLED TONGUE
BDDEEHIINOORSTY	IN BY THE SIDE DOOR
BDDEEHLNOOORTTU	UNBOLTED THE DOOR
BDDEEIILNOPSTTU	BOTTLED UP INSIDE
BDDEEIINSTTVWYY	DIVIDES BY TWENTY
BDDEGGHIIINTVY	DIVIDING BY EIGHT
BDDEGGNNOORRUUY	GO BY UNDERGROUND
BDDEHIIINSSSTUW	DID BUSINESS WITH
BDDGGIIMNNOOORS	BIDS GOOD MORNING
BDEEEEEFLNORSTT	BETTERED ONESELF
BDEEEEELNNOOTUV	DOUBLE SEVENTEEN
BDEEEEEFHLOORSTZ	FREEZES THE BLOOD
BDEEEEEFLNOOORSZ	FREEZE ONE'S BLOOD
BDEEEEEGHKLNOPRT	BROKEN THE PLEDGE
BDEEEEEGIOPRRRTV	BEVERIDGE REPORT
BDEEEEELLNOOSSTV	DO ONES LEVEL BEST
BDEEEENNOORSSST	RESTED ONE'S BONES
BDEEEEFGHINNORTY	BEYOND THE FRINGE
BDEEEEFGHINOORST	BRIDGE OF THE NOSE
BDEEEFGIIINNRTV	DERIVING BENEFIT
BDEEEFHHOOPRSTT	HOPED FOR THE BEST
BDEEEFHLNOOSTTW	SOFTENED THE BLOW
BDEEEGGHINNOSST	HEDGING ONE'S BETS
BDEEEGGHINNSTTT	GETTING THE BENDS
BDEEEGHIINNORTV	GIVEN ONE THE BIRD
BDEEEGHIINORSTV	GIVES ONE THE BIRD
BDEEEFGHILNOPSTT	STOP THE BLEEDING
BDEEEGLNNORSSUY	BOUNDLESS ENERGY
BDEEEHHHINNORTT	BEHIND THE THRONE
BDEEEHIIILLNOTUW	DOUBLE WHITE LINE
BDEEEHIKLOORSTT	STOKED THE BOILER
BDEEEHILNNOORRT	ON THE BORDERLINE
BDEEEHMNNOOSSTU	THUMBED ONE'S NOSE
BDEEEIKLLNOOSTT	LIKED ONE'S BOTTLE
BDEEEILLOOUUVWY	WOULD YOU BELIEVE?
BDEEEILNUOPPSTW	TIPPED ONE'S ELBOW
BDEEEIILNPRRRTUY	REPLIED BY RETURN
BDEEEIMNNOOPRSY	BEYOND ONES PRIME
BDEEEELLNOPRSTUU	UNTROUBLED SLEEP
BDEEFFGGGIINORT	BEGGING TO DIFFER
BDEEFFHLNOOOTTT	FOND OF THE BOTTLE
BDEEFGGINOOTTTU	GETTING OUT OF BED
BDEEFHIILLMORTT	FILLED TO THE BRIM
BDEEFHIIMNOORRTV	THIRD OF NOVEMBER
BDEEFIIIILLNNSTY	INDEFENSIBILITY
BDEEFLNNOOOORSZ	FROZEN ONE'S BLOOD
BDEEGGIINNOTTTT	GETTING INTO DEBT
BDEEGGGLNOOOORRW	LORD GEORGE BROWN
BDEEGHHIINORSTT	ON THE BRIGHT SIDE
BDEEGHIINNNRTWY	WINNING THE DERBY
BDEEGHJNOOOTTTW	GET DOWN TO THE JOB
BDEEGHLLOORSSSU	GOD BLESS HER SOUL
BDEEGIILNNOOPWW	BLOWING WIDE OPEN
BDEEGKNNNOORRUW	BROKEN NEW GROUND
BDEEGLNOOOPSSTU	GETS ONE'S BLOOD UP
BDEEGOOOOOSTTTU	TOO GOOD TO BE TRUE
BDEEHHILOOPRSTT	SPOILED THE BROTH
BDEEHHLMPPSSTTU	PLUMBS THE DEPTHS
BDEEHIIINNNSSTU	UNINHIBITEDNESS
BDEEHIJLNOOSTVW	THE DEVIL'S OWN JOB
BDEEHIMNOSSSSTU	BUSINESS METHODS
BDEEHMNOOOSTTTT	SEND TO THE BOTTOM
BDEEHMOOOORRSTY	SOMEBODY OR OTHER
BDEEIILNOPSSTTU	BOTTLES UP INSIDE
BDEEIILNOSSTVWY	LIVED BY ONE'S WITS
BDEEILMOOPPRRSS	BEDROOM SLIPPERS
BDEEILNNOOPSTTU	BUTTONED ONE'S LIP
BDEEILNOOOPRSTW	BLOW TO ONES PRIDE
BDEEILNOORSTUYY	YOURS OBEDIENTLY
BDEEINORSSSSSTU	BURSTS ONE'S SIDES
BDEELMNOOORUUYY	DOUBLE YOUR MONEY
BDEFGILLNOOOORW	ROBIN GOODFELLOW
BDEFGINOOORSSSU	GOOD FOR BUSINESS
BDEGHIIINNNPPTU	NIPPING IN THE BUD
BDEGHILLOOSSSSU	GOD BLESS HIS SOUL
BDEGHILNNOOORTU	DOUBLE OR NOTHING
BDEGHJNOOOOTTTW	GOT DOWN TO THE JOB
BDEGIIIIILNSTTY	INDIGESTIBILITY
BDEGIILMNNNOOSW	BLOWING ONE'S MIND
BDEGIIMNOORSSTT	BED-SITTING-ROOMS
BDEGIINNNNORTTU	RUNNING INTO DEBT
BDEGIKNNOOOOOSS	IN ONES GOOD BOOKS
BDEHHILNOOSTWWW	HOW THE WIND BLOWS
BDEHIINNOOPSTTY	BEYOND THIS POINT
BDEHIKLNOPRSUUW	UNPUBLISHED WORK
BDEIIILLMPSTUXY	MULTIPLIED BY SIX
BDEIIILLMOPTTUWY	MULTIPLIED BY TWO
BDFHILOORRSSTT	THIRSTS FOR BLOOD
BDGIIKLLNORSTW	KILLING TWO BIRDS
BDIIIILLNOSSTUY	INDISSOLUBILITY
BEEEEEEILNOSSVY	BELIEVE ONE'S EYES
BEEEEEFFHILNSTT	FEELS THE BENEFIT
BEEEEEGHPRSTTUZ	GETS THE BREEZE UP
BEEEEEHILNNSTTW	BETWEEN THE LINES
BEEEEEORRSTWWYZ	EYEBROW TWEEZERS
BEEEEFGHORSTTTT	GETS THE BETTER OF
BEEEEFILNNNOOSS	FEEL IN ONE'S BONES
BEEEEFILNOORRBU	ERRONEOUS BELIEF
BEEEEFINORSTTWW	BETWEEN TWO FIRES
BEEEEGHHILLRTTT	LET THERE BE LIGHT
BEEEEGILLNOSUWY	WE'LL BE SEEING YOU
BFEEEGLNNORSTTT	TEN GREEN BOTTLES
BEEEEHLMNNOPRTU	TELEPHONE NUMBER
BEEEEHNOORRSTTT	SOONER THE BETTER
BEEEEINRSSSTTTW	BITTERSWEETNESS
BEEEEFFHHINOSTTV	BEETHOVENS FIFTH
BEEEEFFLMOOPRTTU	BOTTLE OF PERFUME
BEEEEFGGINORSSSV	BEGS FORGIVENESS
BEEEFGHIMMNNORTT	FOR THE TIME BEING
BEEEEFGHIOSSTTTT	GETS THE BEST OF IT
BEEEEFGIIILLORSU	RELIGIOUS BELIEF
BEEEEFGILRSSTTTU	GETS BUTTERFLIES
BEEEEFHHOOPRSSTT	HOPES FOR THE BEST
BEEEEFHMMNOORTTV	TENTH OF NOVEMBER
BEEEEFHNNOOORTTZ	FROZEN TO THE BONE
BEEEFILNNOSSTTT	FELT IN ONE'S BONES
BEEEGGHILNOTTTW	GETTING THE ELBOW
BEEEGHILLNPRSST	PRESSING THE BELL
BEEEGHILNNOSTTT	TIGHTEN ONES BELT
BEEEGHIMMNNNORRT	REMEMBER NOTHING
BEEEGHINOOPTUVZ	GIVEN UP THE BOOZE
BEEEGHINOQSSTTU	BEGS THE QUESTION
BEEEGHIOOPSTUVZ	GIVES UP THE BOOZE
BEEEGIIMMNSSTTU	BUSINESS MEETING
BEEEGINNOOSSTTU	BITES ONE'S TONGUE
BEEEGNOORRSTUVW	WESTBOURNE GROVE
BEEEHHILLSSTTUY	HITS THE BULL'S-EYE
BEEEEHHINNNOSTTV	BEETHOVENS NINTH
BEEEHIIMMRRSSTV	SHIVER ME TIMBERS!
BEFFHIKLORSSTT	STOKES THE BOILER
BEEEHIMPRRSSTTU	STIR UP THE EMBERS
BEEEEHLLMOOPRSTV	SOLVE THE PROBLEM
BEEEHOOPRSTTUWY	UP TO THE EYEBROWS
BEEEIKLLNOOSSTT	LIKES ONE'S BOTTLE
BEEEILMNNNOSSTT	NOBLE SENTIMENTS

BEEEILNNOPRSSSS	RESPONSIBLENESS	BEGGIILNNOORTUV	GIVING NO TROUBLE
BEEEILNPRRRSTUY	REPLIES BY RETURN	BEGGINNNRSTTTUU	GETTING SUNBURNT
BEEEEINNRSSSTUUV	BUSINESS VENTURE	BEGHHIJNOOOTTTW	GOT ON WITH THE JOB
BEEEELMNOORSSSTU	TROUBLESOMENESS	BEGHIIIKNNOPRST	POKING IN THE RIBS
BEEENNORRRSTTUW	BOW-STREET RUNNER	BEGHIILLMPTTUYY	MULTIPLY BY EIGHT
BEEFFFHIMNOORTV	FIFTH OF NOVEMBER	BEGHIILNOORTTU	BROUGHT INTO LINE
BEEFFGHHIORSTUV	GIVE THE BRUSH-OFF	BEGHILNOOORSTTU	TROUBLESHOOTING
BEEFFIMNOORRSTV	FIRST OF NOVEMBER	BEGHINNOOPRTTTW	POTTING THE BROWN
BEEFGHINNORSTUW	WEIGHT OF NUMBERS	BEGHNNOOOPSSTUU	HUNG UP ONE'S BOOTS
BEEFGHINOORRSTT	BRINGS TO THE FORE	BEGIIIILLLNTTY	INTELLIGIBILITY
BEEFGILNNOORSST	BRINGS TO ONESELF	BEGIIKNNOOOSSTU	SUITING ONE'S BOOK
BEEFGINNNNORRSSU	BURN ONES FINGERS	BEGIINNNOQRSTUU	BURNING QUESTION
BEEFGLOOORTTTUU	GET OUT OF TROUBLE	BEGIJKMNOOSTUUY	YOU MUST BE JOKING
BEEFHIIKNORTTTT	THINK BETTER OF IT	BEGIKLMNNOORSSW	BLOWN SMOKE-RINGS
BEEFHIMNNNOORTV	NINTH OF NOVEMBER	BEGIKLMNOORSSSW	BLOWS SMOKE-RINGS
BEEFHIMNOORSTVX	SIXTH OF NOVEMBER	BEGILLNNOOSTTUU	WELLINGTON BOOTS
BEEFKLORRSTTUY	BUTTERFLY STROKE	BEGIMNNOOOPPRSW	MOPPING ONE'S BROW
BEEFLLOOPRSTTUV	BULLET-PROOF VEST	BEGINNOOORSSTTW	STRING TO ONE'S BOW
	BULLETPROOF VEST	BEHHIKNOOPSSTTU	PUTS THE KIBOSH ON
BEEGGHHOOORRTTTU	BROUGHT TOGETHER	BEHIIINNOOOPRTZ	PROHIBITION ZONE
BEEGGHIILLNTTUV	GIVING THE BULLET	BEHIKMNOOOSTTTT	SINK TO THE BOTTOM
BEEGHHIILNNSTTU	BLUES IN THE NIGHT	BEHKMNOOOSTTTTU	SUNK TO THE BOTTOM
BEEGHHIJNOOOTTTW	GET ON WITH THE JOB	BEIIIILRRSSTTY	IRRESISTIBILITY
BEEGHHIMPSTTUUV	GIVE THE THUMBS UP	BEIIILLMPSSTUXY	MULTIPLIES BY SIX
BEEGHHIMPSSTTTUU	GETS THE THUMBS UP	BEIIILMNNOOSSTU	BENITO MUSSOLINI
BEEGHIILNOPPTTW	TIPPING THE ELBOW	BEIIILPPRSSSTUY	SUPPRESSIBILITY
BEEGHILNNSSSTUY	LENGTHY BUSINESS	BEIILLMPSSTTUWY	MULTIPLIES BY TWO
BEEGHMNOOOOTTTT	GONE TO THE BOTTOM	BEILMNNNRSTTTUU	BLUNT INSTRUMENT
BEEGHMOOOOSTTTT	GOES TO THE BOTTOM	BEILNNOOPSSSTTU	BUTTONS ONE'S LIPS
BEEGHNOORRSTTUY	YOUNGEST BROTHER	BEILNNOORRSTTUU	RUNS INTO TROUBLE
BEEGIIKNNORSSTT	BRING TO ITS KNEES	BEILNOORSTTTUUV	VIOLENT OUTBURST
BEEGILNOORSTTTU	GETS INTO TROUBLE	BEIMNORSSSSTUUU	RUMBUSTIOUSNESS
BEEHHIKNNOORRTV	HOVER ON THE BRINK	BELLLORSSTUUWYY	SLOWLY BUT SURELY
BEEHHILLNOSTTWW	BLOWN THE WHISTLE	BELOPRRSSSSSTUU	BRUSSELS SPROUTS
BEEHHILLOSSTTWW	BLOWS THE WHISTLE	BFGIIINNOORRTTU	BRING TO FRUITION
BEEHHILNOOORTWZ	BELOW THE HORIZON	BFMMOOOOOPRTTTT	FROM TOP TO BOTTOM
BEEHIIIINOPRSSTV	PROHIBITIVENESS	BGGGHHIINNORRTU	BRINGING THROUGH
BEEHIIMMRRSSTVY	SHIVER MY TIMBERS!	BGGHIINNOOPRSTU	BRINGING UP SHORT
BEEHIINNOSSTTWX	IN THE WITNESS-BOX	BHMMNOOORSSTTUU	BUTTON MUSHROOMS
BEEHIJLORRSTUUY	JERRY-BUILT HOUSE	CCCCEEIIILRRTTU	ELECTRIC CIRCUIT
BEEHILLMPRTTUYY	MULTIPLY BY THREE	CCCDEEEEIIMNNOR	MERE COINCIDENCE
BEEHINOOPRSSTTT	STRIPS TO THE BONE	CCCDEEEEILLNOTV	COLLECT EVIDENCE
BEEHKLOOOOTTTTT	TOOK TO THE BOTTLE	CCCDEEEHHKORRST	CHECK THE RECORDS
BEEHLOOORRSSTTU	TROUBLESHOOTERS	CCCDEEEIIMNOSST	DOMESTIC SCIENCE
BEEHMNOOOSTTTTT	SENT TO THE BOTTOM	CCCDEEEIINNOPRU	PURE COINCIDENCE
BEEHMNOOOTTTTTW	WENT TO THE BOTTOM	CCCDEEEIKKNNORS	CRICKED ONE'S NECK
BEEIIIIILRRRSTVY	IRREVERSIBILITY	CCCDEEFIIKNNORT	CONFIDENCE TRICK
BEEIIILNOPRSTVX	INVISIBLE EXPORT	CCCDEEFINOOOORST	DOCTOR OF SCIENCE
BEEIILLMNPSTTUY	MULTIPLIES BY TEN	CCCDEEFFHIIILOTU	DIFFICULT CHOICE
BEEIILNOSSSTVWY	LIVES BY ONE'S WITS	CCCDIIILNORSTTU	DISTRICT COUNCIL
BEEIINNNNOORSSTU	RUB ONE'S NOSE IN IT	CCCEEEEILLOOPRST	COLLECTORS PIECE
BEEILLMNPSTTUY	MULTIPLY BY SEVEN	CCCEEEILNRRRTTU	ELECTRIC CURRENT
BEEILNPRRSTTTUU	TURBULENT PRIEST	CCCEEEIMNNNOOSY	CONSCIENCE MONEY
BEEIMNOPRRRSSUU	SUPERIOR NUMBERS	CCCEEFILLLMORSU	COMES FULL CIRCLE
BEEINNNOOSSSSUW	ONE'S OWN BUSINESS	CCCEEHKNOORTTUU	CHECK-OUT COUNTER
BEEINNORSSSTUUV	UNOBTRUSIVENESS	CCCEEHLMOOSTTYY	CHOLECYSTECTOMY
BEELMOOPRSSSTTU	BOTTOMLESS PURSE	CCCEEIILMNOORRT	MICROELECTRONIC
BEFFHKLMOOOOOTT	TOOK THE BLOOM OFF	CCCEEIILMNORSTU	ELECTRONIC MUSIC
BEFFHMMOOOORTTT	BOTTOM OF THE FORM	CCCEEIIKLLOORTT	TICKET COLLECTOR
BEFGGGIIINNORRT	BRINGING TO GRIEF	CCCEEIKNORRTTUY	COUNTY CRICKETER
BEFGGHILLNOORTU	GOING FOR THE BULL	CCCEFHILOOOORSU	CHOICE OF COLOURS
BEFGHHIIIJNNOST	FINISHING THE JOB	CCCEIIKNOQSSSUU	QUICK SUCCESSION
BEFGIINNOOSSSTU	BUSINESS FOOTING	CCCEIILNORSTUUY	SECURITY COUNCIL
BEFGINOOOSSSTUU	GO OUT OF BUSINESS	CCCIIIMNOPRRSTU	CIRCUMSCRIPTION
BEFGLOOOORTTTUU	GOT OUT OF TROUBLE	CCCIILMNOORSTUU	CIRCUMLOCUTIONS
BEFHHILLMOOOTTT	BOTTOM OF THE HILL	CCCIILMOOORSTUU	CIRCUMLOCUTIOUS
BEFHINOORSSSSUU	HOURS OF BUSINESS	CCDDDEHHILNOOOS	SECOND CHILDHOOD
BEFKLLOOOORRSTU	LOOKS FOR TROUBLE	CCDDEEEIIILNRSUV	SERVICE INCLUDED
BEGGHHHIILRSTTT	THE BRIGHT LIGHTS	CCDDEEGILNNNOSY	CONDESCENDINGLY
BEGGHHINOORSTTU	SOBERING THOUGHT	CCDDEEHIIMNNOPTU	OCCUPIED THE MIND
BEGGHINORRSTTUY	BRIGHT YOUNGSTER	CCDEEEEEFIINOPV	PIECE OF EVIDENCE

CCDEEEEFLNNORSU	FENCED ENCLOSURE
CCDEEEEFNORRRSS	CROSS-REFERENCED
CCDEEEEFFHIMOOOR	FREEDOM OF CHOICE
CCDEEEEFFNOORRTT	CONCERTED EFFORT
CCDEEEFIILNNRTU	DIRECT INFLUENCE
CCDEEEFILNNOOSS	LOSES CONFIDENCE
CCDEEEEHIILLMORT	MICHELLE DOTRICE
CCDEEEHIOPRSSTU	CRUSHED TO PIECES
CCDEEEHMOOPTTUX	EXPECTED TOO MUCH
CCDEEEIIMORSSTV	DOMESTIC SERVICE
CCDEEEIKNOOPRSX	CROOKED SIXPENCE
CCDEEEINORRSTVY	RECENT DISCOVERY
CCDEEEENNNNORSSU	UNCONCERNEDNESS
CCDEEEENNOOPRRSS	CORRESPONDENCES
CCDEEFFIILNORRS	CIRCLE OF FRIENDS
CCDEEFHILLNOOST	INCH OF COLD STEEL
CCDEEFOOOPRRRST	CORRECTED PROOFS
CCDEEGHHILNNOTY	HIGHLY CONNECTED
CCDEEFHIIMNOPSTU	OCCUPIES THE MIND
CCDEEHIKLNOOPSS	LICKED ONE'S CHOPS
CCDEEHILNNORRRS	CHILDRENS CORNER
CCDEEIIIORSTVVY	DECISIVE VICTORY
CCDEEIJLOOPRRUU	COLOUR PREJUDICE
CCDEEIKLNORSTUW	TURNED CLOCKWISE
CCDEEILLNOOPRRT	CONTROLLED PRICE
CCDEEIMMNOOOSTY	DOMESTIC ECONOMY
CCDEEINOORRRSTV	CORONERS VERDICT
CCDEEINOPRSTUUV	SUPERCONDUCTIVE
CCDEELMNNOSTUUY	UNSEEMLY CONDUCT
CCDEFFIIIORRSTT	DISTRICT OFFICER
CCDEGHMNOORRUUV	COVER MUCH GROUND
CCDEGIILNNORSTY	DISCONCERTINGLY
CCDEGINNNOOOOST	GOOD CONNECTIONS
CCDEGINNOPRSTUU	SUPERCONDUCTING
CCDEHIIKKNOOTTU	KICKED INTO TOUCH
CCDEHINOOOPTTUV	PHOTOCONDUCTIVE
CCDEIIOOOORRSSTT	CORTICOSTEROIDS
CCDEILNNOORSSUW	DREW CONCLUSIONS
CCDENOOPRRSSTUU	SUPERCONDUCTORS
CCDGHHILLOOPSYY	CHILD PSYCHOLOGY
CCDGHLOOOPRSWYY	CROWD PSYCHOLOGY
CCEEEEFHIMNORST	SCENE OF THE CRIME
CCEEEEFILNNRSTU	SECRET INFLUENCE
CCEEEEFIMNPPRST	PERFECT SPECIMEN
CCEEEEFNNOPRRSS	PRESS CONFERENCE
CCEEEEFNORRRSSS	CROSS-REFERENCES
CCEEEEHHHOORSTT	CHEERS TO THE ECHO
CCEEEEHHLNNOSTT	CLENCH ONES TEETH
CCEEEEHHMNOOSSTT	COMES TO THE SCENE
CCEEEEHMOORSTTU	COME TO THE RESCUE
CCEEEEILLMNOPST	COMPLETE SILENCE
CCEEEEILMMOSTTT	SELECT COMMITTEE
CCEEEEINNOPRRTT	RECEPTION CENTRE
CCEEEEFHHNRRSTTU	FENCHURCH STREET
CCEEEFLLOORRSTU	REFUSE COLLECTOR
CCEEEEFNNNOOOQSU	OF NO CONSEQUENCE
CCEEEGGHHIKNORT	CHICKEN OR THE EGG
CCEEEGIIINNNORTV	RECEIVING NOTICE
CCEEEGINPSSSSUW	SWEEPING SUCCESS
CCEEEHHHNRRSTTU	ENTERS THE CHURCH
CCEEEHHLOOSSTTT	CLOSE TO THE CHEST
CCEEEHHNOOPPRSS	PHOSPHORESCENCE
CCEEEHIIKPPPSTU	PICK UP THE PIECES
CCEEEHIKLLNOSSS	CLICKS ONE'S HEELS
CCEEEHILOOPRRTT	ELECTROPHORETIC
CCEEEHIOPRSSSTU	CRUSHES TO PIECES
CCEEEIIKLNORSTT	ELECTROKINETICS
CCEEEILNOORRSTX	EXERCISE CONTROL
CCEEEINNOSSSTUV	CONSECUTIVENESS
CCEEFFFHKNORSTU	SCRUFF OF THE NECK
CCEEFFFIILNSSUY	SELF-SUFFICIENCY
CCEEFFHIILLMMOR	CLIFF MICHELMORE
CCEEFGINNORRRUY	FOREIGN CURRENCY
CCEEFHIIMNORSST	FORENSIC CHEMIST
CCEEFHILNNOSSST	CLENCH ONES FISTS
CCEEFHKLOORRTTU	CLERK OF THE COURT
CCEEFIINNOORTTU	COUNTERFEIT COIN
CCEEFILNNOSSSTY	SELF-CONSISTENCY
CCEEFILNOOOPRUU	COUNCIL OF EUROPE
CCEEFIMNNNNOOOR	NO CONCERN OF MINE
CCEEGHHIIKLLNTT	CHECKING THE TILL
CCEEGHIILOPSSTT	TELESCOPIC SIGHT
CCEEGHIINRRRSTU	THREE-RING CIRCUS
CCEEGHINOORSTTV	COVERING THE COST
CCEEGIIKNOPPST	PICKING TO PIECES
CCEEGIIINNNNNNOV	INCONVENIENCING
CCEEGIINNNNORTT	INTERCONNECTING
CCEEGIINOPSTTTU	CUTTING TO PIECES
CCEEHHLNNOORUUV	LUNCHEON VOUCHER
CCEEHHIILNOPTY	CHILLY RECEPTION
CCEEHIINNORTTTY	ETHNOCENTRICITY
CCEEHIKNNOOSTTU	CUCKOO IN THE NEST
CCEEHILNOOOPRTT	PHOTOELECTRONIC
CCEEHILOPRSSTUW	WHITE CORPUSCLES
CCEEHIOPRRSSTTU	SECRET COURTSHIP
CCEEIIKNOPRSTTT	TICKET INSPECTOR
CCEEIILNOOPPRST	POLICE INSPECTOR
CCEEIINNNNOORTT	INTERCONNECTION
CCEEILMOOPRTTVY	COMPLETE VICTORY
CCEEIMMNNORTTUY	COMMUNITY CENTRE
CCEEINNOOSSSSSU	CONSCIOUSNESSES
CCEELLMNOOOPRTT	COMPLETE CONTROL
CCEFGIIMNNOOORT	COMING INTO FORCE
CCEEFILLNOOSSSUY	SELF-CONSCIOUSLY
CCEEFILNOOOPRSUV	CONCLUSIVE PROOF
CCEEFMNOOOPRTTTU	CONTEMPT OF COURT
CCEEGHIIKNNNOPRS	NO SPRING CHICKEN
CCEEGHINNOOSTTU	COUNTING THE COST
CCEEGIIKNRSSSSTU	STRIKING SUCCESS
CCEEHIIILLNOPTUY	NUCLEOPHILICITY
CCEEHIIKLNNOOSTY	CHOLECYSTOKININ
CCEEHIIMNOOORSTY	ECONOMIC HISTORY
CCEEHILNOOOPRSST	SCHOOL INSPECTOR
CCEEHKLNOOPSSTTU	PUTS THE CLOCKS ON
CCEEHMNNOOPRSTYY	SYMPHONY CONCERT
CCEEIIIMMNOOPRSS	PRICE COMMISSION
CCEEIIIMNOOPRSTT	OPEN TO CRITICISM
CCEEIIKLLOORRSST	SOLICITORS CLERK
CCEEIILNOOOORSSU	COLLISION COURSE
CCEEIILMNOOSSSUY	SEMICONSCIOUSLY
CCEEIILNNOOSSTUY	CONSCIENTIOUSLY
CCEEIMOOOPRRRSSS	MICROPROCESSORS
CCEEINNNOOSSSSUU	UNCONSCIOUSNESS
CCEEINNOOPSSSSUU	CONSPICUOUSNESS
CCEEIOOOPPRSSSSTT	SPECTROSCOPISTS
CCGHIIINNORRSTU	SHORT-CIRCUITING
CCGHIINORRSTUVY	CRUSHING VICTORY
CCGIIIILNOOSSTU	SOCIOLINGUISTIC
CCHIIILNNOOSTUV	LUCHINO VISCONTI
CCIIINNOOORSTTT	CONTORTIONISTIC
CCIILLNOOOPRRUVY	PRIVY COUNCILLOR
CCIILNNOOPSSUUY	INCONSPICUOUSLY
CCIIMNNNOOSSTTU	MISCONSTRUCTION
CCIINORSSSTTTUV	CONSTRUCTIVISTS
CCKNOOOPRSTTTUY	STOCKPORT COUNTY
CCNNOORRRSSTUUY	CROSS-COUNTRY RUN
CDDDEEEGINNNORS	DESCENDING ORDER
CDDDEEEIIIMNSTU	STUDIED MEDICINE
CDDDEEEOOOPRRTUW	REDUCED TO POWDER
CDDDEEGHLMNOOTU	DODGED THE COLUMN
CDDDEFHHIILNOOR	CHILDHOOD FRIEND
CDDEEEEEFHNORSW	SHOWED DEFERENCE

CDDEEEEEEFILNOSV	DECEIVED ONESELF
CDDEEEEEEINNNPRT	INTERDEPENDENCE
CDDEEEEEFHINORSV	SHRED OF EVIDENCE
CDDEEEEEIIINOPRVV	PROVIDE EVIDENCE
CDDEEEEEINNNPRTY	INTERDEPENDENCY
CDDEEEEELNNPRTUY	UNPRECEDENTEDLY
CDDEEEEGHOORRTTW	CROWDED TOGETHER
CDDEEEGIMNNORWY	WEDDING CEREMONY
CDDEEEEHIIKNNORS	DICKIE HENDERSON
CDDEEEHIINORSTT	ON THE CREDIT SIDE
CDDEEEEHILOSSTUU	CLOUDED THE ISSUE
CDDEEIIILMNSSTU	STUDIES MEDICINE
CDDEEEOOPRRSTUW	REDUCES TO POWDER
CDDEEFGHHIILNRT	FRIGHTENED CHILD
CDDEEFGHHILLSTU	SCHEDULED FLIGHT
CDDEEFIIILLNPSS	SELF-DISCIPLINED
CDDEEFIIIINNORRT	DIRECTION FINDER
CDDEEGGIKLOSSTT	GILT-EDGED STOCKS
CDDEEGHHILMMNOY	HIGHLY COMMENDED
CDDEEGHLMNOOSTU	DODGES THE COLUMN
CDDEEGHOOOPRSTU	PRODUCE THE GOODS
CDDEEGIIILLNOOSU	GOLDEN DELICIOUS
CDDEEHHILLLOPST	SPOILED THE CHILD
CDDEEHHLLOORSTU	THE COLD SHOULDER
CDDEEHILNOOSTWW	CLOSED THE WINDOW
CDDEEHKLNOOORTU	UNLOCKED THE DOOR
CDDEEIIILNNPRSU	UNDER DISCIPLINE
CDDEEIIMNNNOOSS	SECOND DIMENSION
CDDEEIMMMORRTTU	COMMITTED MURDER
CDDEEIMNNOORSSS	CROSSED ONE'S MIND
CDDEEIMNNOORSSW	MINCED ONE'S WORDS
CDDEEIMNNOORSTU	SECOND TIME ROUND
CDDEEINOPRRTUUV	UNDERPRODUCTIVE
CDDEELOPRRSSTUU	PRODUCED RESULTS
CDDEFHIINOPRSTU	FINISHED PRODUCT
CDDEFILLNOOSTTU	SUTTON COLDFIELD
CDDEGIIIIILNPRS	RIGID DISCIPLINE
CDDEGIINOORRSTU	RECORDING STUDIO
CDDEIILNOPRSTVY	SPLENDID VICTORY
CDDEIINNOOOPRTW	CONDITION POWDER
CDDEIINNORSSSUU	UNDER DISCUSSION
CDDEILMNOOPRUXY	RUDDY COMPLEXION
CDDEINNOOPRRTUU	UNDERPRODUCTION
CDDEEEEEFFNRRTTT	DETERPENT EFFECT
CDDEEEEFGHLLNOT	THE GOLDEN FLEECE
CDDEEEEEFILNOSSV	DECEIVES ONESELF
CDDEEEEEFLLLNOSX	EXCELLED ONESELF
CDDEEEEFLNNSSSS	DEFENCELESSNESS
CDDEEEEFFHMOOPRS	FREEDOM OF SPEECH
CDDEEEEFIILRRTTT	CERTIFIED LETTER
CDDEEEEFIIMNNRST	DEFENCE MINISTER
CDDEEEFIMMORTVY	DEFECTIVE MEMORY
CDDEEEEGGHNOORST	GEORGE THE SECOND
CDDEEEEGHIKNPSTW	SWEEPING THE DECK
CDDEEEEHHIPQRTTU	QUEERED THE PITCH
CDDEEEEHIILMSTTX	EXCEEDS THE LIMIT
CDDEEEEHIIMNRSTX	EXERCISE THE MIND
CDDEEEEHIKKLNOSS	KICKED ONE'S HEELS
CDDEEEEHILOPRRTW	LOWERED THE PRICE
CDDEEEEHLLNOOOSS	COOLED ONE'S HEELS
CDDEEEEIILOPSVVX	EXPLOSIVE DEVICE
CDDEEEEIINNRTTVW	WRITTEN EVIDENCE
CDDEEEEIJNNOSSTU	SEEN JUSTICE DONE
CDDEEEEIJNOSSSTU	SEES JUSTICE DONE
CDDEEEEIMMNRRSSU	SUMMER RESIDENCE
CDDEEEEINNNORTTT	DETENTION CENTRE
CDDEEEEINNNPRSTU	SUPERINTENDENCE
CDDEEEEKLNNOSTTY	KEENLY CONTESTED
CDDEEEENNNPSSSTU	SUSPEND SENTENCE
CDDEEEFFIIILLNOR	FEDERICO FELLINI
CDDEEEFGGILNOTTT	GETTING COLD FEET
CDDEEEFGHIIILNRRS	FRIEDRICH ENGELS
CDDEEEFGHKLOORTT	FLOCKED TOGETHER
CDDEEEFGIIKNNSSS	FEIGNED SICKNESS
CDDEEEFGINOOOPSW	PIECE OF GOOD NEWS
CDDEEEFHNNORTTUY	END OF THE CENTURY
CDDEEEFIIINOSTVV	DEFECTIVE VISION
CDDEEEFIIMNNOOPS	PIECE OF ONES MIND
CDDEEEFILRSSTTUV	SELF-DESTRUCTIVE
CDDEEEFLLNOOPRTW	FOLLOW PRECEDENT
CDDEEEFLMNOOOPSS	COMPOSED ONESELF
CDDEEEFOOORRRSTT	RESORTED TO FORCE
CDDEEEGHHILPRSTY	HIGHLY RESPECTED
CDDEEEGIIINNOSUV	INGENIOUS DEVICE
CDDEEEGIILLNNOSS	SILENCE IS GOLDEN
CDDEEEGIINORRRSV	RECEIVING ORDERS
CDDEEEGKNOOOOOSS	COOKED ONE'S GOOSE
CDDEEEGLNNOSTTUY	NEGLECT ONES DUTY
CDDEEEGLNOORSSSS	CROSSED ONE'S LEGS
CDDEEEHHILPRSTUW	WHITED SEPULCHRE
CDDEEEHHLOORRSTT	DORCHESTER HOTEL
CDDEEEHIIKNNPRTW	PICKED THE WINNER
CDDEEEHIKLLORTTW	ROLLED THE WICKET
CDDEEEHINNNOPPTU	PENCE IN THE POUND
CDDEEEHINNOPSTTT	PITCHED ONE'S TENT
CDDEEEHKLOOPSTTU	KEEPS THE COLD OUT
CDDEEEHNNOOPRSST	THE SECOND PERSON
CDDEEEHNNORRRTTU	TURNED THE CORNER
CDDEEEHNNORRTTUU	UNDER THE COUNTER
	UNDER-THE-COUNTER
CDDEEEHNOOOSSTTU	TOUCHED ONE'S TOES
CDDEEEHNOOPRSSTW	SHOWED NO RESPECT
CDDEEEIIJNPSSSTU	DISPENSE JUSTICE
CDDEEEIILLPSSTVW	TWELVE DISCIPLES
CDDEEEIIMNNNOOSW	ONE'S OWN MEDICINE
CDDEEEIINNPRRSWW	WINDSCREEN WIPER
CDDEEEIINPPRRSST	INSPIRED RESPECT
CDDEEEIINPSTTUVX	UNEXPECTED VISIT
CDDEEEIKLLRRSSVY	DRIVE RECKLESSLY
CDDEEEIKNOOPPRST	POCKET ONE'S PRIDE
CDDEEEIMNNOPPRTTV	TEMPT PROVIDENCE
CDDEEEINNNPRSTUY	SUPERINTENDENCY
CDDEEEINOPPRSSSU	SUPERSONIC SPEED
CDDEEEINRSSSTTUV	DESTRUCTIVENESS
CDDEEEKLLORRSSVY	DROVE RECKLESSLY
CDDEEELLOORSSSTT	SETTLE OLD SCORES
CDDEEELOOOPRRSSU	POOLED RESOURCES
CDDEEEOOPRRTTUVY	REDUCE TO POVERTY
CDDEEFFIIILLOPPRR	CRIPPLED FOR LIFE
CDDEEFGIIIMNNORRU	COMING UNDER FIRE
CDDEEFGIKOOOOPRW	GOOD PIECE OF WORK
CDDEEFGILNRSSTTU	SELF-DESTRUCTING
CDDEEFHIIILNOPRSS	CLOSE FRIENDSHIP
CDDEEFHIMNOOOORRT	CRIED FOR THE MOON
CDDEEFHLOOOORRSST	CROSSED THE FLOOR
CDDEEFIIKNOSTVWW	FIVE WICKETS DOWN
CDDEEFIIILNORSTYY	FRIENDLY SOCIETY
CDDEEFIIILORRSSST	CROSS-FERTILISED
CDDEEFIIILORRSSTZ	CROSS-FERTILIZED
CDDEEFIIKNOPRRSTU	UNFROCKED PRIEST
CDDEEFIILLPRSSTUY	DISRESPECTFULLY
CDDEEFIILNORSSTTU	SELF-DESTRUCTION
CDDEEFNNNOOOOORST	NOT FOR ONE SECOND
CDDEEGGHIIIINNRTTV	GIVING THE CREDIT
CDDEEGHIMNNNOPRU	UNCOMPREHENDING
CDDEEGHINNOORTTU	REDUCE TO NOTHING
CDDEEGHNOORRSTUV	COVERS THE GROUND
CDDEEGIIINNRRRTUV	RECRUITING DRIVE
CDDEEGKLMMNNOOOW	COMMON KNOWLEDGE
CDDEEHHHLOOORSSU	HOUSEHOLD CHORES
CDDEEHHIILLMORSST	MOTHERLESS CHILD
CDDEEHHILLOOOSTT	THE OLD SCHOOL TIE

CDEEHHNOORSTTUU	COUNTED THE HOURS
CDEEHIIIMNNNSTY	TINY CHINESE MIND
CDEEHILNOOSSTWW	CLOSES THE WINDOW
CDEEHKLOORSSTUW	WORKS TO SCHEDULE
CDEEHLLNNOPPSUU	PULLED NO PUNCHES
CDEEHLMNOOOSSTU	CLOSED ONE'S MOUTH
CDEEHNNOOORSSSW	CHOSEN ONE'S WORDS
CDEEHNOOOORSSSW	CHOOSE ONES WORDS
CDEEIIIMMNNRSTT	INDETERMINISTIC
CDEEIIIMNOPRSSU	UMPIRES DECISION
CDEEIIINNSSSTTV	DISTINCTIVENESS
CDEEIIJNNNNORTU	INJURED INNOCENT
CDEEIIKNNNOSTWW	NINE WICKETS DOWN
CDEEIIKNQSSTTUW	QUICK-WITTEDNESS
CDEEIILOQRRSSUU	LIQUID RESOURCES
CDEEIINNOPRSSWZ	WINS SECOND PRIZE
CDEEIKNOOOPRSTZ	TOOK SECOND PRIZE
CDEEILMNNOOPTWY	ENDOWMENT POLICY
CDEEILNOOOPRRSS	SPOIL ONES RECORD
CDEEIMNNOOPSSSU	COMPENDIOUSNESS
CDEEIMNNOORSSSS	CROSSES ONE'S MIND
CDEEIMNNOORSSSW	MINCES ONE'S WORDS
CDEELNOOPRRSSUU	CREDULOUS PERSON
CDEELOPRRSSSTUU	PRODUCES RESULTS
CDEEMNNOOOORSTY	STOOD ON CEREMONY
CDEENNOORSSTTVY	SENDS TO COVENTRY
CDEFFGHHHIILOOS	HOLDS HIGH OFFICE
CDEFFIILNOPRSTU	DIFFICULT PERSON
CDEFFKKNOOOPSST	KNOCKED SPOTS OFF
CDEFGHIIINNNOSS	FINISHING SECOND
CDEFGIINOOORRSUV	SUING FOR DIVORCE
CDEFGJMNOORTTUU	COURT OF JUDGMENT
CDEFHIMNOOSSTUU	THE SOUND OF MUSIC
CDEFHLLOOORSTWW	FOLLOWS THE CROWD
CDEFFIKNOORSTUWW	FOUR WICKETS DOWN
CDEFILLLOORSSUU	COLOURLESS FLUID
CDEFLOOOORRTTUUU	RULED OUT OF COURT
CDEFMOOORSTTTUU	TOUTED FOR CUSTOM
CDEGGHIKLLNTUUY	THE UGLY DUCKLING
CDEGHHIIILNOTTV	DO THE CIVIL THING
CDEGHHMOOOPRSTU	THROUGH-COMPOSED
CDEGHHNNOOOSTTU	ON SECOND THOUGHT
CDEGIIIMMNNOOSS	DECOMMISSIONING
CDEGIIINNOPPPRR	DROPPING IN PRICE
CDEGIIKLLMMNOOT	TILL KINGDOM COME
CDEGIILNNOOORST	ENDOCRINOLOGIST
CDEGILLNOSSTUYY	STUDYING CLOSELY
CDEGILNNOOPRRSY	CORRESPONDINGLY
CDEGINNOOPRRTTU	PUTTING ON RECORD
CDEHIKNOOQTTUUW	WOUND TO THE QUICK
CDEHILMNNOOPSTT	HOLDS IN CONTEMPT
CDEHIMNOOOSSSTU	DICHOTOMOUSNESS
CDEHKKNNOOOOORST	KNOCKS ON THE DOOR
CDEHLNOOOORSTUY	SHOULDER TO CRY ON
CDEIIIJNNOSSSUU	INJUDICIOUSNESS
CDEIIMMNNOOOSS	NONCOMMISSIONED
CDEIKLNNOOSSSUW	LICKS ONE'S WOUNDS
CDEILMNNOOPRSUU	UNDER COMPULSION
CDELOOPRRSSUWZZ	CROSSWORD PUZZLE
CDFIIIKNNNOOOPT	PINK OF CONDITION
CDGHIIIKNNOTTTW	DICK WHITTINGTON
CDGHILNOOOORTTU	OUTDOOR CLOTHING
CDHIILNOPRSTUUU	PULCHRITUDINOUS
CDIIIINOSSSTUUV	VICISSITUDINOUS
CDIILLNORRRSTTU	DRILL INSTRUCTOR
CDIILNNOOSSTUUY	DISCONTINUOUSLY
CDIKLLOOOSSSTTT	STOOD STOCK-STILL
CDIKNOOOOSTTTUY	TOOK INTO CUSTODY
CEEEEEFFMNORRRT	TERM OF REFERENCE
CEEEEEFFNRRRTUU	FUTURE REFERENCE
CEEEEEGHINNPRTT	EIGHTEEN PER CENT
CEEEEEHHNPQSSTU	THE QUEENS SPEECH
CEEEEEHIIPRSTTU	THREE-PIECE SUITE
CEEEEEHINNPPRTY	THREEPENNY PIECE
CEEEEEHIORSTTVX	EXERCISE THE VETO
CEEEEEILNNOPRVX	NOVEL EXPERIENCE
CEEEEEINNNNPRTT	NINETEEN PER CENT
CEEEEEENNNOPSTVY	SEVENTY-ONE PENCE
CEEEEEFFHINPRTTY	FIFTY-THREE PENCE
CEEEEEFFIINNSSTV	INEFFECTIVENESS
CEEEEEFFIINNPSTVY	FIFTY-SEVEN PENCE
CEEEEEFFKNOORRRW	WORK OF REFERENCE
CEEEEEFGHIINPTVY	EIGHTY-FIVE PENCE
CEEEEEFHIILRRTTV	LIFT THE RECEIVER
CEEEEEFHNOPRRTTY	FORTY-THREE PENCE
CEEEEEFHORRRRSSU	REFRESHER COURSE
CEEEEEFIIMNPRSTTV	FIVE CENTIMETRES
CEEEEEFIINNNPTVY	NINETY-FIVE PENCE
CEEEEEFIKLNPRSST	PERFECT LIKENESS
CEEEEEFILNNHSTUX	EXERTS INFLUENCE
CEEEEEFINNNOOPSS	PIECE OF NONSENSE
CEEEEEFINNPTTVWY	TWENTY-FIVE PENCE
CEEEEEFINRSTTIIIX	FUTURE EXISTENCE
CEEEEEFLNOPRSSST	RESPECTS ONESELF
CEEEEEFNNOOOORRSY	CORNER OF ONE'S EYE
CEEEEEFNNOPRRTTU	FOURTEEN PER CENT
CEEEEEFNNOPRSTVY	FORTY-SEVEN PENCE
CEEEEEGHHIIISSTVX	EXCESSIVE HEIGHT
CEEEEEGHIINNNPTY	EIGHTY-NINE PENCE
CEEEEEGHIIISSTVWX	EXCESSIVE WEIGHT
CEEEEEGHINNSSTTT	SETTING THE SCENE
CEEEEEGHNOOORSTTU	GONE TO THE RESCUE
CEEEEEGHOORSSTTU	GOES TO THE RESCUE
CEEEEEGINNNNOPST	OPENING SENTENCE
CEEEEEGINNOOPRRST	ENERGETIC PERSON
CEEEEEGKNOPPRSTU	GET ONE'S PECKER UP
CEEEEEGMNOPRRSWY	EMERGENCY POWERS
CEEEEEHHIMNPSTWY	SWEEP THE CHIMNEY
CEEEEEHHKMRRSTUW	WHERE THERES MUCK
CEEEEEHILLNOOSTT	LOSE THE ELECTION
CEEEEEHINNPRRTTT	THIRTEEN PER CENT
CEEEEEHINPRSTTXY	SIXTY-THREE PENCE
CEEEEEHIOPRSTTWX	EXPECT OTHERWISE
CEEFFHKNOOPRSTU	KEEP ON THE COURSE
CEEEEEHLNNRRTTUVY	ELEVENTH CENTURY
CEEEEEHNNOORSTTTUW	WENT TO THE RESCUE
CEEEEEIILNORSTVX	VIOLENT EXERCISE
CEEEEEIIMNNNNRSTT	NINE CENTIMETRES
CEEEEEIINNNNNPTY	NINETY-NINE PENCE
CEEEEEIKLNORSSTV	SKELETON SERVICE
CEEEEEIKNNOOPPSS	SPOKEN ONE'S PIECE
CEEEEEILORRRSVVV	SERVICE REVOLVER
CEEEEEINNNNPTTWY	TWENTY NINE PENCE
CEEEEEINNPSSTVXY	SEVENTY-SIX PENCE
	SIXTY-SEVEN PENCE
CEEEEEKLNNOOPSSU	KEEP ONES COUNSEL
CEEEEELLLNRSTTUX	EXCELLENT RESULT
CEEEEENNOPSTTVWY	SEVENTY-TWO PENCE
CEEEEFFFIIORRSTTV	STRIVE FOR EFFECT
CEEEEFFFOOORRSTTV	STROVE FOR EFFECT
CEEEEFFGHIINPTTY	FIFTY-EIGHT PENCE
CEEEEFFGHINOOOTT	GONE TO THE OFFICE
CEEEEFFGHIOOOSTT	GOES TO THE OFFICE
CEEEEFFGHINOOSSTT	GET OFF ONE'S CHEST
CEEEEFFHILOPSSTT	SPOILS THE EFFECT
CEEEEFFHINOOTTTW	WENT TO THE OFFICE
CEEEEFFIILLNNRSSU	SUFFER IN SILENCE
CEEEEFFINOOPRSUV	PREVIOUS OFFENCE
CEEEEFGHILNORSTV	LENGTH OF SERVICE
CEEEEFGHINOPRTTY	FORTY-EIGHT PENCE
CEEEEFGHINOPRTUY	EIGHTY-FOUR PENCE
CEEEEFGILNNOSSUX	EXCUSING ONESELF

CEEEFHHKLOORSTU	CLERK OF THE HOUSE
CEEEFHIILNRRSTW	WINCHESTER RIFLE
CEEEFHILNOPSSTU	ECLIPSE OF THE SUN
CEEEFHIMNOOOORTV	THE MOOR OF VENICE
CEEEFHIMOORSTTU	THE COURSE OF TIME
CEEEFHINOSSSTUU	CONFUSE THE ISSUE
CEEEFHLNOPRSTTY	PERFECTLY HONEST
CEEEFHLNORSTTUY	FLEES THE COUNTRY
CEEEFIILMNNOSTU	MINUTE OF SILENCE
CEEEFIIMNORRRTT	INTERFEROMETRIC
CEEEFIMNORRSTTU	FOUR CENTIMETRES
CEEEFINNNOPRTUY	NINETY-FOUR PENCE
CEEEFINNOORTTTU	COUNTERFEIT NOTE
CEEEFINORSSSTUY	SENSE OF SECURITY
CEEEFLLMNOSSSUX	FLEX ONE'S MUSCLES
CEEEFLLNOOOSSTU	CUT ONESELF LOOSE
CEEEFLMNNNOSTTT	SELF-CONTENTMENT
CEEEFLMNOOOPSSS	COMPOSES ONESELF
CEEEFLNORRSSSUU	RESOURCEFULNESS
CEEEFNNOPRTTUWY	TWENTY-FOUR PENCE
CEEEFOOOPRRRVWY	POWER OF RECOVERY
CEEEGGGILNNORSS	GROSS NEGLIGENCE
CEEEGGHIINOPRTT	PIECING TOGETHER
CEEEGGILNNOOSSU	GLUCONEOGENESIS
CEEEGHIIKNNSTTT	GETS IT IN THE NECK
CEEEGHIINPSTTXY	SIXTY-EIGHT PENCE
CEEEGHLNORSSSTT	STRETCH ONES LEGS
CEEEGIIILNPRSVV	GIVEN LIP SERVICE
CEEEGIIILPRSSVV	GIVES LIP SERVICE
CEEEGIINNNNQSUW	WINNING SEQUENCE
CEEEGIINNNOOSTV	GIVEN ONE'S NOTICE
CEEEGIINNOOSSTV	GIVES ONE'S NOTICE
CEEEGIINOPRRSWX	EXERCISING POWER
CEEEGIKLNNOOOPS	KEEPING ONE'S COOL
CEEEGILNNOOSSSY	CLOSING ONE'S EYES
CEEEGIMNNNNOOPRY	OPENING CEREMONY
CEEEGINNNOOSSTV	GIVE ONES CONSENT
CEEEGKNOOPPRSTU	GOT ONE'S PECKER UP
CEEEGLNOORSSSSS	CROSSES ONE'S LEGS
CEEEHHIIKKNSTTT	KICKS IN THE TEETH
CEEEHHIMNPSTTWY	SWEPT THE CHIMNEY
CEEEHHLOOORSSTT	CLOSE TO THE SHORE
CEEEHHMNOOORTTT	COME TO THE THRONE
CEEEHIILLMMOTTW	THE TIME WILL COME
CEEEHIILLNPRTTT	THE LITTLE PRINCE
CEEEHIILNNRSTWZ	WIENER SCHNITZEL
CEEEHIILNPRSSSV	SPEECH IS SILVERN
CEEEHIINNNPRTTY	THIRTY-NINE PENCE
CEEEHIJLNNORTWW	JEWEL IN THE CROWN
CEEEHIJNOPSSTTU	STEPS ON THE JUICE
CEEEHIKKKLNOPSSU	KICK UP ONE'S HEELS
CEEEHIKLNPQSTUU	QUICKEN THE PULSE
CEEEHIKNNOPPSSU	KEEPS ONE'S CHIN UP
CEEEHILLNOOSTTT	LOST THE ELECTION
CEEEHIIMNNOPRSVY	COMPREHENSIVELY
CEEEHILOOPRRSST	ELECTROPHORESIS
CEEEHIMNNOOOPTT	COME INTO THE OPEN
CEEEHIMORRSSTTY	STEREOCHEMISTRY
CEEEHINNOPSSTTT	PITCHES ONE'S TENT
CEEEHINOPQRSSTU	QUEERS ONE'S PITCH
CEEEHKLNOORSSUY	HONEYSUCKLE ROSE
CEEEHKNOOPRSTTU	KEPT ON THE COURSE
CEEEHKNOOPSSTTY	THE KEYSTONE COPS
CEEEHLMMNOOOOPPT	THE COMMON PEOPLE
CEEEHLNOOORSSTT	TORE ONE'S CLOTHES
CEEEHMOOPRSSSTW	SHOW SOME RESPECT
CEEEHNOOORRTTTT	ROTTEN TO THE CORE
CEEEHNOOOSSSTTU	TOUCHES ONE'S TOES
CEEEIIKMNNOOPTT	KEEN COMPETITION
CEEEIILOOPRSTTV	ELECTROPOSITIVE
CEEEIIMNOPSSTTV	COMPETITIVENESS

CEEEIIMNORSTTUX	EXCREMENTITIOUS
CEEEIINPPRRSSST	INSPIRES RESPECT
CEEEIINRRSSSTTV	RESTRICTIVENESS
CEEEIKLNNOOPSST	LINE ONES POCKETS
CEEEILLNORSSTTU	ELECTION RESULTS
CEEEILMNNORSSSY	CROSS ENEMY LINES
CEEEILNOOORSSVW	LOWERS ONE'S VOICE
CEEEILOPRRSTTVY	RETROSPECTIVELY
CEEEILOPRRSTUVX	EXCLUSIVE REPORT
CEEEIMNNOORSSSU	CEREMONIOUSNESS
CEEEINNOSSSSSTU	NECESSITOUSNESS
CEEEINPQRSSSTUU	PICTURESQUENESS
CEEEKLNNOOPSSTU	KEPT ONE'S COUNSEL
CEEEKNOPPPRSTUU	PUT ONE'S PECKER UP
CEEEMNOPPRSSTTX	EXPRESS CONTEMPT
CEEFFGHHIIILNTY	HIGHLY EFFICIENT
CEEFFGHNOOOSSTT	GOT OFF ONE'S CHEST
CEEFFGIMNNOOORT	MOTORING OFFENCE
CEEFFHNOPSSTTTU	PUTS OFF THE SCENT
CEEFFIIOOPRRRSU	SUPERIOR OFFICER
CEEFFIOOOPRSTTW	POST OFFICE TOWER
CEEFFNNOOOSSSTU	CUTS OFF ONE'S NOSE
CEEFGHIIMOPSTTU	GET UP TO MISCHIEF
CEEFGHIINORSSTU	FORCING THE ISSUE
CEEFGHIKNOORRST	CROOKS THE FINGER
CEEFGHIMNOOOORTT	COMING TO THE FORE
CEEFGIIIILLNNRUV	RECEIVING IN FULL
CEEFGIIINOOPRSS	ORIGIN OF SPECIES
CEEFGIIKLNNORSS	LICK ONES FINGERS
CEEFGIKNNOOORRS	CROOK ONE'S FINGER
CEEFGILMNNOOOST	COMING TO ONESELF
CEEFGILNNNORSTU	STRONG INFLUENCE
CEEFGILNNOORSSS	CROSSING ONESELF
CEEFHIIIKMNNOTT	IN THE NICK OF TIME
CEEFHILMNNOOPRSX	FRESH COMPLEXION
CEEFHIMNOOOORRST	CRIES FOR THE MOON
CEEFHINNOPRRTTUY	THIRTY-FOUR PENCE
CEEFHIOOPRTTTUU	OUT OF THE PICTURE
CEEFHKKLOORRSTW	CLERK OF THE WORKS
CEEFHLLNOOSSTTW	FOLLOWS THE SCENT
CEEFHLOOOORRSSST	CROSSES THE FLOOR
CEEFHMNOOOORSTTT	COMES TO THE FRONT
CEEFIILNOOPSTUV	LIFT UP ONES VOICE
CEEFIILORRSSSST	CROSS-FERTILISES
CEEFIILORRSSSTZ	CROSS-FERTILIZES
CEEFINNOPRRSSTU	PERFUNCTORINESS
CEEFLLNNOOOORSST	CONTROLS ONESELF
CEEGHHHIINOPRSS	CHERISHING HOPES
CEEGHHIIIPRRSTT	THE PRICE IS RIGHT
CEEGHHINNORSTTT	ON THE RIGHT SCENT
CEEGHIIILNPRSTW	PIERCING WHISTLE
CEEGHIILNNORSST	CROSSING THE LINE
CEEGHIILRSSTUVX	EXCLUSIVE RIGHTS
CEEGHIINNORSTWZ	SEIZING THE CROWN
CEEGHIMMNNORTVY	VICHY GOVERNMENT
CEEGHNNNOOORSTTW	ON THE WRONG SCENT
CEEGIILNNOOOSSV	LOSING ONE'S VOICE
CEEGIINOPRSTVWY	SWEEPING VICTORY
CEEGIMMNNNNOOSTT	CONSIGNMENT NOTE
CEEHHHIIILMMNNRR	HEINRICH HIMMLER
CEEHHIILRSTTTTU	ELICITS THE TRUTH
CEEHHIKLNOPSTTT	THE PLOT THICKENS
CEEHHIMMORRSTTY	THERMOCHEMISTRY
CEEHHINOPRRRSTW	CHRISTOPHER WREN
CEEHHINOPRSTTTT	STRETCH THE POINT
CEEHIIKLNNSSTTU	KITCHEN UTENSILS
CEEHIIMNNNOOPRS	INCOMPREHENSION
CEEHIIMNOSSSSUV	MISCHIEVOUSNESS
CEEHIINNORRSSTT	SITS IN THE CORNER
CEEHIINOPRRSSTT	HISTORIC PRESENT
CEEHIINPPRTTTUU	PUT IN THE PICTURE

CEEHIIORRRSSTTT	SCOTTISH TERRIER
CEEHIKLNNOPRTUY	PHENYLKETONURIC
CEEHIKLORSSTTTU	STICK TO THE RULES
CEEHIKNNOOSSTTW	SHOWN ONE'S TICKET
CEEHIKNOOSSSTTW	SHOWS ONE'S TICKET
CEEHILNOORSTTUW	THE LOW COUNTRIES
CEEHIMMOORSTTTW	COME TO TERMS WITH
CEEHIMNNOSTTTUU	COUNT THE MINUTES
CEEHIMNOOOPSTTT	COMES TO THE POINT
CEEHIMNOORTTUWY	WITHOUT CEREMONY
CEEHKLORSSTTTUU	STUCK TO THE RULES
CEEHKMNOOPRSTTU	PUT THE MOCKERS ON
CEEHLLNNOPPSSUU	PULL ONES PUNCHES
CEEHLMNNOOOOPUY	HONEYMOON COUPLE
CEEHLMNNOORSSST	LOCH NESS MONSTER
CEEHLMNOOOSSSTU	CLOSES ONE'S MOUTH
CEEHLNNOOOORSST	TORN ONE'S CLOTHES
CEEHMMOOOOORSTT	COME HOME TO ROOST
CEEHNOPRSSSTTUW	PUTS THE SCREWS ON
CEEHOORRSSSTUWW	SUCH SWEET SORROW
CEEIIILLNNOSSUV	LIVE IN SECLUSION
CEEIIILNNNPRTTW	WRITTEN IN PENCIL
CEEIIINOPRSSSTX	EXPRESSIONISTIC
CEEIIKLLNOPSSTT	LICK ONE'S SPITTLE
CEEIIKNNNOOSSST	STICK ONE'S NOSE IN
CEEIIILLMNOOSSTT	TONSILLECTOMIES
CEEIILMNNOOSTTW	WILSON COMMITTEE
CEEIIMNNOOOPPTT	OPEN COMPETITION
CEEIIMNNOPSSSUU	IMPECUNIOUSNESS
CEEIINNRSSSTTUV	INSTRUCTIVENESS
CEEIINOPPRSSSTU	PRECIPITOUSNESS
CEEIINORRRSSTTU	RESURRECTIONIST
CEEIINPSSSTTUUV	INTUSSUSCEPTIVE
CEEIKMNOOORSTTU	COME OUT ON STRIKE
CEEIKNNNOOSSSTU	STUCK ONE'S NOSE IN
CEEIKNOPRRSTTVY	POVERTY-STRICKEN
CEEILLNNOOOSSTU	ELOCUTION LESSON
CEEILMNNOORSUUY	UNCEREMONIOUSLY
CEEIMNNNOOOOSTW	COME INTO ONES OWN
CEEINNNOOSSSTTU	CONTENTIOUSNESS
CEEINNOORRRSSTU	CORONERS INQUEST
CEEINOPPRSSSSUU	PERSPICUOUSNESS
CEELLRRSSTTUUUUV	CULTURE-VULTURES
CEELNOOOPRSSSTU	PLOTS ONE'S COURSE
CEEMNNNOOSSTUY	COUNTS ONE'S MONEY
CEEPRRRSSSTTUUU	SUPERSTRUCTURES
CEFFFGIILLNSSUY	SELF-SUFFICINGLY
CEFFHIIKLORSTTW	FLICK OF THE WRIST
CEFGHHIILLNNOPRS	FRENCH-POLISHING
CEFGHIILNOOSTTV	THE COST OF LIVING
CEFGHIIMOOPSTTU	GOT UP TO MISCHIEF
CEFGIMMNOOOPRRU	COMING UP FOR MORE
CEFGINNNOORRRUV	RUNNING FOR COVER
CEFGNNOORRRSSSU	RUNS FOR CONGRESS
CEFHIIKMNOOOTTT	COME TO THINK OF IT
CEFHINNNOOOPRSU	FRENCH ONION SOUP
CEFHKKLLNOOOSTU	KNOCKS HELL OUT OF
CEFHKKLNOOOORTT	KNOCK TO THE FLOOR
CEFHMMNOOORTTWY	WORTHY OF COMMENT
CEFHNOOORTTTUUY	OUT OF THE COUNTRY
CEFHOOORRTTTUUW	THREW OUT OF COURT
CEFIIILNPPRRSST	FIRST PRINCIPLES
CEFIIMNNOOORST	NONCONFORMITIES
CEFLOOORRSTTUUU	RULES OUT OF COURT
CEGGHHIIKLNNSTT	LIGHTNING SKETCH
CEGGHHIINRSTTT	STRETCHING TIGHT
CEGGHILNOOOORST	GEOCHRONOLOGIST
CEGGIIIKLLNNVY	CLINGING LIKE IVY
CEGHHHIINORTTUW	THE WITCHING HOUR
CEGHHINNOOOOSTT	NOTHING TO CHOOSE
CEGHIIIKNSSTTV	VISITING THE SICK
CEGHIIIKMMNRTTW	TRIMMING THE WICK
CEGHIIIKNNNRTTW	WINNING THE TRICK
CEGHIKNOQSTTTUU	STUNG TO THE QUICK
CEGHILMNOOOSTUY	ETHNOMUSICOLOGY
CEGHILNNOOOSSTU	LOSING ONE'S TOUCH
CEGHILNOOOOPPST	SCOOPING THE POOL
CEGIIILLNNNPRTW	WRITING IN PENCIL
CEGIIIOPRRSSSTV	PROGRESSIVISTIC
CEGIIKLNNOOSSTU	COOKING UTENSILS
CEGIIMMMNOSSTUW	SWIMMING COSTUME
CEGIIMMNNNOOOTY	COMING INTO MONEY
CEGIINNNNOOPRTV	PROVING INNOCENT
CEGIINNNOOPRTTU	COUNTERPOINTING
CEGIKNNOOSSSTTU	STICK TO ONES GUNS
CEGILNNOOPRTUUY	PRONOUNCE GUILTY
CEGINNNOORSSSUU	INCONGRUOUSNESS
CEGKNNOOSSSTTUU	STUCK TO ONE'S GUNS
CEHHHIMNNOPTTUU	PUNCH IN THE MOUTH
CEHHHINORSTTTWW	THROWN THE SWITCH
CEHHHIORSSTTTWW	THROWS THE SWITCH
CEHHIIJNNOORSTU	JOIN IN THE CHORUS
CEHHIIKNNOOOTTT	TOOK IT ON THE CHIN
CEHHIILOSSSTTTT	SCOTTISH THISTLE
CEHHIKNOOPSTTTT	STICK TO THE POINT
CEHIILLMOPPSTYY	POLYPHYLETICISM
CEHIILMMNOPSTTW	WITH COMPLIMENTS
CEHIILNOOOORRRS	RECOILS IN HORROR
CEHIINNOOPRSSSU	CONNOISSEURSHIP
CEHIJLNOOORSSTU	JOINS THE COLOURS
CEHIKNOOPSTTTTU	STUCK TO THE POINT
CEHIKNOPSSTTTTU	PUTS IN THE STOCKS
CEHILLMOOPPRRST	COMPTROLLERSHIP
CEHILMOOPRRSTTY	SHORT-TERM POLICY
CEHIMMNNOOOOPRSW	COMMON OWNERSHIP
CEHKLLOOPRSTTUU	PULLS THE CORK OUT
CEHLNOOOORSSSUW	SHOW ONES COLOURS
CEHMOOOPRSSTTTU	PROTESTS TOO MUCH
CEHNOORRSTTTUUY	TOURS THE COUNTRY
CEIIIIMNOPRSSST	IMPRESSIONISTIC
CEIIIINOSSSTTVV	VIVISECTIONISTS
CEIIINNORRSSTTU	INSURRECTIONIST
CEIILNNOPSSSTUU	PUNCTILIOUSNESS
CEIIMOPRRRSSTTT	RESTRICT IMPORTS
CEIINNOOOOPPSSTU	OPEN TO SUSPICION
CEIINNOPSSSTTUU	INTUSSUSCEPTION
CEIINOOOPPPRRST	PROPRIOCEPTIONS
CEILNORRSTTTTUY	NOT STRICTLY TRUE
CEIMMMMOOORSTTY	COMMITS TO MEMORY
CEIMMNNNOOOPSST	NON COMPOS MENTIS
CEIMNOOOPSSSTTU	COMES OUT IN SPOTS
CEIMNOOOPRSSSSUU	PROMISCUOUSNESS
CEIMNOPRSSSSTUU	SCRUMPTIOUSNESS
CEKLLNOOPPSSSUU	PULL ONES SOCKS UP
CFFGIKKKNNOOORW	PULL UP ONES SOCKS / KNOCKING OFF WORK
CFFIIOORRSTTUVY	FRUITS OF VICTORY
CFGHHHLOOOOSTTU	SCHOOL OF THOUGHT
CFGHHIIILNNOOSS	FINISHING SCHOOL
CFGHIIIKNNRSSTY	CRY STINKING FISH
CFGHINNNOOORTTU	COUNT FOR NOTHING
CFGIIILMNNOORTV	LIVING IN COMFORT
CFGIINNOOOORRTUY	COUNTRY OF ORIGIN
CFHOOOORRTTTUUW	THROW OUT OF COURT
CFIIIMMNNOOOSSS	SIN OF COMMISSION
CFIILOOOPRSSTVY	SPOILS OF VICTORY
CFIIMMNOOOOSSTU	OUT OF COMMISSION
CGGHIIMMNNNOOOT	COMING TO NOTHING
CGGIIILMMNNOPSU	COMING UP SMILING
CGHIIIIKLNNOPTT	PILING IT ON THICK
CGHIIIKKLNNQTUY	THINKING QUICKLY
CGHIIMMNNNNOOOT	NOTHING IN COMMON

CGIIIKKLNRSTTUY	STRIKING IT LUCKY	DDEEIKNNOOOORRTV	DROVE ONE TO DRINK
CGIIIMMNOORTTTW	COMMIT TO WRITING	DDEEINOORRRSSUV	NERVOUS DISORDER
CGIILMNOOPSSSTU	GOSSIP COLUMNIST	DDEEELNNOOOPRSUW	REOPEN OLD WOUNDS
CGIILOOOORRSTUVY	GLORIOUS VICTORY	DDEFGHLNOOOPSSU	SLOUGH OF DESPOND
CHIIKOPRRSSTTUY	TURKISH CYPRIOTS	DDEFGIJNOORSSTU	JUST GOOD FRIENDS
CIIILLRSSSTTUUV	SILVICULTURISTS	DDEGGHHIILNNOST	SHEDDING LIGHT ON
DDDDDDEEEEHIILLY	HEY DIDDLE DIDDLE	DDEGHHINOOSSTTU	SHOUTING THE ODDS
DDDEEEEEEFFLNNOS	DEFENDED ONESELF	DDEGHIIINNSSTUU	UNDISTINGUISHED
DDDEEEGHHLORTTU	HUDDLED TOGETHER	DDEGHIINNNOOSTW	DID ONE'S OWN THING
DDDEEEGLNOOOPRSW	PLEDGED ONE'S WORD	DDEGHLNOOORRTUW	GO ROUND THE WORLD
DDDEEEHILLORSTV	SOLVED THE RIDDLE	DDEGHNNOOORTTUW	DOWN TO THE GROUND
DDDEEEIIKLLNSVY	DEVILLED KIDNEYS	DDEGILNOOORSTWY	LONG-WINDED STORY
DDDEEFILNOOPRSU	DID ONESELF PROUD	DDEGNNOOOORSSTU	STOOD ONE'S GROUND
DDDEEGHHLLOORSUU	HOUSEHOLD DRUDGE	DDEINNOPRSSTUUW	TURNS UPSIDE DOWN
DDDEEGHINNORRUU	HIDE UNDERGROUND	DDGGHHIINOORRSU	RIDING ROUGH-SHOD
DDDEEHLNOORRSUU	ROUND-SHOULDERED		RIDING ROUGHSHOD
DDDEEIIIIMNNRTV	INTERIM DIVIDEND	DDGGHHILMNORTUU	MUDDLING THROUGH
DDDEGHHINOORRSU	RIDDEN ROUGH-SHOD	DEEEEEFHLORTTTV	VEERED TO THE LEFT
	RIDDEN ROUGHSHOD	DEEEEEGPRRRSSTX	EXPRESSED REGRET
DDEEEEEFFGHNOOPT	GO OFF THE DEEP END	DEEEEEHNRRRTVVY	THE VERY REVEREND
DDEEEEGGHILNPST	SIGNED THE PLEDGE	DEEEEELLNPRRSTW	WELL REPRESENTED
DDEEEEHILMPTTTV	TEMPTED THE DEVIL	DEEEEEPRRRSSTUX	EXERTED PRESSURE
DDEEEEHINNNNRTU	NINETEEN HUNDRED	DEEEEFFLLLNOOSS	FEEL ONE'S OLD SELF
DDEEEEHLNOPRRTT	THE OLD PRETENDER	DEEEEFGILNNORSS	RESIGNED ONESELF
DDEEEENOOPPRSSY	DROPPED ONE'S EYES	DEEEEFGKLNOORTW	TREE OF KNOWLEDGE
DDEEEFFHIILNSTU	SHEFFIELD UNITED	DEEEEFHHILNNOTT	THE END OF THE LINE
DDEEEFFIKLNOORT	LOOKED DIFFERENT	DEEEEFHHOPTTTTU	FED UP TO THE TEETH
DDEEEFGILLNNOSU	DELUDING ONESELF	DEEEEFHINNSSTUY	SEE THE FUNNY SIDE
DDEEEFHHLLOORTW	FOLLOWED THE HERD	DEEEEFHNNOORSTT	END OF ONES TETHER
DDEEEGGGHIINSTW	DIGGING THE WEEDS	DEEEEFLLLNNOOSW	DONE ONESELF WELL
DDEEEGHILOORSTV	DELIVER THE GOODS	DEEEEFLLLNOOSSW	DOES ONESELF WELL
DDEEEGIILNPRRUV	UNDERPRIVILEGED	DEEEEGGHIILNNTV	GIVING THE NEEDLE
DDEEEGIJLMNRTUV	DELIVER JUDGMENT	DEEEEGGINPRRRSV	PRESERVED GINGER
DDEEEGLNOOPRSSW	PLEDGES ONE'S WORD	DEEEEGHHILNRSTT	SEEN THE RED LIGHT
DDEEEHIINNNRRTW	RIDDEN THE WINNER	DEEEEGHHILRSSTT	SEES THE RED LIGHT
DDEEEHIINNOOSSS	DIED IN ONE'S SHOES	DEEEEGHKOOOPRSU	GOOD HOUSEKEEPER
DDEEEHILLORSSTV	SOLVES THE RIDDLE	DEEEEGIIMMNNRSSV	DIVINE MESSENGER
DDEEEHILMNOPSTV	DEVELOPS THE MIND	DEEEEGILNORRRTV	GOLDEN RETRIEVER
DDEEEHILNNOOTTT	ON THE DOTTED LINE	DEEEEGKLNOPRTWX	EXPERT KNOWLEDGE
DDEEEHILNOSSTTW	LETS THE SIDE DOWN	DEEEEGNORSSSSTT	GETS ONE'S DESERTS
DDEEEHINNOOPTWW	OPENED THE WINDOW	DEEEEHHNOOSSTTW	SHOWED ONE'S TEETH
DDEEEIIILNRSSTTY	DISINTERESTEDLY	DEEEEHIILNNOSTT	LIED IN ONE'S TEETH
DDEEEIIMNNOPRRT	POINTED REMINDER	DEEEEHIKLNOOSTY	LOOKED IN THE EYES
DDEEEELOPPRRRSSY	PROPERLY DRESSED	DEEEEHKNOOOPPRT	KEEP THE DOOR OPEN
DDEEFFFHIILLOTT	LIFTED THE LID OFF	DEEEEHLORRRTTTW	THREE-LETTER WORD
DDEEFLOOOORRRTUU	RULED OUT OF ORDER	DEEEEHNOPRRSTUY	SUPERHETERODYNE
DDEEFOOOPRRRTTUY	REPORTED FOR DUTY	DEEEEIILNORSSSTU	DELETERIOUSNESS
DDEEGGHHHIILLTY	HIGHLY DELIGHTED	DEEEEIILPRRSSVXY	EXPRESS DELIVERY
DDEEGGHIINOSSTU	DODGING THE ISSUE	DEEEEINNOPSSTTV	VENTED ONE'S SPITE
DDEEGGNNNOORRUU	GONE UNDERGROUND	DEEEENNNOPSSTUV	SEVENTEEN POUNDS
DDEEGGNNOORRSUU	GOES UNDERGROUND	DEEEFFFGILLNRSU	RUFFLED FEELINGS
DDEEGHIILOPRTWW	GLOWED WITH PRIDE	DEEEFFFINORRSTZ	FRENZIED EFFORTS
DDEEGHIIMNNRSST	RIGHT-MINDEDNESS	DEEEFFFLNNOORSS	FENDS FOR ONESELF
DDEEGHIKLMOOSTV	KID-GLOVE METHODS	DEEEFFGIILLLOSZ	ZIEGFELD FOLLIES
DDEEGHIKNORSSTU	KISSED THE GROUND	DEEEFFGIILLNNRY	FRIENDLY FEELING
DDEEGHIMNNOSSTU	TOUGH-MINDEDNESS	DEEEFFGJLNOORSU	JUDGE FOR ONESELF
DDEEGHNOOOOPSST	HOPED TO GOODNESS	DEEEFFIIOPRRSTT	PETRIFIED FOREST
DDEEGNNNNORRTUUW	WENT UNDERGROUND	DEEEFFLLLNOOSST	FELT ONE'S OLD SELF
DDEEHHILNORTTUW	HURLED TO THE WIND	DEEEFFMNORRSSTU	SUFFERED TORMENT
DDEEHHINNOPSTTW	DOWN IN THE DEPTHS	DEEEFGGILLNNOPS	PLEDGING ONESELF
DDEEHIILMNRSSUX	SIX HUNDRED MILES	DEEEFGHINORSSST	FORESIGHTEDNESS
DDEEHIKMNOOORSW	DID ONE'S HOMEWORK	DEEEFGIILMNNRST	SELF-DETERMINING
DDEEHILLNORSTTU	ROLLED IN THE DUST	DEEEFGIILNOSSUU	DISGUISE ONESELF
DDEEHILMNORSTUW	TWO HUNDRED MILES	DEEEFGILNRRSTUY	FRIENDLY GESTURE
DDEEHILOOORRSSUY	DISORDERLY HOUSE	DEEEFHIMNORSTTT	TREND OF THE TIMES
DDEEHNNNOORSSUU	SOUNDED ONE'S HORN	DEEEFHLNORTTTTU	TURNED TO THE LEFT
DDEEIIIKLNNOPRSS	SPOKEN IN RIDDLES	DEEEFIILNNORSSU	INSURED ONE'S LIFE
DDEEIIKNNOOORRTV	DRIVE ONE TO DRINK	DEEEFIILMNOOPRSV	IMPROVED ONESELF
DDEEIILMNORSSUY	SERIOUS-MINDEDLY	DEEEFLLLNOPPSUU	PULLED ONESELF UP
DDEEIINNORSTTUU	TURNED INSIDE OUT	DEEEFLLOPSSSSSY	SELF-POSSESSEDLY
DDEEIKLOOPRRSSU	LOOKED SURPRISED	DEEEFMNOOPRRSSY	PRESSED FOR MONEY

DEEEGGHJMMOORTY	JOGGED THE MEMORY
DEEEGGILNNOORSV	GOLDEN SOVEREIGN
DEEEGHHIIMSSTTW	MISSED THE WEIGHT
DEEEGHHIINOTTTW	GONE WITH THE TIDE
DEEEGHHIIOSTTTW	GOES WITH THE TIDE
DEEEGHIIKLNNOTW	GONE LIKE THE WIND
DEEEGHIIKLNOSTW	GOES LIKE THE WIND
DEEEGHIIKNNRSST	RENDING THE SKIES
DEEEGHIILNNNOST	SIGNED ON THE LINE
DEEEGHIILNNOSSS	DIGS IN ONE'S HEELS
	DIGS ONE'S HEELS IN
DEEEGHIIMMMNSTTT	STEMMING THE TIDE
DEEEGHIKNNOPPSW	WEEK-END SHOPPING
DEEEGHIKNNRSTTU	GET UNDER THE SKIN
DEEEGHINNORSSTT	GRINDS ONE'S TEETH
DEEEGHINNOSTTUV	EVENED THINGS OUT
DEEEGHINNRSTTTT	SETTING THE TREND
DEEEGHINNOOOOTTU	GROUND ONE'S TEETH
DEEEGIIKLNNNSTT	KNITTING NEEDLES
DEEEGIKLLLNOTTW	LITTLE KNOWLEDGE
DEEEGLLMMOOOVVY	LOVE ME, LOVE MY DOG
DEEEGNOOPRRSSTU	TONGUE DEPRESSOR
DEEEHHIINTTTTWW	WENT WITH THE TIDE
DEEEHHIIORSSTWW	WISHED OTHERWISE
DEEEHHLNORSTTTU	STOLE THE THUNDER
DEEEHIIKLNNTTWW	WENT LIKE THE WIND
DEEEHIILNNRSSTW	IN THE WILDERNESS
DEEEHIIMMMMNRTTU	IN THE MEDIUM TERM
DEEEHIINNOOSSSS	DIES IN ONE'S SHOES
DEEEHIINNPPRTTW	TIPPED THE WINNER
DEEEHILNNORRTVW	NEVER IN THE WORLD
DEEEHINNNOOPPSS	PINNED ONE'S HOPES
DEEEHINOOOSTTUU	STOOD IN THE QUEUE
DEEEHKNOOOPPRTT	KEPT THE DOOR OPEN
DEEFHILLOPRSTUW	WELL-UPHOLSTERED
DEEEHLLOOPTTIWY	POTTED THE YELLOW
DEEEHMNNOOOPSTU	OPENED ONE'S MOUTH
DEEEIILNNNOTTW	WELL-INTENTIONED
DEEEIILMMNRRSTU	DELIRIUM TREMENS
DEEEIIMNRSSSTTV	DIVERTISSEMENTS
DEEEIINOPSSSTUX	EXPEDITIOUSNESS
DEEEIINORSSTTTU	OUTSIDE INTEREST
DEEEIKMNNOORSSY	RISKED ONE'S MONEY
DEEEIKNNNOOOPSS	POKED ONE'S NOSE IN
DEEEILOPRRSSTUY	YIELD TO PRESSURE
DEEEINNNOSSSTTU	TENDENTIOUSNESS
DEEEINNNPRSSTTU	SUPERINTENDENTS
DEEEINOPRSSSSTU	PRESSED ONE'S SUIT
DEEEJNORSSSSTTU	ONE'S JUST DESERTS
DEEELMMNNOPRTUY	UNDEREMPLOYMENT
DEEEENOOPRSSSTT	DESERTS ONE'S POST
DEEEOOOPRRRSTTW	RESTORED TO POWER
DEEEOOPRRRSSSWX	EXPRESSED SORROW
DEEFFFGHIMOORRT	FIGHT FOR FREEDOM
DEEFFGGHNOORTTU	GET OFF THE GROUND
DEEFFGHLOOOORTV	FOR THE LOVE OF GOD
DEEFFGIIILNOPRV	DEPRIVING OF LIFE
DEEFFGINNOORSTU	GO FIFTEEN ROUNDS
DEEFFHIOORRRSTT	OF THE FIRST ORDER
DEEFFIINOOPRSST	FIT OF DEPRESSION
DEEFFILOOOPRRVY	PROOF OF DELIVERY
DEEFFLOOOPPRSST	DROPS OFF TO SLEEP
DEEFGHHILLOPSTU	PLOUGH THE FIELDS
DEEFGHHILORRTTU	FILTERED THROUGH
DEEFGHIILLQTTUU	QUITE DELIGHTFUL
DEEFGHINNOORRTU	IN THE FOREGROUND
DEEFGHLLNOORTTU	FELL TO THE GROUND
DEEFGIIINOORTVV	TO FORGIVE DIVINE
DEEFGILNNNOORSW	DROWNING ONESELF
DEEFGINNNOOSSTU	FINDS ONE'S TONGUE
DEEFGINOOPRSUXY	DYING OF EXPOSURE
DEEFGJMNOORRRTU	ERROR OF JUDGMENT
DEEFGNNNOOOSTUU	FOUND ONE'S TONGUE
DEEFHHLMOORRSTU	FROM THE SHOULDER
DEEFHIIKLNORSTW	WORK IN THE FIELDS
DEEFHIILNNOTTUY	IN THE LINE OF DUTY
DEEFHLLNOORTUVY	VOLLEY OF THUNDER
DEEFHLNOORRTTTU	RETURN TO THE FOLD
DEEFIIIMMNOPRSSX	FIXED IMPRESSION
DEEFIINNOPRRRTUU	PERIOD FURNITURE
DEEFIKLLMMOOORS	SMOKE-FILLED ROOM
DEEFILLNOPRSSUY	SPLENDIFEROUSLY
DEEFINNOPRRRSTU	RUN FOR PRESIDENT
DEEFLMNOOOOPRRY	MONEY FOR OLD ROPE
DEEFLNNOOOORSTTU	TOLD ONE'S FORTUNE
DEEFLNOOPRSSSTU	DESSERTSPOONFUL
DEEFLOOOORRRSTUU	RULES OUT OF ORDER
DEEGGHILNNOSSST	LONGSIGHTEDNESS
DEEGGHILNOOPSST	GOOD NIGHTS SLEEP
DEEGGHNOOOORRTUV	GO OVER THE GROUND
DEEGGIILNNOTTVV	GETTING INVOLVED
DEEGGIINNNOSSSW	SINGED ONE'S WINGS
DEEGGIMNOOPNTTT	GETTING PROMOTED
DEEGGIMOOOOPPRSU	GEORGES POMPIDOU
DEEGHHIIINOPRTT	HIGH-PROTEIN DIET
DEEGHHIINNOTTTW	GONE WITH THE WIND
DEEGHHIINOSTTWW	GOES WITH THE WIND
DEEGHHILNNOORTU	HOLE IN THE GROUND
DEEGHHILNNOOSTT	TIGHTEN ONES HOLD
DEEGHIIILOPSTTUY	YIELD UP THE GHOST
DEEGHIIINNNRRTW	RIDING THE WINNER
DEEGHIINNNRSSTW	DRESSING IN WHITE
DEEGIIIKLMMNOOS	HOMOGENISED MILK
DEEGHIILLNSSSTT	LETS THINGS SLIDE
DEEGHIILNNPSTUV	LIVENED THINGS UP
DEEGHIILNNOORSST	ON ONE'S RIGHT SIDE
DEEGHIKNNORSTTU	GOT UNDER THE SKIN
DEEGHIKNORSSSTU	KISSES THE GROUND
DEEGHILNNNOORTW	GET ON IN THE WORLD
DEEGHILNOORRTTX	THE GIRL NEXT DOOR
DEEGHINNNORTTUV	NOTHING VENTURED
DEEGHINOORSSSWW	WEIGHS ONE'S WORDS
DEEGHINOPRRSTVY	DROPS EVERYTHING
DEEGHLNNOOOSSTU	HOLDS ONE'S TONGUE
DEEGHNNOORRUVWY	HUNG ON EVERY WORD
DEEGHNOOOOPSSST	HOPES TO GOODNESS
DEEGIIINNNRSTTV	INVITING TENDERS
DEEGIINNPRRSUV	SERVING UP DINNER
DEEGIINNRSSSSTW	DISTRESSING NEWS
DEEGIINOPPSSTTU	STEPPING OUTSIDE
DEEGILLNNOPSSUY	SLEEPING SOUNDLY
DEEGILNNOOSSTTX	NEXT TO GODLINESS
DEEGINNNOOSSSW	ON ONE'S WRONG SIDE
DEEGLMNNOORRTVW	WORLD GOVERNMENT
DEEHHIIIMSTTTWW	SWIM WITH THE TIDE
DEEHHIIMSTTTUWW	SWUM WITH THE TIDE
DEEHHIINNTTTWWW	WENT WITH THE WIND
DEEHHIKNNOORSTU	DRINK ON THE HOUSE
DEEHHINORSTTTWW	THREW TO THE WINDS
DEEHHLNOOOORSSSS	HOLDS ONE'S HORSES
DEEHHNNOOOOORSTW	SHOWN ONE THE DOOR
DEEHHNOOOORSSTW	SHOWS ONE THE DOOR
DEEHIIKLNNRSTUW	RUNS LIKE THE WIND
DEEHIILLLOSTWWW	WIELDS THE WILLOW
DEEHIILLPRSSTWW	SWELLS WITH PRIDE
DEEHIINNNOORSST	THORN IN ONES SIDE
DEEHIINOOPSSSTT	PHOTOSENSITISED
DEEHIINOOPSSTTZ	PHOTOSENSITIZED
DEEHIKKLLNOORTU	LOOK LIKE THUNDER
DEEHIKLNOOTUVWY	THE DEVIL YOU KNOW
DEEHILNNOPSSSSU	HOLDS IN SUSPENSE
DEEHIMMMNOOOPRST	PROMISED THE MOON

DEEHIMOORRSTTTU	RIDE OUT THE STORM
DEEHINNNOPPTUY	PENNY IN THE POUND
DEEHINNNOORRSSW	DREW IN ONE'S HORNS
DEEHINNOORSSTTW	SWORD IN THE STONE
DEEHMOOORRSTTTU	RODE OUT THE STORM
DEEHNNNOOPRRSTT	PRESTON NORTH END
DEEHOOOOOPRSTTTT	ROOTED TO THE SPOT
DEEIIJMMNNOTUYY	ENJOYED IMMUNITY
DEEIILNNOOSSTVW	LIVED ON ONE'S WITS
DEEIILNOPRSSSTW	LOW-SPIRITEDNESS
DEEIILNOPSSSSST	SPLITS ONE'S SIDES
DEEIIMNOOPRRSVV	IMPROVED VERSION
DEEIINOOOOPPSSTX	EXPOSED POSITION
DEEIKMNNNNOOSWW	KNEW ONE'S OWN MIND
DEEIMNNNOOPRSSY	PREYS ON ONE'S MIND
DEEIMNNNOSSTTUV	SOUND INVESTMENT
DEEINNOOOOPPRSTV	PROVED ONE'S POINT
DEELMNORSSTUVYY	UNSOLVED MYSTERY
DEELNNOOPPRSSTU	LEND ONES SUPPORT
DEENNNNOOOOSSST	STOOD NO NONSENSE
DEENNNNOORSTTUU	NO STONE UNTURNED
DEENNOOOOOSSSTT	STOOD ON ONE'S TOES
DEFFGGHIMOORSTT	GIFT FROM THE GODS
DEFFGGHNOOOORTTU	GOT OFF THE GROUND
DEFFIKMNNOOOOST	TOOK ONE'S MIND OFF
DEFGGHIIKLNNORT	FORKED LIGHTNING
DEFGGIMNOOSTTW	GOD'S GIFT TO WOMEN
DEFGHHILLOORTTW	LIGHT OF THE WORLD
DEFGHHLLOOORTUW	FOLLOWED THROUGH
DEFGHIILNNOSTTW	FLING TO THE WINDS
	FLINGS TO THE WIND
DEFGHILNNOSTTUW	FLUNG TO THE WINDS
DEFGHILNOORSTTU	DUSTING THE FLOOR
DEFGHINNOOORSSTU	SHIFT ONE'S GROUND
DEFGIILNOORSTUY	DOING IT YOURSELF
DEFGIMNORRRRTUY	TRYING FOR MURDER
DEFGJLLLLOOOOWY	JOLLY GOOD FELLOW
DEFHIIMMNNOORSTU	FOURTH DIMENSION
DEFHIKNNOOPRRTU	PROFOUND THINKER
DEFHINOOOORRTTTW	NOT THE WORD FOR IT
DEFHLMOOOORRSTU	HOLDS OUT FOR MORE
DEFHLNOOOOPRTTW	ON TOP OF THE WORLD
DEFHNOOOOOTTTUW	NOT OUT OF THE WOOD
DEFIIMMNNNOOOPR	INFORMED OPINION
DEFIIKLOORSTTUY	DO-IT-YOURSELF KIT
DEFIIKNOOORRRSW	INDOOR FIREWORKS
DEFIILLNOOSTUVW	STOOD IN FULL VIEW
DEFIILMNOSSTTUU	MULTITUDE OF SINS
DEFILNRSSSSTTUU	DISTRUSTFULNESS
DEFILOOOOPRRSST	TROOP OF SOLDIERS
DEFIMMNNOOOORSTT	SIMON DE MONTFORT
DEFNNOOOOPSTTUW	PUT ONES FOOT DOWN
DEGGGHIINOOSTTV	GIVING TO THE DOGS
DEGGHHHIINORTTT	DO THE RIGHT THING
DEGGHHINNOORTTW	DO THE WRONG THING
DEGGHIILMNOOSTY	DEMYTHOLOGISING
DEGGHIILMNOOTYZ	DEMYTHOLOGIZING
DEGGHIILNNNOOTW	LONDON WEIGHTING
DEGGHIILNNSSTUY	STUDYING ENGLISH
DEGGIIIKNNNPRUV	GIVEN UP DRINKING
DEGGIIIKNNPRSUV	GIVES UP DRINKING
DEGGIINNOOTTTTW	GETTING DOWN TO IT
DEGHHIIILNRRSVW	WHIRLING DERVISH
DEGHHINNNOORTTU	THIN ON THE GROUND
DEGHHINNOOOORSTU	DOING THE HONOURS
DEGHHINOORSTTTU	SHUTTING THE DOOR
DEGHHNOOOORSTTTW	THROWN TO THE DOGS
DEGHHOOORSSTTTW	THROWS TO THE DOGS
DEGHIIIMNNNORST	IN ONES RIGHT MIND
DEGHIIILLMOORSTV	OLIVER GOLDSMITH
DEGHIILNNOPTTTU	PUTTING THE LID ON
DEGHIILNNOSSTTY	DO THINGS IN STYLE
DEGHILLLNOSTTWY	LETS DOWN LIGHTLY
DEGHINNOORSSTTU	SITS ON THE GROUND
DEGHINOORSSTTTU	SORTED THINGS OUT
DEGHNNNOOORSSUW	HUNG ON ONE'S WORDS
DEGIIIJNNOPRTUW	JOINED-UP WRITING
DEGIILLLNOPSSTU	DUELLING PISTOLS
DEGIILNNOOPRSSU	GIRD UP ONES LOINS
DEGIINOOPPSSTTU	STOPPING OUTSIDE
DEGIMNNOOOSSTTU	DOING ONE'S UTMOST
DEHHHIILMORTTWW	HOWLED WITH MIRTH
DEHHIIMOPRRSTYY	HYPERTHYROIDISM
DEHHILNORSSTTUW	HURLS TO THE WINDS
DEHHINNOORTTTWW	THROWN TO THE WIND
DEHHINOORSTTTWW	THROW TO THE WINDS
	THROWS TO THE WIND
DEHHIORRSTTTTTU	DISTORT THE TRUTH
DEHHLOOOOPRSSTU	HOUSEHOLD TROOPS
DEHIIINNOPSSTTW	PISS INTO THE WIND
DEHIINNOPRRSTTU	RUSHED INTO PRINT
DEIIILLMNNOSSTU	DISILLUSIONMENT
DEIIMNNNRSSTTUW	WIND INSTRUMENTS
DEIINNORSSSSTUU	INDUSTRIOUSNESS
DEIKMNNNNOOOSWW	KNOW ONES OWN MIND
DEILLNNOOORSTUWY	WOOLLEN INDUSTRY
DFGHHNOOOPRTTUU	PROFOUND THOUGHT
DFGHIIINNRSSTUY	FISHING INDUSTRY
DFILMMNOOOOOSSW	WISDOM OF SOLOMON
DGGGHIIIINNNOOT	GOING INTO HIDING
DGGHHIIINNNOOTT	HIDING TO NOTHING
DGGIIIMNNNOPRST	SPRINGING TO MIND
DGGINNNNOOORRTUU	RUNNING TO GROUND
DGHHIINNOOOTTTW	NOTHING TO DO WITH
DGHIINNOOORSTVY	GO DOWN IN HISTORY
DGIIILLMNPTTTUY	PUTTING IT MILDLY
DGIIINOOPPRRSST	DROOPING SPIRITS
DGIIKLMNNOOTTWY	TOOK IT LYING DOWN
DIILLMNOSTTUUUY	MULTITUDINOUSLY
DIINORRSSTTTUUY	TOURIST INDUSTRY
DILOOOOPRRSSSSTW	SWORDS OR PISTOLS
EEEEEEKNNOOPSY	KEEP ONE'S EYE OPEN
EEEEEFGNORRRSVY	RESERVE OF ENERGY
EEEEEFGNOSSTTTW	GETS ONE'S FEET WET
EEEEEFHHILRRSTW	WHERE THERES LIFE
EEEEEFHKKOPRSTY	KEEPER OF THE KEYS
EEEEEGGHHINNRTT	EIGHTEENTH GREEN
EEEEEGMNNQRSSSU	QUEENS MESSENGER
EEEEEGPRRRSSSTX	EXPRESSES REGRET
EEEEEHHJLNNTTUV	JUNE THE ELEVENTH
EEEEEHHLNOPSTTU	USE THE TELEPHONE
EEEEEHIQRRSTTUV	QUITE THE REVERSE
EEEEEHKMRRSSTTU	THREE MUSKETEERS
EEEEEHNNNORRTVV	ON THE NEVER-NEVER
EEEEEINNNNSTTVY	NINETEEN SEVENTY
EEEEEKMNNOPPRSST	KEEPS ONE'S TEMPER
EEEEEKNNOOPPSTY	KEPT ONE'S EYE OPEN
EEEEFFLLLNOORSV	FELL OVER ONESELF
EEEEFGGILLNNOSS	FEELING ONE'S LEGS
EEEEFGIILLMNOSTV	GIVE ONESELF TIME
EEEEFGILLNNOSST	STEELING ONESELF
EEEEFGILNNNOPRS	PREENING ONESELF
EEEEFGILNNORSTX	EXERTING ONESELF
EEEEFHHIILLRSTW	WHILE THERES LIFE
EEEEFHHIOSSTTWY	WHITES OF THE EYES
EEEEFHHORRSSTTT	THE REST OF ESTHER
EEEEFHHIKNOPPST	HOPE IT KEEPS FINE
EEEEFHLORRSTTUW	THREW OUT FEELERS
EEEEFHMNNRRSTTT	REFRESHMENT TENT
EEEEFIJLMOPRSTY	EPISTLE OF JEREMY
EEEEEFIMNORRRSTT	INTERFEROMETERS
EEEEFINNOORSSTT	RISEN TO ONE'S FEET

EEEEEFINOORSSSTT	RISES TO ONE'S FEET
EEEEEFKNNOORSSTU	SEEK ONES FORTUNE
EEEEEGGLNOORSSTV	GETS ONE'S LEG OVER
EEEEEGGNORRSSTUU	GENEROUS GESTURE
EEEEEGHHINOORTTV	ONE OVER THE EIGHT
EEEEEGHLNOORSTUY	HETEROGENEOUSLY
EEEEEGHNRRRSSTTV	RESERVE STRENGTH
EEEEEGIIIKKLLMNT	LIKE MEETING LIKE
EEEEEGILLMNOPTTV	TOP-LEVEL MEETING
EEEEEGILLNPSSTWY	SLEEPING SWEETLY
EEEEEGNNNOORSSTV	GET ON ONES NERVES
EEEEEHHHLNORTTUV	THE ELEVENTH HOUR
EEEEEHHNNNRSTTVY	HENRY THE SEVENTH
EEEEEHHIKLNOPSTW	SPOKE IN THE WHEEL
EEEEEHHIORRSUWWY	WISH YOU WERE HERE
EEEEEHHIRRSSSTTT	THE THREE SISTERS
EEEEEHHJLLNTTUVY	JULY THE ELEVENTH
EEEEEHIKLMORRSTT	THREE KILOMETRES
EEEEEHILLLOPPTTT	THE LITTLE PEOPLE
EEEEEHILLNPSSTTW	SWEETENS THE PILL
EEEEEHILMMORRRTW	MORTIMER WHEELER
EEEEEHILNOPTTUVY	PUT THE EVIL EYE ON
EEEEEHKLOPRSSTTU	KEEPS TO THE RULES
EEEEEHLMNUPSSTTY	TELEPHONE SYSTEM
EEEEEHLORRTTTTTU	TRUE TO THE LETTER
EEEEEHNNRSSSTTUV	THE SUN NEVER SETS
EEEEEIINNNPSSSVX	INEXPENSIVENESS
EEEEEIKLMNORSSTV	SEVEN KILOMETRES
EEEEEIKMNOOPPRSS	KEEP ONES PROMISE
EEEEEIKNNPPSSSSU	KEEPS IN SUSPENSE
EEEEEILPRRSTTTWY	TELETYPEWRITERS
EEEEEIMOOPPRSTTX	OPPOSITE EXTREME
EEEEELMNOOPRSSST	LOSES ONE'S TEMPER
EEEEELMNORRSSSSS	REMORSELESSNESS
EEEEELNNNOPSSSTV	VENTS ONE'S SPLEEN
EEEEEMNNRSSSTUV	VENTURESOMENESS
EEEEENNOORRSSUVY	RUNS ONE'S EYE OVER
EEEFFFHIJNNOTTU	FIFTEENTH OF JUNE
EEEFFGHIOORRSWY	SIR GEOFFREY HOWE
EEEFFHHKOORTTWY	THREW OFF THE YOKE
EEEFFHIILLNNORT	IN THE LINE OF FIRE
EEEFFIINNNOSSSV	INOFFENSIVENESS
EEEFGGHHOORRTTU	GEORGE THE FOURTH
EEEFGGHIILLNNOSW	WEIGHING ONESELF
EEEFGGIILLMNPST	FLEETING GLIMPSE
EEEFGGIILNRRSST	SELF-REGISTERING
EEEFGIIILLLNNTT	INTELLIGENT LIFE
EEEFGIJLNNNOOSY	ENJOYING ONESELF
EEEFGILLNNOORSW	LOWERING ONESELF
EEEFGIMMNNOORTW	REGIMENT OF WOMEN
EEEFGIMNOPRRSSW	SWEEPING REFORMS
EEEFHHNNOOQSTTUU	QUEEN OF THE SOUTH
EEEFHIINQRSTTUU	FIRST IN THE QUEUE
EEEFHIJNNOSTTUX	SIXTEENTH OF JUNE
EEEFHIJNNOTTTUW	TWENTIETH OF JUNE
EEEFHIKNNOSSTTT	SKIN OF ONES TEETH
EEEFHLOORRSTTUW	THROW OUT FEELERS
EEEFHMMNOORRRST	REFRESHMENT ROOM
EEEFHOOPPRRSSTW	POWER OF THE PRESS
EEEFIILMNSTTVWY	TWENTY-FIVE MILES
EEEFIILLNNORSSSU	INSURES ONE'S LIFE
EEEFILMNOOPRSSV	IMPROVES ONESELF
EEEFILNOPRSSSSX	SELF-EXPRESSIONS
EEEFIMNNORSTTUU	FOURTEEN MINUTES
EEEFLLNNOORSTTU	TELL ONES FORTUNE
EEEFNNOOOSSSSTU	OUT OF ONES SENSES
EEEGGGHINORTTTT	GETTING TOGETHER
EEEGGHHHLNOOOTW	GONE THE WHOLE HOG
EEEGGHHHLOOOSTW	GOES THE WHOLE HOG
EEEGGHHIINSSSTT	SEEING THE SIGHTS
EEEGGHHINNNORST	HERE GOES NOTHING
EEEGGHIIILNNOTV	GIVING ONE THE LIE
EEEGGHIILLNNRST	GREEN IN THE GILLS
EEEGGHIIMNORSTT	GOING THREE TIMES
EEEGGHIINNTTTVW	GETTING EVEN WITH
EEEGGHIINRRSSTT	SIGN THE REGISTER
EEEGGHILNNOPRSU	GENEROUS HELPING
EEEGGHINNOOPRUV	GIVEN ENOUGH ROPE
EEEGGHINNOPRTTT	POTTING THE GREEN
EEEGGHINNOOPRSUV	GIVES ENOUGH ROPE
EEEGGHIPRRRSSTT	PRESS THE TRIGGER
EEEGGIIMNNPRRSU	REIGNING SUPREME
EEEGGILNNORSUVY	GIVEN GENEROUSLY
EEEGGILNORSSUVY	GIVES GENEROUSLY
EEEGGIMNOORSTTX	GOING TO EXTREMES
EEEGHHHHLNOOTTWW	WENT THE WHOLE HOG
EEEGGHIIILLNOSTW	OILING THE WHEELS
EEEGHHIIMSSTTW	MISSES THE WEIGHT
EEEGHHIINRSSTVV	GIVEN THE SHIVERS
EEEGHHIIRSSSTVV	GIVES THE SHIVERS
EEEGHHINNOPSTUV	GIVEN ONE THE PUSH
EEEGHHINOPSSTUV	GIVES ONE THE PUSH
EEEGHHIORRSTTTV	VEERS TO THE RIGHT
EEEGGHHLLLOPRTTU	PULL THE OTHER LEG
EEEGHIIILLNSTW	GIVEN THE WILLIES
EEEGHIIILLSSTVW	GIVES THE WILLIES
EEEGHIIKLMORSTT	EIGHT KILOMETRES
EEEGGHIIKLNNOOTY	LOOKING IN THE EYE
EEEGHIIILLPRSTTT	THREE LITTLE PIGS
EEEGHIILLNNOPSTV	GIVEN ONE THE SLIP
EEEGHILLNNORSTT	THERE'S NO TELLING
EEEGHILLNRSTTVY	TELLS EVERYTHING
EEEGHILNORSSTVY	LOSES EVERYTHING
EEEGHIMNOOOSTTV	GONE TO THE MOVIES
EEEGHIMOOOSSTTV	GOES TO THE MOVIES
EEEGHNNMNOOOSSSU	HOMOGENEOUSNESS
EEEGHNNOOORSSST	GETS ON ONE'S HORSE
EEEGIIINNNSTUVV	INVENTIVE GENIUS
EEEGIIMMNNORSTV	SERVING ONE'S TIME
EEEGIIMNNPRRSST	MISREPRESENTING
EEEGIINNRRSTTVY	VERY INTERESTING
EEEGIKNNOORSTTW	TWO-STROKE ENGINE
EEEGILMNNNOOSVY	LOVING ONE'S ENEMY
EEEGILNNNOORSSV	LOSING ONE'S NERVE
EEEGILORRRSSTVY	RETROGRESSIVELY
EEEGINNOPSSTTUY	SETTING EYES UPON
EEEGINOPRRSSSSV	PROGRESSIVENESS
EEEGINOPRRTTTVY	REVERTING TO TYPE
EEEGKMNNOOPSTUY	GET ONE'S MONKEY UP
EEEGLNNOOOSSSTU	LOSES ONE'S TONGUE
EEEGNNNOOORSSTV	GOT ON ONE'S NERVES
EEEHHHINOORRTTT	HEIR TO THE THRONE
EEEHHINNORTTTVW	WITHER ON THE VINE
EEEHHIIORSSSTTWW	WISHES OTHERWISE
EEEHHILNORTTTWW	THREW IN THE TOWEL
	THREW THE TOWEL IN
EEEHHLLNOOPRTTU	PULL THE OTHER ONE
EEEHHLNOOPRTTTT	OPEN THE THROTTLE
EEEHIILNNOOSTTV	ON THE TELEVISION
EEEHIIMNNRSTTTU	THIRTEEN MINUTES
EEEHIIMPPRRSTUV	HEIR PRESUMPTIVE
EEEHIIKKNNOSTTTY	KITTEN ON THE KEYS
EEEHIKNNOOPRSST	KEEP ONES SHIRT ON
EEEHIKNOOPSPTTT	KEEPS TO THE POINT
EEEHILLPRRSSTUV	SELLS UP THE RIVER
EEEHILNORRSSTTW	NORTHWESTERLIES
EEEHILNOSSSTTWW	WETS ONE'S WHISTLE
EEEHILORSSSTTUW	SOUTHWESTERLIES
EEEHIMMOOORRSTT	SOME TIME OR OTHER
EEEHIMNOOSTTTVW	WENT TO THE MOVIES
EEEHIOOPRRSSTTU	PETER OOSTERHUIS
EEEHKLNOOOSSSTT	TOOK TO ONE'S HEELS

EEEHKLNOPSTTTTU	PUTS THE KETTLE ON
EEEHLNNNOORSSTU	TURN ON ONE'S HEELS
	TURNS ON ONE'S HEEL
EEEHMNOORRSSTVY	EVERY MOTHERS SON
EEEHOORRRSSTTUW	WORE THE TROUSERS
EEEIIINNNSSSSTV	INSENSITIVENESS
EEEIIMMOORRSSST	STEREOISOMERISM
EEEIIMNOOPRSTTX	EXTREME POSITION
EEEIIINNOPSSSSTY	SPITS IN ONE'S EYES
EEEIINOPRSSSTTU	REPETITIOUSNESS
EEEIKKNNNOOSSST	SINK TO ONES KNEES
EEEIKLLNNOOSSTV	SINK TO ONE'S LEVEL
EEEIKMNOOPPRSST	KEPT ONE'S PROMISE
EEEIKNNNOOOPSSS	POKES ONE'S NOSE IN
EEEIILLOOPRRSTTV	LIVERPOOL STREET
EEEILNNOOPPRSTT	POISON-PEN LETTER
EEEILNOPRRSTUUV	PERILOUS VENTURE
EEEINNNOSSSSTTU	SENTENTIOUSNESS
EEEINNOPRSSSTTU	PRETENTIOUSNESS
EEEINOPRSSSSSTU	PRESSES ONE'S SUIT
EEEKKNNNOOSSSTU	SUNK TO ONE'S KNEES
EEEKLLNNOOSSTUV	SUNK TO ONE'S LEVEL
EEELMMNOOOORSSSY	LOSES ONE'S MEMORY
EEEMNOPSSSSTTUU	TEMPESTUOUSNESS
EEEOOOPRRRSSTTW	RESTORES TO POWER
EEEOOPRRRSSSSSWX	EXPRESSES SORROW
EEFFFGILNNOSSTU	STUFFING ONESELF
EEFFFHHLOOSSSTU	SOFT-SHOE SHUFFLE
EEFFFHIJLNOTTUY	FIFTEENTH OF JULY
EEFFFILORRSSTTU	FRUITLESS EFFORT
EEFFGHIMNNOOORT	OFFERING THE MOON
EEFFGHINOOPSTTT	GETS OFF THE POINT
EEFFGIIIILLNRSST	SELF-FERTILISING
EEFFGIIIILLNRSTZ	SELF-FERTILIZING
EEFFGIINOORSTTY	FIT OF GENEROSITY
EEFFHHIKNOOOSTT	TOOK THE SHINE OFF
EEFFHHKOOORTTWY	THROW OFF THE YOKE
EEFFHHLOOOORSTU	FLOOR OF THE HOUSE
EEFFHIIMORRSTTT	FOR THE FIRST TIME
EEFFHNOOPRRTTUW	TURN OFF THE POWER
EEFFIIKLMORSTTY	FIFTY KILOMETRES
EEFFIKLNOOPRSST	SPOKEN FOR ITSELF
EEFFILNNOORRSSU	RUNS FOR ONE'S LIFE
EEFFLNOOOORRSSY	SORRY FOR ONESELF
EEFFNOORRSSTTUU	STRENUOUS EFFORT
EEFGGHIIMNNORTV	THE MOVING FINGER
EEFGGHIJKLNNOTU	KING OF THE JUNGLE
EEFGGIILNNOPSUV	GIVING ONESELF UP
EEFGHHIIILRSSTW	SIGHS WITH RELIEF
EEFGHIIIILNNNRT	IN THE FIRING LINE
EEFGHIINNOPRSTT	POINTS THE FINGER
EEFGHIKOOPSSTTU	KEEPS OUT OF SIGHT
EEFGHILLORSSTUY	SELF-RIGHTEOUSLY
EEFGHILNNOOOSST	SHOOTING ONESELF
EEFGHILNOOPSTTU	SLIP OF THE TONGUE
EEFGHINNOPPRSTU	PUTS THE FINGER ON
EEFGHINOORTTVWY	TWO OF EVERYTHING
EEFGHIOORSTTTTW	GET THE WORST OF IT
EEFGHLLLNNOORWY	HENRY LONGFELLOW
EEFGHNOORRSTTTW	TOWER OF STRENGTH
EEFGIIIIMNNRSTV	VISITING FIREMEN
EEFGIIIMNNORRST	FOREIGN MINISTER
EEFGIILLNNOOPSS	SPOILING ONESELF
EEFGIILMNNOOPSS	IMPOSING ONESELF
EEFGIILNNOOSSTU	SELF-QUESTIONING
EEFGIILNOORRSTT	RESTORING TO LIFE
EEFGIINNOPPRST	POINT ONE'S FINGER
EEFGIINNNOORRTW	TOWERING INFERNO
EEFGILLMNOORSSS	SMELLING OF ROSES
EEFGILNNNOOSSTU	FOULING ONE'S NEST
EEFGILNNOOOOSST	LOSE ONES FOOTING

EEFGIMNNOPRTTU	TEMPTING FORTUNE
EEFGINNNOOPRTU	PUT ONE'S FINGER ON
EEFGINNOOOPSTTU	TIP OF ONES TONGUE
EEFHHHILNNORSTT	THORN IN THE FLESH
EEFHHIIJNORTTTU	THIRTIETH OF JUNE
EEFHHIINORRSTTU	THEIR FINEST HOUR
EEFHHIMOORRSSTW	SWIM FOR THE SHORE
EEFHHIMOORRTTUV	MOUTH OF THE RIVER
EEFHHINOORRRTTV	NORTH OF THE RIVER
EEFHHIOORRSTTUV	SOUTH OF THE RIVER
EEFHHMOOPRRSSTT	HOT FROM THE PRESS
EEFHHMOORRSSTUW	SWUM FOR THE SHORE
EEFHIJLNOSTTUXY	SIXTEENTH OF JULY
EEFHIJLNOTTTUWY	TWENTIETH OF JULY
EEFHIKMOOORRTTT	TOOK IT FROM THERE
EEFHKLOOOORTTTUU	LOOK TO THE FUTURE
EEFHMMNOOOPRSTTU	SPUR OF THE MOMENT
EEFHNOORRRSTTUW	TURN FOR THE WORSE
EEFIIINNOORRRSV	INFERIOR VERSION
EEFIILOPPPRSTTU	LITTER OF PUPPIES
EEFIINOQRRSTTUV	FREQUENT VISITOR
EEFIKLMOORRSTTY	FORTY KILOMETRES
EEFIKLNNOOOOSTW	TOOK ONE'S OWN LIFE
EEFILLLMNOSSSUU	MELLIFLUOUSNESS
EEFIMNNNOOORTTU	NOT FOR ONE MINUTE
EEFLLNNOOOOSSSW	FOLLOWS ONE'S NOSE
EEFLMNNOOOORRVY	FOR LOVE NOR MONEY
EEFLNNNOOOOSSTUW	FOUL ONE'S OWN NEST
EEFMMMOOOOQRRTUY	QUOTE FROM MEMORY
EEFMMNNNOOOORTT	NOT FOR ONE MOMENT
EEFMMNNOORRSSTTT	FROM STEM TO STERN
EEFMNNNOOOORRSUY	RUN FOR ONES MONEY
EEFMNOOOSSSSTTUY	OUT OF ONE'S SYSTEM
EEGGGHHHHINORSTU	HUGGING THE SHORE
EEGGGHIKKNNNOPST	KEEP THINGS GOING
EEGGHHHIIILLMOTT	HOG THE LIMELIGHT
EEGGHHIIKLNNSST	THE KINGS ENGLISH
EEGGHHIILLNNOTTV	LIGHTING THE OVEN
EEGGHHIINORSTTU	SEEING IT THROUGH
EEGGHHINOPRSTUW	SWEEPING THROUGH
EEGGHHINOPSTTUV	GIVEN UP THE GHOST
EEGGHHIOPSSTTUV	GIVES UP THE GHOST
EEGGHIIINNNNRTW	RINGING IN THE NEW
EEGGHIIINNOPPTV	GIVING ONE THE PIP
EEGGHIIKLLNNOTV	LONG LIVE THE KING!
EEGGHIILLMNRRVY	GIVING MERRY HELL
EEGGHIINNOPRSTT	TIGHTEN ONES GRIP
EEGGHIINNOPTTTT	GETTING THE POINT
EEGGHIINNORRSTV	SERVING ONE RIGHT
EEGGHIINNOSSTTW	GETTING ONE'S WISH
EEGGHIINNOSSTUW	USING ONE'S WEIGHT
EEGGHIINNOSTTTW	GET INTO THE SWING
EEGGHIINORSSTTU	SIGHT-SEEING TOUR
	SIGHTSEEING TOUR
EEGGHIKNORSTTTW	GETTING THE WORKS
EEGGHILLPRRSTTU	PULLS THE TRIGGER
EEGGHINOOOPRTTV	GOING OVER THE TOP
EEGGHINOOPTTTTT	GETTING TO THE TOP
EEGGHINOPRTTTTU	PUTTING TOGETHER
EEGGHINOORRSSTT	STRINGS TOGETHER
EEGGHNOOPRRTTUW	GROWN UP TOGETHER
EEGGIIILLNPRRTTZ	GLITTERING PRIZE
EEGGIIINOSSTTW	GETTING WISE TO IT
EEGGIINNNOSSSSW	SINGES ONE'S WINGS
EEGGIINNOOOPRTU	GOING INTO EUROPE
EEGGIINNOPSTTTT	GETTING INTO STEP
EEGGILLNORSTTUV	VIOLENT STRUGGLE
EEGGINOPRRSSTTU	SPORTING GESTURE
EEGHHHIINORTTTT	HIT THE RIGHT NOTE
EEGHHHINNOOORSS	ON ONES HIGH HORSE
EEGHHIIILLNSTTW	WHITE IN THE GILLS

EEGHHIILNNORSTT	ON THE RIGHT LINES
EEGHHIILNNOSTTT	NIGHT ON THE TILES
EEGHHILNNORTTWW	THREW NEW LIGHT ON
EEGHHINOOPRSSTW	SHOWING THE ROPES
EEGHHLNOSSSSTTU	THOUGHTLESSNESS
EEGHIIILNNNTTTW	WINNING THE TITLE
EEGHIIINNNPRTWZ	WINNING THE PRIZE
EEGHIIKLLNSTTTW	WHISTLING KETTLE
EEGHIIKNORSTTVW	GIVEN IT THE WORKS
EEGHIIKNRRSSTVY	RISKS EVERYTHING
EEGHIIKORSSTTVW	GIVES IT THE WORKS
EEGHIILLNNNOSTT	TEN-SHILLING NOTE
EEGHIILMNNOPTTT	IN THE MELTING-POT
EEGHIILNNNSTTTU	LETTING IN THE SUN
EEGHIILNNORSTTU	IN ONE'S TRUE LIGHT
EEGHIILNOPRSTVY	SPOIL EVERYTHING
EEGHIINNNNOPSST	OPENS THE INNINGS
EEGHIKLNOOOTTVW	TOOK THE LONG VIEW
EEGHIKNNNOORSTW	THERE'S NO KNOWING
EEGHIILLNOPSSTUW	PULLS ONE'S WEIGHT
EEGHILMNNNOOOPST	PHENOMENOLOGIST
EEGHILNNNOORSTW	ON THE WRONG LINES
EEGHILNNOOSSSTW	LOSE ON THE SWINGS
EEGHILNOORSSSTW	LOWER ONES SIGHTS
EEGHIMNNOORSTTT	SOMETHING ROTTEN
EEGHNNORRSSTTTY	TRY ONES STRENGTH
EEGIIIMNNOPRSSV	GIVEN PERMISSION
EEGIIIMNNPRRSTT	MISINTERPRETING
EEGIIIMNOPRSSSV	GIVES PERMISSION
EEGIILNNOPSSTTW	WETTING ONE'S LIPS
EEGIIMNNORSSTTT	MOST INTERESTING
EEGIINOPRSSSSTU	PRESTIGIOUSNESS
EEGIJMNNNOORTTV	JOINT GOVERNMENT
EEGIKNNNOOORSTTU	GONE OUT ON STRIKE
EEGIKNOOORSSTTU	GOES OUT ON STRIKE
EEGILMNNNOOOSSY	LOSING ONE'S MONEY
EEGILNOPPRSSSSY	PREPOSSESSINGLY
EEGINNNNORRSSTUV	SERVING ONE'S TURN
EEGKMNNOOOPSTUY	GOT ONE'S MONKEY UP
EEHHIIKLMSSTTTY	THE SKYS THE LIMIT
EEHHIIMOOOOPRRRT	EMPEROR HIROHITO
EEHHILMMNNOSTTTU	MELTS IN THE MOUTH
EEHHILMNOOTTTWY	ON WITH THE MOTLEY
EEHHILNOORSTTTW	THREW TO THE LIONS
EEHHILNOORTTTWW	THROW IN THE TOWEL
	THROW THE TOWEL IN
EEHHINNOORSSSTW	WINS ON THE HORSES
EEHHINNOORSSTTT	SITS ON THE THRONE
EEHHINOOPSSSTTY	PHOTOSYNTHESISE
EEHHINOOPSSTTYZ	PHOTOSYNTHESIZE
EEHHLLOORSSTTUY	YOUTH-HOSTELLERS
EEHHMMNNOORSTTTU	MOUNTS THE THRONE
EEHHMMNNOPSSTVYY	SEVENTH SYMPHONY
EEHHNOPRRSSTTUU	USURPS THE THRONE
EEHIIIILNOOPSSTT	OPEN HOSTILITIES
EEHIIJMNPRRSTUV	JUMPS IN THE RIVER
EEHIIKOPPRRRRSY	YORKSHIRE RIPPER
EEHIINNPRSSTTTY	THIRTY-NINE STEPS
EEHIINOOPSSSSTT	PHOTOSENSITISES
EEHIINOOPSSSTTZ	PHOTOSENSITIZES
EEHIINOPRSTTVWW	INVEST WITH POWER
EEHIINORSTTTTUW	WITHOUT INTEREST
EEHIKNNOOPRSSTT	KEPT ONE'S SHIRT ON
EEHIKNOOPRRSTUY	KEEP YOUR SHIRT ON!
EEHILMMNNOOSTTU	MELT IN ONES MOUTH
EEHILOOOOPPRRRTT	HOTEL PROPRIETOR
EEHIMMNOOOPRSST	PROMISES THE MOON
EEHIMNOOPPRSSTT	TOM,THE PIPERS SON
EEHINNNOOOOPPSSS	PINS ONE'S HOPES ON
EEHINOOPPQSSTTU	POPS THE QUESTION
EEHINOPQSSTTTUU	PUTS THE QUESTION

EEHIOOPSTTTTTUV	PUTS IT TO THE VOTE
EEHIOPSSTTTTTTU	PUTS IT TO THE TEST
EEHJMMNOOOPRTUV	JUMP OVER THE MOON
EEHLMMOOOORSSTT	TOOTHSOME MORSEL
EEHLMNOPRTTUUUV	TURN THE VOLUME UP
	TURN UP THE VOLUME
EEHNNOOPRRSSTTUW	TURNS ON THE POWER
EEHNOORRRSSTTUW	WORN THE TROUSERS
EEIIIIKLLLSSTTT	TELLS IT LIKE IT IS
EEIIIINNQSSSTUV	INQUISITIVENESS
EEIIIMNNNORSTTV	INTERVENTIONISM
EEIIINNNNORSTTTV	INTERVENTIONIST
EEIIKLMORSSTTXY	SIXTY KILOMETRES
EEIILLNOPRTTTVY	VERY LITTLE POINT
EEIILNNOORRTTTU	TRINITROTOLUENE
EEIILNNOOSSSTVW	LIVES ON ONE'S WITS
EEIIMNNOPSSSTTU	PIOUS SENTIMENTS
EEIIMNNOSSTTTUW	WOMENS INSTITUTE
EEIIMNOORRSSSTU	MERITORIOUSNESS
EEIINNNNNOORTTV	NONINTERVENTION
EEIINOOQRSSSTUU	SERIOUS QUESTION
EEIINOPRRRSSSTU	SURPRISE IN STORE
EEIKNNOOPPSSSTU	PUTS ONE'S SPOKE IN
EEIKNNOORSTTTUW	WENT OUT ON STRIKE
EEILLNNOOORTUY	NOT ON YOUR NELLIE!
EEILLOOPPRSTTTU	TO LITTLE PURPOSE
EEILMMNNOOPRSSY	SLIPS ONE'S MEMORY
EEILNNOPRSTTUUY	UNPRETENTIOUSLY
EEIMNNRRSSTTTUV	INVESTMENT TRUST
EEIMNOPPQRSSTTU	SPORTS EQUIPMENT
EEINNNOOOPPRSSTU	INOPPORTUNENESS
EEINNOOOPPRSSTV	PROVES ONE'S POINT
EEINNOQSSTTTUWY	TWENTY QUESTIONS
EELNNOOPPRSSTTU	LENT ONE'S SUPPORT
EEMMNNOOOOPPRTTU	OPPORTUNE MOMENT
EENNNOOPRSSSTUU	TURNS ONE'S NOSE UP
	TURNS UP ONE'S NOSE
EENNOOPRSSSTTUU	TURNS UP ONE'S TOES
EFFGGILLNNORSUY	LONG-SUFFERINGLY
EFFGHHHILNORTTTU	TURN OFF THE LIGHT
	TURN THE LIGHT OFF
EFFGHILMOORRTTT	FROM LEFT TO RIGHT
EFFHHJLOORTTUUY	THE FOURTH OF JULY
EFFHMOOOOPRRSTT	FROM THE ROOF-TOPS
EFFIKMNNNOOOSSY	NO SKIN OFF MY NOSE
EFFILLOPRRSSSUU	FULL OF SURPRISES
EFFNORSSSSTTTUU	STRUTS ONE'S STUFF
EFGGGINNNOOORSU	GOING FOR ONE'S GUN
EFGGHHIINNNTTW	WINNING THE FIGHT
EFGGHINNOOORTTT	GOING TO THE FRONT
EFGGILNOOOSTTUY	GOING OUT OF STYLE
EFGHHIILLNOSTTT	STILL OF THE NIGHT
EFGHHIIORRSSTTV	GIVE SHORT SHRIFT
EFGHHILLOOTTTTU	THOUGHT LITTLE OF
EFGHHILNOOPRSTU	SHOUTING FOR HELP
EFGHHIIOORRSTTUY	FORTY-EIGHT HOURS
EFGHHIORRRSSTTT	GETS SHORT SHRIFT
EFGHHLLLOOOPTUW	FOLLOW THE PLOUGH
EFGHIIIJJNNNNOTU	JOINING IN THE FUN
EFGHIIINNOOOPTW	WEIGHT OF OPINION
EFGHIIINOOPRTTT	PETITION OF RIGHT
EFGHIJNOOPRSSTY	THE JOYS OF SPRING
EFGHILLOORSTTUV	GLORIOUS TWELFTH
EFGHILMNOOOOPPRT	MOPPING THE FLOOR
EFGHILNOOPPSTTW	STOPPING THE FLOW
EFGHIMNNNOOOPRTT	TOP OF THE MORNING
EFGHINNNOOORTTU	OUT OF THE RUNNING
EFGHIOOORSTTTTW	GOT THE WORST OF IT
EFGIIILMNOPRSVY	OVERSIMPLIFYING
EFGIIINNOQRSSTU	FIRING QUESTIONS
EFGIIINORRSTTYZ	TRYING IT FOR SIZE

EFGIIMNNOOOSSST	MISS ONES FOOTING
EFGIINOPRRSTTUX	SPORTING FIXTURE
EFGILNNOOOOSSTT	LOST ONE'S FOOTING
EFHIIILLMNORSTT	THE FIRST MILLION
EFHIILNOPRRSTUU	FURNITURE POLISH
EFHIINOOPTTTTUW	THE TOWN OF TITIPU
EFHIOOPRRRSSTTW	THIRSTS FOR POWER
EFHNOORRSTTUUWY	TWENTY-FOUR HOURS
EFIIIIILNNPSTTV	SPLIT INFINITIVE
EFIIIMNOPRRSSST	FIRST IMPRESSION
EFIIKMNOORRSSTW	MINISTER OF WORKS
EFIINNOOOOPSTTTU	PUT ONES FOOT IN IT
EFIINOOOOPPRSTW	POSITION OF POWER
EFINNNOOOPRRTTU	POINT OF NO RETURN
EFKNNOOOPRSTTUU	SPOKEN OUT OF TURN
EFLNOOOPRRSTTUU	RUNS OUT OF PETROL
EGGGHHLORRSTTUU	STRUGGLE THROUGH
EGGGHIIKNNOPSTT	KEPT THINGS GOING
EGGGHHIINRSSSTTT	SETS THINGS RIGHT
EGGHIIIKLNNRSTT	LIGHTNING STRIKE
EGGHIIILLPSTTTY	THIS LITTLE PIGGY
EGGHIIIINNOTTTTW	GETTING ON WITH IT
EGGHIILMMNNRSTU	SUMMER LIGHTNING
EGGHIILNNOOSSST	LOSING ONE'S SIGHT
EGGHIINNOOSTTTW	GOT INTO THE SWING
EGGHIINNOPTTTUW	PUTTING ON WEIGHT
EGGHIINORSSTTTT	SETTING TO RIGHTS
EGGHILLNOOOPSTT	GOING TO THE POLLS
EGGHILMOOOOPRST	GEOMORPHOLOGIST
EGGHIMNNNNOORTTU	GUNNING THE MOTOR
EGGHIMNNOOOOSTT	SOMETHING TO GO ON
EGGHNNNOOOORSTTU	NOT STRONG ENOUGH
EGGIIIINNSSSTWX	SWINGING SIXTIES
EGGIIKNNNOPSSSU	SPIKING ONE'S GUNS
EGGIILMMMNOSTWY	GET ON SWIMMINGLY
EGGIINNNORSSTWY	TRYING ONE'S WINGS
EGGLNOOOOSSSTTUU	SLOG ONE'S GUTS OUT
EGHHHHIIOPSSTTT	HIT THE HIGH SPOTS
EGHHHIIINNPSSTT	SHIPS IN THE NIGHT
EGHHHOORSTTTTUW	THOUGHT THE WORST
EGHHIIILNOPPSST	SPOILING THE SHIP
EGHHIIKLLNOOSTT	TOOK THE SHILLING
EGHHIIKNNORSTTV	THINK THINGS OVER
EGHHIIKNORRSTTU	STRIKING THE HOUR
EGHHIILMNNPSTTU	LIGHT PUNISHMENT
EGHHIILNOOPRTTT	RIGHT TO THE POINT
EGHHHILLNOOSTTUY	YOUTH HOSTELLING
	YOUTH-HOSTELLING
EGHHILNOORTTWW	THROW NEW LIGHT ON
EGHHILNNORSTTTU	TURNS ON THE LIGHT
EGHHILNOOPRSTTT	PLIGHT ONES TROTH
EGHHILNORTTTTUU	TURN OUT THE LIGHT
	TURN THE LIGHT OUT
EGHHINORRSTTTTU	TURNS TO THE RIGHT
EGHHMNOOOSSTTUW	THE SHOW MUST GO ON
EGHIIIKLNNORSTV	SHRINKING VIOLET
EGHIIIMNNORSSTU	HOUSING MINISTER
EGHIIINNNNOPTTW	WINNING THE POINT
EGHIIINNOPSSTYZ	HYPOSENSITIZING
EGHIILLNOORTTTT	LITTLE OR NOTHING
EGHIILLNNSSTTWY	TWENTY SHILLINGS
EGHIILNNNOOPSTW	WINNING THE POOLS
EGHIILNNOORSSST	LOSING ONE'S SHIRT
EGHIINNNNNORTTU	NOT IN THE RUNNING
EGHIINNRSSTTTUY	UNITY IS STRENGTH
EGHIKNNNOOSSTTU	SOUTH KENSINGTON
EGHILLNPRSSSTTU	PULLS THE STRINGS
EGHILNNOOSSSTTW	LOST ON THE SWINGS
EGHINOOOOSTTTVW	NOT GIVE TWO HOOTS
EGHLLLOPPSTTUUU	PULLS THE PLUG OUT
EGHNNOORSSTTTUW	STUNT ONES GROWTH

EGHNORRRSTTTUYY	TRY YOUR STRENGTH
EGIIILMNNOSTTVY	LIVING TESTIMONY
EGIIILNNOORSTUV	REVOLUTIONISING
EGIIILNNOORTUVZ	REVOLUTIONIZING
EGIIILNNOPRTVVY	LIVING IN POVERTY
EGIIIMNNOOSSSU	IGNOMINIOUSNESS
EGIIIMNNNOOSTTT	SETTING IN MOTION
EGIIINNOPSSTTTW	PITTING ONE'S WITS
EGIIINORRRRTTVY	VIRGIN TERRITORY
EGIIKLLNNORSSTY	TRYING ONE'S SKILL
EGIILNNNOQSTUUY	UNQUESTIONINGLY
EGIILNNOPPRSSSU	PURSING ONE'S LIPS
EGIKLLNNOOOOSSS	LOSING ONE'S LOOKS
EGILLNOOPRRSTWW	STRONG WILL-POWER
	STRONG WILLPOWER
EGINMNNOOOPRSSTT	ONES STRONG POINT
EGKNOOOORSSTTUUW	WORK ONE'S GUTS OUT
EHHIILMNNOOSTTU	IN THE LION'S MOUTH
EHHIKLMNOOOOSTTU	LOOKS IN THE MOUTH
EHHILLORTTTTUUW	THE TRUTH WILL OUT
EHHILNOOORSTTTW	THROW TO THE LIONS
EHIIIKLMMOOPRST	POIKILOTHERMISM
EHIILLMOOPPRTTU	PHOTOMULTIPLIER
EHIIMNNPRRRTTUU	RETURN IN TRIUMPH
EHIINNOOPRRSTTW	THREW INTO PRISON
EHIINNOPRRSSTTU	RUSHES INTO PRINT
EHIINOOQSTTTUUW	WITHOUT QUESTION
EHILLNNNOOPRSSU	PULL IN ONE'S HORNS
EHILMMNNOOPSTUU	PLUM IN ONES MOUTH
EHILNNNOOORSTTW	THROWN IN ONE'S LOT
EHILNNOOORSSTTW	THROWS IN ONE'S LOT
EHILNOOPSSTTTWW	WHISTLESTOP TOWN
EHILOOPRSSTTTUW	WHISTLE-STOP TOUR
	WHISTLESTOP TOUR
EHINOORRRSSSTTU	IN SHORT TROUSERS
EHINORRSSSTTTUW	TRUSTWORTHINESS
EHKNNNOOOPSTTWW	KNOWN WHEN TO STOP
EHKNNOOOOPSSTTWW	KNOWS WHEN TO STOP
EHLLOOPPSSTTTUU	PULL OUT THE STOPS
EIIIMNNOOPPRSSTU	SUPERIMPOSITION
EIIJNNOOOPSSSST	JOINT POSSESSION
EIILLNORSSSSTUU	ILLUSTRIOUSNESS
EIILOPRRSSTTUUY	SURREPTITIOUSLY
EIILOPRSSSTTUUY	SUPERSTITIOUSLY
EIKNNNNNOOOOSSW	KNOWN ONE'S ONIONS
EIKNNNNOOOOSSSW	KNOWS ONE'S ONIONS
EIMNOPRSSSSSTTU	STIRS ONE'S STUMPS
EJLLLLMNOOOORRTY	JELLY ROLL MORTON
FFFFGGIIINOTTYY	GOING FIFTY-FIFTY
FFIIINORRSSTTTU	FIRST IN FIRST OUT
FGGGHIINNNOOORT	GOING FOR NOTHING
FGGHIILNOPTTTTU	PUTTING TO FLIGHT
FGHHIIIKLNNSTUW	WISHFUL THINKING
FGHHIIKNNNOOSTT	THINKS NOTHING OF
FGIILNNNOOOORTUU	RUNNING OUT OF OIL
FGIIMNNNNOORRTU	RUNNING INTO FORM
FIIKMNOORRSSTWY	MINISTRY OF WORKS
FIINOOOPRSSTTTU	POSITION OF TRUST
FINOOOOOOPPRRTTU	OUT OF PROPORTION
GGGIIIKMNNOPSUV	GIVING UP SMOKING
GGGIIILMMMNNOSWY	GOING SWIMMINGLY
GGHHHHIIKNNORTTU	THINKING THROUGH
GGHHHIIOORTTTUW	GO THROUGH WITH IT
GGHHHINOOORSTTU	SHOOTING THROUGH